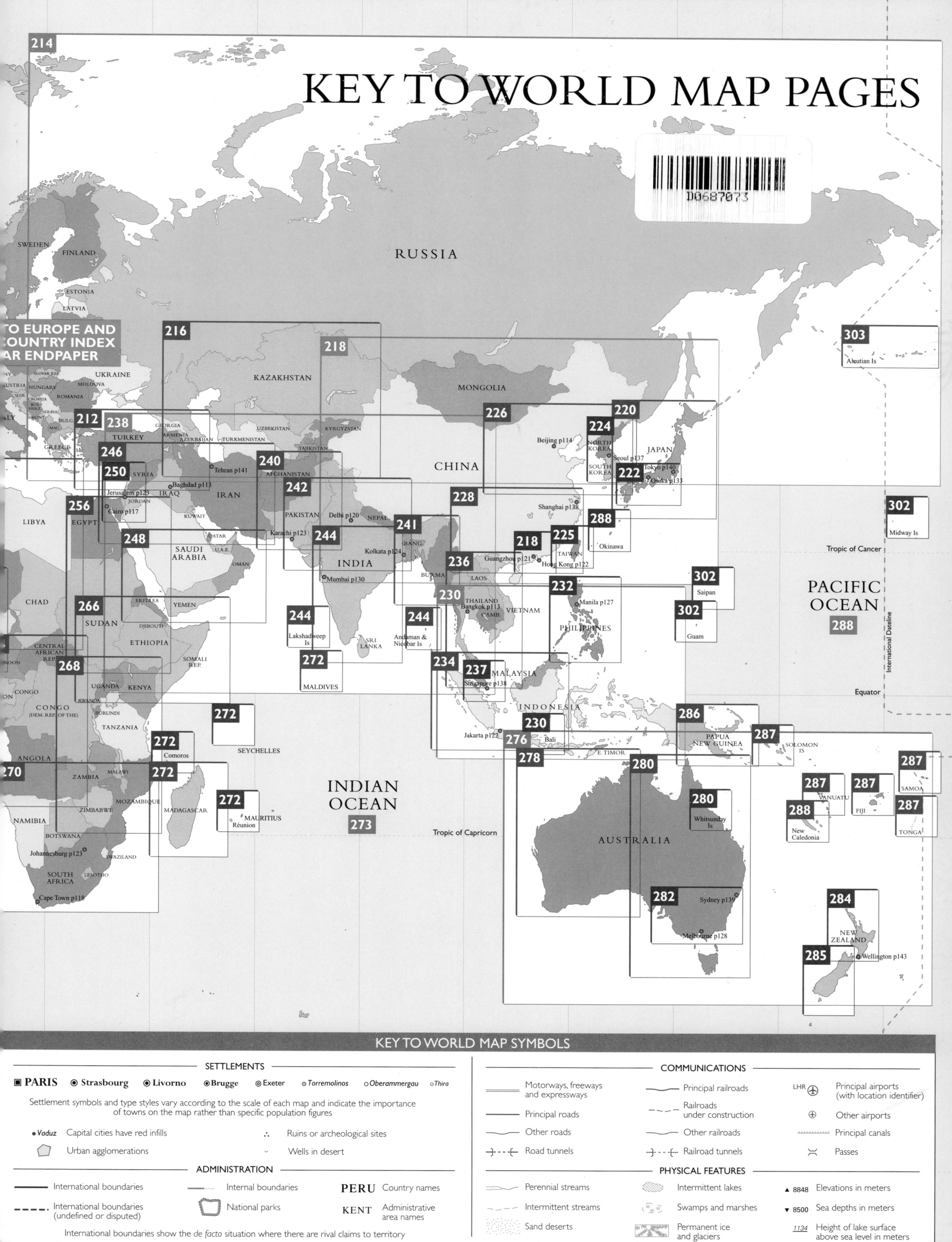

KEY TO WORLD MAP PAGES

RUSSIA

SWEDEN
FINLAND
ESTONIA
LATVIA

TO EUROPE AND
COUNTRY INDEX
AR ENDPAPER

SLOVAK REP.
UKRAINE
AUSTRIA
HUNGARY
MOLDOVA
CROATIA
ROMANIA
BOS.
HERZ.
SERBIA
MONT.
BULG.
MAC.
ITALY
GREECE

KAZAKHSTAN

MONGOLIA

303
Aleutian Is

216

218

226

220
224

Beijing p114

NORTH
KOREA
SOUTH
KOREA
Seoul p137

JAPAN
Tokyo p140
Osaka p133

222

212 238
TURKEY
GEORGIA
ARMENIA
AZERBAIJAN
TURKMENISTAN
UZBEKISTAN
KYRGYZSTAN
TAJIKISTAN

CHINA

246
250 SYRIA
Tehran p141
240
AFGHANISTAN
242

Jerusalem p123
JORDAN
IRAQ
IRAN
Baghdad p113
256
EGYPT
Cairo p117
KUWAIT
PAKISTAN
Delhi p120
NEPAL
241
BANG.

228

Shanghai p138

288

302
Midway Is

LIBYA

248
SAUDI
ARABIA
QATAR
U.A.E.
OMAN
Karachi p123
244
INDIA
Kolkata p124
236
BURMA
LAOS
218
Guangzhou p21
225
TAIWAN
Hong Kong p122

Okinawa

Tropic of Cancer

PACIFIC
OCEAN

288

CHAD
266
SUDAN
ERITREA
YEMEN
DJIBOUTI
Mumbai p130
230
THAILAND
Bangkok p113
VIETNAM
CAMB.
232
Manila p127

302
Saipan

302
Guam

CENTRAL
AFRICAN
REP.
ETHIOPIA
SOMALI
REP.
244
Lakshadweep
Is
SRI
LANKA
244
Andaman &
Nicobar Is
PHILIPPINES

International Dateline

268
UGANDA
KENYA
RWANDA
BURUNDI
272
MALDIVES
234
237
MALAYSIA
Singapore p138

Equator

CONGO
CONGO
(DEM. REP. OF THE)
TANZANIA
272
SEYCHELLES
INDONESIA
286
287
SOLOMON
IS

ANGOLA
272
Comoros
Jakarta p122
230
Bali
276
E. TIMOR
PAPUA
NEW GUINEA
287
287
SAMOA
287
VANUATU

270
ZAMBIA
MALAWI
272
272
MADAGASCAR
278
288
New
Caledonia
287
FIJI
287
TONGA
NAMIBIA
ZIMBABWE
MOZAMBIQUE
272
MAURITIUS
Réunion
INDIAN
OCEAN
273
280
280
Whitsunday
Is

BOTSWANA
Tropic of Capricorn
AUSTRALIA

Johannesburg p123
SWAZILAND
SOUTH
AFRICA
LESOTHO

282
Sydney p139
284

Cape Town p118
Melbourne p128
NEW
ZEALAND

285
Wellington p143

KEY TO WORLD MAP SYMBOLS

SETTLEMENTS

■ **PARIS** ◉ **Strasbourg** ◎ **Livorno** ⊙ **Brugge** ⊚ **Exeter** ⊙ *Torremolinos* ○ *Oberammergau* ○ *Thira*

Settlement symbols and type styles vary according to the scale of each map and indicate the importance
of towns on the map rather than specific population figures

● *Vaduz* Capital cities have red infills   ∴ Ruins or archeological sites

⬠ Urban agglomerations   ˅ Wells in desert

ADMINISTRATION

—— International boundaries   ┈┈ Internal boundaries   **PERU** Country names

--- International boundaries
(undefined or disputed)   ⬠ National parks   KENT Administrative
area names

International boundaries show the *de facto* situation where there are rival claims to territory

COMMUNICATIONS

—— Motorways, freeways
and expressways   —— Principal railroads   LHR ⊕ Principal airports
(with location identifier)

—— Principal roads   --- Railroads
under construction   ⊕ Other airports

—— Other roads   —— Other railroads   ┄┄┄ Principal canals

+-·-+ Road tunnels   +-·-+ Railroad tunnels   ⊃⊂ Passes

PHYSICAL FEATURES

—— Perennial streams   ⬚ Intermittent lakes   ▲ 8848 Elevations in meters

--- Intermittent streams   ⬚ Swamps and marshes   ▼ 8500 Sea depths in meters

⬚ Sand deserts   ⬚ Permanent ice
and glaciers   *1134* Height of lake surface
above sea level in meters

OXFORD

ATLAS
OF THE
WORLD

SEVENTEENTH EDITION

WILL THE WORLD RUN OUT OF FOOD?
The specialist consultant for the "*Will the World Run Out of Food?*" section is **Professor Keith W. T. Goulding**, President of the British Society of Soil Science and Head of the Department of Soil Science, Rothamsted Research, Harpenden, UK (www.rothamsted.ac.uk).

Rothamsted Research is an institute of the Biotechnology and Biological Sciences Research Council.

THE EDITORS are especially grateful to **Professor Goulding** and **Dr Sharon Hall** of Rothamsted Research for their invaluable assistance in preparing this section.

IMAGES OF EARTH
THE EDITORS would like to thank **Richard Chiles** and the staff at Fugro NPA Ltd, Edenbridge, Kent, UK (www.satmaps.com) for sourcing and processing the satellite imagery that appears in the atlas.

GAZETTEER OF NATIONS
TEXT Keith Lye

PHOTOGRAPHIC ACKNOWLEDGEMENTS
Alamy /*Peter Barritt* 10 (right), /*Cultura* 13 (top), /*David R. Frazier Photolibrary, Inc.* 12 (left);
Corbis /*William Caram* 103, /*P. Deliss* 10 (left), /*Nigel J. Dennis/Gallo Images* 86, /*Jay Dickman* 109 (bottom left), /*Paulo Fridman* 8–9, /*Yang Liu* 91, /*Gideon Mendel* 13 (centre), /*Radius Images* 11, /*Royalty-Free* 97, /*Liba Taylor* 104, /*David Turnley* 109 (bottom right);
© Crown copyright 2007. Published by the Met Office, UK 82;
Fugro NPA Ltd 14–31, 32–33, 66–67, 84, 110–111, 144–145, 156–157, 208–209, 252–253, 274–275, 290–291, 324–325 /*Image provided by the USGS EROS Data Center Satellite Systems Branch* 87;
Galaxy Picture Library /*Robin Scagell* 73;
iStockphoto.com 101;
Javier Méndez (ING)/Nik Szymanek (Univ. Herts) 68;
NASA/GSFC 83 (top and bottom), 98, /*Jacques Descloitres, MODIS Rapid Response Team* 81;
Plantagon International 13 (bottom);
Science Photo Library /*Lawrence Migdale* 12 (right).

STAR CHARTS (PAGE 69)
Wil Tirion

CARTOGRAPHY BY PHILIP'S
David Gaylard, Ray Smith, Caroline Rayner, Andy Stephenson, Darren Hildrew, Carl Beddows, Selina Bugby, James Hughes

WORLD CITIES
PAGE 120, DUBLIN: The town plan of Dublin is based on Ordnance Survey Ireland by permission of the Government Permit Number 8621. © Ordnance Survey Ireland and Government of Ireland.

PAGE 121, EDINBURGH, and PAGE 125, LONDON:
This product includes mapping data licensed from Ordnance Survey® with the permission of the Controller of Her Majesty's Stationery Office. © Crown copyright 2010. All rights reserved. Licence number 100011710.

Copyright © 2010 Philip's
www.philips-maps.co.uk

Philip's, a division of Octopus Publishing Group Limited (www.octopusbooks.co.uk)
Endeavour House, 189 Shaftesbury Avenue, London WC2H 8JY
An Hachette UK Company (www.hachette.co.uk)

Published in North America by
Oxford University Press, Inc.
198 Madison Avenue
New York, NY 10016

www.oup.com/us

OXFORD is a registered trademark
UNIVERSITY PRESS of Oxford University Press

All rights reserved. No part of this publication may be reproduced, stored in a retrieval system, or transmitted in any form or by any means, electronic, electrical, chemical, mechanical, optical, photocopying, recording, or otherwise, without the prior permission of the Publisher.

Library of Congress Cataloging-in-Publication Data available

ISBN 978-0-19-975128-0

Printing (last digit): 9 8 7 6 5 4 3 2

Printed in Hong Kong

FOREWORD

A N AUTHORITATIVE AND SERIOUS REFERENCE WORK, the Oxford *Atlas of the World* is one of the finest atlases available anywhere in the world. The atlas incorporates computer-derived maps which have been produced using the very latest in digital cartographic techniques.

The Oxford *Atlas of the World* has been devised with the help of a panel of specialist geography consultants from the United Kingdom and the United States, whose specialties range from the history of cartography, urban and social geography, epidemiology, and the European Union to biogeography and applied geomorphology. The result of their valuable input can be seen in the wealth of maps and data contained in the "*World Geography*" section of this atlas.

Country names are shown in conventional English form and are those that are in common usage. They are the forms used by publications such as *Newsweek* and *The Washington Post,* and by the BBC and the British Foreign Office. Alternative country names appear in parentheses on the maps where space permits – for example, Burma (Myanmar) – and are cross-referenced in the index, for example, Côte d'Ivoire = Ivory Coast.

HOW TO USE THE ATLAS
The atlas is divided into a number of sections which are explained below.

WORLD STATISTICS AND "WILL THE WORLD RUN OUT OF FOOD?"
World statistics on topics such as area and population for every country in the world. Also included in this section is a listing of the world's largest cities by population, arranged in country alphabetical order. This section is followed by the highly topical "Will the World Run Out of Food?" feature, which examines the issues and possible solutions to the world's most pressing problem.

IMAGES OF EARTH
A beautifully illustrated satellite section showing 16 of the world's major regions and cities in the Americas, Europe, Africa, Asia, and Australasia.

GAZETTEER OF NATIONS
A comprehensive A–Z reference providing concise profiles of every country's geography, climate, history, politics, and economy, together with ready-reference tables, and illustrated with flags and locator maps.

WORLD GEOGRAPHY
A richly informative section comprising 42 pages of maps, charts, graphs, and diagrams that explain key themes about the world in which we live. The topics covered include the Solar System, oceans, climate, the natural world, energy, and trade. Explanatory text on each spread describes the patterns shown by the data.

CITY MAPS
A detailed selection of maps for 69 urban areas around the world. These are useful for planning trips abroad as well as for comparative studies of cities worldwide.

WORLD MAPS
An outstanding collection of 179 pages of distinctive Philip's cartography. The highly acclaimed physical world maps combine relief shading with layer-colored contours to give a striking visual picture of the Earth's surface. Roads, railroads, canals, and airports are accurately depicted on the maps, and towns and cities are clearly marked. More information on the key features employed in the construction and presentation of the maps is given on the facing page.

GEOGRAPHICAL GLOSSARY AND INDEX
The 84,000-name index to the world maps includes geographical features as well as towns and cities, with both latitude/longitude and letter/figure grid references. Preceding the index is a list of geographical terms from various foreign languages that may be found in the place names on the maps and also in the index, together with their meanings.

SPECIALIST GEOGRAPHY CONSULTANTS

THE EDITORS are grateful to the following for acting as specialist geography consultants on the "*World Geography*" front section:

Professor D. Brunsden Kings College, University of London, UK
Dr C. Clarke Oxford University, UK
Professor P. Haggett University of Bristol, UK
Professor M-L. Hsu University of Minnesota, Minnesota, USA
Professor K. McLachlan School of Oriental and African Studies, University of London, UK
Professor M. Monmonier Syracuse University, New York, USA

Professor M. J. Tooley University of St Andrews, UK
Dr T. Unwin Royal Holloway, University of London, UK

THE EDITORS would also like to thank:
Dr Dibyesh Anand
John Burden
Peter Grego
Keith Lye
Garrett Nagle
Caroline Ohara
Ross Reynolds
Robin Scagell
John Woodruff

USER GUIDE

The reference maps which form the main body of this atlas have been prepared in accordance with the highest standards of international cartography to provide an accurate and detailed representation of the Earth. The scales and projections used have been carefully chosen to give balanced coverage of the world, while emphasizing the most densely populated and economically significant regions. A hallmark of Philip's mapping is the use of hill shading and relief coloring to create a graphic impression of landforms: this makes the maps exceptionally easy to read. However, knowledge of the key features employed in the construction and presentation of the maps will enable the reader to derive the fullest benefit from the atlas.

MAP SEQUENCE

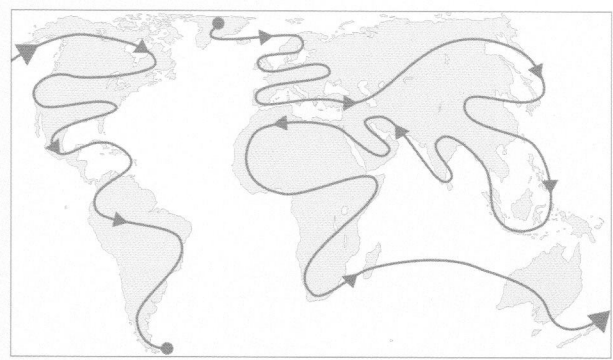

The atlas covers the Earth continent by continent: first Europe; then its land neighbor Asia (mapped north before south, in a clockwise sequence), then Africa, Australia and Oceania, North America, and South America. This is the classic arrangement adopted by most cartographers since the 16th century. For each continent, there are maps at a variety of scales. First, physical relief and political maps of the whole continent; then a series of larger-scale maps of the regions within the continent, each followed, where required, by still larger-scale maps of the most important or densely populated areas. The governing principle is that by turning the pages of the atlas, the reader moves steadily from north to south through each continent, with each map overlapping its neighbors.

MAP PRESENTATION

With very few exceptions (for example, for the Arctic and Antarctica), the maps are drawn with north at the top, regardless of whether they are presented upright or sideways on the page. In the borders will be found the map title; a locator diagram showing the area covered; continuation arrows showing the page numbers for maps of adjacent areas; the scale; the projection used; the degrees of latitude and longitude; and the letters and figures used in the index for locating place names and geographical features. Physical relief maps also have a height reference panel identifying the colors used for each layer of contouring.

MAP SYMBOLS

Each map contains a vast amount of detail which can only be conveyed clearly and accurately by the use of symbols. Points and circles of varying sizes locate and identify the relative importance of towns and cities; different styles of type are employed for administrative, geographical, and regional place names to aid identification. A variety of pictorial symbols denote landforms such as glaciers, marshes, and coral reefs, and man-made structures including roads, railroads, airports, and canals. International borders are shown by red lines. Where neighboring countries are in dispute, for example in parts of the Middle East, the maps show the *de facto* boundary between nations, regardless of the legal or historical situation.

The symbols are explained on the front endpapers of the atlas.

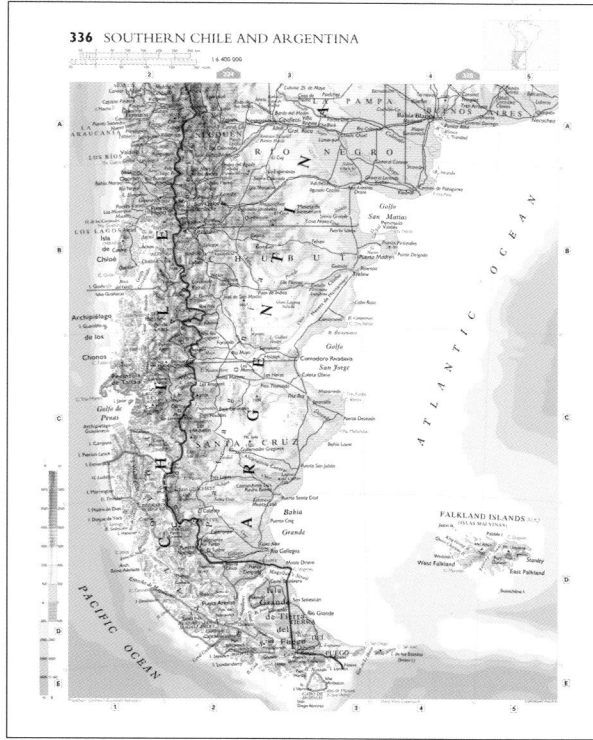

MAP SCALES

1:16 000 000
1 inch = 252 statute miles

The scale of each map is given in the numerical form known as the "representative fraction." The first figure is always one, signifying one unit of distance on the map; the second figure, usually in millions, is the number by which the map unit must be multiplied to give the equivalent distance on the Earth's surface. Calculations can easily be made in centimeters and kilometers, by dividing the Earth units figure by 100 000 (i.e. deleting the last five 0s). Thus 1:1 000 000 means 1 cm = 10 km. The calculation for inches and miles is more laborious, but 1 000 000 divided by 63 360 (the number of inches in a mile) shows that 1:1 000 000 means approximately 1 inch = 16 miles. The table below provides distance equivalents for scales down to 1:50 000 000.

LARGE SCALE		
1:1 000 000	1 cm = 10 km	1 inch = 16 miles
1:2 500 000	1 cm = 25 km	1 inch = 39.5 miles
1:5 000 000	1 cm = 50 km	1 inch = 79 miles
1:6 000 000	1 cm = 60 km	1 inch = 95 miles
1:8 000 000	1 cm = 80 km	1 inch = 126 miles
1:10 000 000	1 cm = 100 km	1 inch = 158 miles
1:15 000 000	1 cm = 150 km	1 inch = 237 miles
1:20 000 000	1 cm = 200 km	1 inch = 316 miles
1:50 000 000	1 cm = 500 km	1 inch = 790 miles
SMALL SCALE		

MEASURING DISTANCES

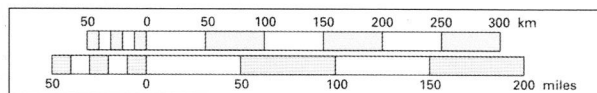

Although each map is accompanied by a scale bar, distances cannot always be measured with confidence because of the distortions involved in portraying the curved surface of the Earth on a flat page. As a general rule, the larger the map scale, the more accurate and reliable will be the distance measured. On small-scale maps such as those of the world and of entire continents, measurement may only be accurate along the "standard parallels," or central axes, and should not be attempted without considering the map projection.

MAP PROJECTIONS

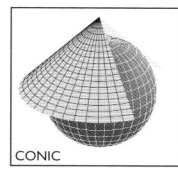 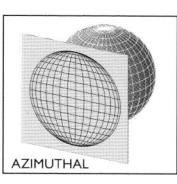 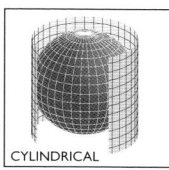

Unlike a globe, no flat map can give a true scale representation of the world in terms of area, shape, and position of every region. Each of the numerous systems that have been devised for projecting the curved surface of the Earth on to a flat page involves the sacrifice of accuracy in one or more of these elements. The variations in shape and position of land masses such as Alaska, Greenland, and Australia, for example, can be quite dramatic when different projections are compared.

For this atlas, the guiding principle has been to select projections that involve the least distortion of size and distance. The projection used for each map is noted in the border. Most fall into one of three categories – conic, azimuthal, or cylindrical – whose basic concepts are shown above. Each involves plotting the forms of the Earth's surface on a grid of latitude and longitude lines, which may be shown as parallels, curves, or radiating spokes.

LATITUDE AND LONGITUDE

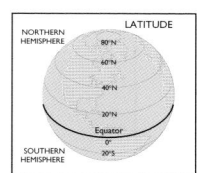 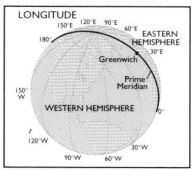 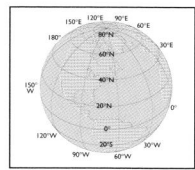

Accurate positioning of individual points on the Earth's surface is made possible by reference to the geometrical system of latitude and longitude. Latitude *parallels* are drawn west–east around the Earth and numbered by degrees north and south of the Equator, which is designated 0° of latitude. Longitude *meridians* are drawn north–south and numbered by degrees east and west of the *prime meridian*, 0° of longitude, which passes through Greenwich in England. By referring to these co-ordinates and their subdivisions of minutes (1/60th of a degree) and seconds (1/60th of a minute), any place on Earth can be located to within a few hundred meters. Latitude and longitude are indicated by blue lines on the maps; they are straight or curved according to the projection employed. Reference to these lines is the easiest way of determining the relative positions of places on different maps, and for plotting compass directions.

NAME FORMS

For ease of reference, both English and local name forms appear in the atlas. Oceans, seas, and countries are shown in English throughout the atlas; country names may be abbreviated to their commonly accepted form (for example, Germany, not The Federal Republic of Germany). Conventional English forms are also used for place names on the smaller-scale maps of the continents. However, local name forms are used on all large-scale and regional maps, with the English form given in brackets only for important cities – the large-scale map of Russia and Northern Asia thus shows Moskva (Moscow). For countries which do not use a Roman script, place names have been transcribed according to the systems adopted by the British and US Geographic Names Authorities. For China, the Pin Yin system has been used, with some more widely known forms appearing in brackets, as with Beijing (Peking). Both English and local names appear in the index, the English form being cross-referenced to the local form.

CONTENTS

WORLD STATISTICS

COUNTRIES	6
CITIES	7

WILL THE WORLD RUN OUT OF FOOD?

THE ISSUES	10–11
THE SOLUTIONS	12–13

IMAGES OF EARTH

LONDON, UK	16
VENICE, ITALY	17
TEHRAN, IRAN	18
KABUL, AFGHANISTAN	19
DHAKA, BANGLADESH	20
SHANGHAI, CHINA	21
NOUAKCHOTT, MAURITANIA	22
CAPE PENINSULA, SOUTH AFRICA	23
NGORONGORO CRATER, TANZANIA	24
SYDNEY, AUSTRALIA	25
WELLINGTON AND THE COOK STRAIT, NZ	26
QUÉBEC, CANADA	27
NEW YORK, USA	28
DENVER, USA	29
PORT-AU-PRINCE, HAITI	30
LIMA, PERU	31

GAZETTEER OF NATIONS

AN A–Z GAZETTEER OF COUNTRIES	34–65

WORLD GEOGRAPHY

THE UNIVERSE	68–69
THE SOLAR SYSTEM	70–71
SEASONS, TIME AND MOTION	72–73
GEOLOGY OF THE EARTH	74–75
OCEANS	76–77
THE ATMOSPHERE	78–79
CLIMATE	80–81
CLIMATE CHANGE AND GLOBAL WARMING	82–83
WATER AND VEGETATION	84–85
BIODIVERSITY AND THE NATURAL WORLD	86–87
POPULATION	88–89
CITIES	90–91
THE HUMAN FAMILY	92–93
CONFLICT AND COOPERATION	94–95
ENERGY	96–97
MINERALS	98–99
EMPLOYMENT AND INDUSTRY	100–101
TRADE	102–103
HEALTH	104–105
WEALTH	106–107
STANDARDS OF LIVING	108–109

WORLD CITIES

AMSTERDAM	112
ATHENS	112
ATLANTA	113
BAGHDAD	113
BANGKOK	113
BARCELONA	114
BEIJING	114
BERLIN	115
BOSTON	116
BRUSSELS	116
BUDAPEST	117
BUENOS AIRES	117
CAIRO	117
CAPE TOWN	118
COPENHAGEN	118
CHICAGO	119
DELHI	120
DUBLIN	120
EDINBURGH	121
GUANGZHOU (CANTON)	121
HELSINKI	121
HONG KONG	122
ISTANBUL	122
JAKARTA	122
JERUSALEM	123
JOHANNESBURG	123
KARACHI	123
KOLKATA (CALCUTTA)	124
LAGOS	124
LAS VEGAS	124
LIMA	124
LONDON	125
LISBON	126
LOS ANGELES	126
MADRID	127
MANILA	127
MELBOURNE	128
MEXICO CITY	128
MIAMI	128
MILAN	129
MOSCOW	129
MONTREAL	130
MUMBAI (BOMBAY)	130
MUNICH	131
NEW ORLEANS	131
NEW YORK	132
ORLANDO	133
OSAKA	133
OSLO	133
PARIS	134
PRAGUE	135
RIO DE JANEIRO	135
ROME	136
SAN FRANCISCO	136
ST PETERSBURG	137
SANTIAGO	137
SÃO PAULO	137
SEOUL	137
SHANGHAI	138
SINGAPORE	138
STOCKHOLM	139
SYDNEY	139
TOKYO	140
TEHRAN	141
TORONTO	141
VIENNA	142
WARSAW	142
WASHINGTON	143
WELLINGTON	143

WORLD MAPS

THE WORLD

MAP SYMBOLS	FRONT ENDPAPER
THE WORLD: PHYSICAL 1:76 000 000	146–147
THE WORLD: POLITICAL 1:76 000 000	148–149
ARCTIC OCEAN 1:28 000 000	150
ANTARCTICA 1:28 000 000	151
ATLANTIC OCEAN 1:41 000 000	152
ISLANDS OF THE ATLANTIC	153
BERMUDA 1:400 000	
NEW PROVIDENCE ISLAND 1:400 000	
MADEIRA 1:800 000	
AZORES 1:1 600 000	
CANARY ISLANDS 1:1 600 000	
FALKLAND ISLANDS 1:6 400 000	
ASCENSION ISLAND 1:400 000	
ST HELENA 1:400 000	
CAPE VERDE ISLANDS 1:8 000 000	
GREENLAND 1:10 000 000	154
ICELAND 1:2 000 000	155

EUROPE

EUROPE: PHYSICAL 1:16 000 000	158
EUROPE: POLITICAL 1:16 000 000	159
SCANDINAVIA 1:4 800 000	160–161
ICELAND 1:4 800 000	
FÆROE ISLANDS 1:4 800 000	
DENMARK AND SOUTHERN SWEDEN 1:2 000 000	162–163
SOUTHERN NORWAY 1:2 000 000	164
BRITISH ISLES 1:4 000 000	165
IRELAND 1:1 600 000	166
SCOTLAND 1:1 600 000	167
ENGLAND AND WALES 1:1 600 000	168–169
NETHERLANDS, BELGIUM AND LUXEMBOURG 1:2 000 000	170
FRANCE 1:4 000 000	171
NORTHERN FRANCE 1:2 000 000	172–173
SOUTHERN FRANCE 1:2 000 000	174–175
CENTRAL EUROPE 1:4 000 000	176–177
GERMANY AND SWITZERLAND 1:2 000 000	178–179
AUSTRIA, CZECH REPUBLIC AND SLOVAK REPUBLIC 1:2 000 000	180–181
HUNGARY, ROMANIA AND THE LOWER DANUBE 1:2 000 000	182–183
POLAND AND THE SOUTHERN BALTIC 1:2 000 000	184–185
EASTERN EUROPE 1:8 000 000	186–187
BALTIC STATES, BELARUS AND UKRAINE 1:4 000 000	188–189
THE VOLGA BASIN AND THE CAUCASUS 1:4 000 000	190–191
SOUTHERN EUROPE 1:8 000 000	192–193
WESTERN SPAIN AND PORTUGAL 1:2 000 000	194–195
EASTERN SPAIN 1:2 000 000	196–197
NORTHERN ITALY, SLOVENIA AND CROATIA 1:2 000 000	198–199
SOUTHERN ITALY 1:2 000 000	200–201
THE BALKANS 1:2 000 000	202–203
SOUTHERN GREECE AND WESTERN TURKEY 1:2 000 000	204–205
MEDITERRANEAN ISLANDS	206–207
IBIZA, MAJORCA, MINORCA 1:800 000	
MALTA 1:400 000	
CORFU 1:800 000	
RHODES 1:800 000	
LEVKAS, ZANTE, CEPHALONIA 1:800 000	
CRETE 1:1 000 000	
CYPRUS 1:1 000 000	

ASIA

ASIA: PHYSICAL 1:40 000 000	210
ASIA: POLITICAL 1:40 000 000	211
TURKEY AND TRANSCAUCASIA 1:4 000 000	212–213

CONTENTS

RUSSIA AND
NORTHERN ASIA 214–215
1:16 000 000

KAZAKHSTAN
AND CENTRAL ASIA 216–127
1:8 000 000

CHINA
AND THE FAR EAST 218–219
1:12 000 000
HONG KONG AND MACAU 1:800 000

JAPAN 220–221
1:4 000 000
RYUKYU ISLANDS 1:4 000 000

SOUTHERN JAPAN 222–223
1:2 000 000

KOREA 224
1:3 100 000

TAIWAN 225
1:1 400 000

NORTHERN CHINA
AND KOREA 226–227
1:4 800 000

SOUTHERN CHINA 228–229
1:4 800 000

SOUTHEAST ASIA 230–231
1:10 000 000
JAVA AND MADURA 1:6 000 000
BALI 1:1 600 000

PHILIPPINES 232–233
1:3 200 000

WESTERN INDONESIA 234–235
1:5 600 000

MAINLAND
SOUTHEAST ASIA 236–237
1:4 800 000
KO PHUKET 1:800 000
KO SAMUI 1:800 000
PINANG 1:800 000
SINGAPORE 1:800 000

SOUTHERN ASIA AND
THE MIDDLE EAST 238–239
1:14 000 000

AFGHANISTAN
AND PAKISTAN 240
1:5 600 000

BANGLADESH,
NORTHEASTERN INDIA
AND BURMA 241
1:4 800 000

NORTHERN INDIA,
PAKISTAN AND
NEPAL 242–243
1:4 800 000

SOUTHERN INDIA AND
SRI LANKA 244–245
1:4 800 000
LAKSHADWEEP ISLANDS 1:4 800 000
ANDAMAN AND
NICOBAR ISLANDS 1:4 800 000

THE MIDDLE EAST 246–247
1:5 600 000

SOUTHERN ARABIAN
PENINSULA 248–249
1:5 600 000

EASTERN
MEDITERRANEAN 250–251
1:2 000 000

AFRICA

AFRICA: PHYSICAL 254
1:33 600 000

AFRICA: POLITICAL 255
1:33 600 000

THE NILE VALLEY 256–257
1:6 400 000
THE NILE DELTA 1:3 200 000

CENTRAL NORTH
AFRICA 258–259
1:6 400 000

NORTHWEST AFRICA 260–261
1:6 400 000

WEST AFRICA 262–263
1:6 400 000

CENTRAL AFRICA 264–265
1:6 400 000
SÃO TOMÉ AND PRÍNCIPE 1:6 400 000

ETHIOPIA AND THE
HORN OF AFRICA 266–267
1:6 400 000

EAST AFRICA 268–269
1:6 400 000

SOUTHERN AFRICA 270–271
1:6 400 000

MADAGASCAR 272
1:6 400 000
COMOROS 1:2 000 000
MAYOTTE 1:800 000
SEYCHELLES 1:2 000 000
RÉUNION 1:800 000
MAURITIUS 1:800 000
MALDIVES 1:6 400 000

INDIAN OCEAN 273
1:40 000 000

AUSTRALIA AND OCEANIA

AUSTRALIA AND OCEANIA:
PHYSICAL
AND POLITICAL 276–277
1:16 000 000

WESTERN AUSTRALIA 278–279
1:6 400 000

EASTERN AUSTRALIA 280–281
1:6 400 000
WHITSUNDAY GROUP 1:2 000 000
TASMANIA 1:6 400 000
TORRES STRAIT 1:6 400 000

SOUTHEAST
AUSTRALIA 282–283
1:3 200 000

NEW ZEALAND –
NORTH ISLAND 284
1:2 800 000

NEW ZEALAND –
SOUTH ISLAND 285
1:2 800 000
CHATHAM ISLANDS 1:2 800 000

PAPUA NEW GUINEA 286
1:5 200 000

ISLANDS OF THE
SOUTHWEST PACIFIC 287
FIJI 1:4 000 000
VANUATU 1:4 000 000
SOLOMON ISLANDS 1:4 000 000
TONGA 1:4 000 000
YAP 1:830 000
CHUUK 1:830 000
SAMOAN ISLANDS 1:4 000 000

PACIFIC OCEAN 288–289
1:43 200 000
OKINAWA 1:1 550 000
IWO JIMA 1:200 000
PALAU 1:1 550 000
NEW CALEDONIA 1:5 750 000
TAHITI 1:1 150 000
FRENCH POLYNESIA 1:26 000 000
NIUE 1:830 000
RAROTONGA 1:415 000

NORTH AMERICA

NORTH AMERICA:
PHYSICAL 292
1:28 000 000

NORTH AMERICA:
POLITICAL 293
1:28 000 000

CANADA 294–295
1:12 000 000

WESTERN CANADA 296–297
1:5 600 000

EASTERN CANADA 298–299
1:5 600 000

UNITED STATES 300–301
1:12 000 000
ALASKA 1:12 000 000
HAWAI'I 1:12 000 000

HAWAI'I 302
1:2 500 000
OAHU 1:500 000
NORTHERN MARIANAS 1:12 800 000
WAKE ISLAND 1:200 000
MIDWAY ISLANDS 1:200 000
GUAM 1:800 000
SAIPAN AND TINIAN 1:800 000
TUTUILA 1:640 000
MANUA ISLANDS 1:640 000

ALASKA 303
1:8 000 000

UNITED STATES –
WEST 304–305
1:5 360 000

CENTRAL AND SOUTHERN
CALIFORNIA AND WESTERN
WASHINGTON 306–307
1:2 000 000

UNITED STATES – MIDWEST
AND NORTHEAST 308–309
1:5 360 000

CHICAGO AND
THE MIDWEST 310–311
1:2 000 000

NORTHEASTERN
UNITED STATES 312–313
1:2 000 000

UNITED STATES –
SOUTH 314–315
1:5 360 000

SOUTHEASTERN
UNITED STATES 316–317
1:2 000 000

MEXICO 318–319
1:6 400 000

CENTRAL AMERICA AND
THE WEST INDIES 320–321
1:6 400 000
PUERTO RICO AND THE
VIRGIN ISLANDS 1:1 600 000
JAMAICA 1:1 600 000
PANAMA CANAL 1:800 000

LESSER ANTILLES 322–323
NORTHERN LEEWARDS 1:600 000
ANTIGUA AND BARBUDA 1:600 000
ST KITTS AND NEVIS 1:600 000
GUADELOUPE 1:600 000
ARUBA 1:600 000
BONAIRE AND CURAÇAO 1:600 000
MARTINIQUE 1:600 000
DOMINICA 1:600 000
ST LUCIA 1:600 000
ST VINCENT AND
THE GRENADINES 1:600 000
MONTSERRAT 1:600 000
GRENADA 1:600 000
BARBADOS 1:600 000
TRINIDAD AND TOBAGO 1:600 000

SOUTH AMERICA

SOUTH AMERICA:
PHYSICAL 326
1:28 000 000

SOUTH AMERICA:
POLITICAL 327
1:28 000 000

SOUTH AMERICA –
NORTHWEST 328–329
1:6 400 000

SOUTH AMERICA –
WEST 330–331
1:6 400 000
GALAPAGOS ISLANDS 1:3 200 000
EASTER ISLAND 1:400 000
ROBINSON CRUSOE ISLAND 1:400 000

EASTERN BRAZIL 332–333
1:6 400 000

CENTRAL
SOUTH AMERICA 334–335
1:6 400 000

SOUTHERN CHILE AND
ARGENTINA 336
1:6 400 000

GEOGRAPHICAL
GLOSSARY 337–338

INDEX TO
WORLD MAPS 339–448

6 WORLD STATISTICS: COUNTRIES

This alphabetical list includes the principal countries and territories of the world. If a territory is not completely independent, the country it is associated with is named. The area figures give the total area of land, inland water, and ice. The population figures are 2009 estimates where available. The annual income is the Gross Domestic Product per capita in US dollars. The figures are the latest available, usually 2009 estimates.

Country/Territory	Area km² Thousands	Area miles² Thousands	Population Thousands	Capital	Annual Income US $
Afghanistan	652	252	28,396	Kabul	800
Albania	28.7	11.1	3,639	Tirana	6,200
Algeria	2,382	920	34,178	Algiers	7,100
American Samoa (US)	0.20	0.08	66	Pago Pago	8,000
Andorra	0.47	0.18	84	Andorra La Vella	42,500
Angola	1,247	481	12,799	Luanda	8,800
Anguilla (UK)	0.10	0.04	14	The Valley	8,800
Antigua & Barbuda	0.44	0.17	86	St John's	18,100
Argentina	2,780	1,074	40,914	Buenos Aires	13,800
Armenia	29.8	11.5	2,967	Yerevan	5,900
Aruba (Netherlands)	0.19	0.07	103	Oranjestad	21,800
Australia	7,741	2,989	21,263	Canberra	38,500
Austria	83.9	32.4	8,210	Vienna	39,400
Azerbaijan	86.6	33.4	8,239	Baku	9,900
Azores (Portugal)	2.2	0.86	236	Ponta Delgada	15,000
Bahamas	13.9	5.4	308	Nassau	29,800
Bahrain	0.69	0.27	729	Manama	38,400
Bangladesh	144	55.6	156,051	Dhaka	1,600
Barbados	0.43	0.17	285	Bridgetown	18,500
Belarus	208	80.2	9,649	Minsk	11,600
Belgium	30.5	11.8	10,414	Brussels	36,600
Belize	23.0	8.9	308	Belmopan	8,200
Benin	113	43.5	8,792	Porto-Novo	1,500
Bermuda (UK)	0.05	0.02	68	Hamilton	69,900
Bhutan	47.0	18.1	691	Thimphu	6,200
Bolivia	1,099	424	9,775	La Paz/Sucre	4,600
Bosnia-Herzegovina	51.2	19.8	4,613	Sarajevo	6,300
Botswana	582	225	1,991	Gaborone	12,100
Brazil	8,514	3,287	198,739	Brasília	10,200
Brunei	5.8	2.2	388	Bandar Seri Begawan	50,100
Bulgaria	111	42.8	7,205	Sofia	12,600
Burkina Faso	274	106	15,746	Ouagadougou	1,200
Burma (Myanmar)	677	261	48,138	Rangoon/Naypyidaw	1,200
Burundi	27.8	10.7	9,511	Bujumbura	300
Cambodia	181	69.9	14,494	Phnom Penh	1,900
Cameroon	475	184	18,879	Yaoundé	2,300
Canada	9,971	3,850	33,487	Ottawa	38,400
Canary Is. (Spain)	7.2	2.8	1,682	Las Palmas/Santa Cruz	19,900
Cape Verde Is.	4.0	1.6	429	Praia	3,900
Cayman Is. (UK)	0.26	0.10	49	George Town	43,800
Central African Republic	623	241	4,511	Bangui	700
Chad	1,284	496	10,329	Ndjaména	1,500
Chile	757	292	16,602	Santiago	14,700
China	9,597	3,705	1,338,613	Beijing	6,500
Colombia	1,139	440	43,677	Bogotá	9,200
Comoros	2.2	0.86	752	Moroni	1,000
Congo	342	132	4,013	Brazzaville	4,200
Congo (Dem. Rep. of the)	2,345	905	68,693	Kinshasa	300
Cook Is. (NZ)	0.24	0.09	12	Avarua	9,100
Costa Rica	51.1	19.7	4,254	San José	11,300
Croatia	56.5	21.8	4,489	Zagreb	17,600
Cuba	111	42.8	11,452	Havana	9,700
Cyprus	9.3	3.6	1,085	Nicosia	21,200
Czech Republic	78.9	30.5	10,212	Prague	25,100
Denmark	43.1	16.6	5,501	Copenhagen	36,200
Djibouti	23.2	9.0	725	Djibouti	2,800
Dominica	0.75	0.29	73	Roseau	10,200
Dominican Republic	48.5	18.7	9,650	Santo Domingo	8,200
East Timor	14.9	5.7	1,132	Dili	2,400
Ecuador	284	109	14,573	Quito	7,300
Egypt	1,001	387	78,867	Cairo	6,000
El Salvador	21.0	8.1	7,185	San Salvador	6,000
Equatorial Guinea	28.1	10.8	633	Malabo	36,100
Eritrea	118	45.4	5,647	Asmara	700
Estonia	45.1	17.4	1,299	Tallinn	18,800
Ethiopia	1,104	426	85,237	Addis Ababa	900
Faroe Is. (Denmark)	1.4	0.54	49	Tórshavn	31,000
Fiji	18.3	7.1	945	Suva	3,800
Finland	338	131	5,250	Helsinki	34,900
France	552	213	64,058	Paris	32,800
French Guiana (France)	90.0	34.7	203	Cayenne	8,300
French Polynesia (France)	4.0	1.5	287	Papeete	18,000
Gabon	268	103	1,515	Libreville	13,700
Gambia, The	11.3	4.4	1,778	Banjul	1,300
Gaza Strip (OPT)*	0.36	0.14	1,552	–	3,100
Georgia	69.7	26.9	4,616	Tbilisi	4,500
Germany	357	138	82,330	Berlin	34,200
Ghana	239	92.1	23,888	Accra	1,500
Gibraltar (UK)	0.006	0.002	29	Gibraltar Town	38,200
Greece	132	50.9	10,737	Athens	32,100
Greenland (Denmark)	2,176	840	58	Nuuk	34,700
Grenada	0.34	0.13	91	St George's	12,700
Guadeloupe (France)	1.7	0.66	453	Basse-Terre	7,900
Guam (US)	0.55	0.21	178	Agana	15,000
Guatemala	109	42.0	13,277	Guatemala City	5,200
Guinea	246	94.9	10,058	Conakry	1,100
Guinea-Bissau	36.1	13.9	1,534	Bissau	600
Guyana	215	83.0	753	Georgetown	3,900
Haiti	27.8	10.7	9,036	Port-au-Prince	1,300
Honduras	112	43.3	7,834	Tegucigalpa	4,200
Hungary	93.0	35.9	9,906	Budapest	18,800
Iceland	103	39.8	307	Reykjavik	39,800
India	3,287	1,269	1,156,898	New Delhi	3,100
Indonesia	1,905	735	240,272	Jakarta	4,000
Iran	1,648	636	66,429	Tehran	12,900
Iraq	438	169	28,946	Baghdad	3,300
Ireland	70.3	27.1	4,203	Dublin	42,200
Israel	20.6	8.0	7,234	Jerusalem	28,400
Italy	301	116	58,126	Rome	30,200
Ivory Coast (Côte d'Ivoire)	322	125	20,617	Yamoussoukro	1,700
Jamaica	11.0	4.2	2,826	Kingston	8,300
Japan	378	146	127,079	Tokyo	32,600
Jordan	89.3	34.5	6,269	Amman	5,300
Kazakhstan	2,725	1,052	15,399	Astana	11,400
Kenya	580	224	39,003	Nairobi	1,600
Kiribati	0.73	0.28	113	Tarawa	5,300
Korea, North	121	46.5	22,665	Pyŏngyang	1,800
Korea, South	99.3	38.3	48,509	Seoul	27,700
Kosovo	10.9	4.2	1,805	Pristina	2,300
Kuwait	17.8	6.9	2,693	Kuwait City	55,800
Kyrgyzstan	200	77.2	5,432	Bishkek	2,100
Laos	237	91.4	6,834	Vientiane	2,100
Latvia	64.6	24.9	2,232	Riga	14,500
Lebanon	10.4	4.0	4,017	Beirut	11,500
Lesotho	30.4	11.7	2,131	Maseru	1,500
Liberia	111	43.0	3,442	Monrovia	500
Libya	1,760	679	6,324	Tripoli	14,600
Liechtenstein	0.16	0.06	35	Vaduz	122,100
Lithuania	65.2	25.2	3,555	Vilnius	15,000
Luxembourg	2.6	1.0	492	Luxembourg	77,600
Macedonia (FYROM)	25.7	9.9	2,067	Skopje	9,000
Madagascar	587	227	20,654	Antananarivo	1,000
Madeira (Portugal)	0.78	0.30	241	Funchal	22,700
Malawi	118	45.7	15,029	Lilongwe	900
Malaysia	330	127	25,716	Kuala Lumpur/Putrajaya	14,700
Maldives	0.30	0.12	396	Malé	4,200
Mali	1,240	479	13,443	Bamako	1,100
Malta	0.32	0.12	405	Valletta	23,800
Marshall Is.	0.18	0.07	65	Majuro	2,500
Martinique (France)	1.1	0.43	436	Fort-de-France	14,400
Mauritania	1,026	396	3,129	Nouakchott	2,100
Mauritius	2.0	0.79	1,284	Port Louis	12,400
Mayotte (France)	0.37	0.14	224	Mamoudzou	4,900
Mexico	1,958	756	111,212	Mexico City	13,200
Micronesia, Fed. States of	0.70	0.27	107	Palikir	2,200
Moldova	33.9	13.1	4,321	Kishinev	2,400
Monaco	0.001	0.0004	33	Monaco	30,000
Mongolia	1,567	605	3,041	Ulan Bator	3,400
Montenegro	14.0	5.4	672	Podgorica	9,800
Morocco	447	172	31,285	Rabat	4,600
Mozambique	802	309	21,669	Maputo	900
Namibia	824	318	2,109	Windhoek	6,400
Nauru	0.02	0.008	14	Yaren	5,000
Nepal	147	56.8	28,563	Katmandu	1,200
Netherlands	41.5	16.0	16,716	Amsterdam/The Hague	39,000
Netherlands Antilles (Neths)†	0.80	0.31	227	Willemstad	16,000
New Caledonia (France)	18.6	7.2	228	Nouméa	15,000
New Zealand	271	104	4,213	Wellington	27,700
Nicaragua	130	50.2	5,891	Managua	2,800
Niger	1,267	489	15,306	Niamey	700
Nigeria	924	357	149,229	Abuja	2,400
Northern Mariana Is. (US)	0.46	0.18	51	Saipan	12,500
Norway	324	125	4,661	Oslo	59,300
Oman	310	119	3,418	Muscat	20,300
Pakistan	796	307	174,579	Islamabad	2,600
Palau	0.46	0.18	21	Melekeok	8,100
Panama	75.5	29.2	3,360	Panamá	11,900
Papua New Guinea	463	179	5,941	Port Moresby	2,300
Paraguay	407	157	6,996	Asunción	4,100
Peru	1,285	496	29,547	Lima	8,600
Philippines	300	116	97,977	Manila	3,300
Poland	323	125	38,483	Warsaw	17,800
Portugal	88.8	34.3	10,708	Lisbon	21,700
Puerto Rico (US)	8.9	3.4	3,966	San Juan	17,100
Qatar	11.0	4.2	833	Doha	121,400
Réunion (France)	2.5	0.97	788	St-Denis	6,200
Romania	238	92.0	22,215	Bucharest	11,500
Russia	17,075	6,593	140,041	Moscow	15,200
Rwanda	26.3	10.2	10,746	Kigali	1,000
St Kitts & Nevis	0.26	0.10	40	Basseterre	18,800
St Lucia	0.54	0.21	160	Castries	10,900
St Vincent & Grenadines	0.39	0.15	105	Kingstown	18,100
Samoa	2.8	1.1	220	Apia	4,700
San Marino	0.06	0.02	30	San Marino	41,900
São Tomé & Príncipe	0.96	0.37	213	São Tomé	1,400
Saudi Arabia	2,150	830	28,687	Riyadh	20,300
Senegal	197	76.0	13,712	Dakar	1,700
Serbia	77.5	29.9	7,379	Belgrade	10,400
Seychelles	0.46	0.18	87	Victoria	19,400
Sierra Leone	71.7	27.7	5,132	Freetown	900
Singapore	0.68	0.26	4,658	Singapore City	50,300
Slovak Republic	49.0	18.9	5,463	Bratislava	21,100
Slovenia	20.3	7.8	2,006	Ljubljana	28,200
Solomon Is.	28.9	11.2	596	Honiara	2,600
Somalia	638	246	9,832	Mogadishu	600
South Africa	1,221	471	49,052	Cape Town/Pretoria	10,000
Spain	498	192	40,525	Madrid	33,700
Sri Lanka	65.6	25.3	21,325	Colombo	4,500
Sudan	2,506	967	41,088	Khartoum	2,300
Suriname	163	63.0	481	Paramaribo	8,800
Swaziland	17.4	6.7	1,337	Mbabane	4,400
Sweden	450	174	9,060	Stockholm	36,800
Switzerland	41.3	15.9	7,604	Bern	41,600
Syria	185	71.5	21,763	Damascus	4,700
Taiwan	36.0	13.9	22,974	Taipei	30,200
Tajikistan	143	55.3	7,349	Dushanbe	1,800
Tanzania	945	365	41,049	Dodoma	1,400
Thailand	513	198	65,998	Bangkok	8,100
Togo	56.8	21.9	6,032	Lomé	900
Tonga	0.65	0.25	121	Nuku'alofa	4,600
Trinidad & Tobago	5.1	2.0	1,230	Port of Spain	23,300
Tunisia	164	63.2	10,486	Tunis	8,000
Turkey	775	299	76,806	Ankara	11,200
Turkmenistan	488	188	4,885	Ashkhabad	6,700
Turks & Caicos Is. (UK)	0.43	0.17	23	Cockburn Town	11,500
Tuvalu	0.03	0.01	12	Fongafale	1,600
Uganda	241	93.1	32,370	Kampala	1,300
Ukraine	604	233	45,700	Kiev	6,400
United Arab Emirates	83.6	32.3	4,798	Abu Dhabi	41,800
United Kingdom	242	93.4	61,113	London	35,400
United States of America	9,629	3,718	307,212	Washington, DC	46,400
Uruguay	175	67.6	3,494	Montevideo	12,600
Uzbekistan	447	173	27,606	Tashkent	2,800
Vanuatu	12.2	4.7	219	Port-Vila	4,800
Venezuela	912	352	26,815	Caracas	13,200
Vietnam	332	128	88,577	Hanoi	2,900
Virgin Is. (UK)	0.15	0.06	24	Road Town	38,500
Virgin Is. (US)	0.35	0.13	110	Charlotte Amalie	14,500
Wallis & Futuna Is. (France)	0.20	0.08	15	Mata-Utu	3,800
West Bank (OPT)*	5.9	2.3	2,416	–	2,900
Western Sahara	266	103	405	El Aaiún	2,500
Yemen	528	204	22,858	Sana'	2,500
Zambia	753	291	11,863	Lusaka	1,500
Zimbabwe	391	151	11,393	Harare	200

*OPT = Occupied Palestinian Territory

† Plans have been announced to dissolve the Netherlands Antilles as a political entity in October 2010. The five islands will then each have a new constitutional status within the Kingdom of the Netherlands.

This list shows the principal cities with more than 750,000 inhabitants. The figures are taken from the most recent census or estimate available, usually 2007, and as far as possible are the population of the metropolitan area or urban agglomeration (for example, greater New York, Mexico, or Paris). All the figures are in thousands. Local name forms have been used for the smaller cities (for example, Thessaloniki).

AFGHANISTAN
Kabul 3,288
ALGERIA
Algiers 3,260
ANGOLA
Luanda 2,839
ARGENTINA
Buenos Aires 13,349
Córdoba 1,592
Rosario 1,312
Mendoza 1,072
San Miguel de Tucumán 837
ARMENIA
Yerevan 1,103
AUSTRALIA
Sydney 4,388
Melbourne 3,663
Brisbane 1,769
Perth 1,484
Adelaide 1,137
AUSTRIA
Vienna 2,260
AZERBAIJAN
Baku 1,856
BANGLADESH
Dhaka 12,560
Chittagong 4,171
Khulna 1,497
Rajshahi 1,035
BELARUS
Minsk 1,778
BELGIUM
Brussels 1,012
BOLIVIA
La Paz 1,533
Santa Cruz 1,352
Cochabamba 797
BRAZIL
São Paulo 18,333
Rio de Janeiro 11,469
Belo Horizonte 5,304
Pôrto Alegre 3,795
Recife 3,527
Brasília 3,341
Salvador 3,331
Fortaleza 3,261
Curitiba 2,871
Campinas 2,640
Belém 2,097
Goiânia 1,878
Manaus 1,673
Santos 1,634
Vitória 1,602
Maceió 1,137
Natal 1,049
São Luís 982
São José dos Campos 972
João Pessoa 931
Teresina 895
Campo Grande 821
BULGARIA
Sofia 1,093
BURKINA FASO
Ouagadougou 870
BURMA (MYANMAR)
Rangoon 4,107
Mandalay 927
CAMBODIA
Phnom Penh 1,364
CAMEROON
Douala 1,980
Yaoundé 1,727
CANADA
Toronto 5,312
Montréal 3,640
Vancouver 2,188
Ottawa 1,156
Calgary 1,058
Edmonton 1,015
CHILE
Santiago 5,683
CHINA
Shanghai 14,503
Beijing 10,717
Guangzhou 8,425
Shenzhen 7,233
Wuhan 7,093
Hong Kong 7,041
Tianjin 7,040
Chongqing 6,363
Shenyang 4,720
Dongguan 4,320
Chengdu 4,065
Xi'an 3,926
Harbin 3,695
Nanjing 3,621
Guiyang 3,447
Dalian 3,073
Changchun 3,046
Zibo 2,982
Kunming 2,837
Hangzhou 2,831
Qingdao 2,817
Taiyuan 2,794
Jinan 2,743
Zhengzhou 2,590
Fuzhou 2,453
Changsha 2,451
Lanzhou 2,411
Xiamen 2,371
Shijiazhuang 2,275
Jinxi 2,268
Jilin 2,255
Wenzhou 2,212
Nanchang 2,188
Zaozhuang 2,096
Nanchong 2,046
Nanning 2,040
Linyi 2,035
Ürümqi 2,025
Yantai 1,991
Wanxian 1,963
Xuzhou 1,960
Baotou 1,920
Hefei 1,916
Suzhou 1,849
Nanyang 1,830
Tangshan 1,825
Ningbo 1,810
Datong 1,763
Yancheng 1,678
Tianmen 1,676
Shangqiu 1,650
Lu'an 1,647
Wuxi 1,646
Luoyang 1,644
Hohhot 1,644
Anshan 1,611
Qiqihar 1,607
Tai'an 1,598
Daqing 1,594
Xinghua 1,587
Pingxiang 1,562
Handan 1,535
Xiantao 1,528
Zhanjiang 1,514
Weifang 1,498
Shantou 1,495
Fushun 1,456
Xianyang 1,450
Luzhou 1,447
Neijiang 1,441
Changde 1,429
Huainan 1,420
Liuzhou 1,409
Suining, Sichuan 1,401
Quanzhou 1,377
Xintai 1,334
Mianyang 1,322
Heze 1,318
Yiyang 1,318
Yueyang 1,286
Suqian 1,258
Changzhou 1,249
Huaian 1,243
Chifeng 1,238
Jingmen 1,228
Yuzhou 1,226
Zaoyang 1,210
Huzhou 1,203
Tianshui 1,199
Yongzhou 1,182
Mudanjiang 1,171
Liupanshui 1,149
Leshan 1,143
Jining, Shandong 1,143
Xiaoshan 1,130
Yixing 1,129
Zigong 1,087
Xianyang 1,072
Fuyu 1,068
Yulin 1,060
Baoding 1,042
Xinyi, Jiangsu 1,022
Zhuzhou 1,016
Jixi 1,012
Linqing 1,009
Jiamusi 1,006
Xiangfan 1,006
Zhangjiakou 1,001
Benxi 967
Xiangxiang 936
Zhangjiagang 936
Xinyu 932
Yichun, Heilongjiang 916
Yichun, Jiangxi 890
Jinzhou 888
Zhaotong 879
Yuyao 876
Anshun 864
Hengyang 853
Xuanzhou 851
Tongliao 847
Huaibei 830
Jiaxing 817
Kaifeng 810
Fuxin 807
Hunjiang 798
COLOMBIA
Bogotá 7,594
Medellín 3,236
Cali 2,583
Barranquilla 1,918
Bucaramanga 1,069
Cartagena 1,002
Cúcuta 883
CONGO
Brazzaville 1,173
CONGO (DEM. REP.)
Kinshasa 6,049
Kolwezi 1,207
Lubumbashi 1,179
Mbuji-Mayi 1,024
COSTA RICA
San José 1,217
CROATIA
Zagreb 1,067
CUBA
Havana 2,192
CZECH REPUBLIC
Prague 1,171
DENMARK
Copenhagen 1,091
DOMINICAN REPUBLIC
Santo Domingo 2,563
Santiago de los Caballeros 804
ECUADOR
Guayaquil 2,387
Quito 1,514
EGYPT
Cairo 11,146
Alexandria 3,760
Shubrâ el Kheima 937
EL SALVADOR
San Salvador 1,517
ETHIOPIA
Addis Ababa 2,899
FINLAND
Helsinki 1,091
FRANCE
Paris 9,820
Lyons 1,403
Marseilles 1,382
Lille 1,029
Nice 889
Toulouse 761
Bordeaux 754
GEORGIA
Tbilisi 1,406
GERMANY
Berlin 3,389
Hamburg 1,740
Munich 1,263
Cologne 963
GHANA
Accra 1,981
Kumasi 1,517
GREECE
Athens 3,238
Thessaloniki 824
GUATEMALA
Guatemala City 3,242
GUINEA
Conakry 1,465
HAITI
Port-au-Prince 2,129
HONDURAS
Tegucigalpa 1,061
HUNGARY
Budapest 1,693
INDIA
Mumbai 18,336
Delhi 15,334
Kolkata 14,299
Chennai 6,915
Bangalore 6,532
Hyderabad 6,145
Ahmedabad 5,171
Pune 4,485
Surat 3,671
Kanpur 3,040
Jaipur 2,796
Lucknow 2,589
Nagpur 2,359
Patna 2,066
Indore 1,941
Vadodara 1,686
Bhopal 1,656
Coimbatore 1,628
Ludhiana 1,583
Agra 1,526
Vishakhapatnam 1,468
Cochin 1,461
Nashik 1,408
Meerut 1,340
Faridabad 1,330
Varanasi 1,300
Ghaziabad 1,277
Asansol 1,272
Jamshedpur 1,246
Madurai 1,245
Jabalpur 1,234
Rajkot 1,205
Dhanbad 1,195
Amritsar 1,162
Allahabad 1,153
Vijayawada 1,093
Srinagar 1,093
Aurangabad 1,065
Bhilainagar-Durg 1,051
Solapur 1,012
Ranchi 999
Jodhpur 954
Guwahati 941
Gwalior 939
Trivandrum 918
Calicut 917
Tiruchchirapalli 913
Chandigarh 896
Hubli-Dharwad 854
Mysore 851
INDONESIA
Jakarta 13,215
Bandung 4,126
Surabaya 2,992
Medan 2,287
Palembang 1,733
Makassar 1,284
Bandar Lampung 915
Malang 898
Tegal 898
Semarang 816
Bogor 761
IRAN
Tehran 7,352
Mashhad 2,147
Esfahan 1,547
Tabriz 1,396
Karaj 1,235
Shiraz 1,230
Qom 1,045
Ahvaz 967
Kermanshah 771
IRAQ
Baghdad 5,910
Mosul 1,236
Basra 1,187
Irbil 840
IRELAND
Dublin 1,037
ISRAEL
Tel Aviv-Yafo 3,025
Haifa 948
ITALY
Rome 3,348
Milan 2,953
Naples 2,245
Turin 1,660
Genoa 803
IVORY COAST (CÔTE D'IVOIRE)
Abidjan 3,516
JAPAN
Tokyo 12,064
Yokohama 6,427
Osaka 2,599
Nagoya 2,172
Sapporo 1,922
Kobe 1,493
Kyoto 1,468
Fukuoka 1,341
Kawasaki 1,250
Hiroshima 1,126
Kitakyushu 1,011
Sendai 1,008
Chiba 887
Sakai 792
JORDAN
Amman 1,292
KAZAKHSTAN
Almaty 1,156
KENYA
Nairobi 2,818
KOREA, NORTH
Pyŏngyang 3,351
N'ampo 1,102
Hamhung 821
KOREA, SOUTH
Seoul 9,888
Busan 3,830
Incheon 2,884
Daegu 2,675
Daejeon 1,522
Gwangju 1,379
Seognam 1,353
Ulsan 1,340
Ansan 984
Pucheon 900
Suwon 876
Pohang 790
KUWAIT
Kuwait City 1,810
KYRGYZSTAN
Bishkek 828
LATVIA
Riga 719
LEBANON
Beirut 2,070
LIBYA
Tripoli 2,098
Benghazi 1,114
MADAGASCAR
Antananarivo 1,808
MALAYSIA
Kuala Lumpur 1,405
MALI
Bamako 1,379
MEXICO
Mexico City 19,013
Guadalajara 3,905
Monterrey 3,517
Toluca 1,987
Puebla 1,880
Tijuana 1,570
Ciudad Juárez 1,469
León 1,438
Torreón 1,057
San Luis Potosí 927
Mérida 919
Querétaro 913
Mexicali 840
Culiacán 799
MONGOLIA
Ulan Bator 842
MOROCCO
Casablanca 3,743
Rabat 1,859
Fès 1,032
Marrakesh 951
MOZAMBIQUE
Maputo 1,316
NEPAL
Katmandu 1,176
NETHERLANDS
Amsterdam 1,157
Rotterdam 1,112
NEW ZEALAND
Auckland 1,152
NICARAGUA
Managua 1,165
NIGER
Niamey 997
NIGERIA
Lagos 11,135
Kano 2,884
Ibadan 2,375
Kaduna 1,329
Benin City 1,022
Ogbomosho 959
Port Harcourt 942
NORWAY
Oslo 808
PAKISTAN
Karachi 11,819
Lahore 6,373
Faisalabad 2,533
Rawalpindi 1,794
Gujranwala 1,466
Multan 1,459
Hyderabad 1,392
Peshawar 1,255
Islamabad 791
PANAMA
Panamá 1,216
PARAGUAY
Asunción 1,858
PERU
Lima 8,180
PHILIPPINES
Manila 10,677
Davao 1,326
POLAND
Warsaw 1,680
Lódz 815
PORTUGAL
Lisbon 2,761
Porto 1,309
PUERTO RICO
San Juan 2,604
ROMANIA
Bucharest 1,934
RUSSIA
Moscow 10,672
Saint Petersburg 5,315
Novosibirsk 1,425
Nizhniy Novgorod 1,288
Yekaterinburg 1,281
Samara 1,140
Omsk 1,132
Kazan 1,108
Rostov 1,081
Chelyabinsk 1,067
Ufa 1,035
Volgograd 1,016
Perm 1,014
Voronezh 918
Saratov 881
Ulyanovsk 864
Krasnoyarsk 840
Togliatti 771
SAUDI ARABIA
Riyadh 5,514
Jedda 3,807
Mecca 1,529
Medina 1,044
Dammam 920
SENEGAL
Dakar 2,313
SERBIA
Belgrade 1,116
SIERRA LEONE
Freetown 1,007
SINGAPORE
Singapore City 4,372
SOMALIA
Mogadishu 1,320
SOUTH AFRICA
Johannesburg 3,254
Cape Town 3,083
Durban 2,631
Pretoria 1,271
Vereeniging 1,027
Port Elizabeth 1,006
SPAIN
Madrid 5,608
Barcelona 4,795
SUDAN
Khartoum 4,518
SWEDEN
Stockholm 1,729
Gothenburg 829
SWITZERLAND
Zürich 1,144
SYRIA
Aleppo 2,505
Damascus 2,317
Homs 915
TAIWAN
Taipei 2,606
Kaohsiung 1,515
T'aichung 1,033
TANZANIA
Dar es Salaam 2,683
THAILAND
Bangkok 6,604
TOGO
Lomé 1,337
TUNISIA
Tunis 2,063
TURKEY
Istanbul 9,712
Ankara 3,573
Izmir 2,487
Bursa 1,414
Adana 1,245
Gaziantep 862
Konya 761
UGANDA
Kampala 1,345
UKRAINE
Kiev 2,621
Kharkov 1,521
Dnepropetrovsk 1,122
Donetsk 1,065
Odessa 1,027
Zaporozhye 863
Lvov 794
UNITED ARAB EMIRATES
Dubai 1,330
Abu Dhabi 928
UNITED KINGDOM
London 8,505
Birmingham 2,280
Manchester 2,228
Liverpool 1,519
Glasgow 1,159
UNITED STATES OF AMERICA
New York 18,718
Los Angeles 12,298
Chicago 8,814
Miami 5,434
Philadelphia 5,392
Dallas–Fort Worth 4,655
Boston 4,361
Houston 4,320
Atlanta 4,304
Washington 4,238
Detroit 4,034
Phoenix–Mesa 3,416
San Francisco 3,385
Seattle 2,989
San Diego 2,852
Minneapolis–St Paul 2,556
Tampa–St Petersburg 2,252
Denver 2,239
Baltimore 2,205
St Louis 2,159
Cleveland 1,855
Portland 1,810
Pittsburgh 1,806
Las Vegas 1,720
San Bernardino 1,690
San Jose 1,631
Cincinnati 1,599
Sacramento 1,555
Norfolk–Virginia Beach 1,460
Kansas City 1,437
San Antonio 1,436
Indianapolis 1,387
Milwaukee 1,316
Orlando 1,306
Providence 1,248
Columbus 1,236
Austin 1,107
Memphis 1,053
New Orleans 1,010
Buffalo 977
Stamford 889
Salt Lake City 888
Jacksonville 882
Louisville 864
Hartford 852
Richmond 819
Charlotte 759
URUGUAY
Montevideo 1,353
UZBEKISTAN
Tashkent 2,181
VENEZUELA
Caracas 3,276
Valencia 2,330
Maracaibo 2,182
Maracay 1,138
Ciudad Guayana 966
Barquisimeto 923
VIETNAM
Ho Chi Minh City 5,065
Hanoi 4,164
Haiphong 1,873
YEMEN
Sana' 1,801
ZAMBIA
Lusaka 1,450
ZIMBABWE
Harare 1,527
Bulawayo 824

In many ways this image represents 21st-century world farming and how it may develop. It shows 25 combine harvesters on a huge farm in Mato Grosso state, western Brazil. They are harvesting soybeans (or soya beans), a crop where much of the world's production is from GM seed. Brazil is the second largest world producer and exporter after the US, followed by Argentina and Paraguay. This crop requires a hot summer to grow well and much land has been cleared in South America in order to grow it on a massive scale. Soybeans contain twice the protein of any other vegetable crop and there is a high demand from Asia as well as the food-processing industry, where it is used as a protein "extender" in pre-prepared meals. But is this type of large-scale farming desirable or sustainable?

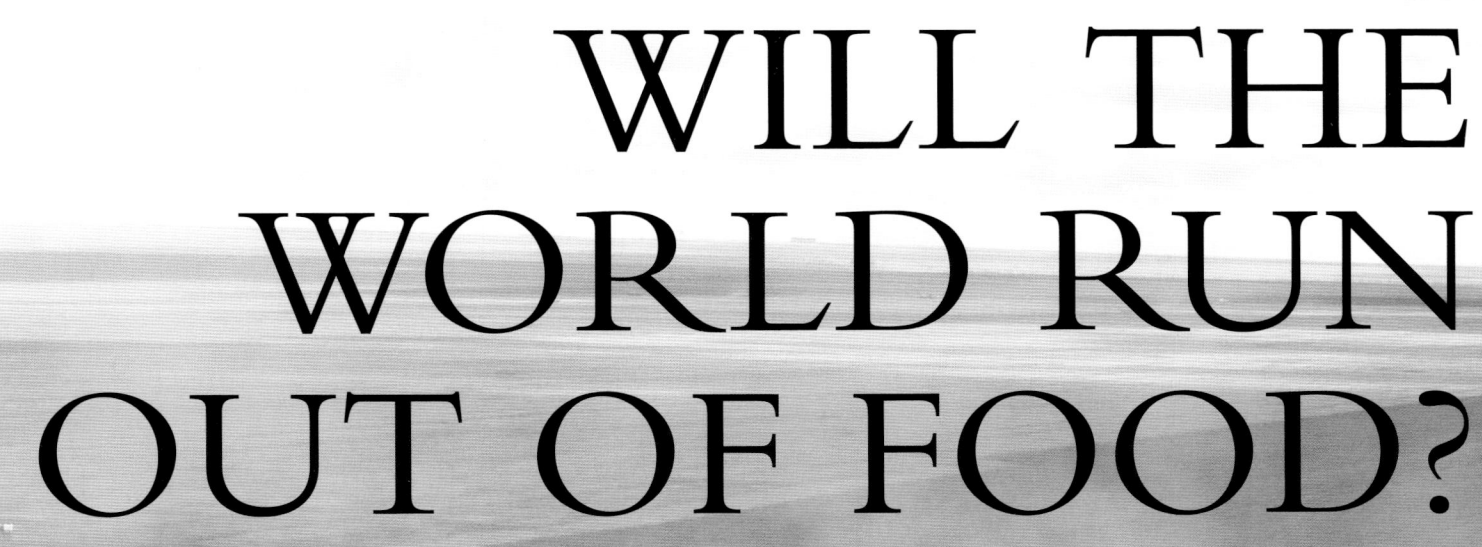

WILL THE WORLD RUN OUT OF FOOD?

For more information:

80 Temperature and precipitation

82 Climate change and global warming

84 Water distribution

88 Population

98 Minerals

▼ Supermarkets in the developed world carry a huge variety of fresh foods from all over the world, much of it out of season. A modern supermarket can often stock in excess of 130 varieties of vegetables and fruit for sale at any one time, much of it flown in chilled from abroad. As well as being extremely costly, these flights produce CO_2 emissions and, because of the high water content of fruit and vegetables, effectively export water and nutrients from countries that can often ill afford to do so. However, they do provide much needed income and employment for the producing country. By comparison, the market in the photograph (below right) only sells produce which can be grown locally and carried there, with no consequent CO_2 cost.

At current rates of growth, the world's population will increase to 9 billion people by 2050, from just over 6.5 billion today. To sustain this population there will have to be a 40% increase in food production which, as now, will have to be grown on the fertile soils irregularly distributed across just 11% of the Earth's surface. In addition, the fast growing and increasingly better-off economies of countries such as China and India are demanding a wider variety and better food in their diets, with many people eating more meat. However, the global trend in population is for people to move off the land toward the cities, resulting in fewer people to produce the food.

Similar conditions have been faced before: in 1898, the eminent Victorian scientist Sir William Crookes predicted that "England and all the civilized nations stand in deadly peril of not having enough to eat." But by 1909 the process to make synthetic nitrogen fertilizer from ammonia (the Haber-Bosch method) had been developed in Germany and Crookes' concerns were forgotten. Artificial nitrogen fixation has been a major factor in enabling the world's population to grow to today's levels. The process uses about 2% of the world's total energy demand to produce more than 100 million tonnes of nitrogen fertilizer, which helps feed about 30% of the world's population.

The issues in the developed world revolve around the quality and quantity of what we eat. The range of food available to consumers in a modern supermarket shows the extent to which food products are transported from around the world to satisfy the perceived need for such a wide variety of choice. There are also huge economic pressures from parts of the processed food industry to entice people in the developed world to eat more than is actually good for them. By comparison, in the developing world many struggle to achieve the minimum food intake to sustain life. Globally, about 1 billion people are malnourished and 1 billion are overweight. One of the biggest problems society faces is balancing this inequality of distribution, not only of food, but also of wealth.

Without the application of fertilizers, we would have been unable to sustain our historic growth rates of agricultural production. Yet the production of these is under pressure. The supply of phosphate rock, which occurs naturally and is currently the major source of phosphorus fertilizer (an essential plant nutrient), is predicted to peak in the 2030s and could be exhausted within 50 years or so, at the current rate of use. More phosphate rock is available but it would cost more to extract and contains cadmium and other contaminants, further increasing the cost of converting it into fertilizer. Nitrogen fertilizer currently uses expensive fossil fuels for its production, although an alternative production process using renewable hydro-electricity has been developed.

At the same time as the demand for food has increased, in recent years the demand for so-called "green" biofuels, derived from plant products, has also had an inflationary effect on prices by reducing the amount of land on which food can be grown.

In addition, because of the increase in the global demand for meat, more agricultural land is being used to grow crops to feed livestock, again pushing up the price of staple foods. This rise in prices disproportionately affects poorer developing economies, where a much higher proportion of family income is spent on food, perhaps as high as 50–70%.

SOIL FERTILITY

The map shows all soils, whether currently used for agriculture or covered by forest, grassland etc.

As much as 90% of all food is grown in soil, but fertile soil irregularly covers only 11% of the global land surface and is a non-renewable asset. Some soils are naturally fertile, such as the Black Earths of Russia and Ukraine. Natural soil fertility results from a combination of a temperate climate and nutrient-rich rocks that slowly weather. Those soils which are not naturally fertile, or which have been degraded by erosion or over-exploitation, require the incorporation of manures and fertilizers to improve soil fertility and maximize production.

This fragile asset is under threat from effects such as erosion and desertification, acidification, salinization, pollution and compaction (modern farm machinery gets heavier each year as its size increases).

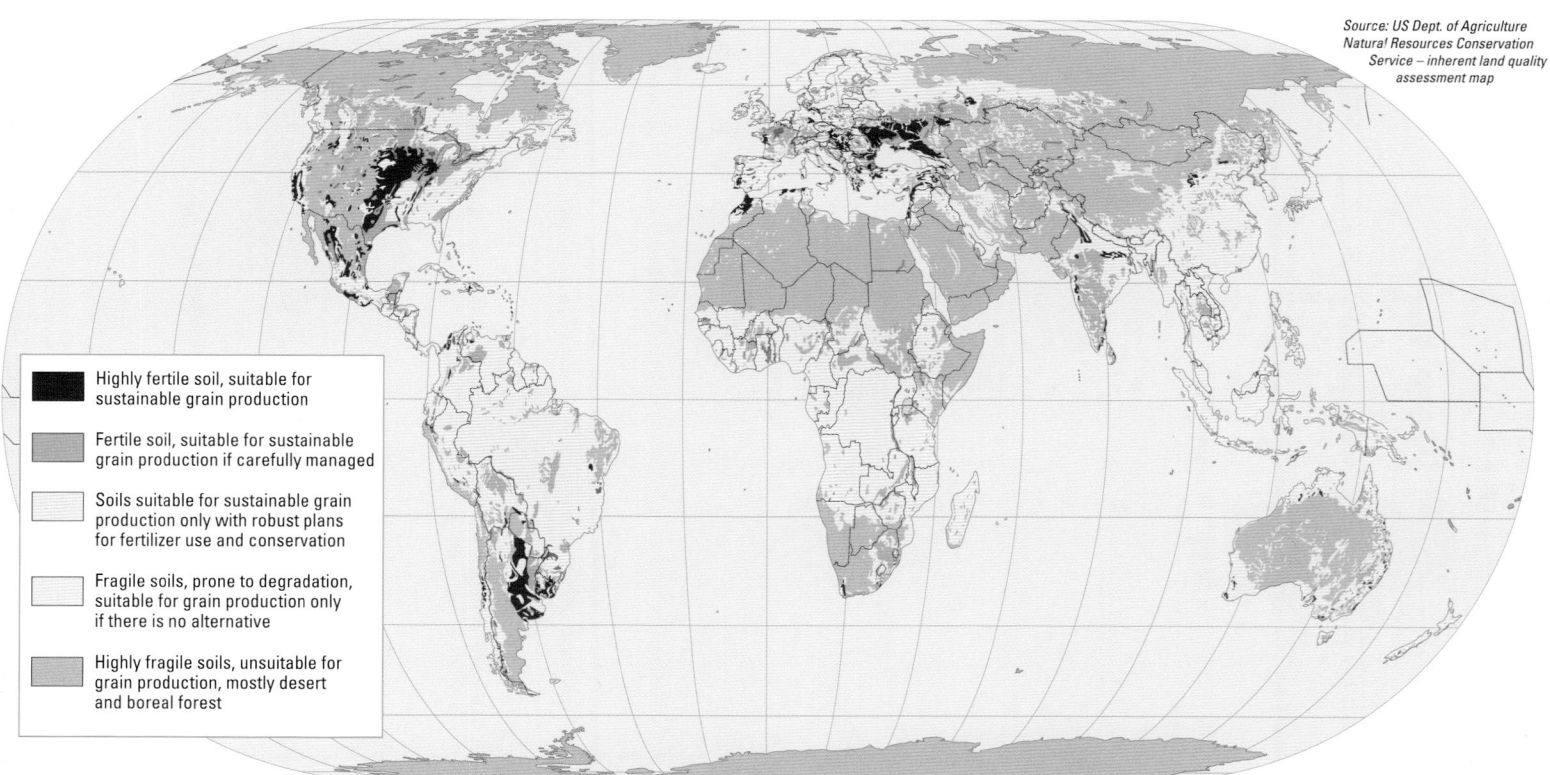

Source: US Dept. of Agriculture Natural Resources Conservation Service – inherent land quality assessment map

Highly fertile soil, suitable for sustainable grain production

Fertile soil, suitable for sustainable grain production if carefully managed

Soils suitable for sustainable grain production only with robust plans for fertilizer use and conservation

Fragile soils, prone to degradation, suitable for grain production only if there is no alternative

Highly fragile soils, unsuitable for grain production, mostly desert and boreal forest

SOIL DEGRADATION

Areas of concern

- Areas of serious concern
- Areas of some concern
- Stable terrain
- Non-vegetated land

Causes of soil degradation (by region)

- Grazing practices
- Other agricultural practices
- Industrialization
- Deforestation
- Fuelwood collection

An estimated 75 billion tonnes of soil comprising 10 million hectares of potentially usable arable land are annually degraded or lost due to erosion. Current rates of loss in China are 57 times the rate of soil creation; in Europe the rate is 17 times and in the US 10 times. There have been frightening predictions of the loss of all fertile soil within 60 years.

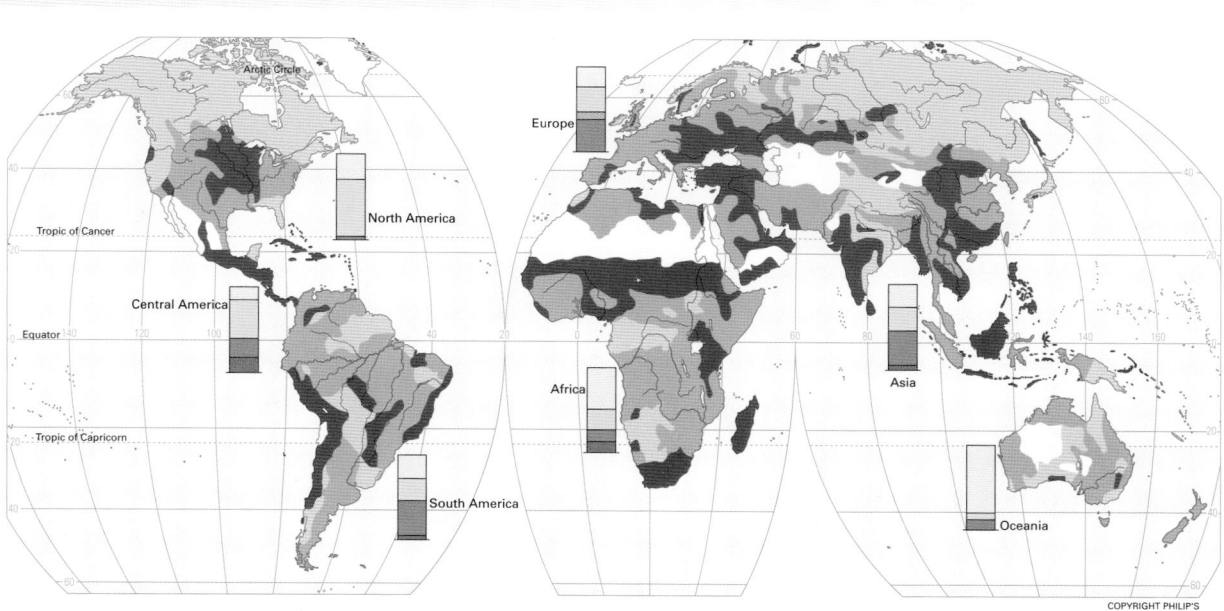

COPYRIGHT PHILIP'S

WORLD CROP PRODUCTION

ROOTS AND TUBERS

- Yams 7.1%
- Other 2.8%
- Sweet potatoes 15.1%
- Potatoes 43.1%
- Cassava 31.9%

World total (2008): 729.6 million tonnes

OIL CROPS

- Olives 2.4%
- Other 3.5%
- Sunflower seeds 4.8%
- Groundnuts 5.2%
- Rapeseed 7.8%
- Coconuts 8.3%
- Seed cotton 8.9%
- Soybeans 31.3%
- Oil palm fruit 27.8%

World total (2008): 738.8 million tonnes

CEREALS

- Rye 0.7%
- Oats 1.0%
- Millet 1.4%
- Sorghum 2.6%
- Barley 6.2%
- Triticale 0.6%
- Other 0.4%
- Maize 32.6%
- Rice paddy 27.1%
- Wheat 27.3%

World total (2008): 2,252.0 million tonnes

BIOFUELS

Industrialized countries, looking to reduce their reliance on fossil fuels such as oil and gas, are setting targets for "bioenergy" production, i.e. energy from renewable sources such as maize, sugarcane, potatoes, or manioc. The EU has decided that 10% of its fuel for transport should be from these sources – mostly bioethanol – by 2020. This demand is resulting in both developed and developing countries converting food crops into bioethanol, jeopardizing food supplies. A major push by the US for bioethanol, coupled with poor harvests in Europe, Australia and the other grain-exporting countries, pushed grain prices up to unusually high levels in late 2007 and 2008; the poor suffered as a result.

This may be overcome as "first generation" biofuels – arable crops, which need fertilizers so the energy balance is not good – are replaced by "second generation" bioenergy crops such as willow and miscanthus grass, which need little if any fertilizer and can be grown on poorer soils not used for food crops.

GLOBAL LAND USAGE

Most suitable land for agriculture is already in use and much is lost to development and erosion each year. The amount of extra land for agriculture is very limited unless we cut down forests or plow up old grasslands, which results in the release of CO_2 into the atmosphere.

- Desert, mountain & ice 31.8%
- Forest 30.3%
- Meadows & pastures 26.0%
- Cereals 4.6%
- Other arable & permanent crops 7.3%

World total (2008): 13,009.1 million hectares

THE GREEN REVOLUTION

Fifty years ago there was a food crisis in the developing world, which was tackled by the so-called "Green Revolution." This combined the breeding of sturdy disease-resistant dwarf crop varieties with the use of irrigation, synthetic fertilizers, and chemical pesticides. Productivity per acre increased by up to 300%. Thus, countries that had only been able to grow enough for their own needs drove down the cost of food and became net exporters of food. Currently, 30–50% of crop yields can be attributed to fertilizer use.

Without fertilizer, under an ideal climate and with adequate pest and disease control, a wheat grain yield of 2–3 tonnes per hectare can be achieved; however, without good pest and disease control, 1 tonne per hectare is more likely. This can be compared with average wheat yields of about 8 tonnes per hectare in the UK, and the current (at the time of going to press) world record wheat yield in New Zealand of 15.6 tonnes per hectare.

The benefits of the Green Revolution plateaued out in the 1990s. There is now the need for a new phase to reinvigorate production to feed 9 billion people.

Using the latest technology to increase the worst yields to match the average, and the average to match the best, would transform food supplies.

YIELDS OF WHEAT GRAIN GROWN IN BROADBALK, ROTHAMSTED, FROM 1852 TO 2005

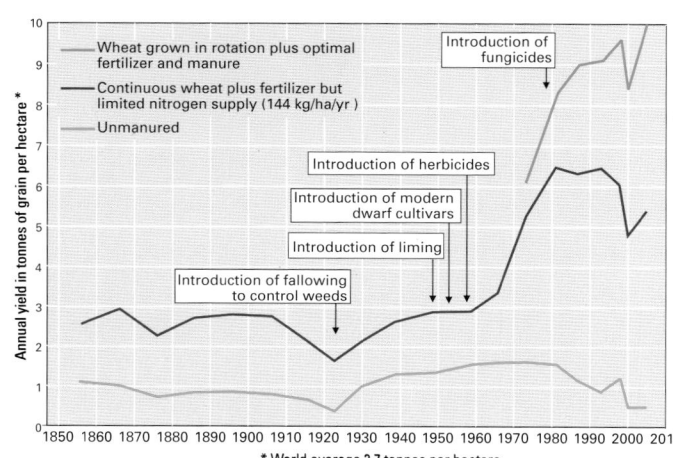

- Wheat grown in rotation plus optimal fertilizer and manure
- Continuous wheat plus fertilizer but limited nitrogen supply (144 kg/ha/yr)
- Unmanured
- Introduction of fungicides
- Introduction of herbicides
- Introduction of modern dwarf cultivars
- Introduction of liming
- Introduction of fallowing to control weeds

Annual yield in tonnes of grain per hectare *

* World average 2.7 tonnes per hectare

LIVESTOCK

As can be seen on the graph below, world livestock production has increased dramatically over the last half century. Currently, over a third of the world's grain is fed to livestock for intensive stock raising, rising to 70% in developed countries where there is higher meat consumption per person.

Animals (and humans) are very inefficient in their utilization of nutrients – generally less than 20% of the nitrogen in their food is used; the rest is excreted, causing problems for recycling and the risk of environmental impact. Methane emissions from cattle are also a major contributor to greenhouse gases in the atmosphere. Additionally, meat is very expensive in terms of water consumption; for example, 1 lb [0.5 kg] of beef requires 1,857 gallons [8,442 liters] of water to produce it, taking account of the water used to grow feed, etc.

The adoption of vegetarianism has been suggested as a possible solution to some of these problems. However, even if this proved acceptable to the majority population, land in many parts of the world is suitable only for livestock production by extensive grazing. In any case, developing countries, which were previously predominantly vegetarian, are demanding more meat, regarded in some societies as a measurement of status. For example, Chinese meat consumption has risen from 9 lb [4 kg] per person in 1960 to 119 lb [54 kg] today. This compares with a figure of 176 lb [80 kg] in the UK and 254 lb [115 kg] in the United States.

WORLD LIVESTOCK PRODUCTION

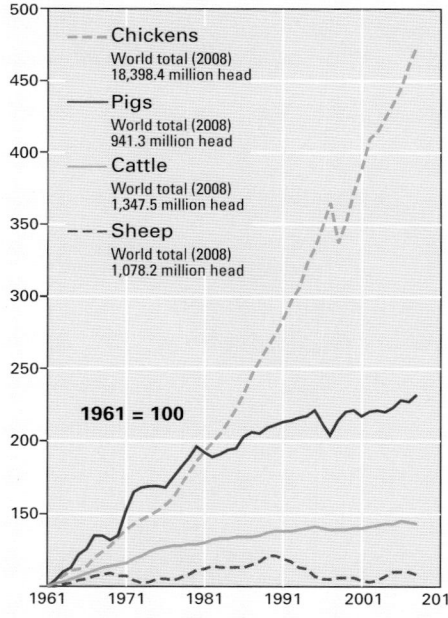

- Chickens
  World total (2008)
  18,398.4 million head
- Pigs
  World total (2008)
  941.3 million head
- Cattle
  World total (2008)
  1,347.5 million head
- Sheep
  World total (2008)
  1,078.2 million head

1961 = 100

◄ The top lines on the graph show the effects of fertilizers and other developments in agricultural practice on wheat production over time, in the longest running trial of this type. The Broadbalk Wheat Experiment at Rothamsted Research in the UK has been running on the same field since 1843. The lower line represents the same crop grown in the same conditions, but with none of these inputs applied – the equivalent of yields in many parts of the developing world.

FOOD & POPULATION

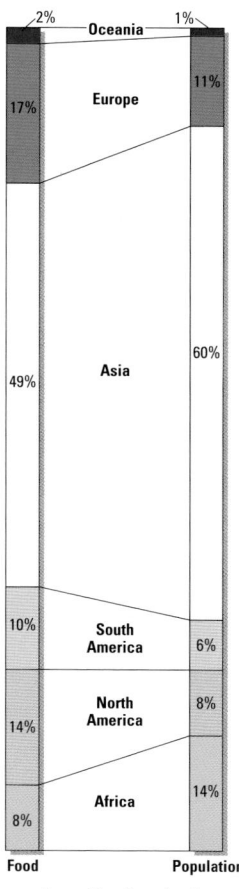

	Food	Population
Oceania	2%	1%
Europe	17%	11%
Asia	49%	60%
South America	10%	6%
North America	14%	8%
Africa	8%	14%

Comparison of food production and population by continent
The left column indicates the proportion of world food production and the right shows population in proportion.

IRRIGATION

By 2030 there will be a 30% increase in water demand to support the world's population and its value will soar, so more efficient methods of collection and delivery will have to be developed.

China currently has 23% of the world's population, but only 11% of its water. The country is therefore building new reservoirs to catch runoff from Himalayan glaciers. Their efforts have, however, already resulted in a conference of the countries downstream on the Mekong River to discuss how to tackle the resultant reduced water flow.

Since over 71% of the Earth's surface is covered in water, it can hardly be said to be in short supply. However, less than 3% of this is fresh water and, of that, over two-thirds is frozen in ice caps and glaciers. The world, therefore, will never run out of water as such, but its over-exploitation in developed areas and availability in regions where it is scarce are major problems.

For more information:

84 Water distribution

85 Natural vegetation

86 Biodiversity and the natural world

▼ If the ever-increasing world demand for food continues, it is likely that more intensive livestock production units will have to be adopted. Pictured below, this battery farm for chickens is in the US. In the past, these units have been synonymous in many people's minds with cruelty to the animals and issues associated with the spread of disease.

The growth of food crops in a protected environment without the use of soil as the growing medium will also become more widespread. In hydroponics the plants grow in nutrient-enriched water, as can be seen in the picture below right, taken at a research establishment in California.

How can we feed 9 billion people adequately and sustainably? There are some simple solutions that we should note before looking at more complicated and technological "fixes." Most agree that we should not be taking more land from forest and other uncropped areas into production because of the release of CO_2 that this would cause and the adverse impacts on predicted climate change and biodiversity. As already noted on page 11, enabling those producing the lowest yields to produce national average yields, and those producing average yields to equal the best, would transform food production. This is likely to involve better pest and disease control, and more widespread and effective use of fertilizers. The Alliance for the Green Revolution in Africa (AGRA), with initial support from the Rockefeller Foundation and the Bill and Melinda Gates Foundation, is looking to achieve this.

It is important to control pests and diseases in growing crops, but post-harvest crop losses from molds, insects, rodents, and birds are 10–40% of the total, according to the FAO. Again, the application of existing technologies could avoid these and make a significant impact on food supplies. Finally, the avoidance of waste would also make an important contribution in developed countries.

But if this is not sufficient, what then? The UK's Royal Society published a report in 2009 entitled "Reaping the benefits. Science and the sustainable intensification of global agriculture." It suggested that we will need to increase crop production but without cultivating more land, while sustaining the environment, preserving natural resources, and supporting farmers' livelihoods: that is, produce more using less and with less of an impact. The Royal Society saw good soil management, maintaining or enhancing crop genetic diversity, and introducing pest and disease resistance, as well as better nitrogen-use efficiency through GM technologies, as key to this.

Research is in progress now at such centers as the International Rice Research Institute in the Philippines and the John Innes Centre in the UK to develop cereals (rice and wheat, for example) that fix their own nitrogen and so do not need nitrogen fertilizer. Possible problems here are the carbon/energy cost to the plant of accommodating the nitrogen-fixing organisms or traits, and the consequent likely reductions in yield. In the longer-term, and even more aspirational, there is the idea of perennial cereals such as wheat, maize, and rice that would not need to be replanted each year, but would regrow and yield each year in the same way as a fruit tree.

However, some reject such technological approaches, saying that reliance on chemical fertilizers and pesticides is a threat to sustainability. They advocate extensive systems that could be viewed as "organic," "biodynamic" or "ecological." But these mostly involve mixed systems rather than the specialist crop or livestock production systems that dominate most developed countries, crop rotations to control pests and diseases, and legumes to supply nitrogen.

Finally, we must note the increasing interest in healthy eating and the efforts of many governments to promote this, mostly with a view to reducing obesity and other diet-induced health problems. This may well drive food production in a particular direction.

NITROGEN – THE KEY TO CROP GROWTH

In most countries, nitrogen is the main yield-determining plant nutrient; exceptions are areas where degraded soils are deficient in phosphorus, such as in parts of Africa and Australia. Adequate inputs of nitrogen are therefore essential for food security.

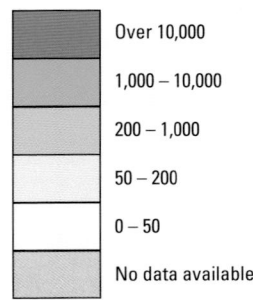

Total nitrogen fertilizer consumption in thousand tonnes (2007)

Over 10,000

1,000 – 10,000

200 – 1,000

50 – 200

0 – 50

No data available

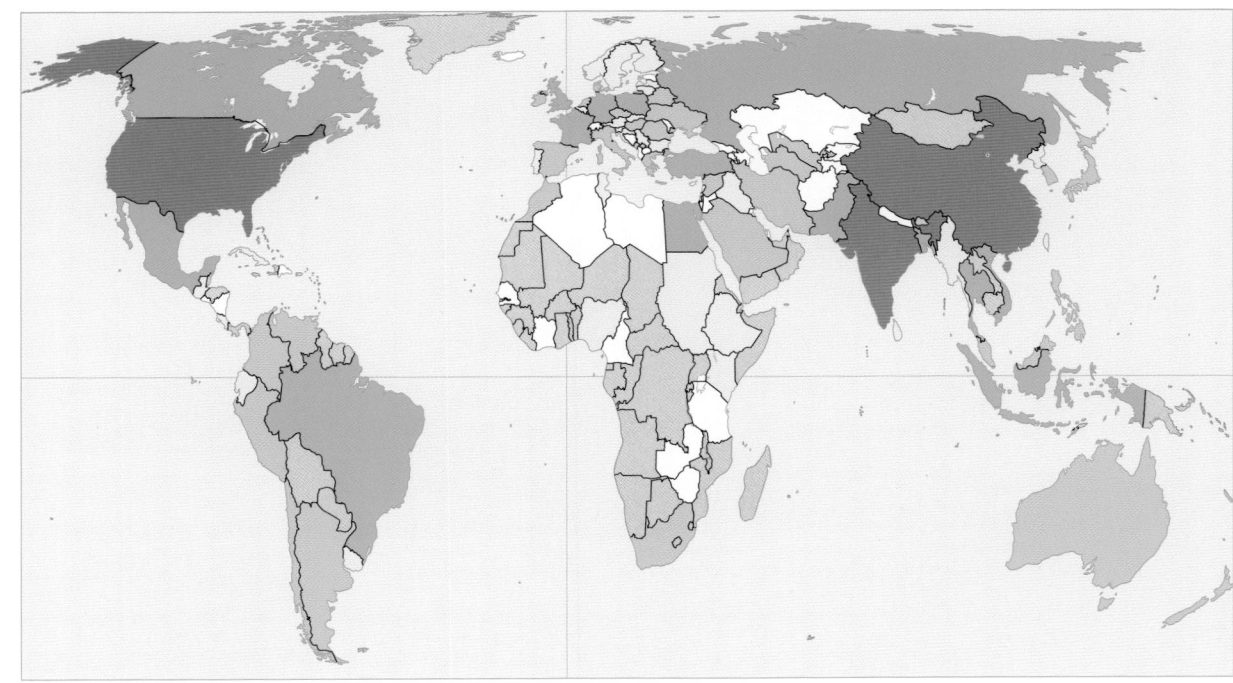

The map shows nitrogen fertilizer inputs across the world. This, in a very real sense, is an index of food production. However, producing nitrogen fertilizer requires energy, so many see a system in which the nitrogen is brought in (or fixed) by legumes such as clover and alfalfa (lucerne) as being more sustainable. However, the problem with such systems is that, in general, while the legume is being grown, a food crop is not being produced (apart from livestock that may graze the legume). In addition, pollution in the form of nitrogen losses to air and water from legume-based systems can be as large as those from fertilizers, and the energy needed to produce fertilizers could be obtained from renewable sources.

PESTS, DISEASES AND WEEDS

Currently, 30% of the world's crop yield is lost because of the effects of pests, diseases, and weeds. Chemical controls (such as herbicides and fungicides) continue to be effective but are disliked by many.

REACH is a new EU regulation on chemicals and their safe use. It deals with the *R*egistration, *E*valuation, *A*uthorization and restriction of *CH*emical substances, and severely limits those chemicals that growers can use.

Because of this, research is focusing on isolating pest and disease resistance genes or traits using molecular methods. Breeding for resistance, transferring these identified traits into crop plants and animals, can be done using conventional plant breeding methods but is much quicker using GM methods (see below right).

Crop rotations can be used to control pests, diseases and weeds, as can mechanical methods, cultivations, and inter-cropping (that is, mixing crops) and trap crops (which protect the main crop from pests).

Although climate change is not accepted by some, whatever happens in the future, changing weather patterns have already caused the movement of pests and diseases around the world.

One example of this is "bluetongue," which has been monitored and action taken to prevent serious impact on food production in Europe. This disease, which affects livestock, has been spread by a species of tiny biting midge from sub-Saharan Africa into north-west Europe since 2006, before which it was never recorded in Europe.

A sustained research program, vector surveillance, restrictions on animal movements, and a vaccination program have helped limit the spread of the disease in the UK.

This map shows the spread of the disease between 2006 and 2009 in Europe as a whole.

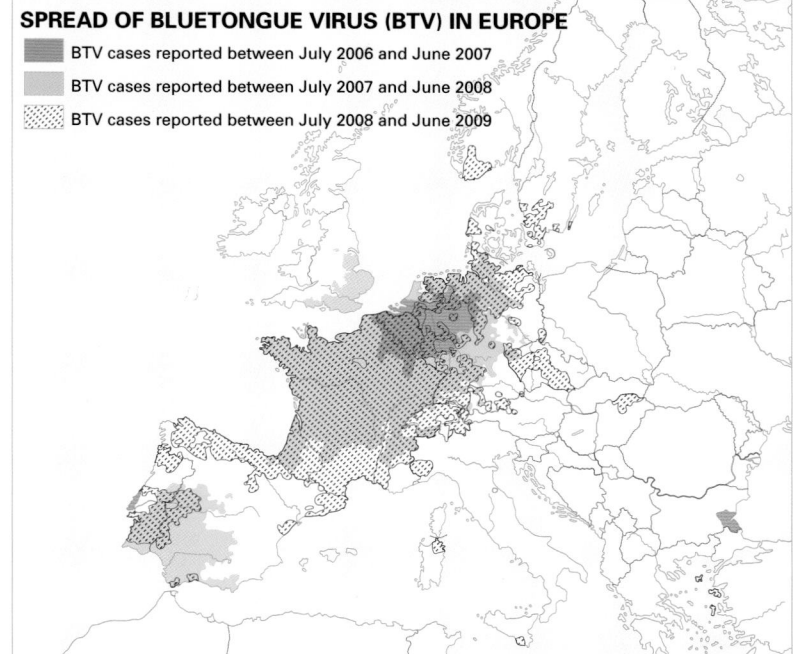

SPREAD OF BLUETONGUE VIRUS (BTV) IN EUROPE
- BTV cases reported between July 2006 and June 2007
- BTV cases reported between July 2007 and June 2008
- BTV cases reported between July 2008 and June 2009

AQUACULTURE

With a greater demand in some western countries for increased fish content in their diets, at the same time as fish stocks in the oceans are becoming depleted from overfishing, fish farming or "aquaculture" has become more important.

The term covers both salt and freshwater fish, and shellfish, but has the same inherent issues as livestock farming in relation to pollution and pest and disease problems. It contributes about a third of the total world fish catch, with carp, oysters, clams, salmon, mussels, and scallops forming some of the major varieties. China, India, and Southeast Asia, where it has always been important for local consumption, are the biggest producers.

It is estimated that 90% of the USA's consumption of shrimps are farmed and imported.

CUTTING BACK ON FOOD WASTE

Major retailers can be fussy because they know that their customers are fussy. Over 30 years ago, the singer Joni Mitchell wrote "Give me spots on my apples, but leave me the birds and bees," but not much has changed. The US Government has estimated that currently 60 million tonnes of food worth $5 billion is left in the fields because it is regarded as being of poor quality and unsaleable. More is left unsold in shops and discarded: in the UK it is estimated that 8.3 million tonnes of food worth £20 billion is sent to landfill each year, and some people now live on the food shops' throwaway ("Dumpster Diving" in the US; "Skipping" in the UK). A further fraction is bought but never consumed. It is estimated that food wasted by the US and Europe could feed the world three times over. Food waste now accounts for more than a quarter of the total freshwater consumption and 300 million barrels of oil per year. Clearly using this waste would make a big impact and must be part of sustainable food supply.

GENETIC MODIFICATION (GM)

Mankind has undertaken selective breeding of crops and livestock for thousands of years, to maintain and improve their most desirable characteristics. In the past 20–30 years, molecular genetics has increasingly been used to guide crop breeding. Biotechnological tools, such as molecular markers and genetic modification (GM), can complement conventional breeding processes to improve almost all important traits, including yield potential, plant structure, tolerance to abiotic stress (that is, salinity, cold, acidity), disease resistances, food and nutritional quality, and market preference.

GM critics suggest that there may be unforeseen effects on human health and the environment. However, in Europe and elsewhere, detailed risk analysis of potential effects of GM crops is made before licences to release the technology are granted. For example, UK Farm Scale Evaluations compared the effects on farmland biodiversity of growing conventional and GM (herbicide-resistant) sugar beet, maize, and oilseed rape. It was found that the species of crop grown (that is, beet, maize or rape) had a greater impact on biodiversity than whether the crop was GM or conventional.

Some would claim proven benefits and GM crops are currently grown in more than 23 countries, on over 114 million hectares worldwide, equivalent to about 5% of global cultivated land. These include eight EU states: Spain, France, Czech Republic, Portugal, Poland, Germany, Slovak Republic, and Romania. In addition, eight countries now grow more than 1 million hectares of GM crops: USA, Canada, China, India, South Africa, Paraguay, Argentina, and Brazil.

A major obstacle for GM acceptance is public perception of the technology. Biotechnology is only part of the solution; research in sustainable agriculture will provide new methods of crop and soil management, and support the development of improved varieties by both conventional breeding and GM.

IMPROVED LAND MANAGEMENT

Improved land management has a large part to play in improving food production. Many soils have been compacted through the use of heavy machinery or by regular plowing, which causes a "plow pan" (a thin compacted layer of soil) to develop just below the bottom of the plow. Other soils have been allowed to become acid or saline through acid rain, the inappropriate use of fertilizers or other amendments, or polluted by toxic metals such as cadmium, nickel, and copper, or by organic pollutants through the use of human and animal "wastes."

Conservation agriculture that includes "no-till" and "min-till" has many benefits in terms of allowing a stable and good soil structure to develop, retaining organic matter, nutrients and moisture. But perennial weeds can be a problem on "heavy" clay soils, requiring a greater use of herbicides.

Strip tillage (cultivating only a narrow strip in which the crop is planted) saves energy use, maintains a soil cover (preventing erosion), and generally carries the benefits of conservation tillage.

In the longer-term, "controlled traffic" in which tractors and other equipment travel along fixed paths, or in which equipment is run from gantries, all linked to GPS, are precision farming systems that would contribute to a high-tech solution to food security.

One matter still to be resolved is the importance of the biodiversity of soil organisms and micro-organisms (for example, earthworms, mycorrhizal fungi, bacteria) to soil fertility and thus sustainable food production. Plants can be grown in sand culture or hydroponics, suggesting that organisms, let alone biodiversity, are not essential. However, for many this is the key to a truly sustainable system based on soil.

THE FUTURE

If we adopt and develop appropriate techniques and practices, and modify our behavior, we stand a good chance of feeding the future, predominantly urban, world population. The image at bottom left shows one of several proposals for a new development currently under discussion: the "vertical farm," this from Plantagon International. Theoretically, this would consist of a giant self-contained production unit, enabling crop production to take place in a controlled environment, regardless of climatic variations, and situated within urban regions, the main areas of consumption.

Its proponents also claim that crops will be able to be grown throughout the year, making one acre in the controlled environment the equivalent of many times more acres grown outdoors. They also say that the units would grow the crops organically, would reduce runoff pollution, and would also ease the pressure on water demand by recycling the water used from evapotranspiration.

However, whether or not we can afford proposals such as these, it still seems likely that parts of the world will still be using subsistence agriculture to feed themselves (such as in the photograph at upper left, taken in southern Africa). Brazil, though, has developed from primarily subsistence agriculture to "modern" intensive methods, and China and India are currently undergoing a similar process. As people move away from the land to live in the growing urban centers, farm sizes can grow and opportunities, created by economies of scale, may evolve to improve the lifestyle of the subsistence farmer.

Whatever develops, it will be our choices that will influence it. What is your concept of a sustainable system of food supply that can feed 9 billion people and provide a livelihood for producers?

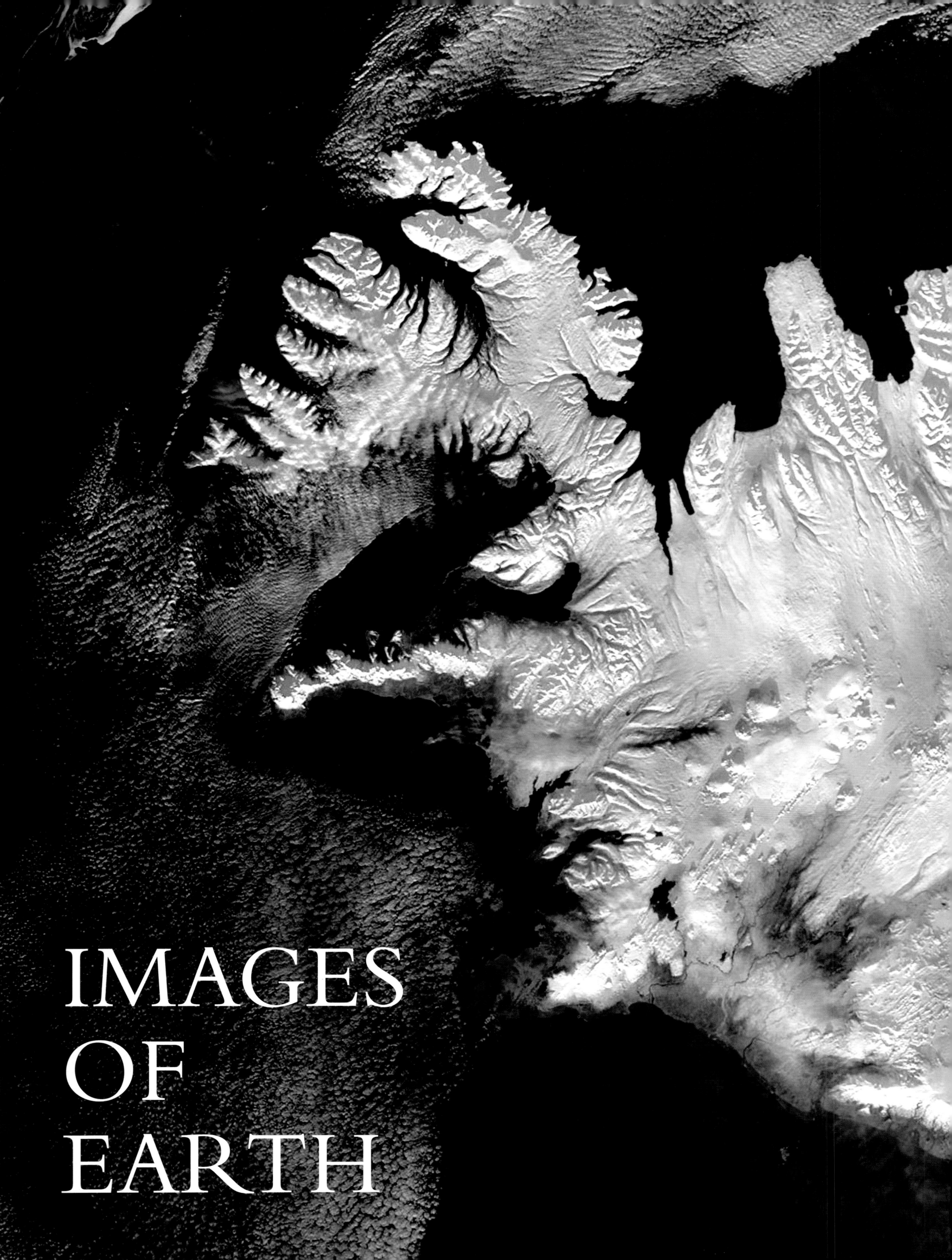

IMAGES
OF
EARTH

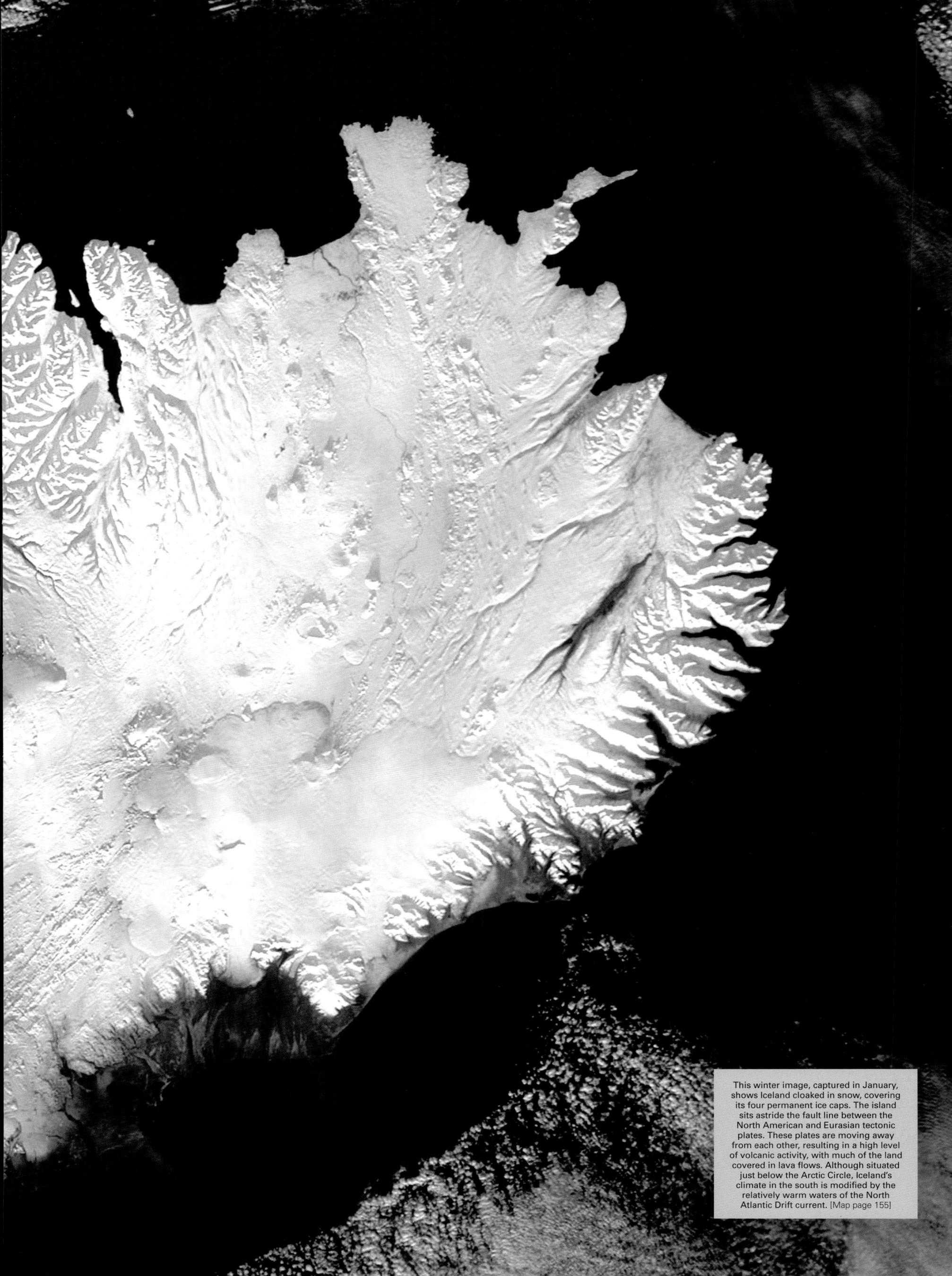

This winter image, captured in January, shows Iceland cloaked in snow, covering its four permanent ice caps. The island sits astride the fault line between the North American and Eurasian tectonic plates. These plates are moving away from each other, resulting in a high level of volcanic activity, with much of the land covered in lava flows. Although situated just below the Arctic Circle, Iceland's climate in the south is modified by the relatively warm waters of the North Atlantic Drift current. [Map page 155]

The River Thames snakes from Chelsea Bridge in the west to Tower Bridge in the east in this image covering both the West End and City of London. Despite having a population in excess of 8 million people, there are still many parks and open spaces around the city center. St James's Park, Green Park and part of Hyde Park, together with Buckingham Palace and its gardens, can be seen center left of the image and farther north the eastern edge of Regent's Park can be seen. Just below the title, the newly developing area around St Pancras, the terminus of the direct high-speed rail link to Europe, can be seen. *(Digital Globe)* [Map page 125]

Built on over 100 small islands in a shallow lagoon, this image shows the largest island on which the main city is built, with the islands of San Michele and Murano to the north. The sinuous Grand Canal connects the train station in the northwest to St Mark's Square in the south, with a network of smaller canals on either side. Since the beginning of the last century the city has been slowly sinking into the mud, due to water extraction on the mainland combined with tidal action. The former has now been stopped and there are plans for a barrage to control tidal surges in the lagoon. *(Satellite image courtesy of Space Imaging)* [Map page 199]

On the sheltered southern slopes of the Elburz (Alborz) Mountains, the street layout of Tehran, the capital city of Iran, with a population of over 7 million people, can be clearly seen toward the bottom left-hand side of this image. However, it is the dissected parallel ridges of the mountains and the spectacular snow-covered peak of Demavend that dominate this scene. At 18,386 ft [5,604 m], the peak is the highest in the Middle East and is an extinct stratovolcano. There have been no eruptions in the recorded past, but there are still active hot springs on its slopes and two small glaciers on its northern side. [Map page 41]

The ancient city of Kabul, believed to
have been founded over 3,000 years ago,
is situated at the head of the triangular-
shaped valley seen just to the left of
center of this image. At a height of 5,900 ft
[1,800 m] above sea level, this capital city of
over 3 million inhabitants sits on an upland
plateau, south of the main Hindu Kush
mountain range. The average summer high
temperature is 90°F [32°C] and the winter
low is 19°F [–7°C], with dry summers and
rainfall concentrated between January
and April. The runways of the international
airport can clearly be seen to the northwest
of the city in this image, but the US airbase
at Bagram is 27 miles [47 km] north of
Kabul, south of Chārīkār. [Map page 240]

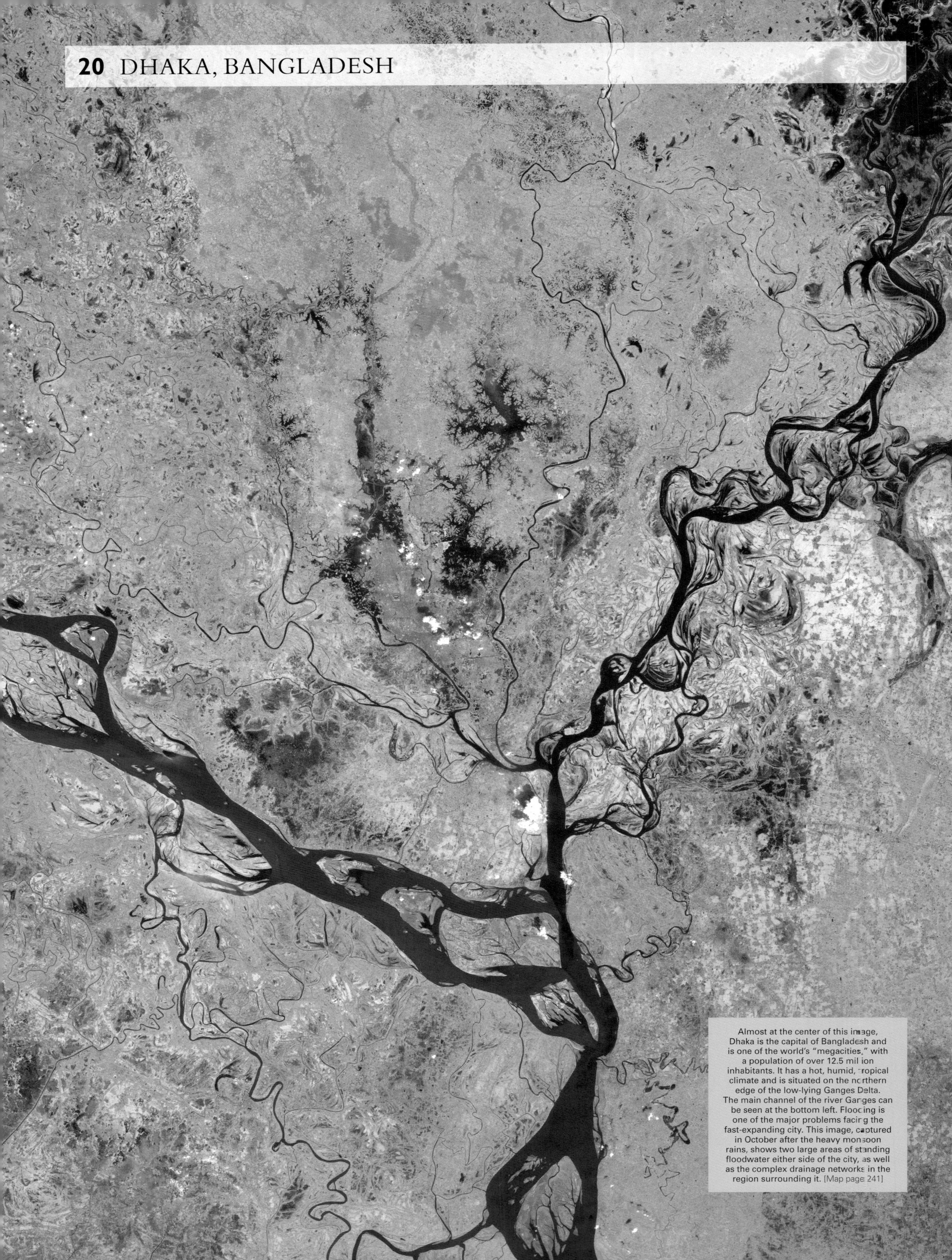

Almost at the center of this image, Dhaka is the capital of Bangladesh and is one of the world's "megacities," with a population of over 12.5 million inhabitants. It has a hot, humid, tropical climate and is situated on the northern edge of the low-lying Ganges Delta. The main channel of the river Ganges can be seen at the bottom left. Flooding is one of the major problems facing the fast-expanding city. This image, captured in October after the heavy monsoon rains, shows two large areas of standing floodwater either side of the city, as well as the complex drainage networks in the region surrounding it. [Map page 241]

This image shows Shanghai, lower left, in its setting on the south bank of the mouth of the Chang Jiang (Yangtse) river. Since it sits at the gateway to one of China's richest regions and the river is navigable for ocean-going vessels up to Hankou, a further 600 miles [1,000 km] inland, it has developed to become the world's largest cargo port. It has grown rapidly with the booming Chinese economy to become the largest city in China, with a population of over 14 million. Much new development has taken place, including the newly expanded airport, which can be seen on the coast at Pudong and which is linked to the city by high-speed Maglev train. [Map page 138]

22 NOUAKCHOTT, MAURITANIA

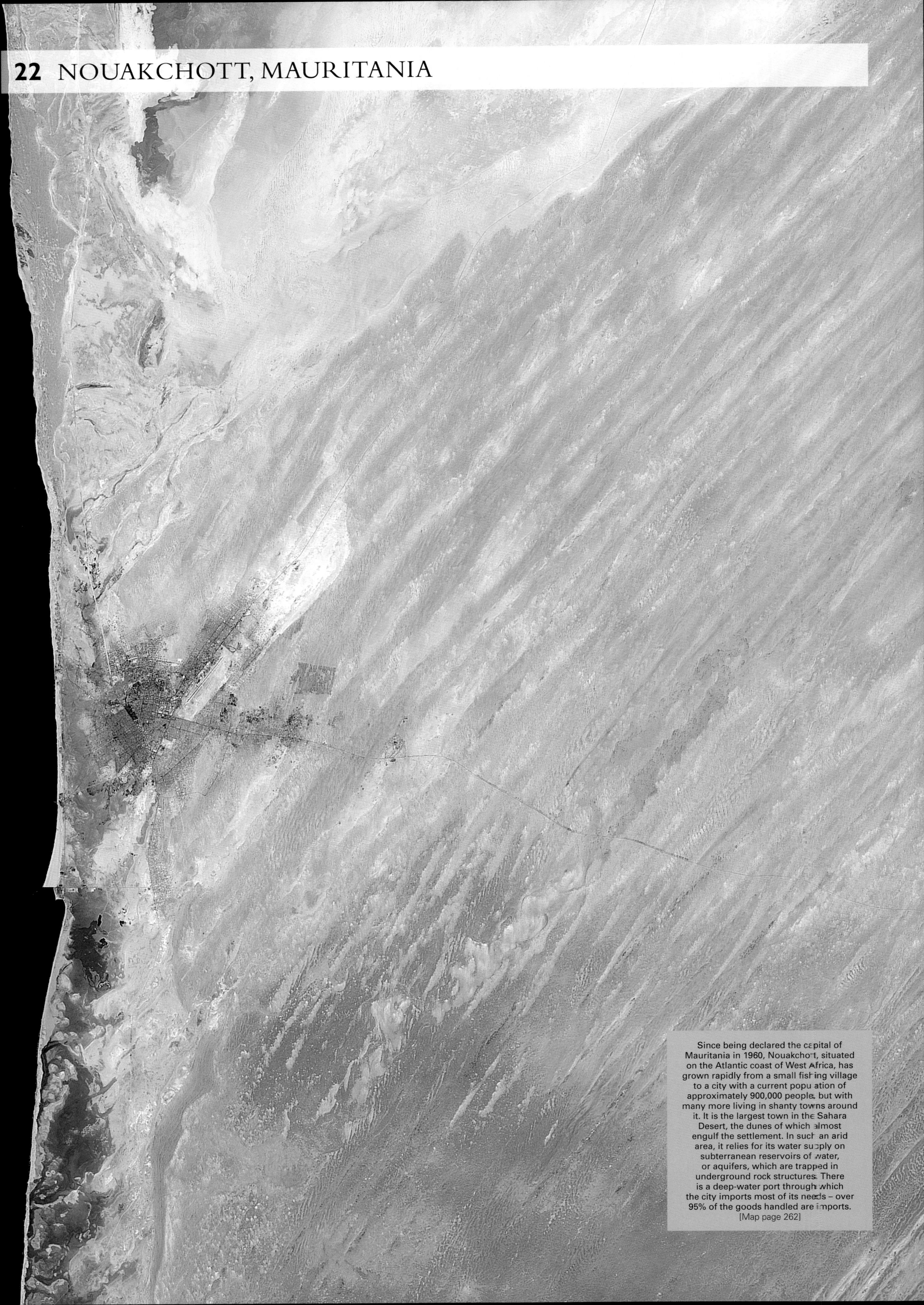

Since being declared the capital of Mauritania in 1960, Nouakchott, situated on the Atlantic coast of West Africa, has grown rapidly from a small fishing village to a city with a current population of approximately 900,000 people, but with many more living in shanty towns around it. It is the largest town in the Sahara Desert, the dunes of which almost engulf the settlement. In such an arid area, it relies for its water supply on subterranean reservoirs of water, or aquifers, which are trapped in underground rock structures. There is a deep-water port through which the city imports most of its needs – over 95% of the goods handled are imports.
[Map page 262]

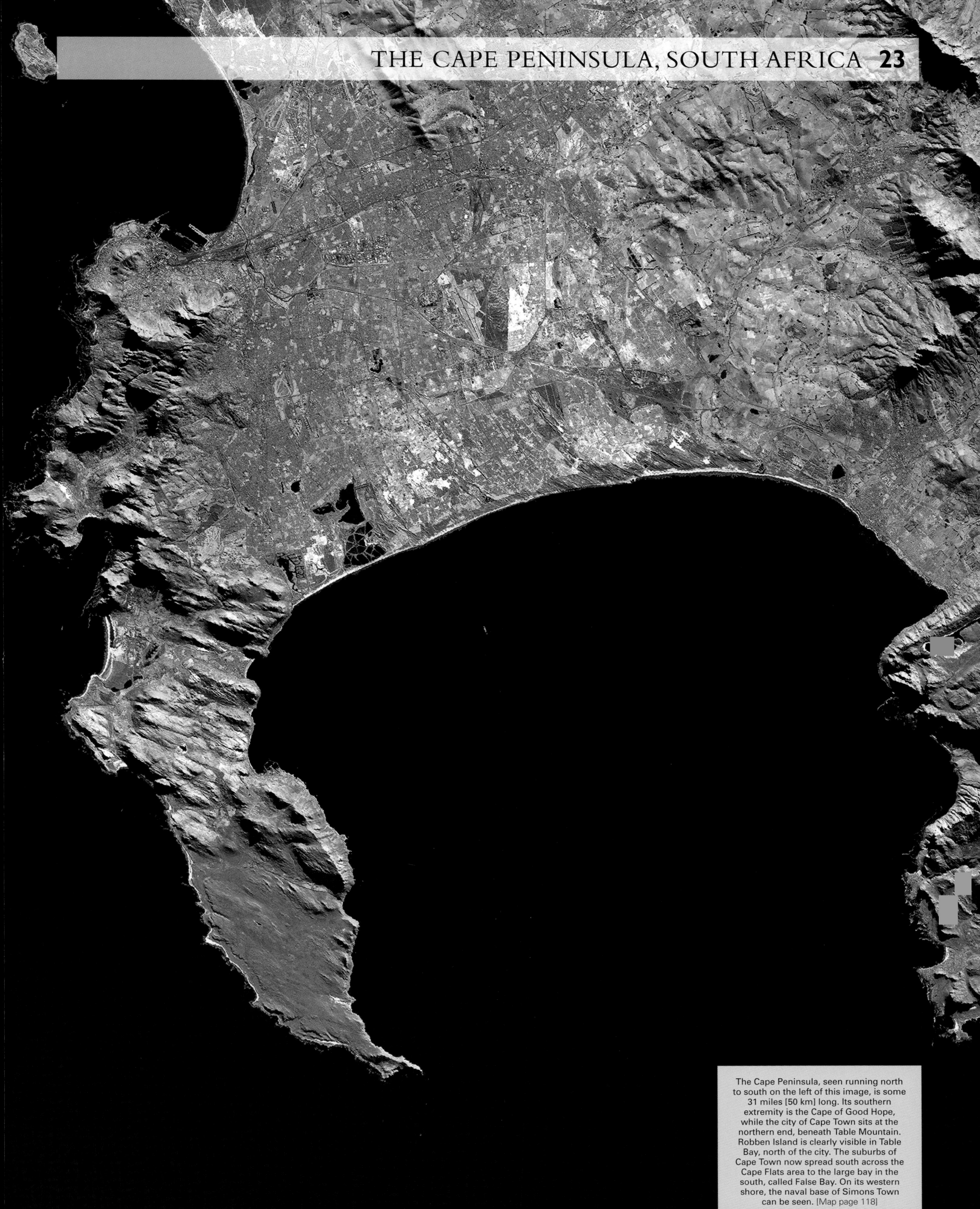

The Cape Peninsula, seen running north to south on the left of this image, is some 31 miles [50 km] long. Its southern extremity is the Cape of Good Hope, while the city of Cape Town sits at the northern end, beneath Table Mountain. Robben Island is clearly visible in Table Bay, north of the city. The suburbs of Cape Town now spread south across the Cape Flats area to the large bay in the south, called False Bay. On its western shore, the naval base of Simons Town can be seen. [Map page 118]

Situated within the Great Rift Valley in northern Tanzania, the crater is the largest complete collapsed volcanic cone, or caldera, in the world. The whole area was one of intense geological activity, as can be seen from the surrounding craters, but currently only one, in the northeast, is active. Ngorongoro is the crater in the south of the image, with Lake Magadi within it. The steep sides of the crater limit normal animal migration, and within it there is a unique ecosystem supporting a wide range of birds and animals. The two lakes in the south are Lake Eyasi (to the west) and Lake Manyara (to the east). [Map page 268]

The largest city in Australia, Sydney was founded at the end of the 18th century on the north shore of Botany Bay. It has since spread inland along the valley of the Parramatta River, but is constrained by the Blue Mountains National Park in the west (the green area in this image). Within this area the reservoir Lake Burragong can be seen, which supplies 80% of the city's water. The runways of Australia's busiest airport are also visible, projecting from the north shore of Botany Bay. [Map page 139]

The Cook Strait separates North Island from South Island in New Zealand, and connects the southern Pacific Ocean with the Tasman Sea. At its narrowest point, it is 14 miles [22 km] wide. The almost circular bay at the southwest corner of North Island is Wellington Harbour. On a restricted site by the hook-shaped peninsula at the harbour mouth, Wellington is the most southerly national capital city in the world and has a population of about 450,000 people. The highly dissected coast toward the top of South Island is called Marlborough Sounds and comprises a series of flooded valleys, or "rias." [Map page 284]

Québec was founded as a trading post in 1608, at the narrowest point of the St Lawrence River, just to the southwest of the Île d'Orléans, and is one of the oldest cities in North America. Strategically, the city controlled the movement of shipping between the Atlantic Ocean and the Great Lakes, and consequently developed fortifications on the cliffs of Cape Diamond, 320 ft [97 m] above the river. The port is 850 miles [1,370 km] from the Atlantic, 1,495 miles [2,404 km] from Duluth, and 1,400 miles [2,252 km] from Chicago. It has a population of over 715,000 people and is the capital city of the province of the same name. [Map page 299]

This image covers the largest urban area in the USA, which has a population of over 18 million people. Flowing from the north, the Hudson River divides the two cities of New York (to the east) and New Jersey (to the west). Toward its mouth on the east bank lies Manhattan Island, with Central Park. Below this is Long Island, with its distinctive offshore spits. At its western end lie the urban areas of Brooklyn and Queens, but further southeast are resorts such as Long Beach and the Fire Island National Seashore. [Map page 132]

As this image shows, the city is situated just to the east of the Front Range, which forms part of the larger Rocky Mountains. Established originally as a frontier town, Denver, Colorado, is known by some as the "Mile-High City" because of its altitude above sea level (5,280 ft [1,609 m]). Denver and its neighboring towns have grown rapidly over the past 50 years to urbanize the area along the foot of the Rockies, forming what is now known as the "Front Range Urban Corridor," which stretches northward from Pueblo in the south to Colorado Springs, Denver and, finally, Cheyenne in Wyoming. [Map page 304]

Situated on the western side of the island of Hispaniola, Port-au-Prince is the capital, chief port and largest town of Haiti. This image, with the city showing as purple near its center, was captured on January 29, 2010, after the catastrophic earthquake of January 12, which killed an estimated 230,000 people, injured over 300,000, and made over 1 million people homeless. The earthquake's epicenter was 18 miles [29 km] southwest of the city at the town of Léogâne, close to the active fault zone between the North American and Caribbean tectonic plates. The valley that can be seen running east to west to the southwest of the city is the axis of this fault zone. [Map page 321]

Peru's largest city and its capital, Lima was founded in the 16th century by the Spanish. Situated at the mouth of the Rimac river, it became one of the pre-eminent cities of the Spanish Empire. On the coast to the north of the distinct Isla San Lorenzo is its port of Callao, a major South American fishing port, whilst behind it lie the foothills of the Andes. With its thriving financial and commercial districts, it is now the major city of the Andean region in South America, and some believe that its current population of over 8 million could reach 10 million by 2015, with people being attracted there from all over the region. [Map page 124]

GAZETTEER
OF
NATIONS

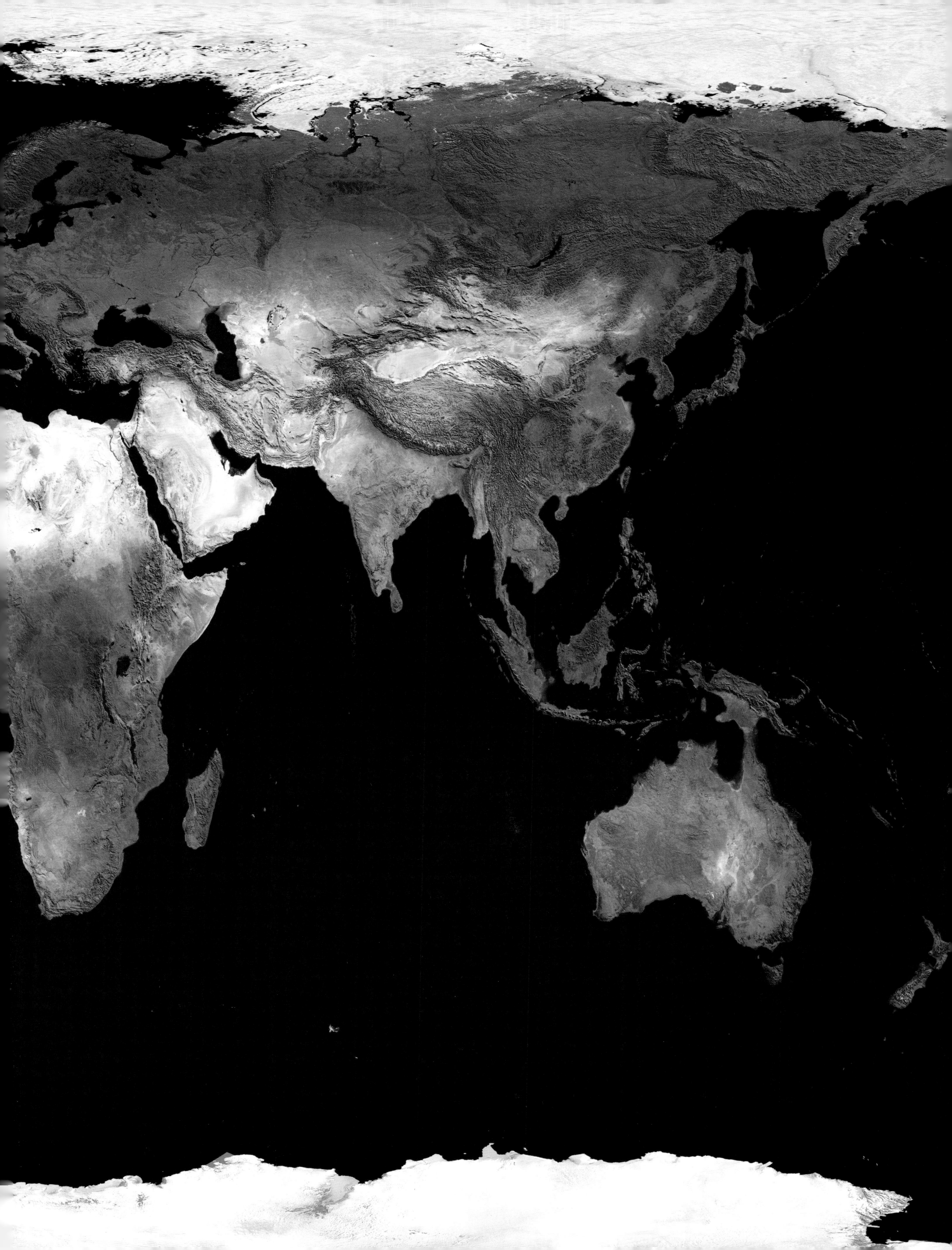

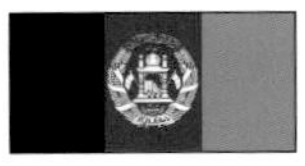
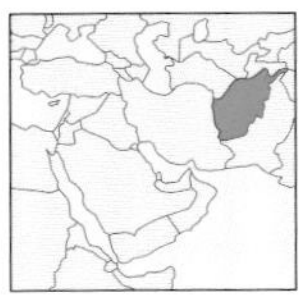

AFGHANISTAN

GEOGRAPHY The Republic of Afghanistan is a landlocked, mountainous country in southern Asia. The central highlands reach a height of more than 22,966 ft [7,000 m] in the east and make up nearly three-quarters of Afghanistan. The main range is the Hindu Kush, which is cut by deep, fertile valleys.

In winter, northerly winds bring cold, snowy weather to the mountains, but summers are hot and dry.

POLITICS & ECONOMY The modern history of Afghanistan began in 1747, when the various tribes in the area united for the first time. In the 19th century, Russia and Britain struggled for control of the country. Following Britain's withdrawal in 1919, Afghanistan became fully independent. Soviet troops invaded in 1979 to support a socialist regime in Kabul, but they withdrew in 1989. By 2001, a group called the Taliban ("Islamic students") controlled 90% of the country. In 2001, following the refusal of the Taliban to hand over the terrorist leader Osama bin Laden, an international force invaded Afghanistan. In 2002, a coalition government was set up under Hamid Karzai, who became president in 2004. Karzai was re-elected in 2009 but conflict with the Taliban continued.

Afghanistan is a poor country and nearly 70% of its people are farmers or nomadic herders. Natural gas is produced, together with some coal, copper, gold, precious stones, and salt.

AREA 251,772 SQ MI [652,090 SQ KM]
POPULATION 28,396,000 **CAPITAL** KABUL
GOVERNMENT ISLAMIC REPUBLIC **ETHNIC GROUPS** PASHTUN (PATHAN) 44%, TAJIK 25%, HAZARA 10%, UZBEK 8%, OTHERS 13%
LANGUAGES PASHTU, DARI/PERSIAN (BOTH OFFICIAL), UZBEK
RELIGIONS ISLAM (SUNNI MUSLIM 84%, SHI'ITE MUSLIM 15%), OTHERS 1%
CURRENCY AFGHANI = 100 PULS

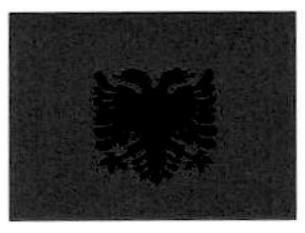
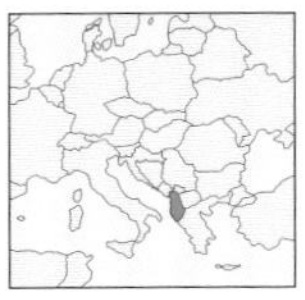

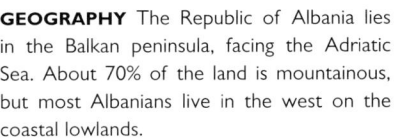

ALBANIA

GEOGRAPHY The Republic of Albania lies in the Balkan peninsula, facing the Adriatic Sea. About 70% of the land is mountainous, but most Albanians live in the west on the coastal lowlands.

The coastal areas of Albania experience a typical Mediterranean climate, with fairly dry, sunny summers and cool, moist winters. The mountains have a severe climate, with heavy winter snowfalls.

POLITICS & ECONOMY Albania is one of Europe's poorest nations. A former Communist country, Albania adopted a multiparty system in the early 1990s. The change proved difficult. But after elections in 1997, a socialist government committed to a market system took office. The transition to democracy has been difficult. However, elections were held in 2005 and again in 2009. They were won by the center-right Democratic Party, led by Sali Berisha.

In 2005, agriculture employed about 50% of the people. Since 1991, private ownership of land has been encouraged, replacing the former state farm and collective system. Albania has some minerals. Chromite, copper, and nickel are exported.

AREA 11,100 SQ MI [28,748 SQ KM] **POPULATION** 3,639,000
CAPITAL TIRANA **GOVERNMENT** MULTIPARTY REPUBLIC
ETHNIC GROUPS ALBANIAN 95%, GREEK 3%, MACEDONIAN, VLACHS, GYPSY **LANGUAGES** ALBANIAN (OFFICIAL) **RELIGIONS** MANY PEOPLE SAY THEY ARE NON-BELIEVERS; OF THE BELIEVERS, 70% FOLLOW ISLAM AND 30% FOLLOW CHRISTIANITY (ORTHODOX 20%, ROMAN CATHOLIC 10%)
CURRENCY LEK = 100 QINDARS

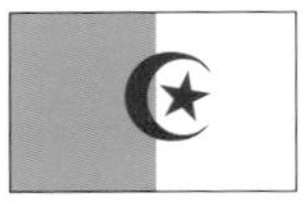
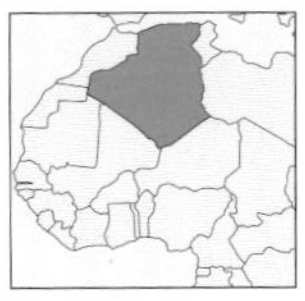

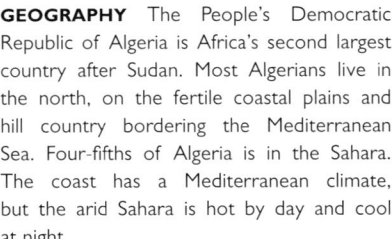

ALGERIA

GEOGRAPHY The People's Democratic Republic of Algeria is Africa's second largest country after Sudan. Most Algerians live in the north, on the fertile coastal plains and hill country bordering the Mediterranean Sea. Four-fifths of Algeria is in the Sahara. The coast has a Mediterranean climate, but the arid Sahara is hot by day and cool at night.

POLITICS & ECONOMY France ruled Algeria from 1830 until 1962, when the socialist FLN (National Liberation Front) formed a one-party government. Following the recognition of opposition parties in 1989, a Muslim group, the FIS (Islamic Salvation Front), won an election in 1991. The FLN canceled the elections and civil conflict broke out. About 100,000 people were killed in the 1990s. Abdelaziz Bouteflika was elected president in 1999 and 2004. Constitutional changes enabled Bouteflika to stand for a third term and he was re-elected in 2009. The scale of violence was reduced under his leadership. In 2005, the government made concessions to the Berber minority.

Algeria is a developing country, whose chief resources are oil and natural gas, which were discovered in the Sahara in 1956. The natural gas reserves are among the world's largest, and gas and oil account for more than 90% of the exports. Cement, iron and steel, textiles, and vehicles are manufactured. Barley, citrus fruits, dates, potatoes, and wheat are major crops.

AREA 919,590 SQ MI [2,381,741 SQ KM]
POPULATION 34,178,000 **CAPITAL** ALGIERS
GOVERNMENT SOCIALIST REPUBLIC **ETHNIC GROUPS** ARAB-BERBER 99%
LANGUAGES ARABIC AND BERBER (OFFICIAL), FRENCH **RELIGIONS** SUNNI MUSLIM 99% **CURRENCY** ALGERIAN DINAR = 100 CENTIMES

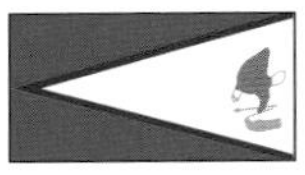
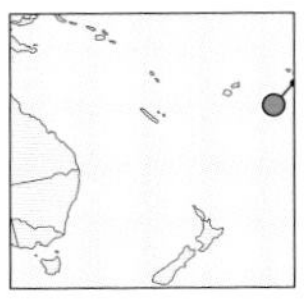

AMERICAN SAMOA

An "unincorporated territory" of the United States, American Samoa lies in the south-central Pacific Ocean.

AREA 77 SQ MI [199 SQ KM]
POPULATION 66,000 **CAPITAL** PAGO PAGO

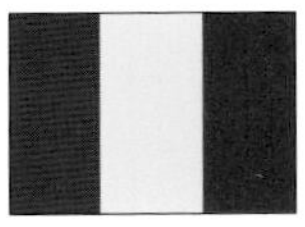
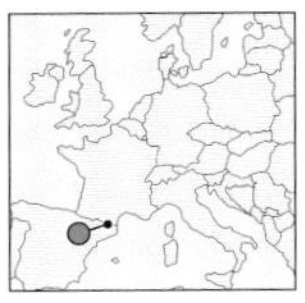

ANDORRA

A mini-state situated in the Pyrenees Mountains, Andorra is a coprincipality whose main activity is tourism. Most Andorrans live in the six valleys (the Valls) that drain into the River Valira.

AREA 181 SQ MI [468 SQ KM]
POPULATION 84,000 **CAPITAL** ANDORRA LA VELLA

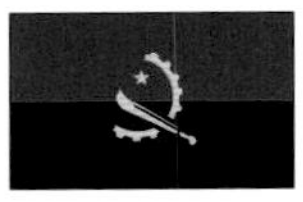
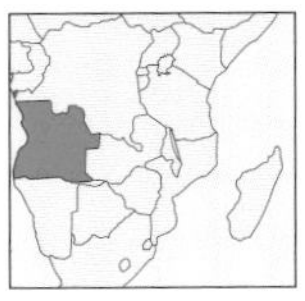

ANGOLA

GEOGRAPHY The Republic of Angola is a large country in southwestern Africa. Much of the country is part of the plateau that forms most of southern Africa, with a narrow coastal plain in the west.

Angola has a tropical climate, with temperatures of over 68°F [20°C] throughout the year, though the highest areas are cooler. The coast is dry, but the rainfall increases to the north and east.

POLITICS & ECONOMY Bantu-speaking people settled in Angola in the 13th century and later founded large kingdoms, such as the Kongo and Mbundu. Portugal controlled the coastal slave trade from the 17th century and extended their control inland in the 19th century. Angola became independent from Portugal in 1975, after which rival nationalist groups struggled for power. Despite a ceasefire in the mid-1990s, conflict finally ended in 2002, when the rebel leader, Jonas Savimbi, was killed. Successful parliamentary elections were held in 2008.

Angola is a developing country, where 70% of the people are poor farmers. The main food crops are cassava and maize. Coffee is exported. Angola has important oil reserves and oil is exported. Angola also produces diamonds and has reserves of copper, manganese, and phosphates.

AREA 481,351 SQ MI [1,246,700 SQ KM]
POPULATION 12,799,000 **CAPITAL** LUANDA
GOVERNMENT MULTIPARTY REPUBLIC
ETHNIC GROUPS OVIMBUNDU 37%, KIMBUNDU 25%, BAKONGO 13%, OTHERS 25% **LANGUAGES** PORTUGUESE (OFFICIAL), MANY OTHERS
RELIGIONS TRADITIONAL BELIEFS 47%, ROMAN CATHOLIC 38%, PROTESTANT 15%
CURRENCY KWANZA = 100 LWEI

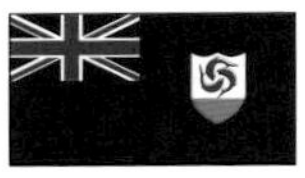
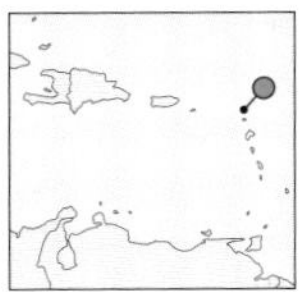

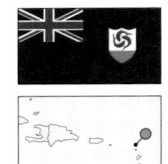

ANGUILLA

Formerly part of St Kitts and Nevis, Anguilla, the most northerly of the Leeward Islands, became a British dependency (now a British overseas territory) in 1980. The main source of revenue is now tourism, although lobster still accounts for half the island's exports.

AREA 37 SQ MI [96 SQ KM]
POPULATION 14,000 **CAPITAL** THE VALLEY

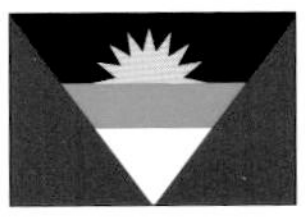
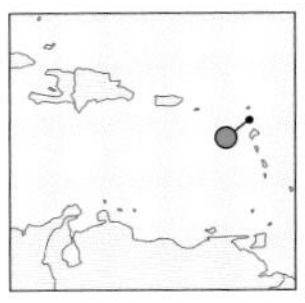

ANTIGUA & BARBUDA

A former British dependency in the Caribbean, Antigua and Barbuda became independent in 1981. Tourism is the main industry, though sugar is an important product.

AREA 171 SQ MI [442 SQ KM]
POPULATION 86,000 **CAPITAL** ST JOHN'S

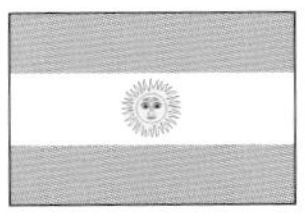
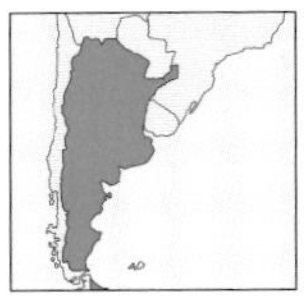

ARGENTINA

GEOGRAPHY The Argentine Republic is South America's second largest and the world's eighth largest country. The high Andes range in the west contains Mount Aconcagua, the highest peak in the Americas. In southern Argentina, the Andes Mountains overlook Patagonia, a plateau region. In east-central Argentina lies a fertile plain called the pampas.

The climate varies from subtropical in the north to temperate in the south. Rainfall is abundant in the north-east but lower to the west and south. Patagonia is largely desert.

POLITICS & ECONOMY The earliest people were American Indians, but 86% of the people are now of European ancestry. Spain took control in the 16th century and ruled until 1816. Argentina later suffered from instability and periods of military rule. In 1982, Argentina's military regime invaded the Falkland (Malvinas) Islands, but Britain regained the islands later that year. Argentina restored civilian rule in 1983. In 2007, Christina Fernández de Kirchner was elected president, succeeding her husband, Néstor Carlos Kirchner, who had served as president from 2003. She was the first woman to be Argentina's directly elected president. The dispute over the Falklands resurfaced in 2010, when drilling for oil began around the islands.

The World Bank classifies Argentina as an "upper-middle-income" developing country. About 90% of the people live in urban areas. Manufactures include food products, cars, electrical equipment, and textiles. Oil is the main resource and the chief farm products are beef, maize, and wheat. Exports include oil, meat, wheat, maize, vegetable oils, hides and skins, and wool. In 1991, Argentina, Brazil, Paraguay, and Uruguay set up an alliance, Mercosur, aimed at creating a common market.

AREA 1,073,512 SQ MI [2,780,400 SQ KM]
POPULATION 40,914,000 **CAPITAL** BUENOS AIRES
GOVERNMENT FEDERAL REPUBLIC **ETHNIC GROUPS** EUROPEAN 97%, MESTIZO, AMERINDIAN **LANGUAGES** SPANISH (OFFICIAL)
RELIGIONS ROMAN CATHOLIC 92%, PROTESTANT 2%, JEWISH 2%, OTHERS **CURRENCY** ARGENTINE PESO = 10,000 AUSTRALS

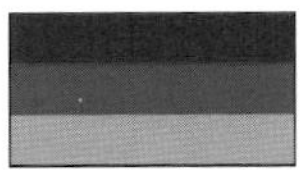
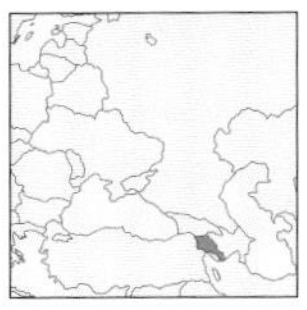

ARMENIA

GEOGRAPHY The Republic of Armenia is a landlocked country in southwestern Asia. Most of Armenia consists of a rugged plateau, crisscrossed by long faults (tracks). Movements along the faults cause earthquakes. The highest point is Mount Aragats, at 13,419 ft [4,090 m] above sea level.

The height of the land, which averages 4,920 ft [1,500 m] above sea level gives rise to severe winters and cool summers. The highest peaks are snow-capped, but the total yearly rainfall is generally low.

POLITICS & ECONOMY In 1920, Armenia became a Communist republic and, in 1922, it became, with Azerbaijan and Georgia, part of the Transcaucasian Republic within the Soviet Union. But the three territories became separate Soviet Socialist Republics in 1936. After the breakup of the Soviet Union in 1991, Armenia became an independent republic. Fighting broke out over Nagorno-Karabakh, an area enclosed by Azerbaijan where most people are Armenians. In 1992, Armenia occupied the land between it and Nagorno-Karabakh. A ceasefire in 1994 left Armenia in control of about 20% of Azerbaijan's land area. Periodic talks with Azerbaijan have ended in failure.

Armenia has a "lower-middle-income" economy. The government has encouraged free enterprise, selling farmland and state-owned businesses.

AREA 11,506 SQ MI [29,800 SQ KM]
POPULATION 2,967,000 **CAPITAL** YEREVAN
GOVERNMENT MULTIPARTY REPUBLIC **ETHNIC GROUPS** ARMENIAN 93%, RUSSIAN 2%, AZERI 1%, OTHERS (MOSTLY KURDS) 4%
LANGUAGES ARMENIAN (OFFICIAL) **RELIGIONS** ARMENIAN APOSTOLIC 94%
CURRENCY DRAM = 100 COUMA

NOTE: This alphabetical list includes the principal countries and territories of the world. The area figures give the total area of land, inland water, and ice. The population figures are 2009 estimates where available.

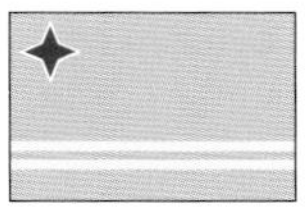

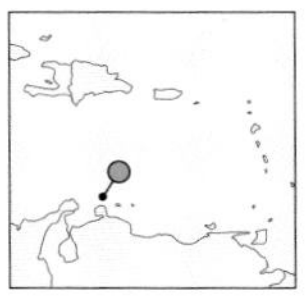

ARUBA

Formerly part of the Netherlands Antilles, Aruba (the most western of the Lesser Antilles) became a separate self-governing Dutch territory in 1986.

AREA 75 SQ MI [193 SQ KM]
POPULATION 103,000 **CAPITAL** ORANJESTAD

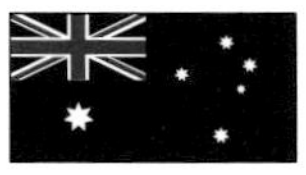

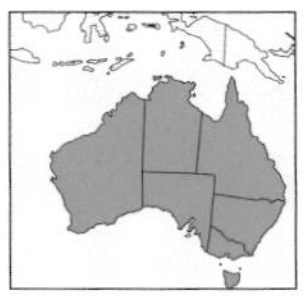

AUSTRALIA

GEOGRAPHY The Commonwealth of Australia, the world's sixth largest country, is also a continent. Australia is the flattest of the continents and the main highland area is in the east. Here the Great Dividing Range separates the eastern coastal plains from the Central Plains. This range extends from the Cape York Peninsula to Victoria in the far south. The longest rivers, the Murray and Darling, drain the southeastern part of the Central Plains. The Western Plateau makes up two-thirds of Australia. A few mountain ranges break the monotony of the generally flat landscape. Only 10% of Australia, notably the tropical north, the northeast coast and the southeast, has an average annual rainfall of more than 39 inches [1,000 mm]. But, in 2001–10, the Murray–Darling basin in the southeast, which produces about 40% of Australia's farm produce, suffered severe and prolonged drought.

POLITICS & ECONOMY The Aboriginal people of Australia entered the continent from Southeast Asia more than 50,000 years ago. The first European explorers were Dutch in the 17th century, but they did not settle. In 1770, the British Captain Cook explored the east coast and, in 1788, the first British settlement was established for convicts on the site of what is now Sydney. Australia has strong ties with the British Isles. But in the last 50 years, people from other parts of Europe and, most recently, from Asia have settled in Australia. Ties with Britain were also weakened by Britain's membership of the European Union. Many Australians believe that they should become more involved with the nations of eastern Asia and the Americas rather than with Europe. In 1999, Australians voted to retain the country's status as a monarchy. In 2003, Australian troops joined in the invasion of Iraq. The Labor Party won the 2007 elections and Kevin Rudd became prime minister. In 2008 Australia ended its combat operations in Iraq.

Australia is a prosperous country. Crops can be grown on only 6% of the land, but dry pasture covers another 58%. Yet the country remains a major producer and exporter of farm products, particularly cattle, wheat, and wool. Grapes grown for wine-making are also important. The country is a major producer of minerals, including bauxite, coal, copper, diamonds, gold, iron ore, manganese, nickel, silver, tin, tungsten, and zinc. Australia also produces oil and natural gas. Metals, minerals, and farm products account for the bulk of exports. Australia's imports are mostly manufactured goods, especially machinery, though industry is now important, especially the manufacture of consumer goods.

AREA 2,988,885 SQ MI [7,741,220 SQ KM] **POPULATION** 21,263,000
CAPITAL CANBERRA **GOVERNMENT** FEDERAL CONSTITUTIONAL MONARCHY
ETHNIC GROUPS CAUCASIAN 92%, ASIAN 7%, ABORIGINAL 1%
LANGUAGES ENGLISH (OFFICIAL) **RELIGIONS** ROMAN CATHOLIC 26%, ANGLICAN 26%, OTHER CHRISTIAN 24%, NON-CHRISTIAN 24%
CURRENCY AUSTRALIAN DOLLAR = 100 CENTS

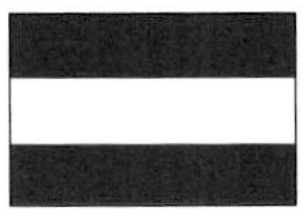

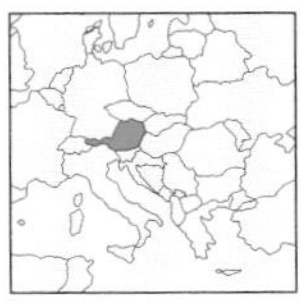

AUSTRIA

GEOGRAPHY Austria is a landlocked country in Europe. Northern Austria contains the valley of the River Danube, which flows from Germany to the Black Sea, and the Vienna basin. Southern Austria contains ranges of the Alps, their highest point at Grossglockner, 12,457 ft [3,797 m] above sea level.

The climate is temperate in the west and more continental in the east. Winters are cold and snowy. Summers are warm and dry in the east.

POLITICS & ECONOMY Formerly part of the monarchy of Austria–Hungary, which collapsed in 1918, Austria was annexed by Germany in 1938. After World War II, the Allies partitioned and occupied the country. In 1955, Austria became a neutral federal republic. It joined the European Union in 1995. In 2000, a coalition government was formed by the right-wing People's Party and the extreme right-wing Freedom Party, which lost much of its support in 2002. In 2008, the Social Democratic/People's Party coalition (formed in 2007) collapsed, but the same parties formed another government after elections, in which far right parties won nearly 29% of the vote.

Austria has a highly developed economy, with plenty of hydroelectric power and some oil, gas, and coal reserves. The country's leading economic activity is manufacturing metals and metal products. Crops are grown on 18% of the land, and another 24% is pasture. Dairy and livestock farming are the leading activities. Major crops include barley, potatoes, rye, sugar beet, and wheat. Tourism is a major activity in this scenic country.

AREA 32,378 SQ MI [83,859 SQ KM] **POPULATION** 8,210,000
CAPITAL VIENNA **GOVERNMENT** FEDERAL REPUBLIC
ETHNIC GROUPS AUSTRIAN 90%, CROATIAN, SLOVENE, OTHERS
LANGUAGES GERMAN (OFFICIAL) **RELIGIONS** ROMAN CATHOLIC 78%, PROTESTANT 5%, ISLAM AND OTHERS 17% **CURRENCY** EURO = 100 CENTS

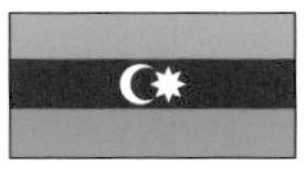

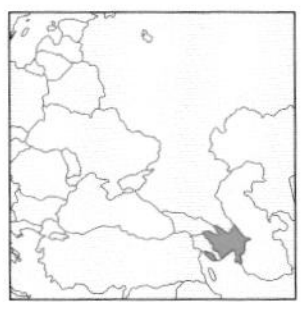

AZERBAIJAN

GEOGRAPHY The Azerbaijani Republic is a country in the southwest of Asia, facing the Caspian Sea to the east. It includes an area called the Naxçivan Autonomous Republic, which is completely cut off from the rest of Azerbaijan by Armenian territory. The Caucasus Mountains border Russia in the north.

Azerbaijan has hot summers and cool winters. The plains are fairly dry, but the mountains are rainy.

POLITICS & ECONOMY After the Russian Revolution of 1917, attempts were made to form a Transcaucasian Federation made up of Armenia, Azerbaijan, and Georgia. When this failed, Azerbaijanis set up an independent state. But Russian forces occupied the area in 1920. In 1922, the Communists set up a Transcaucasian Republic consisting of Armenia, Azerbaijan, and Georgia under Russian control. In 1936, the three areas became separate Soviet Socialist Republics within the Soviet Union. In 1991, following the breakup of the Soviet Union, Azerbaijan became an independent nation. After independence, Azerbaijan clashed with Armenia over the enclave of Nagorno-Karabakh, a region in Azerbaijan where the majority of the people are Armenian. A ceasefire in 1994 left Armenia in control of 20% of Azerbaijan's area, including Nagorno-Karabakh. Tension continued and border clashes occurred in 2006. Ilham Aliyev of the New Azerbaijan Party succeeded his father, Haidar Aliyev, as president in 2003. He was re-elected in 2005 and 2008, though the elections were thought to fall short of full democratic standards.

Azerbaijan has huge oil reserves. Oil extraction and manufacturing, including oil refining and the production of chemicals, machinery, and textiles, are major activities.

AREA 33,436 SQ MI [86,600 SQ KM] **POPULATION** 8,239,000
CAPITAL BAKU **GOVERNMENT** FEDERAL MULTIPARTY REPUBLIC
ETHNIC GROUPS AZERI 90%, DAGESTANI 3%, RUSSIAN, ARMENIAN, OTHERS **LANGUAGES** AZERBAIJANI (OFFICIAL), RUSSIAN, ARMENIAN
RELIGIONS ISLAM 93%, RUSSIAN ORTHODOX 2%, ARMENIAN ORTHODOX 2%
CURRENCY AZERBAIJANI MANAT = 100 GOPIK

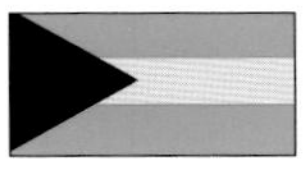

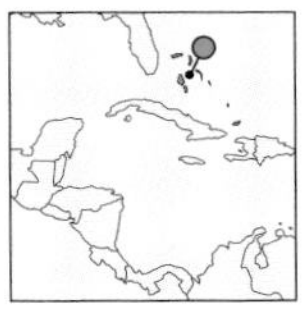

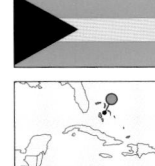

BAHAMAS

A coral-limestone archipelago off the coast of Florida, the Bahamas became independent from Britain in 1973, and has since developed strong ties with the United States. Tourism and banking are major activities.

AREA 5,358 SQ MI [13,878 SQ KM]
POPULATION 308,000 **CAPITAL** NASSAU

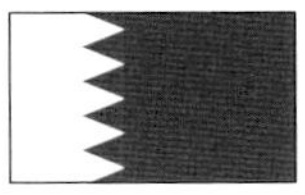

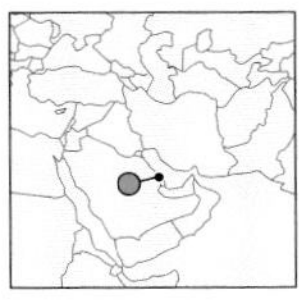

BAHRAIN

The Kingdom of Bahrain, an island nation in the Persian Gulf, became independent from the UK in 1971. Oil accounts for 80% of its exports.

AREA 268 SQ MI [694 SQ KM]
POPULATION 729,000 **CAPITAL** MANAMA

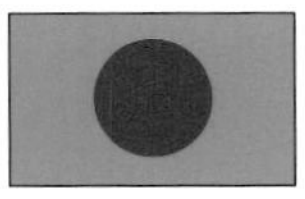

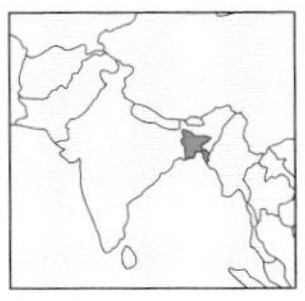

BANGLADESH

GEOGRAPHY The People's Republic of Bangladesh is one of the world's most densely populated countries. Apart from hilly regions in the far northeast and southeast, most of the land is flat and covered by fertile alluvium spread over the land by the Ganges, Brahmaputra and Meghna rivers. These rivers overflow when they are swollen by the annual monsoon rains. Floods also occur along the coast, 357 mi [575 km] long, when cyclones (hurricanes) drive seawater inland. Bangladesh has a tropical monsoon climate. Dry northerly winds blow in winter, but moist southerly winds bring heavy rain in summer.

POLITICS & ECONOMY In 1947, British India was partitioned between the mainly Hindu India and the Muslim Pakistan. Pakistan consisted of two parts, West and East Pakistan, which were separated by about 1,000 mi [1,600 km] of Indian territory. Differences developed between West and East Pakistan. In 1971, the East Pakistanis rebeled. After a nine-month civil war, they declared East Pakistan to be a new nation named Bangladesh. A famine in 1974 and a coup in 1975 were followed by political upheavals. The army seized power in 2007, but elections in 2008 returned Sheikh Hasina's Awami League to power.

Bangladesh is one of the world's poorest countries. Its economy depends mainly on agriculture, which employs nearly half the population. Bangladesh is the world's fourth largest producer of rice.

AREA 55,598 SQ MI [143,998 SQ KM]
POPULATION 156,051,000 **CAPITAL** DHAKA
GOVERNMENT MULTIPARTY REPUBLIC **ETHNIC GROUPS** BENGALI 98%, TRIBAL GROUPS **LANGUAGES** BENGALI (OFFICIAL), ENGLISH
RELIGIONS ISLAM 83%, HINDUISM 16% **CURRENCY** TAKA = 100 PAISAS

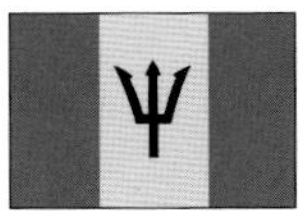

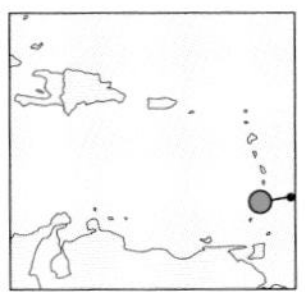

BARBADOS

The most easterly Caribbean country, Barbados became independent from the UK in 1960. A densely populated island, Barbados is prosperous by comparison with most Caribbean countries.

AREA 166 SQ MI [430 SQ KM]
POPULATION 285,000 **CAPITAL** BRIDGETOWN

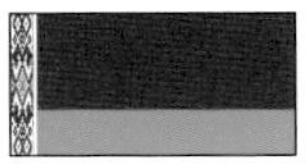

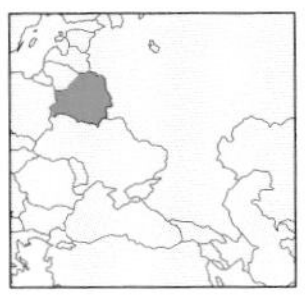

BELARUS

GEOGRAPHY The Republic of Belarus is a landlocked country in Eastern Europe. The land is low-lying and mostly flat. In the south, much of the land is marshy and this area contains Europe's largest marsh and peat bog, the Pripet Marshes. The climate is affected by both the moderating influence of the Baltic Sea and continental conditions to the east. The winters are cold and the summers warm.

POLITICS & ECONOMY In 1918, Belarus (White Russia) became an independent republic, but Russia invaded the country and, in 1919, a Communist state was set up. In 1922, Belarus became a founder republic of the Soviet Union. In 1991, Belarus again became an independent republic, and although Belarus continued to support reunification with Russia, any surrender of sovereignty was not expected. President Alexander Lukashenko, who was elected in flawed elections in 1994, 2001, and 2006, has been criticized for his autocratic rule, his poor record on human rights, and disregard for freedom of speech. In elections in 2008, pro-government candidates won all 110 parliamentary seats.

According to the World Bank, Belarus has an "upper-middle-income" economy. Most economic activities remain under government control and, in the 1990s, the economy declined. Mining and manufacturing are the most valuable activities.

AREA 80,154 SQ MI [207,600 SQ KM]
POPULATION 9,649,000 **CAPITAL** MINSK
GOVERNMENT MULTIPARTY REPUBLIC **ETHNIC GROUPS** BELARUSIAN 81%, RUSSIAN 11%, POLISH, UKRAINIAN, OTHERS **LANGUAGES** BELARUSIAN, RUSSIAN (BOTH OFFICIAL) **RELIGIONS** EASTERN ORTHODOX 80%, OTHERS 20% **CURRENCY** BELARUSIAN ROUBLE = 100 KOPECKS

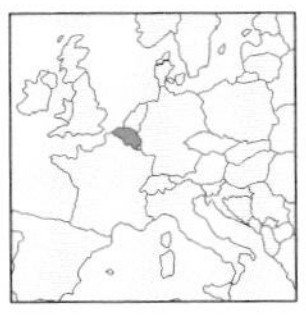

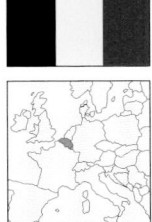

BELGIUM

GEOGRAPHY The Kingdom of Belgium is a densely populated country in western Europe. Behind the coastline on the North Sea, which is 39 mi [63 km] long, lie its coastal plains. Central Belgium consists of low plateaux and the only highland region is the Ardennes in the southeast.

Belgium has a cool, temperate climate. Moist winds from the Atlantic Ocean bring fairly heavy rain, especially in the Ardennes. In January and February much snow falls on the Ardennes.

POLITICS & ECONOMY In 1815, Belgium and the Netherlands united as the "low countries," but Belgium became independent in 1830. Belgium's economy was weakened by the two World

Wars, but, from 1945, the country recovered quickly, first through collaboration with the Netherlands and Luxembourg, which formed a customs union called Benelux, and later through its membership of the European Union.

A central political problem in Belgium has been the tension between the Dutch-speaking Flemings and the French-speaking Walloons. In the 1970s, the government divided the country into three economic regions: Dutch-speaking Flanders, French-speaking Wallonia, and bilingual Brussels. In 1993, Belgium adopted a federal constitution, giving each region its own parliament. Following national elections in 2007, some people thought that Belgium might split apart. In 2009, a coalition government was set up, but differences between the Flemish- and French-speaking parties made government difficult.

Belgium is a major trading nation, though most materials used in manufacturing are imported. Major products include chemicals, processed food, and steel. The textile industry has existed since medieval times in Flanders. Agriculture employs less than 2% of the people, but farmers produce most of the food the country needs. Barley and wheat are major crops, followed by flax, hops, potatoes, and sugar beet. But the most valuable agricultural activities are dairy farming and livestock rearing.

AREA 11,787 SQ MI [30,528 SQ KM]
POPULATION 10,414,000
CAPITAL BRUSSELS
GOVERNMENT FEDERAL CONSTITUTIONAL MONARCHY
ETHNIC GROUPS BELGIAN 89% (FLEMING 58%, WALLOON 31%), OTHERS 11% **LANGUAGES** DUTCH, FRENCH, GERMAN (ALL OFFICIAL)
RELIGIONS ROMAN CATHOLIC 75%, OTHERS 25%
CURRENCY EURO = 100 CENTS

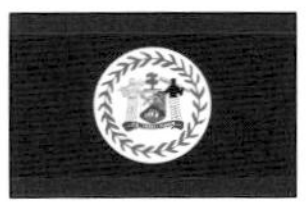
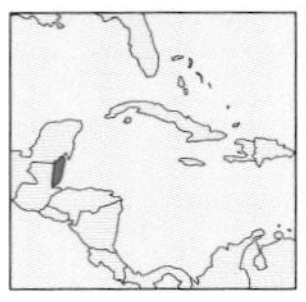

BELIZE

GEOGRAPHY Behind the southern coastal plain, the land rises to the Maya Mountains, which reach 3,674 ft [1,120 m] at Victoria Peak. The north is mostly low-lying and swampy. Temperatures are high all year round, while the average annual rainfall ranges from 51 inches [1,300 mm] in the north to over 150 inches [3,800 mm] in the south. Hurricanes caused much damage in the 1990s and 2000s, but tourist numbers have continued to increase.

POLITICS & ECONOMY From 1862, Belize (then called British Honduras) was a British colony. Full independence was achieved in 1981, but Guatemala, which had claimed the area since the early 19th century, opposed Belize's independence and British troops remained to prevent a possible invasion. In 1983, Guatemala reduced its claim to the southern fifth of Belize. Improved relations in the early 1990s led Guatemala to recognize Belize's independence and, in 1992, Britain agreed to withdraw its troops from the country.

The World Bank classifies Belize as a "lower-middle-income" developing country. Its economy is based on agriculture and sugarcane is the chief commercial crop and export. Other crops include bananas, beans, citrus fruits, maize, and rice. Forestry, fishing, and tourism are other important activities.

AREA 8,867 SQ MI [22,966 SQ KM]
POPULATION 308,000 **CAPITAL** BELMOPAN
GOVERNMENT CONSTITUTIONAL MONARCHY **ETHNIC GROUPS** MESTIZO 49%, CREOLE 25%, MAYAN INDIAN 11%, GARIFUNA 6%, OTHERS 9%
LANGUAGES ENGLISH (OFFICIAL), SPANISH, CREOLE
RELIGIONS ROMAN CATHOLIC 50%, PROTESTANT 27%, OTHERS
CURRENCY BELIZEAN DOLLAR = 100 CENTS

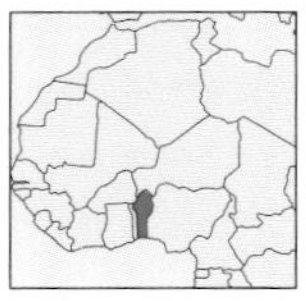

BENIN

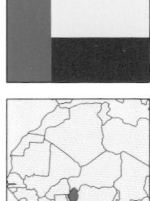

GEOGRAPHY The Republic of Benin is one of Africa's smallest countries. It extends north–south for about 390 mi [620 km]. Lagoons line the short coastline, and the country has no natural harbors.

Benin has a hot, wet climate. The average annual temperature on the coast is about 77°F [25°C], and the average rainfall is about 52 inches [1,330 mm]. The inland plains are wetter than the coast.

POLITICS & ECONOMY After slavery was ended in the 19th century, the French began to gain influence in the area. Benin became self-governing in 1958 and fully independent in 1960. After much instability and many changes of government, a military group took over in 1972. The country, renamed Benin in 1975, became a one-party socialist state. Socialism was abandoned in 1989. Former coup leader Mathieu Kérékou served as president until 2006, when a former banker, Yayi Boni, was elected president.

Benin is a poor developing country. About half of the people live by farming, mainly at subsistence level. Exports include cotton, petroleum, and palm products. Cocoa, coffee, groundnuts (peanuts), tobacco, and shea nuts are also grown for export.

AREA 43,483 SQ MI [112,622 SQ KM]
POPULATION 8,792,000 **CAPITAL** PORTO-NOVO
GOVERNMENT MULTIPARTY REPUBLIC **ETHNIC GROUPS** FON, ADJA, BARIBA, YORUBA, FULANI **LANGUAGES** FRENCH (OFFICIAL), FON, ADJA, YORUBA
RELIGIONS TRADITIONAL BELIEFS 50%, CHRISTIANITY 30%, ISLAM 20%
CURRENCY CFA FRANC = 100 CENTIMES

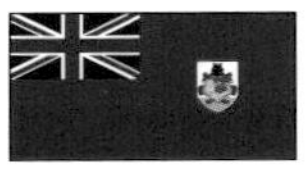
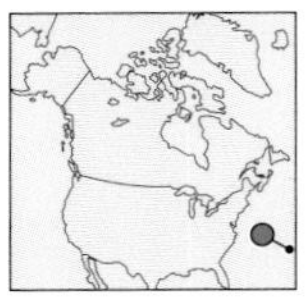

BERMUDA

A group of about 150 small islands situated 570 mi [920 km] east of the USA. Bermuda remains Britain's oldest overseas territory, but it has a long tradition of self-government.

AREA 21 SQ MI [53 SQ KM]
POPULATION 68,000 **CAPITAL** HAMILTON

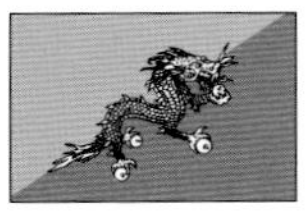
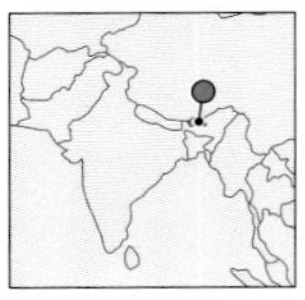

BHUTAN

GEOGRAPHY A mountainous, isolated Himalayan country located between India and Tibet. The climate is similar to that of Nepal, being dependent on altitude and affected by monsoonal winds.

POLITICS & ECONOMY The monarch of Bhutan is head of both state and government, and this predominantly Buddhist country remains, even in the Asian context, both conservative and poor. In 2008, Bhutan held its first ever democratic elections, ending over a century of absolute royal rule and turning Bhutan into a constitutional monarchy.

AREA 18,147 SQ MI [47,000 SQ KM] **POPULATION** 691,000
CAPITAL THIMPHU **GOVERNMENT** CONSTITUTIONAL MONARCHY
ETHNIC GROUPS BHUTANESE 50%, NEPALESE 35%
LANGUAGES DZONGKHA (OFFICIAL) **RELIGIONS** BUDDHISM 75%, HINDUISM 25% **CURRENCY** NGULTRUM = 100 CHETRUM

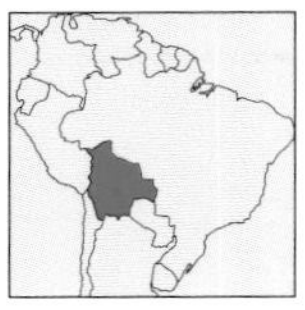

BOLIVIA

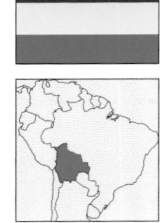

GEOGRAPHY The Republic of Bolivia is a landlocked country which straddles the Andes Mountains in central South America. The Andes rise to a height of 21,391 ft [6,520 m] at Nevado Sajama in the west.

About 40% of Bolivians live on a high plateau called the Altiplano in the Andean region, while the sparsely populated east is essentially a vast lowland plain.

The Bolivian climate is greatly affected by altitude, with the Andean peaks permanently snow-covered, and the eastern plains remaining hot and humid.

POLITICS & ECONOMY American Indians have lived in Bolivia for at least 10,000 years. The main groups today are the Aymara and Quechua people.

In the last 50 years, Bolivia, an independent country since 1825, has been ruled by a succession of civilian and military governments, which violated human rights. Democracy was restored in 1982. Economic problems led a widening of the gap between rich and poor and, in 2005, Evo Morales, a left-wing Aymara farmer, was elected president. His policies of nationalization and redistributing wealth to peasants aroused opposition especially in the richer east. In 2009, Bolivia adopted a new constitution and, in December, Morales was re-elected president.

Bolivia is one of South America's poorest countries. Resources include natural gas, silver, tin, and zinc, but the main activity is agriculture. Soybeans and soybean products are exported.

AREA 424,162 SQ MI [1,098,581 SQ KM]
POPULATION 9,775,000 **CAPITAL** LA PAZ (SEAT OF GOVERNMENT); SUCRE (LEGAL CAPITAL/SEAT OF JUDICIARY)
GOVERNMENT MULTIPARTY REPUBLIC **ETHNIC GROUPS** MESTIZO 30%, QUECHUA 30%, AYMARA 25%, WHITE 15% **LANGUAGES** SPANISH, AYMARA, QUECHUA (ALL OFFICIAL) **RELIGIONS** ROMAN CATHOLIC 95%
CURRENCY BOLIVIANO = 100 CENTAVOS

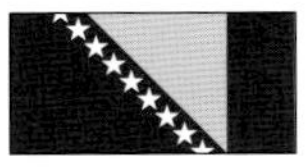
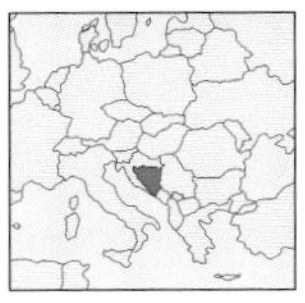

BOSNIA-HERZEGOVINA

GEOGRAPHY The Republic of Bosnia-Herzegovina is one of the five republics to emerge from the former Federal People's Republic of Yugoslavia. Much of the country is mountainous or hilly, with an arid limestone plateau in the southwest. The River Sava, which forms most of the northern border with Croatia, is a tributary of the River Danube. Because of the country's odd shape, the coastline is limited to a short stretch of 13 mi [20 km] on the Adriatic coast.

A Mediterranean climate, with dry, sunny summers and moist, mild winters, prevails only near the coast. Inland, the weather is more severe, with hot, dry summers and bitterly cold snowy winters.

POLITICS & ECONOMY In 1918, Bosnia-Herzegovina became part of the Kingdom of the Serbs, Croats, and Slovenes, which was renamed Yugoslavia in 1929. Germany occupied the area during World War II (1939–45). From 1945, Communist governments ruled Yugoslavia as a federation containing six republics, one of which was Bosnia-Herzegovina. In the 1980s, the country faced problems as Communist policies proved unsuccessful.

In 1990, free elections were held in Bosnia-Herzegovina and the non-Communists won a majority. A Muslim, Alija Izetbegovic, was elected president. In 1991, Croatia and Slovenia, other parts of the former Yugoslavia, declared themselves independent. In 1992, Bosnia-Herzegovina held a vote on independence. Most Bosnian Serbs boycotted the vote, while the Muslims and Bosnian Croats voted in favor. Many Bosnian Serbs, opposed to independence, started a war against the non-Serbs. They soon occupied more than two-thirds of the land. The Bosnian Serbs were accused of "ethnic cleansing" – that is, the killing or expulsion of other ethnic groups from Serb-occupied areas. The war was later extended when Croat forces seized other parts of the country.

In 1995, the conflict was resolved. Under an agreement, the country's boundaries were maintained, but the territory was divided into two self-governing provinces, one Bosnian-Serb and the other Muslim-Croat, under a central government. Stability was restored with the help of NATO. Elections were held in 2006, but in 2009 the Serb leader Milorad Dodik called for a referendum on Serb secession from Bosnia-Herzegovina.

The economy of Bosnia-Herzegovina, the least developed of the six republics of the former Yugoslavia apart from Macedonia, was shattered by the war in the early 1990s. Before the war, manufactures were the main exports, including electrical, machinery and transport equipment, and textiles. Farm products include fruits, maize, tobacco, vegetables, and wheat, but food has to be imported.

AREA 19,767 SQ MI [51,197 SQ KM]
POPULATION 4,613,000 **CAPITAL** SARAJEVO
GOVERNMENT FEDERAL REPUBLIC **ETHNIC GROUPS** BOSNIAN 48%, SERB 37%, CROAT 14% **LANGUAGES** BOSNIAN, SERBIAN, CROATIAN
RELIGIONS ISLAM 40%, SERBIAN ORTHODOX 31%, ROMAN CATHOLIC 15%, OTHERS 14% **CURRENCY** CONVERTIBLE MARKA = 100 CONVERTIBLE PFENNIGA

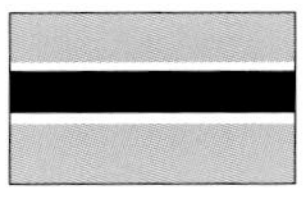
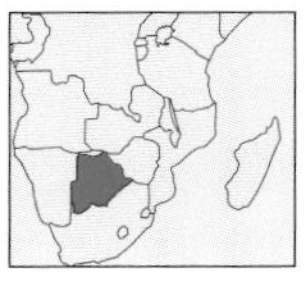

BOTSWANA

GEOGRAPHY The Republic of Botswana is a landlocked country in southern Africa. The Kalahari, a semidesert area covered mostly by grasses and thorn scrub, covers much of the country. Most of the south has no permanent streams. But large depressions in the north are inland drainage basins. In one of them, the Okavango River, which rises in Angola, forms a large, swampy delta.

Temperatures are high in the summer months (October to April), but the winter months are much cooler. In winter, night-time temperatures sometimes drop below freezing point. The average annual rainfall ranges from over 16 inches [400 mm] in the east to less than 8 inches [200 mm] in the southwest.

POLITICS & ECONOMY The earliest inhabitants of the region were the San, who are also called Bushmen. They had a nomadic way of life, hunting wild animals and collecting wild plant foods.

Britain ruled the area as the Bechuanaland Protectorate between 1885 and 1966. When the country became independent, it was renamed Botswana. Since then, the country has been a stable, multiparty democracy. However, a major setback occurred in the early 21st century, when health officials announced that around 25% of the people were infected with HIV/AIDS.

In 1966, Botswana was extremely poor, depending on meat and live cattle for its exports. But the discovery of minerals, including coal, cobalt, copper, diamonds, and nickel, has boosted the economy. About 16% of the people now depend on agriculture, raising cattle, and growing crops. Industries include the processing of farm products.

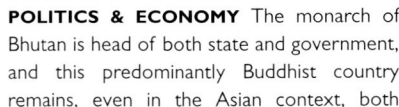

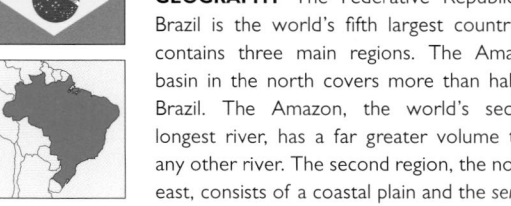

AREA 224,606 sq mi [581,730 sq km]
POPULATION 1,991,000 **CAPITAL** Gaborone
GOVERNMENT Multiparty republic **ETHNIC GROUPS** Tswana (or Setswana) 79%, Kalanga 11%, Basarwa 3%, others
LANGUAGES English (official), Setswana **RELIGIONS** Traditional beliefs 85%, Christianity 15% **CURRENCY** Pula = 100 thebe

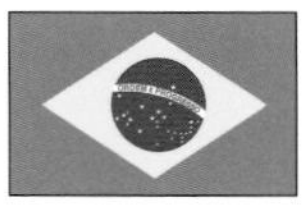
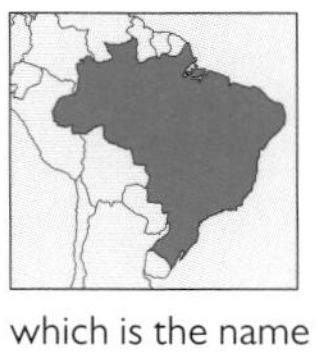

BRAZIL

GEOGRAPHY The Federative Republic of Brazil is the world's fifth largest country. It contains three main regions. The Amazon basin in the north covers more than half of Brazil. The Amazon, the world's second longest river, has a far greater volume than any other river. The second region, the northeast, consists of a coastal plain and the *sertão*, which is the name for the inland plateaux and hill country. The main river in this region is the São Francisco.

The third region is made up of the plateaux in the southeast. This region, which covers about a quarter of the country, is the most developed and densely populated part of Brazil. Its main river is the Paraná, which flows south through Argentina.

Manaus has high temperatures all through the year. The rainfall is heavy, though the period from June to September is drier than the rest of the year. The capital, Brasília, and the city Rio de Janeiro also have tropical climates, with much more marked dry seasons than Manaus. The far south has a temperate climate. The northeastern interior is the driest region, with an average annual rainfall of only 10 inches [250 mm] in places. The rainfall is also unreliable and severe droughts are common in this region.

POLITICS & ECONOMY The Portuguese explorer Pedro Alvarez Cabral claimed Brazil for Portugal in 1500. With Spain occupied in western South America, the Portuguese began to develop their colony, which was more than 90 times as big as Portugal. To do this, they enslaved many local Amerindian people and introduced about 4 million African slaves. Brazil declared itself an independent empire in 1822 and a republic in 1889. From the 1930s, Brazil faced periods of military rule and widespread corruption. Civilian rule was restored in 1985. Brazil adopted a new constitution in 1988.

The United Nations has described Brazil as a "Rapidly Industrializing Country," or RIC. Its total volume of production is one of the largest in the world. But many people, including poor farmers and residents of the *favelas* (city slums), do not share in the country's fast economic growth. Poverty, inflation, and unemployment led to the election as president of Luiz Inácio Lula da Silva (popularly called "Lula") in 2002. In office, he worked to create economic stability. Despite revelations about political corruption, Lula was re-elected president in 2006.

Industry is the most important economic sector. Brazil is among the world's top producers of bauxite, chrome, diamonds, gold, iron ore, manganese, and tin. It is also a major manufacturing country. Its products include aircraft, cars, chemicals, processed food, iron and steel, paper, and textiles. The discovery of a major offshore oilfield was announced in 2007. Brazil is a major farming nation and agriculture employs 18% of the people. Coffee is a leading export. Other products include bananas, citrus fruits, cocoa, maize, rice, soybeans, and sugarcane. Brazil is also South America's top producer of eggs, meat, and milk.

Forestry is a major industry, though many people fear that the destruction of the rain forests, which may accelerate global warming, is an impending disaster for the entire world.

AREA 3,287,338 sq mi [8,514,215 sq km]
POPULATION 198,739,000 **CAPITAL** Brasília
GOVERNMENT Federal republic
ETHNIC GROUPS White 55%, Mulatto 38%, Black 6%, others 1% **LANGUAGES** Portuguese (official)
RELIGIONS Roman Catholic 80%
CURRENCY Real = 100 centavos

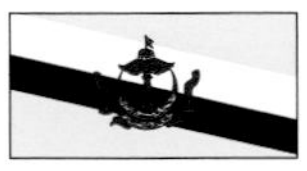
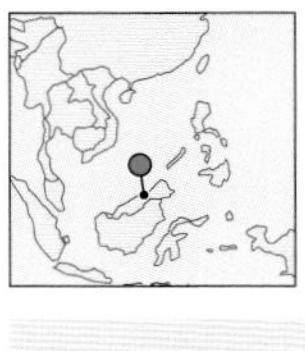

BRUNEI

The Islamic Sultanate of Brunei, a British protectorate until 1984, lies on the north coast of Borneo. The climate is tropical and rain forests cover large areas. Brunei is a prosperous country because of its oil and natural gas production, and the Sultan is said to be among the world's richest men.

AREA 2,226 sq mi [5,765 sq km]
POPULATION 388,000 **CAPITAL** Bandar Seri Begawan

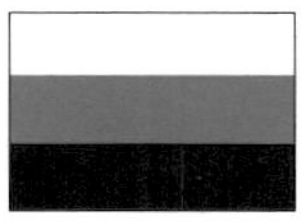
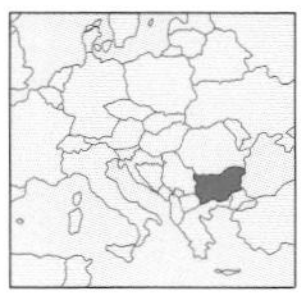

BULGARIA

GEOGRAPHY The Republic of Bulgaria is a country in the Balkan peninsula, facing the Black Sea in the east. The heart of Bulgaria is mountainous. The main ranges are the Balkan Mountains in the center and the Rhodope (or Rhodopi) Mountains in the south.

Summers are hot and winters are cold, though seldom severe. The rainfall is moderate.

POLITICS & ECONOMY Ottoman Turks ruled Bulgaria from 1396 and ethnic Turks still form a sizable minority in the country. In 1879, Bulgaria became a monarchy, and in 1908 it became fully independent. Bulgaria was an ally of Germany in World War I (1914–18) and again in World War II (1939–45). In 1944, Soviet troops invaded Bulgaria and, after the war, the monarchy was abolished and the country became a Communist ally of the Soviet Union. In the late 1980s, reforms in the Soviet Union led Bulgaria's government to introduce a multiparty system in 1990. A non-Communist government was elected in 1991, the first free elections in 44 years. Throughout the 1990s, Bulgaria faced many problems and it sought to become aligned to the West. Bulgaria became a member of NATO in 2004 and a member of the European Union in 2007. In 2009, the center-right GERB party, led by Boiko Borisov, who promised to tackle corruption and the economic crisis, won the parliamentary elections.

Bulgaria has a "lower-middle economy." It has some mineral deposits, including brown coal, manganese, and iron ore. But manufacturing is the leading activity, though, in the early 1990s, much of its industrial plant was out of date. Leading products include chemicals, processed foods, metal products, machinery, and textiles. Manufactures are the leading exports.

AREA 42,823 sq mi [110,912 sq km] **POPULATION** 7,205,000
CAPITAL Sofia **GOVERNMENT** Multiparty republic
ETHNIC GROUPS Bulgarian 84%, Turkish 9%, Gypsy 5%, Macedonian, Armenian, others **LANGUAGES** Bulgarian (official), Turkish **RELIGIONS** Bulgarian Orthodox 83%, Islam 12%, Roman Catholic 2%, others **CURRENCY** Lev = 100 stotinki

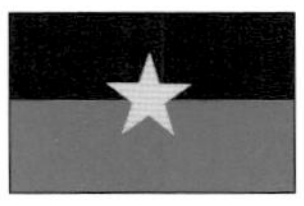
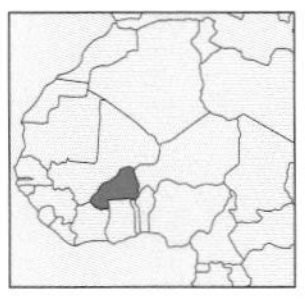

BURKINA FASO

GEOGRAPHY The Democratic People's Republic of Burkina Faso is a landlocked country, a little larger than the United Kingdom, in West Africa. But Burkina Faso has only one-sixth of the population of the UK. The country consists of a plateau, between about 650 ft and 2,300 ft [300 m to 700 m] above sea level. The plateau is cut by several rivers.

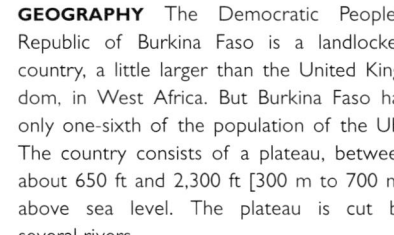

The capital city, Ouagadougou, in central Burkina Faso, has high temperatures throughout the year. Most of the rain falls between May and September, but the rainfall is erratic and droughts are common.

POLITICS & ECONOMY The people of Burkina Faso are divided into two main groups. The Voltaic group includes the Mossi, who form the largest single group, and the Bobo. The French conquered the Mossi capital of Ouagadougou in 1897 and they made the area a protectorate. In 1919, the area became a French colony called Upper Volta. After independence in 1960, Upper Volta became a one-party state. But it was unstable – military groups seized power several times and political killings took place. In 1984, the country's name was changed to Burkina Faso. In 1991, 1998, and 2005, the former coup leader, Captain Blaise Compaoré, was elected president. The military continued to influence government.

Burkina Faso is one of the world's 20 poorest countries and has become very dependent on foreign aid. Most of Burkina Faso is dry with thin soils. The country's main food crops are beans, maize, millet, rice, and sorghum. Cotton, groundnuts, and shea nuts, whose seeds produce a fat used to make cooking oil and soap, are grown for sale abroad. Livestock are also an important export.

The country has few resources and manufacturing is on a small scale. There are some deposits of manganese, zinc, lead, and nickel in the north of the country, but there is not yet a good enough transport system there. Many young men seek jobs abroad in Ghana and Ivory Coast. The money they send home to their families is important to the country's economy.

AREA 105,791 sq mi [274,000 sq km]
POPULATION 15,746,000 **CAPITAL** Ouagadougou
GOVERNMENT Multiparty republic **ETHNIC GROUPS** Mossi 40%, Gurunsi, Senufo, Lobi, Bobo, Mande, Fulani **LANGUAGES** French (official), Mossi, Fulani **RELIGIONS** Islam 50%, traditional beliefs 40%, Christianity 10% **CURRENCY** CFA franc = 100 centimes

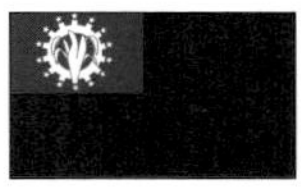
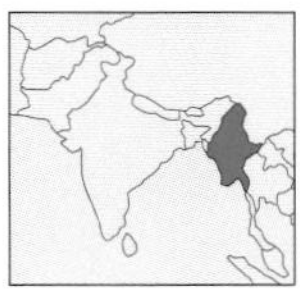

BURMA (MYANMAR)

GEOGRAPHY The Union of Burma has been officially known as the Union of Myanmar since 1989. However, it is more usually referred to as Burma. Mountains border the country in the east and west, with the highest mountains in the north. Burma's highest mountain is Hkakabo Razi, which is 19,294 ft [5,881 m] high. Between these ranges is central Burma, which contains the fertile valleys of the Irrawaddy and Sittang rivers. The Irrawaddy delta is a leading rice-growing area.

Burma has a tropical monsoon climate with three seasons. The rainy season runs from late May to mid-October. A cool, dry season follows, between late October and the middle part of February. The hot season lasts from late February to mid-May. In May 2008, a typhoon devastated the south, including the Irrawaddy delta. More than 80,000 people were reported killed and another 50,000 were missing.

POLITICS & ECONOMY Many groups settled in Burma in ancient times. Some, called the hill peoples, live in remote mountain areas where they have retained their own cultures. The ancestors of the country's main ethnic group today, the Burmese, arrived in the 9th century AD. Britain conquered Burma in the 19th century and made it a province of British India. But, in 1937, the British granted Burma limited self-government. Japan conquered Burma in 1942, but the Japanese were driven out in 1945. Burma became a fully independent country in 1948.

Revolts by Communists and various hill people led to instability in the 1950s. In 1962, Burma became a military dictatorship and, in 1974, a one-party state. Attempts to control minority liberation movements and the opium trade led to repressive rule. The National League for Democracy led by Aung San Suu Kyi won the elections in 1990, but the military continued their repressive rule, earning Burma the reputation for having one of the world's worst human rights records. In 2004, a UN report criticized the regime for failing to release opposition leader Aung San Suu Kyi from house arrest. In 2005, the government announced that a new capital, Naypyidaw ("Abode of Kings"), was being built north of Rangoon (Yangon). In 2010, the military *junta* announced that Aung San Suu Kyi would not be allowed to participate in elections. In 2010, her party announced its dissolution.

Agriculture is the main activity, employing 66% of the people. The chief crop is rice. Maize, pulses, oilseeds, and sugarcane are other major products. Forestry is important. Teak and rice together make up about two-thirds of the total value of the exports. Burma has many mineral resources, though they are mostly undeveloped, but the country is famous for its precious stones, especially rubies. Manufacturing is mostly on a small scale.

AREA 261,227 sq mi [676,578 sq km] **POPULATION** 48,138,000
CAPITAL Rangoon (Yangon); Naypyidaw (administrative capital)
GOVERNMENT Military regime **ETHNIC GROUPS** Burman 68%, Shan 9%, Karen 7%, Rakhine 4%, Chinese, Indian, Mon
LANGUAGES Burmese (official); minority ethnic groups have their own languages **RELIGIONS** Buddhism 89%, Christianity, Islam
CURRENCY Kyat = 100 pyas

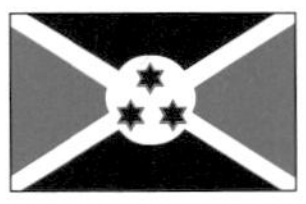
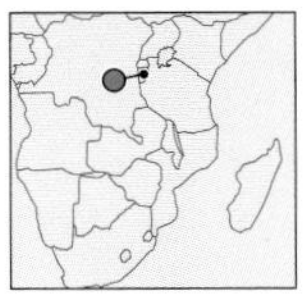

BURUNDI

GEOGRAPHY The Republic of Burundi is the fifth smallest country in mainland Africa. It is also the second most densely populated after its northern neighbor, Rwanda. Part of the Great African Rift Valley, which runs throughout eastern Africa into southwestern Asia, lies in western Burundi. It includes part of Lake Tanganyika. Bujumbura, the capital city, lies on the shore of Lake Tanganyika and has a warm climate. A dry season occurs from June to September, but the other months are fairly rainy. The mountains and plateaux to the east are cooler and wetter, but the rainfall generally decreases to the east.

POLITICS & ECONOMY The Twa, a pygmy people, were the first known inhabitants of Burundi. About 1,000 years ago, the Hutu, a people who speak a Bantu language, gradually began to settle the area, pushing the Twa into remote areas.

From the 15th century, the Tutsi, a cattle-owning people from the northeast, gradually took over the country. The Hutu, though greatly outnumbering the Tutsi, were forced to serve the Tutsi overlords.

Germany conquered the area that is now Burundi and Rwanda in the late 1890s. The area, called Ruanda-Urundi, was taken by Belgium during World War I (1914–18). In 1961, the people of Urundi voted to become a monarchy, while the people of Ruanda voted to become a republic. The two territories became fully independent as Burundi and Rwanda in 1962. After 1962, the rivalries between the Hutu and Tutsi led to periodic outbreaks of

fighting. The Tutsi monarchy was ended in 1966 and Burundi became a republic. Instability continued with coups and massacres as Tutsis and Hutus fought against each other. A power-sharing agreement was reached in 2001, though conflict continued in places. Elections were held in 2005 under a new constitution and the last major rebel group disarmed in 2009.

Burundi is one of the world's poorest countries. About 93% of the people live by farming, mostly at subsistence level. Food crops include beans, cassava, maize, and sweet potatoes. Livestock are raised and fishing is important. But Burundi has to import food.

AREA 10,747 SQ MI [27,834 SQ KM]
POPULATION 9,511,000 **CAPITAL** BUJUMBURA
GOVERNMENT REPUBLIC **ETHNIC GROUPS** HUTU 85%, TUTSI 14%, TWA (PYGMY) 1% **LANGUAGES** FRENCH AND KIRUNDI (BOTH OFFICIAL)
RELIGIONS ROMAN CATHOLIC 62%, TRADITIONAL BELIEFS 23%, ISLAM 10%, PROTESTANT 5% **CURRENCY** BURUNDI FRANC = 100 CENTIMES

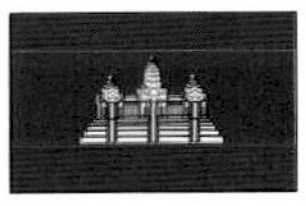
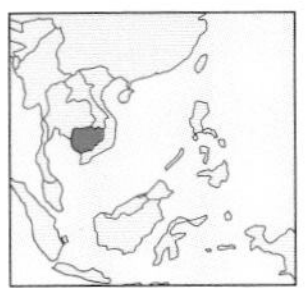

CAMBODIA

GEOGRAPHY The Kingdom of Cambodia is a country in Southeast Asia. Low mountains border the country except in the southeast. But most of Cambodia consists of plains drained by the River Mekong, which enters Cambodia from Laos in the north and exits through Vietnam in the southeast. The northwest contains Tonlé Sap (or Great Lake). In the dry season, this lake drains into the River Mekong. But in the wet season, the level of the Mekong rises and water flows in the opposite direction from the river into Tonlé Sap – the lake then becomes the largest freshwater lake in Asia.

Cambodia has a tropical monsoon climate, with high temperatures throughout the year. The dry season, when winds blow from the north or northeast, runs from November to April. During the rainy season (May to October), moist winds blow from the south or southeast. The high humidity and heat often make conditions unpleasant. Rainfall is heaviest near the coast, and rather lower inland.

POLITICS & ECONOMY From 802 to 1432, the Khmer people ruled a great empire, which reached its peak in the 12th century. The Khmer capital was at Angkor. The Hindu stone temples built there and at nearby Angkor Wat form the world's largest group of religious buildings. France ruled the country between 1863 and 1954, when the country became an independent monarchy. But the monarchy was abolished in 1970 and Cambodia became a republic.

In 1970, US and South Vietnamese troops entered Cambodia but left after destroying North Vietnamese Communist camps in the east. The country became involved in the Vietnamese War, and then in a civil war as Cambodian Communists of the Khmer Rouge organization fought for power. The Khmer Rouge took over Cambodia in 1975 and launched a reign of terror in which between 1 million and 2.5 million people were killed. In 1979, Vietnamese and Cambodian troops overthrew the Khmer Rouge government. But fighting continued between factions. Vietnam withdrew in 1989, and in 1991 Prince Sihanouk was recognized as head of state. Elections were held in May 1993, and in September 1993 the monarchy was restored. Elections were held in 1998, 2003, and 2008. In 2004, King Sihanouk abdicated because of ill health and his son, Prince Norodom Sihamoni, became king. In 2008–9, Cambodia and Thailand clashed over a border dispute involving an area near the ancient Preah Vihear temple, which had been declared a World Heritage site.

Cambodia is a poor country whose economy has been wrecked by war. Farming is the main activity and rice, rubber, and maize are leading products. Manufacturing is on a small scale, but the discovery of oil reserves and an increase in tourism have recently boosted the economy.

AREA 69,898 SQ MI [181,035 SQ KM] **POPULATION** 14,494,000
CAPITAL PHNOM PENH **GOVERNMENT** CONSTITUTIONAL MONARCHY
ETHNIC GROUPS KHMER 90%, VIETNAMESE 5%, CHINESE 1%, OTHERS
LANGUAGES KHMER (OFFICIAL), FRENCH, ENGLISH
RELIGIONS BUDDHISM 95%, OTHERS 5% **CURRENCY** RIEL = 100 SEN

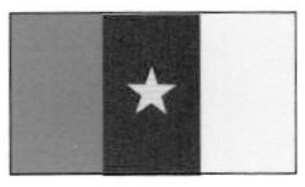
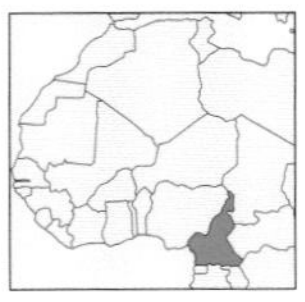

CAMEROON

GEOGRAPHY The Republic of Cameroon in West Africa derived its name from the Portuguese word *camarões*, or prawns. This name was used by Portuguese explorers who fished for prawns along the coast. Behind the narrow coastal plains on the Gulf of Guinea, the land rises to a series of plateaux, with a mountainous region in the southwest where the volcano Mount Cameroun is situated. In the north, the land slopes down toward the Lake Chad basin.

The rainfall is heavy, especially in the highlands. The rainiest months near the coast are June to September. The rainfall decreases to the north and the far north has a hot, dry climate. Temperatures are high on the coast, whereas the inland plateaux are cooler.

POLITICS & ECONOMY Germany lost Cameroon during World War I (1914–18). The country was then divided into two parts, one ruled by Britain and the other by France. In 1960, French Cameroon became the independent Cameroon Republic. In 1961, after a vote in British Cameroon, part of the territory joined the Cameroon Republic to become the Federal Republic of Cameroon – the other part joined Nigeria. In 1972, Cameroon became a unitary state called the United Republic of Cameroon. It adopted the name Republic of Cameroon in 1984, but the country had two official languages. In 1995, partly to placate the English-speaking people, Cameroon became the 52nd member of the Commonwealth.

Like most countries in tropical Africa, Cameroon's economy is based on agriculture, which employs 54% of the people. The chief food crops include cassava, maize, millet, sweet potatoes, and yams. The country also has plantations to produce such crops as cocoa and coffee for export. Cameroon exports oil and bauxite. In 2002, its claim over the oil-rich Bakassi peninsula was upheld by the International Court of Justice. Nigeria finally withdrew in 2006, although it kept control over the southern part of the peninsula until 2008 when it withdrew. Cameroon has few manufacturing industries, but it is self-sufficient in food.

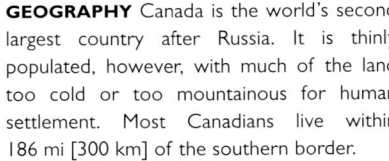

AREA 183,568 SQ MI [475,442 SQ KM] **POPULATION** 18,879,000
CAPITAL YAOUNDÉ **GOVERNMENT** MULTIPARTY REPUBLIC
ETHNIC GROUPS CAMEROON HIGHLANDERS 31%, BANTU 27%, KIRDI 11%, FULANI 10%, OTHERS **LANGUAGES** FRENCH AND ENGLISH (BOTH OFFICIAL)
RELIGIONS CHRISTIANITY 40%, TRADITIONAL BELIEFS 40%, ISLAM 20%
CURRENCY CFA FRANC = 100 CENTIMES

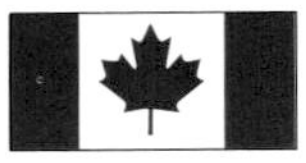
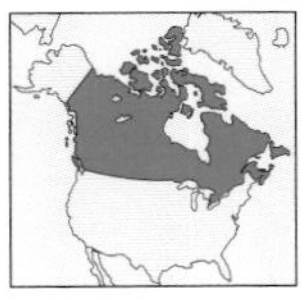

CANADA

GEOGRAPHY Canada is the world's second largest country after Russia. It is thinly populated, however, with much of the land too cold or too mountainous for human settlement. Most Canadians live within 186 mi [300 km] of the southern border.

Western Canada is rugged. It includes the Pacific ranges and the mighty Rocky Mountains. East of the Rockies are the interior plains. In the north lie the bleak Arctic islands, while to the south lie the densely populated lowlands around lakes Erie and Ontario and in the St Lawrence River valley. The melting of Arctic ice, attributed to global warming, has led to concern about international rights over the Arctic waters off northern Canada.

Canada has a cold climate. In winter, temperatures fall below freezing point throughout most of Canada. But the southwestern coast has a relatively mild climate. Along the Arctic Circle, mean temperatures are below freezing for seven months a year. The west and southeast have high rainfall, but the prairies are dry with 10 inches to 20 inches [250 mm to 500 mm] of rain every year.

POLITICS & ECONOMY Canada's first people, the ancestors of the Native Americans, or Indians, arrived in North America from Asia around 40,000 years ago. The Inuit (Eskimos) were later arrivals from Asia. Europeans first reached Canada in 1497 and soon Britain and France began to compete for control.

France gained an initial advantage, and the French founded Québec in 1608. But the British later occupied eastern Canada. In 1867, Britain passed the British North America Act, which set up the Dominion of Canada, which was made up of Québec, Ontario, Nova Scotia, and New Brunswick. Other areas were added, the last being Newfoundland in 1949. Canada fought alongside Britain in both World Wars and many Canadians feel close ties with Britain. Canada is a constitutional monarchy, and the British monarch is Canada's head of state.

In 1995, the people of Québec voted narrowly against a move to make Québec a sovereign state. In 2006, the national parliament voted to recognize Québec as a nation within a united Canada – a symbolic act of reconciliation. Another major issue concerns the rights of Aboriginal minorities. In 1999, Canada created the territory of Nunavut for the Inuit population. Nunavut covers 64% of what was formerly the eastern part of the Northwest Territories. In 2006, the Conservative Party, led by Stephen Harper, was returned to power, ending 12 years of Liberal Party rule. Stephen Harper was re-elected in 2008.

Canada is a highly developed and prosperous country. Although farmland covers only 8% of the country, Canadian farms are highly productive. Canada is one of the world's leading producers of barley, wheat, meat, and milk. Forestry and fishing are other important industries. It is rich in natural resources, especially oil and natural gas, and is a major exporter of minerals. The country also produces copper, gold, iron ore, uranium, and zinc. Manufacturing is important in the cities, where 80% of the people live. Manufactures include processed mineral and farm products, cars, chemicals, electronic goods, machinery, paper, and timber products.

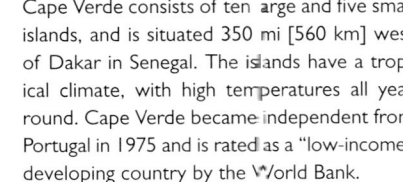

AREA 3,849,653 SQ MI [9,970,610 SQ KM]
POPULATION 33,487,000 **CAPITAL** OTTAWA
GOVERNMENT FEDERAL MULTIPARTY CONSTITUTIONAL MONARCHY
ETHNIC GROUPS BRITISH ORIGIN 28%, FRENCH ORIGIN 23%, OTHER EUROPEAN 15%, AMERINDIAN/INUIT 2%, OTHERS
LANGUAGES ENGLISH AND FRENCH (BOTH OFFICIAL)
RELIGIONS ROMAN CATHOLIC 46%, PROTESTANT 36%, JUDAISM, ISLAM, HINDUISM **CURRENCY** CANADIAN DOLLAR = 100 CENTS

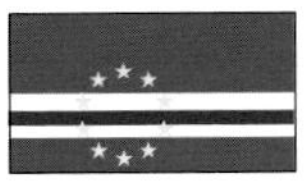
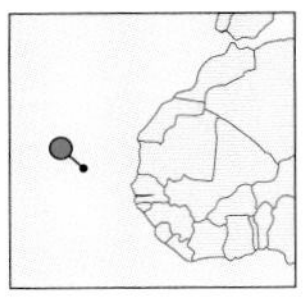

CAPE VERDE

Cape Verde consists of ten large and five small islands, and is situated 350 mi [560 km] west of Dakar in Senegal. The islands have a tropical climate, with high temperatures all year round. Cape Verde became independent from Portugal in 1975 and is rated as a "low-income" developing country by the World Bank.

AREA 1,557 SQ MI [4,033 SQ KM]
POPULATION 429,000 **CAPITAL** PRAIA

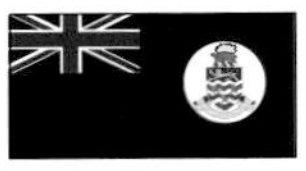
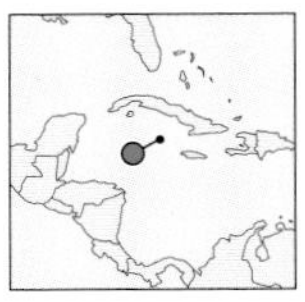

CAYMAN ISLANDS

The Cayman Islands are an overseas territory of the UK, consisting of three low-lying islands. Financial services are the main economic activity and the islands offer a secret tax haven to many companies and banks.

AREA 102 SQ MI [264 SQ KM]
POPULATION 49,000 **CAPITAL** GEORGE TOWN

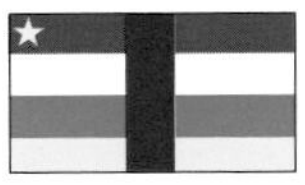
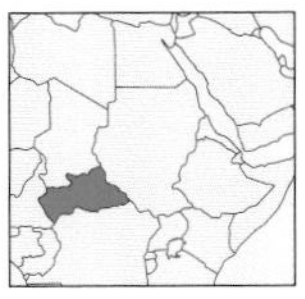

CENTRAL AFRICAN REPUBLIC

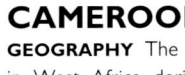

GEOGRAPHY The Central African Republic is a remote, landlocked country in the heart of Africa. It consists mostly of a plateau lying between 1,970 ft and 2,620 ft [600 m to 800 m] above sea level. The Ubangi drains the south, while the Chari (or Shari) River flows from the north to the Lake Chad basin. The climate is warm throughout the year, while the annual average rainfall in the capital Bangui totals 62 inches [1,574 mm]. The north is drier, with an average annual rainfall of about 31 inches [800 mm].

POLITICS & ECONOMY France set up an outpost at Bangui in 1899 and ruled the country as a colony from 1894. Known as Ubangi-Shari, the country was ruled by France as part of French Equatorial Africa until it gained independence in 1960.

Central African Republic became a one-party state in 1962, but army officers seized power in 1966. The head of the army, Jean-Bedel Bokassa, made himself emperor in 1976. The country was renamed the Central African Empire, but Bokassa was removed by a military coup in 1979. The country again became a republic.

The republic adopted a new multiparty constitution in 1991, and elections were held in 1993 and 1998. An army uprising in 2002 ended in the overthrow of the government in 2003. General François Bozize took power. He was elected president in 2005, but rebel activities in 2006–7 led thousands of refugees to flee into Chad and Cameroon. In 2009, the US-based Fund for Peace classified the country as a "failed state."

The World Bank classifies Central African Republic as a "low-income" developing country. Over 80% of the people are farmers, and most of them produce little more than they need to feed their families. The main crops are bananas, maize, manioc, millet, and yams. Coffee, cotton, timber, and tobacco are produced for export. Development has been impeded by the country's remote position, its poor transport system, and its untrained work force. The country depends heavily on aid from France.

AREA 240,534 SQ MI [622,984 SQ KM] **POPULATION** 4,511,000
CAPITAL BANGUI **GOVERNMENT** MULTIPARTY REPUBLIC
ETHNIC GROUPS BAYA 33%, BANDA 27%, MANDJIA 13%, SARA 10%, MBOUM 7%, MBAKA 4%, OTHERS **LANGUAGES** FRENCH (OFFICIAL), SANGHO
RELIGIONS TRADITIONAL BELIEFS 35%, PROTESTANT 25%, ROMAN CATHOLIC 25%, ISLAM 15% **CURRENCY** CFA FRANC = 100 CENTIMES

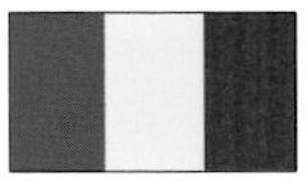

CHAD

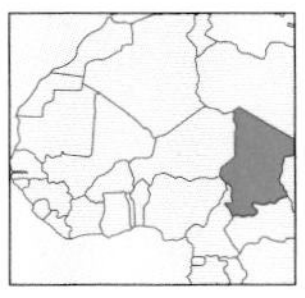

GEOGRAPHY The Republic of Chad is a landlocked country in north-central Africa. It is Africa's fifth largest country and is over twice the size of France, the country which once ruled it as a colony.

Ndjamena in central Chad has a hot, tropical climate, with a marked dry season from November to April. The south of the country is wetter, with an average yearly rainfall of around 39 inches [1,000 mm]. The burning-hot desert in the north has an average yearly rainfall of less than 5 inches [130 mm].

POLITICS & ECONOMY Chad straddles two worlds. The north is populated by Muslim Arab and Berber peoples, while black Africans, who follow traditional beliefs or who have converted to Christianity, live in the south. French explorers were active in the area in the late 19th century. France made Chad a colony in 1902.

Chad became independent in 1960, but the 1970s were marked by ethnic conflict that led to civil wars, coups and conflict with Libya, which supported rebel factions. Chad and Libya agreed a truce in 1987 and, in 1994, the International Court of Justice ruled against Libya's claim on the Aozou Strip. From 2004, Chad forces clashed with pro-Sudanese militias as the conflict in Sudan's Darfur province spilled over the border. In 2010, talks between Chad and Sudan led to hopes of normalization along the border.

Chad is one of the world's poorest countries. Farming and fishing employ 83% of the people. Food crops include groundnuts, millet, rice and sorghum, but cotton is the chief export crop. Chad has few manufacturing industries, but its oil reserves hold out hope for development. Oil production began in 2003.

AREA 495,752 sq mi [1,284,000 sq km]
POPULATION 10,329,000 **CAPITAL** Ndjamena
GOVERNMENT Multiparty republic **ETHNIC GROUPS** 200 distinct groups: mostly Muslim in the north and center; mostly Christian or animist in the south **LANGUAGES** French and Arabic (both official), many others **RELIGIONS** Islam 51%, Christianity 35%, animist 7%
CURRENCY CFA franc = 100 centimes

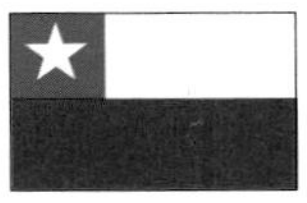

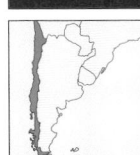

CHILE

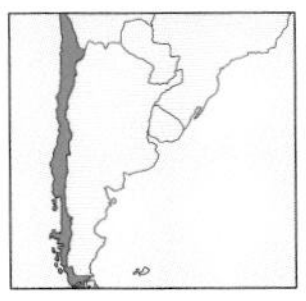

GEOGRAPHY The Republic of Chile stretches about 2,650 mi [4,260 km] from north to south, although the maximum east–west distance is only about 267 mi [430 km]. The high Andes Mountains form Chile's eastern borders with Argentina and Bolivia. To the west are basins and valleys, with coastal uplands overlooking the shore. Most people live in the central valley, where Santiago is situated. Earthquakes are common. In February 2010, an earthquake with a magnitude of 8.8 (the biggest in 50 years) struck central Chile, killing more than 400 people.

Santiago has a Mediterranean climate with hot, dry summers and mild, moist winters. The Atacama Desert in the north is extremely arid, while the south is cold and stormy.

POLITICS & ECONOMY Amerindian people reached the southern tip of South America 8,000 years ago. In 1520, Portuguese navigator Ferdinand Magellan was the first European to sight Chile. The country became a Spanish colony in the 1540s. Chile became independent in 1818. During a war (1879–83), it gained mineral-rich areas from Peru and Bolivia.

In 1970, Salvador Allende became the first Communist leader to be elected democratically. He was overthrown in 1973 by army officers, who were supported by the CIA. General Augusto Pinochet then ruled as a dictator. A new constitution was introduced in 1981. Pinochet remained in power until 1989. In 2006, Michelle Bachelet, a center-left former torture victim under the Pinochet regime, became president. She was succeeded in 2010 by a right-winger, Sebastian Pinera.

According to the World Bank, Chile has a "lower-middle-income" economy. Mining, especially copper, is important and minerals dominate the exports. But manufacturing is the most valuable activity. Products include processed foods, metals, iron and steel, transport equipment, and textiles. The chief crop is wheat, while beans, fruits, maize, and livestock products are also important. Chile's fishing industry is one of the world's largest.

AREA 292,133 sq mi [756,626 sq km]
POPULATION 16,602,000 **CAPITAL** Santiago
GOVERNMENT Multiparty republic **ETHNIC GROUPS** Mestizo 95%, Amerindian 3% **LANGUAGES** Spanish (official)
RELIGIONS Roman Catholic 89%, Protestant 11%
CURRENCY Chilean peso = 100 centavos

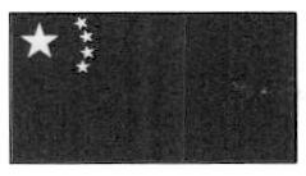

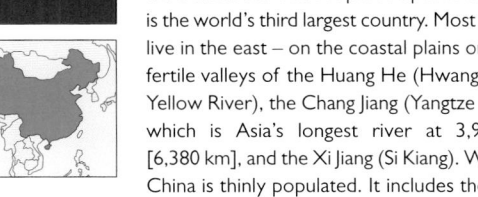

CHINA

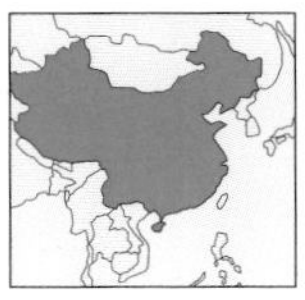

GEOGRAPHY The People's Republic of China is the world's third largest country. Most people live in the east – on the coastal plains or in the fertile valleys of the Huang He (Hwang Ho or Yellow River), the Chang Jiang (Yangtze Kiang), which is Asia's longest river at 3,960 mi [6,380 km], and the Xi Jiang (Si Kiang). Western China is thinly populated. It includes the bleak Tibetan plateau which is bounded by the Himalaya, the world's highest mountain range. Deserts include the Gobi Desert along the Mongolian border and the Taklamakan Desert in the far west. Earthquakes are common. In May 2008, a major earthquake in the southwest killed more than 69,000 people and made millions homeless.

Beijing has cold winters and warm summers with moderate rainfall. To the south, Shanghai has milder winters and more rain. The southeast has a wet, subtropical climate, but the west has a severe climate. Lhasa has very cold winters and a low rainfall.

POLITICS & ECONOMY China is one of the world's oldest civilizations, going back 3,500 years. Under the Han dynasty (202 BC to AD 220), the Chinese empire was as large as the Roman empire. Mongols conquered China in the 13th century, but Chinese rule was restored in 1368. The Manchu people of Mongolia ruled the country from 1644 to 1912, when the country became a republic.

War with Japan (1937–45) was followed by civil war between the nationalists and the Communists. The Communists triumphed in 1949, setting up the People's Republic of China. In the 1980s, following the death of the revolutionary leader Mao Zedong (Mao Tse-tung) in 1976, China encouraged formerly forbidden policies, namely private enterprise and foreign investment. But the Communist leaders have not permitted political freedom. Opponents are still harshly treated, while attempts to negotiate some degree of autonomy for Tibet have been rejected.

China's economy has expanded greatly since the 1970s and many new industries have been set up in the east. Between 1989 and 2008, the economy grew by around 9% per year and China is now one of the world's four largest economies. China has benefited from the return of Hong Kong in 1997 and its admission to the World Trade Organization in 2001. The global financial crisis in 2008 slowed the economic growth rate, though China's economy grew in 2009 by around 8.7%, which was higher than official expectations, making China look likely to become the world's second largest economy before long.

Despite its recent success, China remains a poor country. In 2002, agriculture employed 43% of the work force, although only 10% of the land is farmed. In 2006, plans were announced to help the people living in the countryside catch up economically with people in the cities.

Farm products include rice, sweet potatoes, tea, and wheat, and many fruits and vegetables. Livestock farming is important, and China has more than a third of the world's pigs. Resources include coal, iron ore, and other metals. Manufactures include cement, chemicals, fertilizers, machinery, telecommunications and recording equipment, and textiles. China is now a major producer of consumer goods, including cameras, computer products, refrigerators, and television sets.

AREA 3,705,387 sq mi [9,596,961 sq km]
POPULATION 1,338,613,000 **CAPITAL** Beijing
GOVERNMENT Single-party Communist republic
ETHNIC GROUPS Han Chinese 92%, many others
LANGUAGES Mandarin Chinese (official) **RELIGIONS** Atheist (official)
CURRENCY Renminbi yuan = 10 jiao = 100 fen

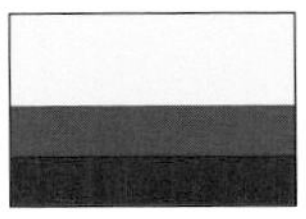

COLOMBIA

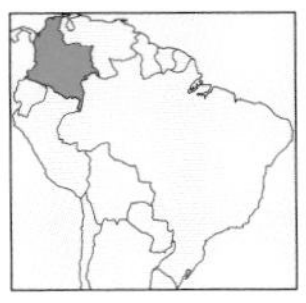

GEOGRAPHY The Republic of Colombia, in northeastern South America, is the only country in the continent to have coastlines on both the Pacific and the Caribbean Sea. Colombia also contains the northernmost ranges of the Andes Mountains.

There is a tropical climate in the lowlands, but the altitude greatly affects the climate of the Andes. The capital, Bogotá, which stands on a plateau in the eastern Andes at about 9,200 ft [2,800 m] above sea level, has mild temperatures throughout the year. The rainfall is heavy, especially on the Pacific coast.

POLITICS & ECONOMY Amerindian people have lived in Colombia for thousands of years. But today, only a small proportion of the people are of unmixed Amerindian ancestry. Mestizos (people of mixed white and Amerindian ancestry) form the largest group, followed by whites and mulattos (people of mixed European and African ancestry). Spaniards opened up the area in the early 16th century. They set up a territory known as the Viceroyalty of the New Kingdom of Granada, including Colombia, Ecuador, Panama, and Venezuela. In 1819, the area became independent, but Ecuador and Venezuela soon split away, followed by Panama in 1903.

Instability has marked its recent history. Colombia faces economic and security problems, notably combating left-wing guerrillas and right-wing paramilitaries, while controlling the illicit drug industry. Andrés Pastrana, president between 1998 and 2002, tried to end the guerrilla war, but peace talks collapsed in 2002 and conflict resumed. His successor, Alvaro Uribe, elected in 2002 and 2006, pursued a tough line against the rebels.

Colombia has a "lower-middle-income" economy. It exports oil, coffee, and chemicals.

AREA 439,735 sq mi [1,138,914 sq km] **POPULATION** 43,677,000
CAPITAL Bogotá **GOVERNMENT** Multiparty republic
ETHNIC GROUPS Mestizo 58%, White 20%, Mulatto 14%, Black 4%
LANGUAGES Spanish (official) **RELIGIONS** Roman Catholic 90%
CURRENCY Colombian peso = 100 centavos

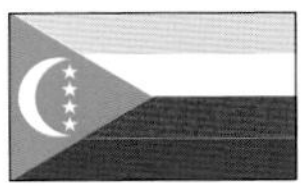

COMOROS

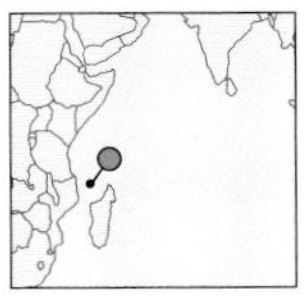

The Union des Isles Comores, as the Comoros is officially called, consists of three large volcanic islands and some smaller ones, lying at the north end of the Mozambique Channel in the Indian Ocean. France took over one of the islands, Mayotte, in 1843, and, in 1886, the other islands came under French protection.

The Comoros became independent in 1974, but Mayotte remained French, becoming fully integrated with France in 2009. In the 1990s, the islands of Anjouan and Mohéli tried to secede, but, in 2004, the large islands were granted autonomy. In 2008, an illegal regime on Anjouan was overthrown. Exports include cloves, perfume oil, and vanilla.

AREA 863 sq mi [2,235 sq km] **POPULATION** 752,000 **CAPITAL** Moroni

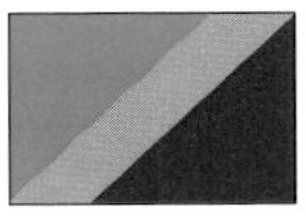

CONGO

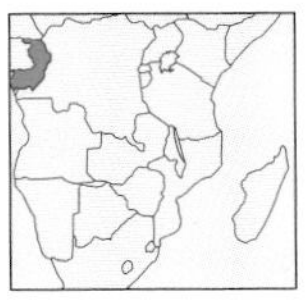

GEOGRAPHY The Republic of Congo is a country on the River Congo in west-central Africa. The Equator runs through the center of the country. Congo has a narrow coastal plain on which its main port, Pointe Noire, stands. Behind the plain are uplands through which the River Niari has carved a fertile valley. Central Congo consists of high plains. The north contains large swampy areas in the valleys of the tributaries of the River Congo.

Congo has a hot, wet equatorial climate. Brazzaville has a dry season between June and September. The coast is drier and cooler than the rest of Congo, because of the cold offshore Benguela ocean current.

POLITICS & ECONOMY Part of the huge Kongo kingdom between the 15th and 18th centuries, the coast of the Congo later became a center of the European slave trade. The area came under French protection in 1880. It was later governed as part of a larger region called French Equatorial Africa. The country remained under French control until 1960.

Congo became a one-party state in 1964 and a military group took over the government in 1968. In 1970, Congo declared itself a Communist country, though it continued to seek aid from Western countries. The government officially abandoned its Communist policies in 1990. Multiparty elections were held in 1992, but the elected president, Pascal Lissouba, was overthrown in 1997 by former president Denis Sassou-Nguesso. Civil war broke out in 1999 but peace was restored in 2002. Sassou-Nguesso was elected president. He was re-elected in 2009.

The World Bank classifies Congo as a "lower-middle-income" developing country. Agriculture is the most important activity, employing about 36% of the people. But many farmers produce little more than they need to feed their families. Major food crops include bananas, cassava, maize, and rice, while the leading cash crops are coffee and cocoa. Congo's main exports are oil (which makes up 90% of the total) and timber. Manufacturing is relatively unimportant at the moment, still hampered by poor transport links, but it is gradually being developed.

AREA 132,046 sq mi [342,000 sq km]
POPULATION 4,013,000 **CAPITAL** Brazzaville
GOVERNMENT Military regime **ETHNIC GROUPS** Kongo 48%, Sangha 20%, Teke 17%, M'Bochi 12% **LANGUAGES** French (official), many others **RELIGIONS** Christianity 50%, animist 48%, Islam 2%
CURRENCY CFA franc = 100 centimes

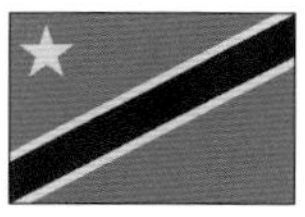

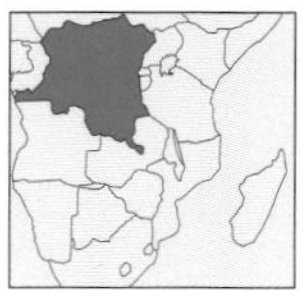

CONGO (DEMOCRATIC REPUBLIC OF THE)

GEOGRAPHY The Democratic Republic of the Congo, formerly known as Zaïre, is the world's 12th largest country. Much of the country lies within the drainage basin of the huge River Congo. The river reaches the sea along the country's coastline, which is 25 mi [40 km] long. Mountains rise in the east, where the country's borders run through lakes Tanganyika, Kivu, Edward, and Albert. The equatorial region has high temperatures and heavy rainfall throughout the year.

POLITICS & ECONOMY Pygmies were the first inhabitants of the region, with Portuguese navigators not reaching the coast until 1482, but the interior was not explored until the late 19th century. In 1885, the country, called Congo Free State, became the personal property of King Léopold II of Belgium. In 1908, the country became a Belgian colony.

The Belgian Congo became independent in 1960 and was renamed Zaïre in 1971. Ethnic rivalries caused instability until 1965, when the country became a one-party state, ruled by President Mobutu. The government allowed the formation of political parties in 1990, but elections were repeatedly postponed. In 1996, fighting broke out in eastern Zaïre, as the Tutsi–Hutu conflict in Burundi and Rwanda spilled over. The rebel leader Laurent Kabila took power in 1997, ousting Mobutu and renaming the country. A rebellion against Kabila broke out in 1998. Rwanda and Uganda supported the rebels, while Angola, Chad, Namibia, and Zimbabwe assisted Kabila. A peace treaty was signed in 1999, but fighting continued. Kabila was assassinated in 2001. His son, Major-General Joseph Kabila, became president. But instability continued into 2010 as various militias, including Tutsi, Hutu, and Ugandan rebels clashed with government forces in the east.

The World Bank classifies the Democratic Republic of the Congo as a "low-income" developing country, despite its reserves of copper, the main export, and other minerals. Agriculture, mainly at subsistence level, employs 62% of the people.

AREA 905,350 sq mi [2,344,858 sq km]
POPULATION 68,693,000 **CAPITAL** Kinshasa
GOVERNMENT Single-party republic
ETHNIC GROUPS Over 200; the largest are Mongo, Luba, Kongo, Mangbetu-Azande
LANGUAGES French (official), tribal languages
RELIGIONS Roman Catholic 50%, Protestant 20%, Islam 10%, others
CURRENCY Congolese franc = 100 centimes

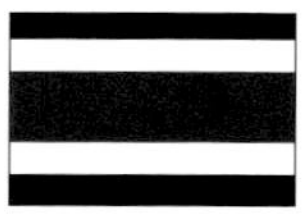

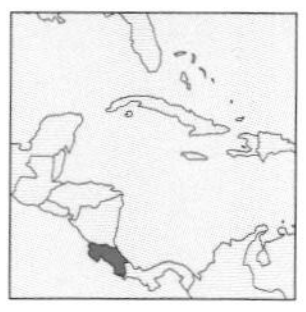

COSTA RICA

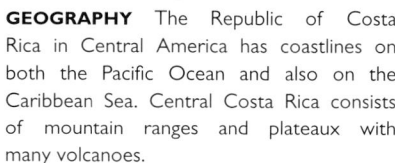

GEOGRAPHY The Republic of Costa Rica in Central America has coastlines on both the Pacific Ocean and also on the Caribbean Sea. Central Costa Rica consists of mountain ranges and plateaux with many volcanoes.

The coolest months are December and January. The northeast trade winds bring heavy rain to the Caribbean coast. There is less rainfall in the highlands and on the Pacific coastlands.

POLITICS & ECONOMY Christopher Columbus reached the Caribbean coast in 1502 and rumors of treasure soon attracted many Spaniards to settle in the country. Spain ruled the country until 1821, when Spain's Central American colonies broke away to join Mexico in 1822. In 1823, the Central American states broke with Mexico and set up the Central American Federation. Later, this large union broke up and Costa Rica became fully independent in 1838.

From the late 19th century, Costa Rica experienced a number of revolutions, with periods of dictatorship and periods of democracy. In 1948, following a revolt, the armed forces were abolished. Since 1948, Costa Rica has enjoyed a long period of stable democracy. In 2010, Costa Ricans elected their first woman president, Laura Chinchilla.

Costa Rica is classified by the World Bank as a "lower-middle-income" developing country and one of the most prosperous countries in Central America. There are high educational standards and a high average life expectancy (about 77 years for men and 81 years for women). Agriculture employs 12% of the people. Costa Rica's natural resources include its forests, but it lacks minerals apart from some bauxite and manganese. Manufacturing is increasing. The United States is Costa Rica's main trading partner. Tourism is a fast-growing industry.

AREA 19,730 sq mi [51,100 sq km] **POPULATION** 4,254,000
CAPITAL San José **GOVERNMENT** Multiparty republic
ETHNIC GROUPS White (including Mestizo) 94%, Black 3%, Amerindian 1%, Chinese 1%, others **LANGUAGES** Spanish (official), English **RELIGIONS** Roman Catholic 76%, Evangelical 14%
CURRENCY Costa Rican colón = 100 céntimos

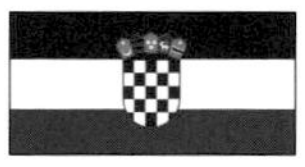

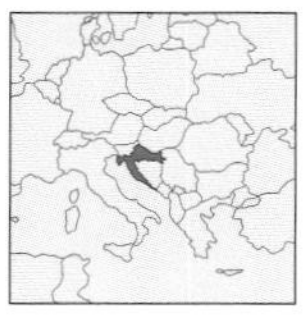

CROATIA

GEOGRAPHY The Republic of Croatia was one of the six republics that made up the former Communist country of Yugoslavia until it became independent in 1991. The region bordering the Adriatic Sea is called Dalmatia. It includes the coastal ranges, which contain large areas of bare limestone. Most of the rest of the country consists of the fertile Pannonian plains.

The coastal area has a typical Mediterranean climate, with hot, dry summers and mild, moist winters. Inland, the climate becomes more continental. Winters are cold, while temperatures often soar to 100°F [38°C] in the summer months.

POLITICS & ECONOMY Slav people settled in the area around 1,400 years ago. In 803, Croatia became part of the Holy Roman empire and the Croats soon adopted Christianity. Croatia was an independent kingdom in the 10th and 11th centuries. In 1102, the king of Hungary also became king of Croatia, creating a union that lasted 800 years. In 1526, part of Croatia came under the Turkish Ottoman empire, while the rest came under the Austrian Habsburgs.

After Austria–Hungary was defeated in World War I (1914–18), Croatia became part of the new Kingdom of the Serbs, Croats, and Slovenes. This kingdom was renamed Yugoslavia in 1929. Germany occupied Yugoslavia during World War II (1939–45). Croatia was proclaimed independent, but it was really ruled by the invaders.

After the war, Communists took power with Josip Broz Tito as the country's leader. Despite ethnic differences between the people, Tito held Yugoslavia together until his death in 1980. In the 1980s, economic and ethnic problems, including a deterioration in relations with Serbia, threatened stability. In the 1990s, Yugoslavia split into five nations, one of which was Croatia, which declared itself independent in 1991.

After Serbia supplied arms to Serbs living in Croatia, war broke out between the two republics, causing great damage. Croatia lost more than 30% of its territory. But in 1992, the United Nations sent a peacekeeping force to Croatia, which effectively ended the war with Serbia.

In 1992, when war broke out in Bosnia-Herzegovina, Bosnian Croats occupied parts of the country. But in 1994, Croatia helped to end Croat–Muslim conflict in Bosnia-Herzegovina and, in 1995, after retaking some areas occupied by Serbs, it helped to draw up the Dayton Peace Accord, ending the civil war. The conflict in the early 1990s disrupted the economy. In 2009, Slovenia lifted its block on Croatia's membership talks with the European Union following the resolution of a border dispute. In 2010, Social Democrat Ivo Josipovic was elected president. Croatia's main exports are manufactures.

AREA 21,829 sq mi [56,538 sq km] **POPULATION** 4,489,000
CAPITAL Zagreb **GOVERNMENT** Multiparty republic
ETHNIC GROUPS Croat 90%, Serb 5%, others
LANGUAGES Croatian 96% **RELIGIONS** Roman Catholic 88%, Orthodox 4%, Islam 1%, others **CURRENCY** Kuna = 100 lipas

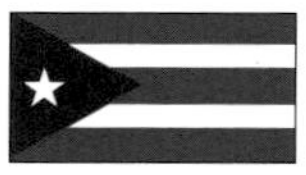

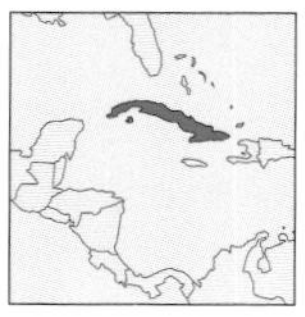

CUBA

GEOGRAPHY The Republic of Cuba is the largest island country in the Caribbean Sea. It consists of one large island, Cuba, the Isle of Youth (Isla de la Juventud), and about 1,600 small islets. Mountains and hills cover about a quarter of Cuba. The highest mountain range, the Sierra Maestra in the southeast, reaches 6,562 ft [2,000 m] above sea level. The rest of the land consists of gently rolling country or coastal plains, crossed by fertile valleys carved by the short, mostly shallow and narrow rivers.

Cuba lies in the tropics. But sea breezes moderate the temperature, warming the land in winter and cooling it in summer.

POLITICS & ECONOMY Christopher Columbus discovered the island in 1492 and Spaniards began to settle there from 1511. Spanish rule ended in 1898, when the United States defeated Spain in the Spanish–American War. American influence in Cuba remained strong until 1959, when revolutionary forces under Fidel Castro overthrew the dictatorial government of Fulgencio Batista.

The United States opposed Castro's policies, when he turned to the Soviet Union for assistance. In 1961, Cuban exiles attempting an invasion were defeated. In 1962, the US learned that nuclear missile bases armed by the Soviet Union had been established in Cuba. The US ordered the Soviet Union to remove the missiles and bases and, after a few days, when many people feared that a world war might break out, the Soviet Union agreed to the American demands.

Cuba's relations with the Soviet Union remained strong until 1991, when the Soviet Union was broken up. The loss of Soviet aid greatly damaged Cuba's economy, but Castro maintained his left-wing policies. Fidel Castro fell ill in 2007 and his brother Raul took over the leadership in 2008. He made some reforms, but in 2009 he insisted that Cuba would remain socialist.

The government runs Cuba's economy and owns 70% of the farmland. Agriculture is important and sugar is the chief export, followed by refined nickel ore. Other exports include cigars, citrus fruits, fish, medical products, and rum.

Before 1959, US companies owned most of Cuba's manufacturing industries. But under Fidel Castro, they became government property. After the collapse of Communist governments in the Soviet Union and its allies, Cuba worked to increase its trade with Latin America and China.

AREA 42,803 sq mi [110,861 sq km]
POPULATION 11,452,000 **CAPITAL** Havana
GOVERNMENT Socialist republic
ETHNIC GROUPS Mulatto 51%, White 37%, Black 11%
LANGUAGES Spanish (official) **RELIGIONS** Christianity
CURRENCY Cuban peso = 100 centavos

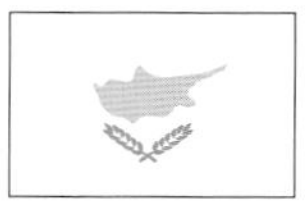

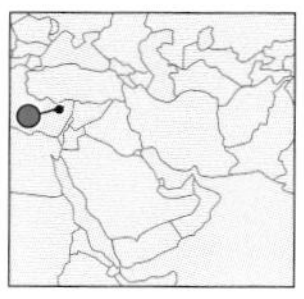

CYPRUS

GEOGRAPHY The Republic of Cyprus is an island nation in the northeastern Mediterranean Sea. Geographers regard it as part of Asia, but it resembles southern Europe in many ways. Its scenic mountain ranges include the southern Troodos Mountains, which reach 6,401 ft [1,951 m] at Mount Olympus, and the Kyrenia range in the north. Between them lies the Mesaoria plain. The climate is Mediterranean, with hot, dry summers and mild, moist winters.

POLITICS & ECONOMY Greeks settled on Cyprus around 3,200 years ago. From AD 330, the island was part of the Byzantine empire. In the 1570s, Cyprus became part of the Turkish Ottoman empire. Turkish rule continued until 1878 when Cyprus was leased to Britain. Britain annexed the island in 1914 and proclaimed it a colony in 1925. In the 1950s, Greek Cypriots, who made up four-fifths of the population, began a campaign for *enosis* (union) with Greece. Their leader was the Greek Orthodox Archbishop Makarios. A secret guerrilla force called EOKA attacked the British, who exiled Makarios in 1956; he returned to Cyprus in 1959.

Cyprus became an independent country in 1960, although Britain retained two military bases. Independent Cyprus had a constitution which provided for power-sharing between the Greek and Turkish Cypriots. But the constitution proved unworkable and fighting broke out between the two communities. In 1964, the United Nations sent in a peacekeeping force, but communal clashes recurred in 1967.

In 1974, Cypriot forces led by Greek officers overthrew Makarios, president since 1966. This led Turkey to invade northern Cyprus, a territory occupying about 40% of the island. Many Greek Cypriots fled from the north, which, in 1979, was proclaimed the Turkish Republic of Northern Cyprus. The only country to recognize this state was Turkey. The United Nations regarded Cyprus as a single unit under the Greek-Cypriot government in the south. In 2002, the European Union invited Cyprus to become a member in 2004. In April 2004, the people voted on a UN plan to reunify the island. The Turkish-Cypriots voted in favor, but the Greek-Cypriots voted against. Hence, only the south was admitted to EU membership on May 1, 2004. In September 2008, Greek and Turkish leaders began an extended series of talks on the reunification of Cyprus as a two-zone federal state.

Cyprus got its name from the Greek word *kypros*, meaning copper. But little copper remains and the chief minerals today are asbestos and chromium. However, the most valuable activity in Cyprus is tourism. Manufactures include cement, clothes, footwear, tiles, and wine.

In the early 1990s, the United Nations reclassified Cyprus as a developed rather than a developing country, reflecting the rapid economic progress in the south. But the north lagged far behind the prosperous Greek-Cypriot south.

AREA 3,572 SQ MI [9,251 SQ KM]
POPULATION 1,085,000 **CAPITAL** NICOSIA
GOVERNMENT MULTIPARTY REPUBLIC **ETHNIC GROUPS** GREEK CYPRIOT 77%, TURKISH CYPRIOT 18%, OTHERS **LANGUAGES** GREEK AND TURKISH (BOTH OFFICIAL), ENGLISH **RELIGIONS** GREEK ORTHODOX 78%, ISLAM 18%
CURRENCY EURO = 100 CENTS

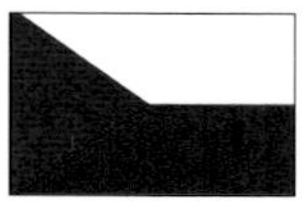

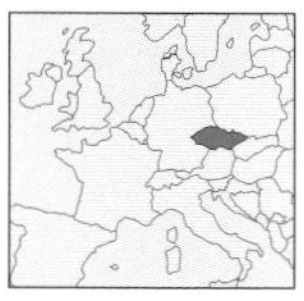

CZECH REPUBLIC

GEOGRAPHY The Czech Republic is the western three-fifths of the former country of Czechoslovakia. It contains two regions: Bohemia in the west and Moravia in the east. Mountains border much of the country in the west. The Bohemian basin in the north-center is a fertile lowland region, with Prague, the capital city, as its main center. Highlands cover much of the center of the country, with lowlands in the southeast.

The climate is influenced by its landlocked position in east-central Europe. Summers are warm and winters cold. The rainfall is moderate.

POLITICS & ECONOMY After World War I (1914–18), Czechoslovakia was created. Germany seized the country in World War II (1939–45). In 1948, Communist leaders took power and Czechoslovakia was allied to the Soviet Union. When democratic reforms were introduced in the Soviet Union in the late 1980s, the Czechs also demanded reforms. Free elections were held in 1990, but differences between the Czechs and Slovaks led to the partitioning of the country on January 1, 1993. The Czech Republic became a member of NATO in 1999 and a member of the European Union on May 1, 2004. In March 2009, Jan Fischer, a little-known economist, took over as interim prime minister from the center-right Mirek Topolanek.

Under Communist rule the Czech Republic became one of the most industrialized parts of Eastern Europe. The country has deposits of coal, uranium, iron ore, magnesite, tin, and zinc. Manufacturing employs about 25% of the Czech Republic's entire work force. Farming is also important. The main crops include barley, fruit, hops for beer-making, maize, potatoes, sugar beet, vegetables, and wheat.

AREA 30,450 SQ MI [78,866 SQ KM]
POPULATION 10,212,000 **CAPITAL** PRAGUE
GOVERNMENT MULTIPARTY REPUBLIC **ETHNIC GROUPS** CZECH 81%, MORAVIAN 13%, SLOVAK 3%, POLISH, GERMAN, SILESIAN, GYPSY, HUNGARIAN, UKRAINIAN **LANGUAGES** CZECH (OFFICIAL) **RELIGIONS** ATHEIST 40%, ROMAN CATHOLIC 39%, PROTESTANT 4%, ORTHODOX 3%, OTHERS
CURRENCY CZECH KORUNA = 100 HALER

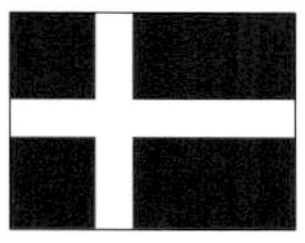

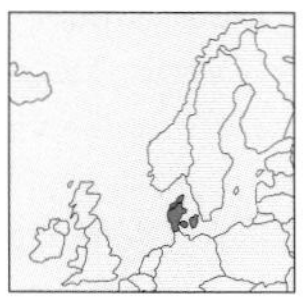

DENMARK

GEOGRAPHY The Kingdom of Denmark is the smallest country in Scandinavia. It consists of a peninsula, called Jutland (or Jylland), which is joined to Germany, and more than 400 islands, 89 of which are inhabited. The land is flat and mostly covered by rocks dropped there by huge ice sheets during the last Ice Age. The highest point in Denmark is on Jutland. It is only 568 ft [173 m] above sea level. Denmark has a mild, moist climate, except during cold spells in winter when The Sound between Sjælland and Sweden may freeze over.

POLITICS & ECONOMY Danish Vikings terrorized much of Western Europe for about 300 years after AD 800. In the late 14th century, Denmark formed a union with Norway and Sweden (which included Finland). Sweden broke away in 1523, while Denmark lost Norway to Sweden in 1814. After 1945, Denmark joined NATO and it became a member of the European Union in 1973. The people of Greenland, a self-governing Danish territory, voted in 2008 for a greater degree of autonomy. This vote could lead to the island's independence, though Greenland still depends on aid from Denmark.

Denmark is a prosperous country. Reources include some oil and gas. Manufacturing employs 15% of the people. Products include furniture, processed food, machinery, television sets, and textiles. Farming employs 3% of the people, but it is highly scientific. Meat and dairy farming are the chief activities.

AREA 16,639 SQ MI [43,094 SQ KM] **POPULATION** 5,501,000
CAPITAL COPENHAGEN **GOVERNMENT** PARLIAMENTARY MONARCHY
ETHNIC GROUPS SCANDINAVIAN, INUIT, FÆROESE **LANGUAGES** DANISH (OFFICIAL), GREENLANDIC, ENGLISH, FÆROESE **RELIGIONS** EVANGELICAL LUTHERAN 95% **CURRENCY** DANISH KRONE = 100 ØRE

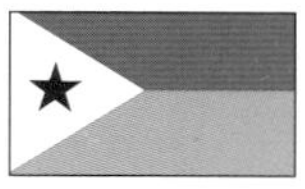

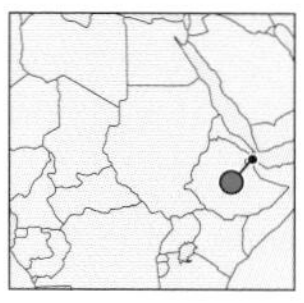

DJIBOUTI

GEOGRAPHY The Republic of Djibouti in eastern Africa occupies a strategic position where the Red Sea meets the Gulf of Aden. Djibouti has one of the world's hottest and driest climates.

POLITICS & ECONOMY France set up a territory called French Somaliland in 1888. Its capital, Djibouti, became important when a railroad was built to Addis Ababa and Djibouti became the main outlet for Ethiopian trade. In 1967, France renamed the dependency the French Territory of the Afars and Issas, but it was renamed Djibouti on independence in 1977. It became a one-party state in 1981, but a new constitution (1992) permitted four parties which had to maintain a balance between the country's ethnic groups. In 2008, a border dispute led to clashes between Djiboutian and Eritrean troops.

Djibouti is a poor country. Its economy is based largely on the revenue it gets from its port and the railroad to Addis Ababa.

AREA 8,958 SQ MI [23,200 SQ KM] **POPULATION** 725,000
CAPITAL DJIBOUTI **GOVERNMENT** MULTIPARTY REPUBLIC
ETHNIC GROUPS SOMALI 60%, AFAR 35% **LANGUAGES** ARABIC AND FRENCH (BOTH OFFICIAL) **RELIGIONS** ISLAM 94%, CHRISTIANITY 6%
CURRENCY DJIBOUTIAN FRANC = 100 CENTIMES

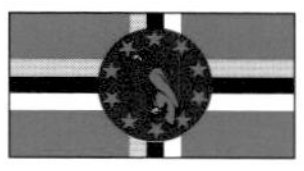

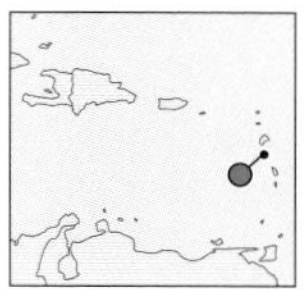

DOMINICA

The Commonwealth of Dominica, a former British colony, became independent in 1978. The island has a mountainous spine and less than 10% of the land is cultivated. But agriculture employs 18% of the people. The manufacture of coconut-based soap is important, while tourism and mining are other economic activities.

AREA 290 SQ MI [751 SQ KM] **POPULATION** 73,000 **CAPITAL** ROSEAU

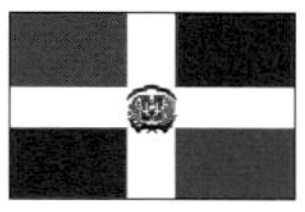

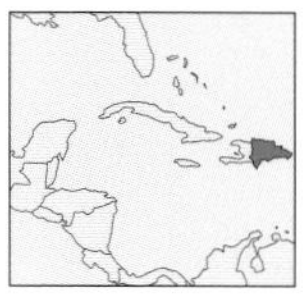

DOMINICAN REPUBLIC

GEOGRAPHY Second largest of the Caribbean nations in both area and population, the Dominican Republic shares the island of Hispaniola with Haiti, with the Dominican Republic occupying the eastern two-thirds. The country is mountainous, and the generally hot and humid climate eases with altitude.

POLITICS & ECONOMY In 1492, Christopher Columbus landed on Hispaniola and Spaniards soon settled the island, followed by the French who occupied the western third of the island (which is now Haiti). The island was held by Haitians from 1822 until 1844, when the Dominican Republic was established. Civil war broke out in 1966 but US intervention ended the conflict. Since 1966, the young democracy has survived violent elections under the watchful eye of the United States.

The Dominican Republic is a developing country and agriculture is the chief activity. Sugarcane, rice, bananas, and cocoa are leading crops. Food processing is also important and some ferronickel is produced.

AREA 18,730 SQ MI [48,511 SQ KM] **POPULATION** 9,650,000
CAPITAL SANTO DOMINGO **GOVERNMENT** MULTIPARTY REPUBLIC
ETHNIC GROUPS MULATTO 73%, WHITE 16%, BLACK 11%
LANGUAGES SPANISH (OFFICIAL) **RELIGIONS** ROMAN CATHOLIC 95%
CURRENCY DOMINICAN PESO = 100 CENTAVOS

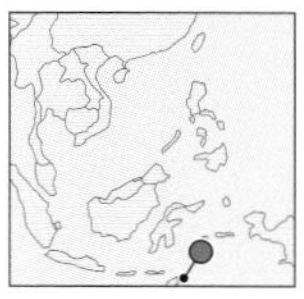

EAST TIMOR

The Republic of East Timor became fully independent on May 20, 2002. The land is mainly rugged. Temperatures are generally high and the rainfall is moderate. Portugal ruled the area from the late 19th century, when it was called Portuguese Timor. Portugal withdrew in 1975 and Indonesia seized the area. Guerrilla activity mounted under Indonesian rule and, in 1999, the people voted for independence. Agriculture is the main activity and East Timor is the poorest country in Southeast Asia. But, in 2006, East Timor and Australia signed a deal to share the revenue from the oil and natural gas deposits under the Timor Sea.

AREA 5,743 SQ MI [14,874 SQ KM] **POPULATION** 1,132,000 **CAPITAL** DILI

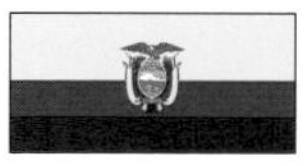

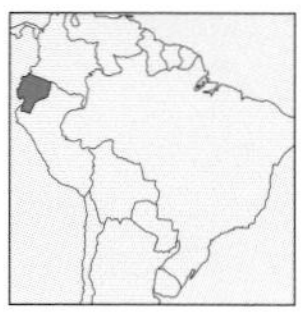

ECUADOR

GEOGRAPHY The Republic of Ecuador straddles the Equator on the west coast of South America. Three ranges of the high Andes Mountains form the backbone of the country. Between the towering, snow-capped peaks of the mountains, some of which are volcanoes, lie a series of high plateaux, or basins. Nearly half of Ecuador's population lives on these plateaux. The coast has a warm tropical climate, despite the cold offshore Peruvian Current. Inland, the altitude gives the plateaux spring-like weather throughout the year.

POLITICS & ECONOMY The Inca people of Peru conquered much of what is now Ecuador in the late 15th century. They introduced their language, Quechua, which is widely spoken today. Spanish forces defeated the Incas in 1533 and took control of Ecuador. The country became independent in 1822, following the defeat of a Spanish force in a battle near Quito.

In the 19th and 20th centuries, Ecuador suffered from political instability, while successive governments failed to tackle the country's social and economic problems. A war with Peru in 1941 led to a loss of territory. Disputes continued until 1995, but a border agreement was signed in January 1998. Economic crises in the early 21st century led to the adoption of the US dollar as the official currency. Political instability marred progress. A coup in 2000 was led by Colonel Lucio Gutiérrez, who was elected president in 2002. He was overthrown in 2005. In 2006, the leftist Rafael Correa was elected president and, in 2008, the people voted in favor of a new constitution.

The World Bank classifies Ecuador as a "lower-middle-income" developing country. Agriculture employs 8% of the people and bananas, cocoa, and coffee are all important crops. Fishing, forestry, mining, and manufacturing are other activities.

AREA 109,483 SQ MI [283,561 SQ KM]
POPULATION 14,573,000 **CAPITAL** QUITO
GOVERNMENT MULTIPARTY REPUBLIC
ETHNIC GROUPS MESTIZO (MIXED WHITE/AMERINDIAN) 65%, AMERINDIAN 25%, WHITE 7%, BLACK 3%
LANGUAGES SPANISH (OFFICIAL), QUECHUA
RELIGIONS ROMAN CATHOLIC 95%
CURRENCY US DOLLAR = 100 CENTS

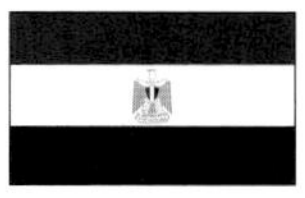

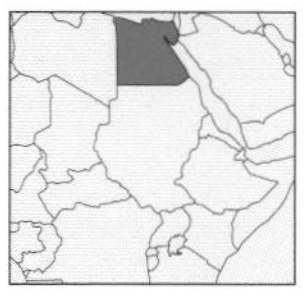

EGYPT

GEOGRAPHY The Arab Republic of Egypt is Africa's second largest country by population after Nigeria, though it ranks 13th in area. Most of Egypt is desert. Almost all the people live either in the Nile Valley and its fertile delta or along the Suez Canal, the artificial waterway between the Mediterranean and Red seas. This canal shortens the sea journey between the United Kingdom and India by 6,027 mi [9,700 km]. Recent attempts have been made to irrigate parts of the western desert and thus redistribute the rapidly growing Egyptian population into previously uninhabited regions.

Apart from the Nile Valley, Egypt has three other main regions. The Western and Eastern deserts are parts of the Sahara. The Sinai peninsula (Es Sina), to the east of the Suez Canal, is a mountainous desert region, geographically within Asia. It contains Egypt's highest peak, Gebel Katherina (8,650 ft [2,637 m]); few people live in this area.

Egypt is a dry country. The low rainfall occurs, if at all, in winter and the country is one of the sunniest places on Earth.

POLITICS & ECONOMY Ancient Egypt, which was founded about 5,000 years ago, was one of the great early civilizations. Throughout the country, pyramids, temples and richly decorated tombs are memorials to its great achievements.

After Ancient Egypt declined, the country came under successive foreign rulers. Arabs occupied Egypt in AD 639–42. They introduced the Arabic language and Islam. Their influence was so great that most Egyptians now regard themselves as Arabs.

Egypt came under British rule in 1882, but it gained partial independence in 1922, becoming a monarchy. The monarchy was abolished in 1952, when Egypt became a republic. The creation of Israel in 1948 led Egypt into a series of wars in 1948–9, 1956, 1967, and 1973. Since the late 1970s, Egypt has sought for peace. In 1979, Egypt signed a peace treaty with Israel and regained the Sinai region which it had lost in a war in 1967. Extremists opposed contacts with Israel and, in 1981, President Sadat, who had signed the treaty, was assassinated.

While Egypt plays a major part in Arab affairs, most of its people are poor. Some Islamic fundamentalists, who dislike Western influences on their way of life, have resorted to violence. In the

1990s, attacks on foreign visitors caused a decline in the valuable tourist industry, as also did the events of September 11, 2001, and the subsequent "war against terrorism." Hosni Mubarak, president since 1981, was re-elected in 2005, though supporters of the banned Muslim Brotherhood made gains in parliamentary elections.

Egypt is Africa's second most industrialized country after South Africa, but most people are poor. Oil and textiles are the country's main exports. In 2007, the government announced plans to build several nuclear power stations to generate electricity.

AREA 386,659 SQ MI [1,001,449 SQ KM]
POPULATION 78,867,000 **CAPITAL** CAIRO
GOVERNMENT REPUBLIC
ETHNIC GROUPS EGYPTIANS/BEDOUINS/BERBERS 99%
LANGUAGES ARABIC (OFFICIAL), FRENCH, ENGLISH
RELIGIONS ISLAM (MAINLY SUNNI MUSLIM) 94%, CHRISTIANITY (MAINLY COPTIC CHRISTIAN) AND OTHERS 6%
CURRENCY EGYPTIAN POUND = 100 PIASTRES

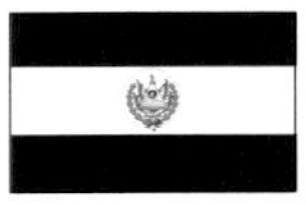
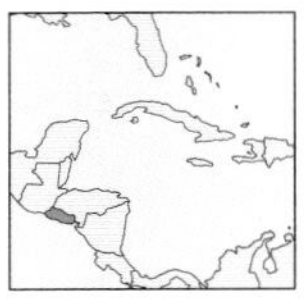

EL SALVADOR

GEOGRAPHY The Republic of El Salvador is the only country in Central America which does not have a coast on the Caribbean Sea. El Salvador has a narrow coastal plain along the Pacific Ocean. Behind the coastal plain, the coastal range is a zone of rugged mountains, including volcanoes, which overlooks a densely populated inland plateau. Beyond the plateau, the land rises to the sparsely populated interior highlands. The coast has a hot, tropical climate. Inland the climate is moderated by the altitude. Rain falls on practically every afternoon between May and October.

POLITICS & ECONOMY Amerindians have lived in El Salvador for thousands of years. The ruins of Mayan pyramids built between AD 100 and 1000 are still found in the western part of the country. Spanish soldiers conquered the area in 1524 and 1525, and Spain ruled until 1821. In 1823, all the Central American countries, except for Panama, set up a Central American Federation. But El Salvador withdrew in 1840 and declared its independence in 1841. El Salvador suffered from instability throughout the 19th century. The 20th century saw a more stable government, but from 1931 military dictatorships alternated with elected governments.

The country remained poor. In the 1970s, protesters demanded that the government introduce reforms to help the poor. Kidnappings and murders committed by left- and right-wing groups caused instability. A civil war broke out in 1979 between the US-backed government forces and left-wing guerrillas. A ceasefire was agreed in 1992. In 2009, Mauricio Funes, a former Marxist rebel and leader of the Farabundo Marti National Liberation Front (FMLN), won the presidential election.

The World Bank classifies El Salvador as a "lower-middle-income" economy. About three-quarters of the country is farmed. Coffee, grown in the highlands, is the main export, followed by sugar and cotton, which grow on the coastal lowlands. Fishing for lobsters and shrimps is important, but manufacturing is on a small scale.

AREA 8,124 SQ MI [21,041 SQ KM]
POPULATION 7,185,000 **CAPITAL** SAN SALVADOR
GOVERNMENT REPUBLIC **ETHNIC GROUPS** MESTIZO (MIXED WHITE AND AMERINDIAN) 90%, WHITE 9%, AMERINDIAN 1%
LANGUAGES SPANISH (OFFICIAL) **RELIGIONS** ROMAN CATHOLIC 83%
CURRENCY US DOLLAR = 100 CENTS

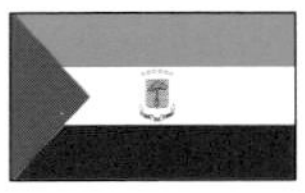
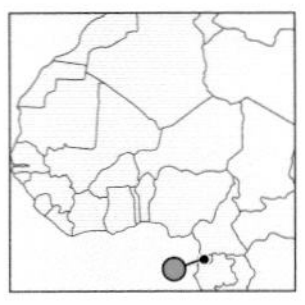

EQUATORIAL GUINEA

GEOGRAPHY The Republic of Equatorial Guinea is a small republic in west-central Africa. It consists of a mainland territory which makes up 90% of the land area, called Rio Muni, between Cameroon and Gabon, and five offshore islands in the Bight of Bonny, the largest of which is Bioko. The island of Annobon lies 350 mi [560 km] southwest of Rio Muni. Rio Muni consists mainly of hills and plateaux behind the coastal plains.

The climate is hot and humid. Bioko is mountainous, with the land rising to 9,869 ft [3,008 m], and hence it is particularly rainy. However, there is a marked dry season between the months of December and February. Mainland Rio Muni has a similar climate, though the rainfall diminishes inland.

POLITICS & ECONOMY Portuguese navigators reached the area in 1471. In 1778, Portugal granted Bioko, together with rights over Rio Muni, to Spain.

In 1959, Spain made Bioko and Rio Muni provinces of overseas Spain and, in 1963, it gave the provinces a degree of self-government. Equatorial Guinea became independent in 1968.

The first president of Equatorial Guinea, Francisco Macias Nguema, proved to be a tyrant. He was overthrown in 1979 and a group of officers, led by Lieutenant-Colonel Teodoro Obiang Nguema Mbasogo, set up a Supreme Military Council to rule the country. In 1991, a democratic system was restored, but alleged human rights abuses continued. In 2004, a coup attempt was foiled. In 2008, one of its leaders, the Briton Simon Mann, was sentenced to 34 years in prison, but he was pardoned in 2009.

Agriculture employs two-thirds of the people. The most valuable crop is coffee. Oil, which has been produced since 1966, accounts for most of the export revenue.

AREA 10,830 SQ MI [28,051 SQ KM] **POPULATION** 633,000
CAPITAL MALABO **GOVERNMENT** MULTIPARTY REPUBLIC (TRANSITIONAL)
ETHNIC GROUPS BUBI (ON BIOKO), FANG (IN RIO MUNI)
LANGUAGES SPANISH AND FRENCH (BOTH OFFICIAL)
RELIGIONS CHRISTIANITY **CURRENCY** CFA FRANC = 100 CENTIMES

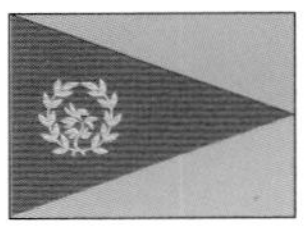
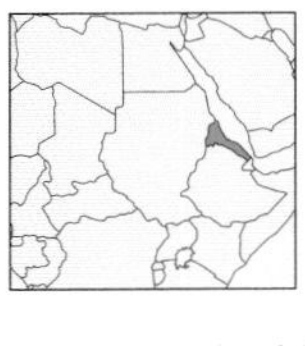

ERITREA

GEOGRAPHY The State of Eritrea consists of a hot, dry coastal plain facing the Red Sea, with a fairly mountainous area in the center. Most people live in the cooler highland area.

POLITICS & ECONOMY From the 1st century AD, Eritrea was part of the ancient Kingdom of Axum, which adopted Christianity in the 4th century AD. It began to decline in the 7th century. The Ottoman Turks took over the area in the 16th century and it became an Italian colony in the 1880s. The Italians were driven out in 1941 and, in 1952, it became part of Ethiopia.

A guerrilla struggle launched in 1961 ended in 1993, when Eritrea became independent. Economic recovery was hampered by conflict with Yemen over three islands in the Red Sea. In 1988–9, clashes occurred along the border with Ethiopia. A peace agreement was signed in 2000, but problems continued. In 2007–8, Eritrea was accused of supporting Islamist forces in Somalia and, in 2008, Eritrean troops clashed with Djiboutian forces over a border dispute.

The main economic activities are farming and livestock rearing. The few manufacturing industries are based mainly in Asmara.

AREA 45,405 SQ MI [117,600 SQ KM] **POPULATION** 5,647,000
CAPITAL ASMARA **GOVERNMENT** TRANSITIONAL GOVERNMENT
ETHNIC GROUPS TIGRINYA 50%, TIGRE AND KUNAMA 40%, AFAR 4%, SAHO 3%, OTHERS **LANGUAGES** AFAR, ARABIC, TIGRE, KUNAMA, TIGRINYA **RELIGIONS** ISLAM, COPTIC CHRISTIAN, ROMAN CATHOLIC
CURRENCY NAKFA = 100 CENTS

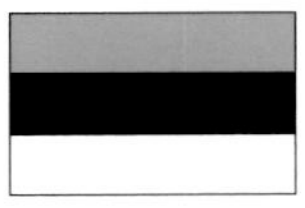
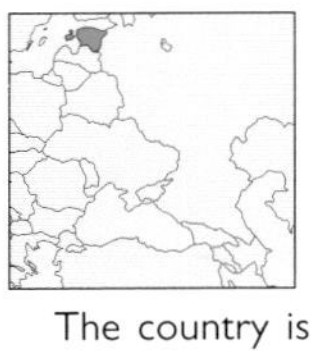

ESTONIA

GEOGRAPHY The Republic of Estonia is the smallest of the three states on the Baltic Sea, which were formerly part of the Soviet Union, but which became independent in the early 1990s. Estonia consists of a generally flat plain which was covered by ice sheets during the Ice Age. The land is strewn with moraine (rocks deposited by the ice).

The country is dotted with more than 1,500 small lakes. The large Lake Peipus (Chudskoye Ozero) and the River Narva together make up much of Estonia's eastern border with Russia. The largest of the islands is Saaremaa (Sarema). The climate is fairly mild because of the moderating effects of the sea.

POLITICS & ECONOMY The ancestors of the Estonians, who are related to the Finns, settled in the area several thousand years ago. German crusaders, known as the Teutonic Knights, introduced Christianity in the early 13th century. By the 16th century, German noblemen owned much of the land in Estonia. In 1561, Sweden took the northern part of the country and Poland the south. From 1625, Sweden controlled the entire country until Sweden handed it over to Russia in 1721.

Estonian nationalists campaigned for their independence from around the mid-19th century. Finally, Estonia was proclaimed independent in 1918. In 1919, the government began to break up the large estates and distribute land among the peasants.

In 1939, Germany and the Soviet Union agreed to take over parts of Eastern Europe. In 1940, Soviet forces occupied Estonia, but they were driven out by the Germans in 1941. Soviet troops returned in 1944 and Estonia became one of the 15 Soviet Socialist Republics of the Soviet Union. The Estonians strongly opposed Soviet rule. Many of them were deported to Siberia.

Political changes in the Soviet Union in the late 1980s led to renewed demands for freedom. In 1990, the Estonian government declared the country independent and, finally, the Soviet Union recognized this act in September 1991, shortly before the Soviet Union was dissolved. Estonia adopted a new constitution in 1992, and elections were held. In 1994, Russian troops withdrew, but anti-Russian sentiment continued. In 2007, ethnic Russians protested at the removal of a Red Army war memorial.

Under Soviet rule, Estonia was the most prosperous of the three Baltic states. Since 1988, Estonia has worked to restructure its economy. Turning increasingly to the West, it became a member of both the North Atlantic Treaty Organization and the European Union in 2004. Estonia's resources include oil shale and its forests. Industries produce fertilizers, processed food, machinery, petrochemical products, wood products, and textiles. Agriculture and fishing are also important activities.

AREA 17,413 SQ MI [45,100 SQ KM] **POPULATION** 1,299,000
CAPITAL TALLINN **GOVERNMENT** MULTIPARTY REPUBLIC
ETHNIC GROUPS ESTONIAN 65%, RUSSIAN 28%, UKRAINIAN 3%, BELARUSIAN 2%, FINNISH 1% **LANGUAGES** ESTONIAN (OFFICIAL), RUSSIAN
RELIGIONS LUTHERAN, RUSSIAN AND ESTONIAN ORTHODOX, METHODIST, BAPTIST, ROMAN CATHOLIC **CURRENCY** ESTONIAN KROON = 100 SENTI

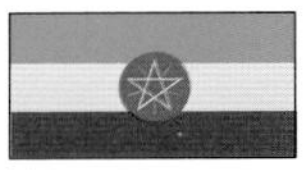
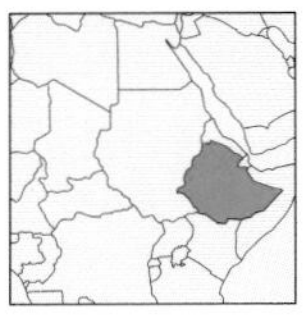

ETHIOPIA

GEOGRAPHY Ethiopia is a landlocked country in northeastern Africa. The land is mainly mountainous, though there are extensive plains in the east, bordering southern Eritrea, and in the south, bordering Somalia. The highlands are divided into two blocks by an arm of the Great Rift Valley which runs throughout eastern Africa. North of the Rift Valley, the land is especially rugged, rising to 15,157 ft [4,620 m] at Ras Dashen. Southeast of Ras Dashen is Lake Tana, source of the River Abay (Blue Nile). The climate is affected by the altitude. The rainfall in the highlands is generally more than 39 inches [1,000 mm]. The lowlands are hot and arid.

POLITICS & ECONOMY Ethiopia was the home of an ancient monarchy, which became Christian in the 4th century. In the 7th century, Muslims gained control of the lowlands, but Christianity survived in the highlands. Ethiopia resisted attempts to colonize it, but Italy invaded the country in 1935. The Italians were driven out in 1941 during World War II.

In 1952, Eritrea, on the Red Sea coast, was federated with Ethiopia. But in 1961, Eritrean nationalists demanded their freedom and began a struggle that ended in their independence in 1993. In 1995, because of Ethiopia's great ethnic diversity, the country was divided into nine provinces, each with its own regional assembly. In 1998, boundary disputes with Eritrea led to conflict. A peace agreement was reached in 2001, but tensions mounted in 2005–6 when Ethiopia failed to accept an international ruling over Badme, a border settlement. In 2006, Ethiopian troops intervened in Somalia on behalf of its provisional government. Ethiopian troops defeated the Islamists, who had taken control of Mogadishu. Ethiopia withdrew its forces in early 2009.

Ethiopia is one of the world's poorest countries and it is heavily dependent on aid. In 2004, a UN report stated that Ethiopia remained on the brink of disaster, with spiraling population growth, slow economic growth, and environmental degradation. Agriculture remains the main activity.

AREA 426,370 SQ MI [1,104,300 SQ KM]
POPULATION 85,237,000 **CAPITAL** ADDIS ABABA
GOVERNMENT FEDERATION OF NINE PROVINCES
ETHNIC GROUPS OROMO 40%, AMHARA AND TIGRE 32%, SIDAMO 9%, SHANKELLA 6%, SOMALI 6%, OTHERS **LANGUAGES** AMHARIC (OFFICIAL), MANY OTHERS **RELIGIONS** ISLAM 47%, ETHIOPIAN ORTHODOX 40%, TRADITIONAL BELIEFS 12% **CURRENCY** BIRR = 100 CENTS

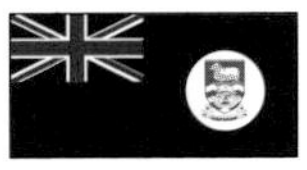
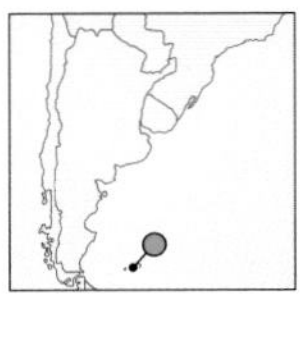

FALKLAND ISLANDS

Comprising two main islands and over 200 small islands, the Falkland Islands (or the Islas Malvinas, as they are called in Argentina) lie 300 mi [480 km] from South America. Sheep farming is the main activity, though the search for oil and diamonds holds out hope for the future of this harsh and virtually treeless environment.

AREA 4,700 SQ MI [12,173 SQ KM]
POPULATION 3,000 **CAPITAL** STANLEY

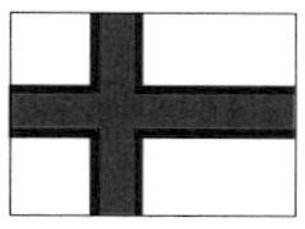
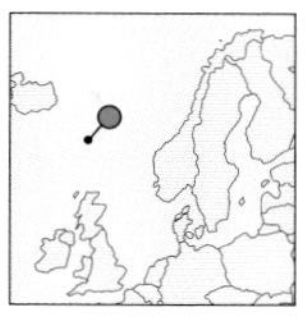

FÆROE ISLANDS

The Færoe Islands are a group of 18 volcanic islands and some reefs in the North Atlantic Ocean. The islands have been Danish since the 1380s, but they became largely self-governing in 1948. In 2001, a referendum on independence was called off after Denmark said that subsidies would end soon after independence.

AREA 540 SQ MI [1,399 SQ KM]
POPULATION 49,000 **CAPITAL** TÓRSHAVN

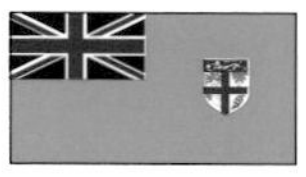
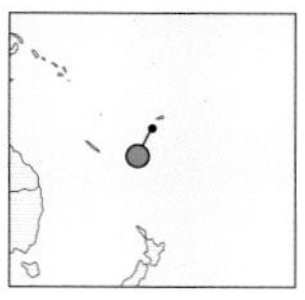

FIJI ISLANDS

The Fiji Islands (the official name of Fiji since 1998) is a republic consisting of more than 800 Melanesian islands, the biggest being Viti Levu and Vanua Levu. The climate is tropical. A former British colony, Fiji became independent in 1970. Its recent history has been marred by efforts by ethnic Fijians to impose their rule, stopping members of the ethnic Indian community from holding senior cabinet posts. Coups have occurred in 1987, 2000, and 2006.

AREA 7,056 SQ MI [18,274 SQ KM] **POPULATION** 945,000 **CAPITAL** SUVA

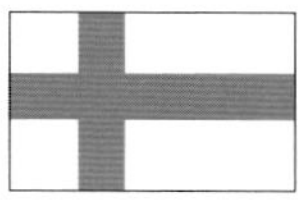
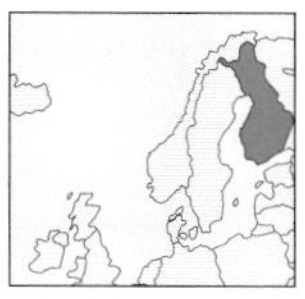

FINLAND

GEOGRAPHY The Republic of Finland is a beautiful country in northern Europe. In the south, behind the coastal lowlands where most Finns live, lies a region of sparkling lakes worn out by ice sheets in the Ice Age. The thinly populated northern uplands cover about two-fifths of the country.

Helsinki, the capital city, has warm summers, but the average temperatures between the months of December and March are below freezing point. Snow covers the land in winter. The north has less precipitation than the south, but it is much colder.

POLITICS & ECONOMY Between 1150 and 1809, Finland was under Swedish rule. The close links between the countries continue today. Swedish remains an official language in Finland and many towns have Swedish as well as Finnish names.

In 1809, Finland became a grand duchy of the Russian empire. It finally declared itself independent in 1917, after the Russian Revolution and the collapse of the Russian empire. But during World War II (1939–45), the Soviet Union declared war on Finland and took part of Finland's territory. Finland allied itself with Germany, but it lost more land to the Soviet Union at the end of the war.

After World War II, Finland became a neutral country and negotiated peace treaties with the Soviet Union. Finland also strengthened its relations with other northern European countries and became an associate member of the European Free Trade Association (EFTA) in 1961. Finland became a full member of EFTA in 1986, but it became a member of the European Union on January 1, 1995. In 2002, Finland adopted the euro as its sole unit of currency. In 2000 and 2006, the Social Democrat Tarja Halonen was elected president. She became the first woman president in Finnish history.

Forests are the chief resource and wood, wood products, and paper once dominated the economy. They still make up about a quarter of the exports, but, since World War II, Finland has set up many new industries, producing machinery and transport equipment. The economy has expanded quickly and machinery and apparatus now account for more than a third of the exports.

AREA 130,558 SQ MI [338,145 SQ KM]
POPULATION 5,250,000 **CAPITAL** HELSINKI
GOVERNMENT MULTIPARTY REPUBLIC **ETHNIC GROUPS** FINNISH 93%, SWEDISH 6% **LANGUAGES** FINNISH AND SWEDISH (BOTH OFFICIAL)
RELIGIONS EVANGELICAL LUTHERAN 89% **CURRENCY** EURO = 100 CENTS

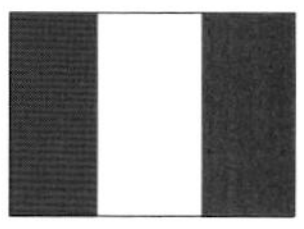
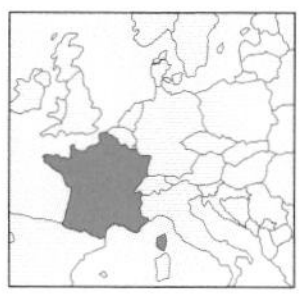

FRANCE

GEOGRAPHY The Republic of France is the largest country in Western Europe. The scenery is extremely varied. The Vosges Mountains overlook the Rhine valley in the northeast, the Jura Mountains and the Alps form the borders with Switzerland and Italy in the southeast, while the Pyrenees straddle France's border with Spain. The only large highland area entirely within France is the Massif Central between the Rhône-Saône valley and the basin of Aquitaine in southern France.

Brittany (Bretagne) and Normandy (Normande) form a scenic hill region. Fertile lowlands cover most of northern France, including the densely populated Paris basin. Another major lowland area, the Aquitanian basin, is in the southwest, while the Rhône-Saône valley and the Mediterranean lowlands are in the southeast.

The climate of France varies from west to east and from north to south. The west comes under the moderating influence of the Atlantic Ocean, giving generally mild weather. To the east, summers are warmer and winters colder. The climate also becomes warmer as one travels from north to south. The Mediterranean Sea coast has hot, dry summers and mild, moist winters. The Alps, Jura, and Pyrenees mountains have snowy winters. Winter sports centers are found in all three areas. Large glaciers occupy high valleys in the Alps.

POLITICS & ECONOMY The Romans conquered France (then called Gaul) in the 50s BC. Roman rule began to decline in the 5th century AD and, in 486, the Frankish realm (as France was called) became independent under a Christian king, Clovis. In 800, Charlemagne, who had been king since 768, became emperor of the Romans. He extended France's boundaries, but, in 843, his empire was divided into three parts and the area of France contracted. After the Norman invasion of England in 1066, large areas of France came under English rule, but this was finally ended in 1453.

France later became a powerful monarchy. But the French Revolution (1789–99) ended absolute rule by French kings. In 1799, Napoleon Bonaparte took power and fought a series of brilliant military campaigns before his final defeat in 1815. The monarchy was restored until 1848, when the Second Republic was founded. In 1852, Napoleon's nephew became Napoleon III, but the Third Republic was established in 1875. France was the scene of much fighting during World War I (1914–18) and World War II (1939–45), causing great loss of life and much damage to the economy.

In 1946, France adopted a new constitution, establishing the Fourth Republic. But political instability and costly colonial wars slowed France's post-war recovery. In 1958, Charles de Gaulle was elected president and he introduced a new constitution, giving the president extra powers and inaugurating the Fifth Republic.

Since the 1960s, France has made rapid economic progress, becoming one of the most prosperous nations in the European Union. But France's government faced a number of problems, including unemployment, pollution, and the growing number of elderly people, who find it difficult to live when inflation rates are high. One social problem concerns the presence in France of large numbers of immigrants from Africa and southern Europe, many of whom live in poor areas.

In 2002, the euro became France's sole unit of currency, replacing the franc. In 2005, France was rocked by inter-ethnic violence and, in 2007, the right-wing Nicolas Sarkozy was elected president. In 2009, he announced that France would rejoin NATO, from which President de Gaulle had withdrawn in 1966.

France is one of the world's most developed countries. Its natural resources include its fertile soil, together with deposits of bauxite, coal, iron ore, oil and natural gas, and potash. France is also one of the world's top manufacturing nations, and it has often innovated in bold and imaginative ways. The TGV and hypermarkets are typical examples. Paris is a world center of fashion industries, but France has many other industrial towns and cities. Major manufactures include aircraft, cars, chemicals, electronic and metal products, machinery, processed food, steel, and textiles.

Agriculture employs about 3% of the people, but France is the largest producer of farm products in Western Europe, producing most of the food it needs. Wheat is the leading crop and livestock farming is of major importance. Fishing and forestry are leading industries, while tourism is a major activity.

AREA 212,934 SQ MI [551,500 SQ KM] **POPULATION** 64,058,000
CAPITAL PARIS **GOVERNMENT** MULTIPARTY REPUBLIC
ETHNIC GROUPS CELTIC, LATIN, ARAB, TEUTONIC, SLAVIC
LANGUAGES FRENCH (OFFICIAL) **RELIGIONS** ROMAN CATHOLIC 85%, ISLAM 8%, OTHERS **CURRENCY** EURO = 100 CENTS

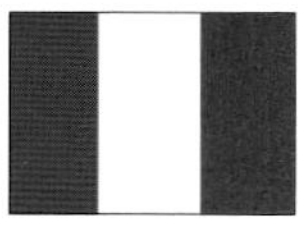
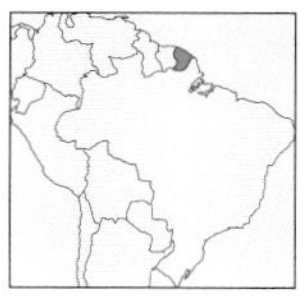

FRENCH GUIANA

GEOGRAPHY French Guiana is the smallest country in mainland South America. The coastal plain is swampy in places, but some dry areas are cultivated. Inland lies a plateau, with the low Tumachumac Mountains in the south. Most of the rivers run north toward the Atlantic Ocean.

French Guiana has a hot, equatorial climate, with high temperatures throughout the year. The rainfall is heavy, especially between December and June, but it is dry between August and October. The northeast trade winds blow constantly across the country.

POLITICS & ECONOMY The first people to live in what is now French Guiana were Amerindians. Today, only a few of them survive in the interior. The first Europeans to explore the coast arrived in 1500, and they were followed by adventurers seeking El Dorado, the mythical city of gold. Cayenne was founded in 1637 by a group of French merchants. The area became a French colony in the late 17th century.

France used the colony as a penal settlement for political prisoners from the times of the French Revolution in the 1790s. From the 1850s to 1945, the country became notorious as a place where prisoners were harshly treated. Many of them died, unable to survive in the tropical conditions.

In 1946, French Guiana became an overseas department of France, and in 1974 it also became an administrative region. An independence movement developed in the 1980s, but most people want to retain their links with France and continue to obtain financial aid to develop their territory.

Although it has rich forest and mineral resources, such as bauxite (aluminum ore), French Guiana is a developing country. It depends greatly on France for money to run its services and the government is the country's biggest employer. Since 1968, Kourou in French Guiana, the European Space Agency's rocket-launching site, has earned money for France by sending communications satellites into space.

AREA 34,749 SQ MI [90,000 SQ KM]
POPULATION 203,000 **CAPITAL** CAYENNE
GOVERNMENT OVERSEAS DEPARTMENT OF FRANCE
ETHNIC GROUPS BLACK OR MULATTO 66%, EAST INDIAN/CHINESE AND AMERINDIAN 12%, WHITE 12%, OTHERS 10% **LANGUAGES** FRENCH (OFFICIAL) **RELIGIONS** ROMAN CATHOLIC **CURRENCY** EURO = 100 CENTS

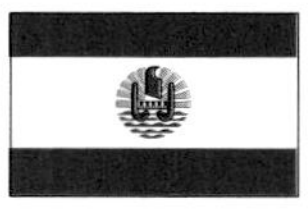
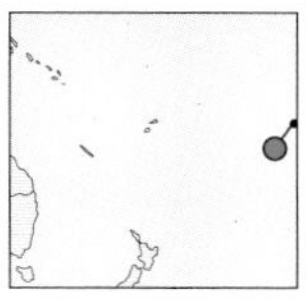

FRENCH POLYNESIA

French Polynesia consists of 130 islands, scattered over 1 million sq mi [2.5 million sq km] of the Pacific Ocean. Tribal chiefs in the area agreed to a French protectorate in 1843. They gained increased autonomy in 1984, but the links with France ensure a high standard of living.

AREA 1,544 SQ MI [4,000 SQ KM]
POPULATION 287,000 **CAPITAL** PAPEETE

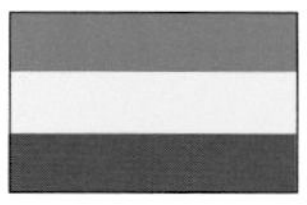
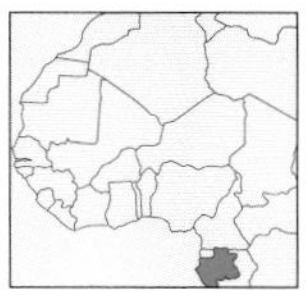

GABON

GEOGRAPHY The Gabonese Republic lies on the Equator in west-central Africa. In area, it is a little larger than the United Kingdom, with a coastline 500 mi [800 km] long. Behind the narrow, partly lagoon-lined coastal plain, the land rises to hills, plateaux and mountains divided by deep valleys carved by the River Ogooué and its tributaries.

Most of Gabon has an equatorial climate, with high temperatures and humidity throughout the year. The rainfall is heavy and the skies are often cloudy.

POLITICS & ECONOMY Gabon became a French colony in the 1880s, but it achieved full independence in 1960. In 1964, an attempted coup was put down when French troops intervened and crushed the revolt. In 1967, Bernard-Albert Bongo, who later renamed himself El Hadj Omar Bongo, became president. He declared Gabon a one-party state in 1968. Opposition parties were legalized in 1991, but Bongo was re-elected president in 1993. He was re-elected in 2005, but, following his death in 2008, he was succeeded by his son Ali Ben Bongo.

Gabon's natural resources include its forests, oil and gas deposits, manganese, and uranium. Its mineral deposits make it one of Africa's better-off countries. But agriculture still employs about one-third of the people and many farmers produce little more than they need to support their families.

AREA 103,347 SQ MI [267,668 SQ KM]
POPULATION 1,515,000 **CAPITAL** LIBREVILLE
GOVERNMENT MULTIPARTY REPUBLIC
ETHNIC GROUPS FOUR MAJOR BANTU TRIBES: FANG, BAPOUNOU, NZEBI AND OBAMBA **LANGUAGES** FRENCH (OFFICIAL), FANG, MYENE, NZEBI, BAPOUNOU/ESCHIRA, BANDJABI
RELIGIONS CHRISTIANITY 75%, ANIMIST, ISLAM
CURRENCY CFA FRANC = 100 CENTIMES

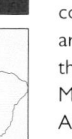

GAMBIA, THE

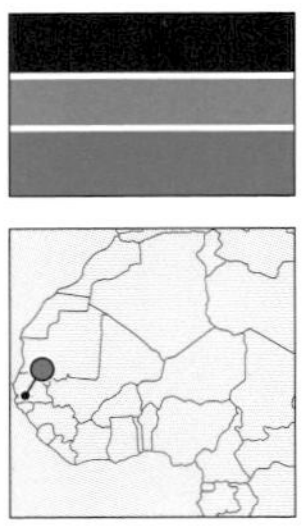

GEOGRAPHY The Republic of The Gambia is the smallest country in mainland Africa. It consists of a narrow strip of land bordering the River Gambia. The Gambia is almost entirely enclosed by Senegal, except along the short Atlantic coastline.

The Gambia has hot and humid summers, but the winter temperatures (November to May) drop to around 61°F [16°C]. In the summer, moist southwesterlies bring rain, which is heaviest on the coast.

POLITICS & ECONOMY English traders bought rights to trade on the River Gambia in 1588, and in 1664 the English established a settlement on an island in the river estuary. In 1765, the British founded Senegambia, which included parts of The Gambia and Senegal. In 1783, Britain handed this colony over to France. In the 19th century, Britain and France discussed the exchange of The Gambia for some other French territory, but an agreement was reached and Britain made The Gambia a British colony in 1888.

The Gambia achieved independence in 1965 and it became a republic in 1970. In 1981, an attempted coup in The Gambia was put down with the help of Senegalese troops. In 1982, The Gambia and Senegal set up a defense alliance, called the Confederation of Senegambia. But this alliance was dissolved in 1989. In 1994, a military group led by Captain Yahya Jammeh overthrew the government of Sir Dawda Jawara. Jammeh became president and was re-elected in 1996, 2001, and 2006.

Agriculture is the chief activity. Food crops include cassava, millet, and sorghum, but groundnuts and groundnut products are the main exports. Tourism is growing and, in 2004, the government announced the discovery of offshore oilfields.

AREA 4,361 SQ MI [11,295 SQ KM]
POPULATION 1,778,000 **CAPITAL** BANJUL
GOVERNMENT MILITARY REGIME
ETHNIC GROUPS MANDINKA 42%, FULA 18%, WOLOF 16%, JOLA 10%, SERAHULI 9%, OTHERS
LANGUAGES ENGLISH (OFFICIAL), MANDINKA, WOLOF, FULA
RELIGIONS ISLAM 90%, CHRISTIANITY 9%, TRADITIONAL BELIEFS 1%
CURRENCY DALASI = 100 BUTUT

GEORGIA

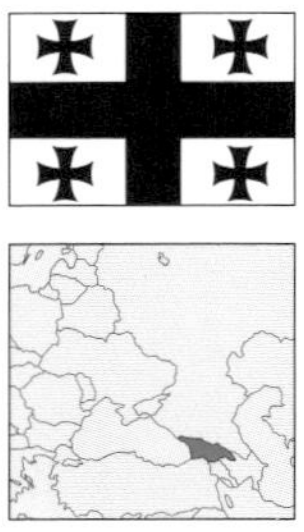

GEOGRAPHY Georgia is a country on the borders of Europe and Asia, facing the Black Sea. The land is rugged with the Caucasus Mountains forming its northern border. The highest mountain in this range, Mount Elbrus (18,510 ft [5,642 m]), lies over the border in Russia.

The Black Sea plains have hot summers and mild winters. The rainfall is heavy, though inland areas are drier.

POLITICS & ECONOMY The first Georgian state was set up nearly 2,500 years ago. But for much of its history, the area was ruled by various conquerors. Christianity was introduced in AD 330. Georgia freed itself of foreign rule in the 11th and 12th centuries, but Mongol armies attacked in the 13th century. From the 16th to the 18th centuries, Iran and the Turkish Ottoman empire struggled for control of the area, and in the late 18th century Georgia sought the protection of Russia, and by the early 19th century Georgia was part of the Russian empire. After the Russian Revolution of 1917, Georgia declared its independence, but Russia invaded, making the country part of the Soviet regime. Georgia declared itself independent in 1991. It became a separate country when the Soviet Union was dissolved in December 1991.

Georgia contains three regions containing minority peoples: Abkhazia in the northwest, South Ossetia in north-central Georgia, and Adjaria (also spelled Adzharia) in the southwest. Civil war broke out in South Ossetia in the early 1990s, while fierce fighting continued in Abkhazia until the late 1990s. In 2000, Georgia agreed to recognize Adjaria's autonomy in the country's constitution. In 2003, the pro-Western Mikhail Saakashvili was elected president following the "Rose Revolution." Following Saakashvili's re-election in 2008, relations with Russia deteriorated. In August 2008, Georgia tried to retake South Ossetia by force. Russian troops counter-attacked and drove Georgian troops out of South Ossetia and Abkhazia. Despite Georgian and Western protests, Russia recognized both of these breakaway regions as independent nations.

Georgia is a developing country. Agriculture, food processing, and perfume-making are important activities. Products include barley, citrus fruits, grapes for wine-making, maize, tea, tobacco, and vegetables. Sheep and cattle are reared.

AREA 26,911 SQ MI [69,700 SQ KM]
POPULATION 4,616,000 **CAPITAL** TBILISI
GOVERNMENT MULTIPARTY REPUBLIC
ETHNIC GROUPS GEORGIAN 70%, ARMENIAN 8%, RUSSIAN 6%, AZERI 6%, OSSETIAN 3%, GREEK 2%, ABKHAZ 2%, OTHERS 3%
LANGUAGES GEORGIAN (OFFICIAL), RUSSIAN
RELIGIONS GEORGIAN ORTHODOX 65%, ISLAM 11%, RUSSIAN ORTHODOX 10%, ARMENIAN APOSTOLIC 8% **CURRENCY** LARI = 100 TETRI

GERMANY

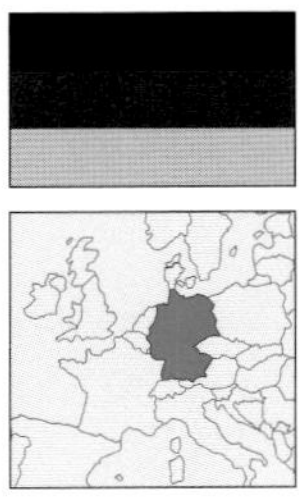

GEOGRAPHY The Federal Republic of Germany is the fourth largest country in Western Europe, after France, Spain, and Sweden. The North German plain borders the North Sea in the northwest and the Baltic Sea in the northeast. Major rivers draining the plain include the Weser, Elbe, and Oder.

The central highlands include the Harz Mountains, the Thuringian Forest (Thüringer Wald), the Ore Mountains (Erzgebirge), and the Bohemian Forest (Böhmerwald) on the Czech border. The Bavarian Alps in the south contain Germany's highest peak, Zugspitze, at 9,718 ft [2,962 m] above sea level. The Black Forest (Schwarzwald) in the southwest overlooks the River Rhine. Northwestern Germany has a mild climate, but the Baltic coasts are cooler. To the south, the climate becomes more continental, especially in the highlands. The precipitation is greatest on the uplands, with snow in winter.

POLITICS & ECONOMY Germany and its allies were defeated in World War I (1914–18) and the country became a republic. Adolf Hitler came to power in 1933 and ruled as a dictator. His order to invade Poland led to the start of World War II (1939–45), which ended with Germany in ruins.

In 1945, Germany was divided into four military zones. In 1949, the American, British, and French zones were amalgamated to form the Federal Republic of Germany (West Germany), while the Soviet zone became the German Democratic Republic (East Germany), a Communist state. Berlin, which had also been partitioned, became a divided city. West Berlin was part of West Germany, while East Berlin became the capital of East Germany. Bonn was the capital of West Germany.

Tension between East and West mounted during the Cold War, but West Germany rebuilt its economy quickly. In East Germany, the recovery was less rapid. In the late 1980s, reforms in the Soviet Union led to unrest in East Germany. Free elections were held in East Germany in 1990 and, on October 3, 1990, Germany was reunited.

The united Germany adopted West Germany's official name, the Federal Republic of Germany. In the 1990s, the government faced many problems, especially those arising from reunification. In 1999, the parliament moved from Bonn to a reconstructed Reichstag building in Berlin. In 2005, Angela Merkel became Germany's first female Chancellor. She was swept back into power in elections in 2009.

West Germany's "economic miracle" after World War II was greatly helped by foreign aid. Today, Germany is one of the world's top economic powers. Manufacturing is the mainstay of the economy and manufactured goods are the chief exports. Cars and other vehicles, cement, chemicals, computers, electrical equipment, processed food, machinery, scientific instruments, ships, steel, textiles, and tools are manufactured. Germany has some coal, potash, and rock salt deposits, but it imports many industrial raw materials. Germany also imports food. Leading products include fruits, grapes for wine-making, potatoes, sugar beet, and vegetables. Livestock include beef and dairy cattle.

AREA 137,846 SQ MI [357,022 SQ KM]
POPULATION 82,330,000 **CAPITAL** BERLIN
GOVERNMENT FEDERAL MULTIPARTY REPUBLIC
ETHNIC GROUPS GERMAN 92%, TURKISH 3%, SERBO-CROATIAN, ITALIAN, GREEK, POLISH, SPANISH **LANGUAGES** GERMAN (OFFICIAL)
RELIGIONS PROTESTANT (MAINLY LUTHERAN) 34%, ROMAN CATHOLIC 34%, ISLAM 4%, OTHERS **CURRENCY** EURO = 100 CENTS

GHANA

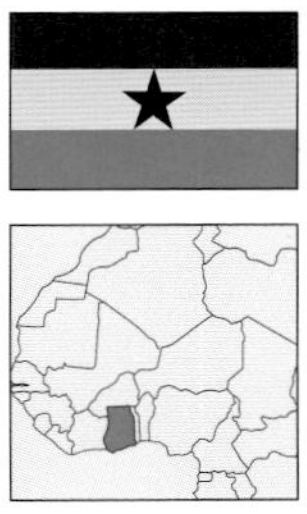

GEOGRAPHY The Republic of Ghana faces the Gulf of Guinea in West Africa. This hot country, just north of the Equator, was formerly called the Gold Coast. Behind the thickly populated southern coastal plains, which are lined with lagoons, lies a plateau region in the southwest.

Accra has a hot, tropical climate. Rain occurs all through the year, though Accra is drier than areas inland.

POLITICS & ECONOMY Portuguese explorers reached the area in 1471 and named it the Gold Coast. The area became a center of the slave trade in the 17th century. The slave trade was ended in the 1860s and, gradually, the British took control of the area. After independence in 1957, attempts were made to develop the economy by creating large state-owned manufacturing industries. But debt and corruption, together with falls in the price of cocoa, the chief export, caused economic problems. This led to instability and frequent coups. In 1981, power was invested in a Provisional National Defense Council, led by Flight-Lieutenant Jerry Rawlings.

The government steadied the economy and introduced reforms. In 1992, a new constitution, allowing for multiparty elections was adopted. Rawlings was elected president in 1992 and 1996. He retired in 2002 and was succeeded as president by John Ageykum Kufuor. In 2008, opposition leader John Atta-Mills was narrowly elected president. The World Bank classifies Ghana as a "low-income" developing country. Most people are poor and farming employs 50% of the population.

AREA 92,098 SQ MI [238,533 SQ KM] **POPULATION** 23,888,000
CAPITAL ACCRA **GOVERNMENT** REPUBLIC
ETHNIC GROUPS AKAN 44%, MOSHI-DAGOMBA 16%, EWE 13%, GA 8%, GURMA 3%, YORUBA 1% **LANGUAGES** ENGLISH (OFFICIAL), AKAN, MOSHI-DAGOMBA, EWE, GA **RELIGIONS** CHRISTIANITY 63%, TRADITIONAL BELIEFS 21%, ISLAM 16% **CURRENCY** CEDI = 100 PESEWAS

GIBRALTAR

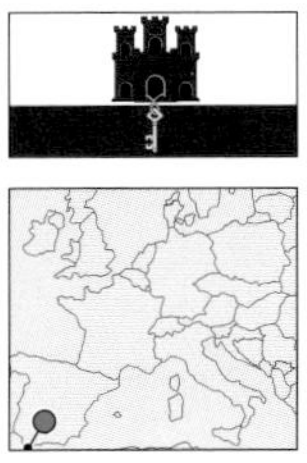

Gibraltar occupies a strategic position on the south coast of Spain where the Mediterranean meets the Atlantic. It was recognized as a British possession in 1713 and, despite Spanish claims, its population has consistently voted to retain its contacts with Britain.

AREA 2.3 SQ MI [6 SQ KM]
POPULATION 29,000 **CAPITAL** GIBRALTAR TOWN

GREECE

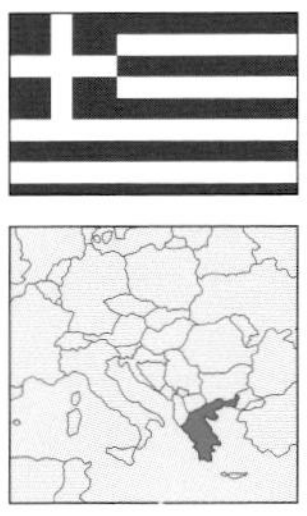

GEOGRAPHY The Hellenic Republic, as Greece is officially called, is a rugged country situated at the southern end of the Balkan peninsula. Olympus, at 9,570 ft [2,917 m] is the highest peak. Islands make up about a fifth of the land.

Low-lying areas in Greece have mild, moist winters and hot, dry summers. The east coast has more than 2,700 hours of sunshine a year and only about half of the rainfall of the west. The mountains have a much more severe climate, with snow on the higher slopes in winter.

POLITICS & ECONOMY Around 2,500 years ago, Greece became the birthplace of Western civilization, and Ancient Greek ruins and art still attract millions of tourists to the country. The first civilization, the Minoan, was centered on Crete. It flourished between about 3000 and 1400 BC. Following the end of the related Mycaenean period on the mainland (1580–1100 BC), a "dark age" lasted until about 800 BC. But from 750 BC, Greeks became rich traders and the city-state of Athens reached its peak in 461–431 BC. Greece became a Roman province in 146 BC and, in AD 365, it became part of the Byzantine Empire.

The Byzantine empire fell to the Turks in 1453. But Greece became an independent monarchy in 1830. After World War II (1939–45), when Germany ruled Greece, a civil war broke out between Greek Communists and nationalists. It ended in 1949 and a military dictatorship seized power in 1967. The monarchy was abolished in 1973 and democracy was restored in 1974. Greece joined the European Community (now the European Union) in 1981 and, on January 1, 2002, the euro became the sole unit of currency in Greece. In 2010, its government faced a debt crisis and was forced to take drastic emergency measures.

Greece is one of the EU's less economically developed members. Manufactured products include processed food, cement, chemicals, metal products, textiles, and tobacco. Greece also mines lignite (brown coal), bauxite, and chromite. Farmland covers about a third of the country and pasture 40%. Crops include barley, grapes, dried fruits, olives, potatoes, sugar beet, and wheat. Livestock farming is important and tourism is a major industry.

AREA 50,949 SQ MI [131,957 SQ KM]
POPULATION 10,737,000 **CAPITAL** ATHENS
GOVERNMENT MULTIPARTY REPUBLIC **ETHNIC GROUPS** GREEK 98%
LANGUAGES GREEK (OFFICIAL) **RELIGIONS** GREEK ORTHODOX 98%
CURRENCY EURO = 100 CENTS

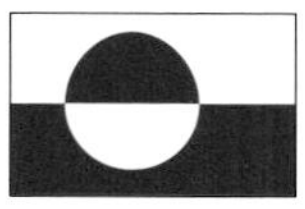
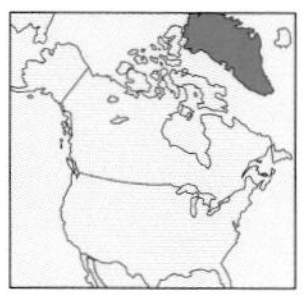

GREENLAND

Greenland is the world's largest island. Settlements are confined to the coast, because an ice sheet covers four-fifths of the land. Greenland became a Danish possession in 1380. Full internal self-government was granted in 1981 and, in 2009, Greenland became a self-governing territory, though it remains dependent on Danish subsidies.

AREA 838,999 sq mi [2,175,600 sq km]
POPULATION 58,000 **CAPITAL** Nuuk

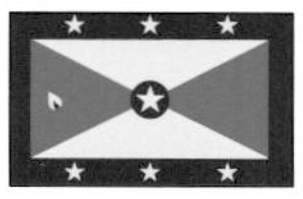
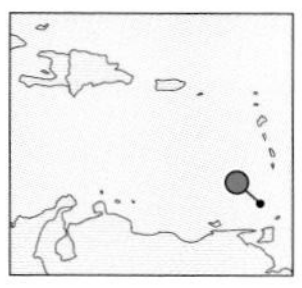

GRENADA

The most southerly of the Windward Islands in the Caribbean Sea, Grenada became independent from the UK in 1974. A military group seized power in 1983, when the prime minister was killed. US troops intervened and restored order and constitutional government.

AREA 133 sq mi [344 sq km]
POPULATION 91,000 **CAPITAL** St George's

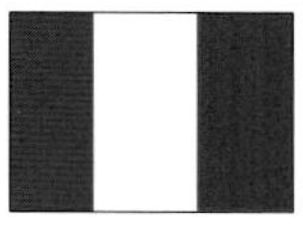
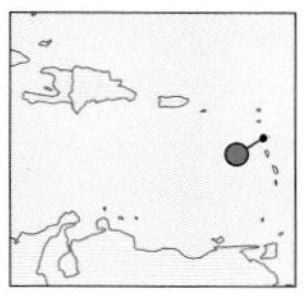

GUADELOUPE

Guadeloupe is a French overseas department which includes seven Caribbean islands, the largest of which is Basse-Terre. French aid has helped to mantain a reasonable standard of living for the people.

AREA 658 sq mi [1,705 sq km]
POPULATION 453,000 **CAPITAL** Basse-Terre

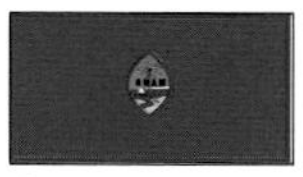
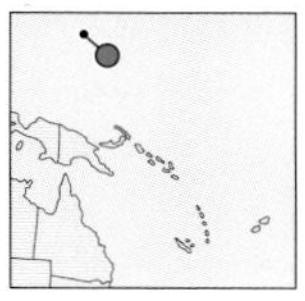

GUAM

Guam, a strategically important "unincorporated territory" of the USA, is the largest of the Mariana Islands in the Pacific Ocean. It is composed of a coralline limestone plateau.

AREA 212 sq mi [549 sq km]
POPULATION 178,000 **CAPITAL** Agana

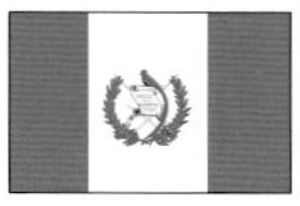
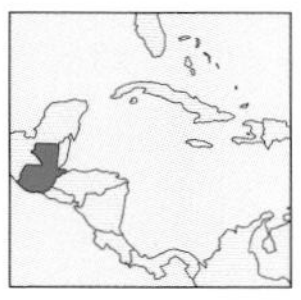

GUATEMALA

GEOGRAPHY The Republic of Guatemala in Central America contains a thickly populated mountain region, with fertile soils. The mountains, which run in an east–west direction, contain many volcanoes, some of which are active. Volcanic eruptions and earthquakes are common in the highlands. South of the mountains lie the thinly populated Pacific coastlands, while a large inland plain occupies the north.

The lowlands of Guatemala are hot and rainy, but the central highlands are cooler and drier. Guatemala City has a pleasant, warm climate with a dry season between November and April.

POLITICS & ECONOMY Much of what is now Guatemala was part of the Maya empire which thrived between AD 300 and 900. Spain ruled the area from the 1520s until 1821. In 1823, Guatemala joined the Central American Federation. But it became fully independent in 1839. Instability and periodic violence have marred its progress. Guatemala has a long-standing claim over Belize, but this was reduced in 1983 to the southern fifth of the country. Between 1960 and 1996, civil war occurred between left-wing groups, including many Amerindians, and government forces. The war claimed perhaps 200,000 lives. In 2004, the government paid US$3.5 million to victims of state-sponsored oppression. In 2007, Alvaro Colom, a center-left politician, became president.

Guatemala is ranked as a "lower-middle-income" economy. Agriculture employs 38% of the population. Coffee, sugar, bananas, and beef are exported, and the spice cardamom and cotton are also important. Maize is the main food crop.

AREA 42,042 sq mi [108,889 sq km]
POPULATION 13,277,000 **CAPITAL** Guatemala City
GOVERNMENT Republic **ETHNIC GROUPS** Ladino (mixed Hispanic and Amerindian) 55%, Amerindian 43%, others 2%
LANGUAGES Spanish (official), Amerindian languages
RELIGIONS Christianity, indigenous Mayan beliefs
CURRENCY US dollar; Quetzal = 100 centavos

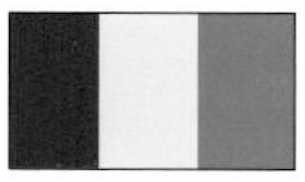
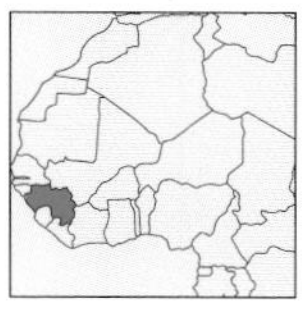

GUINEA

GEOGRAPHY The Republic of Guinea faces the Atlantic Ocean in West Africa. A flat, swampy plain borders the coast. Behind this plain, the land rises to a plateau region called Fouta Djalon. The Upper Niger plains, named after one of Africa's longest rivers, the Niger, which rises there, are in the northeast.

Guinea has a tropical climate and Conakry has its rainy period between May and November, the coolest season. In the dry season, hot harmattan winds blow from the Sahara.

POLITICS & ECONOMY Guinea came under the influence of several medieval African states, including Ancient Ghana and Ancient Mali. France began to control the area in the late 19th century. Guinea became independent in 1958. Its leaders pursued socialist policies but resorted to repressive measures to hold on to power. A military regime under Lansana Conté took over in 1984, but a multiparty system was restored in 1992. Conté was elected president in 1993, 1998, and 2002. But following Conté's death in 2008, an army group led by Captain Mousa Dadis Camara seized power. In 2010, a power-sharing government was set up to oversee a return to civilian rule.

Guinea is a "low-income" developing country. Its resources include bauxite (aluminum ore), diamonds, gold, iron ore, and uranium. Bauxite and alumina (processed bauxite) account for more than half of the exports. Agriculture employs more than 70% of the people, but most farmers are poor. Manufactures include alumina, processed food, and textiles.

AREA 94,925 sq mi [245,857 sq km]
POPULATION 10,058,000 **CAPITAL** Conakry
GOVERNMENT Multiparty republic
ETHNIC GROUPS Peuhl 40%, Malinke 30%, Soussou 20%, others 10% **LANGUAGES** French (official)
RELIGIONS Islam 85%, Christianity 8%, traditional beliefs 7%
CURRENCY Guinean franc = 100 cauris

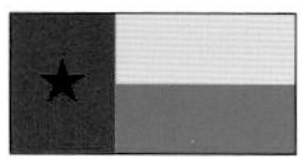
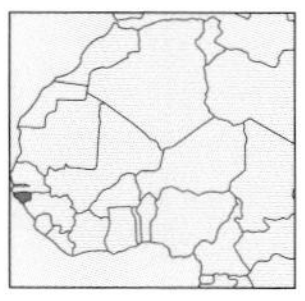

GUINEA-BISSAU

GEOGRAPHY The Republic of Guinea-Bissau, formerly known as Portuguese Guinea, is a small country in West Africa. The land is mostly low-lying, with a broad, swampy coastal plain and many flat offshore islands, including the Bijagós Archipelago.

The country has a tropical climate, with one dry season (December to May) and a rainy season from June to November.

POLITICS & ECONOMY Portuguese explorers reached Guinea-Bissau in 1446 and the area became a center of the slave trade. From 1836, Portugal administered Guinea-Bissau with the Cape Verde Islands but, in 1879, the territories were separated. Guinea-Bissau became a separate colony called Portuguese Guinea. But economic development in the colony was slow.

In 1956, African nationalists in Portuguese Guinea and Cape Verde founded the African Party for the Independence of Guinea and Cape Verde (PAIGC). The PAIGC began a guerrilla war in 1963 and, by 1968, it held two-thirds of the country. In 1972, a rebel National Assembly, elected by the people in the PAIGC-controlled area, voted to make the country independent as Guinea-Bissau.

In 1974, newly independent Guinea-Bissau faced many problems arising from its underdeveloped economy and its lack of trained people to work in the administration. One objective of the leaders of Guinea-Bissau was to unite their country with Cape Verde. But, in 1980, army leaders overthrew Guinea-Bissau's government. The Revolutionary Council, which took over, opposed unification with Cape Verde. Guinea-Bissau ceased to be a one-party state in 1991 and multiparty elections were held in 1994. Civil war broke out in 1998 and a military coup occurred in 1999. Elections were held in 2000. Another coup occurred in 2003, but civilian government was restored in 2004. In 2005, a former military leader, Joao Bernardo Viera, became president but he was assassinated in 2009. A former president, Malam Bacai Sanha, was elected president in July 2009.

Agriculture, mainly at subsistence level, employs 76% of the people. Crops include coconuts, groundnuts, maize, and rice.

AREA 13,948 sq mi [36,125 sq km]
POPULATION 1,534,000 **CAPITAL** Bissau
GOVERNMENT "Interim" government
ETHNIC GROUPS Balanta 30%, Fula 20%, Manjaca 14%, Mandinga 13%, Papel 7% **LANGUAGES** Portuguese (official), Crioulo
RELIGIONS Traditional beliefs 50%, Islam 45%, Christianity 5%
CURRENCY CFA franc = 100 centimes

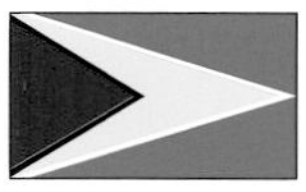
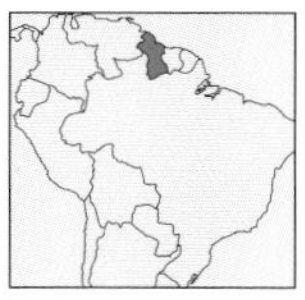

GUYANA

GEOGRAPHY The Cooperative Republic of Guyana is a country facing the Atlantic Ocean in northeastern South America. The coastal plain is flat and much of it is below sea level.

The climate is hot and humid, though the interior highlands are cooler than the coast. The rainfall is heavy, occurring on more than 200 days a year.

POLITICS & ECONOMY Britain gained control of the area in 1814 and ruled British Guiana until it became independent as Guyana in 1966. A black lawyer, Forbes Burnham, was the first prime minister. Under a new constitution adopted in 1980, the president's powers were increased. Burnham became president and served in this post until he died in 1985. He was succeeded by Hugh Desmond Hoyte, who was defeated in 1993 by an ethnic Indian, Cheddi Jagan. Jagan died in 1997 and was succeeded by his wife, Janet. In 1999, Bharrat Jagdeo was elected president. He was re-elected in 2001 and again in 2006.

Guyana is a poor country. Its resources include gold, bauxite (aluminum ore) and other minerals, forests, and fertile soils. Sugarcane and rice are leading crops. Guyana has potential for producing hydroelectricity from its many rivers.

AREA 83,000 sq mi [214,969 sq km]
POPULATION 753,000 **CAPITAL** Georgetown
GOVERNMENT Multiparty republic
ETHNIC GROUPS East Indian 50%, Black 36%, Amerindian 7%, others 7% **LANGUAGES** English (official), Creole, Hindi, Urdu
RELIGIONS Christianity 50%, Hinduism 35%, Islam 10%, others 5%
CURRENCY Guyanese dollar = 100 cents

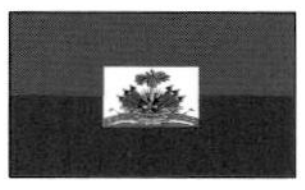
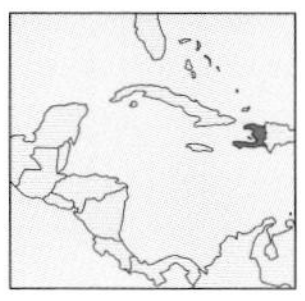

HAITI

GEOGRAPHY The Republic of Haiti occupies the western third of Hispaniola in the Caribbean. The land is mainly mountainous. The climate is hot and humid, though the northern highlands, with about 79 inches [200 mm], have more than twice as much rainfall as the southern coast.

POLITICS & ECONOMY Visited by Christopher Columbus in 1492, Haiti was later developed by the French. The African slaves revolted in 1791 and the country became independent in 1804. Haiti subsequently suffered from instability, violence, and dictatorial rule. Elections in 1990 returned Jean-Bertrand Aristide as president, but he was overthrown in 1991. In 1995, René Préval was elected president, but Aristide was again elected president in 2000. In 2004, rebel activity forced Aristide to flee the country. A US-backed government was set up to restore order and, in 2006, René Préval was re-elected president. In January 2010, an earthquake hit Port-au-Prince, killing about 230,000 people and devastating the economy.

AREA 10,714 sq mi [27,750 sq km]
POPULATION 9,036,000 **CAPITAL** Port-au-Prince
GOVERNMENT Multiparty republic **ETHNIC GROUPS** Black 95%, Mulatto/White 5% **LANGUAGES** French and Creole (both official)
RELIGIONS Roman Catholic 80%, Voodoo
CURRENCY Gourde = 100 centimes

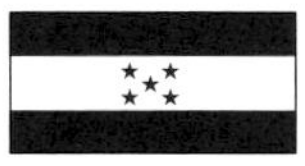
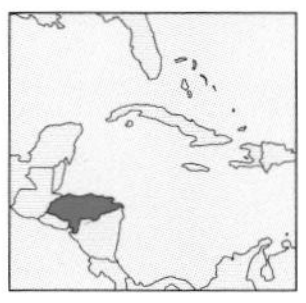

HONDURAS

GEOGRAPHY The Republic of Honduras is the second largest country in Central America. The northern coast on the Caribbean Sea extends more than 373 mi [600 km], but the Pacific coast in the southeast is only about 50 mi [80 km] long. Honduras has a tropical climate, but the highlands are cooler. The rainiest months are between May and November. Hurricanes often hit the north coast. Hurricane Mitch in 1998 caused the worst destruction in modern times.

POLITICS & ECONOMY Western Honduras was part of the Maya empire which flourished between AD 300 and 900. Christopher Columbus claimed the area for Spain in 1502 and Spain ruled from 1625 until 1821. Honduras became part of the Central American Federation but withdrew in 1838.

In the 1890s, American companies developed plantations to grow bananas and Honduras became known as a "banana state." But instability slowed economic progress. Since 1980, civilian governments friendly toward the United States have ruled Honduras, but in 2008 Honduras joined the "Bolivarian Alternative to the Americas," a left-wing alliance headed by Venezuelan President Hugo Chavez. A military coup in 2009 removed

President Manuel Zelaya from office. In elections in November 2009, Porfiro Lobo was elected president.

Honduras is a developing country. Its few resources include silver, lead, and zinc. Agriculture is the main activity. Bananas and coffee are exported and maize is the chief food crop. Honduras is one of Central America's least industrialized countries. Products include processed food, textiles, and wood products.

AREA 43,277 SQ MI [112,088 SQ KM]
POPULATION 7,834,000 **CAPITAL** TEGUCIGALPA
GOVERNMENT REPUBLIC **ETHNIC GROUPS** MESTIZO 90%, AMERINDIAN 7%, BLACK (INCLUDING BLACK CARIB) 2%, WHITE 1% **LANGUAGES** SPANISH (OFFICIAL), AMERINDIAN DIALECTS **RELIGIONS** ROMAN CATHOLIC 97%
CURRENCY HONDURAN LEMPIRA = 100 CENTAVOS

HUNGARY

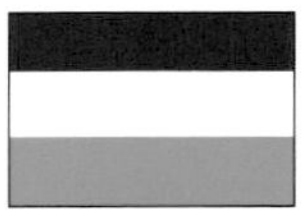

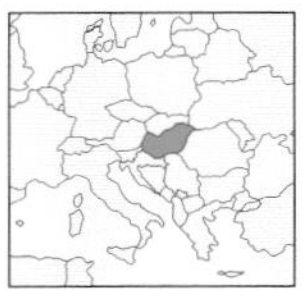

GEOGRAPHY The Hungarian Republic is a landlocked country in central Europe. The land is mostly low-lying and drained by the Danube (Duna) and its tributary, the Tisza. Most of the land east of the Danube belongs to a region called the Great Plain (Nagyalföld), which covers about half of Hungary.

Hungary lies far from the moderating influence of the sea. As a result, summers are warmer and sunnier, and the winters colder than in Western Europe.

POLITICS & ECONOMY Hungary entered World War II (1939–45) in 1941, as an ally of Germany, but the Germans occupied the country in 1944. The Soviet Union invaded Hungary in 1944 and, in 1946, the country became a republic. The Communists gradually took over the government, taking complete control in 1949. From 1949, Hungary was an ally of the Soviet Union. In 1956, Soviet troops crushed an anti-Communist revolt. But in the 1980s, reforms in the Soviet Union led to the growth of anti-Communist groups in Hungary. In 1989, Hungary adopted a new constitution making it a multiparty state. Elections held in 1990 led to a victory for the non-Communist Democratic Forum. In 2002, the Hungarian Socialist Party, in alliance with the liberal Free Democrats, won a majority in parliament. In 2004, Hungary became a member of both the North Atlantic Treaty Organization and the European Union.

Before World War II, Hungary's economy was based mainly on agriculture. But the Communists set up many manufacturing industries. From the late 1980s, private ownership increased. This caused problems, including inflation and high rates of unemployment. Elections in 2010 resulted in victory for the center-right Fidezs Party led by Viktor Oban, though 17% of voters supported the far-right Jobbik Party. Leading manufactures include aluminum, chemicals, electrical and electronic goods, and telecommunications equipment.

AREA 35,920 SQ MI [93,032 SQ KM]
POPULATION 9,906,000 **CAPITAL** BUDAPEST
GOVERNMENT MULTIPARTY REPUBLIC
ETHNIC GROUPS MAGYAR 90%, GYPSY, GERMAN, SERB, ROMANIAN, SLOVAK **LANGUAGES** HUNGARIAN (OFFICIAL)
RELIGIONS ROMAN CATHOLIC 68%, CALVINIST 20%, LUTHERAN 5%, OTHERS **CURRENCY** FORINT = 100 FILLÉR

ICELAND

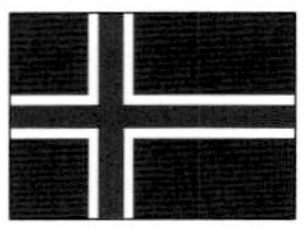

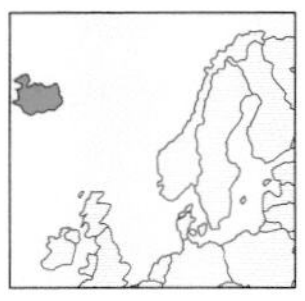

GEOGRAPHY The Republic of Iceland, in the North Atlantic Ocean, is closer to Greenland than Scotland. Iceland sits astride the Mid-Atlantic Ridge. It is slowly getting wider as the ocean is being stretched apart by continental drift.

Iceland has around 200 volcanoes, and eruptions are frequent. An eruption under the Vatnajökull ice cap in 1996 created a subglacial lake which subsequently burst, causing severe flooding. Geysers and hot springs are common, and in 2010 a volcanic eruption and its resulting ash cloud disrupted international air services. Ice caps and glaciers cover about an eighth of the land. The only habitable regions are the coastal lowlands. Despite its northerly position, Iceland's climate is moderated by the warm waters of the Gulf Stream. The port of Reykjavik is ice-free all year round.

POLITICS & ECONOMY Norwegian Vikings colonized Iceland in AD 874, and in 930 the settlers founded the world's oldest parliament, the Althing.

Iceland united with Norway in 1262. But when Norway united with Denmark in 1380, Iceland came under Danish rule. Iceland became a self-governing kingdom, united with Denmark, in 1918. It became a fully independent republic in 1944, following a referendum in which 97% of the people voted to break their country's ties with Denmark. Iceland has played a leading part in European affairs and is a member of the North Atlantic Treaty Organization. But it has been involved in fishing and whaling disputes. Iceland has few resources besides its fishing grounds, and fishing and fish processing dominate Iceland's overseas trade. Barely 1% of the land is used to grow crops, but 23% of the country can be used for grazing sheep and cattle. Vegetables and fruit are grown in greenhouses, heated by water from the hot springs. Iceland's economy was hit by the global financial crisis of 2008–9, causing the collapse of its currency and banking system. In 2009, Johanna Sigurdardottir became Iceland's first female prime minister and Iceland applied for membership of the European Union.

AREA 39,768 SQ MI [103,000 SQ KM]
POPULATION 307,000 **CAPITAL** REYKJAVIK
GOVERNMENT MULTIPARTY REPUBLIC
ETHNIC GROUPS ICELANDIC 97%, DANISH 1%
LANGUAGES ICELANDIC (OFFICIAL) **RELIGIONS** EVANGELICAL LUTHERAN 87%, OTHER PROTESTANT 4%, ROMAN CATHOLIC 2%, OTHERS
CURRENCY ICELANDIC KRÓNA = 100 AURAR

INDIA

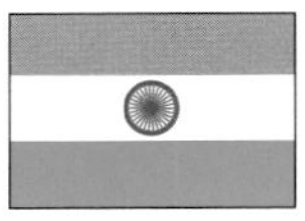

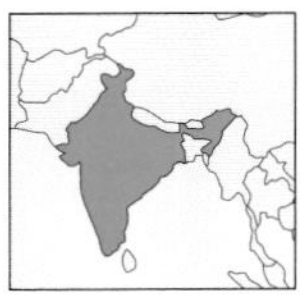

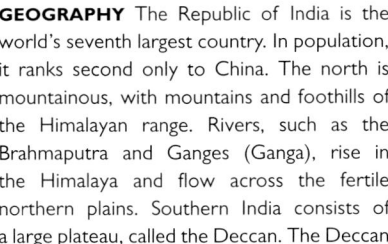

GEOGRAPHY The Republic of India is the world's seventh largest country. In population, it ranks second only to China. The north is mountainous, with mountains and foothills of the Himalayan range. Rivers, such as the Brahmaputra and Ganges (Ganga), rise in the Himalaya and flow across the fertile northern plains. Southern India consists of a large plateau, called the Deccan. The Deccan is bordered by two mountain ranges, the Western Ghats and the Eastern Ghats.

India has three main seasons. The cool season runs from October to February. The hot season runs from March to June. The rainy monsoon season starts in the middle of June and continues into September. Delhi has a moderate rainfall, with about 25 inches [640 mm] a year. The southwestern coast and the northeast have far more rain. Darjeeling in the northeast has an average annual rainfall of 120 inches [3,040 mm]. But parts of the Thar Desert in the northwest have only 2 inches [50 mm] of rain per year.

POLITICS & ECONOMY In southern India, most of the people are descendants of the dark-skinned Dravidians, who were among India's earliest people. Most northerners are descendants of lighter-skinned Aryans who arrived around 3,500 years ago.

India was the birthplace of several major religions, including Hinduism, Buddhism, and Sikhism. Islam was introduced from about AD 1000. The Muslim Mughal empire was founded in 1526. From the 17th century, Britain began to gain influence. From 1858 to 1947, India was ruled as part of the British empire. An independence movement began after the Sepoy Rebellion (1857–9), and in 1885 the Indian National Congress was formed. In 1920, Mohandas K. Gandhi became its leader and it soon became a mass movement. When independence was finally achieved in 1947, British India was divided into modern India and Muslim Pakistan. Partition was marred by mass slaughter as Hindus and Sikhs fled from Pakistan, and Indian Muslims poured into Pakistan. In the ensuing disputes, some 1 million people were killed.

Although India has 15 major languages and hundreds of minor ones, together with many religions, the country remains the world's largest democracy. It has faced many problems, especially with Pakistan, over the disputed territory of Jammu and Kashmir. Two wars in 1965 and 1972 failed to alter greatly the 1948 ceasefire lines. In the late 1980s, Kashmiri nationalists in the Indian-controlled area waged a campaign, demanding either integration into Pakistan or independence. India sent in troops and accused Pakistan of intervention. In the 1990s, Pakistani-backed guerrillas fought to break India's hold on the Srinagar valley, Kashmir's most populous region. Tension mounted following the testing of nuclear devices by both countries in 1998. Relations improved, but an attack on buildings in Mumbai in 2008, allegedly by Pakistanis, caused tension. In 2009–10, the long-running dispute with Maoists in central and eastern India flared up again.

The World Bank classifies India as a "low-income" developing country. To boost the economy, a right-wing government led by the Hindu Bharatiya Janata Party introduced free-enterprise policies. But in 2004, the left-wing United Progressive Alliance was successful at the polls and Manmohan Singh became prime minister.

Agriculture employs 52% of the people. Crops include rice, wheat, millet, sorghum, peas, and beans. India has more cattle than any other country. Milk is produced, but Hindus do not eat beef. Resources include coal, iron ore, and oil. Manufacturing has expanded greatly since 1947. Iron and steel, machinery, refined petroleum, textiles, and transport equipment are major products.

AREA 1,269,212 SQ MI [3,287,263 SQ KM]
POPULATION 1,156,898,000 **CAPITAL** NEW DELHI
GOVERNMENT MULTIPARTY FEDERAL REPUBLIC
ETHNIC GROUPS INDO-ARYAN (CAUCASOID) 72%, DRAVIDIAN (ABORIGINAL) 25%, OTHERS (MAINLY MONGOLOID) 3%
LANGUAGES HINDI, ENGLISH, TELUGU, BENGALI, MARATHI, TAMIL, URDU, GUJARATI, MALAYALAM, KANNADA, ORIYA, PUNJABI, ASSAMESE, KASHMIRI, SINDHI, AND SANSKRIT ARE ALL OFFICIAL LANGUAGES
RELIGIONS HINDUISM 82%, ISLAM 12%, CHRISTIANITY 2%, SIKHISM 2%, BUDDHISM AND OTHERS **CURRENCY** INDIAN RUPEE = 100 PAISA

INDONESIA

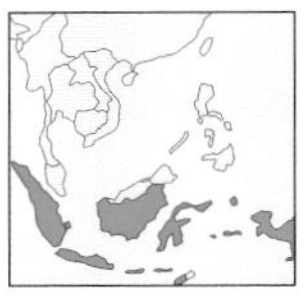

GEOGRAPHY The Republic of Indonesia is an island nation in Southeast Asia. In all, Indonesia contains about 13,600 islands, less than 6,000 of which are inhabited. Three-quarters of the country is made up of five main areas: the islands of Sumatra, Java and Sulawesi (Celebes), together with Kalimantan (southern Borneo) and Irian Jaya (western New Guinea). The islands are generally mountainous and volcanic. The larger islands have extensive coastal lowlands. The climate is hot and humid, with a high rainfall. Only Java and the Sunda Islands have relatively dry seasons.

POLITICS & ECONOMY Indonesia is the world's most populous Muslim nation, though Islam was introduced as recently as the 15th century. The Dutch became active in the area in the early 17th century and Indonesia became a Dutch colony in 1799. After a long struggle, the Netherlands recognized Indonesia's independence in 1949. The economy has expanded, but ethnic and religious conflict have slowed down economic progress.

In the early 21st century, Indonesia was facing many problems, arising from widespread corruption in the government and the army. Separatists were operating in Aceh province in northern Sumatra and in West Papua (formerly Irian Jaya), Christian-Muslim clashes led to loss of life in the Moluccas, and East (formerly Portuguese) Timor became an independent country. Terrorist incidents occurred in the early 21st century. In December 2004, a tsunami killed more than 100,000 people. Worst hit was Aceh, but the tragedy was followed by the granting of autonomy for Aceh province in 2006. Indonesia is a democratic, developing country with a growing industrial sector. It exports oil and natural gas, and also mines tin and other minerals. Timber, textiles, rubber, coffee and tea are also exported. Rice is the main food crop.

AREA 735,354 SQ MI [1,904,569 SQ KM]
POPULATION 240,272,000 **CAPITAL** JAKARTA
GOVERNMENT MULTIPARTY REPUBLIC
ETHNIC GROUPS JAVANESE 45%, SUNDANESE 14%, MADURESE 7%, COASTAL MALAYS 7%, APPROXIMATELY 300 OTHERS
LANGUAGES BAHASA INDONESIAN (OFFICIAL), MANY OTHERS
RELIGIONS ISLAM 88%, ROMAN CATHOLIC 3%, HINDUISM 2%, BUDDHISM 1%
CURRENCY INDONESIAN RUPIAH = 100 SEN

IRAN

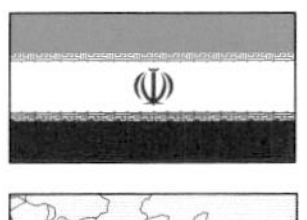

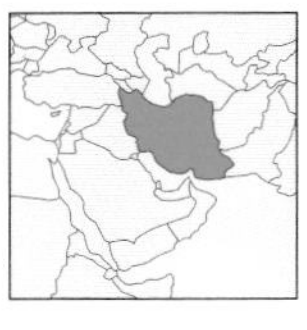

GEOGRAPHY The Republic of Iran contains a barren central plateau which covers about half of the country. It includes the Dasht-e-Kavir (Great Salt Desert) and the Dasht-e-Lut (Great Sand Desert). The Elburz Mountains north of the plateau contain Iran's highest peak, Damavand, while narrow lowlands lie between the mountains and the Caspian Sea. West of the plateau are the Zagros Mountains, beyond which the land descends to the plains bordering the Persian Gulf.

Much of Iran has a severe, dry climate, with hot summers and cold winters. In Tehran, rain falls on only about 30 days in the year and the annual temperature range is more than 45°F [25°C]. The climate in the lowlands, however, is generally milder.

POLITICS & ECONOMY Iran was called Persia until 1935. The empire of Ancient Persia flourished between 550 and 350 BC, when it fell to Alexander the Great. Islam was introduced in AD 641.

Britain and Russia competed for influence in the area in the 19th century, and in the early 20th century the British began to develop the country's oil resources. In 1925, the Pahlavi family took power.

Reza Khan became shah (king) and worked to modernize the country. The Pahlavi dynasty was ended in 1979 when a religious leader, Ayatollah Ruhollah Khomeini, made Iran an Islamic republic. In 1980–8, Iran and Iraq fought a war over disputed borders. Khomeini died in 1989, but his fundamentalist views and anti-Western attitudes continued to dominate politics. In 2005, a hardliner, Mahmoud Ahmadinejad, was elected president. Iran's nuclear policies, which many in the West considered were to develop nuclear weapons, led to the application of international sanctions against Iran in 2009–10.

Iran's prosperity is based on its oil production and oil accounts for more than 70% of the country's exports. However, the economy was severely damaged by the Iran–Iraq war in the 1980s. Oil revenues have been used to develop a growing manufacturing sector. Agriculture is important even though farms cover only a tenth of the land. The main crops are wheat and barley. Livestock farming and fishing are other important activities, although Iran has to import much of the food it needs.

AREA 636,368 sq mi [1,648,195 sq km]
POPULATION 66,429,000 **CAPITAL** Tehran
GOVERNMENT Islamic republic **ETHNIC GROUPS** Persian 51%, Azeri 24%, Gilaki and Mazandarani 8%, Kurd 7%, Arab 3%, Lur 2%, Baluchi 2%, Turkmen 2% **LANGUAGES** Persian 58%, Turkic 26%, Kurdish **RELIGIONS** Islam (Shi'ite Muslim 89%)
CURRENCY Iranian rial = 100 dinars

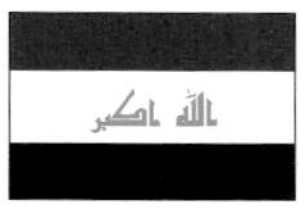

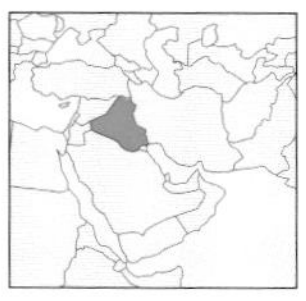

IRAQ

GEOGRAPHY The Republic of Iraq is a southwest Asian country at the head of the Persian Gulf. Rolling deserts cover western and southwestern Iraq, with part of the Zagros Mountains in the northeast, where farming can be practised without irrigation. The northern plains, across which flow the rivers Euphrates (Nahr al Furat) and Tigris (Nahr Dijlah), are dry. But the southern plains, including Mesopotamia and the delta of the Shatt al Arab, contain irrigated farmland, together with marshland.

The climate of Iraq ranges from temperate in the north to subtropical in the south. Baghdad, in central Iraq, has cool winters, with occasional frosts, and hot summers. The rainfall is generally low.

POLITICS & ECONOMY Mesopotamia was the home of several great civilizations, including Sumer, Babylon, and Assyria. It later became part of the Persian empire. Islam was introduced in AD 637 and Baghdad became the brilliant capital of the powerful Arab empire. But Mesopotamia declined after the Mongols invaded it in 1258. From 1534, Mesopotamia became part of the Turkish Ottoman empire. Britain invaded the area in 1916. In 1921, Britain renamed the country Iraq and set up an Arab monarchy. Iraq finally became independent in 1932.

By the 1950s, oil dominated Iraq's economy. In 1952, Iraq agreed to take 50% of the profits of the foreign oil companies. This revenue enabled the government to pay for welfare services and development projects. But many Iraqis felt that they should benefit more from their oil. Since 1958, when army officers killed the king and made Iraq a republic, Iraq has undergone turbulent times. In the 1960s, the Kurds, who live in northern Iraq and also in Iran, Turkey, Syria, and Armenia, asked for self-rule. The government rejected their demands and war broke out. A peace treaty was signed in 1975, but conflict has continued.

In 1979, Saddam Hussein became Iraq's president. Under his leadership, Iraq invaded Iran in 1980, starting an eight-year war. Iraqi Kurds supported Iran and the Iraqi government attacked Kurdish villages with poison gas. In 1990, Iraqi troops occupied Kuwait, but an international force drove them out in 1991. Since 1991, Iraqi troops have attacked Shi'ite Marsh Arabs and Kurds. In 1998, Iraq's failure to permit UN inspectors, charged with disposing of Iraq's deadliest weapons, access to suspect sites led to the Western bombardment of Iraqi military sites. Another major offensive occurred in 2001. In 2002–3, pressure mounted on Iraq to dispose of its alleged weapons of mass destruction. In March–April 2003, a coalition force headed by the United States invaded Iraq, overthrowing Saddam Hussein's regime. Despite ongoing violence, elections were held in 2005, and again in 2010 when former premier Iyad Allawi's bloc was declared to have come first, narrowly defeating Nouri al-Maliki's State of Law Alliance.

Civil war, war damage, mismanagement, and UN sanctions have damaged the economy. Oil remains the main resource. Farmland, including pasture, covers about a fifth of the land. Products include barley, cotton, dates, fruit, livestock, wheat, and wool. But Iraq still has to import food. Manufactures include refined oil, petrochemicals, and consumer goods.

AREA 169,234 sq mi [438,317 sq km]
POPULATION 28,946,000 **CAPITAL** Baghdad
GOVERNMENT Parliamentary democracy **ETHNIC GROUPS** Arab 77%, Kurdish 19%, Assyrian and others **LANGUAGES** Arabic (official), Kurdish (official in Kurdish areas), Assyrian, Armenian **RELIGIONS** Islam 97%, Christianity and others **CURRENCY** New Iraqi dinar

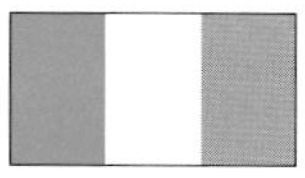

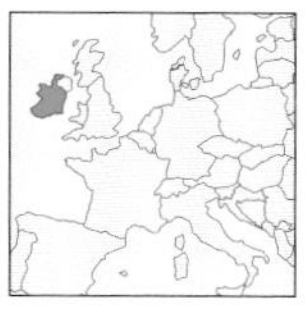

IRELAND

GEOGRAPHY The Republic of Ireland occupies five-sixths of the island of Ireland. The country consists of a large lowland region surrounded by a broken rim of low mountains. The uplands include the Mountains of Kerry where Carrauntoohill, Ireland's highest peak at 3,415 ft [1,041 m], is situated. The River Shannon is the longest in Ireland, flowing through three large lakes, loughs Allen, Ree, and Derg.

Ireland has a mild, rainy climate influenced by the warm Gulf Stream current, whose effects are greatest in the west. However, Dublin in the east is cooler than places on the west coast.

POLITICS & ECONOMY In 1801, the Act of Union created the United Kingdom of Great Britain and Ireland. But Irish discontent intensified in the 1840s when a potato blight caused a famine in which a million people died and nearly a million emigrated. Britain was blamed for not having done enough to help. In 1916, an uprising in Dublin was crushed, but between 1919 and 1922 civil war occurred. In 1922, the Irish Free State was created as a Dominion in the British Commonwealth. But Northern Ireland remained part of the UK.

Ireland became a republic in 1949. In 1973, Ireland became a member of the European Community (now the European Union) and, until the global financial crisis of 2008–9, it prospered. In 1998, Ireland took part in the negotiations to produce a constitutional settlement in Northern Ireland. Ireland agreed to give up its claim on Northern Ireland and, in 2007, a power-sharing government was set up in the north.

Major farm products in Ireland include barley, cattle and dairy products, pigs, potatoes, poultry, sheep, sugar beet, and wheat, while fishing provides another valuable source of food. Farming is now profitable, aided by European Union grants, but manufacturing is the leading economic sector. Many factories produce food and beverages. Chemicals and pharmaceuticals, electronic equipment, machinery, paper, and textiles are also important.

AREA 27,132 sq mi [70,273 sq km]
POPULATION 4,203,000 **CAPITAL** Dublin
GOVERNMENT Multiparty republic **ETHNIC GROUPS** Irish 94%
LANGUAGES Irish (Gaelic) and English (both official)
RELIGIONS Roman Catholic 92%, Protestant 3%
CURRENCY Euro = 100 cents

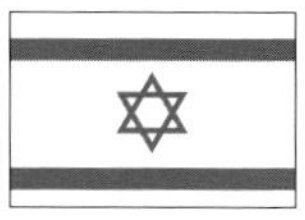

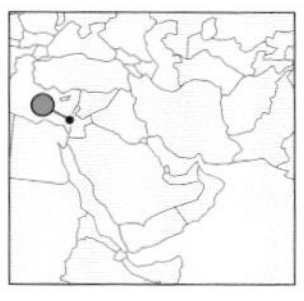

ISRAEL

GEOGRAPHY The State of Israel is a small country in the eastern Mediterranean. It includes a fertile coastal plain, where Israel's main industrial cities, Haifa (Hefa) and Tel Aviv-Jaffa, are situated. Inland lie the Judaeo-Galilean highlands, which run from northern Israel to the northern tip of the Negev Desert. To the east lies part of the Great Rift Valley which contains the River Jordan, the Sea of Galilee, and the Dead Sea. Summers are hot and dry. Winters on the coast are mild and moist, but the rainfall decreases from west to east and from north to south.

POLITICS & ECONOMY Israel is part of a region called Palestine. Some Jews have always lived in the area, though most modern Israelis are descendants of immigrants who began to settle there from the 1880s. Britain ruled Palestine from 1917. Large numbers of Jews escaping Nazi persecution arrived in the 1930s, provoking an Arab uprising against British rule. In 1947, the UN agreed to partition Palestine into an Arab and a Jewish state. Fighting broke out after Arabs rejected the plan. The State of Israel came into being in May 1948, but fighting continued into 1949. Other Arab-Israeli wars in 1956, 1967, and 1973 led to land gains for Israel.

In 1978, Israel signed a treaty with Egypt which led to the return of the occupied Sinai peninsula to Egypt in 1979. But conflict continued between Israel and the PLO (Palestine Liberation Organization). In 1993, the PLO and Israel agreed to establish Palestinian self-rule in two areas: the occupied Gaza Strip, and in the town of Jericho in the occupied West Bank. The agreement was extended in 1995 to include more than 30% of the West Bank. Israel's prime minister, Yitzhak Rabin, was assassinated in 1995. In 1996, Benjamin Netanyahu was elected prime minister. The peace process stalled until Ehud Barak defeated Netanyahu in 1999. In 2001, Ariel Sharon became prime minister. In 2005, he handed over the Gaza Strip to the Palestinian Authority. Sharon formed a new political party, Kadima. After Sharon suffered a stroke, Ehud Olmert became leader of Kadima and prime minister. Between 2005 and 2009, Israeli forces clashed with Palestinians in southern Lebanon and Gaza. In 2009, elections led to the return of Benjamin Netanyahu, heading a right-wing coalition.

Israel's most valuable activity is manufacturing and the country's products include chemicals, electronic equipment, fertilizers, military equipment, plastics, processed food, scientific instruments, and textiles. Fruits and vegetables are leading exports.

AREA 7,954 sq mi [20,600 sq km] **POPULATION** 7,234,000
CAPITAL Jerusalem **GOVERNMENT** Multiparty republic
ETHNIC GROUPS Jewish 80%, Arab and others 20%
LANGUAGES Hebrew and Arabic (both official)
RELIGIONS Judaism 80%, Islam (mostly Sunni) 14%, Christianity 2%, Druze and others 2% **CURRENCY** New Israeli shekel = 100 agorat

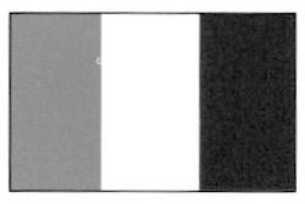

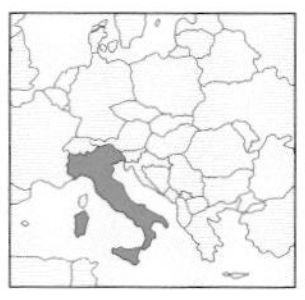

ITALY

GEOGRAPHY The Republic of Italy is famous for its history and traditions, its art and culture, and its beautiful scenery. Northern Italy is bordered in the north by the high Alps, with their many climbing and skiing resorts. The Alps overlook the northern plains – Italy's most fertile and densely populated region – drained by the River Po. The rugged Apennines form the backbone of southern Italy. Bordering the range are scenic hilly areas and coastal plains. Southern Italy contains a string of volcanoes, stretching from Vesuvius, through the Lipari Islands, to Etna on Sicily, the largest Mediterranean island. Northern Italy has cold, often snowy, winters, but the summer months are warm and sunny, with brief summer thunderstorms. Rainfall is abundant. The south has mild, moist winters and warm, dry summers.

POLITICS & ECONOMY Magnificent ruins throughout Italy testify to the glories of the ancient Roman Empire, which was founded, according to legend, in 753 BC. It reached its peak in the AD 100s. It finally collapsed in the 400s, although the Eastern Roman Empire, also called the Byzantine Empire, survived for another 1,000 years.

In the Middle Ages, Italy was split into many tiny states. These states made a great contribution to the revival of art and learning, called the Renaissance, in the 14th to 16th centuries. Beautiful cities, such as Florence (Firenze) and Venice (Venézia), testify to the artistic achievements of this period.

Italy finally became a united kingdom in 1861, although the Papal Territories (a large area ruled by the Roman Catholic Church) was not added until 1870. The Pope and his successors disputed the takeover of the Papal Territories. The dispute was finally resolved in 1929, when the Vatican City was set up in Rome as a fully independent state.

Italy fought in World War I (1914–18) alongside the Allies – Britain, France, and Russia. In 1922, the dictator Benito Mussolini, leader of the Fascist Party, took power. Under Mussolini, Italy conquered Ethiopia. During World War II (1939–45), Italy at first fought on Germany's side against the Allies. But in late 1943, Italy declared war on Germany. Italy became a republic in 1946. It has played an important part in European affairs. It was a founder member of the North Atlantic Treaty Organization (NATO) in 1949 and also, in 1958, of what has since become the European Union.

After the setting up of the European Union, Italy's economy developed quickly. But the country faced many problems. For example, much of the economic development was in the north. This forced many people to leave the poor south to find jobs in the north or abroad. Social problems, corruption at high levels of society, and a succession of weak coalition governments all contributed to instability. From 1998, power shifted between center-left coalitions led by Romano Prodi and center-right coalitions led by media tycoon Silvio Berlusconi. Berlusconi won elections in 2008, and in 2009 he formed a new, broad center-right coalition called People of Freedom, which included his own party, Forza Italia.

Only 50 years ago, Italy was a mainly agricultural society. But today it is a leading industrial power. It lacks mineral resources, and imports most of the raw materials used in industry. Manufactures include textiles and clothing, processed food, machinery, cars, and chemicals. The chief industrial region is in the northwest.

Farmland covers around 42% of the land, pasture 17%, and forest and woodland 22%. Major crops include citrus fruits, grapes which are used to make wine, olive oil, sugar beet, and vegetables. Livestock farming is important, though meat is imported.

AREA 116,339 SQ MI [301,318 SQ KM]
POPULATION 58,126,000 **CAPITAL** ROME
GOVERNMENT MULTIPARTY REPUBLIC **ETHNIC GROUPS** ITALIAN 94%, GERMAN, FRENCH, ALBANIAN, SLOVENE, GREEK **LANGUAGES** ITALIAN (OFFICIAL), GERMAN, FRENCH, SLOVENE **RELIGIONS** PREDOMINANTLY ROMAN CATHOLIC **CURRENCY** EURO = 100 CENTS

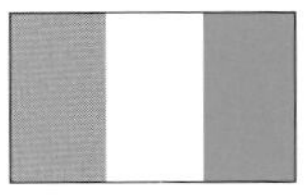

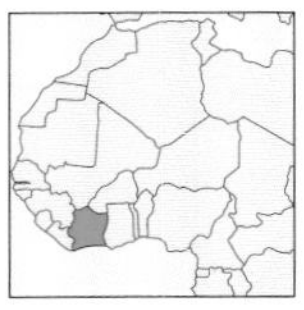

IVORY COAST

GEOGRAPHY The Republic of the Ivory Coast, in West Africa, is officially known as Côte d'Ivoire. The southeast coast is bordered by sand bars that enclose lagoons. The southwest coast is lined by rocky cliffs.

Ivory Coast has a hot and humid tropical climate, with high temperatures all year. The south has two rainy seasons: between May and July, and from October to November. Inland, the rainfall decreases and the north has one dry and one rainy season.

POLITICS & ECONOMY From 1895, Ivory Coast was governed as part of French West Africa, which also included what are now Benin, Burkina Faso, Guinea, Mali, Mauritania, Niger, and Senegal. In 1946, Ivory Coast became a territory in the French Union.

Ivory Coast became fully independent in 1960. Its first president, Félix Houphouët-Boigny, became the longest serving head of state in Africa with an uninterrupted period in office which ended with his death in 1993. Houphouët-Boigny, a pro-Western leader, made Ivory Coast a one-party state. In 1983, the National Assembly voted to make Yamoussoukro, the president's birthplace, the new capital. In 1999, a military coup occurred, but civilian rule was restored in 2000, when Laurent Gbagbo was elected president. An army rebellion began in 2002. By 2004, the government held the south, while mainly Muslim rebels held the north. A peace deal was agreed in 2007, and in 2009 civilian rule was restored in ten formerly rebel-held northern zones.

Agriculture employs 45% of the people. Cocoa beans and farm products, crude oil, and petroleum products make up more than half of the value of the exports.

AREA 124,503 SQ MI [322,463 SQ KM]
POPULATION 20,617,000 **CAPITAL** YAMOUSSOUKRO
GOVERNMENT MULTIPARTY REPUBLIC **ETHNIC GROUPS** AKAN 42%, VOLTAIQUES 18%, NORTHERN MANDES 16%, KROUS 11%, SOUTHERN MANDES 10% **LANGUAGES** FRENCH (OFFICIAL), MANY NATIVE DIALECTS
RELIGIONS ISLAM 40%, CHRISTIANITY 30%, TRADITIONAL BELIEFS 30%
CURRENCY CFA FRANC = 100 CENTIMES

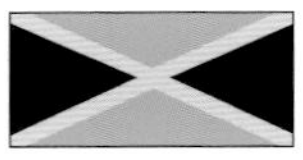

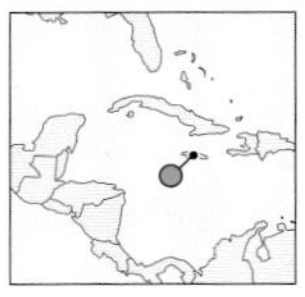

JAMAICA

GEOGRAPHY Third largest of the Caribbean islands, half of Jamaica lies above 1,000 ft [300 m] and moist southeast trade winds bring rain to the central mountain range.

The "cockpit country" in the northwest of the island is an inaccessible limestone area of steep broken ridges and isolated basins.

POLITICS & ECONOMY Britain took Jamaica from Spain in the 17th century, and the island did not gain its independence until 1962. Power has alternated between the People's National Party (PNP) and Jamaica Labor Party. In 2006, Portia Simpson Miller succeeded Percival Patterson as prime minister. In 2007 she was succeeded by Bruce Golding after elections. Tourism and sugarcane farming are important, but alumina and bauxite make up half of the exports.

AREA 4,244 SQ MI [10,991 SQ KM]
POPULATION 2,826,000 **CAPITAL** KINGSTON
GOVERNMENT CONSTITUTIONAL MONARCHY
ETHNIC GROUPS BLACK 91%, MIXED 7%, EAST INDIAN 1%
LANGUAGES ENGLISH (OFFICIAL), PATOIS ENGLISH
RELIGIONS PROTESTANT 61%, ROMAN CATHOLIC 4%
CURRENCY JAMAICAN DOLLAR = 100 CENTS

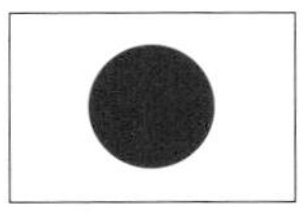

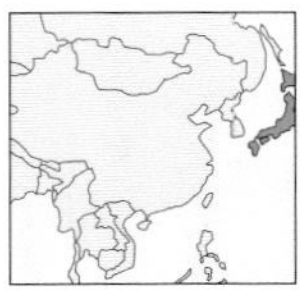

JAPAN

GEOGRAPHY Japan's four largest islands – Honshu, Hokkaido, Kyushu, and Shikoku – make up 98% of the country. But Japan contains thousands of small islands. The four largest islands are mainly mountainous, while many of the small islands are the tips of volcanoes. Japan has more than 150 volcanoes, about 60 of which are active. Volcanic eruptions, earthquakes, and tsunamis (destructive sea waves triggered by underwater earthquakes and eruptions) are common because the islands lie in an unstable part of our planet, where continental plates are always on the move. One powerful recent earthquake killed more than 5,000 people in Kobe in 1995.

The climate of Japan varies greatly from north to south. Hokkaido in the north has cold, snowy winters. At Sapporo, temperatures below 4°F [–20°C] have been recorded between December and March. But summers are warm, with temperatures sometimes exceeding 86°F [30°C]. Rain falls throughout the year, though Hokkaido is one of the driest parts of Japan. Tokyo has higher rainfall and temperatures, while the southern islands of Shikoku and Kyushu have warm temperate climates. Summers are long and hot. Winters are cold.

POLITICS & ECONOMY In the late 19th century, Japan began a program of modernization. Under its new imperial leaders, it began to look for lands to conquer. In 1894–5, it fought a war with China and, in 1904–5, it defeated Russia. Soon its overseas empire included Korea and Taiwan. In 1930, Japan invaded Manchuria (northeast China), and in 1937 it began a war against China. In 1941, Japan launched an attack on the US base at Pearl Harbor in Hawai'i. This drew both Japan and the United States into World War II.

Japan surrendered in 1945 when the Americans dropped atomic bombs on two cities, Hiroshima and Nagasaki. The United States occupied Japan until 1952. During this period, Japan adopted a democratic constitution. The emperor, who had previously been regarded as a god, became a constitutional monarch. Power was vested in the prime minister and cabinet, who are chosen from the Diet (elected parliament).

From the 1960s, Japan experienced many changes as the country rapidly built up new industries. By the early 1990s, Japan had become the world's second richest economic power after the US. But economic success has brought problems. For example, the rapid growth of cities has led to housing shortages and pollution. Another problem is that the proportion of people over 65 years of age is steadily increasing.

Japan has the world's second highest gross domestic product (GDP) after the United States. [The GDP is the total value of all goods and services produced in a country in one year.] The leading activity is manufacturing. Japan imports most of the materials and fuels it needs for its industries, and its success is based on its use of the latest technology, its skilled work force, its vigorous export policies, and relatively low government spending on defense. Exports include machinery, electrical and electronic equipment, iron and steel, chemicals, textiles, and ships. Japan suffered an economic slowdown in the 1990s, which developed into a recession. Signs of recovery from 2005 were shattered by the global financial crisis in 2008–9, when Japan's exports greatly declined.

Japan is one of the world's top fishing nations and fish is an important source of protein. Because the land is so rugged, only 15% of the country can be farmed. Yet Japan produces about 70% of the food it needs. Rice is the chief crop, taking up about half of the total farmland. Other major products include fruits, sugar beet, tea, and vegetables. Livestock farming has increased since the 1950s.

AREA 145,880 SQ MI [377,829 SQ KM]
POPULATION 127,079,000 **CAPITAL** TOKYO
GOVERNMENT CONSTITUTIONAL MONARCHY
ETHNIC GROUPS JAPANESE 99%, CHINESE, KOREAN, BRAZILIAN AND OTHERS
LANGUAGES JAPANESE (OFFICIAL) **RELIGIONS** SHINTOISM AND BUDDHISM 84% (MOST JAPANESE CONSIDER THEMSELVES TO BE BOTH SHINTO AND BUDDHIST), OTHERS **CURRENCY** YEN = 100 SEN

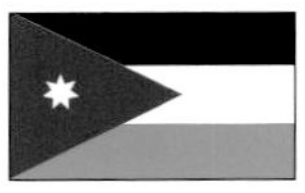

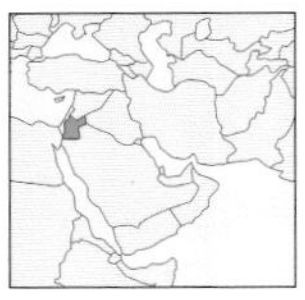

JORDAN

GEOGRAPHY The Hashemite Kingdom of Jordan is an Arab country in southwestern Asia. The Great Rift Valley in the west contains the River Jordan and the Dead Sea, which Jordan shares with Israel. East of the Rift Valley is the Transjordan plateau, where most Jordanians live. To the east and south lie vast areas of desert.

Amman has a much lower rainfall and longer dry season than the Mediterranean lands to the west. The Transjordan plateau, on which Amman stands, is a transition zone between the Mediterranean climate zone and the desert climate to the east.

POLITICS & ECONOMY In 1921, Britain created a territory called Transjordan east of the River Jordan. In 1923, Transjordan became self-governing, but Britain retained control of its defenses, finances, and foreign affairs. This territory became fully independent as Jordan in 1946. Jordan has suffered from instability arising from the Arab–Israeli conflict since the creation of the State of Israel in 1948. After the first Arab–Israeli War in 1948–9, Jordan acquired East Jerusalem and a fertile area called the West Bank. In 1967, Israel occupied this area. In Jordan, the presence of Palestinian refugees led to civil war in 1970–1.

In 1974, Arab leaders declared that the PLO (Palestine Liberation Organization) was the sole representative of the Palestinian people. In 1988, King Hussein of Jordan renounced Jordan's claims to the West Bank and passed responsibility for it to the PLO. Opposition parties were legalized in 1991 and elections were held in 1993. In October 1994, Jordan and Israel signed a peace treaty, ending a state of war that had lasted more than 40 years. Jordan's King Hussein commanded respect for his role in Middle Eastern affairs until his death in 1999. He was succeeded by his eldest son, who became Abdullah II. Jordan supported the US-led war on terrorism. In 2005, suicide bombings on hotels in Amman damaged Jordan's reputation as a stable country. In 2009, the king dissolved parliament and set up a new government to push through economic and political reforms.

Jordan has a "lower-middle-income" economy. It lacks natural resources, apart from phosphates and potash and depends on substantial aid. Less than 6% of the land is farmed or used as pasture. Jordan has an oil refinery and manufactures include cement, pharmaceuticals, processed food, fertilizers, and textiles.

AREA 34,495 SQ MI [89,342 SQ KM]
POPULATION 6,269,000 **CAPITAL** AMMAN
GOVERNMENT CONSTITUTIONAL MONARCHY **ETHNIC GROUPS** ARAB 98%, OF WHICH PALESTINIANS MAKE UP ROUGHLY HALF **LANGUAGES** ARABIC (OFFICIAL) **RELIGIONS** ISLAM (MOSTLY SUNNI) 94%, CHRISTIANITY (MOSTLY GREEK ORTHODOX) 6% **CURRENCY** JORDANIAN DINAR = 1,000 FILS

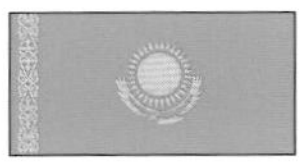

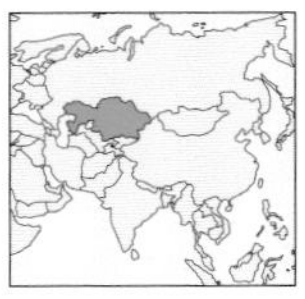

KAZAKHSTAN

GEOGRAPHY Kazakhstan is a large country in west-central Asia. In the west, the Caspian Sea lowlands include the Karagiye depression, which reaches 433 ft [132 m] below sea level. The lowlands extend eastward through the Aral Sea area. The north contains high plains, but the highest land is along the eastern and southern borders. These areas include parts of the Altai and Tian Shan mountain ranges. Eastern Kazakhstan contains several freshwater lakes, the largest of which is Lake Balkhash. The water in the rivers has been used for irrigation, causing ecological problems. For example, the Aral Sea, deprived of water, shrank from 25,830 sq mi [66,900 sq km] in 1960 to 12,989 sq mi [33,642 sq km] in 1993. Large areas are now barren desert.

Kazakhstan has an extreme climate. Winters are cold and snowy. The rainfall is generally low.

POLITICS & ECONOMY After the Russian Revolution of 1917, many Kazakhs wanted to make their country independent. But the Communists prevailed and in 1936 Kazakhstan became a republic of the Soviet Union, called the Kazakh Soviet Socialist Republic. During World War II and also after the war, the Soviet government moved many people from the west into Kazakhstan. From the 1950s, people were encouraged to work on a "Virgin Lands" project, which involved bringing large areas of grassland under cultivation.

Reforms in the Soviet Union in the 1980s led to its breakup in December 1991. Kazakhstan maintained contacts with Russia through the Commonwealth of Independent States (CIS). In 1997, the government moved its capital from Almaty to Aqmola (later renamed Astana), a town in the north. By the mid-2000s, the economy was in better shape than the other ex-Soviet republics in Central Asia. But President Nursultan Nazarbaev was criticized for his authoritarian rule, and the elections in 2004, won by his party, were described as flawed. In 2007, the governing party won all the seats in parliament, taking 88% of the vote.

The World Bank classifies Kazakhstan as a "lower-middle-income" developing country. Livestock farming, especially sheep and cattle, is an important activity, and major crops include barley, cotton, rice, and wheat. The country is rich in mineral resources, including coal and oil reserves, together with bauxite, copper, lead, tungsten, and zinc. Manufactures include chemicals, food products, machinery, and textiles. Oil is exported via a pipeline through Russia. However, to reduce the country's dependence on Russia, in 2009 the Kazakh and Chinese prime ministers unveiled the Kazakh sections of a pipeline linking Central Asia to China. Other exports include metals, chemicals, grain, wool, and meat.

AREA 1,052,084 SQ MI [2,724,900 SQ KM] **POPULATION** 15,399,000
CAPITAL ASTANA **GOVERNMENT** MULTIPARTY REPUBLIC
ETHNIC GROUPS KAZAKH 53%, RUSSIAN 30%, UKRAINIAN 4%, GERMAN 2%, UZBEK 2% **LANGUAGES** KAZAKH (OFFICIAL), RUSSIAN, THE FORMER OFFICIAL LANGUAGE, IS WIDELY SPOKEN **RELIGIONS** ISLAM 47%, RUSSIAN ORTHODOX 44% **CURRENCY** TENGE = 100 TIYN

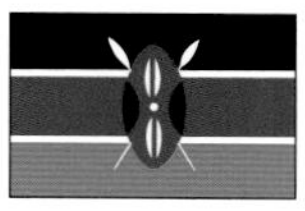

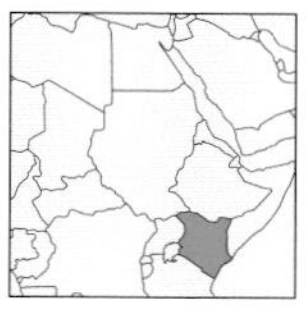

KENYA

GEOGRAPHY The Republic of Kenya is a country in East Africa which straddles the Equator. Behind the narrow coastal plain on the Indian Ocean, the land rises to high plains and highlands, broken by volcanic mountains, including Mount Kenya, the country's highest peak at 17,057 ft [5,199 m]. Crossing the country is an arm of the Great Rift Valley, on the floor of which are several lakes, including Baringo, Magadi, Naivasha, Nakuru and, on the northern frontier, Lake Turkana (formerly Lake Rudolf).

The climate is moderated by the terrain. Nairobi, in the southwestern highlands, has summer temperatures which are 18°C [10°F] lower than humid Mombasa. Only about 15% of Kenya has a reliable annual rainfall of 31 inches [800 mm].

POLITICS & ECONOMY The Kenyan coast has been a trading center for more than 2,000 years. Britain took over the coast in 1895 and soon extended its influence inland. In the 1950s, a secret movement, called Mau Mau, launched an armed struggle against British rule. Although Mau Mau was eventually defeated, Kenya became independent in 1963.

Kenya was a one-party state for much of the time after 1963. Democracy was restored in 1992. But elections in December 2007 sparked off inter-ethnic violence when the opposition refused to accept the declared results. In 2008, a power-sharing deal agreed by President Mwai Kibaki and opposition leader Raila Odinga, who became prime minister, restored peace, though charges of corruption against senior politicians and others persisted.

Kenya remains a "low-income" developing country. Many Kenyans are subsistence farmers. The chief food crop is maize. The main cash crops and the leading exports are coffee and tea. Manufactures include chemicals, leather and footwear, processed food, petroleum products, and textiles.

AREA 224,080 sq mi [580,367 sq km]
POPULATION 39,003,000 **CAPITAL** Nairobi
GOVERNMENT Multiparty republic **ETHNIC GROUPS** Kikuyu 22%, Luhya 14%, Luo 13%, Kalenjin 12%, Kamba 11%, others
LANGUAGES Kiswahili and English (both official)
RELIGIONS Protestant 45%, Roman Catholic 33%, traditional beliefs 10%, Islam 10% **CURRENCY** Kenyan shilling = 100 cents

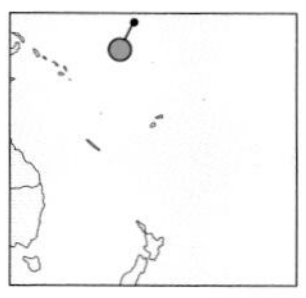

KIRIBATI

The Republic of Kiribati comprises three groups of coral atolls scattered over about 2 million sq mi [5 million sq km]. Kiribati straddles the equator and temperatures are high and the rainfall is abundant.

Formerly part of the British Gilbert and Ellice Islands, Kiribati became independent in 1979. The main export is copra and the country depends heavily on foreign aid.

AREA 280 sq mi [726 sq km] **POPULATION** 113,000 **CAPITAL** Tarawa

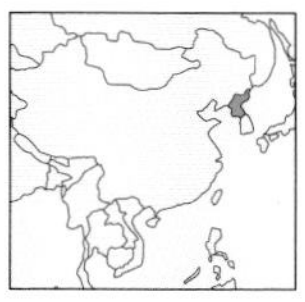

KOREA, NORTH

GEOGRAPHY The Democratic People's Republic of Korea occupies the northern part of the Korean peninsula which extends south from northeastern China. Mountains form the heart of the country, with the highest peak, Paektu-san, reaching 9,003 ft [2,744 m] on the northern border.

North Korea has a fairly severe climate, with cold, snowy winters. In summer, moist winds from the oceans bring rain.

POLITICS & ECONOMY North Korea was created in 1945, when the peninsula, which had been a Japanese colony since 1910, was divided into two parts. Soviet forces occupied the north, with US forces in the south. Soviet occupation led to a Communist government being established in 1948 under the leadership of Kim Il Sung, who effectively became a dictator.

The Korean War began in June 1950 when North Korean troops invaded the south. North Korea, aided by China and the Soviet Union, fought with South Korea, which was supported by troops from the United States and other UN members. The war ended in July 1953. An armistice was signed but no permanent peace treaty was agreed. The end of the Cold War in the late 1990s eased the situation. North and South Korea joined the United Nations in 1991, although North Korea remained isolated from most other countries. In 1993, North Korea withdrew from the Nuclear Non-Proliferation Treaty, arousing suspicions that it was developing nuclear weapons. Kim Il Sung died in 1994 and was succeeded by his son, Kim Jong Il. From 2003, the United States accused North Korea of developing nuclear weapons and, in 2006, the country conducted its first nuclear test. Efforts to achieve a disarmament agreement blew hot and cold through 2007–10.

North Korea's resources include coal, copper, iron ore, lead, tin, tungsten, and zinc. Under Communism, the country developed heavy, state-owned industries. Manufactures include chemicals, iron and steel, machinery, processed food, and textiles. Agriculture employs 27% of the people. Rice is the chief food crop, but food shortages have occurred in recent years.

AREA 46,540 sq mi [120,538 sq km]
POPULATION 22,665,000 **CAPITAL** Pyŏngyang
GOVERNMENT Single-party people's republic
ETHNIC GROUPS Korean 99%
LANGUAGES Korean (official)
RELIGIONS Buddhism and Confucianism
CURRENCY North Korean won = 100 chon

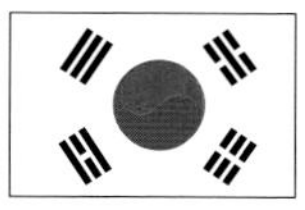

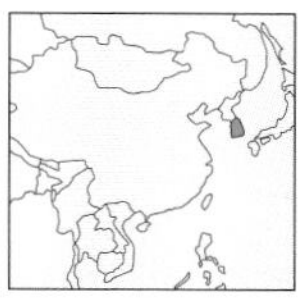

KOREA, SOUTH

GEOGRAPHY The Republic of Korea, as South Korea is officially known, occupies the southern part of the Korean peninsula. Mountains cover much of the country. The southern and western coasts are major farming regions. Many islands are found along the west and south coasts. The largest of these is Cheju-do, which contains South Korea's highest peak, Halla-San, which rises to 6,398 ft [1,950 m].

Like North Korea, South Korea is chilled in winter by cold, dry winds from central Asia. Summers are hot and wet, especially in July and August.

POLITICS & ECONOMY After Japan's defeat in World War II (1939–45), North Korea was occupied by troops from the Soviet Union, while South Korea was occupied by United States forces. A National Assembly elected in 1948 in South Korea created the Republic of Korea, while North Korea became a Communist state. North Korea invaded the South in June 1950, sparking off the Korean War (1950–3). Despite the destruction caused by the war, South Korea under a series of rather authoritarian governments began to industrialize the economy between the 1960s and 1980s. In 1987, a new constitution permitted the election of presidents every five years. In the 2000s, South Korea worked for closer contacts with the North, but relations deteriorated in 2008–10.

Until the onset of the global financial crisis in 2008, South Korea had one of the world's fastest growing economies. Its main manufactures are processed food and textiles. Heavy industries produce chemicals, fertilizers, and iron and steel, together with a wide range of consumer products, such as computers, cars, and television sets.

Farming remains important in South Korea. Rice is the chief crop, together with fruits, grains, and vegetables, while fishing provides a major source of protein.

AREA 38,327 sq mi [99,268 sq km]
POPULATION 48,509,000 **CAPITAL** Seoul
GOVERNMENT Multiparty republic **ETHNIC GROUPS** Korean 99%
LANGUAGES Korean (official) **RELIGIONS** No affiliation 46%, Christianity 26%, Buddhism 26%, Confucianism 1%
CURRENCY South Korean won = 100 chon

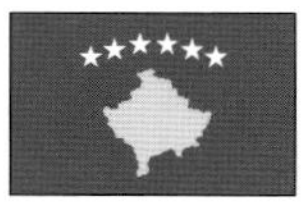

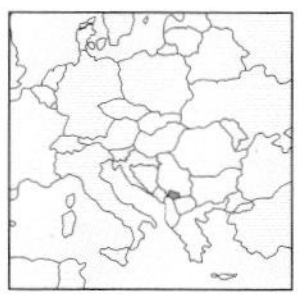

KOSOVO

GEOGRAPHY The Republic of Kosovo, formerly part of Serbia and, before 2003, part of Yugoslavia, declared its independence in February 2008. Its independence was recognized by the United States and major EU countries. But Serbia and its ally Russia refused recognition. It is a landlocked country, consisting of a river basin bounded by uplands in the north and southwest. It has cold, snowy winters and hot, dry summers.

POLITICS & ECONOMY Most people are Albanian-speakers who are Muslims, but there is an important Christian Serb minority. In the early 13th century, Kosovo was part of the Serbian empire but, after 1389, it came under Muslim Turkish Ottoman rule. Serbia regained control of Kosovo in 1912 and, in 1918, it became part of the Kingdom of Serbia. In 1946, it became part of the Socialist Federal Republic of Yugoslavia, becoming an autonomous province within the Republic of Serbia. In 1989, Serbia curtailed Kosovo's autonomy, while Albanian speakers declared their province independent. In 1995, the Albanian speakers set up the Kosovo Liberation Army, which launched an uprising against Serbia. In 1998, Serbia began repressive measures against Kosovo, resulting in massacres and ethnic cleansing of Albanian-speaking Kosovars. In 1999, NATO forces bombed Serbia and placed Kosovo under a temporary administration, pending agreement on Kosovo's future status. Finally, the Kosovo Assembly declared its independence on February 17, 2008. Local elections were held in 2009.

Kosovo is a poor country, with the lowest per capita income in Europe. Many people are subsistence farmers and its industries have declined because of lack of investment. The economy is highly dependent on international aid.

AREA 4,203 sq mi [10,887 sq km]
POPULATION 1,805,000 **CAPITAL** Pristina
GOVERNMENT Republic
ETHNIC GROUPS Albanian 88%, Serb 7%, others 5%
LANGUAGES Albanian and Serbian (both official), Turkish
RELIGIONS Islam, Serbian Orthodox, Roman Catholic
CURRENCY Euro = 100 cents

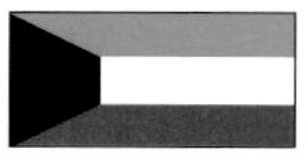

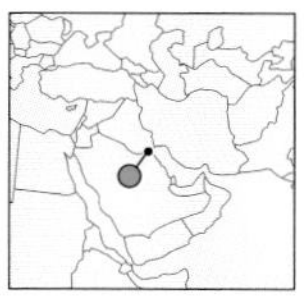

KUWAIT

GEOGRAPHY The State of Kuwait at the north end of the Persian Gulf is an emirate (ruled by an emir, or amir). The land is low-lying and largely desert. Summer temperatures are high but winters are cooler. The rainfall is low.

POLITICS & ECONOMY British influence began in 1775 and, in 1899, the local ruler concluded a treaty with Britain, agreeing to support British interests in return for British protection. Kuwait became independent in 1961. Its revenue from its oil exports made it highly prosperous. Iraq invaded Kuwait in 1990, but it was liberated in 1991 by a coalition force. In 2004, the government announced legislation for women to vote and stand for parliament. Women stood in the 2008 elections, but none was elected.

AREA 6,880 sq mi [17,818 sq km]
POPULATION 2,693,000 **CAPITAL** Kuwait City

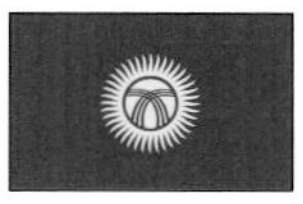

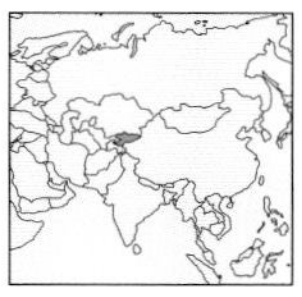

KYRGYZSTAN

GEOGRAPHY The Republic of Kyrgyzstan is a landlocked country between China, Tajikistan, Uzbekistan, and Kazakhstan. The country is mountainous, with spectacular scenery. The highest mountain, Pik Pobedy in the Tian Shan range, reaches 24,406 ft [7,439 m] in the east. The lowlands have warm summers and cold winters. But January temperatures in the mountains plummet to –18°F [–28°C]. Kyrgyzstan has a low annual rainfall.

POLITICS & ECONOMY In 1876, Kyrgyzstan became a province of Russia and Russian settlement in the area began. In 1916, Russia crushed a rebellion among the Kyrgyz, and many subsequently fled to China. In 1922, the area became an autonomous oblast (self-governing region) of the newly formed Soviet Union, but in 1936 it became one of the Soviet Socialist Republics. Under Communist rule, local customs and religious worship were suppressed, but education and health services were greatly improved.

In 1991, Kyrgyzstan became an independent country following the breakup of the Soviet Union. The Communist Party was dissolved, but the country maintained ties with Russia through an organization called the Commonwealth of Independent States. Elections were held under a new constitution adopted in 1994. Massive protests followed elections in 2005. President Askar Akayev fled the country. His successor, Kurmanbek Bakiyev, faced massive protests in 2010 and fled from the country. An interim government was set up.

In the 1990s, Kyrgyzstan sought to reform its Soviet-style economy. Now classified as a "lower-middle income" developing country, agriculture is the main activity. Major products include cotton, eggs, fruits, grain, tobacco, vegetables, and wool. But food is imported. Most industries are concentrated around the capital Bishkek.

AREA 77,181 sq mi [199,900 sq km]
POPULATION 5,432,000 **CAPITAL** Bishkek
GOVERNMENT Multiparty republic
ETHNIC GROUPS Kyrgyz 65%, Russian 13%, Uzbek 13%
LANGUAGES Kyrgyz and Russian (both official)
RELIGIONS Islam 75%, Russian Orthodox 20%
CURRENCY Kyrgyzstani som = 100 tyiyn

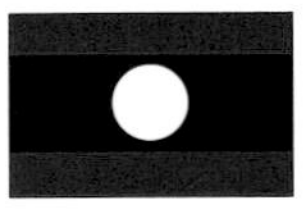
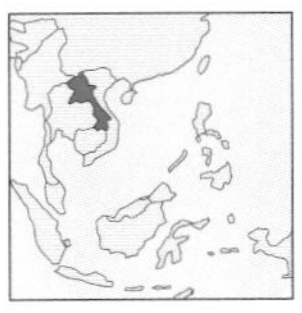

LAOS

GEOGRAPHY The Lao People's Democratic Republic is a landlocked country in Southeast Asia. Mountains and plateaux cover much of the country. Most people live on the plains bordering the River Mekong and its tributaries. This river, one of Asia's longest, forms much of the country's northwestern and southwestern borders.

Laos has a tropical monsoon climate. Winters are dry and sunny, with winds blowing in from the northeast. The temperatures rise until April, when the wind directions are reversed and moist southwesterly winds reach Laos, heralding the start of the wet monsoon season.

POLITICS & ECONOMY France made Laos a protectorate in the late 19th century and ruled it, with Cambodia and Vietnam, as part of French Indochina. Laos became an independent kingdom in 1954. After independence, a power struggle between royalist government forces and a pro-Communist group called Pathet Lao caused instability. A civil war broke out and continued into the 1970s. The Pathet Lao took control in 1975 and the king abdicated. Laos then came under the influence of Communist Vietnam, which had used Laos as a supply base during the Vietnam War (1957–75).

Laos is one of the world's poorest countries. Agriculture employs nearly 80% of the population and accounts for 31% of the gross domestic product. Rice is the main crop. Timber and coffee are exported. But the most valuable export is electricity, which is produced at hydroelectric power stations on the River Mekong and is exported to Thailand. Laos also produces opium.

AREA 91,428 SQ MI [236,800 SQ KM]
POPULATION 6,834,000 **CAPITAL** VIENTIANE
GOVERNMENT SINGLE-PARTY REPUBLIC
ETHNIC GROUPS LAO LOUM 68%, LAO THEUNG 22%, LAO SOUNG 9%
LANGUAGES LAO (OFFICIAL), FRENCH, ENGLISH **RELIGIONS** BUDDHISM 60%, TRADITIONAL BELIEFS AND OTHERS 40% **CURRENCY** KIP = 100 AT

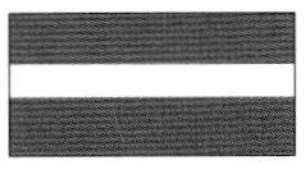
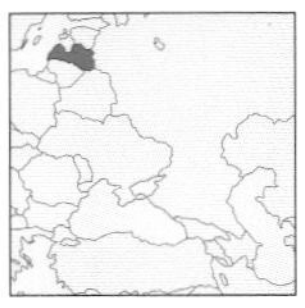

LATVIA

GEOGRAPHY The Republic of Latvia is one of three states on the southeastern corner of the Baltic Sea which were ruled as parts of the Soviet Union between 1940 and 1991. Latvia consists mainly of flat plains separated by low hills, composed of moraine (ice-worn rocks).

Riga has warm summers, but the winter months are subzero. The rainfall is moderate.

POLITICS & ECONOMY In 1800, Russia was in control of Latvia, but Latvians declared their independence after World War I. In 1940, under a German-Soviet pact, Soviet troops occupied Latvia, but they were driven out by the Germans in 1941. Soviet troops returned in 1944 and Latvia became part of the Soviet Union. Under Soviet rule, many Russian immigrants settled in Latvia and many Latvians feared that the Russians would become the dominant ethnic group.

In the late 1980s, when reforms were being introduced in the Soviet Union, Latvia's government ended absolute Communist rule and made Latvian the official language. In 1990, it declared the country to be independent, an act which was finally recognized by the Soviet Union in September 1991.

Latvia held its first free elections to its parliament (the Saeima) in 1993. Voting was limited only to citizens of Latvia on June 17, 1940, and their descendants. This meant that about 34% of Latvian residents were unable to vote. In 1994, Latvia restricted the naturalization of non-Latvians, including many Russian settlers, who were not allowed to vote or own land. However, in 1998, the government agreed that all children born since independence should have automatic citizenship. Its cultivation of closer ties to the West was realized in 2004 when Latvia was admitted to membership of both the North Atlantic Treaty Organization and the European Union.

The World Bank classifies Latvia as a "lower-middle-income" country, and, in 2009, hit by the global financial crisis, the coalition government collapsed. Manufactures include electronic goods, farm machinery, fertilizers, processed food, plastics, radios, and vehicles. Latvia produces only about a tenth of the electricity it needs. It imports the rest from Belarus, Russia, and Ukraine.

AREA 24,942 SQ MI [64,600 SQ KM]
POPULATION 2,232,000 **CAPITAL** RIGA
GOVERNMENT MULTIPARTY REPUBLIC
ETHNIC GROUPS LATVIAN 58%, RUSSIAN 30%, BELARUSIAN, UKRAINIAN, POLISH, LITHUANIAN **LANGUAGES** LATVIAN (OFFICIAL), LITHUANIAN, RUSSIAN **RELIGIONS** LUTHERAN, ROMAN CATHOLIC, RUSSIAN ORTHODOX
CURRENCY LATVIAN LATS = 10 SANTIMI

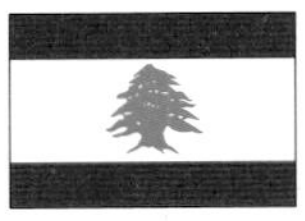
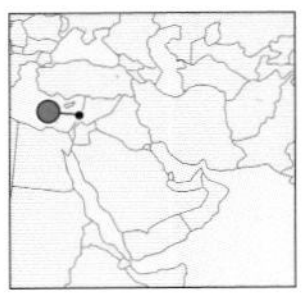

LEBANON

GEOGRAPHY The Republic of Lebanon is a country on the eastern shores of the Mediterranean Sea. Behind the coastal plain are the rugged Lebanon Mountains (Jabal Lubnan), which rise to 10,131 ft [3,088 m]. Another range, the Anti-Lebanon Mountains (Al Jabal Ash Sharqi), form the eastern border with Syria. Between the two ranges is the Bekaa (Beqaa) Valley, a fertile farming region.

The Lebanese coast has hot, dry summers and mild, wet winters. Heavy rain falls on the western slopes of the mountains in winter, with snow at higher altitudes.

POLITICS & ECONOMY Lebanon was ruled by Turkey from 1516 until World War I. France ruled the country from 1923, but Lebanon became independent in 1946. After independence, the Muslims and Christians agreed to share power, and Lebanon made rapid economic progress. But from the late 1950s, development was slowed by periodic conflict between Sunni and Shia Muslims, Druze, and Christians. The situation was further complicated by the presence of Palestinian refugees who used bases in Lebanon to attack Israel.

In 1975, civil war broke out as private armies representing the many factions struggled for power. This led to intervention by Israel in the south and Syria in the north. UN peacekeeping forces arrived in 1978, but violence continued in the 1980s. Peace was restored in the 1990s, but, in 2005, the assassination of Rafik Hariri, former prime minister, was blamed on Syria. Under pressure, Syria withdrew its forces from Lebanon. In 2006, a 34-day conflict between Israeli troops and Hezbollah guerrillas caused devastation in southern Lebanon. In 2008–9, relations with Syria improved and diplomatic relations were restored.

Lebanon's civil war almost destroyed valuable trade and financial services that had been Lebanon's chief source of income, together with tourism. Manufacturing, formerly a major activity, was badly hit.

AREA 4,015 SQ MI [10,400 SQ KM]
POPULATION 4,017,000 **CAPITAL** BEIRUT
GOVERNMENT MULTIPARTY REPUBLIC **ETHNIC GROUPS** ARAB 95%, ARMENIAN 4%, OTHERS **LANGUAGES** ARABIC (OFFICIAL), FRENCH, ENGLISH, ARMENIAN **RELIGIONS** ISLAM 70%, CHRISTIANITY 30%
CURRENCY LEBANESE POUND = 100 PIASTRES

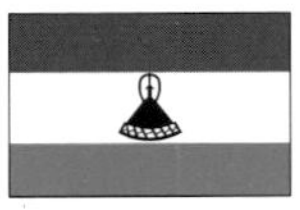
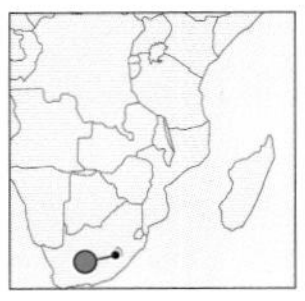

LESOTHO

GEOGRAPHY The Kingdom of Lesotho is a landlocked country, completely enclosed by South Africa. The land is mountainous, rising to 11,424 ft [3,482 m] on the northeastern border. The Drakensberg range covers most of the country.

The climate of Lesotho is greatly affected by the altitude, because most of the country lies above 4,920 ft [1,500 m]. Summers are warm but winters are cold. The rainfall averages about 28 inches [700 mm].

POLITICS & ECONOMY The Basotho nation was founded in the 1820s by King Moshoeshoe I, who united various groups fleeing from tribal wars in southern Africa. Britain made the area a protectorate in 1868 and, in 1871, placed it under the British Cape Colony in South Africa. But in 1884, Basutoland, as the area was called, was reconstituted as a British protectorate, where whites were not allowed to own land.

The country finally became independent in 1966 as the Kingdom of Lesotho, with Moshoeshoe II, great-grandson of Moshoeshoe I, as its king. Since independence, Lesotho has suffered instability. The military seized power in 1986 and stripped Moshoeshoe II of his powers in 1990, installing his son, Letsie III, as monarch. After elections in 1993, Moshoeshoe II was restored to office in 1995. But after his death in a car crash in 1996, Letsie III again became king. In 1998, an army revolt, following an election in which the ruling party won 79 out of the 80 seats, caused much damage to the economy. Lesotho has faced many problems, including drought, while 23.2% of the people were reported to be infected with the HIV virus in 2008.

Lesotho lacks natural resources, and the UN has stated that 40% of the people are "ultra-poor." Agriculture employs 18% of the people, mostly at subsistence level. Remittances sent home by Basotho working abroad are important to the economy.

AREA 11,720 SQ MI [30,355 SQ KM]
POPULATION 2,131,000 **CAPITAL** MASERU
GOVERNMENT CONSTITUTIONAL MONARCHY
ETHNIC GROUPS SOTHO 99% **LANGUAGES** SESOTHO AND ENGLISH (BOTH OFFICIAL) **RELIGIONS** CHRISTIANITY 80%, TRADITIONAL BELIEFS 20%
CURRENCY LOTI = 100 LISENTE

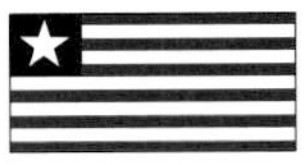
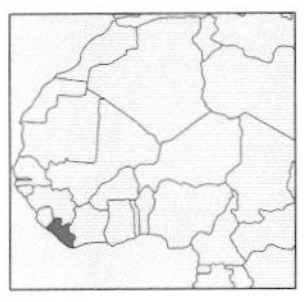

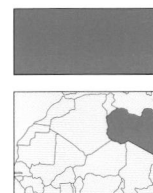

LIBERIA

GEOGRAPHY The Republic of Liberia is a country in West Africa. Behind the coastline, 311 mi [500 km] long, lies a narrow coastal plain. Beyond, the land rises to a plateau region, with the highest land along the border with Guinea. Liberia has a tropical climate with high temperatures and high humidity all through the year. The rainfall is abundant all year round, but there is a particularly wet period from June to November. The rainfall generally increases from east to west.

POLITICS & ECONOMY In the late 18th century, some white Americans in the United States wanted to help freed black slaves to return to Africa. In 1816, they set up the American Colonization Society, which bought land in what is now Liberia.

In 1822, the Society landed former slaves at a settlement on the coast which they named Monrovia. In 1847, Liberia became a fully independent republic with a constitution much like that of the United States. For many years, the Americo-Liberians controlled the country's government. US influence remained strong and the American Firestone Company, which ran Liberia's rubber plantations, was especially influential. Foreign companies were also involved in exploiting Liberia's mineral resources, including its huge iron-ore deposits.

In 1980, a military group composed of people from the local population killed the Americo-Liberian president, William R. Tolbert. An army sergeant, Samuel K. Doe, was made president of Liberia. Elections held in 1985 resulted in victory for Doe. From 1989, the country was plunged into civil war between various ethnic groups. Doe was assassinated in 1990 and the struggle with rebel groups continued. West African peacekeeping forces arrived in Liberia and, in 1995, a ceasefire was agreed. A council of state, composed of former warlords, was set up in 1997 and Charles Taylor became president. Taylor fled the country in 2003, and in 2006 he was extradited and charged with war crimes. Following elections in 2005, Ellen Sirleaf-Johnson was elected president. She became Africa's first woman president.

Liberia's economy was devastated by the civil war. Agriculture is important, but most farmers live at subsistence level. Food crops include cassava, rice, and sugarcane, while rubber, cocoa, and coffee are exported. The most valuable export is rubber.

Liberia also obtains revenue from its "flag of convenience," which is used by about one-sixth of the world's commercial shipping, exploiting low taxes.

AREA 43,000 SQ MI [111,369 SQ KM]
POPULATION 3,442,000 **CAPITAL** MONROVIA
GOVERNMENT MULTIPARTY REPUBLIC **ETHNIC GROUPS** INDIGENOUS AFRICAN TRIBES 95% (INCLUDING KPELLE, BASSA, GREBO, GIO, KRU, MANO)
LANGUAGES ENGLISH (OFFICIAL), ETHNIC LANGUAGES
RELIGIONS CHRISTIANITY 40%, ISLAM 20%, TRADITIONAL BELIEFS AND OTHERS 40% **CURRENCY** LIBERIAN DOLLAR = 100 CENTS

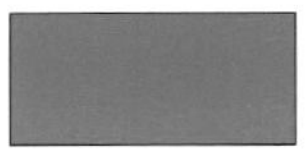
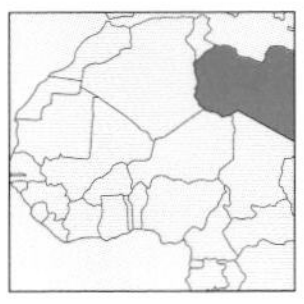

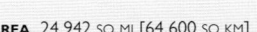

LIBYA

GEOGRAPHY The Socialist People's Libyan Arab Jamahiriya, as Libya is officially called, is a large country in North Africa. Most people live on the coastal plains in the northeast and northwest. The Sahara, the world's largest desert which occupies 95% of Libya, reaches the Mediterranean coast along the Gulf of Sidra (Khalij Surt).

The coastal plains in the northeast and northwest have Mediterranean climates, with hot, dry summers and mild, sometimes wet winters. Inland, the average yearly rainfall drops to 4 inches [100 mm] or less.

POLITICS & ECONOMY Italy took over Libya in 1911, but lost it during World War II. Britain and France jointly ruled Libya until 1951, when the country became an independent kingdom.

In 1969, a military group headed by Colonel Muammar Gaddafi deposed the king and set up a military government. Under Gaddafi, the government took control of the economy and used money from oil exports to finance welfare services and development projects. Gaddafi was criticized for supporting terrorist groups around the world, and Libya became isolated from the mid-1980s. In 1998, he tried to restore Libya's reputation by surrendering for trial two Libyans suspected of planting a bomb on a PanAm plane which exploded over the Scottish town of Lockerbie in 1988. In 2001, one of the Libyans was found guilty and the other acquitted of the bombing. In 2003, Libya announced that it would pay compensation to victims of the bombing. From 2004, relations with the West gradually improved and diplomatic relations with many nations, including the United States, were restored.

The discovery of oil and natural gas in 1959 led to a transformation of Libya's economy. This formerly poor country soon became Africa's richest in terms of its per capita income. But it remains a developing country, because oil accounts for nearly all its export revenues. Agriculture is important, although Libya imports food. Crops include barley, citrus fruits, dates, olives, potatoes, and wheat, while cattle, sheep, and poultry are raised. Libya has oil refineries and petrochemical plants. Other manufactures include cement and steel.

AREA 679,358 SQ MI [1,759,540 SQ KM] **POPULATION** 6,324,000
CAPITAL TRIPOLI **GOVERNMENT** SINGLE-PARTY SOCIALIST STATE
ETHNIC GROUPS LIBYAN ARAB AND BERBER 97%
LANGUAGES ARABIC (OFFICIAL), BERBER **RELIGIONS** ISLAM (SUNNI MUSLIM) 97% **CURRENCY** LIBYAN DINAR = 1,000 DIRHAMS

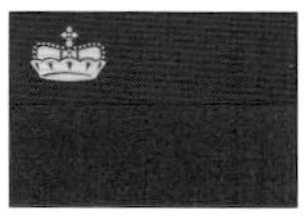
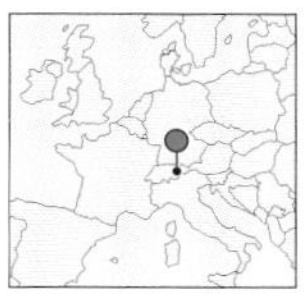

LIECHTENSTEIN

The tiny Principality of Liechtenstein is sandwiched between Switzerland and Austria. The River Rhine flows along its western border, while Alpine peaks rise in the east and south. The climate is relatively mild. Since 1924, Liechtenstein has been in a customs union with Switzerland. Taxation is low and the country is a haven for foreign companies. In 2003, the people voted to give their head of state, Prince Hans Adam II, sovereign powers. However, he later announced his retirement from politics. In 2004, he handed over the running of the country to his son, Prince Alois, although he remained the titular head of state.

AREA 62 SQ MI [160 SQ KM] **POPULATION** 35,000 **CAPITAL** VADUZ

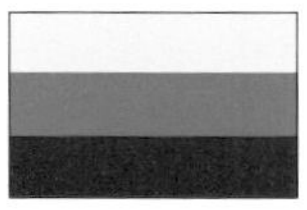
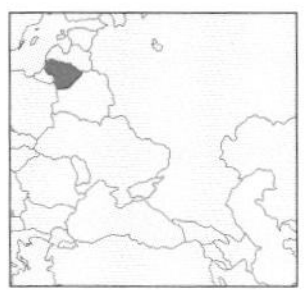

LITHUANIA

GEOGRAPHY The Republic of Lithuania is the southernmost of the three Baltic states which were ruled as part of the Soviet Union between 1940 and 1991. Much of the land is flat or gently rolling, with the highest land in the southeast.

Winters are cold and summers warm. The annual rainfall in the west is about 25 inches [630 mm]. Eastern areas are drier.

POLITICS & ECONOMY The Lithuanian people were united into a single nation in the 12th century, and later joined a union with Poland. In 1795, Lithuania came under Russian rule. After World War I (1914–18), Lithuania declared itself independent, and in 1920 it signed a peace treaty with the Russians, though Poland held Vilnius until 1939. In 1940, the Soviet Union occupied Lithuania, but the Germans invaded in 1941. Soviet forces returned in 1944, and Lithuania was integrated into the Soviet Union. In 1988, when the Soviet Union was introducing reforms, the Lithuanians demanded independence. Their language is one of the oldest in the world, and the country was always the most homogenous of the Baltic states, staunchly Catholic and resistant of attempts to suppress their culture. Pro-independence groups won the national elections in 1990 and, in 1991, the Soviet Union recognized Lithuania's independence.

Since 1991, Lithuania has sought to reform its economy and introduce a private enterprise system. Lithuania has also drawn closer to the West and, in 2004, it became a member of both the North Atlantic Treaty Organization and the European Union.

The World Bank classifies Lithuania as a "lower-middle-income" developing country. Lithuania lacks natural resources, but manufacturing, based on imported materials, is the most valuable activity.

AREA 25,174 SQ MI [65,200 SQ KM]
POPULATION 3,555,000 **CAPITAL** VILNIUS
GOVERNMENT MULTIPARTY REPUBLIC
ETHNIC GROUPS LITHUANIAN 80%, RUSSIAN 9%, POLISH 7%, BELARUSIAN 2% **LANGUAGES** LITHUANIAN (OFFICIAL), RUSSIAN, POLISH
RELIGIONS MAINLY ROMAN CATHOLIC **CURRENCY** LITAS = 100 CENTAI

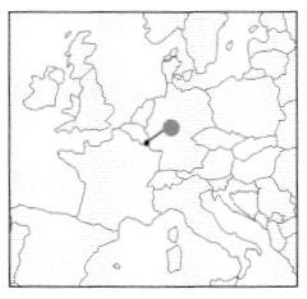

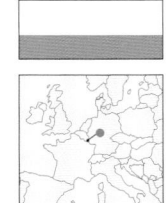

LUXEMBOURG

GEOGRAPHY The Grand Duchy of Luxembourg is one of the smallest and oldest countries in Europe. The north belongs to an upland region which includes the Ardenne in Belgium and Luxembourg, and the Eifel highlands in Germany.

Luxembourg has a temperate climate. The south has warm summers and falls, when grapes ripen in sheltered southeastern valleys. Winters are sometimes severe, especially in upland areas.

POLITICS & ECONOMY Germany occupied Luxembourg in World Wars I and II. In 1944–5, northern Luxembourg was the scene of the Battle of the Bulge. In 1948, Luxembourg joined Belgium and the Netherlands in a union called Benelux. In the 1950s, it was one of the six founders of what is now the European Union. Its capital is a major financial center and contains several international agencies. In 2008, parliament restricted the monarch to a ceremonial role following the grand duke's refusal to sign a law allowing for euthanasia.

Luxembourg has iron-ore reserves and is a major steel producer. It also has many high-technology industries, producing electronic goods and computers. Steel and other manufactures, including chemicals, rubber products, glass, and aluminum, dominate the country's exports. Other major activities include tourism and financial services.

AREA 998 SQ MI [2,586 SQ KM]
POPULATION 492,000 **CAPITAL** LUXEMBOURG
GOVERNMENT CONSTITUTIONAL MONARCHY (GRAND DUCHY)
ETHNIC GROUPS LUXEMBOURGER 71%, PORTUGUESE, ITALIAN, FRENCH, BELGIAN, SLAVS **LANGUAGES** LUXEMBOURGISH (OFFICIAL), FRENCH, GERMAN **RELIGIONS** ROMAN CATHOLIC 87%, OTHERS 13%
CURRENCY EURO = 100 CENTS

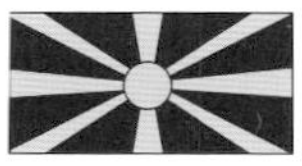
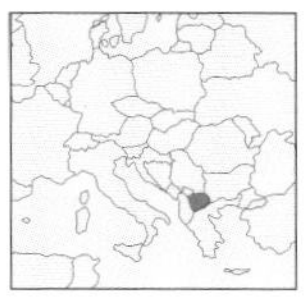

MACEDONIA (FYROM)

GEOGRAPHY The Republic of Macedonia is a country in southeastern Europe, which was once one of the six republics that made up the former Federal People's Republic of Yugoslavia. This landlocked country is largely mountainous or hilly. Macedonia has hot summers, though highland areas are cooler. Winters are cold and snowfalls are often heavy. The climate is fairly continental in character and rain occurs throughout the year.

POLITICS & ECONOMY Until the 20th century, Macedonia's history was closely tied to a larger area, also called Macedonia, which included parts of northern Greece and southwestern Bulgaria. This region reached its peak in power at the time of Philip II (382–336 BC) and his son Alexander the Great (336–323 BC). After Alexander's death, his empire was split up and it gradually declined. The area became a Roman province in the 140s BC and part of the Byzantine Empire from AD 395. In the 6th century, Slavs from eastern Europe settled in the area, followed by Bulgars from central Asia in the 9th century. The Byzantine Empire regained control in 1018, but Serbia took Macedonia in the early 14th century. In 1371, the Ottoman Turks conquered the area and ruled it for more than 500 years.

In 1913, at the end of the Balkan Wars, the area was divided between Serbia, Bulgaria, and Greece. At the end of World War I, Serbian Macedonia became part of the Kingdom of the Serbs, Croats, and Slovenes, which was renamed Yugoslavia in 1929. After World War II, Yugoslavia became a Communist country under ex-partisan leader Josip Broz Tito.

Tito died in 1980 and, in the early 1990s, the country broke up into five separate republics. Macedonia declared its independence in September 1991. Greece objected to this territory using the name Macedonia, which it considered to be a Greek name. It also objected to a symbol on Macedonia's flag and a reference in the constitution to the desire to reunite the three parts of the old Macedonia.

Macedonia adopted a new clause in its constitution rejecting any Macedonian claims on Greek territory and, in 1993, the United Nations accepted the new republic as a member under the name of The Former Yugoslav Republic of Macedonia (FYROM). By the end of 1993, all the countries of the EU, except Greece, were establishing diplomatic relations with the FYROM. In 1995, Greece lifted its trade ban, when Macedonia agreed to redesign its flag and remove territorial claims from its constitution. In 2001, fighting along the Kosovo border was attributed to people who wanted to create a Greater Albania. The uprising ended when Macedonia granted its Albanian-speakers increased rights. In 2009, Macedonia applied to the International Court of Justice for a ruling on its dispute with Greece over its name.

The World Bank describes Macedonia as a "lower-middle-income" economy. Manufactures dominate the country's exports. Coal is mined, but oil and natural gas are imported. The country is self-sufficient in its basic food needs.

AREA 9,928 SQ MI [25,713 SQ KM] **POPULATION** 2,067,000
CAPITAL SKOPJE **GOVERNMENT** MULTIPARTY REPUBLIC
ETHNIC GROUPS MACEDONIAN 64%, ALBANIAN 25%, TURKISH 4%, ROMANIAN 3%, SERB 2% **LANGUAGES** MACEDONIAN AND ALBANIAN (OFFICIAL) **RELIGIONS** MACEDONIAN ORTHODOX 70%, ISLAM 29%
CURRENCY MACEDONIAN DENAR = 100 PARAS

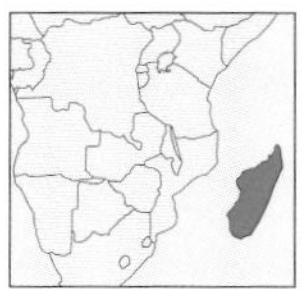

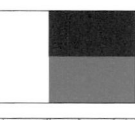

MADAGASCAR

GEOGRAPHY The Democratic Republic of Madagascar, in southeastern Africa, is an island nation, which has a larger area than France. Behind the narrow coastal plains in the east lies a highland zone, mostly between 2,000 ft and 4,000 ft [610 m to 1,220 m] above sea level. Broad plains border the Mozambique Channel in the west.

Temperatures in the highlands are moderated by the altitude. The winters (from April to September) are dry, but heavy rains occur in summer. The eastern coastlands are warm and humid. The west is drier, and the south and southwest are hot and dry.

POLITICS & ECONOMY People from Southeast Asia began to settle on Madagascar around 2,000 years ago. Subsequent influxes from Africa and Arabia added to the island's diverse heritage, culture, and language.

French troops defeated a Malagasy army in 1895 and Madagascar became a French colony. In 1960, it achieved full independence as the Malagasy Republic. In 1972, army officers seized control and, in 1975, under the leadership of Lieutenant-Commander Didier Ratsiraka, the country was renamed Madagascar. Parliamentary elections were held in 1977, but Ratsiraka remained president of a one-party socialist state. In 2002, the country came close to civil war when Ratsiraka and his opponent, Marc Ravalomanana, both claimed victory in presidential elections. Ravalomanana was finally recognized as president. In 2009, he was forced from office by Andry Rajoelina, who declared himself president.

Madagascar is a poor country. Poverty and population growth impose pressure on the dwindling forests and the unique wildlife, as well as causing severe soil erosion. Farming, fishing, and forestry employ about 80% of the people. Food crops include bananas, cassava, rice, and sweet potatoes. Coffee is exported.

AREA 226,657 SQ MI [587,041 SQ KM]
POPULATION 20,654,000 **CAPITAL** ANTANANARIVO
GOVERNMENT REPUBLIC **ETHNIC GROUPS** MERINA, BETSIMISARAKA, BETSILEO, TSIMIHETY, SAKALAVA AND OTHERS
LANGUAGES MALAGASY AND FRENCH (BOTH OFFICIAL)
RELIGIONS TRADITIONAL BELIEFS 52%, CHRISTIANITY 41%, ISLAM 7%
CURRENCY MALAGASY FRANC = 100 CENTIMES

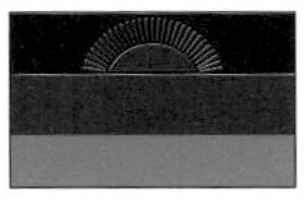
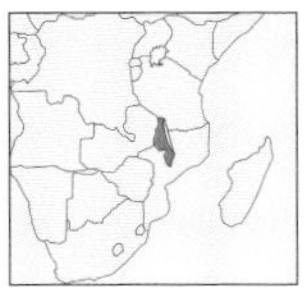

MALAWI

GEOGRAPHY The Republic of Malawi includes part of Lake Malawi, which is drained by the River Shire, a tributary of the River Zambezi. The land is mostly mountainous. The highest peak, Mulanje, reaches 9,843 ft [3,000 m] in the southeast.

While the low-lying areas of Malawi are hot and humid all year round, the uplands have a pleasant climate. Lilongwe has a warm and sunny climate. Frosts sometimes occur in July and August, in the middle of the long dry season.

POLITICS & ECONOMY Malawi, then called Nyasaland, became a British protectorate in 1891. In 1953, Britain established the Federation of Rhodesia and Nyasaland, which also included what are now Zambia and Zimbabwe. Black African opposition, led in Nyasaland by Dr Hastings Kamuzu Banda, led to the dissolution of the federation in 1963. In 1964, Nyasaland became independent as Malawi, with Banda as prime minister. Banda became president when the country became a republic in 1966, and in 1971 he was made president for life. Banda was an autocrat, ruling through the only party, the Malawi Congress Party. But a multiparty system was restored in 1993. Bakili Muluzi became president, and in 2004 he was succeeded by Bingu wa Mutharika, leader of the United Democratic Front (UDF). In 2005, he resigned from the UDF and set up a new Democratic Progressive Party. Mutharika was re-elected president in 2009.

Malawi is one of the world's poorest countries. More than 80% of the people are farmers, but many grow little more than they need to feed their families.

AREA 45,747 SQ MI [118,484 SQ KM]
POPULATION 15,029,000 **CAPITAL** LILONGWE
GOVERNMENT MULTIPARTY REPUBLIC
ETHNIC GROUPS CHEWA, NYANJA, TONGA, TUMBUKA, LOMWE, YAO, NGONI AND OTHERS
LANGUAGES CHICHEWA AND ENGLISH (BOTH OFFICIAL)
RELIGIONS PROTESTANT 55%, ROMAN CATHOLIC 20%, ISLAM 20%
CURRENCY MALAWIAN KWACHA = 100 TAMBALA

MALAYSIA

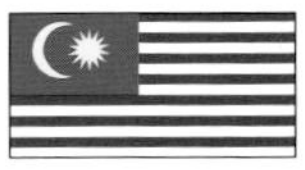

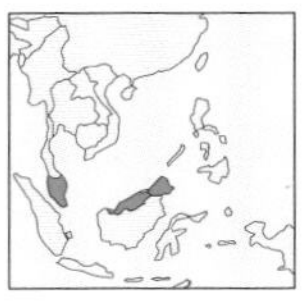

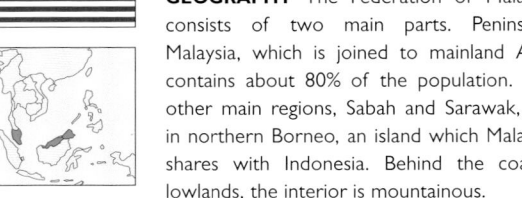

GEOGRAPHY The Federation of Malaysia consists of two main parts. Peninsular Malaysia, which is joined to mainland Asia, contains about 80% of the population. The other main regions, Sabah and Sarawak, are in northern Borneo, an island which Malaysia shares with Indonesia. Behind the coastal lowlands, the interior is mountainous.

Malaysia has a hot equatorial climate. The temperatures are high all through the year, though the mountains are much cooler than the lowland areas. The rainfall is heavy throughout the year.

POLITICS & ECONOMY Around 1,200 years ago, Indian traders introduced Hinduism and Buddhism into the Malay peninsula, while Arabs introduced Islam in the 15th century. Portuguese traders reached Melaka in 1509, but the Dutch took over in 1641. Britain became established in the area in 1786.

Japan occupied the area during World War II (1939–45), but the area reverted to British rule in 1945. In the 1940s and 1950s, Communist guerrillas battled unsuccessfully for power. Malaya (Peninsular Malaysia) became independent in 1957. Malaysia was created in 1963, when Malaya, Singapore, Sabah, and Sarawak agreed to unite, but Singapore withdrew in 1965.

From 1981, under the leadership of Dr Mahathir bin Mohamad, Malaysia achieved rapid economic progress. However, together with other countries in eastern Asia, it experienced an economic recession in 1997. The government initiated measures aimed at restoring confidence. In 2003 Mahathir bin Mohamad was succeeded by Abdullah Ahmad Badawi, who stood down in 2009, following poor parliamentary election results in 2008. His deputy, Najib Razak, took over as prime minister. He faced many economic problems caused by the global financial crisis.

The World Bank classifies Malaysia as an "upper-middle-income" developing country. Palm oil, rubber, and tin are major products. Manufactures include cars, chemicals, a wide range of electronic goods, plastics, textiles, rubber, and wood products.

AREA 127,320 sq mi [329,758 sq km] **POPULATION** 25,716,000
CAPITAL Kuala Lumpur; Putrajaya (administrative capital awaiting completion)
GOVERNMENT Federal constitutional monarchy
ETHNIC GROUPS Malay and other indigenous groups 58%, Chinese 24%, Indian 8%, others **LANGUAGES** Malay (official), Chinese, English **RELIGIONS** Islam, Buddhism, Daoism, Hinduism, Christianity, Sikhism **CURRENCY** Ringgit = 100 cents

MALDIVES

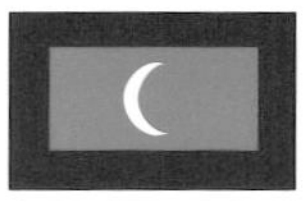

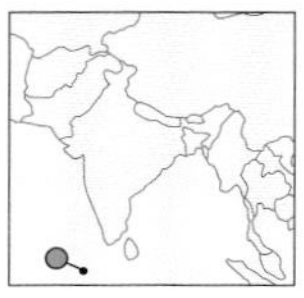

The Republic of the Maldives consists of about 1,200 low-lying coral islands, south of India. The highest point is 79 ft [24 m], but most of the land is only 6 ft [1.8 m] above sea level. The islands became a British territory in 1887 and independence was achieved in 1965. Tourism and fishing are the main industries.

AREA 115 sq mi [298 sq km] **POPULATION** 396,000 **CAPITAL** Malé

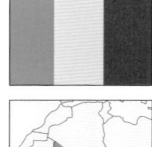

MALI

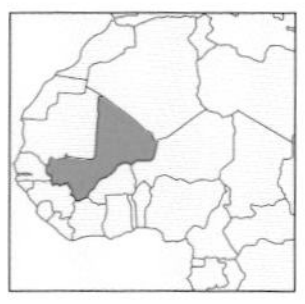

GEOGRAPHY The Republic of Mali is a landlocked country in northern Africa. The land is generally flat, with the highest land in the north. Northern Mali is hot and practically rainless. The south has enough rain for farming.

POLITICS & ECONOMY Between the 4th and 16th centuries, Mali was part of three African empires – ancient Ghana, ancient Mali, and Songhay. However, after 1591, when Songhay was defeated by Morocco, the area was divided into small kingdoms. France ruled the area, then known as French Sudan, from 1893 until the country became independent as Mali in 1960.

The first socialist government was overthrown in 1968 by an army group led by Moussa Traoré, but he was ousted in 1991. Multiparty democracy was restored in 1992 and Alpha Oumar Konaré was elected president. Konaré stood down in 2002 and Ahmadou Toure, who had restored democracy in 1992, was elected president. He was re-elected in 2007.

Mali is one of the world's poorest countries and 70% of the land is desert or semidesert. Only about 2% of the land is used for growing crops, while 25% is used for grazing animals. Agriculture employs more than one-third of the people, many of whom subsist by nomadic livestock rearing.

AREA 478,838 sq mi [1,240,192 sq km]
POPULATION 13,443,000 **CAPITAL** Bamako
GOVERNMENT Multiparty republic **ETHNIC GROUPS** Mande 50% (Bambara, Malinke, Soninke), Peul 17%, Voltaic 12%, Songhai 6%, Tuareg and Moor 10%, others **LANGUAGES** French (official), many African languages **RELIGIONS** Islam 90%, traditional beliefs 9%, Christianity 1% **CURRENCY** CFA franc = 100 centimes

MALTA

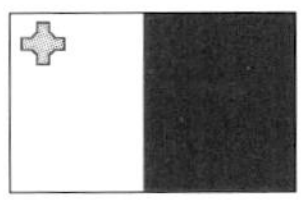

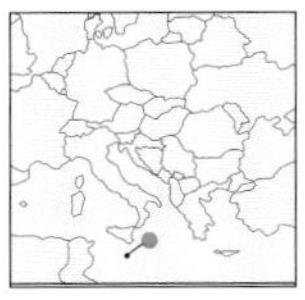

GEOGRAPHY The Republic of Malta consists of two main islands, Malta and Gozo, with a third, much smaller island called Comino lying between the two large islands and two islets. The climate is typically Mediterranean, with hot, dry summers and mild, moist winters.

POLITICS & ECONOMY Malta has fascinating Stone and Bronze age remains. The islands later came under Phoenician, Greek, Carthaginian, Roman, and Arab rule. In about 1090, Malta came under the Norman kings of Sicily and, from 1530, the Knights Hospitallers (also called the Knights of St John of Jerusalem). France took the islands in 1798, but the British drove them out in 1800. British rule was officially recognized in 1815.

During World War I (1914–18), Malta was an important naval base. In World War II (1939–45), Italian and German aircraft bombed the islands. In recognition of the islanders' bravery, the British King George VI awarded the George Cross to Malta in 1942. In 1953, Malta became a base for NATO (North Atlantic Treaty Organization). Malta became independent in 1964 and a republic in 1974. In 1979, Malta ceased to be a British military base. Malta was declared a neutral country in the 1980s. It became a member of the European Union on May 1, 2004, and adopted the euro as its official currency in 2008.

The World Bank classifies Malta as an "upper-middle-income" developing country. It lacks natural resources, and most people work in the former naval dockyards, which are now used for commercial shipbuilding and repair, in manufacturing industries, and in the tourist industry.

Manufactures include processed food and chemicals. Farming is difficult, because of the rocky soils. Crops include barley, fruits, potatoes, and wheat. Malta also has a small fishing industry.

AREA 122 sq mi [316 sq km] **POPULATION** 405,000
CAPITAL Valletta **GOVERNMENT** Multiparty republic
ETHNIC GROUPS Maltese 96%, British 2% **LANGUAGES** Maltese and English (both official) **RELIGIONS** Roman Catholic 98%
CURRENCY Euro = 100 cents

MARSHALL ISLANDS

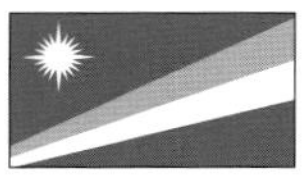

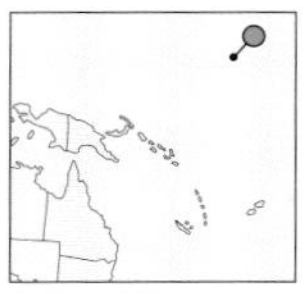

The Republic of the Marshall Islands, a former US territory, became fully independent in 1991. This island nation, lying north of Kiribati in a region known as Micronesia, is heavily dependent on US aid. The main activities are agriculture and tourism.

AREA 70 sq mi [181 sq km]
POPULATION 65,000 **CAPITAL** Majuro

MARTINIQUE

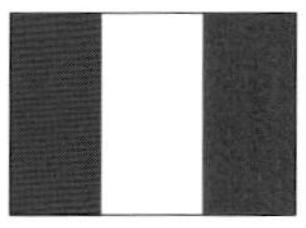

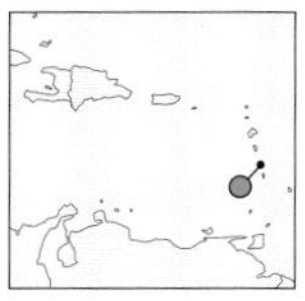

Martinique, a volcanic island nation in the Caribbean, was colonized by France in 1635. It became a French overseas department in 1946. Tourism and agriculture are major activities. About 70% of Martinique's gross domestic product is provided by the French government, allowing for a good standard of living.

AREA 425 sq mi [1,102 sq km]
POPULATION 436,000 **CAPITAL** Fort-de-France

MAURITANIA

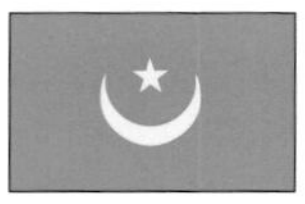

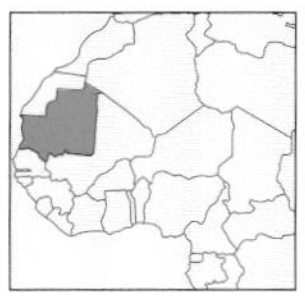

GEOGRAPHY The Islamic Republic of Mauritania in northwestern Africa is nearly twice the size of France. But France has more than 28 times as many people. Part of the world's largest desert, the Sahara, covers northern Mauritania and most Mauritanians live in the southwest. The amount of rainfall and the length of the rainy season increase from north to south. Much of the land is desert, but southwesterly winds bring summer rain to the south.

POLITICS & ECONOMY Originally part of the great African empires of Ghana and Mali, France set up a protectorate in Mauritania in 1903, attempting to exploit the trade in gum arabic. The country became a territory of French West Africa and a French colony in 1920. French West Africa was a huge territory, which included present-day Benin, Burkina Faso, Guinea, Ivory Coast, Mali, Niger, and Senegal, as well as Mauritania. Mauritania became independent in 1960.

In 1976, Spain withdrew from Spanish (now Western) Sahara, a territory bordering Mauritania to the north. Morocco occupied the northern two-thirds of this territory, while Mauritania took the rest. But Saharan guerrillas belonging to POLISARIO (the Popular Front for the Liberation of Saharan Territories) began an armed struggle for independence. In 1979, Mauritania withdrew from the southern part of Western Sahara, which was then occupied by Morocco. Democracy was restored after a new constitution was adopted in 1991. A military group seized power in 2005, but democratic elections were held in 2007. The military again seized control in 2008, and in 2009 its leader, Mohamed Ould Abdelaziz, was elected president.

Mauritania is a "low-income" developing country. Nearly half of the people are engaged in agriculture. In 2006 Mauritania became Africa's newest oil producer, when an offshore platform came online for the first time.

AREA 395,953 sq mi [1,025,520 sq km]
POPULATION 3,129,000 **CAPITAL** Nouakchott
GOVERNMENT Multiparty Islamic republic
ETHNIC GROUPS Mixed Moor/Black 40%, Moor 30%, Black 30%
LANGUAGES Arabic and Wolof (both official), French
RELIGIONS Islam
CURRENCY Ouguiya = 5 khoums

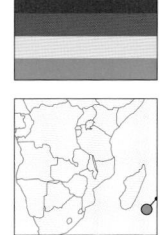

MAURITIUS

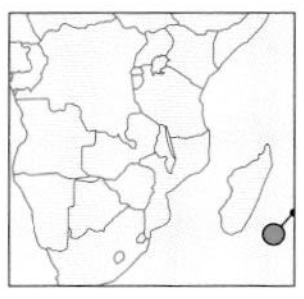

The Republic of Mauritius, an Indian Ocean nation lying east of Madagascar, was previously ruled by France and Britain until it achieved independence in 1968. It became a republic in 1992. Sugar production is in decline but tourism is vital to the economy.

AREA 788 sq mi [2,040 sq km]
POPULATION 1,284,000 **CAPITAL** Port Louis

MEXICO

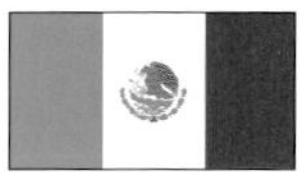

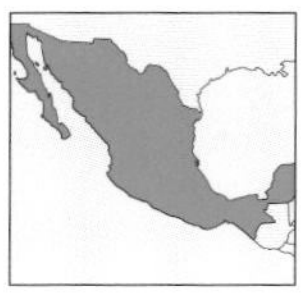

GEOGRAPHY The United Mexican States, as Mexico is officially named, is the world's most populous Spanish-speaking country. Much of the land is mountainous, although most people live on the central plateau. Mexico contains two large peninsulas, Lower (or Baja) California in the northwest and the flat Yucatán peninsula in the southeast.

The climate varies according to the altitude. The resort of Acapulco on the southwest coast has a dry and sunny climate. Mexico City, at about 7,546 ft [2,300 m] above sea level, is much cooler. Most rain occurs between June and September. The rainfall decreases north of Mexico City and northern Mexico is mainly arid.

POLITICS & ECONOMY In the mid-19th century, Mexico lost land to the United States, and between 1910 and 1921 violent revolutions created chaos. Reforms were introduced in the 1920s and, in 1929, the Institutional Revolutionary Party (PRI) was formed. The PRI ruled Mexico effectively as a one-party state until it was finally defeated in 2001. The new president, Vicente Fox, faced many problems. He was succeeded by Felipe Calderón. In 2008–9, killings associated with the illegal drug traffic increased, spreading over the border into the United States.

The World Bank classifies Mexico as an "upper-middle-income" developing country. Agriculture is important. Food crops include beans, maize, rice, and wheat, while cash crops include coffee, cotton, fruits, and vegetables. Beef cattle, dairy cattle, and other livestock are raised and fishing is also important.

But oil and oil products are the chief exports, while manufacturing is the most valuable activity. Mexico is the world's leading silver producer, and it also mines copper, gold, lead, zinc, and other minerals. Many factories near the northern border assemble goods, such as car parts and electrical products, for US companies.

Hopes for the future lie in increasing cooperation with the USA and Canada. However, problems with the United States mounted

from 2008 as drug cartels carried out large numbers of killings, mostly along the US border.

AREA 756,061 SQ MI [1,958,201 SQ KM]
POPULATION 111,212,000 **CAPITAL** MEXICO CITY
GOVERNMENT FEDERAL REPUBLIC
ETHNIC GROUPS MESTIZO 60%, AMERINDIAN 30%, WHITE 9%
LANGUAGES SPANISH (OFFICIAL)
RELIGIONS ROMAN CATHOLIC 90%, PROTESTANT 6%
CURRENCY MEXICAN PESO = 100 CENTAVOS

MICRONESIA

The Federated States of Micronesia, a former US territory covering a vast area in the western Pacific Ocean, became fully independent in 1991. The main export is copra. Fishing and tourism are also important.

AREA 271 SQ MI [702 SQ KM]
POPULATION 107,000 **CAPITAL** PALIKIR

MOLDOVA

GEOGRAPHY The Republic of Moldova is a small country sandwiched between Ukraine and Romania. It was formerly one of the 15 republics that made up the Soviet Union. Much of the land is hilly and the highest areas are near the center of the country.

Moldova has a moderately continental climate, with warm summers and fairly cold winters when temperatures dip below freezing point. Most of the rain comes in the warmer months.

POLITICS & ECONOMY In the 14th century, the Moldavians formed a state called Moldavia. It included part of Romania and Bessarabia (now the modern country of Moldova). The Ottoman Turks took the area in the 16th century, but in 1812 Russia took over Bessarabia. In 1861, Moldavia and Walachia united to form Romania. Russia retook southern Bessarabia in 1878.

After World War I (1914–18), all of Bessarabia was returned to Romania, but the Soviet Union did not recognize this act. From 1944, the Moldovan Soviet Socialist Republic was part of the Soviet Union.

In 1989, the Moldovans asserted their independence and ethnicity by making Romanian the official language and, at the end of 1991, Moldova became an independent nation. But Trans-Dniester, an area east of the River Dniester, has sought autonomy. In 2006, its people voted for independence and union with Russia. This vote was not recognized internationally.

In 2001, Moldovans returned the Communist Party to power in a general election. Under President Vladimir Voronin, Moldova enjoyed a period of economic growth. The Communist Party was re-elected in 2005 and again in 2009. But demonstrators alleged that the 2009 polls were fraudulent.

In terms of its GNP per capita, Moldova is one of Europe's poorest countries. Agriculture is the leading activity and products include fruits, maize, tobacco, and wine. Moldova has few natural resources and it imports materials and fuels for its industries. Light industries, such as food processing and factories making household appliances, are increasing.

AREA 13,070 SQ MI [33,851 SQ KM]
POPULATION 4,321,000 **CAPITAL** KISHINEV
GOVERNMENT MULTIPARTY REPUBLIC
ETHNIC GROUPS MOLDOVAN/ROMANIAN 65%, UKRAINIAN 14%, RUSSIAN 13%, OTHERS
LANGUAGES MOLDOVAN/ROMANIAN AND RUSSIAN (OFFICIAL)
RELIGIONS EASTERN ORTHODOX 98%
CURRENCY MOLDOVAN LEU = 100 BANI

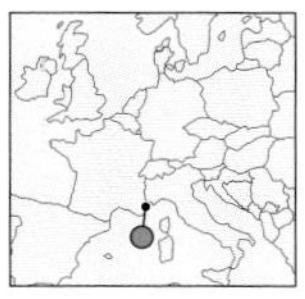

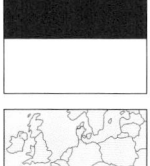

MONACO

The tiny Principality of Monaco consists of a narrow strip of coastline and a rocky peninsula on the French Riviera. Its considerable wealth is derived largely from banking, finance, gambling, and tourism. Monaco's citizens do not pay any state tax. The reigning prince is Albert II. In 2008, plans to extend the area of Monaco by reclaiming land from under the sea were shelved.

AREA 0.4 SQ MI [1 SQ KM] **POPULATION** 33,000 **CAPITAL** MONACO

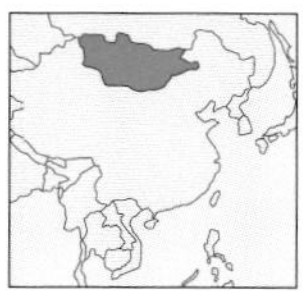

MONGOLIA

GEOGRAPHY The State of Mongolia is the world's largest landlocked country. It consists mainly of high plateaux, with the Gobi Desert in the southeast.

Ulan Bator lies on the northern edge of a desert plateau. It has bitterly cold winters. Summer temperatures are moderated by the altitude.

POLITICS & ECONOMY In the 13th century, Genghis Khan united the Mongolian peoples and built up a great empire. Under his grandson, Kublai Khan, the Mongol empire extended from Korea and China to eastern Europe and present-day Iraq.

The Mongol empire broke up in the late 14th century. In the early 17th century, Inner Mongolia came under Chinese control, and by the late 17th century Outer Mongolia had become a Chinese province. In 1911, the Mongolians drove the Chinese out of Outer Mongolia and made the area a Buddhist kingdom. But in 1924, under Russian influence, the Communist Mongolian People's Republic was set up. From the 1950s, Mongolia supported the Soviet Union in its disputes with China. In 1990, the people demonstrated for more freedom, and free elections in June 1990 were won by the Communist Mongolian People's Revolutionary Party (MPRP). The Democratic Union coalition won power in 1996, but the MPRP regained power in 2000. In 2004, after disputed elections, a coalition government was set up. In 2009, the Democratic Union candidate, Tsakhiagiin Elbegdori, was elected president.

The World Bank classifies Mongolia as a "lower-middle-income" developing country. Most people were once nomads, who moved around with their herds of sheep, cattle, goats, and horses. Under Communist rule, most people were moved into permanent homes on government-owned farms. Livestock and animal products remain important, but minerals and fuels now account for more than three-fifths of Mongolia's exports.

AREA 604,826 SQ MI [1,566,500 SQ KM]
POPULATION 3,041,000 **CAPITAL** ULAN BATOR
GOVERNMENT MULTIPARTY REPUBLIC **ETHNIC GROUPS** KHALKHA MONGOL 85%, KAZAKH 6% **LANGUAGES** KHALKHA MONGOLIAN (OFFICIAL), TURKIC, RUSSIAN **RELIGIONS** TIBETAN BUDDHIST LAMAISM 96%
CURRENCY TUGRIK = 100 MÖNGÖS

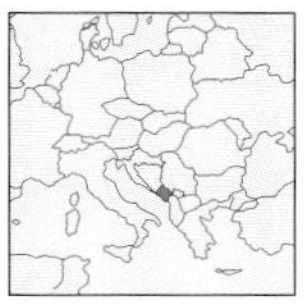

MONTENEGRO

The Republic of Montenegro became a fully independent nation in 2006. It was formerly part of the Union of Serbia and Montenegro and, before 2003, part of Yugoslavia. The coastal region has a Mediterranean climate. However, inland, the Dinaric Alps, which reach a height of 8,274 ft [2,522 m], have a more severe climate.

Serbia fell under Turkish rule in the 14th century, but Montenegro remained Christian. Montenegro was absorbed into Serbia in 1918. It became part of the Kingdom of the Serbs, Croats, and Slovenes, which was renamed Yugoslavia in 1929. After World War II, Montenegro was recognized as one of the six republics in the Federal Republic of Yugoslavia. In 2009, Prime Minister Milo Djukanovic's Coalition for European Montenegro won a landslide victory in parliamentary elections.

Manufacturing is the leading activity, and steel and aluminum are major products. But farming remains important. Forests cover more than half of the land.

AREA 5,415 SQ MI [14,026 SQ KM]
POPULATION 672,000 **CAPITAL** PODGORICA
GOVERNMENT REPUBLIC **ETHNIC GROUPS** MONTENEGRIN 43%, SERB 32%, BOSNIAN 8%, ALBANIAN 5%, OTHERS
LANGUAGES SERBIAN (OFFICIAL), BOSNIAN, ALBANIAN, CROATIAN
RELIGIONS ORTHODOX, ISLAM, ROMAN CATHOLIC
CURRENCY EURO = 100 CENTS

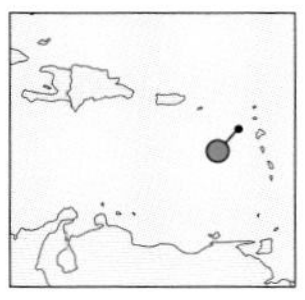

MONTSERRAT

Montserrat is a British overseas territory in the Caribbean Sea. The climate is tropical and hurricanes often cause much damage. Intermittent eruptions of the Soufrière Hills volcano between 1995 and 1998, and again in 2003, led to the emigration of many people and the virtual destruction of Plymouth, the then capital. A new airport was opened in 2005.

AREA 39 SQ MI [102 SQ KM] **POPULATION** 5,000 **CAPITAL** BRADES

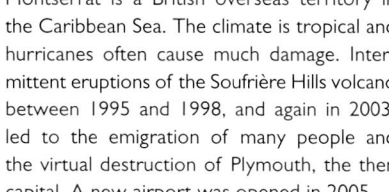

MOROCCO

GEOGRAPHY The Kingdom of Morocco lies in northwestern Africa. Its name comes from the Arabic Maghreb-el-Aksa, meaning "the farthest west." Behind the western coastal plain the land rises to a broad plateau and ranges of the Atlas Mountains. The High (Haut) Atlas contains the highest peak, Djebel Toubkal, at 13,665 ft [4,165 m]. East of the mountains, the land descends to the Sahara. The Canaries Current cools the Atlantic coast. Inland, summers are hot and dry. Winters are mild, with moderate rainfall. Snow often falls on the High Atlas Mountains.

POLITICS & ECONOMY The original people of Morocco were the Berbers. But in the 680s, Arab invaders introduced Islam and the Arabic language. By the early 20th century, France and Spain controlled Morocco, which became an independent kingdom in 1956. Although Morocco is a constitutional monarchy, King Hassan II ruled the country in a generally authoritarian way from the time of his accession to the throne in 1961 to his death in 1999. His successor, Mohamed VI, faced several problems, including that of Western Sahara, which he claimed for Morocco, and the activities of Islamic extremists. In 2009, the alleged al Qaida leader in Morocco was sentenced to imprisonment for life.

Morocco is classified as a "lower-middle-income" developing country. It is the world's third largest producer of phosphate rock, which is used to make fertilizer. One of the reasons why Morocco wants to keep Western Sahara is that it, too, has large phosphate reserves. Farming employs about 40% of Moroccans. Chief crops include barley, beans, citrus fruits, maize, olives, sugar beet, and wheat. Processed phosphates are exported, but most of Morocco's manufactures are for home consumption. Fishing and tourism are also important.

AREA 172,413 SQ MI [446,550 SQ KM]
POPULATION 31,285,000 **CAPITAL** RABAT
GOVERNMENT CONSTITUTIONAL MONARCHY
ETHNIC GROUPS ARAB-BERBER 99%
LANGUAGES ARABIC (OFFICIAL), BERBER DIALECTS, FRENCH
RELIGIONS ISLAM 99% **CURRENCY** MOROCCAN DIRHAM = 100 CENTIMES

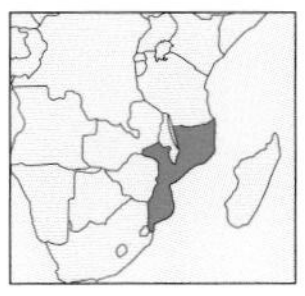

MOZAMBIQUE

GEOGRAPHY The Republic of Mozambique borders the Indian Ocean in southeastern Africa. The coastal plains are narrow in the north but broaden in the south. Inland lie plateaux and hills, which make up another two-fifths of the country. Mozambique has a mostly tropical climate. The capital Maputo, which lies outside the tropics, has hot and humid summers, though the winters are mild and fairly dry.

POLITICS & ECONOMY In 1885, when the European powers divided Africa, Mozambique was recognized as a Portuguese colony. But black African opposition to European rule gradually increased. In 1961, the Front for the Liberation of Mozambique (FRELIMO) was founded to oppose Portuguese rule. In 1964, FRELIMO launched a guerrilla war, which continued for ten years. Mozambique became independent in 1975.

After independence, Mozambique became a one-party state. Its government aided African nationalists in Rhodesia (now Zimbabwe) and South Africa. But the white governments of these countries helped an opposition group, the Mozambique National Resistance Movement (RENAMO) to lead an armed struggle against Mozambique's government. Civil war, combined with droughts, caused much suffering in the 1980s. In 1989, FRELIMO ended one-party rule. The war ended in 1992 and multiparty elections were held in 1994. In 1995 Mozambique became the 53rd member of the Commonwealth. In 2004, and again in 2009, FRELIMO leader Antonio Guebuza was elected president.

In the early 1990s, the UN rated Mozambique as one of the world's poorest countries. The second half of the 1990s saw the start of renewed economic growth, but floods in 2000–1, 2007, and 2008, and prolonged droughts in the mid-2000s and 2008, were major setbacks. About 80% of the people are poor farmers. Crops include cassava, cotton, maize, rice, and tea.

AREA 309,494 SQ MI [801,590 SQ KM]
POPULATION 21,669,000 **CAPITAL** MAPUTO
GOVERNMENT MULTIPARTY REPUBLIC **ETHNIC GROUPS** INDIGENOUS TRIBAL GROUPS (SHANGAAN, CHOKWE, MANYIKA, SENA, MAKUA, OTHERS) 99%
LANGUAGES PORTUGUESE (OFFICIAL), MANY OTHERS
RELIGIONS TRADITIONAL BELIEFS 50%, CHRISTIANITY 30%, ISLAM 20%
CURRENCY METICAL = 100 CENTAVOS

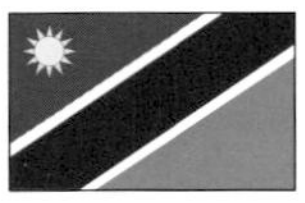
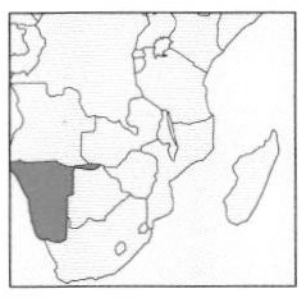

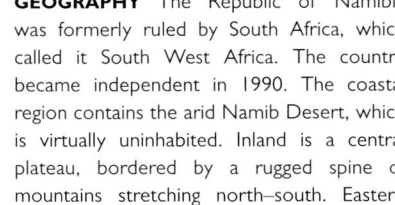

NAMIBIA

GEOGRAPHY The Republic of Namibia was formerly ruled by South Africa, which called it South West Africa. The country became independent in 1990. The coastal region contains the arid Namib Desert, which is virtually uninhabited. Inland is a central plateau, bordered by a rugged spine of mountains stretching north–south. Eastern Namibia contains part of the Kalahari Desert, a semidesert area extending into Botswana. Namibia has a warm and arid climate. Windhoek has an average annual rainfall of 15 inches [370 mm], which often occurs in thunderstorms during the hot summer.

POLITICS & ECONOMY During World War I, South African troops defeated the Germans who ruled what is now Namibia. After World War II, many people challenged South Africa's right to govern the territory and a civil war began in the 1960s between African guerrillas and South African troops. A ceasefire was agreed in 1989 and Namibia became independent in 1990. In the 1990s, the government pursued a policy of "national reconciliation." An enclave on the coast, called Walvis Bay (Walvisbaai), remained part of South Africa until 1994, when it was transferred to Namibia. In 2004, the nationalist leader, Sam Nujoma, president since 1990, retired. He was succeeded by Hifikepunye Pohamba, who was re-elected in 2009.

Namibia has reserves of diamonds, uranium, zinc, and copper. Minerals make up the bulk of the exports, though agriculture employs 20% of the people. Sea fishing is also important. Namibia has few industries, but tourism is expanding.

AREA 318,259 SQ MI [824,292 SQ KM]
POPULATION 2,109,000 **CAPITAL** WINDHOEK
GOVERNMENT MULTIPARTY REPUBLIC **ETHNIC GROUPS** OVAMBO 50%, KAVANGO 9%, HERERO 7%, DAMARA 7%, WHITE 6%, NAMA 5%
LANGUAGES ENGLISH (OFFICIAL), AFRIKAANS, GERMAN, INDIGENOUS DIALECTS **RELIGIONS** CHRISTIANITY 90% (LUTHERAN 51%)
CURRENCY NAMIBIAN DOLLAR = 100 CENTS

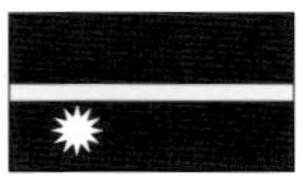
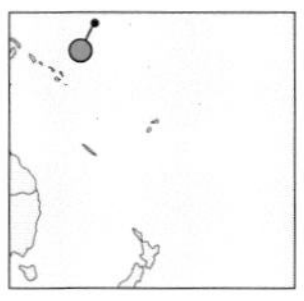

NAURU

Nauru is the world's smallest republic, located in the western Pacific Ocean, close to the equator. Independent since 1968, Nauru's prosperity is based on phosphate mining, but the reserves are running out.

AREA 8 SQ MI [21 SQ KM]
POPULATION 14,000 **CAPITAL** YAREN

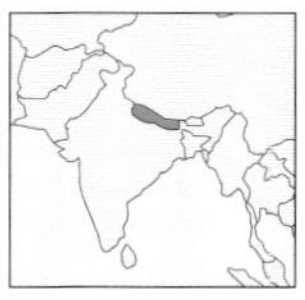

NEPAL

GEOGRAPHY Over three-quarters of Nepal lies in the Himalayan region, culminating in the world's highest peak (Mount Everest, or Chomolongma in Nepali) at 29,035 ft [8,850 m]. As a result, climatic conditions vary widely according to the altitude.

POLITICS & ECONOMY Nepal was united in the late 18th century, although its complex topography has ensured that it remains a diverse patchwork of peoples. From the mid-19th century to 1951, power was held by the royal Rana family. The first democratic elections in 32 years were held in 1991, but, by the early 21st century, Nepal faced many problems, including an uprising of Maoist guerrillas. In 2005, King Gyanendra seized power but failed to stop the conflict. In 2006, the Maoists joined a provisional coalition government. In elections in April 2008, the Maoists became the largest single party. In May, Nepal became a republic, and in August the Maoist leader, named "Prachanda" (meaning "fierce"), became prime minister. He resigned in 2009 and Communist leader Madhav Kumar Nepal replaced him.

Agriculture is the main activity in this overwhelmingly rural country, and Nepal is heavily dependent on aid. Tourism, based on the attractions of the high Himalaya, is growing in importance. There are also ambitious plans to exploit the hydroelectric potential offered by the ferocious Himalayan rivers.

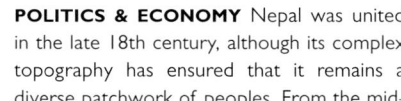

AREA 56,827 SQ MI [147,181 SQ KM] **POPULATION** 28,563,000
CAPITAL KATMANDU **GOVERNMENT** MULTIPARTY REPUBLIC
ETHNIC GROUPS BRAHMAN, CHETRI, NEWAR, GURUNG, MAGAR, TAMANG, SHERPA AND OTHERS
LANGUAGES NEPALI (OFFICIAL), LOCAL LANGUAGES
RELIGIONS HINDUISM 86%, BUDDHISM 8%, ISLAM 4%
CURRENCY NEPALESE RUPEE = 100 PAISA

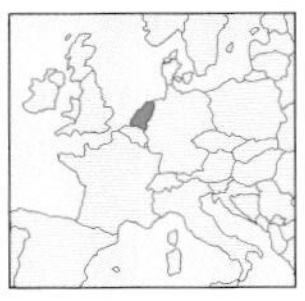

NETHERLANDS

GEOGRAPHY The Netherlands lies at the western end of the North European Plain, which extends to the Ural Mountains in Russia. Except for the far southeastern corner, the Netherlands is flat and about 40% lies below sea level at high tide. To prevent flooding, the Dutch have built dykes (sea walls) to hold back the waves. Large areas which were once under the sea, but which have been reclaimed, are called polders. Because of its position on the North Sea, the Netherlands has a temperate climate, with mild, rainy winters.

POLITICS & ECONOMY Before the 16th century, the area that is now the Netherlands was under a succession of foreign rulers, including the Romans, the Germanic Franks, the French, and the Spanish. The Dutch declared their independence from Spain in 1581 and their status was finally recognized by Spain in 1648. In the 17th century, the Dutch built up a great overseas empire, especially in Southeast Asia. But in the early 18th century, the Dutch lost control of the seas to England.

France controlled the Netherlands from 1795 to 1813. In 1815, the Netherlands, then containing Belgium and Luxembourg, became an independent kingdom. Belgium broke away in 1830 and Luxembourg followed in 1890.

The Netherlands was neutral in World War I (1914–18), but was occupied by Germany in World War II (1939–45). After the war, the Netherlands Indies became independent as Indonesia. The Netherlands became active in West European affairs. With Belgium and Luxembourg, it formed a customs union called Benelux in 1948. In 1949, it joined NATO (the North Atlantic Treaty Organization), and the European Coal and Steel Community (ECSC) in 1953. In 1957, it became a founder member of the European Economic Community (now the European Union), and in 2002 it adopted the euro as its sole unit of currency. Since 2002, four coalition governments, under Prime Minister Jan Peter Balkenende, have collapsed. The cause of the breakup in 2010 was the refusal of Balkenende's center-right Christian Democratic Alliance to withdraw its troops from Afghanistan.

The Netherlands is a highly industrialized country, and industry and commerce are the most valuable activities. Its resources include natural gas, some oil, salt, and china clay. But the Netherlands imports many of the materials needed by its industries and it is, therefore, a major trading country. Industrial products are wide-ranging, including aircraft, chemicals, electronic equipment, machinery, textiles, and vehicles. Farming is scientific and yields are high. Dairy farming is the leading farming activity. Major products include barley, flowers and bulbs, potatoes, sugar beet, and wheat.

AREA 16,033 SQ MI [41,526 SQ KM]
POPULATION 16,716,000
CAPITAL AMSTERDAM; THE HAGUE (SEAT OF GOVERNMENT)
GOVERNMENT CONSTITUTIONAL MONARCHY
ETHNIC GROUPS DUTCH 83%, INDONESIAN, TURKISH, MOROCCAN AND OTHERS **LANGUAGES** DUTCH (OFFICIAL), FRISIAN
RELIGIONS ROMAN CATHOLIC 31%, PROTESTANT 21%, ISLAM 4%, OTHERS
CURRENCY EURO = 100 CENTS

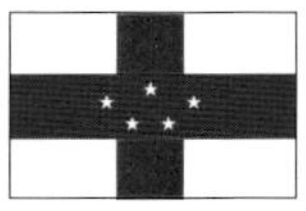
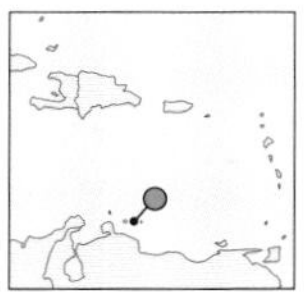

NETHERLANDS ANTILLES

The Netherlands Antilles consists of two different island groups; one off the coast of Venezuela, and the other at the northern end of the Leeward Islands, some 500 mi [800 km] away. In 2006, Curaçao and Saint Maarten voted for autonomy, while the small islands of Bonaire, Saint Eustatius, and Saba voted to become a type of Dutch municipality.

AREA 309 SQ MI [800 SQ KM] **POPULATION** 227,000 **CAPITAL** WILLEMSTAD

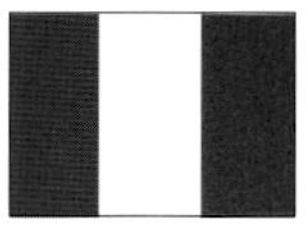
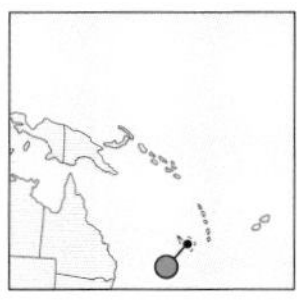

NEW CALEDONIA

New Caledonia is the most southerly of the Melanesian countries in the Pacific. It has been a French possession since 1853 and an Overseas Territory since 1958. In 1998, France announced an agreement with local Melanesians that a vote on independence would be postponed until 2014. The country is rich in mineral resources, especially nickel.

AREA 7,172 SQ MI [18,575 SQ KM] **POPULATION** 228,000 **CAPITAL** NOUMÉA

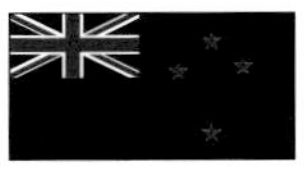
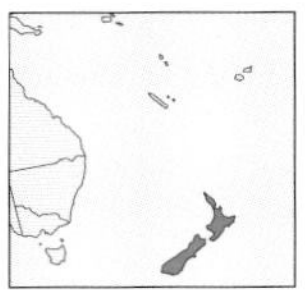

NEW ZEALAND

GEOGRAPHY New Zealand lies about 994 mi [1,600 km] southeast of Australia. It consists of two main islands and several other small ones. Much of North Island is volcanic. Active volcanoes include Ngauruhoe and Ruapehu. Hot springs and geysers are common, and steam from the ground is used to produce electricity. The Southern Alps, which contain the country's highest peak, Aoraki Mount Cook, at 12,313 ft [3,753 m], form the backbone of South Island. The island also has some large, fertile plains.

Auckland in the north has a warm, humid climate throughout the year. Wellington has cooler summers, while in Dunedin, in the southeast, temperatures sometimes dip below freezing in winter. The rainfall is heaviest on the western highlands.

POLITICS & ECONOMY Evidence suggests that early Maori settlers arrived in New Zealand more than 1 000 years ago. The Dutch navigator Abel Tasman reached New Zealand in 1642, but his discovery was not followed up. In 1769, the British Captain James Cook rediscovered the islands. In the early 19th century, British settlers arrived and, in 1840, under the Treaty of Waitangi, Britain took possession of the islands. From the 1870s, the Maoris were gradually integrated into colonial society.

In 1907, New Zealand became a self-governing dominion in the British Commonwealth. The country's economy developed quickly and the people became increasingly prosperous. However, after Britain joined the European Economic Community in 1973, New Zealand's exports to Britain shrank and the country had to reassess its economic and defense strategies and seek new markets. The world recession led the government to cut back on welfare spending in the 1990s. The preservation of Maori culture and Maori rights are major issues. The Maoris, a Polynesian people, make up about 13% of the population. Other mainly Polynesian Pacific people make up another 6%. Ties with Britain have been reduced. Helen Clark, leader of the Labor Party and prime minister from 1999–2008, has expressed the view that New Zealand will eventually abolish the monarchy and become a republic. In November 2008, the center-right National Party defeated the Labor Party in elections. John Key became prime minister.

The economy once depended on agriculture, but manufacturing now employs twice as many people as farming. Meat and dairy products are leading commodities. Sheep rearing has declined as the area under cattle, deer, and vines has expanded. Crops include barley, fruits, potatoes and other vegetables and wheat.

AREA 104,453 SQ MI [270,534 SQ KM]
POPULATION 4,213,000 **CAPITAL** WELLINGTON
GOVERNMENT CONSTITUTIONAL MONARCHY
ETHNIC GROUPS NEW ZEALAND EUROPEAN 74%, NEW ZEALAND MAORI 13%, POLYNESIAN 6% **LANGUAGES** ENGLISH AND MAORI (BOTH OFFICIAL) **RELIGIONS** ANGLICAN 24%, PRESBYTERIAN 18%, ROMAN CATHOLIC 15%, OTHERS
CURRENCY NEW ZEALAND DOLLAR = 100 CENTS

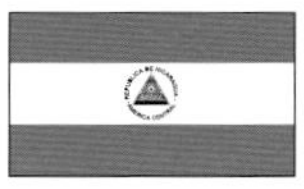
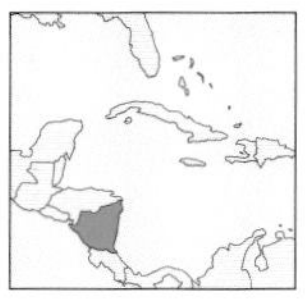

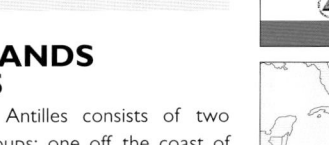

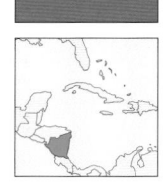

NICARAGUA

GEOGRAPHY The Republic of Nicaragua is a large country in Central America. In the east is a broad plain bordering the Caribbean Sea. The plain is drained by rivers that flow from the Central Highlands. The fertile western Pacific region contains about 40 volcanoes, many of which are active, and earthquakes are common.

Nicaragua has a tropical climate. Managua is hot throughout the year and there is a marked rainy season from May to October. In October 1998, Hurricane Mitch caused great devastation in Nicaragua. The Central Highlands and Caribbean region are cooler and wetter. The wettest region is the humid Caribbean plain.

POLITICS & ECONOMY In 1502, Christopher Columbus claimed the area for Spain, which ruled Nicaragua until 1821. By the early 20th century, the United States had considerable influence in the country and, in 1912, US forces entered Nicaragua to protect US interests. From 1927 to 1933, rebels under General Augusto César Sandino tried to drive US forces out of the country. In 1933, US marines set up a Nicaraguan army, the National Guard, to help to defeat the rebels. Its leader, Anastasio Somoza García, had Sandino murdered in 1934, and from 1937 Somoza ruled as a dictator.

In the mid-1970s, many people began to protest against Somoza's rule. Many joined a guerrilla force, called the Sandinista National Liberation Front, named after General Sandino. The rebels defeated the Somoza regime in 1979. In the 1980s, the US-supported forces, called the "Contras," launched a campaign

against the Sandinista government. The US government opposed the Sandinista regime, under Daniel José Ortega Saavedra, claiming that it was a Communist dictatorship. A coalition, the National Opposition Union, defeated the Sandinistas in 1990. In 2001, the Sandinista candidate, Daniel Ortega, was defeated in presidential elections, but he was re-elected president of Nicaragua in 2006.

In the early 1990s, Nicaragua faced many problems in rebuilding its shattered economy. Agriculture is the main activity, employing more than a third of the population. Coffee, cotton, sugar, and bananas are grown for export, while rice is the main food crop.

AREA 50,193 SQ MI [130,000 SQ KM]
POPULATION 5,891,000 **CAPITAL** MANAGUA
GOVERNMENT MULTIPARTY REPUBLIC
ETHNIC GROUPS MESTIZO 69%, WHITE 17%, BLACK 9%, AMERINDIAN 5%
LANGUAGES SPANISH (OFFICIAL)
RELIGIONS ROMAN CATHOLIC 85%, PROTESTANT
CURRENCY CÓRDOBA ORO (GOLD CÓRDOBA) = 100 CENTAVOS

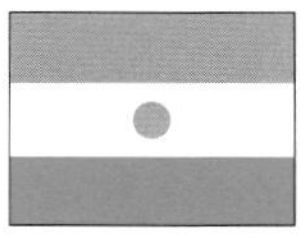
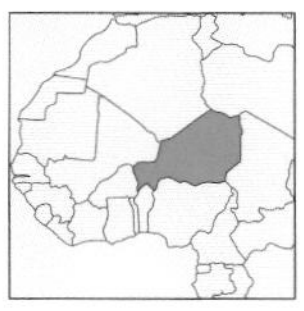

NIGER

GEOGRAPHY The Republic of Niger is a landlocked nation in north-central Africa. The northern plateaux lie in the Sahara Desert, while Central Niger contains the rugged Aïr Mountains. The most fertile, densely populated region is the Niger valley in the southwest.

Niger has a tropical climate and the south has a rainy season between June and September. The north is practically rainless.

POLITICS & ECONOMY Since independence in 1960, Niger, a French territory from 1900, has suffered severe droughts. Food shortages and the collapse of the traditional nomadic way of life of some of Niger's people have caused political instability. After a period of military rule, a multiparty constitution was adopted in 1992, but the military again seized power in 1996. Later that year, the coup leader, Colonel Ibrahim Barre Mainassara, was elected president. He was assassinated in 1999, but parliamentary rule was restored and Mamadou Tandja was elected president. He was re-elected in 2004, but he was overthrown in a coup in 2010. A military government was set up.

Niger's chief resource is uranium and the country is the world's fourth largest producer. Some tin and tungsten are also mined, though other mineral reserves are largely untouched. Despite its considerable resources, Niger remains one of the world's poorest countries. Only 3% of the land can be used for growing crops.

AREA 489,189 SQ MI [1,267,000 SQ KM]
POPULATION 15,306,000 **CAPITAL** NIAMEY
GOVERNMENT MULTIPARTY REPUBLIC **ETHNIC GROUPS** HAUSA 56%, DJERMA 22%, TUAREG 8%, FULA 8%, OTHERS **LANGUAGES** FRENCH (OFFICIAL), HAUSA, DJERMA **RELIGIONS** ISLAM 80%, INDIGENOUS BELIEFS, CHRISTIANITY **CURRENCY** CFA FRANC = 100 CENTIMES

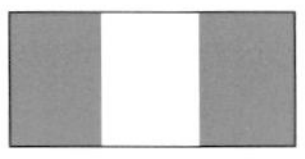
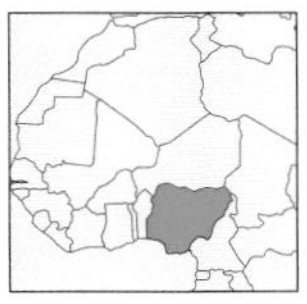

NIGERIA

GEOGRAPHY The Federal Republic of Nigeria is the most populous nation in Africa. The country's main rivers are the Niger and Benue, which meet in central Nigeria. North of the two river valleys are high plains and plateaux. The Lake Chad basin is in the northeast, with the Sokoto plains in the northwest. The south contains hilly uplands and plains. The south has a hot, rainy climate. The north is drier and often hotter than the south.

POLITICS & ECONOMY Nigeria has a long artistic tradition. Major cultures include the Nok (500 BC to AD 200), the Ife, a major Yoruba culture which developed about 1,000 years ago, and the Benin (15th to 17th centuries). Britain gradually extended its influence over the area in the second half of the 19th century.

Nigeria became independent in 1960 and a federal republic in 1963. A federal constitution dividing the country into regions was necessary because Nigeria contains more than 250 ethnic and linguistic groups, as well as several religious ones. Local rivalries have long been a threat to national unity, and six new states were created in 1996 in an attempt to overcome this. Civil war occurred between 1967 and 1970, when the people of the southeast attempted unsuccessfully to secede during the Biafran War. Between 1960 and 1998, Nigeria had only nine years of civilian government.

In 1998–9, civilian rule was restored and Olusegun Obasanjo became president. Nigeria faced many problems, including violence in the Niger delta region and religious conflict. In 2007, Umar Yar'Adua, a northerner, was elected president. However, he died in 2010, and was replaced as head of state by the vice-president, Goodluck Johnson, a southerner.

Nigeria is a developing country with great potential. Its chief natural resource is oil, which accounts for most of its exports. Agriculture employs 59% of the people and the country is a major producer of cocoa, palm oil and palm kernels, groundnuts (peanuts), and rubber. Industry is increasing and manufactures include cement, chemicals, fertilizers, textiles, and timber.

AREA 356,667 SQ MI [923,768 SQ KM]
POPULATION 149,229,000 **CAPITAL** ABUJA
GOVERNMENT FEDERAL MULTIPARTY REPUBLIC
ETHNIC GROUPS HAUSA AND FULANI 29%, YORUBA 21%, IBO (OR IGBO) 18%, IJAW 10%, KANURI 4%, MANY OTHERS
LANGUAGES ENGLISH (OFFICIAL), HAUSA, YORUBA, IBO
RELIGIONS ISLAM 50%, CHRISTIANITY 40%, TRADITIONAL BELIEFS 10%
CURRENCY NAIRA = 100 KOBO

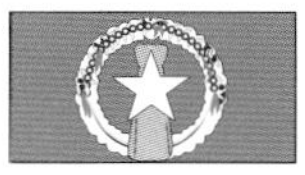
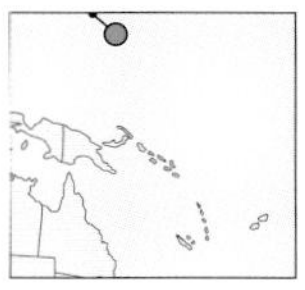

NORTHERN MARIANA ISLANDS

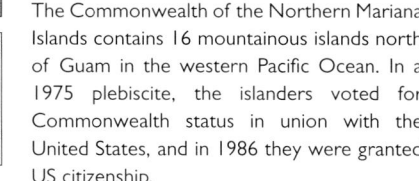

The Commonwealth of the Northern Mariana Islands contains 16 mountainous islands north of Guam in the western Pacific Ocean. In a 1975 plebiscite, the islanders voted for Commonwealth status in union with the United States, and in 1986 they were granted US citizenship.

AREA 179 SQ MI [464 SQ KM] **POPULATION** 51,000 **CAPITAL** SAIPAN

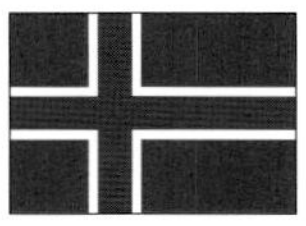
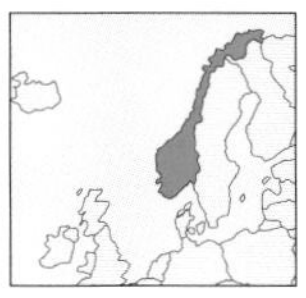

NORWAY

GEOGRAPHY The Kingdom of Norway forms the western part of the rugged Scandinavian peninsula. The deep inlets along the highly indented coastline were worn out by glaciers during the Ice Age. The warm North Atlantic Drift off the coast of Norway moderates the climate, with mild winters and cool summers. Nearly all the ports are ice-free throughout the year. Inland, winters are colder and snow cover lasts for at least three months a year.

POLITICS & ECONOMY Between about AD 800 and 1100, Norwegian Vikings ravaged western Europe. In 1380, Norway was united with Denmark. But in 1814, Denmark handed Norway over to Sweden, though it kept Norway's colonies – Greenland, Iceland, and the Færoe Islands. Norway briefly became independent, but Swedish forces defeated the Norwegians and Norway had to accept Sweden's king as its ruler. The union with Sweden ended in 1903. Germany occupied Norway during World War II (1939–45). Norway recovered quickly after the war and it now has one of the world's highest standards of living. In 1960, Norway and six other countries formed the European Free Trade Association (EFTA). But, in 1994, Norway voted against joining the European Union. In the 1990s and 2000s, Norwegian diplomats sought to broker peace deals in Palestine and Sri Lanka.

Norway's chief resources and exports are oil and natural gas which come from wells under the North Sea. Farmland covers only 3% of the land. Dairy farming and meat production are important, but Norway has to import food. Norway has many industries powered by cheap hydroelectricity.

AREA 125,049 SQ MI [323,877 SQ KM]
POPULATION 4,661,000 **CAPITAL** OSLO
GOVERNMENT CONSTITUTIONAL MONARCHY
ETHNIC GROUPS NORWEGIAN 97%
LANGUAGES NORWEGIAN (OFFICIAL)
RELIGIONS EVANGELICAL LUTHERAN 86%
CURRENCY NORWEGIAN KRONE = 100 ORE

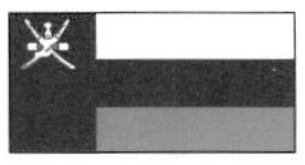
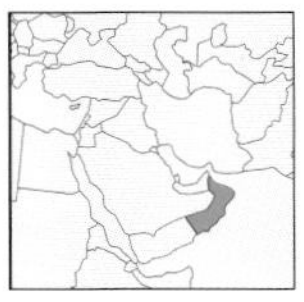

OMAN

GEOGRAPHY The Sultanate of Oman occupies the southeastern corner of the Arabian peninsula. It also includes the tip of the Musandam peninsula, overlooking the strategic Strait of Hormuz.

Oman has a hot tropical climate. In Muscat, temperatures may reach 117°F [47°C] in the summer months.

POLITICS & ECONOMY British influence in Oman dates back to the end of the 18th century, but the country became fully independent in 1971. Since then, using revenue from oil, which was discovered in 1964, the absolute ruler, Qaboos ibn Said, and his government have sought to modernize Oman. In 2000, Oman held elections to its consultative parliament. In 2004, the Sultan appointed Oman's first woman minister without portfolio. Oman has so far escaped the militant Islamic violence that has affected many of its neighbors in the Middle East.

Oil and natural gas make up about 80% of Oman's exports. Agriculture and fishing remain important. Crops include alfalfa, bananas, coconuts, dates, limes, tobacco, vegetables, and wheat. However, Oman has to import food.

AREA 119,498 SQ MI [309,500 SQ KM]
POPULATION 3,418,000 **CAPITAL** MUSCAT
GOVERNMENT MONARCHY WITH CONSULTATIVE COUNCIL
ETHNIC GROUPS ARAB, BALUCHI, INDIAN, PAKISTANI
LANGUAGES ARABIC (OFFICIAL), BALUCHI, ENGLISH
RELIGIONS ISLAM (MAINLY IBADHI), HINDUISM
CURRENCY OMANI RIAL = 100 BAIZAS

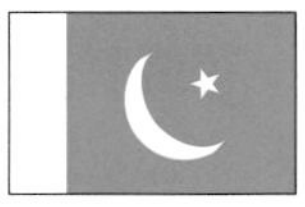
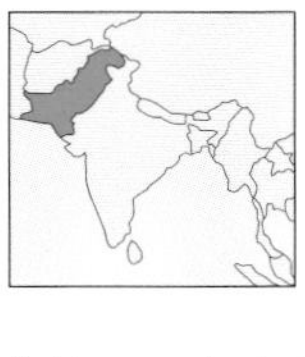

PAKISTAN

GEOGRAPHY The Islamic Republic of Pakistan contains high mountains, fertile plains and rocky deserts. The Karakoram range, which contains K2, the world's second highest peak, lies in the northern part of Jammu and Kashmir, which is occupied by Pakistan but claimed by India. Other mountains rise in the west. Plains, drained by the River Indus and its tributaries, occupy much of eastern Pakistan. Arid areas include the Thar Desert and the Baluchistan plateau. Most of Pakistan has hot summers and mild winters, though the mountains have cold winters. The rainfall is generally sparse.

POLITICS & ECONOMY Pakistan was the site of the Indus Valley civilization which developed about 4,500 years ago. But Pakistan's modern history dates from 1947, when British India was divided into India and Pakistan. Muslim Pakistan was divided into two parts: East and West Pakistan, but East Pakistan broke away in 1971 to become Bangladesh. In 1948–9, 1965, and 1971, Pakistan and India clashed over Kashmir. In 1998, Pakistan responded in kind to India's nuclear weapons tests, but, in 2003–7, Pakistan and India launched a series of initiatives aimed at achieving peace.

Pakistan has been subject to several periods of military rule, but elections in 1988 led to Benazir Bhutto becoming prime minister. She was removed from office in 1990, but she returned as prime minister between 1993 and 1996. In 1997, Narwaz Sharif was elected prime minister, but a military coup in 1999 brought General Pervez Musharraf to power. The security situation deteriorated in 2006–7. In 2007, in the run-up to elections in February 2008, Benazir Bhutto was assassinated, but in the elections, the opposition parties heavily defeated Musharraf's supporters. Musharraf resigned in August 2008 and was succeeded as president by Benazir Bhutto's widower, Asif Ali Zardari. The security situation in the border regions of the northwest worsened. In 2010, parliament approved measures to reduce the powers of the presidency.

According to the World Bank, Pakistan is a "low-income" developing country. The economy is based on farming or rearing goats and sheep. Agriculture employs 40% of the people. Major crops include cotton, fruits, rice, sugarcane, and wheat.

AREA 307,372 SQ MI [796,095 SQ KM]
POPULATION 174,579,000 **CAPITAL** ISLAMABAD
GOVERNMENT MILITARY REGIME **ETHNIC GROUPS** PUNJABI, SINDHI, PASHTUN (PATHAN), BALUCHI, MUHAJIR
LANGUAGES URDU (OFFICIAL), MANY OTHERS
RELIGIONS ISLAM 97%, CHRISTIANITY, HINDUISM
CURRENCY PAKISTANI RUPEE = 100 PAISA

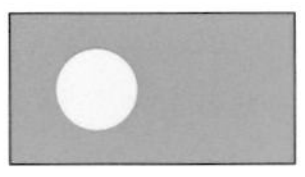
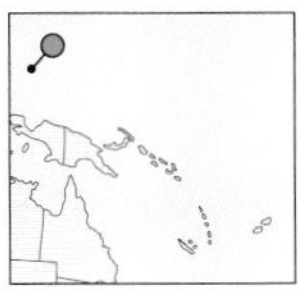

PALAU

The Republic of Palau became fully independent in 1994, after the USA refused to accede to a 1979 referendum that declared this island nation a nuclear-free zone. In December 1994 Palau joined the United Nations. The economy relies heavily on US aid, tourism, fishing, and subsistence agriculture. The main crops include cassava, coconuts, and copra.

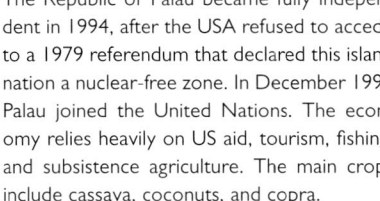

AREA 177 SQ MI [459 SQ KM] **POPULATION** 21,000 **CAPITAL** MELEKEOK

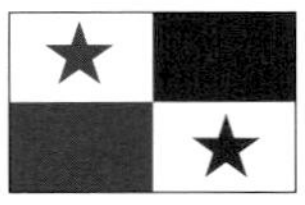
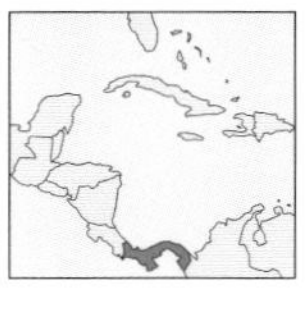

PANAMA

GEOGRAPHY The Republic of Panama forms an isthmus linking Central America to South America. The Panama Canal, which is 50.7 mi [81.6 km] long, cuts across the isthmus. It has made the country a major transport center.

Panama has a tropical climate. Temperatures are high, though the mountains are much cooler than the coastal plains. The main rainy season is between May and December.

POLITICS & ECONOMY Christopher Columbus landed in Panama in 1502 and Spain soon took the area. In 1821, Panama became independent from Spain and a province of Colombia.

In 1903, Colombia refused a request by the United States to build a canal. Panama then revolted against Colombia, and became independent. The United States then began to build the canal, which was opened in 1914. The United States administered the Panama Canal Zone, a strip of land along the canal. But many Panamanians resented US influence and, in 1979, the Canal Zone was returned to Panama. Control of the canal itself was handed over by the USA to Panama on December 31, 1999.

Panama's government has changed many times since independence, and there have been periods of military dictatorships, including that of General Manuel Antonio Noriega in the 1980s. He was finally convicted of drug offences in the United States in 1992. Noriega was released from a Florida prison in 2009. In May 2009, Ricardo Martinelli of the conservative Alliance for Change coalition was elected president.

The World Bank classifies Panama as a "lower-middle-income" developing country. The Panama Canal is an important source of revenue and, in 2006, work began on widening the canal to take giant container ships. Away from the canal, the main activity is agriculture, which employs 14% of the people.

AREA 29,157 sq mi [75,517 sq km] **POPULATION** 3,360,000
CAPITAL Panamá **GOVERNMENT** Multiparty republic
ETHNIC GROUPS Mestizo 70%, Black and Mulatto 14%, White 10%, Amerindian 6% **LANGUAGES** Spanish (official), English **RELIGIONS** Roman Catholic 85%, Protestant 15%
CURRENCY US dollar; Balboa = 100 centésimos

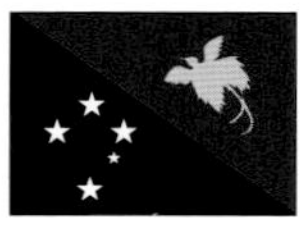
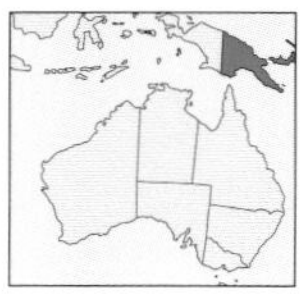

PAPUA NEW GUINEA

GEOGRAPHY Papua New Guinea is an independent country in the Pacific Ocean, north of Australia. It is part of a Pacific island region called Melanesia. Papua New Guinea includes the eastern part of New Guinea, the Bismarck Archipelago, the northern Solomon Islands, the D'Entrecasteaux Islands, and the Louisiade Archipelago. The land is largely mountainous.

Papua New Guinea has a tropical climate, with high temperatures throughout the year. Most of the rain occurs during the monsoon season (from December to April), when the northwesterly winds blow. Winds blow from the southeast during the dry season.

POLITICS & ECONOMY The Dutch took western New Guinea (now part of Indonesia) in 1828, but it was not until 1884 that Germany took northeastern New Guinea and Britain took the southeast. In 1906, Britain handed the southeast over to Australia. It then became known as the Territory of Papua. When World War I broke out in 1914, Australia took German New Guinea and, in 1921, the League of Nations gave Australia a mandate to rule the area, which was named the Territory of New Guinea. Japan invaded New Guinea in 1942, but the Allies reconquered the area in 1944. In 1949, Papua and New Guinea were combined into the Territory of Papua and New Guinea. Papua New Guinea became fully independent in 1975.

Mining is important. An important mine was on Bougainville, where a secessionist group declared the island independent. Under a peace treaty in 2001, Bougainville became autonomous and held elections in 2005. In 2004, Australia sent police to Papua New Guinea to help fight crime. They were withdrawn in 2005, following a Supreme Court ruling that their presence was unconstitutional.

The country has a "lower-middle-income" economy. Agriculture employs 70% of the people, mostly at subsistence level. Petroleum and minerals, notably copper, are major exports.

AREA 178,703 sq mi [462,840 sq km] **POPULATION** 5,941,000
CAPITAL Port Moresby **GOVERNMENT** Constitutional monarchy
ETHNIC GROUPS Papuan, Melanesian, Micronesian **LANGUAGES** English (official), Melanesian Pidgin; more than 700 indigenous languages **RELIGIONS** Traditional beliefs 34%, Roman Catholic 22%, Lutheran 16% **CURRENCY** Kina = 100 toea

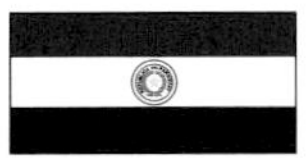
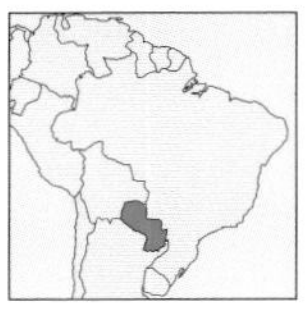

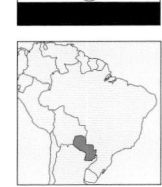

PARAGUAY

GEOGRAPHY The Republic of Paraguay is a landlocked country and rivers, notably the Paraná, Pilcomayo (Brazo Sur), and Paraguay, form most of its borders. A flat region called the Gran Chaco lies in the northwest, while the southeast contains plains, hills, and plateaux. Northern Paraguay lies in the tropics, while the south is subtropical. Most of the country has a warm, humid climate.

POLITICS & ECONOMY In 1776, Paraguay became part of a large colony called the Viceroyalty of La Plata, with Buenos Aires as the capital. Paraguayans opposed this move and the country declared its independence in 1811.

For many years, Paraguay was torn by internal strife and conflict with its neighbors. A war against Brazil, Argentina, and Uruguay (1865–70) led to the deaths of more than half of Paraguay's population, and a great loss of territory.

General Alfredo Stroessner took power in 1954 and ruled as a dictator. His government imprisoned many opponents. Stroessner was overthrown in 1989 (he died in exile in Brazil in 2006). However, the return of democracy in the years that followed often seemed precarious, because of rivalries between politicians and army leaders, together with economic problems arising partly from the severe problems experienced in neighboring Argentina and Brazil in 1999. In 2008, a former Roman Catholic bishop, Fernando Lugo, who was regarded as a champion of the poor, was elected president. His victory ended more than six decades of rule by the Colorado Party.

The World Bank classifies Paraguay as a "lower-middle-income" developing country. Agriculture and forestry, employing about a third of the population, are important. Paraguay produces hydroelectricity and exports power to its neighbors.

AREA 157,047 sq mi [406,752 sq km]
POPULATION 6,996,000 **CAPITAL** Asunción
GOVERNMENT Multiparty republic **ETHNIC GROUPS** Mestizo 95%
LANGUAGES Spanish and Guaraní (both official)
RELIGIONS Roman Catholic 90%, Protestant
CURRENCY Guaraní = 100 céntimos

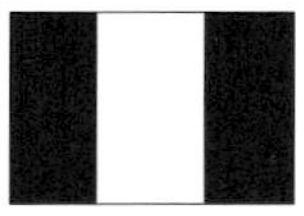
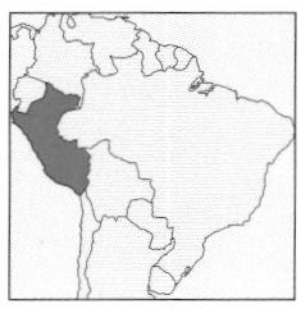

PERU

GEOGRAPHY The Republic of Peru lies in the tropics in western South America. A narrow coastal plain borders the Pacific Ocean in the west. Inland are ranges of the Andes Mountains, which rise to 22,205 ft [6,768 m] at Mount Huascarán, an extinct volcano. East of the Andes lies the Amazon basin.

Lima, on the coastal plain, has an arid climate. The coastal region is chilled by the cold, offshore Humboldt Current. The rainfall increases inland and many mountains in the high Andes are snow-capped.

POLITICS & ECONOMY Spanish *conquistadores* conquered Peru in the 1530s. In 1820, an Argentinian, José de San Martín, led an army into Peru and declared it independent. But Spain still held large areas. In 1823, the Venezuelan Simon Bolívar led another army into Peru and, in 1824, one of his generals defeated the Spaniards at Ayacucho. The Spaniards surrendered in 1826. Peru suffered much instability throughout the 19th century.

Instability continued in the 20th century. In 1980, when civilian rule was restored, a left-wing group called the Sendero Luminoso, or the "Shining Path," began guerrilla warfare against the government. In 1990, Alberto Fujimori, son of Japanese immigrants, became president. In 1992, he suspended the constitution and dismissed the legislature. The guerrilla leader, Abimael Guzmán, was arrested in 1992 and, in 2006, he was sentenced to life imprisonment. Fujimori left Peru but was later extradited, and in 2009 he was found guilty of ordering killings and kidnapping during the conflict and sentenced to 25 years in jail. In 2006, Alan Garcia was elected president. In 2009, tension arose with Chile over a disputed border.

The World Bank classifies Peru as a "lower-middle-income" developing country. Major food crops include beans, maize, potatoes, and rice. Fish products are exported, but the most valuable export is copper. Peru also produces lead, silver, zinc, and iron ore.

AREA 496,222 sq mi [1,285,216 sq km]
POPULATION 29,547,000 **CAPITAL** Lima
GOVERNMENT Constitutional republic **ETHNIC GROUPS** Amerindian 45%, Mestizo 37%, White 15% **LANGUAGES** Spanish and Quechua (both official), Aymara, other Amazonian languages **RELIGIONS** Roman Catholic 90% **CURRENCY** New sol = 100 centavos

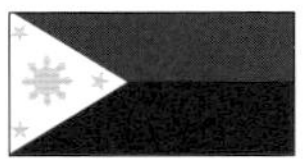
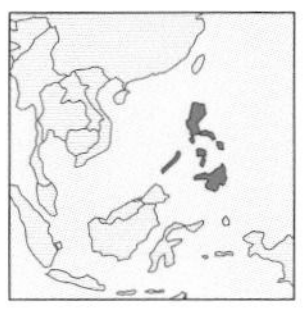

PHILIPPINES

GEOGRAPHY The Republic of the Philippines is an island country in southeastern Asia. It includes about 7,100 islands, of which 2,770 are named and about 1,000 are inhabited. Luzon and Mindanao, the two largest islands, make up more than two-thirds of the country. The land is mainly mountainous.

The country has a hot tropical climate. The dry season runs from December to April. The rest of the year is wet. Much of the rainfall comes from the typhoons which periodically strike the east coast. In November 2006, a powerful typhoon struck Luzon in the Philippines. The typhoon triggered mudslides on the slopes of Mount Mayon, one of the country's many volcanoes. The mudslides destroyed several villages and killed around 1,000 people.

POLITICS & ECONOMY The first European to reach the Philippines was the Portuguese navigator Ferdinand Magellan in 1521. Spanish explorers claimed the region in 1565 when they established a settlement on Cebu. The Spaniards ruled the country until 1898, when the United States took over at the end of the Spanish–American War. Japan invaded the Philippines in 1941, but US forces returned in 1944. The country became fully independent as the Republic of the Philippines in 1946.

Since independence, the country's problems have included armed uprisings by left-wing guerrillas demanding land reform, and Muslim separatist groups, crime, corruption, and unemployment. The dominant figure in recent times was Ferdinand Marcos, who ruled in a dictatorial manner from 1965 to 1986. His successors were Corazon Aquino (1986–92), Fidel Ramos (1992–8), and Joseph Estrada, who resigned following accusations of corruption. He was succeeded by Vice-President Gloria Arroyo, who was re-elected president in 2004. Fighting, killings, and kidnappings continued throughout the 2000s in the southern Philippines despite a series of attempts by the government to agree a peace settlement with Islamic rebel groups.

The Philippines is a developing country. Agriculture employs around 30% of the people. The main foods are rice and maize, while bananas, cocoa, coffee, sugarcane, and tobacco are grown commercially. Shellfish and sea fishing in coastal waters are also important, while manufacturing plays an increasingly significant part in the economy.

AREA 115,830 sq mi [300,000 sq km]
POPULATION 97,977,000 **CAPITAL** Manila
GOVERNMENT Multiparty republic
ETHNIC GROUPS Christian Malay 92%, Muslim Malay 4%, Chinese and others **LANGUAGES** Filipino (Tagalog) and English (both official), Spanish, many others
RELIGIONS Roman Catholic 83%, Protestant 9%, Islam 5%
CURRENCY Philippine peso = 100 centavos

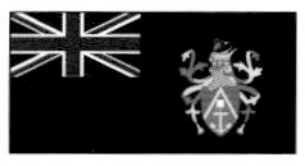
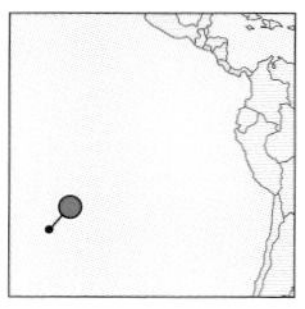

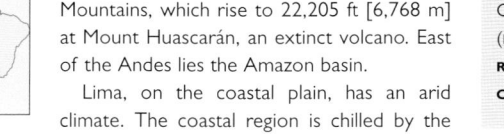

PITCAIRN

Pitcairn Island is a British overseas territory in the Pacific Ocean. Its inhabitants are descendants of the original settlers – nine mutineers from HMS *Bounty* and 18 Tahitians who arrived in 1790.

AREA 21 sq mi [55 sq km]
POPULATION 48 **CAPITAL** Adamstown

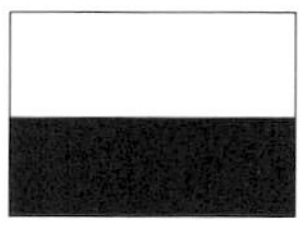
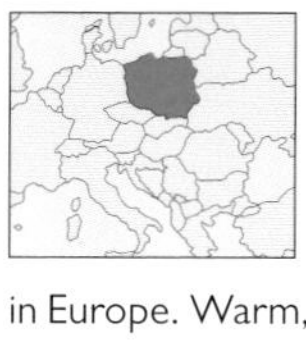

POLAND

GEOGRAPHY The Republic of Poland faces the Baltic Sea and behind its lagoon-fringed coast lies a broad plain. A plateau lies in the southeast, while the Sudeten Highlands straddle part of the border with the Czech Republic. Part of the Carpathian Range (the Tatra) lies in the southeast.

Poland's climate is influenced by its position in Europe. Warm, moist air masses come from the west, while cold air masses come from the north and east. Summers are warm, but winters are cold and snowy.

POLITICS & ECONOMY Poland's boundaries have changed several times in the last 200 years, partly as a result of its geographical location between the powers of Germany and Russia. It disappeared from the map in the late 18th century, when a Polish state called the Grand Duchy of Warsaw was set up. But in 1815, the country was partitioned between Austria, Prussia, and Russia. Poland became independent in 1918, but in 1939 it was divided between Germany and the Soviet Union. The country again became independent in 1945, when it lost land to Russia

but gained some from Germany. Communists took power in 1948, but opposition mounted and eventually became focused through an organization called Solidarity.

Solidarity was led by a trade unionist, Lech Walesa. A coalition government was formed between Solidarity and the Communists in 1989. In 1990, the Communist Party was dissolved and Walesa became president. But Walesa faced many problems in turning Poland toward a market economy, and he was defeated in presidential elections in 1995. But his successor followed westward-looking policies. Poland joined NATO in 1999 and the European Union in 2004. In 2005, a nationalist, Lech Kaczynski, was elected president. But along with other prominent Poles, he was killed in a plane crash in Russia in 2010. He had been due to attend a memorial for the Katyn massacre in World War II.

Poland has large reserves of coal and deposits of various minerals which are used in its factories. Manufactures include chemicals, processed food, machinery, ships, steel, and textiles.

AREA 124,807 SQ MI [323,250 SQ KM]
POPULATION 38,483,000 **CAPITAL** WARSAW
GOVERNMENT MULTIPARTY REPUBLIC
ETHNIC GROUPS POLISH 97%, BELARUSIAN, UKRAINIAN, GERMAN
LANGUAGES POLISH (OFFICIAL) **RELIGIONS** ROMAN CATHOLIC 95%, EASTERN ORTHODOX **CURRENCY** ZLOTY = 100 GROSZY

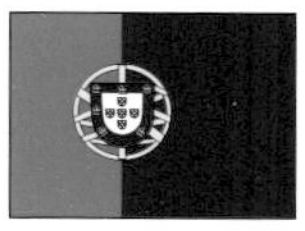

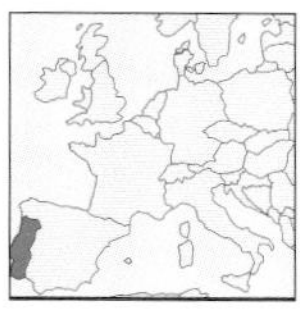

PORTUGAL

GEOGRAPHY The Republic of Portugal is the most westerly of Europe's mainland countries. The land rises from the coastal plains on the Atlantic Ocean to the western edge of the huge plateau, or Meseta, which occupies most of the Iberian peninsula. The climate is moderated by winds blowing from the Atlantic Ocean. Summers are cooler and winters are milder than in other Mediterranean lands. Portugal also contains two autonomous regions, the Azores and Madeira island groups.

POLITICS & ECONOMY Portugal became a separate country, independent of Spain, in 1143. In the 15th century, Portugal led the "Age of European Exploration." This led to the growth of a large Portuguese empire, with colonies in Africa, Asia and, most valuable of all, Brazil in South America. Portuguese power began to decline in the 16th century and, between 1580 and 1640, Portugal was ruled by Spain. Portugal lost Brazil in 1822, and in 1910 Portugal became a republic. Instability hampered progress and army officers seized power in 1926. In 1928, they chose Antonio de Salazar to be minister of finance.

Salazar became prime minister in 1932 and ruled as a dictator from 1933 until 1968. In 1974, army officers mounted a coup. The new regime made most of Portugal's colonies independent and held free elections in 1978. Portugal joined the European Community (now the European Union) in 1986, and in 2002 the euro became the sole unit of currency. In 2009, following national elections, the Socialist party formed a minority government. It announced austerity measures to reduce the country's budget deficit.

Agriculture and fishing were the mainstays of the economy until the mid-20th century, when manufacturing became the most valuable activity.

AREA 34,285 SQ MI [88,797 SQ KM]
POPULATION 10,708,000 **CAPITAL** LISBON
GOVERNMENT MULTIPARTY REPUBLIC **ETHNIC GROUPS** PORTUGUESE 99%
LANGUAGES PORTUGUESE (OFFICIAL) **RELIGIONS** ROMAN CATHOLIC 94%, PROTESTANT **CURRENCY** EURO = 100 CENTS

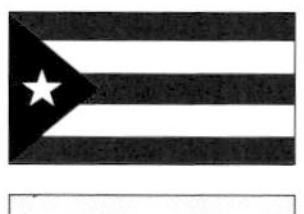

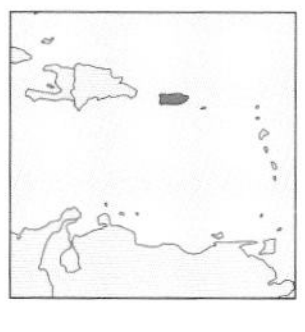

PUERTO RICO

The Commonwealth of Puerto Rico, a mainly mountainous island, is the easternmost of the Greater Antilles chain. The climate is hot and wet. Puerto Rico is a dependent territory of the USA and the people are US citizens. In 1998, 50.2% of the population voted in a referendum on possible statehood to maintain the status quo.

Puerto Rico is the most industrialized country in the Caribbean. Tax exemptions attract US companies to the island and manufacturing is expanding. The chief exports are chemicals and chemical products, machinery, and food.

AREA 3,427 SQ MI [8,875 SQ KM]
POPULATION 3,966,000 **CAPITAL** SAN JUAN

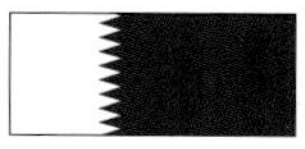

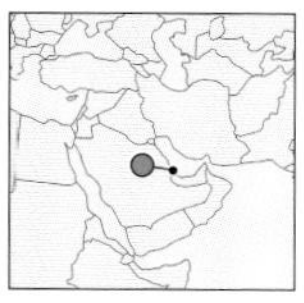

QATAR

The State of Qatar occupies a low, barren peninsula that extends northward from the Arabian peninsula into the Persian Gulf. The climate is hot and dry. Qatar became a British protectorate in 1916, but it became fully independent in 1971. Oil, first discovered in 1939, is the mainstay of the economy of this prosperous nation.

AREA 4,247 SQ MI [11,000 SQ KM] **POPULATION** 833,000 **CAPITAL** DOHA

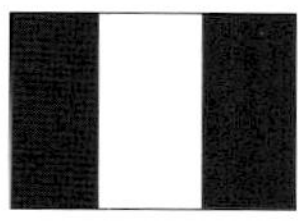

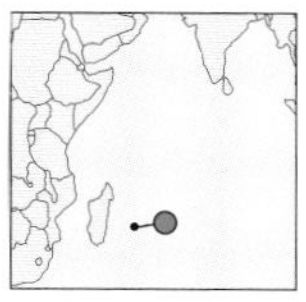

RÉUNION

Réunion is a French overseas department in the Indian Ocean. The land is mainly mountainous, though the lowlands are intensely cultivated. Sugar and sugar products are the main exports, but French aid, given to the island in return for its use as a military base, is important to the economy.

AREA 969 SQ MI [2,510 SQ KM]
POPULATION 788,000 **CAPITAL** ST-DENIS

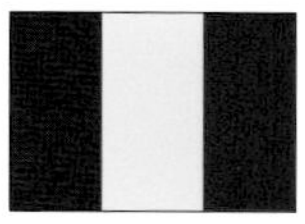

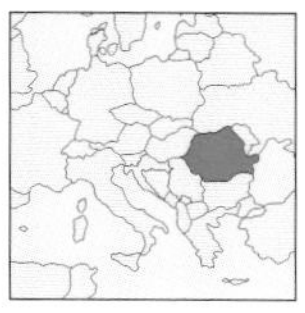

ROMANIA

GEOGRAPHY Romania is a country on the Black Sea in eastern Europe. Eastern and southern Romania form part of the Danube river basin. The delta region, near the mouths of the Danube, where the river flows into the Black Sea, is one of Europe's finest wetlands. The southern part of the coast contains several resorts. The heart of the country is called Transylvania. It is ringed in the east, south, and west by scenic mountains which are part of the Carpathian mountain system. Romania has hot summers and cold winters. The rainfall is heaviest in spring and early summer.

POLITICS & ECONOMY From the late 18th century, the Turkish empire began to break up. The modern history of Romania began in 1861 when Walachia and Moldavia united. After World War I (1914–18), Romania, which had fought on the side of the victorious Allies, obtained large areas, including Transylvania, where most people were Romanians. This almost doubled the country's size and population. In 1939, Romania lost territory to Bulgaria, Hungary, and the Soviet Union. Romania fought alongside Germany in World War II, and Soviet troops occupied the country in 1944. Hungary returned northern Transylvania to Romania in 1945, but Bulgaria and the Soviet Union kept former Romanian territory. In 1947, Romania officially became a Communist country.

In 1990, Romania held its first free elections since the end of World War II. The National Salvation Front, led by Ion Iliescu and containing many former Communist leaders, won a large majority. A new constitution, approved in 1991, made the country a democratic republic. Elections held under this constitution in 1992 again resulted in victory for Ion Iliescu, whose party was renamed the Party of Social Democracy in 1993. Iliescu was defeated in 1996, but he served again as president in 2000–4. Romania joined NATO in 2004 and the European Union in 2007. In 2008, the European Commission warned Romania over its high level of corruption and threatened sanctions unless action was taken.

Romania has a "lower-middle-income" economy. Under Communist rule, industry, including mining and manufacturing, became more important than farming.

AREA 92,043 SQ MI [238,391 SQ KM]
POPULATION 22,215,000 **CAPITAL** BUCHAREST
GOVERNMENT MULTIPARTY REPUBLIC
ETHNIC GROUPS ROMANIAN 89%, HUNGARIAN 7%, ROMA 2%, UKRAINIAN **LANGUAGES** ROMANIAN (OFFICIAL), HUNGARIAN, GERMAN **RELIGIONS** EASTERN ORTHODOX 87%, PROTESTANT 7%, ROMAN CATHOLIC 5% **CURRENCY** LEU = 100 BANI

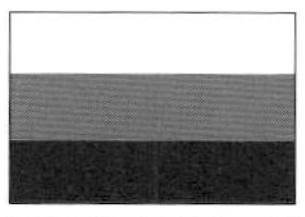

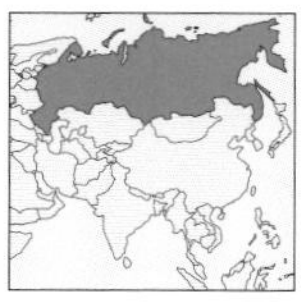

RUSSIA

GEOGRAPHY Russia is the world's largest country. About 25% lies west of the Ural Mountains in European Russia, where 80% of the population lives. It is mostly flat or undulating, but the land rises to the Caucasus Mountains in the south, where Russia's highest peak, Elbrus, at 18,481 ft [5,633 m], is found. Asian Russia, or Siberia, contains vast plains and plateaux, with mountains in the east and south. The Kamchatka peninsula in the far east has many active volcanoes. Russia contains many of the world's longest rivers, including the Yenisey-Angara and the Ob-Irtysh. It also includes part of the world's largest inland body of water, the Caspian Sea, and Lake Baikal, the world's deepest lake.

Moscow has a continental climate with cold and snowy winters and warm summers. Siberia has a harsher, drier climate.

POLITICS & ECONOMY In the 9th century AD, a state called Kievan Rus was formed by a group of people called the East Slavs. Kiev, now capital of Ukraine, became a major trading center, but, in 1237, Mongol armies conquered Russia and destroyed Kiev. Russia was part of the Mongol empire until the late 15th century. Under Mongol rule, Moscow became the leading Russian city.

In the 16th century, Moscow's grand prince was retitled "tsar." The first tsar, Ivan the Terrible, expanded Russian territory. In 1613, after a period of civil war, Michael Romanov became tsar, founding a dynasty which ruled until 1917. In the early 18th century, Tsar Peter the Great began to westernize Russia and, by 1812, when Napoleon failed to conquer the country, Russia was a major European power. But during the 19th century, many Russians demanded reforms and discontent was widespread.

In World War I (1914–18), the Russian people suffered great hardships and, in 1917, Tsar Nicholas II was forced to abdicate. In November 1917, the Bolsheviks seized power under Vladimir Lenin. The Bolsheviks set up the Union of Soviet Socialist Republics (also called the USSR or the Soviet Union).

From 1924, Joseph Stalin introduced a socialist economic program, suppressing all opposition. In 1939, the Soviet Union and Germany signed a non-aggression pact, but Germany invaded the Soviet Union in 1941. Soviet forces pushed the Germans back, occupying eastern Europe. They reached Berlin in May 1945. From the late 1940s, tension between the Soviet Union and its allies and Western nations developed into a "Cold War." This continued until 1991, when the Soviet Union was dissolved.

The Soviet Union collapsed because of the failure of its economic policies. From 1991, President Boris Yeltsin introduced democratic and economic reforms. Yeltsin retired in 1999 and, in 2000, was succeeded by Vladimir Putin. Putin, who was re-elected in 2004, sought to develop contacts with the West. He supported the US-declared "war on terrorism," though he opposed the invasion of Iraq in 2003. The secessionist conflict in Chechenia, including the occupation of a school by Muslim extremists in 2004, causing more than 330 deaths, provoked outrage. In 2005, violent incidents in the republics of Dagestan, Ingushetia, and Kabardino-Balkaria further confirmed that Russia's size and diversity make national unity hard to achieve. From 2006, relations with the West appeared to deteriorate, with Russia criticizing the expansion of NATO in Eastern Europe. In 2008, Putin, having served two terms as president, was replaced by his ally Dmitry Medvedev. But Putin took the post of prime minister. In August 2008, Russia fought a short war against Georgia, which had attacked South Ossetia, one of Georgia's secessionist regions. In 2010, Muslim militants from the North Caucasus were accused of bomb attacks on Moscow's Metro. Also in 2010, Russia and the US signed a strategic arms agreement, reducing their nuclear warheads.

Russia's economy was thrown into disarray after the collapse of the Soviet Union, and in the early 1990s the World Bank described Russia as a "lower-middle-income" economy. Russia was admitted to the Council of Europe in 1997 and was also invited to attend the G7 summit in 1997. Industry is Russia's leading economic activity. Resources include oil and natural gas, coal, timber, metal ores, and hydroelectric power.

Russia is a major producer of farm products, though it imports grains. Major crops include barley, flax, fruits, oats, rye, potatoes, sugar beet, sunflower seeds, vegetables, and wheat.

AREA 6,592,812 SQ MI [17,075,400 SQ KM]
POPULATION 140,041,000 **CAPITAL** MOSCOW
GOVERNMENT FEDERAL MULTIPARTY REPUBLIC
ETHNIC GROUPS RUSSIAN 82%, TATAR 4%, UKRAINIAN 3%, CHUVASH 1%, MORE THAN 100 OTHERS **LANGUAGES** RUSSIAN (OFFICIAL), MANY OTHERS
RELIGIONS MAINLY RUSSIAN ORTHODOX, ISLAM, JUDAISM
CURRENCY RUSSIAN RUBLE = 100 KOPEKS

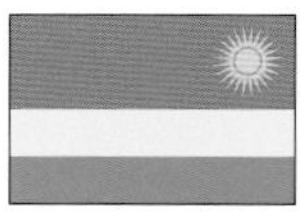

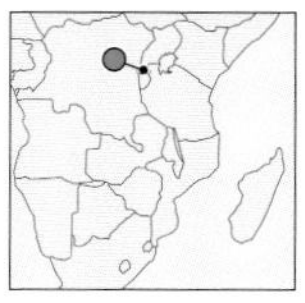

RWANDA

GEOGRAPHY The Republic of Rwanda is a small, landlocked country in east-central Africa. Lake Kivu and the River Ruzizi in the Great African Rift Valley form the country's western border.

Kigali stands on the central plateau of Rwanda. Here, temperatures are moderated by the altitude. The rainfall is abundant, but much

heavier rain falls on the western uplands, while the Rift Valley floor is drier and warmer than the rest of Rwanda.

POLITICS & ECONOMY Germany conquered the area, called Ruanda-Urundi, in the 1890s. However, Belgium occupied the region during World War I (1914–18) and ruled it until 1961, when the people of Ruanda voted for their country to become a republic, called Rwanda. This decision followed a rebellion by the majority Hutu people against the Tutsi monarchy. About 150,000 deaths resulted from this conflict. Many Tutsis fled to Uganda, where they formed a rebel army. Relations between Hutus and Tutsis deteriorated and, in 1994, between 500,000 and 800,000 people were massacred in Rwanda. After the Tutsis had restored order, Hutu rebels fled into the Democratic Republic of the Congo. Rwanda intervened in the Congo in 1996, 2002, and again in 2009. In 2009, Rwanda became the 54th member of the Commonwealth.

According to the World Bank, Rwanda is a "low-income" developing country. Most people are poor farmers. Food crops include bananas, beans, cassava, and sorghum. Some cattle are raised.

AREA 10,169 sq mi [26,338 sq km]
POPULATION 10,746,000 **CAPITAL** Kigali
GOVERNMENT Republic **ETHNIC GROUPS** Hutu 84%, Tutsi 15%, Twa 1% **LANGUAGES** French, English and Kinyarwanda (all official) **RELIGIONS** Roman Catholic 57%, Protestant 26%, Adventist 11%, Islam 5% **CURRENCY** Rwandan franc = 100 centimes

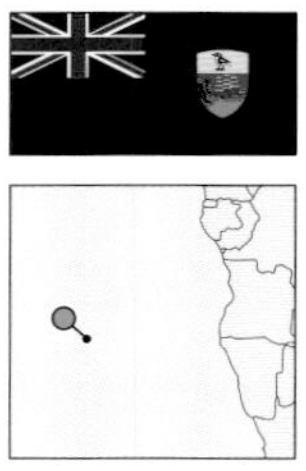

ST HELENA

St Helena, which became a British colony in 1834, is an isolated volcanic island in the south Atlantic Ocean. Now a British overseas territory, it is also the administrative center of Ascension and Tristan da Cunha.

AREA 47 sq mi [122 sq km]
POPULATION 8,000 **CAPITAL** Jamestown

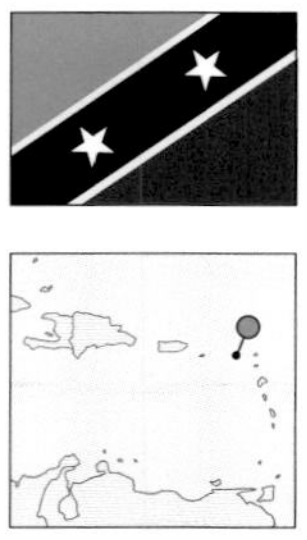

ST KITTS AND NEVIS

The Federation of St Kitts and Nevis comprises two well-watered volcanic islands, with mountains rising to around 3,300 ft [1,000 m]. The islands were the first in the Caribbean to be colonized by Britain (in 1623 and 1628), and they became an independent country in 1983. In 1998, a vote for the secession of Nevis fell short of the two-thirds majority required. Tourism has replaced sugar as the principal earner.

AREA 101 sq mi [261 sq km]
POPULATION 40,000 **CAPITAL** Basseterre

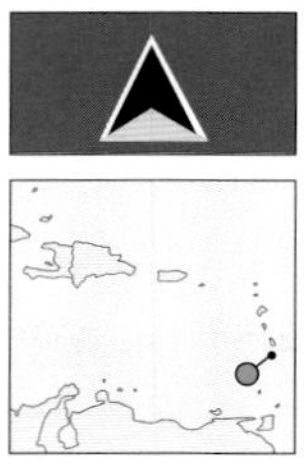

ST LUCIA

St Lucia, which became independent from Britain in 1979, is a mountainous, forested island of extinct volcanoes. It exports bananas and coconuts, and now attracts many tourists.

AREA 208 sq mi [539 sq km]
POPULATION 160,000 **CAPITAL** Castries

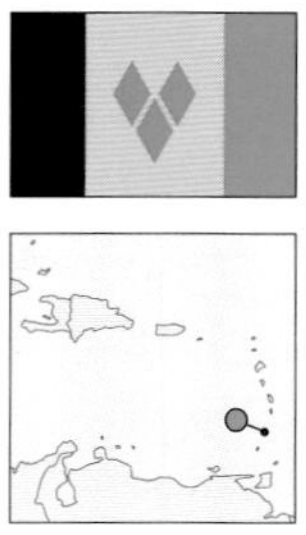

ST VINCENT AND THE GRENADINES

St Vincent and the Grenadines achieved its independence from Britain in 1979. Tourism is growing, but the territory is less prosperous than its neighbors.

AREA 150 sq mi [388 sq km]
POPULATION 105,000 **CAPITAL** Kingstown

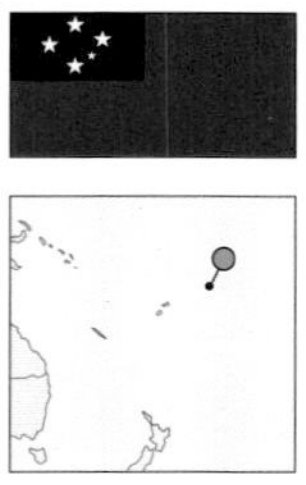

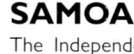

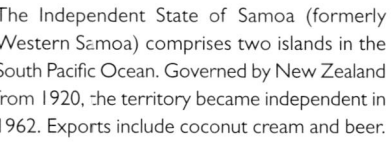

SAMOA

The Independent State of Samoa (formerly Western Samoa) comprises two islands in the South Pacific Ocean. Governed by New Zealand from 1920, the territory became independent in 1962. Exports include coconut cream and beer.

AREA 1,093 sq mi [2,831 sq km]
POPULATION 220,000 **CAPITAL** Apia

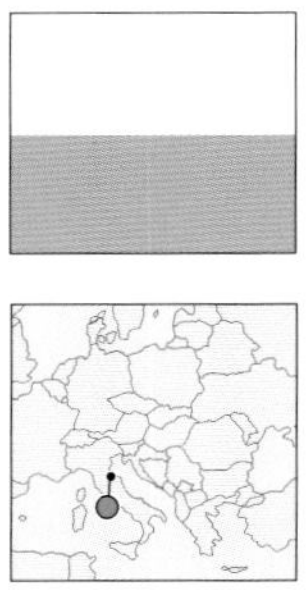

SAN MARINO

San Marino in northern Italy has been independent since 885 and a republic since the 14th century. It is the world's oldest republic. It has a friendship and cooperation treaty with Italy dating back to 1862. The state is governed by an elected council and has its own legal system. It has no armed forces and the police are "hired" from the Italian constabulary. The chief occupations are tourism, limestone quarrying, textiles, and wine-making.

AREA 24 sq mi [61 sq km] **POPULATION** 30,000 **CAPITAL** San Marino

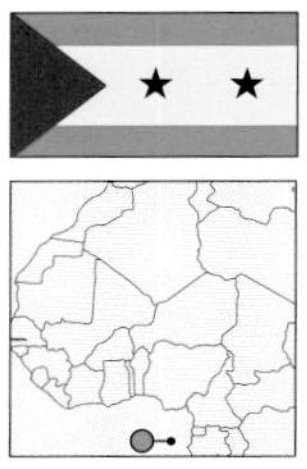

SÃO TOMÉ AND PRÍNCIPE

The Democratic Republic of São Tomé and Príncipe, a mountainous island territory west of Gabon, became a Portuguese colony in 1522. Following independence in 1975, the islands became a one-party Marxist state, but multiparty elections were held from 1991.

AREA 372 sq mi [964 sq km] **POPULATION** 213,000 **CAPITAL** São Tomé

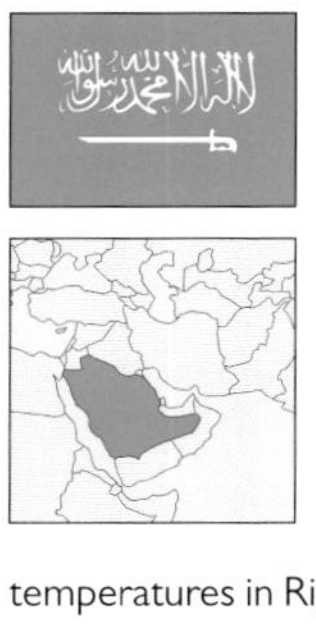

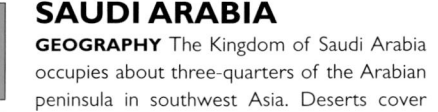

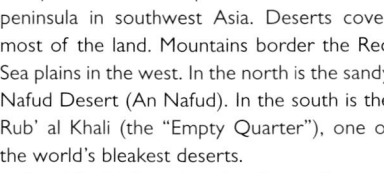

SAUDI ARABIA

GEOGRAPHY The Kingdom of Saudi Arabia occupies about three-quarters of the Arabian peninsula in southwest Asia. Deserts cover most of the land. Mountains border the Red Sea plains in the west. In the north is the sandy Nafud Desert (An Nafud). In the south is the Rub' al Khali (the "Empty Quarter"), one of the world's bleakest deserts.

Saudi Arabia has a hot dry climate. Summer temperatures in Riyadh often exceed 104°F [40°C]. Nights are cool.

POLITICS & ECONOMY Saudi Arabia contains the two holiest places in Islam – Mecca (or Makka), the birthplace of the Prophet Muhammad in AD 570, and Medina (Al Madinah) where Muhammad went in 622. These places are visited by many pilgrims.

Saudi Arabia was poor until the oil industry began to operate on the eastern plains in 1933. Oil revenues have been used to develop the country and Saudi Arabia has given aid to poorer Arab nations. The monarch has supreme authority and Saudi Arabia has no formal constitution. Saudi Arabia supported Iraq against Iran in 1980–8. But when Iraq invaded Kuwait in 1990, it joined the alliance against Iraq. Many of the alleged terrorists involved in the terrorist attacks on the US on September 11, 2001, were Saudi nationals. Saudi Arabia condemned the violence and, from 2003, Islamists launched attacks inside Saudi Arabia. In 2010, about 100 people suspected of links to al Qaida were arrested. In 2009 and 2010, Saudi troops clashed with Yemeni rebels along Yemen's northern border.

Saudi Arabia has about 25% of the world's known oil reserves and oil products make up about 90% of its exports. Agriculture remains important. Irrigation and desalination schemes have increased crop production.

AREA 829,995 sq mi [2,149,690 sq km]
POPULATION 28,687,000 **CAPITAL** Riyadh
GOVERNMENT Absolute monarchy with consultative assembly
ETHNIC GROUPS Arab 90%, Afro-Asian 10%
LANGUAGES Arabic (official)
RELIGIONS Islam 100%
CURRENCY Saudi riyal = 100 halalas

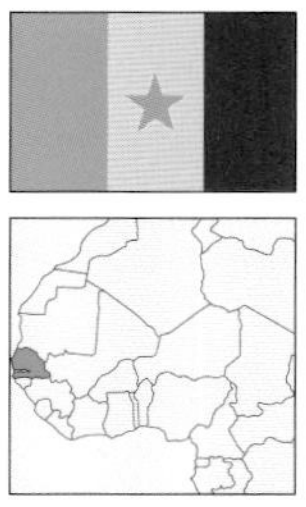

SENEGAL

GEOGRAPHY The Republic of Senegal is on the northwest coast of Africa. The volcanic Cape Verde (Cap Vert), on which Dakar stands, is the most westerly point in Africa. Plains cover most of Senegal, though the land rises gently in the southeast.

Dakar has a tropical climate, with a short rainy season between July and October.

POLITICS & ECONOMY In 1882, Senegal became a French colony, and from 1895 it was ruled as part of French West Africa, the capital of which, Dakar, developed as a major port and city.

In 1959, Senegal joined French Sudan (now Mali) to form the Federation of Mali. But Senegal withdrew in 1960 and became the separate Republic of Senegal. Its first president, Léopold Sédar Senghor, served until 1981, when he was succeeded by Abdou Diouf. However, in 2000, Diouf was defeated in elections by Abdoulaye Wade. In 2001, the government signed a peace treaty with separatist rebels in the southern Casamance province, but sporadic violence continued throughout the 2000s.

In the past, Senegal has usually enjoyed close relations with The Gambia, despite their differing traditions. In 1981, Senegalese troops put down an attempted coup in The Gambia and, in 1982, the countries set up a defense alliance, called the Confederation of Senegambia. But this alliance was dissolved in 1989.

According to the World Bank, Senegal is a "lower-middle-income" developing country. It was badly hit in the 1960s and 1970s by droughts, which caused starvation. Agriculture still employs 65% of the population, though many farmers produce little more than they need to feed their families. Food crops include groundnuts, millet, and rice. Phosphates are the country's chief resource, but Senegal also refines oil which it imports from Gabon and Nigeria. Dakar is a busy port and has many industries.

AREA 75,954 sq mi [196,722 sq km]
POPULATION 13,712,000 **CAPITAL** Dakar
GOVERNMENT Multiparty republic
ETHNIC GROUPS Wolof 44%, Pular 24%, Serer 15%
LANGUAGES French (official), tribal languages
RELIGIONS Islam 94%, Christianity (mainly Roman Catholic) 5%, traditional beliefs 1%
CURRENCY CFA franc = 100 centimes

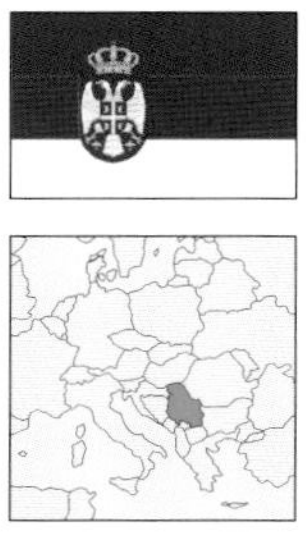

SERBIA

GEOGRAPHY The Republic of Serbia lies in the central Balkan peninsula. A landlocked country, it contains large fertile lowlands drained by the River Danube and its tributaries, with uplands in the south. Most of Serbia has a continental climate, with cold, snowy winters and hot, dry summers. Heavy rains fall in the spring and the fall.

POLITICS & ECONOMY Around 1,500 years ago, South Slavs moved into the Balkan peninsula, and each group founded its own state. Serbia came under the Turkish Ottoman Empire in the 15th century. In the 19th century, many Slavs worked for independence and Slavic unity. In 1914 Austria–Hungary declared war on Serbia, blaming it for the assassination of Archduke Franz Ferdinand of Austria–Hungary. In 1918, the South Slavs united in the Kingdom of the Serbs, Croats, and Slovenes, which was renamed Yugoslavia in 1929. Germany invaded in 1941, but Communist partisans, led by Josip Broz Tito, took power in 1945.

From 1945, the country became the Federal People's Republic of Yugoslavia. In 1991–2, the country split apart, with Bosnia-Herzegovina, Croatia, Macedonia, and Slovenia proclaiming their independence. The remaining republics, Serbia and Montenegro, retained the name Yugoslavia. In 2003, these two republics agreed to form the loose Union of Serbia and Montenegro. In 2006, the Montenegrins voted for full independence, and Serbia and Montenegro became separate republics. In 2008, the province of Kosovo, which had been under a NATO administration since 1999, declared itself independent. Its new status was widely recognized, though not by Serbia and Russia. In 2009, Serbia formally applied to join the European Union.

Serbia's resources include bauxite, coal, copper and other metals, together with oil and natural gas. Manufactured products include aluminum, machinery, plastics, steel, textiles, and vehicles. Crops include fruits, maize, potatoes, tobacco, and wheat. Livestock include cattle, pigs, and sheep.

AREA 29,913 sq mi [77,474 sq km]
POPULATION 7,379,000 **CAPITAL** Belgrade
GOVERNMENT Republic
ETHNIC GROUPS Serb 83%, Hungarian 4%, others
LANGUAGES Serbian (official), Hungarian
RELIGIONS Serbian Orthodox, Roman Catholic, Islam, Protestant
CURRENCY New dinar = 100 paras

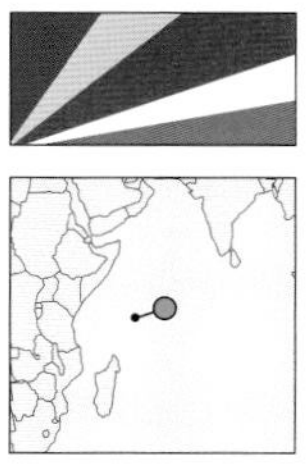

SEYCHELLES

The Republic of Seychelles in the western Indian Ocean achieved independence from Britain in 1976. Coconuts are the main cash crop, and fishing and tourism are important to the country's economy.

AREA 176 sq mi [455 sq km]
POPULATION 87,000 **CAPITAL** Victoria

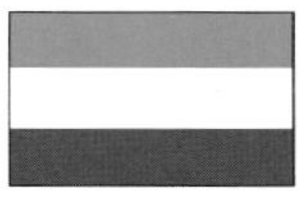
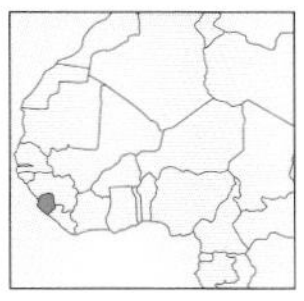

SIERRA LEONE

GEOGRAPHY The Republic of Sierra Leone in West Africa is about the same size as the Republic of Ireland. The coast contains several deep estuaries in the north, with lagoons in the south. The most prominent feature is the mountainous Freetown (or Sierra Leone) peninsula.

Sierra Leone has a tropical climate, with heavy rainfall between April and November.

POLITICS & ECONOMY A former British territory, Sierra Leone became independent in 1961 and a republic in 1971. It became a one-party state in 1978, but, in 1991, the people voted for the restoration of democracy. The military seized power in 1992 and a civil war caused much destruction in 1994–5. Elections in 1996 were followed by another military coup. In 1998, the West African Peace Force restored the deposed President Ahmed Tejan Kabbah. In 1999, a peace agreement followed further conflict. As part of this agreement, Foday Sankoh, one of the rebel leaders, became vice-president. However, he was arrested in 2000 and charged with war crimes. Conflict resumed, but another ceasefire was agreed. In 2004, President Kabbah declared a successful end to the disarmament process. The last of the UN forces left the country in 2005 and national elections were held in 2007.

Sierra Leone has a "low-income" economy. About 58% of the people live by farming, mainly at subsistence level. The leading exports are minerals, including diamonds, bauxite, and rutile (titanium ore). The country has few manufacturing industries.

AREA 27,699 SQ MI [71,740 SQ KM]
POPULATION 5,132,000 **CAPITAL** FREETOWN
GOVERNMENT SINGLE-PARTY REPUBLIC **ETHNIC GROUPS** NATIVE AFRICAN TRIBES 90% **LANGUAGES** ENGLISH (OFFICIAL), MENDE, TEMNE, KRIO
RELIGIONS ISLAM 60%, TRADITIONAL BELIEFS 30%, CHRISTIANITY 10%
CURRENCY LEONE = 100 CENTS

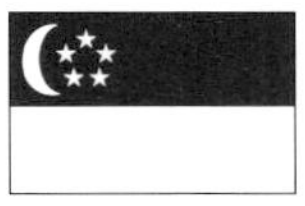
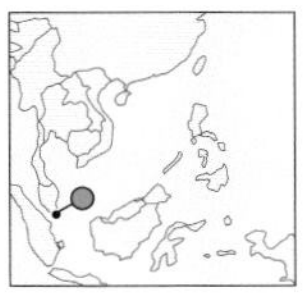

SINGAPORE

GEOGRAPHY The Republic of Singapore is an island country at the southern tip of the Malay peninsula. It consists of the large Singapore Island and 58 small islands, 20 of which are inhabited. The climate is hot and humid. Temperatures are high and rainfall is heavy throughout the year.

POLITICS & ECONOMY In 1819, Sir Thomas Stamford Raffles (1781–1826), agent of the British East India Company, made a treaty with the Sultan of Johor allowing the British to build a settlement on Singapore Island. Singapore soon became the leading British trading center in South-east Asia and it later became a naval base. Japanese forces seized the island in 1942, but British rule was restored in 1945.

In 1963, Singapore became part of the Federation of Malaysia, which also included Malaya and the territories of Sabah and Sarawak on Borneo. In 1965, Singapore broke away and became independent.

The People's Action Party (PAP) has ruled Singapore since 1959. Its leader, Lee Kuan Yew, served as prime minister from 1959 until 1990, when he resigned and was succeeded by Goh Chok Tong. In 2004, Lee Hsien Loong, son of Lee Kuan Yew, became prime minister.

The World Bank classifies Singapore as a "high-income" economy, where a skilled work force has created a fast-growing economy. Trade and finance are major activities. The global financial crisis in 2008–9 caused great concern, but recovery was rapid. Manufactures include electronic products, machinery, scientific instruments, textiles, and ships. Petroleum products and manufactures are the main exports.

AREA 264 SQ MI [683 SQ KM]
POPULATION 4,658,000 **CAPITAL** SINGAPORE CITY
GOVERNMENT MULTIPARTY REPUBLIC
ETHNIC GROUPS CHINESE 77%, MALAY 14%, INDIAN 8%
LANGUAGES CHINESE, MALAY, TAMIL AND ENGLISH (ALL OFFICIAL)
RELIGIONS BUDDHISM, ISLAM, CHRISTIANITY, HINDUISM
CURRENCY SINGAPORE DOLLAR = 100 CENTS

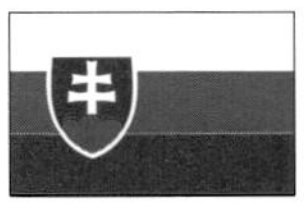
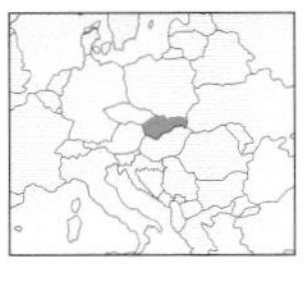

SLOVAK REPUBLIC

GEOGRAPHY The Slovak Republic is a predominantly mountainous country, consisting of part of the Carpathian range. The highest peak is Gerlachovsky in the Tatra Mountains, which reaches 8,711 ft [2,655 m]. The south is a fertile lowland. The Slovak Republic has cold winters and warm summers. Kosice, in the east, has average temperatures ranging from 27°F [–3°C] in January to 68°F [20°C] in July. The highland areas are much colder. Snow or rain falls throughout the year. Kosice has an average annual rainfall of 24 inches [600 mm], the wettest months being July and August.

POLITICS & ECONOMY Slavic peoples settled in the region in the 5th century AD. They were subsequently conquered by Hungary, beginning a millennium of Hungarian rule and suppression of Slovak culture.

In 1867, Hungary and Austria united to form Austria–Hungary, of which the present-day Slovak Republic was a part. Austria–Hungary collapsed at the end of World War I (1914–18). The Czech and Slovak people then united to form a new nation, Czechoslovakia. But Czech domination led to resentment by many Slovaks. In 1939, the Slovak Republic declared itself independent, but Germany occupied the country. At the end of World War II, the Slovak Republic again became part of Czechoslovakia.

The Communist Party took control in 1948. In the 1960s, many people sought reform, but they were crushed by the Russians. In the late 1980s, demands for democracy mounted and a non-Communist government took office in 1990. Elections in 1992 led to victory for the Movement for a Democratic Slovakia headed by a former Communist and nationalist, Vladimir Meciar, and the independent Slovak Republic came into existence on January 1, 1993.

Independence raised national aspirations among Slovakia's Magyar-speaking community, but relations with Hungary deteriorated when the Magyars felt that administrative changes under-represented them politically. The government also made Slovak the only official language. The government's autocratic rule and human rights record provoked international criticism. But the government continued to strengthen its ties with the West, gaining membership of NATO and the European Union in 2004. On January 1, 2009, Slovakia became the 16th country to adopt the euro as its official currency.

Before 1948, the Slovak Republic's economy was based on farming, but Communist governments developed manufacturing industries, producing such things as chemicals, machinery, steel, and weapons. Since the late 1980s, many state-run businesses have been handed over to private owners.

AREA 18,924 SQ MI [49,012 SQ KM]
POPULATION 5,463,000 **CAPITAL** BRATISLAVA
GOVERNMENT MULTIPARTY REPUBLIC
ETHNIC GROUPS SLOVAK 86%, HUNGARIAN 11%
LANGUAGES SLOVAK (OFFICIAL), HUNGARIAN
RELIGIONS ROMAN CATHOLIC 60%, PROTESTANT 8%, ORTHODOX 4%, OTHERS **CURRENCY** EURO = 100 CENTS

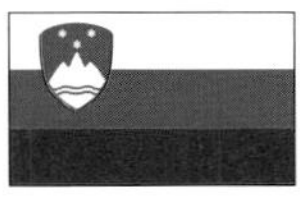
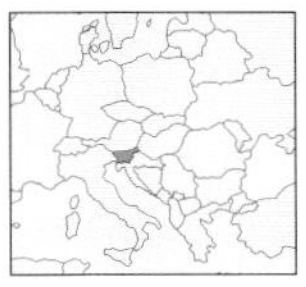

SLOVENIA

GEOGRAPHY The Republic of Slovenia was one of the six republics which made up the former Yugoslavia. Much of the land is mountainous, rising to 9,393 ft [2,863 m] at Mount Triglav in the Julian Alps (Julijske Alpe) in the northwest. Central Slovenia contains the limestone Karst region. The Postojna caves near Ljubljana are among the largest in Europe.

The coast has a mild Mediterranean climate, but inland the climate is more continental. The mountains are snow-capped in winter.

POLITICS & ECONOMY In the last 2,000 years, the Slovene people have been independent as a nation for less than 50 years. The Austrian Habsburgs ruled over the region from the 13th century until World War I. Slovenia became part of the Kingdom of the Serbs, Croats, and Slovenes (later called Yugoslavia) in 1918. During World War II, Slovenia was invaded and partitioned between Italy, Germany, and Hungary, but, after the war, Slovenia again became part of Yugoslavia.

From the late 1960s, some Slovenes demanded independence, but the central government opposed the breakup of the country. In 1990, when Communist governments had collapsed throughout Eastern Europe, elections were held and a non-Communist coalition government was set up. Slovenia then declared itself independent. This led to fighting between Slovenes and the federal army, but Slovenia did not become a battlefield. Slovenia's independence was recognized in 1992 and a coalition led by the Liberal Democrats was elected in 1992, 1996, and 2000. In 2004, Slovenia became a member of the North Atlantic Treaty Organization and the European Union. In 2009, Slovenia became the first former Communist country to assume the presidency of the European Union.

The reform of the formerly state-run economy caused problems for Slovenia. However, it has enjoyed considerable economic progress, with one of Europe's fastest growing economies. In 1992, the World Bank classified Slovenia's economy as "upper-middle-income."

Manufacturing is the leading activity and manufactures are the main exports. Manufactures include chemicals, machinery and transport equipment, metal goods, and textiles. Slovenia mines some iron ore, lead, lignite, and mercury. Agriculture and forestry employ 9% of the people. Fruits, maize, potatoes, and wheat are major crops, and many farmers raise animals.

AREA 7,821 SQ MI [20,256 SQ KM]
POPULATION 2,006,000 **CAPITAL** LJUBLJANA
GOVERNMENT MULTIPARTY REPUBLIC
ETHNIC GROUPS SLOVENE 92%, CROAT 1%, SERB, HUNGARIAN, BOSNIAK
LANGUAGES SLOVENIAN (OFFICIAL), SERBO-CROATIAN
RELIGIONS MAINLY ROMAN CATHOLIC
CURRENCY EURO = 100 CENTS

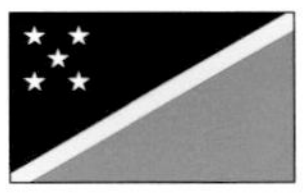
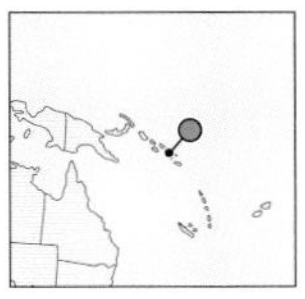

SOLOMON ISLANDS

The Solomon Islands, a chain of mainly volcanic islands in the Pacific Ocean, were a British territory between 1893 and 1978. The chain extends for some 1,400 mi [2,250 km]. They were the scene of fierce fighting during World War II. Most people are Melanesians, and the islands have a young population profile, with 40% of the people aged under 15. Fish, coconuts, and cocoa are leading products, though development is hampered by mountainous, forested terrain.

AREA 11,157 SQ MI [28,896 SQ KM]
POPULATION 596,000 **CAPITAL** HONIARA

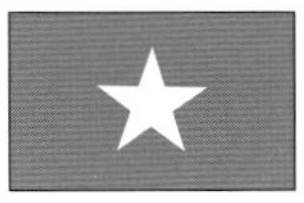
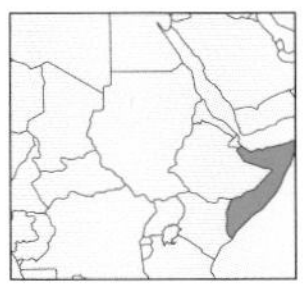

SOMALIA

GEOGRAPHY The Somali Democratic Republic, or Somalia, is in a region known as the "Horn of Africa." It is more than twice the size of Italy, the country which once ruled the southern part of Somalia. The most mountainous part of the country is in the north, behind the narrow coastal plains that border the Gulf of Aden. Rainfall is sparse, with the wettest regions in the south and northern mountains. Droughts are common and temperatures are generally high.

POLITICS & ECONOMY European powers became interested in the Horn of Africa in the 19th century. In 1884, Britain made the northern part of what is now Somalia a protectorate, while Italy took the south in 1905. The new boundaries divided the Somalis into five areas: the two Somalilands, Djibouti (which was taken by France in the 1880s), Ethiopia, and Kenya. Since then, many Somalis have wanted to create a Greater Somalia. Italy invaded British Somaliland in 1940, but was defeated in 1941. Britain ruled both Somalilands until 1950, when the United Nations asked Italy to take over the former Italian Somaliland for ten years. In 1960, the two Somalilands united to become Somalia.

Somalia has faced many problems. Economic difficulties led a military group to seize power in 1969. In the 1970s, Somalia supported an uprising of Somali-speaking people in the Ogaden region of Ethiopia. But, in 1988, Somalia and Ethiopia signed a peace treaty. In the 1990s, Somalia gradually broke apart. In 1991, the people in what was once British Somaliland set up the "Somaliland Republic," but it failed to get international recognition. The northeast, called Puntland, also seceded, while the south was riven by clan warfare. In 2004–5, a Somali parliament was set up in Kenya. In 2006, it moved to Baidoa, in Somalia (Mogadishu was regarded as unsafe). In 2006, Mogadishu was taken over by the Islamist Union of Islamic Courts, but government forces backed by Ethiopian troops defeated the Islamists. Ethiopia finally withdrew all its troops in January 2009. By 2010, the militant group al-Shabab controlled much of central and southern Somalia, while Somali pirates were a major threat to international shipping.

Somalia's economy has been shattered by war, droughts, and periodic floods. Many Somalis are nomads, who raise livestock. Live animals, meat, and hides and skins are exported. Crops include bananas, citrus fruits, cotton, maize, and sugarcane. Mining and manufacturing are relatively unimportant.

AREA 246,199 SQ MI [637,657 SQ KM] **POPULATION** 9,832,000
CAPITAL MOGADISHU **GOVERNMENT** SINGLE-PARTY REPUBLIC, MILITARY DOMINATED **ETHNIC GROUPS** SOMALI 85%, BANTU, ARAB
LANGUAGES SOMALI (OFFICIAL), ARABIC **RELIGIONS** ISLAM (SUNNI MUSLIM)
CURRENCY SOMALI SHILLING = 100 CENTS

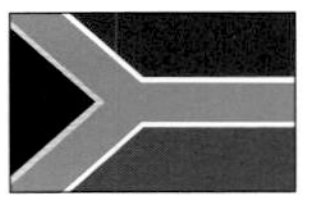

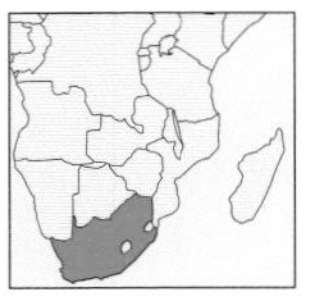

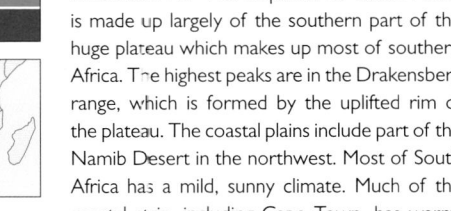

SOUTH AFRICA

GEOGRAPHY The Republic of South Africa is made up largely of the southern part of the huge plateau which makes up most of southern Africa. The highest peaks are in the Drakensberg range, which is formed by the uplifted rim of the plateau. The coastal plains include part of the Namib Desert in the northwest. Most of South Africa has a mild, sunny climate. Much of the coastal strip, including Cape Town, has warm, dry summers and mild, rainy winters. Inland, large areas are arid.

POLITICS & ECONOMY Early inhabitants in South Africa were the Khoisan. In the last 2,000 years, Bantu-speaking people moved into the area. Their descendants include the Zulu, Xhosa, Sotho, and Tswana. The Dutch founded a settlement at the Cape in 1652, but Britain took over in the early 19th century, making the area a colony. The Dutch, called Boers or Afrikaners, resented British rule and moved inland. Rivalry between the groups led to Anglo-Boer Wars in 1880–1 and 1899–1902.

In 1910, the country was united as the Union of South Africa. In 1948, the National Party won power and introduced a policy known as apartheid, under which non-whites had no votes and their human rights were strictly limited. In 1990, Nelson Mandela, leader of the African National Congress (ANC), was released from prison. Multi-racial elections were held in 1994 and Mandela became president. After Mandela's retirement in 1999, his successor, Thabo Mbeki, led the ANC to victory in national elections. In 2004, the ANC won again by a landslide. The government faced many problems, including a health crisis – South Africa has more people infected with the HIV virus than any other country. In 2007, ANC activists defeated Mbeki as president of the ANC, electing Jacob Zuma in his place. In 2008, Mbeki resigned as South Africa's president and Kgalema Motlanthe, the ANC deputy leader, became president. This opened the way for Jacob Zuma to be elected president of South Africa in the 2009 elections.

South Africa is Africa's most developed country. However, most of the black people are poor, with low standards of living. Natural resources include diamonds, gold, and many other metals. Mining and manufacturing are the most valuable activities.

AREA 471,442 sq mi [1,221,037 sq km] **POPULATION** 49,052,000
CAPITAL Cape Town (legislative); Pretoria/Tshwane (administrative); Bloemfontein (judiciary) **GOVERNMENT** Multiparty republic
ETHNIC GROUPS Black 76%, White 13%, Colored 9%, Asian 2%
LANGUAGES Afrikaans, English, Ndebele, Pedi, Sotho, Swazi, Tsonga, Tswana, Venda, Xhosa, and Zulu (all official)
RELIGIONS Christianity 68%, Islam 2%, Hinduism 1%
CURRENCY Rand = 100 cents

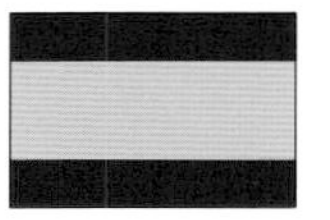

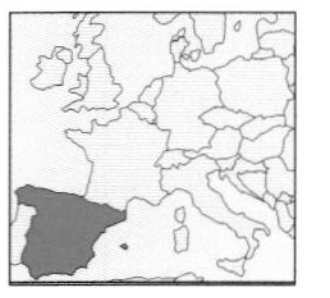

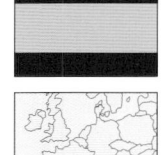

SPAIN

GEOGRAPHY The Kingdom of Spain is the second largest country in Western Europe after France. It shares the Iberian peninsula with Portugal. A large plateau, called the Meseta, covers most of Spain. Much of the Meseta is flat, but it is crossed by several mountain ranges, called sierras.

The northern highlands include the Cantabrian Mountains (Cordillera Cantabrica) and the high Pyrenees, which form Spain's border with France. But Mulhacén, the highest peak on the Spanish mainland, is in the Sierra Nevada in the southeast. Spain also contains fertile coastal plains. Other major lowlands are the Ebro river basin in the northeast and the Guadalquivir river basin in the southwest. Spain also includes the Balearic Islands in the Mediterranean Sea and the Canary Islands off the northwest coast of Africa.

The Meseta has a continental climate, with hot summers and cold winters, when temperatures often fall below freezing point. Snow frequently covers the mountain ranges on the Meseta. The Mediterranean coasts have hot, dry summers and mild winters.

POLITICS & ECONOMY In the 16th century, Spain became a world power. At its peak, it controlled much of Central and South America, parts of Africa, and the Philippines in Asia. Spain began to decline in the late 16th century. Its sea power was destroyed by a British fleet in the Battle of Trafalgar (1805). By the 20th century, it was a poor country.

Spain became a republic in 1931, but the republicans were defeated in the Spanish Civil War (1936–9). General Francisco Franco (1892–1975) became the country's dictator, though, technically, it was a monarchy. When Franco died, the monarchy was restored and Prince Juan Carlos became king.

Spain has several groups with their own languages and cultures. Some of these people want to run their own regional affairs. In the northern Basque region, some nationalists have waged a terrorist campaign. A truce in 1998 was ended in 1999 when talks failed to produce results.

Since the 1970s, regional parliaments with a considerable degree of autonomy have been set up in the Basque Country (called Euskadi in the indigenous language and Pais Vasco in Spanish), in Catalonia in the northeast, and in Galicia in the northwest. From the 1960s, ETA, a Basque terrorist group, waged a violent campaign for the secession of the Basque Country, and in 2003 Batasuna, the Basque separatist party, was banned. In March 2004, bombings attributed to al Qaida terrorists killed about 200 people in Madrid. The opposition socialists won the parliamentary elections that followed. In 2005, the government rejected proposals to make the Basque Country a "free state" associated with Spain. In 2006, ETA declared a permanent ceasefire, but this ended in 2007 and the government's campaign against ETA was intensified.

In the last 50 years, Spain has changed from one of Europe's poorest countries into a prosperous nation and major holiday destination. Agriculture employs 4% of the people, as compared with 14% in mining and manufacturing. Farmland makes up two-thirds of Spain, with forests covering most of the rest. Crops include barley, citrus fruits, grapes for wine-making, olives, potatoes, and wheat. Spain lacks natural resources apart from some high-grade iron ore in the north. Manufactures include cars, chemicals, electronic goods, food, metal goods, and textiles.

AREA 192,103 sq mi [497,548 sq km]
POPULATION 40,525,000 **CAPITAL** Madrid
GOVERNMENT Constitutional monarchy
ETHNIC GROUPS Composite of Mediterranean and Nordic types
LANGUAGES Castilian Spanish (official) 74%, Catalan 17%, Galician 7%, Basque 2%
RELIGIONS Roman Catholic 94%, others
CURRENCY Euro = 100 cents

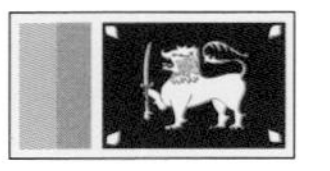

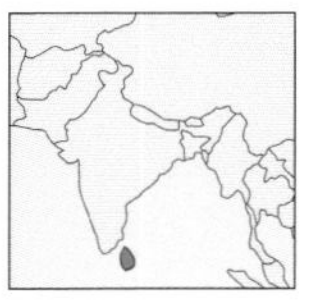

SRI LANKA

GEOGRAPHY The Democratic Socialist Republic of Sri Lanka is an island nation, separated from the southeast coast of India by the Palk Strait. The land is mostly low-lying, but a mountain region dominates the south-central part of the country.

The western part of Sri Lanka has a wet equatorial climate. Temperatures are high and the rainfall is heavy. Eastern Sri Lanka is drier than the west of the country.

POLITICS & ECONOMY From the early 16th century, Ceylon (as Sri Lanka was then known) was ruled successively by the Portuguese, Dutch, and British. Independence was achieved in 1948 and the country was renamed Sri Lanka in 1972.

After independence, rivalries between the two main ethnic groups, the Sinhalese and Tamils, marred progress. In the 1950s, the government made Sinhala the official language. Following protests, the prime minister made provisions for Tamil to be used in some areas. In 1959, the prime minister was assassinated by a Sinhalese extremist and he was succeeded by Sirimavo Bandanaraike, the world's first woman prime minister.

Conflict between Tamils and Sinhalese continued in the 1970s and 1980s. In 1987, India helped to engineer a ceasefire. Indian troops arrived to enforce the agreement, but withdrew in 1990 after failing to subdue the main guerrilla group, the Tamil Tigers, who wanted to set up an independent Tamil homeland in northern Sri Lanka. In 1993, the country's president was assassinated by a suspected Tamil separatist. Offensives against the Tamil Tigers continued until hopes of peace were raised in 2002, with the signing of a ceasefire. In late 2004, a tsunami, caused by a sudden movement of the plates underlying the eastern Indian Ocean, struck parts of the coast of Sri Lanka, killing more than 30,000 people. The Tamil Tigers were finally defeated in May 2009, and in 2010 Mahinda Rajapaksa was re-elected president of Sri Lanka.

Sri Lanka is classed as a "low-income" economy. Agriculture employs about 28% of the people. Coconuts, rubber, and tea are exported, but rice is the main food crop. Factories process farm products and manufacture textiles.

AREA 25,332 sq mi [65,610 sq km]
POPULATION 21,325,000 **CAPITAL** Colombo
GOVERNMENT Multiparty republic
ETHNIC GROUPS Sinhalese 74%, Tamil 18%, Moor 7%
LANGUAGES Sinhala and Tamil (both official)
RELIGIONS Buddhism 70%, Hinduism 15%, Christianity 8%, Islam 7%
CURRENCY Sri Lankan rupee = 100 cents

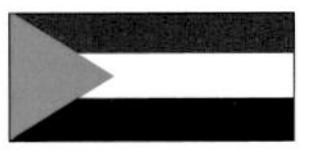

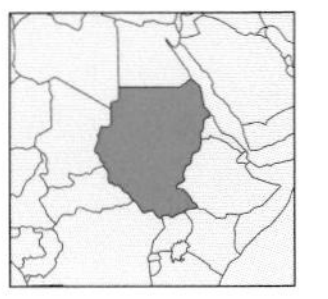

SUDAN

GEOGRAPHY The Republic of Sudan is the largest country in Africa. From north to south, it spans a vast area extending from the arid Sahara in the north to the wet equatorial region in the south. The land is mostly flat, with the highest mountains in the far south. The main physical feature is the River Nile. The north is virtually rainless, while the south has a wet equatorial climate.

POLITICS & ECONOMY In the 19th century, Egypt gradually took over Sudan. In 1881, a Muslim religious teacher, the Mahdi ("divinely appointed guide"), led an uprising. Britain and Egypt put the rebellion down in 1898. In 1899, they agreed to rule Sudan jointly as a condominium. After independence in 1952, the black Africans in the south, who were either Christians or followers of traditional religions, feared domination by the Muslim north. They objected to Arabic becoming the sole official language and, in 1964, civil war broke out. The war ended in 1972, when the south was granted regional self-government.

In 1983, the announcement that Islamic law would apply throughout Sudan sparked off further resistance from the rebel Sudan People's Liberation Army (SPLA) in the south. In 1998, Sudan's government announced that it accepted the idea of a referendum in the south. In 2005, a peace agreement was signed, bringing peace to the south. Since 2003, another conflict has raged in the western province of Darfur, where government-backed militias battled with local rebel forces. In 2008, the International Criminal Court charged Sudan's President Omar al-Bashir with war crimes, but, in 2010, al-Bashir was re-elected president in national elections.

Agriculture employs 57% of the people and cotton is the chief crop. Cotton, gum arabic, and sesame seeds are exported, but the most valuable exports are oil and oil products. Manufacturing industries produce items mainly for home consumption.

AREA 967,494 sq mi [2,505,813 sq km]
POPULATION 41,088,000 **CAPITAL** Khartoum
GOVERNMENT Military regime **ETHNIC GROUPS** Black 52%, Arab 39%, Beja 6%, others **LANGUAGES** Arabic (official), Nubian, Ta Bedawie **RELIGIONS** Islam 70%, traditional beliefs 25%
CURRENCY Sudanese dinar = 10 Sudanese pounds

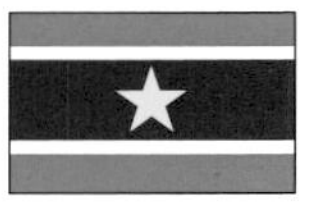

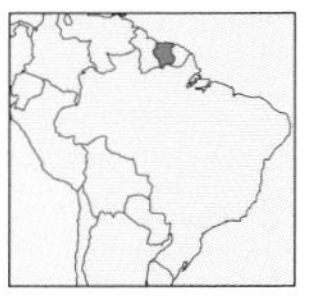

SURINAME

GEOGRAPHY The Republic of Suriname is sandwiched between French Guiana and Guyana in northeastern South America. The narrow coastal plain was once swampy, but it has been drained and now consists mainly of farmland. Inland lie hills and low mountains, which rise to 4,199 ft [1,230 m].

Suriname has a hot, wet and humid climate. Temperatures are high throughout the year.

POLITICS & ECONOMY In 1667, the British handed Suriname to the Dutch in return for New Amsterdam, an area that is now the state of New York. Slave revolts and Dutch neglect hampered development. In the early 19th century, Britain and the Netherlands disputed the ownership of the area. The British gave up their claims in 1813. Slavery was abolished in 1863 and, soon afterward, Indian and Indonesian laborers were introduced to work on the plantations.

Suriname became fully independent in 1975, but the economy was weakened when thousands of skilled people emigrated from Suriname to the Netherlands. Following a coup in 1980, Suriname was ruled by a military dictator, Dési Bouterse. The adoption of a new constitution led to the restoration of democracy in 1988, though another military coup occurred in 1990. Ronald Venetiaan was elected president in 2000 and his government replaced the guilder with the Surinamese dollar in 2004. Venetiaan was re-elected in 2005, when his New Front coalition won a narrow majority in elections.

The World Bank classifies Suriname as an "upper-middle-income" developing country. Its economy is based on mining and metal processing. Suriname is a leading producer of bauxite, from which the metal aluminum is made.

AREA 63,037 sq mi [163,265 sq km]
POPULATION 481,000 **CAPITAL** Paramaribo
GOVERNMENT Multiparty republic
ETHNIC GROUPS Hindustani/East Indian 37%, Creole (mixed White and Black) 31%, Javanese 15%, Black 10%, Amerindian 2%, Chinese 2%, others **LANGUAGES** Dutch (official), Sranang Tonga
RELIGIONS Hinduism 27%, Protestant 25%, Roman Catholic 23%, Islam 20% **CURRENCY** Surinamese dollar = 100 cents

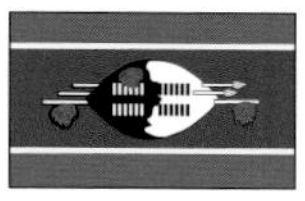

SWAZILAND

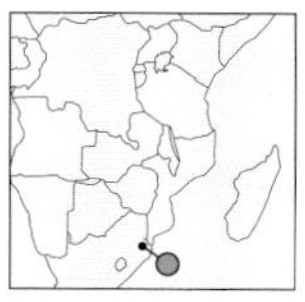

GEOGRAPHY The Kingdom of Swaziland is a small, landlocked country in southern Africa. The country has four regions which run north–south. In the west, the Highveld, with an average height of 3,950 ft [1,200 m], makes up 30% of Swaziland. The Middleveld, between 1,150 ft and 3,280 ft [350 m to 1,000 m], covers 28% of the country. The Lowveld, with an average height of 886 ft [270 m], covers another 33%. Finally, the Lebombo Mountains reach 2,600 ft [800 m] along the eastern border. The Lowveld is almost tropical, with average temperatures of 72°F [22°C] and low rainfall.

POLITICS & ECONOMY In 1894, Britain and the Boers of South Africa agreed to put Swaziland under the control of the South African Republic (the Transvaal). But at the end of the Anglo–Boer War (1899–1902), Britain took control of the country. In 1968, when Swaziland became fully independent as a constitutional monarchy, the head of state was King Sobhuza II. Sobhuza died in 1982 and was succeeded by his son, who, in 1986, became King Mswati III. Political parties were banned in elections in 1993 and 1998. Mswati ruled by decree. In 2005, Mswati signed a new constitution, but Swaziland remained an absolute monarchy. In 2008, oppositions groups boycotted elections in a campaign for multiparty elections.

The World Bank classifies Swaziland as a "lower-middle-income" developing country. Agriculture employs 13% of the people, and farm products and processed foods, including soft drink concentrates, sugar, wood pulp, citrus fruits, and canned fruit, are the leading exports. Many farmers live at subsistence level. Swaziland is heavily dependent on South Africa and the two countries are linked through a customs union. Swaziland shares two major problems with South Africa – the widespread poverty and the high incidence of HIV/AIDS. Experts have reported that Swaziland has the world's highest per capita HIV infection rate.

AREA 6,704 SQ MI [17,364 SQ KM]
POPULATION 1,337,000 **CAPITAL** MBABANE
GOVERNMENT MONARCHY **ETHNIC GROUPS** AFRICAN 97%, EUROPEAN 3% **LANGUAGES** SISWATI AND ENGLISH (BOTH OFFICIAL)
RELIGIONS ZIONIST (A MIX OF CHRISTIANITY AND TRADITIONAL BELIEFS) 40%, ROMAN CATHOLIC 20%, ISLAM 10% **CURRENCY** LILANGENI = 100 CENTS

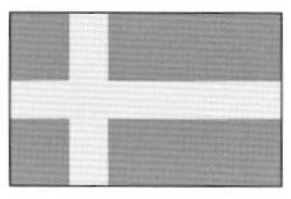

SWEDEN

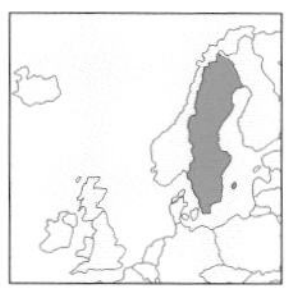

GEOGRAPHY The Kingdom of Sweden is the largest of the countries of Scandinavia in both area and population. It shares the Scandinavian peninsula with Norway. The western part of the country, along the border with Norway, is mountainous. The highest point is Kebnekaise, which reaches 6,946 ft [2,117 m] in the northwest.

The climate of Sweden becomes more severe from south to north. Stockholm has cold winters and cool summers. The far south is much milder.

POLITICS & ECONOMY Swedish Vikings plundered areas to the south and east between the 9th and 11th centuries. Sweden, Denmark, and Norway were united in 1397, but Sweden regained its independence in 1523. In 1809, Sweden lost Finland to Russia, but, in 1814, it gained Norway from Denmark. The union between Sweden and Norway was dissolved in 1905. Sweden was neutral in World Wars I and II. Since 1945, Sweden has become a prosperous country. In 1995, it joined the European Union. However, many people were sceptical about the advantages of EU membership and Sweden did not adopt the euro, the single EU currency, in 1999.

Sweden has wide-ranging welfare services. But many people are concerned about the high cost of these services and the high taxes they must pay. In a general election in 2006, a center-right alliance won 178 out of the 349 seats in parliament, defeating the Social Democrats, who had ruled Sweden for 65 of the past 74 years and introduced most of the welfare services. Fredrick Reinfeldt replaced Göran Persson as prime minister.

Sweden is a highly developed industrial country. Major products include steel and steel goods. Steel is used in the engineering industry to manufacture aircraft, cars, machinery, and ships. Sweden has some of the world's richest iron ore deposits. They are located near Kiruna in the far north. But most of this ore is exported, and Sweden imports most of the materials needed by its industries. Forestry is also important and hydroelectricity is a major source of energy. In 1996, Sweden announced the decommissioning of its nuclear power stations. The first reactor closed in 1999, followed by a second in 2005. But in 2009, the government, under pressure to diversify from fossil fuels, reversed this policy.

AREA 173,731 SQ MI [449,964 SQ KM]
POPULATION 9,060,000 **CAPITAL** STOCKHOLM
GOVERNMENT CONSTITUTIONAL MONARCHY **ETHNIC GROUPS** SWEDISH 91%, FINNISH, SAMI **LANGUAGES** SWEDISH (OFFICIAL), FINNISH, SAMI
RELIGIONS LUTHERAN 87%, ROMAN CATHOLIC, ORTHODOX
CURRENCY SWEDISH KRONA = 100 ÖRE

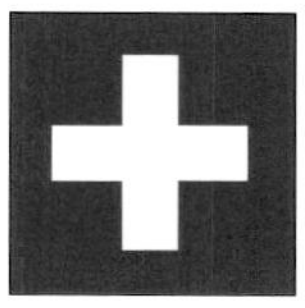

SWITZERLAND

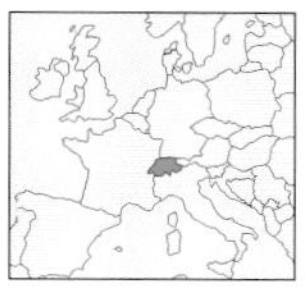

GEOGRAPHY The Swiss Confederation is a landlocked country in Western Europe. Much of the land is mountainous. The Jura Mountains lie along Switzerland's western border with France, while the Swiss Alps make up about 60% of the country in the south and east. Four-fifths of the people of Switzerland live on the fertile Swiss plateau, which contains most of Switzerland's large cities.

The climate of Switzerland varies greatly according to the altitude. The plateau has warm summers and cold, snowy winters. Rain occurs throughout the year.

POLITICS & ECONOMY In 1291, three small cantons (states) united to defend their freedom against the Habsburg rulers of the Holy Roman Empire. They were Schwyz, Uri, and Unterwalden, and they called the confederation they formed "Switzerland." Switzerland expanded and, in the 14th century, defeated Austria in three wars of independence. After a defeat by the French in 1515, the Swiss adopted a policy of neutrality, which they still follow. In 1815, the Congress of Vienna expanded Switzerland to 22 cantons and guaranteed its neutrality. Switzerland's 23rd canton, Jura, was created in 1979 from part of Bern. Neutrality combined with the vigor and independence of its people have made Switzerland prosperous. The Swiss have voted against joining the European Union, although, in 2002, the country joined the United Nations. In 2005, it also joined the Schengen group, a European passport-free zone.

Although lacking in natural resources, Switzerland is a wealthy, industrialized country. Products include chemicals, electrical equipment, machinery and machine tools, precision instruments, processed food, watches, and textiles. Farmers produce about three-fifths of the country's food – the rest is imported. Crops include fruits, potatoes, and wheat. Tourism and banking are also important. Swiss banks attract investors from all over the world. However, in January 2009, the Swiss economy went into recession owing to the global financial crisis.

AREA 15,940 SQ MI [41,284 SQ KM] **POPULATION** 7,604,000
CAPITAL BERN **GOVERNMENT** FEDERAL REPUBLIC
ETHNIC GROUPS GERMAN 65%, FRENCH 18%, ITALIAN 10%, ROMANSCH 1%, OTHERS **LANGUAGES** FRENCH, GERMAN, ITALIAN, AND ROMANSCH (ALL OFFICIAL) **RELIGIONS** ROMAN CATHOLIC 46%, PROTESTANT 40% **CURRENCY** SWISS FRANC = 100 CENTIMES

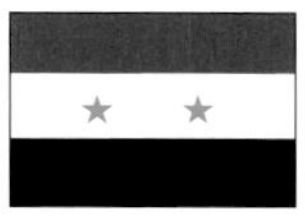

SYRIA

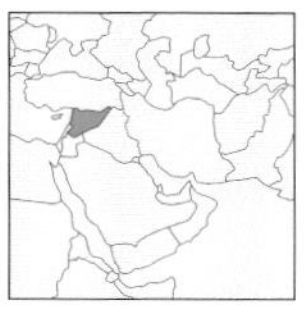

GEOGRAPHY The Syrian Arab Republic is a country in southwestern Asia. The narrow coastal plain is overlooked by a low mountain range which runs north–south. Another range, the Jabal ash Sharqi, runs along the border with Lebanon. South of this range is the Golan Heights, which Israel has occupied since 1967.

The coast has a Mediterranean climate, with dry, warm summers and wet, mild winters. The low mountains cut off Damascus from the sea. It has less rainfall than the coastal areas. To the east, the land becomes drier.

POLITICS & ECONOMY After the collapse of the Turkish Ottoman empire in World War I, Syria was ruled by France. Since independence in 1946, Syria has been involved in the Arab–Israeli wars, and in 1967 it lost a strategic border area, the Golan Heights, to Israel. In 1970, Lieutenant-General Hafez al-Assad took power, establishing a stable but repressive regime. Syria sent troops into Lebanon in 1976 in an effort to halt the civil war there, but, in 2005, following demonstrations, Syria withdrew its troops. Hafez al-Assad died in 2000 and was succeeded by his son, Bashar al-Assad. Tensions with the West continued but, in 2009, as diplomatic relations with Lebanon were restored, hopes were high that Syria's isolation might be coming to an end.

The World Bank classifies Syria as a "lower-middle-income" developing country. But it has great potential for development. Its main resources are oil, hydroelectricity from the dam at Lake Assad, and fertile land. Oil is the main export; farm products, textiles, and phosphates are also important. Agriculture employs about 17% of the work force.

AREA 71,498 SQ MI [185,180 SQ KM]
POPULATION 21,763,000 **CAPITAL** DAMASCUS
GOVERNMENT MULTIPARTY REPUBLIC **ETHNIC GROUPS** ARAB 90%, KURDISH, ARMENIAN, OTHERS **LANGUAGES** ARABIC (OFFICIAL), KURDISH, ARMENIAN **RELIGIONS** SUNNI MUSLIM 74%, OTHER ISLAM 16%
CURRENCY SYRIAN POUND = 100 PIASTRES

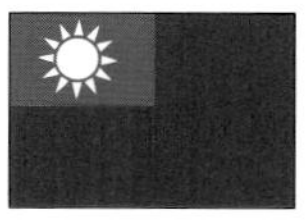

TAIWAN

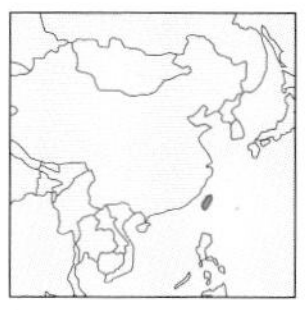

GEOGRAPHY High mountain ranges run down the length of the island, with dense forest in many areas. The climate is warm, moist, and suitable for agriculture.

POLITICS & ECONOMY Chinese settlers occupied Taiwan from the 7th century. In 1895, Japan seized the territory from the Portuguese, who had named it Isla Formosa, or "beautiful island." China regained the island after World War II. In 1949, it became the refuge of the Nationalists who had been driven out of China by the Communists. They set up the Republic of China, which, with US help, began to expand its economy. Today, it produces a wide range of manufactured goods.

In the early 21st century, the Taiwanese declared full nationhood for Taiwan. But the government of mainland China threatened to attack the territory if it did not accept the fact that it was a self-governing province of China. Relations improved in 2009, but reunification still seemed a remote prospect.

AREA 13,900 SQ MI [36,000 SQ KM]
POPULATION 22,974,000 **CAPITAL** TAIPEI
GOVERNMENT UNITARY MULTIPARTY REPUBLIC
ETHNIC GROUPS TAIWANESE 84%, MAINLAND CHINESE 14%
LANGUAGES MANDARIN CHINESE (OFFICIAL), MIN, HAKKA
RELIGIONS BUDDHISM, TAOISM, CONFUCIANISM
CURRENCY NEW TAIWAN DOLLAR = 100 CENTS

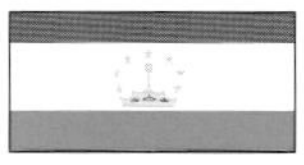

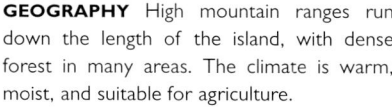

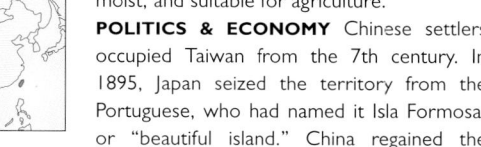

TAJIKISTAN

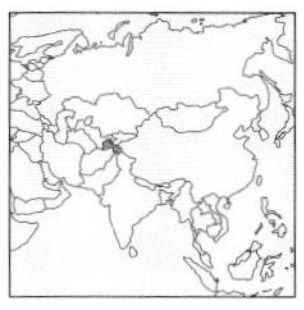

GEOGRAPHY The Republic of Tajikistan is one of the five central Asian republics that formed part of the former Soviet Union. Only 7% of the land is below 3,280 ft [1,000 m], while almost all of eastern Tajikistan is above 9,840 ft [3,000 m]. The highest point is Pik Imeni Ismail Samani (formerly known as Communism Peak or Pik Kommunizma), which reaches 24,590 ft [7,495 m]. The main ranges are the westward extension of the Tian Shan Range in the north and the snow-capped Pamirs in the southeast. Earthquakes are common throughout the country. The climate is continental, with hot, dry summers in the lower valleys and bitterly cold winters, especially in the mountains.

POLITICS & ECONOMY Russia conquered parts of Tajikistan in the late 19th century and, by 1920, Russia took complete control. In 1924, Tajikistan became part of the Uzbek Soviet Socialist Republic, but, in 1929, it was expanded, taking in some areas populated by Uzbeks, becoming the Tajik Soviet Socialist Republic.

While the Soviet Union began to introduce reforms during the 1980s, many Tajiks demanded freedom. In 1989, the Tajik government made Tajik the official language instead of Russian and, in 1990, it stated that its local laws overruled Soviet laws. Tajikistan became fully independent in 1991, following the breakup of the Soviet Union. In 1992, civil war broke out between the government, which was run by former Communists, and an alliance of democrats and Islamic forces. A ceasefire was agreed in 1996. In 2006, President Emomali Rahmon, president since 1994, was re-elected. In 2010, his party won parliamentary elections amid accusations of fraud.

The World Bank classifies Tajikistan as a "low-income" developing country and, in 2009, an international think tank warned that it risked becoming a failed state, with 70% of its people living in abject poverty. Agriculture, mainly on irrigated land, is the main activity and cotton is the chief product. Other crops include fruits, grains, and vegetables. The country has large hydroelectric resources and it produces aluminum.

AREA 55,521 SQ MI [143,100 SQ KM]
POPULATION 7,349,000 **CAPITAL** DUSHANBE
GOVERNMENT TRANSITIONAL DEMOCRACY
ETHNIC GROUPS TAJIK 65%, UZBEK 25%, RUSSIAN
LANGUAGES TAJIK (OFFICIAL), RUSSIAN
RELIGIONS ISLAM (SUNNI MUSLIM 85%)
CURRENCY SOMONI = 100 DIRAMS

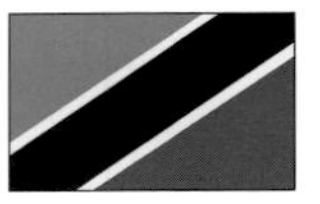

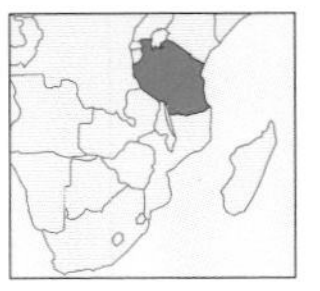

TANZANIA

GEOGRAPHY The United Republic of Tanzania consists of the former mainland country of Tanganyika and the island nation of Zanzibar, which also includes the island of Pemba. Behind a narrow coastal plain, most of Tanzania is a plateau, which is broken by arms of the Great African Rift Valley. In the west, this valley contains lakes Nyasa and Tanganyika. The highest peak is Kilimanjaro, Africa's tallest mountain.

The coast has a hot and humid climate, with the greatest rainfall in April and May. The inland plateaux and mountains are cooler and less humid.

POLITICS & ECONOMY Mainland Tanganyika became a German territory in the 1880s, while Zanzibar and Pemba became a British protectorate in 1890. Following Germany's defeat in World War I, Britain took over Tanganyika, which remained a British territory until its independence in 1961. In 1964, Tanganyika and Zanzibar united to form the United Republic of Tanzania. The country's president, Julius Nyerere, pursued socialist policies of self-help (*ujamaa*) and egalitarianism. Many of its social reforms were successful, though the country failed to make economic progress. Nyerere resigned as president in 1985. His successors followed more liberal economic policies. In 2009, Tanzania joined with Burundi, Kenya, Rwanda, and Uganda in a common market agreement, allowing free movement of goods and people between them.

Tanzania is a poor country. Crops are grown on only 4.2% of the land, yet agriculture employs nearly 80% of the people. Food crops include bananas, cassava, maize, millet, and rice. Minerals, including gold, as well as cashews, tobacco, coffee, and tea are exported.

AREA 364,899 sq mi [945,090 sq km]
POPULATION 41,049,000 **CAPITAL** Dodoma
GOVERNMENT Multiparty republic
ETHNIC GROUPS Native African 99% (of which 95% are Bantu consisting of more than 130 tribes)
LANGUAGES Swahili (Kiswahili) and English (both official)
RELIGIONS Islam 35% (99% in Zanzibar), traditional beliefs 35%, Christianity 30%
CURRENCY Tanzanian shilling = 100 cents

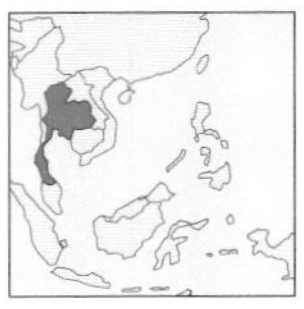

THAILAND

GEOGRAPHY The Kingdom of Thailand is one of the ten countries in Southeast Asia. The highest land is in the north, where Doi Inthanon, the highest peak, reaches 8,415 ft [2,565 m]. The Khorat plateau, in the northeast, makes up about 30% of the country and is the most heavily populated part of Thailand. In the south, Thailand shares the finger-like Malay peninsula with Burma and Malaysia.

Thailand has a tropical climate. Monsoon winds from the southwest bring heavy rains in May to October. Mountains shelter the central plains from the rain-bearing winds.

POLITICS & ECONOMY The first Thai state was set up in the 13th century. By 1350, it included most of what is now Thailand. European contact began in the early 16th century. But, in the late 17th century, the Thais, fearing interference in their affairs, forced all Europeans to leave. This policy continued for 150 years. In 1782, a Thai General, Chao Phraya Chakkri, became king, founding a dynasty which continues today. The country became known as Siam, and Bangkok became its capital. From the mid-19th century, contacts with the West were restored. In World War I, Siam supported the Allies against Germany and Austria–Hungary. But in 1941, the country was conquered by Japan and became its ally. After 1945, it became an ally of the United States.

After 1967, when Thailand became a member of ASEAN (Association of Southeast Asian Nations), its economy expanded rapidly, especially in manufacturing and service industries. In 1997, with other eastern Asian economies, it suffered an economic recession. Thailand has also faced conflict in southern Thailand, where the government has clashed with Muslim groups who feel that the government discriminates against them. In 2001, Thaksin Shinawatra, a businessman, became prime minister. In 2006, his party won a majority, the result of a boycott of opposition parties. Following mass protests, a military *junta* took power. Civilian rule was restored in 2007 and Thaksin was tried in his absence. Huge anti-government protests in 2010 showed that the people of Thailand remained deeply divided.

Agriculture employs 41% of the people and rice is the chief crop. Cassava, cotton, maize, rubber, sugarcane, and tobacco are also grown. Tin is mined, but the chief exports are manufactures and food products. Tourism is also important.

AREA 198,114 sq mi [513,115 sq km]
POPULATION 65,998,000 **CAPITAL** Bangkok
GOVERNMENT Constitutional monarchy
ETHNIC GROUPS Thai 75%, Chinese 14%, others 11%
LANGUAGES Thai (official), English, ethnic and regional dialects
RELIGIONS Buddhism 95%, Islam, Christianity
CURRENCY Baht = 100 satang

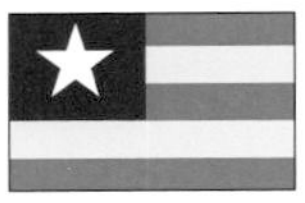

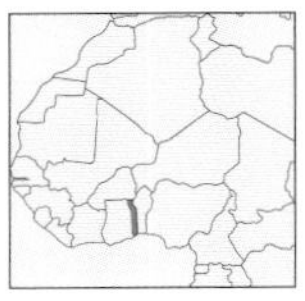

TOGO

GEOGRAPHY The Republic of Togo is a long, narrow country in West Africa. From north to south, it extends about 311 mi [500 km]. Its coastline on the Gulf of Guinea is only 40 mi [64 km] long and it is only 90 mi [145 km] at its widest point.

Togo has high temperatures all through the year. The main wet season is from March to July, with a minor wet season in October and November.

POLITICS & ECONOMY Togo became a German protectorate in 1884 but, in 1919, Britain took over the western third of the territory, while France took over the eastern two-thirds. In 1956, the people of British Togoland voted to join Ghana, while French Togoland became an independent republic in 1960.

A military regime took power in 1963. In 1967, General Gnassingbé Eyadéma became head of state and suspended the constitution. Under a new constitution adopted in 1992, multiparty elections were held in 1994. However, in 1998, the count in the presidential elections was stopped when it became clear that Eyadéma had been defeated. The opposition boycotted subsequent elections. Eyadéma died in 2005. His son, Faure Gnassingbé, took over as president, but international pressure forced him to step down. However, he was elected president in 2005 and 2010.

Togo is a poor, developing country dependent on agriculture. Major food crops include cassava, maize, millet, and yams. Phosphate rock is the leading export.

AREA 21,925 sq mi [56,785 sq km]
POPULATION 6,032,000 **CAPITAL** Lomé
GOVERNMENT Multiparty republic **ETHNIC GROUPS** Native African 99% (largest tribes are Ewe, Mina and Kabre) **LANGUAGES** French (official), African languages **RELIGIONS** Traditional beliefs 51%, Christianity 29%, Islam 20% **CURRENCY** CFA franc = 100 centimes

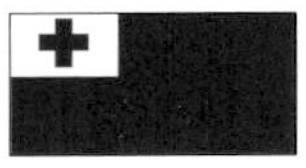

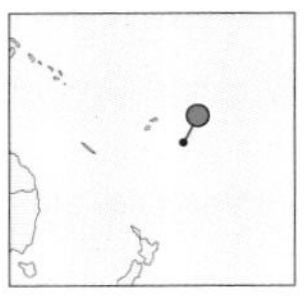

TONGA

The Kingdom of Tonga, a former British protectorate, became independent in 1970. Situated in the South Pacific Ocean, it contains more than 170 islands, 36 of which are inhabited. Agriculture is the main activity; coconuts, copra, fruits, and fish are leading products.

AREA 251 sq mi [650 sq km] **POPULATION** 121,000 **CAPITAL** Nuku'alofa

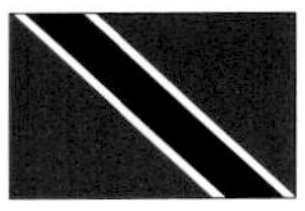

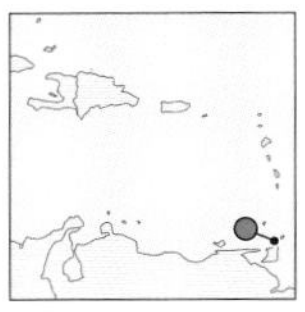

TRINIDAD AND TOBAGO

The Republic of Trinidad and Tobago became independent from Britain in 1962. These tropical islands, populated by people of African, Asian (mainly Indian) and European origin, are hilly and forested, though there are some fertile plains. Oil production is the mainstay of the economy.

AREA 1,981 sq mi [5,130 sq km]
POPULATION 1,230,000 **CAPITAL** Port of Spain

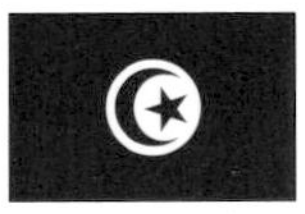

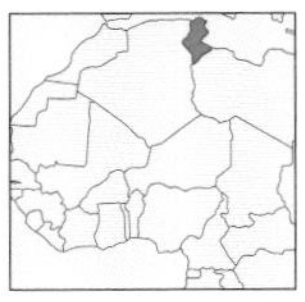

TUNISIA

GEOGRAPHY The Republic of Tunisia is the smallest country in North Africa. The mountains in the north are an eastward and comparatively low extension of the Atlas Mountains. To the north and east of the mountains lie fertile plains, especially between Sfax, Tunis, and Bizerte. In the south, low-lying regions contain a vast salt pan, called the Chott Djerid, and part of the Sahara Desert.

Northern Tunisia has a Mediterranean climate, with dry, sunny summers, and mild winters with a moderate rainfall. The average yearly rainfall decreases toward the south.

POLITICS & ECONOMY In 1881, France established a protectorate over Tunisia and ruled the country until 1956. The new parliament abolished the monarchy and declared Tunisia to be a republic in 1957, with the nationalist leader, Habib Bourguiba, as president. His government introduced many reforms, including votes for women, but various problems arose, including unemployment among the middle class and fears that Western values introduced by tourists might undermine Muslim values. In 1987, the prime minister, Zine el Abidine Ben Ali, removed Bourguiba, and became president. He was re-elected to a fifth term in 2009. In the 2000s, Tunisia's government was widely criticized internationally for its poor human rights record.

The World Bank classifies Tunisia as a "middle-income" developing country. The main resources and chief exports are phosphates and oil. Most industries are concerned with food processing. Agriculture employs 16% of the people, and barley, dates, grapes, olives, and wheat are major crops. Fishing is important, as is tourism.

AREA 63,170 sq mi [163,610 sq km] **POPULATION** 10,486,000
CAPITAL Tunis **GOVERNMENT** Multiparty republic
ETHNIC GROUPS Arab 98%, European 1% **LANGUAGES** Arabic (official), French **RELIGIONS** Islam 98%, Christianity 1%, others
CURRENCY Tunisian dinar = 1,000 millimes

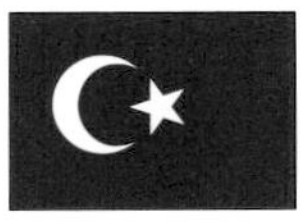

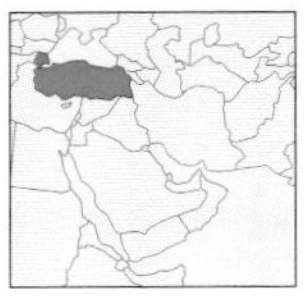

TURKEY

GEOGRAPHY The Republic of Turkey lies in two continents. European Turkey, also called Thrace, lies west of a waterway linking the Mediterranean and Black seas. Most of Asian Turkey consists of plateaux and mountains, which rise to 16,945 ft [5,165 m] at Mount Ararat (Agri Dagi) near the border with Armenia. Earthquakes are common. Central Turkey has a dry climate with hot, sunny summers and cold winters. The west has a Mediterranean climate, but the Black Sea coast has cooler summers.

POLITICS & ECONOMY In AD 330, the Roman empire moved its capital to Byzantium, which it renamed Constantinople. Constantinople became capital of the East Roman (or Byzantine) empire in 395. Muslim Seljuk Turks from central Asia invaded Anatolia in the 11th century. In the 14th century, another group of Turks, the Ottomans, conquered the area. In 1453, the Ottoman Turks took Constantinople, which they called Istanbul. The Ottomans built up a vast empire which finally collapsed during World War I (1914–18). Turkey became a republic in 1923. Its leader, Mustafa Kemal, or Atatürk ("father of the Turks") began to modernize and secularize the country.

Since the 1940s, Turkey has sought to strengthen its ties with Western powers. It joined NATO (North Atlantic Treaty Organization) in 1951 and it applied to join the European Economic Community in 1987. But Turkey's conflict with Greece, together with its invasion of northern Cyprus in 1974, have led many Europeans to treat Turkey's aspirations with caution. Political instability, military coups, conflict with Kurdish nationalists in eastern Turkey, and concern about the country's record on human rights are other problems. Turkey has enjoyed democracy since 1983, though, in 1998, the government banned the Islamist Welfare Party, which it accused of violating secular principles. In 1999, the Muslim Virtue Party (successor to Islamist Welfare Party) lost ground. The largest numbers of parliamentary seats were won by the ruling Democratic Left Party and the far-right National Action Party. However, in the elections in 2002, the moderate Islamic Justice and Development Party (AKP) won 362 of the 500 seats in parliament. Despite its Islamist roots, the AKP was re-elected in 2007. In 2007–8, the activities of the separatist Kurdish Workers Party (PKK) guerrillas lead Turkey to bomb its bases in northern Iraq. In 2009–10, the government accused some military leaders of planning a coup.

The World Bank classifies Turkey as a "lower-middle-income" developing country. Agriculture employs 25% of the people, and barley, cotton, fruits, maize, tobacco, and wheat are major crops. Livestock farming is important and wool is a leading product. Turkey produces chromium, but manufacturing is the chief activity. Manufactures include processed farm products and textiles, cars, fertilizers, iron and steel, machinery, metal products, and paper products.

AREA 299,156 sq mi [774,815 sq km]
POPULATION 76,806,000 **CAPITAL** Ankara
GOVERNMENT Multiparty republic **ETHNIC GROUPS** Turkish 80%, Kurdish 20% **LANGUAGES** Turkish (official), Kurdish, Arabic
RELIGIONS Islam (mainly Sunni Muslim) 99%
CURRENCY New Turkish lira = 100 kurus

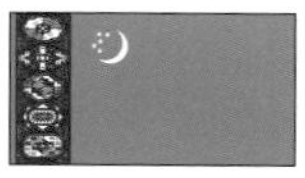
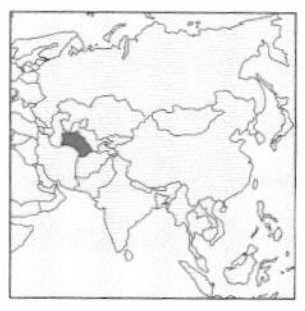

TURKMENISTAN

GEOGRAPHY The Republic of Turkmenistan is one of the five central Asian republics which once formed part of the former Soviet Union. Most of the land is low-lying, with mountains lying on the southern and southwestern borders. In the west lies the salty Caspian Sea. Most of Turkmenistan is arid and the Garagum, Asia's largest sand desert, covers about 80% of the country. Turkmenistan has a continental climate, with average annual rainfall varying from 3 inches [80 mm] in the desert to 12 inches [300 mm] in the mountains. Summer months are hot, but winter temperatures drop well below freezing point.

POLITICS & ECONOMY Just over 1,000 years ago, Turkic people settled in the lands east of the Caspian Sea and the name "Turkmen" comes from this time. Mongol armies conquered the area in the 13th century and Islam was introduced in the 14th century. Russia took over the area in the 1870s and 1880s. The area came under Communist rule in 1917 and, in 1924, it became the Turkmen Soviet Socialist Republic. The Communists controlled all aspects of life, but they raised living standards.

In the 1980s, when the Soviet Union began to introduce reforms, the Turkmen began to demand more freedom. In 1990, the Turkmen government stated that its laws overruled Soviet laws. In 1991, Turkmenistan became fully independent after the breakup of the Soviet Union. But the country kept ties with Russia through the Commonwealth of Independent States (CIS).

In 1992, Turkmenistan adopted a new constitution, allowing for the setting up of political parties, providing that they were not ethnic or religious in character. But, effectively, Turkmenistan remained a one-party state and, in 1992, Saparmurad Niyazov, the former Communist and now Democratic Party leader, was the only presidential candidate. In 1999, parliament declared Niyazov president for life. Niyazov died in 2006 and was succeeded by Gurbanguly Berdymukhammedov. He was formally elected (no opposition candidates were allowed to stand) and was sworn in as president in 2007.

Faced with many economic problems, Turkmenistan began to look south rather than to the CIS for support. As part of this policy, it joined the Economic Cooperation Organization, which had been set up in 1985 by Iran, Pakistan, and Turkey. In 1996, the completion of a rail link from Turkmenistan to the Iranian coast was an important step in the development of Central Asia. Oil and natural gas are the chief resources, and gas pipelines to China and Iran were opened in 2009 and 2010. But agriculture is the main activity. Cotton is the main commercial crop. Manufactures include cement, glass, petrochemicals, and textiles.

AREA 188,455 SQ MI [488,100 SQ KM] **POPULATION** 4,885,000
CAPITAL ASHKHABAD **GOVERNMENT** SINGLE-PARTY REPUBLIC
ETHNIC GROUPS TURKMEN 85%, UZBEK 5%, RUSSIAN 4%
LANGUAGES TURKMEN (OFFICIAL), RUSSIAN, UZBEK **RELIGIONS** ISLAM 89%, EASTERN ORTHODOX 9% **CURRENCY** TURKMEN MANAT = 100 TENESI

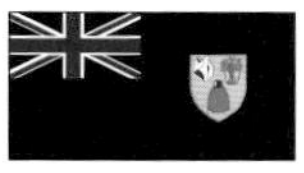
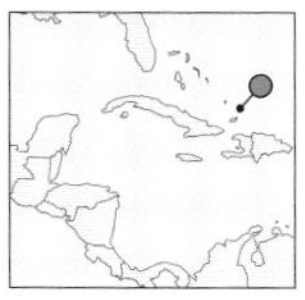

TURKS AND CAICOS ISLANDS

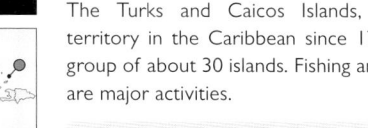

The Turks and Caicos Islands, a British territory in the Caribbean since 1776, are a group of about 30 islands. Fishing and tourism are major activities.

AREA 166 SQ MI [430 SQ KM]
POPULATION 23,000 **CAPITAL** COCKBURN TOWN

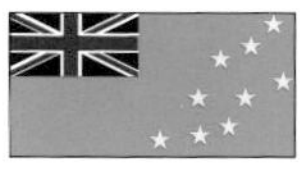
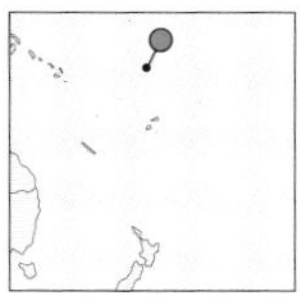

TUVALU

Tuvalu, formerly called the Ellice Islands, was a British territory from the 1890s until it became independent in 1978. It consists of nine low-lying coral atolls in the southern Pacific Ocean. Copra is the chief export.

AREA 10 SQ MI [26 SQ KM]
POPULATION 12,000 **CAPITAL** FONGAFALE

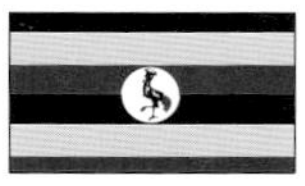
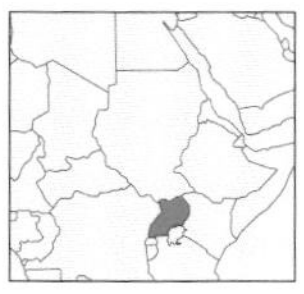

UGANDA

GEOGRAPHY The Republic of Uganda is a landlocked country on the East African plateau. It contains part of Lake Victoria, Africa's largest lake and a source of the River Nile, which occupies a shallow depression in the plateau.

The equator runs through Uganda and the country is warm throughout the year, though the high altitude moderates the temperature. The wettest regions are the lands to the north of Lake Victoria, where Kampala is situated, and the western mountains, especially the high Ruwenzori range.

POLITICS & ECONOMY Little is known of the early history of Uganda. When Europeans first reached the area in the 19th century, many of the people were organized in kingdoms, the most powerful of which was Buganda, the home of the Baganda people. Britain took over the country between 1894 and 1914, and ruled it until independence in 1962.

In 1967, Uganda became a republic and Buganda's Kabaka (king), Sir Edward Mutesa II, was made president. But tensions between the Kabaka and the prime minister, Apollo Milton Obote, led to the dismissal of the Kabaka in 1966. Obote also abolished the traditional kingdoms, including Buganda. Obote was overthrown in 1971 by an army group led by General Idi Amin Dada. Amin ruled as a dictator. He forced most of the Asians who lived in Uganda to leave the country and had many of his opponents killed.

In 1978, a border dispute between Uganda and Tanzania led Tanzanian troops to enter Uganda. With help from Ugandan opponents of Amin, they overthrew Amin's government. In 1980, Obote led his party to victory in national elections. But after charges of fraud, Obote's opponents began guerrilla warfare. A military group overthrew Obote in 1985, though strife continued until 1986, when Yoweri Museveni's National Resistance Movement seized power. In 1993, Museveni restored the traditional kingdoms. Elections were held in 1994, but political parties were forbidden. Museveni was elected in 1996, 2001, and again in 2006, when political parties were permitted. In recent years, Uganda has faced a rebel force in the north, known as the Lord's Resistance Army (LRA). Attempts at a peace settlement in 2006–9 failed, while the LRA staged a violent campaign in the Democratic Republic of the Congo and the Central African Republic.

Internal strife since the 1960s has greatly damaged the economy, but conditions improved during the relative stability of the 1990s and 2000s. Agriculture dominates the economy, employing 66% of the people. The chief export is coffee.

AREA 93,065 SQ MI [241,038 SQ KM]
POPULATION 32,370,000 **CAPITAL** KAMPALA
GOVERNMENT REPUBLIC
ETHNIC GROUPS BAGANDA 17%, ANKOLE 8%, BASOGO 8%, ITESO 8%, BAKIGA 7%, LANGI 6%, RWANDA 6%, BAGISU 5%, ACHOLI 4%, LUGBARA 4% AND OTHERS
LANGUAGES ENGLISH AND SWAHILI (BOTH OFFICIAL), GANDA
RELIGIONS ROMAN CATHOLIC 33%, PROTESTANT 33%, TRADITIONAL BELIEFS 18%, ISLAM 16%
CURRENCY UGANDAN SHILLING = 100 CENTS

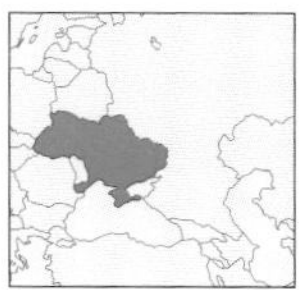

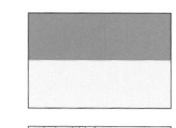

UKRAINE

GEOGRAPHY Ukraine is the second largest country in Europe after Russia. It was formerly part of the Soviet Union, which split apart in 1991. This mostly flat country faces the Black Sea in the south. The Crimean peninsula includes a highland region overlooking Yalta. Ukraine has warm summers, but the winters are cold, becoming more severe from west to east. In the summer, the east is often warmer than the west. Most rain comes in summer.

POLITICS & ECONOMY Kiev was the original capital of the early Slavic civilization known as Kievan Rus. In the 17th and 18th centuries, parts of Ukraine came under Polish and Russian rule. But Russia gained most of Ukraine in the late 18th century. In 1918, Ukraine became independent, but in 1922 it became part of the Soviet Union.

In the 1980s, Ukrainian people demanded more say over their affairs. The country became independent in 1991. Leonid Kuchma, who became president in 1994, came under fire in the early 2000s for maladministration and for his alleged involvement in the murder of a journalist. In 2005, the pro-Western leader Viktor Yushchenko was elected president. Economic problems and political infighting led to a Russian-leaning party, led by Viktor Yanukovych, winning most seats in parliament in 2006. Yanukovych became prime minister, but an election in 2007 resulted in a pro-Western coalition government led by a former prime minister, Yulia Tymoshenko. In 2010, the pro-Russian Viktor Yanukovych was declared winner of the presidential election. Tymoshenko stood down and Yanukovych's ally Mykola Azarov was appointed prime minister.

The World Bank classifies Ukraine as a "lower-middle-income" economy. Agriculture is important. Wheat and sugar are exported. Barley, maize, potatoes, sunflowers, and tobacco are also grown. Livestock rearing and fishing are also important.

Manufacturing is the chief economic activity. Major manufactures include iron and steel, machinery, and vehicles. Ukraine has large coalfields. The country imports oil and natural gas, but it has hydroelectric and nuclear power stations.

AREA 233,089 SQ MI [603,700 SQ KM]
POPULATION 45,700,000 **CAPITAL** KIEV
GOVERNMENT MULTIPARTY REPUBLIC
ETHNIC GROUPS UKRAINIAN 78%, RUSSIAN 17%, BELARUSIAN, MOLDOVAN, BULGARIAN, HUNGARIAN, POLISH
LANGUAGES UKRAINIAN (OFFICIAL), RUSSIAN
RELIGIONS MOSTLY UKRAINIAN ORTHODOX
CURRENCY HRYVNIA = 100 KOPIYKAS

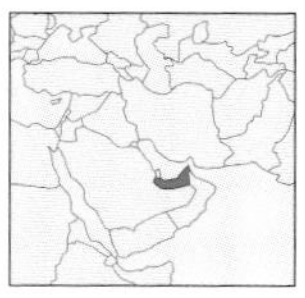

UNITED ARAB EMIRATES

The United Arab Emirates were formed in 1971 when the seven Trucial States of the Persian Gulf (Abu Dhabi, Dubai, Sharjah, Ajman, Umm al Qawayn, Ra's al Khaymah, and Al Fujayrah) opted to join together and form an independent country. The economy of this hot and dry country depends on oil production, and oil revenues give the United Arab Emirates one of the highest per capita GDPs in Asia.

AREA 32,278 SQ MI [83,600 SQ KM]
POPULATION 4,798,000 **CAPITAL** ABU DHABI

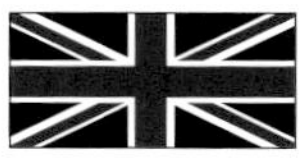
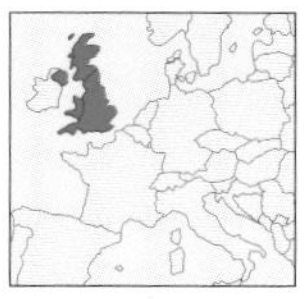

UNITED KINGDOM

GEOGRAPHY The United Kingdom (or UK) is a union of four countries. Three of them – England, Scotland, and Wales – make up Great Britain. The fourth country is Northern Ireland. The Isle of Man and the Channel Islands, including Jersey and Guernsey, are not part of the UK. They are self-governing British dependencies.

The land is highly varied. Much of Scotland and Wales is mountainous, and the highest peak is Scotland's Ben Nevis at 4,404 ft [1,342 m]. England has some highland areas, including the Cumbrian Mountains (or Lake District) and the Pennine range in the north. But England also has large areas of fertile lowland. Northern Ireland is also a mixture of lowlands and uplands. It contains the UK's largest lake, Lough Neagh.

The UK has a mild climate, influenced by the warm Gulf Stream which flows across the Atlantic from the Gulf of Mexico, then past the British Isles. Moist winds from the southwest bring rain, but the rainfall decreases from west to east. Winds from the east and north bring cold weather in winter.

POLITICS & ECONOMY In ancient times, Britain was invaded by many peoples, including Iberians, Celts, Romans, Angles, Saxons, Jutes, Norsemen, Danes, and Normans, who arrived in 1066. The evolution of the United Kingdom spanned hundreds of years. The Normans finally overcame Welsh resistance in 1282, when King Edward I annexed Wales and united it with England. Union with Scotland was achieved by the Act of Union of 1707. This created a country known as the United Kingdom of Great Britain.

Ireland came under Norman rule in the 11th century, and much of its later history was concerned with a struggle against English domination. In 1801, Ireland became part of the United Kingdom of Great Britain and Ireland. But in 1921, southern Ireland broke away to become the Irish Free State. Most of the people in the Irish Free State were Roman Catholics. In Northern Ireland, where the majority of the people were Protestants, most people wanted to remain citizens of the United Kingdom. As a result, the country's official name changed to the United Kingdom of Great Britain and Northern Ireland.

The modern history of the UK began in the 18th century when the British empire began to develop, despite the loss in 1783 of its 13 North American colonies which became the core of the modern United States. The other major event occurred in the late 18th century, when the UK became the first country to industrialize its economy.

The British empire broke up after World War II (1939–45), though the UK still administers many small, mainly island, territories around the world. The empire was transformed into the Commonwealth of Nations, a free association of independent countries which numbered 54 in 2009.

The UK has retained an important world role. For example, in 2001, it played a prominent role in creating a broad alliance to counter international terrorism following the attacks on the United

States. It was also a prominent member of the coalition force which invaded Iraq in 2003. However, the UK has recognized that its economic future lies within Europe. It became a member of the European Economic Community (now the European Union) in 1973. Membership of the EU has been important to the British economy, but some people fear a loss of British identity should the EU ever evolve into a political union. Another matter of public concern is large-scale immigration, both from the EU and outside.

The UK is a major industrial and trading nation. It lacks natural resources apart from coal, iron ore, oil, and natural gas, and has to import most of the materials it needs for its industries. The UK also has to import food, because it produces only about two-thirds of the food it needs. In the first half of the 20th century, Britain was a major exporter of cars, ships, steel, and textiles. But many industries have suffered from competition from other countries, with lower labor costs. In 2008–9, Britain's economy was hit by the global financial crisis, which led the country into recession.

The UK is one of the world's most urbanized countries, and agriculture employs only 1% of the people. Production is high because of the use of scientific methods and modern machinery. However, in the early 21st century, especially following the outbreak of foot-and-mouth disease in 2001, questions were raised about the future of rural industries. Major crops include barley, potatoes, sugar beet, and wheat. Sheep are the leading livestock, but beef and dairy cattle, pigs, and poultry are also important. Fishing is another major activity and the UK is one of the largest fishing countries in the EU. Important catches include cod, haddock, plaice, and mackerel.

Service industries play a major part in the UK's economy. Financial and insurance services bring in much-needed foreign exchange, while tourism has become a major earner.

AREA 93,381 SQ MI [241,857 SQ KM]
POPULATION 61,113,000 **CAPITAL** LONDON
GOVERNMENT CONSTITUTIONAL MONARCHY
ETHNIC GROUPS ENGLISH 82%, SCOTTISH 10%, IRISH 2%, WELSH 2%, ULSTER 2%, WEST INDIAN, INDIAN, PAKISTANI, AND OTHERS **LANGUAGES** ENGLISH (OFFICIAL), WELSH, GAELIC
RELIGIONS CHRISTIANITY (ANGLICAN, ROMAN CATHOLIC, PRESBYTERIAN, METHODIST), ISLAM, SIKHISM, HINDUISM, JUDAISM
CURRENCY POUND STERLING = 100 PENCE

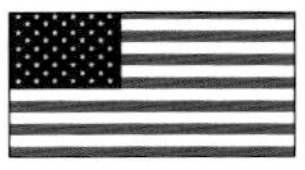
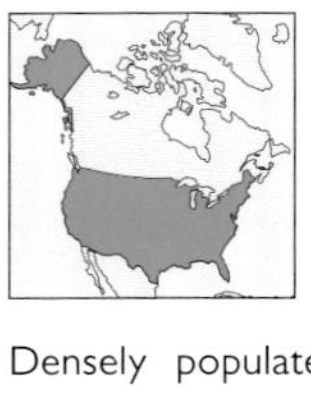

UNITED STATES OF AMERICA

GEOGRAPHY The United States of America is the world's fourth largest country in area and the third largest in population. It contains 50 states, 48 of which lie between Canada and Mexico, plus Alaska in northwestern North America, and Hawai'i, a group of volcanic islands in the North Pacific Ocean. Densely populated coastal plains lie to the east and south of the Appalachian Mountains. The central lowlands, drained by the Mississippi–Missouri rivers, stretch from the Appalachians to the Rocky Mountains in the west. The Pacific region contains fertile valleys, separated by mountain ranges.

The climate varies greatly, ranging from the Arctic cold of Alaska to the intense heat of Death Valley, a bleak desert in California. Of the 48 states between Canada and Mexico, winters are cold and snowy in the north, but mild in the south, a region which is often called the "Sun Belt."

POLITICS & ECONOMY The first people in North America, the ancestors of the Native Americans (or American Indians) arrived perhaps 40,000 years ago from Asia. Although Vikings probably reached North America 1,000 years ago, European exploration proper did not begin until the late 15th century.

The first Europeans to settle in large numbers were the British, who founded settlements on the eastern coast in the early 17th century. British rule ended in the War of Independence (1775–83). The country expanded in 1803 when a vast territory in the south and west was acquired through the Louisiana Purchase, while the border with Mexico was fixed in the mid-19th century. The Civil War (1861–5) ended slavery and the serious threat that the nation might split into two parts. In the late 19th century, the West was opened up, while immigrants flooded in from Europe and elsewhere.

During the late 19th and early 20th centuries, industrialization led to the United States becoming the world's leading economic superpower and a pioneer in science and technology. It took on the mantle of the champion of Western democracy and, following the breakup of the former Soviet Union, it became the world's only superpower. But the attacks on the country on September 11, 2001, revealed its vulnerability to terrorists and rogue states. The response was vigorous. In 2001, it attacked the Taliban government in Afghanistan, which was protecting al Qaida terrorists. Then, in 2003, it led a coalition force to invade Iraq and overthrow Saddam Hussein. President George W. Bush was re-elected in 2004, but the conflicts in Afghanistan and Iraq continued. In 2008, the Democratic Party candidate, Barack Obama, defeated the Republican John McCain in the presidential elections. Obama, the first black president in US history, faced many challenges, including those arising from the global financial crisis and the conflicts in southwestern Asia.

The United States has the world's largest economy in terms of the total value of its production. Although agriculture employs only about 1.5% of the people, farming is highly mechanized and scientific, and the United States leads the world in farm production. Major products include beef and dairy cattle, together with such crops as cotton, fruits, groundnuts, maize, potatoes, soybeans, tobacco, and wheat.

Natural resources include oil, natural gas, coal, a wide range of metal ores, and timber, especially from the Pacific northwest. Manufacturing is the single most valuable activity, employing 10.9% of the people. Major products include vehicles, food products, chemicals, machinery, printed goods, metal products, and scientific instruments. California, with its high-tech electronics industries, is the top manufacturing state.

AREA 3,717,792 SQ MI [9,629,091 SQ KM]
POPULATION 307,212,000 **CAPITAL** WASHINGTON, DC
GOVERNMENT FEDERAL REPUBLIC
ETHNIC GROUPS WHITE 77%, AFRICAN AMERICAN 13%, ASIAN 4%, AMERINDIAN 2%, OTHERS **LANGUAGES** ENGLISH (OFFICIAL), SPANISH, MORE THAN 30 OTHERS **RELIGIONS** PROTESTANT 56%, ROMAN CATHOLIC 28%, ISLAM 2%, JUDAISM 2%
CURRENCY US DOLLAR = 100 CENTS

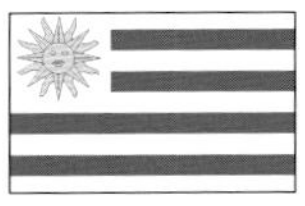
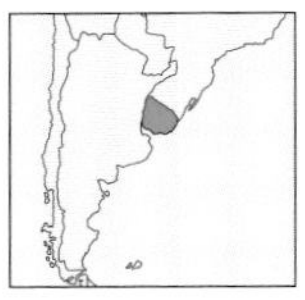

URUGUAY

GEOGRAPHY Uruguay is South America's second smallest independent country after Suriname. The land consists mainly of flat plains and hills. The River Uruguay, which forms the country's western border, flows into the Río de la Plata, a large estuary which leads into the South Atlantic Ocean.

Uruguay has a mild climate, with rain in every month, though droughts sometimes occur. Summers are pleasantly warm and winters relatively mild.

POLITICS & ECONOMY In 1726, Spanish settlers founded Montevideo in order to halt the Portuguese gaining influence in the area. By the late 18th century, Spaniards had settled in most of the country. Uruguay became part of a colony called the Viceroyalty of La Plata, which also included Argentina, Paraguay, and parts of Bolivia, Brazil, and Chile. In 1820 Brazil annexed Uruguay, ending Spanish rule. In 1825, Uruguayans, supported by Argentina, began a struggle for independence. Finally, in 1828, Brazil and Argentina recognized Uruguay as an independent republic. Social and economic developments were slow, but, from 1903, Uruguay became stable and democratic.

From the 1950s, economic problems caused unrest. Terrorist groups, notably the Tupumaros, carried out murders and kidnappings. The army crushed the Tupumaros in 1972, but the army took over the government in 1973. Military rule continued until 1984 when elections were held. In the early 21st century, Uruguay faced many economic problems, many of which were the result of the economic crisis in its neighbor, Argentina, and its imposition of banking controls. In 2009, the former left-wing rebel-turned-moderate Jose Mujica, of the governing Broad Front, was elected president.

The World Bank classifies Uruguay as an "upper-middle-income" developing country. Agriculture employs 10% of the people, but farm products, notably hides and leather goods, beef, and wool, are the main exports, while many manufacturing industries process farm products. Crops include maize, potatoes, wheat, and sugar beet. Uruguay depends largely on hydroelectric power for energy. In 2008, Uruguay announced the discovery of a natural gas field off the country's coast.

AREA 67,574 SQ MI [175,016 SQ KM]
POPULATION 3,494,000 **CAPITAL** MONTEVIDEO
GOVERNMENT MULTIPARTY REPUBLIC
ETHNIC GROUPS WHITE 88%, MESTIZO 8%, MULATTO OR BLACK 4%
LANGUAGES SPANISH (OFFICIAL)
RELIGIONS ROMAN CATHOLIC 66%, PROTESTANT 2%, JUDAISM 1%
CURRENCY URUGUAYAN PESO = 100 CENTÉSIMOS

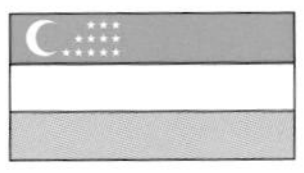
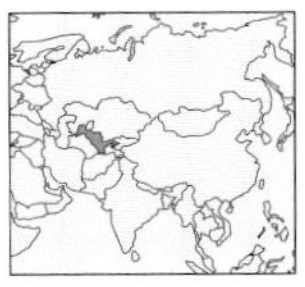

UZBEKISTAN

GEOGRAPHY The Republic of Uzbekistan is one of the five republics in Central Asia which were once part of the Soviet Union. Plains cover most of western Uzbekistan, with highlands in the east. The main rivers, the Amu (or Amu Darya) and Syr (or Syr Darya), drain into the Aral Sea. So much water has been taken from these rivers to irrigate the land that the Aral Sea has now shrunk to about a quarter of its size in 1960. The former lake area is now desert. Uzbekistan has cold winters and hot summers. The largely uninhabited Kyzyl Kum desert lies in central Uzbekistan.

POLITICS & ECONOMY Russia took the area in the 19th century. After the Russian Revolution of 1917, the Communists took over and, in 1924, they set up the Uzbek Soviet Socialist Republic. Under Communism, all aspects of Uzbek life were controlled and religious worship was discouraged. But education, health, housing, and transport were improved. In the late 1980s, the people demanded more freedom, and in 1990 the government stated that its laws overruled those of the Soviet Union. Uzbekistan became independent in 1991 when the Soviet Union broke up, but it retained links with Russia through the Commonwealth of Independent States. Islam Karimov, leader of the People's Democratic Party (formerly the Communist Party), was elected president in December 1991. In 1992–3, many opposition leaders were arrested because the government said that they threatened national stability. In 1994–5, the PDP was victorious in national elections and, in 1995, a referendum extended Karimov's term in office until 2000. He was re-elected in 2001 and 2007. Uzbekistan allowed the United States to use bases in Uzbekistan for its military campaign in Afghanistan, but it asked US troops to leave in 2005. However, in 2009 the government announced that the US could transport supplies through Uzbekistan to its forces in Afghanistan.

The World Bank classifies Uzbekistan as a "lower-middle-income" developing country and the government still controls most economic activity. The country produces coal, copper, gold, oil, and natural gas.

AREA 172,741 SQ MI [447,400 SQ KM]
POPULATION 27,606,000 **CAPITAL** TASHKENT
GOVERNMENT SOCIALIST REPUBLIC **ETHNIC GROUPS** UZBEK 80%, RUSSIAN 5%, TAJIK 5%, KAZAKH 3%, TATAR 2%, KARA-KALPAK 2%
LANGUAGES UZBEK (OFFICIAL), RUSSIAN **RELIGIONS** ISLAM 88%, EASTERN ORTHODOX 9% **CURRENCY** UZBEKISTANI SUM = 100 TYIYN

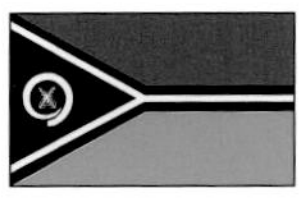
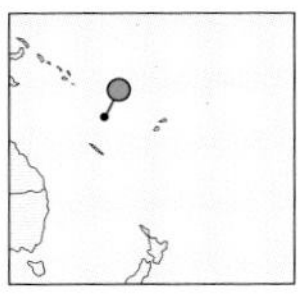

VANUATU

The Republic of Vanuatu, formerly the Anglo-French Condominium of the New Hebrides, became independent in 1980. It consists of a chain of 83 islands in the South Pacific Ocean. Its economy is based on agriculture and it exports copra, beef and veal, timber, and cocoa.

AREA 4,706 SQ MI [12,189 SQ KM]
POPULATION 219,000 **CAPITAL** PORT-VILA

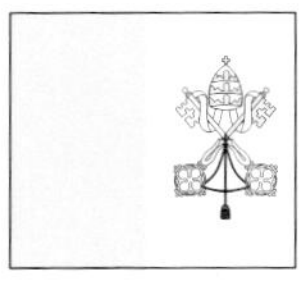
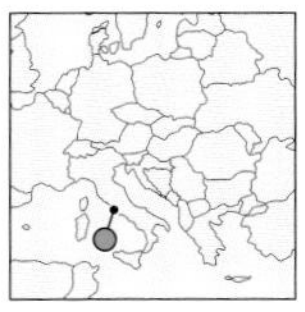

VATICAN CITY

Vatican City State, the world's smallest independent nation, is an enclave on the west bank of the River Tiber in Rome. It forms an independent base for the Holy See, the governing body of the Roman Catholic Church.

AREA 0.17 SQ MI [0.44 SQ KM]
POPULATION 1,000

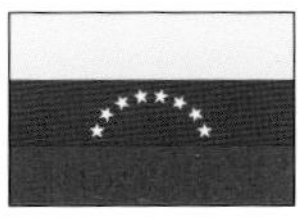
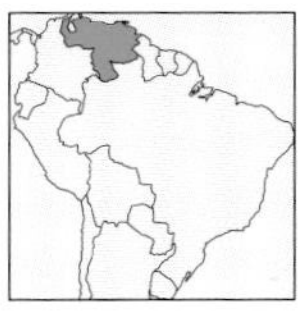

VENEZUELA

GEOGRAPHY The Bolivarian Republic of Venezuela, in northern South America, contains the Maracaibo lowlands around the oil-rich Lake Maracaibo in the west. Andean ranges enclose the lowlands and extend across most of northern Venezuela. The Orinoco river basin, containing tropical grasslands called *llanos*, lies between the northern highlands and the Guiana Highlands in the southeast. The Orinoco is Venezuela's longest river.

Venezuela has a tropical climate. Temperatures are high

throughout the year on the lowlands, though the mountains are cooler. Rainfall is heaviest in the mountains. But much of the country has a dry season between December and April.

POLITICS & ECONOMY In the early 19th century, Venezuelans, such as Simón Bolívar and Francisco de Miranda, began a struggle against Spanish rule. Venezuela declared its independence in 1811. But it only became truly independent in 1821, when the Spanish were defeated in a battle near Valencia.

The development of Venezuela in the 19th and the first half of the 20th centuries was marred by instability, violence, and periods of harsh dictatorial rule. But Venezuela has had elected governments since 1958. The country has greatly benefited from its oil resources which were first exploited in 1917. In 1960, Venezuela helped to form OPEC (the Organization of Petroleum Exporting Countries) and, in 1976, the government of Venezuela took control of the entire oil industry. In 1999, Hugo Chavez, who had staged an unsuccessful coup in 1992, was elected president. In 2004, he won a majority in a referendum that had been intended by the opposition to remove him from office. He was re-elected in 2006, and his left-wing policies continued to arouse US hostility. In 2009, voters approved plans to abolish limits on the number of terms in office for elected officials. This would enable Chavez to stand for re-election in 2012.

With oil accounting for about 90% of its exports, Venezuela has an "upper-middle-income" economy. Other exports include bauxite and aluminum, iron ore, and farm products. Beef cattle, dairy cattle, and poultry are raised. Crops include bananas, cassava, citrus fruits, coffee, and rice. The main industry is petroleum refining. Cement, steel, and textiles are also produced.

AREA 352,143 sq mi [912,050 sq km] **POPULATION** 26,815,000
CAPITAL Caracas **GOVERNMENT** Federal republic
ETHNIC GROUPS Spanish, Italian, Portuguese, Arab, German, African, indigenous people **LANGUAGES** Spanish (official), indigenous dialects **RELIGIONS** Roman Catholic 96%
CURRENCY Bolívar = 100 céntimos

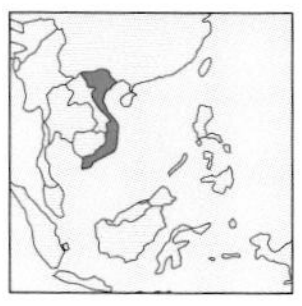

VIETNAM

GEOGRAPHY The Socialist Republic of Vietnam occupies an S-shaped strip of land facing the South China Sea in Southeast Asia. The coastal plains include two densely populated, fertile delta regions: the Red (Hong) delta facing the Gulf of Tonkin in the north, and the Mekong delta in the south.

Vietnam has a tropical climate, though the driest months of January to March are a little cooler than the wet, hot summer months, when monsoon winds blow from the southwest. Typhoons (cyclones or hurricanes) sometimes hit the coast, causing extensive flooding and much damage.

POLITICS & ECONOMY China dominated Vietnam for a thousand years before AD 939, when a Vietnamese state was founded. The French took over the area between the 1850s and 1880s. They ruled Vietnam as part of French Indochina, which also included Cambodia and Laos.

Japan conquered Vietnam during World War II (1939–45). In 1946, war broke out between a nationalist group, called the Vietminh, and the French colonial government. France withdrew in 1954 and Vietnam was divided into a Communist North Vietnam, led by the Vietminh leader, Ho Chi Minh, and a non-Communist South.

A force called the Viet Cong rebeled against South Vietnam's government in 1957 and a war began, which gradually increased in intensity. The United States aided the South, but after it withdrew in 1975, South Vietnam surrendered. In 1976, the united Vietnam became a Socialist Republic.

Vietnamese troops intervened in Cambodia in 1978 to defeat the Communist Khmer Rouge government, but it withdrew its troops in 1989. In the 1990s, Vietnam began to introduce reforms. In 1995, the United States opened an embassy in Hanoi, and in 2002 trade relations with the US were normalized. In 2007, Vietnam became the 150th member of the World Trade Organization. In the late 2000s, the economy grew rapidly. But agriculture remains the main activity. Rice is the chief food crop. Vietnam produces chromium, tin, and phosphates.

AREA 128,065 sq mi [331,689 sq km]
POPULATION 88,577,000 **CAPITAL** Hanoi
GOVERNMENT Socialist republic
ETHNIC GROUPS Vietnamese 87%, Chinese, Hmong, Thai, Khmer, Cham, mountain groups **LANGUAGES** Vietnamese (official), English, Chinese **RELIGIONS** Buddhism, Christianity, indigenous beliefs
CURRENCY Dong = 10 hao = 100 xu

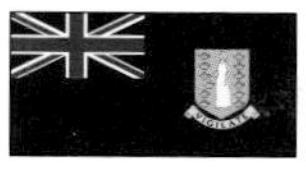
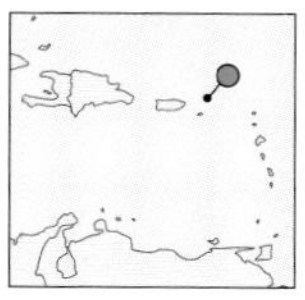

VIRGIN ISLANDS, BRITISH

The British Virgin Islands, the most northerly of the Lesser Antilles, are a British overseas territory, with a substantial measure of self-government.

AREA 58 sq mi [151 sq km]
POPULATION 24,000 **CAPITAL** Road Town

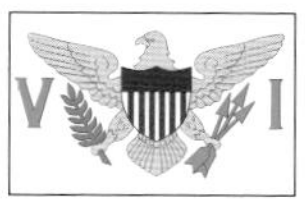
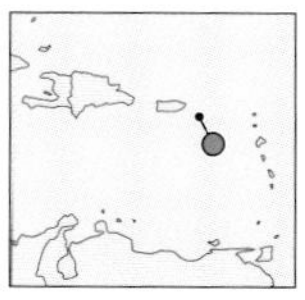

VIRGIN ISLANDS, US

The Virgin Islands of the United States, a group of three islands and 65 small islets, are a self-governing US territory. Purchased from Denmark in 1917, its residents are US citizens and they elect a non-voting delegate to the US House of Representatives.

AREA 134 sq mi [347 sq km]
POPULATION 110,000 **CAPITAL** Charlotte Amalie

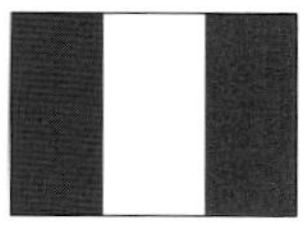
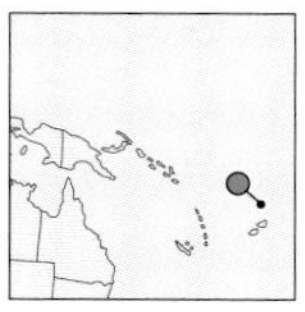

WALLIS AND FUTUNA

Wallis and Futuna, in the South Pacific Ocean, is the smallest and the poorest of France's overseas territories. French aid remains vital to an economy based on subsistence agriculture.

AREA 77 sq mi [200 sq km]
POPULATION 15,000 **CAPITAL** Mata-Utu

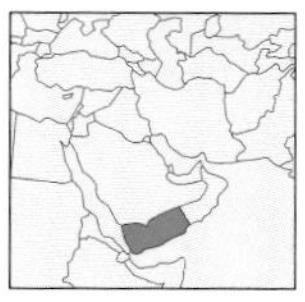

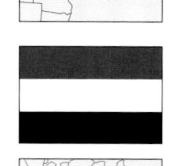

YEMEN

GEOGRAPHY The Republic of Yemen faces the Red Sea and the Gulf of Aden in the southwestern corner of the Arabian peninsula. Behind the narrow coastal plain along the Red Sea, the land rises to a mountain region called High Yemen. The climate ranges from hot and often humid conditions on the coast to the cooler highlands. Most of the country is arid. The south coasts are particularly hot and humid.

POLITICS & ECONOMY After World War I, northern Yemen, which had been ruled by Turkey, began to evolve into a separate state from the south, where Britain was in control. Britain withdrew in 1967 and a left-wing government took power in the south. In North Yemen, the monarchy was abolished in 1962 and the country became a republic.

Clashes occurred between the traditionalist Yemen Arab Republic in the north and the formerly British Marxist People's Democratic Republic of Yemen, but, in 1990, the two Yemens merged to form a single country. Further conflict occurred in 1994, when southern secessionist forces were defeated. In 1998 and 1999, militants in the Aden-Abyan Islamic army sought to destabilize the country. Conflict with northern Shi'ite rebels, called Houthis, which began in 2004, intensified in 2009 and 2010 when it spilled over the border into Saudi Arabia. The Yemeni government also faced conflict with al Qaida supporters and southern separatists.

Yemen is a developing country and agriculture employs about half of the people. Sheep are reared and such crops as barley, fruits, wheat, and vegetables are grown in highland valleys and around oases. Cash crops include coffee and cotton. Since the 1980s, petroleum extraction has been important in the economy, but by 2009, supplies were nearing exhaustion. Manufactures include handicrafts, leather goods, and textiles. Remittances from Yemenis abroad are a major source of revenue.

AREA 203,848 sq mi [527,968 sq km] **POPULATION** 22,858,000
CAPITAL Sana' **GOVERNMENT** Multiparty republic
ETHNIC GROUPS Predominantly Arab **LANGUAGES** Arabic (official)
RELIGIONS Islam **CURRENCY** Yemeni rial = 100 fils

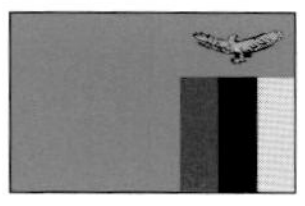
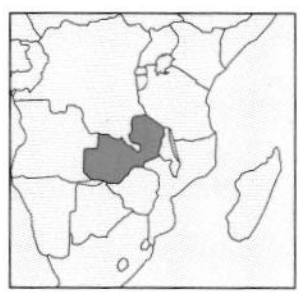

ZAMBIA

GEOGRAPHY The Republic of Zambia is a landlocked country in southern Africa. Zambia lies on the plateau that makes up most of southern Africa. Much of the land is between 2,950 ft and 4,920 ft [900 m to 1,500 m] above sea level. The Muchinga Mountains in the northeast rise above this flat land. Lakes include Bangweulu, which is entirely within Zambia, together with parts of lakes Mweru and Tanganyika in the north. Zambia lies in the tropics, but temperatures are moderated by the altitude.

POLITICS & ECONOMY European contact with Zambia began in the 19th century, when the explorer David Livingstone crossed the River Zambezi. In the 1890s, the British South Africa Company, set up by Cecil Rhodes (1853–1902), the British financier and statesman, made treaties with local chiefs and gradually took over the area. In 1911, the Company named the area Northern Rhodesia. In 1924, Britain took over the government of the country.

In 1953, Britain formed a federation of Northern Rhodesia, Southern Rhodesia (now Zimbabwe), and Nyasaland (now Malawi). Because of African opposition, the federation was dissolved in 1963 and Northern Rhodesia became independent as Zambia in 1964. Kenneth Kaunda became president and one-party rule was introduced in 1972. Under a new constitution, Frederick Chiluba was elected president in 1996. He stood down in 2001 and Levy Mwanawasa became president. But following his death in 2008, he was succeeded by his vice-president, Rupiah Banda.

Copper, the main resource, accounted for 79% of the exports in 2006. Zambia also produces cobalt, lead, zinc, and gemstones. Agriculture employs 62% of the people, as compared with 4% in industry and mining. Food crops include cassava, fruits and vegetables, maize, millet, and sorghum, while cash crops include coffee, sugarcane, and tobacco.

AREA 290,586 sq mi [752,618 sq km]
POPULATION 11,863,000 **CAPITAL** Lusaka
GOVERNMENT Multiparty republic **ETHNIC GROUPS** Native African (Bemba, Tonga, Maravi/Nyanja) **LANGUAGES** English (official), Bemba, Kaonda, Nyanja, and about 70 others **RELIGIONS** Christianity 70%, Islam, Hinduism **CURRENCY** Zambian kwacha = 100 ngwee

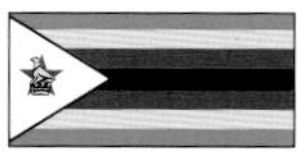
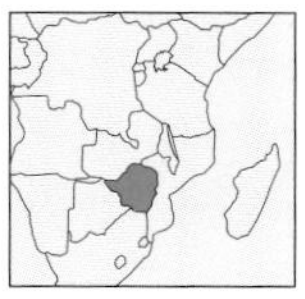

ZIMBABWE

GEOGRAPHY The Republic of Zimbabwe is a landlocked country in southern Africa. Most of the country lies on a high plateau between the Zambezi and Limpopo rivers, ranging from 2,950 ft to 4,920 ft [900 m to 1,500 m] above sea level. From October to March, the weather is hot and wet, but in the winter, daily temperatures can vary greatly.

POLITICS & ECONOMY The Shona people became dominant in the region about 1,000 years ago. The British South Africa Company, under the statesman Cecil Rhodes (1853–1902), occupied the area in the 1890s, after obtaining mineral rights from local chiefs. The area was named Rhodesia and later Southern Rhodesia. It became a self-governing British colony in 1923. Between 1953 and 1963, Southern and Northern Rhodesia (now Zambia) were joined to Nyasaland (Malawi) in the Central African Federation.

In 1965, the European government of Southern Rhodesia (then called Rhodesia) declared their country independent, but Britain refused to accept this. Finally, after a civil war, the country became legally independent in 1980, though rivalries between the Shona and Ndebele people threatened stability. Order was restored when the Shona prime minister, Robert Mugabe, brought his Ndebele rivals into his government. In 1987, Mugabe became the country's executive president, and in 1991 the government renounced its Marxist ideology. Mugabe was re-elected president in 1990 and 1996.

From the late 1990s, Mugabe's government seized white-owned farms and landless "war veterans" began to occupy them. In 2002, Mugabe was re-elected amid accusations of electoral irregularities. In elections in 2008, Mugabe's party was defeated and Mugabe lost to Morgan Tsvangirai in the presidential election. A presidential run-off was ordered, but intimidation of opposition supporters led Tsvangirai to withdraw. In September 2008, a power-sharing agreement was signed and a power-sharing government was set up, with Mugabe as president and Tsvangirai as prime minister. But relations between them proved difficult.

In the 2000s, the economy collapsed. Hyperinflation occurred and many people starved, while the breakdown of public services led to a cholera epidemic. Zimbabwe has valuable mineral reserves and minerals are important exports. Agriculture employs 56% of the people. Maize is the main food crop. Cash crops include cotton, sugar, and tobacco. Cattle ranching is also important.

AREA 150,871 sq mi [390,757 sq km]
POPULATION 11,393,000 **CAPITAL** Harare
GOVERNMENT Multiparty republic **ETHNIC GROUPS** Shona 82%, Ndebele 14%, other African groups 2%, mixed and Asian 1%
LANGUAGES English (official), Shona, Ndebele
RELIGIONS Christianity, traditional beliefs
CURRENCY Zimbabwean new dollar = 100 cents [suspended in 2009]

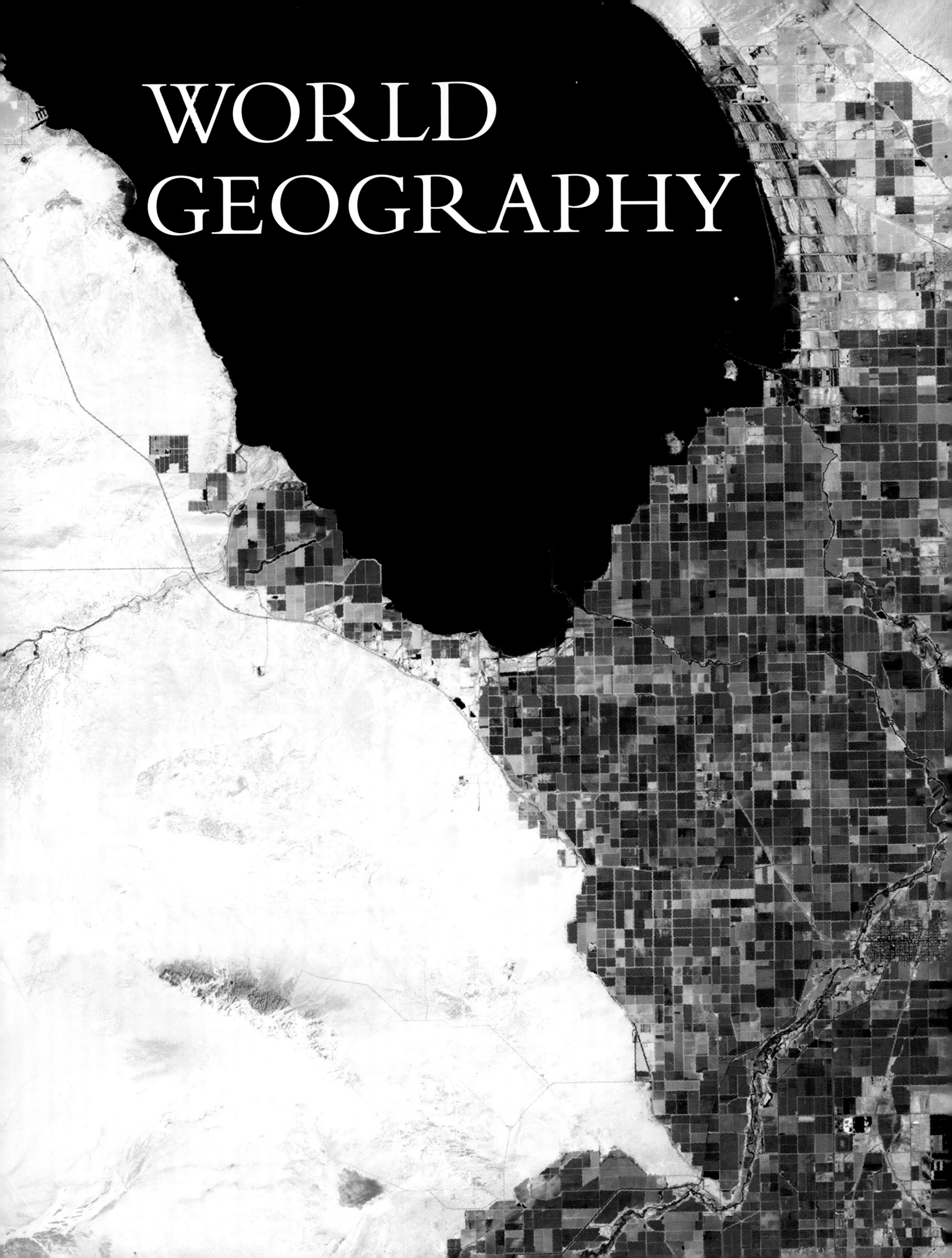

WORLD
GEOGRAPHY

– IMPERIAL VALLEY, USA/MEXICO –
The dark area at top left of this false-color image is the Salton Sea. It is the largest lake in California but was created inadvertently in 1905 during an attempt to divert the flow of the Colorado River for irrigation. The resultant floodwaters filled part of the Imperial Valley. It lies 236 ft [72 m] below sea level and is very saline. To the south is a large area of productive land, which uses irrigated water from the river. The vegetation appears bright red on this image. [Map page 307]

For more information:
70 Orbits of the planets
Planetary data

About 13.7 billion years ago, time and space began with the most colossal explosion in cosmic history: the so-called Big Bang that is believed to have initiated the Universe. According to current theory, in the first millionth of a second of its existence it expanded from a dimensionless point of infinite mass and density into a fireball about the size of our present Solar System – and it has been expanding ever since.

It took about 300,000 years for the primal fireball to cool enough for atoms to form. They were mostly hydrogen which is still the most abundant material in the Universe. The radiation from this era still pervades the Universe, though its subsequent expansion means that we see it at about 3° above absolute zero instead of its original 3,000°C. Observations of this faint background glow reveal slight fluctuations. It is these which appear to have become, over the next billion years or so, the large-scale structures in the present Universe. As well as the matter which we can see, there is evidence of a much greater quantity of dark matter whose nature remains unknown. Within knots of this dark matter, the first stars and galaxies formed, probably within the first billion years of the life of the Universe. Our own Galaxy was among them.

There were several generations of stars, each feeding on the wreckage of its extinct predecessors as well as the original galactic gas swirls. With each new generation, progressively larger atoms were forged in stellar furnaces, and the Galaxy's range of elements, once restricted to hydrogen and helium, grew larger. About 9 billion years after the Big Bang, a star formed on the outskirts of our Galaxy with enough matter left over to create a retinue of planets. Nearly 5 billion years after that, human beings evolved.

The Sun is one of more than 100 billion stars in the Home Galaxy alone. Our Galaxy, in turn, forms part of a local group consisting of approximately 30 similar structures, mostly small "dwarf" galaxies but a few large ones, and one – the Andromeda Galaxy – larger than our own. There are at least 100 billion galaxies in the Universe, many of which are members of huge galaxy clusters.

LIFE OF A STAR

For most of its existence, a star produces energy by the nuclear fusion of hydrogen into helium at its core. The duration of this hydrogen-burning period – known as the *main sequence* – depends on the star's mass; the greater the mass, the higher the core temperatures and the sooner the star's supply of hydrogen is exhausted. Dim, dwarf stars consume their hydrogen slowly, eking it out over billions of years. The Sun, like other stars of its mass, should spend about 10 billion years on the main sequence; since it was formed less than 5 billion years ago, it still has half its life left.

Once all of a star's core hydrogen has been fused into helium, nuclear activity moves outward into layers of unconsumed hydrogen. For a time, energy production sharply increases: the star grows hotter and expands enormously, turning into a so-called red giant. Its energy output will increase a thousandfold, and it will swell to a hundred times its former diameter.

After a few hundred million years, helium in the core will become sufficiently compressed to initiate a new cycle of nuclear fusion: from helium to carbon. The star will contract somewhat, before beginning its last expansion, in the Sun's case engulfing the Earth and perhaps Mars. In this bloated condition, the Sun's outer layers will break off into space, leaving a tiny inner core, mainly of carbon, that shrinks progressively under its own gravity. The white dwarf star thus formed can attain a density more than 10,000 times that of normal matter, with crushing surface gravity to match. Gradually, the nuclear fires will die down, and the Sun will reach its terminal stage: a black dwarf, emitting insignificant amounts of energy.

Black holes

However, stars more massive than the Sun may undergo a different transformation. The additional mass allows gravitational collapse to continue indefinitely: eventually, all the star's remaining matter shrinks to a point, and its density approaches infinity – a state that will not permit even subatomic structures to survive.

The star has become a *black hole*: an anomalous "singularity" in the fabric of space and time. Although vast coruscations of radiation will be emitted by any matter falling into its grasp, the singularity itself has an escape velocity that exceeds the speed of light, and nothing can ever be released from it. Within the boundaries of the black hole, the laws of physics are suspended.

GALACTIC STRUCTURES

Many of the Universe's 100 billion galaxies show clear structural patterns, originally classified by the American astronomer Edwin Hubble in 1925. Spiral galaxies like our own have a central, almost spherical bulge and a surrounding disk composed of spiral arms. Barred spirals have a central bar of stars across the nucleus, with spiral arms trailing from the ends of the bar. Elliptical galaxies have a more uniform appearance, ranging from a flattened disk to a near sphere.

▲ M51, the Whirlpool Nebula, comprises the large spiral galaxy NGC 5194 and its smaller, barred companion NGC 5195. M51 was the first astronomical object in which a spiral structure was identified, in 1845. Although smaller and less massive than our own Galaxy, M51 is much brighter, due to recent star formation.

Most galaxies, however, have no obvious structure at all. Galaxies also vary enormously in size, from dwarf galaxies only 2,000 light-years across to great assemblies of stars 80 or more times larger.

THE NEAREST STARS

The 22 nearest stars, excluding the Sun, with their distance from Earth in light-years*

Proxima Centauri	4.2	UV Ceti A	8.7	61 Cygni A	11.4
Alpha Centauri A	4.4	UV Ceti B	8.7	Procyon A	11.4
Alpha Centauri B	4.4	Ross 154	9.7	Procyon B	11.4
Barnard's Star	5.9	Ross 248	10.3	61 Cygni B	11.4
Wolf 359	7.8	Epsilon Eridani	10.5	HD 173740	11.5
Lalande 21185	8.3	HD 217987	10.7	HD 173739	11.7
Sirius A	8.6	Ross 128	10.9	* A light-year is about 5,900	
Sirius B	8.6	L789-6	11.2	billion miles [9,500 billion km]	

THE HOME GALAXY

The Sun and its planets are located in one of the spiral arms of the Galaxy, about 26,000 light-years from the galactic center and orbiting around it in a period of about 220 million years. The center is invisible from the Earth, masked by vast, light-absorbing clouds of interstellar dust.

The Galaxy is probably around 12 billion years old and, like other spiral galaxies, has three distinct regions. The central bulge is about 30,000 light-years in diameter. The disk in which the Sun is located is not much more than 1,000 light-years thick, but approximately 100,000 light-years from end to end. Around the Galaxy is the halo, a spherical zone 300,000 light-years across, studded with globular star clusters and sprinkled with individual suns.

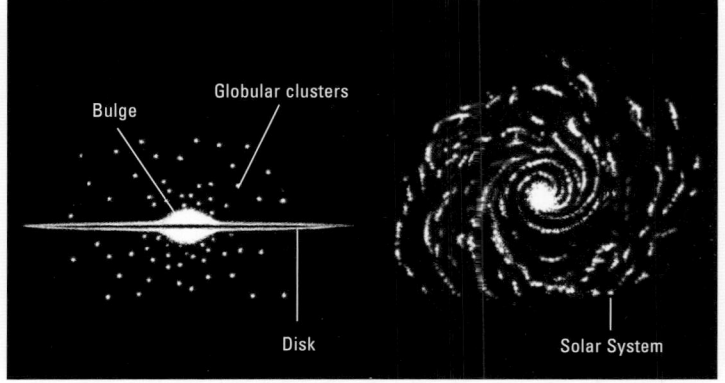

THE END OF THE UNIVERSE

The likely fate of the Universe is disputed. According to one theory (*top of diagram, below*), the expansion begun at the time of the Big Bang will continue "indefinitely," with aging galaxies moving further and further apart in an immense, dark graveyard.

Alternatively, gravity may overcome the expansion (*bottom of diagram*). Galaxies will fall back together until everything is again concentrated at a single point, followed by a new Big Bang and a new expansion, in an endlessly repeated cycle.

The first theory is supported by the amount of visible matter in the Universe; the second theory assumes that there is enough dark material in the Universe to bring about the gravitational collapse.

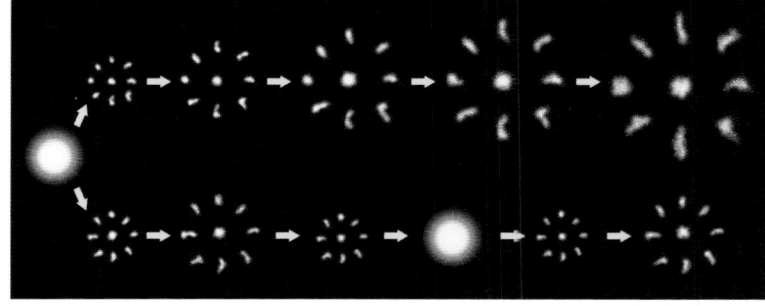

Many of the nearest stars, like Alpha Centauri A and B, are double stars, orbiting about their common center of gravity and to all intents and purposes equidistant from Earth. Many of them are dim objects, with no name other than the designation given to them by the astronomers who first investigated them.

However, they include Sirius, the brightest star in the sky, and Procyon, the seventh brightest. Both are larger than the Sun; of the nearest stars, only Epsilon Eridani is similar in size and luminosity. Most of the other bright stars in the sky are within 500 light-years of the Sun – a small fraction of the diameter of our Galaxy.

STAR CHARTS

NORTHERN
HEMISPHERE SKY

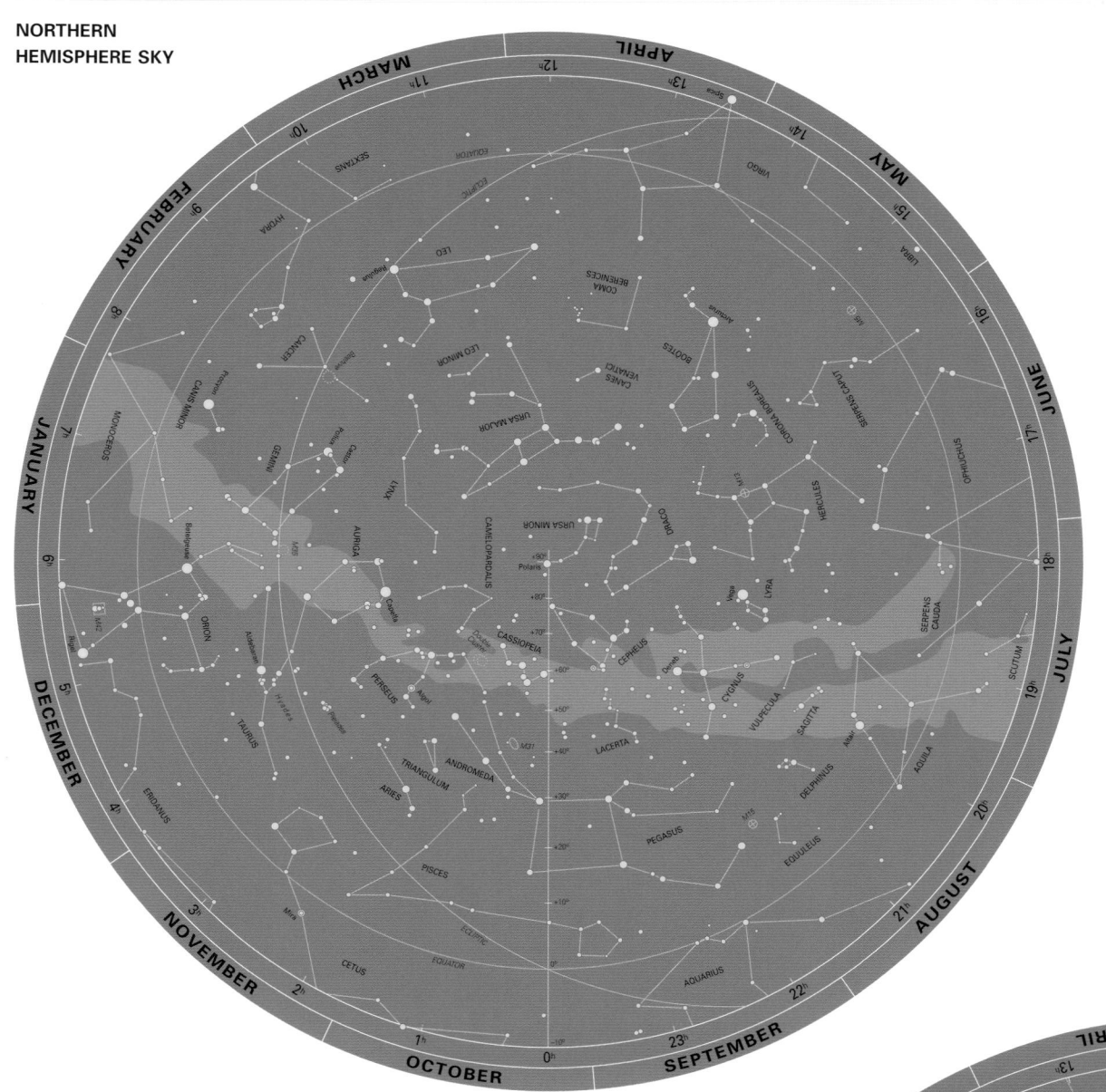

THE CONSTELLATIONS
The constellations and their English names

Andromeda	Andromeda	Lacerta	Lizard
Antlia	Air Pump	Leo	Lion
Apus	Bird of Paradise	Leo Minor	Little Lion
Aquarius	Water Carrier	Lepus	Hare
Aquila	Eagle	Libra	Scales
Ara	Altar	Lupus	Wolf
Aries	Ram	Lynx	Lynx
Auriga	Charioteer	Lyra	Lyre
Boötes	Herdsman	Mensa	Table Mountain
Caelum	Chisel	Microscopium	Microscope
Camelopardalis	Giraffe	Monoceros	Unicorn
Cancer	Crab	Musca	Fly
Canes Venatici	Hunting Dogs	Norma	Level
Canis Major	Great Dog	Octans	Octant
Canis Minor	Little Dog	Ophiuchus	Serpent Bearer
Capricornus	Sea Goat	Orion	Orion
Carina	Ship's Keel	Pavo	Peacock
Cassiopeia	Cassiopeia	Pegasus	Winged Horse
Centaurus	Centaur	Perseus	Perseus
Cepheus	Cepheus	Phoenix	Phoenix
Cetus	Whale	Pictor	Easel
Chamaeleon	Chameleon	Pisces	Fishes
Circinus	Compasses	Piscis Austrinus	Southern Fish
Columba	Dove	Puppis	Ship's Stern
Coma Berenices	Berenice's Hair	Pyxis	Mariner's Compass
Corona Australis	Southern Crown	Reticulum	Net
Corona Borealis	Northern Crown	Sagitta	Arrow
Corvus	Crow	Sagittarius	Archer
Crater	Cup	Scorpius	Scorpion
Crux	Southern Cross	Sculptor	Sculptor
Cygnus	Swan	Scutum	Shield
Delphinus	Dolphin	Serpens	Serpent
Dorado	Swordfish	Sextans	Sextant
Draco	Dragon	Taurus	Bull
Equuleus	Little Horse	Telescopium	Telescope
Eridanus	River Eridanus	Triangulum	Triangle
Fornax	Furnace	Triangulum Australe	Southern Triangle
Gemini	Twins	Tucana	Toucan
Grus	Crane	Ursa Major	Great Bear
Hercules	Hercules	Ursa Minor	Little Bear
Horologium	Clock	Vela	Ship's Sails
Hydra	Water Snake	Virgo	Virgin
Hydrus	Sea Serpent	Volans	Flying Fish
Indus	Indian	Vulpecula	Fox

SOUTHERN
HEMISPHERE SKY

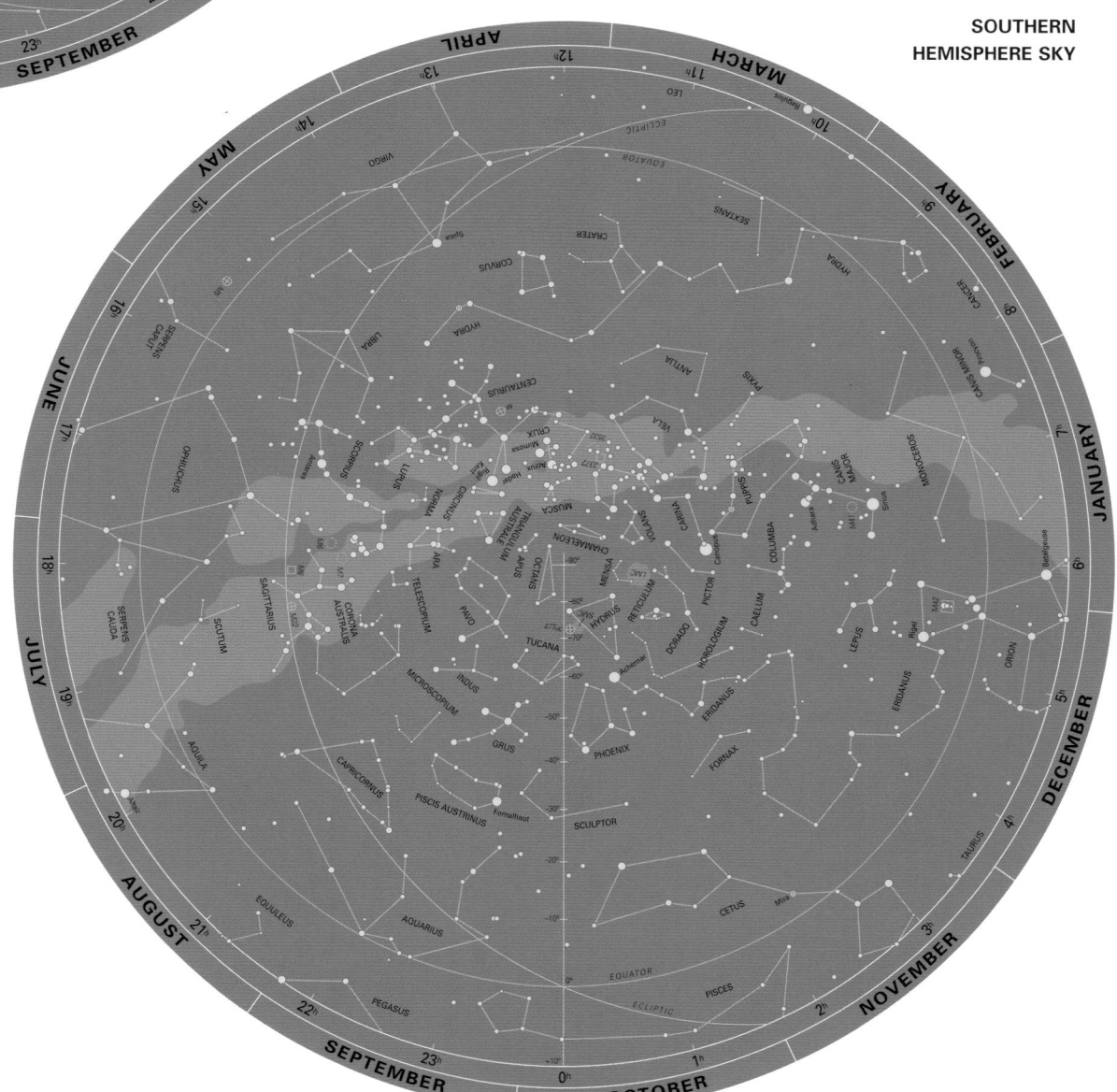

The charts on this page show the entire heavens divided into northern and southern hemispheres, with 10° of overlap between them around the perimeter of each one. However, the view from any particular location on Earth will be different, and will change both hourly as the Earth turns, and throughout the year as the Earth goes around the Sun.

The Sun's annual path through the heavens is known as the "ecliptic," and is shown here by an orange line. When the Sun is in the sky its light drowns out our view of the stars, so only that part of the heavens opposite the Sun is visible at a particular time. The sky's equivalent of longitude is known as "right ascension." As the stars appear to rotate around the Earth once every 24 hours, right ascension is measured eastward in hours and minutes, and is marked around the edge of the maps. The equivalent of latitude is "declination," measured in degrees north or south of the celestial equator, and shown by the vertical line on each chart.

Using the charts

At any place and time you can see half of the whole sky, assuming a flat horizon. If you were at one of the poles your view would be shown as a circle centered on the middle of the map for the appropriate hemisphere, with the horizon marked by the celestial equator. From all other locations the center of your view (your overhead point) will be at some other point on the map whose location changes with time. The closer you are to Earth's equator, the closer the center will be to the edge of the map and more stars in the opposite hemisphere will be visible.

So first choose the appropriate chart for your hemisphere and hold it with the month at the bottom. At 11 p.m., not allowing for Daylight Saving Time (Summer Time), your overhead point will be at the same declination as your geographical latitude and stars lower on the map will be due south (or north in the southern hemisphere). From latitude 50° in mid August, for example, your overhead point will be close to the star Deneb in the constellation of Cygnus. Stars on the opposite side of the map will be below your northern horizon, while stars below Deneb will be due south.

STAR MAGNITUDES
Apparent visual magnitudes

The magnitude scale of star brightnesses is developed from the system used by the Ancient Greeks in which the brightest stars were first magnitude and the faintest visible to the naked eye were sixth. Today the scale has a mathematical basis and extends, at the brightest end, through to negative magnitudes.

The Milky Way is shown in light blue on these charts.

For more information:
68 The Home Galaxy
72 The seasons
    Day and night
73 The Moon

Lying about halfway from the center of one of billions of galaxies that populate the observable Universe, our Solar System contains eight planets and their moons, five dwarf planets, innumerable asteroids, comets and other icy bodies, and a miscellany of dust and gas, all tethered by the immense gravitational field of the Sun, the star whose thermonuclear furnaces provide them all with heat and light.

The Solar System was formed about 5 billion years ago, when a spinning cloud of gas, mostly hydrogen but seeded with other heavier elements, condensed enough to ignite a nuclear reaction and create a star. The Sun still accounts for almost 99.9% of the system's total mass.

By composition as well as distance, the planetary array divides quite neatly in two: an inner system of four small, solid planets, including the Earth, and an outer system, from Jupiter to Neptune, of four much larger planets composed of lighter materials, such as gas, liquid, and ice. Lying mostly between the two groups is a scattering of rocky asteroids, numbering perhaps a million or more. They may be debris left over from the formation of the inner Solar System. In 2006, Pluto was demoted from its former status as a planet and is now regarded as a member of the Kuiper Belt of icy bodies at the fringes of the Solar System.

Much of the early history of science is the story of people trying to make sense of the wandering points of light that were all they knew of the planets. Now, men have themselves stood on the Earth's Moon, space probes have landed on Mars and Venus, and distant landscapes have been mapped with astonishing accuracy, transforming our knowledge of our celestial environment.

In the 1980s, the Voyager space probes skimmed all four major planets of the outer Solar System, bringing new revelations with each close approach. The Magellan (Venus), Galileo (Jupiter) and Cassini–Huygens (Saturn) missions have transformed our knowledge of those planets and the giants' moons, and a host of orbiters and landers have shown us Mars in a new light. A spacecraft is also on its way to visit Pluto.

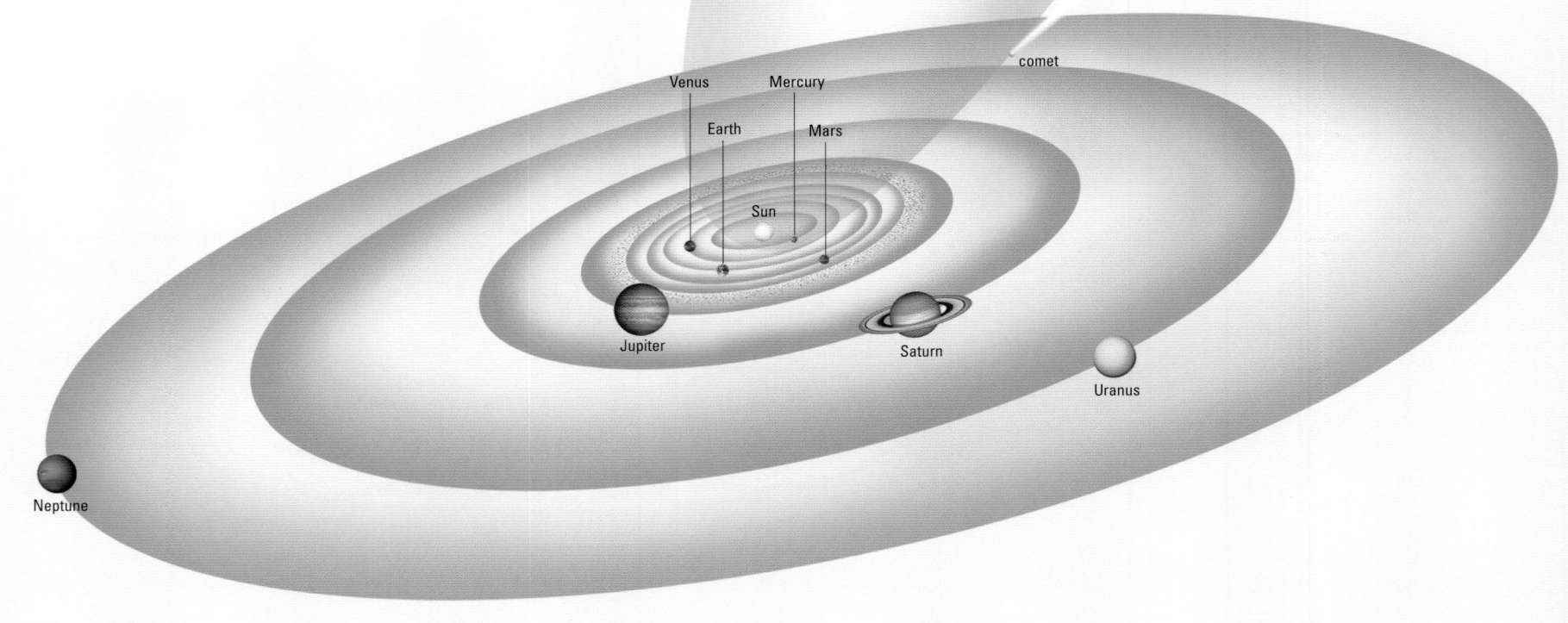

Diagram not drawn to scale

ORBITS OF THE PLANETS

The diagram above shows the Solar System as it might appear to an observer a few light-hours away in the direction of the constellation Hercules. Seen from such a position, above the plane of the ecliptic, all the planets revolve about the Sun in a counterclockwise direction. The perspective view exaggerates the elliptical form of all the planetary orbits: only Mercury follows a path that deviates noticeably from circularity.

The diagram also shows the main swarm of asteroids between Mars and Jupiter, and the orbit of a comet. Comets reside in a vast spherical halo beyond the Solar System, and are occasionally diverted toward the Sun on highly elliptical orbits which may take many thousands of years to complete. Most, therefore, still await discovery, though there are a number of shorter-period comets which return regularly, such as Halley's Comet.

PLANETARY DATA

	Mean distance from Sun (million miles)	Mass (Earth = 1)	Period of orbit (Earth days/years)	Period of rotation (Earth days)	Equatorial diameter (miles)	Average density (water = 1)	Surface gravity (Earth = 1)	Number of known satellites*
Sun	–	332,946	–	25.38	865,000	1.41	27.9	–
Mercury	36.0	0.06	87.97d	58.65	3,032	5.43	0.38	0
Venus	67.2	0.82	224.7d	243.02	7,521	5.24	0.91	0
Earth	93.0	1.00	365.3d	1.00	7,926	5.52	1.00	1
Mars	141.6	0.11	687.0d	1.029	4,220	3.94	0.38	2
Jupiter	483.7	317.8	11.86y	0.411	88,848	1.33	2.36	63
Saturn	886.6	95.2	29.45y	0.428	74,900	0.69	0.91	62
Uranus	1,784.0	14.5	84.02y	0.720	31,764	1.27	0.89	27
Neptune	2,795.2	17.2	164.8y	0.673	30,776	1.64	1.13	13

Planetary days are given in sidereal days – that is, with respect to the stars rather than the Sun. The difference is caused by the movement of the planet in its orbit, so the interval between successive noons is slightly different from that between the rising of a particular star. The Earth's own sidereal day is 23h 56m in solar time. The equatorial diameters of most planets differ from their polar diameters as a consequence of their rotation, which is most marked in the case of Jupiter and Saturn, which are very noticeably flattened at the poles. Strictly speaking, the figures for surface gravity apply to the four inner planets only, as the outer planets have no solid surfaces. In their case, the figure is given for an arbitrary point in the atmosphere where the pressure is 1 bar.

* Number of known satellites at mid-2010

THE PLANETS

Mercury is the closest planet to the Sun and hence the fastest-moving. It is very hot, with a cratered, wrinkled surface very similar to that of Earth's Moon. It is small and has low gravity, so there is no significant atmosphere.

Venus has much the same physical dimensions as Earth. Its dense atmosphere is composed of 97% carbon dioxide resulting in a runaway greenhouse effect that makes the surface, at 890°F, the hottest of all the planets in the Solar System. Radar mapping revealed a terrain consisting of highland regions and vast, rolling plains crossed by volcanic flows and dotted with craters. Discharges from volcanic regions could explain the sulfuric-acid rain detected by spacecraft. Soft-landers last less than an hour in Venus's fierce climate.

Earth seen from space is easily the most beautiful of the inner planets; it is also, and more objectively, the largest, as well as the only known home of life. Living things are the main reason why the Earth is able to retain a substantial proportion of reactive oxygen in its atmosphere; the oxygen in turn supports the life that constantly regenerates it. The Earth's natural satellite, the Moon, is believed to have been created when an asteroid struck our planet in its infancy.

Mars, smaller and cooler than the Earth, is nevertheless the most likely planet other than Earth where life may have formed. The planet was until recently (in astronomical terms) a geologically active world with water on its surface: rivers, lakes, and even an ocean. Liquid water may well exist today, but trapped beneath its dusty, boulder-strewn surface. The Martian landscape features huge extinct volcanoes, a giant canyon system, craters, and sand dunes. Its thin atmosphere is mostly carbon dioxide, and its polar caps are of frozen carbon dioxide and water ice. It has two tiny moons, probably captured asteroids.

Jupiter has about three times the mass of all the other planets combined. The planet is mostly gas, under intense pressure in the lower atmosphere above a core of fiercely compressed hydrogen and helium. The upper layers form strikingly colored rotating belts, the outward sign of the intense storms created by Jupiter's rapid rotation. The Great Red Spot is a storm feature that has persisted for at least 170 years. Jupiter has at least 63 moons. Most are very small, but the four largest – Io, Europa, Ganymede, and Callisto – are fascinating worlds in their own right. Io is the most volcanically active world known, and Europa possesses an ocean deep below its icy surface. The planet also has a system of rings, though nowhere near as prominent as Saturn's.

Saturn is structurally similar to Jupiter, rotating fast enough to produce an obvious bulge at its equator. It is composed of 89% hydrogen and 11% helium, and has wind velocities in the outer atmosphere of 1,600 ft/sec. Ever since the invention of the telescope, Saturn's rings have been the feature that has most attracted observers. The rings consist of thousands of individual ringlets, composed of icy particles ranging in size from 30 feet down to microscopic. Titan, the largest of Saturn's 62 known moons, has a dense atmosphere.

Uranus was unknown to the ancients. Although it is faintly visible to the naked eye, it was not established as a planet until 1781. In its interior is probably a rocky core surrounded by frozen methane, water, and ammonia; the atmosphere is of hydrogen, helium, and some methane, which gives the planet its greenish-blue color. There is a system of thin, dark rings and a retinue of 27 moons, all but five of which are small.

Neptune is always more than 2.5 billion miles from Earth, and despite its diameter of over 31,000 miles, it can only be seen by telescope. Its discovery in 1846 was the result of mathematical predictions by astronomers seeking to explain irregularities in the orbit of Uranus. Like Uranus, it has a ring system; recent observations have revealed a total of 13 moons.

In 2006, following an increasing number of discoveries of objects orbiting the Sun of similar size to Pluto but at a greater distance, the International Astronomical Union issued for the first time a definition of a planet. A planet is defined as "a body orbiting the Sun, which is essentially round as a consequence of its gravity, and which does not share its orbital neighborhood with similar bodies." On this definition, Pluto is no longer classified as a planet, but is instead a member of a new category of "dwarf planet," which relaxes the last criterion but excludes bodies in orbit around another one.

Mean distance from the Sun in millions of miles

Mercury	36.0 Mercury
Venus	67.2 Venus
Earth	93.0 Earth
Mars	141.6 Mars
Jupiter	483.7 Jupiter
Saturn	886.6 Saturn
Uranus	1,784.0 Uranus
Neptune	2,795.2 Neptune

Diagrams not drawn to scale

Uranus

Neptune

For more information:

70 Orbits of the planets

77 Ocean currents

78 Circulation of the air

80 Climate

The basic units of time measurement are the day and the year. The day is one rotation of the Earth on its axis. Our present calendar is based on the solar year of 365.24 days, the time taken by the Earth to orbit the Sun. Calendars based on the movements of the Sun and Moon have been used since ancient times. The length of the year, reckoned by the Julian Calendar introduced by Julius Caesar, was about 11 minutes too long. The cumulative error was rectified in 1582 by the Gregorian Calendar, when Pope Gregory XIII decreed that the day following October 4 was October 15, and that century years did not count as leap years unless they were divisible by 400. England finally adopted the reformed calendar in 1752, when it was 11 days behind the European mainland.

The rotation of the Earth on its axis causes day and night. The Earth rotates through 360° every 24 hours, and the world is divided into 24 time zones centered on lines of longitude at 15° intervals.

The tilt of the Earth's axis, which is also called the "obliquity of the ecliptic," accounts for the seasons which are so familiar in the middle latitudes. However, geological evidence shows that, over long periods of time, climates change, and the advances and retreats of the ice during the Pleistocene Ice Age may have been caused by regular variations in the Earth's tilt, its orbit around the Sun, and changes in the season when it is closest to the Sun (perihelion).

THE SEASONS

Seasons occur because the Earth's axis is tilted at an angle of approximately 23½°. When the northern hemisphere is tilted to a maximum extent toward the Sun, on June 21, the Sun is overhead at the Tropic of Cancer (latitude 23½° North). This is midsummer, or the summer solstice, in the northern hemisphere.

On September 22 or 23, the Sun is overhead at the equator, and day and night are of equal length throughout the world. This is the autumnal equinox in the northern hemisphere.

On December 21 or 22, the Sun is overhead at the Tropic of Capricorn (23½° South), the winter solstice in the northern hemisphere. The overhead Sun then tracks north until, on March 21, it is overhead at the equator. This is the spring (vernal) equinox in the northern hemisphere.

In the southern hemisphere, the seasons are the reverse of those in the north.

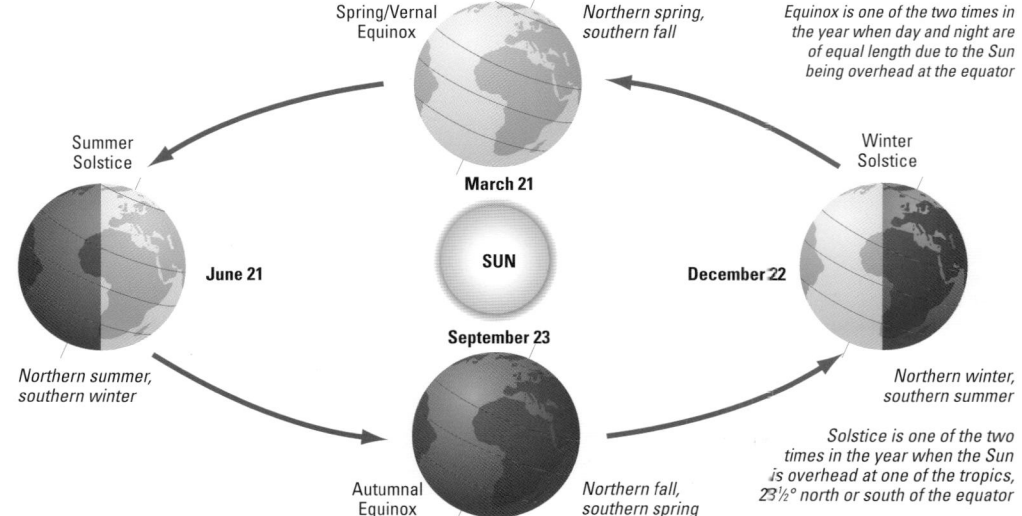

DAY AND NIGHT

The Sun appears to rise in the east, reach its highest point at noon, and then set in the west, to be followed by night. In reality, it is not the Sun that is moving but the Earth rotating from west to east. The moment when the Sun's upper limb first appears above the horizon is termed sunrise; the moment when the Sun's upper limb disappears below the horizon is sunset.

At the summer solstice in the northern hemisphere (June 21), the Arctic has total daylight and the Antarctic total darkness. The opposite occurs at the winter solstice (December 21 or 22). At the equator, the length of day and night are almost equal all year.

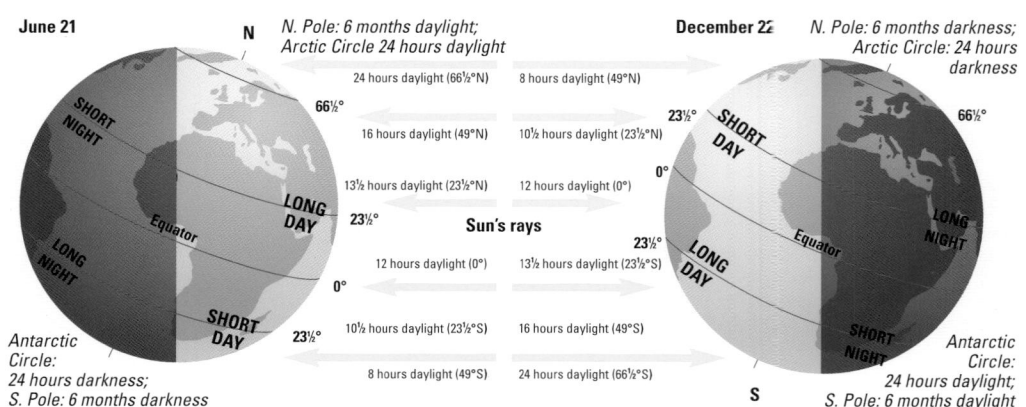

EARTH DATA

Aphelion (maximum distance from Sun):	94,508,166 miles	Length of year:	365 days, 5 hours, 48 minutes, 46 seconds of mean solar time	Polar circumference:	24,860 miles
Perihelion (minimum distance from Sun):	91,403,477 miles			Equatorial diameter:	7,926 miles
		Superficial area:	197,000,000 sq miles	Polar diameter:	7,900 miles
Angle of tilt (obliquity of the ecliptic):	23° 27' 08"	Land surface:	57,500,000 sq miles (29.2%)	Equatorial radius:	3,963 miles
				Polar radius:	3,950 miles
Length of year – solar tropical (equinox to equinox):	365.24 days	Water surface:	139,500,000 sq miles (70.8%)	Volume of the Earth:	259,880 × 10^6 cu miles
		Equatorial circumference:	24,901 miles	Mass of the Earth:	5.97 × 10^{24} kg

SUNRISE AND SUNSET

The term "equinox" comes from the Latin for "equal night." At the spring and autumnal equinoxes, the Sun is vertically overhead at midday at the equator and all places on Earth have 12 hours of darkness and 12 hours of daylight. The graphs of sunrise and sunset show that these occasions occur on March 21 and on September 22 or 23. The graphs also show that, because the Sun remains high in the sky at the equator throughout the year, the length of day and night there remains roughly the same throughout the year, with sunrise around 6 a.m. and sunset around 6 p.m.

The further north or south one travels, the greater the difference between the number of hours of daylight and darkness. For example, the graph (right) shows that at latitude 60°N sunrise varies from just after 9 a.m. in midwinter (on December 22 or 23) to about 2.30 a.m. in midsummer (around the summer solstice on June 21). By contrast, the second graph (far right) shows that sunset at latitude 60°N occurs at about 2.45 p.m. in midwinter and 9.20 p.m. in midsummer.

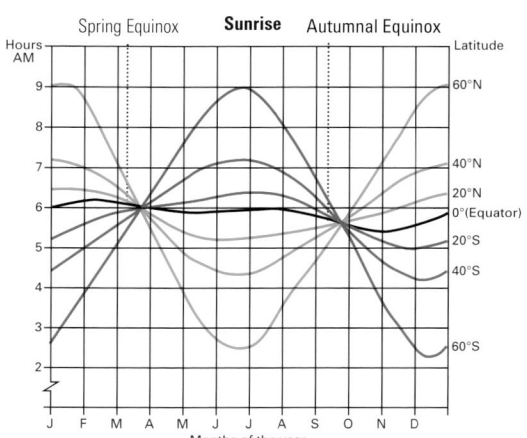

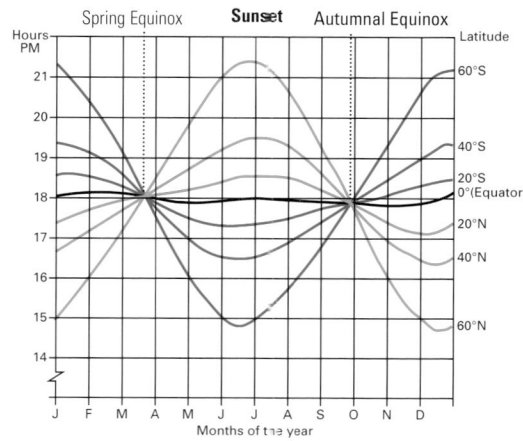

THE MOON

The Moon rotates more slowly than the Earth, taking just over 27 days to make one complete rotation on its axis. This corresponds to the Moon's orbital period around the Earth, and therefore the Moon always presents the same hemisphere toward us; some 41% of the Moon's far side is never visible from the Earth. The interval between one New Moon and the next is 29½ days – this is called a lunation, or lunar month. The Moon shines only by reflected sunlight, and emits no light of its own. During each lunation the Moon displays a complete cycle of phases, caused by the changing angle of illumination from the Sun.

PHASES OF THE MOON

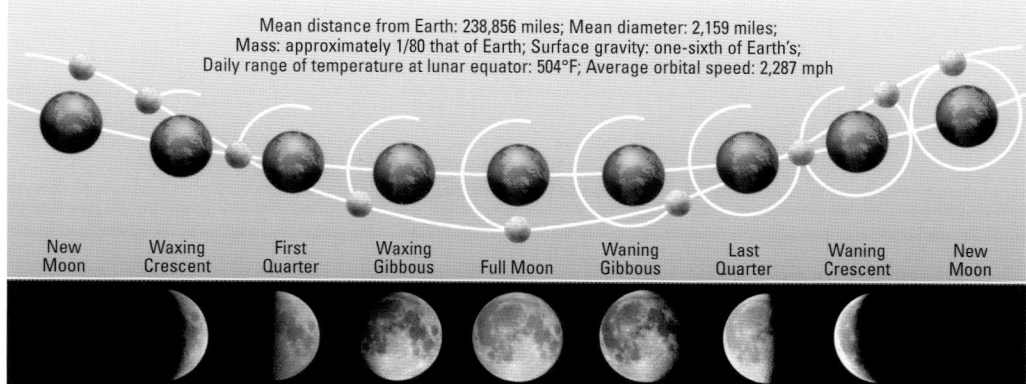

Mean distance from Earth: 238,856 miles; Mean diameter: 2,159 miles;
Mass: approximately 1/80 that of Earth; Surface gravity: one-sixth of Earth's;
Daily range of temperature at lunar equator: 504°F; Average orbital speed: 2,287 mph

New Moon	Waxing Crescent	First Quarter	Waxing Gibbous	Full Moon	Waning Gibbous	Last Quarter	Waning Crescent	New Moon

MOON DATA

Distance from Earth
The Moon orbits at a mean distance of 238,856 miles, at an average speed of 2,287 mph in relation to the Earth.

Size and mass
The average diameter of the Moon is 2,159 miles. It is 400 times smaller than the Sun but is about 400 times closer to the Earth, so we see them as the same size. The Moon has a mass of 7.35×10^{22} kg, with a density 3.344 times that of water.

Visibility
Only 59% of the Moon's surface is visible from the Earth over time. Sunlight reflected from the Moon takes 1.3 seconds to reach the Earth (the Sun itself is around 8½ light-minutes away).

Temperature
With the Sun overhead, the temperature on the lunar equator can reach 243°F [117°C]. At night it can sink to −261°F [−163°C].

ECLIPSES

When the Moon passes between the Sun and the Earth, the Sun becomes partially eclipsed (1). A partial eclipse becomes a total eclipse if the Moon proceeds to cover the Sun completely (2) and the dark central part of the lunar shadow touches the Earth. The broad geographical zone covered by the Moon's outer shadow (P), has only a very small central area (often less than 62 miles wide) that experiences totality. Totality can never last for more than 7½ minutes at maximum, but is usually much briefer than this. Lunar eclipses take place when the Moon moves through the shadow of the Earth, and can be partial or total. Any single location on Earth can experience a maximum of four solar and three lunar eclipses in any single year, while a total solar eclipse occurs an average of once every 360 years for any given location.

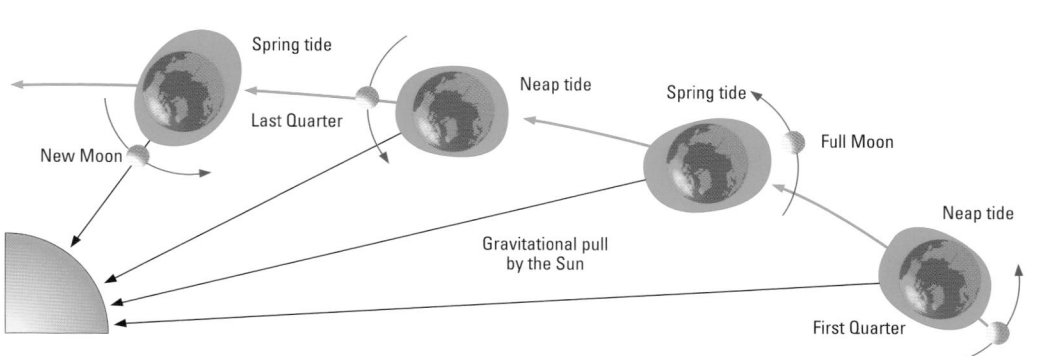

Partial eclipse (1) Solar eclipse Lunar eclipse

P P P

Total eclipse (2)

TIDES

The daily rise and fall of the ocean's tides are the result of the gravitational pull of the Moon and that of the Sun, though the effect of the latter is not as strong as that of the Moon. This effect is greatest on the hemisphere facing the Moon and causes a tidal "bulge." Spring tides occur when the Sun, Earth, and Moon are aligned; high tides are at their highest, and low tides fall to their lowest. When the Moon and Sun are furthest out of line (near the Moon's First and Last Quarters), neap tides occur, producing the smallest range between high and low tides.

TIME ZONES

The Earth rotates through 360° in 24 hours, and so moves 15° every hour. The world is divided into 24 standard time zones, each centered on lines of longitude at 15° intervals. At the center of the first zone is the prime meridian, or Greenwich meridian. All places to the west of Greenwich are one hour behind for every 15° of longitude; places to the east are ahead by one hour for every 15°.

International Date Line
When it is 12 noon on the Greenwich meridian, 180° east it is midnight of the same day – while 180° west the day is just beginning. To overcome this, the International Date Line was established, approximately following the 180° meridian. Thus, if you were to travel eastward from Japan (140°E) to Samoa (170°W), you would pass from Sunday night into Sunday morning.

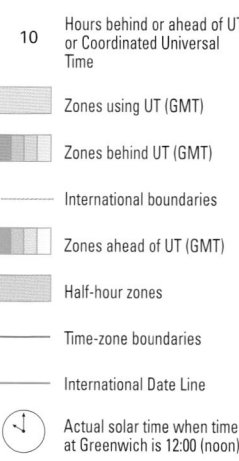

10	Hours behind or ahead of UT or Coordinated Universal Time

Zones using UT (GMT)

Zones behind UT (GMT)

International boundaries

Zones ahead of UT (GMT)

Half-hour zones

Time-zone boundaries

International Date Line

Actual solar time when time at Greenwich is 12:00 (noon)

Note: Some of the above time zones are affected by the incidence of Daylight Saving Time in countries where it is adopted.

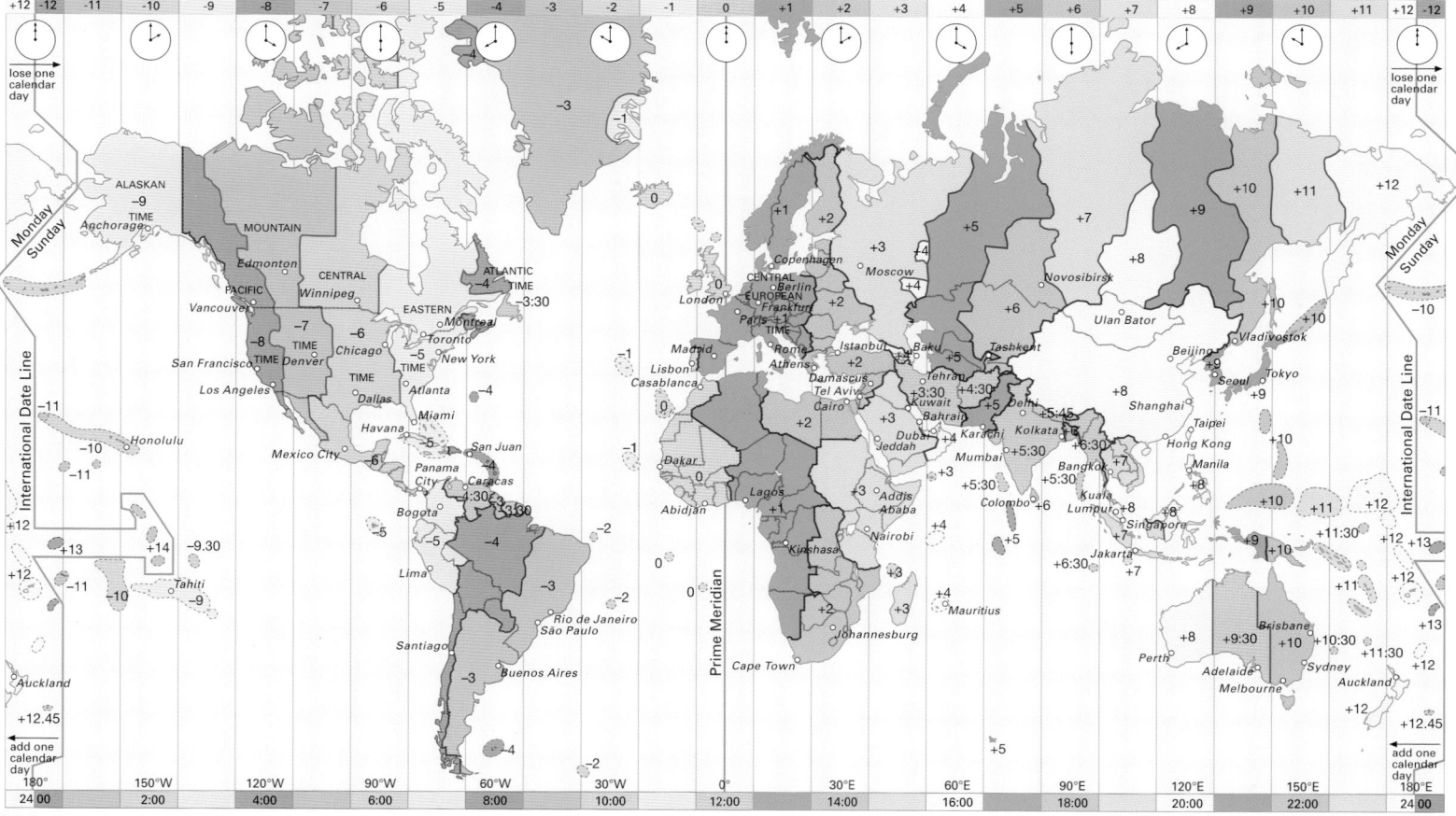

Projection: Mercator

For more information:
98 Minerals

Every year, earthquakes and volcanic eruptions cause much destruction throughout the world. Such phenomena were once thought to be unconnected, but since the late 1960s, scientists have understood that these events are surface manifestations of the tremendous forces operating in the Earth's interior that are slowly but constantly changing the face of our planet.

The Earth is divided into three zones. The crust, a brittle, low-density zone, overlies the dense mantle. Separating the crust from the mantle is a distinct boundary called the Mohorovičić (or Moho) discontinuity. Enclosed by the mantle is the Earth's core, which consists mainly of iron and nickel.

Temperatures inside the Earth range from about 1,600°F in the upper mantle to perhaps 9,000°F in the core. Heat creates convection currents in a semimolten part of the mantle called the asthenosphere. Above the asthenosphere is the lithosphere, a solid layer about 40 miles thick, consisting of the crust and part of the mantle. The lithosphere is divided into rigid plates, moved around by the currents in the asthenosphere, a process named plate tectonics.

The Earth was formed around 4.6 billion years ago. Lighter elements floated toward the surface, where they formed crustal rocks. The oldest rocks so far discovered are about 4 billion years old, while the oldest fossils occur in rocks formed around 3.5 billion years ago. An explosion of life occurred at the start of the Cambrian period, 570 million years ago. The fossil record since the start of the Cambrian has enabled scientists to piece together the story of life on Earth.

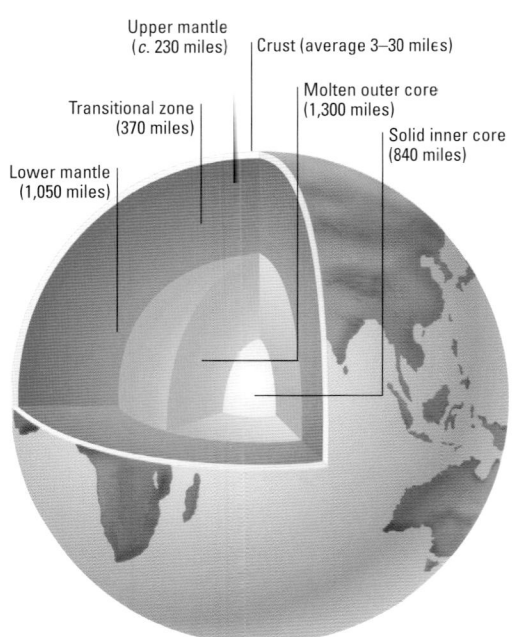

Upper mantle (c. 230 miles) — Crust (average 3–30 miles)
Transitional zone (370 miles)
Lower mantle (1,050 miles)
Molten outer core (1,300 miles)
Solid inner core (840 miles)

CONTINENTAL DRIFT

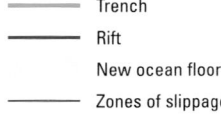

— Trench
— Rift
  New ocean floor
— Zones of slippage

In 1915, Alfred Wegener produced a series of world maps proposing that, around 200 million years ago, the continents had been joined together in a supercontinent that he called Pangaea. This land mass started to break up about 180 million years ago and the parts drifted to their present positions. In the 1950s and 1960s, evidence from studies of the ocean floor suggested that the low-density continents rest on huge slow-moving plates. The arrows on the present-day world map (*below*) show that the continents are still on the move.

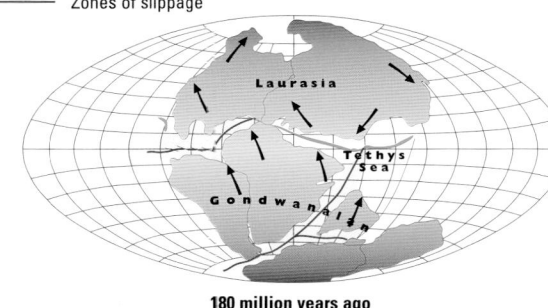

180 million years ago

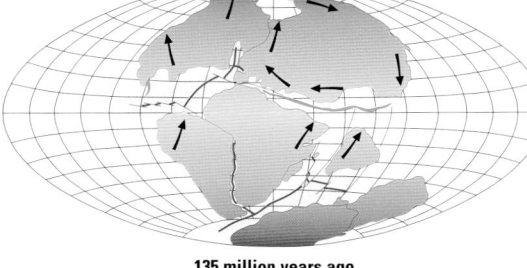

135 million years ago

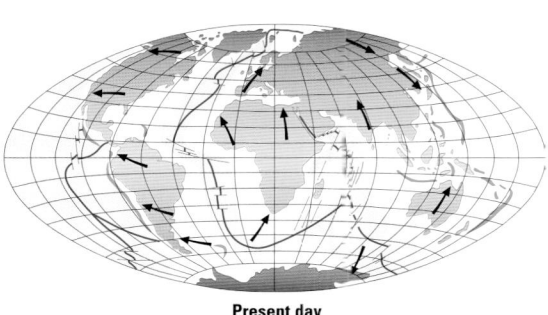

Present day

DISTRIBUTION OF VOLCANOES

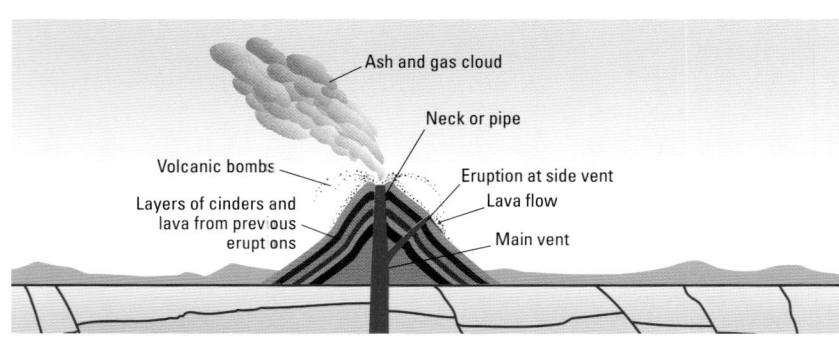

Ash and gas cloud
Neck or pipe
Volcanic bombs
Eruption at side vent
Lava flow
Layers of cinders and lava from previous eruptions
Main vent

Volcanoes occur when hot liquefied rock beneath the Earth's crust is pushed up by pressure to the surface as molten lava. There are some 550 known active volcanoes, around 20 of which are erupting at any one time.

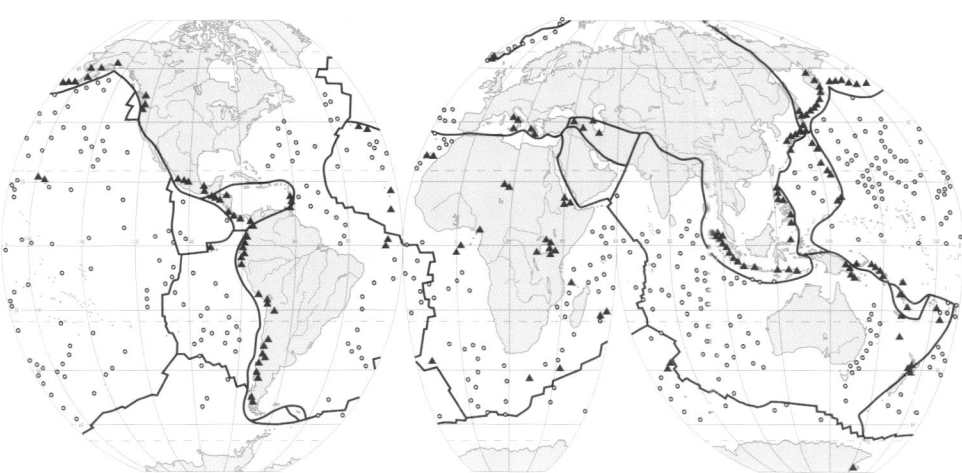

o Submarine volcanoes

▲ Land volcanoes active since 1700

— Boundaries of tectonic plates

PLATE TECTONICS

The huge ridges that run through the oceans represent boundaries between plates. Here plates are diverging and molten magma from the mantle rises along a central rift valley to form new crustal rock. These ocean ridges, which are active zones where earthquakes and volcanic eruptions are common, are called constructive plate margins. Destructive plate margins, which occur when two contrasting plates converge, are marked by deep-ocean trenches as one plate is forced under the other. The descending plate is melted to produce the magma that fuels volcanoes alongside the trenches. Movements of descending plates are often sudden, triggering earthquakes in overlying continental areas.

Sea-floor spreading in the Atlantic Ocean and plate collision

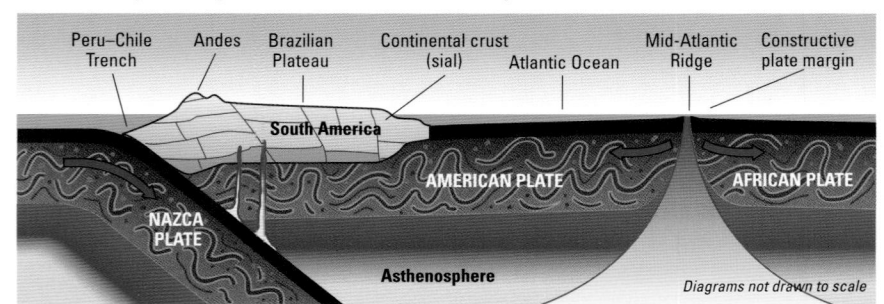

Peru–Chile Trench | Andes | Brazilian Plateau | Continental crust (sial) | Atlantic Ocean | Mid-Atlantic Ridge | Constructive plate margin
South America
AMERICAN PLATE | AFRICAN PLATE
NAZCA PLATE
Asthenosphere
Diagrams not drawn to scale

Sea-floor spreading in the Indian Ocean and continental plate collision

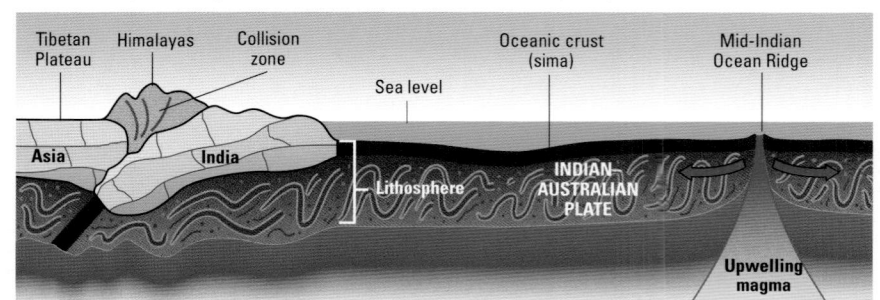

Tibetan Plateau | Himalayas | Collision zone | Oceanic crust (sima) | Mid-Indian Ocean Ridge
Sea level
Asia | India | Lithosphere | INDIAN-AUSTRALIAN PLATE
Upwelling magma

GEOLOGICAL TIME

Time, in millions of years before the present, is shown on a sliding scale, greatly compressed in the distant past.

ERA | PERIOD | EPOCH

PRE-CAMBRIAN		
PALEOZOIC	Cambrian 542	
	Ordovician 488.3	
	Silurian 443.7	
	Devonian 416	
	Carboniferous 359.2	
	Permian 299	
MESOZOIC	Triassic 251	
	Jurassic 199.6	
	Cretaceous 145.5	
CENOZOIC	Tertiary 65.5	Paleocene 55.8
		Eocene 33.9
		Oligocene 23.03
		Miocene 5.33
	Quaternary	Pliocene 1.81
		Pleistocene
		Holocene 10,000 BP to present

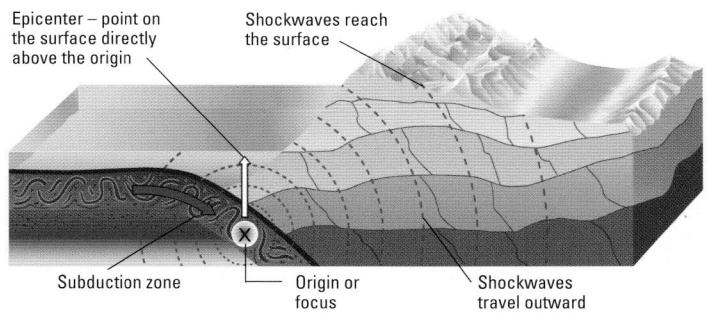

Geologists devised their timescale on the basis of relative, not calendar, ages. Accurate dating was impossible and estimates were often bitterly disputed, but the order in which the rocks were formed could be deduced from careful observation. The advent of radioactive dating – culminating in the 1950s with the development of a mass spectrometer capable of accurately measuring tiny quantities of isotopes – appears to have settled the arguments. The Earth is far older than geologists first imagined, but their painstakingly-created structure of geological time has withstood the advent of high technology.

The 4.6 billion (4,600 million) years since the formation of the Earth are divided into four great eras, further split into periods and, in the case of the most recent era, epochs. The present era is the Cenozoic ("new life"), extending backward through "middle life" and "ancient life" to the Pre-Cambrian, named after the Latin word for Wales, the location of some of the earliest known fossils. Most of the Earth's geological history is encompassed by the Pre-Cambrian: though traces of ancient life have since been found, it was largely the proliferation of fossils from the beginning of the Paleozoic era onward, some 570 million years ago, which first allowed precise subdivisions to be made.

Like the Cambrian, most are named after regions exemplifying a period's geology. Others – such as the Carboniferous ("coal-bearing") or the Cretaceous ("chalk-bearing") – are more directly descriptive.

- Pre-Cambrian shields
- Sedimentary cover on Pre-Cambrian shields
- Paleozoic (Caledonian and Hercynian) folding
- Sedimentary cover on Paleozoic folding
- Mesozoic folding
- Sedimentary cover on Mesozoic folding
- Cenozoic (Alpine) folding
- Sedimentary cover on Cenozoic folding
- Intensive Mesozoic and Cenozoic vulcanism
- ——— Principal faults
- ——— Oceanic marginal troughs
- ——— Mid-oceanic ridges
- ~~~~~ Overthrust faults

EARTHQUAKES

Earthquake magnitude is usually rated according to either the Richter scale or the Modified Mercalli scale, both devised by seismologists in the 1930s. The Richter scale measures absolute earthquake power with mathematical precision: each step upward represents a tenfold increase in the amplitude of the shockwave. Theoretically, there is no upper limit, but most of the largest earthquakes measured have been rated at between 8.8 and 8.9. The 12-point Mercalli scale, based on observed effects, is often more meaningful, ranging from I (earthquakes noticed only by seismographs) to XII (total destruction); intermediate points include V (people awakened at night; unstable objects overturned), VII (collapse of ordinary buildings; chimneys and monuments fall), and IX (conspicuous cracks in ground; serious damage to reservoirs).

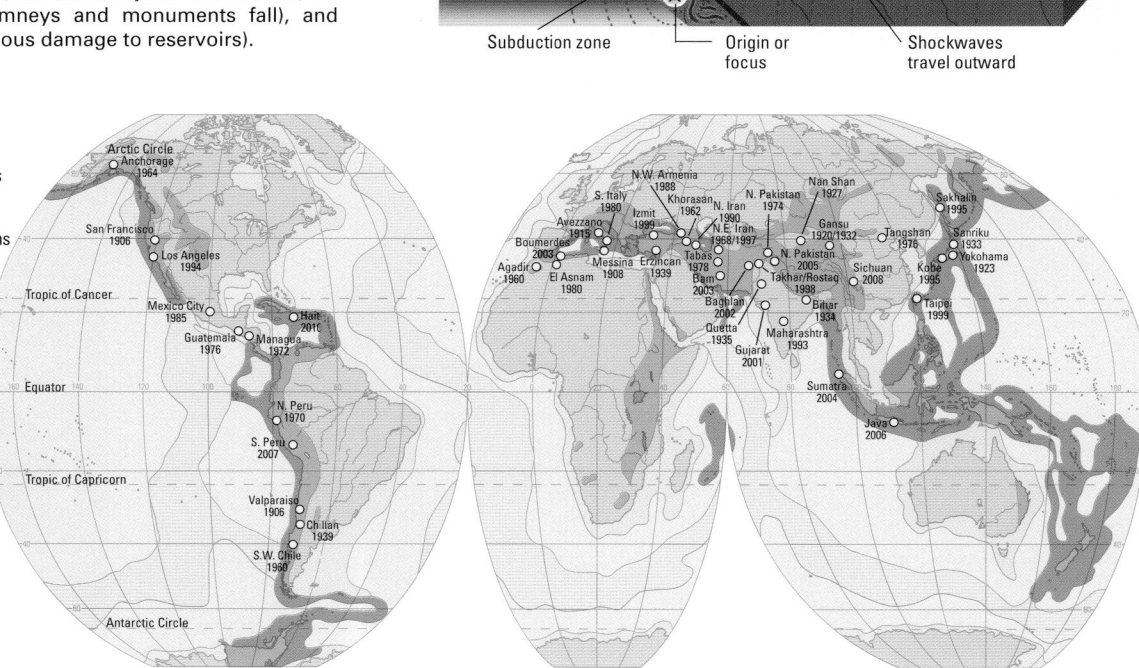

Epicenter – point on the surface directly above the origin

Shockwaves reach the surface

Subduction zone

Origin or focus

Shockwaves travel outward

Notable Earthquakes Since 1900

Year	Location	Mag.	Deaths
1906	San Francisco, USA	8.3	3,000
1906	Valparaiso, Chile	8.6	22,000
1908	Messina, Italy	7.5	83,000
1915	Avezzano, Italy	7.5	30,000
1920	Gansu (Kansu), China	8.6	180,000
1923	Yokohama, Japan	8.3	143,000
1927	Nan Shan, China	8.3	200,000
1932	Gansu (Kansu), China	7.6	70,000
1933	Sanriku, Japan	8.9	2,990
1934	Bihar, India/Nepal	8.4	10,700
1935	Quetta, India*	7.5	60,000
1939	Chillan, Chile	8.3	28,000
1939	Erzincan, Turkey	7.9	30,000
1960	S. W. Chile	9.5	2,200
1960	Agadir, Morocco	5.8	12,000
1962	Khorasan, Iran	7.1	12,230
1964	Anchorage, USA	9.2	125
1968	N. E. Iran	7.4	12,000
1970	N. Peru	7.8	70,000
1972	Managua, Nicaragua	6.2	5,000
1974	N. Pakistan	6.3	5,200
1976	Guatemala	7.5	22,500
1976	Tangshan, China	8.2	255,000
1978	Tabas, Iran	7.7	25,000
1980	El Asnam, Algeria	7.3	20,000
1980	S. Italy	7.2	4,800
1985	Mexico City, Mexico	8.1	4,200
1988	N.W. Armenia	6.8	55,000
1990	N. Iran	7.7	36,000
1993	Maharashtra, India	6.4	30,000
1994	Los Angeles, USA	6.6	51
1995	Kobe, Japan	7.2	5,000
1995	Sakhalin Is., Russia	7.5	2,000
1997	N. E. Iran	7.1	2,400
1998	Takhar, Afghanistan	6.1	4,200
1998	Rostaq, Afghanistan	7.0	5,000
1999	Izmit, Turkey	7.4	15,000
1999	Taipei, Taiwan	7.6	1,700
2001	Gujarat, India	7.7	14,000
2002	Baghlan, Afghanistan	6.1	1,000
2003	Boumerdes, Algeria	6.8	2,200
2003	Bam, Iran	6.6	30,000
2004	Sumatra, Indonesia	9.0	250,000
2005	N. Pakistan	7.6	74,000
2006	Java, Indonesia	6.4	6,200
2007	S. Peru	8.0	600
2008	Sichuan, China	7.9	70,000
2010	Haiti	7.0	230,000

An earthquake off the coast of Sumatra on December 26, 2004, triggered a deadly tsunami that swept across the Indian Ocean, causing devastation in many countries, in particular Sri Lanka, India, Thailand, and Indonesia, where the loss of life was greatest.

* now Pakistan

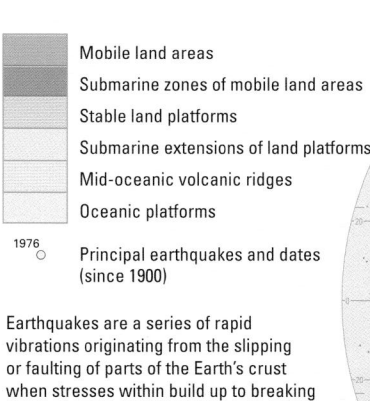

- Mobile land areas
- Submarine zones of mobile land areas
- Stable land platforms
- Submarine extensions of land platforms
- Mid-oceanic volcanic ridges
- Oceanic platforms

1976 ○ Principal earthquakes and dates (since 1900)

Earthquakes are a series of rapid vibrations originating from the slipping or faulting of parts of the Earth's crust when stresses within build up to breaking point. They usually happen at depths varying from 5 to 20 miles. Severe earthquakes cause extensive damage when they take place in populated areas, destroying structures and severing communications. Most initial loss of life occurs due to secondary causes such as falling masonry, fires, and flooding.

For more information:

73 Tides
74 Plate tectonics
78 Atmosphere
84 Hydrological cycle
   Water distribution
85 Watersheds
103 World shipping

The last 40 years have been described as the "Space Age," but another exciting and perhaps even more important area of discovery, proceeding at the same time, has been the exploration of the oceans, which cover more than 70% of our planet. Studies of the ocean floor and oceanic islands have revealed features that help to explain how continents move, and how the movements are related to earthquakes and volcanic activity.

Manned submersibles have established that life exists even in the deepest trenches, where the pressure reaches 1,000 atmospheres, the equivalent of the force of 1 tonne bearing down on every square centimeter. Further exploration in the pitch-black environment of the ocean ridges has revealed strange forms of marine life around scalding hot vents. The creatures include giant tubeworms, blind shrimps, and bacteria, some of which are genetically very different from any other known life forms. In 1996, an analysis of one microorganism revealed that at least half of its 1,700 or so genes were hitherto unknown. This environment, which is based on chemicals, not sunlight, may resemble the places where life on Earth first began.

Another vital area of contemporary research concerns the interactions between the oceans and the atmosphere, as exemplified in the El Niño–Southern Oscillation (ENSO) cycle, and the bearing that these have on climatic change (see below).

Most geographers divide the world's ocean waters into five areas: the Pacific, Atlantic, Indian, Southern, and Arctic oceans. The most active zone in the oceans is the sunlit upper layer, where the water is moved around by wind-blown currents. It is the home of most sea life and acts as a membrane through which the ocean breathes,

ATOLL BUILDING

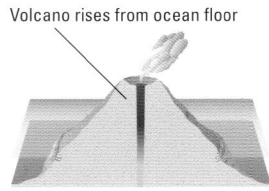

Volcano rises from ocean floor

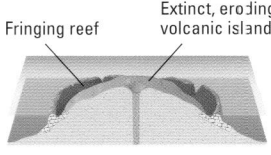

Fringing reef / Extinct, eroding volcanic island

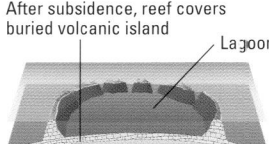

After subsidence, reef covers buried volcanic island — Lagoon

A coral atoll usually begins existence as a bare volcanic peak, thrusting above the surface of the ocean. A colony of coral – organisms with calcium carbonate skeletons – forms itself in the shallow water around the peak. The volcano is eroded and slowly sinks, leaving the coral forming a ring of hard limestone around its remnant. In time, the barrier reef of an atoll is all that remains.

LIFE IN THE OCEANS

An imaginary profile of the typical coastal and oceanic zones is shown, with a selection of the life forms that might occur in the waters off the Pacific Coast of Central America. The animals illustrated are not drawn to scale as the range of sizes is too great. Most marine life is confined to the first 650 feet, the upper sunlit (photic) zone, where sunlight can still penetrate. Plant and animal plankton, the basis of life in the oceans, occur in great quantities in all zones.

In the pelagic environment (open sea), vertical gradients, including those of light, temperature, and salinity, determine the distribution of organisms. From the tidal zone at the coastline, the continental shelf, geologically still part of the continental land mass, drops gently to about 650 feet – the sunlit zone. At the end of the shelf, the seabed falls away in the steeper angle of the continental slope. The subsequent descent to the deep-ocean floor, known as the "continental rise," is more gentle, with gradients between 1 in 100 and 1 in 700 until the abyssal plains and hills between 8,000 and 19,500 feet below the surface.

The deep-sea floor contains seamounts, some of which are capped by coral reefs, ocean ridges – the longest mountain chains on Earth – and deep-ocean trenches, especially in the Pacific Ocean where six trenches reach depths of more than 33,000 feet, including the Mariana Trench at 36,161 feet deep.

Each of these zones contains a distinctive community of species adapted to the different conditions of salinity, temperature, and light intensity. Indeed, a few organisms have been found even in the abyssal darkness of the great ocean trenches.

absorbing great quantities of carbon dioxide and partly exchanging it for oxygen.

As the depth increases, so light fades and temperatures fall until just before 3,000 feet where there is a marked temperature change at the thermocline, the boundary between the warm surface zone and the cold deep zone. Below the thermocline, slow currents are caused by density differences between bodies of water with varying temperatures and salinity.

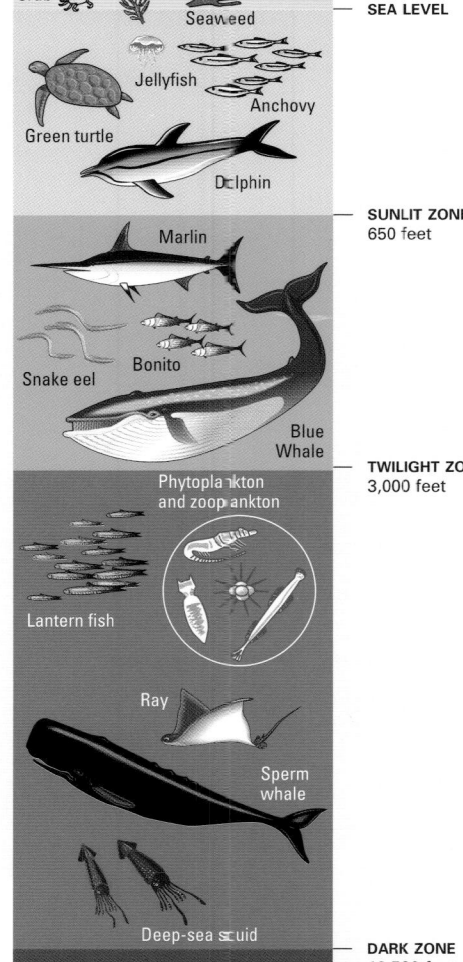

Crab / Seaweed — SEA LEVEL
Jellyfish / Anchovy
Green turtle / Dolphin — SUNLIT ZONE 650 feet
Marlin
Snake eel / Bonito
Blue Whale — TWILIGHT ZONE 3,000 feet
Phytoplankton and zooplankton
Lantern fish
Ray
Sperm whale
Deep-sea squid — DARK ZONE 19,500 feet
Anglerfish
Halosaur
Sea cucumber
Sponge
Isopod — TRENCH ZONE 33,000 feet

EL NIÑO PHENOMENON

Typical air and sea circulation pattern

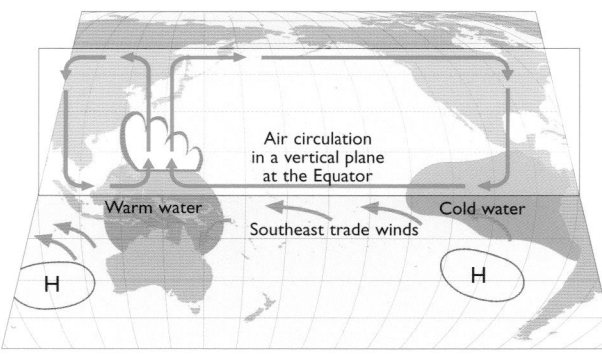

Air circulation in a vertical plane at the Equator
Warm water / Cold water
Southeast trade winds
H   H

El Niño air and sea circulation pattern

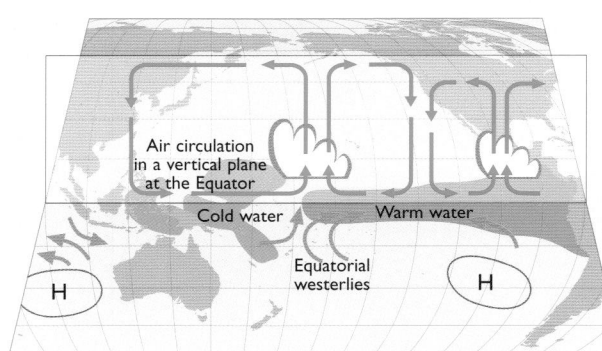

Air circulation in a vertical plane at the Equator
Cold water / Warm water
Equatorial westerlies
H   H

The importance of the ocean–atmosphere interaction is nowhere more dramatically demonstrated than in the El Niño phenomenon of the southern Pacific Ocean. Under normal conditions, called La Niña, cold, nutrient-rich water rises to the surface off South America and spreads westward. In the western Pacific, sea surface temperatures reach 82°F or more and warm air rises, creating a low-pressure air system and causing heavy rains. The rising air spreads out and some of it descends over South America and the eastern Pacific, creating a high-pressure air system from which winds blow westward.

An El Niño event is characterized by a reversal of currents. The upwelling of cold water is greatly reduced and surface water temperatures rise, causing a drastic reduction in fish life. The heaviest rainfall is over the eastern Pacific, while Southeast Asia is drier than usual. However, each El Niño event is unique in terms of its strength as well as its impact.

During an intense El Niño, the effects of the current and wind reversals affect the weather around the world. In the 1997 El Niño event there was a very suppressed hurricane season in the Caribbean but numerous super typhoons in the Pacific. Whilst South America and East Africa were much wetter than average, West Africa and parts of

Indonesia were much drier than normal. Algal blooms occurred in Australia's drought-stricken rivers and there were numerous bush fires in Indonesia.

Scientists have found evidence that the frequency of the El Niño event, which normally occurs every three to seven years, and lasts between 12–18 months, may have increased in recent years.

We do not fully understand the causes of the El Niño event, though some researchers are currently investigating possible connections between major volcanic eruptions in the tropical Pacific region, the El Niño Southern Oscillation (ENSO) cycle, and atmospheric circulation.

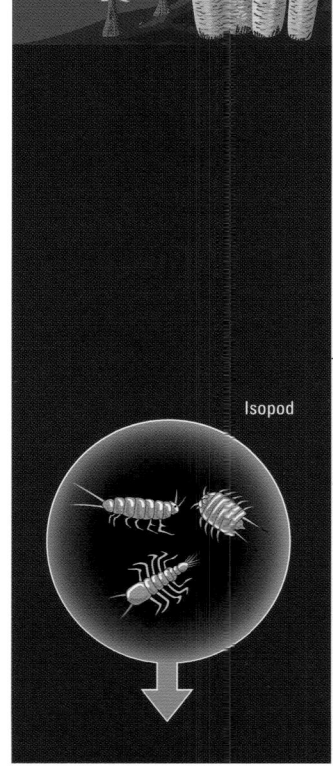

OCEAN CURRENTS

JANUARY CURRENTS
(Northern Hemisphere: winter)

Cold Warm Speed (knots)
- Less than 0.5
- 0.5 – 1.0
- Over 1.0

JULY CURRENTS
(Northern Hemisphere: summer)

Cold Warm Speed (knots)
- Less than 0.5
- 0.5 – 1.0
- Over 1.0

Moving immense quantities of energy as well as billions of tonnes of water every hour, the ocean currents are a vital part of the great heat engine that drives the Earth's climate. They themselves are produced by a twofold mechanism. At the surface, winds push huge masses of water before them; in the deep ocean below, an abrupt temperature gradient separates the churning surface waters from the still depths (see the ocean conveyor belt diagram, below left).

Coriolis effect
The pattern of circulation of the great surface currents is determined by the displacement known as the "Coriolis effect." As the Earth turns, the vast mass of ocean water is deflected to one side. The deflection is most obvious near the equator, where the Earth's surface is spinning eastward at 1,000 mph; currents moving poleward are curved clockwise in the northern hemisphere and counterclockwise in the southern hemisphere.

Ocean currents
The result is a system of spinning circles known as "gyres." Warm currents move constantly from the equator toward the poles, while cold water moves in the reverse direction. In this way, ocean currents act like a thermostat, helping to regulate temperatures around the world.

Depending on the annual movements of the prevailing wind belts, some currents on or near the equator may reverse their direction in the course of the year, a variation on which Asia's monsoon rains depend and whose occasional failure has brought disaster to millions of people.

THE OCEAN CONVEYOR BELT

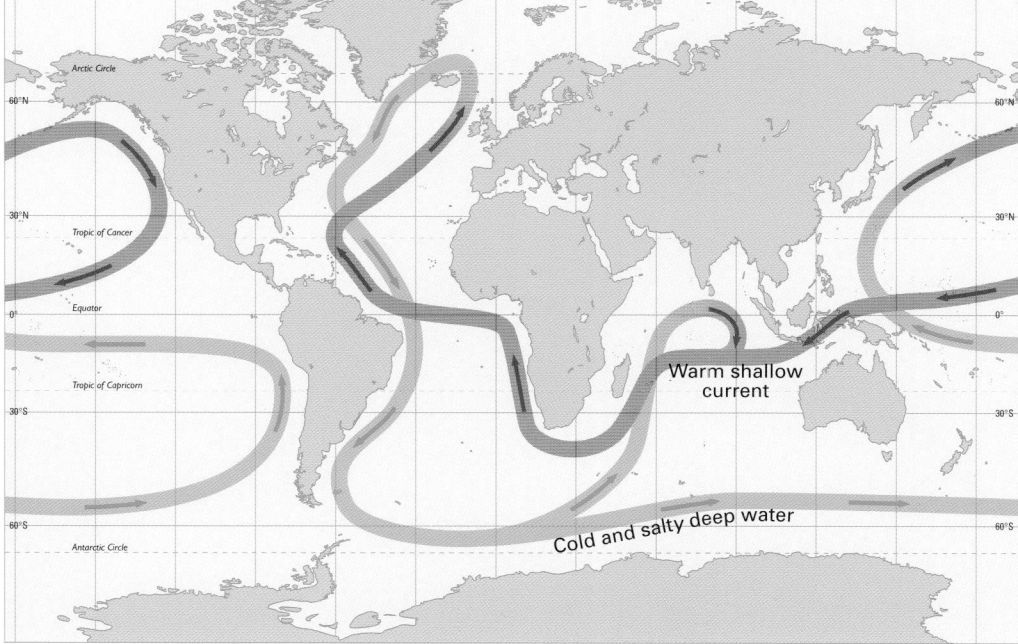

Thermohaline circulation, or the ocean conveyor belt, refers to the global, density-driven circulation of the oceans. The name comes from "thermo," for temperature, and "haline," for salt, which together determine the density of sea water.

The cycle starts near the equator in the Pacific Ocean, where surface currents drive the water westward. This water is warm and not very salty, making it lightweight, so it travels along the surface of the ocean.

As the water progresses west it eventually works its way into the North Atlantic where it cools, increases in salinity and sinks. It slowly circulates southward then eastward toward the Antarctic, where it splits into two routes: one to the Indian Ocean and one into the Pacific.

As the water recycles, it once again becomes warmer, less salty, lighter, and upwells in the Pacific to start the cycle all over again.

WORLD FISH CATCH

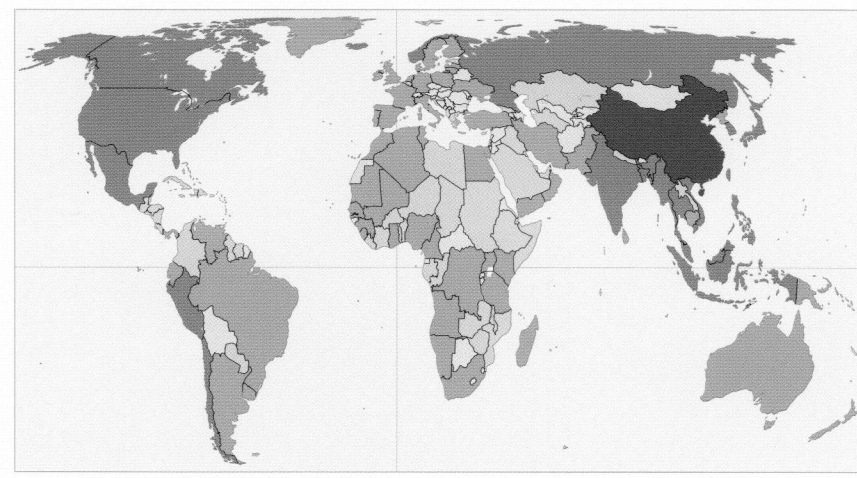

Total world fish catch in metric tonnes (2007)
(inland and marine fishing)

- Over 10 million
- 1 million – 10 million
- 100,000 – 1 million
- 10,000 – 100,000
- Under 10,000
- No data available

Leading fishing nations
(percentage of total world catch in 2007)

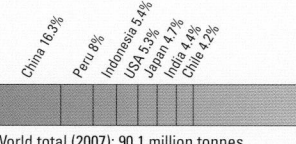

China 16.3% | Peru 8% | Indonesia 5.4% | USA 5.3% | Japan 4.7% | India 4.4% | Chile 4.2%

World total (2007): 90.1 million tonnes
(Marine catch 90.3% : Inland catch 9.7%)

With many marine stocks now fully exploited or over-exploited, future fish supplies are likely to be constrained by resource limits.

For more information:
76 El Niño phenomenon
77 Ocean currents
81 Beaufort wind scale
    Monsoon
82 Climate change
    Global warming

The atmosphere is a meteor shield, a radiation deflector, a thermal blanket, and a source of chemical energy for the Earth's diverse life forms. Five-sixths of its mass is in the lowest layer, the troposphere, which ranges in thickness from 11–6 miles between the equator and the poles. Powered by the Sun, the air is always on the move, flowing generally from high- to low-pressure areas. The troposphere is the layer where virtually all weather phenomena, including clouds, precipitation, and winds, occur. Above the troposphere is the stratosphere, which contains the important ozone layer and extends to about 30 miles above the Earth's surface. Beyond 60 miles, atmospheric density is lower than most laboratory vacuums.

STRUCTURE OF THE ATMOSPHERE

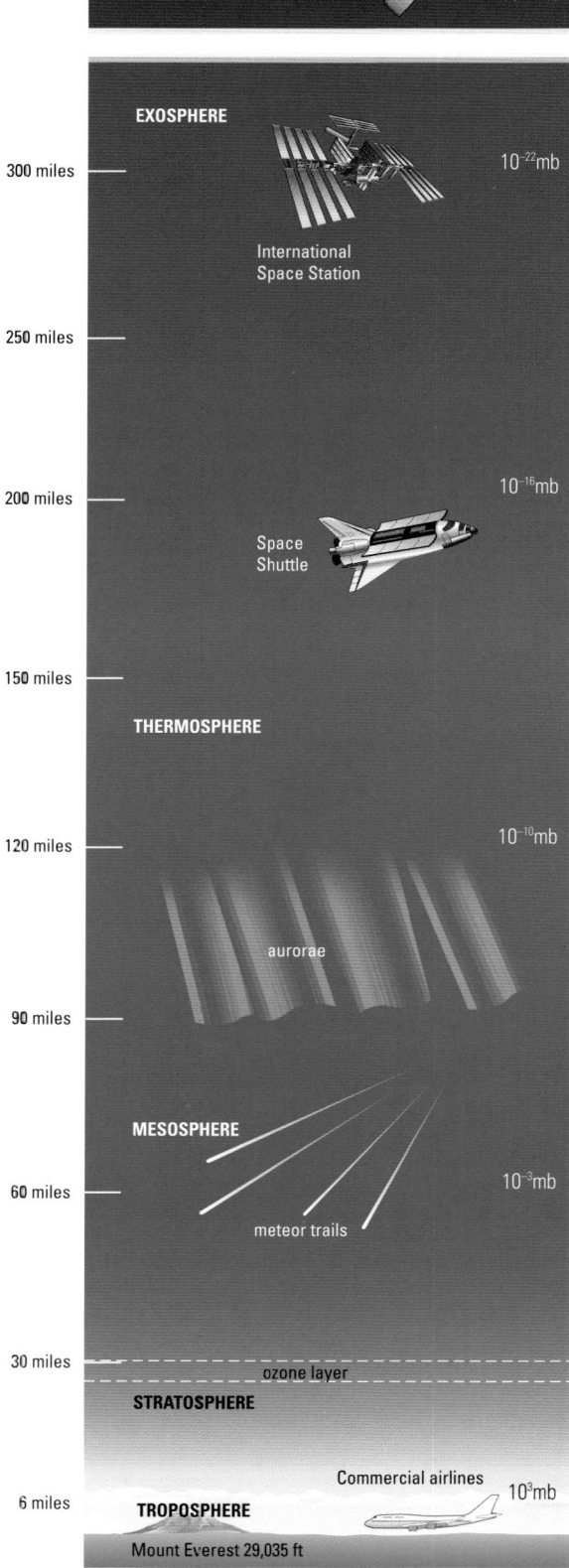

CIRCULATION OF THE AIR

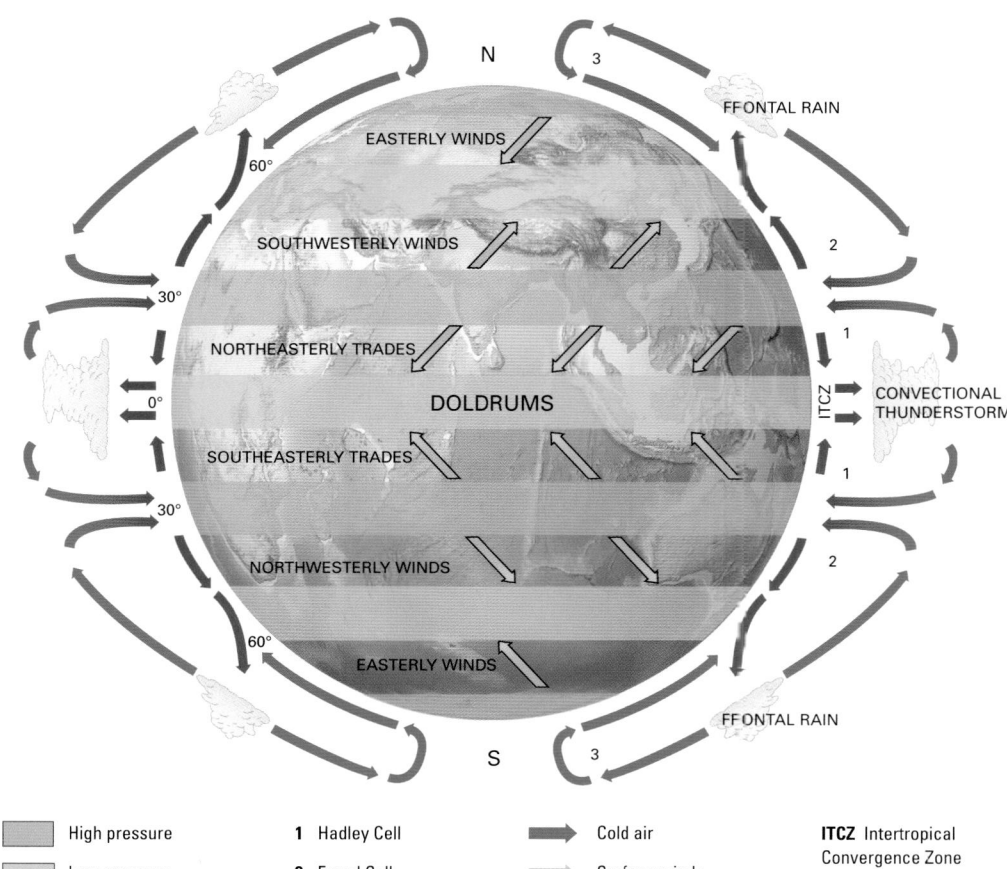

High pressure	**1** Hadley Cell	Cold air	**ITCZ** Intertropical Convergence Zone
Low pressure	**2** Ferrel Cell	Surface winds	
Warm air	**3** Polar Cell	Clouds	

FRONTAL SYSTEMS

Depressions, also known as cyclones or lows, form on the polar front where relatively cold and dry polar air flows alongside warmer, moister subtropical air. They occur when the flow high above the polar front generates a surface inward-swirling circulation that moves along the polar front as a wave.

The warm front is the leading edge of the subtropical air that glides up and over the cooler air ahead of it. This gently ascending flow produces a characteristic sequence of clouds ahead of the warm front and a band of precipitation a few hundred miles wide immediately in advance it. Conditions within the warm sector are often overcast with layer cloud and generally light rain or drizzle. The cloud sometimes breaks up downwind of hills.

Another band of precipitation often occurs just ahead of the cold front that is the leading edge of the cooler polar air. Cumulus clouds tend to occur in the air behind the cold front, producing scattered showers. The changes of temperature, wind direction, and cloud, etc, are illustrated by the diagram below.

CHEMICAL COMPOSITION

Gaseous composition of the principal atmospheric layers

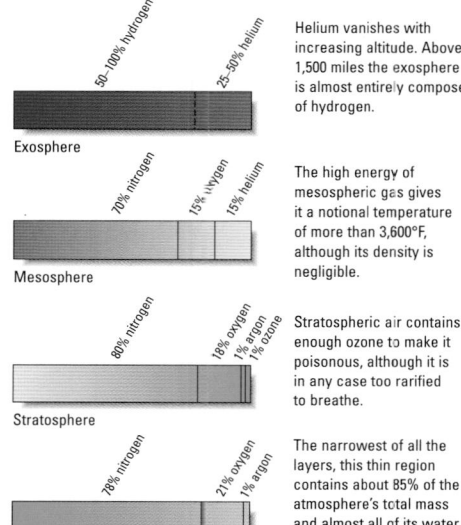

Helium vanishes with increasing altitude. Above 1,500 miles the exosphere is almost entirely composed of hydrogen.

The high energy of mesospheric gas gives it a notional temperature of more than 3,600°F, although its density is negligible.

Stratospheric air contains enough ozone to make it poisonous, although it is in any case too rarified to breathe.

The narrowest of all the layers, this thin region contains about 85% of the atmosphere's total mass and almost all of its water vapor. It is also the realm of the Earth's weather.

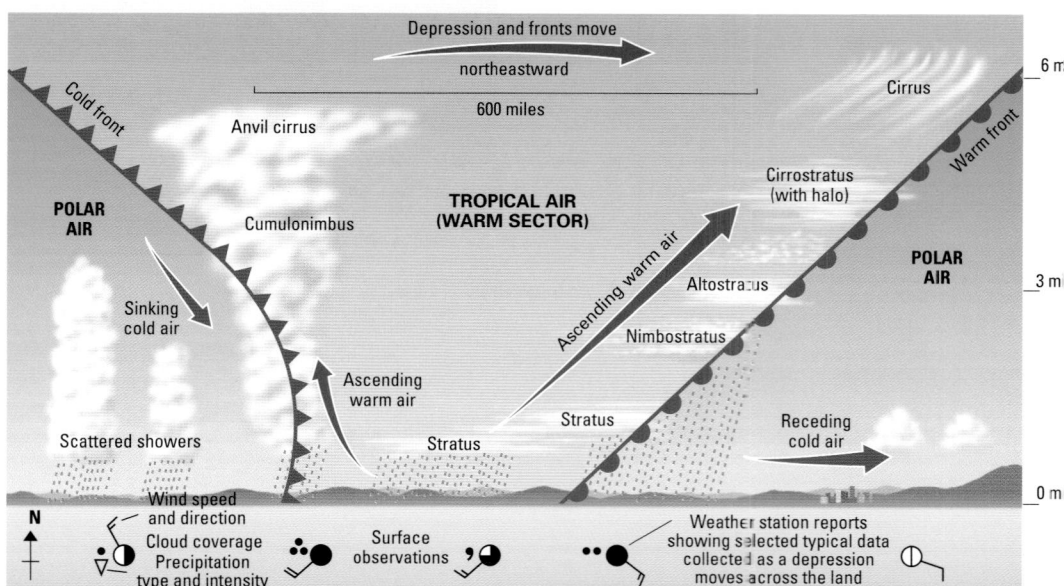

AIR MASSES

Air masses are extensive regions of air, typically a few thousand miles across, that have horizontally gently varying temperature and humidity characteristics produced by the underlying continental or maritime surfaces over which they occur. They can, for example, be warm and moist air or cold and dry air that spiral slowly out from their "source regions." These are the highs marked on the world maps below.

A particular location's weather associated with an air mass depends on the air's source region (for example, the North Atlantic subtropical high), the track it has taken (for example, long maritime or continental track), and the time of year (for example, across a cold or strongly heated continent). The polar front (and its frontal cyclones) is a gently sloping, troposphere-deep surface that separates two air masses – the North Atlantic subtropical high and the North American wintertime anticyclone. The warmer, damper subtropical air rides up and over the cooler, drier polar air to produce widespread frontal cloud and precipitation.

Air masses are classified as, amongst others, "polar continental," "polar maritime" or "tropical maritime." The massive Asian high in January is a source of polar continental, very cold, very dry air, while in contrast the extensive North Pacific and North Atlantic highs are sources of warm and very moist air throughout the year.

CLASSIFICATION OF CLOUDS

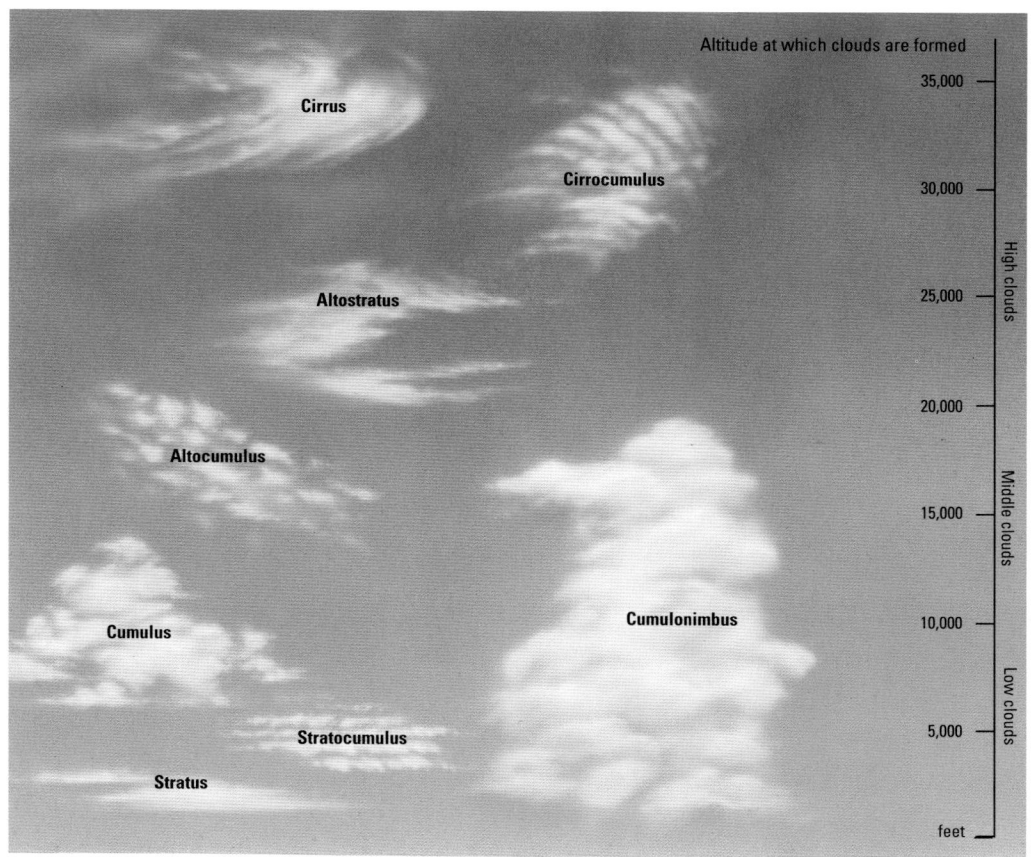

Clouds form when damp, usually rising, air is cooled. Thus they form when a wind rises to cross hills or mountains; when a mass of air rises over, or is pushed up by, another mass of denser air; or when local heating of the ground causes convection currents.

The first classification of clouds was developed by a London chemist, Luke Howard, in 1803, and it was later modified by the World Meteorological Organization. The types of clouds are classified according to altitude as high, middle, or low. The high ones, composed of ice crystals, are cirrus, cirrostratus, and cirrocumulus.

The middle clouds are altostratus – a gray or bluish striated, fibrous or uniform sheet producing light drizzle – and altocumulus, a thicker and fluffier version of cirrocumulus.

Low clouds include nimbostratus, a dark gray layer that brings rain or snow; cumulus, a detached heap, dark at the base; stratus, which forms dull, overcast skies at low levels; and stratocumulus, which consists of fluffy grayish-white layers.

Cumulonimbus, associated with storms and rains, heavy and dense with a flat base and a high, fluffy outline, can be tall enough to occupy middle as well as low altitudes.

PRESSURE AND SURFACE WINDS

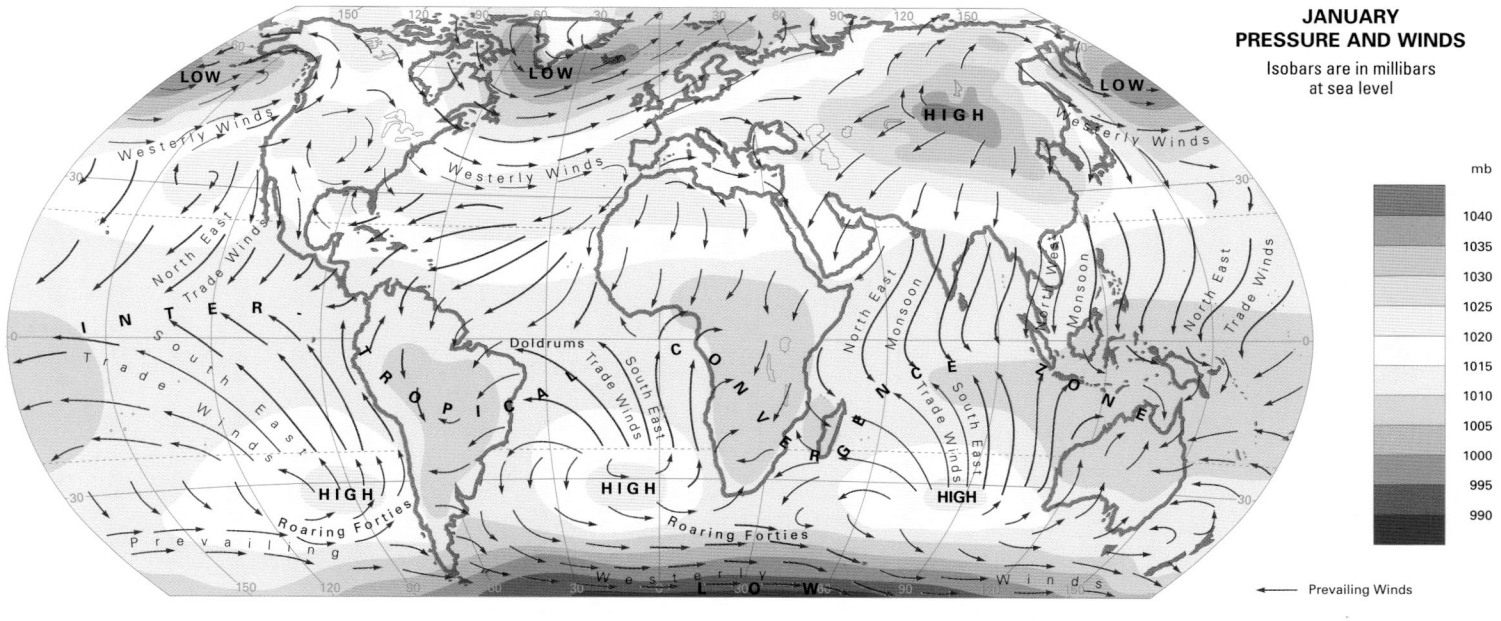

JANUARY PRESSURE AND WINDS

Isobars are in millibars at sea level

JULY PRESSURE AND WINDS

Isobars are in millibars at sea level

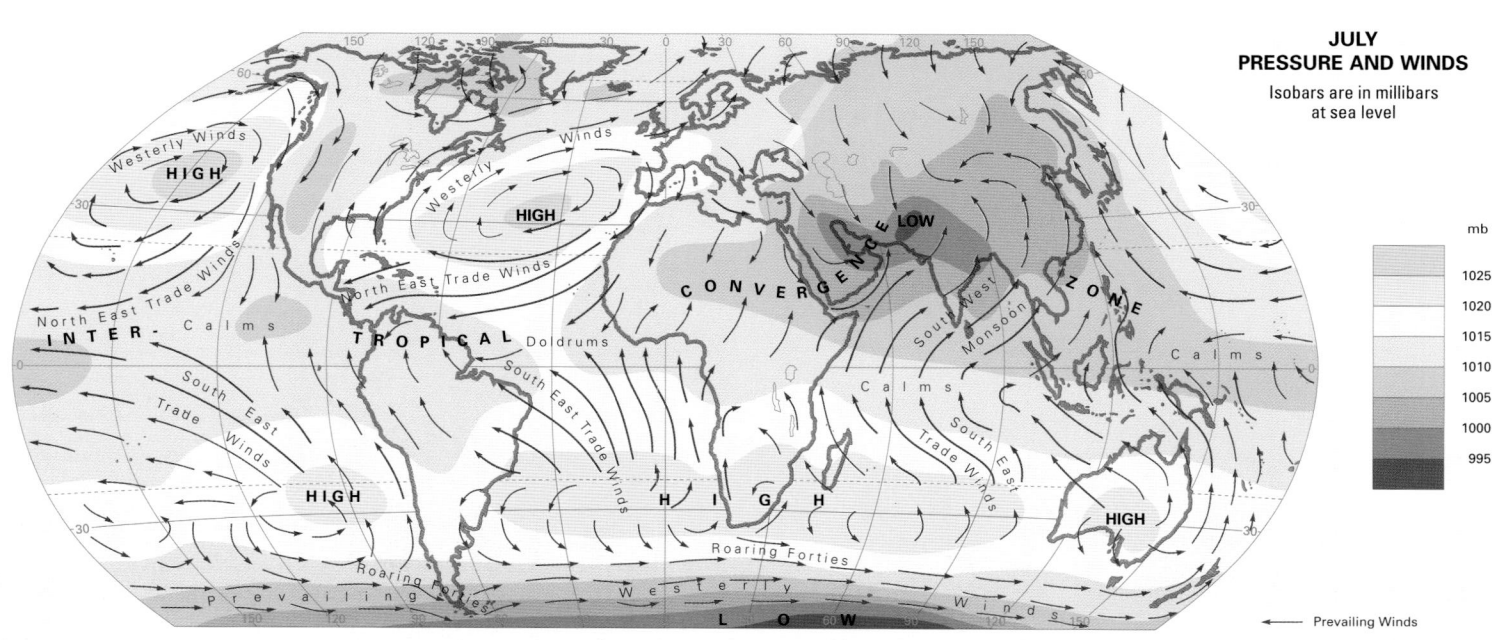

WEATHER RECORDS

Pressure and winds

Highest barometric pressure:
Agata, Siberia, 1,083.8 mb at altitude 862 ft [262 m], December 31, 1968.

Lowest barometric pressure:
Typhoon Tip, 300 mi [480 km] west of Guam, Pacific Ocean, 870 mb, October 12, 1979.

Highest recorded wind speed:
Bridge Creek, Oklahoma, USA, 318 mph [512 km/h], May 3, 1999. Measured by Doppler radar monitoring a tornado.

Windiest place:
Port Martin, Antarctica, where winds of more than 40 mph [64 km/h] occur for not less than 100 days a year.

Worst recorded storm:
Bangladesh (then East Pakistan) cyclone, November 13, 1970 – over 300,000 dead or missing. The 1991 cyclone, Bangladesh's and the world's second worst in terms of loss of life, killed an estimated 138,000 people.

Worst recorded tornado:
Tri-state tornado – Missouri/Illinois/Indiana, USA, March 18, 1925 – 695 deaths, lasted 3 hours with 219 mi [352 km] path length. A suspected tornado in Bangladesh on April 26, 1989, killed approximately 1,300 people.

For more information:

77 Ocean currents
78 Circulation of the air
79 Classification of clouds
   Pressure and winds
82 Climate change
   Global warming
84 Hydrological cycle
85 Natural vegetation

Weather is the day-to-day or hour-to-hour condition of the air, while climate is weather in the long term – the seasonal pattern of hot and cold, wet and dry, averaged over a long period.

Most classifications of climate are based on a system developed in the early 19th century by Vladimir Köppen, a Russian meteorologist. Using a code based on letters and a classification centered on two main features, temperature and precipitation, he identified five main climatic types: tropical (A), dry (B), warm temperate (C), cold temperate (D), and polar (E). A highland mountain climate (H) was added later to account for the variety of altitudinal climatic zones on high mountains. Each of these main regions was then further subdivided.

Latitude is a major factor in determining climate, but other factors add to the complexity. These include the differential heating of land and sea, the distance from the sea, the effect of mountains on winds, and the influence of ocean currents. For example, New York City, Naples, and the Gobi Desert share almost the same latitude, but their climates are very different.

During the last Ice Age, the Earth underwent alternating cold periods, called glacials, separated by warm interglacials. The Milankovich theory suggests such cycles may be caused by variations in the Earth's path around the Sun, changing from almost circular to elliptical every 95,000 years, and variations in the Earth's tilt from 21.5° to 24.5° every 42,000 years. Another factor is that the Earth is now closest to the Sun in the middle of winter in the northern hemisphere and furthest away in summer. But 12,000 years ago, at the height of the last glacial period, the northern winter fell with the Sun at its most distant.

Studies of these cycles suggest that we are now in an interglacial with a new glacial period on the way. However, scientists believe that global warming, largely a result of burning fossil fuels and deforestation, may be occurring much faster than the great, slow cycles of the Solar System.

Tropical rainy climates
All mean monthly temperatures above 64°F.

Af	Rain forest climate
Am	Monsoon climate
Aw	Savanna climate

Dry climates
Low rainfall combined with a wide range of temperatures

| BS | Steppe climate |
| BW | Desert climate |

Warm temperate rainy climates
The mean temperature is below 64°F but above 26°F and that of the warmest month is over 50°F.

Cw	Dry winter climate
Cs	Dry summer climate
Cf	Climate with no dry season

Cold temperate rainy climates
The mean temperature of the coldest month is below 26°F but that of the warmest month is still over 50°F.

| Dw | Dry winter climate |
| Df | Climate with no dry season |

Polar climates
The mean temperature of the warmest month is below 50°F, giving permanently frozen subsoil.

| ET | Tundra climate |

The mean temperature of the warmest month is below 32°F, giving permanent ice and snow.

| EF | Polar climate |

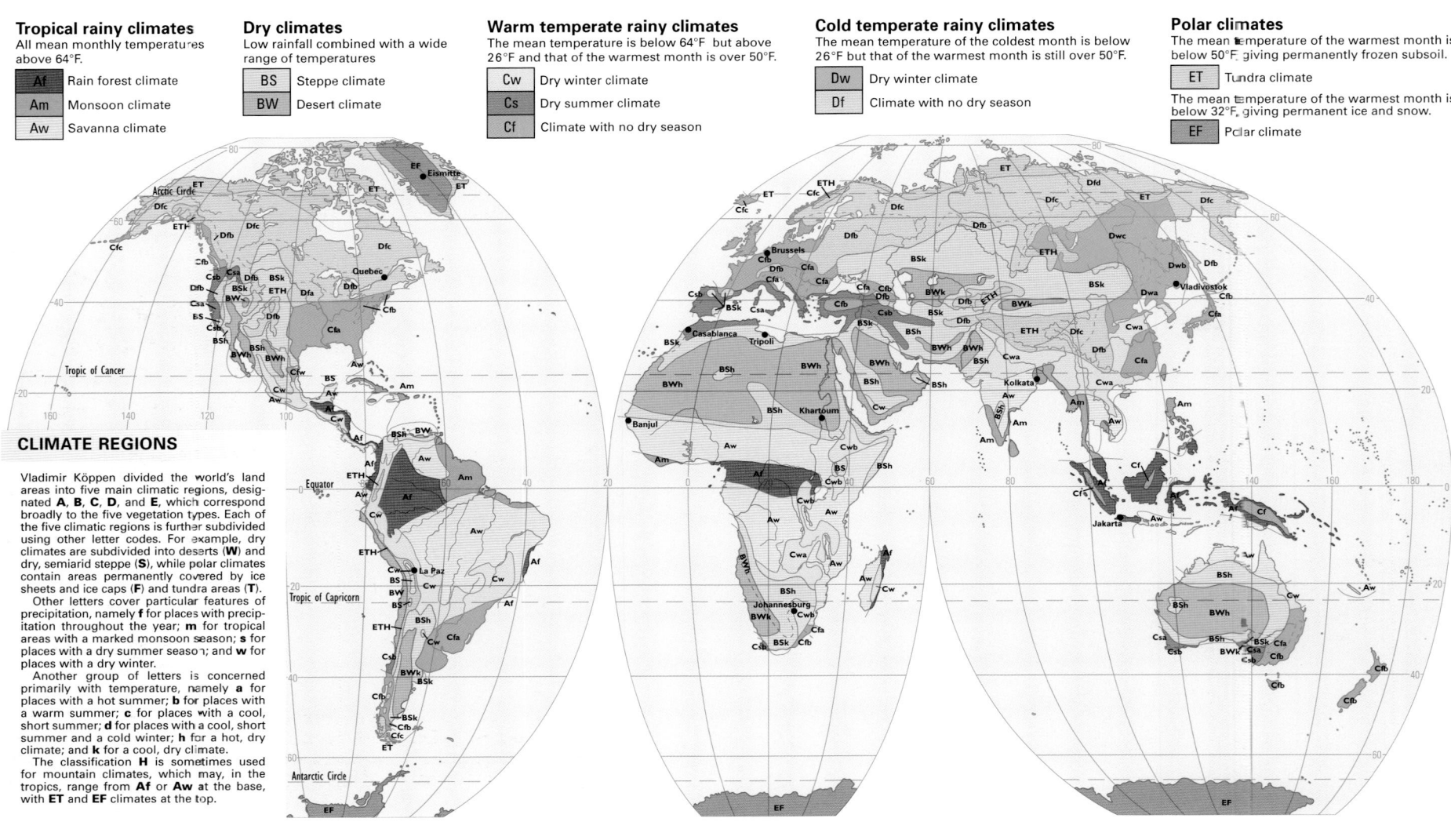

CLIMATE REGIONS

Vladimir Köppen divided the world's land areas into five main climatic regions, designated **A**, **B**, **C**, **D**, and **E**, which correspond broadly to the five vegetation types. Each of the five climatic regions is further subdivided using other letter codes. For example, dry climates are subdivided into deserts (**W**) and dry, semiarid steppe (**S**), while polar climates contain areas permanently covered by ice sheets and ice caps (**F**) and tundra areas (**T**).

Other letters cover particular features of precipitation, namely **f** for places with precipitation throughout the year; **m** for tropical areas with a marked monsoon season; **s** for places with a dry summer season; and **w** for places with a dry winter.

Another group of letters is concerned primarily with temperature, namely **a** for places with a hot summer; **b** for places with a warm summer; **c** for places with a cool, short summer; **d** for places with a cool, short summer and a cold winter; **h** for a hot, dry climate; and **k** for a cool, dry climate.

The classification **H** is sometimes used for mountain climates, which may, in the tropics, range from **Af** or **Aw** at the base, with **ET** and **EF** climates at the top.

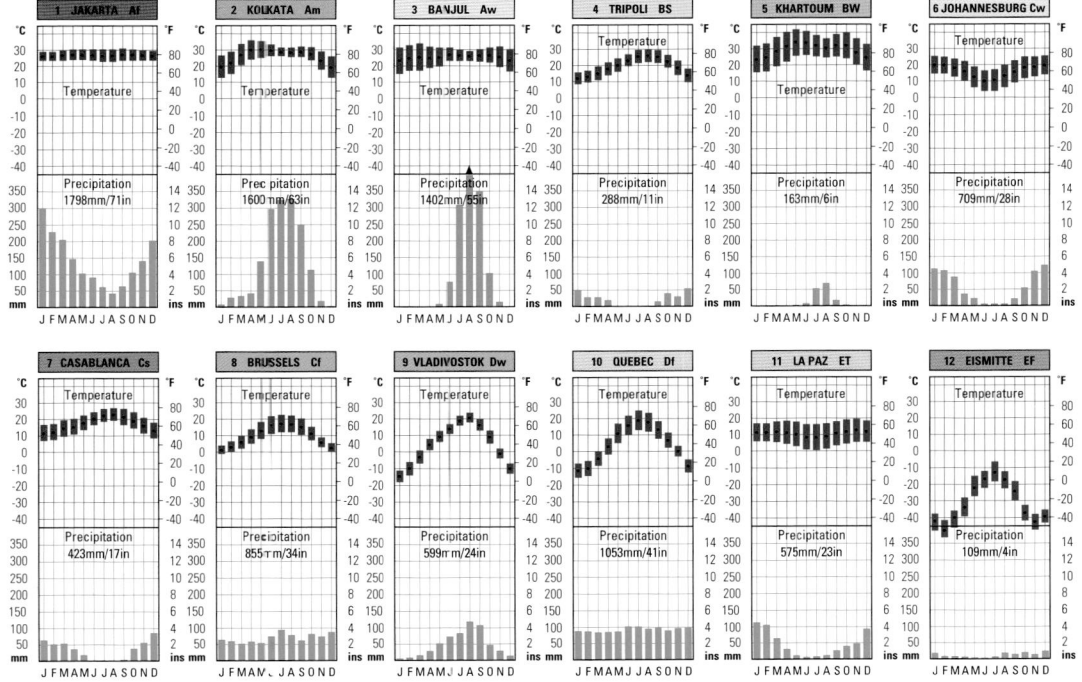

CLIMATE AND WEATHER TERMS

Anticyclone: area of high pressure with light winds and generally quiet weather.

Absolute humidity: mass of water vapor contained in a given volume of air.

Cloud cover: amount of cloud in the sky; measured in oktas (from 0–9), with 0 clear, and 9 "sky obscured."

Condensation: the conversion of water vapor into liquid.

Cyclone: violent storm resulting from counterclockwise rotation of winds in the northern hemisphere and clockwise in the southern: called hurricane in North America, typhoon in the Far East.

Depression: large area of low barometric pressure, a few thousand miles across.

Dew: deposition of small water droplets on the Earth's surface by direct condensation of water vapor.

Dew point: the temperature at which air becomes saturated by cooling at constant barometric pressure and absolute humidity

Drizzle: precipitation drops between 0.01–0.02 inches [0.2 and 0.5 mm] in diameter.

Evaporation: conversion of water from liquid into vapor or moisture in the air.

Front: the dividing line between two air masses.

Frost: the surface deposition of water vapor as minute ice crystals, when temperature reaches the frost point.

Hail: variably-sized pieces of ice that fall in downdrafts from cumulonimbus clouds.

Humidity: amount of water vapor in the air.

Isobar: line joining places with the same barometric pressure.

Isotherm: line connecting places of equal temperature.

Lightning: massive electrical discharge released in thunderstorm from cloud to cloud or cloud to ground, the result of the top becoming positively charged and the bottom negatively charged.

Precipitation: measurable rain, snow, sleet, or hail.

Prevailing wind: most common direction of wind at a given location.

Rain: precipitation of liquid particles with diameter larger than 0.02 inches [0.5 mm].

Relative humidity: observed quantity of water vapor in a mass of air over the saturation value at a given temperature (as a percentage).

Snow: flake-like coagulations of ice crystals that fall from clouds in subzero temperatures.

Thunder: sound produced by the rapid expansion of air heated by lightning.

Tornado: rapidly-rotating funnel-shaped cloud or debris column that must reach the surface and be attached to a parent cumulonimbus cloud.

BEAUFORT WIND SCALE

Named after Admiral Sir Francis Beaufort, the 19th-century British naval officer who devised it, the Beaufort Scale assesses wind speed according to its effects. It was originally designed as an aid for sailors, but has since been adapted for use on the land. It is used internationally.

Scale	Wind speed mph	km/h	Effect
0	0–1	0–1	**Calm** Smoke rises vertically
1	1–3	1–5	**Light air** Wind direction shown only by smoke drift
2	4–7	6–11	**Light breeze** Wind felt on face; leaves rustle; vanes moved by wind
3	8–12	12–19	**Gentle breeze** Leaves and small twigs in constant motion; wind extends small flag
4	13–18	20–28	**Moderate** Raises dust and loose paper; small branches move
5	19–24	29–38	**Fresh** Small trees in leaf sway; crested wavelets on inland waters
6	25–31	39–49	**Strong** Large branches move; difficult to use umbrellas; overhead wires whistle
7	32–38	50–61	**Near gale** Whole trees in motion; difficult to walk against wind
8	39–46	62–74	**Gale** Twigs break from trees; walking very difficult
9	47–54	75–88	**Strong gale** Slight structural damage
10	55–63	89–102	**Storm** Trees uprooted; serious structural damage
11	64–72	103–117	**Violent storm** Widespread damage
12	73+	118+	**Hurricane**

▲ On September 14, 2003, Hurricane Isabel was located over the Atlantic Ocean, 400 miles [640 km] north of Puerto Rico. It moved in a northwestward direction with maximum winds of 155 mph [250 km/h], making it a Category 5 hurricane.

THE MONSOON

Monsoon is the term given to the seasonal reversal of wind direction, most noticeably in Southeast Asia. It results from a combination of factors: the extreme heating and cooling of large land masses in relation to the less marked changes in temperature of the adjacent seas; the northward movement of the Intertropical Convergence Zone (ITCZ); and the effect of the Himalayas on the circulation of the air.

In March, winds blow outward from the mainland. But as the Sun and the ITCZ move northward, the land is intensely heated, and a low-pressure system develops. The southeast trade winds change direction and are sucked into the interior to become southwesterlies, bringing heavy rain. By November, the Sun and the ITCZ have again moved south and the wind directions are again reversed. Cool winds blow from the Asian interior to the sea, losing any moisture on the Himalayas before descending to the coast.

TEMPERATURE

Average temperature in January

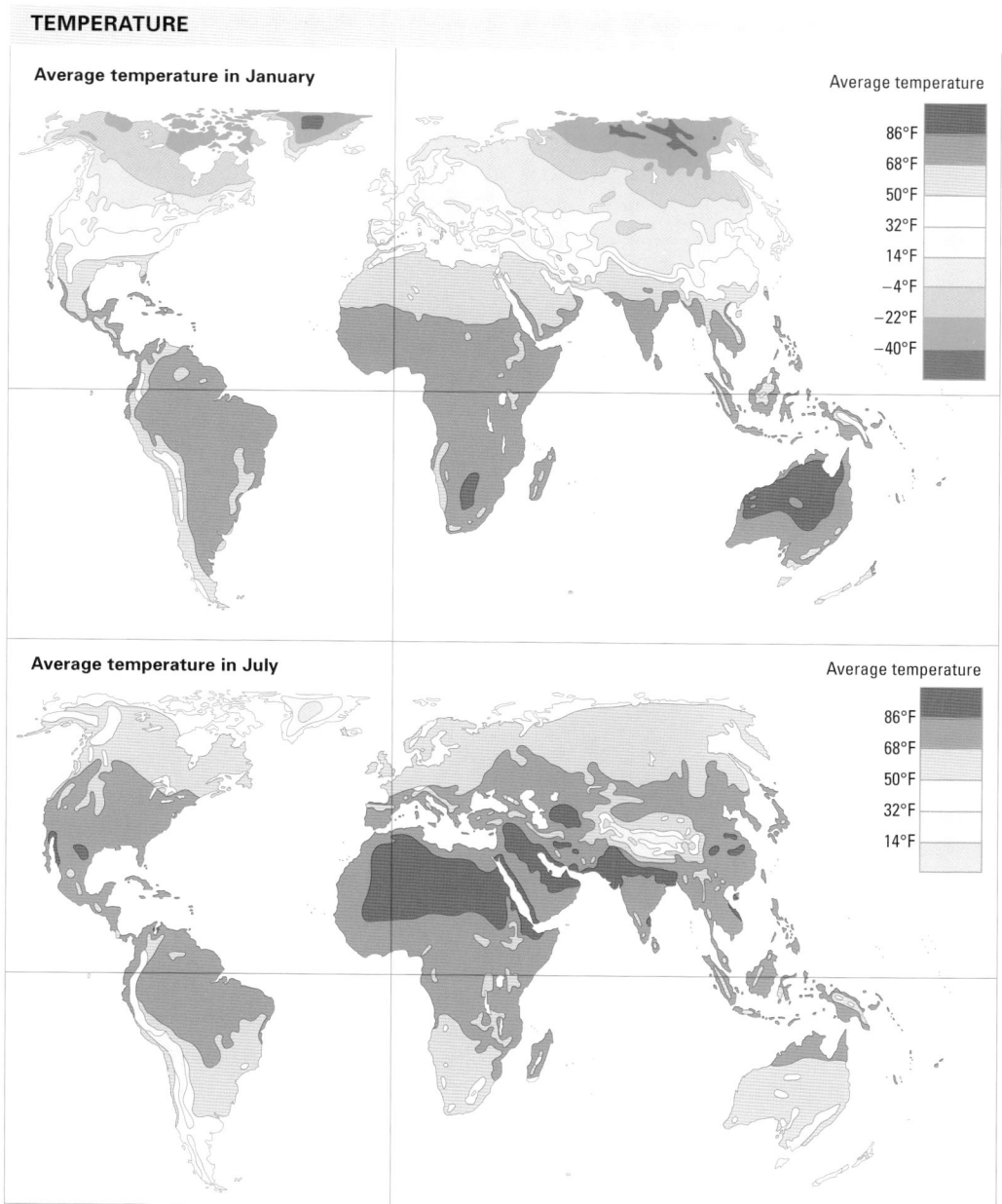

Average temperature
- 86°F
- 68°F
- 50°F
- 32°F
- 14°F
- −4°F
- −22°F
- −40°F

Average temperature in July

Average temperature
- 86°F
- 68°F
- 50°F
- 32°F
- 14°F

PRECIPITATION (RAINFALL AND SNOW)

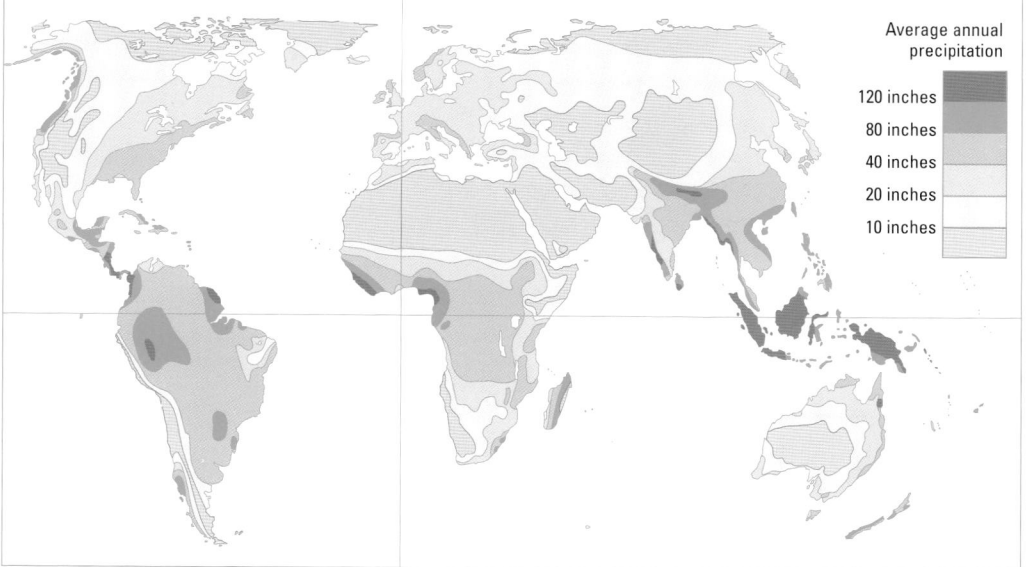

Average annual precipitation
- 120 inches
- 80 inches
- 40 inches
- 20 inches
- 10 inches

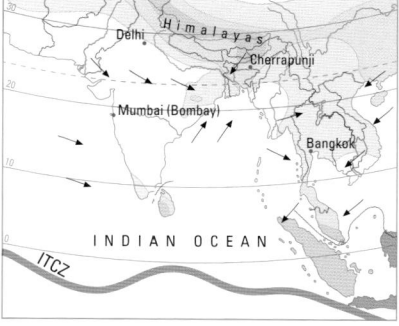

March – Start of the hot, dry season. The ITCZ is over the southern Indian Ocean.

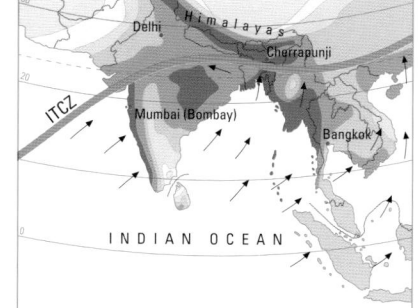

July – The rainy season. The ITCZ has migrated northward; winds blow onshore.

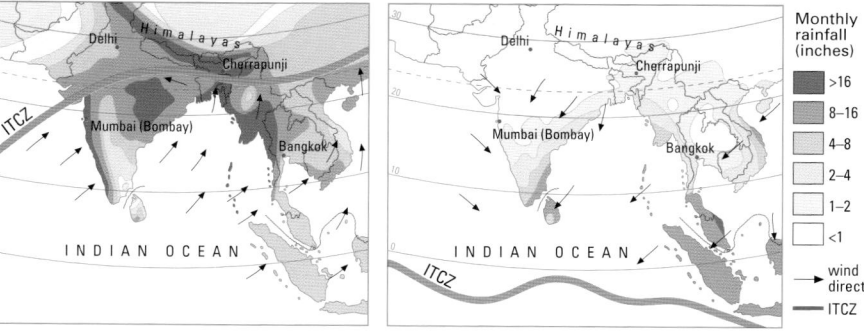

November – The ITCZ has returned south. The offshore winds are cool and dry.

Monthly rainfall (inches)
- >16
- 8–16
- 4–8
- 2–4
- 1–2
- <1

→ wind direction
— ITCZ

CLIMATE RECORDS

TEMPERATURE

Highest recorded temperature:
Al Aziziyah, Libya, 135.9°F [57.7°C], September 13, 1922.

Highest mean annual temperature:
Dallol, Ethiopia, 94°F [34.4°C], 1960–6.

Longest heatwave:
Marble Bar, W. Australia, 162 days over 100°F [38°C], October 23, 1923, to April 7, 1924.

Lowest recorded temperature (outside poles):
Verkhoyansk, Siberia, −93.6°F [−69.8°C], February 7, 1982. Verkhoyansk also registered the greatest annual range of temperature: −90°F to 98°F [−68°C to 37°C].

Lowest mean annual temperature:
Polus Nedostupnosti, Pole of Cold, Antarctica, −72°F [−57.8°C].

PRECIPITATION

Driest place:
Quillagua, N. Chile, mean annual rainfall 0.02 inches [0.5 mm], 1964–2001.

Wettest place (average):
Mt Wai'ale'ale, Hawai'i, USA, mean annual rainfall 459.8 inches [11,680 mm].

Wettest place (12 months):
Cherrapunji, Meghalaya, N.E. India, 1,042 inches [26,461 mm], August 1860 to August 1861. Cherrapunji also holds the record for rainfall in one month: 115 inches [2,930 mm], July 1861. (See Monsoon maps below.)

Wettest place (24 hours):
Fac Fac, Réunion, Indian Ocean, 71.9 inches [1,825 mm], March 15–16, 1952.

Heaviest hailstones:
Gopalganj, Bangladesh, up to 2.25 lb [1.02 kg], April 14, 1986 (killed 92 people).

Heaviest snowfall (continuous):
Bessans, Savoie, France, 68 inches [1,730 mm] in 19 hours, April 5–6. 1969.

Heaviest snowfall (season/year):
Mt Baker, Washington, USA, 1,140 inches [28,956 mm], June 1998 to June 1999.

For more information:

77 Ocean currents
78 Atmosphere
80 Climate

Ever since the Industrial Revolution began, the amount of carbon dioxide in the atmosphere has steadily increased. It is the result of burning fossil fuels – coal, oil, and natural gas, and also the destruction of forests which absorb carbon dioxide. In the late 18th century, carbon dioxide made up about 280 parts per million by volume (ppmv). Since 1958, regular measurements have been made at the Mauna Kea Observatory, Hawai'i, to avoid local pollution. It has since risen from 316 ppmv to 387 ppmv in 2008.

Carbon dioxide is one of the "greenhouse gases," which also include CFCs (which also cause ozone depletion in the upper atmosphere), methane, and nitrous oxides. Water vapor is another greenhouse gas. The volume of vapor in the atmosphere is not changing significantly, though it may increase if the atmosphere warms up, causing an increase in the evaporation of surface waters.

Greenhouse gases are so-called because they slow the escape of heat that is reradiated from the Earth's surface, in much the same way the glass walls and roof of a greenhouse block the escape of heat. The greenhouse effect is essential for life on Earth. Without it, our planet would be some 54°F [30°C] colder than it is. But the increase in the volume of carbon dioxide in particular has caused global temperatures to rise. These changes were detailed by the Intergovernmental Panel on Climate Change (IPCC) report in 2007. While computer projections are difficult to make, the IPCC report concluded that a rise in temperatures of 7°F [4°C] was likely by 2100. Global warming will almost certainly alter weather patterns, causing extreme food and water shortages in vulnerable parts of the world, massive floods, and a rise in sea levels of between 7 inches and 23 inches [18–59 cm].

While an international ban has been imposed on some greenhouse gases, their residence time in the atmosphere may have long-lasting consequences.

CARBON DIOXIDE

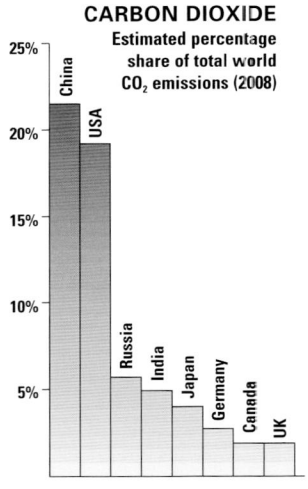

Estimated percentage share of total world CO₂ emissions (2008)

In 2007 it was estimated that China was building two coal-fired power stations every week to support its economic boom. It has since overtaken the USA to become the world's biggest producer of carbon dioxide.

GLOBAL WARMING

High atmospheric concentrations of heat-absorbing gases appear to be causing a rise in average temperatures worldwide – up by approximately 3°F [1.5°C] by the year 2020, according to some estimates. Global warming is also likely to bring about a rise in sea levels that may flood some of the world's densely populated coastal areas.

Evidence of global warming is attributed mainly to the "greenhouse effect," caused by the emission of certain gases, notably carbon dioxide, into the atmosphere. Despite international action to control emissions of some greenhouse gases, carbon dioxide levels are still rising.

Carbon dioxide emissions in tonnes per capita (2008)

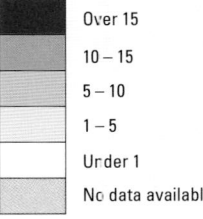

- Over 15
- 10 – 15
- 5 – 10
- 1 – 5
- Under 1
- No data available

CLIMATE CHANGE

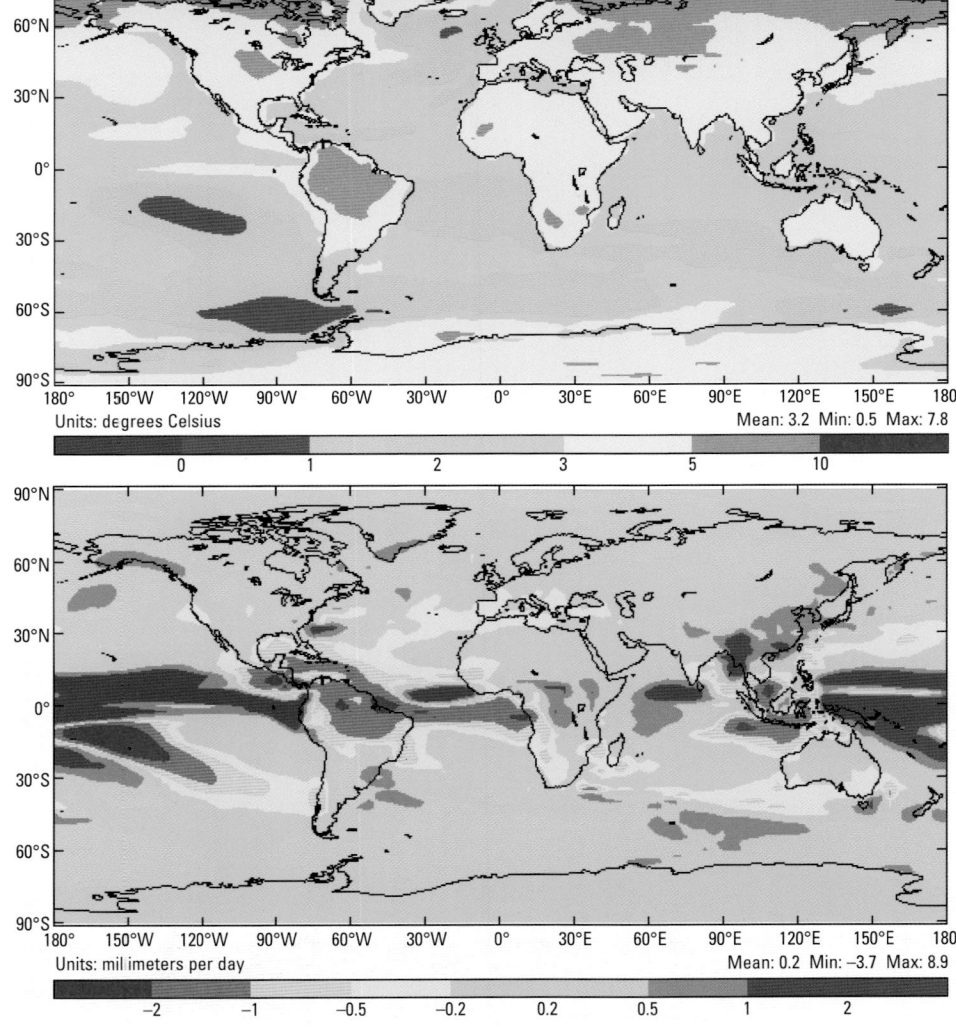

Units: degrees Celsius

Mean: 3.2 Min: 0.5 Max: 7.8

| 0 | 1 | 2 | 3 | 5 | 10 |

Units: millimeters per day

Mean: 0.2 Min: –3.7 Max: 8.9

| –2 | –1 | –0.5 | –0.2 | 0.2 | 0.5 | 1 | 2 |

Annual average surface air temperature

The map summarizes the change in long-term mean values between the predicted average for the period from 2070 to 2100, and the observed average for 1960 to 1990. The predictions are from a long-term "run" of a "coupled" atmosphere-ocean computer model that represents the complex processes in the Earth's climate system. It assumes that the atmospheric concentration of carbon dioxide will increase more than twofold during the 21st century, assuming "medium growth" of the global economy, and that no measures to combat the emission of greenhouse gases are taken. Note that the predicted increase in average surface temperature suggests a warming across Britain and Ireland of between 2°C [3.6°F] in the north and west to possibly 4°C [7.2°F] in the southeast. Very broadly, the oceans and some adjacent continental areas are likely to see the smaller increases.

Annual average precipitation

Predictions from climate models always involve some degree of uncertainty. This is because our understanding of the climate system and its complex workings are imperfect, as are the model representations of the physical system. Additionally, we are unsure quite how the world will evolve economically and politically over the coming decades – although different scenarios are used in this regard. The map of predicted precipitation change indicates broadly, for example, an increase across Britain and Ireland. The largest increases of some 0.01–0.02 inches [0.2–0.5 mm] a day are anticipated to be over northern and western areas. This equates to some 3–7 inches [75–180 mm] a year.

It should be noted that both these maps mask quite significant seasonal detail, which is also predicted by the models.

ANTARCTICA

▶ Between January and March 2002, the 1,255 sq mi [3,250 sq km] Larsen B ice shelf on the Antarctic Peninsula collapsed. The left-hand image shows its area (in blue) in December 2001 before the collapse, while the right-hand image shows the area fragmented in December 2002 after the collapse. The 656 ft [200 m] thick ice sheet had been retreating before this date, but over 500 billion tonnes of ice collapsed in under a month. This was due to rising temperatures of 0.9°F [0.5°C] per year in this part of Antarctica.

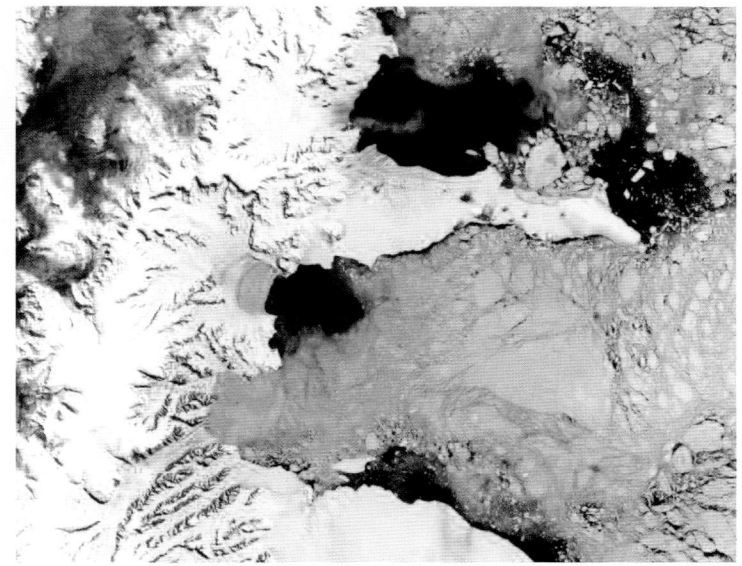

TEMPERATURE CHANGE

Climate modelers have produced simulations of global and continental surface temperature changes over the last century. This is done using only "natural forcing" by modeling the impact on atmospheric temperatures from known solar variability and volcanic eruptions. In addition, the same period of time is simulated by adding to natural forcing the impact of anthropogenic (human) influence due to measured changes in the concentration of greenhouse gases, particulate matter, etc.

The separate model "runs" are then compared with the observed temperature changes to illustrate which of the simulations matches the observations best.

This is a powerful means of verifying the relative roles of natural and human induced changes in atmospheric composition, and known solar output fluctuations on climate change.

▶ Climate model simulations for 1906 to 2005 using "natural forcings only" (blue bands) and "natural plus anthropogenic forcings" (pink bands). Regional decadal averages of observed temperature (black lines) are plotted as anomalies with respect to the 1901 to 1950 average. Blue and pink bands define the 5% to 95% range of possibilities for 19 runs produced by five models (natural forcing) and 58 simulations from 14 models (natural plus anthropogenic forcing).

Models using only natural forcings

Models using both natural and anthropogenic forcings

Observations
(dashed when spatial coverage is less than 50%)

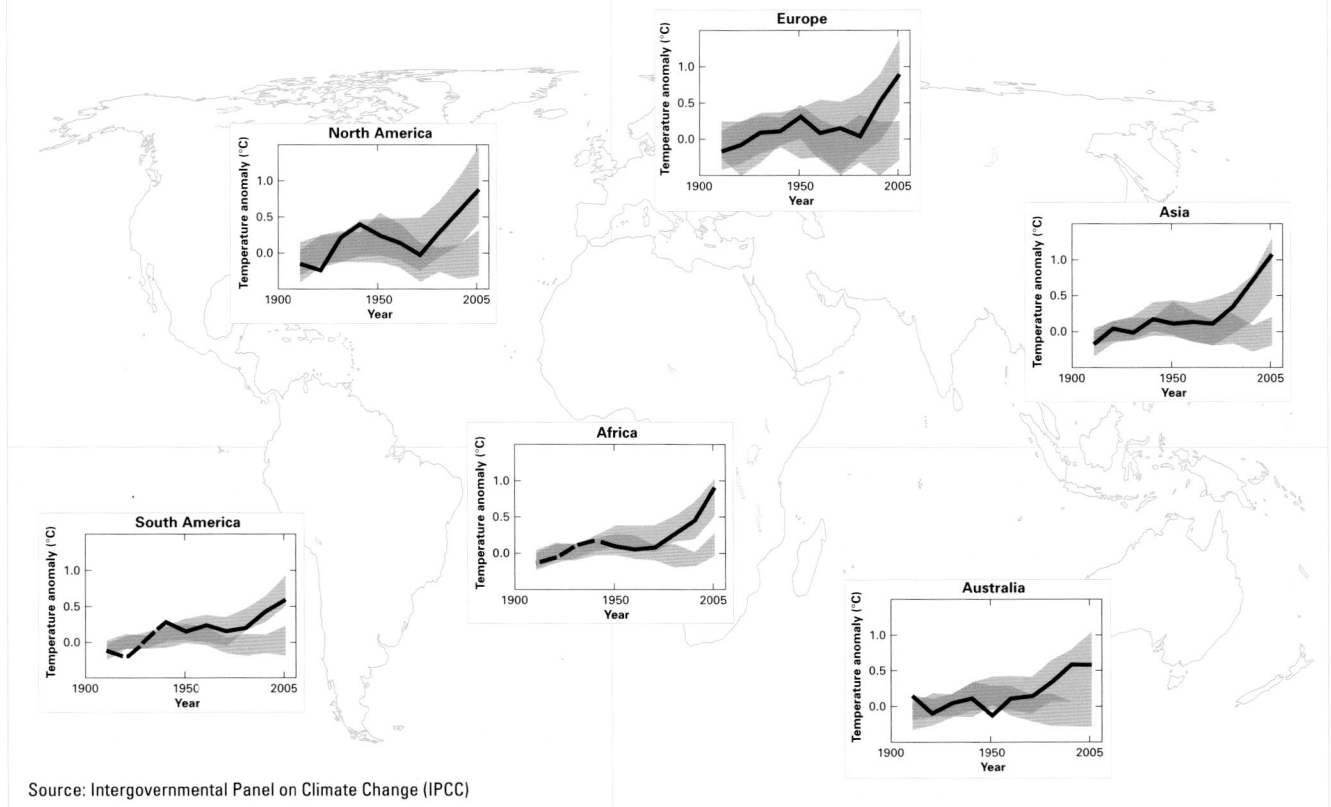

Source: Intergovernmental Panel on Climate Change (IPCC)

PROJECTED CHANGE IN GLOBAL WARMING

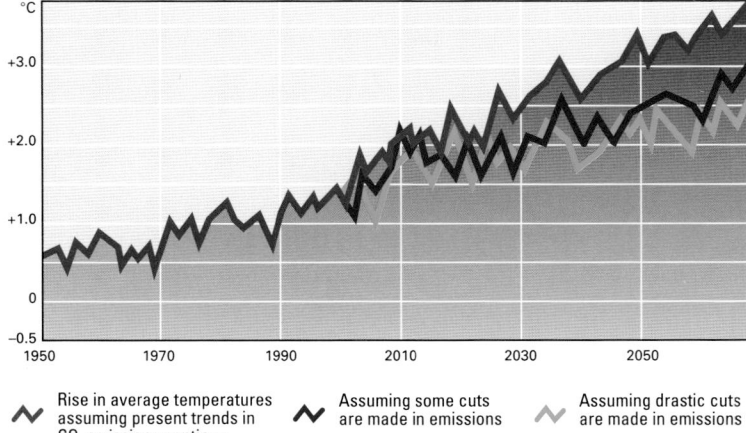

⋀ Rise in average temperatures assuming present trends in CO₂ emissions continue

⋀ Assuming some cuts are made in emissions

⋀ Assuming drastic cuts are made in emissions

Climate models are used to provide the best scientifically-based estimates of the future global climate. A typical method is to run the models for some decades ahead and then to compare the predicted average with a past 30-year period. A range of climate models are used, run with different scenarios that express the breadth of possibilities of, for example, industrial development, and the degree of atmospheric pollution "clean-up" by industrial nations.

The diagram above shows global observed and predicted surface mean temperature change from 1950 to 2080 with three prediction scenarios for this century. The first (red) assumes rapid economic growth and continued population increases. The second (blue) assumes some attempts are made to cut greenhouse gas emissions, while the green line involves the greater use of cleaner technologies, with global population peaking mid-century then declining.

THE OZONE LAYER

Total atmospheric ozone concentration in the southern hemisphere (2009)

In 1985, scientists working in Antarctica discovered a thinning of the ozone layer, resulting in what is commonly known as the "ozone hole." This caused immediate alarm because the ozone layer absorbs most of the Sun's dangerous ultraviolet radiation, which is believed to cause an increase in skin cancer, cataracts, and damage to the immune system.

Between 1985 and 2001 the ozone depletion increased and, by 2002, the ozone hole over the South Pole was estimated to be three times as large as the USA. This false-color image shows the total atmospheric ozone concentration in the southern hemisphere in September 2009, with the ozone hole clearly identifiable in blue at the centre. The data is from NASA's Aura satellite, ESA's ERS-2 satellite, and the NOAA-16 weather-forecasting satellite. The colours represent the ozone concentration in Dobson Units (DU).

Scientists agree that ozone depletion is caused by CFCs, a group of manufactured chemicals that were used in refrigerators and air-conditioning systems. In the Montreal Protocol in 1987, industrial nations agreed to phase out CFCs, and a complete ban on most CFCs was agreed after the end of 1995.

Since 2001 the amount of ozone in the atmosphere has stabilized and so too has the hole. While scientists believe that the chemicals may remain in the atmosphere for 50 to 100 years, if current trends are maintained it is possible that ozone levels may recover by 2050.

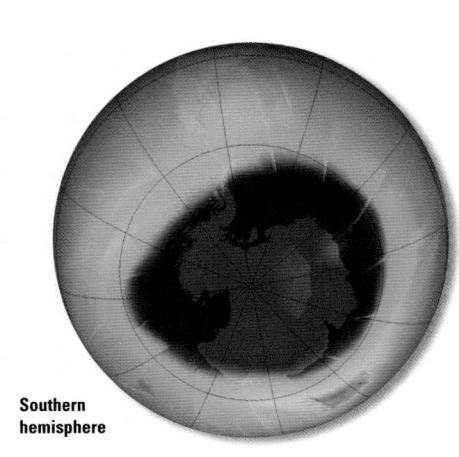

Southern
hemisphere

Ozone (Dobson Units)

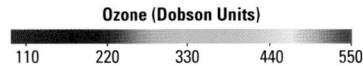

110   220   330   440   550

For more information:
80 Climate regions
81 Precipitation
86 Biodiversity

Without the hydrological cycle, by which water is constantly recycled between the oceans, the atmosphere and the land, the continents would be barren. Precipitation enables plants to grow and soils to form, creating the world's natural vegetation regions and the ecosystems that support animal life.

Running water also plays a major role in shaping landforms. Yet in many parts of the world, people do not have safe water to drink and suffer from diseases caused by water-borne organisms and pollution. In 2008, an estimated 884 million people lacked access to safe water and 2.6 billion people lacked basic sanitation.

Experts argue that world demand for water is increasing at about twice the rate of population growth. It is predicted that, by 2025, half the world's population will face water shortages. This could lead to conflict and even boundary wars – 300 major rivers cross national frontiers and access to their water is likely to be disputed.

THE HYDROLOGICAL CYCLE

The world's water balance is regulated by the constant recycling of water between the oceans, the atmosphere and the land. The movement of water between these three reservoirs is known as the "hydrological cycle." The oceans play a vital role in the hydrological cycle: 74% of the total precipitation falls over the oceans and 84% of the total evaporation comes from the oceans. Water vapor in the atmosphere circulates around the planet, transporting energy as well as the water itself. When the vapor cools, it falls as rain or snow. The whole cycle is driven by the Sun.

WATER DISTRIBUTION

The distribution of planetary water, by percentage. Oceans and ice caps together account for more than 99% of the total; the breakdown of the remainder is estimated.

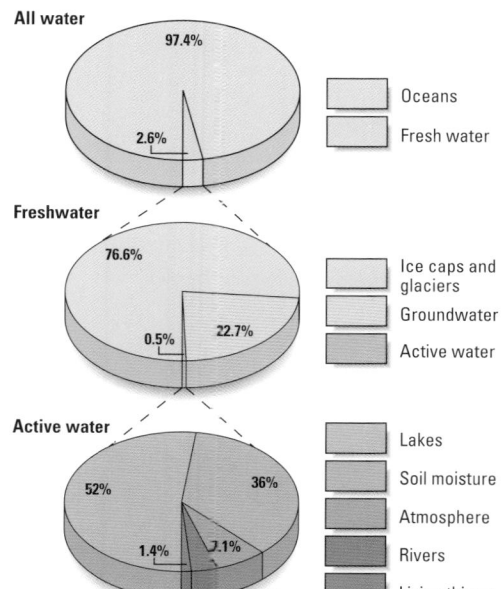

Almost all the world's water is 3,000 million years old, and all of it cycles endlessly through the hydrosphere, though at different rates. Water vapor circulates over days, even hours; deep-ocean water circulates over millennia; and ice-cap water remains solid for millions of years.

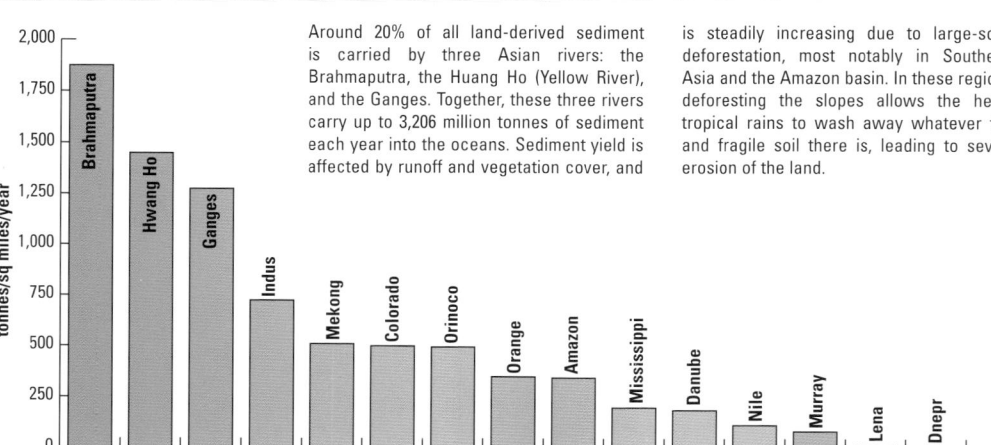

ANNUAL SEDIMENT YIELD

Around 20% of all land-derived sediment is carried by three Asian rivers: the Brahmaputra, the Huang Ho (Yellow River), and the Ganges. Together, these three rivers carry up to 3,206 million tonnes of sediment each year into the oceans. Sediment yield is affected by runoff and vegetation cover, and is steadily increasing due to large-scale deforestation, most notably in Southeast Asia and the Amazon basin. In these regions, deforesting the slopes allows the heavy tropical rains to wash away whatever thin and fragile soil there is, leading to severe erosion of the land.

WATER RUNOFF

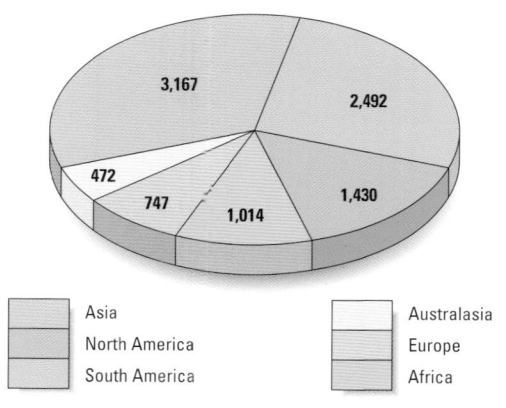

▶ The River Amazon is the world's second-longest river (after the River Nile), draining the vast rain forest basin of northern South America. The Amazon carries by far the greatest volume of water of any river in the world: the average rate of discharge is approximately 3,355,000 cu ft [95,000 cu m] per second, nearly three times as much as its nearest rival, the Congo. The flow is so great that its silt discolors the water up to 125 miles [200 km] into the Atlantic. At approximately 2.7 million sq miles [7 million sq km], the Amazon basin comprises nearly 40% of the whole of South America. Nevertheless, in 2005 large parts of the Amazon rain forest were at their driest in living memory, partly related to the severe hurricane season off the US Gulf coast. Rainfall was significantly below average, causing water levels to drop to record lows. At Tabatinga, 600 miles [970 km] west of Manaus, rainfall was almost 70% down from 2004. Rivers and lakes began to dry up, revealing huge sandbanks and making navigation difficult for boats.

WATERSHEDS

The map below shows the world's major rivers, with the ranking of the 20 longest rivers shown in square brackets after their name, led by the Nile [1] and the Amazon [2].

The map shows the direction of freshwater flow on a continental scale, whereas the water runoff chart on the facing page indicates the quantities involved annually.

The rate of runoff varies seasonally and is affected by the surface vegetation and climate. Most of the world's major rivers discharge into the Atlantic Ocean.

Where the rivers run

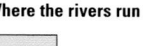

Pacific Ocean

Indian Ocean

Arctic Ocean

Atlantic Ocean

Caribbean Sea—Gulf of Mexico

Mediterranean Sea

Inland basins, ice caps, and deserts

NATURAL VEGETATION

The map below illustrates the natural "climax vegetation" of a region, as dictated by its climate and topography. In most cases, human agricultural activity has drastically altered the pattern of the vegetation. The various vegetation

regions support different kinds of animals and wildlife, and, in an undisturbed state, they are highly developed biological communities, or "biomes."

The blue line on the map represents the northern

limit of tree growth, and the red lines indicate the northern and southern limits of palm growth. The majority of the numerous species are tropical or subtropical. Some, such as the coconut, date, sago, and oil palms, are important economically.

Tropical rain forest

Subtropical and temperate rain forest

Monsoon woodland and open jungle

Subtropical and temperate woodland, scrub, and bush

Tropical savanna, with low trees and bush

Tropical savanna and grasslands

Dry semidesert, with shrub and grass

Desert shrub

Desert

Dry steppe and shrub

Temperate grasslands, prairie, and steppe

Mediterranean hardwood forest and scrub

Temperate deciduous forest and meadow

Temperate deciduous and coniferous forest

Northern coniferous forest (taïga)

Mountainous forest, mainly coniferous

High plateau steppe and tundra

Arctic tundra

Polar and mountainous ice desert

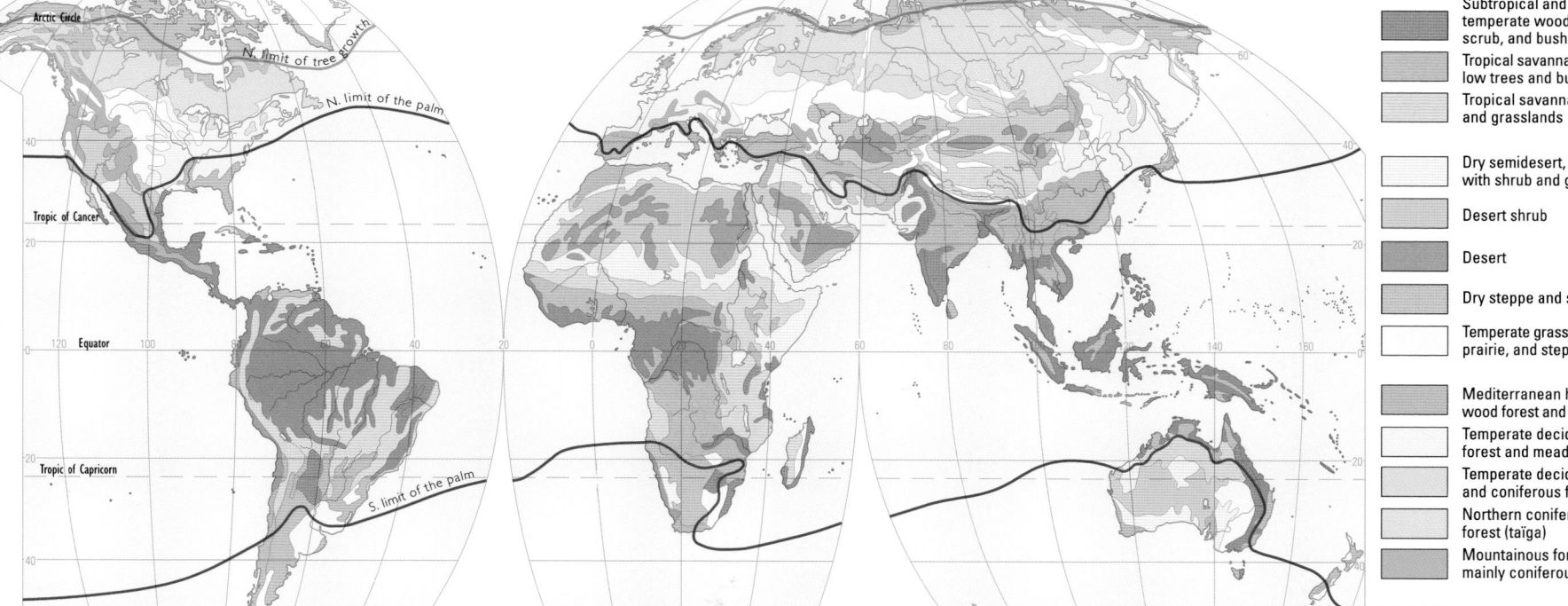

For more information:
76 Life in the oceans
80 Climate
82 Climate change
   Global warming
85 Natural vegetation

Levels of endemism
Known endemic species per
100 sq miles, selected countries (2004)

USA
Congo (Dem. Rep.)
Kenya
Ethiopia
India
Burma (Myanmar)
China
Australia
Italy
Bulgaria
Turkey
Peru
Greece
Japan
Mexico
Venezuela
Indonesia
Malaysia
Madagascar
Colombia
Ecuador
Costa Rica 0.9

0.2   0.4   0.6

Biodiversity refers to the variety of living material. It includes the variety of species, the variety within the same species, and the variety of ecosystems within which species operate. Estimates of the number of species in the world vary from between 7 million and 80 million. The currently accepted total is about 14 million, yet only 2 million species have been formally identified.

Biodiversity is vital for human survival. It remains the basis for our food and most of our medicine. In less economically developed countries (LEDCs), over 20% of the food consumed is gathered from natural sources. At a global level, over 15% of animal protein consumed is from sea fish caught in the wild. More than 60% of the world's population rely on traditional medicines for their health care. In Mexico, the Popoluca Indians "farm" over 250 species of plant. Many medicines come from natural sources. Aspirin, for example, comes from an acid taken from the bark of willow trees. The anti-cancer drug "taxol" originates from the wild Pacific yew tree. It is estimated that

the pharmaceuticals industry gains US $32 billion per year in profits from traditional remedies.

However, the loss of biodiversity is increasing at an accelerating rate. Up to 27,000 species a year may be lost, and the United Nations Environment Program (UNEP) suggests that the current rate of extinction is 50–100 times greater than "normal," and believes that up to 25% of all the world's species may be lost by 2025. The main reasons for the decline are the introduction of alien species and habitat destruction. Human impact on biodiversity has brought about more extinctions than any other single factor since the extinction of the dinosaurs (65 million years ago).

Since 1600, 39% of animal extinctions have been due to the introduction of alien species, 36% from habitat destruction, and 23% from hunting or deliberate extermination. The introduction of rats, cats, and other species has led to the extinction of many flightless birds in Polynesia. Plantation crops, such as rubber, often thrive best when taken away from their natural homes, since in

the new lands there may not be the pests to control them. One noted example of extinction was caused by the introduction of the Nile perch into Lake Victoria, East Africa: introduced in the 1960s, it led to the extinction of some 30 species of cichlid fish within 20 years.

In 2007, a report by the International Union for the Conservation of Nature listed 16,306 organisms facing extinction. Up to 46% of primates are said to be at risk of extinction. Overall, some 25% of mammals are endangered – including "charismatic" species such as the tiger and the panda, but equally less recognizable species of bats, rodents, and marsupials. Up to one-fifth of reptiles, one-third of amphibians, and one-third of bird species are at risk of extinction. The most threatened group are fish (one-third are at risk), largely as a result of overfishing. The World Conservation Union reported that 8% of mammals were threatened in the US, compared with 32% in the Philippines and 44% in Madagascar, two countries where habitat destruction has been proceeding on a large scale.

THREATENED MAMMAL SPECIES

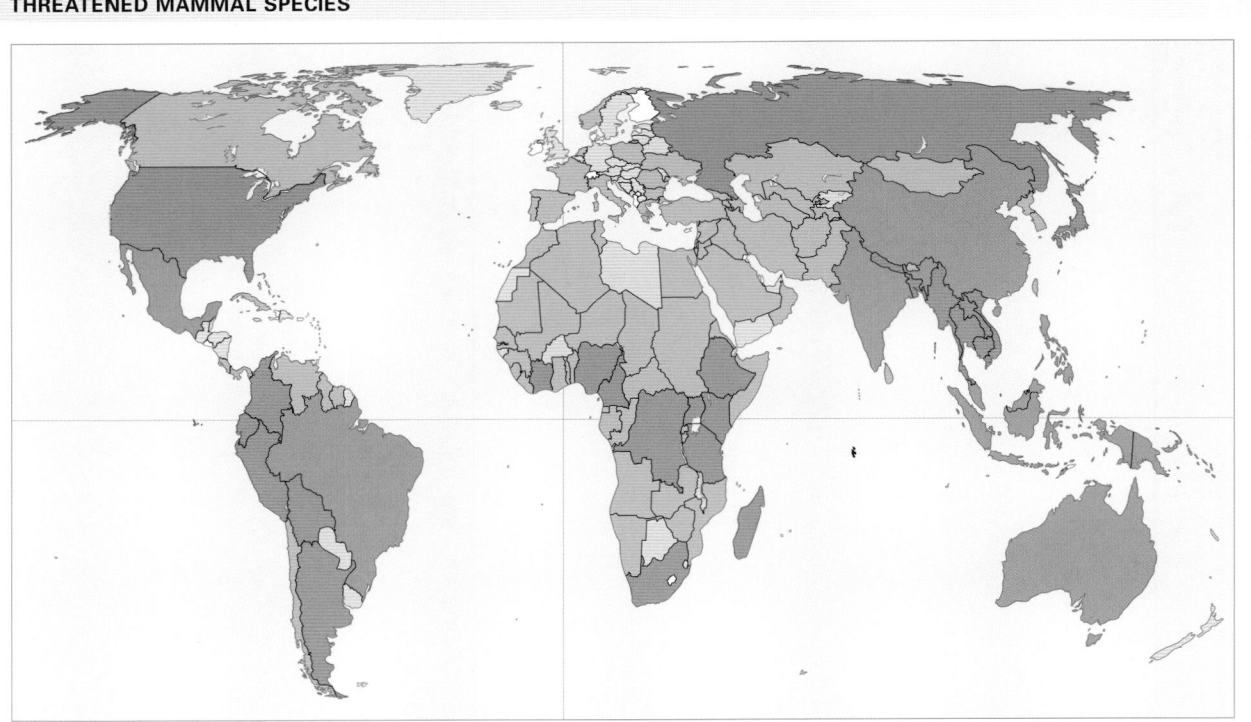

Mammal species threatened with extinction (2007)

	Over 50
	25 – 50
	10 – 25
	5 – 10
	Under 5

Countries with the highest number of mammal species threatened with extinction (2007)

Indonesia	146
India	89
China	83
Brazil	73
Mexico	72
Australia	64
Papua New Guinea	58
Philippines	51
Malaysia	50
Madagascar	47

NATIVE ('ENDEMIC') SPECIES AS A PROPORTION OF TOTAL SPECIES (SELECTED COUNTRIES)

Country	Mammals (2004)		Birds (2004)		Higher Plants (2004)	
	Total	Endemic	Total	Endemic	Total	Endemic
Australia	376	225	851	387	15,638	14,074
Brazil	578	131	1,712	207	56,215	18,000
Burma (Myanmar)	288	4	1,047	24	7,000	1,071
China	502	78	1,221	92	32,200	18,000
Colombia	467	43	1,821	84	51,220	15,000
Congo (Dem. Rep.)	430	26	1,148	24	11,007	1,100
Ecuador	341	26	1,515	56	19,362	4,000
Ethiopia	288	34	839	24	6,603	1,000
India	422	44	1,180	70	18,664	5,000
Indonesia	667	216	1,604	443	29,375	17,500
Japan	171	43	592	55	5,565	2,000
Madagascar	165	102	262	111	9,505	6,500
Malaysia	337	35	746	26	15,500	3,600
Mexico	544	155	1,026	125	26,071	12,500
Peru	441	48	1,781	125	17,144	5,356
Philippines	222	106	590	205	8,931	3,500
South Africa	320	33	829	27	23,420	8,200
Turkey	145	4	436	3	8,650	2,675
USA	468	104	888	122	19,473	4,036
Venezuela	353	18	1,392	46	21,073	8,000

▲ Madagascar has developed in isolation since it split from Africa 150 million years ago. As a result of this isolation, a unique range of plants and animals have evolved, adapted to its own specific conditions. Over 95% of Madagascar's mammals, 90% of its reptiles, over 66% of its plants, and over 40% of its breeding birds do not exist anywhere else in the world.
Madagascar is home to all of the world's lemurs (all of which are endangered, such as the aye-aye pictured above) and two-thirds of the world's chameleons. Its plant species include pitcher plants, orchids, and the Madagascan rosy periwinkle (the most effective known treatment for childhood leukemia). However, large-scale deforestation since the 1970s has reduced Madagascar's cover of rain forest to less than 10% of the island's original forest cover.

ENVIRONMENTAL HOTSPOTS

Up to 75% of the world's most threatened mammals, birds and amphibians live in an area covering just 2.3% of the Earth's surface, and roughly half of all flowering plant species and 42% of land-based vertebrates exist in 34 biological hotspots.

Scientists argue that, with limited financial resources, governments and conservationists should prioritize by protecting the small total land areas that account for a very high percentage of global biodiversity. In 1999, scientists identified 25 such areas, mostly in the tropics, which were the center of global biodiversity.

By 2005, the number of hotspots had risen to 34. These include the mountains of central Asia, the whole of Japan, the Horn of Africa including the Ethiopian highlands, and the Himalayas region. The hotspots once covered 15.7% of the Earth's surface, an area roughly the size of Russia and Australia combined – now they cover only 2.3% of the Earth's surface, an area slightly larger than India.

Over 70% of all mammals, 86% of all birds, and 92% of all amphibians are crammed into this small area of the world's total land mass. Madagascar and the Indian Ocean Islands hotspot was found to have very high concentrations of plant and vertebrate families that are found nowhere else on the globe.

Global warming could have a devastating effect on biodiversity hotspots such as the Amazonian and Indonesian rain forests. By 2100, between 12% and 39% of the land surface of the Earth will have a new climate. There are numerous species that will be unable to move in order to stay within their preferred climate range. These species will either have to evolve rapidly or die out.

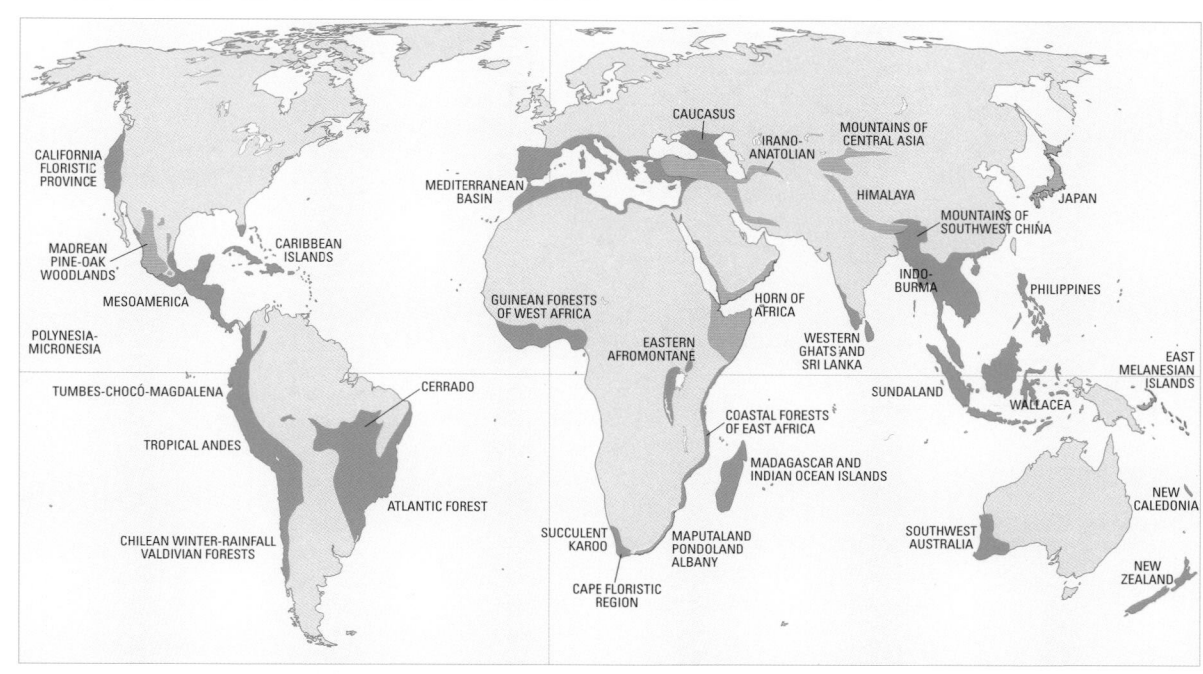

☐ New hotspots   ☐ Recognized environmental areas

AUSTRALIA'S INTRODUCED SPECIES

Australia's native plants and animals adapted to life on an isolated continent over millions of years. Since European settlement in the 18th century they have had to compete with a range of species introduced by the settlers, which impact on the native species by predation, competition for food and shelter, destroying habitat, and by spreading diseases. Introduced species typically have few predators or fatal diseases, and some have very high reproductive rates.

Management and the prevention of the introduction of new invasive species are key environmental and agricultural policy issues for the Australian federal and state governments.

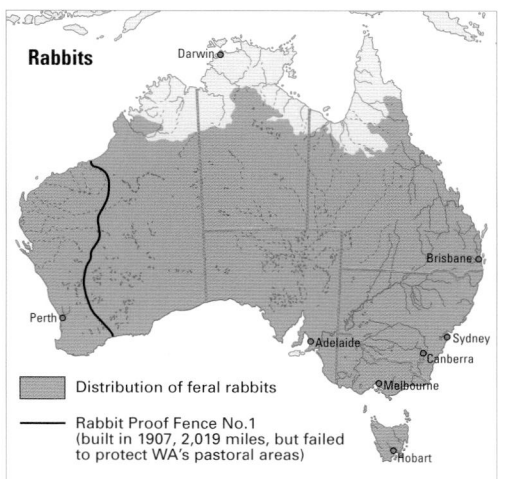

Rabbits

☐ Distribution of feral rabbits

— Rabbit Proof Fence No.1
(built in 1907, 2,019 miles, but failed to protect WA's pastoral areas)

▲ Rabbits were introduced to Australia from England in 1859 for hunting, and quickly spread throughout the country. They are one of the most destructive introduced species in Australia, competing with native wildlife, damaging vegetation, and degrading the land.

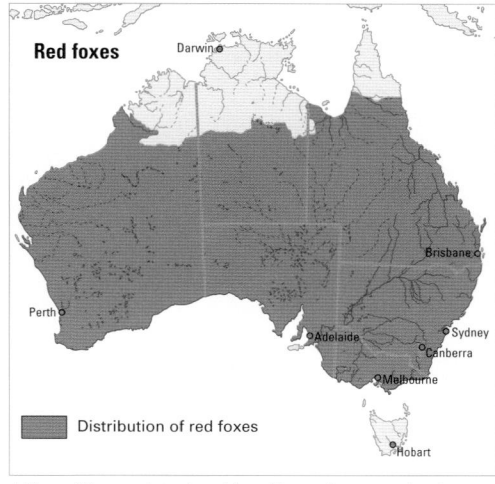

Red foxes

☐ Distribution of red foxes

▲ The red fox was introduced from Europe for recreational hunting in 1855 and populations became established in the wild within 15 years. They prey on newborn lambs and have also been responsible for the decline of a number of native species.

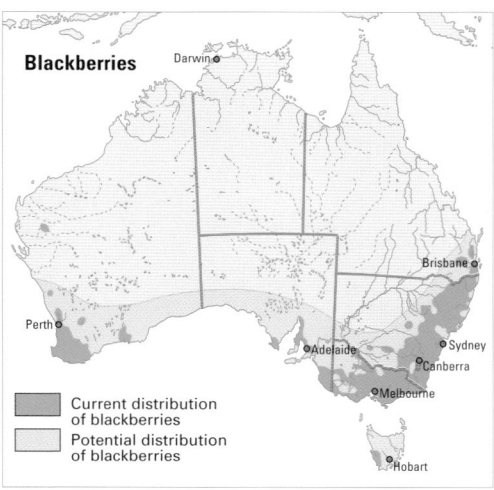

Blackberries

☐ Current distribution of blackberries
☐ Potential distribution of blackberries

▲ The blackberry was introduced from Europe as a source of fresh fruit. It is now regarded as one of the worst weeds in Australia because of its invasiveness, spreading through farmland, forests, and scrub. It out-competes many native plants, prevents light reaching the ground below, and provides food and shelter for pests.

Cane toads

☐ Distribution of cane toads

▲ Cane toads were introduced in 1935 to control beetles which were threatening the sugarcane industry. However, this was a failure and both the toad and the beetle are still thriving. They adapted well to the Australian environment and with no natural predators they quickly spread. They eat small native wildlife and poison any predators.

ESTIMATED VALUE OF WILD RESOURCES IN LESS ECONOMICALLY DEVELOPED COUNTRIES

Tropical non-coniferous forest product exports	US $11 billion per year
Fruit/latex harvesting, Peru	US $6,330 per hectare
Sustainable timber harvesting, Peru	US $490 per hectare
Buffalo range ranching, Zimbabwe	US $3.5–4.5 per hectare
Wetlands fish and fuelwood, Nigeria	US $38–59 per hectare
Viewing value of elephants, Kenya	US $25 million per year
Ecotourism, Costa Rica	US $1,250 per hectare
Tourism, Thailand	US $385,000–860,000 per year
Research/education, Thailand	US $38,000–77,000 per year
Tourism, Cameroon	US $10 per hectare
Genetic value, Cameroon	US $7 per hectare
Pharmaceutical prospecting, Costa Rica	US $4,981 million per product

▲ Bolivia has over 100,000 sq miles [250,000 sq km] of dry tropical forest, home to animals such as jaguars and ocelots. It is, however, being cleared at a rate of over 2% per annum.

This false-color image shows an area that has been almost completely cleared. The darkest areas are remnants of the original forest, some of which have been retained

as wind-breaks between newly created arable fields. The radial patterns are fields with new villages at their centers, part of a government resettlement scheme.

For more information:

11 Food and
    population

90 Urbanization of
    the Earth

    Urban population

91 Largest cities

In 8000 BC, following the development of agriculture, the world had an estimated population of 8 million and by AD 1000 it was about 300 million. The onset of the Industrial Revolution in the late 18th century led to a population explosion. The 1,000 million mark was passed by 1850, it doubled by the 1920s, and doubled again to 4,000 million by 1975.

In the 1990s, demographers estimated that the world's population, which passed the 6 billion mark in 1999, would reach 9.3 billion by 2050 and only level out in 2200, at a peak of around 11 billion. However, in the early 21st century, after the rate of population growth had shown signs of decline, the Institute for Applied Systems Analysis suggested that the world's population might peak at about 9 billion in 2070. Whatever the global projections, everyone agreed that the greatest population growth would be in the developing countries.

The developing world includes what the World Bank (2009) describes as low-income economies (average per capita GNI of US $524), lower-middle-income economies (average per capita GNI of US $2,078) and upper-middle-income economies (average per capita GNI of US $7,878). Most developing countries are in Africa, Asia, and Latin America. The developed world, made up of high-income, industrialized economies (average per capita GNI of US $39,345), contains Australasia, most of Europe and North America, and Japan.

In developing countries, a high proportion of the population is young and so these countries face high expenditure on health and education. In developed countries, the population pyramids are becoming top-heavy, with increasingly aging populations.

LARGEST NATIONS

The world's most populous nations, in millions (2009 est.)

1.	China	1,339
2.	India	1,157
3.	USA	307
4.	Indonesia	240
5.	Brazil	199
6.	Pakistan	175
7.	Bangladesh	156
8.	Nigeria	149
9.	Russia	140
10.	Japan	127
11.	Mexico	111
12.	Philippines	98
13.	Vietnam	89
14.	Ethiopia	85
15.	Germany	82
16.	Egypt	79
17.	Turkey	77
18.	Congo (Dem.Rep.)	69
19.	Iran	66
20.	Thailand	66
21.	France	64
22.	UK	61
23.	Italy	58
24.	South Africa	49
25.	South Korea	49

MOST CROWDED NATIONS

Population per square mile (2009 est.)

1.	Monaco	43,796
2.	Singapore	17,412
3.	Gaza Strip (OPT)	11,158
4.	Samoa	9,343
5.	Maldives	3,423
6.	Malta	3,322
7.	Bahrain	2,339
8.	Bangladesh	2,337
9.	Nauru	1,729
10.	Barbados	1,711

LEAST CROWDED NATIONS

Population per square mile (2009 est.)

1.	Western Sahara	3.9
2.	Mongolia	5.0
3.	Namibia	6.6
4.	Australia	7.2
5.	Suriname	7.6
6.	Iceland	7.7
7.	Mauritania	7.9
8.	Botswana	8.6
9.	Canada	8.7
10.	Guyana	9.1

POPULATION CHANGE

The projected population change for the years 2004–2050

- Over 125% population gain
- 100 – 125% population gain
- 50 – 100% population gain
- 25 – 50% population gain
- 0 – 25% population gain
- No change or population loss
- No data available

Based on estimates for the year 2050, below are listed the ten most populous nations in the world, in millions:

1.	India	1,628	6.	Pakistan	295
2.	China	1,437	7.	Bangladesh	280
3.	USA	420	8.	Brazil	221
4.	Indonesia	308	9.	Congo (Dem. Rep.)	181
5.	Nigeria	307	10.	Ethiopia	173

POPULATION DENSITY

The places marked on the map reflect the size of the urban agglomerations and conurbations, rather than the actual city limits. San Francisco itself, for example, has an official population of less than a million people.

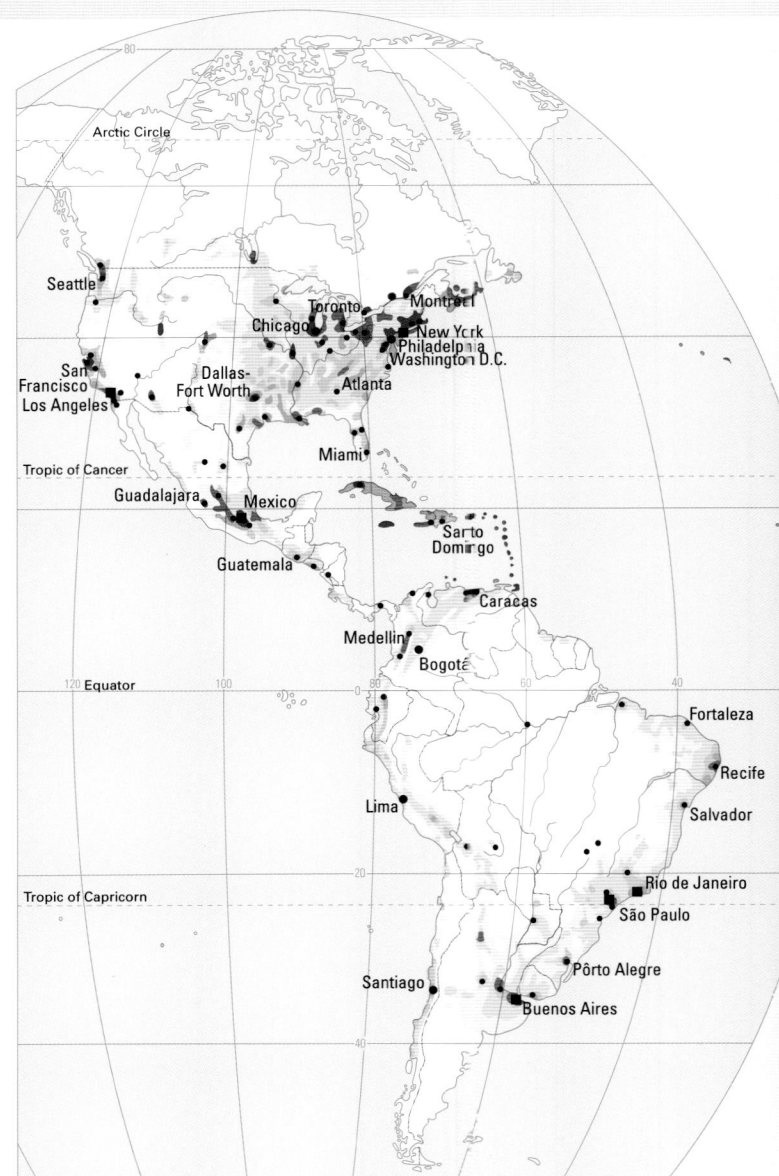

Inhabitants per square mile

- Over 500
- 250 – 500
- 125 – 250
- 65 – 125
- 15 – 65
- 8 – 15
- 3 – 8
- Under 3

Urban population

- ■ Over 10,000,000
- ● 5,000,000 – 10,000,000
- • 1,000,000 – 5,000,000

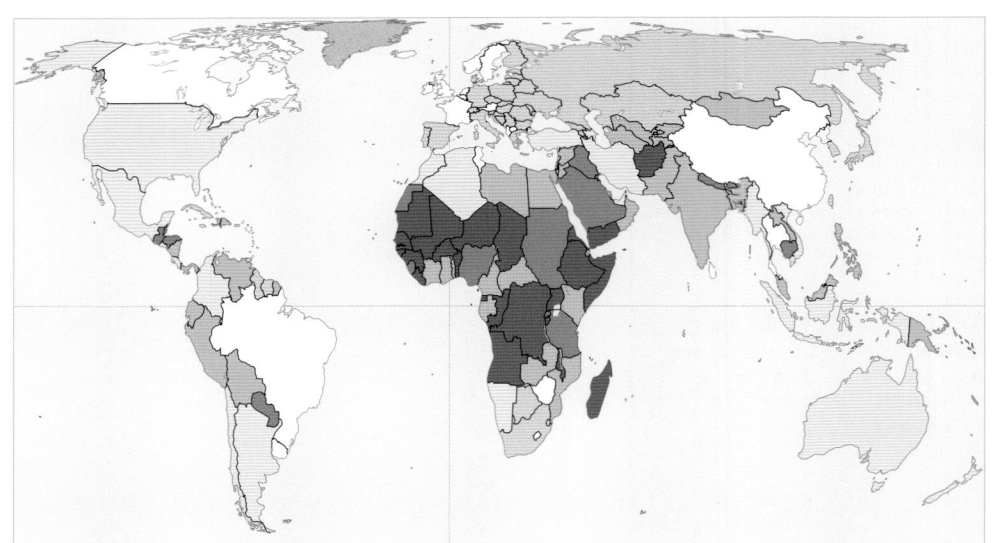

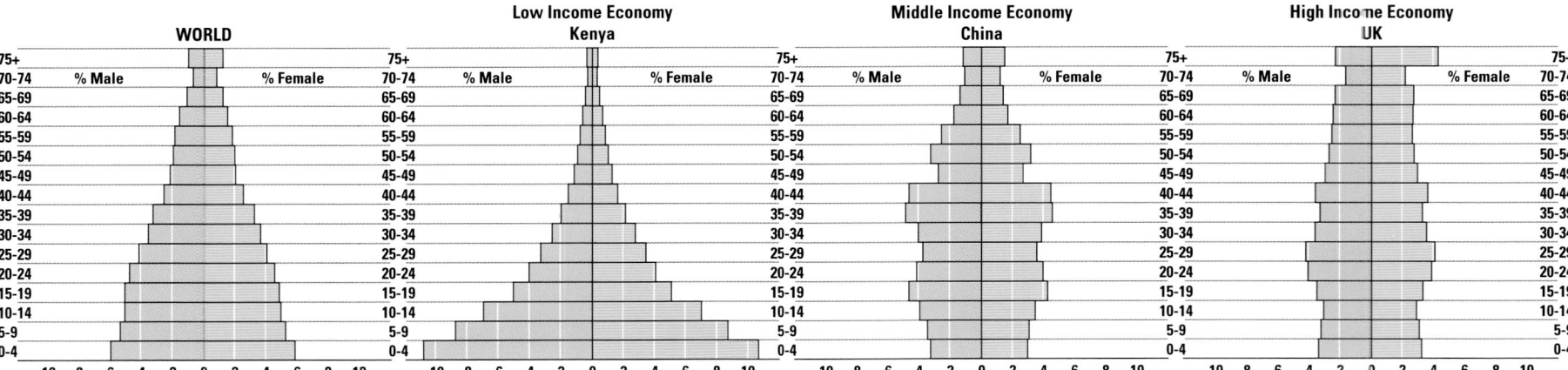

WORLD	Low Income Economy Kenya	Middle Income Economy China	High Income Economy UK

COPYRIGHT PHILIP'S

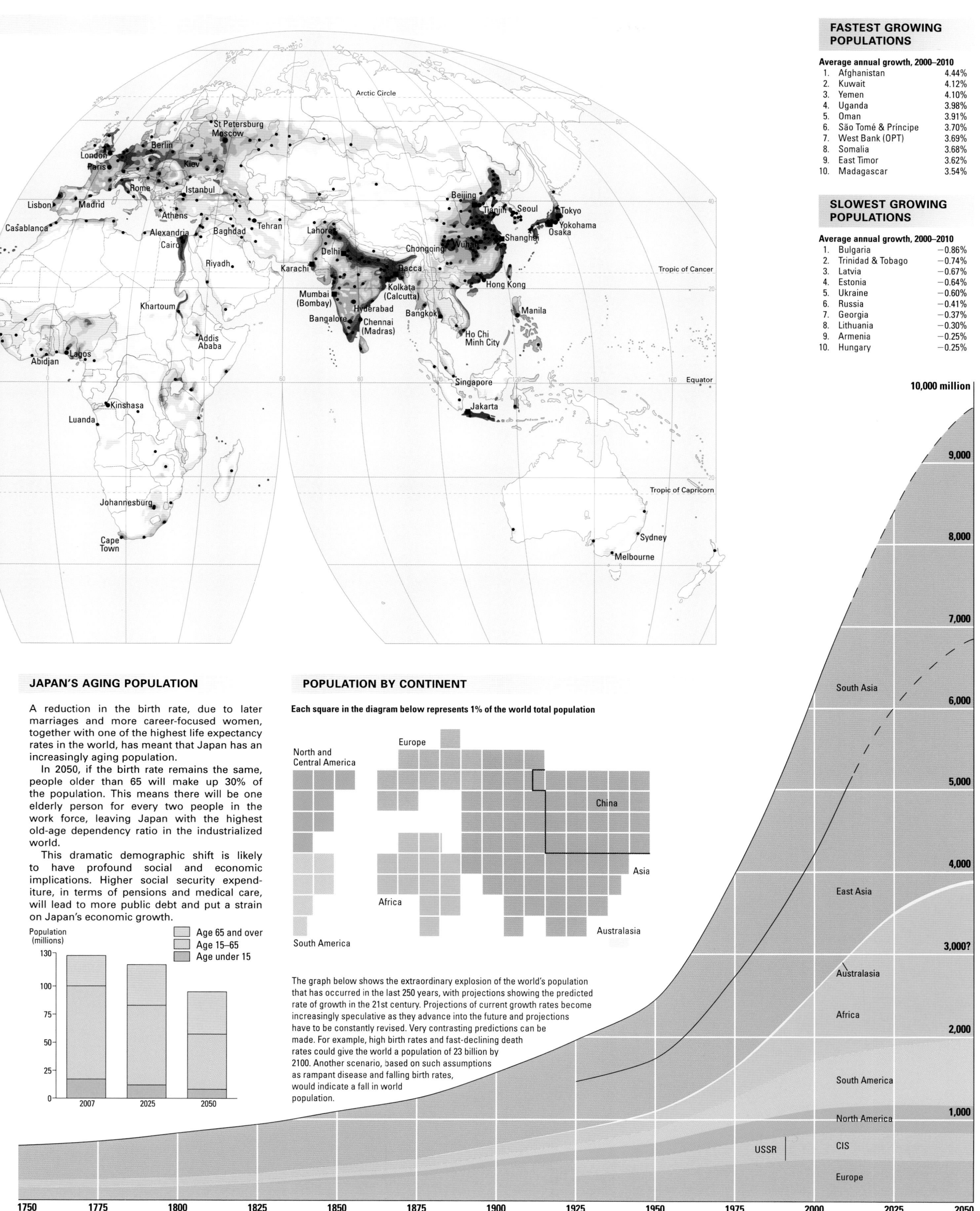

FASTEST GROWING POPULATIONS

Average annual growth, 2000–2010

1.	Afghanistan	4.44%
2.	Kuwait	4.12%
3.	Yemen	4.10%
4.	Uganda	3.98%
5.	Oman	3.91%
6.	São Tomé & Príncipe	3.70%
7.	West Bank (OPT)	3.69%
8.	Somalia	3.68%
9.	East Timor	3.62%
10.	Madagascar	3.54%

SLOWEST GROWING POPULATIONS

Average annual growth, 2000–2010

1.	Bulgaria	−0.86%
2.	Trinidad & Tobago	−0.74%
3.	Latvia	−0.67%
4.	Estonia	−0.64%
5.	Ukraine	−0.60%
6.	Russia	−0.41%
7.	Georgia	−0.37%
8.	Lithuania	−0.30%
9.	Armenia	−0.25%
10.	Hungary	−0.25%

JAPAN'S AGING POPULATION

A reduction in the birth rate, due to later marriages and more career-focused women, together with one of the highest life expectancy rates in the world, has meant that Japan has an increasingly aging population.

In 2050, if the birth rate remains the same, people older than 65 will make up 30% of the population. This means there will be one elderly person for every two people in the work force, leaving Japan with the highest old-age dependency ratio in the industrialized world.

This dramatic demographic shift is likely to have profound social and economic implications. Higher social security expenditure, in terms of pensions and medical care, will lead to more public debt and put a strain on Japan's economic growth.

POPULATION BY CONTINENT

Each square in the diagram below represents 1% of the world total population

The graph below shows the extraordinary explosion of the world's population that has occurred in the last 250 years, with projections showing the predicted rate of growth in the 21st century. Projections of current growth rates become increasingly speculative as they advance into the future and projections have to be constantly revised. Very contrasting predictions can be made. For example, high birth rates and fast-declining death rates could give the world a population of 23 billion by 2100. Another scenario, based on such assumptions as rampant disease and falling birth rates, would indicate a fall in world population.

For more information:
84 Water distribution
88 Population density
102 World trade

Following the development of agriculture more than 10,000 years ago, people began to live in farming villages. Around 5,500 years ago, the world's first cities appeared in the lower Tigris and Euphrates valleys in Mesopotamia. Cities were founded in Ancient Egypt around 5,000 years ago and in China around 3,600 years ago. By contrast with the villages, most people in the early cities were not engaged in farming. Instead, they worked in craft industries, in government services, in religion, and in trade. The cities became centers of early civilizations and, through trade, their influence spread far and wide. However, they were dependent on the surrounding farming communities for their food and other materials.

In 1750, prior to the start of the Industrial Revolution, barely 3% of the world's population lived in urban areas. By 1850, London and Paris had more than a million people, and, by 1900, 14% of the world's population lived in cities. By 1950, the world had 83 cities with more than a million people, and by 1996 there were 280; by 2015, experts predict there will be more than 500.

New York City was the only city with a population in excess of 10 million in 1950; by 2015, experts predict there will be 26 such cities worldwide, the majority located in the developing world. In addition, many of the world's largest cities are now merging to form "mega regions," such as Hong Kong-Shenzhen-Guangzhou in China, and these are becoming major economic drivers, on a world scale.

In 2008, for the first time in history, more than half of the world's population lived in urban areas. By 2050, it is thought that 5.3 billion people in the developing world will be living in an urban environment, with Asia having over 60% of the world's urban population and Africa almost 25%.

Urbanization is greatest in industrialized countries. For example, in 2004, 81% of the people in the US lived in urban areas. However, in low-income countries, which had nearly 40% of the world's population in the early 21st century, only 31% lived in urban areas.

The rapid rate of urbanization has created many social problems, especially in cities that have been unable to provide enough jobs and services for the new arrivals. Many of the new city dwellers come from rural areas and take time to adjust to urban life and employment possibilities.

A typical city in a developing country contains millions of people living, often illegally, in shanty towns (or "informal settlements"), while thousands live on the streets. Yet many of these shanty towns are healthier than the industrial cities of 19th-century Europe and North America. Indeed, surveys have shown that migrants to cities in developing countries are less likely to face poverty than they are in rural areas, while benefiting from greater access to healthcare services and education.

Modern cities face many problems today, including pollution, unemployment, and crime. Yet, with competent government, they are capable of generating the wealth they need to solve them, as well as making a major contribution to the nation's economy.

URBAN POPULATION

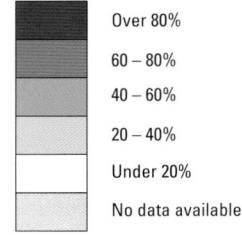

Percentage of total population living in towns and cities (2009)

- Over 80%
- 60 – 80%
- 40 – 60%
- 20 – 40%
- Under 20%
- No data available

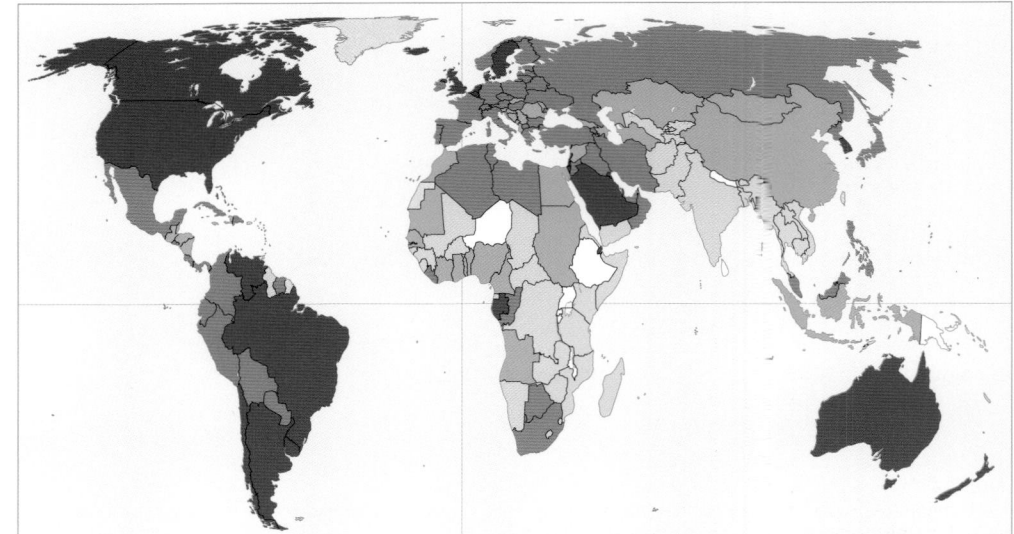

Most urbanized		Least urbanized	
Singapore	100%	Burundi	11%
Kuwait	98%	Papua New Guinea	13%
Belgium	97%	Uganda	13%
Qatar	96%	Trinidad & Tobago	14%
Malta	95%	Sri Lanka	15%

THE URBANIZATION OF THE EARTH

City-building, 1900–2005; each white spot represents a city of at least 1 million inhabitants

1900

1950

1975

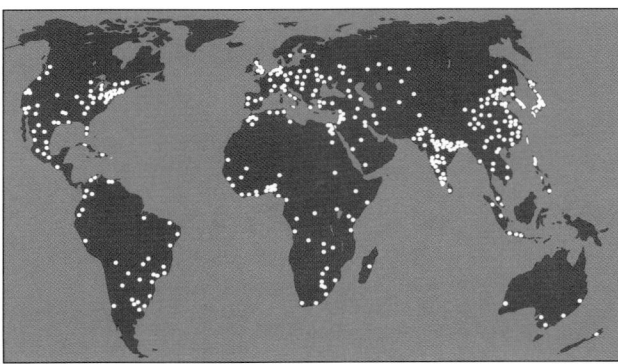

2005

URBANIZATION

The urban population of 3.3 billion people in 2008 was larger than the entire global population in 1947, 61 years earlier. Cities and urban areas are gaining an estimated 60 million people per year – over 1 million every week.

Urbanization rates vary across the world; the US and UK have far lower rates of urbanization compared to less developed countries. This is because a high proportion of their populations already live in cities. The largest percentage increases in the urban population in the next decade will be in Africa and Asia. Dhaka in Bangladesh, for example, nearly doubled in population between 1990 and 2000.

Rapid urban growth reflects three factors:
1. Migration to cities from rural areas.
2. Natural population increases (births minus deaths).
3. Reclassification of previously rural areas as urban as they become built up and engulfed by urban sprawl.

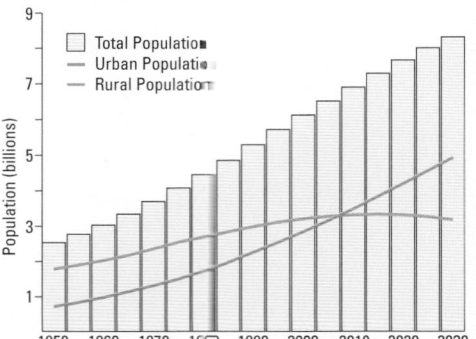

Total Population
Urban Population
Rural Population

SLUM CITIES

The total number of slum dwellers in the world reached 1 billion in 2007, with one in every three city residents living in inadequate housing, with no or few basic services.

Urbanization in most developing countries has been proceeding so rapidly that local governments have been unable to provide the necessary services and housing to meet demand.

In some cities, many people make their homes in squatter settlements, or slums, which are frequently without basic services such as power, water, and sanitation. They are often on hazardous, dangerous, or polluted land, and the building structures are inadequate and sometimes unsafe. Slum dwellers have limited access to credit and formal job markets due to stigmatization, discrimination, and geographical isolation.

Slums have a high concentration of poverty and social and economic deprivation, which may include broken families, unemployment, and economic, physical, and social exclusion. Yet these communities are often a dynamic part of the city's economy, keeping the wheels of the city turning in many different ways. Their inhabitants often take the initiative in setting up their own local government and self-help associations.

Some of the world's richest cities also have a homeless underclass, although calculating the numbers of people involved is problematic. Yet it is the case that homelessness and unemployment are currently affecting an increasing number of people in the developed world.

The locus of poverty is moving from the countryside to cities, in a process now recognized as the "urbanization of poverty."

Efforts to improve the living conditions of slum dwellers peaked during the 1980s. However, renewed concern about poverty has recently led governments to adopt specific targets on slums in the United Nations Millennium Declaration, which aims to improve the lives of at least 100 million slum dwellers by the year 2020.

CITIES IN DANGER

In mid-2002, a "brown haze," stretching 2 miles [3 km] high, covered much of southern Asia. Caused mainly by the burning of coal and biomass, it caused respiratory diseases and many deaths. Alarm concerning urban air pollution had been expressed much earlier, but controls since the 1980s had proved difficult to enforce and expensive to introduce.

Those cities taking part in the United Nation's Global Environment Monitoring System frequently show dangerous levels of pollutants, ranging from soot to sulfur dioxide and photochemical smog. Air in the majority of cities without such sampling equipment is likely to be at least as bad. Traffic, a major source of air pollution worldwide, loses Thailand's work force 44 working days each year. It was also a major cause for concern in the run-up to the 2008 Beijing Olympic Games.

SLUM FACTBOX

• 78% of the urban population in developing countries live in slums.

• The total number of slum dwellers in the world increased by about 36% during the 1990s.

• More than 41% of Kolkata's slum households have lived there for more than 30 years.

• In most African cities between 40% and 70% of the city's population live in slums or squatter settlements.

• Slum populations in some parts of the world (for example, Pune in India and Ibadan in Nigeria) quite often include university lecturers, students, civil servants, and formal private-sector employees.

• All slum households in Bangkok have a color television.

• Singapore is one of the few countries that successfully practises comprehensive public-sector housing development.

CITY GROWTH

The growth of some of the world's largest cities in millions, 1950–2015
Comparisons of city populations over time are problematic due to changes in the definition of the city limits. These figures attempt to take such changes into consideration.

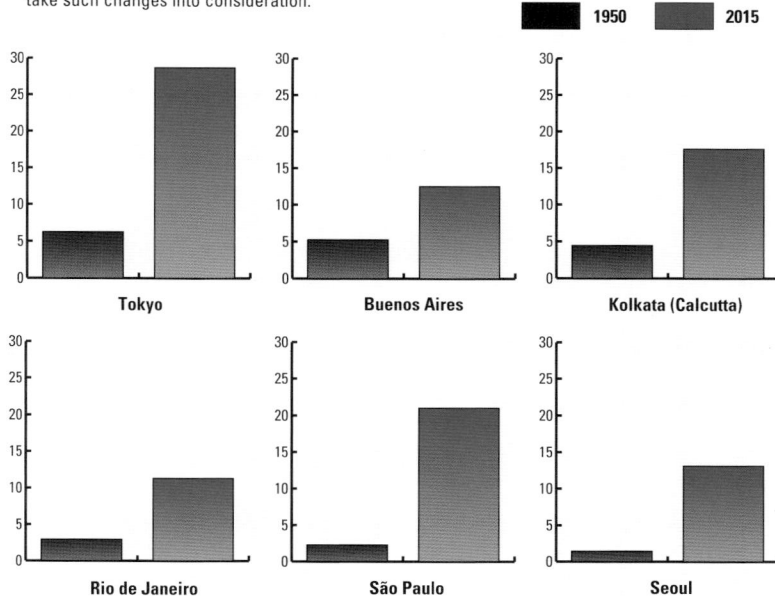

LARGEST CITIES

◄ Originally a fishing village, Shanghai's skyscrapers and modern lifestyle are often seen as representing China's recent economic development. It is now the sixth largest city in the world and home to many of Asia's tallest buildings, including the Jinmao Tower on the right of this image.

In 2008, for the first time in history, the majority of the world's population lived in cities. Below is a list of all the cities that are expected to have more than 10 million inhabitants by the year 2015, based on current estimates:

1.	Tokyo–Yokohama	28.7
2.	Mumbai (Bombay)	27.4
3.	Lagos	24.1
4.	Shanghai	23.2
5.	Jakarta	21.5
6.	São Paulo	21.0
7.	Karachi	20.6
8.	Beijing	19.6
9.	Dhaka	19.2
10.	Mexico City	19.1
11.	Kolkata (Calcutta)	17.6
12.	Delhi	17.5
13.	New York City	17.4
14.	Tianjin	17.1
15.	Manila	14.9
16.	Cairo	14.7
17.	Los Angeles	14.5
18.	Seoul	13.1
19.	Buenos Aires	12.5
20.	Istanbul	12.1
21.	Rio de Janeiro	11.3
22.	Lahore	10.9
23.	Hyderabad	10.6
24.	Bangkok	10.4
25.	Osaka	10.2
26.	Lima	10.1
27.	Tehran	10.0

The city populations above are based on urban agglomerations rather than legal city limits. In some cases, where two adjacent cities have merged into one concentration, such as Tokyo–Yokohama, they have been regarded as a single unit.

URBAN ADVANTAGES

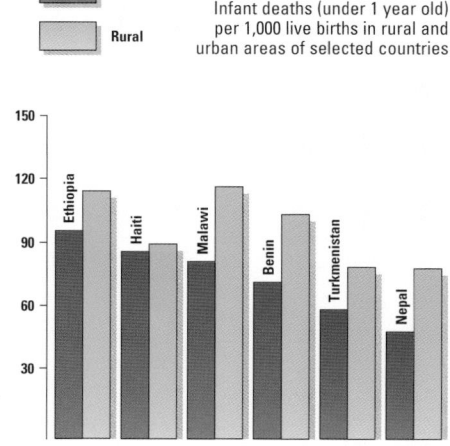

RELATIVE MORTALITY
Infant deaths (under 1 year old) per 1,000 live births in rural and urban areas of selected countries

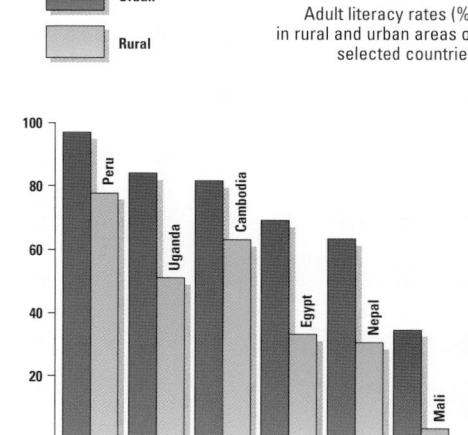

RELATIVE LITERACY
Adult literacy rates (%) in rural and urban areas of selected countries

Despite overcrowding and poor housing, living standards in the developing world's cities are almost invariably better than in the surrounding countryside. Resources – financial, material, and administrative – are concentrated in the towns, which are usually also the centers of political activity and pressure. Governments – frequently unstable, and rarely established on a solid democratic base – are usually more responsive to urban discontent than to rural misery.

In many developing countries, especially in Africa, food prices are kept artificially low, thus appeasing the underemployed urban masses at the expense of agricultural development.

This imbalance encourages further cityward migration, helping to account for the astonishing rate of post-1950 urbanization and putting great strain on the ability of many nations to provide even modest improvements for their people.

Racial, language, and religious differences have led to appalling acts of inhumanity throughout history. Yet, strictly speaking, all human beings belong to one species, *Homo sapiens*, which has no sub-species. The differences between the three racial types which most people identify – Caucasoid, Mongoloid, and Negroid – reflect not so much evolutionary differences as long periods of separation.

Migration has recently mingled the various groups to an unprecedented extent, and most nations now have some degree of racial mixing. For example, the USA has often been called a melting pot, because of the large numbers of people from various geographical locations that make up the population. The country has no official language but, until recently, English was spoken by the vast majority of the people. But in recent years, some of the immigrants from Mexico, Cuba, and other parts of Latin America have not learned English and speak only Spanish. This development disturbs those Americans who believe that the use of English binds the nation together, and several states have passed laws stating that English is their only official language.

Language is fundamental to human culture. Because definitions of languages vary, estimates of the total number range from 3,000 to 6,000, although most are spoken by only a few people. Chinese is spoken by more people as a first language than any other, while English ranks second, but English is the leading international language, because so many people speak it as their second tongue.

Like language, religion encourages cohesion in single human groups and it satisfies a deep human need by assigning people a place in a divinely ordered world. Religion is a way in which a culture can express its individuality. For example, the rise of Islamic fundamentalism in the late 20th century was partly an expression of resentment that secular Western values were being imposed on Muslims.

For more information:
88 Population density
94 The world's refugees
War since 1945
95 United Nations
International
organizations

WORLD MIGRATION

The greatest voluntary migration was the colonization of North America by 30–35 million European settlers during the 19th century. The greatest forced migration involved 9–11 million Africans taken as slaves to America between 1550 and 1860. The migrations shown on the map below are mostly international, as population movements within borders are not usually recorded. Many of the statistics are necessarily estimates as so many refugees and migrant workers enter countries illegally and unrecorded. Emigrants may have a variety of motives for leaving, thus making it difficult to distinguish between voluntary and involuntary migrations.

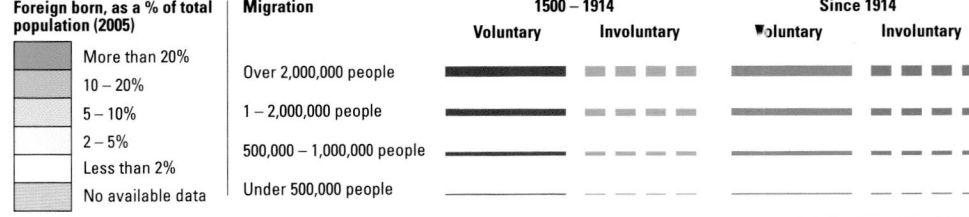

Foreign born, as a % of total population (2005)	Migration		
More than 20%	Over 2,000,000 people		
10 – 20%	1 – 2,000,000 people		
5 – 10%	500,000 – 1,000,000 people		
2 – 5%	Under 500,000 people		
Less than 2%			
No available data			

1500 – 1914: Voluntary, Involuntary
Since 1914: Voluntary, Involuntary

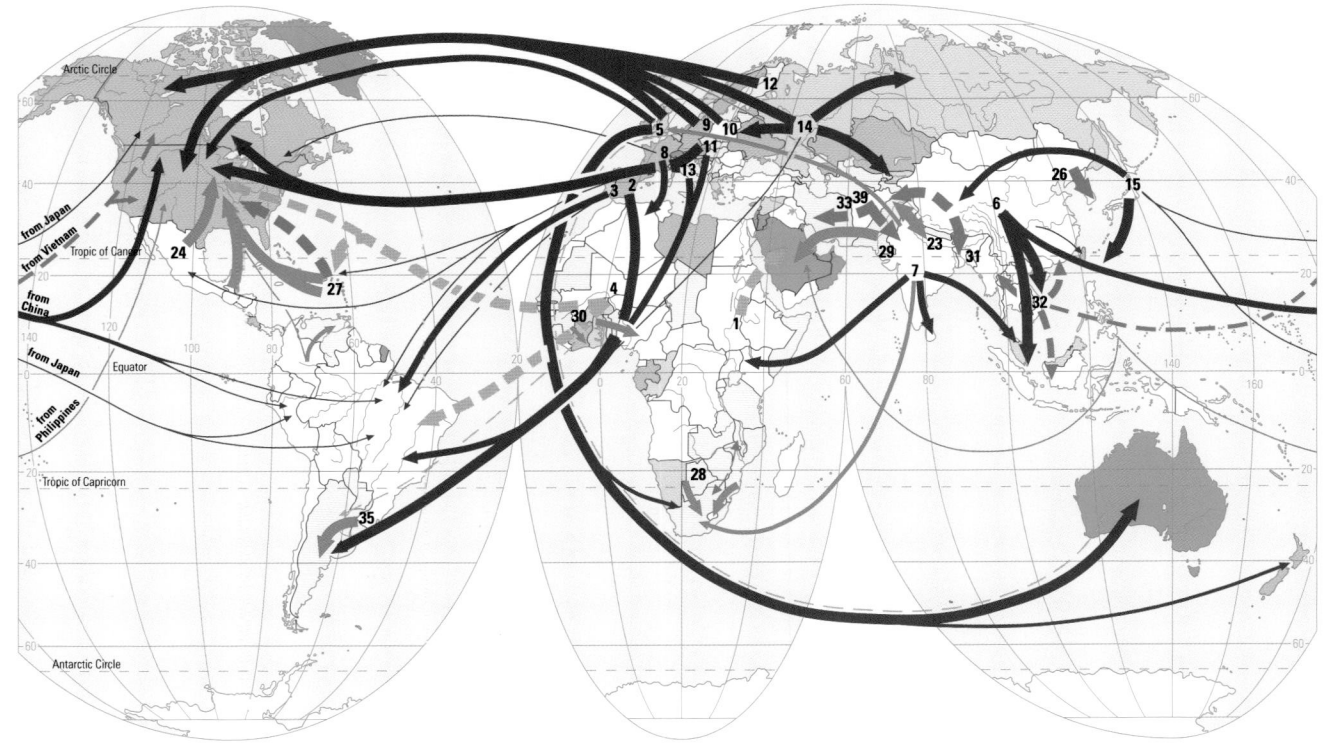

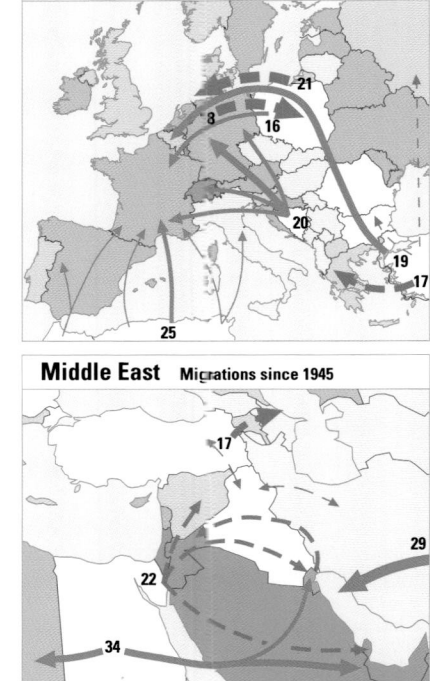

Europe — Migrations since 1914

Middle East — Migrations since 1945

Major world migrations since 1500 (over 1 million people)

1. North and East African slaves to Arabia (4.3m) 1500–1900
2. Spanish to South and Central America (2.3m) 1530–1914
3. Portuguese to Brazil (1.4m) 1530–1914
4. West African slaves to South America (4.6m) 1550–1860
   to Caribbean (4m) 1580–1860
   to North/Central America (1m) 1650–1820
5. British and Irish to North America (13.5m) 1620–1914
   to Australasia and South Africa (3m) 1790–1914
6. Chinese to Southeast Asia (22m) 1820–1914
   to North America (1m) 1880–1914
7. Indian migrant workers (3m) 1850–1914
8. French to North Africa (1.5m) 1850–1914
9. Germans to North America (5m) 1850–1914
10. Poles to North America (3.6m) 1850–1914
11. Austro-Hungarians to North America (3.2m) 1850–1914
   to Western Europe (3.4m) 1850–1914
   to South America (1.8m) 1850–1914

12. Scandinavians to North America (2.7m) 1850–1914
13. Italians to North America (5m) 1860–1914
   to South America (3.7m) 1860–1914
14. Russians to North America (2.2m) 1880–1914
   to Western Europe (2.2m) 1880–1914
   to Siberia (6m) 1880–1914
   to Central Asia (4m) 1880–1914
15. Japanese to Eastern Asia, Southeast Asia and America (8m) 1900–1914
16. Poles to Western Europe (1m) 1920–1940
17. Greeks and Armenians from Turkey (1.6m) 1922–1923
18. European Jews to extermination camps (5m) 1940–1944
19. Turks to Western Europe (1.9m) 1940–
20. Yugoslavs to Western Europe (2m) 1940–
21. Germans to Western Europe (9.8m) 1945–1947
22. Palestinian refugees (2m) 1947–
23. Indian and Pakistani refugees (15m) 1947
24. Mexicans to North America (9m) 1950–

25. North Africans to Western Europe (1.1m) 1950–
26. Korean refugees (5m) 1950–1954
27. Latin Americans and West Indians to North America (4.7m) 1960–
28. Migrant workers to South Africa (1.5m) 1960–
29. Indians and Pakistanis to the Persian Gulf (2.4m) ... 1970–
30. Migrant workers to Nigeria and Ivory Coast (3m) 1970–
31. Bangladeshi and Pakistani refugees (2m) 1972
32. Vietnamese and Cambodian refugees (1.5m) 1975–
33. Afghan refugees (6.1m) 1979–
34. Egyptians to the Persian Gulf and Libya (2.9m) 1980–
35. Migrant workers to Argentina (2m) 1980–
36. Mozambique refugees (1.7m) 1985–
37. Yugoslav/Balkan refugees (1.7m) 1992–
38. Rwanda/Burundi refugees (2.6m) 1994–
39. Afghan refugees (2.1m) 2001–

BUILDING THE USA

US Immigration, 1920 and 2009

For decades the USA was the magnet that attracted millions of immigrants, notably from Central and Eastern Europe, the flow peaking in the early years of the 20th century. By the mid-1990s the proportion of immigrants had increased again to pre-World War II rates, reaching over 12% by 2009. However, the balance of origin had swung from Europe to Latin America and Asia, as the graphs indicate.

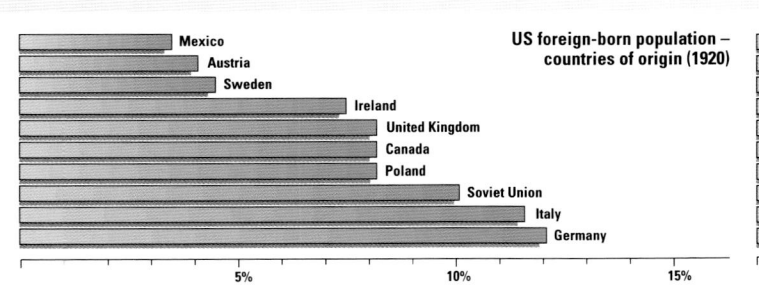

US foreign-born population – countries of origin (1920)

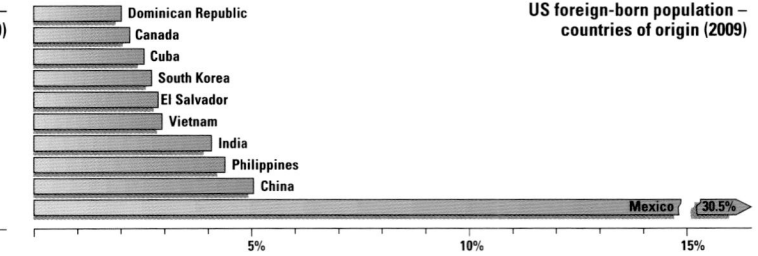

US foreign-born population – countries of origin (2009)

PREDOMINANT LANGUAGES

INDO-EUROPEAN FAMILY

1	Balto-Slavic group (incl. Russian, Ukrainian)
2	Germanic group (incl. English, German)
3	Celtic group
4	Greek
5	Albanian
6	Iranian group
7	Armenian
8	Romance group (incl. Spanish, Portuguese, French, Italian)
9	Indo-Aryan group (incl. Hindi, Bengali, Urdu, Punjabi, Marathi)
10	**CAUCASIAN FAMILY**

AFRO-ASIATIC FAMILY

11	Semitic group (incl. Arabic)
12	Kushitic group
13	Berber group
14	**KHOISAN FAMILY**
15	**NIGER-CONGO FAMILY**
16	**NILO-SAHARAN FAMILY**
17	**URALIC FAMILY**

ALTAIC FAMILY

18	Turkic group (incl. Turkish)
19	Mongolian group
20	Tungus-Manchu group
21	Japanese and Korean

SINO-TIBETAN FAMILY

22	Sinitic (Chinese) languages (incl. Mandarin, Wu, Yue)
23	Tibetic-Burmic languages
24	**TAI FAMILY**

AUSTRO-ASIATIC FAMILY

25	Mon-Khmer group
26	Munda group
27	Vietnamese
28	**DRAVIDIAN FAMILY** (incl. Telugu, Tamil)
29	**AUSTRONESIAN FAMILY** (incl. Malay-Indonesian, Javanese)
30	**OTHER LANGUAGES**

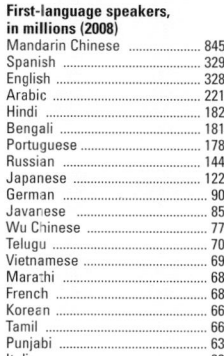

First-language speakers, in millions (2008)

Mandarin Chinese	845
Spanish	329
English	328
Arabic	221
Hindi	182
Bengali	181
Portuguese	178
Russian	144
Japanese	122
German	90
Javarese	85
Wu Chinese	77
Telugu	70
Vietnamese	69
Marathi	68
French	68
Korean	66
Tamil	66
Punjabi	63
Italian	62

Languages form a kind of tree of development, splitting from a few ancient proto-tongues into branches that have grown apart and further divided with the passage of time. English and Hindi, for example, both belong to the great Indo-European family, although the relationship is only apparent after much analysis and comparison with non-Indo-European languages such as Chinese or Arabic. Hindi is part of the Indo-Aryan subgroup, whereas English is a member of Indo-European's Germanic branch. French, another Indo-European tongue, traces its descent through the Latin, or Romance, branch. A few languages – Basque is one example – have no apparent links with any other, living or dead. Most modern languages, of course, have acquired enormous quantities of vocabulary from each other.

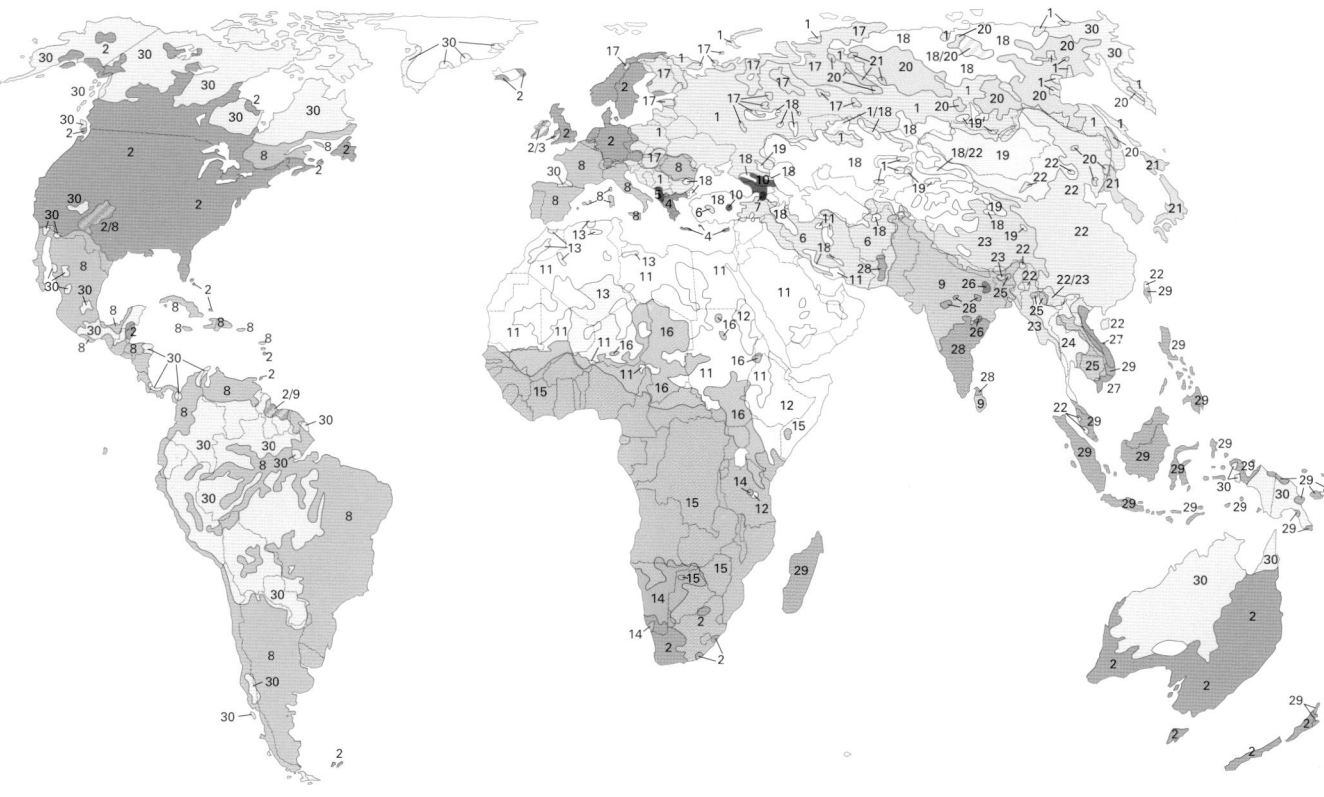

DISTRIBUTION OF LIVING LANGUAGES

The figures refer to the number of languages currently in use in the regions shown

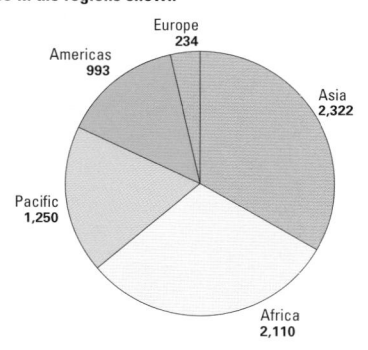

Europe 234
Americas 993
Asia 2,322
Pacific 1,250
Africa 2,110

PREDOMINANT RELIGIONS

- ▲ Roman Catholicism
- Orthodox and other Eastern Churches
- ● Protestantism
- Sunni Islam
- Shia Islam
- Buddhism
- Hinduism
- Confucianism
- ★ Judaism
- Shintoism
- Tribal Religions

Religions are not as easily mapped as the physical contours of the land. Divisions are often blurred and frequently overlapping: most nations include people of many different faiths – or no faith at all. Some religions, like Islam and Christianity, have proselytes worldwide; others, like Hinduism and Confucianism, are restricted to a particular area, though modern migrations have taken some Indians and Chinese very far from their cultural origins. It is also difficult to show the degree to which religion controls daily life: Christian Western Europe, for example, is now far less dominated by its religion than are the Islamic nations of the Middle East. Similarly, figures for the major faiths' adherents make no distinction between nominal believers enrolled at birth and those for whom religion is a vital part of their existence.

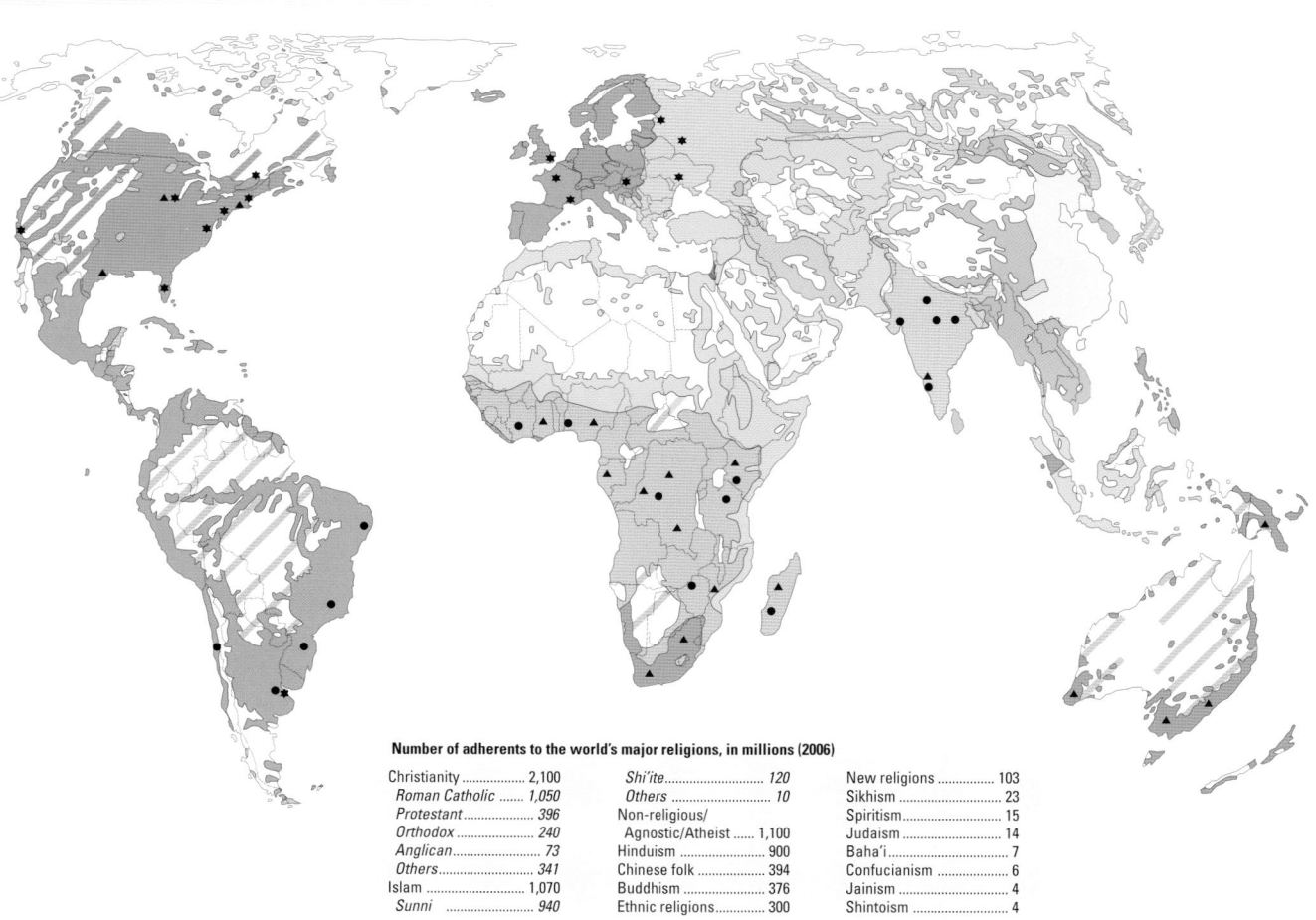

Number of adherents to the world's major religions, in millions (2006)

Christianity	2,100	Shi'ite	120	New religions	103
Roman Catholic	*1,050*	*Others*	*10*	Sikhism	23
Protestant	*396*	Non-religious/		Spiritism	15
Orthodox	*240*	Agnostic/Atheist	1,100	Judaism	14
Anglican	*73*	Hinduism	900	Baha'i	7
Others	*341*	Chinese folk	394	Confucianism	6
Islam	1,070	Buddhism	376	Jainism	4
Sunni	*940*	Ethnic religions	300	Shintoism	4

For more information:
92 Migration
93 Religion

The 20th century witnessed two world wars, followed by a Cold War which several times threatened to erupt into a third world war, fought with nuclear weapons. The Cold War was marked by a great number of conflicts. Some were colonial wars, as the empires of the first half of the century fell apart, some were border wars, and some were civil wars. All the wars have caused great suffering among civilians, many of whom were forced to join the ranks of the world's refugees.

In the late 1980s, many people hoped that the end of the Cold War, following the collapse of Communist regimes in the former Soviet Union and Eastern Europe, would herald a new era of international stability. Instead, old ethnic and religious antagonisms surfaced in many areas, leading to civil war in such places as Chechenia, in Russia, and the former Yugoslavia. Nationalist rivalries, suppressed under Communist rule, replaced ideological factors as the major cause of conflict.

War is a very human activity, with no real equivalent in any other species. Yet humans also function well when they cooperate – evolution has made this so. Hunter-gatherers in cooperative bands were far more effective than animals that prowled. Agriculture, urbanization, and industrialization all depend on the ability of humans to cooperate.

The creation of the United Nations in 1945 held out hope that the world's nations, tired of war, would have the means to control humanity's aggressive instincts. Although the UN lacks the power to halt conflicts, it has often helped to achieve negotiation. Economic pressures have led to another kind of cooperation, resulting in the creation of common markets and economic unions, such as ASEAN in Southeast Asia, the European Union, and NAFTA in North America.

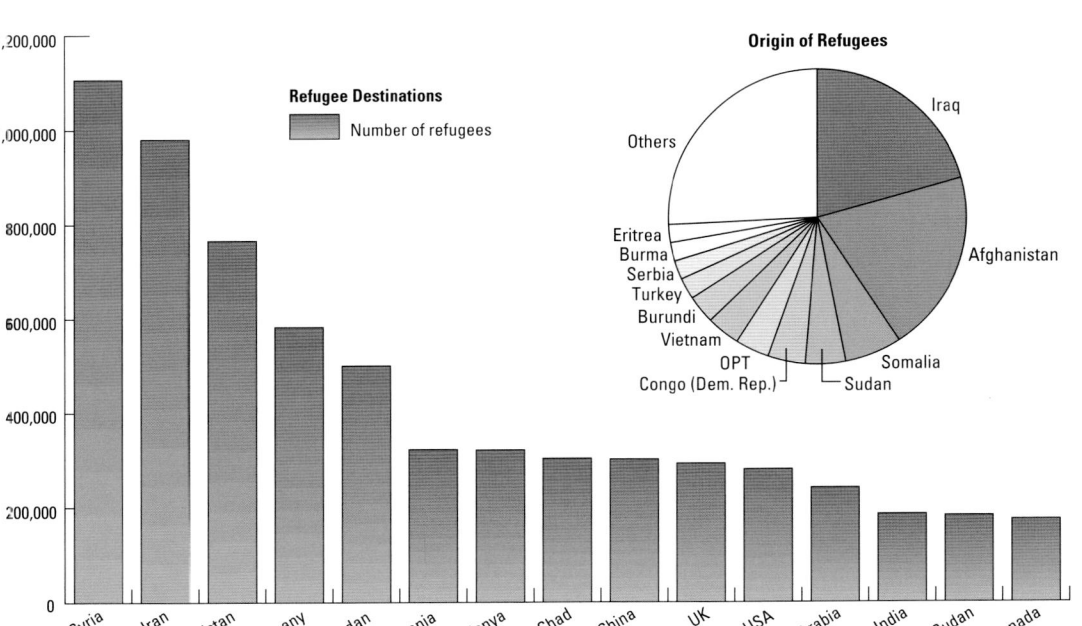

THE WORLD'S REFUGEES

Refugees by host nation (bar-chart, left) and by nation of origin (pie-chart, left) (2008 The source is the United Nations High Commission for Refugees (UNHCR).

The pie-chart shows the origins of the world's refugees, while the bar-chart below shows their destinations. According to the United Nations High Commission for Refugees (UNHCR) in 2009 there were 10.4 million refugees. However, the UNHCR definition of a refugee, "a person who has left or remains outside their own country because they have a well-founded fear of persecution, or because their safety is threatened by events seriously disturbing public order," does not include people who are in a refugee-like situation but who have not been formally recognized. In 2009, there were a further 15.6 million people who were internally displaced, and a total "population of concern" of 36.5 million people, worldwide.

All but a few who cross international boundaries seek asylum in neighboring countries, which are often the least equipped to deal with them. Lacking any rights or power, they frequently become an unwelcome burden to their hosts. Usually, the best any refugee can hope for is rudimentary food and shelter in temporary camps. Many Palestinians have been forced to live in camps since 1948.

WAR SINCE 1945

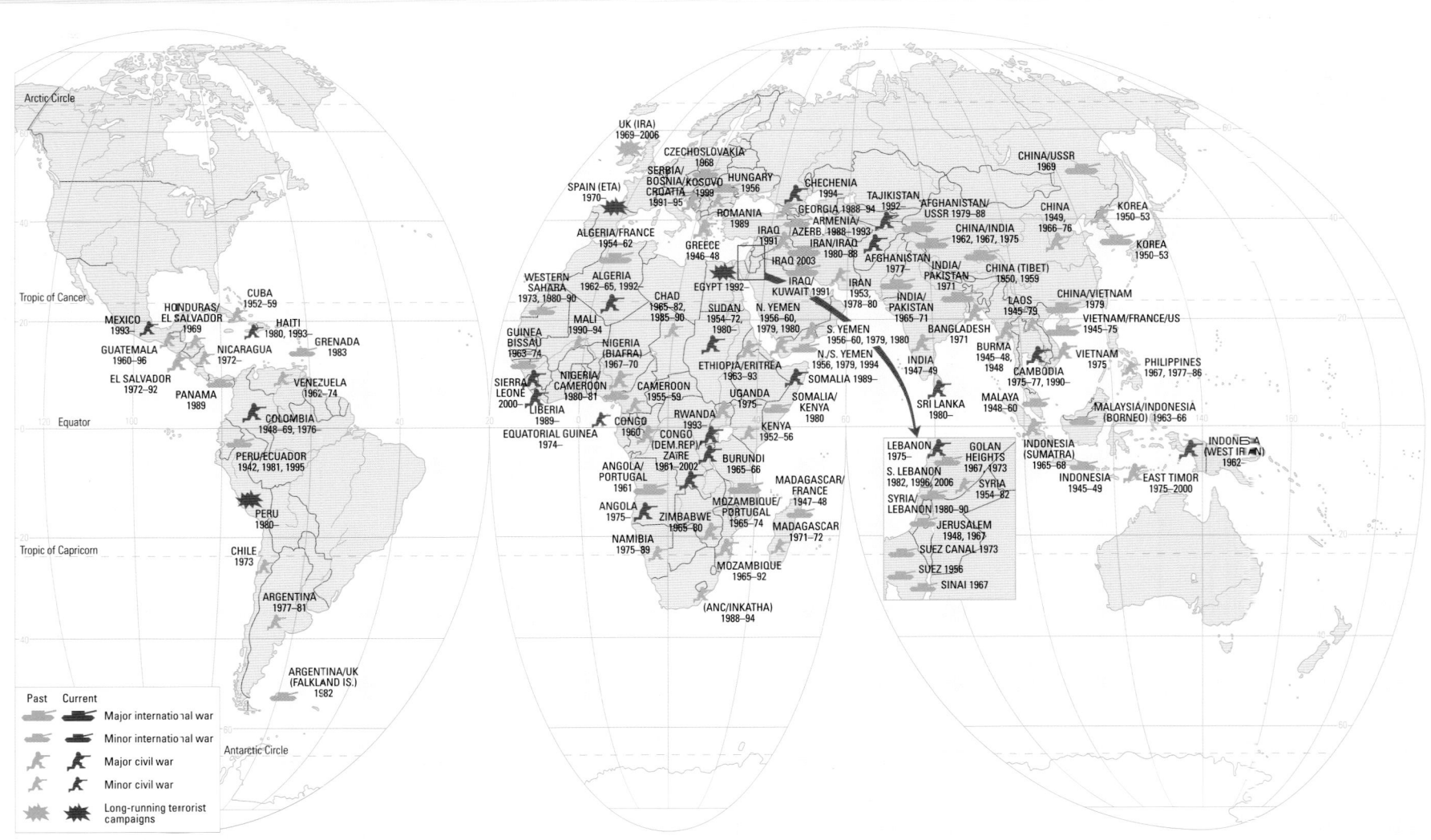

UNITED NATIONS

The United Nations Organization was born as World War II drew to its conclusion. Six years of strife had strengthened the world's desire for peace, but an effective international organization was needed to help achieve it. That body would replace the League of Nations which, since its inception in 1920, had failed to curb the aggression of at least some of its member nations. At the United Nations Conference on International Organization held in San Francisco, the United Nations Charter was drawn up. Ratified by the Security Council and signed by the 51 original members, it came into effect on October 24, 1945.

The Charter set out the aims of the organization: to maintain peace and security, and to develop friendly relations between nations; to achieve international cooperation in solving economic, social, cultural, and humanitarian problems; to promote respect for human rights and fundamental freedoms; and to harmonize the activities of nations in order to achieve these common goals.

Membership From the original 51, membership of the UN has now grown to 192. Recent additions include East Timor, Switzerland, and Montenegro. There are only two independent states which are not members – Taiwan and the Vatican City. Official languages are Chinese, English, French, Russian, Spanish, and Arabic.

Funding The UN budget for 2008–9 was US $4.2 billion. Contributions are assessed by the members' ability to pay, with the maximum 22% of the total (the USA's share), and the minimum 0.001%. The 27-member EU pays nearly 39% of the budget.

Peacekeeping The UN has been involved in 64 peacekeeping operations worldwide since 1948.

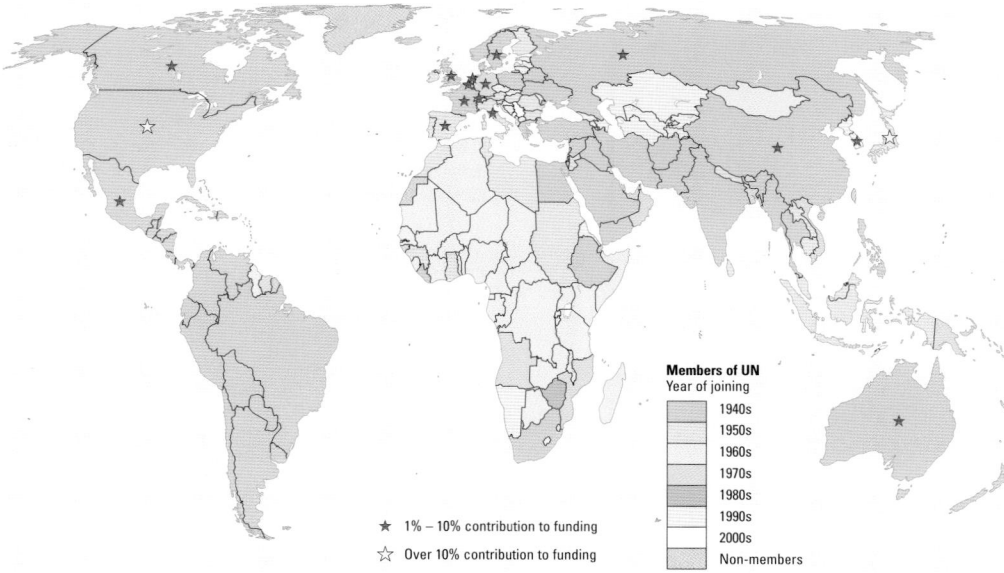

INTERNATIONAL ORGANIZATIONS

OAS Organization of American States (formed in 1948). It aims to promote social and economic cooperation between countries in the developed North America and developing Latin America.
EU European Union (evolved from the European Community in 1993). Cyprus, the Czech Republic, Estonia, Hungary, Latvia, Lithuania, Malta, Poland, the Slovak Republic, and Slovenia joined the EU in May 2004, Bulgaria and Romania joined in 2007. The other 15 members of the EU are Austria, Belgium, Denmark, Finland, France, Germany, Greece, Ireland, Italy, Luxembourg, Netherlands, Portugal, Spain, Sweden, and the UK. Together, the 27 members aim to integrate economies, coordinate social developments, and bring about political union.
AU The African Union was set up in 2002, taking over from the Organization of African Unity (1963). It has 53 members. Working languages are Arabic, English, French, and Portuguese.
COLOMBO PLAN (formed in 1951) Its 25 members aim to promote economic and social development in Asia and the Pacific.

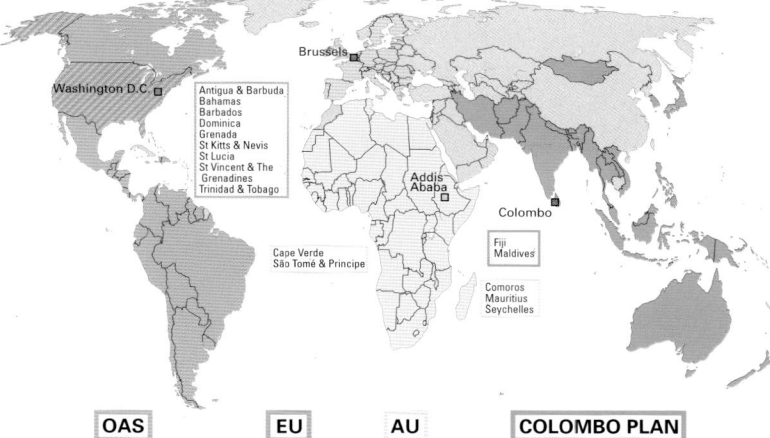

G8 Group of eight leading industrialized nations, comprising Canada, France, Germany, Italy, Japan, Russia, the UK, and the USA. Periodic meetings are held to discuss major world issues, such as world recessions.
APEC Asia-Pacific Economic Cooperation (formed in 1989). It aims to enhance economic growth and prosperity for the region and to strengthen the Asia-Pacific community. APEC is the only intergovernmental grouping in the world operating on the basis of non-binding commitments, open dialogue, and equal respect for the views of all participants. There are 21 member economies.
OECD Organization for Economic Cooperation and Development (formed in 1961). It comprises 30 major free-market economies. The "G8" is its "inner group" of leading industrial nations, comprising Canada, France, Germany, Italy, Japan, Russia, the UK, and the USA.
ACP African-Caribbean-Pacific (formed in 1963). Members enjoy economic ties with the EU.
OPEC Organization of Petroleum Exporting Countries (formed in 1960). It controls about three-quarters of the world's oil supply. Gabon formally withdrew from OPEC in August 1996.

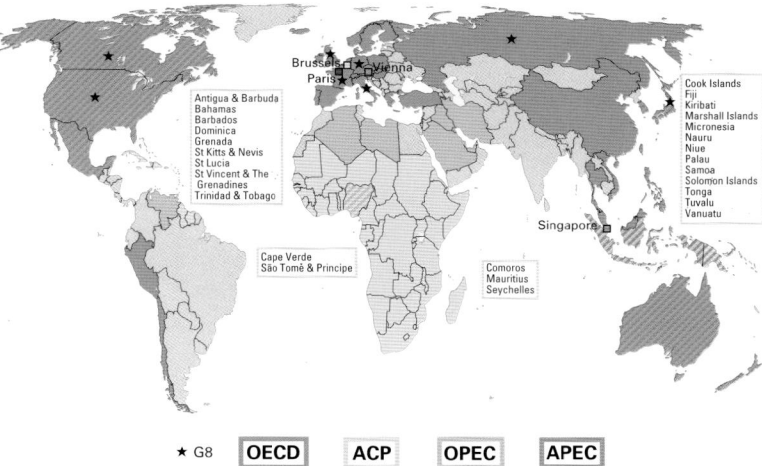

NATO North Atlantic Treaty Organization (formed in 1949). It continues despite the winding-up of the Warsaw Pact in 1991. Bulgaria, Estonia, Latvia, Lithuania, Romania, the Slovak Republic, and Slovenia became members in 2004.
LAIA The Latin American Integration Association (formed in 1980) superceded the Latin American Free Trade Association formed in 1961. Its aim is to promote freer regional trade.
ARAB LEAGUE (1945) Aims to promote economic, social, political, and military cooperation. There are 22 member nations.
COMMONWEALTH The Commonwealth of Nations evolved from the British Empire. Pakistan was suspended in 1999, but reinstated in 2004. Zimbabwe was suspended in 2002 and, in response to its continued suspension, Zimbabwe left the Commonwealth in 2003. Fiji Islands was suspended in 2006 following a military coup. Rwanda joined the Commonwealth in 2009, as the 54th member state, becoming only the second country which was not formerly a British colony to be admitted to the group.
ASEAN Association of Southeast Asian Nations (formed in 1967). Cambodia joined in 1999.

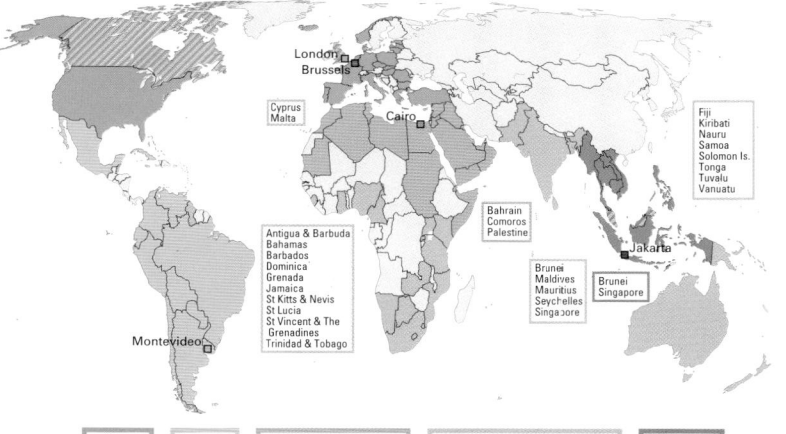

OCEAN PIRACY

Piracy, or the robbing or hijacking of ships, their crews, and their cargoes, has been increasing steadily in certain parts of the world over recent years. In 2009, the International Maritime Bureau recorded 380 attacks on vessels worldwide, compared with 239 attacks in 2006. The most high-profile acts of piracy were off the coasts of Nigeria and Indonesia, and, most particularly, off the Somali coast in the Gulf of Aden (see map right).

Some of the ships involved have been large ocean-going tankers, bulk carriers, and container vessels, and the pirates have proved that they can sail these without the crew. Attacks have taken place up to 1,150 miles [1,852 km] off the Somali coast when larger "mother ships" are used, from which smaller vessels operate. Firearms and rocket-propelled grenades have been used by the hijackers and many millions of pounds paid in ransom by the ships' owners to release their vessels, much of which goes to support terrorist groups.

To counter this very real threat, both the United States and the European Union have introduced naval operations in the area to try to protect their shipping interests, with some success. However, with such a large area of ocean to cover, it is very difficult to police.

As a result of the pirate activity, insurance premiums have risen and, should this continue, shipping will start to avoid the Suez Canal and take the longer and more expensive route around the Cape of Good Hope.

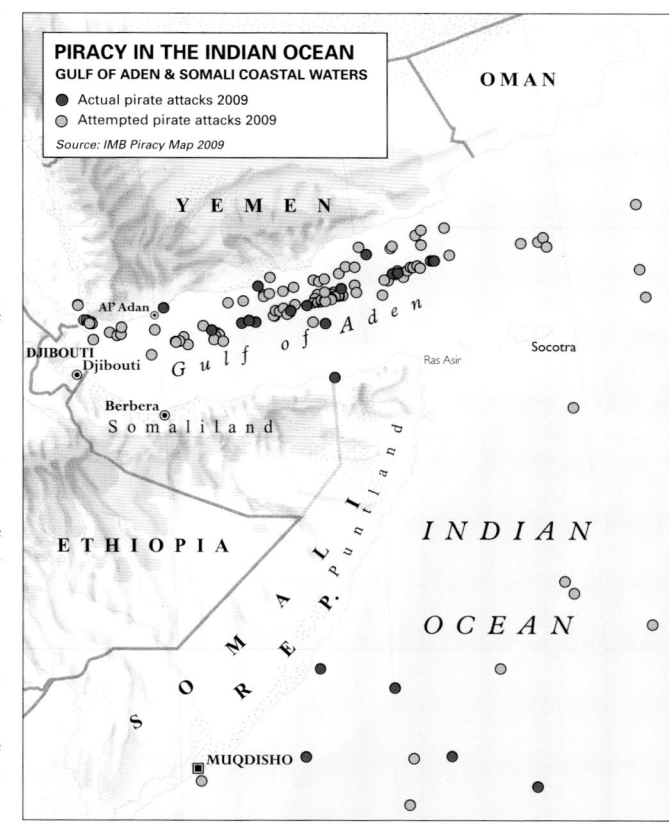

For more information:
82 Global warming
    Carbon dioxide
98 Minerals
103 World shipping

Every year, the world's energy consumption is about the equivalent of what would come from burning 10,000 million tonnes of oil (10,000 MtOe) – a 20-fold increase since 1850. Two-fifths of this total actually comes from burning oil and most of the rest comes from coal and natural gas.

The oil crises in the 1970s precipitated concern over dependence on finite fossil fuels as the primary source of energy, and growing environmental awareness has added impetus to the search for alternative energy resources. Fossil fuel combustion damages the environment through the release of gases and particulate matter, but two other major sources of energy, hydroelectricity and nuclear power, are also controversial. Hydroelectricity production involves flooding large areas to create reservoirs, while nuclear power stations generate dangerous radioactive wastes and can cause major disasters. Nuclear power is now a growing source of energy. By 2009, about 15% of the world's electricity was produced by nuclear plants, compared with 3.3% in 1973.

Alternative energy resources may soon provide a much larger proportion of the world's energy consumption. Solar and wind energy may become important in such countries as China and India, while tidal, wave, and geothermal energy all have potential in appropriate areas. Experts calculate that solar power could, in theory, supply between five and ten times the present electricity supply of developing countries.

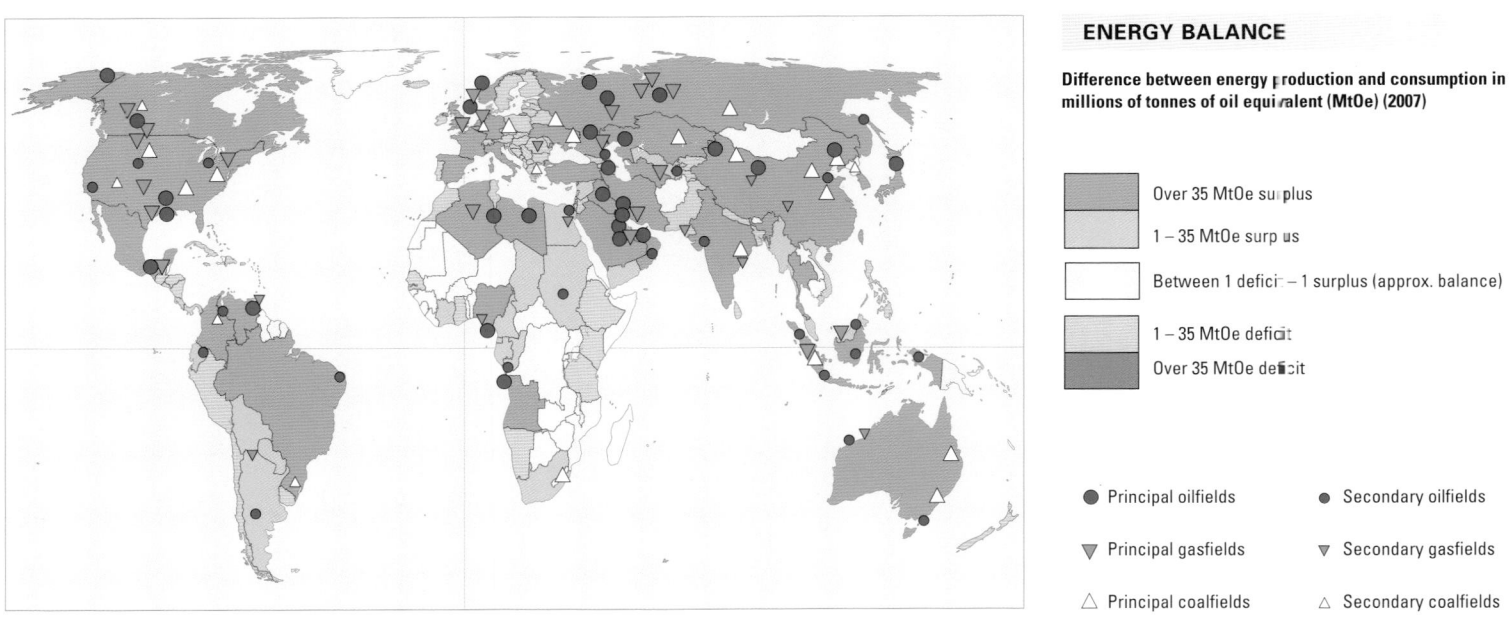

ENERGY BALANCE

Difference between energy production and consumption in millions of tonnes of oil equivalent (MtOe) (2007)

- Over 35 MtOe surplus
- 1 – 35 MtOe surplus
- Between 1 deficit – 1 surplus (approx. balance)
- 1 – 35 MtOe deficit
- Over 35 MtOe deficit

● Principal oilfields   ● Secondary oilfields
▼ Principal gasfields   ▼ Secondary gasfields
△ Principal coalfields   △ Secondary coalfields

ENERGY CONSUMPTION

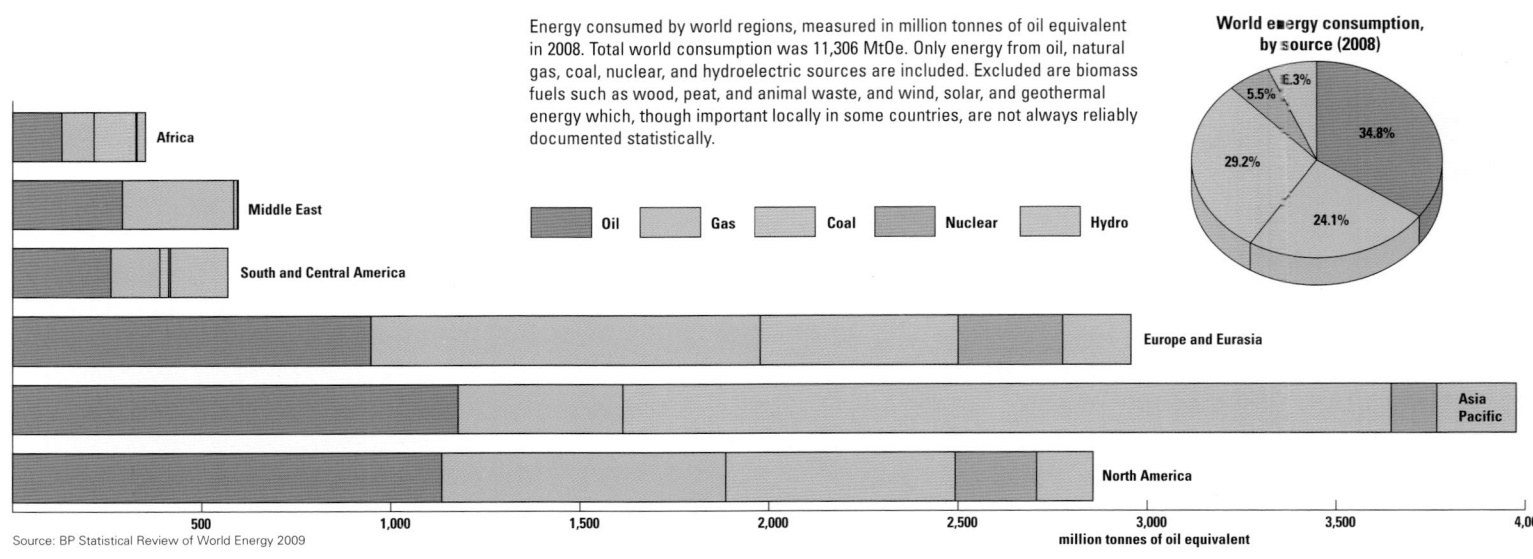

Energy consumed by world regions, measured in million tonnes of oil equivalent in 2008. Total world consumption was 11,306 MtOe. Only energy from oil, natural gas, coal, nuclear, and hydroelectric sources are included. Excluded are biomass fuels such as wood, peat, and animal waste, and wind, solar, and geothermal energy which, though important locally in some countries, are not always reliably documented statistically.

■ Oil   ■ Gas   ■ Coal   ■ Nuclear   ■ Hydro

World energy consumption, by source (2008)

34.8%
24.1%
29.2%
5.5%
6.3%

Africa
Middle East
South and Central America
Europe and Eurasia
Asia Pacific
North America

500   1,000   1,500   2,000   2,500   3,000   3,500   4,000
million tonnes of oil equivalent

Source: BP Statistical Review of World Energy 2009

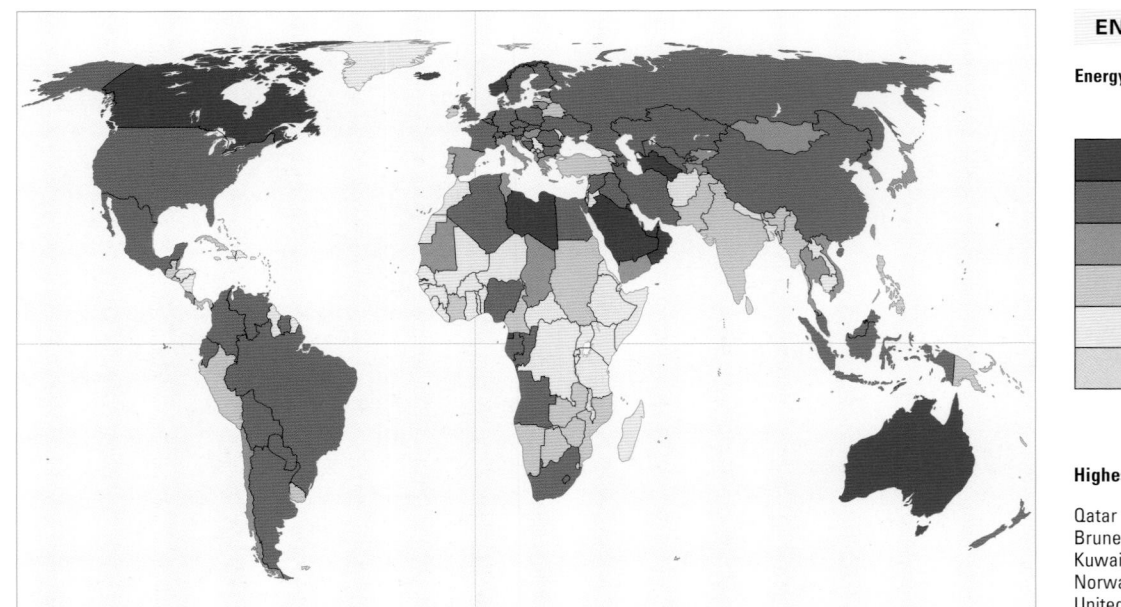

ENERGY PRODUCTION

Energy production in tonnes of oil equivalent per capita (2007)

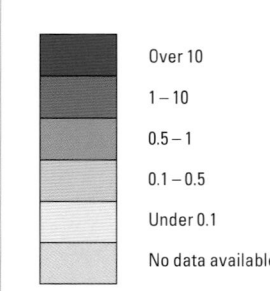

- Over 10
- 1 – 10
- 0.5 – 1
- 0.1 – 0.5
- Under 0.1
- No data available

Highest energy producers, tonnes of oil equivalent per capita

Qatar	111.7
Brunei	65.0
Kuwait	61.3
Norway	55.5
United Arab Emirates	44.3

OIL MOVEMENTS

Major world movements of oil in millions of tonnes (2008)

1.	Middle East to Asia (not China or Japan)	399.0
2.	Former Soviet Union to Europe	318.5
3.	Middle East to Japan	196.9
4.	Middle East to Europe	127.6
5.	Canada to USA	121.7
6.	Middle East to USA	119.7
7.	South and Central America to USA	119.4
8.	North Africa to Europe	101.3
9.	Middle East to China	92.0
10.	West Africa to USA	90.9
11.	Mexico to USA	64.7
Total world imports		**2,697.8 million tonnes**

In 1990, China consumed 120 million tonnes of oil, leaving a surplus for export. In 2009 it consumed 405 million tonnes, of which it had to import around half. It is predicted that by 2030 China will be consuming over 800 million tonnes of oil, importing around three-quarters.

The majority of China's imported oil comes from the Middle East and Africa and has to pass through the narrow and crowded Singapore Strait. The Chinese government is pushing for alternative routes, such as a pipeline from Kazakhstan and a transit route from the Indian Ocean through Burma to Southern China.

◄ With many of the world's onshore oilfields reaching their maturity, exploration and production in ever-deeper ocean waters is taking place to try to satisfy demand. The "Deepwater Horizon" rig in the Gulf of Mexico drilled one of the world's deepest oil wells with a depth of 35,055 ft [10,685 m] before an explosion in April 2010 resulted in a massive oil spill.

ENERGY RESERVES

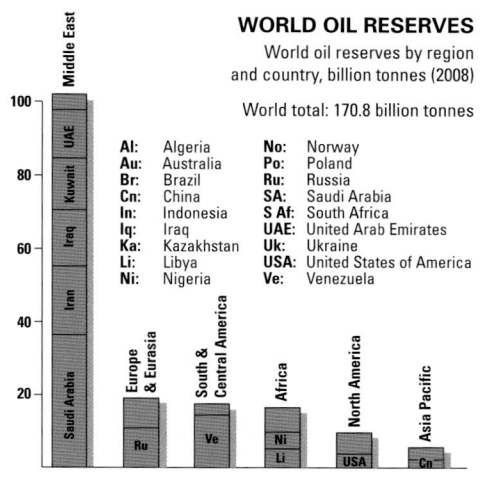

WORLD OIL RESERVES

World oil reserves by region and country, billion tonnes (2008)

World total: 170.8 billion tonnes

Al:	Algeria	No:	Norway
Au:	Australia	Po:	Poland
Br:	Brazil	Ru:	Russia
Cn:	China	SA:	Saudi Arabia
In:	Indonesia	S Af:	South Africa
Iq:	Iraq	UAE:	United Arab Emirates
Ka:	Kazakhstan	Uk:	Ukraine
Li:	Libya	USA:	United States of America
Ni:	Nigeria	Ve:	Venezuela

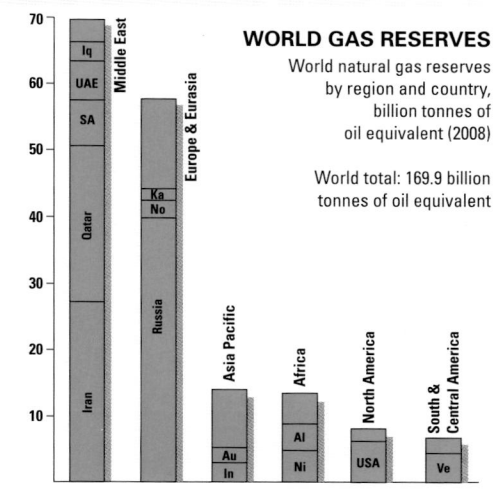

WORLD GAS RESERVES

World natural gas reserves by region and country, billion tonnes of oil equivalent (2008)

World total: 169.9 billion tonnes of oil equivalent

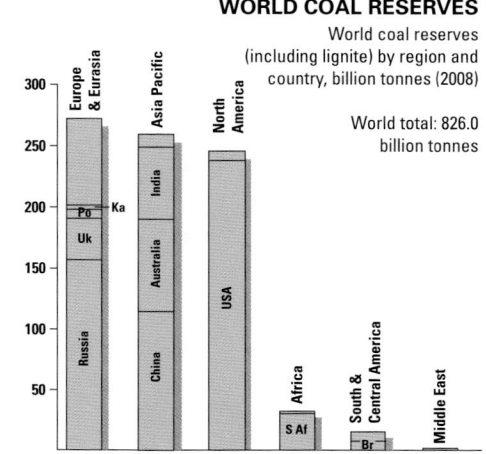

WORLD COAL RESERVES

World coal reserves (including lignite) by region and country, billion tonnes (2008)

World total: 826.0 billion tonnes

NUCLEAR POWER

Major producers by percentage of world total and by percentage of domestic electricity generation (2008)

Country	% of world total production	Country	% of nuclear as proportion of domestic electricity
1. USA	31.0%	1. France	77.5%
2. France	16.1%	2. Lithuania	75.6%
3. Japan	9.4%	3. Slovak Rep.	56.7%
4. Russia	5.9%	4. Belgium	55.4%
5. South Korea	5.5%	5. Ukraine	45.5%
6. Germany	5.4%	6. Slovenia	42.2%
7. Canada	3.4%	7. Sweden	41.9%
8. Ukraine	3.2%	8. Armenia	40.7%
9. China	2.5%	9. Switzerland	40.2%
10. Sweden	2.3%	10. Hungary	37.2%

Although the 1980s were a bad time for the nuclear power industry (fears of long-term environmental damage were heavily reinforced by the 1986 disaster at Chernobyl), the industry picked up in the early 1990s. Sixteen countries currently rely on nuclear power to supply over 25% of their total electricity requirements. There are over 400 operating nuclear power stations worldwide, with over 100 more planned or under construction.

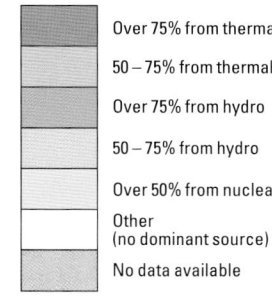

ELECTRICITY PRODUCTION

Percentage of electricity generated by source (2007)

- Over 75% from thermal
- 50 – 75% from thermal
- Over 75% from hydro
- 50 – 75% from hydro
- Over 50% from nuclear
- Other (no dominant source)
- No data available
- ⊙ Selected geothermal plants
- ◇ Selected hydroelectric plants

HYDROELECTRICITY

Major producers by percentage of world total and by percentage of domestic electricity generation (2007)

Country	% of world total production	Country	% of hydroelectric as proportion of domestic electricity
1. China	14.3%	1. Lesotho	100%
2. Brazil	12.3%	= Bhutan	100%
3. Canada	12.2%	= Paraguay	100%
4. USA	8.3%	4. Mozambique	99.9%
5. Russia	5.8%	5. Congo (Rep. Dem.)	99.7%
6. Norway	4.4%	6. Nepal	99.5%
7. India	4.1%	7. Zambia	99.4%
8. Venezuela	2.8%	8. Norway	98.7%
9. Japan	2.4%	9. Tajikistan	97.9%
10. Sweden	2.2%	10. Burundi	97.8%

Countries heavily reliant on hydroelectricity are usually small and non-industrial: a high proportion of hydroelectric power more often reflects a modest energy budget than vast hydroelectric resources. The USA, for instance, produces only 6% of its domestic power requirements from hydroelectricity; yet that 6% amounts to almost half the hydropower generated by the whole of Africa.

ALTERNATIVE ENERGY RESOURCES

Solar: Each year the Sun bestows upon the Earth almost a million times as much energy as is locked up in all the planet's oil reserves, but only an insignificant fraction is trapped and used commercially. In a few installations around the world, mirrors focus the Sun's rays on to boilers, whose steam generates electricity by spinning turbines.

Wind: Caused by uneven heating of the Earth, winds are themselves a form of solar energy. Windmills have been long used for wind power; recent models, often arranged in banks on wind-swept high ground or off coastlines, usually generate electricity. Wind-power figures are given in the table (*right*). Although it currently produces less than 1% of the world's electricity, it contributes 19% of all electricity generated in Denmark.

Tidal: The energy from tides is potentially enormous, although only a few installations have so far been built to exploit it. In theory, at least, waves and currents could also provide almost unimaginable power, and the thermal differences in the ocean depths are another huge well

of potential energy. But work on extracting it is still at the experimental stage.

Geothermal: The Earth's temperature rises by 1°F for every 50 feet descent, with much steeper temperature gradients in geologically active areas. El Salvador, for example, produces 25% of its electricity from geothermal power stations, whilst the USA is the world's leading producer. Some of the oldest and most successful applications are in Iceland, where 86% of all households are heated by geothermal energy.

Biomass: The oldest of human fuels ranges from animal dung, still burned in cooking fires in much of North Africa and elsewhere, to sugarcane plantations feeding high-technology distilleries to produce ethanol for motor-vehicle engines. In Brazil and South Africa, plant ethanol provides up to 25% of motor fuel. Throughout the developing world, most biomass energy comes from firewood: although accurate figures are impossible to obtain, it may yield as much as 10% of the world's total energy consumption.

WIND POWER

World wind energy generating capacity, in megawatts

1984	600
1986	1,270
1988	1,580
1990	1,930
1992	2,510
1994	3,710
1996	6,115
1998	9,600
1999	11,700
2000	17,800
2001	23,300
2002	31,000
2003	39,300
2004	47,671
2005	58,982
2006	74,151
2007	93,927
2008	121,188
2009	157,899

For more information:
74 Geology
101 Patterns of production
103 World shipping

The use of metals played a vital part in the evolving technologies of early peoples. Copper first came into use around 10,000 years ago, bronze about 5,000 years ago, and iron 3,300 years ago. In the early stages of the Industrial Revolution, the location of coal, iron ore, and water power usually determined the location of new industries. But due to continuing improvements in transport, including oil pipelines, industries can now be located almost anywhere.

Minerals are distributed unevenly and some industrial countries, lacking their own mineral resources, import most of the raw materials they need. Some imports come from mineral-rich countries, such as Australia, but others come from developing countries, especially in Africa and South America. Most developing countries export unprocessed ores, losing out on the higher revenues gained from exporting metals.

Most minerals come from land deposits, because undersea deposits, with the exception of oil reserves under the continental shelves, have been inaccessible. But shortages of terrestrial minerals may one day encourage exploitation of the ocean floor.

▶ Bingham Canyon Mine in Utah, USA, is one of the largest open-pit mines in the world. It measures over 2.5 miles [4 km] wide and 3,900 ft [1,200 m] deep. Copper-containing rocks are excavated from the surface downward in terraces. These terraces are 50–80 ft [15–25 m] high and provide access for equipment to work the rock face whilst maintaining stability of the sloping pit walls.

Today's copper market is booming due to global demands from construction, telecommunications, and electronics companies. Over 17 million tonnes of copper have been mined from Bingham Canyon Mine to date.

URANIUM

Uranium was first discovered by the German chemist Martin Klaproth in 1789. In its pure state, uranium is an immensely heavy, white metal. Its main use is as a fuel in nuclear reactors and in nuclear weaponry, although depleted uranium is employed as a projectile in anti-missile cannons, where its mass ensures a lethal punch.

Uranium is very scarce: the main source is the rare ore pitchblende, which itself contains only 0.2% uranium oxide. This blackish, lustrous ore occurs in quartz veins. Only a minute fraction of that is the radioactive U^{235} isotope, though so-called breeder reactors can transmute the more common U^{238} into highly radioactive plutonium.

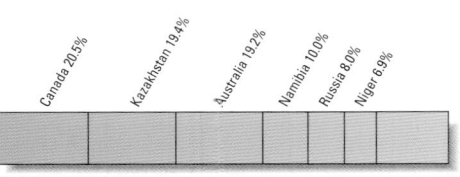

World total (2008): 43,800 tonnes

DIAMOND

Most of the world's diamond is found in kimberlite, or "blue ground," a basic peridotite rock; erosion may wash the diamond from its kimberlite matrix and deposit it with sand or gravel on river beds. Only a small proportion of the world's diamond, the most flawless, is cut into gemstones – "diamonds"; most are used in industry, where the material's remarkable hardness and abrasion resistance finds a use in cutting tools, drills, and dies. In 2008, the world's major producers were the Democratic Republic of the Congo (29.9%), Australia (23.4%), Russia (19.5%), South Africa (11.7%), and Botswana (10.4%). Natural diamonds now account for less than 10% of all industrial diamond output. Synthetic diamond production in centers such as Ireland, Japan, Russia, and the USA far exceeds it.

METALS

Figures refer to ore production unless otherwise specified after the world total figure.

The world's leading producers of aluminum ore (bauxite) in 2008 were as follows:

1. Australia 29.9%
2. China....................................17.1%
3. Brazil 10.7%
4. India 10.3%
5. Guinea 9.0%
6. Jamaica 6.8%
7. Russia 3.1%
8. Venezuela 2.7%
9. Suriname 2.6%
10. Kazakhstan 2.4%

The figures shown above are in stark contrast to the figures showing aluminum production (*see above right*). Australia, for example, produces 29.9% of the world's bauxite but only 5.1% of aluminum. Guinea and Jamaica account for almost 16% of the bauxite mined but have no smelters and export virtually all of it to countries like the USA and Canada.

Aluminum: Produced mainly from its oxide, bauxite, which yields 25% of its weight in aluminum. The cost of refining and production is often too high for producer-countries to bear, so bauxite is largely exported. Lightweight and corrosion resistant, aluminum alloys are widely used in aircraft, vehicles, cans, and packaging.

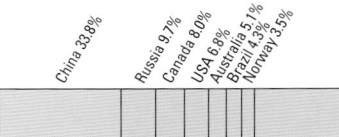

World total (2008): 39,000,000 tonnes

Lead: A soft metal, obtained mainly from galena (lead sulfide), which occurs in veins associated with iron, zinc, and silver sulfides. Its use in vehicle batteries accounts for the USA's prime consumer status; lead is also made into sheeting and piping. Its use as an additive to paints and petrol is decreasing.

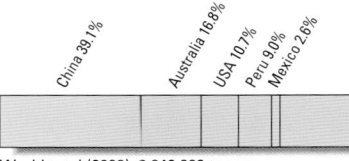

World total (2008): 3,840,000 tonnes

Tin: Soft, pliable and non-toxic, used to coat "tin" (tin-plated steel) cans, in the manufacture of foils and in alloys. The principal tin-bearing mineral is cassiterite (SnO_2), found in ore formed from molten rock. Producers and refiners were hit by a price collapse in 1991.

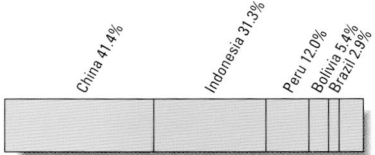

World total (2008): 326,000 tonnes

Gold: Regarded for centuries as the most valuable metal in the world and used to make coins, gold is still recognized as the monetary standard. A soft metal, it is alloyed to make jewelry; the electronics industry values its corrosion resistance and conductivity.

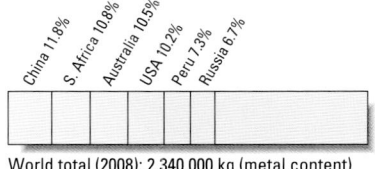

World total (2008): 2,340,000 kg (metal content)

Copper: Derived from low-yielding sulfide ores, copper is an important export for several developing countries. An excellent conductor of heat and electricity, it forms part of most electrical items, and is used in the manufacture of brass and bronze. Major importers include Japan and Germany.

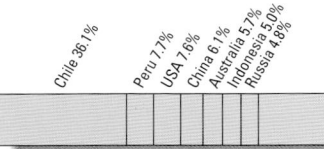

World total (2008): 15,400,000 tonnes

Mercury: The only metal that is liquid at normal temperatures, most is derived from its sulfide, cinnabar, found only in small quantities in volcanic areas. Apart from its value in thermometers and other instruments, most mercury production is used in anti-fungal and anti-fouling preparations, and to make detonators.

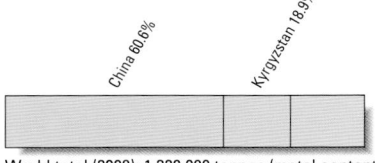

World total (2008): 1,320,000 tonnes (metal content)

Zinc: Often found in association with lead ores, zinc is highly resistant to corrosion, and about 40% of the refined metal is used to plate sheet steel, particularly vehicle bodies – a process known as galvanizing. Zinc is also used in dry batteries, paints, and dyes.

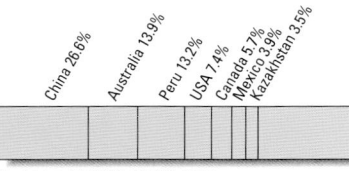

World total (2008): 10,900,000 tonnes

Silver: Most silver comes from ores mined and processed for other metals (including lead and copper). Pure or alloyed with harder metals, it is used for jewelry and ornaments. Industrial use includes dentistry, electronics, photography, and as a chemical catalyst.

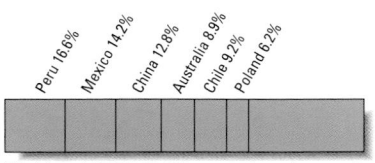

World total (2008): 20,400 tonnes (metal content)

DISTRIBUTION OF MINERALS

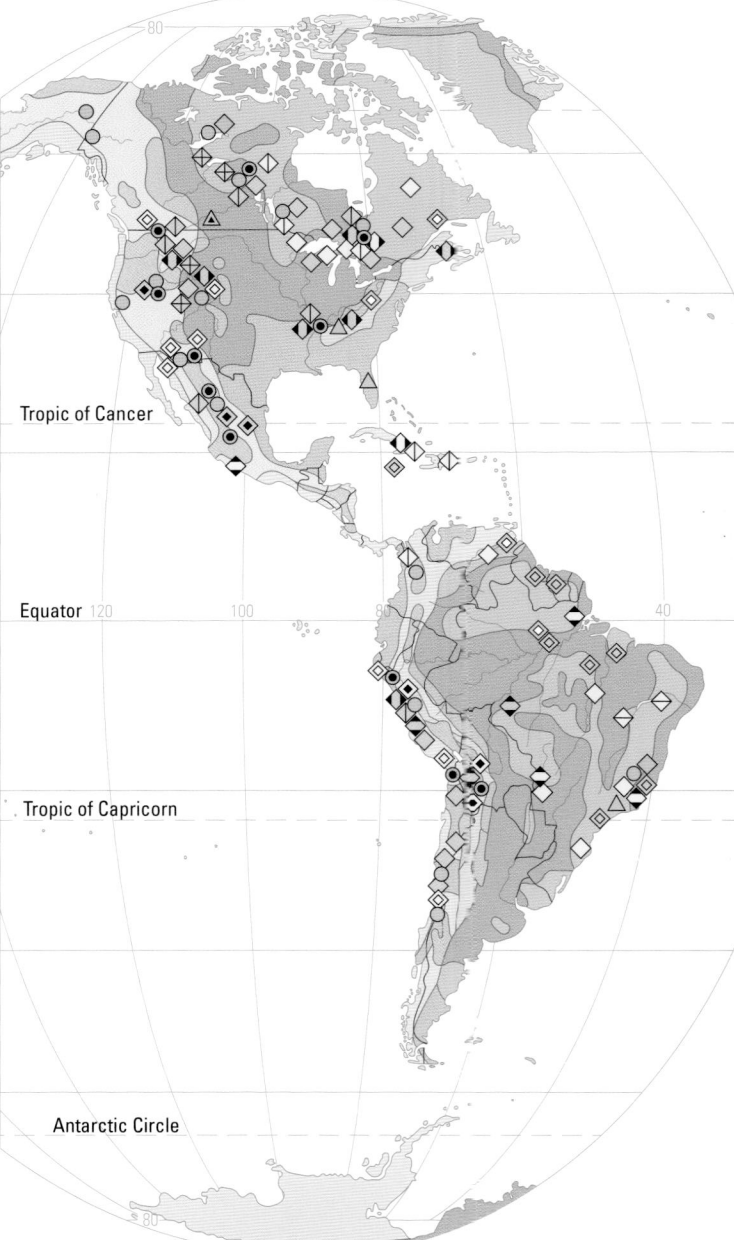

IRON ORE

Ever since the art of high-temperature smelting was discovered, some time in the second millennium BC, iron has been by far the most important metal known to man. The earliest iron plows transformed primitive agriculture and led to the first human population explosion, while iron weapons – or the lack of them – ensured the rise or fall of entire cultures.

Widely distributed around the world, iron ores usually contain 25–60% iron; blast furnaces process the raw product into pig-iron, which is then alloyed with carbon and other minerals to produce steels of various qualities. From the time of the Industrial Revolution, steel has been almost literally the backbone of modern civilization, the prime structural material on which all else is built.

Iron smelting usually developed close to the sources of ore and, later, to the coalfields that fueled the furnaces. Today, most ore comes from a few richly-endowed locations where large-scale mining is possible.

Iron and steel plants are generally built at coastal sites so that giant ore carriers, which account for a sizable proportion of the world's merchant fleet, can easily discharge their cargoes.

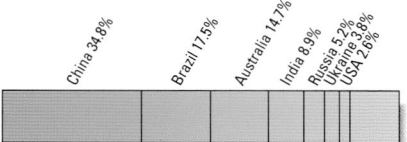

World total (2008): 2,030,000,000 tonnes

World production of pig-iron (2008)

Total world production: 10.9 million tonnes

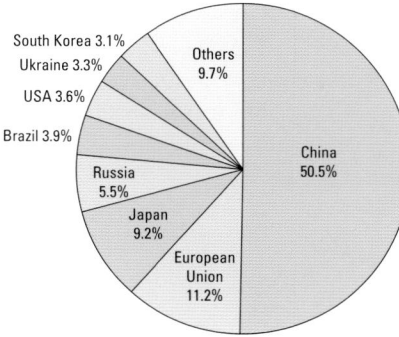

South Korea 3.1%
Ukraine 3.3%
USA 3.6%
Brazil 3.9%
Russia 5.5%
Japan 9.2%
European Union 11.2%
Others 9.7%
China 50.5%

Manganese: In its pure state, manganese is a hard, brittle metal. Alloyed with chromium, iron and nickel, it produces abrasion-resistant steels; manganese-aluminum alloys are light but tough. Found in batteries and inks, manganese is also used in glass production. Manganese ores are frequently found in the same location as sedimentary iron ores. Pyrolusite (MnO_2) and psilomelane are the main economically-exploitable sources.

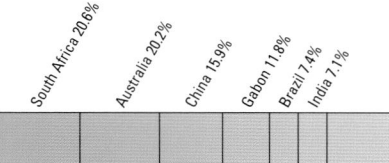

World total (2008): 12,600,000 tonnes

Chromium: Most of the world's chromium production is alloyed with iron and other metals to produce steels with various different properties. Combined with iron, nickel, cobalt, and tungsten, chromium produces an exceptionally hard steel, resistant to heat; chrome steels are used for many household items where utility must be matched with appearance – cutlery, for example. Chromium is also used in the production of refractory bricks, and its salts for tanning and dyeing leather and cloth.

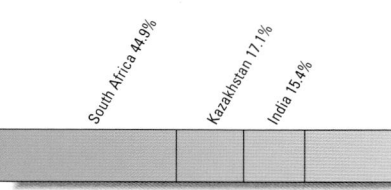

South Africa 44.9% | Kazakhstan 17.1% | India 15.4%

World total (2008): 21,500,000 tonnes

Nickel: Combined with chromium and iron, nickel produces stainless and high-strength steels; similar alloys go to make magnets and electrical heating elements. Nickel combined with copper is widely used to make coins; cupro-nickel alloy is very resistant to corrosion. Its ores yield only modest quantities of nickel – 0.5% to 3% – but also contain copper, iron, and small amounts of precious metals. Japan, USA, UK, Germany, and France are the principal importers.

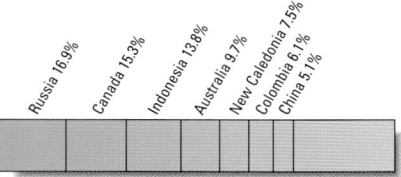

World total (2008): 1,660,000 tonnes

SCRAP METAL

Scrap metal has been an important source material for the manufacturing industry in domestic markets for decades, its value fluctuating according to the state of the local economy. Recently, however, with growing concern for the global environment and the rapid development of the economies in the Far East, the industry has become far more globalized. Container loads of processed-metal scrap from time-expired machinery in the Western world are now being exported to the Far East to be recycled. Processed-steel scrap accounts for almost half of the requirements for "furnace feed" for the world's steelmakers, and 40% of the world's copper requirements are derived from scrap.

Two major advantages of using scrap rather than refining mined ore are the energy and raw material savings that can be made. If 1 tonne of steel scrap is recycled, it saves 120 lb [54 kg] of limestone, 2,500 lb [1,130 kg] of iron ore, and 1,400 lb [635 kg] of coal, with a consequent 86% reduction in air pollution, 40% saving in water use, and 76% reduction in water pollution. Huge energy savings, with consequent cuts in greenhouse-gas emissions, can also be made by using scrap.

As well as bulk minerals, such as those quoted above, alloys using nickel, chromium, tungsten, molybdenum, cobalt, and titanium, which are often only available in limited supplies and are expensive to produce, can also be recycled. The techniques involved to do this work are often very sophisticated, involving X-ray spectrometry and other computer-controlled methods, in order to recover high-value but low-volume metals from devices such as computers and televisions.

With companies having to take increased responsibility for their products, from manufacturing to sale and thence to their ultimate disposal at the end of their useful life, recycling scrap metals will become a much more important method of conserving the world's raw materials and preserving the environment in the future.

STRUCTURAL REGIONS

- Pre-Cambrian shields
- Sedimentary cover on Pre-Cambrian shields
- Paleozoic (Caledonian and Hercynian) folding
- Sedimentary cover on Paleozoic folding
- Mesozoic folding
- Sedimentary cover on Mesozoic folding
- Cenozoic (Alpine) folding
- Sedimentary cover on Cenozoic folding
- Intensive Mesozoic and Cenozoic vulcanism

DISTRIBUTION

Iron and ferro-alloys

- Chromium
- Cobalt
- Iron ore
- Manganese
- Molybdenum
- Nickel ore
- Tungsten

Non-ferrous metals

- Bauxite (Aluminum)
- Copper
- Lead
- Mercury
- Tin
- Zinc
- Uranium

Precious metals and stones

- Diamonds
- Gold
- Silver

Fertilizers

- Phosphates
- Potash

For more information:

84 Water distribution
98 Minerals
99 Iron and ferro-alloys
102 Major exports
   Traded products

The Industrial Revolution, which began in Britain in the late 18th century, represented a major technological advance in the evolution of human society. It enabled a group of countries to become prosperous by replacing expensive human labor with increasingly sophisticated machinery. In economic terms, manufacturing is the transformation of raw materials, energy, labor, and machines into finished goods, which have a higher value than the various elements used in production.

The economies of countries can be compared by reference to their per capita Gross Domestic Products (GDPs), namely, the total value of goods and services produced within a country in a year, divided by the population. The industrialized, or developed, countries accounted for 19% of the world's population in 2009 with an average per capita GDP of more than US $36,000. On the other hand, low-income developing countries, with small industrial sectors, accounted for 38% of the world's population. Their per capita GDPs are less than $2,100, with some as low as $500.

Kenya, with its low-income economy, had a per capita GDP in 2009 of US $1,600. Agriculture employs 75% of the people, while industry together with services employs 25%. The main industries are the processing of agricultural imports and import substitution (making such necessities as cement, footwear, and textiles). Heavy industry plays only a small part. By contrast, Germany had a per capita GDP in 2009 of $34,200. Agriculture employs only 2% of the population, with 30% in industry and 68% in services. Germany's industrial sector differs greatly from Kenya's, with its emphasis on vehicles, machinery, chemicals, and electronics.

Since the 1970s, some former developing countries in eastern Asia achieved rapid economic growth through industrialization. Despite setbacks in the late 1990s, they demonstrated that a developing industrial sector can transform an economy, which starts off with certain advantages, such as low labor costs. But economic success also depends on such factors as education to provide skills, and regulations that attract foreign investors. China, whose economy grew by more than 9% per year between 2001 and 2007, satisfies many of these criteria, though its record on human rights leaves much to be desired.

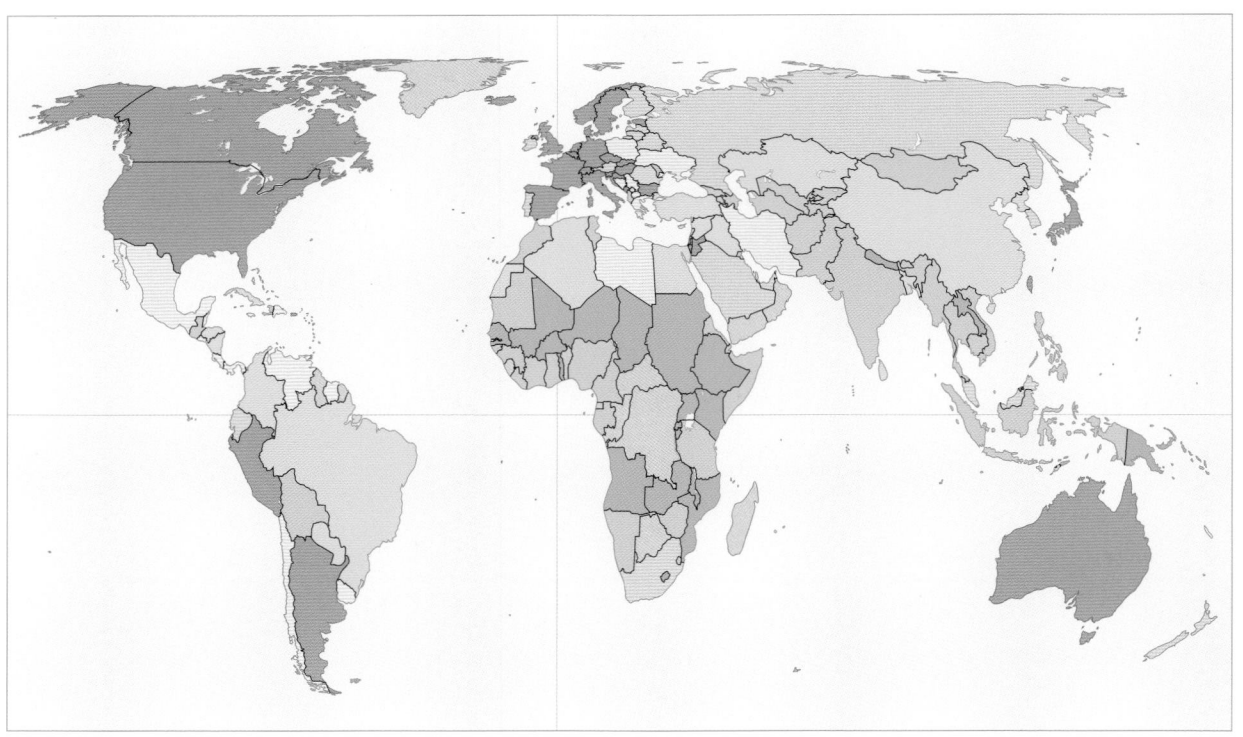

EMPLOYMENT

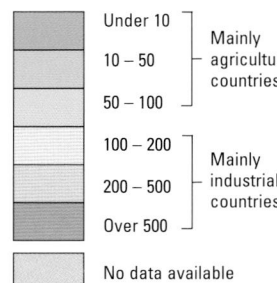

The number of workers employed in manufacturing for every 100 workers engaged in agriculture (2007)

Under 10	Mainly
10 – 50	agricultural countries
50 – 100	
100 – 200	Mainly
200 – 500	industrial countries
Over 500	
No data available	

Countries with the highest number of workers employed in manufacturing per 100 workers in agriculture (2007)

Bahrain	7,900
USA	3,800
San Marino	3,700
Micronesia, Fed. States of	3,400
Sweden	2,800
Peru	2,400
Argentina	2,300
Singapore	2,200
Liechtenstein	2,150
Andorra	2,000

DIVISION OF EMPLOYMENT

Distribution of workers between agriculture, industry and services, selected countries (2006)

The six countries selected illustrate the usual stages of economic development, from dependence on agriculture through industrial growth to the expansion of the service sector.

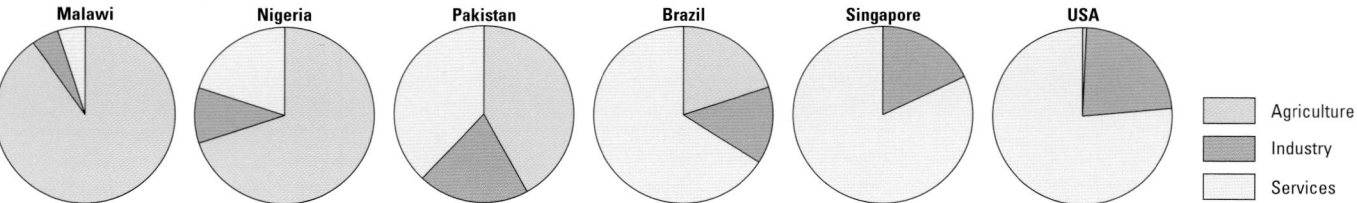

Malawi   Nigeria   Pakistan   Brazil   Singapore   USA

Agriculture
Industry
Services

THE WORK FORCE

Percentages of men and women between 15 and 64 in employment (selected countries)

The figures include employees and the self-employed, who in developing countries are often subsistence farmers. People in full-time education are excluded. Because of the population age structure in developing countries, the employed population has to support a far larger number of non-workers than its industrial equivalent. For example, more than 52% of Kenya's people are under 15, an age group that makes up less than a tenth of the UK population.

Men   Women

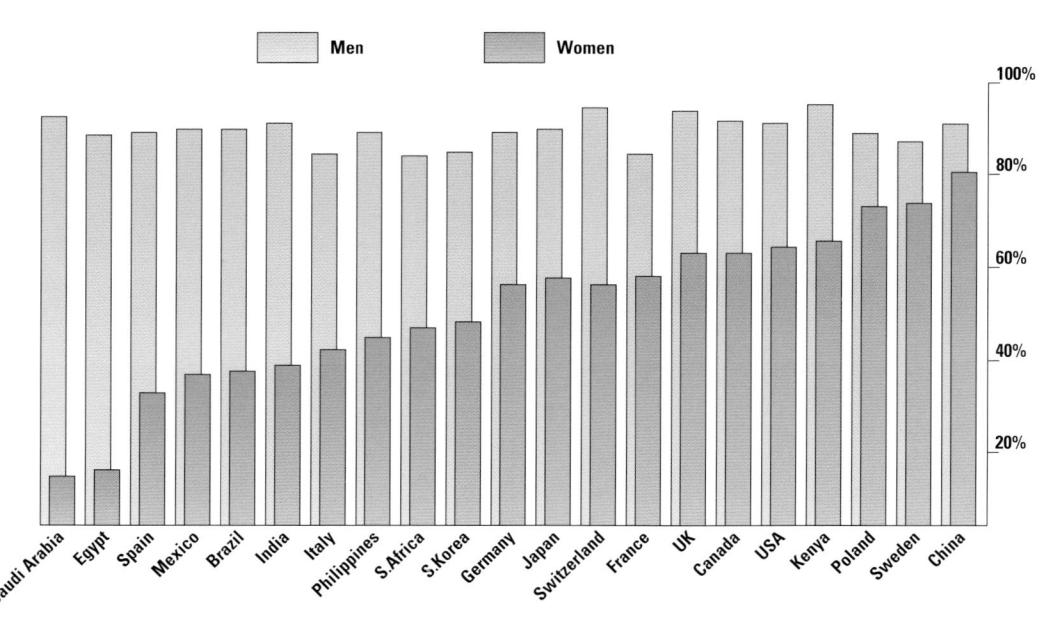

WEALTH CREATION

The Gross National Income (GNI) of the world's largest economies, US $ million (2008)

1.	USA	14,466,100	21.	Indonesia	458,200
2.	Japan	4,879,200	22.	Poland	453,000
3.	China	3,899,300	23.	Norway	415,200
4.	Germany	3,485,700	24.	Austria	386,000
5.	UK	2,787,200	25.	Saudi Arabia	374,300
6.	France	2,702,200	26.	Denmark	325,100
7.	Italy	2,109,100	27.	Greece	322,000
8.	Spain	1,456,500	28.	Argentina	287,200
9.	Brazil	1,411,200	29.	South Africa	283,300
10.	Canada	1,390,000	30.	Venezuela	257,800
11.	Russia	1,364,500	31.	Finland	255,700
12.	India	1,215,500	32.	Iran	251,500
13.	Mexico	1,061,400	33.	Ireland	221,200
14.	South Korea	1,046,300	34.	Hong Kong	219,300
15.	Australia	862,500	35.	Portugal	218,400
16.	Netherlands	824,600	36.	Colombia	207,400
17.	Turkey	690,700	37.	Thailand	191,700
18.	Switzerland	498,500	38.	Malaysia	188,100
19.	Belgium	474,500	39.	Israel	180,500
20.	Sweden	469,700	40.	Nigeria	175,600

INDUSTRIAL OUTPUT

Largest industrial output (mining, manufacturing, construction, energy, and water production), US $ billion (2007)

1.	USA	2,634	
2.	Japan	1,355	
3.	China	1,279	
4.	Germany	783	
5.	UK	508	
6.	Italy	439	
7.	France	417	
8.	Canada	371	
9.	Russia	332	
10.	Spain	324	
11.	South Korea	313	
12.	Brazil	284	
13.	India	231	
14.	Saudi Arabia	227	
15.	Mexico	201	
16.	Australia	190	
17.	Indonesia	172	
18.	Netherlands	144	
19.	Norway	134	
20.	Turkey	103	
21.	Taiwan	100	
22.	Switzerland	98
23.	Sweden	97
24.	Iran	96
25.	Poland	94
26.	Thailand	92
27.	Austria	89
28.	Belgium	85
29.	Malaysia	75
30.	UAE	74
31.	South Africa	70
=	Argentina	70
33.	Chile	66
34.	Ireland	64
35.	Denmark	61
36.	Finland	59
=	Algeria	59
38.	Greece	58
39.	Nigeria	55
40.	Czech Rep.	50
41.	Colombia	49
42.	Israel	48

INDUSTRY AND TRADE

Manufactured goods (including machinery and transport) as a percentage of total exports (2008)

- Over 75%
- 50 – 75%
- 25 – 50%
- 10 – 25%
- Under 10%
- No data available

Countries most dependent on the export of manufactured goods

Cambodia	94%
China	93%
Israel	93%
Malta	90%
Slovenia	90%
Switzerland	89%

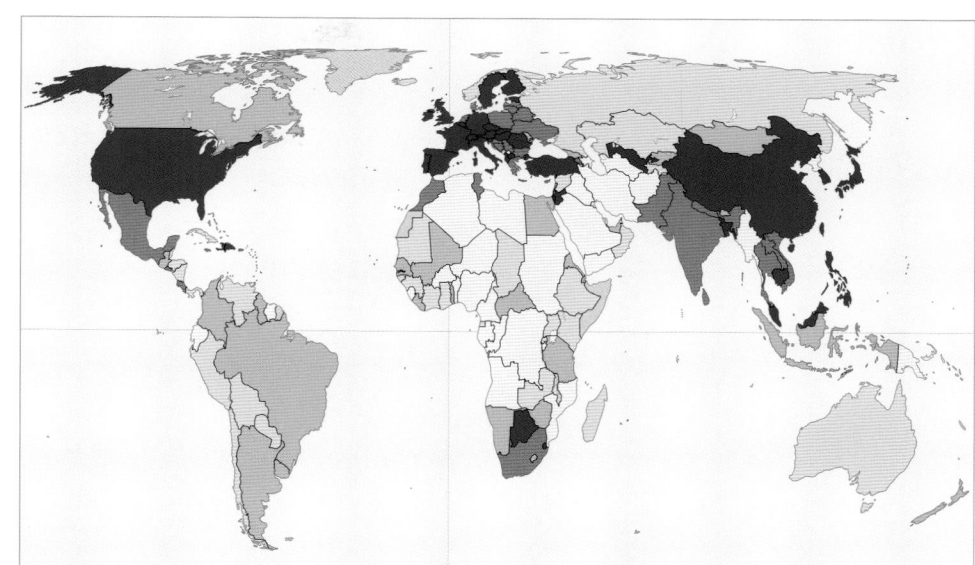

UNEMPLOYMENT

Highest rates of unemployment, percentage of the labor force (2008)

1.	Macedonia	36.0%
2.	Namibia	33.8%
3.	Réunion	29.1%
4.	Guadeloupe	27.3%
5.	Guinea-Bissau	26.3%
6.	South Africa	25.5%
7.	Martinique	25.2%
8.	West Bank and Gaza (OPT)	23.3%
9.	Serbia	20.9%
10.	Dominican Republic	17.9%
11.	Botswana	17.6%
12.	Ethiopia	16.7%
13.	Venezuela	15.8%
14.	Tunisia	14.2%
15.	Burundi	14.0%
16.	Albania	13.8%
=	Georgia	13.8%
=	Poland	13.8%
19.	Slovak Republic	13.3%
20.	Jordan	13.2%

◀ This photograph shows a cement-manufacturing plant in Vác, Hungary. Cement production figures are often an indicator of the relative prosperity of a country, since they show the construction of roads, dams, and other infrastructure projects (*see the graph below*). However, cement manufacture emits high levels of carbon dioxide into the atmosphere.

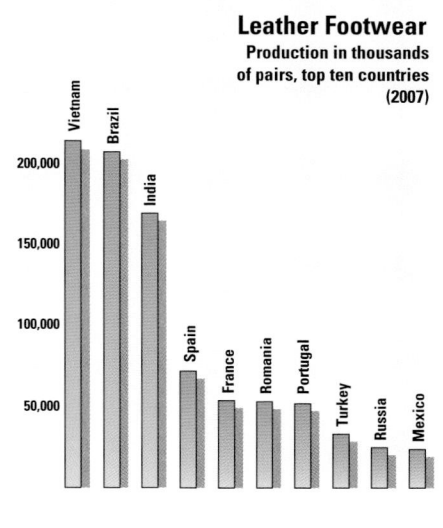

Leather Footwear
Production in thousands of pairs, top ten countries (2007)

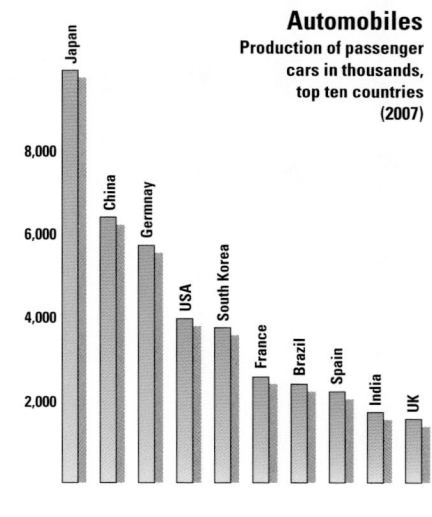

Automobiles
Production of passenger cars in thousands, top ten countries (2007)

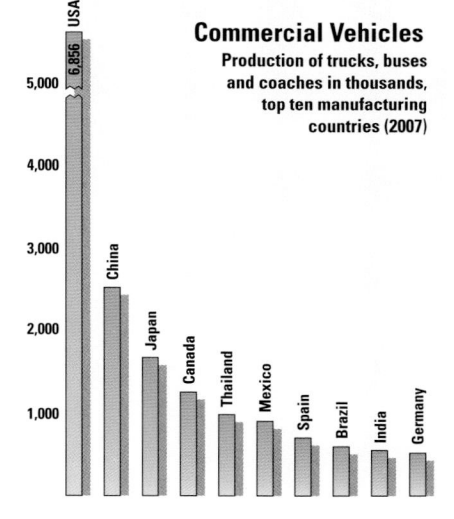

Commercial Vehicles
Production of trucks, buses and coaches in thousands, top ten manufacturing countries (2007)

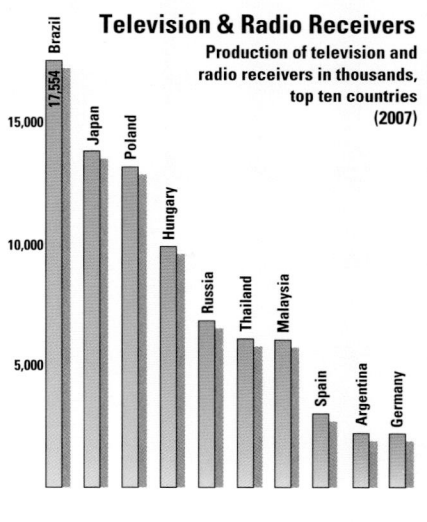

Television & Radio Receivers
Production of television and radio receivers in thousands, top ten countries (2007)

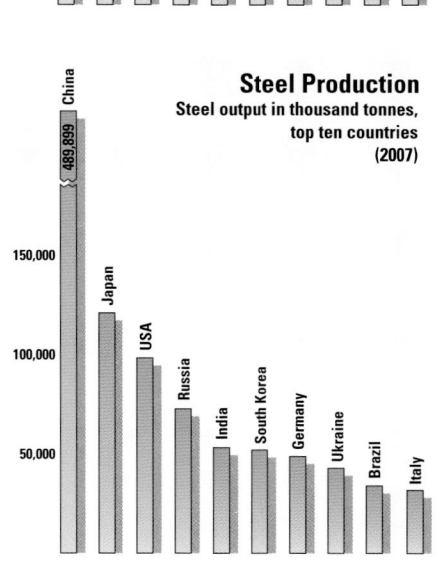

Steel Production
Steel output in thousand tonnes, top ten countries (2007)

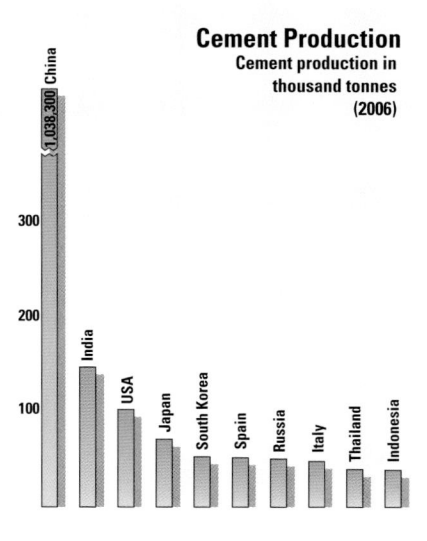

Cement Production
Cement production in thousand tonnes (2006)

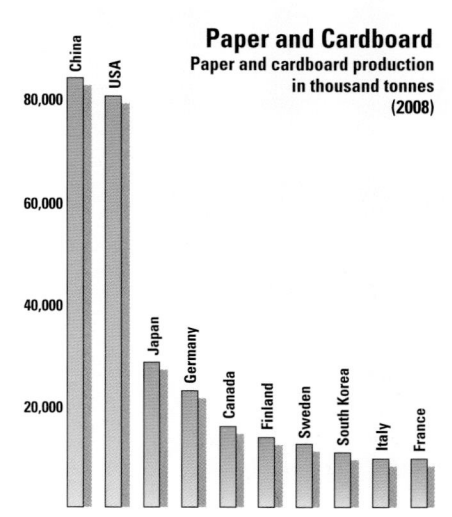

Paper and Cardboard
Paper and cardboard production in thousand tonnes (2008)

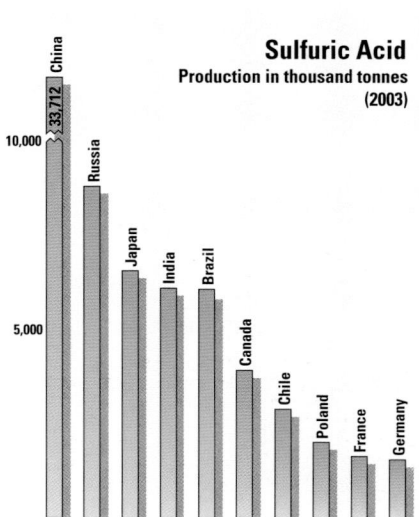

Sulfuric Acid
Production in thousand tonnes (2003)

For more information:

95 International organizations
97 Movements of oil
98 Minerals
100 Wealth creation
101 Industry and trade
107 Air travel and tourism
   Inflation

Trade played a vital role in the growth of early civilizations and it was later a spur to European exploration and colonization. The colonial powers grew rich by exporting cheap manufactures, such as clothing and footwear, while obtaining primary products from their colonies.

From the late 19th century to the early 1950s, as transport technology improved, primary products, especially oil in the later stages of this period, dominated world trade. However, since that time, manufactures have become the chief commodities in world trade, which is dominated by the industrialized countries. Nearly half of all world trade flows between the developed market economies of the European Union, the United States, and Japan, although a number of Asian economies, notably China, Malaysia, Singapore, South Korea, Taiwan, and Thailand, increased their share since the 1990s.

China's remarkable growth means that it has rapidly overtaken countries such as Japan, Mexico, and Germany, to become the second biggest exporter to the United States. China's low production costs, especially its cheap labor, were estimated to be one-twentieth of those of Japan, making its high-quality exports highly competitive in price. Growth in world trade is regarded as a sign of economic health, as is a favorable balance of trade (or trade surplus) in any country.

WORLD TRADE

Percentage share of total world exports by value (2009)

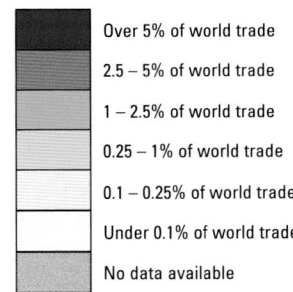

- Over 5% of world trade
- 2.5 – 5% of world trade
- 1 – 2.5% of world trade
- 0.25 – 1% of world trade
- 0.1 – 0.25% of world trade
- Under 0.1% of world trade
- No data available

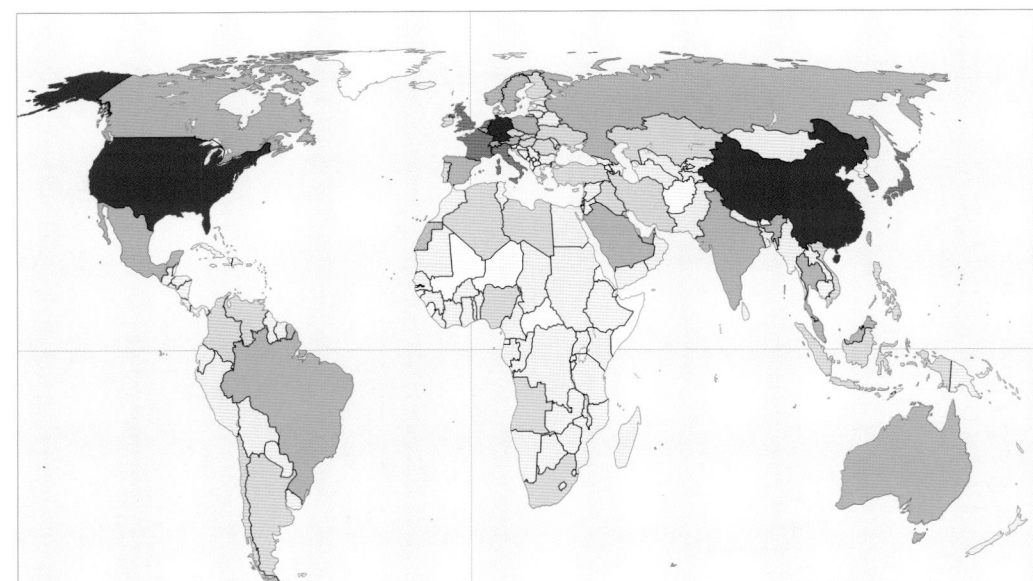

International trade is dominated by a handful of powerful maritime nations. The members of "G8" (Canada, France, Germany, Italy, Japan, Russia, the United Kingdom, and the United States) account for more than one-third of the total. The majority of nations contribute less than a quarter of 1% to the worldwide total of exports.

DEPENDENCE ON TRADE

Exports as a percentage of GDP (2009)

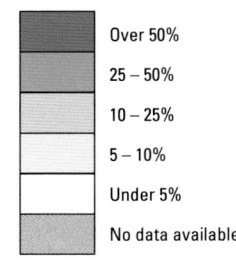

- Over 50%
- 25 – 50%
- 10 – 25%
- 5 – 10%
- Under 5%
- No data available

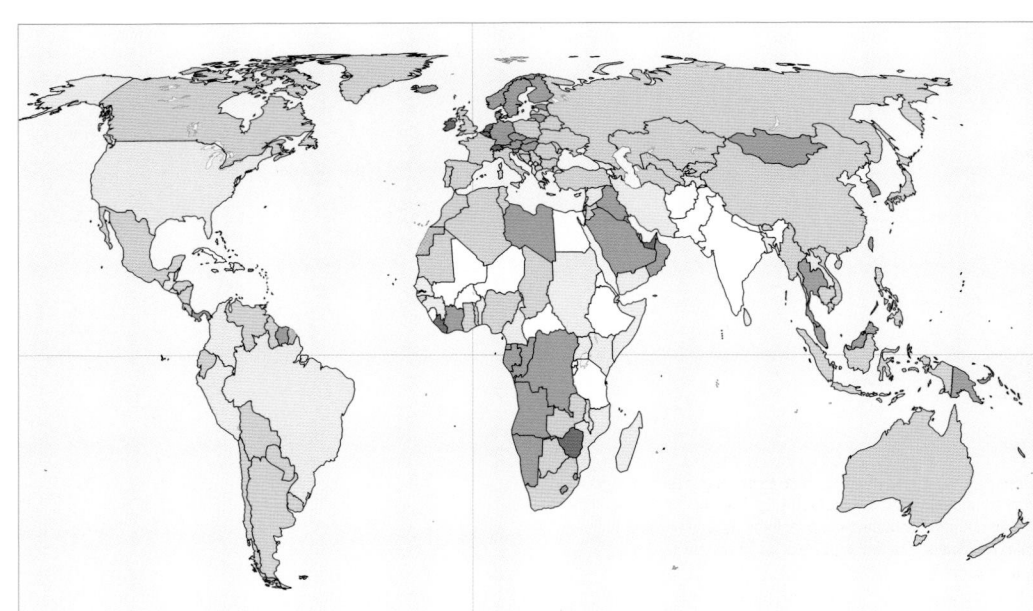

The character of world trade has changed a great deal in the last 50 years or so. While many developing countries still remain heavily dependent on exporting mineral ores, fossil fuels or farm products, such as coffee or cocoa, world trade is now dominated by manufactured goods. Since the 1980s, high-tech products, such as computer equipment, telecommunications gear, and transistors, have become increasingly important.

TRADED PRODUCTS

World merchandise exports by product, percentage of total value (2007)

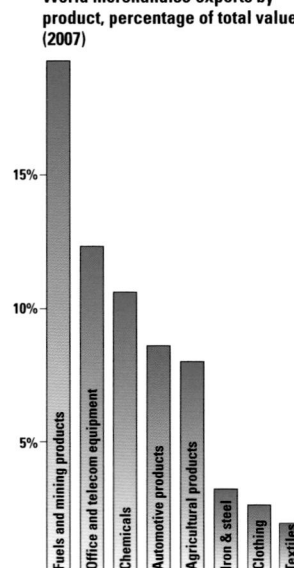

MAJOR EXPORTS

Leading manufactured items and their exporters

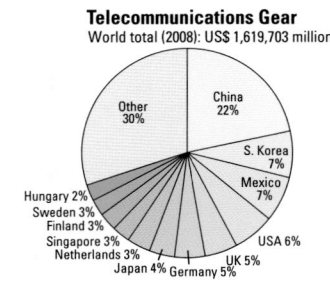

Motor Vehicles
World total (2008): US$ 3,355,798 million

Germany 18%, Japan 14%, USA 9%, France 6%, Canada 6%, Spain 4%, S. Korea 4%, Belgium 4%, Mexico 4%, Italy 3%, China 2%, Sweden 2%, Czech Rep 2%, Other 22%

Telecommunications Gear
World total (2008): US$ 1,619,703 million

China 22%, S. Korea 7%, Mexico 7%, USA 6%, Germany 5%, Japan 4%, Netherlands 3%, Singapore 3%, Finland 3%, Sweden 3%, Hungary 2%, Other 30%

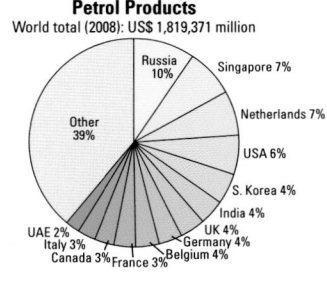

Petrol Products
World total (2008): US$ 1,819,371 million

Russia 10%, Singapore 7%, Netherlands 7%, USA 6%, S. Korea 4%, India 4%, UK 4%, Germany 4%, Belgium 4%, France 3%, Canada 3%, Italy 3%, UAE 2%, Other 39%

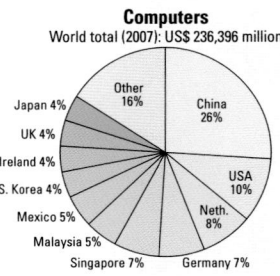

Computers
World total (2007): US$ 236,396 million

China 26%, USA 10%, Neth. 8%, Germany 7%, Singapore 7%, Malaysia 5%, Mexico 5%, S. Korea 4%, Ireland 4%, UK 4%, Japan 4%, Other 16%

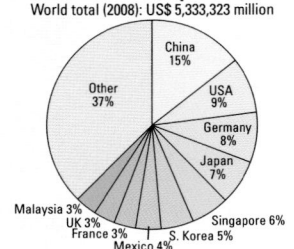

Electrical Components
World total (2008): US$ 5,333,323 million

China 15%, USA 9%, Germany 8%, Japan 7%, Singapore 6%, S. Korea 5%, Mexico 4%, France 3%, UK 3%, Malaysia 3%, Other 37%

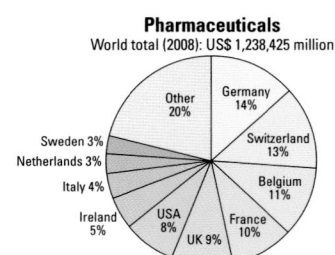

Pharmaceuticals
World total (2008): US$ 1,238,425 million

Germany 14%, Switzerland 13%, Belgium 11%, France 10%, UK 9%, USA 8%, Ireland 5%, Italy 4%, Netherlands 3%, Sweden 3%, Other 20%

WORLD SHIPPING

While ocean passenger traffic is relatively modest nowadays, sea transport still carries most of the world's trade. Oil and bulk carriers make up the majority of the world fleet, although the general cargo category is the fastest growing. Two innovations have revolutionized sea transport. The first is the development of the roll-on/roll-off (Ro-Ro) method where trucks or even trains loaded with freight are driven straight on to the ship, thus saving time. The second is containerization in which goods are packed into containers (the dimensions of which are fixed) at the factory, driven to the port, and loaded on board by specialist machinery.

Almost 30% of world shipping today sails under a "flag of convenience," whereby owners take advantage of low taxes by registering their vessels in a foreign country the ships will never see, notably Panama and Liberia.

TYPES OF VESSELS

World merchant fleet by type of vessel and deadweight tonnage (2009)

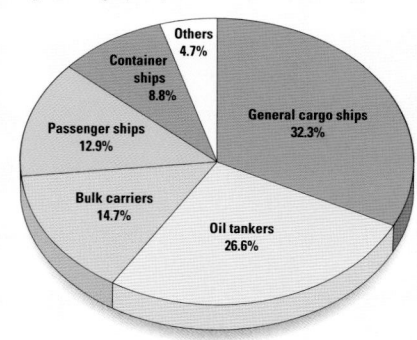

MERCHANT FLEETS

Merchant fleets in thousand gross registered tonnage (2009). Although a large number of vessels are registered in Liberia and Panama, they are not part of the national fleet.

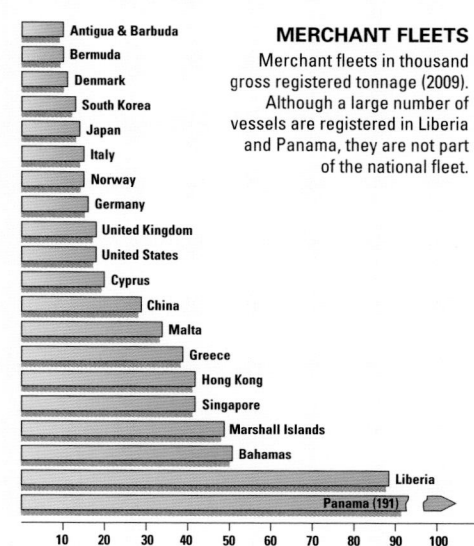

TOP TEN PORTS

Total container traffic, in million TEU (2008)

("TEU" stands for Twenty-foot Equivalent Unit, the equivalent of a standard container)

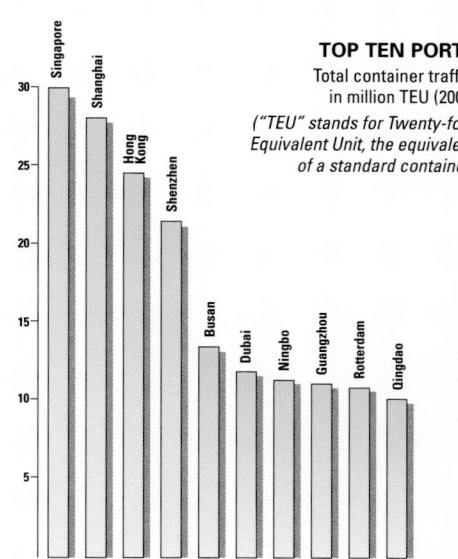

▲ A container ship being unloaded in the port of Melbourne, Australia. World trade depends on transport. Containerization, introduced in the 1950s, reduced the risk of damage to cargo and cut the time and cost of loading and unloading.

TRADE IN PRIMARY EXPORTS

Primary exports as a percentage of total export value (2008)

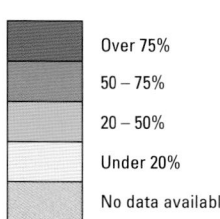

Over 75%

50 – 75%

20 – 50%

Under 20%

No data available

Primary exports are raw materials or partly processed products that form the basis for manufacturing. They are the necessary requirements of industries and include agricultural products, minerals, fuels, and timber, as well as many semimanufactured goods such as cotton, which has been spun but not woven, wood pulp, or flour. Many developed countries have few natural resources and rely on imports for the majority of their primary products. The countries of Southeast Asia export hardwoods to the rest of the world, while many South American countries are heavily dependent on coffee exports.

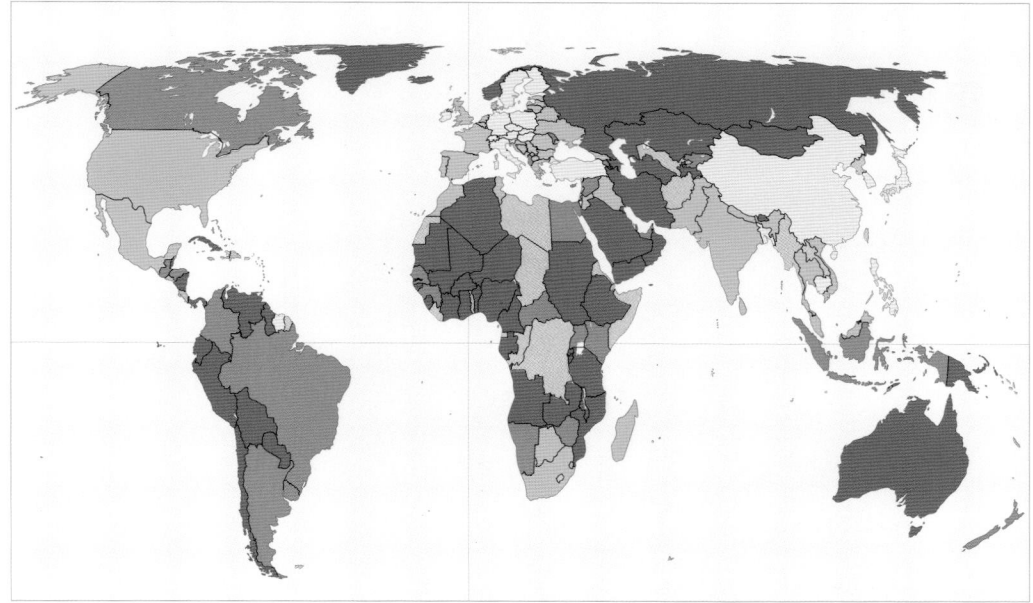

BALANCE OF TRADE

Value of exports in proportion to the value of imports (2009)

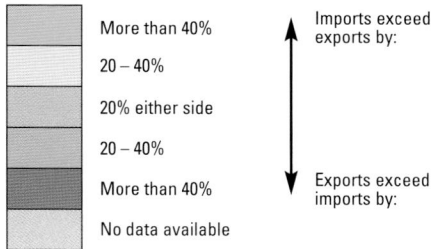

More than 40%

20 – 40%   Imports exceed exports by:

20% either side

20 – 40%

More than 40%   Exports exceed imports by:

No data available

The total world trade balance should amount to zero, since exports must equal imports on a global scale. In practice, though, at least US $100 billion in exports go unrecorded, leaving the world with an apparent deficit and many countries in a better position than public accounting reveals. However, a favorable trade balance is not necessarily a sign of prosperity: many poorer countries must maintain a high surplus in order to service debts, and do so by restricting imports below the levels needed to sustain successful economies.

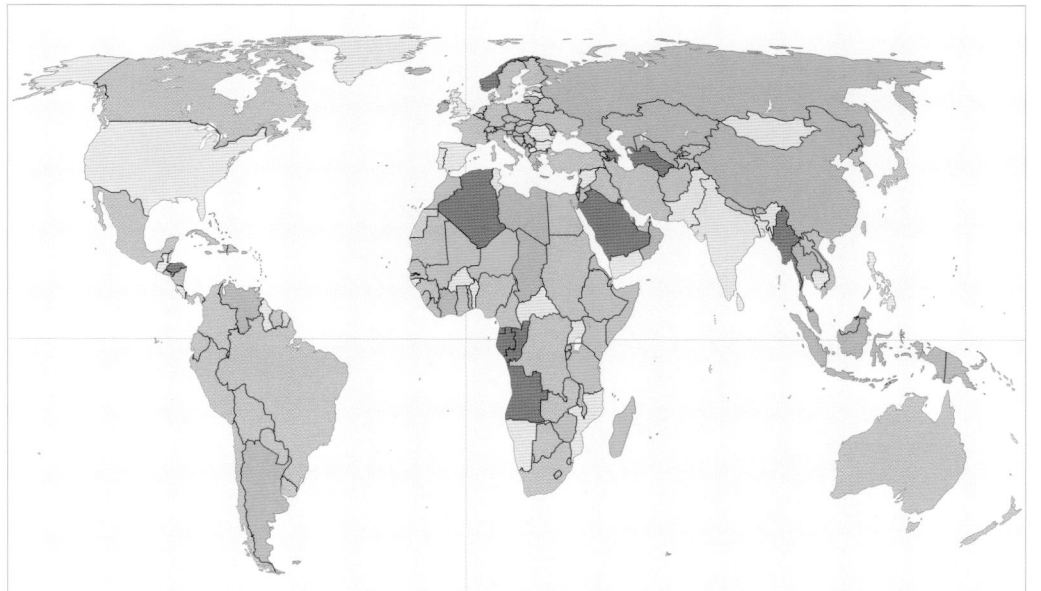

For more information:
84   Water distribution
91   Urban pollution
     Urban advantages
109 Distribution of
     spending

Until the late 1990s, when the full extent of the AIDS crisis emerged, average life expectancies at birth were rising almost everywhere. By 2005, they ranged from 78 years in high-income economies to 46 in sub-Saharan Africa. These figures represented an enormous advance on the situation in 1880, when citizens of Berlin had an estimated life expectancy of 30 years.

The ravages of AIDS have been greatest in southern Africa. One of the worst affected countries is Swaziland, where over 26% of the adult population were thought to be infected in 2007. Life expectancies had fallen to 31 years in 2008, instead of an original estimate of 57 years, and 10,000 people died from AIDS in 2007. However, in much of the world, average life expectancies are still increasing. The rises are attributed to improvements in agriculture and, hence, nutrition, as well as health education, improved sanitation and the quality of drinking water, together with advances in medicine.

Besides AIDS, the people of the developing world are subject to another affliction – malnutrition. The map below shows that in most of Africa, Asia, and Latin America, the average daily calorie supply per person is so low as to cause malnutrition. Malnutrition is a serious condition – among pregnant women it causes high rates of child mortality.

Deficiency diseases occur when people do not have a balanced diet. Protein deficiency causes stunting and kwashiorkor, which can be fatal, especially among young children, while vitamin deficiencies cause such illnesses as beri beri, pellagra, scurvy, and rickets. Iron deficiency causes anemia, while a lack of iodine causes mental retardation.

Infectious diseases, in association with deficient diets, continue to affect people in developing countries. Around the turn of the century, a WHO report stated that infectious diseases cause over 16 million deaths a year. Most of the victims are young and otherwise fit people in developing countries. The major killers are AIDS, cholera, dysentery, malaria, measles, pneumonia, respiratory infections, tuberculosis, and typhoid.

Infectious diseases are much less important as causes of death in developed countries, where cancer and circulatory diseases, such as atherosclerosis and hypertension, which cause strokes and heart attacks, are the most common causes of fatality. Because these diseases tend to kill older people, they are relatively less important in the developing countries where people have shorter lifespans.

Harmful habits are also generally practiced more by the rich than the poor. For example, smoking is an important cause of death in developed countries, while poor diet and high alcohol consumption can badly affect health.

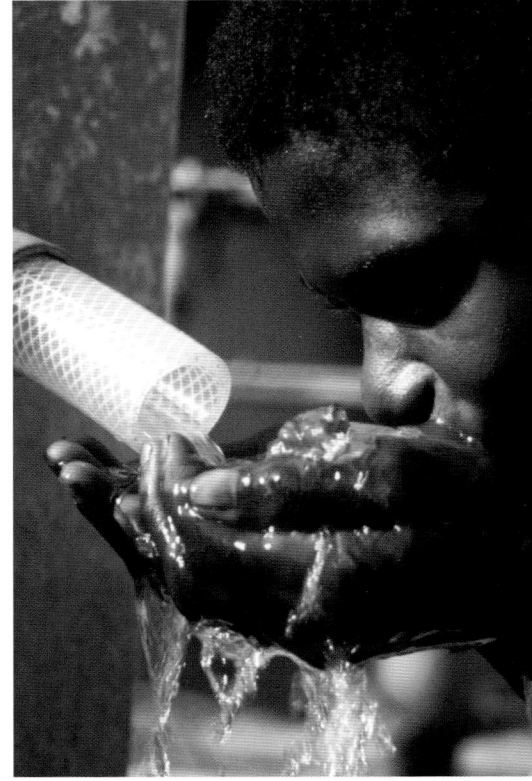

▲ Almost 25% of the world's population does not have access to safe water (the diagram at the bottom left-hand corner of this page shows how this breaks down by continent). This places a huge strain on the millions of mainly women and children who have to walk, collect, and carry drinkable water in order to survive. UNICEF is dedicated to help improve this situation and to react swiftly in the case of emergencies such as civil war, as with the case of this man in Liberia.

FOOD CONSUMPTION

Average daily food intake in calories per person (2005)

- Over 3,500 calories
- 3,000 – 3,500 calories
- 2,500 – 3,000 calories
- 2,000 – 2,500 calories
- Under 2,000 calories
- No data available

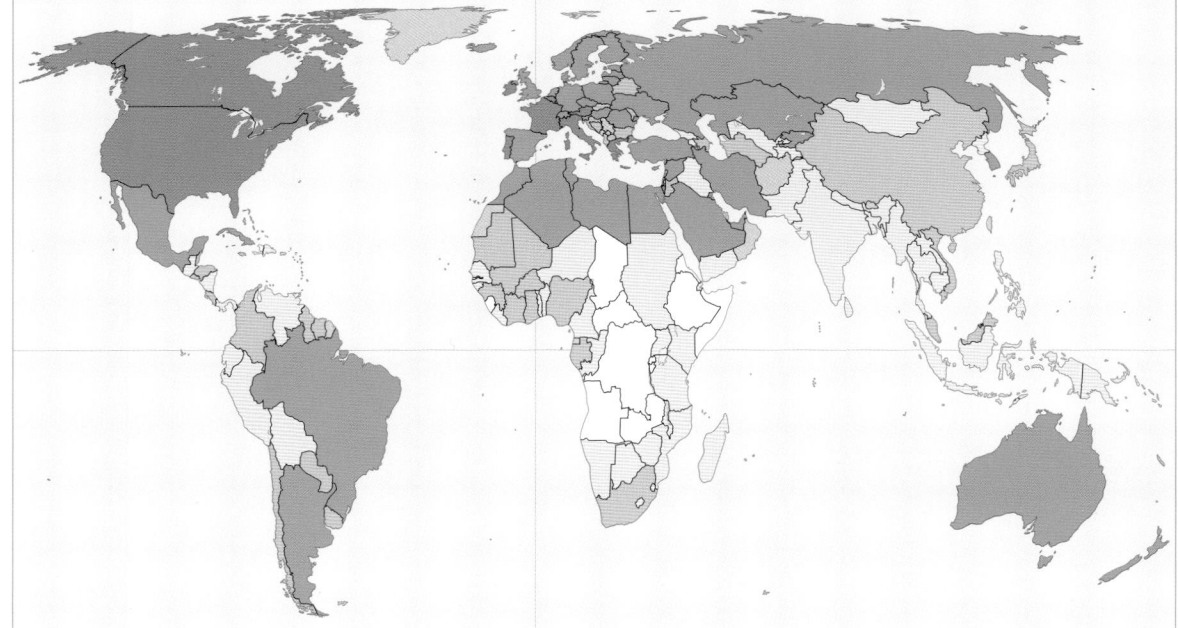

The daily food intake rated adequate by the World Health Organization is between 2,300 and 2,500 calories per day. Approximately 6 million children under the age of 5 years die of starvation each year, the vast majority in Africa. In 2006, the FAO estimated that 854 million people were undernourished, contrasting sharply with the overconsumption of food in some Western cultures.

ACCESS TO SAFE WATER

- Urban
- Rural

Proportion of urban and rural population with access to safe water, by region (2006)

TOBACCO

Up to 1.3 billion people smoke worldwide (1 billion men and 0.3 billion women). According to the World Health Organization, tobacco claims 4.9 million lives each year. At the end of 2007, 29 countries had introduced smoking bans in public places.

Percentage of the population who smoke

	Men	Women
Africa	29%	4%
North America	35%	22%
Eastern Mediterranean	35%	4%
Europe	46%	26%
South-east Asia	44%	4%
Western Pacific	60%	8%

Countries with the highest annual consumption of cigarettes per person

1. Greece	4,313	5. South Korea	2,918
2. Hungary	3,265	6. Slovenia	2,917
3. Kuwait	3,062	7. Spain	2,779
4. Japan	3,023	8. Switzerland	2,720

ALCOHOL

The average Western European and North American drinks over a third more alcohol than the average person living in any other region. Globally, alcohol consumption has increased in recent decades, with all of that increase being found in developing countries. Alcohol consumption has health and social consequences, and is responsible for 1.8 millions deaths per year.

Liters of alcohol consumed per person per year

	1980	1990	2000	2007
Developed countries	11.1	9.5	8.9	8.7
Developing countries	2.0	2.4	2.9	3.1

Countries with the highest annual consumption of alcohol per person (liters)

1. Luxembourg	15.6	6. Croatia	12.3
2. Ireland	13.7	7. Germany	12.0
3. Hungary	13.6	8. UK	11.8
4. Moldova	13.2	9. Denmark	11.7
5. Czech Republic	13.0	= Spain	11.7

INFANT MORTALITY

Number of babies who died under the age of one, per 1,000 live births (2009)

- Over 100 deaths
- 50 – 100 deaths
- 20 – 50 deaths
- 10 – 20 deaths
- Under 10 deaths
- No data available

Highest infant mortality
Angola ....180 deaths
Afghanistan ....153 deaths
Liberia ....138 deaths

Lowest infant mortality
Japan ....3 deaths
Iceland ....3 deaths
France ....3 deaths

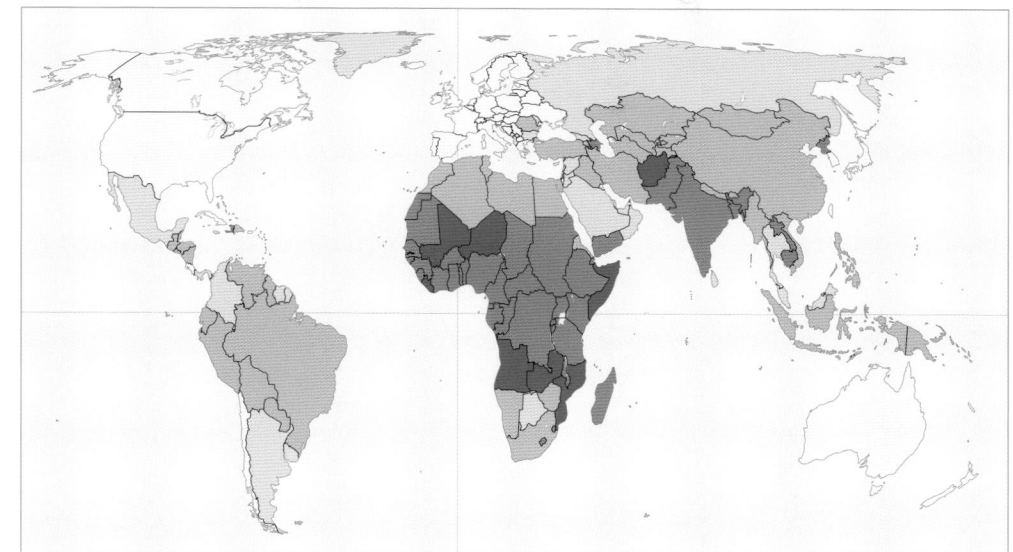

THE AIDS CRISIS

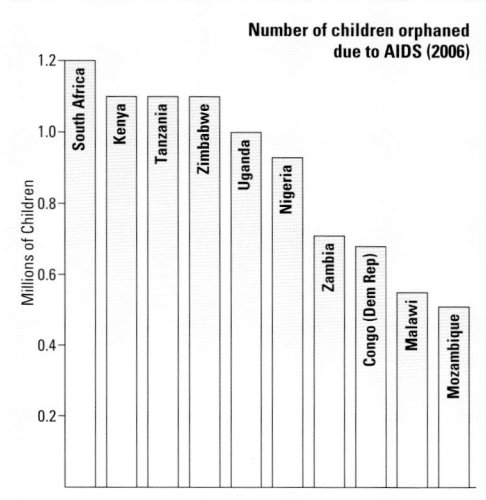

Number of children orphaned due to AIDS (2006)

Millions of Children

South Africa, Kenya, Tanzania, Zimbabwe, Uganda, Nigeria, Zambia, Congo (Dem Rep), Malawi, Mozambique

Percentage of the population infected with HIV/AIDS (2007)

- Over 10 %
- 1 – 10 %
- 0.5 – 1 %
- 0.2 – 0.5 %
- 0.1 – 0.2 %
- Under 0.1 %
- No data available

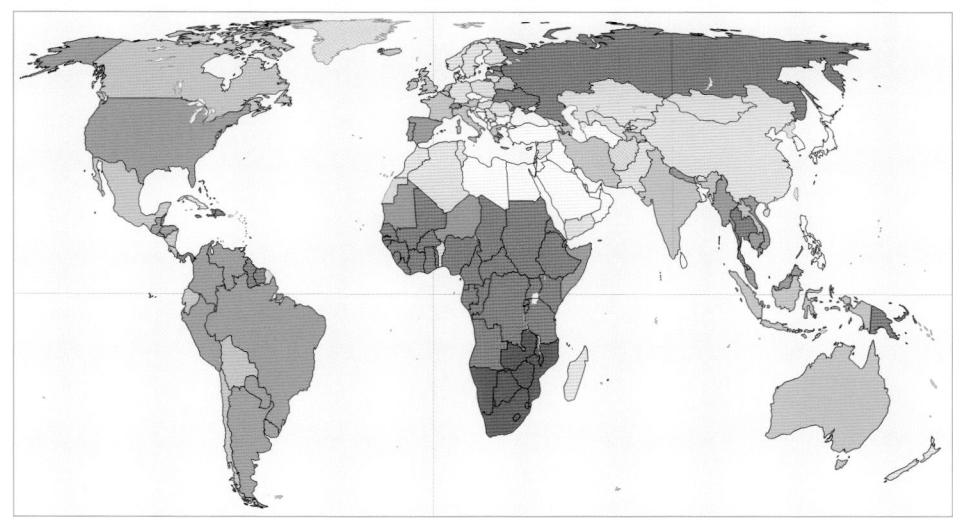

EXPENDITURE ON HEALTH

Public health expenditure per capita, in US $ (2006)

Countries with the highest spending		Countries with the lowest spending	
Monaco	$5,309	Burundi	$4
Luxembourg	$5,233	Congo (Dem. Rep.)	$7
Norway	$3,780	Burma (Myanmar)	$7
USA	$3,074	Somalia	$8
France	$2,833	Afghanistan	$8
Denmark	$2,812	Pakistan	$8
Netherlands	$2,768	Guinea-Bissau	$10
San Marino	$2,765	Eritrea	$10
Iceland	$2,758	Ethiopia	$13
Austria	$2,729	Congo	$13

The allocation of limited funds for health care in developing countries is rarely evenly spread – for example, the quality of treatment can vary enormously from place to place within the same country. Urban dwellers tend to have much better access to health provisions than those living in rural areas.

CAUSES OF DEATH

- Accidents, poisoning, and violence
- Respiratory and digestive diseases
- Nervous and circulatory diseases
- Metabolic disorders
- Cancers
- Infectious and parasitic diseases

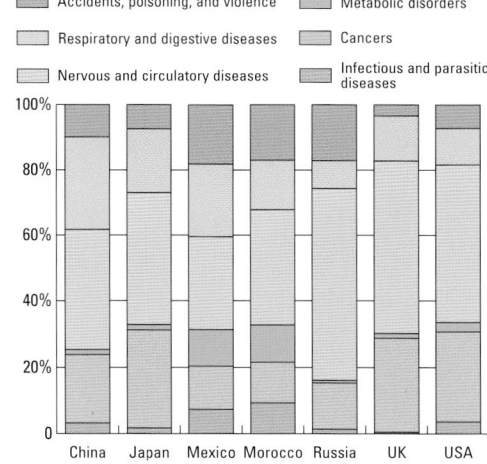

China, Japan, Mexico, Morocco, Russia, UK, USA

MEDICAL PROVISION

Doctors per 100,000 population, selected countries (2006)

Although the ratio of people to doctors gives a good approximation of a country's health provision, it is not an absolute indicator. Raw numbers may mask inefficiency and other weaknesses. The definition of a doctor also varies from nation to nation.

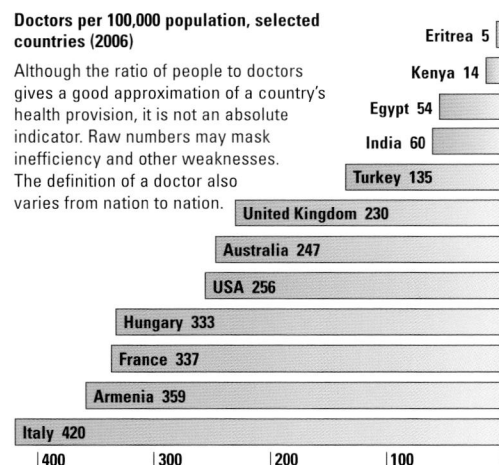

Eritrea 5
Kenya 14
Egypt 54
India 60
Turkey 135
United Kingdom 230
Australia 247
USA 256
Hungary 333
France 337
Armenia 359
Italy 420

OBESITY IN EUROPE

The percentage of adults who are obese (2005)

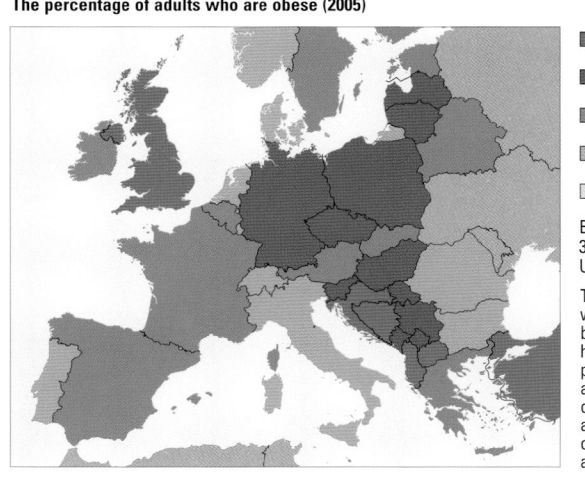

- Over 20%
- 15 – 20%
- 10 – 15%
- Under 10%
- No data available

By comparison, over 32% of people in the USA are obese.

The global epidemic of over-weight and obesity is rapidly becoming a major public health problem in many parts of the world. It is associated with diet-related chronic diseases such as diabetes, strokes, cardiovascular disease, and certain cancers.

SANITATION

Percentage of population with access to sanitation services, selected countries (2006)

- Urban
- Rural

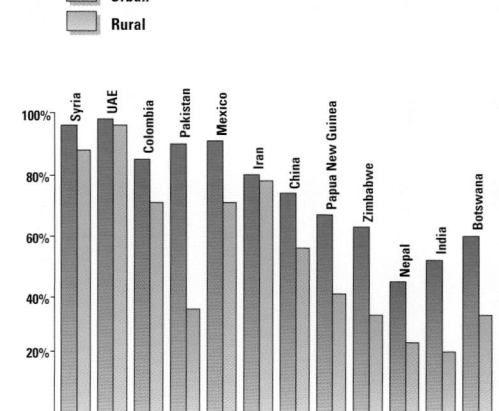

Syria, UAE, Colombia, Pakistan, Mexico, Iran, China, Papua New Guinea, Zimbabwe, Nepal, India, Botswana

MALARIA

Cases of malaria per 100,000 people exposed to malaria-infected environments (2007)

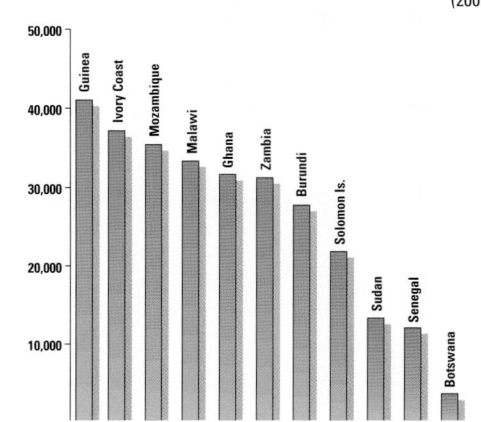

Guinea, Ivory Coast, Mozambique, Malawi, Ghana, Zambia, Burundi, Solomon Is., Sudan, Senegal, Botswana

For more information:
100 Wealth creation
101 Industrial output
102 World trade
    Major exports
103 Balance of trade
109 Distribution of
    spending

Perhaps the most glaring differences in the world today are those between the rich and the poor. The World Bank divides countries into three main groups based on average economic production expressed in terms of per capita GNI (Gross National Income). They are the low-income economies (most African countries and much of Asia), the middle-income economies (most of Latin America and most of the former USSR), and the high-income economies of Canada, the United States, Western Europe, Japan, and Australia.

Per capita GNIs are a measure of the total goods and services produced by a country divided by the population, and then converted into US dollars at official exchange rates. They are useful indicators of a country's prosperity, though, like all statistics, they must be treated with care. For example, the prices for goods and services in China are far cheaper than they are in the United States. China's per capita GNI in 2008 was $2,940 (as compared with $47,930 in the US), but the PPP (Purchasing Power Parity, which adjusts the figure for cost-of-living differences) estimate of China's per capita GNI was considerably higher at $6,010. Another problem with per capita GNIs is that they are averages, which often conceal wide internal variations.

The pattern of poverty varies from region to region. In Latin America, much progress has been made through industrialization, though startling inequalities still exist between rich and poor. China and other countries in eastern Asia, including South Korea and Taiwan, have followed Japan's example in pursuing export-led industrial policies. The success of China's Special Economic Zones, where foreign investment is encouraged, has led to a huge rise in China's per capita GNI.

In contrast to the dynamism of Asia, Africa lags behind as an impoverished continent. Corrupt governments, wasteful expenditures, civil wars, natural disasters, faulty national and international policy environments, high population growth, and the failure to break away from the neo-colonial trading patterns – all these contribute to keeping the majority of Africans impoverished. An initiative in some African countries has been to improve the infrastructure and develop tourism, creating employment and providing much-needed foreign currency. But the social and environmental cost of mass tourism needs to be taken seriously too.

The International Monetary Fund and the World Bank argue that real economic progress in Africa will be achieved only when African countries create market-friendly economies that encourage trade through export-led manufacturing, while at the same time strictly controlling public spending.

CONTINENTAL SHARES

Shares of population and of wealth (GNI) by continent

These generalized continental figures show the startling difference between rich and poor, but mask the successes or failures of individual countries. Japan, for example, with less than 4% of Asia's population, produces almost 40% of the continent's output. Within countries, the difference between rich and poor can also be startling. In Brazil, for example, the richest 20% of the population own 60% of the wealth.

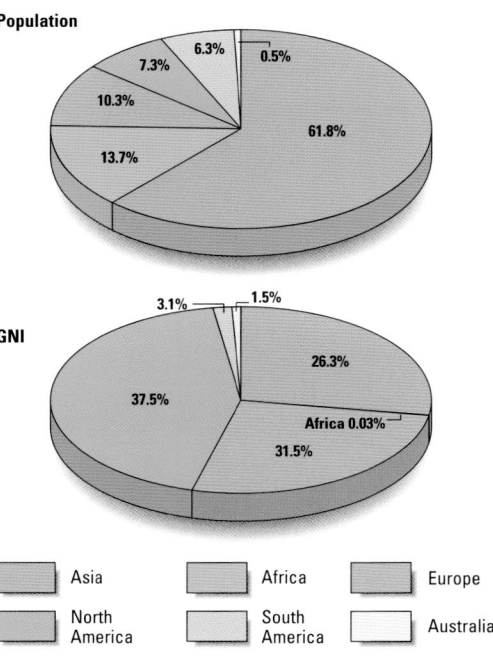

LEVELS OF INCOME

Gross National Income per capita: the value of total production divided by the population (2009)

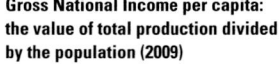
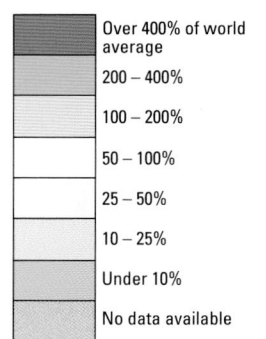

- Over 400% of world average
- 200 – 400%
- 100 – 200%
- 50 – 100%
- 25 – 50%
- 10 – 25%
- Under 10%
- No data available

Richest countries (GNI per capita)
Luxembourg......................US $64,320
Norway.............................US $58,500
Kuwait..............................US $52,610
Brunei...............................US $50,200
Singapore........................US $47,940

Poorest countries (GNI per capita)
Congo (Dem. Rep.)...............US $290
Liberia...............................US $300
Burundi.............................US $380
Guinea-Bissau.....................US $530
Eritrea...............................US $630

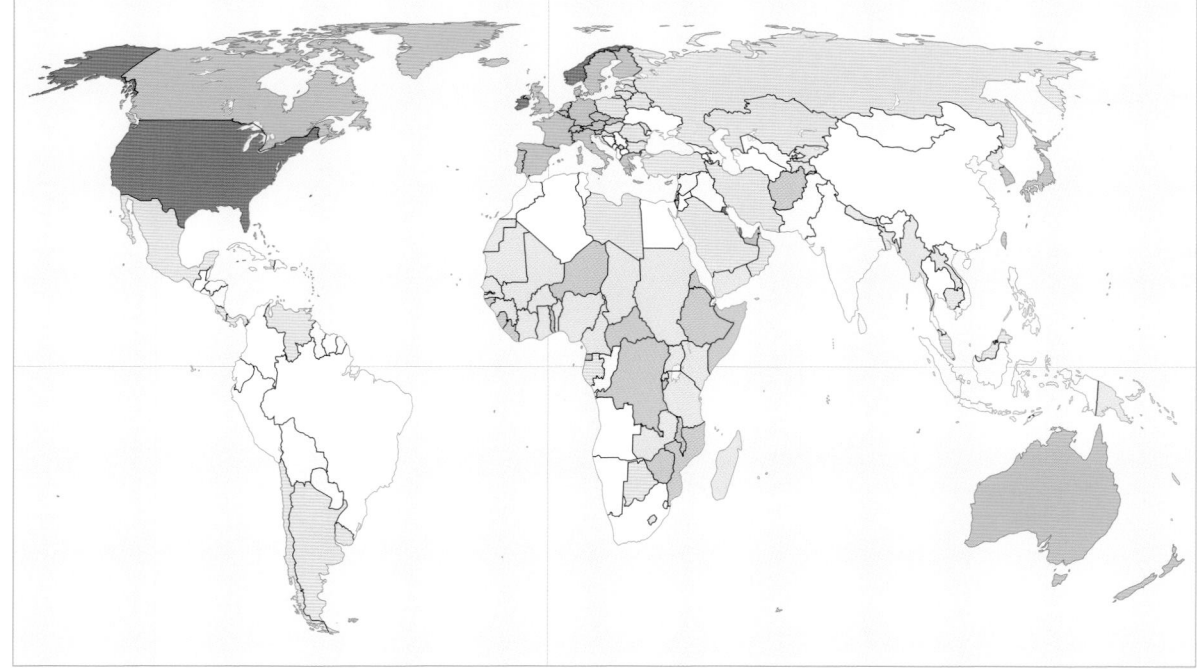

INDICATORS

The gap between the world's rich and poor is now so great that it is difficult to illustrate on a single graph. Within each income group (as defined by the World Bank), however, comparisons have some meaning. The wealth gap in many developing countries, though, is wide, with a small, rich class and a large, impoverished majority, while many high-income countries contain an underclass of unemployed and homeless people.

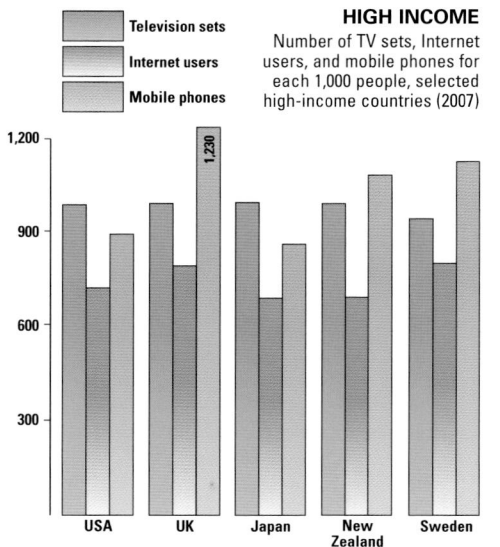
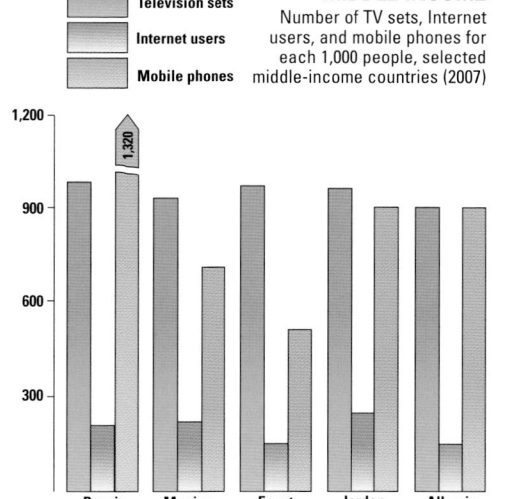
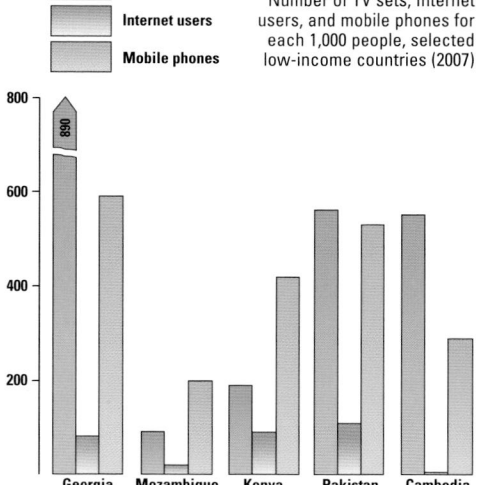

STATE FINANCE

Inflation rates (*shown on the map, right*) are an indication of a country's financial stability and, usually, of its prosperity. Annual inflation rates above 20% are usually marked by slow or even negative growth of the GNI. Above 50%, it becomes hyperinflation and an economy is left reeling.

In the late 1980s and early 1990s, many high-income countries had to contend with annual inflation rates of 10% or more, while Japan, the growth leader, had an average inflation rate of just 1.3% between 1985 and 1994.

Market-friendly policies, including low taxes and state spending, liberal trade policies, and a warm welcome for foreign investors, are major factors in countries that have enjoyed rapid economic growth in the decades since 1980. For example, the setting-up of Special Economic Zones in eastern China has led to a spectacular rise in that country's per capita GNI. However, an effective state remains a crucial factor in economic growth in most countries.

Other successful countries include South Korea and Singapore, although an Asian market crash in 1997 temporarily halted the dramatic economic expansion of these countries.

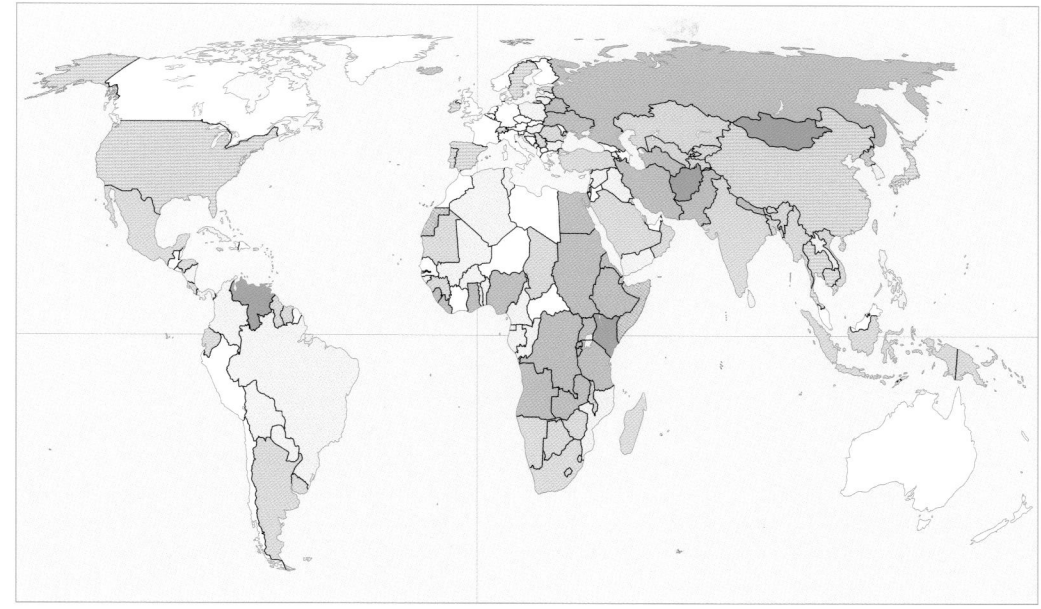

INFLATION

Average annual rate of inflation (2009)

	Over 20%
	10 – 20%
	5 – 10%
	2.5 – 5%
	Under 2.5%
	Negative inflation
	No data available

Highest average inflation
Seychelles 34%
Mongolia 28%
Venezuela 27%

Lowest average inflation
Qatar .... −3.9%
Ireland .... −3.9%
San Marino .... −3.5%

GROWTH IN GNI

GNI average annual change (1999–2008)

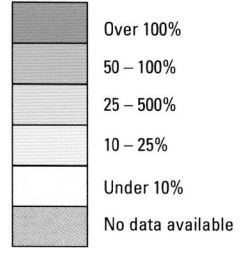

	Over 100%
	50 – 100%
	25 – 500%
	10 – 25%
	Under 10%
	No data available

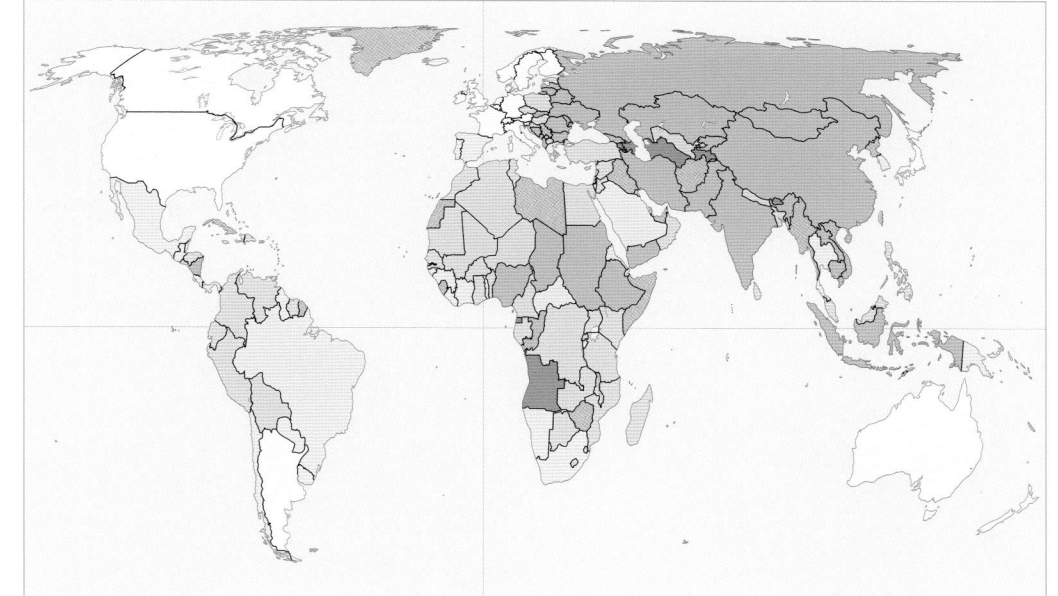

Countries with the highest rate of change
Equatorial Guinea	283%
Azerbaijan	140%
Angola	119%
Tajikistan	110%
Bhutan	104%

WORLD AIR TRAVEL

Leisure and tourism is the world's second largest industry in terms of revenue generated. Small economies in attractive areas are often completely dominated by tourism: in some Caribbean islands, for example, tourist spending provides over 90% of the total income and is the biggest foreign-exchange earner.

In cash terms, the United States is the world leader: its 2006 earnings exceeded US $85 billion, although that sum amounted to approximately 0.6% of its total GNI. Of the 46 million visitors to the US, 29% came from Canada and 20% came from Mexico. Germany spends the most on overseas tourism; this amounts to nearly US $75,000 million. The next biggest spenders are the US, the UK, and France.

The world's travel and tourist industry was predicted to generate 74 million jobs in 2006. If the broader travel and tourist economy is considered, this total would increase to 215 million.

Major airports
Number of passengers (international and domestic) per year
● Over 25 million
● 15 – 25 million
· 10 – 15 million

Major air routes
Number of international flights per year
⟺ Over 50 million
⟹ 10 – 50 million
→ 5 – 10 million

Total world air passenger traffic (2006)

Africa 3%
Middle East 2%
Latin America & Caribbean 6%
Asia Pacific 21%
North America 37%
Europe 31%

WORLD'S BUSIEST AIRPORTS
Total passengers in millions (2009)
1.	Atlanta Hartsfield Intl. (ATL)	88.0
2.	London Heathrow (LHR)	66.0
3.	Beijing Capital Intl. (PEK)	65.3
4.	Chicago O'Hare Intl. (ORD)	64.4
5.	Tokyo Haneda (HND)	61.9
6.	Paris Charles de Gaulle (CDG)	57.9
7.	Los Angeles Intl. (LAX)	56.5
8.	Dallas/Fort Worth Intl. (DFW)	56.0
9.	Frankfurt Intl. (FRA)	50.9
10.	Denver Intl. (DEN)	50.2

For more information:
84 Water supply
88 Population density
90 Urban population
91 Urban advantages
94 World's refugees
   War since 1945
100 Employment
   The work force
105 Infant mortality
106 Wealth

Wealth is a basic factor in determining standards of living. Everywhere, the rich have more of everything, including higher average life expectancies, while the poor have to spend most of their income on basic human needs, such as food and clothing. Yet poverty and wealth are relative terms: slum dwellers living on social security in an industrial society feel their poverty acutely, but have far more resources than an average African living in a rural area.

In 1990 the United Nations Development Program published its first Human Development Index (HDI), an attempt to construct a comparative scale by which a simplified form of well-being might be measured. The HDI, expressed as a value between 0 and 0.999, combines figures for life expectancy and literacy with a wealth scale, based on Purchasing Power Parity.

The world's countries are divided into three groups: those with a high HDI (0.8 and above); those with a medium HDI (0.5 to 0.799); and those with a low HDI (below 0.5). In 2007, Norway and Australia were top in the world rankings and Niger was bottom. In fact, 22 of the 24 countries with a low HDI were from Africa. Besides having low per capita GNIs, the average life expectancy in these

countries was 51 years, while the adult literacy rate was 48%. By comparison, the average life expectancy at birth in countries in the high HDI group was 72 years, while the literacy rate was 94%.

Comparisons between countries with similar per capita GNIs reveal the effects of government actions. For example, the World Bank classifies both India and China as low-income economies, but India's HDI at 0.612 is much lower than that of China, at 0.772. This reflects not only China's economic progress in the 1980s and 1990s, but also differences in average life expectancies (63 years in India and 72 years in China), and adult literacy rates (66% in India and 93% in China).

Disparities in standards of living exist not only between countries but also between individuals, groups, and regions within countries. For example, income distribution figures for 2007 show that, in the United States, the poorest 10% of households received less than 2% of the income.

Other contrasts exist in developing countries between rural communities, where incomes are low and basic services are often in short supply, and urban areas, where even those living in slums are

generally better off than their rural neighbors. Other striking differences exist between men and women. For example, while adult literacy rates for men and women living in developed countries are more or less the same, large differences exist in many developing countries. In 2007, in countries in the lowest HDI category, only 36% of women were literate, as compared with 58% of men.

Female education is a factor in population control, especially as women's fertility rates appear to fall in direct proportion to the amount of secondary education they receive. This point was acknowledged in 2004 by the UN Population Fund, which defined four main objectives relating to women and population control: the reduction of maternal, infant, and child mortality; better education, especially for girls; universal access to reproductive health services; and gender equality.

Statistical analysis presents many problems of interpretation, especially when trying to define such intangible factors as a sense of well-being. For example, education helps create wealth; but are rich countries wealthy because their people are well educated, or are they well educated because they are rich?

HUMAN DEVELOPMENT INDEX

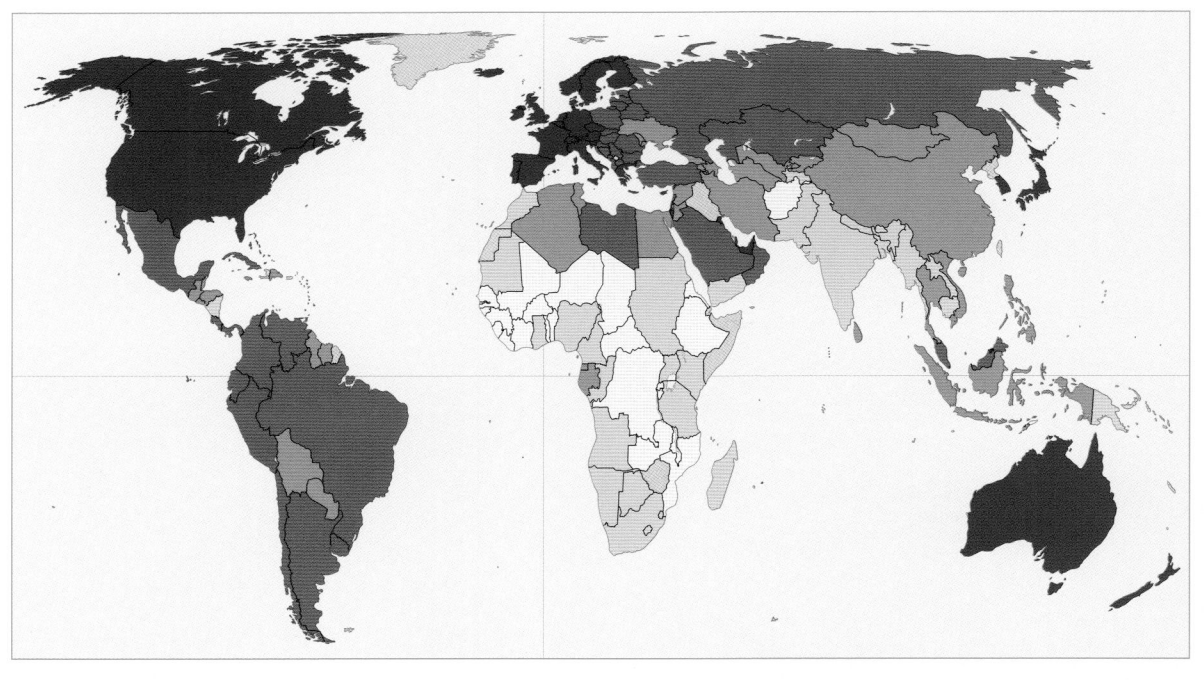

The Human Development Index (HDI), calculated by the UN Development Program (UNDP), gives a value to countries using indicators of life expectancy, education, and standards of living (2007). Higher values show more developed countries.

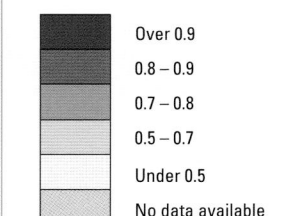

Over 0.9
0.8 – 0.9
0.7 – 0.8
0.5 – 0.7
Under 0.5
No data available

Highest values
Norway 0.971
Australia 0.970
Iceland 0.969
Canada 0.966
Ireland 0.965

Lowest values
Niger 0.340
Afghanistan 0.352
Sierra Leone 0.365
Central African Rep. 0.369
Mali 0.371

EDUCATION

The developing countries made great efforts in the 1970s and 1980s to bring at least a basic education to their people. In all but the poorest nations, primary school enrolments rose above 60%. However, figures often include teenagers or young adults, and there are still 300 million children worldwide who receive no schooling at all. A lack of resources has restricted the development of secondary and higher education. Most primary school education is free in the poorer countries, but fees are often paid for secondary and higher education, thus heightening the differences between rich and poor.

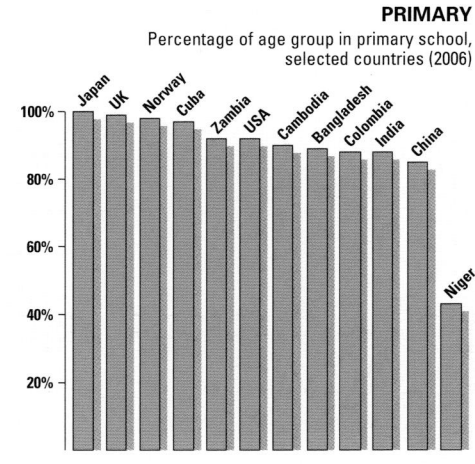

PRIMARY
Percentage of age group in primary school, selected countries (2006)

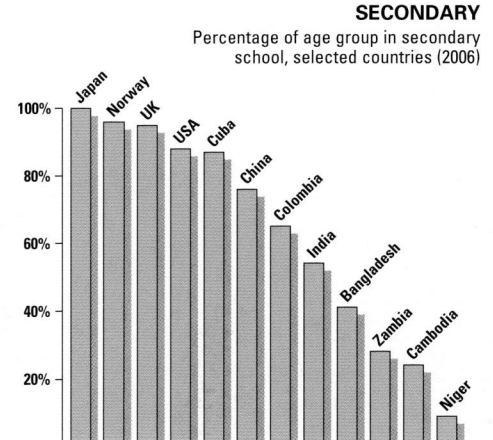

SECONDARY
Percentage of age group in secondary school, selected countries (2006)

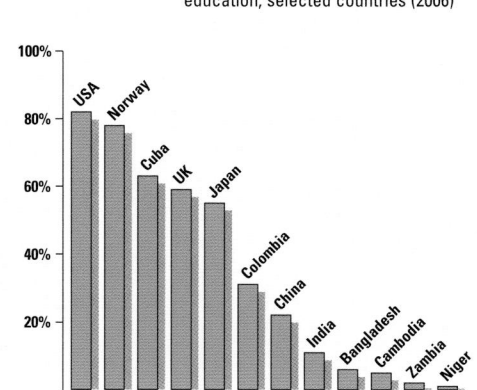

HIGHER
Percentage of age group in higher education, selected countries (2006)

DISTRIBUTION OF SPENDING

Percentage share of household spending

A high proportion of the average income of households in developing nations is spent on basic needs such as food and clothing. In most Western countries food and clothing account for less than 25% of expenditure.

Food
Clothing
Energy & Housing
Medicine & Education
Transport
Other

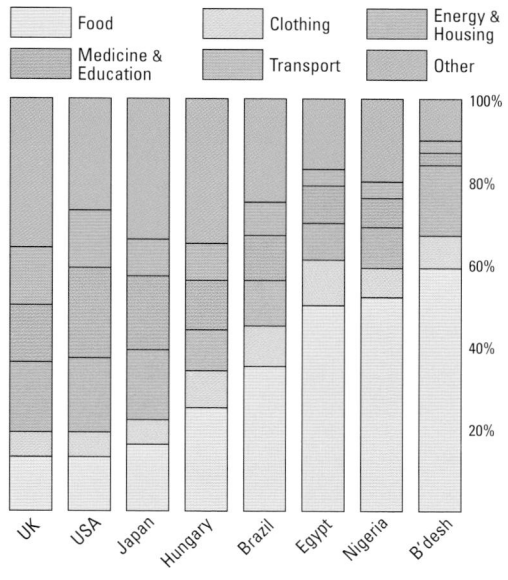

UK   USA   Japan   Hungary   Brazil   Egypt   Nigeria   B'desh

STANDARDS OF LIVING IN THE USA BY RACE, AGE AND REGION

A comparison of measures of income and education, by selected characteristics (2008)

Median income per household (US $), by age and region

15–24 years	27,235
25–44 years	57,154
45–64 years	64,040
65 years and over	33,055
Northeast	57,595
Midwest	50,780
South	48,046
West	56,837

Per capita income (US $), by race and Hispanic origin of householder

ALL RACES	27,466
White	30,299
Black	18,119
Asian and Pacific Is.	30,248
Hispanic (any race)	15,916

The poorest 20% of households received just 2.4% of the income, whereas the richest 20% received 55.4%.

Percentage of persons aged 25 and over who have completed High School, by race or origin

ALL RACES	1975	62.5
	2008	84.5
White	1975	64.5
	2008	86.9
Black	1975	42.5
	2008	80.0
Hispanic	1975	37.9
	2008	60.5

FERTILITY AND EDUCATION

Fertility rates compared with female education, selected countries (2008)

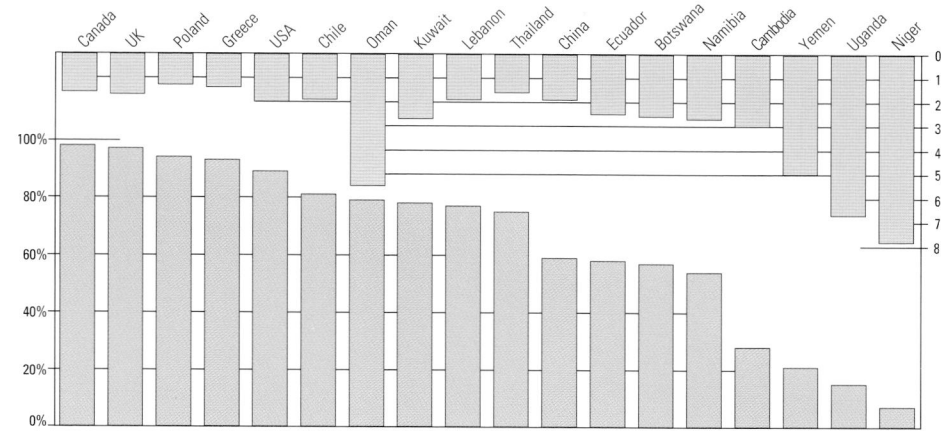

Canada UK Poland Greece USA Chile Oman Kuwait Lebanon Thailand China Ecuador Botswana Namibia Cambodia Yemen Uganda Niger

There seems to be a strong link between access to secondary education and the fertility rate. In developed countries, young girls have a high access to education and a low fertility rate. In contrast, in many developing countries women have a high fertility rate but lack access to education. This can be for a complex mix of social, economic, and cultural reasons. Despite a few high-profile examples of female politicians in different parts of the world, all evidence points to the continuing marginalization of women from the political and economic processes of decision-making. Female wages are, on average, only two-thirds of those of men.

Fertility rate: average number of children borne per woman

Percentage of females aged 12–17 in secondary education

GENDER DEVELOPMENT INDEX

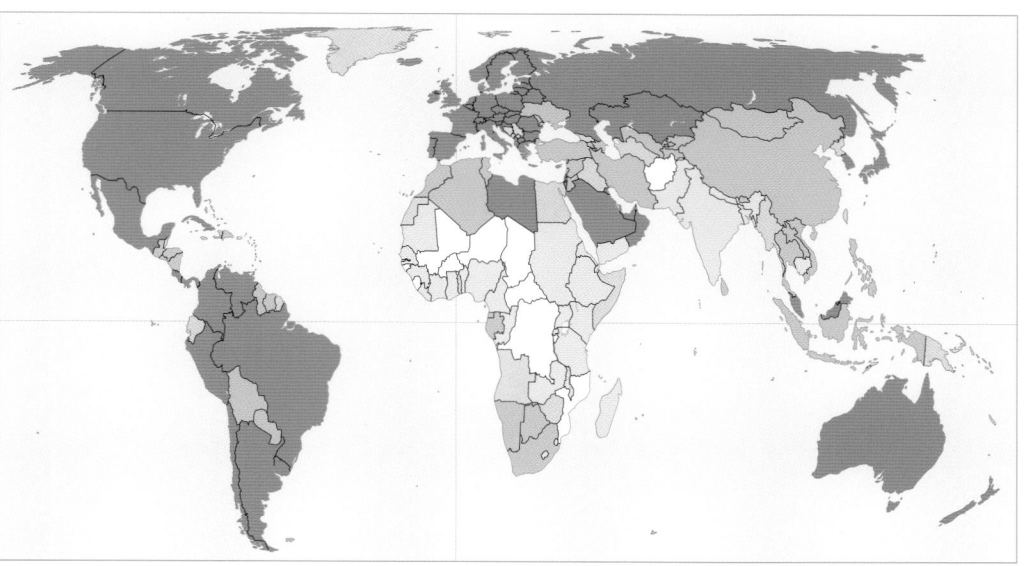

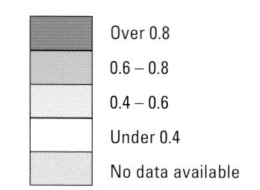

The Gender Development Index (GDI) shows economic and social differences between men and women by using various UNDP indicators (2007). Countries with higher values of GDI have more equality between men and women.

Over 0.8
0.6 – 0.8
0.4 – 0.6
Under 0.4
No data available

Highest values

Australia	0.966
Norway	0.961
Canada	0.959
Iceland	0.959

Lowest values

Niger	0.308
Afghanistan	0.310
Mali	0.353
Sierra Leone	0.354

REGIONAL INEQUALITY IN ITALY

The southern part of Italy, known as the *Mezzogiorno*, has been described as one of the poorest parts of the European Union. It is identifiable on the map (*right*) as all the regions with a GDP per capita of less than US $30,000 (including the two islands of Sicily and Sardinia).

The *Mezzogiorno* region suffers from a lack of energy resources, minerals, industry, commerce, services, and skilled labor. As a result, standards of living in the region are well below the rest of Italy. Employment is predominantly agricultural and small-scale.

The north of Italy accounts for 60% of the population but 80% of the GDP, whereas the *Mezzogiorno* accounts for 40% of the population and only 20% of the GDP. Manpower surpluses in the south led to emigration to other parts of Europe and the Americas.

It has also led, especially in the last 50 years, to inter-regional migration from the islands and the southern mainland to the north. The main regions attracting migrants are the northwest (the prosperous Liguria–Piedmont–Lombardy triangle, with its great industrial cities of Genoa, Milan and Turin) and the Venetia region in the northeast.

As a result, the north has experienced much higher population growth rates than the rest of Italy.

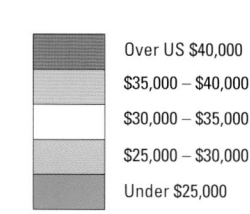

Gross Domestic Product (GDP) per capita in Italy, by region (2007)

Over US $40,000
$35,000 – $40,000
$30,000 – $35,000
$25,000 – $30,000
Under $25,000

The average GDP per capita for Italy is US $29,900. By comparison, the GDP for the UK is $35,200; for the USA $46,100; and for the EU $32,800.

The number of inhabitants per doctor, another social indicator, varies from less than 600 in the northwest of Italy to nearly 800 in the far south (the *Mezzogiorno*), with a national average of 628.

◄ These two images illustrate the reality of suburban life for people at either end of the economic scale. On the far left is part of a huge area of "tract housing" in California, where large houses of a similar design are laid out by a developer, complete with gardens, drives, and swimming pools. On the right is a much more haphazard arrangement of home-built, rudimentary shelters, many without sanitation and most with no electricity, in Crossroads Township, outside Cape Town in South Africa.

– CHICAGO, ILLINOIS, USA –
At the southern end of Lake Michigan,
Chicago is the center of the third largest
metropolitan area in the US, with a total
population of over 8 million people. The
central area of the agglomeration, known in
some quarters as "Chicagoland," can be
seen on the lake shore. The town developed
as a major transport focus for the Midwest,
with a complex road and rail network, and
a large port trading on a global scale. The
runway pattern of the fourth busiest airport
in the world, O'Hare International, which
handles over 64 million passengers a year,
can clearly be seen to the northwest of
the city. [Map page 119]

WORLD
CITIES

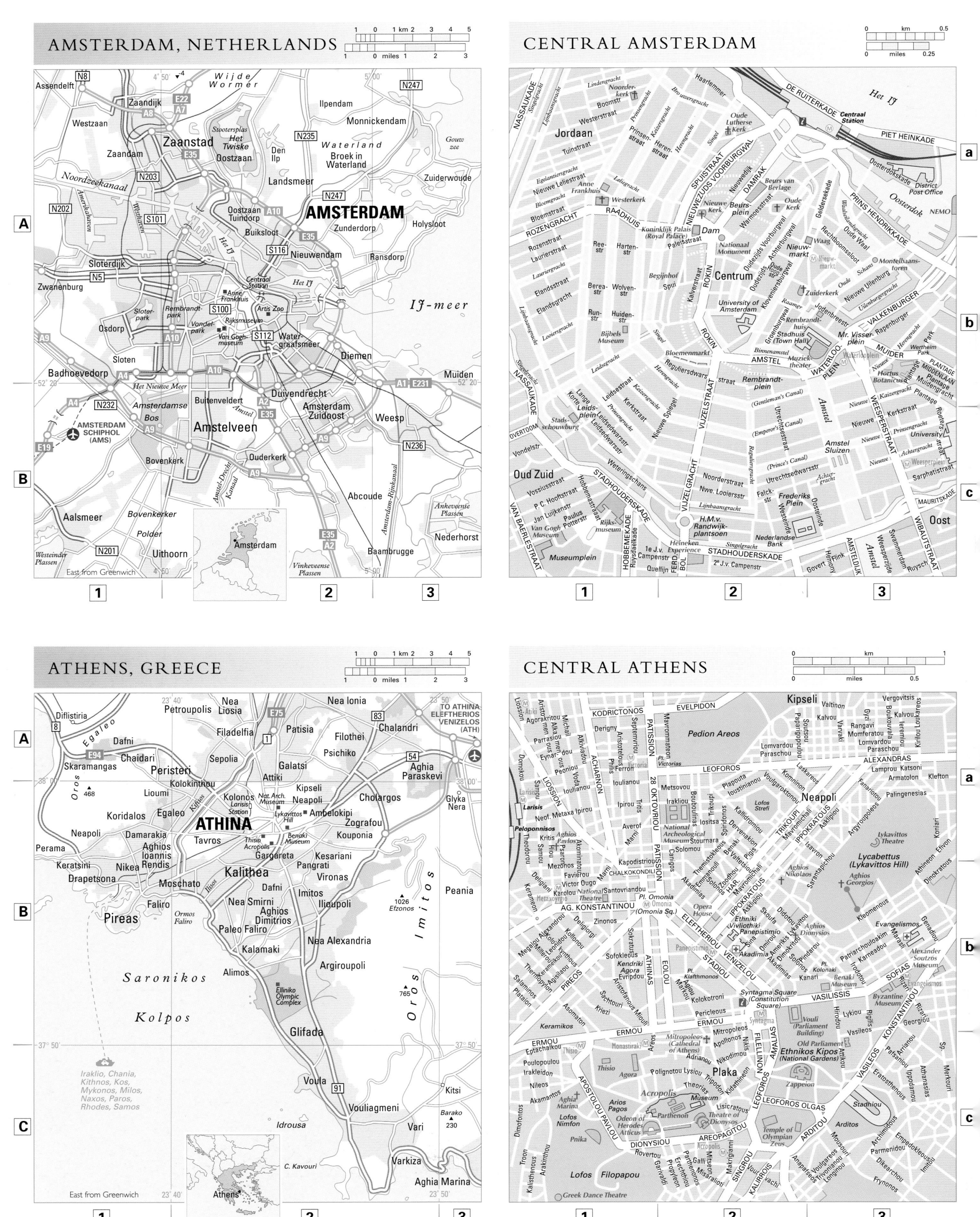

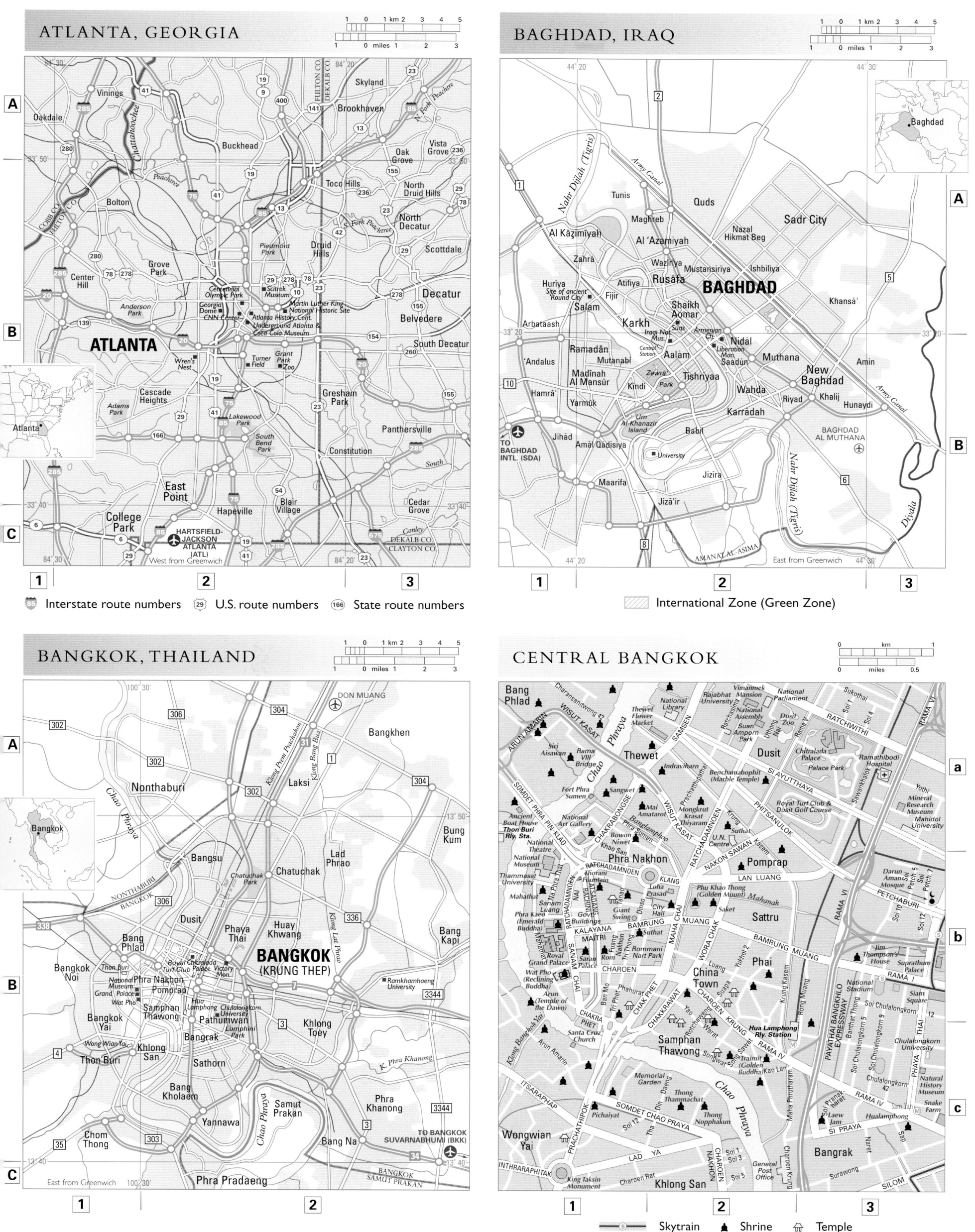

ATLANTA, GEORGIA

Interstate route numbers · **U.S. route numbers** · **State route numbers**

BAGHDAD, IRAQ

International Zone (Green Zone)

BANGKOK, THAILAND

CENTRAL BANGKOK

Skytrain · Shrine · Temple

COPYRIGHT PHILIP'S

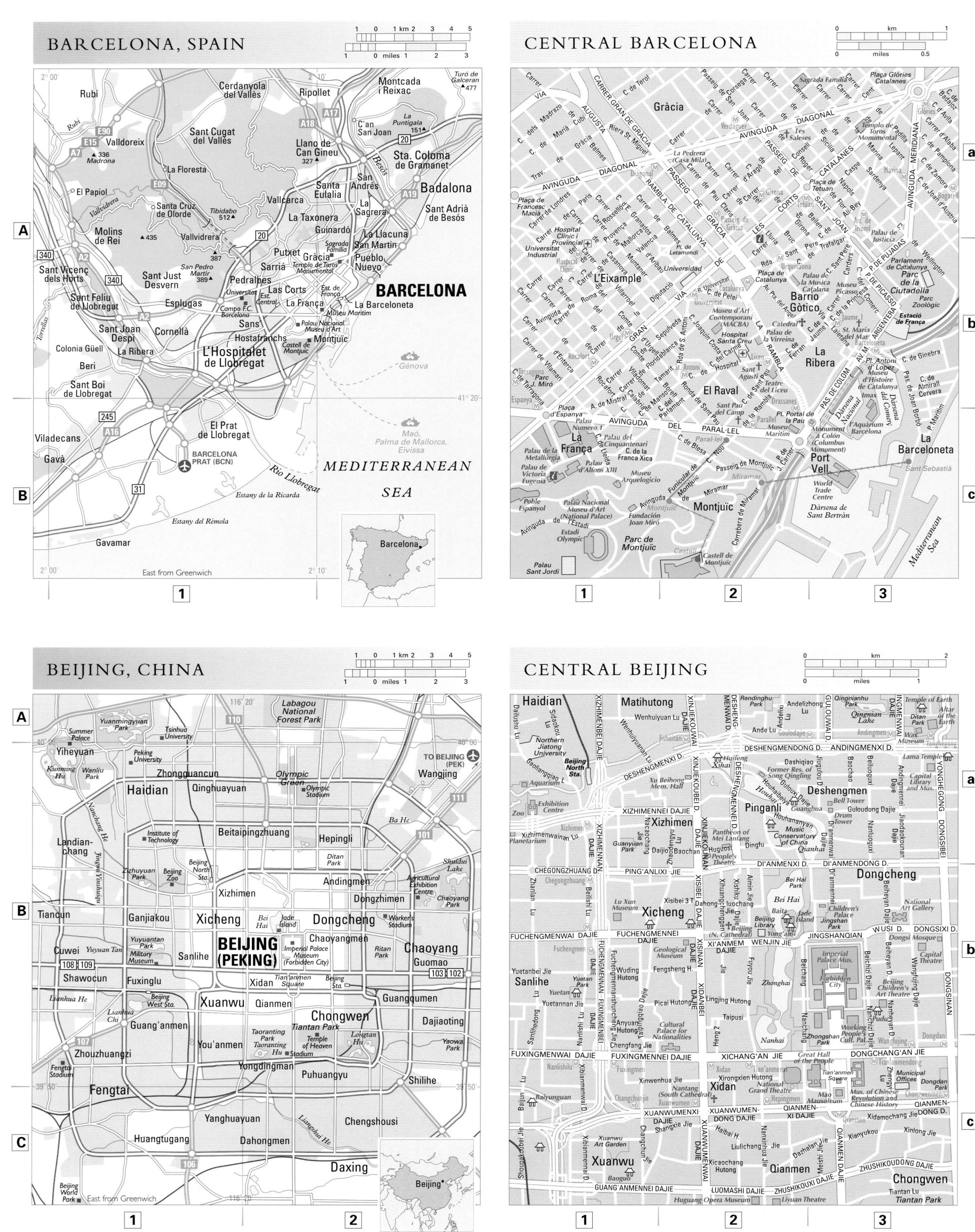

BERLIN, GERMANY

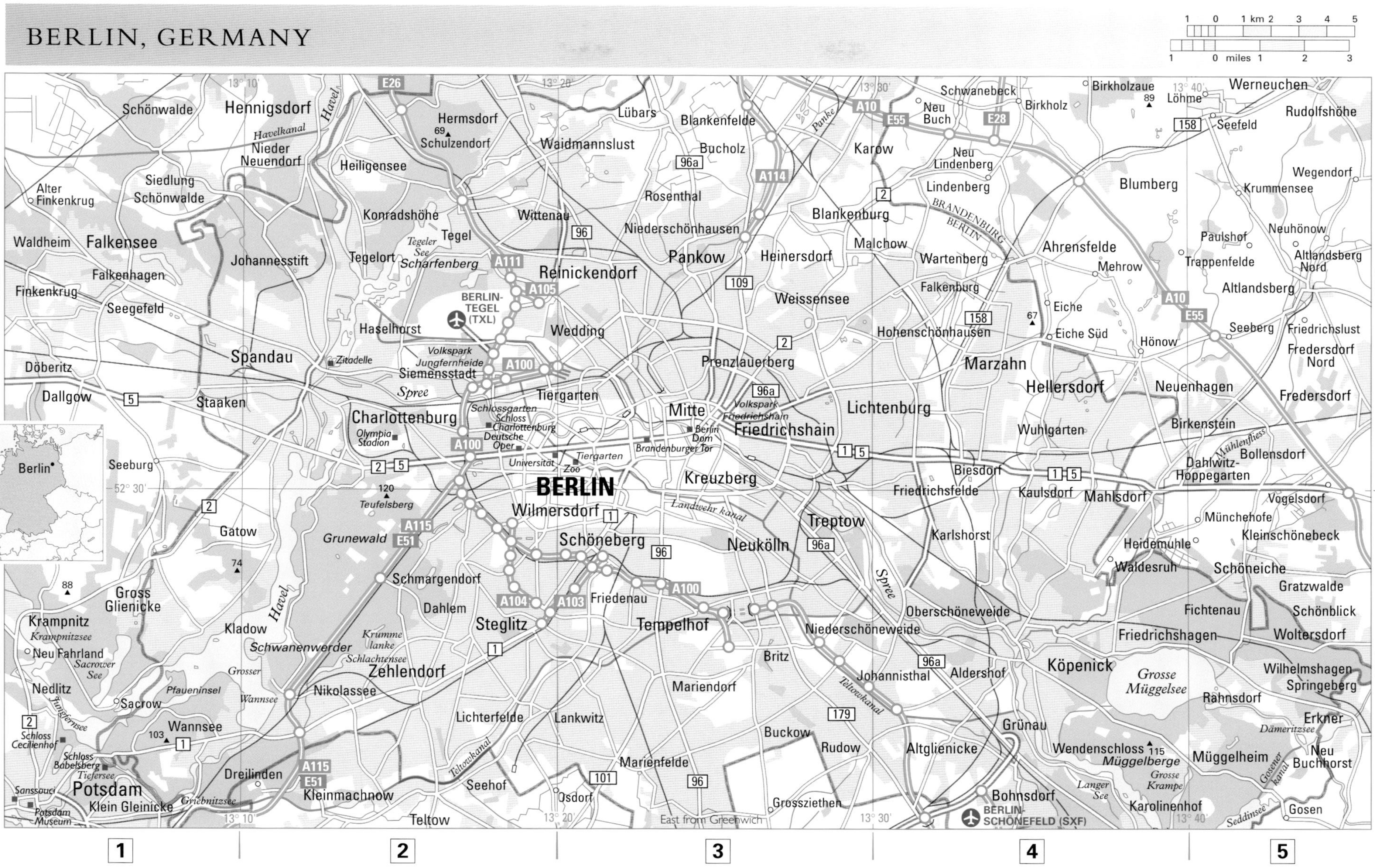
1 0 1 km 2 3 4 5
1 0 miles 1 2 3
Schönwalde
Hennigsdorf
Havelkanal
Nieder Neuendorf
Hermsdorf
Schulzendorf
Lübars
Waidmannslust
Blankenfelde
Bucholz
Schwanebeck
Neu Buch
Birkholz
Birkholzaue
Löhme
Werneuchen
Seefeld
Rudolfshöhe
Karow
Neu Lindenberg
Lindenberg
Heiligensee
Siedlung Schönwalde
Alter Finkenkrug
Konradshöhe
Wittenau
Rosenthal
Niederschönhausen
Blankenburg
Blumberg
Krummensee
Wegendorf
Waldheim
Falkensee
Johannesstift
Tegeler See
Tegel
Scharfenberg
Tegelort
Reinickendorf
Pankow
Heinersdorf
Malchow
Wartenberg
Ahrensfelde
Mehrow
Paulshof
Trappenfelde
Neuhönow
Altlandsberg Nord
Falkenhagen
Finkenkrug
Seegefeld
BERLIN-TEGEL (TXL)
Weissensee
Falkenberg
Altlandsberg
Eiche
Eiche Süd
Haselhorst
Wedding
Hohenschönhausen
Hönow
Seeberg
Fredersdorf Nord
Friedrichslust
Spandau
Zitadelle
Volkspark Jungfernheide
Siemensstadt
Prenzlauer Berg
Marzahn
Döberitz
Dallgow
Staaken
Spree
Tiergarten
Hellersdorf
Neuenhagen
Fredersdorf
Charlottenburg
Schlossgarten
Schloss Charlottenburg
Olympia Stadion
Deutsche Oper
Mitte
Berlin Dom
Volkspark Friedrichshain
Friedrichshain
Lichtenburg
Wuhlgarten
Birkenstein
Bollensdorf
Dahlwitz-Hoppegarten
Berlin
Seeburg
Universität
Tiergarten
Zoo
Brandenburger Tor
BERLIN
Kreuzberg
Biesdorf
Kaulsdorf
Mahlsdorf
Friedrichsfelde
Vogelsdorf
52° 30'
Teufelsberg
Wilmersdorf
Landwehr kanal
Treptow
Karlshorst
Münchehofe
Gatow
Grunewald
Schöneberg
Neukölln
Heidemühle
Waldesruh
Kleinschönebeck
Schöneiche
Schmargendorf
Gratzwalde
Gross Glienicke
Krampnitz
Dahlem
Friedenau
Schönblick
Fichtenau
Oberschöneweide
Steglitz
Tempelhof
Kladow
Niederschöneweide
Woltersdorf
Friedrichshagen
Neu Fahrland
Schwanenwerder
Krumme Lanke
Schlachtensee
Zehlendorf
Britz
Johannisthal
Aldershof
Köpenick
Grosse Müggelsee
Wilhelmshagen
Springeberg
Nedlitz
Sacrow
Pfaueninsel
Nikolassee
Wannsee
Mariendorf
Teltowkanal
Rahnsdorf
Lichterfelde
Lankwitz
Buckow
Rudow
Grünau
Erkner
Schloss Cecilienhof
Wannsee
Altglienicke
Wendenschloss
Müggelberge
Müggelheim
Neu Buchhorst
Schloss Babelsberg
Potsdam
Dreilinden
Marienfelde
Sanssouci
Klein Glienicke
Kleinmachnow
Seehof
Bohnsdorf
Grosse Krampe
Langer See
Karolinenhof
Gosen
Potsdam Museum
Teltow
Osdorf
Grossziethen
BERLIN-SCHÖNEFELD (SXF)
East from Greenwich
13° 10'
13° 20'
13° 30'
13° 40'
A
B
1
2
3
4
5

CENTRAL BERLIN

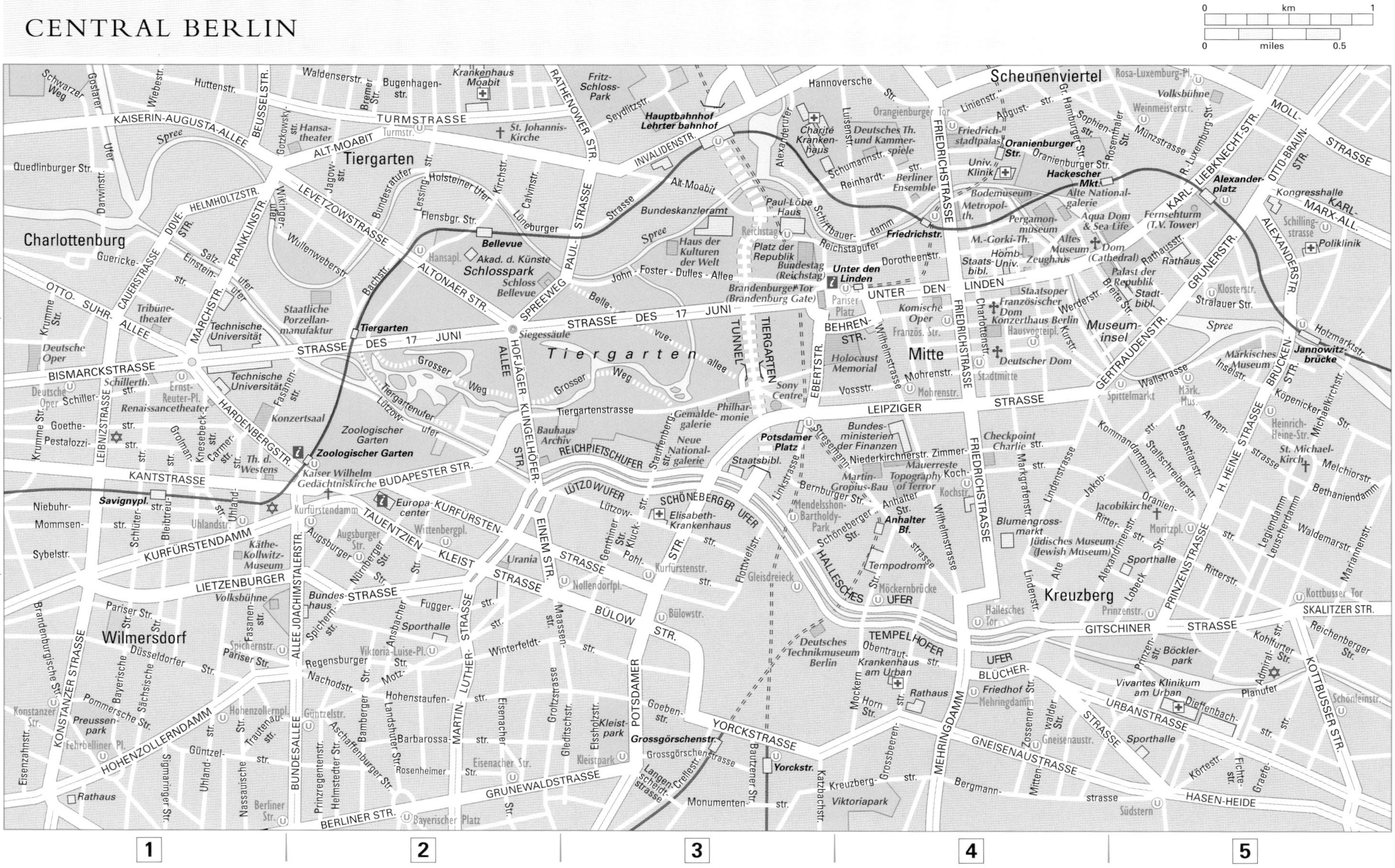
0 km 1
0 miles 0.5
Scheunenviertel
Rosa-Luxemburg-Pl.
Volksbühne
Krankenhaus Moabit
Fritz-Schloss-Park
Hannoversche
Huttenstr.
Waldenserstr.
Bugenhagen-str.
KAISERIN-AUGUSTA-ALLEE
TURMSTRASSE
St. Johannis-Kirche
Hauptbahnhof Lehrter bahnhof
Charité Kranken-haus
Deutsches Th. und Kammer-spiele
Oranienburger Str.
Friedrich-stadtpalast
Hackescher Mkt.
MOLL-STRASSE
Hansa-theater
ALT-MOABIT
Tiergarten
INVALIDENSTR.
Alexander-platz
KARL-MARX-ALL.
Kongresshalle
Charlottenburg
Berliner Ensemble
Bodemuseum
Pergamon-museum
Alte National-galerie
Aqua Dom & Sea Life
Fernsehturm (T.V. Tower)
Bundeskanzleramt
Haus der Kulturen der Welt
Paul-Löbe Haus
Reichstag
Platz der Republik
Bundestag (Reichstag)
Friedrichstr.
Dom (Cathedral)
Rathaus
Poliklinik
Bellevue
Akad. d. Künste
Schlosspark
Schloss Bellevue
Dorotheenstr.
Staats-bibl.
Humb.-Univ.
Zeughaus
Palast der Republik
Stadt-bibl.
Brandenburger Tor (Brandenburg Gate)
Unter den Linden
UNTER DEN LINDEN
Staatsoper
Französischer Dom
Konzerthaus Berlin
Museum-insel
Jannowitz-brücke
Tiergarten
STRASSE DES 17 JUNI
Siegessäule
Tiergarten
Technische Universität
Staatliche Porzellan-manufaktur
Holocaust Memorial
Mitte
Deutscher Dom
Märkisches Museum
Deutsche Oper
BISMARCKSTRASSE
Ernst-Reuter-Pl.
Renaissancetheater
Sony Centre
Philhar-monie
LEIPZIGER STRASSE
Checkpoint Charlie
Konzertsaal
Zoologischer Garten
Bauhaus Archiv
Gemälde-galerie
Neue National-galerie
Potsdamer Platz
Bundes-ministerien der Finanzen
Mauerreste
Topography of Terror
Martin-Gropius-Bau
KANTSTRASSE
Savignypl.
Kaiser Wilhelm Gedächtniskirche
BUDAPESTER STR.
Europa-center
REICHPIETSCHUFER
Staatsbibl.
Anhalter Bf.
Kochstr.
Blumengross-markt
Jüdisches Museum (Jewish Museum)
Jacobikirche
KURFÜRSTENDAMM
Käthe-Kollwitz-Museum
TAUENTZIEN
LÜTZOWUFER
SCHÖNEBERGER UFER
Elisabeth-Krankenhaus
Mendelssohn-Bartholdy-Park
Tempodrom
Urania
KLEIST
HALLESCHES UFER
LIETZENBURGER
Volksbühne
Nollendorfpl.
Gleisdreieck
Möckernbrücke
Kreuzberg
Bundes-haus
BÜLOWSTR.
Sporthalle
Wilmersdorf
Viktoria-Luise-Pl.
Deutsches Technikmuseum Berlin
TEMPELHOFER UFER
GITSCHINER STRASSE
Kottbusser Tor
SKALITZER STR.
Böckler-park
BLÜCHER-
Krankenhaus am Urban
Friedhof der Mehringdamm
Vivantes Klinikum am Urban
Dieffenbach-
URBANSTRASSE
Hohenzollernpl.
Preussen-park
Fehrbelliner Pl.
HOHENZOLLERNDAMM
Kleist park
Grossgörschenstr.
YORCKSTRASSE
Yorckstr.
GNEISENAUSTRASSE
Sporthalle
GRUNEWALDSTRASSE
Viktoriapark
Rathaus
Berliner Str.
BERLINER STR.
Bayerischer Platz
Monumenten-
Südstern
HASEN-HEIDE
KONSTANZER STRASSE
BUNDESALLEE
ALLEE JOACHIMSTALERSTR.
MARTIN-LUTHER-STR.
POTSDAMER
MEHRINGDAMM
FRIEDRICHSTRASSE
PRINZENSTRASSE
KOTTBUSSER STR.
a
b
c
1
2
3
4
5

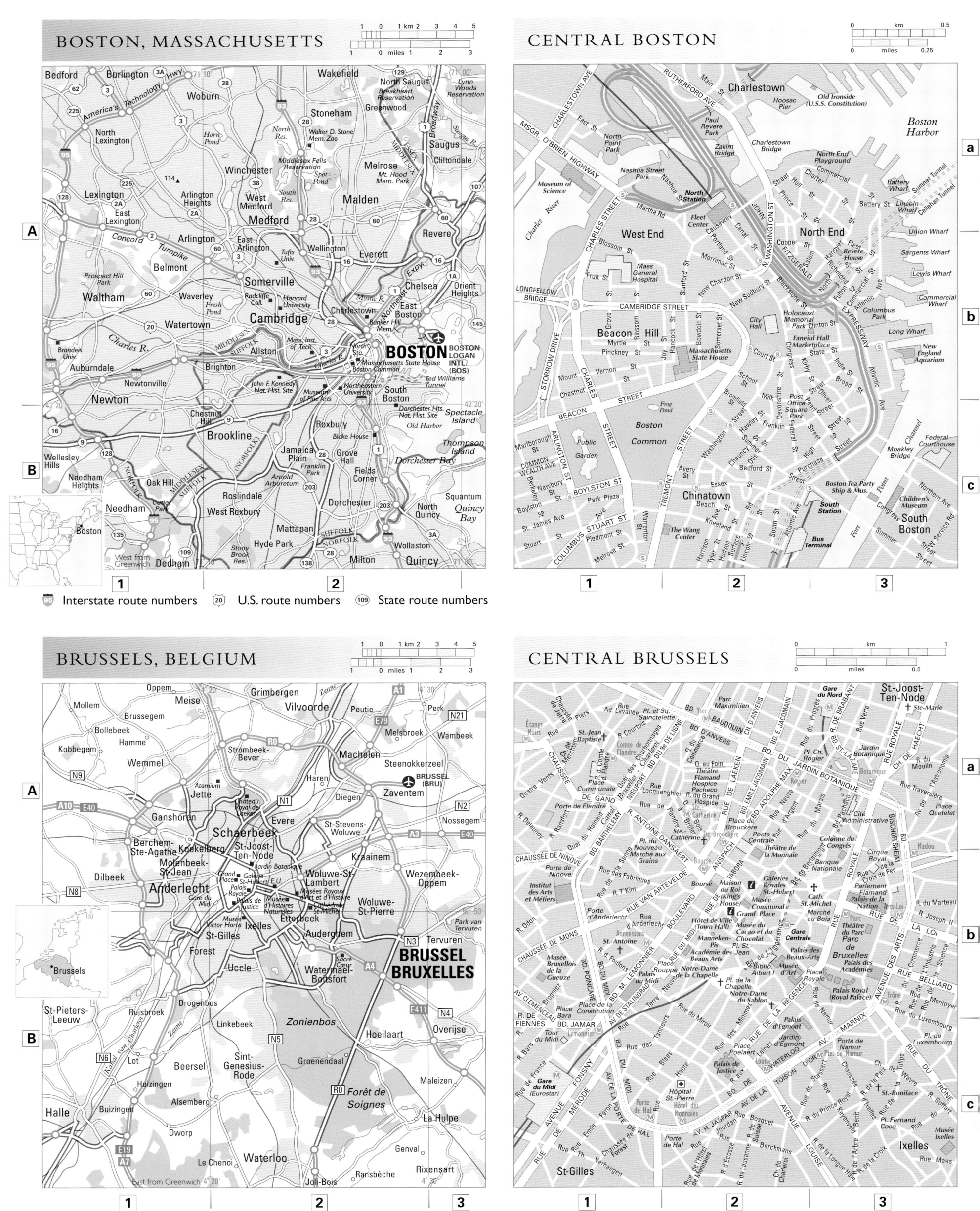

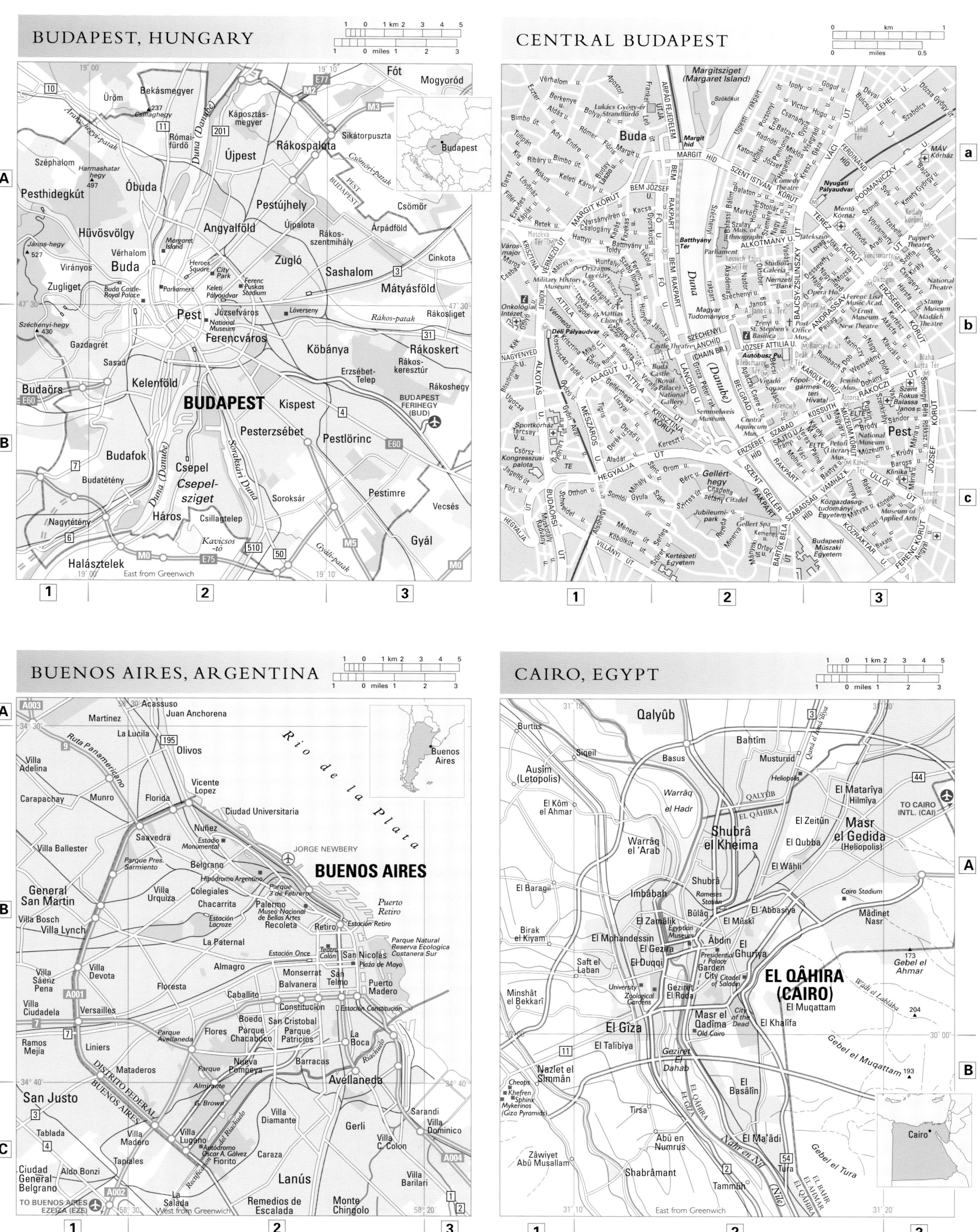

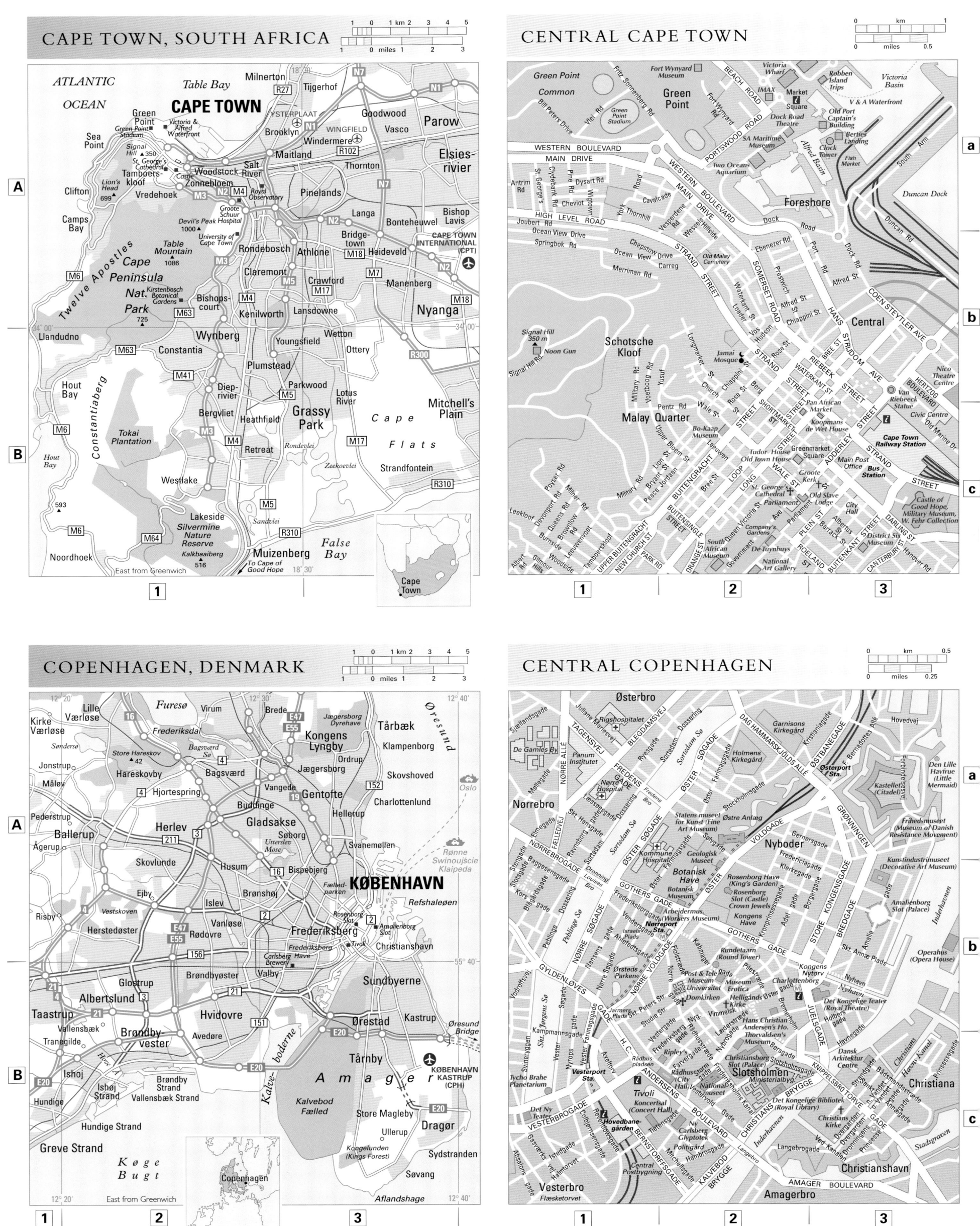

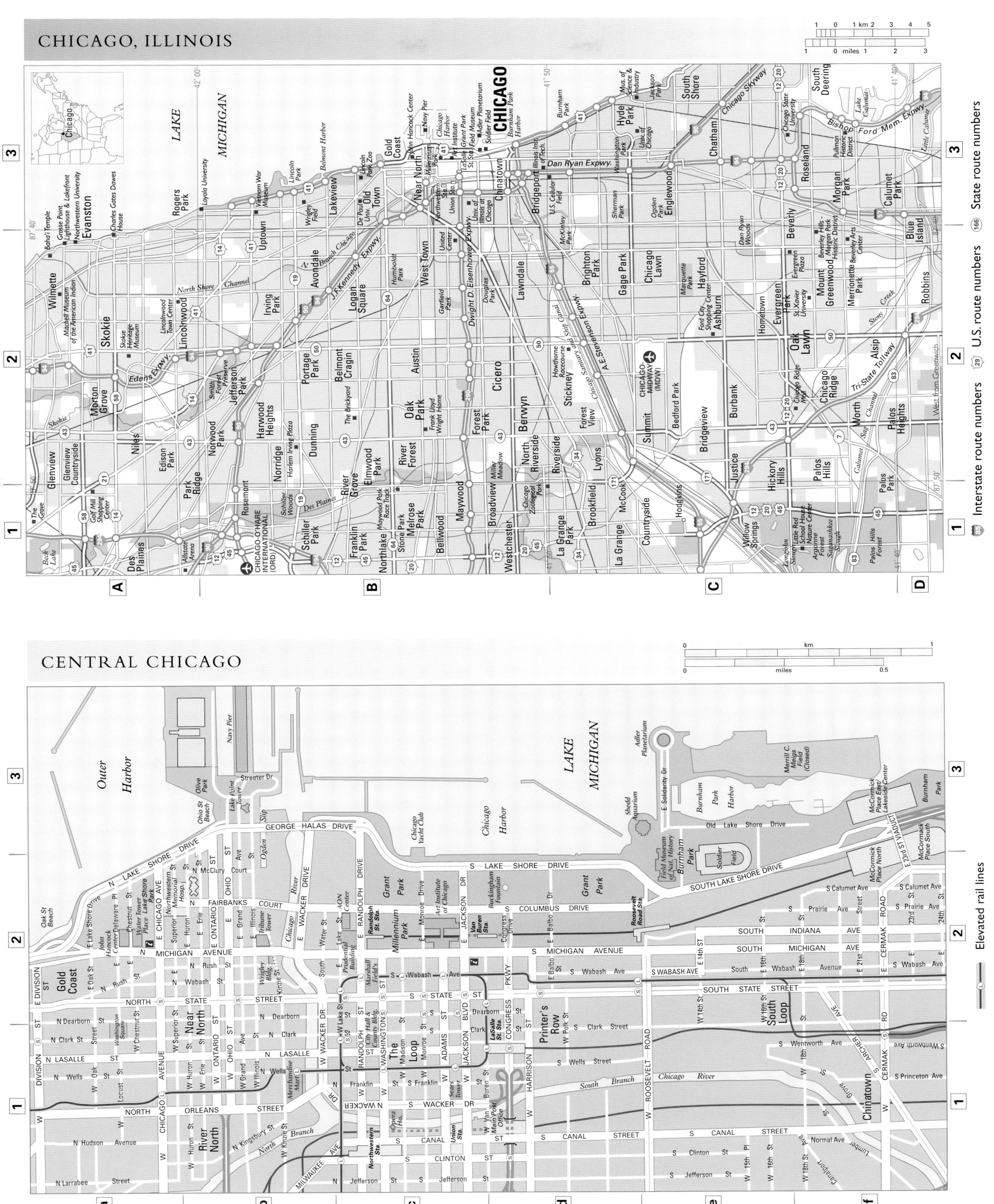

CHICAGO, ILLINOIS

CENTRAL CHICAGO

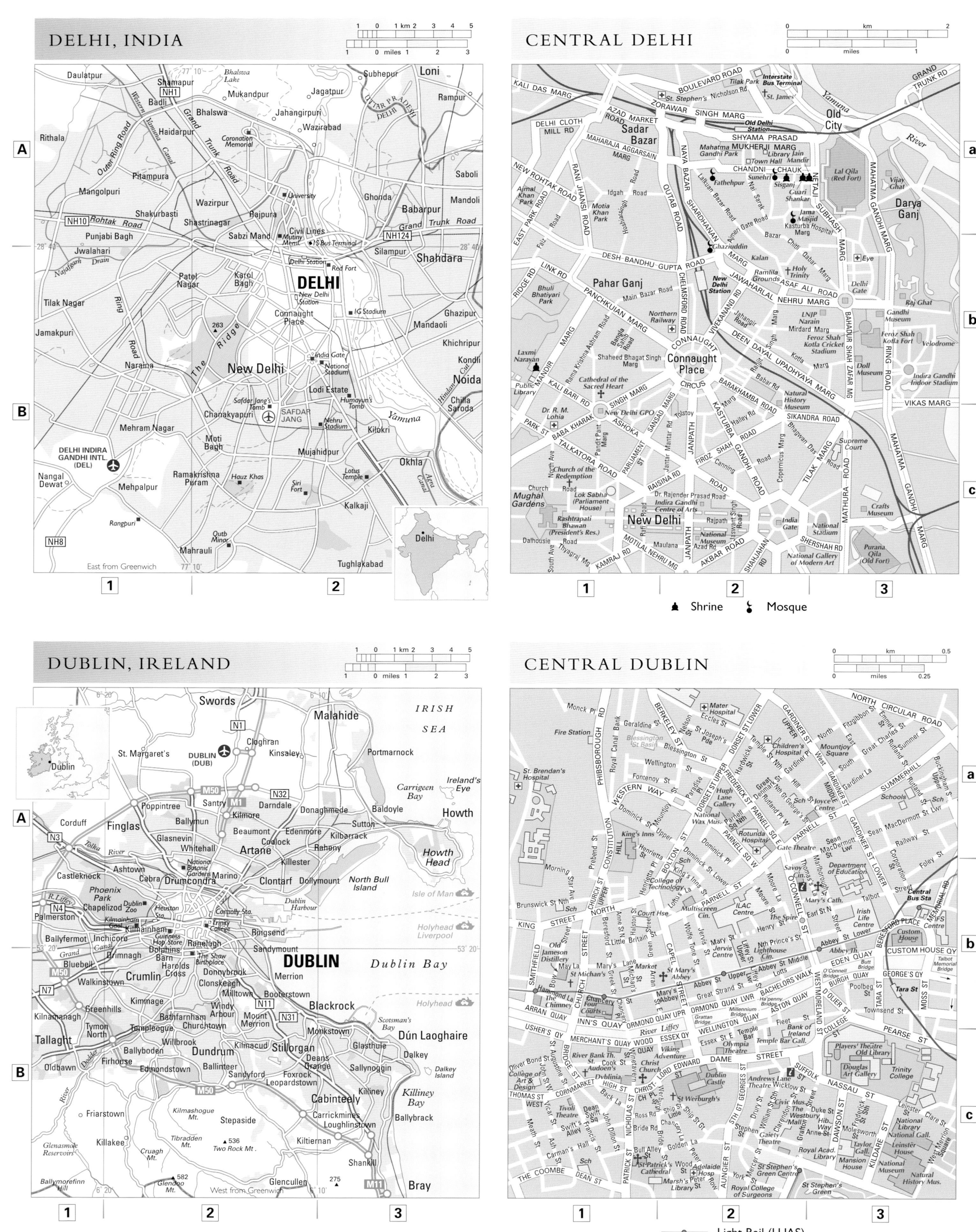

DELHI, INDIA

CENTRAL DELHI

▲ Shrine   ⚲ Mosque

DUBLIN, IRELAND

CENTRAL DUBLIN

Light Rail (LUAS)

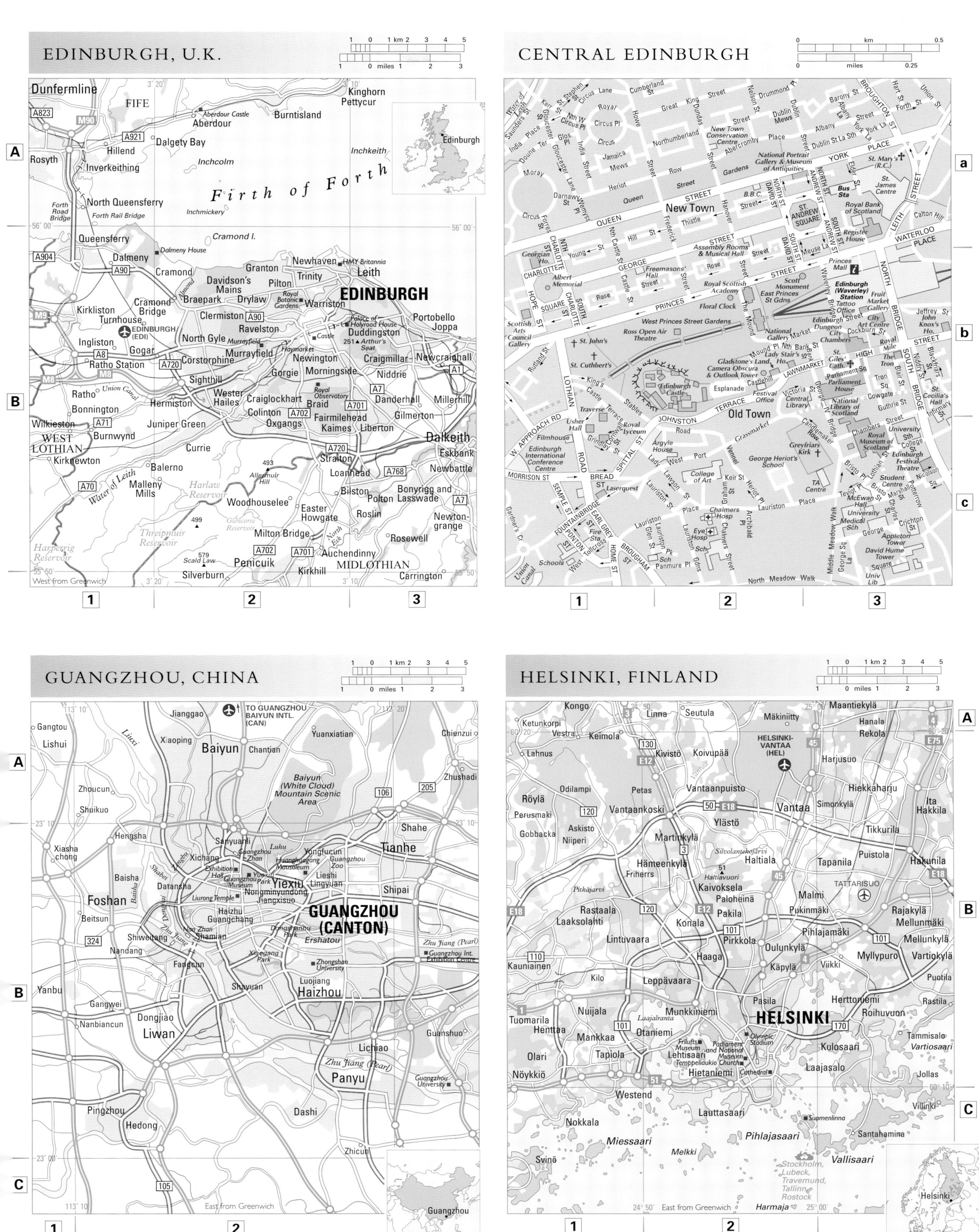

EDINBURGH, U.K.

Dunfermline
FIFE
Rosyth
A823
M90
A921
Aberdour Castle
Aberdour
Burntisland
Kinghorn
Pettycur
Hillend
Dalgety Bay
Inverkeithing
Inchcolm
Inchkeith
Forth Road Bridge
Forth Rail Bridge
Queensferry
Dalmeny House
Cramond I.
Edinburgh
A904
A90
Dalmeny
Cramond
Newhaven
HMY Britannia
Leith
Granton
Trinity
EDINBURGH
Kirkliston
Turnhouse
Cramond Bridge
Davidson's Mains
Pilton
Braepark
Drylaw
Warriston
Gogar
A90
Royal Botanic Gardens
Portobello
Joppa
Ingliston
EDINBURGH (EDI)
North Gyle
Ravelston
Palace of Holyrood House
Duddingston
Ratho Station
Corstorphine
Murrayfield
Haymarket
Castle
251 Arthur's Seat
Craigmillar
Newcraighall
A8
A720
Sighthill
Newington
Gorgie
Morningside
Niddrie
A1
Wester Hailes
Craiglockhart
Braid
A7
Royal Observatory
Danderhall
Millerhill
Ratho
Hermiston
Colinton
A701
Fairmilehead
Kaimes
Gilmerton
WEST LOTHIAN
Burnwynd
Juniper Green
A702
Oxgangs
Liberton
Currie
Balerno
Straiton
A720
Dalkeith
Eskbank
Newbattle
Malleny Mills
493 Allermuir Hill
Loanhead
A768
Woodhouselee
Bilston
Polton
Roslin
A7
Easter Howgate
Milton Bridge
Bonnyrigg and Lasswade
Newton-grange
499
Glencorse Reservoir
Rosewell
579 Scald Law
A702
A701
Auchendinny
Penicuik
Kirkhill
MIDLOTHIAN
Carrington
Silverburn

CENTRAL EDINBURGH

New Town
Old Town

GUANGZHOU, CHINA

Jianggao
TO GUANGZHOU BAIYUN INTL. (CAN)
Gangtou
Lishui
Xiaoping
Yuanxiatian
Chientsui
Baiyun
Chantian
Zhoucun
Baiyun (White Cloud) Mountain Scenic Area
Zhushadi
Shuikuo
106
205
Xiasha chong
Hengsha
Sanyuanli
Shahe
Xichang
Guangzhou Zhan
Luhu
Yongfucun
Tianhe
Foshan
Datansha
Guangzhou Museum
Yuexiu Park
Guangzhou Zoo
Beitsun
Liurong Temple
Yiexiu
Lieshi Lingyuan
Shipai
324
Shiwetang
Huanghuagang Mausoleum
Norigminyundong
Shamian
Jiangxisiou
GUANGZHOU (CANTON)
Nandang
Haizhu
Dongshanfu Park
Yanbu
Shayuan
Ershatou
Zhu Jiang (Pearl)
Gangwei
Dongjiao
Xinganz Park
Zhongshan University
Guangzhou Int.
Exhibition Centre
Nanbiancun
Liwan
Luojiang
Guanshuo
Pingzhou
Lichiao
Guangzhou University
Hedong
Zhu Jiang (Pearl)
Panyu
Dashi
105
Zhicun

HELSINKI, FINLAND

Kongo
Linna
Seutula
Mäkiniitty
Maantiekylä
Ketunkorpi
Vestra
Keimola
Kivistö
Koivupää
HELSINKI-VANTAA (HEL)
Hanala
Rekola
Lahnus
E12
130
Harjusuo
4
E75
Röylä
Odilampi
Petas
Vantaanpuisto
Vantaa
Simonkylä
Hiekkaharju
Perusmaki
120
Vantaankoski
50
E18
Ita Hakkila
Gobbacka
Askisto
Niiperi
Ylästö
Tikkurila
45
E18
Martinkylä
3
Puistola
Hämeenkylä
Friherrs
Silvolantekojärvi
Haltiala
Hakunila
Pitkäjärvi
Haltiavuori
51
Tapanila
Kaivoksela
TATTARISUO
45
E18
Rastaala
Paloheinä
Malmi
Rajakylä
Mellunmäki
Laaksolahti
120
Pakila
Pukinmäki
Pihlajamäki
101
Mellunkylä
Lintuvaara
E12
Konala
101
Vartiokylä
110
Pirkkola
Oulunkylä
4
Myllypuro
Kauniainen
Kilo
Haaga
Käpylä
Viikki
Puotila
Leppävaara
Pasila
Herttoniemi
Rastila
Tuomarila
Nuijala
Laajalranta
Munkkiniemi
Roihuvuori
1
Henttaa
101
Otaniemi
HELSINKI
170
Mankkaa
Frilufts Museum and National Museum
Olympic Stadium
Tammisalo
Olari
Tapiola
Lehtisaari
Parliament
Kulosaari
Vartiosaari
Temppeliaukio Church
Nöykkiö
Hietaniemi
Cathedral
Laajasalo
Jollas
51
Westend
60 10
Lauttasaari
Villinki
Nokkala
Suomenlinna
Svinö
Miessaari
Melkki
Pihlajasaari
Santahamina
Stockholm, Lubeck, Travemund, Tallinn, Rostock
Vallisaari
Harmaja
Helsinki

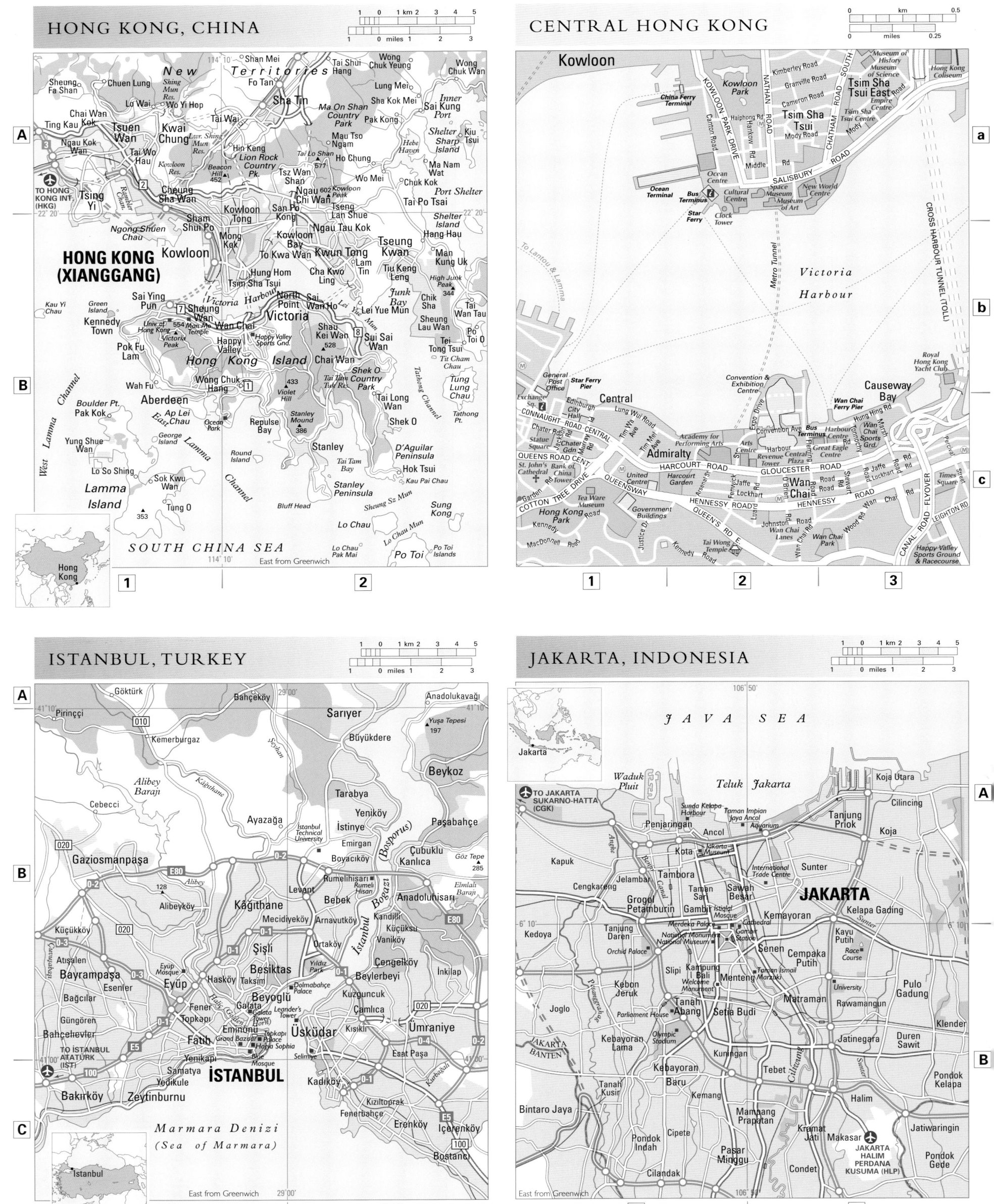

HONG KONG, CHINA

km 2 3 4 5
miles 1 2 3

New Territories
Shan Mei
Fo Tan
Tai Shui Hang
Wong Chuk Yeung
Wong Chuk Wan
Sheung Fa Shan
Chuen Lung
Lo Wai
Shing Mun Res.
Wo Yi Hop
Lung Mei
Sai Kung Port
Inner Port Shelter
Chai Wan Kok
Tsuen Wan
Kwai Chung
Tai Wai
Sha Tin
Ma On Shan Country Park
Ha Kok Mei
Shelter
Kiu Tsui
Ting Kau
Ngau Kok Wan
Tai Wo Hau
Lwr. Shing Mun Res.
Hin Keng
Lion Rock Country Pk.
Pak Kong
Mau Tso Ngam
Ho Chung
Sharp Island
TO HONG KONG INT. (HKG)
Tsing Yi
Cheung Sha Wan
Beacon Hill 452
Tai Lo Shan 577
Tsz Wan Shan
Ngau Chi Wan
Kowloon Peak 602
Wo Mei
Chuk Kok
Ma Nam Wat
Port Shelter
Ngong Shuen Chau
Sham Shui Po
Kowloon Tong
San Po Kong
Kowloon Bay
Ngau Tau Kok
Tseng
Lan Shue
Hang Hau
Shelter Island
HONG KONG (XIANGGANG)
Mong Kok
Kowloon City
Kwun Tong
Tseung Kwan
Man Kung Uk
Kowloon
To Kwa Wan
Tiu Keng Leng
Sai Ying Pun
Hung Hom
Cha Kwo Ling
Lam Tin
High Junk Peak
Kau Yi Chau
Green Island
Tsim Sha Tsui
Victoria Harbour
North Point
Sai Wan Ho
Lei Yue Mun
Junk Bay
Chik Sha 344
Tai Wan Tau
Sheung Wan
Wan Chai
Victoria
Shau Kei Wan
Sheung Lau Wan
Po Toi O
Kennedy Town
Univ. of Hong Kong
Man Mo Temple 554
Happy Valley Sports Gnd.
Sui Sai Wan
Tei Tong Tsui
Pok Fu Lam
Victoria Peak 528
Happy Valley
Chai Wan
Shek O Country Park
Tit Cham Chau
Wah Fu
Wong Chuk Hang
Hong Kong Island
Violet Hill 433
Tai Tam Tuk Res.
Tai Long Wan
Tung Lung Chau
Aberdeen
Ap Lei Chau
Ocean Park
Shek O
Tathong Pt.
Boulder Pt.
Pak Kok
East Chau
George Island
Repulse Bay
Stanley Mound 386
Stanley
Tai Tam Bay
D'Aguilar Peninsula
Hok Tsui
Yung Shue Wan
Lamma Channel
Round Island
Kau Pai Chau
West Lamma Channel
Lo So Shing
Sok Kwu Wan
Stanley Peninsula
Sheung Sz Mun
Sung Kong
Lamma Island
Tung O
Bluff Head
Lo Chau
Lo Chau Mun
Po Toi
SOUTH CHINA SEA
353
Lo Chau Pak Mai
Po Toi Islands
East from Greenwich
114° 10'

Hong Kong

1 **2**

CENTRAL HONG KONG

km
miles 0.25

Kowloon
China Ferry Terminal
Kowloon Park
Kimberley Road
Granville Road
Cameron Road
Museum of History
Museum of Science
Hong Kong Coliseum
Tsim Sha Tsui East
Haiphong Rd
Harbour
Tsim Sha Tsui Centre
Ocean Centre
Middle Rd
Mody Road
Tsim Sha Tsui
Empire Centre
Ocean Terminal
Star Ferry
Bus Terminus
Cultural Centre
Space Museum
Museum of Art
New World Centre
Clock Tower
SALISBURY
CROSS HARBOUR TUNNEL (TOLL)
Victoria Harbour
Metro Tunnel
Royal Hong Kong Yacht Club
General Post Office
Star Ferry Pier
Convention & Exhibition Centre
Exchange Sq.
Edinburgh Place
City Hall
Central
Lung Wui Road
Wan Chai Ferry Pier
Causeway Bay
Statue Square
Chater Gdn
Academy for Performing Arts
Convention Ave
Bus Terminus
Great Eagle Centre
St. John's Cathedral
Bank of China
Admiralty
Arts Centre
Harbour Centre
Central Plaza
Jaffe Rd
Times Square
Queensway
HARCOURT ROAD
GLOUCESTER ROAD
Lockhart Rd
Wan Chai
Hong Kong Park
Government Buildings
QUEEN'S RD E.
HENNESSY ROAD
Johnston Road
Wan Chai Park
Cotton Tree Drive
Tai Wong Temple
Happy Valley Sports Ground & Racecourse

1 **2** **3**

ISTANBUL, TURKEY

km 2 3 4 5
miles 1 2 3

Göktürk
Bahçeköy
Sarıyer
Anadolukavağı
Pirinççi
010
Kemerburgaz
Büyükdere
Yuşa Tepesi 197
Beykoz
Alibey Barajı
Tarabya
Cebecci
Ayazağa
Yeniköy
İstinye
Paşabahçe
İstanbul Technical University
Emirgan
Çubuklu
Göz Tepe 285
Gaziosmanpaşa
Kanlıca
020
E80
Levent
Rumelihisarı
Anadoluhisarı
Elmalı Barajı
Küçükköy
Kağıthane
Bebek
Kandilli
Küçüksu
Atışalen
020
Mecidiyeköy
Arnavutköy
Vaniköy
Şişli
Ortaköy
Çengelköy
İnkilap
Bayrampaşa
Eyüp Mosque
Beşiktaş
Yıldız Park
Beylerbeyi
Esenler
Taksim
Dolmabahçe Palace
Kuzguncuk
Çamlıca
Bağcılar
Eyüp
Hasköy
Beyoğlu
Galata
Leander's Tower
Bahçelievler
Fener
Galata Tower
Üsküdar
Güngören
Topkapı
Kısıklı
Fatih
Grand Bazaar
Topkapı Palace
Ümraniye
Yenikapı
Hagia Sophia
Selimiye
TO İSTANBUL ATATÜRK (IST)
Samatya
Blue Mosque
Esat Paşa
E5
Yedikule
100
Kadıköy
Bakırköy
Zeytinburnu
İSTANBUL
Kızıltoprak
Kurbağalı
E5
Fenerbahçe
Erenköy
İçerenköy
100
Marmara Denizi (Sea of Marmara)
Bostancı
East from Greenwich
29° 00'

Istanbul

1 **2**

JAKARTA, INDONESIA

km 2 3 4 5
miles 1 2 3

Jakarta
JAVA SEA
Waduk Pluit
Teluk Jakarta
Koja Utara
TO JAKARTA SUKARNO-HATTA (CGK)
Penjaringan
Sunda Kelapa Harbour
Taman Impian Jaya Ancol
Aquarium
Tanjung Priok
Cilincing
Koja
Ancol
Kota
Jakarta Museum
International Trade Centre
Sunter
Kapuk
Jelambar
Tambora
Taman Sari
Sawah Besar
JAKARTA
Cengkareng
Grogol Petamburin
Gambir
Istiqlal Mosque
Cathedral
Kemayoran
Kelapa Gading
Kedoya
Tanjung Daren
Merdeka Palace
National Monument National Museum
Gambir Station
Senen
Cempaka Putih
Kayu Putih
Race Course
Orchid Palace
Slipi
Kampung Bali
Welcome Monument
Taman Ismail Marzuki
Menteng
University
Pulo Gadung
Kebon Jeruk
Tanah Abang
Matraman
Rawamangun
Joglo
Parliament House
Setia Budi
Klender
JAKARTA BANTEN
Kebayoran Lama
Olympic Stadium
Kebayoran Baru
Tebet
Jatinegara
Duren Sawit
Bintaro Jaya
Tanah Kusir
Kemang
Kuningan
Pondok Kelapa
Pondok Indah
Cipete
Mampang Prapatan
Kramat Jati
Makasar
Jatiwaringin
Pasar Minggu
Cilandak
Condet
JAKARTA HALIM PERDANA KUSUMA (HLP)
Pondok Gede
East from Greenwich
106° 50'

1 **2**

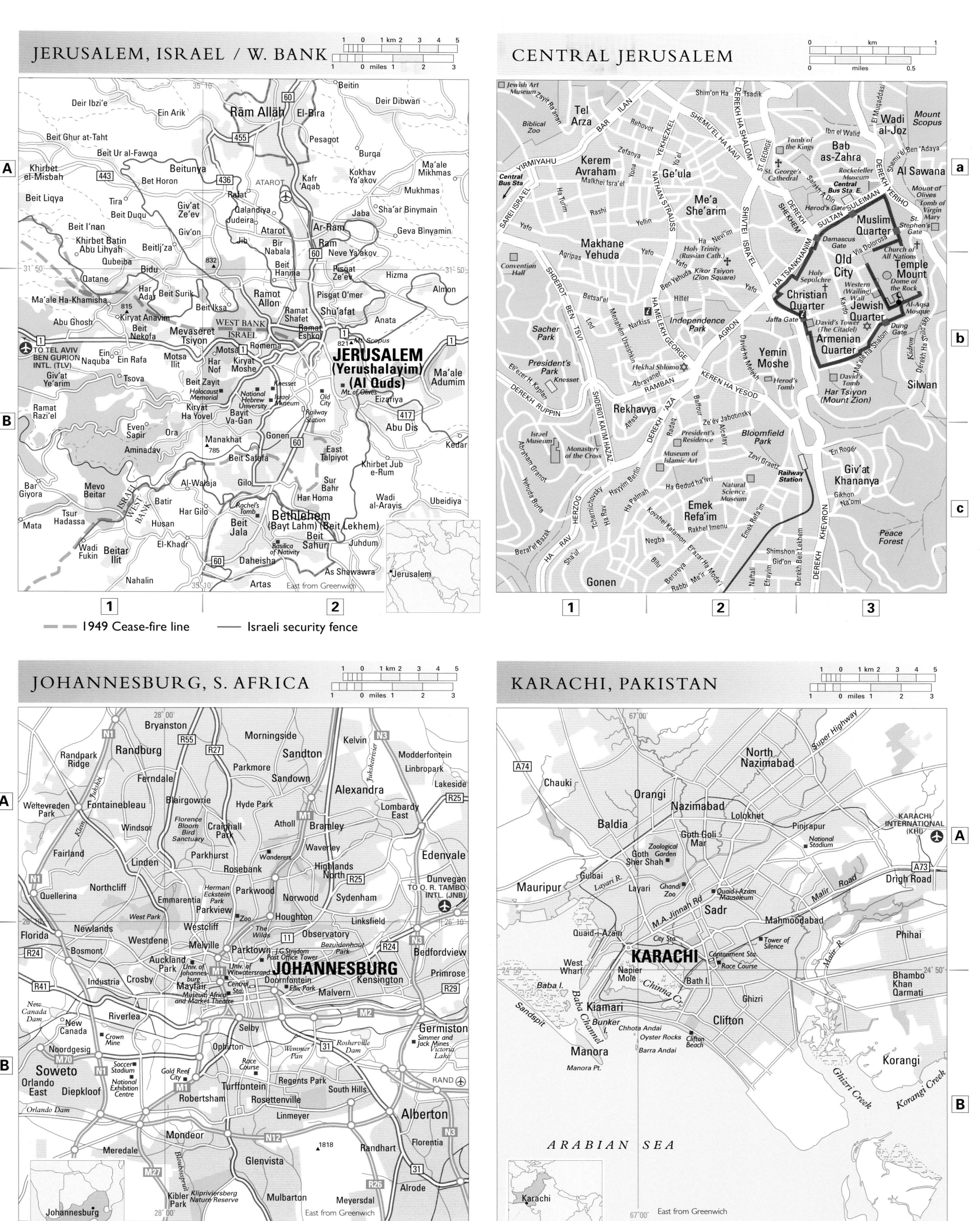

JERUSALEM, ISRAEL / W. BANK

1949 Cease-fire line — — — Israeli security fence

CENTRAL JERUSALEM

JOHANNESBURG, S. AFRICA

KARACHI, PAKISTAN

COPYRIGHT PHILIP'S

KOLKATA, INDIA

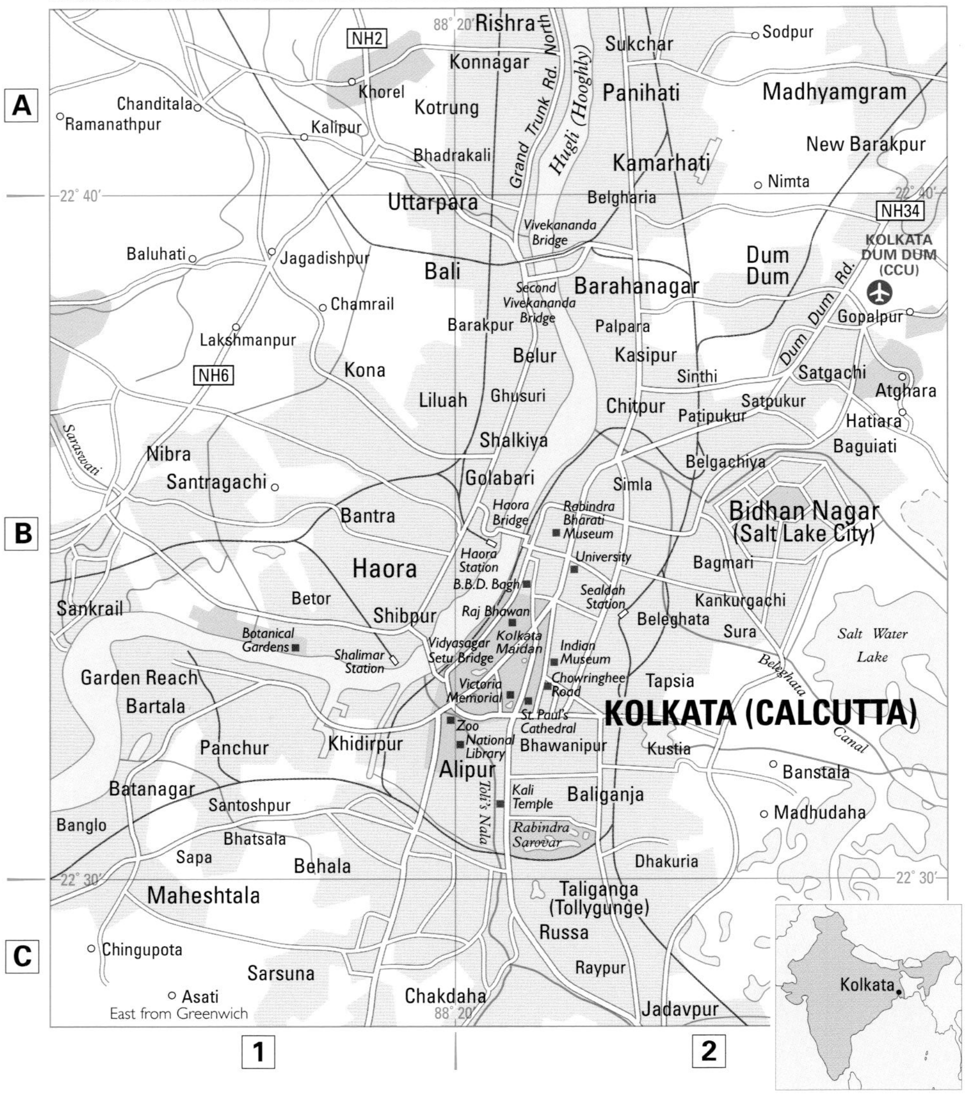

Rishra, Sukchar, Sodpur, Konnagar, Panihati, Madhyamgram, Chanditala, Ramanathpur, Khorel, Kotrung, Kalipur, Bhadrakali, Kamarhati, New Barakpur, Uttarpara, Belgharia, Nimta, Baluhati, Jagadishpur, Vivekananda Bridge, Bali, Barahanagar, Dum Dum, Chamrail, Second Vivekananda Bridge, Barakpur, Belur, Palpara, Kasipur, KOLKATA DUM DUM (CCU), Gopalpur, Lakshmanpur, Kona, Ghusuri, Sinthi, Satgachi, Satpukur, Atghara, Nibra, Santragachi, Golabari, Shalkiya, Chitpur, Patipukur, Hatiara, Baguiati, Haora Bridge, Rabindra Bharati Museum, Simla, Belgachiya, Bidhan Nagar (Salt Lake City), Bantra, Haora, Haora Station, B.B.D. Bagh, University, Bagmari, Betor, Shibpur, Raj Bhawan, Sealdah Station, Kankurgachi, Beleghata, Sura, Sankrail, Botanical Gardens, Shalimar Station, Vidyasagar Setu Bridge, Kolkata Maidan, Indian Museum, Chowringhee Road, Tapsia, Salt Water Lake, Garden Reach, Victoria Memorial, St. Paul's Cathedral, KOLKATA (CALCUTTA), Bartala, Zoo, National Library, Bhawanipur, Kustia, Banstala, Panchur, Khidirpur, Alipur, Kali Temple, Baliganja, Madhudaha, Batanagar, Santoshpur, Rabindra Sarovar, Dhakuria, Banglo, Bhatsala, Behala, Sapa, Maheshtala, Sarsuna, Taliganga (Tollygunge), Russa, Raypur, Chingupota, Asati, Chakdaha, Jadavpur

East from Greenwich

LAGOS, NIGERIA

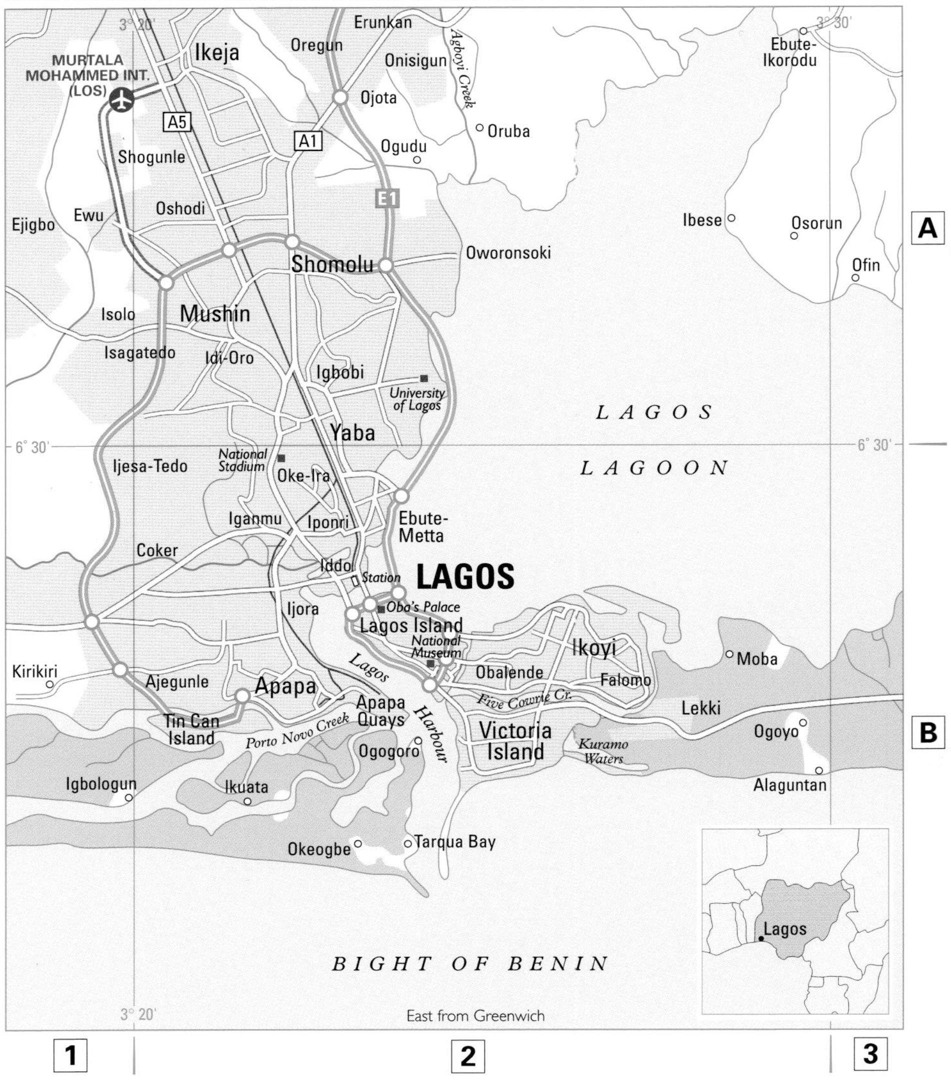

Ikeja, Erunkan, Oregun, Onisigun, Ebute-Ikorodu, MURTALA MOHAMMED INT. (LOS), Shogunle, Ojota, Ogudu, Oruba, Ewu, Oshodi, Igbobi, Ibese, Osorun, Ejigbo, Isolo, Shomolu, Oworonsoki, Ofin, Isagatedo, Mushin, Idi-Oro, University of Lagos, LAGOS LAGOON, Ijesa-Tedo, National Stadium, Yaba, Oke-Ira, Iganmu, Iponri, Ebute-Metta, Coker, Iddo, Station, LAGOS, Kirikiri, Ijora, Oba's Palace, Lagos Island, National Museum, Ikoyi, Moba, Ajegunle, Apapa, Obalende, Falomo, Lekki, Tin Can Island, Apapa Quays, Five Cowrie Cr., Victoria Island, Ogoyo, Igbologun, Ogogoro, Porto Novo Creek, Kuramo Waters, Alaguntan, Ikuata, Okeogbe, Tarqua Bay, Lagos Harbour, BIGHT OF BENIN

East from Greenwich, Lagos

LAS VEGAS, NEVADA

North Las Vegas, NELLIS AFB, City View Park, NORTH LAS VEGAS (VGT), Zoological Botanical Park, Las Vegas Natural History Museum, Cashman Field, Nevada State Museum & Historical Society, LAS VEGAS, Las Vegas Art Museum, The Meadows Mall, Sunrise Mountain Natural Area, Court Ho., Sunrise Manor, Stratosphere Tower, Fashion Show Mall, Sahara, Las Vegas Country Club Convention Center, Boulevard Mall, Desert Wetlands Park, Treasure Island, The Mirage, Caesars Palace, Venetian, Flamingo, Winchester, Spring Valley, Bellagio, Monte Carlo, New York New York, Paris, MGM Grand, University of Nevada L.V., Thomas & Mack Center, Whitney (East Las Vegas), Luxor, Tropicana, Liberace Museum, Paradise, Mandalay Bay, LAS VEGAS McCARRAN INTL. (LAS), Sam Boyd Stadium, Galleria at Sunset, Civic Center, Sunset Park, Las Vegas Outlet Center, Henderson, Enterprise

West from Greenwich

Las Vegas

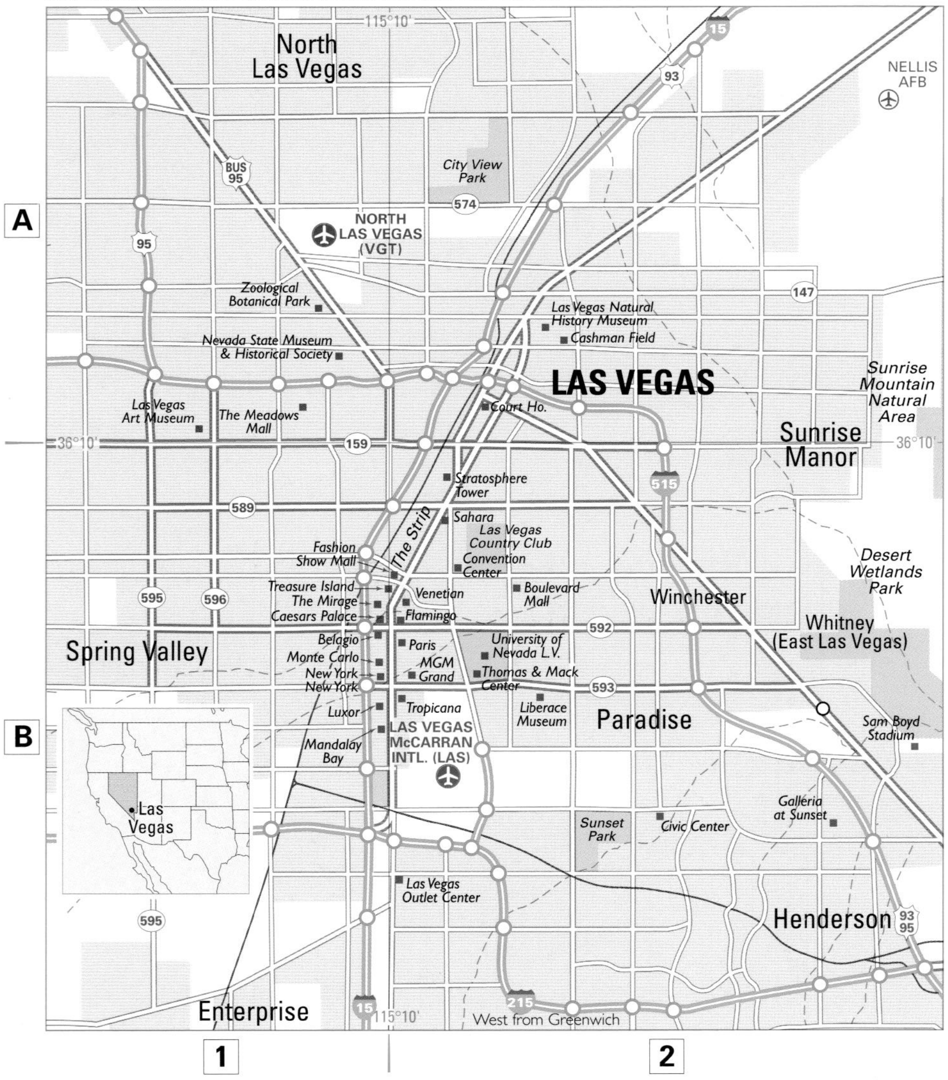

🛈 Interstate route numbers 🛈 U.S. route numbers 🛈 State route numbers

LIMA, PERU

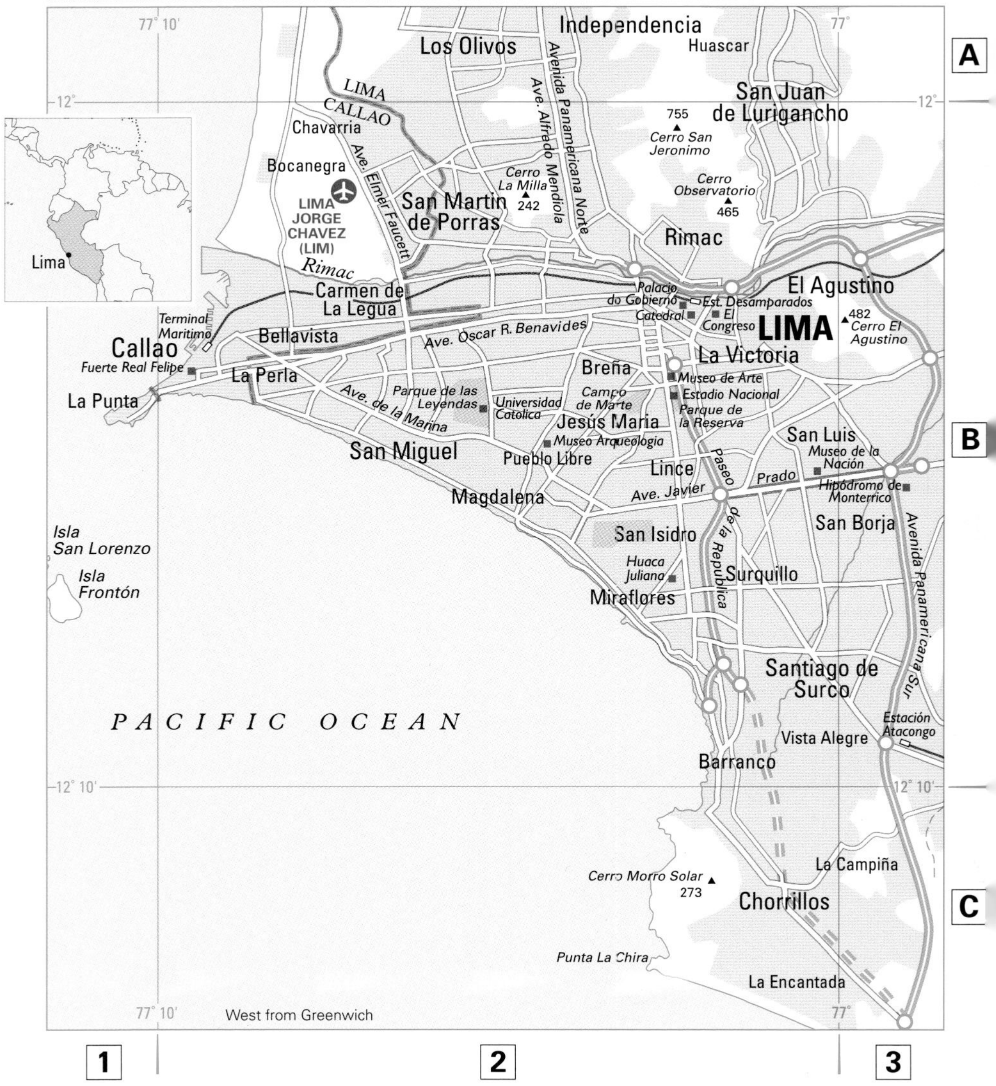

Independencia, Los Olivos, Huascar, LIMA CALLAO, Chavarria, San Juan de Lurigancho, Cerro San Jeronimo, Bocanegra, Cerro Observatorio, Cerro La Milla, San Martin de Porras, Rimac, LIMA JORGE CHAVEZ (LIM), Carmen de La Legua, El Agustino, Palacio do Gobierno, Est. Desamparados, Terminal Maritimo, Bellavista, Catedral, El Congreso, Cerro El Agustino, Callao, Fuerte Real Felipe, Ave. Oscar R. Benavides, LIMA, La Perla, Breña, Museo de Arte, La Victoria, La Punta, Parque de las Leyendas, Universidad Catolica, Campo de Marte, Estadio Nacional, Parque de la Reserva, San Luis, Jesus Maria, Museo Arqueologia, San Miguel, Pueblo Libre, Museo de la Nación, Magdalena, Ave. Javier, Prado, Hipodromo de Monterrico, Isla San Lorenzo, San Isidro, Huaca Juliana, San Borja, Isla Fronton, Miraflores, Surquillo, Santiago de Surco, PACIFIC OCEAN, Vista Alegre, Estación Atacongo, Barranco, Cerro Morro Solar, La Campiña, Chorrillos, Punta La Chira, La Encantada

West from Greenwich

LONDON, U.K.

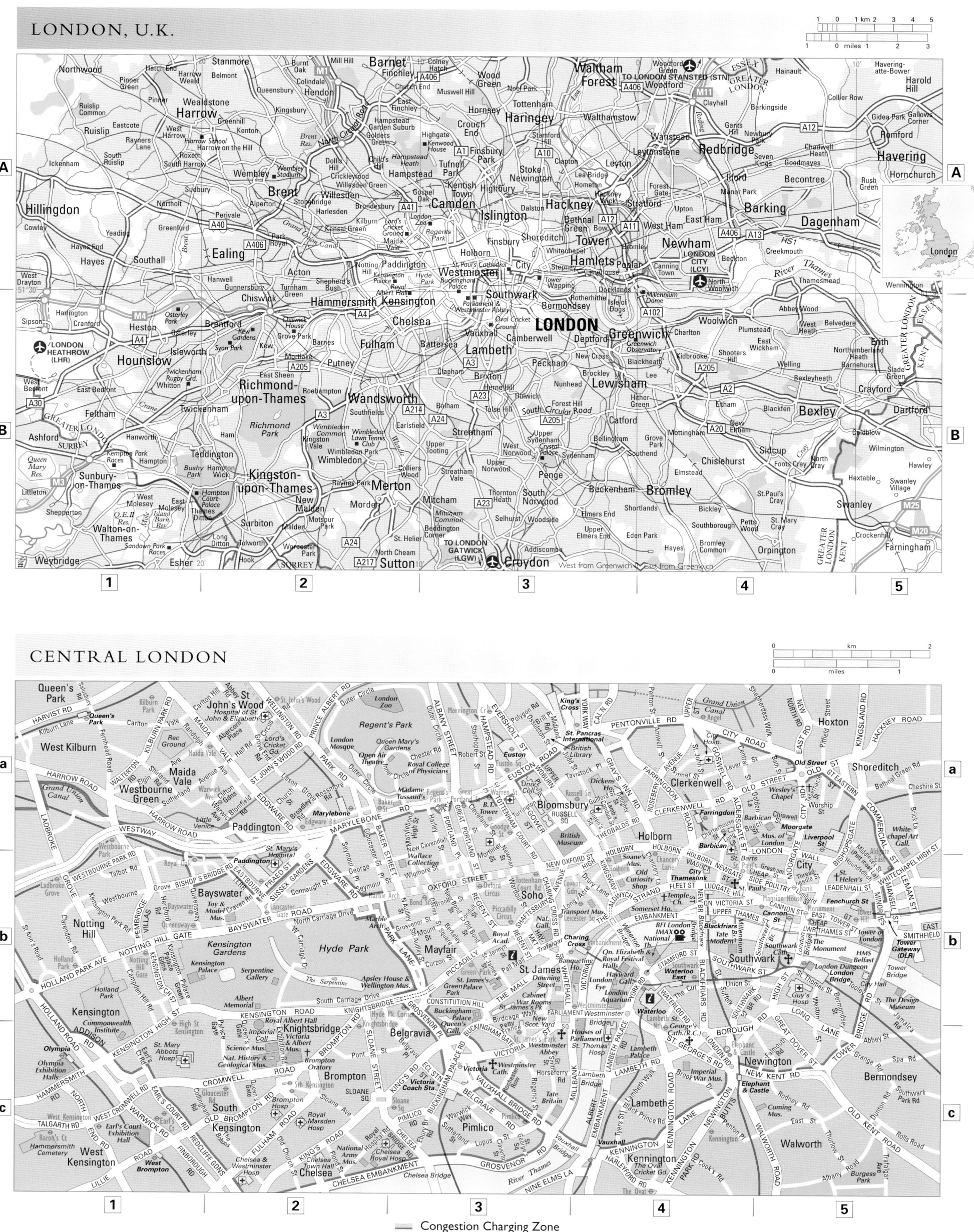

Congestion Charging Zone

LISBON, PORTUGAL

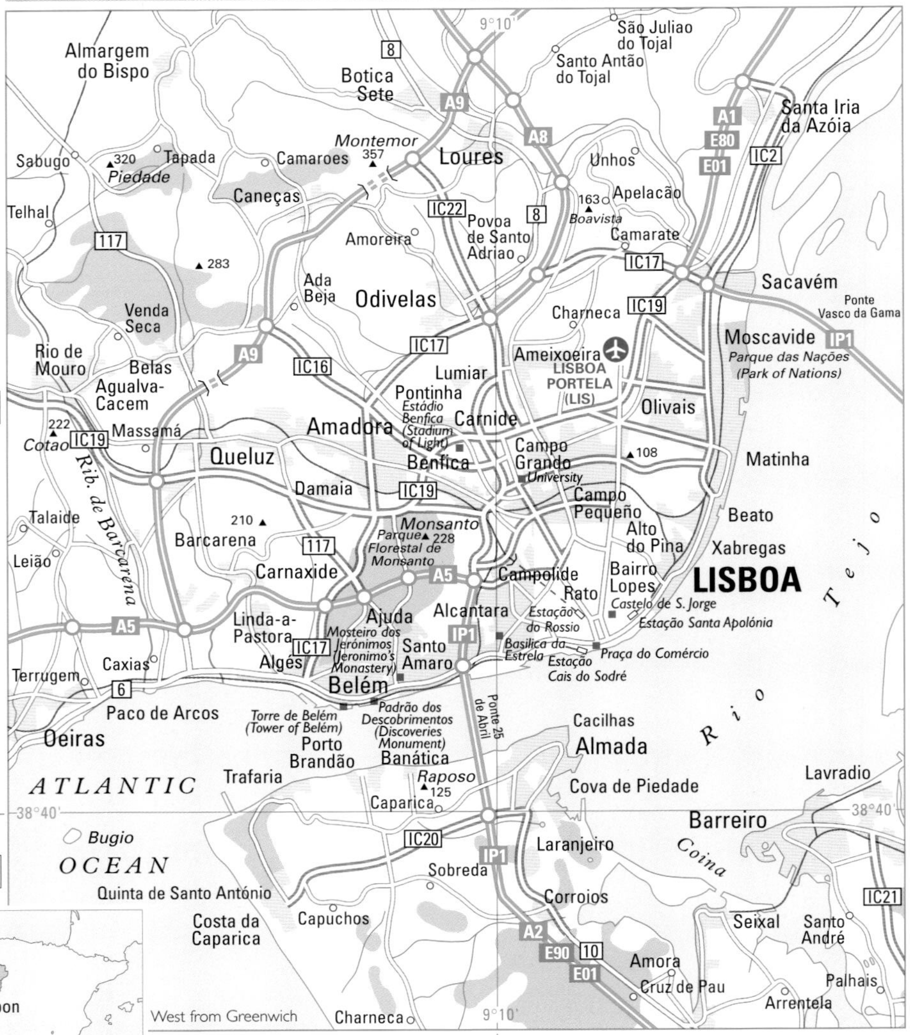

1 0 1 km 2 3 4 5
1 0 miles 1 2 3

Almargem do Bispo • Botica Sete • Santo Antão do Tojal • São Julião do Tojal
Sabugo • Tapada • Piedade • 320 • Montemor 357 • Camarões • Loures • Unhos • Santa Iria da Azóia
Telhal • Caneças • Amoreira • Póvoa de Santo Adrião • Apelação • Camarate
Rio de Mouro • Venda Seca • Ada Beja • Odivelas • Charneca • Sacavém • Ponte Vasco da Gama
Belas • Agualva-Cacem • Massamá • Lumiar • Pontinha • Carnide • Moscavide • Parque das Nações (Park of Nations)
Cotaxo • Queluz • Damaia • Amadora • Benfica • Estádio Benfica (Stadium of Light) • Campo Grande • University • Olivais
Talaide • Barcarena • Carnaxide • Monsanto Parque Florestal de Monsanto • Campo Pequeno • Alto do Pina • Beato • Xabregas • Matinha
Leião • Linda-a-Pastora • Ajuda • Mosteiro dos Jerónimos (Jerónimos Monastery) • Campolide • Rato • Bairro Lopes • Castelo de S. Jorge
Caxias • Algés • Santo Amaro • Belém • Torre de Belém (Tower of Belém) • Estação do Rossio • Estação Santa Apolónia
Terrugem • Paço de Arcos • Oeiras • Padrão dos Descobrimentos (Discoveries Monument) • Banática • Raposo • Cacilhas • Almada
Trafaria • Ponte 25 de Abril • Cova de Piedade • Lavradio
LISBOA
ATLANTIC • Bugio • Quinta de Santo António • Costa de Caparica • Capuchos • Sobreda • Corroios • Seixal • Santo André • Barreiro
OCEAN • Caparica • Laranjeiro • Amora • Cruz de Pau • Palhais • Arrentela • Charneca
Rio Tejo

Lisbon

West from Greenwich

1 2

CENTRAL LISBON

0 km 1
0 miles 0.5

Penitenciária • Palácio de Justiça • M. S. Sebastião • R. Pinheiro Chagas • Instituto Superior Técnico
Praça Duque Saldanha • Estefânia • Praça do Chile • Arroios
Parque Eduardo VII • Pavilhão dos Desportos • Penha França
Amoreiras • Marquês de Pombal • Anjos
Rato • Hospital M. Bombarda • Bairro Lopes
Jardim Botânico • Graça • Castelo de São Jorge (St. George's Castle)
Palácio de Assembleia Nacional • Bairro Alto • Estação do Rossio • Alfama • Estação Santa Apolónia
Baixa • Praça do Comércio • Estação Cais do Sodré • Estação Fluvial
Rio Tejo (Tagus)

1 2 3

LOS ANGELES, CALIFORNIA

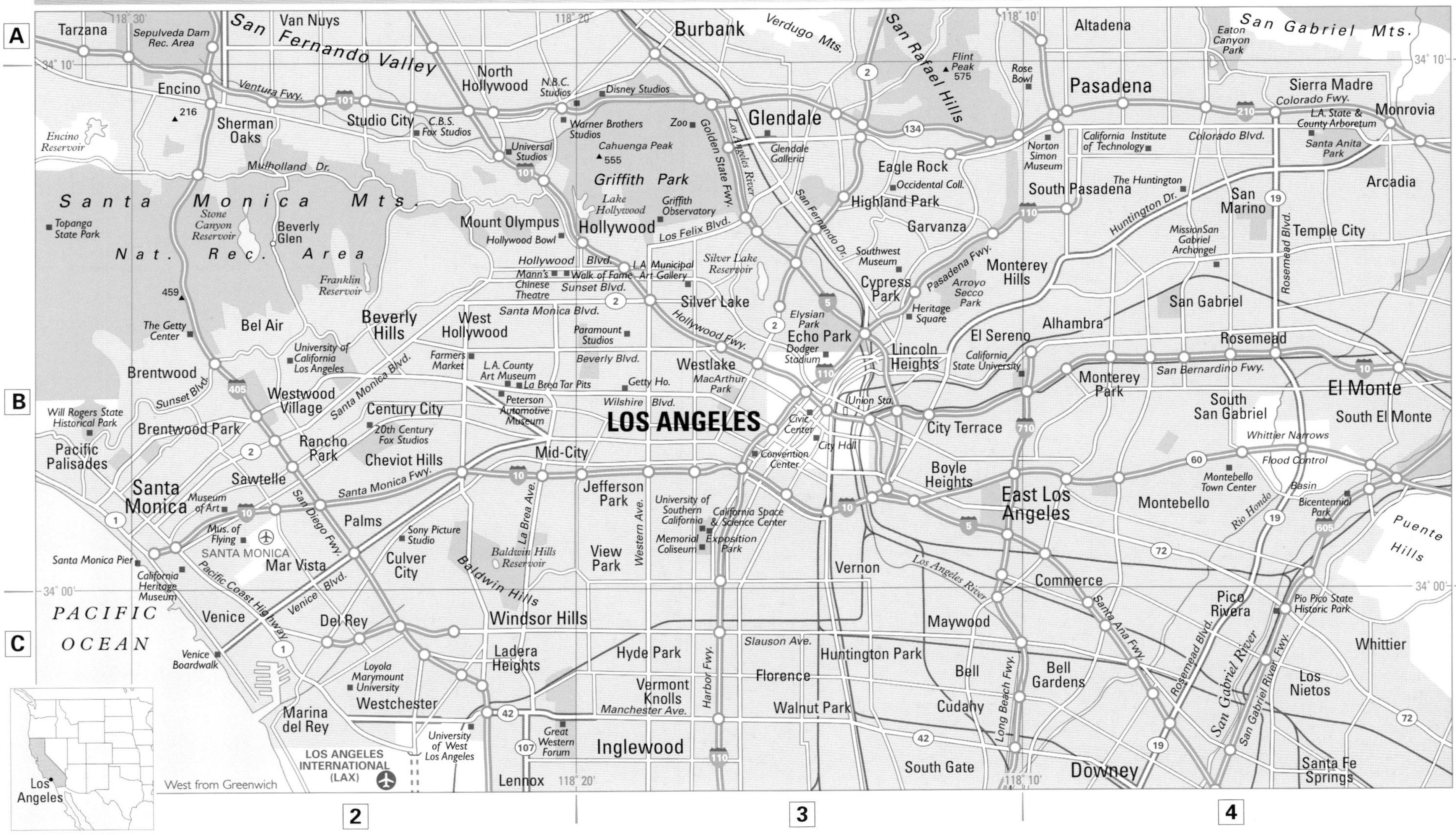

1 0 1 km 2 3 4 5
1 0 miles 1 2 3

Tarzana • Sepulveda Dam Rec. Area • Van Nuys • San Fernando Valley • Burbank • Verdugo Mts. • Altadena • San Gabriel Mts. • Eaton Canyon Park
Encino • Ventura Fwy. • North Hollywood • N.B.C. Studios • Disney Studios • Flint Peak 575 • Rose Bowl • Pasadena • Sierra Madre • Monrovia
Encino Reservoir • Sherman Oaks • Studio City • C.B.S. Fox Studios • Warner Brothers Studios • Zoo • Glendale • San Rafael Hills • L.A. State & County Arboretum • Colorado Fwy.
Santa Monica Mts. • Mulholland Dr. • Universal Studios • Cahuenga Peak 555 • Glendale Galleria • Eagle Rock • Occidental Coll. • California Institute of Technology • Santa Anita Park • Arcadia
Nat. Rec. Area • Topanga State Park • Stone Canyon Reservoir • Beverly Glen • Mount Olympus • Griffith Park • Lake Hollywood • Griffith Observatory • Highland Park • Norton Simon Museum • South Pasadena • The Huntington • San Marino • Temple City
Franklin Reservoir • Hollywood Bowl • Hollywood • Los Felix Blvd. • Silver Lake Reservoir • Garvanza • Monterey Hills • San Gabriel
The Getty Center • Bel Air • Hollywood Blvd. • Mann's Chinese Theatre • Walk of Fame • Art Gallery • L.A. Municipal Art Gallery • Southwest Museum • Cypress Park • Heritage Square • Alhambra • Rosemead
Brentwood • University of California Los Angeles • Beverly Hills • West Hollywood • Sunset Blvd. • Santa Monica Blvd. • Silver Lake • Elysian Park • Echo Park • Lincoln Heights • El Sereno • Monterey Park
Will Rogers State Historical Park • Westwood Village • Century City • Farmers Market • L.A. County Art Museum • Beverly Blvd. • Getty Ho. • Paramount Studios • Westlake • MacArthur Park • Dodger Stadium • California State University • San Bernardino Fwy.
Pacific Palisades • Brentwood Park • Santa Monica • Sawtelle • Rancho Park • 20th Century Fox Studios • Cheviot Hills • Mid-City • Wilshire Blvd. • Peterson Automotive Museum • La Brea Tar Pits • Civic Center • Union Sta. • City Terrace • South San Gabriel • El Monte
LOS ANGELES • City Hall • Boyle Heights • South El Monte
Santa Monica • Museum of Art • Mus. of Flying • Palms • Sony Picture Studios • Culver City • Jefferson Park • University of Southern California • California Space & Science Center • Memorial Coliseum • East Los Angeles • Montebello • Puente Hills
Santa Monica Pier • California Heritage Museum • Mar Vista • Baldwin Hills Reservoir • View Park • Vernon • Commerce • Pico Rivera • Pio Pico State Historic Park
PACIFIC OCEAN • Venice • Del Rey • Windsor Hills • Ladera Heights • Hyde Park • Huntington Park • Maywood • Bell Gardens • Whittier
Venice Boardwalk • Loyola Marymount University • Vermont Knolls • Manchester Ave. • Slauson Ave. • Florence • Bell • Cudahy • Los Nietos
Marina del Rey • Westchester • University of West Los Angeles • Great Western Forum • Walnut Park • South Gate • Downey • Santa Fe Springs
LOS ANGELES INTERNATIONAL (LAX) • Inglewood • Lennox

Los Angeles

West from Greenwich

2 3 4

85 Interstate route numbers   166 State route numbers

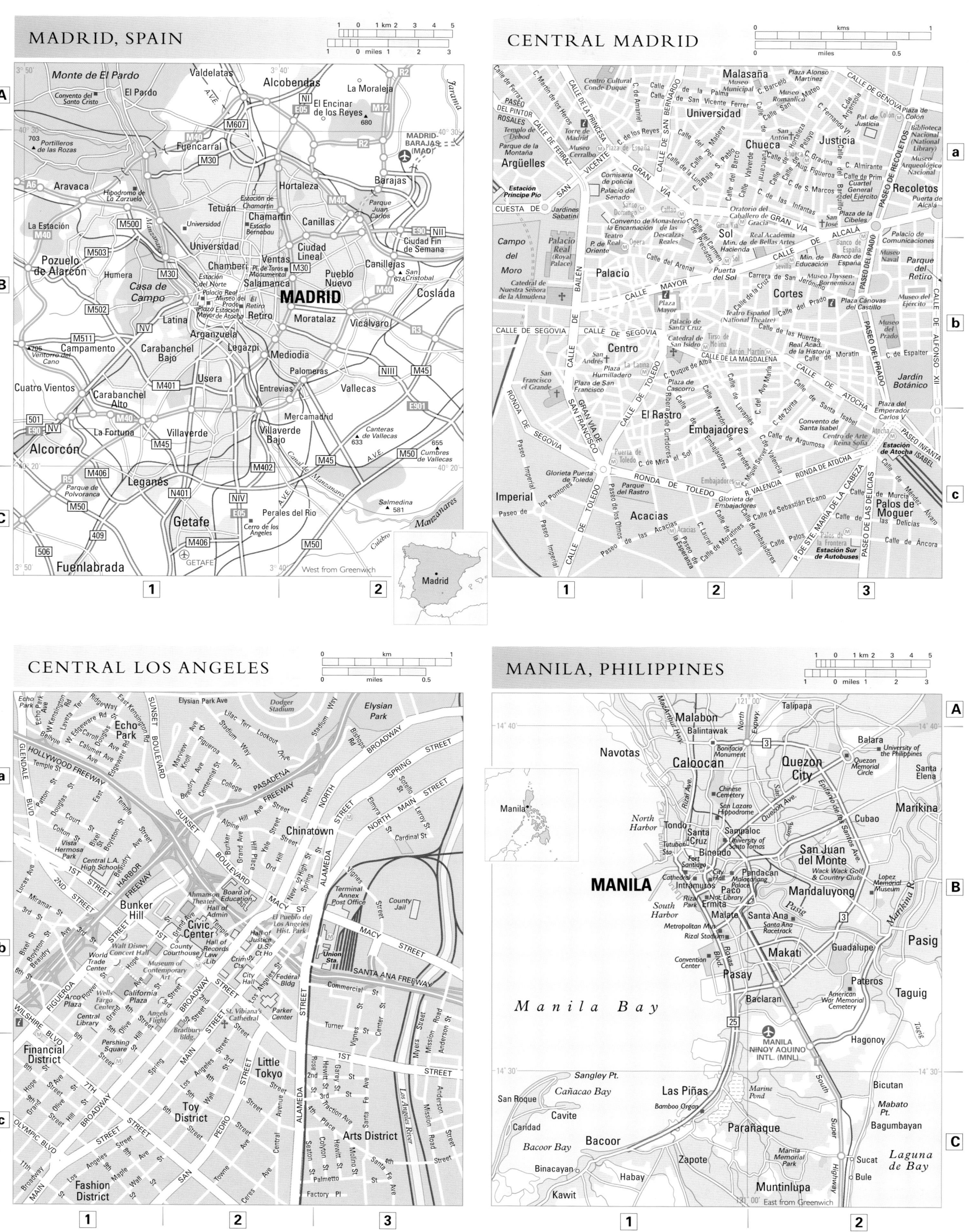

MADRID, SPAIN

CENTRAL MADRID

CENTRAL LOS ANGELES

MANILA, PHILIPPINES

COPYRIGHT PHILIP'S

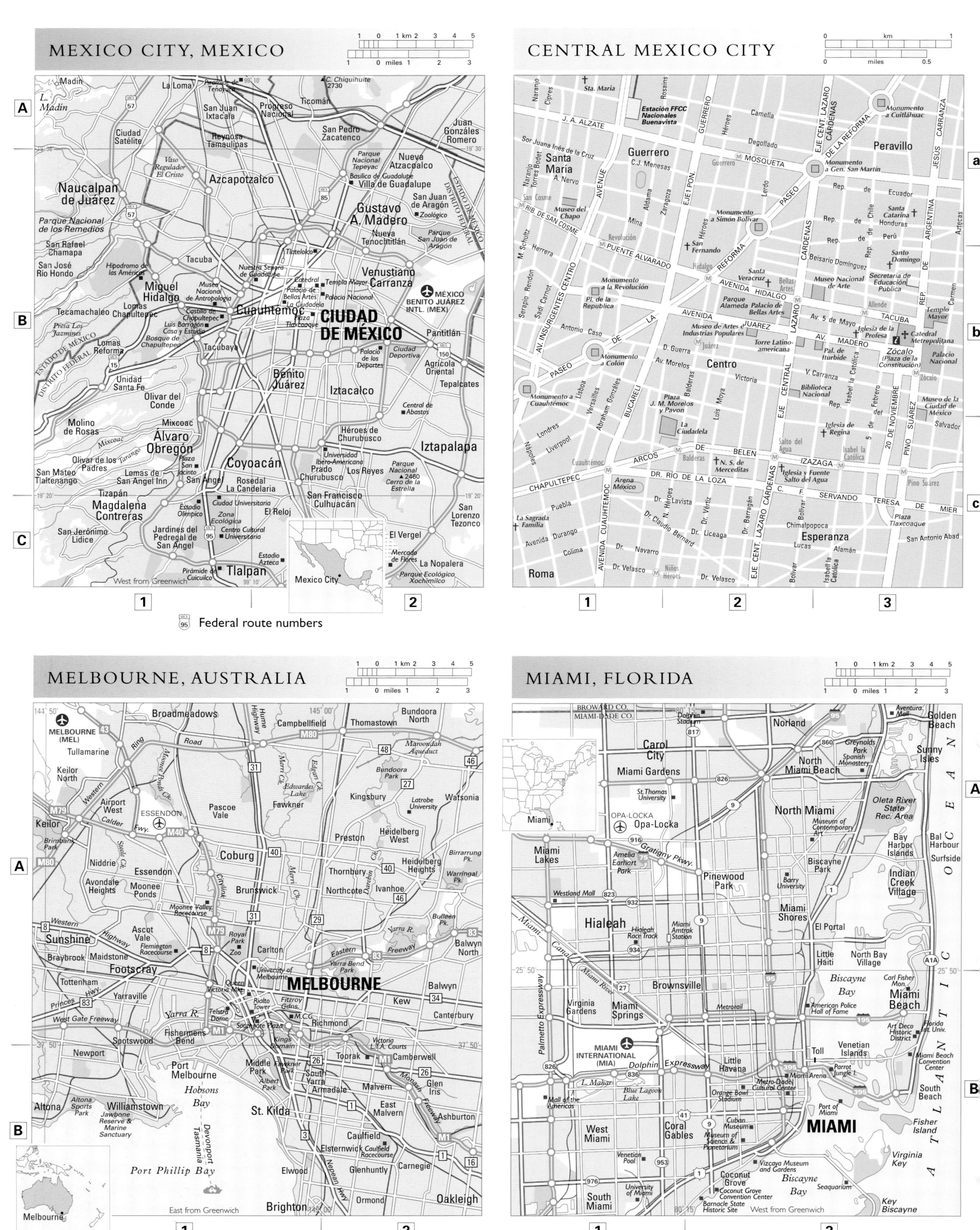

MILAN, ITALY

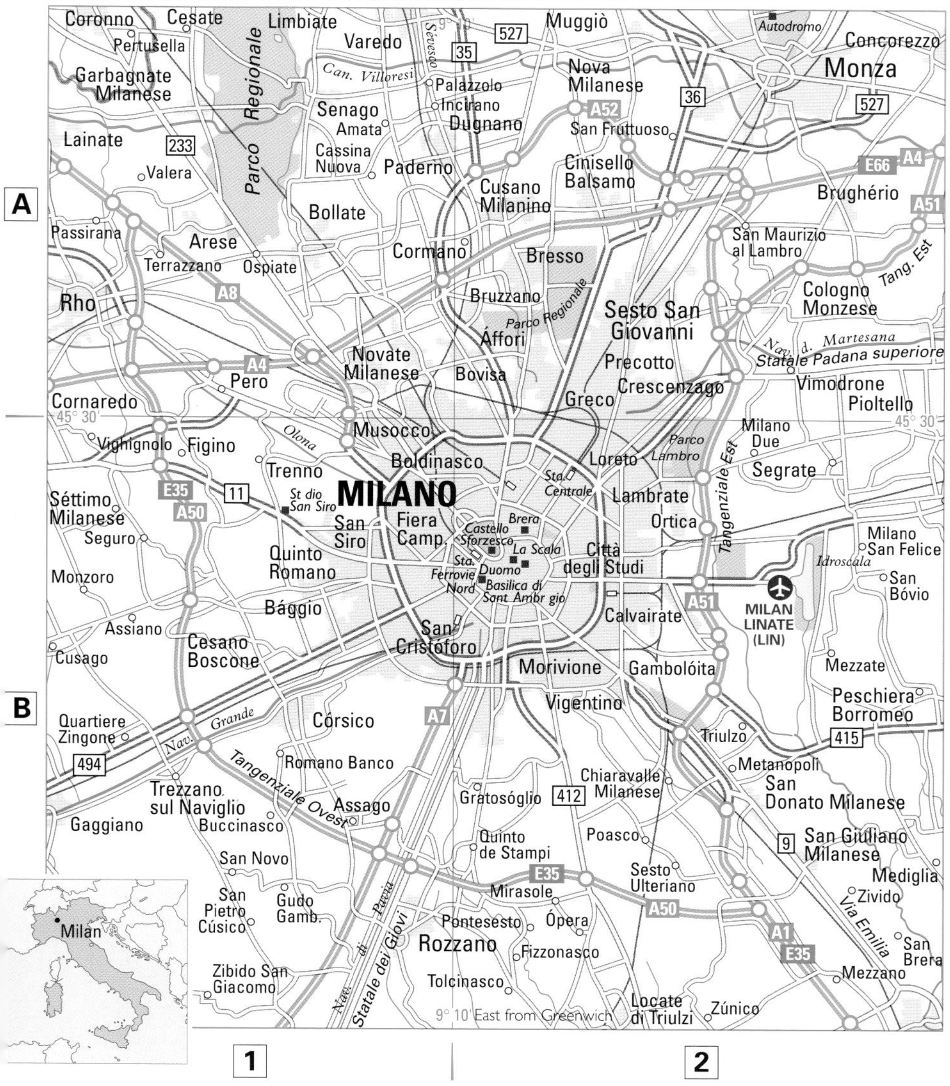

Coronno, Cesate, Pertusella, Limbiate, Varedo, Muggiò, Concorezzo, Autodromo, Garbagnate Milanese, Senago, Palazzolo, Nova Milanese, Monza, Amata, Incirano, Dugnano, Cassina Nuova, Paderno, San Fruttuoso, Lainate, Bollate, Cusano Milanino, Cinisello Balsamo, Brughério, Arese, Cormano, San Maurizio al Lambro, Rho, Terrazzano, Ospiate, Bresso, Bruzzano, Cologno Monzese, Pero, Novate Milanese, Áffori, Sesto San Giovanni, Precotto, Vimodrone, Pioltello, Passirana, Cornaredo, Musocco, Boldinasco, Greco, Crescenzago, Vighignolo, Figino, Trenno, **MILANO**, Loreto, Lambrate, Ortica, Milano Due, Segrate, San Siro, Fiera Camp., Brera, La Scala, Città degli Studi, Milano San Felice, Séttimo Milanese, Seguro, Quinto Romano, Bággio, Duomo, Basílica di Sant'Ambrógio, San Cristoforo, Calvairate, MILAN LINATE (LIN), Monzoro, Cusago, Assiano, Cesano Boscone, Morivione, Gambolóita, Mezzate, San Bóvio, Quartiere Zingone, Córsico, Vigentino, Triulzo, Peschiera Borromeo, Trezzano sul Naviglio, Gaggiano, Buccinasco, Romano Banco, Assago, Chiaravalle Milanese, Metanópoli, San Donato Milanese, San Novo, Grátosóglio, Quinto de Stampi, Poasco, San Giuliano Milanese, San Pietro Cúsico, Gudo Gamb., Mirasole, Ópera, Fizzonasco, Zívido, Mediglia, San Brera, Rozzano, Tolcinasco, Pontesesto, Mezzano, Zibido San Giacomo, Locate di Triulzi, Zúnico

CENTRAL MOSCOW

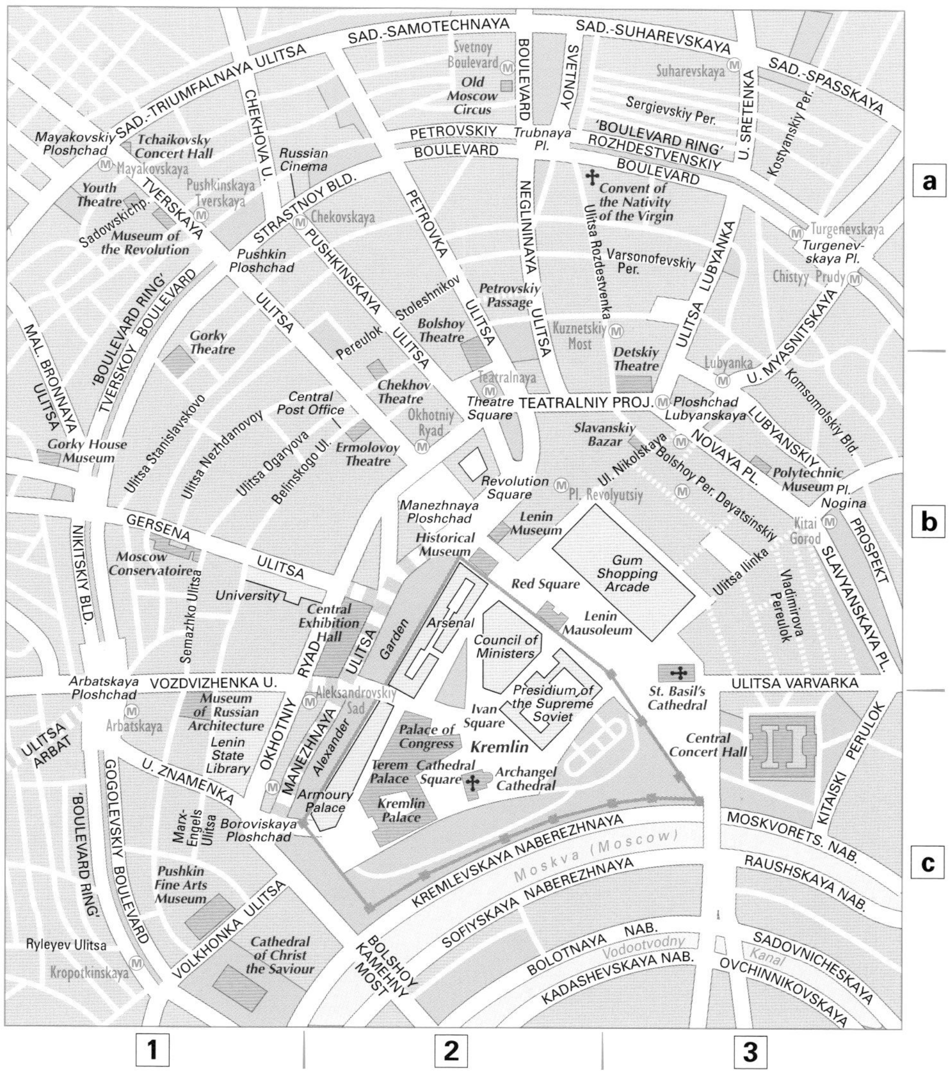

SAD.-SAMOTECHNAYA, SAD.-SUHAREVSKAYA, SAD.-SPASSKAYA, Svetnoy Boulevard, Old Moscow Circus, Mayakovskiy Ploshchad, Tchaikovsky Concert Hall, Chekhova Ulitsa, Russian Cinema, Sergievskiy Per., Sad.-Triumfalnaya Ulitsa, PETROVSKIY BOULEVARD, Trubnaya Pl., ROZHDESTVENSKIY BOULEVARD, U. Sretenka, Convent of the Nativity of the Virgin, Youth Theatre, Museum of the Revolution, Strastnaya, Pushkinskaya, Pushkin Ploshchad, Petrovka, Neglinnaya, U. Rozhdestvenka, Varsonofyevskiy Per., Turgenevskaya, Chistiy Prudy, Gorky Theatre, Bolshoi Theatre, Petrovsky Passage, Kuznetskiy Most, Detskiy Theatre, Lubyanka, U. Myasnitskaya, Central Post Office, Chekhov Theatre, Okhotnmy Ryad, Teatralnaya, Theatre, Slavanskiy Bazar, NOVAYA PL., Polytechnic Museum, Nogina, Gorky House Museum, Revolution Square, Manezhnaya Ploshchad, Historical Museum, Lenin Museum, Gum Shopping Arcade, Kitai Gorod, PROSPEKT, Moscow Conservatoire, Red Square, Arbatskaya Ploshchad, University, Central Exhibition Hall, Alexander Garden, Arsenal, Lenin Mausoleum, Ivan Square, St. Basil's Cathedral, Museum of Russian Architecture, Council of Ministers, Presidium of the Supreme Soviet, Lenin State Library, Palace of Congress, Kremlin, Central Concert Hall, Terem Palace, Cathedral Square, Armoury Palace, Archangel Cathedral, Kremlin Palace, Pushkin Fine Arts Museum, MOSKVORETS. NAB., RAUSHSKAYA NAB., Ryleyev Ulitsa, Kropotkinskaya, VOLKHONKA ULITSA, Cathedral of Christ the Saviour, KREMLEVSKAYA NABEREZHNAYA, Moskva (Moscow), SOFIYSKAYA NABEREZHNAYA, BOLOTNAYA NAB., KADASHEVSKAYA NAB., Vodootvodniy Kanal, OVCHINNIKOVSKAYA, SADOVNICHESKAYA

MOSCOW, RUSSIA

Putilkovo, Degunino, Vladykino, Babushkin, Medvezhiy Ozyora, Novonikolyskoye, Mitino, Bratsevo, TO MOSCOW SHEREMETYEVO INTL. (SVO), Khimki-Khovrino, Losiny Ostrov National Park, Almazova, Chernyovo, Penyagino, Tushino, Nikolskiy, Petrovsko-Razumovskoye, Dzerzhinskiy Park, Abramtsevo, Pekhra-Pokrovskoye, Krasnogorsk, Pavshino, Timiryazev Park, Ostankino, Galyanovo, Vostochnyy, Balashikha, Golyevo, Myakinino, Strogino, Pokrovsko-Sresnevo, Petrovskiy Park, Sokolniki Park, Izmaylovo, Gorenki, Novaya, Arkhangelskoye, Troitse-Lykovo, Leningradskiy Prospekt, Bogorodskoye, Izmayloskiy Park, Vishnyaki, Pekhra-Yakovlevskaya, Zakharkovo, Rublovo, Khorosovo, Frunze, Dzerzhinskiy, Yaroslav Station, Leportovo, Nikolyskoye, Saltykovka, Razdory, Cherepkovo, Mnevniki, **MOSKVA**, Sverdlov, Leningrad Station, Kazan Station, Bauman, Kursk Station, Novogireyevo, Reutov, Kutsino, Barvikha, Krylatskoye, Krasno-Presnenskaya, Bolshoi Theatre, Red Square, St. Basil's Cath., Lenin Museum, Perovo, Kuskovo, Veshnyaki, Serebryanka, Zheleznodorozhnyy, Romashkovo, Kuntsevo, Fili-Mazilovo, Kiev Station, Kremlin, Zhdanov, Plyushchevo, Poduskino, Nemchinovka, Novoivanovskoye, Davydkovo, Novodevichy Convent, Gorky Park, Pavelet Station, Moskvoretskiy, Vykhino, Volgogradskiy Prospekt, Zhulebino, Mikhelysona, Lochino, Aminyevo, Luzhniki Sports Centre, Lenin Stadium, Tekstilyshchik, Kuzyminki, Kosino, Kozhukhovo, Mamonovo, Bakovka, Zarechye, Ochakovo, Ramenki, Leninskiye Gory, Moscow Circus, Oktyabrskiy, Nogatino, Lyublino, Lyubertsy, Nekrasovka, Odintsovo, Meshcherskiy, Lomonosov Moscow State University, Cheryomushki, Yugo-Zarad, Dyakovo, Maryino, Marusino, Nikulino, Troparevo, Zyuzino, Volkhonka-Zil, Kuryanovo, Tomilino, Choboty, Solntsevo, Belyayevo Bogorodskoye, Bittsevsky Forest Park, Lenino, Brateyevo, Kapotnya, Kotelniki, Kraskovo, Malakhovka, Peredelkino, Orlovo, Chertanovo, TO DOMODEDOVO INTL. (DME), Borisovo, Dzerzhinskiy, Vnukovo, Rasskazova, Rumyantsevo

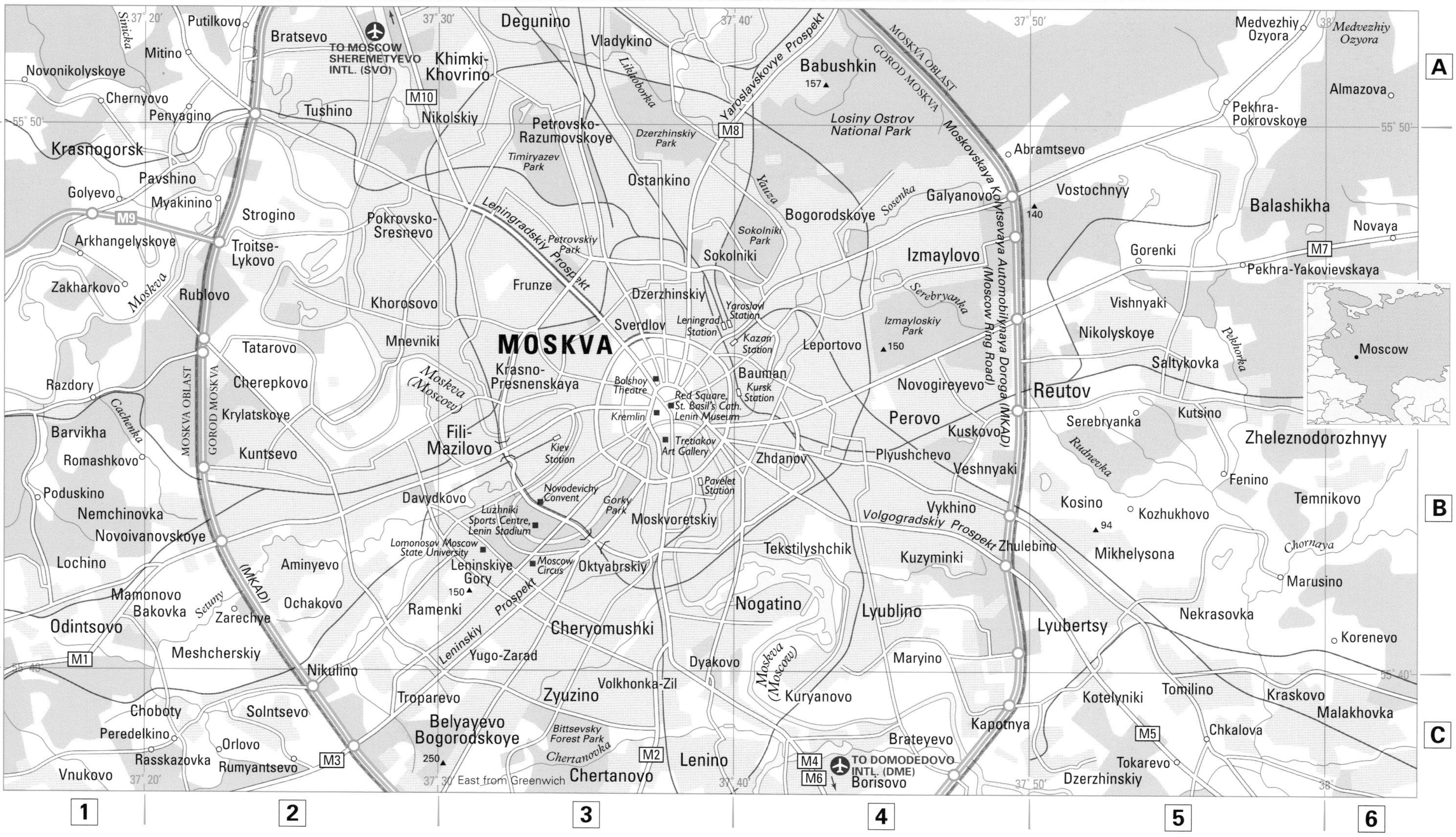

COPYRIGHT PHILIP'S

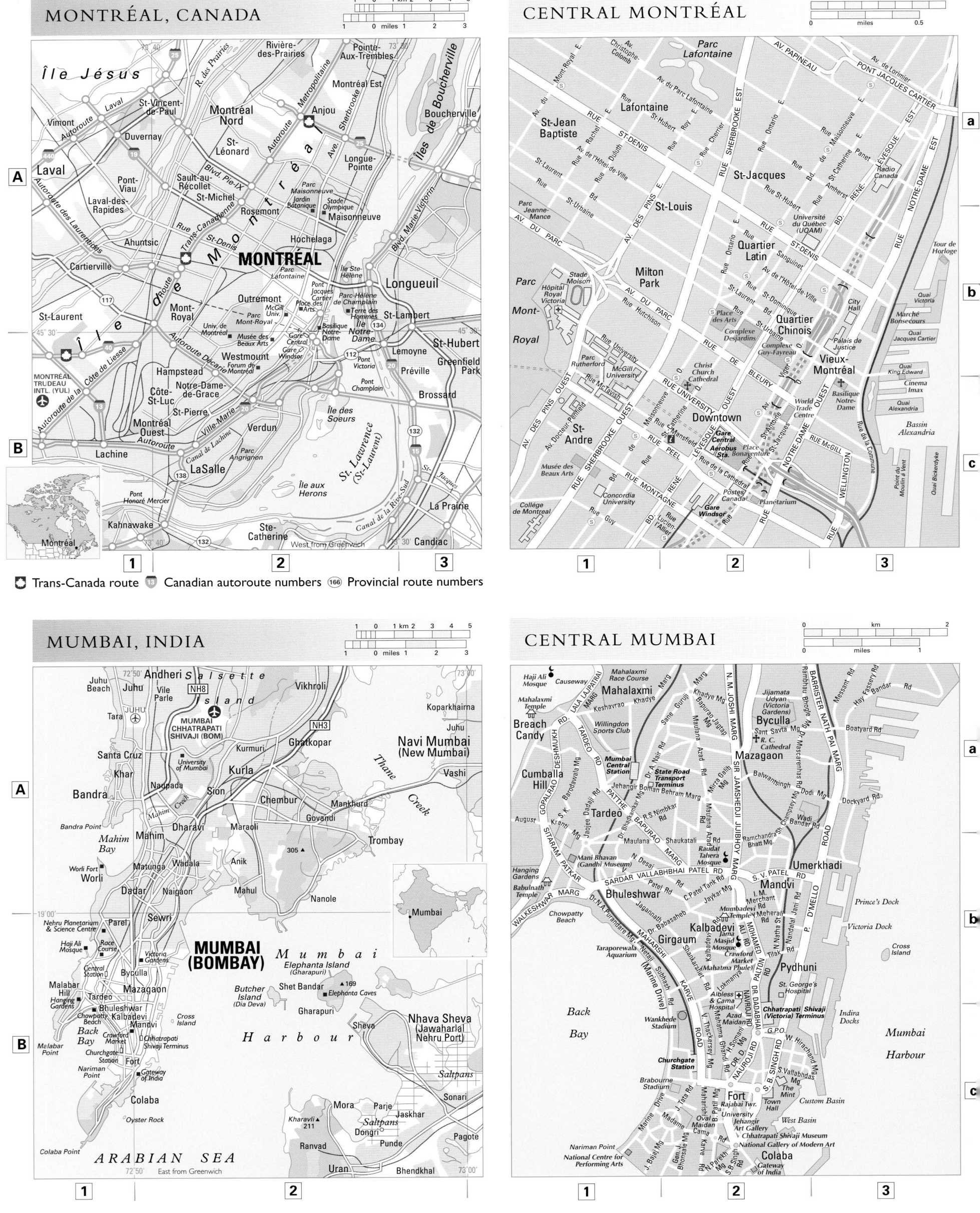

MUNICH, GERMANY

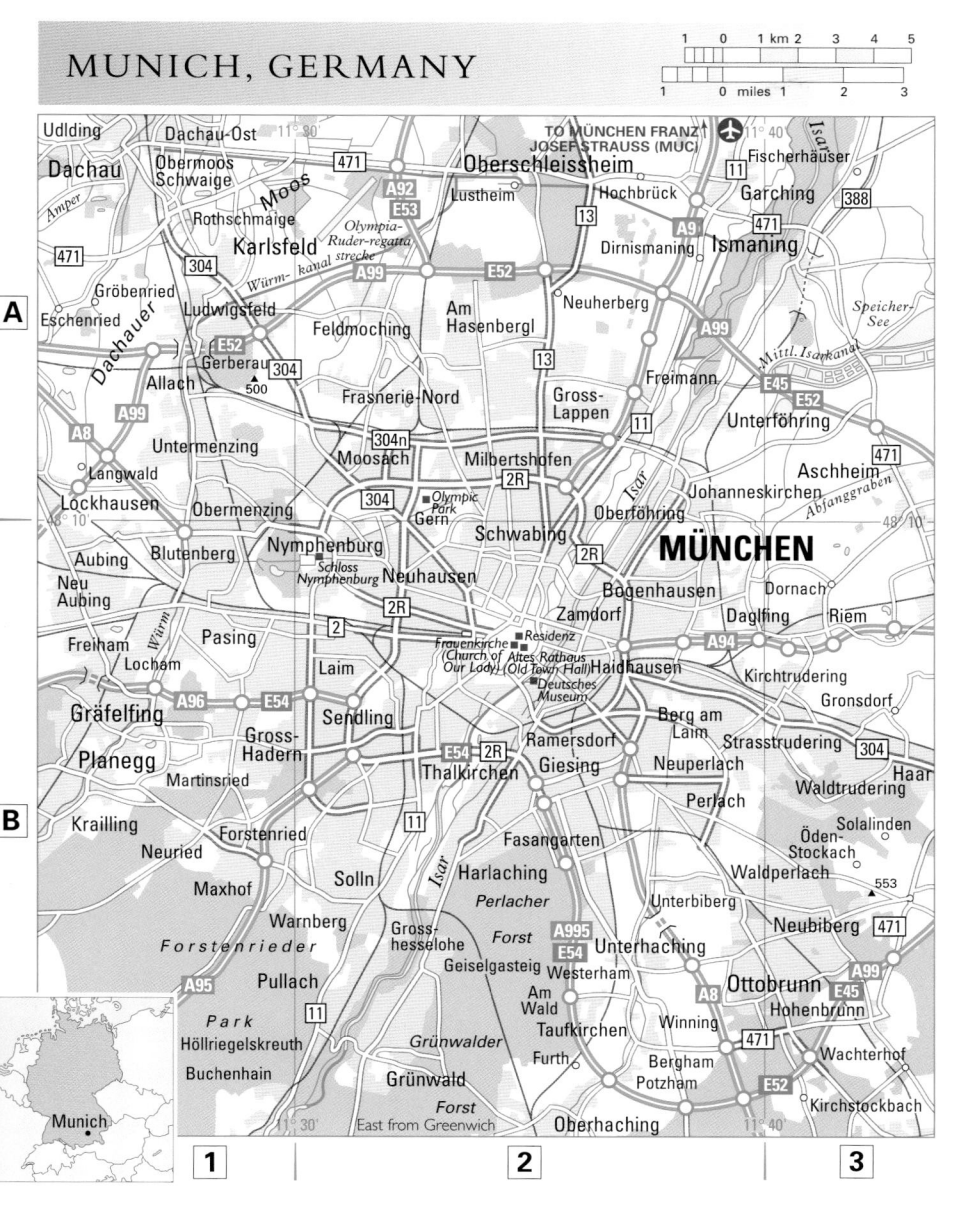

CENTRAL MUNICH

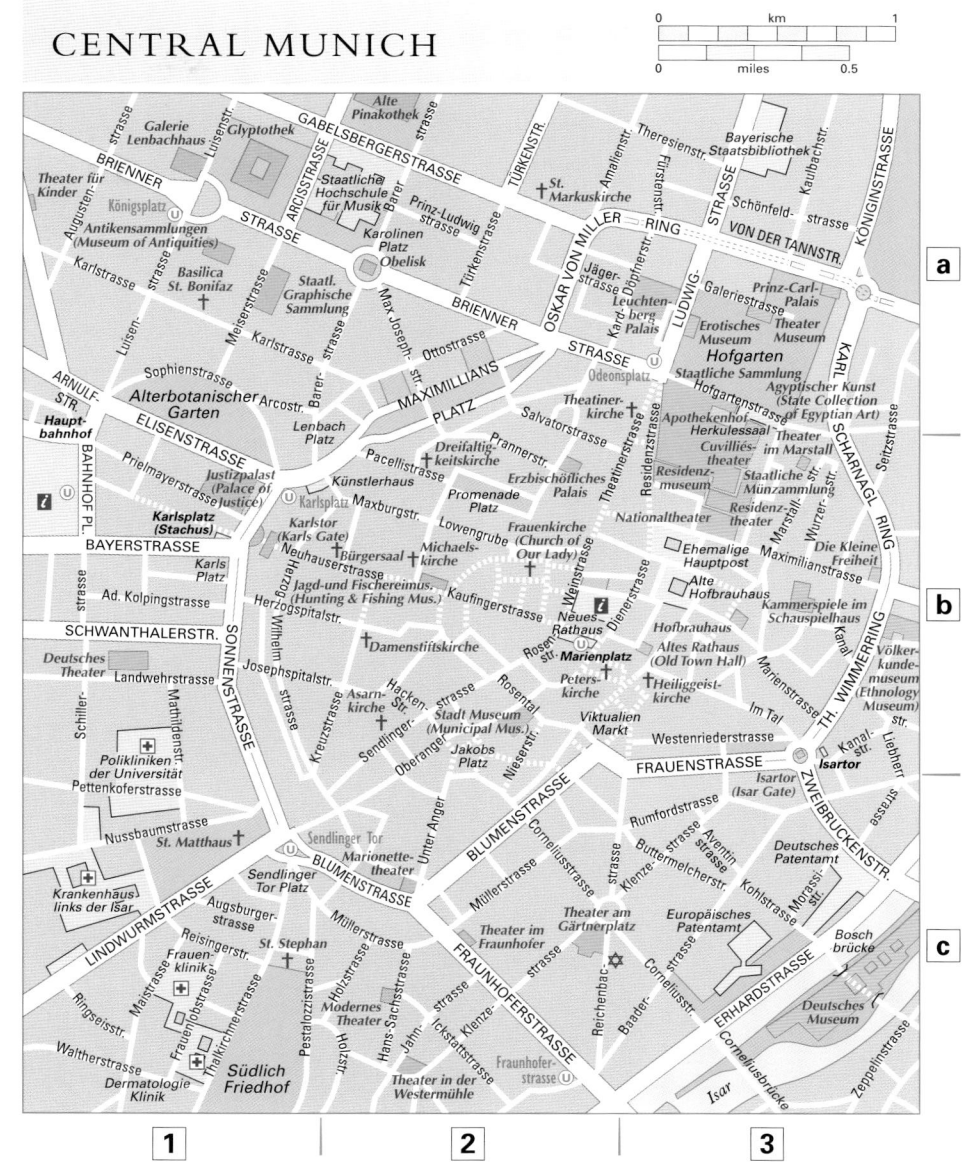

NEW ORLEANS, LOUISIANA

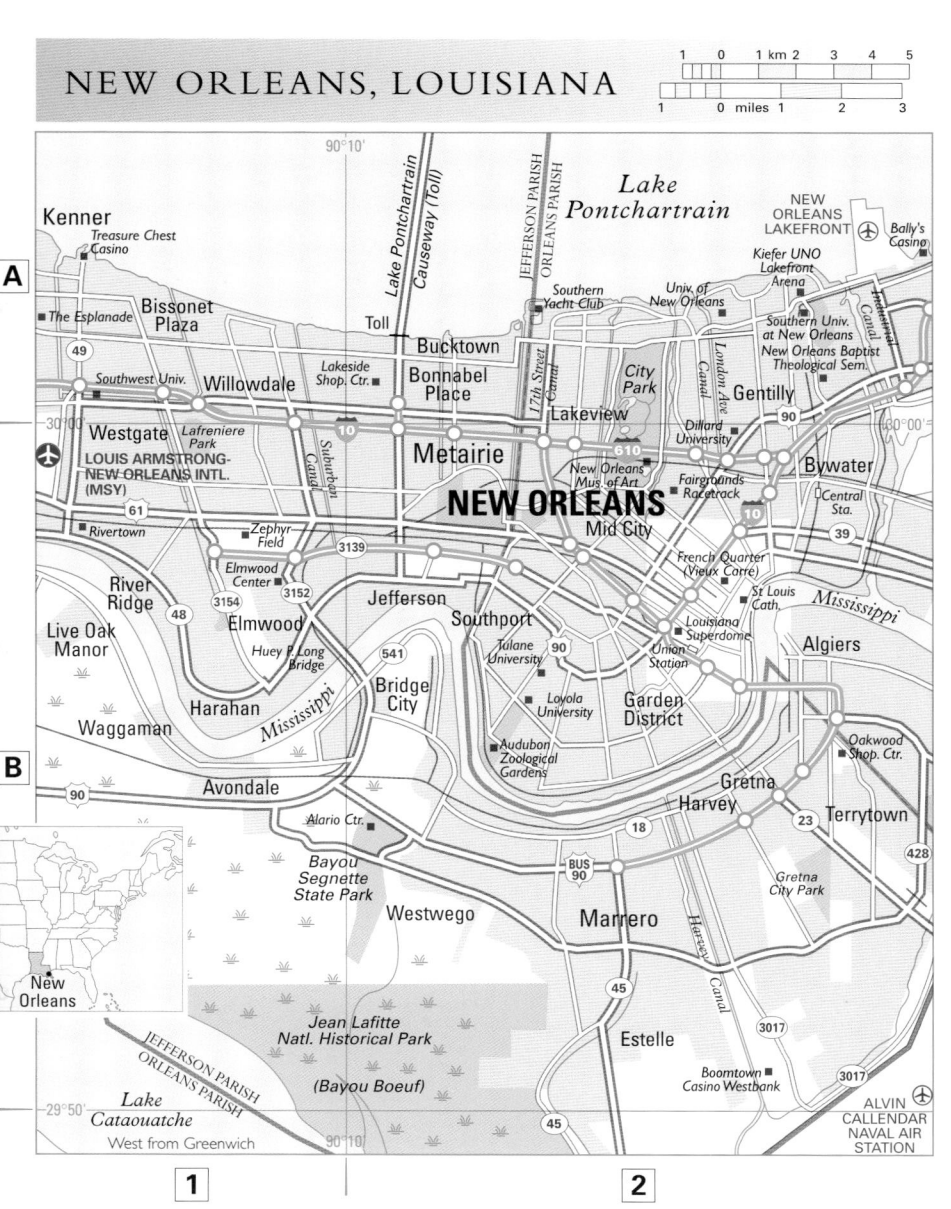

CENTRAL NEW ORLEANS

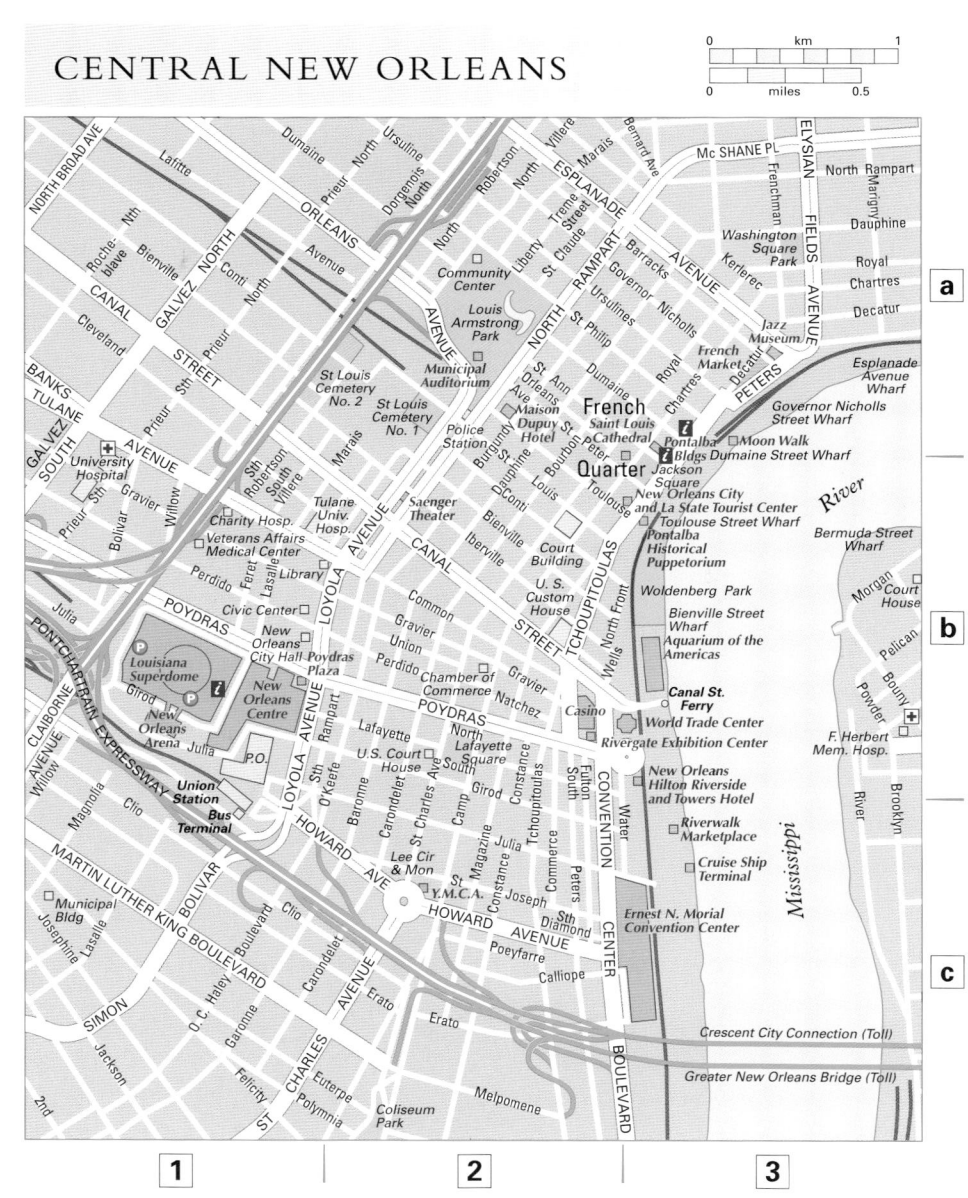

Interstate route numbers ⑰ U.S. route numbers ④¹⁷ State route numbers

NEW YORK, NEW YORK

Interstate route numbers
U.S. route numbers
State route numbers

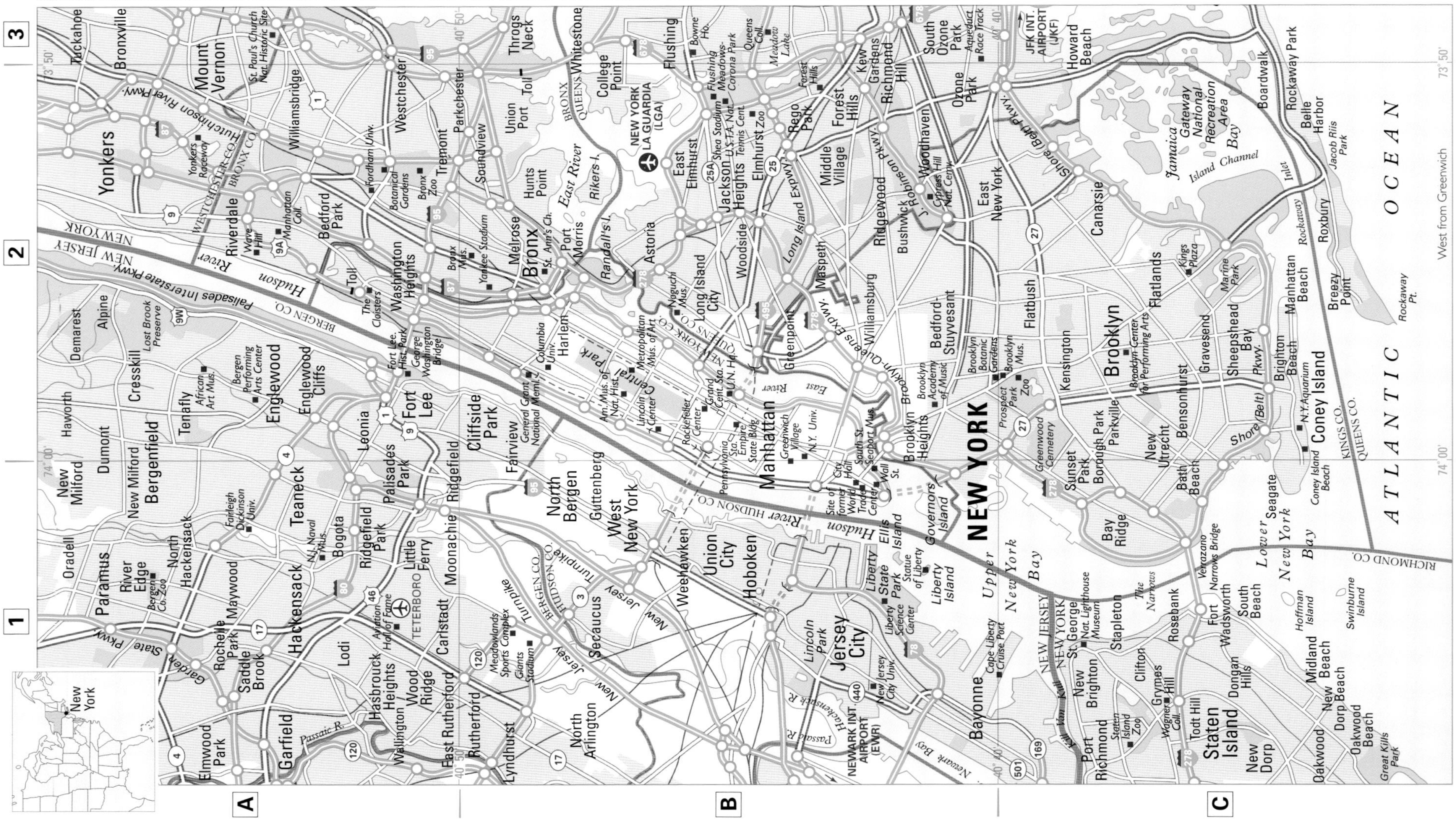

New York

CENTRAL NEW YORK

ATLANTIC OCEAN

West from Greenwich

Yonkers · Mount Vernon · Bronxville · Tuckahoe · Westchester · Throgs Neck · College Point · Whitestone · Flushing · Bowne Pk. · South Ozone Park · JFK INT. AIRPORT (JFK) · Howard Beach · Rockaway Park · Belle Harbor

Riverdale · Washington Heights · Bronx · Melrose · Hunts Point · Astoria · Long Island City · Woodside · Elmhurst · Rego Park · Forest Hills · Kew Gardens · Richmond Hill · Ozone Park · Boardwalk

Englewood · Fort Lee · Harlem · Manhattan · Greenpoint · Williamsburg · Bushwick · Ridgewood · Woodhaven · Jamaica Bay · Gateway National Recreation Area · Rockaway Inlet

Paramus · Hackensack · Teaneck · Cliffside Park · Fairview · North Bergen · West New York · Weehawken · Union City · Hoboken · **NEW YORK** · Brooklyn · Bedford-Stuyvesant · Flatbush · Kensington · Gravesend · Sheepshead Bay · Brighton Beach · Manhattan Beach · Coney Island · Breezy Point

Garfield · Elmwood Park · Lodi · Rutherford · Secaucus · Jersey City · Bayonne · Staten Island · Lower New York Bay

Lyndhurst · North Arlington · NEWARK INT. AIRPORT (EWR) · New Brighton · St. George · Stapleton · Clifton · Dongan Hills · New Dorp · Oakwood · Great Kills Park

ATLANTIC OCEAN · Upper New York Bay · Verrazano-Narrows Bridge · The Narrows · Richmond Co.

Hudson River · East River · New Jersey · New York Co. · Bronx Co. · Queens Co. · Kings Co.

Harlem · Upper West Side · Upper East Side · Central Park · Midtown · Manhattan · Chelsea · Greenwich Village · East Village · Lower East Side · Soho · Little Italy · China Town · Tribeca · Lower Manhattan · Brooklyn Heights

Queens · Long Island City · Greenpoint · Williamsburg · Fort Greene · Brooklyn

West New York · Weehawken · Hoboken · Union City · Guttenberg

Hudson River · East River · Roosevelt Island

United Nations Headquarters · Grand Central Sta. · Empire State Building · Penn Sta. · Port Authority Bus Terminal · Times Square · Rockefeller Center · Lincoln Center for the Performing Arts · American Mus. of Natural History · Metropolitan Mus. of Art · Guggenheim Museum · MoMA · St. Patrick's Cathedral · Carnegie Hall · Flatiron Building · Chrysler Bldg. · Flatiron Building · N.Y. State Bldg. · N.Y. Public Library

World Financial Center · World Trade Center (Site of former) · Ground Zero · Battery Park · Ellis & Statue of Liberty · Staten Island Ferry · Brooklyn-Battery Tunnel · Governors Island

Intrepid Air & Space Museum · Chelsea Piers Sports and Entertainment Complex · Jacob Javits Convention Center · Passenger Ship Terminal

BROADWAY · FIFTH AVE · PARK AVE · MADISON AVE · LEXINGTON AVE · THIRD AVE · SECOND AVE · FIRST AVE · TWELFTH AVENUE · ELEVENTH AVE · WEST STREET · CANAL STREET · HOUSTON ST · BOWERY · DELANCEY ST · FLATBUSH AVE · ADAMS ST · BROOKLYN-QUEENS EXPRESSWAY · BROOKLYN BRIDGE · MANHATTAN BRIDGE · WILLIAMSBURG BRIDGE · QUEENSBORO BRIDGE · FRANKLIN D. ROOSEVELT DRIVE · JOE DIMAGGIO HIGHWAY · HENRY HUDSON PARKWAY · RIVERSIDE DRIVE · J.F. KENNEDY BOULEVARD · HILLSIDE RD · BERGENLINE AVE · Holland Tunnel · Lincoln Tunnel · Queens-Midtown Tunnel

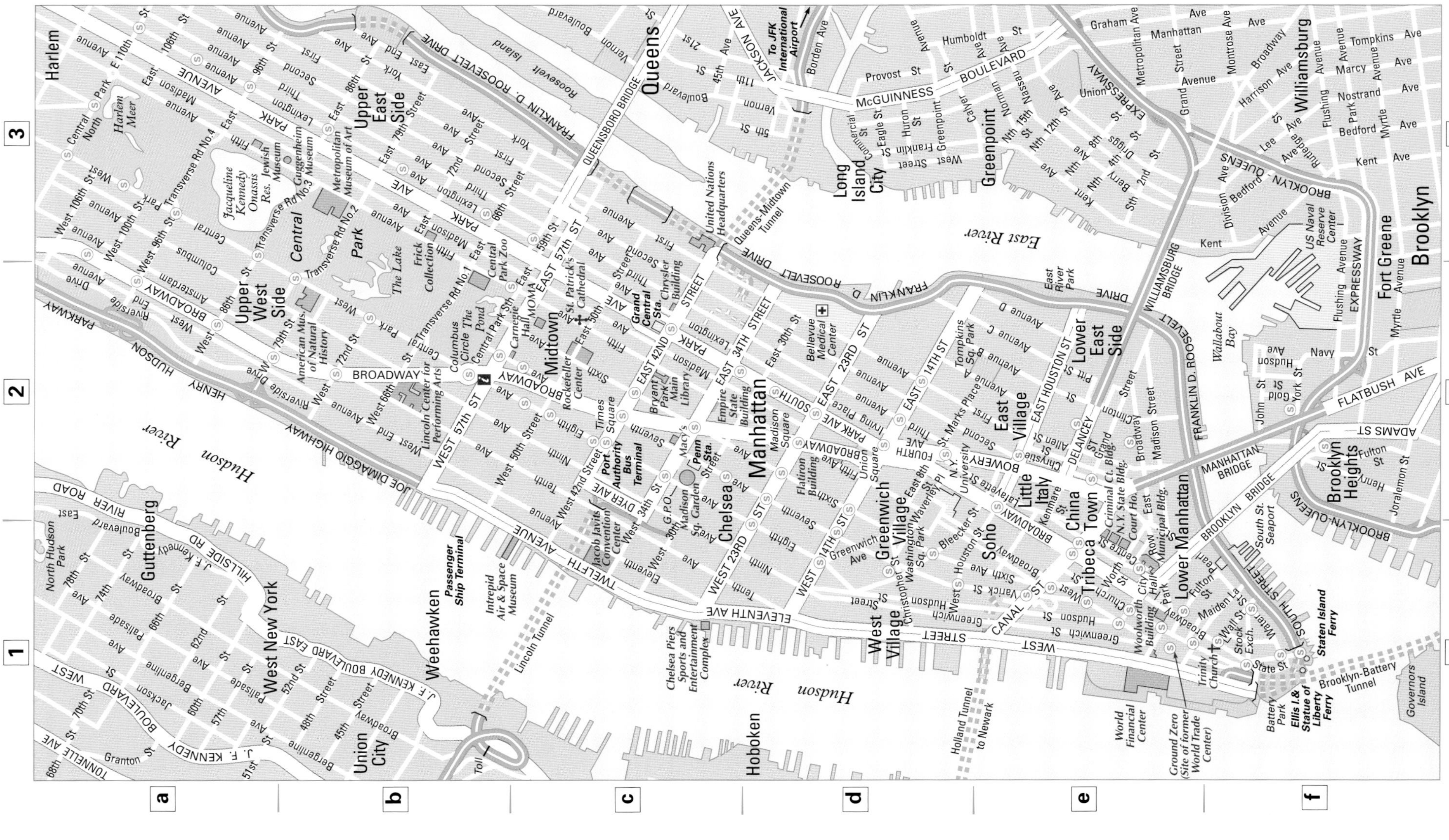

COPYRIGHT PHILIP'S

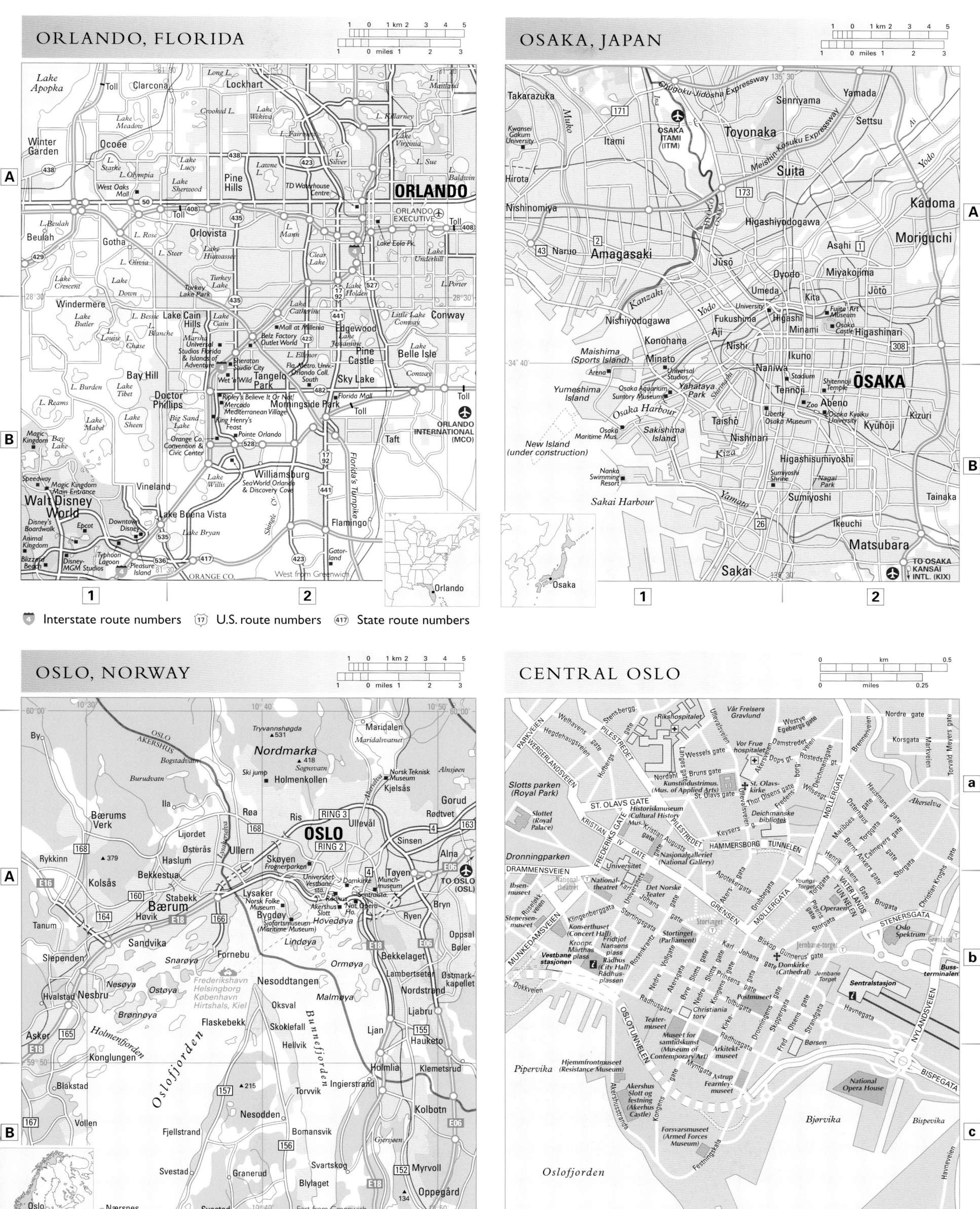

PARIS, FRANCE

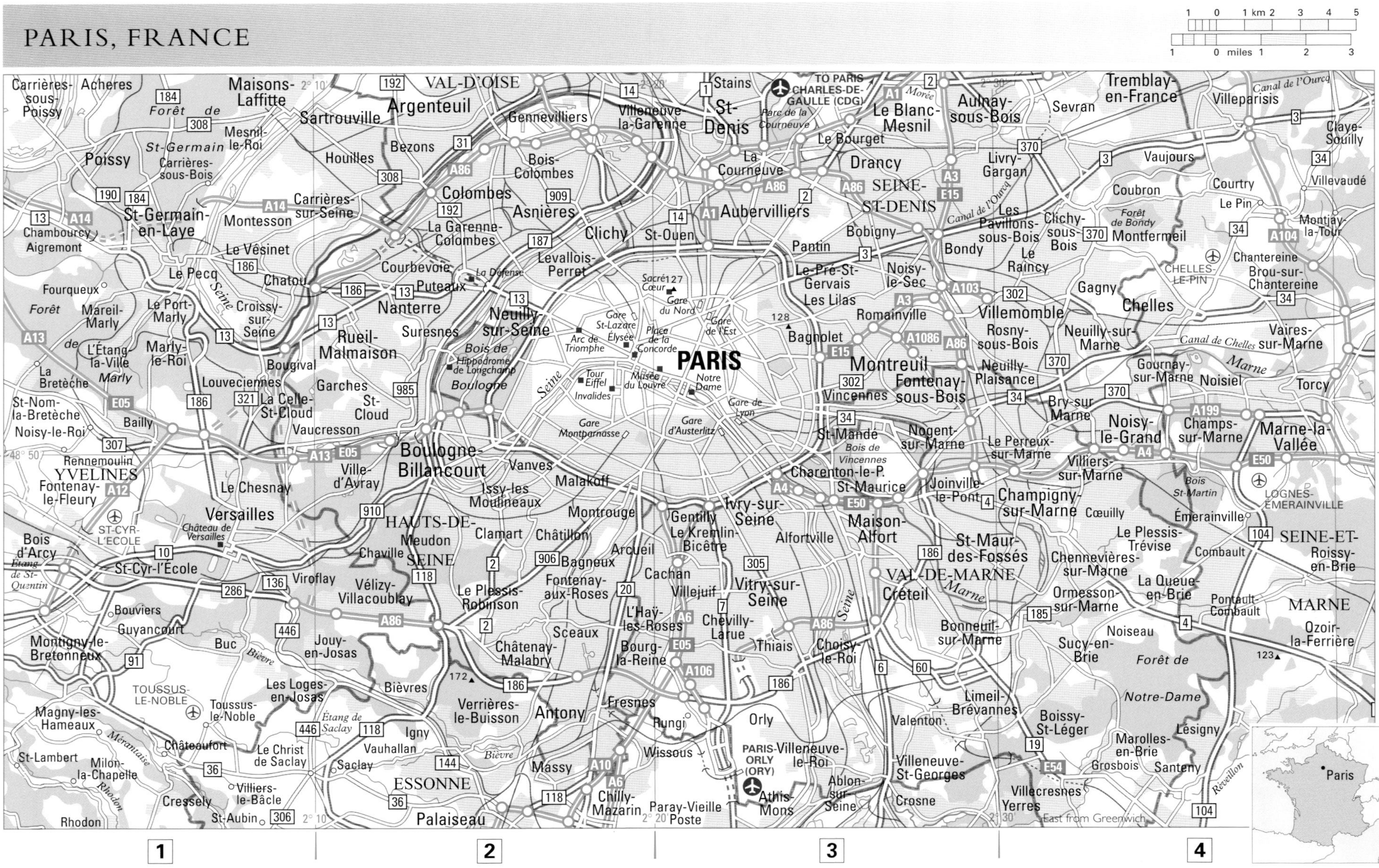

1 0 1 km 2 3 4 5
1 0 miles 1 2 3

Carrières-sous-Poissy · Achères · Maisons-Laffitte · VAL-D'OISE · Argenteuil · Gennevilliers · Villeneuve-la-Garenne · Stains · St-Denis · TO PARIS CHARLES-DE-GAULLE (CDG) · Le Blanc-Mesnil · Aulnay-sous-Bois · Tremblay-en-France · Villeparisis · Canal de l'Ourcq · Claye-Souilly

Sartrouville · Bezons · Houilles · Bois-Colombes · La Courneuve · Le Bourget · Drancy · Livry-Gargan · Sevran · Vaujours · Courtry · Le Pin · Villevaudé

Forêt de St-Germain · Colombes · Asnières · SEINE-ST-DENIS · Bobigny · Les Pavillons-sous-Bois · Clichy-sous-Bois · Montfermeil · Coubron · CHELLES-LE-PIN · Chantereine · Brou-sur-Chantereine

Poissy · St-Germain-en-Laye · Montesson · La Garenne-Colombes · Levallois-Perret · Aubervilliers · St-Ouen · Pantin · Le Pré-St-Gervais · Noisy-le-Sec · Bondy · Gagny · Chelles · Vaires-sur-Marne

Chambourcy · Aigremont · Le Vésinet · Chatou · Courbevoie · Puteaux · La Défense · Gare St-Lazare · Gare du Nord · Gare de l'Est · Romainville · Les Lilas · Le Raincy · Neuilly-sur-Marne · Torcy · Noisiel

Fourqueux · Le Pecq · Nanterre · Suresnes · Neuilly-sur-Seine · Sacré Cœur · Place de la Concorde · Bagnolet · Villemomble · Rosny-sous-Bois · Gournay-sur-Marne · Noisiel

Mareil-Marly · Le Port-Marly · Croissy-sur-Seine · Rueil-Malmaison · Bois de Boulogne · Arc de Triomphe · PARIS · Notre Dame · Montreuil · Fontenay-sous-Bois · Neuilly-Plaisance · Bry-sur-Marne · Noisy-le-Grand · Champs-sur-Marne · Marne-la-Vallée

L'Étang-la-Ville · Marly-le-Roi · Louveciennes · Bougival · Garches · St-Cloud · Tour Eiffel · Musée du Louvre · Invalides · Vincennes · Gare de Lyon · St-Mandé · Nogent-sur-Marne · Le Perreux-sur-Marne · Villiers-sur-Marne

L'Étang de Marly · La Celle-St-Cloud · Vaucresson · Hippodrome de Longchamp · Boulogne · Seine · Gare Montparnasse · Gare d'Austerlitz · Bois de Vincennes · Charenton-le-P. · St-Maurice · Joinville-le-Pont · Champigny-sur-Marne · Émerainville

St-Nom-la-Bretèche · Noisy-le-Roi · Bailly · Rennemoulin · YVELINES · Fontenay-le-Fleury · Versailles · Le Chesnay · Boulogne-Billancourt · Ville-d'Avray · Vanves · Malakoff · Gentilly · Le Kremlin-Bicêtre · Ivry-sur-Seine · Maisons-Alfort · Le Plessis-Trévise · SEINE-ET-MARNE · Roissy-en-Brie

Bois d'Arcy · Étang de St-Quentin · ST-CYR-L'ÉCOLE · Château de Versailles · HAUTS-DE-SEINE · Meudon · Clamart · Châtillon · Montrouge · Arcueil · Alfortville · Chennevières-sur-Marne · La Queue-en-Brie · Combault · MARNE

Montigny-le-Bretonneux · St-Cyr-l'École · Viroflay · Vélizy-Villacoublay · Chaville · Issy-les-Moulineaux · Bagneux · Cachan · Villejuif · Vitry-sur-Seine · Créteil · VAL-DE-MARNE · Ormesson-sur-Marne · Ozoir-la-Ferrière

Bouviers · Guyancourt · Buc · Bièvre · Le Plessis-Robinson · Fontenay-aux-Roses · Sceaux · Châtenay-Malabry · L'Haÿ-les-Roses · Chevilly-Larue · Bourg-la-Reine · Thiais · Choisy-le-Roi · Bonneuil-sur-Marne · Noiseau · Sucy-en-Brie

Magny-les-Hameaux · TOUSSUS-LE-NOBLE · Toussus-le-Noble · Jouy-en-Josas · Les Loges-en-Josas · Bièvres · Verrières-le-Buisson · Antony · Fresnes · Rungis · Orly · Valenton · Limeil-Brévannes · Boissy-St-Léger · Forêt de Notre-Dame · Lésigny

St-Lambert · Milon-la-Chapelle · Châteaufort · Le Christ de Saclay · Igny · Vauhallan · Saclay · Massy · Wissous · PARIS-VILLENEUVE-ORLY (ORY) · Athis-Mons · Ablon-sur-Seine · Villeneuve-St-Georges · Villecresnes · Marolles-en-Brie · Grosbois · Santeny

Cressely · Rhodon · St-Aubin · ESSONNE · Palaiseau · Chilly-Mazarin · Paray-Vieille-Poste · Crosne · Yerres · East from Greenwich

Paris

CENTRAL PARIS

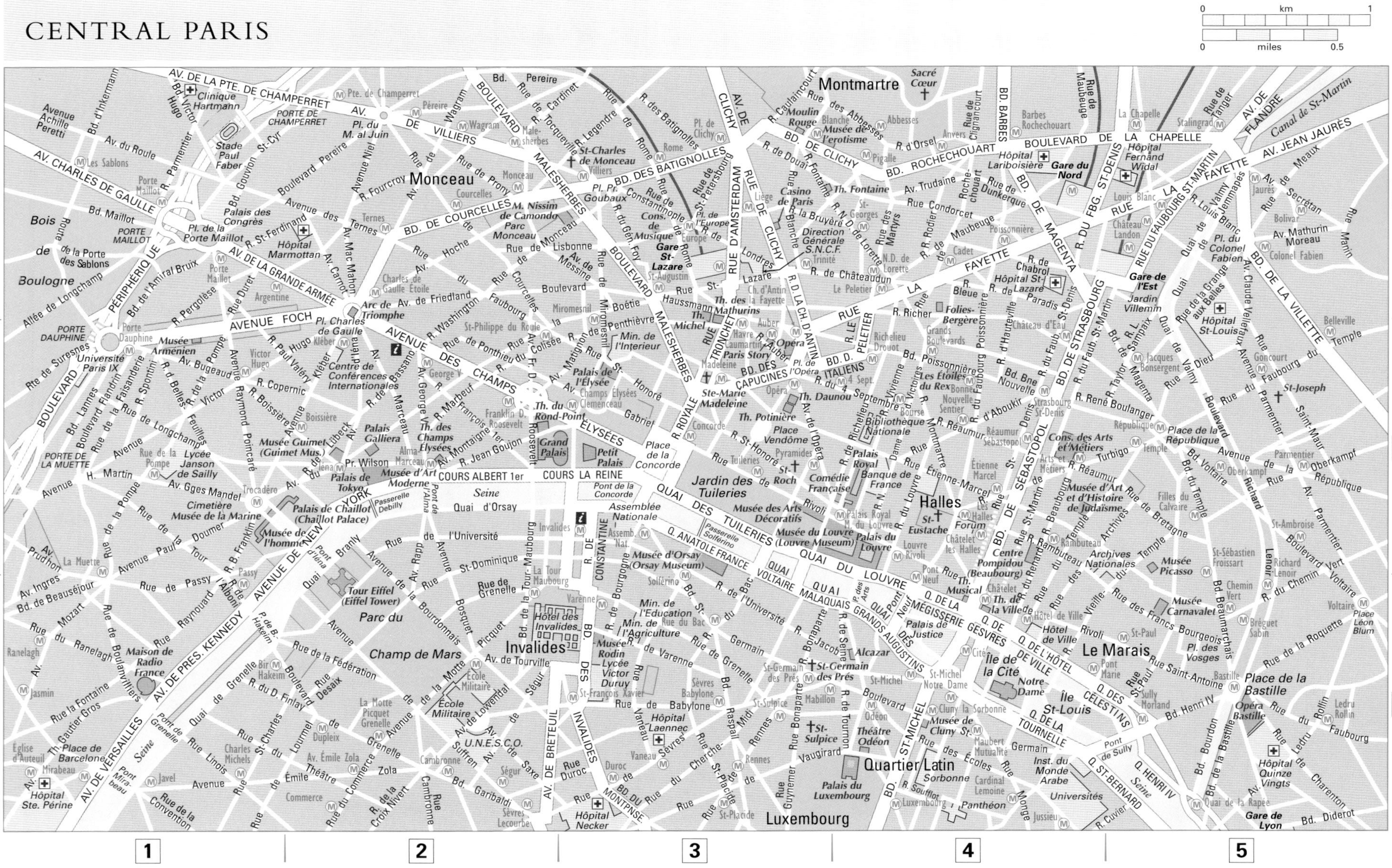

0 km 1
0 miles 0.5

AV. DE LA PTE. DE CHAMPERRET · Montmartre · Sacré Cœur · BD. DE LA CHAPELLE · Canal de St-Martin · AV. DE FLANDRE

Clinique Hartmann · Moulin Rouge · Musée de l'Érotisme · BD. ROCHECHOUART · Gare du Nord · Hôpital Lariboisière · AV. JEAN JAURÈS

Stade Paul Faber · St-Charles de Monceau · Casino de Paris · BD. DE CLICHY · RUE LA FAYETTE · Hôpital St-Louis

Bois de Boulogne · Palais des Congrès · Monceau · Parc Monceau · Th. Fontaine · Direction Générale S.N.C.F. · N.D. de Lorette · Gare de l'Est · Pl. du Colonel Fabien

PORTE MAILLOT · Hôpital Marmottan · BD. DE COURCELLES · M. Nissim de Camondo · Hôpital St-Lazare · RUE DU FBG. ST-MARTIN · Av. Claude Vellefaux

Bois de Boulogne · PORTE MAILLOT · AV. DE LA GRANDE ARMÉE · Arc de Triomphe · RUE DE CHÂTEAUDUN · Folies-Bergère · BD. DE STRASBOURG · BD. DE LA VILLETTE

PÉRIPHÉRIQUE · Av. de la Grande Armée · Pl. Charles de Gaulle · BD. HAUSSMANN · Opéra · Bibliothèque Nationale · Cons. des Arts et Métiers

PORTE DAUPHINE · AVENUE FOCH · Arc de Triomphe · Pl. Charles de Gaulle Étoile · Th. Mathurins · Th. Daunou · St-Joseph

Musée Arménien · Th. des Champs Élysées · Palais de l'Élysée · Ste-Marie Madeleine · Pl. Vendôme · Comédie Française · Th. de la Ville · Musée d'Art et d'Histoire du Judaïsme

Musée Galliera · Palais de Tokyo · AVENUE DES CHAMPS ÉLYSÉES · Grand Palais · Place de la Concorde · Palais Royal · Banque de France · Place de la République

Palais de Chaillot (Chaillot Palace) · Musée d'Art Moderne · Petit Palais · Jardin des Tuileries · Musée du Louvre (Louvre Museum) · Forum · Centre Pompidou (Beaubourg) · Archives Nationales · Musée Picasso

Musée de la Marine · Musée de l'Homme · COURS ALBERT 1er · COURS LA REINE · Musée des Arts Décoratifs · Châtelet · Hôtel de Ville · Musée Carnavalet

Seine · Quai d'Orsay · Assemblée Nationale · Musée d'Orsay (Orsay Museum) · QUAI DU LOUVRE · Palais de Justice · Île de la Cité · Le Marais

Tour Eiffel (Eiffel Tower) · Maison de Radio France · Parc du Champ de Mars · Invalides · Min. de l'Agriculture · St-Germain des Prés · Notre Dame · Île St-Louis · Place de la Bastille

Hôtel des Invalides · Musée Rodin · Hôpital Laennec · Cluny la Sorbonne · Musée de Cluny · St-Louis · Opéra Bastille

École Militaire · U.N.E.S.C.O. · Hôpital Necker · St-Sulpice · Théâtre Odéon · Quartier Latin · Sorbonne · Inst. du Monde Arabe

Hôpital Ste-Périne · Palais du Luxembourg · Luxembourg · Panthéon · Universités · Hôpital Quinze Vingts · Gare de Lyon

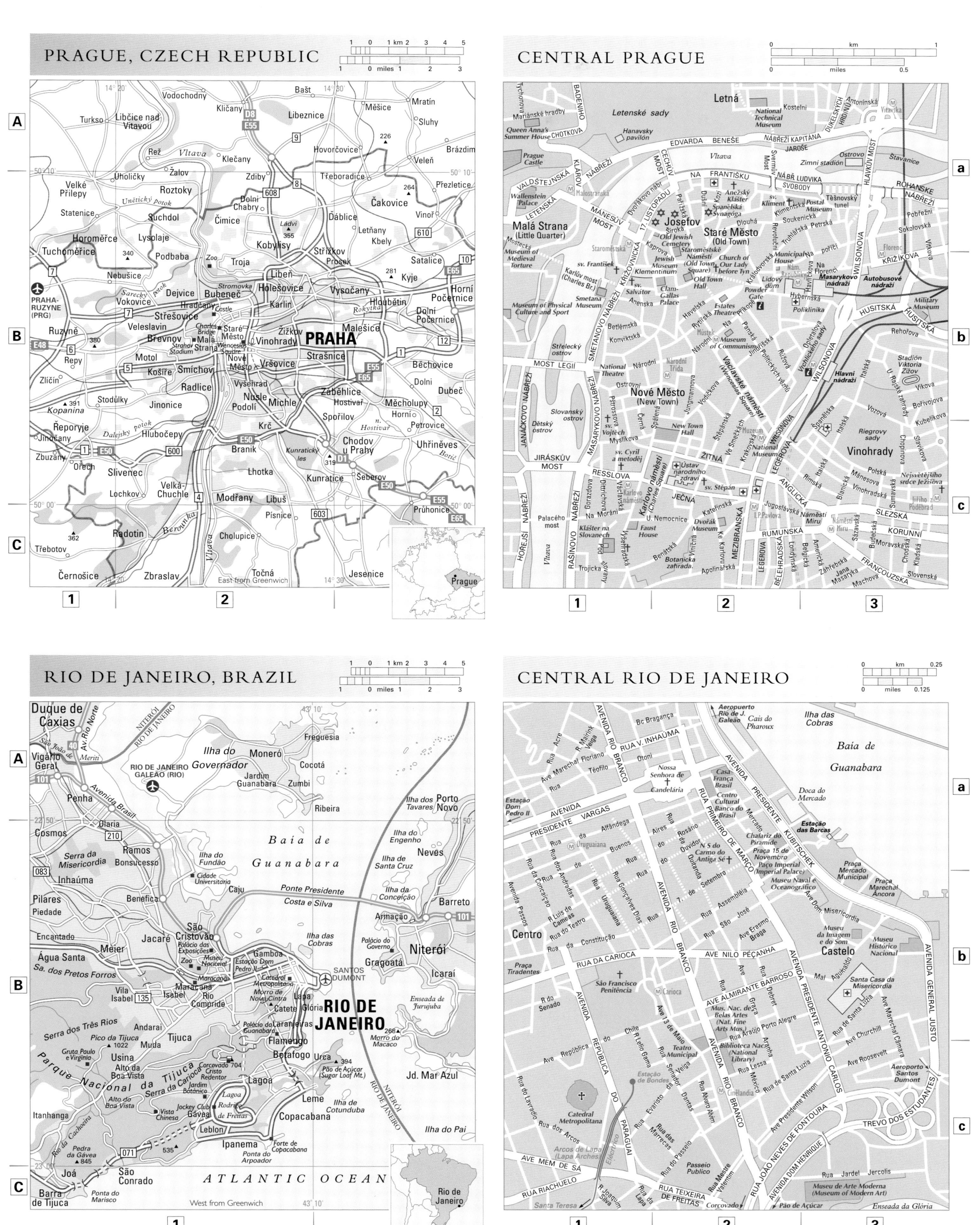

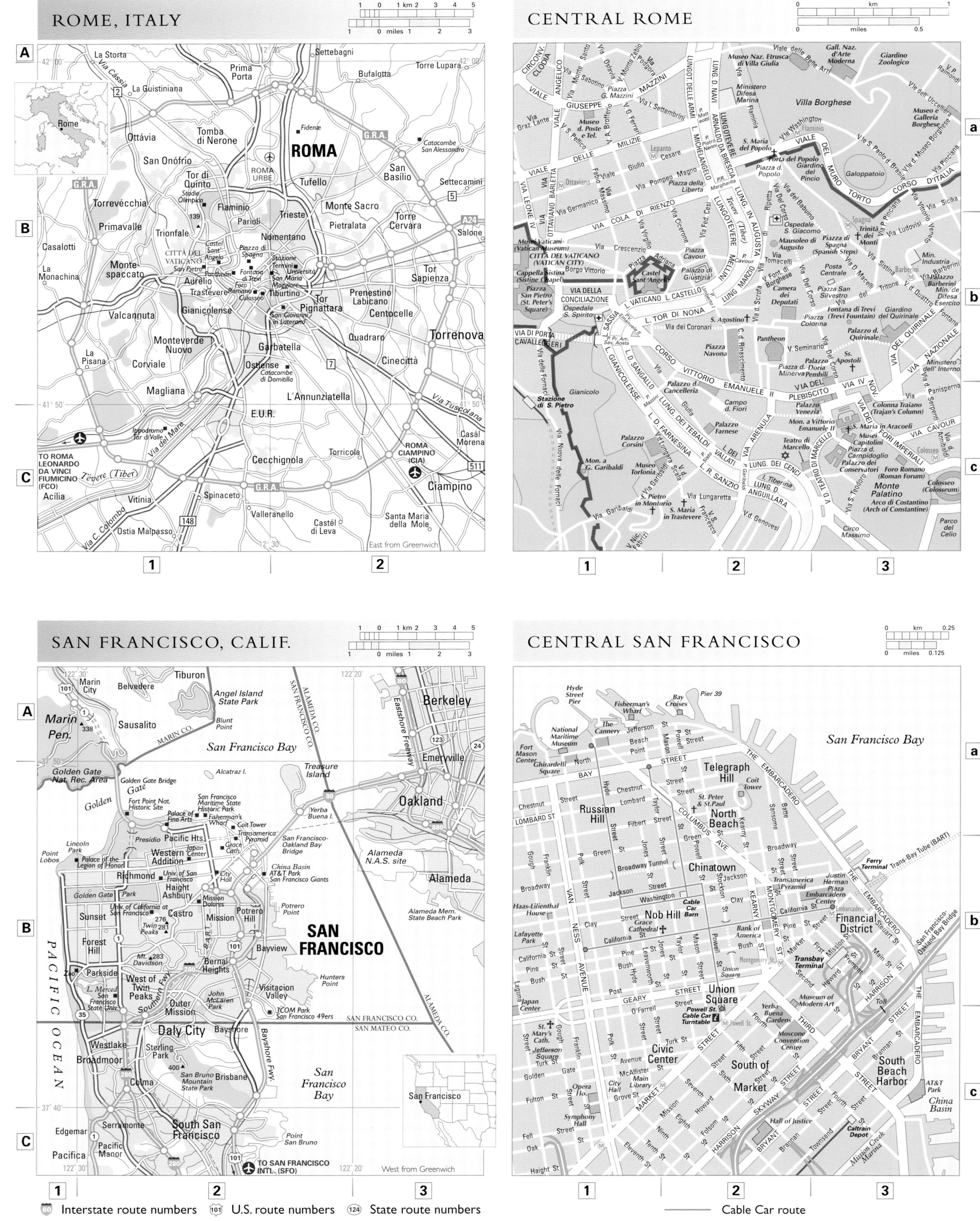

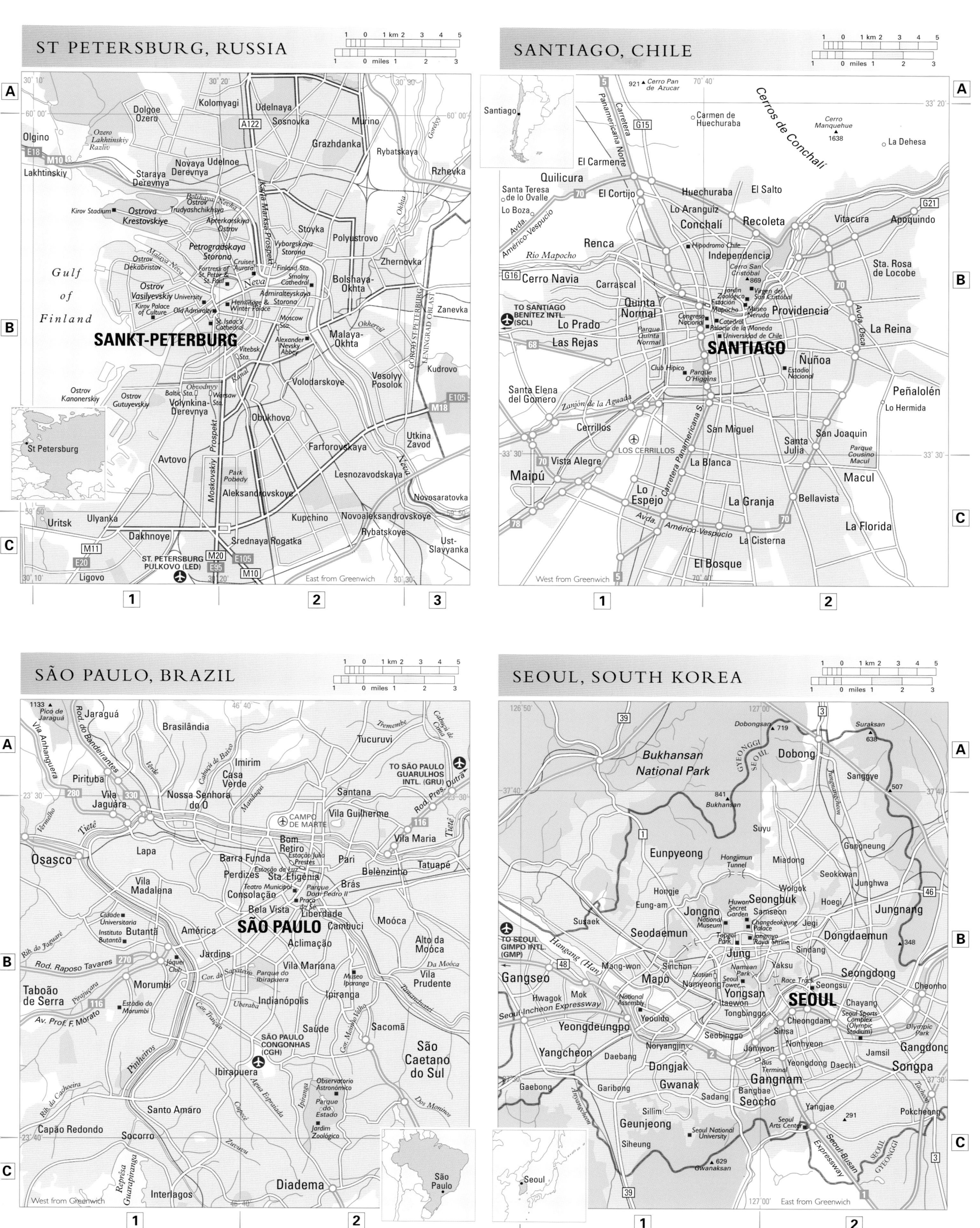

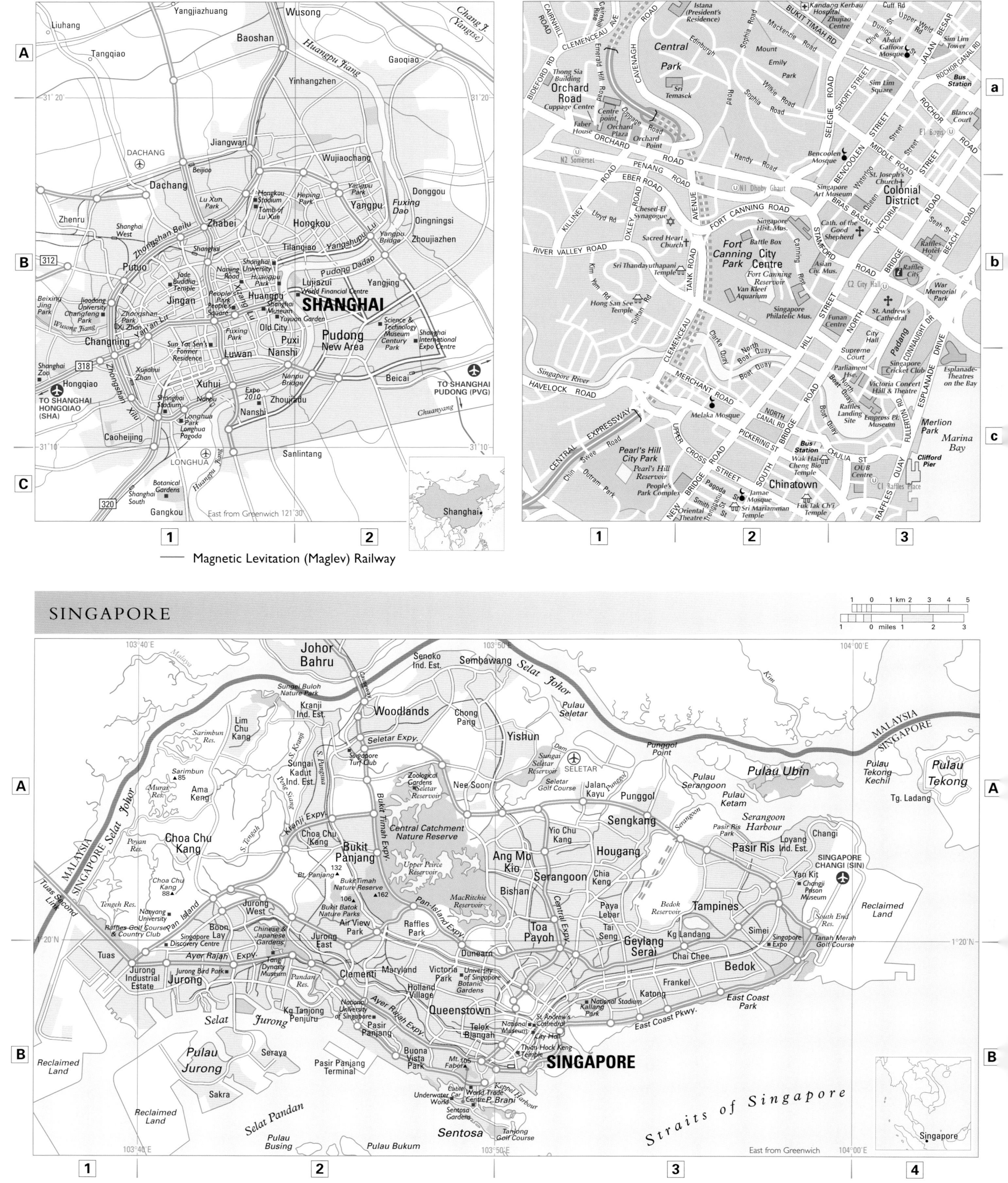

SHANGHAI, CHINA

CENTRAL SINGAPORE

— Magnetic Levitation (Maglev) Railway

SINGAPORE

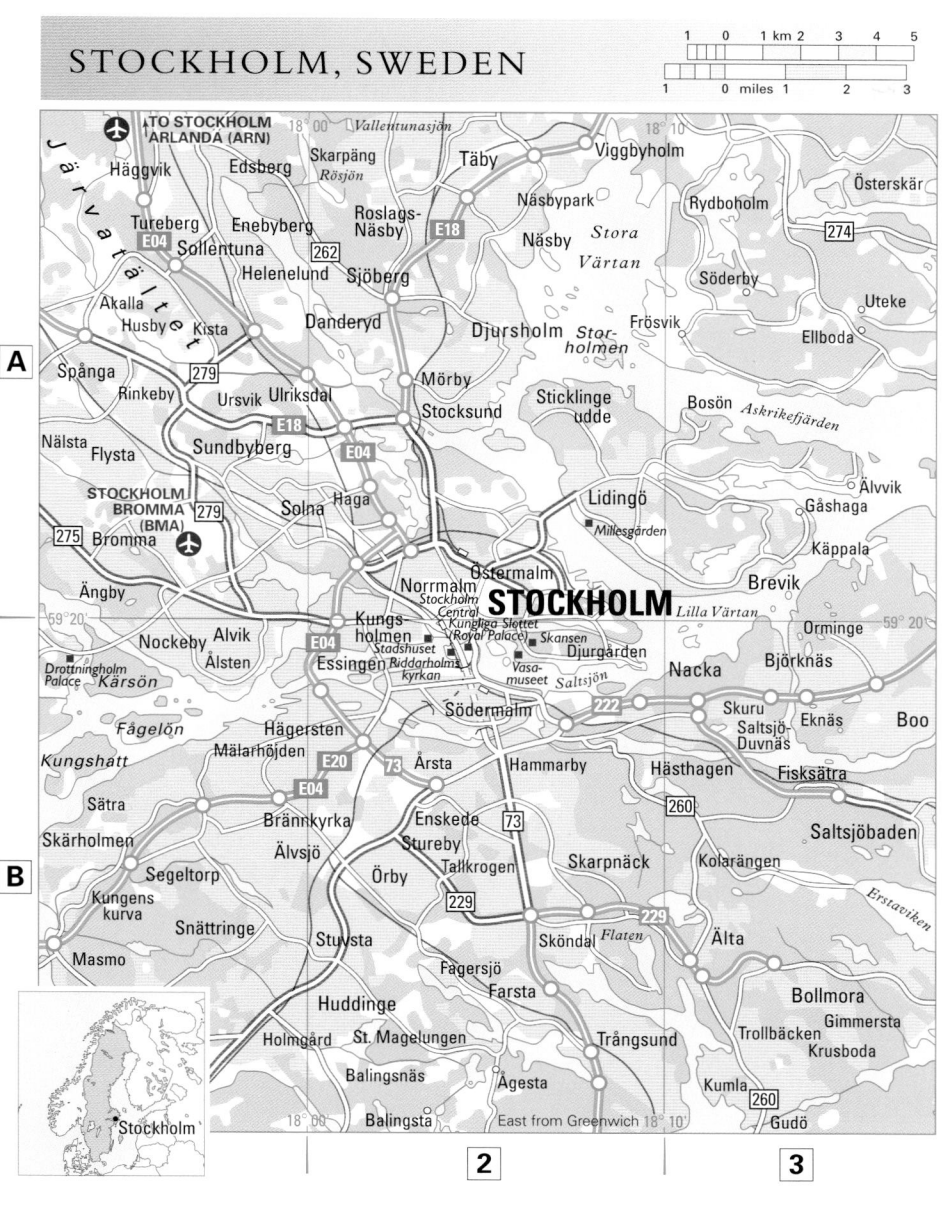

STOCKHOLM, SWEDEN

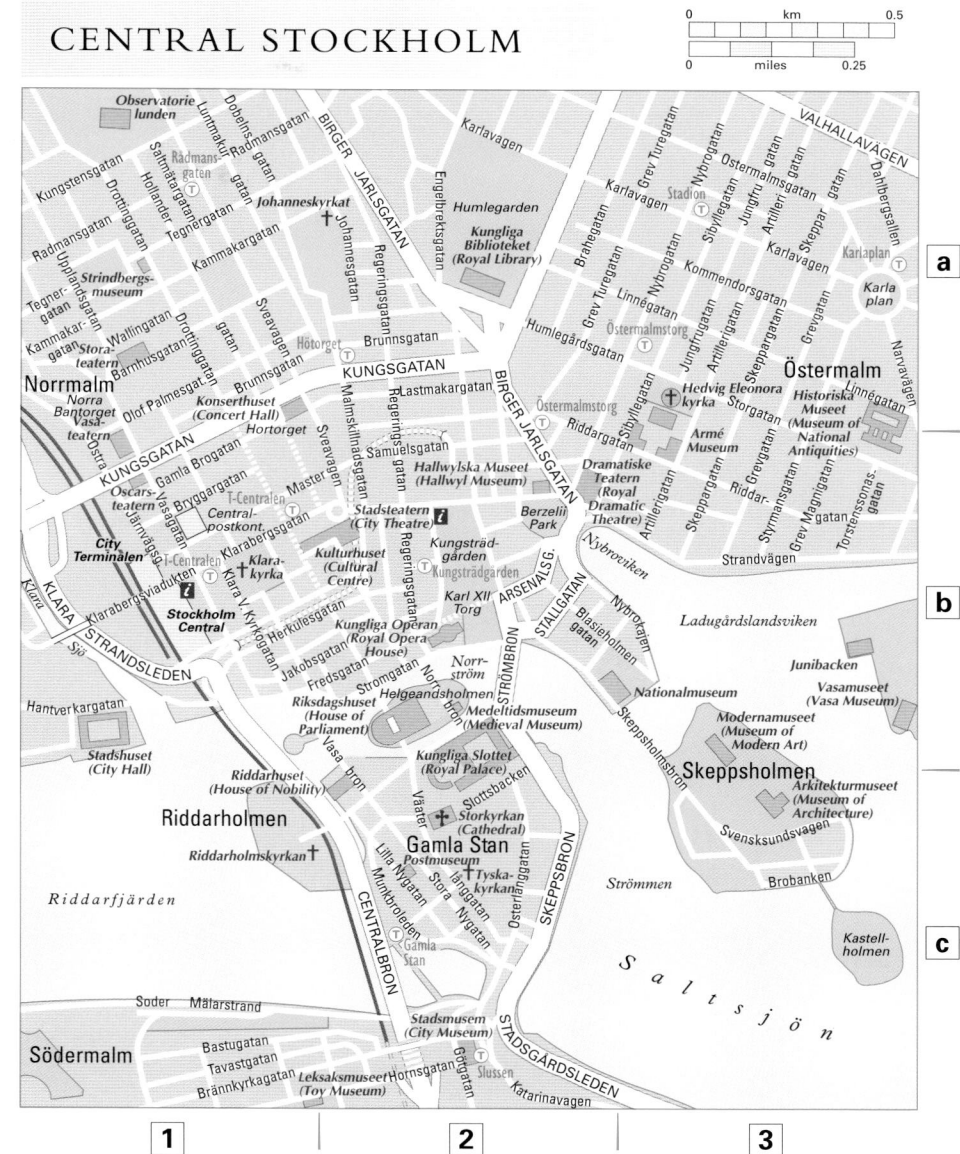

CENTRAL STOCKHOLM

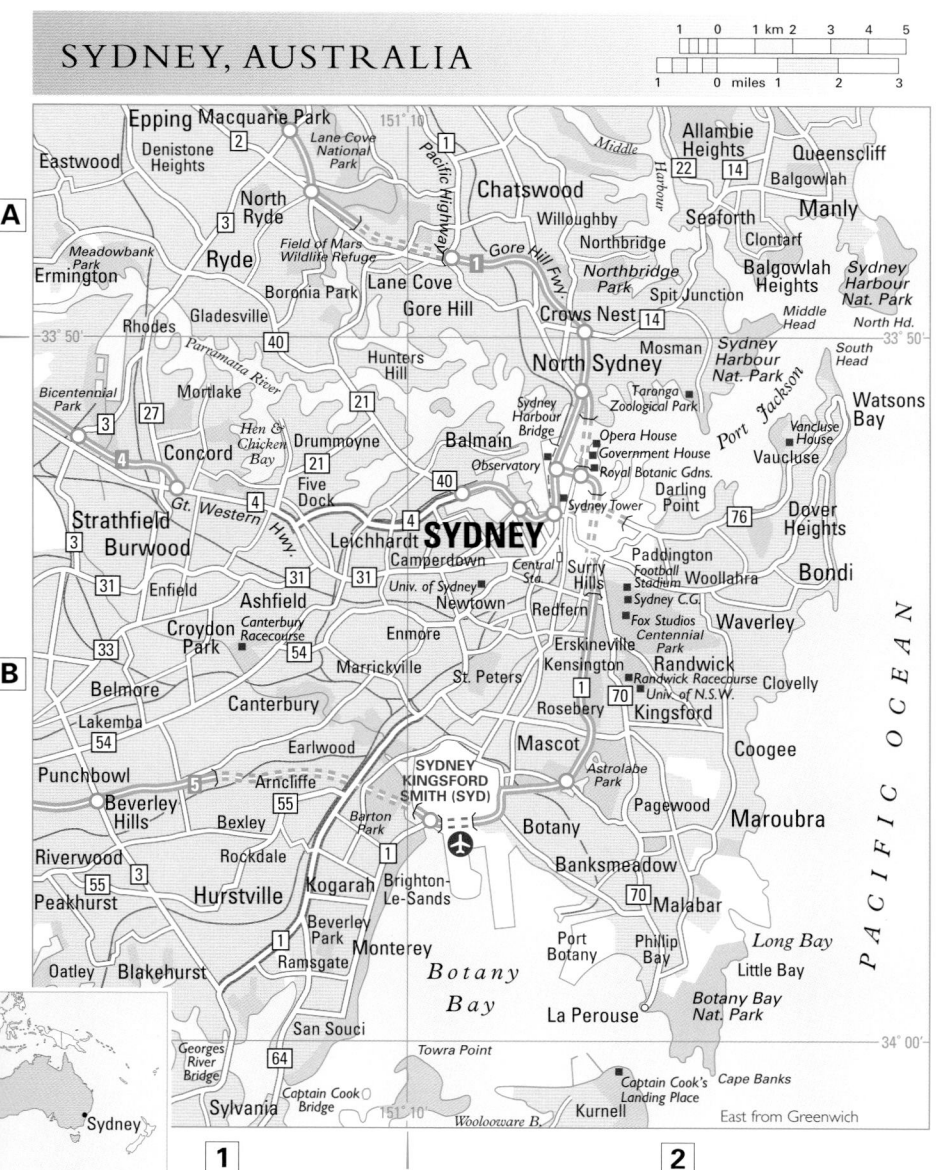

SYDNEY, AUSTRALIA

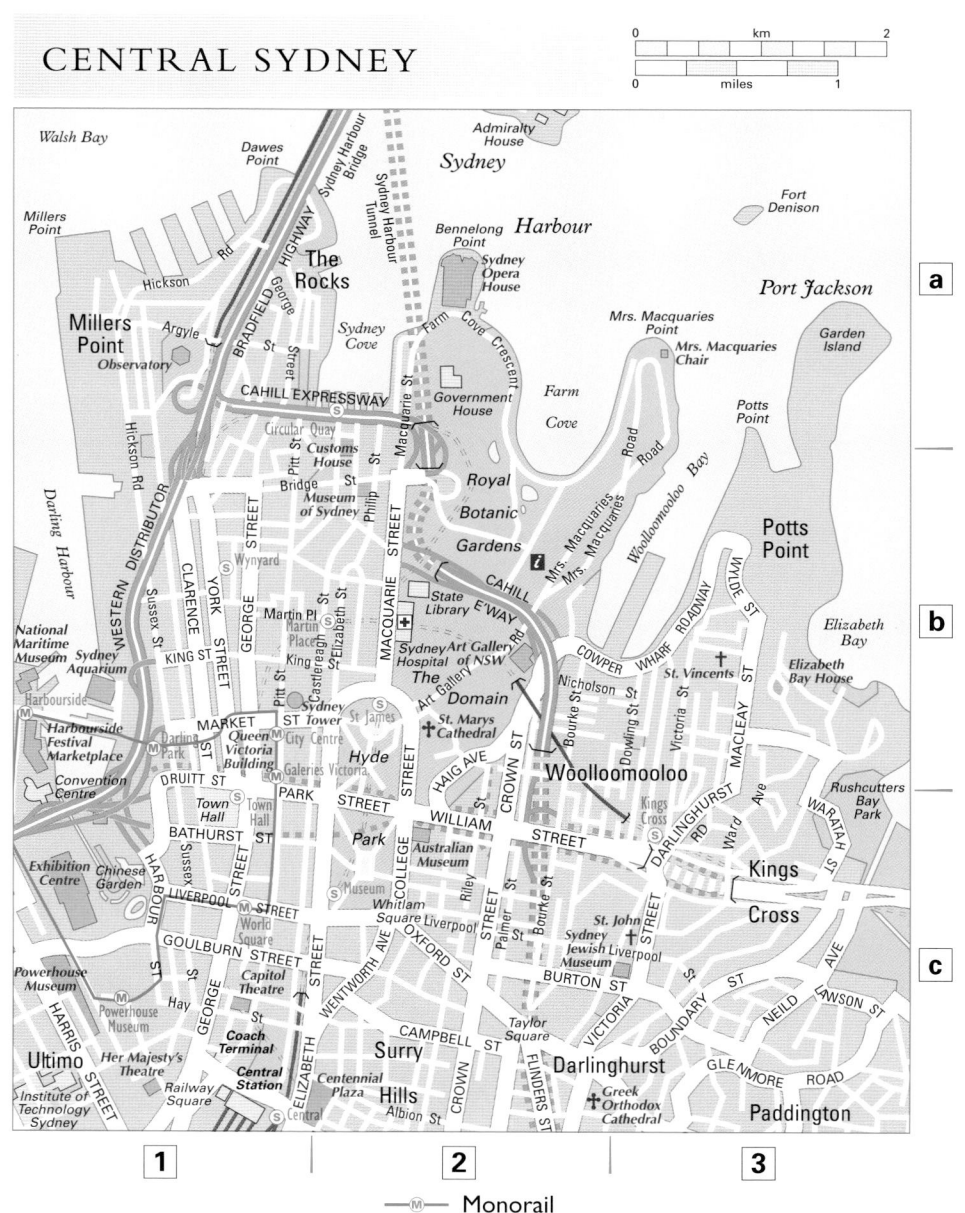

CENTRAL SYDNEY

—Ⓜ— Monorail

TOKYO, JAPAN

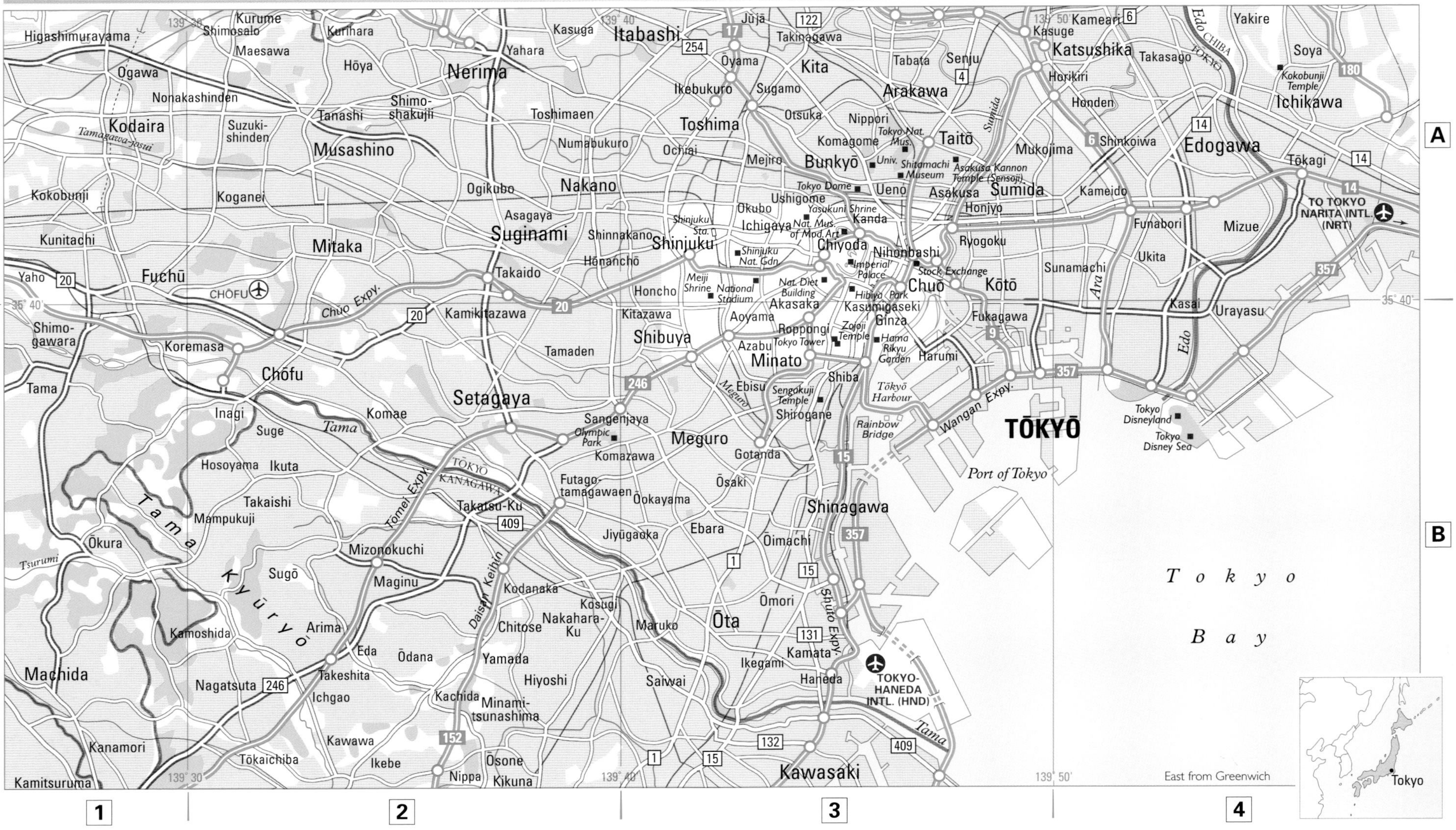

1 0 1 km 2 3 4 5
1 0 miles 1 2 3

Higashimurayama · Shimosato · Kurume · Kunihara · Kasuga · Jūjō · Takinogawa · Kasuge · Kameari · Yakire · Soya
Ogawa · Maesawa · Yahara · Oyama · Itabashi · Kita · Tabata · Senju · Horikiri · Katsushika · Takasago · Kokobunji Temple · Ichikawa
Hōya · Nonakashinden · Shimo-shakuji · Ikebukuro · Sugamo · Otsuka · Nippori · Honden · Shinkoiwa · Edogawa · Tōkagi
Kodaira · Suzuki-shinden · Tanashi · Numabukuro · Toshimaen · Toshima · Komagome · Tokyo Nat. Mus. · Taitō · Mukojima
Kokobunji · Koganei · Ogikubo · Nakano · Asagaya · Mejiro · Bunkyō · Univ. · Shitamachi Museum · Asakusa Kannon Temple (Sensōji) · Sumida · Kameido

A

Kunitachi · Mitaka · Shinnakano · Shinjuku · Ichigaya · Kanda · Nihonbashi · Ryogoku · Funabori · Mizue
Yaho · Fuchū · Takaido · Honancho · Honcho · Chiyoda · Imperial Palace · Stock Exchange · Chūō · Kōtō · Sunamachi · Ukita · TO TOKYO NARITA INTL (NRT)
Kamikitazawa · Kitazawa · Akasaka · Hibiya Park · Ginza · Fukagawa
Chōfu · Koremasa · Tamaden · Shibuya · Aoyama · Roppongi · Zojoji Temple · Kasumigaseki · Harumi · Kasai · Urayasu
Inagi · Komae · Setagaya · Sangenjaya · Meguro · Minato · Azabu · Tokyo Tower · Shiba · Hama Rikyū Garden

B

Hosoyama · Ikuta · Takaishi · Komazawa · Ebisu · Shirogane · Rainbow Bridge · Tōkyō Harbour · Port of Tokyo · Tokyo Disneyland · Tokyo Disney Sea
Mampukuji · Sugō · Maginu · Mizonokuchi · Jiyūgaoka · Gotanda · Ōsaki · TŌKYŌ
Ōkura · Arima · Kodanaka · Ōokayama · Shinagawa · Tokyo Bay
Machida · Kamoshida · Eda · Ōdana · Chitose · Nakahara-Ku · Ōimachi · Ebara
Nagatsuta · Takeshita · Yamada · Kosugi · Maruko · Ōta · Omori · Ikegami · Kamata
Kanamori · Ichgao · Minami-tsunashima · Hiyoshi · Saiwai · Haneda · TOKYO-HANEDA INTL (HND)
Kamitsuruma · Tōkaichiba · Ikebe · Osone · Nippa · Kikuna · Kawasaki

East from Greenwich · Tokyo

1 2 3 4

CENTRAL TOKYO

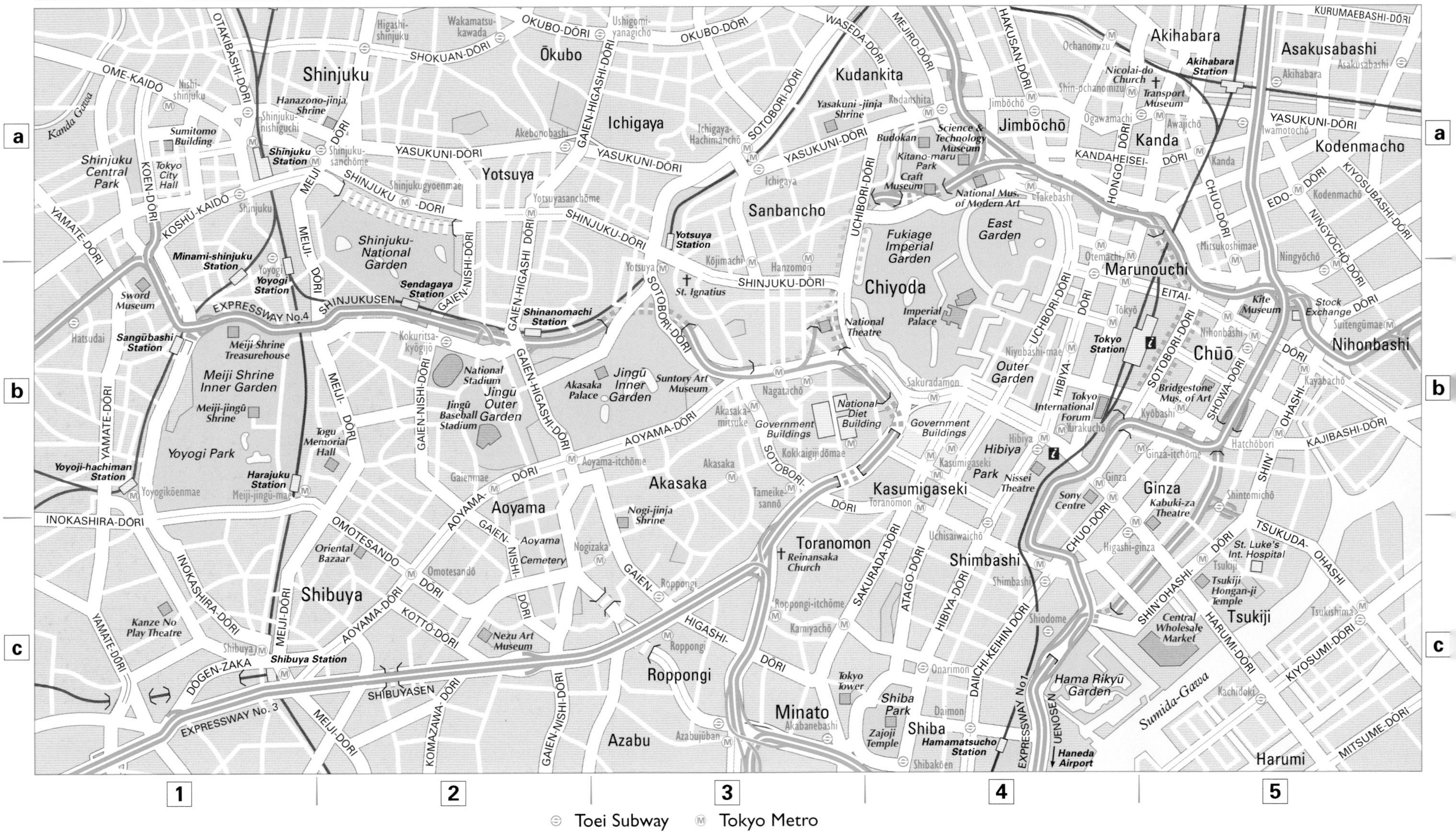

0 km 1
0 miles 0.5

Shinjuku · Ōkubo · Kudankita · Akihabara · Asakusabashi
Hanazono-jinja Shrine · Yasukuni-jinja Shrine · Nicolai-do Church · Akihabara Station
Sumitomo Building · Tokyo City Hall · Shinjuku Station · Ichigaya · Jimbōchō · Kanda · Kodenmacho
Shinjuku Central Park · Shinjuku-sanchome · Yotsuya · Sanbancho · National Mus. of Modern Art · Marunouchi

a

Minami-shinjuku Station · Yoyogi Station · Shinjuku-National Garden · Sendagaya Station · Yotsuya Station · Fukiage Imperial Garden · East Garden · Chiyoda
Sangūbashi Station · Meiji Shrine Treasurehouse · Shinanomachi Station · St. Ignatius · National Theatre · Imperial Palace · Tokyo Station · Chūō · Nihonbashi
Meiji Shrine Inner Garden · National Stadium · Jingū Inner Garden · Suntory Art Museum · Akasaka Palace · Outer Garden · Bridgestone Mus. of Art · Kite Museum · Stock Exchange

b

Yoyogi Park · Togu Memorial Hall · Jingū Baseball Stadium · Nagatachō · Nissei Theatre · Hibiya · Tokyo International Forum · Kyobashi
Yoyogi-hachiman Station · Meiji-jingū-mae · Harajuku Station · Aoyama · Akasaka · Government Buildings · National Diet Building · Kasumigaseki · Ginza
Kanze No Play Theatre · Oriental Bazaar · Nogi-jinja Shrine · Toranomon · Sony Centre · Kabuki-za Theatre
Shibuya · Omotesando · Aoyama Cemetery · Reinansaka Church · Shimbashi · St. Luke's Int. Hospital

c

Shibuya Station · Nezu Art Museum · Roppongi · Tokyo Tower · Shiba Park · Zajoji Temple · Hamamatsucho Station · Central Wholesale Market · Tsukiji · Tsukiji Hongan-ji Temple
Minato · Azabu · Shiba · Haneda Airport · Hama Rikyū Garden · Harumi

1 2 3 4 5

◎ Toei Subway   Ⓜ Tokyo Metro

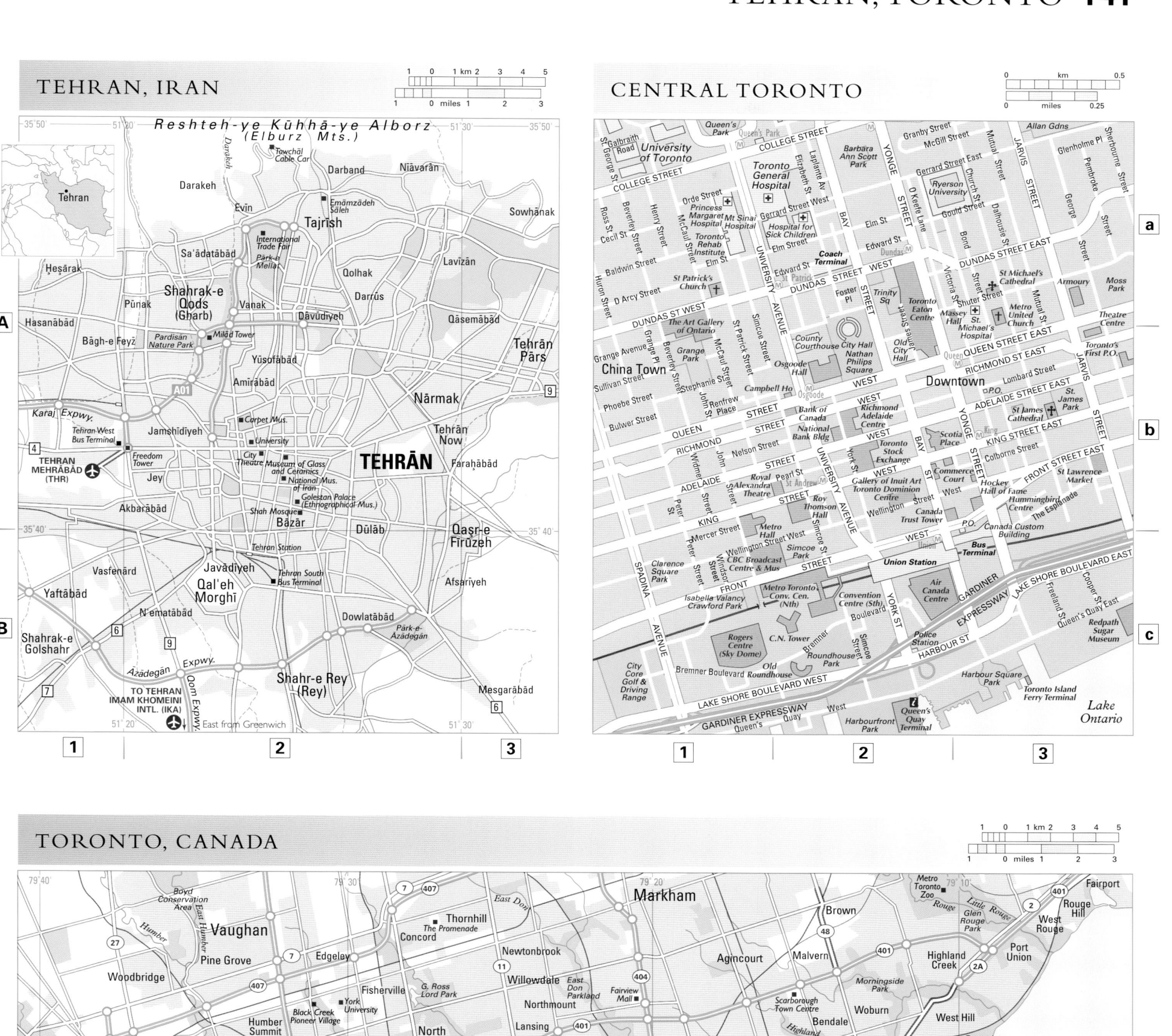

TEHRAN, IRAN

Reshteh-ye Kūhhā-ye Alborz
(Elburz Mts.)

Darakeh
Towchāl Cable Car
Darband
Niāvarān
Darakeh
Emāmzādeh Sāleh
Sowhānak
Sa'ādatābād
Ēvin
Tajrīsh
Lavīzān
International Trade Fair
Pārk-e Mellat
Qolhak
Shahrak-e Qods (Gharb)
Darrūs
Vanak
Dāvūdiyeh
Qāsemābād
Pūnak
Milād Tower
Hesārak
Bāgh-e Feyż
Pardisan Nature Park
Yūsofābād
Amīrābād
Tehrān Pārs
Hasanābād
Jamshīdiyeh
Karaj Expwy.
Tehrān West Bus Terminal
Tehrān Now
TEHRAN MEHRĀBĀD (THR)
Freedom Tower
University
Carpet Mus.
Narmak
Tehrān Now
Farahābād
City Theatre Museum of Glass and Ceramics
Jey
National Mus. of Iran
TEHRĀN
Akbarābād
Golestan Palace (Ethnographical Mus.)
Shah Mosque
Bāzār
Dūlāb
Qasr-e Firūzeh
Tehran Station
Vasfenārd
Javādiyeh
Tehrān South Bus Terminal
Afsariyeh
Yaftābād
Qal'eh Morghī
N'ematābād
Dowlatābād
Pārk-e Azādegān
Shahrak-e Golshahr
Āzādegān Expwy.
Mesgarābād
Qom Expwy.
Shahr-e Rey (Rey)
TO TEHRAN IMAM KHOMEINI INTL. (IKA)
East from Greenwich

CENTRAL TORONTO

Queen's Park
Galbraith Road
University of Toronto
COLLEGE STREET
St George St
Granby Street
McGill Street
Allan Gdns
Barbara Ann Scott Park
Glenholme St
Sherbourne Street
Pembroke St
COLLEGE STREET
Toronto General Hospital
Gerrard Street East
Ryerson University
Gould Street
YONGE
Mutual St
Church St
Dalhousie St
Jarvis Street
George St
Orde Street
Princess Margaret Hospital
Mt Sinai Hospital
Gerrard Street West
Hospital for Sick Children
Elm St
DUNDAS STREET EAST
St Michael's Cathedral
Armoury
Moss Park
Ross Street
Henry Street
McCaul Street
Toronto Rehab Institute
Elm St
Coach Terminal
Edward St
Baldwin Street
Cecil St
D'Arcy Street
St Patrick's Church
DUNDAS STREET WEST
Foster Pl
Trinity Sq
Toronto Eaton Centre
Victoria St
Shuter Street
Metro United Church
St Michael's Hospital
Theatre Centre
Huron Street
The Art Gallery of Ontario
Grange Avenue
McCaul Street
Simcoe Street
County Courthouse City Hall
Nathan Philips Square
Old City Hall
QUEEN STREET EAST
Toronto's First P.O.
China Town
Grange Park
Osgoode Hall
RICHMOND ST EAST
Lombard Street
P.O.
Phoebe Street
Campbell Ho
Bank of Canada
WEST
Richmond Adelaide Centre
ADELAIDE STREET EAST
St James Cathedral
St James Park
Bulwer Street
QUEEN
STREET
National Bank Bldg
Scotia Plaza
King St
Colborne Street
Toronto Stock Exchange
KING STREET EAST
RICHMOND
Wideman St
Nelson Street
UNIVERSITY
York St
FRONT STREET EAST
ADELAIDE
Royal Alexandra Theatre
Pearl St
Gallery of Inuit Art
Commerce Court
Hockey Hall of Fame
St Lawrence Market
Peter St
St Andrew
Roy Thomson Hall
Toronto Dominion Centre
Canada Trust Tower
Hummingbird Centre
The Esplanade
Mercer Street
KING
AVENUE
Wellington
WEST
P.O.
Canada Custom Building
Metro Hall
Wellington Street West
Simcoe Park
WEST
Union
Bus Terminal
Clarence Square Park
CBC Broadcast Centre & Mus
STREET
Air Canada Centre
SPADINA
Windsor St
Simcoe St
Union Station
YORK ST
GARDINER
Isabella Valancy Crawford Park
Metro Toronto Conv. Cen. (Nth)
Convention Centre (Sth)
LAKE SHORE BOULEVARD EAST
Queen's Quay East
Rogers Centre (Sky Dome)
C.N. Tower
Bremner Roundhouse Pk
Police Station
EXPRESSWAY
Redpath Sugar Museum
AVENUE
City Core Golf & Driving Range
Bremner Boulevard
Old Roundhouse
HARBOUR ST
Harbour Square Park
GARDINER EXPRESSWAY
Queen's Quay
Harbourfront Park
Queen's Quay Terminal
Toronto Island Ferry Terminal
Lake Ontario

TORONTO, CANADA

Boyd Conservation Area
East Humber
Markham
Metro Toronto Zoo
Rouge
Little Rouge
Fairport
Rouge Hill
Vaughan
Thornhill
The Promenade
Concord
East Don
Brown
West Rouge
Woodbridge
Pine Grove
Edgeley
Newtonbrook
Glen Rouge Park
Port Union
Fisherville
G. Ross Lord Park
Willowdale
East Don Parkland
Agincourt
Malvern
Highland Creek
Humber Summit
Black Creek Pioneer Village
York University
Northmount
Fairview Mall
Morningside Park
Beaumonte Heights
Blackwood Creek
North York
Lansing
Scarborough Town Centre
Woburn
Thistletown
Northwood Park
Armour Heights
York Mills
Wexford
Bendale
West Hill
Claireville Reservoir
Humberwood Park
Kipling Heights
Downsview
Don Mills
Scarborough
Cliffside
Eastpoint Park
Woodbine Centre
Rexdale
Humberlea
Lawrence Heights
York Univ
Wilket Creek Park
Malton
Humber
Weston
Yorkdale Shopping Centre
Forest Hill
Sunnybrook Health Science Centre
Ontario Science Centre
Thorncliffe
Danforth
Bluffers Park
Woodbine Race Track
Cedarvale Park
Leaside
Scarborough Bluffs
TORONTO LESTER B. PEARSON INTL. (YYZ)
Humber Valley Village
Mount Dennis
York
Dentonia Park
East York
Birch Cliff
Hanlon
Casa Loma
Riverdale Park
Kew Gardens
Etobicoke
Lambton Mills
Swansea
Royal Ontario Museum
Ashbridge's Bay Park
Islington
High Park
University of Toronto
Parliament Buildings
Kingsway
Old City Hall
Union Sta.
Gardiner Expy.
Markland Wood
Humber Bay
C.N. Tower & Rogers Centre
Old Fort York
TORONTO
Burnhamthorpe
Parkdale
Summerville
Exhibition Place
TORONTO CITY CENTRE (ISLAND)
Tommy Thompson Park
Elizabeth
Humber Bay Park
Ontario Place
Island Park
Toronto Harbour
Mimico
New Toronto
Toronto Islands
Gibraltar Point
LAKE ONTARIO
Mississauga
Square One
Dixie Mall
Samuel Smith Park
Cooksville
Long Branch
West from Greenwich
Toronto

427 Provincial route numbers

COPYRIGHT PHILIP'S

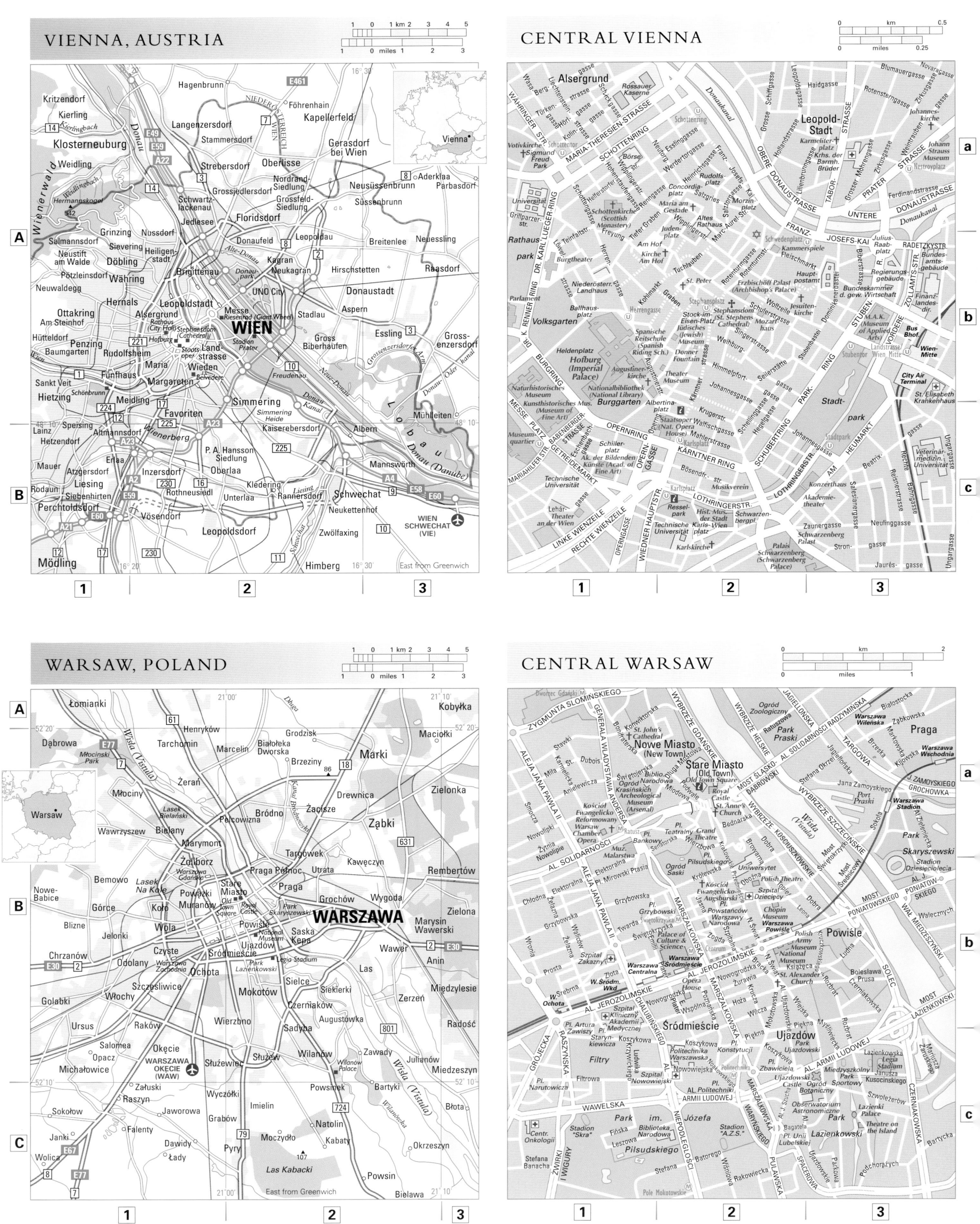

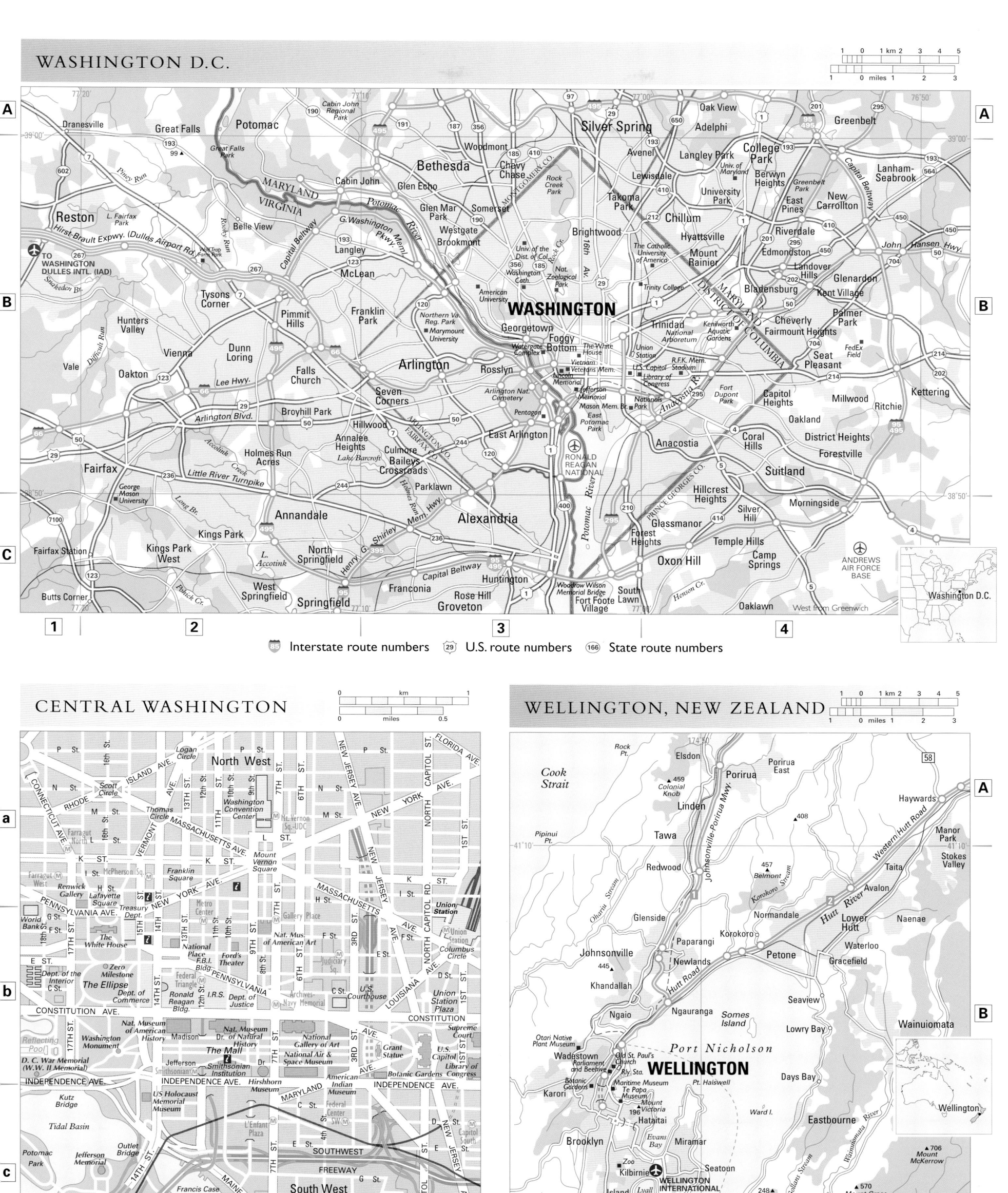

WASHINGTON D.C.

Dranesville, Potomac, Great Falls, Great Falls Park, Cabin John Regional Park, Woodmont, Silver Spring, Oak View, Adelphi, Greenbelt, Bethesda, Chevy Chase, Avenel, Langley Park, College Park, Berwyn Heights, Greenbelt Park, New Carrollton, Lanham-Seabrook, Reston, L. Fairfax Park, Glen Echo, Glen Mar Park, Somerset, Takoma Park, Univ. of Maryland, University Park, East Pines, Hirst-Brault Expwy. (Dulles Airport Rd.), Belle View, G. Washington Meml. Pkwy., Westgate, Brightwood, The Catholic University of America, Mount Rainier, Riverdale, Edmonston, Landover Hills, Glenarden, TO WASHINGTON DULLES INTL. (IAD), Langley, Brookmont, Univ. of the Dist. of Col., Nat. Zoological Park, Hyattsville, John Hansen Hwy., McLean, Chillum, Trinity College, Washington Cath., Tysons Corner, Pimmit Hills, Franklin Park, WASHINGTON, Bladensburg, Kent Village, Hunters Valley, Vienna, Dunn Loring, American University, Georgetown, Foggy Bottom, The White House, Trinidad, National Arboretum, Kenilworth Aquatic Gardens, Cheverly, Fairmount Heights, Seat Pleasant, Palmer Park, FedEx Field, Northern Va. Reg. Park, Marymount University, Watergate Complex, Vietnam Meml., Union Station, U.S. Capitol, R.F.K. Mem. Stadium, Vale, Oakton, Falls Church, Arlington, Rosslyn, Veterans Mem., Lincoln Memorial, Library of Congress, Fort Dupont Park, Kettering, Lee Hwy., Arlington Blvd., Seven Corners, Broyhill Park, Hillwood, Arlington Nat. Cemetery, Jefferson Memorial, Mason Mem. Br., Nationals Park, Fort Park, Capitol Heights, Capitol Hills, Oakland, District Heights, Millwood, Ritchie, Fairfax, Annalee Heights, Holmes Run Acres, Culmore, Baileys Crossroads, Pentagon, East Potomac Park, Anacostia, Coral Hills, Forestville, Little River Turnpike, Lake Barcroft, East Arlington, RONALD REAGAN NATIONAL, Suitland, George Mason University, Annandale, Parklawn, Alexandria, Hillcrest Heights, Morningside, Kings Park, North Springfield, L. Accotink, Huntington, Glassmanor, Silver Hill, Temple Hills, Camp Springs, Fairfax Station, Kings Park West, West Springfield, Franconia, Rose Hill, Forest Heights, Oxon Hill, ANDREWS AIR FORCE BASE, Butts Corner, Springfield, Groveton, Woodrow Wilson Memorial Bridge, Fort Foote Village, South Lawn, Oaklawn, West from Greenwich

MARYLAND, VIRGINIA, DISTRICT OF COLUMBIA, MONTGOMERY CO., PRINCE GEORGES CO.

Washington D.C. (inset)

🛩 Interstate route numbers   🛩 U.S. route numbers   🛩 State route numbers

CENTRAL WASHINGTON

Logan Circle, North West, FLORIDA AVE., Scott Circle, ISLAND AVE., RHODE ISLAND AVE., CONNECTICUT AVE., Thomas Circle, Washington Convention Center, Mt. Vernon Sq.-UDC, NEW JERSEY AVE., NORTH CAPITOL ST., VERMONT AVE., MASSACHUSETTS AVE., Farragut North, Mount Vernon Square, NEW YORK AVE., Farragut West, Renwick Gallery, Lafayette Square, Franklin Square, McPherson Sq., Metro Center, Gallery Place, Union Station, World Bank, Treasury Dept., National Place, F.B.I. Bldg., Nat. Mus. of American Art, Columbus Circle, The White House, Ford's Theater, PENNSYLVANIA AVE., Judiciary Sq., Union Station Plaza, Zero Milestone, The Ellipse, Dept. of Commerce, Federal Triangle, Ronald Reagan Bldg., I.R.S. Bldg., Dept. of Justice, Archives-Navy Memorial, U.S. Courthouse, Dept. of the Interior, Reflecting Pool, D.C. War Memorial (W.W. II Memorial), Washington Monument, Nat. Museum of American History, Madison Dr., National Museum of Natural History, The Mall, Smithsonian Institution, National Gallery of Art, National Air & Space Museum, Grant Statue, U.S. Capitol, Library of Congress, Supreme Court, CONSTITUTION AVE., INDEPENDENCE AVE., Hirshhorn Museum, American Indian Museum, Botanic Gardens, Kutz Bridge, Jefferson Memorial, US Holocaust Memorial Museum, L'Enfant Plaza, Federal Center SW, Tidal Basin, Potomac Park, Francis Case Meml. Bridge, SOUTHWEST FREEWAY, Capitol St., Potomac River, Jefferson Memorial, Outlet Bridge, South West, Navy Yard, East Potomac Park, Washington Channel, Waterfront, MAINE AVE.

WELLINGTON, NEW ZEALAND

Cook Strait, Rock Pt., Elsdon, Porirua, Porirua East, Colonial Knob 459, Linden, Haywards, Pipinui Pt., Tawa, 408, Western Hutt Road, Manor Park, Stokes Valley, Redwood, Belmont 457, Taita, Avalon, Glenside, Normandale, Naenae, Johnsonville, Paparangi, Newlands, Korokoro, Lower Hutt, Waterloo, Gracefield, 445, Khandallah, Petone, Ngaio, Ngauranga, Somes Island, Seaview, Brooklyn, Otari Native Plant Museum, Wadestown, Parliament and the Beehive, Old St. Paul's Church, Rly. Sta., WELLINGTON, Lowry Bay, Wainuiomata, Karori, Botanic Gardens, Maritime Museum, Te Papa Museum, Mount Victoria 196, Hataitai, Port Nicholson, Pt. Halswell, Ward I., Days Bay, Eastbourne, Mount McKerrow 706, Evans Bay, Miramar, Zoo, Kilbirnie, Seatoun, WELLINGTON INTERNATIONAL (WLG), Qwhiro Bay, Island Bay, Lyall Bay, Mount Cameron 248, Mount Grace 570, Picton, Pencarrow Head, East from Greenwich

Wellington (inset)

WORLD MAPS

1 2 3 4 5 6 7 8 9 10

A

B

A

C

D

E

F

G

H

80 160 140 120 100 80 60 40 20 0

Queen Elizabeth Islands Ellesmere I.
North Greenland Greenland
Magnetic Pole Sea
Pt. Barrow Banks I. Devon I.
Beaufort Parry Is. Jan Mayen
Sea Victoria I. Arctic Circle 3350 Denmark Str. Norwegian
Alaska Baffin Island Sea
Mt. McKinley Gr. Bear L. Hudson 2118 Iceland Faroe Is. 2469
6194 Str. Iceland
(Denali) Gr. Slave L. Hudson
Bering Str. Bay Davis Str. British 3342 North
Bering Gulf of Labrador Isles Sea
Sea Alaska L. Winnipeg Labrador C. Farewell B. of Mt. Blanc
Kodiak I. North Great Sea Biscay 4808
Queen America Lakes Laurentian Plateau Newfoundland Iberian Pic d'Aneto
Charlotte Is. St. Lawrence Nova Scotia C. Race Pen. 3404
Vancouver I. Rocky Great Laurentian Plateau Azores Pyrenees
Aleutian Is. Mountains Plains G. of St. Lawrence Str. of Gibraltar Me
C. Mendocino 40 Ohio C. Cod Madeira Atlas Mts.
Mt. Elbert Arkansas Appalachian Mts. J. Toubkal 4165 Maghreb
Hawaiian Is. 4399 C. Hatteras ATLANTIC Canary Is. 3718
Mt. Whitney Mt. Mitchell Bermuda OCEAN Sa
4418 Death Valley 2037 Madeira Tropic of Cancer Ho
Mauna Kea Great Florida Sargasso Canary Is. 3718 A f
4205 Basin Gulf of Sea 1752 G r i c a
Lower Mexico Bahamas C. Verde S a h a
California Florida Str. Hispaniola Milwaukee Deep Is. C. Palmas Gulf of Guinea Mt. Came
C. San Lucas Popocatepetl 3175 9200 C. Verde
Revilla Gigedo Is. 5452 Pico de Orizaba Greater Puerto Equator
PACIFIC 5610 Antilles Rico Lesser
4093 Jamaica Caribbean Sea Antilles Ascension
Central Trinidad
America 5775 Orinoco
Isthmus Guiana Highlands C. de São Roque
of Panama Llanos Mt. Roraima
Galapagos 2964 2810
OCEAN Is. Negro South
Chimborazo Japurá Amazon St. Helena
6310 Selva
Marañón America
6768 Purus Plateau of
Madeira Mato Grosso
Marquesas Is. Tapajós
6425 Tocantins
E L. Titicaca São Francisco Brazilian Highlands 2890
Polynesia Society Is. Bolivian Trindade
Tuamotu Is. Plateau Gran Chaco C. Frio
Tahiti Andes Paraguay Tropic of Capricorn
Cook Is. 20 Chile Trench Paraná ATLANTIC
Tubuai Is. 8050
Pitcairn I. Cerro Ojos del Salado Pampas
6863 40
Easter I. Cerro Aconcagua R. de la Plata Tristan da Cunha
Arch. de 6960
Juan Fernández Negro OCEAN
4058 Patagonia 105
Falkland Is. 2937
Magellan's Str. Tierra del Scotia S. Georgia
C. Horn Fuego Sea South
Drake Passage South Sandwich Is.
Shetland Is. South
Orkney Is. Antarctic Circle
Bellingshausen Antarctic Peninsula Weddell Sea
Sea Alexander I. Palmer Caird Coast
Amundsen Sea Thurston I. Land Que
Ellsworth Land Ronne Berkner I. Coats Land
Roosevelt I. Vinson Massif Ice Shelf
Marie Byrd Land 4897
Ross 80
Sea

Projection: Winkel III 160 140 120 100 80 60 40 20 West from Greenwich

1 2 3 4 5 6 7 8 9 10

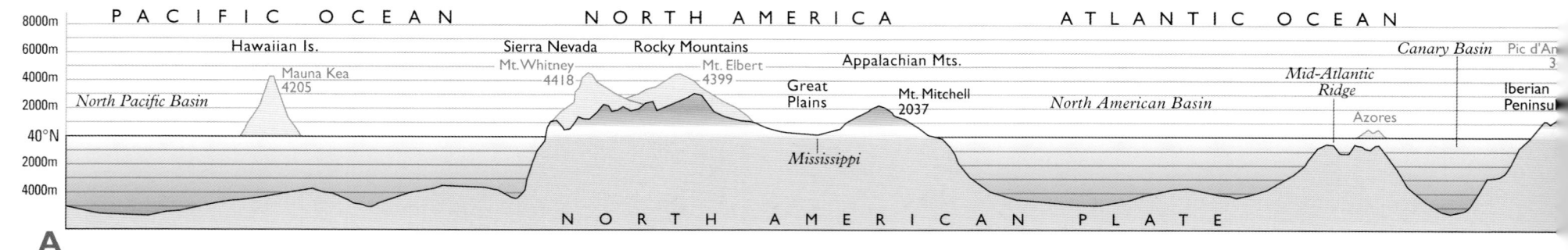

8000m
6000m PACIFIC OCEAN NORTH AMERICA ATLANTIC OCEAN
Hawaiian Is. Sierra Nevada Rocky Mountains Canary Basin Pic d'An
4000m Mauna Kea Mt. Whitney Mt. Elbert Appalachian Mts. Mid-Atlantic 3
4205 4418 4399 Ridge
2000m North Pacific Basin Great Mt. Mitchell North American Basin Iberian
40°N Plains 2037 Azores Peninsula
2000m Mississippi
4000m

A NORTH AMERICAN PLATE

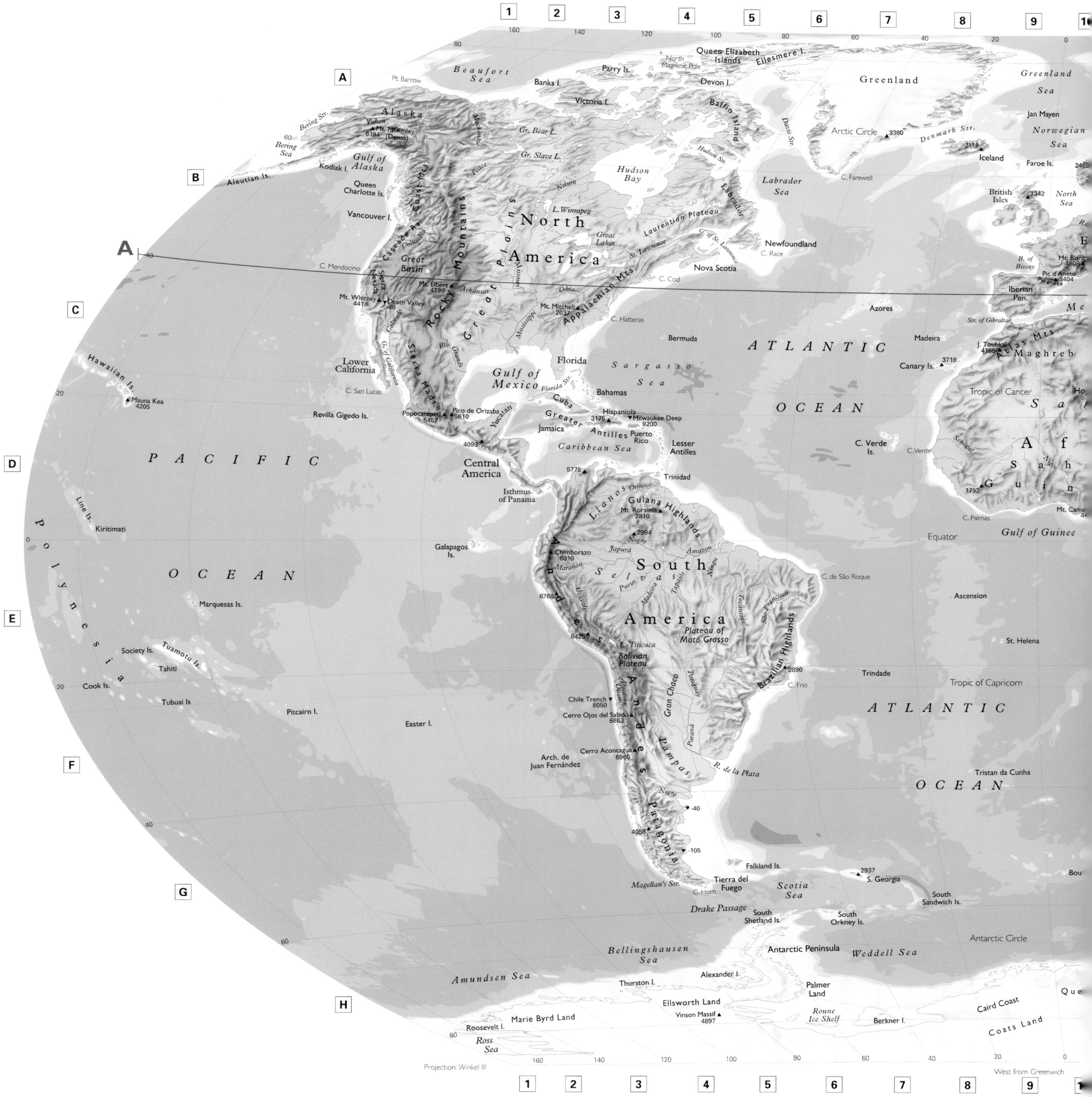

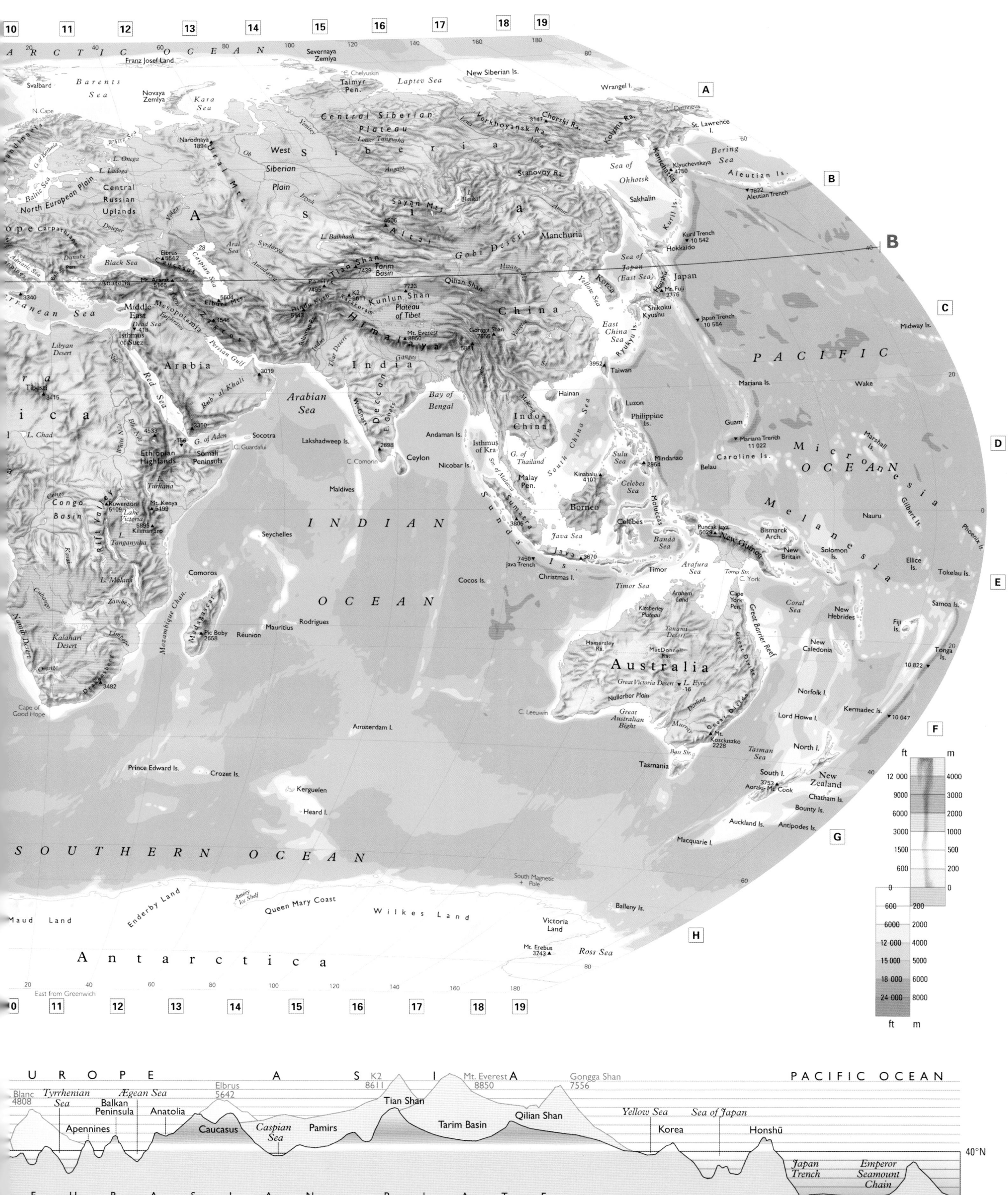

A R C T I C   O C E A N

Svalbard
Franz Josef Land
N. Cape
Barents
Sea
Novaya Zemlya
Kara Sea
Severnaya Zemlya
C. Chelyuskin
Taimyr Pen.
Laptev Sea
New Siberian Is.
Wrangel I.
C. Dezhnev

A

L. Onega
White Sea
L. Ladoga
Baltic Sea
G. of Bothnia
North European Plain
Central Russian Uplands
Ural Mts.
Narodnaya 1894
Ob
West Siberian Plain
Yenisey
Lower Tunguska
Central Siberian Plateau
Angara
Verkhoyansk Ra.
Cherski Ra. 3147
Kolyma Ra.
Stanovoy Ra.
St. Lawrence I.
Kamchatka
Klyuchevskaya 4750
Bering Sea
Aleutian Is.

B

7822
Aleutian Trench

Carpathians
Danube
Dnieper
Volga
Caspian Sea
Elbrus 5642
Caucasus
Black Sea
Aral Sea
Syrdarya
Amudarya
L. Balkhash
Altai 4606
Sayan Mts.
L. Baikal
Lena
Amur
Gobi Desert
Manchuria
Sakhalin
Sea of Okhotsk
Hokkaido
Kuril Is.
Kuril Trench 10 542

B

3340
Aegean Sea
Mediterranean Sea
Anatolia
Mt. Ararat 5165
Mesopotamia
Euphrates
Elbrus 5604
Zagros
4548
Pamir 7495
Tian Shan 7439
Hindu Kush
5121
K2 8611
Karakoram
Kunlun Shan
Tarim Basin
7723
Qilian Shan
Himalaya
Plateau of Tibet
Mt. Everest 8850
Gongga Shan 7556
5881
China
Huang He
Yellow Sea
Korea
Sea of Japan (East Sea)
Japan
Mt. Fuji 3776
Shikoku
Kyushu
Japan Trench 10 554

C

Midway Is.

Libyan Desert
Middle East
Dead Sea
Isthmus of Suez
Red Sea
Arabia
Persian Gulf
Rub' al Khali
3019
India
Deccan
W. Ghats
E. Ghats
Ganges
Indus
Thar Desert
Brahmaputra
3952
Taiwan
Hainan
East China Sea
Ryukyu Is.

P A C I F I C

Mariana Is.
Wake

Tibesti 3415
L. Chad
Blue Nile
White Nile
4533
G. of Aden
156
Socotra
C. Guardafui
Ethiopian Highlands
Somali Peninsula
3350
Arabian Sea
Lakshadweep Is.
2698
Andaman Is.
Nicobar Is.
C. Comorin
Ceylon
Bay of Bengal
Indo-China
Isthmus of Kra
G. of Thailand
Luzon
Philippine Is.
Philippine Is.
Guam
Mariana Trench 11 022
Caroline Is.
Belau

D

M i c r o n e s i a
Marshall Is.

O C E A N

L. Turkana
Ruwenzori 5109
Kilimanjaro 5895
Mt. Kenya 5199
Lake Victoria
Congo Basin
Congo
Tanganyika
Maldives
Seychelles
I N D I A N
Malay Pen.
Str. of Malacca
Sumatra
3806
Sunda Is.
Kinabalu 4101
Borneo
Sulu Sea
Celebes Sea
Mindanao 2954
Celebes
Molucca Sea
Banda Sea
Puncak Jaya 5029
New Guinea
Bismarck Arch.
New Britain
Solomon Is.

M e l a n e s i a
Nauru
Phoenix Is.

E

Namib Desert
Kalahari Desert
Cabora
Zambezi
L. Malawi
Madagascar
Pic Boby 2658
Réunion
Mauritius
Rodrigues
Comoros
Mozambique Chan.
O C E A N
Cocos Is.
7450 Java Trench
Java Is.
3670
Christmas I.
Timor
Timor Sea
Arafura Sea
Torres Str.
C. York
Arnhem Land
Cape York Pen.
Coral Sea
Great Barrier Reef
New Hebrides
New Caledonia
Ellice Is.
Tokelau Is.
Samoa Is.
Fiji Is.
Tonga Is. 10 822

Orange
Kasai
Limpopo
Drakensberg 3482
Cape of Good Hope
Amsterdam I.
Seychelles
Kimberley Plateau
Hamersley Ra.
Tanami Desert
MacDonnell Ra.
Great Victoria Desert
L. Eyre 16
Nullarbor Plain
Great Australian Bight
C. Leeuwin
A u s t r a l i a
Great Dividing Ra.
Darling
Murray
Mt. Kosciuszko 2228
Tasmania
Bass Str.
Tasman Sea
Norfolk I.
Lord Howe I.
North I.
Kermadec Is. 10 047

F

Prince Edward Is.
Crozet Is.
Kerguelen
Heard I.
New Zealand
Aoraki Mt. Cook 3753
South I.
Chatham Is.
Bounty Is.
Antipodes Is.
Auckland Is.
Macquarie I.

G

S O U T H E R N   O C E A N
Amery Ice Shelf
Enderby Land
Queen Mary Coast
Wilkes Land
South Magnetic Pole
Victoria Land
Balleny Is.

H

Maud Land
A n t a r c t i c a
Mt. Erebus 3743
Ross Sea

ft   m
12 000   4000
9000   3000
6000   2000
3000   1000
1500   500
600   200
0   0
600   200
6000   2000
12 000   4000
15 000   5000
18 000   6000
24 000   8000
ft   m

U R O P E   A   S   K2   I   Mt. Everest A   Gongga Shan   P A C I F I C   O C E A N
Blanc   Tyrrhenian   Ægean Sea   Elbrus   8611   8850   7556
4808   Sea   5642
          Balkan   Tian Shan
          Peninsula   Anatolia   Yellow Sea   Sea of Japan
     Apennines   Caucasus   Caspian   Pamirs   Tarim Basin   Qilian Shan
                                               Sea   Korea   Honshū
                                                                                                          40°N
                                                                                              Japan   Emperor
                                                                                              Trench   Seamount
                                                                                                        Chain
E U R A S I A N   P L A T E

COPYRIGHT PHILIP'S   **B**

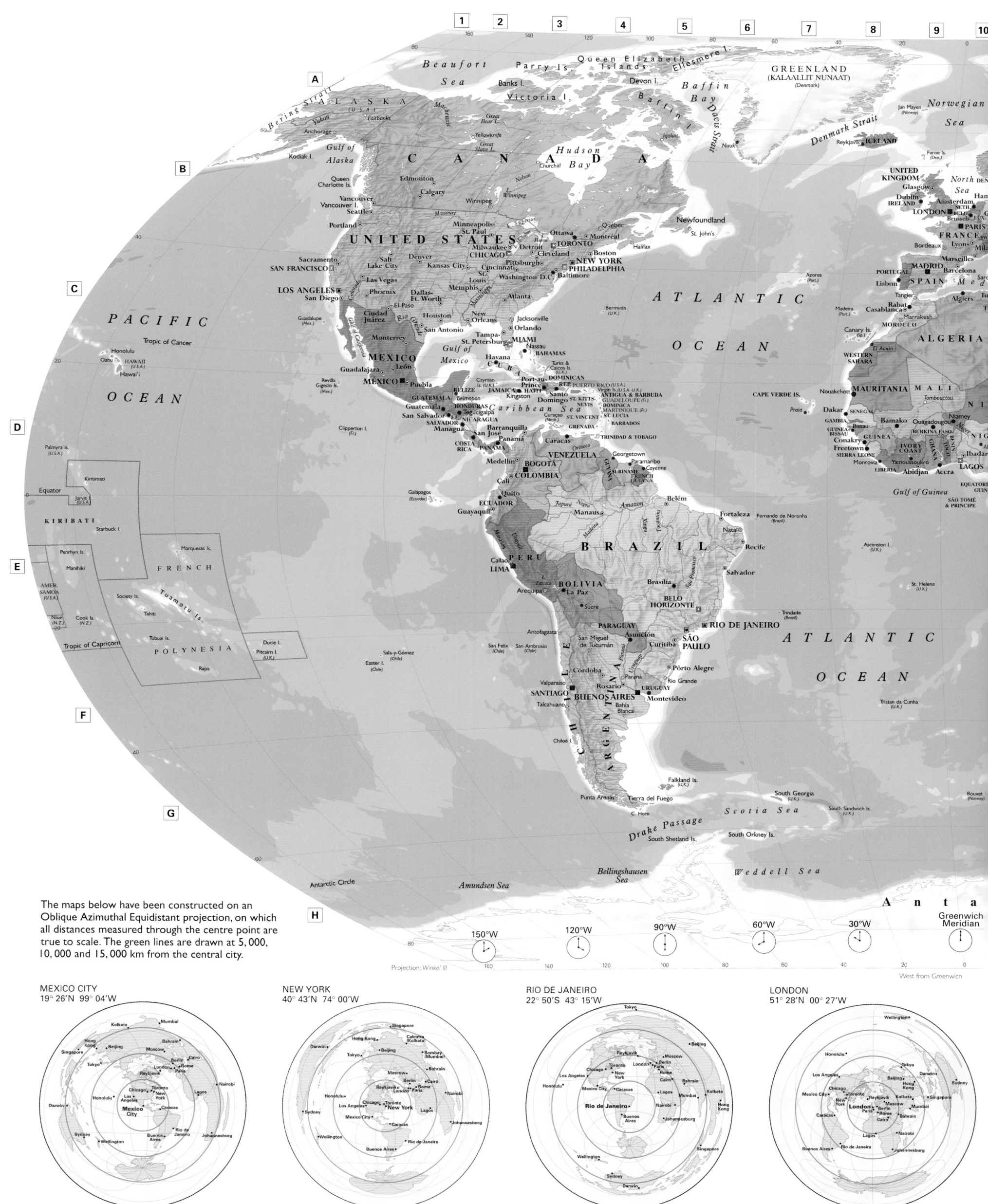

The maps below have been constructed on an Oblique Azimuthal Equidistant projection, on which all distances measured through the centre point are true to scale. The green lines are drawn at 5,000, 10,000 and 15,000 km from the central city.

Projection: Winkel III

West from Greenwich

MEXICO CITY
19° 26'N 99° 04'W

NEW YORK
40° 43'N 74° 00'W

RIO DE JANEIRO
22° 50'S 43° 15'W

LONDON
51° 28'N 00° 27'W

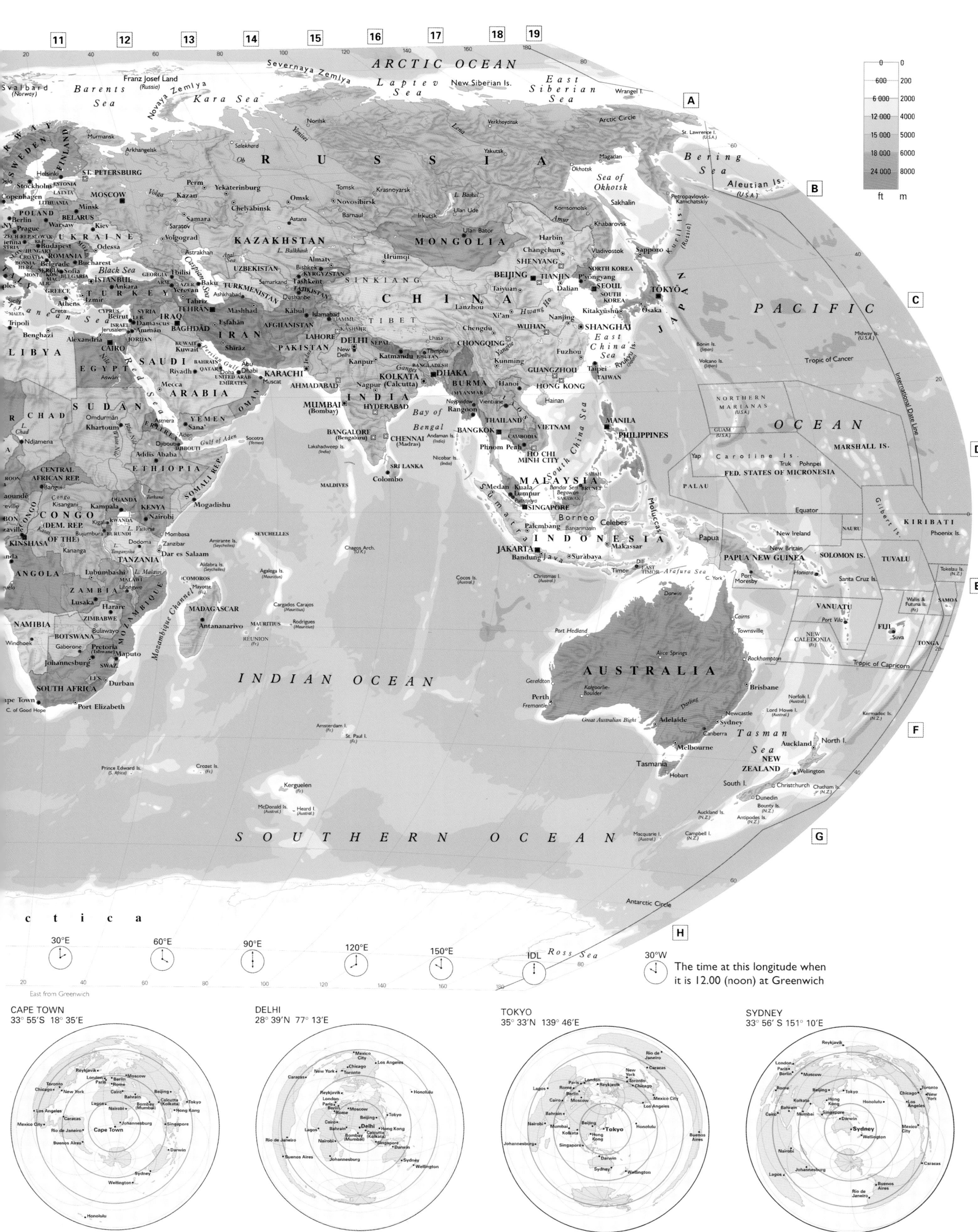

CAPE TOWN
33° 55'S 18° 35'E

DELHI
28° 39'N 77° 13'E

TOKYO
35° 33'N 139° 46'E

SYDNEY
33° 56' S 151° 10'E

The time at this longitude when it is 12.00 (noon) at Greenwich

East from Greenwich

COPYRIGHT PHILIP'S

1:28 000 000

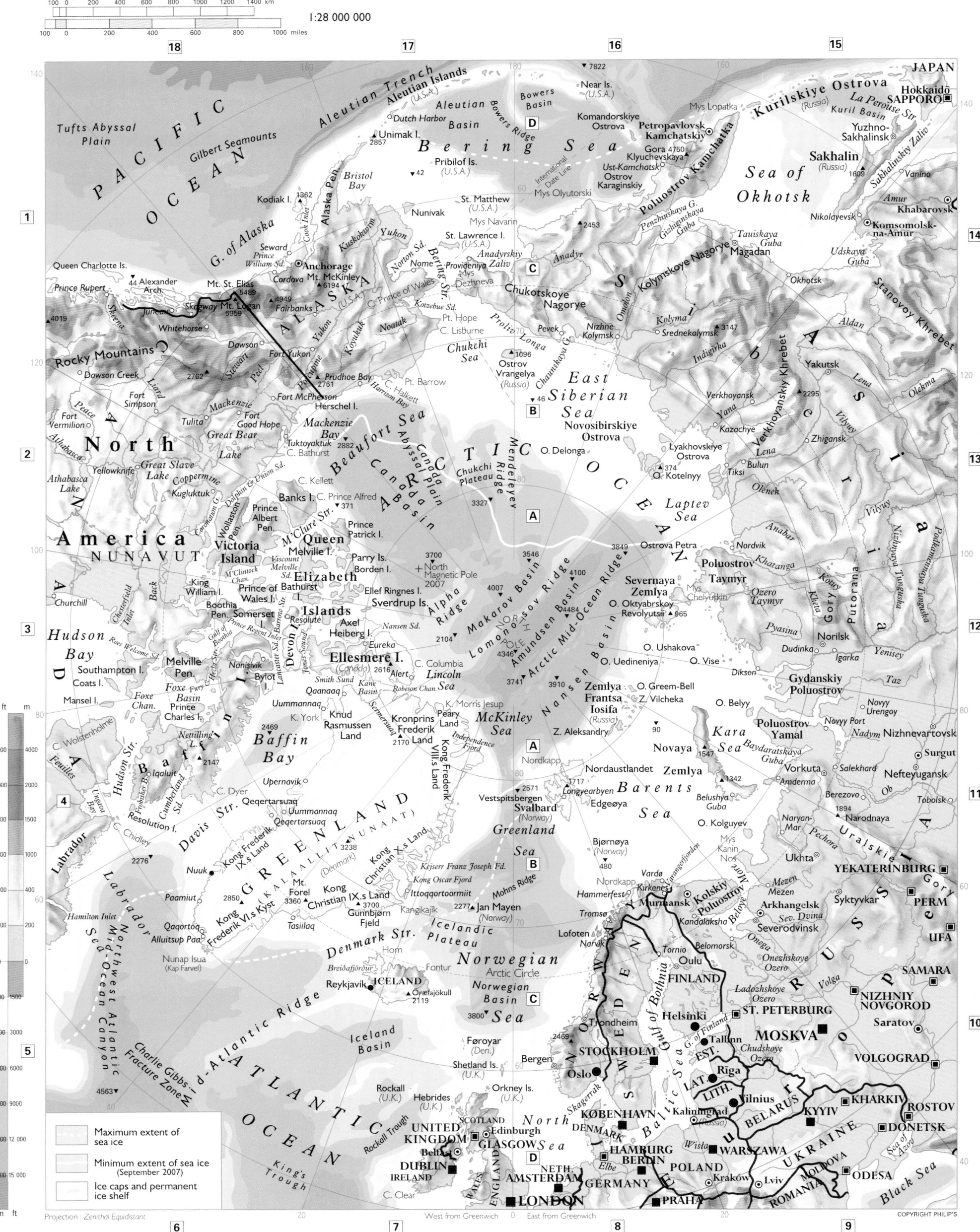

Maximum extent of sea ice

Minimum extent of sea ice (September 2007)

Ice caps and permanent ice shelf

Projection: Zenithal Equidistant

COPYRIGHT PHILIP'S

1:28 000 000

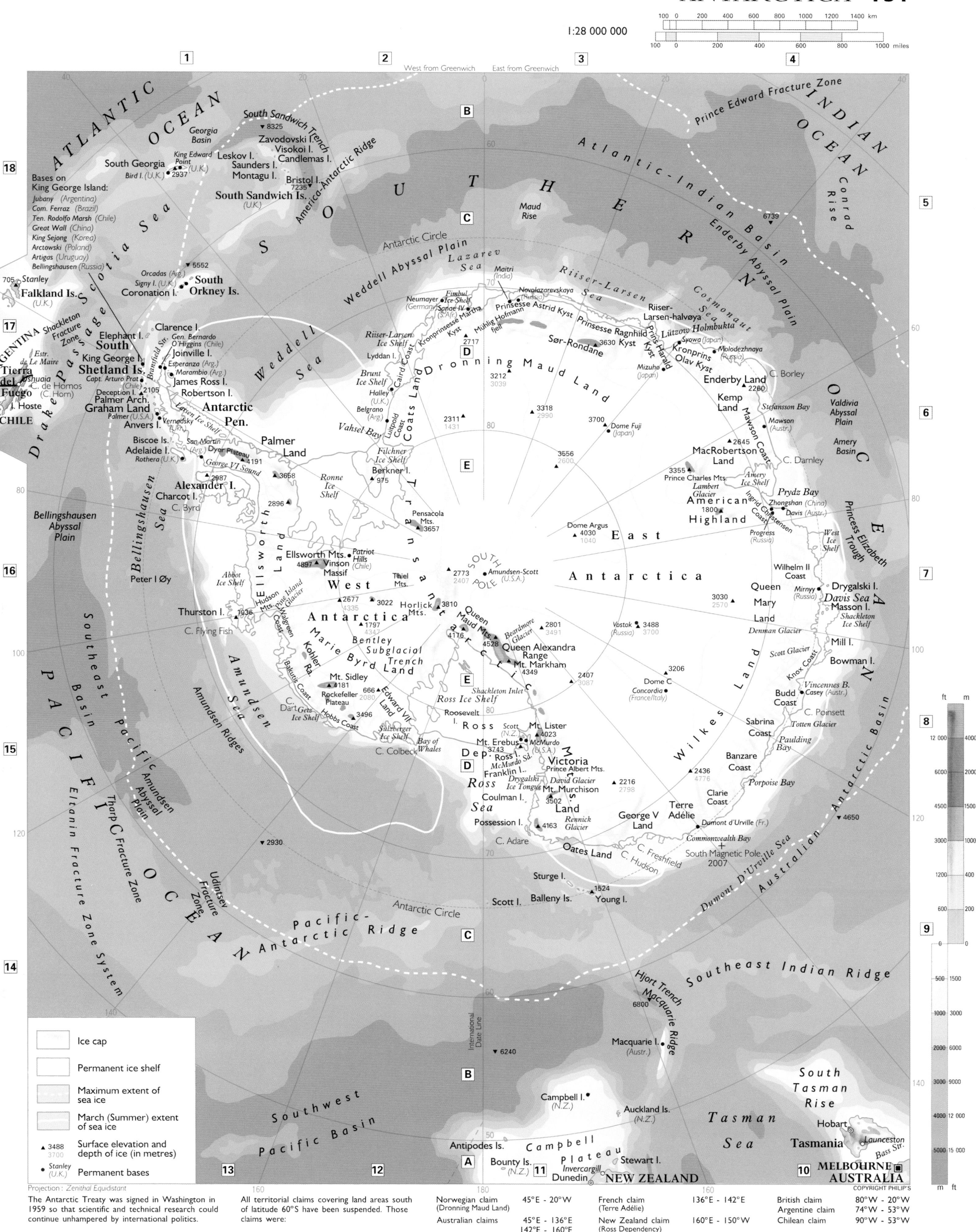

Projection : Zenithal Equidistant

The Antarctic Treaty was signed in Washington in 1959 so that scientific and technical research could continue unhampered by international politics.

All territorial claims covering land areas south of latitude 60°S have been suspended. Those claims were:

Norwegian claim (Dronning Maud Land)	45°E – 20°W
Australian claims	45°E – 136°E 142°E – 160°E
French claim (Terre Adélie)	136°E – 142°E
New Zealand claim (Ross Dependency)	160°E – 150°E
British claim	80°W – 20°W
Argentine claim	74°W – 53°W
Chilean claim	90°W – 53°W

COPYRIGHT PHILIP'S

Equatorial Scale 1:41 000 000

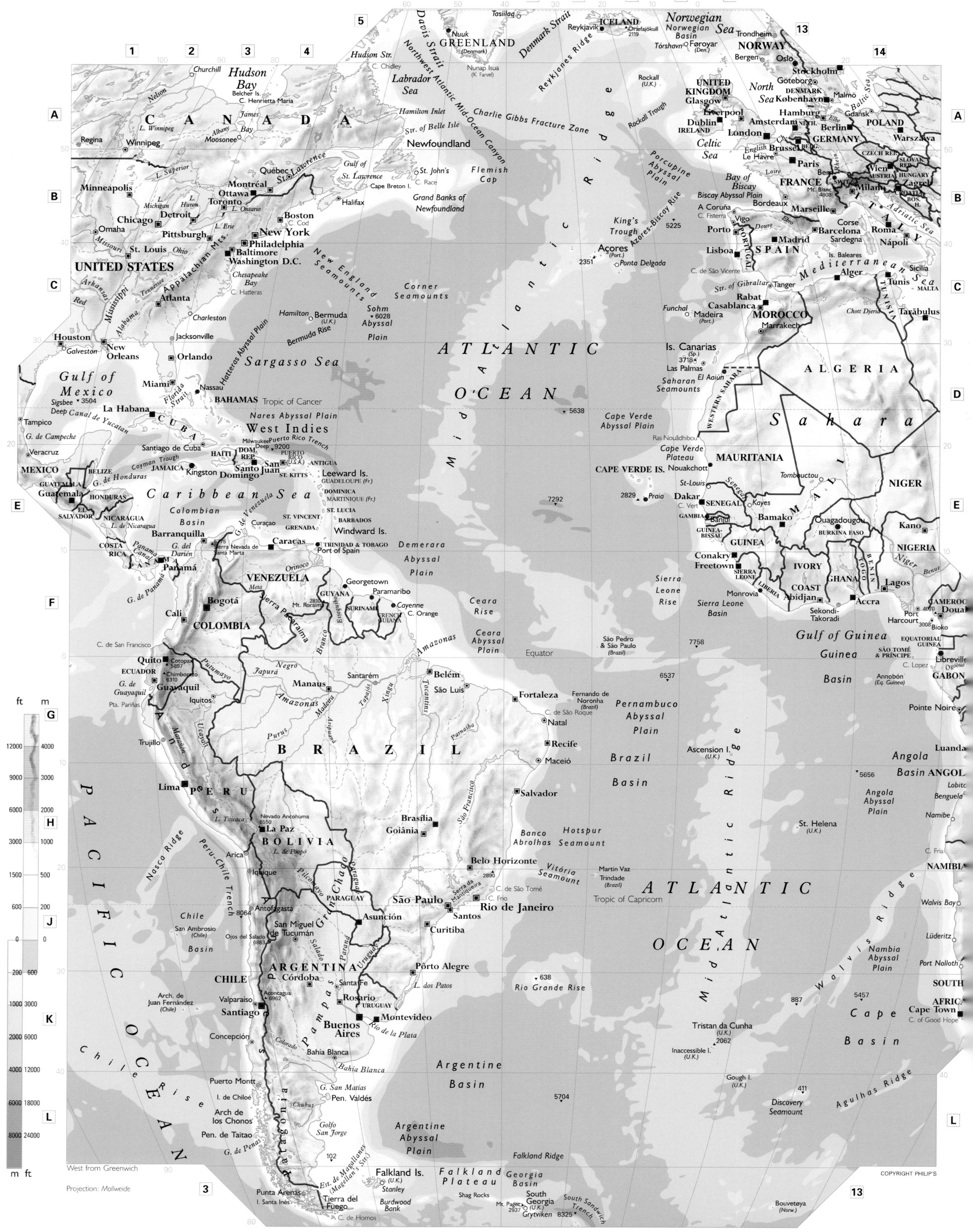

ATLANTIC OCEAN

PACIFIC OCEAN

Countries and regions
CANADA, UNITED STATES, MEXICO, GREENLAND (Denmark), BAHAMAS, CUBA, HAITI, DOM. REP., JAMAICA, BELIZE, GUATEMALA, HONDURAS, EL SALVADOR, NICARAGUA, COSTA RICA, PANAMA, COLOMBIA, VENEZUELA, GUYANA, SURINAME, FRENCH GUIANA, ECUADOR, PERU, BOLIVIA, BRAZIL, PARAGUAY, CHILE, ARGENTINA, URUGUAY

UNITED KINGDOM, IRELAND, NORWAY, DENMARK, FRANCE, GERMANY, POLAND, SPAIN, PORTUGAL, ITALY, MOROCCO, WESTERN SAHARA, ALGERIA, MAURITANIA, CAPE VERDE IS., SENEGAL, GAMBIA, GUINEA-BISSAU, GUINEA, SIERRA LEONE, LIBERIA, IVORY COAST, GHANA, TOGO, BENIN, NIGERIA, NIGER, MALI, BURKINA FASO, CAMEROON, EQUATORIAL GUINEA, GABON, NAMIBIA, SOUTH AFRICA, ANGOLA

Cities and places
Churchill, Nuuk, Reykjavík, ICELAND, Tórshavn, Trondheim, Oslo, Bergen, Stockholm, Göteborg, København, Malmö, Gdańsk, Warszawa, Berlin, Hamburg, Amsterdam, Brussel, London, Dublin, Liverpool, Glasgow, Le Havre, Paris, Bordeaux, Marseille, Wien, Milano, Roma, Barcelona, Madrid, Lisboa, Porto, A Coruña, Vigo

Winnipeg, Regina, Minneapolis, Chicago, Detroit, Toronto, Ottawa, Montréal, Québec, Halifax, Boston, New York, Philadelphia, Baltimore, Washington D.C., Pittsburgh, St. Louis, Omaha, Houston, New Orleans, Galveston, Atlanta, Charleston, Jacksonville, Orlando, Miami, Nassau, La Habana, Tampico, Veracruz, MEXICO, Guatemala, Belize

Caracas, Barranquilla, Bogotá, Cali, Quito, Guayaquil, Iquitos, Trujillo, Lima, Arica, Antofagasta, Valparaíso, Santiago, Concepción, Córdoba, Rosario, Santa Fe, Buenos Aires, Montevideo, Pôrto Alegre, Curitiba, São Paulo, Santos, Rio de Janeiro, Belo Horizonte, Brasília, Goiânia, Salvador, Maceió, Recife, Natal, Fortaleza, São Luís, Belém, Santarém, Manaus, La Paz, Asunción, Punta Arenas

Casablanca, Rabat, Tanger, Tunis, Alger, Tarābulus, Marrakech, El Aaiún, Las Palmas, Nouâdhibou, Nouakchott, Dakar, Banjul, Bissau, Conakry, Freetown, Monrovia, Abidjan, Accra, Lagos, Libreville, Luanda, Lobito, Benguela, Namibe, Lüderitz, Walvis Bay, Cape Town, Bamako, Ouagadougou, Kano, Tombouctou

Seas, oceans and features
Hudson Bay, Labrador Sea, Davis Strait, Denmark Strait, Norwegian Sea, North Sea, Baltic Sea, Celtic Sea, Bay of Biscay, Mediterranean Sea, Adriatic Sea, Gulf of Mexico, Sargasso Sea, Caribbean Sea, West Indies, Gulf of Guinea, Cape Basin, Argentine Basin

Mid Atlantic Ridge, Reykjanes Ridge, Charlie Gibbs Fracture Zone, Northwest Atlantic Mid-Ocean Canyon, Walvis Ridge, Agulhas Ridge, Nasca Ridge, Peru-Chile Trench, Chile Rise, Puerto Rico Trench, Milwaukee Deep 9200, Cayman Trough, South Sandwich Trench

Hatteras Abyssal Plain, Nares Abyssal Plain, Bermuda Rise, Sohm Abyssal Plain, Demerara Abyssal Plain, Ceara Abyssal Plain, Pernambuco Abyssal Plain, Brazil Basin, Argentine Abyssal Plain, Angola Basin, Angola Abyssal Plain, Nambia Abyssal Plain, Cape Verde Abyssal Plain, Guinea Basin, Sierra Leone Basin, Canary Basin, Biscay Abyssal Plain, Porcupine Abyssal Plain, King's Trough

Tropic of Cancer, Equator, Tropic of Capricorn

Projection: Mollweide

West from Greenwich

COPYRIGHT PHILIP'S

ft m

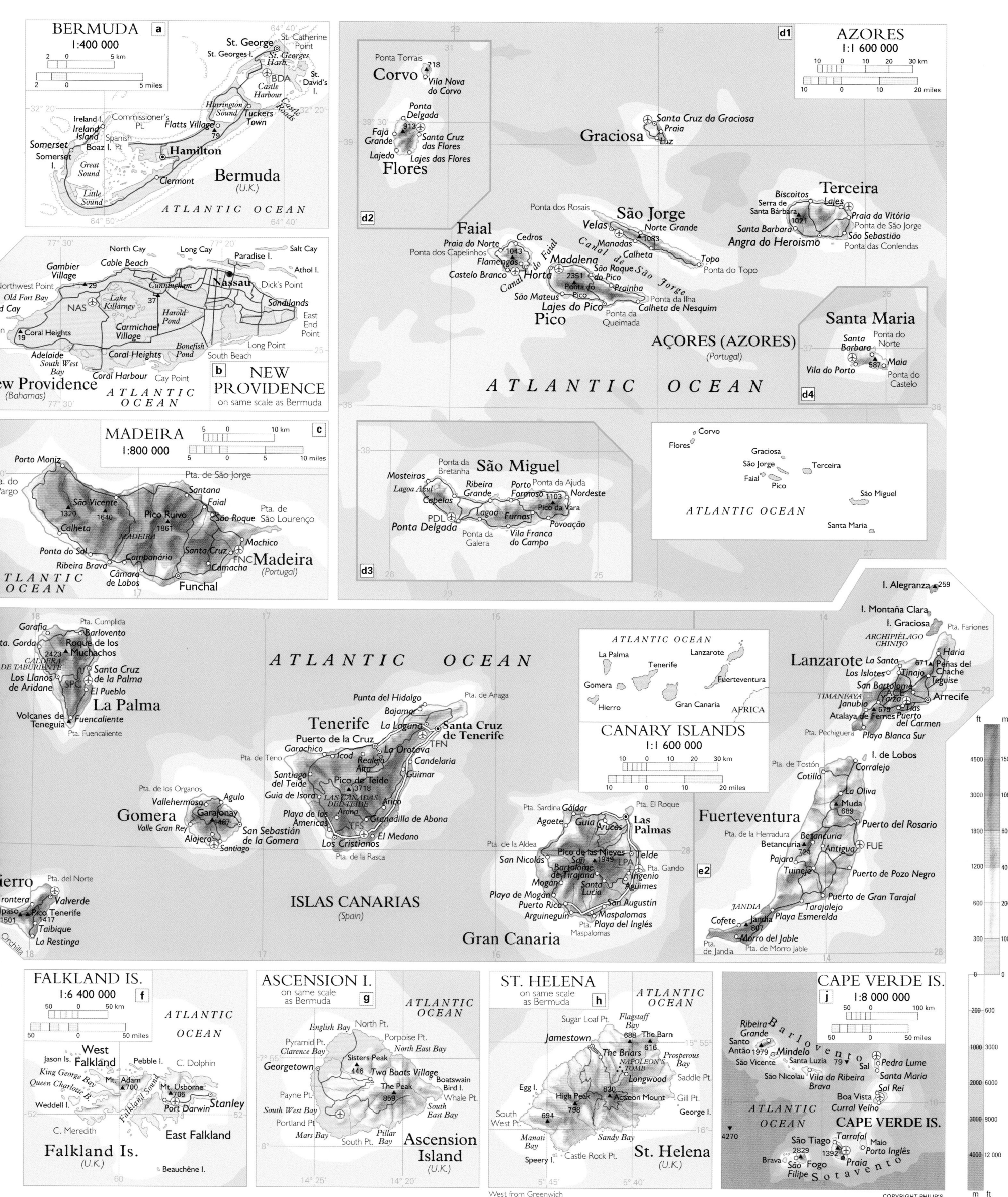

BERMUDA
a
1:400 000

2   0   5 km
2   0   5 miles

St. George
St. Catherine Point
St. Georges I.
St. Georges Harb.
BDA
Castle Harbour
Castle Roads
St. David's I.
Harrington Sound
Tuckers Town
Flatts Village
79
Commissioner's Pt.
Ireland I.
Ireland Island
Boaz I.
Spanish Pt.
Somerset
Somerset I.
Great Sound
Little Sound
Hamilton
Clermont

Bermuda
(U.K.)

ATLANTIC OCEAN

North Cay
Cable Beach
Long Cay
Salt Cay
Paradise I.
Gambier Village
Northwest Point
Old Fort Bay
d Cay
Coral Heights
29
Cunningham
Lake Killarney
NAS
37
Carmichael Village
Coral Heights
Harold Pond
Bonefish Pond
Nassau
Dick's Point
Sandilands
East End Point
19
Adelaide
South West Bay
Coral Harbour
Coral Heights
Cay Point
Long Point
South Beach

b
NEW PROVIDENCE
on same scale as Bermuda

w Providence
(Bahamas)

ATLANTIC OCEAN

MADEIRA
c
1:800 000

5   0   10 km
5   0   5   10 miles

Porto Moniz
a. do argo
Pta. de São Jorge
Santana
São Vicente
1320
1640
Faial
Pico Ruivo
1861
São Roque
Pta. de São Lourenço
MADEIRA
Calheta
Ponta do Sol
Campanário
Santa Cruz
Machico
Ribeira Brava
Câmara de Lobos
Camacha
FNC
Madeira
(Portugal)
Funchal

TLANTIC OCEAN

Ponta Torrais
718
Corvo
Vila Nova do Corvo

Ponta Delgada
913
Fajã Grande
Santa Cruz das Flores
Lajedo
Lajes das Flores
Flores

Santa Cruz da Graciosa
Praia
Graciosa
Luz

Biscoitos
Serra de Santa Bárbara
Terceira
Lajes
Praia da Vitória
Santa Barbara
1021
Ponta de São Jorge
Angra do Heroismo
São Sebastião
Ponta das Conlendas

Ponta dos Rosais
São Jorge
Velas
Norte Grande
Cedros
Manadas
1083
Topo
Faial
Praia do Norte
Calheta
Ponta do Topo
Ponta dos Capelinhos
1043
Flamengos
Madalena
Castelo Branco
Horta
São Roque do Pico
2351
São Mateus
Ponta do Pico
Prainha
Lajes do Pico
Ponta da Ilha
Calheta de Nesquim
Pico
Ponta da Queimada

AÇORES (AZORES)
(Portugal)

AZORES
d1
1:1 600 000

10   0   10   20   30 km
10   0   10   20 miles

Santa Maria
d4
Santa Barbara
Ponta do Norte
587   Maia
Vila do Porto
Ponta do Castelo

ATLANTIC OCEAN

Corvo
Flores
Graciosa
São Jorge
Terceira
Faial
Pico
São Miguel
Santa Maria

ATLANTIC OCEAN

São Miguel
d3
Mosteiros
Ponta da Bretanha
Ribeira Grande
Porto Formoso
Ponta da Ajuda
Nordeste
Lagoa Azul
Capelas
Lagoa
1103
Pico da Vara
PDL
Furnas
Povoação
Ponta Delgada
Vila Franca do Campo
Ponta da Galera

I. Alegranza
259
I. Montaña Clara
I. Graciosa
Pta. Fariones
ARCHIPIÉLAGO CHINIJO
Lanzarote
La Santa
Haria
671
Peñas del Chache
Los Islotes
Tinajo
Teguise
San Bartolomé
Arrecife
TIMANFAYA
Janubio
Yaiza
679
Tías
Atalaya de Femes
Puerto del Carmen
Pta. Pechiguera
Playa Blanca Sur

CANARY ISLANDS
ATLANTIC OCEAN
La Palma
Lanzarote
Tenerife
Gomera
Fuerteventura
Gran Canaria
Hierro
AFRICA
1:1 600 000

10   0   10   20   30 km
10   0   10   20 miles

ATLANTIC OCEAN

Garafia
Pta. Cumplida
Barlovento
ta. Gorda
Roque de los Muchachos
2423
CALDERA DE TABURIENTE
Santa Cruz de la Palma
Los Llanos de Aridane
SPC
El Pueblo
La Palma
Volcanes de Teneguia
Fuencaliente
Pta. Fuencaliente

Punta del Hidalgo
Pta. de Anaga
Bajamar
Tenerife
La Laguna
Santa Cruz de Tenerife
Puerto de la Cruz
La Orotava
TFN
Garachico
Icod
Realejo Alta
Candelaria
Pta. de Teno
Santiago del Teide
Pico de Teide
3718
Güimar
LAS CAÑADAS DEL TEIDE
Pta. de los Organos
Vallehermoso
Agulo
Playa de las Americas
Arico
Gomera
Garajonay
1487
Arona
TFS
Granadilla de Abona
Valle Gran Rey
San Sebastián de la Gomera
El Medano
Alajero
Los Cristianos
Santiago
Pta. de la Rasca

ierro
Pta. del Norte
rontera
Valverde
paso
Pico Tenerife
1501
1417
Taibique
La Restinga
Orchilla

ISLAS CANARIAS
(Spain)

Pta. Sardina
Gáldar
Pta. El Roque
Agaete
Guia
Arucas
Las Palmas
San Nicolás
Telde
Pta. de la Aldea
Pico de las Nieves
1949
San Bartolomé de Tirajana
LPA
Mogan
Ingenio
Pta. Gando
Playa de Mogan
Santa Lucia
Aguimes
Puerto Rico
San Augustin
Arguineguin
Maspalomas
Playa del Inglés
Pta. Maspalomas

Gran Canaria

Fuerteventura
e2
I. de Lobos
Corralejo
Cotillo
La Oliva
Muda
689
Pta. de Tostón
Pta. de la Herradura
Betancuria
Puerto del Rosario
Betancuria
724
Antigua
FUE
Pajara
Tuineje
Puerto de Pozo Negro
JANDIA
Tarajalejo
Puerto de Gran Tarajal
Cofete
Jandia Playa Esmerelda
Pta. de Jandia
Morro del Jable
Pta. de Morro Jable

FALKLAND IS.
f
1:6 400 000

50   0   50 km
50   0   50 miles

ATLANTIC OCEAN

West Falkland
Jason Is.
Pebble I.
C. Dolphin
King George Bay
Queen Charlotte B.
Mt. Adam
700
Mt. Usborne
705
Weddell I.
Falkland Sound
Port Darwin
Stanley
East Falkland
C. Meredith
Falkland Is.
(U.K.)
Beauchêne I.

ASCENSION I.
g
on same scale as Bermuda

English Bay
North Pt.
ATLANTIC OCEAN
Pyramid Pt.
Porpoise Pt.
Clarence Bay
North East Bay
Sisters Peak
446
Two Boats Village
Georgetown
Boatswain Bird I.
The Peak
859
Payne
South West Bay
Whale Pt.
South East Bay
Portland Pt.
Mars Bay
Pillar Bay
South Pt.
Ascension Island
(U.K.)

ST. HELENA
h
on same scale as Bermuda

Sugar Loaf Pt.
ATLANTIC OCEAN
Flagstaff Bay
688
The Barn
Jamestown
616
15° 55'
The Briars
Prosperous Bay
NAPOLEON'S TOMB
Longwood
Saddle Pt.
Egg I.
820
Ackeon Mount
Gill Pt.
High Peak
798
George I.
South West Pt.
694
Manati Bay
Sandy Bay
Castle Rock Pt.
Speery I.
St. Helena
(U.K.)

West from Greenwich

CAPE VERDE IS.
j
1:8 000 000

50   0   100 km
50   0   50 miles

Ribeira Grande
Santo Antão
1979
Mindelo
Barlovento
São Vicente
Santa Luzia
79
Sal
Pedra Lume
São Nicolau
Vila da Ribeira Brava
Santa Maria
Sal Rei
Boa Vista
ATLANTIC OCEAN
Curral Velho
CAPE VERDE IS.
4270
São Tiago
Tarrafal
Maio
Porto Inglês
2829
1392
Praia
Brava
São Fogo
Filipe
Sotavento

COPYRIGHT PHILIP'S

ft   m

4500   1500
3000   1000
1800   600
1200   400
300   100
0   0
200   600
1000   3000
2000   6000
3000   9000
4000   12000

m   ft

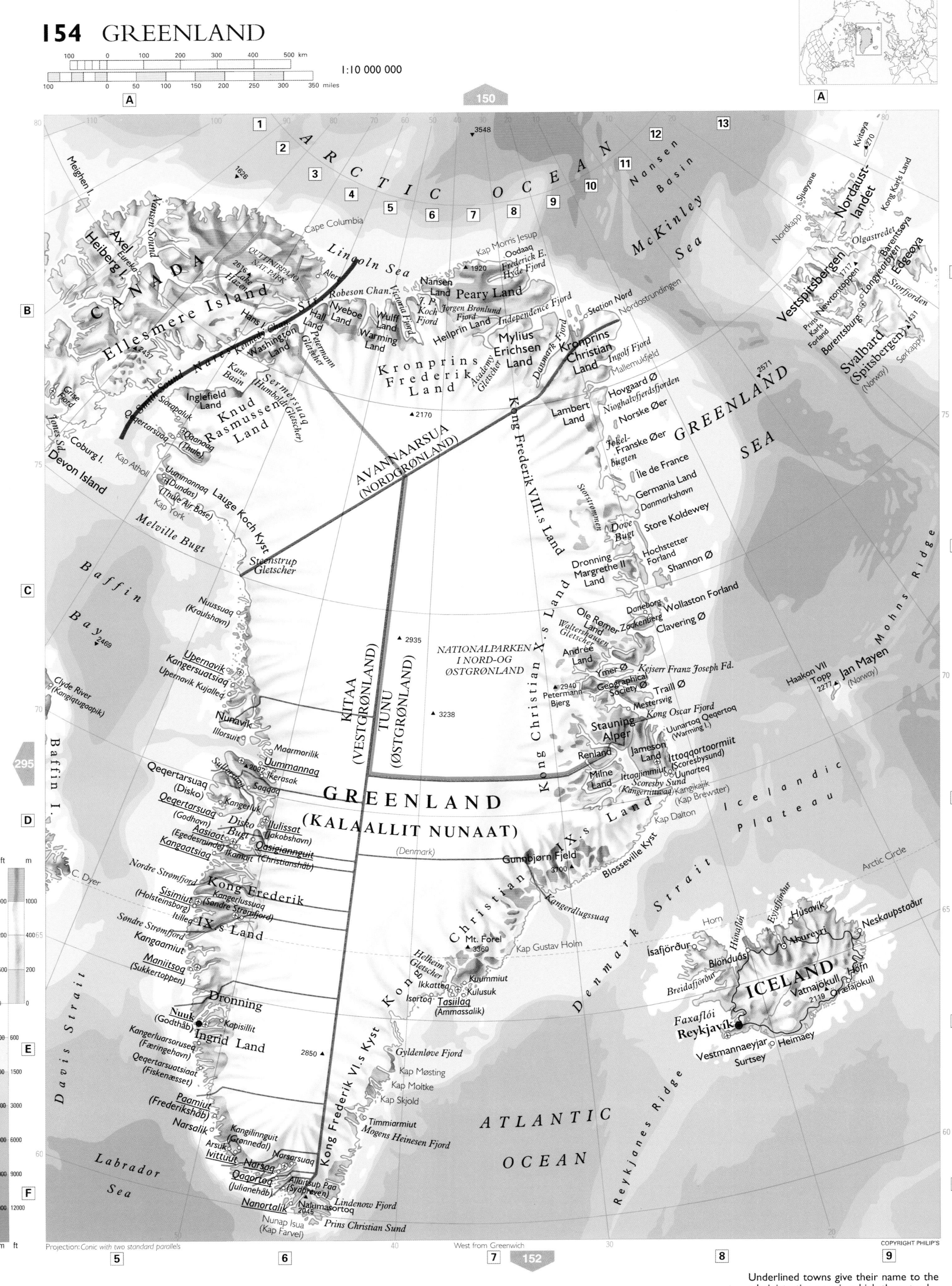

1:10 000 000

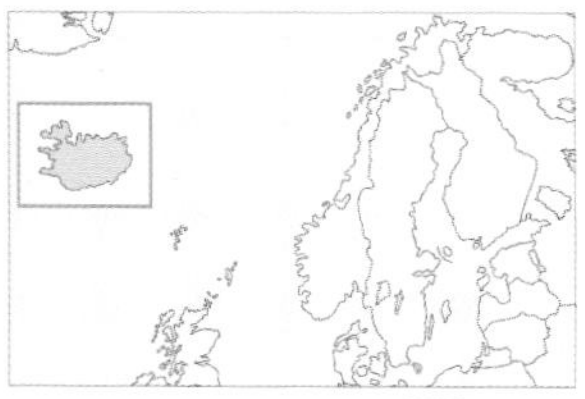

1:2 000 000

10 0 10 20 30 40 50 60 70 80 100 km
10 0 10 20 30 40 50 60 miles

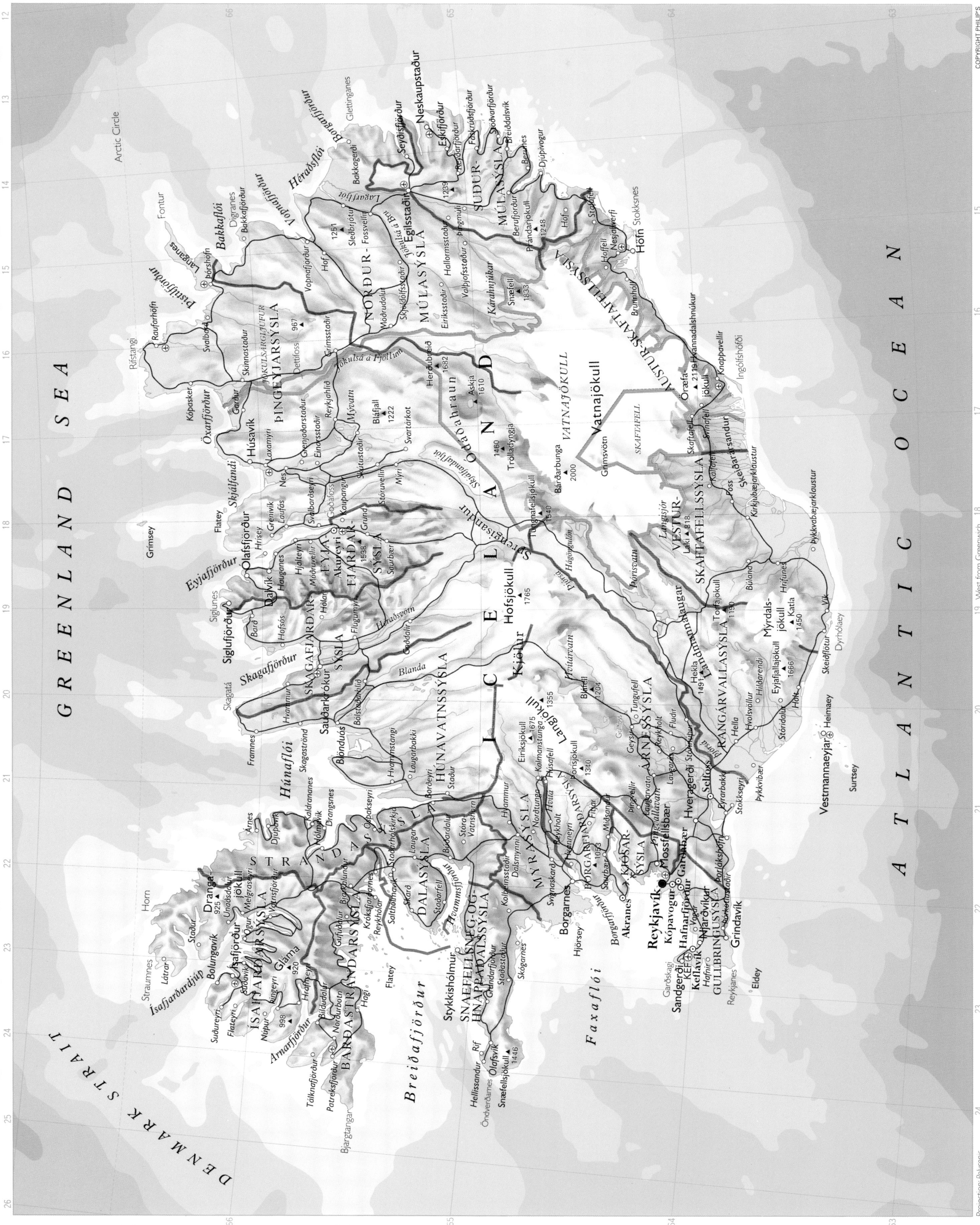

Projection: Polyconic

GREENLAND SEA

DENMARK STRAIT

ATLANTIC OCEAN

ICELAND

Arctic Circle

NORÐUR-

MÚLASÝSLA

SUÐUR-

MÚLASÝSLA

AUSTUR-SKAFTAFELLSSÝSLA

VESTUR-SKAFTAFELLSSÝSLA

VATNAJÖKULL

Vatnajökull

ÞINGEYJARSÝSLA

SKAGAFJARÐAR-SÝSLA

EYJA-FJARÐAR-SÝSLA

HÚNAVATNSSÝSLA

STRANDA-SÝSLA

ÍSAFJARÐARSÝSLA

BARÐASTRANDARSÝSLA

SNÆFELLSNES-OG-HNAPPADALSSÝSLA

DALASÝSLA

MÝRASÝSLA

BORGARFJARÐAR-SÝSLA

ÁRNESSÝSLA

RANGÁRVALLASÝSLA

GULLBRINGUSÝSLA

KJÓSAR-SÝSLA

Reykjavík
Kópavogur
Hafnarfjörður
Garðabær
Mosfellsbær
Keflavík
Njarðvík
Sandgerði
Grindavík

Akureyri
Siglufjörður
Dalvík
Ólafsfjörður
Húsavík
Sauðárkrókur
Blönduós
Ísafjörður
Bolungarvík
Stykkishólmur
Borgarnes
Akranes
Selfoss
Hveragerði
Vestmannaeyjar
Höfn
Egilsstaðir
Seyðisfjörður
Neskaupstaður
Eskifjörður
Djúpivogur
Vík
Heimaey
Surtsey
Eldey

Faxaflói
Breiðafjörður
Húnaflói
Skagafjörður
Eyjafjörður
Öxarfjörður
Skjálfandi
Héraðsflói
Bakkaflói
Vopnafjörður
Þistilfjörður
Bakkafjörður
Berufjörður

Langjökull
Hofsjökull
Mýrdalsjökull
Eyjafjallajökull
Drangajökull

Askja 1610
Herðubreið 1682
Hekla 1491
Katla 1450
Grímsvötn 2000
Bárðarbunga 2000
Öræfajökull 2119

Horn
Langanes
Fontur

1:16 000 000

1:16 000 000

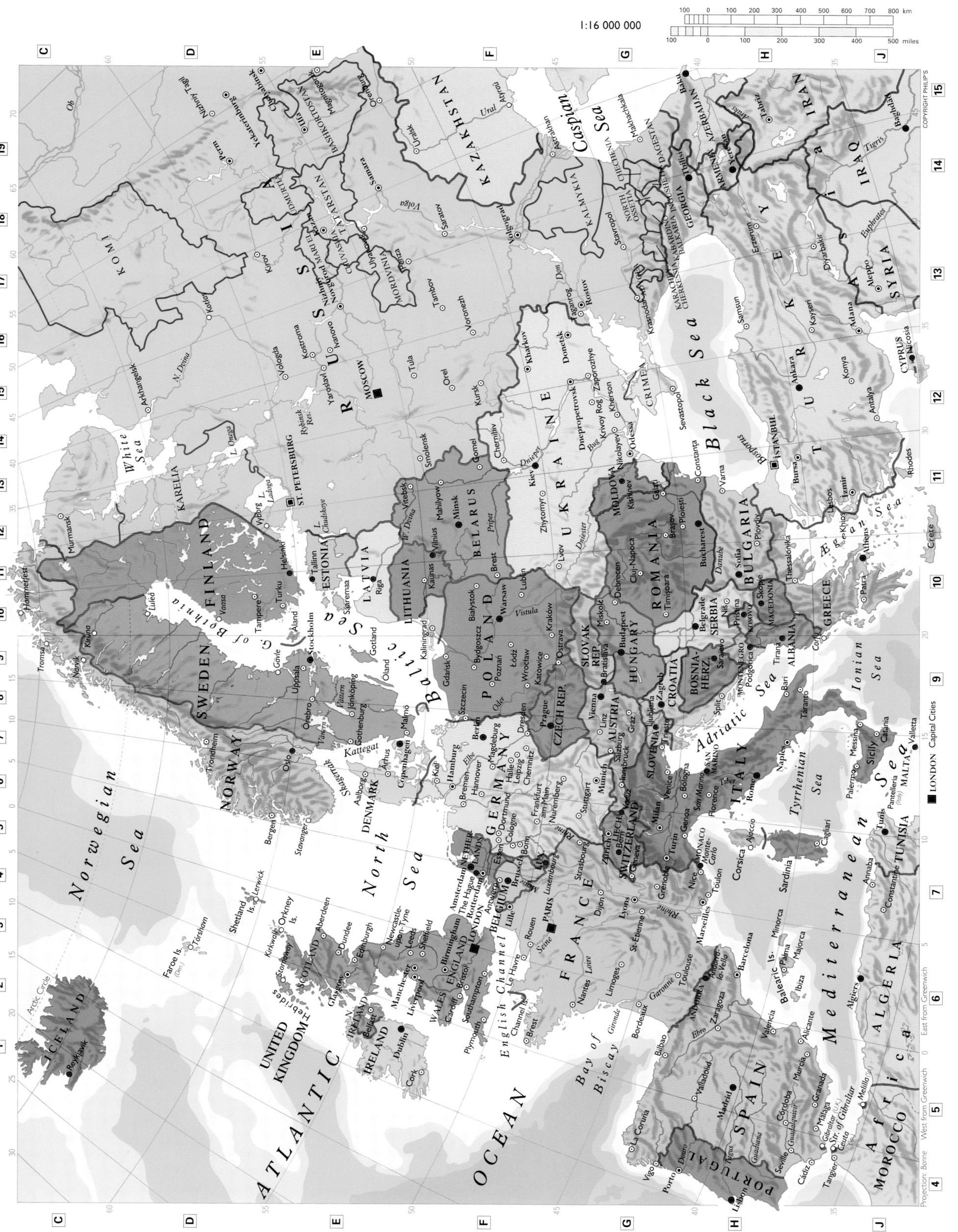

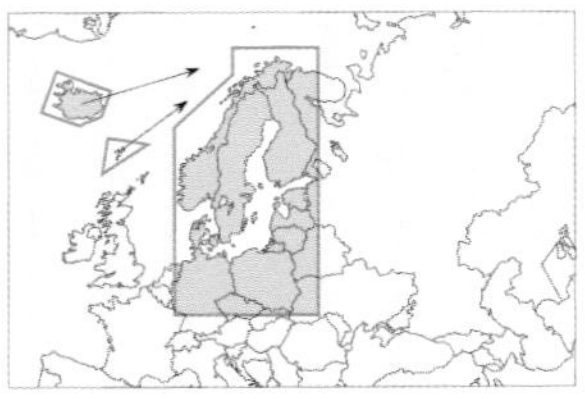

1:4 800 000

50   0 25 50 75 100 125 150 175 km

50   0   25   50   75   100   125 miles

B A R E N T S   S E A

R U S S I A

K A R E L I A

F I N L A N D

N O R W A Y

S W E D E N

Gulf of Bothnia

ATLANTIC OCEAN

NORWEGIAN SEA

L a p l a n d

F i n n m a r k

Murmansk
Kola
Severomorsk
Polyarnyy
Pechenga
Nikel
Kirkenes
Vadsø
Vardø
Varangerfjorden
Varanger-halvøya
Hammerfest
Magerøya
Nordkapp
Sørøya
Tromsø
Narvik
Harstad
Bodø
Mo
Mosjøen
Rovaniemi
Kemi
Tornio
Haparanda
Luleå
Boden
Piteå
Skellefteå
Umeå
Örnsköldsvik
Härnösand
Sundsvall
Hudiksvall
Söderhamn
Östersund
Kiruna
Gällivare
Oulu
Kokkola
Vaasa
Pori
Rauma
Tampere
Kuopio
Joensuu
Mikkeli
Lappeenranta
Vyborg
Trondheim
Steinkjer
Namsos
Levanger
Röros
Lillehammer
Gjøvik
Mora

ICELAND on same scale
Reykjavík
Keflavík
Akureyri
Vatnajökull
Vestmannaeyjar
Vík
Höfn

FÆROE ISLANDS on same scale
Tórshavn
Føroyar (Faroe Is.) (Den.)

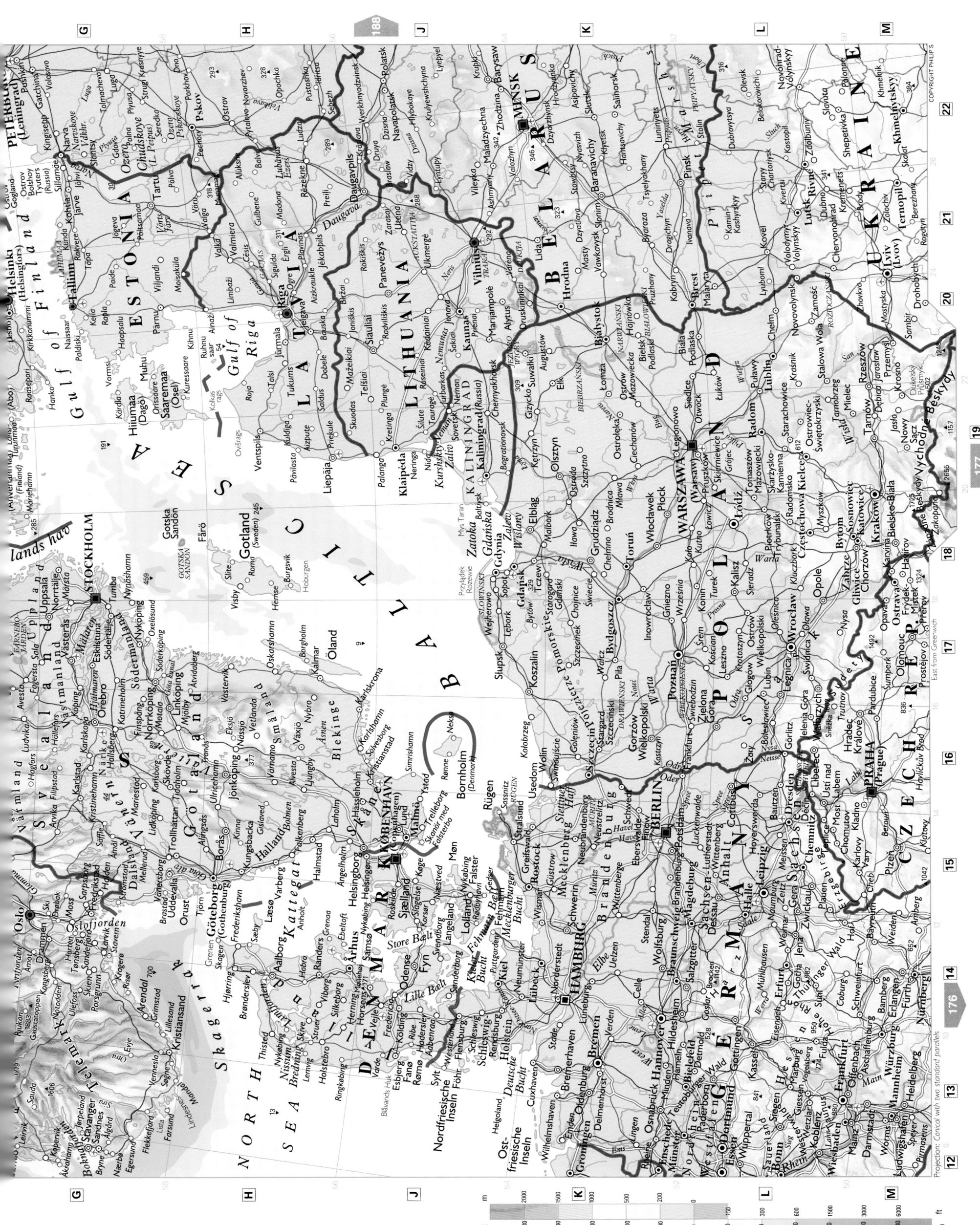

1:2 000 000

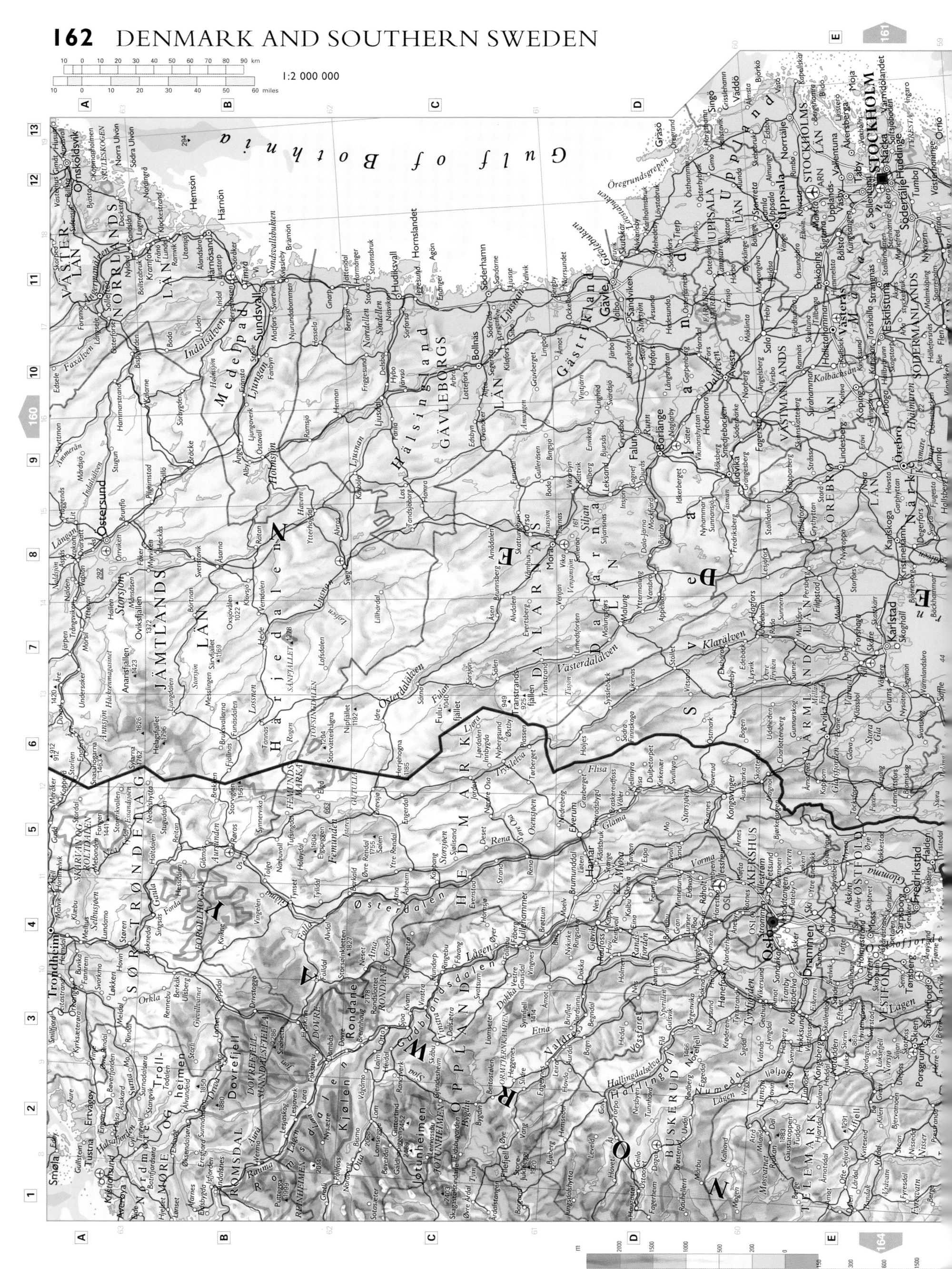

Gulf of Bothnia

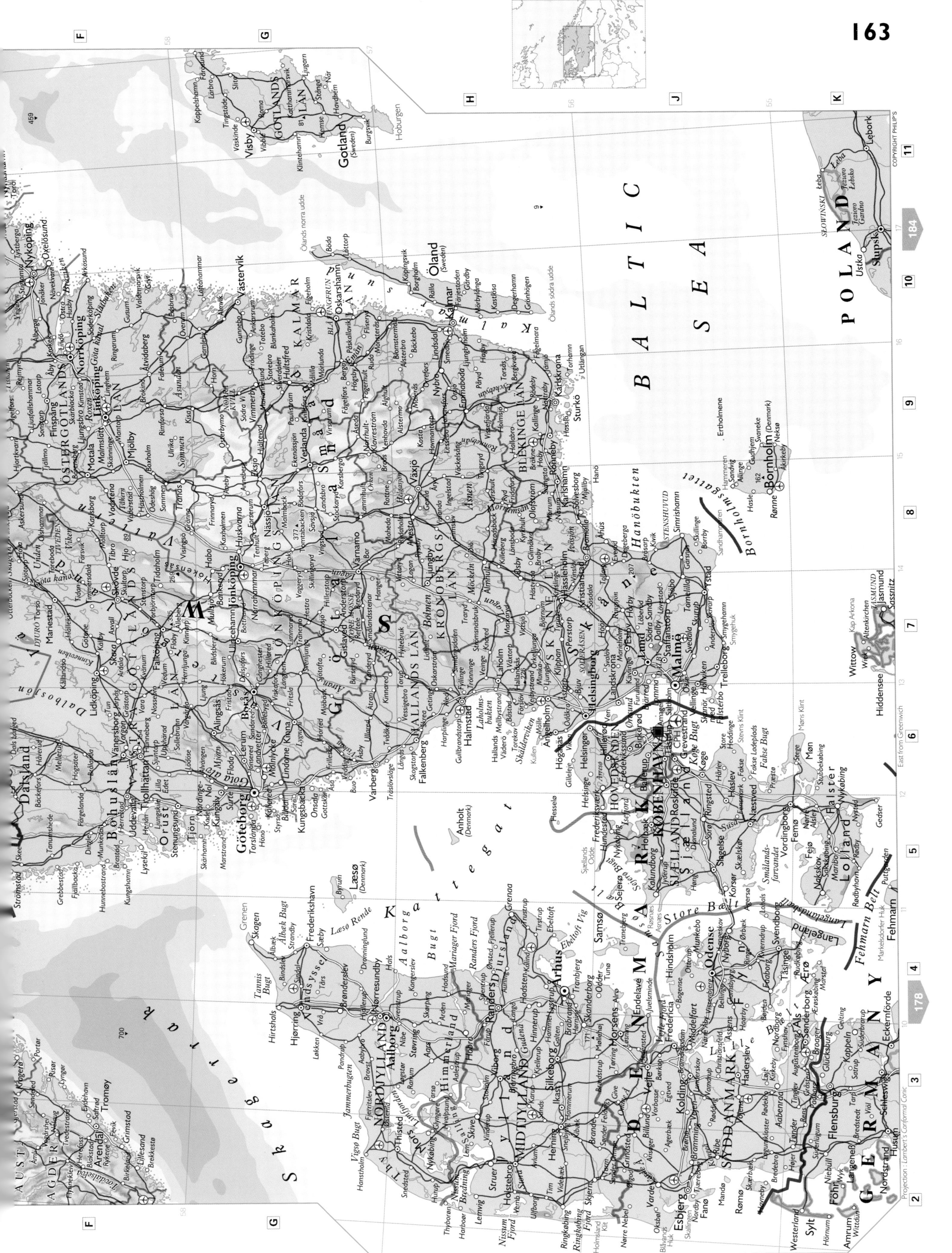

Projection: Lambert's Conformal Conic

1:2 000 000

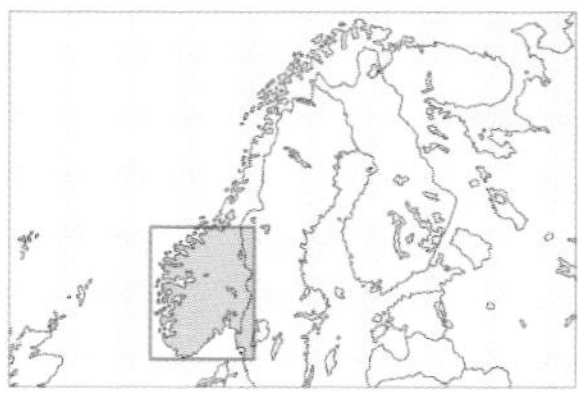

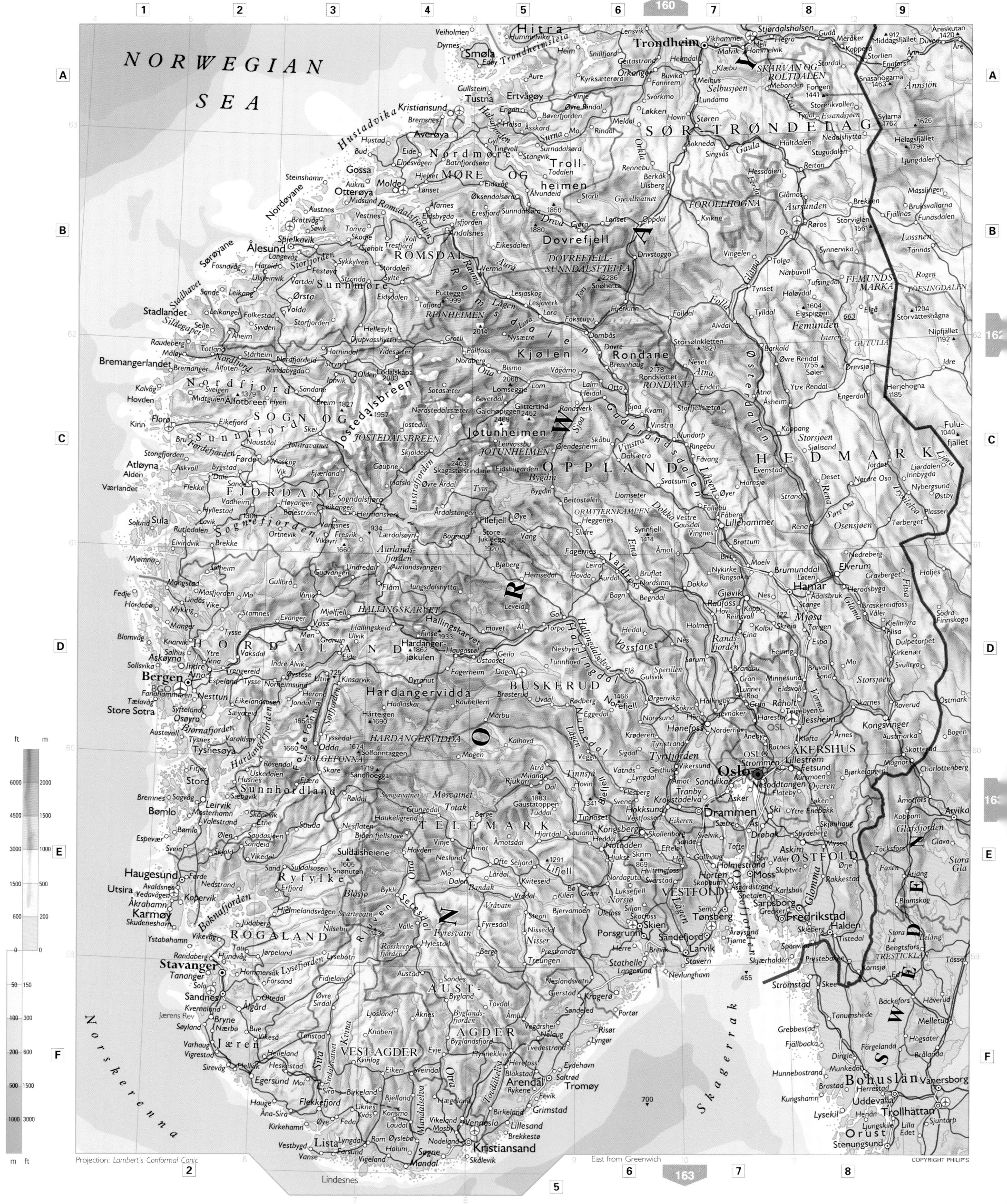

NORWEGIAN SEA
Norskerenna
Skagerrak
SØR-TRØNDELAG
MØRE OG ROMSDAL
SOGN OG FJORDANE
HORDALAND
ROGALAND
VEST-AGDER
AUST-AGDER
TELEMARK
BUSKERUD
OPPLAND
HEDMARK
AKERSHUS
VESTFOLD
ØSTFOLD
SWEDEN
NORWAY
Trondheim
Kristiansund
Molde
Ålesund
Bergen
Haugesund
Stavanger
Kristiansand
Arendal
Larvik
Skien
Drammen
Oslo
Hamar
Lillehammer
Gjøvik
Fredrikstad
Sarpsborg
Halden
Moss
Tønsberg
Hitra
Smøla
Dovrefjell
Jotunheimen
Hardangervidda
Jostedalsbreen
Rondane
Femunden
Mjøsa
Sognefjorden
Hardangerfjorden
Nordfjord
Lindesnes
Projection: Lambert's Conformal Conic
East from Greenwich
COPYRIGHT PHILIP'S
160
162
163

1:4 000 000

50   0 25 50 75 100 125 150 175 km
50   0 25   50   75   100   125 miles

ATLANTIC OCEAN

NORWAY
Askøyna
Bergen
Osøyro
Stord
Bømlo   Leirvik
Haugesund
Kopervik   Boknafjorden
Åkrahamn
Stavanger
Sandnes
Bryne   Nærbø

Shetland Is.
(U.K.)
Yell   Unst
Fetlar
Foula   Mainland
Lerwick

Fair Isle

Orkney Is.
Westray   Sanday
Stronsay
Mainland   Kirkwall
Hoy
South
Ronaldsay

C. Wrath
Pentland Firth
Thurso
Wick
Helmsdale
Lairg
Golspie
Lewis   Stornoway
North Minch
Ullapool   Tain   Golspie
Invergordon   Buckie
Dingwall   Banff   Fraserburgh
Harris   Nairn   Elgin   Peterhead
St. Kilda   North   Inverness   Huntly
(U.K.)   Uist   Aviemore   Inverurie
Benbecula   Glen More   CAIRNGORMS   Don   Aberdeen
South Uist   L. Ness   Dee
Skye   Ben Nevis   SCOTLAND   Ballater   Stonehaven
Barra   Rhum   Fort William   Grampian Mts.   Forfar   Montrose
Eigg   Arbroath
Coll   Oban   Perth   Dundee
Mull   L. LOMOND   St. Andrews
Tiree   Stirling   Glenrothes
Colonsay   L. Awe   L. Lomond   Kirkcaldy
Jura   Dumbarton   Dunfermline   Dunbar
Islay   Greenock   GLASGOW   Edinburgh   Berwick-upon-Tweed
East Kilbride   Motherwell
Campbeltown   Paisley   Hamilton   Galashiels
Arran   Kilmarnock   Southern Uplands   Jedburgh   Alnwick
Ayr   Hawick   Cheviot Hills
Girvan   Dumfries   NORTHUMBERLAND

Outer Hebrides
Inner Hebrides
Sea of the Hebrides
North Channel
Firth of Clyde

NORTH SEA

Malin Hd.
Buncrana   Coleraine
Aran I.   Letterkenny   Ballymena   Larne
Londonderry   Antrim   Bangor
GLENVEAGH   Omagh   NORTHERN IRELAND   Belfast
Donegal   Ulster   Lough Neagh   Lisburn   Lurgan
Bundoran   Enniskillen   Portadown   Newry
Lower L. Erne   Clones   Armagh
Sligo   Leitrim   Cavan   Castleblaney
Ballina   Castlebar   Carlisle
Workington   Hexham   Gateshead   Sunderland
Whitehaven   Durham   Hartlepool
Cumbrian   Redcar
Mts.   Darlington   Middlesbrough
Barrow-   Stockton-on-Tees
LAKE   in-Furness   N. YORK MOORS
DISTRICT   Lancaster   Scarborough
I. of Man   YORKSHIRE DALES   Bridlington
Douglas   Harrogate   York   Beverley
Keighley   Leeds   Kingston upon Hull
Blackpool   Bradford   Humber
Preston   Burnley   Huddersfield   Grimsby
Blackburn   Halifax   Barnsley   Scunthorpe
Bolton   Doncaster   Louth
MANCHESTER   Oldham   Rotherham
LIVERPOOL   Stockport   SHEFFIELD   Lincoln
Warrington   PEAK   Chesterfield   Boston   Skegness
Chester   DISTRICT   Mansfield   THE WASH
Crewe   Derby   Nottingham   King's Lynn   Cromer
Stoke on Trent   Grantham   THE BROADS
Stafford   Trent   Great Yarmouth
Shrewsbury   Telford   Leicester   Peterborough   Norwich   Lowestoft
Welshpool   Nuneaton   Corby   Thetford
BIRMINGHAM   Coventry   Northampton   Ely   Bury St. Edmunds   Ipswich
Wolverhampton   Rugby   Cambridge   Felixstowe
Redditch   Royal   Bedford   Harwich
Worcester   Leamington Spa   Milton Keynes   Colchester
Hereford   Cheltenham   Stevenage   Chelmsford
Gloucester   Oxford   Luton   Harlow
Cardigan Bay   Cotswold Hills   Hemel   Southend-on-Sea
Aberystwyth   High Wycombe   Hempstead   Slough   Watford   Basildon
Cambrian Mts.   Swindon   Reading   LONDON   Chatham   Margate
WALES   Newbury   Basingstoke   Reigate   Maidstone   Canterbury
SNOWDONIA   ENGLAND   Guildford   Crawley   Dover
Snowdon   Newport   Crawley   Ashford   Folkestone
Pwllheli   Bath   Salisbury   Winchester   Hastings
Llanelli   Cardiff   Bristol   Eastbourne   Str. of Dover
Wrexham   Brecon   NEW   Southampton   Fareham   Brighton   Worthing
Bangor   Merthyr Tydfil   FOREST   Havant   Portsmouth
Colwyn Bay   BRECON BEACONS   Bournemouth   Isle of Wight
Anglesey   Swansea   Port Talbot   Poole   Newport
Holyhead   Barry   Weston-super-Mare
Carmarthen   Bristol Channel   Weymouth

UNITED KINGDOM

IRELAND
Achill I.   Westport   Roscommon   Longford
Lough Mask   Connemara   Lough Corrib   Athlone   Mullingar   Boyne   Drogheda
Galway B.   Galway   Ballinasloe   Tullamore   Dundalk
Aran Is.   BURREN   Birr   Liffey   DUBLIN   Dun Laoghaire
Ennis   Lough Derg   Port Laoise   Bray
Kilrush   Nenagh   Athy   Carlow   Arklow
Shannon   Limerick   Thurles   Kilkenny   Wicklow Mts.
Listowel   Tipperary   Carrick-on-Suir   Wexford
Tralee   Clonmel   Waterford   Rosslare
Dingle   Mallow   Blackwater   Dungarvan
Killarney   Cork   Youghal   St. George's Channel
Carrauntoohill   Bandon   Cobh   Fishguard   Milford Haven
Macgillycuddy's Reeks   Kinsale   Haverfordwest   Pembroke
Bantry   PEMBROKESHIRE COAST
C. Clear   Neath
Kenmare

IRISH SEA

CELTIC SEA

Barnstaple   Exmoor   Taunton
Bude   Yeovil
Newquay   DARTMOOR   Exmouth
Truro   Exeter   Dorchester
St. Austell   Torbay   Torquay
Land's End   Plymouth
Penzance   Falmouth
Isles of Scilly

English Channel

NETHERLANDS
Texel
Den Helder
Alkmaar
Haarlem
's-Gravenhage (Den Haag)
Hoek van Holland
ROTTERDAM   Dordrecht

BELGIUM
Vlissingen
Zeebrugge
Oostende   Brugge
Dunkerque   Gent   Mechelen
Calais   Antwerpen
Boulogne-sur-Mer   BRUSSEL (Bruxelles)
St-Omer   LILLE   Tournai
Béthune   Mechelen
C. Gris-Nez   Bruay-la-Buissière   Valenciennes
Le Touquet-   Lens   Cambrai
Paris-Plage   Villeneuve d'Ascq
St. Quentin
FRANCE
Dieppe
Le Tréport   Abbeville   Amiens   Laon
Fécamp   Pays de Caux   Picardie
C. de la Hague   Le Havre   Rouen
Pte. de Barfleur   Seine   Elbeuf
Alderney   Rolbec
St. Peter Port   Guernsey   Cherbourg
Sark   Valognes   Lisieux
St. Helier   Jersey   Bayeux   Caen
Channel Is.   Cotentin   Trouville-sur-Mer
(U.K.)

Projection: Conical with two standard parallels

West from Greenwich   East from Greenwich   COPYRIGHT PHILIP'S

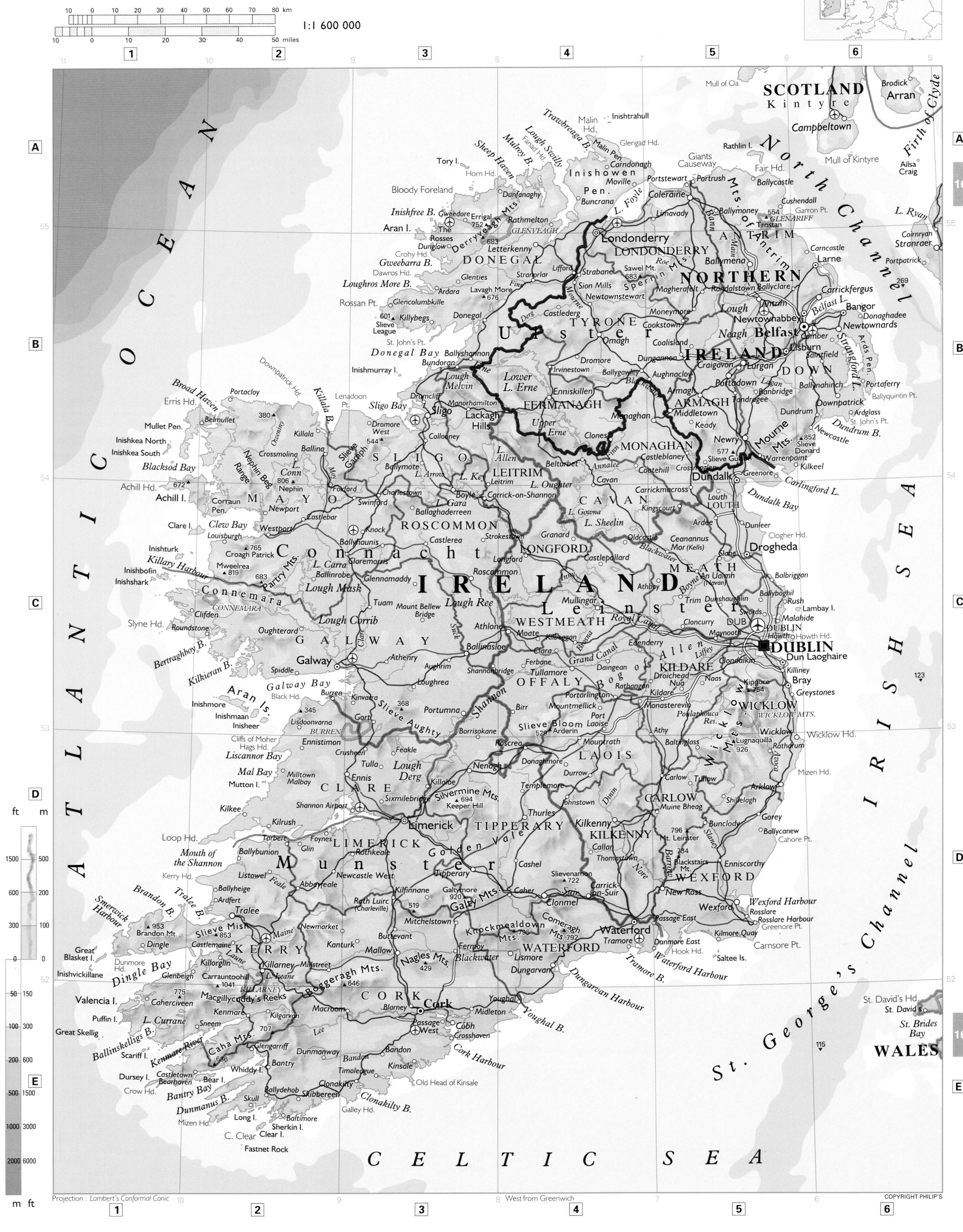

10 10 20 30 40 50 60 70 80 km
10 0 10 20 30 40 50 miles

1:1 600 000

Projection : Lambert's Conformal Conic
West from Greenwich
COPYRIGHT PHILIP'S

ATLANTIC OCEAN

NORTH CHANNEL

IRISH SEA

St. George's Channel

CELTIC SEA

SCOTLAND
Kintyre
Arran
Brodick
Campbeltown
Firth of Clyde
Mull of Oa
Mull of Kintyre
Ailsa Craig
Cairnryan
Stranraer
Portpatrick
L. Ryan

IRELAND

NORTHERN IRELAND

Ulster
Leinster
Munster
Connacht

Counties / regions
DONEGAL
LONDONDERRY
ANTRIM
TYRONE
FERMANAGH
MONAGHAN
ARMAGH
DOWN
CAVAN
LEITRIM
SLIGO
MAYO
ROSCOMMON
LONGFORD
WESTMEATH
MEATH
LOUTH
GALWAY
OFFALY
KILDARE
DUBLIN
WICKLOW
LAOIS
CARLOW
CLARE
TIPPERARY
KILKENNY
WEXFORD
LIMERICK
KERRY
CORK
WATERFORD

Cities and towns
Londonderry
Belfast
Dublin
Dún Laoghaire
Cork
Limerick
Galway
Waterford
Sligo
Drogheda
Dundalk
Newry
Coleraine
Ballymena
Larne
Bangor
Carrickfergus
Lisburn
Armagh
Omagh
Enniskillen
Monaghan
Letterkenny
Donegal
Ballina
Castlebar
Westport
Roscommon
Longford
Mullingar
Athlone
Tullamore
Naas
Bray
Greystones
Wicklow
Arklow
Gorey
Enniscorthy
Wexford
Rosslare
New Ross
Carlow
Kilkenny
Clonmel
Carrick-on-Suir
Dungarvan
Tralee
Killarney
Kenmare
Bantry
Skibbereen
Clonakilty
Kinsale
Cóbh
Midleton
Youghal
Mallow
Fermoy
Tipperary
Cashel
Thurles
Nenagh
Ennis
Kilrush
Listowel

Physical features
Macgillycuddy's Reeks
Carrauntoohill 1041
Mweelrea 819
Croagh Patrick 765
Nephin 806
Errigal 752
Slieve Donard 852
Lugnaquilla 926
Mt. Leinster 796
Galtymore 920
Knockmealdown Mts.
Comeragh Mts.
Slieve Bloom
Wicklow Mts.
Slieve Aughty
Silvermine Mts.
Keeper Hill 694
Slieve Mish
Caha Mts.
Boggeragh Mts.
Nagles Mts.

Lough Neagh
Lough Erne
Lower L. Erne
Upper L. Erne
Lough Corrib
Lough Mask
Lough Ree
Lough Derg
Lough Conn
Lough Allen
L. Key
L. Gara
L. Oughter
L. Sheelin
L. Gowna
L. Ennell

Donegal Bay
Sligo Bay
Clew Bay
Galway Bay
Dingle Bay
Bantry Bay
Cork Harbour
Dundalk Bay
Wexford Harbour
Waterford Harbour
Tramore B.
Youghal B.
Kenmare River
Mouth of the Shannon
Tralee B.
Brandon B.
Smerwick Harbour

Shannon
River Barrow
Blackwater
Boyne
Liffey
Royal Canal
Grand Canal

Malin Head
Bloody Foreland
Horn Hd.
Erris Hd.
Achill Hd.
Loop Hd.
Mizen Hd.
Old Head of Kinsale
Carnsore Pt.
Wicklow Hd.

Aran Is.
Inishmore
Inishmaan
Inisheer
Achill I.
Clare I.
Valencia I.
Great Blasket I.
Fastnet Rock
Clear I.
Rathlin I.
Lambay I.

Giants Causeway
Cliffs of Moher
Golden Vale

WALES
St. David's
St. David's Hd.
St. Brides Bay

1:1 600 000

10 0 10 20 30 40 50 60 70 80 km
10 0 10 20 30 40 50 miles

Key to Scottish unitary authorities on map
1 CITY OF ABERDEEN
2 DUNDEE CITY
3 WEST DUNBARTONSHIRE
4 EAST DUNBARTONSHIRE
5 CITY OF GLASGOW
6 INVERCLYDE
7 RENFREWSHIRE
8 EAST RENFREWSHIRE
9 NORTH LANARKSHIRE
10 FALKIRK
11 CLACKMANNANSHIRE
12 WEST LOTHIAN
13 CITY OF EDINBURGH
14 MIDLOTHIAN

ORKNEY IS. on same scale

North Ronaldsay
Papa Westray
Westray
Rousay
Eday
Sanday
Stronsay
Stromness
Mainland
ORKNEY
Kirkwall
Brough Hd.
481
Hoy
Scapa Flow
St. Mary's
Burray
South Ronaldsay
Shapinsay
Burwick
Dunnet Hd. Stroma
Pentland Firth
Thurso
John o' Groats
Duncansby Head
Sinclair's Bay

SHETLAND IS. on same scale

Muckle Flugga
Unst
Haroldswick
Fetlar
Yell
453
Esha Ness
Yell Sound
Ulsta
Out Skerries
St. Magnus Bay
Sullom Voe
Whalsay
Papa Stour
Voe
Walls
SHETLAND
Lerwick
Foula
Scalloway
Bressay
West Burra
Boddam
Sumburgh Hd.

WESTERN ISLES
Butt of Lewis
Flannan Is.
Gallan Hd.
Broad Bay
Stornoway
Lewis
Scarp
Taransay
799
Clisham
Harris
Toe Hd.
Pabbay
Berneray
Sound of Harris
North Uist
Lochmaddy
Baleshare
Grimsay
Benbecula
Ardivachar Pt.
South Uist
Ben Mhor 620
Lochboisdale
Eriskay
Barra
Castlebay
Vatersay
Sandray
Barra Hd. 268
Outer Hebrides
North Minch
Little Minch
Sea of the Hebrides
Inner Hebrides

C. Wrath
Durness
L. Eriboll
Strathy Pt.
Dunnet Hd.
Dounreay
Thurso
Halkirk
Caithness
Wick
Lybster
Ord of Caithness
Helmsdale
Brora
Golspie
Dornoch
Tain
Tarbat Ness
Moray Firth

Handa
Eddrachillis B.
Pt. of Stoer
L. Laxford
Reay Forest
Ben Hope 927
Tongue
Sutherland
West Highlands
961
705
Strath Oykel
Lairg
Bonar Bridge
Dornoch Firth

Greenstone Pt.
Lochinver
Ben More Assynt 998
L. Assynt
Enard B.
Rubha Coigeach
Ullapool
L. Broom
1081
Ben Dearg 1109
L. Shin
Oykel

Gairloch
L. Ewe
L. Maree 1053
L. Fannich
Ben Wyvis 1045
Strathpeffer
Dingwall
Muir of Ord
Invergordon
Alness
Cromarty
Fortrose
Nairn
Elgin
Forres
Lossiemouth
Burghead
Buckie
Portknockie
Portsoy
Cullen
Banff
Macduff
Rosehearty
Fraserburgh
Rattray Hd.
Kinnairds Hd.

Gruinard B.
Rubha Unish
L. Gairloch
L. Torridon
Inner Sound
Raasay
Rona
L. Carron
Stromeferry
Carn Eige 1182
Beauly
Beauly
Inverness
Loch Ness
MORAY
Rothes
Fochabers
Keith
Aberchirder
Turriff
Huntly
BUCHAN
Peterhead
Buchan Ness
Cruden Bay
Ellon
Deveron
Yhan

Uig
Skye
Portree
L. Snizort
L. Bracadale
Dunvegan
Cuillin Hills 992
Scalpay
Kyle of Lochalsh
Dornie
1068
Glen Affric
Glen Moriston
Fort Augustus
941
Monadhliath Mts.
Carn Ban 1124
Aviemore
Kingussie
Newtonmore
CAIRNGORM Mts.
Strath Spey
Grantown-on-Spey
Tomintoul
Alford
Charlestown of Aberlour
Dufftown
Aberlour
Oldmeldrum
Inverurie
Kintore
Westhill
ABERDEENSHIRE
Dyce
Aberdeen
Girdle Ness
Peterculter
Banchory
Stonehaven

Cuillin Sound
Sd. of Sleat
Mallaig
Knoydart
L. Arkaig
L. Lochy 1128
Glen Spean
Spean
L. Lochy
Fort William
Ben Nevis 1342
Kinlochleven
Lochaber
L. Morar
L. Shiel
L. Eil
Arisaig
Pt. of Ardnamurchan
L. Moidart
L. Sunart
Morvern
Ballachulish
1148
Glen Coe
Rannoch Moor
L. Rannoch
1148
Forest of Atholl 1121
Blair Atholl
Pitlochry
Kirriemuir
Brechin
Montrose
ANGUS
Laurencekirk
Inverbervie
N. Esk
Glen More
Cairn Toul 1291
Ben Macdhui 1309
Braemar
Ballater
Aboyne
Lochnagar 1155
Cairngorms
Grampian Mountains
Forest of Atholl
1154

Coll
Tobermory
Passage of Tiree
Tiree
Staffa
Ulva
Mull
Ben More 966
Iona
Sound of Mull
Lismore
Kerrera
Oban
Lorn
Firth of Lorn
Luing
Scarba
Colonsay
Oronsay
ARGYLL AND BUTE
Ben Cruachan 1126
Crianlarich
Ben More 1174
Ben Lawers 1214
SCOTLAND
Crieff
Comrie
Ben Vorlich 983
Callander
Aberfeldy
Dunkeld
PERTH AND KINROSS
Blairgowrie
Alyth
Coupar
Tay
Strathmore
455
Sidlaw Hills
Forfar
Arbroath
Carnoustie
Monifieth
Dundee
Firth of Tay
Tayport
Leuchars
St. Andrews
Fife Ness
Perth
Scone
Cupar
Auchtermuchty
FIFE
Falkland
Leven
Anstruther
Buckhaven
Glenrothes
Cowdenbeath
Kirkcaldy

Jura
Sd. of Jura
Rubh a' Mhail
Ardnave Pt.
Islay
Bowmore
Port Ellen
Rhinns Pt.
Mull of Oa
Gigha
Kintyre
Tarbert
Loch Fyne
Lochgilphead
Inveraray
Loch Awe
LOCH LOMOND AND THE TROSSACHS
Ben Lomond 973
Loch Lomond
Aberfoyle
Callander
Doune
Dunblane
STIRLING
Stirling
Bannockburn
Alloa
Dollar
Ochil Hills
Kinross
720
Dunfermline
Firth of Forth
North Berwick
Dunbar
EAST LOTHIAN
Haddington
Musselburgh
St. Abb's Head
Eyemouth

Campbeltown
Mull of Kintyre
Kilbrannan Sd.
Goat Fell 874
Brodick
Arran
Firth of Clyde
Rothesay
Bute
Dunoon
Gourock
Greenock
Port Glasgow
Helensburgh
Alexandria
Dumbarton
Kirkintilloch
Cumbernauld
Denny
Falkirk
Grangemouth
Bo'ness
GLASGOW
Paisley
Clydebank
Airdrie
Coatbridge
Motherwell
Hamilton
East Kilbride
Wishaw
Carluke
Lanark
Livingston
Bathgate
Edinburgh
Dalkeith
Penicuik
Bonnyrigg
Peebles
Pentland Hills
Moorfoot Hills
Lammermuir Hills
535
Duns
Coldstream
Tweed
Galashiels
Melrose
Selkirk
Kelso
Jedburgh
Flodden
651
SCOTTISH BORDERS
Hawick
The Cheviot 816
Wooler
Bamburgh
Farne Is.
Holy I.
Berwick-upon-Tweed

Saltcoats
Ardrossan
Kilwinning
Irvine
Troon
Prestwick
Ayr
NORTH AYRSHIRE
Dalry
Kilmarnock
Strathaven
Biggar
EAST AYRSHIRE
SOUTH LANARKSHIRE
Broad Law 840
Moffat
Maybole
Cumnock
Sanquhar
733
Dalmellington
Girvan
Ailsa Craig
SOUTH AYRSHIRE
Merrick 844
New Galloway
Nith
Dumfries
Lockerbie
Langholm
Ettrick Water
Esk
Teviot
Alnwick
Almouth
Amble
Morpeth
NORTHUMBERLAND
Kielder Water
North Tyne

NORTHERN IRELAND
Larne
Cushendall
Garron Pt.
269
Belfast L.
Carrickfergus
Bangor
Donaghadee
Newtownards
Belfast
North Channel
Stranraer
Cairnryan
Loch Ryan
Portpatrick
Luce Bay
Wigtown B.
Mull of Galloway
Whithorn
Burrow Hd.
Newton Stewart
Galloway
Wigtown
Gatehouse of Fleet
Kirkcudbright
Castle Douglas
Dalbeattie
DUMFRIES & GALLOWAY
Annan
Solway Firth
Gretna
Carlisle
Brampton
ENGLAND
Aspatria
Maryport
Workington
Whitehaven
St. Bees Hd.
Cockermouth
Keswick
931
Skiddaw
Derwent Water
Ullswater
Helvellyn 950
CUMBRIA
Penrith
Appleby-in-Westmorland
Brough
893
Cross Fell
Alston
Haltwhistle
Hexham
Consett
Stanley
Blaydon
Gateshead
Newcastle-upon-Tyne
HADRIAN'S WALL
DURHAM
Crook
Bishop Auckland
Barnard Castle
Wear

ATLANTIC OCEAN
NORTH SEA

West from Greenwich

Projection: Lambert's Conformal Conic

COPYRIGHT PHILIP'S

ft m
3000 1000
1500 500
600 200
300 100
0
150 50
100
200 600
1000 3000
m ft

166
168

1:1 600 000

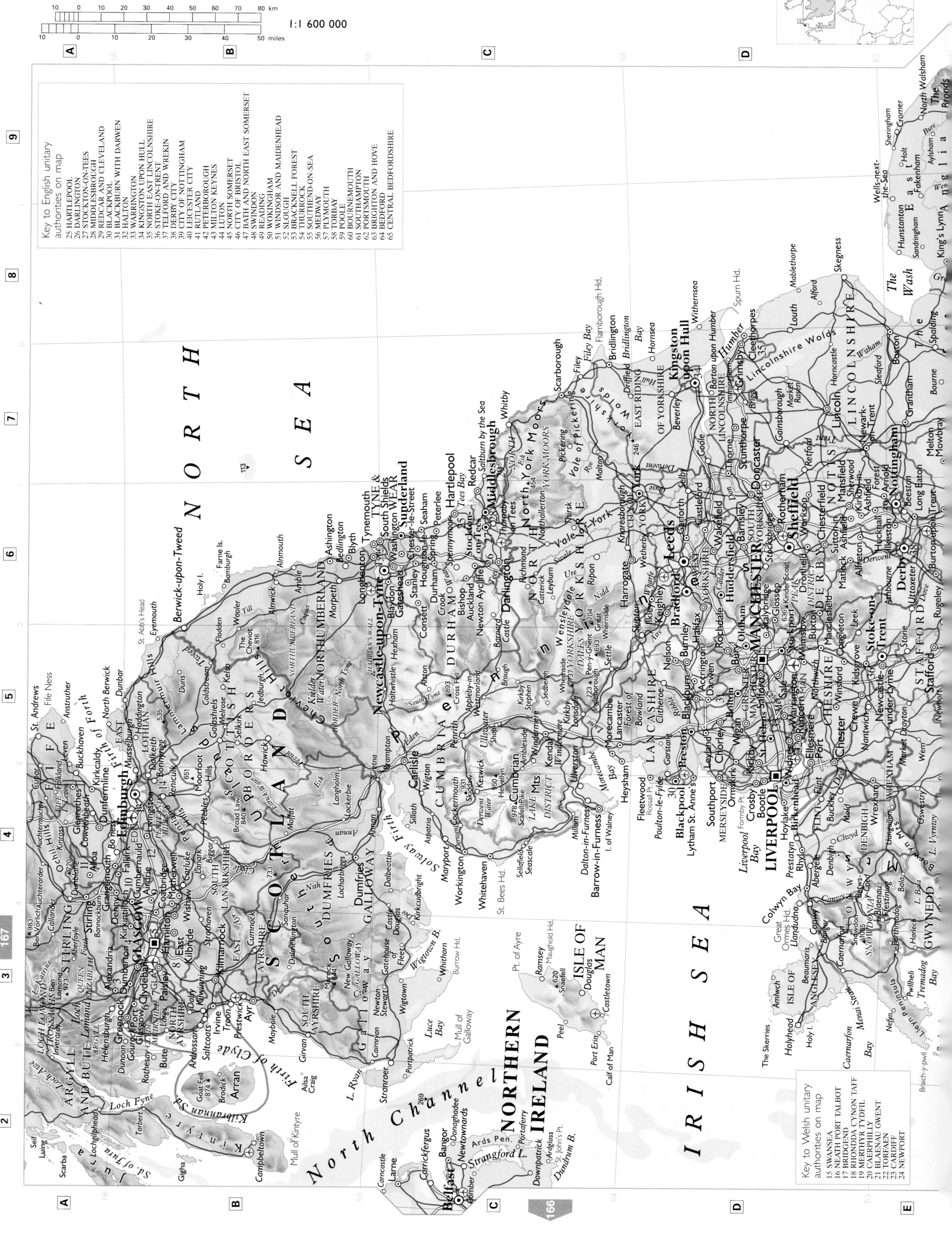

10 0 10 20 30 40 50 60 70 80 km
10 0 10 20 30 40 50 miles

Key to English unitary
authorities on map

25 HARTLEPOOL
26 DARLINGTON
27 STOCKTON-ON-TEES
28 MIDDLESBROUGH
29 REDCAR AND CLEVELAND
30 BLACKPOOL
31 BLACKBURN WITH DARWEN
32 HALTON
33 WARRINGTON
34 KINGSTON UPON HULL
35 NORTH EAST LINCOLNSHIRE
36 STOKE-ON-TRENT
37 TELFORD AND WREKIN
38 DERBY CITY
39 CITY OF NOTTINGHAM
40 LEICESTER CITY
41 RUTLAND
42 PETERBOROUGH
43 MILTON KEYNES
44 LUTON
45 NORTH SOMERSET
46 CITY OF BRISTOL
47 BATH AND NORTH EAST SOMERSET
48 SWINDON
49 READING
50 WOKINGHAM
51 WINDSOR AND MAIDENHEAD
52 SLOUGH
53 BRACKNELL FOREST
54 THURROCK
55 SOUTHEND-ON-SEA
56 MEDWAY
57 PLYMOUTH
58 TORBAY
59 POOLE
60 BOURNEMOUTH
61 SOUTHAMPTON
62 PORTSMOUTH
63 BRIGHTON AND HOVE
64 BEDFORD
65 CENTRAL BEDFORDSHIRE

Key to Welsh unitary
authorities on map

15 SWANSEA
16 NEATH PORT TALBOT
17 BRIDGEND
18 RHONDDA CYNON TAFF
19 MERTHYR TYDFIL
20 CAERPHILLY
21 BLAENAU GWENT
22 TORFAEN
23 CARDIFF
24 NEWPORT

NORTH SEA

IRISH SEA

North Channel

NORTHERN IRELAND

SCOTLAND

ISLE OF MAN

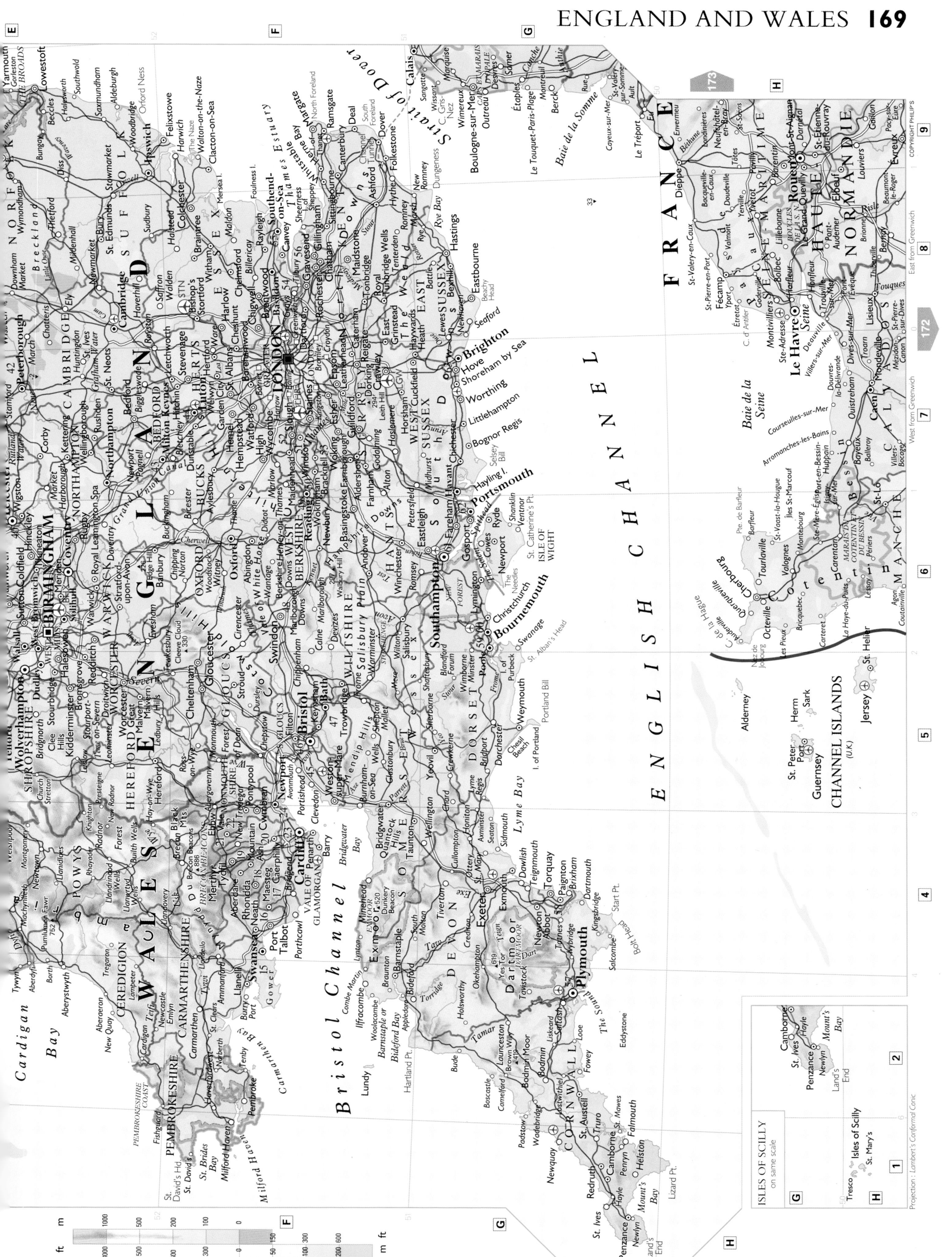

Projection: Lambert's Conformal Conic

1:2 000 000

10 0 10 20 30 40 50 60 70 80 90 km
10 0 10 20 30 40 50 60 miles

NORTH SEA

UNITED KINGDOM

Cromer
North Walsham
THE BROADS
Norwich
Great Yarmouth
Bungay
Beccles
Lowestoft
Southwold
Saxmundham
Aldeburgh
Woodbridge
Orford Ness
Felixstowe

Margate
North Foreland
Ramsgate
Deal
Dover
Calais
Sangatte
Wissant
C. Gris-Nez
Marquise

Dunkerque
St-Pol-sur-Mer
Gravelines
Oostende
De Haan
Blankenberge
Zeebrugge
Knokke-Heist

Boulogne-sur-Mer
Étaples
Berck
Rue
St-Valery-sur-Somme
Le Crotoy
Abbeville

NETHERLANDS

Waddeneilanden
Terschelling
Vlieland
Texel
Den Burg
Den Helder
Schiermonnikoog
Ameland
Holwerd
Dokkum
Leeuwarden
Franeker
Harlingen
Bolsward
Sneek
FRIESLAND
Heerenveen
Drachten
Wolvega
Steenwijk
Emmeloord
Urk
Staveren
Lemmer
Workum

Groningen
GRONINGEN
Delfzijl
Zoutkamp
Bedum
Uithuizen
Winschoten
Hoogezand-Sappemeer
Veendam
Assen
DRENTHE
Hoogeveen
Emmen
Coevorden
Klazienaveen
Beilen

Schagen
Alkmaar
Heerhugowaard
Bergen
Castricum
IJmuiden
Haarlem
Zandvoort
Hillegom
Noordwijk
Katwijk
Leiden
NOORD-HOLLAND
Hoorn
Enkhuizen
Purmerend
Edam
Zaanstad
AMSTERDAM
Almere-Stad
Bussum
Hilversum
Lelystad
FLEVOLAND
Dronten
Kampen
Zwolle
OVERIJSSEL
Hardenberg
Almelo
Hengelo
Enschede
Haaksbergen
Oldenzaal

's-Gravenhage (Den Haag)
Zoetermeer
Delft
Gouda
Vlaardingen
Schiedam
ROTTERDAM
ZUID-HOLLAND
Dordrecht
Gorinchem
Waalwijk
's-Hertogenbosch
Tilburg
Breda
Eindhoven
NOORD-BRABANT
Helmond
Venlo
Roermond
LIMBURG
Weert
Maastricht
Heerlen

Utrecht
Amersfoort
Apeldoorn
Deventer
Zutphen
Arnhem
Nijmegen
GELDERLAND
Ede
Wageningen
Tiel

ZEELAND
Middelburg
Vlissingen
Goes
Terneuzen
Hulst

Oosterhout
Roosendaal
Bergen op Zoom

BELGIUM

BRUSSEL (Bruxelles)
Antwerpen
Gent (Gand)
Brugge
Oostende
Mechelen
Leuven
Hasselt
Genk
Turnhout
Aarschot
Tienen
Sint-Niklaas
Lokeren
Dendermonde
Aalst
Vilvoorde
Waterloo
Nivelles
Namur
Charleroi
Mons
La Louvière
Tournai
Liège
Verviers
Eupen
Huy
Dinant
Marche-en-Famenne
Bastogne
Arlon
St-Hubert
Neufchâteau
Bouillon

VLAANDEREN
WEST-VLAANDEREN
OOST-VLAANDEREN
Roeselare
Kortrijk
Ieper
Menen
Mouscron
Ronse
Oudenaarde
Geraardsbergen
Soignies
Ath
BRABANT
HAINAUT
LIMBURG
Maaseik
Tongeren
St-Truiden
Herentals
Geel
Lommel
Mol
LUXEMBOURG
LIÈGE
 NAMUR

LUXEMBOURG
Luxembourg
Diekirch
Echternach
Wiltz
Esch-sur-Alzette
Grevenmacher
Vianden
Mersch

GERMANY
Bremerhaven
Nordenham
Oldenburg
Emden
Leer
Wilhelmshaven
Aurich
Norden
Papenburg
Cloppenburg
Meppen
Lingen
Nordhorn
Rheine
Osnabrück
Münster
Dortmund
Essen
Duisburg
Düsseldorf
Köln
Bonn
Krefeld
Mönchengladbach
Aachen
Düren
Koblenz
Wiesbaden
Mainz
Saarbrücken
Kaiserslautern
NORDRHEIN-WESTFALEN
RHEINLAND-PFALZ
SAARLAND
Trier
Bitburg

Ostfriesische Inseln
Borkum
Juist
Norderney
Baltrum
Langeoog
Spiekeroog
Wangerooge
Helgoland
Scharhörn
Neuwerk

FRANCE
Paris
Versailles
Beauvais
Amiens
Compiègne
Soissons
Laon
St-Quentin
Cambrai
Arras
Lens
Béthune
Douai
Valenciennes
Maubeuge
Lille
Roubaix
Tourcoing
Armentières
Hazebrouck
St-Omer
Calais
Boulogne-sur-Mer
Reims
Épernay
Châlons-en-Champagne
Charleville-Mézières
Sedan
Verdun
Metz
Thionville
Nancy
Toul
Strasbourg
Saverne
Haguenau
Sarreguemines
Sarrebourg
St-Dizier
NORD
PAS-DE-CALAIS
PICARDIE
SOMME
OISE
AISNE
ARDENNES
MEUSE
MOSELLE
MEURTHE-ET-MOSELLE
LORRAINE
VOSGES
BAS-RHIN
CHAMPAGNE
SEINE-ET-MARNE
VAL-D'OISE
YVELINES
ESSONNE

IJsselmeer
Waddenzee
Niedersächsisches Wattenmeer
Rhein
Maas
Mosel
Meuse
Marne
Seine
Somme

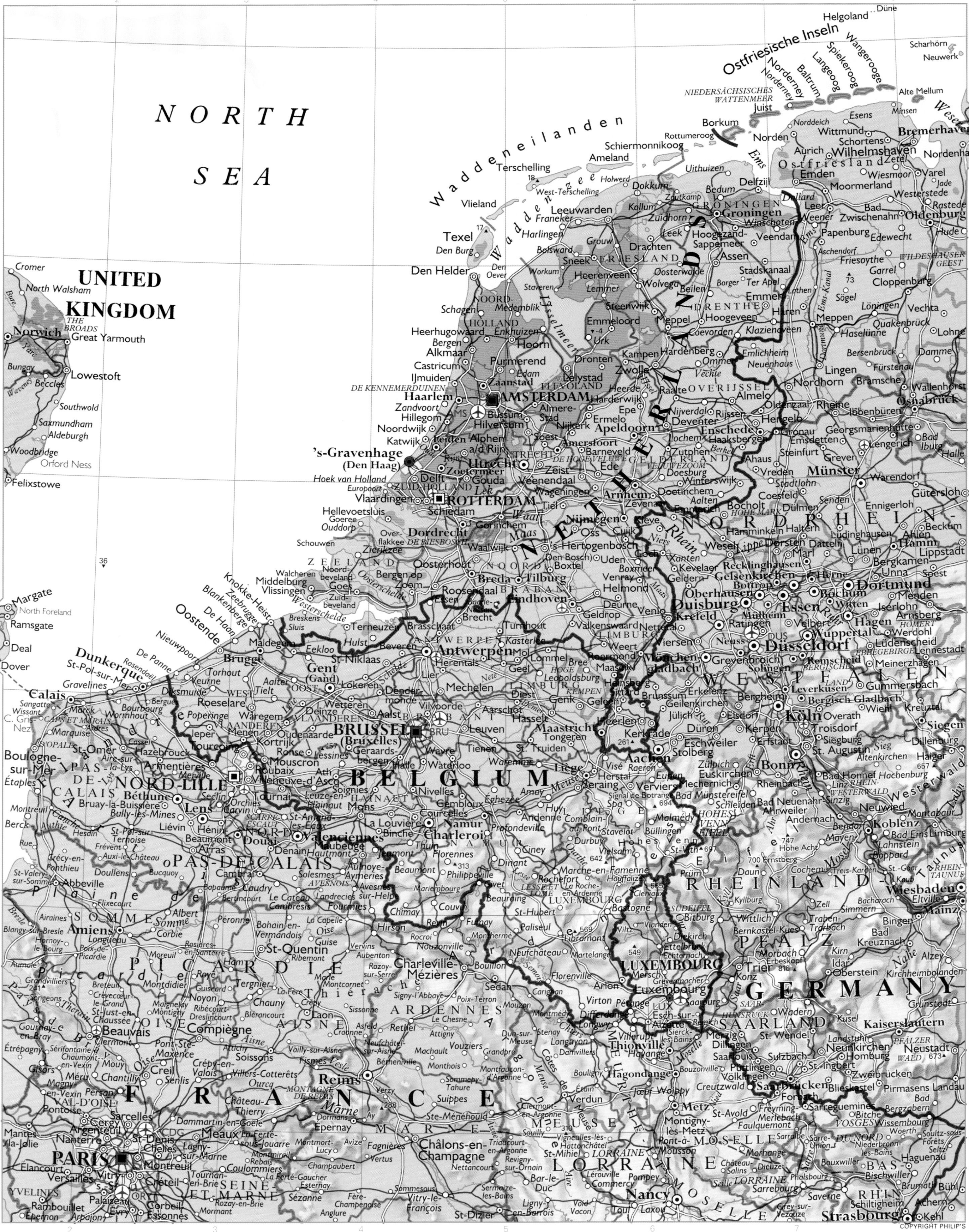

Underlined towns give their name to the administrative area in which they stand.

COPYRIGHT PHILIP'S

169
173
178
173

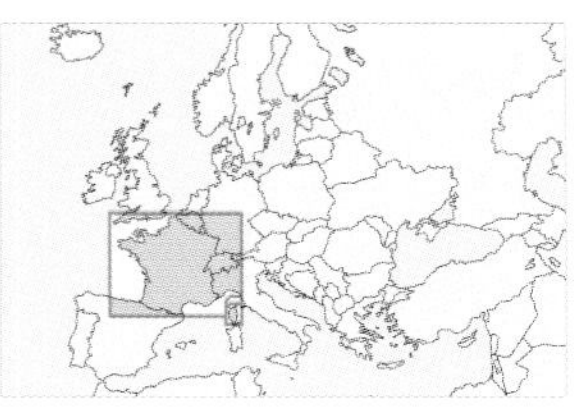

1:4 000 000

50   0   25   50   75   100   125   150   175 km

50   0   25   50   75   100   125 miles

Corse (Corsica)

MEDITERRANEAN SEA

GERMANY

SWITZERLAND

ITALY

BELGIUM

LUXEMBOURG

UNITED KINGDOM

English Channel

FRANCE

Bay of Biscay

Golfe de Gascogne

Massif Central

Golfe du Lion

PARIS

MARSEILLE

Provence

Côte d'Azur

MONACO

ANDORRA

East from Greenwich

West from Greenwich

Projection: Conical with two standard parallels

COPYRIGHT PHILIP'S

m   ft
4000   12000
3000   9000
2000   6000
1500   4500
1000   3000
500   1500
200   600
100   300
0   150
0

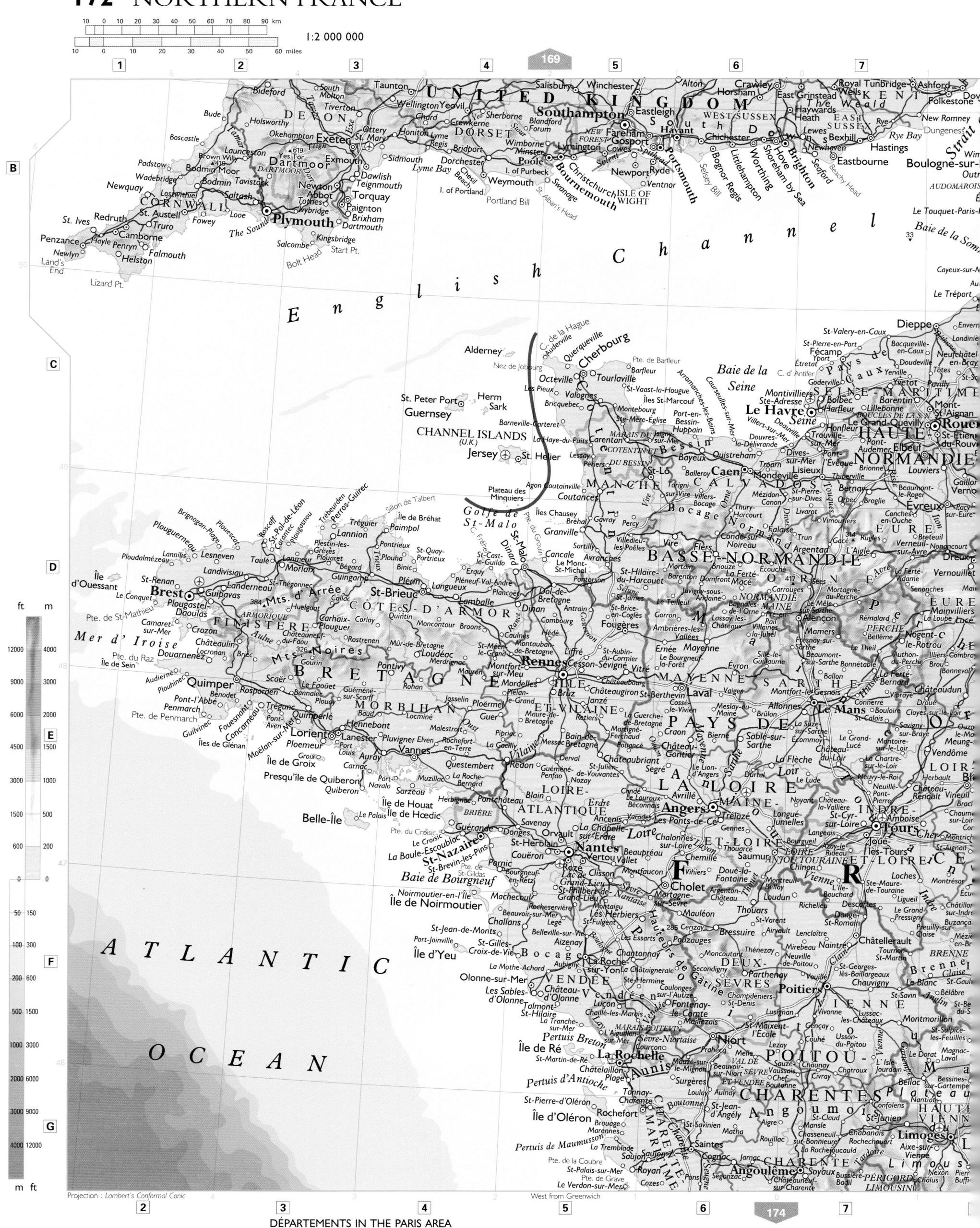

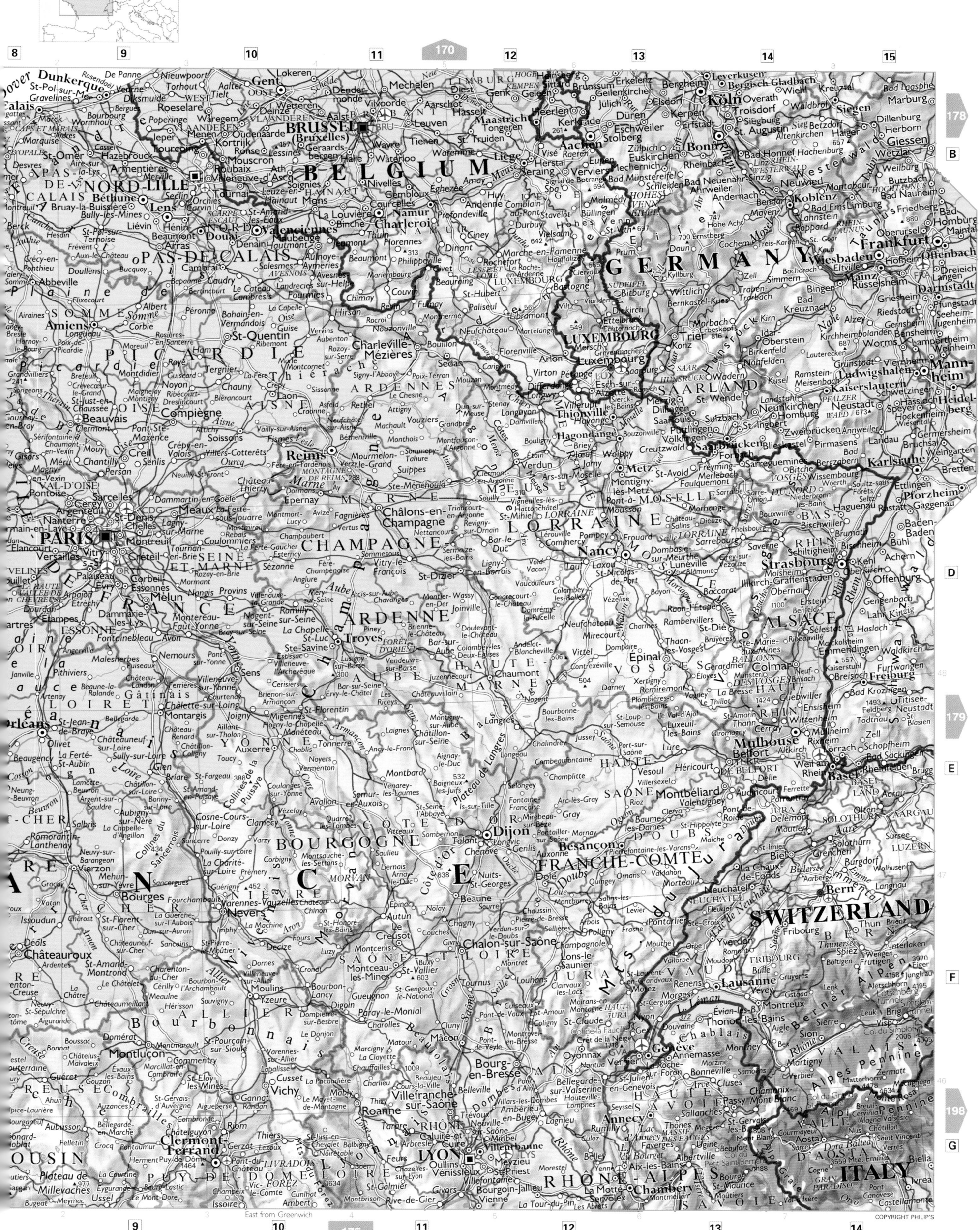

Underlined towns give their name to the administrative area in which they stand.

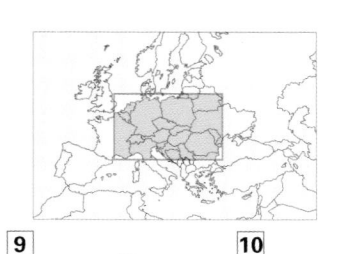

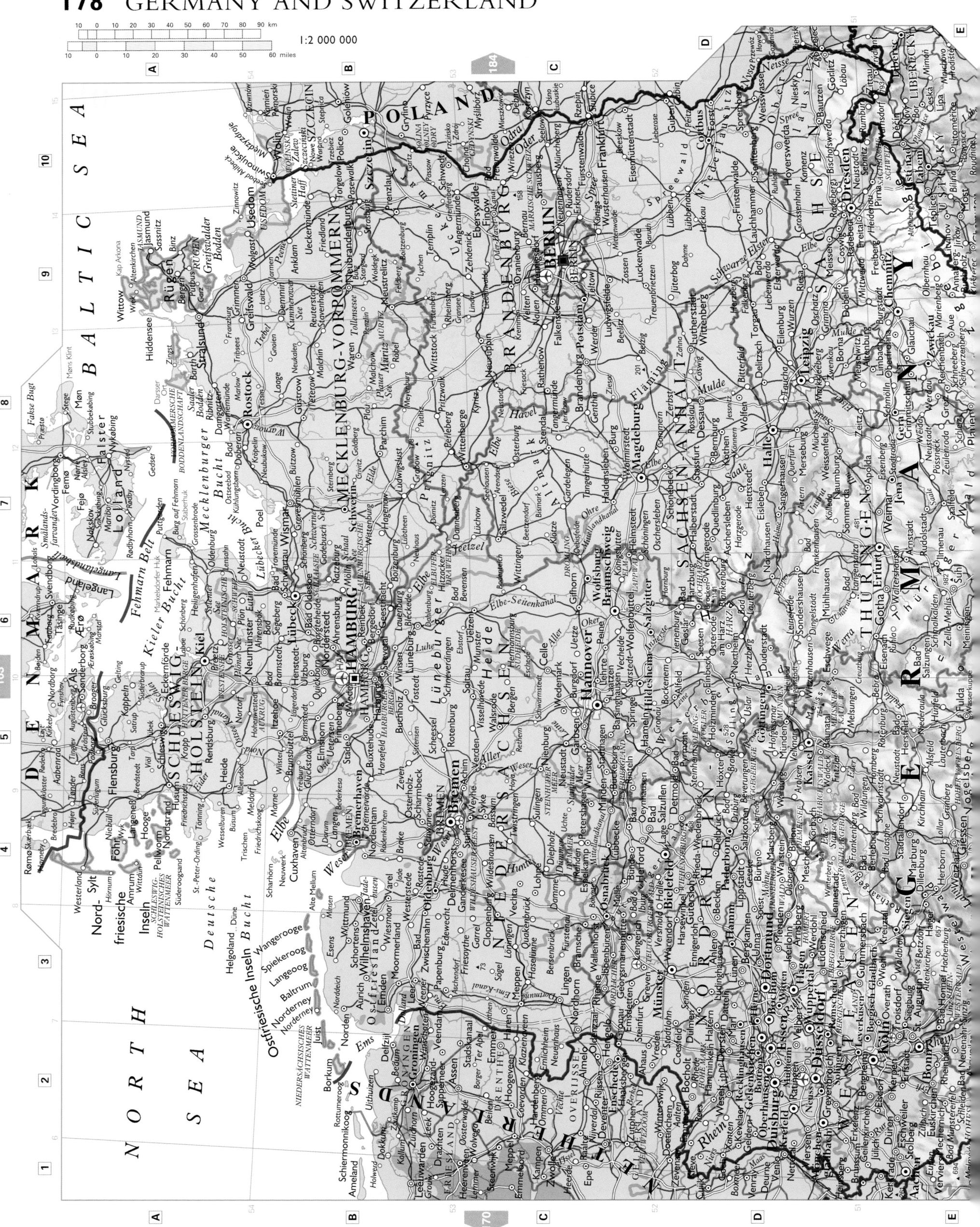

GERMANY
SWITZERLAND
FRANCE
ITALIA
AUSTRIA
SLOVENIA
Projection : Lambert's Conformal Conic
East from Greenwich
COPYRIGHT PHILIP'S

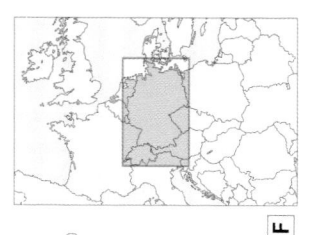

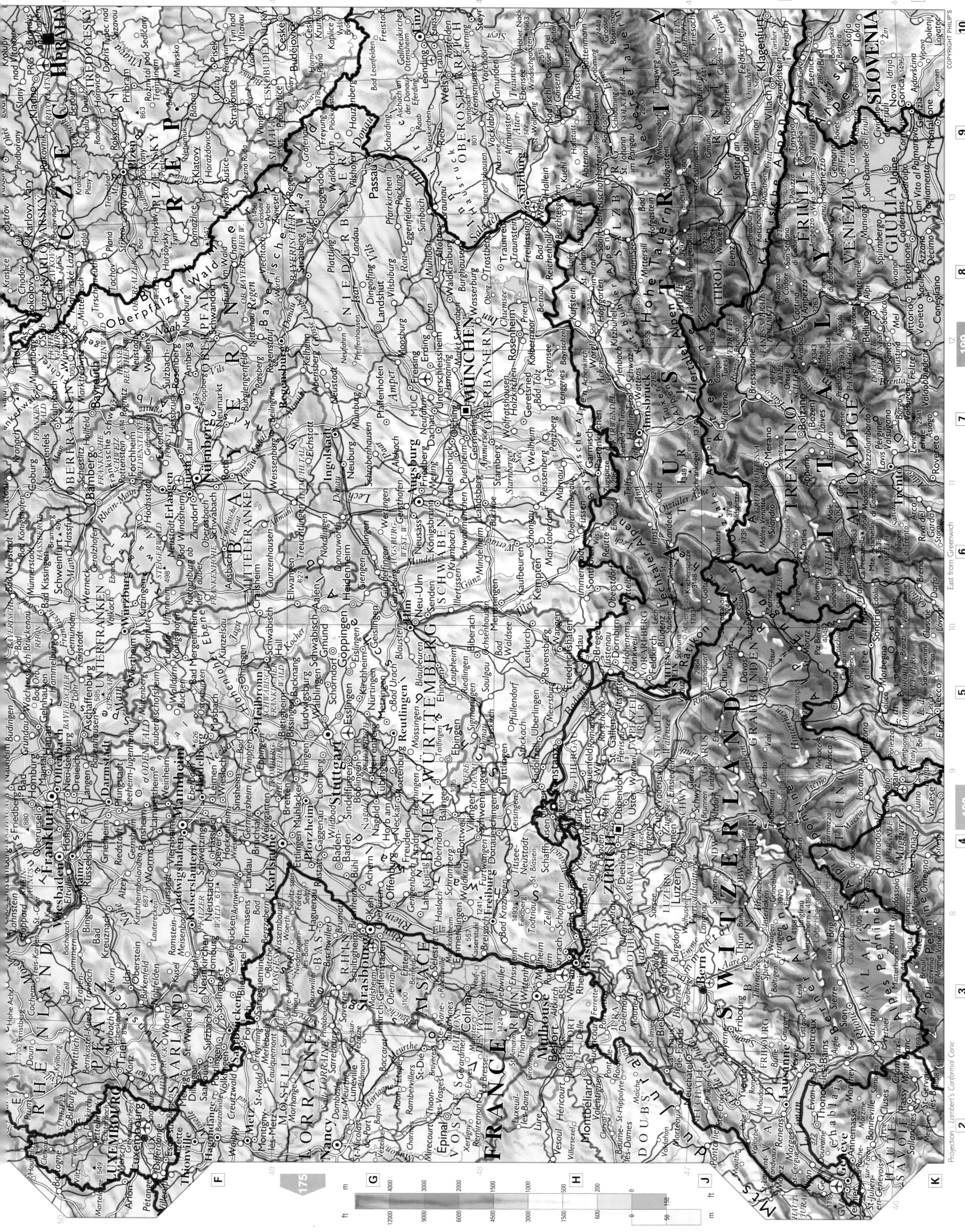

Underlined towns give their name to the administrative area in which they stand.

Underlined towns give their name to the administrative area in which they stand.

COPYRIGHT PHILIP'S

East from Greenwich

1:2 000 000

Administrative divisions in Croatia:

1 Brodsko-Posavska	5 Osječko-Baranjska	9 Vukovarsko-Srijemska
2 Koprivničko-Križevačka	6 Požeško-Slavonska	
4 Medimurska	8 Virovitičko-Podravska	

East from Greenwich

10 0 10 20 30 40 50 60 70 80 90 km

1:2 000 000

10 0 10 20 30 40 50 60 miles

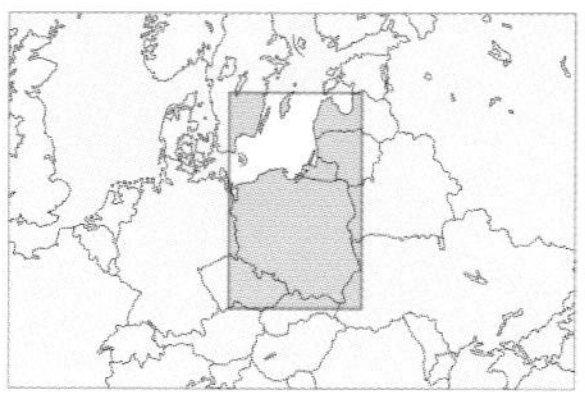

Gulf of Riga

Ruhnu

Kolkas rags

Irbes šaurums (Kur kurk)

LATVIA

Riga
Jūrmala
Olaine
Jelgava
Dobele
Bauska
Tukums
Ventspils
Liepāja
Talsi
Kuldīga
Saldus
Šiauliai
Palanga
Klaipėda
Šventoji

LITHUANIA

Kaunas
Marijampolė
Telšiai
Mažeikiai
Skuodas
Kretinga
Šilutė
Tauragė
Radviliškis

Neman / Nemunas

KALININGRAD (Russia)

Kaliningrad
Sovetsk
Gusev
Chernyakhovsk
Baltiysk
Zelenogradsk
Svetlogorsk
Bagrationovsk

Kuršský Záliv
Neringa
Nida

WARMIŃSKO-MAZURSKIE

Suwałki
Goldap
Węgorzewo
Giżycko
Olsztyn
Kętrzyn
Ełk
Mrągowo
Elbląg

Hrodna

SWEDEN

Jönköping
Kalmar
Karlskrona
Västervik
Oskarshamn
Växjö

Gotland (Sweden)
Visby

Öland (Sweden)

KALMAR LÄN
KRONOBERGS LÄN
BLEKINGE LÄN
JÖNKÖPINGS LÄN
GOTLANDS LÄN
SMÅLAND

BALTIC SEA

Bornholm (Denmark)
Rønne
Nexø

Hanöbukten
Bornholmsgattet

POMORSKIE

Gdańsk
Gdynia
Sopot
Zatoka Gdańska
Władysławowo
Hel
Puck
Rumia
Wejherowo
Lębork
Słupsk
Ustka
Koszalin
Kołobrzeg
Darłowo
Malbork
Tczew
Starogard
Grudziądz
Chojnice

ZACHODNIO-POMORSKIE

Szczecin
Stargard
Świnoujście
Goleniów
Police
Wolin
Międzyzdroje

Wisła

SŁOWIŃSKI

Pojezierze Mazurskie

POLAND
SLOVAK REP.
CZECH REP.
UKRAINE
BELARUS
GERMANY
AUSTRIA
POMORSKIE
MAZOWIECKIE
LUBELSKIE
PODKARPACKIE
MAŁOPOLSKIE
ŚWIĘTOKRZYSKIE
ŁÓDZKIE
ŚLĄSKIE
OPOLSKIE
DOLNOŚLĄSKIE
WIELKOPOLSKIE
LUBUSKIE
WARSZAWA
Kraków
Łódź
Wrocław
Poznań
Lublin
Kielce
Radom
Częstochowa
Katowice
Bydgoszcz
Toruń
Białystok
Brest
Ostrava
Brno
Olomouc
Rzeszów
Projection : Lambert's Conformal Conic
East from Greenwich
COPYRIGHT PHILIP'S

Underlined towns give their name to the administrative area in which they stand.

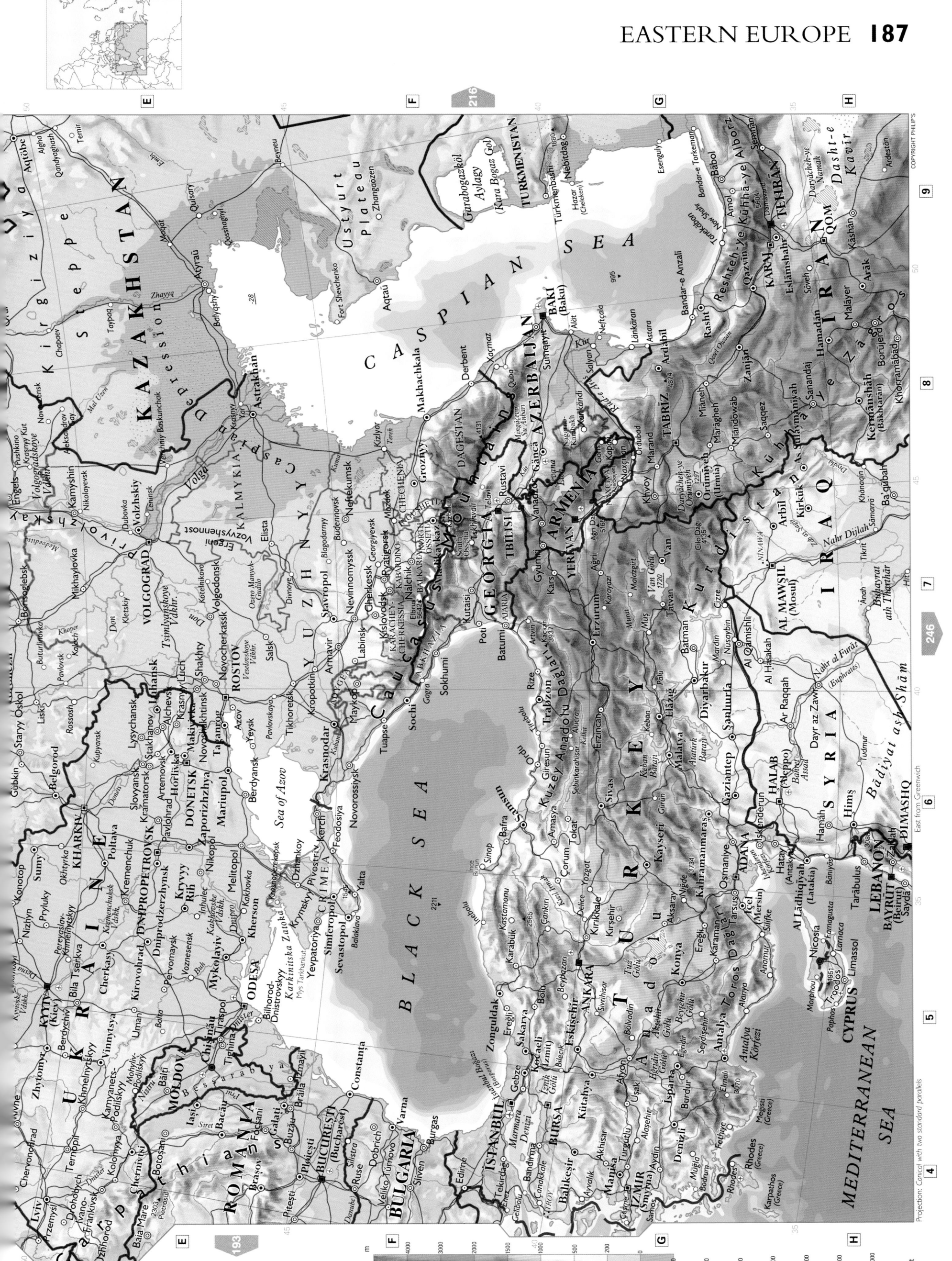

Projection: Conical with two standard parallels

East from Greenwich

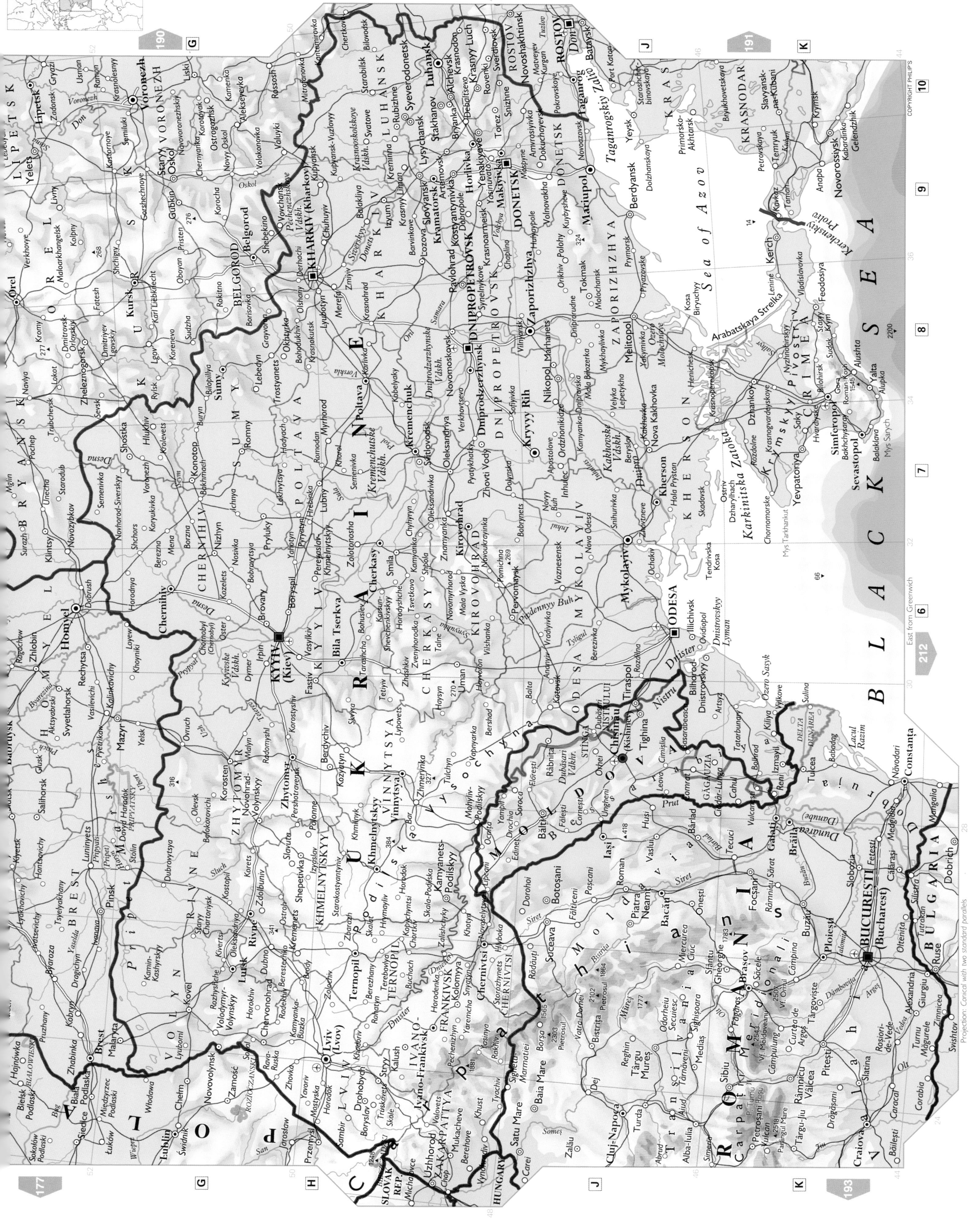

U K R A I N E

B E L A R U S

R O M A N I A

B U L G A R I A

M O L D O V A

Sea of Azov

B L A C K   S E A

C R I M E A

KYIV (Kiev)
KHARKIV (Kharkov)
Luhansk
DONETSK
DNIPROPETROVSK
Zaporizhzhya
Mariupol
ODESA
Mykolayiv
Kherson
Kryvyy Rih
Poltava
Sumy
Chernihiv
Zhytomyr
Vinnytsya
Khmelnytskyy
Ternopil
Rivne
Lutsk
Lviv (Lvov)
Ivano-Frankivsk
Chernivtsi
Kremenchuk
Cherkasy
Kirovohrad

Chişinău (Kishinev)
Tiraspol
Bucureşti (Bucharest)
Constanţa

Homel
Brest
Pinsk
Mazyr

VORONEZH
BELGOROD
KURSK
Orel
Rostov
KRASNODAR

L I P E T S K
B R Y A N S K
O R E L
V O R O N E Z H
K U R S K
B E L G O R O D
S U M Y
P O L T A V A
C H E R N I H I V
K Y Y I V
Z H Y T O M Y R
R I V N E
V O L Y N
L V I V
T E R N O P I L
K H M E L N Y T S K Y
I V A N O - F R A N K I V S K
C H E R N I V T S I
V I N N Y T S Y A
C H E R K A S Y
K I R O V O H R A D
D N I P R O P E T R O V S K
K H A R K I V
L U H A N S K
D O N E T S K
Z A P O R I Z H Z H Y A
K H E R S O N
M Y K O L A Y I V
O D E S A

East from Greenwich

Projection: Conical with two standard parallels

Projection: Conical with two standard parallels

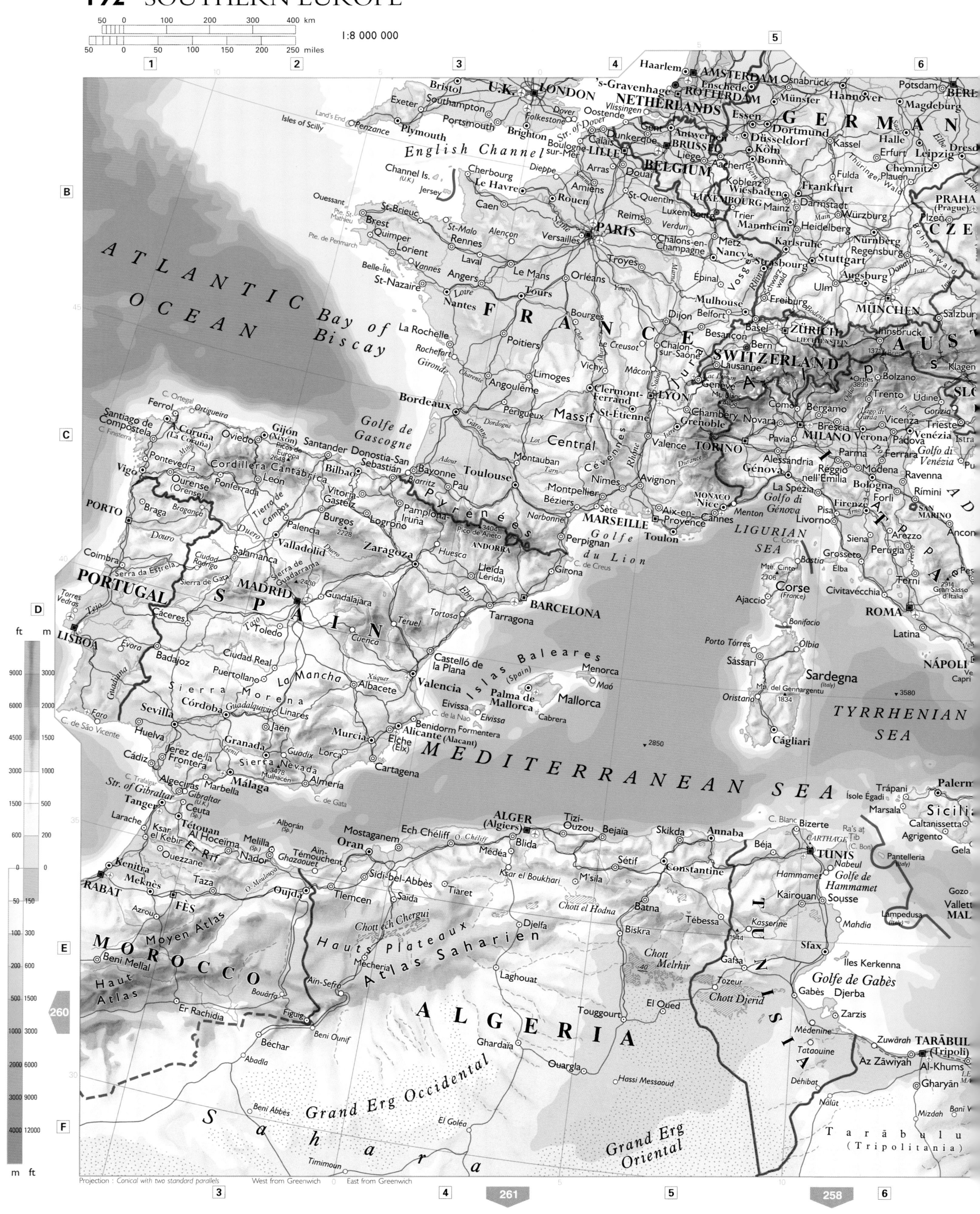

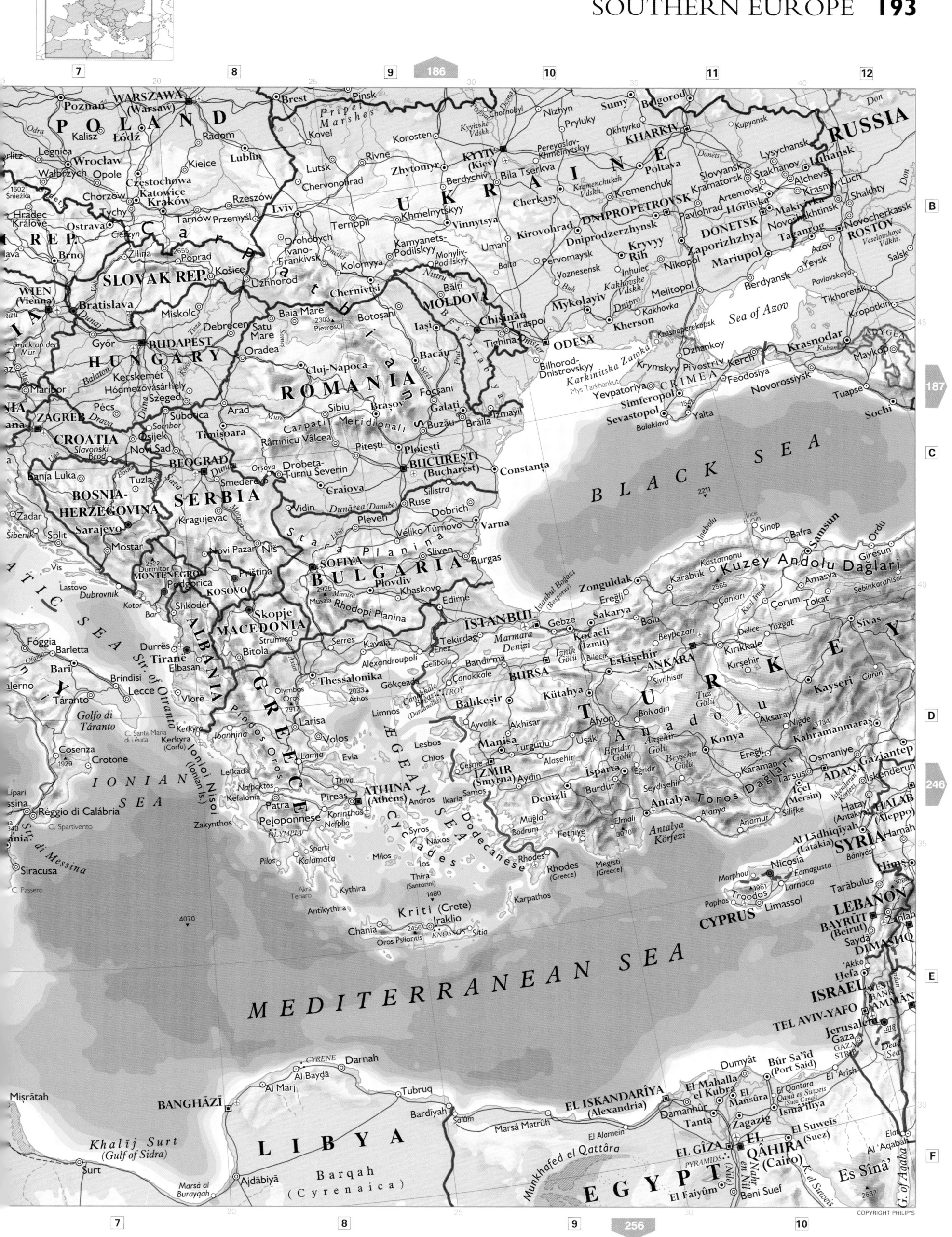

10 0 10 20 30 40 50 60 70 80 90 km

10 0 10 20 30 40 50 60 miles

1:2 000 000

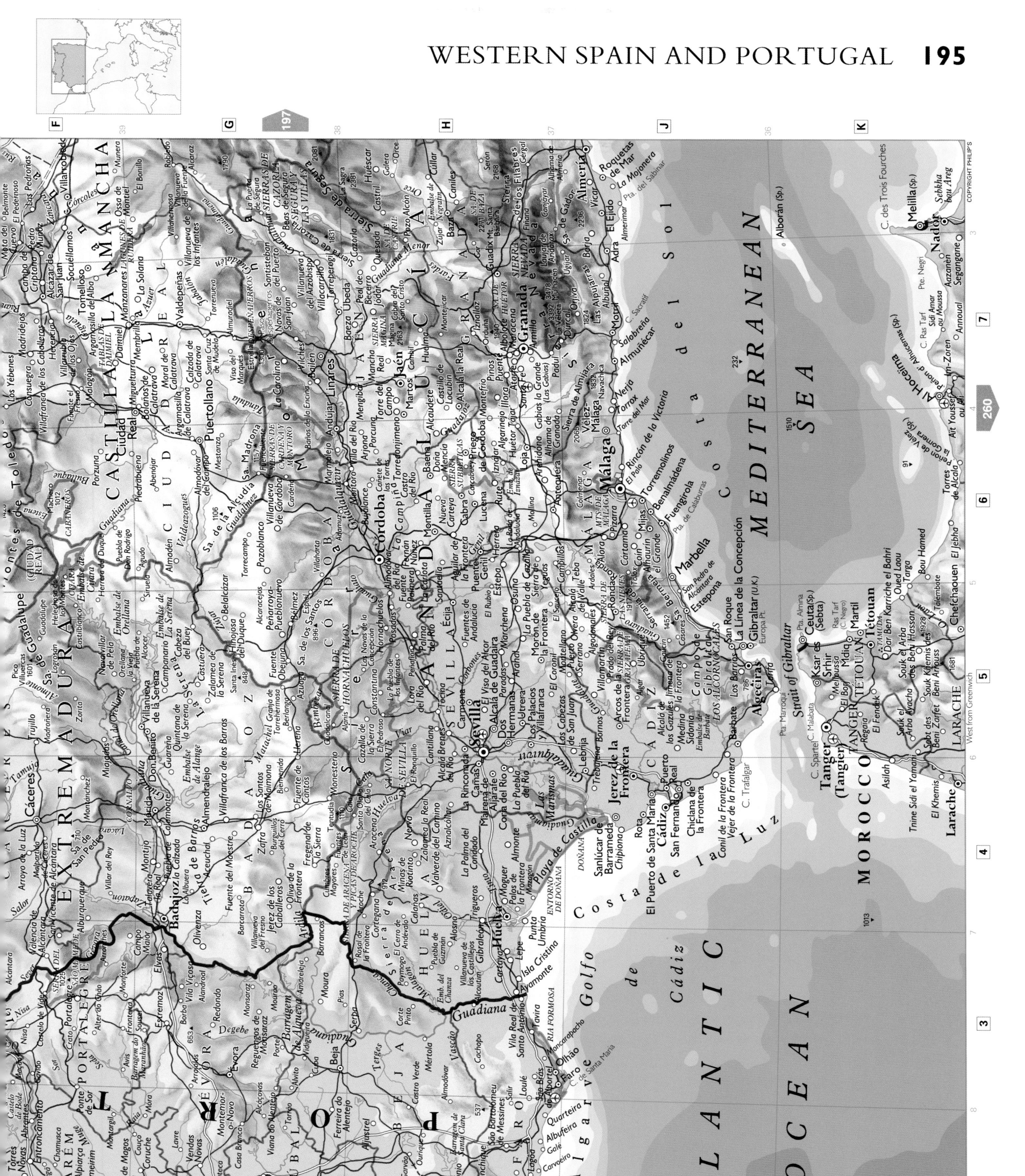

1:2 000 000

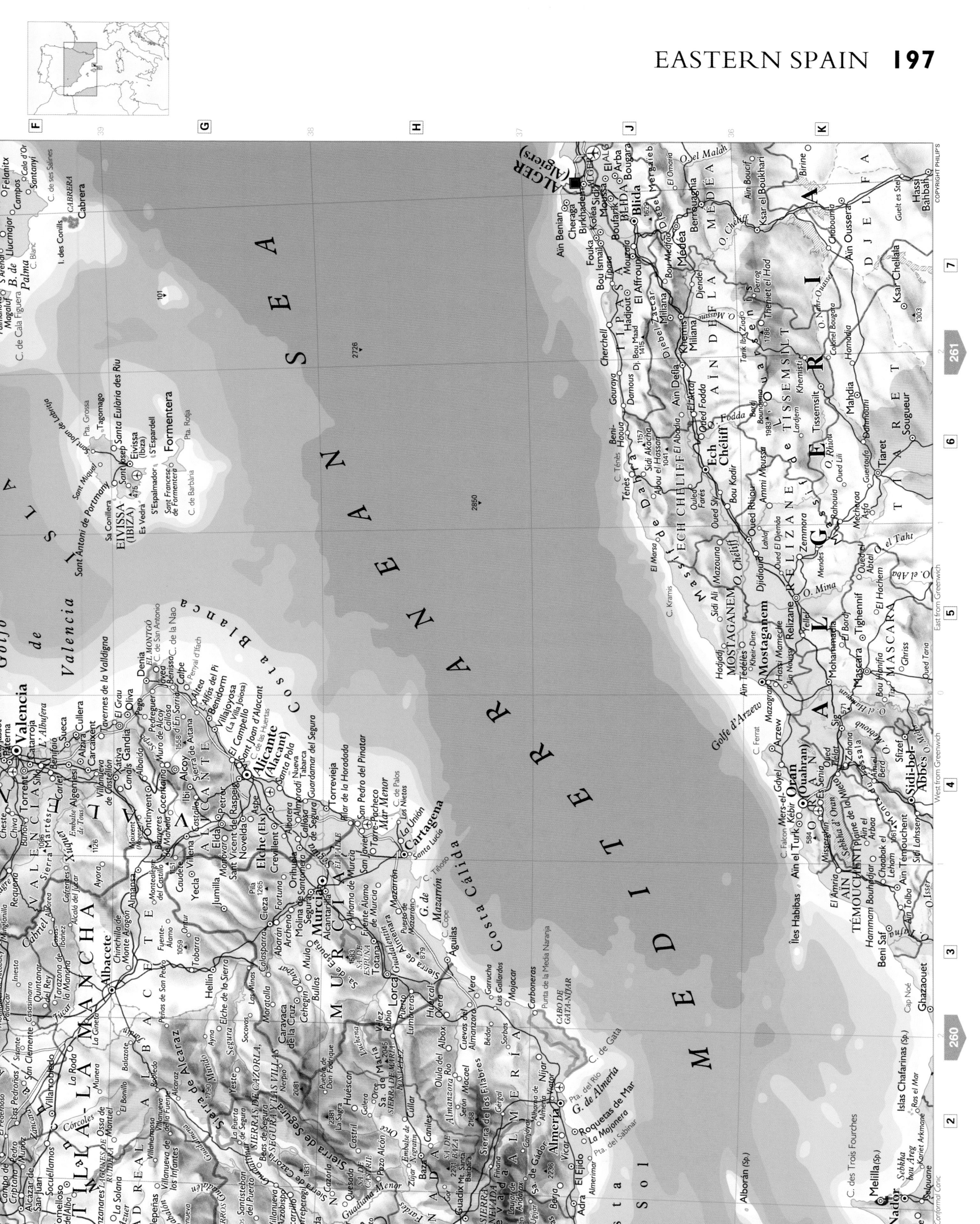

Projection: Lambert's Conformal Conic

East from Greenwich

West from Greenwich

1:2 000 000

Projection: Lambert's Conformal Conic

East from Greenwich

Underlined towns give their name to
administrative area in which they stand

Administrative divisions in Croatia:

Brodsko-Posavska	4 Medimurska	8 Virovitičko-Podravska
Koprivničko-Križevačka	6 Požeško-Slavonska	10 Zagreba čka
Krapinsko-Zagorska	7 Varaždinska	

COPYRIGHT PHILIP'S

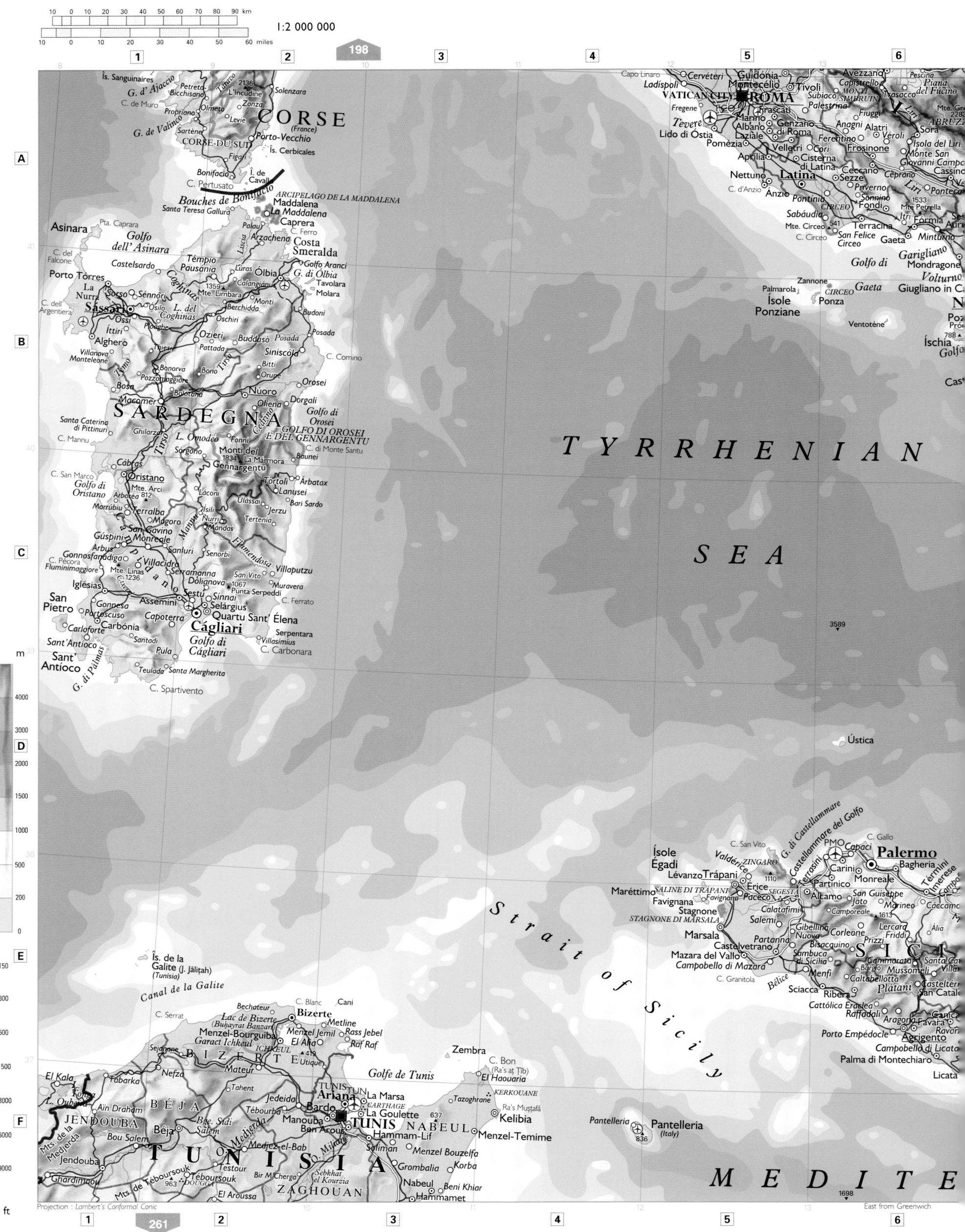

1:2 000 000

10 0 10 20 30 40 50 60 70 80 90 km
10   0   10   20   30   40   50 60 miles

198

261

Projection : Lambert's Conformal Conic

CORSE
(France)
CORSE-DU-SUD

Ìs. Sanguinaires
G. d'Ajaccio
Petreto
Bicchisano
L'Incudine 2136
Solenzara
Olmeto
Levie
Zonza
Propriano
Sartène
Porto-Vecchio
Figari
Ìs. Cerbicales
Bonifacio
Î. de
Cavalli
C. Pertusato
Bouches de Bonifacio

Maddalena
La Maddalena
Santa Teresa Gallura
ARCIPELAGO DE LA MADDALENA
Caprera
Palau
Arzachena
**Costa
Smeralda**
C. Ferro
Golfo Aranci
G. di Òlbia
Asinara
Pta. Caprara
**Golfo
dell' Asinara**
Tavolara
Molara

C. del
Falcone
Castelsardo
Témpio
Pausánia
Lúras
Ólbia
Calangiánus
Budoni
Porto Tòrres
La
Nurra
Sorso
Sénnori
Òsilo
Ploághe
Berchidda
Monti
Posada
Sássari
Ossi
Íttiri
Oschiri
C. dell'
Argentiera
Alghero
Thiesi
Ozieri
Pattada
Buddusò
Posada
Siniscóla
Villanova
Monteleone
Bonorva
Bono
Tirso
Bitti
Orune
C. Comino
Bosa
Pozzomaggiore
Bolotana
Núoro
Orosei
Macomer
Oliena
Dorgali
**Golfo di
Orosei**
SARDEGNA
Ghilarza
L. Omodeo
Sórgono
Fonni
**GOLFO DI OROSEI
E DEL GENNARGENTU**
C. di Monte Santu
Tirso
Séneghe
1834
La
Marmora
Monti del
Gennargentu
Baunei
C. San Marco
Cábras
Oristano
Mte. Arci
812
Árbatax
Tortolì
Lanusei
**Golfo di
Oristano**
Árborea
Mógoro
Terralba
Ísili
Láconi
Bari Sardo
Jerzu
C. Mannu
Marrúbiu
Nurri
Mándas
Tertenia
Sanluri
Senorbì
Guspini
San Gávino
Monreale
Flumendosa
Villaputzu
Arbus
Serramanna
Villacidro
Dólianova
Muravera
Mte. Línas
1236
Sestu
Sinnai
Punta Serpeddì
1067
San Vito
Gonnosfanádiga
Flumínimaggiore
San
Pietro
Assémini
C. Pécora
Gonnesa
Sélargius
Quartu Sant' Élena
C. Ferrato
Iglésias
Portescuso
Capoterra
Cágliari
Serpentara
Carloforte
Carbónia
**Golfo di
Cágliari**
Santadi
Villasimius
San Pietro
Sant'Antioco
Pula
C. Carbonara
**Sant'
Antioco**
Teulada
Santa Margherita
C. Spartivento
G. di Palmas

**T Y R R H E N I A N
S E A**

3589

Capo Linaro
Cervéteri
Guidonia
Montecéllo
Avezzano
Ladispoli
Capistrello
Piana
del Fucino
Pescina
VATICAN CITY
ROMA
Subiaco
MONTI
SIMBRUINI
Trasacco
ABRUZZI
Tivoli
Palestrina
Fiuggi
2285
Frascati
Marino
Anagni
Alatri
Véroli
Sora
Albano
Cisterna
di Roma
Ferentino
Monte San
Giovanni
Lido di Ostia
Laziale
Genzano
di Roma
Cori
Frosinone
Pomézia
Velletri
Sezze
Ceccano
Cassino
Nettuno
Latina
Ceprano
Sonnino
Priverno
Pontecor
Anzio
C. d'Anzio
Pontinia
Fondi
Itri
Formia
Sabáudia
CIRCEO
1533
Terracina
Mte. Petrella
Gaeta
Mte. Circeo
541
Garigliano
C. Circeo
San Felice
Circeo
Mondragone
Volturno
Palmarola
CIRCEO
Zannone
**Golfo di
Gaeta**
Giugliano in C
Ísole
Ponza
Ponziane
Ventoténe
Íschia
Golfo

N

Pozz

Ísole
Égadi
Lévanzo
Maréttimo
Favignana
Palermo
Ústica
C. San Vito
G. di Castellammare
C. Gallo
Capaci
PM
Bagheria
Valdérice
Zingaro
Carini
Érice
Castellammare del Golfo
Termini
Monreale
Imerese
Trápani
Paceci
Partinico
1110
Alcamo
San Giuseppe
Jato
Paceco
SEGESTA
Calatafimi
Marineo
SALINE DI TRÁPANI
Favara
Camporeale
Cáccamo
Stagnone
Salemi
1615
Gibellina
Corleone
Ália
STAGNONE DI MARSALA
Nuova
Partanna
Prizzi
Lercara
Friddi
Marsala
Castelvetrano
Bisacquino
SICI
Mazara del Vallo
Sambuca
di Sicilia
Commam
Santa Car
Campobello di Mazara
Menfi
Bardo
Mussomeli
Villa
C. Granitola
Bélice
Sciacca
Castelter
San Catal
Cámmarata
Plátani
Ribera
Cattólica Eraclea
Raffadali
Favara
Aragona
Porto Empédocle
Canic
Agrigento
Ravan
Campobello di Licata
Palma di Montechiaro
Licata

Strait of Sicily

Ís. de la
Galite (J. Jālițah)
(Tunisia)
Canal de la Galite

C. Blanc
Cani
Béchateur
Bizerte
C. Serrat
Lac de Bizerte
(Buhayrat Banzart)
Metline
Menzel-Bourguiba
Menzel Jemil
Rass Jebel
Garaet Ichkeul
El Alia
Raf Raf
ICHKEUL
B I Z E R T E
Séjnane
419
Utique
Zembra
Nefza
Mateur
Tahent
C. Bon
(Ra's aț Tib)
El Haouaria
Tábarka
El Kala
L. Oubeïra
Aïn Draham
B É J A
Jedeida
Téboursouk
Manouba
TUNIS
Ariana
La Marsa
TUNIS
Bardo
CARTHAGE
KERKOUANE
Mts. de la
Medjerda
JENDOUBA
Béja
Bge. Sidi
Salem
La Goulette
Tazoghrane
Ra's Muṣṭafá
Kelibia
Pantelleria
Bou Salem
Medjerda
Ben Arous
NABEUL
Jendouba
Béja
Medjez-el-Bab
Manouba
Hammam-Lif
Menzel-Temime
Pantelleria
(Italy)
Mts. de Téboursouk
963
Téboursouk
Soliman
Menzel Bouzelfa
836
Ghardimaou
DOUGGA
Bir M'Cherga
Grombalia
Korba
Sebkhat
el Kourzia
T U N I S I A
Nabeul
Beni Khiar
El Aroussa
ZAGHOUAN
Hammamet

M E D I T E

1698
East from Greenwich

Underlined towns give their name to the
administrative area in which they stand.

1:2 000 000

M A R I A — *Romania*
Râmnicu Vâlcea • Curtea de Argeş • Câmpulung • Sinaia • Busteni • BUCEGI

PRAHOVA • BUZĂU • Buzău • Brăila • **Brăila** • BRĂILA
Galaţi • Reni • Giurgiuleşti • Kiliya • Izmayil • Vylkove
Ostrov Letea • Bratul Chilia • Dunay • Măcin • Isaccea • Tulcea • TULCEA
Bratul Sulina • Dunărea • Sulina • DELTA DUNĂREA • Ostrov Sfântu Gheorghe • Bratul Sfântu Gheorghe • Ostrov Dranov • Sfântu Gheorghe

Piteşti • ARGEŞ • Târgovişte • DÂMBOVITA • Ploieşti
Moreni • Titu • Giurgeni • Hârşova • Topalu • Babadag • Lacul Razim • Gura Portiţei

Alexandria • TELEORMAN • Giurgiu • Ruse • RUSE
BUCUREŞTI (Bucharest) • GIURGIU • CĂLĂRAŞI • Slobozia • IALOMIŢA • CONSTANŢA
Lacul Sinoie • Nāvodari • Constanţa • Lacul Siutghiol • Ovidiu • Medgidia • Basarabi
Cernavoda • Corbu

V a l a h i a — Wallachia

Caracal • OLT • Corabia • Nikopol • Svishtov • Zimnicea • Silistra • SILISTRA
Dulovo • DOBRICH • Dobrich • Techirghiol • Eforie • Mangalia • Shabla • Kavarna • Nos Kaliakra

PLEVEN • Pleven • Lovech • LOVECH • RAZGRAD • Razgrad • SHUMEN • Shumen • Novi Pazar • Belogradets • VARNA • Varna • Druzhba
General Toshevo • Negru Vodā • Durankulak • Kardam • Balchik

B U L G A R I A

GABROVO • Gabrovo • VELIKO TÜRNOVO • Veliko Türnovo • TÜRGOVISHTE • Türgovishte
Botev 2376 • Shipchenski Prohod • Sevlievo • Tryavna • Elena • Kotlenska Planina • Kotel
Preslav • Smyadovo • KAMCHIYA • Kamchiya • Staro Oryakhovo • Byala • Obzor • Emona • Nos Emine

B a l k a n

Sliven • SLIVEN • Nova Zagora • Yambol • Aytos • Karnobat • Rudnik • Pomorie • Nesebür • Slünchev Bryag
Kazanlūk • Stara Zagora • STARA ZAGORA • YAMBOL • Burgaski Zaliv • **Burgas** • BURGAS • Sozopol

Plovdiv • PLOVDIV • Pazardzhik • Asenovgrad • Dimitrovgrad • KHASKOVO • Khaskovo • Harmanli
Chirpan • Radnevo • Elkhovo • Topolovgrad • Malko Türnovo • Rezovo • Primorsko • Michurin • Akhtopol

Smolyan • RODOPI • KÜRDZHALI • Kürdzhali • Momchilgrad • Krumovgrad • Svilengrad • **Edirne** • EDIRNE
Demirköy • İğneada Burnu • İğneada

T U R K E Y

ANATOLIKI MAKEDONIA • Xanthi • XANTHI • Komotini • RODOPI • Orestiáda • Didimótikho
KIRKLARELI • Kırklareli • Vize • Saray • Çerkezköy • **İSTANBUL** • ISTANBUL • Üsküdar • Kartal • Pendik • KOCAELI (İzmit)

KAVALA • Kavala • KAI THRAKI • EVROS • Komotini • Soufli • Uzunköprü • TEKIRDAĞ • Tekirdağ • Çorlu • Silivri • Büyükçekmece • Beykoz • Gebze • Darıca • Gölcük

Alexandroúpoli • *Thrace* • Feres • Enez • Keşan • Malkara • Barbaros • Marmaraereğlisi • Gürpınar

T h r a c e — *Thráki*

Sea of Thrace • Thasos • Samothráki • Gökçeada • *Saros Körfezi* • Gelibolu (Gallipoli)
Çanakkale Boğazı (Dardanelles) • **Çanakkale** • ÇANAKKALE

Marmara Denizi (Sea of Marmara) • Marmara • Yalova • Karamürsel • Bandırma • **BURSA** • BURSA • Gemlik Körfezi • Gemlik • İznik Gölü • İznik

Limnos • Bozcaada • TROY • Ezine • Biga • Gönen • Mustafakemalpaşa • İnegöl • Uludağ 2543

B L A C K   S E A

COPYRIGHT PHILIP'S

Underlined towns give their name to the administrative area in which they stand.

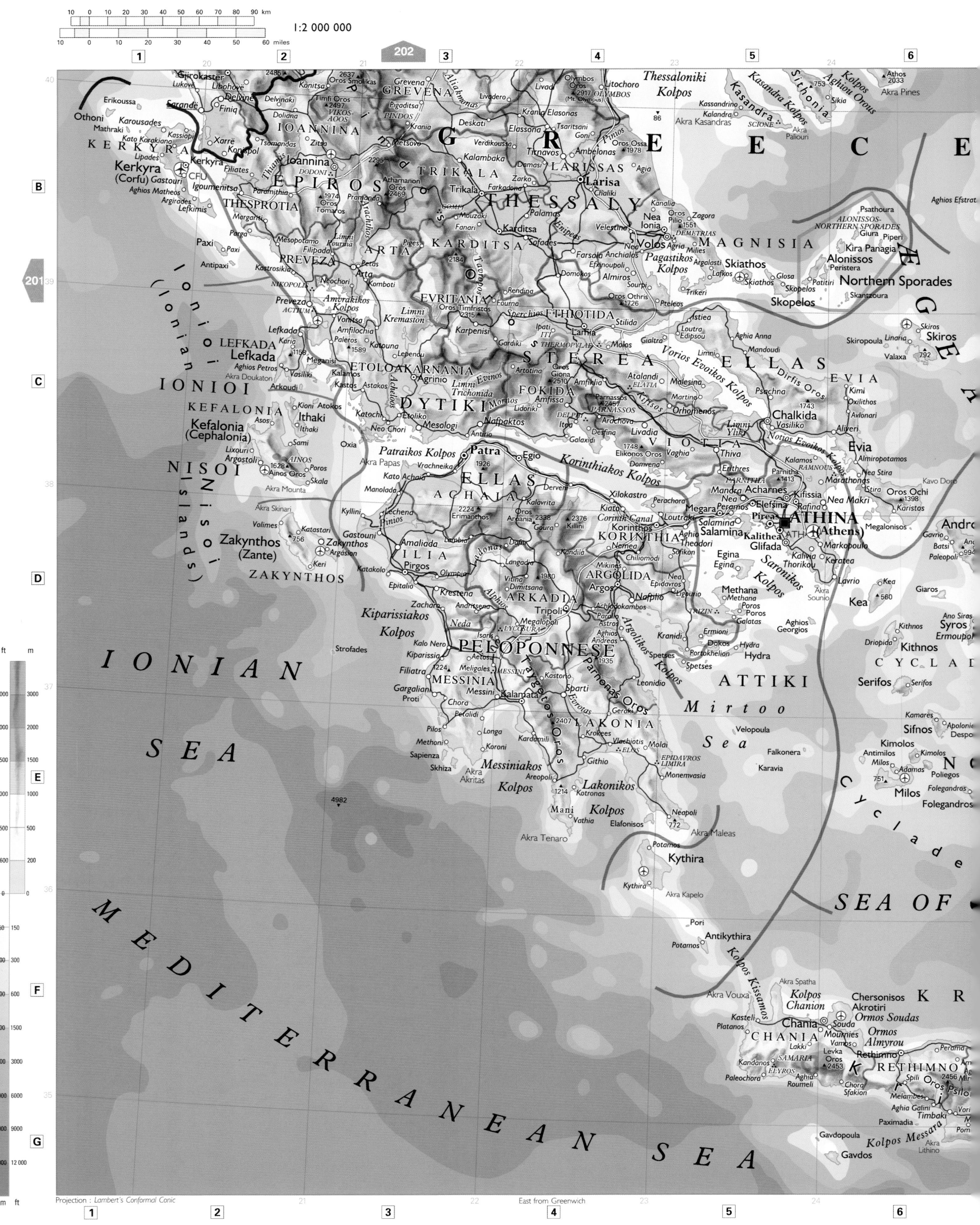

1:2 000 000

Projection : Lambert's Conformal Conic

East from Greenwich

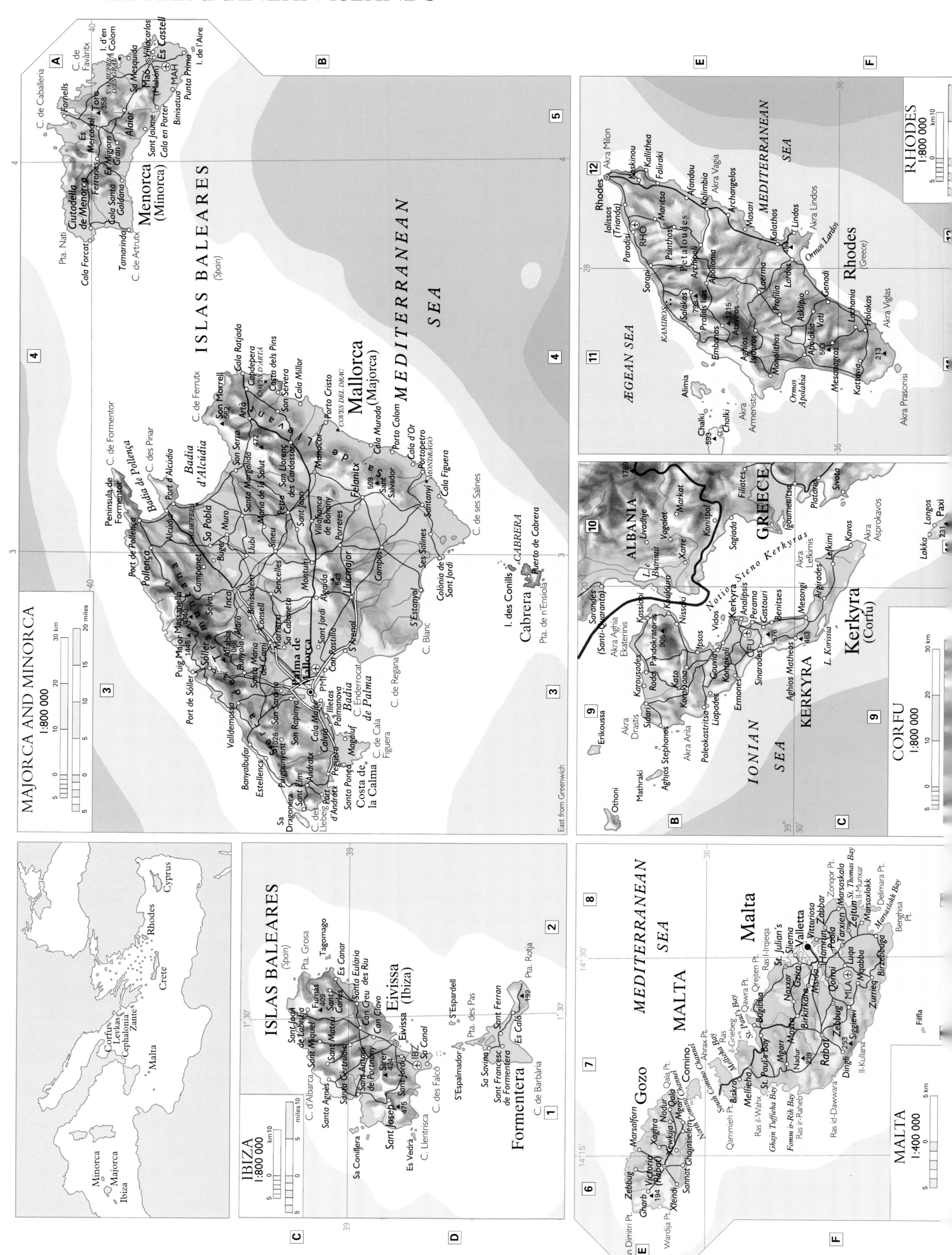

MAJORCA AND MINORCA
1:800 000

MENORCA (Minorca)

C. de Caballeria
Pta. Nati
Ciutadella
C. de Artrutx
Ferreres
Es Mercadal
Es Migjorn Gran
Alaior
Sant Jaume
Cala Santa
Galdana
Cala en Porter
Sant Lluís
Tamarinda
Cala Forcat

Fornells
Toro ▲ 358
I. d'en Colom
MENORCA
SANTUARI D'EN XOROI
C. de Favàritx
Maó (Mahón)
MAH
Binisatua
Punta Prima
Es Castell
Villacarlos
I. de l'Aire

ISLAS BALEARES
(Spain)

MALLORCA (Majorca)

Peninsula de Formentor
C. de Formentor
Badia de Pollença
C. des Pinar
C. d'Alcúdia
Badia d'Alcúdia
Port d'Alcúdia
Alcúdia
Sa Pobla
Muro
Santa Margalida
Son Serra
Son Morrell
Artà
COVES D'ARTÀ
C. de Ferrutx
Capdepera
Cala Ratjada
Costa dels Pins
Son Servera
Cala Millor
Porto Cristo
COVES DEL DRAC
Manacor
Cala Murada
Porto Colom
Cala Figuera
Cala d'Or
Portopetro
Santanyí
C. de ses Salines

Peninsula de Pollença
Port de Pollença
Pollença
Port de Sóller
Sóller
Valldemossa
Banyalbufar
Estellencs
Sa Dragonera
Sant Elm
Port d'Andratx
Andratx
Peguera
Santa Ponça
Costa de la Calma
Sa Figuera
Cala Major
Magaluf
Palmanova
Illetes
Badia de Palma
Palma de Mallorca
PMI
C. de Regana
Inca
Selva
Biniamar
Campanet
Búger
Llubí
Sineu
Llorito
Maria de la Salut
Petra
Sant Joan
Sencelles
Santa Maria del Camí
Bunyola
Santa Eugènia
Consell
Binissalem
Algaida
Montuïri
Porreres
Vilafranca de Bonany
Felanitx
Sant Salvador
S. Salvador 509
Ses Salines
Colònia de Sant Jordi
C. des Salines
C. Blanc
Sant Jordi
Llucmajor
Campos
Santanyí
S'Estanyol
S'Arenal
Cabanes
C. Enderrocat
Puig Major 1445 ▲ 1340
1026
543

CABRERA
I. des Conills
Colònia de Sant Jordi
CABRERA
Puerto de Cabrera
Pta. de n'Ensiola

ISLAS BALEARES (Spain)

EIVISSA (Ibiza)

Pta. Grosa
Tagomago
Es Canar
Santa Eulària des Riu
Santa Creu
Sant Carles
Sant Vicent de sa Cala
Sant Miquel
Santa Agnès
Sant Antoni de Portmany
Sant Mateu
Santa Gertrudis
Can Guasch
Can Clavo
Sant Jordi
Sant Joan de Labritja
Eivissa (Ibiza)
IBZ
Sa Canal
Sant Josep
C. d'Albarca
C. Llentrisca
Es Vedrà
Sa Conillera
475
424

FORMENTERA
S'Espalmador
S'Espardell
Sa Savina
Sant Francesc de Formentera
Sant Ferran
Es Caló
Pta. des Pas
C. de Barbària
Pta. Rotja
192

IBIZA
1:800 000

MEDITERRANEAN SEA
SEA

Minorca
Majorca
Ibiza
Corfu
Levkas
Cephalonia
Zante
Crete
Malta
Rhodes
Cyprus

East from Greenwich

RHODES (Greece)

Akra Milon
Akra Skinou
Muskinou
Kallithea
Faliraki
Afandou
Akra Vaga
Archangelos
Masari
Akra Lindos
Lindos
Kalathos
Lachania
Holakas
Akra Viglas
Akra Prasonisi

Rhodes
RHO
Ialissos (Trianda)
Paradisi
Soroni
KAMIROS
Psinthos
Petaloudes
Archipoli
Apollona
Salakos
Profitis Ilias 798 ▲
Embonas
Laerma
Lardos
Genadi
Asklipio
Vati
Apolakia
Monolithos
Aghios Isidoros
Ebmbonas
Chalki
Chalki 593
Alimia
Akra Armenistis
Ormos Apolakia
Mesanagros 563
Katavia
Ormos Lardos
Profilia
213
215

AEGEAN SEA
MEDITERRANEAN SEA

RHODES
1:800 000

KERKYRA (Corfu)

ALBANIA
GREECE
1769
Filiates
Markat
Vagalat
Konispol
Xarrë
Livadhje
Blerimat
Sagiada
Igoumenitsa
Platonas
Svoa

Sarandë (Santi-Quaranta)
Lefkimi
Ksamil
Butrinti 906
Kassiopi
Akra Agathia
Ekaterinis
Karousades
Sidari
Akra Drastis
Roda
Pandokratoras
Ipsos
Gouvia
Kerkyra (Corfu)
CFU
Perama
Benitses
Moraïtika
Mesongi
Sinarades
Liapades
Paleokastritsa
Ermones
Aghios Matheos
Akra Arila
Akra Lefkimis
Kavos
Akra Asprokavos
Erikoussa
Othoni
Mathraki
Akra Stephanos
Aghios Stephanos
576
463
Vidos

IONIAN SEA
Notia Steno Kerkyras

Lakka
Longos
Paxi
Gaïos

CORFU
1:800 000

MALTA

Marsalforn
Żebbuġ
Xagħra
Victoria
Rabat
Gharb
Nadur
Qala
Xewkija
Xlendi
San Dimitri Pt.
Wardija Pt.
Ta' Ċenċ Pt.
Qala Pt.
194
Gozo
Comino
North Comino Channel
South Comino Channel
Comino Channel

Mellieħa
St. Paul's Bay
Buġibba
Qawra Pt.
St. Paul's Bay
Naxxar
Mosta
Mġarr
Rabat
Dingli
Żebbuġ
Siġġiewi
Qrendi
Żurrieq
Mqabba
Luqa
MLA
Paola
Qormi
Ħamrun
Valletta
Marsa
Sliema
St. Julian's
Birkirkara
Tarxien
Żabbar
Żejtun
Marsaskala
St. Thomas Bay
Marsaxlokk
Birżebbuġa
Delimara Pt.
Benghisa Pt.
Marfa Ras
Qammieħ Pt.
Ahrax Pt.
Ras il-Qawra
Il-Wahx
Ras il-Wardija
Ġnejna Bay
Fomm ir-Riħ Bay
Għajn Tuffieħa Bay
Ras il-Pellegrin
Anchor Bay
Mellieħa Bay
St. George's Bay
Ras id-Dawwara
Il-Munxar
Il-Kullana
253
Filfla
Zonqor Pt.
Marsaskala
Oreiten Pt.

Gozo
MALTA
253
239
Ras il-Ħamrija
Ras il-Raħeb

MALTA
1:400 000

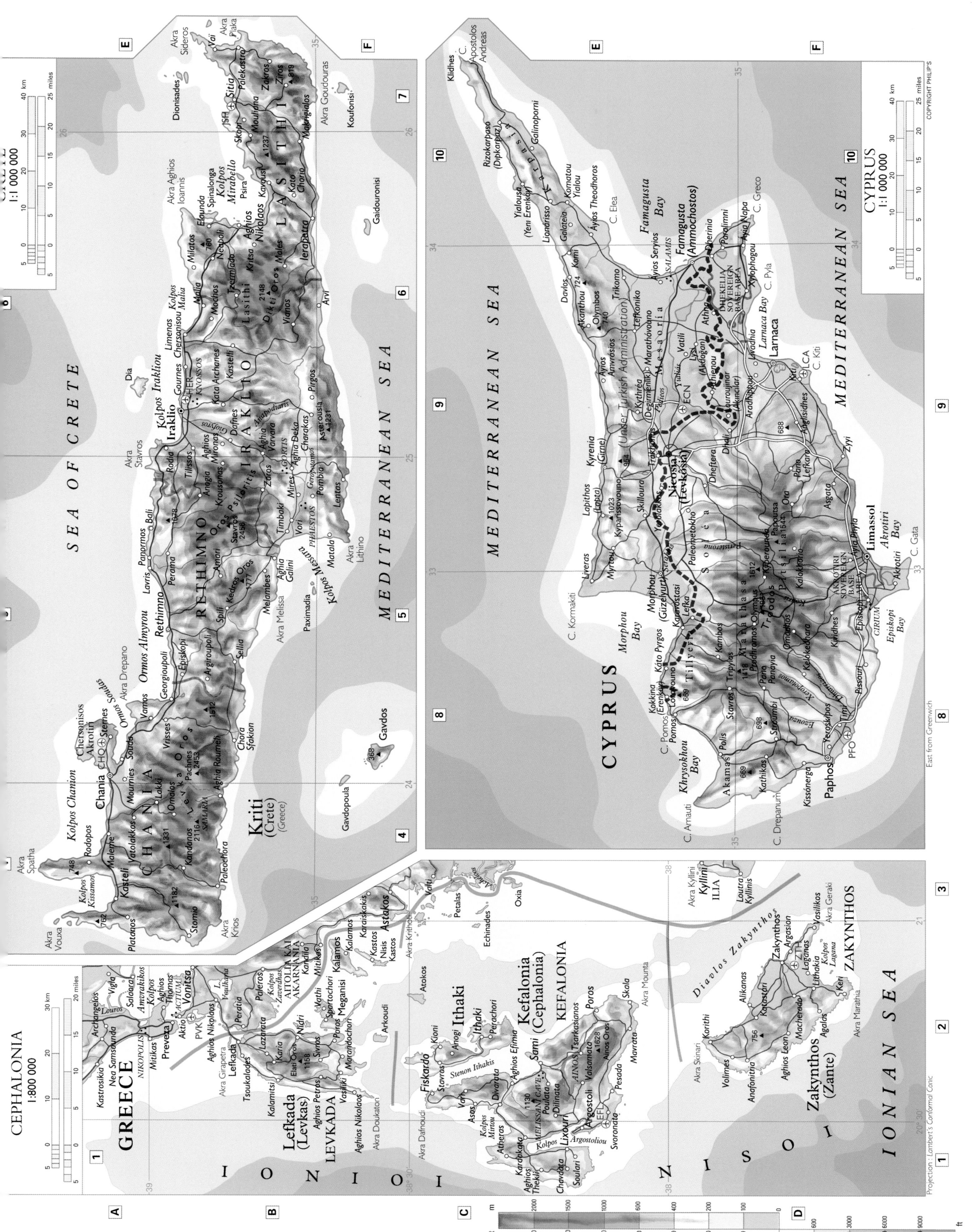

CRETE
1:1 000 000

SEA OF CRETE

Kriti
(Crete)
(Greece)

RETHIMNO

IRAKLIO

LASITHI

CHANIA

MEDITERRANEAN SEA

CYPRUS
1:1 000 000

CYPRUS

MEDITERRANEAN SEA

Famagusta Bay

Larnaca

Limassol

Nicosia (Lefkosia)

Kyrenia (Girne)

Paphos

(Under Turkish Administration)

DHEKELIA SOVEREIGN BASE AREA

AKROTIRI SOVEREIGN BASE

MEDITERRANEAN SEA

East from Greenwich

COPYRIGHT PHILIP'S

CEPHALONIA
1:800 000

GREECE

Lefkada
(Levkas)

LEVKADA

Ithaki

Kefalonia
(Cephalonia)

KEFALONIA

Zakynthos
(Zante)

ZAKYNTHOS

IONIAN SEA

Projection: Lambert's Conformal Conic

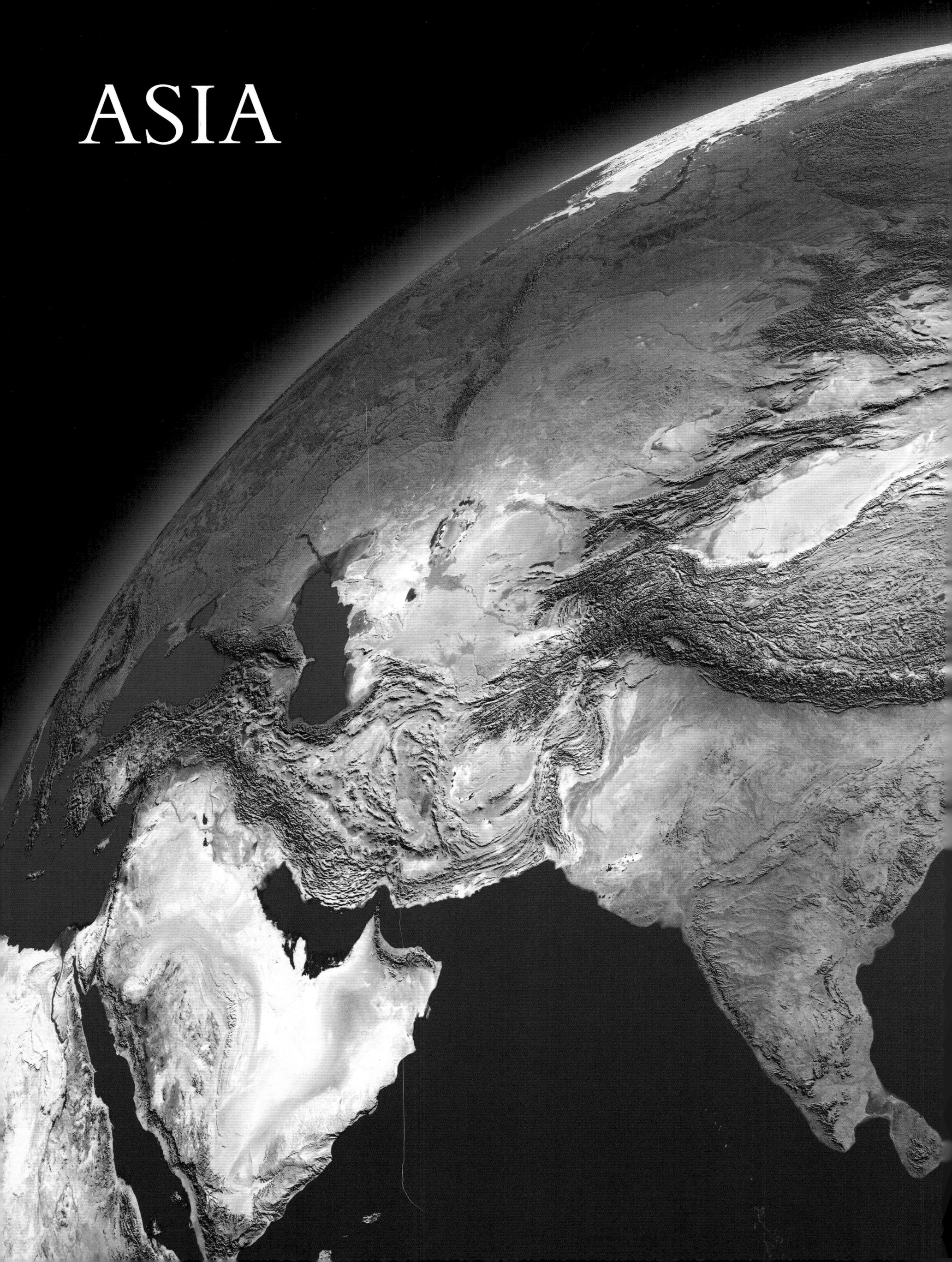

ASIA

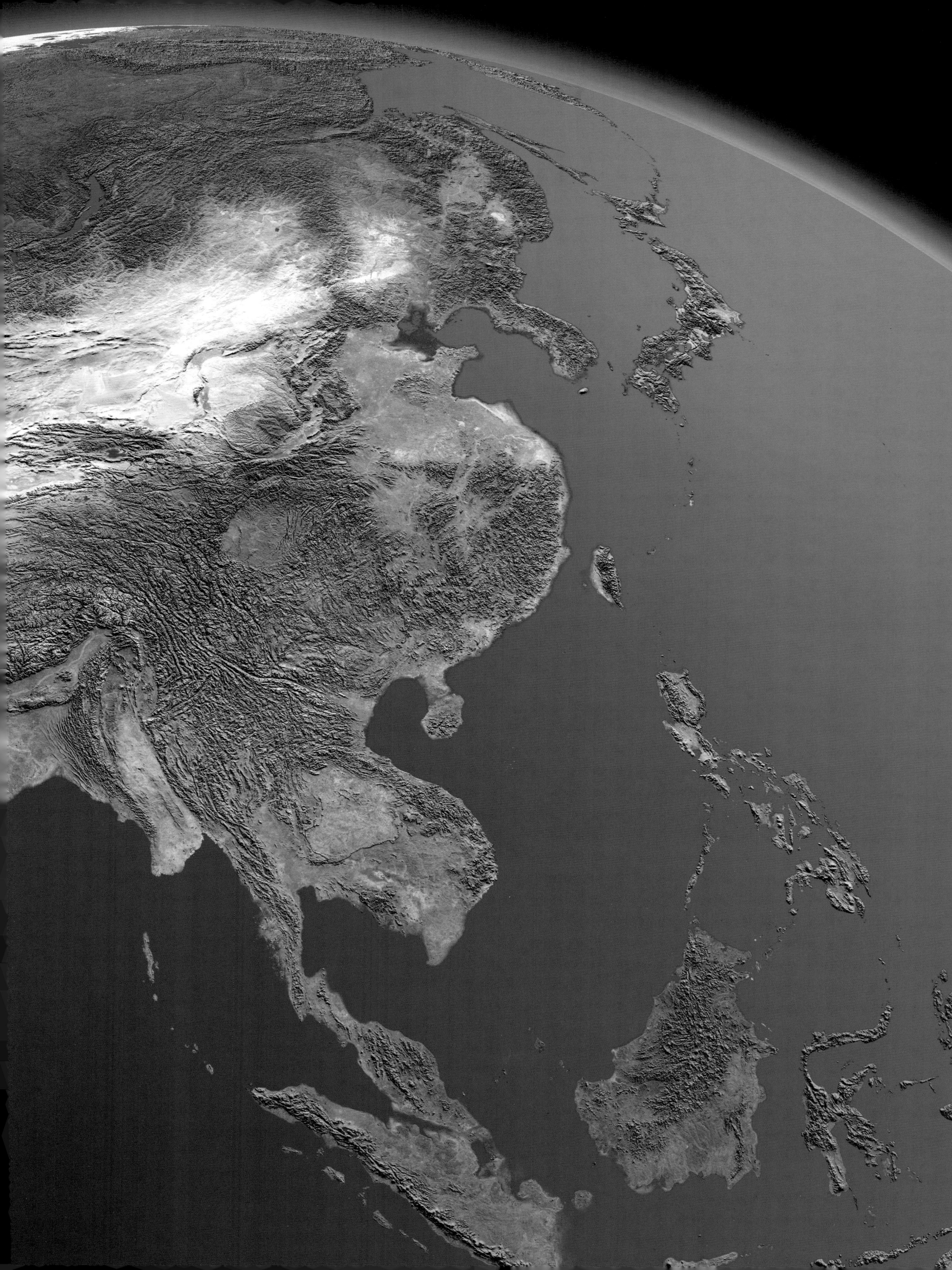

100 0 200 400 600 800 1000 1200 1400 km

100 0 200 400 600 800 1000 miles

1:40 000 000

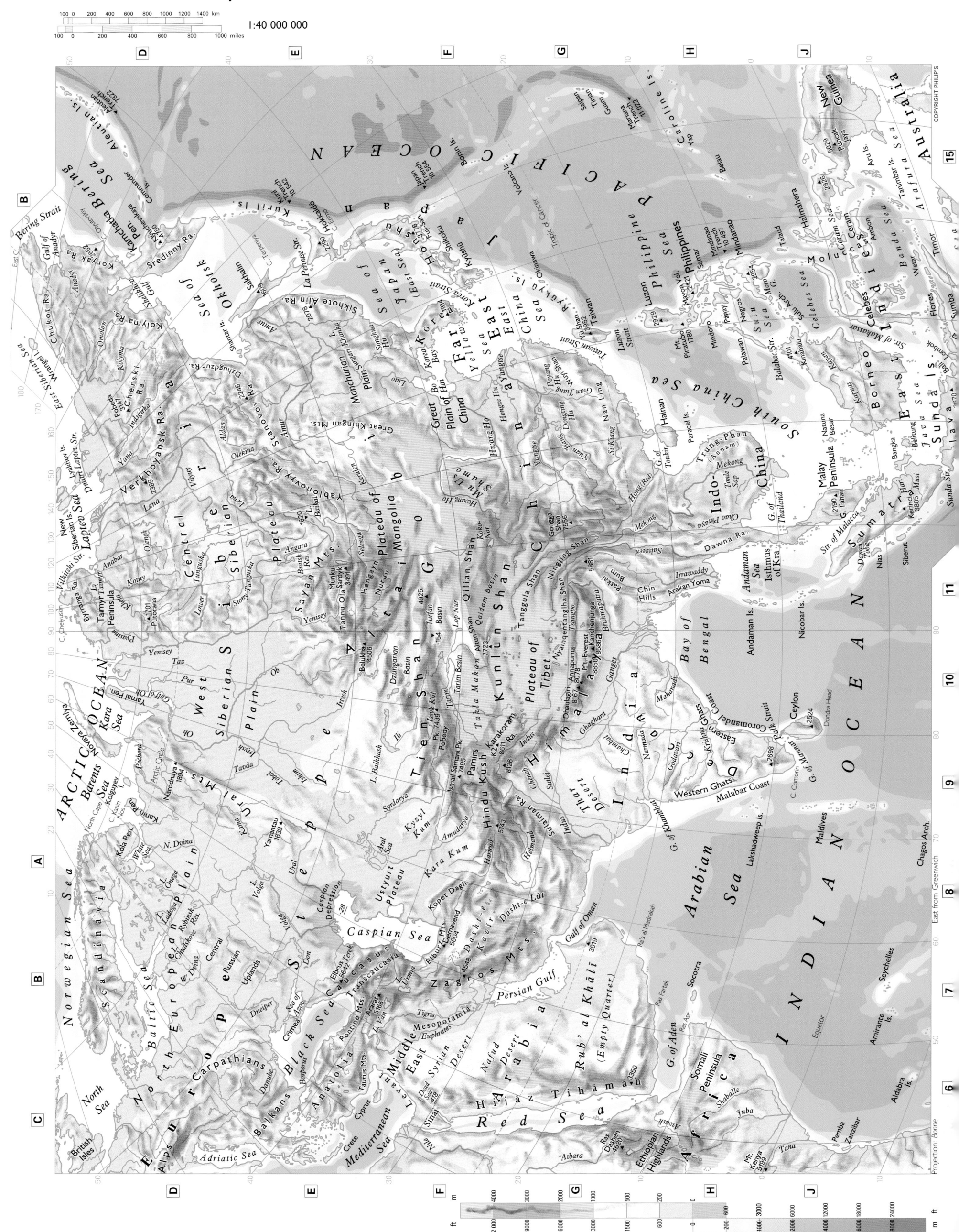

Projection: Bonne

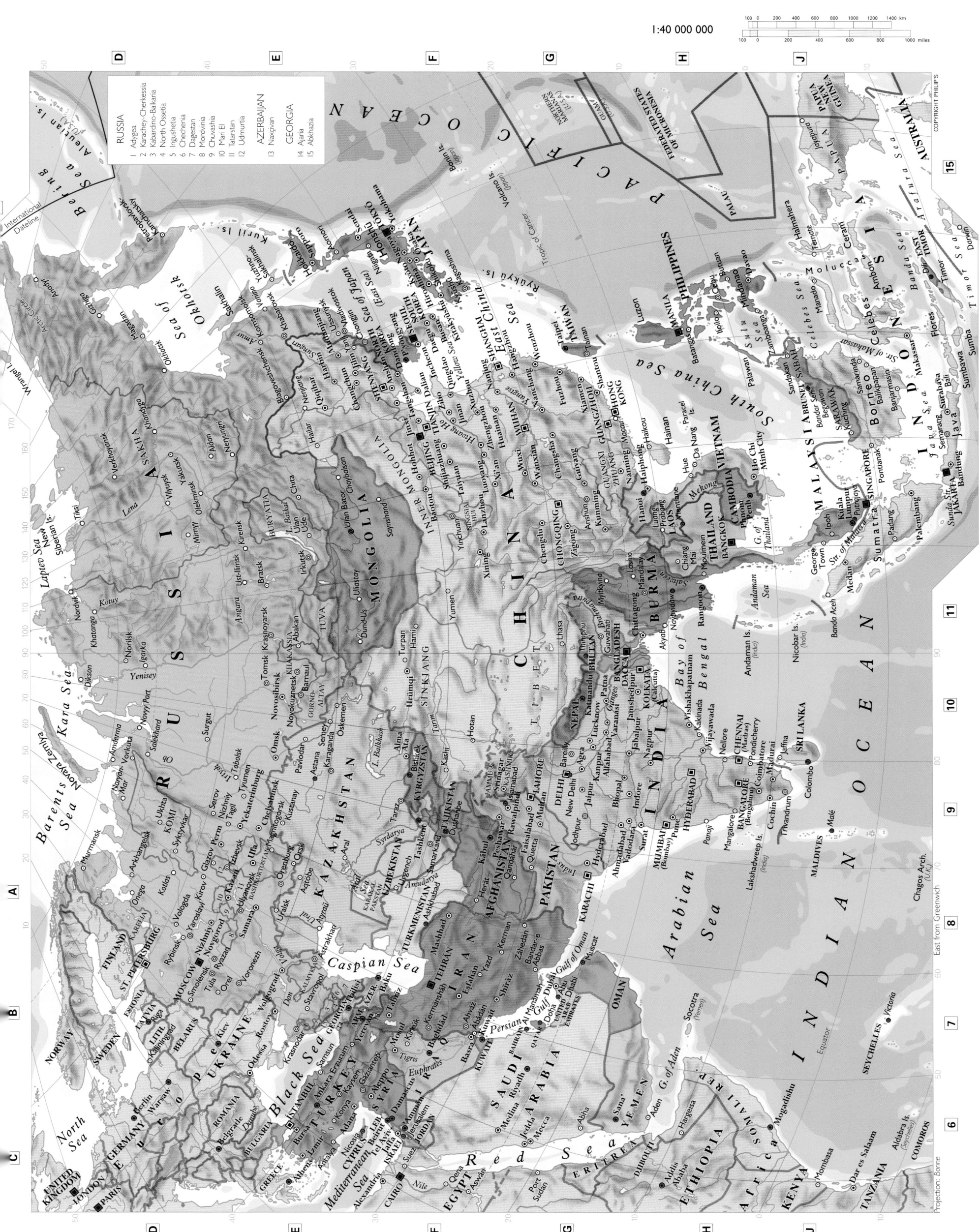

1 : 4 000 000

50 0 25 50 75 100 125 150 175 km
50 0 25 50 75 100 125 miles

BLACK SEA

BULGARIA

Stara Zagora · Yambol · Aytos · Burgas · Nos Emine · Michurin
Elkhovo · Kırklareli · Igneada · İgneada Burnu
Edirne · Pınarhisar · Demirköy
Orestiada · Babaeski · Lüleburgaz · Vize · Saray · Çerkezköy
Uzunköprü · Muratlı · İstanbul Boğazı (Bosporus) · İSTANBUL
Keşan · Tekirdağ · Büyükçekmece · Kartal · Kocaeli (İzmit) (Adapazarı) · Sakarya
Malkara · Şarköy · Marmara · Kapı Dağı · Gebze · Körfez · Darıca · Hendek
Enez · Gelibolu · Marmara Denizi (Sea of Marmara) · Yalova · Gölcük · Sapanca · Akyazı · Düzce
Gökçeada · Çanakkale · Erdek · Bandırma · İznik Gölü · İznik · Geyve · Göynük · Bolu · Gerede · Çerkeş
Bozcaada · TROY · Biga · Gönen · Mudanya · Bursa · İnegöl · Bilecik · Söğüt · Mudurnu · Seben

MEDITERRANEAN SEA

CYPRUS
Morphou · Kyrenia · Nicosia · Famagusta
Polis · Olympus 1961 · Troodos · Larnaca
Paphos · Episkopi · Limassol
Akrotiri

GREECE
Lesbos · Chios · Ikaria · Samos · Dodecanese · Kos · Rhodes (Rhodes) · Karpathos · Kasos

TURKEY
İZMİR (Smyrna) · Manisa · Denizli · Muğla · Antalya · Konya · ANKARA · Kırıkkale · Kayseri · Sivas · ADANA · Gaziantep · Kahramanmaraş

LEBANON
TARĀBULUS (Tripoli) · BAYRŪT (Beirut) · Saydā · Şūr

SYRIA
Al Lādhiqīyah (Latakia) · Hamāh · Himş (Homs) · DIMASHQ (Damascus) · HALAB (Aleppo)

ISRAEL
Hefa (Haifa) · TEL AVIV-YAFO · Jerusalem · WEST BANK

JORDAN
AMMĀN

Projection: Conical with two standard parallels

Division between Greeks and Turks in Cyprus; Turks to the North.

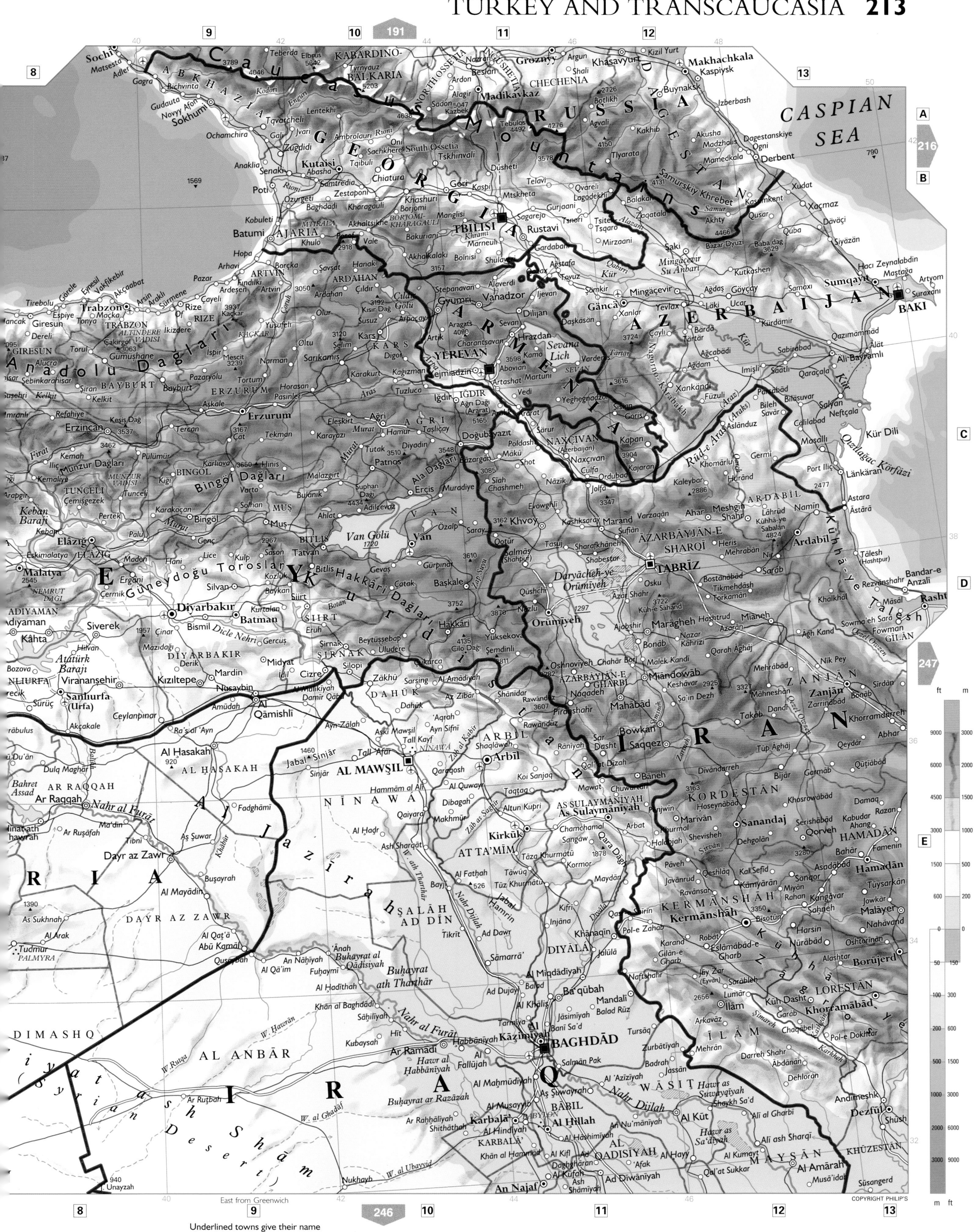

CASPIAN SEA

Sochi · Matsesta · Adler · Gagra · Bichvinta · ABKHAZIA · Gudauta · Novyy Afon · Sukhumi · Ochamchira · Gali · Anaklia · Zugdidi · Senaki · Poti · Kobuleti · Batumi · AJARIA · Khulo · Hopa

KABARDINO-BALKARIA · Tyrnyauz · Teberda · Elbrus 5642 · Nazran · 3789 · 4046 · Kodori · 5203 · NORTH OSSETIA · Vladikavkaz · 5047 · Kazbek · 4638 · Mt'irala · Lentekhi · Ambrolauri · Rioni · Oni · Tqibuli · Sachkhere · South Ossetia · Tskhinvali · Dusheti · 3578 · Gori

Grozny · Argun · Shali · CHECHENIA · Beslan · Ardon · Alagir · Botlikh · 4492 · 4276 · 4150 · Tlyarata · Khasavyurt · Kizil Yurt · Buynaksk · Makhachkala · Kaspiysk · Izberbash · Agvali · Kakhib · DAGESTAN · Akusha · Madzhalis · Ogni · Dagestanskiye Ogni · Derbent · 790

RUSSIA · Caucasus Mountains · 2726 · Botlikh · 4131 · Samurskiy Khrebet · Samur · Xudat · Kas'mkent · Akhty · Baba dag 3629 · Quba · Xaçmaz · Haçı Zeynalabdin · Maştağa · Sumqayıt · Suraxanı · Artyom · BAKI

GEORGIA · Kutaisi · Abasha · Samtredia · Chiatura · Zestaponi · Ozurgeti · Rioni · Khashuri · Baghdadi · Kharagauli · BORJOMI-KHARAGAULI · Borjomi · 1569 · Akhaltsikhe · Manglisi · Bakuriani · TBILISI · Khrami · Marneuli · Rustavi · Mtskheta · Kaspi · Sagarejo · Gurjaani · Telavi · Tsiteli Tsqaro · Qvareli · Lagodekhi · Alazani · Balakan · Zaqatala · Şaki · Bazar Dyuzi · 4466 · Qusar · Siyäzän · 3629

ARMENIA · Vale · 2918 · Arhavi · Pazar · Borçka · Savşat · Hanak · ARDAHAN · Çıldır · Ardahan · Çıldır Gölü · Şavşat · 3157 · 3192 · Stepanavan · Vanadzor · Ijevan · Şamkir · Dilijan · Tovuz · Ağstafa · Tawax · Kür · Mingäçevir Su Anbarı · Mingäçevir · Ağdaş · Göyçay · GÄNCÄ · Xanlar · Yevlax · Bärdä · Tärtär · Kürdämir · Sabirabad · AZERBAIJAN · Älät · Ali-Bayramlı · Qazımämmäd · Qaraçala · Salyan · Neftçala · Qızılağac Körfäzi · Länkäran · Astara

TRABZON · Trabzon · Maçka · Arsin · Araklı · Of · Rize · RIZE · Çayeli · ALTINDERE VADISI · İkizdere · Yusufeli · Çakırgol · 3063 · KAÇKAR · 3937 · Kaçkar · İspir · Artvin · ARTVIN · Fındıklı · Ardeşen · Olur · Oltu · 3050 · Şenkaya · Susuz · Arpaçay · Kısır Dağ · 3192 · Kağızman · Artik · Aragats 4090 · Charentsavan · Hrazdan · Sevan · Sevana Lich · 3598 · Kamo · Martuni · Vardenis · 3724 · 3616 · Xankändi · Naxçıvan · LACHIN · Kälbäcär · 3904 · Qubadlı · Zängilan · Fuzuli · Imişli · Saatlı · Biläsuvar · Masallı · Port İliç · 2477 · 2886 · ARDABIL · Germi · Hürand · Kaleybar · Ahar · Hürand · Namin · Kühhā-ye Sabalān 4824 · Ardabīl · Nir · Mehrabān · Heris · Tälesh · Hoshtpur · Tāsuj · Şabestar · Sufiān · Vazaqān · Marand · Osku · Āzar Shahr · 3722 · Kūh-e Sahand · TABRĪZ

GIRESUN · Giresun · Tirebolu · Görele · Eşpiye · Espiye · Tonya · Gümüşhane · ANADOLU DAĞLARI · Bayburt · BAYBURT · Torul · 3063 · Dereli · Alucra · Şebinkarahisar · Kelkit · Kelkit · ERZURUM · Aşkale · Erzurum · Tortum · Narman · Pasinler · Horasan · Sarıkamış · Selim · Digor · Kağızman · KARS · Kars · Iğdır · İĞDIR · Ağrı Dağı (Ararat) 5165 · Doğubayazıt · Maku · AĞRI · Sürmene

GÜMÜŞHANE · Gümüşhane · 3063 · Refahiye · Kemah · İliç · Kemaliye · İmranlı · Refahiye · Erzincan · ERZINCAN · 3537 · 3462 · Tercan · Çat · Tekman · Karaçoban · Eleşkirt · Taşlıçay · Tutak · Diyadin · 3510 · 3548 · Pötürge · SİİRT · YEREVAN · Ejmiadzin · Abovian · Artashat · Vedi · Sisian · Goris · Kapan · Kajaran · Culfa · Ordubad · Jolfa · Rüde Araz (Araks) · Khomārlu · Hadrūt · Qaradağ · Kaleybar · 3347 · ĀZARBĀYJĀN-E SHARQĪ

Erzincan · Munzur Dağları · MUNZUR VADISI · 3537 · Pülümür · Tuzluca · Ağrı · Hamur · Murat · Karayazı · Patnos · Malazgirt · Ala Dağları 3085 · Siah Chashmeh · 3162 · Khvoy · Ōtūr · Saray · Özalp · Şor · Qotūr · 3610 · Salmās (Shāpūr) · Tasuj · Sharafkhāneh · 3752 · Daryācheh-ye Orūmīyeh · 3870 · Naḡlu · Āzar Shahr · 1297 · Qūshchī

Eskimalatya · ELAZIĞ · Elazığ · Madan · KEBAN BARAJI · Keban · Baraji · Palu · Bingöl · 3650 · Hınıs · Varto · 2967 · Erciş · Muradiye · Adilcevaz · Suphan Dağı 4434 · Ahlat · Tatvan · VAN · Van Gölü 1720 · Van · Gevaş · Gürpınar · Başkale · Başkale · 4135 · Çatak · HAKKÂRİ DAĞLARI · Hakkâri · Yüksekova · Semdinli · 3811 · Oshnovīyeh · Chahār Borj · Naḡadeh · Piranshahr · Rawānduz · Shānīdar · 3607 · Sardasht · Mahābād · Bowkan · Saqqez · Baneh · Divāndarreh

Malatya · 2545 · NEMRUT DAĞI · Ergani · Çermik · Siverek · Hani · Lice · Kulp · Genç · Bingöl · Muş · MUŞ · Bulanık · Bitlis · BİTLİS · Kozluk · Baykan · GÜNEYDOĞU TOROSLARI · Silvan · KÜRDISTAN

Adıyaman · Kâhta · Bozova · NLIURFA · Viranşehir · Şanlıurfa (Urfa) · Süruç · Akçakale · Atatürk Barajı · Siverek · Çınar · Bismil · Dicle Nehri · DIYARBAKIR · Diyarbakır · Batman · Gercüş · Kurtalan · Eruh · Şirnak · Silvan · Midyat · İdil · Cizre · Silopi · Zākhū · Sarsing · Al 'Amādīyah · DAHŪK · Dahūk · Az Zībār · 'Aqrah · Ayn Sifnī · Ayn Zālah · Tall Kayf · Shaqlāwah · ARBĪL · Arbīl · Koi Sanjaq · Rāniyah · Qal'ah Dīzah · Mawat · Chuwārta · 3163 · Penjwīn · AS SULAYMĀNIYAH · As Sulaymāniyah · KORDESTĀN · Marīvān · Hoseynābād · Qorveh · Serīshābād · Ahang

Adıyaman · Kāhta · Hilvan · Mazıdağı · Derik · Kızıltepe · Mardin · Nusaybin · Ceylanpınar · Ra's al 'Ayn · Amūdah · Al Qāmishlī · Ayn Zālah · Ashkī Mawsil · Tall 'Afar · 1460 · Sinjār · NINAWĀ · AL MAWSIL · Qaraqosh · Al Quwayr · Khabūr · Dibagah · Makhmūr · Zāb as Saghīr · Altun Köprü · KIRKŪK · Kirkūk · Taqtaq · Qara Dagh · 3280 · Shevsheh · Dehgolān · Sanandaj · Qeshlāq · Kāmyārān · Dīvāndarreh · HAMADĀN · Hamadān · Bahār

ṢALĀḤ AD DĪN · DAYR AZ ZAWR · Dayr az Zawr · Buşayrah · Al Mayādīn · 1390 · As Sukhnah · Al Arak · Tudmur PALMYRA · Abū Kamāl · Quşaybah · Al Qā'im · 'Ānah · An Nāḥiyah · Buhayrat al Qādisiyah · Fuhaymī · Ḥadīthah · Al Haḍr · Qaiyārah · Al Fatḥah · 526 · Bayjī · Tāwūq · Tūz Khurmātū · Kormor · Maydān · Kifrī · Injānah · Khānaqīn · Jalūlā · Qaşr-e Shīrīn · KERMĀNSHĀH · Kermānshāh · Bīsotūn · 3350 · Javānrud · Ravānsar · Pāveh · Sonqor · Kangāvar · Sahneh · Asadābād · Tūysarkān · Nahāvand

AR RAQQAH · Ar Raqqah · Nahr al Furāt · Ma'din · Ar Ruşāfah · Aş Şuwar · Fadghāmī · AL JAZĪRA · Tibnī · Al Qaţā · Kifri · Tikrīt · Ad Dawr · Sāmarrā' · DIYĀLĀ · Al Miqdādīyah · Ad Dujayl · Balad · Ba'qūbah · Al Khāliş · Mandalī · Balad Rūz · 2656 · Lūmār · Mehrān · Qaşr-e Shīrīn · Pol-e Zahāb · Eslāmābād-e Gharb · Gīlān-e Gharb · Karand · Robāţ · Ṣarpol-e Zahāb · KUHDASHT · Khorramābād · LORESTĀN · Ālashtar · Borūjerd · Nūrābād · Oshtorīnān

Tudmur · DAYR AZ ZAWR · Nukhayb · W. al Ubayyid · 940 · Unayzah · 'Ar Ruţbah · Khān al Baghdādī · Ḥīt · Kubaysah · Ar Ramādī · Al Fallūjah · Al Habbānīyah · Buhayrat al Habbānīyah · Buhayrat ath Tharthār · W. Hawrān · Şāhilīyah · Nahr al Furāt · Al Mahmūdīyah · BAGHDAD · AL ANBĀR · W. Rutga · Ar Rahhālīyah · Shithāthah · Ar Rahhālīyah · Buhayrat ar Razāzah · Al Musayyab · BĀBIL · Al Hindīyah · Al Kifl · KARBALĀ' · Karbalā' · Al Hillah · An Nu'māniyah · AL QĀDISIYAH · Ad Dīwānīyah · Ash Shāmīyah · An Najaf · Al Kūfah

DIMASHQ · SYRIA · Al Hasakah · AL HASAKAH · 920 · Jabal Sinjār · Al Hadr · Hammām al 'Alīl · Qaiyārah · NINAWĀ · Ash Sharqāt · Khabūr · Tall 'Afar · AR RAQQAH · Bālīh · Bahret Assad · Dulq Maghar · Ar Ruşāfah · Şinat ath hawrat · Quşaybah · Abū Kamāl

IRAQ · IRAN · ZANJĀN · Zanjān · Bonāb · Miāndowāb · Malek Kandi · Miāneh · Marāgheh · Bonāb · Takāb · Saqqez · Tūp Āghāj · Hashtrūd · 2925 · 3327 · Māhneshān · Zarrīnābād · Qeydār · Abhar · Ṣā'īn Dezh · Qā'el · Hashtrūd · Qūţīābād · Damaq · Razan · Kabudar Āhang · Famenīn · Hamadān

ILĀM · ĪLĀM · Darreh Shahr · Āsmānābād · Andīmeshk · Dezfūl · Shūsh · Alī ash Sharqī · KHŪZESTĀN · Sūsangerd · Al 'Amārah · MAYSĀN · Qal'at Sukkar · Al Kumayt · Alī al Gharbī · Al Kūt · WĀSIT · Nahr Dijlah · Sa'dīyah · Shaykh Sa'd · Hawr as Suwayqīyah · Al 'Azīzīyah · Aş Şuwayrah · Salmān Pak · BAGHDAD · Al Kāzimīyah · Tarmīya · Banī Sa'd · Balad Rūz · Tursāq · Badrah · Jaşşān · Dehlorān · Arkavāz · Mūsá 'idal

Darband · Qezel Owzan · Sirdān · Māsāl · Rezvānshahr · Bandar-e Anzalī · Rasht · TĀLESH · Fowman · Qezel Owzan · 'Ağh Kand · Nīk Pey · Āb Bar · Garmāb · Bījār

East from Greenwich

ft · m · 9000 · 3000 · 6000 · 2000 · 4500 · 1500 · 3000 · 1000 · 1500 · 500 · 600 · 200 · 0 · 0 · 150 · 50 · 300 · 100 · 600 · 200 · 1500 · 500 · 3000 · 1000 · 6000 · 2000 · 9000 · 3000 · m · ft

1:16 000 000

Projection: Conical Orthomorphic with two standard parallels

East from Greenwich

RUSSIA
1 Adygea
2 Karachey-Cherkessia
3 Kabardino-Balkaria
4 North Ossetia
5 Ingushetia
6 Chechenia
7 Dagestan
8 Mordvinia
9 Chuvashia
10 Mari El
11 Tatarstan
12 Udmurtia
13 Khakassia
AZERBAIJAN
14 Naxçivan
GEORGIA   UKRAINE
15 Ajaria   17 Crimea
16 Abkhazia

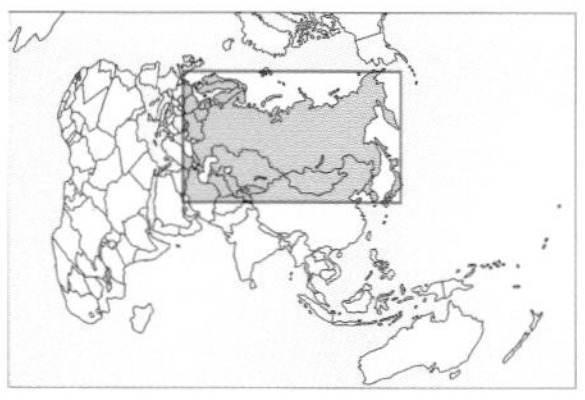

A
150
B
C
D
E
F
8
9
10
11
12
13
14
15
16
17
18
19
ARCTIC OCEAN
Severnaya Zemlya
Ostrov Komsomolets
Ostrov Oktyabrskoy Revolyutsii
Ostrov Bolshevik
Ostrov Malyy Taymyr
Mys Chelyuskin
Mys Arkticheskiy
Ostrov Shmidta
Ostrov Ushakova
Ostrov Pioner
Proliv Vilkitskogo
Ostrova Sergeya Kirova
Ostrov Russkiy
Ostrova Petra
Laptev Sea
Poluostrov Taymyr
Gory Byrranga
Oz. Taymyr
Ostrov Bolshoy Begichev
Nordvik
Novosibirskiye Ostrova
Ostrov Kotelnyy
Ostrov Belkovskiy
Ostrov Stolbovoy
Ostrov Faddeyevskiy
Novaya Sibir
Ostrova Delonga
Ostrov Bennetta
Ostrov Genriyetty
Ostrov Zhannetty
Ostrov Zhokhova
Lyakhovskiye Ostrova
Ostrov Malyy Lyakhovskiy
Ostrov Bolshoy Lyakhovskiy
Proliv Dmitriya Lapteva
East Siberian Sea
Ostrova Medvezhi
Ostrov Vrangelya
Proliv Longa
Chukchi Sea
Mys Dezhneva (East C.)
Bering Str.
St. Lawrence I. (U.S.A.)
International Date Line
Uelen
Provideniya
Anadyrskiy Zaliv
Chukotskoye Nagorye
Vankarem
Pevek
Chaunskaya Guba
Ust Chaun
Bilibino
Anadyr
Beringovskiy
Mys Navarin
Koryakskoye Nagorye
Bering Sea
Mys Olyutorskiy
Kolymskoye Nagorye
Sredinnyy Khrebet
Poluostrov Kamchatka
Petropavlovsk-Kamchatskiy
Vilyuchinsk
Ust-Kamchatsk
Komandorskiye Ostrova
Mys Lopatka
Kurilskiye Ostrova
Sea of Okhotsk
Magadan
Okhotsk
Ayan
Sakhalin
Okha
Nogliki
Aleksandrovsk-Sakhalinskiy
Yuzhno-Sakhalinsk
La Perouse Str.
Tatarskiy Proliv
DALNEVOSTOCHNYY
Khrebet Cherskogo
Verkhoyanskiy Khrebet
Verkhoyansk
Tiksi
Lena
Yakutsk
Mirnyy
Lensk
Olekminsk
Aldan
Neryungri
Tynda
Stanovoy Khrebet
Khrebet Dzhugdzur
Arctic Circle
Norilsk
Talnakh
Dudinka
Gory Putorana
Khatanga
Tura
Nizhnyaya Tunguska
Podkamennaya Tunguska
Vanavara
RUSSIA
Krasnoyarsk
Kansk
Bratsk
Ust-Ilimsk
Ust-Kut
Severobaykalsk
Irkutsk
Angarsk
Ulan Ude
Chita
L. Baykal
Vostochnyy Sayan
Yablonovyy Khrebet
Kyzyl
Abakan
Komsomolsk-na-Amur
Khabarovsk
Birobidzhan
Blagoveshchensk
Heihe
Sikhote Alin
Vladivostok
Nakhodka
Ussuriysk
Amur
Ulaanbaatar
MONGOLIA
Hövsgöl Nuur
Darhan
Erdenet
Choybalsan
Hentiyn Nuruu
Hangayn Nuruu
Gobi
Dalandzadgad
CHINA
Manzhouli
Hailar
Da Hinggan Ling
Dongbei (Manchuria)
QIQIHAR
HARBIN
DAQING
JIAMUSI
JIXI
MUDANJIANG
JILIN
CHANGCHUN
SHENYANG
FUSHUN
ANSHAN
DALIAN
CHIFENG
BEIJING
TANGSHAN
ZHANGJIAKOU
HOHHOT
BAOTOU
Hami
NORTH KOREA
P'YONGYANG
NAMP'O
SOUTH KOREA
SEOUL
INCHEON
DAEJEON
DAEGU
BUSAN
GWANGJU
Sea of Japan (East Sea)
JAPAN
Hokkaidō
SAPPORO
Hakodate
Honshū
Aomori
Akita
Niigata
Sado
Toyama
Kanazawa
KYOTO
KOBE
ŌSAKA
10
218
11
12
219
13
14
COPYRIGHT PHILIP'S

50 0 100 200 300 400 km
50 0 50 100 150 200 250 miles
1:8 000 000

Projection : Modified Miller oblated stereographic

East from Greenwich

RUSSIA

Petukhovo · Isil Kul · OMSK · Tatarsk · NOVOSIBIRSK · Berdsk · Leninsk · Belovo · Chernogorsk · Minusinsk · Shushenskoye · Toora-Khem

Mamlyutka · Petropavl · OMSK · Kalachinsk · Om · Iskitim · Kuznetskiy · Kiselevsk · Abakan · KRASNOYARSK · Turan · Kyzyl

Troebratskiy · Cherlak · Suzun · Prokopyevsk · Novokuznetsk · Mezhdurechensk · Abaza · Sayanogorsk · Khrebet Akademika Obrucheva

SOLTÜSTIK QAZAQSTAN · Tayynsha · Kishkeneköl · Kamen · Novoaltaysk · Tashtagol · TUVA · Tannu Ola

Gergeevka · Kökshetaü · Zaozyorny · Ozero Chany · Ob · BARNAUL · Biysk · Gorno-Altaysk · GORNO-ALTAY · Ak-Dovurak · Kyzyl · Erzin · Dzun

Rüzaevka · Makinsk · Shchüchinsk · Siletitengiz Köli · Slavgorod · Aleysk · Ob Mayma · Belukha 4506 · Ölgiy · Tolbo · Uvs Nuur · Hanhöhiy Uul · Hyargas Nuur

Esil · Atbasar · Stepnogorsk · Kulunda · Rubtsovsk · Zmeinogorsk · Gornyak · ALTAY · MONGOLIA

ASTANA · AQMOLA · Ereymentaü · PAVLODAR · Ekibastuz · Ertis (Irtysh) · Semey (Semipalatinsk) · Öskemen · Zyryan · Qotanqaraghay · Ulaangom · Tögrög · GOVI-ALTAY

Derzhavinsk · Qazaqtyng · Temirtaü · Aqtaü · Kürchatov · Glübokoe · Belousovka · Serebryansk · Georgievka · QAZAQSTAN · Marqaköl · Habahe · Altay · Dund-Us (Hovd)

QARAGHANDY (Karaganda) · Shakhtinsk · Abay · Qarqaraly · Qaraghayly · SHYGHYS QAZAQSTAN · Zaysan Köli (Oz. Zaysan) · Kürshim · Burqin · Fuyun · Qinghe · AERHTAI SHAN (ALTAI)

Ulutau · Qyzylzhar · USAQSHOGYLYGHY · Atasū · Qaynar · Khrebet Tarbagatay · Zaysan · Ertix He · HOVD

ZHAYRANG · Barshatas · Ayaköz · Tacheng (Qoqek) · Emin · Hoxtolgay · Baytik Shan

Qarazhal · Aqshataü · Aqtoghay · Maqanshy · Alakol (Ozero Alakol) · Toli · Karamay · Gurbantünggüt Shamo

BETPAQDALA · Moyynty · Balqash · Üsharal · Dostyq · Bole · Kuytun · Manas · ÜRÜMQI · Bogda Shan

Balqash Köli (L. Balkhash) · Saryesik-Atyrau Qumy · Sarqan · Ala Tau · Ebinur Hu · Uşu · Shihezi · Changji · TIAN SHAN · Turpan · Turpan Pendi

ONGTÜSTIK QAZAQSTAN · Saryshaghan · Ülken · Taldyqorghan · Molaly · Borohoro Shan · Yining (Gulja) · Erbeng Shan · Toksun

Shyghanaq · Bürylbaytal · Tekeli · Zharkent · Huocheng · Gongliu · Hejing · Korla · Kuruktag · Lop Nur

ZHAMBYL · Moyynqum · Qapshaghay · ALMATY · Saryözek · Köktal · Qapqal · Hoxud · Bosten Hu · Konqi He

Sozaq · Qabanbay · Shelek · Bögeni · Shonzhy · Halik Shan · Luntai · Yuli (Lop Nur)

Kentaü · Qaratau · Zhangatas · Shü · Töle Bi · Talghar · Pik Khan-Tengri · Tarim He · Xinhe · Kuqa · Xayar

Türkistan · Taraz (Zhambyl) · Bishkek (Frunze) · Tokmak · Cholpon-Ata · Karakol · Jengish Chokusu (Pik Pobedy) 7439 · Baicheng · Aksu

Baltaköl · Shymkent (Chimkent) · Qazyghurt · KYRGYZSTAN · Ysyk-Köl 1609 · Kyzyl-Suu 6995 · Terskey Ala Too · Wensu · Aksu He

TOSHKENT (Tashkent) · Chirchiq · Talas Ala Too · Toktogul · Kochkor · Naryn · Karateki Shan · Wushi · TARIM PENDI

Angren · Namangan · Andijon · Osh · Baetov · At-Bashy · Takla-Makan · XINJIANG UYGUR ZIZHIQU (SINKIANG)

Qüqon (Kokand) · Marghilon · Farghona · Gülchö · Uluqqat · Sugun · Bachu · Kaxgar He · Shamo

Jizzax · SIRDARYO · Khujand · Farghona · Alai Range · Artux · Kashi · Akto · Yengisar · Shache (Kashgar) · Ruoqiang · Waxxari

Samarqand · SUGHD · Ura-teppa · Batken · Tash · Tash-Kömür · Kashi · Shule · Yengisar · Qiemo · Altun Shan

Pendzhikent · Panjakent · Khrebet Gissarskiy · Gharm · KÜHISTON BADAKHSHON (GORNO-BADAKHSHON) · Xaidulla · Hadilik · Ayakkum Hu

Qarshi · TAJIKISTAN · Turšunzoda · Dushanbe · Kofarnihon · Murghob · Kongur Shan 7719 · Muztagh-Ata · Zepu · Yecheng · Pishan · Qira · Minfeng

SURXON-DARYO · KHATLON · Küleb · Pamir · Taxkorgan · Zizhixian · Yutian · Muz Tag 6723

Denau · Sherabad · Qürghonteppa · Dusti · Feyzābād · Khorugh · Shazud · CHINA · Hotan · Lop · Kokyar · KUNLUN SHAN · Muz Muztag

Termiz · BALKH · Kholm · BADAKHSHAN · Ishkim · HINDU KUSH · KARAKORAM RANGE · Mazar · Xaidulla · Karatax Shan · Karakoram Pass · Aksai Chin · XIZANG ZIZHIQU (TIBET)

Mazar-e Sharif · Āybak · Baghlan · TAKHAR · Murghob · Darkot Pass · Rakaposhi · Gilgit · K2 8611 · Dahongliutan · Chagdo Kangri · Lazhuglung

SAMANGAN · Sar-e Pol · Chārikār · NURISTAN · NORTH WEST FRONTIER · Northern Areas · Nanga Parbat · Kotmul · Sumdo · Sumxi · Duomula · Rutog

KABUL · Jalalabad · Mardan · Chilas · Abbottabad · JAMMU & KASHMIR · Leh · Bangong Co · INDIA

PAKISTAN · SRINAGAR · Khyber Pass

Underlined towns give their name to the administrative area in which they stand.

COPYRIGHT PHILIP'S

1:12 000 000

Projection: Bonne

East from Greenwich

RUSSIA

Oz. Baykal
Ulan Ude
Chita
Bukachacha
Sakhalin
Sretensk
Nerchinsk
Svobodnyy
Aleksandrovsk-Sakhalinskiy
Mys Terpeniya
Olovyannaya
Priargunsk
Blagoveshchensk
Heihe
Bureya
Komsomolsk-na-Amur
Poronaysk
Manzhouli
Krasnokamensk
Heihe
Khabarovsk
Dolinsk
Borzya
Yakeshi
Fuyu
Hailun
Hegang
Tongjiang
Kholmsk
Yuzhno-Sakhalinsk
Hailar
Nenjiang
Nehe
Yichun
Jiamusi
La Perouse Str.
Rebun-Tō
Wakkanai
Buir Nur
Zalantun
Daqing
Anda
Qitaihe
Hulin
Asahikawa
Kitami
Ostrov Kunashir

QIQIHAR
HARBIN
JIAMUSI
JIXI
Mishan
SAPPORO
HOKKAIDŌ
Muroran
Hakodate

SEA OF JAPAN (EAST SEA)

CHIFENG
SHENYANG
NORTH KOREA
P'YONGYANG
SEOUL
SOUTH KOREA
YELLOW SEA
INCHEON
DAEJEON
DAEGU
ULSAN
BUSAN
GWANGJU
TŌKYŌ
KAWASAKI
YOKOHAMA
NAGOYA
ŌSAKA
KYŌTO
KŌBE
HIROSHIMA
KITAKYŪSHŪ
FUKUOKA
Nagasaki
Kumamoto
KYŪSHŪ
Kagoshima
Miyazaki

BEIJING (Peking)
TIANJIN
TANGSHAN
DALIAN
QINGDAO
JINAN
ZHENGZHOU
NANJING
SHANGHAI
WUHAN
HANGZHOU
NINGBO
FUZHOU
XIAMEN
GUANGZHOU
SHENZHEN
HONG KONG (Xianggang)
Macau
TAIPEI
T'AICHUNG
KAOHSIUNG
TAIWAN (FORMOSA)

EAST CHINA SEA
PACIFIC OCEAN
SOUTH CHINA SEA
Hainan Dao
HAINAN
Sanya
PHILIPPINES

Tropic of Cancer

HONG KONG, MACAU AND SHENZHEN
1:800 000

GUANGDONG
SHENZHEN
ZHONGSHAN
ZHUHAI
Macau (Aomen)
HONG KONG (Xianggang)
Kowloon (Jiulong)
Victoria
Hong Kong Island
Lantau Island (Tai Yue Shan)
Pearl River Bridge

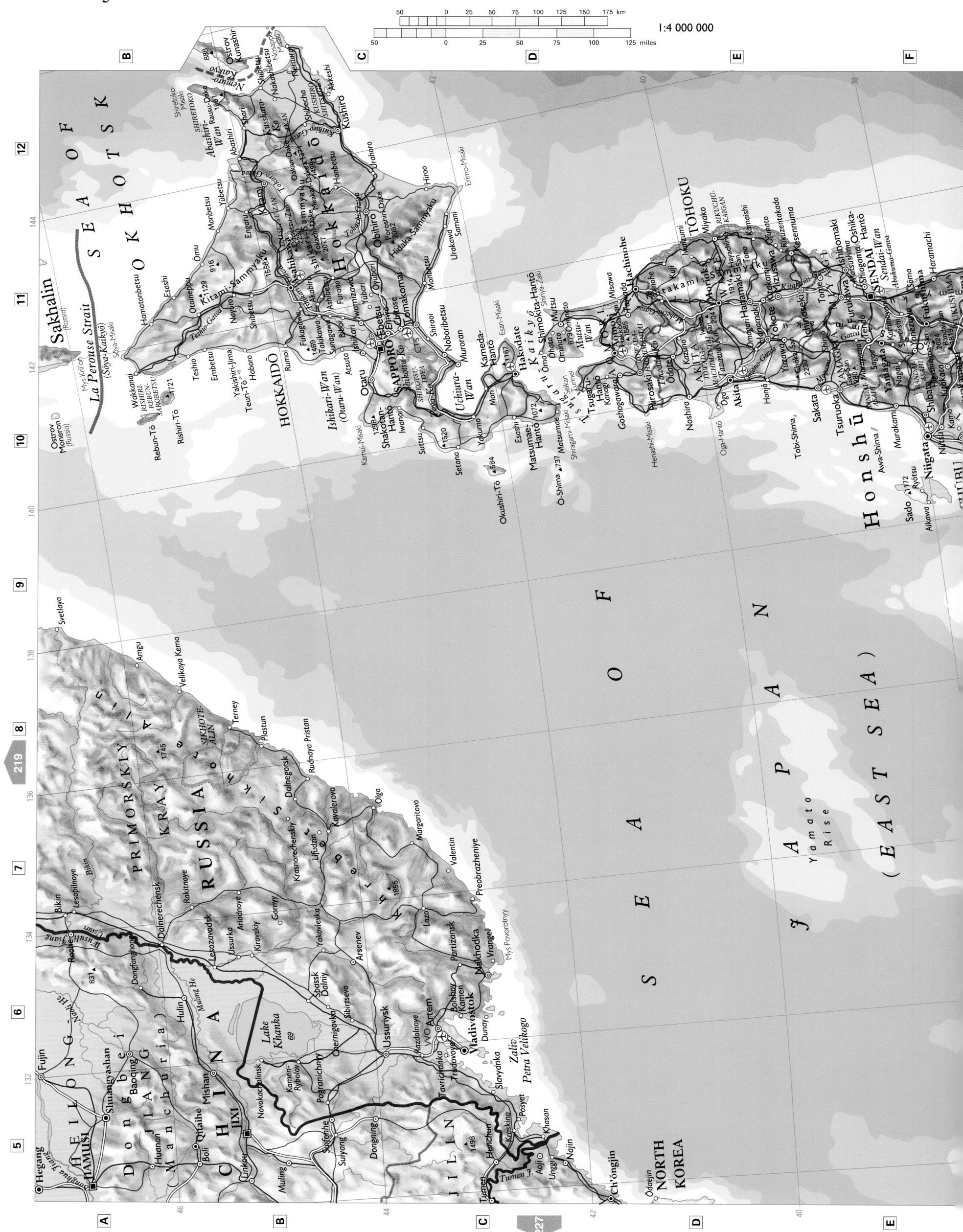

50 0 25 50 75 100 125 150 175 km

50 0 25 50 75 100 125 miles

1:4 000 000

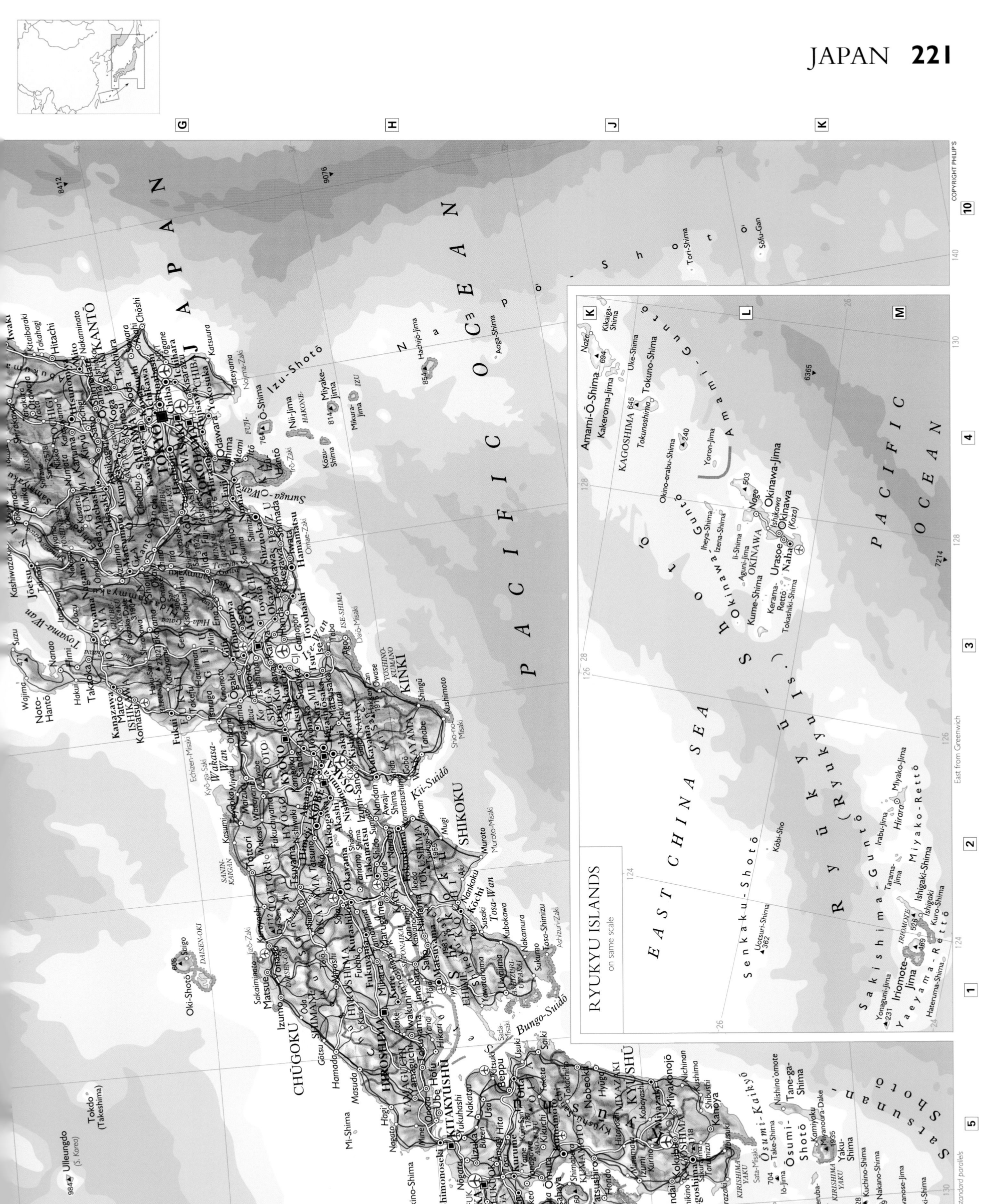

RYUKYU ISLANDS
on same scale

East from Greenwich

Projection: Conical with two standard parallels

SEA OF JAPAN
(EAST SEA)

SOUTH KOREA

Korea Strait

CHŪGOKU-DISTRICT

Tsushima

HONSHU

Kyūshū

Shikoku
SHIKOKU-DISTRICT

Kyūshū
KYŪSHŪ-DISTRICT

Projection:
Lambert's Conformal
Conic

Shinkansen line

CHŪBU-DISTRICT

KANTŌ-DISTRICT

KINKI-DISTRICT

Wakasa-Wan

Enshū-Nada

Kumano-Nada

Sagami-Nada

Suruga-Wan

Ise-Wan

TOKYO
YOKOHAMA
KAWASAKI
NAGOYA
KYOTO
OSAKA
SAKAI

P A C I F I C   O C E A N

East from Greenwich

COPYRIGHT PHILIP'S

20 0 20 40 60 80 100 120 140 160 km
20 0 20 40 60 80 100 miles

1:3 100 000

RUSSIA

CHINA

Dongbei (Manchuria)

Faku Tiefa Kaiyuan Dongfeng Meihekou Huinan Dashahe Tumen Namyang
Yemaotai Shenchengzhen Jingyu Fusong Songjianghe Helong Chongsong
Xinmin SHENYANG FUSHUN Tonghua Hunjiang Linjiang Baihe Paektu-san Hoeryong Aoji Sösura
Xinchengzi SHE Qingyuan Xinbin Chunggang-ŭp Musan Puryŏng Najin
Piao'ertun JILIN Manjiang Pugŏdong Khasan
Liaozhong Tieling Dahuofan Shuiku Morihong Shan Kwardamao Tiechang Chasong Changbai Nanam Ch'ŏngjin
Liaoyang Anping Benxi Tianshifu Huanren Ji'an Manp'o Huch'ang Kimjŏngsugŭp Hyesan Kyŏngsŏng Ödaejin
Dengta Gongchangling Lianshanguan Huanren Shuiku Kanggye Sŏnggan Kasan Sinhŭng Kapsan P'ungsan Kilchu Musudan
Haicheng ANSHAN Guanshui Niumaowu Kuandian Ch'osan CHAGANG-DO YANGGANG-DO HAMGYŎNG-BUK-DO
Caohekou Supung Shuiku Pyoktong Wiwon Koin Pujon-ho Kimch'aek (Sŏngjin)
Xiuyan Fengcheng Sakchu Taegwan Pukchin Huichon Changjin HAMGYŎNGNAM-DO Tanch'ŏn
Dandong Uiju Kusong Kujang Changjin Pukch'ŏng Iwŏn
Zhuanghe Sin-do Yongamp'o Sŏnch'ŏn Unsan Taehung Oro Sinhung Sinch'ang
Gushan Donggou SINŬIJU P'YŎNGANBUK-DO Taedong-gang Hamhŭng Hongwon Sinp'o
Dalu Dao T'an-do Chŏngju Anju Kaech'ŏn Tŏkch'ŏn Chŏngp'yŏng HŬNGNAM
Shicheng Dao Taehwa-do (N. Korea) Sinmi-do Sinanju Hamhŭng-man Hodo-dan
Dawangjin Dao Söhan-man Sukch'ŏn P'YŎNGANNAM-DO Yŏnghŭng Kowŏn Sinsang
Changshan Sunan Sunch'ŏn **NORTH** Munch'ŏn Yŏnghŭng-man
Wumang Dao Qundao P'yŏngsŏng Yangdok Wŏnsan Tongjosŏn-man
Haiyang Dao (China) Kangdong **KOREA** Anbyŏn Kojŏ
P'YŎNGYANG FNJ Hoeyang Changjŏn
Onch'ŏn NAMP'O P'yŏngyang Chunghwa Suan Koksan Kosan T'ongch'on Kosŏng
NAMP'O Songnim Hwangju Sep'o Changdo-ri Gangseong
Cho-do Ullyul Kuwŏl-san Sariwŏn HWANGHAEBUK-DO Sin'gye Ich'ŏn Kimhwa
Songhwa Chaeryŏng Sinmak Nam-ch'ŏn P'yŏnggang Sokcho
Changyŏn HWANGHAENAM-DO Pyŏksŏng Sinch'on Kŭmch'ŏn Cheorwon Sincheorwon Hwacheon-Chuseoul Yang-yang
Taedong-man Pyŏksŏng Haeju Kaesŏng Chŏrwon GANGWON-DO SORAKSAN Seoraksan Jumunjin
Baengnyeongdo (S. Korea) Ongjin Yŏnan KAESŎNG-DO Yeoncheon Soyangho Soyang-ho Gangneung
Daecheongdo (S. Korea) Haeju-man P'anmunjŏm Dongducheon Chuncheon ODAESAN
Sunwi-do Gyodong Munsan Pocheon Hongcheon Jeongseon Donghae
Daeyeonpyeong (S. Korea) Ganghwa Paju Yangju CHIAKSAN Samcheok
Seongmodo Uijeongbu Namyangju Hoengseong Wŏnju Taebaek
GOYANG GMP **SEOUL** Yeoju Jecheon Yeong-wol Taebaeksan
Bucheon ICN Anyang **SEONGNAM** Chungju Uljin
INCHEON Siheung Suwŏn Yong-in Icheon Sangdong
Deokjeokdo Ansan Jeju Eumseong Danyang Uljin
Yeongheungdo Hwaseong GYEONGGI-DO Anseong CHUNGCHEONGBUK-DO WORAKSAN SOBAEKSAN Yeongju
Osan Pyeongtaek Jincheon Goesan Mun-gyeong Pyeonghae
Dangjin Cheonan CHEONGJU Jeungpyeong Yecheon Andong HWANGSAN **SOUTH**
TAE-AN Seosan Hapdeok Asan Boeun SONGNISAN Sangju Cheongsong **KOREA**
Anmyeon Hongseong CHUNGCHEONGNAMDO Gongju DAEJEON Yeongdong GYEONGSANGBUK-DO Yeongdeok
Anmyeondo Yesan Yeon-gi Gagyegyeong Gimcheon Seonsan Uiseong Heunghae
Boryeong Nonsan Gumi Yeongcheon Pohang Ulleungdo (S. Korea)
Daecheon Ganggyeong GYEONGJU YEONGJU SEOKGURAM GROTTO
Gunsan Iksan Deogyusan Waegwan Gyeongju Gampo
Seonyudo Iri Jeonju GAYASAN DAEGU Gyeongsan Oedong
Buan Gimje Geochang HAEINSA Gyeongsan ULSAN
BYEONSAN Jeongeup Hamyang Miryang ULSAN
Wido JEOLLABUK-DO Jangsu GYEONGSANGNAMDO Changwon Yangsan
Gochang Namwon JIRISAN Uiryeong Gimhae Gijang
Yeonggwang Damyang Jinju Haman Masan Jinhae BUSAN
GWANGJU Hadong Jinju BUSAN
Imjado Jido Hwasun Gwang-yang Sacheon Geoje Dongnae
Hampyeong Naju Suncheon Goseong Geojedo Tong-Yeong
Jeungdo Muan JEOLLANAM-DO Yeong-am Boseong Goheung HALLYEO
Ja-eundo Mokpo Yeong-am Jangheung Goheung Yeosu
Heuksando Bigeumdo Jangheung Boseong Geumodo
Hongdo Uido Hwangsan Haenam Geogeumdo Onarodo
Jindo Wando Wando Cheongsando
Haido Nohwado Bogildo Daemodo
Soheuksando DADOHAE Soheuksando

SEA OF JAPAN (EAST SEA)

Korea Bay

YELLOW SEA (HUANG HAI)

Korea Strait

JAPAN Kara-Saki Kamitsushima Mi-Shima Ömi-Shima
Kamiagata Tsuno-Shima Nagato
Tsushima (Japan) Hibiki-Nada Mine
Mitsushima Izuhara Toyoura

JEJU-DO on same scale

a

Jeju Jeju-do (S. Korea)
CJU Hallim Hallasan HALLASAN Namwon
Daejeong Seogwipo Namjeju

Projection : Conical with two standard parallels

East from Greenwich

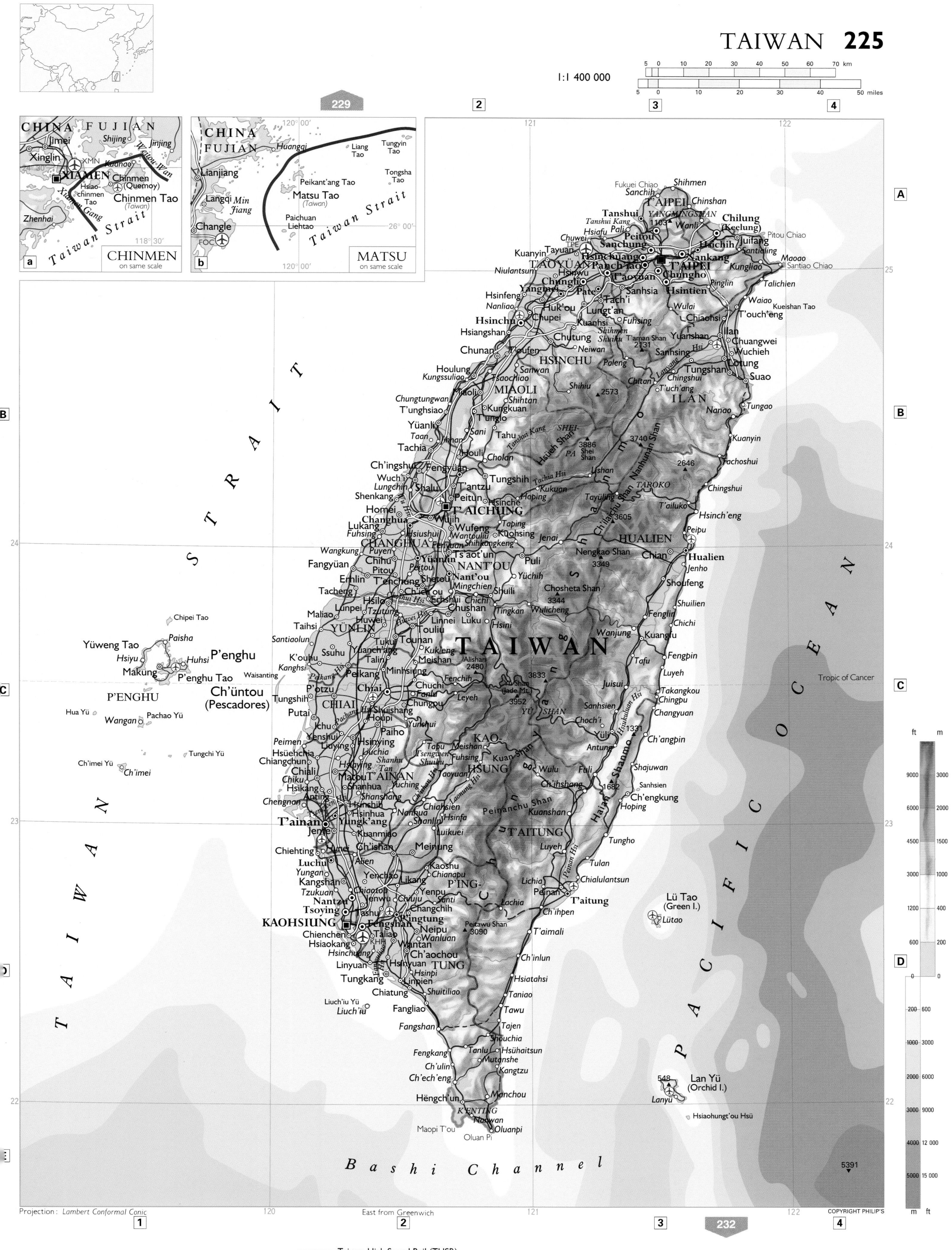

1:1 400 000

5 0   10   20   30   40   50   60   70 km
5 0   10   20   30   40   50 miles

229

CHINMEN

CHINA FUJIAN
Jimei
Shijing Jinjing
Xinglin
Xiamen
XMN Kuahao
Hsiao-chinmen Tao Chinmen (Quemoy)
Zhenhai
Chinmen Tao (Taiwan)
Taiwan Strait
118° 30'

CHINMEN
on same scale a

MATSU

CHINA FUJIAN
Huangqi
Lianjiang Liang Tao Tungyin Tao
Langqi Min Jiang Peikant'ang Tao
Matsu Tao (Taiwan)
Changle Paichuan Tongsha Tao
Liehtao
Taiwan Strait
120° 00' 26° 00'

MATSU
on same scale b

T A I W A N   S T R A I T

Fukuei Chiao Shihmen
Sanchih Chinshan
T'AIPEI
Tanshui YANGMINGSHAN
Tanshui Kang 1103 Wanli Chilung (Keelung)
Hsiafu Pali Peitou Pitou Chiao
Chuwei Sanchung Hsichih Juifang
Kuanyin TPE Nankang Santiaoling
T'AOYÜAN Panchiao T'aipei Maooo
Hsinchuang Chungho Kungliao Santiao Chiao
Chungli Pate T'aoyüan Chinghsia 25
Yangmei Sanhsia Hsintien Waiao Kueishan Tao
Huk'ou Lungt'an Wulai Chiaohsi T'ouch'eng
Hsinfeng Kuanhsi Fuhsing Ilan Chuangwei
Hsinchu Chupei Shihmen Yüanshan Lotung
Hsiangshan Chutung Shuiku 2131 Sanhsing Tungshan Suao
Chunan Youfen Neiwan Poleng T'uch'ang Nanao
HSINCHU Shihtan Chitan Tungao
MIAOLI Shihiu 2573 Tachoshui
Houlung Tsaochiao SHEI-PA Kuanyin
Kungssuliao Shitan 3886 3740 Shan 2646
Chungtungwan T'unghsiao Tahu Hsüeh Shei Shan Chingshui
Yüanli Taan Tunglo Ushan TAROKO
Tachia Sani Tachia Hsi T'ailuko
Ch'ingshui Fengyüan Tungshih Kukuan 3605 Hsinch'eng
Wuch'i Tantzu Peitun Hoping Tayüling Peipu
Lungchin Shalu T'aichung Hsinche HUALIEN 2480
Homei Wujih Taping Kuohsing Hualien
Changhua Wufeng Wantouliu Jenai Nengkao Shan Jenho
Lukang Hsiushui Shihkongkeng 3349 Chian Shoufeng
Fuhsing CHANGHUA Fenyüan Ts'aot'un Puli Fenglin
Wangkung Puyen Yüanlin NANTOU Yüchih Chichi
Chihu Pitou Nant'ou Mingchien Choshata Shan Kuangfu
Fangyüan Ernlin Tenching Shetou Shuili 3344 Wulicheng Wanjung
Tacheng Hsilo Tzutung Echshui Chichi Tafu Kuangfu
Maliao Linpei Huwei Linnei Tingkan Fengpin
Taihsi YÜNLIN Touliu Luku Hsini Chichi
Santiaolun Tuku Yüanch'ang Kuk'eng Alishan Juisui
K'ouhu Talin Meishan 2480 T A I W A N Luyeh
Kanghsi Peikang Minhsiung Fenchih 3833 Takangkou
Waisanting Minhsiung Chuchi Jade Mt. Chingpu
P'otzu Chiai Shuishang Fanlu 3952 Changyuan
Tungshih CHIAI Chungpu Leyeh YÜ SHAN Tropic of Cancer
Putai Holpi Paiho Yünshui KAO- Chich'i
Ichu Yenshui Hsinying Tapu Meishan Antung Ch'angpin
Peimen Liaying Kuchia Shanhu Fuhsing HSUNG Ch'ih'shang
Hsüehchia Chiangchun Hsiaying Tsengwen Shuilu Kuan Shan Wulu Fuli
Chiali Matou T'AINAN Taoyuan 1682 Shajuwan
Chiku Shanshang Yuching Tan Sanhsien
Hsinhua Nankua Chiahsien Hsinfa Ch'engkung
Chengnon Anting Shanlin Peinanchu Shan Hoping
T'ainan Hsinshih Luikuei Kuanshan
Jeni Yingk'ang Chiehting Meinung T'AITUNG Tungho
Ch'ishan Peinan Hsi Tulan
Luchu Alien Kaoshu Luyeh Lichia Tulan Lü Tao (Green I.)
Yungan Yenchao Likang Chianapu Peinan Lütao
Kangshan Likang Yenpu P'ING- Lichia Chialulantsun
Tzukuan Chiaotou Chuju Santi Lanti Peinan
Nantzu Yenwu Chuju Changchih Lachia T'aitung
KAOHSIUNG Yashu Kangshan Peitawu Shan T'aimali
Tsoying Fenghan 3090 Ch'ihpen
Chienchen KHH Taliao Neipu Ch'inlun
Hsiaokang Wanluan TUNG Hsiatahsi
Hsinchuang Wantan Hsiaohungt'ou Hsü
Linyuan Hsiyuan Ch'aochou Taniao
Tungkang Linpien Lan Yü (Orchid I.)
Chiatung Shuitiliao 548 Lanyu
Liuch'iu Yü Tawu
Liuch'iu Fangliao Tajen
Fangshan Shouchia
Fengkang Tanlu Hsühaitsun
Ch'ulin Mutanshe Kangtzu
Ch'ech'eng Manchou
Hengch'un 22
K'ENTING Nanwan
Maopi T'ou Oluanpi 5391
Oluan Pi

Bashi Channel

P A C I F I C O C E A N

T A I W A N   S T R A I T

ft   m
9000 3000
6000 2000
4500 1500
3000 1000
1200 400
600 200
0 0
200 600
1000 3000
2000 6000
3000 9000
4000 12 000
5000 15 000
m ft

—— Taiwan High Speed Rail (THSR)

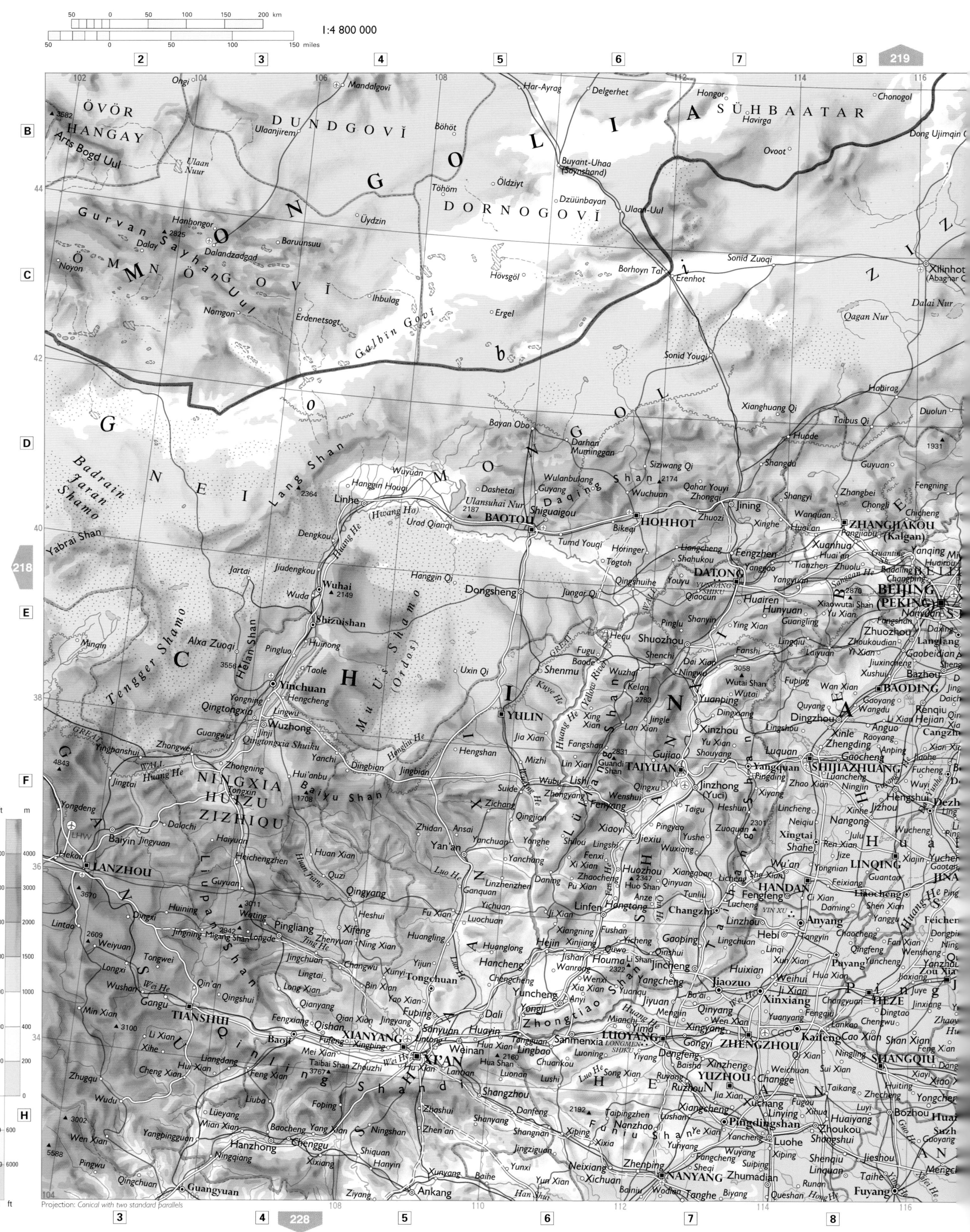

1:4 800 000

Projection: Conical with two standard parallels

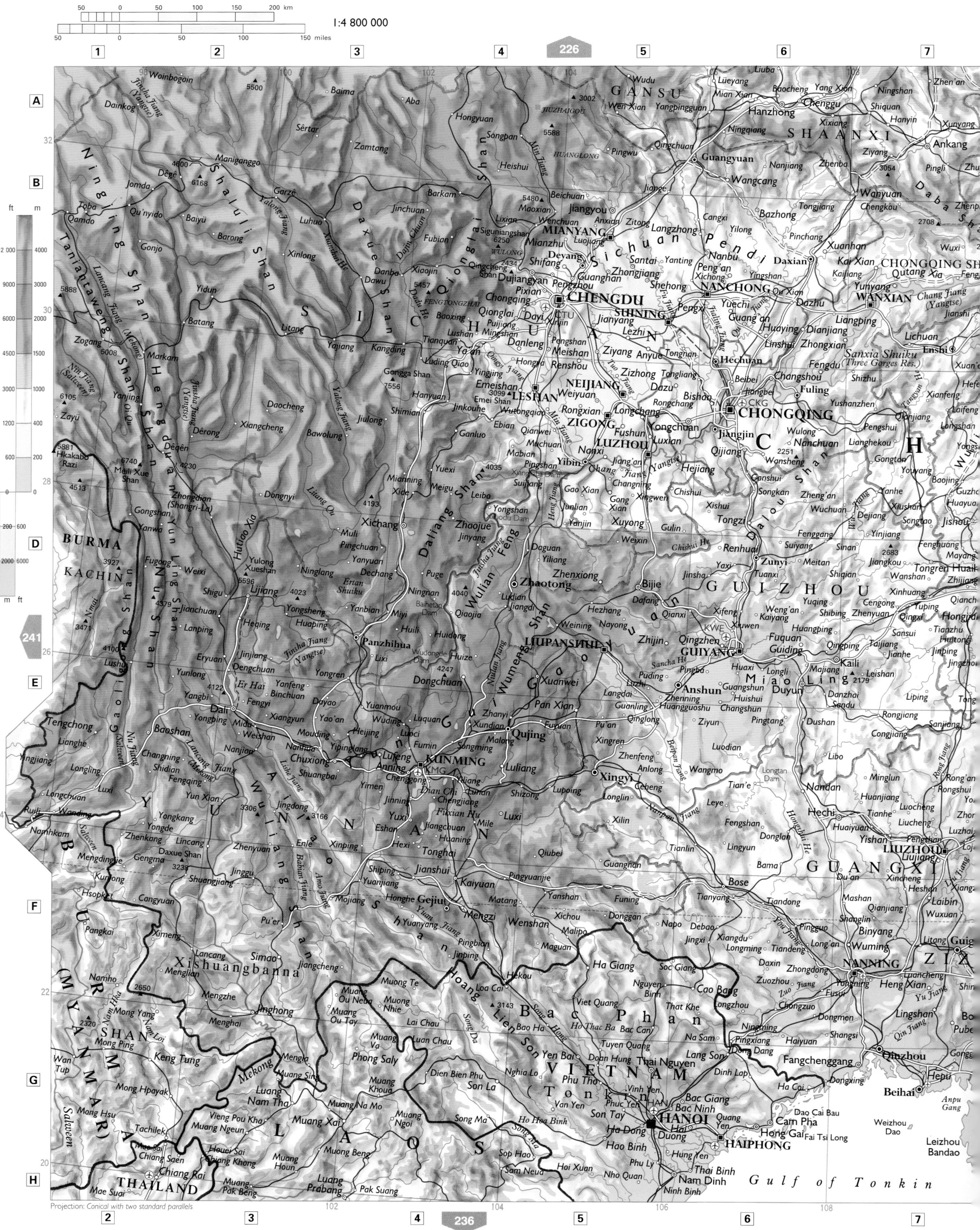

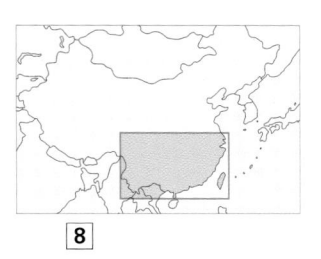

Projection: Mercator

East from Greenwich

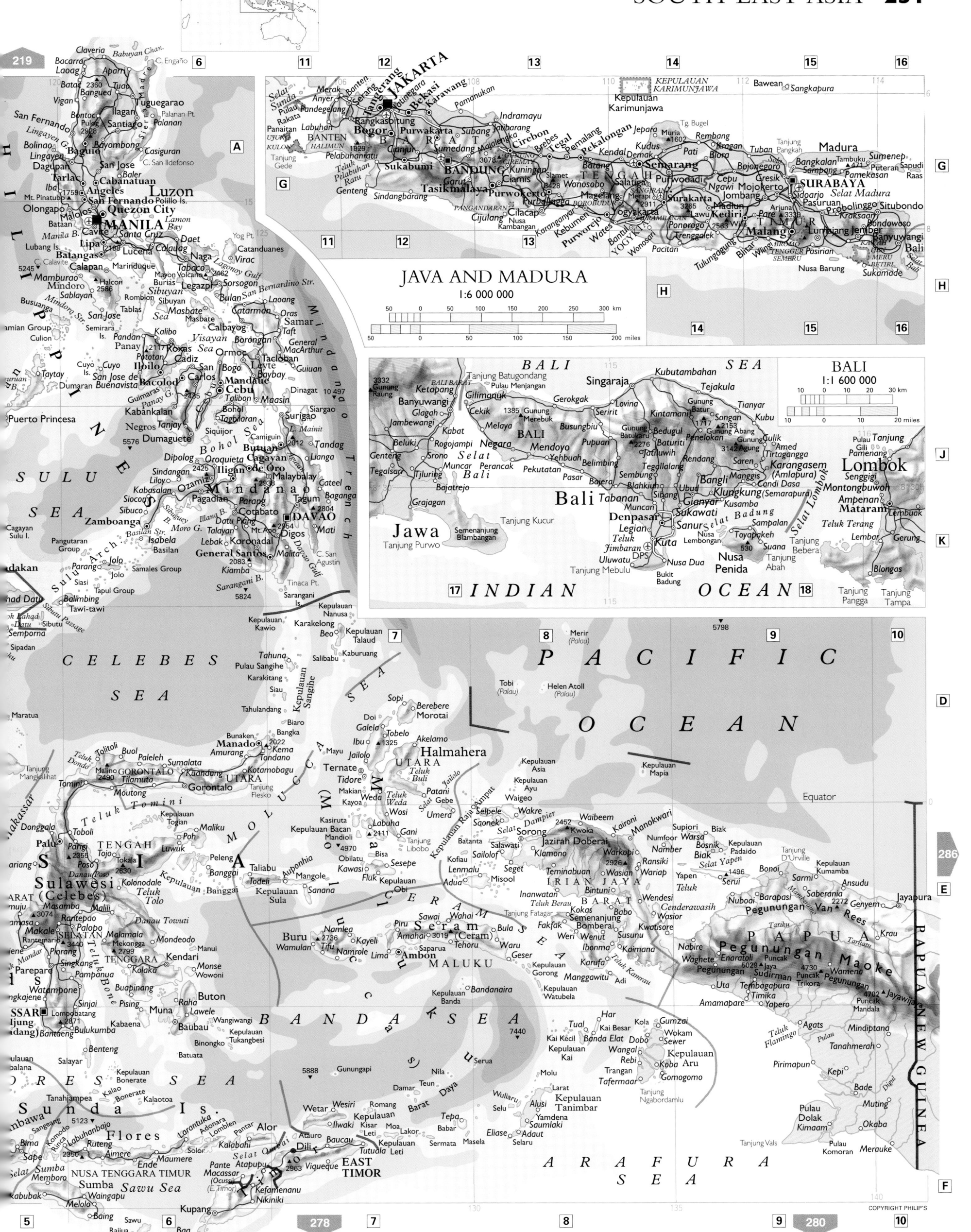

6   11   12   JAKARTA   13   14   15   16

JAVA AND MADURA
1:6 000 000

50   0   50   100   150   200   250   300 km

50   0   50   100   150   200 miles

BALI
1:1 600 000

10   0   10   20   30 km

10   0   10   20 miles

17 *I N D I A N*   *O C E A N* 18

7   8   Merir
(Palau)   9   10

P A C I F I C

O C E A N

Equator

286

Jayapura

E

Bacarra
Laoag   Babuyan Chan.
C. Engaño

Claveria
Aparri

Tuguegarao

Vigan

Bangued   2360 Tuao

Batac

Bontoc   Ilagan

San Fernando   Santiago
Palanan   Palanan Pt.
2928

Baguio   Cabanatuan
Casiguran
S. San Ildefonso

San Jose

Bolinao   Lingayen G.   Tarlac   Baler
Dagupan   Iba   1759   Angeles

Mt. Pinatubo   Cabanatuan

Olongapo   San Fernando
Bataan   **Luzon**
Lubang Is.   Malolos   **MANILA**   Lamon
Bay

Manila B.   **Cavite** ● Santa Cruz
Lipa   Daet

Batangas   Lucena   Calauag   Naga   Virac   Catanduanes

Calapan   Marinduque   Lagonoy Gulf   Yog Pt. 125

5245   **Mamburao**   2462   Mayon Volcano
Mindoro   Tabaco
2586   Legazpi   Sorsogon
Busuanga   Sibuyan   Bulan   Catarman   Laoang

Sablayan   Romblon   Sibuyan   Samar   Oras
Tablas   Masbate   *Sea*   Taft
Culion   Semirara Is.   Masbate   Calbayog   General
MacArthur
Damian Group

Cuyo   *Visayan*   2117   Roxas   Panay   Borongan
Sea   Pandan

Taytay   Cuyo Is.   San Jose del   Iloilo   2425   Bogo   Tacloban
Dumaran   Buenavista   Cebu   Baybay
Guimaras   San Carlos   Mandaue   Guiuan
Puerto Princesa   5576   Negros   Bacolod   Talibon   Maasin   Dinagat 10 497
B.   Dumaguete   Tanjay   Bohol *Sea*   Tagbilaran   Surigao   Siargao
Taytay   Camiguin   2012   Tandag
Siquijor   Dipolog   Oroquieta   Cagayan   Lianga
Sindangan   2425   de Oro

Sibutu   Sibuguey   Ozamiz   Iligan   Malaybalay   Cateel
Passage   Kabasalan   Sibuco   Pagadian   Parang   2938   Tagum   2804

Zamboanga   Ilana B.   Cotabato   Mt. Apu   **DAVAO**
Panguturan   Siocon   Datu Piang   Talayan   2954   Digos
Sulu I.   Isabela   Lebak   Koronadal   Mati

Basilan   **General Santos**   2083   C. San Agustin
Jolo   Jolo   Kiamba   Malita
Samales Group   Kiamba

Siasi   Tapul Group   Sarangani B.   Sarangani
Tawi-tawi   Balimbing   5824   Sarangani Is.

S U L U   S E A

C E L E B E S   *S E A*

219

COPYRIGHT PHILIP'S

5   278   6   7   8   9   280   10

1:3 200 000

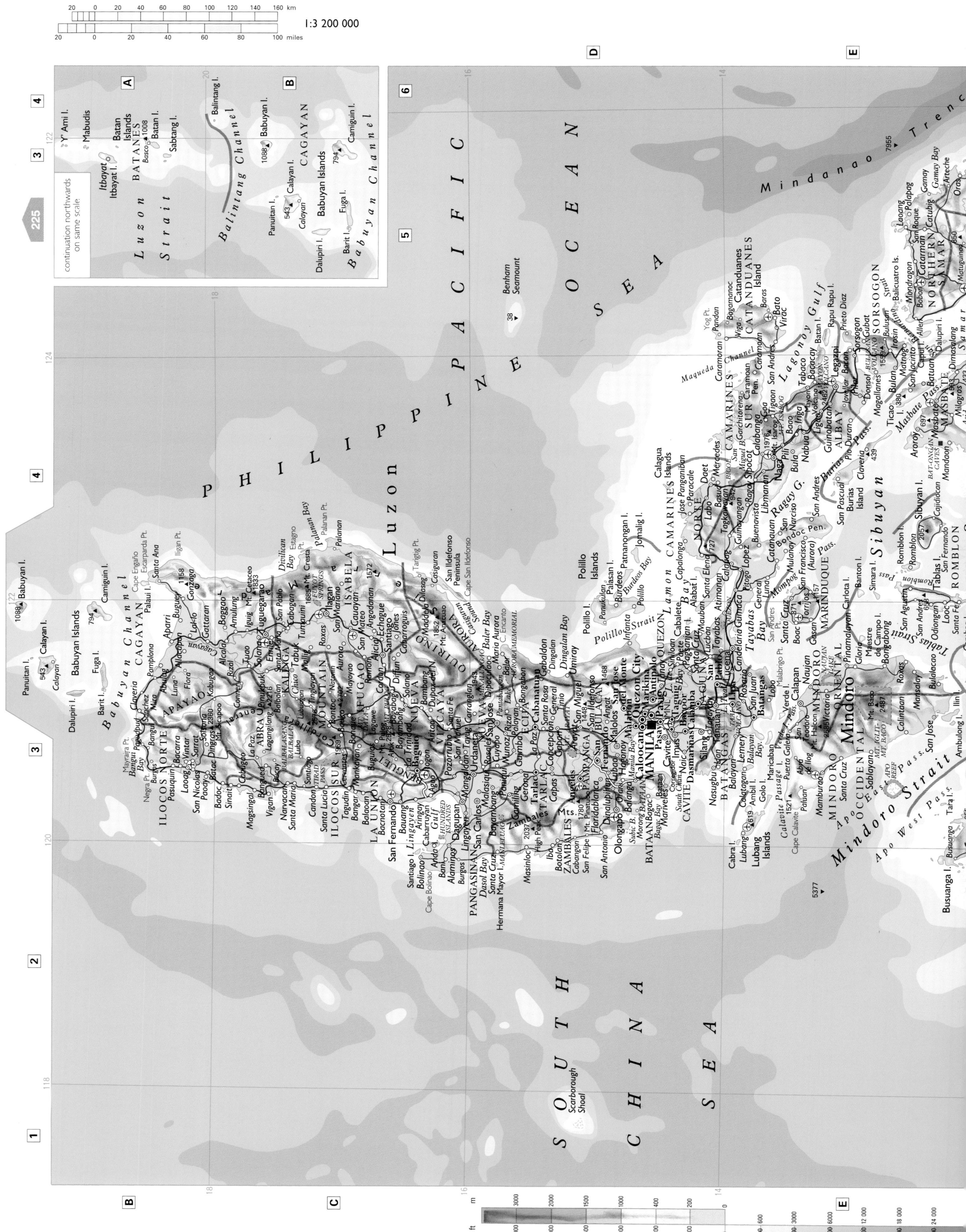

225

continuation northwards
on same scale

A   B

PHILIPPINE OCEAN

PHILIPPINE SEA

Mindanao Trench

PACIFIC

Luzon Strait

BATANES
Islands

CAGAYAN

Babuyan Islands

Babuyan Channel

Balintang Channel

Benham
Seamount

L u z o n

CAGAYAN

ILOCOS
NORTE

ISABELA

AURORA

QUIRINO

NUEVA
VIZCAYA

MOUNTAIN

KALINGA

APAYAO

ABRA

ILOCOS
SUR

LA
UNION

PANGASINAN

ZAMBALES

TARLAC

NUEVA
ECIJA

BULACAN

PAMPANGA

BATAAN

CAVITE

MANILA

BATANGAS

QUEZON

CAMARINES
NORTE

CAMARINES
SUR

ALBAY

SORSOGON

MASBATE

CATANDUANES

NORTHERN
SAMAR

Lagonoy Gulf

Ragay G.

Lamon
Bay

Sibuyan
Sea

ROMBLON

MINDORO
ORIENTAL

MINDORO
OCCIDENTAL

Mindoro

MARINDUQUE

Tablas Strait

Mindoro Strait

Apo West Pass.

SOUTH

CHINA

SEA

Scarborough
Shoal

Polillo
Islands

Polillo I.

Lingayen
Gulf

HUNDRED
ISLANDS

m
3000
2000
1500
1000
400
200
0

ft
9000
6000
4500
3000
1200
600
0
-200
-600
-1000
-2000
-4000
-6000
-8000

-200
-600
-3000
-6000
-12 000
-18 000
-24 000

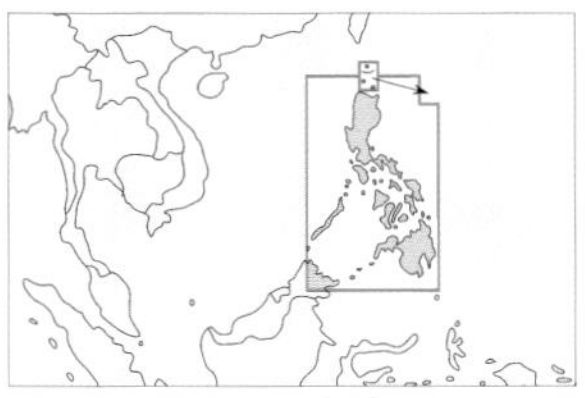

PHILIPPINES

Seas and Major Regions

- VISAYAS
- SULU SEA
- CELEBES SEA
- Visayan Sea
- Bohol Sea
- Moro Gulf
- Leyte Gulf
- Camotes Sea
- Sibuyan Sea
- Panay Gulf
- Davao Gulf
- Illana Bay
- Palawan Passage
- Mindoro Strait
- Cuyo West Pass
- Cuyo East Pass
- Linapacan Strait
- Balabac Str.
- Basilan Strait
- Sibutu Passage
- Sibutu Passage
- Tapiantana Channel

Major Islands and Provinces

- EASTERN SAMAR
- SAMAR
- BILIRAN
- LEYTE
- SOUTHERN LEYTE
- CARAGA
- SURIGAO DEL NORTE
- SURIGAO DEL SUR
- DINAGAT
- AGUSAN DEL NORTE
- AGUSAN DEL SUR
- DAVAO ORIENTAL
- DAVAO DEL NORTE
- DAVAO DEL SUR
- DAVAO
- COMPOSTELA
- BUKIDNON
- LANAO DEL NORTE
- LANAO DEL SUR
- MISAMIS ORIENTAL
- MISAMIS OCCIDENTAL
- CAMIGUIN
- ZAMBOANGA DEL NORTE
- ZAMBOANGA DEL SUR
- ZAMBOANGA
- NORTH COTABATO
- COTABATO
- SULTAN KUDARAT
- SOUTH COTABATO
- SARANGANI
- SOCCSKSARGEN
- MUSLIM MINDANAO (ARMM)
- Mindanao
- BASILAN
- SULU
- TAWI-TAWI
- CEBU
- BOHOL
- SIQUIJOR
- NEGROS
- NEGROS ORIENTAL
- NEGROS OCCIDENTAL
- PANAY
- AKLAN
- CAPIZ
- ANTIQUE
- ILOILO
- GUIMARAS
- Palawan
- PALAWAN
- MALAYSIA
- SABAH
- Borneo

Cities and Towns (selected)

- Davao
- Zamboanga
- Cebu
- Bacolod
- Iloilo
- Cagayan
- Butuan
- Surigao
- Tacloban
- Ormoc
- Puerto Princesa
- Dumaguete
- Dipolog
- General Santos
- Koronadal
- Cotabato
- Marawi
- Malaybalay
- Valencia
- Ozamiz
- Pagadian
- Jolo
- Bongao
- Sandakan

Mountains / Elevations (selected)

- Mt. Apo 2954
- Mt. Kitanglad 2938
- Mt. Matutum 2293
- Mt. Kalatungan 2815
- Mt. Ragang 2815
- Mt. Canlaon 2450
- 2652
- 2012
- 2085
- 2117
- 5207 (depth)

East from Greenwich

Pulau Miangas (Indonesia)

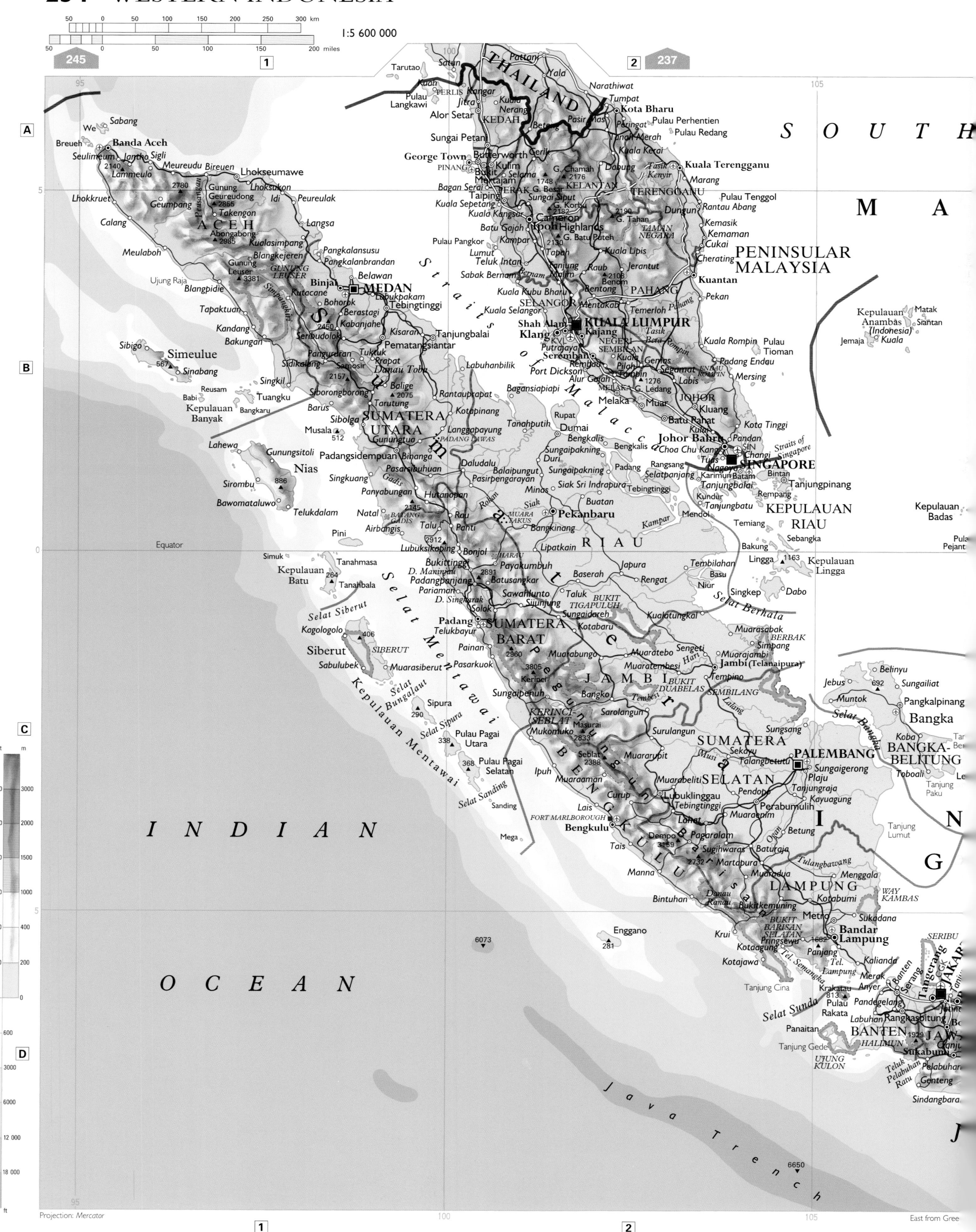

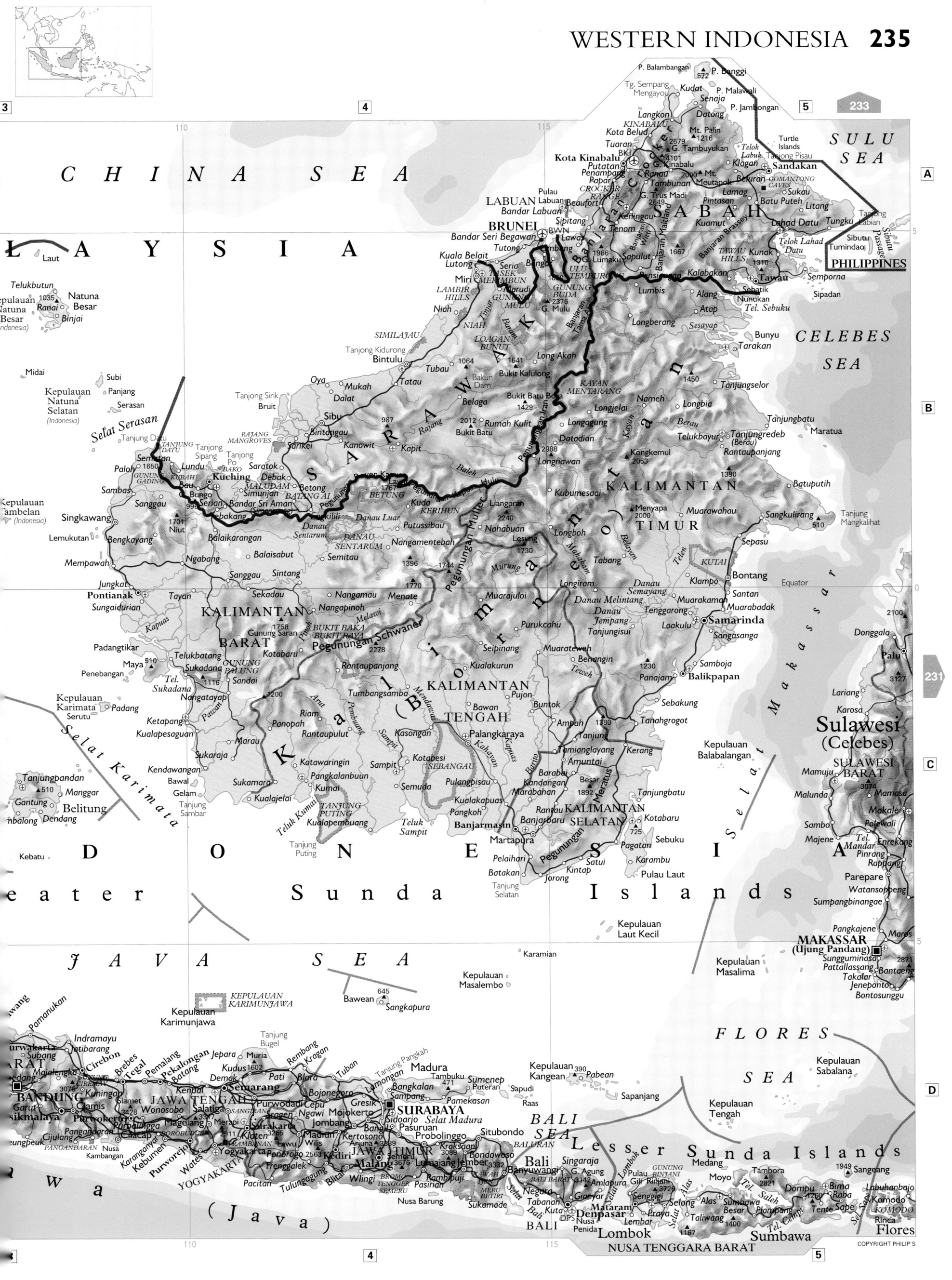

C H I N A   S E A

M A L A Y S I A

Laut

Telukbutun
Kepulauan
Natuna
Besar
(Indonesia)
Ranai
Binjai
Natuna
Besar 1035

Midai

Subi
Panjang
Serasan
Kepulauan
Natuna
Selatan
(Indonesia)

Selat Serasan

Tanjung Datu
TANJUNG
DATU
Tanjong
Sipang
Tanjong
Po
BAKO
Semitan
GUNUNG
GADING
Paloh
Sematan 1650
KUBAH
Batu
Bau
Bungo
Kuching
Lundu
Debak
Sambas
Serian
Singkawang
Sanggau
Niut 1701
Balaikarangan
Bengkayang

Kepulauan
Tambelan
(Indonesia)

Lemukutan

Mempawah

Ngabang
Balaisabut
Sanggau

Jungkat
Pontianak
Sungaidurian
Tayan

KALIMANTAN
BARAT

Padangtikar
Telukbatang
Sukadana
GUNUNG
PALUNG
Sandai
Maya 510
Penebangan
1116

Kepulauan
Karimata
Serutu
Padang
Ketapang
Kualapesaguan
Sukaraja
Kendawangan
Bawal
Gelam
Kumai
Sukamara
Kualajelai

Tanjungpandan
Gantung 510
Manggar
Dendang
Selat Karimata
Belitung
Kebatu
mbalong

I N D O N E S I A

Greater   *Sunda*   *Islands*

J A V A   *S E A*

*KEPULAUAN
KARIMUNJAWA*
Kepulauan
Karimunjawa
Bawean 645
Sangkapura

Kepulauan
Masalembo

Karamian

S A R A W A K

Niah
SIMILAJAU
Bintulu
Tubau
1064
Tatau
Mukah
Dalat
Oya
Bruit
RAJANG
MANGROVES
Sibu
Bintangau
Sarikei
Saratok
Betong
MALUDAM
Simunjan
Bandar Sri Aman
BATANG AI
Lubok
Antu
Engkilili
Balai Ringin
998
Sri
Aman
BETUNG
Pakan
Kanowit
Kapit
987
Rajang
2012
Rumah Kulit
Bukit Batu
Belaga
Bakun
Dam
Baleh
Hulai
KERIHUN
Kuda
Putussibau
Danau Luar
Danau
Sentarum
Nangamentebah
DANAU
SENTARUM
Semitau
Sintang
Nangapinoh
1396
1744
1770
Sekadau
Nangamau
Menate
Melawi
BUKIT BAKA
BUKIT RAYA
1758
Gunung Saran
Kotabaru
Pegunungan Schwaner
2278
Nangatayap
Marau
Riam
Panopah
Rantaupulut
Tumbangsamba
Pembuang
Arut
Kotawaringin
Rantauprapat
Sampit
Kasongan
Kotabesi
Pangkalanbuun
Kumai
Semuda
TANJUNG
PUTING
Kualapembuang
Tanjung
Sambar
Tanjung
Puting
Teluk
Sampit
Teluk Kumai

P. Balambangan
Tg. Sempang
Mengayou
Langkon
Kota Belud
Tuaran
KINABALU
2579
G. Tambuyukon
Penampang
Papar
CROCKER
RANGE
Beaufort
Sipitang
Tenom
BWN
Lawas
Limbang
ULU
TEMBURU
Bangar
GUNUNG
MULU
G. Mulu
2376
Long Akah
LOAGAN
BUNUT
1641
Bukit Kalulong
Datodian
2988
Longnawan
Liangpran
Nahabuan
Lesung
2240
Longboh
Murung
Muarajuloi
Purukcahu
Kualakurun
Seipinang
Muarateweh
Teweh
Buntok
Bawan
Kasongan
Palangkaraya
Pulangpisau
Kualakapuas
Pangkoh
Banjarmasin
Martapura
Pelaihari
Batakan

P. Banggi
572
Kudat
Senaja
Datong
P. Malawali
P. Jambongan
Mt. Palin
1216
G. Kinabalu
4101
Ranau
2000
Mt.
Meutapok
Tambunan
Keningau
1966
Lumaku
Sapulut
Pensiangan
Nunukan
Tel. Sebuku
Sesayap
Longberang
Atap
Lumbis
Alang
Kalabakan
Sebatik
Tawau
Semporna
Sipadan
Malundu
Bunyu
Tarakan
Tanjungselor
Nameh
1450
Longgagung
Longbia
Berau
Telukbayur
Tanjungredeb
(Berau)
Rantaupanjang
Maratua
1390
Batuputih
Tanjung
Mangkalihat
Menyapa
2000
Muarawahau
Sangkulirang 510
Tabang
Longiram
Tanjung
Danau
Semayang
Muarakaman
Tenggarong
Tanjungsui
Danau
Jempang
Danau
Melintang
Loakulu
Sangasanga
Samarinda
Santan
Muarabadak
2100
Sebakung
Penajam
1230
Balikpapan
Tanahgrogot
Amuntai
Kandangan
Marabahan
Barabai
Besar
1892
MERATUS
Tanjungbatu
Kotabaru
725
Sebuku
Pagatan
Satui
Karambu
*KALIMANTAN
SELATAN*
Banjarbaru
Rantau
Pegunungan
Jorong
Kintap
Pulau Laut

S U L U
S E A

Sandakan
Turtle
Islands
Tanjong Pisau
GOMANTONG
CAVES
Batu Puteh
Lahad Datu
Tungku
Tanjong
Labian
Litang
Tomanggong
Kunak
Telok Lahad
Datu
Sibutu
Tumindao
Sibuku
Passage
PHILIPPINES

C E L E B E S
S E A

KALIMANTAN
T I M U R

K a l i m a n t a n
(B o r n e o)

KUTAI
Equator

Selat Makassar

Donggala
Palu
3127
Lariang
Karosa
2100
Sulawesi
(Celebes)
SULAWESI
BARAT
Mamuju
3074
Malunda
Mamasa
Makale
Polewali
Majene
Tel.
Mandar
Pinrang
Sambo
Enrekong
Rappang
Parepare
Watansoppeng
Sumpangbinangae
Pangkajene
MAKASSAR
(Ujung Pandang)
Maros
Sungguminasa
Pattallassang
Takalar
Jeneponto
Bantaeng
Bontosunggu

Kepulauan
Balabalangan

KALIMANTAN
TENGAH

Sunda   *Islands*

Kepulauan
Laut Kecil

Kepulauan
Masalima

FLORES
SEA

Kepulauan
Sabalana

Tanjung
Selatan

Kepulauan
Kangean
390
Pabean
Sapudi
Raas
Sapanjang

Kepulauan
Tengah

BALI
SEA

Lesser   *Sunda*   *Islands*

Kepulauan
Sabalana

J A V A

Indramayu
Pamanukan
Jatibarang
Subang
Cirebon
Brebes
Tegal
Pemalang
Pekalongan
Batang
Kendal
Demak
Kudus
1602
Pati
Blora
Rembang
Kragan
Tuban
Tanjung
Pangkah
Lamongan
Gresik
SURABAYA
Sidoarjo
Bangkalan
Sampang
Pamekasan
Sumenep
Madura
Tambuku
471
Puteran
Selat Madura
Pasuruan
Probolinggo
Situbondo
Bondowoso
Banyuwangi
BALI
BARAT

BANDUNG
3078
CIREMAI
Majalengka
Ciamis
Garut
Slamet
3428
Purwodadi
Cepu
Ngawi
Bojonegoro
Mojokerto
Jombang
Kertosono
Madiun
Nganjuk
Jombang
Ponorogo
2563
Kediri
Semarang
Wonosobo
Magelang
Salatiga
Surakarta
Klaten
Sragen
JAWA TENGAH
Merapi
2911
Borobudur
Lawu
3265
JAWA
TIMUR
Arjuna
3339
Malang
3676
Lumajang
Jember
3332
Kraksaan
*MERU
BETIRI*

Pangandaran
Cilacap
Nusa
Kambangan
Wates
YOGYAKARTA
Pacitan
Trenggalek
Tulungagung
Blitar
Wlingi
SEMERU
TENGGER
BROMO
Pasirian
Nusa Barung

G. Agung
3142
Amlapura
Singaraja
Gili Rinjani
Pulau
GUNUNG
RINJANI
Medang
Tambora
Sumbawa
Besar
2821
Taliwang
1400
Plampang
Empang
Dompu
Bima
1949
Sangeang
Raba
Sape
KOMODO
Komodo
Rinca
Flores
Labuanbajo

Mataram
Tabanan
Gianyar
Kuta
Denpasar
BALI
DPS
Nusa
Penida
Lombok
Senggigi
Selong
Praya
Selat Lombok
Alas
Sumbawa
Taliwang
Moyo
Tel. Saleh
Senggigi
Tente

NUSA TENGGARA BARAT

COPYRIGHT PHILIP'S

233
231
A
B
C
D
3
4
5
110
115

1:4 800 000

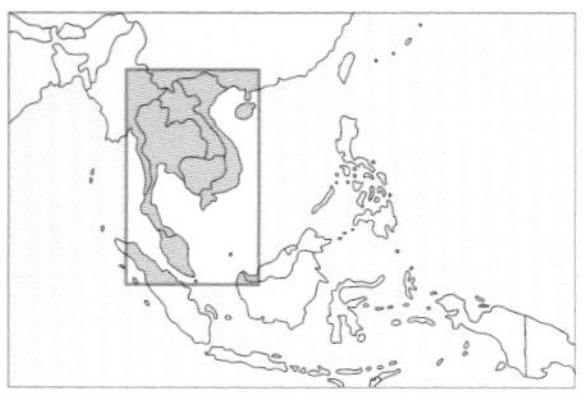

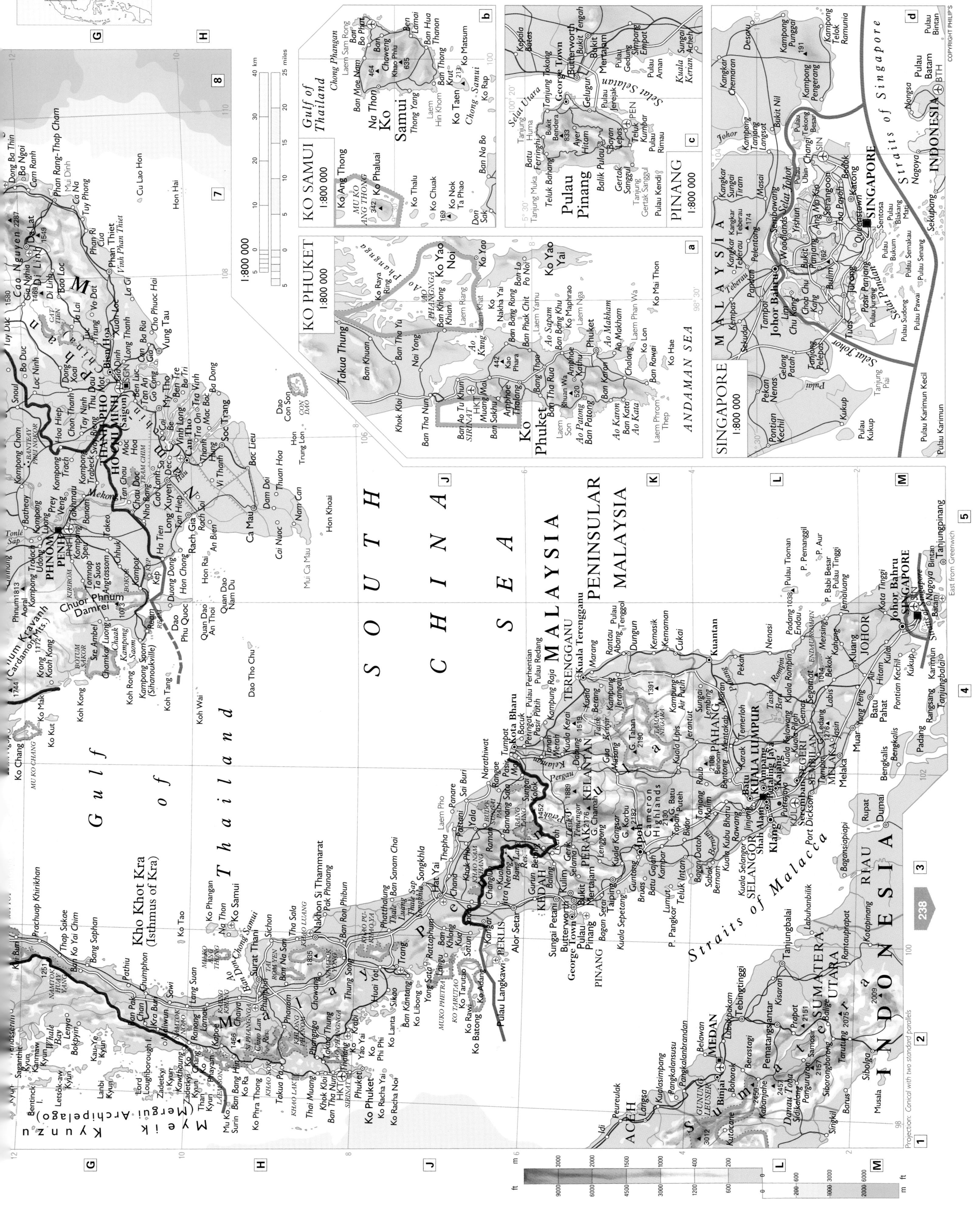

SOUTH CHINA SEA

Gulf of Thailand

Gulf of Thailand (Ko Samui inset)

ANDAMAN SEA

Straits of Malacca

Straits of Singapore

INDONESIA

PENINSULAR MALAYSIA

MALAYSIA

SINGAPORE

Ko Phuket 1:800 000

Ko Samui 1:800 000

Ko Ang Thong (Ko Samui) 1:800 000

Pulau Pinang 1:800 000

Pinang 1:800 000

Singapore 1:800 000

Kho Khot Kra (Isthmus of Kra)

Myeik (Mergui Archipelago) / Kyunzu

Projection: Conical with two standard parallels

East from Greenwich

COPYRIGHT PHILIP'S

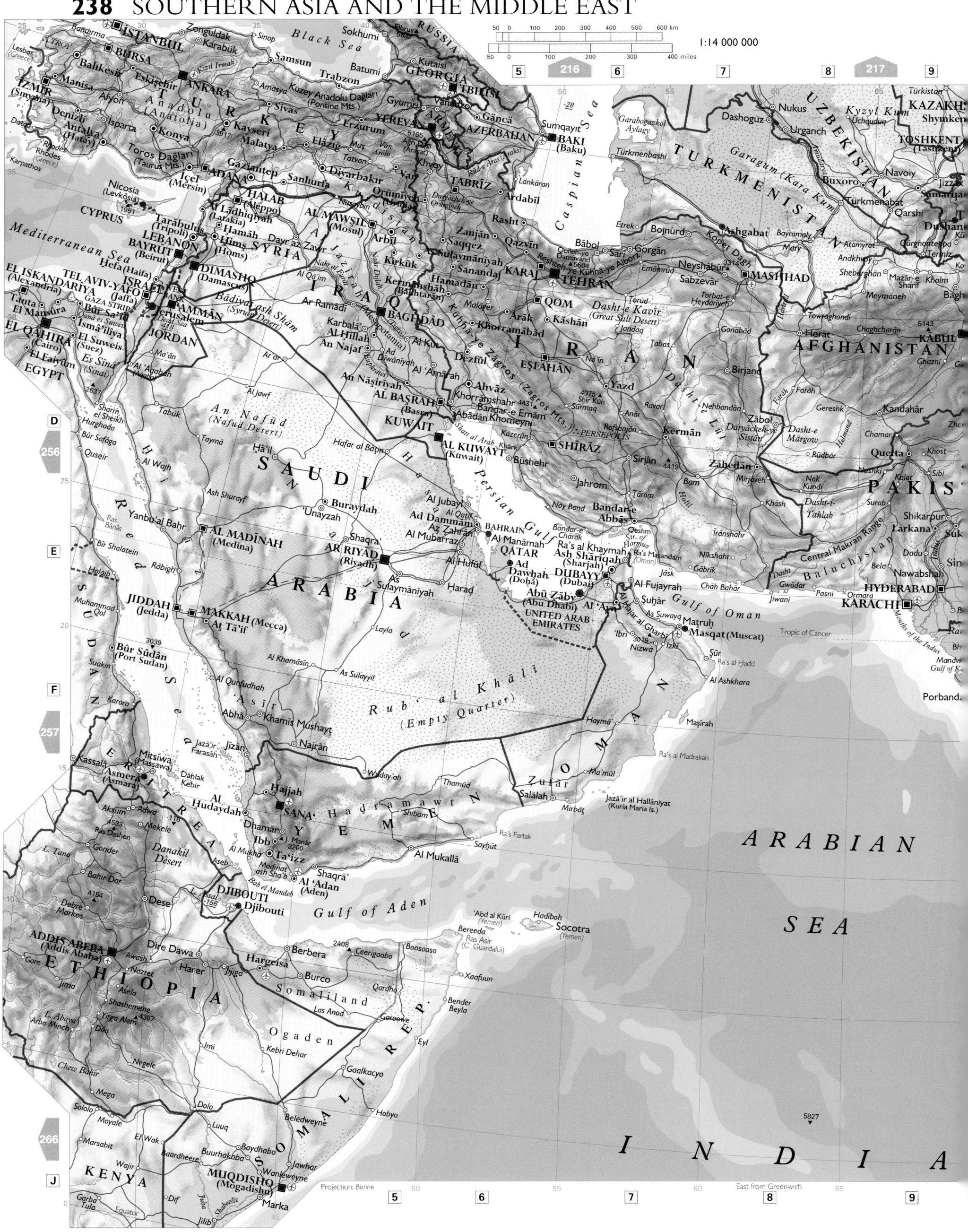

1:14 000 000

1:5 600 000

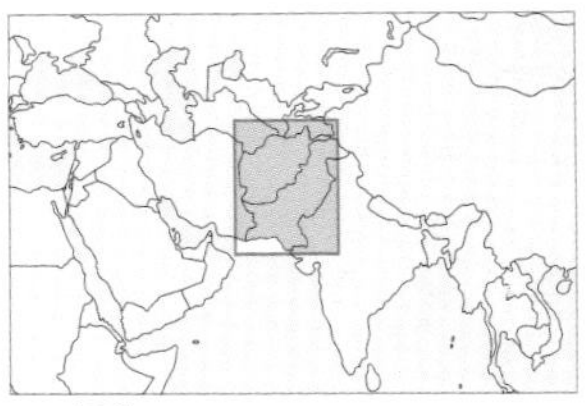

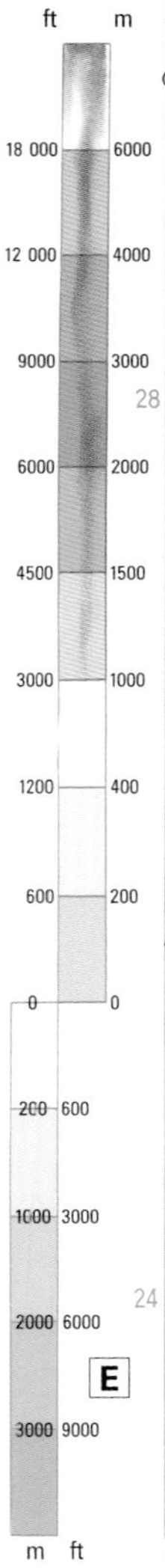

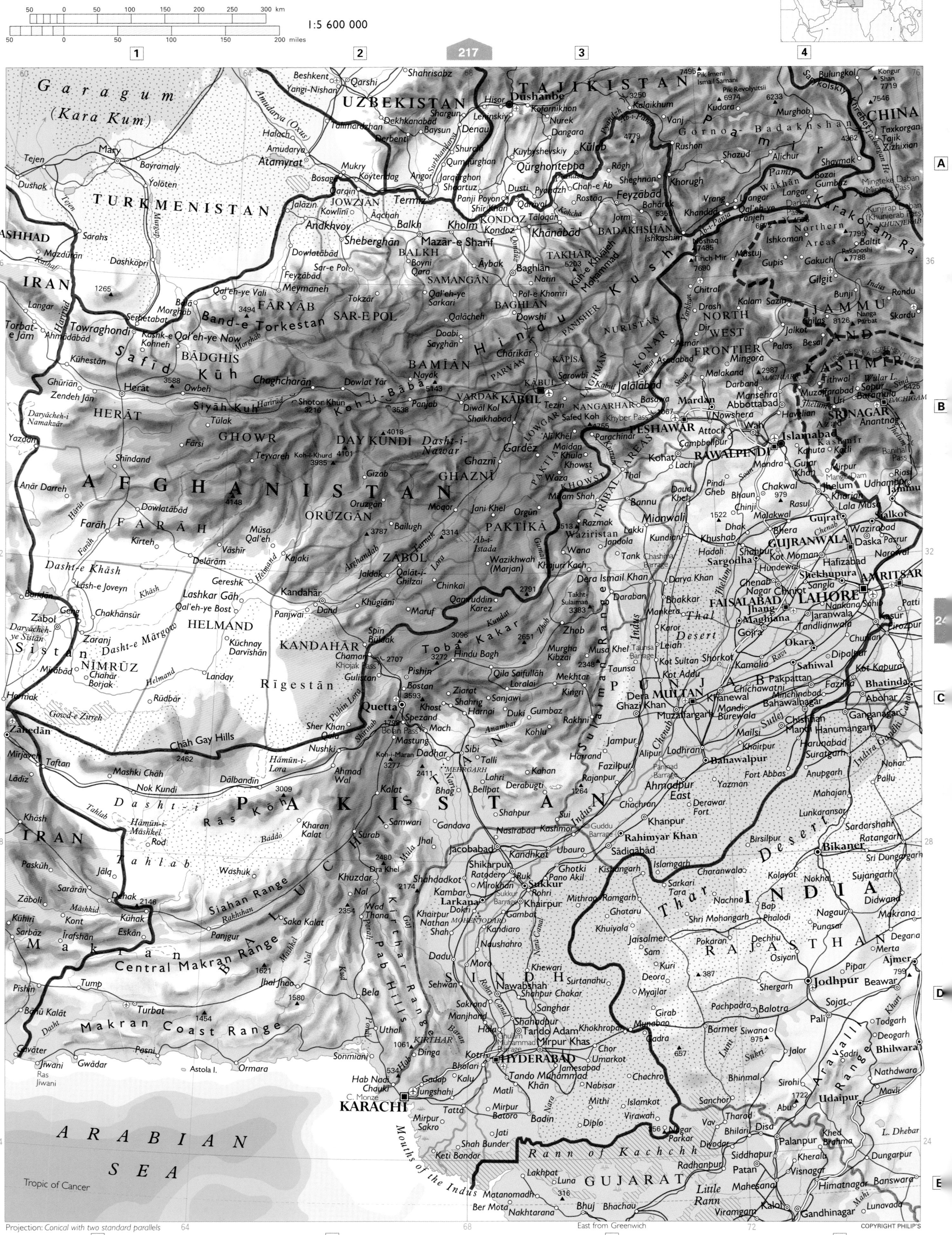

50 0 50 100 150 200 250 300 km
50 0 50 100 150 200 miles

Countries and regions: TURKMENISTAN, UZBEKISTAN, TAJIKISTAN, CHINA, IRAN, AFGHANISTAN, PAKISTAN, INDIA, JAMMU AND KASHMIR

Provinces/regions (Afghanistan): FĀRYĀB, SAR-E POL, BADGHĪS, GHOWR, HERĀT, FARĀH, NĪMRŪZ, HELMAND, KANDAHĀR, ZABOL, ORŪZGĀN, DAY KUNDĪ, GHAZNĪ, VARDAK, PAKTĪKĀ, PAKTIĀ, KHOWST, LOWGAR, NANGARHAR, KONAR, NURISTAN, KĀPĪSĀ, PARVAN, BAMIĀN, BAGHLĀN, SAMANGĀN, BALKH, JOWZJĀN, KONDOZ, TAKHĀR, BADAKHSHĀN

Provinces/regions (Pakistan): NORTH WEST FRONTIER, TRIBAL AREAS, PUNJAB, BALUCHISTAN, SINDH

India: RAJASTHAN, GUJARAT

Physical features: Garagum (Kara Kum), Hindu Kush, Koh-i-Baba, Safīd Kūh, Band-e Torkestan, Siyāh Kūh, Dasht-e Khāsh, Dasht-e Mārgow, Gowd-e Zireh, Rīgestān, Chāh Gay Hills, Sīstān, Makrān, Central Makran Range, Makran Coast Range, Siahan Range, Rās Koh, Pab Hills, Kirthar Range, Sulaiman Range, Toba Kakar, Thar Desert, Thal Desert, Aravalli Range, Rann of Kachchh, Little Rann

Water bodies/rivers: ARABIAN SEA, Mouths of the Indus, Amudarya (Oxus), Harīrūd, Helmand, Indus, Chenab, Jhelum, Ravi, Sutlej, Hāmūn-i-Lora, Hāmūn-i-Māshkel, Daryācheh-ye Sīstān

Major cities: MASHHAD, Herāt, KĀBUL, Kandahar, Quetta, PESHAWAR, ISLAMABAD, RAWALPINDI, SRINAGAR, GUJRANWALA, FAISALABAD, LAHORE, AMRITSAR, MULTAN, HYDERABAD, KARACHI, Zāhedān, Mazār-e Sharīf, Jalālābād, Dushanbe, Bikaner, Jodhpur

Tropic of Cancer

East from Greenwich

Projection: Conical with two standard parallels

COPYRIGHT PHILIP'S

1:4 800 000

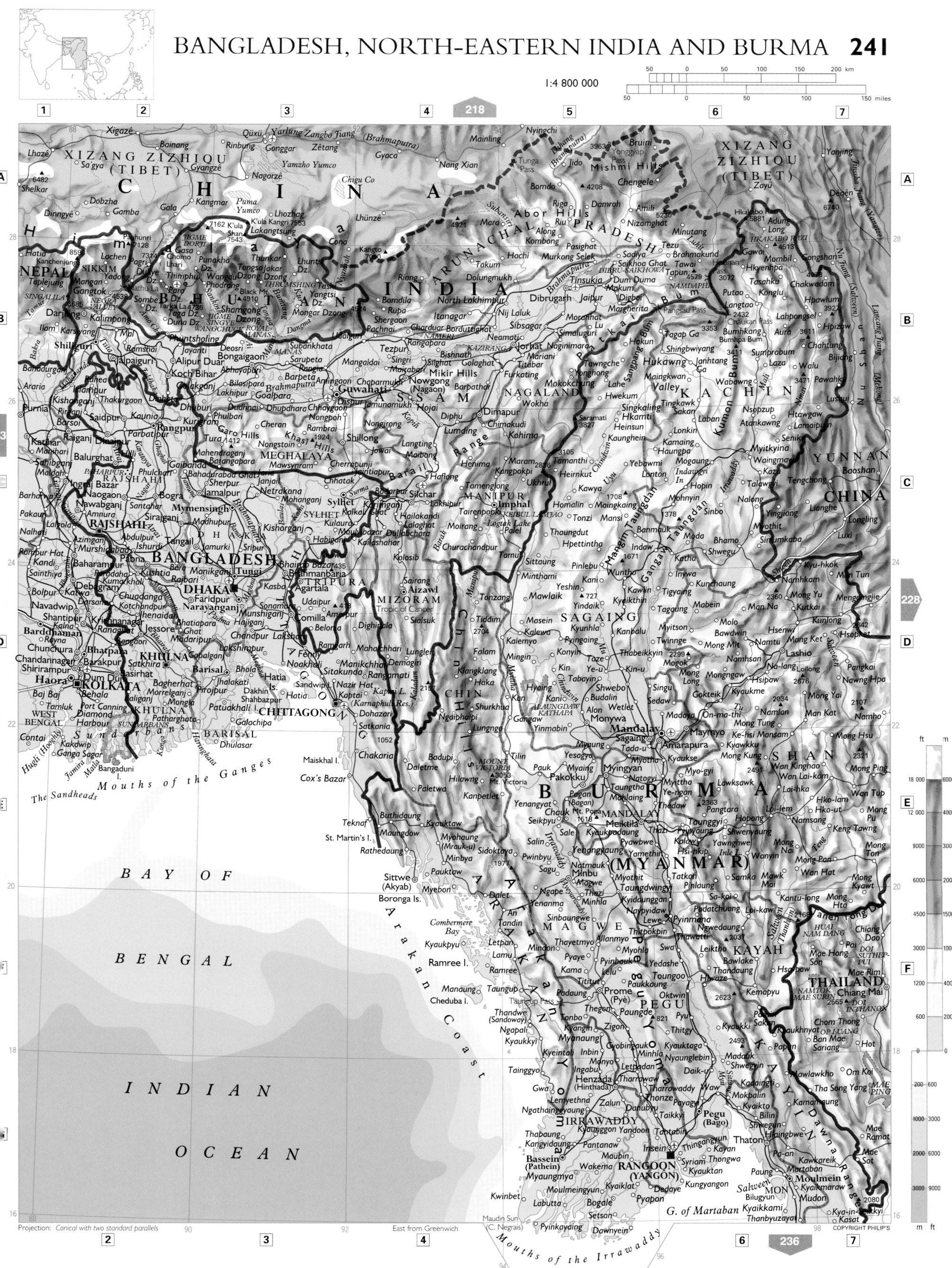

1:4 800 000

Projection: Conical with two standard parallels

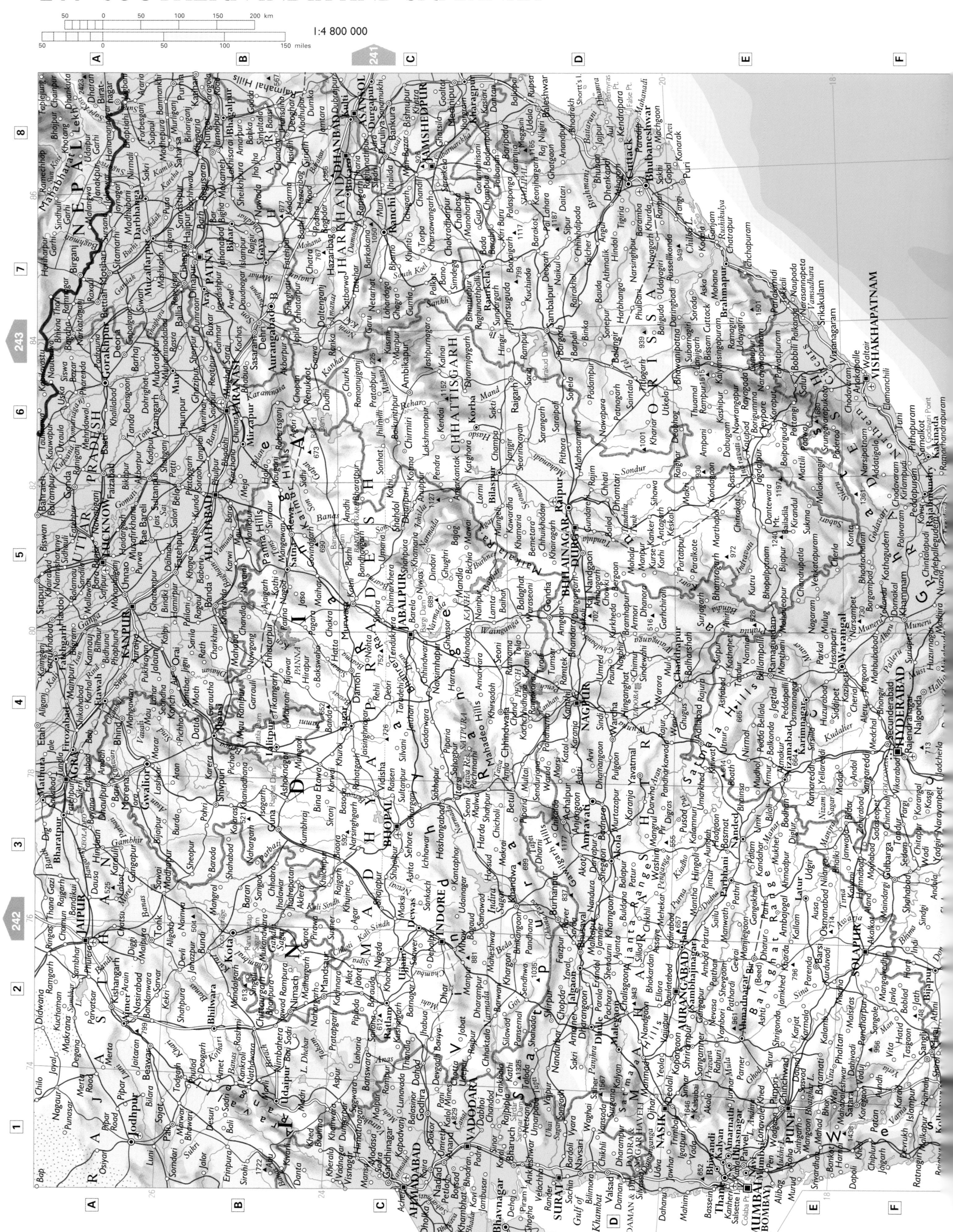

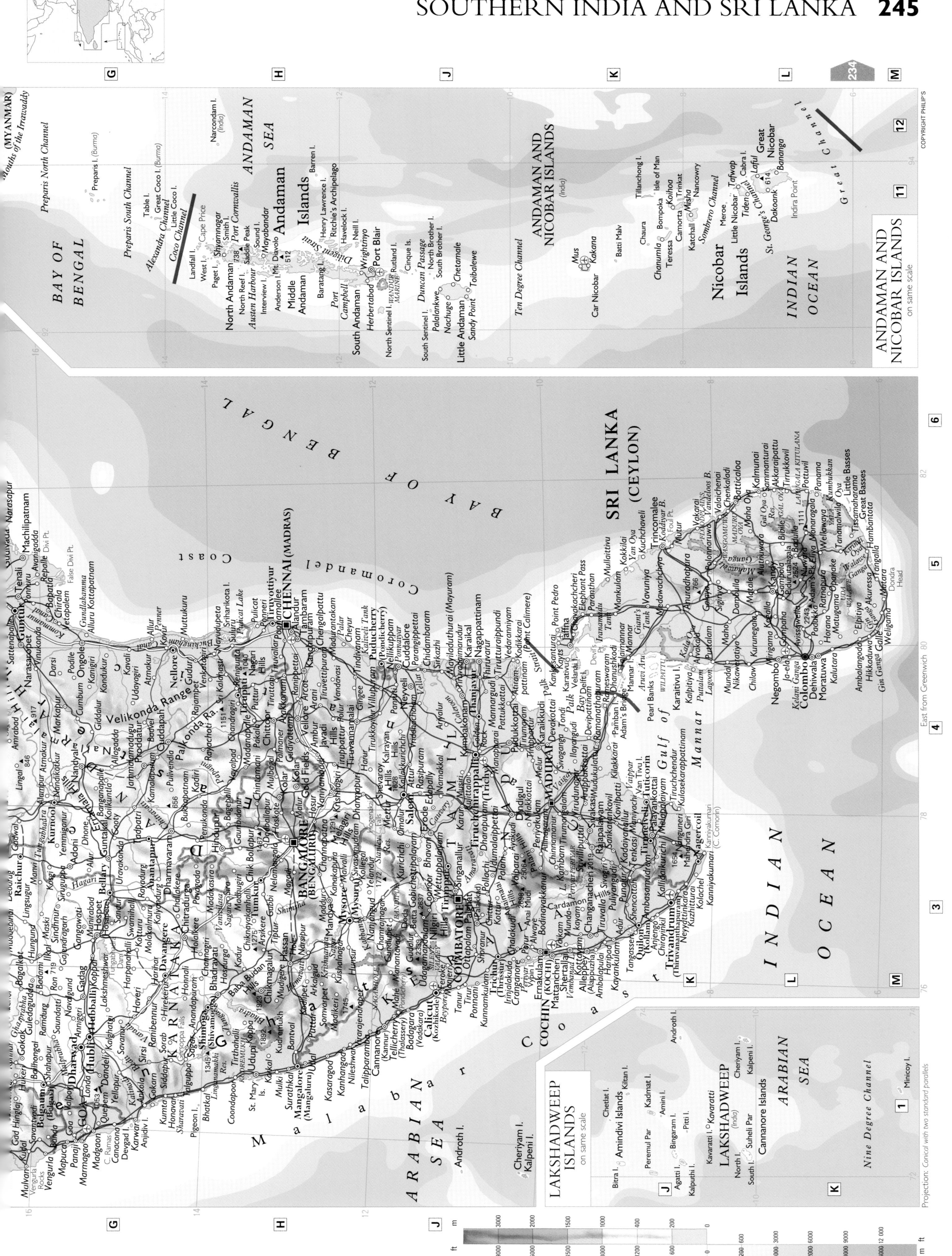

Projection: Conical with two standard parallels

1:5 600 000

Projection: Conical with two standard parallels

Underlined towns in Iraq give their name
to the administrative area in which they stand

Lava fields

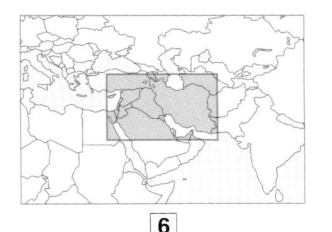

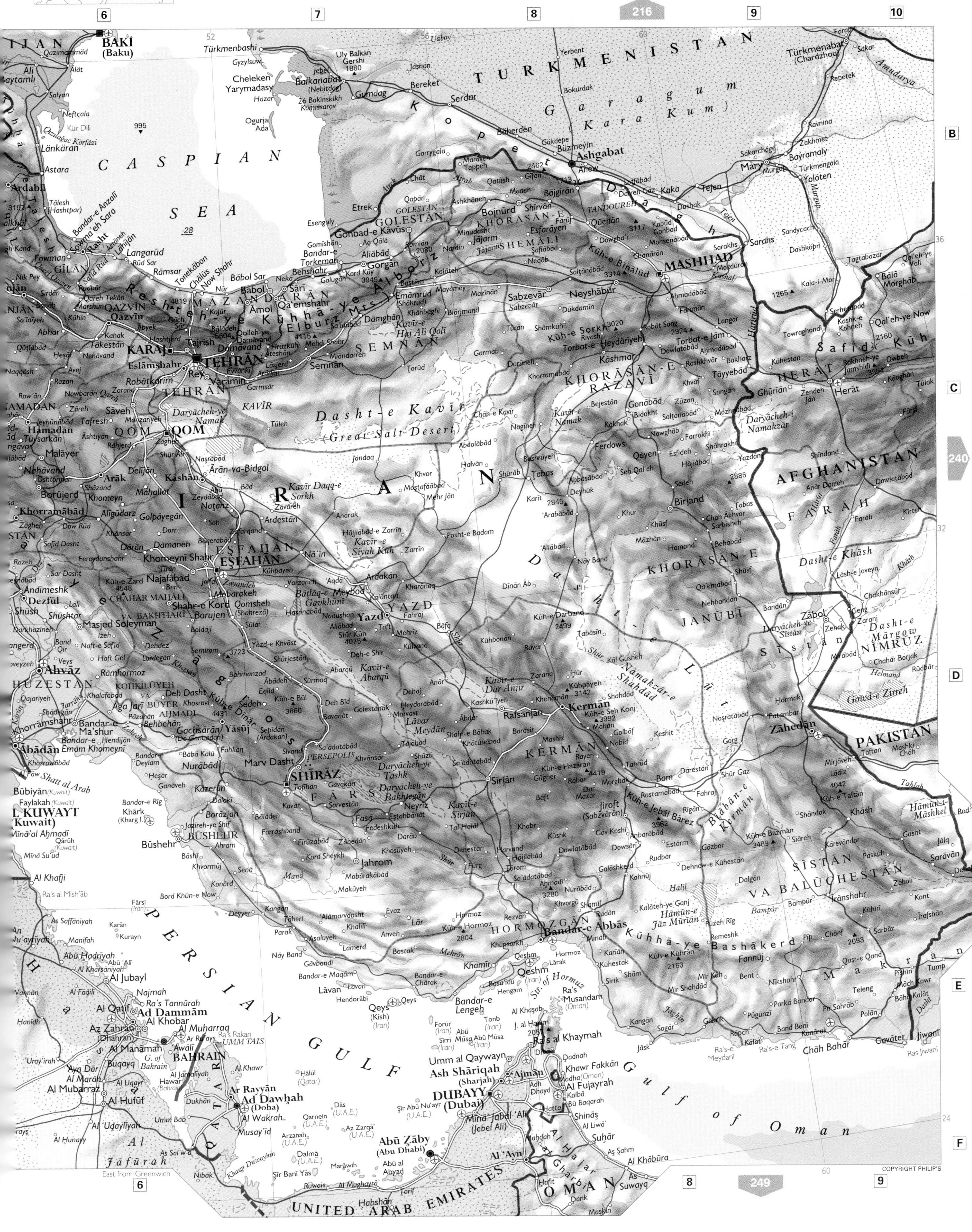

1:5 600 000

50 0 50 100 150 200 250 300 km

50 0 50 100 150 200 miles

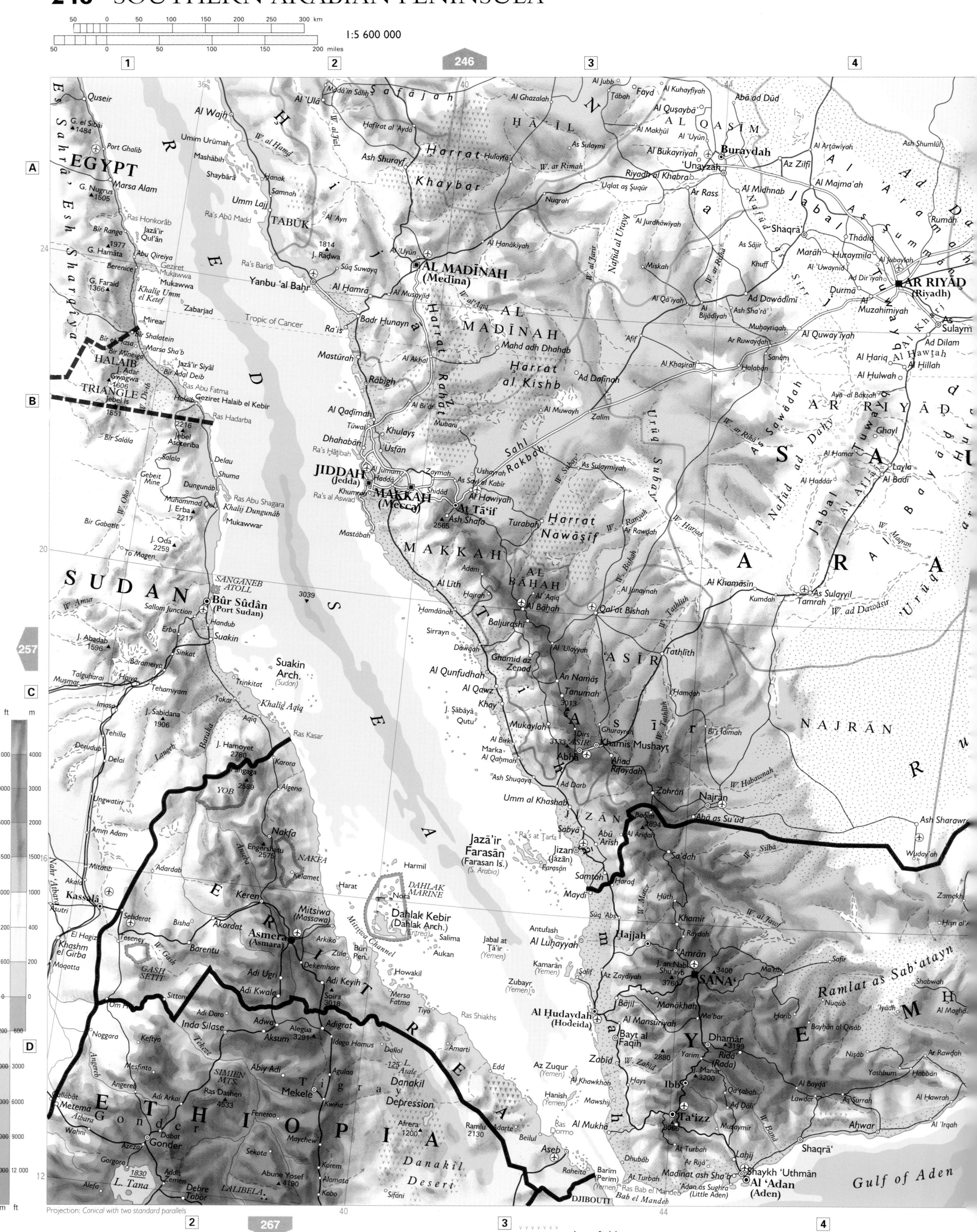

Projection: Conical with two standard parallels

Lava fields

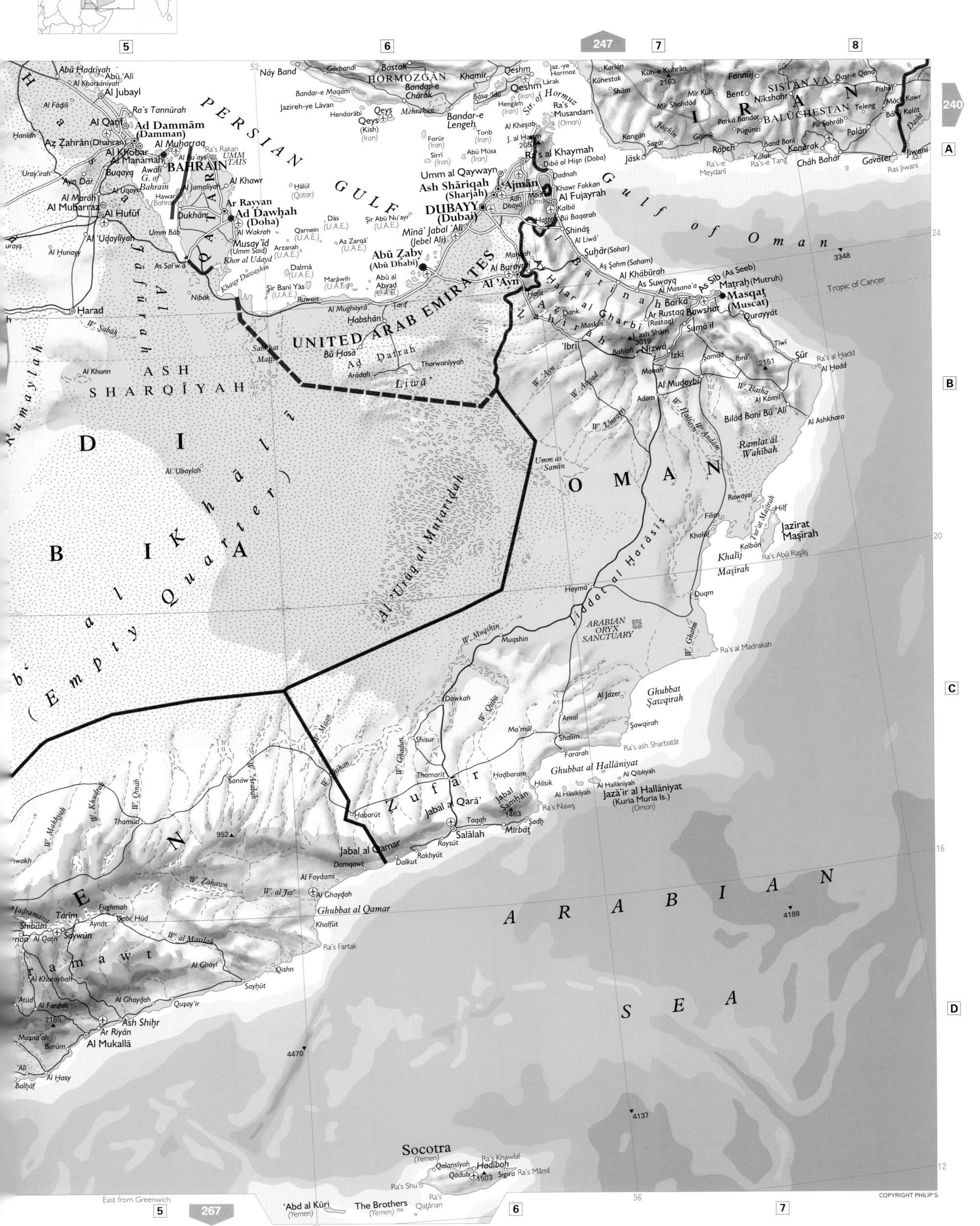

PERSIAN GULF

Gulf of Oman

IRAN

HORMOZGĀN

SISTĀN VA BALŪCHESTAN

Abū Hadrīyah
Abū 'Alī
Al Kharsānīyah
Al Jubayl
Al Fāḍilī
Al Qaṭīf
Ad Dammām (Damman)
Az Zahrān (Dhahran)
Al Khobar
Al Manāmah
BAHRAIN
Hanīdh
Al Mubarraz
Al Hufūf
Al 'Udaylīyah
Al Hunayy
Harad

Ra's Tannūrah
Ra's Rakan
UMM TAIS
Buqayq
Awālī
G. of Bahrain
Dukhān
QATAR
Ar Rayyan
Ad Dawḥah (Doha)
Musay'id (Umm Said)
Khor al Udayd
Nibāk
As Sal'wā

Nāy Band
Bastak
Khamīr
Qeshm
Jaz-ye Hormoz
Kārīān
Kūh-e Kuhrān 2163
Mīr Kūh
Fannūj
Qasr-e Qand
Pishīn
Māch Kawr
Bāmrī Kalāt
Dasht

Gāvbandī
Bandar-e Maqām
Bandar-e Charak
Jazīreh-ye Lāvan
Hendorābī
Qeys (Kish)
Forūr (Iran)
Sirrī (Iran)
Az Zarqā' (U.A.E.)

Bandar-e Lengeh
Mehrābān
Hengam (Iran)
Tonb (Iran)
Abū Mūsa (Iran)

Umm al Qaywayn
Ash Shāriqah (Sharjah)
DUBAYY (Dubai)
Mīnā' Jabal 'Alī (Jebel Ali)
Abū Zaby (Abu Dhabi)
Al 'Ayn

UNITED ARAB EMIRATES

Qeshm
Bāsa'īdū
Str. of Hormuz
Ra's Musandam (Oman)
J. al Harim 2051
Ra's al Khaymah
Dibā al Hiṣn (Doba)
Dadnah
Khawr Fakkan
Al Fujayrah
Kalbā

As Sīb (As Seeb)
Matraḥ (Mutruh)
Masqaṭ (Muscat)
Quryyāt

Tropic of Cancer
3348

OMAN

Ra's al Hadd
Al Hadd
Ṣūr
2151
Tiwī

Ramlat āl Wahībah

Jazīrat Maṣīrah
Maṣīrah
Ra's Abū Raṣāṣ

DI BI KA al Khālī (Empty Quarter)

ARABIAN ORYX SANCTUARY

Ra's al Madrakah

Ghubbat Ṣawqirah

Ghubbat al Hallāniyat
Al Hallāniyah
Jazā'ir al Hallāniyat (Kuria Muria Is.) (Oman)

ARABIAN

SEA

Socotra (Yemen)
Qalansīyah
Ra's Khawlaf
Hadiboh
1503
'Abd al Kūri (Yemen)
The Brothers (Yemen)

COPYRIGHT PHILIP'S

Projection : Polyconic

37 COPYRIGHT PHILIP'S

East from Greenwich

=== 1974 Cease Fire Lines

AFRICA

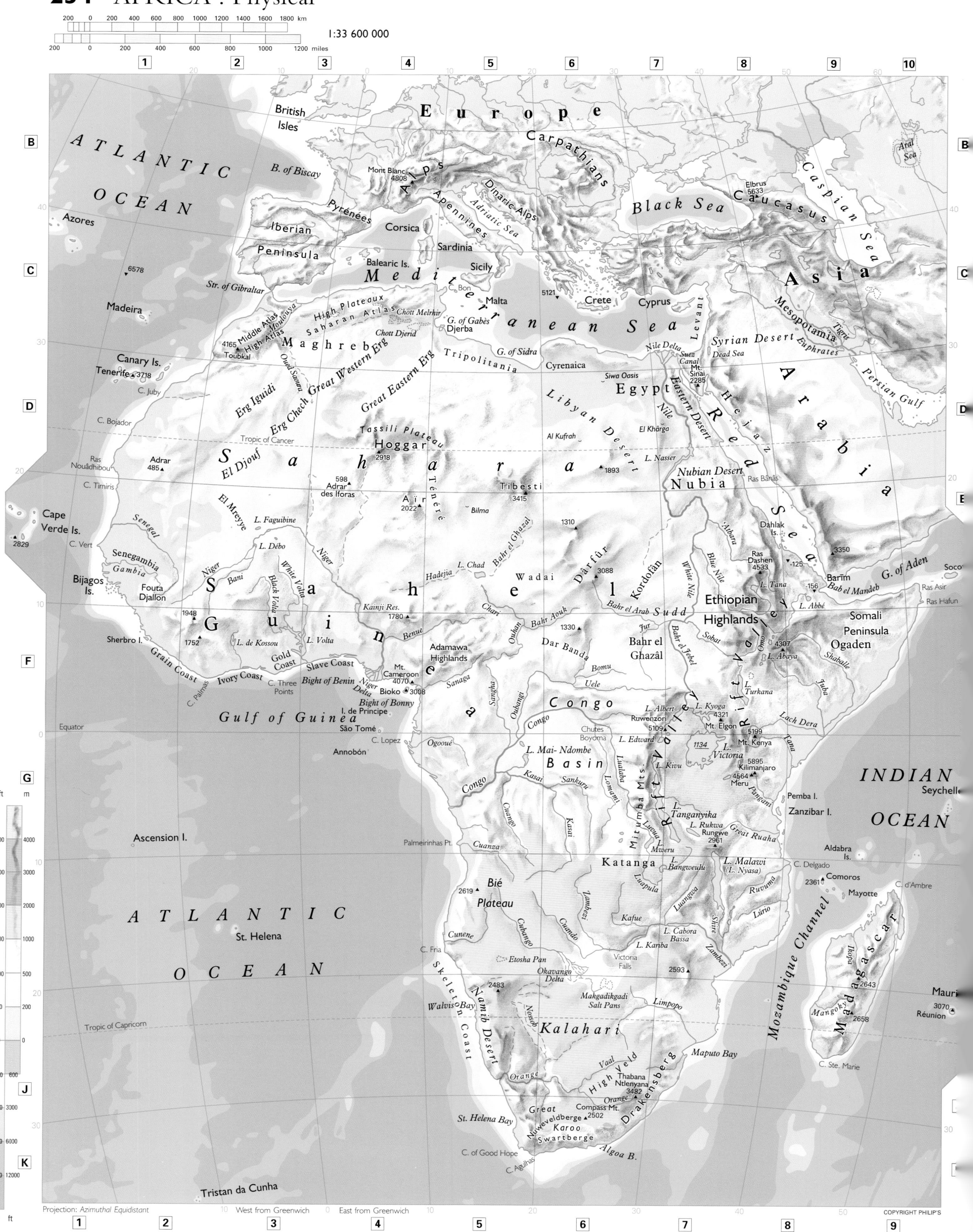

1:33 600 000

Projection: *Azimuthal Equidistant*

COPYRIGHT PHILIP'S

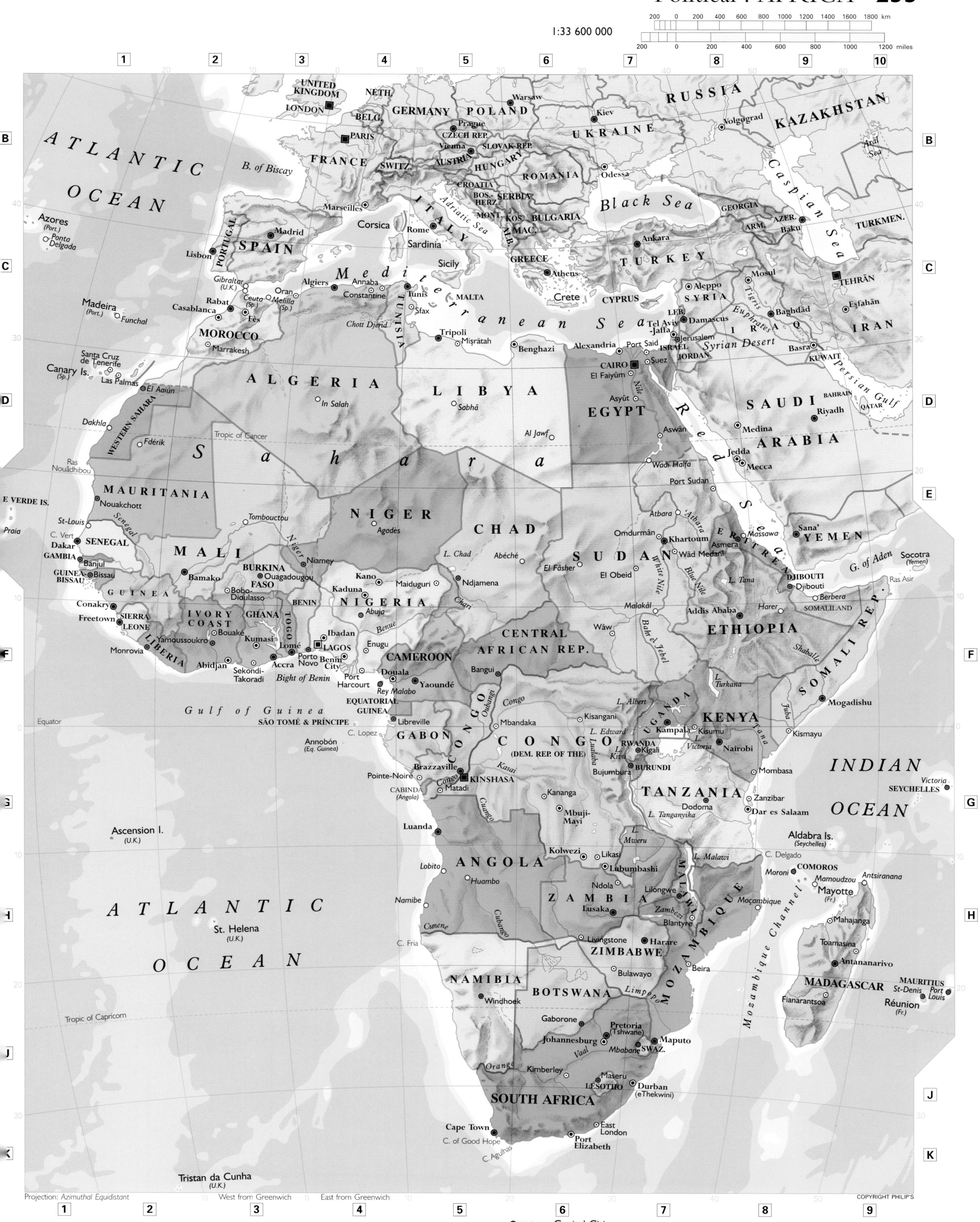

1:33 600 000

200 0 200 400 600 800 1000 1200 1400 1600 1800 km
200 0 200 400 600 800 1000 1200 miles

● Dakar Capital Cities

Projection: Azimuthal Equidistant

West from Greenwich   East from Greenwich

COPYRIGHT PHILIP'S

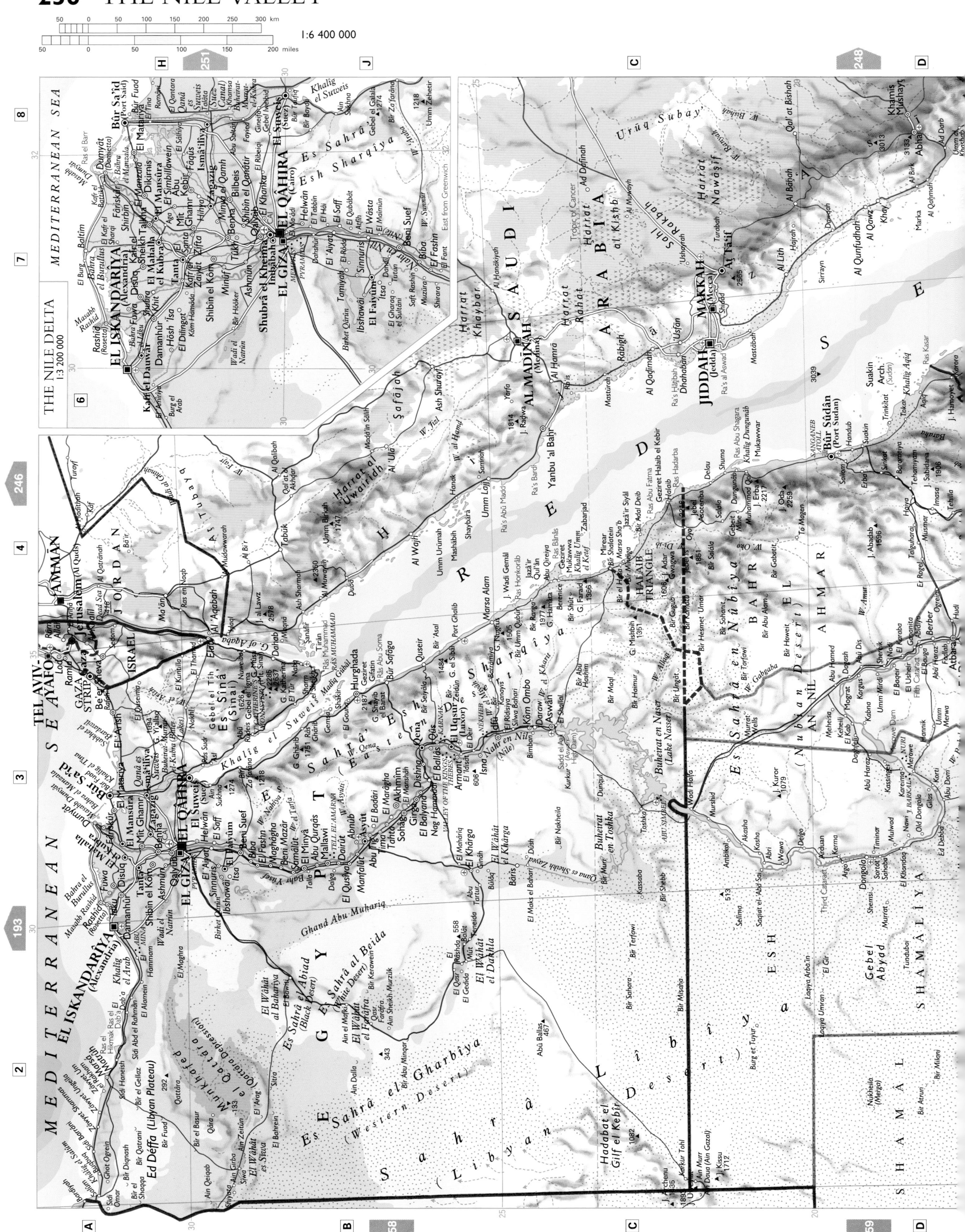

1:6 400 000

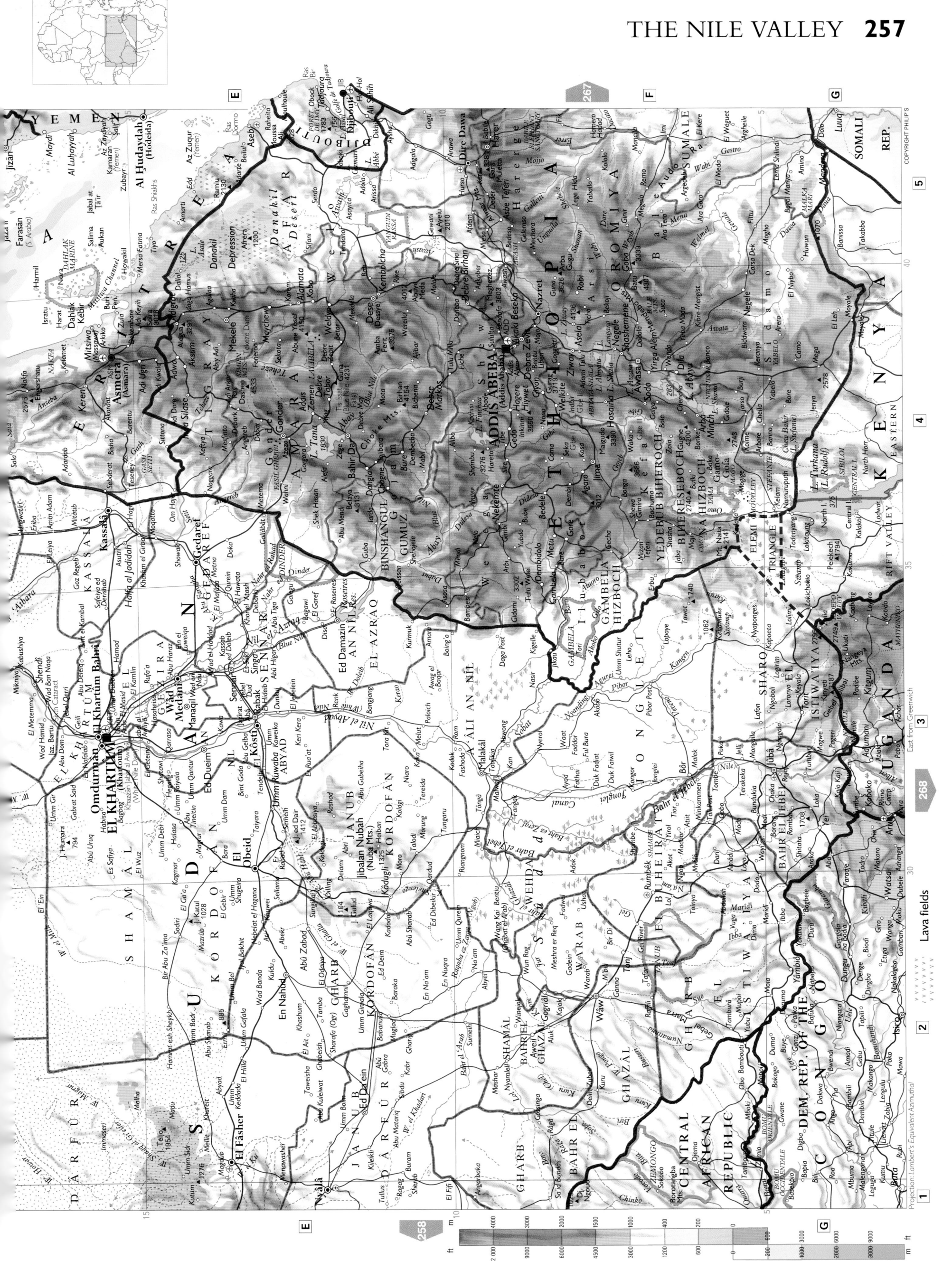

Projection: Lambert's Equivalent Azimuthal

East from Greenwich

Lava fields

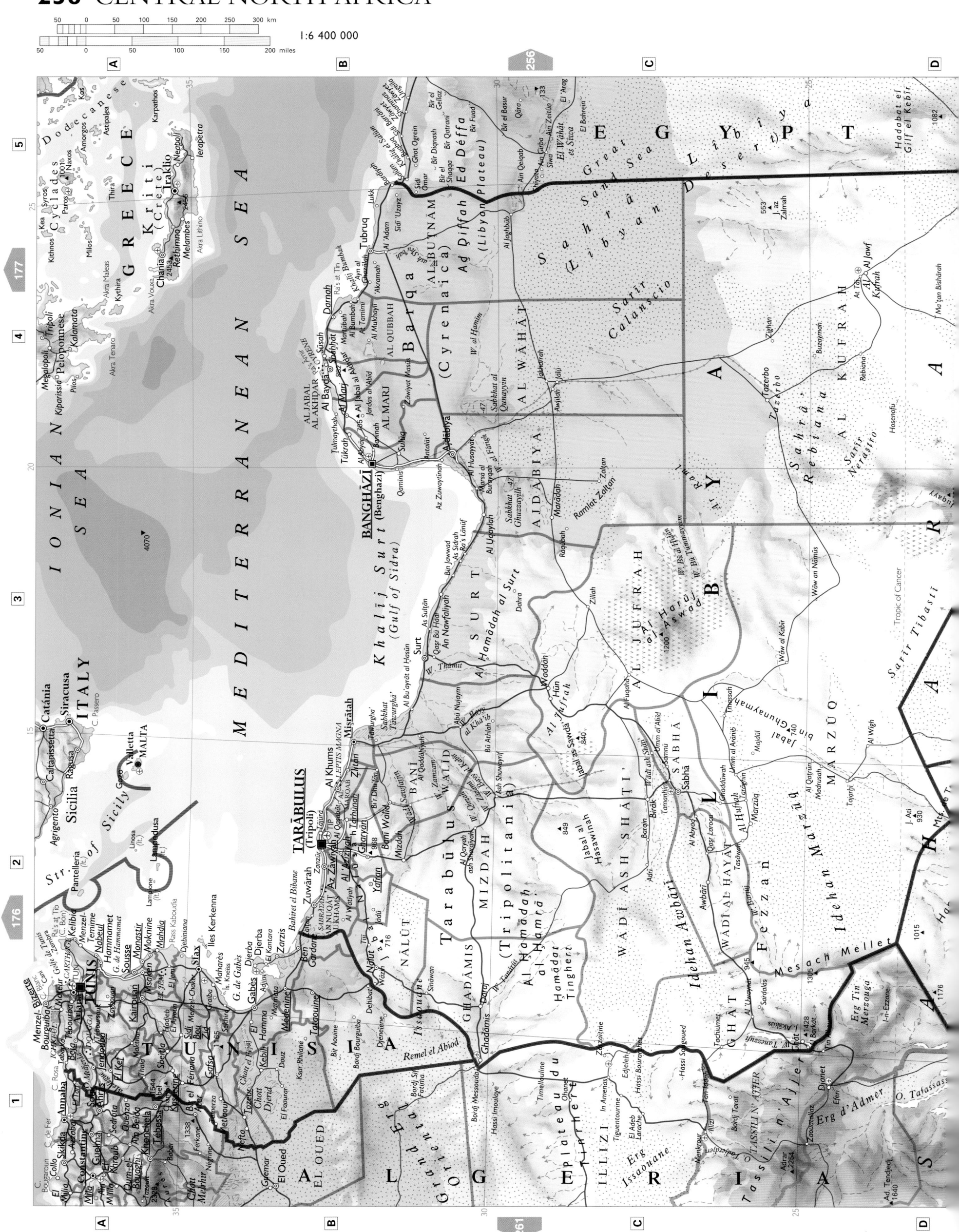

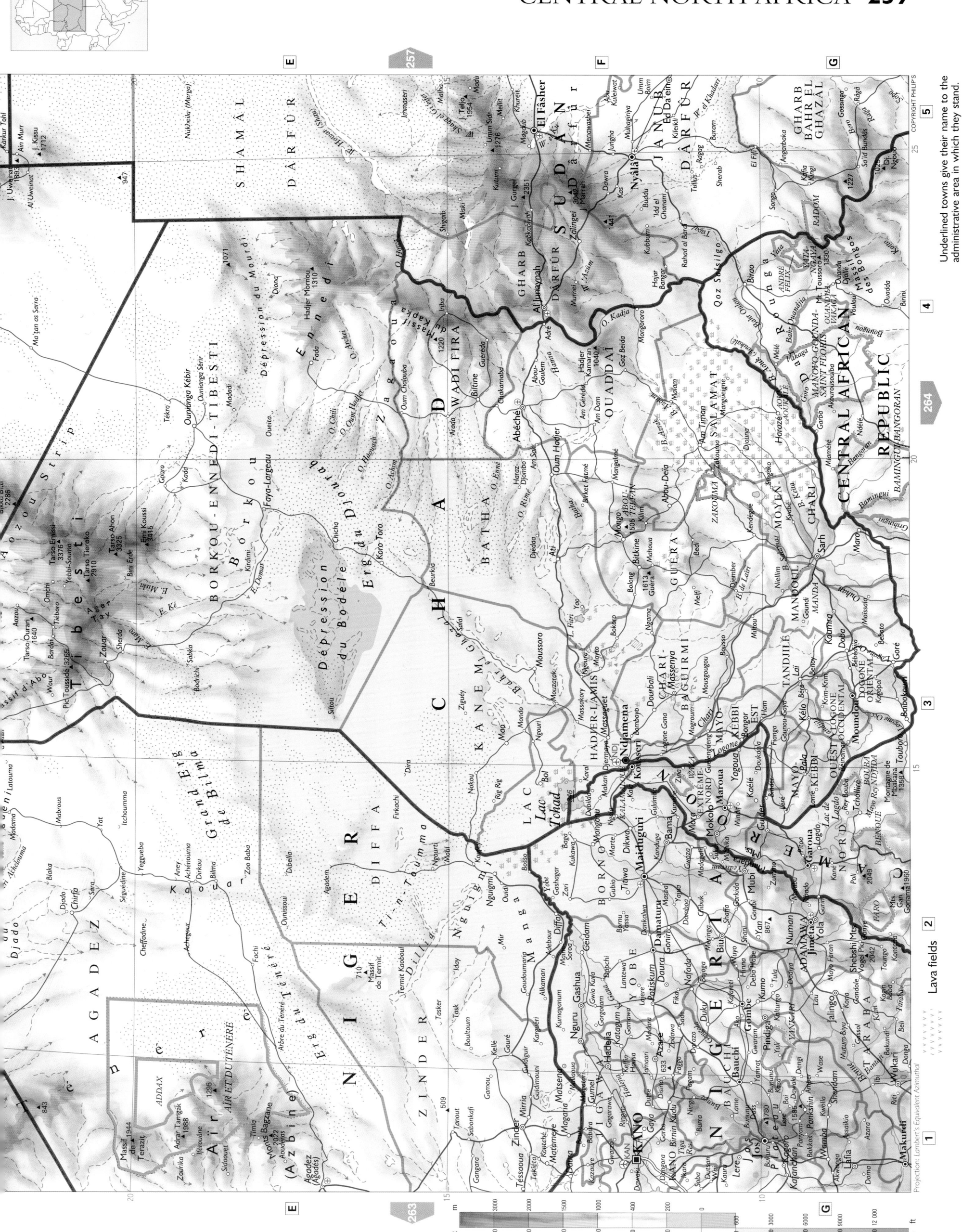

Underlined towns give their name to the
administrative area in which they stand.

Lava fields

Projection: Lambert's Equivalent Azimuthal

50 0   50   100 150 200 250 300 km

1:6 400 000

50   0   50   100   150   200 miles

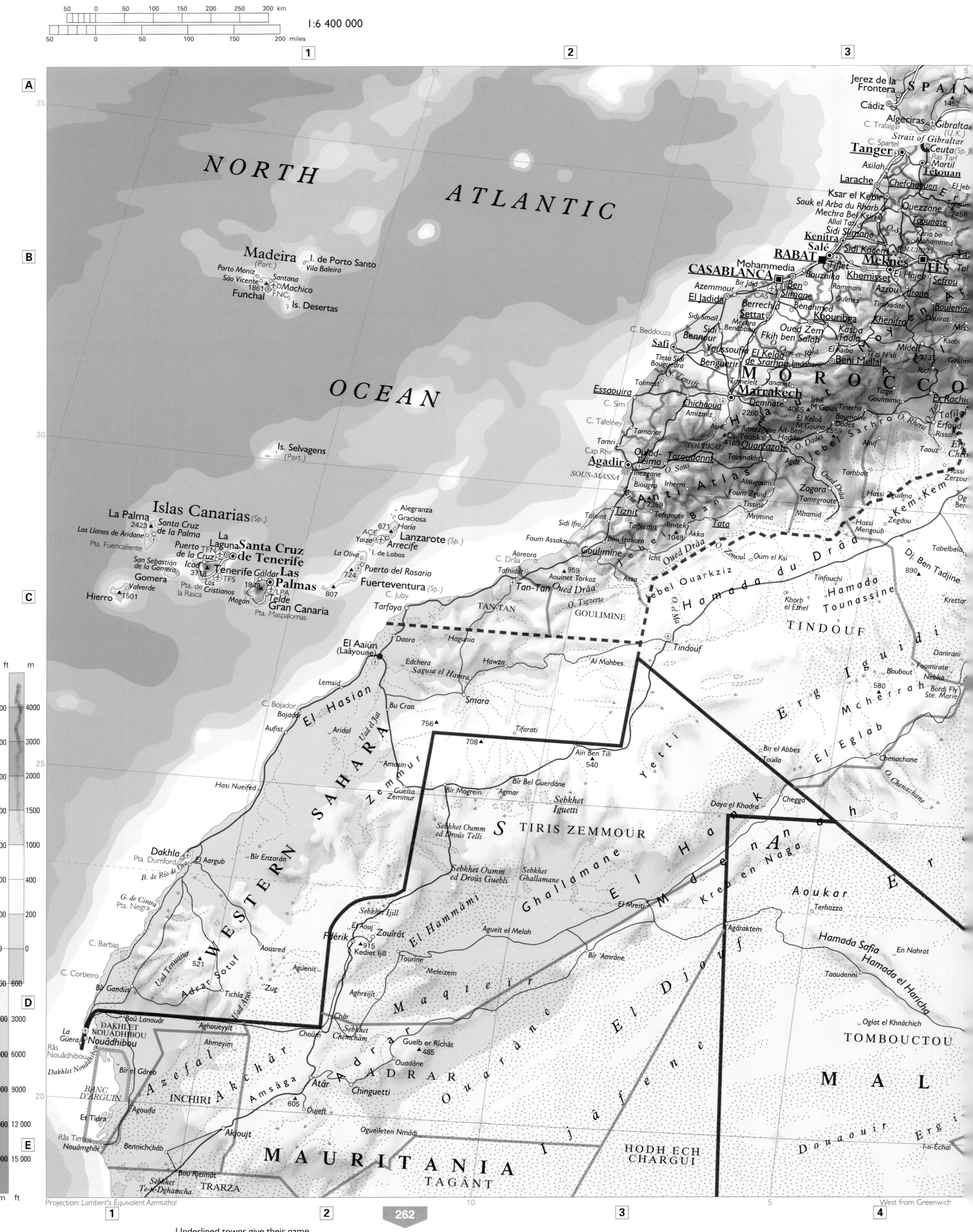

ft   m

12 000   4000

9000   3000

6000   2000

4500   1500

3000   1000

1200   400

600   200

0   0

200   600

600   1000

1000   3000

2000   6000

3000   9000

4000   12 000

5000   15 000

m   ft

Projection: Lambert's Equivalent Azimuthal

West from Greenwich

Underlined towns give their name
to the administrative area in which they stand

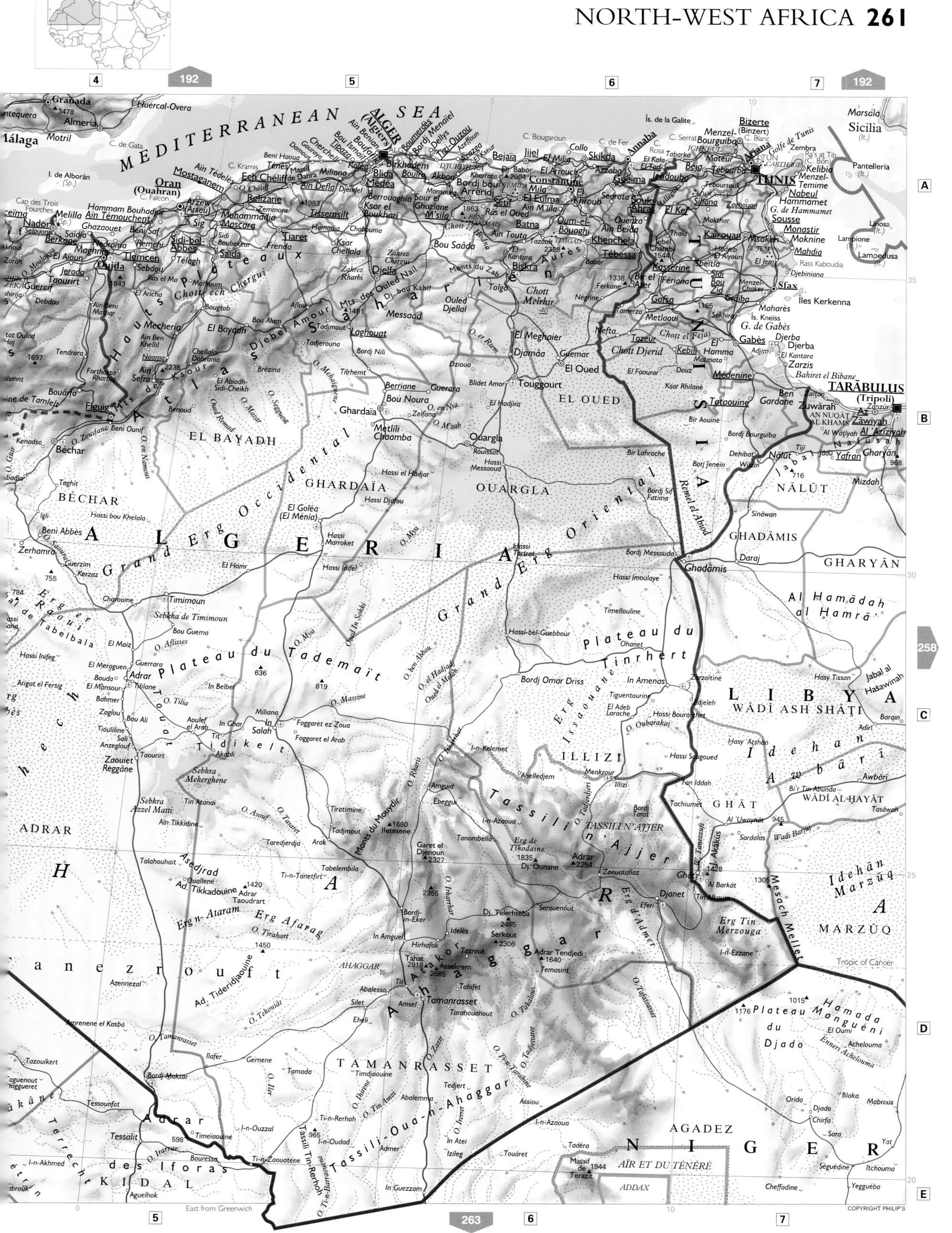

A

MEDITERRANEAN SEA

Granada
Almeria
Motril
Málaga
I. de Alborán (Sp.)
C. de Gata
Huércal-Overa
Cap des Trois
Fourches
Melilla
Nador
Saïdia
Berkane
Maghnia
Oujda
Jerada
Taourirt
Debdou

ALGER (Algiers)
Oran (Ouahran)
Arzew (Arseu)
Mostaganem
Mohammadia
Mascara
Relizane
Ain Témouchent
Sidi-bel-Abbès
Saïda
Tlemcen
Tiaret
Frenda
Télagh
Ksar Chellala

Birkhadem
Blida
Médéa
Berrouaghia
Ksar el Boukhari
Djelfa
Laghouat
Aflou
El Bayadh
Brézina
Mecheria
Aïn Sefra
Figuig
Béchar
Kenadsa
Taghit

MEDITERRANEAN SEA
Bizerte (Binzert)
TUNIS
CARTHAGE
Sfax
Gabès
TARĀBULUS (Tripoli)

ALGERIA
LIBYA
TUNISIA
NIGER
MALI

Tropic of Cancer

East from Greenwich

B

C

D

E

258

35

30

25

20

Projection : Lambert's Equivalent Azimuthal

Underlined towns give their name to the
administrative area in which they stand.

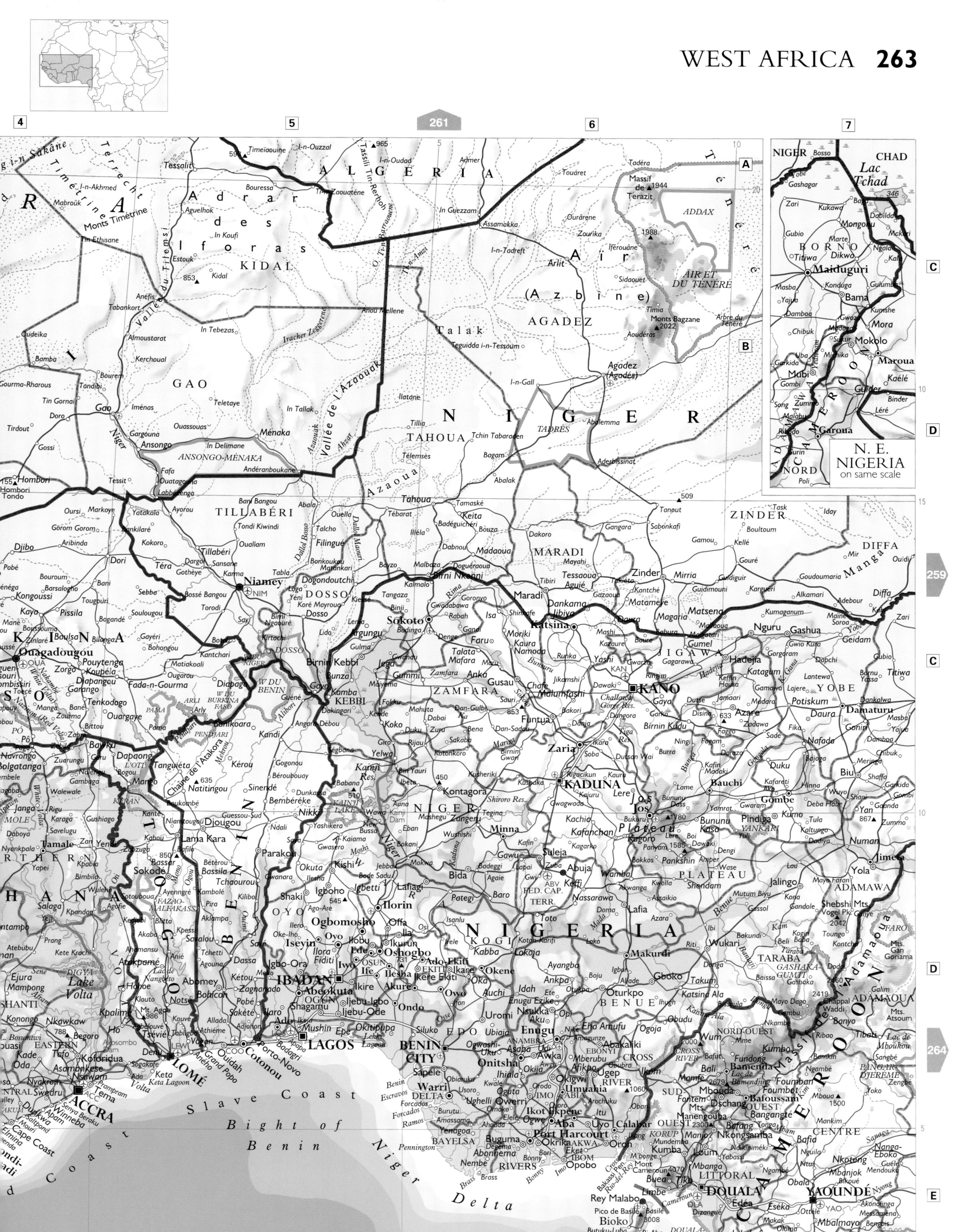

261

259

264

N. E.
NIGERIA
on same scale

East from Greenwich

COPYRIGHT PHILIP'S

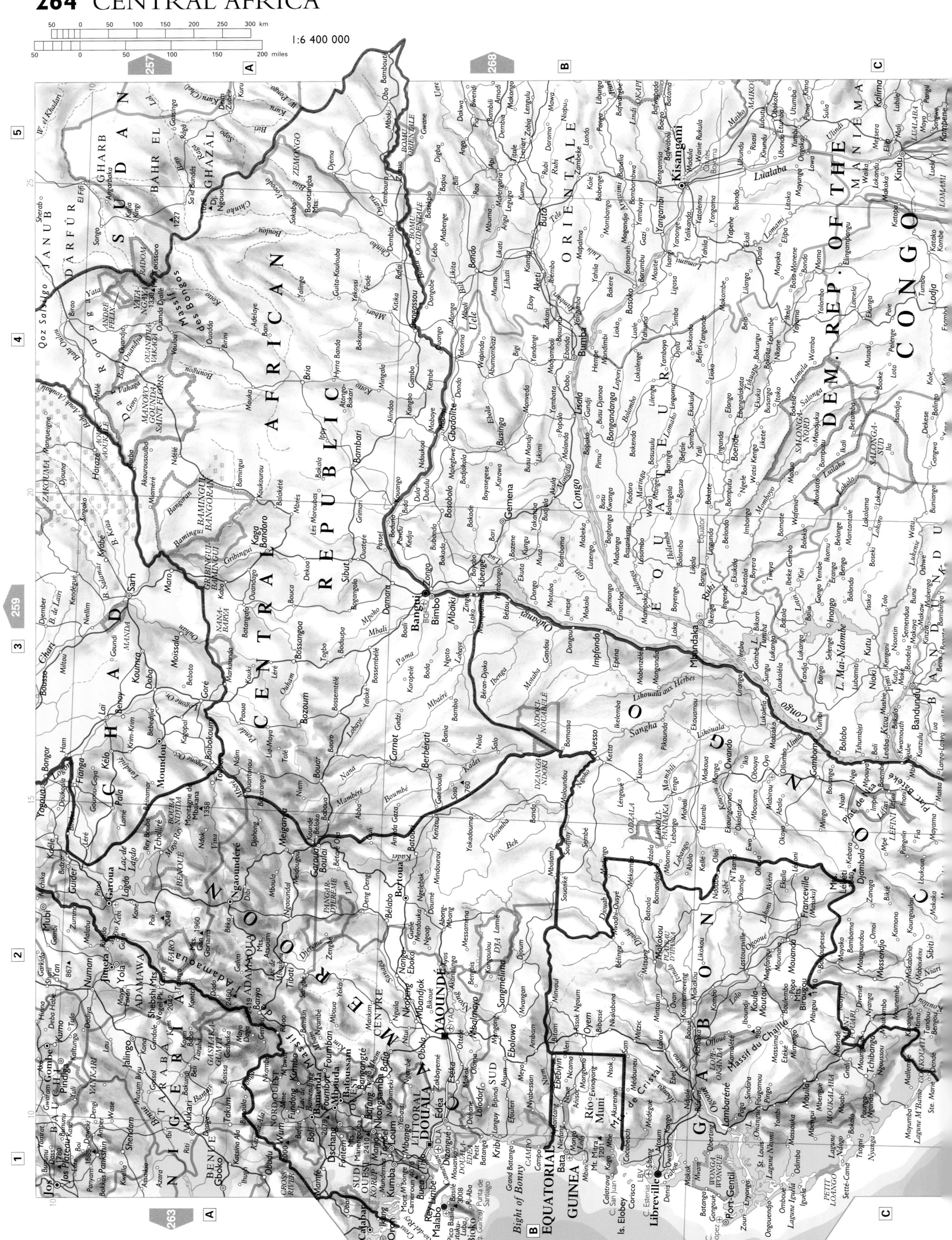

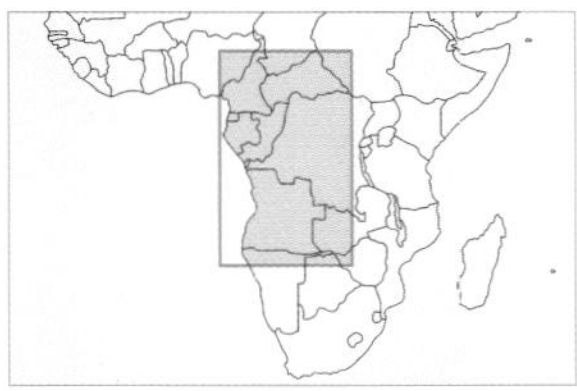

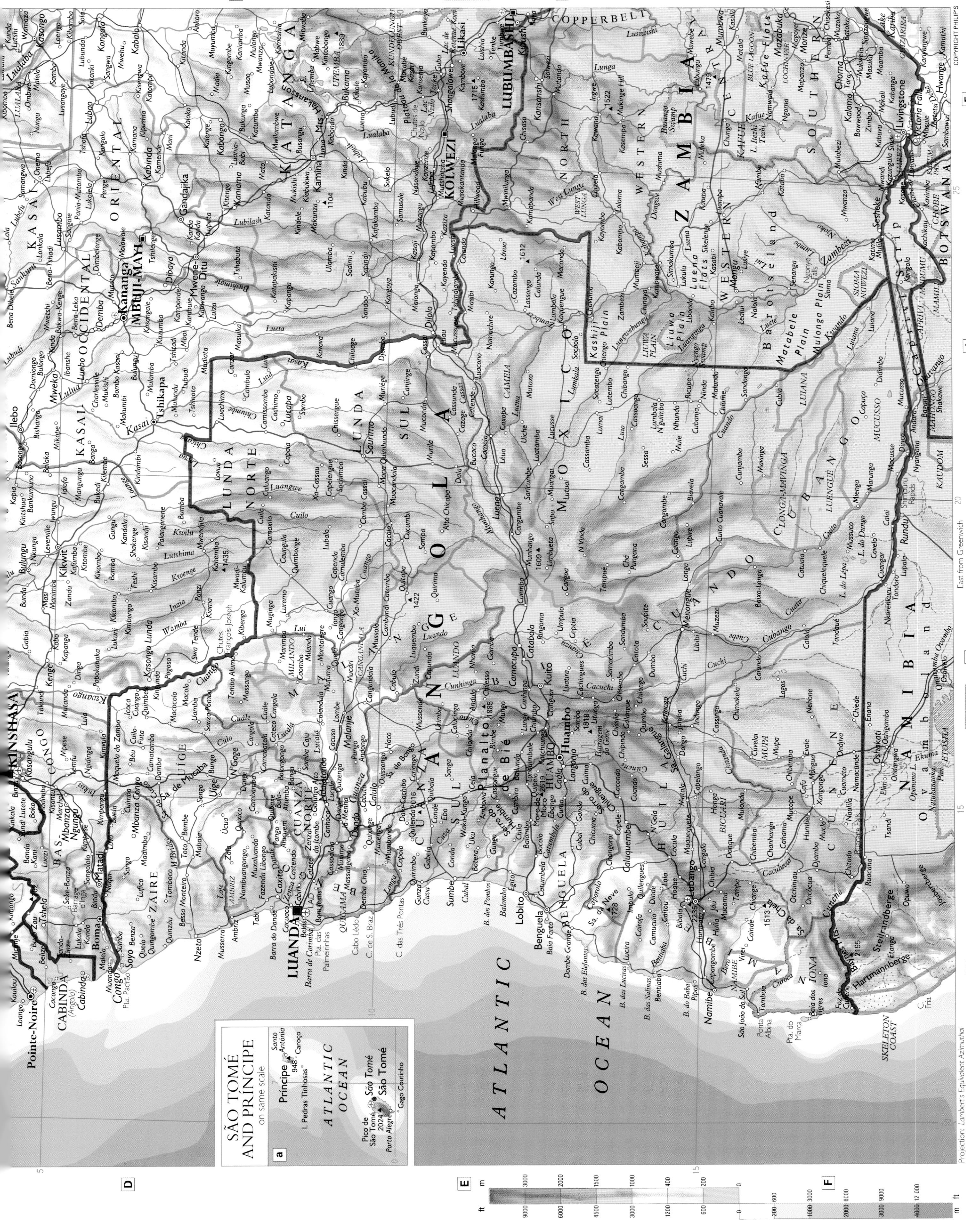

269

270

COPYRIGHT PHILIP'S

Projection: Lambert's Equivalent Azimuthal

East from Greenwich

SÃO TOMÉ AND PRÍNCIPE
on same scale

ATLANTIC OCEAN

Santo António
Príncipe
948
I. Pedras Tinhosas
Caroço

São Tomé
São Tomé
Pico de São Tomé 2024
Porto Alegre
Gago Coutinho

COPPERBELT

KATANGA
KASAI ORIENTAL
KASAI OCCIDENTAL
ORIENTAL
Kananga
MBUJI-MAYI
Mwene-Ditu
KOLWEZI
LUBUMBASHI
Likasi
Kamina

NORTH WESTERN
WESTERN
ZAMBIA
SOUTHERN
CENTRAL
Livingstone
Victoria Falls

BOTSWANA

Pointe-Noire
CABINDA
(Angola)
Cabinda

KINSHASA
CONGO
ZAIRE
BAS-CONGO
Matadi
Boma
Soyo

LUANDA
Benguela
Lobito
Namibe

LUNDA NORTE
LUNDA SUL
MOXICO
ZAIRE
UÍGE
CUANZA NORTE
CUANZA SUL
MALANJE
BENGUELA
HUAMBO
Huambo
BIÉ
Kuito
Planalto de Bié
HUÍLA
Lubango
NAMIBE
CUNENE
CUANDO CUBANGO

A N G O L A

NAMIBIA
ETOSHA
Ovamboland
Caprivi Strip
Okavango

ATLANTIC OCEAN

SKELETON COAST

m ft scale bar

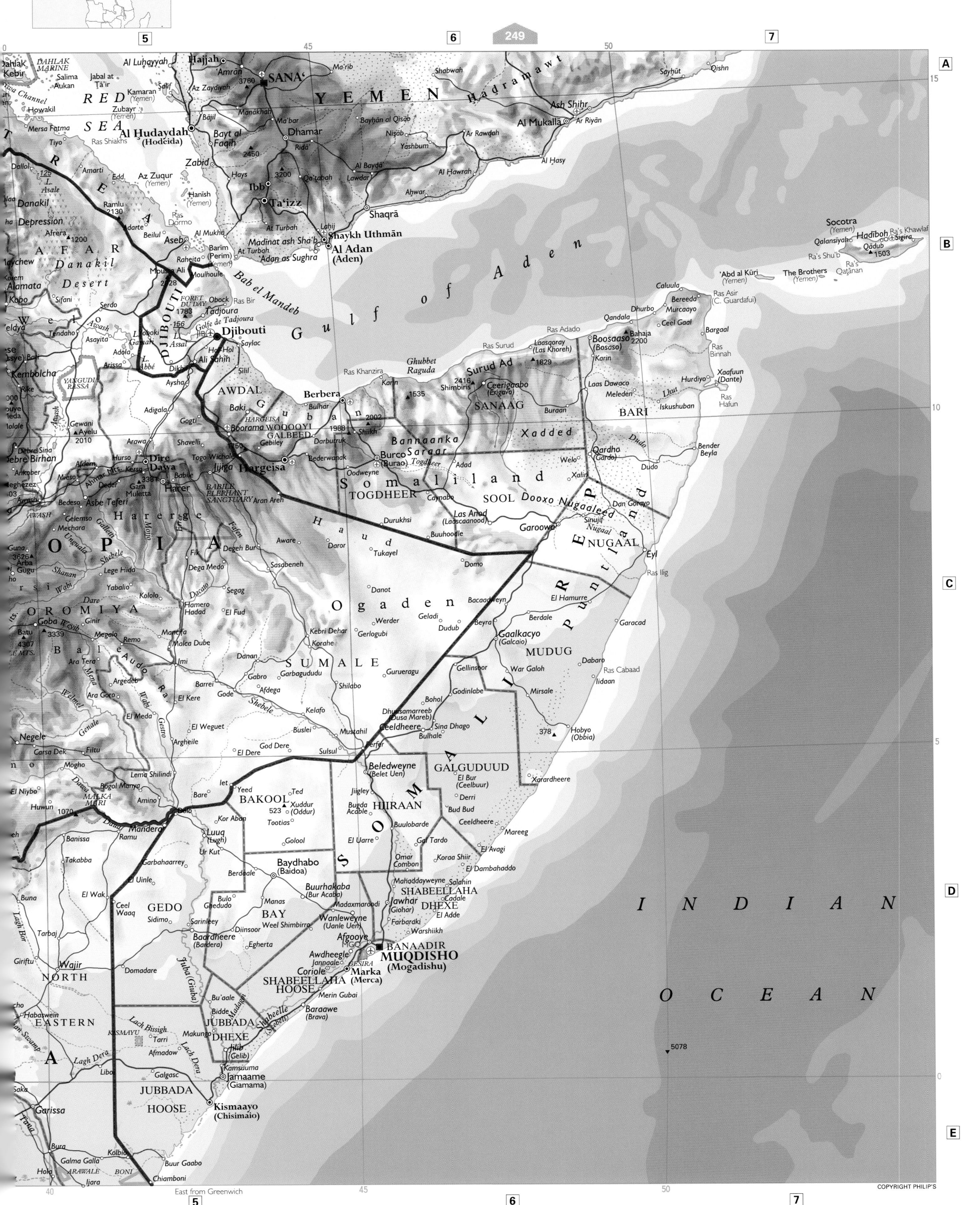

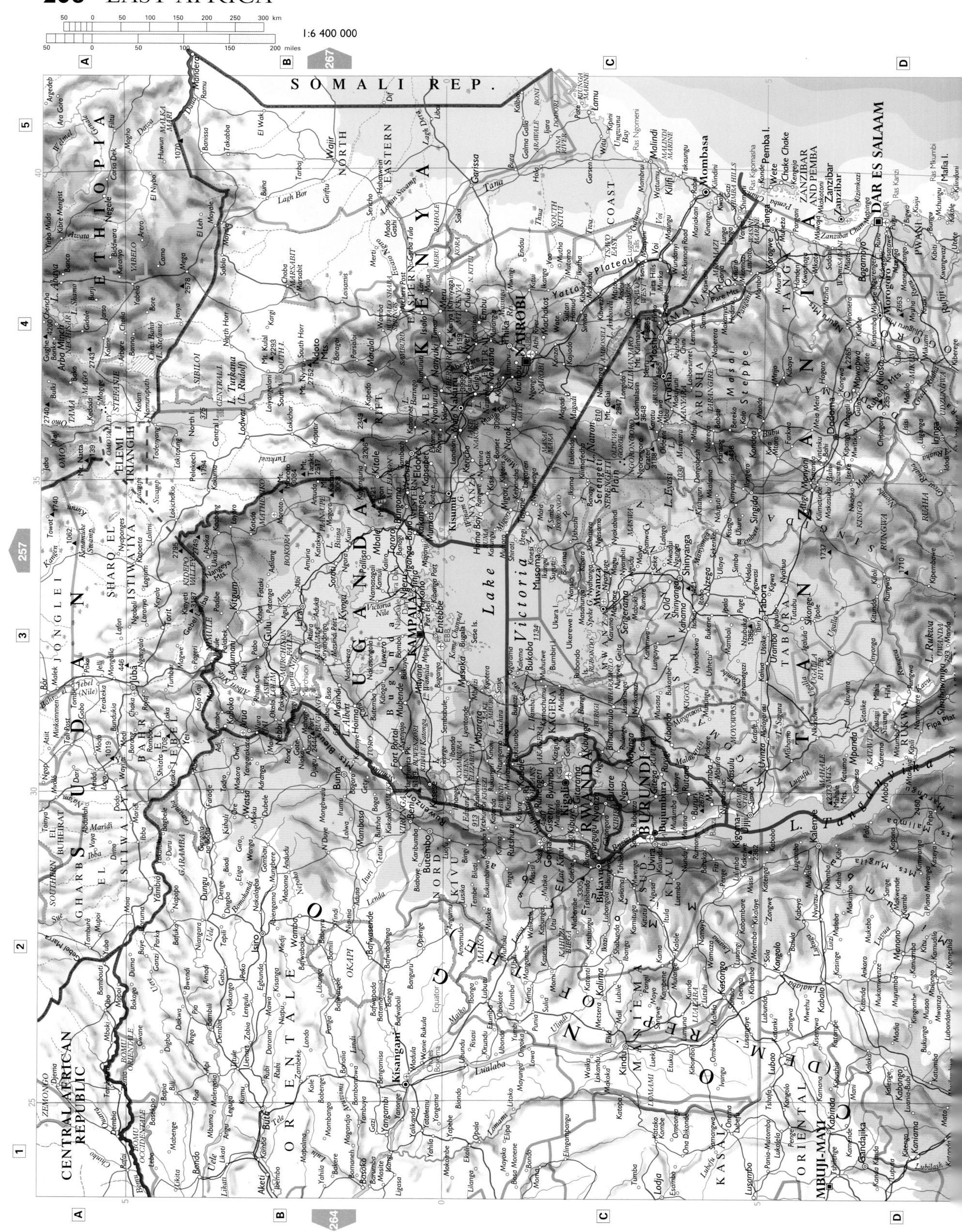

1:6 400 000

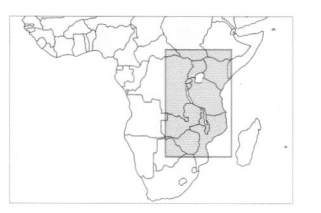

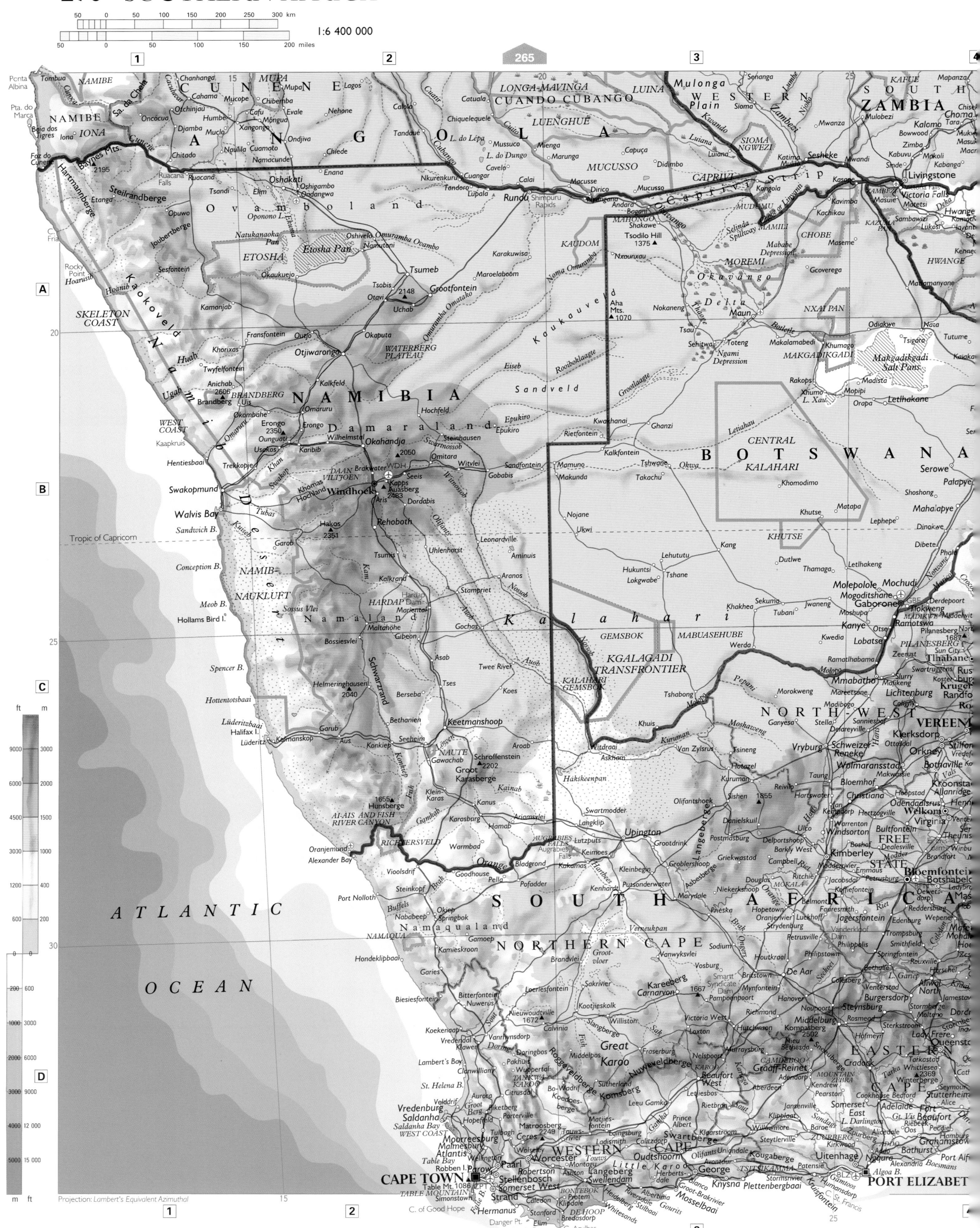

1:6 400 000

265

MOZAMBIQUE

CHANNEL

Île de
Júan de Nova
(Fr.)

Bassas da India
(Fr.)

Île Europa
(Fr.)

Tropic of Capricorn

INDIAN

OCEAN

ZAMBEZIA

MALAWI

ZIMBABWE

MATABELELAND
NORTH

MATABELELAND
SOUTH

MASHONALAND
WEST

MASHONALAND
CENTRAL

MASHONALAND
EAST

MANICALAND

MASVINGO

HARARE
Chitungwiza

Bulawayo

Beira

Quelimane

Mocuba

Angoche
I. Angoche

MOZAMBIQUE

LIMPOPO

Polokwane

MPUMALANGA

PRETORIA
(Tshwane)

JOHANNESBURG

Benoni
Springs
Nigel

SWAZILAND

Mbabane
Manzini

MAPUTO

Maputo

Matola

KWAZULU-NATAL

EASTERN
CAPE

DURBAN

Pietermaritzburg

Richards Bay

East London

East from Greenwich

COPYRIGHT PHILIP'S

5   6   7

269   272

A   B   C   D

30   35   40

20   25   30

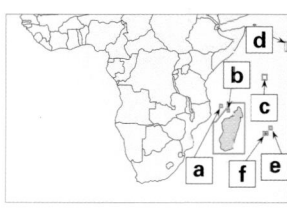

a

COMOROS
1:2 000 000

10 0 10 20 30 40 50 km
10 0 10 20 30 miles

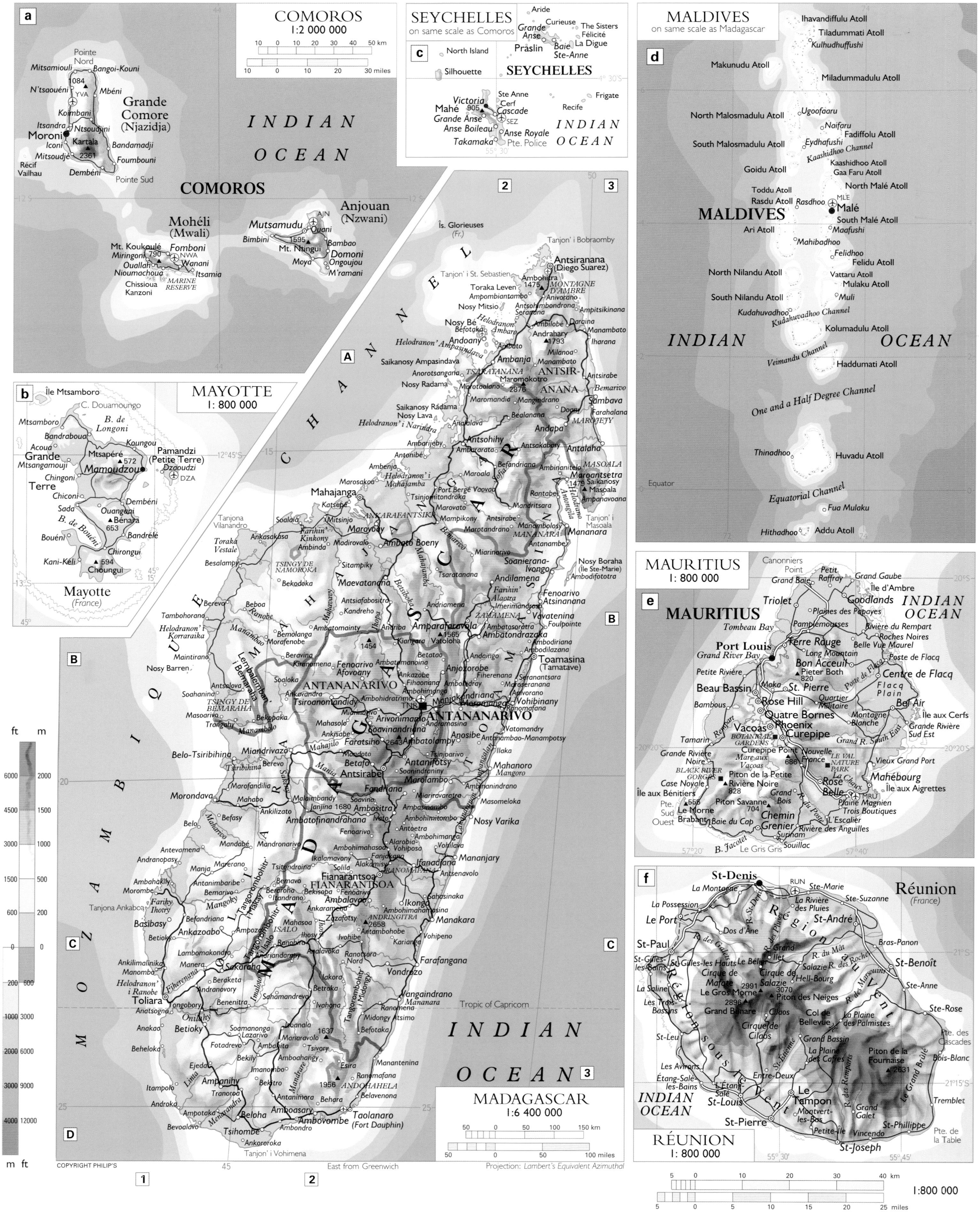

Pointe Nord
Mitsamiouli · Bangoi-Kouni
1084
N'tsaoueni · YVA · Mbéni
Koimbani
Itsandra · Ntsoudjini
Moroni · Iconi · **Grande Comore (Njazidja)**
Kartala · Bandamadji
Mitsoudjé · 2361 · Foumbouni
Récif · Dembéni
Vailhau · Pointe Sud

INDIAN OCEAN

COMOROS

Mohéli (Mwali)
Mt. Koukoulé · NWA · Fomboni
Miringoni 790 · Wanani
Ouallah · Nioumachoua
Chissioua · Itsamia
Kanzoni · MARINE RESERVE

Anjouan (Nzwani)
Mutsamudu · AJN · Ouani
Bimbini · 1595 · Bambao
Mt. Ntingui · Domoni
Moya · Ongoujou
M'ramani

SEYCHELLES
on same scale as Comoros

Aride
Grande Anse · Curieuse · The Sisters
Félicité
Praslin · Baie · La Digue
Ste-Anne

c North Island
Silhouette

SEYCHELLES

Victoria · Ste Anne
Mahé · 905 · Cerf · Cascade
Grande Anse · SEZ
Anse Boileau · Anse Royale
Takamaka · Pte. Police

Frigate · Recife

INDIAN OCEAN

4° 30'S
55° 30'

MALDIVES
on same scale as Madagascar

d

Ihavandiffulu Atoll
Tiladummati Atoll
Kulhuduffushi
Makunudu Atoll
Miladummadulu Atoll
North Malosmadulu Atoll · Ugoofaaru
Naifaru · Fadiffolu Atoll
Eydhafushi · Kaashidhoo Channel
South Malosmadulu Atoll · Kaashidhoo Atoll
Goidu Atoll · Gaa Faru Atoll
Toddu Atoll · North Malé Atoll
Rasdu Atoll · Rasdhoo · MLE
MALDIVES · Male
Ari Atoll · South Malé Atoll · Maafushi
Mahibadhoo
North Nilandu Atoll · Felidhoo
Felidu Atoll
South Nilandu Atoll · Vattaru Atoll
Mulaku Atoll
Kudahuvadhoo · Muli

INDIAN *OCEAN*

Kudahuvadhoo Channel
Kolumadulu Atoll
Veimandu Channel · Haddumati Atoll

One and a Half Degree Channel

Thinadhoo · Huvadu Atoll
Equator
Equatorial Channel · Fua Mulaku
Hithadhoo · Addu Atoll

b

MAYOTTE
1:800 000

Île Mtsamboro
C. Douamoungo
Mtsamboro · B. de Longoni
Bandraboua · Koungou
Acoua
Grande · Mtsapéré · 572 · Pamandzi (Petite Terre)
Mtsangamouji · **Mamoudzou** · Dzaoudzi · DZA
Chingoni
Terre · Chiconi · Dembéni
Sada
Ouangani · B. de Bouéni · 653 · Bénara
Bouéni · Bandrélé
Chirongui
Kani-Kéli · 594 · Choungui

Mayotte
(France)

45°
45°
13°
15°

INDIAN OCEAN

Îs. Glorieuses (Fr.)
Tanjon' i Bobraomby
Tanjon' i St. Sébastien
Antsiranana (Diego Suarez)
Ambohitra · MONTAGNE D'AMBRE
Toraka Leven · 1475
Ampombiantambo · Anivorano
Nosy Mitsio · Antsohimbondrona · Daraina
Serahna · Andrahary · Manambato
Nosy Bé · 1793 · Iharana
Befotaka · Milanoa
Andoany · Helodranon' · Ambato
Saikanosy Ampasindava · Antsirabe
Anorotsangana · Ambanja · Bemarivo
Nosy Radama · Marotolana · Sambava
Saikanosy Rádama · Maromandia · Mangindrano
Nosy Lava · Bealanana · Andapa
Helodranon' i Narindra · Antsohihy · MAROJEŽY
Antalaha
Antonibé · Amburarata · Antsakabary
Ambenja · Befandriana · Ambinanitelo
Helodranon' i · Maroala · Maroantsetra
Marosakoa · 1475 · Saikanosy
Mahajamba · Masoala
Mahajanga · Port Bergé Voavao · Rantabe
Katsepe · Tsinjomitondraka · Antsirabe · Ampanavoana
Marovato · Mandritsara
Soalala · Mitsinjo · Mampikony · Nosy Boraha (Île Ste-Marie)
Maroatra · Antsirabe · Ambodifototra
Farihy · Kinkony · Madirovalo · Marotandrano · Manambolosy
Ambínda · Sitampiky · Antanambe
A · Mitsinjo · Miarinarivo · Mananara
Toraka · Ambato Boeny · Soanierana-Ivongo
Vestale · Besalampy · Andilamena · Nosy Boraha

INDIAN OCEAN

MAURITIUS
1:800 000

Canonniers Point
Grand Baie · Petit Raffray · Grand Gaube
Grand Bois · Île d'Ambre
e · **MAURITIUS** · Triolet · Goodlands · *INDIAN OCEAN*
Tombeau Bay · Plaines des Papayes · Rivière du Rempart
Pamplemousses · Roches Noires
Port Louis · Terre Rouge · Belle Vue Maurel
Grand River Bay · Bon Accueil · Poste de Flacq
Petite Rivière · Pieter Both · Poste de Flacq
820 · Centre de Flacq
Beau Bassin · Moka · Quartier · Flacq
St. Pierre · Militaire · Plain
Bambous · Rose Hill · Bel-Air
Quatre Bornes · Montagne · Île aux Cerfs
Vacoas · Phoenix · Blanche · Grande Rivière
BOTANICAL · Curepipe · Sud Est
Tamarin · GARDENS · Curepipe Point · Rose Belle
Grande Rivière · Nouvelle · Vieux Grand Port
Noire · Mare aux · France · 688
Vacoas · LE VAL · Mahébourg
Case Noyale · BLACK RIVER · NATURE PARK
GORGES · Rivière Noire · Île aux Aigrettes
Île aux Bénitiers · 828 · Grand
Pte. · 655 · Piton Savanne · Bois · Plaine Magnien
Sud · Le Morne · 704 · Trois Boutiques
Ouest · Brabant · Chemin · L'Escalier
Baie du Cap · Grenier · Rivière des Anguilles
B. Jacotet · Le Gris Gris · Suriam · Souillac

57°20' · 57°40'
20°20'S

f · **Réunion** (France)

St-Denis · RUN · Ste-Marie
La Montagne · Ste-Suzanne
La Possession · La Rivière des Pluies · St-André
Le Port · St-Benoît
St-Paul · Dos d'Âne · Salazie · Bras-Panon
St-Gilles-les-Hauts · Le Bélier · Cirque de · Hell-Bourg
St-Gilles-les-Bains · Mafate · Cirque de · Salazie
La Saline · 2991 · Salazie
Les Trois · Le Gros Morne · Piton des Neiges
Bassins · 2896 · 3070
Grand Bénare · Col de · La Plaine
Cirque de · Cilaos · Bellevue · des Palmistes
Cilaos · Ste-Anne
Les Avirons · Grand Bassin · Ste-Rose
St-Leu · La Plaine · Pte. des
Étang-Salé · des Cafres · Cascades
les-Bains · Entre-Deux · Bois-Blanc
Étang- · Le · 2631
Salé · Tampon · Piton de la Fournaise
St-Louis · Montvert- · Grand
INDIAN OCEAN · les-Bas · Galet · Tremblet
St-Pierre · Petite-Île · Vincendo · Pte. de
St-Phillippe · la Table
St-Joseph

RÉUNION
1:800 000

5 0 10 20 30 40 km
5 0 10 15 20 25 miles
1:800 000

MADAGASCAR

A · **B** · **C**

Antsiranana
ANTSIR-ANANA
TSARATANANA · Maromokotro · 2876

MASOALA

MANANARA

Mahajanga
ANKARAFANTSIKA
Maevatanana
TSINGY DE NAMOROKA
Bekodoka

Antananarivo

Tananarive
Antsirabe

Fianarantsoa

Toliara

Toamasina (Tamatave)

Tropic of Capricorn

INDIAN OCEAN

MADAGASCAR
1:6 400 000

50 0 50 100 150 km
50 0 50 100 miles

MOZAMBIQUE CHANNEL

ft   m
6000 2000
4500 1500
3000 1000
1500 500
600   200
0   0
200   600
1000 3000
2000 6000
3000 9000
4000 12000
m ft

D

20°
25°
45°

COPYRIGHT PHILIP'S

East from Greenwich

Projection: Lambert's Equivalent Azimuthal

1 · **2** · **3**

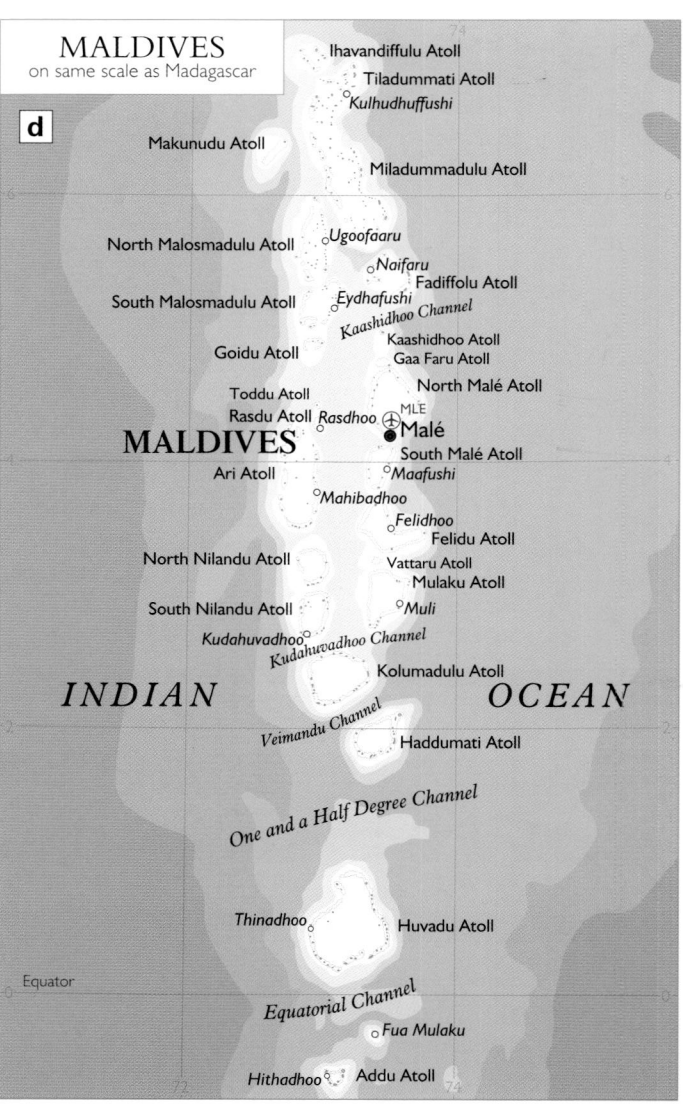

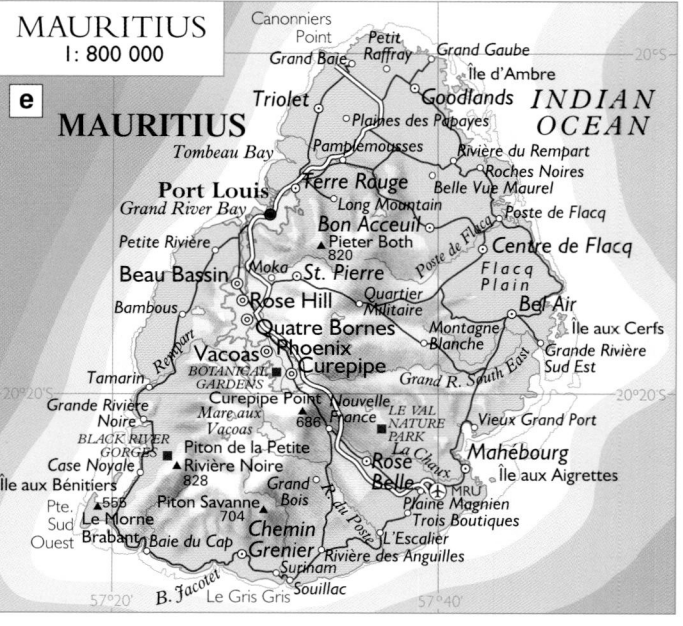

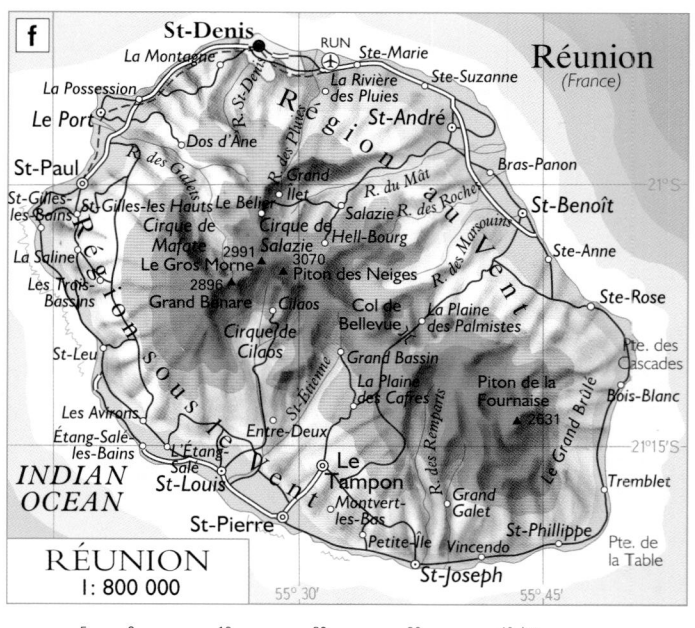

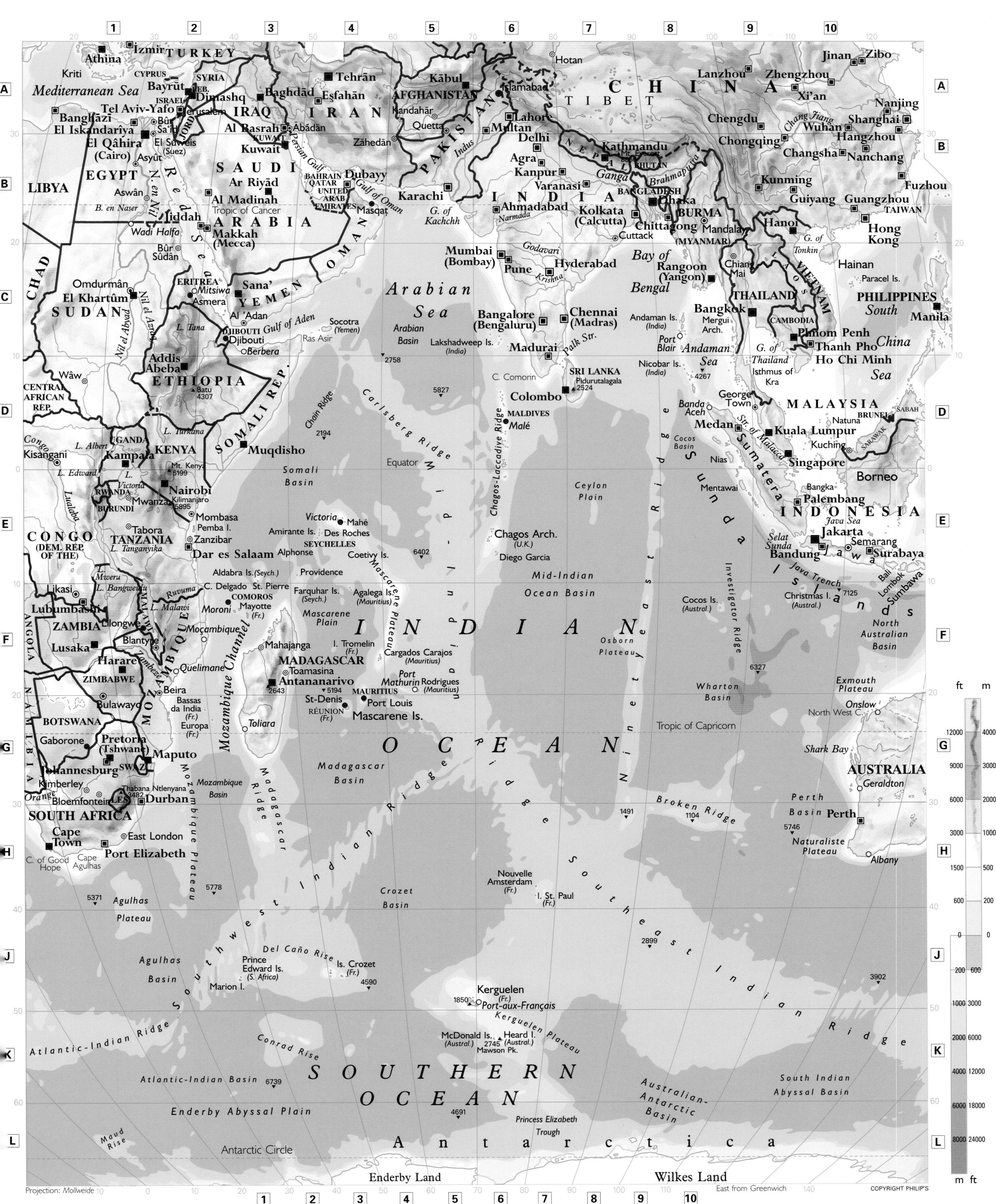

AUSTRALIA AND OCEANIA

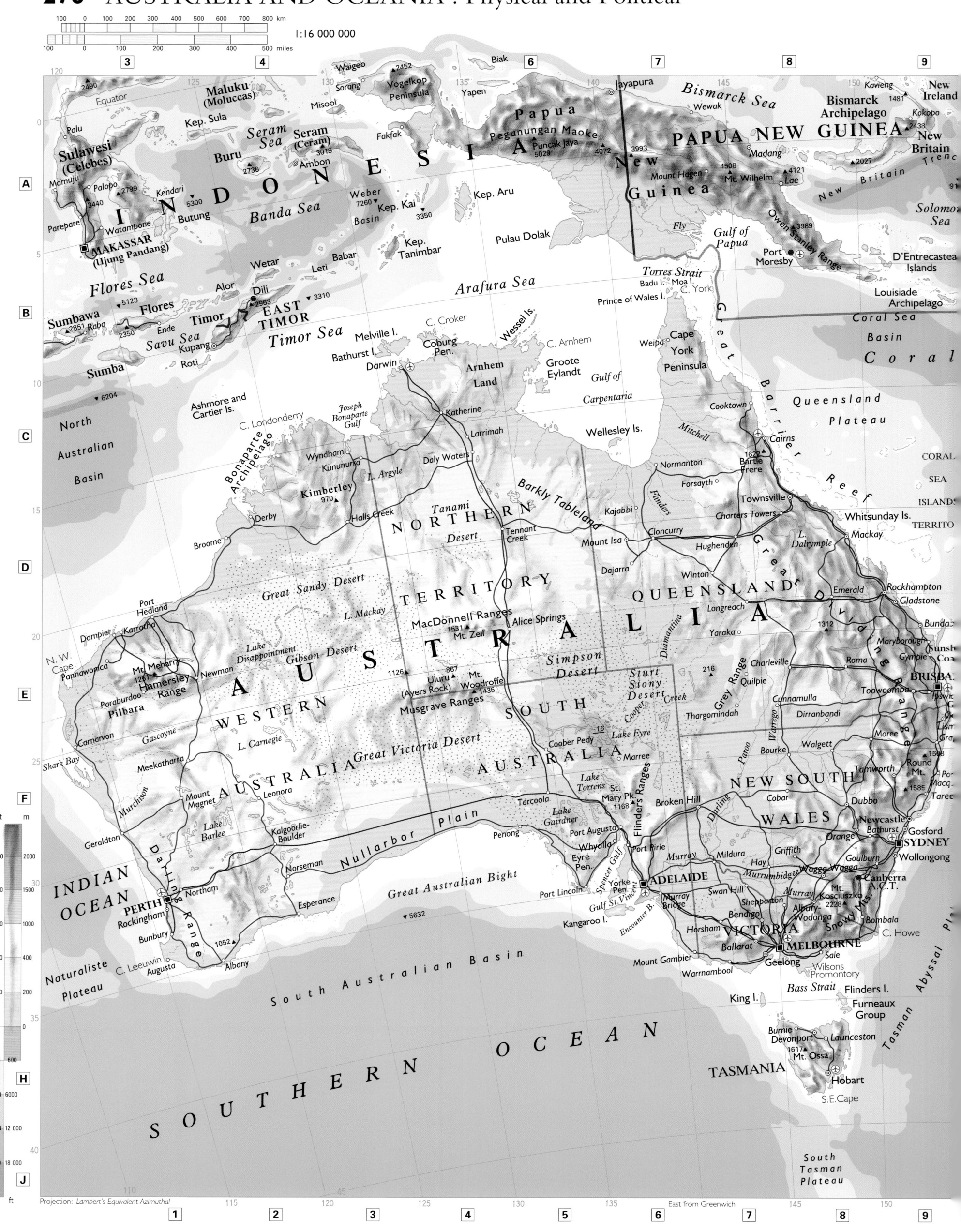

1:16 000 000

Projection: Lambert's Equivalent Azimuthal

East from Greenwich

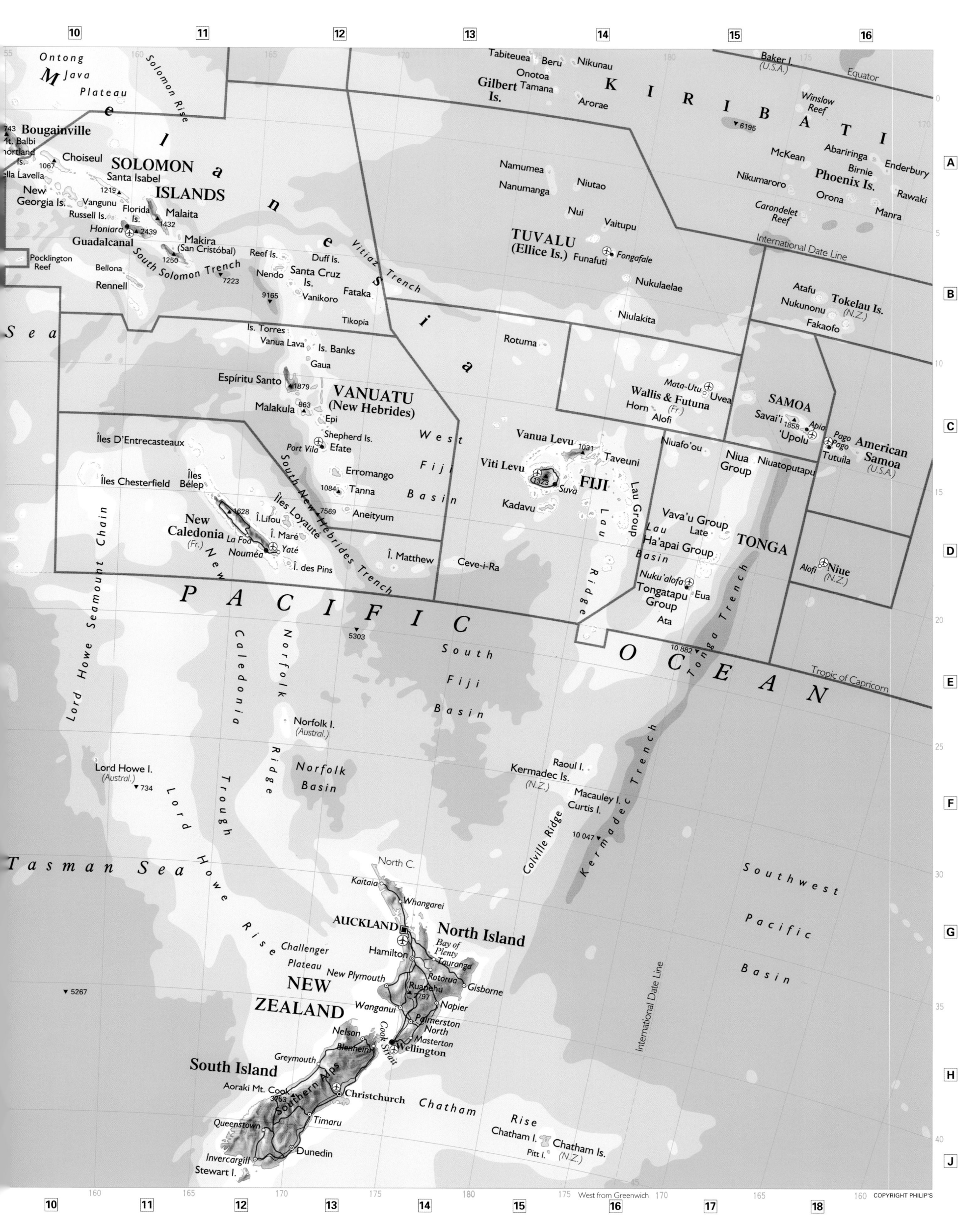

10 **11** **12** **13** **14** **15** **16**

55 160 165 170 175 180

Ontong
M *Java*
Plateau

Solomon Rise

Mel

743 Bougainville
Mt. Balbi
iortland
Is.
Choiseul
ella Lavella
1067
SOLOMON
New
Georgia Is.
Santa Isabel
1219
ISLANDS
Vangunu
Florida
Russell Is.
Is.
1432
Malaita
Honiara
2439
Guadalcanal
1250
Makira
(San Cristóbal)
Bellona
Rennell

Pocklington
Reef
South Solomon Trench
7223

Reef Is.
Nendo
Duff Is.
9165
Santa Cruz
Is.
Vanikoro
Fataka
Tikopia

Is. Torres
Vanua Lava Is. Banks
Gaua

Espíritu Santo
1879
VANUATU
Malakula
863
(New Hebrides)
Epi
Shepherd Is.

Îles D'Entrecasteaux

Îles Chesterfield
Îles Bélep
Port Vila Efate
Erromango
1084
Tanna
7569
Aneityum

Îles Loyauté
1628
Î. Lifou
La Foa
Î. Maré
Nouméa Yaté
Î. des Pins
Î. Matthew
Ceve-i-Ra

New
Caledonia
(Fr.)

Tabiteuea Beru Nikunau
Onotoa
Gilbert Tamana
Is.
Arorae
K
6195

Namumea
Nanumanga
Nui
Vaitupu
TUVALU
(Ellice Is.) Funafuti
Fongafale

Nukulaelae

Niulakita

Rotuma

Mata-Utu Uvea
Wallis & Futuna
Horn Alofi
(Fr.)

Niuafo'ou

Vanua Levu
1031
Viti Levu
Taveuni
1323
Suva
FIJI
Kadavu

Niua
Group
Niuatoputapu

Vava'u Group
Lau Late
Ha'apai Group

Nuku'alofa
Tongatapu Eua
Group
Ata

Baker I.
(U.S.A.) Equator
Winslow
Reef
I R I B A T I
McKean
Abariringa
Birnie Enderbury
Nikumaroro **Phoenix Is.**
Orona
Manra
Carondelet
Reef

Atafu
Nukunonu **Tokelau Is.**
(N.Z.)
Fakaofo

SAMOA
Savai'i 1858
'Upolu Apia
Pago **American**
Tutuila Pago **Samoa**
(U.S.A.)

Alofi Niue
(N.Z.)

International Date Line

A

B

C

D

TONGA

Lau
Ridge

Lau
Basin

10 882
Tonga Trench

P A C I F I C
5303
South
Fiji
Basin
O C E A N
Tropic of Capricorn

E

Lord Howe Seamount Chain

Caledonia

Norfolk
Ridge

Norfolk
Basin

Norfolk I.
(Austral.)

Caledonia
Trough

Lord Howe I.
(Austral.)
734

Lord

Howe
Rise

Kermadec Trench

Southwest

Pacific

Basin

F

G

Tasman Sea

5267

Raoul I.
Kermadec Is.
(N.Z.)
Macauley I.
Curtis I.
10 047

Colville Ridge

North C.
Kaitaia
Whangarei
AUCKLAND
Hamilton
Challenger
Plateau
NEW
ZEALAND
New Plymouth
Wanganui
North Island
Bay of
Plenty Tauranga
Rotorua
Ruapehu
2797
Gisborne
Napier
Palmerston
North
Masterton
Wellington
Nelson
Blenheim
Greymouth
Cook Strait

South Island
Aoraki Mt. Cook
3753
Christchurch
Queenstown *Southern Alps*
Timaru
Invercargill
Dunedin
Stewart I.

Chatham

Rise

Chatham I.
Chatham Is.
Pitt I. *(N.Z.)*

International Date Line

H

J

170

10 **11** **12** **13** **14** **15** **16** **17** **18**

160 165 170 175 180 175 *West from Greenwich* 170 165 160 COPYRIGHT PHILIP'S

50 0 50 100 150 200 250 300 km
1:6 400 000
50 0 50 100 150 200 miles

Projection: Bonne

Aboriginal lands

1. NGALIWURRU/NUNGALI
2. WANIMIYN
3. WAMBARDI
4. LIJALALTUMA
5. RODNA
6. NTARIA
7. ROULPMAULPMA
8. URUNA

East from Greenwich

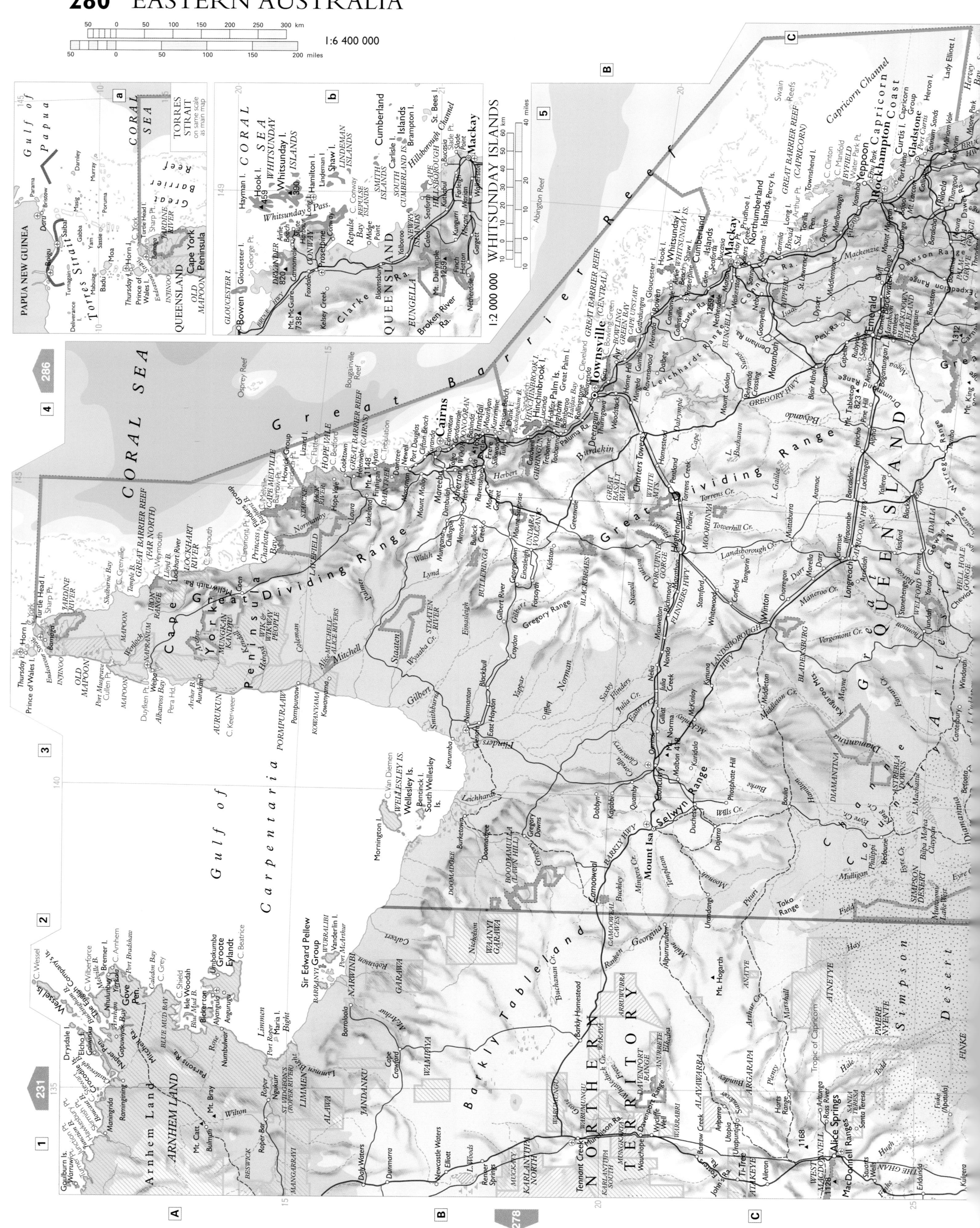

NEW SOUTH WALES
SOUTH AUSTRALIA
TASMANIA
TASMAN SEA
Bass Strait
BRISBANE
SYDNEY
MELBOURNE
ADELAIDE
Hobart
Canberra
Newcastle
Wollongong
Gold Coast
Sunshine Coast
Toowoomba
Broken Hill
Mildura
Wagga Wagga
Albury
Geelong
Ballarat
Bendigo
Launceston
Devonport
Mount Gambier
Port Augusta
Port Pirie
Port Lincoln
Whyalla
Dubbo
Tamworth
Armidale
Lake Eyre (North)
Lake Torrens
Lake Gairdner
Lake Frome
Kangaroo I.
King Island
Flinders Island
Furneaux Group
Eyre Peninsula
Spencer Gulf
Gulf St. Vincent
Sturt Stony Desert
Strzelecki Desert
East from Greenwich
Aboriginal lands
Projection: Bonne
COPYRIGHT PHILIP'S

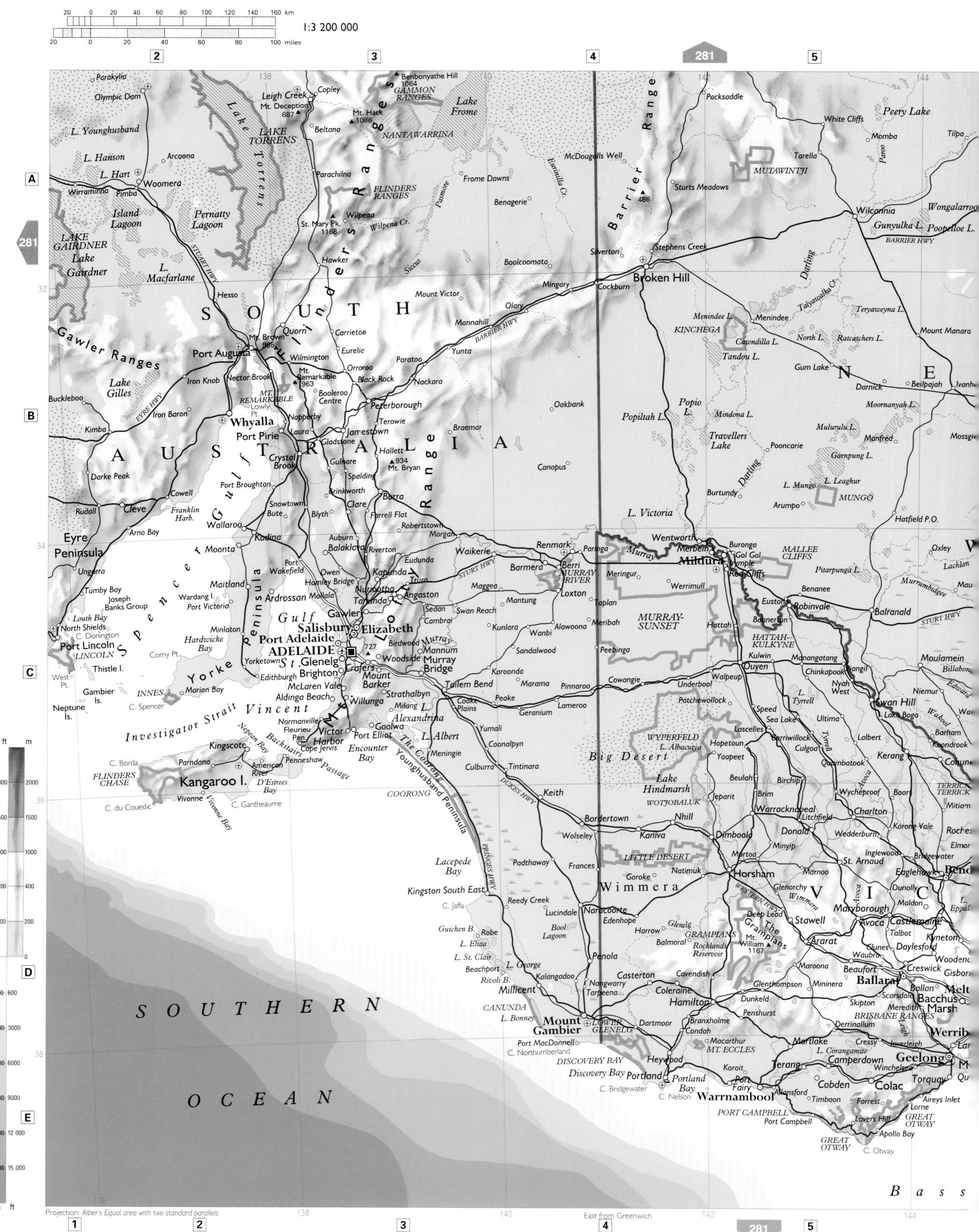

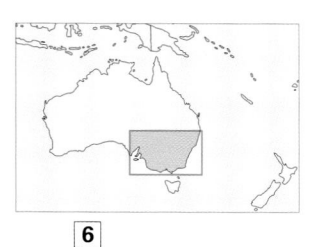

6   7   8   9   281   10

A

B

C

D

E

T A S M A N

S E A

Coffs Harbour
Armidale
Tamworth
Port Macquarie
Taree
Forster
Dubbo
Muswellbrook
Maitland
Cessnock
Newcastle
Gosford
Orange
Bathurst
Penrith
Parramatta
SYDNEY
Liverpool
Campbelltown
Wollongong
Port Kembla
Kiama
Shellharbour
Nowra
Goulburn
Canberra
Queanbeyan
Batemans Bay
Cooma
Wagga Wagga
Albury
Wodonga
Shepparton
Benalla
Bairnsdale
Sale
MELBOURNE
Dandenong
Traralgon
Morwell

Great Dividing Range

KOSCIUSZKO
Mt. Kosciuszko
2228

Strait

Wilsons Promontory

East from Greenwich

6   7   [shaded] Aboriginal lands   8   9   10

10 0 20 40 60 80 100 120 140 km
10 0 20 40 60 80 100 miles

1:2 800 000

PACIFIC OCEAN

TASMAN SEA

NORTHLAND

C. Reinga
C. Maria van Diemen
Waitiki Landing
North C.
Parengarenga Harbour
Houhora Heads
Rangaunu B.
C. Karikari
Doubtless B.
Whangaroa Harb.
Ahipara B.
Awanui
Mongonui
Kaeo
Cavalli Is.
Kaitaia
Kerikeri
Paihia
Russell
Herekino
Okaihau
Waitangi
B. of Islands
C. Brett
744
Opua
Kawakawa
Kohukohu
Kaikohe
Moerewa
Whangaruru Harb.
Rawene
Poor Knights Is.
Hokianga Harbour
781
Omapere
Hikurangi
Waipoua Forest
Kamo
Donnelly's Crossing
Whangarei
Aranga
Onerahi
Whangarei Harb.
Kirikopuni
Bream Hd.
Dargaville
Waikiekie
Paparoa
Bream B.
Hen & Chickens Is.
Te Kopuru
Waipu
Bream Tail
Ruawai
Maungaturoto
Kaipara Harbour
Wellsford
Needles Pt.
Little Barrier I.
Port Fitzroy
Matakana
722
627
Great Barrier I.
Tryphena
C. Rodney
Kawau I.
Warkworth
Matakana I.
Coville Chan.
Snells Beach
C. Colville
Cuvier I.
Helensville
Hauraki G.
892
Port Charles
Whangaparaoa Pen.
Mercury Is.

AUCKLAND
Takapuna
Coromandel
Ostend
Waiheke I.
Mercury B.
Whitianga
AUCKLAND
Mount Wellington
Howick
Coromandel Pen.
Muriwai Beach
Piha
AKL
Onehunga
Otahuhu
Tairua
Papakura
Pauanui
Manukau Harbour
Manukau
846
Thames
Whangamata
Pukekohe
Thames Ra.
Waiuku
Tuakau
Mercer
Mayor I.
Te Kauwhata
Waikato
L. Waikare
Waihi
Waihi Beach

WAIKATO
Huntly
Katikati
Tauranga Harb.
BAY OF PLENTY
Ngaruawahia
Te Aroha
Matakana I.
White I. (Whakaari)
Glen Afton
Waitoa
Mount Maunganui
Glen Massey
Morrinsville
Tauranga
C. Runaway
Hicks Bay
Hamilton
Te Puke
Te Kaha
Te Araroa
Raglan Harbour
Raglan
Cambridge
Paengaroa
Matata
Edgecumbe
East C.
1067
1753
Waharoa
Matamata
Rotoma
Whakatane
Hikurangi
Ruatoria
Aotea Harbour
Leamington
Tirau
L. Rotoiti
Ohiwa Harbour
Opotiki
Raukumara Ra.
Te Awamutu
Karapiro
L. Rotorua
Waipiro Bay
Kawhia
Arapuni
Putaruru
Kawerau
Kawhia Harbour
Kihikihi
Mamaku
Ngongotaha
Te Teko
Taneatua
Tokomaru Bay
Albatross Pt.
Otorohanga
Rotorua
Mt. Tarawera
Matawai
Puha
Tolaga Bay
Waitomo Caves
Tokoroa
1111
GISBORNE
Te Karaka
Tirua Pt.
Te Kuiti
Kinleith
Waiotapu
Ormond
Aria
Mangakino
Atiamuri
Murupara
UREWERA
Ngatapa
Gisborne
Mokau
Ongarue
Mokai
Wairakei
Galatea
Manuoha
Poverty B.
North Taranaki Bight
Okahukura
1392
L. Waikareiti
1165
Waikaremoana
Tuai
Tuaheni Pt.
Pukearuhe
Manunui
Tokaanu
Taupo
Rangitaiki
Waitara
369
L. Taupo
Tarawera
1383

TARANAKI
New Plymouth
Okato
Inglewood
Tahora
Whangamomona
Mt. Tongariro 1968
Ahimanawa Mts.
Frasertown
Nuhaka
C. Egmont
Mt. Taranaki or Mt. Egmont 2518
Midhirst
Mt. Ngauruhoe 2287
Kaweka Ra.
403
Waikokopu
Rahotu
Huiroa
WHANGANUI 746
TONGARIRO
Ruapehu 2797
1726
Mohaka
Putorino
Table C.
Egmont
Stratford
Ohakune
Mahia Pen.
Opunake
Kaponga
Eltham
Ohura
Owhango
L. Rotoaira
Rangataua
Portland I.
Manaia
Kapuni
Normanby
Raetihi
Waiouru
Bay View
Hawke Bay
Hawera
Pipiriki
Napier
South Taranaki Bight
Patea
Taihape
Taradale
Waverley
Maxwell
Mangaweka
Hastings
Clive
Waitotara
Mangawai
1733
C. Kidnappers
Wanganui
Hunterville
Apiti
Havelock North
Castlecliff
Mangaweka
Opapa
Turakina
Waipawa

MANAWATU-WANGANUI
Marton
Halcombe
Norsewood
Waipukurau
Bulls
Feilding
Ormondville
Takapau
112
Rangitikei
Danevirke
Palmerston North
Bunnythorpe
Rongotea
Ashhurst
Porangahau
Foxton
Longburn
Woodville
803
Pahiatua
Weber
Levin
Shannon
Herbertville
Otaki
Eketahuna
Alfredton
Kapiti I.
Tararua Ra.
Mauriceville
1571
Mt. Mere
Tinui
Stephens I.
Paraparaumu
Castlepoint
Golden Bay
C. Farewell
Farewell Spit
Rangitoto ke te tonga (D'Urville I.)
French Pass
Paekakariki
Masterton
Separation Pt.
ABEL TASMAN N.P.
Stephens I.
Porirua
Carterton
Kahurangi Pt.
Collingwood
Takaka
Tasman Bay
1780
Pelorus Sd.
Forsyth I.
Johnsonville
Upper Hutt
Greytown
Lower Hutt
Featherston
WELLINGTON
Riwaka
Motueka
Queen Charlotte Sd.
Arapawa
Wellington
Petone
665
KAHURANGI MTS.
NELSON
Havelock
Picton
Wainuiomata
Flat Pt.
Karamea
Brightwater
Stoke
Eastbourne
L. Wairarapa
Martinborough
Mt. Owen 1875
Wakefield
Nelson
Port Nicholson
L. Onoke
1203
Richmond
Cloudy B.
Aorangi Mts. 981
Tadmor
Mt. Richmond 1756
Renwick
Belgrove
Richmond Ra.
C. Palliser
Glenhope
Blenheim
Palliser B.
Lyell
TASMAN
NELSON LAKES N.P.
2120
Seddon
Murchison
L. Rotoiti
1780
Ward
L. Rotoroa
Awatere
Cook Strait

ft m
9000 3000
6000 2000
3000 1000
1200 400
600 200
0 0

200 600
1000 3000
1500 4500
3000 9000
m ft

Projection: Conical with two standard parallels

East from Greenwich

1:2 800 000

10 0 20 40 60 80 100 120 140 km
10 0 20 40 60 80 100 miles

1 **2** **3** **4** **5** **6** **7** **8** **9**

167 168 169 170 171 172 173 174

TASMAN SEA

C. Farewell
Farewell Spit
Golden Bay
Collingwood
C. Stephens
Stephens I.
Takaka
Rangitoto ke te tonga (D'Urville I.)
Kahurangi Pt.
French Pass
ABEL TASMAN
Devil River Pk.
1780
Forsyth I.
Jackson
KAHURANGI
Tasman Mts
Riwaka
Motueka
Tasman Bay
Pelorus Sd.
1203
Queen Charlotte Sd.
Arapawa I.

Karamea
Karamea
Moteka
NELSON
Picton

Waimarie
Mokihinui
Brightwater
Stoke
Nelson
Havelock
Cloudy B.
Seddon

Granity
Millerton
Wakefield
Tadmor
Mt. Richmond
Richmond
Belgrove
1756
Renwick
Blenheim

Waimangaroa
Seddonville
Glenhope
Richmond Ra.
MARLBOROUGH
Ward

Westport
Lyell
Buller
Murchison
Mt. Owen
1875
TASMAN
C. Campbell

C. Foulwind
Buller Gorge
Inangahua
1780
L. Rotoiti
Molesworth
2885
Tapuae-o-Uenuku
Wharanui

Reefton
Mt. Travers
2337
St. Arnaud Ra.
Inland Kaikoura Ra.
Kenuku

PAPAROA
L. Rotoroa
Mt. Franklin
2340
NELSON LAKES
Clarence
2608

Punakaiki
Maruia
Maruia Springs
Hanmer Springs
Seaward Kaikoura Ra.
Kaikoura

Blackball
Paparoa Ra.
Lewis Pass
Spenser Mts
1747
Kaikoura Pen.

Runanga
Ahaura
Victoria Ra.
1615

Greymouth
L. Kaimata
Mt. Ajax
1834
L. Sumner
Waiau
Parnassus

Hokitika
L. Brunner
Kumara
ARTHUR'S PASS
Mt. Crossley
1980
Waikari
Culverden
Seargill

Ross
Kaniere
Jacksons
Otira
Arthur's Pass
926
Waipara
Domett

Wanganui
Otira Gorge
Mt. Murchison
2408
Waiau
Amberley

Abut Hd.
Harihari
2650
Springston
Oxford
Pegasus Bay

Whataroa
Lake Coleridge
Sheffield
Sefton
Rangiora

Okarito
L. Mapourika
Whatoroa
Whitcombe Pass
Whitecliffs
Darfield
Kaiapoi
Belfast

WESTLAND
Franz Josef Glacier
Arrowsmith
2781
Mt. Taylor
2333
Highbank
Rolleston
New Brighton

Fox Glacier
MT. COOK
North Branch
Methven
Lincoln
Christchurch

Bruce B.
2497
Mt Tasman
South Branch
Rakaia
Hornby
Sumner
Lyttelton

Tititira Hd.
Aoraki Mount Cook 3753
Tasman Gl.
2251
Mount Somers
Leeston
919
Little River
Banks Pen.

Haast
Okuru
Mount Cook
L. Tekapo
Lake Tekapo
Ashburton
Tinwald
Southbridge
L. Ellesmere
Akaroa

Jackson
Jackson Hd.
B.
Haast
Glenmary
2590
Geraldine
Hinds
Akaroa Harbour

Cascade Pt.
Haast Pass
L. Pukaki
McKenzie Plains
Fairlie
Winchester

Awarua Pt.
Awarua B.
MOUNT ASPIRING
3033
L. Ohau
Lake Pukaki
Temuka
Pleasant Point

Yates Pt.
Mt. Tutoko
2723
Mt. Aspiring
Benmore Pk.
1894
The Hunter Hills
Timaru

Milford Sd.
Darran Mts
Mt. Earnslaw
2819
L. Hawea
Hawea
Waitaki Plains
Canterbury Bight

Mitre Peak
1683
Milford Sound
Harris Mts
Hawea Flat
Mt. St. Bathan's
2087
Waihao
St. Andrews

Bligh Sound
George Sound
Sutherland Falls
L. Wanaka
Wanaka
Hakataramea
Kurow
Waimate
Studholme

Caswell Sound
Charles Sound
Franklin Mts
Glenorchy
1936
Duntroon
Waihao
Morven

Thompson Sd.
Stuart Mts
1610
Richardson Mts
Dunstan Mts
St. Bathans
Ngapara
Glenavy

Secretary I.
Murchison Mts
Queenstown
Cromwell
Hawkdun Ra.
Oamaru

Doubtful Sd.
2022
Jane Pk.
The Remarkables
2319
Clyde
Naseby
Kakanui Mts
Maheno

Dagg Sd.
Mt. Lyall
1892
Eyre Mts
Double Cone
Garvie Mts
Rough Ridge
Windsor
Pukeuri

FIORDLAND
Kepler Mts
L. Te Anau
Kingston
Alexandra
Hyde
Dunback

Breaksea Sd.
Heath Mts
L. Manapouri
Athol
Roxburgh
Middlemarch
Palmerston

Resolution I.
Manapouri
Umbrella Mts
Miller's Flat
Sutton
Waikouaiti Downs
Shag Pt.

Dusky Sd.
Mossburn
Waikaia
Edievale
Beaumont
Waikouaiti
Otago Harbour

Kaherekoau Mts
Lumsden
Waimea Plain
Clutha
Otago Pen.

Providence
Chalky Inlet
Hunter Mts
Monowai
Dipton
Mataura
Lawrence
Warrington
Port Chalmers

Preservation Inlet
Cameron Mts
1704
Birchwood
Ohai
Riversdale
Kelso
Taieri
Mosgiel
St. Kilda

Puysegur Pt.
Caroline Pk.
Orawia
Nightcaps
Waikaka
Tapanui
Milton
C. Saunders

Te Waewae B.
Tuatapere
Wairio
Otautau
Winton
Waipahi
Clinton
Stirling

Pahia Pt.
Orepuki
Thornbury
Makarewa
Hedgehope
Edendale
Balclutha
Kaitangata

Centre I.
Riverton
Glenham
Gore
Mataura
Wyndham
Owaka

Wallacetown
Invercargill
Catlins
Tahakopa
Nugget Pt.

Bluff
South Invercargill
Fortrose
Tokanui
Long Pt.

Solander I.
Mt. Anglem
980
Fortrose
Toetoes B.
Waipapa Pt.
Chaslands Mistake

Codfish I.
Foveaux Str.
Bluff Harbour
Ruapuke I.

Mason B.
Halfmoon Bay
Paterson Inlet

Doughboy B.
RAKIURA
Stewart I. (Rakiura)

South West C.
Port Pegasus

TASMAN SEA

PACIFIC OCEAN

4870

33

CHATHAM ISLANDS
on same scale

a

PACIFIC OCEAN

The Sisters
C. Young
Munning Pt.

Western Reef
Te One
Chatham I.
(Rekohu)
The Forty Fours

Waitangi
C. Fournier

Chatham Islands (Wharekauri)

The Horns
Pitt Strait
Mangere I.
Star Keys
Owenga
Pitt I.
The Pyramid
Rangatira I.

178 177 176

West from Greenwich

167 168 169 170 171

ft m
9000 3000
6000 2000
3000 1000
1200 400
600 200
0 0
200 600
1000 3000
1500 4500
3000 9000
4000 12 000
m ft

1:5 200 000

50 0 50 100 150 200 km
50 0 50 100 150 miles

PACIFIC OCEAN

NORTH SOLOMONS

Solomon Islands

Nuguria Is.
Sable I.
Green Is.
Kilinailau Is. (Carteret Is.)
C. Hanpan
Buka I.
Hutjena
Sohano
Kunua
Torokina
Mt. Balbi 2715
Kieta
Arawa
Panguna
Mt. Takuam 2251
Boku
Buin
Shortland I. (Solomon Is.)
Treasury Is. (Solomon Is.)
Toki
Mutupena Pt.
Metlik

Lyra Reef
Tanga Is.
Boang I.
Malendok I.
Feni Is.
Ambitle I.
Babase I.

NEW IRELAND

St. Matthias Group
Mussau I.
Tabalo
Eloaua I.
Emirau I.
Tench I.

New Hanover
Tingwon Group
Noipuos
Taskul
Ungat
Djaul I.
Lambu
Kavieng
North C.
Lokuramau
Tatau I.
Simberi I.
Tabar Is.
Tabar I.
Lihir I.
Lihir Group
Konos
Schleinitz Ra. 1481
Konogogo
Namatanai

Hans Meyer Ra. 2340
Verron Ra. 2021
Lambon
Namatanai
C. St. George
St. George's Channel

Bismarck Sea

BISMARCK ARCHIPELAGO

Admiralty Islands
Hermit Is.
Ninigo Group
Aua I.
Wuvulu I.
Sori
Lorengau
Momote
Manus I.
Tong I.
Rambutyo I.
Lou I.
Baluan I.
MANUS
Kabuli
South West Pt.

Circular Reef
Sherburne Reef

Vokeo I.
Schouten Is.
Tarawai I.
Kairiru I.
Muschu I.
Wewak
Bam I.
Manam I.
Karkar I.
Bagabag I.
Long I.
Crown I.
Tolokiwa I.
Sakar I.
Umboi I.
Sag Sag
C. Gloucester
Whirlwind Reef
Ottilien Reef
Garove I.
Witu Is.
Unea I.
Nukuhu
Williaumez Pen.
Talasea
Hoskins
Kimbe
Kimbe Bay
Ewasse
Ubai
Matong
Kokopo
Gazelle Peninsula
Rabaul
Keravat
Watom I.
Pondo
C. Lambert
Mt. Sinewit 2438
Sampun
Pomio
Jacquinot Bay
Wide Bay
Crater Pt.

NEW BRITAIN
WEST NEW BRITAIN
EAST NEW BRITAIN

Whiteman Ra. 2027
Gasmata
C. Kablungu
C. Anukur
Kandrian
Arawe Is.
Aumo
Waku
Dampier Strait
Vitiaz Strait

Bougainville Trench 9140

Solomon Sea

WEST SOLOMON SEA

8320

NEW GUINEA

WEST SEPIK
EAST SEPIK
MADANG
Bogia
C. Girgir
Watam
Madang
Saidor
Bogadjim
Bibi
Matuka
Finisterre Ra.
Adelbert Range
Amaimon
Annanberg
Ajome
Sepik R.
Angoram
Keram
Yuat
April
Ramu

Torricelli Mts.
West Sepik
Dreikikir
Maprik
Yangoru
Ambunti
Wogamush
Oksapmin
Telefomin
Mt. Capella 3993
Mt. Aiyang 3505
Mt. Alwart
Tabubil
Ningerum
Kiunga
Nomad
Mt. Bosavi 2507
Lake Murray

CENTRAL RANGE
ENGA
Wabag
Porgera
Wapenamanda
Kandep
Laiagam
WESTERN HIGHLANDS
Mt. Hagen 4508
Mt. Giluwe 4368
Mendi
Tari
SOUTHERN HIGHLANDS
Baiyer
Banz
Minj
Wahgi
CHIMBU
Kundiawa
Mt. Wilhelm 4509
Mt. Michael 3647
Goroka
EASTERN HIGHLANDS
Kainantu
Henganofi
Mt. Michael
Okapa
Crater Mt. 3231
Kagua
Erave
Kerabi
Kikori
Kikori
Daru
Darai Hills
Aramia
Balimo
Fly
Wasua
Morehead

PAPUA NEW GUINEA
GULF
Gulf of Papua
Kukipi
Iokea
Malalaua
Kerema
Ihu
Deception Bay
Blackwood Bay
Vailala
Baimuru
Bairuru

MOROBE
Huon Peninsula
Finschhafen
C. Cretin
Tami Is.
Sialum
Wasu
Lasanga I.
Huon Gulf
Morobe
Lae
Mt. Bangeta 4121
Kaiapit
Markham
Erap
Nadzab
Bulolo
Wau
Kabwum
Saruwaged Ra.
Menyamya
Aseki
Kaintiba
Wonenara
Garaina
Mumeng

NORTHERN
C. Ward Hunt
Dyke Ackland Bay
Buna
Popondetta
Kokoda
Afore
Seriri
Gona
Wanigela
Tufi
C. Nelson
Sibium
Kumusi
Mt. Lamington 1680
Mt. Victoria 4036
Mt. Albert Edward 3993
OWEN STANLEY RANGE
Mt. Suckling 3676
Safia
Mt. Simpson 2883
Abau
Amazon Bay
Mullins Harbour
Milne Bay
MILNE BAY

CENTRAL
Port Moresby
Kwikila
Hood Pt.
Kupiano
Kabo
Keppel Pt.
Hula
Marshall Lagoon
Aroma
Kwato

Trobriand Islands
Kiriwina I.
Kitava I.
Kaileuna I.
Losuia
Marshall Bennett Is.
Vakuta I.
Lusancay Is. and Reefs
Egum Atoll
D'Entrecasteaux Islands
Goodenough I.
Fergusson I.
2566
Normanby I.
Bolubolu
Tutubeiao
Esa'ala
Sanaroa I.
Sehulea
Numanuma
Alulului
Dobu
East C.
Samarai
Sariba
Suau
Gadaisu
Bunama
Nuakata I.
Basilaki I.
Dumoulin Is.

Woodlark I.
Guasopa
Madau I.
Laughlan Is.
Kulumadau
Alcester I.
Conflict Group
Engineer Group
Debdyne
Deboyne
Panatinani
Misima I.
Bwagaoia
Louisiade Archipelago
East I.
Tawa Tawa Mal Reef
The Calvados Chain
Rossel I.
Tagula I.
Tagula
Pocklington Reef

Coral Sea

Gulf of Papua
Papua

Great Barrier Reef
Torres Strait
Daru I.
Parama I.
Bristow I.
Kiwai I.
Saibai I. (Australia)
Boigu I. (Australia)
Dauan I.
Bamaga
Cape York
York Peninsula
C. Grenville
Temple Bay
C. York
Turtle Head I.
Prince of Wales I.
Thursday I.
Wednesday I.
Horn I.
Shelburne Bay
Sharp Pt.
Moa I.
Badu I.
AUSTRALIA
QUEENSLAND
Cullen Pt.
Endeavour Strait

WESTERN
NEW GUINEA
PAPUA
INDONESIA

East from Greenwich

Projection: Lambert Conformal Conic

m ft
4000 12 000
2000 6000
1000 3000
400 1200
200 600
0
600 2000
1000 3000
2000 6000
3000 9000
4000 12 000
6000 18 000
ft m

287
231

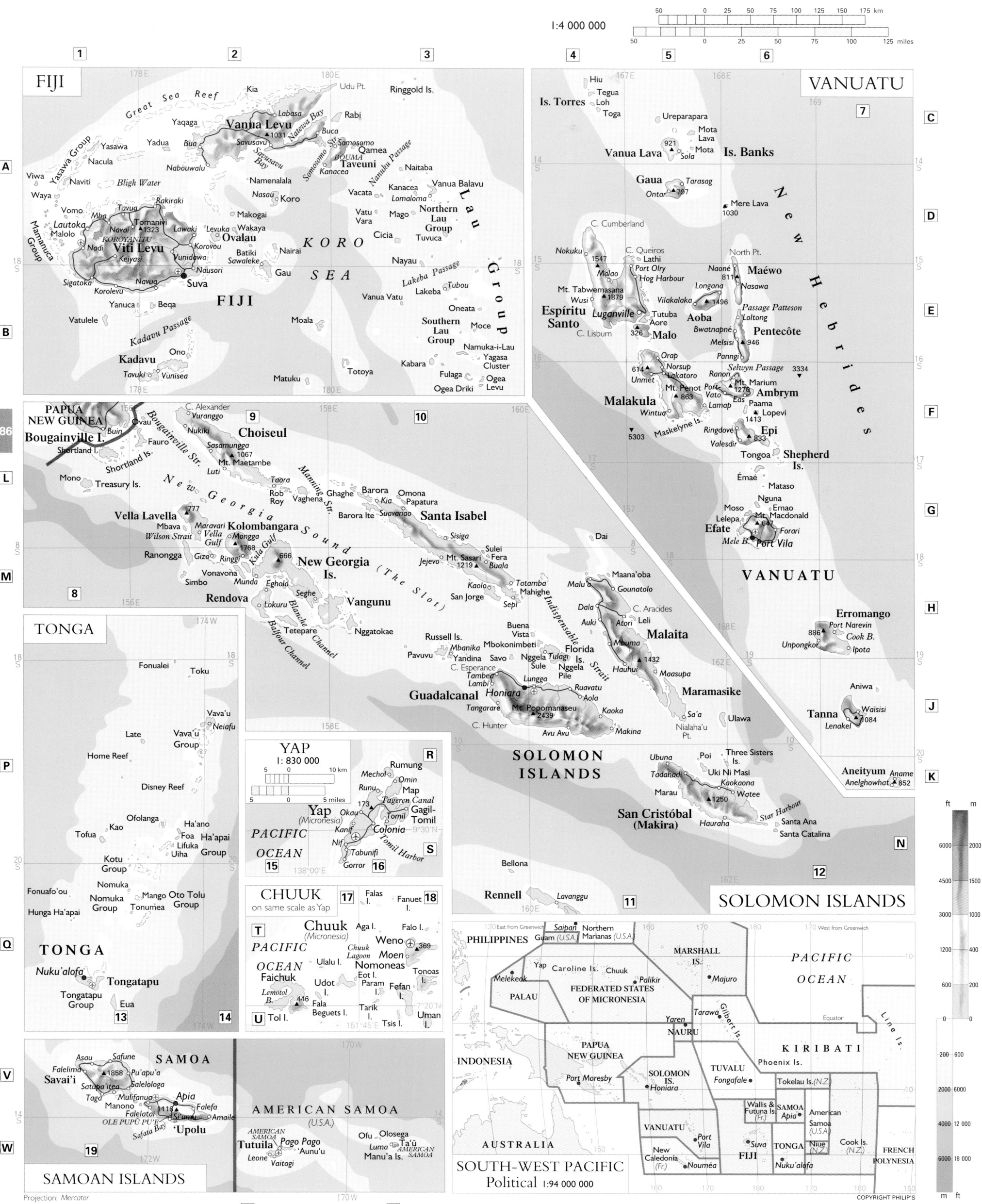

Equatorial Scale 1:43 200 000

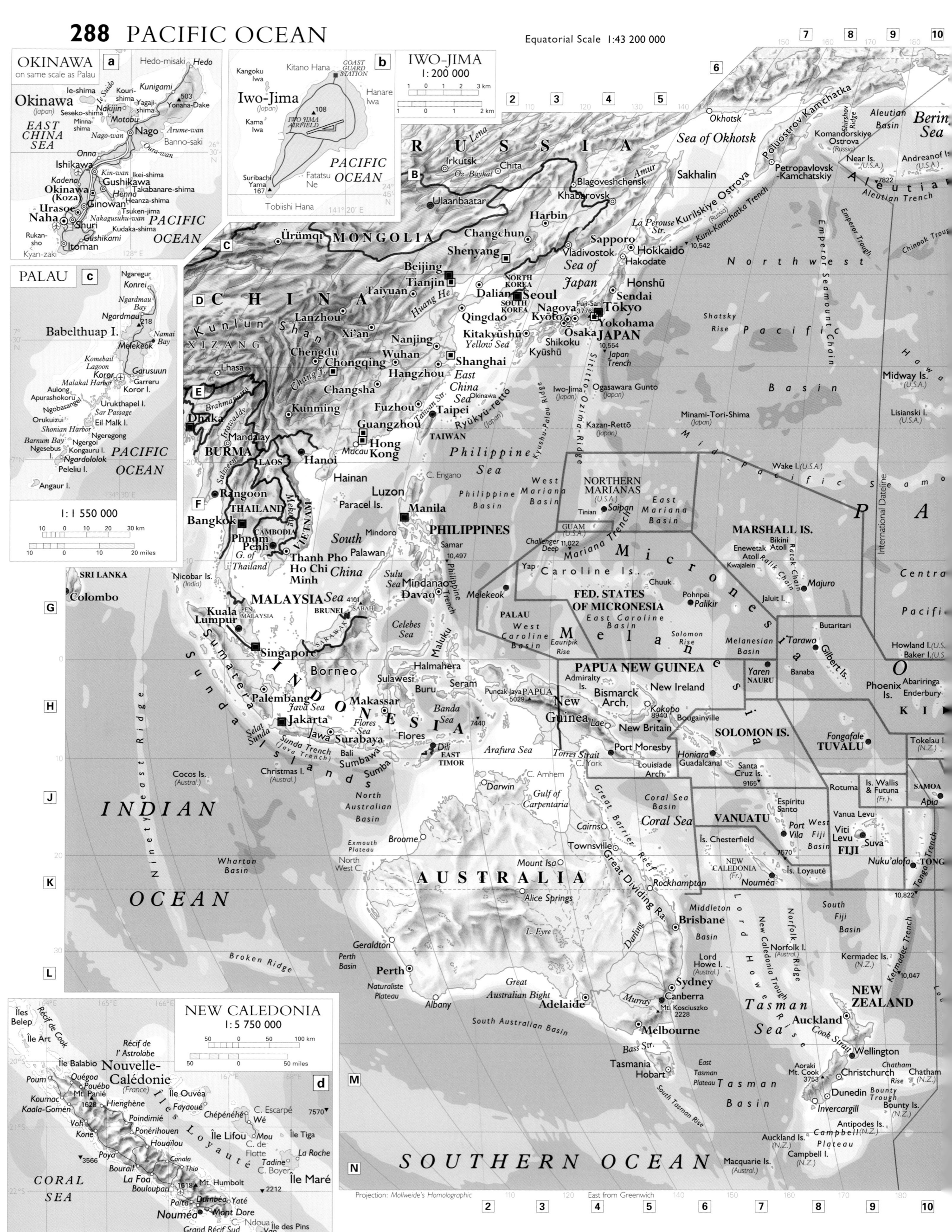

OKINAWA
a
on same scale as Palau

Okinawa
(Japan)

Hedo-misaki · Hedo
Kangoku Iwa
Kitano Hana
COAST GUARD STATION

Ie-shima
Kouri-shima
Yagaji-shima
503
Yonaha-Dake
Kunigami

EAST CHINA SEA

Seseko-shima
Nakijin
Minna-shima
Motobu
Arume-wan
Nago-wan
Banno-saki

Onna
Ikei-shima

Ishikawa
Okinawa (Koza)
Kin-wan
Tsuken-jima

Kadena
Henna
Heanza-shima

Gushikawa
Nakagusuku-wan

Ginowan
Kudaka-shima

Urasoe
Tsuken-jima

Naha
Shuri
Gushikami

Rukan-sho
Kudaka-shima

Itoman

Kyan-zaki

PACIFIC OCEAN

IWO-JIMA
b
Iwo-Jima
(Japan)
Kangoku Iwa
Kitano Hana
COAST GUARD STATION
Hanare Iwa

Kama Iwa

IWO JIMA AIRFIELD
108

Suribachi Yama
167
Fatatsu Ne
PACIFIC OCEAN

Tobiishi Hana

IWO-JIMA
1:200 000
1 0 1 2 3 km
1 0 1 2 km

PALAU
c

Ngaregur
Konrei

Ngardmau Bay

Ngardmau
Namai Bay

Babelthuap I.
218

Melekeok

Komebail Lagoon
Koror
Garusuun
Malakal Harbor
Garreru
Aulong
Koror I.
Apurashokoru
Ngobasangel
Sar Passage
Orukuizui
Eil Malk I.
Shonian Harbor
Barnum Bay
Ngergoi
Ngeregong
Ngesebus
Konauru I.
Ngercoi
Ngdolokol

Peleliu I.

PACIFIC OCEAN

Angaur I.

1:1 550 000
10 0 10 20 30 km
10 0 10 20 miles

RUSSIA

Irkutsk
Oz. Baykal
Chita
Blagoveshchensk
Amur
Khabarovsk
Sakhalin

Ulaanbaatar

MONGOLIA
Ürümqi

Changchun
Shenyang
Harbin
La Perouse Str.
10,542

Sapporo
Hokkaidō
Hakodate

Beijing
Tianjin
NORTH KOREA
Seoul
SOUTH KOREA
Dalian
Sea of Japan
Vladivostok

Taiyuan

CHINA
Lanzhou
Xi'an
Qingdao
Huang He
Yellow Sea
Kyōto
Nagoya
Fuji-San 3776
Tōkyō
Sendai
Honshū

XIZANG
Kunlun Shan
Lhasa
Chengdu
Chongqing
Wuhan
Nanjing
Shanghai
Kitakyūshū
Kyūshū
Shikoku
Ōsaka
JAPAN
10,554
Yokohama

Chang J.
Changsha
Hangzhou
East China Sea

Brahmaputra
Dhaka
Kunming
Fuzhou
Okinawa
Ryūkyū-rettō *(Japan)*

BURMA
Irrawaddy
Mandalay
Guangzhou
Macau
Hong Kong
TAIWAN
Taipei

LAOS
Hanoi
Hainan
C. Engano
Philippine Sea

Rangoon
THAILAND
Luzon
Paracel Is.
Philippine Basin

Bangkok
CAMBODIA
Phnom Penh
VIETNAM
Manila
Mindoro
Samar
PHILIPPINES
Palawan

SRI LANKA
Thanh Pho Ho Chi Minh
South China Sea
4101
Sulu Sea
Mindanao
Davao
Philippine Trench

Nicobar Is. *(India)*

Colombo

MALAYSIA
Kuala Lumpur
PEN. MALAYSIA
BRUNEI
SABAH
Celebes Sea
SARAWAK

Sumatera
Singapore
Borneo
Sulawesi
Halmahera
Seram
Buru

INDONESIA
Palembang
Makassar
Banda Sea
7440

Jakarta
Jawa
Java Sea
Surabaya
Flores
Flores Sea
Bali
Sumbawa
Sumba
Dili
EAST TIMOR

INDIAN OCEAN

Cocos Is. *(Austral.)*
Christmas I. *(Austral.)*

Ninetyeast Ridge

Sunda Trench (Java Trench)

Selat Sunda

Okhotsk
Sea of Okhotsk

Poluostrov Kamchatka

Kurilskiye Ostrova (Russia)

Petropavlovsk-Kamchatskiy

Kuril-Kamchatka Trench

Komandorskiye Ostrova *(Russia)*

Shirshov Ridge
Bering Sea

Aleutian Basin

Near Is. *(U.S.A.)*
Andreanof Is. *(U.S.A.)*

Aleutian
Aleutian Trench

Emperor Trough
Emperor Seamount Chain

Chinook Trough

Northwest
7822

Shatsky Rise
Pacific
Basin

10,542

Ogasawara Gunto *(Japan)*

Iwo-Jima *(Japan)*
Kazan-Rettō *(Japan)*

Minami-Tori-Shima *(Japan)*

Hawaii

Midway Is. *(U.S.A.)*

Lisianski I. *(U.S.A.)*

Kyushu-Palau Ridge

Stretto Ozima Ridge

Wake I. *(U.S.A.)*

Mid Pacific

Seamo...

PA

International Dateline

West Mariana Basin

NORTHERN MARIANAS *(U.S.A.)*

Tinian
Saipan
East Mariana Basin

GUAM *(U.S.A.)*

Mariana Trench

Challenger Deep 11,022

Yap
Caroline Is.

MARSHALL IS.
Bikini Atoll
Enewetak Atoll
Kwajalein
Ratak Chain
Ralik Chain

Majuro

M i c r o n e s i a

PALAU
West Caroline Basin
Eauripik Rise

Melekeok

Chuuk

FED. STATES OF MICRONESIA

Pohnpei
Palikir

Jaluit I.

East Caroline Basin

Butaritari
Tarawa
Gilbert Is.
Banaba

Howland I. *(U.S.)*
Baker I. *(U.S.)*

KI

Phoenix Is.
Abariringa
Enderbury

Central Pacific

O

Solomon Rise
Melanesian Basin

PAPUA NEW GUINEA
Admiralty Is.
New Ireland
Bismarck Arch.

Puncak Jaya 5029
PAPUA
New Guinea
Kokopo 8940
Bougainville
Lae
New Britain

Torres Strait
C. York
Port Moresby

Louisiade Arch.

SOLOMON IS.
Honiara
Guadalcanal

Santa Cruz Is.
9165

Yaren
NAURU

Fongafale
TUVALU

Tokelau *(N.Z.)*

Melanesia

Rotuma
Is. Wallis & Futuna *(Fr.)*
SAMOA
Apia

Espiritu Santo
Vanua Levu
VANUATU
Port Vila
Viti Levu
Suva
FIJI

Îs. Chesterfield
West Fiji Basin
7570

Nuku'alofa
TONG..

Tonga Trench
10,822

Darwin
C. Arnhem

Arafura Sea

Gulf of Carpentaria

North Australian Basin

Broome
Exmouth Plateau

Wharton Basin

North West C.

AUSTRALIA
Mount Isa
Alice Springs
L. Eyre

Cairns
Townsville

Coral Sea Basin
Coral Sea

Great Barrier Reef

Great Dividing Ra.

Rockhampton

NEW CALEDONIA *(Fr.)*
Nouméa
Is. Loyauté

Middleton Reef

Lord Howe Rise
New Caledonia Ridge

Norfolk I. *(Austral.)*

South Fiji Basin

Kermadec Is. *(N.Z.)*
10,047

Kermadec Trench

Lou...

OCEAN
Geraldton
Perth Basin

Perth
Naturaliste Plateau
Albany

Great Australian Bight

South Australian Basin

Adelaide
Murray
Darling

Brisbane

Lord Howe I. *(Austral.)*

Norfolk I. *(Austral.)*

Sydney
Canberra
Mt. Kosciuszko 2228

Melbourne

Bass Str.

Tasmania
Hobart

East Tasman Plateau

South Tasman Rise

Tasman Sea

Norfolk Trough

Auckland

NEW ZEALAND

Cook Strait
Wellington

Aoraki Mt. Cook 3753
Christchurch

Chatham Rise
Chatham Is. *(N.Z.)*

Dunedin
Invercargill
Bounty Trough
Bounty Is. *(N.Z.)*

Auckland Is. *(N.Z.)*
Antipodes Is. *(N.Z.)*

Campbell I. *(N.Z.)*
Campbell Plateau

Macquarie Is. *(Austral.)*

SOUTHERN OCEAN

NEW CALEDONIA
d
1:5 750 000
50 0 50 100 km
50 0 50 miles

Îles Belep
Récif de Cook
Île Art
Récif de l'Astrolabe

Île Balabio
Poum
Quégoa
Pouébo
Mt. Panié 1628
Hienghène
Nouvelle-Calédonie
(France)
Île Ouvéa
Fayaoué
C. Escarpé
Wé
7570

Koumac
Kaala-Gomén
Voh
Koné
Poindimié
Pouembout
Pouérihouen
Île Lifou
Mou
Île Tiga
La Roche

Poya
3566
Bourail
Canala
Thio
Tadine
C. Boyer
Île Maré

La Foa
Boulouparis
1618
Mt. Humbolt 2212

Païta
Yaté
Dumbéa
Nouméa
Mont Dore
CORAL SEA
Île des Pins
Grand Récif Sud
N'Goa

Projection: Mollweide's Homolographic
East from Greenwich

Main map

Arctic Circle
ALASKA (U.S.A.)
Anchorage
Bristol Bay
Gulf of Alaska
Is. (U.S.A.)
CANADA
Juneau
5959
Prince of Wales I. (U.S.A.)
Prince Rupert
Queen Charlotte Is. (Canada)
Edmonton
Vancouver
Vancouver I.
Victoria
Calgary
ROCKY Mts
Seattle
Portland
Boise
Snake
Tufts Abyssal Plain
Northeast
Pacific
Mendocino Fracture Zone
C. Mendocino
Salt Lake City
Denver
Colorado
Sacramento
San Francisco
4418
UNITED STATES
Oklahoma City
Memphis
Atlanta
Murray Fracture Zone
Los Angeles
San Diego
Phoenix
Dallas
Houston
Jacksonville
6741
Ciudad Juárez
San Antonio
New Orleans
Basin
Guadalupe (Mex.)
MEXICO
Monterrey
Gulf of Mexico
Miami
BAHAMAS
Molokai Fracture Zone
Baja California
Gulfo de California
3504
Sigsbee Deep
La Habana
CUBA
Tropic of Cancer
C. San Lucas
Canal de Yucatan
Florida Str.
Honolulu
O'ahu
HAWAI'I
4205
Hawai'i
Basin
Is. de Revillagigedo (Mex.)
Guadalajara
Mexico
5610
Puebla
Mérida
7680
JAMAICA
HAITI
Kingston
Johnston I. (U.S.A.)
Clarion Fracture Zone
Acapulco
BELIZE
GUATEMALA
Guatemala
HONDURAS
Caribbean Sea
Middle America Trench
San Salvador
EL SALVADOR
NICARAGUA
Managua
Barranquilla
Palmyra Is. (U.S.A.)
PACIFIC
Guatemala Basin
COSTA RICA
San José
Colón
Panamá
PANAMA
Cocos Ridge
I. del Coco (Costa Rica)
Panama Basin
Medellín
Cali
COLOMBIA
San Ridge
North West Christmas I. Ridge
Cooper Ridge
Clipperton Fracture Zone
Î. Clipperton (Fr.)
I. de Malpelo (Colombia)
Teraina
Tabuaeran
Kiritimati
Galápagos Fracture Zone
Galápagos (Ecuador)
Quito
ECUADOR
Carnegie Ridge
Jarvis I. (U.S.A.)
OCEAN
Equator
Guayaquil
C. Pariñas
Phoenix Is.
Malden I.
Starbuck I.
KIRIBATI
BASIN
Caroline I. (Millennium I.)
Nuku Hiva
Îs. Marquises
Hiva Oa
Marquesas Fracture Zone
Trujillo
6369
Penrhyn (Tongareva)
Manihiki
Pukapuka
Manihiki
Vostok I.
Flint I.
Yupanqui Basin
Mendaña Fracture Zone
PERU
Lima
Cusco
Plateau
Suwarrow Is.
Îs. de la Société
Bora Bora
Huahine
Raiatea
Papeete
Tahiti
Rangiroa
Îs. Tuamotu
Peru Basin
L. Titicaca
Arequipa
Nevado Ancohuma 6550
Cook Is. (N.Z.)
Aitutaki
Atiu
Austral / Seamount Chain
FRENCH POLYNESIA
Îs. Gambier
Mururoa
Nazca Ridge
6866
Peru-
Arica
LA PAZ
BOLIVIA
Rarotonga
Mangaia
Îs. Tubuaï
Tropic of Capricorn
Iquique
CHILE
Antofagasta
PARAGUAY
Oeno I.
Henderson I.
Ducie I.
Pitcairn I. (U.K.)
Sala y Gómez Ridge
Sala-y-Gómez (Chile)
San Félix (Chile)
San Ambrosio (Chile)
8064
Trench
San Miguel de Tucumán
Asunción
Rapa
Easter Fracture Zone
I. de Pascua (Chile)
Easter Fracture Zone
Nasca Ridge
Chile Basin
Córdoba
Porto Alegre
Roggeveen Basin
Arch. de Juan Fernández (Chile)
Aconcagua 6962
Valparaíso
Rosario
URUGUAY
Santiago
Buenos Aires
Montevideo
Río de la Plata
Challenger Fracture Zone
Chile Rise
Concepción
ARGENTINA
Argentine Basin
Southwest
Pacific
Ridge
Menard Fracture Zone
Nemo Point (furthest point from any land)
114
ATLANTIC OCEAN
Basin
East Pacific
Pacific Antarctic Ridge
Punta Arenas
Est. de Magallanes
C. de Hornos
Tierra del Fuego
Drake Passage
4402
Falkland Plateau
Falkland Is. (U.K.)
6212
Georgia Basin
South Georgia (U.K.)
South Georgia Ridge
Southeast Pacific Basin
West from Greenwich

Inset e — TAHITI (1:1 150 000)

TAHITI
Pte. Aroa
B. de Matavai
Pte. Vénus
Papetoai
Mahina
Poopao
Papeete
Arue
Papenoo
Tiarei
Mt. Tohiea 1207
Pirae
Afareaitu
Faaa
Hitiaa
Tahiti (France)
Haapiti
Pte. Nuupere
Moorea
Mt. Aorai 2060
Mt. Orohena 2241
Faaone
Punaauia
Mt. Tetufera 1799
Lac Vaihiria
Isthme de Taravao
Pte. Tatatua
Paea
Taravao
Maraa
Papara
Pueu
Vairao
Tautira
PACIFIC OCEAN
Atimaono
Mataiea
Rooniu 1332
Teahupoo
Presqu'île de Taiarapu
10 0 10 km
10 0 10 miles

Inset f — FRENCH POLYNESIA (1:26 000 000)

FRENCH POLYNESIA
200 0 200 400 km
200 0 200 400 miles
Hatutu
Eiao
Îles Marquises
Nuku Hiva
Ua Huka
Ua Pu
Hiva Oa
Tahuata
Motané
4884
6513
Flint I. (Kiribati)
Îles Tuamotu
Îles du Désappointement
Puka Puka
Manihi
Takaroa
Tikei
Ahe
Rangiroa
Apataki
Takume
Roi-Georges
Îles Sous-le-Vent
Tikahau
Matahiva
Île
Kauehi
Raraka
Raroia
Fangatau
Maupiti
Bora Bora
Îles du Vent
Palliser
Makemo
Huahine
Fakarava
Maupihaa
Raiatea
Tahiti
Anaa
Île Raeuki
Tekokota
Tatakoto
Moorea
Papeete
Marokau
Amanu
Méhétia
Île Haraiki
Puka Ruha
Îles de la Société
Hereheretue 4616
Ravahere
Nengonengo
Hao
Paraoa
Vahitahi
Réao
Ahunui
Vairaatea
Îles du Duc-de-Gloucester
Vanavana
Turéia
Groupe Actéon
Îles Maria
Rimatara
Tematagi
Mururoa
Fangataufa
Morané
Îles Gambier
Raivavae
Tropic of Capricorn
Tubuaï
Récif Président-Thiers
Récif Portland
Îles Tubuaï (Îles Australes)
PACIFIC OCEAN
Récif Neilson
Rapa
Îlots de Bass

Inset g — NIUE (1:830 000)

NIUE
5 0 10 km
5 0 5 miles
Hikutavake
Mutalau
Namukulu
Toi
Tuapa
Makefu
Lakepa
Alofi Bay
Alofi
Liku
Niue (N.Z.)
Halangingie Pt.
Fonuakula
Tamakautoga
Avatele
Tepa Pt.
Vaiea
Hakupu
PACIFIC OCEAN

Inset h — RAROTONGA (1:415 000)

RAROTONGA
5 km
5 miles
Rarotonga (N.Z.)
Avarua Harbour
Avatiu
Pue
Nikao
Avarua
Matavera
509
Maungaroa
Te Manga
Ngatangiia
Arorangi
588
653
Motu Tapu
222
Te Kou
Oneroa
Maungatongaiti
329
Koromiri
Taruume
Muri
Taakoka
Titikaveka
PACIFIC OCEAN

Elevation scale (right margin)

ft m
12 000 4000
9000 3000
6000 2000
1500
1000
600
500
200 600
0 0
200 600
1000 3000
2000 6000
4000 12 000
6000 18 000
8000 24 000
m ft

NORTH
AMERICA

1:28 000 000

Projection: Bonne

West from Greenwich

COPYRIGHT PHILIP'S

1:28 000 000

100 0 200 400 600 800 1000 1200 1400 km
100 0 200 400 600 800 1000 miles

B **A** **B**

C **C**

RUSSIA
Asia

ARCTIC

OCEAN

GREENLAND

ICELAND
Reykjavík

St. Lawrence I.

Bering Strait

Beaufort
Sea

Queen Elizabeth Is.

Ellesmere I.

Baffin
Bay

Denmark Strait

D

Bering
Sea

Yukon

ALASKA
(USA)
Fairbanks

Porcupine

Anchorage

Kodiak I.

Gulf of Alaska

YUKON
TERRITORY

Whitehorse

Juneau

Arctic Circle

NORTHWEST

Great Bear
L.

Mackenzie

TERRITORIES

Liard

Great
Slave L.

Back

Dubawnt

NUNAVUT

Victoria I.

Hudson Strait

Iqaluit

Baffin Island

Davis Strait

Nuuk

(Denmark)

D

E

70 80

60

50

BRITISH
COLUMBIA

Skeena

Peace

Athabasca

CANADA

Fraser

Athabasca

Edmonton

ALBERTA

Calgary

SASKATCHEWAN

Saskatchewan

Regina

Churchill

Nelson

MANITOBA

L.
Winnipeg

Hudson

B a y

ONTARIO

Eastmain

QUÉBEC

St. Lawrence

LABRADOR

NEWFOUNDLAND &

St-Pierre
et Miquelon
(Fr.)

St. John's

E

50

F

Victoria

Vancouver

Olympia

WASHINGTON

Seattle

Portland

Salem

OREGON

Columbia

Helena

MONTANA

Missouri

IDAHO

Boise

Snake

WYOMING

Bismarck

NORTH
DAKOTA

SOUTH
DAKOTA

MINNESOTA

Minneapolis-
St. Paul

WISCONSIN

Madison

Milwaukee

MICHIGAN

Lansing

L. Superior

L. Huron

Detroit

Toledo

Cleveland

TORONTO

Buffalo

L. Ontario

PA.

Pittsburgh

NEW YORK

Ottawa

Montréal

Québec

Fredericton

NEW
BRUNSWICK

MAINE

Augusta

VER.

N.H.

Concord

MASS.

Boston

Providence

Hartford

NEW YORK

PHILADELPHIA

PRINCE
EDWARD I.

Charlottetown

NOVA SCOTIA

Halifax

F

40

SAN FRANCISCO

Sacramento

San Jose

CALIFORNIA

LOS ANGELES

Carson
City

Salt Lake
City

NEVADA

UTAH

Las Vegas

Denver

COLORADO

NEBRASKA

Lincoln

KANSAS

Kansas City

Topeka

IOWA

ILLINOIS

CHICAGO

St.
Louis

MISSOURI

Springfield

Indianapolis

INDIANA

OHIO

Columbus

Cincinnati

Washington D.C.

W.V.

VIRGINIA

Richmond

KENTUCKY

Nashville

TENNESSEE

DE.

MD.

N.J.

Baltimore

Raleigh

NORTH
CAROLINA

Charlotte

Bermuda
(U.K.)

G

PACIFIC

OCEAN

San Diego

Tijuana

Santa Fe

Albuquerque

NEW MEXICO

ARIZONA

Phoenix

Tucson

Mexicali

El Paso

Ciudad Juárez

Colorado

Oklahoma
City

OKLAHOMA

ARKANSAS

Little Rock

Memphis

MISSISSIPPI

Birmingham

ALABAMA

GEORGIA

Atlanta

Montgomery

Columbia

SOUTH
CAROLINA

Charleston

ATLANTIC

OCEAN

G

30

Guadalupe
(Mex.)

Hermosillo

Rio Grande

Dallas-
Ft. Worth

TEXAS

Austin

Houston

San Antonio

LOUISIANA

Baton
Rouge

Jackson

New
Orleans

Tallahassee

Jacksonville

FLORIDA

Orlando

Tampa-
St. Petersburg

MIAMI

Nassau

BAHAMAS

Turks & Caicos Is.
(U.K.)

San Juan

H

Revilla Gigedo Is.
(Mex.)

Culiacán

Torreón

MÉXICO

San Luis Potosí

León

Guadalajara

Monterrey

Gulf of Mexico

Florida Str.

Havana

CUBA

Cayman Is.
(U.K.)

JAMAICA

Kingston

HAITI

Port-au-
Prince

DOMINICAN
REP.

Santo
Domingo

PUERTO
RICO
(U.S.A.)

Mérida

Tropic of Cancer

MÉXICO

Toluca

Puebla

Acapulco

Belmopan

BELIZE

GUATEMALA

Guatemala

San Salvador

EL SALVADOR

HONDURAS

Tegucigalpa

NICARAGUA

Managua

L. Nicaragua

Caribbean Sea

Barranquilla

Maracaibo

VENEZUELA

J

COSTA
RICA

San José

PANAMA

Panamá

COLOMBIA

Medellín

South

America

J

120 110 West from Greenwich 100 90 80

7 ■ MÉXICO Capital Cities **8** **9** **10** **11** **12**

Projection: Bonne

COPYRIGHT PHILIP'S

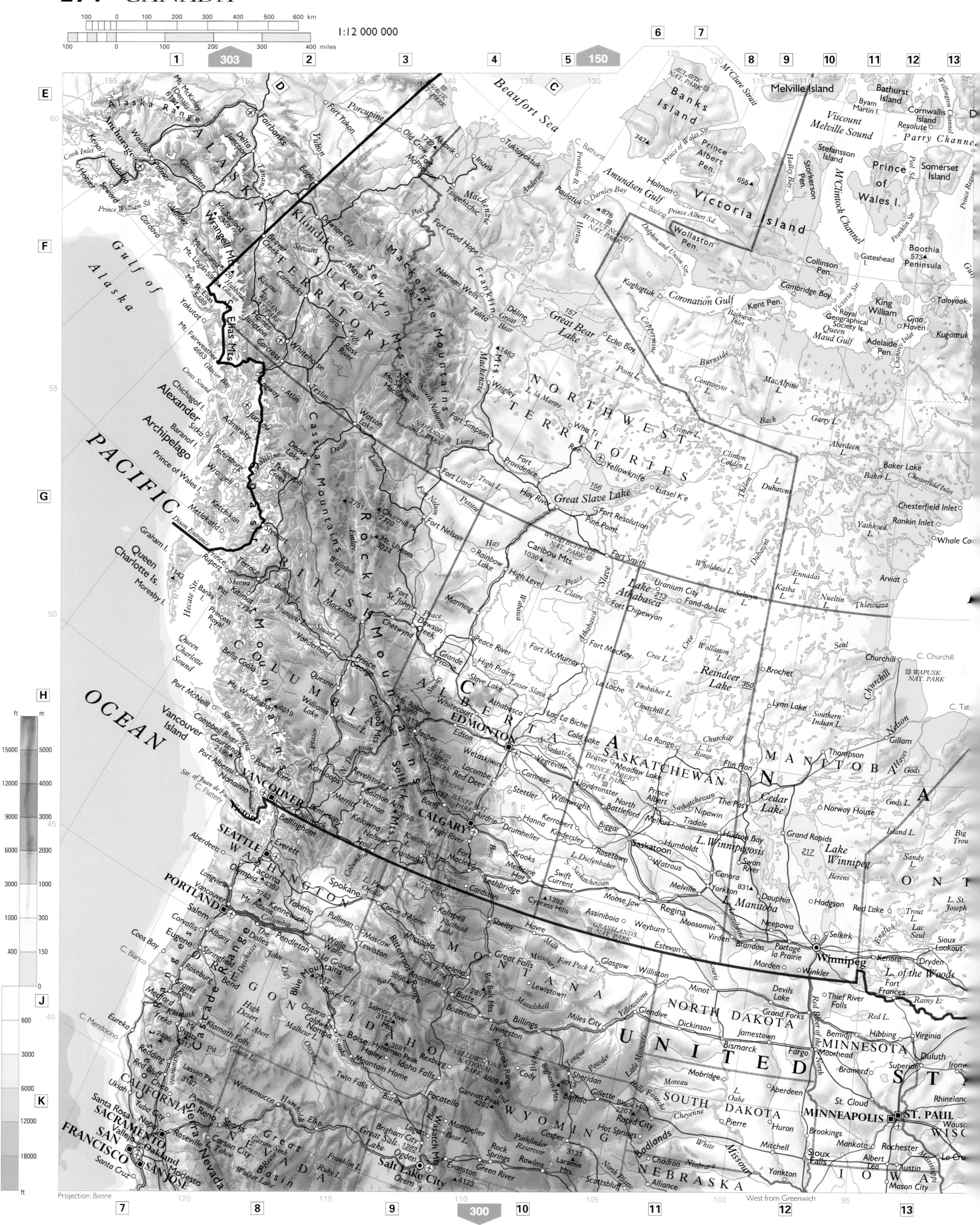

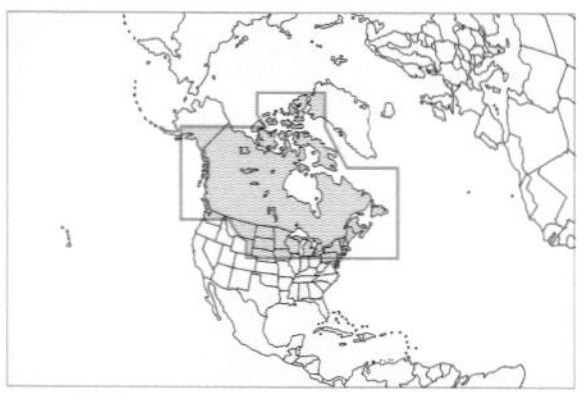

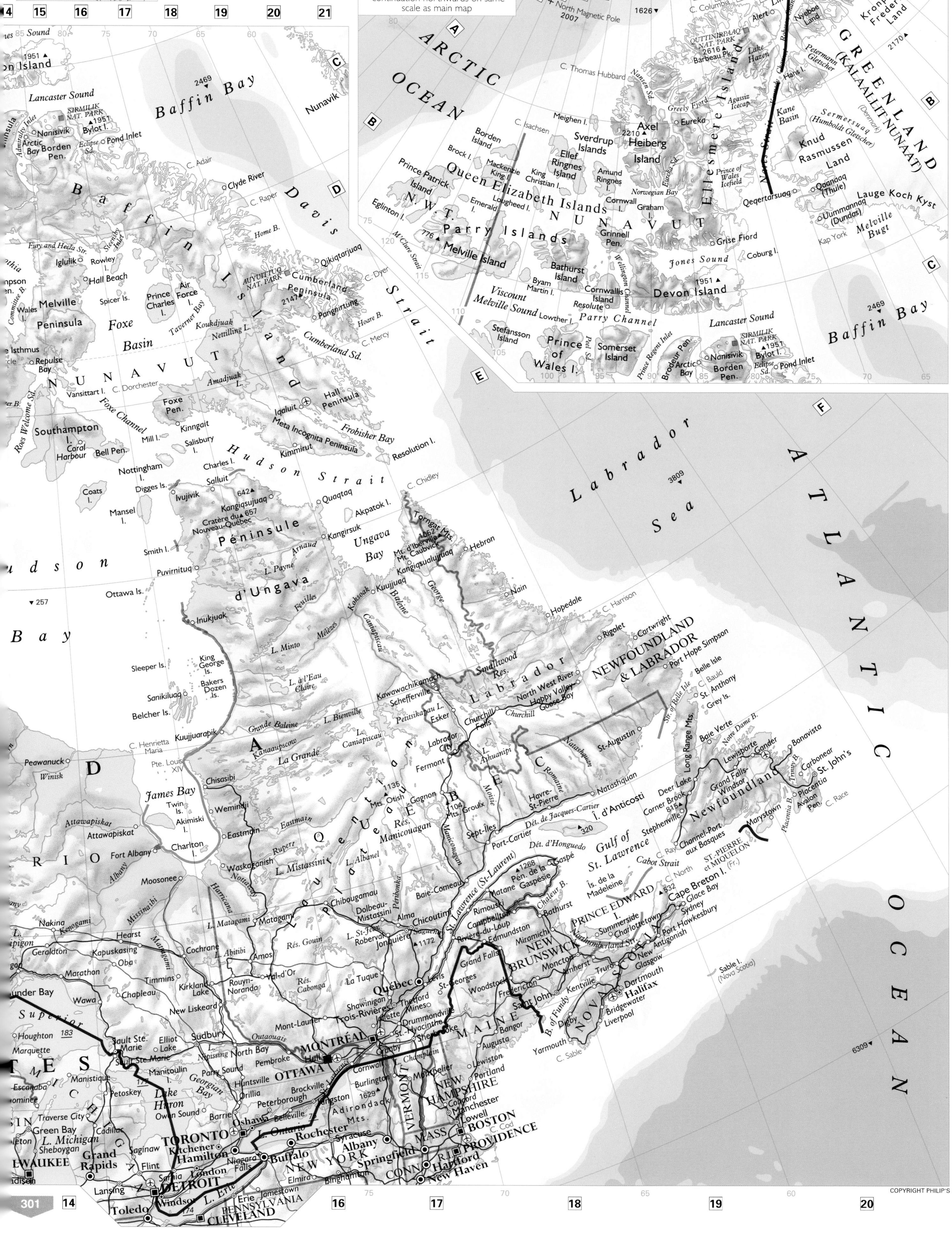
150
NORTHERN CANADA
continuation northwards on same scale as main map
ARCTIC OCEAN
North Magnetic Pole 2007
Queen Elizabeth Islands
N.W.T.
NUNAVUT
Parry Islands
Melville Island
Prince Patrick Island
Borden Island
Sverdrup Islands
Ellef Ringnes Island
Amund Ringnes I.
Axel Heiberg Island
Ellesmere Island
Eureka
Alert
QUTTINIRPAAQ NAT. PARK
Barbeau Pk. 2616
Lake Hazen
Greely Fiord
Agassiz Icecap
Cornwall I.
Grinnell Pen.
Grise Fiord
Jones Sound
Devon Island
Bathurst Island
Cornwallis Island
Resolute
Byam Martin I.
Wellington Channel
Parry Channel
Viscount Melville Sound
Lowther I.
Prince of Wales I.
Stefansson Island
Somerset Island
Peel Sd.
Prince Regent Inlet
Brodeur Pen.
Arctic Bay
Lancaster Sound
SIRMILIK NAT. PARK
Nanisivik
Borden Pen.
Bylot I.
Eclipse Sd.
Pond Inlet
Baffin Bay
GREENLAND (KALAALLIT NUNAAT) (Denmark)
Kronprins Frederik Land
Nyeboe Land
Petermann Gletscher
Hans I.
Kane Basin
Sermersuaq (Humboldt Gletscher)
Knud Rasmussen Land
Qaanaaq (Thule)
Qeqertarsuaq
Lauge Koch Kyst
Uummannaq (Dundas)
Kap York
Melville Bugt
Lincoln Sea
Coburg I.
Baffin Island
Davis Strait
Clyde River
Qikiqtarjuaq
Cumberland Peninsula
AUYUITTUQ NAT. PARK
Pangnirtung
Cumberland Sd.
Hall Peninsula
Iqaluit
Frobisher Bay
Meta Incognita Peninsula
Kimmirut
Resolution I.
Foxe Basin
Foxe Channel
Foxe Pen.
Kinngait
Prince Charles I.
Air Force I.
Igluligaarjuk
Iglulik
Hall Beach
Melville Peninsula
Repulse Bay
Southampton I.
Coral Harbour
Hudson Strait
Salluit
Ivujivik
Kangiqsujuaq
Quaqtaq
Péninsule d'Ungava
Ungava Bay
Kangirsuk
Kangiqsualujjuaq
Kuujjuaq
Torngat Mts.
Mt. Caubvick
Labrador Sea
3809
Hebron
Nain
Hopedale
Puvirnituq
Inukjuak
Hudson Bay
Ottawa Is.
Belcher Is.
Sanikiluaq
Kuujjuarapik
James Bay
Chisasibi
Akimiski I.
Charlton I.
Moosonee
Attawapiskat
Fort Albany
ONTARIO
QUÉBEC
Labrador
NEWFOUNDLAND & LABRADOR
Smallwood Res.
Churchill Falls
Happy Valley-Goose Bay
North West River
Cartwright
Port Hope Simpson
Schefferville
Labrador City
Fermont
L. Mistassini
Rés. Manicouagan
Sept-Îles
Port-Cartier
Havre-St-Pierre
Natashquan
Î. d'Anticosti
Gaspé
Pén. de la Gaspésie
Gulf of St. Lawrence
Newfoundland
St. Anthony
Deer Lake
Corner Brook
Stephenville
Gander
Grand Falls-Windsor
Bonavista
St. John's
Placentia
Marystown
Channel-Port aux Basques
ST-PIERRE et MIQUELON (Fr.)
Cabot Strait
Cape Breton I.
Sydney
Glace Bay
Îs. de la Madeleine
PRINCE EDWARD I.
Charlottetown
Summerside
NEW BRUNSWICK
Bathurst
Miramichi
Moncton
Fredericton
Saint John
Edmundston
B. of Fundy
NOVA SCOTIA
Halifax
Dartmouth
Truro
Amherst
Bridgewater
Liverpool
Yarmouth
Digby
Sable I. (Nova Scotia)
ATLANTIC OCEAN
Chicoutimi
Saguenay
Jonquière
Roberval
Rimouski
Rivière-du-Loup
Québec
Lévis
Trois-Rivières
Sherbrooke
MONTRÉAL
OTTAWA
Hull
Kingston
Belleville
Peterborough
TORONTO
Hamilton
Kitchener
London
Sarnia
DETROIT
Windsor
CLEVELAND
Toledo
Buffalo
Rochester
Syracuse
Albany
Springfield
Hartford
PROVIDENCE
BOSTON
NEW YORK
VERMONT
NEW HAMPSHIRE
MAINE
Augusta
Bangor
Portland
Lake Huron
Lake Superior
L. Michigan
L. Ontario
L. Erie
Sudbury
North Bay
Sault Ste. Marie
Timmins
Kapuskasing
Hearst
Rouyn-Noranda
Val-d'Or
Amos
Chibougamau
Thunder Bay
Marquette
Green Bay
Grand Rapids
Lansing
Flint
Saginaw
PENNSYLVANIA
MASS.
CONN.
R.I.
C. Cod
6309
COPYRIGHT PHILIP'S
301
154

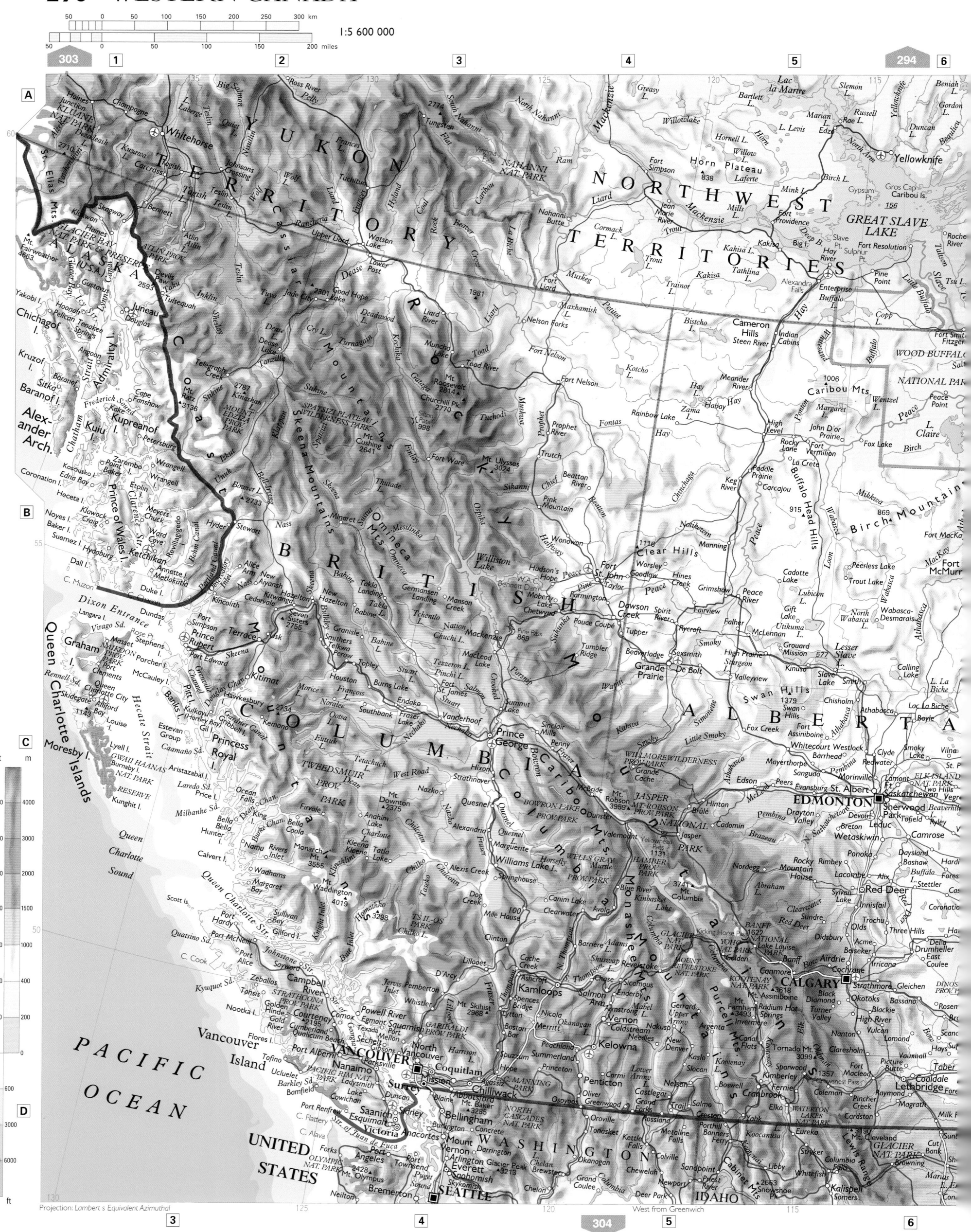

50   0   50   100   150   200   250   300 km

1:5 600 000

50   0   50   100   150   200 miles

Projection: Lambert's Equivalent Azimuthal

West from Greenwich

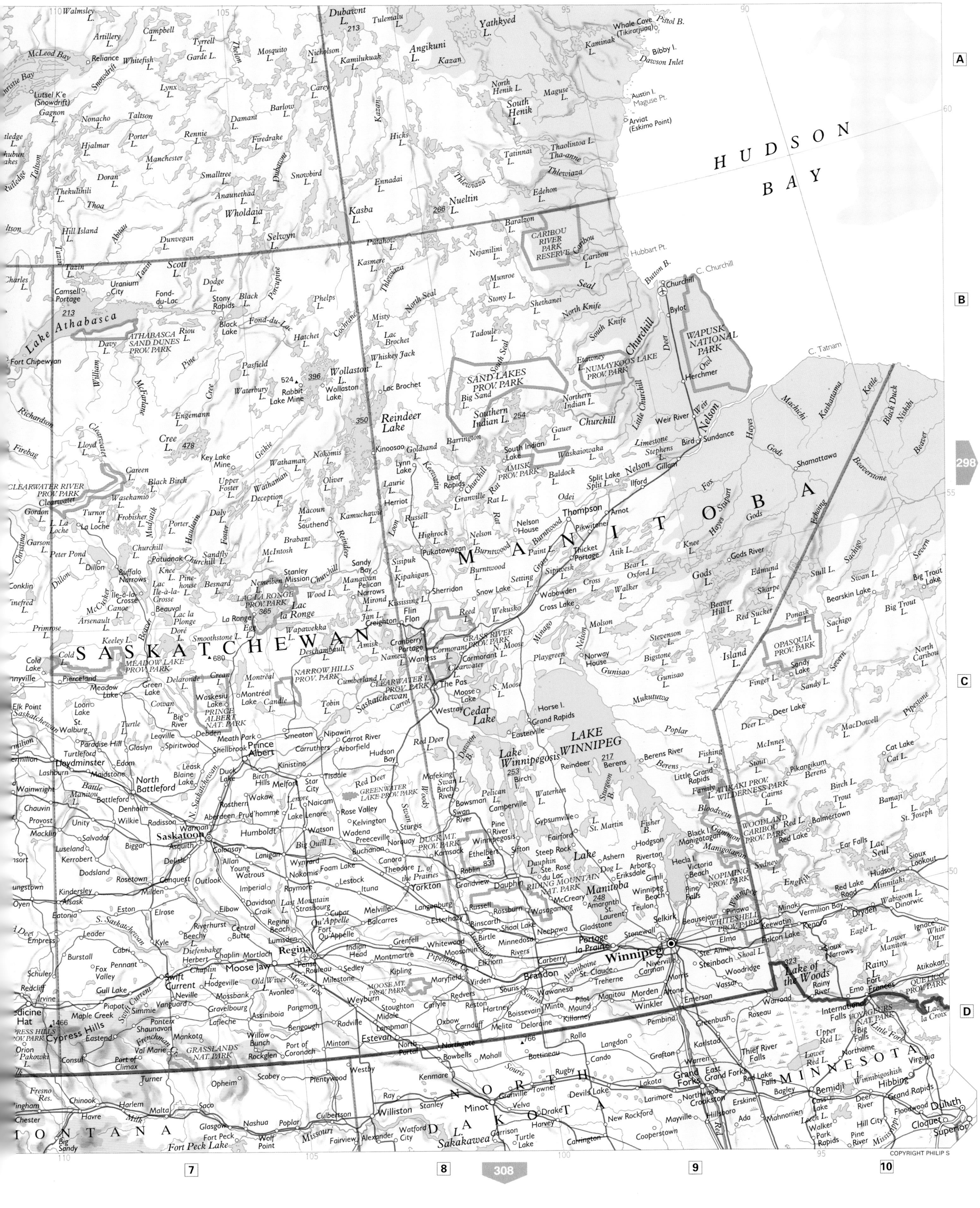

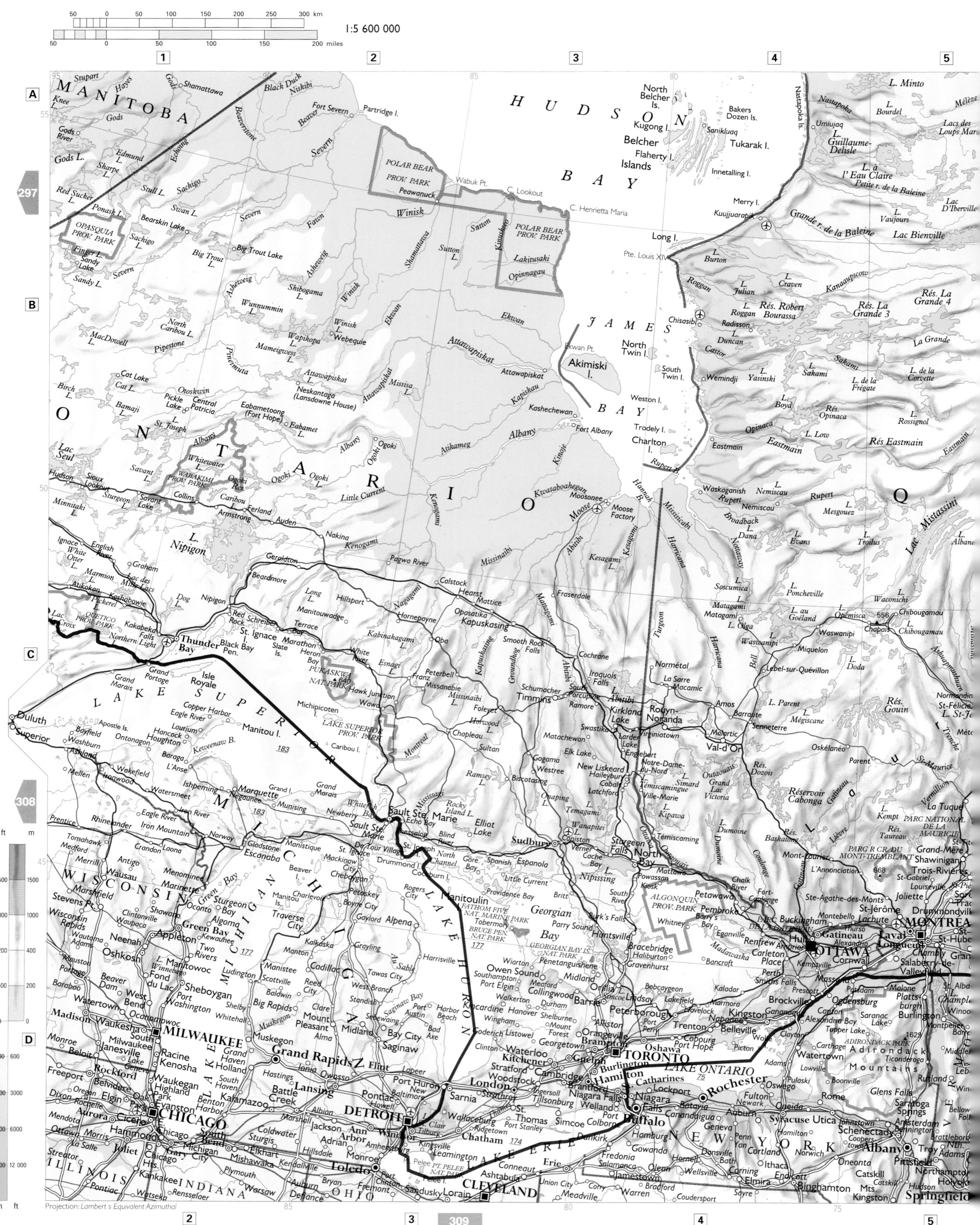

6 | **295** | **7** | **8** | **9**

A

L A B R A D O R

S E A

L. Le
Moyne

L. Nachicapau

L. Châteauguay

L. Chakonipau
Otelnuk

L. Wakuach

L. de la
Hutte
Sauvage

Fraser

George

L. de la
Hutte
Sauvage

Nain

South
Aulatsivik I.
Paul I.

Voisey B.

Kogaluc

Tunungayualok I.

Davis Inlet

Big Bay

Nunaksaluk I.

Hopedale

Kojoluk B.

Aillik

Makkovik

Adlavik
Is.

C. Harrison

55

60

B

L. Néret

Brisay

L. Sérigny

Mistastin
L.

Harp L.

Nipishish

Seal L.

Postville

Holton

Indian Harbour

Groswater
B.

North
River

Sandwich
B.

Cartwright

Table B.

Black Tickle
Island of Ponds

N E W F O U N D L A N D   &

L. Dalmas
Nitchequon

L. Baleine

Champdoré
L.

610

Attikamagen
L.

Kawawachikamach

Schefferville

Petitsikapau
L.

Menihek

Esker
Siding

Menihek
Lakes

Smallwood Reservoir

Churchill Falls

Twin Falls

Churchill

North West River

Goose

Happy Valley-
Goose Bay

Melville 1128

Mealy Mts.

Rigolet

Hamilton Inlet

L a b r a d o r

Paradise
River

Charlottetown

Alexis

Port Hope
Simpson

Square Islands

Williams Harbour

Battle Harbour

Lodge Bay

St. Louis

Mary's
Harbour

Red
Bay

Cook's H.

L'Anse aux Meadows

Belle Isle

St. Anthony

50

U

É

B

E

C

L. Nichicun

L. Naococane

Mts. Otish
1128

L. Opiscotéo

Labrador City

Fermont

Wabush

Shabogamo
L.

Emeril
Joseph

Atikonak
L.

L. Brûlé

Ashuanipi
L.

Natashquan

Winokapau
L.

Minipi
L.

Little Mécatina

St-Augustin

St-Paul

L'Anse
au Loup

Forteau

Lourdes-de-
Blanc-Sablon

St. Barbe

Rivière-
St-Paul

Str. of Belle Isle

L A B R A D O R

Hare B.

Grey

Roddickton

Englee

Groais I.

Bell I. Is.

N e w f o u n d l a n d

C

L. Plétipi

L. Manouane

L. Péribonka

Rés.
Manicouagan

Gagnon

Petit Lac
Manicouagan

1049

L. Magpie

St-Jean

L. Manitou

Nahishpi

L. Musquaro

Olomane

Petit-Mécatina

St-Augustin

I. du
Petit-Mécatina

Harrington Harbour

Daniel's
Harbour

Port au Choix

Hawke's Bay

Harbour
Deep

White B.

Horse Is.

Baie
Verte

La Scie

Notre Dame
B.

Jackson's
Arm

Springdale

South Brook

Lewisporte

Twillingate

Fogo I.

Musgrave Harbour

C. Freels

Funk I.

Long Range Mts.

GROS MORNE
NAT. PARK

Rocky Harbour

Norris Point

Trout River

Deer
Lake

Botwood

Bishop's
Falls

Glenwood

Grand Falls-
Windsor

Badger

Buchans

Gander L.

Gander

Glovertown

Bonavista

C. Bonavista

Catalina

TERRA NOVA
NAT. PARK

Trinity

Trinity B.

45

L. Péribonka

L. Pipmuacan

La Centrale
de la Péribonka

Forestville

Betsiamites

Baie-
Comeau

Chute-aux-
Outardes

Godbout

Baie-Trinité

Cap-Chat

Pte. des Monts

Pointe-
du-Lac

Mingan

Havre-St-Pierre

Sheldrake

Clarke
City

Moisie

Sept-Îles

Port-Cartier

Rivière-Pentecôte

Walker

Sainte-
Anne

Pte.
de l'Ouest

Port-Menier

Île d'Anticosti

320

Pte. Heath

Dét. de Jacques-Cartier

R.S. DE PARC NAT. DE
L'ARCHIPEL-DE-MINGAN

Natashquan

Kegaska

La Romaine

Aguanish

B. of Islands

Pasadena

Corner Brook

814

Port au Port

Port au Port
B.

Stephenville

St. George's

St. George's B.

Long Range Mts.

Red Indian
L.

L. Maelpaeg

Victoria L.

Jeddore L.

Port Blandford

Clarenville

Hearts Content

Carbonear

Bay
Roberts

Heart's
Content

Old Perlican

Conception B.

Torbay

St. John's

Mt
Pearl

376

Mistaribi

Ste-
Marguerite

Manicouagan

Outardes

Bersimis

Rés.
Pipmuacan

Péribonka

Alma

Chicoutimi

Jonquière

La Baie

Saguenay

Les
Escoumins

St-Siméon

La Malbaie

Tadoussac

Rimouski

Le Bic

Trois-Pistoles

Matane

Sayabec

Amqui

Causapscal

Mont-Joli

Matapédia

New
Richmond

Percé

Bonaventure

Miscou I.

Shippagan

Lamèque

Tracadie

Caraquet

Bathurst

Chaleur Bay

Î. Brion

Îs. de la
Madeleine
(Québec)

Grande-Entrée

Cap-aux-Meules

Havre-Aubert

Îs. de la
Fatima

St. Paul I.

Cape North

Cabot Strait

Grande-
Vallée

Mont-Louis

Ste-Anne-
des-Monts

Mt-Jacques-
Cartier 1268

PARC DE
GASPÉSIE

Mts. Chic-Chocs

Pén. de la Gaspésie

Gaspé

PARC NAT. DE
FORILLON

C. de Gaspé

Dét. d'Honguedo

Grande-Rivière

Chandler

GULF OF

ST. LAWRENCE

572

Cape St. George

C. St. George

St. David's

South Branch

Great Codroy

St. Andrew's

Codroy

Granite L.

Burgeo

François

Rose Blanche

Île aux Morts

Channel-Port
aux Basques

St. Alban's

Belleoram

Harbour
Breton

Fortune B.

Terrenceville

Marystown

Grand
Bank

Fortune

Miquelon

St-Pierre

ST-PIERRE-
ET-MIQUELON
(France)

St. Lawrence

Burin

Placentia B.

Argentia

Placentia

St.
Bride's

Trepassey

Holyrood

Avalon
Peninsula

Ferryland

C. St. Mary's

C. Race

C. Freels

50

D

ATLANTIC

OCEAN

Sable I.
(Nova Scotia)

PARC DES
GRANDS-JARDINS

PARC PROV.
DE LA
JACQUES-
CARTIER

1166

Beaupré

Î. d'Orléans

Québec

Lévis

Charny

Montmagny

St-
Pambile

Rivière-du-Loup

Cabano

Dégelis

Edmundston

St-Jean-Port-Joli

La Pocatière

St-Pascal

Grand Falls

Van Buren

St. Léonard 820

Eagle
Lake

Caribou

Presque Isle

Mt. Carleton

Plaster
Rock

Perth-Andover

Kedgwick

St-Quentin

Atholville

Campbellton

Dalhousie

Nepisiguit

Miramichi R.

Newcastle

Miramichi

Rogersville

N E W

B R U N S W I C K

KOUCHIBOUGUAC
NAT. PARK

Richibucto

Bouctouche

Shediac

Moncton

PRINCE EDWARD
ISLAND

Tignish

North Cape

Alberton

North Point

Kensington

Summerside

St.
Peters

Souris

East Pt.

Pleasant Bay

Ingonish

CAPE BRETON
HIGHLANDS
NAT. PARK

532

Chéticamp

Cheticamp

Inverness

Cape North

St. Ann's B.

N. Sydney

Sydney Mines

Glace Bay

New Waterford

Sydney

Louisbourg

Cape Breton
Island

Bras d'Or

St. Peters

Charlottetown

Georgetown

Port
Hood

Port
Hawkesbury

Î. Madame

Chedabucto B.

Canso

St-Georges

Lac-
Mégantic L.

Mooselook-
meguntic L.

Jackman

Mooshead
L.

1605

Millinocket

Fredericton
Junction

Fredericton

Oromocto

Grand L.

Chipman

Minto

Petitcodiac

Sussex

Sackville

Amherst

Springhill

Parrsboro

Minas Basin

Truro

New Glasgow

Stellarton

Pictou

Antigonish

Mulgrave

Sherbrooke

Upper
Musquodoboit

Stewiacke

Enfield

Musquodoboit Harbour

Sheet Harbour

Dartmouth

Halifax

Greenville

Lincoln

St. John

Woodstock

Chamberlain
L.

Chesuncook
L.

Patten

Houlton

Hartland

Chipman

N O V A   S C O T I A

Kentville

Windsor

Middleton

Annapolis
Royal

Bridgetown

Digby

Weymouth

Yarmouth

Wedgeport

Clark's Harbour

C. Sable

Shelburne

Liverpool

Lockeport

KEJIMKUJIK
NAT. PARK

Rossignol

Milton

Bridgewater

Lunenburg

Mahone Bay

L. Rossignol

St. Marys Bay

St. Marys

M A I N E

Bangor

Brewer

Old Town

Skowhegan

Waterville

Belfast

Bar Harbor

Ellsworth

Mount
Desert I.

Camden

Rockland

Bath

Brunswick

Portland

Saco

Biddeford

Berlin

Rumford

Norway

Auburn

Lewiston

Augusta

Bingham

U N I T E D

S T A T E S

West from Greenwich

N E W

H A M P S H I R E

Conway

Hanover

Laconia

Sanford

Rochester

Dover

Concord

Portsmouth

Newport

Island
Pond

St.
Johnsbury

Keene

Nashua

Manchester

Haverhill

Lawrence

Lowell

Lynn

BOSTON

Quincy

Newton

Brockton

Worcester

Woonsocket

Cape Cod

70

65

60

COPYRIGHT PHILIP'S

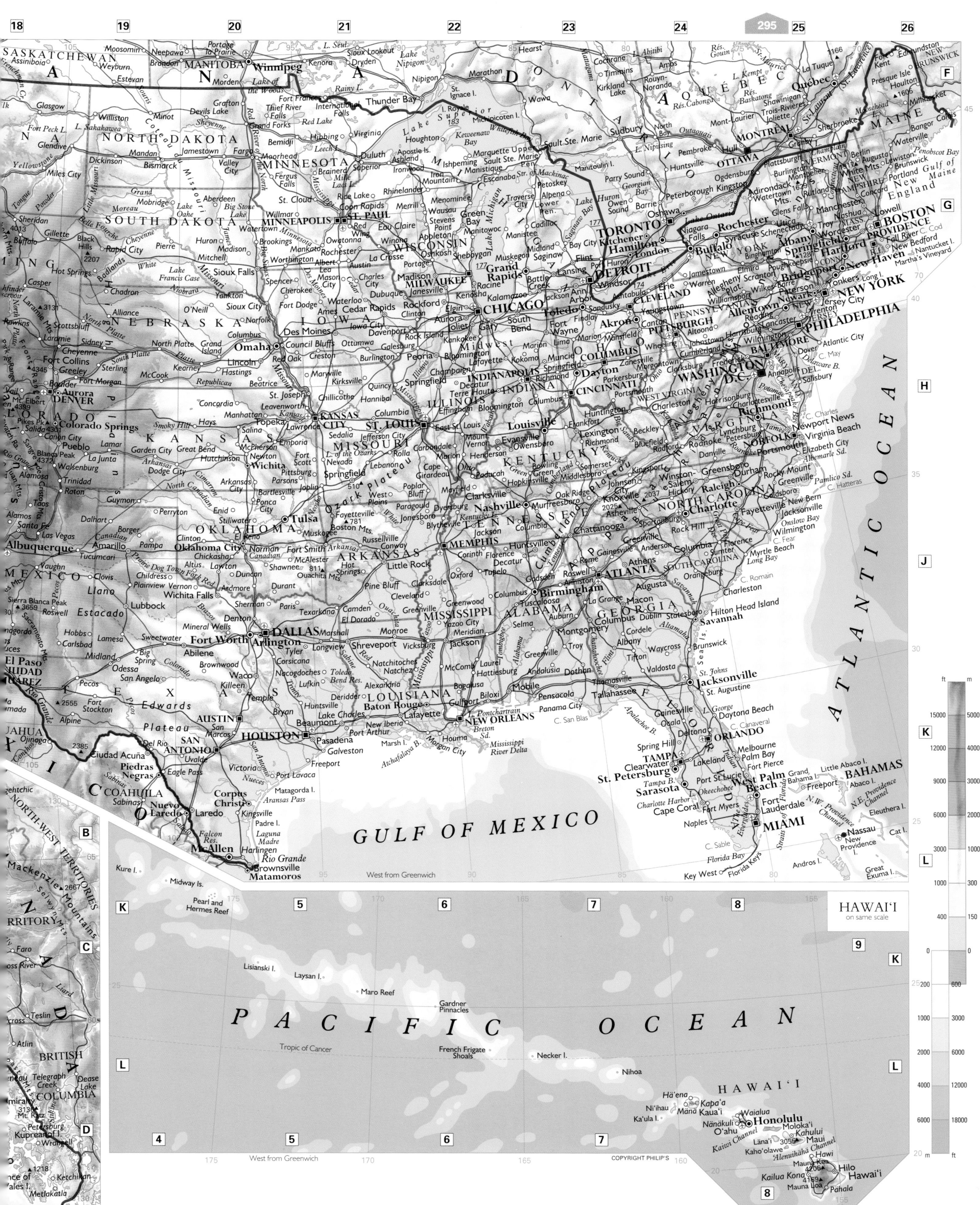

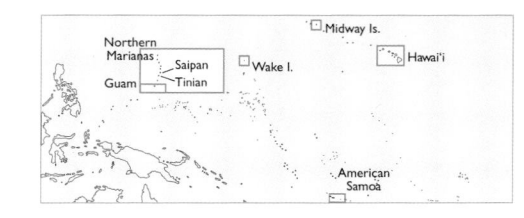

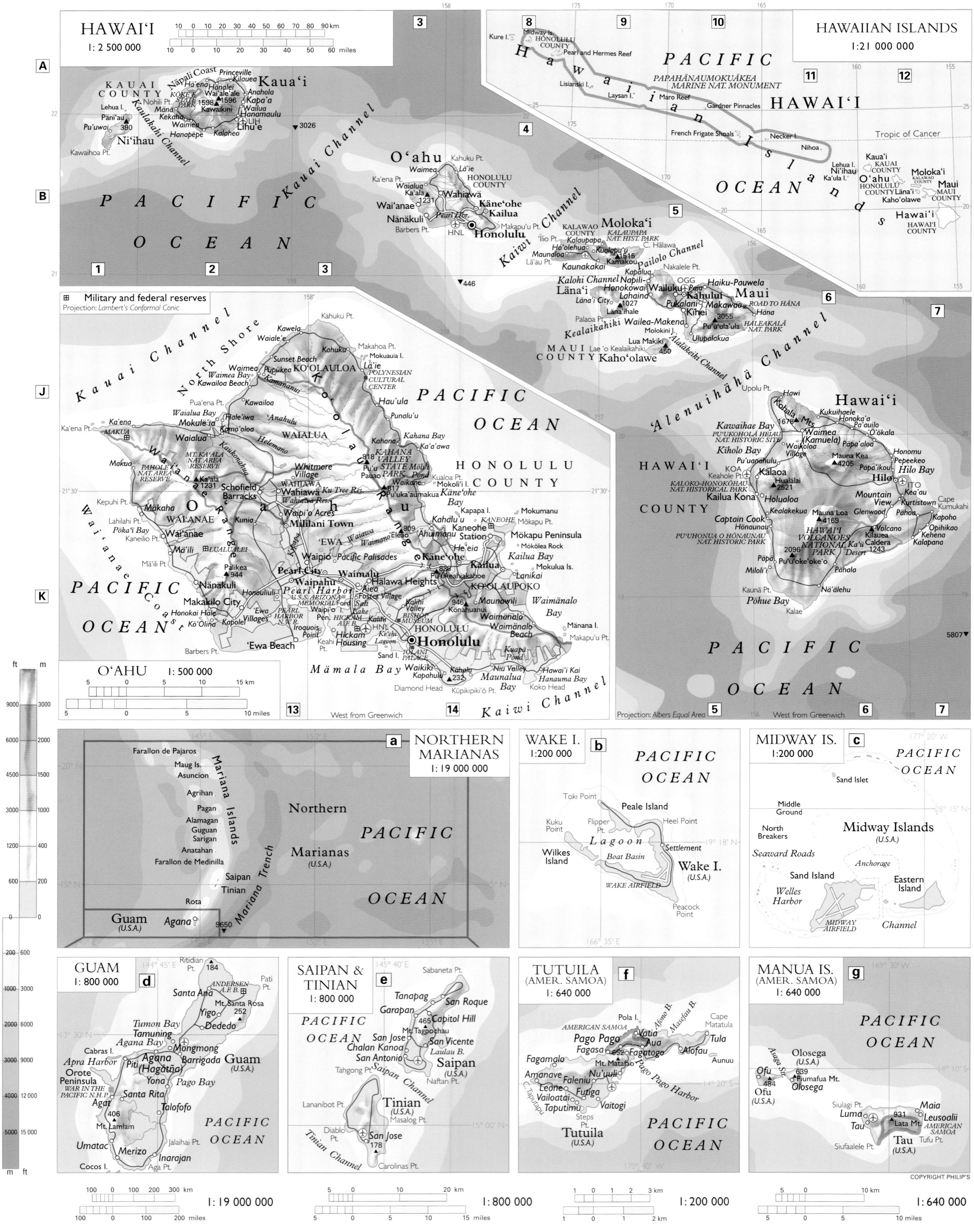

HAWAI'I
1: 2 500 000

10 0 10 20 30 40 50 60 70 80 90 km
10 0   10   20   30   40   50   60 miles

KAUAI COUNTY
Nāpali Coast Princeville Kilauea
Hā'ena Hanalei
Nohili Pt. Māna KŌKE'E Wai'ale'ale Anahola Kaua'i
Lehua I. Kekaha 1596 Kapa'a
Pāni'au Waimea Kawaikini Wailua Kanamaulu
Pu'uwai 390 Kalaheo Līhu'e
Ni'ihau Hanapēpē ▼3026
Kawaihoa Pt.

PACIFIC OCEAN

Kaunakahiki Channel
Kauai Channel

O'ahu
Kahuku Pt.
Waimea Lā'ie
Ka'ena Pt. HONOLULU COUNTY
Waialua Ka'a'la Wahiawā
Wai'anae 1231 Kāne'ohe
Nānākuli Kailua
Barbers Pt. Pearl Hbr. Honolulu
HNL

Kaiwi Channel

HAWAIIAN ISLANDS
1:21 000 000

Kure I. Midway Is. HONOLULU COUNTY
Pearl and Hermes Reef
Lisianski I. Laysan I. Maro Reef
Gardner Pinnacles
French Frigate Shoals Necker I.
Maro Reef Nihoa Tropic of Cancer

PACIFIC HAWAI'I OCEAN
PAPAHĀNAUMOKUĀKEA MARINE NAT. MONUMENT

Hawaiian Islands

Lehua I. Kaua'i KAUAI COUNTY
Ni'ihau Ka'ula I. O'ahu HONOLULU COUNTY Moloka'i
Kaho'olawe Lāna'i Maui MAUI COUNTY
Hawai'i HAWAI'I COUNTY

KALAWAO COUNTY Moloka'i
Kalaupapa KALAUPAPA NAT. HIST. PARK
Kalae 'Ilio Pt. Kaluako'i Ho'olehua C. Hālawa
Maunaloa Kaunakakai Nakalele Pt.
Lā'au Pt. Kapalua Pailolo Channel
Kalohi Channel Napili- Honokōwai Wailuku Pāʻia Haiku-Pāuwela
Lāna'i Lāhainā Kahului ROAD TO HĀNA
Lāna'i City 1027 Pukalani Makawao Hāna
Palaoa Pt. Kīhei ▲3055
Kealaikahiki Channel Wailea-Makena HALEAKALĀ NAT. PARK
Lua Makiki Ulupalakua 450
'Alalākeiki Channel
MAUI COUNTY Lae'o Kealaikahiki Kaho'olawe

'Alenuihāhā Channel

Hawai'i
Kohala Mts. 6764 ▲ Kukuihaele Honoka'a Pa'auilo
Kawaihae Bay Waimea (Kamuela) Papa'aloa
PU'UKOHOLĀ HEIAU NAT. HISTORIC SITE 2521 Papa'ikou Honomū Pepeekeo
Kīholo Bay Pu'uapanulu Mauna Kea ▲4205 Hilo Bay
KOA Kalaoa Hualālai Hilo ITO
Keahole Pt. Kailua Kona Holualoa Kurtistown Kea'au
KALOKO-HONOKŌHAU NAT. HISTORICAL PARK Mountain View Glenwood
HAWAI'I COUNTY Kealakekua Mauna Loa Pāhoa
Captain Cook ▲4169 Pōhakuloa Volcano Kapoho
Hōnaunau HAWAI'I VOLCANOES NATIONAL PARK Kīlauea Caldera Kehena Kalapana
PU'UHONUA O HŌNAUNAU NAT HISTORIC PARK 2096 1243
Pāpā Pu'u 'oke'oke'o Pāhala
Miloli'i Kaunā Pt.
Pōhue Bay Nā'ālehu
Kalae

PACIFIC OCEAN 5807 ▼

O'AHU
1: 500 000

5 0 5 10 15 km
5 0   5   10 miles

Kahuku Pt.
Kawela
Kauai Channel North Shore KO'OLAULOA Kahuku
Waiale'e Makahoa Pt. Mokuauia I. Lā'ie POLYNESIAN CULTURAL CENTER
Sunset Beach Pūpūkea Hau'ula
Waimea Bay Kamananui 'Anahulu Punalu'u
Kawailoa Beach Pua'ena Pt. Hale'iwa Kahana Bay
Ka'ena Ka'ena Pt. MAKUA Kawailoa Kahana Ka'a'awa
MT. KA'ALA NAT. AREA RESERVE Helemano KAHANA VALLEY STATE PARK
Waialua Bay Mōkulē'ia Komo'oloa 818 Kualoa Pt.
Waialua WAIALUA Whitmore Village Pu'u Pauao Waikāne Mokumanu
Makua Pu'uka'aumakua Kapapa I. Kāne'ohe Bay
PAHOLE NAT. AREA RESERVE Ka'ala 1231 WAHIAWĀ Ku Tree Res. Kāne'ohe Mōkapu Peninsula
Mākaha Schofield Barracks Wahiawā Kahalu'u Mōkōlea Rock
Wai'anae Wahiawā Res. Waipi'o Acres KANEOHE He'eia
WAI'ANAE Kunia Mililani Town MARINE STATION Kailua Bay
Mā'ili Waikele Kaneohe Kailua Lanikai
Pōkā'i Bay Kaneili Waipi'o 'EWA Waimano 'Aikahi Mokulua Is.
Mā'ili Pt. LUALUALEI 944 Palikea Pacific Palisades Manana I.
Nānākuli Waipio Pearl City Waimalu KO'OLAUPOKO
Makakilo City Waipahu Halawa Heights Waimānalo
Honokai Hale Pearl Harbor Foster Village 946 Maunawili Waimānalo Bay
Kapolei U.S.S. ARIZONA MEMORIAL Ford Salt BISHOP MUSEUM Konahuanui Waimānalo Beach
Kō 'Ōlina 'Ewa Villages Ford I. Kalihi Valley Manana I.
'Ewa Beach HICKAM A.F.B. Kahili Ka'elepulu Makapu'u Pt.
Barbers Pt. Iroquois Point Keahi Housing ʻIOLANI PALACE Kuapā Pond
Sand I. Honolulu Hawai'i Kai Koko Head
Māmala Bay Lagoon Waikīkī Kahala Niu Valley Hanauma Bay
Diamond Head Maunalua Bay
Kūpikipiki'ō Pt. Kaiwi Channel

West from Greenwich
West from Greenwich

Projection: Albers Equal Area

⊞ Military and federal reserves
Projection: Lambert's Conformal Conic

NORTHERN MARIANAS
1:19 000 000

Farallon de Pajaros
Maug Is.
Asuncion
Agrihan
Pagan
Alamagan Mariana Islands
Guguan
Sarigan
Anatahan
Farallon de Medinilla
Saipan Northern Marianas (U.S.A.)
Tinian
Rota
Guam (U.S.A.) Agana 9650 ▼ Mariana Trench

PACIFIC OCEAN

WAKE I.
1:200 000

PACIFIC OCEAN
Toki Point
Peale Island
Kuku Flipper Heel Point
Point Pt.
Wilkes Lagoon Settlement
Island Boat Basin Wake I. (U.S.A.)
WAKE AIRFIELD
Peacock Point

MIDWAY IS.
1:200 000

PACIFIC OCEAN
Sand Islet
Middle Ground
North Breakers Midway Islands (U.S.A.)
Seaward Roads Anchorage
Welles Harbor Sand Island Eastern Island
MIDWAY AIRFIELD Channel

GUAM
1: 800 000

Ritidian Pt. 184
ANDERSEN A.F.B. ⊞ Pati Pt.
Santa Ana Mt. Santa Rosa 252
Yigo Dededo
Tumon Bay Tamuning
Agana Bay Mongmong
Cabras I. Barrigada Guam (U.S.A.)
Apra Harbor Agana (Hagåtña)
Orote Piti Yona Pago Bay
Peninsula WAR IN THE PACIFIC N.H.P. Santa Rita
Agat 406 Talofofo
Umatac Mt. Lamlam Inarajan
Cocos I. Merizo Aga Pt.

PACIFIC OCEAN

SAIPAN & TINIAN
1: 800 000

Sabaneta Pt.
Tanapag San Roque
Garapan Capitol Hill
PACIFIC OCEAN 465 Mt. Tagpochau San Vicente
San Jose Laulau B.
Chalan Kanoa Saipan (U.S.A.)
San Antonio
Tahgong Pt. Saipan Channel
Lananibot Pt. Tinian (U.S.A.)
Diablo Tinian
San Jose 178
Tinian Channel Carolinas Pt.
Masalog Pt.

TUTUILA
(AMER. SAMOA)
1: 640 000

Pola I. Afono B. Masefau B.
AMERICAN SAMOA Vatia Cape Matatula
Pago Pago Aua Tula
Fagasa 652 Fagatogo Alofau
Fagamalo Mt. Matafao Aunuu
Amanave Nu'uuli Pago Pago Harbor
Leone Faleniu Futiga
Vailoatai Taputimu Vaitogi
Steps
Tutuila (U.S.A.) Siufaalele Pt.

PACIFIC OCEAN

MANUA IS.
(AMER. SAMOA)
1: 640 000

PACIFIC OCEAN
Asaga St. Olosega (U.S.A.)
Ofu 639 Piumafua Mt.
484 Olosega
Ofu (U.S.A.)
Siulagi Pt. Maia
Luma 931 Leusoalii
Tau Lata Mt. AMERICAN SAMOA
Tau (U.S.A.) Tufu Pt.

COPYRIGHT PHILIP'S

---

ft m
9000 3000
6000 2000
4500 1500
3000 1000
1200 400
600 200
0 0
200 600
1000 3000
2000 6000
3000 9000
4000 12 000
5000 15 000
m ft

1: 19 000 000
100 0 100 200 300 km
100 0   100   200 miles

1: 800 000
5 0 5 10 15 20 km
5 0   5   10   15 miles

1: 200 000
1 0 1 2 3 km
1 0   1   2 km

1: 640 000
5 0 5 10 km
5 0   5   10 miles

1:8 000 000

50   0   100   200   300   400 km

50   0   50   100   150   200   250 miles

continuation westwards
on same scale

294
296
215

West from Greenwich
East from Greenwich
West from Greenwich

1 ANCHORAGE
2 BRISTOL BAY
3 HAINES
4 SKAGWAY-HOONAH-
ANGOON
5 KETCHIKAN
GATEWAY

Projection: Bipolar oblique conic conformal

ARCTIC OCEAN

BEAUFORT SEA

CHUKCHI SEA

RUSSIA

CANADA

NORTH WEST TERRITORIES

YUKON TERRITORY

BRITISH COLUMBIA

BERING SEA

PACIFIC OCEAN

Gulf of Alaska

Aleutian Islands

Alexander Archipelago

A L A S K A
(U.S.A.)

Brooks Range

Alaska Range

Kodiak I.

ft   m
18 000   6000
12 000   4000
9000   3000
6000   2000
4500   1500
3000   1000
1500   600
600   200
0   0
200   600
4000   1200
6000   2000
12 000   4000
18 000   6000   ft   m

1:5 360 000

1:2 000 000

WESTERN WASHINGTON REGION
on same scale

PACIFIC OCEAN

BRITISH COLUMBIA
CANADA
Vancouver Island
Strait of Georgia
Strait of Juan de Fuca
VANCOUVER

WASHINGTON
SEATTLE
Olympic Mountains
OLYMPIC NATIONAL PARK
Mt. Olympus 2428
Mt. Rainier 4392
MT. RAINIER NAT. PARK
MT. ST. HELENS NATIONAL VOLCANIC MONUMENT
Mt. St. Helens 2550
OREGON
PORTLAND

Pahute Mesa
Inyo Mts.
White Mts.
DEATH VALLEY

Sierra Nevada
Lake Tahoe
SAN FRANCISCO
SACRAMENTO
SAN JOSE
Fresno
Reno
Carson City
YOSEMITE NATIONAL PARK
KINGS CANYON NAT. PARK
SEQUOIA NATIONAL PARK
Mt. Whitney 4418

Sacramento Valley
San Joaquin Valley
Santa Clara Valley
Salinas Valley
Santa Lucia Range
Diablo Range

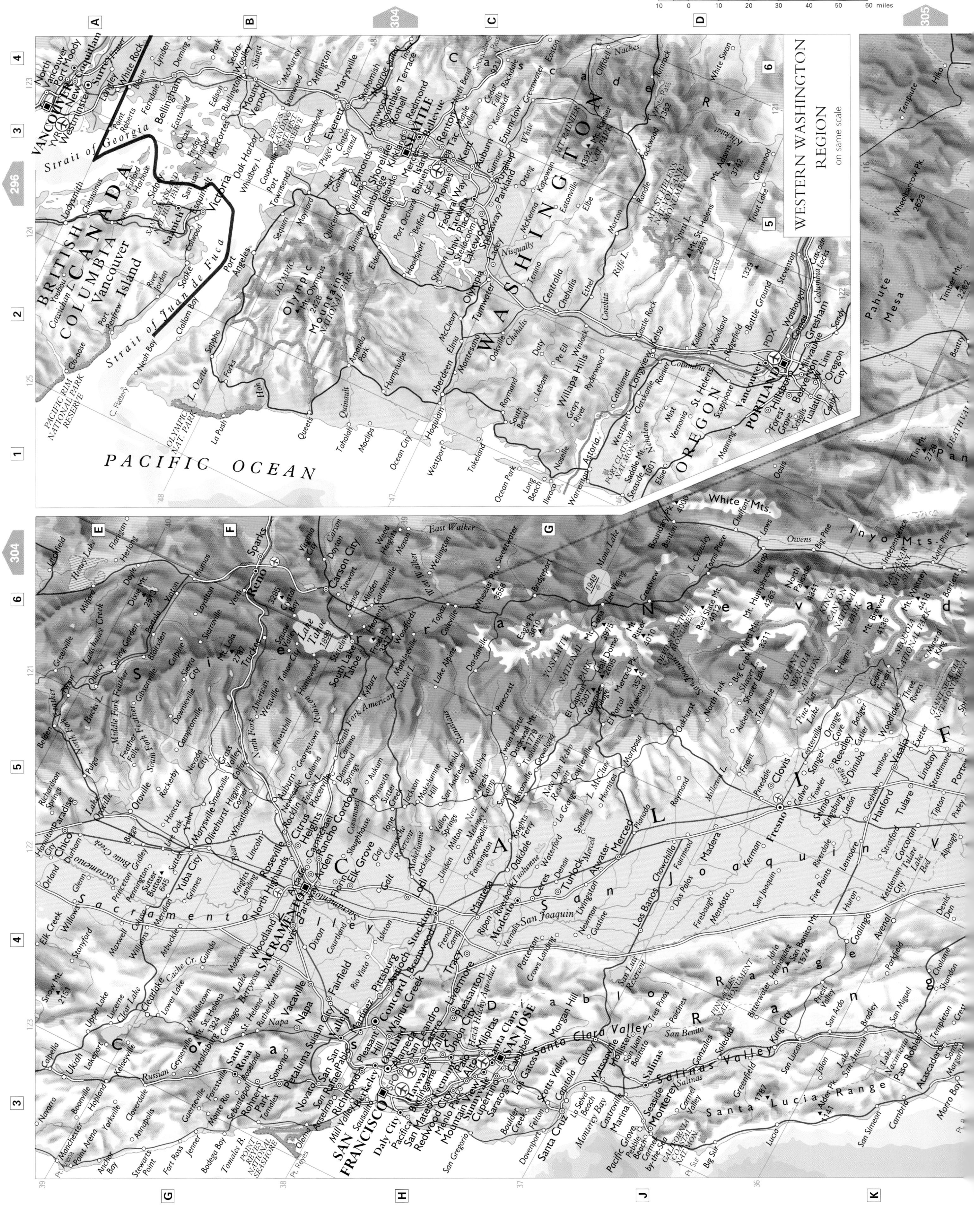

318

Lava fields

West from Greenwich

Projection: Bonne

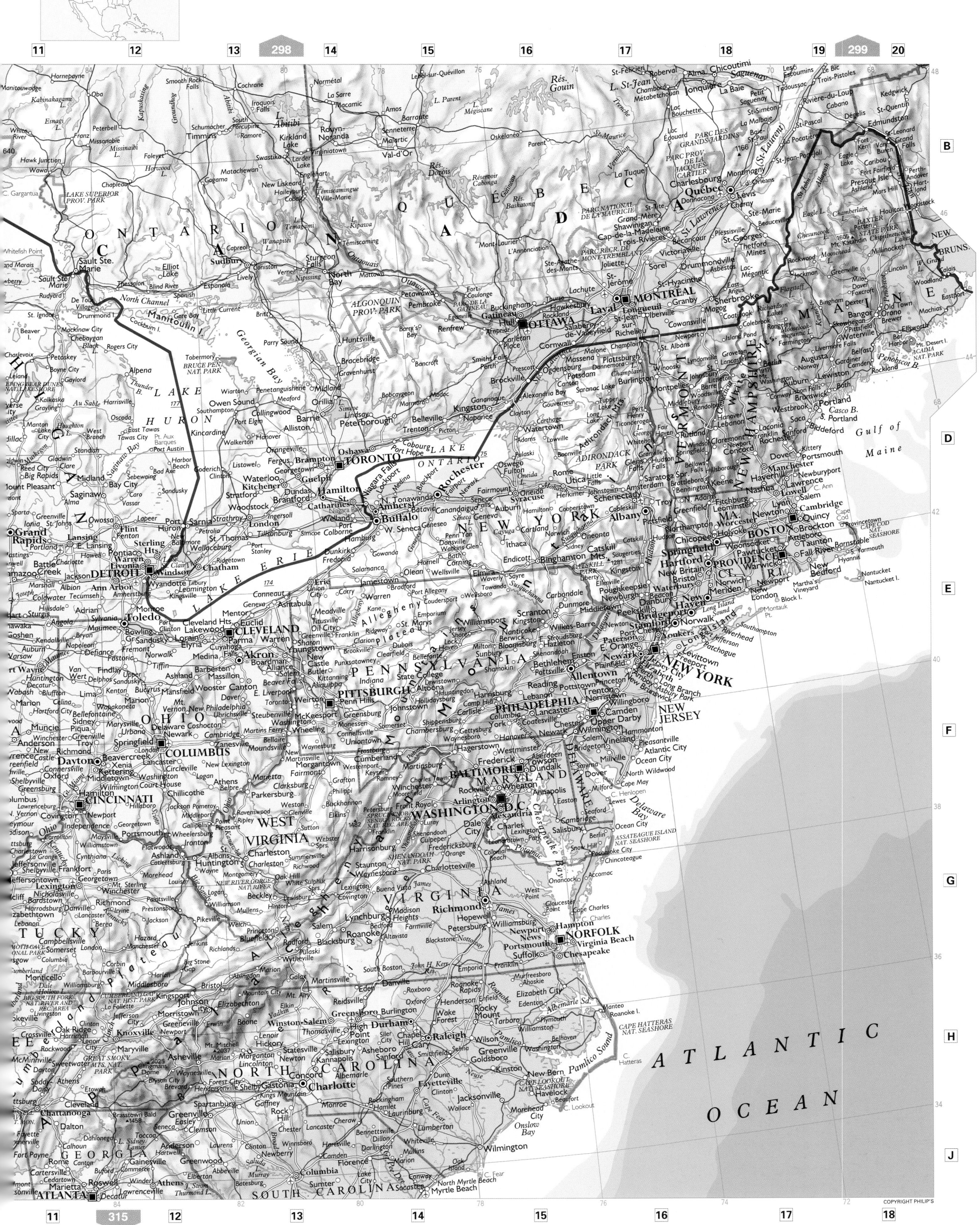

1:2 000 000

Projection: Bonne

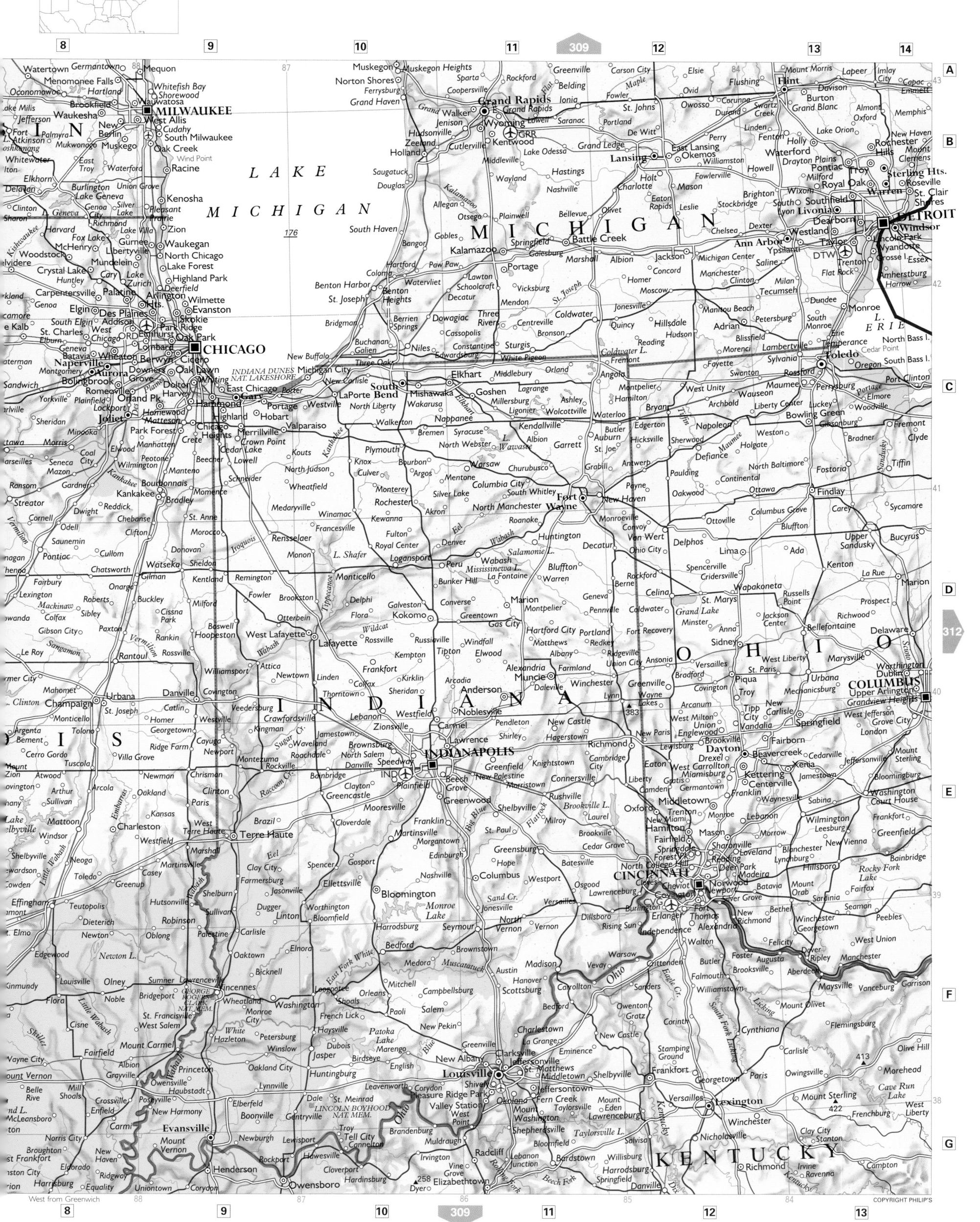

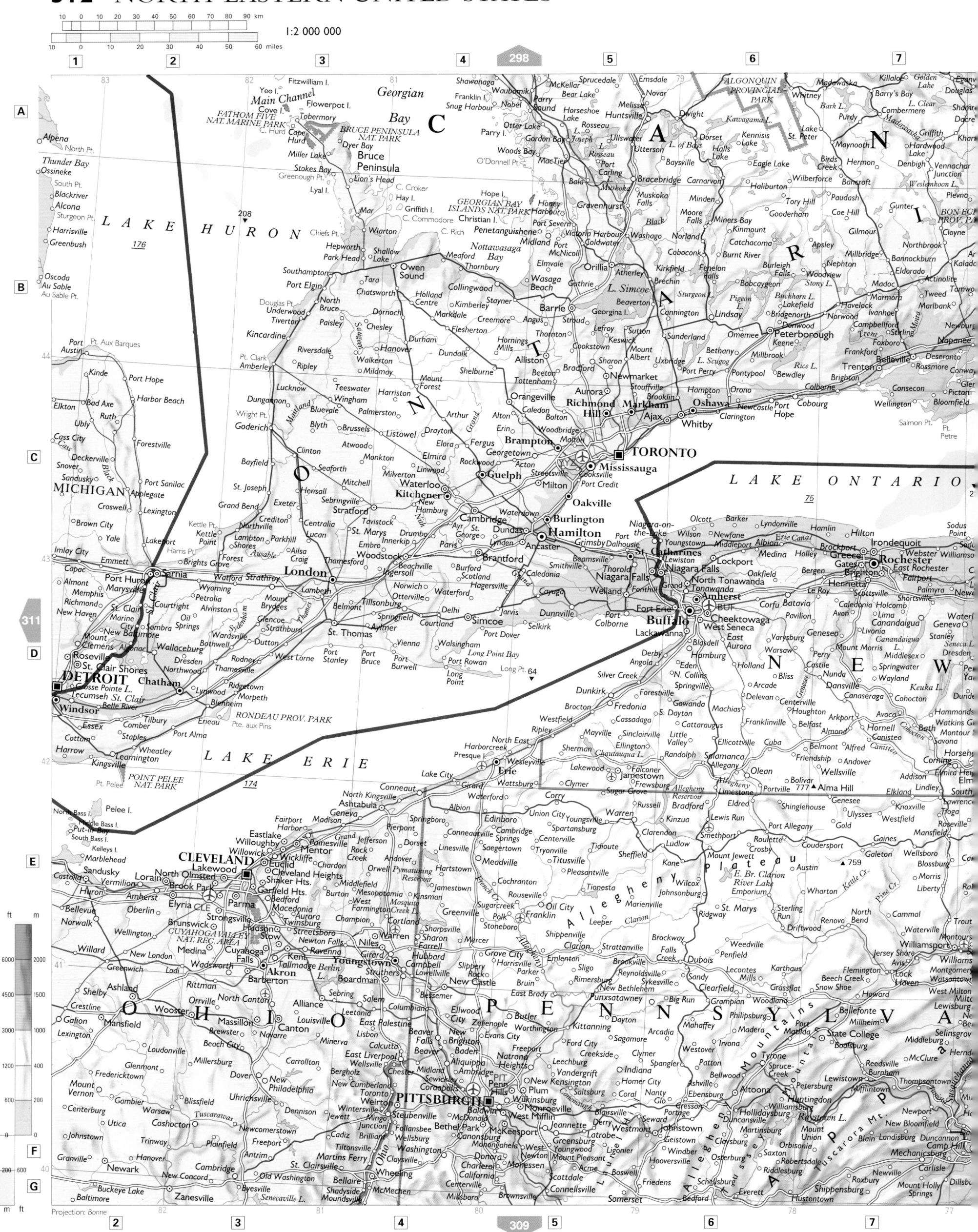

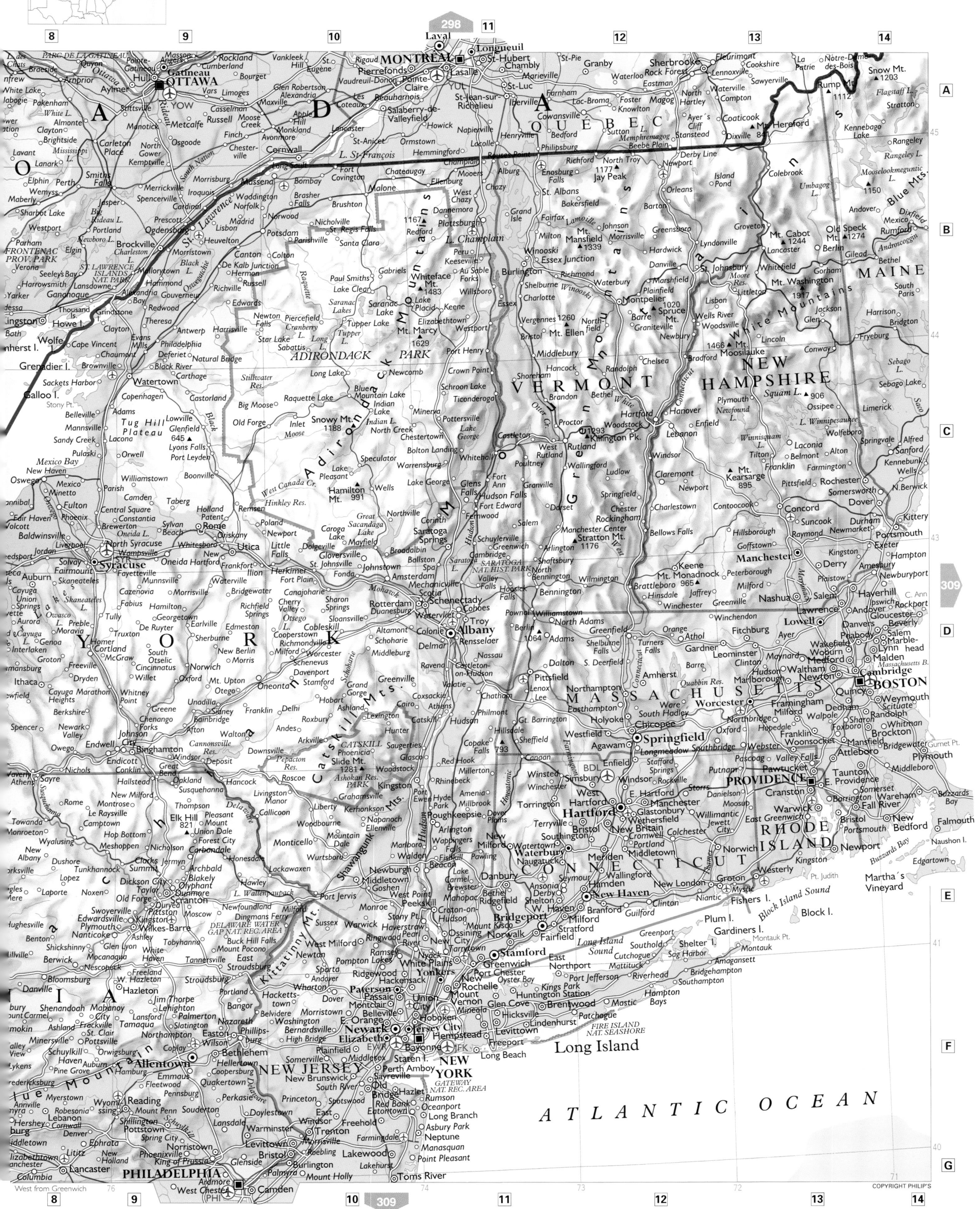

ILLINOIS
INDIANA
OHIO
PENNSYLVANIA
MARYLAND
DELAWARE
WEST VIRGINIA
VIRGINIA
KENTUCKY
TENNESSEE
NORTH CAROLINA
SOUTH CAROLINA
GEORGIA
ALABAMA
MISSISSIPPI
FLORIDA
BAHAMAS
ATLANTIC OCEAN
OF MEXICO
PITTSBURGH
PHILADELPHIA
BALTIMORE
WASHINGTON D.C.
COLUMBUS
INDIANAPOLIS
CINCINNATI
NORFOLK
MEMPHIS
ATLANTA
NEW ORLEANS
ORLANDO
TAMPA
MIAMI
Nashville
Louisville
Charlotte
Richmond
Birmingham
Jacksonville
Chattanooga
Knoxville
Montgomery
Savannah
Charleston
Tallahassee
Jackson
Columbia
Raleigh
Lexington
Huntsville
Augusta
Mobile
West Palm Beach
Fort Lauderdale
St. Petersburg
Sarasota
Nassau
Cumberland Plateau
Appalachian Mts.
Blue Ridge
Okefenokee Swamp
Lake Okeechobee
Florida Bay
Florida Keys
Str. of Florida
Mississippi River Delta
Dry Tortugas
Key West
Sea Islands
Pamlico Sound
Albemarle Sd.
Chesapeake Bay
Delaware Bay
Onslow Bay
Long Bay
Apalachee B.
Chandeleur Sd.
Breton Sd.
Northwest Providence Channel
Northeast Providence Channel
COPYRIGHT PHILIP'S

309

320

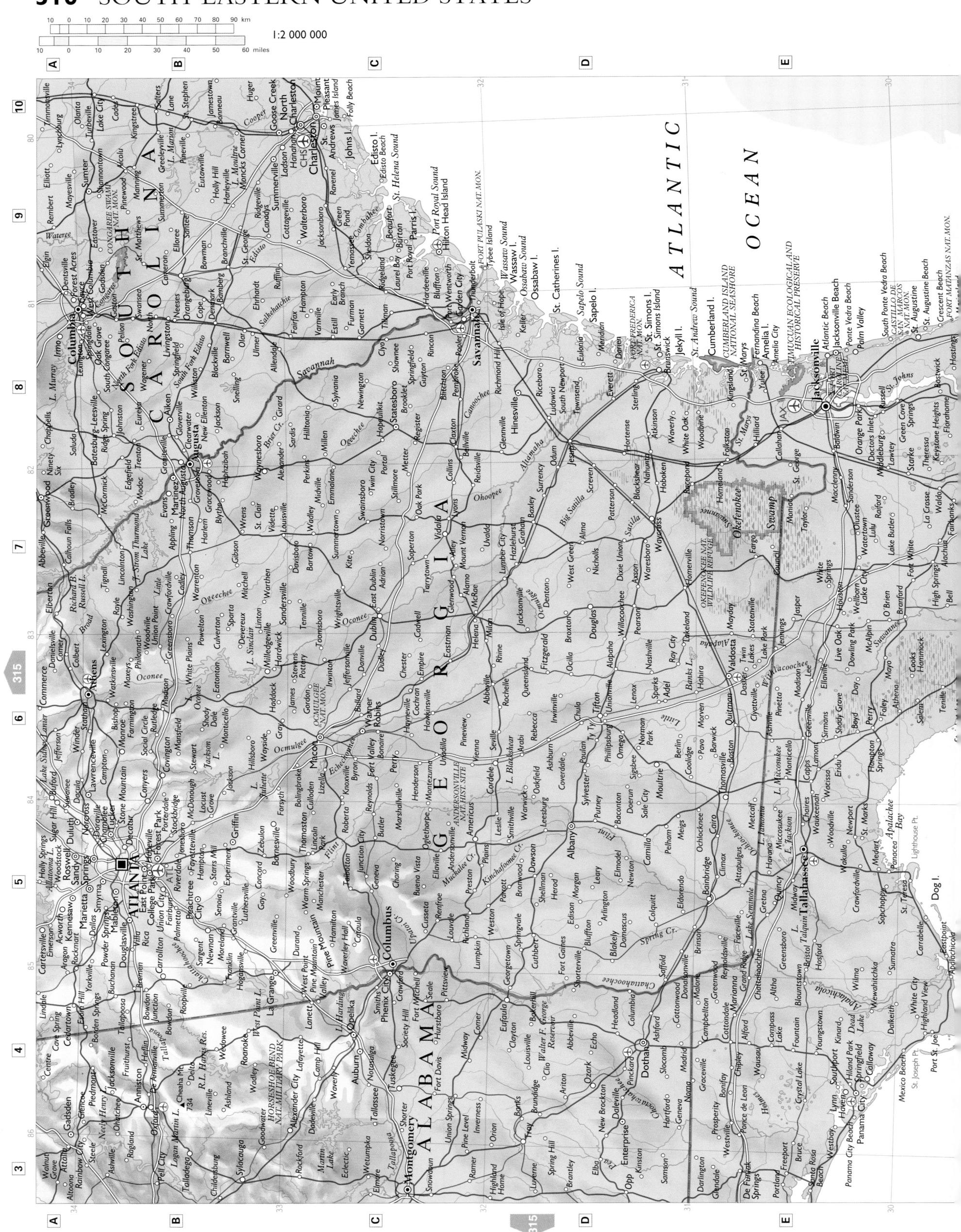

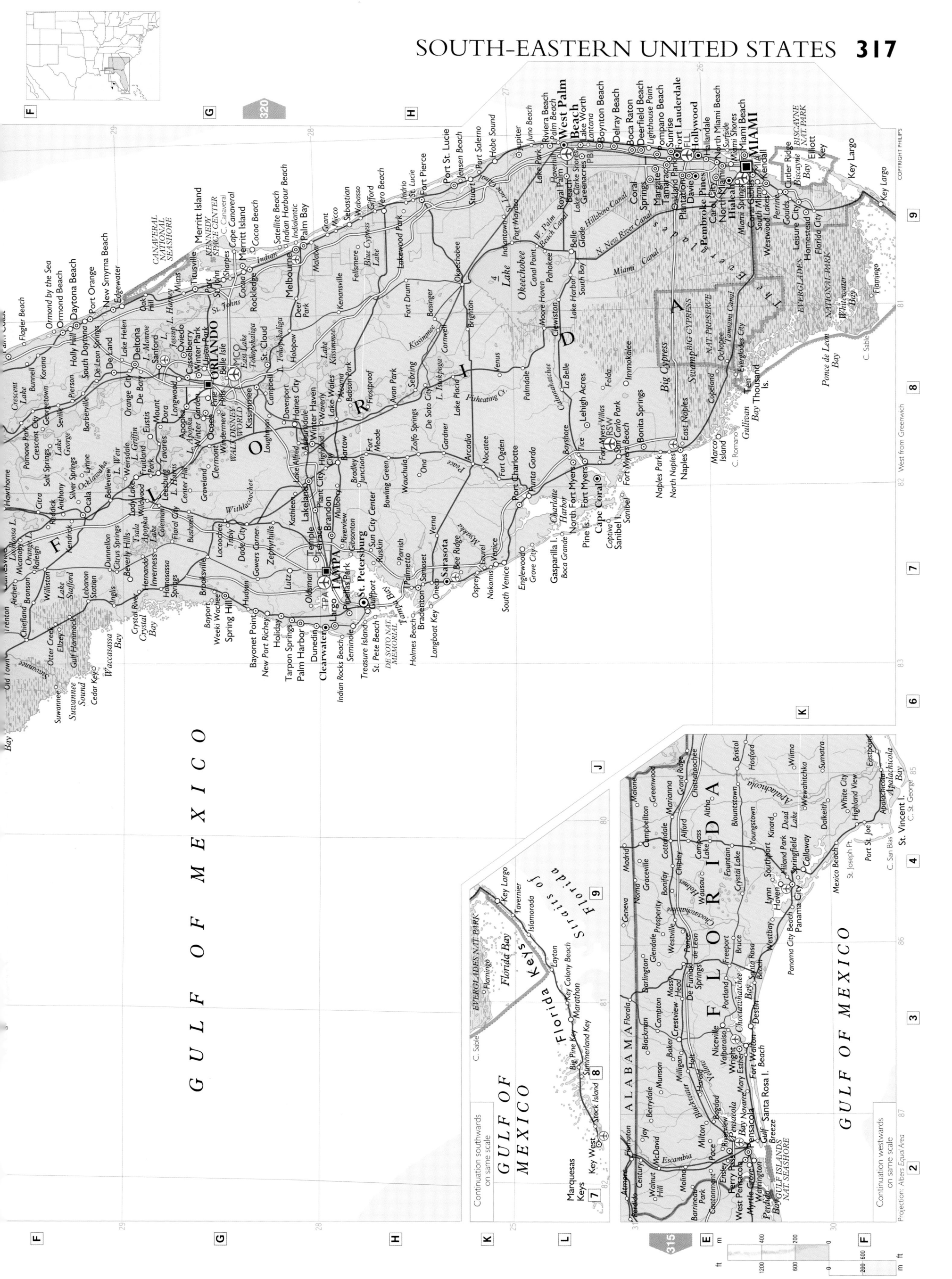

GULF OF MEXICO

F L O R I D A

Bay

Map labels (peninsula Florida)

CANAVERAL
NATIONAL
SEASHORE
Merritt Island
KENNEDY
SPACE CENTER
Cape Canaveral
C. Canaveral
Cocoa Beach
Merritt Island

Flagler Beach
Ormond by the Sea
Ormond Beach
Daytona Beach
Port Orange
New Smyrna Beach
Edgewater

Crescent
Lake
Bunnell
Crescent City
Pomona Park
Georgetown
Seville
Pierson
Holly Hill
South Daytona

Hawthorne
Citra
Reddick
Anthony
Silver Springs
Ocala
Belleview
Ocklawaha

Lake
George
Salt Springs
De Leon Springs
De Land
Deltona
Sanford
Lake Helen
L. Monroe

West Palm
Beach
Riviera Beach
Juno Beach
Palm Beach
Lake Park
Lake Worth
Lantana
Boynton Beach
Delray Beach
Boca Raton
Deerfield Beach
Lighthouse Point
Pompano Beach
Fort Lauderdale
Hollywood
Hallandale
Hialeah
MIAMI
Miami Beach
Miami Springs
South Miami
Coral Gables
Kendall
Perrine
Cutler Ridge
Homestead
Florida City
Key Largo

BISCAYNE
NAT. PARK
Biscayne
Bay
Elliott
Key

EVERGLADES
NATIONAL PARK
BIG CYPRESS
NAT. PRESERVE
Whitewater
Bay
Flamingo
C. Sable

Lake
Okeechobee
Pahokee
Belle Glade
South Bay
Clewiston
Moore Haven
La Belle
Immokalee
Copeland
Ochopee
Everglades City
Ten
Thousand
Is.

Naples Park
North Naples
Naples
Marco
Island
C. Romano

Port St. Lucie
Stuart
Jensen Beach
Port Salerno
Hobe Sound
Jupiter
Fort Pierce
Vero Beach
Sebastian
Micco
Grant
Palm Bay
Melbourne
Indialantic
Indian Harbour Beach
Satellite Beach

Orlando
WALT DISNEY WORLD
Kissimmee
St. Cloud
Winter Park
Casselberry
Oviedo
Apopka
Winter Garden

TAMPA
St. Petersburg
Clearwater
Largo
Tarpon Springs
Dunedin
Palm Harbor
Brandon
Plant City
Lakeland
Bartow
Sarasota
Bradenton
Venice

Fort Myers
Cape Coral
Sanibel
Captiva
Punta Gorda
Port Charlotte
Arcadia
Sebring
Avon Park

GULF OF MEXICO

Inset maps

Continuation southwards
on same scale

GULF OF
MEXICO

Key West
Marquesas
Keys
Florida Keys
Key Largo
Tavernier
Islamorada
Marathon
Big Pine Key
Summerland Key
Florida Bay
EVERGLADES NAT. PARK
Flamingo
C. Sable
Straits of Florida
GULF ISLANDS
NAT. SEASHORE

Continuation westwards
on same scale

A L A B A M A
F L O R I D A
GULF OF MEXICO
Apalachicola
Apalachicola
Bay
Panama City
Panama City Beach
Pensacola
Fort Walton Beach
Destin
St. Joseph Pt.
Port St. Joe
C. San Blas
St. Vincent I.
C. St. George

Projection: Albers Equal Area

COPYRIGHT PHILIP'S

315

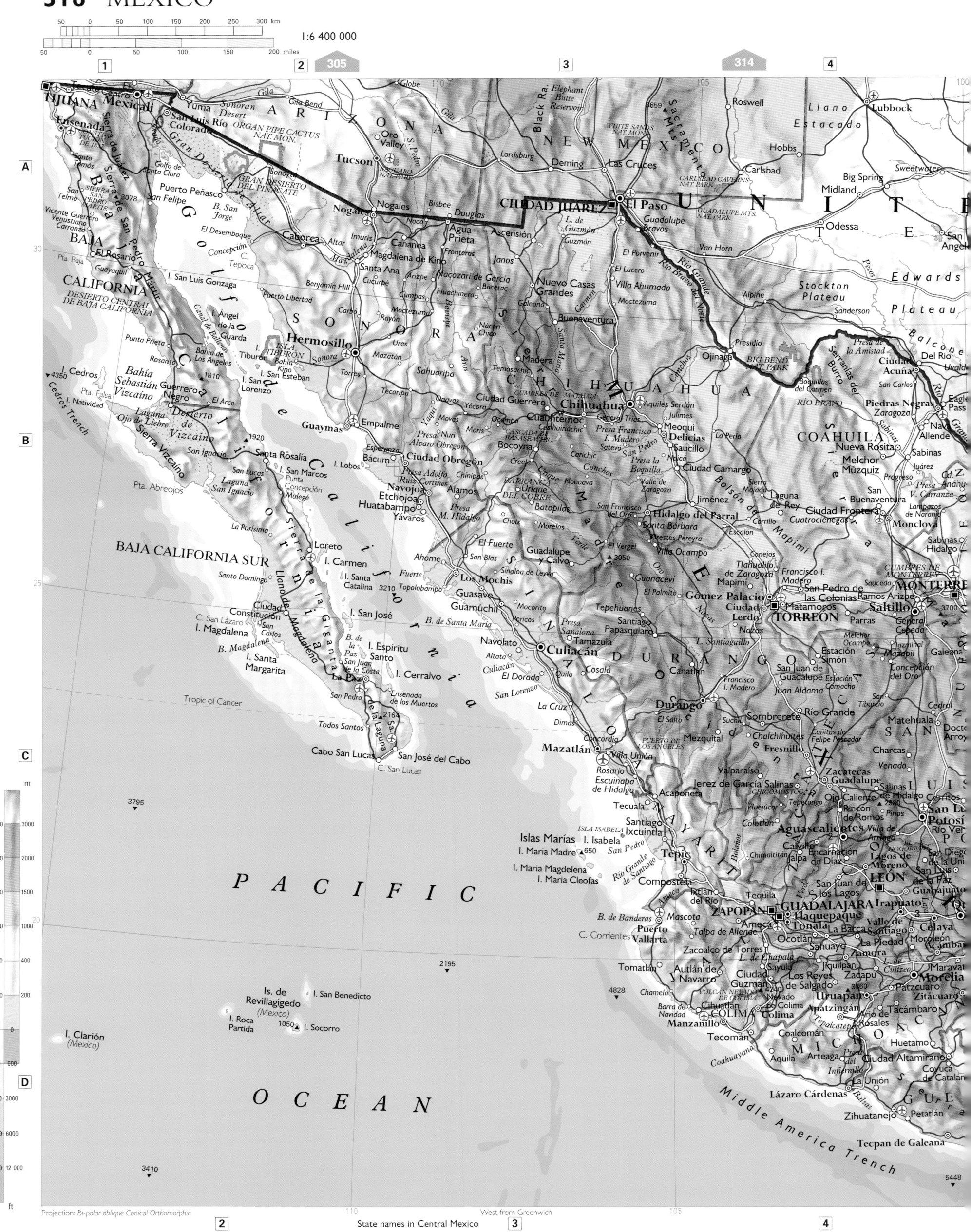

Projection: Bi-polar oblique Conical Orthomorphic

West from Greenwich

State names in Central Mexico

1 DISTRITO FEDERAL   3 GUANAJUATO   5 MÉXICO   7 QUERÉTARO
2 AGUASCALIENTES   4 HIDALGO   6 MORELOS   8 TLAXCALA

1:6 400 000

JAMAICA

CARIBBEAN SEA

JAMAICA
1:1 600 000
a

Gulf of Mexico

MEXICO

FLORIDA
U.S.A.

Straits of Florida

EVERGLADES NAT. PARK

MIAMI

Great Bahama Bank

LA HABANA (Havana)

CUBA

Greater

Yucatan Basin

Cayman Islands (U.K.)

Cayman Trench

Misteriosa Bank

JAMAICA

Pedro Bank

BELIZE

GUATEMALA

HONDURAS

Rosalind Bank

Serranilla Bank

Banco Gorda

Bajo Nuevo (Colombia)

Is. Santanilla (Swan Islands) (Honduras)

Mosquitia

GUATEMALA

EL SALVADOR

TEGUCIGALPA

NICARAGUA

MANAGUA

CARIB

Cayos Miskitos (Nicaragua)

I. de Providencia (Colombia)

Cayos Roncador (Colombia)

I. de San Andrés (Colombia)

Cayos de Albuquerque (Nicaragua)

CARIBBEAN SEA

Colón

PANAMA

Guatemala Trench

PANAMA CANAL
1:800 000
c

PACIFIC OCEAN

COSTA RICA

SAN JOSE

Isthmus of Panama

CARTAG

PANAMÁ

Golfo del Darién

PACIFIC OCEAN

Projection: Conical with two standard parallels

1:6 400 000

328

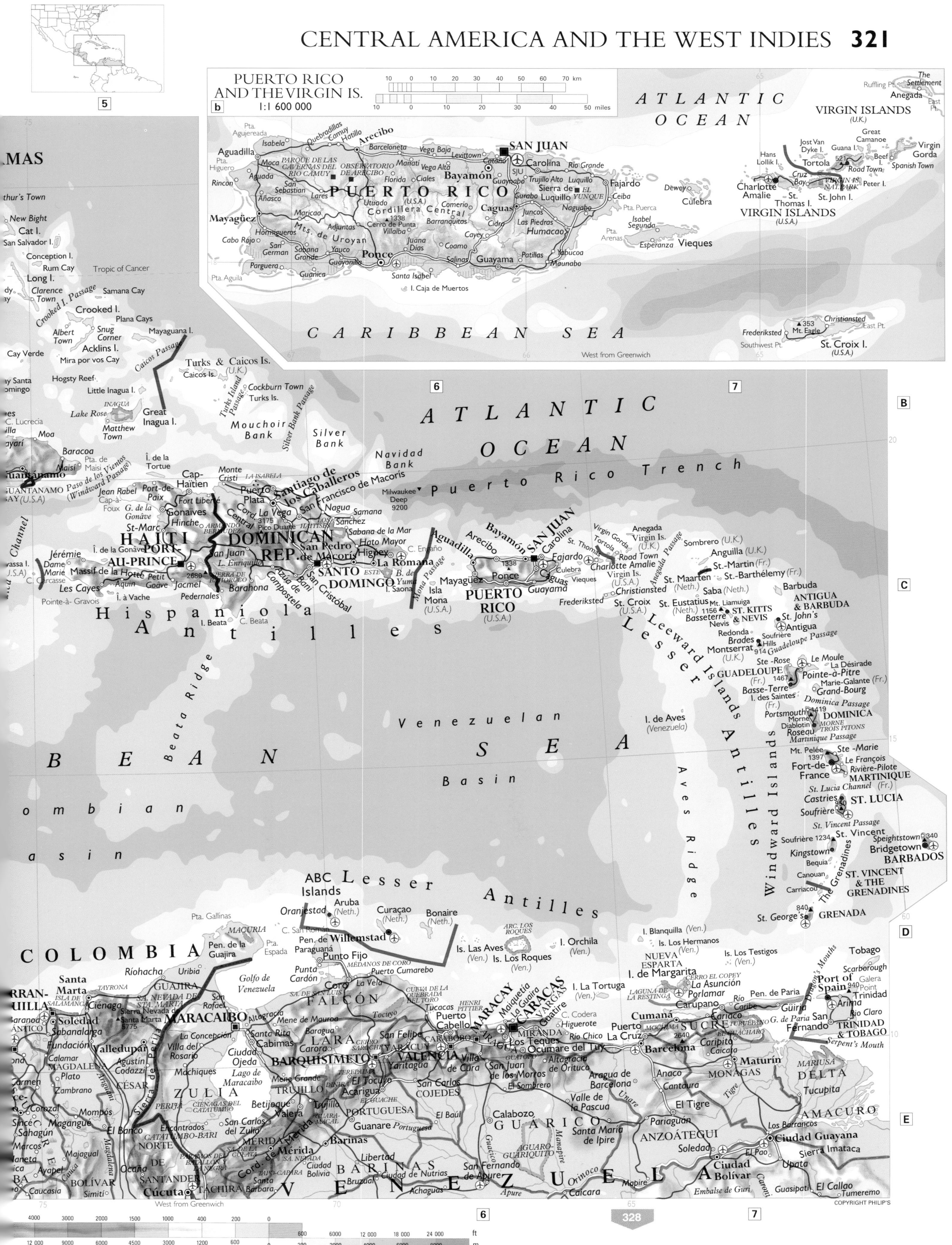

ATLANTIC OCEAN

VIRGIN ISLANDS (U.K.)

VIRGIN ISLANDS (U.S.A.)

PUERTO RICO

San Juan
Bayamón
Mayagüez
Ponce
Guayama

CARIBBEAN SEA

St. Croix I. (U.S.A.)

ATLANTIC OCEAN

Puerto Rico Trench

Milwaukee Deep 9200

HAITI
PORT-AU-PRINCE

DOMINICAN REP.
SANTO DOMINGO

Hispaniola

PUERTO RICO (U.S.A.)

Mona Passage

Anegada Passage

Sombrero (U.K.)
Anguilla (U.K.)
St-Martin (Fr.)
St. Maarten (Neth.)
St-Barthélemy (Fr.)
Saba (Neth.)
Barbuda
St. Eustatius (Neth.)
ST. KITTS & NEVIS
Basseterre
Nevis
Redonda
Montserrat (U.K.)

ANTIGUA & BARBUDA
St. John's
Antigua

Guadeloupe Passage

GUADELOUPE (Fr.)
Basse-Terre
Pointe-à-Pitre
Marie-Galante (Fr.)
Grand-Bourg
I. des Saintes (Fr.)

Dominica Passage

DOMINICA
Portsmouth
Roseau

Martinique Passage

MARTINIQUE
Fort-de-France

St. Lucia Channel (Fr.)

ST. LUCIA
Castries
Soufrière

St. Vincent Passage

ST. VINCENT & THE GRENADINES
Kingstown
The Grenadines
Bequia
Canouan
Carriacou

GRENADA
St. George's

BARBADOS
Bridgetown
Speightstown

Leeward Islands

Windward Islands

Lesser Antilles

Aves Ridge

CARIBBEAN SEA

Venezuelan Basin

Beata Ridge

Colombian Basin

I. de Aves (Venezuela)

ABC Islands

Aruba (Neth.)
Curaçao (Neth.)
Bonaire (Neth.)
Oranjestad
Willemstad

COLOMBIA

MARACAIBO
Lago de Maracaibo

VENEZUELA

CARACAS
VALENCIA
MARACAY
BARQUISIMETO

TRINIDAD & TOBAGO
Port of Spain
Tobago

Ciudad Bolívar

COPYRIGHT PHILIP'S

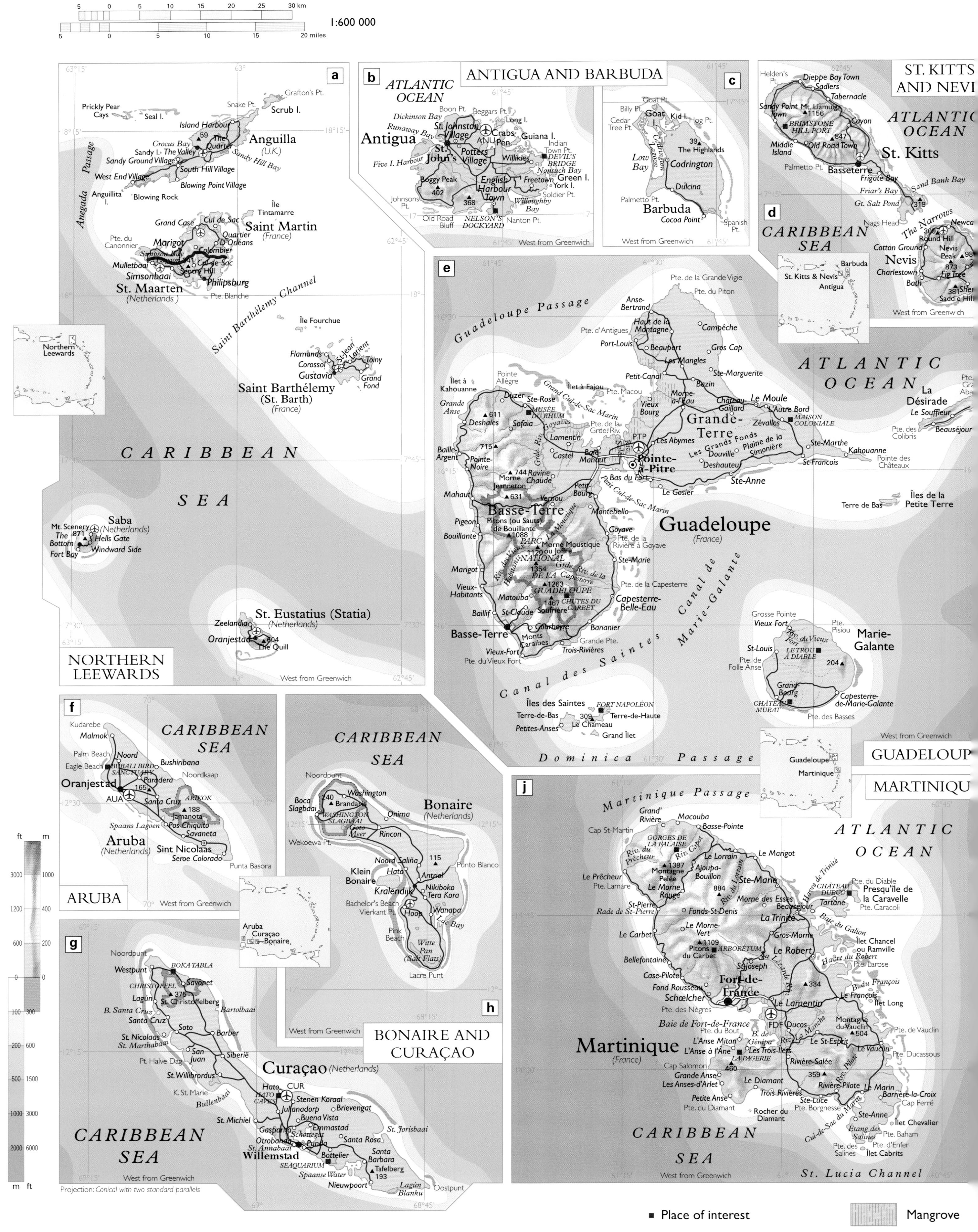

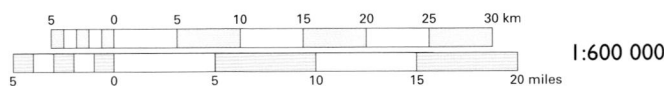

5 0 5 10 15 20 25 30 km

1:600 000

5 0 5 10 15 20 miles

ANTIGUA AND BARBUDA

a

Prickly Pear Cays
Seal I.
Snake Pt.
Grafton's Pt.
Scrub I.
Island Harbour
Crocus Bay
59
The Quarter
Sandy I.
The Valley
Anguilla (U.K.)
West End Village
Sandy Ground Village
South Hill Village
Blowing Point Village
Blowing Rock
Anguillita I.
Île Tintamarre
Grand Case
Cul de Sac
Pte. du Canonnier
Saint Martin (France)
Marigot
Quartier D'Orleans
Colombier
Simpson Bay
Cul de Sac
Mulletbaai
Simsonbaai
Sperry Hill
St. Maarten (Netherlands)
Philipsburg
Pte. Blanche

Anegada Passage
Sandy Hill Bay
Saint Barthélemy Channel

Île Fourchue
Flamands
St-Jean
Lorient
Corossol
Toiny
Gustavia
Grand Fond
Saint Barthélemy (St. Barth) (France)

Northern Leewards

b
ATLANTIC OCEAN
Dickinson Bay
Boon Pt.
Beggars Pt.
Long I.
St. Johnston Village
Crabs Pen.
Guiana I.
Antigua
St. John's
Potters Village
Willikies
Indian Town Pt.
DEVIL'S BRIDGE
Five I. Harbour
English Harbour Town
Freetown
Green I.
York I.
Nonsuch Bay
Soldier Pt.
Boggy Peak
402
368
Willoughby Bay
Johnsons Pt.
Old Road Bluff
NELSON'S DOCKYARD
Nanton Pt.
West from Greenwich

c
Billy Pt.
Goat Pt.
Goat I.
Kid I.
Hog Pt.
Cedar Tree Pt.
Low Bay
Codrington Lagoon
39
The Highlands
Codrington
Dulcina
Palmetto Pt.
Barbuda
Cocoa Point
Spanish Pt.
West from Greenwich

ST. KITTS AND NEVIS

d
Helden's Pt.
Dieppe Bay Town
Sadlers
Sandy Point Town
Mt. Liamuiga 1156
Tabernacle
BRIMSTONE HILL FORT
Cayon
847
Middle Island
Old Road Town
ATLANTIC OCEAN
St. Kitts
Palmetto Pt.
Basseterre
Frigate Bay
Nags Head
Friar's Bay
Sand Bank Bay
Gt. Salt Pond
319
CARIBBEAN SEA
The Narrows
Round Hill
305
Newcastle
Cotton Ground
Nevis Peak 985
Charlestown
Nevis
873
Bath
361
Fig Tree
Sher Sadd.Hill
St. Kitts & Nevis / Antigua
West from Greenwich

e
Anse-Bertrand
Pte. de la Grande Vigie
Pte. du Piton
Haut de la Montagne
Campêche
Port-Louis
Beauport
Gros Cap
Ste-Marguerite
Guadeloupe Passage
Pte. d'Antigues
Les Mangles
Bazin
Îlet à Kahouanne
Pointe Allègre
Île à Fajou
Pte. Macou
Morne-à-l'Eau
Château-Gaillard
Le Moule
L'Autre Bord
Grande Anse
Duzer
Ste-Rose
MUSÉE DU RHUM
611
Goyaves
Grand Cul-de-Sac Marin
Vieux Bourg
Zévallos
MAISON COLONIALE
La Désirade
Le Souffleur
Beauséjour
Deshaies
Sofaia
Les Abymes
Grande-Terre
Pte. de la Grde.Riv.
PTP
Ste-Marthe
Kahouanne
Pte. des Colibris
Baille-Argent
715
Lamentin
Castel
Baie Mahault
Pointe-à-Pitre
Douville
Plaine de la Simonière
Les Grands Fonds
St-François
Pointe-Noire
744 Ravine Chaude
Morne Jeannetton
631
Bas du Fort
Petit-Bourg
Le Gosier
Ste-Anne
Pointe des Châteaux
Mahaut
Petit Cul-de-Sac Marin
Montebello
Îles de la Petite Terre
Pigeon
Pitons (ou Sauts) de Bouillante 1088
PARC NATIONAL
Morne Moustique
Goyave
Pte. de la Rivière à Goyave
Terre de Bas
Guadeloupe (France)
Bouillante
1170 ou Jotre
Grde. Riv. de la Capesterre
Ste-Marie
1354
DE LA GUADELOUPE
Marigot
1265
Capesterre-Belle-Eau
Vieux-Habitants
1467 CHUTES DU CARBET
Matouba
St-Claude
Soufrière
Pte. de la Capesterre
Baillif
Monts Caraïbes
Bananier
Grosse Pointe
Vieux Fort
Basse-Terre
Grande Pte.
Trois-Rivières
Pte. du Vieux Fort
Vieux-Fort
Canal de Marie-Galante
St-Louis
Pte. Pisiou
Pte. du Vieux
LE TROU À DIABLE
Marie-Galante
Pte. de Folle Anse
Grand-Bourg
204
CHÂTEAU MURAT
Capesterre-de-Marie-Galante
Pte. des Basses
Îles des Saintes
FORT NAPOLÉON
Terre-de-Bas
309
Terre-de-Haute
Petites-Anses
Le Chameau
Grand Îlet
Canal des Saintes

St. Kitts & Nevis / Antigua
Barbuda / Antigua

GUADELOUPE
MARTINIQUE
Guadeloupe / Martinique
West from Greenwich
Dominica Passage

f
Kudarebe
Malmok
Noord
Palm Beach
BUBALI BIRD SANCTUARY
Bushiribana
Eagle Beach
Paradera
Noordkaap
Oranjestad
165
Santa Cruz
ARIKOK
AUA
188
Jamanota
Pos Chiquito
Spaans Lagoen
Savaneta
Aruba (Netherlands)
Sint Nicolaas
Seroe Colorado
Punta Basora
CARIBBEAN SEA

ARUBA

Aruba / Curaçao / Bonaire
West from Greenwich

h
CARIBBEAN SEA
Noordpunt
Boca Slagbaai
240
Washington
Brandaris
Onima
Bonaire (Netherlands)
WASHINGTON SLAGBAAI
Goto Meer
Rincon
Wekoewa Pt.
Noord Saliña
Hato
115
Antriol
Klein Bonaire
Nikiboko
Tera Kora
Kralendijk
Wanapa
Lac Bay
Bachelor's Beach
Hoop
Vierkant Pt.
Pink Beach
Witte Pan (Salt Flats)
Lacre Punt
West from Greenwich

BONAIRE AND CURAÇAO

g
Noordpunt
BOKA TABLA
Westpunt
Savonet
CHRISTOFFEL
375 St. Christoffelberg
Lagun
Bartolbaai
B. Santa Cruz
Santa Cruz
Barber
St. Nicolaas
St. Marthabai
Soto
San Juan
Siberië
Pt. Halve Dag
St. Willibrordus
K. St. Marie
Curaçao (Netherlands)
Hato
CUR
Bullenbaai
HATO CAVES
Stenen Koraal
St. Michiel
Jullandorp
Brievengat
Buena Vista
Gasparito
Otrobanda
St. Annabaai
Santa Rosa
Punda
Willemstad
Bottelier
Santa Barbara
St. Jorisbaai
SEAQUARIUM
Tafelberg
193
Spaanse Water
Nieuwpoort
Lagun Blanku
Oostpunt
CARIBBEAN SEA
West from Greenwich
Projection: Conical with two standard parallels

j
Martinique Passage
Grand' Rivière
Macouba
Basse-Pointe
Cap St-Martin
GORGES DE LA FALAISE
Le Lorrain
Le Marigot
Le Prêcheur
1397 Montagne Pelée
Ajoupa-Bouillon
Le Morne Rouge
884
Morne des Esses
Ste-Marie
CHÂTEAU DUBUC
Presqu'île de la Caravelle
Le Carbet
Fonds-St-Denis
Beauséjour
Tartane
Pte. Caracoli
Rade de St-Pierre
St-Pierre
La Trinée
Baie du Galion
Le Morne-Vert
1109
Gros-Morne
Îlet Chancel
Pitons du Carbet
ARBORÉTUM
Le Robert
ou Ramville
Bellefontaine
334
Le François
Îlet Long
Case-Pilote
B. du François
Fond Rousseau
Schœlcher
Fort-de-France
Le Lamentin
Pte. Larose
ATLANTIC OCEAN
FDF
Ducos
Montagne du Vauclin
504
Pte. de Vauclin
Baie de Fort-de-France
L'Anse Mitan
Les Trois-Îlets
St-Joseph
Le St-Esprit
Le Vauclin
L'Anse à l'Âne
LA PAGERIE
Rivière-Salée
Cap Salomon
460
Grande Anse
Le Diamant
Les Anses-d'Arlet
359
Rivière-Pilote
Le Marin
Petite Anse
Trois Rivières
Barrière-la-Croix
Cap Ferré
Rocher du Diamant
Pte. du Diamant
Ste-Luce
Îlet Chevalier
Martinique (France)
Cul-de-Sac du Marin
Étang des Salines
Ste-Anne
CARIBBEAN SEA
Pte. Baham
Pte. d'Enfer
Îlet Cabrits
St. Lucia Channel
West from Greenwich

CARIBBEAN SEA

Mt. Scenery 871
Saba (Netherlands)
Hells Gate
The Bottom
Windward Side
Fort Bay

St. Eustatius (Statia) (Netherlands)
Zeelandia
Oranjestad
504
The Quill

NORTHERN LEEWARDS

ft m
3000 / 1000
1200 / 400
600 / 200
0
100 / 300
200 / 600
500 / 1500
1000 / 3000
2000 / 6000
m ft

■ Place of interest
Mangrove

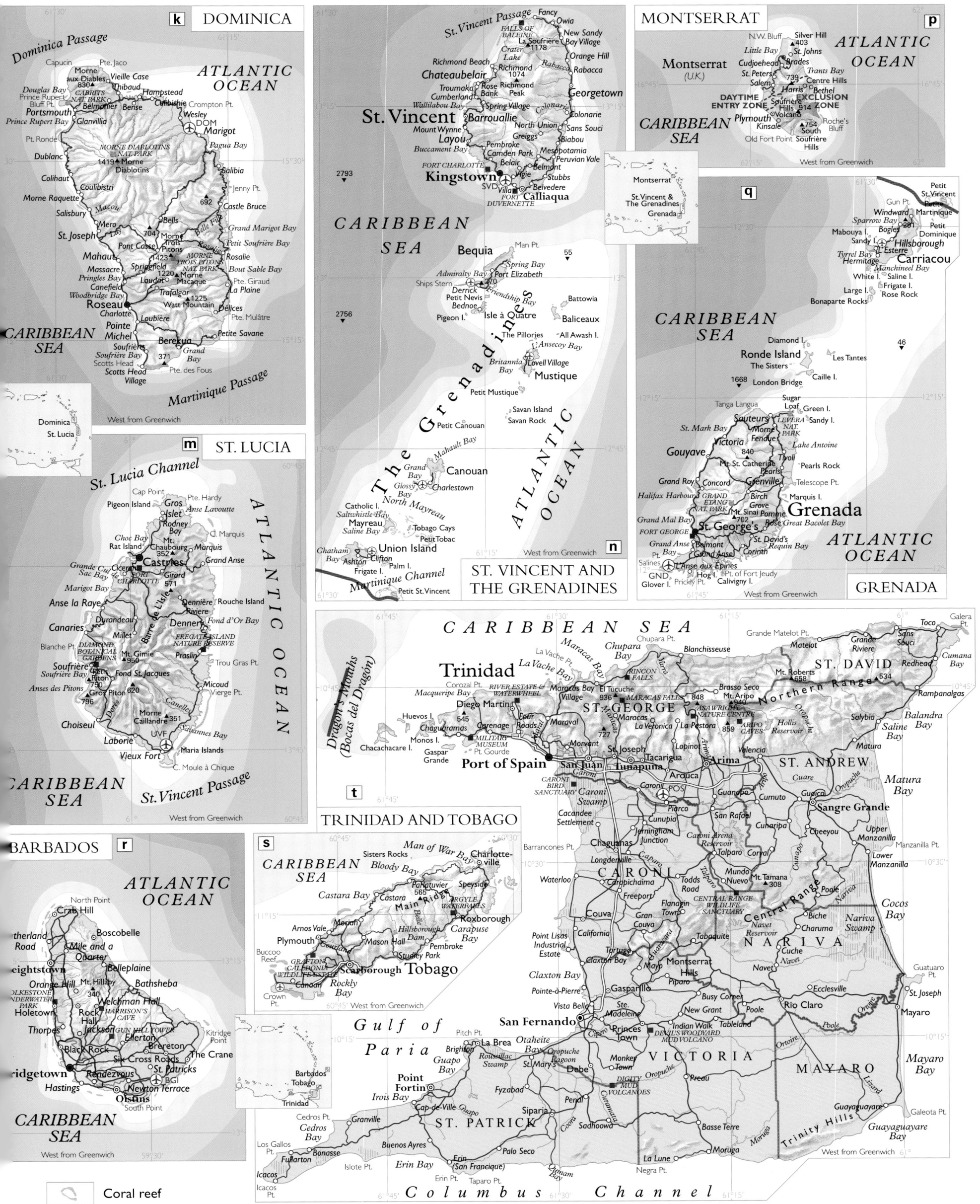

DOMINICA k

Dominica Passage

ATLANTIC OCEAN

Capucin
Pte. Jaco
Morne
aux Diables
Vieille Case
830△
Thibaud
Hampstead
Douglas Bay
Prince Rupert
Bluff Pt.
Belmanier
Bense
CABRITS
NAT. PARK
Wesley
DOM
Portsmouth
Glanvillia
Crompton Pt.
Marigot
Prince Rupert Bay
Pt. Ronde
MORNE DIABLOTINS
NAT. PARK
Pagua Bay
Dublanc
MORNE DIABLOTINS
NAT. PARK
1419△
Morne
Diablotins
Colihaut
692
Castle Bruce
Coulibistri
Macoucheri
Morne Raquette
704△
Bells
Belle Fille
Grand Marigot Bay
St. Joseph
Mero
Pont Casse
Morne
Trois
Pitons
Petit Soufrière Bay
Mahaut
352△
1423△
MORNE
TROIS PITONS
NAT. PARK
Rosalie
Massacre
Springfield
1220△
Morne
Macaque
Bout Sable Bay
Pringles Bay
Laudat
Pte. Giraud
La Plaine
Canefield
Trafalgar
1225△
Woodbridge Bay
Watt Mountain
Pélices
Roseau
Charlotte
Loubière
Pte. Mulâtre
Pointe
Michel
Berekua
Petite Savane
Soufrière
371△
Grand Bay
Soufrière Bay
Scotts Head
Scotts Head Village
Pte. des Fous

CARIBBEAN SEA

Martinique Passage

West from Greenwich

ST. LUCIA m

St. Lucia Channel

Cap Point
Pte. Hardy
Pigeon Island
Anse Lavoutte
Gros Islet
Rodney Bay
C. Marquis
Mt. Chaubourg
352△
Marquis
Choc Bay
Rat Island
Castries
FORT CHARLOTTE
Girard
571△
Dennière
Rivière
Rouche Island
Fond d'Or Bay
Anse la Raye
Durandeau
Dennery
Canaries
Millet
FREGATE ISLAND
NATURE RESERVE
Blanche Pt.
Praslin
Trou Gras Pt.
Soufrière
DIAMOND
BOTANICAL
GARDENS
Mt. Gimie
950△
Soufrière Bay
Petit
Piton
750
Fond St. Jacques
Micoud
Vierge Pt.
Anses des Pitons
Gros Piton 620
796
Canelles
Morne
Caillandre
351△
Choiseul
UVF
Savannes Bay
Laborie
Maria Islands
Vieux Fort
C. Moule à Chique

ATLANTIC OCEAN

CARIBBEAN SEA

St. Vincent Passage

West from Greenwich

BARBADOS r

ATLANTIC OCEAN

North Point
Crab Hill
Boscobelle
Sutherland Road
Mile and a Quarter
Belleplaine
Eightstown
Orange Hill
Mt. Hillaby
340△
Bathsheba
FOLKESTONE
UNDERWATER
PARK
Welchman Hall
HARRISON'S CAVE
Holetown
Rock Hall
GUN HILL TOWER
Thorpes
Jackson
Ellerton
Black Rock
Brereton
The Crane
Six Cross Roads
St. Patricks
Bridgetown
Rendezvous
BGI
Hastings
Newton Terrace
Oistins
South Point

CARIBBEAN SEA

West from Greenwich

St. Vincent / **St. Vincent & The Grenadines**

St. Vincent Passage
Fancy
Owia
FALLS OF BALEINE
New Sandy Bay Village
La Soufrière
1178
Crater Lake
Orange Hill
Rabacca
Richmond Beach
Richmond
1074
Rose Bank
Richmond Peak
Rabacca
Georgetown
Chateaubelair
Troumaka
Cumberland
Wallilabou Bay
Spring Village
Colonarie
Colonarie
St. Vincent
Barrouallie
North Union
Greiggs
Biabou
Sans Souci
Mount Wynne
Layou
Pembroke
Mesopotamia
Buccament Bay
Camden Park
Belair
Peruvian Vale
FORT CHARLOTTE
2793▽
Vigie
Belmont
Stubbs
Kingstown
SVD
Villan
Belvedere
FORT DUVERNETTE
Calliaqua

CARIBBEAN SEA

The Grenadines

Bequia
Spring Bay
Man Pt.
Admiralty Bay
Port Elizabeth
55
Ships Stern
Derrick
Friendship Bay
2756▽
Petit Nevis
Bednoe
Pigeon I.
Isle à Quatre
Battowia
Baliceaux
All Awash I.
The Pillories
L'Ansecoy Bay
Britannia Bay
Lovell Village
Mustique
Petit Mustique
Savan Island
Savan Rock
Petit Canouan
Mahault Bay
Grand Bay
Glossy Bay
Canouan
Charlestown
Catholic I.
Saltwhistle Bay
North Mayreau
Mayreau
Saline Bay
Tobago Cays
Petit Tobac
Chatham Bay
Union Island
Clifton
Palm I.
Ashton
Frigate I.
Martinique Channel
Petit St. Vincent

ATLANTIC OCEAN

West from Greenwich n

ST. VINCENT AND THE GRENADINES

Montserrat
St. Vincent & The Grenadines
Grenada

MONTSERRAT p

N.W. Bluff
Silver Hill
Little Bay
403△
St. Johns
Cudjoehead
Brades
Trants Bay
Montserrat
(U.K.)
St. Peters
Salem
739△
Centre Hills
DAYTIME ENTRY ZONE
Soufrière
914△
EXCLUSION ZONE
Plymouth
Kinsale
Soufrière Volcano
Old Fort Point
754△
South
Roche's Bluff
Soufrière Hills

ATLANTIC OCEAN

CARIBBEAN SEA

West from Greenwich

q

Petit St. Vincent
Gun Pt.
Petite Martinique
Windward
Sparrow Bay
281△
Bogles
Petit Dominique
Mabouya
Sandy I.
Hillsborough
Tyrrel Bay
Esterre
Carriacou
Hermitage
Manchineel Bay
White I.
Saline I.
Large I.
Frigate I.
Rose Rock
Bonaparte Rocks

CARIBBEAN SEA

Diamond I.
46▽
Ronde Island
Les Tantes
The Sisters
Caille I.
1668△
Sugar Loaf
London Bridge
Green I.
Tanga Langua
Sandy I.
St. Mark Bay
Sauteurs
Morne Fendue
LEVERA NAT. PARK
Gouyave
840△
Victoria
Lake Antoine
Tivoli
Mt. St. Catherine
Pearls
Pearls Rock
Grand Roy
Concord
Grenville
Halifax Harbour
GRAND ETANG NAT. PARK
Birch Grove
Telescope Pt.
702△
Mt. Sinai
Marquis I.
Grand Mal Bay
Pomme
Grenada
FORT GEORGE
St. George's
Rose
Great Bacolet Bay
Grand Anse Bay
Belmont
St. David's
Requin Bay
Grand Anse
Corinth
Salines
L'Anse aux Epines
Hog I.
Pt. of Fort Jeudy
GND
Prickly Pt.
Calivigny I.
Glover I.

CARIBBEAN SEA

ATLANTIC OCEAN

GRENADA

West from Greenwich

TRINIDAD AND TOBAGO t

CARIBBEAN SEA

Toco
Galera Pt.
Grande Matelot Pt.
Grande Riviere
Sans Souci
Chupara Pt.
Matelot
Cumana Bay
Maracas Bay
Blanchisseuse
Trinidad
La Vache Bay
RINCON FALLS
Yara
Mt. Roberts
658△
534△
Redhead
La Vache Pt.
936△
MARACAS FALLS
848△
Brasso Seco
Rampanalgas
Corozal Pt.
RIVER ESTATE WATERWHEEL
El Tucuche
Northern Range
Macqueripe Bay
Maracas Bay Village
ST. GEORGE
Mt. Aripo
940△
ASA WRIGHT NATURE CENTRE
Salybia
Diego Martin
545△
Maracas
La Veronica
La Pastora
859△
ARIPO CAVES
Hollis Reservoir
Balandra Bay
Huevos I.
Four Roads
Chaguaramas
Carenage
Maraval
727△
St. Joseph
Lopinot
Arima
Valencia
Matura Bay
Monos I.
MILITARY MUSEUM
Morvant
Tacarigua
Cuare
ST. ANDREW
Chacachacare I.
Gaspar Grande
Pt. Gourde
San Juan
Tunapuna
Arouca
Guanapo
Cumuto
Matura
Port of Spain
POS
Caroni
Garoni
Piarco
San Rafael
Cuaripa
Guaico
Orupouche
Oropuche
Upper Manzanilla
CARONI BIRD SANCTUARY
Caroni Swamp
Cunupia
Jerningham Junction
Caroni Arena Reservoir
Talparo
Corval
Cacandee Settlement
Mundo Nuevo
Cuche
Mt. Tamana
308△
Lower Manzanilla
Manzanilla Pt.
Barrancones Pt.
Chaguanas
Longdenville
CARONI
Todds Road
Flanagin Town
Biche
Nariva Swamp
Waterloo
Carapichaima
Freeport
CENTRAL RANGE
WILDLIFE SANCTUARY
Poole
Central Range
Cocos Bay
Couva
Gran Couva
Tabaquite
Navet Reservoir
Navet
NARIVA
Point Lisas Industrial Estate
California
Tortuga
Claxton Bay
Mayo
Montserrat Hills
Charuma
Ste. Madeleine
San Fernando
New Grant
Rio Claro
St. Joseph
Pointe-à-Pierre
Piparo
Gasparillo
Busy Corner
Guatuaro Pt.
Claxton Bay
Vista Bella
Indian Walk
Tableland
Mayaro
La Brea
Otaheite
Otaheite Bay
DEVIL'S WOODYARD MUD VOLCANO
VICTORIA
Brighton
Guapo Bay
Rousillac
Oropuche Swamp
St. Mary's
Monkey Town
Debe
MAYARO
Mayaro Bay
Point Fortin
Princes Town
Guayaguayare
Irois Bay
Guapo
Cap-de-Ville
Fyzabad
DIGITY MUD VOLCANOES
Penal
Erin Bay
St. Patrick
Siparia
Sadhoowa
Basse Terre
Trinity Hills
Guayaguayare Bay
Cedros Pt.
Cedros Bay
Granville
Buenos Ayres
Palo Seco
Los Gallos Pt.
Fullarton
Bonasse
Erin (San Francique)
Negra Pt.
Moruga
Icacos Bay
Islote Pt.
Erin Bay
La Lune
Icacos Pt.
Taparo Pt.
Guaya Bay
West from Greenwich
Galeota Pt.

Gulf of Paria

Columbus Channel

TOBAGO s

CARIBBEAN SEA

Man of War Bay
Charlotteville
Sisters Rocks
Bloody Bay
Speyside
Parlatuvier
Castara Bay
Castara
ARGYLE WATERFALLS
565△
Main Ridge
Roxborough
Arnos Vale
Moriah
Carapuse Bay
Plymouth
Mason Hall
Hillsborough Dam
Pembroke
Buccoo Reef
Courland
Studley Park
GRAFTON CALEDONIA WILDLIFE SANCTUARY
Scarborough
Tobago
Canaan
Rockly Bay
Crown Pt.
West from Greenwich

Barbados
Tobago
Trinidad

Coral reef

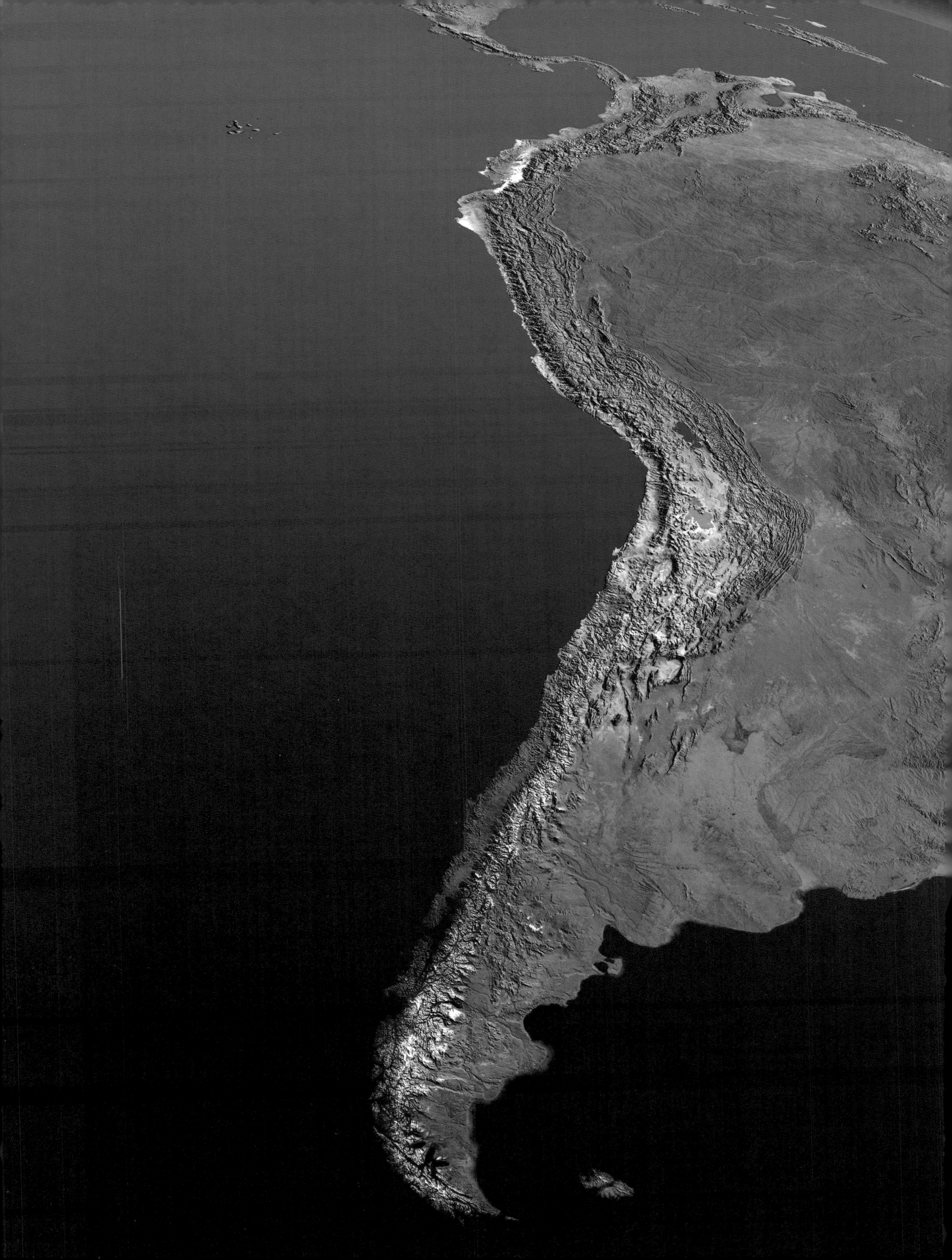

SOUTH AMERICA

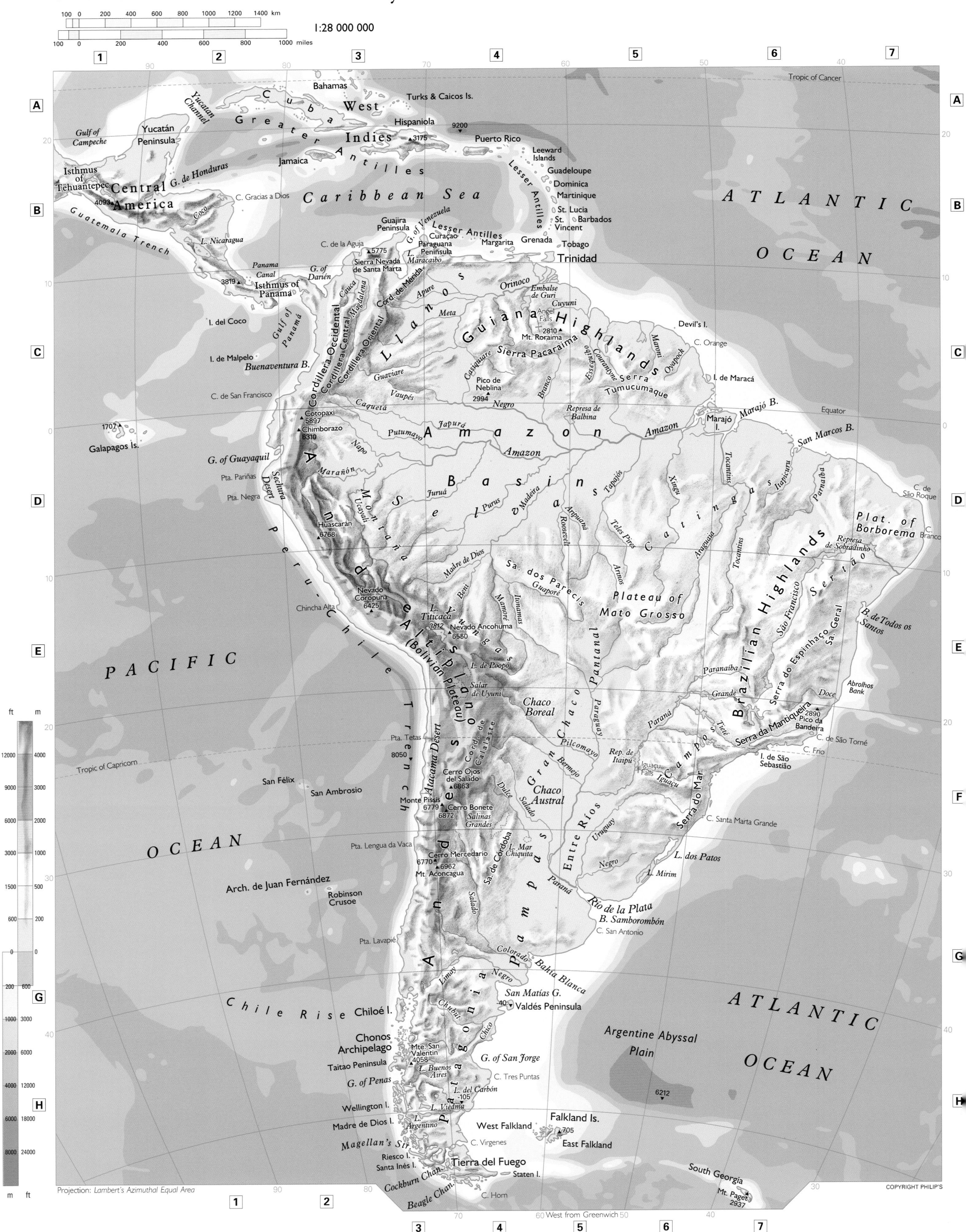

100 0   200 400 600 800 1000 1200 1400 km

100 0   200   400   600   800   1000 miles

1:28 000 000

Projection: Lambert's Azimuthal Equal Area

COPYRIGHT PHILIP'S

ft   m
12000 4000
9000   3000
6000   2000
3000   1000
1500   500
600   200
0   0
200   600
1000   3000
2000   6000
4000   12000
6000   18000
8000   24000
m   ft

1:28 000 000

100 0 200 400 600 800 1000 1200 1400 km
100 0 200 400 600 800 1000 miles

Tropic of Cancer

A

Havana
CUBA
BAHAMAS
Turks & Caicos Is.
(U.K.)

Cayman Is.
(U.K.)
HAITI
DOMINICAN
REP.
San Juan
Virgin Is. (U.S.A. - U.K.)
Anguilla (U.K.)
St. Martin (Fr. - Neth.)
ANTIGUA &
BARBUDA

B

MEXICO
BELIZE
JAMAICA
Kingston
Port-au-
Prince
Santo
Domingo
PUERTO
RICO
(U.S.A.)
ST. KITTS
& NEVIS
Basse-Terre
GUADELOUPE
(Fr.)
DOMINICA
Fort-de-France
MARTINIQUE
(Fr.)

GUATEMALA
HONDURAS
Tegucigalpa
Caribbean Sea
Castries ST. LUCIA
BARBADOS
Bridgetown

Guatemala
San Salvador
EL SALVADOR
NICARAGUA
Managua
ST. VINCENT
Kingstown
GRENADA
St. George's

COSTA
RICA
San José
Panamá
PANAMA
Barranquilla
Maracaibo
Caracas
Port of
Spain
TRINIDAD &
TOBAGO

I. del Coco
(Costa Rica)
Gulf of Panama
Cartagena
Barquísimeto
Valencia
Aruba
(Neth.)
Curaçao
(Neth.)
Oranjestad
Willemstad

C

I. de Malpelo
(Colombia)
Cúcuta
San Cristóbal
Medellín
Bucaramanga
VENEZUELA
Orinoco
Ciudad Guayana
Georgetown
Paramaribo
Cayenne
C. Orange

Cali
BOGOTÁ
GUYANA
SURINAME
FRENCH
GUIANA

COLOMBIA
RORAIMA
AMAPÁ

Equator

Galapagos Is.
(Ecuador)
Quito
Putumayo
Japurá
Amazon
Marajó
I.
Belém

D

ECUADOR
Guayaquil
G. of Guayaquil
Napo
Iquitos
Manaus
Santarém
São Luís
Fortaleza

Marañón
Ucayali
Juruá
Purus
Madeira
AMAZONAS
Amazon
Tapajós
PARÁ
Tocantins
MARANHÃO
Teresina
CEARÁ
RIO G.
DO NORTE
Natal

Chiclayo
Trujillo
ACRE
Pôrto Velho
Xingu
Araguaia
PIAUÍ
Parnaíba
PARAÍBA
Campina Grande
Recife

Chimbote
PERU
RONDÔNIA
PERNAMBUCO
ALAGOAS
Maceió
SERGIPE
Aracaju

E

Callao
LIMA
Cusco
Madre de Dios
Mamoré
TOCANTINS
BRAZIL
BAHÍA
Salvador

L.
Titicaca
BOLIVIA
MATO GROSSO
Cuiabá
GOIÁS
DIS. FED.
Brasília

Arequipa
La Paz
Cochabamba
Santa Cruz
Goiânia
MINAS GERAIS

Iquique
Sucre
Paraguay
MATO GROSSO
DO SUL
São Francisco
Ribeirão
Prêto
Belo
Horizonte
ESPÍRITO
SANTO
Vitória

F

Antofagasta
Salta
PARAGUAY
Paraná
SÃO PAULO
Campinas
Juiz
de Fora
R. DE J.
Campos

San Félix
(Chile)
San Ambrosio
(Chile)
Pilcomayo
ASUNCIÓN
PARANÁ
SÃO
PAULO
Santos
RIO DE
JANEIRO
Niterói

San Miguel
de Tucumán
Resistencia
Corrientes
Curitiba
SANTA CATARINA
Uruguay

ARGENTINA
Salado
RIO GRANDE
DO SUL
Pôrto Alegre

G

Córdoba
San Juan
Santa Fé
Paraná
Pelotas

Viña del Mar
Valparaíso
SANTIAGO
Mendoza
Rosario
URUGUAY
Montevideo

Arch. de Juan Fernández
(Chile)
Robinson
Crusoe
Talca
BUENOS AIRES
La Plata
Río de la Plata

Concepción
Bahía
Blanca
Colorado
Mar del Plata

Valdivia
Negro
Viedma

H

Puerto Montt
CHILE

Comodoro Rivadavia
Gulf of San Jorge

Gulf of Penas

ATLANTIC
OCEAN

West Falkland FALKLAND IS.
(U.K.)
Stanley
East Falkland

Punta Arenas
Magellan's Str.
Tierra del Fuego
South Georgia
(U.K.)

PACIFIC
OCEAN

Tropic of Capricorn

ATLANTIC
OCEAN

C. Horn
West from Greenwich

Projection: Lambert's Azimuthal Equal Area

COPYRIGHT PHILIP'S

■ LIMA Capital Cities

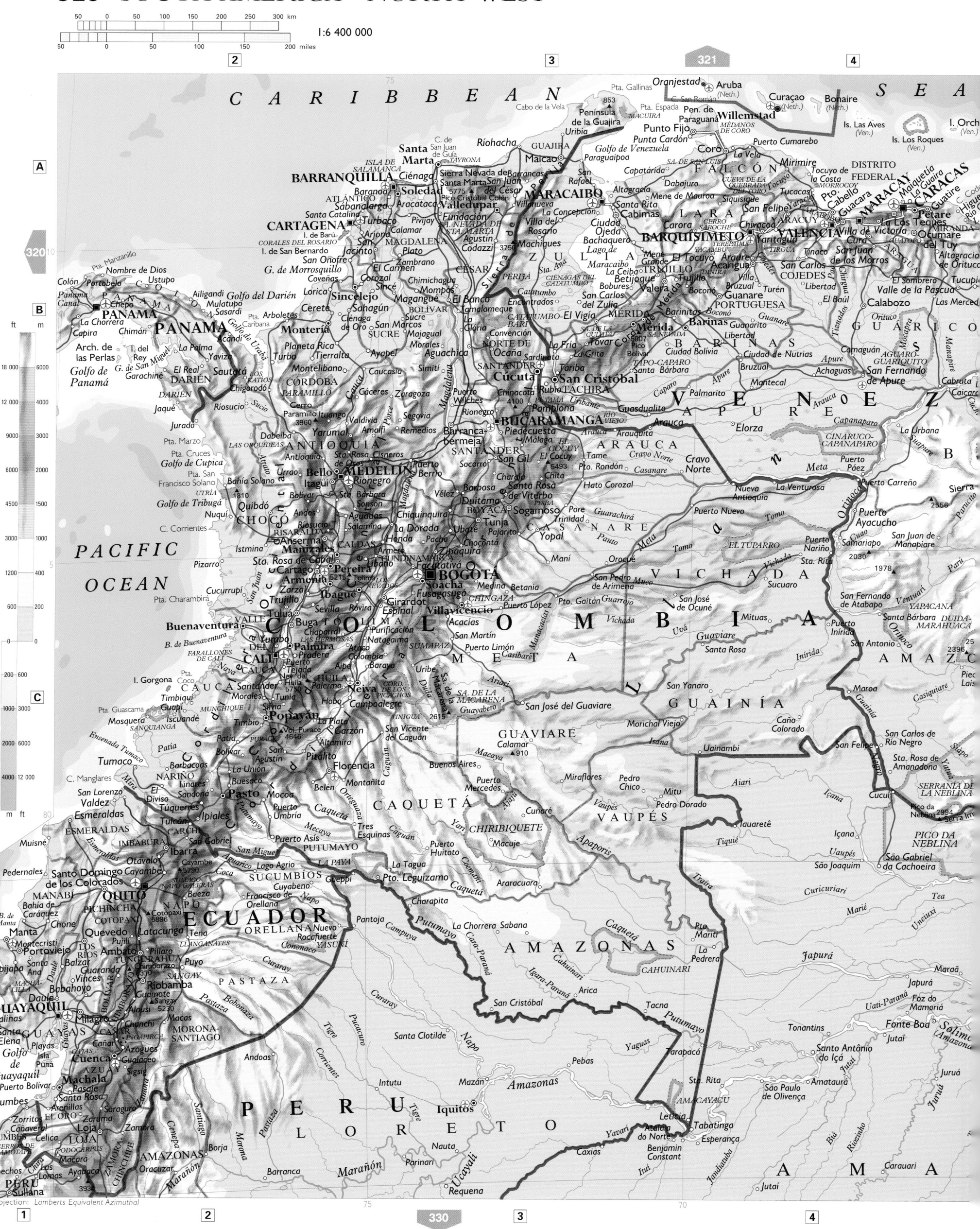

1:6 400 000

Projection: Lamberts Equivalent Azimuthal

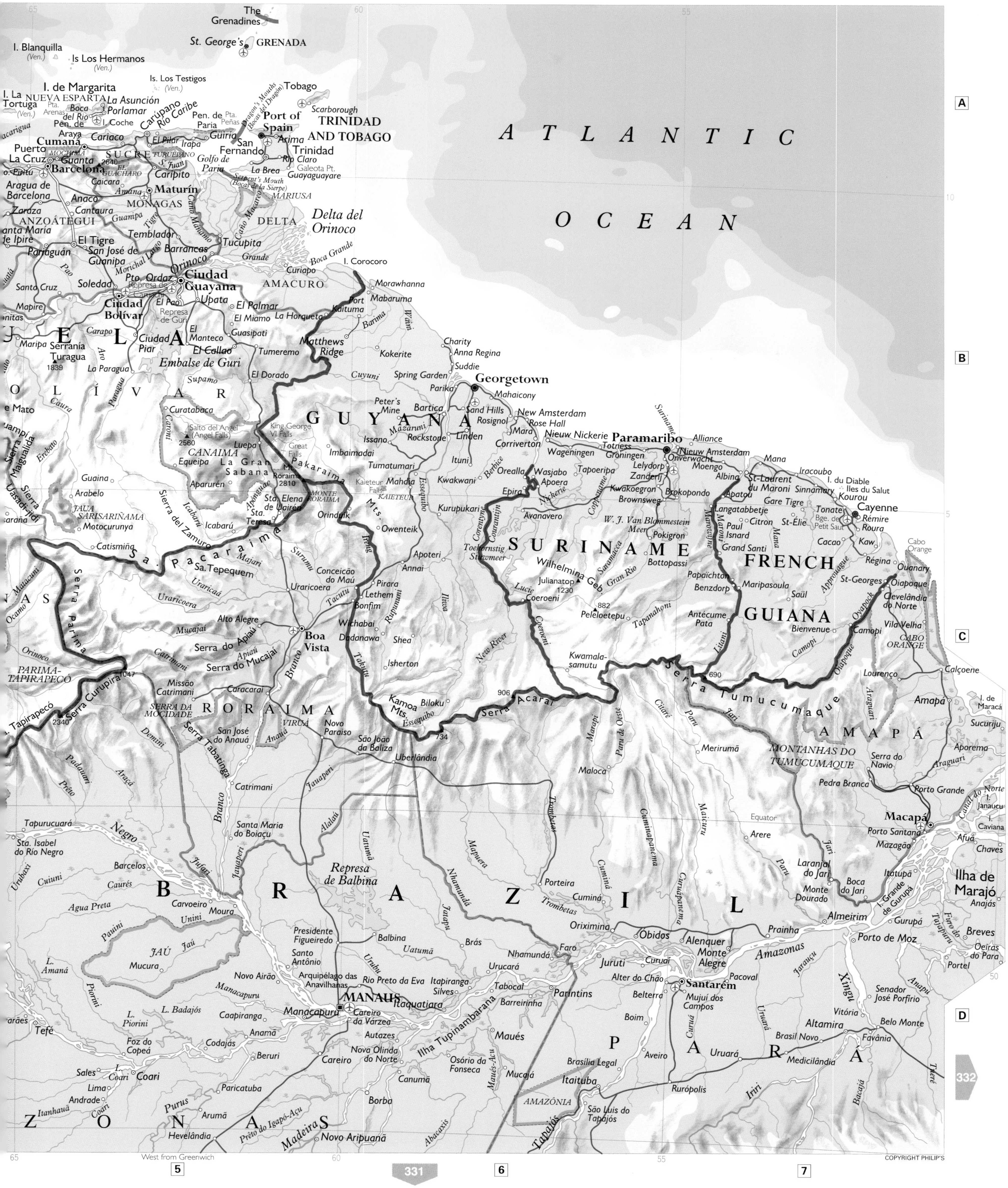

5 **6** **7**

A T L A N T I C

O C E A N

The
Grenadines
St. George's GRENADA
I. Blanquilla
(Ven.) Is Los Hermanos
(Ven.)
I. de Margarita
I. La NUEVA ESPARTA La Asunción
Tortuga Arenas Porlamar Is. Los Testigos
(Ven.) del Río I. Coche (Ven.)
Pen. de Boca Tobago
Puerto del Caribe Scarborough
La Cruz MOCHIMA Carúpano Pta. Peñas Boca Macareo
Guanta Cariaco Río Caribe Paria Pta. de Pen. de Dragon's Mouths
Cumaná SUCRE Carúpano Guíria Paria (Boca del Dragón)
Barcelona Caicara TUREUARO El Pilar Irapa Port of TRINIDAD
Aragua de Amana 2640 EL S. Juan Golfo de San Spain AND TOBAGO
Barcelona Anaco GUACHARO Caripito Paria Fernando Arima Trinidad
Zaraza Cantaura MONAGAS Caripe La Brea Río Claro
ANZOÁTEGUI San José de Maturín Serpent's Mouth Galeota Pt.
Santa María El Tigre Guanipa Temblador (Bocas de la Sierpe) Guayaguayare
de Ipire Paraguán Guanipa Barrancas Caño Manamo MARIUSA
Pao Tigre DELTA Delta del
Paraguán Pao Morichal Tucupita Orinoco
Santa Cruz Soledad Pto. Ordaz Grande Boca Grande
Mapire Ciudad Represa de AMACURO Curiapo I. Corocoro
nitas Guayana Uri Morawhanna
Ciudad El Pao Port Mabaruma
Bolívar Upata Kaituma Wani
Carapo El Palmar El Miamo La Horqueta Barima Charity
Mariposa Ciudad El Manteco Guasipati Matthews Anna Regina GUYANA
Serranía Piar El Callao Ridge Kokerite Suddie
Turagua El Dorado Tumeremo Cuyuni Spring Garden Parika
1839 Embalse de Guri Peter's Bartica Georgetown
La Paragua Supamo Mine Issano Rockstone Mahaicony
Curatabaca Spring Mazaruni Linden New Amsterdam
Caura Caroní King George Garden Rose Hall
Salto del Angel VI Falls Issano Ituni Corriverton
(Angel Falls) Great Imbaimadai Kwakwani Nieuw Nickerie Paramaribo
2560 Falls Mahdia Berbice Totness Onverwacht
CANAIMA Luepa Kaieteur Tumatumari Oreall Wageningen Groningen Alliance
Equeipa La Gran Falls Kaieteur Epira Wasjabo Tapeoriba Zanderij
Guaina Sabana KAIETEUR Nickerie Apoera Kwakoegron Brokopondo Moengo Albina
Arabelo Roraima Orinduik Kurupukari Avanavero Brownsweg Langatabbetje
JAUA 2810 Owenteik W. J. Van Blommestein Paul Gare Tire
SARISARIÑAMA MONTE Apoteri Meer Isnard Citron St-Laurent
Motocurunya RORAIMA Sta. Elena Annai SURINAME Pokigron Grand Santi du Maroni Sinnamary
Catismiña de Uairén Lethem Wilhelmina Geb Bottopassi Papaïchton FRENCH
Sa. Parima Sta. Pirara Julianatop Papaïchton Maripasoula GUIANA
Teresa Bonfim 1230 Benzdorp Antécume
Sa. Pacaraima Icabarú Conceição Lucie Pelēoetepu Pata Bienvenue
do Maú Coeroeni 882
S. Tepequem Uricaá Uraricoera Annai Kwamala- Serra Tumucumaque
Majari Uraricoera Tacutu samutu 690
Serra del Zamuro Alto Alegre Withabai Coeroeni MONTANHAS DO
Mucajaí Dadanawa New River TUMUCUMAQUE
PARIMA- Catrimani Serra do Apiaí Shea AMAPÁ
TAPIRAPECÓ Caracaraí Apiaí Isherton 906
Serra Curupira Serra do Mucajaí Kamoa Biloku Acarai Serra do
1047 Mts Essequibo Serra Acarai Navio
2340 SERRA DA Boa Vista 734 Camopi Pedra Branca
MOCIDADE Novo São João Vila Velha
San José Paraiso da Baliza CABO
Serra Tabatinga de Anauá Uberlândia ORANGE
Demini Anauá RORAIMA Calçoene
Preto San José VIRUA Jauaperi Lourenço Amapá
Padauari Araçá Catrimani Santa Maria I. de Maracá
Branco do Boiaçu Sucuriju
Santa Maria Porto Grande Aporema
do Boiaçu Macapá
Represa Equator Porto Santana
de Balbina Arere Caviana
BRAZIL Presidente Porteira Cuminá Laranjal Boca Chaves
Figueiredo Balbina Trombetas do Jari do Jari Ilha de
Santo Brás Cuminá Monte I. Grande Marajó
Antônio Faro Oriximiná Dourado de Gurupá Anajás
Barcelos Carvoeiro Nhamundá Óbidos Almeirim Breves
Agua Preta Moura Urucará Alenquer Gurupá Oeiras
Unini Monte Porto de Moz do Pará
Cuiuni Caurés Alegre Amazonas Portel
Pauini BRAZIL Juruti Santarém Prainha
L. Jaú JAÚ Novo Airão Rio Preto da Eva Alter do Chão Pacoval Xingu
Amaná Santo Itapiranga Belterra Senador
Mucura António Silves Mujuí dos José Porfírio
Codajás Arquipélago das Tabocal Campos Vitória
L. Anavilhanas Barreirinha Boim Altamira
Tefé Piorini MANAUS Itaquatiara Parintins Belo Monte
L. Manacapuru Careiro Maués Fávánia
Piorini Manacapuru da Várzea Ilha Tupinambarana Osório da Mucajá Medicilândia
L. Anamã Nova Olinda Fonseca Brasil Novo
Badajós Caapiranga do Norte Canumã Aveiro
Foz do Codajás Careiro PARÁ Uruará
Sales Copeá Beruri PA RÁ Ruropólis Irirí
Coari Paricatuba Brasília Legal São Luís do
Lima L. Coari Borba Itaituba Tapajós
Andrade Purus AMAZÔNIA
Coari Arumã Preto do Igapó-Açu Iriri
Itanhauá Hevelândia Madeira Bacajá
A M A Z O N A S Novo Aripuanã
Itanhauá Abacaxis

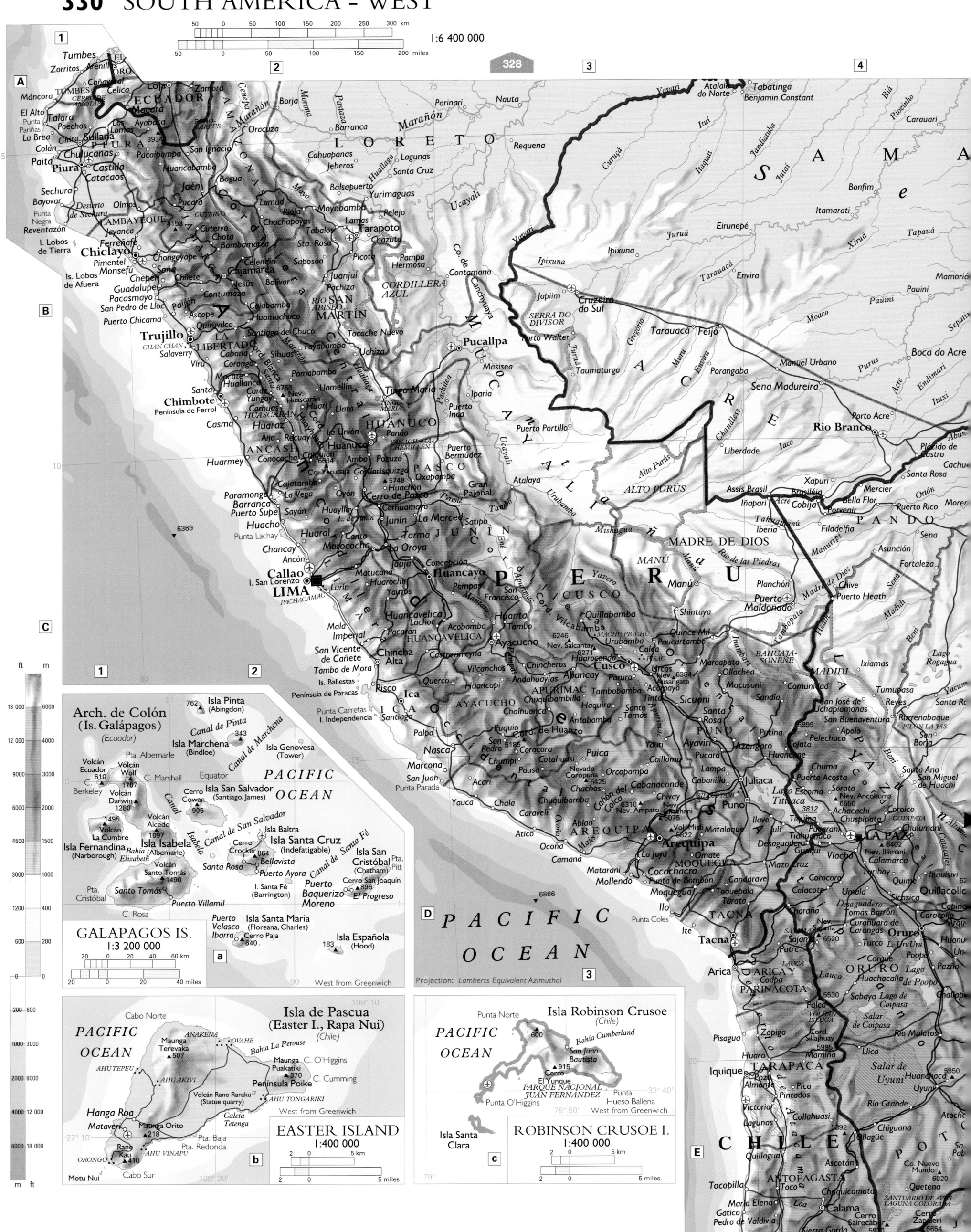

50   0   50   100   150   200   250   300 km
50   0   50   100   150   200 miles

1:6 400 000

328

Arch. de Colón
(Is. Galápagos)
(Ecuador)

GALAPAGOS IS.
1:3 200 000

20   0   20   40   60 km
20   0   20   40 miles

PACIFIC
OCEAN

Equator

West from Greenwich

Isla de Pascua
(Easter I., Rapa Nui)
(Chile)

EASTER ISLAND
1:400 000

2   0   5 km
2   0   5 miles

PACIFIC
OCEAN

West from Greenwich

Isla Robinson Crusoe
(Chile)

PACIFIC
OCEAN

PARQUE NACIONAL
JUAN FERNÁNDEZ

Isla Santa Clara

ROBINSON CRUSOE I.
1:400 000

2   0   5 km
2   0   5 miles

West from Greenwich

PACIFIC
OCEAN

Projection: Lamberts Equivalent Azimuthal

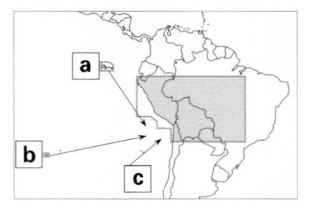

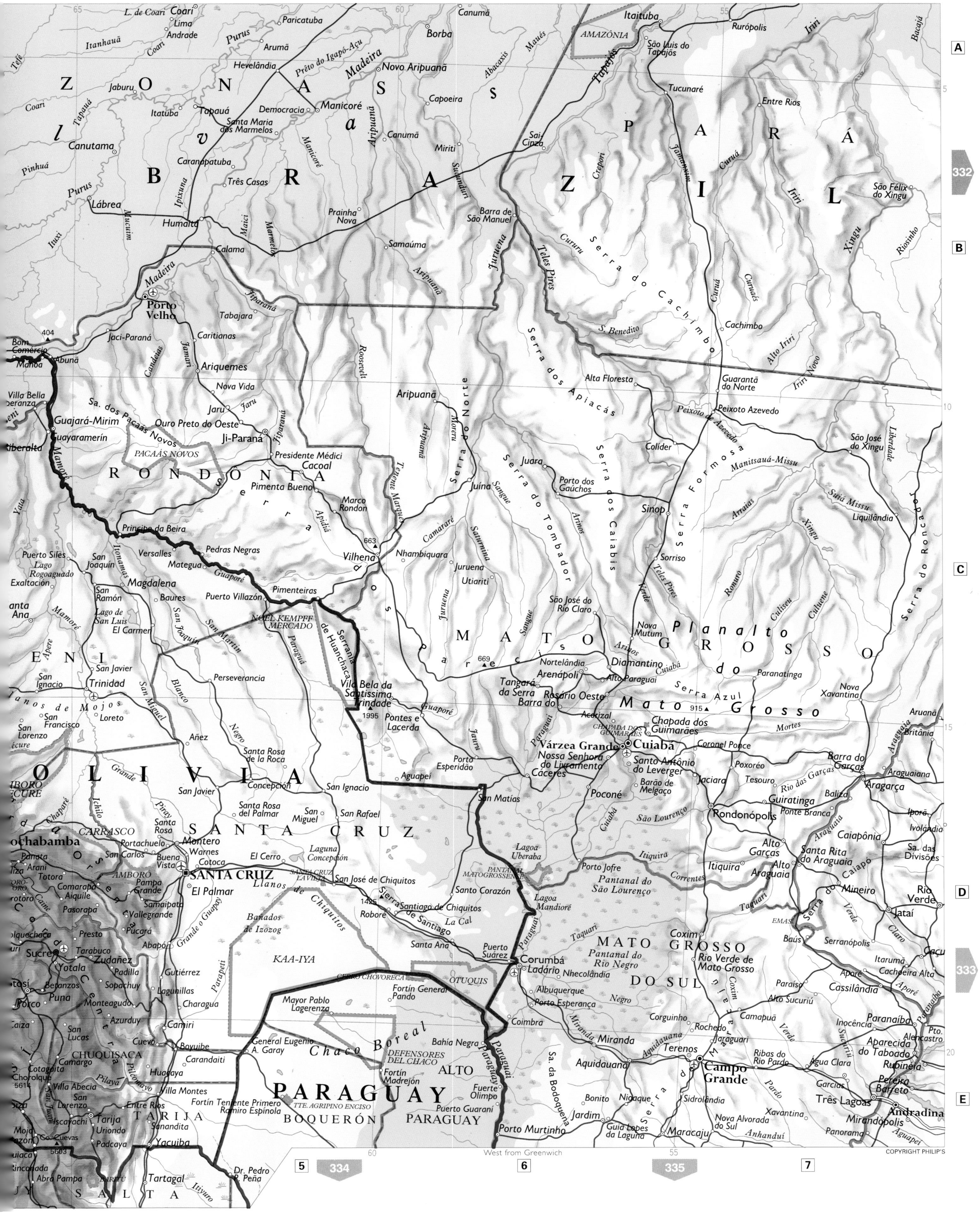

329   332   333   334   335

B R A Z I L

A M A Z O N A S

P A R Á

R O N D Ô N I A

M A T O   G R O S S O

Planalto do Mato Grosso

Mato Grosso

MATO GROSSO DO SUL

B O L I V I A

SANTA CRUZ

BENI

CHUQUISACA

TARIJA

PARAGUAY

BOQUERÓN

ALTO PARAGUAY

Chaco Boreal

Llanos de Mojos

Llanos de Chiquitos

Porto Velho · Guajará-Mirim · Guayaramerín · Ji-Paraná · Vilhena · Cuiabá · Várzea Grande · Corumbá · Campo Grande · Santa Cruz · Cochabamba · Sucre · Trinidad · Cáceres · Rondonópolis

L. de Coari · Coari · Itanhauã · Manicoré · Humaitá · Borba · Canumã · Itaituba · Rurópolis · Iriri · São Félix do Xingu

West from Greenwich

COPYRIGHT PHILIP'S

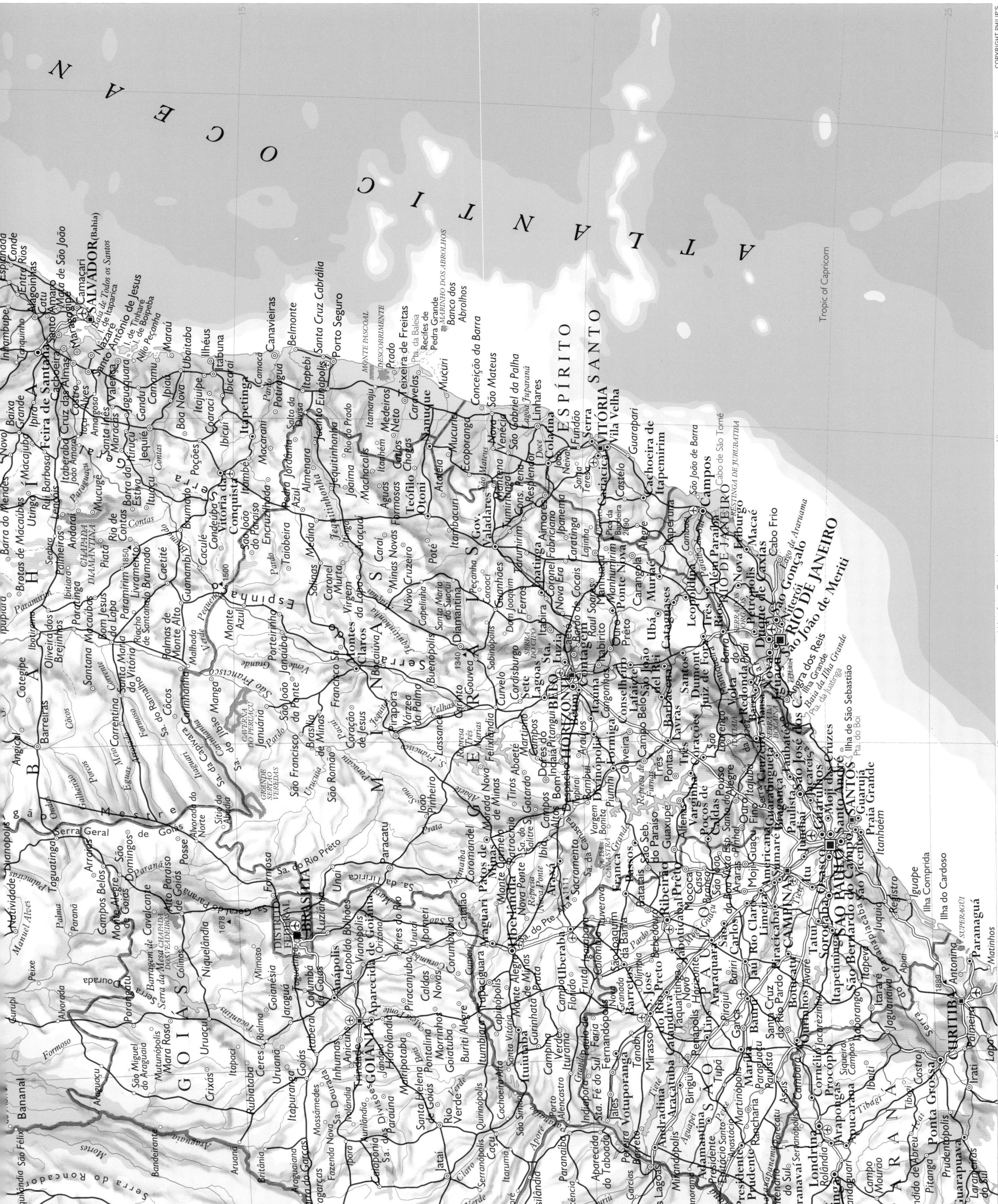

ATLANTIC OCEAN

SALVADOR (Bahia)

ESPÍRITO SANTO

VITÓRIA
Vila Velha

RIO DE JANEIRO

Niterói

BELO HORIZONTE

BRASÍLIA
DISTRITO FEDERAL

GOIÂNIA

GOIÁS

MINAS GERAIS

BAHIA

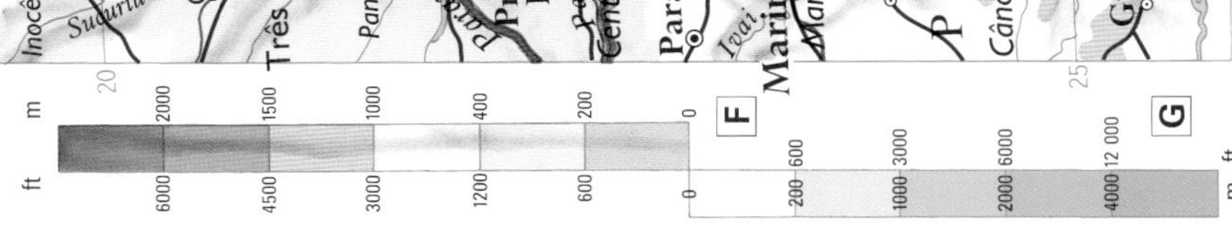

SÃO PAULO

CURITIBA

PARANÁ

Tropic of Capricorn

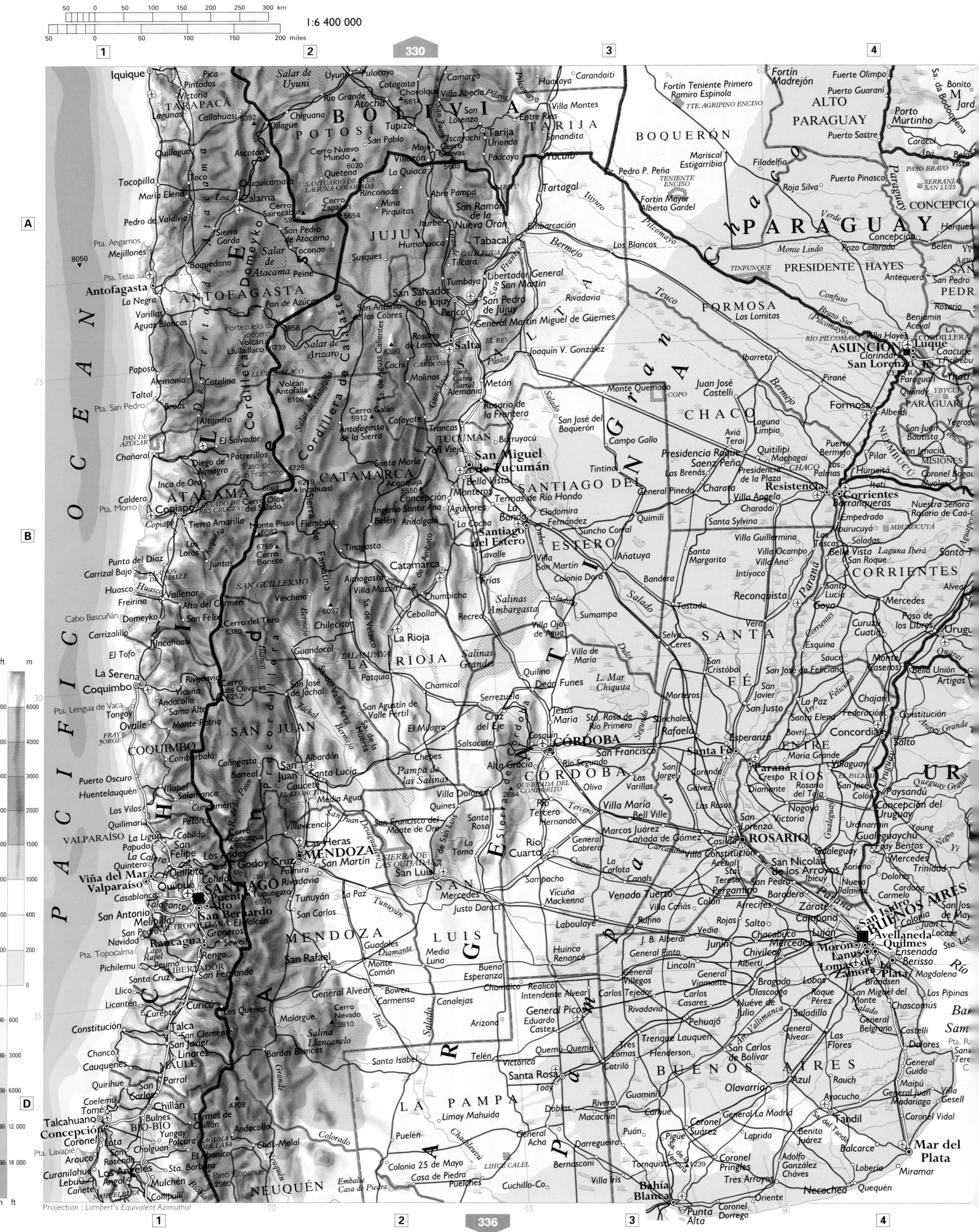

1:6 400 000

Projection : Lambert's Equivalent Azimuthal

331 **5**   **6**   333   **7**

BELO HORIZONTE
Betim Contagem
Itabirito
VITÓRIA
Sidrolândia   Oliveira Conselheiro Ouro Ponte Nova Vila Velha
Nioaque   Olímpia São Sebastião Lafaiete Prêto Carangola Guarapari
MATO GROSSO Três Lagoas Andradina Mirassol São José Passos Campo Belo São João Uba Muriae Cachoeiro
Xavantina Mirandópolis do Rio Preto Bebedouro Represa de del Rei Cataguases de Itapemirim
Maracaju DO SUL Panorama Araçatuba Catanduva Ribeirão Guaxupé Furnas Barbacena
Nova Alvorada Aguapeí Taquaritinga Jaboticabal Prêto Tres Lavras Alem Paraíba Campos
Dourados   Adamantina Lins Mococa Pontas Santos Leopoldina Tres São João
Pardo   Presidente Penápolis SÃO PAULO Casa Alfenas Dumont Juiz de Fora Rios de Barra
Ponta Porã Brilhante Nova Epitácio Novo Branca Varginha Poços de Paraiba do Sul RIO DE JANEIRO
Pedro Juan Caballero Andradina Euclides da Martinópolis Marília São Esp. Santo do Pouso Barra Nova Friburgo Macaé
Porto São José Cunha Paulista Rancharia Paraguaçu Bauru Carlos Araras Pinhal Alegre Itajubá Mansa Nova Duque de Caxias
Navirai Ilha Centenário do Sul Paulista Assis Santa Cruz Rio Claro Moji Americana Guaratinguetá Barra São Gonçalo Cabo Frio
Amambai GRANDE Paranapanema do Rio Pardo Limeira Taubaté Mirim Viterói Cabo de São Tomé
Mundo Novo Rolândia Cambará Piracicaba Sumaré Bragança Jacarei Angra dos Reis RESTINGA DE JURUBATIBA
Salto do Guaíra Maringá Londrina Ourinhos CAMPINAS Paulista São José dos João Tropic of Capricorn
Esperança Cornélio Botucatu Atu Jundiaí Campos de Janeiro
Umuarama Cianorte Procópio Avaré Sorocaba Osasco Guarulhos Ilha Grande
Cruzeiro Mandaguari Apucarana Joaquim São Guaça Moji das Cruzes Bahia da Ilha Grande
Goio-Erê Campo Távora Itaporanga Bernardo do Campo Santo SANTOS André
Guara Mourão Itapeva SÃO PAULO São Vicente Guarujá
PARANÁ Ibaiti Itaparanga Praia Grande
Cândido de Abreu Tibagi Paranapiacaba Juquiá Ilha de São Sebastião
BRAZIL Pitanga Castro Itararé Itanhaém Pta. do Boi
Cascavel Sa. das Araras Jaguariaíva Apiaí Registro
Prudentópolis Iguape
Represa de Itaipú Guarapuava Ponta Iguaçu Ilha Comprida
Medianeira Grossa CURITIBA Antonina
Foz do Iguaçu Larangeiras Irati Palmeira Ilha do Cardoso
Ciudad Francisco do Sul Lapa SUPERAGÜI
del Este Beltrão União da São Mateus Paranaguá
PARANÁ Vitória do Sul Matinhos
Pato Branco Rio Negro Guaratuba
Eldorado   Palmas Joinville
Montecarlo   Clevelândia Caçador São Francisco do Sul
Jardim San Pedro Xanxerê Itajaí
MISIONES América San Pedro Chapecó SANTA Blumenau
Corpus Iruguai Concórdia Joaçaba CATARINA Brusque
Oberá Campos Santa Cecília
Encarnación Monteagudo Frederico Novos Rio do Sul
Candelaria Westphalen Ererhim Lages São José
Leandro Horizontina Palmeira Cutitibanos Ilha de Santa Catarina
N. Alem Santa Rosa das Missões Florianópolis
Santo Angelo Carazinho Vacaria São
São Luís Ijuí Passo Joaquim
Gonzaga Fundo Lagoa SÃO JOAQUIM
Sa. do Espinilho Cruz Alta Vermelha Laguna
São Borja RIO GRANDE Guaporé Tubarão Cabo Santa Marta Grande
Santiago Bento Gonçalves Criciúma
Ibicuí Caxias ARARADOS DA SERRA
Alegrete Santa Maria do Sul Araranguá
Rosário do Sul Santa Cruz Novo Hamburgo Torres
DO SUL Montenegro São Taquara
Canoas Leopoldo Osório
Cachoeira do Sul Viamão PORTO ALEGRE
URUGUAY São Gabriel Caçapava Encantadas
Santana do do Sul Tapes
Livramento Dom Pedrito Camaquã
Rivera Santana Camaquã
Bagé Sa. do Camaquã
Tacuarembó Pinheiro São Lourenço Mostardas
Machado do Sul LAGOA DO PEIXE
L. Rincón Pelotas
Bonete Melo Lagoa
Fraile Rio São José do Norte
Muerto Branco Rio Grande
San Gregorio Jaguarão Lagoa Mangueira
Blanquillo Vergara Mirim
Cerro Treinta y Tres Santa Vitória do Palmar
Chato
Sarandí del Yí Lascano Chuy
Aiguá SANTA TERESA
Tala Minas Rocha
Piedras San Carlos Castillos
Pando Maldonado
MONTEVIDEO Pta. del Este
Plata

bón

Antonio

A T L A N T I C

O C E A N

5304

West from Greenwich   COPYRIGHT PHILIP'S

55   50   45   40

5   **6**   **7**

A
B
C
D

5
6
7

1:6 400 000

FALKLAND ISLANDS (U.K.)
(ISLAS MALVINAS)

GEOGRAPHICAL GLOSSARY

This is a list of the geographical terms from various foreign languages that are found in the place names on the maps and in the index. Each is followed by the language and its English meaning.

Afr. Afrikaans
Alb. Albanian
Amh. Amharic
Ar. Arabic
Belo. Belorussian
Berb. Berber
Bulg. Bulgarian
Burm. Burmese
Cam. Cambodian
Cat. Catalan
Chin. Chinese
Czec. Czech
Dan. Danish
Dut. Dutch
Est. Estonian
Fin. Finnish
Fr. French
Gae. Gaelic
Ger. German
Gr. Greek
Heb. Hebrew
Hin. Hindi
Hung. Hungarian
I.-C. Indo-Chinese
Ice. Icelandic
It. Italian
Indo. Indonesian
Jap. Japanese
Kaz. Kazakh
Kor. Korean
Kyrg. Kyrgyz
Lapp. Lapp (Sami)
Lat. Latvian
Lith. Lithuanian
Malag. Malagasy
Mong. Mongolian
Nor. Norway
Pash. Pashto
Per. Persian
Pol. Polish
Port. Portuguese
Rom. Romanian
Russ. Russian
Sin. Sinhalese
Ser.-Cr. Serbo-Croat
Slov. Slovene
Som. Somali
Span. Spanish
Swe. Swedish
Tib. Tibetan
Turk. Turkish
Ukr. Ukrainian
Viet. Vietnamese

-á *Ice.* river
-å *Dan., Nor., Swe.* stream
-abad *Farsi, Russ.* town
Abyad *Ar.* white mountain
Ada, Adasi *Turk.* island
Addis *Amh.* new
Adrar *Ar., Berb.* mountains
Aiguille *Fr.* peak
Aïn, Aïn (A.) *Ar.* spring
Ákra *Gr.* cape, point
Akrotíri *Gr.* cape, point
Alb *Ger.* mountains
Albufera *Span.* lagoon
-ålen *Nor.* islands
Alpen *Ger.* mountain ranges
Alpes *Fr.* mountains
Alpi *It.* mountains
Alt *Ger.* old
Alta, Alto *Port.* high, upper
Altos *Span.* mountains
-älv, -älven *Swe.* stream, river
Amtskommune (Amt.) *Dan.* first-order administrative division
-ån *Swe.* river
Anse *Fr.* bay
Ao *Thai* bay
Appennino *It.* mountain range
Archipel *Fr.* archipelago
Archipiélago (Arch.) *Span.* archipelago
Arcipélago *It.* archipelago
Arquipélago (Arq.) *Port.* archipelago
Arrecife *Span.* reef
Arroyo (Arr.) *Span.* stream
-ås, -åsen *Nor., Swe.* hill
Ayios *Gr.* island
Ayn *Ar.* well, waterhole

Baai, -baai *Afr., Dut.* bay
Bāb *Ar.* gate, strait
Bäck, -bäcken *Swe.* stream
Back, -backen, *Swe.* hill
Bad, -baden *Ger.* spa
Badia *Cat.* bay
Bādiyah, Bādiyat *Ar.* desert
Bæk *Dan.* stream
Bælt *Dan.* strait
Baharu *Malay* new
Bahia (B.) *Span.* bay
Bahiret *Ar.* lagoon
Bahr *Ar.* sea, lake, river
Bahra Bahrat *Ar.* lake
Baía (B.) *Port.* bay
Baie (B.) *Fr.* bay
Baixa, Baixo *Port.* lower
Baja, Bajo *Span.* lower
Bakke *Nor.* hill
Bala *Farsi* upper
Ballon *Fr.* dome
Baltă *Rom.* marsh, lake
Ban *Lao, Thai* village
-Bana *Jap.* cape
Banc *Fr.* bank
Banco *Span.* bank
Bandao *Chin.* peninsula
Bandar *Ar., Malay* port, harbour
Bandar *Farsi* bay
Banja *Ser.-Cr.* spa, resort
Banjaran *Malay* mountain range
Baraji *Turk.* dam
Barat *Indo., Malay* western
Barrage (Barr.) *Fr.* dam
Barragem (Barr.) *Port.* dam, reservoir
Bas, basse *Fr.* lower
Bassin *Fr.* basin
-batang *Indo.* river
Batlaq *Farsi* marsh
Batu *Malay* mountain
Bayt *Heb.* house, village
Bazar *Hin.* market, bazaar
-beek *Afr., Dut.* river
Be'er *Heb.* well
Bei *Chin.* north, northern
Beinn, Ben *Gae.* mountain
Beit *Heb.* village
Belaya, Belo, Beloye, Belyy *Russ.* white
Belogorye *Russ.* hills, mountain range
Bender *Som.* harbour
Berg(e), -berg(e) *Afr., Ger.* mountain(s)
-berg, -en, -et *Nor., Swe.* hill, mountain, rock
Besar *Indo., Malay* big
Bet *Heb.* house, village
Bir, Bîr, Bi'r *Ar.* well
Birkat, Birket *Ar.* lake, marsh, well
Bishti *Alb.* cape
-bjerg *Dan.* hill, point
Blaenau *Welsh* upland
-bo *Chin.* lake
Boca *Port., Span.* river mouth, inlet
Bodden *Ger.* bay, inlet
Bogaz, Boğazı *Turk.* channel, strait
Bogd *Mong.* mountain range
Bois *Fr.* woods
Boka *Ser.-Cr.* gulf, inlet
Bolshoi, Bolshaya, Bolshoye (Bol.) *Russ.* great, large
Bordj (Bj.) *Ar.* fort
-borg *Dan., Nor., Swe.* castle, fort
Bory *Pol.* woods
Bosque *Span.* woods
-botn *Nor.* valley floor
Bouche(s) *Fr.* mouth(s)
Braţul *Rom.* distributary stream, branch
-bre, -breen *Nor.* glacier
Bredning *Dan.* bay
Brücke *Ger.* bridge
-brug *Dut.* bridge
-brunn *Swe.* well, spring
Bucht *Ger.* bay
Bugt *Dan.* bay
-bugten *Dan.* bay
Buheirat *Ar.* lake, reservoir
Bukit *Malay* hill
-bukt, -a *Nor.* bay
-bukten *Swe.* bay
-bulag *Mong.* spring
Bulag *Chin.* lake
Bulu *Malay* mountain
Bum *Burm.* mountain
Bûr *Ar.* port
Burg. *Ar.* fort
Burg, -burg *Ger.* castle
Burnu, Burun *Turk.* cape
Butt *Gae.* promontory
Büyük *Turk.* big
-by *Dan., Nor., Swe.* town
-byen *Nor., Swe.* town

Cabeza *Span.* peak, hill
Cabo (C.) *Port., Span.* headland, cape
Cachoeira *Port.* waterfall
Cala Cat. *It.* bay
Camp Port. *Span.* land, field
Câmpia *Rom.* plain
Campo *It., Port., Span.* plain
Campos *Span.* upland
Canal (Can.) *Fr., Port., Span.* canal, channel
Canale (Can.) *It.* channel
Canalul (Can.) *Ser.-Cr.* canal
Cao Nguyen *Thai* plateau, tableland
Cap (C.) *Cat., Fr.* cape
Capo (C) *It.* cape
Carn *Gae.* hill
Carse *Gae.* valley
Catarata *Port., Span.* cataract
Cauce *Span.* intermittent stream
Causse *Fr.* limestone plateau
Cay, Cayi, -cay, -cayi *Turk.* river
Cayo(s) *Span.* rock(s), islet(s)
Cefn *Welsh* hill
Cerro *Span.* hill, peak
Česká, Český, České *Czec.* Czech
Chaco *Span.* jungle
Chaîne(s) *Fr.* mountain range(s)
Chang *Chin.* mountain
Chapa *Span.* hills, upland
Chapada *Port.* hills, upland
Chaung *Burm.* stream, river
Chi *Chin.* small lake
-ch'ŏn *Kor.* river
-chŏsuji *Kor.* reservoir
Chott *Ar.* salt lake, depression
Chu *Tib.* river
Chute *Fr.* waterfall
Città *It.* city
Ciudad *Span.* city
Co *Tib.* lake
Cochilla (Coch.) *Port.* hills
Col *Fr., It.* pass
Colina(s) *Span.* hill(s)
Colle *It.* pass
Colline(s) *Fr.* hill(s)
Conca *It.* plain, basin
Cordillera (Cord.) *Span.* mountain range
Costa *It., Port., Span.* coast
Côte *Fr.* coast, slope, hill
Coteaux *Fr.* hills
Cuchilla *Span.* hills
Cuenca *Span.* river basin
Cu-Lao *Viet.* island

Da *Chin.* big
Da *Viet.* river
Daban *Mong.* pass
Dağ(ı) *Turk.* mountain(s)
Dāgh *Farsi* mountain
Dağları *Turk.* mountain range
-dai, -daichi *Jap.* plateau
-Dake *Jap.* mountain
-dal, -e *Dan., Swe.* valley
-dal, -en *Swe., Nor.* valley, stream
Dalay Mong. large lake
-ðalir, -ðalur *Ice.* valley
-damm, -en *Swe.* lake
Danau *Malay* lake
Dao *Chin., Viet.* island
Dar *Ar.* region
Darya *Russ.* river
Daryācheh *Farsi* marshy lake, lake
Dasht *Farsi* desert, steppe
Daung *Burm.* mountain, hill
Dayr *Ar.* monastery
Debre *Amh.* hill
Deli *Ser.-Cr.* mountain
Deniz, -i *Turk.* sea
Département (Dépt.) *Fr.* first-order administrative division
Dere *Turk.* stream
Desierto (Des.) *Span.* desert
Détroit *Fr.* strait
Dhar *Ar.* region, mountain range
Diep *Dut.* channel
Dijk *Dut.* dyke
Ding *Chin.* mountain
Dingzi *Chin.* hill, mountain
Djebel (Dj.) *Ar.* mountain
-djúp *Ice.* fjord
-djupet *Swe.* channel, sound
-Do *Jap., Kor.* island
Dolina *Russ.* valley
Dolna, Dolni *Bulg.* lower
Dolna, Dolne, Dolny *Russ.* lower
Dolní *Czec.* lower
Dolok (D.) *Malay* mountain
-dong *Kor.* village, town
Dong *Chin.* east, eastern
Donja, Donji *Ser.-Cr.* lower
-dorf *Ger.* village
-dorp *Afr.* village
-drif *Afr.* ford
-dybet *Dan.* marine channel
Dzong *Tib.* town, settlement
Dzüün *Mong.* east, eastern

-egga *Nor.* peak
-eiland, -en (eil.) *Afr., Dut.* island(s)
Eilean *Gae.* island
-elv, -a *Nor.* river
Embalse *Span.* reservoir
'Emeq *Heb.* plain, valley
Ensenada *Span.* bay
Erg *Ar.* sand desert
Estero *Span.* estuary
Estrada *Span.* bay
Estrecho *Span.* strait
Estuaire *Fr.* estuary
Estuario *Span.* estuary
Étang *Fr.* lagoon, lake
-ey, -jar *Ice.* island(s)
-ežeras *Lith.* lake
-ezers *Lat.* lake

Falaise *Fr.* cliff
-fallet *Swe.* waterfall
Farihy *Malag.* lake
Faro *Span.* lighthouse
-feld *Ger.* field
-fell *Ice.* mountain, hill
Feng *Chin.* mountain range
Fiume (F.) *It.* river
-fjäll, -en, -et *Swe.* hill(s), mountain(s), ridge
-fjärden *Swe.* fjord
Fjeld *Dan.* mountain
-fjell, -et *Nor.* mountain range
-fjord, -en *Dan., Nor., Swe.* fjord
-fjorður *Ice.* fjord, bay, inlet
Fleuve (Fl.) *Fr.* river
-flói *Ice.* bay, marshy country
Fluss (F.) *Ger.* river
Foce, Foci *It.* mouth(s)
Folyó (F.) *Hung.* river
-fonn *Nor.* glacier
-fontein *Afr.* fountain, spring
Forêt *Fr.* forest
-fors, -en *Swe.* waterfall, rapids
-foss, -en *Ice., Nor.* waterfall
Forst *Ger.* forest
Foum *Ar.* pass
Fuente *Span.* source
-furt *Ger.* ford
Fylke *Nor.* first-order administrative division

-gang *Chin.* bay, harbour
-gang *Kor.* river
Ganga *Hin., Sin.* river
Gangri *Tib.* mountain
Gaoyuan *Chin.* plateau
-gat *Dan.* sound
-Gata *Jap.* lake
-gau *Ger.* district
-Gawa *Jap.* river
Gebel (G.) *Ar.* mountain
Gebirge (Geb.) *Ger.* hills, mountains
Gezirat, Geziret *Ar.* island
Ghat *Hin.* range of hills
Ghiol *Rom.* lake
Ghubbat *Ar.* bay, inlet
Gjiri *Alb.* bay
Gjol *Alb.* lagoon, lake
Glava (Gl.) *Ser.-Cr.* mountain, peak
Glen *Gae.* valley
Gletscher (Gl.) *Ger.* glacier
Gobi *Mong.* desert
Gol *Mong.* river
Göl *Azeri, Turk.* lake
Golfe (G.) *Fr.* gulf
Golfo (G.) *It., Span.* gulf
Gölü *Turk.* lake
Gomba *Tib.* settlement
Gora, Góra *Bulg., Russ., Ser.-Cr., Pol.* mountain
Gorje *Ser.-Cr.* hills, mountains
Gorno *Russ.* mountainous
-gorod *Russ.* small town
Gory, Góry *Pol., Russ.* mountain
-grad *Bulg. Russ., Ser.-Cr.* town, city
-grada *Russ.* ridge
Gran *It., Span.* big, great
Grand, -e *Fr.* big, great
Groot (Gt.) *Afr., Dut.* big, great
Gross, -e, -en, -er *Ger.* big, great(er)
Grupo *Span.* group
Gruppo *It.* group
Guan *Chin.* pass
Guba (G.) *Russ.* bay
-Guntō *Jap.* island group
Gunong, Gunung (G.) *Indo., Malay* mountain
Gură *Rom.* passage

Hadabat *Ar.* plateau
Hadjer *Ar.* mountain
-hafen *Ger.* harbour, port
Haff *Ger.* bay, lagoon
Hai *Chin.* lake, sea
Haixia *Chin.* channel, strait
Halbinsel *Ger.* peninsula
Halvø *Dan.* peninsula
Halvøya *Nor.* peninsula
Hâmad, Hamada, Hammādah, Hammādat *Ar.* stony desert, plateau
-hamn *Swe., Nor.* harbour, anchorage
Hāmūn *Farsi* marsh, lake
-Hantō *Jap.* peninsula
Har(e) *Heb.* hill(s), mountain(s)
Hassi (Hi.) *Ar.* well
-haug *Nor.* hill
Hav, Havet *Nor., Swe.* sea
-havn *Dan., Nor.* bay, harbour
Havre *Fr.* harbour
Hawd *Ar.* oasis
Hawr *Ar.* lake, marsh
He *Chin.* river
-hegység *Hung.* hills, forest
Heide *Ger.* heath, moor
Helodranon' *Malag.* bay
Higashi *Jap.* east, eastern
-ho *Kor.* lake
-hø *Nor.* peak
Hoch *Ger.* high
Hochland *Afr.* highland
Hoek, -hoek *Afr., Dut.* cape, point
-höfn *Ice.* harbour, port
-hög, -en, -högar, -högarna *Swe.* hill(s), peak, mountain
Höhe *Ger.* height
Hohen *Ger.* high, upper
-hoi *Chin.* bay
-høj, -e *Dan.* hills
-holm, -holme, -holmen *Dan., Nor., Swe.* island
Hon *Viet.* island
Hoog *Dut.* high
Hora *Czec., Ukr.* mountain
-horn *Ger.* peak
Hory *Czec.* mountains, hills
-hot *Mong.* town
-hoved *Dan.* point, headland, peninsula
-hrad *Czec.* town
Hraun *Ice.* lava
-hsi *Chin.* river
-hsia *Chin.* gorge, strait
-hsien *Chin.* district
Hu *Chin.* lake, reservoir
Huk *Dan., Ger.* cape
-huk *Swe.* cape
Huken *Nor.* cape

Idd *Ar.* well
Idehan *Ar., Berb.* sandy plain, dunes
-ike *Jap.* lake
Île(s) (I(s).) *Fr.* island(s)
Ilha(s) (I(s).) *Port.* island(s)
imeni *Russ.* 'in the name of'
Inish *Gae.* island
Insel(n) (I.) *Ger.* island(s)
Irmak *Turk.* river
'Irq *Ar.* dunes
Isla(s) (I(s).) *Span.* island(s)
Iso *Fin.* big, great
Isol, -a, -e (I.) *It.* island(s)
Isthme *Fr.* isthmus
Istmo *Span.* isthmus
-iwa *Jap.* island

Jabal *Ar.* mountain range
Järv *Est.* lake
järvi *Fin.* lake, bay, pond
-jaur, -javre *Lapp.* lake
Jazā'ir *Ar.* islands
Jazīra, jazīrat *Ar.* island
Jazireh *Farsi* island
Jebel *Ar.* mountain
Jezero *Ser.-Cr.* lake
Jezioro *Pol.* lake
Jiang *Chin.* river
Jiao *Chin.* cape
-Jima *Jap.* island
Jøkulen *Nor.* glacier, ice cap
-joki *Fin.* river
-jökull *Ice.* glacier, ice cap
Jūras Līcis *Lat.* bay, gulf

Kaap (K.) *Afr.* cape
-kai *Jap.* bay, channel, sea
-kaikyō *Jap.* strait
-kaise *Lapp.* mountain
kalnas *Lith.* hill
Kamennyy *Russ.* stony
Kampong *Cam.* village
Kampung *Malay* village
-kanaal *Dut.* canal
Kanal *Dan.* channel, gulf
Kanal *Ger., Swe.* canal
-kanal *Ser.-Cr.* channel, canal
Kanava *Fin.* canal
Kang *Kor.* river, bay
Kap (K.) *Dan., Ger.* cape, point
-kapp *Nor.* cape, point
-kaupstaður *Ice.* market town
-kaupunki *Fin.* town
Kavīr *Farsi* salt desert
Kébir *Ar.* great
Kecil *Malay* lesser, little
Kefar *Heb.* village, hamlet
-Ken *Jap.* first-order administrative division
Kep, -i (K.) *Alb.* cape
Kepulauan (Kep.) *Indo., Malay* archipelago
Keski- *Fin.* middle, central
Khalīg, Khalīj *Ar.* gulf
-khamba *Tib.* source, spring
Khawr *Ar.* bay, channel, wadi
Khlong *Thai* river
Kho Khot *Thai* isthmus
Khōr *Farsi* bay, estuary
Khrebet *Russ.* mountain range
Kita- *Jap.* north
Klein,-e, -er *Ger.* small
-klint *Dan.* cliff
Klintar *Swe.* hills
-kloof *Afr.* gorge, pass
Knude *Dan.* point
-Ko *Jap.* lake
Ko *Thai* island
-kōchi *Jap.* mountainous region
-kōgen *Jap.* plateau
Kohi *Pash.* mountains
Kol *Kaz., Kyrg.* lake
Kólpos *Gr., Turk.* gulf, bay
Kolymskoye *Russ.* mountain range
Kompong *Malay* landing place
-kop *Afr.* hill
-kopf *Ger.* hill
-köping *Swe.* market town
Körfäzi *Azeri* gulf
Körfezi *Turk.* gulf
Kosa *Russ., Ukr.* spit
-koski *Fin.* rapids
-kraal *Afr.* native village
-kraj *Czec., Pol., Ser.-Cr.* region
Krasnyy *Russ.* red
Kryazh *Russ.* ridge, hills
Kuala *Malay* bay
-kuan *Chin.* pass
Kūh(ha) *Farsi* mountain(s)
Kul *Russ.* lake
-kulle *Swe.* hill
Kum *Russ.* sandy desert
Kumpu *Fin.* hill
Kwe *Burm.* bay, gulf
-kylä *Fin.* village
Kyst, -en *Dan., Nor.* coast
Kyun(zu) *Burm.* island(s)

La *Tib.* pass
-laagte *Afr.* watercourse

Lääni *Fin.* first-order administrative division
Lac (L.) *Fr.* lake
Lacul (L.) *Rom.* lake, lagoon
Lago (L.) *It., Port., Span.* lake, lagoon
Lagoa (L.) *Port.* lagoon
Lagos *Port., Span.* lakes
Laguna (L.) *It., Span.* lagoon, lake
Lagune (L.) *Fr.* lake
-laht *Est.* bay
Lahti *Fin.* bay, gulf, cove
Lakhti *Russ.* bay, gulf
Lam *Thai* river
Lampi *Fin.* lake
Län *Swe.* first-order administrative division
Land *Ger.* first-order administrative division
-land *Dan.* region
-land *Afr., Nor.* land, province
Lande *Fr.* heath
Laut *Indo.* sea
Law *Gae.* hill, mountain
Līcis *Lat.* gulf
Lido *It.* beach, shore
Liedao *Chin.* islands
Lilla *Swe.* small
Lille *Dan., Nor.* small
Liman *Russ.* bay, gulf
Límni (L.) *Gr.* lake
Ling *Chin.* mountain range
-linna *Fin.* fort
Llano *Span.* prairie, plain
Llyn *Welsh* lake
Loch (L.) *Gae.* lake, inlet
Lough (L.) *Gae.* lake, inlet
Lum *Alb.* river
Lund *Dan.* forest
-lund, -en *Swe.* wood(s)
-luoto *Fin.* island

-maa *Est.* island
Madīnat *Ar.* town, city
Madiq *Ar.* strait
Maja *Alb.* mountains
-mäki *Fin.* hill, hillside
Mal *Alb.* mountain
Maloye, Malyy, Malyya *Russ.* little, small
Mala, Mali, Malo *Ser.-Cr.* little, small
Malaya *Belo.* small
Malé *Czec., Slovak* small
Mali *Alb.* mountain
-man *Kor.* bay
Mar *Span.* lagoon, sea
Marais *Fr.* marsh
Mare *It.* sea
Mare *Rom.* great
Marisma *Span.* marsh
-mark *Dan., Nor.* land
Marsâ *Ar.* anchorage, bay, inlet
Masabb *Ar.* river mouth, estuary
Massif *Fr.* upland, mountains
Mato *Port.* forest
Mazar *Farsi* shrine, tomb
Meer, -meer *Afr., Dut., Ger.* lake, sea
-men *Chin.* bay, gorge, channel
Mesto *Ser.-Cr., Czec.* town
Mezzo *It.* middle
Midbar *Heb.* wilderness
Mierzeja *Pol.* spit
Mifraz *Heb.* bay
Mina *Ar.* port
Minami *Jap.* south, southern
-misaki *Jap.* cape, point
Mittel *Ger.* central, middle
-mo *Nor., Swe.* heath, island
-mon *Swe.* heath
Mong *Burm.* town
Mont(s) (Mt(s).) *Fr.* hill(s), mountain(s)
Montagna (Mt.) *It.* mountain
Montagne(s) (Mt(s).) *Fr.* hill(s), mountain(s)
Montaña(s) (Mt(s).) *Span.* mountain(s)
Montanyes *Cat.* mountains
Monte(s) (Mte(s).) *It., Port., Span.* mountain(s)
Monti (Mti.) *It.* mountains
More *Russ.* sea
Mörön *Mong.* river
Moyen *Fr.* central, middle
Muang *Malay* town
Mui *Viet.* cape
Mull *Gae.* promontory
Mund, -mund *Afr.* mouth
Munkhafed *Ar.* depression
Munte (Mte.) *Rom.* mount
Munţi(i) (Mti.) *Rom.* mountain(s)
Muong *Malay* village
Myit *Burm.* river
Myitwanya *Burm.* mouths of river
Mynydd *Welsh* mountain
-myr *Nor., Swe.* swamp
-mýri *Ice.* swamp
Mys (M.) *Russ.* cape

-Nada *Jap.* bay, gulf
-næs *Dan.* point, cape
Nafūd *Ar.* sandy desert
Nagorye *Russ.* hills, mountains
Nagy *Hung.* big
Nahal (N.) *Heb.* river
Nahr (N.) *Ar.* river, stream
Najd *Ar.* plateau, pass
Nakhon *Thai* town
Nam *Kor., Viet.* river
-nam *Kor.* south
Namakzār *Per.* salt flat
Nan *Chin.* south, southern
-nao *Chin.* lake
-näs *Swe.* cape
Neder *Dut.* lower
Nedre *Nor.* lower
Nei *Chin.* inner
Nek *Afr.* pass
-nes *Ice., Nor.* cape
Ness, -ness *Gae.* promontory, cape
Nevada, Nevado *Span.* snow-capped mountain
Nez *Fr.* cape
Nieder *Ger.* lower
-niemi *Fin.* cape, point, peninsula, island
Nieuw, -e *Dut.* new
Nishi *Jap.* west, western
Nisos, Nisoi *Gr.* island(s)
Nizhneye, Nizhniy *Russ.* lower
Nizina *Belo., Pol.* lowland
Nizmennost *Russ.* plain, lowland
Nízní *Czec.* lower
Noord *Dut.* north, northern
Nord *Fr.* north, northern
Norra *Swe.* north, northern
Nørre *Dan.* north, northern
Norte *Port., Span.* north, northern
Nos *Bulg., Russ.* cape, point
Nosy *Malag.* island
Nouveau, Nouvelle *Fr.* new
Nova, Novi *Bulg., Port., Serb.-Cr.* new
Novaya, Novo, Novoye, Novyy *Russ.* new
Nové, Novy *Czec., Slovak* new
Novo *Port.* new
Nowa, Nowe, Nowy *Pol.* new
Nudo *Span.* mountain
Nueva, Nuevo *Span.* new
Nur *Chin.* lake
Nur *Tib.* peak
Nuruu *Mong.* mountain range
Nusa *Indo.* island
Nuur *Mong.* lake
Ny *Dan., Nor., Swe.* new

-ø *Dan., Nor.* island
-ö *Swe.* island
-öar, -na *Swe.* islands
Ober *Ger., Ukr.* upper
Oblast *Russ.* administrative division
Öbor *Mong.* inner
Occidental *Fr., Span.* western
-odde *Dan., Nor.* point, peninsula, cape
Oeste *Span.* west, western
Oglat *Ar.* well
Oji *Alb.* bay
Ojo *Span.* spring
-Oki *Jap.* bay
-ön *Swe.* island
Ondör *Mong.* upper
Oost(er) *Dut.* east(ern)
Oraşu *Rom.* city
Ord *Gae.* point
Óri *Gr.* mountains
Oriental, -e *Fr., Span.* east, eastern
Órmos *Gr.* bay
Óros *Gr.* mountain(s)
Ort *Ger.* point, cape
Ost *Ger.* east
Øst(er) *Den., Nor.* east(ern)
Öst(ra) *Swe.* east(ern)
Ostriv *Ukr.* island
Ostrov(a) *Russ.* island(s)
Otok(i) *Ser.-Cr.* island(s)
Ouabi, Ouadi (O.) *Ar.* dry watercourse, wadi
Oud, -e *Dut.* old
Oued, -i (O.) *Ar.* watercourse
Ouest *Fr.* west, western
Ouzan *Farsi* river
Ova, -si *Turk.* plains, lowlands
Over- *Dan., Dut.* upper
Över-, Övre *Nor., Swe.* upper
-øy, -a *Nor.* island(s)
Oya *Hin.* point
Oya *Sin.* river
Ozero, Ozera (Oz.) *Russ., Ukr.* lake(s)

-pää *Fin.* hill(s), mountain
Pahta *Lapp.* hill
Pampa(s) *Span.* plain(s)
Pantanal *Port.* marsh
Pantano *Span.* reservoir
Pantao *Chin.* peninsula
Parbat *Urdu* mountain
Pas *Fr.* strait
Paso (P.) *Span.* pass
Passage *Fr.* channel
Passe *Fr.* channel
Passo (P.) *It.* pass
Pasul (P.) *Rom.* pass
Patam *Hin.* small village
Patna, -patnam *Hin.* small village
Pegunungan *Indo., Malay* mountain range
Pei, -pei *Chin.* north
Pélagos *Gr.* sea
Pen *Welsh* hill
Peña *Span.* rock, peak
Pendi *Chin.* basin, depression
Péninsule *Fr.* peninsula
Penisola (Pen.) *It.* peninsula
Pereval (Per.) *Russ.* pass
Pervo-, Pervyy- *Russ.* first
Pertuis *Fr.* channel, strait
Peski *Russ.* sand desert
Petit, -e *Fr.* small
Phanom *Thai* mountain
Phnum *Cam.* mountain
Phou *Lao.* mountain
Phu *Thai, Viet.* mountain
Piano *It.* plain
Pic *Cat., Fr.* peak
Pico(s) *Span.* peak(s)
-piggen *Dan.* peak
Pik *Russ.* peak
Pingyuan *Chin.* plain
Pique *Fr.* peak
Piton *Fr.* peak
Pivostriv *Ukr.* peninsula
Piz, Pizzo *It.* peak
Plage *Fr.* beach
Plaine *Fr.* plain
Planalto *Port.* plateau
Planina (Pl.) *Bulg., Ser.-Cr.* mountain range
Plato *Russ., Bulg.* plateau
Playa *Span.* beach
-po *Chin.* lake, wetland
Pointe (Pte.) *Fr.* point, cape
Pojezierze *Pol.* lakes
Polder *Dut.* reclaimed farmland
-pólis *Gr.* city, town
Poluostrov (Pov.) *Russ.* peninsula
Połwysep *Pol.* peninsula
Pont *Fr.* bridge
Ponta (Pta.) *Port.* point, cape
Ponte *Port.* bridge
Poort *Afr.* passage, gate
-poort *Dut.* port
Porta *Port.* pass
Porţile *Rom.* gate
Portillo *Span.* pass
Porto *It., Port., Span.* port
Potámi, Potamós *Gr.* river
Pradesh *Hin.* state
Praia *Port.* beach, shore
Presa *Span.* reservoir
Presqu'île *Fr.* peninsula
Prokhod *Bulg.* pass
Proliv *Russ.* strait
Promontorio *Span.* promontory
Průsmyk (Pr.) *Czec.* pass
Pueblo *Span.* village
Puerto (Pto.) *Span.* port
Puig *Cat.* peak
Pulau (P.) *Indo., Malay* island
Puna *Span.* desert plateau
Puncak *Indo.* peak
Punta (Pta.) *It., Span.* point, peak
Puy *Fr.* peak

Qal'at *Ar.* fort
Qanat *Ar.* canal
Qasr *Ar.* fort
Qiryat *Heb.* town
Qiuling *Chin.* plateau
Qolleh *Farsi* mountain
-qundao *Chin.* islands

Rach *Viet.* river
Rags *Lat.* cape
Rambla *Cat.* river
Ramlat *Ar.* sandy desert
Rão (R.) *Port.* river
Rann *Hin.* swampy region
Rao *I.-C.* river
Ras *Amh., Ar., Farsi* cape, point
Récif(s) *Fr.* reef(s)
Recife(s) *Port.* reef(s)
Reka *Bulg.* river
Repede *Rom.* rapids
Represa *Port.* reservoir
Reshteh *Farsi* mountain range
-rettō *Jap.* group of islands, chain
Ria *Port., Span.* estuary, bay
Ribeirão (R.) *Port.* river
Ribera (R.) *Span.* river bank
Rijeka *Ser.-Cr.* river
Rio (R.) *Port., Span.* river
Rivier (R.) *Afr., Dut.* river
Riviera *It.* coastal plain, coast
Rivière (R.) *Fr.* river
Roca *Span.* rock
Rocca *It.* rock, peak
Roche *Fr.* rock
Rt *Ser.-Cr.* cape, point
Rubh', Rubha *Gae.* cape, point
-rück *Ger.* ridge
Rūd *Farsi* stream, river
Rudohorie *Slovak* mountains
Rzeka (R.) *Pol.* river

-saar *Est.* island
-saari *Fin.* island
Sabkhat, Sabkhet *Ar.* salt flats
Sadd *Ar.* dam
Sagar,-a *Hin., Urdu* lake
Sahrâ *Ar.* desert
-Saki *Jap.* cape, point
Salar *Span.* salt flat
Salina(s) *Span.* salt marsh(es)
-salmi *Fin.* strait, sound, lake, channel
Saltsjöbad *Swe.* resort
-Sammyaku *Jap.* mountain range
Samut *Thai* gulf
San (S.) *It., Port., Span.* saint
-San *Jap., Kor.* hill, mountain
-Sanchi *Jap.* mountain range
Sankt (St.) *Ger., Russ.* saint
-sanmaek *Kor.* mountain range
-sanmyaku *Jap.* mountain range
Santa (Sta.) *It., Port., Span.* saint
Santo (Sto.) *It. Port., Span.* saint
São (S.) *Port.* saint
Sarīr *Ar.* desert
Sasso *It.* mountain
Satu *Rom.* village
Saurums *Lat.* strait
Sebkha, Sebkhet *Ar.* salt flat
See, -see *Ger.* lake
-şehir *Turk.* town
Selat *Indo., Malay* strait
Selatan *Indo.* southern
-selkä *Fin.* bay, lake, ridge, hills
Selo *Ser.-Cr., Russ.* village
Selva *Port., Span.* forest, wood
Seno *Span.* bay, sound
Serir *Ar.* stony desert
Serra (Sa.) *Cat., Port.* range of hills
Serranía *Span.* mountain ridge
Severo, Severnaya, Severnoye, Severnyy (Sev.) *Russ.* north, northern
Sfântu *Rom.* saint
Shahr, -shahr *Farsi* city, town
Shamo *Chin.* desert
Shan *Chin.* hills, mountains
Shankou *Chin.* pass
Shanmo *Chin.* mountain range
Sharm *Ar.* bay
Shatt *Ar.* river mouth, estuary
-Shima *Jap.* island
Shimāli *Ar.* northern
-Shotō *Jap.* group of islands
-shui *Chin.* river
-shuiku *Chin.* reservoir
Sierra (Sa.) *Span.* mountain range
-sjö, -sjön, -sjø *Swe., Nor.* lake
-sjøen *Dan.* sea
-sjór *Ice.* lake
-sker *Ice.* island
-skär *Swe.* island, rock, cape
-skog, -skogen *Nor., Swe.* wood(s)
-skov *Dan.* forest
Slieve *Gae.* hill, mountain
Sø *Dan., Nor.* lake
Söder, Södra *Swe.* south, southern
Sør *Nor.* south, southern
Solonchak *Russ.* salt lake, marsh
Sønder, Søndra *Dan.* south, southern
Song *Viet.* river
Souk *Ar.* market
-spitze *Ger.* peak, mountain
-spruit *Afr.* stream
Sredna, Sredno *Bulg.* middle, central
Sredne, Sredneye *Russ.* middle, central
Srednja *Ser.-Cr.* middle, central
-stad *Afr., Nor., Swe.* town
-stadt *Ger.* town
-staður *Ice.* town
Stara, Stari *Ser.-Cr.* old
Stará, Staré, Stary *Czec.* old
Staraya, Staroye, Staryy *Russ.* old
Stare, Staro, Stary *Ukr.* old
Stausee *Ger.* reservoir
Stenón *Gr.* strait, pass
Step *Russ.* steppe
Stor, -a *Swe.* big
Store *Dan.* big
-strand *Dan., Ger., Nor., Swe.* beach
-strede *Nor.* straits
Strelka *Russ.* spit
-strete *Nor.* straits
Stretto (Str.) *It.* strait
Strædet (Str.) *Dan.* strait
-ström, -strömmen *Swe.* stream(s)
-stroom *Afr.* large river
Sud *Fr.* south, southern
Süd, -er *Ger.* south, southern
Suid *Afr.* south, southern
-Suidō *Jap.* strait, channel
Sul *Port.* south, southern
Sûn *Burm.* cape
-sund, -et *Swe., Nor.* sound, estuary, inlet
Sungai *Indo., Malay* river
Sur *Span.* south, southern
Sveti *Bulg.* saint
Syd *Dan., Swe.* south, southern
Sýsla *Ice.* first-order administrative division

-tag *Uighur* mountain
Tai -tai *Chin.* tower
-Take *Jap.* mountain
Tal *Mong.* plain, steppe
-tal *Ger.* valley
Tall *Ar.* hills
Tanjona *Malag.* cape, point
Tanjung, Tanjong (Tg.) *Indo., Malay.* cape, point
Tao *Chin.* island
Tasik *Malay* lake
Tassili *Ar.* rocky plateau
Tau *Russ.* mountain range
Taung *Burm.* mountain
Taungdan. *Burm.* mountain range
Taunggya *Burm.* pass
-tekojärvi *Fin.* reservoir
Teluk *Indo., Malay* bay, gulf
Ténéré *Berb.* desert
Tengah *Indo.* middle, central
-thal *Ger.* valley
Thok *Tib.* town
Tien *Chin.* lake, marsh
Tierra *Span.* land, country
Timur *Indo.* eastern
-tind *Nor.* peak
-ting *Chin.* mountain
Tjärn, -en, -et *Swe.* lake
-Tō *Jap.* island
Tong *Kor.* village, town
Tong *Burm., Thai, Kor.* mountain range
Tonlé *Cam.* lake
Top *Dut.* peak
-topp, -en *Nor.* peak
-träsk *Swe.* lake, swamp
Tsangpo *Tib.* large river
Tso *Tib.* lake
Tsu *Jap.* entrance, bay
Tsui *Chin.* cape, point
Tulur *Ar.* hill
-tunturi *Fin.* hill(s), mountain(s), ridge

Uad *Ar.* dry watercourse, wadi
Über *Ger.* upper
-udde, -udden *Swe.* point, cape
Uebi *Som.* river
Ujung *Indo., Malay* cape
Unter- *Ger.* lower
Us *Mong.* water
Ust, Ustye *Russ.* river mouth
Utara *Indo.* north, northern
Uttar *Hin.* north, northern
Uul *Mong., Russ.* mountain range

-vaara *Fin.* hill, mountain ridge, peak
Vaart *Dut.* canal
-våg *Nor.* bay
Val *Fr., Port., Span.* valley
Valea *Rom.* valley
-vall, -en *Swe.* mountain
Valle *It., Span.* valley
Vallée *Fr.* valley
Valli *It.* lake, lagoon
-város *Hung.* town
-varre *Nor.* mountain
Väst, Västra *Swe.* west, western
-vatn *Ice., Nor.* lake
-vatnet *Nor.* lake
-vatten, vattnet *Swe.* lake
-vecchio *It.* old
Vechi *Rom.* old
-ved, -veden *Swe.* hills
Veld, -veld *Afr.* field
Velha, Velho *Port.* old
Velika, Velike, Veliki, Veliko *Ser.-Cr., Slov.* big, large
Velikaya, Velikiy *Russ.* big, large
Velká, Velké, Velký *Czec.* big, large
Verkhne, Verkhniy *Russ.* upper
-vesi *Fin.* water, lake, bay, sound, strait
Vest, Vester, Vestre *Dan., Nor.* west, western
-vidda *Nor.* plateau
Vieille, Vieux *Fr.* old
Vieja, Vejo *Span.* old
Vig *Dan.* bay, inlet, cove, lagoon, lake
-vik *Ice.* bay
-vik, -a, -en *Nor., Swe.* bay, gulf, inlet, lake
Vila *Port.* small town
Villa *Span.* town
Ville *Fr.* town
Vinh *Viet.* bay
Vîrful (Vf.) *Rom.* peak, mountain
-viz *Hung.* river
-víztároló *Hung.* reservoir
-vlei *Afr.* lake, salt pan
-vliet *Dut.* canal
-vloer *Afr.* salt pan
Vodokhranilishche (Vdkhr.) *Russ.* reservoir
Vodoskovyshche (Vdskh.) *Ukr.* reservoir
Volcán (Vol.) *Span.* volcano, mountain
Vorota *Russ.* pass, channel, strait
Vostochno, Vostochnyy *Russ.* east, eastern
-vötn *Ice.* lakes
Vozvyshennost *Russ.* heights, uplands
Vozyera *Belo.* lake
Vrata *Bulg.* gate, pass
Vrchovina *Czec.* mountainous country
Vrch(y) *Czec.* mountain (range)
Vung *Viet.* bay, gulf
-vuori *Fin.* mountain, hill
Vychodné *Slovak* east, eastern
Vysochyna *Ukr.* upland

-waard *Dut.* polder
Wadi (W.) *Ar.* dry watercourse
Wâhât *Ar.* oasis
Wald *Ger.* forest, mountains
-Wan *Chin., Jap.* bay, harbour
Wāw *Ar.* well
Webi *Amh.* river
Wes *Afr.* west, western
Wielka, Wielki, Wielko *Pol.* big, large
Woestyn *Afr.* desert
Wysoka, Wysoki *Pol.* upper
Wyżyna *Pol.* plateau

Xi *Chin.* river
Xia *Chin.* gorge, strait
Xiao *Chin.* small

Yam *Heb.* sea
-Yama *Jap.* mountain
-yan *Chin.* gorge, island
Yang *Chin.* bay, sea, sound
Yangi *Russ.* new
Yazovir *Bulg.* reservoir
Yeni *Turk.* new
Yli *Fin.* upper
Ynys *Welsh* island
Yoma *Burm.* mountain range
Ytre-, Ytter- *Nor., Swe.* outer
-yuan *Chin.* stream
Yugo- *Ser.-Cr.* south, southern
Yunhe *Chin.* canal
Yuzhni, Yuzhno *Russ.* south, southern

-Zaki *Jap.* point
Zalew *Pol.* lagoon, swamp
Zaliv *Russ.* bay, gulf
-Zan *Jap.* mountain
Zangbo *Tib.* stream, river
Zapadnaya, Zapadno, Zapadnyi (Zap.) *Russ.* west, western
Zatoka *Pol., Ukr.* bay, gulf
-zee *Dut.* lake, sea
Zemlya *Russ.* land, island(s)
Zhang *Chin.* mountain
-zhou *Chin.* island
Zhong *Chin.* middle, central
Zhou *Chin.* island
Zizhiqu *Chin.* autonomous region
Zuid, Zuider *Dut.* south, southern

INDEX TO WORLD MAPS

HOW TO USE THE INDEX

The index contains the names of all the principal places and features shown on the World and City Maps. Each name is followed by an additional entry in italics giving the country or region within which it is located. The alphabetical order of names composed of two or more words is governed primarily by the first word, then by the second, and then by the country or region name that follows. This is an example of the rule:

Mir *Niger*	14°5N 11°59E	**259**	F2
Mīr Kūh *Iran*	26°22N 58°55E	**247**	E8
Mīr Shahdād *Iran*	26°15N 58°29E	**247**	E8
Mira *Italy*	45°26N 12°8E	**199**	C9

Physical features composed of a proper name (Erie) and a description (Lake) are positioned alphabetically by the proper name. The description is positioned after the proper name and is usually abbreviated:

Erie, L. *N. Amer.*	42°15N 81°0W	**312**	D4

Where a description forms part of a settlement or administrative name, however, it is always written in full and put in its true alphabetical position:

Mount Olive *U.S.A.*	39°4N 89°44W	**310**	E7

Names beginning with M' and Mc are indexed as if they were spelled Mac. Names beginning St. are alphabetized under Saint, but Sankt, Sint, Sant', Santa and San are all spelt in full and are alphabetized accordingly. If the same place name occurs two or more times in the index and all are in the same country, each is followed by the name of the administrative subdivision in which it is located.

The geographical co-ordinates which follow each name in the index give the latitude and longitude of each place. The first co-ordinate indicates latitude – the distance north or south of the Equator. The second co-ordinate indicates longitude – the distance east or west of the Greenwich Meridian. Both latitude and longitude are measured in degrees and minutes (there are 60 minutes in a degree). Latitude and longitude references are not used on the Central Area City Maps.

The latitude is followed by N(orth) or S(outh) and the longitude by E(ast) or W(est).

The number in bold type which follows the geographical co-ordinates refers to the number of the map page where that feature or place will be found. This is usually the largest scale at which the place or feature appears.

The letter and figure that are immediately after the page number give the grid square on the map page, within which the feature is situated. The letter represents the latitude and the figure the longitude. A lower-case letter immediately after the page number refers to an inset map on that page.

In some cases the feature itself may fall within the specified square, while the name is outside. This is usually the case only with features that are larger than a grid square.

Rivers are indexed to their mouths or confluences, and carry the symbol → after their names. The following symbols are also used in the index: ■ country, ☑ overseas territory or dependency, ☐ first-order administrative area, ☆ U.S. county, △ national park, ⌒ other park (provincial park, nature reserve or game reserve), ۞Australian aboriginal land, ▲ U.S. Indian reservation ✈ (LHR) principal airport (and location identifier).

HOW TO PRONOUNCE PLACE NAMES

English-speaking people usually have no difficulty in reading and pronouncing correctly English place names. However, foreign place name pronunciations may present many problems. Such problems can be minimized by following some simple rules. However, these rules cannot be applied to all situations, and there will be many exceptions.

1. In general, stress each syllable equally, unless your experience suggests otherwise.
2. Pronounce the letter 'a' as a broad 'a' as in 'arm'.
3. Pronounce the letter 'e' as a short 'e' as in 'elm'.
4. Pronounce the letter 'i' as a cross between a short 'i' and long 'e', as the two 'i's in 'California'.
5. Pronounce the letter 'o' as an intermediate 'o' as in 'soft'.
6. Pronounce the letter 'u' as an intermediate 'u' as in 'sure'.
7. Pronounce consonants hard, except in the Romance-language areas where 'g's are likely to be pronounced softly like 'j' in 'jam'; 'j' itself may be pronounced as 'y'; and 'x's may be pronounced as 'h'.
8. For names in mainland China, pronounce 'q' like the 'ch' in 'chin', 'x' like the 'sh' in 'she', 'zh' like the 'j' in 'jam', and 'z' as if it were spelled 'dz'. In general, pronounce 'a' as in 'father', 'e' as in 'but', 'i' as in 'keep', 'o' as in 'or', and 'u' as in 'rule'.

Moreover, English has no diacritical marks (accent and pronunciation signs), although some languages do. The following is a brief and general guide to the pronunciation of those most frequently used in the principal Western European languages.

		Pronunciation as in
French	é	day and shows that the 'e' is to be pronounced; e.g. Orléans.
	è	mare
	î	used over any vowel and does not affect pronunciation; shows contraction of the name, usually omission of 's' following a vowel.
	ç	's' before 'a', 'o' and 'u'.
	ë, ï, ü	over 'e', 'i' and 'u' when they are used with another vowel and shows that each is to be pronounced.
German	ä	fate
	ö	fur
	ü	no English equivalent; like French 'tu'.
Italian	à, é	over vowels and indicates stress.
Portuguese	ã, õ	vowels pronounced nasally.
	ç	boss
	á	shows stress.
	ô	shows that a vowel has an 'i' or 'u' sound combined with it.
Spanish	ñ	canyon
	ü	pronounced as 'w' and separately from adjoining vowels.
	á	usually indicates that this is a stressed vowel.

ABBREVIATIONS

A.C.T. – Australian Capital Territory
A.R. – Autonomous Region
Afghan. – Afghanistan
Afr. – Africa
Ala. – Alabama
Alta. – Alberta
Amer. – America(n)
Ant. – Antilles
Arch. – Archipelago
Ariz. – Arizona
Ark. – Arkansas
Atl. Oc. – Atlantic Ocean
B. – Baie, Bahía, Bay, Bucht, Bugt
B.C. – British Columbia
Bangla. – Bangladesh
Barr. – Barrage
Bos.-H. – Bosnia-Herzegovina
C. – Cabo, Cap, Cape, Coast
C.A.R. – Central African Republic
C. Prov. – Cape Province
Calif. – California
Cat. – Catarata
Cent. – Central
Chan. – Channel
Colo. – Colorado
Conn. – Connecticut
Cord. – Cordillera
Cr. – Creek
Czech. – Czech Republic
D.C. – District of Columbia
Del. – Delaware
Dem. – Democratic
Dep. – Dependency
Des. – Desert
Dét. – Détroit
Dist. – District
Dj. – Djebel
Dom. Rep. – Dominican Republic
E. – East

El Salv. – El Salvador
Eq. Guin. – Equatorial Guinea
Est. – Estrecho
Falk. Is. – Falkland Is.
Fd. – Fjord
Fla. – Florida
Fr. – French
G. – Golfe, Golfo, Gulf, Guba, Gebel
Ga. – Georgia
Gt. – Great, Greater
Guinea-Biss. – Guinea-Bissau
H.K. – Hong Kong
H.P. – Himachal Pradesh
Hants. – Hampshire
Harb. – Harbor, Harbour
Hd. – Head
Hts. – Heights
I. (s). – Île, Ilha, Insel, Isla, Island, Isle
Ill. – Illinois
Ind. – Indiana
Ind. Oc. – Indian Ocean
Ivory C. – Ivory Coast
J. – Jabal, Jebel
Jaz. – Jazīrah
Junc. – Junction
K. – Kap, Kapp
Kans. – Kansas
Kep. – Kepulauan
Ky. – Kentucky
L. – Lac, Lacul, Lago, Lagoa, Lake, Limni, Loch, Lough
La. – Louisiana
Ld. – Land
Liech. – Liechtenstein
Lux. – Luxembourg
Mad. P. – Madhya Pradesh
Madag. – Madagascar

Man. – Manitoba
Mass. – Massachusetts
Md. – Maryland
Me. – Maine
Medit. S. – Mediterranean Sea
Mich. – Michigan
Minn. – Minnesota
Miss. – Mississippi
Mo. – Missouri
Mont. – Montana
Mozam. – Mozambique
Mt.(s) – Mont, Montaña, Mountain
Mte. – Monte
Mti. – Monti
N. – Nord, Norte, North, Northern, Nouveau, Nahal, Nahr
N.B. – New Brunswick
N.C. – North Carolina
N. Cal. – New Caledonia
N. Dak. – North Dakota
N.H. – New Hampshire
N.I. – North Island
N.J. – New Jersey
N. Mex. – New Mexico
N.S. – Nova Scotia
N.S.W. – New South Wales
N.W.T. – North West Territory
N.Y. – New York
N.Z. – New Zealand
Nac. – Nacional
Nat. – National
Nebr. – Nebraska
Neths. – Netherlands
Nev. – Nevada
Nfld & L.. – Newfoundland and Labrador
Nic. – Nicaragua
O. – Oued, Ouadi
Occ. – Occidentale

Okla. – Oklahoma
Ont. – Ontario
Or. – Orientale
Oreg. – Oregon
Os. – Ostrov
Oz. – Ozero
P. – Pass, Passo, Pasul, Pulau
P.E.I. – Prince Edward Island
Pa. – Pennsylvania
Pac. Oc. – Pacific Ocean
Papua N.G. – Papua New Guinea
Pass. – Passage
Peg. – Pegunungan
Pen. – Peninsula, Péninsule
Phil. – Philippines
Pk. – Peak
Plat. – Plateau
Prov. – Province, Provincial
Pt. – Point
Pta. – Ponta, Punta
Pte. – Pointe
Qué. – Québec
Queens. – Queensland
R. – Rio, River
R.I. – Rhode Island
Ra. – Range
Raj. – Rajasthan
Recr. – Recreational, Récréatif
Reg. – Region
Rep. – Republic
Res. – Reserve, Reservoir
Rhld-Pfz. – Rheinland-Pfalz
S. – South, Southern, Sur
Si. Arabia – Saudi Arabia
S.C. – South Carolina
S. Dak. – South Dakota
S.I. – South Island
S. Leone – Sierra Leone
Sa. – Serra, Sierra

Sask. – Saskatchewan
Scot. – Scotland
Sd. – Sound
Sev. – Severnaya
Sib. – Siberia
Sprs. – Springs
St. – Saint
Sta. – Santa
Ste. – Sainte
Sto. – Santo
Str. – Strait, Stretto
Switz. – Switzerland
Tas. – Tasmania
Tenn. – Tennessee
Terr. – Territory, Territoire
Tex. – Texas
Tg. – Tanjung
Trin. & Tob. – Trinidad & Tobago
U.A.E. – United Arab Emirates
U.K. – United Kingdom
U.S.A. – United States of America
Univ. – University, Université, Universidad
Ut. P. – Uttar Pradesh
Va. – Virginia
Vdkhr. – Vodokhranilishche
Vdskh. – Vodoskhovyshche
Vf. – Vírful
Vic. – Victoria
Vol. – Volcano
Vt. – Vermont
W. – Wadi, West
W. Va. – West Virginia
Wall. & F. Is. – Wallis and Futuna Is.
Wash. – Washington
Wis. – Wisconsin
Wlkp. – Wielkopolski
Wyo. – Wyoming
Yorks. – Yorkshire

340 A 'Âli an Nîl
INDEX

A

A 'Âli an Nîl □ *Sudan* 9°30N 33°0E **257** F3
A Baña *Spain* 42°58N 8°46W **194** C2
A Cañiza *Spain* 42°13N 8°16W **194** C2
A Coruña *Spain* 43°20N 8°25W **194** B2
A Coruña □ *Spain* 43°10N 8°30W **194** B2
A Cruz do Incio *Spain* 42°39N 7°21W **194** C3
A Estrada *Spain* 42°43N 8°27W **194** C2
A Fonsagrada *Spain* 43°8N 7°4W **194** B3
A Guarda *Spain* 41°56N 8°52W **194** D2
A Gudiña *Spain* 42°4N 7°8W **194** C3
A Pobre *Spain* 42°58N 7°3W **194** C3
A Ramallosa *Spain* 42°45N 8°30W **194** C2
A Rúa *Spain* 42°24N 7°6W **194** C3
A Serra de Outes *Spain* 42°52N 8°55W **194** C2
A Shau *Vietnam* 16°6N 107°22E **236** D6
Aabenraa *Denmark* 55°3N 9°25E **163** J3
Aabybro *Denmark* 57°10N 9°44E **163** G3
Aachen *Germany* 50°45N 6°6E **178** E2
Aalām *Iraq* 33°19N 44°23E **113** B2
Aalborg *Denmark* 57°2N 9°54E **163** G3
Aalborg Bugt *Denmark* 56°50N 10°35E **163** H4
Aalen *Germany* 48°51N 10°6E **179** G6
Aalestrup *Denmark* 56°42N 9°29E **163** H3
Aalsmeer *Neths.* 52°16N 4°46E **112** B1
Aalst *Belgium* 50°56N 4°2E **170** D4
Aalten *Neths.* 51°56N 6°35E **170** C6
Aalter *Belgium* 51°5N 3°28E **170** C3
Äänekoski *Finland* 62°36N 25°44E **160** E21
Aarau *Switz.* 47°23N 8°4E **179** H4
Aarberg *Switz.* 47°2N 7°16E **179** H3
Aare → *Switz.* 47°33N 8°14E **179** H4
Aargau □ *Switz.* 47°26N 8°10E **179** H4
Aarhus = Århus *Denmark* 56°8N 10°11E **163** H4
Aarlen = Arlon *Belgium* 49°42N 5°49E **170** E5
Aars *Denmark* 56°48N 9°30E **163** H3
Aarschot *Belgium* 50°59N 4°49E **170** D4
Aasiaat *Greenland* 68°43N 52°56W **154** D5
Ab-i-Istada *Afghan.* 32°29N 67°55E **240** B3
Ab-i-Panja = Pyandzh → *Asia* 37°6N 68°20E **240** A2
Aba *Sichuan, China* 32°59N 101°42E **228** A3
Aba *Dem. Rep. of the Congo* 3°58N 30°17E **268** B3
Aba *Nigeria* 5°10N 7°19E **263** D6
Âbâ, Jazîrat *Sudan* 13°30N 32°31E **257** E3
Abacaxis → *Brazil* 3°54S 58°47W **329** D6
Abaco I. *Bahamas* 26°25N 77°10W **320** A4
Abadab, J. *Sudan* 18°54N 35°56E **256** D4
Ābādān *Iran* 30°22N 48°20E **247** D6
Abade *Ethiopia* 9°22N 38°3E **257** F4
Ābādeh *Iran* 31°8N 52°40E **247** D7
Abadín *Spain* 43°21N 7°29W **194** B3
Abadla *Algeria* 31°2N 2°45W **261** B4
Abaeté *Brazil* 19°9S 45°27W **333** E2
Abaeté → *Brazil* 18°2S 45°12W **333** E2
Abaetetuba *Brazil* 1°40S 48°50W **332** B2
Abagnar Qi = Xilinhot *China* 43°52N 116°2E **226** C9
Abah, Tanjung *Indonesia* 8°46S 115°38E **231** K18
Abai *Paraguay* 25°58S 55°54W **335** B4
Abakaliki *Nigeria* 6°22N 8°2E **263** D6
Abakan *Russia* 53°40N 91°10E **217** B12
Abala *Congo* 1°17S 15°35E **264** C3
Abala *Niger* 14°56N 3°22E **263** C5
Abalak *Niger* 15°22N 6°21E **263** B6
Abalemma *Algeria* 20°51N 5°59E **261** D6
Abalemma *Niger* 16°12N 7°50E **263** B6
Abalessa *Algeria* 22°58N 4°47E **261** D5
Abana *Turkey* 41°59N 34°1E **212** B6
Abancay *Peru* 13°35S 72°55W **330** C3
Abang, Gunung *Indonesia* 8°16S 115°25E **231** J18
Abanga → *Gabon* 0°20S 10°30E **264** C2
Abano Terme *Italy* 45°22N 11°46E **199** C8
Abapó *Bolivia* 18°48S 63°25W **331** D5
Abarán *Spain* 38°12N 1°23W **197** G3
Abariringa *Kiribati* 2°50S 171°40W **277** A16
Abarqū *Iran* 31°10N 53°20E **247** D7
Abasha *Georgia* 42°11N 42°13E **191** J6
Abashiri *Japan* 44°0N 144°15E **220** B12
Abashiri-Wan *Japan* 44°0N 144°30E **220** C12
Abau *Papua N. G.* 10°11S 148°46E **286** F5
Abaújszántó *Hungary* 48°16N 21°12E **182** B6
Abava → *Latvia* 57°6N 21°54E **184** A8
Ābay = Nîl el Azraq → *Sudan* 15°38N 32°31E **257** D3
Abay *Kazakhstan* 49°38N 72°53E **217** C8
Abaya, L. *Ethiopia* 6°30N 37°50E **257** F4
Abaza *Russia* 52°39N 90°6E **217** B12
Abba *C.A.R.* 5°20N 15°11E **264** A3
Abbadia di Fiastra ⌓ *Italy* 43°12N 13°24E **199** E10
Abbadia San Salvatore *Italy* 42°53N 11°41E **199** F8
'Abbāsābād *Iran* 33°34N 58°23E **247** C8
Abbay = Nîl el Azraq → *Sudan* 15°38N 32°31E **257** D3
Abbaye, Pt. *U.S.A.* 46°58N 88°8W **308** B9
Abbazia = Opatija *Croatia* 45°21N 14°17E **199** C11
Abbé, L. *Ethiopia* 11°8N 41°47E **257** E5
Abbeville *Somme, France* 50°6N 1°49E **173** B8
Abbeville *Ala., U.S.A.* 31°34N 85°15W **316** D4
Abbeville *Ga., U.S.A.* 31°59N 83°18W **316** D6
Abbeville *La., U.S.A.* 29°58N 92°8W **314** G8
Abbeville *S.C., U.S.A.* 34°11N 82°23W **316** A7
Abbey Wood *U.K.* 51°29N 0°7E **125** B4
Abbeyfeale *Ireland* 52°23N 9°18W **166** D2
Abbiategrasso *Italy* 45°24N 8°54E **198** C5
Abbot Ice Shelf *Antarctica* 73°0S 92°0W **151** D16
Abbotsford *Canada* 49°5N 122°20W **296** D4
Abbottabad *Pakistan* 34°10N 73°15E **242** B5
Abbou, O. ben → *Algeria* 28°32N 5°14E **261** C5
ABC Islands *W. Indies* 12°15N 69°0W **321** D6
Abcoude *Neths.* 52°17N 4°59E **112** B2
Abd al Kūrī *Yemen* 12°5N 52°20E **249** D6
Ābdānān *Iran* 32°56N 47°28E **213** F12
Ābdar *Iran* 30°16N 55°19E **247** D7
Âbdin *Egypt* 30°2N 31°14E **117** A2
'Abdolābād *Iran* 34°12N 56°30E **247** C8
Abdulino *Russia* 53°42N 53°40E **216** B4
Abdulpur *Bangla.* 24°15N 88°59E **241** C2
Abéché *Chad* 13°50N 20°35E **259** F4
Abejar *Spain* 41°48N 2°47W **196** D2
Abekr *Sudan* 12°45N 28°50E **257** E2
Abel Tasman △ *N.Z.* 40°59S 173°3E **285** A8
Abengourou *Ivory C.* 6°42N 3°27W **262** D4
Abeno *Japan* 34°38N 135°31E **133** B2
Abenójar *Spain* 38°53N 4°21W **195** G6
Åbenrå = Aabenraa *Denmark* 55°3N 9°25E **163** J3
Abensberg *Germany* 48°48N 11°51E **179** G7
Abeokuta *Nigeria* 7°3N 3°19E **263** D5
Aberaeron *U.K.* 52°15N 4°15W **169** E3
Aberayron = Aberaeron *U.K.* 52°15N 4°15W **169** E3
Aberchirder *U.K.* 57°34N 2°37W **167** D6
Abercorn = Mbala *Zambia* 8°46S 31°24E **269** D3
Abercorn *Australia* 25°12S 151°5E **281** D5
Abercrombie River △ *Australia* 34°5S 149°40E **283** C8
Aberdare *U.K.* 51°43N 3°27W **169** F4
Aberdare △ *Kenya* 0°22S 36°44E **268** C4
Aberdare Ra. *Kenya* 0°15S 36°50E **268** C4
Aberdeen *N.S.W., Australia* 32°9S 150°56E **283** B9
Aberdeen *Sask., Canada* 52°20N 106°8W **297** C7
Aberdeen *Hong Kong, China* 22°14N 114°8E **122** B1
Aberdeen *Eastern Cape, S. Africa* 32°28S 24°2E **270** D3
Aberdeen *C. of Aberd., U.K.* 57°9N 2°5W **167** D6
Aberdeen *Idaho, U.S.A.* 42°57N 112°50W **304** E7
Aberdeen *Md., U.S.A.* 39°31N 76°10W **309** F15
Aberdeen *Miss., U.S.A.* 33°49N 88°33W **315** E10
Aberdeen *Ohio, U.S.A.* 38°39N 83°46W **311** F13
Aberdeen *S. Dak., U.S.A.* 45°28N 98°29W **308** C4
Aberdeen *Wash., U.S.A.* 46°59N 123°50W **306** D3
Aberdeen, City of □ *U.K.* 57°10N 2°10W **167** D6
Aberdeen L. *Canada* 64°30N 99°0W **294** E12
Aberdeenshire □ *U.K.* 57°17N 2°36W **167** D6
Aberdour *U.K.* 56°3N 3°18W **121** A2
Aberdour Castle *U.K.* 56°3N 3°18W **121** A2
Aberdovey = Aberdyfi *U.K.* 52°33N 4°3W **169** E3
Aberdyfi *U.K.* 52°33N 4°3W **169** E3
Aberfeldy *U.K.* 56°37N 3°51W **167** E5
Aberfoyle *U.K.* 56°11N 4°23W **167** E4
Abergavenny *U.K.* 51°49N 3°1W **169** F4
Abergele *U.K.* 53°17N 3°35W **168** D4
Abernathy *U.S.A.* 33°50N 101°51W **314** E4
Abert, L. *U.S.A.* 42°38N 120°14W **304** E3
Aberystwyth *U.K.* 52°25N 4°5W **169** E3
Abfanggraben → *Germany* 48°10N 11°41E **131** A3
Abhā *Si. Arabia* 18°0N 42°34E **248** C3
Abhar *Iran* 36°9N 49°13E **213** D13
Abhayapuri *India* 26°24N 90°38E **241** B3
Abia □ *Nigeria* 5°30N 7°35E **263** D6
Abide *Turkey* 38°55N 29°20E **205** C11
Abidiya *Sudan* 18°18N 34°3E **256** D3
Abidjan *Ivory C.* 5°26N 3°58W **262** D4
Abilene *Kans., U.S.A.* 38°55N 97°13W **308** F5
Abilene *Tex., U.S.A.* 32°28N 99°43W **314** E5
Abingdon *Oxon., U.K.* 51°40N 1°17W **169** F6
Abingdon *Ill., U.S.A.* 40°48N 90°24W **310** D6
Abingdon *Va., U.S.A.* 36°43N 81°59W **309** G13
Abingdon, I. = Pinta, I. *Ecuador* 0°35N 90°44W **330** a
Abington Reef *Australia* 18°0S 149°35E **280** B4
Abiod, Remel el *Tunisia* 31°45N 9°35E **261** B6
Abitau → *Canada* 59°53N 109°3W **297** B7
Abitibi → *Canada* 51°3N 80°55W **298** B3
Abitibi, L. *Canada* 48°40N 79°40W **298** C4
Abiy Adi *Ethiopia* 13°39N 39°3E **257** E4
Abiyata, L. *Ethiopia* 7°37N 38°36E **266** C4
Abiyata-Shala △ *Ethiopia* 7°40N 38°37E **257** F4
Abkhaz Republic = Abkhazia □ *Georgia* 43°12N 41°5E **191** J5
Abkhazia □ *Georgia* 43°12N 41°5E **191** J5
Ablon-sur-Seine *France* 48°43N 2°25E **134** B3
Abminga *Australia* 26°8S 134°51E **281** D1
Abnûb *Egypt* 27°18N 31°4E **256** B3
Åbo = Turku *Finland* 60°30N 22°19E **188** B2
Abo, Massif d' *Chad* 21°41N 16°8E **259** D3
Abohar *India* 30°10N 74°10E **242** D6
Aboisso *Ivory C.* 5°30N 3°5W **262** D4
Abolo *Congo* 0°8N 14°16E **264** B2
Abomey *Benin* 7°10N 2°5E **263** D5
Abong-Mbang *Cameroon* 4°0N 13°8E **264** B2
Abongabong *Indonesia* 4°15N 96°48E **234** B1
Abonnema *Nigeria* 4°41N 6°49E **263** E6
Abony *Hungary* 47°12N 20°3E **182** C5
Abor Hills *India* 28°25N 94°46E **241** A5
Aborlan *Phil.* 9°26N 118°33E **233** G2
Aboso *Ghana* 5°23N 1°57W **262** D4
Abou-Deïa *Chad* 11°20N 19°20E **259** F3
Abou-Goulem *Chad* 13°37N 21°38E **259** F4
Abou-Telfan ⌓ *Chad* 12°2N 18°58E **259** F3
Abovian *Armenia* 40°16N 44°37E **191** K7
Aboyne *U.K.* 57°4N 2°47W **167** D6
Abra □ *Phil.* 17°35N 120°45E **232** C3
Abra de Ilog *Phil.* 13°27N 120°44E **232** E3
Abra Pampa *Argentina* 22°43S 65°42W **334** A2
Abraham L. *Canada* 52°15N 116°35W **296** C5
Abramtsevo *Russia* 55°49N 37°49E **129** B4
Abrantes *Portugal* 39°24N 8°7W **195** F2
Abreojos, Pta. *Mexico* 26°50N 113°40W **318** B2
Abri *Esh Shamâliya, Sudan* 20°50N 30°27E **256** C3
Abri *Janub Kordofân, Sudan* 11°40N 30°21E **257** E3
Abrolhos, Banco dos *Brazil* 18°0S 38°0W **333** E4
Abrud *Romania* 46°19N 23°5E **182** D8
Abruzzo □ *Italy* 42°15N 14°0E **199** F10
Absaroka Range *U.S.A.* 44°45N 109°50W **304** D9
Abtenau *Austria* 47°33N 13°21E **180** D6
Abu *India* 24°41N 72°50E **242** G5
Abū aḍ Ḍuhūr *Syria* 35°44N 37°2E **250** C8
Abū al Abyaḍ *U.A.E.* 24°11N 53°50E **247** E7
Abū al Khaṣīb *Iraq* 30°25N 48°0E **246** D5
Abū 'Alī *Si. Arabia* 27°20N 49°27E **247** E6
Abū 'Alī → *Lebanon* 34°25N 35°50E **250** D6
Abū 'Arīsh *Si. Arabia* 16°53N 42°48E **248** C3
Abu 'Aweigîla *Egypt* 30°50N 34°7E **251** H5
Abû Ballas *Egypt* 24°26N 27°36E **256** C2
Abu Deleiq *Sudan* 15°57N 33°48E **257** D3
Abu Dhabi = Abū Ẓāby *U.A.E.* 24°28N 54°22E **247** E7
Abû Dis *Sudan* 19°12N 33°38E **256** D3
Abu Dis *West Bank* 31°46N 35°16E **123** B2
Abu Dom *Sudan* 16°18N 32°25E **257** D3
Abū Du'ān *Syria* 36°25N 38°15E **213** D8
Abu el Gaīn, W. → *Egypt* 29°35N 33°30E **251** J4
Abû en Numrus *Egypt* 29°57N 31°12E **117** B2
Abu Fatma, Ras *Sudan* 22°25N 36°25E **256** C4
Abû Gabra *Sudan* 11°2N 26°50E **257** E2
Abu Ga'da, W. → *Egypt* 29°15N 32°53E **251** J3
Abu Gelba *Sudan* 13°11N 31°52E **257** E3
Abu Ghosh *Israel* 31°48N 35°6E **123** B1
Abu Gubeiha *Sudan* 11°30N 31°15E **257** E3
Abu Habl, Khawr → *Sudan* 12°37N 31°0E **257** E3
Abū Ḥadrīyah *Si. Arabia* 27°20N 48°58E **247** E6
Abu Hamed *Sudan* 19°32N 33°13E **256** D3
Abû Haraz *An Nîl el Azraq, Sudan* 18°1N 33°58E **256** D3
Abu Haraz *El Gezira, Sudan* 14°35N 33°30E **257** E3
Abû Haraz *Esh Shamâliya, Sudan* 19°8N 32°18E **256** D3
Abû Higar *Sudan* 12°50N 33°59E **257** E3
Abū Kamāl *Syria* 34°30N 41°0E **213** E9
Abu Kebîr *Egypt* 30°43N 31°40E **251** H2
Abu Kuleiwat *Sudan* 12°20N 26°0E **257** E2
Abū Madd, Ra's *Si. Arabia* 24°50N 37°7E **246** E3
Abu Matariq *Sudan* 10°59N 26°9E **257** E2
Abu Mendi *Ethiopia* 11°48N 35°42E **257** E4
Abū Mūsā *U.A.E.* 25°52N 55°3E **247** E7
Abū Qaṣr *Si. Arabia* 30°21N 38°34E **246** D3
Abu Qireiya *Egypt* 24°5N 35°28E **256** C4
Abu Qurqâs *Egypt* 28°1N 30°44E **256** B3
Abū Rašāş, Ra's *Oman* 20°10N 58°38E **249** B7
Abu Rudeis *Egypt* 28°54N 33°11E **251** K4
Abu Shagara, Ras *Sudan* 21°4N 37°19E **256** C4
Abû Shanab *Janub Kordofân, Sudan* 10°47N 29°32E **266** B2
Abû Shanab *Shamâl Kordofân, Sudan* 13°58N 27°49E **257** E2
Abu Simbel *Egypt* 22°18N 31°40E **256** C3
Abū Şukhayr *Iraq* 31°54N 44°30E **213** G11
Abu Sultân *Egypt* 30°24N 32°21E **256** H8
Abu Tabari *Sudan* 17°32N 28°32E **256** D2
Abu Tig *Egypt* 27°4N 31°15E **256** B3
Abu Tiga *Sudan* 12°47N 34°12E **257** E3
Abu Tineitin *Sudan* 14°24N 31°1E **257** E3
Abû Uruq *Sudan* 15°52N 30°25E **257** D3
Abû Zabad *Sudan* 12°25N 29°10E **257** E2
Abū Ẓāby *U.A.E.* 24°28N 54°22E **247** E7
Abū Zeydābād *Iran* 33°54N 51°45E **247** C6
Abufari *Brazil* 5°25S 62°59W **331** B5
Abuja *Nigeria* 9°5N 7°32E **263** D6
Abukuma-Gawa → *Japan* 38°6N 140°52E **220** E10
Abukuma-Sammyaku *Japan* 37°30N 140°45E **220** F10
Abulug *Phil.* 18°27N 121°27E **232** B3
Abumombazi *Dem. Rep. of the Congo* 3°42N 22°10E **264** B4
Abunã *Brazil* 9°40S 65°20W **331** B4
Abunã → *Brazil* 9°41S 65°20W **331** B4
Abune Yosef *Ethiopia* 12°5N 39°12E **257** E4
Aburatsu *Japan* 31°34N 131°24E **222** F3
Aburo *Dem. Rep. of the Congo* 2°4N 30°53E **268** B3
Abut Hd. *N.Z.* 43°7S 170°15E **285** D5
Abuye Meda *Ethiopia* 10°30N 39°49E **257** E4
Abuyog *Phil.* 10°45N 125°0E **233** F5
Abwong *Sudan* 9°2N 32°14E **257** F3
Åby *Sweden* 58°40N 16°10E **163** F10
Aby, Lagune *Ivory C.* 5°15N 3°14W **262** D4
Abyad *Sudan* 13°47N 26°24E **257** E2
Abyei *Sudan* 9°36N 28°26E **257** F2
Ābyek *Iran* 36°4N 50°33E **247** B6
Acacías *Colombia* 3°59N 73°46W **328** C3
Acacias *Madrid, Spain* **127** c2
Academy Gletscher *Greenland* 82°2N 34°0W **154** A7
Acadia △ *U.S.A.* 44°20N 68°13W **309** C19
Açailandia *Brazil* 5°0S 47°30W **332** C2
Acajutla *El Salv.* 13°36N 89°50W **320** D2
Acámbaro *Mexico* 20°2N 100°44W **318** D4
Acandí *Colombia* 8°32N 77°14W **328** B2
Acanthus *Greece* 40°27N 23°47E **202** F7
Acaponeta *Mexico* 22°30N 105°22W **318** C3
Acapulco *Mexico* 16°51N 99°55W **319** D5
Acapulco Trench *Pac. Oc.* 12°0N 88°0W **320** D2
Acará *Brazil* 1°57S 48°11W **332** B2
Acaraí, Serra *Brazil* 1°50N 57°50W **329** C6
Acaraú *Brazil* 2°53S 40°7W **332** B3
Acari *Brazil* 6°31S 36°38W **332** C4
Acarí *Peru* 15°25S 74°36W **330** D3
Acarigua *Venezuela* 9°33N 69°12W **328** B4
Acassuso *Argentina* 34°29S 58°30W **117** A2
Acatlán *Mexico* 18°12N 98°3W **319** D5
Acayucán *Mexico* 17°57N 94°55W **319** D6
Accéglio *Italy* 44°28N 7°0E **198** D4
Accomac *U.S.A.* 37°43N 75°40W **309** G16
Accotink, L. *U.S.A.* 38°47N 77°13W **143** C2
Accotink Cr. → *U.S.A.* 38°51N 77°15W **143** B2
Accous *France* 43°0N 0°36W **174** E3
Accra *Ghana* 5°35N 0°6W **263** D4
Accrington *U.K.* 53°45N 2°22W **168** D5
Acebal *Argentina* 33°20S 60°50W **334** C3
Aceh □ *Indonesia* 4°15N 97°30E **234** B1
Acerra *Italy* 40°57N 14°22E **201** B7
Aceuchal *Spain* 38°39N 6°30W **195** G4
Achacachi *Bolivia* 16°3S 68°43W **330** D4
Achaguas *Venezuela* 7°46N 68°14W **328** B4
Achaia □ *Greece* 38°5N 21°45E **204** C3
Achalpur *India* 21°22N 77°32E **244** D3
Achao *Chile* 42°28S 73°30W **336** B2
Acharnes *Greece* 38°5N 23°44E **204** C5
Achegour *Niger* 19°10N 11°54E **259** E2
Acheloos → *Greece* 38°19N 21°7E **204** C3
Achelouma *Niger* 22°12N 12°50E **259** D2
Achelouma, Enneri → *Niger* 21°55N 13°35E **259** D2
Acheng *China* 45°30N 126°58E **227** B14
Achenkirch *Austria* 47°32N 11°45E **180** D4
Achénouma *Niger* 19°7N 12°55E **259** E2
Achensee *Austria* 47°26N 11°45E **180** D4
Achentrias *Greece* 34°59N 25°13E **205** G7
Acher *India* 23°10N 72°32E **242** H5
Achères *France* 48°57N 2°3E **134** A1
Achern *Germany* 48°37N 8°4E **179** G4
Acheron → *N.Z.* 42°16S 173°4E **285** C8
Achill Hd. *Ireland* 53°58N 10°15W **166** C1
Achill I. *Ireland* 53°58N 10°1W **166** C1
Achim *Germany* 53°1N 9°3E **178** B5
Achinsk *Russia* 56°20N 90°20E **215** D10
Achladokambos *Greece* 37°31N 22°35E **204** D4
Achouka *Gabon* 0°52S 9°45E **264** C2
Acıgöl *Turkey* 37°50N 29°50E **205** D11
Acília *Italy* 41°47N 12°21E **136** C1
Acıpayam *Turkey* 37°26N 29°22E **205** D11
Acireale *Italy* 37°37N 15°10E **201** E8
Ackerman *U.S.A.* 33°19N 89°11W **315** E10
Ackley *U.S.A.* 42°33N 93°3W **310** B3
Acklins I. *Bahamas* 22°30N 74°0W **321** B5
Aclimação *Brazil* 23°34S 46°37W **137** B2
Acme *Alta., Canada* 51°33N 113°30W **296** C6
Acme *Pa., U.S.A.* 40°8N 79°26W **312** F5
Acobamba *Peru* 12°52S 74°35W **330** C3
Acomayo *Peru* 13°55S 71°38W **330** C3
Aconcagua, Cerro *Argentina* 32°39S 70°0W **334** C2
Aconquija, Mt. *Argentina* 27°0S 66°0W **334** B2
Acopiara *Brazil* 6°6S 39°27W **332** C4
Açores, Is. dos *Atl. Oc.* 38°0N 27°0W **153** d1
Acorizal *Brazil* 15°12S 56°22W **331** D6
Acornhoek *S. Africa* 24°37S 31°2E **271** B5
Acoua *Mayotte* 12°43S 45°4E **272** b
Acquapendente *Italy* 42°44N 11°52E **199** F8
Acquasanta Terme *Italy* 42°46N 13°24E **199** F10
Acquasparta *Italy* 42°41N 12°33E **199** F9
Acquaviva delle Fonti *Italy* 40°54N 16°50E **201** B9
Ácqui Terme *Italy* 44°41N 8°28E **198** D5
Acraman, L. *Australia* 32°2S 135°23E **281** E2
Acre = 'Akko *Israel* 32°55N 35°4E **250** F6
Acre □ *Brazil* 9°1S 71°0W **330** B3
Acre → *Brazil* 8°45S 67°22W **330** B4
Acri *Italy* 39°29N 16°23E **201** C9
Acropolis *Athens, Greece* **112** c2
Acs *Hungary* 47°42N 18°2E **182** C3
Actæon Mt. *St. Helena* 15°58S 5°42W **153** h
Actéon, Groupe *French Polynesia* 21°20S 136°30W **289** f
Actinolite *Canada* 44°32N 77°19W **312** B7
Actium *Greece* 38°57N 20°45E **207** B2
Acton *Ont., Canada* 43°38N 80°3W **312** C4
Acton *London, U.K.* 51°30N 0°16W **125** A2
Açu *Brazil* 5°34S 36°54W **332** C4
Açúcar, Pão de *Brazil* 22°56S 43°9W **135** B2
Acul = Vidin *Bulgaria* 43°59N 22°50E **202** C6
Acworth *U.S.A.* 34°4N 84°41W **316** A5
Ad Dafinah *Si. Arabia* 23°18N 41°58E **248** B3
Aḍ Ḍafrah *U.A.E.* 23°30N 54°30E **249** B6
Ad Daghghāran *Iraq* 32°8N 44°55E **213** G11
Ad Dahnā *Si. Arabia* 24°30N 48°10E **249** A5
Aḍ Ḍāli' *Yemen* 13°42N 44°44E **248** D4
Ad Dammām *Si. Arabia* 26°20N 50°5E **247** E6
Ad Dāmūr *Lebanon* 33°43N 35°27E **250** E6
Ad Darb *Si. Arabia* 18°2N 43°7E **248** C3
Ad Dawādimī *Si. Arabia* 24°35N 44°15E **246** E5
Ad Dawḥah *Qatar* 25°15N 51°35E **247** E6
Ad Dawr *Iraq* 34°27N 43°47E **213** E10
Aḍ Ḍiffah *Libya* 30°30N 24°30E **258** B4
Ad Dilam *Si. Arabia* 23°55N 47°10E **248** B4
Ad Dir'īyah *Si. Arabia* 24°44N 46°35E **246** E5
Ad Dīwānīyah *Iraq* 32°0N 45°0E **213** F11
Ad Dujayl *Iraq* 33°51N 44°14E **213** F11
Ad Duwayd *Si. Arabia* 30°15N 42°17E **246** D4
Ada *Ghana* 5°44N 0°40E **263** D5
Ada *Serbia* 45°49N 20°9E **182** E5
Ada *Minn., U.S.A.* 47°18N 96°31W **308** B5
Ada *Ohio, U.S.A.* 40°46N 83°49W **311** D13
Ada *Okla., U.S.A.* 34°46N 96°41W **314** D6
Ada Beja *Portugal* 38°47N 9°13W **126** A1
Adad *Somali Rep.* 9°27N 46°49E **267** C6
Adado, Ras *Somali Rep.* 11°19N 48°39E **267** B6
Adair, C. *Canada* 71°30N 71°34W **295** C17
Adaja → *Spain* 41°32N 4°52W **194** D6
Adak *U.S.A.* 51°45N 176°45W **303** L3
Adak I. *U.S.A.* 51°45N 176°45W **303** L3
Ådalsbruk *Norway* 60°43N 11°19E **164** D8
Adam *Oman* 22°15N 57°28E **249** B7
Adam, Mt. *Falk. Is.* 51°34S 60°4W **153** f
Adamantina *Brazil* 21°42S 51°4W **333** F1
Adamaoua □ *Cameroon* 6°30N 13°30E **263** D7
Adamaoua, Massif de l' *Cameroon* 7°20N 12°20E **263** D7
Adamawa □ *Nigeria* 9°20N 12°30E **263** D7
Adamawa Highlands = Adamaoua, Massif de l' *Cameroon* 7°20N 12°20E **263** D7
Adamello, Mte. *Italy* 46°9N 10°30E **198** B7
Adamello ⌓ *Italy* 46°4N 10°28E **198** B7
Adami Tulu *Ethiopia* 7°53N 38°41E **257** F4
Adaminaby *Australia* 36°0S 148°45E **283** D8
Adams *Mass., U.S.A.* 42°38N 73°7W **313** D11
Adams *N.Y., U.S.A.* 43°49N 76°1W **313** C8
Adams *Wis., U.S.A.* 43°57N 89°49W **308** D9
Adams, Mt. *U.S.A.* 46°12N 121°30W **306** D5
Adam's Bridge *Sri Lanka* 9°15N 79°40E **245** K4
Adams L. *Canada* 51°10N 119°40W **296** C5
Adams Park *U.S.A.* 33°43N 84°27W **113** B2
Adam's Peak *Sri Lanka* 6°48N 80°30E **245** L5
Adamuz *Spain* 38°2N 4°32W **195** G6
Adana *Turkey* 37°0N 35°16E **250** B6
Adana □ *Turkey* 37°0N 35°30E **250** B6
Adanero *Spain* 40°56N 4°36W **194** E6
Adang, Ko *Thailand* 6°33N 99°18E **237** J2
Adapazarı = Sakarya *Turkey* 40°48N 30°25E **212** B4
Adar Gwagwa, J. *Sudan* 22°15N 35°20E **256** C4
Adarama *Sudan* 17°10N 34°52E **257** D3
Adare, C. *Antarctica* 71°0S 171°0E **151** D11
Adarte *Eritrea* 13°18N 42°8E **257** E5
Adaut *Indonesia* 8°8S 131°7E **231** F8
Adavale *Australia* 25°52S 144°32E **281** D3
Adda → *Italy* 45°8N 9°53E **198** C6
Addatigala *India* 17°31N 82°3E **244** F6
Addax ⌓ *Niger* 19°17N 9°22E **259** E1
Addis Ababa = Addis Abeba *Ethiopia* 9°2N 38°42E **257** F4
Addis Abeba *Ethiopia* 9°2N 38°42E **257** F4
Addis Alem *Ethiopia* 9°0N 38°17E **257** F4
Addis Zemen *Ethiopia* 12°7N 37°47E **257** E4
Addiscombe *U.K.* 51°22N 0°4W **125** B3
Addison *Ill., U.S.A.* 41°55N 88°0W **311** C8
Addison *N.Y., U.S.A.* 42°1N 77°14W **312** D7
Addo *S. Africa* 33°32S 25°45E **270** D4
Addo △ *S. Africa* 33°30S 25°50E **270** D4
Addu Atoll *Maldives* 0°38S 73°10E **272** d
Adebour *Niger* 13°17N 11°50E **259** F2
Ādeh *Iran* 37°42N 45°11E **246** B5
Adel *Ga., U.S.A.* 31°8N 83°25W **316** D6
Adel *Iowa, U.S.A.* 41°37N 94°1W **310** C2
Adel Bagrou *Mauritania* 15°29N 6°57W **262** B3
Adelaide *S. Austral., Australia* 34°52S 138°30E **282** C3
Adelaide *Eastern Cape, S. Africa* 32°42S 26°20E **270** D4
Adelaide I. *Antarctica* 67°15S 68°30W **151** C17
Adelaide Pen. *Canada* 68°15N 97°30W **294** D12
Adelaide River *Australia* 13°15S 131°7E **278** B5
Adelaide Village *Bahamas* 25°0N 77°31W **153** b
Adelanto *U.S.A.* 34°35N 117°22W **307** L9
Adelaye *C.A.R.* 7°7N 22°49E **264** A4
Adele I. *Australia* 15°32S 123°9E **278** C3
Adélie, Terre *Antarctica* 68°0S 140°0E **151** C10
Adelie Land = Adélie, Terre *Antarctica* 68°0S 140°0E **151** C10
Adelong *Australia* 35°16S 148°4E **283** C8
Adelphi *U.S.A.* 39°0N 76°58W **143** A4
Adelsk *Belarus* 53°24N 23°47E **184** E10
Ademuz *Spain* 40°5N 1°13W **196** E3
Aden = Al 'Adan *Yemen* 12°45N 45°0E **248** D4
Aden, G. of *Ind. Oc.* 12°30N 47°30E **267** B6
Adendorp *S. Africa* 32°15S 24°30E **270** D3
Aderbissinat *Niger* 15°34N 7°54E **263** B6
Aderklaa *Austria* 48°17N 16°32E **142** A3
Adh Dhayd *U.A.E.* 25°17N 55°53E **247** E7
Adhoi *India* 23°26N 70°32E **242** H4
Adi *Indonesia* 4°15S 133°30E **231** E8
Adi Arkai *Ethiopia* 13°35N 37°57E **257** E4
Adi Daro *Ethiopia* 14°20N 38°14E **257** E4
Adi Keyih *Eritrea* 14°51N 39°22E **257** E4
Adi Kwala *Eritrea* 14°38N 38°48E **257** E4
Adi Ugri *Eritrea* 14°58N 38°48E **257** E4
Adieu, C. *Australia* 32°0S 132°10E **279** F5
Adieu Pt. *Australia* 15°14S 124°35E **278** C3
Adigala *Ethiopia* 10°24N 42°15E **257** E5
Adige → *Italy* 45°9N 12°20E **199** C9
Adigrat *Ethiopia* 14°20N 39°26E **257** E4
Adıgüzel Barajı *Turkey* 38°13N 29°14E **205** C11
Adilabad *India* 19°33N 78°20E **244** E4
Adilcevaz *Turkey* 38°47N 42°43E **213** C10
Adīrī *Libya* 27°32N 13°2E **258** C2
Adirondack ⌓ *U.S.A.* 44°0N 74°20W **313** C10
Adirondack Mts. *U.S.A.* 44°0N 74°0W **313** C10
Adis Abeba = Addis Abeba *Ethiopia* 9°2N 38°42E **257** F4
Adıyaman *Turkey* 37°45N 38°16E **213** D8
Adıyaman □ *Turkey* 37°30N 38°10E **213** D8
Adjim *Tunisia* 33°47N 10°50E **258** B2
Adjohon *Benin* 6°41N 2°32E **263** D5
Adjud *Romania* 46°7N 27°10E **183** D12
Adjumani *Uganda* 3°20N 31°50E **268** B3
Adjuntas *Puerto Rico* 18°10N 66°43W **321** b
Adlavik Is. *Canada* 55°0N 58°40W **299** B8
Adler *Russia* 43°28N 39°52E **191** J4
Adler Planetarium *Chicago, U.S.A.* **119** e3
Admer *Algeria* 20°21N 5°27E **261** D6
Admer, Erg d' *Algeria* 24°0N 9°5E **261** D6
Admiralteyskaya Storona *Russia* 59°56N 30°20E **137** B2
Admiralty G. *Australia* 14°20S 125°55E **278** B4
Admiralty Gulf ☼ *Australia* 14°16S 125°52E **278** B4
Admiralty I. *U.S.A.* 57°30N 134°30W **296** B2
Admiralty Inlet *Canada* 72°30N 86°0W **295** C14
Admiralty Is. *Papua N. G.* 2°0S 147°0E **286** B4
Admiralty Island ⌓ *U.S.A.* 57°40N 134°10W **303** H14
Adnan Menderes, İzmir ✕ (ADB) *Turkey* 38°23N 27°6E **205** C9
Ado *Nigeria* 6°36N 2°56E **263** D5
Ado-Ekiti *Nigeria* 7°38N 5°12E **263** D6
Adok *Sudan* 8°10N 30°20E **257** F3
Adola *Ethiopia* 11°14N 41°44E **257** E5
Adolfo González Chaves *Argentina* 38°2S 60°5W **334** D3
Adolfo Ruiz Cortines, Presa *Mexico* 27°15N 109°6W **318** B3
Adonara *Indonesia* 8°15S 123°5E **231** F6
Adoni *India* 15°33N 77°18E **245** G3
Adony *Hungary* 47°6N 18°52E **182** C3
Adour → *France* 43°32N 1°32W **174** E2
Adra *India* 23°30N 86°42E **243** H12
Adra *Spain* 36°43N 3°3W **195** J7
Adrano *Italy* 37°40N 14°50E **201** E7
Adrar *Algeria* 27°51N 0°11E **261** C4
Adrar □ *Algeria* 25°45N 1°0E **261** C5
Adrar □ *Mauritania* 21°0N 10°0W **260** D3
Adrar des Iforas *Africa* 19°40N 1°40E **261** D5
Adré *Chad* 13°40N 22°20E **259** F4
Ádria *Italy* 45°3N 12°3E **199** C9
Adrian *Ga., U.S.A.* 32°33N 82°35W **316** C7
Adrian *Mich., U.S.A.* 41°54N 84°2W **311** C12
Adrian *Mo., U.S.A.* 38°24N 94°21W **310** F2
Adrian *Tex., U.S.A.* 35°16N 102°40W **314** D3
Adrianople = Edirne *Turkey* 41°40N 26°34E **203** E10
Adriatic Sea *Medit. S.* 43°0N 16°0E **193** C7
Adua *Indonesia* 1°45S 129°50E **231** E7
Adung Long *Burma* 28°7N 97°42E **241** A6
Adur *India* 9°8N 76°40E **245** K3
Adwa *Ethiopia* 14°15N 38°52E **257** E4
Adygea □ *Russia* 45°0N 40°0E **191** H5
Adzhar Republic = Ajaria □ *Georgia* 41°30N 42°0E **191** K6
Adzhibakul = Qazımämmäd *Azerbaijan* 40°3N 49°0E **191** K9
Adzopé *Ivory C.* 6°7N 3°49W **262** D4
Ægean Sea *Medit. S.* 38°30N 25°0E **205** C7
Aerhtai Shan *Mongolia* 46°40N 92°45E **217** C12
Ærø *Denmark* 54°52N 10°25E **163** K4
Ærøskøbing *Denmark* 54°53N 10°24E **163** K4
Aetos *Greece* 37°15N 21°50E **204** D3
Afaahiti *Tahiti* 17°45S 149°17W **289** e
Afafi, Massif d' *Niger* 22°11N 15°10E **259** D3
'Afak *Iraq* 32°4N 45°15E **213** F11
Afandou *Greece* 36°18N 28°12E **206** E12
Afar □ *Ethiopia* 12°0N 41°0E **257** E5
Afarag, Erg *Algeria* 23°50N 2°47E **261** D5
Afareaitu *Moorea* 17°33S 149°47W **289** e
Åfarnes *Norway* 62°40N 7°32E **164** B4
Afdega *Ethiopia* 6°4N 43°30E **267** C5
Afdem *Ethiopia* 9°28N 41°0E **267** C5
Áffori *Italy* 45°31N 9°10E **129** A2
Affton *U.S.A.* 38°33N 90°20W **310** F6
Afghanistan ■ *Asia* 33°0N 65°0E **240** B2
Afgooye *Somali Rep.* 2°7N 44°59E **267** D5
'Afif *Si. Arabia* 23°53N 42°56E **248** B3
Afikpo *Nigeria* 5°53N 7°54E **263** D6
Aflandshage *Denmark* 55°33N 12°35E **118** B3
Aflisses, O. → *Algeria* 28°40N 0°50E **261** C5
Aflou *Algeria* 34°7N 2°3E **261** B5
Afmadow *Somali Rep.* 0°31N 42°4E **267** D5
Afogados da Ingàzeira *Brazil* 7°45S 37°39W **332** C4
Afognak I. *U.S.A.* 58°15N 152°30W **303** G9
Afono B. *Amer. Samoa* 14°15S 170°38W **302** f
Afore *Papua N. G.* 9°9S 148°23E **286** E5
Afragóla *Italy* 40°55N 14°18E **201** B7
Afram → *Ghana* 7°0N 0°52W **263** D4
Afrera *Ethiopia* 13°16N 41°5E **257** E5
Africa 10°0N 20°0E **254** E6
'Afrīn *Syria* 36°32N 36°50E **250** B7
'Afrīn → *Syria* 36°20N 36°35E **250** B7
Afşar → *Turkey* 37°2N 32°35E **250** A3
Afsarīyeh *Iran* 35°39N 51°30E **141** B2
Afşin *Turkey* 38°14N 36°55E **212** C7
Afton *Iowa, U.S.A.* 41°2N 94°12W **310** C2
Afton *N.Y., U.S.A.* 42°14N 75°32W **313** D9
Afton *Wyo., U.S.A.* 42°44N 110°56W **304** E8
Afuá *Brazil* 0°15S 50°20W **329** D7
'Afula *Israel* 32°37N 35°17E **250** F6
Afumba *Zambia* 15°38S 24°56E **265** F4
Afyon *Turkey* 38°45N 30°33E **205** C12
Afyon □ *Turkey* 38°25N 30°30E **205** C12
Afyonkarahisar = Afyon *Turkey* 38°45N 30°33E **205** C12
Aga *Egypt* 30°55N 31°10E **256** H7
Aga I. *Micronesia* 7°29N 151°43E **287** T18
Āgā Jarī *Iran* 30°42N 49°50E **247** D6
Agadem *Niger* 16°50N 13°11E **259** E2
Agadés = Agadez *Niger* 16°58N 7°59E **259** E1
Agadez *Niger* 16°58N 7°59E **259** E1
Agadir *Morocco* 30°28N 9°55W **260** B3
Agadir □ *Morocco* 30°42N 9°0W **260** B3
Agaete *Canary Is.* 28°6N 15°43W **153** e1
Agaie *Nigeria* 9°1N 6°18E **263** D6
Agalas *Greece* 37°43N 20°47E **207** D2
Agalega Is. *Mauritius* 11°0S 57°0E **273** F4
Agana *Guam* 13°28N 144°45E **302** d
Agana B. *Guam* 13°29N 144°45E **302** d
Ağapınar *Turkey* 39°48N 30°47E **205** B12
Agar *India* 23°40N 76°2E **242** H7
Agar → *India* 21°0N 82°57E **244** D6
Agâraktem *Mali* 23°8N 6°22W **260** D3
Agaro *Ethiopia* 7°50N 36°38E **257** F4
Agartala *India* 23°50N 91°23E **241** D3
Agăş *Romania* 46°28N 26°15E **183** D11
Agassiz *Canada* 49°14N 121°46W **296** D4
Agassiz Icecap *Canada* 80°15N 76°0W **295** A16
Agat *Guam* 13°25N 144°40E **302** d
Agats *Indonesia* 5°33S 138°0E **231** F9
Agatti I. *India* 10°50N 72°12E **245** J1
Agattu I. *U.S.A.* 52°25N 173°35E **303** K1
Agawam *U.S.A.* 42°5N 72°37W **313** D12
Agbélouvé *Togo* 6°35N 1°14E **263** D5
Agboville *Ivory C.* 5°55N 4°15W **262** D4
Agboyi Cr. → *Nigeria* 6°33N 3°24E **124** A2
Ağcabädi *Azerbaijan* 40°5N 47°27E **191** K8
Ağdam *Azerbaijan* 40°0N 46°58E **191** L8
Ağdaş *Azerbaijan* 40°44N 47°22E **191** K8
Agde *France* 43°19N 3°28E **174** E7
Agde, C. d' *France* 43°16N 3°28E **174** E7
Agdz *Morocco* 30°47N 6°30W **260** B3
Agdzhabedi = Ağcabädi *Azerbaijan* 40°5N 47°27E **191** K8
Agen *France* 44°12N 0°38E **174** D4
Ageo *Japan* 35°58N 139°36E **223** B11
Ager Tay *Chad* 20°0N 17°41E **259** E3
Agerbæk *Denmark* 55°36N 8°48E **163** J2
Agersø *Denmark* 55°13N 11°12E **163** J5
Ågerup *Denmark* 55°43N 12°19E **118** A1
Ågesta *Sweden* 59°12N 18°6E **139** B2
Ageyevo *Russia* 54°10N 36°27E **188** E9
Aggteleki △ *Hungary* 48°27N 20°36E **182** B5
Āgh Kand *Iran* 37°15N 48°4E **213** D13
Aghathonisi *Greece* 37°28N 27°0E **205** D8
Aghia Anna *Greece* 38°52N 23°24E **204** C5
Aghia Deka *Greece* 35°3N 24°58E **207** E5
Aghia Ekaterinis, Akra *Greece* 39°50N 19°50E **206** B9
Aghia Galini *Greece* 35°6N 24°41E **207** E5
Aghia Marina *Athina, Greece* 37°48N 23°51E **112** C3
Aghia Marina *Kasos, Greece* 35°27N 26°53E **205** F8
Aghia Marina *Leros, Greece* 37°11N 26°48E **205** D8
Aghia Paraskevi *Athina, Greece* 38°1N 23°49E **112** A2
Aghia Paraskevi *Voreio Aigaio, Greece* 39°14N 26°21E **205** B8
Aghia Roumeli *Greece* 35°14N 23°58E **207** E4
Aghia Varvara *Greece* 35°8N 25°1E **207** E6
Aghiasos *Greece* 39°5N 26°23E **205** B8
Aghio Theodori *Greece* 37°55N 23°9E **204** D5
Aghion Oros □ *Greece* 40°25N 24°6E **203** F8
Aghios Andreas *Greece* 37°21N 22°45E **204** D4
Aghios Dimitrios *Greece* 37°53N 23°44E **112** B2
Aghios Efimia *Greece* 38°18N 20°36E **207** C2
Aghios Efstratios *Greece* 39°34N 24°58E **204** B6
Aghios Georgios *Greece* 37°28N 23°57E **204** D5
Aghios Ioannis, Akra *Greece* 35°20N 25°40E **207** E6
Aghios Ioannis Rendis *Greece* 37°57N 23°39E **112** B1
Aghios Isidoros *Greece* 36°9N 27°51E **206** E11
Aghios Kirikos *Greece* 37°34N 26°17E **205** D8
Aghios Leon *Greece* 37°47N 20°43E **207** D2
Aghios Matheos *Greece* 39°30N 19°47E **206** C9
Aghios Mironas *Greece* 35°15N 25°1E **207** E6
Aghios Nikolaos *Etoloakarnania, Greece* 38°52N 20°48E **207** B2
Aghios Nikolaos *Kriti, Greece* 35°11N 25°41E **207** E6
Aghios Nikolaos *Lefkada, Greece* 38°36N 20°34E **207** B2
Aghios Oros = Athos *Greece* 40°9N 24°22E **203** F8
Aghios Petros *Greece* 38°40N 20°36E **207** B2
Aghios Stephanos *Greece* 39°46N 19°39E **206** B9
Aghios Thekli *Greece* 38°15N 20°23E **207** C1
Aghios Thomas *Greece* 38°58N 20°47E **207** B2
Aghiou Orous, Kolpos *Greece* 40°6N 24°0E **202** F7
Aghireşu *Romania* 46°53N 23°15E **183** D8
Aghoueyyît *Mauritania* 21°10N 15°6W **260** D1
Aghreïjît *Mauritania* 21°58N 12°11W **260** D2
Agia *Greece* 39°43N 22°45E **204** B4
Agincourt *Canada* 43°47N 79°16W **141** A3
Aginskoye *Russia* 51°6N 114°32E **215** D12
Agjert *Mauritania* 16°23N 9°17W **262** B3
Ağlasun *Turkey* 37°39N 30°31E **205** D12
Agly → *France* 42°46N 3°3E **174** F7
Agmar *Mauritania* 25°18N 10°50W **260** C2
Agnew *Australia* 28°1S 120°31E **279** E3
Agnibilékrou *Ivory C.* 7°10N 3°11W **262** D4
Agnita *Romania* 45°59N 24°40E **183** E9
Agnone *Italy* 41°48N 14°22E **199** G11
Ago *Japan* 34°20N 136°51E **223** C8
Ago-Are *Nigeria* 8°30N 3°25E **263** D5
Agofie *Ghana* 8°27N 0°15E **263** D5
Agogna → *Italy* 45°4N 8°54E **198** C5
Agoitz = Aoiz *Spain* 42°46N 1°22W **196** C3
Agön *Sweden* 61°34N 17°23E **162** C11
Agon Coutainville *France* 49°2N 1°34W **172** C5
Agoo *Phil.* 16°20N 120°22E **232** C3
Agora *Athens, Greece* **112** c1
Ágordo *Italy* 46°18N 12°2E **199** B9
Agori *India* 24°33N 82°57E **243** G10
Agouifa *Mauritania* 19°57N 16°10W **260** E1
Agouna *Benin* 7°39N 1°47E **263** D5
Agout → *France* 43°47N 1°41E **174** E5
Agra *India* 27°17N 77°58E **242** F7
Agra Canal *India* 28°33N 77°17E **120** B2
Agrakhanskiuy Poluostrov *Russia* 43°42N 47°36E **191** J8
Agram = Zagreb *Croatia* 45°50N 15°58E **199** C12
Agramunt *Spain* 41°48N 1°6E **196** D6
Ágreda *Spain* 41°51N 1°55W **196** D3
Ağri *Turkey* 39°44N 43°3E **213** C10
Ağri □ *Turkey* 39°45N 43°5E **213** C10
Agri → *Italy* 40°13N 16°44E **201** B9
Ağrı Dağı *Turkey* 39°50N 44°15E **213** C11
Ağri Karakose = Ağri *Turkey* 39°44N 43°3E **213** C10
Agria *Greece* 39°20N 23°1E **204** B5
Agricola Oriental *Mexico* 19°23N 99°4W **128** B2
Agrigento *Italy* 37°19N 13°34E **200** E6
Agrihan *N. Marianas* 18°46N 145°40E **302** a
Agrinio *Greece* 38°37N 21°27E **204** C3
Agrópoli *Italy* 40°21N 14°59E **201** B7
Ağstafa *Azerbaijan* 41°7N 45°27E **191** K7
Água Branca *Brazil* 5°50S 42°40W **332** C3
Agua Caliente *Mexico* 32°29N 116°59W **307** N10
Agua Caliente Springs *U.S.A.* 32°56N 116°19W **307** N10
Água Clara *Brazil* 20°25S 52°45W **331** E7
Água Espraiada → *Brazil* 23°36S 46°41W **137** B2
Agua Fria ⌓ *U.S.A.* 34°14N 112°0W **305** J8
Agua Hechicera *Mexico* 32°28N 116°15W **307** N10
Água Preta → *Brazil* 1°41S 63°48W **329** D5
Agua Prieta *Mexico* 31°18N 109°34W **318** A3
Aguachica *Colombia* 8°19N 73°38W **328** B3
Aguada *Puerto Rico* 18°23N 67°11W **321** b
Aguada Cecilio *Argentina* 40°51S 65°51W **336** B3
Aguadas *Colombia* 5°40N 75°38W **328** B2
Aguadilla *Puerto Rico* 18°26N 67°10W **321** C6
Aguadulce *Panama* 8°15N 80°32W **320** E3
Agualva-Cacem *Portugal* 38°46N 9°15W **126** A1
Aguanga *U.S.A.* 33°27N 116°51W **307** M10
Aguanish *Canada* 50°14N 62°2W **299** B7
Aguanish → *Canada* 50°13N 62°5W **299** B7
Aguapeí *Brazil* 16°12S 59°43W **331** D6
Aguapeí → *Brazil* 21°0S 51°0W **333** F1
Aguapey → *Argentina* 29°7S 56°36W **334** B4
Aguaray Guazú → *Paraguay* 24°47S 57°19W **334** A4
Aguarico → *Ecuador* 0°59S 75°11W **328** D2
Aguaro-Guariquito △ *Venezuela* 8°20N 66°35W **328** B4
Aguas → *Spain* 41°20N 0°30W **196** D4
Aguas Blancas *Chile* 24°15S 69°55W **334** A2
Aguas Calientes, Sierra de *Argentina* 25°26S 66°40W **334** B2
Águas Formosas *Brazil* 17°5S 40°57W **333** E3
Aguascalientes *Mexico* 21°53N 102°18W **318** C4
Aguascalientes □ *Mexico* 22°0N 102°20W **318** C4
Agudo *Spain* 38°59N 4°52W **195** G6
Águeda *Portugal* 40°34N 8°27W **194** E2
Agueda → *Spain* 41°2N 6°56W **194** D4
Aguelhok *Mali* 19°29N 0°52E **261** E5
Aguelt el Melah *Mauritania* 23°3N 10°40W **260** D2
Agüenit *W. Sahara* 22°11N 13°8W **260** D2
Aguié *Niger* 13°31N 7°46E **263** C6
Aguila, Punta *Puerto Rico* 17°57N 67°13W **321** b
Aguilafuente *Spain* 41°13N 4°7W **194** D6
Aguilar de Campóo *Spain* 42°47N 4°15W **194** C6
Aguilar de la Frontera *Spain* 37°31N 4°40W **195** H6
Aguilares *Argentina* 27°26S 65°35W **334** B2
Águilas *Spain* 37°23N 1°35W **197** H3
Agüimes *Canary Is.* 27°58N 15°27W **153** e1
Aguja, C. de la *Colombia* 11°18N 74°12W **328** A3
Agujereada, Pta. *Puerto Rico* 18°30N 67°8W **321** b
Agulaa *Ethiopia* 13°40N 39°40E **257** E4
Agulhas, C. *S. Africa* 34°52S 20°0E **270** D3
Agulhas Ridge *Atl. Oc.* 42°0S 15°0E **152** L13
Agulo *Canary Is.* 28°11N 17°12W **153** e1
Agung, Gunung *Indonesia* 8°20S 115°28E **231** J18
Aguni-Jima *Japan* 26°30N 127°10E **221** L3

Agur Uganda 2°28N 32°55E 268 B3
Agusan → Phil. 9°0N 125°30E 233 G5
Agusan del Norte □ Phil. 9°20N 125°10E 233 G5
Agusan del Sur □ Phil. 8°30N 125°30E 233 G5
Agustín Codazzi Colombia 10°2N 73°14W 328 A3
Agutaya I. Phil. 11°9N 120°58E 233 F3
Ağva Turkey 41°8N 29°51E 203 E13
Agvali Russia 42°36N 46°8E 191 J8
Aha Mts. Botswana 19°45S 21°0E 270 A3
Ahad Rifaydah Si. Arabia 17°50N 42°50E 248 C3
Ahaggar Algeria 23°0N 6°30E 261 D6
Ahaggar △ Algeria 23°0N 4°50E 261 D5
Ahal □ Turkmenistan 37°0N 57°0E 216 E5
Ahamansu Ghana 7°38N 0°35E 263 D5
Ahar Iran 38°35N 47°0E 213 C12
Ahat Turkey 38°39N 29°47E 205 C11
Ahaura → N.Z. 42°21S 171°34E 285 C6
Ahaus Germany 52°4N 7°0E 178 C2
Ahé French Polynesia 14°30S 146°18W 289 f
Åheim Norway 62°2N 5°13E 164 B2
Ahelledjem Algeria 26°37N 6°58E 261 C6
Ahimanawa Ra. N.Z. 39°3S 176°30E 284 F5
Ahioma Papua N. G. 10°20S 150°33E 286 F6
Ahipara B. N.Z. 35°5S 173°5E 284 B2
Ahir Dağı Turkey 38°45N 30°10E 205 C12
Ahiri India 19°30N 80°0E 244 E5
Ahlat Turkey 38°45N 42°29E 213 C10
Ahlen Germany 51°45N 7°53E 178 D3
Ahmad Wal Pakistan 29°18N 65°58E 242 E1
Ahmadabad India 23°0N 72°40E 242 H5
Aḩmadābād Khorāsān, Iran 35°3N 60°50E 247 C9
Aḩmadābād Khorāsān, Iran 35°49N 59°42E 247 C8
Aḩmadī Iran 27°56N 56°42E 247 E8
Ahmadnagar India 19°7N 74°46E 244 E2
Ahmadpur India 18°40N 76°57E 244 E3
Ahmadpur East Pakistan 29°12N 71°10E 242 E4
Ahmadpur Lamma Pakistan 28°19N 70°3E 242 E4
Ahmanson Theater Los Angeles, U.S.A. 127 b2
Ahmar, Mts. Ethiopia 9°20N 41°15E 257 F5
Ahmedabad = Ahmadabad India 23°0N 72°40E 242 H5
Ahmednagar = Ahmadnagar India 19°7N 74°46E 244 E2
Ahmetbey Turkey 41°26N 27°34E 203 E11
Ahmetler Turkey 38°28N 29°5E 205 C11
Ahmetli Turkey 38°32N 27°57E 205 C9
Ahmeyim Mauritania 20°51N 14°25W 260 D2
Ahoada Nigeria 5°8N 6°36E 263 D6
Ahome Mexico 25°55N 109°11W 318 B3
Ahon, Tarso Chad 20°23N 18°18E 259 D3
Ahoskie U.S.A. 36°17N 76°59W 315 C16
Ahr → Germany 50°32N 7°16E 178 E3
Ahram Iran 28°52N 51°16E 247 D6
Ahrax Pt. Malta 36°0N 14°22E 206 F7
Ahrensbök Germany 54°2N 10°35E 178 A6
Ahrensburg Germany 53°40N 10°13E 178 B6
Ahrensfelde Germany 52°34N 13°34E 115 A4
Ahu Akivi Chile 27°7S 109°24W 330 b
Ahu Tepeu Chile 27°6S 109°25W 330 b
Ahu Tongariki Chile 27°8S 109°17W 330 b
Ahu Vinapu Chile 27°10S 109°25W 330 b
Ahuachapán El Salv. 13°54N 89°52W 320 D2
'Āhuimanu U.S.A. 21°26N 157°50W 302 K14
Ahun France 46°4N 2°5E 173 F9
Ahuntsic Canada 45°32N 73°41W 130 A1
Ahunui French Polynesia 19°39S 140°25W 289 f
Ahuriri → N.Z. 44°31S 170°12E 285 E5
Åhus Sweden 55°56N 14°18E 163 J8
Ahvāz Iran 31°20N 48°40E 247 D6
Ahvenanmaa = Åland Finland 60°15N 20°0E 161 F19
Aḩwar Yemen 13°30N 46°40E 248 D4
Ahzar → Mali 15°30N 3°20E 263 B5
Ai → India 26°26N 90°44E 241 B3
Ai → Ōsaka, Japan 34°46N 135°35E 133 A2
Ai-Ais Namibia 27°54S 17°59E 270 C2
Ai-Ais and Fish River Canyon △ Namibia 24°45S 17°15E 270 B2
Aiari → Brazil 1°22N 68°36W 328 C4
Aichach Germany 48°27N 11°8E 179 G7
Aichi □ Japan 35°0N 137°15E 223 C9
'Aiea U.S.A. 21°23N 157°56W 302 K14
Aigle Switz. 46°18N 6°58E 179 J2
Aignay-le-Duc France 47°40N 4°43E 173 E11
Aigoual, Mt. France 44°8N 3°35E 174 D7
Aigre France 45°54N 0°1E 174 C4
Aigremont France 48°54N 2°1E 134 A1
Aigrettes, Île aux Mauritius 20°25S 57°43E 272 e
Aiguá Uruguay 34°13S 54°46W 335 C5
Aigueperse France 46°3N 3°13E 173 F10
Aigues → France 44°7N 4°43E 175 D8
Aigues-Mortes France 43°35N 4°12E 175 E8
Aigues-Mortes, G. d' France 43°31N 4°3E 175 E8
Aigües-Tortes i Estany de St. Maurici △ Spain 42°38N 0°31E 196 C4
Aiguilles France 44°47N 6°51E 175 D10
Aiguillon France 44°18N 0°21E 174 D4
Aigurande France 46°27N 1°49E 173 F8
Aihui = Heihe China 50°10N 127°30E 219 A14
Aija Peru 9°50S 77°45W 330 B2
Aikawa Japan 38°2N 138°15E 220 E9
Aiken U.S.A. 33°34N 81°43W 316 B8
Ailao Shan China 24°0N 101°20E 228 F3
Aileron Australia 22°39S 133°20E 280 C1
Ailey U.S.A. 32°11N 82°34W 316 C7
Ailigandí Panama 9°14N 78°1W 328 B2
Aillant-sur-Tholon France 47°52N 3°20E 173 E10
Aillik Canada 55°11N 59°18W 299 A8
Ailsa Craig Ont., Canada 43°8N 81°33W 312 C3
Ailsa Craig S. Ayrs., U.K. 55°15N 5°6W 167 F3
Ailuluai Papua N. G. 9°38S 150°35E 286 E6
'Aim Russia 59°0N 133°55E 215 D14
Aimere Indonesia 8°45S 121°3E 231 F6
Aimogasta Argentina 28°33S 66°50W 334 B2
Aimorés Brazil 19°30S 41°4W 333 E3
Ain □ France 46°5N 5°20E 173 F12
Ain → France 45°45N 5°11E 175 C9
Aïn Beïda Algeria 35°50N 7°29E 261 A6
Aïn Ben Khellil Algeria 33°15N 0°49W 261 B4
Aïn Ben Tili Mauritania 25°59N 9°27W 260 C3
Aïn Beni Mathar Morocco 34°1N 2°0W 261 B4
Aïn Benian Algeria 36°48N 2°55E 261 A5
Ain Dalla Egypt 27°20N 27°23E 256 B2
Aïn Defla Algeria 36°16N 1°58E 261 A5
Aïn Defla □ Algeria 36°10N 2°0E 261 A5
Ain el Akhdar Egypt 28°50N 33°55E 251 K4
Ain el Mafki Egypt 27°30N 28°15E 256 B2
Ain Girba Egypt 29°20N 25°14E 256 B2
Aïn M'lila Algeria 36°2N 6°35E 261 A6
Ain Murr Sudan 21°50N 25°9E 256 C2
Ain Qeiqab Egypt 29°42N 24°55E 256 B1
Ain Salah = In Salah Algeria 27°10N 2°32E 261 C5
Aïn-Sefra Algeria 32°47N 0°37W 261 B4
Ain Sheikh Murzûk Egypt 26°47N 27°45E 256 B2
Ain Sudr Egypt 29°50N 33°6E 251 J4
Ain Sukhna Egypt 29°32N 32°20E 256 J8
Aïn Tédelès Algeria 36°0N 0°21E 261 A5
Aïn Témouchent Algeria 35°16N 1°8W 261 A4
Aïn Témouchent □ Algeria 35°20N 1°5W 261 A4
Aïn Tikkidine Algeria 25°33N 1°24E 261 C5
Aïn Touta Algeria 35°26N 5°54E 261 A6
Ain Zeitûn Egypt 29°10N 25°48E 256 B2
Aïn Zorah Morocco 34°37N 3°32W 261 B4
Ainaži Latvia 57°50N 24°24E 188 D3
Ainos Oros Greece 38°9N 20°40E 207 C2
Ainsworth U.S.A. 42°33N 99°52W 308 D4
Aintab = Gaziantep Turkey 37°6N 37°23E 250 A8
Aioi Japan 34°48N 134°28E 222 C6
Aiome Papua N. G. 5°8S 144°44E 286 C3
Aipe Colombia 3°13N 75°15W 328 C2
Aiquile Bolivia 18°10S 65°10W 331 D4
Aïr Niger 18°30N 8°0E 259 E1
Air Canada Centre Toronto, Canada 141 c2
Aïr et Ténéré △ Niger 18°12N 9°56E 263 B6
Air Force I. Canada 67°58N 74°5W 295 D17
Air Hitam Malaysia 1°55N 103°11E 237 M4
Air View Park Singapore 1°20N 103°46E 138 A2
Aira Japan 31°43N 130°43E 222 F2
Airaines France 49°58N 1°55E 173 C8
Airão Brazil 1°56S 61°22W 329 D5
Airbangis Indonesia 0°12N 99°22E 234 B1
Airdrie Alta., Canada 51°18N 114°2W 296 C6
Airdrie N. Lanarks., U.K. 55°52N 3°57W 167 F5
Aire → Meuse, France 49°18N 4°49E 173 C11
Aire → N. Yorks., U.K. 53°43N 0°55W 168 D7
Aire, I. de l' Spain 39°48N 4°16E 206 B5
Aire-sur-la-Lys France 50°37N 2°22E 173 B9
Aire-sur-l'Adour France 43°42N 0°15W 174 E3
Aireys Inlet Australia 38°29S 144°5E 282 E6
Airlie Beach Australia 20°16S 148°43E 280 b
Airport West Australia 37°42S 144°52E 128 A1
Airvault France 46°50N 0°8W 172 F6
Aisch → Germany 49°49N 10°58E 179 F6
Aisen □ Chile 46°30S 73°0W 336 C2
Aisne □ France 49°42N 3°40E 173 C10
Aisne → France 49°26N 2°50E 173 C9
Ait India 25°54N 79°14E 243 G8
Ait Ben Haddou Morocco 31°3N 7°7W 260 B3
Aitana, Sierra de Spain 38°35N 0°24W 197 G4
Aitape Papua N. G. 3°11S 142°22E 286 B2
Aitkin U.S.A. 46°32N 93°42W 308 B7
Aitutaki Cook Is. 18°52S 159°45W 289 J12
Aiuaba Brazil 6°38S 40°7W 332 C3
Aiud Romania 46°19N 23°44E 183 D8
Aix-en-Provence France 43°32N 5°27E 175 E9
Aix-la-Chapelle = Aachen Germany 50°45N 6°6E 178 E2
Aix-les-Bains France 45°41N 5°53E 175 C9
Aixe-sur-Vienne France 45°47N 1°9E 174 C5
Aiyang, Mt. Papua N. G. 5°10S 141°20E 286 C1
Aíyina = Egina Greece 37°45N 23°26E 204 D5
Aizawl India 23°40N 92°44E 241 D4
Aizenay France 46°44N 1°38W 172 F5
Aizkraukle Latvia 56°36N 25°11E 188 D3
Aizpute Latvia 56°43N 21°40E 184 B8
Aizuwakamatsu Japan 37°30N 139°56E 220 F9
Ajabshir Iran 37°28N 45°54E 213 D11
Ajaccio France 41°55N 8°40E 175 G12
Ajaccio, G. d' France 41°52N 8°40E 175 G12
Ajai ⌂ Uganda 2°52N 31°16E 268 B3
Ajaigarh India 24°52N 80°16E 243 G9
Ajajú → Colombia 0°59N 72°20W 328 C3
Ajalpan Mexico 18°22N 97°15W 319 D5
Ajanta India 20°30N 75°48E 244 D2
Ajanta Ra. India 20°28N 75°50E 244 D2
Ajari Rep. = Ajaria □ Georgia 41°30N 42°0E 191 K6
Ajaria □ Georgia 41°30N 42°0E 191 K6
Ajax Canada 43°50N 79°1W 312 C5
Ajax, Mt. N.Z. 42°35S 172°5E 285 C7
Ajdābiyā Libya 30°54N 20°4E 258 B4
Ajdābiyā □ Libya 29°0N 20°0E 258 C4
Ajdovščina Slovenia 45°54N 13°54E 199 C10
Ajegunle Nigeria 6°26N 3°20E 124 B2
Aji Japan 34°40N 135°27E 133 A1
Ajibar Ethiopia 10°35N 38°36E 257 E4
Ajka Hungary 47°4N 17°31E 182 C2
'Ajlūn Jordan 32°18N 35°47E 251 F6
'Ajmān U.A.E. 25°25N 55°30E 247 E7
Ajmer India 26°28N 74°37E 242 F6
Ajnala India 31°50N 74°48E 242 D6
Ajo U.S.A. 32°22N 112°52W 305 K7
Ajo, C. de Spain 43°31N 3°35W 194 B7
Ajoupa-Bouillon Martinique 14°49N 61°7W 322 j
Ajuda Portugal 38°42N 9°12W 126 A1
Ajuda, Pta. da Azores 37°52N 25°19W 153 d3
Ajuy Phil. 11°10N 123°1E 233 F4
Ak Dağ Turkey 36°30N 29°32E 205 E11
Ak Dağlar Turkey 39°32N 36°12E 212 C7
Ak Dağları Turkey 36°30N 29°30E 205 E11
Ak-Dovurak Russia 51°11N 90°36E 217 B12
Ak-Mechet = Qyzylorda Kazakhstan 44°48N 65°28E 217 D7
Ak-Mednet = Chornomorske Ukraine 45°31N 32°40E 189 K7
Ak-Sheikh = Razdolnoye Ukraine 45°46N 33°29E 189 K7
Akaba Togo 8°10N 1°2E 263 D5
Akabira Japan 43°33N 142°5E 220 C11
Akabli Algeria 26°49N 1°31E 261 C5
Akademika Obrucheva, Khrebet Russia 51°50N 96°0E 217 B13
Akagera △ Rwanda 1°31S 30°33E 268 C3
Akaishi-Dake Japan 35°27N 138°9E 223 B10
Akaishi-Sammyaku Japan 35°25N 138°10E 223 B10
Akaki Beseka Ethiopia 8°55N 38°45E 257 F4
Akäküs, J. Libya 25°20N 10°30E 258 C2
Akalkot India 17°32N 76°13E 244 F3
Akalla Sweden 59°24N 17°55E 139 A1
Akamas Cyprus 35°3N 32°18E 207 E8
Akan △ Japan 43°20N 144°20E 220 C12
Akanthou Cyprus 35°22N 33°45E 207 D12
Akarca Turkey 38°35N 29°35E 205 C11
Akaroa N.Z. 43°49S 172°59E 285 D7
Akaroa Harbour N.Z. 43°50S 172°55E 285 D7
Akasaka Tokyo, Japan 140 b3
Akasha Sudan 21°10N 30°32E 256 C3
Akashi Japan 34°45N 134°58E 222 C6
Akbarābād Iran 35°40N 51°20E 141 A2
Akbarpur Bihar, India 24°39N 83°58E 243 G10
Akbarpur Ut. P., India 26°25N 82°32E 243 F10
Akbou Algeria 36°31N 4°31E 261 A5
Akbulak Russia 51°1N 55°37E 216 B5
Akçaabat Turkey 41°1N 39°34E 213 B8
Akçadağ Turkey 38°27N 37°43E 212 C7
Akçakale Turkey 36°41N 38°56E 213 D8
Akçakoca Turkey 41°5N 31°8E 212 B4
Akçalı Dağları Turkey 36°18N 33°21E 250 B4
Akçaova Turkey 41°3N 29°57E 203 E13
Akçay Turkey 36°36N 29°45E 205 E11
Akçay → Turkey 37°50N 28°15E 205 D10
Akchâr Mauritania 20°20N 14°28W 260 D2
Akchi-Karasu = Toktogul Kyrgyzstan 41°50N 72°50E 217 D8
Akdağ Antalya, Turkey 37°0N 32°0E 250 B3
Akdağ İzmir, Turkey 38°33N 26°30E 205 C8
Akdağmadeni Turkey 39°39N 35°53E 212 C6
Akdere Turkey 36°14N 33°46E 250 B4
Akdoğan = Lysi Cyprus 35°6N 33°41E 207 E9
Akechi Japan 35°18N 137°23E 223 B9
Akelamo Indonesia 1°35N 129°40E 231 D7
Åkernes = Åknes Norway 58°45N 7°30E 164 F4
Åkers styckebruk Sweden 59°15N 17°5E 162 E11
Åkersberga Sweden 59°29N 18°18E 162 E12
Akershus □ Norway 60°0N 11°10E 164 D8
Akershus Slott Oslo, Norway 133 c1
Akeru → India 17°25N 80°5E 244 F5
Aketi Dem. Rep. of the Congo 2°38N 23°47E 264 B4
Akhalkalaki Georgia 41°27N 43°25E 191 K6
Akhaltsikhe Georgia 41°40N 43°0E 191 K6
Akhḑar, W. al → Si. Arabia 28°36N 36°36E 251 K7
Akhiok U.S.A. 56°57N 154°10W 303 H9
Akhisar Turkey 38°56N 27°48E 205 C9
Akhmîm Egypt 26°31N 31°47E 256 B3
Akhnur India 32°52N 74°45E 243 C6
Akhtarīn Syria 36°31N 37°20E 250 B8
Akhtopol Bulgaria 42°6N 27°56E 203 D11
Akhtuba → Russia 47°41N 46°55E 191 G8
Akhtubinsk Russia 48°13N 46°7E 191 F8
Akhty Russia 41°30N 47°45E 191 K8
Akhtyrka = Okhtyrka Ukraine 50°25N 35°0E 189 G8
Aki Japan 33°30N 133°54E 222 D5
Aki-Nada Japan 34°5N 132°40E 222 C4
Akiachak U.S.A. 60°55N 161°26W 303 F7
Akiak U.S.A. 60°55N 161°13W 303 F7
Akiéni Gabon 1°11S 13°53E 264 C2
Akihabara Tokyo, Japan 140 a5
Akimiski I. Canada 52°50N 81°30W 298 B3
Akıncı Burnu Turkey 36°19N 35°46E 250 B6
Akincilar = Louroujina Cyprus 35°0N 33°28E 207 F9
Åkirkeby Denmark 55°4N 14°55E 163 J8
Akita Japan 39°45N 140°7E 220 E10
Akita □ Japan 39°40N 140°30E 220 E10
Akjoujt Mauritania 19°45N 14°15W 262 B2
Akka Mali 15°24N 4°11W 262 B4
Akka Morocco 29°22N 8°9W 260 C3
Akkaraipattu Sri Lanka 7°13N 81°51E 245 L5
Akkaya Tepesi Turkey 37°25N 29°38E 205 D11
Akkerman = Bilhorod-Dnistrovskyy Ukraine 46°11N 30°23E 189 J6
Akkeshi Japan 43°2N 144°51E 220 C12
'Akko Israel 32°55N 35°4E 250 F6
Akköy Turkey 37°29N 27°15E 205 D9
Akkuş Turkey 40°47N 37°0E 212 B7
Aklampa Benin 8°15N 2°10E 263 D5
Aklan □ Phil. 11°50N 122°30E 233 F4
Aklavik Canada 68°12N 135°0W 294 D4
Aklera India 24°26N 76°32E 242 G7
Akmenė Lithuania 56°15N 22°45E 184 B9
Akmenrags Latvia 56°50N 21°4E 184 B8
Akmolinsk = Astana Kazakhstan 51°10N 71°30E 217 B8
Akmonte = Almonte Spain 37°13N 6°38W 195 H4
Åknes Norway 58°45N 7°30E 164 F4
Aknoul Morocco 34°40N 3°55W 261 B4
Akō Japan 34°45N 134°24E 222 C6
Ako Nigeria 10°19N 10°48E 263 C7
Akôbô Sudan 7°47N 33°1E 257 F3
Akobo → Ethiopia 7°48N 33°3E 257 F3
Akola Maharashtra, India 20°42N 77°2E 244 D3
Akola Maharashtra, India 19°32N 74°3E 244 E2
Akolmiut U.S.A. 60°55N 162°20W 303 F7
Akonolinga Cameroon 3°50N 12°18E 263 E7
Akor Mali 14°59N 6°58W 262 C3
Akordat Eritrea 15°30N 37°40E 257 D4
Akosombo Dam Ghana 6°20N 0°5E 263 D5
Akot India 21°10N 77°10E 244 D3
Akot Sudan 6°31N 30°9E 257 F3
Akoupé Ivory C. 6°23N 3°54W 262 D4
Akourousoulba C.A.R. 8°58N 20°46E 264 A4
Akpatok I. Canada 60°25N 68°8W 295 E18
Åkrahamn Norway 59°15N 5°10E 164 E2
'Akramah Libya 32°2N 23°41E 258 B4
Akranes Iceland 64°19N 22°5W 155 C4
Akreïjit Mauritania 18°19N 9°11W 262 B3
Akritas, Akra Greece 36°43N 21°54E 204 E3
Akron Colo., U.S.A. 40°10N 103°13W 304 F12
Akron Ind., U.S.A. 41°2N 86°1W 311 C10
Akron Ohio, U.S.A. 41°5N 81°31W 312 E3
Akrotiri Cyprus 34°36N 32°57E 207 F8
Akrotiri, Akra Greece 40°26N 25°27E 203 F9
Akrotiri Bay Cyprus 34°35N 33°10E 207 F9
Aksai Chin China 35°15N 79°55E 243 B8
Aksaray Turkey 38°25N 34°2E 212 C6
Aksaray □ Turkey 38°20N 33°45E 212 C5
Aksay = Aqsay Kazakhstan 51°11N 53°0E 187 D9
Akşehir Turkey 38°18N 31°30E 212 C4
Akşehir Gölü Turkey 38°30N 31°25E 212 C4
Akseki Turkey 37°2N 31°47E 250 A2
Akstafa = Ağstafa Azerbaijan 41°7N 45°27E 191 K7
Aksu Xinjiang Uygur, China 41°5N 80°10E 217 D10
Aksu Turkey 36°57N 30°50E 250 B1
Aksu → Turkey 36°52N 30°57E 250 B1
Aksu He → China 40°26N 80°59E 217 D10
Aksum Ethiopia 14°5N 38°40E 257 E4
Aktash Russia 55°2N 52°3E 190 C11
Aktepe Turkey 36°42N 36°27E 250 B7
Aktio Greece 38°57N 20°46E 207 B2
Akto China 39°5N 75°59E 217 E9
Aktsyabrski Belarus 52°38N 28°53E 177 B15
Aktyubinsk = Aqtöbe Kazakhstan 50°17N 57°10E 187 D10
Aku Nigeria 6°40N 7°18E 263 D6
Akula Dem. Rep. of the Congo 2°22N 20°12E 264 B4
Akun I. U.S.A. 54°11N 165°32W 303 J6
Akune Japan 32°1N 130°12E 222 E2
Akure Nigeria 7°15N 5°5E 263 D6
Akurenan Eq. Guin. 1°2N 10°40E 264 B2
Akuressa Sri Lanka 6°5N 80°29E 245 L5
Akureyri Iceland 65°40N 18°6W 155 B8
Akuseki-Shima Japan 29°27N 129°37E 221 K4
Akusha Russia 42°18N 47°30E 191 J8
Akutan U.S.A. 54°8N 165°46W 303 J6
Akutan I. U.S.A. 54°7N 165°55W 303 J6
Akwa-Ibom □ Nigeria 4°30N 7°30E 263 E6
Akwanga Nigeria 8°55N 8°23E 263 D6
Akyab = Sittwe Burma 20°18N 92°45E 241 E4
Akyazı Turkey 40°40N 30°38E 212 B4
Al → Norway 60°38N 8°33E 164 D5
Al Abyaḑ Libya 26°49N 14°13E 258 C2
Al Abyār Libya 32°9N 20°29E 258 B4
Al 'Adam Libya 31°51N 23°55E 258 B4
Al 'Adan Yemen 12°45N 45°0E 248 D4
Al Aḩsā = Hasa Si. Arabia 25°50N 49°0E 247 E6
Al Ajfar Si. Arabia 27°26N 43°0E 246 E4
Al Amādīyah Iraq 37°5N 43°30E 213 D10
Al 'Amārah Iraq 31°55N 47°15E 246 D5
Al Anbār □ Iraq 33°25N 42°0E 246 C4
Al 'Aqabah Jordan 29°31N 35°0E 251 J6
Al 'Aqabah □ Jordan 29°30N 35°0E 251 J6
Al 'Aqīq Si. Arabia 20°39N 41°25E 248 B3
Al 'Arak Syria 34°38N 38°35E 213 E8
Al 'Aramah Si. Arabia 25°30N 46°0E 246 E5
Al 'Ariḑah Si. Arabia 17°3N 43°5E 248 C3
Al 'Arţāwīyah Si. Arabia 26°31N 45°20E 246 E5
Al Ashkhara Oman 21°50N 59°30E 249 B7
Al 'Āşimah = 'Ammān □ Jordan 31°40N 36°30E 251 G7
Al 'Assāfiyah Si. Arabia 28°17N 38°59E 246 D3
Al Atārib Syria 36°9N 36°49E 250 B7
Al 'Awdah Si. Arabia 25°32N 45°29E 246 E5
Al 'Ayn Si. Arabia 25°4N 38°6E 246 E3
Al 'Ayn U.A.E. 24°15N 55°45E 247 E7
Al 'Azamīyah Iraq 33°22N 44°22E 213 F11
Al 'Azīzīyah Iraq 32°54N 45°4E 213 F11
Al 'Azīzīyah Libya 32°30N 13°1E 258 B2
Al 'Azīzīyah □ Libya 32°31N 13°1E 261 B7
Al Bāb Syria 36°23N 37°29E 250 B8
Al Bad' Si. Arabia 28°28N 35°1E 246 D2
Al Bādī Iraq 35°56N 41°32E 246 C4
Al Badī' Si. Arabia 22°0N 46°35E 248 B4
Al Bāḩah Si. Arabia 20°1N 41°28E 256 C5
Al Bāḩah □ Si. Arabia 20°30N 41°30E 248 B3
Al Baḩrah Kuwait 29°40N 47°52E 246 D5
Al Baḩral Mayyit = Dead Sea Asia 31°30N 35°30E 251 G6
Al Balqā' □ Jordan 32°5N 35°45E 251 F6
Al Barkāt Libya 24°56N 10°14E 258 D2
Al Bārūk, J. Lebanon 33°39N 35°40E 250 E6
Al Başrah Iraq 30°30N 47°50E 246 D5
Al Baţḩā Iraq 31°6N 45°53E 246 D5
Al Batinah Oman 24°10N 56°50E 249 A7
Al Batrūn Lebanon 34°15N 35°40E 250 D6
Al Bayāḑ Si. Arabia 22°0N 47°0E 248 B4
Al Bayḑā Libya 32°50N 21°44E 258 B4
Al Bayḑā' Yemen 14°5N 45°42E 248 D4
Al Bi'ār Si. Arabia 22°39N 39°40E 248 B2
Al Biqā Lebanon 34°10N 36°10E 250 D7
Al Biqā □ Lebanon 34°0N 36°5E 250 E7
Al Bi'r Si. Arabia 28°51N 36°16E 251 K7
Al Birk Si. Arabia 18°13N 41°33E 248 C3
Al Bu'ayrāt al Ḩasūn Libya 31°24N 15°44E 258 B3
Al Bukayrīyah Si. Arabia 26°9N 43°40E 246 E4
Al Bumbah Libya 32°24N 23°8E 258 B4
Al Burayj Syria 34°15N 36°46E 250 D7
Al Buţnān □ Libya 30°0N 24°0E 258 B4
Al Buţnān □ Libya 31°40N 24°30E 258 B4
Al Faḑilī Si. Arabia 26°58N 49°10E 247 E6
Al Fallūjah Iraq 33°20N 43°55E 213 F10
Al Fatḩah Iraq 35°3N 43°33E 213 E10
Al Fāw Iraq 30°0N 48°30E 247 D6
Al Faydamī Yemen 16°25N 52°26E 249 C6
Al Fujayrah U.A.E. 25°7N 56°18E 247 E8
Al Ghadaf, W. → Jordan 31°26N 36°43E 251 G7
Al Ghammās Iraq 31°45N 44°37E 246 D5
Al Gharīb Libya 32°35N 21°11E 258 B4
Al Ghayḑah Ḩaḑramaut, Yemen 14°55N 50°0E 249 D5
Al Ghayḑah Qamar, Yemen 16°13N 52°11E 249 C6
Al Ghayl Yemen 15°30N 50°54E 249 D5
Al Ghazālah Si. Arabia 26°48N 41°19E 246 E4
Al Ḩadd Oman 22°32N 59°48E 249 B7
Al Ḩaddār Si. Arabia 21°58N 45°57E 248 B4
Al Ḩadīthah Iraq 34°0N 41°13E 213 E10
Al Ḩadīthah Si. Arabia 31°28N 37°8E 246 D3
Al Ḩaḑr Iraq 35°35N 42°44E 213 E10
Al Ḩaffah Syria 35°36N 36°1E 250 C7
Al Ḩājānah Syria 33°20N 36°33E 250 E7
Al Ḩajar al Gharbī Oman 24°10N 56°15E 247 E8
Al Ḩallānīyah Oman 17°30N 56°1E 249 C7
Al Ḩāmad Si. Arabia 31°30N 39°30E 246 D3
Al Ḩamādah al Ḩamrā' Libya 29°30N 12°0E 258 C2
Al Ḩamar Si. Arabia 22°26N 46°12E 248 B4
Al Ḩamdānīyah Syria 35°25N 36°50E 250 C7
Al Ḩamīdīyah Syria 34°42N 35°57E 250 D6
Al Ḩammār Iraq 30°57N 46°51E 246 D5
Al Ḩamrā' Si. Arabia 24°2N 38°55E 246 E3
Al Ḩamrā' Syria 35°19N 37°5E 250 C8
Al Ḩamzah Iraq 31°43N 44°58E 246 D5
Al Ḩanākīyah Si. Arabia 24°51N 40°31E 246 E4
Al Ḩarīq Si. Arabia 23°29N 46°27E 248 B4
Al Ḩarūj al Aswad Libya 27°0N 17°10E 258 C3
Al Ḩasakah Syria 36°35N 40°45E 213 D9
Al Ḩasakah □ Syria 36°40N 40°50E 213 D9
Al Hāshimīyah Iraq 32°22N 44°39E 213 G11
Al Ḩāsikīyah Oman 17°28N 55°36E 249 C6
Al Ḩasy Yemen 14°3N 48°40E 249 D5
Al Hawīyah Ash Sharqīyah, Si. Arabia 24°45N 49°6E 249 A5
Al Hawīyah Makkah, Si. Arabia 21°26N 40°30E 248 B3
Al Ḩawrah Yemen 13°50N 47°35E 248 D4
Al Ḩawtah = Laḩij Yemen 13°4N 44°53E 248 D4
Al Ḩawţah Si. Arabia 23°30N 47°0E 248 B4
Al Ḩayy Iraq 32°5N 46°5E 213 F12
Al Ḩijarah Asia 30°0N 44°0E 246 D4
Al Ḩillah Iraq 32°30N 44°25E 213 F11
Al Ḩillah Si. Arabia 23°35N 46°50E 248 B4
Al Hindīyah Iraq 32°30N 44°10E 213 F11
Al Hirmil Lebanon 34°26N 36°24E 250 D7
Al Hoceïma Morocco 35°8N 3°58W 261 A4
Al Ḩudaydah Yemen 14°50N 43°0E 248 D3
Al Ḩudūd ash Shamālīyah □ Si. Arabia 29°10N 42°30E 246 D4
Al Ḩufrah Libya 25°32N 14°1E 258 C2
Al Hufūf Si. Arabia 25°25N 49°45E 247 E6
Al Ḩulwah Si. Arabia 23°24N 46°48E 248 B4
Al Ḩumayḑah Si. Arabia 29°14N 34°56E 251 J5
Al Ḩunayy Si. Arabia 25°58N 48°45E 247 E6
Al Husayyāt Libya 30°24N 20°37E 258 B4
Al 'Irqah Yemen 13°39N 47°22E 248 D4
Al 'Īsāwīyah Si. Arabia 30°43N 37°59E 246 D3
Al Ittihad = Madīnat ash Sha'b Yemen 12°50N 45°0E 248 D4
Al Jabal al Akhḑar Libya 32°30N 21°30E 258 B4
Al Jabal al Akhḑar □ Libya 32°30N 21°41E 258 B4
Al Jafr Jordan 30°18N 36°14E 251 H7
Al Jāfūrah Si. Arabia 25°0N 50°15E 247 E7
Al Jaghbūb Libya 29°42N 24°38E 258 C4
Al Jahrah Kuwait 29°25N 47°40E 246 D5
Al Jalāmīd Si. Arabia 31°20N 40°6E 246 D3
Al Jamalīyah Qatar 25°37N 51°5E 247 E6
Al Janūb □ Lebanon 33°20N 35°20E 250 E6
Al Jawf Libya 24°10N 23°24E 258 D4
Al Jawf Si. Arabia 29°55N 39°40E 246 D3
Al Jawf □ Si. Arabia 29°30N 39°30E 246 D3
Al Jazair = Algeria ■ Africa 28°30N 2°0E 261 C5
Al Jazirah Iraq 33°30N 44°0E 213 E10
Al Jithāmīyah Si. Arabia 27°41N 41°43E 246 E4
Al Jubayl Si. Arabia 27°0N 49°50E 247 E6
Al Jubaylah Si. Arabia 24°55N 46°25E 246 E5
Al Jubb Si. Arabia 27°11N 42°17E 246 E4
Al Jufrah Libya 29°10N 16°0E 258 C3
Al Jufrah □ Libya 29°0N 16°0E 258 C3
Al Jumūm Si. Arabia 21°37N 39°42E 248 B2
Al Junaynah Sudan 13°27N 22°45E 259 F4
Al Kabā'ish Iraq 30°58N 47°0E 246 D5
Al Kāmil Oman 22°13N 59°12E 249 B7
Al Karak Jordan 31°11N 35°42E 251 G6
Al Karak □ Jordan 31°0N 36°0E 251 H7
Al Kāẓimīyah Iraq 33°22N 44°18E 213 F11
Al Khābūrah Oman 23°57N 57°5E 247 F8
Al Khafjī Si. Arabia 28°24N 48°29E 247 E6
Al Khalīl West Bank 31°32N 35°6E 251 G6
Al Khāliş Iraq 33°49N 44°32E 213 F11
Al Khamāsīn Si. Arabia 20°29N 44°46E 248 B4
Al Kharj Si. Arabia 24°0N 47°0E 248 B4
Al Kharsānīyah Si. Arabia 27°13N 49°18E 247 E6
Al Khaşab Oman 26°14N 56°15E 247 E8
Al Khāşirah Si. Arabia 23°30N 43°47E 248 B3
Al Khawr Qatar 25°41N 51°30E 247 E6
Al Khiḑr Iraq 31°12N 45°33E 246 D5
Al Khiyām Lebanon 33°20N 35°36E 250 E6
Al Khobar Si. Arabia 26°17N 50°12E 247 E6
Al Khums Libya 32°40N 14°17E 258 B2
Al Kifl Iraq 32°13N 44°22E 213 G11
Al Kiswah Syria 33°23N 36°14E 250 E7
Al Kūfah Iraq 32°2N 44°24E 213 F11
Al Kufrah Libya 24°17N 23°15E 258 D4
Al Kuhayfiyah Si. Arabia 27°12N 43°3E 246 E4
Al Kumayt Iraq 32°2N 46°52E 213 G12
Al Kūt Iraq 32°30N 46°0E 213 F11
Al Kuwayt Kuwait 29°30N 48°0E 246 D5
Al Labwah Lebanon 34°11N 36°20E 250 D7
Al Lādhiqīyah Syria 35°30N 35°45E 250 C6
Al Lādhiqīyah □ Syria 35°45N 36°0E 250 C7
Al Līth Si. Arabia 20°9N 40°15E 248 B3
Al Liwā' Oman 24°31N 56°36E 247 E8
Al Luḩayyah Yemen 15°45N 42°40E 248 D3
Al Madīnah Iraq 30°57N 47°16E 246 D5
Al Madīnah Si. Arabia 24°35N 39°52E 246 E3
Al Madīnah □ Si. Arabia 25°0N 40°30E 248 B3
Al Mafraq Jordan 32°17N 36°14E 251 F7
Al Mafraq □ Jordan 32°17N 36°15E 251 F7
Al Maghārīm Yemen 15°1N 47°49E 248 D4
Al Maghreb = Morocco ■ N. Afr. 32°0N 5°50W 260 B3
Al Mahbes W. Sahara 27°10N 9°50W 260 C3
Al Maḩmūdīyah Iraq 33°3N 44°21E 213 F11
Al Majma'ah Si. Arabia 25°57N 45°22E 246 E5
Al Makhruq, W. → Jordan 31°28N 37°0E 251 G8
Al Makḩūl Si. Arabia 26°37N 42°39E 246 E4
Al Mālikīyah Syria 37°10N 42°8E 213 D10
Al Manāmah Bahrain 26°10N 50°30E 247 E6
Al Maqwa' Kuwait 29°10N 47°59E 246 D5
Al Marāḩ Si. Arabia 25°35N 49°35E 247 E6
Al Marj Libya 32°25N 20°30E 258 B4
Al Marj □ Libya 32°0N 21°0E 258 B4
Al Marqab □ Libya 32°32N 14°35E 258 B2
Al Maţlā Kuwait 29°24N 47°40E 246 D5
Al Mawşil Iraq 36°15N 43°5E 213 D10
Al Mayādin Syria 35°1N 40°27E 213 E9
Al Mazār Jordan 31°4N 35°41E 251 G6
Al Midhnab Si. Arabia 25°50N 44°18E 246 E5
Al Minā' Lebanon 34°24N 35°49E 250 D6
Al Miqdādīyah Iraq 34°0N 45°0E 213 E11
Al Mubarraz Si. Arabia 25°30N 49°40E 247 E6
Al Mudawwarah Jordan 29°19N 36°0E 251 J7
Al Muḑaybī Oman 22°34N 58°7E 249 B7
Al Mughayrā' U.A.E. 24°5N 53°32E 247 E7
Al Muḩarraq Bahrain 26°15N 50°40E 247 E6
Al Mukallā Yemen 14°33N 49°2E 249 D5
Al Mukhā Yemen 13°18N 43°15E 248 D3
Al Mukhaylī Libya 32°10N 22°17E 258 B4
Al Musayjīd Si. Arabia 24°5N 39°5E 246 E3
Al Musayyib Iraq 32°49N 44°20E 213 F11
Al Muthannā □ Iraq 30°30N 45°15E 246 D5
Al Muwayh Si. Arabia 22°41N 41°37E 256 C5
Al Muwayliḩ Si. Arabia 27°40N 35°30E 246 E2
Al Muzāḩimīyah Si. Arabia 24°29N 46°18E 248 A4
Al Owuho = Otukpa Nigeria 7°9N 7°41E 263 D6
Al Qaddāḩīyah Libya 31°15N 15°9E 258 B3
Al Qaḑīmah Si. Arabia 22°20N 39°13E 248 B2
Al Qādisīyah □ Iraq 32°0N 45°0E 246 D5
Al Qadmūs Syria 35°5N 36°10E 250 C7
Al Qaḩmah Si. Arabia 18°0N 41°41E 248 C3
Al Qā'im Iraq 34°21N 41°7E 213 E9
Al Qā'iyah Si. Arabia 24°33N 43°15E 248 A3
Al Qalībah Si. Arabia 28°24N 37°42E 246 D3
Al Qāmishlī Syria 37°2N 41°14E 213 D9
Al Qardāḩah Syria 35°27N 36°3E 250 C7
Al Qaryah ash Sharqīyah Libya 30°28N 13°40E 258 B2
Al Qaryatayn Syria 34°12N 37°13E 250 D8
Al Qaşabāt Libya 32°39N 14°1E 258 B2
Al Qaşīm □ Si. Arabia 26°0N 43°0E 246 E4
Al Qaţ'ā Syria 34°40N 40°48E 213 E9
Al Qaţīf Si. Arabia 26°35N 50°0E 247 E6
Al Qaţn Yemen 15°51N 48°26E 249 D5
Al Qatrānah Jordan 31°12N 36°6E 251 G7
Al Qaţrūn Libya 24°56N 15°3E 258 D3
Al Qawz Si. Arabia 18°58N 41°26E 248 C3
Al Qayşūmah Si. Arabia 28°20N 46°7E 246 D5
Al Qiblīyah Oman 17°30N 56°20E 249 C7
Al Qubbah □ Libya 31°0N 23°40E 258 B4
Al Quds = Jerusalem Israel/West Bank 31°47N 35°10E 123 B2
Al Qunayţirah Syria 33°5N 35°45E 250 F6
Al Qunfudhah Si. Arabia 19°3N 41°4E 248 C3
Al Qurayyāt Oman 23°17N 58°53E 249 B7
Al Qurḩ Yemen 16°44N 51°29E 249 C5
Al Qurnah Iraq 31°1N 47°25E 246 D5
Al Quşayr Iraq 30°39N 45°50E 246 D5
Al Quşayr Syria 34°31N 36°34E 250 D7
Al Qutayfah Syria 33°44N 36°36E 250 E7
Al Quway'īyah Si. Arabia 24°3N 45°15E 248 A4
Al Quwayr Iraq 36°2N 43°29E 213 D10
Al 'Ubaylah Si. Arabia 21°59N 50°57E 249 B5
Al 'Uḑaylīyah Si. Arabia 25°8N 49°18E 247 E6
Al 'Ulā Si. Arabia 26°35N 38°0E 246 E3
Al 'Ulayyah Si. Arabia 19°39N 41°54E 248 C3
Al Uqaylah ash Sharqīgah Libya 30°12N 19°10E 258 B3
Al 'Uqayr Si. Arabia 25°40N 50°15E 247 E6
Al 'Urūq al Mutariḑah Si. Arabia 21°0N 53°30E 249 B6
Al 'Uwaynāt Libya 25°47N 10°33E 261 C7
Al 'Uwaynid Si. Arabia 24°50N 46°0E 246 E5
Al 'Uwayqīlah Si. Arabia 30°30N 42°10E 246 D4
Al Uweinat Libya 21°34N 24°50E 259 D4
Al 'Uyūn Ḩijāz, Si. Arabia 24°33N 39°35E 246 E3
Al 'Uyūn Najd, Si. Arabia 26°30N 43°50E 246 E4
Al 'Uzayr Iraq 31°19N 47°25E 246 D5
Al Wāhāt □ Libya 29°0N 22°0E 258 C4
Al Wajh Si. Arabia 26°10N 36°30E 246 E3
Al Wakrah Qatar 25°10N 51°40E 247 E6
Al-Walaja West Bank 31°44N 35°9E 123 B1
Al Waqbah Si. Arabia 28°48N 45°33E 246 D5
Al Wari'āh Si. Arabia 27°51N 47°25E 246 E5
Al Wāţīyah Libya 32°28N 11°57E 258 B2
Al Wīgh Libya 24°16N 14°58E 258 D2
Al Yaman = Yemen ■ Asia 15°0N 44°0E 248 D4
Ala Italy 45°45N 11°0E 198 C8
Ala Dağ Turkey 37°44N 35°9E 246 B2
Ala Dağları Turkey 39°15N 43°33E 213 C10
Ala Tau Asia 45°30N 80°40E 217 C10
Ala Tau Shankou = Dzungarian Gate Asia 45°10N 82°0E 217 C10
Alabama □ U.S.A. 33°0N 87°0W 315 E11
Alabama → U.S.A. 31°8N 87°57W 315 F11
Alabaster U.S.A. 33°15N 86°49W 315 E11
Alabat I. Phil. 14°7N 122°3E 232 D4
Alabel Phil. 6°4N 125°16E 233 H5
Alabule → Papua N. G. 8°31S 146°56E 286 E4
Alaca Turkey 40°10N 34°51E 212 B6
Alacaatlı Turkey 39°15N 28°3E 205 B10
Alaçam Turkey 41°36N 35°36E 212 B6
Alaçam Dağları Turkey 39°18N 28°49E 205 B10
Alacant = Alicante Spain 38°23N 0°30W 197 G4
Alaçatı Turkey 38°15N 26°22E 205 C8
Alachua U.S.A. 29°47N 82°30W 316 F7
Alaejos Spain 41°18N 5°13W 194 D5
Alagir Russia 43°3N 44°14E 191 J7
Alagna Valsésia Italy 45°51N 7°56E 198 C4
Alagoa de Baixo = Sertânia Brazil 8°5S 37°20W 332 C4
Alagoa Grande Brazil 7°3S 35°35W 332 C4
Alagoas = Marechal Deodoro Brazil 9°43S 35°54W 332 C4
Alagoas □ Brazil 9°0S 36°0W 332 C4
Alagoinhas Brazil 12°7S 38°20W 333 D4
Alagón Spain 41°46N 1°12W 196 D3
Alagón → Spain 39°44N 6°53W 194 F4
Alaguntan Nigeria 6°25N 3°29E 124 B2
Alagyoz = Aragats Armenia 40°30N 44°15E 191 K7
Alahan Turkey 36°46N 33°19E 250 B4
Alaheaieatnu = Altaelva → Norway 69°54N 23°17E 160 B20
Alai Range Asia 39°45N 72°0E 217 E8
Alaior Spain 39°57N 4°8E 206 B5
Alajero Canary Is. 28°3N 17°13W 153 e1
Alajuela Costa Rica 10°2N 84°8W 320 D3
Alajuela, L. Panama 9°14N 79°34W 320 c
Alakamisy Madag. 21°19S 47°14E 272 C2
Alakanuk U.S.A. 62°41N 164°37W 303 E6
Alaknanda → India 30°8N 78°36E 243 D8
Alaköl Kazakhstan 46°0N 81°5E 217 C10
Alakurtti Russia 66°58N 30°25E 160 C24
'Alaläkeiki Channel U.S.A. 20°30N 156°30W 302 C5
Alalapura Suriname 2°20N 56°25W 329 C6
Alalaú → Brazil 0°30S 61°9W 329 D5
Alamagan N. Marianas 17°36N 145°50E 302 a
Alamarvdasht Iran 27°37N 52°59E 247 E7
Alamata Ethiopia 12°25N 39°33E 257 E4
Alameda Calif., U.S.A. 37°46N 122°15W 136 B3
Alameda N. Mex., U.S.A. 35°11N 106°37W 305 J10
Alameda, Parque Mexico City, Mexico 128 b2
Alameda Memorial State Beach Park U.S.A. 37°45N 122°16W 136 B3
Alaminos Phil. 16°10N 119°59E 232 C2
Alamo Ga., U.S.A. 32°9N 82°47W 316 C7
Alamo Nev., U.S.A. 37°22N 115°10W 307 H11
Alamogordo U.S.A. 32°54N 105°57W 305 K11
Alamos Mexico 27°1N 108°56W 318 B3
Alamosa U.S.A. 37°28N 105°52W 305 H11
Alampur India 15°55N 78°6E 245 G4
Åland Finland 60°15N 20°0E 161 F19
Aland India 17°36N 76°35E 244 F3
Alandroal Portugal 38°41N 7°24W 195 G3
Ålands hav Europe 60°0N 19°30E 161 G18
Älandsbro Sweden 62°40N 17°51E 162 B11
Alandur India 13°0N 80°15E 245 H5
Alang Indonesia 4°7N 117°0E 235 B5
Alange, Embalse d' Spain 38°45N 6°18W 195 G4
Alania = North Ossetia □ Russia 43°30N 44°30E 191 J7
Alanís Spain 38°3N 5°43W 195 G5
Alanya Turkey 36°38N 32°0E 250 B3
Alaotra, Farihin' Madag. 17°30S 48°30E 272 B2
Alapaha U.S.A. 31°23N 83°13W 316 D6
Alapayevsk Russia 57°52N 61°42E 214 D7
Alappuzha = Alleppey India 9°30N 76°28E 245 K3
'Alāqān Si. Arabia 29°10N 35°21E 251 J6
Alar del Rey Spain 42°38N 4°20W 194 C6
Alara → Turkey 36°38N 31°39E 250 B2
Alaraz Spain 40°45N 5°17W 194 E5
Alarcón, Embalse de Spain 39°36N 2°10W 196 F2
Alaró Spain 39°42N 2°47E 206 B3
Alarobia-Vohiposa Madag. 20°59S 47°9E 272 C2
Alas Indonesia 8°29S 117°0E 235 D5
Alas, Selat Indonesia 8°40S 116°40E 235 D5
Alaşehir Turkey 38°23N 28°30E 205 C10
Alashtar Iran 33°51N 48°15E 213 F13
Alaska □ U.S.A. 64°0N 154°0W 303 D9
Alaska, G. of Pac. Oc. 58°0N 145°0W 303 G11
Alaska Maritime Nat. Wildlife Refuge ⌂ U.S.A. 52°0N 174°0W 303 L4
Alaska Peninsula U.S.A. 56°0N 159°0W 303 H8
Alaska Peninsula Nat. Wildlife Refuge ⌂ U.S.A. 56°0N 159°0W 303 J8
Alaska Range U.S.A. 62°50N 151°0W 303 E10
Alássio Italy 44°0N 8°10E 198 E5
Älät Azerbaijan 39°58N 49°25E 191 L9
Alatau Shan = Ala Tau Asia 45°30N 80°40E 217 C10
Alatri Italy 41°43N 13°21E 199 G10
Alatyr Russia 54°55N 46°35E 190 C8
Alatyr → Russia 54°52N 46°36E 190 C8
Alaungdaw Kathapa △ Burma 22°30N 94°30E 241 D5
Alausi Ecuador 2°0S 78°50W 328 D2
Álava □ Spain 42°48N 2°28W 196 C2
Alava, C. U.S.A. 48°10N 124°44W 304 B1
Alaverdi Armenia 41°15N 44°37E 191 K7
Alavo = Alavus Finland 62°35N 23°36E 160 E20
Alavus Finland 62°35N 23°36E 160 E20
Alawa ◎ Australia 15°42S 134°39E 280 B1
Alawoona Australia 34°45S 140°30E 282 C4
Alayawarra ◎ Australia 22°0S 134°30E 280 C1
'Alayh Lebanon 33°46N 35°33E 250 E6
Alazani → Azerbaijan 41°5N 46°40E 191 K8
Alba Italy 44°42N 8°2E 198 D5
Alba □ Romania 46°10N 23°30E 183 D8
Alba Adriática Italy 42°50N 13°56E 199 F10
Alba de Tormes Spain 40°50N 5°30W 194 E5
Alba-Iulia Romania 46°8N 23°39E 183 D8
Albac Romania 46°28N 22°58E 182 D7
Albacete Spain 39°0N 1°50W 197 F3
Albacete □ Spain 38°50N 2°0W 197 G3
Albacutya, L. Australia 35°45S 141°58E 282 C4
Ålbæk Denmark 57°36N 10°25E 163 G4
Ålbæk Bugt Denmark 57°35N 10°40E 163 G4
Albaida Spain 38°51N 0°31W 197 G4
Albalate de las Nogueras Spain 40°22N 2°18W 196 E2
Albalate del Arzobispo Spain 41°6N 0°31W 196 D4
Alban France 43°53N 2°28E 174 E6
Albanel, L. Canada 50°55N 73°12W 298 B5
Albania ■ Europe 41°0N 20°0E 202 E4
Albano Laziale Italy 41°44N 12°39E 199 G9
Albany W. Austral., Australia 35°1S 117°58E 279 G2
Albany Ga., U.S.A. 31°35N 84°10W 316 D5
Albany Ind., U.S.A. 40°18N 85°14W 311 D11
Albany Mo., U.S.A. 40°15N 94°20W 310 D2
Albany N.Y., U.S.A. 42°39N 73°45W 313 D11
Albany Oreg., U.S.A. 44°38N 123°6W 304 D2
Albany Tex., U.S.A. 32°44N 99°18W 314 E5
Albany Wis., U.S.A. 42°42N 89°26W 310 B7
Albany → Canada 52°17N 81°31W 298 B3
Albarca, C. d' Spain 39°4N 1°22E 206 C1
Albardón Argentina 31°20S 68°30W 334 C2
Albarracín Spain 40°25N 1°26W 196 E3
Albarracín, Sierra de Spain 40°30N 1°30W 196 E3
Albatera Spain 38°11N 0°52W 197 G4
Albatross B. Australia 12°45S 141°30E 280 A3
Albatross Pt. N.Z. 38°7S 174°44E 284 E3
Albay □ Phil. 13°13N 123°33E 232 E4
Albegna → Italy 42°30N 11°11E 199 F8
Albemarle U.S.A. 35°21N 80°12W 315 D14
Albemarle, I. = Isabela, I. Ecuador 0°30S 91°4W 330 a
Albemarle, Pta. Ecuador 0°11N 91°21W 330 a
Albemarle Sd. U.S.A. 36°5N 76°0W 315 C16
Albenga Italy 44°3N 8°13E 198 D5
Alberche → Spain 39°58N 4°46W 194 F6
Alberdi Paraguay 26°14S 58°20W 334 B4
Albères, Mts. France 42°28N 2°56E 174 F6
Ålberga Sweden 58°44N 16°35E 163 F10
Alberga → Australia 27°6S 135°33E 281 D2

Albern *Austria* 48°9N 16°29E **142** B2
Albersdorf *Germany* 54°8N 9°17E **178** A5
Albert *France* 50°0N 2°38E **173** C9
Albert, L. *Africa* 1°30N 31°0E **268** B3
Albert, L. *S. Austral., Australia* 35°30S 139°10E **282** C3
Albert Edward, Mt. *Papua N. G.* 8°20S 147°24E **286** E4
Albert Edward Ra. *Australia* 18°17S 127°57E **278** C4
Albert Lea *U.S.A.* 43°39N 93°22W **308** D7
Albert Nat. Park = Virunga △ *Dem. Rep. of the Congo* 0°5N 29°38E **268** B2
Albert Nile → *Uganda* 3°36N 32°2E **268** B3
Albert Park *Australia* 37°51S 144°58E **128** B1
Albert Town *Bahamas* 22°37N 74°33W **321** B5
Albert Town *Jamaica* 18°17N 77°33W **320** a
Alberta □ *Canada* 54°40N 115°0W **296** C6
Alberti *Argentina* 35°1S 60°16W **334** D3
Albertinia *S. Africa* 34°11S 21°34E **270** D3
Albertirsa *Hungary* 47°14N 19°37E **182** C4
Alberto de Agostini △ *Chile* 54°38S 71°37W **336** D2
Alberton *P.E.I., Canada* 46°50N 64°0W **299** C7
Alberton *Gauteng, S. Africa* 26°15S 28°7E **123** B2
Albertslund *Denmark* 55°39N 12°21E **118** B2
Albertville = Kalemie *Dem. Rep. of the Congo* 5°55S 29°9E **268** D2
Albertville *Savoie, France* 45°40N 6°22E **175** C10
Albertville *Ala., U.S.A.* 34°16N 86°13W **315** D11
Albi *France* 43°56N 2°9E **174** E6
Albia *U.S.A.* 41°2N 92°48W **310** C4
Albina *Suriname* 5°37N 54°15W **329** B7
Albina, Ponta *Angola* 15°52S 11°44E **265** F2
Albino *Italy* 45°46N 9°47E **198** C6
Albion *Ill., U.S.A.* 38°23N 88°4W **311** F8
Albion *Ind., U.S.A.* 41°24N 85°25W **311** C11
Albion *Mich., U.S.A.* 42°15N 84°45W **311** B12
Albion *Nebr., U.S.A.* 41°42N 98°0W **308** E4
Albion *Pa., U.S.A.* 41°53N 80°22W **312** E4
Albocásser *Spain* 40°21N 0°1E **196** E5
Albolote *Spain* 37°14N 3°39W **195** H7
Alborán *Medit. S.* 35°57N 3°0W **195** K7
Alborea *Spain* 39°17N 1°24W **197** F3
Ålborg = Aalborg *Denmark* 57°2N 9°54E **163** G3
Ålborg Bugt = Aalborg Bugt *Denmark* 56°50N 10°35E **163** H4
Alborz, Reshteh-ye Kūhhā-ye *Iran* 36°0N 52°0E **247** C7
Albox *Spain* 37°23N 2°8W **197** H2
Albuera *Phil.* 10°55N 124°42E **233** F5
Albufeira *Portugal* 37°5N 8°15W **195** H2
Albula → *Switz.* 46°38N 9°28E **179** J5
Albuñol *Spain* 36°48N 3°11W **195** J7
Albuquerque *Brazil* 19°23S 57°26W **331** D6
Albuquerque *N. Mex., U.S.A.* 35°5N 106°39W **305** J10
Albuquerque, Cayos de *Caribbean* 12°10N 81°50W **320** D3
Alburg *U.S.A.* 44°59N 73°18W **313** B11
Alburno, Mte. *Italy* 40°33N 15°17E **201** B8
Alburquerque *Spain* 39°15N 6°59W **195** F4
Albury *Australia* 36°3S 146°56E **283** D7
Alby *Sweden* 62°30N 15°28E **162** B9
Alcácer do Sal *Portugal* 38°22N 8°33W **195** G2
Alcáçovas *Portugal* 38°23N 8°9W **195** G2
Alcala *Phil.* 17°54N 121°39E **232** C3
Alcalá de Guadaira *Spain* 37°20N 5°50W **195** H5
Alcalá de Henares *Spain* 40°28N 3°22W **194** E7
Alcalá de los Gazules *Spain* 36°29N 5°43W **195** J5
Alcalá de Xivert *Spain* 40°19N 0°13E **196** E5
Alcalá del Júcar *Spain* 39°12N 1°26W **197** F3
Alcalá del Río *Spain* 37°31N 5°59W **195** H5
Alcalá del Valle *Spain* 36°54N 5°10W **195** J5
Alcalá la Real *Spain* 37°27N 3°57W **195** H7
Álcamo *Italy* 37°59N 12°55E **200** E5
Alcanadre *Spain* 42°24N 2°7W **196** C2
Alcanadre → *Spain* 41°43N 0°12W **196** D4
Alcanar *Spain* 40°33N 0°28E **196** E5
Alcanede *Portugal* 39°25N 8°49W **195** F2
Alcanena *Portugal* 39°27N 8°40W **195** F2
Alcañices *Spain* 41°41N 6°21W **194** D4
Alcañiz *Spain* 41°2N 0°8W **196** D4
Alcântara *Brazil* 2°20S 44°30W **332** B3
Alcantara *Lisboa, Portugal* 38°43N 9°10W **126** A1
Alcántara *Spain* 39°41N 6°57W **194** F4
Alcántara, Embalse de *Spain* 39°44N 6°50W **194** F4
Alcantarilla *Spain* 37°59N 1°12W **197** H3
Alcaracejos *Spain* 38°24N 4°58W **195** G6
Alcaraz *Spain* 38°40N 2°29W **197** G2
Alcaraz, Sierra de *Spain* 38°40N 2°20W **197** G2
Alcatraz I. *U.S.A.* 37°49N 122°25W **136** B2
Alcaudete *Spain* 37°35N 4°5W **195** H6
Alcázar de San Juan *Spain* 39°24N 3°12W **195** F7
Alcazarquivir = Ksar el Kebir *Morocco* 35°0N 6°0W **260** B3
Alcedo, Volcán *Ecuador* 0°24S 91°6W **330** a
Alchevsk *Ukraine* 48°30N 38°45E **189** H10
Alcira = Alzira *Spain* 39°9N 0°30W **197** F4
Alcobaça = Tucuruí *Brazil* 3°42S 49°44W **332** B2
Alcobaça *Portugal* 39°32N 8°58W **195** F2
Alcobendas *Spain* 40°32N 3°38W **127** A2
Alcolea del Pinar *Spain* 41°2N 2°28W **196** D2
Alcoma *U.S.A.* 27°54N 81°29W **317** H8
Alcorcón *Spain* 40°20N 3°48W **127** B1
Alcoutim *Portugal* 37°25N 7°28W **195** H3
Alcova *U.S.A.* 42°34N 106°43W **304** E10
Alcoy *Spain* 38°43N 0°30W **197** G4
Alcubierre, Sierra de *Spain* 41°45N 0°22W **196** D4
Alcublas *Spain* 39°48N 0°43W **196** F4
Alcúdia *Spain* 39°51N 3°7E **206** B4
Alcúdia, B. d' *Spain* 39°47N 3°15E **206** B4
Alcúdia, Sierra de la *Spain* 38°34N 4°30W **195** G6
Aldabra Is. *Seychelles* 9°22S 46°28E **255** G8
Aldama *Mexico* 22°55N 98°4W **319** C5
Aldan *Russia* 58°40N 125°30E **215** D13
Aldan → *Russia* 63°28N 129°35E **215** C13
Aldea, Pta. de la *Canary Is.* 28°0N 15°50W **153** e1
Aldeburgh *U.K.* 52°10N 1°37E **169** E9
Alden *Norway* 61°19N 4°45E **164** C1
Alder Pk. *U.S.A.* 35°53N 121°22W **306** K5
Alderney *U.K.* 49°42N 2°11W **169** H5
Aldershof *Germany* 52°26N 13°33E **115** B4
Aldershot *U.K.* 51°15N 0°44W **169** F7
Aldinga Beach *Australia* 35°17S 138°27E **282** C3
Aldo Bonzi *Argentina* 34°42S 58°31W **117** C1
Åled *Sweden* 56°44N 12°57E **163** H6
Aledo *U.S.A.* 41°12N 90°45W **310** C6
Alefa *Ethiopia* 11°55N 36°55E **257** E4
Aleg *Mauritania* 17°3N 13°55W **262** B2
Alegranza *Canary Is.* 29°23N 13°32W **260** C2
Alegranza, I. *Canary Is.* 29°23N 13°32W **153** e2
Alegre *Brazil* 20°50S 41°30W **333** F3
Alegrete *Brazil* 29°40S 56°0W **335** B4
Aleknagik *U.S.A.* 59°17N 158°36W **303** G8
Aleksandriya = Oleksandriya *Kirovohrad, Ukraine* 48°42N 33°3E **189** H7
Aleksandriya = Oleksandriya *Rivne, Ukraine* 50°37N 26°19E **177** C14
Aleksandriyskaya *Russia* 43°58N 47°14E **191** J8
Aleksandropol = Gyumri *Armenia* 40°47N 43°50E **191** K6
Aleksandrov *Russia* 56°23N 38°44E **188** D10
Aleksandrov Gay *Russia* 50°9N 48°34E **190** E9
Aleksandrovac *Serbia* 43°28N 21°3E **202** C5
Aleksandrovac *Serbia* 44°28N 21°13E **202** B5
Aleksandrovka = Oleksandrivka *Ukraine* 48°55N 32°20E **189** H7
Aleksandrovka = Ordzhonikīdze *Ukraine* 47°39N 34°3E **189** J8
Aleksandrovo *Bulgaria* 43°14N 24°51E **203** C8
Aleksandrovsk = Belogorsk *Russia* 51°0N 128°20E **215** D13
Aleksandrovsk = Polyarny *Russia* 69°8N 33°20E **160** B25
Aleksandrovsk = Zaporizhzhya *Ukraine* 47°50N 35°10E **189** J8
Aleksandrovsk-Grushevsky = Shakhty *Russia* 47°40N 40°16E **191** G5
Aleksandrovsk-Sakhalinskiy *Russia* 50°50N 142°20E **219** A17
Aleksandrovskoye *Russia* 59°51N 30°20E **137** B2
Aleksandrów Kujawski *Poland* 52°53N 18°43E **185** F5
Aleksandrów Łódźki *Poland* 51°49N 19°17E **185** G6
Aleksandry, Zemlya *Russia* 80°25N 48°0E **214** A5
Alekseyevka *Samara, Russia* 52°35N 51°17E **190** D10
Alekseyevka *Voronezh, Russia* 50°43N 38°40E **189** G10
Alekseyevsk = Svobodnyy *Russia* 51°20N 128°0E **215** D13
Alekseyevskoye = Qazyghurt *Kazakhstan* 41°45N 69°23E **217** D7
Aleksin *Russia* 54°31N 37°9E **188** E9
Aleksinac *Serbia* 43°31N 21°42E **202** C5
Além Paraíba *Brazil* 21°52S 42°41W **333** F3
Alemania *Argentina* 25°40S 65°30W **334** B2
Alemania *Chile* 25°10S 69°55W **334** B2
Alen *Eq. Guin.* 1°58N 11°19E **264** B2
Alençon *France* 48°27N 0°4E **172** D7
'Alenuihähä Channel *U.S.A.* 20°30N 156°0W **302** C5
Alépé *Ivory C.* 5°29N 3°40W **262** D4
Aleppo = Ḩalab *Syria* 36°10N 37°15E **250** B8
Alerce Andino △ *Chile* 41°33S 72°29W **336** B2
Aléria *France* 42°5N 9°26E **175** F13
Alert *Canada* 83°2N 60°0W **295** A20
Aleru *India* 17°39N 79°3E **244** F4
Alès *France* 44°9N 4°5E **175** D8
Aleşd *Romania* 47°3N 22°22E **182** C7
Alessándria *Italy* 44°54N 8°37E **198** D5
Ålesund *Norway* 62°28N 6°12E **164** B3
Alet-les-Bains *France* 42°59N 2°14E **174** F6
Aletschhorn *Switz.* 46°28N 8°0E **179** J4
Aleutian Basin *Pac. Oc.* 57°0N 177°0E **288** B9
Aleutian Is. *Pac. Oc.* 52°0N 175°0W **303** K3
Aleutian Range *U.S.A.* 60°0N 154°0W **303** G9
Aleutian Trench *Pac. Oc.* 48°0N 180°0E **150** D17
Alexander *Ga., U.S.A.* 33°1N 81°53W **316** B8
Alexander *N. Dak., U.S.A.* 47°51N 103°39W **308** B2
Alexander, C. *Solomon Is.* 6°34S 156°32E **287** L9
Alexander, Mt. *Australia* 28°58S 120°16E **279** E3
Alexander Arch. *U.S.A.* 56°0N 136°0W **303** J14
Alexander Bay *S. Africa* 28°40S 16°30E **270** C2
Alexander City *U.S.A.* 32°56N 85°58W **316** C4
Alexander I. *Antarctica* 69°0S 70°0W **151** C17
Alexander Nevsky Abbey *Russia* 59°54N 30°23E **137** B2
Alexander Soutzos Museum *Athens, Greece* **112** b3
Alexandra *Vic., Australia* 37°8S 145°40E **283** D6
Alexandra *N.Z.* 45°14S 169°25E **285** F4
Alexandra *Singapore, Singapore* 1°17N 103°49E **138** B2
Alexandra *Gauteng, S. Africa* 26°6S 28°5E **123** A2
Alexandra Channel *Burma* 14°7N 93°13E **245** G11
Alexandra Falls *Canada* 60°29N 116°18W **296** A5
Alexandretta = İskenderun *Turkey* 36°32N 36°10E **250** B7
Alexandria = El Iskandarîya *Egypt* 31°13N 29°58E **256** H7
Alexandria *B.C., Canada* 52°35N 122°27W **296** C4
Alexandria *Ont., Canada* 45°19N 74°38W **313** A10
Alexandria *Romania* 43°57N 25°24E **183** G10
Alexandria *Eastern Cape, S. Africa* 33°38S 26°28E **270** D4
Alexandria *W. Dunb., U.K.* 55°59N 4°35W **167** F4
Alexandria *Ind., U.S.A.* 40°16N 85°41W **311** D11
Alexandria *Ky., U.S.A.* 38°58N 84°23W **311** F12
Alexandria *La., U.S.A.* 31°18N 92°27W **314** F8
Alexandria *Minn., U.S.A.* 45°53N 95°22W **308** C6
Alexandria *Mo., U.S.A.* 40°27N 91°28W **310** D5
Alexandria *S. Dak., U.S.A.* 43°39N 97°47W **308** D5
Alexandria *Va., U.S.A.* 38°49N 77°5W **143** C3
Alexandria Bay *U.S.A.* 44°20N 75°55W **313** B9
Alexandrina, L. *Australia* 35°25S 139°10E **282** C3
Alexandroupoli *Greece* 40°50N 25°54E **203** F9
Alexis *U.S.A.* 41°4N 90°33W **310** C6
Alexis → *Canada* 52°33N 56°8W **299** B8
Alexis Creek *Canada* 52°10N 123°20W **296** C4
Aley → *Russia* 52°51N 83°36E **217** B10
Aleysk *Russia* 52°40N 83°0E **217** B10
Alfabia *Spain* 39°44N 2°44E **206** B3
Alfama *Lisbon, Portugal* **126** c3
Alfambra *Spain* 40°33N 1°5W **196** E3
Alfândega da Fé *Portugal* 41°20N 6°59W **194** D4
Alfaro *Spain* 42°10N 1°50W **196** C3
Alfatar *Bulgaria* 43°59N 27°13E **203** C11
Alfeld *Germany* 51°59N 9°50E **178** D5
Alfenas *Brazil* 21°20S 46°10W **335** A6
Alföld *Hungary* 46°30N 20°0E **182** D5
Alfonsine *Italy* 44°30N 12°3E **199** D9
Alford *Aberds., U.K.* 57°14N 2°41W **167** D6
Alford *Lincs., U.K.* 53°15N 0°10E **168** D8
Alford *Fla., U.S.A.* 30°42N 85°24W **316** E4
Alfortville *France* 48°48N 2°24E **134** B3
Ålfotbreen *Norway* 61°45N 5°39E **164** C2
Ålfoten *Norway* 61°51N 5°41E **164** C2
Alfred *Maine, U.S.A.* 43°29N 70°43W **313** C14
Alfred *N.Y., U.S.A.* 42°16N 77°48W **312** D7
Alfredton *N.Z.* 40°41S 175°54E **284** G4
Alfreton *U.K.* 53°6N 1°24W **168** D6
Alfta *Sweden* 61°21N 16°4E **162** C10
Algaida *Spain* 39°33N 2°53E **206** B3
Algar *Spain* 36°40N 5°39W **195** J5
Ålgård *Norway* 58°46N 5°53E **164** F2
Algarinejo *Spain* 37°19N 4°9W **195** H6
Algarve *Portugal* 36°58N 8°20W **195** J2
Algeciras *Spain* 36°9N 5°28W **195** J5
Algemesí *Spain* 39°11N 0°27W **197** F4
Alger *Algeria* 36°42N 3°8E **261** A5
Alger □ *Algeria* 36°45N 3°10E **197** J8
Alger ✈ (ALG) *Algeria* 36°39N 3°13E **197** J8
Algeria ■ *Africa* 28°30N 2°0E **261** C5
Algés *Portugal* 38°42N 9°13W **126** A1
Algha *Kazakhstan* 49°53N 57°20E **187** E10
Alghero *Italy* 40°33N 8°19E **200** B1
Älghult *Sweden* 57°0N 15°35E **163** G9
Algiers = Alger *Algeria* 36°42N 3°8E **261** A5
Algiers *U.S.A.* 29°56N 90°2W **131** B2
Algoa B. *S. Africa* 33°50S 25°45E **270** D4
Algodonales *Spain* 36°54N 5°24W **195** J5
Algodor → *Spain* 39°55N 3°53W **194** F7
Algoma *U.S.A.* 44°36N 87°26W **308** C10
Algona *U.S.A.* 43°4N 94°14W **310** A2
Algonac *U.S.A.* 42°37N 82°32W **312** D2
Algonquin ⌂ *Canada* 45°50N 78°30W **298** C4
Alhama de Almería *Spain* 36°57N 2°34W **195** J8
Alhama de Aragón *Spain* 41°18N 1°54W **196** D3
Alhama de Granada *Spain* 37°0N 3°59W **195** H7
Alhama de Murcia *Spain* 37°51N 1°25W **197** H3
Alhambra *U.S.A.* 34°5N 118°7W **126** B4
Alhaurín el Grande *Spain* 36°39N 4°41W **195** J6
Alhucemas = Al Hoceïma *Morocco* 35°8N 3°58W **261** A4
'Alī al Gharbī *Iraq* 32°30N 46°45E **213** F12
'Alī ash Sharqī *Iraq* 32°7N 46°44E **213** F12
Äli Bayramlı *Azerbaijan* 39°59N 48°52E **191** L9
'Alī Khēl *Afghan.* 33°57N 69°43E **242** C3
Ali Sahîh *Djibouti* 11°10N 42°44E **257** E5
Alī Shāh *Iran* 38°9N 45°50E **246** B5
Ália *Italy* 37°47N 13°43E **200** E6
'Alīābād *Golestān, Iran* 36°40N 54°33E **247** B7
'Alīābād *Khorāsān, Iran* 32°30N 57°30E **247** C8
'Alīābād *Kordestān, Iran* 35°4N 46°58E **246** C5
'Alīābād *Yazd, Iran* 31°41N 53°49E **247** D7
Aliade *Nigeria* 7°18N 8°29E **263** D6
Aliaga *Spain* 40°40N 0°42W **196** E4
Aliağa *Turkey* 38°47N 26°59E **205** C8
Aliakmonas → *Greece* 40°30N 22°36E **202** F6
Alibag *India* 18°38N 72°56E **244** E1
Alibey → *Turkey* 41°3N 28°56E **122** B1
Alibey Barajı *Turkey* 41°8N 28°53E **122** B1
Alibeyköy *Turkey* 41°4N 28°56E **122** B1
Alibo *Ethiopia* 9°52N 37°5E **257** F4
Alibori → *Benin* 11°56N 3°17E **263** C5
Alibunar *Serbia* 45°5N 20°57E **182** E5
Alicante *Spain* 38°23N 0°30W **197** G4
Alicante □ *Spain* 38°30N 0°37W **197** G4
Alicante ✈ (ALC) *Spain* 38°14N 0°36W **197** G4
Alice *Eastern Cape, S. Africa* 32°48S 26°55E **270** D4
Alice *Tex., U.S.A.* 27°45N 98°5W **314** H5
Alice → *Queens., Australia* 24°2S 144°50E **280** C3
Alice → *Queens., Australia* 15°35S 142°20E **280** B3
Alice → *Papua N. G.* 6°10S 141°8E **286** D1
Alice, Punta *Italy* 39°24N 17°9E **201** C10
Alice Arm *Canada* 55°29N 129°31W **296** B3
Alice Springs *Australia* 23°40S 133°50E **280** C1
Alicedale *S. Africa* 33°15S 26°4E **270** D4
Aliceville *U.S.A.* 33°8N 88°9W **315** E10
Alicia *Bohol, Phil.* 9°54N 124°26E **233** G5
Alicia *Isabela, Phil.* 16°46N 121°42E **232** C3
Alicudi *Italy* 38°33N 14°20E **201** D7
Alien *Taiwan* 22°52N 120°19E **225** D2
Aliganj *India* 27°30N 79°10E **243** F8
Aligarh *Raj., India* 25°55N 76°15E **242** G7
Aligarh *Ut. P., India* 27°55N 78°10E **242** F8
Alīgūdarz *Iran* 33°25N 49°45E **247** C6
Alijó *Portugal* 41°16N 7°27W **194** D3
Alikanas *Greece* 37°51N 20°47E **207** D2
Alima → *Congo* 1°35S 16°37E **264** C3
Alimia *Greece* 36°16N 27°43E **206** E11
Alimodian *Phil.* 10°49N 122°26E **233** F4
Alimos *Greece* 37°52N 23°43E **112** B2
Alindao *C.A.R.* 5°2N 21°13E **264** A4
Alingsås *Sweden* 57°56N 12°31E **163** G6
Alipur *W. Bengal, India* 22°43N 88°12E **124** B1
Alipur *Pakistan* 29°25N 70°55E **242** E4
Alipur Duar *India* 26°30N 89°35E **241** B2
Aliquippa *U.S.A.* 40°37N 80°15W **312** F4
Alishan *Taiwan* 23°31N 120°48E **225** C2
Aliste → *Spain* 41°34N 5°58W **194** D5
Alitus = Alytus *Lithuania* 54°24N 24°3E **188** E3
Aliveri *Greece* 38°24N 24°2E **204** C6
Aliwal North *S. Africa* 30°45S 26°45E **270** D4
Alix *Canada* 52°24N 113°11W **296** C6
Aljezur *Portugal* 37°18N 8°49W **195** H2
Aljustrel *Portugal* 37°55N 8°10W **195** H2
Alkamari *Niger* 13°27N 11°10E **259** F2
Alkmaar *Neths.* 52°37N 4°45E **170** B4
All American Canal *U.S.A.* 32°45N 115°15W **305** K6
Allacapan *Phil.* 18°15N 121°35E **232** B3
Allach *Germany* 48°11N 11°27E **131** A1
Allada *Benin* 6°41N 2°9E **263** D5
Allagadda *India* 15°8N 78°30E **245** G4
Allagash → *U.S.A.* 47°5N 69°3W **309** B19
Allah Dad *Pakistan* 25°38N 67°34E **242** G2
Allahabad *India* 25°25N 81°58E **243** G9
Allakaket *U.S.A.* 66°34N 152°39W **303** C9
Allal Tazi *Morocco* 34°30N 6°20W **260** B3
Allambie Heights *Australia* 33°46S 151°15E **139** A2
Allan *Canada* 51°53N 106°4W **297** C7
Allanche *France* 45°14N 2°57E **174** C6
Allanmyo *Burma* 19°30N 95°17E **241** F5
Allanridge *S. Africa* 27°45S 26°40E **270** C4
Allansford *Australia* 38°26S 142°39E **282** E5
Allanton *N.Z.* 45°55S 170°15E **285** F5
Allaqi, Wadi → *Egypt* 23°7N 32°47E **256** C3
Allariz *Spain* 42°11N 7°50W **194** C3
Allassac *France* 45°15N 1°29E **174** C5
Allatoona L. *U.S.A.* 34°10N 84°44W **316** A5
Ålleberg *Sweden* 58°8N 13°36E **163** F7
Allegan *U.S.A.* 42°32N 85°51W **311** B11
Allegany *U.S.A.* 42°6N 78°30W **312** D6
Allegheny → *U.S.A.* 40°27N 80°1W **312** F5
Allegheny Mts. *U.S.A.* 38°15N 80°10W **309** F13
Allegheny Plateau *U.S.A.* 41°30N 78°30W **309** E14
Allegheny Res. *U.S.A.* 41°50N 79°0W **312** E6
Allègre *France* 45°12N 3°41E **174** C7
Allègre, Pte. *Guadeloupe* 16°22N 61°46W **322** e
Allen *Argentina* 38°58S 67°50W **336** A3
Allen *Phil.* 12°30N 124°17E **232** E5
Allen, Bog of *Ireland* 53°15N 7°0W **166** C5
Allen, L. *Ireland* 54°8N 8°4W **166** B3
Allendale *U.S.A.* 33°1N 81°18W **316** B8
Allende *Mexico* 28°20N 100°51W **318** B4
Allenstein = Olsztyn *Poland* 53°48N 20°29E **184** E7
Allentown *U.S.A.* 40°37N 75°29W **313** F9
Allentsteig *Austria* 48°41N 15°20E **180** C8
Alleppey *India* 9°30N 76°28E **245** K3
Allepuz *Spain* 40°29N 0°44W **196** E4
Aller → *Germany* 52°56N 9°12E **178** C5
Allermuir Hill *U.K.* 55°53N 3°14W **121** B2
Alley, The *Jamaica* 17°48N 77°17W **320** a
Alliance *Suriname* 5°50N 54°50W **329** B7
Alliance *Nebr., U.S.A.* 42°6N 102°52W **308** D2
Alliance *Ohio, U.S.A.* 40°55N 81°6W **312** F3
Allier □ *France* 46°25N 2°40E **173** F9
Allier → *France* 46°57N 3°4E **173** F10
Alliford Bay *Canada* 53°12N 131°58W **296** C2
Alligator Pond *Jamaica* 17°52N 77°34W **320** a
Allinagaram *India* 10°2N 77°30E **245** J3
Allinge *Denmark* 55°17N 14°50E **163** J8
Allison *U.S.A.* 42°45N 92°48W **310** B4
Alliston *Canada* 44°9N 79°52W **312** B5
Alloa *U.K.* 56°7N 3°47W **167** E5
Allones *France* 48°20N 1°40E **172** D8
Allora *Australia* 28°2S 152°0E **281** D5
Allos *France* 44°15N 6°38E **175** D10
Allstate Arena *U.S.A.* 42°2N 87°54W **119** A1
Allston *U.S.A.* 42°21N 71°7W **116** A2
Alluitsup Paa *Greenland* 60°30N 45°35W **154** E6
Allur *India* 14°40N 80°4E **245** G5
Alluru Kottapatnam *India* 15°24N 80°7E **245** G5
Alma *Qué., Canada* 48°35N 71°40W **299** C5
Alma *Ga., U.S.A.* 31°33N 82°28W **316** D7
Alma *Kans., U.S.A.* 39°1N 96°17W **308** F5
Alma *Mich., U.S.A.* 43°23N 84°39W **309** D11
Alma *Nebr., U.S.A.* 40°6N 99°22W **308** E4
Alma *Wis., U.S.A.* 44°20N 91°55W **308** C8
Alma Ata = Almaty *Kazakhstan* 43°15N 76°57E **217** D9
Alma Hill *U.S.A.* 42°2N 78°0W **312** D7
Almacelles *Spain* 41°43N 0°27E **196** D5
Almada *Portugal* 38°41N 9°8W **126** A2
Almaden *Queens., Australia* 17°22S 144°40E **280** B3
Almadén *Spain* 38°49N 4°52W **195** G6
Almagro *Argentina* 34°38S 58°24W **117** B2
Almagro I. *Phil.* 11°55N 124°18E **233** F5
Almalyk = Olmaliq *Uzbekistan* 40°50N 69°35E **217** D7
Almanor, L. *U.S.A.* 40°14N 121°9W **304** F3
Almansa *Spain* 38°51N 1°5W **197** G3
Almanza *Spain* 42°39N 5°3W **194** C5
Almanzor, Pico *Spain* 40°15N 5°18W **194** E5
Almanzora → *Spain* 37°14N 1°46W **197** H3
Almargem do Bispo *Portugal* 38°49N 9°17W **126** A1
Almas *Brazil* 11°33S 47°9W **333** D2
Almaş, Munţii *Romania* 44°49N 22°12E **182** F7
Almassora *Spain* 39°57N 0°3W **196** F4
Almaty *Kazakhstan* 43°15N 76°57E **217** D9
Almaty □ *Kazakhstan* 44°30N 78°0E **217** D9
Almazán *Spain* 41°30N 2°30W **196** D2
Almazovo *Russia* 55°50N 38°3E **129** A6
Almeirim *Brazil* 1°30S 52°34W **329** D7
Almeirim *Portugal* 39°12N 8°37W **195** F2
Almelo *Neths.* 52°22N 6°42E **170** B6
Almenar de Soria *Spain* 41°43N 2°12W **196** D2
Almenara *Brazil* 16°11S 40°42W **333** E3
Almenara *Spain* 39°46N 0°14W **196** F4
Almenara, Sierra de *Spain* 37°34N 1°32W **197** H3
Almendra, Embalse de *Spain* 41°10N 6°5W **194** D4
Almendralejo *Spain* 38°41N 6°26W **195** G4
Almere-Stad *Neths.* 52°20N 5°15E **170** B5
Almería *Spain* 36°52N 2°27W **195** J8
Almería □ *Spain* 37°20N 2°20W **197** H2
Almería, G. de *Spain* 36°41N 2°28W **197** J2
Almetyevsk *Russia* 54°53N 52°20E **190** C11
Älmhult *Sweden* 56°33N 14°8E **163** H8
Almirante *Panama* 9°10N 82°30W **320** E3
Almirante G. Brown, Parque *Argentina* 34°40S 58°28W **117** C2
Almirante Montt, G. *Chile* 51°52S 72°50W **336** D2
Almiropotamos *Greece* 38°16N 24°11E **204** C6
Almiros *Greece* 39°11N 22°45E **204** B4
Almodôvar *Portugal* 37°31N 8°2W **195** H2
Almodóvar del Campo *Spain* 38°43N 4°10W **195** G6
Almodóvar del Río *Spain* 37°48N 5°1W **195** H5
Almon *West Bank* 31°49N 35°17E **123** B2
Almond *U.S.A.* 42°19N 77°44W **312** D7
Almond → *U.K.* 55°58N 3°18W **121** B2
Almont *U.S.A.* 42°55N 83°3W **312** D1
Almonte *Ont., Canada* 45°14N 76°12W **313** A8
Almonte *Spain* 37°13N 6°38W **195** H4
Almora *India* 29°38N 79°40E **243** E8
Almoradí *Spain* 38°7N 0°46W **197** G4
Almorox *Spain* 40°14N 4°24W **194** E6
Almoustarat *Mali* 17°35N 0°8E **263** B5
Älmsta *Sweden* 59°58N 18°50E **162** E12
Almudévar *Spain* 42°3N 0°35W **196** C4
Almuñécar *Spain* 36°43N 3°41W **195** J7
Almunge *Sweden* 59°53N 18°3E **162** E12
Almuradiel *Spain* 38°32N 3°28W **195** G7
Almus *Turkey* 40°22N 36°54E **212** B7
Almvik *Sweden* 57°49N 16°30E **163** G10
Almyrou, Ormos *Greece* 35°23N 24°20E **207** E5
Alna *Norway* 59°55N 10°50E **133** A4
Alness *U.K.* 57°41N 4°16W **167** D4
Alnif *Morocco* 31°10N 5°8W **260** B3
Alnmouth *U.K.* 55°24N 1°37W **168** B6
Alnsjøen *Norway* 59°57N 10°51E **133** A4
Alnwick *U.K.* 55°24N 1°42W **168** B6
Alofau *Amer. Samoa* 14°16S 170°36W **302** f
Alofi *Niue* 19°1S 169°55W **289** g
Alofi, I. *Wall. & F. Is.* 14°27S 178°5W **277** C15
Alofi B. *Niue* 19°1S 169°56W **289** g
Aloi *Uganda* 2°16N 33°10E **268** B3
Alon *Burma* 22°12N 95°5E **241** D5
Along *India* 28°10N 94°46E **241** A5
Alonissos *Greece* 39°12N 23°50E **204** B5
Alonissos-Northern Sporades △ *Greece* 39°15N 24°5E **204** B6
Alor *Indonesia* 8°15S 124°30E **231** F6
Alor Setar *Malaysia* 6°7N 100°22E **237** J3
Álora *Spain* 36°49N 4°46W **195** J6
Alosno *Spain* 37°33N 7°7W **195** H3
Alost = Aalst *Belgium* 50°56N 4°2E **170** D4
Alot *India* 23°56N 75°40E **242** H6
Alotau *Papua N. G.* 10°16S 150°30E **286** F6
Alougoum *Morocco* 30°17N 6°56W **260** B3
Aloum *Cameroon* 2°16N 10°34E **264** B2
Aloysius, Mt. *Australia* 26°0S 128°38E **279** E4
Alpaugh *U.S.A.* 35°53N 119°29W **306** K7
Alpe Apuane ⌂ *Italy* 44°4N 10°15E **198** D7
Alpedrinha *Portugal* 40°6N 7°27W **194** E3
Alpena *U.S.A.* 45°4N 83°27W **309** C12
Alpercatas → *Brazil* 6°2S 44°19W **332** C3
Alperton *U.K.* 51°32N 0°17W **125** A2
Alpes-de-Haute-Provence □ *France* 44°8N 6°10E **175** D10
Alpes-Maritimes □ *France* 43°55N 7°10E **175** E11
Alpha *Queens., Australia* 23°39S 146°37E **280** C4
Alpha *Ill., U.S.A.* 41°12N 90°23W **310** C6
Alpha Ridge *Arctic* 84°0N 118°0W **150** A2
Alphen aan den Rijn *Neths.* 52°7N 4°40E **170** B4
Alphios → *Greece* 37°40N 21°33E **204** D3
Alphonse *Seychelles* 7°0S 52°45E **273** E4
Alpiarça *Portugal* 39°15N 8°35W **195** F2
Alpine *Ariz., U.S.A.* 33°51N 109°9W **305** K9
Alpine *Calif., U.S.A.* 32°50N 116°46W **307** N10
Alpine *N.J., U.S.A.* 40°57N 73°57W **132** A2
Alpine *Tex., U.S.A.* 30°22N 103°40W **314** F3
Alpine △ *Australia* 36°56S 148°10E **283** D7
Alps *Europe* 46°30N 9°30E **171** C8
Alpu *Turkey* 39°46N 30°58E **212** C4
Alpurrurulam *Australia* 20°59S 137°50E **280** C2
Alqueta, Barragem do *Portugal* 38°20N 7°25W **195** G3
Alrø *Denmark* 55°52N 10°5E **163** J4
Alrode *S. Africa* 26°17S 28°7E **123** B2
Als *Denmark* 54°59N 9°55E **163** K3
Alsace □ *France* 48°15N 7°25E **173** D14
Alsask *Canada* 51°21N 109°59W **297** C7
Alsasua *Spain* 42°54N 2°10W **196** C2
Alsek → *U.S.A.* 59°10N 138°12W **296** B1
Alsemberg *Belgium* 50°44N 4°20E **116** B2
Alsergrund *Austria* 48°13N 16°21E **142** A2
Alsfeld *Germany* 50°44N 9°16E **178** E5
Alsip *U.S.A.* 41°40N 87°44W **119** C2
Alsta *Norway* 65°58N 12°40E **160** D15
Ålsten *Sweden* 59°19N 17°57E **139** B1
Alsterbro *Sweden* 56°57N 15°55E **163** H9
Alstermo *Sweden* 56°58N 15°38E **163** H9
Alston *U.K.* 54°49N 2°25W **168** C5
Alta *Finnmark, Norway* 69°57N 23°10E **160** B20
Älta *Sweden* 59°15N 18°11E **139** B3
Alta, Sierra *Spain* 40°31N 1°30W **196** E3
Alta Floresta *Brazil* 9°57S 55°58W **331** B6
Alta Gracia *Argentina* 31°40S 64°30W **334** C3
Alta Sierra *U.S.A.* 35°42N 118°33W **307** K8
Altadena *U.S.A.* 34°11N 118°8W **126** A4
Altaelva → *Norway* 69°54N 23°17E **160** B20
Altafjorden *Norway* 70°5N 23°5E **160** A20
Altagracia *Venezuela* 10°45N 71°30W **328** A3
Altagracia de Orituco *Venezuela* 9°52N 66°23W **328** B4
Altai = Aerhtai Shan *Mongolia* 46°40N 92°45E **217** C12
Altai = Gorno-Altay □ *Russia* 51°0N 86°0E **217** B11
Altamachi → *Bolivia* 16°8S 66°50W **330** D4
Altamaha → *U.S.A.* 31°20N 81°20W **316** D8
Altamira *Brazil* 3°12S 52°10W **329** D7
Altamira *Chile* 25°47S 69°51W **334** B2
Altamira *Colombia* 2°3N 75°47W **328** C2
Altamira *Tamaulipas, Mexico* 22°24N 97°55W **319** C5
Altamira, Cuevas de *Spain* 43°20N 4°5W **194** B6
Altamont *Ill., U.S.A.* 39°4N 88°45W **311** E8
Altamont *N.Y., U.S.A.* 42°42N 74°2W **313** D10
Altamura *Italy* 40°49N 16°33E **201** B9
Altanbulag *Mongolia* 50°16N 106°30E **218** A10
Altar *Mexico* 30°43N 111°44W **318** A2
Altar, Gran Desierto de *Mexico* 31°50N 114°10W **318** B2
Altata *Mexico* 24°40N 107°55W **318** C3
Altavas *Phil.* 11°32N 122°29E **233** F4
Altavista *U.S.A.* 37°6N 79°17W **309** G14
Altay *Xinjiang Uygur, China* 47°48N 88°10E **217** C11
Altay *Mongolia* 46°22N 96°15E **218** B8
Altdorf *Switz.* 46°52N 8°36E **179** J4
Alte-Donau → *Austria* 48°14N 16°25E **142** A2
Alte Mellum *Germany* 53°43N 8°10E **178** B4
Altea *Spain* 38°38N 0°2W **197** G4
Altenberg *Germany* 50°45N 13°45E **178** E9
Altenbruch *Germany* 53°49N 8°46E **178** B4
Altenburg *Germany* 50°59N 12°25E **178** E8
Altenkirchen *Mecklenburg-Vorpommern, Germany* 54°38N 13°22E **178** A9
Altenkirchen *Rhld-Pfz., Germany* 50°41N 7°39E **178** E3
Altenmarkt *Austria* 47°43N 14°39E **180** D7
Alter do Chão *Brazil* 2°31S 54°57W **329** D6
Alter do Chão *Portugal* 39°12N 7°40W **195** F3
Alter Finkenkrug *Germany* 52°35N 13°3E **115** A1
Altes Rathaus *Munich, Germany* **131** b3
Altglienicke *Germany* 52°25N 13°32E **115** B4
Altha *U.S.A.* 30°34N 85°8W **316** E4
Altınkaya Barajı *Turkey* 41°18N 35°30E **212** B6
Altınoluk *Turkey* 39°34N 26°45E **205** B8
Altınova *Turkey* 39°12N 26°47E **205** B8
Altınözü *Turkey* 36°7N 36°14E **250** B7
Altıntaş *Turkey* 39°4N 30°7E **205** B12
Altınyaka *Turkey* 36°33N 30°20E **205** E12
Altınyayla *Turkey* 37°0N 29°33E **205** D11
Altiplano *Bolivia* 17°0S 68°0W **330** D4
Altkirch *France* 47°37N 7°15E **173** E14
Altlandsberg *Germany* 52°33N 13°43E **115** A5
Altlandsberg Nord *Germany* 52°34N 13°43E **115** A5
Altmannsdorf *Austria* 48°9N 16°18E **142** B1
Altmark *Germany* 52°45N 11°30E **178** C7
Altmühl → *Germany* 48°54N 11°52E **179** G7
Altmühltal ⌂ *Germany* 48°55N 11°15E **179** G7
Altmunster *Austria* 47°54N 13°45E **180** D6
Alto Adige = Trentino-Alto Adige □ *Italy* 46°30N 11°20E **199** B8
Alto Alegre *Brazil* 2°50N 61°20W **329** C5
Alto Araguaia *Brazil* 17°15S 53°20W **331** D7
Alto Chicapa *Angola* 10°52S 19°17E **265** E3
Alto Cuchumatanes = Cuchumatanes, Sierra de los *Guatemala* 15°35N 91°25W **320** C1
Alto Cuito = Tempué *Angola* 13°27S 18°49E **265** E3
Alto da Boa Vista *Brazil* 22°57S 43°16W **135** B1
Alto da Moóca *Brazil* 23°34S 46°33W **137** B2
Alto del Carmen *Chile* 28°46S 70°30W **334** B1
Alto do Pina *Portugal* 38°44N 9°7W **126** A2
Alto Garças *Brazil* 16°56S 53°32W **331** D7
Alto Garda Bresciano ⌂ *Italy* 45°42N 10°38E **198** C7
Alto Iriri → *Brazil* 8°50S 53°25W **331** B7
Alto Ligonha *Mozam.* 15°30S 38°11E **269** F4
Alto Molocue *Mozam.* 15°50S 37°35E **269** F4
Alto Paraguai *Brazil* 14°30S 56°31W **331** C6
Alto Paraguay □ *Paraguay* 21°0S 58°30W **334** A4
Alto Paraiso de Goiás *Brazil* 14°7S 47°31W **333** D2
Alto Paraná □ *Paraguay* 25°30S 54°50W **335** B5
Alto Parnaíba *Brazil* 9°6S 45°57W **332** C2
Alto Purús → *Peru* 9°12S 70°28W **330** B3
Alto Río Senguerr *Argentina* 45°2S 70°50W **336** C2
Alto Santo *Brazil* 5°31S 38°15W **332** C4
Alto Sucuriú *Brazil* 19°19S 52°47W **331** D7
Alton *Ont., Canada* 43°54N 80°5W **312** C4
Alton *Hants., U.K.* 51°9N 0°59W **169** F7
Alton *Ill., U.S.A.* 38°53N 90°11W **310** F6
Alton *N.H., U.S.A.* 43°27N 71°13W **313** C13
Altona *Vic., Australia* 37°51S 144°49E **128** B1
Altona *Man., Canada* 49°6N 97°33W **297** D9
Altoona *Ala., U.S.A.* 34°2N 86°20W **316** A3
Altoona *Iowa, U.S.A.* 41°39N 93°28W **310** C3
Altoona *Pa., U.S.A.* 40°31N 78°24W **312** F6
Altos *Brazil* 5°3S 42°28W **332** C3
Altötting *Germany* 48°12N 12°39E **179** G8
Altstätten *Switz.* 47°22N 9°33E **179** H5
Altun Kupri *Iraq* 35°45N 44°9E **213** E11
Altun Shan *Xinjiang Uygur, China* 38°30N 88°0E **217** E11
Altun Shan *Xinjiang Uygur, China* 39°18N 93°42E **218** D7
Alturas *U.S.A.* 41°29N 120°32W **304** F3
Altus *U.S.A.* 34°38N 99°20W **314** D5
Alubijid *Phil.* 8°35N 124°29E **233** G5
Alucra *Turkey* 40°22N 38°47E **213** B8
Aluk *Sudan* 8°25N 27°30E **257** F2
Alūksne *Latvia* 57°24N 27°3E **188** D4
Alunda *Sweden* 60°4N 18°5E **162** D12
Alunite *U.S.A.* 35°59N 114°55W **307** K12
Aluoro → *Ethiopia* 8°26N 33°24E **257** F3
Alupka *Ukraine* 44°23N 34°2E **189** K8
Alur *India* 15°24N 77°15E **245** E3
Alur Gajah *Malaysia* 2°23N 102°13E **234** B2
Alushta *Ukraine* 44°40N 34°25E **189** K8
Alusi *Indonesia* 7°35S 131°40E **231** F8
Alustante *Spain* 40°36N 1°40W **196** E3
Alutgama *Sri Lanka* 6°26N 79°59E **245** L4
Alutnuwara *Sri Lanka* 7°19N 80°59E **245** L5
Aluva = Alwaye *India* 10°8N 76°24E **245** J3
Alva *U.S.A.* 36°48N 98°40W **314** C5
Alvaiázere *Portugal* 39°49N 8°23W **194** F2
Älvängen *Sweden* 57°58N 12°8E **163** G6
Alvão ⌂ *Portugal* 41°22N 7°48W **194** D3
Alvarado *Veracruz, Mexico* 18°46N 95°46W **319** D5
Alvarado *Tex., U.S.A.* 32°24N 97°13W **314** E6
Alvarães *Brazil* 3°12S 64°50W **329** D5
Alvaro Obregón, Presa *Mexico* 27°52N 109°52W **318** B3
Alvdal *Norway* 62°6N 10°37E **164** B7
Älvdalen *Sweden* 61°13N 14°4E **162** C8
Alvear *Argentina* 29°5S 56°30W **334** B4
Alverca *Portugal* 38°56N 9°1W **195** G1
Alvesta *Sweden* 56°54N 14°35E **163** H8
Alvik *Sweden* 59°19N 17°58E **139** B1
Alvin *U.S.A.* 29°26N 95°15W **314** G7
Alvin Callendar Naval Air Station *U.S.A.* 29°50N 90°1W **131** B2
Alvinston *Canada* 42°49N 81°52W **312** D3
Alvito *Portugal* 38°15N 7°58W **195** G3
Älvkarleby *Sweden* 60°34N 17°26E **162** D11
Alvorado *Brazil* 12°28S 49°6W **333** D2
Alvord Desert *U.S.A.* 42°30N 118°25W **304** E4
Älvros *Sweden* 62°3N 14°38E **162** B8
Älvsbyn *Sweden* 65°40N 21°0E **160** D19
Älvsjo *Sweden* 59°16N 18°0E **139** B2
Ålvundeid *Norway* 62°45N 8°33E **164** B5
Älvvik *Sweden* 59°21N 18°15E **139** A3
Alwar *India* 27°38N 76°34E **242** F7
Alwaye *India* 10°8N 76°24E **245** J3
Alxa Zuoqi *China* 38°50N 105°40E **226** E3
Alyangula *Australia* 13°55S 136°30E **280** A2
Alyata = Älät *Azerbaijan* 39°58N 49°25E **191** L9
Alyth *U.K.* 56°38N 3°13W **167** E5
Alytus *Lithuania* 54°24N 24°3E **188** E3
Alzada *U.S.A.* 45°2N 104°25W **304** D11
Alzamay *Russia* 55°33N 98°39E **215** D10
Alzey *Germany* 49°45N 8°7E **179** F4
Alzira *Spain* 39°9N 0°30W **197** F4
Am Dam *Chad* 12°40N 20°35E **259** F4
Am Géréda *Chad* 12°53N 21°14E **259** F4
Am Hasenbergl *Germany* 48°12N 11°33E **131** A2
Am Sak *Chad* 13°39N 20°8E **259** F4
Am Steinhof *Austria* 48°12N 16°17E **142** A1
Am Timan *Chad* 11°0N 20°10E **259** F4
Am Wald *Germany* 48°3N 11°36E **131** B2
Ama Keng *Singapore* 1°23N 103°41E **138** A2
Amacayacu △ *Colombia* 3°21S 70°8W **328** D3
Amada Gaza *C.A.R.* 4°46N 15°9E **264** B3
Amådalen *Sweden* 61°20N 14°44E **162** C8
Amadeus, L. *Australia* 24°54S 131°0E **279** D5
Amadi *Dem. Rep. of the Congo* 3°40N 26°40E **268** B2
Amâdi *Sudan* 5°29N 30°25E **257** F3
Amadjuak L. *Canada* 65°0N 71°8W **295** E17
Amadora *Portugal* 38°45N 9°13W **126** A1
Amagansett *U.S.A.* 40°59N 72°9W **313** F12
Amagasaki *Japan* 34°42N 135°23E **133** A1
Amager *Denmark* 55°36N 12°35E **118** B3
Amagi *Japan* 33°25N 130°39E **222** D2
Amagunze *Nigeria* 6°20N 7°40E **263** D6
Amahai *Indonesia* 3°20S 128°55E **231** E7
Amaile *Samoa* 13°59S 171°22W **287** V20
Amaimon *Papua N. G.* 5°12S 145°30E **286** C3
Amaiun-Maia *Spain* 43°12N 1°29W **196** B3
Amakusa-Nada *Japan* 32°35N 130°5E **222** E2
Amakusa-Shotō *Japan* 32°15N 130°10E **222** E2
Amal *Oman* 18°21N 55°39E **249** C6
Åmål *Sweden* 59°3N 12°42E **162** E6
Amāl Qādisiya *Iraq* 33°16N 44°20E **113** B2
Amalapuram *India* 16°35N 81°55E **245** F5
Amalfi *Colombia* 6°55N 75°4W **328** B2
Amalfi *Italy* 40°38N 14°36E **201** B7
Amaliada *Greece* 37°47N 21°22E **204** D3
Amalienborg Slot *Copenhagen, Denmark* **118** b3
Amalner *India* 21°5N 75°5E **244** D2
Amamapare *Indonesia* 4°53S 136°38E **231** E9
Amambaí *Brazil* 23°5S 55°13W **335** A4
Amambaí → *Brazil* 23°22S 53°56W **335** A5
Amambay □ *Paraguay* 23°0S 56°0W **335** A4
Amambay, Cordillera de *S. Amer.* 23°0S 55°45W **335** A4
Amami-Guntō *Japan* 27°16N 129°21E **221** L4
Amami-Ō-Shima *Japan* 28°16N 129°21E **221** K4
Aman, Pulau *Malaysia* 5°16N 100°24E **237** c
Amana → *Venezuela* 9°45N 62°39W **329** B5
Amaná, L. *Brazil* 2°35S 64°40W **329** D5
Amanab *Papua N. G.* 3°40S 141°14E **286** B1
Amanat → *India* 24°7N 84°4E **243** G11
Amanave *Amer. Samoa* 14°20S 170°50W **302** f
Amanda Park *U.S.A.* 47°28N 123°55W **306** C3
Amankeldi *Kazakhstan* 50°10N 65°10E **217** B7
Amanohashidate *Japan* 35°40N 135°15E **223** B7
Amantea *Italy* 39°8N 16°4E **201** C9
Amanu *French Polynesia* 17°48S 140°46W **289** f
Amapá *Brazil* 2°5N 50°50W **329** C7
Amapá □ *Brazil* 1°40N 52°0W **329** C7
Amapari = Ferreira Gomes *Brazil* 0°48N 51°8W **332** A1
Amapari *Brazil* 0°37N 51°39W **329** C7
Amara *Sudan* 10°25N 34°10E **257** E3
Amara □ *Ethiopia* 12°30N 37°30E **257** E4
Amaração = Luís Correia *Brazil* 3°0S 41°35W **332** B3
Amarante *Brazil* 6°14S 42°50W **332** C3
Amarante *Portugal* 41°16N 8°5W **194** D2
Amarante do Maranhão *Brazil* 5°36S 46°45W **332** C2
Amaranth *Canada* 50°36N 98°43W **297** C9
Amarapura *Burma* 21°54N 96°3E **241** E6
Amaravati → *India* 11°0N 78°15E **245** J4
Amareleja *Portugal* 38°12N 7°13W **195** G3
Amargosa *Brazil* 13°2S 39°36W **333** D4
Amargosa → *U.S.A.* 36°14N 116°51W **307** J10
Amargosa Desert *U.S.A.* 36°40N 116°30W **307** J10
Amargosa Range *U.S.A.* 36°20N 116°45W **307** J10
Amari *Greece* 35°13N 24°40E **207** E5
Amarillo *U.S.A.* 35°13N 101°50W **314** D4
Amarkantak *India* 22°40N 81°45E **243** H9
Amârna, Tell el' *Egypt* 27°38N 30°52E **256** B3
Amarnath *India* 19°12N 73°22E **244** E1
Amaro, Mte. *Italy* 42°5N 14°5E **199** F11
Amarpur *Bihar, India* 25°5N 87°0E **243** G12
Amarpur *Tripura, India* 23°31N 91°39E **241** D3
Amarti *Eritrea* 14°17N 41°6E **257** E5
Amarwara *India* 22°18N 79°10E **243** H8
Amasin *W. Sahara* 25°45N 13°20W **260** C2
Amasra *Turkey* 41°45N 32°23E **212** B5
Amassama *Nigeria* 5°1N 6°2E **263** D6
Amasya *Turkey* 40°40N 35°50E **212** B6
Amasya □ *Turkey* 40°40N 35°50E **212** B6
Amata *S. Austral., Australia* 26°9S 131°9E **279** E5
Amata *Piemonte, Italy* 45°34N 9°8E **129** A1
Amataurá *Brazil* 3°29S 68°6W **328** D4
Amatignak I. *U.S.A.* 51°16N 179°6W **303** L3
Amatikulu *S. Africa* 29°3S 31°33E **271** C5
Amatitlán *Guatemala* 14°29N 90°38W **320** D1
Amatrice *Italy* 42°38N 13°17E **199** F10
Amau *Papua N. G.* 10°2S 148°34E **286** F5
Amay *Belgium* 50°33N 5°19E **170** D5
Amazon = Amazonas → *S. Amer.* 0°5S 50°0W **329** D8
Amazonas □ *Brazil* 5°0S 65°0W **331** B5
Amazonas □ *Peru* 5°0S 78°0W **330** B2
Amazonas □ *Venezuela* 3°30N 66°0W **328** C4
Amazonas → *S. Amer.* 0°5S 50°0W **329** D8
Amba Ferit *Ethiopia* 10°55N 38°50E **257** E4
Ambad *India* 19°38N 75°50E **244** E2
Ambagarh Chowki *India* 20°47N 80°43E **244** D5

INDEX
Anti-Lebanon 343

Ambah India 26°43N 78°13E 242 F8
Ambahakily Madag. 21°36S 43°41E 272 C1
Ambahita Madag. 24°1S 45°16E 272 C2
Ambajogal India 18°44N 76°23E 244 E3
Ambala India 30°23N 76°56E 242 D7
Ambalangoda Sri Lanka 6°15N 80°5E 245 L5
Ambalapulai India 9°25N 76°25E 245 K3
Ambalavao Madag. 21°50S 46°56E 272 C2
Ambam Cameroon 2°20N 11°15E 264 B2
Ambanja Madag. 13°40S 48°27E 272 A2
Ambararata Madag. 15°3S 48°33E 272 B2
Ambarchik Russia 69°40N 162°20E 215 C17
Ambarijeby Madag. 14°56S 47°41E 272 A2
Ambaro, Helodranon' Madag. 13°23S 48°38E 272 A2
Ambasamudram India 8°43N 77°25E 245 K3
Ambato Ecuador 1°5S 78°42W 328 D2
Ambato Madag. 13°24S 48°29E 272 A2
Ambato, Sierra de Argentina 28°25S 66°10W 334 B2
Ambato Boeny Madag. 16°28S 46°43E 272 B2
Ambatofinandrahana Madag. 20°33S 46°48E 272 C2
Ambatolampy Madag. 19°20S 47°35E 272 B2
Ambatomainty Madag. 17°41S 45°40E 272 B2
Ambatomanoina Madag. 18°18S 47°37E 272 B2
Ambatondrazaka Madag. 17°55S 48°28E 272 B2
Ambatosoratra Madag. 17°37S 48°31E 272 B2
Ambelokipi Greece 37°58N 23°47E 112 B2
Ambelonas Greece 39°45N 22°22E 204 B4
Ambenja Madag. 15°17S 46°58E 272 B2
Amberg Germany 49°26N 11°52E 179 F7
Ambergris Cay Belize 18°0N 87°55W 320 C2
Ambérieu-en-Bugey France 45°57N 5°20E 175 C9
Amberley Ont., Canada 44°2N 81°42W 312 B3
Amberley N.Z. 43°9S 172°44E 285 D7
Ambert France 45°33N 3°44E 174 C7
Ambidédi Mali 14°35N 11°47W 262 C2
Ambikapur India 23°15N 83°15E 243 H10
Ambikol Sudan 21°20N 30°50E 256 C3
Ambil I. Phil. 13°48N 120°18E 232 E3
Ambilobé Madag. 13°10S 49°3E 272 A2
Ambinanindrano Madag. 20°5S 48°23E 272 C2
Ambinanitelo Madag. 15°21S 49°35E 272 B2
Ambinda Madag. 16°25S 45°52E 272 B2
Ambitle I. Papua N. G. 4°5S 153°37E 286 C7
Amble U.K. 55°20N 1°36W 168 B6
Ambler U.S.A. 67°5N 157°52W 303 C8
Ambleside U.K. 54°26N 2°58W 168 C5
Ambo Peru 10°5S 76°10W 330 C2
Amboahangy Madag. 24°15S 46°22E 272 C2
Amboasary Madag. 25°1S 46°45E 272 D2
Ambodifototra Madag. 16°59S 49°52E 272 B2
Ambodilazana Madag. 18°6S 49°10E 272 B2
Ambodiriana Madag. 17°55S 49°18E 272 B2
Ambohidratrimo Madag. 18°50S 47°26E 272 B2
Ambohidray Madag. 18°36S 48°18E 272 B2
Ambohimahamasina Madag. 21°56S 47°11E 272 C2
Ambohimahasoa Madag. 21°7S 47°13E 272 C2
Ambohimanga Madag. 20°52S 47°36E 272 C2
Ambohimitombo Madag. 20°43S 47°26E 272 C2
Ambohitra Madag. 12°30S 49°10E 272 A2
Amboise France 47°24N 1°2E 172 E8
Amboiva Angola 11°33S 14°43E 265 E2
Ambon Indonesia 3°43S 128°12E 231 E7
Ambondro Madag. 25°13S 45°44E 272 D2
Amboró △ Bolivia 17°39S 64°3W 331 D5
Amboseli, L. Kenya 2°40S 37°10E 268 C4
Amboseli △ Kenya 2°37S 37°13E 268 C4
Ambositra Madag. 20°31S 47°25E 272 C2
Ambovombe Madag. 25°11S 46°5E 272 D2
Amboy Calif., U.S.A. 34°33N 115°45W 307 L11
Amboy Ill., U.S.A. 41°44N 89°20W 310 C7
Amboyna Cay S. China Sea 7°50N 112°50E 230 C4
Ambre, Île d' Mauritius 20°2S 57°41E 272 e
Ambridge U.S.A. 40°36N 80°14W 312 F4
Ambriz Angola 7°48S 13°8E 265 D2
Ambriz ⌓ Angola 7°56S 10°27E 265 D2
Ambrolauri Georgia 42°31N 43°9E 213 A10
Ambrym Vanuatu 16°15S 168°10E 287 F6
Ambulong I. Phil. 12°13N 121°1E 232 E3
Ambunti Papua N. G. 4°13S 142°52E 286 C2
Ambur India 12°48N 78°43E 245 H4
Amchitka I. U.S.A. 51°32N 179°0E 303 L2
Amderma Russia 69°45N 61°30E 214 C7
Amdhi India 23°51N 81°27E 243 H9
Amdo China 32°20N 91°40E 218 E7
Ameca Mexico 20°33N 104°2W 318 C4
Ameca → Mexico 20°41N 105°18W 318 C3
Amecameca de Juárez Mexico 19°8N 98°46W 319 D5
Amed Indonesia 8°19S 115°39E 231 J18
Ameixoeira Portugal 38°46N 9°8W 126 A2
Ameland Neths. 53°27N 5°45E 170 A5
Amélia Italy 42°33N 12°25E 199 F9
Amelia City U.S.A. 30°35N 81°28W 316 E8
Amelia I. U.S.A. 30°40N 81°25W 316 E8
Amendolara Italy 39°57N 16°35E 201 C9
Amenia U.S.A. 41°51N 73°33W 313 E11
América Brazil 23°35S 46°41W 137 B1
America-Antarctica Ridge S. Ocean 59°0S 16°0W 151 B2
American Falls U.S.A. 42°47N 112°51W 304 E7
American Falls Res. U.S.A. 42°47N 112°52W 304 E7
American Fork U.S.A. 40°23N 111°48W 304 F8
American Highland Antarctica 73°0S 75°0E 151 D6
American Indian Museum Washington, D.C., U.S.A. 143 b3
American Museum of Natural History New York, U.S.A. 132 b2
American Police Hall of Fame U.S.A. 25°49N 80°11W 128 B2
American River Australia 35°47S 137°46E 282 C2
American Samoa ⊠ Pac. Oc. 14°20S 170°0W 302 f
American Samoa △ Amer. Samoa 14°15S 170°28W 302 g
American Univ. U.S.A. 38°56N 77°15W 143 B3
Americana Brazil 22°45S 47°20W 335 A6
Americus U.S.A. 32°4N 84°14W 316 C5
Amerigo Vespucci, Firenze ✈ (FLR) Italy 43°49N 11°13E 199 E8
Amerika = Nakhodka Russia 42°53N 132°54E 220 C6
Amersfoort Neths. 52°9N 5°23E 170 B5
Amersfoort Mpumalanga, S. Africa 26°59S 29°53E 271 C4
Amery Basin S. Ocean 68°15S 74°30E 151 C6
Amery Ice Shelf Antarctica 69°30S 72°0E 151 C6
Amerzgane Morocco 31°4N 7°14W 260 B3
Ames = Bertamirans Spain 42°54N 8°38W 194 C2
Ames U.S.A. 42°2N 93°37W 310 C3
Amesbury U.S.A. 42°51N 70°56W 313 D14
Amet India 25°18N 73°56E 242 G5
Amfiklia Greece 38°38N 22°35E 204 C4
Amfilochia Greece 38°52N 21°9E 204 C3
Amfipoli Greece 40°48N 23°52E 202 F7
Amfissa Greece 38°32N 22°22E 204 C4
Amga Russia 60°50N 132°0E 215 C14
Amga → Russia 62°38N 134°32E 215 C14
Amgaon India 21°22N 80°22E 244 D5
Amgu Russia 45°45N 137°15E 220 B8
Amguid Algeria 26°26N 5°22E 261 C6
Amgun → Russia 52°56N 139°38E 215 D14
Amherst = Kyaikkami Burma 16°4N 97°34E 241 G6
Amherst N.S., Canada 45°48N 64°8W 299 C7
Amherst Mass., U.S.A. 42°23N 72°31W 313 D12
Amherst N.Y., U.S.A. 42°59N 78°48W 312 D6
Amherst Ohio, U.S.A. 41°24N 82°14W 312 E2
Amherst I. Canada 44°8N 76°43W 313 B8
Amherstburg Canada 42°6N 83°6W 311 B13
Amiata, Mte. Italy 42°53N 11°37E 199 F8
Amidon U.S.A. 46°29N 103°19W 308 B2
Amiens France 49°54N 2°16E 173 C9
Amik Gölü Turkey 36°22N 36°17E 250 B7
Amili India 28°25N 95°52E 241 A5
Amin Iraq 33°19N 44°29E 113 B2
Aminadav Israel 31°45N 35°8E 123 B1
Amindeo Greece 40°42N 21°42E 202 F5
Amindivi Is. India 11°23N 72°23E 245 J1
Amingaon India 26°11N 91°40E 241 B3
Amini I. India 11°6N 72°45E 245 J1
Amino Ethiopia 4°25N 41°52E 257 G5
Aminuis Namibia 23°43S 19°21E 270 B2
Aminyevo Russia 55°41N 37°25E 129 B2
Āmir, Ra's Libya 32°57N 21°43E 258 B4
Amīrābād Īlām, Iran 33°20N 46°16E 246 C5
Amīrābād Tehrān, Iran 35°43N 51°24E 141 A2
Amirante Is. Seychelles 6°0S 53°0E 210 J7
Amisk ⌓ Canada 56°43N 98°0W 297 B9
Amisk L. Canada 54°35N 102°15W 297 C8
Amistad, Presa de la Mexico 29°26N 101°3W 318 B4
Amistad ⌓ U.S.A. 29°32N 101°12W 314 G4
Amite U.S.A. 30°44N 90°30W 315 F9
Amizmiz Morocco 31°12N 8°15W 260 B3
Amla India 21°56N 78°7E 242 J8
Amlapura Indonesia 8°27S 115°37E 231 J18
Åmli Norway 58°45N 8°32E 164 F5
Amlia I. U.S.A. 52°4N 173°30W 303 K4
Amlwch U.K. 53°24N 4°20W 168 D3
Amm Adam Sudan 16°20N 36°1E 257 D4
'Ammān Jordan 31°57N 35°52E 251 G6
'Ammān □ Jordan 31°40N 36°30E 251 G7
Ammanford U.K. 51°48N 3°59W 169 F4
Ammassalik = Tasiilaq Greenland 65°40N 37°20W 154 D7
Ammerån → Sweden 63°9N 16°13E 162 A10
Ammersee Germany 48°0N 11°7E 179 G7
Ammochostos = Famagusta Cyprus 35°8N 33°55E 207 E9
Ammon U.S.A. 43°28N 111°58W 304 E8
Amnat Charoen Thailand 15°51N 104°38E 236 E5
Amnura Bangla. 24°37N 88°25E 243 G13
Amo Jiang → China 23°0N 101°50E 228 F3
Āmol Iran 36°23N 52°20E 247 B7
Amora Portugal 38°37N 9°6W 126 B2
Amoreira Portugal 38°48N 9°11W 126 A1
Amoret U.S.A. 38°15N 94°35W 310 F2
Amorgos Greece 36°50N 25°57E 205 E7
Amory U.S.A. 33°59N 88°29W 315 E10
Amos Canada 48°35N 78°5W 298 C4
Åmot Buskerud, Norway 59°57N 9°54E 164 E6
Åmot Oppland, Norway 61°0N 10°2E 164 D7
Åmot Telemark, Norway 59°34N 8°0E 164 E5
Åmot Sweden 60°58N 16°27E 162 D10
Åmotfors Sweden 59°47N 12°22E 162 E6
Åmotsdal Norway 59°37N 8°26E 164 E5
Amour, Djebel Algeria 33°42N 1°37E 261 B5
Amoy = Xiamen China 24°25N 118°4E 229 E12
Ampah Indonesia 1°46S 115°7E 235 C5
Ampanavoana Madag. 15°41S 50°22E 272 B3
Ampang Malaysia 3°8N 101°45E 237 L3
Ampangalana, Lakandranon' Madag. 22°48S 47°50E 272 C2
Ampani India 19°35N 82°38E 244 E6
Ampanihy Madag. 24°40S 44°45E 272 C1
Amparafaravola Madag. 17°35S 48°13E 272 B2
Ampasinambo Madag. 20°31S 48°0E 272 C2
Ampasindava, Helodranon' Madag. 13°40S 48°15E 272 A2
Ampasindava, Saikanosy Madag. 13°42S 47°55E 272 A2
Ampato, Nevado Peru 15°40S 71°56W 330 D3
Ampenan Indonesia 8°34S 116°4E 231 K18
Amper Nigeria 9°25N 9°40E 263 D6
Amper → Bayern, Germany 48°29N 11°55E 179 G7
Amper → Oberbayern, Germany 48°14N 11°25E 131 A1
Ampezzo Italy 46°25N 12°48E 199 B9
Amphoe Kathu Thailand 7°55N 98°21E 237 a
Amphoe Thalang Thailand 8°1N 98°20E 237 a
Ampitsikinana Madag. 12°57S 49°49E 272 A2
Ampombiantambo Madag. 12°42S 48°57E 272 A2
Amposta Spain 40°43N 0°34E 196 E5
Ampotaka Madag. 25°3S 44°41E 272 D1
Ampoza Madag. 22°20S 44°44E 272 C1
Amqui Canada 48°28N 67°27W 299 C6
Amrabad India 16°23N 78°50E 245 F4
'Amrān Yemen 15°41N 43°55E 248 D3
Amraoti = Amravati India 20°55N 77°45E 244 D3
Amravati India 20°55N 77°45E 244 D3
Amreli India 21°35N 71°17E 242 J4
Amrenene el Kasba Algeria 22°10N 0°30E 261 D5
Amritsar India 31°35N 74°57E 242 D6
Amroha India 28°53N 78°30E 243 E8
Amrum Germany 54°38N 8°22E 178 A4
Amsâga Mauritania 20°7N 14°10W 260 D2
Amsel Algeria 22°47N 5°29E 261 D6
Amstel Amsterdam, Neths. 112 b2
Amstel → Amsterdam, Neths. 112 b3
Amstel-Drecht-Kanaal Neths. 52°18N 4°54E 112 B2
Amstelveen Neths. 52°18N 4°51E 112 B2
Amsterdam Neths. 52°23N 4°54E 112 A2
Amsterdam N.Y., U.S.A. 42°56N 74°11W 313 D10
Amsterdam ✈ (AMS) Neths. 52°18N 4°45E 112 B1
Amsterdam, I. = Nouvelle Amsterdam, Î. Ind. Oc. 38°30S 77°30E 273 H6
Amsterdam-Rijnkanaal Neths. 51°53N 5°28E 112 B3
Amsterdam Zuidoost Neths. 52°18N 4°58E 112 B2
Amsterdamse Bos Neths. 52°19N 4°50E 112 B1
Amstetten Austria 48°7N 14°51E 180 C7
'Amūdah Syria 37°6N 40°55E 213 D9
Amudarya Turkmenistan 37°53N 65°15E 216 E7
Amudarya → Uzbekistan 43°58N 59°34E 216 D5
Amukta I. U.S.A. 52°30N 171°16W 303 K5
Amukta Pass U.S.A. 52°0N 171°0W 303 K5
Amulung Phil. 17°50N 121°43E 232 C3
Amund Ringnes I. Canada 78°20N 96°25W 295 B12
Amundsen Abyssal Plain S. Ocean 65°0S 125°0W 151 C14
Amundsen Basin Arctic 87°30N 80°0E 150 A
Amundsen Gulf Canada 71°0N 124°0W 294 C7
Amundsen Ridges S. Ocean 69°15S 123°0W 151 C14
Amundsen-Scott Antarctica 90°0S 166°0E 151 E
Amundsen Sea Antarctica 72°0S 115°0W 151 D15
Amungen Sweden 61°10N 15°40E 162 C9
Amuntai Indonesia 2°28S 115°25E 235 C5
Amur → Russia 52°56N 141°10E 215 D15
Amur, W. → Sudan 18°56N 33°34E 256 D3
Amurang Indonesia 1°5N 124°40E 231 D6
Amurrio Spain 43°3N 3°0W 196 B1
Amursk Russia 50°14N 136°54E 215 D14
Amusco Spain 42°10N 4°28W 194 C6
Amvrakikos Kolpos Greece 39°0N 20°55E 204 C2
Amvrosiyivka Ukraine 47°43N 38°30E 189 J10
Amyderya = Amudarya → Uzbekistan 43°58N 59°34E 216 D5
An Burma 19°48N 94°0E 241 F5
An Bien Vietnam 9°45N 105°0E 237 H5
An Cabhán = Cavan Ireland 54°0N 7°22W 166 B4
An Cóbh = Cóbh Ireland 51°51N 8°17W 166 E3
An Daingean = Dingle Ireland 52°9N 10°17W 166 D1
An Hoa Vietnam 15°40N 108°5E 236 E7
An Khe Vietnam 13°57N 108°51E 236 F7
An Longfort = Longford Ireland 53°43N 7°49W 166 C4
An Muileann gCearr = Mullingar Ireland 53°31N 7°21W 166 C4
An Nabatīyah at Tahta Lebanon 33°23N 35°27E 250 E6
An Nabk Si. Arabia 31°20N 37°20E 246 D3
An Nabk Syria 34°2N 36°44E 250 D7
An Nafūd Si. Arabia 28°15N 41°0E 246 D4
An Nāḩīyah Iraq 34°26N 41°33E 213 E9
An Najaf Iraq 32°3N 44°15E 213 G11
An Namāş Si. Arabia 19°7N 42°8E 248 C3
An Nás = Naas Ireland 53°12N 6°40W 166 C5
An Nāşirīyah Iraq 31°0N 46°15E 246 D5
An Nawfaliyah Libya 30°54N 17°58E 258 B3
An Nhon = Binh Dinh Vietnam 13°55N 109°7E 236 F7
An Nîl □ Sudan 19°30N 33°0E 256 D3
An Nîl el Abyad □ Sudan 14°0N 32°15E 257 E3
An Nîl el Azraq □ Sudan 11°30N 34°30E 257 E3
An Nu'ayrīyah Si. Arabia 27°30N 48°30E 247 E6
An Nu'mānīyah Iraq 32°32N 45°25E 213 F11
An Nuqat Alkhams □ Libya 32°42N 11°57E 261 B7
An Ros = Rush Ireland 53°31N 6°6W 166 C5
An tAonach = Nenagh Ireland 52°52N 8°11W 166 D3
An Thoi, Quan Dao Vietnam 9°58N 104°0E 237 H5
An tInbhear Mór = Arklow Ireland 52°48N 6°10W 166 D5
An Uaimh Ireland 53°39N 6°41W 166 C5
Åna-Sira Norway 58°17N 6°25E 164 F3
Anaa French Polynesia 17°25S 145°30W 289 f
Anabar → Russia 73°8N 113°36E 215 B12
Anaco Venezuela 9°27N 64°28W 329 B5
Anaconda U.S.A. 46°8N 112°57W 304 C7
Anacortes U.S.A. 48°30N 122°37W 306 B4
Anacosta → U.S.A. 38°52N 77°1W 143 B4
Anacostia U.S.A. 38°51N 76°59W 143 B4
Anacuao, Mt. Phil. 16°16N 121°53E 232 C3
Anadarko U.S.A. 35°4N 98°15W 314 D5
Anadia Brazil 9°42S 36°18W 332 C4
Anadia Portugal 40°26N 8°27W 194 E2
Anadolu Turkey 39°0N 30°0E 212 C5
Anadoluhisarı Turkey 41°4N 29°3E 122 B2
Anadolukavağı Turkey 41°10N 29°7E 122 A2
Anadyr Russia 64°35N 177°20E 215 C18
Anadyr → Russia 64°55N 176°5E 215 C18
Anadyrskiy Zaliv Russia 64°0N 180°0E 215 C19
Anafi Greece 36°22N 25°48E 205 E7
Anafonitria Greece 37°51N 20°39E 207 D2
Anaga, Pta. de Canary Is. 28°34N 16°9W 153 e1
Anagni Italy 41°44N 13°9E 199 G10
'Ānah Iraq 34°25N 42°0E 213 E10
Anaheim U.S.A. 33°50N 117°55W 307 M9
Anahim Lake Canada 52°28N 125°18W 296 C3
Anahola U.S.A. 22°9N 159°19W 302 A2
'Anahulu → U.S.A. 21°37N 158°6W 302 J13
Anai Mudi India 10°12N 77°4E 245 J3
Anaichak ⌓ U.S.A. 56°50N 158°15W 303 H8
Anaimalai Hills India 10°20N 76°40E 245 J3
Anajás Brazil 0°59S 49°57W 332 B2
Anajatuba Brazil 3°16S 44°37W 332 B3
Anakao Madag. 23°40S 43°39E 272 C1
Anakapalle India 17°42N 83°6E 244 F6
Anakena Chile 27°5S 109°20W 330 b
Anakie Australia 23°32S 147°45E 280 C4
Anaklia Georgia 42°22N 41°35E 191 J5
Anaktuvuk Pass U.S.A. 68°8N 151°45W 303 B10
Analalava Madag. 14°35S 48°0E 272 A2
Analavoka Madag. 22°23S 46°30E 272 C2
Analipsis Greece 39°36N 19°55E 206 B9
Anamã Brazil 3°35S 61°22W 329 D5
Anambar → Pakistan 30°15N 68°50E 242 D3
Anambas, Kepulauan Indonesia 3°20N 106°30E 234 B3
Anambas Is. = Anambas, Kepulauan Indonesia 3°20N 106°30E 234 B3
Anambra □ Nigeria 6°20N 7°0E 263 D6
Aname Vanuatu 20°8S 169°47E 287 K7
Anamosa U.S.A. 42°7N 91°17W 310 B5
Anamur Turkey 36°8N 32°58E 250 B3
Anamur → Turkey 36°5N 32°53E 250 B3
Anamur Burnu Turkey 36°2N 32°47E 250 B3
Anan Japan 33°54N 134°40E 222 D6
Anand India 22°32N 72°59E 242 H5
Anandapuram India 14°5N 75°12E 245 G2
Anandpur India 21°16N 86°13E 244 D8
Ananes Greece 36°33N 24°9E 204 E6
Anangu Pitjantjatjara ✿ Australia 27°0S 132°0E 279 E5
Anantapur India 14°39N 77°42E 245 G3
Anantnag India 33°45N 75°10E 243 C6
Ananyiv Ukraine 47°44N 29°58E 183 C14
Anapa Russia 44°55N 37°25E 189 K9
Anapodiaris → Greece 34°59N 25°20E 207 F6
Anápolis = Simão Dias Brazil 10°44S 37°49W 332 D4
Anápolis Brazil 16°15S 48°50W 333 E2
Anapu → Brazil 1°53S 50°53W 329 D7
Anār Iran 30°55N 55°13E 247 D7
Anār Darreh Afghan. 32°46N 61°39E 240 B1
Anārak Iran 33°25N 53°40E 247 C7
Anarisfjällen Sweden 63°6N 13°10E 162 A7
Anas → India 23°26N 74°0E 242 H5
Añasco Puerto Rico 18°17N 67°8W 321 b
Anata West Bank 31°49N 35°16E 123 B2
Anatahan N. Marianas 16°21N 145°40E 302 a
Anatolia = Anadolu Turkey 39°0N 30°0E 212 C5
Anatsogno Madag. 23°33S 43°46E 272 C1
Añatuya Argentina 28°20S 62°50W 334 B3
Anatye ✿ Australia 22°29S 137°3E 280 C2
Anauá → Brazil 0°58N 61°21W 329 C5
Anaunethad L. Canada 60°55N 104°25W 297 A8
Anavilhanas, Arquipélago das Brazil 2°42S 60°45W 329 D5
Anbyŏn N. Korea 39°1N 127°35E 224 C3
Ancares, Sierra dos Spain 42°51N 6°52W 194 C4
Ancares ⌓ Spain 42°50N 6°40W 194 C4
Ancash □ Peru 9°30S 77°45W 330 B2
Ancaster Canada 43°13N 79°59W 312 C5
Ancenis France 47°21N 1°10W 172 E5
Anchieta = Piatã Brazil 13°9S 41°48W 333 D3
Anch'ing = Anqing China 30°30N 117°3E 229 B11
Ancho, Canal Chile 50°0S 74°20W 336 D2
Anchor Bay U.S.A. 38°48N 123°34W 306 G3
Anchorage U.S.A. 61°13N 149°54W 303 F10
Anchorage ✈ (ANC) U.S.A. 61°10N 150°0W 303 F10
Anci China 39°20N 116°40E 226 E9
Ancohuma, Nevado Bolivia 16°0S 68°50W 330 D4
Ancol Indonesia 6°7S 106°49E 122 A1
Ancón Peru 11°50S 77°10W 330 C2
Ancona Italy 43°38N 13°30E 199 E10
Ancud Chile 42°0S 73°50W 336 B2
Ancud, G. de Chile 42°0S 73°0W 336 B2
Ancy-le-Franc France 47°46N 4°10E 173 E11
Anda Heilongjiang, China 46°24N 125°19E 219 B14
Anda Phil. 16°17N 119°57E 232 C2
Andacollo Argentina 37°10S 70°42W 334 D1
Andacollo Chile 30°14S 71°6W 334 C1
Andahuaylas Peru 13°40S 73°25W 330 C3
Andaingo Madag. 18°12S 48°17E 272 B2
Andalgalá Argentina 27°40S 66°30W 334 B2
Åndalsnes Norway 62°35N 7°43E 164 B4
Andalucía □ Spain 37°35N 5°0W 195 H6
'Andalus Iraq 33°19N 44°18E 113 B1
Andalusia = Andalucía □ Spain 37°35N 5°0W 195 H6
Andalusia U.S.A. 31°18N 86°29W 315 F11
Andaman & Nicobar Is. □ India 10°0N 93°0E 245 K11
Andaman Is. Ind. Oc. 12°30N 92°45E 245 H11
Andaman Sea Ind. Oc. 13°0N 96°0E 230 B1
Andamooka Australia 30°27S 137°9E 281 E2
Andapa Madag. 14°39S 49°39E 272 A2
Andara Namibia 18°2S 21°9E 270 A3
Andaraí Bahia, Brazil 12°48S 41°20W 333 D3
Andaraí Rio de J., Brazil 22°56S 43°14W 135 B1
Andelot-Blancheville France 48°15N 5°18E 173 D12
Andenes Norway 69°19N 16°18E 160 B17
Andenne Belgium 50°28N 5°5E 170 D5
Andéranboukane Mali 15°26N 3°2E 263 B5
Anderlecht Belgium 50°50N 4°19E 116 A1
Andermatt Switz. 46°38N 8°35E 179 J4
Andernach Germany 50°26N 7°24E 178 E3
Andernos-les-Bains France 44°44N 1°6W 174 D2
Andersen Air Force Base Guam 13°35N 144°55E 302 d
Anderslöv Sweden 55°26N 13°19E 163 J7
Anderson Vic., Australia 38°31S 145°26E 283 E6
Anderson Alaska, U.S.A. 64°25N 149°15W 303 D10
Anderson Calif., U.S.A. 40°27N 122°18W 304 F2
Anderson Ind., U.S.A. 40°10N 85°41W 311 D11
Anderson Mo., U.S.A. 36°39N 94°27W 308 G6
Anderson S.C., U.S.A. 34°31N 82°39W 315 D13
Anderson → Canada 69°42N 129°0W 294 D6
Anderson I. India 12°46N 92°43E 245 H11
Anderson Park U.S.A. 33°45N 84°27W 113 B2
Andersonville U.S.A. 32°12N 84°9W 316 C5
Andersonville ⌓ U.S.A. 32°12N 84°1W 316 C5
Anderstorp Sweden 57°19N 13°39E 163 G7
Andes Colombia 5°39N 75°54W 328 B2
Andes N.Y., U.S.A. 42°12N 74°47W 313 D10
Andes, Cord. de los S. Amer. 20°0S 68°0W 330 E4
Andfjorden Norway 69°10N 16°20E 160 B17
Andhra, L. India 18°54N 73°32E 244 E1
Andhra Pradesh □ India 18°0N 79°0E 244 F4
Andijon Uzbekistan 41°10N 72°15E 217 D8
Andijon □ Uzbekistan 40°45N 72°20E 217 D8
Andikíthira = Antikythira Greece 35°52N 23°15E 204 F5
Andilamena Madag. 17°1S 48°35E 272 B2
Andīmeshk Iran 32°27N 48°21E 213 F13
Andímilos = Antimilos Greece 36°47N 24°12E 204 E6
Andingmen China 39°55N 116°23E 114 B2
Andíparos = Antiparos Greece 37°0N 25°3E 205 D7
Andípaxoi = Antipaxi Greece 39°9N 20°13E 204 B2
Andipsara Greece 38°30N 25°29E 205 C7
Andizhan = Andijon Uzbekistan 41°10N 72°15E 217 D8
Andkhvoy Afghan. 36°52N 65°8E 240 A2
Andoain Spain 43°13N 2°1W 196 B2
Andoany Madag. 13°25S 48°16E 272 A2
Andoas Peru 2°55S 76°25W 328 D2
Andohahela ⌓ Madag. 24°4S 46°44E 272 C2
Andol India 17°51N 78°4E 244 F4
Andola India 16°57N 76°50E 244 F3
Andong S. Korea 36°40N 128°43E 224 D4
Andorra Spain 40°59N 0°28W 196 E4
Andorra ■ Europe 42°30N 1°30E 174 F5
Andorra La Vella Andorra 42°31N 1°32E 174 F5
Andover Hants., U.K. 51°12N 1°29W 169 F6
Andover Maine, U.S.A. 44°38N 70°45W 313 B14
Andover Mass., U.S.A. 42°40N 71°8W 313 D13
Andover N.J., U.S.A. 40°59N 74°45W 313 F10
Andover N.Y., U.S.A. 42°10N 77°48W 312 D7
Andover Ohio, U.S.A. 41°36N 80°34W 312 E4
Andøya Norway 69°10N 15°50E 160 B16
Andrade Brazil 4°40S 63°45W 329 D5
Andradina Brazil 20°54S 51°23W 333 F1
Andrahary Madag. 13°37S 49°17E 272 A2
Andramasina Madag. 19°11S 47°35E 272 B2
Andranopasy Madag. 21°17S 43°44E 272 C1
Andranovory Madag. 23°8S 44°10E 272 C1
Andratx Spain 39°39N 2°25E 206 B3
André Félix △ C.A.R. 9°29N 23°18E 264 A4
Andreanof Is. U.S.A. 51°30N 176°0W 303 L4
Andreapol Russia 56°40N 32°17E 188 D7
Andrée Land Greenland 73°40N 26°0W 154 C8
Andrews S.C., U.S.A. 33°27N 79°34W 315 E15
Andrews Tex., U.S.A. 32°19N 102°33W 314 E3
Andreyev = Jędrzejów Poland 50°35N 20°15E 185 H7
Andreyevka Russia 52°19N 51°55E 190 D10
Ándria Italy 41°13N 16°17E 201 A9
Andriamena Madag. 17°26S 47°30E 272 B2
Andriandampy Madag. 22°45S 45°41E 272 C2
Andriba Madag. 17°30S 46°58E 272 B2
Andrijevica Montenegro 42°45N 19°48E 202 D3
Andringitra ⌓ Madag. 22°13S 46°5E 272 C2
Andritsena Greece 37°29N 21°52E 204 D3
Androka Madag. 24°58S 44°2E 272 C1
Andropov = Rybinsk Russia 58°5N 38°50E 188 C10
Andros Greece 37°50N 24°57E 204 D6
Andros I. Bahamas 24°30N 78°0W 320 B4
Andros Town Bahamas 24°43N 77°47W 320 B4
Androscoggin → U.S.A. 43°58N 69°52W 313 C14
Androth I. India 10°50N 73°41E 245 J1
Andrychów Poland 49°51N 19°18E 185 J6
Andselv Norway 69°4N 18°34E 160 B18
Andújar Spain 38°3N 4°5W 195 G6
Andulo Angola 11°25S 16°45E 265 E3
Åneby Akershus, Norway 60°5N 10°51E 164 D7
Aneby Sweden 57°48N 14°49E 163 G8
Anéfis Mali 18°2N 0°36E 263 B5
Anegada Br. Virgin Is. 18°45N 64°20W 321 C7
Anegada, B. Argentina 40°20S 62°20W 336 B4
Anegada Passage W. Indies 18°15N 63°45W 321 C7
Aného Togo 6°12N 1°34E 263 D5
Aneityum Vanuatu 20°12S 169°45E 287 K7
Anelghowhat Vanuatu 20°19S 169°43E 287 K7
Añelo Argentina 38°20S 68°45W 336 A3
Anenni-Noi Moldova 46°53N 29°15E 183 D14
Aneto, Pico de Spain 42°37N 0°40E 196 C5
Änew Turkmenistan 37°52N 58°31E 216 E5
Aney Niger 19°15N 12°50E 259 E2
Añez Bolivia 15°40S 63°10W 331 D5
Anfu China 27°21N 114°40E 229 D10
Ang Mo Kio Singapore 1°23N 103°50E 138 A3
Ang Thong Thailand 14°35N 100°31E 236 E3
Ang Thong, Ko Thailand 9°37N 99°41E 237 b
Ang Thong, Mu Ko △ Thailand 9°40N 99°43E 237 H2
Angadanan Phil. 16°45N 121°45E 232 C3
Angamos, Punta Chile 23°1S 70°32W 334 A1
Angara → Russia 58°5N 94°20E 215 D10
Angara-Débou Benin 11°19N 3°3E 263 C5
Angarbaka Sudan 9°44N 24°44E 257 F1
Angarsk Russia 52°30N 104°0E 218 A9
Angas Hills Australia 23°0S 127°50E 278 D4
Angaston Australia 34°30S 139°8E 282 C3
Angat Phil. 14°56N 121°2E 232 D3
Angaur I. Palau 6°54N 134°9E 288 c
Ängby Sweden 59°20N 17°53E 139 A1
Ånge Sweden 62°31N 15°35E 162 B9
Ángel, Salto = Angel Falls Venezuela 5°57N 62°30W 329 B5
Ángel de la Guarda, I. Mexico 29°20N 113°25W 318 B2
Angel Falls Venezuela 5°57N 62°30W 329 B5
Angel I. U.S.A. 37°52N 122°25W 136 A2
Angel Island State Park ⌓ U.S.A. 37°52N 122°25W 136 A2
Angeles Phil. 15°9N 120°33E 232 D3
Ängelholm Sweden 56°15N 12°50E 163 H6
Angels Camp U.S.A. 38°4N 120°32W 306 G6
Ängelsberg Sweden 59°58N 16°0E 162 E10
Anger → Ethiopia 9°37N 36°6E 257 F4
Angerburg = Węgorzewo Poland 54°13N 21°43E 184 D8
Angereb Ethiopia 13°11N 37°7E 257 E4
Angereb → Ethiopia 13°45N 36°40E 257 E4
Ångermanälven → Sweden 64°0N 17°20E 162 A11
Ångermanland Sweden 63°36N 17°45E 160 E17
Angermünde Germany 53°0N 14°0E 178 B9
Angers Qué., Canada 45°31N 75°29W 313 A9
Angers Maine-et-Loire, France 47°30N 0°35W 172 E6
Angerville France 48°19N 2°0E 173 D9
Ängesån → Sweden 66°16N 22°47E 160 C20
Angical Brazil 12°0S 44°42W 333 D3
Angikuni L. Canada 62°12N 99°59W 297 A9
Angke, Kali → Indonesia 6°6S 106°46E 122 A1
Angkor Cambodia 13°22N 103°50E 236 F4
Angledool Australia 29°5S 147°55E 281 D4
Anglem, Mt. N.Z. 46°45S 167°53E 285 G2
Anglès Spain 41°57N 2°38E 196 D7
Anglesey U.K. 53°17N 4°20W 168 D3
Anglesey, Isle of □ U.K. 53°16N 4°18W 168 D3
Anglet France 43°29N 1°31W 174 E2
Angleton U.S.A. 29°10N 95°26W 314 G7
Anglin → France 46°42N 0°52E 174 B4
Anglisidhes Cyprus 34°51N 33°27E 207 F9
Anglure France 48°35N 3°50E 173 D10
Angmagssalik = Tasiilaq Greenland 65°40N 37°20W 154 D7
Ango Dem. Rep. of the Congo 4°10N 26°5E 268 B2
Angoche Mozam. 16°8S 39°55E 269 F4
Angoche, I. Mozam. 16°20S 39°50E 269 F4
Angol Chile 37°56S 72°45W 334 D1
Angola Ind., U.S.A. 41°38N 85°0W 311 C12
Angola N.Y., U.S.A. 42°38N 79°2W 312 D5
Angola ■ Africa 12°0S 18°0E 265 E3
Angola Abyssal Plain Atl. Oc. 15°0S 2°0E 152 H12
Angola Basin Atl. Oc. 15°0S 3°0E 152 H12
Angoon U.S.A. 57°30N 134°35W 303 H14
Angora = Ankara Turkey 39°57N 32°54E 212 C5
Angoram Papua N. G. 4°4S 144°4E 286 C3
Angoulême France 45°39N 0°10E 174 C4
Angoumois France 45°50N 0°25E 174 C4
Angra do Heroismo Azores 38°39N 27°13W 153 d1
Angra dos Reis Brazil 23°0S 44°10W 335 A7
Angrapa → Russia 54°37N 21°54E 184 D8
Angren Uzbekistan 41°1N 70°12E 217 D8
Angtassom Cambodia 11°1N 104°41E 237 G5
Angu Dem. Rep. of the Congo 3°23N 24°30E 264 B4
Anguang China 45°15N 123°45E 227 B12
Anguilla ⊠ W. Indies 18°14N 63°5W 322 a
Anguillita I. Anguilla 18°9N 63°11W 322 a
Angul India 20°51N 85°6E 244 D7
Anguo China 38°28N 115°15E 226 E8
Angurugu Australia 14°0S 136°25E 280 A2
Angus Canada 44°19N 79°53W 312 B5
Angus □ U.K. 56°46N 2°56W 167 E6
Angwa → Zimbabwe 16°0S 30°23E 271 A5
Angyalföld Hungary 47°32N 19°5E 117 A2
Anhanduí → Brazil 21°46S 52°9W 335 A5
Anholt Denmark 56°42N 11°33E 163 H5
Anhua China 28°23N 111°12E 229 C8
Anhui □ China 32°0N 117°0E 229 B11
Anhwei = Anhui □ China 32°0N 117°0E 229 B11
Aniak U.S.A. 61°35N 159°32W 303 F8
Anichab Namibia 21°0S 14°46E 270 B1
Anicuns Brazil 16°28S 49°58W 333 E2
Anidros Greece 36°38N 25°43E 205 E7
Anié Togo 7°42N 1°8E 263 D5
Anik India 19°1N 72°53E 130 A2
Anil Brazil 2°32S 44°14W 332 B3
Animas → U.S.A. 36°43N 108°13W 305 H9
Anin Burma 15°36N 97°50E 236 E1
Anin Warszawa, Poland 52°13N 21°9E 142 B2
Anina Romania 45°6N 21°51E 182 E6
Anini-y Phil. 10°25N 121°55E 233 F3
Aninoasa Romania 44°47N 24°10E 183 F9
Añisoc Eq. Guin. 1°51N 10°46E 264 B2
Anita U.S.A. 41°27N 94°46W 310 C2
Anivorano Antsiranana, Madag. 12°44S 49°14E 272 A2
Anivorano Toamasina, Madag. 18°44S 48°58E 272 B2
Aniwa Vanuatu 19°17S 169°35E 287 J7
Anjalankoski Finland 60°45N 26°51E 188 B4
Anjangaon India 21°10N 77°20E 244 D3
Anjar India 23°6N 70°10E 242 H4
Anjengo India 8°40N 76°46E 245 K3
Anji China 30°46N 119°40E 229 B12
Anjidiv I. India 14°40N 74°10E 245 G2
Anjō Japan 34°57N 137°5E 223 C9
Anjou Qué., Canada 45°36N 73°33W 130 A2
Anjou Maine-et-Loire, France 47°20N 0°15W 172 E6
Anjouan Comoros Is. 12°15S 44°20E 272 a
Anjouan ✈ (AJN) Comoros Is. 12°9S 44°26E 272 a
Anjozorobe Madag. 18°22S 47°52E 272 B2
Anju N. Korea 39°36N 125°40E 224 C2
Anka Nigeria 12°13N 5°58E 263 C6
Ankaboa, Tanjona Madag. 21°58S 43°20E 272 C1
Ankang China 32°40N 109°1E 226 H5
Ankara Turkey 39°57N 32°54E 212 C5
Ankara □ Turkey 39°55N 32°50E 212 C5
Ankarafantsika ⌓ Madag. 16°8S 47°5E 272 B2
Ankaramena Madag. 21°57S 46°39E 272 C2
Ankarsrum Sweden 57°41N 16°20E 163 G10
Ankasakasa Madag. 16°21S 44°52E 272 B1
Ankavandra Madag. 18°46S 45°18E 272 B2
Ankazoabo Madag. 22°18S 44°31E 272 C1
Ankazobe Madag. 18°20S 47°10E 272 B2
Ankeny U.S.A. 41°44N 93°36W 310 C3
Ankhialo = Pomorie Bulgaria 42°32N 27°41E 203 D11
Ankilimalinika Madag. 22°58S 43°45E 272 C1
Ankilizato Madag. 20°25S 45°1E 272 C2
Anking = Anqing China 30°30N 117°3E 229 B11
Ankisabe Madag. 19°17S 46°29E 272 B2
Anklam Germany 53°51N 13°41E 178 B9
Ankleshwar India 21°38N 73°3E 244 D1
Ankober Ethiopia 9°35N 39°40E 257 F4
Ankola India 14°40N 74°18E 245 G2
Ankoro Dem. Rep. of the Congo 6°45S 26°55E 268 D2
Ankororoka Madag. 25°30S 45°11E 272 D2
Ankpa Nigeria 7°22N 7°38E 263 D6
Anlong China 25°2N 105°27E 228 E5
Anlong Veng Cambodia 14°14N 104°5E 236 E5
Anlu China 31°15N 113°45E 229 B9
Anmyeondo S. Korea 36°25N 126°25E 224 D3
Ånn Sweden 63°19N 12°33E 162 A6
Ann, C. U.S.A. 42°38N 70°35W 313 D14
Ann Arbor U.S.A. 42°17N 83°45W 311 B13
Anna Russia 51°28N 40°23E 190 E5
Anna Ill., U.S.A. 37°28N 89°15W 308 G9
Anna Ohio, U.S.A. 40°24N 84°11W 311 D12
Anna Regina Guyana 7°10N 58°30W 329 B6
Annaba Algeria 36°50N 7°46E 261 A6
Annaba □ Algeria 36°12N 7°45E 261 A6
Annaberg-Buchholz Germany 50°34N 13°0E 178 E9
Annai Guyana 3°57N 59°8W 329 C6
Annaka Japan 36°19N 138°54E 223 A10
Annalee → Ireland 54°2N 7°24W 166 B4
Annalee Heights U.S.A. 38°51N 77°10W 143 B2
Annam = Trung-Phan Vietnam 17°0N 109°0E 236 D6
Annamitique, Chaîne Asia 17°0N 106°40E 236 D6
Annan U.K. 54°59N 3°16W 167 G5
Annan → U.K. 54°58N 3°16W 167 G5
Annanberg Papua N. G. 4°52S 144°42E 286 C3
Annandale U.S.A. 38°50N 77°11W 143 C2
Annapolis U.S.A. 38°59N 76°30W 309 F15
Annapolis Royal Canada 44°44N 65°32W 299 D6
Annapurna Nepal 28°34N 83°50E 243 E10
Anne Frankhuis Amsterdam, Neths. 112 a1
Annean, L. Australia 26°54S 118°14E 279 E2
Anneberg Sweden 57°44N 14°49E 163 G8
Annecy France 45°55N 6°8E 175 C10
Annecy, Lac d' France 45°52N 6°10E 175 C10
Annemasse France 46°12N 6°16E 173 F13
Annenfeld = Şämkir Azerbaijan 40°50N 46°0E 191 K8
Annenskiy Most Russia 60°45N 37°10E 188 B9
Annette I. U.S.A. 55°9N 131°28W 296 B2
Annette Island ▲ U.S.A. 55°9N 131°28W 303 J15
Annigeri India 15°26N 75°26E 245 G2
Anning China 24°55N 102°26E 228 E4
Anniston U.S.A. 33°39N 85°50W 316 B4
Annobón Atl. Oc. 1°25S 5°36E 255 G4
Annonay France 45°15N 4°40E 175 C8
Annot France 43°58N 6°38E 175 E10
Annotto B. Jamaica 18°17N 76°45W 320 a
Annotto Bay Jamaica 18°16N 76°47W 320 a
Ånnsjön Sweden 63°19N 12°34E 162 A6
Annville U.S.A. 40°20N 76°31W 313 F8
Annweiler Germany 49°12N 7°57E 179 F3
Ano Poroia Greece 41°17N 23°2E 202 E7
Ano Siros Greece 37°29N 24°56E 204 D6
Anogi Greece 38°25N 20°40E 207 C2
Anogia Greece 35°16N 24°52E 207 E5
Anorotsangana Madag. 13°56S 47°55E 272 A2
Anosibe Madag. 19°26S 48°13E 272 B2
Anou Mellene Mali 17°29N 0°33E 263 B5
Anoumaba Ivory C. 6°23N 4°38W 262 D4
Anping Hebei, China 38°15N 115°30E 226 E8
Anping Liaoning, China 41°5N 123°30E 224 B1
Anpu Gang China 21°25N 109°50E 228 G7
Anqing China 30°30N 117°3E 229 B11
Anqiu China 36°25N 119°10E 227 F10
Anren China 26°43N 113°18E 229 D9
Ansager Denmark 55°43N 8°45E 163 J2
Ansai China 36°50N 109°20E 226 F5
Ansan S. Korea 37°21N 126°52E 224 D3
Ansbach Germany 49°28N 10°34E 179 F6
Anse-Bertrand Guadeloupe 16°28N 61°32W 322 e
Anse Boileau Seychelles 4°43S 55°29E 272 c
Anse Royale Seychelles 4°44S 55°31E 272 c
Anseba → Eritrea 16°0N 38°30E 257 D4
Anseong S. Korea 37°0N 127°16E 224 D3
Anserma Colombia 5°13N 75°48W 328 B2
Ansfelden Austria 48°12N 14°17E 180 C7
Anshan China 41°5N 122°58E 224 B1
Anshun China 26°18N 105°57E 228 D5
Ansião Portugal 39°56N 8°27W 194 F2
Ansley U.S.A. 41°18N 99°23W 308 E4
Ansó Spain 42°51N 0°48W 196 C4
Ansoáin Spain 42°50N 1°38W 196 C3
Anson U.S.A. 32°45N 99°54W 314 E5
Anson B. Australia 13°20S 130°6E 278 B5
Ansongo Mali 15°25N 0°35E 263 B5
Ansongo-Ménaka ⌓ Mali 15°3N 1°37E 263 B5
Ansonia Conn., U.S.A. 41°21N 73°5W 313 E11
Ansonia Ohio, U.S.A. 40°13N 84°38W 311 D12
Anstruther U.K. 56°14N 2°41W 167 E6
Ansudu Indonesia 2°11S 139°22E 231 E9
Antabamba Peru 14°40S 73°0W 330 C3
Antagarh India 20°6N 81°9E 244 D5
Antakya = Hatay Turkey 36°14N 36°10E 250 B7
Antalaha Madag. 14°57S 50°20E 272 A3
Antalāt Libya 31°8N 20°42E 258 B4
Antalya Turkey 36°52N 30°45E 250 B1
Antalya □ Turkey 36°50N 30°45E 250 B1
Antalya Körfezi Turkey 36°15N 31°30E 250 B2
Antambohobe Madag. 22°20S 46°47E 272 C2
Antanambao-Manampotsy Madag. 19°29S 48°34E 272 B2
Antanambe Madag. 16°26S 49°52E 272 B2
Antananarivo Madag. 18°55S 47°31E 272 B2
Antananarivo □ Madag. 19°0S 47°0E 272 B2
Antanifotsy Madag. 19°39S 47°19E 272 B2
Antanimbaribe Madag. 21°30S 44°48E 272 C1
Antanimora Madag. 24°49S 45°40E 272 C2
Antarctic Pen. Antarctica 67°0S 60°0W 151 C18
Antarctica 90°0S 0°0 151 E3
Antécume Pata Fr. Guiana 3°17N 54°4W 329 C7
Antelope Zimbabwe 21°2S 28°31E 269 G2
Antequera Paraguay 24°8S 57°7W 334 A4
Antequera Spain 37°5N 4°33W 195 H6
Antero, Mt. U.S.A. 38°41N 106°15W 304 G10
Antevamena Madag. 21°2S 44°8E 272 C1
Anthony Fla., U.S.A. 29°18N 82°7W 317 F7
Anthony Kans., U.S.A. 37°9N 98°2W 308 G4
Anthony N. Mex., U.S.A. 32°0N 106°36W 305 K10
Anti Atlas Morocco 30°0N 8°30W 260 C3
Anti-Lebanon = Sharqi, Al Jabal ash Lebanon 33°40N 36°10E 250 E7

344 Antibes INDEX

Antibes France 43°34N 7°6E 175 E11
Antibes, C. d' France 43°31N 7°7E 175 E11
Anticosti, Î. d' Canada 49°30N 63°0W 299 C7
Antifer, C. d' France 49°41N 0°10E 172 C7
Antigo U.S.A. 45°9N 89°9W 308 C9
Antigonish Canada 45°38N 61°58W 299 C7
Antigua Canary Is. 28°24N 14°1W 153 e2
Antigua Guatemala 14°34N 90°41W 320 D1
Antigua W. Indies 17°0N 61°50W 322 b
Antigua & Barbuda ■ W. Indies 17°20N 61°48W 322 b
Antigua Int. ✕ (ANU) Antigua & B. 17°8N 61°47W 322 b
Antigues, Pte. d' Guadeloupe 16°26N 61°32W 322 e
Antikythira Greece 35°52N 23°15E 204 F5
Antilla Cuba 20°40N 75°50W 320 B4
Antilles = West Indies Cent. Amer. 15°0N 65°0W 321 D7
Antimilos Greece 36°47N 24°12E 204 E6
Anting Taiwan 23°7N 120°14E 225 C2
Antioch = Hatay Turkey 36°14N 36°10E 250 B7
Antioch U.S.A. 38°1N 121°48W 306 G5
Antioche, Pertuis d' France 46°6N 1°20W 174 B2
Antioquia Colombia 6°40N 75°55W 328 B2
Antioquia □ Colombia 7°0N 75°30W 328 B2
Antiparos Greece 37°0N 25°3E 205 D7
Antipaxi Greece 39°9N 20°13E 204 B2
Antipodes Is. Pac. Oc. 49°45S 178°40E 288 M9
Antipolo Phil. 14°35N 121°10E 232 D3
Antique □ Phil. 11°10N 122°5E 233 F4
Antirio Greece 38°20N 21°46E 204 C3
Antlers U.S.A. 34°14N 95°37W 314 D7
Antoetra Madag. 20°46S 47°20E 272 C2
Antofagasta Chile 23°50S 70°30W 334 A1
Antofagasta □ Chile 24°0S 69°0W 334 A2
Antofagasta de la Sierra Argentina 26°5S 67°20W 334 B2
Antofalla Argentina 25°30S 68°5W 334 B2
Antofalla, Salar de Argentina 25°40S 67°45W 334 B2
Antoine, L. Grenada 12°11N 61°36W 323 q
Anton U.S.A. 33°49N 102°10W 314 E3
Antongila, Helodrano Madag. 15°30S 49°50E 272 B2
Antonibé Madag. 15°7S 47°24E 272 B2
Antonina Brazil 25°26S 48°42W 335 B6
Antonio B. Won Pat Int. ✕ (GUM) Guam 13°29N 144°48E 322 d
Antônio Enes = Angoche Mozam. 16°8S 39°55E 269 F4
Antony France 48°44N 2°17E 134 B2
Antrain France 48°28N 1°30W 172 D5
Antrim Antrim, U.K. 54°43N 6°14W 166 B5
Antrim Ohio, U.S.A. 40°7N 81°21W 312 F3
Antrim □ U.K. 54°56N 6°25W 166 B5
Antrim, Mts. of U.K. 55°3N 6°14W 166 A5
Antrim Plateau Australia 18°8S 128°20E 278 C4
Antriol Bonaire 12°12N 68°16W 322 h
Antrodoco Italy 42°25N 13°5E 199 F10
Antropovo Russia 58°24N 43°6E 190 A6
Antsakabary Madag. 15°3S 48°56E 272 B2
Antsalova Madag. 18°40S 44°37E 272 B1
Antsenavolo Madag. 21°24S 48°3E 272 C2
Antsiafabositra Madag. 17°18S 46°57E 272 B2
Antsirabe Antananarivo, Madag. 19°55S 47°2E 272 B2
Antsirabe Antsiranana, Madag. 14°0S 49°59E 272 A2
Antsirabe Mahajanga, Madag. 15°57S 48°58E 272 B2
Antsiranana Madag. 12°25S 49°20E 272 A2
Antsiranana □ Madag. 12°16S 49°17E 272 A2
Antsohihy Madag. 14°50S 47°59E 272 A2
Antsohimbondrona Seranana Madag. 13°7S 48°48E 272 A2
Antu China 42°30N 128°20E 227 C15
Antufash Yemen 15°42N 42°25E 248 D3
Antung Taiwan 23°18N 121°20E 225 C3
Antwerp = Antwerpen Belgium 51°13N 4°25E 170 C4
Antwerp N.Y., U.S.A. 44°12N 75°37W 313 B9
Antwerp Ohio, U.S.A. 41°11N 84°45W 311 C12
Antwerpen Belgium 51°13N 4°25E 170 C4
Antwerpen □ Belgium 51°15N 4°40E 170 C4
Anukur, C. Papua N. G. 6°18S 149°37E 286 D5
Anupgarh India 29°10N 73°10E 242 E5
Anuppur India 23°6N 81°41E 243 H9
Anuradhapura Sri Lanka 8°22N 80°28E 245 K5
Anurrete ✪ Australia 20°50S 135°38E 280 C2
Anveh Iran 27°23N 54°11E 247 E7
Anvers = Antwerpen Belgium 51°13N 4°25E 170 C4
Anvers I. Antarctica 64°30S 63°40W 151 C17
Anvik U.S.A. 62°39N 160°13W 303 E7
Anwen China 29°4N 120°26E 229 C13
Anxi Fujian, China 25°2N 118°12E 229 E12
Anxi Gansu, China 40°30N 95°43E 218 C8
Anxian China 31°40N 104°25E 228 B5
Anxiang China 29°27N 112°11E 229 C9
Anxious B. Australia 33°24S 134°45E 281 E1
Anyama Ivory C. 5°30N 4°3W 262 D4
Anyang Henan, China 36°5N 114°21E 226 F8
Anyang S. Korea 37°23N 126°55E 224 D3
Anyer Indonesia 6°4S 105°53E 234 D3
Anyi Jiangxi, China 28°49N 115°25E 229 C10
Anyi Shanxi, China 35°2N 111°2E 226 G6
Anyuan China 25°9N 115°21E 229 E10
Anyue China 30°9N 105°50E 228 B5
Anza U.S.A. 33°35N 116°39W 307 M10
Anze China 36°10N 112°12E 226 F7
Anzegfouf Algeria 26°50N 0°1E 261 C5
Anzhero-Sudzhensk Russia 56°10N 86°0E 214 D9
Ánzio Italy 41°27N 12°37E 200 A5
Anzoátegui □ Venezuela 9°0N 64°30W 329 B5
Ao Makham Thailand 7°50N 98°24E 237 a
Ao Phangnga △ Thailand 8°10N 98°32E 237 a
Aoba Vanuatu 15°25S 167°50E 287 E5
Aoga-Shima Japan 32°28N 139°46E 223 E11
Aohan Qi China 43°18N 119°43E 227 C10
Aoiz Spain 42°46N 1°22W 196 C3
Aoji N. Korea 42°31N 130°23E 224 A5
Aola Solomon Is. 9°30S 160°30E 287 M11
Aomen = Macau China 22°12N 113°33E 229 F9
Aomori Japan 40°45N 140°45E 220 D10
Aomori □ Japan 40°45N 140°40E 220 D10
AON Center Chicago, U.S.A. 119 b2
Aonla India 28°16N 79°11E 243 E8
Aono-Yama Japan 34°28N 131°48E 222 C3
Aorai, Mt. Tahiti 17°34S 149°30W 289 e
Aoraki Mount Cook N.Z. 43°36S 170°9E 285 D5
Aoral, Phnum Cambodia 12°0N 104°15E 237 G5
Aorangi Ra. N.Z. 41°28S 175°22E 284 H4
Aore Vanuatu 15°35S 167°10E 287 E5
Aoreora Morocco 28°51N 10°53W 260 C2
Aosta Italy 45°45N 7°20E 198 C4
Aotea Harbour N.Z. 38°0S 174°50E 284 E3
Aotearoa = New Zealand ■ Oceania 40°0S 176°0E 284 G5
Aoudéras Niger 17°45N 8°20E 259 E1
Aouinet Torkoz Morocco 28°31N 9°46W 260 C3
Aouk, Bahr → Africa 8°51N 18°53E 259 G3
Aouk-Aoukalé △ C.A.R. 9°52N 21°25E 264 A4
Aoukar Mali 23°50N 2°45W 260 D4
Aoukâr Mauritania 17°40N 10°0W 262 B3
Aoulef el Arab Algeria 26°55N 1°2E 261 C5
Aousred W. Sahara 22°32N 14°17W 260 D2
Aoyama Tokyo, Japan 140 b2
Aozou Chad 21°45N 17°28E 259 D3
Aozou, Couloir d' Chad 22°0N 19°0E 259 D3
Ap Lei Chau China 22°14N 114°9E 122 B1
Apá → S. Amer. 22°6S 58°2W 334 A4
Apache U.S.A. 34°54N 98°22W 314 D5
Apache Junction U.S.A. 33°25N 111°33W 305 K8
Apalachee B. U.S.A. 30°0N 84°0W 316 E5
Apalachicola U.S.A. 29°43N 84°59W 316 F5
Apalachicola → U.S.A. 29°43N 84°58W 316 F5
Apalachicola B. U.S.A. 29°40N 85°0W 316 F3
Apam Ghana 5°19N 0°42W 263 D4
Apamea Syria 35°31N 36°28E 250 C7
Apapa Nigeria 6°26N 3°21E 124 B2
Apapa Quays Nigeria 6°26N 3°23E 124 B2
Apaporis → Colombia 1°23S 69°25W 328 D4
Aparados da Serra △ Brazil 29°10S 50°8W 335 B5
Aparecida = Bertolínia Brazil 7°38S 43°57W 332 C3
Aparecida de Goiânia Brazil 16°45S 49°16W 333 E2
Aparecida do Taboado Brazil 20°5S 51°5W 333 F1
Aparri Phil. 18°22N 121°38E 232 B3
Aparurén Venezuela 5°6N 62°8W 329 B5
Apataki French Polynesia 15°26S 146°20W 289 f
Apateu Romania 46°36N 21°47E 182 D6
Apatin Serbia 45°40N 19°0E 182 E4
Apatity Russia 67°34N 33°22E 160 C25
Apatou Fr. Guiana 5°9N 54°20W 329 B7
Apatula = Finke Australia 25°34S 134°35E 280 D1
Apatzingán Mexico 19°5N 102°21W 318 D4
Apayao □ Phil. 18°10N 121°10E 232 B3
Apelacão Portugal 38°48N 9°7W 126 A2
Apeldoorn Neths. 52°13N 5°57E 170 B5
Apen Germany 53°13N 7°48E 178 B3
Apennines = Appennini Italy 44°30N 10°0E 198 D7
Apenrade = Aabenraa Denmark 55°3N 9°25E 163 J3
Apere → Bolivia 13°44S 65°18W 331 C4
Aphrodisias Turkey 37°42N 28°46E 205 D10
Api Nepal 30°0N 80°57E 218 F5
Apia Samoa 13°50S 171°50W 287 V20
Apiacás, Serra dos Brazil 9°50S 57°0W 331 B6
Apiaí Brazil 24°31S 48°50W 333 F2
Apiaú → Brazil 2°39N 61°12W 329 C5
Apiaú, Serra do Brazil 2°30N 62°0W 329 C5
Apidiá → Brazil 11°39S 61°11W 331 C5
Apies → S. Africa 25°15S 28°8E 271 C4
Apinajé Brazil 11°31S 48°18W 333 D2
Apiti N.Z. 39°58S 175°54E 284 F4
Apizaco Mexico 19°25N 98°8W 319 D5
Aplao Peru 16°0S 72°40W 330 D3
Apo, Mt. Phil. 6°53N 125°14E 233 H5
Apo East Pass. Phil. 12°40N 120°40E 232 E3
Apo Reef △ Phil. 12°50N 120°50E 232 E3
Apo West Pass. Phil. 12°31N 120°22E 232 E3
Apodi Brazil 5°39S 37°48W 332 C4
Apoera Suriname 5°12N 57°10W 329 B6
Apolakia Greece 36°5N 27°48E 206 E11
Apolakia, Ormos Greece 36°5N 27°45E 206 E11
Apolda Germany 51°2N 11°32E 178 D7
Apollo Bay Australia 38°45S 143°40E 282 E5
Apollonia = Marsá Súsah Libya 32°52N 21°59E 258 B4
Apollonia Greece 36°15N 27°58E 206 E11
Apolo Bolivia 14°30S 68°30W 330 C4
Apolonia Greece 36°58N 24°43E 204 E6
Apónguao → Venezuela 4°48N 61°36W 329 C5
Apopa El Salv. 13°48N 89°10W 320 D2
Apopka U.S.A. 28°40N 81°31W 317 G8
Apopka, L. U.S.A. 28°37N 81°37W 133 A1
Apoquindo Chile 33°24S 70°32W 137 B2
Aporé Brazil 18°58S 52°1W 331 D7
Aporé → Brazil 19°27S 50°57W 333 E1
Aporema Brazil 1°14N 50°49W 332 A1
Apostle Is. U.S.A. 47°0N 90°40W 308 B8
Apostle Islands △ U.S.A. 46°55N 91°0W 308 B8
Apóstoles Argentina 28°0S 56°0W 335 B4
Apostolos Andreas, C. Cyprus 35°42N 34°35E 207 E10
Apostolovo Ukraine 47°39N 33°39E 189 J7
Apoteri Guyana 4°2N 58°32W 329 C6
Appalachian Mts. U.S.A. 38°0N 80°0W 309 G14
Äppelbo Sweden 60°29N 14°1E 162 D8
Appennini Italy 44°30N 10°0E 198 D7
Appennino Ligure Italy 44°30N 9°0E 198 D6
Appenzell-Ausser Rhoden □ Switz. 47°23N 9°23E 179 H5
Appenzell-Inner Rhoden □ Switz. 47°20N 9°25E 179 H5
Appiano Italy 46°28N 11°15E 199 B8
Apple Hill Canada 45°13N 74°46W 313 A10
Apple Valley U.S.A. 34°32N 117°14W 307 L9
Appleby-in-Westmorland U.K. 54°35N 2°29W 168 C5
Appledore U.K. 51°3N 4°13W 169 F3
Appleton U.S.A. 44°16N 88°25W 308 C9
Appleton City U.S.A. 38°11N 94°2W 310 F2
Appleton Rum Distillery Jamaica 18°10N 77°44W 320 a
Appling U.S.A. 33°33N 82°19W 316 B7
Approuague Fr. Guiana 4°20N 52°0W 329 C7
Apra Harbor Guam 13°26N 144°40E 302 d
Apra Heights Guam 13°23N 144°42E 302 d
Apricena Italy 41°47N 15°27E 199 G12
April → Papua N. G. 4°18S 142°26E 286 C2
Aprilia Italy 41°36N 12°39E 200 A5
Apsheronsk Russia 44°28N 39°42E 191 H4
Apsley Canada 44°45N 78°6W 312 B6
Apt France 43°53N 5°24E 175 E9
Apterkarskiy Ostrov Russia 59°57N 30°20E 137 B2
Apuane, Alpi Italy 44°7N 10°14E 198 D7
Apuaú Brazil 2°25S 60°53W 329 D5
Apucarana Brazil 23°55S 51°33W 335 A5
Apulia = Púglia □ Italy 41°15N 16°15E 201 A9
Apurashokoru Palau 7°16N 134°17E 288 c
Apurauan Phil. 9°35N 118°20E 233 G2
Apure □ Venezuela 7°10N 68°50W 328 B4
Apure → Venezuela 7°37N 66°25W 328 B4
Apurímac □ Peru 14°0S 73°0W 330 C3
Apurímac → Peru 12°17S 73°56W 330 C3
Apuseni, Munţii Romania 46°30N 22°45E 182 D7
Āq Qālā Iran 37°10N 54°30E 247 B7
Aqaba = Al 'Aqabah Jordan 29°31N 35°0E 251 J6
Aqaba, G. of Red Sea 29°0N 34°40E 251 K5
'Aqabah, Khalīj al = Aqaba, G. of Red Sea 29°0N 34°40E 251 K5
Aqadyr Kazakhstan 48°17N 74°50E 217 C8
Āqchah Afghan. 36°56N 66°11E 240 A2
'Aqdā Iran 32°26N 53°37E 247 C7
Aqiq Sudan 18°14N 38°12E 256 D4
Aqīq, Khalīg Sudan 18°20N 38°10E 256 D4
'Aqiq, W. al → Si. Arabia 20°16N 41°40E 248 B3
Aqköl Kazakhstan 51°59N 70°56E 217 B8
Aqmola = Astana Kazakhstan 51°10N 71°30E 217 B8
Aqmola □ Kazakhstan 51°30N 70°0E 217 B8
'Aqrah Iraq 36°46N 43°45E 213 D10
Aqsay Kazakhstan 51°11N 53°0E 187 D9
Aqshataū Kazakhstan 47°59N 74°3E 217 C8
Aqsū Ongtüstik Qazaqstan, Kazakhstan 42°25N 69°50E 217 D7
Aqsū Pavlodar, Kazakhstan 52°2N 76°55E 217 B9
Aqsūgek Kazakhstan 44°37N 74°30E 217 D8
Aqtaū Mangghystaū, Kazakhstan 43°39N 51°12E 187 F9
Aqtaū Qaraghandy, Kazakhstan 50°17N 73°6E 217 B8
Aqtöbe Kazakhstan 50°17N 57°10E 187 D10
Aqtoghay Kazakhstan 46°57N 79°40E 217 C9
Aquarium of the Americas New Orleans, U.S.A. 131 b3
Aquidauana Brazil 20°30S 55°50W 331 E6
Aquidauana → Brazil 19°44S 56°50W 331 D6
Aquila Mexico 18°36N 103°30W 318 D4
Aquiles Serdán Mexico 28°36N 105°53W 318 B3
Aquin Haiti 18°16N 73°24W 321 C5
Aquitain, Bassin France 44°0N 0°30W 171 D3
Aquitaine □ France 44°25N 0°30W 174 D3
Ar Horqin Qi China 43°45N 120°0E 227 C11
Ar Kazimiyah Iraq 33°22N 44°20E 113 B1
Ar Rafid Syria 32°57N 35°52E 250 F6
Ar Raḥḥālīyah Iraq 32°44N 43°23E 213 F10
Ar Ram West Bank 31°51N 35°15E 123 A2
Ar Ramādī Iraq 33°25N 43°20E 213 F10
Ar Raml Libya 26°45N 19°40E 258 C3
Ar Ramthā Jordan 32°34N 36°0E 251 F7
Ar Raqqah Syria 35°59N 39°8E 213 E8
Ar Raqqah □ Syria 36°20N 39°10E 213 D8
Ar Rashidiya = Er Rachidia Morocco 31°58N 4°20W 260 B4
Ar Rass Si. Arabia 25°50N 43°40E 246 E4
Ar Rastan Syria 34°55N 36°43E 250 D7
Ar Rawḍah Si. Arabia 21°16N 42°50E 248 B3
Ar Rawḍah Yemen 14°28N 47°17E 248 D4
Ar Rayyan Qatar 25°17N 51°25E 247 E6
Ar Rifā'ī Iraq 31°50N 46°10E 246 D5
Ar Rijā' Yemen 13°1N 44°35E 248 D4
Ar Riyāḍ Si. Arabia 24°41N 46°42E 246 E5
Ar Riyāḍ □ Si. Arabia 23°0N 45°50E 248 B4
Ar Riyān Yemen 14°39N 49°19E 267 B6
Ar Rmās, W. → Syria 35°47N 36°50E 250 C7
Ar Ru'ays Qatar 26°8N 51°12E 247 E6
Ar Rukhaymīyah Iraq 29°22N 45°38E 246 D5
Ar Rumaythah Iraq 31°31N 45°12E 246 D5
Ar Ruṣāfah Syria 35°45N 38°49E 213 E8
Ar Ruṭbah Iraq 33°0N 40°15E 213 F9
Ar Ruwayḍah Si. Arabia 23°40N 44°40E 248 B4
Ara India 25°35N 84°32E 243 G11
Ara → Japan 35°41N 139°50E 140 A4
Ara Goro Ethiopia 5°48N 41°18E 257 F5
Ara Tera Ethiopia 6°38N 40°57E 257 F5
Arab U.S.A. 34°19N 86°30W 315 D11
'Arab, Bahr el → Sudan 9°0N 29°30E 257 F2
Arab, Khalîg el Egypt 30°55N 29°0E 256 A2
Arab, Shatt al → Asia 29°57N 48°34E 247 D6
'Araba, W. → Egypt 28°19N 33°31E 256 J8
'Arabābād Iran 33°2N 57°41E 247 C8
'Arabah, W. → Yemen 18°5N 51°26E 249 C5
Araban Turkey 37°28N 37°44E 212 D7
Arabatskaya Strelka Ukraine 45°40N 35°0E 189 K8
Arabba Italy 46°30N 11°52E 199 B8
Arabelo Venezuela 4°55N 64°13W 329 C5
Arabi U.S.A. 31°50N 83°44W 316 D6
Arabia Asia 25°0N 45°0E 210 F6
Arabian Basin Ind. Oc. 11°30N 65°0E 273 C5
Arabian Desert = Es Sahrâ' Esh Sharqîya Egypt 27°30N 32°30E 256 B3
Arabian Gulf = Persian Gulf Asia 27°0N 50°0E 247 E6
Arabian Sea Ind. Oc. 16°0N 65°0E 238 F9
Arabistan = Khūzestān □ Iran 31°0N 49°0E 247 D6
Araç Turkey 41°15N 33°21E 212 B5
Aracaju Brazil 10°55S 37°4W 332 D4
Aracataca Colombia 10°38N 74°9W 328 A3
Aracati Brazil 4°30S 37°44W 332 B4
Araçatuba Brazil 21°10S 50°30W 335 A5
Araceli Phil. 10°33N 119°59E 233 F2
Aracena Spain 37°53N 6°38W 195 H4
Aracena, Sierra de Spain 37°50N 6°50W 195 H4
Arachova Greece 38°28N 22°35E 204 C4
Arachthos → Greece 39°20N 21°4E 204 B3
Aracides, C. Solomon Is. 8°21S 161°0E 287 M11
Aračinovo Macedonia 42°1N 21°34E 202 D5
Araçuaí Brazil 16°52S 42°4W 333 E3
Araçuaí → Brazil 16°46S 42°2W 333 E3
'Arad Israel 31°15N 35°12E 251 G6
Arad Romania 46°10N 21°20E 182 D6
Arad □ Romania 46°20N 22°0E 182 D6
Arada Chad 15°0N 20°20E 259 E4
Arādān Iran 35°21N 52°30E 247 C7
Aradhippou Cyprus 34°57N 33°36E 207 F9
Arafura Sea E. Indies 9°0S 135°0E 288 H5
Aragarças Brazil 15°55S 52°15W 331 D7
Aragats Armenia 40°30N 44°15E 191 K7
Aragon U.S.A. 34°2N 85°3W 316 A4
Aragón □ Spain 41°25N 0°40W 196 D4
Aragón → Spain 42°13N 1°44W 196 C3
Aragona Italy 37°24N 13°27E 200 E6
Aragua □ Venezuela 10°0N 67°10W 328 B4
Aragua de Barcelona Venezuela 9°28N 64°49W 329 B5
Araguacema Brazil 8°50S 49°20W 332 C2
Araguaçu = Paraguaçu Paulista Brazil 22°22S 50°35W 335 A5
Araguaçu Brazil 12°49S 49°51W 333 D2
Araguaia → Brazil 5°21S 48°41W 332 C2
Araguaia △ Brazil 10°30S 50°0W 332 D1
Araguaiana Brazil 15°43S 51°51W 331 D7
Araguaína Brazil 7°12S 48°12W 332 C2
Araguari Brazil 18°38S 48°11W 333 E2
Araguari → Brazil 1°15N 49°55W 329 C8
Araguatins Brazil 5°38S 48°7W 332 C2
Arahal Spain 37°15N 5°33W 195 H5
Arain India 26°27N 75°2E 242 F6
Araioses Brazil 2°53S 41°55W 332 B3
Arak Algeria 25°20N 3°45E 261 C5
Arāk Iran 34°0N 49°40E 247 C6
Araka Sudan 4°20N 30°23E 257 G3
Arakan □ Burma 19°0N 94°15E 241 F5
Arakan Coast Burma 19°0N 94°0E 241 F5
Arakan Yoma Burma 20°0N 94°40E 241 F5
Arakawa Japan 35°44N 139°48E 140 A3
Arakkonam India 13°7N 79°43E 245 H4
Araklı Turkey 41°6N 40°2E 213 B9
Araks = Aras, Rūd-e → Asia 40°5N 48°29E 213 B13
Araks → Iran 39°10N 47°10E 216 E3
Aral Kazakhstan 46°41N 61°45E 216 C6
Aral Mangy Qaraqumy Kazakhstan 46°50N 63°10E 216 C6
Aral Sea Asia 44°30N 60°0E 216 C5
Aral Tengizi = Aral Sea Asia 44°30N 60°0E 216 C5
Aralık Turkey 39°52N 44°31E 213 C11
Aralqum Asia 44°30N 60°35E 216 D6
Aralsk = Aral Kazakhstan 46°41N 61°45E 216 C6
Aralskoye More = Aral Sea Asia 44°30N 60°0E 216 C5
Aralsor, Ozero = Aralsor Köli Kazakhstan 49°5N 48°12E 191 F9
Aralsor Köli Kazakhstan 49°5N 48°12E 191 F9
Aramac Australia 22°58S 145°14E 280 C4
Aramia → Papua N. G. 7°55S 143°22E 286 D2
Aran → India 19°55N 78°12E 244 E4
Aran Areh Ethiopia 9°2N 43°54E 267 C5
Aran I. Ireland 55°0N 8°30W 166 A3
Aran Is. Ireland 53°6N 9°38W 166 C2
Aranda de Duero Spain 41°39N 3°42W 194 D7
Arandān Iran 35°23N 46°55E 246 C5
Aranđelovac Serbia 44°18N 20°34E 202 B4
Aranga N.Z. 35°44S 173°40E 284 B2
Arani Bolivia 17°34S 65°46W 331 D4
Arani India 12°43N 79°19E 245 H4
Aranjuez Spain 40°1N 3°40W 194 E7
Aranos Namibia 24°9S 19°7E 270 B2
Aransas Pass U.S.A. 27°55N 97°9W 314 H6
Arany-hegyi-patak → Hungary 47°34N 19°4E 117 A2
Aranyaprathet Thailand 13°41N 102°30E 236 F4
Arao Japan 32°59N 130°25E 222 E2
Araouane Mali 18°55N 3°30W 262 B4
Arapahoe U.S.A. 40°18N 99°54W 308 E4
Arapari Brazil 5°34S 49°15W 332 C2
Arapawa I. N.Z. 41°11S 174°17E 285 B9
Arapey Grande → Uruguay 30°55S 57°49W 334 C4
Arapgir Turkey 39°5N 38°30E 213 C8
Arapiraca Brazil 9°45S 36°39W 332 C4
Arapis, Akra Greece 40°27N 24°0E 203 F8
Arapongas Brazil 23°29S 51°28W 335 A5
Arapuni N.Z. 38°4S 175°39E 284 E4
Ar'ar Si. Arabia 30°59N 41°2E 246 D4
Araracuara Colombia 0°24S 72°17W 328 D3
Araranguá Brazil 29°0S 49°30W 335 B6
Araraquara Brazil 21°50S 48°0W 333 F2
Araras Brazil 22°22S 47°23W 333 F2
Ararás, Serra das Brazil 25°0S 53°10W 335 B5
Ararat Armenia 39°48N 44°50E 213 C11
Ararat Vic., Australia 37°16S 142°58E 282 D5
Ararat, Mt. = Ağrı Dağı Turkey 39°50N 44°15E 213 C11
Arari Brazil 3°28S 44°47W 332 B3
Araria India 26°9N 87°33E 243 F12
Araripe, Chapada do Brazil 7°20S 40°0W 332 C4
Araripina Brazil 7°33S 40°34W 332 C3
Araruama, L. de Brazil 22°53S 42°12W 333 F3
Araruna Brazil 6°52S 35°44W 332 C4
Aras, Rūd-e → Asia 40°5N 48°29E 213 B13
Aratâne Mauritania 18°24N 8°32W 262 B3
Araticu = Oeiras do Pará Brazil 1°58S 49°51W 329 D8
Arauca Colombia 7°0N 70°40W 328 B3
Arauca □ Colombia 6°40N 71°0W 328 B3
Arauca → Venezuela 7°24N 66°35W 328 B4
Arauco Chile 37°16S 73°25W 334 D1
Araújos Brazil 19°56S 45°14W 333 E2
Arauquita Colombia 7°2N 71°25W 328 B3
Araure Venezuela 9°34N 69°13W 328 B4
Aravaca Spain 40°27N 3°47W 127 B1
Aravalli Range India 25°0N 73°30E 242 G5
Arawa Ethiopia 9°57N 41°58E 257 F5
Arawale △ Kenya 1°24S 40°9E 268 C5
Arawe Is. Papua N. G. 6°6S 149°0E 286 D5
Arawhata → N.Z. 44°0S 168°40E 285 E3
Araxá Brazil 19°35S 46°55W 333 E2
Araya, Pen. de Venezuela 10°40N 64°0W 329 A5
Arayat Phil. 15°10N 120°46E 232 D3
Arba Gugu Ethiopia 8°40N 40°15E 257 F5
Arba Minch Ethiopia 6°0N 37°30E 257 F4
Arbat Iraq 35°25N 45°35E 213 E11
Arbataash Iraq 33°20N 44°19E 113 A1
Árbatax Italy 39°56N 9°42E 200 C2
Arbi Ethiopia 9°4N 35°7E 257 F4
Arbīl Iraq 36°15N 44°5E 213 D11
Arbīl □ Iraq 36°20N 44°20E 213 D11
Arboga Sweden 59°24N 15°52E 162 E9
Arbois France 46°55N 5°46E 173 F12
Arboletes Colombia 8°51N 76°26W 328 B2
Arbore Ethiopia 5°3N 36°50E 257 F4
Arborea Italy 39°46N 8°35E 200 C1
Arborfield Canada 53°6N 103°39W 297 C8
Arborg Canada 50°54N 97°13W 297 C9
Arbre du Ténéré Niger 17°50N 10°4E 259 E2
Arbroath U.K. 56°34N 2°35W 167 E6
Arbuckle U.S.A. 39°1N 122°3W 306 F4
Arbus Italy 39°30N 8°33E 200 C1
Arc → France 45°34N 6°12E 175 C10
Arc de Triomphe Paris, France 134 a2
Arc-lès-Gray France 47°28N 5°34E 173 E12
Arcachon France 44°40N 1°10W 174 D2
Arcachon, Bassin d' France 44°42N 1°10W 174 D2
Arcade U.S.A. 42°32N 78°25W 312 D6
Arcadia Calif., U.S.A. 34°7N 118°1W 126 B4
Arcadia Fla., U.S.A. 27°13N 81°52W 317 H8
Arcadia Ind., U.S.A. 40°11N 86°1W 311 D10
Arcadia Iowa, U.S.A. 42°5N 95°3W 310 B1
Arcadia La., U.S.A. 32°33N 92°55W 314 E8
Arcadia Pa., U.S.A. 40°47N 78°51W 312 F6
Arcanum U.S.A. 39°59N 84°33W 311 E12
Arcata U.S.A. 40°52N 124°5W 304 F1
Arcévia Italy 43°30N 12°56E 199 E9
Archanes Greece 35°16N 25°11E 205 F7
Archangel = Arkhangelsk Russia 64°38N 40°36E 186 B7
Archangelos Preveza, Greece 39°6N 20°42E 207 A2
Archangelos Rhodes, Greece 36°13N 28°7E 206 E12
Archar Bulgaria 43°50N 22°54E 202 C6
Archbald U.S.A. 41°30N 75°32W 313 E9
Archbold U.S.A. 41°31N 84°18W 311 C12
Archena Spain 38°9N 1°16W 197 G3
Archenu, J. Libya 22°15N 24°45E 259 D4
Archer U.S.A. 29°32N 82°32W 317 F7
Archer → Australia 13°28S 141°41E 280 A3
Archer B. Australia 13°20S 141°30E 280 A3
Archer Bend = Mungkan Kandju △ Australia 13°35S 142°52E 280 A3
Archers Post Kenya 0°35N 37°35E 268 B4
Arches △ U.S.A. 38°45N 109°25W 304 G9
Archidona Spain 37°6N 4°22W 195 H6
Archipel-de-Mingan △ Canada 50°13N 63°10W 299 B7
Archipiélago Chinijo △ Canary Is. 29°20N 13°30W 153 e2
Archipiélago Los Roques △ Venezuela 11°50N 66°44W 321 D6
Archives Navy Memorial Washington, D.C., U.S.A. 143 b2
Arci, Mte. Italy 39°47N 8°45E 200 C1
Arcidosso Italy 42°52N 11°32E 199 F8
Arcila = Asilah Morocco 35°29N 6°0W 260 A3
Arcipelago de la Maddalena △ Italy 41°14N 9°24E 200 A2
Arcipelago Toscano △ Italy 42°45N 10°15E 198 F7
Arcis-sur-Aube France 48°32N 4°10E 173 D11
Arckaringa Cr. → Australia 28°10S 135°22E 281 D2
Arco Italy 45°55N 10°53E 198 C7
Arco Idaho, U.S.A. 43°38N 113°18W 304 E7
Arco Plaza Los Angeles, U.S.A. 127 b1
Arcola U.S.A. 39°41N 88°19W 311 E8
Arcoona Australia 31°2S 137°1E 282 A2
Arcos de Jalón Spain 41°12N 2°16W 196 D2
Arcos de la Frontera Spain 36°45N 5°49W 195 J5
Arcos de Valdevez Portugal 41°55N 8°22W 194 D2
Arcot India 12°53N 79°20E 245 H4
Arcoverde Brazil 8°25S 37°4W 332 C4
Arcozelo Portugal 40°32N 7°47W 194 E3
Arctic Bay Canada 73°1N 85°7W 295 C14
Arctic Mid-Ocean Ridge Arctic 87°0N 90°0E 150 A
Arctic Ocean Arctic 78°0N 160°0W 150 B18
Arctic Red River = Tsiigehtchic Canada 67°15N 134°0W 294 D5
Arctic Village U.S.A. 68°8N 145°32W 303 B11
Arctowski Antarctica 62°30S 58°0W 151 C18
Arcueil France 48°48N 2°19E 134 B2
Arda → Bulgaria 41°40N 26°30E 203 E10
Arda → Italy 45°2N 10°2E 198 C7
Ardabīl Iran 38°15N 48°18E 213 C13
Ardabīl □ Iran 38°15N 48°20E 247 B6
Ardahan Turkey 41°7N 42°41E 213 B10
Ardahan □ Turkey 41°10N 42°50E 213 B10
Ardakān = Sepīdān Iran 30°20N 52°5E 247 D7
Ardakān Iran 32°19N 53°59E 247 C7
Ardala Sweden 58°22N 13°19E 163 F7
Ardales Spain 36°53N 4°51W 195 J6
Årdalstangen Norway 61°14N 7°43E 164 C4
Ardara Ireland 54°46N 8°25W 166 B3
Ardas → Greece 41°40N 26°30E 203 E10
Ardèche □ France 44°42N 4°16E 175 D8
Ardèche → France 44°16N 4°39E 175 D8
Ardee Ireland 53°52N 6°33W 166 C5
Arden Ont., Canada 44°43N 76°56W 312 B8
Arden Denmark 56°46N 9°52E 163 H3
Arden Calif., U.S.A. 38°36N 121°33W 306 G5
Arden Nev., U.S.A. 36°1N 115°14W 307 J11
Ardenne Belgium 49°50N 5°5E 170 E5
Ardennes = Ardenne Belgium 49°50N 5°5E 170 E5
Ardennes □ France 49°35N 4°40E 173 C11
Ardentes France 46°45N 1°50E 173 F8
Arderin Ireland 53°2N 7°39W 166 C4
Ardeşen Turkey 41°12N 41°2E 213 B9
Ardestān Iran 33°20N 52°25E 247 C7
Ardfert Ireland 52°20N 9°47W 166 D2
Ardglass U.K. 54°17N 5°36W 166 B6
Ardhéa = Aridea Greece 40°58N 22°3E 202 F6
Ardila → Portugal 38°12N 7°28W 195 G3
Ardino Bulgaria 41°34N 25°9E 203 E9
Ardivachar Pt. U.K. 57°23N 7°26W 167 D1
Ardlethan Australia 34°22S 146°53E 283 C7
Ardmore Okla., U.S.A. 34°10N 97°8W 314 D6
Ardmore Pa., U.S.A. 40°2N 75°17W 313 F9
Ardnamurchan, Pt. of U.K. 56°43N 6°14W 167 E2
Ardnave Pt. U.K. 55°53N 6°20W 167 F2
Ardon Russia 43°10N 44°18E 191 J7
Ardore Italy 38°11N 16°10E 201 D9
Ardres France 50°50N 1°59E 173 B8
Ardrossan S. Austral., Australia 34°26S 137°53E 282 C2
Ardrossan N. Ayrs., U.K. 55°39N 4°49W 167 F4
Ards Pen. U.K. 54°33N 5°34W 166 B6
Arduan Sudan 19°54N 30°20E 256 D3
Ardud Romania 47°37N 22°52E 182 C7
Åre Sweden 63°22N 13°15E 162 A7
Arecibo Puerto Rico 18°29N 66°43W 321 C6
Areia Branca Brazil 5°0S 37°0W 332 C4
Arena, Pt. U.S.A. 38°57N 123°44W 306 G3
Arena I. Phil. 9°14N 120°45E 233 G3
Arenal Honduras 15°21N 86°50W 320 C2
Arenales, Cerro Chile 47°5S 73°40W 336 C2
Arenápolis Brazil 14°26S 56°49W 331 C6
Arenas = Las Arenas Spain 43°17N 4°50W 194 B6
Arenas, Pta. Venezuela 10°31N 64°14W 329 A5
Arenas de San Pedro Spain 40°12N 5°5W 194 E5
Arendal Norway 58°28N 8°46E 164 F5
Arendsee Germany 52°52N 11°27E 178 C7
Arenillas Ecuador 3°33S 80°10W 328 D1
Arensburg = Kuressaare Estonia 58°15N 22°30E 188 C2
Arenys de Mar Spain 41°35N 2°33E 196 D7
Arenzano Italy 44°24N 8°41E 198 D5
Arenzville U.S.A. 39°53N 90°22W 310 E6
Areopoli Greece 36°40N 22°22E 204 E4
Arequipa Peru 16°20S 71°30W 330 D3
Arequipa □ Peru 16°0S 72°50W 330 D3
Arere Brazil 0°16S 53°52W 329 D7
Arero Ethiopia 4°41N 38°50E 257 G4
Arès France 44°47N 1°8W 174 D2
Arese Italy 45°32N 9°4E 129 A1
Arévalo Spain 41°3N 4°43W 194 D6
Arezzo Italy 43°25N 11°53E 199 E8
Arga Turkey 38°21N 37°59E 246 B3
Arga → Spain 42°18N 1°47W 196 C3
Argalasti Greece 39°13N 23°13E 204 B5
Argamasilla de Alba Spain 39°8N 3°5W 195 F7
Argamasilla de Calatrava Spain 38°44N 4°4W 195 G6
Arganda del Rey Spain 40°19N 3°26W 194 E7
Arganil Portugal 40°13N 8°3W 194 E2
Arganzuela Spain 40°23N 3°42W 127 B1
Argao Phil. 9°52N 123°36E 233 G4
Argarapa ✪ Australia 22°20S 134°58E 280 C1
Argasi Greece 37°45N 20°56E 207 D2
Argedeb Ethiopia 6°11N 41°13E 257 F5
Argelès-Gazost France 43°0N 0°6W 174 E3
Argelès-sur-Mer France 42°34N 3°1E 174 F7
Argens → France 43°24N 6°44E 175 E10
Argent-sur-Sauldre France 47°33N 2°25E 173 E9
Argenta = North Little Rock U.S.A. 34°45N 92°16W 314 D8
Argenta B.C., Canada 50°11N 116°56W 296 C5
Argenta Italy 44°37N 11°50E 199 D8
Argenta Ill., U.S.A. 39°59N 88°49W 311 E8
Argentan France 48°45N 0°1W 172 D6
Argentário, Mte. Italy 42°24N 11°9E 199 F8
Argentat France 45°6N 1°56E 174 C5
Argentera Italy 44°24N 6°56E 198 D4
Argenteuil France 48°56N 2°15E 134 A2
Argentia Canada 47°18N 53°58W 299 C9
Argentiera, C. dell' Italy 40°44N 8°8E 200 B1
Argentina ■ S. Amer. 35°0S 66°0W 327 G4
Argentine Abyssal Plain Atl. Oc. 47°0S 50°0W 152 L6
Argentine Basin Atl. Oc. 45°0S 45°0W 152 L7
Argentino, L. Argentina 50°10S 73°0W 336 D2
Argenton-Château France 46°59N 0°27W 172 F6
Argenton-sur-Creuse France 46°36N 1°30E 173 F8
Argeş □ Romania 45°0N 24°45E 183 F9
Argeş → Romania 44°5N 26°38E 183 F11
Arghandab → Afghan. 31°30N 64°15E 242 D1
Argheile Ethiopia 5°19N 42°4E 257 F5
Argirades Greece 39°27N 19°58E 206 C9
Argiroupoli Athina, Greece 37°52N 23°44E 112 B2
Argiroupoli Kriti, Greece 35°17N 24°20E 207 E5
Argo Sudan 19°28N 30°30E 256 D3
Argolida □ Greece 37°38N 22°50E 204 D4
Argolikos Kolpos Greece 37°20N 22°52E 204 D4
Argonne France 49°10N 5°0E 173 C12
Argonne Forest U.S.A. 41°42N 87°53W 119 C1
Argos Greece 37°40N 22°43E 204 D4
Argos Ind., U.S.A. 41°14N 86°15W 311 C10
Argos Orestiko Greece 40°27N 21°18E 202 F5
Argostoli Greece 38°11N 20°29E 207 C2
Argostoliou, Kolpos Greece 38°10N 20°27E 207 C1
Arguedas Spain 42°11N 1°36W 196 C3
Argüelles Madrid, Spain 127 a1
Arguello, Pt. U.S.A. 34°35N 120°39W 307 L6
Arguineguín Canary Is. 27°46N 15°41W 153 e1
Argun Russia 43°18N 45°52E 191 J7
Argun → Russia 53°20N 121°28E 219 A13
Argungu Nigeria 12°40N 4°31E 263 C5
Argus Pk. U.S.A. 35°52N 117°26W 307 K9
Argyle, L. Australia 16°20S 128°40E 278 C4
Argyle Waterfalls Trin. & Tob. 11°15N 60°35W 323 s
Argyll U.K. 56°6N 5°0W 167 E4
Argyll & Bute □ U.K. 56°13N 5°28W 167 E3
Arhavi Turkey 41°21N 41°18E 213 B9
Århus Denmark 56°8N 10°11E 163 H4
Ari Atoll Maldives 3°53N 72°50E 272 d
Aria N.Z. 38°33S 175°0E 284 E4
Ariadnoye Russia 45°8N 134°25E 220 B7
Ariamsvlei Namibia 28°9S 19°51E 270 C2
Ariana Tunisia 36°52N 10°12E 258 A2
Ariana □ Tunisia 36°50N 9°52E 261 A6
Ariano Irpino Italy 41°9N 15°5E 201 A8
Ariari → Colombia 2°35N 72°47W 328 C3
Aribinda Burkina Faso 14°17N 0°52W 263 C4
Arica Chile 18°32S 70°20W 330 D3
Arica Colombia 2°0S 71°50W 328 D3
Arica y Parinacota □ Chile 17°40S 69°50W 330 D4
Arico Canary Is. 28°9N 16°29W 153 e1
Arid, C. Australia 34°1S 123°10E 279 F3
Arida Japan 34°5N 135°8E 223 C7
Aridal W. Sahara 25°59N 13°54W 260 C2
Aride Seychelles 4°13S 55°40E 272 c
Aridea Greece 40°58N 22°3E 202 F6
Ariège □ France 42°56N 1°30E 174 F5
Ariège → France 43°30N 1°25E 174 E5
Arieş → Romania 46°24N 23°20E 183 D8
Arigat el Fersig Algeria 27°35N 2°7W 261 C4
Arīḥā Israel 31°51N 35°27E 256 A4
Arīḥā Syria 35°49N 36°35E 250 C7
Arikok △ Aruba 12°31N 69°56W 322 f
Arila, Akra Greece 39°43N 19°39E 206 B9
Arilje Serbia 43°44N 20°7E 202 C4
Arima Kanagawa, Japan 35°33N 139°33E 140 B2
Arima Trin. & Tob. 10°38N 61°17W 323 t
Arima → Trin. & Tob. 10°35N 61°16W 323 t
Aringay Phil. 16°26N 120°21E 232 C3
Arinos → Brazil 10°25S 58°20W 331 C6
Ario de Rosales Mexico 19°12N 101°43W 318 D4
Ariogala Lithuania 55°16N 23°28E 184 C10
Arios Pagos Athens, Greece 112 c1
Aripo → Trin. & Tob. 10°35N 61°14W 323 t
Aripo, Mt. Trin. & Tob. 10°45N 61°15W 323 t
Aripo Caves Trin. & Tob. 10°43N 61°14W 323 t
Aripuanã Brazil 9°25S 60°30W 331 B5
Aripuanã → Brazil 5°7S 60°25W 331 B5
Ariquemes Brazil 9°55S 63°6W 331 B5
Arisaig U.K. 56°55N 5°51W 167 E3
Arish, W. el → Egypt 31°9N 33°49E 256 A3
Arissa Ethiopia 11°10N 41°35E 257 E5
Aristazabal I. Canada 52°40N 129°10W 296 C3
Arita Japan 33°11N 129°54E 222 D1
Aritao Phil. 16°18N 121°2E 232 C3
Ariton U.S.A. 31°36N 85°43W 316 D4
Arivonimamo Madag. 19°1S 47°11E 272 B2
Ariyalur India 11°8N 79°8E 245 J4
Ariza Spain 41°19N 2°3W 196 D2
Arizaro, Salar de Argentina 24°40S 67°50W 334 A2
Arizona Argentina 35°45S 65°25W 334 D2
Arizona □ U.S.A. 34°0N 112°0W 305 J8
Arizpe Mexico 30°20N 110°10W 318 A2
'Arjah Si. Arabia 24°43N 44°17E 246 E5
Årjäng Sweden 59°24N 12°8E 162 E6
Arjeplog Sweden 66°3N 17°54E 160 C17
Arjepluovve = Arjeplog Sweden 66°3N 17°54E 160 C17
Arjona Colombia 10°14N 75°22W 328 A2
Arjona Spain 37°56N 4°4W 195 H6
Arjuna Indonesia 7°49S 112°34E 235 D4
Arka Russia 60°15N 142°0E 215 C15
Arkadak Russia 51°58N 43°30E 190 E6
Arkadelphia U.S.A. 34°7N 93°4W 314 D8
Arkadia □ Greece 37°30N 22°20E 204 D4
Arkaig, L. U.K. 56°59N 5°10W 167 E3
Arkalgud India 12°46N 76°3E 245 H3
Arkalyk = Arqalyk Kazakhstan 50°13N 66°50E 217 B7
Arkansas □ U.S.A. 35°0N 92°30W 314 D8
Arkansas → U.S.A. 33°47N 91°4W 314 E9
Arkansas City U.S.A. 37°4N 97°2W 308 G5
Arkaroola Australia 30°20S 139°22E 281 E2
Arkavāz Iran 33°22N 46°35E 213 F12
Arkhangelsk Russia 64°38N 40°36E 186 B7
Arkhangelskoye Russia 51°32N 40°58E 190 E5
Arkhangelskoye Russia 55°47N 37°17E 129 B1
Arki Greece 37°24N 26°44E 205 D8
Arki India 31°9N 76°58E 242 D7
Arkiko Eritrea 15°33N 39°30E 257 D4
Arklow Ireland 52°48N 6°10W 166 D5
Arkona, Kap Germany 54°42N 13°26E 178 A9
Arkösund Sweden 58°29N 16°56E 163 F10
Arkoudi Greece 38°33N 20°43E 207 B2
Arkport U.S.A. 42°24N 77°42W 312 D7
Arkticheskiy, Mys Russia 81°10N 95°0E 215 A10
Arkul Russia 57°17N 50°3E 190 B10
Arkville U.S.A. 42°9N 74°37W 313 D10
Årla Sweden 59°17N 16°40E 162 E10
Arlanda, Stockholm ✕ (ARN) Sweden 59°41N 17°56E 139 A1
Arlanza → Spain 42°6N 4°9W 194 C6
Arlanzón → Spain 42°3N 4°17W 194 C6
Arlbergpass Austria 47°9N 10°12E 180 D3
Arlbergtunnel Austria 47°9N 10°12E 180 D3
Arles France 43°41N 4°40E 175 E8
Arli Burkina Faso 11°35N 1°28E 263 C5
Arli △ Burkina Faso 11°35N 1°28E 263 C5
Arlington Free State, S. Africa 28°1S 27°53E 271 C4
Arlington Ga., U.S.A. 31°26N 84°44W 316 D5
Arlington Mass., U.S.A. 42°24N 71°10W 116 A1
Arlington N.Y., U.S.A. 41°42N 73°54W 313 E11
Arlington Oreg., U.S.A. 45°43N 120°12W 304 D3
Arlington S. Dak., U.S.A. 44°22N 97°8W 308 C5
Arlington Tex., U.S.A. 32°44N 97°6W 314 E6
Arlington Va., U.S.A. 38°53N 77°7W 143 B3
Arlington Vt., U.S.A. 43°5N 73°9W 313 C11
Arlington Wash., U.S.A. 48°12N 122°8W 306 B4
Arlington Heights Ill., U.S.A. 42°5N 87°59W 311 B9
Arlington Heights Mass., U.S.A. 42°25N 71°10W 116 A1
Arlington Nat. Cemetery U.S.A. 38°52N 77°4W 143 B3
Arlon Belgium 49°42N 5°49E 170 E5
Arlparra Australia 22°11S 134°30E 280 C1
Arltunga Australia 23°26S 134°41E 280 C1
Armação Brazil 22°52S 43°6W 135 B2
Armadale Vic., Australia 37°51S 145°0E 128 B2
Armadale W. Austral., Australia 32°9S 116°0E 279 F2
Armagh U.K. 54°21N 6°39W 166 B5

INDEX
Augathella 345

Armagh □ U.K. 54°18N 6°37W 166 B5
Armagnac France 43°50N 0°10E 174 E4
Armançon → France 47°59N 3°30E 173 E10
Armando Bermudez △ Dom. Rep. 19°3N 71°0W 321 C5
Armant Egypt 25°37N 32°32E 256 B3
Armatree Australia 31°26S 148°28E 283 A8
Armavir Russia 45°2N 41°7E 191 H5
Armenia Colombia 4°35N 75°45W 328 C2
Armenia ■ Asia 40°20N 45°0E 191 K7
Armenian Quarter Jerusalem 123 b3
Armeniş Romania 45°13N 22°17E 182 E7
Armenistis, Akra Greece 36°8N 27°42E 206 E11
Armentières France 50°40N 2°50E 173 B9
Armero Colombia 4°58N 74°54W 328 C3
Armidale Australia 30°30S 151°40E 283 A9
Armilla Spain 37°9N 3°37W 195 H7
ARMM = Muslim Mindanao □ Phil. 8°0N 123°0E 233 H3
Armori India 20°28N 79°59E 244 D4
Armorique ⌓ France 48°22N 3°50W 172 D3
Armour U.S.A. 43°19N 98°21W 308 D4
Armour Heights Canada 43°45N 79°25W 141 A2
Armstrong B.C., Canada 50°25N 119°10W 296 C5
Armstrong Ont., Canada 50°18N 89°4W 298 B2
Armur India 18°48N 78°16E 244 E4
Armutlu Bursa, Turkey 40°31N 28°50E 203 F12
Armutlu İzmir, Turkey 38°24N 27°34E 205 C9
Arnarfjörður Iceland 65°48N 23°40W 155 B3
Arnaud → Canada 59°59N 69°46W 295 F18
Arnauti, C. Cyprus 35°6N 32°17E 207 E8
Arnay-le-Duc France 47°10N 4°27E 173 E11
Arncliffe Australia 33°56S 151°8E 139 B1
Arnea Greece 40°30N 23°38E 202 F7
Arnedillo Spain 42°13N 2°14W 196 C2
Arnedo Spain 42°12N 2°5W 196 C2
Árnes Iceland 66°1N 21°31W 155 A5
Årnes Akershus, Norway 60°7N 11°28E 164 D8
Árnessýsla □ Iceland 64°15N 20°30W 155 C6
Arnett U.S.A. 36°8N 99°46W 314 C5
Arnhem Neths. 51°58N 5°55E 170 C5
Arnhem, C. Australia 12°20S 137°30E 280 A2
Arnhem B. Australia 12°20S 136°10E 280 A2
Arnhem Land Australia 13°10S 134°30E 280 A1
Arnhem Land ◎ Australia 12°50S 134°50E 280 A1
Arnissa Greece 40°47N 21°49E 202 F5
Arno → Italy 43°41N 10°17E 198 E7
Arno Bay Australia 33°54S 136°34E 282 B2
Arnold Notts., U.K. 53°1N 1°7W 168 D6
Arnold Calif., U.S.A. 38°15N 120°21W 306 G6
Arnold Mo., U.S.A. 38°26N 90°23W 310 F6
Arnold Arboretum U.S.A. 42°18N 71°8W 116 B2
Arnoldstein Austria 46°33N 13°43E 180 E6
Arnon → France 47°13N 2°1E 173 E9
Arnos Vale Trin. & Tob. 11°13N 60°45W 323 s
Arnot Canada 55°56N 96°41W 297 B9
Arnøya Norway 70°9N 20°40E 160 A19
Arnprior Canada 45°26N 76°21W 313 A8
Arnsberg Germany 51°24N 8°5E 178 D4
Arnsberger Wald ⌓ Germany 51°25N 8°20E 178 D4
Arnstadt Germany 50°50N 10°56E 178 E6
Arnswalde = Choszczno Poland 53°7N 15°25E 185 E2
Aro → Venezuela 8°1N 64°11W 329 B5
Aroa, Pte. Moorea 17°28S 149°46W 289 e
Aroab Namibia 26°41S 19°39E 270 C2
Aroania Oros Greece 37°56N 22°12E 204 D4
Aroche Spain 37°56N 6°57W 195 H4
Arochuku Nigeria 5°21N 7°54E 263 D6
Aroeiras Brazil 7°31S 35°41W 332 C4
Arolsen Germany 51°23N 9°2E 178 D5
Aron India 25°57N 77°56E 242 G6
Aron → France 46°50N 3°28E 173 F10
Arona Canary Is. 28°6N 16°40W 153 e1
Arona Italy 45°46N 8°34E 198 C5
Arorae Kiribati 2°38S 176°49E 277 A14
Arorangi Cook Is. 21°13S 159°49W 289 h
Aroroy Phil. 12°31N 123°24E 232 E4
Aros → Mexico 29°9N 107°57W 318 B3
Arouca Trin. & Tob. 10°38N 61°20W 323 t
Arousa, Ría de → Spain 42°28N 8°57W 194 C2
Årøysund Norway 59°10N 10°27E 164 E7
Arpa → Asia 39°28N 44°56E 213 C11
Arpaçay Turkey 40°50N 43°19E 213 B10
Árpádföld Hungary 47°32N 19°8E 117 A3
Arpajon France 48°36N 2°15E 173 D9
Arpajon-sur-Cère France 44°53N 2°28E 174 D6
Arpaşu de Jos Romania 45°47N 24°37E 183 E9
Arqalyk Kazakhstan 50°13N 66°50E 217 B7
Arque Bolivia 17°48S 66°23W 330 D4
Arrah = Ara India 25°35N 84°32E 243 G11
Arrah Ivory C. 6°40N 3°58W 262 D4
Arraias Brazil 12°56S 46°57W 333 D2
Arraias → Mato Grosso, Brazil 11°10S 53°35W 331 C7
Arraias → Pará, Brazil 7°30S 49°20W 332 C2
Arraijan Panama 8°56N 79°36W 320 c
Arraiolos Portugal 38°44N 7°59W 195 G3
Arran U.K. 55°34N 5°12W 167 F3
Arras France 50°17N 2°46E 173 B9
Arrasate Spain 43°4N 2°30W 196 B2
Arrats → France 44°6N 0°52E 174 D4
Arreau France 42°54N 0°22E 174 F4
Arrecife Canary Is. 28°57N 13°37W 153 e2
Arrecifes Argentina 34°6S 60°9W 334 C3
Arrée, Mts. d' France 48°26N 3°55W 172 D3
Arrentela Portugal 38°37N 9°6W 126 B2
Arresø Denmark 55°58N 12°6E 163 J6
Arriaga Mexico 16°14N 93°54W 319 D6
Arribes del Duero ⌓ Spain 41°11N 6°39W 194 D4
Arrilalah Australia 23°43S 143°54E 280 C3
Arrino Australia 29°30S 115°40E 279 E2
Arriondas Spain 43°23N 5°11W 194 B5
Arrojado → Brazil 13°24S 44°20W 333 D3
Arromanches-les-Bains France 49°20N 0°38W 172 C6
Arronches Portugal 39°8N 7°16W 195 F3
Arros → France 43°40N 0°2W 174 E3
Arrow, L. Ireland 54°3N 8°19W 166 B3
Arrowsmith, Mt. N.Z. 43°20S 170°55E 285 D5
Arrowtown N.Z. 44°57S 168°50E 285 E3
Arroyo de la Luz Spain 39°30N 6°38W 195 F4
Arroyo del Puerco = Arroyo de la Luz Spain 39°30N 6°38W 195 F4
Arroyo Grande U.S.A. 35°7N 120°35W 307 K6
Arroyo Seco Park U.S.A. 34°6N 118°11W 126 B3
Ars Iran 37°9N 47°46E 246 B5
Ars-sur-Moselle France 49°5N 6°4E 173 C13
Arsenault L. Canada 55°6N 108°32W 297 B7
Arsenev Russia 44°10N 133°15E 220 B6
Arsi Ethiopia 7°45N 39°0E 257 F4
Arsiero Italy 45°48N 11°21E 199 C8
Arsikere India 13°15N 76°15E 245 H3
Arsin Turkey 41°8N 39°55E 213 B8
Arsk Russia 56°10N 49°50E 190 B9
Arslanköy Turkey 37°0N 34°17E 250 B5
Årsta Sweden 59°17N 18°3E 139 B2
Årsunda Sweden 60°31N 16°45E 162 D10
Art, Î. N. Cal. 19°43S 163°38E 288 d
Arta Greece 39°8N 21°2E 204 B3
Artà Spain 39°41N 3°21E 206 B4
Arta □ Greece 39°15N 21°5E 204 B3
Artà, Coves d Spain 39°40N 3°24E 206 B4
Artane Ireland 53°22N 6°12W 120 A2
Artas West Bank 31°41N 35°11E 123 B2
Artashat Armenia 40°0N 44°35E 213 B11
Arteaga Mexico 18°28N 102°25W 318 D4
Arteche Phil. 12°17N 125°22E 232 E5
Arteijo = Arteixo Spain 43°19N 8°29W 194 B2
Arteixo Spain 43°19N 8°29W 194 B2
Artem = Artyom Azerbaijan 40°28N 50°20E 191 K10
Artem Russia 43°22N 132°13E 220 C6
Artemovsk Sib., Russia 54°45N 93°35E 215 D10
Artemovsk Ukraine 48°35N 38°0E 189 H9
Artemovskiy Russia 47°45N 40°16E 191 G5
Artenay France 48°5N 1°50E 173 D8
Artern Germany 51°22N 11°18E 178 D7
Artesa de Segre Spain 41°54N 1°3E 196 D6
Artesia = Mosomane Botswana 24°2S 26°19E 270 B4
Artesia U.S.A. 32°51N 104°24W 305 K11
Arthington Liberia 6°35N 10°45W 262 D2
Arthur Ont., Canada 43°50N 80°32W 312 C4
Arthur Ill., U.S.A. 39°43N 88°28W 311 E8
Arthur → Australia 41°2S 144°40E 281 G3
Arthur Cr. → Australia 22°30S 136°25E 280 C2
Arthur Pt. Australia 22°7S 150°3E 280 C5
Arthur River Australia 33°20S 117°2E 279 F2
Arthur's Pass N.Z. 42°54S 171°35E 285 C6
Arthur's Pass △ N.Z. 42°53S 171°42E 285 C6
Arthur's Seat U.K. 55°56N 3°9W 121 B3
Arthur's Town Bahamas 24°38N 75°42W 321 B4
Artigas = Río Branco Uruguay 32°40S 53°40W 335 C5
Artigas Antarctica 62°30S 58°0W 151 C18
Artigas Uruguay 30°20S 56°30W 334 C4
Artik Armenia 40°38N 43°58E 191 K6
Artillery L. Canada 63°9N 107°52W 297 A7
Artois France 50°20N 2°30E 173 B9
Artotina Greece 38°42N 22°2E 204 C4
Artova Turkey 40°5N 36°28E 212 B7
Artrutx, C. de Spain 39°55N 3°49E 206 B4
Arts, Place des Montréal, Canada 130 b2
Arts Bogd Uul Mongolia 44°40N 102°20E 226 B2
Artsyz Ukraine 46°4N 29°26E 183 D14
Artux China 39°40N 76°10E 217 E9
Artvin Turkey 41°14N 41°44E 213 B9
Artvin □ Turkey 41°10N 41°50E 213 B9
Artyk Russia 64°12N 145°6E 215 C15
Artyom Azerbaijan 40°28N 50°20E 191 K10
Aru, Kepulauan Indonesia 6°0S 134°30E 231 F8
Aru Is. = Aru, Kepulauan Indonesia 6°0S 134°30E 231 F8
Arua Uganda 3°1N 30°58E 268 B3
Aruanã Brazil 14°54S 51°10W 333 D1
Aruba ☑ W. Indies 12°30N 70°0W 322 f
Arudy France 43°7N 0°28W 174 E3
Arué Tahiti 17°31S 149°30W 289 e
Arumã Brazil 4°44S 62°8W 329 D5
Arume-wan Japan 26°35N 128°8E 288 a
Arumpo Australia 33°48S 142°55E 282 B5
Arun Bangkok, Thailand 113 b1
Arun → Nepal 26°55N 87°10E 243 F12
Arun → W. Susx., U.K. 50°49N 0°33W 169 G7
Arunachal Pradesh □ India 28°0N 95°0E 241 B5
Aruppukkottai India 9°31N 78°8E 245 K4
Arusha Tanzania 3°20S 36°40E 268 C4
Arusha □ Tanzania 4°0S 36°30E 268 C4
Arusha △ Tanzania 3°16S 36°47E 268 C4
Arusha Chini Tanzania 3°32S 37°20E 268 C4
Arut → Indonesia 2°42S 111°34E 235 C4
Aruvi → Sri Lanka 8°48N 79°53E 245 K4
Aruwimi → Dem. Rep. of the Congo 1°13N 23°36E 264 B4
Arvada Colo., U.S.A. 39°48N 105°5W 304 G11
Arvada Wyo., U.S.A. 44°39N 106°8W 304 D10
Arvakalu Sri Lanka 8°20N 79°58E 245 K4
Arvayheer Mongolia 46°15N 102°48E 218 B9
Arve → France 46°11N 6°8E 173 F13
Arvi Kriti, Greece 34°59N 25°28E 207 F6
Arvi India 20°59N 78°16E 244 D4
Arviat Canada 61°6N 93°59W 297 A10
Arvidsjaur Sweden 65°35N 19°10E 160 D18
Arvika Sweden 59°40N 12°36E 162 E6
Arvin U.S.A. 35°12N 118°50W 307 K8
Arwad Syria 34°51N 35°51E 250 D6
Arwal India 25°15N 84°41E 243 G11
Arxan China 47°11N 119°57E 219 B12
Åryd Sweden 56°49N 14°59E 163 H8
Arys Kazakhstan 42°26N 68°48E 217 D7
Arzachena Italy 41°5N 9°23E 200 A2
Arzamas Russia 55°27N 43°55E 190 C6
Arzanah U.A.E. 24°47N 52°34E 247 E7
Arzew Algeria 35°50N 0°23W 261 A4
Arzgir Russia 45°18N 44°23E 191 H7
Arzignano Italy 45°31N 11°20E 199 C8
Arzúa Spain 42°56N 8°9W 194 C2
Aš Czech Rep. 50°13N 12°12E 180 A5
Ås Akershus, Norway 59°40N 10°48E 164 E7
Ås Sweden 63°15N 14°34E 162 A8
As Pontes de García Rodríguez Spain 43°27N 7°50W 194 B3
As Sa'an Syria 35°16N 37°22E 250 C8
Aş Şafā Syria 33°10N 37°0E 250 E8
As Saffānīyah Si. Arabia 27°55N 48°50E 247 E6
As Safīrah Syria 36°5N 37°21E 250 B8
Aş Şahm Oman 24°10N 56°53E 247 E8
As Sājir Si. Arabia 25°11N 44°36E 246 E5
As Salamīyah Syria 35°1N 37°2E 250 C8
As Salmān Iraq 30°30N 44°32E 246 D5
As Salţ Jordan 32°2N 35°43E 251 F6
As Sal'w'a Qatar 24°23N 50°50E 247 E6
As Samāwah Iraq 31°15N 45°15E 246 D5
As Sanamayn Syria 33°3N 36°10E 250 E7
As Sawāḑah Si. Arabia 22°24N 44°28E 248 B4
As Sayl al Kabīr Si. Arabia 21°38N 40°25E 248 B3
As Shawawra West Bank 31°41N 35°15E 123 B2
As Sohar = Şuḩār Oman 24°20N 56°40E 247 E8
As Sukhnah Syria 34°52N 38°52E 213 E8
As Sulaymānīyah Iraq 35°35N 45°29E 213 E11
As Sulaymānīyah Si. Arabia 24°9N 47°18E 248 A4
As Sulaymānīyah □ Iraq 35°50N 45°30E 213 E11
As Sulaymī Si. Arabia 26°17N 41°21E 246 E4
As Sulayyil Si. Arabia 20°27N 45°34E 248 B4
As Sulţān Libya 31°4N 17°8E 258 B3
As Summān Si. Arabia 25°0N 47°0E 246 E5
Aş Şurrah Yemen 13°57N 46°14E 248 D4
Aş Şuwar Syria 35°30N 40°38E 213 E9
As Suwaydā' Syria 32°40N 36°30E 250 F7
As Suwaydā' □ Syria 32°45N 36°45E 250 F7
As Suwayq Oman 23°51N 57°26E 247 F8
Aş Şuwayrah Iraq 32°55N 45°0E 213 F11
Åsa Sweden 57°21N 12°8E 163 G6
Asa Wright Nature Centre Trin. & Tob. 10°43N 61°17W 323 t
Asab Namibia 25°30S 18°0E 270 C2
Asaba Nigeria 6°12N 6°38E 263 D6
Asad, Buḩayrat al Syria 36°0N 38°15E 213 D8
Asadābād Iran 34°47N 48°7E 213 E13
Asafo Ghana 6°20N 2°40W 262 D4
Asaga Str. Amer. Samoa 14°10S 169°37W 302 g
Asagaya Japan 35°41N 139°38E 140 A2
Asahi Chiba, Japan 35°43N 140°39E 223 B12
Asahi Ōsaka, Japan 34°43N 135°31E 133 A2
Asahi-Gawa → Japan 34°36N 133°58E 222 C5
Asahigawa = Asahikawa Japan 43°46N 142°22E 220 C11
Asahikawa Japan 43°46N 142°22E 220 C11
Asakusa Japan 35°42N 139°47E 140 A3
Asakusabashi Tokyo, Japan 140 a5
Asale, L. Ethiopia 14°0N 40°20E 257 E5
Asaluyeh Iran 27°29N 52°37E 247 E7
Asama-Yama Japan 36°24N 138°31E 223 A10
Asamankese Ghana 5°50N 0°40W 263 D4
Asan S. Korea 36°48N 127°1E 224 D3
Asan → India 26°37N 78°24E 243 F8
Asansol India 23°40N 87°1E 243 H12
Åsarna Sweden 62°39N 14°22E 162 B8
Asati India 22°28N 88°15E 124 C1
Asau Samoa 13°27S 172°33W 287 V19
Asayita Ethiopia 11°35N 41°23E 257 E5
Asba Littoria = Asbe Teferi Ethiopia 9°4N 40°49E 257 F5
Asbe Teferi Ethiopia 9°4N 40°49E 257 F5
Asbesberge S. Africa 29°0S 23°0E 270 C3
Asbestos Canada 45°47N 71°58W 299 C5
Asbury Park U.S.A. 40°13N 74°1W 313 F10
Åsby Sweden 57°14N 12°18E 163 G6
Ascea Italy 40°8N 15°11E 201 B8
Ascensión Mexico 31°6N 107°59W 318 A3
Ascensión, B. de la Mexico 19°40N 87°30W 319 D7
Ascension I. Atl. Oc. 7°57S 14°23W 153 g
Aschach an der Donau Austria 48°22N 14°2E 180 C7
Aschaffenburg Germany 49°58N 9°6E 179 F5
Aschendorf Germany 53°3N 7°19E 178 B3
Aschersleben Germany 51°45N 11°29E 178 D7
Aschheim Germany 48°10N 11°42E 131 A3
Asciano Italy 43°14N 11°33E 199 E8
Áscoli Piceno Italy 42°51N 13°34E 199 F10
Áscoli Satriano Italy 41°11N 15°32E 201 A8
Ascope Peru 7°46S 79°8W 330 B2
Ascot Vale Australia 37°46S 144°53E 128 A1
Ascotán Chile 21°45S 68°17W 334 A2
Ascuncion Phil. 7°35N 125°45E 233 H5
Aseb Eritrea 13°0N 42°40E 257 E5
Åseda Sweden 57°10N 15°20E 163 G9
Asedjrad Algeria 24°51N 1°29E 261 D5
Aseki Papua N. G. 7°21S 146°12E 286 D4
Asela Ethiopia 8°0N 39°0E 257 F4
Åsen Sweden 61°17N 13°50E 162 C7
Asenovgrad Bulgaria 42°1N 24°51E 203 D8
Asfeld France 49°27N 4°5E 173 C11
Asfûn el Matâ'na Egypt 25°26N 32°30E 256 B3
Aşgabat = Ashgabat Turkmenistan 38°0N 57°50E 247 B8
Åsgårdstrand Norway 59°22N 10°27E 164 E7
Asgata Cyprus 34°46N 33°15E 207 F9
Ash Fork U.S.A. 35°13N 112°29W 305 J7
Ash Grove U.S.A. 37°19N 93°35W 308 G7
Ash Shabakah Iraq 30°49N 43°39E 246 D4
Ash Shafa Si. Arabia 21°27N 39°49E 248 B2
Ash Shamāl □ Lebanon 34°25N 36°0E 250 D7
Ash Shāmīyah Iraq 31°55N 44°35E 213 G11
Ash Sha'rā' Si. Arabia 24°16N 44°11E 248 A4
Ash Shāriqah U.A.E. 25°23N 55°26E 247 E7
Ash Sharmah Si. Arabia 28°1N 35°16E 251 K6
Ash Sharqāt Iraq 35°27N 43°16E 213 E10
Ash Sharqīyah □ Si. Arabia 23°0N 50°30E 249 B6
Ash Shāţi Libya 27°30N 12°30E 258 C2
Ash Shaţrah Iraq 31°30N 46°10E 246 D5
Ash Shawbak Jordan 30°32N 35°34E 246 D2
Ash Shaykh Ḩumayd Si. Arabia 28°6N 34°33E 251 K5
Ash Shifā' Si. Arabia 28°30N 35°30E 251 K6
Ash Shiḩr Yemen 14°45N 49°36E 249 D5
Ash Shināfīyah Iraq 31°35N 44°39E 246 D5
Ash Shu'bah Si. Arabia 28°54N 44°44E 246 D5
Ash Shumlūl Si. Arabia 26°31N 47°20E 246 E5
Ash Shuqayq Si. Arabia 17°44N 42°1E 248 C3
Ash Shūr'a Iraq 35°58N 43°13E 246 C4
Ash Shurayf Si. Arabia 25°43N 39°14E 246 E3
Ash Shuwayfāt Lebanon 33°45N 35°30E 250 E6
Ash Shuwayrif Libya 29°59N 14°16E 258 C2
Asha Russia 55°0N 57°16E 186 D10
Ashanti □ Ghana 7°30N 1°30W 263 D4
Ashbourne U.K. 53°2N 1°43W 168 D6
Ashbridge's Bay Park Canada 43°40N 79°18W 141 B3
Ashburn Ga., U.S.A. 31°43N 83°39W 316 D6
Ashburn Ill., U.S.A. 41°45N 87°43W 119 C2
Ashburton Vic., Australia 37°51S 145°4E 128 B2
Ashburton N.Z. 43°53S 171°48E 285 D6
Ashburton → Australia 21°40S 114°56E 278 D1
Ashburton, North Branch → N.Z. 43°54S 171°44E 285 D6
Ashburton, South Branch → N.Z. 43°54S 171°44E 285 D6
Ashcroft Canada 50°40N 121°20W 296 C4
Ashdod Israel 31°49N 34°35E 251 G5
Ashdown U.S.A. 33°40N 94°8W 314 E7
Asheboro U.S.A. 35°43N 79°49W 315 D15
Åsheim Norway 61°42N 11°11E 164 C8
Ashern Canada 51°11N 98°21W 297 C9
Asherton U.S.A. 28°27N 99°46W 314 G5
Asheville U.S.A. 35°36N 82°33W 315 D13
Ashewat Pakistan 31°22N 68°32E 242 D3
Asheweig → Canada 54°17N 87°12W 298 B2
Ashfield Australia 33°53S 151°7E 139 B1
Ashford N.S.W., Australia 29°15S 151°3E 281 D5
Ashford Kent, U.K. 51°8N 0°53E 169 F8
Ashford Surrey, U.K. 51°25N 0°26W 125 B1
Ashford Ala., U.S.A. 31°11N 85°14W 316 D4
Ashgabat Turkmenistan 38°0N 57°50E 247 B8
Ashhurst N.Z. 40°16S 175°45E 284 G4
Ashibetsu Japan 43°31N 142°11E 220 C11
Ashikaga Japan 36°28N 139°29E 223 A11
Ashington U.K. 55°11N 1°33W 168 B6
Ashio Japan 36°38N 139°27E 223 A11
Ashizuri-Uwakai △ Japan 32°56N 132°32E 222 E4
Ashizuri-Zaki Japan 32°44N 133°0E 222 E5
Ashkarkot Afghan. 33°3N 67°58E 242 C2
Ashkhabad = Ashgabat Turkmenistan 38°0N 57°50E 247 B8
Āshkhāneh Iran 37°26N 56°55E 247 B8
Ashland Ala., U.S.A. 33°16N 85°50W 316 B4
Ashland Ill., U.S.A. 39°53N 90°1W 310 E7
Ashland Kans., U.S.A. 37°11N 99°46W 308 G4
Ashland Ky., U.S.A. 38°28N 82°38W 309 F12
Ashland Maine, U.S.A. 46°38N 68°24W 309 B19
Ashland Mont., U.S.A. 45°36N 106°16W 304 D10
Ashland Ohio, U.S.A. 40°52N 82°19W 312 F2
Ashland Oreg., U.S.A. 42°12N 122°43W 304 E2
Ashland Pa., U.S.A. 40°45N 76°22W 313 F8
Ashland Va., U.S.A. 37°46N 77°29W 309 G15
Ashland Wis., U.S.A. 46°35N 90°53W 308 B8
Ashley Ill., U.S.A. 38°20N 89°11W 310 F7
Ashley Ind., U.S.A. 41°32N 85°4W 311 C11
Ashley N. Dak., U.S.A. 46°2N 99°22W 308 B4
Ashley Pa., U.S.A. 41°12N 75°55W 313 E9
Ashley → N.Z. 43°17S 172°44E 285 D7
Ashmore and Cartier Is. Ind. Oc. 12°15S 123°0E 278 B3
Ashmore Reef Australia 12°14S 123°5E 278 B3
Ashmûn Egypt 30°18N 30°58E 251 H1
Ashmyany Belarus 54°26N 25°52E 177 A13
Ashokan Res. U.S.A. 41°56N 74°13W 313 E10
Ashoknagar India 24°34N 77°43E 244 B3
Ashqelon Israel 31°42N 34°35E 251 G5
Ashraf = Behshahr Iran 36°45N 53°35E 247 B7
Ashta India 23°1N 76°43E 242 H7
Ashtabula U.S.A. 41°52N 80°47W 312 E4
Ashti Maharashtra, India 21°12N 78°11E 244 D4
Ashti Maharashtra, India 18°50N 75°15E 244 E2
Āshtiyān Iran 34°31N 50°0E 247 C6
Ashton Western Cape, S. Africa 33°50S 20°5E 270 D3
Ashton Idaho, U.S.A. 44°4N 111°27W 304 D8
Ashtown Ireland 53°22N 6°19W 120 A2
Ashuanipi, L. Canada 52°45N 66°15W 299 B6
Ashuapmushuan → Canada 48°37N 72°20W 298 C5
Ashville Ala., U.S.A. 33°50N 86°15W 316 B3
Ashville Fla., U.S.A. 30°37N 83°39W 316 E6
Ashville Pa., U.S.A. 40°34N 78°33W 312 F6
'Āşī → Asia 36°1N 35°59E 250 B6
Asia 45°0N 75°0E 210 E9
Asia, Kepulauan Indonesia 1°0N 131°13E 231 D8
Asiago Italy 45°52N 11°30E 199 C8
Asid G. Phil. 12°10N 123°29E 232 E4
Asidonhoppo Suriname 3°50N 55°30W 329 C6
Asifabad India 19°20N 79°24E 244 E4
Asilah Morocco 35°29N 6°0W 260 A3
Asinara Italy 41°4N 8°16E 200 A1
Asinara, G. dell' Italy 41°0N 8°30E 200 A1
Asino Russia 57°0N 86°0E 214 D9
Asipovichy Belarus 53°19N 28°33E 177 B15
'Asir Si. Arabia 18°40N 42°30E 248 C3
Asir, Ras Somali Rep. 11°55N 51°10E 267 B7
Aska India 19°2N 84°42E 244 E7
Aşkale Turkey 39°55N 40°41E 213 C9
Asker Norway 59°50N 10°29E 164 E7
Askersund Sweden 58°53N 14°55E 163 F8
Askham S. Africa 26°59S 20°47E 270 C3
Askī Mawşil Iraq 36°30N 42°44E 213 D10
Askim Norway 59°35N 11°10E 164 E8
Askio, Oros Greece 40°25N 21°35E 202 F5
Askisto Finland 60°16N 24°47E 121 B1
Askja Iceland 65°3N 16°48W 155 B10
Asklipio Greece 36°4N 27°56E 206 E11
Askøyna Norway 60°29N 5°10E 164 D2
Askrikefjärden Sweden 59°22N 18°13E 139 A3
Askvoll Norway 61°21N 5°4E 164 C2
Asl Egypt 29°33N 32°44E 256 B3
Aslan Burnu Turkey 38°44N 26°45E 205 C8
Aslanapa Turkey 39°13N 29°52E 205 B11
Aslānduz Iran 39°26N 47°24E 213 C12
Āsmār Afghan. 35°10N 71°27E 240 B3
Asmara = Asmera Eritrea 15°19N 38°55E 257 D4
Asmera Eritrea 15°19N 38°55E 257 D4
Asnæs Denmark 55°40N 11°0E 163 J4
Åsnen Sweden 56°37N 14°45E 163 H8
Asni Morocco 31°17N 7°58W 260 B3
Asnières France 48°54N 2°16E 134 A2
Aso Japan 32°55N 131°5E 222 E3
Aso Kujū △ Japan 32°53N 131°6E 222 E3
Aso-Zan Japan 32°53N 131°6E 222 E3
Ásola Italy 45°13N 10°24E 198 C7
Asos Greece 38°22N 20°33E 207 C2
Asosa Ethiopia 10°3N 34°32E 257 E3
Asoteriba, Jebel Sudan 21°51N 36°30E 256 C4
Asouf, O. → Algeria 25°40N 2°8E 261 C5
Aspatria U.K. 54°47N 3°19W 168 C4
Aspe Spain 38°20N 0°40W 197 G4
Aspen U.S.A. 39°11N 106°49W 304 G10
Aspendos Turkey 36°54N 31°7E 250 B2
Aspermont U.S.A. 33°8N 100°14W 314 E4
Aspern Austria 48°13N 16°29E 142 A2
Aspet France 43°1N 0°48E 174 E4
Aspiring, Mt. N.Z. 44°23S 168°46E 285 E3
Aspres-sur-Buëch France 44°32N 5°44E 175 D9
Asprokavos, Akra Greece 39°21N 20°6E 206 C10
Aspromonte △ Italy 38°9N 15°58E 201 D8
Aspur India 23°58N 74°7E 242 H6
Asquith Canada 52°8N 107°13W 297 C7
Assa Morocco 28°35N 9°6W 260 C3
Assab = Aseb Eritrea 13°0N 42°40E 257 E5
Assâba □ Mauritania 16°40N 11°40W 262 B2
Assâba, Massif de l' Mauritania 16°10N 11°45W 262 B2
Assagny △ Ivory C. 5°10N 4°48W 262 D4
Assago Italy 45°24N 9°7E 129 B1
Assaikio Nigeria 8°34N 8°55E 263 D6
Assal, L. Djibouti 11°40N 42°26E 257 E5
Assam □ India 26°0N 93°0E 241 C4
Assamakka Niger 19°21N 5°38E 263 B6
Assateague Island ⌓ U.S.A. 38°15N 75°10W 309 F16
Assaye India 20°15N 75°53E 244 D2
Asse Belgium 50°24N 4°10E 170 D4
Assekrem Algeria 23°16N 5°49E 261 D6
Assémini Italy 39°17N 9°0E 200 C1
Assen Neths. 53°0N 6°35E 170 A6
Assendelft Neths. 52°28N 4°45E 112 A1
Assens Denmark 55°16N 9°55E 163 J3
Assiano Italy 45°27N 9°3E 129 B1
Assini Ivory C. 5°9N 3°17W 262 D4
Assiniboia Canada 49°40N 105°59W 297 D7
Assiniboine → Canada 49°53N 97°8W 297 D9
Assiniboine, Mt. Canada 50°52N 115°39W 296 C5
Assiou Algeria 21°7N 7°36E 261 D6
Assis Brazil 22°40S 50°20W 335 A5
Assis Brasil Brazil 10°55S 69°32W 330 C4
Assisi Italy 43°4N 12°37E 199 E9
Åsskard Norway 63°1N 8°30E 164 A5
Assok Ngoum Gabon 1°45N 11°39E 264 B2
Assumption U.S.A. 39°31N 89°3W 310 E7
Assynt, L. U.K. 58°10N 5°3W 167 C3
Astaffort France 44°4N 0°40E 174 D4
Astakida Greece 35°53N 26°50E 205 F8
Astakos Greece 38°32N 21°5E 207 B3
Astana Kazakhstan 51°10N 71°30E 217 B8
Āstāneh Iran 37°17N 49°59E 247 B6
Astapovo = Lev Tolstoy Russia 53°13N 39°29E 188 F10
Astara Azerbaijan 38°30N 48°50E 213 C13
Āstārā Iran 38°20N 48°52E 213 C13
Astarabad = Gorgān Iran 36°55N 54°30E 247 B7
Asterousia Greece 34°59N 25°3E 207 F6
Asti Italy 44°54N 8°12E 198 D5
Astipalea Greece 36°32N 26°22E 205 E8
Astola I. Pakistan 25°7N 63°51E 240 D1
Astorga Davao del S., Phil. 6°54N 125°27E 233 H5
Astorga Spain 42°29N 6°8W 194 C4
Astoria Ill., U.S.A. 40°14N 90°21W 310 D6
Astoria N.Y., U.S.A. 40°46N 73°55W 132 B2
Astoria Oreg., U.S.A. 46°11N 123°50W 306 D3
Åstorp Sweden 56°6N 12°55E 163 H6
Astrakhan Russia 46°25N 48°5E 191 G9
Astrakhan □ Russia 47°45N 46°20E 191 G8
Astrebla Downs Australia 24°12S 140°34E 280 C3
Astrolabe, Récifs de l' N. Cal. 19°48S 165°37E 288 d
Astrolabe Park Australia 33°57S 151°12E 139 B2
Astudillo Spain 42°12N 4°22W 194 C6
Asturias □ Spain 43°15N 6°0W 194 B5
Asturias ✈ (OVD) Spain 43°33N 6°3W 194 B4
Asumman S. Korea 37°4N 126°40E 224 D3
Asunción Bolivia 11°46S 67°50W 330 C4
Asuncion N. Marianas 19°40N 145°24E 302 a
Asunción Paraguay 25°10S 57°30W 334 B4
Asunción Nochixtlán Mexico 17°28N 97°14W 319 D5
Åsunden Sweden 58°0N 15°51E 163 F9
Asutri Sudan 15°25N 35°45E 257 D4
Aswa → Uganda 3°43N 31°55E 268 B3
Aswa-Lolim ⌓ Uganda 2°43N 31°35E 268 B3
Aswad, Ra's al Si. Arabia 21°20N 39°0E 248 B2
Aswân Egypt 24°4N 32°57E 256 C3
Aswan High Dam = Sadd el Aali Egypt 23°54N 32°54E 256 C3
Asyût Egypt 27°11N 31°4E 256 B3
Asyûti, Wadi → Egypt 27°11N 31°16E 256 B3
Aszód Hungary 47°39N 19°28E 182 C4
At-Bashy Kyrgyzstan 41°10N 75°48E 217 D9
At Ţafīlah Jordan 30°45N 35°30E 251 H6
At Ţafīlah □ Jordan 30°45N 35°30E 251 H6
Aţ Tā'if Si. Arabia 21°5N 40°27E 248 B3
At Tāj Libya 24°13N 23°18E 258 D4
At Ta'mīm □ Iraq 35°30N 44°20E 246 C5
At Tamīmī Libya 32°20N 23°4E 258 B4
Aţ Ţirāq Si. Arabia 27°19N 44°33E 246 E5
Aţ Tubayq Si. Arabia 29°30N 37°0E 251 J8
Aţ Ţunayb Jordan 31°48N 35°57E 251 G6
At Turbah Laḩij, Yemen 12°40N 43°30E 248 D3
At Turbah Ta'izz, Yemen 13°13N 44°7E 248 D4
Atabey Turkey 37°57N 30°39E 205 D12
Atacama □ Chile 27°30S 70°0W 334 B2
Atacama, Desierto de Chile 24°0S 69°20W 334 A2
Atacama, Salar de Chile 23°30S 68°20W 334 A2
Ataco Colombia 3°35N 75°23W 328 C2
Atafu Pac. Oc. 8°32S 172°31W 277 B16
Atakeye ◎ Australia 22°30S 133°45E 278 D5
Atakor Algeria 23°27N 5°31E 261 D6
Atakpamé Togo 7°31N 1°13E 263 D5
Atalaia do Norte Brazil 4°20S 70°12W 328 D3
Atalandi Greece 38°39N 22°58E 204 C4
Atalaya Peru 10°45S 73°50W 330 C3
Atalaya de Femes Canary Is. 28°56N 13°47W 153 e2
Ataléia Brazil 18°3S 41°6W 333 E3
Atami Japan 35°5N 139°4E 223 B11
Atamyrat Turkmenistan 37°50N 65°12E 217 E7
Atankawng Burma 25°50N 97°47E 241 C6
Atap Indonesia 3°51N 117°1E 235 B5
Atapupu Indonesia 9°0S 124°51E 231 F6
Atâr Mauritania 20°30N 13°5W 260 D2
Ataram, Erg n- Algeria 23°57N 2°0E 261 D5
Atarfe Spain 37°13N 3°40W 195 H7
Atari Pakistan 30°56N 74°2E 242 D6
Atarot West Bank 31°52N 35°13E 123 A2
Atarot ✈ (JRS) West Bank 31°52N 35°14E 123 A2
Atascadero U.S.A. 35°29N 120°40W 306 K6
Atasū Kazakhstan 48°30N 71°0E 217 C8
Atatürk, İstanbul ✈ (IST) Turkey 40°59N 28°49E 203 F12
Atatürk Barajı Turkey 37°28N 38°30E 213 D8
Atauro E. Timor 8°10S 125°30E 231 F7
Ataviros Greece 36°12N 27°50E 206 E11
Atbara Sudan 17°42N 33°59E 256 D3
'Atbara, Nahr → Sudan 17°40N 33°56E 256 D3
Atbasar Kazakhstan 51°48N 68°20E 217 B7
Atbashi = At-Bashy Kyrgyzstan 41°10N 75°48E 217 D9
Atça Turkey 37°53N 28°13E 205 D10
Atchafalaya B. U.S.A. 29°25N 91°25W 314 G9
Atchison U.S.A. 39°34N 95°7W 308 F6
Atebubu Ghana 7°47N 1°0W 263 D4
Ateca Spain 41°20N 1°49W 196 D3
Aterno → Italy 42°11N 13°51E 199 F10
Āteshān Iran 35°35N 52°37E 247 C7
Atesine, Alpi Italy 46°55N 11°30E 199 B8
Atessa Italy 42°4N 14°27E 199 F11
Atfîh Egypt 29°25N 31°15E 256 J7
Atghara India 22°37N 88°26E 124 B2
Ath Belgium 50°38N 3°47E 170 D3
Athabasca Canada 54°45N 113°20W 296 C6
Athabasca → Canada 58°40N 110°50W 297 B6
Athabasca, L. Canada 59°15N 109°15W 297 B7
Athabasca Sand Dunes ⌓ Canada 59°4N 108°43W 297 B7
Athagarh India 20°32N 85°37E 244 D7
Athamanon Oros Greece 39°30N 21°26E 204 B3
Athboy Ireland 53°37N 6°56W 166 C5
Athena U.S.A. 29°59N 83°30W 316 F6
Athenry Ireland 53°18N 8°44W 166 C3
Athens = Athina Greece 37°58N 23°43E 112 B2
Athens Ala., U.S.A. 34°48N 86°58W 315 D11
Athens Ga., U.S.A. 33°57N 83°23W 316 B6
Athens N.Y., U.S.A. 42°16N 73°49W 313 D11
Athens Ohio, U.S.A. 39°20N 82°6W 309 F12
Athens Pa., U.S.A. 41°57N 76°31W 313 E8
Athens Tenn., U.S.A. 35°27N 84°36W 315 D12
Athens Tex., U.S.A. 32°12N 95°51W 314 E7
Atheras Greece 38°19N 20°25E 207 C1
Atherley Canada 44°37N 79°20W 312 B5
Atherton Australia 17°17S 145°30E 280 B4
Athi River Kenya 1°28S 36°58E 268 C4
Athiéme Benin 6°37N 1°40E 263 D5
Athienou Cyprus 35°3N 33°32E 207 E9
Athina Greece 37°58N 23°43E 112 B2
Athina ✈ (ATH) Greece 37°56N 23°56E 112 A3
Athínai = Athina Greece 37°58N 23°43E 112 B2
Athis-Mons France 48°42N 2°23E 134 B3
Athlone Westmeath, Ireland 53°25N 7°56W 166 C4
Athlone Western Cape, S. Africa 33°57S 18°30E 118 A2
Athmalik India 20°43N 84°32E 244 D7
Athna Cyprus 35°3N 33°47E 207 E9
Athni India 16°44N 75°6E 244 F2
Athol N.Z. 45°30S 168°35E 285 F3
Athol Mass., U.S.A. 42°36N 72°14W 313 D12
Athol I. Bahamas 25°5N 77°16W 153 b
Atholl S. Africa 26°7S 28°3E 123 A2
Atholl, Forest of U.K. 56°51N 3°50W 167 E5
Atholl, Kap Greenland 76°25N 69°30W 154 B4
Atholville Canada 47°59N 66°43W 299 C6
Athos Greece 40°9N 24°22E 203 F8
Athy Ireland 53°0N 7°0W 166 C5
Ati Chad 13°13N 18°20E 259 F3
Ati Sudan 13°5N 29°2E 257 E2
Ati, J. Libya 23°24N 14°21E 258 D2
Atiak Uganda 3°12N 32°2E 268 B3
Atiamuri N.Z. 38°24S 176°5E 284 E5
Atico Peru 16°14S 73°40W 330 D3
Atienza Spain 41°12N 2°52W 196 D2
Atīfīya Iraq 33°21N 44°21E 113 A2
Atiit Sudan 6°10N 30°35E 257 F3
Atik L. Canada 55°15N 96°0W 297 B9
Atikaki ⌓ Canada 51°30N 95°31W 297 C9
Atikameg → Canada 52°30N 82°46W 298 B3
Atikokan Canada 48°45N 91°37W 298 C1
Atikonak L. Canada 52°40N 64°32W 299 B7
Atimaono Tahiti 17°46S 149°28W 289 e
Atimonan Phil. 14°0N 121°55E 232 D3
'Ātinah, W. → Oman 18°23N 53°28E 249 C6
Atirampattinam India 10°28N 79°20E 245 J4
Atişalen Turkey 41°3N 28°52E 122 B1
Atitlán △ Cent. Amer. 14°38N 91°10W 320 D1
Atiu Cook Is. 20°0S 158°10W 289 J12
Atka Russia 60°50N 151°48E 215 C16
Atka Alaska, U.S.A. 52°12N 174°12W 303 K4
Atka I. U.S.A. 52°7N 174°30W 303 K4
Atkarsk Russia 51°55N 45°2E 190 E7
Atkinson Ga., U.S.A. 31°13N 81°47W 316 D8
Atkinson Ill., U.S.A. 41°25N 90°1W 310 C6
Atkinson Nebr., U.S.A. 42°32N 98°59W 308 D4
Atlanta Ga., U.S.A. 33°45N 84°23W 113 B2
Atlanta Ill., U.S.A. 40°16N 89°14W 310 D7
Atlanta Mo., U.S.A. 39°54N 92°29W 310 E4
Atlanta Tex., U.S.A. 33°7N 94°10W 314 E7
Atlanta Hartsfield Int. ✈ (ATL) U.S.A. 33°38N 84°26W 113 C2
Atlanta History Center U.S.A. 33°45N 84°22W 113 B2
Atlanta Zoo U.S.A. 33°44N 84°22W 113 B2
Atlantic U.S.A. 41°24N 95°1W 310 C2
Atlantic Beach U.S.A. 30°20N 81°24W 316 E8
Atlantic City U.S.A. 39°21N 74°27W 309 F16
Atlantic-Indian Basin Antarctica 60°0S 30°0E 151 B4
Atlantic Ocean 0°0 20°0W 152 F8
Atlántico □ Colombia 10°45N 75°0W 328 A3
Atlantis S. Africa 33°34S 18°29E 270 D2
Atlas Mts. = Haut Atlas Morocco 32°30N 5°0W 260 B4
Atlin Canada 59°31N 133°41W 296 B2
Atlin, L. Canada 59°26N 133°45W 296 B2
Atlin ⌓ Canada 59°10N 134°30W 296 B2
Atløyna Norway 61°21N 4°58E 164 C1
Atmakur Andhra Pradesh, India 18°45N 78°39E 244 E4
Atmakur Andhra Pradesh, India 14°37N 79°40E 245 G4
Atmakur Andhra Pradesh, India 15°53N 78°35E 245 G4
Atmore U.S.A. 31°2N 87°29W 315 F11
Atna Norway 61°44N 10°49E 164 C7
Atna → Norway 61°44N 10°49E 164 C7
Atō Japan 34°25N 131°40E 222 C3
Atocha Bolivia 20°56S 66°14W 330 E4
Atok Phil. 16°35N 120°41E 232 C3
Atoka U.S.A. 34°23N 96°8W 314 D6
Atokos Greece 38°28N 20°49E 207 C2
Atolia U.S.A. 35°19N 117°37W 307 K9
Atomium Belgium 50°54N 4°20E 116 A2
Atongo-Bakari C.A.R. 5°49N 21°35E 264 A4
Atori Solomon Is. 8°42S 160°59E 287 M11
Atqasuk U.S.A. 70°28N 157°24W 303 A8
Atqasuk → U.S.A. 70°52N 155°55W 303 A9
Atrå Norway 59°59N 8°45E 164 E5
Atrai → Bangla. 24°7N 89°22E 241 C2
Atrak = Atrek → Turkmenistan 37°35N 53°58E 247 B8
Ätran Sweden 57°7N 12°57E 163 G6
Ätran → Sweden 56°53N 12°30E 163 H6
Atrato → Colombia 8°17N 76°58W 328 B2
Atrauli India 28°2N 78°20E 242 E8
Atrek → Turkmenistan 37°35N 53°58E 247 B8
Atri Italy 42°35N 13°58E 199 F10
Atsiki Greece 39°56N 25°13E 205 B7
Atsoum, Mts. Cameroon 6°41N 12°57E 263 D7
Atsugi Japan 35°25N 139°21E 223 B11
Atsumi Japan 34°35N 137°4E 223 C9
Atsuta Japan 43°24N 141°26E 220 C10
Attalla U.S.A. 34°1N 86°6W 316 A3
Attapeu Laos 14°48N 106°50E 236 E6
Attapulgus U.S.A. 30°45N 84°29W 316 E5
Attawapiskat Canada 52°56N 82°24W 298 B3
Attawapiskat → Canada 52°57N 82°18W 298 B3
Attawapiskat L. Canada 52°18N 87°54W 298 B2
Attersee Austria 47°55N 13°32E 180 D6
Attica Ind., U.S.A. 40°18N 87°15W 311 D9
Attica Ohio, U.S.A. 41°4N 82°53W 312 E2
Attichy France 49°25N 3°3E 173 C10
Attigny France 49°28N 4°35E 173 C11
Attika = Attiki □ Greece 37°10N 23°40E 204 D5
Attikamagen L. Canada 55°0N 66°30W 299 B6
Attiki Greece 38°0N 23°43E 112 A2
Attiki □ Greece 37°10N 23°40E 204 D5
Attleboro U.S.A. 41°57N 71°17W 313 E13
Attock Pakistan 33°52N 72°20E 242 C5
Attopu = Attapeu Laos 14°48N 106°50E 236 E6
Attu U.S.A. 52°56N 173°15E 303 K1
Attu I. U.S.A. 52°55N 172°55E 303 K1
Attunga Australia 30°55S 150°50E 283 A9
Attur India 11°35N 78°30E 245 J4
'Atūd Yemen 14°53N 48°10E 249 D5
Atuel → Argentina 36°17S 66°50W 334 D2
Atura Uganda 2°7N 32°20E 268 B3
Åtvidaberg Sweden 58°12N 16°0E 163 F10
Atwater U.S.A. 37°21N 120°37W 306 H6
Atwood Ont., Canada 43°40N 81°1W 312 C3
Atwood Ill., U.S.A. 39°48N 88°28W 311 E8
Atwood Kans., U.S.A. 39°48N 101°3W 308 F3
Atyraū Kazakhstan 47°5N 52°0E 187 E9
Atzgersdorf Austria 48°8N 16°18E 142 B1
Au Sable U.S.A. 44°25N 83°20W 312 B1
Au Sable → U.S.A. 44°25N 83°20W 309 C12
Au Sable Forks U.S.A. 44°27N 73°41W 313 B11
Au Sable Pt. U.S.A. 44°20N 83°20W 312 B1
Au Vent, Région Réunion 21°0S 55°35E 272 f
Aua Amer. Samoa 14°17S 170°40W 302 f
Auas Honduras 15°29N 84°20W 320 C3
Auasberg Namibia 22°37S 17°13E 270 B2
Aubagne France 43°17N 5°37E 175 E9
Aube □ France 48°15N 4°10E 173 D11
Aube → France 48°34N 3°43E 173 D10
Aubenas France 44°37N 4°24E 175 D8
Aubenton France 49°50N 4°12E 173 C11
Auberry U.S.A. 37°7N 119°29W 306 H7
Aubervilliers France 48°54N 2°22E 134 A3
Aubigny-sur-Nère France 47°30N 2°24E 173 E9
Aubin France 44°33N 2°15E 174 D6
Aubing Germany 48°9N 11°25E 131 B1
Aubrac, Mts. d' France 44°40N 3°2E 174 D7
Auburn S. Austral., Australia 34°1S 138°42E 282 C3
Auburn Ala., U.S.A. 32°36N 85°29W 316 C4
Auburn Calif., U.S.A. 38°54N 121°4W 306 G5
Auburn Ill., U.S.A. 39°36N 89°45W 310 E7
Auburn Ind., U.S.A. 41°22N 85°4W 311 C11
Auburn Maine, U.S.A. 44°6N 70°14W 309 C18
Auburn N.Y., U.S.A. 42°56N 76°34W 313 D8
Auburn Nebr., U.S.A. 40°23N 95°51W 308 E6
Auburn Pa., U.S.A. 40°36N 76°6W 313 F8
Auburn Wash., U.S.A. 47°18N 122°14W 306 C4
Auburn Ra. Australia 25°15S 150°30E 281 D5
Auburndale Fla., U.S.A. 28°4N 81°48W 317 G8
Auburndale Mass., U.S.A. 42°20N 71°14W 116 A1
Aubusson France 45°57N 2°11E 174 C6
Auce Latvia 56°28N 22°53E 184 B9
Auch France 43°39N 0°36E 174 E4
Auchendinny U.K. 55°51N 3°11W 121 B2
Auchi Nigeria 7°6N 6°13E 263 D6
Auchterarder U.K. 56°18N 3°41W 167 E5
Auchtermuchty U.K. 56°18N 3°13W 167 E5
Auckland N.Z. 36°52S 174°46E 284 C3
Auckland □ N.Z. 36°50S 175°0E 284 C3
Auckland Is. Pac. Oc. 50°40S 166°5E 288 N8
Auckland Park S. Africa 26°11S 28°0E 123 B2
Aude □ France 43°8N 2°28E 174 E6
Aude → France 43°13N 3°14E 174 E7
Auden Canada 50°14N 87°53W 298 B2
Auderghem Belgium 50°49N 4°26E 116 B2
Auderville France 49°43N 1°57W 172 C5
Audierne France 48°1N 4°34W 172 D2
Audincourt France 47°30N 6°50E 173 E13
Audo Ra. Ethiopia 6°20N 41°50E 257 F5
Audubon U.S.A. 41°43N 94°56W 310 C2
Aue Germany 50°35N 12°41E 178 E8
Auerbach Germany 50°30N 12°24E 178 E8
Aufist W. Sahara 25°44N 14°39W 260 C2
Augathella Australia 25°48S 146°35E 281 D4

Aughnacloy U.K. 54°25N 6°59W 166 B5
Aughrim Ireland 53°18N 8°19W 166 C3
Augrabies Falls S. Africa 28°35S 20°20E 270 C3
Augrabies Falls △ S. Africa 28°40S 20°22E 270 C3
Augsburg Germany 48°25N 10°52E 179 G6
Augsburg-Westliche Wälder ⌂ Germany 48°22N 10°40E 179 G6
August Town Jamaica 17°59N 76°44W 320 a
Augusta W. Austral., Australia 34°19S 115°9E 279 F2
Augusta Italy 37°13N 15°13E 201 E8
Augusta Ark., U.S.A. 35°17N 91°22W 314 D9
Augusta Ga., U.S.A. 33°28N 81°58W 316 B8
Augusta Ill., U.S.A. 40°14N 90°57W 310 D6
Augusta Kans., U.S.A. 37°41N 96°59W 308 G5
Augusta Ky., U.S.A. 38°47N 84°0W 311 F12
Augusta Maine, U.S.A. 44°19N 69°47W 309 C19
Augusta Mont., U.S.A. 47°30N 112°24W 304 C7
Augusta, Mausoleo di Rome, Italy 136 b2
Augustenborg Denmark 54°57N 9°53E 163 K3
Augustine I. U.S.A. 59°22N 153°26W 303 G9
Augusto Cardosa = Metangula Mozam. 12°40S 34°50E 269 E3
Augustów Poland 53°51N 23°0E 184 E9
Augustówka Poland 52°11N 21°52E 142 B2
Augustus, Mt. Australia 24°20S 116°50E 279 D2
Augustus I. Australia 15°20S 124°30E 278 C3
Aujuittuq = Grise Fiord Canada 76°25N 82°57W 295 B15
Aukan Eritrea 15°29N 40°50E 257 D5
Auki Solomon Is. 8°45S 160°42E 287 M11
Aukra Norway 62°47N 6°55E 164 B3
Aukrug ⌂ Germany 54°5N 9°45E 178 A5
Aukštaitija △ Lithuania 55°15N 26°0E 161 J22
Aukum U.S.A. 38°34N 120°43W 306 G6
Aul India 20°41N 86°39E 244 D8
Aulavik △ Canada 73°42N 119°55W 294 C8
Auld, L. Australia 22°25S 123°50E 278 D3
Äüliekōl Kazakhstan 52°32N 62°45E 216 B6
Aulifeltet Norway 60°30N 11°21E 162 D5
Auliye-Ata = Taraz Kazakhstan 42°54N 71°22E 217 D8
Aulla Italy 44°12N 9°58E 198 D6
Aulnay France 46°2N 0°22W 174 B3
Aulnay-sous-Bois France 48°56N 2°29E 134 A3
Aulne → France 48°17N 4°16W 172 D2
Aulnoye-Aymeries France 50°12N 3°50E 173 B10
Aulong Palau 7°16N 134°17E 288 c
Ault Somme, France 50°8N 1°26E 172 B8
Ault Colo., U.S.A. 40°35N 104°44W 304 F11
Ault-les-Bains France 42°49N 1°19E 174 F5
Aumale = Sour el Ghozlane Algeria 36°10N 3°45E 261 A5
Aumale France 49°46N 1°46E 173 C8
Aumo Papua N. G. 5°44S 148°30E 286 C5
Aumont-Aubrac France 44°43N 3°17E 174 D7
Auna Nigeria 10°9N 4°42E 263 C5
Aundah India 19°32N 77°3E 244 E3
Aundh India 17°33N 74°23E 244 F2
Auning Denmark 56°26N 10°22E 163 H4
Aunis France 46°5N 0°50W 174 B3
Aunu'u Amer. Samoa 14°20S 170°31W 302 f
Auponhia Indonesia 1°58S 125°27E 231 E7
Aups France 43°37N 6°15E 175 E10
Aur, Pulau Malaysia 2°35N 104°10E 237 L5
Aura Burma 26°59N 97°57E 241 B6
Auraiya India 26°28N 79°33E 243 F8
Aurangabad Bihar, India 24°45N 84°18E 243 G11
Aurangabad Maharashtra, India 19°50N 75°23E 244 E2
Auray France 47°40N 2°59W 172 E4
Aurdal Norway 60°55N 9°26E 164 D6
Aure Norway 63°16N 8°33E 164 A5
Aurelio Italy 41°54N 12°26E 136 B1
Aurès Algeria 35°8N 6°30E 261 A6
Aurich Germany 53°28N 7°28E 178 B3
Aurilândia Brazil 16°44S 50°28W 333 E1
Aurillac France 44°55N 2°26E 174 D6
Aurlandsfjorden Norway 61°3N 7°1E 164 C4
Aurlandsvangen Norway 60°55N 7°12E 164 D4
Auronzo di Cadore Italy 46°33N 12°26E 199 B9
Aurora = Maéwo Vanuatu 15°10S 168°10E 287 E6
Aurora = San Francisco Phil. 13°21N 122°31E 232 E4
Aurora Ont., Canada 44°0N 79°28W 312 C5
Aurora Isabela, Phil. 16°59N 121°38E 232 C3
Aurora Zamboanga del S., Phil. 7°57N 123°36E 233 H4
Aurora Western Cape, S. Africa 32°40S 18°29E 270 D2
Aurora Colo., U.S.A. 39°43N 104°49W 304 G11
Aurora Ill., U.S.A. 41°45N 88°19W 311 C8
Aurora Mo., U.S.A. 36°58N 93°43W 308 G7
Aurora N.Y., U.S.A. 42°45N 76°42W 313 D8
Aurora Nebr., U.S.A. 40°52N 98°0W 308 E5
Aurora Ohio, U.S.A. 41°21N 81°20W 312 E3
Aurora □ Phil. 15°30N 121°30E 232 D3
Aurora Memorial △ Phil. 15°40N 121°20E 232 D3
Aursmoen Norway 59°55N 11°26E 164 E8
Aursunden Norway 62°40N 11°40E 164 B8
Aurukun Australia 13°20S 141°45E 280 A3
Aurukun ◎ Australia 13°36S 141°48E 280 A3
Aus Namibia 26°35S 16°12E 270 C2
Ausa India 18°15N 76°30E 244 E3
Ausable → Canada 43°19N 81°46W 312 C3
Auschwitz = Oświęcim Poland 50°2N 19°11E 185 H6
Ausīm Egypt 30°7N 31°8E 117 A1
Auski Roadhouse Australia 22°22S 118°41E 278 D2
Auspitz = Hustopeče Czech Rep. 48°57N 16°43E 181 C9
Aussig = Ústí nad Labem Czech Rep. 50°41N 14°3E 180 A7
Aust-Agder □ Norway 58°55N 7°40E 164 F4
Austad Norway 58°58N 7°37E 164 F4
Austen Harbour India 12°55N 92°45E 245 H11
Austerlitz = Slavkov u Brna Czech Rep. 49°10N 16°52E 181 B9
Austerlitz, Gare d' France 48°50N 2°22E 134 A3
Austevoll Norway 60°5N 5°13E 164 D2
Austin Ill., U.S.A. 41°53N 87°45W 119 B2
Austin Ind., U.S.A. 38°45N 85°49W 311 F11
Austin Minn., U.S.A. 43°40N 92°58W 308 D7
Austin Nev., U.S.A. 39°30N 117°4W 304 G5
Austin Pa., U.S.A. 41°38N 78°6W 312 E6
Austin Tex., U.S.A. 30°17N 97°45W 314 F6
Austin, L. Australia 27°40S 118°0E 279 E2
Austin I. Canada 61°10N 94°0W 297 A10
Austmarka Norway 60°6N 12°21E 164 D9
Austnes Norway 62°38N 6°16E 164 B3
Austra Norway 65°8N 11°55E 160 D14
Austral Is. = Tubuaï, Îs. French Polynesia 25°0S 150°0W 289 f
Austral Seamount Chain Pac. Oc. 24°0S 150°0W 289 K13
Australia ■ Oceania 23°0S 135°0E 276 E3
Australian-Antarctic Basin S. Ocean 60°0S 120°0E 151 C9
Australian Capital Territory □ Australia 35°30S 149°0E 283 C8
Australind Australia 33°17S 115°42E 279 F2
Austria ■ Europe 47°0N 14°0E 180 E7
Austur-Skaftafellssýsla □ Iceland 64°15N 16°0W 155 C10
Austvågøya Norway 68°20N 14°40E 160 B16
Autazes Brazil 3°35S 59°8W 329 D6
Auterive France 43°21N 1°29E 174 E5
Authie → France 50°22N 1°38E 173 B8
Authon-du-Perche France 48°12N 0°54E 172 D7
Autlán de Navarro Mexico 19°46N 104°22W 318 D4
Autun France 46°58N 4°17E 173 F11
Auvergne □ France 45°20N 3°15E 174 C7
Auvergne, Mts. d' France 45°20N 2°55E 174 C6
Auvézère → France 45°12N 0°50E 174 C4
Auxerre France 47°48N 3°32E 173 E10
Auxi-le-Château France 50°15N 2°8E 173 B9
Auxonne France 47°10N 5°20E 173 E12
Auxvasse U.S.A. 39°1N 91°54W 310 E5
Auyuittuq △ Canada 67°30N 66°0W 295 D18
Auzances France 46°2N 2°30E 173 F9
Auzangate, Nevado Peru 13°47S 71°13W 330 C3
Av-Dovurak Russia 51°17N 91°35E 215 D10
Ava Ill., U.S.A. 37°53N 89°30W 310 G7
Ava Mo., U.S.A. 36°57N 92°40W 308 G7
Avaldsnes Norway 59°21N 5°20E 164 E2
Avallon France 47°30N 3°53E 173 E10
Avalon N.Z. 41°12S 174°56E 143 B2
Avalon Calif., U.S.A. 33°21N 118°20W 307 M8
Avalon Pen. Canada 47°30N 53°20W 299 C9
Avana → Cook Is. 21°14S 159°43W 289 h
Avanavero Suriname 4°51N 57°22W 329 C6
Avanigadda India 16°0N 80°56E 245 G5
Avannaarsua □ Greenland 80°0N 55°0W 154 B5
Avanos Turkey 38°43N 34°51E 212 C6
Avantas Greece 40°57N 25°56E 203 F9
Avaré Brazil 23°4S 48°58W 335 A6
Avarua Cook Is. 21°12S 159°46W 289 h
Avarua Harb. Cook Is. 21°12S 159°46W 289 h
Avatele Cook Is. 19°6S 169°55W 289 g
Avatiu Cook Is. 21°12S 159°47W 289 h
Avawatz Mts. U.S.A. 35°40N 116°30W 307 K10
Avdan Dağı Turkey 40°23N 29°46E 203 F13
Avedøre Denmark 55°37N 12°27E 118 B2
Aveiro Brazil 3°10S 55°5W 329 D6
Aveiro Portugal 40°37N 8°38W 194 E2
Aveiro □ Portugal 40°40N 8°35W 194 E2
Āvej Iran 35°40N 49°15E 247 C6
Avellaneda Argentina 34°40S 58°22W 117 C2
Avellino Italy 40°54N 14°47E 201 B7
Avenal U.S.A. 36°0N 120°8W 306 K6
Avenel U.S.A. 38°59N 76°59W 143 B4
Averøya Norway 63°0N 7°35E 164 A4
Aversa Italy 40°58N 14°12E 201 B7
Avery U.S.A. 47°15N 115°49W 304 C6
Aves, I. de W. Indies 15°45N 63°55W 321 C7
Aves, Is. las Venezuela 12°0N 67°30W 321 D6
Aves Laguna Colorada, Santuario de ⌂ Bolivia 22°30S 67°30W 330 E4
Aves Ridge W. Indies 14°0N 63°30W 321 D7
Avesnes-sur-Helpe France 50°8N 3°55E 173 B10
Avesnois ⌂ France 50°5N 3°45E 173 B10
Avesta Sweden 60°9N 16°10E 162 D10
Aveyron □ France 44°22N 2°45E 174 D6
Aveyron → France 44°5N 1°16E 174 D5
Avezzano Italy 42°2N 13°25E 199 F10
Avgo Greece 35°33N 25°37E 205 F7
Aviá Terai Argentina 26°45S 60°50W 334 B3
Aviano Italy 46°4N 12°36E 199 B9
Aviatu → Cook Is. 21°12S 159°49W 289 h
Aviemore U.K. 57°12N 3°50W 167 D5
Aviemore, L. N.Z. 44°37S 170°18E 285 E5
Avigliana Italy 45°5N 7°23E 198 C4
Avigliano Italy 40°44N 15°43E 201 B8
Avignon France 43°57N 4°50E 175 E8
Ávila Spain 40°39N 4°43W 194 E6
Ávila □ Spain 40°30N 5°0W 194 E6
Ávila, Sierra de Spain 40°40N 5°15W 194 E5
Avila Beach U.S.A. 35°11N 120°44W 307 K6
Avilés Spain 43°35N 5°57W 194 B5
Avintes Portugal 41°7N 8°33W 194 D2
Avis Portugal 39°4N 7°53W 195 F3
Avis Pa., U.S.A. 41°11N 77°19W 312 E7
Avísio → Italy 46°7N 11°5E 198 B8
Avissawella Sri Lanka 6°56N 80°11E 245 L5
Aviston U.S.A. 38°36N 89°36W 310 F7
Aviz = Avis Portugal 39°4N 7°53W 195 F3
Avize France 48°59N 4°1E 173 D11
Avlona = Vlorë Albania 40°32N 19°28E 202 F3
Avlonari Greece 38°31N 24°8E 204 C6
Avlum Denmark 56°16N 8°47E 163 H2
Avoca Vic., Australia 37°5S 143°26E 282 D5
Avoca N.Y., U.S.A. 42°25N 77°25W 312 D7
Avoca → Vic., Australia 35°40S 143°43E 282 C5
Avoca → Wicklow, Ireland 52°48N 6°10W 166 D5
Avola B.C., Canada 51°45N 119°19W 296 C5
Avola Italy 36°56N 15°7E 201 F8
Avon Ill., U.S.A. 40°40N 90°26W 310 D6
Avon N.Y., U.S.A. 42°55N 77°45W 312 D7
Avon → W. Austral., Australia 31°40S 116°7E 279 F2
Avon → Bristol, U.K. 51°29N 2°41W 169 F5
Avon → Dorset, U.K. 50°44N 1°46W 169 G6
Avon → Warks., U.K. 52°0N 2°8W 169 E5
Avon Park U.S.A. 27°36N 81°31W 317 H8
Avondale Ill., U.S.A. 41°56N 87°41W 119 B2
Avondale La., U.S.A. 29°54N 90°12W 131 B1
Avondale Zimbabwe 17°43S 30°58E 269 F3
Avondale Heights Australia 37°45S 144°52E 128 A1
Avonlea Canada 50°0N 105°0W 297 D8
Avonmore Canada 45°10N 74°58W 313 A10
Avonmouth U.K. 51°30N 2°42W 169 F5
Avramov Bulgaria 42°45N 26°38E 203 D10
Avranches France 48°40N 1°20W 172 D5
Avre → France 48°47N 1°22E 172 D8
Avrig Romania 45°43N 24°21E 183 E9
Avrillé France 47°30N 0°35W 172 E6
Avtovac Bos.-H. 43°9N 18°35E 202 C2
Avtovo Russia 59°51N 30°16E 137 B1
Avu Avu Solomon Is. 9°50S 160°22E 287 M11
Awa-Shima Japan 38°27N 139°14E 220 E9
Awag el Baqar Sudan 10°10N 33°10E 257 E3
A'waj → Syria 33°23N 36°20E 250 E7
Awaji Japan 34°32N 135°1E 223 C7
Awaji-Shima Japan 34°30N 134°50E 222 C6
'Awālī Bahrain 26°0N 50°30E 247 E6
Awantipur India 33°55N 75°3E 243 C6
Awanui N.Z. 35°4S 173°17E 284 B2
Aware Ethiopia 8°15N 44°10E 257 F5
Awarja → India 17°5N 76°15E 244 F3
Awarua B. N.Z. 44°28S 168°4E 285 E3
Awarua Pt. N.Z. 44°15S 168°5E 285 E3
Awasa Ethiopia 7°2N 38°28E 257 F4
Awasa, L. Ethiopia 7°0N 38°30E 257 F4
Awash Ethiopia 9°1N 40°10E 257 F5
Awash → Ethiopia 11°45N 41°5E 257 E5
Awash △ Ethiopia 9°8N 40°0E 257 F4
Awaso Ghana 6°15N 2°22W 262 D4
Awat China 40°35N 80°24E 217 C10
Awatere → N.Z. 41°37S 174°10E 285 B9
Awbārī Libya 26°46N 12°57E 258 C2
Awbārī, Idehan Libya 27°10N 11°30E 258 C2
Awdal □ Somali Rep. 10°30N 43°30E 267 B5
Awdheegle Somali Rep. 1°59N 44°50E 267 D5
Awe, L. U.K. 56°17N 5°16W 167 E3
Aweil Sudan 8°42N 27°20E 257 F2
Awgu Nigeria 6°4N 7°24E 263 D6
Awjilah Libya 29°8N 21°7E 258 C4
Awka Nigeria 6°12N 7°5E 263 D6
Aworro Papua N. G. 7°43S 143°11E 286 D2
Awsard Mauritania 22°37N 14°22W 260 D2
Ax-les-Thermes France 42°44N 1°50E 174 F5
Axat France 42°48N 2°13E 174 F6
Axe → U.K. 50°42N 3°4W 169 F5
Axel Heiberg I. Canada 80°0N 90°0W 295 B14
Axim Ghana 4°51N 2°15W 262 E4
Axinim Brazil 4°2S 59°22W 329 D6
Axintele Romania 44°37N 26°47E 183 F11
Axiōma Brazil 6°45S 64°31W 331 B5
Axios → Greece 40°57N 22°35E 202 F6
Axminster U.K. 50°46N 3°0W 169 G4
Axson U.S.A. 31°17N 82°44W 316 D7
Axvall Sweden 58°23N 13°34E 163 F7
Ay France 49°3N 4°1E 173 C11
Ayaantang Eq. Guin. 1°58N 10°24E 264 B2
Ayabaca Peru 4°40S 79°53W 330 A2
Ayabe Japan 35°20N 135°20E 223 B7
Ayacucho Argentina 37°5S 58°20W 334 D4
Ayacucho Peru 13°0S 74°0W 330 C3
Ayacucho □ Peru 14°0S 74°0W 330 C3
Ayaguz = Ayaköz Kazakhstan 48°10N 80°10E 217 C10
Ayakkum Hu China 37°30N 89°20E 217 E11
Ayaköz Kazakhstan 48°10N 80°10E 217 C10
Ayaköz → Kazakhstan 46°40N 79°14E 217 C9
Ayakudi India 10°28N 77°56E 245 J3
Ayala Phil. 6°57N 121°57E 233 H3
Ayamé Ivory C. 5°35N 3°9W 262 D4
Ayamonte Spain 37°12N 7°24W 195 H3
Ayan Russia 56°30N 138°16E 215 D14
Ayancık Turkey 41°57N 34°35E 212 B6
Ayangba Nigeria 7°31N 7°8E 263 D6
Ayapel Colombia 8°19N 75°9W 328 B2
Ayas Turkey 40°2N 32°21E 212 B5
Ayaviri Peru 14°50S 70°35W 330 C3
Ayazağa Turkey 41°6N 28°59E 122 B1
Aybak Afghan. 36°15N 68°5E 240 A3
Aybastı Turkey 40°41N 37°23E 212 B7
Aydarköl Uzbekistan 40°50N 67°10E 217 D7
Aydın Turkey 37°51N 27°51E 212 D2
Aydın □ Turkey 37°50N 28°0E 205 D9
Aydın Dağları Turkey 38°0N 28°0E 205 D10
Aydıncık Turkey 36°9N 33°21E 250 B4
Aydingkol Hu China 42°40N 89°15E 217 D11
Ayelu Ethiopia 10°5N 40°42E 257 E5
Ayenngré Togo 8°40N 1°1E 263 D5
Ayer U.S.A. 42°34N 71°35W 313 D13
Ayer Chawan, Pulau Singapore 1°16N 103°41E 138 B2
Ayer Hitam Malaysia 5°24N 100°16E 237 c
Ayer Merbau, Pulau Singapore 1°16N 103°42E 138 B2
Ayerbe Spain 42°17N 0°41W 196 C4
Ayer's Cliff Canada 45°10N 72°3W 313 A12
Ayers Rock = Uluru Australia 25°23S 131°5E 279 E5
Ayeyarwady = Irrawaddy → Burma 15°50N 95°6E 241 G5
Áyia Napa Cyprus 34°59N 34°0E 207 F10
Áyia Phyla Cyprus 34°43N 33°1E 207 F9
Áyios Amvrósios Cyprus 35°20N 33°35E 207 E9
Áyios Seryios Cyprus 35°12N 33°53E 207 E9
Áyios Theodhoros Cyprus 35°22N 34°1E 207 E10
Áyios Yeóryios = Aghios Georgios Greece 37°28N 23°57E 204 D5
Aykhal Russia 66°0N 111°30E 215 C12
Aykino Russia 62°15N 49°56E 186 B8
Aykirikçi Turkey 39°8N 30°9E 205 B12
Aylesbury U.K. 51°49N 0°49W 169 F7
Aylmer Canada 42°46N 80°59W 312 D4
Aylmer, L. Canada 64°5N 108°30W 294 E10
'Ayn, Wādī al Oman 22°15N 55°28E 247 F7
'Ayn al Ghazālah Libya 32°10N 23°20E 258 B4
Ayn Dār Si. Arabia 25°55N 49°10E 247 E7
Ayn Sifnī Iraq 36°41N 43°20E 213 D10
Ayn Zālah Iraq 36°45N 42°35E 213 D10
Ayna Spain 38°34N 2°3W 197 G2
Aynāt Yemen 16°4N 49°9E 249 C5
'Aynūnah Si. Arabia 28°5N 35°8E 251 K6
Ayod Sudan 8°7N 31°26E 257 F3
Ayolas Paraguay 27°10S 56°59W 334 B4
Ayon, Ostrov Russia 69°50N 169°0E 215 C17
Ayora Spain 39°3N 1°3W 197 F3
Ayorou Niger 14°53N 1°0E 263 C5
Ayos Cameroon 3°53N 12°31E 264 B2
'Ayoûn el 'Atroûs Mauritania 16°38N 9°37W 262 B3
Ayr Queens., Australia 19°35S 147°25E 280 B4
Ayr Ont., Canada 43°17N 80°27W 312 C4
Ayr S. Ayrs., U.K. 55°28N 4°38W 167 F4
Ayr → U.K. 55°28N 4°38W 167 F4
Ayrancı Turkey 37°21N 33°41E 212 D5
Ayrancılar Turkey 38°15N 27°18E 205 C9
Ayre, Pt. of I. of Man 54°25N 4°21W 168 C3
Ayribaba Turkmenistan 37°50N 66°34E 217 E7
Aysha Ethiopia 10°50N 42°23E 257 E5
Ayton Australia 15°56S 145°22E 280 B4
Aytos Bulgaria 42°42N 27°16E 203 D11
Aytoska Planina Bulgaria 42°45N 27°30E 203 D11
Ayu, Kepulauan Indonesia 0°35N 131°5E 231 D8
Ayutla Guatemala 14°40N 92°10W 320 D1
Ayutla de los Libres Mexico 16°54N 99°13W 319 D5
Ayvacık Turkey 39°36N 26°24E 212 C2
Ayvalık Turkey 39°20N 26°46E 205 B8
Az Zabadānī Syria 33°43N 36°5E 250 E7
Az Ẓāhirah Asia 23°40N 56°10E 249 B7
Az Ẓāhirīyah West Bank 31°25N 34°58E 251 G3
Az Ẓahrān Si. Arabia 26°10N 50°7E 247 E6
Az Zarqā Jordan 32°5N 36°4E 251 F7
Az Zarqā' U.A.E. 24°53N 53°4E 247 E7
Az Zāwiyah Libya 32°52N 12°56E 258 B2
Az Zāwiyah □ Libya 32°44N 12°43E 261 B7
Az Zaydīyah Yemen 15°20N 43°1E 248 D3
Az Zībār Iraq 36°52N 44°4E 213 D11
Az Zilfī Si. Arabia 26°12N 44°52E 246 E5
Az Zubayr Iraq 30°26N 47°40E 246 D5
Az Zuqur Yemen 14°0N 42°45E 248 D3
Az Zuwaytīnah Libya 30°58N 20°7E 258 B4
Azabu Tokyo, Japan 140 c3
Azad Kashmir □ Pakistan 33°50N 73°50E 243 C5
Azambuja Portugal 39°4N 8°51W 195 F2
Azamgarh India 26°5N 83°13E 243 F10
Azangaro Peru 14°55S 70°13W 330 C3
Azaouad Mali 19°0N 3°0W 262 B4
Azaouak → Mali 15°30N 3°18E 263 B5
Azaouak, Vallée de l' Mali 15°30N 3°20E 263 B5
Āzār Shahr Iran 37°45N 45°59E 213 D11
Azara Nigeria 8°22N 9°12E 263 D6
Azarān Iran 37°25N 47°16E 213 D12
Azärbayjan = Azerbaijan ■ Asia 40°20N 48°0E 191 K9
Āzarbāyjān-e Gharbī □ Iran 37°0N 44°30E 246 B5
Āzarbāyjān-e Sharqī □ Iran 37°20N 47°0E 246 B5
Azare Nigeria 11°55N 10°10E 263 C7
Azay-le-Rideau France 47°16N 0°30E 172 E7
A'zāz Syria 36°36N 37°4E 250 B8
Azazga Algeria 36°48N 4°22E 261 A5
Azbine = Aïr Niger 18°30N 8°0E 259 E1
Azcapotzalco Mexico 19°28N 99°10W 128 B1
Azefal Mauritania 21°0N 14°45W 260 D2
Azeffoun Algeria 36°51N 4°26E 261 A5
Azemmour Morocco 33°20N 9°20W 260 B3
Azennezal Algeria 22°58N 0°43E 261 D5
Azerbaijan ■ Asia 40°20N 48°0E 191 K9
Azezo Ethiopia 12°28N 37°15E 257 E4
Azimganj India 24°14N 88°16E 243 G13
Aznalcóllar Spain 37°32N 6°17W 195 H4
Azogues Ecuador 2°35S 78°0W 328 D2
Azores = Açores, Is. dos Atl. Oc. 38°0N 27°0W 153 d1
Azores-Biscay Rise Atl. Oc. 42°0N 20°0W 152 B9
Azoum, B. → Chad 10°53N 20°15E 259 F4
Azov Russia 47°3N 39°25E 191 G4
Azov, Sea of Europe 46°0N 36°30E 189 J9
Azovskoye More = Azov, Sea of Europe 46°0N 36°30E 189 J9
Azpeitia Spain 43°12N 2°19W 196 B2
Azrak, B. → Chad 10°52N 20°35E 259 F4
Azraq ash Shīshān Jordan 31°50N 36°49E 251 G7
Azrou Morocco 33°28N 5°19W 260 B3
Aztec U.S.A. 36°49N 107°59W 305 H10
Azteca, Estadia Mexico 19°19N 99°9W 128 C2
Azúa de Compostela Dom. Rep. 18°25N 70°44W 321 C5
Azuaga Spain 38°16N 5°39W 195 G5
Azuara Spain 41°15N 0°53W 196 D4
Azuay □ Ecuador 2°55S 79°0W 328 D2
Azucar, Cerro Pan de Chile 33°19S 70°41W 137 A1
Azuer → Spain 39°8N 3°36W 195 F7
Azuero, Pen. de Panama 7°30N 80°30W 320 E3
Azuga Romania 45°27N 25°33E 183 E10
Azul Argentina 36°42S 59°43W 334 D4
Azul, Lagoa Azores 37°52N 25°47W 153 d3
Azul, Serra Brazil 14°50S 54°50W 331 C7
Azumino Japan 36°20N 137°50E 223 A9
Azurduy Bolivia 19°59S 64°29W 331 D5
Azusa U.S.A. 34°8N 117°52W 307 L9
Azzaba Algeria 36°48N 7°6E 261 A6
Azzano Décimo Italy 45°52N 12°56E 199 C9
Azzel Matti, Sebkra Algeria 26°10N 0°43E 261 C5

B

Ba Be △ Vietnam 22°25N 105°37E 236 A5
Ba Don Vietnam 17°45N 106°26E 236 D6
Ba Dong Vietnam 9°40N 106°33E 237 H6
Ba Ngoi Vietnam 11°54N 109°10E 237 G7
Ba Ria Vietnam 10°30N 107°10E 237 G6
Ba Tri Vietnam 10°2N 106°36E 237 G6
Ba Vi △ Vietnam 21°1N 105°22E 236 B5
Ba Xian = Bazhou China 39°8N 116°22E 226 E9
Baa Indonesia 10°50S 123°0E 278 B3
Baambrugge Neths. 52°15N 4°59E 112 B2
Baamonde Spain 43°7N 7°44W 194 B3
Baao Phil. 13°27N 123°22E 232 E4
Baardheere Somali Rep. 2°20N 42°27E 267 D5
Baarle-Nassau Belgium 51°27N 4°56E 170 C4
Bab el Mandeb Red Sea 12°35N 43°25E 248 D3
Baba Bulgaria 42°44N 23°59E 202 D7
Baba, B. do Angola 14°50S 12°14E 265 E2
Bābā, Koh-i- Afghan. 34°30N 67°0E 240 B2
Baba Budan Hills India 13°30N 75°44E 245 H2
Baba Burnu Turkey 39°29N 26°2E 205 B8
Baba Channel Pakistan 24°48N 66°58E 123 B1
Baba dag Azerbaijan 41°0N 48°19E 191 K9
Baba I. Pakistan 24°49N 66°57E 123 B1
Bābā Kalū Iran 30°7N 50°49E 247 D6
Babaçulândia Brazil 7°13S 47°46W 332 C2
Babadag Romania 44°53N 28°44E 183 F13
Babadağ Turkey 37°49N 28°52E 205 D10
Babaeski Turkey 41°26N 27°6E 203 E11
Babahoyo Ecuador 1°40S 79°30W 328 D2
Babai = Sarju → India 27°21N 81°23E 243 F9
Babak Phil. 7°8N 125°41E 233 H5
Babana Nigeria 10°31N 3°46E 263 C5
Babanusa Sudan 11°20N 27°48E 257 E2
Babar Algeria 35°10N 7°6E 261 A6
Babar Indonesia 8°0S 129°30E 231 F7
Babar Pakistan 31°7N 69°32E 242 D3
Babarkach Pakistan 29°45N 68°0E 242 E3
Babarpur India 28°41N 77°16E 120 A2
Babase I. Papua N. G. 4°0S 153°42E 286 B7
Babayevo Russia 59°24N 35°55E 188 C8
Babb U.S.A. 48°51N 113°27W 304 B7
Babelthuap Palau 7°30N 134°30E 288 c
Babenhausen Germany 49°57N 8°57E 179 F4
Băbeni Romania 44°58N 24°11E 183 F9
Baberu India 25°33N 80°43E 243 G9
Babi Indonesia 2°5N 96°39E 234 B1
Babi Besar, Pulau Malaysia 2°25N 103°59E 237 L4
Babia Gora Europe 49°38N 19°38E 185 J6
Babian Jiang → China 22°55N 101°47E 228 F3
Bābil □ Iraq 32°30N 44°30E 246 C5
Babile Ethiopia 9°16N 42°11E 257 F5
Babile ⌂ Ethiopia 8°45N 42°20E 267 C5
Babimost Poland 52°10N 15°49E 185 F2
Babinda Australia 17°20S 145°56E 280 B4
Babine Canada 55°22N 126°37W 296 B3
Babine → Canada 55°45N 127°44W 296 B3
Babine L. Canada 54°48N 126°0W 296 C3
Babiogórski △ Poland 49°38N 19°39E 185 J6
Babo Indonesia 2°30S 133°30E 231 E8
Babócsa Hungary 46°2N 17°21E 182 D2
Bābol Iran 36°40N 52°50E 247 B7
Bābol Sar Iran 36°45N 52°45E 247 B7
Babor, Dj. Algeria 36°31N 5°25E 261 A6
Baborów Poland 50°7N 18°1E 185 H5
Baboua C.A.R. 5°49N 14°58E 264 A2
Babruysk Belarus 53°10N 29°15E 177 B15
Babson Park U.S.A. 27°49N 81°32W 317 H8
Babuhri India 26°49N 69°43E 242 F3
Babuna Macedonia 41°30N 21°40E 202 E5
Babura Nigeria 12°51N 8°59E 263 C6
Babusar Pass Pakistan 35°12N 73°59E 243 B5
Babushkin Russia 55°51N 37°42E 129 A4
Babušnica Serbia 43°7N 22°27E 202 C6
Babuyan Phil. 10°0N 118°54E 233 F2
Babuyan Chan. Phil. 18°40N 121°30E 232 B3
Babuyan I. Phil. 19°32N 121°57E 232 B3
Babuyan Is. Phil. 19°10N 121°40E 232 B3
Babylon Iraq 32°34N 44°22E 213 F11
Bač Serbia 45°29N 19°17E 182 E4
Bâc → Moldova 46°55N 29°26E 183 D14
Bac Can Vietnam 22°8N 105°49E 228 F5
Bac Giang Vietnam 21°16N 106°11E 236 B6
Bac Lieu Vietnam 9°17N 105°43E 237 H5
Bac Ninh Vietnam 21°13N 106°4E 236 B6
Bac Phan Vietnam 22°0N 105°0E 228 G5
Bacaadweyn Somali Rep. 7°15N 47°40E 267 C6
Bacabal Brazil 4°15S 44°45W 332 B3
Bacacay Phil. 13°18N 123°47E 232 E4
Bacajá → Brazil 3°25S 51°50W 329 D7
Bacalar Mexico 18°43N 88°27W 319 D7
Bacan, Kepulauan Indonesia 0°35S 127°30E 231 E7
Bacarra Phil. 18°15N 120°37E 232 B3
Bacău Romania 46°35N 26°55E 183 D11
Bacău □ Romania 46°30N 26°45E 183 D11
Baccarat France 48°28N 6°42E 173 D13
Bacchus Marsh Australia 37°43S 144°27E 282 D6
Bacerac Mexico 30°18N 108°50W 318 A3
Băceşti Romania 46°50N 27°11E 183 D12
Bach Long Vi, Dao Vietnam 20°10N 107°40E 236 B6
Bach Ma △ Vietnam 16°11N 107°49E 236 D6
Bachaquero Venezuela 9°56N 71°8W 328 B3
Bacharach Germany 50°3N 7°44E 179 E3
Bachelor's Beach Bonaire 12°11N 68°17W 322 h
Bachhwara India 25°35N 85°54E 243 G11
Bachu China 39°46N 78°34E 217 E9
Bachuma Ethiopia 6°48N 35°53E 257 F4
Bačina Serbia 43°42N 21°23E 202 C5
Back → Canada 65°10N 104°0W 294 D11
Back B. India 18°56N 72°48E 130 B1
Bačka Palanka Serbia 45°17N 19°27E 182 E4
Bačka Topola Serbia 45°49N 19°39E 182 E4
Bäckebo Sweden 56°53N 16°4E 163 H10
Bäckefors Sweden 58°48N 12°9E 163 F6
Bäckhammar Sweden 59°10N 14°11E 162 E8
Bački Petrovac Serbia 45°29N 19°32E 182 E4
Backnang Germany 48°56N 9°26E 179 G5
Backstairs Passage Australia 35°40S 138°5E 282 C3
Baclaran Phil. 14°31N 121°0E 127 B2
Bacnotan Phil. 16°43N 120°21E 232 C3
Baco, Mt. Phil. 12°49N 121°10E 232 E3
Bacolod Phil. 10°40N 122°57E 233 F4
Bacon Phil. 13°3N 124°3E 232 E5
Baconton U.S.A. 31°23N 84°10W 316 D5
Bacoor Phil. 14°27N 120°56E 127 C1
Bacoor B. Phil. 14°27N 120°54E 127 C1
Bacqueville-en-Caux France 49°47N 1°0E 172 C8
Bács-Kiskun □ Hungary 46°43N 19°30E 182 D4
Bácsalmás Hungary 46°8N 19°17E 182 D4
Bacuag = Placer Phil. 9°36N 125°38E 233 G5
Bacuit = El Nido Phil. 11°10N 119°25E 233 F2
Bacuk Malaysia 6°4N 102°25E 237 J4
Bácum Mexico 27°33N 110°5W 318 B2
Bād Iran 33°41N 52°1E 247 C7
Bad → U.S.A. 44°21N 100°22W 308 C3
Bad Aussee Austria 47°43N 13°45E 180 D6
Bad Axe U.S.A. 43°48N 83°0W 312 C2
Bad Bergzabern Germany 49°6N 7°59E 179 F3
Bad Berleburg Germany 51°2N 8°26E 178 D4
Bad Bevensen Germany 53°5N 10°35E 178 B6
Bad Bramstedt Germany 53°55N 9°53E 178 B5
Bad Brückenau Germany 50°18N 9°47E 179 E5
Bad Doberan Germany 54°6N 11°53E 178 A7
Bad Driburg Germany 51°43N 9°1E 178 D5
Bad Ems Germany 50°20N 7°43E 179 E3
Bad Frankenhausen Germany 51°21N 11°5E 178 D7
Bad Freienwalde Germany 52°46N 14°1E 178 C10
Bad Goisern Austria 47°38N 13°38E 180 D6
Bad Harzburg Germany 51°52N 10°34E 178 D6
Bad Hersfeld Germany 50°52N 9°42E 178 E5
Bad Hofgastein Austria 47°17N 13°6E 180 D6
Bad Homburg Germany 50°13N 8°38E 179 E4
Bad Honnef Germany 50°38N 7°13E 178 E3
Bad Iburg Germany 52°10N 8°3E 178 C4
Bad Ischl Austria 47°44N 13°38E 180 D6
Bad Kissingen Germany 50°11N 10°4E 179 E6
Bad Königshofen Germany 50°17N 10°28E 179 E6
Bad Kreuznach Germany 49°50N 7°51E 179 F3
Bad Krozingen Germany 47°54N 7°42E 179 H3
Bad Kudowa = Kudowa-Zdrój Poland 50°27N 16°15E 185 H3
Bad Laasphe Germany 50°56N 8°25E 178 E4
Bad Landeck = Lądek-Zdrój Poland 50°21N 16°53E 185 H3
Bad Langensalza Germany 51°5N 10°38E 178 D6
Bad Lauterberg Germany 51°38N 10°28E 178 D6
Bad Leonfelden Austria 48°31N 14°18E 180 C7
Bad Liebenwerda Germany 51°31N 13°24E 178 D9
Bad Mergentheim Germany 49°28N 9°42E 179 F5
Bad Münstereifel Germany 50°33N 6°46E 178 E2
Bad Nauheim Germany 50°21N 8°43E 179 E4
Bad Neuenahr-Ahrweiler Germany 50°32N 7°5E 178 E3
Bad Neustadt Germany 50°18N 10°13E 179 E6
Bad Oeynhausen Germany 52°12N 8°46E 178 C4
Bad Oldesloe Germany 53°48N 10°22E 178 B6
Bad Orb Germany 50°12N 9°22E 179 E5
Bad Polzin = Polanica-Zdrój Poland 50°24N 16°32E 185 H3
Bad Pyrmont Germany 51°59N 9°16E 178 D5
Bad Reichenhall Germany 47°43N 12°54E 179 H8
Bad Reinerz = Duszniki-Zdrój Poland 50°24N 16°24E 185 H3
Bad Säckingen Germany 47°33N 7°56E 179 H3
Bad St. Leonhard Austria 46°58N 14°47E 180 E7
Bad Salzuflen Germany 52°5N 8°45E 178 C4
Bad Salzungen Germany 50°48N 10°14E 178 E6
Bad Schönfliess = Trzcińsko Zdrój Poland 52°58N 14°35E 185 F1
Bad Schwartau Germany 53°55N 10°41E 178 B6
Bad Segeberg Germany 53°56N 10°17E 178 B6
Bad Tölz Germany 47°45N 11°34E 179 H7
Bad Urach Germany 48°29N 9°23E 179 G5
Bad Vöslau Austria 47°58N 16°12E 181 D9
Bad Waldsee Germany 47°55N 9°45E 179 H5
Bad Wildungen Germany 51°6N 9°7E 178 D5
Bad Wimpfen Germany 49°13N 9°11E 179 F5
Bad Windsheim Germany 49°30N 10°25E 179 F6
Bad Zwischenahn Germany 53°12N 8°1E 178 B4
Bada Barabil India 22°7N 85°24E 243 H11
Badagara India 11°35N 75°40E 245 J2
Badagri Nigeria 6°25N 2°55E 263 D5
Badain Jaran Shamo China 40°23N 102°0E 218 C9
Badajós, L. Brazil 3°15S 62°50W 329 D5
Badajoz Spain 38°50N 6°59W 195 G4
Badajoz □ Spain 38°40N 6°30W 195 G4
Badakhshān □ Afghan. 36°30N 71°0E 240 A3
Badaling China 40°20N 116°0E 226 D9
Badalona Spain 41°26N 2°15E 114 A2
Badalzai Afghan. 29°50N 65°35E 242 E1
Badampahar India 22°10N 86°10E 244 C8
Badanah Si. Arabia 30°58N 41°30E 246 D4
Badarinath India 30°45N 79°30E 243 D8
Badarpur India 24°54N 92°36E 241 C4
Badas, Kepulauan Indonesia 0°45N 107°5E 234 B3
Baddo → Pakistan 28°0N 64°20E 240 D2
Bade Indonesia 7°10S 139°35E 231 F9
Badeggi Nigeria 9°4N 6°8E 263 D6
Badéguichéri Niger 14°30N 5°22E 263 C6
Baden Austria 48°1N 16°13E 181 C9
Baden Switz. 47°28N 8°18E 179 H4
Baden U.S.A. 40°38N 80°14W 312 F4
Baden-Baden Germany 48°44N 8°13E 179 G4
Baden-Württemberg □ Germany 48°20N 8°40E 179 G4
Badgam India 34°1N 74°45E 243 B6
Badgastein Austria 47°7N 13°9E 180 D6
Badger Nfld. & L., Canada 49°0N 56°4W 299 C8
Badger Calif., U.S.A. 36°38N 119°1W 306 J7
Bādghīs □ Afghan. 35°0N 63°0E 240 B1
Badgingarra △ Australia 30°23S 115°22E 279 F2
Badhoevedorp Neths. 52°20N 4°47E 112 A1
Badia Polésine Italy 45°5N 11°29E 199 C8
Badian Phil. 9°55N 123°24E 233 G4
Badiar △ Guinea 13°37N 13°11W 262 C2
Badin Pakistan 24°38N 68°54E 242 G3
Badinka ⌂ Mali 13°31N 9°28W 262 C3
Badjokola Dem. Rep. of the Congo 3°54N 20°17E 264 B4
Badlands U.S.A. 43°55N 102°30W 308 D2
Badlands △ U.S.A. 43°38N 102°56W 308 D2
Badlī India 28°44N 77°8E 120 A1
Badnera India 20°48N 77°44E 244 D3
Badoc Phil. 17°56N 120°28E 232 C3
Badogo Mali 11°2N 8°13W 262 C3
Badoumbé Mali 13°42N 10°15W 262 C2
Badr Ḥunayn Si. Arabia 23°44N 38°46E 248 B2
Badrah Iraq 33°6N 45°58E 213 F11
Badrain Jaran Shamo China 40°40N 103°20E 226 D2
Badrinath India 30°44N 79°29E 243 D8
Badu Australia 10°7S 142°11E 280 a
Badulla Sri Lanka 7°1N 81°7E 245 L5
Badung, Bukit Indonesia 8°49S 115°10E 231 K18
Badung, Selat Indonesia 8°40S 115°22E 231 K18
Badupi Burma 21°36N 93°27E 241 E4
Badvel India 14°45N 79°3E 245 G4
Baena Spain 37°37N 4°20W 195 H6
Baengnyeongdo S. Korea 37°57N 124°40E 224 D2
Baerami Australia 32°27S 150°27E 283 B9
Bærum Norway 59°54N 10°36E 133 A2
Baetov Kyrgyzstan 41°13N 74°54E 217 D8
Baeza Ecuador 0°25S 77°53W 328 D2
Baeza Spain 37°57N 3°25W 195 H7
Bafang Cameroon 5°9N 10°11E 263 D7
Bafatá Guinea-Biss. 12°8N 14°40W 262 C2
Baffin B. N. Amer. 72°0N 64°0W 292 B13
Baffin I. Canada 68°0N 75°0W 295 D17
Bafia Cameroon 4°40N 11°10E 263 E7
Bafilo Togo 9°22N 1°22E 263 D5
Bafing → Mali 13°49N 10°50W 262 C2
Bafing △ Mali 12°38N 10°28W 262 C2
Bafliyūn Syria 36°37N 36°59E 246 B3
Bafoulabé Mali 13°50N 10°55W 262 C2
Bafoussam Cameroon 5°28N 10°25E 263 D7
Bāfq Iran 31°40N 55°25E 247 D7
Bafra Turkey 41°34N 35°54E 212 B6
Bafra Burnu Turkey 41°45N 36°2E 212 B7
Bāft Iran 29°15N 56°38E 247 D8
Bafut Cameroon 6°6N 10°2E 263 D7
Bafwasende Dem. Rep. of the Congo 1°3N 27°5E 268 B2
Bagabag Phil. 16°30N 121°16E 232 C3
Bagabag I. Papua N. G. 4°48S 146°14E 286 C4
Bagac Phil. 14°36N 120°23E 232 D3
Bagac B. Phil. 14°36N 120°20E 232 D3
Bagaha India 27°6N 84°5E 244 A7
Bagalkot India 16°10N 75°40E 245 F2
Bagam Niger 15°43N 6°35E 263 B6
Bagamanoc Phil. 13°57N 124°17E 232 E5
Bagamoyo Tanzania 6°28S 38°55E 268 D4
Bagan = Pagan Burma 21°10N 94°52E 241 E5
Bagan Datoh Malaysia 3°59N 100°47E 237 L3
Bagan Serai Malaysia 5°1N 100°32E 237 K3
Baganga Phil. 7°34N 126°33E 233 H6
Bagani Namibia 18°7S 21°41E 270 A3
Bagansiapiapi Indonesia 2°12N 100°50E 234 B2
Bagasra India 21°30N 71°0E 242 J4
Bagata Dem. Rep. of the Congo 3°44S 17°57E 264 C3
Bagaud India 22°19N 75°53E 242 H6
Bagawi Sudan 12°20N 34°18E 257 E3
Bagbag Sudan 15°23N 31°30E 257 D3
Bağcılar Turkey 41°2N 28°49E 122 B1
Bagdad Calif., U.S.A. 34°35N 115°53W 307 L11
Bagdad Fla., U.S.A. 30°36N 87°2W 317 E2
Bagdarin Russia 54°26N 113°36E 215 D12
Bagé Brazil 31°20S 54°15W 335 C5
Bagenalstown = Muine Bheag Ireland 52°42N 6°58W 166 D5
Bagepalli India 13°47N 77°47E 245 H3
Bagevadi India 16°35N 75°58E 244 F2
Baggao Phil. 17°56N 121°46E 232 C3
Baggio Italy 45°27N 9°6E 129 B1
Baggs U.S.A. 41°2N 107°39W 304 F10
Bagh Pakistan 33°59N 73°45E 243 C5
Bāgh-e Feyz Iran 35°44N 51°19E 141 A1
Baghain → India 25°32N 81°1E 243 G9
Baghdād Iraq 33°20N 44°23E 113 A2
Baghdād al Muthana ✈ (BGW) Iraq 33°17N 44°30E 113 B2
Baghdad Int. ✈ (SDA) Iraq 33°15N 44°14E 113 B1
Baghdadi Georgia 42°5N 42°49E 213 A10
Bagherhat Bangla. 22°40N 89°47E 241 D2
Bagheria Italy 38°5N 13°30E 200 D6
Baghlān Afghan. 32°12N 68°46E 240 A3
Baghlān □ Afghan. 36°0N 68°30E 240 B3
Bagley U.S.A. 47°32N 95°24W 308 B6
Bagmari India 22°34N 88°23E 124 B2
Bagn Norway 60°49N 9°34E 164 D6
Bagnara Cálabra Italy 38°17N 15°48E 201 D8
Bagnasco Italy 44°18N 8°2E 198 D5
Bagnell Dam U.S.A. 38°14N 92°36W 310 F4
Bagnères-de-Bigorre France 43°5N 0°9E 174 E4
Bagnères-de-Luchon France 42°47N 0°38E 174 F4
Bagneux France 48°47N 2°18E 134 B2
Bagni di Lucca Italy 44°1N 10°35E 198 D7
Bagno di Romagna Italy 43°50N 11°57E 199 E8
Bagnoles-de-l'Orne France 48°32N 0°25W 172 D6
Bagnolet France 48°52N 2°25E 134 A3
Bagnols-sur-Cèze France 44°10N 4°36E 175 D8
Bagnorea = Bagnoregio Italy 42°37N 12°5E 199 F9
Bagnorégio Italy 42°37N 12°5E 199 F9
Bago = Pegu Burma 17°20N 96°29E 241 G6
Bago Phil. 10°32N 122°50E 233 F4
Bagodar India 24°5N 85°52E 243 G11
Bagrationovsk Russia 54°23N 20°39E 184 D7
Bagrdan Serbia 44°5N 21°11E 202 B5
Bagsværd Denmark 55°45N 12°27E 118 A2
Bagsværd Sø Denmark 55°46N 12°28E 118 A2
Bagua Peru 5°35S 78°22W 330 B2
Baguiati India 22°36N 88°25E 124 B2
Baguio Phil. 16°26N 120°34E 232 C3
Bagumbayan Phil. 14°28N 121°2E 127 C2
Bağyurdu Turkey 38°25N 27°41E 205 C9
Bagzane, Monts Niger 17°43N 8°45E 263 B6
Bah India 26°53N 78°36E 243 F8
Bahabón de Esgueva Spain 41°52N 3°43W 194 D7
Bahadurabad Ghat Bangla. 25°11N 89°44E 241 C2
Bahadurganj India 26°16N 87°49E 243 F12
Bahadurgarh India 28°40N 76°57E 242 E7
Baha'i Temple U.S.A. 42°4N 87°41W 119 A2
Bahaïa Somali Rep. 11°16N 49°50E 267 B6
Baham, Pte. Martinique 14°24N 60°50W 322 j
Bahama, Canal Viejo de W. Indies 22°10N 77°30W 320 B4
Bahamas ■ N. Amer. 24°0N 75°0W 321 B5
Bahār Iran 34°54N 48°26E 213 E13
Baharak Afghan. 37°0N 70°53E 240 A3
Baharampur India 24°2N 88°27E 243 G13
Baharîya, El Wâhât al Egypt 28°0N 28°50E 256 B2

Baharu Pandan = Pandan
  Malaysia 1°32N 103°46E **237** d
Bahawalnagar *Pakistan* 30°0N 73°15E **242** E5
Bahawalpur *Pakistan* 29°24N 71°40E **242** E4
Bahçe *Turkey* 37°13N 36°34E **212** D7
Bahçecik *Turkey* 40°41N 29°44E **203** F13
Bahçeköy *Turkey* 41°10N 28°59E **122** A1
Bahçelievler *Turkey* 41°0N 28°50E **122** B1
Baheli *Phil.* 10°0N 118°47E **232** F2
Bäherden *Turkmenistan* 38°25N 57°26E **247** B8
Baheri *India* 28°45N 79°34E **243** E8
Bahgul → *India* 27°45N 79°36E **243** F8
Bahi *Tanzania* 5°58S 35°21E **268** D4
Bahi Swamp *Tanzania* 6°10S 35°0E **268** D4
Bahía = Salvador *Brazil* 13°0S 38°30W **333** D4
Bahía □ *Brazil* 12°0S 42°0W **333** D3
Bahía, Is. de la *Honduras* 16°45N 86°15W **320** C2
Bahía Blanca *Argentina* 38°35S 62°13W **334** D3
Bahía de Caráquez
  Ecuador 0°40S 80°27W **328** D1
Bahía Kino *Mexico* 28°47N 111°58W **318** B2
Bahía Laura *Argentina* 48°10S 66°30W **336** C3
Bahía Mansa *Chile* 40°35S 73°46W **336** B2
Bahía Negra *Paraguay* 20°5S 58°5W **331** E6
Bahía Solano *Colombia* 6°14N 77°25W **328** B2
Bahir Dar *Ethiopia* 11°37N 37°10E **257** E4
Bahlah *Oman* 22°58N 57°18E **249** F8
Bahmanzād *Iran* 31°15N 51°47E **247** D6
Bahmer *Algeria* 27°32N 0°10W **261** C4
Bahr el Ahmar □ *Egypt* 28°40N 31°30E **251** K2
Bahr el Ahmar □ *Sudan* 20°0N 35°0E **256** D4
Bahr el Jabal □ *Sudan* 4°0N 31°0E **257** G3
Bahraich *India* 27°38N 81°37E **243** F9
Bahrain ■ *Asia* 26°0N 50°35E **247** E6
Bahror *India* 27°51N 76°20E **242** F7
Bahtīm *Egypt* 30°8N 31°16E **117** A2
Bāhū Kalāt *Iran* 25°43N 61°25E **247** E9
Bai *Mali* 13°35N 3°28W **262** C4
Bai Bung, Mui = Ca Mau, Mui
  Vietnam 8°38N 104°44E **237** H5
Bai Thuong *Vietnam* 19°54N 105°23E **236** C5
Baia de Aramă *Romania* 45°0N 22°50E **182** E7
Baia Farta *Angola* 12°40S 13°11E **265** G2
Baia Mare *Romania* 47°40N 23°35E **183** C8
Baia-Sprie *Romania* 47°41N 23°43E **183** C8
Baião *Brazil* 2°40S 49°40W **332** B2
Baïbokoum *Chad* 7°46N 15°43E **259** G3
Baicheng *Jilin, China* 45°38N 122°42E **227** B12
Baicheng *Xinjiang Uygur,*
  China 41°46N 81°52E **217** D10
Băicoi *Romania* 45°3N 25°52E **183** E10
Baidoa = Baydhabo
  Somali Rep. 3°8N 43°30E **267** D5
Baie-Comeau *Canada* 49°12N 68°10W **299** D6
Baie du Cap *Mauritius* 20°29S 57°22E **272** e
Baie-Mahault *Guadeloupe* 16°16N 61°35W **322** e
Baie-St-Paul *Canada* 47°28N 70°32W **299** C5
Baie Ste-Anne *Seychelles* 4°18S 55°45E **272** c
Baie-Trinité *Canada* 49°25N 67°20W **299** C6
Baie Verte *Canada* 49°55N 56°12W **299** C8
Baignes-Ste-Radegonde
  France 45°23N 0°25W **174** C3
Baigneux-les-Juifs *France* 47°31N 4°39E **173** E11
Baihar *India* 22°6N 80°33E **243** H9
Baihe *Hubei, China* 32°50N 110°5E **228** H6
Baihe *Jilin, China* 42°27N 128°9E **227** C15
Baihetan Dam *China* 27°11N 102°54E **228** D4
Ba'iji *Iraq* 35°0N 43°30E **213** E10
Baijnath *India* 29°55N 79°37E **243** E8
Baikal, L. = Baykal, Oz.
  Russia 53°0N 108°0E **215** D11
Baikonur = Bayqongyr
  Kazakhstan 47°50N 66°3E **216** C6
Baikunthpur *India* 23°15N 82°33E **243** H10
Bailadila, Mt. *India* 18°43N 81°15E **244** E5
Baile Átha Cliath = Dublin
  Ireland 53°21N 6°15W **120** A2
Baile Átha Fhirdhia = Ardee
  Ireland 53°52N 6°33W **166** C5
Baile Átha I = Athy *Ireland* 53°0N 7°0W **166** D5
Baile Átha Luain = Athlone
  Ireland 53°25N 7°56W **166** C4
Baile Átha Troim = Trim
  Ireland 53°33N 6°48W **166** C5
Baile Brigín = Balbriggan
  Ireland 53°37N 6°11W **166** C5
Băile Govora *Romania* 45°5N 24°11E **183** E9
Băile Herculane *Romania* 44°53N 22°26E **182** F7
Băile Olăneşti *Romania* 45°12N 24°14E **183** E9
Băile Tuşnad *Romania* 46°9N 25°51E **183** D10
Bailén *Spain* 38°8N 3°48W **195** G7
Băileşti *Romania* 44°1N 23°20E **183** F8
Baileys Crossroads *U.S.A.* 38°50N 77°6W **143** B3
Bailing *Indonesia* 15°55N 74°53E **246** G2
Bailique, Ilha *Brazil* 0°54N 49°58W **332** A2
Baille-Argent *Guadeloupe* 16°15N 61°48W **322** e
Bailläf *Guadeloupe* 16°1N 61°44W **322** e
Bailly *France* 48°50N 2°4E **134** A1
Bailulgh *Afghan.* 32°40N 66°47E **240** B2
Bailundo = Luau *Angola* 10°40S 22°10E **265** G4
Bailundo *Angola* 12°10S 15°50E **265** G3
Baima *China* 33°0N 100°26E **228** H3
Baimuru *Papua N. G.* 7°35S 144°51E **286** D3
Bain-de-Bretagne *France* 47°50N 1°40W **172** E5
Bainbridge *Ga., U.S.A.* 30°55N 84°35W **316** E5
Bainbridge *Ind., U.S.A.* 39°46N 86°49W **311** E10
Bainbridge *N.Y., U.S.A.* 42°18N 75°29W **313** D9
Bainbridge *Ohio, U.S.A.* 39°14N 83°16W **311** F13
Bainbridge Island *U.S.A.* 47°38N 122°32W **306** C4
Baine *China* 42°0N 128°0E **219** C14
Baing *Indonesia* 10°14S 120°34E **231** F6
Bainiu *China* 32°50N 112°15E **228** H7
Bainiyk *Papua N. G.* 3°40S 143°4E **286** B2
Baiona *Spain* 42°6N 8°52W **194** C2
Ba'ir *Jordan* 30°45N 36°55E **251** H7
Baird Mts. *U.S.A.* 67°0N 160°0W **303** C7
Bairiki = Tarawa *Kiribati* 1°30N 173°0E **288** G9
Bairin Youqi *China* 43°30N 118°35E **227** C10
Bairnsdale *Australia* 37°48S 147°36E **283** D7
Bairro Alto Lisbon, *Portugal* **126** b1
Bairro Lopes *Lisbon, Portugal* **126** b3
Bais *Phil.* 9°35N 123°7E **233** G4
Baisha *Guangdong, China* 23°8N 113°11E **121** B2
Baisha *Henan, China* 34°20N 112°32E **228** G7
Baisha Li *China* 19°12N 109°20E **236** C7
Baishan *China* 42°43N 127°14E **227** C14
Baissa *Nigeria* 7°14N 10°38E **263** D8
Baitadi *Nepal* 29°35N 80°25E **243** E9
Baitarani → *India* 20°45N 86°48E **240** c2
Baixa *Lisbon, Portugal* **126** c2
Baixa Grande *Brazil* 11°57S 40°11W **333** D3
Baixa Limia-Sierra do Xurés △
  Spain 41°55N 8°4W **194** D2
Baixo-Longa *Angola* 15°41S 18°45E **265** F3
Baiyer River *Papua N. G.* 5°32S 144°9E **286** C3
Baiyin *China* 36°45N 104°14E **226** F3
Baiyü *China* 31°16N 98°50E **228** E2
Baiyu Shan *China* 37°15N 107°30E **226** F4
Baiyu *Sudan* 17°35N 32°7E **256** D3
Baiyun *China* 23°11N 113°16E **121** A2
Baiyun Int'l Airport *China* 23°11N 113°15E **121** A2
Baiyun Mountain Scenic Area
  China 23°11N 113°17E **121** A2

Baj Baj *India* 22°30N 88°5E **243** H13
Baja *Hungary* 46°12N 18°59E **182** D3
Baja, Pta. *Easter I., Chile* 27°10S 109°22W **330** b
Baja, Pta. *Baja Calif.,*
  Mexico 29°58N 115°49W **318** B1
Baja California *Mexico* 31°10N 115°12W **318** A1
Baja California □ *Mexico* 30°0N 115°0W **318** B2
Baja California Sur □
  Mexico 25°50N 111°50W **318** B2
Bajag *India* 22°40N 81°21E **243** H9
Bajamar *Canary Is.* 28°33N 16°20W **153** e1
Bajana *India* 23°7N 71°49E **242** H4
Bajatrejo *Indonesia* 8°29S 114°19E **231** J17
Bajera *Indonesia* 8°31S 115°2E **231** J18
Bäjgīrān *Iran* 37°36N 58°24E **247** B8
Bājil *Yemen* 15°4N 43°17E **248** D3
Bajimba, Mt. *Australia* 29°17S 152°6E **281** D5
Bajina Bašta *Serbia* 43°58N 19°35E **202** C3
Bajmok *Serbia* 45°57N 19°24E **182** B3
Bajo Boquete *Panama* 8°46N 82°27W **320** E3
Bajo Caracoles *Argentina* 47°27S 70°56W **336** C2
Bajo Nuevo *Caribbean* 15°40N 78°50W **320** C4
Bajoga *Nigeria* 10°57N 11°20E **263** C7
Bajool *Australia* 23°40S 150°35E **280** C5
Bak *Hungary* 46°43N 16°51E **182** D1
Bakel *C.A.R.* 6°15N 20°20E **264** A4
Bakar *Croatia* 45°18N 14°32E **199** C11
Bakassi Pen. *Cameroon* 4°42N 8°20E **263** E6
Bakel *Senegal* 14°56N 12°20W **262** C2
Baker *Calif., U.S.A.* 35°16N 116°4W **307** K10
Baker *Fla., U.S.A.* 30°48N 86°41W **317** E3
Baker *Mont., U.S.A.* 46°22N 104°17W **304** C11
Baker, Canal *Chile* 47°45S 74°45W **336** C2
Baker, L. *Canada* 64°0N 96°0W **294** C12
Baker, Mt. *U.S.A.* 48°50N 121°49W **304** B3
Baker City *U.S.A.* 44°47N 117°50W **304** D5
Baker I. *Pac. Oc.* 0°10N 176°35W **277** A15
Baker I. *Alaska, U.S.A.* 55°20N 133°40W **296** B2
Baker I. *Australia* 26°54S 126°5E **279** E4
Baker Lake *Canada* 64°20N 96°3W **294** C12
Bakere
  Dem. Rep. of the Congo 1°36N 23°50E **264** B4
Bakerhill *U.S.A.* 31°47N 85°18W **316** D4
Bakers Creek *Australia* 21°13S 149°7E **280** C4
Bakers Dozen Is. *Canada* 56°45N 78°45W **298** A4
Bakersfield *Calif., U.S.A.* 35°23N 119°1W **307** K8
Bakersfield *Vt., U.S.A.* 44°45N 72°48W **313** B12
Bakharden = Bäherden
  Turkmenistan 38°25N 57°26E **247** B8
Bakhchysaray *Ukraine* 44°40N 33°45E **189** F7
Bakhmach *Ukraine* 51°10N 32°45E **189** G7
Bakhmut = Artemovsk
  Ukraine 48°35N 38°0E **189** H9
Bākhtarān = Kermānshāh
  Iran 34°23N 47°0E **213** E12
Bākhtarān = Kermānshāh □
  Iran 34°0N 46°30E **246** C5
Baki = Krasnyye Baki
  Russia 57°40N 45°10E **190** B7
Bakı *Azerbaijan* 40°29N 49°56E **191** K9
Bakı *Somali Rep.* 10°30N 43°8E **267** B5
Bakır → *Turkey* 38°55N 27°0E **205** C9
Bakırdaği *Turkey* 38°13N 35°46E **212** C6
Bakırköy *Turkey* 40°58N 28°52E **122** C1
Bakkafjörður *Iceland* 66°2N 14°48W **155** A12
Bakkaflói *Iceland* 66°10N 14°45W **155** A12
Bakkagerði *Iceland* 65°31N 13°49W **155** B13
Baklan *Turkey* 38°0N 29°36E **205** C11
Bako *Ethiopia* 5°51N 36°23E **257** F4
Bako *Ivory C.* 9°8N 7°40W **262** D3
Bako △ *Malaysia* 1°43N 110°28E **235** B4
Bakony *Hungary* 47°10N 17°30E **182** C2
Bakony Forest = Bakony
  Hungary 47°10N 17°30E **182** C2
Bakool □ *Somali Rep.* 4°0N 44°0E **267** D5
Bakori *Nigeria* 11°34N 7°25E **263** C6
Bakovka *Russia* 55°40N 37°19E **129** B2
Baksan *Russia* 43°42N 43°32E **191** J6
Bakswaho *India* 24°15N 79°18E **243** G8
Baku = Bakı *Azerbaijan* 40°29N 49°56E **191** K9
Bakun Dam *Malaysia* 2°50N 113°50E **235** B4
Bakundi *Nigeria* 8°2N 10°45E **263** D7
Bakung *Indonesia* 0°5N 104°26E **234** B2
Bakungan *Indonesia* 0°0N 104°26E **234** B2
Bakuriani *Georgia* 41°44N 43°31E **213** B10
Bakutis Coast *Antarctica* 74°0S 120°0W **151** D11
Bakwa-Kenge
  Dem. Rep. of the Congo 4°51S 22°4E **265** C4
Bakwanga = Mbuji-Mayi
  Dem. Rep. of the Congo 6°9S 23°40E **265** D4
Baky = Bakı *Azerbaijan* 40°29N 49°56E **191** K9
Bal Harbor *U.S.A.* 25°53N 80°7W **318** b
Bala *Ont., Canada* 45°1N 79°37W **312** A5
Bala *Senegal* 14°1N 13°8W **262** C2
Balá *Turkey* 39°32N 33°7E **212** C5
Bala *Gwynedd, U.K.* 52°54N 3°36W **168** E4
Bala, L. *U.K.* 52°53N 3°37W **168** E4
Balá Morghāb *Afghan.* 35°35N 63°20E **240** B3
Balabac I. *Phil.* 7°59N 117°4E **233** H1
Balabac I. *Phil.* 8°0N 117°0E **233** H1
Balabac Str. *E. Indies* 7°53N 117°5E **230** C5
Balabagh *Afghan.* 34°25N 70°12E **242** B4
Ba'labakk *Lebanon* 34°0N 36°10E **250** E7
Balabalangan, Kepulauan
  Indonesia 2°20S 117°30E **235** C5
Balabio, Î. *N. Cal.* 20°7S 164°11E **288** d
Bălăcița *Romania* 44°23N 23°8E **183** F8
Balad *Iraq* 34°0N 44°5E **213** F11
Balad Rūz *Iraq* 33°42N 45°5E **213** F11
Bālādeh *Fārs, Iran* 29°17N 51°56E **247** D6
Bālādeh *Māzandaran, Iran* 36°12N 51°48E **247** B6
Balaghat *India* 21°49N 80°12E **244** D5
Balaghat Ra. *India* 18°50N 76°30E **244** E3
Balaguer *Spain* 41°50N 0°50E **196** D5
Balaikarangan *Indonesia* 0°49N 110°25E **234** B3
Balaipungut *Indonesia* 1°3N 101°17E **234** B2
Balaisabut *Indonesia* 0°28N 110°49E **235** B4
Balaka
  Dem. Rep. of the Congo 4°52S 19°57E **265** C3
Balakän *Azerbaijan* 41°43N 46°24E **191** K8
Balakété *C.A.R.* 6°56N 19°56E **264** A3
Balakhna *Russia* 56°25N 43°32E **190** B6
Balaklava *S. Austral.,*
  Australia 34°7S 138°22E **282** E2
Balaklava *Ukraine* 44°30N 33°30E **189** K7
Balakliya *Ukraine* 49°28N 36°55E **189** H9
Balakovo *Russia* 52°4N 47°55E **190** D8
Balamau *India* 27°10N 80°21E **243** F9
Balamban *Phil.* 10°30N 123°43E **233** F4

Balashikha *Russia* 55°48N 37°58E **129** B5
Balashov *Russia* 51°30N 43°10E **190** E6
Balasore = Baleshwar
  India 21°35N 87°3E **244** D8
Balassagyarmat *Hungary* 48°4N 19°15E **182** D4
Balāt *Egypt* 25°36N 29°19E **256** B2
Balaton *Hungary* 46°50N 17°40E **182** D2
Balaton-Felvidéki △
  Hungary 46°52N 17°30E **182** D2
Balatonboglár *Hungary* 46°46N 17°40E **182** D2
Balatonfüred *Hungary* 46°58N 17°54E **182** D2
Balatonszentgyörgy
  Hungary 46°41N 17°19E **182** D2
Balayan *Phil.* 13°57N 120°44E **232** E3
Balayan B. *Phil.* 13°51N 120°48E **232** E3
Balazote *Spain* 38°54N 2°9W **197** G2
Balbalan *Phil.* 17°27N 121°12E **232** C3
Balbalasang-Balbalan △
  Phil. 17°23N 121°1E **232** C3
Balbi, Mt. *Papua N. G.* 5°55S 154°58E **286** C8
Balbieriskis *Lithuania* 54°32N 23°53E **184** D10
Balbigny *France* 45°49N 4°11E **175** C8
Balbina *Brazil* 1°58S 59°29W **329** D6
Balbina, Represa de *Brazil* 2°0S 59°30W **329** D6
Balboa *Panama* 8°57N 79°34W **320** C5
Balbriggan *Ireland* 53°37N 6°11W **166** C5
Balcarce *Argentina* 38°0S 58°10W **334** D4
Balcarres *Canada* 50°50N 103°35W **297** C8
Bălceşti *Romania* 44°37N 23°57E **183** F8
Balchik *Bulgaria* 43°28N 28°11E **203** C12
Balchuta *N.Z.* 46°15S 169°45E **285** G4
Balcones Escarpment
  U.S.A. 29°30N 99°15W **314** G5
Balçova *Turkey* 38°22N 27°4E **205** C9
Bald I. *Australia* 34°57S 118°27E **279** F2
Bald Knob *U.S.A.* 35°19N 91°34W **314** D9
Baldenburg = Biały Bór
  Poland 53°53N 16°51E **184** E3
Baldock L. *Canada* 56°33N 97°57W **297** B9
Baldoyle *Ireland* 53°24N 6°8W **166** C5
Baldwin *Fla., U.S.A.* 30°18N 81°59W **316** E8
Baldwin *Mich., U.S.A.* 43°54N 85°51W **309** D11
Baldwin *La., U.S.A.* 40°21N 79°58W **133** A3
Baldwin, L. *U.S.A.* 28°34N 81°19W **133** A3
Baldwin Hills *U.S.A.* 34°0N 118°21W **126** B2
Baldwin Hills Res. *U.S.A.* 34°0N 118°21W **126** B2
Baldwinsville *U.S.A.* 43°10N 76°20W **313** C8
Baldy Peak *U.S.A.* 33°54N 109°34W **315** D9
Bale *Croatia* 45°4N 13°46E **199** C10
Bale *Oromiya, Ethiopia* 6°57N 40°8E **257** F5
Bale *Oromiya, Ethiopia* 6°59N 39°52E **257** F4
Baleares, Is. *Spain* 39°30N 3°0E **206** B4
Baleares, Is. = Baleares, Is.
  Spain 39°30N 3°0E **206** B4
Baleh → *Malaysia* 2°1N 113°1E **235** B4
Baleia, Pta. da *Brazil* 17°40S 39°7W **333** E4
Baleine → *Canada* 58°15N 67°40W **299** A6
Baleine, Petite R. de la →
  Canada 56°0N 76°45W **298** A4
Băleni *Romania* 45°48N 27°51E **183** E12
Baler *Phil.* 15°46N 121°34E **232** D3
Baler B. *Phil.* 15°50N 121°35E **232** D3
Baleshare *U.K.* 57°31N 7°22W **167** D1
Baleshwar *India* 21°35N 87°3E **244** D8
Balestrand *Norway* 61°11N 6°31E **164** C3
Baley *Russia* 51°36N 116°37E **215** D12
Balezino *Russia* 58°2N 53°6E **190** B11
Balfate *Honduras* 15°48N 86°25W **320** C2
Balfour Channel
  Solomon Is. 8°43S 157°27E **287** M9
Balgo *Australia* 20°9S 127°58E **278** D4
Balgowlah *Australia* 33°47S 151°16E **139** A2
Balgowlah Heights
  Australia 33°48S 151°16E **139** A2
Balham *U.K.* 51°26N 0°8W **125** B3
Balharshah *India* 19°50N 79°23E **244** E4
Bali *Cameroon* 5°54N 10°0E **263** D7
Bali *Dem. Rep. of the Congo* 5°25S 16°12E **264** C3
Bali *Kriti, Greece* 35°25N 24°47E **207** C5
Bali *Raj., India* 25°11N 73°17E **242** G5
Bali *W. Bengal, India* 22°39N 88°20E **243** a2
Bali *Indonesia* 8°20S 115°0E **231** J18
Bali □ *Indonesia* 8°20S 115°0E **231** J18
Bali, Selat *Indonesia* 8°18N 114°35E **231** J17
Bali Barat △ *Indonesia* 8°12S 114°35E **231** J17
Bali Sea *Indonesia* 8°0S 115°0E **231** J17
Balia *S. Leone* 8°30N 11°1W **262** D2
Baliapal *India* 21°40N 87°17E **243** J12
Baliceaux *St. Vincent* 12°57N 61°8W **323** a
Balicuatro Is. *Phil.* 12°39N 124°24E **232** E5
Baliganja *India* 22°31N 88°22E **124** B2
Balige *Indonesia* 2°14N 99°7E **234** B1
Baligród *Poland* 49°20N 22°17E **185** J9
Baliguda *India* 20°12N 83°55E **244** D6
Balik Pulau *Malaysia* 5°21N 100°14E **237** c
Balikesir *Turkey* 39°39N 27°53E **205** B9
Balikesir □ *Turkey* 39°45N 28°0E **205** B9
Balikpapan *Indonesia* 1°10S 116°55E **235** C5
Balimbing *Phil.* 5°5N 119°58E **233** J2
Balimo *Papua N. G.* 8°6S 142°57E **286** D3
Baling *Malaysia* 5°41N 100°55E **237** K3
Balingasag *Phil.* 8°45N 124°47E **233** G5
Bälinge *Sweden* 59°57N 17°33E **162** G11
Balingen *Germany* 48°16N 8°51E **179** G4
Balingsnäs *Sweden* 59°13N 18°10E **139** B2
Balingsta *Sweden* 59°12N 18°13E **139** B2
Balini *Romania* 45°8N 28°43E **124** B2
Balintang Channel *Phil.* 19°49N 121°40E **232** B3
Balintang I. *Phil.* 19°58N 122°9E **232** B4
Balintawak *Phil.* 14°39N 120°59E **127** B1
Baliza *Brazil* 16°0S 52°20W **331** D7
Baljurashi *Si. Arabia* 19°51N 41°33E **248** C3
Balkan □ *Turkmenistan* 40°0N 54°30E **216** D5
Balkan Mts. = Stara Planina
  Bulgaria 43°15N 23°0E **202** C7
Balkanabat *Turkmenistan* 39°30N 54°22E **216** F6
Balkh □ *Afghan.* 36°30N 67°0E **240** A2
Balkhash = Balqash
  Kazakhstan 46°50N 74°50E **216** E8
Balkhash, Ozero = Balqash Köli
  Kazakhstan 46°0N 74°50E **217** E8
Balkonda *India* 18°52N 78°21E **244** E4
Ballachulish *U.K.* 56°41N 5°8W **167** E3
Balladonia *Australia* 32°27S 123°51E **279** F3
Ballaghaderreen *Ireland* 53°55N 8°34W **166** C3
Ballan *Australia* 37°33S 144°2E **283** D6
Ballarat *Australia* 37°33S 143°50E **283** D6
Ballard, L. *Australia* 29°20S 120°40E **279** E3
Ballater *U.K.* 57°3N 3°3W **167** D5
Ballé *Mali* 15°18N 8°33W **262** B3
Ballena, Canal de
  Mexico 29°10N 113°29W **318** B2
Balleny Is. *Antarctica* 66°30S 163°0E **151** C11
Balleroy *France* 49°11N 0°50W **172** C6
Ballestas, Is. *Peru* 13°44S 76°25W **330** C2
Balli *Turkey* 40°50N 27°3E **203** F11

Ballia *India* 25°46N 84°12E **243** G11
Ballina *N.S.W., Australia* 28°50S 153°31E **281** D5
Ballina *Mayo, Ireland* 54°7N 9°9W **166** B2
Ballinasloe *Ireland* 53°20N 8°13W **166** C3
Ballindine *U.S.A.* 31°45N 99°57W **314** F5
Ban Chiang *Thailand* 17°30N 103°10E **236** D4
Ban Chiang Klang
  Thailand 19°25N 100°55E **236** C3
Ballinger *U.S.A.* 31°45N 99°57W **314** F5
Ballinrobe *Ireland* 53°38N 9°13W **166** C2
Ballinskelligs B. *Ireland* 51°48N 10°13W **166** E1
Ballinteer *Ireland* 53°17N 6°15W **120** B2
Ballon *France* 48°10N 0°14E **172** D7
Ballons des Vosges △ *France* 48°0N 7°0E **173** E14
Ballsh *Albania* 40°36N 19°44E **202** F3
Ballston Spa *U.S.A.* 43°0N 73°51W **313** D11
Ballybofey *Ireland* 53°17N 6°18W **120** B2
Ballyboghil *Ireland* 53°32N 6°16W **166** C5
Ballybrack *Ireland* 53°15N 6°7W **120** B3
Ballybunion *Ireland* 52°31N 9°40W **166** D2
Ballycanew *Ireland* 52°37N 6°19W **166** D5
Ballycastle *U.K.* 55°12N 6°15W **166** A5
Ballyclare *U.K.* 54°46N 6°0W **166** B5
Ballydehob *Ireland* 51°34N 9°28W **166** E2
Ballyfermot *Ireland* 53°20N 6°21W **120** A1
Ballygawley *U.K.* 54°27N 7°2W **166** B4
Ballyhaunis *Ireland* 53°46N 8°46W **166** C3
Ballyheige *Ireland* 52°23N 9°49W **166** D2
Ballymena *U.K.* 54°52N 6°17W **166** B5
Ballymoney *U.K.* 55°5N 6°31W **166** A5
Ballymorefinn Hill *Ireland* 53°14N 6°22W **120** B1
Ballymote *Ireland* 54°5N 8°31W **166** B3
Ballymun *Ireland* 53°23N 6°16W **120** A2
Ballynahinch *U.K.* 54°24N 5°54W **166** B6
Ballyquintin Pt. *U.K.* 54°20N 5°30W **166** B6
Ballyshannon *Ireland* 54°30N 8°11W **166** B3
Balmaceda *Chile* 46°0S 71°50W **336** C2
Balmain *Australia* 33°51S 151°11E **139** B2
Balmaseda *Spain* 43°11N 3°12W **196** B1
Balmertown *Canada* 51°4N 93°41W **297** C10
Balmoral *Australia* 37°15S 141°48E **282** D4
Balmorhea *U.S.A.* 30°59N 103°45W **314** F3
Baln Mi *Thailand* 15°3N 100°32E **236** E3
Ban Mae Chedi *Thailand* 19°11N 99°31E **236** C2
Ban Mae Nam *Thailand* 9°34N 100°0E **237** b
Ban Mae Sariang *Thailand* 18°10N 97°56E **236** C1
Ban Mê Thuột = Buon Ma Thuot
  Vietnam 12°40N 108°3E **237** F7
Ban Mi *Thailand* 15°3N 100°32E **236** E3
Ban Muang Mo *Laos* 19°4N 99°48E **236** C2
Ban Na Bo *Thailand* 9°19N 99°41E **237** b
Ban Na San *Thailand* 8°53N 99°52E **237** H2
Ban Na Tong *Laos* 20°56N 101°47E **236** B3
Ban Nam Bac *Laos* 20°38N 102°20E **236** B4
Ban Nammi *Thailand* 17°7N 105°40E **236** D5
Ban Nong Bok *Laos* 17°5N 104°48E **236** D5
Ban Nong Pling *Thailand* 15°40N 100°10E **236** E3
Ban Pak Chan *Thailand* 10°32N 98°51E **237** G2
Ban Patong *Thailand* 7°54N 98°18E **237** a
Ban Phai *Thailand* 16°4N 102°44E **236** D4
Ban Phak Chit *Thailand* 8°0N 98°24E **237** a
Ban Pong *Thailand* 13°50N 99°55E **236** F2
Ban Ron Phibun *Thailand* 8°9N 99°51E **237** H2
Ban Sakhu *Thailand* 8°4N 98°18E **237** a
Ban Sanam Chai *Thailand* 7°33N 100°25E **237** J3
Ban Tak *Thailand* 17°2N 99°4E **236** D2
Ban Tako *Thailand* 14°5N 102°40E **236** E4
Ban Tha Nun *Thailand* 8°12N 98°18E **237** a
Ban Tha Rua *Thailand* 7°59N 98°22E **237** a
Ban Tha Yu *Thailand* 8°17N 98°22E **237** a
Ban Thong Krut *Thailand* 9°25N 99°57E **237** b
Ban Xien Kok *Laos* 20°54N 100°39E **236** B3
Ban Yen Nhan *Vietnam* 20°57N 106°2E **236** B6
Banaba *Kiribati* 0°45S 169°50E **288** H8
Banalia
  Dem. Rep. of the Congo 1°32N 25°5E **268** B2
Banam *Cambodia* 11°20N 105°17E **237** G5
Banamba *Mali* 13°29N 7°22W **262** C3
Banana Is. *S. Leone* 8°7N 13°15W **262** D2
Bananal, I. do *Brazil* 11°30S 50°30W **333** D1
Banaras = Varanasi *India* 25°22N 83°0E **243** G10
Banas → *Gujarat, India* 23°45N 71°25E **242** H4
Banas → *Mad. P., India* 24°15N 81°30E **243** G9
Bânâs, Ras *Egypt* 23°57N 35°59E **256** C4
Banática *Portugal* 38°40N 9°11W **126** A1
Banaue *Phil.* 16°55N 121°4E **232** C3
Banaz *Turkey* 38°44N 29°46E **205** C11
Banaz → *Turkey* 38°12N 29°41E **205** C11
Banbridge *U.K.* 54°22N 6°16W **166** B5
Banbury *U.K.* 52°4N 1°20W **169** E6
Banc d'Arguin △
  Mauritania 20°10N 16°20W **260** D1
Banchory *U.K.* 57°3N 2°29W **167** D6
Banco do Brasil, Centro Cultural
  Rio de J., Brazil **135** a2
Bancoran *Phil.* 7°45N 118°30E **233** H1
Bancroft = Chililabombwe
  Zambia 12°18S 27°43E **269** G5
Bancroft *Canada* 45°3N 77°51W **312** A7
Band *Romania* 46°30N 24°25E **183** D9
Band Boni *Iran* 25°30N 59°33E **247** E8
Band-e Torkestan *Afghan.* 35°30N 64°0E **240** B2
Band Qīr *Iran* 31°39N 48°53E **247** D6
Banda *Cameroon* 3°58N 14°32E **263** E8
Banda *Mad. P., India* 24°3N 78°57E **243** G8
Banda *Ut. P., India* 25°30N 80°26E **243** G9
Banda, Kepulauan
  Indonesia 4°37S 129°50E **231** E7
Banda, La *Argentina* 27°45S 64°10W **334** B3
Banda Aceh *Indonesia* 5°35N 95°20E **234** A1
Banda Banda, Mt.
  Australia 31°10S 152°28E **283** A10
Banda Elat *Indonesia* 5°40S 133°5E **231** F8
Banda Is. = Banda, Kepulauan
  Indonesia 4°37S 129°50E **231** E7
Banda Kani
  Dem. Rep. of the Congo 4°48S 13°52E **265** C2
Banda Sea *Indonesia* 6°0S 130°0E **231** F7
Bandai-Asahi △ *Japan* 37°38N 140°2E **220** F10
Bandai-San *Japan* 37°36N 140°4E **220** F10
Bandak *Norway* 59°23N 8°9E **164** E5
Bandama → *Ivory C.* 6°32N 5°30W **262** D3
Bandama Blanc → *Ivory C.* 6°55N 5°30W **262** D4
Bandama Rouge →
  Ivory C. 6°55N 5°30W **262** C4
Bandamadji *Comoros Is.* 11°47S 43°26E **272** a
Bandanwara *India* 26°9N 74°38E **242** F6
Bandar = Machilipatnam
  India 16°12N 81°8E **245** F5
Bandar-e Abbās *Iran* 27°15N 56°15E **247** E7
Bandar-e Anzalī *Iran* 37°30N 49°30E **213** D13
Bandar-e Büshehr = Büshehr
  Iran 28°55N 50°55E **247** D6
Bandar-e Chārak *Iran* 26°45N 54°20E **247** E7
Bandar-e Deylam *Iran* 30°5N 50°10E **247** D6
Bandar-e Emām Khomeynī
  Iran 30°30N 49°5E **247** D6
Bandar-e Lengeh *Iran* 26°35N 54°58E **247** E7
Bandar-e Ma'shur *Iran* 30°35N 49°10E **247** D6
Bandar-e Torkeman *Iran* 37°0N 54°10E **247** B7
Bandar Labuan *Malaysia* 5°20N 115°14E **235** A5
Bandar Lampung *Indonesia* 5°20S 105°10E **234** F3
Bandar Maharani = Muar
  Malaysia 2°3N 102°34E **237** L4
Bandar Penggaram = Batu Pahat
  Malaysia 1°50N 102°56E **237** M4

Bandar Seri Begawan
  Brunei 4°52N 115°0E **235** B4
Bandar Sri Aman
  Malaysia 1°15N 111°32E **235** B4
Bandawe *Malawi* 11°58S 34°5E **269** G6
Bande *Spain* 42°3N 7°58W **194** C3
Bandeira, Pico da *Brazil* 20°26S 41°47W **333** F3
Bandeirante *Brazil* 13°41S 50°48W **333** D1
Bandera *Argentina* 28°55S 62°20W **334** B3
Banderas, B. de *Mexico* 20°40N 105°25W **318** C3
Bandhavgarh *India* 23°40N 81°2E **243** H9
Bandhavgarh △ *India* 23°45N 81°10E **244** C5
Bandi → *India* 26°12N 75°47E **242** F6
Bandia → *India* 19°2N 80°28E **244** E5
Bandiagara *Mali* 14°12N 3°29W **262** C4
Bandikui *India* 27°3N 76°34E **242** F7
Bandipur △ *India* 11°45N 76°30E **245** H3
Bandırma *Turkey* 40°20N 28°0E **203** F11
Bandjarmasin = Banjarmasin
  Indonesia 3°20S 114°35E **235** C4
Bandol *France* 43°8N 5°46E **175** E9
Bandon *Ireland* 51°44N 8°44W **166** E3
Bandon → *Ireland* 51°43N 8°37W **166** E3
Bandra *India* 19°3N 72°49E **130** A1
Bandra Pt. *India* 19°2N 72°49E **130** A1
Bandraboua *Mayotte* 12°42S 45°8E **272** b
Bandrélé *Mayotte* 12°54S 45°11E **272** b
Bandula *Mozam.* 19°0S 33°7E **269** F3
Bandundu
  Dem. Rep. of the Congo 3°15S 17°22E **264** C3
Bandundu □
  Dem. Rep. of the Congo 3°30S 17°30E **264** C3
Bandung *Indonesia* 6°54S 107°36E **235** D3
Bané *Burkina Faso* 11°42N 0°15W **263** C4
Băneasa *Romania* 45°56N 27°55E **183** E12
Băneh *Iran* 35°59N 45°53E **213** E11
Banes *Cuba* 21°0N 75°42W **320** B4
Banff *Canada* 51°10N 115°34W **296** C5
Banff *Aberds., U.K.* 57°40N 2°33W **167** D6
Banff □ *Canada* 51°30N 116°15W **296** C5
Banfora *Burkina Faso* 10°40N 4°40W **262** C4
Bang Fai → *Laos* 16°57N 104°45E **236** D5
Bang Hieng → *Laos* 16°10N 105°10E **236** D5
Bang Kapi *Thailand* 13°45N 100°38E **113** B2
Bang Krathum *Thailand* 16°34N 100°18E **236** D3
Bang Lang *Thailand* 5°58N 101°19E **237** K3
Bang Lang Res. *Thailand* 6°6N 101°17E **237** K3
Bang Mun Nak *Thailand* 16°2N 100°23E **236** D3
Bang Na *Thailand* 13°40N 100°36E **113** B2
Bang Pa In *Thailand* 14°14N 100°35E **236** E3
Bang Phlad *Bangkok, Thailand* **113** a1
Bang Rakam *Thailand* 16°45N 100°7E **236** D3
Bang Saphan *Thailand* 11°14N 99°28E **237** G2
Bang Thao *Thailand* 7°59N 98°18E **237** a
Banga *Angola* 8°43S 15°13E **265** D3
Banga *Dem. Rep. of the Congo* 5°25S 20°28E **265** D4
Banga *Aklan, Phil.* 11°38N 122°24E **233** F4
Banga *S. Cotabato, Phil.* 6°21N 124°47E **233** H5
Bangaduni I. *India* 21°34N 88°52E **241** E2
Bangala Dam *Zimbabwe* 21°7S 31°25E **269** G3
Bangalore *India* 12°59N 77°40E **245** H3
Banganapalle *India* 15°19N 78°14E **245** G4
Banganga → *India* 27°6N 77°25E **242** F7
Bangaoti *Cameroon* 5°8N 10°32E **263** D7
Bangaon *India* 23°0N 88°47E **243** H13
Bangar *Brunei* 4°43N 115°4E **235** B4
Bangar *La Union, Phil.* 16°54N 120°25E **232** C3
Bangassou *C.A.R.* 4°55N 23°7E **264** B4
Bangbae *S. Korea* 37°29N 126°59E **137** C1
Banggai *Indonesia* 1°34S 123°30E **231** E6
Banggai, Kepulauan
  Indonesia 1°40S 123°30E **231** E6
Banggai Arch. = Banggai,
  Kepulauan *Indonesia* 1°40S 123°30E **231** E6
Banggi, Pulau *Malaysia* 7°17N 117°12E **235** A5
Banghāzī *Libya* 32°11N 20°3E **258** B4
Banghāzī □ *Libya* 32°7N 20°4E **258** B4
Bangil *Indonesia* 7°36S 112°50E **235** D4
Bangjang *Sudan* 11°23N 32°41E **257** E3
Bangka *Sulawesi, Indonesia* 1°50N 125°5E **231** D7
Bangka *Sumatera, Indonesia* 2°0S 105°50E **234** E3
Bangka, Selat *Indonesia* 2°30S 105°30E **234** E3
Bangka-Belitung □
  Indonesia 2°30S 107°0E **234** E3
Bangkalan *Indonesia* 7°2S 112°46E **235** D4
Bangkaru *Indonesia* 2°4N 97°7E **234** B1
Bangkhen *Thailand* 13°52N 100°36E **113** A2
Bangko *Indonesia* 0°18N 101°5E **234** B2
Bangkok *Thailand* 13°45N 100°35E **113** B2
Bangkok, Bight of
  Thailand 12°55N 100°30E **236** F3
Bangkok Don Muang Int. ✈ (BKK)
  Thailand 13°55N 100°36E **113** a2
Bangkok Noi *Thailand* 13°45N 100°28E **113** B1
Bangkok Yai *Thailand* 13°43N 100°29E **113** B1
Bangla = West Bengal □
  India 23°0N 88°0E **243** H13
Bangladesh ■ *Asia* 24°0N 90°0E **241** G17
Bangli *Indonesia* 8°27S 115°21E **231** J18
Banglo *India* 23°18N 88°14E **124** b2
Bangoi-Kouni *Comoros Is.* 11°22S 43°21E **272** a
Bangolo *Ivory C.* 7°1N 7°29W **262** D3
Bangong Co *China* 35°50N 78°43E **243** B8
Bangor *Down, U.K.* 54°40N 5°40W **166** B6
Bangor *Gwynedd, U.K.* 53°14N 4°8W **168** D3
Bangor *Maine, U.S.A.* 44°48N 68°46W **309** C19
Bangor *Mich., U.S.A.* 42°19N 86°7W **311** D10
Bangor *N.Y., U.S.A.* 40°52N 75°13W **313** E10
Bangor *Pa., U.S.A.* 40°52N 75°13W **313** E10
Bangrak *Thailand* 13°43N 100°31E **113** a2
Bangsu *Thailand* 13°48N 100°32E **113** a2
Bangu *Dem. Rep. of the Congo* 0°3S 19°12E **264** C3
Bangued *Phil.* 17°40N 120°37E **232** C3
Bangui *Phil.* 18°32N 120°46E **232** B3
Bangui *C.A.R.* 4°23N 18°35E **264** B3
Bangui B. *Phil.* 18°33N 120°43E **232** B3
Banguru
  Dem. Rep. of the Congo 0°30N 27°10E **268** B2
Bangweulu, L. *Zambia* 11°0S 30°0E **269** E3
Bangweulu Swamp
  Zambia 11°20S 30°15E **269** E3
Banhine △ *Mozam.* 22°49S 32°55E **271** B5
Bani *Burkina Faso* 13°4N 0°10W **263** C4
Bani *C.A.R.* 7°6N 22°50E **264** A4
Bani *Dom. Rep.* 18°16N 70°22E **321** C5
Bani *Phil.* 16°11N 119°52E **232** C2
Bani → *Mali* 14°30N 4°12W **262** C4
Bani, Jebel *Morocco* 29°16N 8°0W **260** C3
Bani Bangou *Niger* 15°3N 2°42E **263** B5
Banī Sa'd *Iraq* 33°34N 44°32E **213** F11
Banī Walīd *Libya* 31°49N 13°4E **258** B2
Banī Walīd □ *Libya* 30°45N 13°0E **258** B2
Bania *C.A.R.* 4°1N 16°7E **264** B3
Baniara *Papua N. G.* 9°44S 149°54E **286** E5
Banihal Pass *India* 33°30N 75°12E **243** C6
Banikoara *Benin* 11°18N 2°26E **263** C5
Baninah *Libya* 32°0N 20°12E **258** B4
Banissa *Kenya* 3°55N 40°19E **257** G5
Bāniyās *Syria* 35°10N 36°0E **250** D6
Banja Luka *Bos.-H.* 44°49N 17°11E **182** F2
Banjar *India* 31°38N 77°21E **242** D7

Bauko Phil. 17°0N 120°52E 232 C3
Baulai → Bangla. 24°22N 91°1E 241 C3
Bauld, C. Canada 51°38N 55°26W 295 G20
Bauman Russia 55°45N 37°40E 129 B4
Baume-les-Dames France 47°22N 6°22E 173 E13
Baumgarten Austria 48°12N 16°17E 142 A1
Baunatal Germany 51°14N 9°24E 178 D5
Baunei Italy 40°2N 9°40E 200 B2
Baure Nigeria 12°52N 8°50E 264 B3
Baures Bolivia 13°35S 63°35W 331 C5
Bauru Brazil 22°10S 49°0W 335 A6
Baús Brazil 18°22S 52°47W 331 D7
Bausi India 24°48N 87°1E 243 G12
Bauska Latvia 56°24N 24°15E 184 B11
Bautino Kazakhstan 44°35N 50°14E 191 H10
Bautzen Germany 51°10N 14°26E 178 D10
Bauya S. Leone 8°12N 12°38W 262 D2
Bavānāt Iran 30°28N 53°27E 247 D7
Bavānište Serbia 44°49N 20°55E 182 F5
Bavaria = Bayern □
Germany 48°50N 12°0E 179 G7
Båven Sweden 59°0N 16°56E 162 E10
Bavispe → Mexico 29°15N 109°11W 318 B3
Baw Baw △ Australia 37°50S 146°17E 283 D7
Bawal Indonesia 7°52S 111°13E 235 D4
Bawan Indonesia 1°42S 113°55E 235 C4
Bawdwin Burma 23°5N 97°20E 241 D6
Bawean Indonesia 5°46S 112°35E 235 D4
Bawku Ghana 11°3N 0°19W 263 C4
Bawlake Burma 19°11N 97°21E 241 H6
Bawolung China 28°50N 101°16E 228 C3
Bawomataluwo Indonesia 0°38N 97°44E 241 H6
Baxley U.S.A. 31°47N 82°21W 316 D7
Baxter Iowa, U.S.A. 41°49N 93°9W 310 C3
Baxter Minn., U.S.A. 46°21N 94°17W 308 B6
Baxter Springs U.S.A. 37°2N 94°44W 310 G7
Baxter State △ U.S.A. 46°5N 68°57W 309 B19
Bay □ Somali Rep. 3°0N 43°30E 267 D5
Bay, L. U.S.A. 28°25N 81°34W 133 A2
Bay, Laguna de Phil. 14°20N 121°11E 232 D3
Bay City Mich., U.S.A. 43°36N 83°54W 309 D12
Bay City Tex., U.S.A. 28°59N 95°58W 311 E6
Bay Harbor Islands U.S.A. 25°53N 80°7W 128 A2
Bay Hill U.S.A. 28°28N 81°30W 133 B1
Bay Minette U.S.A. 30°53N 87°46W 315 F11
Bay of Plenty □ N.Z. 38°0S 177°0E 284 D5
Bay Ridge U.S.A. 40°37N 74°1W 132 C1
Bay Roberts Canada 47°36N 53°16W 299 C9
Bay St. Louis U.S.A. 30°19N 89°20W 315 F10
Bay Springs U.S.A. 31°59N 89°17W 315 F10
Bay View N.Z. 39°25S 176°50E 284 F5
Baya Dem. Rep. of the Congo 11°53S 27°25E 269 G2
Bayambang Phil. 15°49N 120°27E 232 D3
Bayamo Cuba 20°20N 76°40W 320 B4
Bayamón Puerto Rico 18°24N 66°9W 321 C6
Bayan Har Shan China 34°0N 98°0E 218 E8
Bayan Hot = Alxa Zuoqi
China 38°50N 105°40E 226 E3
Bayan Lepas Malaysia 5°17N 100°16E 237 c
Bayan Obo China 41°52N 109°59E 226 D5
Bayan-Ovoo = Erdenetsogt
Mongolia 42°55N 106°5E 226 C4
Bayan-Tumen = Choybalsan
Mongolia 48°4N 114°30E 219 B11
Bayana India 26°55N 77°18E 242 F7
Bayanaūyl Kazakhstan 50°45N 75°45E 217 B9
Bayanhongor Mongolia 46°8N 102°43E 218 B9
Bayard N. Mex., U.S.A. 32°46N 108°8W 305 K9
Bayard Nebr., U.S.A. 41°45N 103°20W 308 E2
Bayawan Phil. 9°46N 122°45E 233 G4
Baybay Phil. 10°40N 124°55E 233 F5
Bayburt Turkey 40°15N 40°20E 213 B9
Bayburt □ Turkey 40°35N 39°25E 213 B9
Baydaratskaya Guba
Russia 69°0N 67°30E 214 C7
Baydhabo Somali Rep. 3°8N 43°30E 267 D5
Bayelsa □ Nigeria 4°30N 6°0E 263 E6
Bayerische Alpen
Germany 47°35N 11°30E 179 H7
Bayerische Rhön △
Germany 50°15N 10°5E 179 E6
Bayerischer Spessart △
Germany 49°58N 10°11E 179 F6
Bayerischer Wald
Germany 48°58N 12°50E 179 G8
Bayern □ Germany 48°50N 12°0E 179 G7
Bayeux France 49°17N 0°42W 172 C6
Bayfield Ont., Canada 43°34N 81°42W 312 C3
Bayfield Wis., U.S.A. 46°49N 90°49W 308 B8
Baybān al Qisāb Yemen 15°48N 45°44E 248 D4
Bayndır Turkey 38°13N 27°39E 205 C9
Bayit Va-Gan Israel 31°46N 35°11E 123 B2
Baykal, Oz. Russia 53°0N 108°0E 215 D11
Baykan Turkey 38°7N 41°44E 213 C9
Baymak Russia 52°36N 58°19E 186 E10
Baynes Mts. Namibia 17°15S 13°0E 270 A1
Bayombong Phil. 16°30N 121°10E 232 C3
Bayon France 48°30N 6°20E 173 D13
Bayona = Baiona Spain 42°6N 8°52W 194 C2
Bayonet Point U.S.A. 28°20N 82°41W 317 D7
Bayonne Pyrénées-Atlantiques,
France 43°30N 1°28W 174 E2
Bayonne N.J., U.S.A. 40°40N 74°6W 132 B1
Bayou Boeuf U.S.A. 29°50N 90°10W 131 B1
Bayou Segnette State Park □
U.S.A. 29°53N 90°10W 131 B2
Bayovar Peru 5°50S 81°0W 330 B1
Bayport U.S.A. 28°32N 82°39W 317 D7
Bayqongyr Kazakhstan 45°40N 63°20E 216 C6
Bayram-Ali = Baýramaly
Turkmenistan 37°37N 62°10E 247 B9
Baýramaly Turkmenistan 37°37N 62°10E 247 B9
Bayramiç Turkey 39°48N 26°36E 205 B8
Bayrampaşa Turkey 41°1N 28°52E 205 E12
Bayreuth Germany 49°56N 11°35E 179 F7
Bayrischzell Germany 47°41N 12°0E 179 H8
Bayrūt Lebanon 33°53N 35°31E 250 B6
Bays, L. of Canada 45°15N 79°4W 312 A5
Bayshore Calif., U.S.A. 37°42N 122°24W 136 B2
Bayshore Fla., U.S.A. 26°43N 81°50W 312 A5
Baysville Canada 45°9N 79°7W 312 A5
Bayswater London, U.K. 125 b2
Bayt al Faqīh Yemen 14°31N 43°19E 248 D3
Bayt Lahm West Bank 31°43N 35°12E 123 B2
Baytown U.S.A. 29°43N 94°59W 311 E12
Bayugan Phil. 8°43N 125°42E 233 G5
Bayview U.S.A. 37°44N 122°23W 136 B2
Bayville = Kirkwood
S. Africa 33°22S 25°15E 270 D4
Bayy al Kabir, W. Libya 31°10N 15°53E 258 B8
Bayy al Khā'ib, Wādī →
Libya 30°55N 15°29E 258 B3
Bayzo Niger 13°52N 4°35E 263 C5
Baza Spain 37°30N 2°47W 195 H8
Bāzār Iran 35°40N 51°0E 141 A2
Bazar Dyuzi Russia 41°12N 47°50E 191 K8
Bazardüzü = Bazar Dyuzi
Russia 41°12N 47°50E 191 K8
Bazargic = Dobrich
Bulgaria 43°37N 27°49E 203 C11
Bazarnyy Syzgan Russia 53°45N 46°40E 190 D8

Bazaruto, I. do Mozam. 21°40S 35°28E 271 C6
Bazaruto △ Mozam. 21°42S 35°26E 271 B6
Bazas France 44°27N 0°13W 174 D3
Bazhong China 31°52N 106°46E 228 B6
Bazhou China 39°8N 116°22E 226 E9
Bazin Guadeloupe 16°22N 61°26W 322 e
Bazmān, Kūh-e Iran 28°4N 60°1E 247 D9
Beach U.S.A. 46°58N 104°0W 308 B2
Beach City U.S.A. 40°39N 81°35W 312 F3
Beachport Australia 37°29S 140°0E 282 D4
Beachville Canada 43°5N 80°49W 312 C4
Beachy Hd. U.K. 50°44N 0°15E 169 G8
Beacon N. Austral.,
Australia 30°26S 117°52E 279 F2
Beacon N.Y., U.S.A. 41°30N 73°58W 313 E11
Beacon Hill Hong Kong,
China 22°21N 114°10E 122 A2
Beacon Hill Boston, U.S.A. 116 b1
Beaconsfield Australia 41°11S 146°48E 281 G4
Beagle, Canal S. Amer. 55°0S 68°30W 336 E3
Beagle Bay Australia 16°58S 122°40E 278 C3
Beagle Bay ○ Australia 16°53S 122°40E 278 C3
Beagle G. Australia 12°15S 130°25E 278 B5
Béal an Átha = Ballina
Ireland 54°7N 9°9W 166 B2
Béal Átha na Sluaighe = Ballinasloe
Ireland 53°20N 8°13W 166 C3
Bealanana Madag. 14°33S 48°44E 272 A2
Beals Cr. → U.S.A. 32°10N 100°51W 314 E4
Beamsville Canada 43°12N 79°28W 312 C5
Bear → Calif., U.S.A. 38°56N 121°36W 306 G5
Bear → Utah, U.S.A. 41°30N 112°8W 300 G17
Bear, C. France 42°31N 3°8E 174 F7
Bear I. Ireland 51°38N 9°50W 166 E2
Bear I. Man., Canada 55°8N 96°0W 297 B9
Bear L. Utah, U.S.A. 41°59N 111°21W 304 F8
Bear Lake Canada 45°27N 79°35W 312 A5
Beardmore Canada 49°36N 87°57W 298 C2
Beardmore Glacier
Antarctica 84°30S 170°0E 151 E11
Beardstown U.S.A. 40°1N 90°26W 310 E8
Bearma → India 24°20N 79°51E 243 G8
Bearpaw Mts. U.S.A. 48°12N 109°30W 304 B9
Bearskin Lake Canada 53°58N 91°2W 298 B1
Beas → India 31°10N 74°59E 242 D6
Beas de Segura Spain 38°15N 2°53W 195 G8
Beasain Spain 43°3N 2°11W 196 B2
Beata, C. Dom. Rep. 17°40N 71°30W 321 C5
Beata, I. Dom. Rep. 17°34N 71°31W 321 C5
Beata Ridge W. Indies 16°0N 72°30W 321 C5
Beato Portugal 38°44N 9°5W 126 A2
Beatrice Nebr., U.S.A. 40°16N 96°45W 308 E5
Beatrice Zimbabwe 18°15S 30°55E 269 F3
Beatrice, C. Australia 14°20S 136°55E 280 A2
Beatton → Canada 56°15N 120°45W 296 B4
Beatton River Canada 57°26N 121°20W 296 B4
Beatty U.S.A. 36°54N 116°46W 306 J10
Beau Bassin Mauritius 20°13S 57°27E 272 e
Beaucaire France 43°48N 4°39E 175 E8
Beauce, Plaine de la France 48°10N 1°45E 173 D8
Beauceville Canada 46°13N 70°46W 299 C5
Beauchêne, I. Falk. Is. 52°55S 59°15W 153 f
Beaudesert Australia 27°59S 153°0E 281 D5
Beaufort Vic., Australia 37°25S 143°25E 282 D5
Beaufort Savoie, France 45°44N 6°34E 175 C10
Beaufort Malaysia 5°30N 115°40E 235 A5
Beaufort N.C., U.S.A. 34°43N 76°40W 315 D16
Beaufort S.C., U.S.A. 32°26N 80°40W 316 C9
Beaufort Sea Arctic 72°0N 140°0W 292 B5
Beaufort West S. Africa 32°18S 22°36E 270 D3
Beaugency France 47°47N 1°38E 173 E8
Beauharnois Canada 45°20N 73°52W 313 A11
Beaujeu France 46°10N 4°35E 173 F11
Beaujolais France 46°0N 4°22E 173 F11
Beaulieu → Canada 62°3N 113°11W 296 A6
Beaulieu France 44°58N 1°50E 175 E8
Beaulieu-sur-Dordogne
France 44°58N 1°50E 175 D5
Beaulieu-sur-Mer France 43°42N 7°20E 175 E11
Beauly U.K. 57°30N 4°28W 167 D4
Beauly → U.K. 57°29N 4°27W 167 D4
Beaumaris U.K. 53°16N 4°6W 168 D3
Beaumont Belgium 50°15N 4°14E 170 D4
Beaumont Dordogne, France 44°45N 0°46E 174 D4
Beaumont Dublin, Ireland 53°23N 6°13W 120 A2
Beaumont N.Z. 45°50S 169°33E 285 F4
Beaumont Tex., U.S.A. 30°5N 94°6W 314 F7
Beaumont-de-Lomagne
France 43°53N 1°0E 174 E5
Beaumont-le-Roger France 49°4N 0°47E 172 C7
Beaumont-sur-Sarthe
France 48°13N 0°8E 172 D7
Beaumonte Heights
Canada 43°45N 79°34W 141 A1
Beaune France 47°2N 4°50E 173 E11
Beaune-la-Rolande France 48°4N 2°25E 173 D9
Beauport Guadeloupe 16°25N 61°30W 322 e
Beaupré Canada 47°3N 70°54W 299 C5
Beaupréau France 47°12N 1°0W 172 E6
Beauraing Belgium 50°7N 4°57E 170 D4
Beauraipaire France 45°22N 5°1E 175 C9
Béhâbâd Iran 32°24N 59°47E 247 C8
Behala India 22°30N 88°18E 124 B1
Behara Madag. 24°55S 46°20E 272 C2
Behbehan Iran 30°30N 50°15E 247 D6
Beheloka Madag. 23°54S 43°40E 272 C1
Behm Canal U.S.A. 55°10N 131°0W 296 D2
Behshahr Iran 36°45N 53°35E 247 B7
Bei Hai Beijing, China 114 b2
Bei Hai Park Beijing, China 114 b2
Bei Jiang → China 23°2N 112°58E 229 F9
Bei'an China 48°10N 126°20E 219 B14
Beibei China 29°47N 106°22E 228 B6
Beicai China 31°11N 121°32E 138 B2
Beichuan China 31°55N 104°39E 228 B5
Beihai China 21°28N 109°6E 228 G7
Beijing China 39°53N 116°21E 114 B1
Beijing □ China 39°55N 116°20E 226 C8
Beijing Zoo Beijing, China 114 a1
Beilen Neths. 52°52N 6°27E 170 B6
Beilngries Germany 49°2N 11°28E 179 F7
Beilpajah Australia 32°54S 143°52E 282 B5
Beilul Eritrea 13°2N 42°20E 257 E5
Béinamar Chad 8°40N 15°22E 259 G3
Beinn na Faoghla = Benbecula
U.K. 57°26N 7°21W 167 D1
Beipan Jiang → China 24°55N 106°58E 228 D6
Beipiao China 41°52N 120°32E 227 D11
Beira Mozam. 19°50S 34°52E 269 F3
Beirut = Bayrūt Lebanon 33°53N 35°31E 250 B6
Beiseker Canada 51°23N 113°32W 296 D6
Beit Duqu West Bank 31°51N 35°7E 123 B1
Beit el-Taht
West Bank 31°54N 35°5E 123 A1
Beit Guvrin el-Fawqa
West Bank 31°31N 35°5E 123 A1
Beit Hanina West Bank 31°49N 35°1E 123 B2
Beit I'ja West Bank 31°49N 35°11E 123 B2
Beit Iksa West Bank 31°49N 35°11E 123 B2

Beit I'nan West Bank 31°51N 35°7E 123 A1
Beit Jala West Bank 31°43N 35°11E 123 B2
Beit Lekhem = Bayt Lahm
West Bank 31°43N 35°12E 123 B2
Beit Liqya West Bank 31°52N 35°4E 123 A1
Beit Nekofa Israel 31°49N 35°7E 123 B1
Beit Sahur West Bank 31°42N 35°13E 123 B2
Beit Sofafa West Bank 31°45N 35°12E 123 B2
Beit Surik West Bank 31°50N 35°9E 123 B1
Beit Ur al-Fawqa
West Bank 31°53N 35°7E 123 A1
Beit Zayit Israel 31°47N 35°9E 123 B1
Beitaipingzhuan China 39°57N 116°20E 114 B1
Beitaolaizhao China 44°58N 125°58E 227 B13
Beitar Ilit West Bank 31°42N 35°7E 123 B1
Beitbridge Zimbabwe 22°12S 30°0E 269 G3
Beitin West Bank 31°56N 35°14E 123 A2
Beitsun China 23°7N 113°10E 121 B2
Beitunya West Bank 31°54N 35°9E 123 B1
Beiuş Romania 46°40N 22°21E 182 D7
Beixing Jing Park China 31°14N 121°21E 138 B2
Beizhen = Binzhou China 37°20N 118°2E 227 F10
Beizhen China 41°38N 121°54E 227 D11
Beizhengzhen China 44°31N 123°30E 227 B12
Beja Portugal 38°2N 7°53W 195 G3
Bêja Tunisia 36°43N 9°12E 258 A1
Beja □ Portugal 37°55N 7°55W 195 H3
Beja □ Tunisia 36°40N 9°29E 261 A6
Bejaïa Algeria 36°42N 5°2E 261 A6
Bejaïa □ Algeria 36°40N 4°55E 261 A6
Béjar Spain 40°23N 5°46W 194 E5
Bejestān Iran 34°30N 58°5E 247 C8
Bek-Budi = Qarshi
Uzbekistan 38°53N 65°48E 217 E7
Bekaa Valley = Al Biqā
Lebanon 34°10N 36°10E 250 D7
Bekasi Indonesia 6°14S 106°59E 234 D3
Békásmegyer Hungary 47°35N 19°3E 117 A2
Bekçiler Turkey 36°56N 29°40E 205 E11
Bekdash Turkmenistan 41°34N 52°32E 216 D4
Békés Hungary 46°47N 21°9E 182 D6
Békés □ Hungary 46°45N 21°0E 182 D6
Békéscsaba Hungary 46°40N 21°0E 182 D6
Bekilli Turkey 38°17N 29°27E 205 C11
Bekily Madag. 24°13S 45°19E 272 C2
Bekisopa Madag. 21°40S 45°54E 272 C2
Bekitro Madag. 24°33S 45°18E 272 C2
Bekkelaget Norway 59°53N 10°47E 133 A3
Bekkestua Norway 59°55N 10°35E 133 A2
Bekodoka Madag. 16°58S 45°7E 272 B2
Bekoji Ethiopia 7°40N 39°17E 257 F4
Bekok Malaysia 2°20N 103°7E 237 L4
Bekopaka Madag. 19°9S 44°48E 272 B1
Bekwai Ghana 6°30N 1°34W 263 D4
Bel Air Mauritius 20°15S 57°44E 272 e
Bel Air Calif., U.S.A. 34°4N 118°27W 126 B2
Bela India 25°50N 82°0E 243 G10
Bela Pakistan 26°12N 66°20E 242 F2
Bela Aliança = Rio do Sul
Brazil 27°13S 49°37W 335 B6
Bela Bela S. Africa 24°51S 28°19E 271 B4
Bela Crkva Serbia 44°55N 21°27E 182 F6
Bela Palanka Serbia 43°13N 22°17E 202 C6
Bela Vista Mato Grosso do Sul,
Brazil 22°12S 56°20W 334 A4
Bela Vista São Paulo,
Brazil 23°33S 46°38W 137 B2
Bela Vista Mozam. 26°10S 32°44E 271 B5
Bélabo Cameroon 4°56N 13°18E 264 B2
Bélâbre France 46°34N 1°8E 174 F4
Belaga Malaysia 2°42N 113°47E 235 B4
Belalcázar Spain 38°35N 5°10W 195 G5
Belan → India 24°2N 81°45E 243 G9
Bélanger → Canada 45°35N 73°42W 130 A1
Belanovica Serbia 44°15N 20°23E 182 F5
Belarus ■ Europe 53°30N 27°0E 177 B14
Belau = Palau ■ Palau 7°30N 134°30E 288 c
Belavenona Madag. 24°50S 47°4E 272 C2
Belawan Indonesia 3°33N 98°32E 234 B1
Belaya Ethiopia 11°25N 36°8E 257 E4
Belaya → Russia 54°40N 56°0E 186 D9
Belaya Glina Russia 46°5N 40°48E 191 G5
Belaya Kalitva Russia 48°13N 40°50E 191 F5
Belaya Tserkov = Bila Tserkva
Ukraine 49°45N 30°10E 177 D16
Belaya Zemlya, Ostrova
Russia 81°36N 62°18E 214 A7
Belayan → Indonesia 0°14S 116°36E 235 C5
Belcești Romania 47°19N 27°7E 183 C12
Belchatów Poland 51°21N 19°22E 185 G6
Belcher Is. Canada 56°15N 78°45W 298 A4
Belchite Spain 41°18N 0°43W 196 D4
Belden U.S.A. 40°2N 121°17W 306 D5
Beldıbi Turkey 36°25N 32°26E 250 B3
Belding U.S.A. 43°6N 85°14W 311 A11
Beledweyne Somali Rep. 4°30N 45°5E 267 F4
Beleghata India 22°33N 88°22E 124 B2
Belém = Palmeirais Brazil 6°0S 43°0W 332 D2
Belém Brazil 1°20S 48°30W 332 B2
Belém, Torre de Portugal 38°41N 9°12W 126 A1
Belém de São Francisco
Brazil 8°46S 38°58W 332 C4
Belén Argentina 27°40S 67°5W 334 B2
Belén Colombia 1°26N 75°56W 328 C2
Belén Paraguay 23°30S 57°6W 334 A4
Belén Turkey 36°31N 36°10E 250 B7
Belen U.S.A. 34°40N 106°46W 305 J10
Belene Bulgaria 43°39N 25°10E 203 C9
Belènzinho Brazil 23°33S 46°37W 137 B2
Belep, Îs. N. Cal. 19°45S 163°40E 288 d
Bélesta France 42°55N 1°56E 174 F5
Belet Uen = Beledweyne
Somali Rep. 4°30N 45°5E 267 D6
Belev Russia 53°50N 36°5E 188 F9
Belevi Turkey 38°0N 27°28E 205 C9
Belfair U.S.A. 47°27N 122°50W 306 C4
Belfast Mpumalanga,
S. Africa 25°42S 30°2E 271 B5
Belfast U.K. 54°37N 5°56W 166 B6
Belfast Maine, U.S.A. 44°26N 69°1W 309 C14
Belfast N.Y., U.S.A. 42°21N 78°7W 312 D6
Belfast L. U.K. 54°40N 5°50W 166 B6
Belfast □ U.K. 54°35N 5°56W 166 B6
Belfort France 47°38N 6°50E 173 E13
Belfort, Territoire de □
France 47°40N 6°55E 173 E13
Belfry U.S.A. 45°9N 109°1W 304 D9
Belgaum India 15°55N 74°35E 245 G2
Belgern Germany 51°29N 13°0E 178 D9
Belgium ■ Europe 50°30N 5°0E 170 D4
Belgodère France 42°35N 9°0E 203 F13
Belgorod Russia 50°35N 36°35E 189 G9
Belgorod-Dnestrovskiy = Bilhorod-
Dnistrovskyy Ukraine 46°11N 30°23E 189 J6

Belgrade = Beograd Serbia 44°50N 20°37E 202 B4
Belgrade U.S.A. 45°47N 111°11W 304 D8
Belgrano Antarctica 77°52S 34°37W 151 D1
Belgrano B. Aires,
Argentina 34°33S 58°27W 117 B2
Belgrove N.Z. 41°27S 172°59E 285 D7
Belhaven U.S.A. 35°33N 76°37W 315 D16
Béli Guinea-Biss. 11°51N 13°56W 262 C2
Beli Nigeria 7°52N 10°56E 263 D7
Beli Drim → Europe 42°6N 20°25E 202 D4
Beli Manastir Croatia 45°45N 18°36E 182 E3
Beli Timok → Serbia 43°53N 22°14E 202 C6
Bélice → Italy 37°35N 12°55E 200 E5
Belimbing Indonesia 8°24S 115°12E 231 J18
Belinskiy Russia 53°0N 43°25E 190 D6
Belinyu Indonesia 1°35S 105°50E 234 C3
Beliton Is. = Belitung
Indonesia 3°10S 107°50E 235 C3
Belitung Indonesia 3°10S 107°50E 235 C3
Belize ■ Cent. Amer. 17°0N 88°30W 320 C2
Belize Angola 4°39S 12°46E 265 C2
Belize City Belize 17°25N 88°0W 320 C2
Beljakovci Macedonia 42°6N 21°59E 202 E5
Beljanica Serbia 44°8N 21°43E 202 B5
Belkovskiy, Ostrov
Russia 75°32N 135°44E 215 B14
Bell → Canada 33°58N 118°11W 126 C3
Bell Calif., U.S.A. 29°45N 82°52W 316 F7
Bell Fla., U.S.A. 51°30N 56°30W 299 B8
Bell → Canada 49°48N 77°38W 298 C4
Bell Gardens U.S.A. 33°58N 118°9W 126 C4
Bell I. Canada 50°46N 55°35W 299 B8
Bell-Irving → Canada 56°12N 129°5W 296 B3
Bell Peninsula Canada 63°50N 82°0W 295 C15
Bell Tower Beijing, China 114 a3
Bell Ville Argentina 32°40S 62°40W 334 C3
Bella Italy 40°45N 15°32E 201 B8
Bella Bella Canada 52°10N 128°10W 296 C3
Bella Coola Canada 52°25N 126°40W 296 C3
Bella Flor Bolivia 11°9S 67°30W 330 C4
Bella Unión Uruguay 30°15S 57°40W 334 C4
Bella Vista Corrientes,
Argentina 28°33S 59°0W 334 B4
Bella Vista Tucuman,
Argentina 27°10S 65°25W 334 B2
Bellac France 46°7N 1°3E 174 F5
Bellágio Italy 45°59N 9°15E 198 C6
Bellaire U.S.A. 40°1N 80°45W 312 F4
Bellária Italy 44°9N 12°28E 199 D9
Bellary India 15°10N 76°56E 245 G3
Bellata Australia 29°53S 149°46E 281 D4
Bellavista Santiago, Chile 33°31S 70°35W 137 C2
Bellavista Galápagos Is.,
Ecuador 0°41S 90°18W 330 a
Bellavista Lima, Peru 12°4S 77°8W 124 B2
Belle → U.S.A. 38°17N 91°43W 310 F5
Belle → Trin. & Tob. 11°14N 60°37W 323 s
Belle Fille → Dominica 15°25N 61°16W 323 k
Belle Fourche U.S.A. 44°40N 103°51W 308 C2
Belle Fourche →
U.S.A. 44°26N 102°18W 301 C19
Belle Glade U.S.A. 26°41N 80°40W 317 A9
Belle-Île France 47°20N 3°10W 172 E3
Belle Isle Nfld. & L.,
Canada 51°57N 55°25W 299 B8
Belle Isle, Str. of Canada 51°30N 56°30W 299 B8
Belle Plaine U.S.A. 41°54N 92°17W 310 C4
Belle River Canada 42°18N 82°43W 132 D2
Belle View U.S.A. 38°57N 77°4W 143 B2
Belle Vue Maurel Mauritius 20°7S 57°39E 272 e
Belle Yella Liberia 7°24N 10°0W 262 D3
Belledonne France 45°20N 6°10E 175 C10
Bellefontaine Martinique 14°39N 61°10W 322 j
Bellefontaine Ohio,
U.S.A. 40°22N 83°46W 311 D13
Bellefonte U.S.A. 40°55N 77°47W 312 F7
Bellegarde France 47°59N 2°18E 174 C6
Bellegarde-en-Marche
France 45°59N 2°18E 174 F6
Bellegarde-sur-Valserine
France 46°4N 5°50E 173 F12
Bellême France 48°22N 0°34E 172 D7
Belleoram Canada 47°31N 55°25W 299 C8
Belleplaine Barbados 13°15N 59°34W 323 r
Belleview U.S.A. 29°4N 82°3W 317 F7
Belleville Canada 44°10N 77°23W 312 B7
Belleville Rhône, France 46°7N 4°45E 173 F11
Belleville Ill., U.S.A. 38°31N 89°59W 310 F7
Belleville Kans., U.S.A. 39°50N 97°38W 308 F5
Belleville N.J., U.S.A. 40°47N 74°9W 313 F10
Belleville N.Y., U.S.A. 43°46N 76°10W 313 C8
Belleville-sur-Vie France 46°46N 1°25E 172 E6
Bellevue Idaho, U.S.A. 43°28N 114°16W 304 E6
Bellevue Iowa, U.S.A. 42°16N 90°26W 310 B6
Bellevue Mich., U.S.A. 42°27N 85°1W 311 A12
Bellevue Nebr., U.S.A. 41°9N 95°54W 308 E6
Bellevue Ohio, U.S.A. 41°17N 82°51W 312 E2
Bellevue Wash., U.S.A. 47°37N 122°12W 306 C4
Bellevue, Col de Réunion 21°9S 55°36E 272 f
Bellevue, Schloss Berlin, Germany 115 a2
Belley France 45°46N 5°41E 175 C9
Bellin = Kangirsuk Canada 60°0N 70°0W 295 F18
Bellingen Australia 30°25S 152°50E 283 A10
Bellingham London, U.K. 51°26N 0°1W 125 b3
Bellingham Wash.,
U.S.A. 48°46N 122°29W 306 B4
Bellinzona Switz. 46°11N 9°1E 179 J5
Bello Colombia 6°20N 75°41W 328 B1
Bellona Solomon Is. 11°17S 159°47E 287 N10
Bellows Falls U.S.A. 43°8N 72°27W 313 C12
Bellpat Pakistan 29°0N 68°5E 242 E3
Bellpuig Spain 41°37N 1°1E 196 D6
Bells U.S.A. 33°37N 96°25W 311 J6
Belluno Dominica 15°25N 61°21W 323 k
Belluno Italy 46°9N 12°13E 199 B9
Bellville U.S.A. 32°9N 81°59W 316 E8
Bellwood Pa., U.S.A. 40°36N 78°20W 312 F6
Belmanier Dominica 15°25N 61°24W 323 k
Belmez Spain 38°17N 5°17W 195 G5
Belmont Australia 33°4S 151°42E 283 B10
Belmont Canada 42°53N 81°5W 312 D3
Belmont N.S.W., Australia 33°4S 151°42E 283 B10
Belmont Ont., Canada 42°53N 81°5W 312 D3
Belmont S. Africa 29°28S 24°22E 270 C3
Belmont U.S.A. 42°14N 78°2W 312 D6
Belmont Northern Cape,
S. Africa 29°28S 24°22E 270 C3
Belmont London, U.K. 51°21N 0°10W 125 c3
Belmont Mass., U.S.A. 42°24N 71°10W 116 A2
Belmont N.C., U.S.A. 35°15N 81°2W 315 D14
Belmont N.Y., U.S.A. 42°14N 78°2W 312 D6
Belmonte Brazil 16°0S 39°0W 333 E6
Belmonte Portugal 40°21N 7°20W 194 E3
Belmonte Spain 39°34N 2°43W 195 F8
Belmopan Belize 17°18N 88°30W 320 C2

Belmore 33°55S 151°5E 139 B1
Belmullet Ireland 54°14N 9°58W 166 B2
Belo Dem. Rep. of the Congo 0°32S 23°13E 264 C4
Belo Madag. 20°44S 44°0E 272 C1
Belo Horizonte Brazil 19°55S 43°56W 333 E3
Belo Jardim Brazil 8°20S 36°26W 332 C4
Belo Monte Brazil 3°35S 51°46W 329 D7
Belo-Tsiribihina Madag. 19°40S 44°30E 272 B1
Belogorsk = Bilohirsk
Ukraine 45°4N 34°35E 189 K8
Belogorsk Russia 51°0N 128°20E 215 D13
Belogradchik Bulgaria 43°53N 22°42E 202 C6
Belogradets Bulgaria 43°22N 27°18E 203 C11
Beloha Madag. 25°10S 45°3E 272 C2
Beloit Kans., U.S.A. 39°28N 98°6W 308 F4
Beloit Wis., U.S.A. 42°31N 89°2W 310 B7
Belokalitvenskaya = Belaya Kalitva
Russia 48°13N 40°50E 191 F5
Belokorovichi Ukraine 51°7N 28°2E 177 C15
Belomorsk Russia 64°35N 34°54E 188 D6
Belondo
Dem. Rep. of the Congo 0°19S 19°31E 264 C3
Belonge
Dem. Rep. of the Congo 2°7S 19°33E 264 C3
Belonia India 23°15N 91°30E 241 D3
Belopolye = Bilopillya
Ukraine 51°14N 34°20E 189 G8
Belorechensk Russia 44°46N 39°52E 191 H4
Beloretsk Russia 53°58N 58°24E 186 D10
Belorussia = Belarus ■
Europe 53°30N 27°0E 177 B14
Beloshchelye = Naryan-Mar
Russia 67°42N 53°12E 186 A9
Beloslav Bulgaria 43°11N 27°42E 203 C11
Belotsarsk = Kyzyl
Russia 51°50N 94°30E 217 B12
Belovárska Kazakhstan 50°8N 82°31E 217 B10
Belovo Bulgaria 42°13N 24°1E 203 D8
Belovo Russia 54°30N 86°0E 217 B11
Beloyarskiy Russia 63°42N 66°40E 214 C7
Beloye, Ozero Russia 60°10N 37°35E 188 B9
Beloye More Russia 66°30N 38°0E 186 A6
Belozem Russia 42°12N 25°2E 203 D9
Belozersk Russia 60°1N 37°45E 188 B9
Belpasso Italy 37°35N 14°58E 201 E7
Belpre U.S.A. 39°17N 81°34W 309 F13
Belrain India 28°23N 80°55E 243 E9
Belt U.S.A. 47°23N 110°55W 304 C8
Beltana Australia 30°48S 138°25E 282 A3
Belterra Brazil 2°45S 55°0W 329 D7
Beltinci Slovenia 46°37N 16°20E 199 B13
Belton Mo., U.S.A. 38°49N 94°32W 310 F2
Belton Tex., U.S.A. 31°3N 97°28W 314 F6
Belton L. U.S.A. 31°6N 97°28W 314 F6
Beltsy = Bălți Moldova 47°48N 27°58E 183 C12
Beltsy Moldova 47°48N 27°58E 183 C12
Belturbet Ireland 54°6N 7°26W 166 B4
Belukha Russia 49°50N 86°50E 217 C11
Belur India 22°37N 88°21E 124 B2
Beluran Malaysia 5°48N 117°35E 235 A5
Beluša Slovak Rep. 49°5N 18°17E 181 B11
Belushya Russia 71°32N 52°19E 214 B6
Belušić Serbia 43°50N 21°10E 202 C5
Belvedere St. Vincent 13°8N 61°11W 323 n
Belvedere London, U.K. 51°29N 0°9E 125 b4
Belvedere Calif., U.S.A. 37°52N 122°28W 136 A2
Belvedere Georgia, U.S.A. 33°45N 84°16W 113 B2
Belvedere Maríttimo Italy 39°37N 15°52E 201 C8
Belvès France 44°46N 1°0E 174 D4
Belvidere Ill., U.S.A. 42°15N 88°50W 311 B8
Belvidere N.J., U.S.A. 40°50N 75°5W 313 F9
Belvis de la Jara Spain 39°45N 4°57W 194 F6
Bely Bychek = Chagoda
Russia 59°10N 35°15E 188 B8
Belyando → Australia 21°38S 146°50E 280 C4
Belyando Crossing
Australia 21°32S 146°51E 280 C4
Belyayevka Bogorodskoye
Russia 55°39N 37°31E 129 C3
Belyuen Australia 12°34S 130°42E 278 B5
Belyy Russia 55°49N 33°3E 188 F7
Belyy, Ostrov Russia 73°30N 71°0E 214 B8
Belyy Yar Russia 58°26N 84°39E 214 D9
Belye Vody = Aqsū
Kazakhstan 42°25N 69°50E 217 D7
Belz Ukraine 50°23N 24°1E 185 H10
Belzec Poland 50°23N 23°26E 185 H10
Belzig Germany 52°8N 12°35E 178 C8
Belzoni U.S.A. 33°11N 90°29W 315 E9
Belżyce Poland 51°11N 22°17E 185 G9
Bemaraha, Lembalemban' i
Madag. 18°40S 44°45E 272 B1
Bemarivo Madag. 21°45S 44°45E 272 C1
Bemarivo → Antsiranana,
Madag. 14°9S 50°9E 272 A3
Bemarivo → Mahajanga,
Madag. 15°27S 47°40E 272 B2
Bemavo Madag. 21°33S 45°25E 272 C2
Bembe Angola 7°0S 14°20E 265 C2
Bembéréke Benin 10°11N 2°43E 263 C5
Bembesi Zimbabwe 20°0S 28°58E 269 G2
Bembesi → Zimbabwe 18°57S 27°47E 269 F2
Bembézar → Spain 42°37N 0°5W 196 B4
Bembibre Spain 42°37N 6°28W 194 C4
Bemboka ○ Australia 36°35S 149°41E 283 D8
Bemetara India 39°55N 88°34W 311 E8
Bemidji U.S.A. 47°28N 94°53W 308 B6
Bemolanga Madag. 17°45S 45°6E 272 B2
Bemowo Poland 52°15N 20°53E 142 B1
Ben Boyd △ Australia 37°0S 149°55E 283 D8
Ben Cruachan U.K. 56°26N 5°8W 167 E3
Ben Dearg U.K. 57°47N 4°56W 167 D4
Ben Dc △ Vietnam 19°37N 105°30E 236 C5
Ben Gardane Tunisia 33°11N 11°11E 258 B2
Ben Halls Gap △ Australia 31°37S 151°1E 283 B9
Ben Hope U.K. 58°25N 4°36W 167 C4
Ben Lawers U.K. 56°32N 4°14W 167 E4
Ben Lomond N.S.W.,
Australia 30°1S 151°43E 281 D5
Ben Lomond Tas.,
Australia 41°38S 147°42E 281 G4
Ben Lomond Stirling, U.K. 56°11N 4°38W 167 E4
Ben Lomond △ Australia 41°33S 147°25E 281 G4
Ben Luc Vietnam 10°39N 106°29E 237 G6
Ben Macdhui U.K. 57°4N 3°40W 167 D5
Ben Mhor U.K. 57°15N 7°18W 167 D1
Ben More Argyll & Bute,
U.K. 56°26N 6°1W 167 E2
Ben More Stirling, U.K. 56°23N 4°32W 167 E4
Ben More Assynt U.K. 58°8N 4°52W 167 C4
Ben Nevis U.K. 56°48N 5°1W 167 E3
Ben Ohau Ra. N.Z. 44°15S 170°4E 285 E3
Ben Quang Vietnam 17°3N 106°55E 236 D6
Ben Slimane □ Morocco 33°38N 7°6W 260 B4
Ben Slimane Morocco 33°38N 7°6W 260 B4
Ben Tre Vietnam 10°14N 106°23E 237 G6
Ben Wyvis U.K. 57°40N 4°35W 167 D4
Bena Nigeria 11°20N 5°50E 263 C6
Bena-Dibele
Dem. Rep. of the Congo 4°4S 22°50E 265 C4
Bena-Leka
Dem. Rep. of the Congo 5°8S 22°10E 265 D4

Bena-Tshadi Dem. Rep. of the Congo 4°40S 22°49E 265 C4
Benagerie Australia 31°25S 140°22E 282 A4
Benahmed Morocco 33°4N 7°9W 260 B3
Benaki Museum Athens, Greece 112 b3
Benalla Australia 36°30S 146°0E 283 D7
Benalmádena Spain 36°36N 4°34W 195 J6
Benambra, Mt. Australia 36°31S 147°34E 283 D7
Benanee Australia 34°31S 142°52E 282 C5
Benangin Indonesia 0°58S 115°19E 235 C5
Bénara Mayotte 12°53S 45°9E 272 b
Benares = Varanasi India 25°22N 83°0E 243 G10
Bénat, C. France 43°5N 6°22E 175 E10
Benavente Portugal 38°59N 8°49W 195 G2
Benavente Spain 42°2N 5°43W 194 C5
Benavides U.S.A. 27°36N 98°25W 314 H5
Benavides de Órbigo Spain 42°30N 5°54W 194 C5
Benbecula U.K. 57°26N 7°21W 167 D1
Benbonyathe Hill Australia 30°25S 139°11E 282 A3
Bend U.S.A. 44°4N 121°19W 304 D3
Bendale Canada 43°45N 79°13W 141 A3
Bendela Dem. Rep. of the Congo 3°18S 17°36E 264 C3
Bendemeer Australia 30°53S 151°8E 283 A9
Bender Beyla Somali Rep. 9°30N 50°48E 267 C7
Bendery = Tighina Moldova 46°50N 29°30E 183 D14
Bendigo Australia 36°40S 144°15E 282 D6
Bendin = Będzin Poland 50°19N 19°7E 185 H6
Bendorf Germany 50°25N 7°35E 178 E3
Bendsburg = Będzin Poland 50°19N 19°7E 185 H6
Benē Beraq Israel 32°6N 34°51E 251 F5
Beneditinos Brazil 5°27S 42°22W 332 C3
Benedito Leite Brazil 7°13S 44°34W 332 C3
Benefica Brazil 22°52S 43°14W 135 B1
Bénéna Mali 13°9N 4°17W 262 C4
Benenitra Madag. 23°27S 45°5E 272 C2
Benešov Czech Rep. 49°46N 14°41E 180 B7
Benevento Italy 41°8N 14°45E 201 A7
Benfeld France 48°22N 7°34E 173 D14
Benfica Portugal 38°45N 9°11W 126 A1
Beng Mealea Cambodia 13°28N 104°14E 236 F5
Benga Mozam. 16°11S 33°40E 269 F3
Bengal = West Bengal □ India 23°0N 88°0E 243 H13
Bengal, Bay of Ind. Oc. 15°0N 90°0E 239 F14
Bengaluru = Bangalore India 12°59N 77°40E 245 H3
Bengbis Cameroon 3°27N 12°36E 263 E7
Bengbu China 32°58N 117°20E 227 H9
Benghazi = Banghāzī Libya 32°11N 20°3E 258 B4
Benghisa Point Malta 35°49N 14°33E 206 F8
Bengkalis Indonesia 1°30N 102°10E 237 M4
Bengkayang Indonesia 0°49N 109°28E 235 B3
Bengkulu Indonesia 3°50S 102°12E 234 C2
Bengkulu □ Indonesia 3°48S 102°16E 234 C2
Bengo Dem. Rep. of the Congo 2°11S 19°5E 264 C3
Bengo □ Angola 9°0S 13°10E 265 D2
Bengough Canada 49°25N 105°10W 297 D7
Bengtsfors Sweden 59°2N 12°14E 162 E6
Benguela Angola 12°37S 13°25E 265 E2
Benguela □ Angola 13°0S 13°30E 265 E2
Benguerir Morocco 32°16N 7°56W 260 B3
Benguérua, I. Mozam. 21°58S 35°28E 271 B6
Benguet □ Phil. 16°30N 120°40E 232 C3
Benha Egypt 30°26N 31°8E 256 H7
Benham Seamount Pac. Oc. 15°40N 124°30E 232 D5
Beni Dem. Rep. of the Congo 0°30N 29°27E 268 B2
Beni □ Bolivia 14°0S 65°0W 331 C5
Beni → Bolivia 10°23S 65°24W 331 C4
Beni Abbès Algeria 30°5N 2°5W 261 B4
Beni Hammad Algeria 35°49N 4°47E 261 A5
Beni Haoua Algeria 36°30N 1°30E 261 A5
Beni Mazâr Egypt 28°32N 30°44E 256 B3
Beni Mellal Morocco 32°21N 6°21W 260 B3
Beni Mellal □ Morocco 32°0N 6°30W 260 B3
Beni Ounif Algeria 32°0N 1°10W 261 B4
Beni Saf Algeria 35°17N 1°15W 261 A4
Beni Suef Egypt 29°5N 31°6E 256 J7
Beniah L. Canada 63°23N 112°17W 296 A6
Benicarló Spain 40°23N 0°23E 196 E5
Benicássim Spain 40°3N 0°4E 196 E5
Benidorm Spain 38°33N 0°9W 197 G4
Benin ■ Africa 10°0N 2°0E 263 D5
Benin → Nigeria 5°45N 5°4E 263 D6
Benin, Bight of W. Afr. 5°0N 3°0E 263 E5
Benin City Nigeria 6°20N 5°31E 263 D6
Benissa Spain 38°43N 0°3E 197 G5
Benitez Int. ✈ (SCL) Chile 33°33S 70°42W 137 B1
Bénitiers, Île aux Mauritius 20°24S 57°20E 272 e
Benito Juárez Argentina 37°40S 59°43W 334 D4
Benito Juárez, Int. ✈ (MEX) Mexico 19°25N 99°5W 128 B2
Benitses Greece 39°32N 19°55E 206 B9
Benjamin Aceval Paraguay 24°58S 57°34W 334 A4
Benjamin Constant Brazil 4°40S 70°15W 328 D3
Benjamin Hill Mexico 30°9N 111°7W 318 A2
Benkelman U.S.A. 40°3N 101°32W 308 E3
Benkovac Croatia 44°2N 15°37E 199 D12
Benmore Pk. N.Z. 44°25S 170°8E 285 E5
Bennett Canada 59°51N 135°0W 296 B2
Bennett, L. Australia 22°50S 131°2E 278 D5
Bennetta, Ostrov Russia 76°21N 148°56E 215 B15
Bennettsville U.S.A. 34°37N 79°41W 315 D15
Bennichchāb Mauritania 19°32N 15°12W 262 B1
Bennington N.H., U.S.A. 43°0N 71°55W 313 D11
Bennington Vt., U.S.A. 42°53N 73°12W 313 D11
Beno Dem. Rep. of the Congo 3°41S 17°49E 264 C3
Bénodet France 47°53N 4°7W 172 E2
Benom Malaysia 3°50N 102°6E 237 L4
Benoni S. Africa 26°11S 28°18E 271 C4
Benoud Algeria 32°20N 0°16E 261 B5
Bénoué △ Cameroon 8°30N 13°55E 264 A2
Benoy Chad 8°59N 16°19E 259 G3
Benque Viejo Belize 17°5N 89°8W 320 C2
Bense Dominica 15°35N 61°22W 323 k
Bensheim Germany 49°40N 8°38E 179 F4
Benson Ariz., U.S.A. 31°58N 110°18W 305 L8
Benson Minn., U.S.A. 45°19N 95°36W 308 C6
Bensonhurst U.S.A. 40°35N 73°59W 132 C2
Bent Iran 26°20N 59°31E 247 E8
Benteng Indonesia 6°10S 120°30E 231 F6
Bentiaba Angola 14°15S 12°21E 265 E2
Bentinck I. Queens., Australia 17°3S 139°35E 280 B2
Bentinck I. Burma 11°45N 98°3E 237 G2
Bentiu Sudan 9°10N 29°55E 257 F2
Bentley Subglacial Trench Antarctica 80°0S 115°0W 151 E15
Bento Gonçalves Brazil 29°10S 51°31W 335 B5
Benton Ark., U.S.A. 34°34N 92°35W 314 D8
Benton Calif., U.S.A. 37°48N 118°32W 306 H8
Benton Ill., U.S.A. 38°0N 88°55W 310 G8
Benton Pa., U.S.A. 41°12N 76°23W 313 E8
Benton Harbor U.S.A. 42°6N 86°27W 311 B10
Benton Heights U.S.A. 42°7N 86°24W 311 B10
Bentong Malaysia 3°31N 101°55E 237 L3
Bentonville U.S.A. 36°22N 94°13W 314 C7
Bentu Liben Ethiopia 8°32N 38°21E 257 F4
Benue □ Nigeria 7°20N 8°45E 263 D6
Benue → Nigeria 7°48N 6°46E 263 D6
Benxi China 41°20N 123°48E 224 B1
Benza Dem. Rep. of the Congo 4°49S 13°17E 265 D2
Benzdorp Suriname 3°44N 54°5W 329 C7
Beo Indonesia 4°25N 126°50E 231 D7
Beograd Serbia 44°50N 20°37E 202 B4
Beograd ✈ (BEG) Serbia 43°49N 20°17E 202 C4
Beolgyo S. Korea 34°51N 127°21E 224 E3
Beoumi Ivory C. 7°45N 5°23W 262 D3
Beppu Japan 33°15N 131°30E 222 D3
Beppu-Wan Japan 33°18N 131°34E 222 D3
Beqa Fiji 18°23S 178°8E 287 B2
Beqaa Valley = Al Biqā Lebanon 34°10N 36°10E 250 D7
Bequia St. Vincent 13°0N 61°15W 323 n
Ber Mota India 23°27N 68°34E 242 H3
Bera Bangla. 24°5N 89°37E 241 C2
Bera, Tasik Malaysia 3°5N 102°38E 237 L4
Berach → India 25°15N 75°2E 242 G6
Beraketa Madag. 23°7S 44°25E 272 C1
Béran-Djoko Congo 3°15N 17°0E 264 B3
Berane Montenegro 42°51N 19°52E 202 D3
Berastagi Indonesia 3°11N 98°31E 237 L2
Berat Albania 40°43N 19°59E 202 F3
Berau = Tanjungredeb Indonesia 2°9N 117°29E 235 B5
Berau → Indonesia 2°10N 117°42E 235 B5
Berau, Teluk Indonesia 2°30S 132°30E 231 E8
Beravina Madag. 18°10S 45°14E 272 B2
Berbak △ Indonesia 1°27S 104°19E 234 C2
Berber Sudan 18°0N 34°0E 256 D3
Berbera Somali Rep. 10°30N 45°2E 267 B6
Berbérati C.A.R. 4°15N 15°40E 264 B3
Berbice → Guyana 6°20N 57°32W 329 B6
Berceto Italy 44°31N 9°51E 198 D6
Berchem-Ste-Agathe Belgium 50°52N 4°17E 116 A1
Berchidda Italy 40°47N 9°10E 200 B2
Berchtesgaden Germany 47°38N 13°0E 179 H8
Berchtesgaden △ Germany 47°34N 12°55E 179 H8
Berck France 50°25N 1°36E 173 B8
Berdaale Somali Rep. 3°14N 43°11E 267 D5
Berdale Somali Rep. 7°4N 47°51E 267 C6
Berdichev = Berdychiv Ukraine 49°57N 28°30E 177 D15
Berdsk Russia 54°47N 83°2E 217 B10
Berdyansk Ukraine 46°45N 36°50E 189 J9
Berdychiv Ukraine 49°57N 28°30E 177 D15
Béré Chad 9°20N 16°9E 259 G3
Berea U.S.A. 37°34N 84°17W 309 G11
Berebere Indonesia 2°25N 128°45E 231 D7
Bereda Somali Rep. 11°45N 51°0E 267 B7
Berehomet Ukraine 48°10N 25°19E 183 B10
Berehove Ukraine 48°15N 22°35E 182 B7
Bereina Papua N. G. 8°39S 146°30E 286 E4
Berekat Turkmenistan 39°16N 55°32E 247 B7
Berekua Dominica 15°14N 61°20W 323 k
Berekum Ghana 7°29N 2°34W 262 D4
Berenice Egypt 24°2N 35°25E 256 C4
Berens → Canada 52°25N 97°2W 297 C9
Berens I. Canada 52°18N 97°18W 297 C9
Berens River Canada 52°25N 97°0W 297 C9
Beresfield Australia 32°50S 151°40E 283 B9
Beresford U.S.A. 43°5N 96°47W 308 D5
Berestechko Ukraine 50°22N 25°5E 177 C13
Bereşti Romania 46°6N 27°50E 183 D12
Beretău → Romania 47°10N 21°50E 182 C6
Berettyó → Hungary 46°59N 21°7E 182 D6
Berettyóújfalu Hungary 47°13N 21°33E 182 C6
Berevo Mahajanga, Madag. 17°14S 44°17E 272 B1
Berevo Toliara, Madag. 19°44S 44°58E 272 B1
Bereza = Byaroza Belarus 52°31N 24°51E 177 B13
Berezhany Ukraine 49°26N 24°58E 177 D13
Berezina = Byarezina → Belarus 52°33N 30°14E 177 B16
Berezivka Ukraine 47°14N 30°55E 189 J6
Berezna Ukraine 51°35N 31°46E 189 G6
Bereznik Russia 62°51N 42°40E 186 B7
Berezniki Russia 59°24N 56°46E 186 C10
Berezovo Russia 64°0N 65°0E 214 C7
Berezyne Ukraine 46°14N 29°12E 183 D14
Berg am Laim Germany 48°7N 11°38E 131 B2
Berga Spain 42°6N 1°48E 196 C6
Berga Kalmar, Sweden 57°14N 16°3E 163 G10
Bergama Turkey 39°8N 27°11E 205 B9
Bérgamo Italy 45°41N 9°43E 198 C6
Bergaon India 20°41N 80°27E 244 D5
Bergara Spain 43°9N 2°28W 196 B2
Bergby Sweden 60°57N 17°2E 162 D11
Berge Norway 59°34N 8°10E 162 E2
Bergedorf Germany 53°28N 10°12E 178 B6
Bergeforsen Sweden 62°32N 17°23E 162 B11
Bergen Mecklenburg-Vorpommern, Germany 54°25N 13°25E 178 A9
Bergen Niedersachsen, Germany 52°49N 9°57E 178 C5
Bergen Neths. 52°40N 4°43E 170 B4
Bergen Hordaland, Norway 60°20N 5°20E 164 D2
Bergen N.Y., U.S.A. 43°5N 77°57W 312 C7
Bergen ✈ (BGO) Norway 60°17N 5°19E 164 D2
Bergen op Zoom Neths. 51°28N 4°18E 170 C4
Bergenfield U.S.A. 40°55N 73°59W 132 A2
Bergerac France 44°51N 0°30E 174 D4
Bergham Germany 48°2N 11°37E 131 B2
Bergheim Germany 50°57N 6°38E 178 E2
Bergholz U.S.A. 40°31N 80°53W 312 F4
Bergisch Gladbach Germany 50°59N 7°8E 170 D7
Bergisches Land ⌓ Germany 51°0N 7°30E 178 E3
Bergkamen Germany 51°37N 7°38E 178 D3
Bergkvara Sweden 56°23N 16°5E 163 H10
Bergshamra Sweden 59°38N 18°37E 162 E12
Bergsjö Sweden 61°59N 17°3E 162 C11
Bergstadt = Leśnica Poland 50°26N 18°11E 185 H5
Bergstrasse-Odenwald ⌓ Germany 49°45N 5°55E 179 F1
Bergues France 50°58N 2°24E 173 B9
Bergviken Sweden 61°15N 16°40E 162 C10
Bergville S. Africa 28°52S 29°18E 271 C4
Bergvliet S. Africa 34°2S 18°25E 118 B1
Berhala, Selat Indonesia 1°0S 104°15E 234 C2
Berhampore = Baharampur India 24°2N 88°27E 243 G13
Berhampur = Brahmapur India 19°15N 84°54E 244 E7
Berheci → Romania 45°58N 27°28E 183 E12
Beri Spain 41°20N 2°1E 114 A1
Berikat, Tanjung Indonesia 2°34S 106°52E 234 C3
Bering Glacier U.S.A. 60°20N 143°30W 303 F12
Bering Land Bridge ⌓ U.S.A. 66°20N 165°0W 303 C6
Bering Sea Pac. Oc. 58°0N 171°0W 292 D2
Bering Strait Pac. Oc. 65°30N 169°0W 303 C6
Beringovskiy Russia 63°3N 179°19E 215 C18
Berisso Argentina 34°56S 57°50W 334 C4
Berja Spain 36°50N 2°56W 195 J8
Berkåk Norway 62°50N 10°0E 164 B6
Berkane Morocco 34°52N 2°20W 261 B4
Berkeley U.S.A. 37°51N 122°16W 136 A3
Berkeley, C. Ecuador 0°1N 91°35W 330 a
Berkner I. Antarctica 79°30S 50°0W 151 D18
Berkovitsa Bulgaria 43°16N 23°8E 202 C7
Berkshire U.S.A. 42°19N 76°11W 313 D8
Berkshire Downs U.K. 51°33N 1°29W 169 F6
Berlanga Spain 38°17N 5°50W 195 G5
Berlenga, I. Portugal 39°25N 9°30W 195 F1
Berlengas = Valença do Piauí Brazil 6°20S 41°45W 332 C3
Berlin = Kitchener Canada 43°27N 80°29W 312 C4
Berlin Berlin, Germany 52°31N 13°23E 115 A3
Berlin Ga., U.S.A. 31°4N 83°37W 316 D6
Berlin Md., U.S.A. 38°20N 75°13W 309 F16
Berlin N.H., U.S.A. 44°28N 71°11W 313 B13
Berlin N.Y., U.S.A. 42°42N 73°23W 313 D11
Berlin Wis., U.S.A. 43°58N 88°57W 308 D9
Berlin □ Germany 52°30N 13°20E 178 C9
Berlin Dom Germany 52°31N 13°24E 115 A3
Berlin L. U.S.A. 41°3N 81°0W 312 E4
Berlin Tegel ✈ (TXL) Germany 52°35N 13°14E 115 A2
Berlinchen = Barlinek Poland 53°0N 15°15E 185 F2
Bermagui Australia 36°25S 150°4E 283 D9
Bermeja, Sierra Spain 36°30N 5°11W 195 J5
Bermejo → Formosa, Argentina 26°51S 58°23W 334 B4
Bermejo → San Juan, Argentina 32°30S 67°30W 334 C2
Bermejo, Paso = Uspallata, P. de Argentina 32°37S 69°22W 334 C2
Bermen, L. Canada 53°35N 68°55W 299 B6
Bermeo Spain 43°25N 2°47W 196 B2
Bermillo de Sayago Spain 41°22N 6°8W 194 D4
Bermondsey U.K. 51°29N 0°3W 125 B3
Bermuda ⊘ Atl. Oc. 32°18N 64°45W 153 a
Bermuda Int. ✈ (BDA) Bermuda 32°22N 64°41W 153 a
Bermuda Rise Atl. Oc. 32°30N 65°0W 152 C5
Bern Switz. 46°57N 7°28E 179 J3
Bern □ Switz. 46°45N 7°40E 179 J3
Bernabeu, Estadio Spain 40°27N 3°41W 127 B1
Bernal Heights U.S.A. 37°44N 122°24W 136 B2
Bernalda Italy 40°24N 16°41E 201 B9
Bernalillo U.S.A. 35°18N 106°33W 305 J10
Bernam → Malaysia 3°45N 101°5E 234 B2
Bernardo de Irigoyen Argentina 26°15S 53°40W 335 B5
Bernardo O'Higgins △ Chile 48°50S 75°36W 336 C1
Bernardsville U.S.A. 40°43N 74°34W 313 F10
Bernasconi Argentina 37°55S 63°44W 334 D3
Bernau Bayern, Germany 47°47N 12°22E 179 H8
Bernau Brandenburg, Germany 52°40N 13°35E 178 C9
Bernay France 49°5N 0°35E 172 C7
Bernburg Germany 51°47N 11°44E 178 D7
Berndorf Austria 47°59N 16°1E 180 D9
Berne = Bern Switz. 46°57N 7°28E 179 J3
Berne = Bern □ Switz. 46°45N 7°40E 179 J3
Berne U.S.A. 40°39N 84°57W 311 D12
Berner Alpen Switz. 46°27N 7°35E 179 J3
Berneray U.K. 57°43N 7°11W 167 D1
Bernier I. Australia 24°50S 113°12E 279 D1
Bernina, Piz Switz. 46°20N 9°54E 179 J5
Bernkastel-Kues Germany 49°55N 7°3E 179 F3
Bernstadt = Bierutów Poland 51°7N 17°32E 185 G4
Bernstein = Pełczyce Poland 53°3N 15°16E 185 E2
Bero → Angola 15°10S 12°9E 265 F2
Beroroha Madag. 21°40S 45°10E 272 C2
Béroubouay Benin 10°34N 2°46E 263 C5
Beroun Czech Rep. 49°57N 14°5E 180 B7
Berounka → Czech Rep. 50°0N 14°22E 180 B7
Berovo Macedonia 41°38N 22°51E 202 E6
Berre, Étang de France 43°27N 5°5E 175 E9
Berre-l'Étang France 43°28N 5°10E 175 E9
Berrechid Morocco 33°18N 7°36W 260 B3
Berri Australia 34°14S 140°35E 282 C4
Berriane Algeria 32°50N 3°46E 261 B5
Berridale Australia 36°22S 148°48E 283 D8
Berrien Springs U.S.A. 41°57N 86°20W 311 C10
Berrigan Australia 35°38S 145°49E 283 C6
Berriwillock Australia 35°36S 142°59E 282 C5
Berrouaghia Algeria 36°10N 2°53E 261 A5
Berry N.S.W., Australia 34°46S 150°43E 283 C9
Berry Indre, France 46°50N 2°0E 173 F8
Berry Is. Bahamas 25°40N 77°50W 320 A4
Berrydale U.S.A. 30°53N 87°3W 317 E2
Berryessa, L. U.S.A. 38°31N 122°6W 306 G4
Berryville U.S.A. 36°22N 93°34W 314 C8
Berseba Namibia 26°0S 17°46E 270 C2
Bersenbrück Germany 52°34N 7°56E 178 C3
Bershad Ukraine 48°22N 29°31E 183 B14
Bertamirans Spain 42°54N 8°38W 194 C2
Berthold U.S.A. 48°19N 101°44W 308 A3
Berthoud U.S.A. 40°19N 105°5W 304 F11
Bertincourt France 50°5N 2°58E 173 B9
Bertolínia Brazil 7°38S 43°57W 332 C3
Bertoua Cameroon 4°30N 13°45E 264 B2
Bertraghboy B. Ireland 53°22N 9°54W 166 C2
Bertys = Balqash Kazakhstan 46°50N 74°50E 214 E8
Beru Kiribati 1°20S 176°0E 277 A14
Berufjörður Iceland 64°48N 14°29W 155 C12
Berunes Iceland 64°42N 14°16W 155 C12
Beruni Uzbekistan 41°41N 60°45E 216 D6
Beruri Brazil 3°54S 61°22W 329 D5
Berwick U.S.A. 41°3N 76°14W 313 E8
Berwick-upon-Tweed U.K. 55°46N 2°0W 168 B6
Berwyn U.S.A. 41°50N 87°47W 119 B2
Berwyn Heights U.S.A. 38°59N 76°55W 143 B4
Berwyn Mts. U.K. 52°54N 3°26W 168 D4
Beryslav Ukraine 46°50N 33°30E 189 J7
Berzasca Romania 44°39N 21°58E 182 F6
Berzence Hungary 46°12N 17°11E 182 D2
Besal Pakistan 35°4N 73°56E 243 B5
Besalampy Madag. 16°43S 44°29E 272 B1
Besançon France 47°15N 6°2E 173 E13
Besar Indonesia 2°40S 116°0E 235 C5
Besar, Gunung Malaysia 5°10N 101°18E 234 A2
Beshenkovichi Belarus 55°2N 29°29E 188 E5
Besiktas Turkey 41°2N 29°0E 122 B2
Beška Serbia 45°8N 20°6E 182 E5
Beslan Russia 43°15N 44°28E 191 J7
Besna Kobila Serbia 42°31N 22°10E 202 D6
Besnard L. Canada 55°25N 106°0W 297 B7
Besni Turkey 37°41N 37°52E 212 D7
Besor, N. → Egypt 31°28N 34°22E 251 G5
Besós → Spain 41°24N 2°13E 114 A2
Bessa Monteiro Angola 7°7S 13°44E 265 D2
Bessarabiya Moldova 47°0N 28°10E 177 E15
Bessarabka = Basarabeasca Moldova 46°21N 28°58E 183 D13
Bessèges France 44°18N 4°8E 175 D8
Bessemer Ala., U.S.A. 33°24N 86°58W 315 E11
Bessemer Mich., U.S.A. 46°29N 90°3W 308 B8
Bessemer Pa., U.S.A. 40°59N 80°30W 312 F4
Bessie, L. U.S.A. 28°29N 81°31W 133 B1
Bessin France 49°18N 1°0W 172 C6
Bessines-sur-Gartempe France 46°6N 1°22E 174 B5
Beswick Australia 14°34S 132°53E 278 B5
Beswick ⌓ Australia 14°31S 132°51E 278 B5
Bet Horon West Bank 31°52N 35°7E 123 A1
Bet She'an Israel 32°30N 35°30E 251 F6
Bet Shemesh Israel 31°44N 35°0E 251 G6
Betafo Madag. 19°50S 46°51E 272 B2
Betamba Dem. Rep. of the Congo 2°17S 21°24E 264 C4
Betancuria Canary Is. 28°25N 14°3W 153 e2
Betancuria, Mt. Canary Is. 28°25N 14°6W 153 e2
Betania Colombia 4°22N 72°54W 328 C3
Betanzos Bolivia 19°34S 65°27W 331 D4
Betanzos Spain 43°15N 8°12W 194 B2
Bétaré Oya Cameroon 5°40N 14°5E 264 A2
Betatao Madag. 18°11S 47°52E 272 B2
Bétera Spain 39°35N 0°28W 197 F4
Bétérou Benin 9°12N 2°16E 263 D5
Bethal S. Africa 26°27S 29°28E 271 C4
Bethalto U.S.A. 38°55N 90°2W 310 F6
Bethanien Namibia 26°31S 17°8E 270 C2
Bethany Ont., Canada 44°11N 78°34W 312 B6
Bethany Ill., U.S.A. 39°39N 88°45W 311 E8
Bethany Mo., U.S.A. 40°16N 94°2W 310 D2
Bethany Okla., U.S.A. 35°31N 97°38W 314 D6
Bethel Montserrat 16°44N 62°9W 323 p
Bethel Alaska, U.S.A. 60°48N 161°45W 303 F7
Bethel Conn., U.S.A. 41°22N 73°25W 313 E11
Bethel Maine, U.S.A. 44°25N 70°47W 313 B14
Bethel Ohio, U.S.A. 38°58N 84°5W 311 F12
Bethel Vt., U.S.A. 43°50N 72°38W 313 C12
Bethel Park U.S.A. 40°19N 80°2W 312 F4
Béthenville France 49°18N 4°23E 173 C11
Bethesda U.S.A. 38°59N 77°6W 143 B3
Bethlehem = Bayt Lahm West Bank 31°43N 35°12E 123 B2
Bethlehem Free State, S. Africa 28°14S 28°18E 271 C4
Bethlehem Pa., U.S.A. 40°37N 75°23W 313 F9
Bethnal Green U.K. 51°31N 0°2W 125 A3
Bethulie S. Africa 30°30S 25°59E 270 D4
Béthune France 50°30N 2°38E 173 B9
Béthune → France 49°53N 1°4E 172 C8
Bethungra Australia 34°45S 147°51E 283 C7
Betijoque Venezuela 9°23N 70°44W 328 B3
Betim Brazil 19°58S 44°13W 333 E3
Betioky Toliara, Madag. 23°48S 44°20E 272 C1
Betioky Toliara, Madag. 22°27S 43°43E 272 C1
Betong Malaysia 1°24N 111°31E 235 B4
Betong Thailand 5°45N 101°5E 237 K3
Betoota Australia 25°45S 140°42E 280 D3
Betor Ethiopia 11°37N 39°2E 257 E4
Betor W. Bengal, India 22°34N 88°17E 124 B1
Bétou Congo 3°2N 18°32E 264 B3
Betpaqdala Kazakhstan 45°45N 70°30E 217 C8
Betroka Madag. 23°16S 46°0E 272 C2
Betsiamites Canada 48°56N 68°40W 299 C6
Betsiamites → Canada 48°56N 68°38W 299 C6
Betsiboka → Madag. 16°3S 46°36E 272 B2
Bettendorf U.S.A. 41°32N 90°30W 310 C6
Bettiah India 26°48N 84°33E 243 F11
Bettna Sweden 58°55N 16°38E 163 F10
Béttola Italy 44°47N 9°36E 198 D6
Betul India 21°58N 77°59E 244 D3
Betung Indonesia 3°58S 104°34E 234 C2
Betung Kerihun △ Indonesia 1°11N 113°38E 235 B4
Betws-y-Coed U.K. 53°5N 3°48W 168 D4
Betxi Spain 39°56N 0°12W 196 F4
Betzdorf Germany 50°46N 7°52E 178 E3
Béu Angola 6°15S 15°32E 265 D3
Beuil France 44°6N 6°59E 175 D10
Beulah Vic., Australia 35°58S 142°29E 282 C5
Beulah Fla., U.S.A. 28°32N 81°34W 133 A1
Beulah Mich., U.S.A. 44°38N 86°6W 308 C10
Beulah N. Dak., U.S.A. 47°16N 101°47W 308 B3
Beulah, L. U.S.A. 28°32N 81°33W 133 A1
Beurkia Chad 15°20N 17°56E 259 E3
Beurs van Berlage Amsterdam, Neths. 112 a2
Beuthen = Bytom Poland 50°25N 18°54E 185 H5
Beuthen an der Oder = Bytom Odrzański Poland 51°44N 15°48E 185 G2
Beuvron → France 47°29N 1°15E 172 E8
Beveren Belgium 51°12N 4°16E 170 C4
Beverley W. Austral., Australia 32°9S 116°56E 279 F2
Beverley E. Riding, U.K. 53°51N 0°26W 168 D7
Beverley Hills Australia 33°56S 151°5E 139 B1
Beverley Park Australia 33°58S 151°8E 139 B1
Beverly Ill., U.S.A. 41°42N 87°39W 119 C2
Beverly Mass., U.S.A. 42°33N 70°53W 313 D14
Beverly Arts Center U.S.A. 41°41N 87°40W 119 C2
Beverly Glen U.S.A. 34°6N 118°26W 126 B2
Beverly Hills Calif., U.S.A. 34°5N 118°24W 126 B2
Beverly Hills Fla., U.S.A. 28°55N 82°28W 317 G7
Beverly Hills -Morgan Park Historic District U.S.A. 41°41N 87°40W 119 C2
Beverungen Germany 51°39N 9°22E 178 D5
Bevoalavo Madag. 25°13S 44°26E 272 D2
Bewas → India 23°59N 79°21E 243 H8
Bewdley Canada 44°5N 78°19W 312 B6
Bex Switz. 46°15N 7°1E 179 J3
Bexhill U.K. 50°51N 0°29E 169 G8
Bexley Australia 33°56S 151°7E 139 B1
Bexley □ U.K. 51°27N 0°9E 125 B4
Bexleyheath U.K. 51°27N 0°8E 125 B4
Bey Dağları Turkey 36°38N 30°29E 205 E12
Beyānlū Iran 36°0N 47°51E 246 C5
Beyazköy Turkey 41°21N 27°42E 203 E11
Beyçayırı Turkey 40°15N 26°35E 203 F10
Beydağ Turkey 38°5N 28°13E 205 C10
Beyeğaç Turkey 37°14N 28°53E 205 D10
Beyin Ghana 5°1N 2°41W 262 D4
Beykoz Turkey 41°7N 29°7E 122 B2
Beyla Guinea 8°30N 8°38W 262 D3
Beylerbeyi Turkey 41°2N 29°2E 122 B2
Beynat France 45°8N 1°44E 174 C5
Beyneu Kazakhstan 45°18N 55°9E 187 E10
Beyoba Turkey 38°48N 27°47E 205 C9
Beyoğlu Turkey 41°1N 28°58E 122 B1
Beyoneisu Retsugan Japan 31°55N 139°55E 223 F11
Beypazarı Turkey 40°10N 31°56E 212 B4
Beypore → India 11°10N 75°47E 245 J2
Beyra Somali Rep. 6°57N 47°19E 267 C6
Beyşehir Turkey 37°41N 31°45E 212 D4
Beyşehir Gölü Turkey 37°41N 31°33E 212 D4
Beytüşşebap Turkey 37°35N 43°10E 213 D10
Bezdan Serbia 45°50N 18°57E 182 E3
Bezhetsk Russia 57°47N 36°39E 188 D9
Béziers France 43°20N 3°12E 174 E7
Bezons France 48°56N 2°13E 134 A2
Bezuidenhout Park S. Africa 26°10S 28°5E 123 B2
Bezwada = Vijayawada India 16°31N 80°39E 244 F5
Bhabua India 25°3N 83°37E 243 G10
Bhachau India 23°20N 70°16E 242 H4
Bhadar → Gujarat, India 22°17N 72°20E 242 H5
Bhadar → Gujarat, India 21°27N 69°47E 242 J3
Bhadarwah India 32°58N 75°46E 243 C6
Bhadgaon = Bhaktapur Nepal 27°38N 85°24E 243 F11
Bhadohi India 25°25N 82°34E 243 G10
Bhadra India 29°8N 75°14E 242 E6
Bhadra → India 14°0N 75°20E 245 H2
Bhadrachalam India 17°40N 80°53E 244 F5
Bhadrakali India 22°40N 88°20E 124 A2
Bhadrakh India 21°10N 86°30E 244 D8
Bhadran India 22°19N 72°6E 242 H5
Bhadravati India 13°49N 75°40E 245 H2
Bhag Pakistan 29°2N 67°49E 242 E2
Bhagalpur India 25°10N 87°0E 243 G12
Bhagirathi → Uttarakhand, India 30°8N 78°35E 243 D8
Bhagirathi → W. Bengal, India 23°25N 88°23E 243 H13
Bhainsa India 19°10N 77°58E 244 E3
Bhairab → Bangla. 22°51N 89°34E 241 D2
Bhairab Bazar Bangla. 24°4N 90°58E 241 C3
Bhakkar Pakistan 31°40N 71°5E 242 D4
Bhakra Dam India 31°30N 76°45E 242 D7
Bhaktapur Nepal 27°38N 85°24E 243 F11
Bhalki India 18°2N 77°13E 244 E3
Bhalswa India 28°44N 77°10E 120 A2
Bhambo Khan Qarmati Pakistan 24°49N 67°7E 123 B2
Bhamo Burma 24°15N 97°15E 241 C6
Bhamragarh India 19°30N 80°40E 244 E5
Bhandara India 21°5N 79°42E 244 D4
Bhanpura India 24°31N 75°44E 242 G6
Bhanrer Ra. India 23°40N 79°45E 243 H8
Bhaptiahi India 26°19N 86°44E 243 F12
Bharat = India ■ Asia 20°0N 78°0E 239 F11
Bharatpur Chhattisgarh, India 23°44N 81°46E 243 H9
Bharatpur Raj., India 27°15N 77°30E 242 F7
Bharatpur Nepal 27°34N 84°10E 243 F11
Bharno India 23°14N 84°53E 243 H11
Bharuch India 21°47N 73°0E 244 D1
Bhatghar L. India 18°10N 73°48E 244 E1
Bhatiapara Ghat Bangla. 23°13N 89°42E 241 D2
Bhatinda India 30°15N 74°57E 242 D6
Bhatkal India 13°58N 74°35E 245 H2
Bhatpara India 22°50N 88°25E 243 H13
Bhatsala India 22°30N 88°16E 124 B1
Bhattu India 29°36N 75°19E 242 E6
Bhaun Pakistan 32°55N 72°40E 242 C5
Bhaunagar = Bhavnagar India 21°45N 72°10E 244 D1
Bhavani India 11°27N 77°43E 245 J3
Bhavnagar India 21°45N 72°10E 244 D1
Bhawanipatna India 19°55N 83°10E 244 E5
Bhawanipur India 22°32N 88°21E 124 B2
Bhawari India 25°42N 73°4E 242 G5
Bhayavadar India 21°51N 70°15E 242 J4
Bhendkhal India 18°52N 72°59E 130 B2
Bhera Pakistan 32°29N 72°57E 242 C5
Bhikangaon India 21°52N 75°57E 242 J6
Bhilai = Bhilainagar-Durg India 21°13N 81°26E 244 D5
Bhilainagar-Durg India 21°13N 81°26E 244 D5
Bhilsa = Vidisha India 23°28N 77°53E 242 H7
Bhilwara India 25°25N 74°38E 242 G6
Bhima → India 16°25N 77°17E 244 F3
Bhimavaram India 16°30N 81°30E 245 F5
Bhimbar Pakistan 32°59N 74°3E 243 C6
Bhind India 26°30N 78°46E 243 F8
Bhinga India 27°43N 81°56E 243 F9
Bhinmal India 25°0N 72°15E 242 G5
Bhisho S. Africa 32°50S 27°23E 270 D4
Bhiwandi India 19°20N 73°0E 244 E1
Bhiwani India 28°50N 76°9E 242 E7
Bhogava → India 22°26N 72°20E 242 H5
Bhokardan India 20°16N 75°46E 244 D2
Bhola Bangla. 22°45N 90°35E 241 D3
Bholari Pakistan 25°19N 68°13E 242 G3
Bhongir India 17°30N 78°56E 244 F4
Bhopal India 23°20N 77°30E 242 H7
Bhopalpatnam India 18°52N 80°23E 244 E5
Bhor India 18°12N 73°53E 244 E1
Bhuban India 20°53N 85°50E 244 D7
Bhubaneshwar India 20°15N 85°50E 244 D7
Bhuj India 23°15N 69°49E 242 H3
Bhuleshwar Mumbai, India 130 b2
Bhumiphol Res. Thailand 17°20N 98°40E 236 D2
Bhusawal India 21°3N 75°46E 244 D2
Bhutan ■ Asia 27°25N 90°30E 241 B3
Biá → Brazil 3°28S 67°23W 328 D4
Biafra, B. of = Bonny, Bight of Africa 3°30N 9°20E 263 E6
Biak Indonesia 1°10S 136°6E 231 E9
Biała Poland 50°24N 17°40E 185 H4
Biała → Poland 50°3N 20°55E 185 H7
Biała Piska Poland 53°37N 22°5E 184 E9
Biała Podlaska Poland 52°4N 23°6E 185 F10
Biała Rawska Poland 51°48N 20°29E 185 G7
Białobrzegi Poland 51°39N 20°57E 185 G7
Białogard Poland 54°2N 15°58E 184 D2
Białołęka Dworska Poland 52°19N 21°1E 142 B2
Białowieski △ Poland 52°43N 23°50E 185 F10
Białowieża Poland 52°41N 23°49E 185 F10
Biały Bór Poland 53°53N 16°51E 184 E3
Białystok Poland 53°10N 23°10E 185 E10
Biancavilla Italy 37°38N 14°52E 201 E7
Bianco Italy 38°5N 16°9E 201 D9
Biankouma Ivory C. 7°50N 7°40W 262 D3
Biaora India 23°56N 76°56E 242 H7
Bīārjmand Iran 36°6N 55°53E 247 B7
Biaro Indonesia 2°5N 125°26E 231 D7
Biarritz France 43°29N 1°33W 174 E2
Biasca Switz. 46°22N 8°58E 179 J4
Biavela Angola 14°43S 19°47E 265 E3
Biba Egypt 28°55N 31°0E 256 J7
Bibai Japan 43°19N 141°52E 220 C10
Bibala Angola 14°44S 13°24E 265 E2
Bibane, Bahiret el Tunisia 33°16N 11°13E 258 B2
Bibassé Gabon 1°27N 11°37E 264 B2
Bibbiena Italy 43°42N 11°49E 199 E8
Bibby I. Canada 61°55N 93°0W 297 A10
Bibei → Spain 42°24N 7°13W 194 C3
Biberach Germany 48°5N 9°47E 179 G5
Bibi Papua N. G. 5°30S 146°2E 286 C4
Bibiani Ghana 6°30N 2°8W 262 D4
Bibile Sri Lanka 7°10N 81°25E 245 L5
Bibungwa Dem. Rep. of the Congo 2°40S 28°15E 268 C2
Bicaj Albania 41°58N 20°25E 202 E4
Bicaz Romania 46°53N 26°5E 183 D11
Bicazu Ardelean Romania 46°51N 25°56E 183 D10
Biccari Italy 41°23N 15°12E 201 A8
Bicentennial Park N.S.W., Australia 33°51S 151°5E 139 B1
Bicentennial Park Calif., U.S.A. 34°1N 118°1W 126 B4
Bicester U.K. 51°54N 1°9W 169 F6
Biche Trin. & Tob. 10°26N 61°8W 323 t
Bichena Ethiopia 10°28N 38°10E 257 E4
Bicheno Australia 41°52S 148°18E 281 G4
Bichia India 22°27N 80°42E 243 H9
Bichvinta Georgia 43°9N 40°21E 191 J5
Bickerton I. Australia 13°45S 136°10E 280 A2
Bickley U.K. 51°23N 0°3E 125 B4
Bicknell U.S.A. 38°47N 87°19W 311 F9
Bicol △ Phil. 13°55N 122°58E 232 E4
Bicske Hungary 47°29N 18°38E 182 C3
Bicuari △ Angola 15°14S 14°45E 265 F2
Bicutan Phil. 14°30N 121°3E 127 C2
Bid = Bir India 19°4N 75°46E 244 E2
Bida Dem. Rep. of the Congo 4°55N 19°56E 264 B3
Bida Nigeria 9°3N 5°58E 263 D6
Bidar India 17°55N 77°35E 244 F3
Bidde Somali Rep. 0°58N 42°37E 267 D5
Biddeford U.S.A. 43°30N 70°28W 309 D18
Biddwara Ethiopia 5°11N 38°34E 257 F4
Bideford U.K. 51°1N 4°13W 169 F3
Bideford Bay U.K. 51°5N 4°20W 169 F3
Bidhan Nagar India 22°35N 88°25E 124 B2
Bidhuna India 26°49N 79°31E 243 F8
Bīdokht Iran 34°20N 58°46E 247 C8
Bidor Malaysia 4°6N 101°15E 237 K3
Bidu West Bank 31°50N 35°9E 123 B1
Bidyadanga Australia 18°45S 121°43E 278 C3
Bidzar Cameroon 9°54N 14°7E 264 A2
Bie Sweden 59°5N 16°12E 162 E10
Bié □ Angola 12°30S 17°0E 265 E3
Bié, Planalto de Angola 12°0S 16°0E 265 E3
Bieber U.S.A. 41°7N 121°8W 304 F3
Biebrza → Poland 53°13N 22°25E 185 E9
Biebrzański △ Poland 53°36N 22°45E 184 E9
Biecz Poland 49°44N 21°15E 185 J8
Biel Switz. 47°8N 7°14E 179 H3
Bielany Poland 52°17N 20°57E 142 B1
Bielawa Dolnośląskie, Poland 50°43N 16°37E 185 H3
Bielawa Warszawa, Poland 52°8N 21°9E 142 C2
Bielefeld Germany 52°1N 8°33E 178 C4
Bielersee Switz. 47°6N 7°5E 179 H3
Bielitz = Bielsko-Biała Poland 49°50N 19°2E 185 J6
Biella Italy 45°34N 8°3E 198 C5
Bielsk Podlaski Poland 52°47N 23°12E 185 F10
Bielsko-Biała Poland 49°50N 19°2E 185 J6
Bien Hoa Vietnam 10°57N 106°49E 237 G6
Bienne = Biel Switz. 47°8N 7°14E 179 H3
Bienvenida Spain 38°18N 6°12W 195 G4
Bienvenue Fr. Guiana 3°0N 52°30W 329 C7
Bienville, L. Canada 55°5N 72°40W 298 A5
Bierné France 47°48N 0°33W 172 E6
Bierun Poland 50°6N 19°6E 185 H6
Bierutów Poland 51°7N 17°32E 185 G4
Biescas Spain 42°37N 0°20W 196 C4
Biesdorf Germany 52°30N 13°33E 115 A4
Biese → Germany 52°53N 11°46E 178 C7
Biesiesfontein S. Africa 30°57S 17°58E 270 D2
Bieszczadzki △ Poland 49°5N 22°43E 185 J9
Bietigheim-Bissingen Germany 48°58N 9°8E 179 G5
Bièvre → France 48°44N 2°9E 134 B1
Bièvres France 48°45N 2°13E 134 B2
Bieżuń Poland 52°58N 19°55E 185 F6
Biferno → Italy 41°59N 15°2E 199 G12
Bifoum Gabon 0°20S 10°23E 264 C2
Big → Nfld. & L., Canada 54°50N 58°55W 299 B8
Big → Mo., U.S.A. 38°28N 90°37W 310 F6
Big B. = Awarua B. N.Z. 44°28S 168°4E 285 E3
Big B. Canada 55°43N 60°35W 299 A7
Big Bear City U.S.A. 34°16N 116°51W 307 L10
Big Bear Lake U.S.A. 34°15N 116°56W 307 L10
Big Belt Mts. U.S.A. 46°30N 111°25W 304 C8
Big Bend Swaziland 26°50S 31°58E 271 C5
Big Bend △ U.S.A. 29°20N 103°5W 314 G3
Big Black → U.S.A. 32°3N 91°4W 315 E9
Big Blue → Ind., U.S.A. 39°12N 85°56W 311 E11
Big Blue → Kans., U.S.A. 39°35N 96°34W 308 F5
Big Creek U.S.A. 37°11N 119°14W 306 H7
Big Cypress ⌓ U.S.A. 26°0N 81°10W 317 J8
Big Cypress Swamp U.S.A. 26°15N 81°30W 317 J8
Big Delta U.S.A. 64°10N 145°51W 303 D11
Big Desert Australia 35°45S 141°10E 281 F3
Big Falls U.S.A. 48°12N 93°48W 308 A7
Big Fork → U.S.A. 48°31N 93°43W 308 A7
Big Horn Mts. = Bighorn Mts. U.S.A. 44°25N 107°0W 304 D10
Big I. Canada 61°7N 116°45W 296 A5
Big Lake Alaska, U.S.A. 61°20N 150°20W 303 F10
Big Lake Tex., U.S.A. 31°12N 101°28W 314 F4
Big Moose U.S.A. 43°49N 74°58W 313 C10
Big Muddy → U.S.A. 37°33N 89°32W 310 G8
Big Muddy Cr. → U.S.A. 48°8N 104°36W 304 B11
Big Pine U.S.A. 37°10N 118°17W 306 H8
Big Pine Key U.S.A. 24°40N 81°21W 317 L8
Big Piney U.S.A. 42°32N 110°7W 304 E8
Big Quill L. Canada 51°55N 104°30W 297 C8
Big Rapids U.S.A. 43°42N 85°29W 309 D11
Big Rideau L. Canada 44°40N 76°15W 313 B8
Big River Canada 53°50N 107°0W 297 C7
Big Run U.S.A. 40°57N 78°55W 312 F6
Big Sable Pt. U.S.A. 44°3N 86°1W 308 C10
Big Salmon → Canada 61°52N 134°55W 296 A2
Big Sand L. Canada 57°45N 99°45W 297 B9
Big Sand Lake U.S.A. 28°25N 81°29W 133 B2
Big Sandy U.S.A. 48°11N 110°7W 304 B8
Big Sandy → U.S.A. 38°25N 82°36W 309 F12
Big Sandy Cr. = Sandy Cr. → U.S.A. 41°51N 109°47W 304 F9
Big Sandy Cr. → U.S.A. 38°7N 102°29W 304 G12
Big Satilla Cr. → U.S.A. 31°27N 82°3W 316 D7
Big Sioux → U.S.A. 42°29N 96°27W 308 D5
Big South Fork ⌓ U.S.A. 36°27N 84°47W 315 C12
Big Spring U.S.A. 32°15N 101°28W 314 E4
Big Stone City U.S.A. 45°18N 96°28W 308 C5
Big Stone Gap U.S.A. 36°52N 82°47W 309 G12
Big Stone L. U.S.A. 45°18N 96°27W 308 C5
Big Sur U.S.A. 36°15N 121°48W 306 J5
Big Timber U.S.A. 45°50N 109°57W 304 D9
Big Trout L. Canada 53°40N 90°0W 298 B2
Big Trout Lake Canada 53°45N 90°0W 298 B2
Biga Turkey 40°13N 27°14E 203 F11
Biga → Turkey 40°20N 27°14E 203 F11
Bigadiç Turkey 39°22N 28°7E 205 B10
Biganos France 44°39N 0°59W 174 D3
Bigeumdo S. Korea 34°45N 125°56E 224 E3
Biggar Sask., Canada 52°4N 108°0W 297 C7
Biggar S. Lanarks., U.K. 55°38N 3°32W 167 F5
Bigge I. Australia 14°35S 125°10E 278 B4
Biggenden Australia 25°31S 152°4E 281 D5
Biggleswade U.K. 52°5N 0°14W 169 E7
Biggs U.S.A. 39°25N 121°43W 306 F5
Bighorn U.S.A. 46°10N 107°27W 304 C10
Bighorn → U.S.A. 46°10N 107°28W 304 C10
Bighorn Canyon ⌓ U.S.A. 45°10N 108°0W 304 D10
Bighorn L. U.S.A. 44°55N 108°15W 304 D9
Bighorn Mts. U.S.A. 44°25N 107°0W 304 D10
Bigi Dem. Rep. of the Congo 3°2N 22°25E 264 B4
Bignona Senegal 12°52N 16°14W 262 C1
Bigorre France 43°10N 0°5E 174 E4
Bigstone L. Canada 53°42N 95°44W 297 C9
Biguglia, Étang de France 42°36N 9°29E 175 F13
Bigwa Tanzania 7°10S 39°10E 268 D4
Bihać Bos.-H. 44°49N 15°57E 199 D12
Bihar India 25°5N 85°40E 243 G11
Bihar □ India 25°0N 86°0E 243 G12
Biharamulo Tanzania 2°25S 31°25E 268 C3
Biharamulo ⌓ Tanzania 2°24S 31°26E 268 C3
Bihariganj India 25°44N 86°59E 243 G12
Biharkeresztes Hungary 47°8N 21°44E 182 C6
Bihor □ Romania 47°0N 22°10E 182 D7
Bihor, Munții Romania 46°29N 22°47E 182 D7
Bijagós, Arquipélago dos Guinea-Biss. 11°15N 16°10W 262 C1
Bijaipur India 26°2N 77°20E 242 F7
Bijapur Chhattisgarh, India 18°50N 80°50E 244 E5
Bijapur Karnataka, India 16°50N 75°55E 244 F2
Bījār Iran 35°52N 47°35E 246 C5
Bijawar India 24°38N 79°30E 243 G8
Bijbels Museum Amsterdam, Neths. 112 b1
Bijela Montenegro 42°28N 18°39E 202 D2
Bijeljina Bos.-H. 44°46N 19°14E 182 F4

Bijelo Polje *Montenegro* 43°1N 19°45E **202** C3
Bijie *China* 27°20N 105°16E **228** D5
Bijnor *India* 29°27N 78°11E **242** E8
Bikaner *India* 28°2N 73°18E **242** E5
Bikapur *India* 26°30N 82°7E **243** F10
Bikeqi *China* 40°43N 111°20E **226** D6
Bikfayyā *Lebanon* 33°55N 35°41E **250** E6
Bikié *Congo* 3°7S 13°52E **264** C2
Bikin *Russia* 46°50N 134°20E **220** A7
Bikin ➔ *Russia* 46°51N 134°2E **220** A7
Bikini Atoll *Marshall Is.* 12°0N 167°30E **288** F8
Bikita *Zimbabwe* 20°6S 31°41E **271** B5
Bīkkū Bīttī *Libya* 22°0N 19°12E **259** D3
Bikoro
Dem. Rep. of the Congo 0°48S 18°15E **264** C3
Bikoué *Cameroon* 3°55N 11°50E **263** E7
Bila Tserkva *Ukraine* 49°45N 30°10E **177** D16
Bilanga *Burkina Faso* 12°40N 0°1W **263** C4
Bilara *India* 26°14N 73°53E **242** F5
Bilasipara *India* 26°13N 90°14E **241** B3
Bilaspur *Chhattisgarh, India* 22°2N 82°15E **243** H10
Bilaspur *Punjab, India* 31°19N 76°50E **242** D7
Bilăsuvar *Azerbaijan* 39°27N 48°32E **213** C13
Bilauk Taungdan *Thailand* 13°0N 99°0E **236** F2
Bilbao *Spain* 43°16N 2°56W **196** B2
Bilbao ✈ **(BIO)** *Spain* 43°18N 2°57W **196** B2
Bilbeis *Egypt* 30°25N 31°34E **256** H7
Bilbo = Bilbao *Spain* 43°16N 2°56W **196** B2
Bilbor *Romania* 47°6N 25°30E **183** C10
Bilche-Zolote *Ukraine* 48°47N 25°53E **183** B10
Bilciureşti *Romania* 44°44N 25°48E **183** F10
Bíldudalur *Iceland* 65°41N 23°36W **155** B3
Bílé Karpaty *Europe* 49°5N 18°0E **181** B11
Bileća *Bos.-H.* 42°53N 18°27E **202** D2
Bilecik *Turkey* 40°5N 30°5E **212** B4
Bilecik ☐ *Turkey* 40°0N 30°0E **212** B3
Bilećko Jezero *Bos.-H.* 42°48N 18°28E **202** D2
Bileh Savār *Iran* 39°21N 48°21E **213** C13
Biłgoraj *Poland* 50°33N 22°42E **185** H9
Bilgram *India* 27°11N 80°2E **243** F9
Bilhaur *India* 26°51N 80°5E **243** F9
Bilhorod-Dnistrovskyy
Ukraine 46°11N 30°23E **189** J6
Bili ➔ *Dem. Rep. of the Congo* 4°9N 22°29E **264** B4
Bilibino *Russia* 68°3N 166°20E **215** C17
Bilibiza *Mozam.* 12°30S 40°20E **269** E5
Bilimora *India* 20°45N 72°57E **244** D1
Bilin *Burma* 17°14N 97°15E **241** G6
Biliran *Phil.* 11°28N 124°28E **233** F5
Biliran ☐ *Phil.* 11°35N 124°28E **233** F5
Bilisht *Albania* 40°37N 21°2E **202** F5
Billabong Cr. ➔ *Australia* 35°5S 144°2E **282** C6
Billdal *Sweden* 57°35N 11°57E **163** G5
Billiluna *Australia* 19°37S 127°41E **278** C4
Billings *U.S.A.* 45°47N 108°30W **304** D9
Billiton Is. = Belitung
Indonesia 3°10S 107°50E **235** C3
Billsta *Sweden* 63°20N 18°28E **162** A12
Billund *Denmark* 55°44N 9°6E **163** J3
Billy Pt. *Antigua & B.* 17°44N 61°52W **322** c
Bilma *Niger* 18°50N 13°30E **259** E2
Bilo Gora *Croatia* 45°53N 17°15E **182** E2
Biloela *Australia* 24°24S 150°31E **280** C5
Bilohirsk *Ukraine* 45°3N 34°35E **189** K8
Biloku *Guyana* 1°50N 58°25W **329** C6
Biloli *India* 18°46N 77°44E **244** E3
Bilopillya *Ukraine* 51°14N 34°20E **189** G8
Bilovodsk *Ukraine* 49°13N 39°36E **189** H10
Biloxi *U.S.A.* 30°24N 88°53W **315** F10
Bilpa Morea Claypan
Australia 25°0S 140°0E **280** D3
Bilqās Qism Auwal *Egypt* 31°12N 31°21E **251** G2
Bilston *U.K.* 55°52N 3°10W **121** B2
Biltine *Chad* 14°40N 20°50E **259** F4
Bilugyun *Burma* 16°24N 97°32E **241** G6
Bilyarsk *Russia* 54°58N 50°22E **190** C10
Bim Son *Vietnam* 20°4N 105°51E **236** B5
Bima *Indonesia* 8°22S 118°49E **235** D5
Bimban *Egypt* 24°24N 32°54E **256** C3
Bimbe *Angola* 11°50S 15°50E **265** E3
Bimberi Pk. *Australia* 35°44S 148°51E **283** C8
Bimbila *Ghana* 8°54N 0°5E **263** D5
Bimbini *Comoros Is.* 12°11S 44°17E **272** a
Bimbo *C.A.R.* 4°15N 18°33E **264** B3
Bimini Is. *Bahamas* 25°42N 79°25W **320** A4
Bin Ghunaymah, Jabal
Libya 25°0N 15°30E **258** D3
Bin Jawwād *Libya* 30°47N 18°4E **258** B3
Bin Xian *Heilongjiang, China* 45°42N 127°32E **227** B14
Bin Xian *Shaanxi, China* 35°2N 108°4E **226** G5
Bin Yauri *Nigeria* 10°46N 4°45E **263** C5
Bina-Etawah *India* 24°13N 78°14E **242** G8
Binacayan *Phil.* 14°27N 120°55E **127** C1
Binalbagan *Phil.* 10°12N 122°50E **233** F4
Binalong *Australia* 34°40S 148°39E **283** C8
Bīnālūd, Kūh-e *Iran* 36°30N 58°30E **247** B8
Binanga *Indonesia* 1°24N 99°46E **234** B1
Binangonan de Lampon = Infanta
Phil. 14°45N 121°39E **232** D3
Binatang = Bintangau
Malaysia 2°10N 111°40E **235** B4
Binche *Belgium* 50°26N 4°10E **170** D4
Binchuan *China* 25°42N 100°38E **228** E3
Binda *Dem. Rep. of the Congo* 5°52S 13°14E **265** D2
Binder *Chad* 9°56N 14°27E **259** G2
Bindki *India* 26°2N 80°36E **243** F9
Bindloe, I. = Marchena, I.
Ecuador 0°19N 90°29W **330** a
Bindoy *Phil.* 9°48N 123°5E **233** G4
Bindslev *Denmark* 57°33N 10°11E **163** G4
Bindura *Zimbabwe* 17°18S 31°18E **269** F3
Binéfar *Spain* 41°51N 0°18E **196** D5
Bingara *Australia* 29°52S 150°36E **281** D5
Bingaram I. *India* 10°56N 72°17E **245** J1
Bingen *Germany* 49°57N 7°55E **179** F3
Bingerau = Węgrów
Poland 52°24N 22°0E **185** F9
Bingerville *Ivory C.* 5°18N 3°49W **262** D4
Bingham *U.S.A.* 45°3N 69°53W **309** C19
Binghamton *U.S.A.* 42°6N 75°55W **313** D9
Bingo-Ochiai *Japan* 34°59N 133°8E **222** C4
Bingöl *Turkey* 38°53N 40°29E **213** C9
Bingöl ☐ *Turkey* 38°55N 40°30E **213** C9
Bingöl Dağları *Turkey* 39°16N 41°9E **213** C9
Bingsjö *Sweden* 61°1N 15°39E **162** C9
Binh Dinh *Vietnam* 13°55N 109°7E **236** F7
Binh Son *Vietnam* 15°20N 108°40E **236** E7
Binhai *China* 34°2N 119°49E **227** G10
Bini Erde *Chad* 20°6N 18°5E **259** D3
Binic *France* 48°46N 2°50W **172** D4
Binisatua *Spain* 39°50N 4°11E **206** B5
Binissalem *Spain* 39°41N 2°50E **206** B3
Binjai *Kepulauan Riau, Indonesia* 3°48N 108°13E **235** B3
Binjai *Sumatera Utara, Indonesia* 3°20N 98°30E **234** B1
Binji *Nigeria* 13°10N 4°55E **263** C5
Binka *India* 21°2N 83°48E **244** D6
Binnah, Ras *Somali Rep.* 11°9N 51°10E **267** F5
Binnaway *Australia* 31°28S 149°24E **283** A8
Binondo *Phil.* 14°36N 120°58E **127** B1
Binongko *Indonesia* 5°57S 124°2E **231** F6
Binscarth *Canada* 50°37N 101°17W **297** C8
Binshangul Gumuz ☐
Ethiopia 11°0N 35°30E **257** E4
Bint Goda *Sudan* 13°17N 31°33E **257** E3
Bintan *Indonesia* 1°0N 104°0E **234** B2
Bintangau *Malaysia* 2°10N 111°40E **235** B4
Bintaro Jaya *Indonesia* 6°16S 106°44E **122** B1
Bintuhan *Indonesia* 4°48S 103°22E **234** C2
Bintulu *Malaysia* 3°10N 113°0E **235** B4
Bintuni *Indonesia* 2°7S 133°32E **231** E8
Binyang *China* 23°12N 108°47E **228** F7
Binz *Germany* 54°24N 13°35E **178** A9
Binza *Dem. Rep. of the Congo* 4°21S 15°14E **265** C3
Binzert = Bizerte *Tunisia* 37°15N 9°50E **258** A1
Binzhou *China* 37°20N 118°2E **227** F10
Bío Bío ☐ *Chile* 37°35S 72°0W **334** D1
Biobío ➔ *Chile* 36°49S 73°10W **334** D1
Biograd na Moru *Croatia* 43°56N 15°29E **199** E12
Biogradska Gora △
Montenegro 42°55N 19°40E **202** D3
Bioko *Eq. Guin.* 3°30N 8°40E **263** E6
Biokovo *Croatia* 43°23N 17°0E **199** E14
Biougra *Morocco* 30°15N 9°14W **260** B3
Bipindi *Cameroon* 3°6N 10°30E **263** E7
Bir *India* 19°4N 75°46E **244** E2
Bir, Ras *Djibouti* 12°0N 43°20E **257** E5
Bîr Abu Hashim *Egypt* 23°42N 34°6E **256** C3
Bîr Abu Minqar *Egypt* 26°33N 27°33E **256** B2
Bîr Abu Muḥammad
Egypt 29°44N 34°14E **251** J5
Bîr Abu Sandûq *Egypt* 29°24N 32°30E **251** J3
Bir Adal Deib *Sudan* 22°35N 36°10E **256** C4
Bi'r al Butayyihāt *Jordan* 29°47N 35°20E **251** J6
Bi'r al Ḩamḑah *Si. Arabia* 28°30N 34°55E **251** K5
Bi'r al Mārī *Jordan* 30°4N 35°33E **251** H6
Bi'r al Musallam *Si. Arabia* 28°56N 35°38E **251** K6
Bi'r al Qattār *Jordan* 29°47N 35°32E **251** J6
Bir 'Ali *Yemen* 14°1N 48°20E **249** D5
Bir 'Amrâne *Mauritania* 22°45N 8°39W **260** D3
Bir Aouine *Tunisia* 32°25N 9°18E **258** B1
Bi'r 'Asal *Egypt* 25°55N 34°20E **256** B3
Bi'r ash Shakkūsīyah
Syria 35°23N 37°26E **250** C8
Bir Atrun *Sudan* 18°15N 26°40E **256** D2
Bîr Beiḍa *Egypt* 30°25N 34°29E **251** H5
Bir Bel Guerdâne
Mauritania 25°24N 10°31W **260** C2
Bîr Bireida *Egypt* 29°8N 32°7E **251** J3
Bîr Buerât *Egypt* 28°59N 32°11E **251** K3
Bi'r Dhu'fān *Libya* 31°59N 14°32E **258** B2
Bîr Di *Sudan* 7°34N 28°49E **257** F2
Bîr Diqnash *Egypt* 31°3N 25°23E **256** A2
Bir el Abbes *Algeria* 26°7N 6°9W **260** C3
Bîr el 'Abd *Egypt* 31°2N 33°0E **251** G4
Bir el 'Agramîya *Egypt* 29°38N 31°50E **251** J2
Bir el Ater *Algeria* 34°46N 8°3E **261** B6
Bîr el Basur *Egypt* 29°51N 25°49E **256** B2
Bîr el Biarât *Egypt* 29°30N 34°43E **251** J5
Bîr el Dakhal *Egypt* 28°39N 32°23E **251** K3
Bîr el Duweidar *Egypt* 30°56N 32°32E **251** H3
Bîr el Garârât *Egypt* 31°3N 33°34E **251** G4
Bir el Gâreb *Mauritania* 20°33N 16°12W **260** D1
Bîr el Gellaz *Egypt* 30°50N 26°40E **256** A2
Bîr el Ghamr *Egypt* 28°43N 31°20E **251** K2
Bîr el Heisi *Egypt* 29°22N 34°36E **251** J5
Bîr el Jafir *Egypt* 30°50N 32°41E **251** H3
Bîr el Mâlḥi *Egypt* 30°38N 33°19E **251** H4
Bîr el Manâyif *Egypt* 30°31N 32°12E **251** H3
Bîr el-Naṣb *Egypt* 29°3N 33°2E **251** J4
Bîr el Şafra *Egypt* 28°45N 34°21E **251** K5
Bîr el-Saura *Egypt* 29°9N 34°30E **251** J5
Bîr el Shaqqa *Egypt* 30°54N 25°1E **256** A2
Bîr el Thamâda *Egypt* 30°12N 33°27E **251** H4
Bir Enzarân *W. Sahara* 23°53N 14°32W **260** D2
Bîr Fuad *Egypt* 30°35N 26°28E **256** A2
Bir Gandûs *W. Sahara* 21°36N 16°30W **260** D1
Bîr Gebeil Ḩişn *Egypt* 30°2N 33°18E **251** H4
Bi'r Ghadīr *Syria* 34°6N 37°3E **250** D8
Bîr Ghalla *Egypt* 28°23N 32°19E **251** K3
Bi'r Gharr *Si. Arabia* 28°7N 35°32E **251** K6
Bîr Gindali *Egypt* 29°55N 31°40E **251** J2
Bîr Haimur *Egypt* 22°45N 33°40E **256** C3
Bîr Ḩasana *Egypt* 30°29N 33°46E **251** H4
Bîr Hôôker *Egypt* 30°22N 30°21E **256** H7
Bi'r Īdīmah *Si. Arabia* 18°31N 44°12E **248** C4
Bi'r Jadīd *Si. Arabia* 29°10N 35°6E **251** J6
Bir Jdid *Morocco* 33°26N 8°0W **260** B3
Bîr Kanayis *Egypt* 24°59N 33°15E **256** C3
Bîr Kaseiba *Egypt* 31°0N 33°17E **251** H4
Bîr Kerawein *Egypt* 27°10N 28°25E **256** B2
Bîr Lahfân *Egypt* 31°0N 33°51E **251** H4
Bir Lahrache *Algeria* 32°1N 8°12E **261** B6
Bîr Madkûr *Egypt* 30°44N 32°33E **251** H3
Bîr Maql *Egypt* 23°7N 33°40E **256** C3
Bîr Mîneiga *Sudan* 22°47N 35°12E **256** C4
Bîr Misaha *Egypt* 22°13N 27°59E **256** C2
Bir Mogreïn *Mauritania* 25°10N 11°25W **260** C2
Bîr Mureir *Egypt* 28°25N 31°15E **251** K2
Bîr Murr *Egypt* 23°28N 30°10E **256** C3
Bi'r Muṭribah *Kuwait* 29°54N 47°17E **246** D5
Bîr Nabala *West Bank* 31°51N 35°12E **123** A2
Bîr Nakheila *Egypt* 24°1N 30°50E **256** C3
Bîr Nakhul *Egypt* 29°33N 33°16E **251** J4
Bîr Qatia *Egypt* 30°58N 32°45E **251** H3
Bîr Qatrani *Egypt* 30°55N 26°10E **256** A2
Bîr Ranga *Egypt* 24°25N 35°15E **256** C4
Bîr Sahara *Egypt* 22°54N 28°40E **256** C2
Bîr Sa'îd *Egypt* 29°38N 31°24E **251** J2
Bîr Seiyâla *Egypt* 26°10N 33°50E **256** B3
Bîr Shalatein *Egypt* 23°5N 35°25E **256** C4
Bîr Shebb *Egypt* 22°25N 29°40E **256** C2
Bîr Shût *Egypt* 23°50N 35°15E **256** C4
Bîr Sidri *Egypt* 28°53N 33°28E **251** K4
Bîr Tâba *Egypt* 29°29N 34°53E **251** J5
Bîr Terfawi *Egypt* 22°57N 28°55E **256** C2
Bi'r Tin Abunda *Libya* 26°28N 12°27E **261** C7
Bîr Umm Qubûr *Egypt* 24°35N 34°2E **256** C3
Bîr Ungât *Egypt* 22°8N 33°48E **256** C3
Bîr Wuseit *Egypt* 29°14N 33°1E **251** J4
Bîr Za'farâna *Egypt* 29°10N 32°40E **256** J8
Bîr Zeidûn *Egypt* 25°45N 33°40E **256** B3
Birâk *Libya* 27°31N 14°20E **258** C2
Birak el Kiyam *Egypt* 30°2N 31°9E **117** A1
Biramféro *Guinea* 11°40N 9°10W **262** C3
Birao *C.A.R.* 10°20N 22°47E **264** A4
Biratnagar *Nepal* 26°27N 87°17E **243** F12
Birawa
Dem. Rep. of the Congo 2°20S 28°48E **268** C2
Birch ➔ *Canada* 58°28N 112°17W **296** B6
Birch Cliff *Canada* 43°41N 79°16W **141** A3
Birch Grove *Grenada* 12°6N 61°40W **323** q
Birch Hills *Canada* 52°59N 105°25W **297** C7
Birch I. *Canada* 52°26N 99°54W **297** C9
Birch L. *N.W.T., Canada* 62°4N 116°33W **296** A5
Birch L. *Ont., Canada* 51°23N 92°18W **298** B1
Birch Mts. *Canada* 57°30N 113°10W **296** B6
Birch River *Canada* 52°24N 101°6W **297** C8
Birchip *Australia* 35°56S 142°55E **282** C5
Birchiş *Romania* 45°58N 22°9E **182** E7
Birchwood *N.Z.* 45°55S 167°53E **285** F2
Birchwood *Alaska, U.S.A.* 61°24N 149°28W **303** F10
Bird *Canada* 56°30N 94°13W **297** B10
Bird I. = Aves, I. de
W. Indies 15°45N 63°55W **321** C7
Bird I. *S. Georgia* 54°0S 38°3W **151** B1
Birds Creek *Canada* 45°6N 77°52W **312** A7
Birdseye *U.S.A.* 38°19N 86°42W **311** F10
Birdsville *Australia* 25°51S 139°20E **280** D2
Birdum Cr. ➔ *Australia* 15°14S 133°0E **278** C5
Birdwood *Australia* 34°51S 138°58E **282** C3
Birecik *Turkey* 37°2N 38°0E **213** D8
Birein *Israel* 30°50N 34°28E **251** H5
Bireuen *Indonesia* 5°14N 96°39E **234** A1
Birganj *Nepal* 27°1N 84°52E **243** F11
Birgu = Vittoriosa *Malta* 35°54N 14°31E **206** F8
Birhan *Ethiopia* 10°45N 38°4E **266** B4
Biri *Norway* 60°58N 10°35E **164** D7
Biri ➔ *Sudan* 7°56N 26°33E **257** F2
Birifo *Gambia* 13°30N 14°0W **262** C2
Birigüi *Brazil* 21°18S 50°16W **335** A5
Birini *C.A.R.* 7°51N 22°24E **264** A4
Bīrjand *Iran* 32°53N 59°13E **247** C8
Birkeland *Norway* 58°24N 7°12E **164** F4
Birkenfeld *Germany* 49°38N 7°9E **179** F3
Birkenhead *U.K.* 53°23N 3°2W **168** D4
Birkenstein *Germany* 52°31N 13°40E **115** A5
Birkerød *Denmark* 55°50N 12°25E **163** J6
Birket Fatmé *Chad* 12°55N 19°7E **259** F3
Birket Qârûn *Egypt* 29°30N 30°40E **256** J7
Birkfeld *Austria* 47°21N 15°45E **180** D8
Birkhadem *Algeria* 36°43N 3°3E **261** A5
Birkholz *Germany* 52°37N 13°34E **115** A4
Birkholzaue *Germany* 52°38N 13°36E **115** A4
Birkirkara *Malta* 35°54N 14°28E **206** F7
Bîrlad = Bârlad *Romania* 46°15N 27°38E **183** D12
Birmingham *W. Mids., U.K.* 52°29N 1°52W **169** E6
Birmingham *Ala., U.S.A.* 33°31N 86°48W **315** E11
Birmingham *Iowa, U.S.A.* 40°53N 91°57W **310** D5
Birmingham Int. ✈ **(BHX)**
U.K. 52°26N 1°45W **169** E6
Birmitrapur *India* 22°24N 84°46E **244** C7
Birni Ngaouré *Niger* 13°5N 2°51E **263** C5
Birni Nkonni *Niger* 13°55N 5°15E **263** C6
Birnie *Kiribati* 3°35S 171°31W **277** A16
Birnin Gwari *Nigeria* 11°0N 6°45E **263** C6
Birnin Kebbi *Nigeria* 12°32N 4°12E **263** C5
Birnin Kudu *Nigeria* 11°30N 9°29E **263** C6
Birobidzhan *Russia* 48°50N 132°50E **219** B15
Birougou, Mts. *Gabon* 1°51S 12°20E **264** C2
Birr *Ireland* 53°6N 7°54W **166** C4
Birrarrung Park *Australia* 37°45S 145°4E **128** A2
Birrie ➔ *Australia* 29°43S 146°37E **281** D4
Birsilpur *India* 28°11N 72°15E **242** E5
Birsk *Russia* 55°25N 55°30E **186** C10
Birtle *Canada* 50°30N 101°5W **297** C8
Biryuchiy *Ukraine* 46°10N 35°0E **189** J8
Biržai *Lithuania* 56°11N 24°45E **188** D3
Birżebbugga *Malta* 35°50N 14°32E **206** F8
Birzuli = Madona *Latvia* 56°53N 26°5E **188** D4
Birzula = Kotovsk
Ukraine 47°45N 29°35E **177** E15
Bisa *Indonesia* 1°15S 127°28E **231** E7
Bisáccia *Italy* 41°1N 15°22E **201** A8
Bisacquino *Italy* 37°42N 13°15E **200** E6
Bisai *Japan* 35°16N 136°44E **223** B8
Bisalpur *India* 28°14N 79°48E **243** E8
Bisbee *U.S.A.* 31°27N 109°55W **305** L9
Biscarrosse *France* 44°22N 1°20W **174** D2
Biscarrosse et de Parentis, Étang de
France 44°21N 1°10W **174** D2
Biscay, B. of *Atl. Oc.* 45°0N 2°0W **171** D1
Biscay Abyssal Plain
Atl. Oc. 45°0N 8°0W **152** B11
Biscayne ⌓ *U.S.A.* 25°25N 80°12W **317** K9
Biscayne B. *U.S.A.* 25°40N 80°12W **317** K9
Biscayne Park *U.S.A.* 25°52N 80°10W **128** A2
Biscéglie *Italy* 41°14N 16°30E **201** A9
Bischheim *France* 48°37N 7°46E **173** D14
Bischoflack = Škofja Loka
Slovenia 46°9N 14°19E **199** B11
Bischofsburg = Biskupiec
Poland 53°53N 20°58E **184** E7
Bischofshofen *Austria* 47°26N 13°14E **180** D6
Bischofstal = Ujazd *Poland* 50°23N 18°21E **185** H5
Bischofstein = Bisztynek
Poland 54°8N 20°53E **184** D7
Bischofswerda *Germany* 51°7N 14°10E **178** D10
Bischwiller *France* 48°46N 7°50E **173** D14
Biscoe Is. *Antarctica* 66°0S 67°0W **151** C17
Biscoitos *Azores* 38°47N 27°15W **153** d1
Biscostasing *Canada* 47°18N 82°9W **298** C3
Biševo *Croatia* 42°57N 16°3E **199** F13
Bisha *Eritrea* 15°30N 37°31E **257** D4
Bishah, W. ➔ *Si. Arabia* 21°24N 43°26E **248** B3
Bishan *China* 29°33N 106°12E **228** C6
Bishanga
Dem. Rep. of the Congo 4°31S 21°2E **265** C4
Bishkek *Kyrgyzstan* 42°54N 74°46E **218** E8
Bishnath *India* 26°40N 93°10E **241** B4
Bishnupur *India* 23°8N 87°20E **243** H12
Bisho = Bhisho *S. Africa* 32°50S 27°23E **270** D4
Bishop *Calif., U.S.A.* 37°22N 118°24W **306** H8
Bishop *Ga., U.S.A.* 33°49N 83°26W **316** B6
Bishop *Tex., U.S.A.* 27°35N 97°48W **314** H6
Bishop Auckland *U.K.* 54°39N 1°40W **168** C6
Bishop Lavis *S. Africa* 33°56S 18°35E **118** A2
Bishop Museum *U.S.A.* 21°20N 157°52W **302** K14
Bishop's Falls *Canada* 49°2N 55°30W **299** C8
Bishop's Stortford *U.K.* 51°52N 0°10E **169** F8
Bishopscourt *S. Africa* 33°59S 18°27E **118** A1
Bisignano *Italy* 39°31N 16°17E **201** C9
Bisina, L. *Uganda* 1°38N 33°56E **268** B3
Biskra *Algeria* 34°50N 5°44E **261** B6
Biskra *Malta* 35°58N 14°21E **206** F7
Biskra ☐ *Algeria* 34°40N 5°25E **261** B6
Biskupiec *Poland* 53°53N 20°58E **184** E7
Bislig *Phil.* 8°12N 126°18E **233** G6
Bismarck *Mo., U.S.A.* 37°46N 90°38W **310** G6
Bismarck *N. Dak., U.S.A.* 46°48N 100°47W **308** B3
Bismarck Arch. *Papua N. G.* 2°30S 150°0E **286** B6
Bismarck Ra. *Papua N. G.* 5°35S 145°0E **286** C3
Bismarck Sea *Papua N. G.* 4°10S 146°50E **286** C4
Bismarckburg = Kasanga
Tanzania 8°30S 31°10E **269** D3
Bismark *Germany* 52°40N 11°33E **178** C7
Bismil *Turkey* 37°51N 40°40E **213** D9
Bismo *Norway* 61°54N 8°15E **164** C5
Biso *Uganda* 1°44N 31°26E **268** B3
Bison *U.S.A.* 45°31N 102°28W **308** C2
Bīsotūn *Iran* 34°23N 47°26E **213** E12
Bispebjerg *Denmark* 55°42N 12°32E **118** A2
Bispgården *Sweden* 63°2N 16°40E **162** A10
Bissagos = Bijagós, Arquipélago dos
Guinea-Biss. 11°15N 16°10W **262** C1
Bissam Cuttack *India* 19°31N 83°31E **244** E6
Bissau *Guinea-Biss.* 11°45N 15°45W **262** C1
Bissaula *Nigeria* 7°0N 10°27E **263** D7
Bissigh, Lach ➔
Somali Rep. 0°45N 41°30E **267** D5
Bissikrima *Guinea* 10°50N 10°58W **262** C2
Bissonet Plaza *U.S.A.* 30°1N 90°13W **131** A1
Bissorã *Guinea-Biss.* 12°16N 15°35W **262** C1
Bistcho L. *Canada* 59°45N 118°50W **296** B5
Bistreţ *Romania* 43°54N 23°23E **183** G8
Bistrica = Ilirska-Bistrica
Slovenia 45°34N 14°14E **199** C11
Bistriţa *Romania* 47°9N 24°35E **183** C9
Bistriţa ➔ *Romania* 46°30N 26°57E **183** D11
Bistriţa Năsăud ☐
Romania 47°15N 24°30E **183** C9
Bistriţei, Munţii *Romania* 47°15N 25°40E **183** C10
Biswan *India* 27°29N 81°2E **243** F9
Bisztynek *Poland* 54°8N 20°53E **184** D7
Bita ➔ *C.A.R.* 6°26N 24°43E **264** A4
Bitam *Gabon* 2°5N 11°25E **264** B2
Bitburg *Germany* 49°58N 6°31E **179** F2
Bitche *France* 49°2N 7°25E **173** C14
Bithynia *Turkey* 40°40N 31°0E **212** B4
Bitkine *Chad* 11°59N 18°13E **259** F3
Bitlis *Turkey* 38°20N 42°3E **213** C10
Bitlis ☐ *Turkey* 38°20N 42°10E **213** C10
Bitola *Macedonia* 41°1N 21°20E **202** E5
Bitolj = Bitola *Macedonia* 41°1N 21°20E **202** E5
Bitonto *Italy* 41°6N 16°41E **201** A9
Bitra I. *India* 11°33N 72°9E **245** J1
Bitter Creek *U.S.A.* 41°33N 108°33W **304** F9
Bitter L. = Buheirat-Murrat-el-Kubra *Egypt* 30°18N 32°26E **256** H8
Bitterfeld *Germany* 51°37N 12°20E **178** D8
Bitterfontein *S. Africa* 31°1S 18°32E **270** D2
Bitterroot ➔ *U.S.A.* 46°52N 114°7W **304** C6
Bitterroot Range *U.S.A.* 46°0N 114°20W **304** C6
Bitterwater *U.S.A.* 36°23N 121°0W **306** J6
Bitti *Italy* 40°29N 9°23E **200** B2
Bittou *Burkina Faso* 11°17N 0°18W **263** C4
Biu *Nigeria* 10°40N 12°3E **263** C7
Bivolari *Romania* 47°31N 27°27E **183** C12
Bivolu, Vf. *Romania* 47°16N 25°58E **183** C10
Biwa-Ko *Japan* 35°15N 136°10E **223** B8
Biwabik *U.S.A.* 47°32N 92°21W **308** B7
Bixad *Romania* 47°56N 23°28E **183** C8
Bixby *U.S.A.* 35°57N 95°53W **314** D7
Biya ➔ *Russia* 52°25N 85°0E **217** B11
Biyala *Egypt* 31°10N 31°13E **251** G2
Biyang *China* 32°38N 113°21E **226** H7
Biysk *Russia* 52°40N 85°0E **217** B11
Bizana *S. Africa* 30°50S 29°52E **271** D4
Bizen *Japan* 34°43N 134°8E **222** C6
Bizerte *Tunisia* 37°15N 9°50E **258** A1
Bizerte ☐ *Tunisia* 37°5N 9°35E **258** A1
Bjåen fjellstove *Norway* 59°37N 7°26E **164** E4
Bjargtangar *Iceland* 65°30N 24°30W **155** B2
Bjarkalundur *Iceland* 65°33N 22°9W **155** B4
Bjärnum *Sweden* 56°17N 13°43E **163** H7
Bjästa *Sweden* 63°12N 18°29E **162** A12
Bjelasica *Montenegro* 42°50N 19°40E **202** D3
Bjelašnica *Bos.-H.* 43°43N 18°9E **182** G3
Bjelovar *Croatia* 45°56N 16°49E **199** C13
Bjerringbro *Denmark* 56°23N 9°39E **163** H3
Bjervamoen *Norway* 59°17N 9°5E **164** E6
Bjøberg *Norway* 60°56N 8°13E **164** D5
Björbo *Sweden* 60°27N 14°44E **162** D8
Bjørkelangen *Norway* 59°53N 11°34E **164** E8
Björklinge *Sweden* 60°2N 17°33E **162** D11
Björknäs *Sweden* 59°19N 18°12E **139** B3
Björkö *Sweden* 59°52N 19°2E **162** E13
Bjørnafjorden *Norway* 60°7N 5°28E **164** D2
Björneborg = Pori *Finland* 61°29N 21°48E **188** B1
Björneborg *Sweden* 59°14N 14°16E **162** E8
Bjørnevatn *Norway* 69°40N 30°0E **160** B24
Bjørnøya *Arctic* 74°30N 19°0E **150** B8
Bjursås *Sweden* 60°44N 15°25E **162** D9
Bjuv *Sweden* 56°5N 12°55E **163** H6
Bla *Mali* 12°56N 5°47W **262** C3
Blå Jungfrun △ *Sweden* 57°16N 16°47E **163** G10
Blace *Serbia* 43°18N 21°17E **202** C5
Blachownia *Poland* 50°49N 18°56E **185** H5
Black = Da ➔ *Vietnam* 21°15N 105°20E **228** G5
Black ➔ *Ont., Canada* 44°42N 79°19W **312** B5
Black ➔ *Alaska, U.S.A.* 66°42N 144°42W **303** C11
Black ➔ *Ariz., U.S.A.* 33°44N 110°13W **305** K8
Black ➔ *Ark., U.S.A.* 35°38N 91°20W **314** D9
Black ➔ *La., U.S.A.* 31°16N 91°50W **314** F9
Black ➔ *Mich., U.S.A.* 42°59N 82°27W **312** D2
Black ➔ *N.Y., U.S.A.* 43°59N 76°4W **313** C8
Black ➔ *Wis., U.S.A.* 43°57N 91°22W **308** D8
Black Bay Pen. *Canada* 48°38N 88°21W **298** C2
Black Birch L. *Canada* 56°53N 107°45W **297** B7
Black Canyon of the Gunnison ⌓
U.S.A. 38°40N 107°35W **304** G10
Black Cr. ➔ *Canada* 43°40N 79°30W **141** A2
Black Creek Pioneer Village
Canada 43°46N 79°31W **141** A1
Black Diamond = Pittsburg
U.S.A. 38°2N 121°53W **306** G5
Black Diamond *Canada* 50°45N 114°14W **296** C6
Black Duck ➔ *Canada* 56°51N 89°2W **298** A2
Black Forest = Schwarzwald
Germany 48°30N 8°20E **179** G4
Black Forest *U.S.A.* 39°0N 104°43W **304** G11
Black Hd. *Ireland* 53°9N 9°16W **166** C2
Black Hills *U.S.A.* 44°0N 103°45W **308** D2
Black I. *Canada* 51°12N 96°30W **297** C9
Black L. *Sask., Canada* 59°12N 105°15W **297** B7
Black L. *Mich., U.S.A.* 45°28N 84°16W **309** C11
Black L. *N.Y., U.S.A.* 44°31N 75°36W **313** B9
Black Lake *Canada* 59°11N 105°20W **297** B7
Black Mesa *U.S.A.* 36°58N 102°58W **314** C3
Black Mountain
Australia 30°18S 151°39E **283** A9
Black Mt. = Mynydd Du
U.K. 51°52N 3°50W **169** F4
Black Mt. *Bhutan* 27°20N 90°25E **241** B3
Black Mts. *U.K.* 51°55N 3°7W **169** F4
Black Range *U.S.A.* 33°15N 107°50W **305** K10
Black River *Jamaica* 18°0N 77°50W **320** a
Black River *N.Y., U.S.A.* 44°0N 75°47W **313** C9
Black River B. *Jamaica* 18°0N 77°51W **320** a
Black River Falls *U.S.A.* 44°18N 90°51W **308** C8
Black River Gorges
Mauritius 20°24S 57°25E **272** e
Black Rock *S. Austral., Australia* 32°50S 138°44E **282** B3
Black Rock *Barbados* 13°7N 59°37W **323** r
Black Rock Desert
U.S.A. 41°10N 118°50W **304** F4
Black Sea *Eurasia* 43°30N 35°0E **187** F6
Black Tickle *Canada* 53°28N 55°45W **299** B8
Black Volta ➔ *Africa* 8°41N 1°33W **262** D4
Black Warrior ➔
U.S.A. 32°32N 87°51W **315** E11
Blackall *Australia* 24°25S 145°45E **280** C4
Blackball *N.Z.* 42°22S 171°26E **285** D3
Blackbraes △ *Australia* 19°10S 144°10E **280** B3
Blackbull *Australia* 17°55S 141°45E **280** B3
Blackburn *U.K.* 53°45N 2°29W **168** D5
Blackburn, Mt. *U.S.A.* 61°44N 143°26W **303** F12
Blackburn with Darwen ☐
U.K. 53°45N 2°29W **168** D5
Blackdown Tableland △
Australia 23°52S 149°8E **280** C4
Blackfen *U.K.* 51°26N 0°6E **125** B4
Blackfoot *U.S.A.* 43°11N 112°21W **304** E7
Blackfoot ➔ *U.S.A.* 46°52N 113°53W **304** C7
Blackfoot Res. *U.S.A.* 42°55N 111°39W **304** E8
Blackheath *U.K.* 51°28N 0°0 **125** B4
Blackman *U.S.A.* 30°56N 86°38W **317** E3
Blackpool *U.K.* 53°49N 3°3W **168** D4
Blackpool ☐ *U.K.* 53°49N 3°3W **168** D4
Blackriver *U.S.A.* 44°46N 83°17W **312** B1
Blackrock *Ireland* 53°18N 6°11W **120** B2
Blacks Harbour *Canada* 45°3N 66°49W **299** C6
Blacksburg *U.S.A.* 37°14N 80°25W **309** G13
Blackshear *U.S.A.* 31°18N 82°14W **316** D7
Blackshear, L. *U.S.A.* 31°51N 83°56W **316** D6
Blacksod B. *Ireland* 54°6N 10°0W **166** B1
Blackstairs Mt. *Ireland* 52°33N 6°48W **166** D5
Blackstone *U.S.A.* 37°5N 78°0W **309** G14
Blackstone Ra. *Australia* 26°0S 128°30E **279** E4
Blackville *U.S.A.* 33°22N 81°16W **316** B8
Blackwater = West Road ➔
Canada 53°18N 122°53W **296** C4
Blackwater *Australia* 23°35S 148°53E **280** C4
Blackwater ➔ *Meath, Ireland* 53°39N 6°41W **166** C5
Blackwater ➔ *Waterford, Ireland* 52°4N 7°52W **166** D4
Blackwater ➔ *Armagh, U.K.* 54°31N 6°35W **166** B5
Blackwater ➔ *Fla., U.S.A.* 30°36N 87°2W **317** E2
Blackwater ➔ *Mo., U.S.A.* 38°56N 92°57W **310** F4
Blackwell *U.S.A.* 36°48N 97°17W **314** C6
Blackwells Corner
U.S.A. 35°37N 119°47W **307** K7
Blackwood, C. *Papua N. G.* 7°49S 144°31E **286** D3
Bladensburg *U.S.A.* 38°55N 76°55W **143** B4
Bladensburg △ *Australia* 22°30S 142°59E **280** C3
Blaenau Ffestiniog *U.K.* 53°0N 3°56W **168** E4
Blaenau Gwent ☐ *U.K.* 51°48N 3°12W **169** F4
Blåfell *Iceland* 64°30N 19°51W **155** D6
Blåfjall *Iceland* 65°26N 16°50W **155** B10
Blagaj *Bos.-H.* 43°16N 17°55E **202** C1
Blagnac *France* 43°38N 1°24E **174** E5
Blagnac, Toulouse ✈ **(TLS)**
France 43°37N 1°22E **174** E5
Blagodarnoye = Blagodarnyy
Russia 45°7N 43°37E **191** H6
Blagodarnyy *Russia* 45°7N 43°37E **191** H6
Blagoevgrad *Bulgaria* 42°2N 23°5E **202** D7
Blagoevgrad ☐ *Bulgaria* 42°2N 23°5E **202** D7
Blagoveshchensk
Russia 50°20N 127°30E **219** A14
Blahkiuh *Indonesia* 8°31S 115°12E **231** J18
Blain *Loire-Atlantique, France* 47°29N 1°45W **172** E5
Blain *Pa., U.S.A.* 40°20N 77°31W **312** F7
Blaine *Minn., U.S.A.* 45°10N 93°13W **308** C7
Blaine *Wash., U.S.A.* 48°59N 122°45W **306** B4
Blaine Lake *Canada* 52°51N 106°52W **297** C7
Blair *U.S.A.* 41°33N 96°8W **308** E5
Blair Athol *Australia* 22°42S 147°31E **280** C4
Blair Atholl *U.K.* 56°46N 3°50W **167** E5
Blair Village *U.S.A.* 33°40N 84°23W **113** C2
Blairgowrie *Gauteng, S. Africa* 26°6S 28°0E **123** A2
Blairgowrie *Perth & Kinr., U.K.* 56°35N 3°21W **167** E5
Blairsden *U.S.A.* 39°47N 120°37W **306** F6
Blairsville *U.S.A.* 40°26N 79°16W **312** F5
Blaj *Romania* 46°10N 23°57E **183** D8
Blaka *Niger* 21°21N 12°47E **259** D2
Blakang Mati, Pulau
Singapore 1°15N 103°50E **237** d
Blake House *U.S.A.* 42°19N 71°3W **116** B2
Blake Pt. *U.S.A.* 48°11N 88°25W **308** A9
Blakehurst *Australia* 33°59S 151°6E **139** B1
Blakely *Ga., U.S.A.* 31°23N 84°56W **316** D5
Blakely *Pa., U.S.A.* 41°28N 75°37W **313** E9
Blakesburg *U.S.A.* 40°58N 92°38W **310** D4
Blakstad *Akershus, Norway* 59°49N 10°28E **133** B1
Blakstad *Aust-Agder, Norway* 58°30N 8°39E **164** F5
Blambangan, Semenanjung
Indonesia 8°42S 114°29E **231** K17
Blâmont *France* 48°35N 6°50E **173** D13
Blanc, C. *Spain* 39°21N 2°51E **206** B3
Blanc, C. *Tunisia* 37°15N 9°56E **258** A1
Blanc, Mont *Europe* 45°48N 6°50E **175** C10
Blanca, B. *Argentina* 39°10S 61°30W **336** A4
Blanca Peak *U.S.A.* 37°35N 105°29W **305** H11
Blanchardville *U.S.A.* 42°49N 89°52W **310** B7
Blanche, C. *Australia* 33°1S 134°9E **281** E1
Blanche, L. *S. Austral., Australia* 29°15S 139°40E **281** D2
Blanche, L. *W. Austral., Australia* 22°25S 123°17E **278** D3
Blanche, L. *Fla., U.S.A.* 28°28N 81°30W **133** B1
Blanche, Pte. *St. Lucia* 13°53N 61°5W **323** m
Blanche, Pte. *St.-Maarten* 18°0N 63°0W **322** a
Blanche Channel
Solomon Is. 8°30S 157°30E **287** M9
Blanchester *U.S.A.* 39°17N 83°59W **311** E13
Blanchisseuse *Trin. & Tob.* 10°48N 61°18W **323** t
Blanco *Western Cape, S. Africa* 33°55S 22°23E **270** D3
Blanco *Tex., U.S.A.* 30°6N 98°25W **314** F5
Blanco ➔ *Argentina* 30°20S 68°42W **334** C2
Blanco ➔ *Bolivia* 12°30S 64°18W **331** C5
Blanco, C. *Costa Rica* 9°34N 85°8W **320** E2
Blanco, C. *Oreg., U.S.A.* 42°51N 124°34W **304** E1
Blanco, Pta. *Bonaire* 12°13N 68°14W **322** h
Blanda ➔ *Iceland* 65°37N 20°9W **155** B6
Blandford Forum *U.K.* 50°51N 2°9W **169** G5
Blanding *U.S.A.* 37°37N 109°29W **305** H9
Blandinsville *U.S.A.* 40°33N 90°52W **310** D6
Blanes *Spain* 41°40N 2°48E **196** D7
Blangkejeren *Indonesia* 3°59N 97°20E **234** B1
Blangpidie *Indonesia* 3°44N 96°49E **234** B1
Blangy-sur-Bresle *France* 49°55N 1°37E **173** C8
Blanice ➔ *Czech Rep.* 49°10N 14°5E **180** B7
Blankaholm *Sweden* 57°36N 16°31E **163** G10
Blankenberge *Belgium* 51°20N 3°9E **170** C3
Blankenburg *Berlin, Germany* 52°35N 13°27E **115** A3
Blankenburg *Sachsen-Anhalt, Germany* 51°47N 10°57E **178** D6
Blankenfelde *Germany* 52°37N 13°23E **115** A3
Blanku, L. *Curaçao* 12°2N 68°47W **322** g
Blanquefort *France* 44°55N 0°38W **174** D3
Blanquilla *Venezuela* 11°51N 64°37W **321** D7
Blanquillo *Uruguay* 32°53S 55°37W **335** C4
Blansko *Czech Rep.* 49°22N 16°40E **181** B9
Blantyre *Malawi* 15°45S 35°0E **269** F4
Blarney *Ireland* 51°56N 8°33W **166** E3
Blasdell *U.S.A.* 42°48N 78°50W **312** D6
Blåsjø *Norway* 59°20N 6°50E **164** E3
Błaszki *Poland* 51°38N 18°30E **185** G5
Blatná *Czech Rep.* 49°25N 13°52E **180** B6
Blato *Croatia* 42°56N 16°48E **199** F13
Blaubeuren *Germany* 48°24N 9°46E **179** G5
Blaustein *Germany* 48°25N 9°53E **179** G5
Blåvands Huk *Denmark* 55°33N 8°4E **163** J2
Blaydon *U.K.* 54°58N 1°42W **168** C6
Blaye *France* 45°8N 0°40W **174** C3
Blaye-les-Mines *France* 44°1N 2°8E **174** D6
Blayney *Australia* 33°32S 149°14E **283** B8
Blaze, Pt. *Australia* 12°56S 130°11E **278** B5
Błażowa *Poland* 49°53N 22°7E **185** J9
Blechhammer = Blachownia
Poland 50°49N 18°56E **185** H5
Bleckede *Germany* 53°17N 10°43E **178** B6
Bled *Slovenia* 46°27N 14°7E **199** B11
Blefjell *Norway* 59°48N 9°10E **164** E6
Bleiburg *Austria* 46°35N 14°49E **180** E7
Blejeşti *Romania* 44°19N 25°27E **183** F10
Blekinge *Sweden* 56°25N 15°20E **161** H16
Blekinge län ☐ *Sweden* 56°20N 15°20E **163** H9
Blenheim *Ont., Canada* 42°20N 82°0W **312** D3
Blenheim *N.Z.* 41°38S 173°57E **285** B8
Bléone ➔ *France* 44°5N 6°0E **175** D10
Blérancourt *France* 49°31N 3°9E **173** C10
Bletchley *U.K.* 51°59N 0°44W **169** F7
Bleus, Monts
Dem. Rep. of the Congo 1°30N 30°30E **268** B3
Blida *Algeria* 36°30N 2°49E **261** A5
Blida ☐ *Algeria* 36°35N 3°0E **261** A5
Blidet Amor *Algeria* 32°59N 5°58E **261** B6
Blidö *Sweden* 59°37N 18°53E **162** E12
Blidsberg *Sweden* 57°56N 13°30E **163** G7
Blieskastel *Germany* 49°14N 7°12E **179** F3
Bligh Sound *N.Z.* 44°47S 167°32E **285** E2
Bligh Water *Fiji* 17°0S 178°0E **287** A2
Blind River *Canada* 46°10N 82°58W **298** C3
Blinisht *Albania* 41°52N 19°59E **202** E3
Bliss *Idaho, U.S.A.* 42°56N 114°57W **304** E6
Bliss *N.Y., U.S.A.* 42°34N 78°15W **312** D6
Blissfield *Mich., U.S.A.* 41°50N 83°52W **311** C13
Blissfield *Ohio, U.S.A.* 40°24N 81°58W **312** F3
Blitar *Indonesia* 8°5S 112°11E **235** D4
Blitchton *U.S.A.* 32°12N 81°26W **316** C8
Blitta *Togo* 8°23N 1°6E **263** D5
Blizne *Poland* 52°14N 20°52E **142** B1
Block I. *U.S.A.* 41°11N 71°35W **313** E13
Block Island Sd. *U.S.A.* 41°15N 71°40W **313** E13
Bloemenmarkt *Amsterdam, Neths.* **112** b2
Bloemfontein *S. Africa* 29°6S 26°7E **270** C4
Bloemhof *S. Africa* 27°38S 25°32E **270** C4
Blois *France* 47°35N 1°20E **172** E8
Blomskog *Sweden* 59°16N 12°2E **162** E6
Blomstermåla *Sweden* 56°59N 16°21E **163** H10
Blomvåg *Norway* 60°32N 4°50E **164** D1
Blönduós *Iceland* 65°40N 20°12W **155** B6
Blongas *Indonesia* 8°53S 116°2E **231** K19
Błonie *Poland* 52°12N 20°37E **185** F7
Bloodvein ➔ *Canada* 51°47N 96°43W **297** C9
Bloody B. *Trin. & Tob.* 11°18N 60°38W **323** s
Bloody Foreland *Ireland* 55°10N 8°17W **166** A3
Bloom = Chicago Heights
U.S.A. 41°30N 87°38W **311** C9
Bloomer *U.S.A.* 45°6N 91°29W **308** C8
Bloomfield *Ont., Canada* 43°59N 77°14W **312** C7
Bloomfield *Ind., U.S.A.* 39°1N 86°57W **311** E10
Bloomfield *Iowa, U.S.A.* 40°45N 92°25W **310** D4
Bloomfield *Ky., U.S.A.* 37°55N 85°19W **311** G11
Bloomfield *N. Mex., U.S.A.* 36°43N 107°59W **305** H10
Bloomfield *Nebr., U.S.A.* 42°36N 97°39W **308** D5
Bloomingburg *U.S.A.* 39°36N 83°24W **311** E13
Bloomington *Ill., U.S.A.* 40°28N 89°0W **310** D8
Bloomington *Ind., U.S.A.* 39°10N 86°32W **311** E10
Bloomington *Minn., U.S.A.* 44°50N 93°17W **308** C7
Bloomington *Wis., U.S.A.* 42°53N 90°55W **310** B6
Bloomsburg *U.S.A.* 41°0N 76°27W **313** F8
Bloomsbury *Australia* 20°48S 148°38E **280** b
Bloomsbury *London, U.K.* **125** a3
Blora *Indonesia* 6°57S 111°25E **235** D4
Blossburg *U.S.A.* 41°41N 77°4W **312** E7
Blosseville Kyst *Greenland* 68°50N 26°30W **154** D8
Błota *Poland* 52°9N 21°11E **142** C3
Blouberg *S. Africa* 23°8S 28°59E **271** B4
Blountstown *U.S.A.* 30°27N 85°3W **316** E4
Blowing Point Village
Anguilla 18°11N 63°6W **322** a
Blowing Rock *Anguilla* 18°9N 63°10W **322** a
Bludenz *Austria* 47°10N 9°50E **180** D2
Blue ➔ *U.S.A.* 38°11N 86°19W **311** F10
Blue Cypress L. *U.S.A.* 27°44N 80°45W **317** H9
Blue Earth *U.S.A.* 43°38N 94°6W **308** D6
Blue Hole *Jamaica* 18°10N 76°24W **320** a
Blue Hole △ *Belize* 17°24N 88°30W **320** C2
Blue Island *U.S.A.* 41°40N 87°40W **119** D2
Blue Lagoon △ *Zambia* 15°28S 27°26E **269** F2
Blue Mesa Res. *U.S.A.* 38°28N 107°20W **304** G10
Blue Mosque = Sultanahme Camil
Turkey 41°0N 28°58E **122** B1
Blue Mound *U.S.A.* 39°42N 89°7W **310** E7
Blue Mountain Lake
U.S.A. 43°51N 74°27W **313** C10
Blue Mountain Pk. *Jamaica* 18°3N 76°36W **320** a
Blue Mountains and John Crow Mountains Nat. Park △
Jamaica 18°5N 76°34W **320** a
Blue Mt. *U.S.A.* 40°30N 76°30W **313** F8
Blue Mts. *N.S.W., Australia* 33°40S 150°15E **283** B9
Blue Mts. *Jamaica* 18°3N 76°36W **320** a
Blue Mts. *Maine, U.S.A.* 44°50N 70°35W **313** B14
Blue Mts. *Oreg., U.S.A.* 45°0N 118°20W **304** D4
Blue Mts. △ *Australia* 34°2S 150°15E **283** C9
Blue Mud B. *Australia* 13°30S 136°0E **280** A2
Blue Mud Bay ✪ *Australia* 13°25S 136°2E **280** A2
Blue Nile = Nîl el Azraq ➔
Sudan 15°38N 32°31E **257** D3
Blue Nile Falls = Tis Issat
Ethiopia 11°25N 37°45E **257** E4
Blue Rapids *U.S.A.* 39°41N 96°39W **308** F5
Blue Ridge *U.S.A.* 36°40N 80°50W **309** G13
Blue River *Canada* 52°6N 119°18W **296** C5
Blue Springs *U.S.A.* 39°1N 94°17W **310** E2
Bluefield *U.S.A.* 37°15N 81°17W **309** G13
Bluefield *Ireland* 53°19N 6°21W **120** B1
Bluefields *Nic.* 12°20N 83°50W **320** D3
Bluevale *Canada* 43°51N 81°15W **312** C3
Bluff *Queens., Australia* 23°35S 149°4E **280** C4
Bluff *N.Z.* 46°37S 168°20E **285** G3
Bluff *Utah, U.S.A.* 37°17N 109°33W **305** H9
Bluff Harbour *N.Z.* 46°36S 168°21E **285** G3
Bluff Hd. *China* 22°11N 114°12E **122** B2
Bluff Knoll *Australia* 34°24S 118°15E **279** F2
Bluff Pt. *Australia* 27°50S 114°5E **279** E1
Bluffers Park *Canada* 43°43N 79°14W **141** A3
Bluffs *U.S.A.* 39°45N 90°32W **310** E6
Bluffton *Ga., U.S.A.* 31°31N 84°52W **316** D5
Bluffton *Ind., U.S.A.* 40°44N 85°11W **311** D11
Bluffton *Ohio, U.S.A.* 40°54N 83°54W **311** D13
Bluffton *S.C., U.S.A.* 32°14N 80°52W **316** C9
Blumberg *Germany* 52°36N 13°39E **115** A4
Blumenau = Stettler
Canada 52°19N 112°40W **296** C6
Blumenau *Brazil* 27°0S 49°0W **335** B6
Blunt *U.S.A.* 44°31N 99°59W **308** C4
Blunt Pt. *U.S.A.* 37°51N 122°25W **136** A2
Blutenburg *Germany* 48°9N 11°27E **131** B1
Bly *U.S.A.* 42°24N 121°3W **304** E3
Blyde River Canyon ⌓
S. Africa 24°37S 31°2E **271** B5
Blyhaget *Norway* 59°46N 10°41E **133** B3
Blyth *S. Austral., Australia* 33°49S 138°28E **282** B3
Blyth *Ont., Canada* 43°44N 81°26W **312** C3
Blyth *Northumberland, U.K.* 55°8N 1°31W **168** B6
Blythe *Calif., U.S.A.* 33°37N 114°36W **307** M12
Blythe *Ga., U.S.A.* 33°17N 82°12W **316** B7
Blytheville *U.S.A.* 35°56N 89°55W **315** D10
Bø *Telemark, Norway* 59°25N 9°3E **164** E6
Bo *S. Leone* 7°55N 11°50W **262** D2
Bo Duc *Vietnam* 11°58N 106°50E **237** G6
Bo-eun *S. Korea* 36°29N 127°43E **224** D3
Bo Hai *China* 39°0N 119°0E **227** E10
Bo Hai Haixia *Asia* 38°25N 121°10E **227** E11
Bo-Kaap Museum *Cape Town, S. Africa* **118** c2
Bō-no-Misaki *Japan* 31°15N 130°13E **222** F2
Bo Xian = Bozhou *China* 33°55N 115°41E **226** H8
Boa Esperança *Brazil* 3°21N 61°23W **329** C5
Boa Esperança, Represa
Brazil 6°50S 43°50W **332** C3

Boa Nova Brazil 14°22S 40°10W 333 D3
Boa Viagem Brazil 5°7S 39°44W 332 C4
Boa Vista = Tocantinópolis
　Brazil 6°20S 47°25W 332 C2
Boa Vista Brazil 2°48N 60°30W 329 C5
Boa Vista C. Verde Is. 16°0N 22°49W 153 j
Boa Vista, Alto do Brazil 12°38S 43°16W 135 B1
Boa Vista do Erechim = Erechim
　Brazil 27°35S 52°15W 335 B5
Boac Phil. 13°27N 121°50E 232 E3
Boaco Nic. 12°29N 85°35W 320 D2
Bo'ai China 35°10N 113°3E 226 G7
Boal Spain 43°25N 6°49W 194 B4
Boali C.A.R. 4°48N 18°7E 264 B3
Boalsburg U.S.A. 40°47N 77°49W 312 F7
Boane Mozam. 26°6S 32°19E 271 C5
Boang I. Papua N. G. 3°23S 153°18E 286 B7
Boao China 19°8N 110°34E 236 C8
Boardman U.S.A. 41°2N 80°40W 312 E4
Boardwalk U.S.A. 40°34N 73°49W 132 C3
Boath India 19°20N 78°20E 244 E4
Boatswain Bird I.
　Ascension I. 7°56S 14°18W 153 g
Boavista Portugal 38°48N 9°8W 126 A2
Boayan I. Phil. 10°34N 119°9E 233 F2
Boaz I. Bermuda 32°18N 64°51W 153 a
Bob Marley Mausoleum
　Jamaica 18°18N 77°18W 320 a
Bobadah Australia 32°19S 146°41E 283 B7
Bobai China 22°17N 109°59E 228 F7
Bobbili India 18°35N 83°30E 244 E6
Bóbbio Italy 44°46N 9°23E 198 D6
Bobcaygeon Canada 44°33N 78°33W 312 B6
Bobigny France 48°54N 2°26E 134 A3
Boblad India 17°13N 75°26E 244 F2
Böblingen Germany 48°40N 9°1E 179 G5
Bobo-Dioulasso
　Burkina Faso 11°8N 4°13W 262 C4
Bobolice Poland 53°58N 16°37E 184 E3
Bobon Phil. 12°32N 124°34E 232 E5
Bobonaza → Ecuador 2°36S 76°38W 328 D2
Bobonong Botswana 21°58S 28°20E 271 B4
Boboshevo Bulgaria 42°9N 23°0E 202 D7
Bobov Dol Bulgaria 42°20N 23°0E 202 D6
Bóbr → Poland 52°4N 15°4E 185 F2
Bobraomby, Tanjon' i
　Madag. 12°40S 49°10E 272 A2
Bobrov Russia 51°5N 40°2E 190 E5
Bobrovytsya Ukraine 50°44N 31°23E 189 G6
Bobruysk = Babruysk
　Belarus 53°10N 29°15E 177 B15
Bobrynets Ukraine 48°4N 32°5E 189 H7
Bobures Venezuela 9°15N 71°11W 328 B3
Boca del Río Mexico 19°5N 96°4W 319 D5
Boca do Acre Brazil 8°50S 67°27W 328 B4
Boca do Jari Brazil 1°7S 51°58W 329 D7
Boca Grande Fla., U.S.A. 26°45N 82°16W 317 J7
Boca Grande Venezuela 8°40N 60°40W 329 B5
Boca Raton U.S.A. 26°21N 80°5W 317 J9
Boca Slagbaai Bonaire 12°16N 68°24W 322 h
Bocaiúva Brazil 17°7S 43°49W 333 E3
Bocanda Ivory C. 7°5N 4°31W 262 D4
Bocanegra Peru 12°1S 77°7W 124 B2
Bocaranga C.A.R. 7°0N 15°35E 264 A3
Bocas del Dragón = Dragon's
　Mouths Venezuela 11°0N 61°50W 323 t
Bocas del Toro Panama 9°15N 82°20W 320 E3
Boceguillas Spain 41°20N 3°39W 194 D7
Bochkarevo = Belogorsk
　Russia 51°0N 128°20E 215 D13
Bochmanivka Ukraine 47°40N 29°34E 183 C14
Bochnia Poland 49°58N 20°27E 185 J7
Bocholt Germany 51°50N 6°36E 178 D2
Bochum = Senwabarana
　S. Africa 23°17S 29°7E 271 B4
Bochum Germany 51°28N 7°13E 178 D3
Bockenem Germany 52°1N 10°8E 178 C6
Bočki Phil. 52°39N 23°3E 185 E10
Bocognano France 42°5N 9°4E 175 F13
Bocoio Angola 12°28S 14°10E 265 E2
Boconó Venezuela 9°15N 70°16W 328 B3
Boconó → Venezuela 8°43N 69°34W 328 B3
Boçna Romania 45°21N 21°47E 182 E6
Boda C.A.R. 4°19N 17°26E 264 B3
Boda Dalarna, Sweden 61°1N 15°13E 162 C9
Böda Kalmar, Sweden 57°15N 17°3E 163 G11
Boda Västernorrland,
　Sweden 62°52N 16°39E 162 B10
Bodafors Sweden 57°48N 14°23E 163 F9
Bodaybo Russia 57°50N 114°0E 215 D12
Boddam U.K. 59°56N 1°17W 167 B7
Boddington Australia 32°50S 116°30E 279 F2
Bode Sadu Nigeria 9°0N 4°47E 263 D5
Bodega Bay U.S.A. 38°20N 123°3W 306 G3
Boden Sweden 65°50N 21°42E 160 D19
Bodensee Europe 47°35N 9°25E 179 H5
Bodenteich Germany 52°49N 10°41E 178 C6
Bodhan India 18°40N 77°44E 244 E3
Bodinayakkanur India 10°2N 77°10E 245 K3
Bodinga Nigeria 12°58N 5°10E 263 C6
Bodmin U.K. 50°28N 4°43W 169 G3
Bodmin Moor U.K. 50°33N 4°36W 169 G3
Bodø Norway 67°17N 14°24E 160 C16
Bodoquena, Serra da
　Brazil 21°0S 56°50W 331 E6
Bodoupa C.A.R. 5°43N 17°26E 264 A3
Bodrichi Chad 19°11N 15°54E 259 E3
Bodrog → Hungary 48°11N 21°22E 182 B6
Bodrum Turkey 37°3N 27°30E 205 D9
Boduna
　Dem. Rep. of the Congo 2°30N 19°44E 264 A3
Bódva → Hungary 48°19N 20°45E 182 B5
Boedo → Argentina 34°38S 58°26W 117 B2
Boembé Congo 2°54S 15°39E 264 C3
Boën France 45°44N 4°1E 175 C8
Boende
　Dem. Rep. of the Congo 0°24S 21°12E 264 C4
Boerne U.S.A. 29°47N 98°44W 314 G5
Boesmans → S. Africa 33°42S 26°39E 270 D4
Boffa Guinea 10°16N 14°3W 262 C2
Bog Walk Jamaica 18°6N 77°1W 320 a
Bogal, Lagh → Kenya 0°41N 40°57E 267 D5
Bogale Burma 16°17N 95°24E 241 G5
Bogalusa U.S.A. 30°47N 89°52W 325 F10
Bogan → Australia 30°20S 146°55E 283 A7
Bogan Gate Australia 33°7S 147°49E 283 B7
Bogandé Burkina Faso 13°2N 0°8W 263 C4
Bogangolo C.A.R. 5°36N 18°30E 264 B3
Bogantungan Australia 23°41S 147°17E 280 C4
Bogata U.S.A. 33°28N 95°13W 314 E7
Bogazkale Turkey 40°0N 34°37E 218 F6
Boğazlıyan Turkey 39°11N 35°14E 212 C6
Bogbonga
　Dem. Rep. of the Congo 1°36N 19°24E 264 B3
Bogda Shan China 43°35N 89°40E 217 E10
Bogen Sweden 60°4N 12°33E 162 D6
Bogenhausen Germany 48°9N 11°36E 182 G4
Bogense Denmark 55°34N 10°5E 163 J4
Bogetići Montenegro 42°43N 18°56E 202 D6
Boggabilla Australia 28°36S 150°24E 281 D5
Boggabri Australia 30°45S 150°5E 283 B8
Boggeragh Mts. Ireland 52°2N 8°55W 166 D3
Boggy Peak Antigua & B. 17°2N 61°52W 322 b

Boghari = Ksar el Boukhari
　Algeria 35°51N 2°52E 261 A5
Bogia Papua N. G. 4°9S 145°0E 286 C3
Bogildi S. Korea 34°9N 126°32E 224 E3
Bogian = Solhan Turkey 38°57N 41°3E 213 C9
Bogles Grenada 12°30N 61°26W 323 q
Bognor Regis U.K. 50°47N 0°40W 169 G7
Bogo Phil. 11°3N 124°0E 233 F4
Bogodukhov = Bohodukhiv
　Ukraine 50°9N 35°33E 189 G8
Bogol Manya Ethiopia 4°34N 41°29E 257 G5
Bogong, Mt. Australia 36°47S 147°17E 283 D7
Bogor Indonesia 6°36S 106°48E 234 D3
Bogoroditsk Russia 53°47N 38°8E 188 F10
Bogorodsk = Noginsk
　Russia 55°50N 38°25E 188 E10
Bogorodsk Russia 56°4N 43°30E 190 B6
Bogorodskoye = Kamskoye Ustye
　Russia 55°10N 49°20E 190 C9
Bogorodskoye = Leninskoye
　Russia 53°28N 47°3E 190 A8
Bogorodskoye Russia 55°48N 37°42E 129 B4
Bogoslovsky = Karpinsk
　Russia 59°45N 60°1E 186 C11
Bogoso Ghana 5°38N 2°3W 262 D4
Bogotá Colombia 4°34N 74°0W 328 C3
Bogotol Russia 56°15N 89°50E 214 D9
Bogou Togo 10°40N 0°12E 263 C5
Bogra Bangla. 24°51N 89°22E 241 C2
Bogstadvatnet Norway 59°58N 10°37E 133 A2
Boguchany Russia 58°40N 97°30E 215 D10
Boguchar Russia 49°55N 40°32E 190 F5
Bogué Mauritania 16°45N 14°10W 262 B2
Boguszów-Gorce Poland 50°45N 16°12E 185 H3
Bohain-en-Vermandois
　France 49°59N 3°28E 173 C10
Bohdan Ukraine 48°2N 24°22E 183 B9
Bohena Cr. → Australia 30°17S 149°42E 283 A8
Bohinjska Bistrica
　Slovenia 46°17N 14°1E 199 B11
Böhmerwald Germany 49°8N 13°14E 179 F9
Böhmisch-Brod = Český Brod
　Czech Rep. 50°4N 14°52E 180 A7
Böhmisch-Leipa = Česká Lípa
　Czech Rep. 50°45N 14°30E 180 A7
Böhmisch-Trübau = Česká Třebová
　Czech Rep. 49°54N 16°27E 181 B9
Bohmte Germany 52°22N 8°19E 178 C4
Bohodukhiv Ukraine 50°9N 35°33E 189 G8
Bohol Somali Rep. 5°45N 46°9E 267 C6
Bohol Phil. 9°50N 124°10E 233 G5
Bohol Sea Phil. 9°0N 124°0E 233 G5
Bohol Str. Phil. 9°45N 123°40E 233 G4
Bohongou Burkina Faso 12°30N 0°40E 263 C5
Böhönye Hungary 46°25N 17°28E 182 D2
Bohorodchany Ukraine 48°48N 24°32E 183 B9
Bohorok Indonesia 3°30N 98°12E 237 L2
Böhöt Mongolia 45°13N 108°16E 226 B5
Bohu China 41°58N 86°37E 217 D11
Bohuslän Sweden 58°25N 12°0E 163 F5
Bohuslav Ukraine 49°33N 30°56E 189 H6
Boi Nigeria 9°35N 9°27E 263 D6
Boi, Pta. do Brazil 23°55S 45°15W 334 B6
Boiaçu Brazil 0°27S 61°46W 329 D5
Boileau, C. Australia 17°40S 122°7E 278 C3
Boim Brazil 2°49S 55°10W 329 D6
Boing'o Sudan 9°58N 33°44E 257 F3
Boipariguda India 18°46N 82°26E 244 E6
Boipeba, I. de Brazil 13°39S 38°55W 333 D4
Boiro Spain 42°39N 8°54W 194 C2
Bois → Brazil 18°35S 50°2W 333 E1
Bois-Blanc Réunion 21°11S 55°49E 272 f
Bois-Colombes France 48°55N 2°16E 134 A2
Bois-d'Arcy France 48°48N 2°1E 134 B1
Boise U.S.A. 43°37N 116°13W 304 E5
Boise City U.S.A. 36°44N 102°31W 314 C3
Boissevain Canada 49°15N 100°5W 297 D8
Boissy-St-Léger France 48°44N 2°31E 134 B4
Bóite → Italy 46°5N 12°5E 199 B9
Boitzenburg Germany 53°16N 13°35E 178 B9
Boizenburg Germany 53°23N 10°43E 178 B6
Bojador C. W. Sahara 26°0N 14°30W 262 C2
Bojana → Albania 41°52N 19°22E 202 E3
Bojano Italy 41°29N 14°29E 201 A7
Bojanowo Poland 51°43N 16°42E 185 G3
Bøjden Denmark 55°6N 10°7E 163 J4
Bojnūrd Iran 37°30N 57°20E 247 B8
Bojonegoro Indonesia 7°11S 111°54E 235 D4
Boju Nigeria 7°22N 7°55E 263 D6
Boka Serbia 45°22N 20°52E 182 E5
Boka Kotorska
　Montenegro 42°23N 18°32E 202 D2
Boka Tabla Curaçao 12°22N 69°8W 322 g
Bokada
　Dem. Rep. of the Congo 4°8N 17°4E 264 A3
Bokala Dem. Rep. of the Congo 3°8S 17°4E 264 C3
Bokani Ivory C. 8°31N 4°33W 262 D4
Bokani Nigeria 9°28N 5°10E 263 D6
Bokaro India 23°46N 85°55E 243 H11
Bokatola
　Dem. Rep. of the Congo 0°38S 18°46E 264 C3
Boké Guinea 10°56N 14°17W 262 C2
Bokela
　Dem. Rep. of the Congo 1°10S 21°59E 264 C4
Bokenda
　Dem. Rep. of the Congo 1°16N 21°22E 264 B4
Bokhara → Australia 29°55S 146°42E 281 D4
Bokkos Nigeria 9°17N 9°1E 263 D6
Boklar Dağları Turkey 37°5N 33°5E 250 A4
Boklarkfjorden Norway 59°14N 5°40E 164 E2
Boko Congo 4°46S 14°50E 265 C2
Bokode
　Dem. Rep. of the Congo 3°55N 19°30E 264 B3
Bokolo Gabon 2°40S 10°10E 264 C2
Bokondo
　Dem. Rep. of the Congo 0°15N 22°32E 264 B4
Bokor △ Cambodia 10°50N 104°1E 237 G5
Bokoro △ Chad 2°12N 31°32E 264 B3
Bokoro Chad 12°25N 17°14E 259 F3
Bokota
　Dem. Rep. of the Congo 0°56S 22°24E 264 C4
Bokote Dem. Rep. of the Congo 0°12S 21°8E 264 C4
Bokpyin Burma 11°18N 98°42E 237 G2
Boksitogorsk Russia 59°22N 33°50E 188 C7
Boku Phil. 6°34S 155°21E 286 D8
Bokungu
　Dem. Rep. of the Congo 0°35S 22°50E 264 C4
Bol Croatia 43°18N 16°38E 199 E13
Bolama Guinea-Biss. 11°30N 15°30W 262 C1
Bolan → Pakistan 28°38N 67°42E 242 E2
Bolan Pass Pakistan 29°50N 67°20E 240 C2
Bolaños → Mexico 21°12N 104°5W 318 C4
Bolayır Turkey 40°31N 26°45E 203 F10
Bolbec France 49°30N 0°30E 172 C7
Boldājī Iran 31°56N 51°3E 247 D6

Boldești-Scăeni Romania 45°3N 26°2E 183 E11
Boldinasco Italy 45°29N 9°8E 129 B1
Bole Xinjiang Uygur, China 44°55N 81°37E 217 C10
Bole Ethiopia 6°36N 37°20E 257 F4
Bole Ghana 9°3N 2°23W 262 D4
Bolekhiv Ukraine 49°0N 23°57E 177 D12
Boleko
　Dem. Rep. of the Congo 1°35S 19°50E 264 C3
Bøler Norway 59°53N 10°50E 133 B4
Bolesławiec Poland 51°17N 15°37E 185 G2
Bolgatanga Ghana 10°44N 0°53W 263 C4
Bolgrad = Bolhrad
　Ukraine 45°40N 28°32E 183 E13
Bolhrad Ukraine 45°40N 28°32E 183 E13
Bolia Dem. Rep. of the Congo 1°35S 18°22E 264 C3
Bolinao Phil. 16°23N 119°54E 232 C2
Bolinao, C. Phil. 16°23N 119°55E 232 C2
Bolingbroke U.S.A. 32°57N 83°48W 316 C6
Bolingbrook U.S.A. 41°42N 88°4W 311 C8
Bolingo
　Dem. Rep. of the Congo 3°31S 21°43E 264 C4
Bolintin-Vale Romania 44°27N 25°46E 183 F10
Bolívar Antioquia, Colombia 5°50N 76°1W 328 B2
Bolívar Cauca, Colombia 2°0N 77°0W 328 C2
Bolívar Peru 7°18S 77°48W 330 B2
Bolívar Mo., U.S.A. 37°37N 93°25W 308 G7
Bolívar N.Y., U.S.A. 42°4N 78°10W 312 D6
Bolívar Tenn., U.S.A. 35°12N 89°0W 315 D10
Bolívar □ Colombia 9°0N 74°40W 328 B3
Bolívar □ Ecuador 1°15S 79°5W 328 D2
Bolívar □ Venezuela 6°20N 63°30W 329 B5
Bolivia ■ S. Amer. 17°6S 64°0W 331 D5
Bolivian Plateau = Altiplano
　Bolivia 17°0S 68°0W 330 D4
Boljevac Serbia 43°51N 21°58E 202 C5
Bolkhov Russia 53°25N 36°0E 188 F9
Bolków Poland 50°55N 16°6E 185 H3
Bollate Italy 45°32N 9°7E 129 B1
Bollebeek Belgium 50°55N 4°14E 116 A1
Bollebygd Sweden 57°40N 12°35E 163 B3
Bollmora Sweden 59°14N 18°14E 139 B3
Bollnäs Sweden 61°21N 16°24E 162 C10
Bollon Australia 28°2S 147°29E 281 D4
Bolmen Sweden 56°55N 13°40E 163 H7
Bolnisi Georgia 41°26N 44°32E 191 K7
Bolobo
　Dem. Rep. of the Congo 2°6S 16°20E 264 C3
Bologna Italy 44°29N 11°20E 199 D8
Bologna ✈ (BLQ) Italy 44°34N 11°16E 199 D8
Bologoye Russia 57°55N 34°5E 188 D8
Bolomba
　Dem. Rep. of the Congo 0°35N 19°0E 264 B3
Bolombo →
　Dem. Rep. of the Congo 1°32N 21°14E 264 B4
Bolonchén Mexico 20°1N 89°45W 319 D7
Bolondo
　Dem. Rep. of the Congo 1°25S 18°42E 264 C3
Bolong Chad 12°3N 17°45E 259 F3
Bolong Phil. 7°6N 122°14E 233 H4
Bolongongo Angola 8°28S 15°16E 265 E3
Bolótana Italy 40°20N 8°52E 200 B1
Boloven, Cao Nguyen
　Laos 15°10N 106°30E 236 E6
Bolpur India 23°40N 87°45E 243 H12
Bolsena Italy 42°39N 11°59E 199 F8
Bolsena, L. di Italy 42°36N 11°56E 199 F8
Bolshakovo Russia 54°53N 21°40E 184 D8
Bolshaya Chernigovka
　Russia 52°6N 50°52E 190 D10
Bolshaya Garmanda = Evensk
　Russia 62°12N 159°30E 215 C16
Bolshaya Glushitsa
　Russia 52°28N 50°30E 190 D10
Bolshaya Martynovka
　Russia 47°19N 41°37E 191 G5
Bolshaya Okhta Russia 59°56N 30°26E 137 B2
Bolshaya Tsaryovshchina =
　Volzhskiy Russia 48°56N 44°46E 191 F7
Bolshaya Vradiyevka
　Ukraine 47°50N 30°40E 189 J6
Bolshevik, Ostrov Russia 78°30N 102°0E 215 B11
Bolshoy Anyuy →
　Russia 68°30N 160°49E 215 C17
Bolshoy Begichev, Ostrov
　Russia 74°20N 112°30E 215 B12
Bolshoy Kamen Russia 43°11N 132°19E 220 C6
Bolshoy Kavkaz = Caucasus
　Mountains Eurasia 42°50N 44°0E 191 J7
Bolshoy Lyakhovskiy, Ostrov
　Russia 73°35N 142°0E 215 B15
Bolshoy Theatre Moscow, Russia 129 B2
Bolshoy Tokmak = Tokmak
　Kyrgyzstan 42°49N 75°15E 217 D9
Bolshoy Tyuters, Ostrov
　Russia 59°51N 27°13E 188 C4
Bólstaðarhlíð Iceland 65°31N 19°49W 155 B7
Bolsward Neths. 53°3N 5°32E 170 A5
Bolt Head U.K. 50°23N 3°48W 169 G4
Boltaña Spain 42°28N 0°4E 196 C5
Boltigen Switz. 46°38N 7°24E 179 J3
Bolton, Ont., Canada 43°54N 79°45W 312 C5
Bolton Gt. Man., U.K. 53°35N 2°26W 168 D5
Bolton Georgia, U.S.A. 33°48N 84°28W 113 B2
Bolton Landing U.S.A. 43°32N 73°35W 313 C11
Bolu Turkey 40°45N 31°35E 212 B4
Bolu □ Turkey 40°40N 31°30E 212 B4
Bolubolu Papua N. G. 9°21S 150°20E 286 E6
Bolungavík Iceland 66°9N 23°15W 155 A3
Boluo China 23°3N 114°21E 229 F10
Bolvadin Turkey 38°45N 31°4E 212 C4
Bolzano Italy 46°31N 11°22E 198 B8
Bom Comércio Brazil 9°45S 65°54W 331 B4
Bom Conselho Brazil 9°10S 36°41W 332 C6
Bom Despacho Brazil 19°43S 45°15W 333 E2
Bom Jesus Angola 9°9S 13°34E 265 D2
Bom Jesus Brazil 9°4S 44°22W 332 C2
Bom Jesus da Gurguéia, Serra
　Brazil 9°0S 43°0W 332 C2
Bom Jesus da Lapa Brazil 13°15S 43°25W 333 D3
Bom Retiro Brazil 27°45S 49°42W 335 B6
Boma Dem. Rep. of the Congo 5°50S 13°4E 265 F2
Bomaderry Australia 34°52S 150°37E 283 B9
Bomandjokou Sudan 3°39N 24°32E 264 B4
Bomaneh
　Dem. Rep. of the Congo 1°18N 23°47E 264 B4
Bomassa Congo 2°12N 16°12E 264 B3
Bomate
　Dem. Rep. of the Congo 2°14N 25°15E 264 B5
Bombala Australia 36°56S 149°15E 283 D8
Bombarral Portugal 39°15N 9°9W 195 F1
Bombay = Mumbai India 18°55N 72°50E 244 E1
Bombay India 44°56N 74°34W 313 B10
Bombedor, Pta. Venezuela 9°53N 61°37W 329 B5
Bomberai, Semenanjung
　Indonesia 3°0S 133°0E 231 E8
Bombo Kasani
　Dem. Rep. of the Congo 5°51S 21°54E 265 D4
Bomboma
　Dem. Rep. of the Congo 2°25N 18°55E 264 B3
Bombombwa
　Dem. Rep. of the Congo 1°40N 25°40E 264 B5
Bomboyo Chad 12°1N 15°24E 259 F2
Bomdila India 27°18N 92°22E 241 B4

Bomdo India 28°44N 94°54E 241 E4
Bomet Kenya 0°47S 35°21E 266 C4
Bomi China 29°50N 95°45E 218 F8
Bomi Hills Liberia 7°1N 10°38W 262 D2
Bomili
　Dem. Rep. of the Congo 1°45N 27°5E 268 B2
Bomlo Norway 59°37N 5°13E 164 E2
Bomokandi →
　Dem. Rep. of the Congo 3°39N 26°8E 268 B2
Bomongo
　Dem. Rep. of the Congo 1°27N 18°21E 264 B3
Bompoka India 8°15N 93°13E 245 K11
Bomputu
　Dem. Rep. of the Congo 1°40S 18°22E 264 C3
Bomu → C.A.R. 4°40N 22°30E 264 B4
Bomu Occidentale □
　Dem. Rep. of the Congo 4°48N 24°17E 264 B4
Bomu Orientale □
　Dem. Rep. of the Congo 5°0N 25°50E 264 B5
Bon, C. = Ra's aṭ Ṭīb Tunisia 37°1N 11°2E 258 A2
Bon Acceuil Mauritius 20°10S 57°39E 272 e
Bon Echo △ Canada 44°55N 77°16W 312 B7
Bon Sar Pa Vietnam 12°24N 107°35E 236 F6
Bona, Mt. U.S.A. 61°23N 141°45W 303 F12
Bonāb Āzarbāijān-e Sharqī,
　Iran 37°20N 46°4E 213 D12
Bonāb Zanjān, Iran 36°35N 48°41E 213 D13
Bonaigarh India 21°50N 84°57E 243 J11
Bonaire Ga., U.S.A. 32°33N 83°36W 316 C6
Bonaire W. Indies 12°10N 68°15W 322 h
Bonampak Mexico 16°44N 91°9W 319 D6
Bonanza Argentina 37°11S 148°41E 283 D8
Bonanza Nic. 13°54N 84°35W 320 D3
Bonaparte Arch. Australia 14°0S 124°30E 278 B3
Bonaparte Rocks Grenada 12°24N 61°39W 323 q
Boñar Spain 42°52N 5°19W 194 C5
Bonar Bridge U.K. 57°54N 4°20W 167 D4
Bonasse Trin. & Tob. 10°5N 61°54W 323 t
Bonaventure Canada 48°5N 65°32W 299 C6
Bonaventure, Place Montréal, Canada 130 c2
Bonavista Canada 48°40N 53°5W 299 C9
Bonavista, C. Canada 48°42N 53°5W 299 C9
Bonavista B. Canada 48°45N 53°25W 299 C9
Bondeno Italy 44°53N 11°25E 199 D8
Bondi Australia 33°53S 151°16E 139 B2
Bondo Équateur,
　Dem. Rep. of the Congo 1°22S 23°54E 264 C4
Bondo Orientale,
　Dem. Rep. of the Congo 3°55N 23°53E 264 B4
Bondoc Pen. Phil. 13°26N 122°33E 232 E4
Bondoukou Ivory C. 8°2N 2°47W 262 D4
Bondowoso Indonesia 7°55S 113°49E 235 D4
Bondy France 48°54N 2°28E 134 A4
Bône = Annaba Algeria 36°50N 7°46E 261 A6
Bone, Teluk Indonesia 4°10S 120°50E 231 E6
Bonefish Pond Bahamas 25°59N 77°23W 153 b
Bord Khūn-e Now Iran 28°3N 51°28E 247 D6
Borda, C. Australia 35°45S 136°34E 282 C2
Bordeaux France 44°50N 0°36W 174 D3
Bordeaux ✈ (BOD) France 44°50N 0°35W 174 D3
Borden Australia 34°3S 118°12E 279 F2
Borden-Carleton Canada 46°18N 63°47W 299 C7
Borden I. Canada 78°30N 111°30W 295 B9
Borden Pen. Canada 73°0N 83°0W 295 C15
Borden Springs U.S.A. 33°56N 85°28W 316 B4
Border Ranges △
　Australia 28°24S 152°56E 281 D5
Borders = Scottish Borders □
　U.K. 55°35N 2°50W 167 F6
Bordertown Australia 36°19S 140°45E 282 C4
Borðeyri Iceland 65°12N 21°6W 155 B5
Bordighera Italy 43°46N 7°39E 198 E4
Bordj bou Arreridj Algeria 36°4N 4°45E 261 A6
Bordj Bou Guiba Tunisia 32°12N 10°25E 258 B2
Bordj Fly Ste. Marie
　Algeria 27°19N 2°32W 260 C5
Bordj-in-Eker Algeria 24°9N 5°3E 261 D6
Bordj Menaïel Algeria 36°46N 3°43E 261 A5
Bordj Messouda Algeria 30°12N 9°25E 261 B6
Bordj Mokhtar Algeria 21°20N 0°56E 261 D5
Bordj Nili Algeria 33°28N 3°2E 261 B5
Bordj Omar Driss Algeria 28°10N 6°40E 261 C6
Bordj Sif Fatima Algeria 31°6N 8°41E 261 B6
Bordj Tarat Algeria 25°55N 9°3E 261 C6
Bordj Tindjillet Algeria 26°57N 9°15E 261 C6
Bordjga Norway 61°48N 9°50E 164 C3
Borduttighat India 26°57N 93°58E 241 E4
Bore Ethiopia 4°39N 37°39E 257 G4
Borehamwood U.K. 51°40N 0°15W 169 F7
Borek Wielkopolski
　Poland 51°54N 17°11E 185 G4
Borensberg Sweden 58°34N 15°17E 163 F9
Borgå = Porvoo Finland 60°24N 25°40E 163 B21
Borgampad India 17°39N 80°52E 244 F5
Borgarfjarðarsýsla □
　Iceland 64°30N 21°30W 155 C4
Borgarfjörður Borgarfjarðarsýsla,
　Iceland 64°30N 21°30W 155 C4
Borgarfjörður Norður-Múlasýsla,
　Iceland 65°33N 13°47W 155 B13
Borgarnes Iceland 64°32N 21°55W 155 C3
Borger Neths. 52°54N 6°44E 170 B6
Borger U.S.A. 35°39N 101°24W 314 D4
Borgholm Sweden 56°52N 16°39E 163 H10
Bórgia Italy 38°49N 16°30E 201 D9
Borgo San Dalmazzo Italy 44°20N 7°31E 198 D4
Borgo San Donnino = Fidenza
　Italy 44°52N 10°3E 198 D7
Borgo San Lorenzo Italy 43°57N 11°23E 199 E8
Borgo Val di Taro Italy 44°29N 9°46E 198 D6
Borgo Valsugana Italy 46°3N 11°27E 198 B8
Borgomanero Italy 45°42N 8°28E 198 C5
Borgorose Italy 42°12N 13°8E 199 F10
Borgosésia Italy 45°43N 8°16E 198 C5
Borgund Norway 61°3N 7°48E 164 C2
Borgyo Norway 61°37N 7°48E 164 C2
Boria → Italy 41°4N 9°2E 200 B2
Borikhane Laos 18°33N 103°43E 236 C4
Borisoglebsk Russia 51°27N 42°5E 190 E6
Borisov = Barysaw
　Belarus 54°17N 28°28E 177 A15
Borisovgrad = Pŭrvomay
　Bulgaria 42°8N 25°17E 203 D9
Borisovka Russia 50°36N 36°1E 189 G9
Borislav Russia 55°38N 37°44E 129 C4
Borja Peru 4°20S 77°40W 330 B2
Borja Spain 41°48N 1°34W 196 D3
Borjas Blancas = Les Borges
　Blanques Spain 41°31N 0°52E 196 D6
Borkou Chad 18°15N 18°50E 259 D4
Borkou-Ennedi-Tibesti □
　Chad 18°15N 18°50E 259 D4
Borkum Germany 53°34N 6°40E 178 B2
Borlänge Sweden 60°29N 15°26E 163 D9
Borley, C. Antarctica 66°15N 52°30E 5 C5
Bormida → Italy 44°49N 8°13E 198 D5

Bormio Italy 46°28N 10°22E 198 B7
Borna Germany 51°7N 12°29E 178 D8
Borne Sulinowo Poland 53°32N 16°36E 184 E3
Borneo E. Indies 1°0N 115°0E 235 B4
Bornholm Denmark 55°10N 15°0E 163 J8
Borno □ Nigeria 12°30N 13°0E 263 C7
Bornos Spain 36°48N 5°42W 195 J5
Bornova Turkey 38°27N 27°14E 205 C9
Bornu Yassa Nigeria 12°14N 12°25E 263 C7
Boro → Spain 8°52N 26°11E 257 G4
Boromo Burkina Faso 11°45N 2°58W 262 C4
Boron U.S.A. 35°0N 117°39W 307 L9
Boronga Is. Burma 19°58N 93°6E 241 F4
Borongan Phil. 11°37N 125°26E 233 F6
Boronia Park Australia 33°49S 151°8E 139 A1
Borotangba Mts. C.A.R. 6°30N 25°0E 257 C4
Borotou Ivory C. 8°46N 7°30W 262 D3
Borovan Bulgaria 43°27N 23°45E 202 C8
Borovichi Russia 58°25N 33°55E 188 C7
Borovsk Russia 55°12N 36°24E 188 E9
Borovskoy Kazakhstan 53°48N 64°9E 216 B6
Borrby Sweden 55°27N 14°10E 163 J8
Borrego Springs U.S.A. 33°15N 116°23W 307 M10
Borriol Spain 40°4N 0°4W 196 E4
Borrisokane Ireland 53°0N 8°7W 166 D3
Borroloola Australia 16°4S 136°17E 280 B2
Borsa Cluj, Romania 46°56N 23°40E 183 D8
Borșa Maramureș, Romania 47°41N 24°50E 183 D9
Borsad India 22°25N 72°54E 242 H5
Borsec Romania 46°57N 25°34E 183 D10
Borshchiv Ukraine 48°48N 26°3E 183 B11
Borsod-Abaúj-Zemplén □
　Hungary 48°20N 21°0E 182 B6
Bort-les-Orgues France 45°24N 2°29E 174 C6
Borth U.K. 52°29N 4°2W 169 E3
Börtnan Sweden 62°45N 13°50E 162 B7
Borūjerd Iran 33°55N 48°50E 213 F13
Boryeong S. Korea 36°21N 126°36E 224 F3
Borynya Ukraine 49°4N 23°0E 185 J10
Boryslav Ukraine 49°18N 23°28E 185 J10
Boryspil Ukraine 50°21N 30°59E 189 G6
Borzhomi = Borjomi
　Georgia 41°48N 43°28E 191 K6
Borzna Ukraine 51°18N 32°26E 189 G7
Borzya Russia 50°24N 116°31E 219 A12
Bosa Italy 40°18N 8°30E 200 B1
Bosa Monene
　Dem. Rep. of the Congo 1°1S 23°40E 264 C4
Bosaga Turkmenistan 37°33N 65°41E 240 A2
Bosambi
　Dem. Rep. of the Congo 2°24N 22°39E 264 B4
Bosanska Dubica
　Bos.-H. 45°10N 16°50E 199 C13
Bosanska Gradiška
　Bos.-H. 45°10N 17°15E 182 E2
Bosanska Kostajnica
　Bos.-H. 45°11N 16°33E 199 C13
Bosanska Krupa Bos.-H. 44°53N 16°10E 199 C13
Bosanski Brod Bos.-H. 45°10N 18°0E 182 E2
Bosanski Novi Bos.-H. 45°2N 16°22E 199 C13
Bosanski Petrovac
　Bos.-H. 44°35N 16°21E 199 C13
Bosanski Šamac Bos.-H. 45°3N 18°29E 182 E3
Bosansko Grahovo
　Bos.-H. 44°12N 16°26E 199 D13
Bosavi, Mt. Papua N. G. 6°30S 142°49E 286 D2
Boscastle U.K. 50°41N 4°42W 169 G3
Boscobel Barbados 13°17N 59°33E 323 r
Bose China 23°53N 106°35E 228 F7
Boseki Dem. Rep. of the Congo 2°34S 19°38E 264 C3
Boseong S. Korea 34°46N 127°5E 224 G3
Boshan China 36°28N 117°49E 227 F9
Boshof S. Africa 28°31S 25°13E 270 C4
Boshrūyeh Iran 33°50N 57°30E 247 C8
Bosilegrad Serbia 42°30N 22°27E 202 D6
Boskovice Czech Rep. 49°29N 16°40E 181 B9
Bosmont S. Africa 26°10S 27°57E 123 B1
Bosna → Bos.-H. 45°4N 18°29E 182 E3
Bosna i Hercegovina = Bosnia-
　Herzegovina ■ Europe 44°0N 18°0E 182 G2
Bosnia-Herzegovina ■
　Europe 44°0N 18°0E 182 G2
Bosnik Indonesia 1°5S 136°10E 231 E9
Bösö-Hantö Japan 35°20N 140°20E 223 B12
Bosobolo
　Dem. Rep. of the Congo 4°15N 19°50E 264 B3
Boson China 59°22N 18°11E 139 A3
Bosporus = İstanbul Boğazı
　Turkey 41°10N 29°10E 203 F13
Bosque Farms U.S.A. 35°51N 106°42W 305 J10
Bossangoa C.A.R. 6°35N 17°30E 264 A3
Bossé Bangou Niger 13°20N 1°18E 263 C5
Bossembélé C.A.R. 5°25N 17°40E 264 A3
Bossemtélé C.A.R. 5°41N 16°38E 264 A3
Bossier City U.S.A. 32°31N 93°44W 314 E8
Bossiesvlei Namibia 25°1S 16°44E 270 C2
Bosso Niger 13°43N 13°19E 259 F2
Bosso, Dallol → Niger 12°25N 2°50E 263 C5
Bostan Pakistan 30°26N 67°2E 242 D2
Bostānābād Iran 37°50N 46°50E 213 D12
Bostancı Turkey 40°57N 29°5E 122 C2
Bosten Hu China 41°55N 87°40E 217 D11
Boston U.K. 52°59N 0°2W 168 E7
Boston Ga., U.S.A. 30°47N 83°47W 316 E6
Boston Lincs., U.K. 52°59N 0°2W 168 E7
Boston Mass., U.S.A. 42°22N 71°3W 313 D13
Boston Bar Canada 49°52N 121°30W 296 C4
Boston Bay Jamaica 18°9N 76°22W 320 a
Boston Common Boston, U.S.A. 116 c1
Boston Logan Int. ✈ (BOS)
　U.S.A. 42°22N 71°1W 116 A2
Boston Tea Party Ship & Museum
　Boston, U.S.A. 116 c3
Bostwick U.S.A. 29°46N 81°38W 316 F8
Bosumtwi, L. Ghana 6°40N 1°27W 262 D4
Bosusulu
　Dem. Rep. of the Congo 0°50N 20°45E 264 B4
Bosut → Croatia 45°20N 18°45E 182 E3
Boswell B.C., Canada 49°28N 116°45W 296 D5
Boswell Okla., U.S.A. 40°31N 79°2W 314 E7
Boswell Pa., U.S.A. 40°10N 79°2W 312 F5
Bosworth U.S.A. 39°28N 93°33W 308 F7
Botad India 22°15N 71°39E 242 H4
Botafogo Brazil 22°56S 43°11W 136 B1
Botan → Turkey 37°57N 42°2E 213 D10
Botanic Gardens
　Washington, D.C., U.S.A. 143 b3
Botanisk Have Copenhagen, Denmark 118 b2
Botany Australia 33°56S 151°12E 139 B2
Botany B. Australia 33°58S 151°11E 139 B2
Botany Bay △ Australia 34°0S 151°14E 139 B2
Botene Laos 17°55N 101°12E 236 D3
Botera Angola 9°40S 16°0E 265 D3
Boteti → Botswana 20°10S 23°15E 271 A3
Botev Bulgaria 42°44N 24°15E 203 D8
Botevgrad Bulgaria 42°55N 23°47E 202 D7

Bothaville *S. Africa* 27°23S 26°34E **270** C4
Bothnia, G. of *Europe* 62°0N 20°0E **160** F19
Bothwell *Tas., Australia* 42°20S 147°1E **281** G4
Bothwell *Ont., Canada* 42°38N 81°52W **312** D3
Botič ➞ *Czech Rep.* 50°4N 14°26E **135** B3
Botica Sete *Portugal* 38°49N 9°10W **126** A1
Boticas *Portugal* 41°41N 7°40W **194** D3
Botlele ➞ *Botswana* 20°10S 23°15E **270** B3
Botlikh *Russia* 42°39N 46°11E **191** J8
Botna ➞ *Moldova* 46°45N 29°34E **183** D14
Botola *Dem. Rep. of the Congo* 1°17S 18°13E **264** C3
Botolan *Phil.* 15°17N 120°1E **232** D3
Botoroaga *Romania* 44°8N 25°32E **183** F10
Botoşani *Romania* 47°42N 26°41E **183** C11
Botoşani □ *Romania* 47°50N 26°50E **183** C11
Botou *Burkina Faso* 12°42N 1°59E **263** C5
Botou *China* 38°4N 116°34E **226** E9
Botricello *Italy* 38°56N 16°51E **201** D9
Botro *Ivory C.* 7°51N 5°19W **262** D3
Botshabelo *S. Africa* 29°14S 26°44E **270** C4
Botswana ■ *Africa* 22°0S 24°0E **270** B3
Bottelier *Curaçao* 12°6N 68°54W **322** g
Bottineau *U.S.A.* 48°50N 100°27W **308** A3
Bottnaryd *Sweden* 57°47N 13°50E **163** G7
Bottom, The *Saba* 17°38N 63°15W **322** a
Bottopassi *Suriname* 4°14N 55°27W **329** C6
Bottrop *Germany* 51°31N 6°58E **170** C6
Botucatu *Brazil* 22°55S 48°30W **335** A6
Botum Sakor △ *Cambodia* 11°5N 103°15E **237** G4
Botwood *Canada* 49°6N 55°23W **299** C8
Bou Alam *Algeria* 33°50N 1°26E **261** B5
Bou Ali *Algeria* 27°11N 0°4W **261** C4
Bou Djébéha *Mali* 18°25N 2°45W **262** B4
Bou Guema *Algeria* 28°49N 0°19E **261** C5
Bou Ismaïl *Algeria* 36°38N 2°42E **261** A5
Bou Izakarn *Morocco* 29°12N 9°46W **260** C3
Boû Lanouâr *Mauritania* 21°12N 16°34W **260** D1
Bou Naga *Mauritania* 18°49N 13°20W **262** B2
Bou Noura *Algeria* 32°29N 3°43E **261** B5
Boû Rjeïmât *Mauritania* 19°4N 15°39W **262** B1
Bou Saâda *Algeria* 35°11N 4°9E **261** A5
Bou Salem *Tunisia* 36°45N 9°2E **258** A1
Bouaflé *Ivory C.* 7°1N 5°47W **262** D3
Bouaké *Ivory C.* 7°40N 5°2W **262** D3
Bouanga *Congo* 2°7S 16°8E **264** C3
Bouar *C.A.R.* 6°0N 15°40E **264** A3
Bouârfa *Morocco* 32°32N 1°58W **261** B4
Bouba Ndjida △ *Cameroon* 8°50N 14°45E **264** A2
Boubout *Algeria* 27°26N 4°30W **260** C4
Bouca *C.A.R.* 6°45N 18°25E **264** A3
Boucaut B. *Australia* 12°0S 134°25E **280** A1
Boucherville *Canada* 45°36N 73°28W **130** A3
Boucherville, Îs. de *Canada* 45°36N 73°28W **130** A3
Bouches-du-Rhône □ *France* 43°37N 5°2E **175** E9
Boucle de Baoulé △ *Mali* 13°53N 9°0W **262** C3
Boucles de la Seine Normande ⌂ *France* 49°32N 0°35E **172** C7
Bouctouche *Canada* 46°30N 64°45W **299** C7
Bouda *Algeria* 27°50N 0°27W **261** C4
Boudenib *Morocco* 31°59N 3°31W **260** B4
Bouéni *Mayotte* 12°54S 45°4E **272** b
Bouéni, B. de *Mayotte* 12°55S 45°7E **272** b
Boufarik *Algeria* 36°34N 2°58E **261** A5
Bougainville, C. *Australia* 13°57S 126°4E **278** B4
Bougainville I. *Papua N. G.* 6°0S 155°0E **287** L8
Bougainville Reef *Australia* 15°30S 147°5E **280** B4
Bougainville Str. *Solomon Is.* 6°40S 156°10E **287** L9
Bougaroun, C. *Algeria* 37°6N 6°30E **261** A6
Bougie = Bejaïa *Algeria* 36°42N 5°2E **261** A6
Bougival *France* 48°51N 2°8E **134** A1
Bougouni *Mali* 11°30N 7°20W **262** C3
Bougtob *Algeria* 34°2N 0°5E **261** B5
Bouillante *Guadeloupe* 16°8N 61°46W **322** e
Bouillante, Pitons de *Guadeloupe* 16°8N 61°43W **322** e
Bouillon *Belgium* 49°44N 5°3E **170** E5
Bouïra *Algeria* 36°20N 3°59E **261** A5
Bouïra □ *Algeria* 36°15N 3°55E **261** A5
Boukombé *Benin* 10°13N 1°9E **263** C5
Boulal *Mali* 15°8N 8°21W **262** B3
Boulazac *France* 45°10N 0°47E **174** C4
Boulder *Colo., U.S.A.* 40°1N 105°17W **304** F11
Boulder *Mont., U.S.A.* 46°14N 112°7W **304** C7
Boulder City *U.S.A.* 35°58N 114°49W **307** K12
Boulder Creek *U.S.A.* 37°7N 122°7W **306** H4
Boulder Dam = Hoover Dam *U.S.A.* 36°1N 114°44W **307** K12
Boulder Pt. *China* 22°14N 114°6E **122** B1
Boulemane □ *Morocco* 33°10N 4°0W **260** B4
Boulembo *Gabon* 1°26S 12°0E **264** C2
Bouli *Mauritania* 15°17N 12°18W **262** B2
Boulia *Australia* 22°52S 139°51E **280** C2
Bouligny *France* 49°17N 5°45E **173** C12
Boulogne ➞ *France* 47°12N 1°47W **172** E5
Boulogne, Bois de *France* 48°51N 2°14E **134** A2
Boulogne-Billancourt *France* 48°50N 2°14E **134** A2
Boulogne-sur-Gesse *France* 43°18N 0°38E **174** E4
Boulogne-sur-Mer *France* 50°42N 1°36E **173** B8
Bouloire *France* 47°59N 0°45E **172** E7
Boulou ➞ *C.A.R.* 6°45N 24°16E **264** A4
Boulouli *Mali* 15°30N 9°25W **262** B3
Bouloupari *N. Cal.* 21°52S 166°4E **288** d
Bouloupesse *Congo* 1°58S 12°40E **264** C2
Boulsa *Burkina Faso* 12°39N 0°34W **263** C4
Boultoum *Niger* 14°45N 10°25E **259** F2
Bouma △ *Fiji* 16°50S 179°52E **287** A2
Boumalne Dadès *Morocco* 31°25N 6°0W **260** B3
Boumba ➞ *Cameroon* 2°2N 15°12E **264** B2
Boumbé ➞ *C.A.R.* 4°4N 15°23E **264** B3
Boûmdeïd *Mauritania* 17°25N 11°50W **262** B2
Boumerdès *Algeria* 36°46N 3°28E **261** A5
Boumerdès □ *Algeria* 36°45N 3°40E **261** A5
Boun Neua *Laos* 21°38N 101°54E **236** B3
Boun Tai *Laos* 21°23N 101°58E **236** B3
Bouna *Ivory C.* 9°10N 3°0W **262** D4
Boundary *U.S.A.* 64°5N 141°1W **303** D12
Boundary Peak *U.S.A.* 37°51N 118°21W **306** H8
Boundiali *Ivory C.* 9°30N 6°20W **262** D3
Boungou ➞ *C.A.R.* 8°21N 23°48E **264** A4
Bountiful *U.S.A.* 40°53N 111°52W **304** F8
Bounty Is. *Pac. Oc.* 48°0S 178°30E **288** M9
Bounty Trough *Pac. Oc.* 46°0S 178°0E **288** M9
Boura *Mali* 12°25N 4°33W **262** C4
Bourail *N. Cal.* 21°34S 165°30E **288** d
Bourbeuse ➞ *U.S.A.* 38°24N 90°53W **310** F6
Bourbon *U.S.A.* 41°18N 86°7W **311** C10
Bourbon-Lancy *France* 46°37N 3°45E **173** F10
Bourbon-l'Archambault *France* 46°36N 3°4E **173** F10
Bourbon Street *New Orleans, U.S.A.* **131** b2
Bourbonnais *Allier, France* 46°28N 3°0E **173** F10
Bourbonnais *Ill., U.S.A.* 41°9N 87°52W **311** C9
Bourbonne-les-Bains *France* 47°54N 5°45E **173** E12
Bourbourg *France* 50°56N 2°12E **173** B9
Bourdel L. *Canada* 56°43N 74°10W **298** A5
Bourem *Mali* 17°0N 0°24W **263** B4
Bouressa *Mali* 20°0N 2°15E **261** E5
Bourg *France* 45°3N 0°34W **174** C3
Bourg-Argental *France* 45°18N 4°32E **175** C8
Bourg-de-Péage *France* 45°2N 5°3E **175** C9
Bourg-en-Bresse *France* 46°13N 5°12E **173** F12
Bourg-la-Reine *France* 48°46N 2°19E **134** B2
Bourg-Lastic *France* 45°39N 2°35E **174** C6
Bourg-Madame *France* 42°26N 1°55E **174** F5
Bourg-St-Andéol *France* 44°23N 4°39E **175** D8
Bourg-St-Maurice *France* 45°35N 6°46E **175** C10
Bourganeuf *France* 45°57N 1°45E **174** C5
Bourgas = Burgas *Bulgaria* 42°33N 27°29E **203** D11
Bourges *France* 47°9N 2°25E **173** E9
Bourget *Canada* 45°26N 75°9W **313** A9
Bourget, Lac du *France* 45°44N 5°52E **175** C9
Bourgneuf, B. de *France* 47°3N 2°10W **172** E4
Bourgneuf-en-Retz *France* 47°2N 1°58W **172** E5
Bourgogne □ *France* 47°0N 4°50E **173** F11
Bourgoin-Jallieu *France* 45°36N 5°17E **175** C9
Bourgueil *France* 47°17N 0°10E **172** E7
Bourke *Australia* 30°8S 145°55E **281** E4
Bourne *U.K.* 52°47N 0°22W **168** E7
Bournemouth *U.K.* 50°43N 1°52W **169** G6
Bournemouth □ *U.K.* 50°43N 1°52W **169** G6
Bouroum *Burkina Faso* 13°37N 0°39W **263** C4
Bouse *U.S.A.* 33°56N 114°0W **307** M13
Boussac *France* 46°22N 2°13E **173** F9
Boussé *Burkina Faso* 12°39N 1°53W **263** C4
Bousso *Chad* 10°34N 16°52E **259** F3
Boussouma *Burkina Faso* 12°52N 1°13W **263** C4
Bout, Pte. du *Martinique* 14°33N 61°3W **322** j
Bout Stable Bay *Dominica* 15°21N 61°15W **323** k
Boutilimit *Mauritania* 17°45N 14°40W **262** B2
Boutonne ➞ *France* 45°54N 0°50W **174** C3
Bouvet I. = Bouvetøya *Antarctica* 54°26S 3°24E **152** M12
Bouvetøya *Antarctica* 54°26S 3°24E **152** M12
Bouviers *France* 48°46N 2°4E **134** B1
Bouxwiller *France* 48°49N 7°27E **173** D14
Bouza *Niger* 14°29N 6°2E **263** C6
Bouznika *Morocco* 33°46N 7°6W **260** B3
Bouzonville *France* 49°17N 6°32E **173** C13
Bova Marina *Italy* 37°56N 15°55E **201** E8
Bovalino Marina *Italy* 38°10N 16°10E **201** D9
Bovec *Slovenia* 46°20N 13°33E **199** B10
Boven Kapuas, Pegunungan *Malaysia* 1°25N 113°15E **235** B4
Bovenkerk *Neths.* 52°18N 4°51E **112** B2
Bovenkerker Polder *Neths.* 52°16N 4°52E **112** B2
Bøverdal *Norway* 61°44N 8°20E **164** C5
Bøverfjorden *Norway* 63°1N 8°32E **164** A5
Bovill *U.S.A.* 46°51N 116°24W **304** C5
Bovino *Italy* 41°15N 15°20E **201** A8
Bovisa *Italy* 45°30N 9°10E **129** A2
Bovril *Argentina* 31°21S 59°26W **334** C4
Bow *U.K.* 51°31N 0°1W **125** A3
Bow ➞ *Canada* 49°57N 111°41W **296** C6
Bow Island *Canada* 49°50N 111°23W **304** B8
Bowbells *U.S.A.* 48°48N 102°15W **308** A2
Bowdle *U.S.A.* 45°27N 99°39W **308** C4
Bowdon *U.S.A.* 33°32N 85°15W **316** B4
Bowdon Junction *U.S.A.* 33°40N 85°9W **316** B4
Bowelling *Australia* 33°25S 116°30E **279** F2
Bowen *Argentina* 35°0S 67°31W **334** D2
Bowen *Queens., Australia* 20°0S 148°16E **280** J6
Bowen Mts. *Australia* 37°0S 147°50E **283** D7
Bowers Basin *Pac. Oc.* 53°45N 176°0E **150** D16
Bowers Ridge *Pac. Oc.* 54°0N 180°0E **150** D17
Bowery *New York, U.S.A.* **132** e2
Bowie *Ariz., U.S.A.* 32°19N 109°29W **305** K9
Bowie *Tex., U.S.A.* 33°34N 97°51W **314** E6
Bowkān *Iran* 36°31N 46°12E **213** D12
Bowland, Forest of *U.K.* 54°0N 2°30W **168** D5
Bowling Green *Fla., U.S.A.* 27°38N 81°50W **317** H8
Bowling Green *Ky., U.S.A.* 36°59N 86°27W **308** G10
Bowling Green *Mo., U.S.A.* 39°21N 91°12W **310** E5
Bowling Green *Ohio, U.S.A.* 41°23N 83°39W **311** C13
Bowling Green, C. *Australia* 19°19S 147°25E **280** B4
Bowling Green Bay △ *Australia* 19°26S 146°57E **280** B4
Bowman *N. Dak., U.S.A.* 46°11N 103°24W **308** B2
Bowman *S.C., U.S.A.* 33°21N 80°41W **316** B9
Bowman I. *Antarctica* 65°0S 104°0E **151** C8
Bowmanville = Clarington *Canada* 43°55N 78°41W **312** C6
Bowmore *U.K.* 55°45N 6°17W **167** F2
Bowral *Australia* 34°26S 150°27E **283** C9
Bowraville *Australia* 30°37S 152°52E **281** E5
Bowron ➞ *Canada* 54°3N 121°50W **296** C4
Bowron Lake ⌂ *Canada* 53°10N 121°5W **296** C4
Bowser L. *Canada* 56°30N 129°30W **296** B3
Bowsman *Canada* 52°14N 101°12W **297** C8
Bowutu Mts. *Papua N. G.* 7°45S 147°10E **286** D4
Bowwood *Zambia* 17°5S 26°20E **269** F2
Box Cr. ➞ *Australia* 34°10S 143°50E **281** E3
Boxholm *Sweden* 58°12N 15°3E **163** F9
Boxmeer *Neths.* 51°38N 5°56E **170** C5
Boxtel *Neths.* 51°36N 5°20E **170** C5
Boyabat *Turkey* 41°28N 34°47E **212** B6
Boyabo *Dem. Rep. of the Congo* 3°43N 18°46E **264** B3
Boyacá □ *Colombia* 5°30N 73°20W **328** B3
Boyacıköy *Turkey* 41°5N 29°2E **122** B2
Boyalıca *Turkey* 40°29N 29°33E **203** F13
Boyang *China* 29°0N 116°38E **229** C11
Boyanup *Australia* 33°29S 115°40E **279** F2
Boyarka *Ukraine* 48°17N 26°8E **183** B11
Boyasegese *Dem. Rep. of the Congo* 3°29N 20°33E **264** B4
Boyce *U.S.A.* 31°23N 92°40W **314** F8
Boyd *U.S.A.* 30°11N 83°37W **316** E6
Boyd Conservation Area *Canada* 43°49N 79°35W **141** A1
Boyd L. *Canada* 52°46N 76°42W **298** B4
Boyenge *Dem. Rep. of the Congo* 0°14N 18°55E **264** B3
Boyer, C. *N. Cal.* 21°37S 168°6E **288** d
Boyera *Dem. Rep. of the Congo* 0°40S 19°23E **264** C3
Boyle *Alta., Canada* 54°35N 112°49W **296** C6
Boyle *Roscommon, Ireland* 53°59N 8°18W **166** C3
Boyle Heights *U.S.A.* 34°1N 118°12W **126** B3
Boyne ➞ *Ireland* 53°43N 6°15W **166** C5
Boyne City *U.S.A.* 45°13N 85°1W **309** C11
Boyni Qara *Afghan.* 36°20N 67°0E **240** A2
Boynitsa *Bulgaria* 43°58N 22°32E **202** C6
Boynton Beach *U.S.A.* 26°32N 80°4W **317** J9
Boyoma, Chutes *Dem. Rep. of the Congo* 0°35N 25°23E **264** B5
Boysen Res. *U.S.A.* 43°25N 108°11W **304** E9
Boyup Brook *Australia* 33°50S 116°23E **279** F2
Boz Burun *Turkey* 40°32N 28°46E **203** F12
Boz Dağ *Turkey* 37°18N 29°11E **205** D11
Boz Dağları *Turkey* 38°20N 28°0E **205** C10
Bozai Gumbaz *Afghan.* 37°8N 74°0E **240** A4
Bozburun *Turkey* 36°43N 28°4E **205** E10
Bozcaada *Turkey* 39°49N 26°3E **212** C2
Bozdağ *Turkey* 36°50N 36°22E **250** B7
Bozdoğan *Turkey* 37°40N 28°17E **205** D10
Boze *Papua N. G.* 9°3S 143°3E **286** E2
Bozeman *U.S.A.* 45°41N 111°2W **304** D8
Bozen = Bolzano *Italy* 46°31N 11°22E **199** B8
Bozene *Dem. Rep. of the Congo* 2°56N 19°12E **264** B3
Boževac *Serbia* 44°32N 21°24E **202** B5
Bozhou *China* 33°55N 115°41E **226** H8
Bozkır *Turkey* 37°11N 32°14E **212** D5
Bozkurt *Turkey* 37°50N 29°37E **205** D11
Bozouls *France* 44°28N 2°43E **174** D6
Bozoum *C.A.R.* 6°25N 16°35E **264** A3
Bozova *Antalya, Turkey* 37°13N 30°18E **205** D12
Bozova *Sanlıurfa, Turkey* 37°21N 38°32E **213** D8
Bozovici *Romania* 44°56N 22°0E **182** F7
Bozüyük *Turkey* 39°54N 30°3E **205** B12
Bozyazı *Turkey* 36°6N 33°0E **250** B4
Bra *Italy* 44°42N 7°51E **198** D4
Braås *Sweden* 57°4N 15°3E **163** G9
Brabant □ *Belgium* 50°46N 4°30E **170** D4
Brabant L. *Canada* 55°58N 103°43W **297** B8
Brabrand *Denmark* 56°9N 10°7E **163** H4
Brač *Croatia* 43°20N 16°40E **199** E13
Bracadale, L. *U.K.* 57°20N 6°30W **167** D2
Bracciano *Italy* 42°6N 12°10E **199** F9
Bracciano, L. di *Italy* 42°7N 12°14E **199** F9
Bracebridge *Canada* 45°2N 79°19W **312** A5
Bracieux *France* 47°30N 1°30E **172** E8
Bräcke *Sweden* 62°45N 15°26E **162** B9
Brackettville *U.S.A.* 29°19N 100°25W **314** G4
Brački Kanal *Croatia* 43°24N 16°40E **199** E13
Bracknell *U.K.* 51°25N 0°43W **169** F7
Bracknell Forest □ *U.K.* 51°25N 0°44W **169** F7
Brad *Romania* 46°10N 22°50E **182** D7
Brádano ➞ *Italy* 40°23N 16°51E **201** B9
Bradbury Building *Los Angeles, U.S.A.* **127** b2
Bradenton *U.S.A.* 27°30N 82°34W **317** H7
Brades *Montserrat* 16°47N 62°13W **321** C7
Bradford *Ont., Canada* 44°7N 79°34W **312** B5
Bradford *W. Yorks., U.K.* 53°47N 1°45W **168** D6
Bradford *Ill., U.S.A.* 41°11N 89°39W **310** C7
Bradford *Ohio, U.S.A.* 40°8N 84°27W **311** D12
Bradford *Pa., U.S.A.* 41°58N 78°38W **312** E6
Bradford *Vt., U.S.A.* 43°59N 72°9W **313** C12
Bradley *Ark., U.S.A.* 33°6N 93°39W **314** E8
Bradley *Calif., U.S.A.* 35°52N 120°48W **306** K6
Bradley *Ill., U.S.A.* 41°9N 87°52W **311** C9
Bradley Institute *Zimbabwe* 17°7S 31°25E **269** F3
Bradley Junction *U.S.A.* 27°48N 81°59W **317** H8
Bradner *U.S.A.* 41°20N 83°26W **311** C13
Brady *U.S.A.* 31°9N 99°20W **314** F5
Brædstrup *Denmark* 55°58N 9°37E **163** J3
Braemar *Australia* 33°12S 139°35E **282** B3
Braepark *U.K.* 55°58N 3°18W **121** B2
Braeside *Canada* 45°28N 76°24W **313** A8
Braeton *Jamaica* 17°57N 76°53W **320** a
Braga *Portugal* 41°35N 8°25W **194** D2
Braga □ *Portugal* 41°30N 8°30W **194** D2
Bragadiru *Romania* 43°46N 25°31E **183** G10
Bragado *Argentina* 35°2S 60°27W **334** D3
Bragança *Brazil* 1°0S 47°2W **332** B2
Bragança *Portugal* 41°48N 6°50W **194** D4
Bragança □ *Portugal* 41°30N 6°45W **194** D4
Bragança Paulista *Brazil* 22°55S 46°32W **335** A6
Bragg's Spur = West Memphis *U.S.A.* 35°8N 90°10W **315** D9
Brahestad = Raahe *Finland* 64°40N 24°28E **160** D21
Brahmakund *India* 27°52N 96°22E **241** B6
Brahmanbaria *Bangla.* 23°58N 91°15E **241** D3
Brahmani ➞ *India* 20°39N 86°46E **244** D8
Brahmapur *India* 19°15N 84°54E **244** E7
Brahmaputra ➞ *Asia* 23°40N 90°35E **241** D3
Braich-y-pwll *U.K.* 52°47N 4°46W **168** E3
Braid *U.K.* 55°55N 3°11W **121** B2
Braidwood *Australia* 35°27S 149°49E **283** C8
Brăila *Romania* 45°19N 27°59E **183** E12
Brăila □ *Romania* 45°5N 27°30E **183** E12
Brainerd *U.S.A.* 46°22N 94°12W **308** B6
Braintree *Essex, U.K.* 51°53N 0°34E **169** F8
Braintree *Mass., U.S.A.* 42°13N 71°0W **313** D14
Brak ➞ *S. Africa* 29°35S 22°55E **270** C3
Brake *Germany* 53°20N 8°28E **178** B4
Brakel *Germany* 51°42N 9°11E **178** D5
Brakna □ *Mauritania* 17°0N 13°20W **262** B2
Bräkne-Hoby *Sweden* 56°14N 15°6E **163** H9
Brakwater *Namibia* 22°28S 17°3E **270** B2
Brålanda *Sweden* 58°34N 12°21E **163** F6
Bramberg *Germany* 50°6N 10°40E **179** E6
Bramdrupdam *Denmark* 55°31N 9°28E **163** J3
Bramhapuri *India* 20°36N 79°52E **244** D4
Bramley *S. Africa* 26°7S 28°4E **123** A2
Bramming *Denmark* 55°28N 8°42E **163** J2
Brämön *Sweden* 62°14N 17°40E **162** B11
Brampton *Ont., Canada* 43°45N 79°45W **312** C5
Brampton *Cumb., U.K.* 54°57N 2°44W **168** C5
Brampton I. *Australia* 20°49S 149°16E **280** b
Bramsche *Germany* 52°24N 7°59E **178** C3
Branchville *U.S.A.* 33°15N 80°49W **316** B9
Branco ➞ *Brazil* 1°20S 61°50W **329** D5
Branco, C. *Brazil* 7°9S 34°47W **332** C5
Brandaris *Bonaire* 12°16N 68°23W **322** h
Brandberg *Namibia* 21°10S 14°33E **270** B1
Brandberg △ *Namibia* 21°10S 14°30E **270** B1
Brandbu *Norway* 60°26N 10°28E **164** D7
Brande *Denmark* 55°57N 9°8E **163** J3
Brandeis Univ. *U.S.A.* 42°21N 71°17W **116** A1
Brandenburg = Neubrandenburg *Germany* 53°33N 13°15E **178** B9
Brandenburg *Brandenburg, Germany* 52°25N 12°33E **178** C8
Brandenburg *Ky., U.S.A.* 38°0N 86°10W **311** G10
Brandenburg □ *Germany* 52°50N 13°0E **178** C9
Brandenburger Tor *Germany* 52°30N 13°21E **115** A3
Brandfort *S. Africa* 28°40S 26°30E **270** C4
Brando *France* 42°47N 9°27E **175** F13
Brandon *Man., Canada* 49°50N 99°57W **297** D9
Brandon *Fla., U.S.A.* 27°56N 82°17W **317** H7
Brandon *Vt., U.S.A.* 43°48N 73°6W **313** C11
Brandon B. *Ireland* 52°17N 10°8W **166** D1
Brandon Mt. *Ireland* 52°15N 10°15W **166** D1
Brandsen *Argentina* 35°10S 58°15W **334** D4
Brandvlei *S. Africa* 30°25S 20°30E **270** D3
Brandýs nad Labem *Czech Rep.* 50°10N 14°40E **180** A7
Brănești *Romania* 44°27N 26°20E **183** F11
Branford *Conn., U.S.A.* 41°17N 72°49W **313** E12
Branford *Fla., U.S.A.* 29°58N 82°56W **316** F7
Brani, Pulau *Singapore* 1°15N 103°50E **138** B3
Braniewo *Poland* 54°25N 19°50E **184** D6
Branik *Czech Rep.* 50°1N 14°25E **135** B2
Brännkyrka *Sweden* 59°17N 18°0E **139** B2
Bransfield Str. *Antarctica* 63°0S 59°0W **151** C18
Brańsk *Poland* 52°45N 22°50E **185** F9
Branson *U.S.A.* 36°39N 93°13W **308** G7
Brantford *Canada* 43°10N 80°15W **312** C4
Brantley *U.S.A.* 31°35N 86°16W **316** D3
Brantôme *France* 45°22N 0°39E **174** C4
Branxholme *Australia* 37°52S 141°49E **282** D4
Branxton *Australia* 32°38S 151°21E **283** B9
Branzi *Italy* 46°1N 9°46E **198** B6
Brás *Amazonas, Brazil* 2°5S 58°10W **329** D6
Brás *São Paulo, Brazil* 23°32S 46°36W **137** B2
Bras d'Or L. *Canada* 45°50N 60°50W **299** C7
Bras-Panon *Réunion* 20°59S 55°41E **272** f
Brasher Falls *U.S.A.* 44°49N 74°47W **313** B10
Brasil = Brazil ■ *S. Amer.* 12°0S 50°0W **327** E6
Brasil, Planalto *Brazil* 18°0S 46°30W **326** E6
Brasil Novo *Brazil* 3°19S 52°38W **329** D7
Brasilândia *Brazil* 23°28S 46°42W **137** A1
Brasiléia *Brazil* 11°0S 68°45W **330** C4
Brasília *Distrito Federal, Brazil* 15°47S 47°55W **333** E2
Brasília *Minas Gerais, Brazil* 16°12S 44°26W **333** E3
Brasília △ *Brazil* 15°41S 48°8W **333** E2
Brasília Legal *Brazil* 3°49S 55°36W **329** D6
Braskereidfoss *Norway* 60°44N 11°46E **164** D8
Braslaw *Belarus* 55°38N 27°0E **188** E4
Braslovče *Slovenia* 46°21N 15°3E **199** B12
Brașov *Romania* 45°38N 25°35E **183** E10
Brașov □ *Romania* 45°45N 25°15E **183** E10
Brass *Nigeria* 4°35N 6°14E **263** E6
Brass ➞ *Nigeria* 4°15N 6°13E **263** E6
Brassac-les-Mines *France* 45°24N 3°20E **174** C7
Brasschaat *Belgium* 51°19N 4°27E **170** C4
Brassey, Banjaran *Malaysia* 5°0N 117°15E **235** B5
Brassey Ra. *Australia* 25°8S 122°15E **279** E3
Brasso Seco *Trin. & Tob.* 10°45N 61°16W **323** t
Brasstown Bald *U.S.A.* 34°53N 83°49W **315** D13
Brastad *Sweden* 58°23N 11°30E **163** F5
Brastavățu *Romania* 43°55N 24°24E **183** G9
Bratan = Morozov *Bulgaria* 42°30N 25°10E **203** D9
Brateș *Romania* 45°50N 26°4E **183** E11
Brateyevo *Russia* 55°39N 37°45E **129** C4
Bratislava *Slovak Rep.* 48°10N 17°7E **181** C10
Bratislava M.R. Stefanik ✕ **(BTS)** *Slovak Rep.* 48°11N 17°9E **181** C10
Bratislavský □ *Slovak Rep.* 48°15N 17°20E **181** C10
Bratsberg = Telemark □ *Norway* 59°25N 8°30E **164** E5
Bratsevo *Russia* 55°51N 37°24E **129** A2
Bratsigovo *Bulgaria* 42°1N 24°22E **203** D8
Bratsk *Russia* 56°10N 101°30E **215** D11
Brattleboro *U.S.A.* 42°51N 72°34W **313** D12
Brattvåg *Norway* 62°37N 6°25E **164** B3
Bratunac *Bos.-H.* 44°13N 19°21E **182** F4
Braunau *Austria* 48°15N 13°3E **180** C6
Braunsberg = Braniewo *Poland* 54°25N 19°50E **184** D6
Braunschweig *Germany* 52°15N 10°31E **178** C6
Braunton *U.K.* 51°7N 4°10W **169** F3
Brava = Baraawe *Somali Rep.* 1°20N 44°8E **267** D5
Brava *C. Verde Is.* 15°0N 24°40W **153** j
Bravicea *Moldova* 47°22N 28°27E **183** C13
Bråviken *Sweden* 58°38N 16°32E **163** F10
Bravo del Norte, Rio = Grande, Rio ➞ *N. Amer.* 25°58N 97°9W **314** J6
Brawley *U.S.A.* 32°59N 115°31W **307** N11
Bray *Ireland* 53°13N 6°7W **166** C5
Bray, Mt. *Australia* 14°0S 134°30E **280** A1
Bray, Pays de *France* 49°46N 1°26E **171** B4
Bray-sur-Seine *France* 48°25N 3°14E **173** D10
Braybrook *Australia* 37°46S 144°51E **128** A1
Braymer *U.S.A.* 39°35N 93°48W **310** E3
Brázdim *Czech Rep.* 50°10N 14°35E **135** A3
Brazeau ➞ *Canada* 52°55N 115°14W **296** C5
Brazil *U.S.A.* 39°32N 87°8W **311** E9
Brazil ■ *S. Amer.* 12°0S 50°0W **327** E6
Brazil Basin *Atl. Oc.* 15°0S 25°0W **152** H9
Brazilian Highlands = Brasil, Planalto *Brazil* 18°0S 46°30W **326** E6
Brazo Sur ➞ *S. Amer.* 25°21S 57°42W **334** B4
Brazos ➞ *U.S.A.* 28°53N 95°23W **314** G7
Brazzaville *Congo* 4°9S 15°12E **265** C3
Brčko *Bos.-H.* 44°54N 18°46E **182** F3
Brda ➞ *Poland* 53°8N 18°8E **185** E5
Brdy *Czech Rep.* 49°43N 13°55E **180** B6
Bré = Bray *Ireland* 53°13N 6°7W **166** C5
Breach Candy *Mumbai, India* **130** a1
Bream Bay *Australia* 25°51S 125°28E **279** E4
Breakheart Reservation *U.S.A.* 42°28N 71°1W **116** A2
Breaksea Sd. *N.Z.* 45°35S 166°35E **285** F1
Bream B. *N.Z.* 35°56S 174°28E **284** B3
Bream Hd. *N.Z.* 35°51S 174°36E **284** B3
Bream Tail *N.Z.* 36°3S 174°36E **284** C3
Breas *Chile* 25°29S 70°24W **334** B1
Breaza *Romania* 45°11N 25°40E **183** E10
Brebes *Indonesia* 6°52S 109°3E **235** D3
Brechin *Ont., Canada* 44°32N 79°10W **312** B5
Brechin *Angus, U.K.* 56°44N 2°39W **167** E6
Brecht *Belgium* 51°21N 4°38E **170** C4
Breckenridge *Colo., U.S.A.* 39°29N 106°3W **304** G10
Breckenridge *Minn., U.S.A.* 46°16N 96°35W **308** B5
Breckenridge *Tex., U.S.A.* 32°45N 98°54W **314** E5
Breckland *U.K.* 52°30N 0°40E **169** E8
Brecknock, Pen. *Chile* 54°35S 71°30W **336** D2
Břeclav *Czech Rep.* 48°46N 16°53E **181** C9
Brecon *U.K.* 51°57N 3°23W **169** F4
Brecon Beacons *U.K.* 51°53N 3°26W **169** F4
Brecon Beacons △ *U.K.* 51°50N 3°30W **169** F4
Breda *Neths.* 51°35N 4°45E **170** C4
Bredaryd *Sweden* 57°10N 13°45E **163** G7
Bredasdorp *S. Africa* 34°33S 20°2E **270** D3
Bredbo *Australia* 35°58S 149°10E **283** C8
Brede *Denmark* 55°47N 12°30E **118** A3
Bredebro *Denmark* 55°4N 8°50E **163** J2
Bredstedt *Germany* 54°37N 8°55E **178** A4
Bredy *Russia* 52°26N 60°21E **216** B6
Bree *Belgium* 51°8N 5°35E **170** C5
Breezy Point *U.S.A.* 40°33N 73°56W **132** C2
Bregalnica ➞ *Macedonia* 41°43N 22°9E **202** E6
Bregenz *Austria* 47°30N 9°45E **180** D2
Bregovo *Bulgaria* 44°9N 22°39E **202** B6
Bréhal *France* 48°53N 1°30W **172** D5
Bréhat, Î. de *France* 48°51N 3°0W **172** D4
Breiðafjörður *Iceland* 65°15N 23°15W **155** B3
Breiðdalsvík *Iceland* 64°44N 14°0W **155** C13
Breil-sur-Roya *France* 43°56N 7°31E **175** E11
Breim *Norway* 61°44N 6°25E **164** C3
Breisach *Germany* 48°1N 7°36E **179** G3
Breitenlee *Austria* 48°15N 16°30E **142** A3
Brejinho de Nazaré *Brazil* 11°1S 48°34W **332** D2
Brejo *Brazil* 3°41S 42°47W **332** B3
Brekke *Norway* 61°1N 5°26E **164** C2
Brekken *Norway* 62°40N 11°51E **164** B8
Brekkestø *Norway* 58°11N 8°22E **164** F5
Bremanger *Norway* 61°51N 4°58E **164** C1
Bremangerlandet *Norway* 61°51N 5°0E **164** C1
Bremen *Bremen, Germany* 53°4N 8°47E **178** B4
Bremen *Ga., U.S.A.* 33°43N 85°9W **316** B4
Bremen *Ind., U.S.A.* 41°27N 86°9W **311** C10
Bremen □ *Germany* 53°4N 8°50E **178** B4
Bremer Bay *Australia* 34°21S 119°20E **279** F2
Bremer I. *Australia* 12°5S 136°45E **280** A2
Bremerhaven *Germany* 53°33N 8°36E **178** B4
Bremersdorp = Manzini *Swaziland* 26°30S 31°25E **271** C5
Bremerton *U.S.A.* 47°34N 122°37W **306** C4
Bremervörde *Germany* 53°29N 9°8E **178** B5
Bremnes *Norway* 59°47N 5°8E **164** E2
Bremsnes *Norway* 63°6N 7°40E **164** A4
Breña *Peru* 12°3S 77°3W **124** B2
Brenes *Spain* 37°32N 5°54W **195** H5
Brenham *U.S.A.* 30°10N 96°24W **314** F6
Brenne *France* 46°44N 1°14E **174** B5
Brenne ⌂ *France* 46°40N 1°15E **174** B5
Brennerpass *Austria* 47°2N 11°30E **180** D4
Brennhaug *Norway* 61°54N 9°21E **164** C6
Breno *Italy* 45°57N 10°18E **198** C7
Brent *U.S.A.* 32°56N 87°10W **315** E11
Brent □ *U.K.* 51°33N 0°16W **125** A2
Brent Res. *U.K.* 51°34N 0°14W **125** A2
Brenta ➞ *Italy* 45°11N 12°18E **199** C9
Brentford *U.K.* 51°28N 0°18W **125** B2
Brentwood *Essex, U.K.* 51°37N 0°19E **169** F8
Brentwood *Calif., U.S.A.* 34°3N 118°28W **126** B2
Brentwood *Calif., U.S.A.* 37°56N 121°42W **306** H5
Brentwood *N.Y., U.S.A.* 40°47N 73°15W **313** F11
Brentwood Park *U.S.A.* 34°3N 118°29W **126** B2
Brera *Italy* 45°28N 9°11E **129** B2
Brereton *Barbados* 13°7N 59°30W **323** r
Bréscia *Italy* 45°33N 10°15E **198** C7
Breskens *Neths.* 51°23N 3°33E **170** C3
Breslau = Wrocław *Poland* 51°5N 17°5E **185** G4
Bresle ➞ *France* 50°4N 1°22E **172** B8
Bressanone *Italy* 46°43N 11°39E **199** B8
Bressay *U.K.* 60°9N 1°6W **167** A7
Bresse *France* 46°50N 5°10E **173** F12
Bresso *Italy* 45°32N 9°11E **129** A2
Bressuire *France* 46°51N 0°30W **172** F6
Brest *Belarus* 52°10N 23°40E **177** B12
Brest *Finistère, France* 48°24N 4°31W **172** D2
Brest □ *Belarus* 52°30N 26°10E **177** B13
Brest-Litovsk = Brest *Belarus* 52°10N 23°40E **177** B12
Bretagne □ *France* 48°10N 3°0W **172** D3
Betanha, Pta. da *Azores* 37°54N 25°47W **153** d3
Brețcu *Romania* 46°7N 26°18E **183** D11
Bretenoux *France* 44°54N 1°51E **174** D5
Breteuil *Eure, France* 48°50N 0°57E **172** D7
Breteuil *Oise, France* 49°38N 2°18E **173** C9
Breton *Canada* 53°7N 114°28W **296** C6
Breton, Pertuis *France* 46°17N 1°25W **174** B2
Breton Sd. *U.S.A.* 29°35N 89°15W **315** G10
Brett, C. *N.Z.* 35°10S 174°20E **284** B3
Bretten *Germany* 49°2N 8°42E **179** F4
Breueh *Indonesia* 5°44N 95°2E **234** B1
Breuil-Cervínia *Italy* 45°56N 7°38E **198** C4
Brevard *U.S.A.* 35°14N 82°44W **315** D13
Breves *Brazil* 1°40S 50°29W **332** B1
Brevig Mission *U.S.A.* 65°20N 166°29W **303** D6
Brevik *Telemark, Norway* 59°4N 9°42E **164** E6
Brevik *Stockholm, Sweden* 59°20N 18°12E **139** A3
Břevnov *Czech Rep.* 50°4N 14°22E **135** B2
Brewarrina *Australia* 30°0S 146°51E **281** E4
Brewer *U.S.A.* 44°48N 68°46W **309** C19
Brewer, Mt. *U.S.A.* 36°44N 118°28W **306** J8
Brewerville *Liberia* 6°26N 10°47W **262** D2
Brewster *N.Y., U.S.A.* 41°24N 73°36W **313** E11
Brewster *Ohio, U.S.A.* 40°43N 81°36W **312** F3
Brewster *Wash., U.S.A.* 48°6N 119°47W **304** B4
Brewster, Kap = Kangikajik *Greenland* 70°7N 22°0W **154** C8
Brewton *U.S.A.* 31°7N 87°4W **315** F11
Breyten *S. Africa* 26°16S 30°0E **271** C5
Breza *Bos.-H.* 44°2N 18°16E **182** F3
Brežice *Slovenia* 45°54N 15°35E **199** C12
Bréziina *Algeria* 33°4N 1°14E **261** B5
Březnice *Czech Rep.* 49°32N 13°57E **180** B6
Breznik *Bulgaria* 42°44N 22°55E **202** D6
Brezno *Slovak Rep.* 48°50N 19°40E **181** C12
Brezoi *Romania* 45°21N 24°15E **183** E9
Brezovica *Kosovo* 42°15N 21°3E **202** D5
Brezovo *Bulgaria* 42°21N 25°5E **203** D9
Bria *C.A.R.* 6°30N 21°58E **264** A4
Briançon *France* 44°54N 6°39E **175** D10
Briare *France* 47°38N 2°45E **173** E9
Briars, The *St. Helena* 15°56S 5°43W **153** h
Briático *Italy* 38°43N 16°2E **201** D9
Bribie I. *Australia* 27°0S 153°10E **281** D5
Bribri *Costa Rica* 9°38N 82°50W **320** E3
Briceni *Moldova* 48°22N 27°6E **183** B12
Brickyard, The *U.S.A.* 41°55N 87°47W **119** B2
Bricquebec *France* 49°28N 1°38W **172** C5
Bridge City *U.S.A.* 29°55N 90°9W **131** B2
Bridgehampton *U.S.A.* 40°56N 72°19W **313** F12
Bridgend *U.K.* 51°30N 3°34W **169** F4
Bridgend □ *U.K.* 51°36N 3°36W **169** F4
Bridgenorth *Canada* 44°23N 78°23W **312** B6
Bridgeport *Calif., U.S.A.* 38°15N 119°14W **306** G7
Bridgeport *Conn., U.S.A.* 41°11N 73°12W **313** E11
Bridgeport *Ill., U.S.A.* 41°50N 87°38W **119** B3
Bridgeport *Ill., U.S.A.* 38°43N 87°46W **311** F9
Bridgeport *N.Y., U.S.A.* 43°9N 75°58W **313** C9
Bridgeport *Nebr., U.S.A.* 41°40N 103°6W **308** E2
Bridgeport *Tex., U.S.A.* 33°13N 97°45W **314** E6
Bridger *U.S.A.* 45°18N 108°55W **304** D9
Bridgeton *U.S.A.* 39°26N 75°14W **309** F16
Bridgetown *W. Austral., Australia* 33°58S 116°7E **279** F2
Bridgetown *Barbados* 13°6N 59°37W **323** r
Bridgetown *N.S., Canada* 44°55N 65°18W **299** D6
Bridgetown *Western Cape, S. Africa* 33°58S 18°33E **118** A2
Bridgeview *U.S.A.* 41°45N 87°48W **119** C2
Bridgewater *Tas., Australia* 42°44S 147°14E **281** G4
Bridgewater *Vic., Australia* 36°36S 143°59E **282** D5
Bridgewater *N.S., Canada* 44°25N 64°31W **299** D7
Bridgewater *Mass., U.S.A.* 41°59N 70°58W **313** E14
Bridgewater *N.Y., U.S.A.* 42°53N 75°15W **313** D9
Bridgewater, C. *Australia* 38°23S 141°23E **282** E4
Bridgman *U.S.A.* 41°57N 86°33W **311** C10
Bridgnorth *U.K.* 52°32N 2°25W **169** E5
Bridgton *U.S.A.* 44°3N 70°42W **313** B14
Bridgwater *U.K.* 51°8N 2°59W **169** F5
Bridgwater B. *U.K.* 51°15N 3°15W **169** F4
Bridlington *U.K.* 54°5N 0°12W **168** C7
Bridlington B. *U.K.* 54°4N 0°10W **168** C7
Bridport *Tas., Australia* 40°59S 147°23E **281** G4
Bridport *Dorset, U.K.* 50°44N 2°45W **169** G5
Briec *France* 48°6N 4°0W **172** D2
Brieg = Brzeg *Poland* 50°52N 17°30E **185** H4
Brienne-le-Château *France* 48°24N 4°30E **173** D11
Brienon-sur-Armançon *France* 47°59N 3°38E **173** E10
Brienz *Switz.* 46°46N 8°2E **179** J4
Brienzersee *Switz.* 46°44N 7°53E **179** J3
Brier Cr. ➞ *U.S.A.* 32°44N 81°26W **316** C8
Brière ⌂ *France* 47°22N 2°13W **172** E4
Brievengat *Curaçao* 12°9N 68°54W **322** g
Brig *Switz.* 46°18N 7°59E **179** J3
Brigg *U.K.* 53°34N 0°28W **168** D7
Brigham City *U.S.A.* 41°31N 112°1W **304** F7
Bright *Australia* 36°42S 146°56E **283** D7
Brighton *S. Austral., Australia* 35°5S 138°30E **282** C3
Brighton *Vic., Australia* 37°55S 144°59E **128** B1
Brighton *Ont., Canada* 44°2N 77°44W **312** B7
Brighton *Trin. & Tob.* 10°13N 61°39W **323** t
Brighton *Brighton & Hove, U.K.* 50°49N 0°7W **169** G7
Brighton *Fla., U.S.A.* 27°14N 81°6W **317** H8
Brighton *Ill., U.S.A.* 39°2N 90°8W **310** E6
Brighton *Iowa, U.S.A.* 41°10N 91°49W **310** C5
Brighton *Mass., U.S.A.* 42°21N 71°9W **116** A2
Brighton *Mich., U.S.A.* 42°32N 83°47W **311** B13
Brighton *N.Y., U.S.A.* 43°8N 77°34W **312** C7
Brighton Beach *U.S.A.* 40°34N 73°57W **132** C2
Brighton-Le-Sands *Australia* 33°57S 151°9E **139** B1
Brighton Park *U.S.A.* 41°48N 87°41W **119** C2
Brightside *Canada* 45°7N 76°29W **313** A8
Brightwater *N.Z.* 41°22S 173°9E **285** B8
Brightwood *U.S.A.* 38°57N 77°1W **143** B3
Brigittenau *Austria* 48°14N 16°22E **142** A2
Brignogan-Plage *France* 48°40N 4°20W **172** D2
Brignoles *France* 43°25N 6°5E **175** E10
Brihuega *Spain* 40°45N 2°52W **196** E2
Brikama *Gambia* 13°15N 16°45W **262** C1
Brilliant *U.S.A.* 40°15N 80°39W **312** F4
Brilon *Germany* 51°23N 8°35E **178** D4
Brim *Australia* 36°3S 142°27E **282** D5
Brimbank Park *Australia* 37°43S 144°50E **128** A1
Brimfield *U.S.A.* 40°50N 89°53W **310** D7
Brimstone Hill Fort *St. Kitts & Nevis* 17°20N 62°50W **322** d
Brindabella △ *Australia* 35°14S 148°5E **283** C8
Brindisi *Italy* 40°39N 17°55E **201** B10
Brinje *Croatia* 44°59N 15°9E **199** D12
Brinkley *U.S.A.* 34°53N 91°12W **314** D9
Brinkworth *Australia* 33°42S 138°26E **282** B3
Brinnon *U.S.A.* 47°41N 122°54W **306** C4
Brinson *U.S.A.* 30°59N 84°44W **316** E5
Brion, Î. *Canada* 47°46N 61°26W **299** C7
Brionne *France* 49°11N 0°43E **172** C7
Brionski *Croatia* 44°55N 13°45E **199** D10
Brioude *France* 45°18N 3°24E **174** C7
Briouze *France* 48°42N 0°23W **172** D6
Brisay *Canada* 54°26N 70°31W **299** B5
Brisbane *Queens., Australia* 27°25S 153°2E **281** D5
Brisbane *Calif., U.S.A.* 37°40N 122°23W **136** B2
Brisbane ➞ *Australia* 27°24S 153°9E **281** D5
Brisbane Ranges △ *Australia* 37°47S 144°16E **282** D6
Brisbane Water △ *Australia* 33°26S 151°13E **283** B9
Brisighella *Italy* 44°13N 11°46E **199** D8
Bristol *Bristol, U.K.* 51°26N 2°35W **169** F5
Bristol *Conn., U.S.A.* 41°40N 72°57W **313** E12
Bristol *Fla., U.S.A.* 30°26N 84°59W **316** E5
Bristol *Pa., U.S.A.* 40°6N 74°51W **313** F10
Bristol *R.I., U.S.A.* 41°40N 71°16W **313** E13
Bristol *Tenn., U.S.A.* 36°36N 82°11W **315** C13
Bristol *Vt., U.S.A.* 44°8N 73°4W **313** B11
Bristol, City of □ *U.K.* 51°27N 2°36W **169** F5
Bristol B. *U.S.A.* 58°0N 160°0W **303** H8
Bristol Channel *U.K.* 51°18N 4°30W **169** F3
Bristol I. *Antarctica* 58°45S 28°0W **151** B1
Bristol L. *U.S.A.* 34°28N 115°41W **305** J6
Bristow *U.S.A.* 35°50N 96°23W **314** D6
Bristow I. *Papua N. G.* 9°8S 143°14E **286** E2
Britain = Great Britain *Europe* 54°0N 2°15W **158** E5
Britânia *Brazil* 15°14S 51°9W **331** D7
British Central Africa = Malawi ■ *Africa* 11°55S 34°0E **269** E3
British Columbia □ *Canada* 55°0N 125°15W **296** C3
British East Africa = Kenya ■ *Africa* 1°0N 38°0E **268** B4
British Guiana = Guyana ■ *S. Amer.* 5°0N 59°0W **329** C6
British Honduras = Belize ■ *Cent. Amer.* 17°0N 88°30W **320** C2
British Indian Ocean Terr. = Chagos Arch. ☑ *Ind. Oc.* 6°0S 72°0E **211** J9
British Isles *Europe* 54°0N 4°0W **165** D5
British Mts. *N. Amer.* 68°50N 140°0W **300** B12
British Museum *London, U.K.* **125** a3
British Virgin Is. ☑ *W. Indies* 18°30N 64°30W **321** C7
Brits *S. Africa* 25°37S 27°48E **271** C4
Britstown *S. Africa* 30°37S 23°30E **270** D3
Britt *Ont., Canada* 45°46N 80°34W **298** C3
Britt *Iowa, U.S.A.* 43°6N 93°48W **310** A3
Brittany = Bretagne □ *France* 48°10N 3°0W **172** D3
Britton *U.S.A.* 45°48N 97°45W **308** C5
Britz *Germany* 52°26N 13°27E **115** B3
Brive-la-Gaillarde *France* 45°10N 1°32E **174** C5
Briviesca *Spain* 42°32N 3°19W **194** C7
Brixen = Bressanone *Italy* 46°43N 11°39E **199** B8
Brixham *U.K.* 50°23N 3°31W **169** G4
Brixton *U.K.* 51°27N 0°8W **125** B3
Brnaze *Croatia* 43°41N 16°40E **199** E13
Brněnský □ *Czech Rep.* 49°10N 16°40E **181** B9
Brno *Czech Rep.* 49°10N 16°35E **181** B9
Broach = Bharuch *India* 21°47N 73°0E **244** D1
Broad ➞ *Ga., U.S.A.* 33°59N 82°39W **316** B7
Broad ➞ *S.C., U.S.A.* 34°1N 81°4W **315** D14
Broad Arrow *Australia* 30°23S 121°15E **279** F3
Broad B. *U.K.* 58°14N 6°18W **167** C2
Broad Haven *Ireland* 54°20N 9°55W **166** B2
Broad Law *U.K.* 55°30N 3°21W **167** F5
Broad Pk. = Faichan Kangri *India* 35°48N 76°34E **243** B7
Broad Sd. *Australia* 22°0S 149°45E **280** C4
Broadalbin *U.S.A.* 43°4N 74°12W **313** C10
Broadback ➞ *Canada* 51°21N 78°52W **298** B4
Broadford *Australia* 37°14S 145°4E **283** D6
Broadhurst Ra. *Australia* 22°30S 122°30E **278** D3
Broadmeadows *Australia* 37°40S 144°55E **128** A1
Broadmoor *U.S.A.* 37°41N 122°29W **136** B2
Broads, The *U.K.* 52°45N 1°30E **168** E9
Broadus *U.S.A.* 45°27N 105°25W **304** D11
Broadview *U.S.A.* 41°51N 87°52W **119** B2
Broadway *New York, U.S.A.* **132** d2
Broager *Denmark* 54°53N 9°40E **163** K3
Broby *Sweden* 56°15N 14°4E **163** H8
Broceni *Latvia* 56°42N 22°32E **184** B9
Brochet *Canada* 57°53N 101°40W **297** B8
Brochet, L. *Canada* 58°36N 101°35W **297** B8
Brock I. *Canada* 77°52N 114°19W **295** B9
Brocken *Germany* 51°47N 10°37E **178** D6
Brocklehurst *Australia* 32°9S 148°38E **283** B8
Brocklesby *Australia* 35°48S 146°40E **283** C7
Brockley *U.K.* 51°27N 0°2W **125** B3
Brockport *U.S.A.* 43°13N 77°56W **312** C7
Brockton *U.S.A.* 42°5N 71°1W **313** D13
Brockville *Canada* 44°35N 75°41W **313** B9
Brockway *Mont., U.S.A.* 47°18N 105°45W **304** C11
Brockway *Pa., U.S.A.* 41°15N 78°47W **312** E6
Brocton *U.S.A.* 42°23N 79°26W **312** D5
Brod *Macedonia* 41°32N 21°17E **202** E5
Brodarevo *Serbia* 43°14N 19°44E **202** C3
Brodeur Pen. *Canada* 72°30N 88°10W **295** C14
Brodhead *U.S.A.* 42°37N 89°22W **310** B7
Brodick *U.K.* 55°35N 5°9W **167** F3
Brodnica *Poland* 53°15N 19°25E **185** E6
Bródno *Poland* 52°17N 21°2E **142** B2
Bródnowski, Kanal *Poland* 52°17N 21°3E **142** B2
Brody *Ukraine* 50°5N 25°10E **177** C13
Broek *Neths.* 52°26N 5°0E **112** A2
Brogan *U.S.A.* 44°15N 117°31W **304** D5
Broglie *France* 49°2N 0°30E **172** C7
Brok *Poland* 52°43N 21°52E **185** F8
Broken Arrow *U.S.A.* 36°3N 95°48W **314** C7
Broken Bow *Nebr., U.S.A.* 41°24N 99°38W **308** E4
Broken Bow *Okla., U.S.A.* 34°2N 94°44W **314** D7
Broken Bow Lake *U.S.A.* 34°9N 94°40W **314** D7
Broken Hill = Kabwe *Zambia* 14°30S 28°29E **269** E2

Broken Hill *Australia* 31°58S 141°29E **282** A4
Broken River Ra. *Australia* 21°0S 148°22E **280** b
Brokind *Sweden* 58°13N 15°42E **163** F9
Brokopondo *Suriname* 5°3N 54°59W **329** B7
Bromberg = Bydgoszcz
Poland 53°10N 18°0E **185** E5
Bromley □ *U.K.* 51°24N 0°2E **125** B4
Bromley Common *U.K.* 51°22N 0°2E **125** B4
Bromma *Sweden* 59°21N 17°55E **139** A1
Bromma ✕ (BMA) *Sweden* 59°21N 17°56E **139** A1
Bromo Tengger Semeru △
Indonesia 7°56S 112°57E **235** D4
Bromölla *Sweden* 56°5N 14°28E **163** H8
Brompton *London, U.K.* **125** c2
Bromsgrove *U.K.* 52°21N 2°2W **169** E5
Bronaugh *U.S.A.* 37°41N 94°28W **310** G2
Brøndby Strand *Denmark* 55°36N 12°25E **118** B2
Brøndbyøster *Denmark* 55°39N 12°26E **118** B2
Brøndbyvester *Denmark* 55°37N 12°23E **118** B2
Brønderslev *Denmark* 57°16N 9°57E **163** G3
Brondesbury *U.K.* 51°32N 0°12W **125** A2
Brong-Ahafo □ *Ghana* 7°50N 2°0W **262** D4
Broni *Italy* 45°4N 9°16E **198** C6
Bronkhorstspruit *S. Africa* 25°46S 28°45E **271** C4
Brønnøya *Norway* 59°51N 10°32E **133** A2
Brønnøysund *Norway* 65°28N 12°14E **160** D15
Brønshøj *Denmark* 55°41N 12°29E **118** A2
Bronson *Fla., U.S.A.* 29°27N 82°39W **317** F7
Bronson *Mich., U.S.A.* 41°52N 85°12W **311** C11
Bronte *Italy* 37°47N 14°50E **201** E7
Bronwood *U.S.A.* 31°50N 84°22W **316** D5
Bronxville *U.S.A.* 40°56N 73°49W **132** A3
Brook Park *U.S.A.* 41°23N 81°48W **312** E4
Brooke's Point *Phil.* 8°47N 117°50E **233** G1
Brookfield *Ill., U.S.A.* 41°48N 87°50W **119** C1
Brookfield *Mo., U.S.A.* 39°47N 93°4W **310** E3
Brookfield *Wis., U.S.A.* 43°4N 88°9W **311** A8
Brookhaven *Georgia,*
U.S.A. 33°52N 84°19W **113** A2
Brookhaven *Miss., U.S.A.* 31°35N 90°26W **315** F9
Brookings *Oreg., U.S.A.* 42°3N 124°17W **304** E1
Brookings *S. Dak., U.S.A.* 44°19N 96°48W **308** C5
Brookland = West Columbia
U.S.A. 33°59N 81°4W **316** B8
Brooklet *U.S.A.* 32°23N 81°40W **316** C8
Brooklin *Canada* 43°55N 78°55W **312** C6
Brookline *U.S.A.* 42°19N 71°8W **116** B2
Brooklyn *N.Z.* 41°18S 174°46E **143** B1
Brooklyn *Western Cape,*
S. Africa 33°54S 18°29E **118** A1
Brooklyn *Iowa, U.S.A.* 41°44N 92°27W **310** C4
Brooklyn *New York, U.S.A.* **132** f3
Brooklyn-Battery Tunnel
New York, U.S.A. **132** f1
Brooklyn Bridge *New York, U.S.A.* **132** f2
Brooklyn Heights *New York, U.S.A.* **132** f2
Brooklyn Park *U.S.A.* 45°6N 93°23W **308** C7
Brookmont *U.S.A.* 38°57N 77°7W **143** B3
Brooks *Canada* 50°35N 111°55W **296** C6
Brooks Range *U.S.A.* 68°0N 152°0W **303** C9
Brookston *U.S.A.* 40°36N 86°52W **311** D10
Brooksville *Fla., U.S.A.* 28°33N 82°23W **317** G7
Brooksville *Ky., U.S.A.* 38°41N 84°4W **311** F12
Brookton *Australia* 32°22S 117°0E **279** F2
Brookville *Ind., U.S.A.* 39°25N 85°1W **311** E12
Brookville *Ohio, U.S.A.* 39°50N 84°24W **311** E12
Brookville *Pa., U.S.A.* 41°10N 79°5W **312** E5
Brookville L. *U.S.A.* 39°28N 85°0W **311** E11
Broom, L. *U.K.* 57°55N 5°15W **167** D3
Broome *Australia* 18°0S 122°15E **278** C3
Broons *France* 48°20N 2°16W **172** D4
Brora *U.K.* 58°0N 3°52W **167** C5
Brora ➜ *U.K.* 58°0N 3°51W **167** C5
Brørup *Denmark* 55°29N 9°1E **163** J2
Brösarp *Sweden* 55°43N 14°6E **163** J8
Brosna ➜ *Ireland* 53°14N 7°58W **166** C4
Brossard *Canada* 45°27N 73°28W **130** B3
Broşteni *Mehedinţi,*
Romania 44°45N 22°59E **182** F7
Broşteni *Suceava, Romania* 47°14N 25°43E **183** C10
Brøsterud *Norway* 60°18N 8°34E **164** D5
Brotas de Macaúbas *Brazil* 12°0S 42°38W **333** D3
Brothers *U.S.A.* 43°49N 120°36W **304** E3
Brothers, The *Yemen* 12°8N 53°10E **249** D6
Brøttum *Norway* 61°2N 10°34E **164** C7
Brou *France* 48°13N 1°11E **172** D8
Brou-sur-Chantereine
France 48°53N 2°37E **134** A4
Brouage *France* 45°52N 1°4W **174** C2
Brough *U.K.* 54°32N 2°18W **168** C5
Brough Hd. *U.K.* 59°8N 3°20W **167** B5
Broughton *U.S.A.* 37°56N 88°27W **311** G8
Broughton Island = Qikiqtarjuaq
Canada 67°33N 63°0W **295** D19
Broumov *Czech Rep.* 50°35N 16°20E **181** A9
Brovary *Ukraine* 50°34N 30°48E **189** G6
Brovst *Denmark* 57°6N 9°31E **163** G3
Brown *Canada* 43°48N 79°14W **141** A3
Brown, L. *Australia* 31°5S 118°15E **279** F2
Brown, Mt. *Australia* 32°30S 138°0E **282** B3
Brown, Pt. *Australia* 32°32S 133°50E **281** E1
Brown City *U.S.A.* 43°13N 82°59W **312** C2
Brown Willy *U.K.* 50°35N 4°37W **169** G3
Brownfield *U.S.A.* 33°11N 102°17W **314** E3
Browning *Ill., U.S.A.* 40°8N 90°22W **310** D6
Browning *Mo., U.S.A.* 40°3N 93°12W **310** D3
Browning *Mont., U.S.A.* 48°34N 113°1W **304** B7
Browns Town *Jamaica* 18°24N 77°22W **320** a
Brownsburg *U.S.A.* 39°51N 86°24W **311** E10
Brownstown *U.S.A.* 38°53N 86°3W **311** F10
Brownsville *Oreg.,*
U.S.A. 44°24N 122°59W **304** D2
Brownsville *Pa., U.S.A.* 40°1N 79°53W **312** F5
Brownsville *Tenn.,*
U.S.A. 35°36N 89°16W **315** D10
Brownsville *Tex., U.S.A.* 25°54N 97°30W **314** J6
Brownsweg *Suriname* 5°5N 55°15W **329** B6
Brownville *U.S.A.* 44°0N 75°59W **313** C9
Brownwood *U.S.A.* 31°43N 98°59W **314** F5
Browse I. *Australia* 14°7S 123°33E **278** B3
Broxton *U.S.A.* 31°38N 82°53W **316** D7
Broyhill Park *U.S.A.* 38°52N 77°12W **143** B2
Bru *Norway* 61°32N 5°11E **164** C2
Bruas *Malaysia* 4°30N 100°47E **237** K3
Bruay-la-Buissière *France* 50°29N 2°33E **173** B9
Bruce *U.S.A.* 30°28N 85°58W **316** E4
Bruce, Mt. *Australia* 22°37S 118°8E **278** D2
Bruce B. *N.Z.* 43°35S 169°42E **285** D4
Bruce Pen. *Canada* 45°0N 81°30W **312** B3
Bruce Peninsula △
Canada 45°14N 81°36W **312** A3
Bruce Rock *Australia* 31°52S 118°8E **279** F2
Bruche ➜ *France* 48°34N 7°43E **173** D14
Bruchsal *Germany* 49°7N 8°35E **179** F4
Bruck an der Leitha
Austria 48°1N 16°47E **181** C9
Bruck an der Mur *Austria* 47°24N 15°16E **180** D8
Brue ➜ *U.K.* 51°13N 2°59W **169** F5
Bruflat *Norway* 60°53N 9°37E **164** D6
Bruges = Brugge *Belgium* 51°13N 3°13E **170** C3
Brugg *Switz.* 47°29N 8°11E **179** H4
Brugge *Belgium* 51°13N 3°13E **170** C3
Brughério *Italy* 45°33N 9°17E **129** A2
Bruin *U.S.A.* 41°3N 79°43W **312** E5
Bruini *India* 29°10N 96°11E **241** A6
Bruit, Pulau *Malaysia* 2°35N 111°20E **235** B4
Brûk, W. el ➜ *Egypt* 30°15N 33°50E **251** H4
Bruksvallarna *Sweden* 62°38N 12°27E **162** B6
Brûlé *Canada* 53°15N 117°58W **296** C5
Brûlé, L. *Canada* 53°35N 64°4W **299** B7
Brûlon *France* 47°58N 0°15W **172** E6
Brumado *Brazil* 14°14S 41°40W **333** D3
Brumado ➜ *Brazil* 14°13S 41°40W **333** D3
Brumath *France* 48°43N 7°40E **173** D14
Brumunddal *Norway* 60°53N 10°56E **164** D7
Brundidge *U.S.A.* 31°43N 85°49W **316** D4
Bruneau *U.S.A.* 42°53N 115°48W **304** E6
Bruneau ➜ *U.S.A.* 42°56N 115°57W **304** E6
Bruneck = Brunico *Italy* 46°48N 11°56E **199** B8
Brunei = Bandar Seri Begawan
Brunei 4°52N 115°0E **235** B4
Brunei ■ *Asia* 4°50N 115°0E **235** B4
Brunflo *Sweden* 63°5N 14°50E **162** A8
Brunico *Italy* 46°48N 11°56E **199** B8
Brünn = Brno *Czech Rep.* 49°10N 16°35E **181** B9
Brunnen *Switz.* 46°59N 8°37E **179** J4
Brunner, L. *N.Z.* 42°37S 171°27E **285** C6
Brunnhóll *Iceland* 64°17N 15°26W **155** C11
Brunnsberg *Sweden* 61°17N 13°56E **162** C8
Brunsbüttel *Germany* 53°53N 9°6E **178** B5
Brunssum *Neths.* 50°57N 5°59E **170** D5
Brunswick = Braunschweig
Germany 52°15N 10°31E **178** C6
Brunswick *Vic., Australia* 37°45S 144°57E **128** A1
Brunswick *Ga., U.S.A.* 31°10N 81°30W **316** D8
Brunswick *Maine, U.S.A.* 43°55N 69°58W **309** D19
Brunswick *Md., U.S.A.* 39°19N 77°38W **309** F15
Brunswick *Mo., U.S.A.* 39°26N 93°8W **310** E3
Brunswick *Ohio, U.S.A.* 41°14N 81°51W **312** E3
Brunswick, Pen. de *Chile* 53°30S 71°30W **336** D2
Brunswick B. *Australia* 15°15S 124°50E **278** C3
Brunswick Junction
Australia 33°15S 115°50E **279** F2
Brunt Ice Shelf *Antarctica* 75°30S 25°0W **151** D2
Bruntál *Czech Rep.* 49°59N 17°27E **181** B10
Brus Laguna *Honduras* 15°47N 84°35W **320** C3
Brusa = Bursa *Turkey* 40°15N 29°5E **203** F13
Brusartsi *Bulgaria* 43°40N 23°5E **202** C7
Brush *U.S.A.* 40°15N 103°37W **304** F12
Brushton *U.S.A.* 44°50N 74°31W **313** B10
Brusio *Switz.* 46°14N 10°8E **179** J6
Brusque *Brazil* 27°5S 49°0W **335** B6
Brussegem *Belgium* 50°56N 4°16E **116** A1
Brussel *Belgium* 50°51N 4°21E **116** A2
Brussel ✕ (BRU) *Belgium* 50°54N 4°29E **116** A2
Brussels = Brussel *Belgium* 50°51N 4°21E **116** A2
Brussels *Canada* 43°44N 81°15W **312** C3
Brusy *Poland* 53°53N 17°43E **184** E4
Bruthen *Australia* 37°42S 147°50E **283** D7
Bruvoll *Norway* 60°27N 11°29E **164** D8
Bruxelles = Brussel
Belgium 50°51N 4°21E **116** A2
Bruyères *France* 48°10N 6°40E **173** D13
Bruz *France* 48°1N 1°46W **172** D5
Bruzzano *Italy* 45°31N 9°10E **129** A2
Brwinów *Poland* 52°9N 20°40E **185** F7
Bry-sur-Marne *France* 48°50N 2°32E **134** A4
Bryagovo *Bulgaria* 41°58N 25°8E **203** E9
Bryan *Ohio, U.S.A.* 41°28N 84°33W **311** C12
Bryan *Tex., U.S.A.* 30°40N 96°22W **314** F6
Bryan, L. *U.S.A.* 28°22N 81°29W **133** B2
Bryan, Mt. *Australia* 33°30S 139°5E **282** B3
Bryanka *Ukraine* 48°32N 38°45E **189** H10
Bryansk *Bryansk, Russia* 53°13N 34°25E **189** F8
Bryansk *Dagestan, Russia* 44°20N 47°10E **191** H8
Bryansk □ *Russia* 53°10N 33°10E **189** F7
Bryanskoye = Bryansk
Russia 44°20N 47°10E **191** H8
Bryanston *S. Africa* 26°4S 28°0E **123** A1
Bryant Park *New York, U.S.A.* **132** c2
Bryce Canyon △ *U.S.A.* 37°30N 112°10W **305** H7
Bryn *Norway* 59°55N 10°27E **133** A1
Bryne *Norway* 58°44N 5°38E **164** F2
Bryson City *U.S.A.* 35°26N 83°27W **315** D13
Bryukhovetskaya *Russia* 45°48N 39°0E **189** K10
Brza Palanka *Serbia* 44°28N 22°27E **202** B6
Brzeg *Poland* 50°52N 17°30E **185** H4
Brzeg Dolny *Poland* 51°16N 16°41E **185** G3
Brześć Kujawski *Poland* 52°36N 18°55E **185** F5
Brzešč nad Bugiem = Brest
Belarus 52°10N 23°40E **177** B12
Brzesko *Poland* 49°59N 20°34E **185** J7
Brzeziny *Łódzkie, Poland* 51°49N 19°42E **185** G6
Brzeziny *Warszawa, Poland* 52°19N 21°2E **142** B2
Brzozów *Poland* 49°41N 22°3E **185** J9
Bsharri *Lebanon* 34°15N 36°0E **250** D7
Bû al Ḥîdân, W. ➜ *Libya* 27°25N 19°22E **258** C3
Bû Athlah *Libya* 30°9N 15°39E **258** B3
Bû Baqarah *U.A.E.* 25°35N 56°25E **247** E8
Bu Craa *W. Sahara* 26°45N 12°50W **260** C2
Bû Ḥasā *U.A.E.* 23°30N 53°20E **247** F7
Bû Tummayyim, W. ➜
Libya 26°56N 19°13E **258** C3
Bua *Fiji* 16°48S 178°37E **287** A2
Bua *Sweden* 57°14N 12°7E **163** G6
Bua ➜ *Malaysia* 12°45S 34°16E **269** E3
Bua Yai *Thailand* 15°33N 102°26E **236** E4
Bu'aale *Somali Rep.* 1°3N 42°35E **267** D5
Buad I. *Phil.* 11°40N 124°51E **233** F5
Buala *Solomon Is.* 8°10S 159°35E **287** M10
Buan *S. Korea* 35°44N 126°44E **224** E3
Buapinang *Indonesia* 4°40S 121°30E **231** E6
Buatan *Indonesia* 0°44N 101°49E **234** B2
Buayan = General Santos
Phil. 6°5N 125°14E **233** H5
Buba *Guinea-Biss.* 11°40N 14°59W **262** C2
Bubali Bird Sanctuary
Aruba 12°33N 70°2W **322** f
Bubanda
Dem. Rep. of the Congo 4°14N 19°38E **264** B3
Bubanza *Burundi* 3°6S 29°23E **268** C2
Bubaque *Guinea-Biss.* 11°16N 15°51W **262** C1
Bube *Ethiopia* 8°46N 35°48E **257** F4
Bubeneč *Czech Rep.* 50°6N 14°24E **135** B2
Bubi ➜ *Zimbabwe* 22°20S 31°7E **271** B5
Būbiyān *Kuwait* 29°45N 48°15E **247** D6
Buc *France* 48°46N 2°7E **134** B1
Buca *Fiji* 16°38S 179°52E **287** A2
Buca *Turkey* 38°22N 27°11E **205** C9
Bucaco *Angola* 11°26S 20°10E **265** E4
Bucak *Turkey* 37°28N 30°36E **205** D12
Bucakkışla *Turkey* 36°57N 33°1E **250** B4
Bucaramanga *Colombia* 7°0N 73°0W **328** B3
Bucas Grande I. *Phil.* 9°40N 125°57E **233** G5
Bucasia *Australia* 21°2S 149°10E **280** b
Bucay *Phil.* 17°32N 120°43E **232** C3
Buccaneer Arch. *Australia* 16°7S 123°20E **278** C3
Buccino *Italy* 40°38N 15°22E **201** B8
Buccoo Reef *Trin. & Tob.* 11°10N 60°51W **323** J16
Bucecea *Romania* 47°47N 26°28E **183** C11
Bucegi △ *Romania* 45°25N 25°25E **183** E10
Buchach *Ukraine* 49°5N 25°25E **177** D13
Buchan *Vic., Australia* 37°30S 148°12E **283** D8
Buchan *Aberds., U.K.* 57°32N 2°21W **167** D6
Buchan Ness *U.K.* 57°29N 1°46W **167** D7
Buchanan *Sask., Canada* 51°40N 102°45W **297** C8
Buchanan *Liberia* 5°57N 10°2W **262** D2
Buchanan *Ga., U.S.A.* 33°48N 85°11W **316** B4
Buchanan *Mich., U.S.A.* 41°50N 86°22W **311** C10
Buchanan, L. *Queens.,*
Australia 21°35S 145°52E **280** C4
Buchanan, L. *W. Austral.,*
Australia 25°33S 123°2E **279** E3
Buchanan, L. *Tex., U.S.A.* 30°45N 98°25W **314** F5
Buchanan Cr. ➜
Australia 19°13S 136°33E **280** B2
Buchans *Canada* 48°50N 56°52W **299** C8
Bucharest = Bucureşti
Romania 44°27N 26°10E **183** F11
Buchen *Germany* 49°32N 9°20E **179** F5
Buchenhain *Germany* 48°1N 11°29E **131** B1
Bucheon *S. Korea* 37°28N 126°45E **224** D3
Buchholz *Berlin, Germany* 52°36N 13°25E **115** A3
Buchholz *Niedersachsen,*
Germany 53°19N 9°52E **178** B5
Buchloe *Germany* 48°1N 10°44E **179** G6
Buchon, Pt. *U.S.A.* 35°15N 120°54W **306** K6
Buciumi *Romania* 47°3N 23°4E **182** C8
Buck Hill Falls *U.S.A.* 41°11N 75°16W **313** E9
Bückeburg *Germany* 52°16N 9°7E **178** C5
Buckeye Lake *U.S.A.* 39°55N 82°29W **312** G2
Buckhannon *U.S.A.* 39°0N 80°8W **309** F13
Buckhaven *U.K.* 56°11N 3°3W **167** E5
Buckhead *U.S.A.* 33°51N 84°24W **113** A2
Buckhorn L. *Canada* 44°29N 78°23W **312** B6
Buckie *U.K.* 57°41N 2°58W **167** D6
Buckingham *Qué., Canada* 45°37N 75°24W **298** C4
Buckingham *Bucks., U.K.* 51°59N 0°57W **169** F7
Buckingham B. *Australia* 12°10S 135°40E **280** A2
Buckingham Canal *India* 14°0N 80°5E **245** H5
Buckingham Fountain *Chicago, U.S.A.* **119** d2
Buckingham Palace *London, U.K.* **125** b3
Buckinghamshire □ *U.K.* 51°53N 0°55W **169** F7
Buckland *U.S.A.* 65°59N 161°8W **303** D7
Buckle Hd. *Australia* 14°26S 127°52E **278** B4
Buckleboo *Australia* 32°54S 136°12E **282** B2
Buckley *Flints., U.K.* 53°10N 3°5W **168** D4
Buckley *Ill., U.S.A.* 40°36N 88°2W **311** D8
Buckley ➜ *Australia* 20°10S 138°49E **280** C2
Bucklin *Kans., U.S.A.* 37°33N 99°38W **308** G4
Bucklin *Mo., U.S.A.* 39°47N 92°53W **310** E4
Buckow *Germany* 52°25N 13°26E **115** B3
Bucks L. *U.S.A.* 39°54N 121°12W **306** F5
Bucktown *U.S.A.* 30°1N 90°8W **311** G10
Buco Zau *Angola* 4°46S 12°33E **265** C2
Bucquoy *France* 50°9N 2°43E **173** B9
Bucureşti *Romania* 44°27N 26°10E **183** F11
Bucureşti Otopeni ✕ (OTP)
Romania 44°30N 26°11E **183** F11
Bucyrus *U.S.A.* 40°48N 82°59W **311** D14
Bud *Norway* 62°55N 6°55E **164** B3
Bud Bud *Somali Rep.* 4°11N 46°28E **267** D6
Buda *Hungary* 47°30N 19°2E **117** A2
Buda Castle = Budavári palota
Budapest, Hungary **117** b2
Budacu, Vf. *Romania* 47°7N 25°41E **183** C10
Budafok *Hungary* 47°25N 19°2E **117** B2
Budalin *Burma* 22°20N 95°10E **241** D5
Budaörs *Hungary* 47°27N 18°57E **117** B1
Budapest *Hungary* 47°29N 19°3E **117** B2
Budapest □ *Hungary* 47°29N 19°5E **182** C4
Budapest ✕ (BUD)
Hungary 47°26N 19°14E **117** B3
Budatétény *Hungary* 47°25N 19°1E **117** B2
Budaun *India* 28°5N 79°10E **243** E8
Budavári palota *Budapest, Hungary* **117** b2
Budawang △ *Australia* 35°10S 150°12E **283** C9
Budd Coast *Antarctica* 68°0S 112°0E **151** C8
Buddenbrock = Brodnica
Poland 53°15N 19°25E **185** E6
Budderoo △ *Australia* 35°40S 150°41E **283** C9
Budding *Denmark* 55°44N 12°30E **118** A3
Buddusò *Italy* 40°35N 9°15E **200** B2
Bude *U.K.* 50°49N 4°34W **169** G3
Budennovsk *Russia* 44°50N 44°10E **191** H7
Budeşti *Romania* 44°13N 26°30E **183** F11
Budeyi *Ukraine* 48°3N 29°16E **183** B14
Budge Budge = Baj Baj
India 22°30N 88°5E **243** H13
Budgewoi *Australia* 33°13S 151°34E **283** B9
Búðardalur *Iceland* 65°7N 21°46W **155** B5
Budia *Spain* 40°38N 2°46W **196** E2
Büdingen *Germany* 50°16N 9°7E **179** E5
Budjala
Dem. Rep. of the Congo 2°50N 19°40E **264** B3
Budo-Sungai Padi △
Thailand 6°19N 101°42E **237** J3
Budokan *Tokyo, Japan* **140** a4
Budoni *Italy* 40°40N 9°45E **200** B2
Búdrio *Italy* 44°32N 11°32E **199** D8
Büdszentmihály = Tiszavasvári
Hungary 47°58N 21°18E **182** C6
Budva *Montenegro* 42°17N 18°50E **202** D2
Budweis = České Budějovice
Czech Rep. 48°55N 14°25E **180** C7
Budyonnovka = Novoazovsk
Ukraine 47°15N 38°4E **189** J10
Budzyń *Poland* 52°54N 16°59E **185** F3
Bue *Norway* 58°40N 5°58E **164** F2
Buea *Cameroon* 4°10N 9°9E **263** E6
Buela *Angola* 5°54S 14°50E **267** D6
Buellton *U.S.A.* 34°37N 120°12W **307** L6
Buena Esperanza
Argentina 34°45S 65°15W **334** C2
Buena Park *U.S.A.* 33°52N 117°59W **307** M9
Buena Vista *Bolivia* 17°27S 63°40W **331** D5
Buena Vista *Curaçao* 12°8N 68°57W **322** g
Buena Vista *Solomon Is.* 8°52S 160°3E **287** M11
Buena Vista *Colo., U.S.A.* 38°51N 106°8W **304** G10
Buena Vista *Ga., U.S.A.* 32°19N 84°31W **316** C5
Buena Vista *Va., U.S.A.* 37°44N 79°21W **309** G14
Buena Vista Lake Bed
U.S.A. 35°12N 119°18W **307** K7
Buenaventura *Colombia* 3°53N 77°4W **328** C2
Buenaventura *Chihuahua,*
Mexico 29°51N 107°29W **318** B3
Buenaventura, B. de
Colombia 3°48N 77°17W **328** C2
Buenavista *Agusan del N.,*
Phil. 8°59N 125°24E **233** G5
Buenavista *Quezon, Phil.* 13°35N 122°34E **232** E4
Buendia, Embalse de *Spain* 40°25N 2°43W **196** E2
Buenópolis *Brazil* 17°54S 44°11W **333** E3
Buenos Aires *Argentina* 34°36S 58°22W **117** B2
Buenos Aires *Colombia* 1°36N 73°18W **328** C3
Buenos Aires *Costa Rica* 9°10N 83°20W **320** E3
Buenos Aires □ *Argentina* 36°30S 60°0W **334** D4
Buenos Aires, L.
Argentina 46°35S 72°30W **336** C2
Buenos Aires Ezeiza ✕ (EZE)
Argentina 34°49S 58°32W **117** C1
Buenos Ayres *Trin. & Tob.* 10°6N 61°4W **323** t
Buesaco *Colombia* 1°23N 77°9W **328** C2
Bufalotta *Italy* 41°59N 12°33E **136** B2
Buff Bay *Jamaica* 18°14N 76°40W **320** a
Buffalo *Mo., U.S.A.* 37°39N 93°6W **310** G3
Buffalo *N.Y., U.S.A.* 42°53N 78°53W **312** D6
Buffalo *Okla., U.S.A.* 36°50N 99°38W **314** C5
Buffalo *S. Dak., U.S.A.* 45°35N 103°33W **308** C2
Buffalo *Wyo., U.S.A.* 44°21N 106°42W **304** D10
Buffalo ➜ *Alta., Canada* 60°5N 115°5W **296** A5
Buffalo ➜ *S. Africa* 28°43S 30°37E **271** C5
Buffalo △ *U.S.A.* 36°14N 92°36W **314** C8
Buffalo Head Hills
Canada 57°25N 115°55W **296** B5
Buffalo L. *Alta., Canada* 52°27N 112°54W **296** C6
Buffalo L. *N.W.T., Canada* 60°12N 115°25W **296** A5
Buffalo Narrows *Canada* 55°51N 108°29W **297** B7
Buffalo Springs ⌂ *Kenya* 0°32N 37°35E **268** B4
Buffels ➜ *S. Africa* 29°36S 17°3E **270** C2
Buford *U.S.A.* 34°10N 84°0W **315** D12
Bug = Buh ➜ *Ukraine* 46°59N 31°58E **189** J6
Bug ➜ *Poland* 52°31N 21°5E **185** F8
Buga *Colombia* 4°0N 76°15W **328** C2
Bugala I. *Uganda* 0°40S 32°20E **268** C3
Buganda *Uganda* 0°0 31°30E **268** C3
Buganga *Uganda* 0°3S 32°0E **268** C3
Bugasong *Phil.* 11°3N 122°4E **233** F4
Bugeat *France* 45°36N 1°55E **174** C5
Bugel, Tanjung *Indonesia* 6°26S 111°3E **235** D4
Bûğer *Spain* 39°45N 2°59E **206** B3
Bugibba *Malta* 35°57N 14°25E **206** F7
Bugio *Portugal* 38°39N 9°18W **126** B1
Bugojno *Bos.-H.* 44°2N 17°25E **182** F2
Bugsuk I. *Phil.* 8°12N 117°18E **233** G1
Buguey *Phil.* 18°17N 121°50E **232** B3
Buguias *Phil.* 16°43N 120°50E **232** C3
Bugulma *Russia* 54°33N 52°48E **186** D9
Buguma *Nigeria* 4°42N 6°55E **263** E6
Bugungu ⌂ *Uganda* 2°17N 31°50E **268** B3
Buguruslan *Russia* 53°39N 52°26E **186** D9
Buh ➜ *Ukraine* 46°59N 31°58E **189** J6
Buharkent *Turkey* 37°58N 28°44E **205** D10
Buheirat-Murrat-el-Kubra
Egypt 30°18N 32°26E **256** H8
Buhera *Zimbabwe* 19°18S 31°29E **271** A5
Bühl *Baden-W., Germany* 48°40N 8°8E **179** G4
Buhl *Idaho, U.S.A.* 42°36N 114°46W **304** E6
Buhuşi *Romania* 46°41N 26°45E **183** D11
Bui △ *Ghana* 8°21N 2°21W **262** D4
Buiksloot *Neths.* 52°24N 4°55E **112** A2
Builth Wells *U.K.* 52°9N 3°25W **169** E4
Buin *Papua N. G.* 6°48S 155°42E **287** L8
Buinsk *Russia* 55°0N 48°18E **190** C9
Buique *Brazil* 8°37S 37°9W **332** C4
Buir Nur *Mongolia* 47°50N 117°42E **219** B12
Buis-les-Baronnies *France* 44°17N 5°16E **175** D9
Buitenveldert *Neths.* 52°20N 4°53E **112** B2
Buitenzorg = Bogor
Indonesia 6°36S 106°48E **234** D3
Buitrago del Lozoya *Spain* 40°58N 3°38W **194** E7
Buizingen *Belgium* 50°44N 4°15E **116** B1
Bujalance *Spain* 37°54N 4°23W **195** H6
Bujanovac *Serbia* 42°28N 21°44E **202** D5
Bujaraloz *Spain* 41°29N 0°10W **196** D4
Buje *Croatia* 45°24N 13°39E **199** C10
Buji *China* 22°37N 114°5E **219** a
Bujumbura *Burundi* 3°16S 29°18E **268** C2
Bük *Hungary* 47°22N 16°45E **182** C1
Buk *Poland* 52°21N 16°30E **185** F3
Buka I. *Papua N. G.* 5°10S 154°35E **286** C8
Bukachacha *Russia* 52°55N 116°50E **215** D12
Bukama
Dem. Rep. of the Congo 9°10S 25°50E **269** D2
Bukavu
Dem. Rep. of the Congo 2°20S 28°52E **268** C2
Bukene *Tanzania* 4°15S 32°48E **268** C3
Bukhansan *S. Korea* 37°38N 126°58E **137** B1
Bukhara = Buxoro
Uzbekistan 39°48N 64°25E **216** E6
Bukhoro = Buxoro
Uzbekistan 39°48N 64°25E **216** E6
Bukhtarma Res. = Zaysan Köli
Kazakhstan 48°0N 83°0E **217** C10
Bukidnon □ *Phil.* 8°0N 125°0E **233** G5
Bukima *Tanzania* 1°50S 33°25E **268** C3
Bukit Baka Bukit Raya △
Indonesia 0°43S 112°40E **235** C4
Bukit Barisan Selatan △
Indonesia 5°8S 104°4E **234** D2
Bukit Bendera *Malaysia* 5°25N 100°15E **237** c
Bukit Duabelas △ *Indonesia* 2°3S 102°48E **234** C2
Bukit Mertajam *Malaysia* 5°22N 100°28E **237** c
Bukit Nil *Malaysia* 1°22N 104°12E **237** d
Bukit Panjang *Singapore* 1°23N 103°46E **237** d
Bukit Panjang Nature Reserve
Singapore 1°22N 103°45E **138** A2
Bukit Tengah *Malaysia* 5°22N 100°25E **237** c
Bukit Tigapuluh △
Indonesia 1°15S 102°25E **234** C2
Bukit Timah Nature Reserve
Singapore 1°20N 103°47E **138** A2
Bukitkemuning *Indonesia* 4°51S 104°33E **234** C2
Bukittinggi *Indonesia* 0°20S 100°20E **234** C2
Bükk *Hungary* 48°0N 20°30E **182** B5
Bukkapatnam *India* 14°14N 77°46E **245** G3
Bükki △ *Hungary* 48°3N 20°30E **182** B5
Bukoba *Tanzania* 1°20S 31°49E **268** C3
Bukom, Pulau *Singapore* 1°14N 103°46E **138** B2
Bukuru *Nigeria* 9°42N 8°48E **263** D6
Bukuya *Uganda* 0°40N 31°52E **268** B3
Būl, Kuh-e *Iran* 30°48N 52°45E **247** D7
Bula *Guinea-Biss.* 12°7N 15°43W **262** C1
Bula *Indonesia* 3°6S 130°30E **231** E8
Bula *Camarines S., Phil.* 13°28N 123°16E **232** E4
Bula-Atumba *Angola* 8°41S 14°52E **265** D2
Bulabog-Putian △ *Phil.* 11°2N 122°4E **233** F4
Bulacan □ *Phil.* 15°0N 121°5E **232** D3
Bülach *Switz.* 47°31N 8°32E **179** H4
Bülaevo *Kazakhstan* 54°54N 70°26E **217** B8
Bulahdelah *Australia* 32°23S 152°13E **283** B10
Bulalacao *Phil.* 12°31N 121°26E **232** E3
Bulan *Phil.* 12°40N 123°52E **232** E4
Bulancak *Turkey* 40°56N 38°14E **213** B8
Búland *Iceland* 63°46N 18°30W **155** D8
Bulandshahr *India* 28°28N 77°51E **242** E7
Bulanık *Turkey* 39°4N 42°14E **213** C10
Bûlâq *El Khârga, Egypt* 25°10N 30°38E **256** B3
Bûlâq *El Qâhira, Egypt* 30°3N 31°14E **117** A2
Bulawayo *Zimbabwe* 20°7S 28°32E **269** G2
Buldan *Turkey* 38°2N 28°50E **205** C10
Buldana *India* 20°30N 76°18E **244** D3
Buldir I. *U.S.A.* 52°21N 175°56E **303** K1
Buldon *Phil.* 7°33N 124°25E **233** H5
Bule *Phil.* 14°26N 121°2E **127** C2
Bulenga *Ghana* 9°56N 2°12W **262** D4
Bulgan *Mongolia* 48°45N 103°34E **218** B9
Bulgar *Russia* 54°57N 49°4E **190** C9
Bulgaria ■ *Europe* 42°35N 25°30E **203** D9
Bulgheria, Monte *Italy* 40°4N 15°26E **201** B8
Bulgurca *Turkey* 38°9N 27°9E **205** C9
Bulhale *Somali Rep.* 5°20N 46°29E **267** C6
Bulhar *Somali Rep.* 10°25N 44°30E **267** B6
Buli, Teluk *Indonesia* 0°48N 128°25E **231** D7
Buliluyan, C. *Phil.* 8°20N 117°15E **233** G1
Bulim *Singapore* 1°22N 103°43E **138** A2
Bulki *Ethiopia* 6°11N 36°31E **257** F4
Bulkley ➜ *Canada* 55°15N 127°40W **296** B3
Bull Head *Jamaica* 18°10N 77°16W **320** a
Bull Savanna *Jamaica* 17°53N 77°35W **320** a
Bull Shoals L. *U.S.A.* 36°22N 92°35W **314** C8
Bullaque ➜ *Spain* 38°59N 4°17W **195** G6
Bullard *U.S.A.* 32°38N 83°30W **316** C6
Bullas *Spain* 38°2N 1°40W **197** G3
Bulle *Switz.* 46°37N 7°3E **179** J3
Bullen Park *Australia* 37°46S 145°4E **128** A2
Bullenbaai *Curaçao* 12°11N 69°2W **322** g
Buller ➜ *N.Z.* 41°44S 171°36E **285** B6
Buller, Mt. *Australia* 37°10S 146°28E **283** D7
Buller Gorge *N.Z.* 41°40S 172°10E **285** B7
Bulleringa △ *Australia* 17°39S 143°56E **280** B3
Bullhead City *U.S.A.* 35°8N 114°32W **307** K12
Bulli *Australia* 34°15S 150°57E **283** C9
Büllingen *Belgium* 50°25N 6°16E **170** D6
Bullock Creek *Australia* 17°43S 144°31E **280** B3
Bulloo ➜ *Australia* 28°43S 142°30E **281** D3
Bulloo L. *Australia* 28°43S 142°25E **281** D3
Bulls *N.Z.* 40°10S 175°24E **284** G4
Bully-les-Mines *France* 50°27N 2°44E **173** B9
Bulman *Australia* 13°39S 134°20E **280** A1
Bulnes *Chile* 36°42S 72°19W **334** D1
Bulo Gheduudo *Somali Rep.* 2°52N 43°1E **267** D5
Bulolo *Papua N. G.* 7°10S 146°40E **286** D4
Bulongo
Dem. Rep. of the Congo 4°45S 21°30E **265** C4
Bulqizë *Albania* 41°30N 20°21E **202** E4
Bulsar = Valsad *India* 20°40N 72°58E **244** D1
Bultfontein *S. Africa* 28°18S 26°10E **270** C4
Buluan *Phil.* 6°44N 124°47E **233** H5
Buluan, L. *Phil.* 6°40N 124°49E **233** H5
Bulukumba *Indonesia* 5°33S 120°11E **231** F6
Bulun *Russia* 70°37N 127°30E **215** B13
Bulungkol *China* 38°36N 74°58E **217** E8
Bulungu *Bandundu,*
Dem. Rep. of the Congo 4°33S 18°36E **265** C3
Bulungu *Kasai-Occ.,*
Dem. Rep. of the Congo 6°4S 21°54E **265** D4
Bulusan *Phil.* 12°45N 124°8E **232** E5
Bulusan Vol. *Phil.* 12°46N 124°3E **232** E5
Bumba *Bandundu,*
Dem. Rep. of the Congo 6°58S 19°19E **265** D3
Bumba *Équateur,*
Dem. Rep. of the Congo 2°13N 22°30E **264** B4
Bumbah, Khalīj *Libya* 32°20N 23°15E **258** B4
Bumbeşti-Jiu *Romania* 45°10N 23°24E **183** E8
Bumbiri I. *Tanzania* 1°40S 31°55E **268** C3
Bumbuna *S. Leone* 9°2N 11°49W **262** D2
Bumhkang *Burma* 26°51N 97°40E **241** B6
Bumhpa Bum *Burma* 26°51N 97°14E **241** B6
Bumi ➜ *Zimbabwe* 17°0S 28°20E **269** F2
Bumtang ➜ *Bhutan* 26°56N 90°53E **241** B3
Bumthang = Jakar Dzong
Bhutan 27°33N 90°43E **241** B3
Buna *Dem. Rep. of the Congo* 3°14S 18°59E **264** C3
Buna *North Eastern, Kenya* 2°58N 39°30E **268** B4
Buna *Papua N. G.* 8°42S 148°27E **286** E5
Bunaken *Indonesia* 1°37N 124°46E **231** D6
Bunama *Papua N. G.* 10°9S 151°9E **286** F6
Bunawan *Phil.* 8°12N 125°57E **233** G5
Bunazi *Tanzania* 1°3S 31°23E **268** C3
Bunbury *Australia* 33°20S 115°35E **279** F2
Bunclody *Ireland* 52°39N 6°40W **166** D5
Buncrana *Ireland* 55°8N 7°27W **166** A4
Bund, The *China* 31°14N 121°30E **138** B1
Bunda *Dem. Rep. of the Congo* 4°58S 14°29E **265** C3
Bundaberg *Australia* 24°54S 152°22E **281** C5
Bundanoon *Australia* 34°40S 150°16E **283** C9
Bünde *Germany* 52°11N 8°35E **178** C4
Bundestag = Reichstag *Berlin, Germany* **115** a3
Bundey ➜ *Australia* 21°46S 135°37E **280** C2
Bundi *India* 25°30N 75°35E **242** G6
Bundjalung △ *Australia* 29°16S 153°21E **281** D5
Bundoora North *Australia* 37°41S 145°2E **128** A2
Bundoora Park *Australia* 37°42S 145°2E **128** A2
Bundoran *Ireland* 54°28N 8°16W **166** B3
Bundukia *Sudan* 5°14N 30°55E **257** F3
Bundure *Australia* 35°10S 146°1E **283** C7
Bung Kan *Thailand* 18°23N 103°37E **236** C4
Bunga ➜ *Nigeria* 11°23N 9°56E **263** C6
Bungalaut, Selat *Indonesia* 2°0S 99°25E **234** C1
Bungay *U.K.* 52°27N 1°28E **169** E9
Bungendore *Australia* 35°14S 149°30E **283** C8
Bungil Cr. ➜ *Australia* 27°5S 149°5E **281** D4
Bungle Bungle = Purnululu △
Australia 17°20S 128°20E **278** C4
Bungo *Angola* 7°26S 15°33E **265** D3
Bungo, Gunung *Malaysia* 1°16N 110°9E **235** B4
Bungo-Suidō *Japan* 33°0N 132°15E **222** E4
Bungoma *Kenya* 0°34N 34°34E **268** B3
Bungotakada *Japan* 33°35N 131°25E **222** D3
Bungu *Tanzania* 7°35S 39°0E **268** D4
Bunia *Dem. Rep. of the Congo* 1°35N 30°20E **268** B3
Bunianga
Dem. Rep. of the Congo 3°28S 20°11E **264** C4
Bunji *Pakistan* 35°45N 74°40E **243** B6
Bunker Hill *Ill., U.S.A.* 39°3N 89°57W **310** E7
Bunker Hill *Ind., U.S.A.* 40°40N 86°6W **311** D10
Bunker Hill Memorial
U.S.A. 42°22N 71°4W **116** A2
Bunker I. *Pakistan* 24°48N 66°57E **123** B1
Bunkie *U.S.A.* 30°57N 92°11W **314** F8
Bunkyō *Japan* 35°42N 139°45E **140** A3
Bunnefjorden *Norway* 59°50N 10°44E **133** A3
Bunnell *U.S.A.* 29°28N 81°16W **317** F8
Bunnythorpe *N.Z.* 40°16S 175°39E **284** G4
Buñol *Spain* 39°25N 0°47W **197** F4
Bunsuru ➜ *Nigeria* 13°21N 6°23E **263** C5
Buntok *Indonesia* 1°40S 114°58E **235** C4
Bununu Dass *Nigeria* 10°5N 9°31E **263** C6
Bununu Kasa *Nigeria* 9°51N 9°32E **263** D6
Bunya Mts. △ *Australia* 26°51S 151°34E **281** D5
Bünyan *Turkey* 38°51N 35°51E **212** C6
Bunyola *Spain* 39°41N 2°42E **206** B3
Bunyu *Indonesia* 3°35N 117°50E **235** B5
Bunza *Nigeria* 12°8N 4°0E **263** C5
Bunzlau = Bolesławiec
Poland 51°17N 15°37E **185** G2
Buol *Indonesia* 1°15N 121°32E **231** D6
Buon Brieng *Vietnam* 13°9N 108°12E **236** F7
Buon Ho *Vietnam* 12°57N 108°18E **236** F7
Buon Ma Thuot *Vietnam* 12°40N 108°3E **236** F7
Buona Vista Park
Singapore 1°16N 103°47E **138** B2
Buong Long *Cambodia* 13°44N 106°59E **236** F6
Buorkhaya, Mys *Russia* 71°50N 132°40E **215** B14
Buqayq *Si. Arabia* 26°0N 49°45E **247** E6
Buqbuq *Egypt* 31°29N 25°29E **256** A2
Bur Acaba = Buurhakaba
Somali Rep. 3°12N 44°20E **267** D5
Bûr Fuad *Egypt* 31°15N 32°20E **256** H8
Bûr Safâga *Egypt* 26°43N 33°57E **246** E2
Bûr Sa'îd *Egypt* 31°16N 32°18E **256** H8
Bûr Sûdân *Sudan* 19°32N 37°9E **256** D4
Bûr Taufiq *Egypt* 29°54N 32°32E **256** J8
Bura *Kenya* 1°4S 39°58E **268** C4
Buraan *Somali Rep.* 10°14N 48°44E **267** B6
Burakin *Australia* 30°31S 117°10E **279** F2
Buram *Sudan* 10°51N 25°9E **257** E2
Buran = Buraan
Somali Rep. 10°14N 48°44E **267** B6
Burang *China* 30°15N 81°10E **218** E5
Burao = Burco *Somali Rep.* 9°32N 45°32E **267** C6
Burāq *Syria* 33°11N 36°29E **250** E7
Burauen *Phil.* 10°58N 124°53E **233** F5
Buraydah *Si. Arabia* 26°20N 43°59E **246** E5
Burbank *Calif., U.S.A.* 34°12N 118°18W **126** A3
Burbank *Ill., U.S.A.* 41°44N 87°46W **119** C2
Burç *Turkey* 36°59N 37°8E **250** B6
Burcher *Australia* 33°30S 147°16E **283** B7
Burco *Somali Rep.* 9°32N 45°32E **267** C6
Burda *India* 25°50N 77°35E **242** G7
Burdekin ➜ *Australia* 19°38S 147°25E **280** B4
Burden, L. *U.S.A.* 28°27N 81°33W **133** B1
Burdeos *Phil.* 14°50N 121°58E **232** D4
Burdeos B. *Phil.* 14°44N 122°6E **232** D4
Burdur *Turkey* 37°45N 30°17E **205** D12
Burdur □ *Turkey* 37°45N 30°0E **205** D12
Burdur Gölü *Turkey* 37°44N 30°10E **205** D12
Burdwan = Barddhaman
India 23°14N 87°39E **243** H12
Burdwood Bank *Atl. Oc.* 54°0S 59°0W **152** M6
Bure *Gojam, Ethiopia* 10°40N 37°4E **257** E4
Bure *Ilubabor, Ethiopia* 8°19N 35°8E **257** F4
Bure ➜ *U.K.* 52°38N 1°43E **168** E9
Büren *Germany* 51°33N 8°35E **178** D4
Bureya ➜ *Russia* 49°27N 129°30E **215** E13
Burford *Canada* 43°7N 80°27W **312** C4
Burg *Germany* 52°16N 11°51E **178** C7
Burg auf Fehmarn
Germany 54°28N 11°9E **178** A7
Burg el Arab *Egypt* 30°54N 29°32E **256** H6
Burg et Tuyur *Sudan* 20°55N 27°56E **256** C2
Burg Stargard *Germany* 53°29N 13°18E **178** B9
Burgas *Bulgaria* 42°33N 27°29E **203** D11
Burgas □ *Bulgaria* 42°30N 27°29E **203** D11
Burgaski Zaliv *Bulgaria* 42°30N 27°39E **203** D11
Burgdorf *Niedersachsen,*
Germany 52°27N 10°1E **178** C6
Burgdorf *Switz.* 47°3N 7°37E **179** H3
Burgenland □ *Austria* 47°20N 16°20E **181** D9
Burgeo *Canada* 47°37N 57°38W **299** C8
Burgersdorp *S. Africa* 31°0S 26°20E **270** D4
Burgess, Mt. *Australia* 30°50S 121°5E **279** F3
Burghausen *Germany* 48°9N 12°49E **179** G8
Burghead *U.K.* 57°43N 3°30W **167** D5
Búrgio *Italy* 37°36N 13°17E **200** E6
Burglengenfeld *Germany* 49°12N 12°2E **179** F8
Burgohondo *Spain* 40°26N 4°47W **194** E6
Burgos *Ilocos N., Phil.* 18°31N 120°39E **232** B3
Burgos *Pangasinan, Phil.* 16°4N 119°52E **232** C2
Burgos *Spain* 42°21N 3°41W **194** C7
Burgos □ *Spain* 42°21N 3°42W **194** C7
Burgstädt *Germany* 50°54N 12°49E **178** E8
Burgsvik *Sweden* 57°3N 18°19E **163** G12
Burguillos del Cerro *Spain* 38°23N 6°35W **195** G4
Burgundy = Bourgogne □
France 47°0N 4°50E **173** F11
Burhaniye *Turkey* 39°30N 26°58E **205** B8
Burhanpur *India* 21°18N 76°14E **244** D3
Burhi Gandak ➜ *India* 25°20N 86°37E **243** G12
Burhner ➜ *India* 22°43N 80°31E **243** H9
Buri Pen. *Eritrea* 15°25N 39°55E **257** D4
Burias I. *Phil.* 12°55N 123°5E **232** E4
Burias Pass. *Phil.* 13°0N 123°15E **232** E4
Burica, Pta. *Costa Rica* 8°3N 82°51W **320** E3
Burien *U.S.A.* 47°28N 122°20W **306** C4
Burigi, L. *Tanzania* 2°2S 31°22E **268** C3
Burigi ⌂ *Tanzania* 2°20S 31°6E **268** C3
Burin *Canada* 47°1N 55°14W **299** C8
Buriram *Thailand* 15°0N 103°0E **236** E4
Buriti Alegre *Brazil* 18°9S 49°3W **333** E2
Buriti Bravo *Brazil* 5°50S 43°50W **332** C3
Buriti dos Lopes *Brazil* 3°10S 41°52W **332** B3
Burji *Ethiopia* 5°29N 37°51E **257** F4
Burkburnett *U.S.A.* 34°6N 98°34W **314** D5
Burke ➜ *Australia* 23°12S 139°33E **280** C2
Burke Chan. *Canada* 52°10N 127°30W **296** C3
Burketown *Australia* 17°45S 139°33E **280** B2
Burkina Faso ■ *Africa* 12°0N 1°0W **262** C4
Burk's Falls *Canada* 45°37N 79°24W **298** C4
Burlada *Spain* 42°49N 1°36W **196** C3
Burleigh Falls *Canada* 44°33N 78°12W **312** B6
Burley *U.S.A.* 42°32N 113°48W **304** E7
Burlingame *U.S.A.* 37°35N 122°21W **306** H4
Burlington *Ont., Canada* 43°18N 79°45W **312** C5
Burlington *Colo., U.S.A.* 39°18N 102°16W **304** G12
Burlington *Iowa, U.S.A.* 40°49N 91°14W **310** D5
Burlington *Kans., U.S.A.* 38°12N 95°45W **308** F6
Burlington *Ky., U.S.A.* 39°2N 84°43W **311** E12
Burlington *Mass., U.S.A.* 42°30N 71°13W **116** A1
Burlington *N.C., U.S.A.* 36°6N 79°26W **315** C15
Burlington *N.J., U.S.A.* 40°4N 74°51W **313** F10
Burlington *Vt., U.S.A.* 44°29N 73°12W **313** B11
Burlington *Wash.,*
U.S.A. 48°28N 122°20W **306** B4
Burlington *Wis., U.S.A.* 42°41N 88°17W **311** B8
Burma ■ *Asia* 21°0N 96°30E **241** E6
Burnaby I. *Canada* 52°25N 131°19W **296** C2
Burnet *U.S.A.* 30°45N 98°14W **314** F5
Burney *U.S.A.* 40°53N 121°40W **304** F3
Burnham *U.S.A.* 40°38N 77°34W **312** F7
Burnham-on-Sea *U.K.* 51°14N 3°0W **169** F5
Burnham Park *U.S.A.* 41°49N 87°35W **119** C3
Burnham Park Harbor *Chicago, U.S.A.* **119** e3
Burnhamthorpe *Canada* 43°37N 79°35W **141** B1
Burnie *Australia* 41°4S 145°56E **281** G4
Burnley *U.K.* 53°47N 2°14W **168** D5
Burns *U.S.A.* 43°35N 119°3W **304** E4
Burns Junction *U.S.A.* 42°47N 117°51W **304** E5
Burns Lake *Canada* 54°14N 125°45W **296** C3
Burnside ➜ *Canada* 66°51N 108°4W **294** D10
Burnside, L. *Australia* 25°22S 123°0E **279** E3
Burnsville *U.S.A.* 44°47N 93°17W **308** C7
Burnt Oak *U.K.* 51°36N 0°15W **125** A2
Burnt Paw *U.S.A.* 66°54N 143°44W **303** C12
Burnt River *Canada* 44°41N 78°42W **312** B6
Burntisland *U.K.* 56°4N 3°13W **167** E5
Burntwood ➜ *Canada* 56°8N 96°34W **297** B9
Burntwood L. *Canada* 55°22N 100°26W **297** B8
Burnwynd *U.K.* 55°54N 3°23W **121** B1
Burongá *Australia* 34°18S 142°20E **282** C5
Burqa *West Bank* 31°54N 35°15E **123** A2
Burqān *Kuwait* 29°0N 47°57E **246** D5
Burqin *China* 47°43N 87°0E **217** C11
Burra *S. Austral., Australia* 33°40S 138°55E **282** B3
Burra *Nigeria* 11°0N 8°56E **263** C6
Burragorang, L. *Australia* 33°52S 150°37E **283** B9
Burray *U.K.* 58°51N 2°54W **167** C6
Burrel *Albania* 41°36N 20°1E **202** E4
Burren *Ireland* 53°9N 9°5W **166** C2
Burren △ *Ireland* 53°1N 8°58W **166** C3
Burren Junction *Australia* 30°7S 148°58E **281** E4
Burrendong, L. *Australia* 32°45S 149°10E **283** B8
Burriana *Spain* 39°50N 0°4W **196** F4
Burrinjuck, L. *Australia* 35°0S 148°36E **283** C8
Burro, Serranías del
Mexico 28°56N 102°5W **318** B4
Burrow Hd. *U.K.* 54°41N 4°24W **167** G4
Burrowa-Pine Mountain △
Australia 36°6S 147°45E **283** D7
Burrum Coast △
Australia 25°13S 152°36E **281** D5
Burruyacú *Argentina* 26°30S 64°40W **334** B3
Burry Port *U.K.* 51°41N 4°15W **169** F3
Bursa *Turkey* 40°15N 29°5E **203** F13
Bursa □ *Turkey* 40°10N 29°0E **203** F13
Burseryd *Sweden* 57°12N 13°17E **163** G7
Burstall *Canada* 50°39N 109°54W **297** C7
Burton *Mich., U.S.A.* 43°0N 83°40W **311** B13
Burton *Ohio, U.S.A.* 41°28N 81°8W **312** E3
Burton *S.C., U.S.A.* 32°26N 80°43W **315** E14
Burton, L. *Canada* 54°45N 78°20W **298** B4
Burton upon Trent *U.K.* 52°48N 1°38W **168** E6
Burtundy *Australia* 33°45S 142°15E **282** B5
Burtus *Egypt* 30°8N 31°8E **117** A1
Buru *Indonesia* 3°30S 126°30E **231** E7
Buruanga *Phil.* 11°51N 121°53E **233** F3
Burudvatn *Norway* 59°58N 10°35E **133** A2
Burullus, Bahra el *Egypt* 31°25N 31°0E **256** H7
Burūm *Yemen* 14°22N 48°59E **249** D5

Burûn, Râs Egypt 31°14N 33°7E 251 G4
Burundi ■ Africa 3°15S 30°0E 268 C3
Burunny = Tsagan Aman Russia 47°34N 46°43E 191 G8
Bururi Burundi 3°57S 29°37E 268 C2
Burutu Nigeria 5°20N 5°29E 263 D6
Burwell U.S.A. 41°47N 99°8W 308 E4
Burwick U.K. 58°45N 2°58W 167 C5
Burwood Australia 33°52S 151°5E 139 B1
Bury U.K. 53°35N 2°17W 168 D5
Bury St. Edmunds U.K. 52°15N 0°43E 169 E8
Buryatia □ Russia 53°0N 110°0E 215 D12
Bürylbaytal Kazakhstan 44°56N 74°0E 217 D8
Buryn Ukraine 51°13N 33°50E 189 G7
Burzenin Poland 51°28N 18°47E 185 G5
Busa, Mt. Phil. 6°8N 124°39E 233 H5
Busalla Italy 44°34N 8°57E 198 D5
Busan S. Korea 35°5N 129°0E 224 E4
Busanga Dem. Rep. of the Congo 0°53S 22°7E 264 C4
Busango Swamp Zambia 14°15S 25°45E 269 E2
Busaso = Boosaaso Somali Rep. 11°12N 49°18E 267 B6
Buşayrah Syria 35°9N 40°26E 213 E9
Busca Italy 44°31N 7°29E 198 D4
Bûsh Egypt 29°9N 31°8E 251 J2
Bushat Albania 41°58N 19°34E 202 E3
Būshehr Iran 28°55N 50°55E 247 D6
Būshehr □ Iran 28°20N 51°45E 247 D6
Bushenyi Uganda 0°35S 30°10E 268 C3
Bushimaie → Dem. Rep. of the Congo 6°2S 23°45E 265 D4
Bushire = Būshehr Iran 28°55N 50°55E 247 D6
Bushiribana Aruba 12°33N 69°58W 322 f
Bushnell Fla., U.S.A. 28°40N 82°7W 317 G7
Bushnell Ill., U.S.A. 40°33N 90°31W 310 D6
Bushtyna Ukraine 48°3N 23°28E 183 B8
Bushwick U.S.A. 40°41N 73°54W 132 B2
Bushy Park U.K. 51°24N 0°20W 125 B1
Busie Ghana 10°29N 2°22W 262 C4
Businga Dem. Rep. of the Congo 3°16N 20°59E 264 B4
Büsingen Germany 47°42N 8°41E 179 H4
Buskerud □ Norway 60°20N 9°0E 164 D5
Busko-Zdrój Poland 50°28N 20°42E 185 H7
Buslei Ethiopia 5°28N 44°25E 267 C5
Busovača Bos.-H. 44°6N 17°53E 182 F2
Buşra ash Shām Syria 32°30N 36°25E 251 F7
Busselton Australia 33°42S 115°15E 279 F2
Busseri → Sudan 7°41N 28°3E 257 F2
Busseto Italy 44°59N 10°2E 198 D7
Bussière-Badil France 45°39N 0°36E 174 C4
Bussolengo Italy 45°28N 10°51E 198 C7
Bussum Neths. 52°16N 5°10E 170 B5
Bustamante, B. Argentina 45°5S 66°18W 336 C3
Buşteni Romania 45°24N 25°32E 183 E10
Busto, C. Spain 43°34N 6°28W 194 B4
Busto Arsízio Italy 45°37N 8°51E 198 C5
Busu Djanoa Dem. Rep. of the Congo 1°43N 21°23E 264 B4
Busu Kwanga Dem. Rep. of the Congo 1°48N 20°21E 264 B4
Busu Mandji Dem. Rep. of the Congo 2°52N 21°14E 264 B4
Busuanga Phil. 12°14N 119°52E 232 E2
Busuanga I. Phil. 12°10N 120°0E 232 E2
Büsum Germany 54°7N 8°51E 178 A4
Busungbiu Indonesia 8°16S 114°58E 231 J17
Busy Corner Trin. & Tob. 10°18N 61°17W 323 t
Buta Dem. Rep. of the Congo 2°50N 24°53E 264 B4
Butantã Brazil 23°34S 46°42W 137 B1
Butare Rwanda 2°31S 29°52E 268 C2
Butaritari Kiribati 3°30N 174°0E 288 G9
Butcher I. India 18°57N 72°53E 130 B2
Bute S. Austral., Australia 33°51S 138°0E 282 B3
Bute Scotland, U.K. 55°48N 5°2W 167 F3
Bute Inlet Canada 50°40N 124°53W 296 C4
Butemba Uganda 1°9N 31°37E 268 B3
Butembo Dem. Rep. of the Congo 0°9N 29°18E 268 B2
Buteni Romania 46°19N 22°7E 182 D7
Butera Italy 37°11N 14°11E 201 E7
Butere Kenya 0°13N 34°30E 268 B3
Butha-Buthe Lesotho 28°47S 28°14E 271 C4
Butha Qi China 48°0N 122°32E 219 B13
Buthidaung Burma 20°52N 92°32E 241 E4
Butiaba Uganda 1°50N 31°20E 268 B3
Butler Ga., U.S.A. 32°33N 84°14W 316 C5
Butler Ind., U.S.A. 41°26N 84°52W 311 C12
Butler Ky., U.S.A. 38°47N 84°22W 311 F12
Butler Mo., U.S.A. 38°16N 94°20W 310 F2
Butler Pa., U.S.A. 40°52N 79°54W 312 F5
Butler, L. U.S.A. 28°29N 81°33W 133 B1
Buton Indonesia 5°0S 122°45E 231 E6
Bütow = Bytów Poland 54°10N 17°30E 184 D4
Butrintit, L. e Albania 39°43N 20°5E 206 B10
Butte Mont., U.S.A. 46°0N 112°32W 304 C7
Butte Nebr., U.S.A. 42°58N 98°51W 308 D4
Butte Creek → U.S.A. 39°12N 121°56W 306 F5
Butterworth = Gcuwa S. Africa 32°20S 28°11E 271 D4
Butterworth Malaysia 5°24N 100°23E 237 c
Buttevant Ireland 52°14N 8°40W 166 D3
Buttfield, Mt. Australia 24°45S 128°9E 279 D4
Button B. Canada 58°45N 94°23W 297 B10
Buttonwillow U.S.A. 35°24N 119°28W 307 K7
Butts Corner U.S.A. 38°46N 77°19W 143 C2
Butty Hd. Australia 33°54S 121°39E 279 F3
Butuan Phil. 8°57N 125°33E 233 G5
Butuan B. Phil. 9°4N 125°21E 233 G5
Butuku-Luba Eq. Guin. 3°29N 8°33E 263 E6
Butung = Buton Indonesia 5°0S 122°45E 231 E6
Buturlinovka Russia 50°50N 40°35E 190 E5
Butwal Nepal 27°33N 83°31E 243 F10
Butzbach Germany 50°25N 8°40E 179 E4
Bützow Germany 53°50N 11°58E 178 B7
Buuhoodle Somali Rep. 8°20N 46°25E 267 C6
Buulobarde Somali Rep. 3°50N 45°33E 267 D6
Buur Gaabo Somali Rep. 1°13S 41°51E 267 E5
Buurhakaba Somali Rep. 3°12N 44°20E 267 D5
Buvika Norway 63°18N 10°11E 164 A7
Buxa Duar India 27°45N 89°35E 243 F13
Buxar India 25°34N 83°58E 243 G10
Buxoro Uzbekistan 39°48N 64°25E 216 E6
Buxtehude Germany 53°28N 9°39E 178 B5
Buxton U.K. 53°16N 1°54W 168 D6
Buxy France 46°44N 4°40E 173 F11
Buy Russia 58°28N 41°28E 190 A5
Buyant-Uhaa Mongolia 44°55N 110°11E 226 B6
Buynaksk Russia 42°48N 47°7E 191 J8
Buyo Ivory C. 6°21N 7°5W 262 D3
Buyo, L. de Ivory C. 6°16N 7°10W 262 D3
Büyük Menderes → Turkey 37°28N 27°11E 205 D9
Büyükçekmece Turkey 41°2N 28°35E 203 E12
Büyükdere Turkey 41°9N 29°2E 122 B2
Büyükeğri Dağı Turkey 36°45N 33°33E 250 B4
Büyükkarıştıran Turkey 41°18N 27°33E 203 E11
Büyükkemikli Burnu Turkey 40°18N 26°14E 203 F10
Büyükorhan Turkey 39°46N 28°56E 205 B10
Büyükyoncalı Turkey 41°20N 27°55E 203 E11
Buyun Shan China 40°4N 122°43E 227 D12
Buzançais France 46°54N 1°25E 172 F8
Buzău Romania 45°10N 26°50E 183 E11
Buzău □ Romania 45°20N 26°30E 183 E11
Buzău → Romania 45°26N 27°44E 183 E12
Buzău, Pasul Romania 45°35N 26°12E 183 E11
Buzaymah Libya 24°55N 22°2E 258 D4
Buzen Japan 33°35N 131°5E 222 D3
Buzet Croatia 45°24N 13°58E 199 C10
Buzi → Mozam. 19°50S 34°43E 269 F3
Buziaş Romania 45°38N 21°36E 182 E6
Büzmeýin Turkmenistan 38°3N 58°12E 247 B8
Buzuluk Russia 52°48N 52°12E 186 D9
Buzuluk → Russia 50°15N 42°7E 190 E6
Buzzards Bay U.S.A. 41°45N 70°37W 313 E14
Bwagaoia Papua N. G. 10°40S 152°52E 286 F7
Bwana Mkubwa Zambia 13°8S 28°38E 269 E2
Bwasa Dem. Rep. of the Congo 3°55S 18°24E 264 C3
Bwatnapné Vanuatu 15°41S 168°9E 287 E6
Bwindi △ Uganda 1°2S 29°42E 268 C2
Byakar Dzong = Jakar Dzong Bhutan 27°33N 90°43E 241 B3
Byala Ruse, Bulgaria 43°28N 25°44E 203 C9
Byala Varna, Bulgaria 42°53N 27°55E 203 D11
Byala Slatina Bulgaria 43°26N 23°58E 202 C7
Byam Martin I. Canada 75°15N 104°15W 295 B11
Byarezina → Belarus 52°33N 30°14E 177 B16
Byaroza Belarus 52°31N 24°51E 177 B13
Bychawa Poland 51°1N 22°36E 185 G9
Byculla India 18°58N 72°50E 130 B2
Byczyna Poland 51°7N 18°12E 185 G5
Bydgoszcz Poland 53°10N 18°0E 185 E5
Byelorussia = Belarus ■ Europe 53°30N 27°0E 177 B14
Byeonsan △ S. Korea 35°40N 126°30E 224 E3
Byers U.S.A. 39°43N 104°14W 304 G11
Byesville U.S.A. 39°58N 81°32W 312 G3
Byfield △ Australia 22°52S 150°45E 280 C5
Bygdin Norway 61°21N 8°32E 164 C5
Bygdøy Norway 59°54N 10°40E 133 A3
Bygland Norway 58°50N 7°48E 164 F4
Byglandsfjorden Norway 58°44N 7°50E 164 F4
Bygstad Norway 61°23N 5°40E 164 C2
Bykhaw Belarus 53°31N 30°14E 177 B16
Bykhov = Bykhaw Belarus 53°31N 30°14E 177 B16
Bykle Norway 59°20N 7°22E 164 E4
Bykovo Russia 49°50N 45°25E 190 F7
Bylas U.S.A. 33°8N 110°7W 305 K8
Bylot Canada 58°25N 94°8W 297 B10
Bylot I. Canada 73°13N 78°34W 295 C16
Byrd, C. Antarctica 69°38S 76°7W 151 C17
Byrock Australia 30°40S 146°27E 283 A7
Byron Ga., U.S.A. 32°39N 83°46W 316 C6
Byron Ill., U.S.A. 42°8N 89°15W 310 B7
Byron, C. Australia 28°43S 153°38E 281 D5
Byron Bay Australia 28°43S 153°37E 281 D5
Byrranga, Gory Russia 75°0N 100°0E 215 B11
Byrranga Mts. = Byrranga, Gory Russia 75°0N 100°0E 215 B11
Byrum Denmark 57°16N 11°0E 163 G5
Byske Sweden 64°57N 21°11E 160 D19
Byskeälven → Sweden 64°57N 21°13E 160 D19
Bystrytsya Ukraine 48°27N 24°14E 183 B9
Bystrzyca → Dolnośląskie, Poland 51°12N 16°55E 185 G3
Bystrzyca → Lubelskie, Poland 51°21N 22°46E 185 G9
Bystrzyca Kłodzka Poland 50°19N 16°39E 185 H3
Bytča Slovak Rep. 49°13N 18°34E 181 B11
Bytkiv Ukraine 48°38N 24°28E 183 B9
Bytom Poland 50°25N 18°54E 185 H5
Bytom Odrzański Poland 51°44N 15°48E 185 G2
Bytów Poland 54°10N 17°30E 184 D4
Byumba Rwanda 1°35S 30°4E 268 C3
Bywater U.S.A. 29°58N 90°2W 131 B2
Bzenec Czech Rep. 48°58N 17°18E 181 C10
Bzura → Poland 52°25N 20°15E 185 F7

C

C.B.S. Fox Studios U.S.A. 34°9N 118°24W 126 B2
C.N.N. Center U.S.A. 33°45N 84°23W 113 B2
C.N. Tower Toronto, Canada 141 c1
C.W. McConaughy, L. U.S.A. 41°14N 101°40W 308 E3
Ca → Vietnam 18°45N 105°45E 236 C5
Ca Mau Vietnam 9°7N 105°8E 237 H5
Ca Mau, Mui Vietnam 8°38N 104°44E 237 H5
Ca Na Vietnam 11°20N 108°54E 237 G7
Caacupé Paraguay 25°23S 57°5W 334 B4
Caaguazú △ Paraguay 26°5S 55°31W 335 B4
Caála Angola 12°46S 15°30E 265 E3
Caamaño Sd. Canada 52°55N 129°25W 296 C3
Caapiranga Brazil 3°18S 61°13W 329 D5
Caazapá Paraguay 26°8S 56°19W 334 B4
Caazapá □ Paraguay 26°10S 56°0W 335 B4
Cabaad, Ras Somali Rep. 6°18N 49°4E 267 C6
Cabadbaran Phil. 9°10N 125°38E 233 G5
Cabagan Phil. 17°26N 121°46E 232 C3
Cabalete I. Phil. 14°16N 121°49E 232 D3
Cabalian = San Juan Phil. 10°16N 125°10E 233 F5
Caballeria, C. de Spain 40°5N 4°5E 206 A5
Caballito Argentina 34°37S 58°25W 117 B2
Cabana Peru 8°25S 78°5W 330 B2
Cabana de Bergantiños Spain 43°13N 8°54W 194 B2
Cabanaconde Peru 15°38S 71°58W 330 D3
Cabañaquinta Spain 43°10N 5°38W 194 B5
Cabanatuan Phil. 15°30N 120°58E 232 D3
Cabañeros ⌂ Spain 39°18N 4°35W 195 F6
Cabanes Spain 40°9N 0°2E 196 E5
Cabangon Phil. 15°10N 120°3E 232 D3
Cabanilla Peru 15°36S 70°28W 330 D3
Cabano Canada 47°40N 68°56W 299 C6
Čabar Croatia 45°36N 14°39E 199 C11
Cabarroguis Phil. 16°50N 121°30E 232 C3
Cabarruyan I. Phil. 16°18N 119°59E 232 C2
Cabazon U.S.A. 33°55N 116°47W 307 M10
Cabedelo Brazil 7°0S 34°50W 332 C5
Cabeza del Buey Spain 38°44N 5°13W 195 G5
Cabezón de la Sal Spain 43°18N 4°14W 194 B6
Cabildo Chile 32°30S 71°5W 334 C1
Cabimas Venezuela 10°23N 71°25W 328 A3
Cabin John U.S.A. 38°58N 77°10W 143 B2
Cabin John Regional Park ⌂ U.S.A. 39°0N 77°10W 143 A2
Cabinda Angola 5°33S 12°11E 265 D2
Cabinda □ Angola 5°0S 12°30E 265 D2
Cabinet Mts. U.S.A. 48°10N 115°50W 304 B6
Cabinteely Ireland 53°16N 6°9W 120 B3
Cabiri Angola 8°52S 13°39E 265 D2
Cable Beach Bahamas 25°4N 77°24W 153 b
Cabo Blanco Argentina 47°15S 65°47W 336 C3
Cabo de Gata-Níjar ⌂ Spain 36°51N 2°6W 197 J2
Cabo de Hornos △ Chile 55°42S 67°20W 336 E3
Cabo de Santo Agostinho Brazil 8°20S 34°55W 332 C5
Cabo Frio Brazil 22°51S 42°3W 333 F3
Cabo Pantoja Peru 1°0S 75°10W 328 D2
Cabo Raso Argentina 44°20S 65°15W 336 B3
Cabo Rojo Puerto Rico 18°5N 67°9W 321 b
Cabo San Lucas Mexico 22°53N 109°54W 318 C3
Cabo Verde = Cape Verde Is. ■ Atl. Oc. 16°0N 24°0W 153 j
Cabo Yubi = Tarfaya Morocco 27°55N 12°55W 260 C2
Cabonga, Réservoir Canada 47°20N 76°40W 298 C4
Cabool U.S.A. 37°7N 92°6W 308 G7
Caboolture Australia 27°5S 152°58E 281 D5
Cabora Bassa Dam = Cahora Bassa, Lago de Mozam. 15°20S 32°50E 269 F3
Caborca Mexico 30°37N 112°6W 318 A2
Cabot, Mt. U.S.A. 44°30N 71°25W 313 B13
Cabot Hd. Canada 45°14N 81°17W 312 A3
Cabot Str. Canada 47°15N 59°40W 299 C8
Cabra Dublin, Ireland 53°21N 6°18W 120 A2
Cabra Spain 37°30N 4°28W 195 H6
Cabra del Santo Cristo Spain 37°42N 3°16W 195 H7
Cabra I. India 7°18N 93°50E 245 L11
Cabra I. Phil. 13°53N 120°2E 232 E3
Cábras Italy 39°56N 8°32E 200 C1
Cabras I. Guam 13°27N 144°44E 302 d
Cabrera Spain 39°8N 2°57E 206 B3
Cabrera, Sierra Spain 42°12N 6°40W 194 C4
Cabrera △ Spain 39°13N 2°53E 197 F7
Cabri Canada 50°35N 108°25W 297 C7
Cabriel → Spain 39°14N 1°3W 197 F3
Cabrits, Î. Martinique 14°23N 60°52W 322 j
Cabrits △ Dominica 15°35N 61°26W 323 k
Cabruta Venezuela 7°50N 66°10W 328 B4
Cabuçú de Baixo → Brazil 23°30S 46°40W 137 A1
Cabuçú de Cima → Brazil 23°30S 46°33W 137 A2
Cabugao Phil. 17°48N 120°27E 232 C3
Cabulauan Is. Phil. 11°25N 120°8E 233 F3
Cabulo Angola 10°18S 16°22E 265 E3
Caburan = Jose Abad Santos Phil. 5°55N 125°39E 233 J5
Cabuta Angola 9°48S 14°58E 265 D2
Cabuyaro Colombia 4°18N 72°49W 328 C3
Cacabelos Spain 42°36N 6°44W 194 C4
Caçador Brazil 26°47S 51°0W 335 B5
Čačak Serbia 43°54N 20°20E 202 C4
Cacandee Settlement Trin. & Tob. 10°33N 61°26W 323 t
Cacao Fr. Guiana 4°33N 52°26W 329 C7
Caçapava do Sul Brazil 30°30S 53°30W 335 C5
Cáccamo Italy 37°56N 13°40E 200 E6
Cacém Portugal 38°46N 9°18W 195 G1
Cáceres Brazil 16°5S 57°40W 331 D6
Cáceres Colombia 7°35N 75°20W 328 B2
Cáceres Spain 39°26N 6°23W 195 F4
Cáceres □ Spain 39°45N 6°0W 194 F5
Cachan France 48°47N 2°19E 134 B2
Cache Bay Canada 46°22N 80°0W 298 C4
Cache Cr. → U.S.A. 38°42N 121°42W 306 G5
Cache Creek Canada 50°48N 121°19W 296 C4
Cachenka → Russia 55°46N 37°17E 129 B1
Cacheu Guinea-Biss. 12°14N 16°8W 262 C1
Cachi Argentina 25°5S 66°10W 334 B2
Cachimbo Brazil 8°57S 54°54W 331 B7
Cachimbo, Serra do Brazil 9°30S 55°30W 331 B6
Cachimo Angola 8°21S 21°24E 265 D4
Cachinal de la Sierra Chile 24°58S 69°32W 334 A2
Cachingues Angola 13°5S 16°43E 265 E3
Cachoeira = Solonópole Brazil 5°44S 39°1W 332 C4
Cachoeira Brazil 12°30S 39°0W 333 D4
Cachoeira, Rib. da → Brazil 23°38S 46°43W 137 B1
Cachoeira Alta Brazil 18°48S 50°58W 333 E1
Cachoeira do Sul Brazil 30°3S 52°53W 335 C5
Cachoeiro de Itapemirim Brazil 20°51S 41°7W 333 F3
Cachoeiro do Arari Brazil 1°1S 48°58W 332 B2
Cachopo Portugal 37°20N 7°49W 195 H3
Cachuela Esperanza Bolivia 10°32S 65°38W 331 C4
Cacilhas Portugal 38°41N 9°8W 126 A2
Cacine Guinea-Biss. 11°8N 14°57W 262 C1
Cacoal Brazil 11°32S 61°18W 331 C5
Cacólo Angola 10°9S 19°21E 265 E3
Caconda Angola 13°48S 15°8E 265 E3
Cacongo Angola 5°11S 12°5E 265 D2
Caçu Brazil 18°37S 51°4W 333 E1
Cacuaco Angola 8°47S 13°21E 265 D2
Cacuchi → Angola 14°26S 16°46E 265 E3
Cacula Angola 14°29S 14°10E 265 E2
Caculé Brazil 14°30S 42°13W 333 D3
Caculuvar → Angola 16°47S 14°56E 265 F2
Cacuso Angola 9°25S 15°45E 265 D3
Cadale Somali Rep. 2°45N 46°19E 267 D6
Čadca Slovak Rep. 49°26N 18°45E 181 B11
Caddo U.S.A. 34°7N 96°16W 314 D6
Cader Idris U.K. 52°42N 3°53W 169 E4
Cadereyta de Jiménez Mexico 25°36N 100°0W 318 B5
Cades U.S.A. 33°47N 79°47W 316 B10
Cadí, Sierra del Spain 42°17N 1°42E 196 C6
Cadí-Moixeró ⌂ Spain 42°17N 1°44W 196 C3
Cadibarrawirracanna, L. Australia 28°52S 135°27E 281 D2
Cadillac Gironde, France 44°38N 0°20W 174 D3
Cadillac Mich., U.S.A. 44°15N 85°24W 309 C11
Cadiz Phil. 10°57N 123°15E 233 F4
Cádiz Spain 36°30N 6°20W 195 J4
Cadiz Calif., U.S.A. 34°30N 115°28W 307 L11
Cadiz Ohio, U.S.A. 40°22N 81°0W 312 F4
Cádiz □ Spain 36°36N 5°45W 195 J5
Cádiz, G. de Spain 36°40N 7°0W 195 J3
Cadiz L. U.S.A. 34°18N 115°24W 305 J6
Cadley U.S.A. 33°32N 82°40W 316 B7
Cadney Park Australia 27°55S 134°3E 281 D1
Cadomin Canada 53°2N 117°20W 296 C5
Cadotte Lake Canada 56°26N 116°23W 296 B5
Cadours France 43°44N 1°2E 174 E5
Cadoux Australia 30°46S 117°7E 279 F2
Cadwell U.S.A. 32°20N 83°3W 316 C6
Caen France 49°10N 0°22W 172 C6
Caernarfon U.K. 53°8N 4°16W 168 D3
Caernarfon B. U.K. 53°4N 4°40W 168 D3
Caernarvon = Caernarfon U.K. 53°8N 4°16W 168 D3
Caerphilly U.K. 51°35N 3°13W 169 F4
Caerphilly □ U.K. 51°37N 3°12W 169 F4
Caesarea Israel 32°30N 34°53E 251 F5
Caeté Brazil 19°55S 43°40W 333 E3
Caetité Brazil 13°50S 42°32W 333 D3
Cafayate Argentina 26°2S 66°0W 334 B2
Cafu Angola 16°30S 15°8E 265 F3
Cagayan □ Phil. 18°0N 121°50E 232 C3
Cagayan → Phil. 18°25N 121°42E 232 B3
Cagayan de Oro Phil. 8°30N 124°40E 233 G5
Cagayan Is. Phil. 9°40N 121°16E 233 G3
Cagayan Sulu I. Phil. 7°1N 118°30E 233 H2
Cagli Italy 43°33N 12°39E 199 E9
Cágliari Italy 39°13N 9°7E 200 C2
Cágliari, G. di Italy 39°8N 9°11E 200 C2
Cagnano Varano Italy 41°49N 15°47E 199 G12
Cagnes-sur-Mer France 43°40N 7°9E 175 E11
Caguán → Colombia 0°8S 74°18W 328 D3
Caguas Puerto Rico 18°14N 66°2W 321 C6
Caha Mts. Ireland 51°45N 9°40W 166 E2
Cahama Angola 16°17S 14°19E 265 F2
Caher Ireland 52°22N 7°56W 166 D4
Cahersiveen Ireland 51°56N 10°14W 166 E1
Cahora Bassa, Lago de Mozam. 15°20S 32°50E 269 F3
Cahore Pt. Ireland 52°33N 6°12W 166 D5
Cahors France 44°27N 1°27E 174 D5
Cahuapanas Peru 5°15S 77°0W 330 B2
Cahuenga Park U.S.A. 34°8N 118°19W 126 B3
Cahuinari → Colombia 1°21S 70°44W 328 D3
Cahuinari △ Colombia 1°20S 71°10W 328 D3
Cahul Moldova 45°50N 28°15E 183 E13
Cai Bau, Dao Vietnam 21°10N 107°27E 228 G6
Cai Be Vietnam 10°20N 106°2E 237 G6
Cai Nuoc Vietnam 8°56N 105°1E 237 H5
Caia Mozam. 17°51S 35°24E 269 F4
Caiabis, Serra dos Brazil 11°30S 56°30W 331 C6
Caianda Angola 11°2S 23°31E 265 E4
Caiapó, Serra do Brazil 17°0S 52°0W 331 D7
Caiapônia Brazil 16°57S 51°49W 331 D7
Caibarién Cuba 22°30N 79°30W 320 B4
Caibiran Phil. 11°34N 124°35E 233 F5
Caiçara = Alvarães Brazil 3°12S 64°50W 329 D5
Caicara Bolívar, Venezuela 7°38N 66°10W 328 B4
Caicara Monagas, Venezuela 9°52N 63°38W 329 B5
Caicó Brazil 6°20S 37°0W 332 C4
Caicos Is. Turks & Caicos 21°40N 71°40W 321 B5
Caicos Passage W. Indies 22°45N 72°45W 321 B5
Caidian China 30°35N 114°2E 229 B10
Caiguna Australia 32°16S 125°29E 279 F4
Caillandre, Morne St. Lucia 13°46N 60°57W 323 m
Caille I. Grenada 12°16N 61°34W 323 q
Cailloma Peru 15°9S 71°45W 330 D3
Cain, L. U.S.A. 28°28N 81°28W 133 B2
Căinari Moldova 46°41N 29°3E 183 D14
Cainde Angola 15°29S 13°24E 265 F2
Caine → Bolivia 18°23S 65°21W 331 D4
Caird Coast Antarctica 75°0S 25°0W 151 D1
Cairn Gorm U.K. 57°7N 3°39W 167 D5
Cairngorm Mts. U.K. 57°6N 3°42W 167 D5
Cairngorms △ U.K. 57°10N 3°50W 167 D5
Cairnryan U.K. 54°59N 5°1W 167 G3
Cairns Australia 16°57S 145°45E 280 B4
Cairns L. Canada 51°42N 94°30W 297 C10
Cairo = El Qâhira Egypt 30°2N 31°13E 117 A2
Cairo Ga., U.S.A. 30°52N 84°13W 316 E5
Cairo Ill., U.S.A. 37°0N 89°11W 308 G9
Cairo N.Y., U.S.A. 42°18N 74°0W 313 D10
Cairo Int. ✈ (CAI) Egypt 30°7N 31°24E 117 A3
Cairo Montenotte Italy 44°23N 8°16E 198 D5
Cairofa Angola 14°3S 12°54E 265 E2
Caiseal = Cashel Ireland 52°30N 7°53W 166 D4
Caisleán an Bharraigh = Castlebar Ireland 53°52N 9°18W 166 C2
Caithness U.K. 58°25N 3°35W 167 C5
Caithness, Ord of U.K. 58°8N 3°36W 167 C5
Caitou Angola 14°28S 13°7E 265 E2
Caiuás = Rio Brilhante Brazil 21°48S 54°33W 335 A5
Caiundo Angola 15°50S 17°28E 265 F3
Caiza Bolivia 20°2S 65°40W 331 E4
Caja de Muertos, I. Puerto Rico 17°54N 66°32W 321 b
Cajabamba Peru 7°38S 78°4W 330 B2
Cajamarca Peru 7°5S 78°28W 330 B2
Cajamarca □ Peru 6°15S 78°50W 330 B2
Cajamarquilla = Bolívar Peru 7°18S 77°48W 330 B2
Cajapió Brazil 2°58S 44°48W 332 B3
Cajarc France 44°29N 1°50E 174 D5
Cajas △ Ecuador 2°48S 79°15W 328 D2
Cajatambo Peru 10°30S 77°2W 330 C2
Cajazeiras Brazil 6°52S 38°30W 332 C4
Čajetina Serbia 43°47N 19°42E 202 C3
Cajidiocan Phil. 12°22N 122°41E 232 E4
Caju Brazil 22°52S 43°12W 135 B1
Çakirgol Turkey 40°33N 39°40E 213 B8
Çakırlar Turkey 36°52N 30°33E 205 E12
Čakovec Croatia 46°23N 16°26E 199 B13
Čakovice Czech Rep. 50°9N 14°31E 135 B3
Çal Turkey 38°4N 29°23E 205 C11
Cala Spain 37°59N 6°21W 195 H4
Cala → Spain 37°38N 6°5W 195 H4
Cala Cadolar, Punta de = Rotja, Pta. Spain 38°38N 1°35E 206 D2
Cala d'Or Spain 39°23N 3°14E 206 B4
Cala en Porter Spain 39°52N 4°8E 206 B5
Cala Figuera Spain 39°20N 3°10E 206 B4
Cala Figuera, C. de Spain 39°27N 2°31E 206 B3
Cala Forcat Spain 40°0N 3°47E 206 B4
Cala Major Spain 39°33N 2°37E 206 B3
Cala Mezquida = Sa Mesquida Spain 39°55N 4°16E 206 B5
Cala Millor Spain 39°35N 3°22E 206 B4
Cala Murada Spain 39°27N 3°17E 206 B4
Cala Ratjada Spain 39°43N 3°27E 206 B4
Cala Santa Galdana Spain 39°56N 3°58E 206 B4
Calabanga Phil. 13°42N 123°17E 232 E4
Calabar Nigeria 4°57N 8°20E 263 E6
Calabogie Canada 45°18N 76°43W 313 A8
Calabozo Venezuela 9°0N 67°28W 328 B4
Calábria □ Italy 39°0N 16°30E 201 C9
Calábria △ Italy 39°6N 16°35E 201 C9
Calaburras, Pta. de Spain 36°30N 4°38W 195 J6
Calaceite Spain 41°1N 0°11E 196 D5
Calacoto Bolivia 17°16S 68°38W 330 D4
Calacuccia France 42°21N 9°1E 175 F13
Calafat Romania 43°58N 22°59E 182 G7
Calafell Spain 41°11N 1°34E 196 D6
Calagnaan I. Phil. 11°29N 123°12E 233 F4
Calagua Is. Phil. 14°30N 122°55E 232 D4
Calahorra Spain 42°18N 1°59W 196 C3
Calai Angola 17°47S 19°41E 265 F3
Calais Pas-de-Calais, France 50°57N 1°56E 173 B8
Calais Maine, U.S.A. 45°11N 67°17W 309 C20
Calakmul ⌂ Mexico 18°14N 89°48W 319 D7
Calalaste, Cord. de Argentina 25°0S 67°0W 334 B2
Calama Brazil 8°0S 62°50W 331 B5
Calama Chile 22°30S 68°55W 334 A2
Calamar Bolívar, Colombia 10°15N 74°55W 328 A3
Calamar Vaupés, Colombia 1°58N 72°32W 328 C3
Calamarca Bolivia 16°55S 68°9W 330 D4
Calamba Cavite, Phil. 14°13N 121°10E 232 D3
Calamba Mis. Occ., Phil. 8°35N 123°39E 233 G4
Calamian Group Phil. 11°50N 119°55E 233 F2
Calamocha Spain 40°50N 1°17W 196 E3
Calamonte Spain 38°53N 6°23W 195 G4
Călan Romania 45°44N 22°59E 182 E7
Calañas Spain 37°40N 6°53W 195 H4
Calanda Spain 40°56N 0°15W 196 E4
Calandagan I. Phil. 10°39N 120°15E 233 F3
Calandula Angola 9°6S 15°57E 265 D3
Calang Indonesia 4°37N 95°37E 234 B1
Calangiánus Italy 40°56N 9°11E 200 B2
Calanscio, Sarīr Libya 27°30N 21°30E 258 C4
Calapan Phil. 13°25N 121°7E 232 E3
Călăraşi Moldova 47°16N 28°19E 183 C13
Călăraşi Romania 44°12N 27°20E 183 F12
Călăraşi □ Romania 44°10N 27°0E 183 F12
Calasparra Spain 38°14N 1°41W 197 G3
Calatafimi Italy 37°55N 12°52E 200 E5
Calatagan Phil. 13°50N 120°38E 232 E3
Calatayud Spain 41°20N 1°40W 196 D3
Călăţele Romania 46°46N 23°1E 182 D8
Calato = Kalathos Greece 36°9N 28°8E 206 E12
Calatrava Eq. Guin. 1°6N 9°25E 264 B1
Calatrava Phil. 10°35N 123°28E 233 F4
Calauag Phil. 13°55N 122°15E 232 E4
Calavà, C. Italy 38°11N 14°55E 201 D7
Calavite, C. Phil. 13°26N 120°20E 232 E3
Calavite Pass. Phil. 13°36N 120°25E 232 E3
Calayan Phil. 19°16N 121°28E 232 B3
Calayan I. Phil. 19°20N 121°27E 232 B3
Calbayog Phil. 12°4N 124°38E 232 E5
Calbiga Phil. 11°38N 125°0E 233 F5
Calca Peru 13°22S 72°0W 330 C3
Calcasieu L. U.S.A. 29°55N 93°18W 314 G8
Calcium U.S.A. 44°1N 75°50W 313 B9
Calcutta = Kolkata India 22°34N 88°21E 124 B2
Calcutta U.S.A. 40°40N 80°34W 312 F4
Caldaro Italy 46°25N 11°14E 199 B8
Caldas □ Colombia 5°15N 75°30W 328 B2
Caldas da Rainha Portugal 39°24N 9°8W 195 F1
Caldas de Reis Spain 42°36N 8°39W 194 C2
Caldas Novas Brazil 17°45S 48°38W 333 E2
Calder → U.K. 53°44N 1°22W 168 D6
Caldera Chile 27°5S 70°55W 334 B1
Caldera de Taburiente △ Canary Is. 28°43N 17°52W 153 e1
Caldwell Idaho, U.S.A. 43°40N 116°41W 304 E5
Caldwell Kans., U.S.A. 37°2N 97°37W 308 G5
Caldwell Tex., U.S.A. 30°32N 96°42W 314 F6
Caledon Ont., Canada 43°51N 79°51W 312 C5
Caledon Western Cape, S. Africa 34°14S 19°26E 270 D2
Caledon → S. Africa 30°31S 26°5E 270 D4
Caledon B. Australia 12°45S 137°0E 280 A2
Caledonia Ont., Canada 43°7N 79°58W 312 C5
Caledonia Mo., U.S.A. 37°45N 90°46W 310 G6
Caledonia N.Y., U.S.A. 42°58N 77°51W 312 D7
Calella Spain 41°37N 2°40E 196 D7
Calemba Angola 16°0S 15°44E 270 A2
Calen Australia 20°56S 148°48E 280 b
Calenzana France 42°31N 8°51E 175 F12
Caleta Olivia Argentina 46°25S 67°25W 336 C3
Caletones Chile 34°6S 70°27W 334 C1
Calexico U.S.A. 32°40N 115°30W 307 N11
Calf of Man I. of Man 54°3N 4°48W 168 C3
Calgary Canada 51°0N 114°10W 296 C6
Calheta Azores 38°36N 28°1W 153 d1
Calheta Madeira 32°44N 17°11W 153 c
Calheta de Nesquim Azores 38°24N 28°5W 153 d1
Calhoun U.S.A. 34°30N 84°57W 315 D12
Calhoun Falls U.S.A. 34°6N 82°36W 316 A7
Cali Colombia 3°25N 76°35W 328 C2
Calibishie Dominica 15°35N 61°21W 323 k
Calicoan I. Phil. 10°59N 125°48E 233 F5
Calicut India 11°15N 75°43E 245 J2
Caliente U.S.A. 37°37N 114°31W 305 H6
California Trin. & Tob. 10°24N 61°28W 323 t
California Mo., U.S.A. 38°38N 92°34W 310 F4
California Pa., U.S.A. 40°4N 79°54W 312 F5
California □ U.S.A. 37°30N 119°30W 306 H7
California, Baja, T.N. = Baja California □ Mexico 30°0N 115°0W 318 B2
California, Baja, T.S. = Baja California Sur □ Mexico 25°50N 111°50W 318 B2
California, G. de Mexico 27°0N 111°0W 318 B2
California City U.S.A. 35°10N 117°55W 307 K9
California Hot Springs U.S.A. 35°51N 118°41W 307 K8
California Inst. of Tech. U.S.A. 34°8N 118°8W 126 B4
California Los Angeles, Univ. of U.S.A. 34°4N 118°27W 126 B2
California Plaza Los Angeles, U.S.A. 127 b1
California State Univ. U.S.A. 34°4N 118°10W 126 B3
Cälilabad Azerbaijan 39°12N 48°29E 213 C13
Calilegua △ Argentina 25°36S 64°50W 334 B3
Călimăneşti Romania 45°14N 24°20E 183 E9
Călimani, Munţii Romania 47°12N 25°0E 183 C10
Calingasta Argentina 31°15S 69°30W 334 C2
Calinog Phil. 11°7N 122°32E 233 F4
Calintaan Phil. 12°35N 120°57E 232 E3
Calipatria U.S.A. 33°8N 115°31W 307 M11
Calistoga U.S.A. 38°35N 122°35W 306 G4
Calitri Italy 40°54N 15°26E 201 B8
Calitzdorp S. Africa 33°33S 21°42E 270 D3
Calivigny I. Grenada 12°0N 61°43W 323 q
Callabonna, L. Australia 29°40S 140°5E 281 D3
Callac France 48°25N 3°27W 172 D3
Callahan U.S.A. 30°34N 81°50W 316 E8
Callahan Tunnel Boston, U.S.A. 116 a3
Callan Ireland 52°32N 7°24W 166 D4
Callander U.K. 56°15N 4°13W 167 E4
Callang = San Manuel Phil. 16°4N 120°40E 232 C3
Callao Peru 12°3S 77°8W 124 B2
Callaway U.S.A. 30°8N 85°36W 316 E4
Calliaqua St. Vincent 13°8N 61°12W 323 n
Callicoon U.S.A. 41°46N 75°3W 313 E9
Calling Lake Canada 55°15N 113°12W 296 B6
Calliope Australia 24°0S 151°16E 280 C5
Callosa de Segura Spain 38°7N 0°53W 197 G4
Callosa d'En Sarrià Spain 38°40N 0°8W 197 G4
Calma, Costa de la Spain 39°28N 2°26E 206 B3
Calmar U.S.A. 43°11N 91°52W 310 A5
Calne U.K. 51°26N 2°0W 169 F6
Calola Angola 16°25S 17°48E 265 F3
Calolbon = San Andres Phil. 13°36N 124°6E 232 E5
Calonge Spain 41°52N 3°5E 196 D8
Caloocan Phil. 14°39N 120°58E 127 B1
Caloosahatchee → U.S.A. 26°31N 82°1W 317 J7
Calore → Italy 41°11N 14°28E 201 A7
Caloundra Australia 26°45S 153°10E 281 D5
Calpe Spain 38°39N 0°3E 197 G5
Calpella U.S.A. 39°14N 123°12W 306 F3
Calpine U.S.A. 39°40N 120°27W 306 F6
Calstock Canada 49°47N 84°9W 298 C3
Caltabellotta Italy 37°34N 13°13E 200 E6
Caltagirone Italy 37°14N 14°31E 201 E7
Caltanissetta Italy 37°29N 14°4E 201 E7
Çaltılıbük Turkey 39°57N 28°36E 203 G12
Caluango Angola 8°20S 19°39E 265 D3
Calubian Phil. 11°27N 124°26E 233 F5
Calucinga Angola 11°18S 16°12E 265 E3
Caluire-et-Cuire France 45°48N 4°52E 173 G11
Calulo Angola 10°1S 14°56E 265 E2
Calumet L. U.S.A. 41°41N 87°35W 119 C3
Calumet Park U.S.A. 41°40N 87°39W 119 C3
Calumet Sag Channel → U.S.A. 41°40N 87°47W 119 C2
Calunda Angola 12°7S 23°36E 265 E4
Caluquembe Angola 13°47S 14°44E 265 E2
Caluso Italy 45°18N 7°53E 198 C4
Caluula Somali Rep. 11°50N 50°45E 267 B7
Caluya I. Phil. 11°55N 121°34E 233 F3
Calvados □ France 49°5N 0°15W 172 C6
Calvados Chain, The Papua N. G. 11°10S 152°45E 286 F7
Calvairate Italy 45°27N 9°13E 129 B2
Calvert → Australia 16°17S 137°44E 280 B2
Calvert I. Canada 51°30N 128°0W 296 C3
Calvert Ra. Australia 24°0S 122°30E 278 D3
Calvi France 42°34N 8°45E 175 F12
Calvià Spain 39°34N 2°31E 206 B3
Calvillo Mexico 21°51N 102°43W 318 C4
Calvinia S. Africa 31°28S 19°45E 270 D2
Calvo, Mte. Italy 41°44N 15°46E 199 G12
Calwa U.S.A. 36°42N 119°46W 306 J7
Calzada Almuradiel = Almuradiel Spain 38°32N 3°28W 195 G7
Calzada de Calatrava Spain 38°42N 3°46W 195 G7
Cam → U.K. 52°21N 0°16E 169 E8
Cam Lam = Ba Ngoi Vietnam 11°54N 109°10E 237 G7
Cam Pha Vietnam 21°7N 107°18E 228 G6
Cam Ranh Vietnam 11°54N 109°12E 237 G7
Cam Xuyen Vietnam 18°15N 106°0E 236 C6
Camabatela Angola 8°20S 15°26E 265 D3
Camacã Brazil 15°24S 39°30W 333 E4
Camaçari Brazil 12°41S 38°18W 333 D4
Camacha Madeira 32°41N 16°49W 153 c
Camacupa Angola 11°58S 17°22E 265 E3
Camaguán Venezuela 8°6N 67°36W 328 B4
Camagüey Cuba 21°20N 77°55W 320 B4
Camagüey, Arch. de Cuba 22°18N 78°0W 320 B4
Camaiore Italy 43°56N 10°18E 198 E7
Camamu Brazil 13°57S 39°7W 333 D4
Camaná Peru 16°30S 72°50W 330 D3
Camanche U.S.A. 41°47N 90°15W 310 C6
Camanche Res. U.S.A. 38°14N 121°1W 306 G6
Camapuã Brazil 19°30S 54°5W 331 D7
Camaquã Brazil 30°51S 51°49W 335 C5
Camaquã → Brazil 31°17S 51°47W 335 C5
Câmara de Lobos Madeira 32°39N 16°59W 153 c
Camararé → Brazil 12°15S 58°55W 331 C6
Camarat, C. France 43°12N 6°41E 175 E10
Camarate Portugal 38°48N 9°7W 126 A2
Çamardı Turkey 37°49N 34°58E 212 D6
Camarès France 43°49N 2°53E 174 E6
Camaret-sur-Mer France 48°16N 4°37W 172 D2
Camargo Bolivia 20°38S 65°15W 331 E4
Camargo Tamaulipas, Mexico 26°19N 98°50W 319 B5
Camargue France 43°34N 4°34E 175 E8
Camargue ⌂ France 43°30N 4°40E 175 E8
Camarillo U.S.A. 34°13N 119°2W 307 L7
Camariñas Spain 43°8N 9°12W 194 B1
Camarines Norte □ Phil. 14°10N 122°45E 232 D4
Camarines Sur □ Phil. 13°40N 123°20E 232 E4
Camaroes Portugal 38°49N 9°14W 126 A1
Camarón, C. Honduras 16°0N 85°5W 320 C2
Camarones Argentina 44°50S 65°40W 336 B3
Camarones, B. Argentina 44°45S 65°35W 336 B3
Camas Spain 37°24N 6°2W 195 H4
Camas Wash., U.S.A. 45°35N 122°24W 306 E4
Camas Valley U.S.A. 43°2N 123°40W 304 E2
Camatambo Angola 6°31S 15°21E 265 D3
Camataquí = Villa Abecia Bolivia 21°0S 68°18W 334 A2
Camaxilo Angola 8°21S 18°56E 265 D3
Camba Cassai Angola 9°47S 19°9E 265 D3
Camballin Australia 17°59S 124°12E 278 C3
Cambamba Angola 8°53S 14°44E 265 D2
Cambará Brazil 23°2S 50°5W 335 A5
Cambay = Khambhat India 22°23N 72°33E 242 H5
Cambay, G. of = Khambhat, G. of India 20°45N 72°30E 239 E10
Camberwell Vic., Australia 37°50S 145°5E 128 B2
Camberwell London, U.K. 51°28N 0°5W 125 B3
Cambil Spain 37°40N 3°33W 195 H7
Cambo Angola 10°55S 20°6E 265 D3
Cambo-les-Bains France 43°22N 1°23W 174 E2
Cambodia ■ Asia 12°15N 105°0E 236 F5
Camborne U.K. 50°12N 5°19W 169 G2
Cambrai S. Austral., Australia 34°40S 139°16E 282 C3
Cambrai Nord, France 50°11N 3°14E 173 B10
Cambre Spain 43°17N 8°20W 194 B2
Cambria U.S.A. 35°34N 121°5W 306 K5
Cambrian Mts. U.K. 52°3N 3°57W 169 E4
Cambridge Ont., Canada 43°23N 80°15W 312 C4
Cambridge Jamaica 18°18N 77°54W 320 a
Cambridge N.Z. 37°54S 175°29E 284 D4
Cambridge Cambs., U.K. 52°12N 0°8E 169 E8
Cambridge Ill., U.S.A. 41°18N 90°12W 310 C6
Cambridge Iowa, U.S.A. 41°54N 93°32W 310 C3
Cambridge Mass., U.S.A. 42°23N 71°7W 116 A2
Cambridge Minn., U.S.A. 45°34N 93°13W 308 C7
Cambridge N.Y., U.S.A. 43°2N 73°22W 313 C11
Cambridge Nebr., U.S.A. 40°17N 100°10W 308 E3
Cambridge Ohio, U.S.A. 40°2N 81°35W 312 F3
Cambridge Bay Canada 69°10N 105°0W 294 D11
Cambridge City U.S.A. 39°49N 85°10W 311 E11
Cambridge G. Australia 14°55S 128°15E 278 B4
Cambridge Springs U.S.A. 41°48N 80°4W 312 E4
Cambridgeshire □ U.K. 52°25N 0°7W 169 E7
Cambrils Spain 41°8N 1°3E 196 D6
Cambuci Rio de J., Brazil 21°35S 41°55W 333 F3
Cambuci São Paulo, Brazil 23°33S 46°47W 137 B2
Cambulo Angola 7°49S 21°15E 265 D4
Cambundi-Catembo Angola 10°10S 17°35E 265 E3
Camdeboo △ S. Africa 32°28S 24°25E 270 D3
Camden N.S.W., Australia 34°1S 150°43E 283 C9
Camden Ala., U.S.A. 31°59N 87°17W 315 F11
Camden Ark., U.S.A. 33°35N 92°50W 314 E8
Camden Maine, U.S.A. 44°13N 69°4W 309 C19
Camden N.J., U.S.A. 39°55N 75°7W 313 G9
Camden N.Y., U.S.A. 43°20N 75°45W 313 C9
Camden Ohio, U.S.A. 39°38N 84°39W 311 E12
Camden S.C., U.S.A. 34°16N 80°36W 315 D14
Camden □ U.K. 51°32N 0°8W 125 A3
Camden Bay U.S.A. 70°10N 145°15W 303 A11
Camden Sd. Australia 15°27S 124°25E 278 C3
Camdenton U.S.A. 38°1N 92°45W 310 F4
Cameia △ Angola 12°5S 21°40E 265 E4
Camelford U.K. 50°37N 4°42W 169 G3
Çameli Turkey 37°5N 29°24E 205 D11
Camenca Moldova 48°3N 28°42E 183 B13
Camerino Italy 43°8N 13°4E 199 E10
Camerón Chile 53°38S 69°39W 336 D3
Cameron Ariz., U.S.A. 35°53N 111°25W 305 J8
Cameron La., U.S.A. 29°48N 93°20W 314 G8
Cameron Mo., U.S.A. 39°44N 94°14W 310 E2
Cameron S.C., U.S.A. 33°34N 80°43W 316 B9
Cameron Tex., U.S.A. 30°51N 96°59W 314 F6
Cameron, Mt. N.Z. 41°20S 174°52E 143 B2
Cameron Highlands Malaysia 4°27N 101°22E 237 K3
Cameron Hills Canada 59°48N 118°0W 296 B5
Cameron Mts. N.Z. 46°1S 167°0E 285 G2
Cameroon ■ Africa 6°0N 12°30E 264 A2
Camerota Italy 40°2N 15°22E 201 B8
Cameroun → Cameroon 4°0N 9°35E 263 E6
Cameroun, Mt. Cameroon 4°13N 9°10E 263 E6
Cametá Brazil 2°12S 49°30W 332 B2
Çamiçi Gölü Turkey 37°29N 27°28E 205 D9
Camiguin □ Phil. 9°11N 124°42E 233 G5
Camiguin I. Phil. 18°56N 121°55E 232 B3
Camiling Phil. 15°42N 120°24E 232 D3
Camilla U.S.A. 31°14N 84°12W 316 D5
Caminha Portugal 41°50N 8°50W 194 D2
Camino U.S.A. 38°44N 120°41W 306 G6
Camiranga Brazil 1°48S 46°17W 332 B2
Camiri Bolivia 20°3S 63°31W 331 E5
Camissombo Angola 8°7S 20°38E 265 D4
Çamlıca Turkey 41°1N 29°3E 122 B2
Çamlıyayla Turkey 37°10N 34°36E 250 A5
Cammal U.S.A. 41°24N 77°28W 312 E7
Cammarata Italy 37°38N 13°38E 200 E6

Cammin = Kamień Pomorski Poland 53°57N 14°43E 184 E1
Camo Ethiopia 4°29N 38°24E 266 D4
Camocim Brazil 2°55S 40°50W 332 B3
Camooweal Australia 19°56S 138°7E 280 B2
Camooweal Caves △ Australia 20°1S 138°11E 280 C2
Camopi Fr. Guiana 3°12N 52°17W 329 C7
Camopi → Fr. Guiana 3°10N 52°20W 329 C7
Camorta India 8°8N 93°30E 245 K11
Camotes Is. Phil. 10°40N 124°24E 233 F5
Camotes Sea Phil. 10°30N 124°15E 233 F5
Camp Coulter = Powell U.S.A. 44°45N 108°46W 304 D9
Camp Hill Ala., U.S.A. 32°48N 85°39W 316 C4
Camp Hill Pa., U.S.A. 40°14N 76°55W 312 F8
Camp Nelson U.S.A. 36°8N 118°39W 307 J8
Camp Pendleton U.S.A. 33°13N 117°24W 307 M9
Camp Point U.S.A. 40°3N 91°4W 310 D5
Camp Springs U.S.A. 38°48N 76°55W 143 C4
Camp Verde U.S.A. 34°34N 111°51W 305 J8
Camp Wood U.S.A. 29°40N 100°1W 314 G4
Campagna Italy 40°40N 15°6E 201 B8
Campamento Spain 40°23N 3°46W 127 B1
Campana Argentina 34°10S 58°55W 334 C4
Campana, I. Chile 48°20S 75°20W 336 C1
Campanário Madeira 32°39N 17°2W 153 c
Campanario Spain 38°52N 5°36W 195 G5
Campanet Spain 39°46N 2°58E 206 B3
Campánia ☐ Italy 41°0N 14°30E 201 B7
Campbell Northern Cape, S. Africa 28°48S 23°44E 270 C3
Campbell Calif., U.S.A. 37°17N 121°57W 306 H5
Campbell Fla., U.S.A. 28°16N 81°27W 317 G8
Campbell Ohio, U.S.A. 41°5N 80°37W 312 E4
Campbell, C. N.Z. 41°47S 174°18E 285 B9
Campbell I. Pac. Oc. 52°30S 169°0E 288 N8
Campbell L. Canada 63°14N 106°55W 297 A7
Campbell Plateau S. Ocean 50°0S 170°0E 151 A11
Campbell River Canada 50°5N 125°20W 296 C3
Campbellfield Australia 37°41S 144°57E 128 A1
Campbellford Canada 44°18N 77°48W 312 B7
Campbellpur Pakistan 33°46N 72°26E 242 C5
Campbellsburg U.S.A. 38°39N 86°16W 311 F10
Campbellsville U.S.A. 37°21N 85°20W 309 G11
Campbellton N.B., Canada 47°57N 66°43W 299 C6
Campbellton Fla., U.S.A. 30°57N 85°24W 316 E4
Campbelltown = Bluff N.Z. 46°37S 168°20E 285 G3
Campbelltown Australia 34°4S 150°49E 283 C9
Campbeltown U.K. 55°26N 5°36W 167 F3
Campêche Guadeloupe 16°26N 61°26W 322 e
Campeche Campeche, Mexico 19°51N 90°32W 319 D6
Campeche ☐ Mexico 19°0N 90°30W 319 D6
Campeche, Banco Mexico 22°30N 88°0W 320 B2
Campeche, Golfo de Mexico 19°30N 93°0W 319 D6
Câmpeni Romania 46°22N 23°3E 182 D8
Camperdown N.S.W., Australia 33°53S 151°11E 139 B2
Camperdown Vic., Australia 38°14S 143°9E 282 E5
Camperville Canada 51°59N 100°9W 297 C8
Campi Salentina Italy 40°24N 18°1E 201 B11
Câmpia Turzii Romania 46°34N 23°53E 183 D8
Campidano Italy 39°30N 8°47E 200 C1
Campidoglio, Piazza de Rome, Italy 136 c3
Campíglia Maríttima Italy 43°4N 10°37E 198 E7
Campillo de Altobuey Spain 39°36N 1°49W 197 F3
Campillos Spain 37°4N 4°51W 195 H6
Câmpina Romania 45°10N 25°45E 183 E10
Campina Grande Brazil 7°20S 35°47W 332 C4
Campina Verde Brazil 19°31S 49°28W 333 E2
Campinas Brazil 22°50S 47°0W 335 A6
Campione Italy 45°58N 8°58E 175 C12
Campli Italy 42°43N 13°41E 199 F10
Campo = Ntem → Cameroon 2°21N 9°49E 264 B2
Campo Cameroon 2°22N 9°50E 264 B1
Campo Spain 42°25N 0°24E 196 C5
Campo, Casa de Spain 40°25N 3°45W 127 B1
Campo ⌓ Cameroon 2°23N 10°5E 264 B2
Campo Belo Brazil 20°52S 45°16W 333 F2
Campo de Criptana Spain 39°24N 3°7W 195 F7
Campo de Diauarum Brazil 11°12S 53°14W 331 C7
Campo de Gibraltar Spain 36°15N 5°25W 195 J5
Campo F.C. Barcelona Spain 41°22N 2°7E 114 A1
Campo Florido Brazil 19°47S 48°35W 333 E2
Campo Formoso = Campo Florido Brazil 19°47S 48°35W 333 E2
Campo Formoso Brazil 10°30S 40°20W 332 D3
Campo Grande Brazil 20°25S 54°40W 331 E7
Campo Grando Portugal 38°45N 9°9W 126 A2
Campo Maior Brazil 4°50S 42°12W 332 B3
Campo Maior Portugal 39°2N 7°7W 195 F3
Campo Mourão Brazil 24°3S 52°22W 335 A5
Campo Pequeño Portugal 38°44N 9°8W 126 A2
Campo Túres Italy 46°53N 11°55E 199 B8
Campoalegre Colombia 2°41N 75°20W 328 C2
Campobasso Italy 41°34N 14°39E 201 A7
Campobello di Licata Italy 37°15N 13°55E 200 E6
Campobello di Mazara Italy 37°38N 12°45E 200 E5
Campofelice di Roccella Italy 37°59N 13°53E 200 E6
Campolide Portugal 38°43N 9°9W 126 A2
Campomarino Italy 41°57N 15°2E 199 G12
Camporeale Italy 37°54N 13°6E 200 E6
Camporrobles Spain 39°39N 1°24W 196 F3
Campos Brazil 21°50S 41°20W 333 F3
Campos Spain 39°26N 3°1E 206 B4
Campos Altos Brazil 19°47S 46°10W 333 E2
Campos Belos Brazil 13°10S 47°3W 333 D2
Campos del Paraíso = Carrascosa del Campo Spain 40°2N 2°45W 196 E2
Campos Novos Brazil 27°21S 51°50W 335 B5
Campos Sales Brazil 7°4S 40°23W 332 C3
Camprodon Spain 42°19N 2°23E 196 C7
Camps Bay S. Africa 33°57S 18°23E 118 A1
Campton Fla., U.S.A. 30°53N 86°31W 317 E3
Campton Ga., U.S.A. 33°52N 83°43W 316 B6
Campton Ky., U.S.A. 37°44N 83°33W 311 G13
Camptonville U.S.A. 39°27N 121°3W 306 F5
Camptown U.S.A. 41°44N 76°14W 313 E8
Câmpulung Argeş, Romania 45°17N 25°3E 183 E10
Câmpulung Suceava, Romania 47°32N 25°30E 183 C10
Câmpuri Romania 46°0N 26°50E 183 D11
Campuya → Peru 1°40S 73°30W 328 D3
Campville U.S.A. 29°40N 82°7W 316 F7
Camrose Canada 53°0N 112°50W 296 C6
Camsell Portage Canada 59°37N 109°15W 297 B7
Camucuio Angola 14°7S 13°15E 265 E2
Camuy Puerto Rico 18°29N 66°51W 321 b
Çamyuva Turkey 36°30N 30°30E 205 E12
Çan Turkey 40°2N 27°3E 203 F11
Can Clavo Spain 38°57N 1°27E 206 D1
Can Creu Spain 38°58N 1°28E 206 D1
Can Gio Vietnam 10°25N 106°58E 237 G6
Can Pastilla Spain 39°32N 2°42E 206 B3
C'an San Joan Spain 41°28N 2°11E 114 A2
Can Tho Vietnam 10°2N 105°46E 237 G5
Canaan Trin. & Tob. 11°9N 60°49W 323 s
Canaan Conn., U.S.A. 42°2N 73°20W 313 D11
Canaan Hill Jamaica 18°23N 77°14W 320 a
Cañacao B. Phil. 14°29N 120°54E 127 C1
Canacona India 15°1N 74°4E 245 G2
Canada ■ N. Amer. 60°0N 100°0W 294 G11
Canada Abyssal Plain Arctic 80°0N 140°0W 150 B18
Canada Basin Arctic 80°0N 145°0W 150 B18
Cañada de Gómez Argentina 32°40S 61°30W 334 C3
Canadian U.S.A. 35°55N 100°23W 314 D4
Canadian → U.S.A. 35°28N 95°3W 314 D7
Canadian Shield Canada 53°0N 75°0W 292 D12
Canadys U.S.A. 33°3N 80°37W 316 B9
Canajoharie U.S.A. 42°54N 74°35W 313 D10
Çanakkale Turkey 40°8N 26°24E 203 F10
Çanakkale ☐ Turkey 40°10N 26°25E 203 F10
Çanakkale Boğazı Turkey 40°17N 26°32E 203 F10
Canal Flats Canada 50°10N 115°48W 296 C5
Canal Point U.S.A. 26°52N 80°38W 317 J9
Canal Street New Orleans, U.S.A. 131 b2
Canala N. Cal. 21°32S 165°57E 288 d
Canalejas Argentina 35°15S 66°34W 334 D2
Canals Argentina 33°35S 62°53W 334 C3
Canals Spain 38°58N 0°35W 197 G4
Canandaigua U.S.A. 42°54N 77°17W 312 D7
Canandaigua L. U.S.A. 42°47N 77°19W 312 D7
Cananea Mexico 31°0N 110°18W 318 A2
Cañar Ecuador 2°33S 78°56W 328 D2
Cañar ☐ Ecuador 2°30S 79°0W 328 D2
Canarias, Is. Atl. Oc. 28°30N 16°0W 153 e1
Canaries St. Lucia 13°55N 61°4W 323 m
Canarreos, Arch. de los Cuba 21°35N 81°40W 320 B3
Canarsie U.S.A. 40°38N 73°53W 132 C2
Canary Is. = Canarias, Is. Atl. Oc. 28°30N 16°0W 153 e1
Canaseraga U.S.A. 42°27N 77°45W 312 D7
Canastra, Serra da Brazil 20°0S 46°20W 333 F2
Canatlán Mexico 24°31N 104°47W 318 C4
Cañaveral Peru 3°56S 80°39W 328 D1
Canaveral, C. U.S.A. 28°27N 80°32W 317 G9
Canaveral ⌓ U.S.A. 28°28N 80°34W 317 G9
Cañaveruelas Spain 40°24N 2°38W 196 E2
Canavieiras Brazil 15°39S 39°0W 333 E4
Canbelego Australia 31°32S 146°18E 283 A7
Canberra Australia 35°15S 149°8E 283 C8
Canby Calif., U.S.A. 41°27N 120°52W 304 F3
Canby Minn., U.S.A. 44°43N 96°16W 308 C5
Canby Oreg., U.S.A. 45°16N 122°42W 306 E4
Cancale France 48°40N 1°50W 172 D5
Cancelleria, Palazzo dei Rome, Italy 136 c2
Canche → France 50°31N 1°39E 173 B8
Canchungo = Teixeira Pinto Guinea-Biss. 12°3N 16°0W 262 C1
Canchungo Guinea-Biss. 12°26N 16°5W 262 C1
Canchyuaya, Cordillera de Peru 7°30S 74°0W 330 B3
Cancún Mexico 21°8N 86°44W 319 C7
Candanchú Spain 42°47N 0°32W 196 C4
Candarave Peru 17°15S 70°13W 330 D3
Çandarlı Turkey 38°56N 26°56E 205 C8
Çandarlı Körfezi Turkey 38°52N 26°55E 205 C8
Candás Spain 43°35N 5°45W 194 B5
Candé France 47°34N 1°2W 172 E5
Candeias → Brazil 8°39S 63°31W 331 B5
Candela Italy 41°8N 15°31E 201 A8
Candelaria Argentina 27°29S 55°44W 335 B4
Candelaria Canary Is. 28°22N 16°22W 153 e1
Candelaria Phil. 13°56N 121°25E 232 E3
Candelario ⌓ Spain 40°20N 5°46W 194 E5
Candeleda Spain 40°10N 5°14W 194 E5
Candelo Australia 36°47S 149°43E 283 D8
Candi Dasa Indonesia 8°30S 115°34E 231 J18
Candia = Iraklio Greece 35°20N 25°12E 207 E6
Candia, Sea of = Crete, Sea of Greece 36°0N 25°0E 205 E7
Candiac Canada 45°23N 73°29W 130 B3
Cândido de Abreu Brazil 24°35S 51°20W 333 F1
Cândido Mendes Brazil 1°27S 45°43W 332 B2
Candle U.S.A. 65°55N 161°56W 303 D7
Candle L. Canada 53°50N 105°18W 297 C7
Candlemas I. Antarctica 57°3S 26°40W 151 B1
Cando U.S.A. 48°32N 99°12W 308 A4
Candon Phil. 17°12N 120°27E 232 C3
Canea = Chania Greece 35°30N 24°4E 207 E5
Caneças Portugal 38°48N 9°13W 126 A1
Canefield Dominica 15°20N 61°24W 323 k
Canela Brazil 10°15S 48°25W 332 D2
Canelles → St. Lucia 13°47N 60°55W 323 m
Canelli Italy 44°43N 8°17E 198 D5
Canelones Uruguay 34°32S 56°17W 335 C4
Canet-Plage France 42°41N 3°2E 174 F7
Cañete Chile 37°50S 73°30W 334 D1
Cañete Spain 40°3N 1°54W 196 E3
Cañete de las Torres Spain 37°53N 4°19W 195 H6
Cangamba Angola 13°40S 19°54E 265 E3
Cangandala Angola 9°45S 16°33E 265 D3
Cangandala △ Angola 9°53S 16°42E 265 D3
Cangas Spain 42°16N 8°47W 194 C2
Cangas de Onís Spain 43°21N 5°8W 194 B5
Cangas de Tineo = Cangas del Narcea Spain 43°10N 6°32W 194 B4
Cangas del Narcea Spain 43°10N 6°32W 194 B4
Cangnan China 27°30N 120°23E 229 D13
Cangoa Angola 13°8S 18°30E 265 E3
Cangola Angola 7°58S 15°53E 265 D3
Cangolo Angola 15°0S 13°52E 265 E2
Cangombe Angola 14°24S 19°59E 265 E3
Cangongo Angola 9°24S 17°30E 265 D3
Cangshan China 34°50N 118°2E 227 G10
Canguaretama Brazil 6°20S 35°5W 332 C4
Canguçu Brazil 31°22S 52°43W 335 C5
Canguçu, Serra do Brazil 31°20S 52°40W 335 C5
Cangumbe Angola 11°58S 19°12E 265 E3
Cangxi China 31°47N 105°59E 228 B5
Cangyuan China 23°12N 99°14E 228 F2
Cangzhou China 38°19N 116°52E 226 E9
Canhoca Angola 9°15S 14°41E 265 D2
Cani, I. Tunisia 36°21N 10°5E 258 A2
Caniapiscau → Canada 56°40N 69°30W 299 A6
Caniapiscau, L. Canada 54°10N 69°55W 299 B6
Canicattì Italy 37°21N 13°51E 200 E6
Canicattini Bagni Italy 37°2N 15°4E 201 E8
Canigao Channel Phil. 10°15N 124°42E 233 F5
Caniles Spain 37°26N 2°43W 195 H8
Canillas Spain 40°27N 3°38W 127 B2
Canillejas Spain 40°26N 3°36W 127 B2
Canim Lake Canada 51°47N 120°54W 296 C4
Canindé Brazil 4°22S 39°19W 332 B4
Canindé → Brazil 6°15S 42°52W 332 C3
Canindeyu ☐ Paraguay 24°10S 55°0W 335 A5
Canino Italy 42°28N 11°45E 199 F8
Canisteo U.S.A. 42°16N 77°36W 312 D7
Canisteo → U.S.A. 42°7N 77°8W 312 D7
Cañitas de Felipe Pescador Mexico 23°36N 102°43W 318 C4
Cañizal Spain 41°12N 5°22W 194 D5
Canjáyar Spain 37°1N 2°44W 195 H8
Canjinge Angola 10°12S 21°17E 265 E4
Çankırı Turkey 40°40N 33°37E 212 B5
Çankırı ☐ Turkey 40°40N 33°30E 212 B5
Cankuzo Burundi 3°10S 30°31E 268 C3
Canlaon Phil. 10°22N 123°12E 233 F4
Canlaon Volcano Phil. 10°25N 123°8E 233 F4
Canmore Canada 51°7N 115°18W 296 C5
Cann River Australia 37°35S 149°7E 283 D8
Canna U.K. 57°3N 6°33W 167 D2
Cannanore India 11°53N 75°27E 245 J2
Cannanore Is. India 10°30N 72°30E 245 J1
Cannelton U.S.A. 37°55N 86°45W 311 G10
Cannery, The San Francisco, U.S.A. 136 a1
Cannes France 43°32N 7°1E 175 E11
Canning Town = Port Canning India 22°23N 88°40E 243 H13
Canning Town U.K. 51°30N 0°1E 125 A4
Cannington Canada 44°20N 79°2W 312 B5
Cannóbio Italy 46°4N 8°42E 198 B5
Cannock U.K. 52°41N 2°1W 169 E5
Cannonball → U.S.A. 46°26N 100°35W 308 B3
Cannondale Mt. Australia 25°13S 148°57E 280 D4
Cannonsville Res. U.S.A. 42°4N 75°22W 313 D9
Cannonvale Australia 20°17S 148°43E 280 b
Caño Colorado Colombia 2°18N 68°22W 328 C4
Canoas Brazil 29°56S 51°11W 335 B5
Canoe L. Canada 55°10N 108°15W 297 B7
Cañon City U.S.A. 38°27N 105°14W 304 G11
Cañón de Río Blanco △ Mexico 18°43N 97°15W 319 D5
Cañón del Río Lobos ⌓ Spain 41°46N 3°28W 194 D7
Cañón del Sumidero △ Mexico 19°22N 96°24W 319 D5
Canonnier, Pte. du St.-Martin 18°4N 63°7W 322 a
Canonniers Pt. Mauritius 20°2S 57°32E 272 e
Canoochee → U.S.A. 31°59N 81°19W 316 D8
Canopus Australia 33°29S 140°42E 282 B4
Canora Canada 51°40N 102°30W 297 C8
Canosa di Púglia Italy 41°13N 16°4E 201 A9
Canouan St. Vincent 12°43N 61°20W 323 n
Canowindra Australia 33°35S 148°38E 283 B8
Canso Canada 45°20N 61°0W 299 C7
Canta Peru 11°29S 76°37W 330 C2
Cantabria ☐ Spain 43°10N 4°0W 194 B7
Cantabria, Sierra de Spain 42°40N 2°30W 196 C2
Cantabrian Mts. = Cantábrica, Cordillera Spain 43°0N 5°10W 194 C5
Cantábrica, Cordillera Spain 43°0N 5°10W 194 C5
Cantal ☐ France 45°5N 2°45E 174 C6
Cantal, Plomb du France 45°3N 2°45E 174 C6
Cantanhede Portugal 40°20N 8°36W 194 E2
Cantaura Venezuela 9°19N 64°21W 329 B5
Cantavieja Spain 40°31N 0°25W 196 E4
Čantavir Serbia 45°55N 19°46E 182 E4
Cantemir Moldova 46°17N 28°14E 183 D13
Canteras de Vallecas Spain 40°20N 3°37W 127 B2
Canterbury = Invermere Canada 50°30N 116°2W 296 C5
Canterbury N.S.W., Australia 33°55S 151°7E 139 B1
Canterbury Queens., Australia 25°23S 141°53E 280 D3
Canterbury Vic., Australia 37°49S 145°4E 128 A2
Canterbury Kent, U.K. 51°16N 1°6E 169 F9
Canterbury ☐ N.Z. 43°45S 171°19E 285 D6
Canterbury Bight N.Z. 44°16S 171°55E 285 E6
Canterbury Plains N.Z. 43°55S 171°22E 285 D6
Cantil U.S.A. 35°18N 117°58W 307 K9
Cantilan Phil. 9°20N 125°58E 233 G5
Cantillana Spain 37°36N 5°50W 195 H5
Canto do Buriti Brazil 8°7S 42°58W 332 C3
Canton = Guangzhou China 23°6N 113°13E 121 B2
Canton Ga., U.S.A. 34°14N 84°29W 315 D12
Canton Ill., U.S.A. 40°33N 90°2W 310 D6
Canton Miss., U.S.A. 32°37N 90°2W 315 E9
Canton Mo., U.S.A. 40°8N 91°32W 310 D5
Canton N.Y., U.S.A. 44°36N 75°10W 313 B9
Canton Ohio, U.S.A. 40°48N 81°23W 312 F3
Canton Pa., U.S.A. 41°39N 76°51W 312 E8
Canton S. Dak., U.S.A. 43°18N 96°35W 308 D5
Canton L. U.S.A. 36°6N 98°35W 314 C5
Cantonment U.S.A. 30°37N 87°20W 317 E2
Cantù Italy 45°44N 9°8E 198 C6
Cantwell U.S.A. 63°24N 148°57W 303 E10
Canudos Brazil 7°13S 58°5W 331 B6
Canumã Amazonas, Brazil 4°2S 59°4W 329 D6
Canumã Amazonas, Brazil 6°8S 60°10W 331 B5
Canumã → Brazil 3°55S 59°10W 331 A6
Canunda △ Australia 37°42S 140°16E 282 D4
Canutama Brazil 6°30S 64°20W 331 B5
Canutillo U.S.A. 31°55N 106°36W 314 F1
Canvey U.K. 51°31N 0°37E 169 F8
Canyon U.S.A. 34°59N 101°55W 314 D4
Canyon De Chelly ⌓ U.S.A. 36°10N 109°20W 305 H9
Canyonlands △ U.S.A. 38°15N 110°0W 305 G9
Canyons of the Ancients ⌓ U.S.A. 37°30N 108°55W 305 H9
Canyonville U.S.A. 42°56N 123°17W 304 E2
Canzar Angola 7°35S 21°34E 265 D4
Cao Bang Vietnam 22°40N 106°15E 228 F6
Cao He → China 40°10N 124°32E 227 D13
Cao Lanh Vietnam 10°27N 105°38E 237 G5
Cao Xian China 34°50N 115°35E 226 G8
Caoheijing China 31°10N 121°25E 138 B1
Caombo Angola 8°42S 16°33E 265 D3
Cáorle Italy 45°36N 12°53E 199 C9
Cap-aux-Meules Canada 47°23N 61°52W 299 C7
Cap-Chat Canada 49°6N 66°40W 299 C6
Cap-de-la-Madeleine Canada 46°22N 72°31W 298 C5
Cap de Ville Trin. & Tob. 10°9N 61°42W 323 t
Cap-Haïtien Haiti 19°40N 72°20W 321 C5
Cap I. Phil. 5°57N 120°6E 233 J3
Cap Pt. St. Lucia 14°7N 60°57W 323 m
Capac U.S.A. 43°1N 82°56W 312 C2
Capáccio Italy 40°25N 15°5E 201 B8
Capaci Italy 38°10N 13°14E 200 D6
Capaia Angola 8°27S 20°13E 265 D4
Capalonga Phil. 14°20N 122°30E 232 D4
Capanaparo → Venezuela 7°1N 67°7W 328 B4
Capanema Brazil 1°12S 47°11W 332 B2
Capangombe Angola 15°6S 13°8E 265 F2
Capánnori Italy 43°50N 10°34E 198 E7
Capão Redondo Brazil 23°39S 46°45W 137 B1
Caparaó △ Brazil 20°25S 41°46W 333 F3
Caparica Portugal 38°40N 9°9W 126 A2
Caparica, Costa da Portugal 38°38N 9°15W 126 B1
Caparo → Trin. & Tob. 10°31N 61°28W 323 t
Capas Phil. 15°38N 120°28E 232 D3
Capatárida Venezuela 11°11N 70°37W 328 A3
Capayas Phil. 10°28N 119°39E 233 F2
Capbreton France 43°39N 1°26W 174 E2
Capdenac France 44°34N 2°5E 174 D6
Capdepera Spain 39°42N 3°26E 206 B4
Cape → Australia 20°59S 146°51E 280 C4
Cape Arid △ Australia 33°58S 123°13E 279 F3
Cape Barren I. Australia 40°25S 148°15E 281 G4
Cape Basin Atl. Oc. 34°0S 7°0W 152 K12
Cape Breton Highlands △ Canada 46°50N 60°40W 299 C7
Cape Breton I. Canada 46°0N 60°30W 299 C7
Cape Canaveral U.S.A. 28°24N 80°36W 317 G9
Cape Charles U.S.A. 37°16N 76°1W 309 G15
Cape Coast Ghana 5°5N 1°15W 263 D4
Cape Cod ⌓ U.S.A. 41°56N 70°6W 309 E18
Cape Coral U.S.A. 26°33N 81°57W 317 J8
Cape Crawford Australia 16°41S 135°43E 280 B2
Cape Dorset = Kinngait Canada 64°14N 76°32W 295 E16
Cape Fear → U.S.A. 33°53N 78°1W 315 E15
Cape Flats S. Africa 34°3S 18°33E 118 B2
Cape Girardeau U.S.A. 37°19N 89°32W 308 G9
Cape Hatteras ⌓ U.S.A. 35°30N 75°28W 315 D17
Cape Hillsborough △ Australia 20°54S 149°2E 280 b
Cape Jervis Australia 35°40S 138°5E 282 C3
Cape Krusenstern ⌓ U.S.A. 67°30N 163°30W 303 C7
Cape Le Grand △ Australia 33°54S 122°26E 279 F3
Cape Lisburne = Wevok U.S.A. 68°53N 166°13W 303 B6
Cape Lookout ⌓ U.S.A. 35°45N 76°25W 315 D16
Cape May U.S.A. 38°56N 74°56W 309 F16
Cape May Point U.S.A. 38°56N 74°58W 309 F16
Cape Melville △ Australia 14°26S 144°28E 280 A3
Cape Mount △ Liberia 6°44N 11°24W 262 D2
Cape Pole U.S.A. 55°58N 133°48W 303 J14
Cape Range △ Australia 22°3S 114°0E 278 D1
Cape St. George Canada 48°28N 59°14W 299 C8
Cape Tormentine Canada 46°8N 63°47W 299 C7
Cape Town S. Africa 33°55S 18°22E 118 A1
Cape Town Int. ✕ (CPT) S. Africa 33°58S 18°35E 118 A2
Cape Upstart △ Australia 19°45S 147°48E 280 B4
Cape Verde Abyssal Plain Atl. Oc. 23°0N 26°0W 152 D9
Cape Verde Is. ■ Atl. Oc. 16°0N 24°0W 153 j
Cape Verde Plateau Atl. Oc. 18°0N 20°0W 152 E10
Cape Vincent U.S.A. 44°8N 76°20W 313 B8
Cape Yakataga U.S.A. 60°4N 142°26W 303 F12
Cape York Peninsula Australia 12°0S 142°30E 286 F2
Capela Brazil 10°30S 37°0W 332 D4
Capelas Azores 37°50N 25°41W 153 d3
Capele Angola 13°39S 14°53E 265 E2
Capelengue Angola 8°53S 19°42E 265 D3
Capelinha Brazil 17°42S 42°31W 333 E3
Capelinhos, Pta. dos Azores 38°36N 28°50W 153 d1
Capella Australia 23°2S 148°1E 280 C4
Capella, Mt. Papua N. G. 5°4S 141°8E 286 C1
Capelongo Angola 14°54S 15°8E 265 E3
Capenda Camulemba Angola 9°24S 18°27E 265 D3
Capendu France 43°11N 2°31E 174 E6
Capertree Australia 33°6S 149°58E 283 B8
Capestang France 43°20N 3°2E 174 E7
Capesterre, Grande Rivière de la → Guadeloupe 16°3N 61°33W 322 e
Capesterre, Pte. de la Guadeloupe 16°3N 61°33W 322 e
Capesterre-Belle-Eau Guadeloupe 16°4N 61°36W 322 e
Capesterre-de-Marie-Galante Guadeloupe 15°53N 61°14W 322 e
Capim → Brazil 1°40S 47°47W 332 B2
Capinópolis Brazil 18°41S 49°35W 333 E2
Capinota Bolivia 17°43S 66°14W 330 D4
Capira Panama 8°45N 79°53W 328 B2
Capistrello Italy 41°57N 13°23E 199 G10
Capitan U.S.A. 33°35N 105°35W 305 K11
Capitán Aracena, I. Chile 54°10S 71°20W 336 D2
Capitán Arturo Prat Antarctica 63°0S 61°0W 151 C17
Capitán Pastene Chile 38°13S 73°1W 336 A2
Capitão de Campos Brazil 4°40S 41°55W 332 B3
Capitol Heights U.S.A. 38°52N 76°55W 143 B4
Capitol Hill N. Marianas 15°13N 145°45E 302 e
Capitol Reef △ U.S.A. 38°15N 111°10W 305 G8
Capitola U.S.A. 36°59N 121°57W 306 J5
Capitolini, Musei Rome, Italy 136 c3
Capivara, Serra da Brazil 14°35S 45°0W 333 D3
Capiz ☐ Phil. 11°35N 122°30E 233 F4
Capizzi Italy 37°51N 14°29E 201 E7
Capoche → Mozam. 15°35S 33°0E 269 F3
Capodichino, Nápoli ✕ (NAP) Italy 40°53N 14°16E 201 B7
Capoeira Brazil 5°37S 59°33W 331 B6
Capolo Angola 10°22S 14°7E 265 E2
Caporetto = Kobarid Slovenia 46°15N 13°30E 199 B10
Caporolo → Angola 12°56S 12°58E 265 E2
Capot → Martinique 14°50N 61°5W 322 j
Capoterra Italy 39°11N 8°58E 200 C1
Cappadocia Turkey 39°0N 35°0E 212 C6
Capps U.S.A. 30°24N 83°54W 316 E6
Capraia Italy 43°2N 9°50E 198 E6
Caprara, Pta. Italy 41°7N 8°19E 200 A1
Caprarola Italy 42°19N 12°14E 199 F9
Caprera Italy 41°12N 9°28E 200 A2
Capri Italy 40°33N 14°14E 201 B7
Capricorn Coast Australia 23°16S 150°49E 280 C5
Capricorn Group Australia 23°30S 151°55E 280 C5
Capricorn Ra. Australia 23°20S 116°50E 278 D2
Caprino Veronese Italy 45°36N 10°47E 198 C7
Caprivi ⌓ Namibia 17°55S 22°37E 270 A3
Caprivi Strip Namibia 18°0S 23°0E 270 A3
Caps et Marais d'Opale ⌓ France 50°40N 2°0E 173 B9
Captain Cook U.S.A. 19°30N 155°55W 302 D6
Captain Cook Bridge Australia 34°0S 151°7E 139 C1
Captain Cook Landing Place Park Australia 34°1S 151°14E 139 C2
Captains Flat Australia 35°35S 149°27E 283 C8
Captieux France 44°18N 0°16W 174 D3
Captiva U.S.A. 26°31N 82°11W 317 J7
Capuça Angola 17°22S 21°18E 265 F4
Capuchos Portugal 38°38N 9°16W 126 B1
Capucin Dominica 15°38N 61°28W 323 k
Capul I. Phil. 12°26N 124°10E 232 E5
Capulin Volcano ⌓ U.S.A. 36°47N 103°58W 314 C3
Capunda Angola 10°41S 17°23E 265 E3
Caquetá ☐ Colombia 1°0N 74°0W 328 C3
Caquetá → Colombia 1°15S 69°15W 328 D4
Car Nicobar India 9°10N 92°47E 245 K11
Cara-Paraná → Colombia 1°45S 73°13W 328 D3
Carabanchel Alto Spain 40°22N 3°44W 127 B1
Carabanchel Bajo Spain 40°23N 3°44W 127 B1
Carabao I. Phil. 12°4N 121°56E 232 E3
Carabobo ☐ Venezuela 10°10N 68°5W 328 A4
Caracal Romania 44°8N 24°22E 183 F9
Caracaraí Brazil 1°50N 61°8W 329 C5
Caracas Venezuela 10°30N 66°55W 328 A4
Caracol Belize 16°45N 89°6W 320 C2
Caracol Mato Grosso do Sul, Brazil 22°18S 57°1W 334 A4
Caracol Piauí, Brazil 9°15S 43°22W 332 C3
Caracoli, Pte. Martinique 14°45N 60°52W 322 j
Caracollo Bolivia 17°39S 67°10W 330 D4
Caraga Phil. 7°20N 126°34E 233 H6
Caraga ☐ Phil. 9°40N 125°30E 233 G6
Caragabal Australia 33°49S 147°45E 283 B7
Caráglio Italy 44°25N 7°26E 198 D4
Carahue Chile 38°43S 73°12W 336 A2
Caraí Brazil 17°12S 41°42W 333 E3
Caraïbes, Mts. Guadeloupe 15°58N 61°41W 322 e
Carajás Brazil 2°57S 51°22W 332 C1
Carajás, Serra dos Brazil 6°0S 51°30W 332 C1
Caramoan Phil. 13°46N 123°52E 232 E4
Caramoan Pen. Phil. 13°47N 123°44E 232 E4
Caramoran Phil. 14°0N 124°8E 232 D5
Caranapatuba Brazil 6°38S 62°34W 331 B5
Carandaiti Bolivia 20°45S 63°4W 331 E5
Carangola Brazil 20°44S 42°5W 333 F3
Caransebeş Romania 45°28N 22°18E 182 E7
Carantec France 48°40N 3°55W 172 D3
Carapachay Argentina 34°31S 58°32W 117 B1
Carapichaima Trin. & Tob. 10°28N 61°27W 323 t
Carapo → Barinas, Venezuela 7°46N 70°23W 328 B3
Carapo → Bolívar, Venezuela 7°30N 64°0W 329 B5
Carapuse B. Trin. & Tob. 11°14N 60°35W 323 s
Caraquet Canada 47°48N 64°57W 299 C6
Caraş Severin ☐ Romania 45°10N 22°10E 182 E7
Caraşova Romania 45°11N 21°51E 182 E6
Caratasca, L. de Honduras 15°20N 83°40W 320 C3
Caratinga Brazil 19°50S 42°10W 333 E3
Carauaí Brazil 4°52S 66°54W 328 D4
Caraúbas Brazil 5°43S 37°33W 332 C4
Caravaca de la Cruz Spain 38°8N 1°52W 197 G3
Caravággio Italy 45°30N 9°38E 198 C6
Caravela Guinea-Biss. 11°30N 16°30W 262 C1
Caravelas Brazil 17°45S 39°15W 333 E4
Caraveli Peru 15°45S 73°25W 330 D3
Caravelle, Presqu'île de la Martinique 14°46N 60°48W 322 j
Caraz Peru 9°3S 77°47W 330 B2
Caraza Argentina 34°41S 58°25W 117 C2
Carazinho Brazil 28°16S 52°46W 335 B5
Carballino = O Carballiño Spain 42°26N 8°5W 194 C2
Carballo Spain 43°13N 8°41W 194 B2
Carberry Canada 49°50N 99°25W 297 D9
Carbet, Chutes du Guadeloupe 16°2N 61°38W 322 e
Carbet, Pitons du Martinique 14°42N 61°7W 322 j
Carbó Mexico 29°42N 110°58W 318 B2
Carbón, L. del Argentina 49°35S 68°21W 336 C3
Carbonara, C. Italy 39°6N 9°31E 200 C2
Carbondale Colo., U.S.A. 39°24N 107°13W 304 G10
Carbondale Ill., U.S.A. 37°44N 89°13W 310 G7
Carbondale Pa., U.S.A. 41°35N 75°30W 313 E9
Carbonear Canada 47°42N 53°13W 299 C9
Carboneras Spain 36°59N 1°53W 197 J3
Carboneras de Guadazaón Spain 39°54N 1°50W 196 F3
Carbónia Italy 39°10N 8°30E 200 C1
Carcabuey Spain 37°27N 4°17W 195 H6
Carcagente = Carcaixent Spain 39°8N 0°28W 197 F4
Carcaixent Spain 39°8N 0°28W 197 F4
Carcajou Canada 57°47N 117°6W 296 B5
Carcar Phil. 10°6N 123°38E 233 F4
Carcarana → Argentina 32°27S 60°48W 334 C3
Carcasse, C. Haiti 18°30N 74°28W 321 C5
Carcassonne France 43°13N 2°20E 174 E6
Carchi ☐ Ecuador 0°45N 78°0W 328 C2
Carcoar Australia 33°36S 149°8E 283 B8
Carcross Canada 60°13N 134°45W 296 A2
Çardak Çanakkale, Turkey 40°22N 26°43E 203 F10
Çardak Denizli, Turkey 37°49N 29°39E 205 D11
Cardamon Hills India 9°30N 77°15E 245 K3
Cardamon Mts. = Kravanh, Chuor Phnum Cambodia 12°0N 103°32E 237 G4
Cardeña Spain 38°16N 4°20W 195 G6
Cárdenas Cuba 23°0N 81°30W 320 B3
Cárdenas San Luis Potosí, Mexico 22°0N 99°38W 319 C5
Cárdenas Tabasco, Mexico 17°59N 93°22W 319 D6
Cardener → Spain 41°41N 1°51E 196 D6
Cardenete Spain 39°46N 1°41W 196 F3
Cardiel, L. Argentina 48°55S 71°10W 336 C2
Cardiff U.K. 51°29N 3°10W 169 F4
Cardiff ☐ U.K. 51°31N 3°12W 169 F4
Cardiff-by-the-Sea U.S.A. 33°1N 117°17W 307 M9
Cardigan U.K. 52°5N 4°40W 169 E3
Cardigan B. U.K. 52°30N 4°30W 169 E3
Cardinal Canada 44°47N 75°23W 313 B9
Cardón, Punta Venezuela 11°37N 70°14W 328 A3
Cardona Spain 41°56N 1°40E 196 D6
Cardona Uruguay 33°53S 57°18W 334 C4
Cardoso, Ilha do Brazil 25°8S 47°58W 335 B5
Cardston Canada 49°15N 113°20W 296 D6
Cardwell Australia 18°14S 146°2E 280 B4
Careen L. Canada 57°0N 108°11W 297 B7
Carei Romania 47°40N 22°29E 182 C7
Careiro Brazil 3°12S 59°45W 329 D6
Carenage Trin. & Tob. 10°41N 61°36W 323 t
Carentan France 49°19N 1°15W 172 C5
Carey Idaho, U.S.A. 43°19N 113°57W 304 E7
Carey Ohio, U.S.A. 40°57N 83°23W 311 D13
Carey, L. Australia 29°0S 122°15E 279 E3
Carey L. Canada 62°12N 102°55W 297 A8
Careysburg Liberia 6°34N 10°30W 262 D2
Cargados Carajos Ind. Oc. 17°0S 59°0E 273 F4
Cargèse France 42°7N 8°35E 175 F12
Carhaix-Plouguer France 48°18N 3°36W 172 D3
Carhuamayo Peru 10°51S 76°4W 330 C2
Carhuas Peru 9°15S 77°39W 330 B2
Carhué Argentina 37°10S 62°50W 334 D3
Caria Turkey 37°20N 28°10E 205 D10
Cariacica Brazil 20°16S 40°25W 333 F3
Cariaco Venezuela 10°29N 63°33W 329 A5
Cariango Angola 10°37S 15°20E 265 E3
Cariati Italy 39°30N 16°57E 201 C9
Caribbean Sea W. Indies 15°0N 75°0W 320 C4
Cariboo Mts. Canada 53°0N 121°0W 296 C4
Caribou U.S.A. 46°52N 68°1W 309 B19
Caribou → Man., Canada 59°20N 94°44W 297 B10
Caribou → N.W.T., Canada 61°27N 125°45W 296 A3
Caribou I. Canada 47°22N 85°49W 298 C2
Caribou Is. Canada 61°55N 113°15W 296 A6
Caribou L. Man., Canada 59°21N 96°10W 297 B9
Caribou L. Ont., Canada 50°25N 89°5W 298 B2
Caribou Mts. Canada 59°12N 115°40W 296 B5
Caribou River ⌓ Canada 59°35N 96°35W 297 B9
Caribrod = Dimitrovgrad Serbia 43°2N 22°48E 202 C6
Carichic Mexico 27°56N 107°3W 318 B3
Caridad Phil. 14°28N 120°53E 127 C1
Carigara Phil. 11°18N 124°41E 233 F5
Carigara B. Phil. 11°22N 124°37E 233 F5
Carignan France 49°38N 5°10E 173 C12
Carignano Italy 44°55N 7°40E 198 D4
Carinda Australia 30°28S 147°41E 283 A7
Cariñena Spain 41°20N 1°13W 196 D3
Carinhanha Brazil 14°15S 44°46W 333 D3
Carinhanha → Brazil 14°20S 43°47W 333 D3
Carini Italy 38°8N 13°11E 200 D6
Cariño Spain 43°45N 7°52W 194 B3
Carínola Italy 41°11N 13°58E 200 A6
Carinthia = Kärnten ☐ Austria 46°52N 13°30E 180 E6
Carioca, Sa. da Brazil 22°57S 43°13W 135 B1
Caripito Venezuela 10°8N 63°6W 329 A5
Cariré Brazil 3°57S 40°27W 332 B3
Caritianas Brazil 9°20S 63°6W 331 B5
Carles Phil. 11°34N 123°8E 233 F4
Carlet Spain 39°14N 0°31W 197 F4
Carleton, Mt. Canada 47°23N 66°53W 299 C6
Carleton Place Canada 45°8N 76°9W 313 A8
Carletonville S. Africa 26°23S 27°22E 270 C4
Cârlibaba Romania 47°35N 25°8E 183 C10
Carlin U.S.A. 40°43N 116°7W 304 F5
Carlingford L. U.K. 54°3N 6°9W 166 B5
Carlinville U.S.A. 39°17N 89°53W 310 E7
Carlisle Cumb., U.K. 54°54N 2°56W 168 C5
Carlisle Ind., U.S.A. 38°58N 87°24W 311 F9
Carlisle Ky., U.S.A. 38°19N 84°1W 311 F12
Carlisle Pa., U.S.A. 40°12N 77°12W 312 F7
Carlisle I. Australia 20°49S 149°18E 280 b
Carlit, Pic France 42°35N 1°55E 174 F5
Carloforte Italy 39°8N 8°18E 200 C1
Carlos Casares Argentina 35°32S 61°20W 334 D3
Carlos Chagas Brazil 17°43S 40°45W 333 E3
Carlos Tejedor Argentina 35°25S 62°25W 334 D3
Carlota I. Phil. 13°1N 121°53E 232 E3
Carlow Ireland 52°50N 6°56W 166 D5
Carlow ☐ Ireland 52°43N 6°50W 166 D5
Carlsbad = Karlovy Vary Czech Rep. 50°13N 12°51E 180 A5
Carlsbad Calif., U.S.A. 33°10N 117°21W 307 M9
Carlsbad N. Mex., U.S.A. 32°25N 104°14W 305 K11
Carlsbad Caverns △ U.S.A. 32°10N 104°35W 305 K11
Carlsberg Ridge Ind. Oc. 1°0N 66°0E 273 D5
Carlstadt U.S.A. 40°50N 74°6W 132 A1
Carlton Australia 37°47S 144°57E 128 A1
Carluke U.K. 55°45N 3°50W 167 F5
Carlyle Sask., Canada 49°40N 102°20W 297 D8
Carlyle Ill., U.S.A. 38°37N 89°22W 310 F7
Carlyle L. U.S.A. 38°37N 89°21W 310 F7
Carmacks Canada 62°5N 136°16W 294 E4
Carmagnola Italy 44°51N 7°43E 198 D4
Carman Canada 49°30N 98°0W 297 D9
Carmarthen U.K. 51°52N 4°19W 169 F3
Carmarthen B. U.K. 51°40N 4°30W 169 F3
Carmarthenshire ☐ U.K. 51°55N 4°13W 169 F3
Carmaux France 44°3N 2°10E 174 D6
Carmel Ind., U.S.A. 39°58N 86°7W 311 E10
Carmel N.Y., U.S.A. 41°26N 73°41W 313 E11
Carmel-by-the-Sea U.S.A. 36°33N 121°55W 306 J5
Carmel Valley U.S.A. 36°29N 121°43W 306 J5
Carmelo Uruguay 34°0S 58°20W 334 C4
Carmen Bolivia 11°40S 67°51W 330 C4
Carmen Paraguay 27°13S 56°12W 335 B4
Carmen Bohol, Phil. 9°50N 124°12E 233 G5
Carmen Cebu, Phil. 10°35N 124°1E 233 F5
Carmen N. Cotabato, Phil. 7°13N 124°45E 233 H5
Carmen Venezuela 1°16N 66°52W 328 C4
Carmen → Mexico 30°42N 106°29W 318 A3
Carmen, I. Mexico 25°57N 111°12W 318 B2
Carmen de Huechuraba Chile 33°20S 70°40W 137 B1
Carmen de la Legua Peru 12°3S 77°7W 124 B2
Carmen de Patagones Argentina 40°50S 63°0W 336 B4
Cármenes Spain 42°58N 5°34W 194 C5
Carmensa Argentina 35°15S 67°40W 334 D2
Carmi B.C., Canada 49°36N 119°8W 296 D5
Carmi Ill., U.S.A. 38°5N 88°10W 311 F8
Carmichael U.S.A. 38°38N 121°19W 306 G5
Carmichael Village Bahamas 25°0N 77°26W 153 b
Carmila Australia 21°55S 149°24E 280 C4
Carmona Costa Rica 10°0N 85°15W 320 E2
Carmona Spain 37°28N 5°42W 195 H5
Carn Ban U.K. 57°7N 4°15W 167 D4
Carn Eige U.K. 57°17N 5°8W 167 D3
Carnac France 47°35N 3°6W 172 E3
Carnamah Australia 29°41S 115°53E 279 E2
Carnarvon W. Austral., Australia 24°51S 113°42E 279 D1
Carnarvon Ont., Canada 45°3N 78°41W 312 A6
Carnarvon Northern Cape, S. Africa 30°56S 22°8E 270 D3
Carnarvon △ Australia 24°54S 148°2E 280 C4
Carnarvon Ra. Queens., Australia 25°15S 148°30E 280 D4
Carnarvon Ra. W. Austral., Australia 25°20S 120°45E 279 E3
Carnatic India 9°40N 77°50E 245 K3
Carnation U.S.A. 47°39N 121°55W 306 C5
Carnaxide Portugal 38°43N 9°14W 126 A1
Carncastle U.K. 54°54N 5°53W 166 B6
Carndonagh Ireland 55°16N 7°15W 166 A4
Carnduff Canada 49°10N 101°50W 297 D8
Carnegie Vic., Australia 37°53S 145°3E 128 B2
Carnegie Pa., U.S.A. 40°24N 80°5W 312 F4
Carnegie, L. Australia 26°5S 122°30E 279 E3
Carnegie Hall New York, U.S.A. 132 c2
Carnegie Ridge Pac. Oc. 1°0S 87°0W 289 H19
Carnic Alps = Karnische Alpen Europe 46°36N 13°0E 180 E6
Carniche Alpi = Karnische Alpen Europe 46°36N 13°0E 180 E6
Carnide Portugal 38°45N 9°10W 126 A1
Carnot C.A.R. 4°59N 15°56E 264 B3
Carnot, C. Australia 34°57S 135°38E 281 E2
Carnot B. Australia 17°20S 122°15E 278 C3
Carnoustie U.K. 56°30N 2°42W 167 E6
Carnsore Pt. Ireland 52°10N 6°22W 166 D5
Caro U.S.A. 43°29N 83°24W 309 D12
Caroço São Tomé & Príncipe 1°32N 7°27E 265 a
Caroga Lake U.S.A. 43°8N 74°28W 313 C10
Carol City U.S.A. 25°56N 80°14W 128 A1
Carolina Brazil 7°10S 47°30W 332 C2
Carolina Puerto Rico 18°23N 65°58W 321 C6
Carolina Mpumalanga, S. Africa 26°5S 30°6E 271 C5
Carolinas Pt. N. Marianas 14°55N 145°38E 302 e
Caroline I. Kiribati 9°58S 150°13W 289 H12
Caroline Is. Micronesia 8°0N 150°0E 288 G6
Caroline Pk. N.Z. 45°57S 167°15E 285 F2
Carondelet Reef Kiribati 5°33S 173°50E 277 B16
Caroni Trin. & Tob. 10°34N 61°23W 323 t
Caroni ☐ Trin. & Tob. 10°30N 61°22W 323 t
Caroni → Trin. & Tob. 10°37N 61°30W 323 t
Caroní → Venezuela 8°21N 62°43W 329 B5
Caroni Arena Res. Trin. & Tob. 10°33N 61°15W 323 t
Caroni Bird Sanctuary Trin. & Tob. 10°36N 61°28W 323 t
Caroni Swamp Trin. & Tob. 10°36N 61°27W 323 t
Caronie = Nébrodi, Monti Italy 37°54N 14°35E 201 E7
Caroona Australia 31°24S 150°26E 283 A9
Carora Venezuela 10°11N 70°5W 328 A3
Carpathians Europe 49°30N 21°0E 177 D11
Carpaţii Meridionali Romania 45°30N 25°0E 183 E9
Carpentaria, G. of Australia 14°0S 139°0E 280 A2
Carpentersville U.S.A. 42°6N 88°17W 311 B8
Carpentras France 44°3N 5°2E 175 D9
Carpi Italy 44°47N 10°53E 198 D7
Carpina Brazil 7°51S 35°15W 332 C4
Cărpineni Moldova 46°46N 28°22E 183 D13
Carpinteria U.S.A. 34°24N 119°31W 307 L7

Carpio Spain 41°13N 5°7W 194 D5
Carr Boyd Ra. Australia 16°15S 128°35E 278 C4
Carra, L. Ireland 53°41N 9°14W 166 C2
Carrabelle U.S.A. 29°51N 84°40W 316 F5
Carraig Mhachdhire Rois = Carrickmacross Ireland 53°59N 6°43W 166 C5
Carraig na Siúire = Carrick-on-Suir Ireland 52°21N 7°24W 166 D4
Carral Spain 43°14N 8°21W 194 B2
Carranglan Phil. 15°58N 121°4E 232 D3
Carranya ۞ Australia 19°13S 127°46E 278 C4
Carranza, Presa V. Mexico 27°20N 100°50W 318 B4
Carrara Italy 44°5N 10°6E 198 D7
Carrascal Santiago, Chile 33°25S 70°42W 137 B1
Carrascal Phil. 9°22N 125°56E 233 G5
Carrasco △ Bolivia 17°23S 64°59W 331 D5
Carrascosa del Campo Spain 40°2N 2°45W 196 E2
Carrauntoohill Ireland 52°0N 9°45W 166 D2
Carretas, Punta Peru 14°12S 76°17W 330 C2
Carriacou Grenada 12°29N 61°26W 323 q
Carrick-on-Shannon Ireland 53°57N 8°5W 166 C3
Carrick-on-Suir Ireland 52°21N 7°24W 166 D4
Carrickfergus U.K. 54°43N 5°49W 166 B6
Carrickmacross Ireland 53°59N 6°43W 166 C5
Carrickmines Ireland 53°15N 6°10W 120 B3
Carrières-sous-Bois France 48°55N 2°6E 134 A1
Carrières-sous-Poissy France 48°56N 2°2E 134 A1
Carrières-sur-Seine France 48°55N 2°11E 134 A2
Carrieton Australia 32°25S 138°31E 282 B3
Carrigeen B. Ireland 53°24N 6°5W 120 A3
Carrillo Mexico 26°54N 103°55W 318 B4
Carrington U.S.A. 47°27N 99°8W 308 B4
Carrión → Spain 41°53N 4°32W 194 D6
Carrión de los Condes Spain 42°20N 4°37W 194 C6
Carrizal Bajo Chile 28°5S 71°20W 334 B1
Carrizalillo Chile 29°5S 71°30W 334 B1
Carrizo Cr. → U.S.A. 36°55N 103°55W 305 H12
Carrizo Plain ⌓ U.S.A. 35°11N 119°47W 306 K7
Carrizo Springs U.S.A. 28°31N 99°52W 314 G5
Carrizozo U.S.A. 33°38N 105°53W 305 K11
Carroll U.S.A. 42°4N 94°52W 310 B2
Carrollton Ga., U.S.A. 33°35N 85°5W 316 B4
Carrollton Ill., U.S.A. 39°18N 90°24W 310 E6
Carrollton Ky., U.S.A. 38°41N 85°11W 311 F11
Carrollton Mo., U.S.A. 39°22N 93°30W 310 E3
Carrollton Ohio, U.S.A. 40°34N 81°5W 312 F3
Carron → U.K. 57°53N 4°22W 167 D4
Carron, L. U.K. 57°22N 5°35W 167 D3
Carrot → Canada 53°50N 101°17W 297 C8
Carrot River Canada 53°17N 103°35W 297 C8
Carrouges France 48°34N 0°10W 172 D6
Carrù Italy 44°29N 7°52E 198 D4
Carruthers Canada 52°52N 109°16W 297 C7
Carsa Dek Ethiopia 5°13N 39°50E 257 F4
Çarşamba Turkey 41°11N 36°44E 212 B7
Carsóli Italy 42°6N 13°5E 199 F10
Carson Calif., U.S.A. 33°49N 118°16W 307 M8
Carson N. Dak., U.S.A. 46°25N 101°34W 308 B3
Carson → U.S.A. 39°45N 118°40W 306 F8
Carson City Mich., U.S.A. 43°11N 84°51W 311 A12
Carson City Nev., U.S.A. 39°10N 119°46W 306 F7
Carson Sink U.S.A. 39°50N 118°25W 304 G4
Carstensz Pyramid = Jaya, Puncak Indonesia 3°57S 137°17E 231 E9
Cartagena Colombia 10°25N 75°33W 328 A2
Cartagena Spain 37°38N 0°59W 197 H4
Cartago Colombia 4°45N 75°55W 328 C2
Cartago Costa Rica 9°50N 83°55W 320 E3
Cártama Spain 36°43N 4°39W 195 J6
Cartaxo Portugal 39°10N 8°47W 195 F2
Cartaya Spain 37°16N 7°9W 195 H3
Carteret Is. = Kilinailau Is. Papua N. G. 4°45S 155°20E 286 C8
Cartersville U.S.A. 34°10N 84°48W 316 A5
Carterton N.Z. 41°2S 175°31E 284 H4
Carterville U.S.A. 37°46N 89°5W 310 G7
Carthage Tunisia 36°52N 10°20E 200 F3
Carthage Ill., U.S.A. 40°25N 91°8W 310 D5
Carthage Mo., U.S.A. 37°11N 94°19W 308 G6
Carthage N.Y., U.S.A. 43°59N 75°37W 309 D16
Carthage Tex., U.S.A. 32°9N 94°20W 314 E7
Cartier I. Australia 12°31S 123°29E 278 B3
Cartierville Canada 45°31N 73°42W 130 A1
Cartwright Canada 53°41N 56°58W 299 B8
Caruachi, Represa de Venezuela 8°9N 62°50W 248 B5
Caruaru Brazil 8°15S 35°55W 332 C4
Carúpano Venezuela 10°39N 63°15W 329 A5
Caruray Phil. 10°20N 119°0E 233 F2
Carutapera Brazil 1°13S 46°1W 332 B2
Caruthersville U.S.A. 36°11N 89°39W 308 G9
Carvalho Brazil 2°16S 51°29W 329 D7
Carvin France 50°30N 2°57E 173 B9
Carvoeiro Brazil 1°30S 61°59W 329 D5
Carvoeiro, C. Portugal 39°21N 9°24W 195 F1
Cary Ill., U.S.A. 42°13N 88°14W 311 B8
Cary N.C., U.S.A. 35°47N 78°46W 315 D15
Casa, Pas de la = Envalira, Port d' Europe 42°33N 1°43E 196 C6
Casa Branca Brazil 21°46S 47°4W 333 F2
Casa Branca Portugal 38°29N 8°12W 195 G2
Casa de Piedra Argentina 38°5S 67°28W 334 D2
Casa de Piedra, Embalse Argentina 38°5S 67°32W 334 D2
Casa Grande U.S.A. 32°53N 111°45W 305 K8
Casa Loma Canada 43°41N 79°24W 141 A2
Casa Nova Brazil 9°25S 41°5W 332 C3
Casa Verde Brazil 23°29S 46°40W 137 A1
Casablanca Chile 33°20S 71°25W 334 C1
Casablanca Morocco 33°36N 7°36W 260 B3
Casablanca □ Morocco 33°38N 7°30W 260 B3
Casacalenda Italy 41°44N 14°51E 199 G11
Casál Morena Italy 41°49N 12°37E 136 C2
Casalbordino Italy 42°9N 14°35E 199 F11
Casale Monferrato Italy 45°8N 8°27E 198 C5
Casalmaggiore Italy 44°59N 10°26E 198 D7
Casalotti Italy 41°54N 12°22E 136 B1
Casalpusterlengo Italy 45°11N 9°39E 198 C6
Casamance → Senegal 12°33N 16°46W 262 C1
Casanare □ Colombia 5°30N 72°0W 328 B3
Casanare → Colombia 6°2N 69°51W 328 B4
Casarano Italy 40°0N 18°10E 201 B11
Casares Spain 36°27N 5°16W 195 J5
Casas Ibáñez Spain 39°17N 1°30W 197 F3
Casasimarro Spain 39°22N 2°3W 197 F2
Casatejada Spain 39°54N 5°40W 194 F5
Casavieja Spain 40°17N 4°46W 194 E6
Cascada de Basaseachic △ Mexico 28°9N 108°15W 318 B3
Cascade Seychelles 4°39S 55°29E 272 c
Cascade Idaho, U.S.A. 44°31N 116°2W 304 D5
Cascade Iowa, U.S.A. 42°18N 91°0W 310 B6
Cascade Mont., U.S.A. 47°16N 111°42W 304 C8
Cascade Heights U.S.A. 33°43N 84°26W 113 B2
Cascade Locks U.S.A. 45°40N 121°54W 306 E5
Cascade Pt. N.Z. 44°1S 168°20E 285 E3
Cascade Ra. U.S.A. 47°0N 121°30W 306 D5
Cascade Res. U.S.A. 44°32N 116°3W 304 D5
Cascades, Pte. des Réunion 21°9S 55°51E 272 f
Cascais Portugal 38°41N 9°25W 195 G1
Cascavel Ceará, Brazil 4°7S 38°14W 332 B4
Cascavel Paraná, Brazil 24°57S 53°28W 335 A5
Cáscina Italy 43°41N 10°33E 198 E7
Casco B. U.S.A. 43°45N 70°0W 309 D19
Case Noyale Mauritius 20°23S 57°22E 272 e
Case-Pilote Martinique 14°38N 61°9W 322 j
Caselle Torinese Italy 45°10N 7°39E 198 C4
Caserta Italy 41°4N 14°20E 201 A7
Casey Antarctica 66°0S 76°0E 151 C8
Casey Ill., U.S.A. 39°18N 87°59W 311 E9
Caseyr, Raas = Asir, Ras Somali Rep. 11°55N 51°10E 267 B7
Cashel Ireland 52°30N 7°53W 166 D4
Casibare → Colombia 3°48N 72°18W 328 C3
Casiguran Phil. 16°22N 122°7E 232 C4
Casiguran Sound Phil. 16°6N 121°58E 232 C3
Casilda Argentina 33°10S 61°10W 334 C3
Casim = General Toshevo Bulgaria 43°42N 28°6E 203 C12
Casimcea Romania 44°45N 28°23E 183 F13
Casino N.S.W., Australia 28°52S 153°3E 281 D5
Casino New Orleans, U.S.A. 131 b2
Casiquiare → Venezuela 2°1N 67°7W 328 C4
Casitas Peru 3°54S 80°39W 330 A1
Čáslav Czech Rep. 49°54N 15°22E 180 B8
Casma Peru 9°30S 78°20W 330 B2
Casmalia U.S.A. 34°50N 120°32W 307 L6
Cásola Valsénio Italy 44°12N 11°40E 199 D8
Cásoli Italy 42°7N 14°18E 199 F11
Caspe Spain 41°14N 0°1W 196 D4
Casper U.S.A. 42°51N 106°19W 304 E10
Caspian Depression Eurasia 47°0N 48°0E 191 G9
Caspian Sea Eurasia 43°0N 50°0E 187 F9
Cass City U.S.A. 43°36N 83°10W 312 C1
Cass Lake U.S.A. 47°23N 94°37W 308 B6
Cassà de la Selva Spain 41°53N 2°52E 196 D7
Cassadaga U.S.A. 42°20N 79°19W 312 D5
Cassai Angola 10°33S 21°59E 265 E4
Cassai → Angola 3°2S 16°57E 265 E4
Cassamba Angola 13°6S 20°18E 265 E4
Cassano allo Iónio Italy 39°47N 16°20E 201 C9
Cassel France 50°48N 2°30E 173 B9
Casselberry U.S.A. 28°41N 81°20W 317 G8
Casselman Canada 45°19N 75°5W 313 A9
Casselton U.S.A. 46°54N 97°13W 308 B5
Cassiar Mts. Canada 59°30N 130°30W 296 B2
Cassilândia Brazil 19°9S 51°45W 331 D7
Cassilis Australia 32°3S 149°58E 283 B8
Cassinga Angola 15°5S 16°4E 265 F3
Cassino Italy 41°30N 13°49E 200 A6
Cassis France 43°14N 5°32E 175 E9
Cassoalala Angola 9°30S 14°22E 265 D2
Cassoango Angola 13°42S 20°56E 265 E4
Cassongue Angola 11°53S 15°2E 265 E3
Cassopolis U.S.A. 41°55N 86°1W 311 C10
Cassunda Angola 10°57S 21°3E 265 E4
Cassville Mo., U.S.A. 36°41N 93°52W 308 G7
Cassville Wis., U.S.A. 42°43N 90°59W 310 B6
Castagneto Carducci Italy 43°9N 10°36E 198 E7
Castaic U.S.A. 34°30N 118°38W 307 L8
Castalia U.S.A. 41°24N 82°49W 312 E2
Castanhal Brazil 1°18S 47°55W 332 B2
Castara Trin. & Tob. 11°17N 60°42W 323 s
Castara B. Trin. & Tob. 11°17N 60°42W 323 s
Castéggio Italy 45°0N 9°7E 198 C6
Castejón de Monegros Spain 41°37N 0°15W 196 D4
Castel Guadeloupe 16°15N 61°35W 322 e
Castèl di Leva Italy 41°46N 12°33E 136 C2
Castèl di Sangro Italy 41°47N 14°6E 199 G11
Castèl San Giovanni Italy 45°4N 9°26E 198 C6
Castèl San Pietro Terme Italy 44°24N 11°35E 199 D8
Castèl Sant'Angelo Rome, Italy 136 b1
Castelbuono Italy 37°56N 14°5E 201 E7
Castelfidardo Italy 43°28N 13°33E 199 E10
Castelfiorentino Italy 43°36N 10°58E 198 E7
Castelfranco Emília Italy 44°37N 11°3E 198 D8
Castelfranco Véneto Italy 45°40N 11°55E 199 C8
Casteljaloux France 44°19N 0°6E 174 D4
Castellabate Italy 40°17N 14°57E 201 B7
Castellammare, G. di Italy 38°8N 12°54E 200 D5
Castellammare del Golfo Italy 38°1N 12°53E 200 D5
Castellammare di Stábia Italy 40°42N 14°29E 201 B7
Castellamonte Italy 45°23N 7°42E 198 C4
Castellane France 43°50N 6°31E 175 E10
Castellaneta Italy 40°38N 16°56E 201 B9
Castelli Argentina 36°7S 57°47W 334 D4
Castelló de la Plana Spain 39°58N 0°3W 196 F4
Castellón de la Plana □ Spain 40°15N 0°5W 196 E4
Castellote Spain 40°48N 0°15W 196 E4
Castelmáuro Italy 41°50N 14°43E 199 G11
Castelnau-de-Médoc France 45°2N 0°48W 174 C3
Castelnau-Magnoac France 43°17N 0°31E 174 E4
Castelnaudary France 43°20N 1°58E 174 E5
Castelnovo ne' Monti Italy 44°26N 10°24E 198 D7
Castelnuovo di Val di Cécina Italy 43°12N 10°59E 198 E7
Castelo = Manuel Urbano Brazil 8°53S 69°18W 330 B4
Castelo Brazil 20°33S 41°14W 333 F3
Castelo, Pta. do Azores 36°56N 25°1W 153 d4
Castelo Branco Azores 38°31N 28°44W 153 d1
Castelo Branco Portugal 39°50N 7°31W 194 F3
Castelo Branco □ Portugal 39°52N 7°45W 194 F3
Castelo de Paiva Portugal 41°2N 8°16W 194 D2
Castelo de Vide Portugal 39°25N 7°27W 195 F3
Castelo do Piauí Brazil 5°20S 41°33W 332 C3
Castelrosso = Megisti Greece 36°8N 29°34E 205 E11
Castelsardo Italy 40°55N 8°43E 200 B1
Castelsarrasin France 44°2N 1°7E 174 D5
Casteltérmini Italy 37°32N 13°39E 200 E6
Castelvetrano Italy 37°41N 12°47E 200 E5
Castendo Angola 8°39S 14°10E 265 D2
Casterton Australia 37°30S 141°30E 282 D4
Castets France 43°52N 1°6W 174 E2
Castiglion Fiorentino Italy 43°20N 11°55E 199 E8
Castiglione = Bou Ismaïl Algeria 36°38N 2°42E 261 A5
Castiglione del Lago Italy 43°7N 12°3E 199 E9
Castiglione della Pescáia Italy 42°46N 10°53E 198 F7
Castiglione delle Stiviere Italy 45°23N 10°29E 198 C7
Castilblanco Spain 39°17N 5°5W 195 F5
Castile U.S.A. 42°38N 78°3W 312 D6
Castilla Peru 5°12S 80°38W 330 B1
Castilla, Playa de Spain 37°0N 6°33W 195 J4
Castilla-La Mancha □ Spain 39°30N 3°30W 195 F7
Castilla y Leon □ Spain 42°0N 5°0W 194 D6
Castillo de Locubín Spain 37°32N 3°56W 195 H7
Castillo de San Marcos ⌓ U.S.A. 29°54N 81°19W 316 F8
Castillon-en-Couserans France 42°56N 1°1E 174 F5
Castillonès France 44°39N 0°37E 174 D4
Castillos Uruguay 34°12S 53°52W 335 C5
Castle Bruce Dominica 15°26N 61°16W 323 k
Castle Dale U.S.A. 39°13N 111°1W 304 G8
Castle Douglas U.K. 54°56N 3°56W 167 G5
Castle Harbour Bermuda 32°21N 64°40W 153 a
Castle Mt. Jamaica 18°8N 76°22W 320 a
Castle of Good Hope Cape Town, S. Africa 118 c3
Castle Roads Bermuda 32°20N 64°40W 153 a
Castle Rock Colo., U.S.A. 39°22N 104°51W 304 G11
Castle Rock Wash., U.S.A. 46°17N 122°54W 306 D4
Castle Rock Pt. St. Helena 16°1S 5°45W 153 h
Castlebar Ireland 53°52N 9°18W 166 C2
Castlebay U.K. 56°57N 7°31W 167 E1
Castleblaney Ireland 54°7N 6°44W 166 B5
Castlecliff N.Z. 39°57S 175°5E 284 F4
Castlederg U.K. 54°42N 7°35W 166 B4
Castleford U.K. 53°43N 1°21W 168 D6
Castlegar Canada 49°20N 117°40W 296 D5
Castleknock Ireland 53°22N 6°21W 120 A1
Castlemaine Vic., Australia 37°2S 144°12E 282 D6
Castlemaine Kerry, Ireland 52°10N 9°42W 166 D2
Castlepoint N.Z. 40°54S 176°15E 284 G5
Castlepollard Ireland 53°41N 7°19W 166 C4
Castlerea Ireland 53°46N 8°29W 166 C3
Castlereagh → Australia 30°12S 147°32E 283 A7
Castlereagh B. Australia 12°10S 135°10E 280 A2
Castleton U.S.A. 43°37N 73°11W 313 C11
Castleton Corners U.S.A. 40°36N 74°8W 132 C1
Castleton-on-Hudson U.S.A. 42°31N 73°45W 313 D11
Castletown I. of Man 54°5N 4°38W 168 C3
Castletown Bearhaven Ireland 51°39N 9°55W 166 E2
Castor Canada 52°15N 111°50W 296 C6
Castor → Canada 53°24N 78°58W 298 B4
Castorland U.S.A. 43°53N 75°31W 313 C9
Castres France 43°37N 2°13E 174 E6
Castricum Neths. 52°33N 4°40E 170 B4
Castries St. Lucia 14°2N 60°58W 323 m
Castril Spain 37°48N 2°46W 195 H8
Castro Brazil 24°45S 50°0W 335 A6
Castro Chile 42°30S 73°50W 336 B2
Castro Alves Brazil 12°46S 39°33W 333 D4
Castro del Río Spain 37°41N 4°29W 195 H6
Castro-Urdiales Spain 43°23N 3°11W 194 B7
Castro Valley U.S.A. 37°41N 122°5W 306 H4
Castro Verde Portugal 37°41N 8°4W 195 H2
Castrogiovanni = Enna Italy 37°34N 14°16E 201 E7
Castrojeriz Spain 42°17N 4°9W 194 C6
Castropol Spain 43°32N 7°0W 194 B4
Castroreale Italy 38°6N 15°12E 201 D8
Castrovíllari Italy 39°49N 16°12E 201 C9
Castroville U.S.A. 36°46N 121°45W 306 J5
Castrovirreyna Peru 13°20S 75°18W 330 C2
Castuera Spain 38°43N 5°37W 195 G5
Caswell Sound N.Z. 44°59S 167°8E 285 E2
Çat Turkey 39°40N 41°3E 213 C9
Cat Ba, Dao Vietnam 20°50N 107°0E 236 B6
Cat Ba △ Vietnam 20°47N 107°3E 236 B6
Cat I. Bahamas 24°30N 75°30W 321 B4
Cat L. Canada 51°40N 91°50W 298 B1
Cat Lake Canada 51°40N 91°50W 298 B1
Cat Tien △ Vietnam 11°25N 107°17E 237 G6
Čata Slovak Rep. 47°58N 18°38E 181 D11
Catabola Angola 12°9S 17°16E 265 E3
Catacamas Honduras 14°54N 85°56W 320 D2
Catacaos Peru 5°20S 80°45W 330 B1
Cataguases Brazil 21°23S 42°39W 333 F3
Catagupan Phil. 8°1N 116°58E 233 G1
Cataingan Phil. 12°0N 124°0E 232 E4
Çatak Turkey 38°1N 43°8E 213 C10
Çatalağzı Turkey 41°30N 31°59E 212 B4
Catalão Brazil 18°10S 47°57W 333 E2
Çatalca Turkey 41°8N 28°27E 203 E12
Catalina Nfld. & L., Canada 48°31N 53°4W 299 C9
Catalina Chile 25°13S 69°43W 334 B2
Catalina Ariz., U.S.A. 32°30N 110°50W 305 K8
Catalonia = Cataluña □ Spain 41°40N 1°15E 196 D6
Cataluña □ Spain 41°40N 1°15E 196 D6
Çatalzeytin Turkey 41°57N 34°12E 212 B6
Catamarca Argentina 28°30S 65°50W 334 B2
Catamarca □ Argentina 27°0S 65°50W 334 B2
Catanauan Phil. 13°36N 122°19E 232 E4
Catanduanes □ Phil. 13°50N 124°20E 232 E5
Catanduva Brazil 21°5S 48°58W 335 A6
Catánia Italy 37°30N 15°6E 201 E8
Catánia, G. di Italy 37°24N 15°9E 201 E8
Cataño Puerto Rico 18°27N 66°7W 321 b
Catanzaro Italy 38°54N 16°35E 201 D9
Cataouatche, L. U.S.A. 29°50N 90°14W 131 B1
Catarman Camiguin, Phil. 9°8N 124°40E 233 G5
Catarman N. Samar, Phil. 12°28N 124°35E 232 E5
Catatumbo → Venezuela 9°21N 71°45W 328 B3
Cataula U.S.A. 32°39N 84°52W 316 C5
Catbalogan Phil. 11°46N 124°53E 233 F5
Catchacoma Canada 44°44N 78°19W 312 B6
Cateco Cangola Angola 8°28S 15°51E 265 D3
Cateel Phil. 7°47N 126°24E 233 H6
Cateel B. Phil. 7°54N 126°25E 233 H6
Catembe Mozam. 26°0S 32°33E 271 C5
Catende Angola 11°14S 21°30E 265 E4
Catende Brazil 8°40S 35°43W 332 C4
Caterham U.K. 51°15N 0°4W 169 F7
Catete Angola 9°6S 13°43E 265 D2
Catete Rio de J., Brazil 22°54S 43°10W 135 B1
Catford U.K. 51°26N 0°1W 125 B3
Cathair na Mart = Westport Ireland 53°48N 9°31W 166 C2
Cathair Saidhbhín = Cahersiveen Ireland 51°56N 10°14W 166 E1
Cathcart N.S.W., Australia 36°52S 149°24E 283 D8
Cathcart Eastern Cape, S. Africa 32°18S 27°10E 270 D4
Cathedral City U.S.A. 33°47N 116°28W 307 M10
Cathedral Rock △ Australia 30°24S 152°15E 283 A10
Catherine, L. U.S.A. 28°30N 81°24W 133 B2
Cathlamet U.S.A. 46°12N 123°23W 306 D3
Catió Guinea-Biss. 11°17N 15°15W 262 C1
Catismiña Venezuela 4°5N 63°40W 329 C5
Catita Brazil 9°31S 43°1W 332 C3
Cativa Panama 9°21N 79°49W 320 c
Catlettsburg U.S.A. 38°25N 82°36W 309 F12
Catlin U.S.A. 40°4N 87°42W 311 D9
Catlins N.Z. 46°22S 169°17E 285 G4
Çatma Dağı Turkey 38°25N 29°50E 205 C11
Catmon Phil. 10°43N 124°1E 233 F5
Catoche, C. Mexico 21°35N 87°5W 319 C7
Catolé do Rocha Brazil 6°21S 37°45W 332 C4
Catota Angola 13°57S 17°30E 265 E3
Cátria, Mte. Italy 43°28N 12°42E 199 E9
Catriló Argentina 36°26S 63°24W 334 D3
Catrimani Brazil 0°27N 61°41W 329 C5
Catrimani → Brazil 0°28N 61°44W 329 C5
Catskill U.S.A. 42°14N 73°52W 313 D11
Catskill ⌓ U.S.A. 42°8N 74°39W 313 D10
Catskill Mts. U.S.A. 42°10N 74°25W 313 D10
Catt, Mt. Australia 13°49S 134°23E 280 A1
Cattaraugus U.S.A. 42°20N 78°52W 312 D6
Cattaro = Kotor Montenegro 42°25N 18°47E 202 D2
Catterick U.K. 54°23N 1°37W 168 C6
Cattólica Italy 43°58N 12°44E 199 E9
Cattólica Eraclea Italy 37°26N 13°24E 200 E6
Catu Brazil 12°21S 38°23W 333 D4
Catuala Angola 16°25S 19°2E 265 F3
Catuane Mozam. 26°48S 32°18E 271 C5
Catubig Phil. 12°24N 125°3E 232 E5
Catumbela Angola 12°25S 13°34E 265 E2
Catumbela → Angola 12°29S 13°28E 265 E2
Catur Mozam. 13°45S 35°30E 269 E4
Catwick Is. = Hon Hai Vietnam 10°0N 109°0E 237 H7
Cauayan Isabela, Phil. 16°56N 121°46E 232 C3
Cauayan Neg. Occ., Phil. 9°58N 122°37E 233 G4
Caubvick, Mt. = Iberville, Mt. d' Canada 58°50N 63°50W 295 F19
Cauca □ Colombia 2°30N 76°50W 328 C2
Cauca → Colombia 8°54N 74°28W 328 B3
Caucaia Brazil 3°40S 38°35W 332 B4
Caucasia Colombia 8°0N 75°12W 328 B2
Caucasus Mountains Eurasia 42°50N 44°0E 191 J7
Caucete Argentina 31°38S 68°20W 334 C2
Caudete Spain 38°42N 1°2W 197 G3
Caudry France 50°7N 3°22E 173 B10
Cauese Mts. Mozam. 15°14S 30°33E 269 F3
Caulfield Australia 37°52S 145°1E 128 B2
Caulnes France 48°18N 2°10W 172 D4
Caulónia Italy 38°23N 16°24E 201 D9
Caungula Angola 8°26S 18°38E 265 D3
Cauquenes Chile 36°0S 72°22W 334 D1
Caura → Venezuela 7°38N 64°53W 329 B5
Caurés → Brazil 1°21S 62°20W 329 D5
Cauresi → Mozam. 17°8S 33°0E 269 F3
Căuşani Moldova 46°38N 29°25E 183 D14
Causapscal Canada 48°19N 67°12W 299 C6
Causeway Bay Hong Kong, China 122 c3
Caussade France 44°10N 1°33E 174 D5
Causse-Méjean France 44°18N 3°42E 174 D7
Causses du Quercy ⌓ France 44°35N 1°35E 174 D5
Cauterets France 42°52N 0°8W 174 F3
Cauvery → India 11°9N 78°52E 245 J4
Caux, Pays de France 49°38N 0°35E 172 C7
Cava de' Tirreni Italy 40°42N 14°42E 201 B7
Cávado → Portugal 41°32N 8°48W 194 D2
Cavagrande del Cassibile ⌓ Italy 36°58N 15°6E 201 F8
Cavaillon France 43°50N 5°2E 175 E9
Cavalaire-sur-Mer France 43°10N 6°33E 175 E10
Cavalcante Brazil 13°48S 47°30W 333 D2
Cavalese Italy 46°17N 11°27E 199 B8
Cavalier U.S.A. 48°48N 97°37W 308 A5
Cavalla = Cavally → Africa 4°22N 7°32W 262 E3
Cavalla △ Liberia 5°8N 7°20W 262 D3
Cavalli Is. N.Z. 35°0S 173°58E 284 B2
Cavallo, Î. de France 41°22N 9°16E 175 G13
Cavally → Africa 4°22N 7°32W 262 E3
Cavan Ireland 54°0N 7°22W 166 B4
Cavan □ Ireland 54°1N 7°16W 166 C4
Cavárzere Italy 45°8N 12°5E 199 C9
Cavazuccherina = Iésolo Italy 45°32N 12°38E 199 C9
Çavdarhisar Turkey 39°12N 29°37E 205 B11
Çavdır Turkey 37°10N 29°42E 205 D11
Cave Creek U.S.A. 33°50N 111°57W 305 K8
Cave Run L. U.S.A. 38°5N 83°25W 311 F13
Cave Spring U.S.A. 34°6N 85°20W 316 A4
Cavenagh Ra. Australia 26°12S 127°55E 279 E4
Cavendish Australia 37°31S 142°2E 282 D5
Caverna do Peruaçu Brazil 15°0S 44°45W 333 E3
Caverna do Peruaçu △ Brazil 15°0S 44°35W 333 E3
Caviana, I. Brazil 0°10N 50°10W 329 C7
Cavili I. Phil. 9°16N 120°49E 233 G3
Cavite Phil. 14°29N 120°54E 127 C1
Cavite □ Phil. 14°15N 120°50E 232 D3
Caviúna = Rolândia Brazil 23°18S 51°23W 335 A5
Cavnic Romania 47°40N 23°52E 183 C8
Cavour Italy 44°47N 7°22E 198 D4
Cavtat Croatia 42°35N 18°13E 202 D2
Cawayan Phil. 11°56N 123°46E 233 F4
Cawayanon = Vintar Phil. 18°14N 120°39E 232 B3
Cawndilla L. Australia 32°30S 142°15E 282 B5
Cawnpore = Kanpur India 26°28N 80°20E 243 F9
Caxias Brazil 4°55S 43°20W 332 B3
Caxias Lisboa, Portugal 38°42N 9°16W 126 A1
Caxias do Sul Brazil 29°10S 51°10W 335 B5
Caxito Angola 8°30S 13°30E 265 D2
Caxopa Angola 11°52S 20°52E 265 E4
Çay Turkey 38°35N 31°1E 212 C4
Cay Pt. Bahamas 25°59N 77°25W 153 b
Cay Sal Bank Bahamas 23°45N 80°0W 320 B4
Cayambe Napo, Ecuador 0°2N 77°59W 328 C2
Cayambe Quito, Ecuador 0°3N 78°8W 328 C2
Cayce U.S.A. 33°58N 81°4W 316 B8
Çaycuma Turkey 41°25N 32°4E 212 B5
Çayeli Turkey 41°5N 40°45E 213 B9
Cayenne Fr. Guiana 5°5N 52°18W 329 B7
Cayenne □ Fr. Guiana 5°0N 53°0W 329 C7
Cayey Puerto Rico 18°7N 66°10W 321 b
Caygören Barajı Turkey 39°15N 28°12E 205 B10
Cayiralan Turkey 39°17N 35°38E 212 C6
Çaylı Azerbaijan 40°20N 46°49E 191 K8
Caylus France 44°15N 1°47E 174 D5
Cayman Brac Cayman Is. 19°43N 79°49W 320 C4
Cayman Is. ☒ W. Indies 19°40N 80°30W 320 C3
Cayman Trench Caribbean 17°0N 83°0W 320 C3
Caynabo Somali Rep. 9°0N 46°25E 267 C6
Cayon St. Kitts & Nevis 17°21N 62°52W 322 d
Cayres France 44°55N 3°48E 174 D7
Cayuga Ont., Canada 42°59N 79°50W 312 D5
Cayuga Ind., U.S.A. 39°57N 87°28W 311 E9
Cayuga N.Y., U.S.A. 42°54N 76°44W 313 D8
Cayuga Heights U.S.A. 42°27N 76°29W 313 D8
Cayuga L. U.S.A. 42°41N 76°41W 313 D8
Cazage Angola 11°2S 20°45E 265 E4
Cazalla de la Sierra Spain 37°56N 5°45W 195 H5
Căzăneşti Romania 44°36N 27°3E 183 F12
Cazaubon France 43°56N 0°3W 174 E3
Cazaux et de Sanguinet, Étang de France 44°29N 1°10W 174 D2
Cazenovia U.S.A. 42°56N 75°51W 313 D9
Cazères France 43°13N 1°5E 174 E5
Cazin Bos.-H. 44°57N 15°57E 199 D12
Čazma Croatia 45°45N 16°39E 199 C13
Cazombo Angola 11°54S 22°56E 265 E4
Cazorla Spain 37°55N 3°2W 195 H7
Cazorla, Sierra de Spain 38°5N 2°55W 195 G8
Cea → Spain 42°0N 5°36W 194 C5
Ceamurlia de Jos Romania 44°43N 28°47E 183 F13
Ceanannus Mor Ireland 53°44N 6°53W 166 C5
Ceará = Fortaleza Brazil 3°45S 38°35W 332 B4
Ceará □ Brazil 5°0S 40°0W 332 C4
Ceara Abyssal Plain Atl. Oc. 0°0 36°30W 152 F7
Ceará-Mirim Brazil 5°38S 35°25W 332 C4
Ceara Rise Atl. Oc. 4°30N 43°30W 152 F7
Ceatharlach = Carlow Ireland 52°50N 6°56W 166 D5
Ceauru, L. Romania 44°58N 23°11E 183 F8
Cébaco, I. de Panama 7°33N 81°9W 320 E3
Cebeccı Turkey 41°7N 28°52E 122 B1
Cebollar Argentina 29°10S 66°35W 334 B2
Cebollera, Sierra de Spain 42°0N 2°30W 196 D2
Cebreros Spain 40°27N 4°28W 194 E6
Cebu Phil. 10°18N 123°54E 233 F4
Cebu □ Phil. 10°20N 123°40E 233 F4
Čečava Bos.-H. 44°42N 17°44E 182 F2
Ceccano Italy 41°34N 13°20E 200 A6
Cecchignola Italy 41°48N 12°29E 136 C2
Cece Hungary 46°46N 18°39E 182 D3
Cechi Ivory C. 6°15N 4°25W 262 D4
Cecil Plains Australia 27°30S 151°11E 281 D5
Cecilienhof, Schloss Germany 52°35N 13°5E 115 B1
Cécina Italy 43°19N 10°31E 198 E7
Cécina → Italy 43°18N 10°29E 198 E7
Ceclavín Spain 39°50N 6°45W 194 F4
Cedar → U.S.A. 41°17N 91°21W 310 C5
Cedar City U.S.A. 37°41N 113°4W 305 H7
Cedar Creek Res. U.S.A. 32°11N 96°4W 314 E6
Cedar Falls Iowa, U.S.A. 42°32N 92°27W 310 B4
Cedar Falls Wash., U.S.A. 47°25N 121°45W 306 C5
Cedar Grove Georgia, U.S.A. 33°40N 84°16W 113 C3
Cedar Grove Ind., U.S.A. 39°22N 84°56W 311 E12
Cedar Key U.S.A. 29°8N 83°2W 317 F6
Cedar L. Canada 53°10N 100°0W 297 C9
Cedar Lake U.S.A. 41°22N 87°26W 311 C9
Cedar Park U.S.A. 30°30N 97°49W 314 F6
Cedar Point U.S.A. 41°44N 83°21W 311 C13
Cedar Rapids U.S.A. 41°59N 91°40W 310 C5
Cedar Tree Pt. Antigua & B. 17°42N 61°53W 322 c
Cedartown U.S.A. 34°1N 85°15W 316 A4
Cedarvale Canada 55°1N 128°22W 296 B3
Cedarvale Park Canada 43°42N 79°36W 141 A2
Cedarville KwaZulu Natal, S. Africa 30°23S 29°3E 271 D4
Cedarville Ill., U.S.A. 42°23N 89°38W 310 B7
Cedarville Ohio, U.S.A. 39°44N 83°49W 311 E13
Cedeira Spain 43°39N 8°2W 194 B2
Cedral Mexico 23°50N 100°45W 318 C4
Cedrino → Italy 40°11N 9°24E 200 B2
Cedro Brazil 6°34S 39°3W 332 C4
Cedros Azores 38°38N 28°42W 153 d1
Cedros, I. Mexico 28°12N 115°15W 318 B1
Cedros B. Trin. & Tob. 10°16N 61°54W 323 t
Cedros Pt. Trin. & Tob. 10°7N 61°49W 323 t
Ceduna Australia 32°7S 133°46E 281 E1
Cedynia Poland 52°53N 14°12E 185 F1
Cée Spain 42°57N 9°10W 194 C1
Ceel Gaal Somali Rep. 10°58N 50°20E 267 B7
Ceel Waaq Kenya 2°49N 40°56E 267 D5
Ceelbuur = El Bur Somali Rep. 4°40N 46°37E 267 D6
Ceeldheere Galguduud, Somali Rep. 3°50N 47°8E 267 D6
Ceeldheere Galguduud, Somali Rep. 5°22N 46°11E 267 C6
Ceerigaabo Somali Rep. 10°35N 47°20E 267 B6
Cefalù Italy 38°2N 14°1E 201 D7
Cega → Spain 41°33N 4°46W 194 D6
Cegléd Hungary 47°11N 19°47E 182 C4
Céglie Messápico Italy 40°39N 17°31E 201 B10
Cehegín Spain 38°6N 1°48W 197 G3
Ceheng China 24°58N 105°48E 228 E5
Cehu-Silvaniei Romania 47°24N 23°9E 183 C8
Ceiba Puerto Rico 18°16N 65°39W 321 b
Ceica Romania 46°53N 22°10E 182 D7
Ceira → Portugal 40°13N 8°16W 194 E2
Çekerek Turkey 40°4N 35°29E 212 B6
Cekik Indonesia 8°12S 114°27E 231 J17
Cela Angola 11°25S 15°7E 265 E3
Čelákovice Czech Rep. 50°10N 14°46E 180 A7
Celano Italy 42°5N 13°33E 199 F10
Celanova Spain 42°9N 7°58W 194 C3
Celaque △ Honduras 14°30N 88°43W 320 D2
Celaya Mexico 20°31N 100°37W 318 C4
Celebes = Sulawesi Indonesia 2°0S 120°0E 235 C5
Celebes Sea Indonesia 3°0N 123°0E 231 D6
Celendín Peru 6°52S 78°10W 330 B2
Celestial Mts. = Tian Shan Asia 40°30N 76°0E 217 D9
Čelić Bos.-H. 44°43N 18°49E 182 F3
Celica Ecuador 4°7S 79°59W 328 D2
Celina U.S.A. 40°33N 84°35W 311 D12
Celinac Bos.-H. 44°44N 17°22E 182 F2
Celje Slovenia 46°16N 15°18E 199 B12
Celldömölk Hungary 47°16N 17°10E 182 C2
Celle Germany 52°37N 10°4E 178 C6
Celorico da Beira Portugal 40°38N 7°24W 194 E3
Celtic Sea Atl. Oc. 50°9N 9°34W 165 F2
Çeltikçi Turkey 37°32N 30°29E 205 D12
Çemişgezek Turkey 39°3N 38°56E 213 C8
Cempaka Putih Indonesia 6°10S 106°51E 122 B2
Cempi, Teluk Indonesia 8°44S 118°22E 235 D5
Cenderwasih, Teluk Indonesia 3°0S 135°20E 231 E9
Cenepa → Peru 4°40S 78°10W 328 D2
Çengelköy Turkey 41°2N 29°3E 122 B2
Cengkareng Indonesia 6°9S 106°45E 122 A1
Cengong China 27°13N 108°44E 228 D7
Ceno → Italy 44°43N 10°5E 198 D7
Centallo Italy 44°30N 7°35E 198 D4
Centelles Spain 41°50N 2°14E 196 D7
Centenário do Sul Brazil 22°48S 51°36W 333 F1
Centennial Olympic Park U.S.A. 33°46N 84°23W 113 B2
Centennial Park Australia 33°53S 151°14E 139 B2
Center N. Dak., U.S.A. 47°7N 101°18W 308 B3
Center Tex., U.S.A. 31°48N 94°11W 314 F7
Center Hill Fla., U.S.A. 28°38N 82°3W 317 G7
Center Hill Georgia, U.S.A. 33°46N 84°29W 113 B2
Center Point U.S.A. 42°12N 91°46W 310 B5
Centerburg U.S.A. 40°18N 82°42W 312 F2
Centerville Calif., U.S.A. 36°44N 119°30W 306 J7
Centerville Iowa, U.S.A. 40°44N 92°52W 310 D4
Centerville Ohio, U.S.A. 39°38N 84°8W 311 E12
Centerville Pa., U.S.A. 40°3N 79°59W 312 F5
Centerville Tenn., U.S.A. 35°47N 87°28W 315 D11
Centerville Tex., U.S.A. 31°16N 95°59W 314 F7
Cento Italy 44°43N 11°17E 199 D8
Centocelle Italy 41°52N 12°34E 136 B2
Centraal Station Amsterdam, Neths. 112 a3
Central = Tsentralnyy □ Russia 52°0N 40°0E 190 D3
Central Brazil 11°8S 42°8W 332 D3
Central Alaska, U.S.A. 65°35N 144°48W 303 D11
Central □ Ghana 5°30N 1°0W 263 D4
Central □ Kenya 0°30S 37°30E 268 C4
Central □ Malawi 13°30S 33°30E 269 E3
Central □ Papua N. G. 10°0S 148°0E 286 F5
Central □ Zambia 14°25S 28°50E 269 E2
Central, Cordillera Bolivia 18°30S 64°55W 331 D5
Central, Cordillera Colombia 5°0N 75°0W 328 C3
Central, Cordillera Costa Rica 10°10N 84°5W 320 D3
Central, Cordillera Dom. Rep. 19°15N 71°0W 321 C5
Central, Cordillera Peru 7°0S 77°30W 330 B2
Central, Cordillera Phil. 17°20N 120°57E 232 C3
Central, Cordillera Puerto Rico 18°8N 66°35W 321 b
Central, Gare Montréal, Canada 130 c2
Central African Empire = Central African Rep. ■ Africa 7°0N 20°0E 264 A4
Central African Rep. ■ Africa 7°0N 20°0E 264 A4
Central America America 12°0N 85°0W 292 H11
Central Australia ۞ Australia 22°30S 128°30E 278 D4
Central Bedfordshire □ U.K. 52°5N 0°20W 169 E7
Central Butte Canada 50°48N 106°31W 297 C7
Central City Colo., U.S.A. 39°48N 105°31W 304 G11
Central City Iowa, U.S.A. 42°12N 91°32W 310 B5
Central City Ky., U.S.A. 37°18N 87°7W 308 G10
Central City Nebr., U.S.A. 41°7N 98°0W 308 E4
Central Desert ۞ Australia 19°56S 130°46E 278 C5
Central I. Kenya 3°30N 36°0E 268 B4
Central Island △ Kenya 2°33N 36°1E 268 B4
Central Japan Int. ✕ (CJI) Japan 34°53N 136°45E 223 C8
Central Kalahari ⌓ Botswana 22°36S 23°58E 270 B3
Central Makran Range Pakistan 26°30N 64°15E 240 D2
Central Pacific Basin Pac. Oc. 8°0N 175°0W 288 G10
Central Park New York, U.S.A. 132 a3
Central Park Zoo New York, U.S.A. 132 b2
Central Patricia Canada 51°30N 90°9W 298 B1
Central Point U.S.A. 42°23N 122°55W 304 E2
Central Provinces = Madhya Pradesh □ India 22°50N 78°0E 242 J8
Central Ra. Papua N. G. 5°0S 143°0E 286 C2
Central Ra. Trin. & Tob. 10°25N 61°15W 323 t
Central Range Wildlife Sanctuary Trin. & Tob. 10°27N 61°14W 323 t
Central Russian Uplands Europe 54°0N 36°0E 158 E13
Central Siberian Plateau Russia 65°0N 105°0E 210 B12
Central Square U.S.A. 43°17N 76°9W 313 C8
Central Village Jamaica 17°59N 76°55W 320 a
Centralia Ont., Canada 43°17N 81°28W 312 C3
Centralia Ill., U.S.A. 38°32N 89°8W 310 F7
Centralia Mo., U.S.A. 39°13N 92°8W 310 E4
Centralia Wash., U.S.A. 46°43N 122°58W 306 D4
Centre U.S.A. 34°9N 85°41W 316 A4
Centre □ Cameroon 4°45N 12°0E 263 E7
Centre de Flacq Mauritius 20°12S 57°43E 272 e
Centreville Mich., U.S.A. 41°55N 85°32W 311 C11
Centreville N.Y., U.S.A. 42°28N 78°14W 312 D6
Centreville Pa., U.S.A. 41°44N 79°45W 312 E5
Century U.S.A. 30°58N 87°16W 317 E2
Century City U.S.A. 34°3N 118°25W 126 B2
Cenxi China 22°57N 110°57E 229 F8
Čeotina → Bos.-H. 43°36N 18°50E 202 C2
Cephalonia = Kefalonia Greece 38°15N 20°30E 207 C2
Čepin Croatia 45°32N 18°34E 182 E3
Ceprano Italy 41°33N 13°31E 200 A6
Ceptia Angola 12°56S 17°35E 265 E3
Ceptura Romania 45°1N 26°21E 183 E11
Cepu Indonesia 7°9S 111°35E 235 D4
Ceram = Seram Indonesia 3°10S 129°0E 231 E7
Ceram Sea = Seram Sea Indonesia 2°30S 128°30E 231 E7
Cerbère France 42°26N 3°10E 174 F7
Cerbicales, Îs. France 41°33N 9°22E 175 G13
Cercal Portugal 37°48N 8°40W 195 H2
Cerdaña Spain 42°22N 1°35E 196 C6
Cerdanyola del Vallès Spain 41°27N 2°8W 114 A1
Cère → France 44°55N 1°49E 174 D5
Cerea Italy 45°12N 11°13E 199 C8
Ceredigion □ U.K. 52°16N 4°15W 169 E3
Ceres Argentina 29°55S 61°55W 334 B3
Ceres Brazil 15°17S 49°35W 333 E2
Ceres Western Cape, S. Africa 33°21S 19°18E 270 D2
Ceres Calif., U.S.A. 37°35N 120°57W 306 H6
Céret France 42°30N 2°42E 174 F6
Cereté Colombia 8°53N 75°48W 328 B2
Cerf Seychelles 4°38S 55°40E 272 c
Cerfs, Îs. aux Mauritius 20°16S 57°47E 272 e
Cergy France 49°2N 2°4E 173 C9
Cerignola Italy 41°17N 15°53E 201 A8
Cerigo = Kythira Greece 36°8N 23°0E 204 E5
Cerillos Chile 33°29S 70°42W 137 B1
Cérilly France 46°37N 2°50E 173 F9
Cerisiers France 48°8N 3°30E 173 D10
Cerizay France 46°50N 0°40W 172 F6
Çerkeş Turkey 40°49N 32°52E 212 B5
Çerkezköy Turkey 41°17N 28°0E 203 E12
Cerknica Slovenia 45°48N 14°21E 199 C11
Cerkovica Bulgaria 43°41N 24°50E 203 C8
Cermerno Serbia 43°35N 20°25E 202 C4
Çermik Turkey 38°8N 39°26E 213 C8
Cerna Romania 45°4N 28°17E 183 E13
Cerna → Romania 44°38N 23°58E 183 F8
Cernauti = Chernivtsi Ukraine 48°15N 25°52E 183 B10
Cernavodă Romania 44°22N 28°3E 183 F13
Cernay France 47°44N 7°10E 173 E14
Cernik Croatia 45°17N 17°22E 182 E2
Cerralvo, I. Mexico 24°15N 109°55W 318 C3
Cërrik Albania 41°2N 19°58E 202 E3
Cerritos Mexico 22°25N 100°16W 318 C4
Cerro Chato Uruguay 33°6S 55°8W 335 C4
Cerro Chovoreca △ Paraguay 19°19S 59°7W 331 D6
Cerro Cofre de Perote △ Mexico 19°29N 97°8W 319 D5
Cerro Corá △ Paraguay 22°35S 56°2W 335 A4
Cerro de la Estrella △ Mexico 19°23N 99°5W 128 B2
Cerro de los Angeles Spain 40°18N 3°41W 127 C1
Cerro de Pasco Peru 10°45S 76°10W 330 C2
Cerro Gordo U.S.A. 39°53N 88°44W 311 E8
Cerro Hoya △ Panama 7°17N 80°45W 320 E3
Cerro Navia Chile 33°25S 70°42W 137 B1
Cerro Saroche △ Venezuela 10°8N 69°38W 328 A4
Cerro Sombrero Chile 52°45S 69°15W 336 D3
Certaldo Italy 43°33N 11°2E 198 E8
Cervantes Phil. 17°0N 120°44E 232 C3
Cervaro → Italy 41°30N 15°52E 201 A8
Cervati, Monte Italy 40°17N 15°29E 201 B8
Cerventes Australia 30°31S 115°3E 279 F2
Cervera Spain 41°40N 1°16E 196 D6
Cervera de Pisuerga Spain 42°51N 4°30W 194 C6
Cervera del Río Alhama Spain 42°2N 1°58W 196 C3
Cervéteri Italy 42°0N 12°6E 199 F9
Cérvia Italy 44°15N 12°22E 199 D9
Cervignano del Friuli Italy 45°49N 13°20E 199 C10
Cervinara Italy 41°1N 14°37E 201 A7
Cervione France 42°20N 9°29E 175 F13
Cervo Spain 43°40N 7°24W 194 B3
Cesano Boscone Italy 45°26N 9°5E 129 B1
César □ Colombia 9°0N 73°30W 328 B3
Cesarò Italy 37°50N 14°38E 201 E7
Cesate Italy 45°35N 9°4E 129 A1
Cesena Italy 44°8N 12°15E 199 D9
Cesenático Italy 44°12N 12°24E 199 D9
Cēsis Latvia 57°18N 25°15E 188 D3
Česká Lípa Czech Rep. 50°45N 14°30E 180 A7
Česká Rep. = Czech Rep. ■ Europe 50°0N 15°0E 180 B8

Česká Třebová Czech Rep. 49°54N 16°27E 181 B9
České Budějovice Czech Rep. 48°55N 14°25E 180 C7
České Velenice Czech Rep. 48°45N 14°57E 180 C7
Českobudějovický □ Czech Rep. 49°10N 14°30E 180 B7
Českomoravská Vrchovina Czech Rep. 49°30N 15°40E 180 B8
Český Brod Czech Rep. 50°4N 14°52E 180 A7
Český Krumlov Czech Rep. 48°43N 14°21E 180 C7
Český Těšín Czech Rep. 49°45N 18°39E 181 B11
Česma → Croatia 45°35N 16°29E 199 C13
Çeşme Turkey 38°20N 26°23E 205 C8
Cessnock Australia 32°50S 151°21E 283 B9
Cesson-Sévigné France 48°7N 1°36W 172 D5
Cestas France 44°44N 0°41W 174 D3
Cestos → Liberia 5°40N 9°10W 262 D3
Cestos Sehnkwehn △ Liberia 5°40N 9°10W 262 D3
Cetaceo, Mt. Phil. 17°42N 122°3E 232 C4
Cetate Romania 44°7N 23°2E 182 F8
Cetatea-Albă = Bilhorod-Dnistrovskyy Ukraine 46°11N 30°23E 189 J6
Cetin Grad Croatia 45°9N 15°45E 199 C12
Cetina → Croatia 43°26N 16°42E 199 E13
Cetinje Montenegro 42°23N 18°59E 202 D2
Çetmı Turkey 36°52N 32°38E 250 B3
Cetraro Italy 39°31N 15°55E 201 C8
Ceuta N. Afr. 35°52N 5°18W 260 A3
Ceva Italy 44°23N 8°2E 198 D5
Ceve-i-Ra Fiji 21°46S 174°31E 277 E13
Cévennes France 44°10N 3°50E 174 D7
Cévennes △ France 44°15N 3°45E 174 D7
Ceyhan Turkey 37°4N 35°47E 250 A6
Ceyhan → Turkey 36°38N 35°40E 250 B6
Ceylanpınar Turkey 36°50N 40°2E 213 D9
Ceylon = Sri Lanka ■ Asia 7°30N 80°50E 245 L5
Ceylon Plain Ind. Oc. 4°0S 82°0E 273 E7
Cèze → France 44°6N 4°43E 175 D8
Cha-am Thailand 12°48N 99°58E 236 F2
Cha Kwo Ling China 22°18N 114°13E 122 B2
Chá Pungana Angola 13°44S 18°39E 265 E3
Chabanais France 45°52N 0°48E 174 C4
Chabeuil France 44°54N 5°3E 175 D9
Chablais France 46°20N 6°36E 173 F13
Chablis France 47°47N 3°48E 173 E10
Chabounia Algeria 35°30N 2°38E 261 A5
Chacabuco Argentina 34°40S 60°27W 334 C3
Chacachacare I. Trin. & Tob. 10°41N 61°45W 323 t
Chacao, Canal Chile 41°47S 73°42W 336 B2
Chacarrita Argentina 34°35S 58°27W 117 B2
Chachani, Nevado Peru 16°11S 71°31W 330 D3
Chachapoyas Peru 6°15S 77°50W 330 B2
Chachasp Peru 15°30S 72°15W 330 D3
Chachoengsao Thailand 13°42N 101°5E 236 F3
Chachran Pakistan 28°55N 70°30E 242 E4
Chachro Pakistan 25°5N 70°15E 242 G4
Chaco □ Argentina 26°30S 61°0W 334 B3
Chaco □ Paraguay 26°0S 60°0W 334 B4
Chaco → U.S.A. 36°46N 108°39W 305 H9
Chaco △ Argentina 27°0S 59°30W 334 B4
Chaco Culture ⌂ U.S.A. 36°3N 107°58W 305 H10
Chacon, C. U.S.A. 54°42N 132°0W 296 C2
Chad ■ Africa 15°0N 17°15E 259 F3
Chad, L. = Tchad, L. Chad 13°30N 14°30E 259 F2
Chadileuvú → Argentina 37°46S 66°0W 334 D2
Chadiza Zambia 14°45S 32°27E 269 E3
Chadron U.S.A. 42°50N 103°0W 308 D2
Chadwell Heath U.K. 51°34N 0°8E 125 A4
Chadyr-Lunga = Ciadâr-Lunga Moldova 46°3N 28°51E 183 D13
Chae Hom Thailand 18°43N 99°35E 236 C2
Chae Son △ Thailand 18°42N 99°20E 236 C2
Chaem → Thailand 18°11N 98°38E 236 C2
Chaeryŏng N. Korea 38°24N 125°36E 224 C2
Chafe Nigeria 11°59N 6°50E 263 C6
Chagai Hills = Chāh Gay Hills Afghan. 29°30N 64°0E 240 C2
Chagang-do □ N. Korea 40°50N 126°30E 224 B3
Chagda Russia 58°45N 130°38E 215 D14
Chagdo Kangri China 34°15N 84°10E 217 F10
Chaghcharān Afghan. 34°31N 65°15E 240 B2
Chagne Ethiopia 10°57N 36°30E 266 B4
Chagny France 46°57N 4°45E 173 F11
Chagoda Russia 59°10N 35°15E 188 C8
Chagos Arch. ⊠ Ind. Oc. 6°0S 72°0E 211 J9
Chagos-Laccadive Ridge Ind. Oc. 3°0N 73°0E 273 D6
Chagres → Panama 9°10N 79°40W 320 c
Chagres △ Panama 9°33N 79°37W 320 c
Chaguanas Trin. & Tob. 10°30N 61°26W 323 t
Chaguaramas Trin. & Tob. 10°41N 61°38W 323 t
Chāh Ākhvor Iran 32°41N 59°40E 247 C8
Chāh Bahar Iran 25°20N 60°40E 247 E9
Chāh-e Āb Afghan. 37°23N 69°48E 240 A3
Chāh-e Kavīr Iran 34°29N 56°52E 247 C8
Chāh Gay Hills Afghan. 29°30N 64°0E 240 C2
Chahār Borj Iran 37°6N 45°59E 213 D11
Chahār Borjak Afghan. 30°17N 62°3E 240 C1
Chahār Mahāll va Bakhtīarī □ Iran 32°0N 49°0E 247 C6
Chahtung Burma 26°41N 98°10E 241 B7
Chai Badan Thailand 15°12N 101°8E 236 E3
Chai Chee Singapore 1°19N 103°46E 138 B3
Chai Wan China 22°16N 114°14E 122 B2
Chai Wan Kok China 22°22N 114°6E 122 A1
Chaibasa India 22°42N 85°49E 243 H11
Chaidari Greece 38°2N 23°38E 112 A1
Chaillé-les-Marais France 46°25N 1°2W 174 B2
Chaillot, Palais de Paris, France 134 b2
Chaillu, Massif du Gabon 2°32S 11°10E 264 C2
Chain Ridge Ind. Oc. 6°0N 54°0E 273 D4
Chainat Thailand 15°11N 100°8E 236 E3
Chaires U.S.A. 30°26N 84°7W 316 E5
Chaitén Chile 42°55S 72°43W 336 B2
Chaiya Thailand 9°23N 99°14E 237 H2
Chaiyaphum Thailand 15°48N 102°2E 236 E4
Chaj Doab Pakistan 32°15N 73°0E 242 C5
Chajari Argentina 30°42S 58°0W 334 C4
Chak Amru Pakistan 32°22N 75°11E 242 C6
Chaka Sudan 4°49N 31°14E 257 G3
Chakar → Pakistan 29°29N 68°2E 242 E3
Chakari Zimbabwe 18°5S 29°51E 271 A4
Chakaria Bangla. 21°45N 92°5E 241 E4
Chakarnaba Chad 14°13N 20°51E 259 F4
Chakdaha India 22°28N 88°19E 124 C1
Chake Chake Tanzania 5°15S 39°45E 268 D4
Chakhānsūr Afghan. 31°10N 62°0E 240 C1
Chakonipau, L. Canada 56°18N 68°30W 299 A6
Chakradharpur India 22°45N 85°40E 243 H11
Chakrata India 30°42N 77°51E 242 D7
Chakwadam Burma 27°29N 98°31E 241 B7
Chakwal Pakistan 32°56N 72°53E 242 C5
Chala Peru 15°48S 74°20W 330 D3
Chalais France 45°16N 0°3E 174 C4
Chalakudi India 10°18N 76°20E 245 J3
Chalan Kanoa N. Marianas 15°9N 145°42E 302 e
Chalandri Greece 38°3N 23°48E 112 A2
Chalchihuites Mexico 23°29N 103°53W 318 C4
Chalcis = Chalkida Greece 38°27N 23°42E 204 C5
Châlette-sur-Loing France 48°1N 2°44E 173 D9
Chaleur B. Canada 47°55N 65°30W 299 C6
Chalfant U.S.A. 37°32N 118°21W 306 H8
Chalhuanca Peru 14°15S 73°15W 330 C3
Chaliki Greece 39°36N 22°30E 204 B4
Chalindrey France 47°43N 5°26E 173 E12
Chaling China 26°58N 113°30E 229 D9
Chalisgaon India 20°30N 75°10E 244 D2
Chalk River Canada 46°1N 77°27W 298 C4
Chalkar, Ozero = Shalkar Köli Kazakhstan 50°35N 51°47E 190 E10
Chalki Greece 36°17N 27°35E 205 E9
Chalkida Greece 38°27N 23°42E 204 C5
Chalkidiki □ Greece 40°25N 23°20E 202 F7
Chalky Inlet N.Z. 46°3S 166°31E 285 G1
Chalkyitsik U.S.A. 66°39N 143°43W 303 C12
Challakere India 14°19N 76°39E 245 G3
Challans France 46°50N 1°52W 172 F5
Challapata Bolivia 18°53S 66°50W 330 D4
Challawa Gorge Res. Nigeria 11°54N 8°25E 263 C6
Challenger Deep Pac. Oc. 11°30N 142°0E 288 F6
Challenger Fracture Zone Pac. Oc. 35°0S 105°0W 289 L17
Challis U.S.A. 44°30N 114°14W 304 D6
Chalmette U.S.A. 29°56N 89°57W 315 G10
Chaloem Rattanakosin △ Thailand 14°40N 99°17E 236 E2
Chalon-sur-Saône France 46°48N 4°50E 173 F11
Chalong Thailand 7°50N 98°22E 237 a
Chalonnes-sur-Loire France 47°20N 0°45W 172 E6
Châlons-en-Champagne France 48°58N 4°20E 173 D11
Chálten, Cerro = Fitz Roy, Cerro Argentina 49°17S 73°5W 336 C2
Châlus Haute-Vienne, France 45°39N 0°58E 174 C4
Chālūs Iran 36°38N 51°26E 247 B6
Cham Germany 49°13N 12°39E 179 F8
Cham, Cu Lao Vietnam 15°57N 108°30E 236 E7
Chama U.S.A. 36°54N 106°35W 305 H10
Chamah, Gunung Malaysia 5°13N 101°35E 234 A2
Chamaicó Argentina 35°3S 64°58W 334 D3
Chaman Pakistan 30°58N 66°25E 240 C2
Chamartin Spain 40°27N 3°40W 127 B1
Chamba India 32°35N 76°10E 242 C7
Chamba Tanzania 11°37S 37°0E 269 E4
Chambal → India 26°29N 79°15E 243 F8
Chamberi Spain 40°26N 3°42W 127 B1
Chamberlain U.S.A. 43°49N 99°20W 308 D4
Chamberlain → Australia 15°30S 127°54E 278 C4
Chamberlain L. U.S.A. 46°14N 69°19W 309 B19
Chambers U.S.A. 35°11N 109°26W 305 J9
Chambersburg U.S.A. 39°56N 77°40W 309 F15
Chambéry France 45°34N 5°55E 175 C9
Chambi, Jebel Tunisia 35°11N 8°39E 261 A6
Chamblee U.S.A. 33°53N 84°18W 316 B5
Chambly Canada 45°27N 73°17W 313 A11
Chambord Canada 48°25N 72°6W 299 C5
Chamboulive France 45°26N 1°42E 174 C5
Chambourcy France 48°54N 2°2E 134 A1
Chambri L. Papua N. G. 4°15S 143°10E 286 C2
Chamchamal Iraq 35°32N 44°50E 213 E11
Chamela Mexico 19°32N 105°5W 318 D3
Chamical Argentina 30°22S 66°27W 334 C2
Chamili Greece 35°50N 26°15E 205 F8
Chamkar Luong Cambodia 11°0N 103°45E 237 G4
Chamois U.S.A. 38°41N 91°46W 310 F5
Chamoli India 30°24N 79°21E 243 D8
Chamonix-Mont Blanc France 45°55N 6°51E 175 C10
Chamouchuane = Ashuapmushuan → Canada 48°37N 72°20W 298 C5
Champ de Mars, Parc du Paris, France 134 c2
Champa India 22°2N 82°43E 243 H10
Champagne Canada 60°49N 136°30W 296 A1
Champagne France 48°40N 4°20E 173 D11
Champagnole France 46°45N 5°55E 173 F12
Champaign U.S.A. 40°7N 88°15W 311 D8
Champassak Laos 14°53N 105°52E 236 E5
Champaubert France 48°50N 3°45E 173 D10
Champawat India 29°20N 80°6E 243 E9
Champdeniers-St-Denis France 46°29N 0°25W 174 B3
Champdoré, L. Canada 55°55N 65°49W 299 A6
Champeix France 45°37N 3°8E 174 C7
Champigny-sur-Marne France 48°49N 2°30E 134 B4
Champion U.S.A. 41°19N 80°51W 312 E4
Champlain U.S.A. 44°59N 73°27W 313 B11
Champlain, L. U.S.A. 44°40N 73°20W 313 B11
Champlain, Pont Canada 45°28N 73°31W 130 B2
Champlitte France 47°32N 5°31E 173 E12
Champotón Mexico 19°21N 90°43W 319 D6
Champs Elysées, Avenue des Paris, France 134 b2
Champs-sur-Marne France 48°50N 2°34E 134 A4
Champua India 22°5N 85°40E 243 H11
Chamrail India 22°38N 88°17E 124 B1
Chamrajnagar India 11°52N 76°52E 245 J3
Chamusca Portugal 39°21N 8°29W 195 F2
Chan Chan Peru 8°7S 79°0W 330 B2
Chana Thailand 6°55N 100°44E 237 J3
Chanakyapuri India 28°35N 77°11E 120 B2
Chañaral Chile 26°23S 70°40W 334 B1
Chanārān Iran 36°39N 59°6E 247 B8
Chanasma India 23°44N 72°5E 242 H5
Chancay Peru 11°32S 77°25W 330 C2
Chancel, Î. Martinique 14°41N 60°53W 322 j
Chanchiang = Zhanjiang China 21°15N 110°20E 229 G8
Chanco Chile 35°44S 72°32W 334 D1
Chand India 21°57N 79°7E 243 J8
Chandalar → U.S.A. 66°37N 146°0W 303 C11
Chandan India 24°38N 86°40E 243 G12
Chandan Chauki India 28°33N 80°47E 243 E9
Chandannagar India 22°52N 88°24E 243 H13
Chandausi India 28°27N 78°49E 243 E8
Chandeleur Is. U.S.A. 29°55N 88°57W 315 G10
Chandeleur Sd. U.S.A. 29°55N 89°0W 315 G10
Chandigarh India 30°43N 76°47E 242 D7
Chandil India 22°58N 86°3E 243 H12
Chanditala India 22°41N 88°15E 124 A1
Chandler S. Austral., Australia 27°0S 133°19E 281 D1
Chandler Qué., Canada 48°18N 64°46W 299 C7
Chandler Ariz., U.S.A. 33°18N 111°50W 305 K8
Chandler Okla., U.S.A. 35°42N 96°53W 314 D6
Chandless → Brazil 9°8S 69°51W 330 B4
Chandod India 21°59N 73°28E 242 J5
Chandpur Bangla. 23°8N 90°45E 241 D3
Chandra Greece 35°3N 26°8E 205 F8
Chandragiri India 13°35N 79°19E 245 H4
Chandrapur India 19°57N 79°25E 244 E4
Chandrupatla India 18°33N 80°24E 244 E5
Chānf Iran 26°38N 60°29E 247 E9
Chang Pakistan 26°59N 68°30E 242 F3
Chang, Ko Thailand 12°0N 102°23E 237 G4
Chang, Ko Thailand 9°50N 98°27E 237 H2
Ch'ang Chiang = Chang Jiang → China 31°48N 121°10E 229 B13
Chang Jiang → China 31°48N 121°10E 229 B13
Chang-won S. Korea 35°16N 128°37E 224 E4
Changan = Xi'an China 34°15N 109°0E 226 G5
Changan China 22°48N 113°48E 219 a
Changanacheri India 9°25N 76°31E 245 K3
Changanassery = Changanacheri India 9°25N 76°31E 245 K3
Changane → Mozam. 24°30S 33°30E 271 B5
Changbai China 41°25N 128°5E 224 B4
Changbai Shan China 42°20N 129°0E 224 A4
Changchiak'ou = Zhangjiakou China 40°48N 114°55E 226 D8
Changchih = Changzhi China 36°10N 113°6E 226 F7
Changchih Taiwan 22°41N 120°32E 225 D2
Ch'angchou = Changzhou China 31°47N 119°58E 229 B12
Changchow = Changzhou China 31°47N 119°58E 229 B12
Changchun China 43°57N 125°17E 227 C13
Changchunling China 45°18N 125°27E 227 B13
Changde China 29°4N 111°35E 229 C8
Changdo-ri N. Korea 38°30N 127°40E 224 C3
Changfeng China 32°28N 117°10E 229 A11
Changfeng Park China 31°14N 121°24E 138 B1
Changge China 34°13N 113°46E 226 G7
Changhai = Shanghai China 31°15N 121°26E 138 B2
Changhua Zhejiang, China 30°12N 119°12E 229 B12
Changhua Taiwan 24°2N 120°30E 225 B2
Changhua □ Taiwan 24°15N 120°55E 225 B2
Changhŭngni N. Korea 40°24N 128°19E 224 B4
Changi Singapore 1°23N 103°59E 138 A3
Changi, Singapore ✕ (SIN) Singapore 1°23N 103°59E 138 A3
Changji China 44°1N 87°19E 217 D11
Changjiang China 19°20N 108°55E 236 C7
Changjiang Shuiku China 22°29N 113°27E 219 a
Changjin N. Korea 40°23N 127°15E 224 B3
Changjin-ho N. Korea 40°30N 127°15E 224 B3
Changle China 25°59N 119°27E 229 E12
Changli China 39°40N 119°13E 227 E10
Changling China 44°20N 123°58E 227 B12
Changlun Malaysia 6°25N 100°26E 237 J3
Changning Hunan, China 26°28N 112°22E 229 D9
Changning Shanghai, China 31°13N 121°24E 138 B1
Changning Sichuan, China 28°40N 104°56E 228 C5
Changning Yunnan, China 24°45N 99°30E 228 E2
Ch'angpin Taiwan 23°19N 121°27E 225 C3
Changping China 40°14N 116°12E 226 D9
Changsha China 28°12N 113°0E 229 C9
Changshan China 28°55N 118°27E 229 C12
Changshan Qundao China 39°11N 122°32E 227 E12
Changshou China 29°50N 107°4E 228 C6
Changshu China 31°38N 120°43E 229 B13
Changshun China 26°3N 106°25E 228 D6
Changtai China 24°35N 117°42E 229 E11
Changt'e = Chongde China 30°32N 120°26E 229 B13
Changting China 25°50N 116°22E 229 E11
Changtu China 42°46N 124°6E 227 C13
Changuinola Panama 9°26N 82°31W 320 E3
Changwu Guangxi Zhuangzu, China 23°25N 111°17E 229 F8
Changwu Shaanxi, China 35°10N 107°45E 226 G4
Changxing China 31°0N 119°55E 229 B12
Changyang China 30°30N 111°10E 229 B8
Changyi China 36°40N 119°30E 227 F10
Changyŏn N. Korea 38°15N 125°6E 224 C2
Changyuan Henan, China 35°15N 114°42E 226 G8
Changyuan Taiwan 23°25N 121°29E 225 C3
Changzhi China 36°10N 113°6E 226 F7
Changzhou China 31°47N 119°58E 229 B12
Chanhanga Angola 16°0S 14°8E 265 F2
Chania Greece 35°30N 24°4E 207 E5
Chania □ Greece 35°30N 24°0E 207 E5
Chania ✕ (CHQ) Greece 35°30N 24°6E 207 E5
Chanion, Kolpos Greece 35°33N 23°55E 207 E4
Chanlar = Xanlar Azerbaijan 40°37N 46°12E 191 K8
Channagiri India 14°2N 75°56E 245 G2
Channapatna India 12°40N 77°15E 245 H3
Channel Is. U.K. 49°19N 2°24W 169 H5
Channel Is. Calif., U.S.A. 33°40N 119°15W 307 M7
Channel Islands △ U.S.A. 34°0N 119°24W 307 L7
Channel-Port aux Basques Canada 47°30N 59°9W 299 C8
Channel Tunnel Europe 51°0N 1°30E 169 F9
Channing U.S.A. 35°41N 102°20W 314 D3
Chantada Spain 42°36N 7°46W 194 C3
Chantereine France 48°53N 2°37E 134 A4
Chanthaburi Thailand 12°38N 102°12E 236 F4
Chantian China 23°12N 113°16E 121 A2
Chantilly France 49°12N 2°29E 173 C9
Chantonnay France 46°40N 1°3W 172 F5
Chantrey Inlet Canada 67°48N 96°20W 294 D12
Chanumla India 8°19N 93°5E 245 K11
Chanute U.S.A. 37°41N 95°27W 308 G6
Chany, Ozero Russia 54°49N 77°29E 217 B9
Chanza → Spain 37°32N 7°30W 195 H3
Chao Hu China 31°30N 117°30E 229 B11
Chao Phraya → Thailand 13°40N 100°31E 236 F3
Chao Phraya Lowlands Thailand 15°30N 100°0E 236 E3
Chaocheng China 36°4N 115°37E 226 F8
Ch'aochou Taiwan 22°33N 120°32E 225 D2
Chaohu China 31°38N 117°50E 229 B11
Chaoyang Beijing, China 39°53N 116°26E 114 B2
Chaoyang Guangdong, China 23°17N 116°30E 229 F11
Chaoyang Liaoning, China 41°35N 120°22E 227 D11
Chaoyangmen China 39°54N 116°23E 114 B2
Chaozhou China 23°42N 116°32E 229 F11
Chapada Diamantina △ Brazil 12°52S 41°30W 333 D3
Chapada dos Guimarães Brazil 15°26S 55°45W 331 D6
Chapada dos Guimarães △ Brazil 15°18S 55°54W 331 D6
Chapada dos Veadeiros △ Brazil 14°0S 47°30W 333 D2
Chapaev Kazakhstan 50°25N 51°10E 190 E10
Chapais Canada 49°47N 74°51W 298 C5
Chapala Mozam. 15°50S 37°35E 269 F4
Chapala, L. de Mexico 20°15N 103°0W 318 C4
Chaparé → Bolivia 15°58S 64°42W 331 D5
Chaparmukh India 26°12N 92°31E 241 B4
Chaparral Colombia 3°43N 75°28W 328 C2
Chapayev = Chapaev Kazakhstan 50°25N 51°10E 190 E10
Chapayevsk Russia 53°0N 49°40E 190 D9
Chapecó Brazil 27°14S 52°41W 335 B5
Chapel Hill U.S.A. 35°55N 79°4W 315 D15
Chapelizod Ireland 53°21N 6°21W 120 A1
Chapelton Jamaica 18°5N 77°16W 320 a
Chapin = Edinburg U.S.A. 26°18N 98°10W 314 H5
Chapin U.S.A. 39°46N 90°24W 310 E6
Chapleau Canada 47°50N 83°24W 298 C3
Chaplin Canada 50°28N 106°40W 297 C7
Chaplin L. Canada 50°22N 106°36W 297 C7
Chaplino Ukraine 48°8N 36°15E 189 H9
Chaplygin Russia 53°15N 40°0E 188 F11
Chappell U.S.A. 41°6N 102°28W 308 E2
Chappells U.S.A. 34°11N 81°52W 316 A8
Chapra = Chhapra India 25°48N 84°44E 243 G11
Chapultepec, Bosque de Mexico 19°25N 99°11W 128 B1
Chapultepec, Castillo de Mexico 19°25N 99°10W 128 B1
Chaqābel Iran 33°16N 47°30E 213 F12
Châr Mauritania 21°32N 12°45W 260 D2
Chara Russia 56°54N 118°20E 215 D12
Charadai Argentina 27°35S 59°55W 334 B4
Charagua Bolivia 19°45S 63°10W 331 D5
Charakas Greece 35°1N 25°7E 207 E6
Charalá Colombia 6°17N 73°10W 328 B3
Charambirá, Punta Colombia 4°16N 77°32W 328 C2
Charaña Bolivia 17°30S 69°25W 330 D4
Charantsavan Armenia 40°35N 44°41E 191 K7
Charanwala India 27°51N 72°10E 242 F5
Charapita Colombia 0°37S 74°21W 328 D3
Charata Argentina 27°13S 61°14W 334 B3
Charcas Mexico 23°8N 101°7W 318 C4
Charcot I. Antarctica 70°0S 70°0W 151 C17
Chard U.K. 50°52N 2°58W 169 G5
Chardon U.S.A. 41°35N 81°12W 312 E3
Charduar India 26°51N 92°46E 241 B4
Chardzhou = Türkmenabat Turkmenistan 39°6N 63°34E 247 B9
Charente □ France 45°50N 0°16E 174 C4
Charente → France 45°57N 1°5W 174 C2
Charente-Inférieure = Charente-Maritime □ France 45°45N 0°45W 174 C3
Charente-Maritime □ France 45°45N 0°45W 174 C3
Charenton-du-Cher France 46°44N 2°39E 173 F9
Charenton-le-Pont France 48°49N 2°25E 134 B3
Chari → Chad 12°58N 14°31E 259 F2
Chari-Baguirmi □ Chad 11°0N 17°0E 259 F3
Chārīkār Afghan. 35°0N 69°10E 240 B3
Charing U.S.A. 32°28N 84°22W 316 C5
Charing Cross London, U.K. 125 b4
Chariton U.S.A. 41°1N 93°19W 310 C3
Chariton → U.S.A. 39°19N 92°58W 310 E4
Charity Guyana 7°24N 58°36W 329 B6
Chärjew = Türkmenabat Turkmenistan 39°6N 63°34E 247 B9
Charkhari India 25°24N 79°45E 243 G8
Charkhi Dadri India 28°37N 76°17E 242 E7
Charleroi Belgium 50°24N 4°27E 170 D4
Charleroi Pa., U.S.A. 40°9N 79°57W 312 F5
Charleroi, Kanal de → Belgium 50°51N 4°19E 116 B1
Charles, C. U.S.A. 37°7N 75°58W 309 G16
Charles, I. = Santa María, I. Ecuador 1°17S 90°26W 330 a
Charles, Peak Australia 32°52S 121°11E 279 F3
Charles Bridge = Karlův most Prague, Czech Rep. 135 b1
Charles City U.S.A. 43°4N 92°41W 310 A4
Charles de Gaulle, Paris ✕ (CDG) France 49°0N 2°32E 173 D9
Charles Gates Dawes House U.S.A. 42°2N 87°40W 119 A2
Charles I. Canada 62°39N 74°15W 295 E17
Charles L. Canada 59°50N 110°33W 297 B6
Charles Sound N.Z. 45°2S 167°4E 285 F2
Charles Square = Karlovo náměstí Prague, Czech Rep. 135 c1
Charles Town U.S.A. 39°17N 77°52W 309 F15
Charlesbourg Canada 46°51N 71°16W 309 B18
Charleston Ill., U.S.A. 39°30N 88°10W 311 E8
Charleston Miss., U.S.A. 34°1N 90°4W 315 D9
Charleston Mo., U.S.A. 36°55N 89°21W 308 G9
Charleston S.C., U.S.A. 32°46N 79°56W 316 C10
Charleston W. Va., U.S.A. 38°21N 81°38W 309 F13
Charleston L. Canada 44°32N 76°0W 313 B9
Charleston Peak U.S.A. 36°16N 115°42W 307 J11
Charlestown Mayo, Ireland 53°58N 8°48W 166 C3
Charlestown St. Kitts & Nevis 17°8N 62°37W 322 d
Charlestown KwaZulu Natal, S. Africa 27°26S 29°53E 271 C4
Charlestown Ind., U.S.A. 38°27N 85°40W 311 F11
Charlestown Mass., U.S.A. 42°22N 71°4W 116 A2
Charlestown N.H., U.S.A. 43°14N 72°25W 313 C12
Charlestown Bridge Boston, U.S.A. 116 a2
Charlestown of Aberlour U.K. 57°28N 3°14W 167 D5
Charleville = Rath Luirc Ireland 52°21N 8°40W 166 D3
Charleville Australia 26°24S 146°15E 281 D4
Charleville-Mézières France 49°44N 4°40E 173 C11
Charlevoix U.S.A. 45°19N 85°16W 309 C11
Charlie Gibbs Fracture Zone Atl. Oc. 52°45N 35°30W 152 A8
Charlieu France 46°10N 4°10E 173 F11
Charlotte Dominica 15°17N 61°24W 323 k
Charlotte Mich., U.S.A. 42°34N 84°50W 311 B12
Charlotte N.C., U.S.A. 35°13N 80°50W 315 D14
Charlotte Vt., U.S.A. 44°19N 73°16W 313 B11
Charlotte Amalie U.S. Virgin Is. 18°21N 64°56W 321 C7
Charlotte Harbor U.S.A. 26°57N 82°4W 317 J7
Charlotte L. Canada 52°12N 125°19W 296 C3
Charlottenberg Sweden 59°54N 12°17E 162 E6
Charlottenburg Germany 52°31N 13°14E 115 A2
Charlottenburg, Schloss Germany 52°31N 13°18E 115 A2
Charlottenlund Denmark 55°44N 12°35E 118 A3
Charlottesville U.S.A. 38°2N 78°30W 309 F14
Charlottetown Nfld. & L., Canada 52°46N 56°7W 299 B8
Charlottetown P.E.I., Canada 46°14N 63°8W 299 C7
Charlotteville Trin. & Tob. 11°20N 60°33W 323 s
Charlton Vic., Australia 36°16S 143°24E 282 D5
Charlton London, U.K. 51°29N 0°1E 125 B4
Charlton I. Canada 52°0N 79°20W 298 B4
Charmes France 48°22N 6°17E 173 D13
Charneca Lisboa, Portugal 38°47N 9°8W 126 A2
Charneca Setúbal, Portugal 38°37N 9°12W 126 B1
Charny Canada 46°43N 71°15W 299 C5
Charnyany Belarus 51°59N 24°12E 185 G11
Charolles France 46°27N 4°16E 173 F11
Chârost France 47°0N 2°7E 173 F9
Charouine Algeria 29°0N 0°15W 261 C4
Charre Mozam. 17°13S 35°10E 269 F4
Charroux France 46°9N 0°25E 174 B4
Charsadda Pakistan 34°7N 71°45E 242 B4
Charshanga = Köýtendag Turkmenistan 37°30N 66°1E 240 A2
Charters Towers Australia 20°5S 146°13E 280 C4
Chartres France 48°29N 1°30E 172 D8
Chartreuse ⌂ France 45°22N 5°42E 175 C9
Charuma Trin. & Tob. 10°24N 61°9W 323 t
Charysh → Russia 52°22N 83°45E 217 B10
Chascomús Argentina 35°30S 58°0W 334 D4
Chase Canada 50°50N 119°41W 296 C5
Chase, L. U.S.A. 28°28N 81°31W 133 B1
Chasefu Zambia 11°55S 33°8E 269 E3
Chashma Barrage Pakistan 32°27N 71°20E 242 C4
Chaslands Mistake N.Z. 46°38S 169°22E 285 G4
Chasong N. Korea 41°27N 126°38E 224 B3
Chasseneuil-sur-Bonnieure France 45°52N 0°29E 174 C4
Chāt Iran 37°59N 55°16E 247 B7
Chatal Balkan = Udvoy Balkan Bulgaria 42°50N 26°50E 203 D10
Chatanika U.S.A. 65°7N 147°28W 303 D11
Château-Arnoux-St-Auban France 44°6N 6°0E 175 D10
Château-Chinon France 47°4N 3°56E 173 E10
Château-d'Olonne France 46°30N 1°44W 174 B2
Château-du-Loir France 47°40N 0°25E 172 E7
Château Dubug Martinique 14°46N 60°55W 322 j
Château Gaillard Guadeloupe 16°18N 61°23W 322 e
Château-Gontier France 47°50N 0°48W 172 E6
Château-la-Vallière France 47°30N 0°20E 172 E7
Château-Landon France 48°8N 2°40E 173 D9
Château Murat Guadeloupe 15°52N 61°17W 322 e
Château-Renard France 47°56N 2°55E 173 E9
Château-Renault France 47°36N 0°56E 172 E7
Château-Salins France 48°50N 6°30E 173 D13
Château-Thierry France 49°3N 3°20E 173 C10
Chateaubelair St. Vincent 13°17N 61°15W 323 n
Châteaubourg France 48°7N 1°25W 172 D5
Châteaubriant France 47°43N 1°23W 172 E5
Châteaudun France 48°3N 1°20E 172 D8
Châteaufort France 48°44N 2°5E 134 B1
Chateaugay U.S.A. 44°56N 74°5W 313 B10
Châteaugiron France 48°3N 1°30W 172 D5
Châteauguay, L. Canada 56°26N 70°3W 299 A5
Châteaulin France 48°11N 4°8W 172 D2
Châteaumeillant France 46°35N 2°12E 173 F9
Châteauneuf-du-Faou France 48°11N 3°50W 172 D3
Châteauneuf-sur-Charente France 45°36N 0°3W 174 C3
Châteauneuf-sur-Cher France 46°52N 2°18E 173 F9
Châteauneuf-sur-Loire France 47°52N 2°13E 173 E9
Châteaurenard France 43°53N 4°51E 175 E8
Châteauroux France 46°50N 1°40E 173 F8
Châteauvillain France 48°2N 4°55E 173 D11
Châteaux, Pte. des Guadeloupe 16°15N 61°10W 322 e
Châtelaillon-Plage France 46°5N 1°5W 174 B2
Châtelguyon France 45°55N 3°4E 174 C7
Châtellerault France 46°50N 0°30E 172 F7
Châtelus-Malvaleix France 46°18N 2°1E 173 F9
Châtenay-Malabry France 48°46N 2°16E 134 B2
Chatham = Miramichi Canada 47°2N 65°28W 299 C6
Chatham Ont., Canada 42°24N 82°11W 312 D2
Chatham Medway, U.K. 51°22N 0°32E 169 F8
Chatham Ill., U.S.A. 41°45N 87°36W 119 C3
Chatham Ill., U.S.A. 39°40N 89°42W 310 E7
Chatham N.Y., U.S.A. 42°21N 73°36W 313 D11
Chatham, I. = San Cristóbal, I. Ecuador 0°50S 89°26W 330 a
Chatham, I. Chile 50°40S 74°25W 336 D2
Chatham I. N.Z. 43°50S 176°20W 285 a
Chatham Is. Pac. Oc. 44°0S 176°40W 285 a
Chatham Rise Pac. Oc. 43°30S 180°0E 288 M10
Châtillon Hauts-de-Seine, France 48°48N 2°17E 134 B2
Châtillon Italy 45°45N 7°37E 198 C4
Châtillon-Coligny France 47°50N 2°51E 173 E9
Châtillon-en-Diois France 44°41N 5°29E 175 D9
Châtillon-sur-Indre France 46°59N 1°10E 172 F8
Châtillon-sur-Loire France 47°35N 2°44E 173 E9
Châtillon-sur-Seine France 47°50N 4°33E 173 E11
Chatmohar Bangla. 24°15N 89°15E 243 G13
Chatou France 48°53N 2°9E 134 A1
Chatpur India 22°36N 88°22E 124 B2
Chatra India 24°12N 84°56E 243 G11
Chatrapur India 19°22N 85°2E 244 E7
Chats, L. des Canada 45°30N 76°20W 313 A8
Chatsu India 26°36N 75°57E 242 F6
Chatswood Australia 33°47S 151°11E 139 A2
Chatsworth Ont., Canada 44°27N 80°54W 312 B4
Chatsworth Ill., U.S.A. 40°45N 88°18W 311 D8
Chatsworth Zimbabwe 19°38S 31°13E 269 F3
Chatta-Hantō Japan 34°45N 136°55E 223 C8
Châttagâm = Chittagong Bangla. 22°19N 91°48E 241 D3
Chattahoochee U.S.A. 30°42N 84°51W 316 E5
Chattahoochee → U.S.A. 30°54N 84°57W 316 E5
Chattanooga U.S.A. 35°3N 85°19W 315 D12
Chatteris U.K. 52°28N 0°2E 169 E8
Chatturat Thailand 15°40N 101°51E 236 E3
Chatuchak Thailand 13°48N 100°33E 113 B2
Chatuchak Park Thailand 13°48N 100°32E 113 B2
Chau Doc Vietnam 10°42N 105°7E 237 G5
Chaubourg, Mt. St. Lucia 14°2N 60°57W 323 m
Chaudes-Aigues France 44°51N 3°1E 174 D7
Chauffailles France 46°13N 4°20E 173 F11
Chauk Burma 20°53N 94°49E 241 E5
Chaukan Pass Burma 27°8N 97°10E 241 B6
Chauki Pakistan 24°55N 66°56E 123 A1
Chaumont Haute-Marne, France 48°7N 5°8E 173 D12
Chaumont N.Y., U.S.A. 44°4N 76°8W 313 B8
Chaumont-en-Vexin France 49°16N 1°53E 173 C8
Chaumont-sur-Loire France 47°29N 1°11E 172 E8
Chaunay France 46°13N 0°9E 174 B4
Chaunskaya G. Russia 69°0N 169°0E 215 C17
Chauny France 49°37N 3°12E 173 C10
Chaura India 8°27N 93°2E 245 K11
Chausey, Îs. France 48°52N 1°49W 172 D5
Chaussin France 46°59N 5°22E 173 F12
Chautauqua L. U.S.A. 42°10N 79°24W 312 D5
Chauvigny France 46°34N 0°39E 172 F7
Chauvin Canada 52°45N 110°10W 297 C6
Chavakachcheri Sri Lanka 9°39N 80°9E 245 K5
Chavanges France 48°30N 4°35E 173 D11
Chavantina Brazil 14°40S 52°21W 331 C7
Chavarria Peru 12°0S 77°7W 124 B2
Chavdata Greece 38°12N 20°23E 207 D1
Chaves Brazil 0°15S 49°55W 332 B2
Chaves Portugal 41°45N 7°32W 194 D3
Chaville France 48°48N 2°11E 134 B2
Chavuma Zambia 13°4S 22°40E 265 E4
Chawang Thailand 8°25N 99°30E 237 H2
Chayang S. Korea 37°32N 127°3E 137 B2
Chaykovskiy Russia 56°47N 54°9E 186 C9
Chazelles-sur-Lyon France 45°39N 4°22E 175 C8
Chazuta Peru 6°30S 76°0W 330 B2
Chazy U.S.A. 44°53N 73°26W 313 B11
Cheaha Mt. U.S.A. 33°29N 85°49W 316 B4
Cheb Czech Rep. 50°9N 12°28E 180 A5
Chebanse U.S.A. 41°0N 87°54W 311 D9
Chebbi, Erg Africa 31°12N 3°58W 260 B4
Cheboksarskoye Vdkhr. Russia 56°13N 46°58E 190 B8
Cheboksary Russia 56°8N 47°12E 190 B8
Cheboygan U.S.A. 45°39N 84°29W 309 C11
Chebsara Russia 59°10N 38°59E 188 C10
Chech, Erg Africa 25°0N 2°15W 260 D4
Chechelnyk Ukraine 48°13N 29°22E 183 B14
Chechen, Ostrov Russia 43°59N 47°40E 191 H8
Ch'ech'eng Taiwan 22°5N 120°42E 225 D2
Chechenia □ Russia 43°30N 45°29E 191 J7
Checheno-Ingush Republic = Chechenia □ Russia 43°30N 45°29E 191 J7
Chechnya = Chechenia □ Russia 43°30N 45°29E 191 J7
Chęciny Poland 50°46N 20°28E 185 H7
Checotah U.S.A. 35°28N 95°31W 314 D7
Chedabucto B. Canada 45°25N 61°8W 299 C7
Cheduba I. Burma 18°45N 93°40E 241 F4
Cheektowaga U.S.A. 42°54N 78°45W 312 D6
Cheepie Australia 26°33S 145°0E 281 D4
Cheeyou Trin. & Tob. 10°33N 61°8W 323 t
Chef-Boutonne France 46°7N 0°4W 174 B3
Chefchaouen Morocco 35°9N 5°15W 260 A3
Chefchaouen □ Morocco 35°10N 5°15W 260 A3
Cheffadine Niger 19°57N 12°11E 259 D2
Chefoo = Yantai China 37°34N 121°22E 227 F11
Chefornak U.S.A. 60°13N 164°12W 303 F6
Chegdomyn Russia 51°7N 133°1E 215 D14
Chegga Mauritania 25°27N 5°40W 260 C3
Chegutu Zimbabwe 18°10S 30°14E 269 F3
Chehalis U.S.A. 46°40N 122°58W 306 D4
Chehalis → U.S.A. 46°57N 123°50W 306 D3
Cheile Nerei-Beusnita △ Romania 44°56N 21°52E 182 F6
Cheiron, Mt. France 43°49N 6°58E 175 E10
Cheju = Jeju S. Korea 33°31N 126°32E 224 a
Cheju-do = Jeju-do S. Korea 33°29N 126°34E 224 a
Chek Lap Kok China 22°18N 113°56E 219 a
Chekalin Russia 54°10N 36°10E 188 E9
Chekhovo Russia 54°33N 20°43E 184 D7
Chekiang = Zhejiang □ China 29°0N 120°0E 229 C13
Chel = Kuru, Bahr el → Sudan 8°10N 26°50E 257 F2
Chela, Sa. da Angola 16°20S 13°20E 265 F2
Chelan U.S.A. 47°51N 120°1W 304 C3
Chelan, L. U.S.A. 48°11N 120°30W 304 B3
Cheleken = Hazar Turkmenistan 39°34N 53°16E 187 G9
Cheleken Yarymadasy Turkmenistan 39°30N 53°15E 247 B7
Chelforó Argentina 39°0S 66°33W 336 A3
Chéliff, O. → Algeria 36°0N 0°8E 261 A5
Chelkar = Shalqar Kazakhstan 47°48N 59°39E 216 C5
Chella Ethiopia 5°0N 37°26E 257 F4
Chellala Dahrania Algeria 33°2N 0°1E 261 B5
Chelles France 48°53N 2°35E 134 A4
Chelles, Canal de France 48°51N 2°35E 134 A4
Chells-le-Pin ✕ France 48°53N 2°36E 134 A4
Chełm Poland 51°8N 23°30E 185 G10
Chełmno Poland 53°20N 18°30E 185 E5
Chelmsford U.K. 51°44N 0°29E 169 F8
Chełmża Poland 53°10N 18°39E 185 E5
Chelny = Naberezhnyye Chelny Russia 55°42N 52°19E 190 C11
Chelsea Vic., Australia 38°5S 145°8E 283 E6
Chelsea London, U.K. 51°29N 0°10W 125 B2
Chelsea Mass., U.S.A. 42°23N 71°1W 116 A2
Chelsea Mich., U.S.A. 42°19N 84°1W 311 B12
Chelsea New York, U.S.A. 132 c1
Chelsea Vt., U.S.A. 43°59N 72°27W 313 C12
Cheltenham U.K. 51°54N 2°4W 169 F5
Chelva Spain 39°45N 1°0W 196 F4
Chelyabinsk Russia 55°10N 61°24E 216 A6
Chelyakobi = Kopeysk Russia 55°7N 61°37E 216 A6
Chelyuskin, C. = Chelyuskin, Mys Russia 77°30N 103°0E 215 B11
Chelyuskin, Mys Russia 77°30N 103°0E 215 B11
Chemainus Canada 48°55N 123°42W 306 B3
Chembar = Belinskiy Russia 53°0N 43°25E 190 D6
Chembur India 19°3N 72°53E 130 A2
Chemchâm, Sebkhet Mauritania 21°2N 12°4W 260 D2
Chemillé France 47°14N 0°45W 172 E6
Chemin Grenier Mauritius 20°29S 57°28E 272 e
Chemnitz Germany 50°51N 12°54E 178 E8
Chemulpho = Incheon S. Korea 37°27N 126°40E 224 D3
Chemult U.S.A. 43°14N 121°47W 304 E3
Chen, Gora Russia 65°16N 141°50E 215 C15
Chenab → Pakistan 30°23N 71°2E 242 D4
Chenab Nagar Pakistan 31°45N 72°55E 242 D5
Chenachane Algeria 26°0N 4°15W 260 C4
Chenachane, O. → Algeria 25°20N 3°20W 260 C4
Chenango Forks U.S.A. 42°15N 75°51W 313 D9
Chencha Ethiopia 6°15N 37°32E 257 F4
Chenchiang = Zhenjiang China 32°11N 119°26E 229 A12
Cheney U.S.A. 47°30N 117°35W 304 C5
Cheng Xian China 33°43N 105°42E 226 H3
Chengalpattu India 12°42N 79°58E 245 H4
Chengbu China 26°18N 110°16E 229 D8
Chengcheng China 35°8N 109°56E 226 G5
Chengchou = Zhengzhou China 34°45N 113°34E 226 G7
Chengde China 40°59N 117°58E 227 D9
Chengdong Hu China 32°15N 116°20E 229 A11
Chengdu China 30°38N 104°2E 228 B5
Chengele India 28°47N 96°16E 241 A6
Chenggong China 24°52N 102°56E 228 E4
Chenggu China 33°10N 107°21E 228 A6
Chenghai China 23°30N 116°42E 229 F11
Chengjiang China 24°39N 103°0E 228 E4
Chengkou China 31°54N 108°31E 228 B7
Ch'engkung Taiwan 23°6N 121°22E 225 C3
Chengmai China 19°50N 109°58E 236 C7
Chengnan Taiwan 23°3N 120°7E 225 C2
Chengshan Jiao China 37°25N 122°44E 227 F12
Chengshousi China 39°49N 116°24E 114 C2
Chengteh = Chengde China 40°59N 117°58E 227 D9
Ch'engtu = Chengdu China 30°38N 104°2E 228 B5
Chengwu China 34°58N 115°50E 226 G8
Chengxi Hu China 32°15N 116°10E 229 A11
Chengyang China 36°18N 120°21E 227 F11
Chenjiagang China 34°23N 119°47E 227 G10
Chenkaladi Sri Lanka 7°47N 81°35E 245 L5
Chennai India 13°8N 80°19E 245 H5
Chennevières-sur-Marne France 48°47N 2°31E 134 B4
Chenoa U.S.A. 40°45N 88°43W 311 D8
Chenôve France 47°16N 5°1E 173 E12
Chenxi China 28°2N 110°12E 229 C8
Chenzhou China 25°47N 113°1E 229 E9
Cheò, Eilean a' = Skye U.K. 57°15N 6°10W 167 D2
Cheo Reo Vietnam 13°20N 108°25E 236 F7
Cheom Ksan Cambodia 14°13N 104°56E 236 E5
Cheonan S. Korea 36°48N 127°9E 224 D3
Cheongdam S. Korea 37°31N 127°2E 137 B2
Cheongdo S. Korea 35°38N 128°42E 224 E4
Cheongju S. Korea 36°39N 127°27E 224 D3
Cheongsando S. Korea 34°11N 126°53E 224 E3
Cheongsong S. Korea 36°25N 129°3E 224 D4
Cheonho S. Korea 37°32N 127°6E 137 B2
Cheonsumman S. Korea 36°33N 126°25E 224 D3
Cheops Egypt 29°58N 31°8E 117 B1
Cheorwon S. Korea 38°15N 127°10E 224 C3

Chepelare Bulgaria 41°44N 24°40E 203 E8
Chepén Peru 7°15S 79°23W 330 B2
Chépénéhé N. Cal. 20°47S 167°9E 288 d
Chepes Argentina 31°20S 66°35W 334 C2
Chepo Panama 9°10N 79°6W 320 E4
Chepstow U.K. 51°38N 2°41W 169 F5
Chequamegon B. U.S.A. 46°39N 90°51W 308 B8
Cher ☐ France 47°10N 2°30E 173 E9
Cher → France 47°21N 0°29E 172 E7
Chéradi Italy 40°27N 17°10E 201 B10
Cheran India 25°45N 90°44E 241 C3
Cherasco Italy 44°39N 7°51E 198 D4
Cherating Malaysia 3°35N 103°5E 234 B2
Cheraw U.S.A. 34°42N 79°53W 315 D15
Cherbourg France 49°39N 1°40W 172 C5
Cherchell Algeria 36°35N 2°12E 261 A5
Cherdakly Russia 54°25N 48°50E 190 C9
Cherdyn Russia 60°24N 56°29E 186 B10
Cheremkhovo Russia 53°8N 103°1E 218 A9
Cherepanovo Russia 54°15N 83°30E 217 B10
Cherepkovo Russia 55°45N 37°21E 129 B2
Cherepovets Russia 59°5N 37°55E 188 C9
Chergui, Chott ech Algeria 34°21N 0°25E 261 B5
Chergui, Zahrez Algeria 35°11N 3°31E 261 B5
Cherial India 17°55N 78°59E 244 F4
Cheribon = Cirebon Indonesia 6°45S 108°32E 235 D3
Cherikov = Cherykaw Belarus 53°32N 31°20E 177 B16
Cheriyam I. India 10°9N 73°40E 245 J1
Cherkasy Ukraine 49°27N 32°4E 189 H7
Cherkasy ☐ Ukraine 48°55N 30°50E 189 H6
Cherkessk Russia 44°15N 42°5E 191 H6
Cherla India 18°5N 80°49E 244 E5
Cherlak Russia 54°15N 74°55E 217 B8
Chernaya Russia 70°30N 89°10E 215 B9
Chernelytsya Ukraine 48°49N 25°26E 183 B10
Cherni Bulgaria 42°35N 23°18E 202 D7
Chernigov = Chernihiv Ukraine 51°28N 31°20E 189 G6
Chernigovka Russia 44°19N 132°34E 220 B6
Chernihiv Ukraine 51°28N 31°20E 189 G6
Chernihiv ☐ Ukraine 51°10N 32°5E 189 G7
Chernivtsi Chernivtsi, Ukraine 48°15N 25°52E 183 B10
Chernivtsi Vinnyts'ka, Ukraine 48°32N 28°9E 183 B13
Chernivtsi ☐ Ukraine 48°5N 25°30E 183 B10
Chernobyl = Chornobyl Ukraine 51°20N 30°15E 177 C16
Chernogorsk Russia 53°49N 91°18E 217 B12
Chernomorskoye = Chornomorske Ukraine 45°31N 32°40E 189 K7
Chernorechye = Dzerzhinsk Russia 56°14N 43°30E 190 B6
Chernovtsy = Chernivtsi Ukraine 48°15N 25°52E 183 B10
Chernyakhovsk Russia 54°36N 21°48E 184 D8
Chernyanka Russia 50°56N 37°49E 189 G9
Chernyovo Russia 55°50N 37°17E 129 A1
Chernysheyskiy Russia 63°0N 112°30E 215 C12
Chernyye Zemli Russia 46°10N 46°0E 191 H8
Cherokee Iowa, U.S.A. 42°45N 95°33W 308 D6
Cherokee Okla., U.S.A. 36°45N 98°21W 314 C5
Cherokee Village U.S.A. 36°18N 91°31W 314 C9
Cherokees, Grand Lake O' The U.S.A. 36°28N 94°55W 314 C7
Cherquenco Chile 38°35S 72°0W 336 A2
Cherrapunji India 25°17N 91°47E 241 C3
Cherry Valley U.S.A. 42°48N 74°45W 313 D10
Cherryville U.S.A. 37°51N 91°16W 310 G5
Cherskiy Russia 68°45N 161°18E 215 C17
Cherskogo Khrebet Russia 65°0N 143°0E 215 C15
Cherso Greece 41°5N 22°47E 202 E6
Chersonisos Akrotiri Greece 35°30N 24°10E 207 E5
Chertanovka → Russia 55°38N 37°48E 129 C3
Chertanovo Russia 55°38N 37°36E 129 C3
Cherthala = Shertallai India 9°42N 76°20E 245 K3
Chertkov = Chortkiv Ukraine 49°2N 25°46E 177 D13
Chertkovo Russia 49°25N 40°19E 189 H11
Cherven Belarus 53°45N 28°28E 177 B15
Cherven-Bryag Bulgaria 43°17N 24°7E 203 C8
Chervonoarmiyske Ukraine 45°47N 28°44E 183 E13
Chervonohrad Ukraine 50°25N 24°10E 177 C13
Cherwell → U.K. 51°44N 1°14W 169 F6
Cherykaw Belarus 53°32N 31°20E 177 B16
Cheryomushki Russia 55°40N 37°35E 129 B3
Chesapeake U.S.A. 36°49N 76°16W 309 G15
Chesapeake B. U.S.A. 38°0N 76°10W 309 F14
Cheshire ☐ U.K. 53°14N 2°30W 168 D5
Cheshskaya Guba Russia 67°20N 47°0E 186 A8
Cheshunt U.K. 51°43N 0°1W 169 F7
Chesil Beach U.K. 50°37N 2°33W 169 G5
Chesley Canada 44°17N 81°5W 312 B3
Chesnokovka = Novoaltaysk Russia 53°30N 84°0E 217 B10
Cheste Spain 39°30N 0°41W 197 F4
Chester Ches., U.K. 53°12N 2°53W 168 D5
Chester Calif., U.S.A. 40°19N 121°14W 304 F3
Chester Ga., U.S.A. 32°24N 83°9W 316 C6
Chester Ill., U.S.A. 37°55N 89°49W 310 G7
Chester Mont., U.S.A. 48°31N 110°58W 304 B8
Chester Pa., U.S.A. 39°51N 75°22W 309 F16
Chester S.C., U.S.A. 34°43N 81°12W 315 D14
Chester Vt., U.S.A. 43°16N 72°36W 313 C12
Chester W. Va., U.S.A. 40°37N 80°34W 312 F4
Chester-le-Street U.K. 54°51N 1°34W 168 C6
Chesterfield Derby, U.K. 53°15N 1°25W 168 D6
Chesterfield Mo., U.S.A. 38°40N 90°35W 310 F6
Chesterfield, Îs. N. Cal. 19°52S 158°15E 277 D10
Chesterfield Inlet Canada 63°30N 90°45W 294 E13
Chesterton Ra. Australia 25°30S 147°27E 281 D4
Chesterton Range △ Australia 26°16S 147°22E 281 D4
Chestertown U.S.A. 43°40N 73°48W 313 C11
Chesterville Canada 45°6N 75°14W 313 A9
Chestnut Hill U.S.A. 42°19N 71°10W 116 B1
Chesuncook L. U.S.A. 46°0N 69°21W 309 C19
Chetamale India 10°43N 92°33E 245 J11
Chéticamp Canada 46°37N 60°59W 299 C7
Chetlat I. India 11°42N 72°42E 245 J1
Chetrosu Moldova 48°5N 27°55E 183 B12
Chetumal Mexico 18°30N 88°20W 319 D7
Chetumal, B. de Cent. Amer. 18°40N 88°10W 319 D7
Chetwynd Canada 55°45N 121°36W 296 B4
Cheung Chau China 22°13N 114°1E 219 a
Cheung Sha Wan China 22°20N 114°8E 122 A1
Chevak U.S.A. 61°32N 165°35W 303 F6
Chevalier, Î. de Martinique 14°25N 60°50W 322 j
Chevanceaux France 45°18N 0°14W 174 C3
Cheverly U.S.A. 38°55N 76°54W 143 B4
Chevilly-Larue France 48°46N 2°21E 134 B3
Cheviot U.S.A. 39°9N 84°36W 311 E12
Cheviot, The U.K. 55°29N 2°9W 168 B5
Cheviot Hills Northumberland, U.K. 55°20N 2°30W 168 B5
Cheviot Hills Calif., U.S.A. 34°2N 118°24W 126 B2
Cheviot Ra. Australia 25°20S 143°45E 280 D3
Chevy Chase U.S.A. 38°59N 77°4W 143 B3
Chew Bahir Ethiopia 4°40N 36°50E 257 G4
Chewelah U.S.A. 48°17N 117°43W 304 B5
Chewore △ Zimbabwe 16°0S 29°52E 269 F2
Cheyenne Okla., U.S.A. 35°37N 99°40W 314 D5
Cheyenne Wyo., U.S.A. 41°8N 104°49W 304 F11
Cheyenne → U.S.A. 44°41N 101°18W 308 C3
Cheyenne Wells U.S.A. 38°49N 102°21W 304 G12
Cheyne B. Australia 34°35S 118°50E 279 F2
Cheyur India 12°21N 80°0E 245 H5
Chhabra India 24°40N 76°54E 242 G7
Chhaktala India 22°6N 74°11E 242 H6
Chhapra India 25°48N 84°44E 243 G11
Chhata India 27°42N 77°30E 242 F7
Chhatak Bangla. 25°5N 91°37E 241 C3
Chhatarpur Jharkhand, India 24°23N 84°11E 243 G11
Chhatarpur Mad. P., India 24°55N 79°35E 243 G8
Chhati India 20°47N 81°40E 244 D5
Chhatrapati Shivaji, Mumbai ✈ (BOM) India 19°5N 72°51E 130 A2
Chhattisgarh ☐ India 22°0N 82°0E 243 J10
Chhaygaon India 26°3N 91°24E 241 B3
Chhep Cambodia 13°45N 105°24E 236 F5
Chhindwara Mad. P., India 23°3N 79°29E 243 H8
Chhindwara Mad. P., India 22°2N 78°59E 243 H8
Chhinhdipada India 21°6N 84°52E 244 D7
Chhlong Cambodia 12°15N 105°58E 237 F5
Chhota Tawa → India 22°14N 76°36E 242 H7
Chhoti Kali Sindh → India 24°2N 75°31E 242 G6
Chhuikhadan India 21°32N 80°59E 243 J9
Chhuk Cambodia 10°46N 104°28E 237 G5
Chi → Thailand 15°11N 104°43E 236 E5
Chi Thanh Vietnam 13°17N 109°16E 236 F7
Chia Keng Singapore 1°21N 103°52E 138 A3
Chiahsien Taiwan 23°5N 120°35E 225 C2
Chiai Taiwan 23°29N 120°25E 225 C2
Chiai ☐ Taiwan 23°30N 120°30E 225 C2
Chiaksan △ S. Korea 37°15N 128°0E 224 D4
Chiali Taiwan 23°9N 120°10E 225 C2
Chialuiantsun Taiwan 22°49N 121°11E 225 D3
Chiamboni Somali Rep. 1°39S 41°35E 267 E5
Chiamussu = Jiamusi China 46°40N 130°26E 219 B15
Chian Taiwan 23°59N 121°33E 225 C3
Chianpu Taiwan 22°47N 120°36E 225 D2
Chianciano Terme Italy 43°2N 11°49E 199 E8
Chiang Dao Thailand 19°22N 98°58E 236 C2
Chiang Dao, Doi Thailand 19°23N 98°54E 236 C2
Chiang Kham Thailand 19°32N 100°18E 236 C3
Chiang Khan Thailand 17°52N 101°36E 236 D3
Chiang Khong Thailand 20°17N 100°24E 228 G3
Chiang Mai Thailand 18°47N 98°59E 236 C2
Chiang Rai Thailand 19°52N 99°50E 228 H2
Chiang Saen Thailand 20°16N 100°5E 228 G3
Chiangchun Taiwan 23°12N 120°9E 225 C2
Chiange Angola 15°35S 13°40E 265 F2
Chianti Italy 43°32N 11°25E 199 E8
Chiaohsi Taiwan 24°49N 121°46E 225 B3
Chiaotou Taiwan 22°45N 120°18E 225 D2
Chiapa → Mexico 16°42N 93°0W 319 D6
Chiapa de Corzo Mexico 16°42N 93°0W 319 D6
Chiapas ☐ Mexico 16°30N 92°30W 319 D6
Chiapas, Sa. Madre de Mexico 15°40N 93°0W 319 D6
Chiaramonte Gulfi Italy 37°2N 14°42E 201 E7
Chiaravalle Italy 43°36N 13°19E 199 E10
Chiaravalle Centrale Italy 38°41N 16°25E 201 D9
Chiaravalle Milanese Italy 45°24N 9°16E 129 B2
Chiari Italy 45°32N 9°56E 198 C6
Chiatung Taiwan 22°25N 120°32E 225 D2
Chiatura Georgia 42°15N 43°17E 191 J6
Chiautla de Tapia Mexico 18°18N 98°36W 319 D5
Chiávari Italy 44°19N 9°19E 198 D6
Chiavenna Italy 46°19N 9°24E 198 B6
Chiba Japan 35°30N 140°7E 223 B12
Chiba ☐ Japan 35°30N 140°20E 223 B12
Chibabava Mozam. 20°17S 33°35E 271 B5
Chibango Angola 13°38S 21°56E 265 E4
Chibemba Cunene, Angola 15°48S 14°8E 265 F2
Chibemba Huila, Angola 16°20S 15°20E 265 F3
Chibi Zimbabwe 20°18S 30°25E 271 B5
Chibia Angola 15°10S 13°42E 265 F2
Chibizovka = Zherdevka Russia 51°56N 41°29E 190 E5
Chibougamau Canada 49°56N 74°24W 298 C5
Chibougamau, L. Canada 49°50N 74°20W 298 C5
Chibuk Nigeria 10°52N 12°50E 263 C7
Chibuto Mozam. 24°40S 33°33E 271 B5
Chibyu = Ukhta Russia 63°34N 53°41E 186 B9
Chic-Chocs, Mts. Canada 48°55N 66°0W 299 C6
Chicacole = Srikakulam India 18°14N 83°58E 244 E6
Chicago U.S.A. 41°52N 87°38W 119 B3
Chicago, Univ. of U.S.A. 41°47N 87°35W 119 C3
Chicago Harbor Chicago, U.S.A. 119 d3
Chicago Heights U.S.A. 41°30N 87°38W 311 C9
Chicago Lawn U.S.A. 41°47N 87°40W 119 C2
Chicago-Midway ✈ (MDW) U.S.A. 41°47N 87°45W 119 C2
Chicago O'Hare Int. ✈ (ORD) U.S.A. 41°59N 87°54W 119 B1
Chicago Ridge U.S.A. 41°41N 87°46W 119 C2
Chicago River → Chicago, U.S.A. 119 b2
Chicago River, North Branch → U.S.A. 41°53N 87°42W 119 B2
Chicago Sanitary and Ship Canal U.S.A. 41°49N 87°45W 119 C2
Chicago State Univ. U.S.A. 41°43N 87°36W 119 C3
Chicago Zoo U.S.A. 41°50N 87°50W 119 B1
Chicapa → Dem. Rep. of the Congo 6°25S 20°48E 265 D4
Chicha Chad 16°57N 18°34E 259 E3
Chichagof I. U.S.A. 57°30N 135°30W 303 H14
Chichaoua Morocco 31°32N 8°44W 260 B3
Chichaoua ☐ Morocco 31°32N 8°45W 260 B3
Chichawatni Pakistan 30°32N 72°42E 242 D5
Chichén-Itzá Mexico 20°37N 88°35W 319 C7
Chicheng China 40°55N 115°55E 226 D8
Chichester U.K. 50°50N 0°47W 169 G7
Chichester Ra. Australia 22°12S 119°15E 278 D2
Chichi Hualien, Taiwan 23°44N 121°33E 225 C3
Chichi Nant'ou, Taiwan 23°49N 120°47E 225 C2
Chichibu Japan 35°59N 139°10E 223 A11
Chichibu-Tama-Kai △ Japan 35°52N 138°42E 223 B10
Ch'ich'ihaerh = Qiqihar China 47°26N 124°0E 219 B13
Chicholi India 22°1N 77°40E 242 H8
Ch'ich'ou Taiwan 23°45N 120°33E 225 C2
Chickasaw △ U.S.A. 34°26N 97°0W 314 D6
Chickasha U.S.A. 35°3N 97°58W 314 D6
Chicken U.S.A. 64°5N 141°56W 303 D12
Chiclana de la Frontera Spain 36°26N 6°9W 195 J4
Chiclayo Peru 6°42S 79°50W 330 B2
Chico U.S.A. 39°44N 121°50W 306 F5
Chico → Chubut, Argentina 44°0S 67°0W 336 B3
Chico → Santa Cruz, Argentina 50°0S 68°30W 336 D3
Chico → Phil. 17°57N 121°36E 232 C3
Chicoa Mozam. 15°36S 32°20E 269 F3
Chicomba Angola 14°10S 14°52E 265 E2
Chicomo Mozam. 24°31S 34°6E 271 B5
Chicomostoc Mexico 22°28N 102°46W 318 C4
Chiconi Mayotte 12°50S 45°7E 272 b
Chicontepec Mexico 20°58N 98°10W 319 C5
Chicopee U.S.A. 42°9N 72°37W 313 D12
Chicoutimi Canada 48°28N 71°5W 299 C5
Chicualacuala Mozam. 22°6S 31°42E 271 B5
Chicuma Angola 13°26S 14°50E 265 E2
Chidambaram India 11°20N 79°45E 245 J4
Chidenguele Mozam. 24°55S 34°11E 271 B5
Chidley, C. Canada 60°23N 64°26W 295 E19
Chiducuane Mozam. 24°35S 34°25E 271 B5
Chiede Angola 17°15S 16°22E 265 F3
Chiefland U.S.A. 29°29N 82°52W 317 F7
Chiefs Pt. Canada 44°41N 81°18W 312 B3
Chiehting Taiwan 22°54N 120°11E 225 D2
Chiem Hoa Vietnam 22°12N 105°17E 236 A5
Chiemsee Germany 47°53N 12°28E 179 H8
Chienchen Taiwan 22°35N 120°18E 225 D2
Chiengi Zambia 8°45S 29°10E 269 D2
Chiengmai = Chiang Mai Thailand 18°47N 98°59E 236 C2
Chiengo Angola 13°20S 21°55E 265 E4
Chienti → Italy 43°18N 13°45E 199 E10
Chienzui China 23°12N 113°22E 121 A3
Chieri Italy 45°1N 7°49E 198 C4
Chiers → France 49°39N 4°59E 173 C11
Chiesa in Valmalenco Italy 46°16N 9°51E 198 B6
Chiese → Italy 45°8N 10°25E 198 C7
Chieti Italy 42°21N 14°10E 199 F11
Chifeng China 42°18N 118°58E 227 C10
Chigasaki Japan 35°19N 139°24E 223 B11
Chigirin Ukraine 49°4N 32°38E 189 H7
Chignecto B. Canada 45°30N 64°40W 299 C7
Chignik U.S.A. 56°18N 158°24W 303 H8
Chigorodó Colombia 7°41N 76°42W 328 B2
Chiguana Bolivia 21°0S 67°58W 334 A2
Chigwell U.K. 51°37N 0°6E 169 F8
Chigwell, G. of = Bo Hai China 39°0N 119°0E 227 E10
Ch'ihpen Taiwan 22°42N 121°2E 225 D3
Ch'ihshang Taiwan 23°7N 121°12E 225 C3
Chihsi = Jixi China 45°20N 130°50E 227 B16
Chihu Taiwan 23°54N 120°24E 225 C2
Chihuahua Mexico 28°38N 106°5W 318 B3
Chihuahua ☐ Mexico 28°30N 106°0W 318 B3
Chiili = Shīeli Kazakhstan 44°20N 66°15E 217 D7
Chik Bollapur India 13°25N 77°45E 245 H3
Chik Sha China 22°17N 114°16E 122 B2
Chikalda India 21°24N 77°19E 244 D3
Chikhli Ahmadabad, India 20°45N 73°4E 244 D1
Chikhli Maharashtra, India 20°20N 76°18E 244 D3
Chikmagalur India 13°15N 75°45E 245 H2
Chiknayakanhalli India 13°26N 76°37E 245 H3
Chikodi India 16°26N 74°38E 245 F2
Chiku Taiwan 23°8N 120°7E 225 C2
Chikugo Japan 33°14N 130°28E 222 D2
Chikuma-Gawa → Japan 36°59N 138°35E 223 A10
Chikura Japan 34°55N 139°57E 223 C11
Chikushino Japan 33°30N 130°30E 222 D2
Chikwawa Malawi 16°2S 34°50E 269 F3
Chila Angola 12°3S 14°29E 265 E2
Ch'ilaichu Shan Taiwan 24°5N 121°20E 225 B3
Chilanga Zambia 15°33S 28°16E 269 F2
Chilapa Mexico 17°36N 99°10W 319 D5
Chilas Pakistan 35°25N 74°5E 243 B6
Chilaw Sri Lanka 7°30N 79°50E 245 L4
Chilcotin → Canada 51°44N 122°23W 296 C4
Childers Australia 25°15S 152°17E 281 D5
Childersburg U.S.A. 33°16N 86°21W 316 B3
Children's Museum Boston, U.S.A. 116 c3
Children's Palace Beijing, China 114 b2
Childress U.S.A. 34°25N 100°13W 314 D4
Child's Hill U.K. 51°33N 0°12W 125 A2
Chile ■ S. Amer. 35°0S 72°0W 327 G3
Chile, Univ. de Chile 33°26S 70°39W 137 B2
Chile Basin Pac. Oc. 33°0S 80°0W 289 L20
Chile Chico Chile 46°33S 71°44W 336 C2
Chile Rise Pac. Oc. 38°0S 92°0W 289 L18
Chilecito Argentina 29°10S 67°30W 334 B2
Chilengue, Serra do Angola 13°18S 15°22E 265 E2
Chilesso Angola 11°35S 16°34E 265 E3
Chilete Peru 7°10S 78°50W 330 B2
Chilhowee U.S.A. 38°36N 93°51W 310 F3
Chilia, Braţul → Romania 45°14N 29°42E 183 E14
Chilibre Panama 9°9N 79°37W 320 c
Chilik = Shelek Kazakhstan 43°33N 78°17E 217 D9
Chililabombwe Zambia 12°18S 27°43E 269 E2
Chilim Pakistan 35°5N 75°5E 243 B6
Chilin = Jilin China 43°44N 126°30E 227 C14
Chiliomodi Greece 37°48N 22°51E 204 D4
Chilka L. India 19°40N 85°25E 244 E7
Chilko → Canada 52°0N 123°40W 296 C4
Chilko L. Canada 51°20N 124°10W 296 C4
Chilla Saroda India 28°35N 77°18E 120 B2
Chillagoe Australia 17°7S 144°33E 280 B3
Chillán Chile 36°40S 72°10W 334 D1
Chillicothe Ill., U.S.A. 40°55N 89°29W 310 D7
Chillicothe Mo., U.S.A. 39°48N 93°33W 310 E3
Chillicothe Ohio, U.S.A. 39°20N 82°59W 309 F12
Chilliwack Canada 49°10N 121°54W 296 D4
Chillum U.S.A. 38°56N 76°58W 143 B4
Chilly-Mazarin France 48°42N 2°17E 134 B2
Chilo India 27°25N 73°32E 242 F5
Chiloane, I. Mozam. 20°40S 34°55E 271 B5
Chiloé, I. de Chile 42°30S 73°50W 336 B2
Chiloé △ Chile 42°11S 73°59W 336 B2
Chilonda Angola 11°19S 16°12E 265 E3
Chilongo Angola 13°55S 16°35E 265 E3
Chilpancingo Mexico 17°33N 99°30W 319 D5
Chiltern Australia 36°10S 146°36E 283 D7
Chiltern Hills U.K. 51°40N 0°53W 169 F7
Chilton U.S.A. 44°2N 88°10W 308 C9
Chiluage Angola 9°30S 21°50E 265 D4
Chilubi Zambia 11°5S 29°58E 269 E2
Chilubula Zambia 10°14S 30°51E 269 E3
Chilumba Malawi 10°28S 34°12E 269 E3
Chilung Taiwan 25°3N 121°45E 225 A3
Chilwa, L. Malawi 15°15S 35°40E 269 F4
Chimakela Angola 15°24S 16°58E 265 F3
Chimakudi India 25°47N 93°48E 241 C4
Chimaltitán Mexico 21°35N 103°50W 318 C4
Chimán Panama 8°45N 78°40W 320 E4
Chimanimani Zimbabwe 19°48S 32°52E 271 A5
Chimanimani △ Zimbabwe 19°48S 33°5E 271 A5
Chimay Belgium 50°3N 4°20E 170 D4
Chimayo U.S.A. 36°0N 105°56W 305 J11
Chimba Zambia 9°54S 31°28E 269 D3
Chimborazo Ecuador 1°29S 78°55W 328 D2
Chimborazo ☐ Ecuador 1°0S 78°40W 328 D2
Chimbote Peru 9°0S 78°35W 330 B2
Chimboy Uzbekistan 42°57N 59°47E 216 D5
Chimbu ☐ Papua N. G. 6°15S 144°50E 288 D3
Ch'imei Taiwan 23°12N 119°25E 225 C1
Ch'imei Yü Taiwan 23°13N 119°26E 225 C1
Chimichagua Colombia 9°15N 73°49W 328 B3
Chimkent = Shymkent Kazakhstan 42°18N 69°36E 217 D7
Chimoio Mozam. 19°4S 33°30E 269 F3
Chimpembe Zambia 9°31S 29°33E 269 D2
Chimur India 20°30N 79°23E 244 D4
Chin ☐ Burma 22°0N 93°0E 241 E4
Chin Hills Burma 22°30N 93°30E 241 D4
Chin Ling Shan = Qinling Shandi China 33°50N 108°10E 226 H5
China Mexico 25°42N 99°14W 319 B5
China ■ Asia 30°0N 110°0E 219 E11
China, Great Plain of Asia 35°0N 115°0E 210 E13
China Basin San Francisco, U.S.A. 136 c3
China Lake U.S.A. 35°44N 117°37W 307 K9
China Town Toronto, Canada 141 b1
Chinacota Colombia 7°37N 72°36W 328 B3
Chinan = Jinan China 36°38N 117°1E 226 F9
Chinandega Nic. 12°35N 87°12W 320 D2
Chinati Peak U.S.A. 29°57N 104°29W 314 G2
Chinatown Singapore 138 c2
Chinatown Boston, U.S.A. 116 c2
Chinatown Chicago, U.S.A. 119 f1
Chinatown Los Angeles, U.S.A. 127 a3
Chinatown New York, U.S.A. 132 e2
Chinatown San Francisco, U.S.A. 136 b2
Chincha Alta Peru 13°25S 76°7W 330 C2
Chinchaga → Canada 58°53N 118°20W 296 B5
Chincheros Peru 13°30S 73°44W 330 C3
Chinchilla Australia 26°45S 150°38E 281 D5
Chinchilla de Monte Aragón Spain 38°53N 1°40W 197 G3
Chincholi India 17°28N 77°26E 244 E3
Chinchorro, Banco Mexico 18°35N 87°22W 319 D7
Chinchou = Jinzhou China 41°5N 121°3E 227 D11
Chinchoua Gabon 0°1N 9°48E 264 B1
Chincoteague U.S.A. 37°56N 75°23W 309 G16
Chinde Mozam. 18°35S 36°30E 269 F4
Chindwin → Burma 21°26N 95°15E 241 E5
Chineni India 33°2N 75°15E 243 C6
Chinga Mozam. 15°13S 38°35E 269 F4
Chingaza △ Colombia 4°30N 73°40W 328 C3
Chingola Zambia 12°31S 27°53E 269 E2
Chingole Malawi 13°4S 34°17E 269 E3
Chingoni Mayotte 12°48S 45°8E 272 b
Chingpu Taiwan 23°28N 121°29E 225 C3
Ch'ingshui Changhua, Taiwan 24°16N 120°34E 225 B2
Chingshui Hualien, Taiwan 24°13N 121°41E 225 B3
Chingshui Ilan, Taiwan 24°39N 121°35E 225 B3
Ch'ingtao = Qingdao China 36°5N 120°20E 227 F11
Chinguar Angola 12°25S 16°45E 265 E3
Chinguetti Mauritania 20°25N 12°24W 260 D2
Chingune Mozam. 20°33S 34°58E 271 B5
Chingupota India 22°29N 88°14E 124 C1
Chinhanguanine Mozam. 25°21S 32°30E 271 C5
Chinhoyi Zimbabwe 17°20S 30°8E 269 F3
Chinhsien = Jinxian China 28°26N 116°17E 229 C11
Chini India 31°32N 78°15E 242 D8
Chiniot Pakistan 31°45N 73°0E 242 D5
Chínipas Mexico 27°23N 108°32W 318 B3
Chinji Pakistan 32°42N 72°22E 242 C5
Chinju = Jinju S. Korea 35°12N 128°2E 224 E4
Chinkai Afghan. 31°57N 67°26E 240 C2
Chinkapook Australia 35°11S 142°57E 282 C5
Chinkiang = Zhenjiang China 32°11N 119°26E 229 A12
Chinko → C.A.R. 4°50N 23°53E 264 B4
Chinle U.S.A. 36°9N 109°33W 305 H9
Ch'inlun Taiwan 22°32N 120°57E 225 D2
Chinmen Taiwan 24°26N 118°19E 225 a
Chinmen Tao Taiwan 24°26N 118°22E 225 a
Chinna Cr. → Pakistan 24°50N 67°0E 123 B2
Chinnamanur India 9°50N 77°24E 245 K3
Chinnampo = Namp'o N. Korea 38°52N 125°10E 224 C2
Chino Japan 35°59N 138°9E 223 B10
Chino Calif., U.S.A. 34°1N 117°41W 307 L9
Chino Valley U.S.A. 34°45N 112°27W 305 J7
Chinois, Quartier Montréal, Canada 130 b2
Chinon France 47°10N 0°15E 172 E7
Chinook U.S.A. 48°35N 109°14W 304 B9
Chinook Trough Pac. Oc. 44°0N 175°0W 288 C10
Chinoya Zambia 13°55S 23°16E 265 E4
Chinsali Zambia 10°30S 32°2E 269 E3
Chinshan Taiwan 25°13N 121°38E 225 A3
Chinsura = Chunchura India 22°53N 88°27E 243 H13
Chintalapudi India 17°4N 80°59E 244 F5
Chintamani India 13°26N 78°3E 245 H4
Chinwangtao = Qinhuangdao China 39°56N 119°30E 227 E10
Chióggia Italy 45°13N 12°17E 199 C9
Chios Greece 38°27N 26°9E 205 C8
Chios ☐ Greece 38°27N 26°9E 205 C8
Chipata Zambia 13°38S 32°28E 269 E3
Chipei Tao Taiwan 23°45N 119°37E 225 C1
Chiperceni Moldova 47°31N 28°50E 183 C13
Chipindo Angola 13°49S 15°48E 265 E3
Chipinge Zimbabwe 20°13S 32°28E 269 G3
Chipinge △ Zimbabwe 20°14S 33°0E 269 G3
Chipiona Spain 36°44N 6°26W 195 J4
Chipley U.S.A. 30°47N 85°32W 316 E4
Chiplun India 17°31N 73°34E 244 F1
Chipman Canada 46°6N 65°53W 299 C6
Chipoka Malawi 13°57S 34°28E 269 E3
Chippenham U.K. 51°27N 2°6W 169 F5
Chippewa → U.S.A. 44°25N 92°5W 308 C7
Chippewa Falls U.S.A. 44°56N 91°24W 308 C8
Chipping Norton U.K. 51°56N 1°32W 169 F6
Chiprovtsi Bulgaria 43°24N 22°52E 202 C6
Chiputneticook Lakes N. Amer. 45°35N 67°35W 309 C20
Chiputo = Vila Vasco da Gama Mozam. 14°54S 32°14E 269 E3
Chiquelequele Angola 16°44S 19°5E 265 F3
Chiquián Peru 10°10S 77°0W 330 C2
Chiquibul △ Belize 16°49N 88°52W 320 C2
Chiquihuite, Cerro Mexico 19°32N 99°8W 128 A2
Chiquimula Guatemala 14°51N 89°37W 320 D2
Chiquinquira Colombia 5°37N 73°50W 328 B3
Chiquitos, Llanos de Bolivia 18°0S 61°30W 331 D5
Chir → Russia 48°30N 43°0E 191 F6
Chira → Peru 4°54S 81°8W 328 D1
Chirala India 15°50N 80°26E 245 G5
Chiramba Mozam. 16°55S 34°39E 269 F3
Chirawa India 28°14N 75°42E 242 E6
Chirayinkil India 8°41N 76°49E 245 K3
Chirchiq Uzbekistan 41°29N 69°35E 217 D7
Chiredzi Zimbabwe 21°0S 31°38E 271 B5
Chirfa Niger 20°55N 12°22E 259 D2
Chirgua → Venezuela 8°54N 67°58W 328 B4
Chiribiquete △ Colombia 0°31N 72°50W 328 C3
Chiricahua △ U.S.A. 32°0N 109°20W 305 K9
Chiricahua Peak U.S.A. 31°51N 109°18W 305 L9
Chirikof I. U.S.A. 55°50N 155°40W 300 D8
Chiriquí, G. de Panama 8°0N 82°10W 320 E3
Chiriquí, L. de Panama 9°10N 82°0W 320 E3
Chirisa △ Zimbabwe 17°53S 28°15E 269 F2
Chirivira Falls Zimbabwe 21°10S 32°12E 269 G3
Chirmiri India 23°15N 82°20E 243 H10
Chirnogi Romania 44°7N 26°32E 183 F11
Chirongui Mayotte 12°55S 45°9E 272 b
Chirpan Bulgaria 42°10N 25°19E 203 D9
Chirripó Grande, Cerro Costa Rica 9°29N 83°29W 320 E3
Chirundu Zimbabwe 16°3S 28°50E 271 A4
Chisamba Zambia 14°55S 28°20E 269 E2
Chisapani Nepal 28°37N 81°16E 243 E9
Chisasa Zambia 12°6S 25°30E 265 E5
Chisasibi Canada 53°50N 79°0W 298 B4
Ch'ishan Taiwan 22°44N 120°31E 225 D2
Ch'ishan Hsi → Taiwan 22°51N 120°28E 225 C2
Chisholm Alta., Canada 54°55N 114°10W 296 C6
Chisholm Minn., U.S.A. 47°29N 92°53W 308 B7
Chishtian Mandi Pakistan 29°50N 72°55E 242 E5
Chishui China 28°30N 105°42E 228 C5
Chishui He → China 28°49N 105°50E 228 C5
Chisimaio = Kismaayo Somali Rep. 0°22S 42°32E 267 E5
Chisimba Falls Zambia 10°12S 30°56E 269 E3
Chişinău Moldova 47°2N 28°50E 183 C13
Chişinău ✈ (KIV) Moldova 47°3N 28°46E 183 C13
Chişineu Criş Romania 46°32N 21°37E 182 D6
Chislehurst U.K. 51°24N 0°6E 125 B4
Chisone → Italy 44°49N 7°25E 198 D4
Chisos Mts. U.S.A. 29°5N 103°15W 314 G3
Chissengue Angola 9°13S 20°34E 265 D4
Chissilo Angola 13°48S 16°31E 265 E3
Chistochina U.S.A. 62°34N 144°40W 303 E11
Chistopol Russia 55°25N 50°38E 190 C10
Chiswick U.K. 51°29N 0°16W 125 B2
Chiswick House U.K. 51°28N 0°15W 125 B2
Chita Colombia 6°11N 72°28W 328 B3
Chita Russia 52°0N 113°35E 219 A11
Chitado Angola 17°10S 14°8E 265 F2
Chitaldrug = Chitradurga India 14°14N 76°24E 245 G3
Chitan Taiwan 24°35N 121°29E 225 B3
Chitanda → Angola 16°1S 15°12E 265 F3
Chitapur India 17°10N 77°5E 244 F3
Chitembo Angola 13°30S 16°50E 265 E3
Chitina U.S.A. 61°31N 144°26W 303 F11
Chitipa Malawi 9°41S 33°19E 269 D3
Chitose Hokkaidō, Japan 42°49N 141°39E 220 C10
Chitose Kanagawa, Japan 35°33N 139°37E 140 B2
Chitradurga India 14°14N 76°24E 245 G3
Chitrakot India 19°10N 81°40E 244 E5
Chitral Pakistan 35°50N 71°56E 240 B3
Chitralada Palace Thailand 13°45N 100°31E 113 B2
Chitravati → India 14°45N 78°15E 245 G4
Chitré Panama 7°59N 80°27W 320 E3
Chittagong Bangla. 22°19N 91°48E 241 D3
Chittagong ☐ Bangla. 24°5N 91°0E 241 C3
Chittaurgarh India 24°52N 74°38E 242 G6
Chittoor India 13°15N 79°5E 245 H4
Chittur India 10°40N 76°45E 245 J3
Chitungwiza Zimbabwe 18°0S 31°6E 269 F3
Chiuju Taiwan 22°44N 120°32E 225 D2
Chiumbe → Dem. Rep. of the Congo 6°59S 21°12E 265 D4
Chiumbo Angola 12°29S 16°8E 265 E3
Chiume Angola 15°3S 21°14E 265 F4
Chiusi Italy 43°1N 11°57E 199 E8
Chiva Spain 39°27N 0°41W 197 F4
Chivacoa Venezuela 10°10N 68°54W 328 A4
Chivasso Italy 45°11N 7°53E 198 C4
Chivay Peru 15°40S 71°35W 330 D3
Chive Bolivia 12°23S 68°35W 330 C4
Chivhu Zimbabwe 19°2S 30°52E 269 F3
Chivilcoy Argentina 34°55S 60°0W 334 C4
Chiwanda Tanzania 11°23S 34°55E 269 E3
Chixi China 22°0N 112°58E 229 G9
Chiyoda Tokyo, Japan 140 b4
Chizarira Zimbabwe 17°36S 27°45E 269 F2
Chizarira △ Zimbabwe 17°44S 27°52E 269 F2
Chizela Zambia 13°8S 25°0E 265 E4
Chizu Japan 35°16N 134°14E 222 B6
Chkalov = Orenburg Russia 51°45N 55°6E 186 D10
Chkalova Russia 55°39N 37°56E 129 C5
Chkolovsk Russia 56°50N 43°10E 190 B6
Chloride U.S.A. 35°25N 114°12W 307 K12
Chlumec nad Cidlinou Czech Rep. 50°9N 15°29E 180 A8
Chmielnik Poland 50°37N 20°43E 185 H7
Cho-do N. Korea 38°30N 124°40E 224 C2
Cho Phuoc Hai Vietnam 10°26N 107°18E 237 G6
Choa Chu Kang Singapore 1°22N 103°41E 138 A2
Choba Kenya 2°30N 38°5E 266 D4
Chobe △ Botswana 18°37S 24°23E 270 A4
Choboty Russia 55°39N 37°21E 129 C2
Choc B. St. Lucia 14°3N 60°59W 323 m
Choch'i Taiwan 23°20N 121°16E 225 C3
Chocianów Poland 51°27N 15°55E 185 G2
Chociwel Poland 53°29N 15°21E 184 E2
Chocó ☐ Colombia 6°0N 77°0W 328 B2
Chocolate Hills Phil. 9°55N 124°10E 233 G5
Chocolate Mts. U.S.A. 33°15N 115°15W 307 M11
Chocontá Colombia 5°9N 73°41W 328 B3
Choctawhatchee → U.S.A. 30°25N 86°8W 316 E3
Choctawhatchee B. U.S.A. 30°20N 86°20W 317 E3
Chodavaram Andhra Pradesh, India 17°50N 82°57E 244 F6
Chodavaram Andhra Pradesh, India 17°27N 81°46E 244 F5
Chodecz Poland 52°24N 19°2E 185 F6
Chodov Czech Rep. 50°15N 12°45E 180 A5
Chodov u Prahy Czech Rep. 50°1N 14°30E 135 B3
Chodziez Poland 52°58N 16°58E 185 F3
Choele Choel Argentina 39°11S 65°40W 336 A3
Chōfu Japan 35°38N 139°32E 140 B2
Choiseul St. Lucia 13°47N 61°3W 323 m
Choiseul Solomon Is. 7°0S 156°40E 287 L9
Choisy-le-Roi France 48°46N 2°24E 134 B3
Choix Mexico 26°43N 108°17W 318 B3
Chojna Poland 52°58N 14°25E 185 F1
Chojnice Poland 53°42N 17°32E 184 E4
Chojnów Poland 51°18N 15°58E 185 G2
Chok Chai Thailand 14°44N 102°10E 236 E4
Chōkai-San Japan 39°6N 140°3E 220 E10
Choke Canyon Res. U.S.A. 28°30N 98°20W 314 G5
Choke Mts. Ethiopia 11°18N 37°15E 257 E4
Chokurdakh Russia 70°38N 147°55E 215 B15
Chokwé Mozam. 24°32S 32°59E 271 B5
Cholame U.S.A. 35°44N 120°18W 306 K6
Cholan Taiwan 24°18N 120°49E 225 B2
Cholargos Greece 37°59N 23°48E 112 B2
Cholet France 47°4N 0°52W 172 E6
Cholguan Chile 37°10S 72°3W 334 D1
Choloma Honduras 15°37N 87°57W 320 C2
Cholpon-Ata Kyrgyzstan 42°40N 77°6E 217 D9
Cholupice Czech Rep. 49°59N 14°27E 135 C2
Choluteca Honduras 13°20N 87°14W 320 D2
Choluteca → Honduras 13°0N 87°20W 320 D2
Chom Bung Thailand 13°37N 99°36E 236 F2
Chom Thong Bangkok, Thailand 13°41N 100°29E 113 B1
Chom Thong Chiang Mai, Thailand 18°25N 98°41E 236 C2
Choma Zambia 16°48S 26°59E 269 F2
Chomolungma = Everest, Mt. Nepal 28°5N 86°58E 243 E12
Chomun India 27°15N 75°40E 242 F6
Chomutov Czech Rep. 50°28N 13°23E 180 A6
Chon Buri Thailand 13°21N 101°1E 236 F3
Chon Thanh Vietnam 11°24N 106°36E 237 G6
Chone Ecuador 0°40S 80°0W 328 D2
Chong Kai Cambodia 13°57N 103°35E 236 F4
Chong Mek Thailand 15°10N 105°27E 236 E5
Chong Pang Singapore 1°26N 103°49E 138 A2
Chong Phangan Thailand 9°39N 100°0E 237 b
Chong Samui Thailand 9°21N 99°50E 237 b
Chongde China 30°32N 120°26E 229 B13
Ch'ŏngjin N. Korea 41°47N 129°50E 224 B4
Chŏngju N. Korea 39°40N 125°5E 224 C2
Chongli China 40°58N 115°15E 226 D8
Chongming China 31°38N 121°23E 229 B13
Chongming Dao China 31°40N 121°30E 229 B13
Chongoroi Angola 13°37S 14°1E 265 E2
Chongoyape Peru 6°35S 79°25W 330 B2
Chŏngp'yŏng N. Korea 39°47N 127°23E 224 C3
Chongqing Chongqing, China 29°35N 106°25E 228 C6
Chongqing Sichuan, China 30°38N 103°40E 228 B4
Chongqing Shi ☐ China 30°0N 108°0E 228 C6
Chongren China 27°46N 116°3E 229 D11
Chonguene Mozam. 25°3S 33°49E 271 C5
Chongwe Zambia 15°21S 28°42E 269 F2
Chongwen Beijing, China 114 c2
Chongyi China 25°45N 114°29E 229 E10
Chongzuo China 22°23N 107°20E 228 F6
Chonogol Mongolia 45°54N 115°22E 226 B8
Chonos, Arch. de los Chile 45°0S 75°0W 336 C2
Chop Ukraine 48°26N 22°12E 182 B7
Chopda India 21°20N 75°15E 244 D2
Chopim → Brazil 25°35S 53°5W 335 B5
Chopin Museum Warsaw, Poland 142 b2
Chor Pakistan 25°31N 69°46E 242 G3
Chora Greece 37°3N 21°42E 204 D3
Chora Sfakion Greece 35°15N 24°9E 207 E5
Chorbat La India 34°42N 76°37E 243 B7
Chorley U.K. 53°39N 2°38W 168 D5
Chorna Ukraine 47°36N 29°20E 183 C14
Chornaya → Russia 55°41N 38°0E 129 B6
Chornobyl Ukraine 51°20N 30°15E 177 C16
Chornomorske Ukraine 45°31N 32°40E 189 K7
Chorolque, Cerro Bolivia 20°59S 66°5W 334 A2
Choroszcz Poland 53°10N 22°59E 185 E9
Chorregon Australia 22°40S 143°32E 280 C3
Chorrillos Peru 12°10S 77°1W 124 C2
Chortkiv Ukraine 49°2N 25°46E 177 D13
Chorzele Poland 53°15N 20°55E 185 E7
Chorzów Poland 50°18N 18°57E 185 H5
Chos-Malal Argentina 37°20S 70°15W 334 D1
Ch'osan N. Korea 40°50N 125°47E 224 B2
Chosheta Shan Taiwan 23°50N 121°6E 225 C3
Chōshi Japan 35°45N 140°51E 223 B12
Choshui Hsi → Taiwan 23°50N 120°15E 225 C2
Choszczno Poland 53°7N 15°25E 185 E2
Chota Peru 6°33S 78°39W 330 B2
Choteau U.S.A. 47°49N 112°11W 304 C7
Chotěboř Czech Rep. 49°43N 15°40E 180 B8
Chotila India 22°23N 71°15E 242 H4
Chotta Udepur India 22°19N 74°1E 242 H6
Choûm Mauritania 21°11N 13°3W 260 D2
Choungui Mayotte 12°57S 45°8E 272 b
Chowchilla U.S.A. 37°7N 120°16W 306 H6
Chowpatty Beach Mumbai, India 130 b1
Choybalsan Mongolia 48°4N 114°30E 219 B11
Choyr Mongolia 46°24N 108°30E 219 B10
Chrisman U.S.A. 39°48N 87°41W 311 E9
Chrisoupoli Greece 40°58N 24°42E 203 F8
Christ Church Cathedral Montréal, Canada 130 c2
Christburg = Dzierzgoń Poland 53°58N 19°20E 184 E6
Christchurch N.Z. 43°33S 172°47E 285 D7
Christchurch Dorset, U.K. 50°44N 1°47W 169 G6
Christian I. Canada 44°50N 80°12W 312 B4
Christian Quarter Jerusalem 123 b3
Christian Sd. U.S.A. 55°56N 134°40W 303 J14
Christiana Greece 36°14N 25°13E 205 E7
Christiana Jamaica 18°10N 77°29W 320 a
Christiana North West, S. Africa 27°52S 25°8E 270 C4
Christiansborg Slot Copenhagen, Denmark 118 c2
Christiansfeld Denmark 55°21N 9°29E 163 J3
Christianshåb = Qasigiannguit Greenland 68°50N 51°18W 154 D5
Christianshavn Denmark 55°40N 12°35E 118 A3
Christiansted U.S. Virgin Is. 17°45N 64°42W 321 C7
Christie B. Canada 62°32N 111°10W 297 A6
Christina → Canada 56°40N 111°3W 297 B6
Christmas Cr. → Australia 18°29S 125°23E 278 C4
Christmas I. = Kiritimati Kiribati 1°58N 157°27W 289 G12
Christmas I. Ind. Oc. 10°30S 105°40E 273 F9
Christoffel △ Curaçao 12°21N 69°8W 322 g
Christopher U.S.A. 37°59N 89°3W 310 G7
Christopher, L. Australia 24°49S 127°42E 279 D4
Christyakovo = Thorez Ukraine 48°4N 38°34E 189 H10
Chrudim Czech Rep. 49°58N 15°43E 180 B8
Chrysler Building New York, U.S.A. 132 c2
Chrzanów Małopolskie, Poland 50°10N 19°21E 185 H6
Chrzanów Warszawa, Poland 52°13N 20°53E 142 B1
Chtapodia Greece 37°24N 25°34E 205 D7
Chtimba Malawi 10°35S 34°13E 269 E3
Chū = Shū Kazakhstan 43°36N 73°42E 217 D8
Chū = Shū → Kazakhstan 45°0N 67°44E 217 D7
Chu → Vietnam 19°53N 105°45E 236 C5
Chu Lai Vietnam 15°28N 108°45E 236 E7
Chu Mom Ray △ Vietnam 14°29N 107°38E 236 E6
Chu Se Vietnam 13°40N 108°8E 236 F7
Chuadanga Bangla. 23°38N 88°51E 241 D2
Chuak, Ko Thailand 9°28N 99°41E 237 b
Ch'uanchou = Quanzhou China 24°55N 118°34E 229 E12
Chūanchow = Quanzhou China 24°55N 118°34E 229 E12
Chuangwei Taiwan 24°45N 121°47E 225 B3
Chuankou China 34°20N 110°59E 226 G6
Chuathbaluk U.S.A. 61°40N 159°15W 303 F8
Chubarovka = Pology Ukraine 47°29N 36°15E 189 J9
Chubbuck U.S.A. 42°55N 112°28W 304 E7
Chūbu ☐ Japan 36°45N 137°30E 223 A9
Chūbu-Sangaku △ Japan 36°30N 137°40E 223 A9
Chubut ☐ Argentina 43°30S 69°0W 336 B3
Chubut → Argentina 43°20S 65°5W 336 B3
Chuch'i Taiwan 23°31N 120°33E 225 C2
Chuchi L. Canada 55°12N 124°30W 296 B4
Chuchow = Zhuzhou China 27°49N 113°12E 229 D9
Chuda India 22°29N 71°41E 242 H4
Chudovo Russia 59°10N 31°41E 188 C6
Chudskoye, Ozero Russia 58°13N 27°30E 188 C4
Chuen Lung China 22°23N 114°6E 122 A1
Chugach Mts. U.S.A. 60°45N 147°0W 303 E11
Chuginadak I. U.S.A. 52°50N 169°45W 303 K5
Chūgoku ☐ Japan 35°0N 133°0E 222 C5
Chūgoku-Sanchi Japan 35°0N 133°0E 222 B5
Chuguyev = Chuhuyiv Ukraine 49°55N 36°45E 189 H9
Chugwater U.S.A. 41°46N 104°50W 304 F11

Chuhuyiv *Ukraine* 49°55N 36°45E **189** H9
Chuk Kok *China* 22°20N 114°15E **122** A2
Chuka *Kenya* 0°20S 37°39E **268** C4
Chukchi Plateau *Arctic* 78°0N 165°0W **150** B17
Chukchi Sea *Russia* 68°0N 175°0W **215** C19
Chukotskiy Mys *Russia* 64°14N 173°8W **300** C5
Chukotskiy Poluostrov *Russia* 66°0N 174°0W **300** B5
Chukotskoye Nagorye *Russia* 68°0N 175°0E **215** C18
Chula *U.S.A.* 31°33N 83°32W **316** D6
Chula Vista *U.S.A.* 32°38N 117°5W **307** N9
Chulalongkom Univ. *Thailand* 13°44N 100°31E **113** B2
Chulband → *India* 20°40N 79°54E **244** D4
Ch'ulin *Taiwan* 22°8N 120°42E **225** D2
Chulucanas *Peru* 5°8S 80°10W **330** B1
Chulumani *Bolivia* 16°24S 67°31W **330** D4
Chulym → *Russia* 57°43N 83°51E **214** D9
Chum Phae *Thailand* 16°40N 102°6E **236** D4
Chum Saeng *Thailand* 15°55N 100°15E **236** E3
Chuma *Bolivia* 15°24S 68°56W **330** D4
Chumar *India* 32°40N 78°35E **243** C8
Chumbicha *Argentina* 29°0S 66°10W **334** B2
Chumerna *Bulgaria* 42°45N 25°55E **203** D9
Chumikan *Russia* 54°40N 135°10E **215** D14
Chumphon *Thailand* 10°35N 99°14E **237** G2
Chumpi *Peru* 15°4S 73°46W **330** D3
Chumuare *Mozam.* 14°31S 31°50E **269** E3
Chuna → *Russia* 57°47N 94°37E **215** D10
Chun'an *Zhejiang, China* 29°35N 119°3E **229** C12
Chunan *Taiwan* 24°41N 120°52E **225** B2
Chuncheon *S. Korea* 37°58N 127°44E **224** D3
Chunchura *India* 22°53N 88°27E **243** H13
Chunga *Zambia* 15°0S 26°2E **269** F2
Chungcheongbuk-do □ *S. Korea* 36°45N 128°0E **224** D4
Chungcheonnam-do □ *S. Korea* 36°30N 127°0E **224** D3
Ch'ungch'ing = Chongqing *China* 29°35N 106°25E **228** C6
Chunggang-ŭp *N. Korea* 41°48N 126°48E **224** B3
Chungho *Taiwan* 25°0N 121°28E **225** A3
Chunghwa *N. Korea* 38°52N 125°47E **224** C2
Chungju *S. Korea* 36°58N 127°58E **224** D3
Chungking = Chongqing *China* 29°35N 106°25E **228** C6
Chungli *Taiwan* 24°57N 121°13E **225** B3
Chungpu *Taiwan* 23°26N 120°31E **225** C2
Chungt'iaoshan = Zhongtiao Shan *China* 35°0N 111°10E **226** G6
Chungtungwan *Taiwan* 24°31N 120°40E **225** B2
Chungyang Shanmo *Taiwan* 23°10N 121°0E **225** C3
Chunian *Pakistan* 30°57N 74°0E **242** D6
Chunya *Tanzania* 8°30S 33°27E **269** D3
Chunyang *China* 43°38N 129°23E **227** C15
Chuō *Tokyo, Japan* **140** b5
Chupara B. *Trin. & Tob.* 10°48N 61°22W **323** t
Chupara Pt. *Trin. & Tob.* 10°49N 61°22W **323** t
Chupei *Taiwan* 24°50N 121°0E **225** B3
Chuquibamba *Peru* 15°47S 72°44W **330** D3
Chuquibambilla *Peru* 14°7S 72°41W **330** C3
Chuquicamata *Chile* 22°15S 69°0W **334** A2
Chuquisaca □ *Bolivia* 20°30S 63°30W **331** E5
Chur *Switz.* 46°52N 9°32E **179** J5
Churachandpur *India* 24°20N 93°40E **241** C4
Church End *U.K.* 51°35N 0°11W **125** A2
Church of our Lady = Frauenkirche *Munich, Germany* **131** b2
Church Stretton *U.K.* 52°32N 2°48W **169** E5
Churchill *Vic., Australia* 38°19S 146°25E **283** E7
Churchill *Man., Canada* 58°47N 94°11W **297** B10
Churchill → *Man., Canada* 58°47N 94°12W **297** B10
Churchill → *Nfld. & L., Canada* 53°19N 60°10W **299** B7
Churchill, C. *Canada* 58°46N 93°12W **297** B10
Churchill Falls *Canada* 53°36N 64°19W **299** B7
Churchill L. *Canada* 55°55N 108°20W **297** B7
Churchill Pk. *Canada* 58°10N 125°10W **296** B3
Churchtown *Ireland* 53°18N 6°16W **120** B2
Churdan *U.S.A.* 42°9N 94°29W **310** B2
Churki *India* 23°50N 83°12E **243** H10
Churu *India* 28°20N 74°50E **242** E6
Churubusco *U.S.A.* 41°14N 85°19W **311** C11
Churún Merú = Angel Falls *Venezuela* 5°57N 62°30W **329** B5
Chushal *India* 33°40N 78°40E **243** C8
Chushan *Taiwan* 23°45N 120°40E **225** C2
Chuska Mts. *U.S.A.* 36°15N 108°50W **305** H9
Chusovoy *Russia* 58°22N 57°50E **186** C10
Chusovskoy Zavod = Chusovoy *Russia* 58°22N 57°50E **186** C10
Chuspipata *Bolivia* 16°18S 67°48W **330** D4
Chust = Khust *Ukraine* 48°10N 23°18E **183** B8
Chust *Uzbekistan* 41°0N 71°13E **217** D8
Chute-aux-Outardes *Canada* 49°7N 68°24W **299** C6
Chutung *Taiwan* 24°44N 121°5E **225** B3
Chuuk = Truk *Micronesia* 7°25N 151°46E **287** T17
Chuuk Lagoon *Micronesia* 7°24N 151°45E **287** T18
Chuvash Republic = Chuvashia □ *Russia* 55°30N 47°0E **190** C8
Chuvashia □ *Russia* 55°30N 47°0E **190** C8
Chuwārtah *Iraq* 35°43N 45°34E **213** E11
Chuwei *Taiwan* 25°6N 121°14E **225** A3
Chuxiong *China* 25°2N 101°28E **228** E3
Chüy *Kyrgyzstan* 42°55N 75°15E **217** D9
Chuy *Uruguay* 33°41S 53°27W **335** C5
Chüy □ *Kyrgyzstan* 42°25N 75°16E **217** D9
Chuzenji-Ko *Japan* 36°44N 139°27E **223** A11
Chuzhou *China* 32°19N 118°20E **229** A12
Chynadiyeve *Ukraine* 48°29N 22°50E **182** B7
Ci Xian *China* 36°20N 114°25E **226** F8
Ciacova *Romania* 45°35N 21°10E **182** E6
Ciadâr-Lunga *Moldova* 46°3N 28°51E **183** D13
Ciales *Puerto Rico* 18°20N 66°28W **321** b
Ciamis *Indonesia* 7°20S 108°21E **235** D3
Ciampino *Italy* 41°47N 12°36E **136** C2
Ciampino ✕ (CIA) *Italy* 41°47N 12°35E **136** C2
Cianjur *Indonesia* 6°49S 107°8E **234** D3
Cianorte *Brazil* 23°37S 52°37W **335** A5
Cibola *U.S.A.* 33°17N 114°42W **307** M12
Çiçekdağı *Turkey* 39°36N 34°24E **212** C6
Cicero *U.S.A.* 41°51N 87°44W **119** B2
Cícero Dantas *Brazil* 10°36S 38°23W **332** D4
Ciceron *St. Lucia* 13°59N 61°1W **323** m
Cicia *Fiji* 17°45S 179°18W **287** A3
Cidacos → *Spain* 42°21N 1°38W **196** C3
Cidade de Minas = Belo Horizonte *Brazil* 19°55S 43°56W **333** E3
Cide *Turkey* 41°53N 33°1E **212** B5
Cidra *Puerto Rico* 18°11N 66°10W **321** b
Ciechanów *Poland* 52°52N 20°38E **185** F7
Ciechanowiec *Poland* 52°40N 22°31E **185** F9
Ciechocinek *Poland* 52°53N 18°45E **185** F5
Ciego de Ávila *Cuba* 21°50N 78°50W **320** B4
Ciénaga *Colombia* 11°1N 74°15W **328** A3
Ciénaga de Oro *Colombia* 8°53N 75°37W **328** B2
Ciénagas del Catatumbo △ *Venezuela* 9°26N 72°8W **328** B3
Cienfuegos *Cuba* 22°10N 80°30W **320** B3
Cierp-Gaud *France* 42°55N 0°40E **174** F4
Cíes, Is. *Spain* 42°12N 8°55W **194** C2
Cieszanów *Poland* 50°14N 23°8E **185** H10
Cieszyn *Poland* 49°45N 18°35E **185** J5
Cieza *Spain* 38°17N 1°23W **197** G3
Çifteler *Turkey* 39°22N 31°2E **212** C4
Cifuentes *Spain* 40°47N 2°37W **196** E2
Cihanbeyli *Turkey* 38°40N 32°55E **212** C5
Cihuatlán *Mexico* 19°14N 104°35W **318** D4
Cijara, Embalse de *Spain* 39°18N 4°52W **195** F6
Cijara ⌓ *Spain* 39°18N 4°35W **195** F6
Cijulang *Indonesia* 7°42S 108°27E **235** D3
Cilacap *Indonesia* 7°43S 109°0E **235** D3
Cilandak *Indonesia* 6°17S 106°47E **122** B1
Cilao, Cirque de *Réunion* 21°7S 55°28E **272** f
Cilaos *Réunion* 21°8S 55°27E **272** f
Çıldır *Turkey* 41°7N 43°8E **213** B10
Çıldır Gölü *Turkey* 41°5N 43°15E **213** B10
Cilento e Vallo di Diano △ *Italy* 40°15N 15°20E **201** B8
Cili *China* 29°30N 111°8E **229** C8
Cilibia *Romania* 45°4N 27°4E **183** E12
Cilicia *Turkey* 36°30N 35°0E **250** B5
Cilincing *Indonesia* 6°6S 106°54E **122** A2
Ciliwung → *Indonesia* 6°6S 106°47E **122** B2
Cill Airne = Killarney *Ireland* 52°4N 9°30W **166** D2
Cill Chainnigh = Kilkenny *Ireland* 52°39N 7°15W **166** D4
Cill Dara = Kildare *Ireland* 53°9N 6°55W **166** C5
Cill Mhantáin = Wicklow *Ireland* 52°59N 6°3W **166** D5
Cilo Dağı *Turkey* 37°28N 43°55E **213** D10
Cima *U.S.A.* 35°14N 115°30W **307** K11
Cimarron *Kans., U.S.A.* 37°48N 100°21W **308** G3
Cimarron *N. Mex., U.S.A.* 36°31N 104°55W **305** H11
Cimarron → *U.S.A.* 36°10N 96°16W **314** C6
Čimice *Czech Rep.* 50°8N 14°25E **135** B2
Cimişlia *Moldova* 46°34N 28°44E **183** D13
Cimone, Mte. *Italy* 44°12N 10°42E **198** D7
Cina, Tanjung *Indonesia* 5°55S 104°45E **234** D2
Çinar *Turkey* 37°46N 40°19E **213** D9
Çınarcık *Turkey* 40°38N 29°5E **203** F13
Cinaruco-Capanaparo △ *Venezuela* 6°51N 67°32W **328** B4
Cinca → *Spain* 41°26N 0°21E **196** D5
Cincar *Bos.-H.* 43°55N 17°5E **182** G2
Cincinnati *Iowa, U.S.A.* 40°38N 92°56W **310** D4
Cincinnati *Ohio, U.S.A.* 39°9N 84°27W **311** E12
Cincinnati-Northern Kentucky Int. ✕ (CVG) *U.S.A.* 39°3N 84°40W **311** E12
Cincinnatus *U.S.A.* 42°33N 75°54W **313** D9
Çine *Turkey* 37°37N 28°2E **205** D10
Cinecittà *Italy* 41°51N 12°34E **136** B2
Ciney *Belgium* 50°18N 5°5E **170** D5
Cíngoli *Italy* 43°23N 13°10E **199** E10
Cinigiano *Italy* 42°53N 11°24E **199** F8
Cinisello Bálsamo *Italy* 45°33N 9°13E **129** A2
Cinkota *Hungary* 47°31N 19°14E **117** A3
Cinque I. *India* 11°16N 92°42E **245** J11
Cinto, Mte. *France* 42°24N 8°54E **175** F12
Cintra, G. de *W. Sahara* 23°0N 16°15W **260** D1
Cintruénigo *Spain* 42°5N 1°49W **196** C3
Ciocile *Romania* 44°49N 27°14E **183** F12
Ciolăneşti din Deal *Romania* 44°19N 25°5E **183** F10
Ciorani *Romania* 44°45N 26°25E **183** F11
Čiovo *Croatia* 43°30N 16°17E **199** E13
Cipero → *Trin. & Tob.* 10°16N 61°28W **323** t
Cipete *Indonesia* 6°15S 106°47E **122** B1
Cipó *Brazil* 11°6S 38°31W **332** D4
Cipolletti *Argentina* 38°56S 67°59W **336** A3
Circeo, Mte. *Italy* 41°14N 13°3E **200** A6
Çirçir *Turkey* 40°3N 36°47E **212** C7
Circle *Alaska, U.S.A.* 65°50N 144°4W **303** D11
Circle *Mont., U.S.A.* 47°25N 105°35W **304** C11
Circleville *U.S.A.* 39°36N 82°57W **309** F12
Circular Reef *Papua N. G.* 3°25S 147°47E **286** B4
Cirebon *Indonesia* 6°45S 108°32E **235** D3
Cirencester *U.K.* 51°43N 1°57W **169** F6
Cireşu *Romania* 44°47N 22°31E **182** F7
Cirey-sur-Vezouze *France* 48°35N 6°57E **173** D13
Ciriè *Italy* 45°14N 7°36E **198** C4
Cirium *Cyprus* 34°40N 32°53E **207** F8
Cirò *Italy* 39°23N 17°4E **201** C10
Cirò Marina *Italy* 39°22N 17°8E **201** C10
Ciron → *France* 44°36N 0°18W **174** D3
Cisco *U.S.A.* 32°23N 98°59W **314** E5
Cislău *Romania* 45°14N 26°20E **183** E11
Cisna *Poland* 49°12N 22°20E **185** J9
Cisnădie *Romania* 45°42N 24°9E **183** E9
Cisne *U.S.A.* 38°31N 88°26W **311** F8
Cisneros *Colombia* 6°33N 75°4W **328** B2
Cissna Park *U.S.A.* 40°34N 87°54W **311** D9
Cisterna di Latina *Italy* 41°35N 12°49E **200** A5
Cisternino *Italy* 40°44N 17°25E **201** B10
Cistierna *Spain* 42°48N 5°7W **194** C5
Citadel = Kastellet *Copenhagen, Denmark* **118** a3
Citadel *Budapest, Hungary* **117** c2
Citaré → *Brazil* 1°11N 54°41W **329** C7
Citeli-Ckaro = Tsiteli-Tsqaro *Georgia* 41°33N 46°0E **191** K8
Citlaltépetl = Orizaba, Pico de *Mexico* 18°58N 97°15W **319** D5
Citra *U.S.A.* 29°25N 82°7W **317** F7
Citron *Fr. Guiana* 4°44N 53°57W **329** C7
Citrus Heights *U.S.A.* 38°42N 121°17W **306** G5
Citrus Springs *U.S.A.* 29°2N 82°27W **317** F7
Citrusdal *S. Africa* 32°35S 19°0E **270** D2
Citta degli Studi *Italy* 45°28N 9°12E **129** B2
Città del Vaticano = Vatican City ■ *Europe* 41°54N 12°27E **136** B1
Città della Pieve *Italy* 42°57N 12°1E **199** F9
Città di Castello *Italy* 43°27N 12°14E **199** E9
Città Sant' Angelo *Italy* 42°32N 14°5E **199** F11
Cittadella *Italy* 45°39N 11°47E **199** C8
Cittaducale *Italy* 42°23N 12°57E **199** F9
Cittanova *Italy* 38°21N 16°5E **201** D9
City, The *U.K.* 51°30N 0°6W **125** A3
City Hall = Rådhus *Oslo, Norway* **133** b1
City Hall = Stadshuset *Stockholm, Sweden* **139** b1
City of the Dead *Egypt* 30°0N 31°15E **117** A2
City Park *U.S.A.* 30°0N 90°5W **131** A2
City Terrace *U.S.A.* 34°3N 118°11W **126** B3
Ciuc, Munţii *Romania* 46°25N 26°5E **183** D11
Ciucaş, Vf. *Romania* 45°31N 25°56E **183** E10
Ciucea *Romania* 46°57N 22°49E **182** D7
Ciuciulea *Moldova* 47°40N 27°29E **183** C12
Ciuciuleni *Moldova* 47°2N 28°25E **183** C13
Ciudad Acuña *Mexico* 29°18N 100°55W **318** B4
Ciudad Altamirano *Mexico* 18°20N 100°40W **318** D4
Ciudad Anáhuac *Mexico* 27°14N 100°7W **318** B4
Ciudad Bolívar *Venezuela* 8°5N 63°36W **329** B5
Ciudad Bolívia *Venezuela* 8°21N 70°34W **328** B3
Ciudad Camargo *Mexico* 27°40N 105°10W **318** B3
Ciudad Cortés *Costa Rica* 8°55N 84°0W **320** E3
Ciudad de México *Mexico* 19°24N 99°9W **128** B2
Ciudad de Nutrias *Venezuela* 8°5N 69°18W **328** B4
Ciudad de Valles *Mexico* 22°0N 99°0W **319** C5
Ciudad del Carmen *Mexico* 18°38N 91°50W **319** D6
Ciudad del Este *Paraguay* 25°30S 54°50W **335** B5
Ciudad Delicias = Delicias *Mexico* 28°13N 105°28W **318** B3
Ciudad Deportiva *Mexico* 19°24N 99°5W **128** B2
Ciudad Fin de Semana *Spain* 40°26N 3°34W **127** B2
Ciudad Frontera *Mexico* 26°56N 101°27W **318** B4
Ciudad General Belgrano *Argentina* 34°43S 58°33W **117** C1
Ciudad Guayana *Venezuela* 8°0N 62°30W **329** B5
Ciudad Guerrero *Mexico* 28°33N 107°30W **318** B3
Ciudad Guzmán *Mexico* 19°41N 103°29W **318** D4
Ciudad Juárez *Mexico* 31°44N 106°29W **318** A3
Ciudad Lerdo *Mexico* 25°32N 103°32W **318** B4
Ciudad Lineál *Spain* 40°26N 3°38W **127** B2
Ciudad Madero *Mexico* 22°19N 97°50W **319** C5
Ciudad Mante *Mexico* 22°44N 98°59W **319** C5
Ciudad Obregón *Mexico* 27°29N 109°56W **318** B3
Ciudad Ojeda *Venezuela* 10°12N 71°19W **328** A3
Ciudad Piar *Venezuela* 7°27N 63°19W **329** B5
Ciudad Porfirio Díaz = Piedras Negras *Mexico* 28°42N 100°31W **318** B4
Ciudad Real *Spain* 38°59N 3°55W **195** G7
Ciudad Real □ *Spain* 38°50N 4°0W **195** G7
Ciudad Rodrigo *Spain* 40°35N 6°32W **194** E4
Ciudad Satélite *Mexico* 19°30N 99°13W **128** A1
Ciudad Trujillo = Santo Domingo *Dom. Rep.* 18°30N 69°59W **321** C6
Ciudad Universitaria *B. Aires, Argentina* 34°33S 58°27W **117** B2
Ciudad Universitaria *México, Mexico* 19°20N 99°11W **128** C1
Ciudad Victoria *Mexico* 23°44N 99°8W **319** C5
Ciudadela *Spain* 40°0N 3°50E **206** B4
Ciulniţa *Romania* 44°26N 27°22E **183** F12
Ciumeghiu *Romania* 46°44N 21°35E **182** D6
Ciuperceni *Romania* 44°54N 23°4E **182** F8
Ciutadella, Parc de la *Barcelona, Spain* **114** b3
Civa Burnu *Turkey* 41°21N 36°38E **212** B7
Civic Center *Los Angeles, U.S.A.* **127** b2
Cividale del Friuli *Italy* 46°6N 13°25E **199** B10
Civita Castellana *Italy* 42°18N 12°24E **199** F9
Civitanova Marche *Italy* 43°18N 13°44E **199** E10
Civitavécchia *Italy* 42°6N 11°48E **199** F8
Civray *France* 46°10N 0°17E **174** B4
Çivril *Turkey* 38°20N 29°43E **205** C11
Cixerri → *Italy* 39°17N 8°59E **200** C1
Cixi *China* 30°17N 121°9E **229** B13
Cizre *Turkey* 37°19N 42°10E **213** D10
Clackmannanshire □ *U.K.* 56°10N 3°43W **167** E5
Clacton-on-Sea *U.K.* 51°47N 1°11E **169** F9
Clain → *France* 46°47N 0°33E **172** F7
Claire, L. *Canada* 58°35N 112°5W **296** B6
Claireville Res. *Canada* 43°45N 79°39W **141** A1
Clairton *U.S.A.* 40°18N 79°53W **312** F5
Clairvaux-les-Lacs *France* 46°35N 5°45E **173** F12
Claise → *France* 46°56N 0°42E **174** B5
Clallam Bay *U.S.A.* 48°15N 124°16W **306** B2
Clam Gulch *U.S.A.* 60°15N 151°23W **303** F10
Clamart *France* 48°48N 2°15E **134** B2
Clamecy *France* 47°28N 3°30E **173** E10
Clanton *U.S.A.* 32°51N 86°38W **315** E11
Clanwilliam *S. Africa* 32°11S 18°52E **270** D2
Clapham *U.K.* 51°27N 0°8W **125** B3
Clapton *U.K.* 51°33N 0°3W **125** A3
Clara *Ireland* 53°21N 7°37W **166** C4
Claraville *U.S.A.* 35°24N 118°20W **307** K8
Clare *S. Austral., Australia* 33°50S 138°37E **282** B3
Clare *Mich., U.S.A.* 43°49N 84°46W **309** D11
Clare □ *Ireland* 52°45N 9°0W **166** D3
Clare → *Ireland* 53°20N 9°2W **166** C2
Clare I. *Ireland* 53°49N 10°0W **166** C1
Claremont *Jamaica* 18°19N 77°11W **320** a
Claremont *Western Cape, S. Africa* 34°8S 18°28E **118** A1
Claremont *Calif., U.S.A.* 34°6N 117°43W **307** L9
Claremont *N.H., U.S.A.* 43°23N 72°20W **313** C12
Claremont Pt. *Australia* 14°1S 143°41E **280** A3
Claremore *U.S.A.* 36°19N 95°36W **314** C7
Claremorris *Ireland* 53°45N 9°0W **166** C3
Clarence *U.S.A.* 39°45N 92°16W **310** E4
Clarence → *N.S.W., Australia* 29°25S 153°22E **281** D5
Clarence → *N.Z.* 42°10S 173°56E **285** C8
Clarence, I. *Chile* 54°0S 72°0W **336** D2
Clarence, Port *U.S.A.* 65°15N 166°40W **303** D6
Clarence B. *Ascension I.* 7°55S 14°25W **153** g
Clarence I. *Antarctica* 61°10S 54°0W **151** C18
Clarence Str. *Australia* 12°0S 131°0E **278** B5
Clarence Town *Bahamas* 23°6N 74°59W **321** B5
Clarendon *Pa., U.S.A.* 41°47N 79°6W **312** E5
Clarendon *Tex., U.S.A.* 34°56N 100°53W **314** D4
Clarenville *Canada* 48°10N 54°1W **299** C9
Claresholm *Canada* 50°2N 113°33W **296** D6
Clarie Coast *Antarctica* 68°0S 135°0E **151** C9
Clarinda *U.S.A.* 40°44N 95°2W **308** E6
Clarington *Canada* 43°55N 78°41W **312** C6
Clarion *Iowa, U.S.A.* 42°44N 93°44W **310** B3
Clarion *Pa., U.S.A.* 41°13N 79°23W **312** E5
Clarion → *U.S.A.* 41°7N 79°41W **312** E5
Clarion Fracture Zone *Pac. Oc.* 20°0N 120°0W **292** H7
Clark *Mo., U.S.A.* 39°17N 92°21W **310** E4
Clark *S. Dak., U.S.A.* 44°53N 97°44W **308** C5
Clark, Pt. *Canada* 44°4N 81°45W **312** B3
Clark Fork *U.S.A.* 48°9N 116°11W **304** B5
Clark Fork → *U.S.A.* 48°9N 116°15W **304** B5
Clarkdale *U.S.A.* 34°46N 112°3W **305** J7
Clarke City *Canada* 50°12N 66°38W **299** B6
Clarke I. *Australia* 40°32S 148°10E **281** G4
Clarke Ra. *Australia* 20°40S 148°30E **280** b
Clarks Fork Yellowstone → *U.S.A.* 45°32N 108°50W **304** D9
Clark's Harbour *Canada* 43°25N 65°38W **299** D6
Clarks Hill L. = J. Strom Thurmond L. *U.S.A.* 33°40N 82°12W **316** B7
Clarks Point *U.S.A.* 58°51N 158°33W **303** G8
Clarks Summit *U.S.A.* 41°30N 75°42W **313** E9
Clarks Town *Jamaica* 18°25N 77°33W **320** a
Clarksburg *U.S.A.* 39°17N 80°30W **309** F13
Clarksdale *U.S.A.* 34°12N 90°35W **315** D9
Clarkston *U.S.A.* 46°25N 117°3W **304** C5
Clarksville *Ark., U.S.A.* 35°28N 93°28W **314** D8
Clarksville *Ind., U.S.A.* 38°17N 85°45W **311** F11
Clarksville *Iowa, U.S.A.* 42°47N 92°40W **310** B4
Clarksville *Mo., U.S.A.* 39°22N 90°54W **310** E6
Clarksville *Tenn., U.S.A.* 36°32N 87°21W **315** C11
Clarksville *Tex., U.S.A.* 33°37N 95°3W **314** E7
Claro → *Brazil* 19°8S 50°40W **333** E1
Clatskanie *U.S.A.* 46°6N 123°12W **306** D3
Claude *U.S.A.* 35°7N 101°22W **314** D4
Claveria *Cagayan, Phil.* 18°37N 121°4E **232** B3
Claveria *Masbate, Phil.* 12°54N 123°15E **232** E4
Claveria *Mis. Or., Phil.* 8°38N 124°55E **233** G5
Clavering Ø *Greenland* 74°15N 21°0W **154** C8
Claxton *U.S.A.* 32°10N 81°55W **316** C8
Claxton B. *Trin. & Tob.* 10°21N 61°28W **323** t
Claxton Bay *Trin. & Tob.* 10°21N 61°28W **323** t
Clay *U.S.A.* 38°17N 121°10W **306** G5
Clay Center *U.S.A.* 39°23N 97°8W **308** F5
Clay City *Ind., U.S.A.* 39°17N 87°7W **311** E9
Clay City *Ky., U.S.A.* 37°52N 83°55W **311** G13
Clayhall *U.K.* 51°35N 0°3E **125** A4
Claypool *U.S.A.* 33°25N 110°51W **305** K8
Claysburg *U.S.A.* 40°17N 78°27W **312** F6
Claysville *U.S.A.* 40°7N 80°25W **312** F4
Clayton *Ont., Canada* 45°11N 76°19W **313** A8
Clayton *Ala., U.S.A.* 31°53N 85°27W **316** D4
Clayton *Ind., U.S.A.* 39°41N 86°31W **311** E10
Clayton *N. Mex., U.S.A.* 36°27N 103°11W **305** H12
Clayton *N.Y., U.S.A.* 44°14N 76°5W **313** B8
Clear, C. *Ireland* 51°25N 9°32W **166** E2
Clear, L. *Ont., Canada* 45°26N 77°12W **312** A7
Clear, L. *Fla., U.S.A.* 28°31N 81°24W **133** A2
Clear Hills *Canada* 56°40N 119°30W **296** B5
Clear I. *Ireland* 51°26N 9°30W **166** E2
Clear L. *U.S.A.* 39°2N 122°47W **306** F4
Clear Lake *Iowa, U.S.A.* 43°8N 93°23W **310** A3
Clear Lake *S. Dak., U.S.A.* 44°45N 96°41W **308** C5
Clear Lake Res. *U.S.A.* 41°56N 121°5W **304** F3
Clearfield *Pa., U.S.A.* 41°2N 78°27W **312** E6
Clearfield *Utah, U.S.A.* 41°7N 112°2W **304** F7
Clearlake *U.S.A.* 38°57N 122°38W **306** G4
Clearwater *B.C., Canada* 51°38N 120°2W **296** C4
Clearwater *Fla., U.S.A.* 27°59N 82°48W **317** H7
Clearwater → *Alta., Canada* 52°22N 114°57W **296** C6
Clearwater → *Alta., Canada* 56°44N 111°23W **297** B6
Clearwater L. *Canada* 53°34N 99°49W **297** C9
Clearwater Lake ⌓ *Canada* 54°0N 101°0W **297** C8
Clearwater Mts. *U.S.A.* 46°5N 115°20W **304** C6
Clearwater River ⌓ *Canada* 56°55N 109°10W **297** B7
Cleburne *U.S.A.* 32°21N 97°23W **314** E6
Clee Hills *U.K.* 52°26N 2°35W **169** E5
Cleethorpes *U.K.* 53°33N 0°3W **168** D7
Cleeve Cloud *U.K.* 51°56N 2°0W **169** F6
Clelles *France* 44°50N 5°38E **175** D9
Clemson *U.S.A.* 34°41N 82°50W **315** D13
Cleopatra Needle *Phil.* 10°7N 118°58E **233** F2
Clerke Reef *Australia* 17°22S 119°20E **278** C2
Clerkenwell *London, U.K.* **125** a4
Clermiston *U.K.* 55°57N 3°17W **121** B2
Clermont *Queens., Australia* 22°49S 147°39E **280** C4
Clermont *Oise, France* 49°23N 2°24E **173** C9
Clermont *Fla., U.S.A.* 28°33N 81°46W **317** G8
Clermont-en-Argonne *France* 49°5N 5°4E **173** C12
Clermont-Ferrand *France* 45°46N 3°4E **174** C7
Clermont-l'Hérault *France* 43°38N 3°26E **174** E7
Clerval *France* 47°25N 6°30E **173** E13
Clervaux *Lux.* 50°4N 6°2E **170** D6
Cles *Italy* 46°22N 11°2E **198** B8
Cleve *Australia* 33°43S 136°30E **282** B2
Clevedon *U.K.* 51°26N 2°52W **169** F5
Cleveland *Miss., U.S.A.* 33°45N 90°43W **315** E9
Cleveland *Ohio, U.S.A.* 41°29N 81°41W **312** E3
Cleveland *Okla., U.S.A.* 36°19N 96°28W **314** C6
Cleveland *Tenn., U.S.A.* 35°10N 84°53W **315** D12
Cleveland *Tex., U.S.A.* 30°21N 95°5W **314** F7
Cleveland, C. *Australia* 19°11S 147°1E **280** B4
Cleveland, Mt. *U.S.A.* 48°56N 113°51W **304** B7
Cleveland Heights *U.S.A.* 41°31N 81°33W **312** E3
Clevelândia *Brazil* 26°24S 52°23W **335** B5
Clevelândia do Norte *Brazil* 3°49N 51°52W **329** C7
Cleves *U.S.A.* 39°10N 84°45W **311** E12
Clew B. *Ireland* 53°50N 9°49W **166** C2
Clewiston *U.S.A.* 26°45N 80°56W **317** J9
Clichy *France* 48°54N 2°18E **134** A2
Clichy-sous-Bois *France* 48°54N 2°32E **134** A4
Clifden *Galway, Ireland* 53°29N 10°1W **166** C1
Clifden *N.Z.* 46°1S 167°42E **285** G2
Cliffdell *U.S.A.* 46°56N 121°5W **306** D5
Cliffside *Canada* 43°44N 79°14W **141** A3
Cliffside Park *U.S.A.* 40°49N 73°59W **132** B2
Cliffy Hd. *Australia* 35°1S 116°29E **279** G2
Clifton *Queens., Australia* 27°59S 151°53E **281** D5
Clifton *Sindh, Pakistan* 24°48N 67°1E **123** B2
Clifton *Western Cape, S. Africa* 33°56S 18°22E **118** A1
Clifton *Ariz., U.S.A.* 33°3N 109°18W **305** K9
Clifton *Colo., U.S.A.* 39°7N 108°25W **304** G9
Clifton *Ill., U.S.A.* 40°56N 87°56W **311** D9
Clifton *N.J., U.S.A.* 40°37N 74°4W **132** C1
Clifton *Tex., U.S.A.* 31°47N 97°35W **314** F6
Clifton Beach *Queens., Australia* 16°46S 145°39E **280** B4
Clifton Beach *Sindh, Pakistan* 24°48N 67°2E **123** B2
Clifton Pt. *Bahamas* 25°1N 77°34W **153** b
Cliftondale *U.S.A.* 42°26N 71°0W **116** A2
Climax *U.S.A.* 30°53N 84°26W **316** E5
Clinch → *U.S.A.* 35°53N 84°29W **315** D12
Clingmans Dome *U.S.A.* 35°34N 83°30W **315** D13
Clint *U.S.A.* 31°35N 106°14W **314** F1
Clinton *B.C., Canada* 51°6N 121°35W **296** C4
Clinton *Ont., Canada* 43°37N 81°32W **312** C3
Clinton *N.Z.* 46°12S 169°23E **285** G4
Clinton *Ark., U.S.A.* 35°36N 92°28W **314** D8
Clinton *Conn., U.S.A.* 41°17N 72°32W **313** E12
Clinton *Ill., U.S.A.* 40°9N 88°57W **310** D8
Clinton *Ind., U.S.A.* 39°40N 87°24W **311** E9
Clinton *Iowa, U.S.A.* 41°51N 90°12W **310** C6
Clinton *Mass., U.S.A.* 42°25N 71°41W **313** D13
Clinton *Mich., U.S.A.* 42°4N 83°58W **311** B13
Clinton *Miss., U.S.A.* 32°20N 90°20W **315** E9
Clinton *Mo., U.S.A.* 38°22N 93°46W **310** F3
Clinton *N.C., U.S.A.* 35°0N 78°22W **315** D15
Clinton *Okla., U.S.A.* 35°31N 98°58W **314** D5
Clinton *S.C., U.S.A.* 34°29N 81°53W **315** D14
Clinton *Tenn., U.S.A.* 36°6N 84°8W **315** C12
Clinton *Wash., U.S.A.* 47°59N 122°21W **306** C4
Clinton *Wis., U.S.A.* 42°34N 88°52W **311** B8
Clinton, C. *Australia* 22°30S 150°45E **280** C5
Clinton, L. *U.S.A.* 40°15N 88°45W **311** D8
Clinton Colden L. *Canada* 63°58N 107°27W **294** E10
Clintonville *U.S.A.* 44°37N 88°46W **308** C9
Clio *U.S.A.* 31°43N 85°37W **316** D4
Clipperton, I. *Pac. Oc.* 10°18N 109°13W **289** F17
Clipperton Fracture Zone *Pac. Oc.* 19°0N 122°0W **289** G16
Clisham *U.K.* 57°58N 6°49W **167** D2
Clisson *France* 47°5N 1°16W **172** E5
Clitheroe *U.K.* 53°53N 2°22W **168** D5
Clive *N.Z.* 39°36S 176°58E **284** F5
Clive *Iowa, U.S.A.* 41°36N 93°43W **310** C3
Cliza *Bolivia* 17°36S 65°56W **331** D4
Clo-oose *Canada* 48°39N 124°49W **306** B2
Cloates, Pt. *Australia* 22°43S 113°40E **278** D1
Clocolan *S. Africa* 28°55S 27°34E **271** C4
Clodomira *Argentina* 27°35S 64°14W **334** B3
Clogher Hd. *Ireland* 53°48N 6°14W **166** C5
Cloghran *Ireland* 53°27N 6°14W **120** A2
Clonakilty *Ireland* 51°37N 8°53W **166** E3
Clonakilty B. *Ireland* 51°35N 8°51W **166** E3
Cloncurry *Queens., Australia* 20°40S 140°28E **280** C3
Cloncurry *Kildare, Ireland* 53°25N 6°48W **166** C5
Cloncurry → *Australia* 18°37S 140°40E **280** B3
Clondalkin *Ireland* 53°19N 6°25W **166** C5
Clones *Ireland* 54°11N 7°15W **166** B4
Clonmel *Ireland* 52°21N 7°42W **166** D4
Clonskeagh *Ireland* 53°19N 6°14W **120** B2
Clontarf *N.S.W., Australia* 33°48S 151°16E **139** A2
Clontarf *Dublin, Ireland* 53°22N 6°11W **120** A2
Cloppenburg *Germany* 52°51N 8°1E **178** C4
Cloquet *U.S.A.* 46°43N 92°28W **308** B7
Clorinda *Argentina* 25°16S 57°45W **334** B4
Cloud Peak *U.S.A.* 44°23N 107°11W **304** D10
Cloudcroft *U.S.A.* 32°58N 105°45W **305** K11
Cloudy B. *N.Z.* 41°25S 174°10E **285** B9
Clovelly *Australia* 33°54S 151°15E **139** B2
Cloverdale *Calif., U.S.A.* 38°48N 123°1W **306** G4
Cloverdale *Ind., U.S.A.* 39°31N 86°48W **311** E10
Cloverport *U.S.A.* 37°50N 86°38W **311** G10
Clovis *Calif., U.S.A.* 36°49N 119°42W **306** J7
Clovis *N. Mex., U.S.A.* 34°24N 103°12W **305** J12
Cloyes-sur-le-Loir *France* 48°0N 1°14E **172** E8
Cloyne *Canada* 44°49N 77°11W **312** B7
Cluain Meala = Clonmel *Ireland* 52°21N 7°42W **166** D4
Club Terrace *Australia* 37°35S 148°58E **283** D8
Cluj □ *Romania* 46°45N 23°30E **183** D8
Cluj-Napoca *Romania* 46°47N 23°38E **183** D8
Clunes *Australia* 37°20S 143°45E **282** D5
Cluny *France* 46°26N 4°38E **173** F11
Cluses *France* 46°5N 6°35E **173** F13
Clusone *Italy* 45°53N 9°57E **198** C6
Clutha → *N.Z.* 46°20S 169°49E **285** G4
Clwyd → *U.K.* 53°19N 3°31W **168** D4
Clyattville *U.S.A.* 30°42N 83°19W **316** E6
Clyde *Alta., Canada* 54°9N 113°39W **296** C6
Clyde *N.Z.* 45°12S 169°20E **285** F4
Clyde *N.Y., U.S.A.* 43°5N 76°52W **312** C8
Clyde *Ohio, U.S.A.* 41°18N 82°59W **311** C14
Clyde → *U.K.* 55°55N 4°30W **167** F4
Clyde, Firth of *U.K.* 55°22N 5°1W **167** F3
Clyde Muirshiel ⌓ *U.K.* 55°50N 4°40W **167** F4
Clyde River *Canada* 70°30N 68°30W **295** C18
Clydebank *U.K.* 55°54N 4°23W **167** F4
Clymer *N.Y., U.S.A.* 42°1N 79°37W **312** D5
Clymer *Pa., U.S.A.* 40°40N 79°1W **312** D5
Clyo *U.S.A.* 32°29N 81°16W **316** C8
Ćmielów *Poland* 50°53N 21°31E **185** H8
Côa → *Portugal* 41°5N 7°6W **194** D3
Coachella *U.S.A.* 33°41N 116°10W **307** M10
Coachella Canal *U.S.A.* 32°43N 114°57W **307** N12
Coahoma *U.S.A.* 32°18N 101°18W **314** E4
Coahuayana → *Mexico* 18°41N 103°45W **318** D4
Coahuila □ *Mexico* 27°20N 102°0W **318** B4
Coal → *Canada* 59°39N 126°57W **296** B3
Coal City *U.S.A.* 41°17N 88°17W **311** C8
Coal I. *N.Z.* 46°8S 166°40E **285** G1
Coalane *Mozam.* 17°48S 37°2E **269** F4
Coalcomán *Mexico* 18°47N 103°9W **318** D4
Coaldale *Canada* 49°45N 112°35W **296** D6
Coalgate *U.S.A.* 34°32N 96°13W **314** D6
Coalinga *U.S.A.* 36°9N 120°21W **306** J6
Coalisland *U.K.* 54°33N 6°42W **166** B5
Coalville *Leics., U.K.* 52°44N 1°23W **168** E6
Coalville *Utah, U.S.A.* 40°55N 111°24W **304** F8
Coamo *Puerto Rico* 18°5N 66°22W **321** b
Coaraci *Brazil* 14°38S 39°32W **333** D4
Coari *Brazil* 4°8S 63°7W **329** D5
Coari → *Brazil* 4°30S 63°33W **329** D5
Coari, L. *Brazil* 4°15S 63°22W **329** D5
Coast □ *Kenya* 2°40S 39°45E **268** C4
Coast Mts. *Canada* 55°0N 129°20W **296** C3
Coast Ranges *U.S.A.* 39°0N 123°0W **306** G4
Coatbridge *U.K.* 55°52N 4°6W **167** F4
Coatepec *Mexico* 19°27N 96°58W **319** D5
Coatepeque *Guatemala* 14°46N 91°55W **320** D1
Coatesville *U.S.A.* 39°59N 75°50W **309** F16
Coaticook *Canada* 45°10N 71°46W **313** A13
Coats I. *Canada* 62°30N 83°0W **295** E15
Coats Land *Antarctica* 77°0S 25°0W **151** D1
Coatzacoalcos *Mexico* 18°7N 94°25W **319** D6
Cobá *Mexico* 20°31N 87°45W **319** C7
Cobadin *Romania* 44°5N 28°13E **183** F13
Cobalt *Canada* 47°25N 79°42W **298** C4
Cobán *Guatemala* 15°30N 90°21W **320** C1
Çobanlar *Turkey* 38°41N 30°47E **205** C12
Cobar *Australia* 31°27S 145°48E **283** A6
Cobargo *Australia* 36°20S 149°55E **283** D8
Cobbannah *Australia* 37°37S 147°13E **283** D7
Cobberas, Mt. *Australia* 36°53S 148°12E **283** D8
Cobden *Australia* 38°20S 143°3E **282** E5
Cóbh *Ireland* 51°51N 8°17W **166** E3
Cobija *Bolivia* 11°0S 68°50W **330** C4
Cobleskill *U.S.A.* 42°41N 74°29W **313** D10
Coboconk *Canada* 44°39N 78°48W **312** B6
Cobourg *Canada* 43°58N 78°10W **312** C6
Cobourg Pen. *Australia* 11°20S 132°15E **278** B5
Cobram *Australia* 35°54S 145°40E **283** C6
Cobras, I. das *Brazil* 22°53S 43°9W **135** B2
Cóbué *Mozam.* 12°0S 34°58E **269** E3
Coburg *Vic., Australia* 37°44S 144°56E **128** A1
Coburg *Bayern, Germany* 50°15N 10°58E **179** E6
Coburg I. *Canada* 75°57N 79°26W **295** B16
Coca *Spain* 41°13N 4°32W **194** D6
Coca → *Ecuador* 0°29S 76°58W **328** D2
Cocachacra *Peru* 17°5S 71°45W **330** D3
Cocal *Brazil* 3°28S 41°34W **332** B3
Cocanada = Kakinada *India* 16°57N 82°11E **244** F6
Cocentaina *Spain* 38°45N 0°27W **197** G4
Cochabamba *Bolivia* 17°26S 66°10W **331** D4
Coche, I. *Venezuela* 10°47N 63°56W **329** A5
Cochem *Germany* 50°9N 7°9E **179** E3
Cochemane *Mozam.* 17°0S 32°54E **269** F3
Cochin *India* 9°58N 76°20E **245** K3
Cochin China = Nam-Phan *Vietnam* 10°30N 106°0E **237** G6
Cochran *U.S.A.* 32°23N 83°21W **316** C6
Cochrane *Alta., Canada* 51°11N 114°30W **296** C6
Cochrane *Ont., Canada* 49°0N 81°0W **298** C3
Cochrane *Chile* 47°15S 72°33W **336** C2
Cochrane → *Canada* 59°0N 103°40W **297** B8
Cochrane, L. *Chile* 47°10S 72°0W **336** C2
Cochranton *U.S.A.* 41°31N 80°3W **312** E4
Cockburn *Australia* 32°5S 141°0E **282** B4
Cockburn, Canal *Chile* 54°30S 72°0W **336** D2
Cockburn I. *Canada* 45°55N 83°22W **298** C3
Cockburn Ra. *Australia* 15°46S 128°0E **278** C4
Cockermouth *U.K.* 54°40N 3°22W **168** C4
Cocklebiddy *Australia* 32°0S 126°3E **279** F4
Cockpit *Jamaica* 18°16N 77°39W **320** a
Cockpit Country, The *Jamaica* 18°15N 77°45W **320** a
Côco → *Brazil* 9°27S 50°2W **332** C2
Coco → *Cent. Amer.* 15°0N 83°8W **320** D3
Coco, I. del *Pac. Oc.* 5°25N 87°55W **289** G19
Coco, Pta. *Colombia* 2°58N 77°43W **328** C2
Coco Channel *Asia* 13°45N 93°10E **245** H11
Cocoa *U.S.A.* 28°21N 80°44W **317** G9
Cocoa Beach *U.S.A.* 28°19N 80°37W **317** G9
Cocoa Point *Antigua & B.* 17°33N 61°46W **322** c
Cocobeach *Gabon* 0°59N 9°34E **264** B1
Cocoparra △ *Australia* 34°10S 146°12E **283** C7
Cocora *Romania* 44°45N 27°3E **183** F12
Côcos *Brazil* 14°10S 44°33W **333** D3
Côcos → *Brazil* 12°44S 44°48W **333** D3
Cocos B. *Trin. & Tob.* 10°25N 61°2W **323** t
Cocos Basin *Ind. Oc.* 1°0N 94°0E **273** D8
Cocos I. *Guam* 13°14N 144°39E **302** d
Cocos Is. *Ind. Oc.* 12°10S 96°55E **273** F8
Cocos Ridge *Pac. Oc.* 4°0N 88°0W **289** G19
Cocotá *Brazil* 22°48S 43°11W **135** A1
Cod, C. *U.S.A.* 42°5N 70°10W **309** D18
Codajás *Brazil* 3°55S 62°0W **329** D5
Codera, C. *Venezuela* 10°35N 66°4W **328** A4
Codfish I. *N.Z.* 46°47S 167°38E **285** G2
Codigoro *Italy* 44°49N 12°8E **199** D9
Codlea *Romania* 45°42N 25°27E **183** E10
Codó *Brazil* 4°30S 43°55W **332** B3
Codogno *Italy* 45°9N 9°42E **198** C6
Codpa *Chile* 18°50S 69°44W **330** D4
Codrington *Antigua & B.* 17°38N 61°50W **322** c
Codrington Lagoon *Antigua & B.* 17°39N 61°50W **322** c
Codróipo *Italy* 45°58N 13°0E **199** C10
Codru, Munţii *Romania* 46°30N 22°15E **182** D7
Cody *U.S.A.* 44°32N 109°3W **304** D9
Coe Hill *Canada* 44°52N 77°50W **312** B7
Coelemu *Chile* 36°30S 72°48W **334** D1
Coelho Neto *Brazil* 4°15S 43°0W **332** B3
Coen *Australia* 13°52S 143°12E **280** A3
Coeroeni *Suriname* 3°22N 57°21W **329** C6
Coeroeni → *Suriname* 3°21N 57°31W **329** C6
Coesfeld *Germany* 51°56N 7°10E **178** D3
Coetivy Is. *Seychelles* 7°8S 56°16E **273** E4
Cœuilly *France* 48°48N 2°32E **134** B4
Coeur d'Alene *U.S.A.* 47°41N 116°46W **304** C5
Coeur d'Alene L. *U.S.A.* 47°32N 116°49W **304** C5
Coevorden *Neths.* 52°40N 6°44E **170** B6
Cofete *Canary Is.* 28°6N 14°23W **153** e2
Coffeyville *U.S.A.* 37°2N 95°37W **308** G6
Coffin B. *Australia* 34°38S 135°28E **281** E2
Coffin Bay *Australia* 34°37S 135°29E **281** E2
Coffin Bay △ *Australia* 34°34S 135°19E **281** E2
Coffin Bay Peninsula *Australia* 34°32S 135°15E **281** E2
Coffs Harbour *Australia* 30°16S 153°5E **283** A10
Cofrentes *Spain* 39°13N 1°5W **197** F3
Cogalnic = Kohylnyk → *Ukraine* 45°49N 29°40E **183** E14
Cogealac *Romania* 44°36N 28°36E **183** F13
Coghinas → *Italy* 40°55N 8°48E **200** B1
Coghinas, L. del *Italy* 40°46N 9°3E **200** B2
Cognac *France* 45°41N 0°20W **174** C3
Cogne *Italy* 45°37N 7°21E **198** C4
Cogolin *France* 43°15N 6°32E **175** E10
Cogolludo *Spain* 40°59N 3°10W **196** E1
Cohocton *U.S.A.* 42°30N 77°30W **312** D7
Cohocton → *U.S.A.* 42°9N 77°6W **312** D7
Cohoes *U.S.A.* 42°46N 73°42W **313** D11
Cohuna *Australia* 35°45S 144°15E **282** C6
Coiba, I. de *Panama* 7°30N 81°40W **320** E3
Coig → *Argentina* 51°0S 69°10W **336** D3
Coigeach, Rubha *U.K.* 58°6N 5°26W **167** C3
Coihaique *Chile* 45°30S 71°45W **336** C2
Coimbatore *India* 11°2N 76°59E **245** J3
Coimbra *Mato Grosso, Brazil* 19°55S 57°48W **331** D6
Coimbra *Portugal* 40°15N 8°27W **194** E2
Coimbra □ *Portugal* 40°12N 8°25W **194** E2
Coín *Spain* 36°40N 4°48W **195** J6
Coina *Portugal* 38°39N 9°5W **126** B2
Coipasa, L. de *Bolivia* 19°12S 68°7W **330** D4
Coipasa, Salar de *Bolivia* 19°26S 68°9W **330** D4
Coit Tower *San Francisco, U.S.A.* **136** a2
Cojata *Peru* 15°2S 69°25W **330** D4
Cojedes □ *Venezuela* 9°20N 68°20W **328** B4
Cojedes → *Venezuela* 8°34N 68°5W **328** B4
Cojimies *Ecuador* 0°20N 80°0W **328** C1
Cojocna *Romania* 46°45N 23°50E **183** D8
Cojutepequé *El Salv.* 13°41N 88°54W **320** D2
Čoka *Serbia* 45°57N 20°12E **182** E5
Coker *Nigeria* 6°28N 3°20E **124** B2
Cokeville *U.S.A.* 42°5N 110°57W **304** E8
Colaba *India* 18°53N 72°48E **130** B1
Colaba Pt. *India* 18°53N 72°48E **130** B1
Colac *Australia* 38°21S 143°35E **282** E5
Colachel = Kolachel *India* 8°10N 77°15E **245** K3
Colán *Peru* 5°0S 81°0W **330** B1
Colatina *Brazil* 19°32S 40°37W **333** E3
Colbeck, C. *Antarctica* 77°6S 157°48W **151** D13
Colbert *U.S.A.* 34°2N 83°13W **316** A6
Colborne *Canada* 44°0N 77°53W **312** C7
Colby *U.S.A.* 39°24N 101°3W **308** F3
Colca, Cañón del *Peru* 15°50S 72°20W **330** D3
Colchester *Essex, U.K.* 51°54N 0°55E **169** F8
Colchester *Conn., U.S.A.* 41°35N 72°20W **313** E12
Cold Bay *U.S.A.* 55°12N 162°42W **303** J7
Cold L. *Canada* 54°33N 110°5W **297** C7
Cold Lake *Canada* 54°27N 110°10W **297** C6
Coldstream *B.C., Canada* 50°13N 119°11W **296** C5
Coldstream *Borders, U.K.* 55°39N 2°15W **167** F6
Coldwater *Ont., Canada* 44°42N 79°40W **312** B5
Coldwater *Kans., U.S.A.* 37°16N 99°20W **308** G4
Coldwater *Mich., U.S.A.* 41°57N 85°0W **311** C11
Coldwater *Ohio, U.S.A.* 40°29N 84°38W **311** D12
Coldwater, L. *U.S.A.* 41°48N 84°59W **311** C12
Cole Camp *U.S.A.* 38°28N 93°12W **310** F3
Coleambally *Australia* 34°49S 145°52E **283** C6
Colebrook *U.S.A.* 44°54N 71°30W **313** B13
Colegiales *Argentina* 34°34S 58°27W **117** B2
Coleman *Alta., Canada* 49°40N 114°30W **296** D6
Coleman *Fla., U.S.A.* 28°48N 82°4W **317** G7
Coleman *Tex., U.S.A.* 31°50N 99°26W **314** F5
Coleman → *Australia* 15°6S 141°38E **280** B3
Colenso *S. Africa* 28°44S 29°50E **271** C4
Coleraine *Vic., Australia* 37°36S 141°40E **282** D4
Coleraine *L'derry., U.K.* 55°8N 6°41W **166** A5
Coleridge, L. *N.Z.* 43°17S 171°30E **285** D6
Coleroon → *India* 11°25N 79°50E **245** J4
Colesberg *S. Africa* 30°45S 25°5E **270** D4
Coleville *U.S.A.* 38°34N 119°30W **306** G7
Colfax *Calif., U.S.A.* 39°6N 120°57W **306** F6
Colfax *Ill., U.S.A.* 40°34N 88°37W **311** D8
Colfax *Ind., U.S.A.* 40°12N 86°40W **311** D10
Colfax *Iowa, U.S.A.* 41°41N 93°14W **310** C3
Colfax *La., U.S.A.* 31°31N 92°42W **314** F8
Colfax *Wash., U.S.A.* 46°53N 117°22W **304** C5
Colhué Huapi, L. *Argentina* 45°30S 69°0W **336** C3
Colibaşi *Moldova* 45°43N 28°11E **183** E13
Colibaşi *Romania* 44°56N 24°54E **183** F9
Colibris, Pte. des *Guadeloupe* 16°17N 61°5W **322** e
Cólico *Italy* 46°8N 9°22E **198** B6
Colíder *Brazil* 10°45S 55°25W **331** C6
Coligny *Ain, France* 46°23N 5°21E **173** F12
Coligny *North West, S. Africa* 26°17S 26°15E **271** C4
Colihaut *Dominica* 15°29N 61°29W **323** k
Colima *Mexico* 19°14N 103°43W **318** D4
Colima □ *Mexico* 19°10N 104°0W **318** D4
Colima, Nevado de *Mexico* 19°33N 103°38W **318** D4
Colina *Chile* 33°13S 70°45W **334** C1
Colina do Norte *Guinea-Biss.* 12°28N 15°0W **262** C2
Colinas *Goiás, Brazil* 14°15S 48°2W **333** D2
Colinas *Maranhão, Brazil* 6°0S 44°10W **332** C3
Colindale *U.K.* 51°35N 0°15W **125** A2
Colindres *Spain* 43°24N 3°27W **194** B7
Colinton *U.K.* 55°55N 3°14W **121** B2
Coll *U.K.* 56°39N 6°34W **167** E2
Collahuasi *Chile* 21°5S 68°45W **334** A2
Collarada, Peña *Spain* 42°43N 0°29W **196** C4
Collarenebri *Australia* 29°33S 148°34E **281** D4
Colle di Val d'Elsa *Italy* 43°25N 11°7E **198** E8
Collécchio *Italy* 44°45N 10°13E **198** D7
Colleen Bawn *Zimbabwe* 21°0S 29°12E **269** G2
College *U.S.A.* 64°52N 147°49W **303** D11
College Park *Ga., U.S.A.* 33°39N 84°27W **113** C2
College Park *Md., U.S.A.* 38°59N 76°55W **143** B4

College Point *U.S.A.* 40°47N 73°50W **132** B2
College Station *U.S.A.* 30°37N 96°21W **314** F6
Collégien *France* 48°50N 2°41E **134** A4
Collesalvetti *Italy* 43°34N 10°27E **198** E7
Colli Euganei ⌓ *Italy* 45°18N 11°43E **199** C8
Collie *N.S.W., Australia* 31°41S 148°18E **283** A8
Collie *W. Austral., Australia* 33°22S 116°8E **279** F2
Collier B. *Australia* 16°10S 124°15E **278** C3
Collier Ra. *Australia* 24°45S 119°10E **279** D2
Collier Range △ *Australia* 24°39S 119°7E **279** D2
Collier Row *U.K.* 51°35N 0°9E **125** A4
Colliers Wood *U.K.* 51°24N 0°10W **125** B2
Collierville *U.S.A.* 35°3N 89°40W **315** D10
Collina, Passo di *Italy* 44°2N 10°56E **198** D7
Collingwood *Ont., Canada* 44°29N 80°13W **312** B4
Collingwood *N.Z.* 40°41S 172°40E **285** A7
Collins *Ont., Canada* 50°17N 89°27W **298** B2
Collins *Ga., U.S.A.* 32°11N 82°7W **316** C7
Collins *Mo., U.S.A.* 37°54N 93°37W **310** G3
Collins Bay *Canada* 44°14N 76°36W **313** B8
Collinson Pen. *Canada* 69°58N 101°24W **294** D11
Collinsville *Queens., Australia* 20°30S 147°56E **280** C4
Collinsville *Ill., U.S.A.* 38°40N 89°59W **310** F7
Collipulli *Chile* 37°55S 72°30W **334** D1
Collo *Algeria* 36°58N 6°37E **261** A6
Collooney *Ireland* 54°11N 8°29W **166** B3
Colma *U.S.A.* 37°40N 122°27W **136** B2
Colmar *France* 48°5N 7°20E **173** D14
Colmars *France* 44°11N 6°39E **175** D10
Colmenar *Spain* 36°54N 4°20W **195** J6
Colmenar de Oreja *Spain* 40°6N 3°25W **194** E7
Colmenar Viejo *Spain* 40°39N 3°47W **194** E7
Colney Hatch *U.K.* 51°36N 0°9W **125** A3
Colo → *Australia* 33°25S 150°52E **283** B9
Cologne = Köln *Germany* 50°56N 6°57E **178** E2
Cologno Monzese *Italy* 45°31N 9°16E **129** A2
Colom, I. d'en *Spain* 39°58N 4°16E **206** B5
Coloma *Calif., U.S.A.* 38°48N 120°53W **306** G6
Coloma *Mich., U.S.A.* 42°11N 86°19W **311** B10
Colomb-Béchar = Béchar *Algeria* 31°38N 2°18W **261** B4
Colombes *France* 48°55N 2°15E **134** A2
Colombey-les-Belles *France* 48°32N 5°54E **173** D12
Colombey-les-Deux-Églises *France* 48°13N 4°50E **173** D11
Colômbia *Brazil* 20°10S 48°40W **333** F2
Colombia ■ *S. Amer.* 3°45N 73°0W **328** C3
Colombian Basin *Caribbean* 14°0N 76°0W **321** D5
Colombier *St.-Martin* 18°5N 63°4W **322** a
Colombo *Sri Lanka* 6°56N 79°58E **245** L4
Colomiers *France* 43°36N 1°21E **174** E5
Colón *B. Aires, Argentina* 33°53S 61°7W **334** C3
Colón *Entre Ríos, Argentina* 32°12S 58°10W **334** C4
Colón *Cuba* 22°42N 80°54W **320** B3
Colón *Panama* 9°20N 79°54W **320** c
Colón, Arch. de *Ecuador* 0°0 91°0W **330** a
Colón, Monumente a *Barcelona, Spain* **114** c3
Colon, Plaza de *Madrid, Spain* **127** a3
Colón Ridge *Pac. Oc.* 2°0N 96°0W **289** G18
Colonarie *St. Vincent* 13°14N 61°8W **323** n
Colonia *Micronesia* 9°30N 138°10E **287** R16
Colonia 25 de Mayo *Argentina* 37°48S 67°41W **336** A3
Colònia de Sant Jordi *Spain* 39°19N 2°59E **206** B3
Colonia del Sacramento *Uruguay* 34°25S 57°50W **334** C4
Colonia Dora *Argentina* 28°34S 62°59W **334** B3
Colonia Güell *Spain* 41°21N 2°2E **114** A1
Colonial Beach *U.S.A.* 38°15N 76°58W **309** F15
Colonial Knob *N.Z.* 41°9S 174°48E **143** A1
Colonie *U.S.A.* 42°43N 73°50W **313** D11
Colonna, C. *Italy* 39°2N 17°12E **201** C10
Colonsay *Sask., Canada* 51°59N 105°52W **297** C7
Colonsay *Argyll & Bute, U.K.* 56°5N 6°12W **167** E2
Colorado □ *U.S.A.* 39°30N 105°30W **304** G11
Colorado → *Argentina* 39°50S 62°8W **336** A4
Colorado → *N. Amer.* 31°45N 114°40W **305** L6
Colorado → *Tex., U.S.A.* 28°36N 95°59W **314** G7
Colorado City *U.S.A.* 32°24N 100°52W **314** E4
Colorado Plateau *U.S.A.* 37°0N 111°0W **305** H8
Colorado River Aqueduct *U.S.A.* 33°50N 117°23W **307** L12
Colorado Springs *U.S.A.* 38°50N 104°49W **304** G11
Colorno *Italy* 44°56N 10°23E **198** D7
Colosseo *Rome, Italy* **136** c3
Colosseum = Colosseo *Rome, Italy* **136** c3
Colotlán *Mexico* 22°6N 103°16W **318** C4
Colquechaca *Bolivia* 18°40S 66°1W **331** D4
Colquitt *U.S.A.* 31°10N 84°44W **316** D5
Colstrip *U.S.A.* 45°53N 106°38W **304** D10
Colton *U.S.A.* 44°33N 74°56W **313** B10
Columbia *Ala., U.S.A.* 31°18N 85°7W **316** D4
Columbia *Ill., U.S.A.* 38°27N 90°12W **310** F6
Columbia *Ky., U.S.A.* 37°6N 85°18W **309** G11
Columbia *La., U.S.A.* 32°6N 92°5W **314** E8
Columbia *Miss., U.S.A.* 31°15N 89°50W **315** F10
Columbia *Mo., U.S.A.* 38°57N 92°20W **310** F4
Columbia *Pa., U.S.A.* 40°2N 76°30W **313** F8
Columbia *S.C., U.S.A.* 34°0N 81°2W **316** A8
Columbia *Tenn., U.S.A.* 35°37N 87°2W **315** D11
Columbia → *N. Amer.* 46°15N 124°5W **306** D2
Columbia, C. *Canada* 83°6N 69°57W **295** A18
Columbia, District of □ *U.S.A.* 38°55N 77°0W **309** F15
Columbia, Mt. *Canada* 52°8N 117°20W **296** C5
Columbia Basin *U.S.A.* 46°45N 119°5W **304** C4
Columbia City *U.S.A.* 41°10N 85°29W **311** C11
Columbia Falls *U.S.A.* 48°23N 114°11W **304** B6
Columbia Mts. *Canada* 52°0N 119°0W **296** C5
Columbia Plateau *U.S.A.* 44°0N 117°30W **304** E5
Columbiana *U.S.A.* 40°53N 80°42W **312** F4
Columbretes, Is. *Spain* 39°50N 0°50E **196** F5
Columbus *Ga., U.S.A.* 32°28N 84°59W **316** C5
Columbus *Ind., U.S.A.* 39°13N 85°55W **311** E11
Columbus *Kans., U.S.A.* 37°10N 94°50W **308** G6
Columbus *Miss., U.S.A.* 33°30N 88°25W **315** E10
Columbus *Mont., U.S.A.* 45°38N 109°15W **304** D9
Columbus *N. Mex., U.S.A.* 31°50N 107°38W **305** L10
Columbus *Nebr., U.S.A.* 41°26N 97°22W **308** E5
Columbus *Ohio, U.S.A.* 39°58N 83°0W **311** E13
Columbus *Tex., U.S.A.* 29°42N 96°33W **314** G6
Columbus Circle *Washington, D.C., U.S.A.* **143** b3
Columbus Circle *New York, U.S.A.* **132** b2
Columbus Grove *U.S.A.* 40°55N 84°4W **311** D12
Columbus Junction *U.S.A.* 41°17N 91°22W **310** C5
Columbus Monument = Colón, Monumente a *Barcelona, Spain* **114** c3
Columbus Park *Jamaica* 18°28N 77°25W **320** a
Columbus Park *Boston, U.S.A.* **116** b3
Colunga *Spain* 43°29N 5°16W **194** B5
Colusa *U.S.A.* 39°13N 122°1W **306** F4
Colville *U.S.A.* 48°33N 117°54W **304** B5
Colville → *U.S.A.* 70°25N 150°30W **303** A10
Colville, C. *N.Z.* 36°29S 175°21E **284** C4
Colville Channel *N.Z.* 36°25S 175°27E **284** C4
Colville Ridge *Pac. Oc.* 30°0S 180°0E **277** G15
Colwood *Canada* 48°26N 123°29W **306** B3
Colwyn Bay *U.K.* 53°18N 3°44W **168** D4
Coma *Ethiopia* 8°29N 36°53E **257** F4
Comácchio *Italy* 44°42N 12°11E **199** D9
Comalcalco *Mexico* 18°16N 93°13W **319** D6
Comallo *Argentina* 41°0S 70°5W **336** B2
Comana *Romania* 44°10N 26°10E **183** F11
Comanche *U.S.A.* 31°54N 98°36W **314** F5
Comandante Arbues = Mirandópolis *Brazil* 21°9S 51°6W **335** A5
Comandante Ferraz *Antarctica* 62°30S 58°0W **151** C18
Comandante Luis Piedrabuena *Argentina* 49°59S 68°54W **336** C3
Comănești *Romania* 46°25N 26°26E **183** D11
Comarapa *Bolivia* 17°54S 64°29W **331** D5
Comarnic *Romania* 45°15N 25°38E **183** E10
Comayagua *Honduras* 14°25N 87°37W **320** D2
Combahee → *U.S.A.* 32°31N 80°31W **315** E14
Combara *Australia* 31°10S 148°22E **283** A8
Combarbalá *Chile* 31°11S 71°2W **334** C1
Combault *France* 48°48N 2°37E **134** B4
Combe Martin *U.K.* 51°12N 4°3W **169** F3
Combeaufontaine *France* 47°38N 5°54E **173** E12
Comber *Ont., Canada* 42°14N 82°33W **312** D2
Comber *Down, U.K.* 54°33N 5°45W **166** B6
Combermere *Canada* 45°22N 77°37W **312** A7
Combermere Bay *Burma* 19°37N 93°34E **241** F4
Comblain-au-Pont *Belgium* 50°29N 5°35E **170** D5
Combourg *France* 48°25N 1°46W **172** D5
Comboyne *Australia* 31°34S 152°27E **283** A10
Combrailles *France* 46°8N 2°8E **173** F9
Combronde *France* 45°58N 3°5E **174** C7
Comer *Ala., U.S.A.* 32°2N 85°23W **316** C4
Comer *Ga., U.S.A.* 34°4N 83°8W **316** A6
Comeragh Mts. *Ireland* 52°18N 7°34W **166** D4
Comércio, Praça do *Portugal* 38°41N 9°9W **126** A2
Comerío *Puerto Rico* 18°12N 66°12W **321** b
Comet *Australia* 23°36S 148°38E **280** C4
Comilla *Bangla.* 23°28N 91°10E **241** D3
Comino *Malta* 36°1N 14°20E **206** E7
Comino, C. *Italy* 40°32N 9°49E **200** B2
Cómiso *Italy* 36°56N 14°36E **201** F7
Comitán de Domínguez *Mexico* 16°15N 92°8W **319** D6
Commentry *France* 46°20N 2°46E **173** F9
Commerce *Calif., U.S.A.* 34°0N 118°9W **126** B4
Commerce *Ga., U.S.A.* 34°12N 83°28W **315** D13
Commerce *Tex., U.S.A.* 33°15N 95°54W **314** E7
Commercy *France* 48°43N 5°34E **173** D12
Commissioner's Pt. *Bermuda* 32°19N 64°49W **153** a
Committee B. *Canada* 68°30N 86°30W **295** D14
Commodore, C. *Canada* 44°47N 80°54W **312** B4
Commonwealth B. *Antarctica* 67°0S 144°0E **151** C10
Commoron Cr. → *Australia* 28°22S 150°8E **281** D5
Communism Pk. = imeni Ismail Samani, Pik *Tajikistan* 39°0N 72°2E **217** E8
Como *Italy* 45°47N 9°5E **198** C6
Como, Lago di *Italy* 46°0N 9°11E **198** B6
Comodoro Rivadavia *Argentina* 45°50S 67°40W **336** C3
Comoé → *Ivory C.* 5°12N 3°44W **262** D4
Comoé △ *Ivory C.* 9°0N 3°35W **262** D4
Comorâște *Romania* 45°10N 21°35E **182** E6
Comorin, C. = Kannyakumari *India* 8°3N 77°40E **245** K3
Comoros ■ *Ind. Oc.* 12°10S 44°15E **272** a
Comox *Canada* 49°42N 124°55W **296** D4
Company's Gardens *Cape Town, S. Africa* **118** c2
Compass Lake *U.S.A.* 30°36N 85°24W **316** E4
Compiègne *France* 49°24N 2°50E **173** C9
Comporta *Portugal* 38°22N 8°46W **195** G2
Compostela *Nayarit, Mexico* 21°14N 104°55W **318** C4
Compostela *Phil.* 7°40N 126°2E **233** H6
Comprida, I. *Brazil* 24°50S 47°42W **335** A6
Compton *Qué., Canada* 45°14N 71°49W **313** A13
Compton *Calif., U.S.A.* 33°53N 118°13W **307** M8
Comrat *Moldova* 46°18N 28°40E **183** D13
Comunidad *Peru* 13°59S 69°20W **330** C4
Con Cuong *Vietnam* 19°2N 104°54E **236** C5
Con Dao △ *Vietnam* 8°42N 106°35E **237** H6
Con Son, Dao *Vietnam* 8°41N 106°37E **237** H6
Cona Niyeu *Argentina* 41°58S 67°0W **336** B3
Conakry *Guinea* 9°29N 13°49W **262** D2
Conara *Australia* 41°50S 147°26E **281** G4
Conargo *Australia* 35°16S 145°10E **283** C6
Concarneau *France* 47°52N 3°56W **172** E3
Conceição *Paraíba, Brazil* 7°33S 38°31W **332** C4
Conceição *Mozam.* 18°47S 36°7E **269** F4
Conceição, I. da *Brazil* 22°52S 43°6W **135** B2
Conceição da Barra *Brazil* 18°35S 39°45W **333** E4
Conceição do Araguaia *Brazil* 8°0S 49°2W **332** C2
Conceição do Canindé *Brazil* 7°54S 41°34W **332** C3
Conceição do Maú *Brazil* 3°35N 59°53W **329** C6
Conceição do Paraíba = Capela *Brazil* 10°30S 37°0W **332** D4
Concepción *Argentina* 27°20S 65°35W **334** B2
Concepción *Bolivia* 16°15S 62°8W **331** D5
Concepción *Chile* 36°50S 73°0W **334** D1
Concepción *Mexico* 18°15N 90°5W **319** D6
Concepción *Paraguay* 23°22S 57°26W **334** A4
Concepción *Peru* 11°54S 75°19W **330** C2
Concepcion *Tarlac, Phil.* 15°27N 120°47E **232** D3
Concepción □ *Chile* 37°0S 72°30W **334** D1
Concepción → *Mexico* 30°32N 113°2W **318** A2
Concepción, Est. de *Chile* 50°30S 74°55W **336** D2
Concepción, L. *Bolivia* 17°20S 61°20W **331** D5
Concepción, Pta. *Mexico* 26°53N 111°50W **318** B2
Concepción del Oro *Mexico* 24°38N 101°25W **318** C4
Concepción del Uruguay *Argentina* 32°35S 58°20W **334** C4
Conception, Pt. *U.S.A.* 34°27N 120°28W **307** L6
Conception B. *Nfld. & L., Canada* 47°45N 53°0W **299** C9
Conception B. *Namibia* 23°55S 14°22E **270** B1
Conception I. *Bahamas* 23°52N 75°9W **321** B4
Concession *Zimbabwe* 17°27S 30°56E **269** F3
Conchalí *Chile* 33°22S 70°39W **137** B2
Conchas Dam *U.S.A.* 35°22N 104°11W **305** J11
Conches-en-Ouche *France* 48°58N 0°56E **172** D7
Concho *U.S.A.* 34°28N 109°36W **305** J9
Concho → *U.S.A.* 31°34N 99°43W **314** F5
Conchos → *Chihuahua, Mexico* 29°35N 104°25W **318** B4
Conchos → *Chihuahua, Mexico* 27°29N 106°45W **318** B3
Conchos → *Tamaulipas, Mexico* 24°55N 97°38W **319** B5
Concord *N.S.W., Australia* 33°51S 151°6E **139** B1
Concord *Ont., Canada* 43°48N 79°29W **141** A2
Concord *Grenada* 12°11N 61°44W **323** q
Concord *Calif., U.S.A.* 37°59N 122°2W **306** H4
Concord *Ga., U.S.A.* 33°5N 84°27W **316** B5
Concord *Mich., U.S.A.* 42°11N 84°38W **311** B12
Concord *Mo., U.S.A.* 38°32N 90°23W **310** F6
Concord *N.C., U.S.A.* 35°25N 80°35W **315** D14
Concord *N.H., U.S.A.* 43°12N 71°32W **313** C13
Concorde, Place de la *Paris, France* **134** b3
Concordia *Antarctica* 75°6S 123°23E **151** D9
Concordia *Argentina* 31°20S 58°2W **334** C4
Concórdia *Amazonas, Brazil* 4°36S 66°36W **328** D4
Concórdia *Sta. Catarina, Brazil* 27°14S 52°1W **335** B5
Concordia *Sinaloa, Mexico* 23°17N 106°4W **318** C3
Concordia *Kans., U.S.A.* 39°34N 97°40W **308** F5
Concordia *Mo., U.S.A.* 38°59N 93°34W **310** F3
Concordia Univ. *Montréal, Canada* **130** c1
Concorezzo *Italy* 45°35N 9°19E **129** A2
Concrete *U.S.A.* 48°32N 121°45W **304** B3
Conda *Angola* 11°9S 14°20E **265** E2
Condah *Australia* 37°57S 141°44E **282** D4
Condamine *Australia* 26°56S 150°9E **281** D5
Condat *France* 45°21N 2°46E **174** C6
Condé *Angola* 10°50S 14°37E **265** E2
Conde *Brazil* 11°49S 37°37W **333** D4
Conde *S. Dak., U.S.A.* 45°9N 98°6W **308** C4
Condé-sur-Noireau *France* 48°51N 0°33W **172** D6
Condet *Indonesia* 6°17S 106°51E **122** A2
Condeúba *Brazil* 14°52S 42°0W **333** D3
Condobolin *Australia* 33°4S 147°6E **283** B7
Condom *France* 43°57N 0°22E **174** E4
Condon *U.S.A.* 45°14N 120°11W **304** D3
Conegliano *Italy* 45°53N 12°18E **199** C9
Conejera, I. = Conills, I. des *Spain* 39°11N 2°58E **206** B3
Conejos *Mexico* 26°14N 103°53W **318** B4
Conemaugh → *U.S.A.* 40°28N 79°19W **312** F5
Conero ⌓ *Italy* 43°32N 13°35E **199** E10
Coney Island *U.S.A.* 40°34N 74°0W **132** C2
Conflict Group *Papua N. G.* 10°47S 151°45E **286** F6
Confolens *France* 46°2N 0°40E **174** B4
Confuso → *Paraguay* 25°9S 57°34W **334** B4
Congaree → *U.S.A.* 33°44N 80°38W **316** B9
Congaree △ *U.S.A.* 33°47N 80°47W **316** B9
Congaz *Moldova* 46°7N 28°36E **183** D13
Congerville *U.S.A.* 40°38N 89°12W **310** D7
Conghua *China* 23°36N 113°31E **229** F9
Congjiang *China* 25°43N 108°52E **228** E7
Congleton *U.K.* 53°10N 2°13W **168** D5
Congo *Brazil* 7°48S 36°40W **332** C4
Congo (Brazzaville) = Congo ■ *Africa* 1°0S 16°0E **264** C3
Congo (Kinshasa) = Congo, Dem. Rep. of the ■ *Africa* 3°0S 23°0E **265** C4
Congo ■ *Africa* 1°0S 16°0E **264** C3
Congo → *Africa* 6°4S 12°24E **265** D2
Congo, Dem. Rep. of the ■ *Africa* 3°0S 23°0E **265** C4
Congo Basin *Africa* 0°10S 24°30E **254** G6
Congo Free State = Congo, Dem. Rep. of the ■ *Africa* 3°0S 23°0E **265** C4
Congonhas *Brazil* 20°30S 43°52W **333** F3
Congonhas São Paulo ✕ **(CGH)** *Brazil* 23°38S 46°39W **137** B2
Congress *U.S.A.* 34°9N 112°51W **305** J7
Conguillio △ *Chile* 38°40S 71°42W **336** A2
Conil de la Frontera *Spain* 36°17N 6°10W **195** J4
Conills, I. des *Spain* 39°11N 2°58E **206** B3
Conimbla △ *Australia* 33°45S 148°28E **283** B8
Coniston *Canada* 46°29N 80°51W **298** C3
Conjeeveram = Kanchipuram *India* 12°52N 79°45E **245** H4
Conklin *Alta., Canada* 55°38N 111°5W **297** B6
Conklin *N.Y., U.S.A.* 42°2N 75°49W **313** D9
Conkouati ⌓ *Congo* 3°50S 11°28E **264** C2
Conlendas, Pta. das *Azores* 38°38N 27°14W **153** d1
Conley → *U.S.A.* 33°40N 84°17W **113** C3
Conn, L. *Ireland* 54°3N 9°15W **166** B2
Connacht □ *Ireland* 53°43N 9°12W **166** C2
Connaught Place *Delhi, India* **120** b2
Conneaut *U.S.A.* 41°57N 80°34W **312** E4
Conneautville *U.S.A.* 41°45N 80°22W **312** E4
Connecticut □ *U.S.A.* 41°30N 72°45W **313** E12
Connecticut → *U.S.A.* 41°16N 72°20W **313** E12
Connell *U.S.A.* 46°40N 118°52W **304** C4
Connellsville *U.S.A.* 40°1N 79°35W **312** F5
Connemara *Ireland* 53°29N 9°45W **166** C2
Connemara △ *Ireland* 53°32N 9°52W **166** C2
Conner *Phil.* 17°48N 121°19E **232** C3
Connerré *France* 48°3N 0°30E **172** D7
Connersville *U.S.A.* 39°39N 85°8W **311** E11
Connors Ra. *Australia* 21°40S 149°10E **280** C4
Conoble *Australia* 32°55S 144°33E **283** B6
Conococha *Peru* 10°7S 77°18W **330** C2
Cononaco → *Ecuador* 1°32S 75°35W **328** D3
Conques *France* 44°36N 2°23E **174** D6
Conquest *Canada* 51°32N 107°14W **297** C7
Conquista = Vitória da Conquista *Brazil* 14°51S 40°51W **333** D3
Conrad *Iowa, U.S.A.* 42°14N 92°52W **310** B4
Conrad *Mont., U.S.A.* 48°10N 111°57W **304** B8
Conrad Rise *S. Ocean* 53°0S 41°0E **151** B5
Conran, C. *Australia* 37°49S 148°44E **283** D8
Conroe *U.S.A.* 30°19N 95°27W **314** F7
Consecon *Canada* 44°0N 77°31W **312** C7
Conselheiro Lafaiete *Brazil* 20°40S 43°48W **333** F3
Conselheiro Pena *Brazil* 19°10S 41°30W **333** E3
Consell *Spain* 39°40N 2°49E **206** B3
Conselve *Italy* 45°14N 11°52E **199** C8
Conservatori, Palazzo dei *Rome, Italy* **136** c3
Consett *U.K.* 54°51N 1°50W **168** C6
Consolação *Brazil* 23°32S 46°38W **137** B2
Consort *Canada* 52°1N 110°46W **297** C6
Constance = Konstanz *Germany* 47°40N 9°10E **179** H5
Constance, L. = Bodensee *Europe* 47°35N 9°25E **179** H5
Constanța *Romania* 44°14N 28°38E **183** F13
Constanța □ *Romania* 44°15N 28°15E **183** F13
Constantia *S. Africa* 34°2S 18°26E **118** B1
Constantina *Spain* 37°51N 5°40W **195** H5
Constantine *Algeria* 36°25N 6°42E **261** A6
Constantine *Mich., U.S.A.* 41°50N 85°40W **311** C11
Constantine □ *Algeria* 36°30N 6°40E **261** A6
Constantine, Arch of = Costantino, Arco di *Rome, Italy* **136** c3
Constantine, C. *U.S.A.* 58°24N 158°54W **303** G8
Constantinople = İstanbul *Turkey* 41°0N 28°58E **122** C1
Constitución *B. Aires, Argentina* 34°38S 58°23W **117** B2
Constitución *Chile* 35°20S 72°30W **334** D1
Constitución *Uruguay* 31°0S 57°50W **334** C4
Constitución de 1857 △ *Mexico* 32°4N 115°55W **318** A1
Constitution *U.S.A.* 33°42N 84°20W **113** B2
Constitution Avenue *Washington, D.C., U.S.A.* **143** b2
Constitution Square = Syntagma Square *Athens, Greece* **112** b2
Consuegra *Spain* 39°28N 3°36W **195** F7
Consul *Canada* 49°20N 109°30W **297** D7
Contact *U.S.A.* 41°46N 114°45W **304** F6
Contagem *Brazil* 19°55S 44°5W **333** E3
Contai *India* 21°54N 87°46E **243** J12
Contamana *Peru* 7°19S 74°55W **330** B3
Contarina *Italy* 45°1N 12°13E **199** C9
Contas → *Brazil* 14°17S 39°1W **333** D4
Contes *France* 43°49N 7°19E **175** E11
Continental *U.S.A.* 41°6N 84°16W **311** C12
Contoocook *U.S.A.* 43°13N 71°45W **313** C13
Contra Costa *Mozam.* 25°9S 33°30E **271** C5
Contres *France* 47°24N 1°26E **172** E8
Contrexéville *France* 48°10N 5°53E **173** D12
Controller B. *U.S.A.* 60°7N 144°15W **303** F11
Contumaza *Peru* 7°23S 78°57W **330** B2
Contwoyto L. *Canada* 65°42N 110°50W **294** D9
Convención *Colombia* 8°28N 73°21W **328** B3
Convention Center *U.S.A.* 34°3N 118°16W **126** B3
Conversano *Italy* 40°58N 17°7E **201** B10
Converse *U.S.A.* 40°35N 85°52W **311** D11
Convoy *U.S.A.* 40°55N 84°43W **311** D12
Conway = Conwy *U.K.* 53°17N 3°50W **168** D4
Conway = Conwy → *U.K.* 53°17N 3°50W **168** D4
Conway *Australia* 20°24S 148°41E **280** b
Conway *Ont., Canada* 44°6N 76°54W **312** B8
Conway *Ark., U.S.A.* 35°5N 92°26W **314** D8
Conway *Fla., U.S.A.* 28°30N 81°19W **133** B2
Conway *N.H., U.S.A.* 43°59N 71°7W **313** C13
Conway *S.C., U.S.A.* 33°51N 79°3W **315** E15
Conway, C. *Australia* 20°34S 148°46E **280** b
Conway, L. *S. Austral., Australia* 28°17S 135°35E **281** D2
Conway, L. *Fla., U.S.A.* 28°28N 81°21W **133** B2
Conwy *U.K.* 53°17N 3°50W **168** D4
Conwy □ *U.K.* 53°10N 3°44W **168** D4
Conwy → *U.K.* 53°17N 3°50W **168** D4
Conyers *U.S.A.* 33°40N 84°1W **316** B5
Coober Pedy *Australia* 29°1S 134°43E **281** D1
Cooch Behar = Koch Bihar *India* 26°22N 89°29E **241** B2
Coogee *Australia* 33°55S 151°16E **139** B2
Cooinda *Australia* 13°15S 130°5E **278** B5
Cook *S. Austral., Australia* 30°37S 130°25E **279** F5
Cook *Minn., U.S.A.* 47°51N 92°41W **308** B7
Cook, B. *Chile* 55°10S 70°0W **336** E3
Cook, C. *Canada* 50°8N 127°55W **296** C3
Cook, Mt. = Aoraki Mount Cook *N.Z.* 43°36S 170°9E **285** D5
Cook, Récif de *N. Cal.* 19°25S 163°50E **288** d
Cook B. *Vanuatu* 18°46S 169°15E **287** H7
Cook Inlet *U.S.A.* 60°0N 152°0W **303** G10
Cook Is. ☒ *Pac. Oc.* 17°0S 160°0W **289** J12
Cook Strait *N.Z.* 41°15S 174°29E **284** H3
Cooke Plains *Australia* 35°23S 139°34E **282** C3
Cookeville *U.S.A.* 36°10N 85°30W **315** C12
Cookhouse *S. Africa* 32°44S 25°47E **270** D4
Cooks Hammock *U.S.A.* 29°56N 83°17W **316** F6
Cooks Harbour *Canada* 51°36N 55°52W **299** B8
Cookshire *Canada* 45°25N 71°38W **313** A13
Cookstown *Ont., Canada* 44°11N 79°42W **312** B5
Cookstown *Tyrone, U.K.* 54°39N 6°45W **166** B5
Cooksville *Canada* 43°35N 79°38W **141** B1
Cooktown *Australia* 15°30S 145°16E **280** B4
Coolabah *Australia* 31°1S 146°43E **283** A7
Cooladdi *Australia* 26°37S 145°23E **281** D4
Coolah *Australia* 31°48S 149°41E **283** A8
Coolah Tops △ *Australia* 31°52S 150°0E **283** A9
Coolamon *Australia* 34°46S 147°8E **283** C7
Coolgardie *Australia* 30°55S 121°8E **279** F3
Coolidge *Ariz., U.S.A.* 32°59N 111°31W **305** K8
Coolidge *Ga., U.S.A.* 31°1N 83°52W **316** D6
Coolidge Dam *U.S.A.* 33°10N 110°32W **305** K8
Coolock *Ireland* 53°22N 6°12W **120** A2
Cooma *Australia* 36°12S 149°8E **283** D8
Coon Rapids *Iowa, U.S.A.* 41°53N 94°41W **310** C2
Coon Rapids *Minn., U.S.A.* 45°9N 93°19W **308** C7
Coonabarabran *Australia* 31°14S 149°18E **283** A8
Coonalpyn *Australia* 35°43S 139°52E **282** C3
Coonamble *Australia* 30°56S 148°27E **283** A8
Coonana *Australia* 31°0S 123°0E **279** F3
Coonana ☼ *Australia* 30°51S 122°53E **279** F3
Condapoor *India* 13°42N 74°40E **245** H2
Coondapoor *India* 13°42N 74°40E **245** H2
Coongie L. *Australia* 27°9S 140°8E **281** D3
Coonninie, L. *Australia* 26°4S 139°59E **281** D2
Coonoor *India* 11°21N 76°45E **245** J3
Cooper *U.S.A.* 33°23N 95°42W **314** E7
Cooper → *U.S.A.* 32°50N 79°56W **316** C10
Cooper Cr. → *Australia* 28°29S 137°46E **281** D2
Cooper Ridge *Pac. Oc.* 10°0N 150°30W **289** G12
Cooper's Hill *Jamaica* 18°4N 76°51W **320** a
Cooperstown *N. Dak., U.S.A.* 47°27N 98°8W **308** B4
Cooperstown *N.Y., U.S.A.* 42°42N 74°56W **313** D10
Coopersville *U.S.A.* 43°4N 85°57W **311** A11
Coopracambra △ *Australia* 37°20S 149°20E **283** D8
Coora → *Trin. & Tob.* 10°10N 61°28W **323** t
Coorabie *Australia* 31°54S 132°18E **279** F5
Coorong, The *Australia* 35°50S 139°20E **282** C3
Coorong △ *Australia* 36°0S 139°29E **282** D3
Coorow *Australia* 29°53S 116°2E **279** E2
Cooroy *Australia* 26°22S 152°54E **281** D5
Coos Bay *U.S.A.* 43°22N 124°13W **304** E1
Coosa → *U.S.A.* 32°30N 86°16W **315** E11
Cootamundra *Australia* 34°36S 148°1E **283** C8
Cootehill *Ireland* 54°4N 7°5W **166** B4
Copacabana *Brazil* 22°58S 43°11W **135** B1
Copahue Paso *Argentina* 37°49S 71°8W **334** D1
Copainalá *Mexico* 17°4N 93°12W **319** D6
Copake *U.S.A.* 42°7N 73°31W **313** D11
Copalnic Mănăștur *Romania* 47°30N 23°41E **183** C8
Copán *Honduras* 14°50N 89°9W **320** D2
Copatana *Brazil* 2°48S 67°4W **328** D4
Cope *Colo., U.S.A.* 39°40N 102°51W **304** G12
Cope *S.C., U.S.A.* 33°23N 81°0W **316** B8
Cope, C. *Spain* 37°26N 1°28W **197** H3
Copeland *U.S.A.* 25°57N 81°22W **317** K8
Copenhagen = København *Denmark* 55°40N 12°26E **118** A2
Copenhagen *U.S.A.* 43°54N 75°41W **313** C9
Copertino *Italy* 40°16N 18°3E **201** B11
Copiapó *Chile* 27°30S 70°20W **334** B1
Copiapó → *Chile* 27°19S 70°56W **334** B1
Coplay *U.S.A.* 40°44N 75°29W **313** F9
Copley *Australia* 30°36S 138°26E **282** A3
Copo △ *Argentina* 25°53S 61°41W **334** B3
Copp L. *Canada* 60°14N 114°40W **296** A6
Copparo *Italy* 44°54N 11°49E **199** D8
Coppename → *Suriname* 5°48N 55°55W **329** B6
Copper → *U.S.A.* 60°18N 145°3W **303** F11
Copper Canyon = Barranca del Cobre ⌓ *Mexico* 27°18N 107°40W **318** B3
Copper Center *U.S.A.* 61°58N 145°18W **303** F11
Copper City = Invermere *Canada* 50°30N 116°2W **296** C5
Copper Harbor *U.S.A.* 47°28N 87°53W **308** B10
Copper Queen *Zimbabwe* 17°29S 29°18E **269** F2
Copperas Cove *U.S.A.* 31°8N 97°54W **314** F6
Copperbelt □ *Zambia* 13°15S 27°30E **269** E2
Coppermine = Kugluktuk *Canada* 67°50N 115°5W **294** D8
Coppermine → *Canada* 67°49N 116°4W **294** D8
Copperopolis *U.S.A.* 37°58N 120°38W **306** H6
Copșa Mică *Romania* 46°7N 24°15E **183** D9
Coquet → *U.K.* 55°20N 1°32W **168** B6
Coquilhatville = Mbandaka *Dem. Rep. of the Congo* 0°1N 18°18E **264** B3
Coquille *U.S.A.* 43°11N 124°11W **304** E1
Coquimbo *Chile* 30°0S 71°20W **334** C1
Coquimbo □ *Chile* 31°0S 71°0W **334** C1
Coquitlam *Canada* 49°17N 122°45W **296** D4
Corabia *Romania* 43°48N 24°30E **183** G9
Coração de Jesus *Brazil* 16°43S 44°22W **333** E3
Coracora *Peru* 15°5S 73°45W **330** D3
Coraki *Australia* 28°59S 153°17E **281** D5
Coral *U.S.A.* 40°29N 79°10W **312** F5
Coral B. *Phil.* 8°25N 117°20E **233** G1
Coral Bay *Australia* 23°8S 113°46E **278** D1
Coral Gables *U.S.A.* 25°43N 80°16W **128** B2
Coral Harbour *Bahamas* 24°58N 77°28W **153** b
Coral Harbour *Nunavut, Canada* 64°8N 83°10W **295** E15
Coral Heights *Bahamas* 25°0N 77°27W **153** b
Coral Hills *U.S.A.* 38°51N 76°55W **143** B4
Coral Sea *Pac. Oc.* 15°0S 150°0E **286** F4
Coral Sea Basin *Pac. Oc.* 14°0S 152°0E **288** J7
Coral Sea Islands Terr. □ *Australia* 20°0S 155°0E **276** D9
Coral Springs *U.S.A.* 26°16N 80°16W **317** J9
Corales del Rosario △ *Colombia* 10°8N 75°46W **328** A2
Coralville *U.S.A.* 41°40N 91°35W **310** C5
Coralville L. *U.S.A.* 41°42N 91°33W **310** C5
Corangamite, L. *Australia* 38°5S 143°30E **282** E5
Corantijn → *Suriname* 5°50N 57°8W **329** B6
Coraopolis *U.S.A.* 40°31N 80°10W **312** F4
Corato *Italy* 41°9N 16°25E **201** A9
Corbeil-Essonnes *France* 48°36N 2°26E **173** D9
Corbeiro, C. *W. Sahara* 21°50N 17°0W **260** D1
Corbett △ *India* 29°20N 79°0E **243** E8
Corbie *France* 49°54N 2°30E **173** C9
Corbières *France* 42°55N 2°35E **174** F6
Corbigny *France* 47°16N 3°40E **173** E10
Corbin *U.S.A.* 36°57N 84°6W **309** G11
Corbones → *Spain* 37°36N 5°39W **195** H5
Corbu *Romania* 44°25N 28°39E **183** F13
Corby *U.K.* 52°30N 0°41W **169** E7
Corcaigh = Cork *Ireland* 51°54N 8°29W **166** E3
Corcoran *U.S.A.* 36°6N 119°33W **306** J7
Corcovado, Cristo Redentor *Brazil* 22°57S 43°12W **135** B1
Corcovado △ *Costa Rica* 8°33N 83°35W **320** E3
Cordele *U.S.A.* 31°58N 83°47W **316** D6
Cordell *U.S.A.* 35°17N 98°59W **314** D5
Cordenòns *Italy* 45°59N 12°42E **199** C9
Cordes-sur-Ciel *France* 44°5N 1°57E **174** D5
Cordillera Azul △ *Peru* 7°30S 76°30W **330** B2
Cordillera de los Picachos △ *Colombia* 2°39N 74°30W **328** C3
Cordisburgo *Brazil* 19°7S 44°21W **333** E3
Córdoba *Argentina* 31°20S 64°10W **334** C3
Córdoba *Veracruz, Mexico* 18°53N 96°56W **319** D5
Córdoba *Spain* 37°50N 4°50W **195** H6
Córdoba □ *Argentina* 31°22S 64°15W **334** C3
Córdoba □ *Colombia* 8°20N 75°40W **328** B2
Córdoba □ *Spain* 38°5N 5°0W **195** G6
Córdoba, Sierra de *Argentina* 31°10S 64°25W **334** C3
Cordon *Phil.* 16°42N 121°32E **232** C3
Cordova *U.S.A.* 60°33N 145°45W **303** F11
Corduff *Ireland* 53°23N 6°21W **120** A1
Corella *Spain* 42°7N 1°48W **196** C3
Corella → *Australia* 19°34S 140°47E **280** B3
Coremas *Brazil* 7°1S 37°58W **332** C4
Corentyne → *Guyana* 5°50N 57°8W **329** B6
Corfield *Australia* 21°40S 143°21E **280** C3
Corfu = Kerkyra *Greece* 39°38N 19°50E **206** B9
Corfu *U.S.A.* 42°57N 78°24W **312** D6
Corfu ✕ **(CFU)** *Greece* 39°35N 19°54E **204** B1
Corfu, Str. of = Kerkyras, Notio Steno *Greece* 39°34N 20°0E **206** B10
Corgo = O Corgo *Spain* 42°56N 7°25W **194** C3
Corguinho *Brazil* 19°53S 54°52W **331** D7
Cori *Italy* 41°39N 12°55E **200** A5
Coria *Spain* 39°58N 6°33W **194** F4
Coria del Río *Spain* 37°16N 6°3W **195** H4
Coricudgy *Australia* 32°51S 150°24E **283** B9
Corigliano Cálabro *Italy* 39°36N 16°31E **201** C9
Corimba, Barra de *Angola* 8°52S 13°9E **265** D2
Coringa Is. *Australia* 16°58S 149°58E **280** B4
Corinth = Korinthos *Greece* 37°56N 22°55E **204** D4
Corinth *Grenada* 12°2N 61°40W **323** q
Corinth *Ky., U.S.A.* 38°30N 84°34W **311** F12
Corinth *Miss., U.S.A.* 34°56N 88°31W **315** D10
Corinth *N.Y., U.S.A.* 43°15N 73°49W **313** C11
Corinth, G. of = Korinthiakos Kolpos *Greece* 38°16N 22°30E **204** C4
Corinth Canal *Greece* 37°58N 23°0E **204** D4
Corinto *Brazil* 18°20S 44°30W **333** E3
Corinto *Nic.* 12°30N 87°10W **320** D2
Corisco *Eq. Guin.* 0°55N 9°18E **264** B1
Cork *Ireland* 51°54N 8°29W **166** E3
Cork □ *Ireland* 51°57N 8°40W **166** E3
Cork Harbour *Ireland* 51°47N 8°16W **166** E3
Corlay *France* 48°20N 3°5W **172** D3
Corleone *Italy* 37°49N 13°18E **200** E6
Corleto Perticara *Italy* 40°23N 16°2E **201** B9
Çorlu *Turkey* 41°11N 27°49E **203** E11
Cormack L. *Canada* 60°56N 121°37W **296** A4
Cormano *Italy* 45°32N 9°10E **129** A2
Cormòns *Italy* 45°58N 13°28E **199** C10
Cormorant *Canada* 54°14N 100°35W **297** C8
Cormorant L. *Canada* 54°15N 100°50W **297** C8
Corn Is. = Maíz, Is. del *Nic.* 12°15N 83°4W **320** D3
Cornalvo ⌓ *Spain* 39°1N 6°13W **195** F4
Cornaredo *Italy* 45°30N 9°1E **129** A1
Cornélio Procópio *Brazil* 23°7S 50°40W **335** A5
Cornell *U.S.A.* 41°0N 88°44W **311** B8
Corner Brook *Canada* 48°57N 57°58W **299** C8
Corner Inlet *Australia* 38°45S 146°20E **283** E7
Corner Seamounts *Atl. Oc.* 35°0N 52°0W **152** C6
Cornești *Moldova* 47°21N 28°1E **183** C13
Corneto = Tarquínia *Italy* 42°15N 11°45E **199** F8
Corniglio *Italy* 44°29N 10°5E **198** D7
Corning *Ark., U.S.A.* 36°25N 90°35W **315** C9
Corning *Calif., U.S.A.* 39°56N 122°11W **304** G2
Corning *Iowa, U.S.A.* 40°59N 94°44W **310** D2
Corning *N.Y., U.S.A.* 42°9N 77°3W **312** D7
Corno Grande *Italy* 42°28N 13°34E **199** F10
Cornwall *Ont., Canada* 45°2N 74°44W **313** A10
Cornwall *Pa., U.S.A.* 40°17N 76°25W **313** F8
Cornwall □ *Jamaica* 18°15N 77°54W **320** a
Cornwall □ *U.K.* 50°26N 4°40W **169** G3
Cornwall I. *Canada* 77°37N 94°38W **295** B13
Cornwallis I. *Canada* 75°8N 95°0W **295** B13
Cornwell *U.S.A.* 27°23N 81°6W **317** H8
Corny Pt. *Australia* 34°55S 137°0E **282** C2
Coro *Venezuela* 11°25N 69°41W **328** A4
Coroaci *Brazil* 18°35S 42°17W **333** E3
Coroatá *Brazil* 4°8S 44°0W **332** B3
Corocoro *Bolivia* 17°15S 68°28W **330** D4
Corocoro, I. *Venezuela* 8°30N 60°10W **329** B5
Coroico *Bolivia* 16°0S 67°50W **330** D4
Coromandel *Brazil* 18°28S 47°13W **333** E2
Coromandel *N.Z.* 36°45S 175°31E **284** C4
Coromandel Coast *India* 12°30N 81°0E **245** H5
Coromandel Pen. *N.Z.* 37°0S 175°45E **284** D4
Coromandel Ra. *N.Z.* 37°0S 175°40E **284** D4
Coron *Phil.* 12°1N 120°12E **232** E3
Coron B. *Phil.* 11°54N 120°8E **233** F3
Coron I. *Phil.* 11°55N 120°14E **233** F3
Corona *Calif., U.S.A.* 33°53N 117°34W **307** M9
Corona *N. Mex., U.S.A.* 34°15N 105°36W **305** J11
Coronado *U.S.A.* 32°41N 117°10W **307** N9
Coronado, B. de *Costa Rica* 9°0N 83°40W **320** E3
Coronados, G. de los *Chile* 41°40S 74°0W **336** B2
Coronados, Is. los *Mexico* 32°26N 117°19W **307** N9
Coronation *Canada* 52°5N 111°27W **296** C6
Coronation Gulf *Canada* 68°25N 110°0W **294** D10
Coronation I. *Antarctica* 60°45S 46°0W **151** C18
Coronation Is. *Australia* 14°57S 124°55E **278** B3
Coronda *Argentina* 31°58S 60°56W **334** C3
Coronel *Chile* 37°0S 73°10W **334** D1
Coronel Bogado *Paraguay* 27°11S 56°18W **334** B4
Coronel Dorrego *Argentina* 38°40S 61°10W **334** D3
Coronel Fabriciano *Brazil* 19°31S 42°38W **333** E3
Coronel Murta *Brazil* 16°37S 42°11W **333** E3
Coronel Oviedo *Paraguay* 25°24S 56°30W **334** B4
Coronel Ponce *Brazil* 15°34S 55°1W **331** D6
Coronel Pringles *Argentina* 38°0S 61°30W **334** D3
Coronel Suárez *Argentina* 37°30S 61°52W **334** D3
Coronel Vidal *Argentina* 37°28S 57°45W **334** D4
Corongo *Peru* 8°30S 77°53W **330** B2
Coropuna, Nevado *Peru* 15°30S 72°41W **330** D3
Corossol *St.-Martin* 17°54N 62°51W **322** a
Çorovodë *Albania* 40°31N 20°14E **202** F4
Corowa *Australia* 35°58S 146°21E **283** C7
Corozal *Colombia* 9°19N 75°18W **328** B2
Corozal *Puerto Rico* 18°21N 66°19W **321** b
Corozal □ *Belize* 18°23N 88°23W **319** D7
Corozal Pt. *Trin. & Tob.* 10°45N 61°37W **323** t
Corps *France* 44°50N 5°56E **175** D9
Corpus *Argentina* 27°10S 55°30W **335** B4
Corpus Christi *U.S.A.* 27°47N 97°24W **314** H6
Corpus Christi, L. *U.S.A.* 28°2N 97°52W **314** G6
Corque *Bolivia* 18°20S 67°41W **330** D4
Corral *Chile* 39°52S 73°26W **336** A2
Corral de Almaguer *Spain* 39°45N 3°10W **194** F7
Corralejo *Canary Is.* 28°43N 13°53W **153** e2
Corraun Pen. *Ireland* 53°54N 9°54W **166** C2
Corrèggio *Italy* 44°46N 10°47E **198** D7
Corregidor *Phil.* 14°23N 120°35E **232** D3
Corrente *Brazil* 10°27S 45°10W **332** D2
Corrente → *Brazil* 13°8S 43°28W **333** D3
Correntes → *Brazil* 17°38S 55°8W **331** D6
Correntes, C. das *Mozam.* 24°6S 35°34E **271** B6
Correntina *Brazil* 13°20S 44°39W **333** D3
Corrèze □ *France* 45°20N 1°45E **174** C5
Corrèze → *France* 45°10N 1°28E **174** C5
Corrib, L. *Ireland* 53°27N 9°16W **166** C2
Corridónia *Italy* 43°15N 13°30E **199** E10
Corrientes *Argentina* 27°30S 58°45W **334** B4
Corrientes □ *Argentina* 28°0S 57°0W **334** B4
Corrientes → *Argentina* 30°42S 59°38W **334** C4
Corrientes → *Peru* 3°43S 74°35W **328** D3
Corrientes, C. *Colombia* 5°30N 77°34W **328** B2
Corrientes, C. *Cuba* 21°43N 84°30W **320** B3
Corrientes, C. *Jalisco, Mexico* 20°25N 105°42W **318** C3
Corrigan *U.S.A.* 31°0N 94°52W **314** F7
Corrigin *Australia* 32°20S 117°53E **279** F2
Corriverton *Guyana* 5°55N 57°20W **329** B6
Corry *U.S.A.* 41°55N 79°39W **312** E5
Corryong *Australia* 36°12S 147°53E **283** D7
Corse □ *France* 42°0N 9°0E **175** G13
Corse, C. *France* 43°1N 9°25E **175** E13
Corse ⌓ *France* 42°14N 9°10E **175** F13
Corse-du-Sud □ *France* 41°45N 9°0E **175** G13
Corsica = Corse □ *France* 42°0N 9°0E **175** G13
Corsicana *U.S.A.* 32°6N 96°28W **314** E6
Córsico *Italy* 45°25N 9°6E **129** B1
Corsini, Palazzo *Rome, Italy* **136** c1
Corstorphine *U.K.* 55°56N 3°17W **121** B2
Corte *France* 42°19N 9°11E **175** F13
Corte Pinto *Portugal* 37°42N 7°29W **195** H3
Cortegana *Spain* 37°52N 6°49W **195** H4
Cortes *Phil.* 9°17N 126°11E **233** G6
Cortés, Mar de = California, G. de *Mexico* 27°0N 111°0W **318** B2
Cortez *U.S.A.* 37°21N 108°35W **305** H9
Cortina d'Ampezzo *Italy* 46°32N 12°8E **199** B9
Cortland *N.Y., U.S.A.* 42°36N 76°11W **313** D8
Cortland *Ohio, U.S.A.* 41°20N 80°44W **312** E4
Cortona *Italy* 43°16N 11°59E **199** E8
Corubal → *Guinea-Biss.* 11°57N 15°5W **262** C2
Coruche *Portugal* 38°57N 8°30W **195** G2
Çoruh → *Turkey* 41°38N 41°38E **191** K5
Çorum *Turkey* 40°30N 34°57E **212** B6
Çorum □ *Turkey* 40°40N 35°0E **212** B6
Corumbá *Brazil* 19°0S 57°30W **331** D6
Corumbá → *Brazil* 18°19S 48°55W **333** E2
Corumbá de Goiás *Brazil* 16°0S 48°50W **333** E2
Corumbaíba *Brazil* 18°9S 48°34W **333** E2
Corund *Romania* 46°30N 25°13E **183** D10
Corunna = A Coruña *Spain* 43°20N 8°25W **194** B2
Corunna *U.S.A.* 42°59N 84°7W **311** B12
Corvallis *U.S.A.* 44°34N 123°16W **304** D2
Corvette, L. de la *Canada* 53°25N 74°3W **298** B5
Corviale *Italy* 41°51N 12°25E **136** B1
Corvo *Azores* 39°42N 31°6W **153** d2
Coryal *Trin. & Tob.* 10°30N 61°11W **323** t
Corydon *Ind., U.S.A.* 38°13N 86°7W **311** F10
Corydon *Iowa, U.S.A.* 40°46N 93°19W **310** D3
Corydon *Ky., U.S.A.* 37°44N 87°43W **311** G9
Cosalá *Mexico* 24°23N 106°41W **318** C3
Cosamaloapan de Carpio *Mexico* 18°22N 95°48W **319** D5
Cosenza *Italy* 39°18N 16°15E **201** C9
Coșereni *Romania* 44°38N 26°35E **183** F11
Coshocton *U.S.A.* 40°16N 81°51W **312** F3
Coslada *Spain* 40°25N 3°35W **127** B2
Cosmo Newberry *Australia* 28°0S 122°54E **279** E3
Cosmo Newberry ☼ *Australia* 27°59S 122°53E **279** E3
Cosmonaut Sea *S. Ocean* 66°30S 40°0E **151** C5
Cosne-Cours-sur-Loire *France* 47°24N 2°54E **173** E9
Coso Junction *U.S.A.* 36°3N 117°57W **307** J9
Coso Pk. *U.S.A.* 36°13N 117°44W **307** J9
Cospeito *Spain* 43°12N 7°34W **194** B3
Cosquín *Argentina* 31°15S 64°30W **334** C3
Cossato *Italy* 45°34N 8°10E **198** C5
Cossé-le-Vivien *France* 47°57N 0°54W **172** E6
Cossigny *France* 48°43N 2°40E **134** B4
Cosson → *France* 47°30N 1°15E **172** E8
Costa Blanca *Spain* 38°25N 0°10W **197** G4
Costa Brava *Spain* 41°30N 3°0E **196** D8
Costa Cálida *Spain* 37°30N 1°30W **197** H3
Costa Daurada *Spain* 41°12N 1°15E **196** D6
Costa del Sol *Spain* 36°30N 4°30W **195** J6
Costa dels Pins *Spain* 39°38N 3°26E **206** B4
Costa Mesa *U.S.A.* 33°38N 117°55W **307** M9
Costa Rica ■ *Cent. Amer.* 10°0N 84°0W **320** E3
Costa Smeralda *Italy* 41°5N 9°35E **200** A2
Costantino, Arco di *Rome, Italy* **136** c3
Costermansville = Bukavu *Dem. Rep. of the Congo* 2°20S 28°52E **266** C2
Costești *Romania* 44°40N 24°53E **183** F9
Costigliole d'Asti *Italy* 44°47N 8°11E **198** D5
Cosumnes → *U.S.A.* 38°16N 121°26W **306** G5
Coswig *Sachsen, Germany* 51°7N 13°34E **178** D9
Coswig *Sachsen-Anhalt, Germany* 51°53N 12°27E **178** D8
Cotabato *Phil.* 7°14N 124°15E **233** H5
Cotacajes → *Bolivia* 16°0S 67°1W **330** D4

Cotagaita *Bolivia* 20°45S 65°40W **334** A2
Cotahuasi *Peru* 15°12S 72°50W **330** D3
Cotao *Portugal* 38°45N 9°17W **126** A1
Côte d'Azur *France* 43°25N 7°10E **175** E11
Côte-d'Ivoire = Ivory Coast ■ *Africa* 7°30N 5°0W **262** D4
Côte d'Or *France* 47°10N 4°50E **173** E11
Côte-d'Or □ *France* 47°30N 4°50E **173** E11
Côte-St-Luc *Canada* 45°28N 73°39W **130** B2
Coteau des Prairies *U.S.A.* 45°20N 97°50W **308** C5
Coteau du Missouri *U.S.A.* 47°0N 100°0W **308** B4
Cotegipe *Brazil* 12°2S 44°15W **333** D3
Cotentin *France* 49°15N 1°30W **172** C5
Côtes-d'Armor □ *France* 48°25N 2°40W **172** D4
Côtes de Meuse *France* 49°15N 5°22E **173** C12
Côtes-du-Nord = Côtes-d'Armor □ *France* 48°25N 2°40W **172** D4
Cotiella *Spain* 42°31N 0°19E **196** C5
Cotillo *Canary Is.* 28°41N 14°1W **153** e2
Cotiujeni *Moldova* 47°51N 28°33E **183** C13
Cotoca *Bolivia* 17°49S 63°3W **331** D5
Cotonou *Benin* 6°20N 2°25E **263** D5
Cotopaxi *Ecuador* 0°40S 78°30W **328** D2
Cotopaxi □ *Ecuador* 0°5S 78°55W **328** D2
Cotopaxi △ *Ecuador* 0°39S 78°24W **328** D2
Cotronei *Italy* 39°9N 16°47E **201** C9
Cotswold Hills *U.K.* 51°42N 2°10W **169** F5
Cottage Grove *U.S.A.* 43°48N 123°3W **304** E2
Cottageville *U.S.A.* 32°56N 80°29W **316** C9
Cottam *Canada* 42°8N 82°45W **312** D2
Cottbus *Germany* 51°45N 14°20E **178** D10
Cotton Ground *St. Kitts & Nevis* 17°11N 62°36W **322** d
Cottondale *U.S.A.* 30°48N 85°23W **316** E4
Cottonwood *Ala., U.S.A.* 31°3N 85°18W **316** D4
Cottonwood *Ariz., U.S.A.* 34°45N 112°1W **305** J7
Cotulla *U.S.A.* 28°26N 99°14W **314** G5
Cotunduba, I. de *Brazil* 22°57S 43°8W **135** B2
Coubre, Pte. de la *France* 45°42N 1°15W **174** C2
Coubron *France* 48°54N 2°34E **134** A4
Couches *France* 46°53N 4°30E **173** F11
Couço *Portugal* 38°59N 8°17W **195** G2
Coudersport *U.S.A.* 41°46N 78°1W **312** E6
Couedic, C. du *Australia* 36°5S 136°40E **282** D2
Couëron *France* 47°13N 1°44W **172** E5
Couesnon → *France* 48°38N 1°32W **172** D5
Couhé *France* 46°17N 0°11E **174** B4
Coulanges-sur-Yonne *France* 47°31N 3°33E **173** E10
Coulee City *U.S.A.* 47°37N 119°17W **304** C4
Coulee Dam Nat. Recr. Area = Lake Roosevelt ⌓ *U.S.A.* 48°5N 118°14W **304** B4
Coulibistri *Dominica* 15°27N 61°28W **323** k
Coulman I. *Antarctica* 73°35S 170°0E **151** D11
Coulommiers *France* 48°50N 3°3E **173** D10
Coulon → *France* 43°51N 5°6E **175** E9
Coulonge → *Canada* 45°52N 76°46W **298** C4
Coulonges-sur-l'Autize *France* 46°29N 0°36W **174** B3
Coulounieix-Chamiers *France* 45°11N 0°42E **174** C4
Coulterville *Calif., U.S.A.* 37°43N 120°12W **306** H6
Coulterville *Ill., U.S.A.* 38°11N 89°36W **310** F7
Council *Alaska, U.S.A.* 64°53N 163°41W **303** D7
Council *Ga., U.S.A.* 30°37N 82°31W **316** E7
Council *Idaho, U.S.A.* 44°44N 116°26W **304** D5
Council Bluffs *U.S.A.* 41°16N 95°52W **308** E6
Council Grove *U.S.A.* 38°40N 96°29W **308** F5
Countryside *U.S.A.* 41°47N 87°52W **119** C1
County Art Museum *U.S.A.* 34°4N 118°21W **126** B2
Coupeville *U.S.A.* 48°13N 122°41W **306** B4
Courantyne → *S. Amer.* 5°55N 57°5W **329** B6
Courbevoie *France* 48°53N 2°14E **134** A2
Courcelles *Belgium* 50°28N 4°22E **170** D4
Courchevel *France* 45°25N 6°36E **175** C10
Courçon *France* 46°15N 0°50W **174** B3
Courland → *Trin. & Tob.* 11°13N 60°47W **323** s
Courmayeur *Italy* 45°47N 6°58E **198** C3
Couronne, C. *France* 43°19N 5°3E **175** E9
Cours-la-Ville *France* 46°7N 4°19E **173** F11
Coursan *France* 43°14N 3°4E **174** E7
Courseulles-sur-Mer *France* 49°20N 0°29W **172** C6
Courtenay *B.C., Canada* 49°45N 125°0W **296** D4
Courtenay *Loiret, France* 48°2N 3°3E **173** D10
Courtland *Ont., Canada* 42°51N 80°38W **312** D4
Courtland *Calif., U.S.A.* 38°20N 121°34W **306** G5
Courtrai = Kortrijk *Belgium* 50°50N 3°17E **170** D3
Courtright *Canada* 42°49N 82°28W **312** D2
Courtry *France* 48°55N 2°35E **134** A4
Coushatta *U.S.A.* 32°1N 93°21W **314** E8
Coutances *France* 49°3N 1°28W **172** C5
Coutras *France* 45°3N 0°8W **174** C3
Coutts Crossing *Australia* 29°49S 152°55E **281** D5
Couva *Trin. & Tob.* 10°25N 61°27W **323** t
Couvin *Belgium* 50°3N 4°29E **170** D4
Covarrubias *Spain* 42°4N 3°31W **194** C7
Covasna *Romania* 45°50N 26°10E **183** E11
Covasna □ *Romania* 45°50N 26°0E **183** E10
Cove I. *Canada* 45°17N 81°44W **312** A3
Coveñas *Colombia* 9°24N 75°44W **328** B2
Covent Garden *London, U.K.* **125** b4
Coventry *U.K.* 52°25N 1°28W **169** E6
Coverdale *U.S.A.* 31°38N 83°58W **316** D6
Covilhã *Portugal* 40°17N 7°31W **194** E3
Covington *Ga., U.S.A.* 33°36N 83°51W **316** B6
Covington *Ind., U.S.A.* 40°9N 87°24W **311** D9
Covington *Ky., U.S.A.* 39°5N 84°30W **311** E12
Covington *Ohio, U.S.A.* 40°7N 84°21W **311** D12
Covington *Tenn., U.S.A.* 35°34N 89°39W **315** D10
Covington *Va., U.S.A.* 37°47N 79°59W **309** G14
Cowal, L. *Australia* 33°40S 147°25E **283** B7
Cowan, Cerro *Ecuador* 0°12S 90°48W **330** a
Cowan, L. *Australia* 31°45S 121°45E **279** F3
Cowan L. *Canada* 54°0N 107°15W **297** C7
Cowangie *Australia* 35°12S 141°26E **282** C4
Cowansville *Canada* 45°14N 72°46W **313** A12
Coward Springs *Australia* 29°24S 136°49E **281** D2
Cowcowing Lakes *Australia* 30°55S 117°20E **279** F2
Cowden *U.S.A.* 39°15N 88°52W **311** E8
Cowdenbeath *U.K.* 56°7N 3°21W **167** E5
Cowell *Australia* 33°39S 136°56E **282** B2
Cowes *Vic., Australia* 38°28S 145°14E **283** E6
Cowes *I. of W., U.K.* 50°45N 1°18W **169** G6
Cowgate *Edinburgh, U.K.* **121** b3
Cowichan L. *Canada* 48°53N 124°17W **306** B2
Cowley *U.K.* 51°31N 0°28W **125** A1
Cowlitz → *U.S.A.* 46°6N 122°55W **306** D4
Cowra *Australia* 33°49S 148°42E **283** B8
Cox *Spain* 38°8N 0°53W **197** G4
Coxilha Grande *Brazil* 28°18S 51°30W **335** B5
Coxim *Brazil* 18°30S 54°55W **331** D7
Coxim → *Brazil* 18°34S 54°46W **331** D7
Cox's Bazar *Bangla.* 21°26N 91°59E **241** E3
Coyah *Guinea* 9°42N 13°22W **262** D2
Coyoacán *Mexico* 19°21N 99°9W **128** B2
Coyote Wells *U.S.A.* 32°44N 115°58W **307** N11
Coyuca de Benitez *Mexico* 17°2N 100°4W **319** D4
Coyuca de Catalán *Mexico* 18°20N 100°39W **318** D4
Cozad *U.S.A.* 40°52N 99°59W **308** E4
Cozes *France* 45°34N 0°49W **174** C3
Cozumel *Mexico* 20°31N 86°55W **319** C7
Cozumel, Isla *Mexico* 20°30N 86°40W **319** C7
Crab Hill *Barbados* 13°19N 59°38W **323** r
Crabs Pen. *Antigua & B.* 17°7N 61°45W **322** b
Cracow = Kraków *Poland* 50°4N 19°57E **185** H6
Cracow *Australia* 25°17S 150°17E **281** D5
Craddock Channel *N.Z.* 36°10S 175°13E **284** C4
Cradle Mt.-Lake St. Clair △ *Australia* 41°49S 147°56E **281** G4
Cradock *S. Austral., Australia* 32°6S 138°31E **281** E2
Cradock *Eastern Cape, S. Africa* 32°8S 25°36E **270** D4
Crafers *Australia* 35°0S 138°42E **282** C3
Craig *Alaska, U.S.A.* 55°29N 133°9W **303** J14
Craig *Colo., U.S.A.* 40°31N 107°33W **304** F10
Craigavon *U.K.* 54°27N 6°23W **166** B5
Craighall Park *S. Africa* 26°7S 28°1E **123** A2
Craigieburn *Australia* 37°36S 144°56E **283** D6
Craiglockhart *U.K.* 55°55N 3°14W **121** B2
Craigmillar *U.K.* 55°56N 3°9W **121** B3
Craigmore *Zimbabwe* 20°28S 32°50E **269** G3
Craik *Canada* 51°3N 105°49W **297** C7
Crailsheim *Germany* 49°8N 10°5E **179** F6
Craiova *Romania* 44°21N 23°48E **183** F8
Cramond *U.K.* 55°58N 3°18W **121** B2
Cramond Bridge *U.K.* 55°57N 3°19W **121** B1
Cramond I. *U.K.* 55°59N 3°17W **121** B2
Cramsie *Australia* 23°20S 144°15E **280** C3
Cranberry L. *U.S.A.* 44°11N 74°50W **313** B10
Cranberry Portage *Canada* 54°35N 101°23W **297** C8
Cranbrook *W. Austral., Australia* 34°18S 117°33E **279** F2
Cranbrook *B.C., Canada* 49°30N 115°46W **296** D5
Crandon *U.S.A.* 45°34N 88°54W **308** C9
Crane *Oreg., U.S.A.* 43°25N 118°35W **304** E4
Crane *Tex., U.S.A.* 31°24N 102°21W **314** F3
Crane, The *Barbados* 13°6N 59°27W **323** r
Cranford *U.K.* 51°29N 0°25W **125** B1
Cranganore *India* 10°13N 76°13E **245** J3
Cranston *U.S.A.* 41°47N 71°26W **313** E13
Craon *France* 47°50N 0°58W **172** E6
Craonne *France* 49°27N 3°46E **173** C10
Craponne-sur-Arzon *France* 45°19N 3°51E **174** C7
Crasna *Romania* 46°32N 27°51E **183** D12
Crasna → *Romania* 47°44N 22°35E **182** C7
Crasnei, Munţii *Romania* 47°0N 23°20E **183** C8
Crater L. *St. Vincent* 13°17N 61°13W **323** n
Crater L. *Oreg., U.S.A.* 42°56N 122°6W **304** E2
Crater Lake △ *U.S.A.* 42°55N 122°10W **304** E2
Crater Mt. *Papua N. G.* 6°37S 145°7E **286** D3
Crater Pt. *Papua N. G.* 5°25S 152°9E **286** C7
Craters of the Moon ⌓ *U.S.A.* 43°25N 113°30W **304** E7
Crateús *Brazil* 5°10S 40°39W **332** C3
Crati → *Italy* 39°43N 16°31E **201** C9
Crato *Brazil* 7°10S 39°25W **332** C4
Crato *Portugal* 39°16N 7°39W **195** F3
Craven, L. *Canada* 54°20N 76°56W **298** B4
Cravo Norte *Colombia* 6°18N 70°12W **328** B3
Cravo Norte → *Colombia* 6°18N 70°12W **328** B3
Crawford *Western Cape, S. Africa* 33°59S 18°30E **118** A2
Crawford *Ala., U.S.A.* 32°27N 85°11W **316** C4
Crawford *Nebr., U.S.A.* 42°41N 103°25W **308** D2
Crawfordsville *Ind., U.S.A.* 40°2N 86°54W **311** D10
Crawfordsville *Iowa, U.S.A.* 41°12N 91°32W **310** C5
Crawfordville *Fla., U.S.A.* 30°11N 84°23W **316** E5
Crawfordville *Ga., U.S.A.* 33°33N 82°54W **316** B7
Crawley *U.K.* 51°7N 0°11W **169** F7
Crayford *U.K.* 51°27N 0°11E **125** B5
Crazy Mts. *U.S.A.* 46°12N 110°20W **304** C8
Crean L. *Canada* 54°5N 106°9W **297** C7
Crécy-en-Ponthieu *France* 50°15N 1°53E **173** B8
Crediton *Ont., Canada* 43°17N 81°33W **312** C3
Crediton *Devon, U.K.* 50°47N 3°40W **169** G4
Cree → *Sask., Canada* 58°57N 105°47W **297** B7
Cree → *Dumf. & Gall., U.K.* 54°55N 4°25W **167** G4
Cree L. *Canada* 57°30N 106°30W **297** B7
Creede *U.S.A.* 37°51N 106°56W **305** H10
Creekmouth *U.K.* 51°30N 0°6E **125** A4
Creekside *U.S.A.* 40°40N 79°11W **312** F5
Creel *Mexico* 27°45N 107°38W **318** B3
Creemore *Canada* 44°19N 80°6W **312** B4
Creighton *Sask., Canada* 54°45N 101°54W **297** C8
Creighton *Nebr., U.S.A.* 42°28N 97°54W **308** D5
Creil *France* 49°15N 2°29E **173** C9
Crema *Italy* 45°22N 9°41E **198** C6
Cremona *Italy* 45°7N 10°2E **198** C7
Crepaja *Serbia* 45°1N 20°38E **182** E5
Crepori → *Brazil* 5°42S 57°8W **331** B6
Crépy *France* 49°35N 3°32E **173** C10
Crépy-en-Valois *France* 49°14N 2°54E **173** C9
Cres *Croatia* 44°58N 14°25E **199** D11
Crescent, L. *U.S.A.* 28°30N 81°33W **133** A1
Crescent Beach *U.S.A.* 29°46N 81°15W **316** F8
Crescent City *Calif., U.S.A.* 41°45N 124°12W **304** F1
Crescent City *Fla., U.S.A.* 29°26N 81°31W **317** F8
Crescent Hd. *Australia* 31°11S 152°59E **283** A10
Crescent L. *U.S.A.* 29°28N 81°30W **317** F8
Crescentino *Italy* 45°11N 8°6E **198** C5
Crescenzago *Italy* 45°30N 9°14E **129** A2
Crespo *Argentina* 32°2S 60°19W **334** C3
Cressely *France* 48°44N 2°6E **134** B1
Cresskill *U.S.A.* 40°56N 73°57W **132** A2
Cresson *U.S.A.* 40°28N 78°36W **312** F6
Cressy *Australia* 38°2S 143°40E **282** E5
Crest *France* 44°44N 5°2E **175** D9
Cresta, Mt. *Phil.* 17°17N 122°6E **232** C4
Crestline *Calif., U.S.A.* 34°14N 117°18W **307** L9
Crestline *Ohio, U.S.A.* 40°47N 82°44W **312** F2
Creston *B.C., Canada* 49°10N 116°31W **296** D5
Creston *Calif., U.S.A.* 35°32N 120°33W **306** K6
Creston *Iowa, U.S.A.* 41°4N 94°22W **310** C2
Crestview *Calif., U.S.A.* 37°46N 118°58W **306** H8
Crestview *Fla., U.S.A.* 30°46N 86°34W **317** E3
Creswick *Australia* 37°25S 143°58E **282** D5
Crêt de la Neige *France* 46°16N 5°58E **173** F12
Crete = Kriti *Greece* 35°15N 25°0E **207** E6
Crete *Ill., U.S.A.* 41°27N 87°38W **311** C9
Crete *Nebr., U.S.A.* 40°38N 96°58W **308** E5
Crete, Sea of *Greece* 36°0N 25°0E **205** E7
Créteil *France* 48°47N 2°27E **134** B3
Cretin, C. *Papua N. G.* 6°40S 147°53E **286** D4
Creus, C. de *Spain* 42°20N 3°19E **196** C8
Creuse □ *France* 46°10N 2°0E **173** F9
Creuse → *France* 47°0N 0°34E **174** B4
Creutzwald *France* 49°12N 6°42E **173** C13
Creuzburg *Germany* 51°3N 10°14E **178** D6
Crèvecœur-le-Grand *France* 49°37N 2°5E **173** C9
Crevillent *Spain* 38°12N 0°48W **197** G4
Crewe *U.K.* 53°6N 2°26W **168** D5
Crewkerne *U.K.* 50°53N 2°48W **169** G5
Crianlarich *U.K.* 56°24N 4°37W **167** E4
Criciúma *Brazil* 28°40S 49°23W **335** B6
Cricklewood *U.K.* 51°33N 0°13W **125** A2
Cricova *Moldova* 47°8N 28°52E **183** C13
Cridersville *U.S.A.* 40°39N 84°9W **311** D12
Crieff *U.K.* 56°22N 3°50W **167** E5
Crikvenica *Croatia* 45°11N 14°40E **199** C11
Crimea □ *Ukraine* 45°30N 33°10E **189** K8
Crimean Pen. = Krymskyy Pivostriv *Ukraine* 45°0N 34°0E **189** K8
Crimmitschau *Germany* 50°48N 12°24E **178** E8
Cristal, Mts. de *Gabon* 0°30N 10°30E **264** B2
Cristalândia *Brazil* 10°36S 49°11W **332** D2
Cristino Castro *Brazil* 8°49S 44°13W **332** C3
Cristo Redentor, Corcovado *Brazil* 22°56S 43°12W **135** B1
Cristobal *Panama* 9°19N 79°54W **320** c
Cristóbal, Pta. *Ecuador* 0°54S 91°31W **330** a
Cristuru Secuiesc *Romania* 46°17N 25°2E **183** D10
Crişul Alb → *Romania* 46°42N 21°17E **182** D6
Crişul Negru → *Romania* 46°42N 21°16E **182** D6
Crişul Repede → *Romania* 46°55N 20°59E **182** D5
Crittenden *U.S.A.* 38°47N 84°36W **311** F12
Criuleni *Moldova* 47°13N 29°10E **183** C14
Crivitz *Germany* 53°34N 11°39E **178** B7
Crixás *Brazil* 14°27S 49°58W **333** D2
Crna → *Macedonia* 41°33N 21°59E **202** E5
Crna Gora = Montenegro ■ *Europe* 42°40N 19°20E **202** D3
Crna Gora *Macedonia* 42°10N 21°30E **202** D5
Crna Reka = Crna → *Macedonia* 41°33N 21°59E **202** E5
Crna Trava *Serbia* 42°49N 22°19E **202** D6
Crni Drim → *Macedonia* 41°17N 20°40E **202** E4
Crni Timok → *Serbia* 43°53N 22°15E **202** C6
Crnoljeva Planina *Kosovo* 42°20N 21°0E **202** D5
Črnomelj *Slovenia* 45°33N 15°10E **199** C12
Croagh Patrick *Ireland* 53°46N 9°40W **166** C2
Croajingolong △ *Australia* 37°45S 149°26E **283** D8
Croatia ■ *Europe* 45°20N 16°0E **199** C13
Crockenhill *U.K.* 51°22N 0°9E **125** B4
Crocker *U.S.A.* 37°57N 92°16W **310** G4
Crocker, Banjaran *Malaysia* 5°40N 116°30E **235** A5
Crocker, Cerro *Ecuador* 0°36S 90°21W **330** a
Crocker Range △ *Malaysia* 5°33N 116°8E **235** A5
Crockett *U.S.A.* 31°19N 95°27W **314** F7
Crocodile = Umgwenya → *Mozam.* 25°14S 32°18E **271** C5
Crocodile → *S. Africa* 24°12S 26°53E **270** B4
Crocodile Is. *Australia* 12°3S 134°58E **280** A1
Crocq *France* 45°52N 2°21E **174** C6
Crocus B. *Anguilla* 18°13N 63°5W **322** a
Crodo *Italy* 46°13N 8°19E **198** B5
Crohy Hd. *Ireland* 54°55N 8°26W **166** B3
Croisette, C. *France* 43°14N 5°22E **175** E9
Croisic, Pte. du *France* 47°19N 2°31W **172** E4
Croissy-Beaubourg *France* 48°49N 2°39E **134** B4
Croissy-sur-Seine *France* 48°52N 2°8E **134** A1
Croix, L. la *Canada* 48°20N 92°15W **298** C1
Croker, C. *N. Terr., Australia* 10°58S 132°35E **278** B5
Croker, C. *Ont., Canada* 44°58N 80°59W **312** B4
Croker I. *Australia* 11°12S 132°32E **278** B5
Croker Islands Seas ✪ *Australia* 11°20S 132°30E **278** B5
Cromarty *U.K.* 57°40N 4°2W **167** D4
Cromer *U.K.* 52°56N 1°17E **168** E9
Crompton Pt. *Dominica* 15°35N 61°19W **323** k
Cromwell *N.Z.* 45°3S 169°14E **285** F4
Cromwell *Conn., U.S.A.* 41°36N 72°39W **313** E12
Cronat *France* 46°43N 3°40E **173** F10
Crook *U.K.* 54°43N 1°45W **168** C6
Crooked → *B.C., Canada* 54°50N 122°54W **296** C4
Crooked → *Oreg., U.S.A.* 44°32N 121°16W **304** D3
Crooked Creek *U.S.A.* 61°52N 158°7W **303** F8
Crooked I. *Bahamas* 22°50N 74°10W **321** B5
Crooked Island Passage *Bahamas* 22°55N 74°35W **321** B5
Crookston *Minn., U.S.A.* 47°47N 96°37W **308** B5
Crookston *Nebr., U.S.A.* 42°56N 100°45W **308** D3
Crookwell *Australia* 34°28S 149°24E **283** C8
Cropane-Micone ⌓ *Italy* 38°31N 16°18E **201** D9
Crosby *Gauteng, S. Africa* 26°11S 27°59E **123** B1
Crosby *Mersey., U.K.* 53°30N 3°3W **168** D4
Crosby *N. Dak., U.S.A.* 48°55N 103°18W **308** A2
Crosby *Pa., U.S.A.* 41°45N 78°23W **312** E6
Crosbyton *U.S.A.* 33°40N 101°14W **314** E4
Crosía *Italy* 39°35N 16°45E **201** C9
Crosne *France* 48°43N 2°27E **134** B3
Cross → *Nigeria* 4°42N 8°21E **263** E6
Cross City *U.S.A.* 29°38N 83°7W **317** F6
Cross Fell *U.K.* 54°43N 2°28W **168** C5
Cross I. *India* 18°56N 72°51E **130** B2
Cross L. *Canada* 54°45N 97°30W **297** C9
Cross Lake *Canada* 54°37N 97°47W **297** C9
Cross River □ *Nigeria* 6°0N 8°0E **263** D6
Cross River △ *Nigeria* 5°50N 9°50E **263** D6
Cross Sound *U.S.A.* 58°0N 135°0W **303** G14
Cross Timbers *U.S.A.* 38°1N 93°14W **310** F3
Crossen = Krosno Odrzańskie *Poland* 52°3N 15°7E **185** F2
Crossett *U.S.A.* 33°8N 91°58W **314** E9
Crosshaven *Ireland* 51°47N 8°17W **166** E3
Crossley, Mt. *N.Z.* 42°50S 172°5E **285** C7
Crossmaglen *U.K.* 54°5N 6°36W **166** B5
Crossmolina *Ireland* 54°6N 9°20W **166** B2
Crossville *Ill., U.S.A.* 38°10N 88°4W **311** F8
Crossville *Tenn., U.S.A.* 35°57N 85°2W **315** D12
Croswell *U.S.A.* 43°16N 82°37W **312** C2
Croton-on-Hudson *U.S.A.* 41°12N 73°55W **313** E11
Crotone *Italy* 39°5N 17°8E **201** C10
Crouch End *U.K.* 51°34N 0°7W **125** A3
Crow → *Canada* 59°41N 124°20W **296** B4
Crow Agency *U.S.A.* 45°36N 107°28W **304** D10
Crow Hd. *Ireland* 51°35N 10°9W **166** E1
Crowdy Bay △ *Australia* 31°45S 152°45E **283** A10
Crowell *U.S.A.* 33°59N 99°43W **314** E5
Crowl Cr. → *Australia* 32°0S 145°30E **283** B6
Crowley *U.S.A.* 30°13N 92°22W **314** F8
Crowley, L. *U.S.A.* 37°35N 118°42W **306** H8
Crown I. *Papua N. G.* 5°7S 146°58E **286** C4
Crown Mine *S. Africa* 26°12S 27°57E **123** B1
Crown Point *Ind., U.S.A.* 41°25N 87°22W **311** C9
Crown Point *N.Y., U.S.A.* 43°57N 73°26W **313** C11
Crown Point ✈ (TAB) *Trin. & Tob.* 11°9N 60°50W **323** s
Crown Pt. *Trin. & Tob.* 11°18N 60°51W **323** s
Crownpoint *U.S.A.* 35°41N 108°9W **305** J9
Crows Landing *U.S.A.* 37°23N 121°6W **306** H5
Crows Nest *N.S.W., Australia* 33°49S 151°12E **139** A2
Crows Nest *Queens., Australia* 27°16S 152°4E **281** D5
Crowsnest Pass *Canada* 49°40N 114°40W **296** D6
Croydon *Queens., Australia* 18°13S 142°14E **280** B3
Croydon *London, U.K.* 51°22N 0°5W **125** B3
Croydon □ *U.K.* 51°22N 0°5W **169** F7
Croydon Park *Australia* 33°55S 151°7E **139** B1
Crozet, Îs. *Ind. Oc.* 46°27S 52°0E **273** J4
Crozet Basin *Ind. Oc.* 39°0S 60°0E **273** H5
Crozon *France* 48°15N 4°30W **172** D2
Cruagh Mt. *Ireland* 53°14N 6°17W **120** B2
Cruces, Punta *Colombia* 6°39N 77°32W **328** B2
Crumlin *Ireland* 53°19N 6°19W **120** B2
Crusheen *Ireland* 52°57N 8°53W **166** D3
Cruz, C. *Cuba* 19°50N 77°50W **320** C4
Cruz Alta *Brazil* 28°45S 53°40W **335** B5
Cruz Bay *U.S. Virgin Is.* 18°20N 64°48W **321** b
Cruz das Almas *Brazil* 12°0S 39°6W **333** D4
Cruz de Pau *Portugal* 38°37N 9°7W **126** B2
Cruz del Eje *Argentina* 30°45S 64°50W **334** C3
Cruzeiro *Brazil* 22°33S 45°0W **333** F3
Cruzeiro do Oeste *Brazil* 23°46S 53°4W **335** A5
Cruzeiro do Sul = Joaçaba *Brazil* 27°5S 51°31W **335** B5
Cruzeiro do Sul *Brazil* 7°35S 72°35W **330** B3
Cry L. *Canada* 58°45N 129°0W **296** B3
Crystal B. *U.S.A.* 28°50N 82°45W **317** G7
Crystal Bay *U.S.A.* 39°15N 120°0W **306** F7
Crystal Brook *Australia* 33°21S 138°12E **282** B3
Crystal City *Mo., U.S.A.* 38°13N 90°23W **310** F6
Crystal City *Tex., U.S.A.* 28°41N 99°50W **314** G5
Crystal Falls *U.S.A.* 46°5N 88°20W **308** B9
Crystal Lake *Fla., U.S.A.* 30°26N 85°42W **316** E4
Crystal Lake *Ill., U.S.A.* 42°14N 88°19W **311** B8
Crystal Palace *U.K.* 51°25N 0°4W **125** B3
Crystal River *U.S.A.* 28°54N 82°35W **317** G7
Crystal Springs *U.S.A.* 31°59N 90°21W **315** F9
Csenger *Hungary* 47°50N 22°41E **182** C7
Csepel *Hungary* 47°25N 19°4E **117** B2
Csepelsziget *Hungary* 47°25N 19°4E **117** B2
Csillaghegy *Hungary* 47°35N 19°2E **117** A2
Csillagtelep *Hungary* 47°24N 19°5E **117** B2
Csömör *Hungary* 47°33N 19°14E **117** A3
Csömöri-patak → *Hungary* 47°35N 19°5E **117** A3
Csongrád *Hungary* 46°43N 20°12E **182** D5
Csongrád □ *Hungary* 46°32N 20°15E **182** D5
Csorna *Hungary* 47°38N 17°18E **182** C2
Csurgo *Hungary* 46°16N 17°9E **182** D2
Cu Lao Hon *Vietnam* 10°54N 108°18E **237** G7
Cua Rao *Vietnam* 19°16N 104°27E **236** C5
Cuácua → *Mozam.* 17°54S 37°0E **269** F4
Cuále *Angola* 8°22S 16°10E **265** D3
Cuále → *Angola* 8°29S 15°1E **265** D3
Cuamato *Angola* 17°2S 15°7E **265** F3
Cuamba *Mozam.* 14°45S 36°22E **269** E4
Cuando *Angola* 14°34S 19°1E **265** E3
Cuando → *Angola* 17°30S 23°15E **265** F4
Cuando Cubango □ *Angola* 16°25S 20°0E **265** F4
Cuangar *Angola* 17°36S 18°39E **265** F3
Cuango = Kwango → *Dem. Rep. of the Congo* 3°14S 17°22E **264** C3
Cuango *Lunda Norte, Angola* 9°8S 18°3E **265** D3
Cuango *Moxico, Angola* 14°30S 19°0E **265** E3
Cuango *Uíge, Angola* 6°15S 16°42E **265** D3
Cuanza → *Angola* 9°21S 13°9E **265** D2
Cuanza Norte □ *Angola* 8°50S 14°30E **265** D2
Cuanza Sul □ *Angola* 10°50S 14°50E **265** E2
Cuao → *Venezuela* 4°55N 67°40W **328** C4
Cuare → *Trin. & Tob.* 10°36N 61°6W **323** t
Cuarto → *Argentina* 33°25S 63°2W **334** C3
Cuatir → *Angola* 17°1S 18°9E **265** F3
Cuatro Vientos *Spain* 40°22N 3°47W **127** B1
Cuatrociénegas *Mexico* 26°59N 102°5W **318** B4
Cuauhtémoc *Chihuahua, Mexico* 28°25N 106°52W **318** B3
Cuauhtémoc *México, Mexico* 19°25N 99°9W **128** B2
Cuba *Portugal* 38°10N 7°54W **195** G3
Cuba *Mo., U.S.A.* 38°4N 91°24W **310** F5
Cuba *N. Mex., U.S.A.* 36°1N 107°4W **305** H10
Cuba *N.Y., U.S.A.* 42°13N 78°17W **312** D6
Cuba ■ *W. Indies* 22°0N 79°0W **320** B4
Cuba City *U.S.A.* 42°36N 90°26W **310** B6
Cubal *Angola* 12°26S 14°3E **265** E2
Cubal → *Angola* 15°9S 12°9E **265** F2
Cuban Museum *U.S.A.* 25°45N 80°13W **128** B2
Cubango → *Africa* 18°50S 22°25E **265** F4
Cubanja *Angola* 14°49S 21°20E **265** E4
Cubao *Phil.* 14°37N 121°3E **127** B2
Cubia *Angola* 15°58S 21°42E **265** F4
Çubuk *Turkey* 40°14N 33°3E **212** B5
Çubuklu *Turkey* 41°5N 29°4E **122** B2
Cuc Phuong △ *Vietnam* 20°17N 105°38E **236** B5
Cuche *Trin. & Tob.* 10°22N 61°10W **323** t
Cuchi *Angola* 14°37S 16°58E **265** E3
Cuchi → *Angola* 15°13S 17°20E **265** F3
Cuchillo-Co *Argentina* 38°20S 64°37W **336** A4
Cuchivero → *Venezuela* 7°40N 65°57W **328** B4
Cuchumatanes, Sierra de los *Guatemala* 15°35N 91°25W **320** C1
Cuckfield *U.K.* 51°1N 0°8W **169** F7
Cucuí *Brazil* 1°12N 66°50W **328** C4
Cucumbi *Angola* 10°17S 19°5E **265** E3
Cucurpé *Mexico* 30°20N 110°43W **318** A2
Cucurrupí *Colombia* 4°23N 76°56W **328** C2
Cúcuta *Colombia* 7°54N 72°31W **328** B3
Cudahy *Calif., U.S.A.* 33°57N 118°11W **126** C3
Cudahy *Wis., U.S.A.* 42°57N 87°51W **311** B9
Cudalbi *Romania* 45°46N 27°41E **183** E12
Cudarebe = Kudarebe *Aruba* 12°37N 70°4W **322** f
Cuddalore *India* 11°46N 79°45E **245** J4
Cuddapah *India* 14°30N 78°47E **245** G4
Cuddapan, L. *Australia* 25°45S 141°26E **280** D3
Cudgewa *Australia* 36°10S 147°42E **283** D7
Cudillero *Spain* 43°33N 6°9W **194** B4
Cudjoehead *Montserrat* 16°47N 62°12W **323** p
Cue *Australia* 27°25S 117°54E **279** E2
Cuebe → *Angola* 15°46S 17°32E **265** F3
Cuéllar *Spain* 41°23N 4°21W **194** D6
Cuemba *Angola* 11°50S 17°42E **265** E3
Cuenca *Ecuador* 2°50S 79°9W **328** D2
Cuenca *Spain* 40°5N 2°10W **196** E2
Cuenca □ *Spain* 40°0N 2°0W **196** F3
Cuenca, Serranía de *Spain* 39°55N 1°50W **196** F3
Cuenca Alta del Manzanares ⌓ *Spain* 40°40N 3°55W **194** E7
Cuerda del Pozo, Embalse de la *Spain* 41°51N 2°44W **196** D2
Cuernavaca *Mexico* 18°55N 99°15W **319** D5
Cuero *U.S.A.* 29°6N 97°17W **314** G6
Cuers *France* 43°14N 6°5E **175** E10
Cueva de la Quebrada del Toro △ *Venezuela* 10°46N 69°3W **328** A4
Cueva de los Guácharos △ *Colombia* 1°35N 76°1W **328** C2
Cuevas, Cerro *Bolivia* 22°0S 65°12W **331** E4
Cuevas de Vera = Cuevas del Almanzora *Spain* 37°18N 1°58W **197** H3
Cuevas del Almanzora *Spain* 37°18N 1°58W **197** H3
Cuevo *Bolivia* 20°15S 63°30W **331** E5
Cugir *Romania* 45°48N 23°25E **183** E8
Cugnaux *France* 43°32N 1°20E **174** E5
Cuhai-Bakony → *Hungary* 47°35N 17°54E **182** C2
Cuiabá *Brazil* 15°30S 56°0W **331** D6
Cuiabá → *Brazil* 17°5S 56°36W **331** D6
Cuicuilco, Pirámide de *Mexico* 19°18N 99°11W **128** C1
Cuihangcun *China* 22°27N 113°32E **219** a
Cuijk *Neths.* 51°44N 5°50E **170** C5
Cuilco *Guatemala* 15°24N 91°58W **320** C1
Cuillin Hills *U.K.* 57°13N 6°15W **167** D2
Cuillin Sd. *U.K.* 57°4N 6°20W **167** D2
Cuilo = Kwilu → *Dem. Rep. of the Congo* 3°22S 17°22E **265** C3
Cuilo *Angola* 8°12S 19°28E **265** D3
Cuilo-Futa *Angola* 6°28S 15°51E **265** D3
Cuima *Angola* 13°25S 15°45E **265** E3
Cuimba *Angola* 6°10S 14°41E **265** D2
Cuiseaux *France* 46°30N 5°22E **173** F12
Cuité *Brazil* 6°29S 36°9W **332** C4
Cuito → *Angola* 18°1S 20°48E **265** F4
Cuito Cuanavale *Angola* 15°10S 19°10E **265** F3
Cuitzeo, L. de *Mexico* 19°55N 101°5W **318** D4
Cuiuni → *Brazil* 0°45S 63°7W **329** D5
Cuivre → *U.S.A.* 38°56N 90°41W **310** F6
Cujmir *Romania* 44°13N 22°57E **182** F7
Cukai *Malaysia* 4°13N 103°25E **237** K4
Çukurca *Turkey* 37°14N 43°36E **213** D10
Cul-de-Sac *St.-Maarten* 18°2N 63°4W **322** a
Cul de Sac *St.-Martin* 18°6N 63°2W **322** a
Culasi *Phil.* 11°26N 122°3E **233** F4
Culbertson *U.S.A.* 48°9N 104°31W **304** B11
Culburra *N.S.W., Australia* 34°56S 150°46E **283** C9
Culburra *S. Austral., Australia* 35°50S 139°58E **282** C3
Culcairn *Australia* 35°41S 147°3E **283** C7
Culebra *Puerto Rico* 18°19N 65°18W **321** b
Culebra, Sierra de la *Spain* 41°55N 6°20W **194** D4
Culfa *Azerbaijan* 38°57N 45°38E **213** C11
Culgoa *Australia* 35°44S 143°6E **282** C5
Culgoa → *Australia* 29°56S 146°20E **281** D4
Culgoa Flood Plain △ *Australia* 28°58S 147°5E **281** D4
Culiacán *Mexico* 24°50N 107°23W **318** C3
Culiacán → *Mexico* 24°30N 107°42W **318** C3
Culik *Indonesia* 8°21S 115°37E **231** J18
Culion *Phil.* 11°54N 119°58E **233** F3
Culion I. *Phil.* 11°50N 120°0E **233** F2
Culiseu → *Brazil* 12°14S 53°17W **331** C7
Cúllar *Spain* 37°35N 2°34W **195** H8
Cullarin Ra. *Australia* 34°30S 149°30E **283** C8
Cullen *U.K.* 57°42N 2°49W **167** D6
Cullen Bullen *Australia* 33°18S 150°2E **283** B9
Cullen Pt. *Australia* 11°57S 141°54E **286** F1
Cullera *Spain* 39°9N 0°17W **197** F4
Cullman *U.S.A.* 34°11N 86°51W **315** D11
Culloden *U.S.A.* 32°52N 84°6W **316** C5
Cullom *U.S.A.* 40°53N 88°16W **311** D8
Cullompton *U.K.* 50°51N 3°24W **169** G4
Culmore *U.S.A.* 38°51N 77°8W **143** B3
Culo → *Angola* 6°13S 15°34E **265** D3
Culoz *France* 45°47N 5°46E **175** C9
Culpeper *U.S.A.* 38°30N 78°0W **309** F14
Culuene → *Brazil* 12°56S 52°51W **331** C7
Culver *U.S.A.* 41°13N 86°25W **311** C10
Culver, Pt. *Australia* 32°54S 124°43E **279** F3
Culver City *U.S.A.* 34°1N 118°24W **126** B2
Culverden *N.Z.* 42°47S 172°49E **285** C7
Culverton *U.S.A.* 33°19N 82°54W **316** B7
Cuma *Angola* 12°52S 15°5E **265** E3
Cumaná *Venezuela* 10°30N 64°5W **329** A5
Cumana B. *Trin. & Tob.* 10°48N 60°56W **323** t
Cumaovası *Turkey* 38°15N 27°9E **205** C9
Cumari *Brazil* 18°16S 48°11W **333** E2
Cumballa Hill *Mumbai, India* **130** a1
Cumbe = Euclides da Cunha *Brazil* 10°31S 39°1W **332** D4
Cumberland *B.C., Canada* 49°40N 125°0W **296** D4
Cumberland *Ont., Canada* 45°29N 75°24W **313** A9
Cumberland *St. Vincent* 13°16N 61°16W **323** n
Cumberland *Iowa, U.S.A.* 41°16N 94°52W **310** C2
Cumberland *Md., U.S.A.* 39°39N 78°46W **309** F14
Cumberland → *U.S.A.* 37°9N 88°25W **308** G9
Cumberland, B. *Chile* 33°37S 78°49W **330** c
Cumberland, C. *Vanuatu* 14°39S 166°37E **287** D4
Cumberland, L. *U.S.A.* 36°52N 85°9W **309** G11
Cumberland Gap ⌓ *U.S.A.* 36°36N 83°40W **309** G12
Cumberland I. *U.S.A.* 30°50N 81°25W **316** E8
Cumberland Is. *Australia* 20°35S 149°10E **280** b
Cumberland Island ⌓ *U.S.A.* 30°12N 81°24W **316** E8
Cumberland L. *Canada* 54°3N 102°18W **297** C8
Cumberland Pen. *Canada* 67°0N 64°0W **295** D19
Cumberland Plateau *U.S.A.* 36°0N 85°0W **315** D12
Cumberland Sd. *Canada* 65°30N 66°0W **295** D18
Cumbernauld *U.K.* 55°57N 3°58W **167** F5
Cumbira *Angola* 12°11S 15°8E **265** E3
Cumborah *Australia* 29°40S 147°45E **281** D4
Cumbres de Majalca △ *Mexico* 28°48N 106°30W **318** B3
Cumbres de Monterrey △ *Mexico* 25°26N 100°25W **318** B4
Cumbres Mayores *Spain* 38°4N 6°39W **195** G4
Cumbria □ *U.K.* 54°42N 2°52W **168** C5
Cumbrian Mts. *U.K.* 54°30N 3°0W **168** C5
Cumbum *India* 15°40N 79°10E **245** G4
Cuminá *Brazil* 1°57S 56°2W **329** D6
Cuminá → *Brazil* 1°30S 56°0W **329** D6
Cuminapanema → *Brazil* 1°9S 54°54W **329** D7
Cumming, C. *Chile* 27°6S 109°14W **330** b
Cummings Mt. *U.S.A.* 35°2N 118°34W **307** K8
Cummins *Australia* 34°16S 135°43E **281** E2
Cumnock *N.S.W., Australia* 32°59S 148°46E **283** B8
Cumnock *E. Ayrs., U.K.* 55°28N 4°17W **167** F4
Cumpas *Mexico* 30°2N 109°48W **318** B3
Cumplida, Pta. *Canary Is.* 28°50N 17°48W **153** e1
Çumra *Turkey* 37°34N 32°45E **212** D5
Cumuto *Trin. & Tob.* 10°35N 61°12W **323** t
Cunapo → *Trin. & Tob.* 10°35N 61°8W **323** t
Cuñare *Colombia* 0°49N 72°32W **328** C3
Cunaripa *Trin. & Tob.* 10°33N 61°10W **323** t
Cuncumén *Chile* 31°53S 70°38W **334** C1
Cundeelee ✪ *Australia* 30°43S 123°25E **279** F3
Cunderdin *Australia* 31°37S 117°12E **279** F2
Cundinamarca □ *Colombia* 5°0N 74°0W **328** C3
Cunene □ *Angola* 16°30S 15°0E **265** F3
Cunene → *Angola* 17°20S 11°50E **265** F2
Cúneo *Italy* 44°23N 7°32E **198** D4
Cung Son *Vietnam* 13°2N 108°58E **236** F7
Çüngüş *Turkey* 38°13N 39°17E **246** B3
Cunhinga *Angola* 12°11S 16°47E **265** E3
Cunhinga → *Angola* 10°42S 16°41E **265** E3
Cunillera, I. = Sa Conillera *Spain* 38°59N 1°13E **206** D1
Cunjamba *Angola* 15°27S 20°10E **265** F4
Cunlhat *France* 45°38N 3°32E **174** C7
Cunnamulla *Australia* 28°2S 145°38E **281** D4
Cunningham *Bahamas* 25°5N 77°26W **153** b
Cunupia *Trin. & Tob.* 10°32N 61°22W **323** t
Cuorgnè *Italy* 45°23N 7°39E **198** C4
Cupar *Sask., Canada* 50°57N 104°10W **297** C8
Cupar *Fife, U.K.* 56°19N 3°1W **167** E5
Cupcini *Moldova* 48°6N 27°23E **183** B12
Cupecé → *Brazil* 23°39S 46°40W **137** B1
Cupertino *U.S.A.* 37°19N 122°2W **306** H4
Cupica, G. de *Colombia* 6°25N 77°30W **328** B2
Ćuprija *Serbia* 43°57N 21°26E **202** C5
Curaçá *Brazil* 8°59S 39°54W **332** C4
Curaçao *W. Indies* 12°10N 69°0W **322** g
Curaçao Int. ✈ (CUR) *Curaçao* 12°11N 68°57W **322** g
Curacautín *Chile* 38°26S 71°53W **336** A2
Curador = Presidente Dutra *Brazil* 5°15S 44°30W **332** C3
Curahuara de Carangas *Bolivia* 17°52S 68°26W **330** D4
Curalhinho = Coelho Neto *Brazil* 4°15S 43°0W **332** B3
Curamata → *Trin. & Tob.* 10°11N 61°28W **323** t
Curanilahue *Chile* 37°29S 73°28W **334** D1
Curaray → *Peru* 2°20S 74°5W **328** D3
Curatabaca *Venezuela* 6°19N 62°51W **329** B5
Cure → *France* 47°40N 3°41E **173** E10
Curepipe *Mauritius* 20°19S 57°31E **272** e
Curepipe Point *Mauritius* 20°21S 57°31E **272** e
Curepto *Chile* 35°8S 72°1W **334** D1
Curiapo *Venezuela* 8°33N 61°5W **329** B5
Curicó *Chile* 34°55S 71°20W **334** C1
Curicuriari → *Brazil* 0°14S 66°48W **328** D4
Curieuse *Seychelles* 4°15S 55°44E **272** c
Curimatá *Brazil* 10°2S 44°17W **332** D3
Curinga *Italy* 38°49N 16°19E **201** D9
Curiplaya *Colombia* 0°16N 74°52W **328** C3
Curitiba *Brazil* 25°20S 49°10W **335** B6
Curitibanos *Brazil* 27°18S 50°36W **335** B5
Curlewis *Australia* 31°7S 150°16E **283** A9
Curoca → *Angola* 15°43S 11°55E **265** F2
Currabubula *Australia* 31°16S 150°44E **283** A9
Currais Novos *Brazil* 6°13S 36°30W **332** C4
Curral Velho *C. Verde Is.* 16°8N 22°48W **153** j
Curralinho *Brazil* 1°45S 49°46W **332** B2
Currane, L. *Ireland* 51°49N 10°4W **166** E1
Currant *U.S.A.* 38°44N 115°28W **304** G6
Curraweena *Australia* 30°47S 145°54E **283** A5
Currawinya △ *Australia* 28°55S 144°27E **281** D3
Current → *U.S.A.* 36°15N 90°55W **314** C9
Currie *Tas., Australia* 39°56S 143°53E **281** F3
Currie *Edinburgh, U.K.* 55°54N 3°17W **121** B2
Currie *Nev., U.S.A.* 40°16N 114°45W **304** F6
Curt-Bunar = Tervel *Bulgaria* 43°45N 27°28E **203** C11
Curtea de Argeş *Romania* 45°12N 24°42E **183** E9
Curtici *Romania* 46°21N 21°18E **182** D6
Curtin Springs *Australia* 25°20S 131°45E **279** E5
Curtis *U.S.A.* 40°38N 100°31W **308** E3
Curtis Group *Australia* 39°30S 146°37E **281** F4
Curtis I. *Queens., Australia* 23°35S 151°10E **280** C5
Curtis I. *Pac. Oc.* 30°30S 178°34W **277** G15
Curuá → *Pará, Brazil* 2°24S 54°5W **329** D7
Curuá → *Pará, Brazil* 5°23S 54°22W **331** B7
Curuá, I. *Brazil* 0°48N 50°10W **332** A1
Curuaés → *Brazil* 7°30S 54°45W **331** B7
Curuaí *Brazil* 2°17S 55°29W **329** D6
Curuápanema → *Brazil* 2°25S 55°2W **329** D6
Curuçá *Brazil* 0°43S 47°50W **332** B2
Curuçá → *Brazil* 4°27S 71°23W **330** B3
Curuguaty *Paraguay* 24°31S 55°42W **335** A4
Çürüksu Çayi = Büyük Menderes → *Turkey* 37°28N 27°11E **205** D9
Curup *Indonesia* 3°26S 102°13E **234** C2
Curupira, Serra *S. Amer.* 1°25N 64°30W **329** C5
Cururu → *Brazil* 7°12S 58°3W **331** B6
Cururupu *Brazil* 1°50S 44°50W **332** B3
Curuzú Cuatiá *Argentina* 29°50S 58°5W **334** B4
Curvelo *Brazil* 18°45S 44°27W **333** E3
Cusago *Italy* 45°26N 9°1E **129** B1
Cusano Milanino *Italy* 45°33N 9°11E **129** A2
Cusco = Cuzco *Peru* 13°32S 72°0W **330** C3
Cushendall *U.K.* 55°5N 6°4W **166** A5
Cushing *U.S.A.* 35°59N 96°46W **314** D6
Cushing, Mt. *Canada* 57°35N 126°57W **296** B3
Cusihuiriáchic *Mexico* 28°14N 106°50W **318** B3
Cusna, Mte. *Italy* 44°17N 10°23E **198** D7
Cussabat = Al Qaşabāt *Libya* 32°39N 14°1E **258** B2
Cusset *France* 46°8N 3°28E **173** F10
Cusseta *U.S.A.* 32°18N 84°47W **316** C5
Cusso, Sa. do *Angola* 6°30S 14°58E **265** D2
Custer *U.S.A.* 43°46N 103°36W **308** D2
Custom House *Dublin, Ireland* **120** b3
Cut Bank *U.S.A.* 48°38N 112°20W **304** B7
Cutchogue *U.S.A.* 41°1N 72°30W **313** E12
Cutervo *Peru* 6°25S 78°55W **330** B2
Cuthbert *U.S.A.* 31°46N 84°48W **316** D5
Cutler *U.S.A.* 36°31N 119°17W **306** J7
Cutler Park *U.S.A.* 42°17N 71°12W **116** B1
Cutler Ridge *U.S.A.* 25°35N 80°20W **317** K9
Cutlerville *U.S.A.* 42°50N 85°40W **311** B11
Cutral-Có *Argentina* 38°58S 69°15W **336** A3
Cutro *Italy* 39°2N 16°59E **201** C9
Cuttaburra → *Australia* 29°43S 144°22E **281** D3
Cuttack *India* 20°25N 85°57E **244** D7
Cuva → *Angola* 11°42S 14°52E **265** E2
Cuvelai *Angola* 15°44S 15°50E **265** F3
Cuvier, C. *Australia* 23°14S 113°22E **279** D1
Cuvier I. *N.Z.* 36°27S 175°50E **284** C4
Çuvuşabaşi → *Turkey* 40°58N 28°51E **122** B1
Cuwei *China* 39°54N 116°15E **114** B1
Cuxhaven *Germany* 53°51N 8°41E **178** B4
Cuyabeno *Ecuador* 0°16S 75°53W **328** D2
Cuyahoga Falls *U.S.A.* 41°8N 81°29W **312** E3
Cuyahoga Valley △ *U.S.A.* 41°24N 81°33W **312** E3
Cuyapo *Phil.* 15°46N 120°40E **232** D3
Cuyo *Phil.* 10°51N 121°2E **233** F3
Cuyo East Pass. *Phil.* 11°0N 121°28E **233** F3
Cuyo Islands *Phil.* 11°4N 120°57E **233** F3
Cuyo West Pass. *Phil.* 11°0N 120°30E **233** F3
Cuyuni → *Guyana* 6°23N 58°41W **329** B6
Cuzco *Bolivia* 20°0S 66°50W **330** E4
Cuzco *Peru* 13°32S 72°0W **330** C3
Cuzco □ *Peru* 13°31S 71°59W **330** C3
Čvrsnica *Bos.-H.* 43°36N 17°35E **182** G2
Cwmbran *U.K.* 51°39N 3°2W **169** F4
Cyangugu *Rwanda* 2°29S 28°54E **268** C2
Cybinka *Poland* 52°12N 14°46E **185** F1
Cyclades *Greece* 37°0N 24°30E **204** E6
Cyclades □ *Greece* 37°0N 25°0E **204** D6
Cygnet *Australia* 43°8S 147°1E **281** G4
Cynthiana *U.S.A.* 38°23N 84°18W **311** F12
Cypress Hills *Sask., Canada* 49°40N 109°30W **297** D7
Cypress Hills *N.Y., U.S.A.* 40°41N 73°53W **132** B2
Cypress Hills ⌓ *Canada* 49°40N 109°30W **297** D7
Cypress Park *U.S.A.* 34°6N 118°13W **126** B3
Cyprus ■ *Asia* 35°0N 33°0E **207** F9
Cyrenaica = Barqa *Libya* 27°0N 23°0E **258** B4
Cyrene *Libya* 32°53N 21°52E **258** B4
Czaplinek *Poland* 53°34N 16°14E **184** E3
Czar *Canada* 52°27N 110°50W **297** C6
Czarna → *Łódzkie, Poland* 51°18N 19°55E **185** G6
Czarna → *Świętokrzyskie, Poland* 50°28N 21°21E **185** H8
Czarna Białostocka *Poland* 53°18N 23°17E **185** E10
Czarna Woda *Poland* 53°51N 18°6E **184** E5
Czarne *Poland* 53°42N 16°58E **184** E3
Czarnków *Poland* 52°55N 16°38E **185** F3
Czaslau = Čáslav *Czech Rep.* 49°54N 15°22E **180** B8
Czech Rep. ■ *Europe* 50°0N 15°0E **180** B8
Czechowice-Dziedzice *Poland* 49°54N 18°59E **185** J5
Czempiń *Poland* 52°9N 16°43E **185** F3
Czeremcha *Poland* 52°31N 23°21E **185** F10
Czerniejewo *Poland* 52°26N 17°30E **185** F4
Czernowitz = Chernivtsi *Ukraine* 48°15N 25°52E **183** B10
Czernriaków *Poland* 52°11N 21°3E **142** B2
Czersk *Poland* 53°46N 17°58E **184** E4
Czerwieńsk *Poland* 52°1N 15°23E **185** F2

Czerwionka-Leszczyny
 Poland 50°7N 18°37E **185** H5
Częstochowa Poland 50°49N 19°7E **185** H6
Człopa Poland 53°6N 16°6E **185** E3
Człuchów Poland 53°41N 17°22E **184** E4
Czortków = Chortkiv
 Ukraine 49°2N 25°46E **177** D13
Cyste Poland 52°13N 20°57E **142** B1
Czyżew-Osada Poland 52°48N 22°19E **185** F9

D

D.C. War Memorial
 Washington, D.C., U.S.A. **143** b1
Da → Vietnam 21°15N 105°20E **228** G5
Da Hinggan Ling China 48°0N 121°0E **219** B13
Da Lat Vietnam 11°56N 108°25E **237** G7
Da Móoca → Brazil 23°35S 46°35W **137** B2
Da Nang Vietnam 16°4N 108°13E **236** D7
Da Qaidam China 37°50N 95°15E **218** D8
Da Yunhe → Hopei,
 China 39°10N 117°10E **227** E9
Da Yunhe → Jiangsu,
 China 34°25N 120°5E **227** G11
Da'an China 45°30N 124°7E **227** B13
Daan Viljoen △ Namibia 22°2S 16°45E **270** B2
Daanbantayan Phil. 11°17N 124°2E **233** F5
Dab'a, Ras el Egypt 31°3N 28°31E **256** H6
Daba Shan China 32°0N 109°0E **228** B7
Dabai Nigeria 11°25N 5°15E **263** C6
Dabajuro Venezuela 11°2N 70°40W **328** A3
Dabakala Ivory C. 8°15N 4°20W **262** D4
Dabaro Somali Rep. 6°21N 48°43E **267** G4
Dabas Hungary 47°11N 19°19E **182** C4
Dabat Ethiopia 12°58N 37°41E **254** E2
Dabbagh, Jabal Si. Arabia 27°52N 35°45E **246** E2
Dabeiba Colombia 7°1N 76°16W **328** B2
Daber = Dobra Poland 53°34N 15°20E **184** E2
Dabhoi India 22°10N 73°20E **242** H5
Dąbie Poland 52°5N 18°50E **185** F5
Dabie Shan China 31°20N 115°20E **229** B10
Dabilda Cameroon 12°45N 14°35E **259** F2
Dabl, W. → Si. Arabia 29°5N 36°16E **251** J7
Dąblice Czech Rep. 50°8N 14°29E **135** B2
Dabnou Niger 14°10N 5°22E **263** C6
Dabo Indonesia 0°30S 104°33E **234** C2
Dabola Guinea 10°50N 11°5W **262** C2
Dabou Ivory C. 5°20N 4°23W **262** D4
Daboya Ghana 9°30N 1°20W **263** D4
Dabravolya Belarus 52°55N 23°59E **185** F10
Dąbrowa Poland 52°19N 20°52E **142** B1
Dąbrowa Białostocka
 Poland 53°40N 23°21E **184** E10
Dąbrowa Górnicza Poland 50°15N 19°10E **185** H6
Dąbrowa Tarnowska
 Poland 50°10N 20°59E **185** H7
Dabu China 24°22N 116°41E **229** E11
Dabugam India 19°27N 82°26E **244** E6
Dabung Malaysia 5°23N 102°1E **237** K4
Dabus → Ethiopia 10°48N 35°10E **257** E4
Dacato → Ethiopia 7°25N 42°40E **257** F5
Dacca = Dhaka Bangla. 23°43N 90°26E **241** D3
Dacca = Dhaka □ Bangla. 24°25N 90°25E **241** D3
Dachang Jiangsu, China 32°13N 118°45E **229** A12
Dachang Shanxi, China 31°17N 121°24E **138** B3
Dachang ✕ China 31°18N 121°25E **138** B3
Dachau Germany 48°15N 11°26E **131** A1
Dachau-Ost Germany 48°15N 11°27E **131** A1
Dachauer Moos Germany 48°13N 11°27E **131** A1
Dachigam, Hoher Austria 47°28N 13°35E **180** B6
Dačice Czech Rep. 49°5N 15°26E **180** B8
Dacre Canada 45°22N 76°57W **312** A8
Dacula U.S.A. 33°59N 83°54W **316** B6
Dadanawa Guyana 2°50N 59°30W **334** C3
Dadar India 19°0N 72°49E **130** A1
Daday Turkey 41°28N 33°27E **205** C6
Dade City U.S.A. 28°22N 82°11W **317** G7
Dadès, Oued → Morocco 30°58N 6°44W **260** B3
Dadeville U.S.A. 32°50N 85°46W **316** C4
Dadhar Pakistan 29°28N 67°39E **242** E2
Dadiya Nigeria 9°35N 11°24E **263** D7
Dadnah U.A.E. 25°32N 56°22E **247** E8
Dadohae Maritime Nat. Park △
 S. Korea 34°0N 126°0E **224** E3
Dadra = Achalpur India 21°22N 77°32E **244** D3
Dadra & Nagar Haveli □
 India 20°5N 73°0E **244** D1
Dadri = Charki Dadri
 India 28°37N 76°17E **242** E7
Dadu Pakistan 26°45N 67°45E **242** F2
Dadu He → China 29°31N 103°46E **228** C4
Daebang S. Korea 37°30N 126°55E **137** B1
Daebudo S. Korea 37°14N 126°35E **224** G2
Daecheongdo S. Korea 37°49N 124°42E **224** G2
Daechi S. Korea 37°30N 127°2E **137** B2
Daegu S. Korea 35°50N 128°37E **224** G4
Daejeon S. Korea 36°20N 127°28E **224** G2
Daejeong S. Korea 33°8N 126°17E **224** a
Daemodo S. Korea 34°11N 126°22E **224** H2
Daet Phil. 14°2N 122°55E **232** D4
Dafdal, J. Si. Arabia 28°16N 35°25E **246** E3
Dafeng China 33°3N 120°45E **227** H11
Dafines Greece 35°13N 25°3E **207** D6
Dafini Athina, Greece 37°55N 23°44E **112** B2
Dafini Peloponnese, Greece 37°48N 22°1E **204** D4
Dafnoudi, Akra Greece 38°28N 20°32E **207** C2
Dağ Turkey 37°12N 30°31E **205** D12
Daga Post Sudan 9°13N 33°58E **246** D3
Dagali Norway 60°25N 8°28E **164** D5
Dagana Senegal 16°30N 15°35W **262** D1
Dagash Sudan 19°19N 33°25E **256** D3
Dagenham U.K. 51°32N 0°8E **125** A4
Dagestan □ Russia 42°30N 47°0E **191** J8
Dagestanskiye Ogni Russia 42°6N 48°12E **191** J9
Dagg Sd. N.Z. 45°23S 166°45E **285** F1
Daggett U.S.A. 34°52N 116°52W **307** L10
Daghestan Republic = Dagestan □
 Russia 42°30N 47°0E **191** J8
Daghfeli Sudan 19°18N 32°40E **256** D3
Daglfing Germany 48°8N 11°39E **131** B2
Dağlıq Qarabağ =
 Nagorno-Karabakh □
 Azerbaijan 39°55N 46°45E **213** C12
Dağö = Hiiumaa Estonia 58°50N 22°45E **188** C2
Dagu China 38°59N 117°42E **138** E2
Dagua Papua N. G. 3°27S 143°20E **286** B2
Daguan China 27°43N 103°56E **228** C4
Dagupan Phil. 16°3N 120°20E **232** C3
Daguragu Australia 17°33S 130°49E **278** C5
Daguragu ○ Australia 17°24S 130°48E **278** C5
Dahab Egypt 28°31N 34°31E **261** A5
Dahab, Geziret el Egypt 30°3N 31°14E **117** D2
Dahanu India 19°58N 72°44E **244** D1
Daheisha West Bank 31°42N 35°11E **123** B2
Dahivadi India 17°43N 74°33E **244** F2
Dahlak Kebir Eritrea 15°50N 40°10E **257** D5
Dahlak Marine △ Eritrea 15°35N 40°1E **257** D5
Dahlem Germany 52°27N 13°16E **115** B2
Dahlenburg Germany 53°11N 10°44E **178** B6
Dahlonega U.S.A. 34°32N 83°59W **316** A6
Dahlwitz-Hoppegarten
 Germany 52°30N 13°41E **115** A5

Dahme Germany 51°52N 13°25E **178** D9
Dahod India 22°50N 74°15E **242** H6
Dahomey = Benin ■ Africa 10°0N 2°0E **263** D5
Dahong Shan China 31°25N 113°0E **229** B9
Dahongliutan China 35°45N 79°20E **243** B8
Dahongmen China 39°48N 116°21E **114** C2
Dahra Libya 29°30N 17°50E **258** C3
Dahra Senegal 15°22N 15°30W **262** B1
Dahra, Massif de Algeria 36°7N 1°21E **261** A5
Dahshūr Egypt 29°45N 31°14E **256** J7
Dahūk Iraq 36°50N 43°1E **213** D10
Dahūk □ Iraq 36°50N 42°50E **213** D10
Dahuofan Shuiku China 41°52N 124°12E **224** B2
Daby, Nafūd al Si. Arabia 22°0N 45°25E **248** B4
Dai Solomon Is. 7°54S 160°40E **287** L11
Dai Hao Vietnam 18°1N 106°25E **236** C6
Dai-Sen Japan 35°22N 133°32E **222** B5
Dai Shan China 30°25N 122°10E **229** B14
Dai Xian China 39°4N 112°58E **226** E7
Daicheng China 38°42N 116°38E **226** E9
Daigo Japan 36°46N 140°21E **223** A12
Daik-u Burma 17°47N 96°40E **241** G6
Daikondi = Day Kundī □
 Afghan. 34°0N 66°0E **240** B2
Daimanji-San Japan 36°14N 133°20E **222** A5
Daingean Ireland 53°18N 7°17W **166** C4
Dainkog China 32°30N 97°58E **228** A1
Daintree Australia 16°20S 145°20E **280** B4
Daintree △ Australia 16°8S 145°2E **280** B4
Daiō-Misaki Japan 34°15N 136°45E **223** C8
Dair, J. ed Sudan 12°27N 30°42E **257** E3
Dairen = Dalian China 38°50N 121°40E **227** E11
Dairūt Egypt 27°34N 30°43E **256** B3
Daisen-Oki △ Japan 35°23N 133°34E **222** B5
Daisetsu-Zan Japan 43°30N 142°57E **220** C11
Daisetsu-Zan △ Japan 43°30N 142°55E **220** C11
Daitari India 21°10N 85°46E **244** D7
Daitō Japan 35°19N 132°58E **222** B4
Daiyun Shan China 25°50N 118°12E **229** E12
Dajarra Australia 21°42S 139°30E **280** C2
Dajiaoting China 39°51N 116°27E **114** B2
Dajiawa China 37°9N 119°0E **227** F10
Dajin Chuan → China 31°16N 101°59E **228** B3
Dak Dam Cambodia 12°20N 107°21E **236** F6
Dak Nhe Vietnam 15°28N 107°48E **236** E6
Dak Pek Vietnam 15°4N 107°44E **236** E6
Dak Song Vietnam 12°19N 107°35E **237** F6
Dak Sui Vietnam 14°55N 107°43E **236** E6
Dakar Senegal 14°34N 17°29E **262** C1
Dakar □ Senegal 14°45N 17°20E **262** C1
Dakhal, W. el → Egypt 28°48N 32°47E **251** K3
Dakhin Bangla. 22°30N 90°45E **241** D3
Dakhla W. Sahara 23°50N 15°53W **260** D1
Dakhla, El Wâhât el
 Egypt 25°30N 28°50E **256** B2
Dakhnoye Russia 59°49N 30°15E **137** C1
Dakingari Nigeria 11°37N 4°1E **263** C5
Dakoank India 7°2N 93°43E **245** L11
Dakor India 22°45N 73°11E **242** H5
Dakoro Niger 14°31N 6°46E **263** C6
Dakota City Iowa, U.S.A. 42°43N 94°12W **310** B2
Dakota City Nebr., U.S.A. 42°25N 96°25W **308** D5
Đakovica Kosovo 42°22N 20°26E **202** D4
Đakovo Croatia 45°19N 18°24E **182** B3
Dal Norway 59°53N 8°40E **164** E5
Dala Lunda Sul, Angola 11°3S 20°17E **265** E4
Dala Uíge, Angola 8°5S 15°49E **265** D3
Dalaba Guinea 8°30S 160°41E **287** M11
Dala-Cachoio Angola 10°30S 14°41E **265** E2
Dala-Järna Sweden 60°33N 14°26E **162** D8
Dalaba Guinea 10°47N 12°12W **262** C2
Dalachi China 37°48N 105°0E **226** F3
Dalagan = San Antonio
 Phil. 14°57N 120°5E **232** D3
Dalai Nur China 43°20N 116°45E **226** C8
Dālakī Iran 29°26N 51°17E **247** D6
Dalälven → Sweden 60°12N 16°43E **162** D10
Dalaman Turkey 36°48N 28°47E **205** E10
Dalaman → Turkey 36°41N 28°43E **205** E10
Dalandzadgad Mongolia 43°27N 104°30E **226** C5
Dalanganem Is. Phil. 10°40N 120°17E **233** F3
Dalap-Uliga-Darrit = Majuro
 Marshall Is. 7°9N 171°12E **288** G9
Dalarna Sweden 61°0N 14°0E **162** D8
Dalarnas län □ Sweden 61°0N 14°15E **162** D8
Dalasýsla □ Iceland 65°15N 22°0W **155** B4
Dalat Malaysia 2°44N 111°56E **235** B4
Dalay Mongolia 43°28N 103°30E **226** C2
Đalbandin Pakistan 29°0N 64°23E **240** C2
Dalbeattie U.K. 54°56N 3°50W **167** G5
Dalby Australia 20°16S 147°18E **280** C4
Dalby Queens., Australia 27°10S 151°17E **281** D5
Dalby Skåne, Sweden 55°40N 13°22E **163** J7
Dalby Söderskog △
 Sweden 55°41N 13°21E **163** J7
Dale Sogn og Fjordane,
 Norway 61°22N 5°23E **164** C22
Dale U.S.A. 38°10N 86°59W **311** F10
Dale City U.S.A. 38°38N 77°19W **309** F15
Dale Hollow L. U.S.A. 36°32N 85°27W **315** C12
Dalej́ov potok →
 Czech Rep. 50°2N 14°24E **135** B2
Dalen Norway 59°26N 8°0E **164** E4
Dalet Burma 19°59N 93°51E **241** F4
Daletme Burma 21°36N 92°46E **241** E4
Daleville Ala., U.S.A. 31°19N 85°43W **316** D4
Daleville Ind., U.S.A. 40°7N 85°33W **311** D11
Dalga Egypt 27°39N 30°41E **256** B3
Dalgán Iran 27°31N 59°19E **247** E8
Dalgety Bay U.K. 56°2N 3°20W **121** A1
Dalhart U.S.A. 36°4N 102°31W **314** C2
Dalhousie N.B., Canada 48°5N 66°26W **299** C6
Dalhousie India 32°38N 75°58E **242** C6
Dali Shaanxi, China 34°48N 109°58E **226** G5
Dali Yunnan, China 25°40N 100°10E **228** E3
Dalian China 38°50N 121°40E **227** E11
Daliang Shan China 28°0N 102°45E **228** D4
Dāliyat el Karmel Israel 32°43N 35°2E **123** C4
Dalj Croatia 45°29N 18°59E **182** B3
Dalkeith Midloth., U.K. 55°54N 3°4W **121** B3
Dalkeith S. Africa 30°0N 85°9W **316** H4
Dalkey I. Ireland 53°16N 6°5W **120** B3
Dalmau India 26°4N 81°2E **243** F9
Dalmellington U.K. 55°19N 4°23W **167** F4
Dalmeny N.S.W., Australia 36°10S 150°8E **283** D9
Dalmeny Edinburgh, U.K. 55°59N 3°22W **121** B1

Dangouadougou
 Burkina Faso 10°9N 4°56W **262** D4
Dangrek, Mts. = Dangrek, Phnom
 Thailand 14°20N 104°0E **236** E5
Dangrek, Phnom Thailand 14°20N 104°0E **236** E5
Dangshan China 34°27N 116°22E **226** G9
Dangtu China 31°32N 118°25E **229** B12
Dangyang China 30°52N 111°44E **229** B8
Daniel U.S.A. 42°52N 110°4W **304** E8
Daniel's Harbour Canada 50°13N 57°35W **299** B8
Daniel's Ra. Australia 33°52S 151°15E **139** B2
Danielskuil S. Africa 28°11S 23°33E **270** C3
Danielson U.S.A. 41°48N 71°53W **313** E13
Danielsville U.S.A. 34°8N 83°13W **316** A6
Danilov Russia 58°16N 40°13E **188** C11
Danilov S.C., U.S.A. 34°18N 79°52W **315** D15
Danilovgrad Montenegro 42°38N 19°4E **202** D3
Danilovka Russia 50°25N 44°12E **190** E7
Daning China 36°28N 110°45E **226** F6
Danish West Indies = Virgin Is.
 (U.S.) ☑ W. Indies 18°20N 65°0W **321** C7
Danissa Kenya 3°17N 40°59E **267** D5
Danja Nigeria 11°21N 7°30E **263** C6
Danje-la-Menha Angola 9°32S 14°39E **265** D2
Danjiangkou China 32°31N 111°30E **229** A8
Danjiangkou Shuiku
 China 32°37N 111°30E **229** A8
Dank Oman 23°33N 56°16E **247** F8
Dankalwa Nigeria 11°52N 12°12E **263** C7
Dankama Nigeria 13°20N 7°44E **263** C6
Dankhar Gompa India 32°10N 78°10E **242** C8
Dankov Russia 53°20N 39°5E **188** F10
Danleng China 30°1N 103°31E **228** B4
Danli Honduras 14°4N 86°35W **320** D2
Danmark = Denmark ■
 Europe 55°45N 10°0E **163** J3
Danmark Fjord Greenland 81°30N 22°0W **154** A8
Danmarkshavn
 Greenland 76°45N 18°50W **154** B9
Dannemora U.S.A. 44°43N 73°44W **313** B11
Dannenberg Germany 53°6N 11°5E **178** B7
Dannevirke N.Z. 40°12S 176°8E **284** G5
Dannhauser S. Africa 28°0S 30°3E **271** C5
Danot Ethiopia 7°33N 45°17E **267** C6
Dansalan = Marawi City
 Phil. 8°0N 124°21E **233** G5
Dansville U.S.A. 42°34N 77°42W **312** D7
Danta India 24°11N 72°46E **242** G5
Dantan India 21°57N 87°20E **243** J12
Dantewara India 18°54N 81°21E **244** E5
Danube = Dunărea →
 Europe 45°20N 29°40E **183** E14
Danubyu Burma 17°15N 95°35E **241** G5
Danvers U.S.A. 42°34N 70°56W **313** D14
Danville Ga., U.S.A. 32°37N 83°15W **316** C6
Danville Ill., U.S.A. 40°8N 87°37W **311** D9
Danville Ind., U.S.A. 39°46N 86°32W **311** E10
Danville Ky., U.S.A. 37°39N 84°46W **311** G12
Danville Pa., U.S.A. 40°58N 76°37W **313** F8
Danville Va., U.S.A. 36°36N 79°23W **309** G14
Danville Vt., U.S.A. 44°25N 72°9W **313** B12
Danyang China 32°0N 119°31E **229** B12
Danzhou China 19°31N 109°33E **228** E8
Danzhou China 19°31N 109°33E **228** E8
Danzig = Gdańsk Poland 54°22N 18°40E **184** D5
Danzig B. = Gdańsk, G. of
 Poland 54°30N 19°20E **184** D5
Dao Antique, Phil. 10°30N 121°57E **233** F3
Dao Capiz, Phil. 11°24N 122°41E **233** F4
Đào = Portugal 40°20N 8°11W **194** E2
Dao Xian China 25°36N 111°31E **229** E8
Daocheng China 29°0N 100°10E **228** C3
Daora W. Sahara 27°5N 12°59W **260** C2
Daoud = Aïn Beïda Algeria 35°50N 7°29E **261** A6
Daoukro Ivory C. 7°0N 3°58W **262** D4
Dapa Phil. 9°46N 126°3E **233** G6
Dapaong Togo 10°55N 0°16E **263** C5
Dapchi Nigeria 12°32N 11°31E **263** C7
Dapiak, Mt. Phil. 8°15N 123°28E **233** G4
Dapitan Phil. 8°39N 123°25E **233** G4
Dapoli India 17°46N 73°11E **244** F1
Daqahlīya □ Egypt 30°55N 31°30E **251** H2
Daqing China 46°35N 125°0E **219** B13
Daqing Shan China 40°40N 111°0E **226** D6
Daqq-e Sorkh, Kavīr Iran 33°45N 52°50E **247** C7
Dar Banda Africa 8°0N 23°0E **254** F6
Dar el Beida = Casablanca
 Morocco 33°36N 7°36W **260** B3
Dar es Salaam Tanzania 6°50S 39°12E **268** D4
Dar Mazār Iran 29°14N 57°20E **247** D8
Dar Rounga C.A.R. 0°45N 22°20E **264** A4
Dãr Ta'izzah Syria 36°20N 36°52E **250** B7
Dar'ā Syria 32°36N 36°7E **250** F7
Dar'ā □ Syria 32°55N 36°10E **250** F7
Dara Dere = Zlatograd
 Bulgaria 41°22N 25°7E **203** E9
Đārāb Iran 28°50N 54°30E **247** D7
Daraban Pakistan 31°44N 70°20E **242** D4
Darabani Romania 48°10N 26°39E **183** B11
Darai Hills Papua N. G. 7°8S 143°33E **286** B2
Daraina Madag. 13°12S 49°40E **272** A2
Daraj Libya 30°10N 10°28E **258** B2
Darakeh Iran 35°49N 51°22E **141** A2
Daram Phil. 11°38N 124°48E **233** F5
Dārān Iran 32°59N 50°24E **247** C6
Daravica Kosovo 42°32N 20°8E **202** D4
Daraw Egypt 24°22N 32°51E **256** C3
Dārayyā Syria 33°28N 36°15E **250** G7
Darazo Nigeria 11°1N 10°24E **263** C7
Darband Tehrãn, Iran 35°49N 51°25E **141** A2
Darband, Kūh-e Iran 31°34N 57°8E **247** D8
Darbhanga India 26°15N 85°55E **243** F11
Darby U.S.A. 64°19N 162°47W **303** D7
D'Arcy Croatia 55°40N 18°41E **182** B3
Dardanelle Calif., U.S.A. 38°20N 119°50W **306** G7
Dardanelle Ark., U.S.A. 35°13N 93°9W **314** D8
Dardanelles = Çanakkale Boğazı
 Turkey 40°17N 26°32E **203** F10
Dare → Ethiopia 7°20N 42°11E **257** F5
Darende Turkey 38°31N 37°30E **212** C7
Dãrestãn Iran 29°9N 58°42E **247** D8
Darfield N.Z. 43°29S 172°7E **285** D7
Darfo Italy 45°53N 10°11E **198** C7
Dãrfūr Sudan 13°40N 24°0E **259** F4
Dargai Pakistan 34°25N 71°55E **242** B4
Dargan Ata = Darganata
 Turkmenistan 40°29N 62°10E **240** A3
Dargaville N.Z. 35°57S 173°52E **284** A4
Dargan China 33°45N 110°50E **226** H6
Dargol Niger 13°13N 1°27E **263** C5
Darhan Mongolia 49°37N 106°21E **218** B10
Darhan Muminggan
 China 41°40N 110°28E **226** D6
Dari Sudan 5°48N 30°26E **257** F3
Darica Turkey 40°45N 29°23E **212** B4
Darién □ Panama 8°0N 77°30W **320** E4
Darién, G. del Colombia 9°0N 77°0W **328** B3
Darién, Serranía del
 Colombia 8°30N 77°30W **320** E4
Darién ○ Panama 7°36N 77°57W **320** E4
Darīeh Iran 30°5N 50°21E **141** A2
Daribadi Nigeria 11°54N 10°24E **263** C7
Dariganga = Ovoot
 Mongolia 45°21N 113°45E **226** B7
Darini Dere → Turkey 36°30N 27°34E **205** F9
Dario Nicaragua 12°44N 86°9W **320** D2
Darjeeling = Darjiling
 India 27°3N 88°18E **241** C7

Darjiling India 27°3N 88°18E **241** B2
Darkan Australia 33°20S 116°43E **279** F2
Darke Peak Australia 33°27S 136°12E **282** B2
Darkhana Pakistan 30°39N 72°11E **242** D5
Darkhazīneh Iran 31°54N 48°39E **247** D6
Darkot Pass Pakistan 36°45N 73°26E **243** A5
Darling → Australia 34°4S 141°54E **282** C4
Darling Downs Australia 27°30S 150°30E **281** D5
Darling Harbour Sydney, Australia **139** b1
Darling Point Australia 33°52S 151°15E **139** B2
Darling Ra. Australia 32°30S 116°0E **279** F2
Darlington Durham, U.K. 54°32N 1°33W **168** C6
Darlington Fla., U.S.A. 30°47N 86°3W **316** E2
Darlington S.C., U.S.A. 34°18N 79°52W **315** D15
Darlington Wis., U.S.A. 42°41N 90°7W **310** D8
Darlington, L. S. Africa 33°10S 25°9E **270** D4
Darlington Point Australia 34°37S 146°1E **283** C7
Darlot, L. Australia 27°48S 121°35E **279** E3
Darlowo Poland 54°25N 16°25E **184** D3
Dārmānești Bacău,
 Romania 46°21N 26°33E **183** D11
Dārmānești Suceava,
 Romania 47°44N 26°9E **183** C11
Darmstadt Germany 49°51N 8°39E **179** F4
Darnah Libya 32°45N 22°45E **258** B4
Darnall S. Africa 29°23S 31°18E **271** C5
Darndale Ireland 53°23N 6°12W **120** A2
Darney France 48°5N 6°2E **173** D13
Darnétal France 49°25N 1°10E **172** C4
Darney France 48°5N 6°2E **173** D13
Darnick Australia 32°48S 143°38E **282** B5
Darnley Australia 9°35S 143°46E **280** a
Darnley, C. Antarctica 68°0S 69°0E **151** C6
Darnley B. Canada 69°30N 123°30W **294** D7
Daroca Spain 41°9N 1°25W **196** D3
Daror Ethiopia 8°14N 44°42E **267** C5
Darou-Mousti Senegal 15°3N 16°3W **262** B1
Darr → Australia 23°39S 143°50E **280** C3
Darra Pezu Pakistan 32°19N 70°44E **242** C4
Darran Mts. N.Z. 44°37S 167°59E **285** E2
Darreh Shahr Iran 33°7N 47°22E **213** F12
Darrequeira Argentina 37°42S 63°10W **334** D3
Darrington U.S.A. 48°15N 121°36W **304** B3
Darrūs Iran 35°46N 51°27E **141** A2
Darsana Bangla. 23°35N 88°48E **241** D2
Darsi India 15°46N 79°44E **245** G4
Darsser Ort Germany 54°28N 12°32E **178** A8
Dart → U.K. 50°24N 3°39W **169** G4
Dart, C. Antarctica 73°6S 126°20W **151** D14
Dartford U.K. 51°26N 0°13E **125** B5
Dartmoor Vic., Australia 37°56S 141°19E **282** D4
Dartmoor Devon, U.K. 50°38N 3°57W **169** G4
Dartmoor △ U.K. 50°37N 3°59W **169** G4
Dartmouth N.S., Canada 44°40N 63°30W **299** D7
Dartmouth Devon, U.K. 50°21N 3°36W **169** G4
Dartmouth, Res.
 Australia 34°35S 147°32E **283** D7
Dartmouth Res. Australia 26°4S 145°18E **281** D4
Dartuch, C. = Artrutx, C. de
 Spain 39°55N 3°49E **206** B10
Daru Papua N. G. 9°3S 143°13E **286** C2
Daruvar Croatia 45°35N 17°14E **182** C2
Darvaza = Içoguz
 Turkmenistan 40°11N 58°24E **216** D5
Darvel, Teluk = Lahad Datu, Telok
 Malaysia 4°50N 118°20E **235** B5
Darwen U.K. 53°42N 2°29W **168** D5
Darwendale Zimbabwe 17°41S 30°33E **271** A5
Darwha India 20°15N 77°45E **244** D3
Darwin N. Terr., Australia 12°25S 130°51E **278** B5
Darwin Calif., U.S.A. 36°15N 117°35W **307** J9
Darwin, Mt. Chile 54°47S 69°55W **336** D3
Darwin, Volcán Ecuador 0°10S 91°18W **330** a
Darwin Ganj Delhi, India **120** A3
Darwin Khan Pakistan 31°48N 71°6E **242** D4
Daryācheh-ye Bakhtegãn
 Iran 29°40N 53°50E **247** D7
Daryapur India 20°55N 77°20E **244** D3
Daryoi Amu = Amudarya →
 Uzbekistan 43°58N 59°34E **216** D5
Dãs U.A.E. 25°20N 53°30E **247** E7
Dashahe China 42°44N 128°12E **224** D4
Dashen, Ras Ethiopia 13°8N 38°26E **257** E4
Dasher S. Africa 30°45N 83°13W **316** E6
Dashetai China 41°0N 109°5E **226** D5
Dashkesan = Daşkäsän
 Azerbaijan 40°25N 46°0E **191** K7
Dashköpri Turkmenistan 36°16N 62°8E **247** B9
Dashoguz Turkmenistan 41°49N 59°58E **216** D5
Dasht → Pakistan 25°10N 61°40E **240** D2
Dasht-i-Tahlab Pakistan 28°40N 62°20E **240** C1
Daşkäsän Azerbaijan 40°25N 46°0E **191** K7
Daşkäsän Azerbaijan 40°25N 46°0E **191** K7
Daşmariñas Phil. 14°20N 120°58E **232** D3
Dasol B. Phil. 15°52N 119°50E **232** D3
Dassa Benin 7°46N 2°14E **263** D5
Dassua India 31°49N 75°38E **242** D6
Datadian Indonesia 2°1N 115°13E **235** B5
Datanga China 28°13N 112°1E **182** B2
Datça Turkey 36°46N 27°40E **205** E9
Datia India 25°40N 78°27E **243** G8
Datian China 25°40N 117°40E **229** E11
Datong Anhui, China 30°48N 117°44E **229** B11
Datong Shanxi, China 40°6N 113°18E **226** D7
Datong Shanxi, China 40°6N 113°18E **226** D7
Dattapur = Dhamangaon
 India 20°48N 78°9E **244** D4
Datteln Germany 51°39N 7°21E **170** D3
Datu Piang Phil. 7°2N 124°30E **233** H5
Datuk, Tanjong = Datu, Tanjong
 Indonesia 2°5N 109°39E **235** B3
Datum China 30°0N 116°23E **114** B2
Daua → Dawa → Africa 4°11N 42°6E **257** G5
Daud Khel Pakistan 32°53N 71°34E **242** C4
Daudnagar India 25°2N 84°24E **243** G11
Daugava → Latvia 57°4N 24°3E **188** E3
Daugavpils Latvia 55°53N 26°32E **188** E4
Daulatabad India 19°57N 75°15E **244** E2
Daulatpur India 28°44N 77°6E **120** A1
Daule Ecuador 1°51S 79°52W **330** D2
Daule → Ecuador 2°10S 79°52W **330** D2
Daule-Peripa, Presa
 Ecuador 1°0S 79°35W **330** D2
Daulpur Germany 50°11N 6°49E **170** E2
Daund India 18°26N 74°40E **244** E2
Daung Kyun Burma 12°13N 98°4E **237** F2
Dauphin Man., Canada 51°9N 100°5W **297** C8
Dauphin L. Canada 51°20N 99°45W **297** C8
Dauphin France 45°15N 5°25E **173** D9
Dauphin I. U.S.A. 30°15N 88°11W **316** E2
Dauphin Island U.S.A. 30°15N 88°6W **316** E2
Dauphiné France 45°15N 5°25E **173** D9
Daura Borno, Nigeria 11°31N 11°24E **263** C7
Daura Katsina, Nigeria 13°2N 8°21E **263** C6
Dãusa India 26°52N 76°20E **242** F7
Däväçi Azerbaijan 41°15N 48°57E **191** K9
Davangere India 14°25N 75°55E **245** M9
Davao Phil. 7°0N 125°40E **233** H6
Davao □ Phil. 7°0N 125°40E **233** H6
Davao, G. of Phil. 6°30N 125°48E **233** H6
Davao del Sur □ Phil. 6°50N 125°20E **233** H6
Davao G. Phil. 6°30N 125°48E **233** H6
Davao Oriental □ Phil. 7°10N 126°30E **233** H6

Dāvar Panāh = Sarāvān
 Iran 27°25N 62°15E **247** E9
Davenport Calif., U.S.A. 37°1N 122°12W **306** H4
Davenport Fla., U.S.A. 28°10N 81°36W **317** G7
Davenport Iowa, U.S.A. 41°32N 90°35W **310** E9
Davenport Wash., U.S.A. 47°39N 118°9W **304** C4
Davenport Ra. Australia 20°28S 134°0E **280** C1
Davenport Range △
 Australia 20°36S 134°12E **280** C1
Daventry U.K. 52°16N 1°10W **169** E6
David Panama 8°30N 82°30W **320** E3
David City U.S.A. 41°15N 97°8W **308** E5
David Glacier Antarctica 75°20S 162°0E **151** D11
David Gorodok = Davyd Haradok
 Belarus 52°4N 27°8E **177** B14
David's Citadel Jerusalem **123** b3
David's Tomb Jerusalem **123** b3
Davidson Canada 51°16N 105°59W **297** C7
Davidson, Mt. U.S.A. 37°44N 122°27W **136** B2
Davidson Mts. U.S.A. 68°41N 142°22W **303** B12
Davidson's Mains U.K. 55°58N 3°16W **121** B2
Davie U.S.A. 26°4N 80°15W **317** H8
Davie City U.S.A. 26°4N 80°15W **317** H8
Daviot U.K. 57°25N 4°8W **167** D5
Davis Antarctica 68°34S 77°55E **151** C6
Davis Calif., U.S.A. 38°33N 121°44W **306** G5
Davis Dam U.S.A. 35°12N 114°34W **307** K12
Davis Inlet Canada 55°50N 60°59W **299** F7
Davis Mts. U.S.A. 30°50N 103°55W **314** F3
Davis Sea Antarctica 66°0S 92°0E **151** C7
Davis Str. N. Amer. 65°0N 58°0W **295** D19
Davisboro U.S.A. 32°59N 82°36W **316** C6
Davison U.S.A. 43°2N 83°31W **311** A13
Davlos Cyprus 35°25N 33°54E **207** D9
Davo → Ivory C. 5°0N 6°10W **262** D3
Davos Switz. 46°48N 9°49E **179** J5
Dāvūdiyeh Iran 35°45N 51°25E **141** A2
Davulca Turkey 37°43N 27°17E **205** D9
Davy L. Canada 58°53N 108°18W **297** B7
Davyd Haradok Belarus 52°4N 27°8E **177** B14
Davydkovo Russia 55°43N 37°29E **129** B2
Dawa → Africa 4°11N 42°6E **257** G5
Dawaki Bauchi, Nigeria 9°25N 9°33E **263** D6
Dawaki Kano, Nigeria 12°5N 8°23E **263** C6
Dawei = Tavoy Burma 14°2N 98°12E **236** E2
Dawes Ra. Australia 24°40S 150°40E **280** C5
Dawidy Poland 52°8N 20°58E **142** C1
Dawkah Oman 18°39N 54°5E **249** D6
Dawley = Telford U.K. 52°40N 2°27W **169** E5
Dawlish U.K. 50°35N 3°28W **169** G4
Dawna Ra. Burma 16°30N 98°30E **236** D2
Dawnyein Burma 15°54N 95°36E **241** G5
Dawqah Si. Arabia 19°36N 45°54E **248** C3
Dawros Hd. Ireland 54°50N 8°33W **166** B3
Dawson U.S.A. 31°46N 84°27W **316** D5
Dawson, L. Canada 53°50N 57°50W **299** B8
Dawson B. Canada 52°53N 100°49W **297** C8
Dawson City Canada 64°10N 139°30W **294** E4
Dawson Creek Canada 55°45N 120°15W **296** B4
Dawson Inlet Canada 61°50N 93°25W **297** A10
Dawson Ra. Australia 24°30S 149°48E **280** C4
Dawu Hubei, China 31°34N 114°7E **229** B9
Dawu Sichuan, China 30°55N 101°10E **228** B3
Dawwah Oman 20°33N 58°48E **249** C6
Dawwara, Ras id- Malta 35°52N 14°21E **207** D1
Dax France 43°44N 1°3W **174** E2
Daxian China 31°15N 107°23E **228** B6
Daxin China 22°50N 107°11E **228** F6
Daxindian China 37°30N 120°50E **227** F11
Daxing China 39°47N 116°24E **114** C2
Daxinggou China 43°25N 129°40E **227** C15
Daxue Shan Sichuan,
 China 30°30N 101°30E **228** B3
Daxue Shan Yunnan,
 China 23°42N 99°48E **228** F2
Day U.S.A. 30°12N 83°17W **316** E6
Day Kundī □ Afghan. 34°0N 66°0E **240** B2
Daya el Khadra Mauritania 25°14N 6°2W **260** D2
Dayang He → China 39°51N 123°38E **224** D3
Dayao China 25°43N 101°20E **228** E3
Daye China 30°6N 114°58E **229** B10
Dayet en Naharat Mali 17°39N 3°10W **262** B4
Dayi China 30°42N 103°30E **228** B4
Daylesford Australia 37°21S 144°9E **282** D6
Dayong China 29°11N 110°30E **229** C8
Dayr az Zawr Syria 35°20N 40°5E **213** E9
Dayr az Zawr □ Syria 35°20N 40°0E **213** E9
Days Bay N.Z. 41°17S 174°54E **143** B2
Daysland Canada 52°50N 112°20W **296** C6
Dayton Iowa, U.S.A. 42°16N 94°4W **310** B2
Dayton Nev., U.S.A. 39°14N 119°36W **306** F7
Dayton Ohio, U.S.A. 39°45N 84°12W **311** E12
Dayton Pa., U.S.A. 40°53N 79°15W **312** F5
Dayton Tenn., U.S.A. 35°30N 85°1W **315** D12
Dayton Wash., U.S.A. 46°19N 117°59W **304** D5
Dayton Wyo., U.S.A. 44°53N 107°16W **304** D10
Daytona Beach U.S.A. 29°13N 81°1W **317** F7
Dayu China 25°24N 114°22E **229** E10
Dayville U.S.A. 44°28N 119°32W **304** D4
Dazaifu Japan 33°32N 130°32E **222** D2
Dazhu China 30°41N 107°15E **228** B6
Dazkırı Turkey 37°57N 29°55E **205** D11
De Aar S. Africa 30°39S 24°0E **270** D3
De Armanville U.S.A. 33°38N 85°45W **316** B4
De Bary U.S.A. 28°54N 81°18W **317** F7
De Biesbosch △ Neths. 51°45N 4°48E **170** C4
De Forest U.S.A. 43°15N 89°20W **310** D8
De Funiak Springs U.S.A. 30°43N 86°7W **316** E2
De Grey → Australia 20°12S 119°13E **278** D2
De Haan Belgium 51°16N 3°2E **170** B3
De Hoge Veluwe △ Neths. 52°5N 5°50E **170** B5
De Hoop △ S. Africa 34°30S 20°28E **270** E3
De Kalb Junction U.S.A. 44°30N 75°16W **313** B9
De Kennemerduinen △
 Neths. 52°27N 4°33E **170** B4
De Land U.S.A. 29°2N 81°18W **317** F7
De Leon U.S.A. 32°7N 98°32W **314** E5
De Leon Springs U.S.A. 29°7N 81°21W **317** F7
De Long Mts. U.S.A. 68°10N 163°30E **303** B8
De Panne Belgium 51°6N 2°34E **170** C2
De Pere U.S.A. 44°27N 88°4W **310** C7
De Queen U.S.A. 34°2N 94°21W **314** D7
De Quincy U.S.A. 30°27N 93°26W **314** F7
De Ruyters U.S.A. 42°45N 75°53W **313** D9
De Smet U.S.A. 44°23N 97°33W **308** C5
De Soto U.S.A. 38°8N 90°34W **310** F8
De Soto City U.S.A. 27°11N 81°26W **317** H7
De Tour Village U.S.A. 46°0N 83°56W **309** B11
De Witt U.S.A. 34°18N 91°20W **314** D9
De Witt Iowa, U.S.A. 41°46N 90°33W **310** E9
De Witt Mich., U.S.A. 42°51N 84°34W **311** B12
Dead I. U.S.A. 43°58N 122°37W **304** E2
Dead Sea Asia 31°30N 35°30E **250** D4
Deadman B. U.S.A. 70°11N 148°27W **303** A10
Deadwood U.S.A. 44°23N 103°44W **308** C2
Deadwood L. Canada 59°10N 128°30W **296** B3
Deal U.K. 51°13N 1°25E **169** F9
Deal I. U.S.A. 39°35N 147°20E **283** F4
Dealesville S. Africa 28°41S 25°44E **270** C3
De'an China 29°21N 115°46E **229** C10
Dean → Canada 52°49N 126°58W **296** C3
Dean, Forest of U.K. 51°45N 2°33W **169** F5
Dean Chan. Canada 52°30N 127°15W **296** C3
Deán Funes Argentina 30°20S 64°20W **334** C3
Dearborn Mich., U.S.A. 42°19N 83°10W **311** B13

Dearborn *Mo., U.S.A.* 39°32N 94°46W **310** E2
Dease → *Canada* 59°56N 128°32W **296** B3
Dease Inlet *U.S.A.* 71°2N 155°26W **303** A9
Dease L. *Canada* 58°40N 130°5W **296** B2
Dease Lake *Canada* 58°25N 130°6W **296** B2
Death Valley *U.S.A.* 36°15N 116°50W **307** J10
Death Valley △ *U.S.A.* 36°29N 117°6W **307** J9
Death Valley Junction
U.S.A. 36°20N 116°25W **307** J10
Deatnu = Tana →
Norway 70°30N 28°14E **160** A23
Deauville *France* 49°23N 0°2E **172** C7
Deba *Spain* 43°18N 2°21W **196** B2
Deba Habe *Nigeria* 10°14N 11°20E **263** C7
Debagram *India* 23°51N 90°33E **243** H14
Debak *Malaysia* 1°34N 111°25E **235** B4
Debaltsevo *Ukraine* 48°22N 38°26E **189** H10
Debao *China* 23°21N 106°46E **228** F6
Debar *Macedonia* 41°31N 20°30E **202** E4
Debark *Ethiopia* 13°1N 37°48E **257** E4
Debden *Canada* 53°30N 106°50W **297** C7
Debdou *Morocco* 33°59N 3°0W **261** B4
Debe *Trin. & Tob.* 10°22N 61°27W **323** t
Dębica *Poland* 50°2N 21°25E **185** H8
Dęblin *Poland* 51°34N 21°50E **185** G8
Dębno *Poland* 52°44N 14°41E **185** F1
Débo, L. *Mali* 15°14N 4°15W **262** B4
DeBolt *Canada* 55°12N 118°1W **296** B5
Deborah East, L.
Australia 30°45S 119°0E **279** F2
Deborah West, L.
Australia 30°45S 119°5E **279** F2
Deboyne Is. *Papua N. G.* 10°43S 152°22E **286** F7
Debrc *Serbia* 44°38N 19°53E **202** B3
Debre Birhan *Ethiopia* 9°41N 39°31E **257** F4
Debre Markos *Ethiopia* 10°20N 37°40E **257** E4
Debre May *Ethiopia* 11°20N 37°25E **257** E4
Debre Sina *Ethiopia* 9°51N 39°50E **257** F4
Debre Tabor *Ethiopia* 11°50N 38°26E **257** E4
Debre Zebit *Ethiopia* 11°48N 38°30E **257** E4
Debre Zevit *Ethiopia* 8°50N 39°0E **257** F4
Debrecen *Hungary* 47°33N 21°42E **182** C6
Debrzno *Poland* 53°31N 17°14E **184** E4
Dečani *Kosovo* 42°30N 20°18E **202** D4
Decatur *Ala., U.S.A.* 34°36N 86°59W **315** D11
Decatur *Ga., U.S.A.* 33°46N 84°16W **113** B3
Decatur *Ill., U.S.A.* 39°51N 88°57W **310** E8
Decatur *Ind., U.S.A.* 40°50N 84°56W **311** D12
Decatur *Mich., U.S.A.* 42°7N 85°58W **311** B11
Decatur *Tex., U.S.A.* 33°14N 97°35W **314** E6
Decazeville *France* 44°34N 2°15E **174** D6
Deccan *India* 18°0N 79°0E **244** F4
Deception, Mt. *Australia* 30°42S 138°16E **282** A3
Deception B. *Papua N. G.* 7°45S 144°40E **286** D3
Deception Bay *Australia* 27°10S 153°5E **281** D5
Deception I. *Antarctica* 63°0S 60°15W **151** C17
Deception L. *Canada* 56°33N 104°13W **297** B8
Dechang *China* 27°25N 102°11E **228** D4
Dechhu *India* 26°46N 72°20E **242** F5
Děčín *Czech Rep.* 50°47N 14°12E **180** A7
Decize *France* 46°50N 3°28E **173** F10
Deckerville *U.S.A.* 43°32N 82°44W **312** C2
Decollatura *Italy* 39°3N 16°21E **201** C9
Decorah *U.S.A.* 43°18N 91°48W **308** D8
Deda *Romania* 46°56N 24°50E **183** D9
Dedaye *Burma* 16°24N 95°53E **241** G5
Dedéagach = Alexandroupoli
Greece 40°50N 25°54E **203** F9
Dededo *Guam* 13°31N 144°50E **302** d
Deder *Ethiopia* 9°19N 41°27E **257** F5
Dedham *U.S.A.* 42°15N 71°10W **116** B1
Dedoplis Tskaro = Tsiteli-Tsqaro
Georgia 41°33N 46°0E **191** K8
Dédougou *Burkina Faso* 12°30N 3°25W **262** C4
Dedovichi *Russia* 57°32N 29°56E **188** D5
Dedza *Malawi* 14°20S 34°20E **269** E3
Dee → *Aberds., U.K.* 57°9N 2°5W **167** D6
Dee → *Dumf. & Gall., U.K.* 54°51N 4°3W **167** G4
Dee → *Wales, U.K.* 53°22N 3°17W **168** D4
Deep B. *Canada* 61°15N 116°35W **296** A5
Deep Bay = Chilumba
Malawi 10°28S 34°12E **269** E3
Deep Bay = Shenzhen Wan
China 22°27N 113°55E **219** a
Deep Lead *Australia* 37°0S 142°43E **282** D5
Deepwater *N.S.W.,*
Australia 29°25S 151°51E **281** D5
Deepwater *Mo., U.S.A.* 38°16N 93°47W **310** F3
Deer → *Canada* 58°23N 94°13W **297** B10
Deer I. *U.S.A.* 54°55N 162°18W **303** J7
Deer L. *Canada* 52°40N 94°20W **297** C10
Deer Lake *Nfld. & L.,*
Canada 49°11N 57°27W **299** C8
Deer Lake *Ont., Canada* 52°36N 94°20W **297** C10
Deer Lodge *U.S.A.* 46°24N 112°44W **304** C7
Deer Park *Fla., U.S.A.* 28°6N 80°54W **317** G9
Deer Park *Ohio, U.S.A.* 39°12N 84°23W **311** E12
Deer Park *Wash., U.S.A.* 47°57N 117°28W **304** C5
Deer River *U.S.A.* 47°20N 93°48W **308** B7
Deeragun *Australia* 19°16S 146°33E **280** B4
Deerfield *Ill., U.S.A.* 42°10N 87°51W **311** B9
Deerfield *Mo., U.S.A.* 37°50N 94°30W **310** G2
Deerfield Beach *U.S.A.* 26°19N 80°6W **317** J9
Deering *U.S.A.* 66°4N 162°42W **303** C7
Defensores del Chaco △
Paraguay 20°13S 60°27W **331** E5
Defiance *U.S.A.* 41°17N 84°22W **311** C12
Dega Medo *Ethiopia* 7°59N 43°1E **257** F5
Degana *India* 26°50N 74°20E **242** F6
Dêgê *China* 31°44N 98°39E **228** B2
Degebe → *Portugal* 38°13N 7°29W **195** G3
Degeberga *Sweden* 55°51N 14°5E **163** J8
Degeh Bur *Ethiopia* 8°11N 43°31E **257** F5
Dégelis *Canada* 47°30N 68°35W **299** C6
Degema *Nigeria* 4°50N 6°48E **263** E6
Degerfors *Sweden* 59°15N 14°27E **162** E8
Degerhamn *Sweden* 56°20N 16°24E **163** H10
Deggendorf *Germany* 48°50N 12°57E **179** G8
Degh → *Pakistan* 31°3N 73°21E **242** D5
Değirmendere *Turkey* 40°42N 29°47E **203** F13
Degirmenlik = Kythréa
Cyprus 35°15N 33°29E **207** E9
Degunino *Russia* 55°52N 37°33E **129** A3
Deh Bīd *Iran* 30°39N 53°11E **247** D7
Deh Dasht *Iran* 30°47N 50°33E **247** D6
Deh-e Shīr *Iran* 31°29N 53°45E **247** D7
Deh Nugaled = Nugaaleed, Dooxo
Somali Rep. 8°35N 48°35E **267** C6
Dehaj *Iran* 30°42N 54°53E **247** D7
Dehak *Iran* 27°11N 62°37E **240** D1
Déhane *Cameroon* 3°30N 10°5E **264** B2
Dehdez *Iran* 31°43N 50°17E **247** D6
Dehej *India* 21°44N 72°40E **242** J5
Dehestān *Iran* 28°30N 55°35E **247** D7
Dehgolān *Iran* 35°17N 47°25E **213** E12
Dehibat *Tunisia* 32°0N 10°47E **258** B2
Dehiwala *Sri Lanka* 6°50N 79°51E **245** L4
Dehlorān *Iran* 32°41N 47°16E **213** F12
Dehnow-e Kūhestān *Iran* 27°58N 58°32E **247** E8
Dehra Dun *India* 30°20N 78°4E **242** D8
Dehri *India* 24°50N 84°15E **243** G11
Dehua *China* 25°26N 118°14E **229** E12
Dehui *China* 44°30N 125°40E **227** B13
Deim Zubeir *Sudan* 7°49N 26°16E **257** F2
Deinze *Belgium* 50°59N 3°32E **170** D3
Deir Dibwan *West Bank* 31°55N 35°16E **123** A2
Deir Ibzi'e *West Bank* 31°55N 35°7E **123** A1
Dej *Romania* 47°10N 23°52E **183** C8
Deje *Sweden* 59°35N 13°29E **162** E7
Dejiang *China* 28°18N 108°7E **228** C7
Dejvice *Czech Rep.* 50°6N 14°23E **135** B2
Deka → *Zimbabwe* 18°4S 26°42E **270** A4
Dekabristov, Ostrov
Russia 59°56N 30°15E **137** B1
DeKalb *U.S.A.* 41°56N 88°46W **311** C8
Dekemhare *Eritrea* 15°6N 39°0E **257** D4
Dekese
Dem. Rep. of the Congo 3°24S 21°24E **264** C4
Dekoa *C.A.R.* 6°19N 19°4E **264** A3
Del Caño Rise *Ind. Oc.* 45°15S 44°15E **273** J3
Del Carmen *Phil.* 9°50N 126°0E **233** G6
Del Mar *U.S.A.* 32°58N 117°16W **307** N9
Del Norte *U.S.A.* 37°41N 106°21W **305** H10
Del Rey *U.S.A.* 33°59N 118°25W **126** C2
Del Rio *U.S.A.* 29°22N 100°54W **314** G4
Delai *Sudan* 17°21N 36°6E **256** D4
Delambre I. *Australia* 20°26S 117°5E **278** D2
Delami *Sudan* 11°38N 30°23E **257** E3
Delano *U.S.A.* 35°46N 119°15W **307** K7
Delano Peak *U.S.A.* 38°22N 112°22W **304** G7
Delārām *Afghan.* 32°9N 63°25E **240** B1
Delareyville *S. Africa* 26°41S 25°26E **270** C4
Delaronde L. *Canada* 54°3N 107°3W **297** C7
Delavan *Ill., U.S.A.* 40°22N 89°33W **310** D7
Delavan *Wis., U.S.A.* 42°38N 88°39W **311** B8
Delaware *U.S.A.* 40°18N 83°4W **311** D13
Delaware □ *U.S.A.* 39°0N 75°20W **309** F16
Delaware → *U.S.A.* 39°15N 75°20W **313** G9
Delaware B. *U.S.A.* 39°0N 75°10W **309** F16
Delaware Water Gap ⌂
U.S.A. 41°10N 74°55W **313** E10
Delay → *Canada* 56°56N 71°28W **299** A5
Delbrück *Germany* 51°46N 8°34E **178** D4
Delčevo *Macedonia* 41°58N 22°46E **202** E6
Delegate *Australia* 37°4S 148°56E **283** D8
Delémont *Switz.* 47°22N 7°20E **179** H3
Delevan *U.S.A.* 42°29N 78°29W **312** D6
Delft *Neths.* 52°1N 4°22E **170** B4
Delft I. *Sri Lanka* 9°30N 79°40E **245** K4
Delfzijl *Neths.* 53°20N 6°55E **170** A6
Delgada, Punta *Chile* 52°28S 69°32W **336** D3
Delgado, C. *Mozam.* 10°45S 40°40E **269** E5
Delgerhet *Mongolia* 45°50N 110°30E **226** B6
Delgo *Sudan* 20°6N 30°40E **256** C3
Delhi *Ont., Canada* 42°51N 80°30W **312** D4
Delhi *India* 28°39N 77°13E **120** B2
Delhi *La., U.S.A.* 32°28N 91°30W **314** E9
Delhi *N.Y., U.S.A.* 42°17N 74°55W **313** D10
Delhi Gate *Delhi, India* **120** b3
Delhi Indira Gandhi Int. ✈ (DEL)
India 28°34N 77°5E **120** B1
Deli Jovan *Serbia* 44°13N 22°9E **202** B6
Delia *Canada* 51°38N 112°23W **296** C6
Delice *Turkey* 39°54N 34°2E **212** C6
Délices *Dominica* 15°17N 61°17W **323** k
Delicias *Mexico* 28°13N 105°28W **318** B3
Delījān *Iran* 33°59N 50°40E **247** C6
Delimara Point *Malta* 35°49N 14°34E **206** F8
Déline *Canada* 65°11N 123°25W **294** D7
Delingha *China* 37°23N 97°23E **218** D8
Delisle *Canada* 51°55N 107°8W **297** C7
Delitzsch *Germany* 51°31N 12°20E **178** D8
Deliverance I. *Australia* 9°31S 141°34E **280** a
Dell City *U.S.A.* 31°56N 105°12W **314** F2
Dell Rapids *U.S.A.* 43°50N 96°43W **308** D5
Delle *France* 47°30N 7°2E **173** E14
Dellys *Algeria* 36°57N 3°57E **261** A5
Delmar *Iowa, U.S.A.* 42°0N 90°37W **310** C6
Delmar *N.Y., U.S.A.* 42°37N 73°47W **313** D11
Delmenhorst *Germany* 53°3N 8°37E **178** B4
Delmiro Gouveia *Brazil* 9°24S 38°6W **332** C4
Delnice *Croatia* 45°23N 14°50E **199** C11
Delonga, Ostrova
Russia 76°40N 149°20E **215** B15
Deloraine *Tas., Australia* 41°30S 146°40E **281** G4
Deloraine *Man., Canada* 49°15N 100°29W **297** D8
Delphi *Greece* 38°28N 22°30E **204** C4
Delphi *Ind., U.S.A.* 40°36N 86°41W **311** D10
Delphos *U.S.A.* 40°51N 84°21W **311** D12
Delportshoop *S. Africa* 28°22S 24°20E **270** C3
Delray Beach *U.S.A.* 26°28N 80°4W **317** J9
Delsbo *Sweden* 61°48N 16°32E **162** C10
Delta *Ala., U.S.A.* 33°26N 85°42W **316** B4
Delta *Colo., U.S.A.* 38°44N 108°4W **304** G9
Delta *Utah, U.S.A.* 39°21N 112°35W **304** G7
Delta □ *Nigeria* 5°30N 6°0E **263** D6
Delta Amacuro □
Venezuela 8°30N 61°30W **329** B5
Delta del Ebre ⌂ *Spain* 40°43N 0°43E **196** E5
Delta del Po ⌂ *Italy* 44°50N 12°15E **199** D9
Delta du Saloum △
Senegal 13°42N 16°43W **262** C1
Delta Dunărea ⌂
Romania 45°15N 29°25E **183** E14
Delta Junction *U.S.A.* 64°2N 145°44W **303** D11
Deltona *U.S.A.* 28°54N 81°16W **317** G8
Delungra *Australia* 29°39S 150°51E **281** D5
Delvada *India* 20°46N 71°2E **242** J4
Delvinaki *Greece* 39°57N 20°32E **204** B2
Delvinë *Albania* 39°59N 20°6E **202** G4
Delyatyn *Ukraine* 48°32N 24°38E **183** B9
Demagiri *India* 22°55N 92°28E **241** D4
Demak *Indonesia* 6°53S 110°38E **235** D4
Demanda, Sierra de la
Spain 42°15N 3°0W **196** C2
Demarcation Pt. *U.S.A.* 69°41N 141°18W **303** B12
Demarest *U.S.A.* 40°57N 73°57W **132** A2
Demavend = Damāvand, Qolleh-ye
Iran 35°56N 52°10E **247** C7
Demba
Dem. Rep. of the Congo 5°28S 22°15E **265** D4
Demba Chio *Angola* 9°41S 13°41E **265** D2
Dembecha *Ethiopia* 10°32N 37°30E **257** E4
Dembéni *Comoros Is.* 11°52S 43°23E **272** a
Dembéni *Mayotte* 12°50S 45°11E **272** b
Dembi *Ethiopia* 8°5N 36°25E **257** F4
Dembia *C.A.R.* 4°56N 23°53E **264** B4
Dembia
Dem. Rep. of the Congo 3°33N 25°48E **268** B2
Dembica = Dębica *Poland* 50°2N 21°25E **185** H8
Dembidolo *Ethiopia* 8°34N 34°50E **257** F3
Demchok *India* 32°42N 79°29E **243** C8
Demer → *Belgium* 50°57N 4°42E **170** D4
Demerara Abyssal Plain
Atl. Oc. 10°0N 48°0W **152** F7
Demetrias *Greece* 39°22N 23°1E **204** B5
Demidov *Russia* 55°16N 31°30E **188** E6
Deming *N. Mex., U.S.A.* 32°16N 107°46W **305** K10
Deming *Wash., U.S.A.* 48°50N 122°13W **306** B4
Demini → *Brazil* 0°46S 62°56W **329** D5
Demirci *Turkey* 39°2N 28°38E **205** B10
Demirköprü Barajı
Turkey 38°42N 28°25E **205** C10
Demirköy *Turkey* 41°49N 27°45E **203** E11
Demirtas *Turkey* 36°25N 32°11E **250** B3
Demmin *Germany* 53°54N 13°2E **178** B9
Demnate *Morocco* 31°44N 6°59W **260** B3
Democracia *Brazil* 5°48S 61°26W **331** B5
Demonte *Italy* 44°19N 7°17E **198** D4
Demopolis *U.S.A.* 32°31N 87°50W **315** E11
Dempo *Indonesia* 4°2S 103°15E **234** C2
Demyansk *Russia* 57°40N 32°27E **188** D7
Den Bosch = 's-Hertogenbosch
Neths. 51°42N 5°17E **170** C5
Den Burg *Neths.* 53°3N 4°47E **170** A4
Den Chai *Thailand* 17°59N 100°4E **236** D3
Den Haag = 's-Gravenhage
Neths. 52°7N 4°17E **170** B4
Den Helder *Neths.* 52°57N 4°45E **170** B4
Den Ilp *Neths.* 52°27N 4°55E **112** A2
Den Lille Havfrue *Copenhagen, Denmark* **118** a3
Den Oever *Neths.* 52°56N 5°2E **170** B5
Denain *France* 50°20N 3°22E **173** B10
Denair *U.S.A.* 37°32N 120°48W **306** H6
Denali = McKinley, Mt.
U.S.A. 63°4N 151°0W **303** E10
Denali △ *U.S.A.* 63°30N 152°0W **303** E10
Denau *Uzbekistan* 38°16N 67°54E **217** E7
Denbigh *Ont., Canada* 45°8N 77°15W **312** A7
Denbigh *Denbs., U.K.* 53°12N 3°25W **168** D4
Denbigh, C. *U.S.A.* 64°23N 161°32W **303** D7
Denbighshire □ *U.K.* 53°8N 3°22W **168** D4
Dendang *Indonesia* 3°7S 107°56E **235** C3
Dendé = Ndindi *Gabon* 3°46S 11°9E **264** C2
Dendermonde *Belgium* 51°2N 4°5E **170** C4
Deneba *Ethiopia* 9°47N 39°10E **257** F4
Deng Deng *Cameroon* 5°12N 13°31E **264** A2
Dengchuan *China* 25°59N 100°3E **228** E3
Denge *Nigeria* 12°52N 5°21E **263** C6
Dengfeng *China* 34°25N 113°2E **226** G7
Dengi *Nigeria* 9°25N 9°55E **263** D6
Dengkou *China* 40°18N 106°55E **226** D4
Dengzhou *China* 32°34N 112°4E **229** A9
Denham *Australia* 25°56S 113°31E **279** E1
Denham, Mt. *Jamaica* 18°13N 77°32W **320** a
Denham Ra. *Australia* 21°55S 147°46E **280** C4
Denham Sd. *Australia* 25°45S 113°15E **279** E1
Denholm *Canada* 52°39N 108°1W **297** C7
Denia *Spain* 38°49N 0°8E **197** G5
Denial B. *Australia* 32°14S 133°32E **281** E1
Deniliquin *Australia* 35°30S 144°58E **283** C6
Denimoo = Fort Resolution
Canada 61°10N 113°40W **296** A6
Denis *Gabon* 0°19N 9°22E **264** B1
Denison *Iowa, U.S.A.* 42°1N 95°21W **308** D6
Denison *Tex., U.S.A.* 33°45N 96°33W **314** E6
Denison Plains *Australia* 18°35S 128°0E **278** C4
Denīsovka *Kazakhstan* 52°27N 61°39E **216** B6
Denistone Heights
Australia 33°48S 151°8E **139** A1
Deniyaya *Sri Lanka* 6°21N 80°33E **245** L5
Denizli *Turkey* 37°42N 29°2E **205** D11
Denizli □ *Turkey* 37°45N 29°5E **205** D11
Denman *Australia* 32°24S 150°42E **283** B9
Denman Glacier
Antarctica 66°45S 100°0E **151** C8
Denmark *W. Austral.,*
Australia 34°59S 117°25E **279** F2
Denmark *S.C., U.S.A.* 33°19N 81°9W **316** B8
Denmark ■ *Europe* 55°45N 10°0E **163** J3
Denmark Str. *Atl. Oc.* 66°0N 30°0W **154** B8
Dennery *St. Lucia* 13°55N 60°54W **323** m
Dennison *U.S.A.* 40°24N 81°19W **312** F3
Denny *U.K.* 56°1N 3°55W **167** E5
Denpasar *Indonesia* 8°39S 115°13E **231** K18
Denpasar ✈ (DPS)
Indonesia 8°44S 115°10E **231** K18
Denton *Ga., U.S.A.* 31°44N 82°42W **316** D7
Denton *Mont., U.S.A.* 47°19N 109°57W **304** C9
Denton *Tex., U.S.A.* 33°13N 97°8W **314** E6
Denton Harbour *Canada* 43°42N 79°17W **141** A3
D'Entrecasteaux, Ís.
N. Cal. 18°0S 163°0E **277** D11
D'Entrecasteaux, Pt.
Australia 34°50S 115°57E **279** F2
D'Entrecasteaux △
Australia 34°20S 115°33E **279** F2
D'Entrecasteaux Is.
Papua N. G. 9°0S 151°0E **286** E6
Dentsville *U.S.A.* 34°4N 80°58W **316** A9
Denu *Ghana* 6°4N 1°8E **263** D5
Denver *Colo., U.S.A.* 39°42N 104°59W **304** G11
Denver *Ind., U.S.A.* 40°52N 86°5W **311** D10
Denver *Iowa, U.S.A.* 42°40N 92°20W **310** B4
Denver *Pa., U.S.A.* 40°14N 76°8W **313** F8
Denver City *U.S.A.* 32°58N 102°50W **314** E3
Denwood = Wainwright
Canada 52°50N 110°50W **297** C6
Deoband *India* 29°42N 77°43E **242** E7
Deobhog *India* 19°53N 82°44E **244** E6
Deodrug *India* 16°26N 76°55E **245** F3
Deogarh *Orissa, India* 21°32N 84°45E **244** D7
Deogarh *Raj., India* 25°32N 73°54E **242** G5
Deoghar *India* 24°30N 86°42E **243** G12
Deogyusan △ *S. Korea* 35°45N 127°40E **224** E3
Deokjeokdo *S. Korea* 37°13N 126°7E **224** D3
Deolali *India* 19°58N 73°50E **244** E1
Deoli = Devli *India* 25°50N 75°20E **242** G6
Déols *France* 46°50N 1°43E **173** F8
Deora *India* 26°22N 70°55E **242** F4
Deorha = Jubbal *India* 31°5N 77°40E **242** D7
Deori *India* 23°24N 79°1E **243** H8
Deoria *India* 26°31N 83°48E **243** F10
Deosai Mts. *Pakistan* 35°40N 75°0E **243** B6
Deosri *India* 26°46N 90°29E **241** B3
Depalpur *India* 22°51N 75°33E **242** H6
DePaul Univ. *U.S.A.* 41°55N 87°39W **119** B3
Deposit *U.S.A.* 42°4N 75°25W **313** D9
Deptford *U.K.* 51°28N 0°1W **125** B3
Depuch I. *Australia* 20°37S 117°44E **278** D2
Deputati, Camera dei *Rome, Italy* **136** b2
Deputatskiy *Russia* 69°18N 139°54E **215** C14
Dêqên *China* 28°34N 98°51E **228** C2
Deqing *China* 23°8N 111°42E **229** F8
Dera, Lach → *Somali Rep.* 0°15N 42°17E **267** D5
Dera Ghazi Khan *Pakistan* 30°5N 70°43E **242** D4
Dera Ismail Khan
Pakistan 31°50N 70°50E **242** D4
Derabugti *Pakistan* 29°2N 69°9E **242** E3
Derawar Fort *Pakistan* 28°46N 71°20E **242** E4
Derbent *Russia* 42°5N 48°15E **191** J9
Derbent *Turkey* 38°11N 28°33E **205** C10
Derby *W. Austral.,*
Australia 17°18S 123°38E **278** C3
Derby *Derby City, U.K.* 52°56N 1°28W **168** E6
Derby *Conn., U.S.A.* 41°19N 73°5W **313** E11
Derby *Kans., U.S.A.* 37°33N 97°16W **308** G5
Derby *N.Y., U.S.A.* 42°41N 78°58W **312** D6
Derby City □ *U.K.* 52°56N 1°28W **168** E6
Derby Line *U.S.A.* 45°0N 72°6W **313** B12
Derbyshire □ *U.K.* 53°11N 1°38W **168** D6
Derdap △ *Serbia* 44°40N 22°23E **202** B6
Derdepoort *S. Africa* 24°38S 26°24E **270** B4
Derecske *Hungary* 47°20N 21°33E **182** C6
Dereham *U.K.* 52°41N 0°57E **169** E8
Dereköy *Turkey* 41°55N 27°21E **203** E11
Dereli *Turkey* 40°44N 38°26E **213** B8
Derg → *U.K.* 54°44N 7°26W **166** B4
Derg, L. *Ireland* 53°0N 8°20W **166** D3
Dergachi = Derhaci
Ukraine 50°9N 36°11E **189** G9
Derhaci *Ukraine* 50°9N 36°11E **189** G9
Derider *U.S.A.* 30°51N 93°17W **314** F8
Derik *Turkey* 37°21N 40°18E **213** D9
Derinkuyu *Turkey* 38°22N 34°45E **212** C6
Dermantsi *Bulgaria* 43°8N 24°17E **203** C8
Dermott *U.S.A.* 33°32N 91°26W **314** E9
Dernière Rivière *St. Lucia* 13°57N 60°55W **323** m
Dêrong *China* 28°44N 99°9E **228** C2
Derri *Somali Rep.* 4°20N 46°32E **267** D6
Derrinallum *Australia* 37°57S 143°15E **282** D5
Derry = Londonderry *U.K.* 55°0N 7°20W **166** B4
Derry = Londonderry □
U.K. 55°0N 7°20W **166** B4
Derry *N.H., U.S.A.* 42°53N 71°19W **313** D13
Derry *Pa., U.S.A.* 40°20N 79°18W **312** F5
Derryveagh Mts. *Ireland* 54°56N 8°11W **166** B3
Derudub *Sudan* 17°31N 36°7E **256** D4
Derval *France* 47°40N 1°41W **172** E5
Derveni *Greece* 38°8N 22°25E **204** C4
Derventa *Bos.-H.* 44°59N 17°55E **182** F2
Derwent → *Cumb., U.K.* 54°39N 3°33W **168** C4
Derwent → *Derby, U.K.* 52°57N 1°28W **168** E6
Derwent → *N. Yorks.,*
U.K. 53°45N 0°58W **168** D7
Derwent Water *U.K.* 54°35N 3°9W **168** C4
Derzhavīnsk *Kazakhstan* 51°6N 66°19E **217** B7
Des Moines *Iowa, U.S.A.* 41°35N 93°37W **310** C3
Des Moines *N. Mex.,*
U.S.A. 36°46N 103°50W **305** H12
Des Moines *Wash.,*
U.S.A. 47°24N 122°19W **306** C4
Des Moines → *U.S.A.* 40°23N 91°25W **310** D5
Des Moines ✈ (DSM)
U.S.A. 41°32N 93°40W **310** C3
Des Plaines *U.S.A.* 42°2N 87°54W **119** A1
Des Plaines → *U.S.A.* 41°23N 88°15W **310** C8
Desa *Romania* 43°52N 23°2E **182** G8
Desaguadero *Peru* 16°34S 69°3W **330** D4
Desaguadero →
Argentina 34°30S 66°46W **334** C2
Desaguadero → *Bolivia* 16°35S 69°5W **330** D4
Desantne *Ukraine* 45°34N 29°32E **183** E14
Désappointement, Is. du
French Polynesia 14°10S 141°20W **289** f
Desaru *Malaysia* 1°31N 104°17E **237** d
Descanso, Pta. *Mexico* 32°21N 117°3W **307** N9
Descartes *France* 46°59N 0°42E **174** B4
Deschaillons-sur-St-Laurent
Canada 46°32N 72°7W **299** C5
Deschambault L. *Canada* 54°50N 103°30W **297** C8
Deschutes → *U.S.A.* 45°38N 120°55W **304** D3
Descobrimento △ *Brazil* 16°53S 39°21W **333** E4
Dese *Ethiopia* 11°5N 39°40E **257** E4
Deseado, C. *Chile* 52°45S 74°42W **336** D2
Desenzano del Garda
Italy 45°28N 10°32E **198** C7
Deseronto *Canada* 44°12N 77°3W **312** B7
Desert Center *U.S.A.* 33°43N 115°24W **307** M11
Desert Hot Springs
U.S.A. 33°58N 116°30W **307** M10
Desert Wetlands Park
U.S.A. 36°7N 115°2W **124** B2
Desertas, Ilhas *Madeira* 32°30N 16°30W **260** B1
Deset *Norway* 61°20N 11°26E **164** C8
Desfina *Greece* 38°25N 22°31E **204** C4
Deshaies *Guadeloupe* 16°18N 61°47W **322** e
Deshauteur *Guadeloupe* 16°15N 61°25W **322** e
Deshnok *India* 27°48N 73°21E **242** F5
Desierto Central de Baja
California ⌂ *Mexico* 29°40N 114°50W **318** B2
Desjardins, Complexe *Montréal, Canada* **130** b2
Deskati *Greece* 39°55N 21°49E **202** G5
Desna → *Ukraine* 50°33N 30°32E **177** C16
Desnătui → *Romania* 43°53N 23°35E **183** G8
Desolación, I. *Chile* 53°0S 74°0W **336** D2
Despeñaperros, Paso
Spain 38°24N 3°30W **195** G7
Despeñaperros ⌂ *Spain* 38°23N 3°32W **195** G7
Despotiko *Greece* 36°57N 24°58E **204** E6
Despotovac *Serbia* 44°6N 21°30E **202** B5
Dessau *Germany* 51°51N 12°14E **178** D8
Dessye = Dese *Ethiopia* 11°5N 39°40E **257** E4
Destin *U.S.A.* 30°24N 86°30W **317** E3
D'Estrees B. *Australia* 35°55S 137°45E **282** C2
Desuri *India* 25°18N 73°35E **242** G5
Desvres *France* 50°40N 1°48E **173** B8
Det Udom *Thailand* 14°54N 105°5E **236** E5
Deta *Romania* 45°24N 21°13E **182** E6
Dete *Zimbabwe* 18°38S 26°50E **270** A4
Detinja → *Serbia* 43°51N 20°5E **202** C4
Detmold *Germany* 51°56N 8°52E **178** D4
Detour, Pt. *U.S.A.* 45°40N 86°40W **308** C10
Detroit *U.S.A.* 42°19N 83°12W **312** D1
Detroit Lakes *U.S.A.* 46°49N 95°51W **308** B6
Detroit Metropolitan Wayne
County ✈ (DTW)
U.S.A. 42°13N 83°21W **311** B13
Detskoye Selo = Pushkin
Russia 59°45N 30°25E **188** C6
Dettifoss *Iceland* 65°48N 16°24W **155** B10
Detva *Slovak Rep.* 48°34N 19°25E **181** C12
Deua △ *Australia* 35°32S 149°46E **283** C8
Deurne *Neths.* 51°27N 5°49E **170** C5
Deutsch = Przemyśl
Poland 49°50N 22°45E **185** J9
Deutsch Brod = Havlíčkův Brod
Czech Rep. 49°36N 15°33E **180** B8
Deutsch-Eylau = Iława
Poland 53°36N 19°34E **184** E6
Deutsch Krone = Wałcz
Poland 53°17N 16°27E **185** E3
Deutsch-Luxemburgischer ⌂
Germany 49°58N 6°12E **179** F2
Deutsche Bucht *Germany* 54°15N 8°0E **178** A4
Deutsche Oper *Germany* 52°30N 13°19E **115** A2
Deutsches Museum
Germany 48°7N 11°35E **131** B2
Deutschland = Germany ■
Europe 51°0N 10°0E **178** E6
Deutschlandsberg *Austria* 46°49N 15°14E **180** E8
Deux-Sèvres □ *France* 46°35N 0°20W **172** F6
Deva *Romania* 45°53N 22°55E **182** E7
Devakottai *India* 9°55N 78°45E **245** K4
Devaprayag *India* 30°13N 78°35E **243** D8
Devarkonda *India* 16°42N 78°56E **244** F4
Dévaványa *Hungary* 47°2N 20°59E **182** C5
Deveci Dağları *Turkey* 40°6N 36°15E **212** B7
Devecikonağı *Turkey* 39°55N 28°34E **203** G12
Devecser *Hungary* 47°6N 17°26E **182** C2
Develi *Turkey* 38°23N 35°29E **212** C6
Deventer *Neths.* 52°15N 6°10E **170** B6
Devereux *U.S.A.* 33°13N 83°5W **316** B6
Deveron → *U.K.* 57°41N 2°32W **167** D6
Devesel *Romania* 44°28N 22°41E **182** F7
Devgad I. *India* 14°48N 74°5E **245** G2
Devgadh Bariya *India* 22°40N 73°55E **242** H5
Devgarh *India* 16°23N 73°23E **245** F1
Devi → *India* 19°59N 86°24E **244** E8
Devikot *India* 26°42N 71°12E **242** F4
Devil River Pk. *N.Z.* 40°56S 172°37E **285** A7
Devil's Bridge *Antigua & B.* 17°6N 61°41W **322** b
Devils Den *U.S.A.* 35°46N 119°58W **306** K7
Devils Hole = Death Valley △
U.S.A. 36°29N 117°6W **307** J9
Devils Island, I. = Diable, Île du
Fr. Guiana 5°16N 52°34W **329** B7
Devils Lake *U.S.A.* 48°7N 98°52W **308** A4
Devils Paw *Canada* 58°47N 134°0W **296** B2
Devil's Peak *S. Africa* 33°57S 18°27E **118** A1
Devils Postpile ⌂ *U.S.A.* 37°37N 119°5W **306** H7
Devil's Pt. *Sri Lanka* 9°26N 80°6E **245** K5
Devils Tower *U.S.A.* 44°35N 104°42W **304** D11
Devils Tower △ *U.S.A.* 44°48N 104°55W **304** D11
Devils Woodyard Mud Volcano
Trin. & Tob. 10°16N 61°22W **323** t
Devin *Bulgaria* 41°44N 24°24E **203** E8
Devine *U.S.A.* 29°8N 98°54W **314** G5
Devipattinam *India* 9°29N 78°54E **245** K4
Devizes *U.K.* 51°22N 1°58W **169** F6
Devli *India* 25°50N 75°20E **242** G6
Devnya *Bulgaria* 43°13N 27°33E **203** C11
Devoll → *Albania* 40°57N 20°15E **202** F4
Devon *Canada* 53°24N 113°44W **296** C6
Devon □ *U.K.* 50°50N 3°40W **169** G4
Devon I. *Canada* 75°10N 85°0W **295** B15
Devonport *Australia* 41°10S 146°22E **281** G4
Devonport *N.Z.* 36°49S 174°49E **284** C5
Devrek *Turkey* 41°13N 31°57E **212** B4
Devrekâni *Turkey* 41°36N 33°50E **212** B5
Devrez → *Turkey* 41°6N 34°25E **212** B6
Devrukh *India* 17°3N 73°37E **244** F1
Dewas *India* 22°59N 76°3E **242** H7
Dewetsdorp *S. Africa* 29°33S 26°39E **270** C4
Dewey *Puerto Rico* 18°18N 65°18W **321** b
Dexing *China* 28°46N 117°30E **229** C11
Dexter *Maine, U.S.A.* 45°1N 69°18W **309** C19
Dexter *Mich., U.S.A.* 42°20N 83°53W **311** B13
Dexter *Mo., U.S.A.* 36°48N 89°57W **308** G9
Dexter *N. Mex., U.S.A.* 33°12N 104°22W **305** K11
Dey-Dey, L. *Australia* 29°12S 131°4E **279** E5
Deyang *China* 31°3N 104°27E **228** B5
Deyhūk *Iran* 33°15N 57°30E **247** C8
Deyyer *Iran* 27°55N 51°55E **247** E6
Dez → *Iran* 31°39N 48°52E **213** F13
Dezadeash L. *Canada* 60°28N 136°58W **296** A1
Dezfūl *Iran* 32°20N 48°30E **213** F13
Dezhneva, Mys *Russia* 66°5N 169°40W **215** C19
Dezhou *China* 37°26N 116°18E **226** F9
Dhadhar → *India* 24°56N 85°24E **243** G11
Dhahaban *Si. Arabia* 21°58N 39°3E **248** B2
Dhahiriya = Az̧ Z̧āhirīyah
West Bank 31°25N 34°58E **251** G5
Dhahran = Az̧ Z̧ahrān
Si. Arabia 26°10N 50°7E **247** E6
Dhak *Pakistan* 32°25N 72°33E **242** C5
Dhaka *Bangla.* 23°43N 90°26E **241** D3
Dhaka □ *Bangla.* 24°25N 90°25E **241** C3
Dhakuria *India* 22°30N 88°22E **124** B2
Dhali *Cyprus* 35°1N 33°25E **207** E9
Dhamangaon *India* 20°48N 78°9E **244** D4
Dhamār *Yemen* 14°30N 44°20E **248** D4
Dhampur *India* 29°19N 78°33E **243** E8
Dhamra → *India* 20°47N 86°58E **244** D8
Dhamtari *India* 20°42N 81°35E **244** D5
Dhanbad *India* 23°50N 86°30E **243** H12
Dhangarhi *Nepal* 28°55N 80°40E **243** E9
Dhankuta *Nepal* 26°55N 87°40E **243** F12
Dhanora *India* 20°20N 80°22E **244** D5
Dhanpuri *India* 23°13N 81°30E **244** C5
Dhanushkodi *India* 9°11N 79°24E **245** K4
Dhar *India* 22°35N 75°26E **242** H6
Dharampur *Gujarat, India* 20°32N 73°17E **244** D1
Dharampur *Mad. P., India* 22°13N 75°18E **242** H6
Dharamsala = Dharmsala
India 32°16N 76°23E **242** C7
Dharan *Nepal* 26°49N 87°17E **243** F12
Dharangaon *India* 21°1N 75°16E **244** D2
Dharapuram *India* 10°45N 77°34E **245** J3
Dharavi *India* 19°1N 72°51E **130** A2
Dhariwal *India* 31°57N 75°19E **242** D6
Dharla → *Bangla.* 25°46N 89°42E **243** G13
Dharmapuri *India* 12°10N 78°10E **245** H4
Dharmavaram *India* 14°29N 77°44E **245** G3
Dharmjaygarh *India* 22°28N 83°13E **243** H10
Dharmsala *India* 32°16N 76°23E **242** C7
Dharni *India* 21°33N 76°53E **242** J7
Dharug △ *Australia* 33°20S 151°2E **283** B9
Dharur *India* 18°3N 76°8E **244** E3
Dharwad *India* 15°30N 75°4E **245** G2
Dhasan → *India* 25°48N 79°24E **243** G8
Dhaulagiri *Nepal* 28°39N 83°28E **243** E10
Dhebar, L. *India* 24°10N 74°0E **242** G6
Dheftera *Cyprus* 35°5N 33°16E **207** E9
Dhenkanal *India* 20°45N 85°35E **244** D7
Dherinia *Cyprus* 35°3N 33°57E **207** E9
Dheskáti = Deskati
Greece 39°55N 21°49E **202** G5
Dhī Qār □ *Iraq* 31°0N 46°15E **246** D5
Dhiarrizos → *Cyprus* 34°41N 32°34E **207** F8
Dhībān *Jordan* 31°30N 35°46E **251** G6
Dhilwan *India* 31°31N 75°21E **242** D6
Dhimarkhera *India* 23°28N 80°22E **243** H9
Dhodhekánisos = Dodecanese
Greece 36°35N 27°0E **205** E8
Dholka *India* 22°44N 72°29E **242** H5
Dhomokós = Domokos
Greece 39°10N 22°18E **204** B4
Dhond = Daund *India* 18°26N 74°40E **244** E2
Dhone *India* 15°25N 77°53E **245** G3
Dhoraji *India* 21°45N 70°37E **242** J4
Dhragonísi = Tragonhsi
Greece 37°27N 25°29E **205** D7
Dhrangadhra *India* 22°59N 71°31E **242** H4
Dhrol *India* 22°33N 70°25E **242** H4
Dhubāb *Yemen* 12°56N 43°25E **248** D3
Dhuburi *India* 26°2N 89°59E **241** B2
Dhulasar *Bangla.* 21°52N 90°14E **241** E3
Dhule *India* 20°58N 74°50E **244** D2
Dhupdhara *India* 26°10N 91°4E **241** B3
Dhurbo *Somali Rep.* 11°37N 50°20E **267** B7
Dhuusamarreeb
Somali Rep. 5°30N 46°15E **267** C6
Di-ib, W. → *Sudan* 22°38N 36°6E **256** C4
Di Linh *Vietnam* 11°35N 108°4E **237** G7
Di Linh, Cao Nguyen
Vietnam 11°30N 108°0E **237** G7
Dia *Greece* 35°28N 25°14E **207** E6
Diabakania *Guinea* 10°38N 10°58W **262** C2
Diable, Île du *Fr. Guiana* 5°16N 52°34W **329** B7
Diable, Pte. du *Martinique* 14°46N 60°53W **322** j
Diables, Morne aux
Dominica 15°37N 61°27W **323** k
Diablo Pt. *N. Marianas* 15°0N 145°35E **302** e
Diablo Range *U.S.A.* 37°20N 121°25W **306** J5
Diablotins, Morne
Dominica 15°30N 61°24W **323** k
Diadema *Brazil* 23°41S 46°37W **137** C2
Diafarabé *Mali* 14°9N 4°57W **262** C4
Diala *Mali* 14°10N 9°58W **262** C3
Dialakoro *Mali* 12°18N 7°54W **262** C3
Dialakoto *Senegal* 13°21N 13°19W **262** C2
Diallassagou *Mali* 13°47N 3°41W **262** C4
Diamant, Pte. du *Martinique* 14°27N 61°3W **322** j
Diamant, Rocher du
Martinique 14°27N 61°2W **322** j
Diamante *Argentina* 32°5S 60°40W **334** C3
Diamante *Italy* 39°41N 15°49E **201** C8
Diamante → *Argentina* 34°30S 66°46W **334** C2
Diamantina *Brazil* 18°17S 43°40W **333** E3
Diamantina → *Australia* 26°45S 139°10E **281** D2
Diamantina △ *Australia* 23°33S 141°23E **280** C3
Diamantino *Brazil* 14°30S 56°30W **331** C6
Diamond Bar *U.S.A.* 34°1N 117°48W **307** L9
Diamond Harbour *India* 22°11N 88°14E **243** H13
Diamond Head *U.S.A.* 21°16N 157°49W **302** K14
Diamond I. *Grenada* 12°20N 61°35W **323** c
Diamond Is. *Australia* 17°25S 151°5E **280** B5
Diamond Mts. *U.S.A.* 39°40N 115°50W **304** G6
Diamond Springs *U.S.A.* 38°42N 120°49W **306** G6
Diamou *Mali* 14°5N 11°16W **262** C2
Dian Chi *China* 24°50N 102°43E **228** E4
Dianalund *Denmark* 55°32N 11°30E **163** J5
Dianbai *China* 21°33N 111°0E **229** G8
Diancheng *China* 21°30N 111°4E **229** G8
Dianjiang *China* 30°24N 107°20E **228** B6
Diano Marina *Italy* 43°54N 8°5E **198** E5
Dianópolis *Brazil* 11°38S 46°50W **333** D2
Dianra *Ivory C.* 8°45N 6°14W **262** D3
Diaoyu Dao = Senkaku-Shotō
E. China Sea 25°45N 123°30E **221** M1
Diaoyu Tai = Senkaku-Shotō
E. China Sea 25°45N 123°30E **221** M1
Diapaga *Burkina Faso* 12°5N 1°46E **263** C5
Diapangou *Burkina Faso* 12°5N 0°10E **263** C5
Diariguila *Guinea* 10°35N 10°2W **262** C2
Diavolo, Mt. *India* 12°40N 92°56E **245** H11
Dibā *U.A.E.* 25°45N 56°16E **247** E8
Dibagah *Iraq* 35°52N 43°48E **213** E10
Dibai *India* 28°13N 78°15E **242** E8
Dibaya
Dem. Rep. of the Congo 6°30S 22°57E **265** D4
Dibaya-Lubue
Dem. Rep. of the Congo 4°12S 19°54E **265** C3
Dibbeen △ *Jordan* 32°20N 35°45E **251** F6
Dibella *Niger* 17°32N 13°6E **259** E2
D'Iberville, Lac *Canada* 55°55N 73°15W **298** A5
Dibete *Botswana* 23°45S 26°32E **270** B4
Dibi *Cameroon* 7°8N 13°43E **264** A2
Dibru-Saikhowa △ *India* 27°40N 95°25E **241** B5
Dibrugarh *India* 27°29N 94°55E **241** B5
Diciosânmartin = Târnăveni
Romania 46°19N 24°13E **183** D9
Dickens *U.S.A.* 33°37N 100°50W **314** E4
Dickeyville *U.S.A.* 42°38N 90°36W **310** B6
Dickinson *U.S.A.* 46°53N 102°47W **308** B2
Dickinson B. *Antigua & B.* 17°10N 61°51W **322** b
Dick's Pt. *Bahamas* 25°4N 77°18W **153** b
Dickson = Dikson *Russia* 73°40N 80°5E **214** B9
Dickson *U.S.A.* 36°5N 87°23W **315** C11
Dickson City *U.S.A.* 41°28N 75°36W **313** E9
Dicle Barajı *Turkey* 38°20N 40°11E **213** C9
Dicle Nehri → *Turkey* 37°44N 41°10E **213** D9
Dicomano *Italy* 43°53N 11°31E **199** E8
Didesa, W. → *Ethiopia* 10°2N 35°32E **257** E4
Didiéni *Mali* 13°53N 8°6W **262** C3
Didimbo *Angola* 17°30S 21°45E **265** F4
Didimoticho *Greece* 41°22N 26°29E **203** E10
Didsbury *Canada* 51°35N 114°10W **296** C6
Didwana *India* 27°23N 74°36E **242** F6
Die *France* 44°47N 5°22E **175** D9
Diébougou *Burkina Faso* 11°0N 3°15W **262** C4
Diecke *Guinea* 7°27N 8°54W **262** D3
Diedenhofen = Thionville
France 49°20N 6°10E **173** C13
Diefenbaker, L. *Canada* 51°0N 106°55W **297** C7
Diegen *Belgium* 50°53N 4°26E **116** A2
Diego de Almagro *Chile* 26°22S 70°3W **334** B1
Diego Garcia *Ind. Oc.* 7°50S 72°50E **273** E6
Diego Martin *Trin. & Tob.* 10°43N 61°34W **323** t
Diego Ramírez, Islas *Chile* 56°30S 68°44W **336** E3
Diego Suarez = Antsiranana
Madag. 12°25S 49°20E **272** A2
Diekirch *Lux.* 49°52N 6°10E **170** E6
Diéma *Mali* 14°32N 9°12W **262** C3
Diembéring *Senegal* 12°29N 16°47W **262** C1
Diemelsee ⌂ *Germany* 51°20N 8°43E **178** D4
Diemen *Neths.* 52°21N 4°58E **112** A2
Dien Ban *Vietnam* 15°53N 108°16E **236** E7
Dien Bien Phu *Vietnam* 21°20N 103°0E **228** G4
Dien Chau, Vinh *Vietnam* 19°0N 105°55E **236** C5
Dien Khanh *Vietnam* 12°15N 109°6E **237** F7
Diepholz *Germany* 52°37N 8°22E **178** C4
Diepkloof *S. Africa* 26°14S 27°57E **123** B1
Dieppe *France* 49°54N 1°4E **172** C8
Dieppe Bay Town
St. Kitts & Nevis 17°25N 62°48W **322** d
Dieprivier *S. Africa* 34°2S 18°27E **118** B1
Dierks *U.S.A.* 34°7N 94°1W **314** D7
Diest *Belgium* 50°58N 5°4E **170** D5
Dieterich *U.S.A.* 39°4N 88°23W **311** E8
Dietikon *Switz.* 47°24N 8°24E **179** H4
Dieulefit *France* 44°32N 5°4E **175** D9
Dieuze *France* 48°49N 6°43E **173** D13
Dievenow = Dziwnów
Poland 54°2N 14°45E **184** D1
Dif *Somali Rep.* 0°59N 40°58E **267** D5
Diffa *Niger* 13°18N 12°36E **263** C7
Diffa □ *Niger* 14°0N 12°30E **263** C7
Differdange *Lux.* 49°31N 5°54E **170** E5
Difficult Run → *U.S.A.* 38°55N 77°18W **143** B2
Diffun *Phil.* 16°36N 121°33E **232** C3
Dig *India* 27°28N 77°20E **242** F7
Digba *Dem. Rep. of the Congo* 4°25N 25°48E **268** B2
Digboi *India* 27°23N 95°38E **241** B5
Digby *Canada* 44°38N 65°50W **299** D6
Digges Is. *Canada* 62°40N 77°50W **295** E16
Diggi *India* 26°22N 75°26E **242** F6
Dighinala *Bangla.* 23°15N 92°5E **241** D4
Dighton *U.S.A.* 38°29N 100°28W **308** F3
Digity Mud Volcanoes
Trin. & Tob. 10°12N 61°25W **323** t
Diglur *India* 18°34N 77°33E **244** E3
Digna *Mali* 14°48N 8°10W **262** C3
Digne-les-Bains *France* 44°5N 6°12E **175** D10
Digoin *France* 46°29N 4°1E **173** F11
Digor *Turkey* 40°22N 43°25E **213** B10
Digos *Phil.* 6°45N 125°20E **233** H5
Digranes *Iceland* 66°4N 14°44W **155** A12
Digras *India* 20°6N 77°45E **244** D3
Digul → *Indonesia* 7°7S 138°42E **231** F9
Digya △ *Ghana* 7°15N 0°5E **263** D5
Dihang = Brahmaputra →
Asia 23°40N 90°35E **241** D3
Diinsoor *Somali Rep.* 2°24N 42°59E **267** D5
Dijlah, Nahr → *Asia* 31°0N 47°25E **246** D5
Dijon *France* 47°20N 5°3E **173** E12
Dikhil *Djibouti* 11°8N 42°20E **257** E5
Dikili *Turkey* 39°4N 26°53E **205** B8
Dikirnis *Egypt* 31°6N 31°35E **256** H7
Dikkil = Dikhil *Djibouti* 11°8N 42°20E **257** E5
Dikodougou *Ivory C.* 9°4N 5°45W **262** D3
Diksmuide *Belgium* 51°2N 2°52E **170** C2
Dikson *Russia* 73°40N 80°5E **214** B9
Dikti Oros *Greece* 35°8N 25°30E **207** E6
Dikwa *Nigeria* 12°4N 13°30E **263** C7
Dila *Ethiopia* 6°21N 38°22E **257** F4
Dilasag *Phil.* 16°25N 122°11E **232** C4
Dilbeek *Belgium* 50°51N 4°17E **116** A1
Dilek Yarimadisi △
Turkey 37°40N 27°10E **205** D9
Dili *E. Timor* 8°39S 125°34E **231** F7
Diligent Strait *India* 12°11N 92°57E **245** H11
Dilijan *Armenia* 40°46N 44°57E **191** K7
Dilinata *Greece* 38°13N 20°31E **207** C2
Dilizhan = Dilijan
Armenia 40°46N 44°57E **191** K7
Dilj *Croatia* 45°29N 18°1E **182** E3
Dillenburg *Germany* 50°43N 8°17E **178** E4
Dilley *U.S.A.* 28°40N 99°10W **314** G5
Dilli = Delhi *India* 28°39N 77°13E **120** B2

366 Dover, Pt. INDEX

Dover, Pt. Australia 32°32S 125°32E 279 F4
Dover, Str. of Europe 51°0N 1°30E 169 G9
Dover-Foxcroft U.S.A. 45°11N 69°13W 309 C19
Dover Heights Australia 33°52S 151°16E 139 B2
Dover Plains U.S.A. 41°43N 73°35W 313 E11
Dovey = Dyfi → U.K. 52°32N 4°3W 169 E3
Dovhe Ukraine 48°22N 23°17E 183 B8
Dovlen = Devin Bulgaria 41°44N 24°24E 203 E8
Dovre Norway 61°58N 9°15E 164 C6
Dovre △ Norway 62°10N 9°30E 164 B6
Dovrefjell Norway 62°15N 9°33E 164 B6
Dovrefjell △ Norway 62°20N 9°25E 164 B6
Dovrefjell-Sunndalsfjella △ Norway 62°23N 9°11E 164 B6
Dow Rūd Iran 33°28N 49°4E 247 C6
Dowa Malawi 13°38S 33°58E 269 E3
Dowagiac U.S.A. 41°59N 86°6W 311 C10
Dowerin Australia 31°12S 117°2E 279 F2
Dowgha'i Iran 36°54N 58°32E 247 B8
Dowlat Yār Afghan. 34°30N 65°45E 240 B2
Dowlatābād Farāh, Afghan. 32°47N 62°40E 240 B1
Dowlatābād Fāryāb, Afghan. 36°26N 64°55E 240 A2
Dowlatābād Kermān, Iran 28°20N 56°40E 247 D8
Dowlatābād Khorāsān, Iran 35°16N 59°29E 247 C8
Dowlatābād Tehrān, Iran 35°38N 51°27E 141 B2
Dowling Park U.S.A. 30°15N 83°15W 316 E6
Down □ U.K. 54°23N 6°2W 166 B5
Down, L. U.S.A. 28°30N 81°31W 133 A1
Downers Grove U.S.A. 41°48N 88°1W 311 C8
Downey Calif., U.S.A. 33°56N 118°9W 126 C4
Downey Idaho, U.S.A. 42°26N 112°7W 304 E7
Downham Market U.K. 52°37N 0°23E 169 E8
Downieville U.S.A. 39°34N 120°50W 306 F6
Downing U.S.A. 40°29N 92°22W 310 D4
Downpatrick U.K. 54°20N 5°43W 166 B6
Downpatrick Hd. Ireland 54°20N 9°21W 166 B2
Downsview Canada 43°43N 79°30W 141 A1
Downsville U.S.A. 42°5N 75°0W 313 D10
Downton, Mt. Canada 52°42N 124°52W 296 C4
Dowsārī Iran 28°25N 57°59E 247 D8
Dowshī Afghan. 35°35N 68°43E 240 B3
Doxato Greece 41°9N 24°16E 203 E8
Doyle U.S.A. 40°2N 120°6W 306 E6
Doylestown U.S.A. 40°21N 75°10W 313 F9
Dōzen Japan 36°5N 133°5E 222 A5
Dozois, Rés. Canada 47°30N 77°5W 298 C4
Dra Khel Pakistan 27°58N 66°45E 242 F2
Drâa, C. Morocco 28°47N 11°0W 260 C3
Drâa, Hamada du Algeria 28°0N 7°0W 260 C3
Drâa, Oued → Morocco 28°40N 11°10W 260 C2
Drac → France 45°12N 5°42E 175 C9
Drac, Coves del Spain 39°31N 3°19E 206 B4
Dračevo Macedonia 41°56N 21°31E 202 E5
Drachten Neths. 53°7N 6°5E 170 A6
Drăgănești Moldova 47°43N 28°15E 183 C13
Drăgănești-Olt Romania 44°9N 24°32E 183 F9
Drăgănești-Vlașca Romania 44°5N 25°33E 183 F10
Dragaš Kosovo 42°5N 20°41E 202 D4
Drăgășani Romania 44°39N 24°17E 183 F9
Dragichyn Belarus 52°15N 25°8E 177 B13
Dragocvet Serbia 43°58N 21°15E 202 C5
Dragon's Mouths Venezuela 11°0N 61°50W 323 t
Dragør Denmark 55°35N 12°38E 118 B3
Dragovishtitsa Bulgaria 42°22N 22°39E 202 D6
Draguignan France 43°32N 6°27E 175 E10
Drahove Ukraine 48°14N 23°33E 183 B8
Drain U.S.A. 43°40N 123°19W 304 E2
Drake U.S.A. 47°55N 100°23W 308 B3
Drake Passage S. Ocean 58°0S 68°0W 151 B17
Drakensberg S. Africa 31°0S 28°0E 271 D4
Drama Greece 41°9N 24°10E 203 E8
Drama □ Greece 41°20N 24°0E 203 E8
Dramburg = Drawsko Pomorskie Poland 53°35N 15°50E 184 E2
Drammen Norway 59°42N 10°12E 164 E7
Drancy France 48°55N 2°26E 134 A3
Dranesville U.S.A. 39°0N 77°20W 143 A1
Drangajökull Iceland 66°9N 22°15W 155 A4
Drangedal Norway 59°6N 9°3E 164 E6
Drangsnes Iceland 65°41N 21°27W 155 B5
Dranov, Ostrov Romania 44°55N 29°30E 183 F14
Drapetsona Greece 37°56N 23°37E 112 B1
Dras India 34°25N 75°48E 243 B6
Drasis, Akra Greece 39°48N 19°40E 206 B9
Drau = Drava → Croatia 45°33N 18°55E 182 E3
Drava → Croatia 45°33N 18°55E 182 E3
Dravograd Slovenia 46°36N 15°5E 199 B12
Drawa → Poland 52°52N 15°59E 185 F2
Drawieński △ Poland 53°6N 15°58E 185 E2
Drawno Poland 53°13N 15°46E 185 E2
Drawsko Pomorskie Poland 53°35N 15°50E 184 E2
Drayton Canada 43°46N 80°40W 312 C4
Drayton Plains U.S.A. 42°41N 83°23W 311 B13
Drayton Valley Canada 53°12N 114°58W 296 C6
Dreieich Germany 50°1N 8°41E 179 E4
Dreikikir Papua N. G. 3°35S 142°46E 286 B2
Dreilinden Germany 52°24N 13°10E 115 B2
Dren Kosovo 43°8N 20°46E 202 C4
Drenthe □ Neths. 52°52N 6°40E 170 B6
Drepano, Akra Greece 35°28N 24°14E 207 E5
Drepanum, C. Cyprus 34°54N 32°19E 207 F8
Dresden Ont., Canada 42°35N 82°11W 312 D2
Dresden Sachsen, Germany 51°3N 13°44E 178 D9
Dresden N.Y., U.S.A. 42°41N 76°57W 312 D8
Dreux France 48°44N 1°23E 172 D8
Drevsjø Norway 61°53N 12°1E 164 C9
Drewnica Poland 52°18N 21°6E 142 B2
Drexel U.S.A. 39°45N 84°18W 311 E12
Drezdenko Poland 52°50N 15°49E 185 F2
Driesen = Drezdenko Poland 52°50N 15°49E 185 F2
Driffield U.K. 54°0N 0°26W 168 C7
Driftwood U.S.A. 41°20N 78°8W 312 E6
Driggs U.S.A. 43°44N 111°6W 304 E8
Drigh Road Pakistan 24°52N 67°7E 123 A2
Drimnagh Ireland 53°19N 6°19W 120 B2
Drin → Albania 42°1N 19°38E 202 D3
Drin i Zi → Albania 41°37N 20°28E 202 E4
Drina → Bos.-H. 44°53N 19°21E 202 B3
Drincea → Romania 44°20N 22°55E 182 F7
Drinjača → Bos.-H. 44°15N 19°8E 182 F4
Driopida Greece 37°25N 24°26E 204 D6
Drissa = Vyerkhnyadzvinsk Belarus 55°45N 27°58E 188 E4
Driva → Norway 62°41N 9°31E 164 B6
Drivstoggo Norway 62°26N 9°47E 164 B6
Drniš Croatia 43°51N 16°10E 199 E13
Drøbak Norway 59°39N 10°39E 164 E7
Drobeta-Turnu Severin Romania 44°39N 22°41E 182 F7
Drobin Poland 52°42N 19°58E 185 F6
Drochia Moldova 48°2N 27°48E 183 B12
Drogenbos Belgium 50°47N 4°19E 116 B1
Drogheda Ireland 53°43N 6°22W 166 C5
Drogichin = Dragichyn Belarus 52°15N 25°8E 177 B13
Drogobych = Drohobych Ukraine 49°20N 23°30E 185 J10
Drohiczyn Poland 52°24N 22°39E 185 F9
Drohobych Ukraine 49°20N 23°30E 185 J10
Droichead Atha = Drogheda Ireland 53°43N 6°22W 166 C5
Droichead na Bandan = Bandon Ireland 51°44N 8°44W 166 E3
Droichead Nua Ireland 53°11N 6°48W 166 C5
Droitwich U.K. 52°16N 2°8W 169 E5
Drôme □ France 44°38N 5°15E 175 D9
Drôme → France 44°46N 4°46E 175 D8
Dromedary, C. Australia 36°17S 150°10E 283 D9
Drömling △ Germany 52°29N 11°5E 178 C7
Dromore U.K. 54°31N 7°28W 166 B4
Dromore West Ireland 54°15N 8°52W 166 B3
Dronero Italy 44°28N 7°22E 198 D4
Dronfield U.K. 53°19N 1°27W 168 D6
Dronne → France 45°2N 0°9W 174 C3
Dronning Ingrid Land Greenland 64°25N 52°5W 154 E5
Dronning Maud Land Antarctica 72°30S 12°0E 151 D3
Dronninglund Denmark 57°10N 10°19E 163 G4
Dronten Neths. 52°32N 5°43E 170 B5
Dropt → France 44°35N 0°6W 174 D3
Drosendorf Austria 48°52N 15°37E 180 C8
Drosh Pakistan 35°33N 71°48E 240 B3
Droué France 48°3N 1°6E 172 D8
Drouin Australia 38°10S 145°53E 283 E6
Druid Hills U.S.A. 33°47N 84°21W 113 B2
Drujba Uzbekistan 41°13N 61°18E 216 D6
Druk Yul = Bhutan ■ Asia 27°25N 90°30E 241 B3
Drum Tower Beijing, China 114 a3
Drumbo Canada 43°16N 80°35W 312 C4
Drumcliff Ireland 54°20N 8°29W 166 B3
Drumcondra Ireland 53°21N 6°16W 120 A2
Drumheller Canada 51°25N 112°40W 296 C6
Drummond U.S.A. 46°40N 113°9W 304 C7
Drummond I. U.S.A. 46°1N 83°39W 309 B12
Drummond Pt. Australia 34°9S 135°16E 281 E2
Drummond Ra. Australia 23°45S 147°10E 280 C4
Drummondville Canada 45°55N 72°25W 298 C5
Drummoyne Australia 33°51S 151°8E 139 B1
Drumright U.S.A. 35°59N 96°36W 314 D6
Druskeniki = Druskininkai Lithuania 54°3N 23°58E 188 E2
Druskininkai Lithuania 54°3N 23°58E 188 E2
Drut → Belarus 53°8N 30°5E 177 B16
Druya Belarus 55°45N 27°28E 188 E4
Druzhba Bulgaria 43°15N 28°1E 203 C12
Druzhina Russia 68°14N 145°18E 215 C15
Drvar Bos.-H. 44°21N 16°23E 199 D13
Drvenik Croatia 43°27N 16°3E 199 E13
Drwęca → Poland 53°0N 18°42E 185 E5
Dry Harbour Mts. Jamaica 18°19N 77°24W 320 a
Dry Tortugas U.S.A. 24°38N 82°55W 315 F13
Dryander △ Australia 20°13S 148°34E 280 b
Dryanovo Bulgaria 42°59N 25°28E 203 D9
Dryden Ont., Canada 49°47N 92°50W 297 D10
Dryden N.Y., U.S.A. 42°30N 76°18W 313 D8
Drygalski I. Antarctica 66°0S 92°0E 151 C7
Drygalski Ice Tongue Antarctica 75°24S 163°30E 151 D11
Drylaw U.K. 55°58N 3°15W 121 B2
Drysdale → Australia 13°59S 126°51E 278 B4
Drysdale I. Australia 11°41S 136°0E 280 A2
Drysdale River △ Australia 14°56S 127°2E 278 B4
Drzewica Poland 51°27N 20°29E 185 G7
Drzewiczka → Poland 51°36N 20°36E 185 G7
Dschang Cameroon 5°32N 10°3E 263 D7
Du Gué → Canada 57°21N 70°45W 298 A5
Du He → China 32°48N 110°40E 229 A8
Du Quoin U.S.A. 38°1N 89°14W 310 G7
Du'an China 23°59N 108°3E 228 F7
Duanesburg U.S.A. 42°45N 74°11W 313 D10
Duaringa Australia 23°42S 149°42E 280 C4
Duarte, Pico Dom. Rep. 19°2N 70°59W 321 C5
Dubai = Dubayy U.A.E. 25°18N 55°20E 247 E7
Dubăsari Moldova 47°15N 29°10E 183 C14
Dubăsari Vdkhr. Moldova 47°30N 29°0E 183 C13
Dubawnt → Canada 64°33N 100°6W 297 A8
Dubawnt L. Canada 63°8N 101°28W 297 A8
Dubayy U.A.E. 25°18N 55°20E 247 E7
Dubbo Australia 32°11S 148°35E 283 B8
Dube → Liberia 5°16N 7°29W 262 D3
Dubeč Czech Rep. 50°3N 14°35E 135 B3
Dubele Dem. Rep. of the Congo 2°56N 29°35E 268 B2
Dübendorf Switz. 47°24N 8°37E 179 H4
Dubica Croatia 45°11N 16°48E 199 C13
Dublanc Dominica 15°31N 61°28W 323 k
Dublin Dublin, Ireland 53°21N 6°15W 120 A2
Dublin Ga., U.S.A. 32°32N 82°54W 316 C7
Dublin Ohio, U.S.A. 40°5N 83°7W 311 D13
Dublin Tex., U.S.A. 32°5N 98°21W 314 E5
Dublin □ Ireland 53°24N 6°20W 166 C5
Dublin ✕ (DUB) Ireland 53°26N 6°15W 120 A2
Dublin B. Ireland 53°19N 6°7W 120 B3
Dublin Castle Dublin, Ireland 120 c2
Dublin Harbour Ireland 53°21N 6°11W 120 A2
Dubna Russia 56°44N 37°10E 188 D9
Dubnica nad Váhom Slovak Rep. 48°58N 18°11E 181 C11
Dubno Ukraine 50°25N 25°45E 177 C13
Dubois Idaho, U.S.A. 44°10N 112°14W 304 D7
Dubois Ind., U.S.A. 38°27N 86°48W 311 F10
DuBois Pa., U.S.A. 41°7N 78°46W 312 E6
Dubossary = Dubăsari Moldova 47°15N 29°10E 183 C14
Dubossary Vdkhr. = Dubăsari Vdkhr. Moldova 47°30N 29°0E 183 C13
Dubove Ukraine 48°10N 23°53E 183 B8
Dubovka Russia 49°5N 44°50E 191 F7
Dubovskoye Russia 47°28N 42°46E 191 G6
Dubrajpur India 23°48N 87°25E 243 H12
Dubréka Guinea 9°46N 13°31W 262 D2
Dubrovitsa = Dubrovytsya Ukraine 51°31N 26°35E 177 C14
Dubrovnik Croatia 42°39N 18°6E 202 D2
Dubrovytsya Ukraine 51°31N 26°35E 177 C14
Dubulu Dem. Rep. of the Congo 4°18N 20°16E 264 B4
Dubuque U.S.A. 42°30N 90°41W 310 B6
Dubysa → Lithuania 55°5N 23°26E 184 C10
Duc de Gloucester, Îs. French Polynesia 20°38S 143°20W 289 f
Duc Tho Vietnam 18°32N 105°35E 236 C5
Ducassous, Pte. Martinique 14°32N 60°50W 322 j
Duchang China 29°18N 116°12E 229 C11
Duchesne U.S.A. 40°10N 110°24W 304 F8
Duchess Australia 21°20S 139°50E 280 C2
Ducie I. Pac. Oc. 24°40S 124°48W 289 K15
Duck → U.S.A. 36°2N 87°52W 315 C11
Duck Cr. → Australia 22°37S 116°53E 278 D2
Duck Lake Canada 52°50N 106°16W 297 C7
Duck Mountain △ Canada 51°45N 101°0W 297 C8
Duckwall, Mt. U.S.A. 37°58N 120°7W 306 H6
Ducos Martinique 14°33N 60°59W 322 j
Duda → Colombia 2°34N 74°3W 328 C3
Duddington U.K. 55°56N 3°8W 121 B3
Duderstadt Germany 51°31N 10°15E 178 D6
Dudhi India 24°15N 83°10E 243 G10
Dudhnai India 25°59N 90°47E 241 C3
Dudinka Russia 69°30N 86°13E 215 C9
Dudley W. Mids., U.K. 52°31N 2°5W 169 E5
Dudley Ga., U.S.A. 32°32N 83°5W 316 C6
Dudna → India 19°17N 76°54E 244 E3
Dudo Somali Rep. 9°20N 50°12E 267 C7
Dudo, W. → Somali Rep. 9°14N 50°14E 267 C7
Dudub Ethiopia 6°55N 46°43E 267 D6
Dudwa India 28°30N 80°41E 243 E9
Dudwa △ India 28°30N 80°40E 243 E9
Duékoué Ivory C. 6°40N 7°15W 262 D3
Dueñas Phil. 11°4N 122°37E 233 F4
Dueñas Spain 41°52N 4°33W 194 D6
Duerê Brazil 11°20S 49°17W 333 D2
Duero = Douro → Europe 41°8N 8°40W 194 D2
Duff Is. Pac. Oc. 9°50S 167°10E 277 B12
Dufftown U.K. 57°27N 3°8W 167 D5
Dufourspitz Switz. 45°56N 7°52E 179 K3
Dugger U.S.A. 39°4N 87°18W 311 E9
Dugi Otok Croatia 44°0N 15°3E 199 D11
Duguima Somali Rep. 1°15N 42°34E 267 D5
Dugnano Italy 45°33N 9°11E 129 A2
Dugo Selo Croatia 45°51N 16°18E 199 C13
Duida-Marahuaca △ Venezuela 3°33N 65°33W 328 C4
Duisburg Germany 51°26N 6°45E 178 D2
Duitama Colombia 5°50N 73°2W 328 B3
Duivendrecht Neths. 52°20N 4°55E 112 B2
Duiwelskloof = Modjadjiskloof S. Africa 23°42S 30°10E 271 B5
Dujiangyan China 31°2N 103°38E 228 B4
Duk Fadiat Sudan 7°45N 31°25E 257 F3
Duk Faiwil Sudan 7°30N 31°29E 257 F3
Dukat Albania 40°16N 19°32E 202 F3
Dūkdamīn Iran 35°59N 57°43E 247 C8
Dukelský Průsmyk Slovak Rep. 49°25N 21°42E 181 B14
Dukhān Qatar 25°25N 50°50E 247 E6
Dukhovshchina Russia 55°15N 32°27E 188 E7
Duki Pakistan 30°14N 68°25E 240 C3
Dukla Poland 49°30N 21°35E 185 J8
Duku Bauchi, Nigeria 10°43N 10°43E 263 C7
Duku Sokoto, Nigeria 11°11N 4°55E 263 C5
Dula Dem. Rep. of the Congo 4°40N 20°21E 264 B4
Dūlāb Iran 35°39N 51°27E 141 B2
Dulag Phil. 10°57N 125°2E 233 F5
Dulan China 36°0N 97°11E 218 D8
Dulawan = Datu Piang Phil. 7°2N 124°30E 233 H5
Dulce U.S.A. 36°56N 107°0W 305 H10
Dulce → Argentina 30°32S 62°33W 334 C3
Dulce, G. Costa Rica 8°40N 83°20W 320 E3
Dulcina Antigua & B. 17°5N 61°49W 322 c
Dulf Iraq 35°7N 45°51E 246 C5
Dŭlgopol Bulgaria 43°3N 27°22E 203 C11
Duliu China 39°2N 116°55E 226 E9
Dullabchara India 24°30N 92°26E 241 C4
Dulles Int. ✕ (IAD) U.S.A. 38°57N 77°27W 143 B1
Dullewala Pakistan 31°50N 71°25E 242 D4
Dullstroom S. Africa 25°27S 30°7E 271 C5
Dülmen Germany 51°49N 7°17E 178 D3
Dulovo Bulgaria 43°48N 27°9E 203 C11
Dulpetorpet Norway 60°34N 12°19E 164 D9
Dulq Maghār Syria 36°22N 38°39E 213 D8
Duluth Ga., U.S.A. 34°0N 84°9W 316 A5
Duluth Minn., U.S.A. 46°47N 92°6W 308 B7
Dulwich U.K. 51°26N 0°5W 125 B3
Dum Dum India 22°39N 88°26E 124 B2
Dum Dum Int. ✕ (CCU) India 22°38N 88°26E 124 B2
Dum Duma India 27°40N 95°40E 241 B5
Dūmā Syria 33°34N 36°24E 250 E7
Dumaguete Phil. 9°17N 123°15E 233 G4
Dumai Indonesia 1°35N 101°28E 234 B2
Dumalinao Phil. 7°49N 123°23E 233 H4
Dumanjug Phil. 10°4N 123°26E 233 F4
Dumanquilas B. Phil. 7°34N 123°4E 233 H4
Dumaran Phil. 10°33N 119°50E 233 F2
Dumaran I. Phil. 10°33N 119°51E 233 F2
Dumarao Phil. 11°16N 122°41E 233 F4
Dumas Ark., U.S.A. 33°53N 91°29W 314 E9
Dumas Tex., U.S.A. 35°52N 101°58W 314 D4
Ḑumayr Syria 33°39N 36°42E 250 F7
Dumbarton U.K. 55°57N 4°33W 167 F4
Dumbéa N. Cal. 22°10S 166°27E 288 d
Ďumbier Slovak Rep. 48°56N 19°38E 181 C12
Dumbleyung Australia 33°17S 117°42E 279 F2
Dumbo Angola 14°6S 17°24E 265 E3
Dumbrăveni Romania 46°14N 24°34E 183 D9
Dumfries U.K. 55°4N 3°37W 167 F5
Dumfries & Galloway □ U.K. 55°9N 3°58W 167 F5
Dumingag Phil. 8°20N 123°20E 233 G4
Dumitrești Romania 45°33N 26°55E 183 E11
Dumka India 24°12N 87°15E 243 G12
Dumlupınar Turkey 38°53N 30°0E 205 C12
Dümmer Germany 52°31N 8°20E 178 C4
Dümmer △ Germany 52°31N 8°21E 178 C4
Dumoine → Canada 46°13N 77°51W 298 C4
Dumoine, L. Canada 46°55N 77°55W 298 C4
Dumont U.S.A. 40°56N 73°59W 132 A2
Dumont d'Urville Antarctica 66°40S 140°0E 151 C10
Dumont d'Urville Sea S. Ocean 63°30S 138°0E 151 C9
Dumoulin Is. Papua N. G. 10°54S 150°46E 286 F6
Dumpu Papua N. G. 5°53S 145°44E 286 C3
Dumraon India 25°33N 84°8E 243 G11
Dumyât Egypt 31°24N 31°48E 251 G2
Dumyât, Far → Egypt 31°31N 31°51E 251 G2
Dumyât, Masabb Egypt 31°28N 31°51E 251 G2
Dún Dealgan = Dundalk Ireland 54°1N 6°24W 166 B5
Dún Garbhán = Dungarvan Ireland 52°5N 7°37W 166 D4
Dún Laoghaire Ireland 53°17N 6°8W 120 B3
Dun-le-Palestel France 46°18N 1°39E 173 F8
Dun-sur-Auron France 46°53N 2°33E 173 F9
Dun-sur-Meuse France 49°23N 5°11E 173 C12
Duna = Dunărea → Europe 45°20N 29°40E 183 E14
Duna-Drava △ Hungary 46°15N 18°50E 182 D3
Duna-völgyi-főcsatorna Hungary 46°40N 19°14E 182 D4
Dünaburg = Daugavpils Latvia 55°53N 26°32E 188 E4
Dunaföldvár Hungary 46°50N 18°57E 182 D3
Dunagiri India 30°31N 79°52E 243 D8
Dunaj = Dunărea → Europe 45°20N 29°40E 183 E14
Dunajec → Poland 50°15N 20°44E 185 H7
Dunajská Streda Slovak Rep. 48°0N 17°37E 181 C10
Dunakeszi Hungary 47°37N 19°8E 182 C4
Dunapataj Hungary 46°39N 19°4E 182 D4
Dunărea → Europe 45°20N 29°40E 183 E14
Dunaszekcső Hungary 46°6N 18°45E 182 D3
Dunaújváros Hungary 46°58N 18°57E 182 D3
Dunav = Dunărea → Europe 45°20N 29°40E 183 E14
Dunavațu de Jos Romania 44°59N 29°13E 183 F14
Dunavtsi Bulgaria 43°57N 22°53E 202 C6
Dunay Russia 42°52N 132°22E 220 C6
Dunayivtsi Ukraine 48°54N 26°50E 183 B11
Dunback N.Z. 45°23S 170°36E 285 F5
Dunbar U.K. 56°0N 2°31W 167 E6
Dunblane U.K. 56°11N 3°58W 167 E5
Duncan B.C., Canada 48°45N 123°40W 306 B3
Duncan Ariz., U.S.A. 32°43N 109°6W 305 K9
Duncan Okla., U.S.A. 34°30N 97°57W 314 D6
Duncan, L. Canada 53°29N 77°58W 298 B4
Duncan Dock Cape Town, S. Africa 118 a3
Duncan L. Canada 62°51N 113°58W 296 A6
Duncan Passage India 11°0N 92°0E 245 J11
Duncan Town Bahamas 22°15N 75°45W 320 B4
Duncannon U.S.A. 40°23N 77°2W 312 F7
Duncans Jamaica 18°27N 77°32W 320 a
Duncansby Head U.K. 58°38N 3°1W 167 C5
Duncansville U.S.A. 40°25N 78°26W 312 F6
Dund-Us Mongolia 48°1N 91°38E 217 C12
Dundaga Latvia 57°31N 22°21E 184 A9
Dundalk Ont., Canada 44°10N 80°24W 312 B4
Dundalk Louth, Ireland 54°1N 6°24W 166 B5
Dundalk Md., U.S.A. 39°15N 76°31W 309 F15
Dundalk Bay Ireland 53°55N 6°15W 166 C5
Dundas = Uummannaq Greenland 77°33N 68°52W 154 B4
Dundas Canada 43°17N 79°59W 312 C5
Dundas, L. Australia 32°35S 121°50E 279 F3
Dundas I. Canada 54°30N 130°50W 296 C2
Dundas Str. Australia 11°15S 131°35E 278 B5
Dundee KwaZulu Natal, S. Africa 28°11S 30°15E 271 C5
Dundee Dundee C., U.K. 56°28N 2°59W 167 E6
Dundee Mich., U.S.A. 41°57N 83°40W 311 C13
Dundee N.Y., U.S.A. 42°32N 76°59W 312 D8
Dundee City □ U.K. 56°30N 2°58W 167 E6
Dundgovĭ □ Mongolia 45°10N 106°0E 226 B4
Dundrum Dublin, Ireland 53°18N 6°14W 120 B2
Dundrum Down, U.K. 54°16N 5°52W 166 B6
Dundrum B. U.K. 54°13N 5°47W 166 B6
Dunearn Singapore 1°19N 103°49E 138 B2
Dunedin N.Z. 45°50S 170°33E 285 F5
Dunedin Fla., U.S.A. 28°1N 82°46W 317 G7
Dunedoo Australia 32°0S 149°25E 283 A8
Dunfanaghy Ireland 55°11N 7°58W 166 A4
Dunfermline U.K. 56°5N 3°27W 167 E5
Dungannon Ont., Canada 43°51N 81°36W 312 C3
Dungannon Tyrone, U.K. 54°31N 6°46W 166 B5
Dungarpur India 23°52N 73°45E 242 H5
Dungarvan Ireland 52°5N 7°37W 166 D4
Dungarvan Harbour Ireland 52°4N 7°35W 166 D4
Dungeness U.K. 50°54N 0°59E 169 G8
Dunglow Ireland 54°57N 8°21W 166 B3
Dungo, L. do Angola 17°15S 19°0E 265 F3
Dungog Australia 32°22S 151°46E 283 B9
Dungu Dem. Rep. of the Congo 3°40N 28°32E 268 B2
Dungun Malaysia 4°45N 103°25E 237 K4
Dungunāb Sudan 21°10N 37°9E 256 C4
Dungunâb, Khalîg Sudan 21°5N 37°12E 256 C4
Dunhua China 43°20N 128°14E 227 C15
Dunhuang China 40°8N 94°36E 218 C7
Dunk I. Australia 17°59S 146°29E 280 B4
Dunkassa Benin 10°21N 3°10E 263 C5
Dunkeld Queens., Australia 33°25S 149°29E 281 E4
Dunkeld Vic., Australia 37°40S 142°22E 282 D5
Dunkeld Perth & Kinr., U.K. 56°34N 3°35W 167 E5
Dunkerque France 51°2N 2°20E 173 A9
Dunkery Beacon U.K. 51°9N 3°36W 169 F4
Dunkirk = Dunkerque France 51°2N 2°20E 173 A9
Dunkirk U.S.A. 42°29N 79°20W 312 D5
Dunkuj Sudan 12°50N 32°49E 257 E3
Dunkwa Central, Ghana 6°0N 1°47W 262 D4
Dunkwa Central, Ghana 5°30N 1°0W 263 D4
Dúnleary = Dún Laoghaire Ireland 53°17N 6°8W 120 B3
Dunleer Ireland 53°50N 6°24W 166 C5
Dunmanus B. Ireland 51°31N 9°50W 166 E2
Dunmanway Ireland 51°43N 9°6W 166 E2
Dunmarra Australia 16°42S 133°25E 280 B1
Dunmore U.S.A. 41°25N 75°38W 313 E9
Dunmore East Ireland 52°9N 7°0W 166 D5
Dunmore Hd. Ireland 52°10N 10°35W 166 D1
Dunmore Town Bahamas 25°30N 76°39W 320 A4
Dunn U.S.A. 35°19N 78°37W 315 D15
Dunn Loring U.S.A. 38°54N 77°13W 143 B2
Dunnellon U.S.A. 29°3N 82°28W 317 F7
Dunnet Hd. U.K. 58°40N 3°21W 167 C5
Dunning Ill., U.S.A. 41°56N 87°48W 119 B2
Dunning Nebr., U.S.A. 41°50N 100°6W 308 E3
Dunn's River Falls Jamaica 18°25N 77°8W 320 a
Dunnville Canada 42°54N 79°36W 312 D5
Dunolly Australia 36°51S 143°44E 282 D5
Dunoon U.K. 55°57N 4°56W 167 F4
Dunqul Egypt 23°26N 31°37E 256 C3
Duns U.K. 55°47N 2°20W 167 F6
Dunseith U.S.A. 48°50N 100°3W 308 A3
Dunshaughlin Ireland 53°31N 6°33W 166 C5
Dunsmuir U.S.A. 41°13N 122°16W 304 F2
Dunstable U.K. 51°53N 0°32W 169 F7
Dunstan Mts. N.Z. 44°53S 169°35E 285 E4
Dunster Canada 53°8N 119°50W 296 C5
Duntroon N.Z. 44°51S 170°40E 285 E5
Dunvegan Gauteng, S. Africa 26°9S 28°9E 123 A2
Dunvegan Highl., U.K. 57°27N 6°35W 167 D2
Dunvegan L. Canada 60°8N 107°10W 297 A7
Duolun China 42°12N 116°28E 226 C9
Duomo Italy 45°28N 9°11E 129 B2
Duomula China 34°8N 82°29E 217 F10
Duong Dong Vietnam 10°13N 103°58E 237 G4
Dupax del Norte Phil. 16°17N 121°5E 232 C3
Dupree U.S.A. 45°4N 101°35W 308 C3
Dupuyer U.S.A. 48°13N 112°30W 304 B7
Duqm Oman 19°39N 57°42E 249 C7
Duque de Caxias Brazil 22°46S 43°18W 135 A1
Duque de York, I. Chile 50°37S 75°25W 336 D1
Durack → Australia 15°33S 127°52E 278 C4
Durack Ra. Australia 16°50S 127°40E 278 C4
Durack River Australia 15°32S 127°39E 278 C4
Durağan Turkey 41°25N 35°3E 212 B6
Durak Turkey 39°42N 28°17E 205 B10
Đurakovac Kosovo 42°43N 20°29E 202 D4
Durance → France 43°55N 4°45E 175 E8
Durand Ga., U.S.A. 32°55N 84°46W 316 C5
Durand Ill., U.S.A. 42°26N 89°20W 310 B7
Durand Mich., U.S.A. 42°55N 83°59W 311 B13
Durand Wis., U.S.A. 44°38N 91°58W 308 C8
Durandeau St. Lucia 13°56N 60°59W 323 m
Durango Mexico 24°3N 104°39W 318 C4
Durango Colo., U.S.A. 37°16N 107°53W 305 H10
Durango □ Mexico 25°0N 105°0W 318 C4
Durankulak Bulgaria 43°41N 28°32E 203 C12
Durant Iowa, U.S.A. 41°36N 90°54W 310 C6
Durant Miss., U.S.A. 33°4N 89°51W 315 E10
Durant Okla., U.S.A. 33°59N 96°25W 314 E6
Duratón → Spain 41°37N 4°7W 194 D6
Durazno Uruguay 33°25S 56°31W 334 C4
Durazzo = Durrës Albania 41°19N 19°28E 202 E3
Durban Aude, France 42°59N 2°49E 174 F6
Durban KwaZulu Natal, S. Africa 29°49S 31°1E 271 C5
Durbuy Belgium 50°21N 5°28E 170 D5
Dúrcal Spain 36°59N 3°34W 195 J7
Đurđevac Croatia 46°2N 17°3E 182 D2
Düren Germany 50°48N 6°29E 178 E2
Duren Sawit Indonesia 6°13S 106°54E 122 A2
Durg = Bhilainagar-Durg India 21°13N 81°26E 244 D5
Durgapur India 23°30N 87°20E 243 H12
Durham Ont., Canada 44°10N 80°49W 312 B4
Durham Darlington, U.K. 54°47N 1°34W 168 C6
Durham Calif., U.S.A. 39°39N 121°48W 306 F5
Durham N.C., U.S.A. 35°59N 78°54W 315 D15
Durham N.H., U.S.A. 43°8N 70°56W 313 C14
Durham □ U.K. 54°42N 1°45W 168 C6
Duri Indonesia 1°27N 101°15E 234 B2
Durlas = Thurles Ireland 52°41N 7°49W 166 D4
Durlești Moldova 47°1N 28°46E 183 C13
Ḑurmā Si. Arabia 24°37N 46°8E 246 E5
Durmitor Montenegro 43°10N 19°0E 202 C2
Durmitor △ Montenegro 43°15N 19°5E 202 C3
Durness U.K. 58°34N 4°45W 167 C4
Durnford, Pta. W. Sahara 23°37N 16°0W 260 D1
Durrës Albania 41°19N 19°28E 202 E3
Durrow Ireland 52°51N 7°24W 166 D4
Dursey I. Ireland 51°36N 10°12W 166 E1
Dursley U.K. 51°40N 2°21W 169 F5
Dursunbey Turkey 39°35N 28°37E 205 B10
Durtal France 47°40N 0°18W 172 E6
Duru Dem. Rep. of the Congo 4°14N 28°50E 268 B2
Duru Gölü Turkey 41°20N 28°35E 203 E12
Durukhsi Ethiopia 8°31N 45°28E 267 C6
Durusu Turkey 41°17N 28°41E 203 E12
Durūz, Jabal ad Jordan 32°35N 36°40E 250 F7
D'Urville, Tanjung Indonesia 1°28S 137°54E 231 E9
D'Urville I. N.Z. 40°50S 173°55E 285 A8
Duryea U.S.A. 41°20N 75°45W 313 E9
Dusa Mareb = Dhuusamarreeb Somali Rep. 5°30N 46°15E 267 C6
Dûsh Egypt 24°35N 30°41E 256 C3
Dushak Turkmenistan 37°13N 60°1E 247 B9
Dushan China 25°48N 107°30E 228 E6
Dushanbe Tajikistan 38°33N 68°48E 217 E7
Dusheti Georgia 42°10N 44°42E 191 J7
Dushore U.S.A. 41°31N 76°24W 313 E8
Dusit Bangkok, Thailand 113 a2
Dusit Zoo Bangkok, Thailand 113 a2
Dusky Sd. N.Z. 45°47S 166°30E 285 F1
Dussejour, C. Australia 14°45S 128°13E 278 B4
Düsseldorf Germany 51°14N 6°47E 178 D2
Düsseldorf Rhein-Ruhr ✕ (DUS) Germany 51°17N 6°46E 178 D2
Dusti Tajikistan 37°20N 68°40E 217 E7
Duszniki-Zdrój Poland 50°24N 16°24E 185 H3
Dutch East Indies = Indonesia ■ Asia 5°0S 115°0E 235 C4
Dutch Guiana = Suriname ■ S. Amer. 4°0N 56°0W 329 C6
Dutch Harbor U.S.A. 53°53N 166°32W 303 K6
Dutlwe Botswana 23°58S 23°46E 270 B3
Dutsan Wai Nigeria 10°50N 8°10E 263 C6
Dutse Nigeria 11°46N 9°20E 263 C6
Dutton Canada 42°39N 81°30W 312 D3
Dutton → Australia 20°44S 143°10E 280 C3
Dutywa S. Africa 32°8S 28°18E 271 D4
Duved Sweden 63°23N 12°55E 162 A6
Düvertepe Turkey 39°14N 28°27E 205 B10
Dúvida = Roosevelt → Brazil 7°35S 60°20W 331 B5
Duwayhin, Khawr U.A.E. 24°20N 51°25E 247 E6
Duyfken Pt. Australia 12°33S 141°38E 280 A3
Duyun China 26°18N 107°29E 228 D6
Düzağac Turkey 38°48N 30°10E 205 C12
Düzce Turkey 40°50N 31°10E 212 B4
Düzce □ Turkey 40°50N 31°10E 212 B4
Duzdab = Zāhedān Iran 29°30N 60°50E 247 D9
Duzer Guadeloupe 16°20N 61°44W 322 e
Dve Mogili Bulgaria 43°35N 25°55E 203 C9
Dvigatelstroy = Kaspiysk Russia 42°52N 47°40E 191 J8
Dvina, Severnaya → Russia 64°32N 40°30E 186 B7
Dvinsk = Daugavpils Latvia 55°53N 26°32E 188 E4
Dvinskaya Guba Russia 65°0N 39°0E 186 B6
Dvor Croatia 45°4N 16°22E 199 C13
Dvůr Králové nad Labem Czech Rep. 50°27N 15°50E 180 A8
Dwarka India 22°18N 69°8E 242 H3
Dwellingup Australia 32°43S 116°4E 279 F2
Dwight Ont., Canada 45°20N 79°1W 312 A5
Dwight Ill., U.S.A. 41°5N 88°26W 311 C8
Dworp Belgium 50°44N 4°18E 116 B1
Dyakove Ukraine 48°1N 23°2E 182 B7
Dyakovo Russia 55°40N 37°39E 129 B3
Dyatkovo Russia 53°40N 34°27E 188 F8
Dyatlovo = Dzyatlava Belarus 53°28N 25°28E 177 B13
Dyce U.K. 57°13N 2°12W 167 D6
Dyer, C. Canada 66°37N 61°16W 295 D19
Dyer Bay Canada 45°10N 81°20W 312 A3
Dyer Plateau Antarctica 70°45S 65°30W 151 D17
Dyersburg U.S.A. 36°3N 89°23W 315 C10
Dyersville U.S.A. 42°29N 91°8W 310 B5
Dyfi → U.K. 52°32N 4°3W 169 E3
Dyhernfurth = Brzeg Dolny Poland 51°16N 16°41E 185 G3
Dyje → Czech Rep. 48°37N 16°56E 181 C9
Dyke Ackland B. Papua N. G. 9°0S 148°45E 286 E5
Dyker Beach Park U.S.A. 40°36N 74°1W 132 C1
Dymer Ukraine 50°47N 30°18E 177 C16
Dynów Poland 49°50N 22°11E 185 J9
Dyranut Norway 60°22N 7°31E 164 D4
Dyrhólaey Iceland 63°24N 19°8W 155 D7
Dyrnes Norway 63°25N 7°52E 164 A4
Dysart Queens., Australia 22°32S 148°23E 280 C4
Dysart Iowa, U.S.A. 42°10N 92°18W 310 B4
Dyushambe = Dushanbe Tajikistan 38°33N 68°48E 217 E7
Dyviziya Ukraine 45°55N 29°59E 183 E14
Dzamin Üüd = Borhoyn Tal Mongolia 43°50N 111°58E 226 C6
Dzaoudzi Mayotte 12°47S 45°16E 272 b
Dzaoudzi ✕ (DZA) Mayotte 12°48S 45°18E 272 b
Dzaudzhikau = Vladikavkaz Russia 43°0N 44°35E 191 J7
Dzavhan □ Mongolia 48°0N 96°0E 217 C13
Dzavhan Gol → Mongolia 48°54N 93°23E 218 B7
Dzerzhinsk Russia 56°14N 43°30E 190 B6
Dzerzhinskiy Moskva, Russia 55°38N 37°51E 129 C5
Dzerzhinskiy Moskva, Russia 55°47N 37°37E 129 B3
Dzerzhinskiy Park Russia 55°50N 37°37E 129 B3
Dzhalal-Abad = Jalal-Abad Kyrgyzstan 40°56N 73°0E 217 D8
Dzhalal-Ogly = Stepanavan Armenia 41°1N 44°23E 191 K7
Dzhalinda Russia 53°26N 124°0E 215 D13
Dzhambeyty = Zhympity Kazakhstan 50°16N 52°35E 216 B4
Dzhambul = Taraz Kazakhstan 42°54N 71°22E 217 D8
Dzhankoy Ukraine 45°40N 34°20E 189 K8
Dzhanybek = Zhänibek Kazakhstan 49°25N 46°50E 190 F8
Dzhargalantu = Hovd □ Mongolia 48°2N 91°37E 217 C12
Dzharkent = Zharkent Kazakhstan 44°10N 80°0E 217 D10
Dzharylhach, Ostriv Ukraine 46°2N 32°55E 189 J7
Dzhezkazgan = Zhezqazghan Kazakhstan 47°44N 67°40E 217 C7
Dzhibkhalantu = Uliastay Mongolia 47°56N 97°28E 218 B8
Dzhizak = Jizzax Uzbekistan 40°6N 67°50E 217 D7
Dzhugdzur, Khrebet Russia 57°30N 138°0E 215 D14
Dzhulynk Ukraine 48°26N 29°45E 183 B14
Dzhumgoltau, Khrebet Kyrgyzstan 42°15N 74°30E 217 D8
Dzhungarskiye Vorota = Dzungarian Gate Asia 45°10N 82°0E 217 C10
Dzhuryn Ukraine 48°41N 28°18E 183 B13
Dzhvari = Jvari Georgia 42°42N 42°4E 191 J6
Działdowo Poland 53°15N 20°15E 185 E7
Działoszyce Poland 50°22N 20°20E 185 H7
Działoszyn Poland 51°6N 18°50E 185 G5
Dzibilchaltún Mexico 21°10N 89°35W 319 C7
Dzierzgoń Poland 53°58N 19°20E 184 E6
Dzierżoniów Poland 50°45N 16°39E 185 H3
Dzilam de Bravo Mexico 21°24N 88°53W 319 C7
Dzioua Algeria 33°14N 5°14E 261 B6
Dzisna Belarus 55°34N 28°12E 188 E5
Dzisna → Belarus 55°34N 28°12E 188 E5
Dziwnów Poland 54°2N 14°45E 184 D1
Džūkija △ Lithuania 54°10N 24°30E 161 J21
Dzungarian Basin = Junggar Pendi China 44°30N 86°0E 217 D11
Dzungarian Gate Asia 45°10N 82°0E 217 C10
Dzüünbayan Mongolia 44°29N 110°2E 226 B6
Dzüünharaa Mongolia 48°52N 106°28E 218 B10
Dzüünmod Mongolia 47°45N 106°58E 218 B10
Dzyarzhynsk Belarus 53°40N 27°1E 177 B14
Dzyatlava Belarus 53°28N 25°28E 177 B13

E

E.C. Manning △ Canada 49°5N 120°45W 296 D4
E.T. Joshua ✕ (SVD) St. Vincent 13°8N 61°13W 323 n
E.U.R. = Esposizione Universale di Roma Italy 41°49N 12°28E 136 C1
Eabamet L. Canada 51°30N 87°46W 298 B2
Eabametoong Canada 51°30N 88°0W 298 B2
Éadan Doire = Edenderry Ireland 53°21N 7°4W 166 C4
Eads U.S.A. 38°29N 102°47W 304 G12
Eagar U.S.A. 34°6N 109°17W 305 J9
Eagle Alaska, U.S.A. 64°47N 141°12W 303 D12
Eagle Colo., U.S.A. 39°39N 106°50W 304 G10
Eagle → Canada 53°36N 57°26W 299 B8
Eagle, Mt. U.S. Virgin Is. 17°46N 64°49W 321 b
Eagle Beach Aruba 12°32N 70°3W 322 f
Eagle Butte U.S.A. 45°0N 101°10W 308 C3
Eagle Cr. → U.S.A. 38°36N 85°4W 311 F11
Eagle Grove U.S.A. 42°40N 93°54W 310 B3
Eagle L. Ont., Canada 49°42N 93°13W 297 D10
Eagle L. Calif., U.S.A. 40°39N 120°45W 304 F3
Eagle L. Maine, U.S.A. 46°20N 69°22W 309 B19
Eagle Lake Ont., Canada 45°8N 78°29W 312 A6
Eagle Lake Maine, U.S.A. 47°3N 68°36W 309 B19
Eagle Lake Tex., U.S.A. 29°35N 96°20W 314 G6
Eagle Mountain U.S.A. 33°49N 115°27W 307 M11
Eagle Nest U.S.A. 36°33N 105°16W 305 H11
Eagle Pass U.S.A. 28°43N 100°30W 314 G4
Eagle Pk. U.S.A. 38°10N 119°25W 306 G7
Eagle Pt. Australia 16°11S 124°23E 278 C3
Eagle River Mich., U.S.A. 47°25N 88°18W 308 B9
Eagle River Wis., U.S.A. 45°55N 89°15W 308 C9
Eagle Rock U.S.A. 34°8N 118°12W 126 B3
Eaglehawk Australia 36°44S 144°15E 282 D6
Eagles Mere U.S.A. 41°25N 76°33W 313 E8
Eagleville U.S.A. 40°28N 93°59W 310 D3
Ealing □ U.K. 51°31N 0°20W 125 A2
Ear Falls Canada 50°38N 93°13W 297 C10
Earle U.S.A. 35°16N 90°28W 315 D9
Earlimart U.S.A. 35°53N 119°16W 307 K7
Earl's Court London, U.K. 125 c1
Earlsfield U.K. 51°26N 0°10W 125 B2
Earlville Ill., U.S.A. 41°35N 88°55W 311 C8
Earlville N.Y., U.S.A. 42°44N 75°32W 313 D9
Earlwood Australia 33°55S 151°8E 139 B1
Early Branch U.S.A. 32°45N 80°55W 316 C9
Earn → U.K. 56°21N 3°18W 167 E5
Earn, L. U.K. 56°23N 4°13W 167 E4
Earnslaw, Mt. N.Z. 44°32S 168°27E 285 E3
Earth U.S.A. 34°14N 102°24W 314 D3
Eas Vanuatu 16°20S 168°15E 287 F6
Easley U.S.A. 34°50N 82°36W 315 D13
East Anglia U.K. 52°30N 1°0E 168 E9
East Angus Canada 45°30N 71°40W 299 C5
East Antarctica Antarctica 80°0S 90°0E 151 D7
East Arlington Mass., U.S.A. 42°24N 71°8W 116 A2
East Arlington Va., U.S.A. 38°51N 77°4W 143 B3
East Aurora U.S.A. 42°46N 78°37W 312 D6
East Ayrshire □ U.K. 55°26N 4°11W 167 F4
East Bedfont U.K. 51°26N 0°28W 125 B1
East Beskids = Vychodné Beskydy Europe 49°20N 22°0E 181 B15
East Boston U.S.A. 42°22N 71°1W 116 A2
East Brady U.S.A. 40°59N 79°37W 312 F5
East Branch Clarion River L. U.S.A. 41°35N 78°35W 312 E6
East C. = Dezhneva, Mys Russia 66°5N 169°40W 215 C19
East C. N.Z. 37°42S 178°35E 284 D7
East C. Papua N. G. 10°13S 150°53E 286 F6
East Caroline Basin Pac. Oc. 4°0N 146°45E 288 G6
East Chicago U.S.A. 41°38N 87°27W 311 C9
East China Sea Asia 30°0N 126°0E 219 F14
East Coulee Canada 51°23N 112°27W 296 C6
East Dereham = Dereham U.K. 52°41N 0°57E 169 E8
East Don → Canada 43°48N 79°25W 141 A2
East Don Parkland Canada 43°47N 79°22W 141 A2
East Dublin U.S.A. 32°32N 82°52W 316 C7
East Dubuque U.S.A. 42°30N 90°39W 310 B6
East Dunbartonshire □ U.K. 55°57N 4°13W 167 F4
East Elmhurst U.S.A. 40°45N 73°52W 132 B2
East End Pt. Bahamas 25°37N 77°16W 153 b
East Falkland Falk. Is. 51°30S 58°30W 153 f
East Finchley U.K. 51°35N 0°10W 125 A2
East Flatbush U.S.A. 40°39N 73°55W 132 B2
East Fork White → U.S.A. 38°33N 87°14W 311 F9
East Grand Forks U.S.A. 47°56N 97°1W 308 B5
East Grand Rapids U.S.A. 42°58N 85°37W 311 B11
East Greenwich U.S.A. 41°40N 71°27W 313 E13
East Grinstead U.K. 51°7N 0°0 169 F8
East Ham U.K. 51°32N 0°3E 125 A4
East Hartford U.S.A. 41°46N 72°39W 313 E12
East Haydon Australia 18°0S 141°30E 280 B3
East Helena U.S.A. 46°35N 111°56W 304 C8
East Humber → Canada 43°47N 79°35W 141 A1
East Indies Asia 0°0 120°0E 210 J14
East Kilbride U.K. 55°47N 4°11W 167 F4

East Lamma Channel *China* 22°14N 114°9E **122** B1
East Lansing *U.S.A.* 42°44N 84°29W **311** B12
East Las Vegas = Whitney *U.S.A.* 36°4N 115°5W **124** B2
East Lexington *U.S.A.* 42°25N 71°12W **116** A1
East Livermore = Livermore Falls *U.S.A.* 44°29N 70°11W **309** C18
East Liverpool *U.S.A.* 40°37N 80°35W **312** F4
East London *S. Africa* 33°0S 27°55E **271** D4
East Los Angeles *U.S.A.* 34°1N 118°10W **126** B3
East Lothian □ *U.K.* 55°58N 2°44W **167** F6
East Main = Eastmain *Canada* 52°10N 78°30W **298** B4
East Mariana Basin *Pac. Oc.* 12°0N 153°0E **288** F7
East Milwaukee = Shorewood *U.S.A.* 43°5N 87°53W **311** A9
East Molesey *U.K.* 51°24N 0°21W **125** B1
East Moline *U.S.A.* 41°32N 90°26W **310** C6
East Naples *U.S.A.* 26°8N 81°46W **317** J8
East New Britain □ *Papua N. G.* 6°30S 152°30E **286** D7
East New York *U.S.A.* 40°40N 73°53W **132** B2
East Northport *U.S.A.* 40°53N 73°20W **313** F11
East Orange *U.S.A.* 40°46N 74°12W **313** F10
East Pacific Rise *Pac. Oc.* 15°0S 110°0W **289** J17
East Pakistan = Bangladesh ■ *Asia* 24°0N 90°0E **241** D3
East Palatka *U.S.A.* 29°39N 81°36W **316** F8
East Palestine *U.S.A.* 40°50N 80°33W **312** F4
East Peoria *U.S.A.* 40°40N 89°34W **310** D7
East Pine *Canada* 55°48N 120°12W **296** B4
East Pines *U.S.A.* 38°57N 76°54W **143** B4
East Point *U.S.A.* 33°41N 84°25W **113** B2
East Potomac Park *Washington, D.C., U.S.A.* **143** c1
East Providence *U.S.A.* 41°49N 71°23W **313** E13
East Pt. *Br. Virgin Is.* 18°40N 64°18W **321** b
East Pt. *N.S., Canada* 46°27N 61°58W **299** C7
East Pt. *U.S. Virgin Is.* 17°45N 64°34W **321** b
East Renfrewshire □ *U.K.* 55°46N 4°21W **167** F4
East Retford = Retford *U.K.* 53°19N 0°56W **168** D7
East Riding of Yorkshire □ *U.K.* 53°55N 0°30W **168** D7
East River ➔ *New York, U.S.A.* **132** e3
East Rochester *U.S.A.* 43°7N 77°29W **312** C7
East Rutherford *U.S.A.* 40°50N 74°5W **132** A1
East St. Louis *U.S.A.* 38°37N 90°9W **310** F6
East Schelde = Oosterschelde ➔ *Neths.* 51°33N 4°0E **170** C4
East Sea = Japan, Sea of *Asia* 40°0N 135°0E **220** E7
East Sepik □ *Papua N. G.* 4°0S 143°45E **286** C2
East Sheen *U.K.* 51°27N 0°16W **125** B2
East Siberian Sea *Russia* 73°0N 160°0E **215** B17
East Stroudsburg *U.S.A.* 41°1N 75°11W **313** E9
East Sussex □ *U.K.* 50°56N 0°19E **169** G8
East Talpiyot *West Bank* 31°45N 35°13E **123** B2
East Tasman Plateau *Pac. Oc.* 43°30S 152°0E **288** M7
East Tawas *U.S.A.* 44°17N 83°29W **309** C12
East Timor ■ *Asia* 8°50S 126°0E **231** F7
East Toorale *Australia* 30°27S 145°28E **281** E4
East Troy *U.S.A.* 42°47N 88°24W **311** B8
East Village *New York, U.S.A.* **132** e2
East Walker ➔ *U.S.A.* 38°52N 119°10W **306** G7
East Wickham *U.K.* 51°28N 0°5E **125** B4
East Windsor *U.S.A.* 40°17N 74°34W **313** F10
East York *Canada* 43°40N 79°22W **141** A2
East Youngstown = Campbell *U.S.A.* 41°5N 80°37W **312** E4
Eastbourne *N.Z.* 41°19S 174°55E **143** B2
Eastbourne *E. Sussex, U.K.* 50°46N 0°18E **169** G8
Eastcote *U.K.* 51°34N 0°23W **125** A1
Eastend *Canada* 49°32N 108°50W **297** D7
Easter Fracture Zone *Pac. Oc.* 25°0S 115°0W **289** K16
Easter Howgate *U.K.* 55°52N 3°12W **121** B2
Easter I. = Pascua, I. de *Chile* 27°7S 109°23W **330** b
Eastern □ *Ghana* 6°30N 0°30W **263** D4
Eastern □ *Kenya* 0°0 38°30E **268** C4
Eastern □ *S. Leone* 8°15N 11°0W **262** D2
Eastern Cape □ *S. Africa* 32°0S 26°0E **270** D4
Eastern Cr. ➔ *Australia* 20°40S 141°35E **280** C3
Eastern Desert = Es Sahrâ' Esh Sharqîya *Egypt* 27°30N 32°30E **256** B3
Eastern Ghats *India* 14°0N 78°50E **245** H4
Eastern Group = Lau Group *Fiji* 17°0S 178°30W **287** A3
Eastern Group *Australia* 33°30S 124°30E **279** F3
Eastern Guruma ◎ *Australia* 22°0S 117°30E **278** D2
Eastern Highlands □ *Papua N. G.* 6°30S 145°35E **286** D3
Eastern I. *Midway Is.* 28°12N 177°19W **302** c
Eastern Samar □ *Phil.* 11°40N 125°40E **233** F5
Eastern Transvaal = Mpumalanga □ *S. Africa* 26°0S 30°0E **271** C5
Easterville *Canada* 53°8N 99°49W **297** C9
Easthampton *U.S.A.* 42°16N 72°40W **313** D12
Eastlake *U.S.A.* 41°40N 81°26W **312** E3
Eastland *U.S.A.* 32°24N 98°49W **314** E5
Eastleigh *U.K.* 50°58N 1°21W **169** G6
Eastmain *Canada* 52°10N 78°30W **298** B4
Eastmain ➔ *Canada* 52°27N 78°26W **298** B4
Eastman *Qué., Canada* 45°18N 72°19W **313** A12
Eastman *Ga., U.S.A.* 32°12N 83°11W **316** C6
Eastman *Wis., U.S.A.* 43°10N 91°1W **310** A5
Easton *Md., U.S.A.* 38°47N 76°5W **309** F15
Easton *Pa., U.S.A.* 40°41N 75°13W **313** F9
Easton *Wash., U.S.A.* 47°14N 121°11W **306** C5
Eastover *U.S.A.* 33°52N 80°41W **316** B9
Eastpoint *U.S.A.* 29°44N 84°53W **316** F5
Eastpoint Park *Canada* 43°46N 79°10W **141** A4
Eastport *U.S.A.* 44°56N 67°0W **309** C20
Eastsound *U.S.A.* 48°42N 122°55W **306** B4
Eastwood *Australia* 33°47S 151°4E **139** A1
Eaton *Colo., U.S.A.* 40°32N 104°42W **304** F11
Eaton *Ohio, U.S.A.* 39°45N 84°38W **311** E12
Eaton Canyon Park *U.S.A.* 34°10N 118°7W **126** A4
Eaton Centre *Toronto, Canada* **141** a2
Eaton Rapids *U.S.A.* 42°31N 84°39W **311** B12
Eatonia *Canada* 51°13N 109°25W **297** C7
Eatonton *U.S.A.* 33°20N 83°23W **316** B6
Eatontown *U.S.A.* 40°19N 74°4W **313** F10
Eatonville *U.S.A.* 46°52N 122°16W **306** D4
Eau Claire *Fr. Guiana* 3°30N 53°40W **329** C7
Eau Claire *Wis., U.S.A.* 44°49N 91°30W **308** C8
Eau Claire, L. à l' *Canada* 56°10N 74°25W **298** A5
Eauripik Rise *Pac. Oc.* 2°0N 142°0E **288** G6
Eauze *France* 43°53N 0°7E **174** E4
Eban *Nigeria* 9°40N 4°50E **263** D5
Ebanga *Angola* 12°45S 14°45E **265** E2
Ebangalakata *Dem. Rep. of the Congo* 0°29S 21°29E **264** C4
Ebano *Mexico* 22°13N 98°24W **319** C5
Ebara *Japan* 35°35N 139°42E **140** B3
Ebbegebirge ⌓ *Germany* 51°10N 7°55E **178** D3
Ebbw Vale *U.K.* 51°46N 3°12W **169** F4
Ebebiyín *Eq. Guin.* 2°9N 11°20E **264** B2
Ebel *Gabon* 0°7N 11°5E **264** B2
Ebeltoft *Denmark* 56°12N 10°41E **163** H4
Ebeltoft Vig *Denmark* 56°10N 10°35E **163** H4
Ebensburg *U.S.A.* 40°29N 78°44W **312** F6
Ebensee *Austria* 47°48N 13°46E **180** D6
Eber Gölü *Turkey* 38°38N 31°11E **212** C4
Eberbach *Germany* 49°28N 8°59E **179** F4
Eberswalde-Finow *Germany* 52°50N 13°49E **178** C9
Ebetsu *Japan* 43°7N 141°34E **220** C10
Ebey's Landing ⌓ *U.S.A.* 48°12N 122°41W **306** B4
Ebian *China* 29°11N 103°13E **228** C4
Ebingen *Germany* 48°13N 9°1E **179** G5
Ebino *Japan* 32°2N 130°48E **222** E2
Ebinur Hu *China* 44°55N 82°55E **217** D10
Ebisu *Japan* 35°38N 139°42E **140** B3
Ebla *Syria* 35°50N 36°48E **250** C7
Ebo *Angola* 11°40S 14°40E **265** E2
Ebola ➔ *Dem. Rep. of the Congo* 3°20N 20°57E **264** B4
Éboli *Italy* 40°39N 15°2E **201** B8
Ebolowa *Cameroon* 2°55N 11°10E **263** E7
Ebonda *Dem. Rep. of the Congo* 2°12N 22°21E **264** B4
Ebonyi □ *Nigeria* 6°20N 8°0E **263** D6
Eboy *Dem. Rep. of the Congo* 2°50N 23°11E **264** B4
Ebrach *Germany* 49°51N 10°29E **179** F6
Ebre = Ebro ➔ *Spain* 40°43N 0°54E **196** E5
Ébrié, Lagune *Ivory C.* 5°12N 4°26W **262** D4
Ebro ➔ *Spain* 40°43N 0°54E **196** E5
Ebro, Embalse del *Spain* 43°0N 3°58W **194** C7
Ebstorf *Germany* 53°2N 10°24E **178** B6
Ebute-Ikorodu *Nigeria* 6°35N 3°29E **124** A2
Ebute-Metta *Nigeria* 6°28N 3°23E **124** B2
Ecatepec de Morelos *Mexico* 19°36N 99°3W **319** D5
Ecbatana = Hamadān *Iran* 34°52N 48°32E **213** E13
Ecclesville *Trin. & Tob.* 10°19N 61°8W **323** t
Eceabat *Turkey* 40°11N 26°21E **203** F10
Ech Chéliff *Algeria* 36°10N 1°20E **261** A5
Ech Chéliff □ *Algeria* 36°15N 1°30E **261** A5
Echague *Phil.* 16°42N 121°38E **232** C3
Echechonnee ➔ *U.S.A.* 32°39N 83°36W **316** C6
Echigo-Sammyaku *Japan* 36°50N 139°50E **221** F9
Echinades *Greece* 38°25N 21°2E **207** C3
Echinos *Greece* 41°16N 25°1E **203** E9
Échirolles *France* 45°8N 5°44E **175** C9
Echizen-Misaki *Japan* 35°59N 135°57E **223** B7
Echmiadzin = Yejmiadzin *Armenia* 40°12N 44°19E **191** K7
Echo *U.S.A.* 31°29N 85°28W **316** D4
Echo Bay *N.W.T., Canada* 66°5N 117°55W **294** D8
Echo Bay *Ont., Canada* 46°29N 84°4W **298** C3
Echo Park *Los Angeles, U.S.A.* **127** a1
Echoing ➔ *Canada* 55°51N 92°5W **298** B1
Echterdingen, Stuttgart ✈ **(STR)** *Germany* 48°42N 9°11E **179** G5
Echternach *Lux.* 49°49N 6°25E **170** E6
Echuca *Australia* 36°10S 144°45E **283** D6
Écija *Spain* 37°30N 5°10W **195** H5
Eckental *Germany* 49°35N 11°12E **179** F7
Eckernförde *Germany* 54°28N 9°50E **178** A5
Eclectic *U.S.A.* 32°38N 86°2W **316** C3
Eclipse I. *Australia* 35°5S 117°58E **279** G2
Eclipse Is. *Australia* 13°54S 126°19E **278** B4
Eclipse Sd. *Canada* 72°38N 79°0W **295** C16
Écommoy *France* 47°50N 0°17E **172** E7
Economy = Ambridge *U.S.A.* 40°36N 80°14W **312** F4
Ecoporanga *Brazil* 18°23S 40°50W **333** E3
Écouché *France* 48°42N 0°10W **172** D6
Ecrins △ *France* 44°54N 6°18E **175** D10
Ecuador ■ *S. Amer.* 2°0S 78°0W **328** D2
Ecuador, Volcán *Ecuador* 1°1S 91°32W **330** a
Écueillé *France* 47°5N 1°21E **172** E8
Ed *Sweden* 58°55N 11°55E **163** F5
Ed Dabbura *Sudan* 17°40N 34°15E **256** D3
Ed Da'ein *Sudan* 11°26N 26°9E **257** E2
Ed Damazin *Sudan* 11°46N 34°21E **266** B3
Ed Dâmer *Sudan* 17°27N 34°0E **256** D3
Ed Dar el Beida = Casablanca *Morocco* 33°36N 7°36W **260** B3
Ed Debba *Sudan* 18°0N 30°51E **256** D3
Ed Déffa *Egypt* 30°40N 26°30E **256** A2
Ed Deim *Sudan* 10°10N 28°20E **257** E2
Ed Dibeikir *Sudan* 10°23N 29°9E **266** B2
Ed Dueim *Sudan* 14°0N 32°10E **257** E3
Eda *Japan* 35°33N 139°33E **140** B2
Edam *Sask., Canada* 53°11N 108°46W **297** C7
Edam *Neths.* 52°31N 5°3E **170** B5
Edane *Sweden* 59°38N 12°49E **162** E6
Edapally *India* 11°19N 78°3E **245** J4
Eday *U.K.* 59°11N 2°47W **167** B6
Edchera *W. Sahara* 27°2N 13°4W **260** C2
Edd *Eritrea* 14°0N 41°38E **257** E5
Eddrachillis B. *U.K.* 58°17N 5°14W **167** C3
Eddystone *U.K.* 50°11N 4°16W **169** G3
Eddystone Pt. *Australia* 40°59S 148°20E **281** G4
Eddyville *U.S.A.* 41°9N 92°38W **310** C4
Ede *Neths.* 52°4N 5°40E **170** B5
Ede *Nigeria* 7°45N 4°29E **263** D5
Édéa *Cameroon* 3°51N 10°9E **263** E7
Edebäck *Sweden* 60°4N 13°32E **162** D7
Edehon L. *Canada* 60°25N 97°15W **297** A9
Edelény *Hungary* 48°18N 20°44E **182** B5
Eden = Bar Harbor *U.S.A.* 44°23N 68°13W **309** C19
Eden *N.S.W., Australia* 37°3S 149°55E **283** D8
Eden *N.C., U.S.A.* 36°29N 79°53W **315** C15
Eden *N.Y., U.S.A.* 42°39N 78°55W **312** D6
Eden *Tex., U.S.A.* 31°13N 99°51W **314** F5
Eden ➔ *U.K.* 54°57N 3°1W **168** C4
Edenburg *S. Africa* 29°43S 25°58E **270** C4
Edendale *N.Z.* 46°19S 168°48E **285** G3
Edendale *Gauteng, S. Africa* 26°8S 28°9E **123** A2
Edendale *KwaZulu Natal, S. Africa* 29°39S 30°18E **271** C5
Edenderry *Ireland* 53°21N 7°4W **166** C4
Edenhope *Australia* 37°4S 141°19E **282** D4
Edenmore *Ireland* 53°22N 6°11W **120** A2
Edenton *U.S.A.* 36°4N 76°39W **315** C16
Edenville *S. Africa* 27°37S 27°34E **271** C4
Eder ➔ *Germany* 51°12N 9°28E **178** D5
Eder-Stausee *Germany* 51°10N 8°57E **178** D4
Edessa *Greece* 40°48N 22°5E **202** F6
Edewecht *Germany* 53°8N 7°58E **178** B3
Edfu = Idfû *Egypt* 24°55N 32°49E **256** C3
Edgar *U.S.A.* 40°22N 97°58W **308** E5
Edgars Cr. ➔ *Australia* 37°43S 144°58E **128** A1
Edgartown *U.S.A.* 41°23N 70°31W **313** E14
Edge Hill *U.K.* 52°8N 1°26W **169** E6
Edgecumbe *N.Z.* 37°59S 176°47E **284** D5
Edgefield *U.S.A.* 33°47N 81°56W **316** B8
Edgeley *Ont., Canada* 43°47N 79°31W **141** A1
Edgeley *N. Dak., U.S.A.* 46°22N 98°43W **308** B4
Edgemar *U.S.A.* 37°39N 122°29W **136** C2
Edgemont *U.S.A.* 43°18N 103°50W **308** D2
Edgeøya *Svalbard* 77°45N 22°30E **150** B9
Edgerton *Ohio, U.S.A.* 41°27N 84°45W **311** C12
Edgerton *Wis., U.S.A.* 42°50N 89°4W **310** B7
Edgewater *Fla., U.S.A.* 28°59N 80°54W **317** G9
Edgewater *N.J., U.S.A.* 40°49N 73°58W **132** B2
Edgewood *Fla., U.S.A.* 28°29N 81°22W **133** B2
Edgewood *Ill., U.S.A.* 38°55N 88°40W **311** F8
Édhessa = Edessa *Greece* 40°48N 22°5E **202** F6
Edievale *N.Z.* 45°49S 169°22E **285** F4
Edina *Liberia* 6°0N 10°10W **262** D2
Edina *Mo., U.S.A.* 40°10N 92°11W **310** D4
Edinboro *U.S.A.* 41°52N 80°8W **312** E4
Edinburg *Ill., U.S.A.* 39°39N 89°23W **310** E7
Edinburg *Tex., U.S.A.* 26°18N 98°10W **314** H5
Edinburgh *Edinburgh, U.K.* 55°57N 3°13W **121** B2
Edinburgh *Ind., U.S.A.* 39°21N 85°58W **311** E11
Edinburgh ✈ **(EDI)** *U.K.* 55°54N 3°22W **121** B1
Edinburgh, City of □ *U.K.* 55°57N 3°17W **167** F5
Edinburgh Castle *Edinburgh, U.K.* **121** b2
Edineț *Moldova* 48°9N 27°18E **183** B12
Edirne *Turkey* 41°40N 26°34E **203** E10
Edirne □ *Turkey* 41°12N 26°30E **203** E10
Edison *Ga., U.S.A.* 31°34N 84°44W **316** D5
Edison *Wash., U.S.A.* 48°33N 122°27W **306** B4
Edison Park *U.S.A.* 42°1N 87°48W **119** A2
Edisto ➔ *U.S.A.* 32°29N 80°21W **316** C9
Edisto Beach *U.S.A.* 32°29N 80°20W **316** C9
Edisto I. *U.S.A.* 32°35N 80°20W **316** C9
Edithburgh *Australia* 35°5S 137°43E **282** C2
Edjeleh *Algeria* 28°38N 9°50E **261** C6
Edmeston *U.S.A.* 42°42N 75°15W **313** D9
Edmond *U.S.A.* 35°39N 97°29W **314** D6
Edmonds *U.S.A.* 47°48N 122°22W **306** C4
Edmondston *U.S.A.* 38°56N 76°54W **143** B4
Edmondstown *Ireland* 53°17N 6°18W **120** B2
Edmonton *Queens., Australia* 17°2S 145°46E **280** B4
Edmonton *Alta., Canada* 53°30N 113°30W **296** C6
Edmund L. *Canada* 54°45N 93°17W **298** B1
Edmundston *Canada* 47°23N 68°20W **299** C6
Edna *U.S.A.* 28°59N 96°39W **314** G6
Edo □ *Nigeria* 6°30N 6°0E **263** D6
Edo ➔ *Japan* 35°38N 139°52E **140** B4
Edogawa *Japan* 35°43N 139°52E **140** A4
Edolo *Italy* 46°10N 10°21E **198** B7
Edøya *Norway* 63°18N 8°10E **164** A5
Edremit *Turkey* 39°34N 27°0E **205** B9
Edremit Körfezi *Turkey* 39°30N 26°45E **205** B8
Edsberg *Sweden* 59°26N 17°57E **139** A1
Edsbro *Sweden* 59°54N 18°29E **162** E12
Edsbruk *Sweden* 58°1N 16°29E **163** F10
Edsbyn *Sweden* 61°23N 15°49E **162** C9
Edson *Canada* 53°35N 116°28W **296** C5
Eduardo Castex *Argentina* 35°50S 64°18W **334** D3
Edward ➔ *Australia* 35°5S 143°30E **282** C5
Edward, L. *Africa* 0°25S 29°40E **268** C2
Edward VII Land *Antarctica* 80°0S 150°0W **151** E13
Edwardesabad = Bannu *Pakistan* 33°0N 70°18E **240** B3
Edwards *Calif., U.S.A.* 34°50N 117°40W **307** L9
Edwards *N.Y., U.S.A.* 44°20N 75°15W **313** B9
Edwards ➔ *U.S.A.* 41°9N 90°59W **310** C6
Edwards L. *Australia* 37°42S 144°59E **128** A1
Edwards Plateau *U.S.A.* 30°45N 101°20W **314** F4
Edwardsburg *U.S.A.* 41°48N 86°6W **311** C10
Edwardsville *Ill., U.S.A.* 38°49N 89°58W **310** F7
Edwardsville *Pa., U.S.A.* 41°15N 75°56W **313** E9
Edzná *Mexico* 19°39N 90°19W **319** D6
Edzo *Canada* 62°49N 116°4W **296** A5
Eek *U.S.A.* 60°14N 162°2W **303** F7
Eeklo *Belgium* 51°11N 3°33E **170** C3
Eel ➔ *Ind., U.S.A.* 39°7N 86°57W **311** E10
Eel ➔ *Ind., U.S.A.* 40°45N 86°22W **311** D10
Eesti = Estonia ■ *Europe* 58°30N 25°30E **188** C3
Efate, I. *Vanuatu* 17°40S 168°25E **287** G6
Eferding *Austria* 48°18N 14°1E **180** C7
Effigy Mounds ⌓ *U.S.A.* 43°5N 91°11W **310** A5
Effingham *U.S.A.* 39°7N 88°33W **311** E8
Eforie *Romania* 44°1N 28°37E **183** F13
Efoulen *Cameroon* 2°46N 10°43E **264** B2
Efteløt *Norway* 59°33N 9°49E **164** E6
Efxinoupoli *Greece* 39°12N 22°42E **204** B4
Efzonos *Greece* 37°55N 23°49E **112** B2
Ega ➔ *Spain* 42°19N 1°55W **196** C3
Égadi, Ísole *Italy* 37°55N 12°16E **200** E5
Egaleo *Greece* 37°59N 23°40E **112** B2
Egaleo, Oros *Greece* 38°0N 23°36E **112** B1
Egan Range *U.S.A.* 39°35N 114°55W **304** G6
Eganville *Canada* 45°32N 77°5W **312** A7
Egedesminde = Aasiaat *Greenland* 68°43N 52°56W **154** D5
Egegik *U.S.A.* 58°13N 157°22W **303** G8
Eger = Cheb *Czech Rep.* 50°9N 12°28E **180** A5
Eger *Hungary* 47°53N 20°27E **182** C5
Eger ➔ *Hungary* 47°38N 20°50E **182** C5
Egersund *Norway* 58°26N 6°1E **164** F3
Egg I. *St. Helena* 15°58S 5°47W **153** h
Egg L. *Canada* 55°5N 105°30W **297** B7
Eggedal *Norway* 60°14N 9°22E **164** D6
Eggegebirge Südlicher Teutoburger Wald ⌓ *Germany* 51°40N 8°59E **178** D4
Eggenburg *Austria* 48°38N 15°50E **180** C8
Eggenfelden *Germany* 48°23N 12°46E **179** G8
Egherta *Somali Rep.* 2°4N 43°11E **267** D5
Éghezée *Belgium* 50°35N 4°55E **170** D4
Egholo *Solomon Is.* 8°25S 157°25E **287** M9
Egilsstaðir *Iceland* 65°16N 14°25W **155** B12
Egina *Greece* 37°45N 23°26E **204** D5
Eginio *Greece* 40°28N 22°28E **202** F6
Egio *Greece* 38°15N 22°5E **204** C4
Egito *Angola* 12°4S 13°58E **265** E2
Égletons *France* 45°24N 2°3E **174** C6
Eglinton I. *Canada* 75°48N 118°30W **295** B8
Egmont *Canada* 49°45N 123°56W **296** D4
Egmont, C. *N.Z.* 39°16S 173°45E **284** F2
Egmont, Mt. = Taranaki, Mt. *N.Z.* 39°17S 174°5E **284** F3
Egmont △ *N.Z.* 39°17S 174°4E **284** F3
Egra *India* 21°54N 87°32E **243** J12
Eğridir *Turkey* 37°52N 30°51E **212** D4
Eğridir Gölü *Turkey* 37°53N 30°50E **212** D4
Egtved *Denmark* 55°38N 9°18E **163** J3
Éguas ➔ *Brazil* 13°26S 44°14W **333** D3
Egum Atoll *Papua N. G.* 9°25S 152°0E **286** E7
Éguzon-Chantôme *France* 46°27N 1°33E **173** F8
Egvekinot *Russia* 66°19N 179°50W **215** C19
Egyek *Hungary* 47°39N 20°52E **182** C5
Egypt ■ *Africa* 28°0N 31°0E **256** B3
Eha Amufu *Nigeria* 6°30N 7°46E **263** D6
Eheli *Algeria* 22°26N 4°40E **261** D5
Ehime □ *Japan* 33°30N 132°40E **222** D4
Ehingen *Germany* 48°16N 9°43E **179** G5
Ehrenberg *U.S.A.* 33°36N 114°31W **307** M12
Ehrhardt *U.S.A.* 33°6N 81°1W **316** B8
Ehrwald *Austria* 47°24N 10°56E **180** D3
Eiao *French Polynesia* 8°0S 140°40W **289** f
Eibar *Spain* 43°11N 2°28W **196** B2
Eibenschitz = Ivančice *Czech Rep.* 49°6N 16°23E **181** B9
Eiche *Germany* 52°33N 13°35E **115** A4
Eiche Süd *Germany* 52°33N 13°35E **115** A4
Eichstätt *Germany* 48°54N 11°11E **179** G7
Eide *Hordaland, Norway* 60°31N 6°44E **164** D3
Eide *Møre og Romsdal, Norway* 62°55N 7°27E **164** B4
Eider ➔ *Germany* 54°19N 8°57E **178** A4
Eidsbugarden *Norway* 61°23N 8°16E **164** C5
Eidsbygda *Norway* 62°36N 7°30E **164** B4
Eidsdalen *Norway* 62°16N 7°10E **164** B4
Eidsvåg *Norway* 62°46N 8°2E **164** B5
Eidsvold *Australia* 25°25S 151°12E **281** D5
Eidsvoll *Norway* 60°19N 11°14E **164** D8
Eielson *U.S.A.* 64°40N 147°4W **303** D11
Eifel *Germany* 50°15N 6°50E **179** E2
Eiffel, Tour *Paris, France* **134** c2
Eiffel Flats *Zimbabwe* 18°20S 30°0E **269** F3
Eiger *Switz.* 46°34N 8°1E **198** B5
Eigg *U.K.* 56°54N 6°10W **167** E2
Eighty Mile Beach *Australia* 19°30S 120°40E **278** C3
Eikefjord *Norway* 61°35N 5°27E **164** C2
Eikelandsosen *Norway* 60°15N 5°43E **164** D2
Eiken *Norway* 58°29N 7°14E **164** F4
Eikeren *Norway* 59°38N 9°58E **164** E6
Eikesdalen *Norway* 62°28N 8°12E **164** B5
Eil, L. *U.K.* 56°51N 5°16W **167** E3
Eil Malk *Palau* 7°10N 134°23E **288** c
Eildon *Australia* 37°14S 145°55E **283** D6
Eildon, L. *Australia* 37°10S 146°0E **283** D7
Eilean Sar = Western Isles □ *U.K.* 57°30N 7°10W **167** D1
Eilenburg *Germany* 51°27N 12°36E **178** D8
Ein Arik *West Bank* 31°54N 35°8E **123** A1
Ein el Luweiqa *Sudan* 14°5N 33°50E **257** E3
Ein Naquba *Israel* 31°47N 35°7E **123** B1
Ein Rafa *Israel* 31°47N 35°7E **123** B1
Eina *Norway* 60°38N 10°35E **164** D7
Einarsstaðir *Iceland* 65°44N 17°24W **155** B9
Einasleigh *Australia* 18°32S 144°5E **280** B3
Einasleigh ➔ *Australia* 17°30S 142°17E **280** B3
Einbeck *Germany* 51°49N 9°53E **178** D5
Eindhoven *Neths.* 51°26N 5°28E **170** C5
Einsiedeln *Switz.* 47°7N 8°46E **179** H4
Eire = Ireland ■ *Europe* 53°50N 7°52W **166** C4
Eiríksjökull *Iceland* 64°46N 20°24W **155** C6
Eiríksstaðir *Iceland* 65°7N 15°25W **155** B11
Eirunepé *Brazil* 6°35S 69°53W **330** B4
Eiseb ➔ *Namibia* 20°33S 20°59E **270** B2
Eisenach *Germany* 50°58N 10°19E **178** E6
Eisenberg *Germany* 50°58N 11°54E **178** E7
Eisenerz *Austria* 47°32N 14°54E **180** D7
Eisenhüttenstadt *Germany* 52°9N 14°38E **178** C10
Eisenkappel *Austria* 46°29N 14°36E **180** E7
Eisenstadt *Austria* 47°51N 16°31E **181** D9
Eisenstein = Železná Ruda *Czech Rep.* 49°8N 13°15E **180** B6
Eisfeld *Germany* 50°25N 10°54E **179** E6
Eisleben *Germany* 51°32N 11°32E **178** D7
Eislingen *Germany* 48°41N 9°42E **179** G5
Eivindvik *Norway* 60°59N 5°5E **164** D2
Eivissa *Spain* 38°54N 1°26E **206** D1
Eixe, Serra do *Spain* 42°24N 6°54W **194** C4
Eizariya *West Bank* 31°46N 35°16E **123** B2
Ejby *Denmark* 55°41N 12°24E **118** A2
Ejea de los Caballeros *Spain* 42°7N 1°9W **196** C3
Ejeda *Madag.* 24°20S 44°31E **272** C1
Ejigbo *Nigeria* 6°33N 3°18E **124** A1
Ejura *Ghana* 7°23N 1°15W **263** D4
Ejutla *Mexico* 16°34N 96°44W **319** D5
Ekalaka *U.S.A.* 45°53N 104°33W **304** D11
Ekalla *Gabon* 1°27S 14°0E **264** C2
Ekanga *Dem. Rep. of the Congo* 2°23S 23°14E **264** C4
Ekaterinburg = Yekaterinburg *Russia* 56°50N 60°30E **214** D7
Ekeberg *Norway* 59°53N 10°46E **133** A3
Ekenäs = Raasepori *Finland* 60°0N 23°26E **188** B2
Ekenässjön *Sweden* 57°28N 15°1E **163** G9
Ekerö *Sweden* 59°16N 17°45E **162** E11
Eket *Nigeria* 4°38N 7°56E **263** E6
Eketahuna *N.Z.* 40°38S 175°43E **284** G4
Ekibastuz *Kazakhstan* 51°50N 75°10E **217** B9
Ekiti □ *Nigeria* 7°25N 5°20E **263** D6
Eklutna *U.S.A.* 61°27N 149°22W **303** F10
Eknäs *Sweden* 59°18N 18°13E **139** B3
Ekoli *Dem. Rep. of the Congo* 0°23S 24°13E **264** C4
Ekoln *Sweden* 59°45N 17°37E **162** E11
Ekouamou *Congo* 0°8N 16°31E **264** B3
Ekoungounou *Congo* 1°10S 15°52E **264** C3
Ekshärad *Sweden* 60°10N 13°30E **162** D7
Eksjö *Sweden* 57°40N 14°58E **163** G8
Ekukola *Dem. Rep. of the Congo* 0°31S 18°56E **264** C3
Ekuku *Dem. Rep. of the Congo* 0°41S 21°42E **264** C4
Ekukula *Dem. Rep. of the Congo* 0°15N 21°30E **264** B4
Ekuma ➔ *Namibia* 18°40S 16°2E **270** A2
Ekuta *Dem. Rep. of the Congo* 3°0N 18°50E **264** B3
Ekwan ➔ *Canada* 53°12N 82°15W **298** B3
Ekwan Pt. *Canada* 53°16N 82°7W **298** B3
Ekwok *U.S.A.* 59°22N 157°30W **303** G8
El Aaiún *W. Sahara* 27°9N 13°12W **260** C2
El Aargub *Mauritania* 23°37N 15°52W **260** D1
El Abanico *Chile* 37°20S 71°31W **334** D1
El 'Abbasiya *El Qâhira, Egypt* 30°3N 31°16E **117** A2
El Abbasiya *Sudan* 12°10N 31°18E **257** E3
El Abiodh-Sidi-Cheikh *Algeria* 32°53N 0°31E **261** B5
El Adde *Somali Rep.* 2°35N 46°9E **267** D6
El Adeb Larache *Algeria* 27°22N 8°52E **261** C6
El 'Agrûd *Egypt* 30°14N 34°24E **251** H5
El Agustino *Peru* 12°2S 77°0W **124** B2
El Agustino, Cerro *Peru* 12°3S 76°59W **124** B3
El Aïoun *Morocco* 34°33N 2°30W **261** B4
El Ait *Sudan* 12°22N 27°27E **257** E2
El 'Aiyat *Egypt* 29°36N 31°15E **256** J7
El Alamein *Egypt* 30°48N 28°58E **256** A2
El Alto *Peru* 4°15S 81°14W **330** A1
El Aouj *Mauritania* 22°53N 12°49W **260** D2
El 'Aqaba, W. ➔ *Egypt* 30°7N 33°54E **251** H4
El 'Arag *Egypt* 28°40N 26°20E **256** B2
El Aricha *Algeria* 34°13N 1°10W **261** B4
El Arīḥā *West Bank* 31°52N 35°27E **251** G6
El 'Arîsh *Egypt* 31°8N 33°50E **251** G4
El 'Arîsh, W. ➔ *Egypt* 31°8N 33°47E **251** G4
El Arrouch *Algeria* 36°37N 6°53E **261** A6
El Asnam = Ech Chéliff *Algeria* 36°10N 1°20E **261** A5
El Astillero *Spain* 43°24N 3°49W **194** B7
El Avagi *Somali Rep.* 3°36N 46°57E **267** D6
El Badâri *Egypt* 27°4N 31°25E **256** B3
El Badrshein *Egypt* 29°51N 31°16E **251** J2
El Bagur *Egypt* 30°25N 31°2E **251** H2
El Bahrein *Egypt* 28°30N 26°25E **256** B2
El Ballâs *Egypt* 26°2N 32°43E **256** B3
El Balyana *Egypt* 26°10N 32°3E **256** B3
El Banco *Colombia* 9°0N 73°58W **328** B3
El Baqeir *Sudan* 18°40N 33°40E **256** D3
El Baragil *Egypt* 30°4N 31°9E **117** A1
El Barco de Ávila *Spain* 40°21N 5°31W **194** E5
El Barco de Valdeorras = O Barco *Spain* 42°23N 6°58W **194** C4
El Basâlîn *Egypt* 29°58N 31°16E **117** B2
El Bauga *Sudan* 18°18N 33°52E **256** D3
El Baúl *Venezuela* 8°57N 68°17W **328** B4
El Bawiti *Egypt* 28°25N 28°45E **256** B2
El Bayadh *Algeria* 33°40N 1°1E **261** B5
El Bayadh □ *Algeria* 32°30N 1°10E **261** B5
El Bierzo *Spain* 42°45N 6°30W **194** C4
El Bira *West Bank* 31°54N 35°13E **123** A2
El Bluff *Nic.* 11°59N 83°40W **320** D3
El Bolsón *Argentina* 41°55S 71°30W **336** B2
El Bonillo *Spain* 38°57N 2°35W **197** G2
El Bosque *Chile* 33°32S 70°40W **137** C2
El Buheirat □ *Sudan* 7°0N 30°0E **257** F3
El Bur *Somali Rep.* 4°40N 46°37E **267** D6
El Burgo de Osma *Spain* 41°35N 3°4W **196** D1
El Caín *Argentina* 41°38S 68°19W **336** B3
El Cajon *U.S.A.* 32°48N 116°58W **307** N10
El Calafate *Argentina* 50°19S 72°15W **336** D2
El Callao *Venezuela* 7°18N 61°50W **329** B5
El Campello *Spain* 38°26N 0°24W **197** G4
El Campo *U.S.A.* 29°12N 96°16W **314** G6
El Capitan *U.S.A.* 37°44N 119°38E **306** H7
El Carbón *Honduras* 15°25N 85°32W **320** C2
El Carmen *Bolivia* 13°40S 63°55W **331** C5
El Carmen *Santiago, Chile* 33°22S 70°43W **137** B1
El Carmen *Colombia* 9°43N 75°8W **328** B2
El Centro *U.S.A.* 32°48N 115°34W **307** N11
El Cerro *Bolivia* 17°30S 61°40W **331** D5
El Cerro de Andévalo *Spain* 37°45N 6°57W **195** H4
El Cocuy *Colombia* 6°25N 72°27W **328** B3
El Cocuy △ *Colombia* 6°33N 72°5W **328** B3
El Compadre *Mexico* 32°20N 116°14W **307** N10
El Corcovado *Argentina* 43°25S 71°35W **336** B2
El Coronil *Spain* 37°5N 5°38W **195** H5
El Cortijo *Chile* 33°22S 70°42W **137** B1
El Cristo, Vaso Regulador *Mexico* 19°30N 99°5W **128** B1
El Cuy *Argentina* 39°55S 68°25W **336** A3
El Cuyo *Mexico* 21°31N 87°41W **319** C7
El Dab'a *Egypt* 31°0N 28°27E **256** H6
El Daheir *Egypt* 31°13N 34°10E **251** G5
El Dambahaddo *Somali Rep.* 3°17N 46°40E **267** D6
El Deir *Egypt* 25°25N 32°20E **256** B3
El Dere = Ceeldheere *Somali Rep.* 5°22N 46°11E **267** C6
El Dere *Ethiopia* 5°6N 43°5E **267** C5
El Descanso *Mexico* 32°12N 116°58W **307** N10
El Desemboque *Mexico* 30°33N 113°1W **318** A2
El Dilingat *Egypt* 30°50N 30°31E **256** H7
El Diviso *Colombia* 1°22N 78°14W **328** C2
El Djouf *Africa* 21°25N 6°40W **260** D3
El Djouf *Mauritania* 20°0N 9°0W **260** C3
El Dorado *Sinaloa, Mexico* 24°17N 107°21W **318** C3
El Dorado *Ark., U.S.A.* 33°12N 92°40W **314** E8
El Dorado *Kans., U.S.A.* 37°49N 96°52W **308** G5
El Dorado *Venezuela* 6°55N 61°37W **329** B5
El Dorado Springs *U.S.A.* 37°52N 94°1W **310** G2
El Duqqi *Egypt* 30°1N 31°12E **117** A2
El Eglab *Algeria* 26°20N 4°30W **260** C4
El 'Ein *Sudan* 16°35N 29°22E **257** D2
El Ejido *Spain* 36°47N 2°49W **195** J8
El Encinar de los Reyes *Spain* 40°30N 3°39W **127** A2
El Escorial *Spain* 40°35N 4°7W **194** E6
El Espinar *Spain* 41°43N 4°15W **194** D6
El Eulma *Algeria* 36°9N 5°42E **261** A6
El Faiyûm *Egypt* 29°19N 30°50E **256** J7
El Faourar *Tunisia* 33°22N 8°45E **258** B1
El Fâsher *Sudan* 13°33N 25°26E **257** E2
El Fashn *Egypt* 28°50N 30°54E **256** J7
El Ferrol = Ferrol *Spain* 43°29N 8°15W **194** B2
El Fifi *Sudan* 10°4N 25°0E **257** E2
El Fud *Ethiopia* 7°15N 42°52E **267** C5
El Fuerte *Mexico* 26°25N 108°39W **318** B3
El Ga'a *Sudan* 14°16N 29°59E **257** E2
El Gamâlîya *Egypt* 31°10N 31°52E **251** G2
El Garef *Sudan* 12°3N 34°19E **257** E3
El Gebir *Sudan* 13°40N 29°40E **257** E2
El Gedida *Egypt* 25°40N 28°30E **256** B2
El Geneina = Al Junaynah *Sudan* 13°27N 22°45E **259** F4
El Geteina *Sudan* 14°50N 32°27E **257** E3
El Gezira *Egypt* 30°2N 31°13E **117** A2
El Gezira □ *Sudan* 15°0N 33°0E **257** E3
El Gharbîya □ *Egypt* 30°50N 31°0E **251** H2
El Ghurîya *Egypt* 30°2N 31°15E **117** A2
El Gir *Sudan* 19°50N 28°18E **256** D2
El Gîza *Egypt* 30°0N 31°12E **117** A2
El Gîza □ *Egypt* 29°46N 31°18E **251** J2
El Gogorrón △ *Mexico* 21°49N 100°57W **318** C4
El Goléa *Algeria* 30°30N 2°50E **261** B5
El Golfo de Santa Clara *Mexico* 31°42N 114°30W **318** A2
El Gouna *Egypt* 27°5N 33°47E **256** B3
El Grau *Spain* 39°0N 0°7W **197** G4
El Hadjira *Algeria* 32°36N 5°30E **261** B6
El Hagiz *Sudan* 15°15N 35°50E **257** D4
El Hâi *Egypt* 29°39N 31°18E **256** J7
El Hajeb *Morocco* 33°43N 5°13W **260** B3
El Hamma *Tunisia* 33°54N 9°48E **258** B1
El Hammam *Egypt* 30°52N 29°25E **256** A2
El Hammâmi *Mauritania* 23°3N 11°30W **260** D2
El Hâmûl *Egypt* 31°18N 31°9E **251** G2
El Hamurre *Somali Rep.* 7°13N 48°54E **267** C6
El Hank *Mauritania* 24°30N 7°0W **260** D3
El Hasian *W. Sahara* 26°20N 14°0W **260** C2
El Hawata *Sudan* 13°25N 34°42E **257** E3
El Hideib *Sudan* 13°0N 32°50E **257** E3
El Hilla *Sudan* 13°24N 27°2E **257** E2
El Homr *Algeria* 29°43N 1°45E **261** C5
El 'Idisât *Egypt* 25°30N 32°35E **256** B3
El Iskandarîya *Egypt* 31°13N 29°58E **256** H7
El Jadida *Morocco* 33°11N 8°17W **260** B3
El Jadida □ *Morocco* 32°45N 8°30W **260** B3
El Jardal *Honduras* 14°54N 88°50W **320** D2
El Jebelein *Sudan* 12°40N 32°55E **257** E3
El Jebha *Morocco* 35°11N 4°43W **260** A4
El Jem *Tunisia* 35°19N 10°41E **258** A2
El Kab *Sudan* 19°27N 32°46E **256** D3
El Kafr el Sharqi *Egypt* 31°16N 31°10E **256** H7
El Kala *Algeria* 36°53N 8°26E **261** A6
El Kamlin *Sudan* 15°3N 33°11E **257** D3
El Kantara *Algeria* 35°14N 5°45E **261** A6
El Kantara *Tunisia* 33°45N 10°58E **258** B2
El Karaba *Sudan* 18°32N 33°41E **256** D3
El Kef *Tunisia* 36°12N 8°47E **258** A1
El Kef □ *Tunisia* 36°0N 9°0E **261** A6
El Kelâa de Srahna *Morocco* 32°4N 7°27W **260** B3
El Kelâa de Srahna □ *Morocco* 32°10N 7°45W **260** B3
El Kelaâ M'Gouna *Morocco* 31°14N 6°7W **260** B3
El Kere *Ethiopia* 5°50N 42°5E **257** F5
El Khadr *West Bank* 31°42N 35°10E **123** B1
El Khalîfa *Egypt* 30°0N 31°15E **117** A2
El Khandaq *Sudan* 18°30N 30°30E **256** D3
El Khanka *Egypt* 30°13N 31°21E **251** H2
El Khârga *Egypt* 25°30N 30°33E **256** B3
El Khartûm *Sudan* 15°31N 32°35E **257** D3
El Khartûm □ *Sudan* 16°0N 33°0E **257** D3
El Khartûm Bahrî *Sudan* 15°40N 32°31E **257** D3
El Khroub *Algeria* 36°10N 6°55E **261** A6
El Kôm el Ahmar *Egypt* 30°6N 31°10E **117** A2
El Kseur *Algeria* 36°46N 4°49E **261** A5
El Ksiba *Morocco* 32°45N 6°1W **260** B3
El Kuntilla *Egypt* 30°1N 34°45E **251** H5
El Laqâwa *Sudan* 11°25N 29°1E **257** E2
El Leh *Ethiopia* 3°46N 39°13E **257** G4
El Leiya *Sudan* 16°15N 35°28E **257** D4
El Leoncito △ *Argentina* 31°58S 69°10W **334** C2
El Limón *Panama* 9°15N 79°49W **320** c
El Lucero *Mexico* 30°37N 106°31W **318** A3
El Ma'âdi *Egypt* 29°57N 31°15E **117** B2
El Maestrazgo *Spain* 40°30N 0°25W **196** E4
El Mafâza *Sudan* 13°38N 34°30E **257** E3
El Maghra *Egypt* 30°15N 28°55E **256** A2
El Mahalla el Kubra *Egypt* 31°0N 31°0E **256** H7
El Mahârîq *Egypt* 25°35N 30°35E **256** B3
El Maîmûn *Egypt* 29°14N 31°12E **256** J7
El Maitén *Argentina* 42°3S 71°10W **336** B2
El Maiz *Algeria* 28°19N 0°9W **261** C4
El Maks el Bahari *Egypt* 24°30N 30°40E **256** C3
El Malpais ⌓ *U.S.A.* 34°53N 108°0W **305** J10
El Manshâh *Egypt* 26°26N 31°50E **256** B3
El Mansour *Algeria* 27°47N 0°14W **261** C4
El Mansûra *Egypt* 31°0N 31°19E **256** H7
El Manteco *Venezuela* 7°38N 62°45W **329** B5
El Manzala *Egypt* 31°10N 31°50E **256** H7
El Marâgha *Egypt* 26°35N 31°10E **256** B3
El Masid *Sudan* 15°15N 33°0E **257** D3
El Masnou *Spain* 41°28N 2°20E **196** D7
El Matarîya *El Mansûra, Egypt* 31°15N 32°0E **256** H8
El Matarîya *El Qâhira, Egypt* 30°7N 31°18E **117** A2
El Meda *Ethiopia* 5°39N 41°47E **257** F5
El Medano *Canary Is.* 28°3N 16°32W **153** e1
El Meghaier *Algeria* 33°55N 5°58E **261** B6
El Ménia = El Goléa *Algeria* 30°30N 2°50E **261** B5
El Meraguen *Algeria* 28°0N 0°7W **261** C4
El Metemma *Sudan* 16°50N 33°10E **257** D3
El Miamo *Venezuela* 7°39N 61°46W **329** B5
El Milagro *Argentina* 30°59S 65°59W **334** C2
El Milia *Algeria* 36°51N 6°13E **261** A6
El Minufîya □ *Egypt* 30°30N 31°0E **251** H2
El Minyâ *Egypt* 28°7N 30°33E **256** B3
El Mohandessin *Egypt* 30°2N 31°11E **117** A2
El Monte *U.S.A.* 34°4N 118°1W **126** B4
El Montseny *Spain* 41°55N 2°25E **196** D7
El Mreiti *Mauritania* 23°29N 7°51W **260** D3
El Mreyye *Mauritania* 18°0N 6°0W **262** B3
El Muqattam *Egypt* 30°1N 31°17E **117** A2
El Mûskî *Egypt* 30°3N 31°15E **117** A2
El Nido *Phil.* 11°10N 119°25E **233** F2
El Niybo *Ethiopia* 4°40N 39°55E **257** G4
El Obeid *Sudan* 13°8N 30°10E **257** E3
El Odaiya *Sudan* 12°8N 28°12E **257** E2
El Oro *Mexico* 19°51N 100°7W **319** D4
El Oro □ *Ecuador* 3°30S 79°50W **328** D2
El Oued *Algeria* 33°20N 6°58E **261** B6
El Oued □ *Algeria* 33°10N 7°15E **261** B6
El Palmar *Bolivia* 17°50S 63°9W **331** D5
El Palmar *Venezuela* 7°58N 61°53W **329** B5
El Palmar △ *Argentina* 32°10S 58°31W **334** C4
El Palmito, Presa *Mexico* 25°40N 105°30W **318** B3
El Pardo *Spain* 40°30N 3°46W **127** A1
El Paso = Derby *U.S.A.* 37°33N 97°16W **308** G5
El Paso *Ill., U.S.A.* 40°44N 89°1W **310** D7
El Paso *Tex., U.S.A.* 31°45N 106°29W **314** F1
El Pedernoso *Spain* 39°29N 2°45W **197** F2
El Pedroso *Spain* 37°51N 5°45W **195** H5
El Pilar *Venezuela* 10°32N 63°9W **329** A5
El Pinacate y Gran Desierto de Altar = Gran Desierto del Pinacate ⌓ *Mexico* 31°51N 113°32W **318** A2
El Pobo de Dueñas *Spain* 40°46N 1°39W **196** E3
El Portal *Calif., U.S.A.* 37°41N 119°47W **306** H7
El Portal *Fla., U.S.A.* 25°51N 80°11W **128** A2
El Porvenir *Mexico* 31°15N 105°51W **318** A3
El Prat de Llobregat *Spain* 41°19N 2°5E **114** B1
El Progreso *Galápagos Is., Ecuador* 0°54S 89°33W **330** a
El Progreso *Honduras* 15°26N 87°51W **320** C2
El Pueblito *Mexico* 29°6N 105°7W **318** B3
El Pueblo *Canary Is.* 28°36N 17°47W **153** e1
El Pueblo de Los Angeles Historic Park *Los Angeles, U.S.A.* **127** b2
El Puente del Arzobispo *Spain* 39°48N 5°10W **194** F5
El Puerto de Santa María *Spain* 36°36N 6°13W **195** J4
El Qâhira *Egypt* 30°2N 31°13E **117** A2
El Qâhira □ *Egypt* 30°2N 31°13E **251** H2
El Qanâyat *Egypt* 30°37N 31°27E **251** H2
El Qantara *Egypt* 30°51N 32°20E **251** H3
El Qasr *Egypt* 25°44N 28°42E **256** B2
El Qassâsîn *Egypt* 30°33N 31°55E **251** H2
El Qubâbât *Egypt* 29°28N 31°16E **256** J7
El Qubba *Egypt* 30°4N 31°16E **117** A2
El Quseima *Egypt* 30°40N 34°15E **251** H5
El Qusîya *Egypt* 27°29N 30°44E **256** B3
El Râshda *Egypt* 25°36N 28°57E **256** B2
El Reloj *Mexico* 19°19N 99°9W **128** C2
El Reno *U.S.A.* 35°32N 97°57W **301** H20
El Retiro *Spain* 40°25N 3°41W **127** B1
El Rey △ *Argentina* 24°40S 64°34W **334** A3
El Rîdisiya *Egypt* 24°56N 32°51E **256** C3
El Rio *U.S.A.* 34°14N 119°10W **307** L7
El Ronquillo *Spain* 37°44N 6°10W **195** H4
El Roque, Pta. *Canary Is.* 28°10N 15°25W **153** e1
El Rosarito *Mexico* 28°38N 114°4W **318** B2
El Rubio *Spain* 37°22N 5°0W **195** H5
El Saff *Egypt* 29°34N 31°16E **256** J7
El Salto *Santiago, Chile* 33°22S 70°38W **137** B2
El Salto *Durango, Mexico* 23°47N 105°22W **318** C3
El Salvador ■ *Cent. Amer.* 13°50N 89°0W **320** D2
El Sauce *Nic.* 13°0N 86°40W **320** D2
El Saucejo *Spain* 37°4N 5°6W **195** H5
El Sereno *U.S.A.* 34°4N 118°10W **126** B3
El Shallal *Egypt* 24°0N 32°53E **256** C3
El Simbillawein *Egypt* 30°48N 31°13E **256** H7
El Sombrero *Venezuela* 9°23N 67°3W **328** B4
El Sueco *Mexico* 29°54N 106°24W **318** B3
El Suweis *Egypt* 29°58N 32°31E **256** B3
El Suweis □ *Egypt* 29°30N 32°15E **251** J3
El Tabbîn *Egypt* 29°47N 31°18E **256** J7
El Talibîya *Egypt* 29°59N 31°10E **117** B2
El Tamá △ *S. Amer.* 7°25N 72°25W **328** B3
El Tamarâni, W. ➔ *Egypt* 30°7N 34°43E **251** H5
El Tarf *Algeria* 36°46N 8°19E **261** A6
El Tarf □ *Algeria* 36°45N 8°10E **261** A6
El Thamad *Egypt* 29°40N 34°28E **251** J5
El Tigre *Venezuela* 8°44N 64°15W **329** B5
El Tîh, Gebel *Egypt* 29°40N 33°50E **251** J4
El Tîna *Egypt* 31°3N 32°22E **256** H8
El Tocuyo *Venezuela* 9°47N 69°48W **328** B4
El Tofo *Chile* 29°22S 71°18W **334** B1
El Tránsito *Chile* 28°52S 70°17W **334** B1
El Tucuche *Trin. & Tob.* 10°43N 61°25W **323** t
El Tuparro △ *Colombia* 5°19N 68°28W **328** B4
El Tûr *Egypt* 28°14N 33°36E **251** K4
El Turbio *Argentina* 51°45S 72°5W **336** D2
El Uarre *Somali Rep.* 3°4N 45°20E **267** D6
El Uqsur *Egypt* 25°41N 32°38E **256** B3
El Valle ⌓ *Spain* 37°56N 1°6W **197** H3
El Vendrell *Spain* 41°10N 1°30E **196** D6
El Vergel *Chihuahua, Mexico* 26°28N 106°22W **318** B3
El Vergel *Distrito Federal, Mexico* 19°18N 99°5W **128** C2
El Vigía *Venezuela* 8°38N 71°39W **328** B3
El Viso del Alcor *Spain* 37°23N 5°43W **195** H5
El Wabeira *Egypt* 29°34N 33°6E **251** J4
El Wâhli *Egypt* 30°3N 31°16E **117** A2
El Wak *Somali Rep.* 2°44N 41°1E **267** D5
El Weguet *Ethiopia* 5°28N 42°17E **257** F5
El Wuz *Sudan* 15°5N 30°7E **257** D3
El Yunque, Cerro *Chile* 33°39S 78°50W **330** c
El Yunque *Puerto Rico* 18°19N 65°48W **321** b
El Zamâlik *Egypt* 30°3N 31°12E **117** A2
El Zeitûn *Egypt* 30°6N 31°18E **117** A2

Elafonisos Greece 36°29N 22°56E 204 E4
Elamanchili India 17°33N 82°50E 244 F6
Élancourt France 48°47N 1°58E 173 D8
Elands Australia 31°37S 152°20E 283 A10
Elandsfontein Junc. = Germiston S. Africa 26°13S 28°10E 123 B2
Elasa Greece 35°18N 26°21E 205 F8
Elassona Greece 39°53N 22°12E 204 B4
Elat Israel 29°30N 34°56E 251 J5
Elati Oros Greece 38°43N 20°39E 207 B2
Elatia Greece 38°37N 22°46E 204 C4
Elâzığ Turkey 38°37N 39°14E 213 C8
Elâzığ □ Turkey 38°40N 39°15E 213 C8
Elba Italy 42°46N 10°17E 198 F7
Elba Ala., U.S.A. 31°25N 86°4W 316 D3
Elbasan Albania 41°9N 20°9E 202 E4
Elbe U.S.A. 46°45N 122°10W 306 D4
Elbe → Europe 53°50N 9°0E 178 B4
Elbe-Seitenkanal Germany 52°45N 10°32E 178 C6
Elberfeld U.S.A. 38°10N 87°27W 311 F9
Elbert, Mt. U.S.A. 39°7N 106°27W 304 G10
Elberton U.S.A. 34°7N 82°52W 316 A7
Elbeuf France 49°17N 1°2E 172 C8
Elbeyli Turkey 36°40N 37°27E 250 B8
Elbing = Elbląg Poland 54°10N 19°25E 184 D6
Elbistan Turkey 38°13N 37°15E 212 C7
Elbląg Poland 54°10N 19°25E 184 D6
Elbow Canada 51°7N 106°35W 297 C7
Elbrus Russia 43°21N 42°30E 191 J6
Elbufer-Drawehn ⌓ Germany 53°8N 10°58E 178 B6
Elburn U.S.A. 41°54N 88°28W 311 C8
Elburz Mts. = Alborz, Reshteh-ye Kūhhā-ye Iran 36°0N 52°0E 247 C7
Elche Spain 38°15N 0°42W 197 G4
Elche de la Sierra Spain 38°27N 2°3W 197 G2
Elcho I. Australia 11°55S 135°45E 280 A2
Elda Spain 38°29N 0°47W 197 G4
Eldama Ravine Kenya 0°3N 35°43E 268 B4
Elde → Germany 53°7N 11°15E 178 B7
Eldey Iceland 63°45N 22°55W 155 D4
Eldon Iowa, U.S.A. 40°55N 92°13W 310 D4
Eldon Mo., U.S.A. 38°21N 92°35W 310 F4
Eldon Wash., U.S.A. 47°33N 123°3W 306 C3
Eldora U.S.A. 42°22N 93°5W 310 B3
Eldorado = Echo Bay Canada 66°5N 117°55W 294 D8
Eldorado Argentina 26°28S 54°43W 335 B5
Eldorado Ont., Canada 44°35N 77°31W 312 B7
Eldorado Ill., U.S.A. 37°49N 88°26W 311 G8
Eldorado Tex., U.S.A. 30°52N 100°36W 314 F4
Eldorendo U.S.A. 31°3N 84°39W 316 D5
Eldoret Kenya 0°30N 35°17E 268 B4
Eldred U.S.A. 41°58N 78°23W 312 E6
Eldridge U.S.A. 41°39N 90°35W 310 C6
Elea, C. Cyprus 35°19N 34°4E 207 E10
Eleanora, Pk. Australia 32°57S 121°9E 279 F3
Eleao U.S.A. 21°27N 157°52W 302 K14
Elefantes → Africa 24°10S 32°40E 271 B5
Elefantes, B. das Angola 13°13S 12°44E 265 E2
Elefantes, G. Chile 46°28S 73°49W 336 C2
Elefsina Greece 38°4N 23°26E 204 C5
Eleftherios Venizelos ✈ (ATH) Greece 37°56N 23°56E 112 A3
Elektrogorsk Russia 55°56N 38°50E 188 E10
Elektroperedacha = Elektrogorsk Russia 55°56N 38°50E 188 E10
Elektrostal Russia 55°41N 38°32E 188 E10
Elektrovoz = Stupino Russia 54°57N 38°2E 188 E10
Elele Nigeria 5°5N 6°50E 263 D6
Elemi Triangle Africa 5°0N 35°20E 257 G4
Elena Bulgaria 42°55N 25°53E 203 D9
Elephant Butte Res. U.S.A. 33°9N 107°11W 305 K10
Elephant I. Antarctica 61°0S 55°0W 151 C18
Elephant Pass Sri Lanka 9°35N 80°25E 245 K5
Elephanta Caves India 18°57N 72°57E 130 B2
Elephanta I. India 18°57N 72°56E 130 B2
Elesbão Veloso Brazil 6°13S 42°8W 332 C3
Eleshnitsa Bulgaria 41°52N 23°36E 202 E7
Eleşkirt Turkey 39°50N 42°50E 213 C10
Eleuthera Bahamas 25°0N 76°20W 320 B4
Eleutheroupoli Greece 40°52N 24°20E 203 F8
Elfin Cove U.S.A. 58°12N 136°22W 303 G13
Elgå Norway 62°10N 11°56E 164 B8
Elgin Ont., Canada 44°36N 76°13W 313 B8
Elgin Moray, U.K. 57°39N 3°19W 167 D5
Elgin Ill., U.S.A. 42°2N 88°17W 311 B8
Elgin N. Dak., U.S.A. 46°24N 101°51W 308 B3
Elgin Oreg., U.S.A. 45°34N 117°55W 304 D5
Elgin S.C., U.S.A. 34°10N 80°48W 316 A9
Elgin Tex., U.S.A. 30°21N 97°22W 314 F6
Elgoibar Spain 43°13N 2°24W 196 B2
Elgon, Mt. Africa 1°10N 34°30E 268 B3
Elgspiggen Norway 62°10N 11°21E 164 B8
Eliase Indonesia 8°21S 130°48E 231 F8
Elikonos Oros Greece 38°18N 22°45E 204 C4
Elim Namibia 17°48S 15°31E 270 A2
Elim Western Cape, S. Africa 34°35S 19°45E 270 D2
Elim Alaska, U.S.A. 64°37N 162°15W 303 D7
Elin Pelin Bulgaria 42°40N 23°36E 202 D7
Elingampangu Dem. Rep. of the Congo 2°0S 24°4E 264 C4
Elipa Dem. Rep. of the Congo 1°3S 24°20E 264 C4
Eliseu Martins Brazil 8°13S 43°42W 332 C3
Elista Russia 46°16N 44°14E 191 G7
Eliza, L. Australia 37°15S 139°50E 282 D3
Elizabeth S. Austral., Australia 34°42S 138°41E 282 C3
Elizabeth Ill., U.S.A. 42°19N 90°13W 310 B6
Elizabeth N.J., U.S.A. 40°39N 74°12W 313 F10
Elizabeth, B. Ecuador 0°36S 91°12W 330 a
Elizabeth City U.S.A. 36°18N 76°14W 315 C16
Elizabethton U.S.A. 36°21N 82°13W 315 C13
Elizabethtown Ky., U.S.A. 37°42N 85°52W 311 G11
Elizabethtown N.Y., U.S.A. 44°13N 73°36W 313 B11
Elizabethtown Pa., U.S.A. 40°9N 76°36W 313 F8
Elizabethville = Lubumbashi Dem. Rep. of the Congo 11°40S 27°28E 269 E2
Elizondo Spain 43°12N 1°30W 196 B3
Ełk Poland 53°50N 22°21E 184 E9
Elk → B.C., Canada 49°11N 115°14W 296 C5
Ełk → Poland 53°41N 22°28E 184 E9
Elk → Ala., U.S.A. 34°46N 87°16W 315 D11
Elk City U.S.A. 35°25N 99°25W 314 D5
Elk Creek U.S.A. 39°36N 122°32W 306 F4
Elk Grove U.S.A. 38°25N 121°22W 306 G5
Elk Island △ Canada 53°35N 112°59W 296 C6
Elk Lake Canada 47°40N 80°25W 298 C3
Elk Point Canada 53°54N 110°55W 297 C6
Elk River Idaho, U.S.A. 46°47N 116°11W 304 C5
Elk River Minn., U.S.A. 45°18N 93°35W 308 C7
Elkader U.S.A. 42°51N 91°24W 310 B5
Elkedra → Australia 21°8S 136°22E 280 C2
Elkhart Ind., U.S.A. 41°41N 85°58W 311 C11
Elkhart Kans., U.S.A. 37°0N 101°54W 308 G3
Elkhart → U.S.A. 41°41N 85°58W 311 C11
Elkhorn Man., Canada 49°59N 101°14W 297 D8
Elkhorn Wis., U.S.A. 42°40N 88°33W 311 B8
Elkhorn → U.S.A. 41°8N 96°19W 308 E5
Elkhovo Bulgaria 42°10N 26°35E 203 D10
Elkin U.S.A. 36°15N 80°51W 315 C14
Elkins U.S.A. 38°55N 79°51W 309 F14
Elkland U.S.A. 41°59N 77°19W 312 E7
Elko B.C., Canada 49°20N 115°10W 296 D5
Elko Nev., U.S.A. 40°50N 115°46W 304 F6
Elkton U.S.A. 43°49N 83°11W 312 C1
Ellas = Greece ■ Europe 40°0N 23°0E 204 B3
Ellaville Fla., U.S.A. 30°23N 83°10W 316 E6
Ellaville Ga., U.S.A. 32°14N 84°19W 316 C5
Ellboda Sweden 59°24N 18°15E 139 A3
Ellef Ringnes I. Canada 78°30N 102°2W 295 B11
Ellen, Mt. U.S.A. 44°9N 72°56W 313 B12
Ellenburg U.S.A. 44°54N 73°48W 313 B11
Ellendale U.S.A. 46°0N 98°32W 308 B4
Ellenor, L. U.S.A. 28°28N 81°25W 133 B2
Ellensburg U.S.A. 46°59N 120°34W 304 C3
Ellenville U.S.A. 41°43N 74°24W 313 E10
Ellerton Barbados 13°7N 59°33W 323 r
Ellery, Mt. Australia 37°28S 148°47E 283 D8
Ellesmere = Scottsdale Australia 41°9S 147°31E 281 G4
Ellesmere, L. N.Z. 43°47S 172°28E 285 H7
Ellesmere I. Canada 79°30N 80°0W 295 B16
Ellesmere Island = Quttinirpaaq △ Canada 82°13N 72°13W 295 A17
Ellesmere Port U.K. 53°17N 2°54W 168 D5
Ellettsville U.S.A. 39°14N 86°38W 311 E10
Ellice Is. = Tuvalu ■ Pac. Oc. 8°0S 178°0E 277 B14
Ellicottville U.S.A. 42°17N 78°40W 312 D6
Ellington U.S.A. 42°13N 79°6W 312 D5
Elliniko Olympic Complex Greece 37°50N 23°45E 112 B2
Elliot N. Terr., Australia 17°33S 133°32E 280 B1
Elliot Eastern Cape, S. Africa 31°22S 27°48E 271 D4
Elliot Lake Canada 46°25N 82°35W 298 C3
Elliotdale = Xhora S. Africa 31°55S 28°38E 271 D4
Elliott U.S.A. 34°6N 80°10W 316 A9
Elliott Key U.S.A. 25°27N 80°12W 317 K9
Ellipse, The Washington, D.C., U.S.A. 143 b1
Ellis U.S.A. 38°56N 99°34W 308 F4
Ellis I. U.S.A. 40°41N 74°2W 132 B1
Elliston Australia 33°39S 134°53E 281 E1
Ellisville U.S.A. 31°36N 89°12W 315 F10
Ellon U.K. 57°22N 2°4W 167 D6
Ellora India 20°1N 75°10E 244 D2
Ellore = Eluru India 16°48N 81°8E 244 F5
Elloree U.S.A. 33°32N 80°34W 316 B9
Ellsworth Kans., U.S.A. 38°44N 98°14W 308 F4
Ellsworth Maine, U.S.A. 44°33N 68°25W 309 C19
Ellsworth Land Antarctica 76°0S 89°0W 151 D16
Ellsworth Mts. Antarctica 78°30S 85°0W 151 D16
Ellwangen Germany 48°57N 10°8E 179 G6
Ellwood City U.S.A. 40°52N 80°17W 312 F4
Ellzey U.S.A. 29°19N 82°48W 317 F7
Elm Switz. 46°54N 9°10E 179 J5
Elm-Lappwald ⌓ Germany 52°15N 10°50E 178 C6
Elma Man., Canada 49°52N 95°55W 297 D9
Elma Wash., U.S.A. 47°0N 123°25W 306 D3
Elmadağ Turkey 39°55N 33°14E 212 C5
Elmalı Turkey 36°44N 29°56E 205 E11
Elmers End U.K. 51°23N 0°2W 125 B3
Elmhurst Ill., U.S.A. 41°53N 87°56W 311 C9
Elmhurst N.Y., U.S.A. 40°44N 73°53W 132 B2
Elmina Ghana 5°5N 1°21W 263 D4
Elmira Ont., Canada 43°36N 80°33W 312 C4
Elmira N.Y., U.S.A. 42°6N 76°48W 312 D8
Elmira Heights U.S.A. 42°8N 76°50W 312 D8
Elmodel U.S.A. 31°21N 84°29W 316 D5
Elmore Vic., Australia 36°30S 144°37E 282 D6
Elmore Ala., U.S.A. 32°32N 86°19W 316 C3
Elmore Ohio, U.S.A. 41°29N 83°18W 311 C13
Elmshorn Germany 53°43N 9°40E 178 B5
Elmstead U.K. 51°24N 0°2E 125 B4
Elmvale Canada 44°35N 79°52W 312 B5
Elmwood Ill., U.S.A. 40°47N 89°58W 310 D7
Elmwood La., U.S.A. 29°57N 90°11W 131 B1
Elmwood Park Ill., U.S.A. 41°55N 87°48W 119 B2
Elmwood Park N.J., U.S.A. 40°54N 74°7W 132 A1
Elne France 42°36N 2°58E 174 F6
Elnesvågen Norway 62°52N 7°10E 164 B4
Elnora U.S.A. 38°53N 87°5W 311 F9
Eloaua I. Papua N. G. 1°38S 149°40E 286 A5
Elobey, Is. Eq. Guin. 1°1N 9°29E 264 B1
Elongo Dem. Rep. of the Congo 0°19S 21°39E 264 C4
Elora Canada 43°41N 80°26W 312 C4
Elorza Venezuela 7°3N 69°31W 328 B4
Elos Greece 36°46N 22°43E 204 E4
Elounda Greece 35°16N 25°42E 207 E6
Eloy U.S.A. 32°45N 111°33W 305 K8
Éloyes France 48°6N 6°36E 173 D13
Elphin Canada 44°55N 76°37W 313 B8
Elpitiya Sri Lanka 6°17N 80°10E 245 L5
Elrose Canada 51°12N 108°0W 297 C7
Elsberry U.S.A. 39°10N 90°47W 310 E6
Elsby △ Australia 14°55S 133°10E 278 B5
Elsdon N.Z. 41°8S 174°50E 143 A1
Elsdorf Germany 50°55N 6°34E 178 E2
Elsie Mich., U.S.A. 43°5N 84°23W 311 A12
Elsie Oreg., U.S.A. 45°52N 123°36W 306 E3
Elsiesrivier S. Africa 33°55S 18°35E 118 A2
Elsinore = Helsingør Denmark 56°2N 12°35E 163 H6
Elster → Germany 51°25N 11°57E 178 D7
Elsternwick Australia 37°52S 145°0E 128 B2
Elsterwerda Germany 51°27N 13°31E 178 D9
Eltanin Fracture Zone System S. Ocean 54°0S 130°0W 151 B14
Eltham N.Z. 39°26S 174°19E 284 F3
Eltham London, U.K. 51°27N 0°3E 125 B4
Elton Russia 49°5N 46°52E 191 F8
Elton, Ozero Russia 49°5N 46°42E 191 F8
Eltville Germany 50°2N 8°7E 179 E4
Eluru India 16°48N 81°8E 244 F5
Elvas Portugal 38°50N 7°10W 195 G3
Elven France 47°44N 2°36W 172 E4
Elverum Norway 60°53N 11°34E 164 D8
Elvire → Australia 17°51S 128°11E 278 C4
Elvire, Mt. Australia 29°22S 119°36E 279 E2
Elvo → Italy 45°23N 8°21E 198 C5
Elwell, L. = Tiber Res. U.S.A. 48°19N 111°6W 304 B8
Elwood Vic., Australia 37°53S 144°59E 128 B1
Elwood Ill., U.S.A. 41°24N 88°7W 311 C8
Elwood Ind., U.S.A. 40°17N 85°50W 311 D11
Elwood Nebr., U.S.A. 40°36N 99°52W 308 E4
Elx = Elche Spain 38°15N 0°42W 197 G4
Ely Cambs., U.K. 52°24N 0°16E 169 E8
Ely Minn., U.S.A. 47°55N 91°51W 308 B8
Ely Nev., U.S.A. 39°15N 114°54W 304 G6
Elyria U.S.A. 41°22N 82°7W 312 E2
Elyros Greece 35°15N 23°45E 204 F5
Élysée France 48°52N 2°19E 134 A2
Elysian Park Los Angeles, U.S.A. 127 a3
Elz → Germany 48°18N 7°44E 179 G3
Émaé Vanuatu 17°4S 168°24E 287 G6
eMalahleni S. Africa 25°51S 29°14E 271 C4
Emāmrūd Iran 36°30N 55°0E 247 B7
Emāmzādeh Sāleh Iran 35°48N 51°26E 141 A2
Emån → Sweden 57°8N 16°30E 163 G10
Emao Vanuatu 17°29S 168°30E 287 G6
Emas △ Brazil 18°2S 52°50W 331 D7
Emateloa Dem. Rep. of the Congo 1°16N 18°42E 264 B3
Embajadores Madrid, Spain 127 c2
Embalenhle S. Africa 26°32S 29°4E 271 C4
Embarcación Argentina 23°10S 64°0W 334 A3
Embarcadero, The San Francisco, U.S.A. 136 b3
Embarras → U.S.A. 38°39N 87°37W 311 F9
Embetsu Japan 44°44N 141°47E 220 B10
Embi Kazakhstan 48°50N 58°8E 216 C5
Embi → Kazakhstan 46°55N 53°28E 187 E9
Embonas Greece 36°13N 27°51E 206 E11
Embro Canada 43°9N 80°54W 312 C4
Embrun France 44°34N 6°30E 175 D10
Embu Kenya 0°32S 37°38E 268 C4
Emden Germany 53°21N 7°12E 178 B3
Emecik Turkey 36°46N 27°49E 205 E9
Emei Shan China 29°30N 103°18E 228 C4
Emeishan China 29°31N 103°23E 228 C4
Emek Refa'im Jerusalem 123 c2
Émerainville France 48°48N 2°37E 134 B4
Emerald Queens., Australia 23°32S 148°10E 280 C4
Emerald Vic., Australia 37°56S 145°29E 276 E8
Emerald Buddha = Phra Kaeo Bangkok, Thailand 113 b1
Emerald I. Canada 76°48N 114°10W 295 B9
Emerson Man., Canada 49°0N 97°10W 297 D9
Emerson Ga., U.S.A. 34°8N 84°45W 316 A5
Emeryville U.S.A. 37°49N 122°17W 136 A3
Emet Turkey 39°20N 29°15E 205 B11
Emeti Papua N. G. 7°53S 143°15E 286 D2
Emi Koussi Chad 19°45N 18°55E 259 E3
Emília-Romagna □ Italy 44°45N 11°0E 198 D8
Emilius, Mte. Italy 45°45N 7°20E 198 C4
Emin China 46°34N 83°36E 217 C10
Eminabad Pakistan 32°2N 74°8E 242 C6
Emine, Nos Bulgaria 42°40N 27°56E 203 D11
Eminence U.S.A. 38°22N 85°11W 311 F11
Eminönü Turkey 41°0N 28°57E 122 B1
Emirau I. Papua N. G. 1°40S 150°0E 286 A6
Emirdağ Turkey 39°2N 31°8E 212 C4
Emirgan Turkey 41°6N 29°2E 122 B2
Emissi, Tarso Chad 21°27N 18°36E 259 D3
Emlenton U.S.A. 41°11N 79°43W 312 E5
Emlichheim Germany 52°37N 6°51E 178 C2
Emmaboda Sweden 56°37N 15°32E 163 H9
Emmalane U.S.A. 32°46N 82°0W 316 C7
Emmarentia S. Africa 26°9S 28°0E 123 A2
Emmastad Curaçao 12°8N 68°55W 322 g
Emmaus S. Africa 29°2S 25°15E 270 C4
Emmaus Pa., U.S.A. 40°32N 75°30W 313 F9
Emme → Switz. 47°14N 7°32E 179 H3
Emmeloord Neths. 52°44N 5°46E 170 B5
Emmen Neths. 52°48N 6°57E 170 B6
Emmen Switz. 47°5N 8°18E 179 H4
Emmendingen Germany 48°6N 7°51E 179 G3
Emmental Switz. 46°55N 7°40E 179 J3
Emmerich Germany 51°50N 6°14E 178 D2
Emmet Australia 24°45S 144°30E 280 C3
Emmetsburg U.S.A. 43°7N 94°41W 310 A2
Emmett Idaho, U.S.A. 43°52N 116°30W 304 E5
Emmett Mich., U.S.A. 42°59N 82°46W 312 D2
Emmiganuru = Yemmiganur India 15°44N 77°29E 245 G3
Emmonak U.S.A. 62°47N 164°31W 303 E6
Emo Canada 48°38N 93°50W 297 D10
Emőd Hungary 47°57N 20°47E 182 C5
Emona Bulgaria 42°43N 27°53E 203 D11
Empalme Mexico 27°58N 110°51W 318 B2
Empangeni S. Africa 28°50S 31°52E 271 C5
Empedrado Argentina 28°0S 58°46W 334 B4
Emperor Seamount Chain Pac. Oc. 40°0N 170°0E 288 D9
Emperor Trough Pac. Oc. 43°0N 175°30E 288 C9
Empingham Res. = Rutland Water U.K. 52°39N 0°38W 169 E7
Empire U.S.A. 32°21N 83°18W 316 C6
Empire State Building New York, U.S.A. 132 c2
Empoli Italy 43°43N 10°57E 198 E7
Emporia Kans., U.S.A. 38°25N 96°11W 308 F5
Emporia Va., U.S.A. 36°42N 77°32W 309 G15
Emporium U.S.A. 41°31N 78°14W 312 E6
Empress Canada 50°57N 110°0W 297 C7
Empty Quarter = Rub' al Khālī Si. Arabia 19°0N 48°0E 249 C5
Ems → Germany 53°20N 7°12E 178 B3
Emsdale Canada 45°32N 79°19W 312 A5
Emsdetten Germany 52°10N 7°32E 178 C3
Emu China 43°40N 128°6E 227 C15
Emu Park Australia 23°13S 150°50E 280 C5
eMuziwezinto S. Africa 30°15S 30°45E 271 D5
'En 'Avrona Israel 29°43N 35°0E 251 J6
'En Boqeq Israel 31°12N 35°21E 251 G6
En Gannim = Ramat Gan Israel 32°4N 34°48E 251 F5
'En Gedi Israel 31°28N 35°25E 251 G6
En Na'am Sudan 10°21N 27°58E 266 B2
En Nahrat Mali 22°55N 3°36W 260 D4
En Nahud Sudan 12°45N 28°25E 257 E2
En Nofalab Sudan 15°52N 32°32E 257 D3
En Nuqra Sudan 10°4N 28°10E 266 B2
Ena Japan 35°25N 137°25E 223 B9
Ena-San Japan 35°26N 137°36E 223 B9
Enambú Colombia 1°1N 70°17W 328 C3
Enana Namibia 17°30S 16°23E 270 A2
Enånger Sweden 61°30N 17°9E 162 C11
Enard B. U.K. 58°5N 5°20W 167 C3
Enare träsk = Inarijärvi Finland 69°0N 28°0E 160 B23
Enarotali Indonesia 3°55S 136°21E 231 E9
Encampment U.S.A. 41°12N 106°47W 304 F10
Encantadas, Serra Brazil 30°40S 53°0W 335 C5
Encantado Brazil 22°53S 43°19W 135 B1
Encarnación Paraguay 27°15S 55°50W 335 B4
Encarnación de Díaz Mexico 21°31N 102°14W 318 C4
Enchi Ghana 5°53N 2°48W 262 D4
Encinitas U.S.A. 33°3N 117°17W 307 M9
Encino Calif., U.S.A. 34°9N 118°28W 126 B2
Encino N. Mex., U.S.A. 34°39N 105°28W 305 J11
Encino Res. U.S.A. 34°8N 118°30W 126 B1
Encontrados Venezuela 9°3N 72°14W 328 B3
Encounter B. Australia 35°45S 138°45E 282 C3
Encruzilhada Brazil 15°31S 40°54W 333 E3
Encs Hungary 48°20N 21°8E 182 B6
Endako Canada 54°6N 125°2W 296 C3
Endau Kenya 1°18S 38°31E 268 C4
Endau Rompin △ Malaysia 2°27N 103°45E 237 L4
Ende Indonesia 8°45S 121°40E 231 F6
Endeavour Str. Australia 10°45S 142°0E 286 F2
Endelave Denmark 55°46N 10°18E 163 J4
Enden Norway 61°47N 10°15E 164 C7
Enderbury Kiribati 3°8S 171°5W 277 A16
Enderby Canada 50°35N 119°10W 296 C5
Enderby Abyssal Plain S. Ocean 60°0S 40°0E 151 C5
Enderby I. Australia 20°35S 116°30E 278 D2
Enderby Land Antarctica 66°0S 53°0E 151 C5
Enderlin U.S.A. 46°38N 97°36W 308 B5
Enderrocat, C. Spain 39°28N 2°43E 206 B3
Endicott U.S.A. 42°6N 76°4W 313 D8
Endicott Mts. U.S.A. 68°0N 152°0W 303 C9
Endimari → Brazil 8°46S 66°7W 330 B4
Endwell U.S.A. 42°6N 76°2W 313 D8
Endyalgout I. Australia 11°40S 132°35E 278 B5
Ené → Peru 11°10S 74°18W 330 C3
Eneabba Australia 29°49S 115°16E 279 E2
Enebyberg Sweden 59°25N 17°59E 139 A1
Enewetak Atoll Marshall Is. 11°30N 162°15E 288 F8
Enez Turkey 40°45N 26°5E 203 F10
Enfer, Pte. d' Martinique 14°22N 60°54W 322 j
Enfield N.S.W., Australia 33°53S 151°6E 139 B1
Enfield N.S., Canada 44°56N 63°32W 299 D7
Enfield Conn., U.S.A. 41°58N 72°36W 313 E12
Enfield Ill., U.S.A. 38°6N 88°20W 311 F8
Enfield N.C., U.S.A. 36°11N 77°41W 315 C16
Enfield N.H., U.S.A. 43°39N 72°9W 313 C12
Enga □ Papua N. G. 5°30S 143°30E 286 C2
Engadin Switz. 46°45N 10°10E 179 J6
Engan Norway 63°8N 8°31E 164 A5
Engaño, C. Dom. Rep. 18°30N 68°20W 321 C6
Engaño, C. Phil. 18°35N 122°23E 232 B4
Engaru Japan 44°3N 143°31E 220 B11
Engcobo = Ngcobo S. Africa 31°37S 28°0E 271 D4
Engelberg Switz. 46°48N 8°26E 179 J4
Engels Russia 51°28N 46°6E 190 E8
Engemann L. Canada 58°0N 106°55W 297 B7
Engenho, I. do Brazil 22°50S 43°6W 135 B2
Engerdal Norway 61°45N 11°58E 164 C8
Engershatu Eritrea 16°7N 38°34E 257 D4
Enggano Indonesia 5°20S 102°40E 234 D2
Engineer Group Papua N. G. 10°35S 151°20E 286 F6
Engkilili Malaysia 1°3N 111°42E 235 B4
England U.S.A. 34°33N 91°58W 314 D9
England □ U.K. 53°0N 2°0W 169 E5
Englee Canada 50°45N 56°5W 299 B8
Englehart Canada 47°49N 79°52W 298 C4
Englewood Colo., U.S.A. 39°38N 104°59W 304 G11
Englewood Fla., U.S.A. 26°58N 82°21W 317 J7
Englewood Ill., U.S.A. 41°46N 87°38W 119 C3
Englewood N.J., U.S.A. 40°54N 73°58W 132 A2
Englewood Ohio, U.S.A. 39°53N 84°18W 311 E12
Englewood Cliffs U.S.A. 40°53N 73°59W 132 A2
English U.S.A. 38°20N 86°28W 311 F10
English → Ont., Canada 49°12N 91°5W 297 C10
English → Iowa, U.S.A. 41°29N 91°32W 310 C5
English B. Ascension I. 7°54S 14°23W 153 g
English Bazar = Ingraj Bazar India 24°58N 88°10E 243 G13
English Channel Europe 50°0N 2°0W 169 G6
English Company's Is., The Australia 11°50S 136°32E 280 A2
English Harbour Town Antigua & B. 17°1N 61°46W 322 b
English River Canada 49°14N 91°0W 298 C1
Engures ezers Latvia 57°16N 23°6E 184 A10
Enguri → Georgia 42°27N 41°38E 191 J5
Enid U.S.A. 36°24N 97°53W 314 C6
Enipeas → Greece 39°22N 22°17E 204 B4
Eniwa Japan 43°0N 141°30E 220 C10
Enkhuizen Neths. 52°42N 5°17E 170 B5
Enköping Sweden 59°37N 17°4E 162 E11
Enle China 24°0N 101°9E 228 F3
Enmore Australia 33°54S 151°10E 139 B2
Enna Italy 37°34N 14°16E 201 E7
Ennadai L. Canada 60°58N 101°20W 297 A8
Enné, O. → Chad 14°24N 18°45E 259 F4
Ennedi Chad 17°15N 22°0E 259 E4
Enneri Achelouma → Niger 21°55N 13°35E 261 D7
Enngonia Australia 29°21S 145°50E 281 D4
Ennigerloh Germany 51°50N 8°2E 178 D4
Ennis Clare, Ireland 52°51N 8°59W 166 D3
Ennis Mont., U.S.A. 45°21N 111°44W 304 D8
Ennis Tex., U.S.A. 32°20N 96°38W 314 E6
Enniscorthy Ireland 52°30N 6°34W 166 D5
Enniskillen U.K. 54°21N 7°39W 166 B4
Ennistimon Ireland 52°57N 9°17W 166 D2
Enns Austria 48°12N 14°28E 180 C7
Enns → Austria 48°14N 14°32E 180 C7
Eno Finland 62°47N 30°10E 160 E24
Enontekiö Finland 68°23N 23°37E 160 B20
Enosburg Falls U.S.A. 44°55N 72°48W 313 B12
Enping China 22°16N 112°21E 229 F9
Enrekang Indonesia 3°34S 119°47E 235 C5
Enrile Phil. 17°34N 121°42E 232 C3
Enriquillo, L. Dom. Rep. 18°20N 72°5W 321 C5
Enschede Neths. 52°13N 6°53E 170 B6
Ensenada Argentina 34°55S 57°55W 334 C4
Ensenada Chile 41°12S 72°33W 336 B2
Ensenada Baja Calif., Mexico 31°52N 116°37W 318 A1
Ensenada de los Muertos Mexico 23°59N 109°51W 318 C2
Enshi China 30°18N 109°29E 228 B7
Enshū-Nada Japan 34°27N 137°38E 223 C9
Ensiola, Pta. de n' Spain 39°7N 2°55E 206 B3
Ensisheim France 47°50N 7°20E 173 E14
Enskede Sweden 59°17N 18°4E 139 B2
Ensley U.S.A. 30°31N 87°16W 317 E2
Entebbe Uganda 0°4N 32°28E 268 B3
Enterprise N.W.T., Canada 60°47N 115°45W 296 A5
Enterprise Ala., U.S.A. 31°19N 85°51W 316 D4
Enterprise Nev., U.S.A. 36°13N 115°14W 124 B1
Enterprise Oreg., U.S.A. 45°25N 117°17W 304 D5
Entorno de Doñana ⌓ Spain 37°0N 6°26W 195 J4
Entrance, The Australia 33°21S 151°30E 283 B9
Entraygues-sur-Truyère France 44°38N 2°35E 174 D6
Entre-Deux Réunion 21°14S 55°28E 272 f
Entre Rios = Rio Brilhante Brazil 21°48S 54°33W 335 A5
Entre Rios = Três Rios Brazil 22°6S 43°15W 333 F3
Entre Ríos Bolivia 21°30S 64°25W 334 A3
Entre Rios Bahia, Brazil 11°56S 38°5W 333 D4
Entre Rios Pará, Brazil 5°24S 54°21W 331 B7
Entre Ríos □ Argentina 30°30S 58°30W 334 C4
Entrepeñas, Embalse de Spain 40°34N 2°42W 196 E2
Entrevias Spain 40°22N 3°40W 127 B1
Entroncamento Portugal 39°28N 8°28W 195 F2
Enugu Nigeria 6°30N 7°30E 263 D6
Enugu □ Nigeria 6°30N 7°45E 263 D6
Enugu Ezike Nigeria 7°0N 7°29E 263 D6
Enumclaw U.S.A. 47°12N 121°59W 306 C5
Envalira, Port d' Europe 42°33N 1°43E 196 C6
Envermeu France 49°53N 1°15E 172 C8
Envigado Colombia 6°10N 75°35W 328 B2
Enviken Sweden 60°49N 15°46E 162 D9
Envira Brazil 7°18S 70°13W 330 B3
Envira → Brazil 7°19S 70°15W 330 B3
Enying Hungary 46°56N 18°15E 182 D3
Enyonga Gabon 0°59S 9°22E 264 C1
Enza → Italy 44°54N 10°31E 198 D7
Enzan Japan 35°42N 138°44E 223 B10
Eochail = Youghal Ireland 51°56N 7°52W 166 E4
Eólie, Ís. Italy 38°30N 14°57E 201 D7
Eot I. Micronesia 7°23N 151°44E 287 T17
Epanomi Greece 40°25N 22°59E 202 F6
Epcot U.S.A. 28°21N 81°32W 133 B1
Epe Neths. 52°21N 5°59E 170 B5
Epe Nigeria 6°36N 3°59E 263 D5
Epéna Congo 1°22N 17°29E 264 B3
Épernay France 49°3N 3°56E 173 C10
Épernon France 48°35N 1°40E 173 D8
Ephesus Turkey 37°55N 27°22E 205 D9
Ephraim U.S.A. 39°22N 111°35W 304 G8
Ephrata Pa., U.S.A. 40°11N 76°11W 313 F8
Ephrata Wash., U.S.A. 47°19N 119°33W 304 C4
Epi Vanuatu 16°43S 168°15E 287 F6
Epidavros Limira Greece 36°46N 23°0E 204 E5
Épila Spain 41°36N 1°17W 196 D3
Épinac France 46°59N 4°31E 173 F11
Épinal France 48°10N 6°27E 173 D13
Epira Guyana 5°5N 57°20W 329 B6
Epiros □ Greece 39°30N 20°30E 204 B2
Episkopi Cyprus 34°40N 32°54E 207 F8
Episkopi Kriti, Greece 35°20N 24°20E 207 E5
Episkopi Bay Cyprus 34°35N 32°50E 207 F8
Epitalio Greece 37°37N 21°30E 204 D3
Eppalock, L. Australia 36°52S 144°34E 282 D6
Eppan = Appiano Italy 46°28N 11°15E 199 B8
Epping Australia 33°46S 151°5E 139 A1
Eppingen Germany 49°8N 8°53E 179 F4
Epsom U.K. 51°19N 0°16W 169 F7
Epukiro Namibia 21°40S 19°9E 270 B2
Equality U.S.A. 37°44N 88°20W 311 G8
Équateur □ Dem. Rep. of the Congo 2°0N 21°0E 264 B4
Equatorial Channel Maldives 0°0 73°10E 272 d
Equatorial Guinea ■ Africa 2°0N 8°0E 264 B1
Equeipa Venezuela 5°22N 62°43W 329 B5
Er Hai China 25°48N 100°11E 228 E3
Er Rachidia Morocco 31°58N 4°20W 260 B4
Er Rachidia □ Morocco 31°45N 4°30W 260 B4
Er Rahad Sudan 12°45N 30°32E 257 E3
Er Rif Morocco 35°1N 4°1W 261 A4
Er Rogel Sudan 18°10N 35°25E 256 D4
Er Roseires Sudan 11°55N 34°30E 257 E3
Er Rua'at Sudan 12°21N 32°17E 257 E3
Eraclea Italy 45°35N 12°40E 199 C9
Eran Phil. 9°4N 117°42E 233 G1
Eran B. Phil. 9°5N 117°43E 233 G1
Erandol India 20°56N 75°20E 244 D2
Eranga Dem. Rep. of the Congo 1°52S 18°56E 264 C3
Erap Papua N. G. 6°37S 146°51E 286 D4
Erasmus = Bronkhorstspruit S. Africa 25°46S 28°45E 271 C4
Erave Papua N. G. 6°39S 144°0E 286 D2
Erave → Papua N. G. 6°54S 144°47E 286 D3
Erāwadī Myit = Irrawaddy → Burma 15°50N 95°6E 241 G5
Erāwadī Myitwanya = Irrawaddy, Mouths of the Burma 15°30N 95°0E 241 H5
Erawan △ Thailand 14°25N 98°58E 236 E2
Erba Italy 45°48N 9°15E 198 C6
Erba Sudan 19°5N 36°51E 256 D4
Erba, J. Sudan 20°48N 36°47E 256 C4
Erbaa Turkey 40°42N 36°36E 212 B7
Erbeng Shan China 42°50N 84°59E 217 D10
Erbeskopf Germany 49°44N 7°2E 179 F3
Erbil = Arbīl Iraq 36°15N 44°5E 213 D11
Erbu Ethiopia 6°44N 34°53E 257 E3
Ercan, Nicosia ✈ (ECN) Cyprus 35°10N 33°30E 207 E9
Erçek Turkey 38°39N 43°36E 246 B4
Erçis Turkey 39°2N 43°21E 213 C10
Erciyaş Dağı Turkey 38°30N 35°30E 246 B2
Érd Hungary 47°22N 18°56E 182 C3
Erdao Jiang → China 42°37N 128°0E 224 A3
Erdek Turkey 40°23N 27°47E 203 F11
Erdély = Transilvania Romania 46°30N 24°0E 183 D9
Erdemli Turkey 36°36N 34°19E 250 B5
Erdene = Ulaan-Uul Mongolia 46°4N 100°49E 226 B6
Erdenet Mongolia 49°2N 104°5E 218 B9
Erdenetsogt Mongolia 42°55N 106°5E 226 C4
Erding Germany 48°18N 11°54E 179 G7
Erdre → France 47°13N 1°32W 172 E5
Erebato → Venezuela 5°54N 64°16W 329 B5
Erebus, Mt. Antarctica 77°35S 167°0E 151 D11
Erechim Brazil 27°35S 52°15W 335 B5
Ereğli Konya, Turkey 37°31N 34°4E 212 D6
Ereğli Zonguldak, Turkey 41°15N 31°24E 212 B4
Erei, Monti Italy 37°20N 14°20E 201 E7
Erenhot China 43°48N 112°2E 226 C7
Erenköy = Kokkina Cyprus 35°11N 32°36E 207 E8
Erenköy Turkey 40°58N 29°3E 122 C2
Eresfjord Norway 62°40N 8°8E 164 B5
Eresma → Spain 41°26N 4°45W 194 D6
Eresos Greece 39°11N 25°57E 205 B7
Ereymentaū Kazakhstan 51°37N 73°6E 217 B8
Erfelek Turkey 41°53N 34°55E 212 B6
Erfenisdam S. Africa 28°30S 26°50E 270 C4
Erfjord Norway 59°20N 6°14E 164 E3
Erfoud Morocco 31°30N 4°15W 260 B4
Erfstadt Germany 50°50N 6°50E 178 E2
Erft → Germany 51°11N 6°44E 178 D2
Erfurt Germany 50°58N 11°2E 178 E7
Ergani Turkey 38°17N 39°49E 213 C8
Ergel Mongolia 43°8N 109°5E 226 C5
Ergene → Turkey 41°1N 26°22E 203 E10
Ergeni Vozvyshennost Russia 47°0N 44°0E 191 G7
Ērgli Latvia 56°54N 25°38E 188 D3
Erhlin Taiwan 23°54N 120°22E 225 C2
Erhshui Taiwan 23°45N 120°37E 225 C2
Eria → Spain 42°3N 5°44W 194 C5
Eriba Sudan 16°40N 36°10E 257 D4
Eriboll, L. U.K. 58°30N 4°42W 167 C4
Érice Italy 38°2N 12°35E 200 D5
Eridu U.S.A. 30°18N 83°45W 316 E6
Erie Mich., U.S.A. 41°47N 83°31W 311 C13
Erie Pa., U.S.A. 42°8N 80°5W 312 D4
Erie, L. N. Amer. 42°15N 81°0W 312 D4
Erie Canal U.S.A. 43°5N 78°43W 312 C7
Erieau Canada 42°16N 81°57W 312 D3
Erigavo = Ceerigaabo Somali Rep. 10°35N 47°20E 267 B6
Erikoussa Greece 39°53N 19°34E 206 B9
Eriksdale Canada 50°52N 98°7W 297 C9
Erimanthos Greece 37°57N 21°50E 204 D3
Erimo-misaki Japan 41°50N 143°15E 220 D11
Erin Ont., Canada 43°45N 80°7W 312 C4
Erin Trin. & Tob. 10°5N 61°39W 323 t
Erin B. Trin. & Tob. 10°4N 61°43W 323 t
Erin Pt. Trin. & Tob. 10°3N 61°39W 323 t
Erinpura India 25°9N 73°3E 242 G5
Eriskay U.K. 57°4N 7°18W 167 D1
Erith U.K. 51°28N 0°11E 125 B5
Erithres Greece 38°13N 23°20E 204 C5
Eritrea ■ Africa 14°0N 38°30E 257 E4
Erivan = Yerevan Armenia 40°10N 44°31E 191 K7
Erjas → Portugal 39°40N 7°1W 194 F3
Erkech-Tam Pass Asia 39°46N 74°2E 217 E8
Erkelenz Germany 51°4N 6°19E 178 D2
Erkner Germany 52°25N 13°44E 178 C9
Erlaa Austria 48°9N 16°19E 142 B1
Erlangen Germany 49°36N 11°0E 179 F6
Erlanger U.S.A. 39°1N 84°36W 311 E12
Erldunda Australia 25°14S 133°12E 280 D1
Ermelo Neths. 52°18N 5°35E 170 B5
Ermelo Mpumalanga, S. Africa 26°31S 29°59E 271 C4
Ermenek Turkey 36°38N 33°0E 250 B4
Ermenek → Turkey 36°35N 33°23E 250 B4
Ermil Sudan 13°35N 27°40E 257 E2
Ermington Australia 33°48S 151°4E 139 A1
Ermioni Greece 37°23N 23°15E 204 D5
Ermita Phil. 14°35N 120°59E 127 B1
Ermones Greece 39°37N 19°46E 206 B9
Ermoupoli Greece 37°28N 24°57E 204 D6
Ernakulam India 9°59N 76°22E 245 K3
Erne → Ireland 54°30N 8°16W 166 B3
Erne, Lower L. U.K. 54°28N 7°47W 166 B4
Erne, Upper L. U.K. 54°14N 7°32W 166 B4
Ernée France 48°18N 0°56W 172 D6
Ernest Giles Ra. Australia 27°0S 123°45E 279 E3
Ernest N. Morial Convention Center New Orleans, U.S.A. 131 c3
Ernstberg Germany 50°13N 6°47E 179 E2
Erode India 11°24N 77°45E 245 J3
Eromanga Australia 26°40S 143°11E 281 D3
Erongo Namibia 21°39S 15°58E 270 B2
Erquy France 48°38N 2°29W 172 D4
Erramala Hills India 15°30N 78°15E 245 G4
Errentería Spain 43°19N 1°54W 196 B3
Errer → Ethiopia 7°32N 42°35E 257 F5
Errigal Ireland 55°2N 8°6W 166 A3
Errinundra △ Australia 37°20S 148°47E 283 D8
Erris Hd. Ireland 54°19N 10°0W 166 B1
Erromango Vanuatu 18°45S 169°5E 287 H7
Ersekë Albania 40°22N 20°40E 202 F4
Ersekújvár = Nové Zámky Slovak Rep. 48°2N 18°8E 181 C11
Ershatou China 23°6N 113°18E 121 B2
Erskine U.S.A. 47°40N 96°0W 308 B6
Erskineville Australia 33°54S 151°12E 139 B2
Erstein France 48°25N 7°38E 173 D14
Ertai China 46°3N 90°5E 217 C12
Ertan Shuiku China 27°5N 101°52E 228 D3
Ertholmene Denmark 55°19N 15°11E 163 J9
Ertil Russia 51°55N 40°50E 190 E5
Ertis = Irtysh → Russia 61°4N 68°52E 214 C7
Ertis Kazakhstan 53°20N 75°27E 217 B9
Ertis → Kazakhstan 47°52N 84°16E 217 C10
Ertvågøy Norway 63°13N 8°26E 164 A5
Eruh Turkey 37°46N 42°13E 213 D10
Erunkan Nigeria 6°36N 3°23E 124 A2
Ervy-le-Châtel France 48°2N 3°55E 173 D10
Erwin U.S.A. 36°9N 82°25W 315 C13
Eryuan China 26°7N 99°57E 228 D2
Erzgebirge Germany 50°27N 12°55E 178 E8
Erzin Russia 50°15N 95°10E 217 B13
Erzin Turkey 36°57N 36°11E 250 B7
Erzincan Turkey 39°46N 39°30E 213 C8
Erzincan □ Turkey 39°45N 39°30E 213 C8
Erzsébet-Telep Hungary 47°27N 19°10E 117 B3
Erzurum Turkey 39°57N 41°15E 213 C9
Erzurum □ Turkey 39°55N 41°15E 213 C9
Es Caló Spain 38°40N 1°30E 206 D2
Es Canar Spain 39°2N 1°36E 206 C2
Es Mercadal Spain 39°59N 4°5E 206 B5
Es Migjorn Gran Spain 39°57N 4°3E 206 B5
Es Safiya Sudan 15°31N 30°7E 257 D3
Es Sahrâ al Beida Egypt 27°50N 28°45E 256 B2
Es Sahrâ' Esh Sharqîya Egypt 27°30N 32°30E 256 B3
Es Sînâ' Egypt 29°0N 34°0E 246 D2
Es Sûkî Sudan 13°20N 33°58E 257 E3
Es Vedrà Spain 38°52N 1°12E 206 D1
Esa'ala Papua N. G. 9°45S 150°49E 286 E6
Esambo Dem. Rep. of the Congo 3°48S 23°30E 264 C4
Esan-Misaki Japan 41°40N 141°10E 220 D10
Esashi Hokkaidō, Japan 44°56N 142°35E 220 B11
Esashi Hokkaidō, Japan 41°52N 140°7E 220 D10
Esbjerg Denmark 55°29N 8°29E 163 J2
Esbo = Espoo Finland 60°12N 24°40E 188 B3
Escada Brazil 8°22S 35°8W 332 C4
Escalante Phil. 10°50N 123°33E 233 F4
Escalante Utah, U.S.A. 37°47N 111°36W 305 H8
Escalante → U.S.A. 37°24N 110°57W 305 H8
Escalón Mexico 26°45N 104°20W 318 B4
Escambia → U.S.A. 30°32N 87°11W 317 E2
Escanaba U.S.A. 45°45N 87°4W 308 C10
Escarparda Pt. Phil. 18°31N 122°13E 232 B4
Escarpé, C. N. Cal. 20°41S 167°13E 288 d
Escaut = Schelde → Belgium 51°15N 4°16E 170 C4
Esch-sur-Alzette Lux. 49°32N 6°0E 170 E6
Eschede Germany 52°44N 10°14E 178 C6
Eschenried Germany 48°13N 11°24E 131 A1
Eschwege Germany 51°11N 10°2E 178 D6
Eschweiler Germany 50°49N 6°15E 178 E2
Escobal Panama 9°6N 80°1W 320 c
Escoma Bolivia 15°40S 69°8W 330 D4
Escondido U.S.A. 33°7N 117°5W 307 M9
Escravos → Nigeria 5°35N 5°10E 263 D6
Escuinapa de Hidalgo Mexico 22°50N 105°50W 318 C3
Escuintla Guatemala 14°20N 90°48W 320 D1
Eséka Cameroon 3°41N 10°44E 263 E7
Eşen → Turkey 36°27N 29°16E 205 E11
Esenguly Turkmenistan 37°37N 53°59E 216 E4
Esenler Turkey 41°1N 28°52E 122 B1
Esens Germany 53°38N 7°36E 178 B3
Esenyurt Turkey 41°3N 28°48E 203 E12
Esera → Spain 42°6N 0°15E 196 C5
Eşfahān Iran 32°39N 51°43E 247 C6
Eşfahān □ Iran 32°50N 51°50E 247 C6
Esfarāyen Iran 37°4N 57°30E 247 B8
Esfideh Iran 33°39N 59°46E 247 C8
Esgueva → Spain 41°40N 4°43W 194 D6
Esh Sham = Dimashq Syria 33°30N 36°18E 250 E7
Esh Shamâlîya □ Sudan 19°0N 29°0E 256 D2
Esha Ness U.K. 60°29N 1°38W 167 A7
Eshan China 24°11N 102°24E 228 E4
Esher U.K. 51°21N 0°20W 125 B1
Eshkāshem = Ishkashim Tajikistan 36°44N 71°37E 217 E8
Eshkol △ Israel 31°20N 34°30E 251 G5
Eshowe S. Africa 28°50S 31°30E 271 C5
Esiama Ghana 4°56N 2°25W 262 E4
Esigodini Zimbabwe 20°18S 28°56E 271 B4
Esil = Ishim → Russia 57°45N 71°10E 214 D8
Esil Kazakhstan 51°57N 66°24E 217 B7
Esino → Italy 43°39N 13°22E 199 E10
Esira Madag. 24°20S 46°42E 272 C2
Esk → Dumf. & Gall., U.K. 54°58N 3°2W 167 G5
Esk → N. Yorks., U.K. 54°30N 0°37W 168 C7
Eskān Iran 26°48N 63°9E 240 D1
Eskbank U.K. 55°52N 3°4W 121 B3
Esker Siding Canada 53°53N 66°25W 299 B6
Eskifjörður Iceland 65°3N 13°55W 155 B13
Eskije = Xanthi Greece 41°10N 24°58E 203 E8
Eskilsäter Sweden 58°57N 13°10E 163 F7
Eskilstuna Sweden 59°22N 16°32E 162 E10
Eskimalatya Turkey 38°24N 38°22E 213 C8
Eskimo Point = Arviat Canada 61°6N 93°59W 297 A10
Eskişehir Turkey 39°50N 30°30E 205 B12
Eskişehir □ Turkey 39°40N 31°0E 205 B12
Esla → Spain 41°29N 6°3W 194 D4
Eslāmābād-e Gharb Iran 34°10N 46°30E 213 E12
Eslāmshahr Iran 35°40N 51°10E 247 C6
Eslöv Sweden 55°50N 13°20E 163 J7
Eşme Turkey 38°23N 28°58E 205 C10
Esmeralda, I. Chile 48°55S 75°25W 336 C1
Esmeraldas Ecuador 1°0N 79°40W 328 C2
Esmeraldas □ Ecuador 0°40N 79°30W 328 C2

Esmeraldas ➔ *Ecuador* 0°58N 79°38W 328 C2
Esna = Isna *Egypt* 25°17N 32°30E 256 B3
Esnagi L. *Canada* 48°36N 84°33W 298 C3
Esom Hill *U.S.A.* 33°57N 85°23W 316 B4
Espa *Norway* 60°34N 11°16E 164 D8
Espada, Pta. *Colombia* 12°5N 71°7W 328 A3
Espalion *France* 44°32N 2°47E 174 D6
España = Spain ■ *Europe* 39°0N 4°0W 192 D3
Espanola *Ont., Canada* 46°15N 81°46W 298 C3
Espanola *N. Mex., U.S.A.* 35°59N 106°5W 305 J10
Española, I. *Ecuador* 1°23S 89°39W 330 a
Espanya, Plaça d' *Barcelona, Spain* 114 c1
Esparreguera *Spain* 41°33N 1°52E 196 D6
Esparza *Costa Rica* 9°59N 84°40W 320 E3
Espeland *Norway* 60°23N 5°28E 164 D2
Espelkamp *Germany* 52°24N 8°36E 178 C4
Espenberg, C. *U.S.A.* 66°33N 163°36W 303 C7
Esperança *Amazonas, Brazil* 4°24S 69°52W 328 D4
Esperança *Paraíba, Brazil* 7°1S 35°51W 332 C4
Esperance *Australia* 33°45S 121°55E 279 F3
Esperance, C. *Solomon Is.* 9°15S 159°43E 287 M10
Esperance B. *Australia* 33°48S 121°55E 279 F3
Esperantinópolis *Brazil* 4°53S 44°53W 332 B3
Esperanza *Antarctica* 65°0S 55°0W 151 C18
Esperanza *Santa Cruz, Argentina* 51°1S 70°49W 336 D2
Esperanza *Santa Fe, Argentina* 31°29S 61°3W 334 C3
Esperanza *Mexico City, Mexico* 128 c3
Esperanza *Agusan del S., Phil.* 8°43N 125°36E 233 G5
Esperanza *Masbate, Phil.* 11°45N 124°3E 233 F5
Esperanza *Puerto Rico* 18°6N 65°28W 321 b
Espéraza *France* 42°56N 2°14E 174 F6
Espevær *Norway* 59°35N 5°7E 164 E2
Espichel, C. *Portugal* 38°22N 9°16W 195 G1
Espiel *Spain* 38°11N 5°1W 195 G5
Espigão, Serra do *Brazil* 26°35S 50°30W 335 B5
Espinal *Colombia* 4°9N 74°53W 328 C3
Espinar *Peru* 14°51S 71°24W 330 C3
Espinazo, Sierra del = Espinhaço, Serra do *Brazil* 17°30S 43°30W 333 E3
Espinhaço, Serra do *Brazil* 17°30S 43°30W 333 E3
Espinho *Portugal* 41°1N 8°38W 194 D2
Espinilho, Serra do *Brazil* 28°30S 55°0W 335 B5
Espinosa de los Monteros *Spain* 43°5N 3°34W 194 B7
Espírito Santo □ *Brazil* 20°0S 40°45W 333 F3
Espírito Santo do Pinhal *Brazil* 22°10S 46°46W 335 A6
Espíritu Santo *Vanuatu* 15°15S 166°50E 287 E4
Espíritu Santo, B. del *Mexico* 19°20N 87°35W 319 D7
Espíritu Santo, I. *Mexico* 24°30N 110°22W 318 C2
Espita *Mexico* 21°1N 88°19W 319 C7
Espiye *Turkey* 40°56N 38°43E 213 B8
Esplanada *Brazil* 11°47S 37°57W 333 D4
Esplugas *Spain* 41°22N 2°5E 114 A1
Espoo *Finland* 60°12N 24°40E 188 B3
Esposizione Universale di Roma *Italy* 41°49N 12°28E 136 C1
Espuña, Sierra de *Spain* 37°51N 1°35W 197 H3
Espungabera *Mozam.* 20°29S 32°45E 271 B5
Esquel *Argentina* 42°55S 71°20W 336 B2
Esquimalt *Canada* 48°26N 123°25W 306 B3
Esquina *Argentina* 30°0S 59°30W 334 C4
Essandsjøen *Norway* 63°0N 12°0E 164 A8
Essaouira *Morocco* 31°32N 9°42W 260 B3
Essaouira □ *Morocco* 31°25N 9°30W 260 B3
Essen *Belgium* 51°28N 4°28E 170 C4
Essen *Nordrhein-Westfalen, Germany* 51°28N 7°2E 178 D3
Essendon *Australia* 37°44S 144°55E 128 A1
Essendon ✕ (MEB) *Australia* 37°43S 144°54E 128 A1
Essendon, Mt. *Australia* 25°0S 120°29E 279 E3
Essequibo ➔ *Guyana* 6°50N 58°30W 329 B6
Essex *Ont., Canada* 42°10N 82°49W 312 D2
Essex *Calif., U.S.A.* 34°44N 115°15W 307 L11
Essex *N.Y., U.S.A.* 44°19N 73°21W 313 B11
Essex □ *U.K.* 51°54N 0°27E 169 F8
Essex Junction *U.S.A.* 44°29N 73°7W 313 B11
Essingen *Sweden* 59°19N 17°59E 139 B1
Essling *Austria* 48°12N 16°30E 142 A3
Esslingen *Germany* 48°44N 9°18E 179 G5
Essonne □ *France* 48°30N 2°20E 173 D9
Est, Gare de l' *Paris, France* 134 a5
Estaca de Bares, C. de *Spain* 43°46N 7°42W 194 B3
Estación Camacho *Mexico* 24°25N 102°18W 318 C4
Estación Simón *Mexico* 24°42N 102°35W 318 C4
Estadilla *Spain* 42°4N 0°16E 196 C5
Estado, Parque do *Brazil* 23°38S 46°38W 137 B2
Estados, I. de Los *Argentina* 54°40S 64°30W 336 D4
Estagel *France* 42°47N 2°40E 174 F6
Estagno Pt. *Phil.* 17°20N 122°24E 232 C4
Eşţahbānāt *Iran* 29°8N 54°4E 247 D7
Estância *Brazil* 11°16S 37°26W 332 D4
Estancia *N. Mex., U.S.A.* 34°46N 106°4W 305 J10
Estancia Monte León *Argentina* 50°14S 68°55W 336 D3
Estārm *Iran* 28°21N 58°21E 247 D8
Estarreja *Portugal* 40°45N 8°35W 194 E2
Estats, Pic d' *Spain* 42°40N 1°24E 196 C6
Estcourt *S. Africa* 29°0S 29°53E 271 C4
Este *Italy* 45°14N 11°39E 199 C8
Este △ *Dom. Rep.* 18°14N 68°42W 321 C6
Estefânia *Lisbon, Portugal* 126 a2
Estelí *Nic.* 13°9N 86°22W 320 D2
Estella *Spain* 42°40N 2°2W 196 C2
Estelle *U.S.A.* 29°50N 90°6W 131 B2
Estellencs *Spain* 39°39N 2°29E 206 B3
Estena ➔ *Spain* 39°23N 4°44W 195 F6
Estepa *Spain* 37°17N 4°52W 195 H6
Estepona *Spain* 36°24N 5°7W 195 J5
Esterhazy *Canada* 50°37N 102°5W 297 C8
Esterias, C. *Gabon* 0°40N 9°20E 264 B1
Esternay *France* 48°44N 3°33E 173 D10
Esterri d'Aneu *Spain* 42°38N 1°5E 196 C6
Estevan *Canada* 49°10N 102°59W 297 D8
Estevan Group *Canada* 53°3N 129°38W 296 C3
Estherville *U.S.A.* 43°24N 94°50W 308 D6
Estill *U.S.A.* 32°45N 81°15W 316 C8
Estissac *France* 48°16N 3°48E 173 D10
Eston *Canada* 51°8N 108°40W 297 C7
Estonia ■ *Europe* 58°30N 25°30E 188 C3
Estoril *Portugal* 38°42N 9°23W 195 G1
Estouk *Mali* 18°14N 1°2E 263 B5
Estrela, Basilica da *Portugal* 38°42N 9°9W 126 A2
Estrela, Serra da *Portugal* 40°10N 7°45W 194 E3
Estrella *Spain* 38°25N 3°35W 195 G7
Estremoz *Portugal* 38°51N 7°39W 195 G3
Estrondo, Serra do *Brazil* 7°20S 48°0W 332 C2
Esutoru = Uglegorsk *Russia* 49°5N 142°2E 215 E15
Esztergom *Hungary* 47°47N 18°44E 182 C3
Et Tîdra *Mauritania* 19°45N 16°20W 262 B1
Etah *India* 27°35N 78°40E 243 F8
Étain *France* 49°13N 5°38E 173 C12
Étampes *France* 48°26N 2°10E 173 D9
Étang-Salé-les-Bains *Réunion* 21°15S 55°20E 272 f
Etanga *Namibia* 17°55S 13°0E 270 A1
Étaples *France* 50°30N 1°39E 173 B8
Etawah *India* 26°48N 79°6E 243 F8
Etawney L. *Canada* 57°50N 96°50W 297 B9
Etchojoa *Mexico* 26°55N 109°38W 318 B3
Ete *Nigeria* 7°2N 7°28E 263 D6
Etéké *Gabon* 1°29S 11°35E 264 C2
eThekwini = Durban *S. Africa* 29°49S 31°1E 271 C5
Ethel *U.S.A.* 46°32N 122°46W 306 D4
Ethelbert *Canada* 51°32N 100°25W 297 C8
Ethiopia ■ *Africa* 8°0N 40°0E 267 C4
Ethiopian Highlands *Ethiopia* 10°0N 37°0E 254 E7
Etili *Turkey* 39°59N 26°54E 203 G10
Etive, L. *U.K.* 56°29N 5°10W 167 E3
Etna *Italy* 37°50N 14°55E 201 E7
Etna ➔ *Norway* 60°49N 10°7E 164 C6
Etne *Norway* 59°40N 5°58E 164 E2
Etobicoke *Canada* 43°39N 79°34W 141 B1
Etobicoke Cr. ➔ *Canada* 43°35N 79°32W 141 B1
Etoile *Dem. Rep. of the Congo* 11°33S 27°30E 269 E2
Etoliko *Greece* 38°26N 21°21E 204 C3
Etolin Strait *U.S.A.* 60°20N 165°15W 303 F6
Etoloakarnania □ *Greece* 38°45N 21°18E 204 C3
Etosha △ *Namibia* 19°0S 16°0E 270 A2
Etosha Pan *Namibia* 18°40S 16°30E 270 A2
Etoumbi *Congo* 0°1S 14°57E 264 C2
Etowah *U.S.A.* 35°20N 84°32W 315 D12
Étréchy *France* 48°30N 2°12E 173 D9
Etrek *Turkmenistan* 37°36N 54°46E 247 B7
Étrépagny *France* 49°18N 1°36E 173 C8
Étretat *France* 49°42N 0°12E 172 C7
Etropole *Bulgaria* 42°50N 24°0E 203 D8
Ettelbruck *Lux.* 49°51N 6°5E 170 E6
Etterbeek *Belgium* 50°50N 4°23E 116 B2
Ettlingen *Germany* 48°56N 8°25E 179 G4
Ettrick Water ➔ *U.K.* 55°31N 2°55W 167 F6
Etuku *Dem. Rep. of the Congo* 3°42S 25°45E 264 C5
Etulia *Moldova* 45°32N 28°27E 183 E13
Etzná-Tixmucuy = Edzná *Mexico* 19°39N 90°19W 319 D6
Eu *France* 50°3N 1°26E 172 B8
Eua *Tonga* 21°22S 174°56W 287 Q13
Euboea = Evia *Greece* 38°30N 24°0E 204 C6
Eucaliptus = Tomás Barrón *Bolivia* 17°35S 67°31W 330 D4
Euchareena *Australia* 32°57S 149°6E 283 B8
Eucla *Australia* 31°41S 128°52E 279 F4
Euclid *U.S.A.* 41°34N 81°32W 312 E3
Euclides da Cunha *Brazil* 10°31S 39°1W 332 D4
Eucumbene, L. *Australia* 36°2S 148°40E 283 D8
Eudora *U.S.A.* 33°7N 91°16W 314 E9
Eudunda *Australia* 34°12S 139°7E 282 C3
Eufaula *Ala., U.S.A.* 31°54N 85°9W 316 D4
Eufaula *Okla., U.S.A.* 35°17N 95°35W 314 D7
Eufaula L. *U.S.A.* 35°18N 95°21W 314 D7
Eugene *U.S.A.* 44°5N 123°4W 304 D2
Eugowra *Australia* 33°22S 148°24E 283 B8
Eulo *Australia* 28°10S 145°3E 281 D4
Eulonia *U.S.A.* 31°32N 81°26W 316 D8
Eumungerie *Australia* 31°56S 148°36E 283 A8
Eun-gam *S. Korea* 37°34N 126°55E 137 B1
Eunice *La., U.S.A.* 30°30N 92°25W 314 F8
Eunice *N. Mex., U.S.A.* 32°26N 103°10W 305 K12
Eunpyeong *S. Korea* 37°36N 126°56E 137 B1
Eupen *Belgium* 50°37N 6°3E 170 D6
Euphrates = Furāt, Nahr al ➔ *Asia* 31°0N 47°25E 246 D5
Eure □ *France* 49°10N 1°0E 172 C8
Eure ➔ *France* 49°18N 1°12E 172 C8
Eure-et-Loir □ *France* 48°22N 1°30E 172 D8
Eureka *Nunavut, Canada* 80°0N 85°56W 295 B14
Eureka *Calif., U.S.A.* 40°47N 124°9W 304 F1
Eureka *Ill., U.S.A.* 40°43N 89°16W 310 D7
Eureka *Kans., U.S.A.* 37°49N 96°17W 308 G5
Eureka *Mo., U.S.A.* 38°30N 90°38W 310 F6
Eureka *Mont., U.S.A.* 48°53N 115°3W 304 B6
Eureka *Nev., U.S.A.* 39°31N 115°58W 304 G6
Eureka *S.C., U.S.A.* 33°42N 81°46W 316 B8
Eureka *S. Dak., U.S.A.* 45°46N 99°38W 308 C4
Eureka, Mt. *Australia* 26°35S 121°35E 279 E3
Eureka Sd. *Canada* 79°0N 85°0W 295 B15
Eurelia *Australia* 32°33S 138°35E 282 B3
Eurinilla Cr. ➔ *Australia* 30°53S 140°11E 282 A4
Euroa *Australia* 36°44S 145°35E 283 D6
Europa, Île *Ind. Oc.* 22°20S 40°22E 271 B7
Europa, Picos de *Spain* 43°10N 4°49W 194 B6
Europa, Pt. *Gib.* 36°3N 5°21W 195 J5
Europe 50°0N 20°0E 158 E10
Europoort *Neths.* 51°57N 4°10E 170 C4
Euskirchen *Germany* 50°39N 6°48E 178 E2
Eustis *U.S.A.* 28°51N 81°41W 317 G8
Euston *N.S.W., Australia* 34°30S 142°46E 282 C5
Euston *London, U.K.* 125 a3
Eutawville *U.S.A.* 33°24N 80°21W 316 B9
Eutin *Germany* 54°8N 10°36E 178 A6
Eutsuk L. *Canada* 53°20N 126°45W 296 C3
Eva Perón = La Pampa □ *Argentina* 36°50S 66°0W 334 D2
Eva Perón = La Plata *Argentina* 35°0S 57°55W 334 C4
Evale *Angola* 16°33S 15°44E 265 F3
Evanger *Norway* 60°39N 6°7E 164 D3
Evanlı *Turkey* 36°46N 34°26E 250 B3
Evans *U.S.A.* 40°23N 104°41W 304 F11
Evans, L. *Canada* 50°50N 77°0W 298 B4
Evans City *U.S.A.* 40°46N 80°4W 312 F4
Evans Head *Australia* 29°7S 153°27E 281 D5
Evansburg *Canada* 53°36N 114°59W 296 C5
Evansdale *U.S.A.* 42°30N 92°17W 310 B4
Evanston *Ill., U.S.A.* 42°3N 87°40W 119 A2
Evanston *Wyo., U.S.A.* 41°16N 110°58W 304 F8
Evansville *Ill., U.S.A.* 38°5N 89°56W 310 F7
Evansville *Ind., U.S.A.* 37°58N 87°35W 311 G9
Evansville *Wis., U.S.A.* 42°47N 89°18W 310 B7
Évaux-les-Bains *France* 46°12N 2°29E 173 F9
Evaz *Iran* 27°46N 53°59E 247 E7
Evciler *Afyon, Turkey* 38°4N 29°54E 205 C11
Evciler *Çanakkale, Turkey* 39°47N 26°44E 205 B8
Eveleth *U.S.A.* 47°28N 92°32W 308 B7
Even Sapir *Israel* 31°46N 35°8E 123 B1
Evensk *Russia* 62°12N 159°30E 215 C16
Evenstad *Norway* 61°25N 11°7E 164 C8
Everard, L. *Australia* 31°30S 135°0E 281 E2
Everard Ranges *Australia* 27°5S 132°28E 279 E5
Evere *Belgium* 50°52N 4°25E 116 A2
Everest, Mt. *Nepal* 28°5N 86°58E 243 E12
Everett *Ga., U.S.A.* 31°24N 81°38W 316 D8
Everett *Mass., U.S.A.* 42°24N 71°3W 116 A2
Everett *Pa., U.S.A.* 40°1N 78°23W 312 F6
Everett *Wash., U.S.A.* 47°59N 122°12W 306 C4
Everglades, The *U.S.A.* 25°50N 81°0W 317 K9
Everglades △ *U.S.A.* 25°30N 81°0W 317 K9
Everglades City *U.S.A.* 25°52N 81°23W 317 K8
Evergreen *Ala., U.S.A.* 31°26N 86°57W 315 F11
Evergreen *Mont., U.S.A.* 48°14N 114°17W 304 B6
Evergreen Park *U.S.A.* 41°43N 87°42W 119 C2
Everöd *Sweden* 55°53N 14°5E 163 J8
Everton *Australia* 36°25S 146°33E 283 D7
Evertsberg *Sweden* 61°8N 13°58E 162 C7
Evesham *U.K.* 52°6N 1°56W 169 E6
Evia *Greece* 38°30N 24°0E 204 C6
Evia □ *Greece* 38°40N 23°40E 204 C5
Évian-les-Bains *France* 46°24N 6°35E 173 F13
Evīn *Iran* 35°47N 51°23E 141 A2
Evinayong *Eq. Guin.* 1°26N 10°35E 264 B2
Evinos ➔ *Greece* 38°27N 21°40E 204 C3
Évisa *France* 42°15N 8°48E 175 F12
Evje *Norway* 58°36N 7°51E 164 F4
Évora *Portugal* 38°33N 7°57W 195 G3
Évora □ *Portugal* 38°33N 7°50W 195 G3
Evowghlī *Iran* 38°43N 45°13E 213 C11
Évreux *France* 49°3N 1°8E 172 C8
Evritania □ *Greece* 39°5N 21°30E 204 B3
Évron *France* 48°10N 0°24W 172 D6
Evros □ *Greece* 41°10N 26°0E 203 E10
Evros ➔ *Greece* 41°40N 26°34E 203 F10
Evrotas ➔ *Greece* 36°50N 22°40E 204 E4
Évry *France* 48°38N 2°27E 173 D9
Évvoia = Evia *Greece* 38°30N 24°0E 204 C6
'Ewa Beach *U.S.A.* 21°19N 158°1W 302 K13
'Ewa District *U.S.A.* 21°25N 158°0W 302 K14
'Ewa Villages *U.S.A.* 21°20N 158°3W 302 K13
Ewarton *Jamaica* 18°11N 77°6W 320 a
Ewasse *Papua N. G.* 5°19S 151°1E 286 C6
Ewe, L. *U.K.* 57°49N 5°38W 167 D3
Ewing *Mo., U.S.A.* 40°6N 91°43W 310 E5
Ewing *Nebr., U.S.A.* 42°16N 98°21W 308 D4
Ewo *Congo* 0°48S 14°45E 264 C2
Ewu *Nigeria* 6°33N 3°19E 124 A1
Exaltación *Bolivia* 13°10S 65°20W 331 C4
Excelsior Springs *U.S.A.* 39°20N 94°13W 310 E2
Exchange Square *Hong Kong, China* 122 c1
Excideuil *France* 45°20N 1°4E 174 C5
Exe ➔ *U.K.* 50°41N 3°29W 169 G4
Exeter *Ont., Canada* 43°21N 81°29W 312 C3
Exeter *Devon, U.K.* 50°43N 3°31W 169 G4
Exeter *Calif., U.S.A.* 36°18N 119°9W 306 J7
Exeter *N.H., U.S.A.* 42°59N 70°57W 313 D14
Exhibition Place *Canada* 43°38N 79°25W 141 B2
Exira *U.S.A.* 41°35N 94°52W 310 C2
Exmoor *U.K.* 51°12N 3°45W 169 F4
Exmoor △ *U.K.* 51°8N 3°42W 169 F4
Exmouth *W. Austral., Australia* 21°54S 114°10E 278 D1
Exmouth *Devon, U.K.* 50°37N 3°25W 169 G4
Exmouth G. *Australia* 22°15S 114°15E 278 D1
Exmouth Plateau *Ind. Oc.* 19°0S 114°0E 288 J3
Expedition △ *Australia* 25°41S 149°7E 281 D4
Expedition Ra. *Australia* 24°30S 149°12E 280 C4
Experiment = Highland Mills *U.S.A.* 33°17N 84°17W 316 B5
Expo 2010 *China* 31°11N 121°29E 138 B1
Exposições, Palácio das *Brazil* 22°53S 43°13W 135 B1
Extremadura □ *Spain* 39°30N 6°5W 195 F4
Extrême-Nord □ *Cameroon* 11°0N 14°30E 259 F2
Exuma Sound *Bahamas* 24°30N 76°20W 320 B4
Eyak *U.S.A.* 60°32N 145°36W 303 F11
Eyasi, L. *Tanzania* 3°30S 35°0E 268 C4
Eydehavn *Norway* 58°30N 8°53E 164 F5
Eydhafushi *Maldives* 5°7N 73°2E 272 d
Eye Pen. *U.K.* 58°13N 6°10W 167 C2
Eyemouth *U.K.* 55°52N 2°5W 167 F6
Eygues = Aigues ➔ *France* 44°7N 4°43E 175 D8
Eygurande *France* 45°40N 2°26E 173 G9
Eyjafjallajökull *Iceland* 63°38N 19°36W 155 D7
Eyjafjarðarsýsla □ *Iceland* 65°30N 18°30W 155 B8
Eyjafjörður *Iceland* 66°15N 18°30W 155 A8
Eyl *Somali Rep.* 8°0N 49°50E 267 C6
Eymet *France* 44°40N 0°25E 174 D4
Eymoutiers *France* 45°40N 1°45E 174 C5
Eynesil *Turkey* 41°4N 39°9E 213 B8
Eyrarbakki *Iceland* 63°52N 21°9W 155 D5
Eyre (North), L. *Australia* 28°30S 137°20E 281 D2
Eyre (South), L. *Australia* 29°18S 137°25E 281 D2
Eyre, L. *Australia* 29°30S 137°26E 276 F6
Eyre Mts. *N.Z.* 45°25S 168°25E 285 F3
Eyre Pen. *Australia* 33°30S 136°17E 282 C1
Eysturoy *Færoe Is.* 62°13N 6°54W 160 E9
Eyüp *Turkey* 41°2N 28°55E 122 B1
Eyvān = Jūy Zar *Iran* 33°50N 46°18E 213 F12
Eyvānkī *Iran* 35°24N 51°56E 247 C6
Ez Zeidab *Sudan* 17°25N 33°55E 256 D3
Ezcaray *Spain* 42°19N 3°0W 196 C1
Ezeiza ✕ (EZE) *Argentina* 34°49S 58°32W 117 C1
Ežerėlis *Lithuania* 54°53N 23°37E 184 D10
Ezhou *China* 30°23N 114°50E 229 B10
Ezine *Turkey* 39°48N 26°20E 205 B8
Ezouza ➔ *Cyprus* 34°44N 32°27E 207 F8

F

F.Y.R.O.M. = Macedonia ■ *Europe* 41°53N 21°40E 202 E5
Faaa *Tahiti* 17°34S 149°35W 289 e
Faaborg *Denmark* 55°6N 10°15E 163 J4
Faaone *Tahiti* 17°40S 149°21W 289 e
Fabala *Guinea* 9°44N 9°5W 262 D3
Fabens *U.S.A.* 31°30N 106°10W 314 F1
Fåberg *Norway* 61°10N 10°25E 164 C7
Fabero *Spain* 42°46N 6°37W 194 C4
Fabius *U.S.A.* 42°50N 75°59W 313 D9
Fabour, Mt. *Singapore* 1°16N 103°49E 138 B2
Fabriano *Italy* 43°20N 12°54E 199 E9
Făcăeni *Romania* 44°32N 27°53E 183 F12
Facatativá *Colombia* 4°49N 74°22W 328 C3
Faceville *U.S.A.* 30°45N 84°38W 316 E5
Fachi *Niger* 18°6N 11°34E 259 E2
Facundo *Argentina* 45°18S 69°58W 336 C3
Fada *Chad* 17°13N 21°34E 259 E4
Fada-n-Gourma *Burkina Faso* 12°10N 0°30E 263 C5
Fadd *Hungary* 46°28N 18°49E 182 D3
Faddeyevskiy, Ostrov *Russia* 76°0N 144°0E 215 B15
Faddor *Sudan* 8°7N 32°17E 257 F3
Fadghāmī *Syria* 35°53N 40°52E 213 E9
Fadhiffolu Atoll *Maldives* 5°23N 73°29E 272 d
Fadlab *Sudan* 17°42N 34°2E 256 D3
Fadwel *Sudan* 8°11N 29°20E 266 C2
Fælledparken *Denmark* 55°42N 12°34E 118 A3
Faenza *Italy* 44°17N 11°53E 199 D8
Færingehavn = Kangerluarsoruseq *Greenland* 63°45N 51°27W 154 E5
Færoe Is. = Føroyar ☑ *Atl. Oc.* 62°0N 7°0W 160 F9
Fafa *Mali* 15°22N 0°48E 263 B5
Fafe *Portugal* 41°27N 8°11W 194 D2
Fafen ➔ *Ethiopia* 5°59N 44°25E 267 C5
Fagam *Nigeria* 11°1N 10°1E 263 C7
Fagamalo *Amer. Samoa* 14°18S 170°48W 302 f
Făgăraş *Romania* 45°48N 24°58E 183 E9
Făgăraş, Munţii *Romania* 45°40N 24°40E 183 E9
Fagasa *Amer. Samoa* 14°17S 170°43W 302 f
Fagatogo *Amer. Samoa* 14°16S 170°41W 302 f
Fågelfors *Sweden* 57°12N 15°51E 163 H9
Fågelmara *Sweden* 56°16N 15°58E 163 H9
Fågelön *Sweden* 59°18N 17°55E 139 B1
Fagerheim *Norway* 60°26N 7°46E 164 D4
Fagerhult *Sweden* 57°8N 15°40E 163 G9
Fagernes *Norway* 60°59N 9°14E 164 D6
Fagersjö *Sweden* 59°14N 18°4E 139 B2
Fagersta *Sweden* 60°1N 15°46E 162 D9
Faget *Romania* 45°52N 22°10E 182 E7
Făget, Munţii *Romania* 47°40N 23°10E 183 C8
Faggo *Nigeria* 11°21N 9°57E 263 C6
Fagnano, L. *Argentina* 54°30S 68°0W 336 D3
Fagnières *France* 48°58N 4°20E 173 D11
Faguibine, L. *Mali* 16°45N 4°0W 262 B4
Fahlīān *Iran* 30°11N 51°28E 247 D6
Fahraj *Kermān, Iran* 29°0N 59°0E 247 D8
Fahraj *Yazd, Iran* 31°46N 54°36E 247 D7
Fai Tsi Long *Vietnam* 21°0N 107°30E 228 G6
Faial *Azores* 38°34N 28°42W 153 d1
Faial *Madeira* 32°47N 16°53W 153 c
Faial, Canal do *Azores* 38°33N 28°35W 153 d1
Faichan Kangri *India* 35°48N 76°34E 243 B7
Faichuk *Micronesia* 7°21N 151°38E 287 T17
Fair Haven *N.Y., U.S.A.* 43°18N 76°42W 313 C8
Fair Haven *Vt., U.S.A.* 43°36N 73°16W 309 D17
Fair Hd. *U.K.* 55°14N 6°9W 166 A5
Fair Isle *U.K.* 59°32N 1°38W 165 B6
Fair Oaks *U.S.A.* 38°39N 121°16W 306 G5
Fairbank *U.S.A.* 42°38N 92°3W 310 B4
Fairbanks *Alaska, U.S.A.* 64°51N 147°43W 303 D11
Fairbanks *Fla., U.S.A.* 29°44N 82°16W 316 F7
Fairborn *U.S.A.* 39°49N 84°2W 311 E12
Fairburn *U.S.A.* 33°34N 84°35W 316 B5
Fairbury *Ill., U.S.A.* 40°45N 88°31W 311 D8
Fairbury *Nebr., U.S.A.* 40°8N 97°11W 308 E5
Fairfax *Ohio, U.S.A.* 39°5N 83°37W 311 E13
Fairfax *S.C., U.S.A.* 32°59N 81°15W 316 C8
Fairfax *Va., U.S.A.* 38°50N 77°19W 143 B2
Fairfax *Vt., U.S.A.* 44°40N 73°1W 313 B11
Fairfax Station *U.S.A.* 38°48N 77°19W 143 C2
Fairfield *N.S.W., Australia* 33°53S 150°57E 283 B9
Fairfield *Ala., U.S.A.* 33°29N 86°55W 315 E11
Fairfield *Calif., U.S.A.* 38°15N 122°3W 306 G4
Fairfield *Conn., U.S.A.* 41°9N 73°16W 313 E11
Fairfield *Idaho, U.S.A.* 43°21N 114°44W 304 E6
Fairfield *Ill., U.S.A.* 38°23N 88°22W 311 F8
Fairfield *Iowa, U.S.A.* 40°56N 91°57W 310 D5
Fairfield *Ohio, U.S.A.* 39°20N 84°34W 311 E12
Fairfield *Tex., U.S.A.* 31°44N 96°10W 314 F6
Fairford *Canada* 51°37N 98°38W 297 C9
Fairhope *U.S.A.* 30°31N 87°54W 315 F11
Fairland *S. Africa* 26°8S 27°57E 123 A1
Fairlie *N.Z.* 44°5S 170°49E 285 E5
Fairmead *U.S.A.* 37°5N 120°10W 306 H6
Fairmilehead *U.K.* 55°54N 3°11W 121 B2
Fairmont *Minn., U.S.A.* 43°39N 94°28W 308 D6
Fairmont *W. Va., U.S.A.* 39°29N 80°9W 309 F13
Fairmount *Calif., U.S.A.* 34°45N 118°26W 307 L8
Fairmount *N.Y., U.S.A.* 43°5N 76°12W 313 C8
Fairmount Heights *U.S.A.* 38°54N 76°54W 143 B4
Fairplay *U.S.A.* 39°15N 106°2W 304 G10
Fairport *Ont., Canada* 43°49N 79°4W 141 A4
Fairport *N.Y., U.S.A.* 43°6N 77°27W 312 C7
Fairport Harbor *U.S.A.* 41°45N 81°17W 312 E3
Fairview *Alta., Canada* 56°5N 118°25W 296 B5
Fairview *Mont., U.S.A.* 47°51N 104°3W 304 C11
Fairview *N.J., U.S.A.* 40°48N 73°59W 132 B2
Fairview *Okla., U.S.A.* 36°16N 98°29W 314 C5
Fairview, L. *U.S.A.* 28°35N 81°24W 133 A2
Fairweather, Mt. *U.S.A.* 58°55N 137°32W 296 B1
Faisalabad *Pakistan* 31°30N 73°5E 242 D5
Faith *U.S.A.* 45°2N 102°2W 308 C2
Faizabad *India* 26°45N 82°10E 243 F10
Faizpur *India* 21°14N 75°49E 244 D2
Fajã Grande *Azores* 39°27N 31°16W 153 d2
Fajardo *Puerto Rico* 18°20N 65°39W 321 C6
Fajou, Îlet à *Guadeloupe* 16°21N 61°35W 322 e
Fajr, W. ➔ *Si. Arabia* 29°10N 38°10E 246 D3
Fakaofo *Pac. Oc.* 9°23S 171°15W 277 B16
Fakarava *French Polynesia* 16°20S 145°37W 289 f
Fakenham *U.K.* 52°51N 0°51E 168 E8
Fåker *Sweden* 63°0N 14°34E 162 A8
Fakfak *Indonesia* 2°55S 132°18E 231 E8
Fakiya *Bulgaria* 42°10N 27°6E 203 D11
Fakobli *Ivory C.* 7°23N 7°23W 262 D3
Fakse *Denmark* 55°15N 12°8E 163 J6
Fakse Bugt *Denmark* 55°11N 12°15E 163 J6
Fakse Ladeplads *Denmark* 55°11N 12°9E 163 J6
Faku *China* 42°32N 123°21E 224 A1
Fala Beguets I. *Micronesia* 7°21N 151°41E 287 U17
Falaba *S. Leone* 9°54N 11°22W 262 D2
Falaise *France* 48°54N 0°12W 172 D6
Falakro Oros *Greece* 41°15N 23°58E 202 E7
Falam *Burma* 23°0N 93°45E 241 D4
Falas I. *Micronesia* 7°31N 151°44E 287 T18
Falces *Spain* 42°24N 1°48W 196 C3
Fălciu *Romania* 46°17N 28°7E 183 D13
Falcó, C. des *Spain* 38°50N 1°23E 206 D1
Falcón □ *Venezuela* 11°0N 69°50W 328 A4
Falcon, C. *Algeria* 35°50N 0°50W 261 A4
Falcón, Presa *Mexico* 26°35N 99°10W 319 B5
Falcon Lake *Canada* 49°42N 95°15W 297 D9
Falcon Res. *U.S.A.* 26°34N 99°10W 314 H5
Falconara Marittima *Italy* 43°37N 13°24E 199 E10
Falcone, C. del *Italy* 40°58N 8°12E 200 B1
Falconer *U.S.A.* 42°7N 79°12W 312 D5
Faléa *Mali* 12°16N 11°17W 262 C2
Falefa *Samoa* 13°54S 171°31W 287 V20
Falelatai *Samoa* 13°55S 171°59W 287 V20
Falelima *Samoa* 13°32S 172°41W 287 V19
Falémé ➔ *Senegal* 14°46N 12°14W 262 C2
Faleniu *Amer. Samoa* 14°19S 170°44W 302 f
Falenty *Poland* 52°8N 20°55E 142 C1
Falerum *Sweden* 58°8N 16°13E 163 F10
Faleshty = Făleşti *Moldova* 47°32N 27°44E 183 C12
Făleşti *Moldova* 47°32N 27°44E 183 C12
Falfurrias *U.S.A.* 27°14N 98°9W 314 H5
Falher *Canada* 55°44N 117°15W 296 B5
Faliraki *Greece* 36°22N 28°12E 206 E12
Faliro *Greece* 37°55N 23°39E 141 B2
Faliro, Ormos *Greece* 37°54N 23°40E 141 B2
Falkenberg *Brandenburg, Germany* 51°35N 13°14E 178 D9
Falkenberg *Sweden* 56°54N 12°30E 163 H6
Falkenburg = Niemodlin *Poland* 50°38N 17°38E 185 H4
Falkenburg *Germany* 52°34N 13°32E 115 A4
Falkenhagen *Germany* 52°34N 13°5E 115 A1
Falkensee *Germany* 52°34N 13°4E 178 C9
Falkirk *U.K.* 56°0N 3°47W 167 F5
Falkirk □ *U.K.* 55°58N 3°49W 167 F5
Falkland *U.K.* 56°16N 3°12W 167 E5
Falkland, East, I. *Falk. Is.* 51°40S 58°30W 336 D5
Falkland, West, I. *Falk. Is.* 51°40S 60°0W 336 D4
Falkland Is. ☑ *Atl. Oc.* 51°30S 59°0W 153 f
Falkland Plateau *Atl. Oc.* 51°0S 50°0W 152 M7
Falkland Ridge *Atl. Oc.* 49°20S 40°0W 152 L8
Falkland Sd. *Falk. Is.* 52°0S 60°0W 153 f
Falknov nad Ohří = Sokolov *Czech Rep.* 50°12N 12°40E 180 A5
Falkonera *Greece* 36°50N 23°52E 204 E5
Falköping *Sweden* 58°12N 13°33E 163 F7
Fall River *U.S.A.* 41°43N 71°10W 313 E13
Fallbrook *U.S.A.* 33°23N 117°15W 307 M9
Fallon *U.S.A.* 39°28N 118°47W 304 G4
Falls Church *U.S.A.* 38°53N 77°12W 143 B2
Falls City *U.S.A.* 40°3N 95°36W 308 E6
Falls Creek *U.S.A.* 41°9N 78°48W 312 E6
Falmouth *Jamaica* 18°30N 77°40W 320 a
Falmouth *Corn., U.K.* 50°9N 5°5W 169 G2
Falmouth *Ky., U.S.A.* 38°41N 84°20W 311 F12
Falmouth *Mass., U.S.A.* 41°33N 70°37W 313 E14
Falo I. *Micronesia* 7°28N 151°52E 287 T18
Falomo *Nigeria* 6°26N 3°26E 124 B2
Falsa, Pta. *Mexico* 27°51N 115°3W 318 B1
False B. *S. Africa* 34°15S 18°40E 270 D2
False Bay *S. Africa* 34°6S 18°33E 118 B2
False Divi Pt. *India* 15°43N 80°50E 245 G5
False Pass *U.S.A.* 54°51N 163°25W 303 J7
False Pt. *India* 20°18N 86°48E 244 D8
Falso, C. *Honduras* 15°12N 83°21W 320 C3
Falster *Denmark* 54°45N 11°55E 163 K5
Fălticeni *Romania* 47°21N 26°20E 183 C11
Falun *Sweden* 60°37N 15°37E 162 D9
Famagusta *Cyprus* 35°8N 33°55E 207 E9
Famagusta Bay *Cyprus* 35°15N 34°0E 207 E10
Famatina, Sierra de *Argentina* 27°30S 68°0W 334 B2
Famenin *Iran* 35°5N 48°58E 213 E13
Family L. *Canada* 51°54N 95°27W 297 C9
Famoso *U.S.A.* 35°37N 119°12W 307 K7
Fan Xian *China* 35°55N 115°38E 226 G8
Fana *Mali* 13°0N 6°56W 262 C3
Fanad Hd. *Ireland* 55°17N 7°38W 166 A4
Fanahammaren *Norway* 60°16N 5°20E 164 D2
Fanari *Greece* 39°24N 21°47E 204 B3
Fandriana *Madag.* 20°14S 47°21E 272 C2
Faneuil Hall Marketplace *Boston, U.S.A.* 116 b3
Fânes-Sènnes e Braies ⌂ *Italy* 46°38N 12°4E 199 B9
Fang *Thailand* 19°55N 99°13E 236 C2
Fang Xian *China* 32°3N 110°40E 229 A8
Fangaga *Sudan* 17°40N 37°50E 256 D4
Fangak *Sudan* 9°4N 30°53E 257 F3
Fangatau *French Polynesia* 15°22S 138°45W 289 f
Fangataufa *French Polynesia* 15°50S 140°52W 289 f
Fangchang *China* 31°5N 118°4E 229 B12
Fangcheng *China* 33°18N 112°59E 226 H7
Fangchenggang *China* 21°42N 108°21E 228 G7
Fangcun *China* 23°6N 113°13E 121 B2
Fangliao *Taiwan* 22°22N 120°38E 225 D2
Fangshan *Beijing, China* 39°41N 116°0E 226 E9
Fangshan *Shanxi, China* 38°3N 111°25E 226 E6
Fangshan *Taiwan* 22°15N 120°39E 225 D2
Fangyüan *Taiwan* 23°56N 120°19E 225 C2
Fangzi *China* 36°33N 119°10E 227 F10
Fani i Madh ➔ *Albania* 41°56N 20°16E 202 E4
Fanjakana *Madag.* 21°10S 46°53E 272 C2
Fanjiatun *China* 43°40N 125°15E 227 C13
Fanling *China* 22°30N 114°8E 219 a
Fannich, L. *U.K.* 57°38N 4°59W 167 D4
Fannrem *Norway* 63°16N 9°50E 164 A6
Fannūj *Iran* 26°35N 59°38E 247 E8
Fanø *Denmark* 55°25N 8°25E 163 J2
Fano *Italy* 43°50N 13°1E 199 E10
Fanshi *China* 39°12N 113°20E 226 E7
Fantzuliao Hsi ➔ *Taiwan* 22°42N 120°28E 225 D2
Fanuet I. *Micronesia* 7°32N 151°48E 287 T18
Fao = Al Fāw *Iraq* 30°0N 48°30E 247 D6
Faqirwali *Pakistan* 29°27N 73°0E 242 E5
Fâqûs *Egypt* 30°44N 31°47E 256 H7
Far East = Dalnevostochnyy □ *Russia* 67°0N 140°0E 215 C14
Far East *Asia* 40°0N 130°0E 210 E14
Fara in Sabina *Italy* 42°12N 12°43E 199 F9
Faradje *Dem. Rep. of the Congo* 3°50N 29°45E 268 B2
Farafangana *Madag.* 22°49S 47°50E 272 C2
Farafenni *Gambia* 13°34N 15°36W 262 C1
Farâfra, El Wâhât el *Egypt* 27°15N 28°20E 256 B2
Farāh *Afghan.* 32°20N 62°7E 240 B1
Farāh □ *Afghan.* 32°25N 62°10E 240 B1
Farāh ➔ *Afghan.* 31°27N 61°28E 240 C1
Farahabad *Iran* 35°41N 51°30E 141 A2
Farahalana *Madag.* 14°26S 50°10E 272 A3
Faraid, Gebel *Egypt* 23°33N 35°19E 256 C4
Farako *Ivory C.* 10°45N 6°50W 262 D4
Farallon de Medinilla *N. Marianas* 16°1N 146°4E 302 a
Farallon de Pajaros *N. Marianas* 20°32N 144°54E 302 a
Farallones de Cali △ *Colombia* 3°13N 76°46W 328 C2
Faramana *Burkina Faso* 11°56N 4°45W 262 C4
Faranah *Guinea* 10°3N 10°45W 262 C2
Farap *Turkmenistan* 39°9N 63°36E 216 E6
Fararah *Oman* 17°55N 55°38E 249 C6
Farasān, Jazā'ir *Si. Arabia* 16°45N 41°55E 248 C3
Farasan Is. = Farasān, Jazā'ir *Si. Arabia* 16°45N 41°55E 248 C3
Faratsiho *Madag.* 19°24S 46°57E 272 B2
Farbaraki *Somali Rep.* 2°30N 45°30E 267 D6
Fardes ➔ *Spain* 37°35N 3°0W 195 H7
Fareham *U.K.* 50°51N 1°11W 169 G6
Farewell *U.S.A.* 62°31N 153°54W 303 E9
Farewell, C. *N.Z.* 40°29S 172°43E 285 A7
Farewell C. = Nunap Isua *Greenland* 59°48N 43°55W 154 F6
Farewell Spit *N.Z.* 40°35S 173°0E 285 A8
Farforovskaya *Russia* 59°52N 30°27E 137 B2
Färgelanda *Sweden* 58°34N 12°0E 163 F5
Farghona *Uzbekistan* 40°23N 71°19E 217 D8
Farghona □ *Uzbekistan* 40°23N 71°19E 217 D8
Farghona Vodiysi *Asia* 40°46N 71°30E 217 D8
Fargo *Ga., U.S.A.* 30°41N 82°34W 316 E7
Fargo *N. Dak., U.S.A.* 46°53N 96°48W 308 B5
Fār'iah, W. al ➔ *West Bank* 32°12N 35°27E 251 F6
Faribault *U.S.A.* 44°18N 93°16W 308 C7
Faridabad *India* 28°26N 77°19E 242 E6
Faridkot *India* 30°44N 74°45E 242 D6
Faridpur *Bangla.* 23°15N 89°55E 241 D2
Faridpur *India* 28°13N 79°33E 243 E8
Färigh, W. al ➔ *Libya* 30°28N 20°44E 258 B3
Färila *Sweden* 61°48N 15°50E 162 C9
Farim *Guinea-Biss.* 12°27N 15°9W 262 C1
Farīmān *Iran* 35°40N 59°49E 247 C8
Farinha ➔ *Brazil* 6°51S 47°30W 332 C2
Fariones, Pta. *Canary Is.* 29°13N 13°28W 153 e2
Fâriskûr *Egypt* 31°20N 31°43E 256 H7
Färjestaden *Sweden* 56°39N 16°27E 163 H10
Farkadona *Greece* 39°36N 22°4E 204 B4
Farleigh *Australia* 21°4S 149°8E 280 b
Farley *U.S.A.* 42°27N 91°0W 310 B5
Farmakonisi *Greece* 37°17N 27°5E 205 D9
Farmer City *U.S.A.* 40°15N 88°39W 311 D8
Farmersburg *U.S.A.* 39°15N 87°23W 311 E9
Farmerville *U.S.A.* 32°47N 92°24W 314 E8
Farmingdale *U.S.A.* 40°12N 74°10W 313 F10
Farmington *B.C., Canada* 55°54N 120°30W 296 B4
Farmington *Calif., U.S.A.* 37°55N 120°59W 306 H6
Farmington *Ga., U.S.A.* 33°47N 83°26W 316 B6
Farmington *Ill., U.S.A.* 40°42N 90°0W 310 D7
Farmington *Iowa, U.S.A.* 40°38N 91°44W 310 D5
Farmington *Maine, U.S.A.* 44°40N 70°9W 309 C18
Farmington *Mo., U.S.A.* 37°47N 90°25W 310 G6
Farmington *N.H., U.S.A.* 43°24N 71°4W 313 C13
Farmington *N. Mex., U.S.A.* 36°44N 108°12W 305 H9
Farmington *Utah, U.S.A.* 40°59N 111°53W 304 F8
Farmington ➔ *U.S.A.* 41°51N 72°38W 313 E12
Farmland *U.S.A.* 40°15N 85°5W 311 D11
Farmville *U.S.A.* 37°18N 78°24W 309 G14
Färnäs *Sweden* 61°0N 14°39E 162 D8
Farne Is. *U.K.* 55°38N 1°37W 168 B6
Färnebofjärden △ *Sweden* 60°10N 16°48E 162 D10
Farnham *Canada* 45°17N 72°59W 313 A12
Farnham, Mt. *Canada* 50°29N 116°30W 296 C5
Farningham *U.K.* 51°23N 0°12E 125 B5
Faro *Brazil* 2°10S 56°39W 329 D6
Faro *Yukon, Canada* 62°11N 133°22W 294 E5
Faro *Portugal* 37°2N 7°55W 195 H3
Fårö *Gotland, Sweden* 57°55N 19°5E 163 G13
Faro □ *Portugal* 37°12N 8°10W 195 H2
Faro ✕ (FAO) *Portugal* 37°2N 7°57W 195 H3
Faro ⌂ *Cameroon* 8°15N 12°37E 264 A2
Fårösund *Sweden* 57°52N 19°2E 163 G13
Farquhar, C. *Australia* 23°50S 113°36E 279 D1
Farquhar Is. *Seychelles* 11°0S 52°0E 273 F4
Farrars Cr. ➔ *Australia* 25°35S 140°43E 280 D3
Farrāshband *Iran* 28°57N 52°5E 247 D7
Farrell *U.S.A.* 41°13N 80°30W 312 E4
Farrell Flat *Australia* 33°48S 138°48E 282 B3
Farrokhī *Iran* 33°50N 59°31E 247 C8
Farruch, C. = Ferrutx, C. de *Spain* 39°47N 3°21E 206 B4
Farrukhabad *India* 27°24N 79°34E 244 A4
Fārs □ *Iran* 29°30N 55°0E 247 D7
Farsala *Greece* 39°17N 22°23E 204 B4
Farsī *Afghan.* 33°47N 63°15E 240 B1
Fārsī *Iran* 27°58N 50°11E 247 E6
Farsø *Denmark* 56°46N 9°19E 163 H3
Farson *U.S.A.* 42°7N 109°26W 304 E9
Farsta *Sweden* 59°14N 18°5E 139 B2
Farsund *Norway* 58°5N 6°55E 164 F3
Fartak, Râs *Si. Arabia* 28°5N 34°34E 246 D2
Fartak, Ra's *Yemen* 15°38N 52°15E 249 D6
Fârţăneşti *Romania* 45°49N 27°59E 183 E12
Fartura, Serra da *Brazil* 26°21S 52°52W 335 B5
Faru *Nigeria* 12°48N 6°12E 263 C6
Fārūj *Iran* 37°14N 58°14E 247 B8
Fårup *Denmark* 56°33N 9°51E 163 H3
Farvel, Kap = Nunap Isua *Greenland* 59°48N 43°55W 154 F6
Farwell *U.S.A.* 34°23N 103°2W 314 D3
Fāryāb □ *Afghan.* 36°0N 65°0E 240 B2
Fasā *Iran* 29°0N 53°39E 247 D7
Fasanerie-Nord *Germany* 48°11N 11°32E 131 A2
Fasangarten *Germany* 48°5N 11°36E 131 B2
Fasano *Italy* 40°50N 17°22E 201 B10
Fashoda *Sudan* 9°50N 32°2E 257 F3
Fasil Ghebbi *Ethiopia* 12°36N 37°28E 266 B4
Fáskrúðsfjörður *Iceland* 64°56N 14°1W 155 C12
Fassa *Mali* 13°26N 8°15W 262 C3
Fastiv *Ukraine* 50°7N 29°57E 177 C15
Fastnet Rock *Ireland* 51°22N 9°37W 166 E2
Fastov = Fastiv *Ukraine* 50°7N 29°57E 177 C15
Fatagar, Tanjung *Indonesia* 2°46S 131°57E 231 E8
Fataka *Solomon Is.* 11°55S 170°12E 277 C12
Fatatsu Ne Iwo Jima 24°45N 141°18E 288 b
Fatehabad *Haryana, India* 29°31N 75°27E 242 E6
Fatehabad *Ut. P., India* 27°1N 78°19E 242 F8
Fatehgarh *India* 27°25N 79°35E 243 F8
Fatehpur *Bihar, India* 24°38N 85°14E 243 G11
Fatehpur *Raj., India* 28°0N 74°40E 242 F6
Fatehpur *Ut. P., India* 25°56N 81°13E 243 G9
Fatehpur *Ut. P., India* 27°10N 81°13E 243 F9
Fatehpur Sikri *India* 27°6N 77°40E 242 F6
Fatesh *Russia* 52°8N 35°57E 189 F8
Fathai *Sudan* 8°5N 31°48E 257 F3
Fathom Five ⌂ *Canada* 45°17N 81°40W 312 A3
Fatick *Senegal* 14°19N 16°27W 262 C1
Fatick □ *Senegal* 14°15N 16°30W 262 C1
Fatih *Turkey* 41°0N 28°56E 122 B1
Fatima *Qué., Canada* 47°24N 61°53W 299 C7
Fátima *Portugal* 39°37N 8°39W 195 F2
Fatoya *Guinea* 11°37N 9°10W 262 C3
Fatsa *Turkey* 41°2N 37°31E 212 B7
Fatshan = Foshan *China* 23°6N 113°9E 121 B2
Faucille, Col de la *France* 46°22N 6°2E 173 F13
Faulkton *U.S.A.* 45°2N 99°8W 308 C4
Faulquemont *France* 49°3N 6°36E 173 C13
Faure I. *Australia* 25°52S 113°50E 279 E1
Fauresmith *S. Africa* 29°44S 25°17E 270 C4
Făurei *Romania* 45°6N 27°19E 183 E12
Fauro *Solomon Is.* 6°55S 156°7E 287 L9
Fauske *Norway* 67°17N 15°25E 160 C16
Fåvang *Norway* 61°27N 10°11E 164 C7
Favânia *Brazil* 3°7S 51°49W 329 D7
Favara *Italy* 37°19N 13°39E 200 E6
Favàritx, C. de *Spain* 40°0N 4°15E 206 B5
Faverges *France* 45°45N 6°17E 175 C10
Favignana *Italy* 37°56N 12°20E 200 E5
Favignana, I. *Italy* 37°56N 12°19E 200 E5
Favoriten *Austria* 48°9N 16°23E 142 B2
Fawcett, Pt. *Australia* 11°46S 130°2E 278 B5
Fawkner *Australia* 37°42S 144°58E 128 A1
Fawkner Park *Australia* 37°50S 144°58E 128 B1
Fawn ➔ *Canada* 55°20N 87°35W 298 A2
Fawnskin *U.S.A.* 34°16N 116°56W 307 L10
Faxaflói *Iceland* 64°29N 23°0W 155 C3
Faxälven ➔ *Sweden* 63°13N 17°13E 162 A10
Faya-Largeau *Chad* 17°58N 19°6E 259 E3
Fayaoué *N. Cal.* 20°38S 166°33E 288 d
Fayd *Si. Arabia* 27°1N 42°52E 246 E4
Fayence *France* 43°38N 6°42E 175 E10
Fayette *Ala., U.S.A.* 33°41N 87°50W 315 E11
Fayette *Iowa, U.S.A.* 42°51N 91°48W 310 B5
Fayette *Mo., U.S.A.* 39°9N 92°41W 310 E4
Fayette *N.Y., U.S.A.* 42°48N 76°48W 313 D8
Fayette *Ohio, U.S.A.* 41°40N 84°20W 311 C12
Fayetteville *Ark., U.S.A.* 36°4N 94°10W 314 C7
Fayetteville *Ga., U.S.A.* 33°27N 84°27W 316 B5
Fayetteville *N.C., U.S.A.* 35°3N 78°53W 315 D15
Fayetteville *N.Y., U.S.A.* 43°1N 76°0W 313 C9
Fayetteville *Tenn., U.S.A.* 35°9N 86°34W 315 D11
Fayied *Egypt* 30°18N 32°16E 256 H8
Faylakah *Kuwait* 29°27N 48°20E 247 D6
Fayón *Spain* 41°15N 0°20E 196 D5
Fazao-Malfakassa △ *Togo* 8°45N 0°50E 263 D5
Fazenda Libongo *Angola* 8°23S 13°24E 265 D2
Fazenda Nova *Brazil* 16°11S 50°48W 333 E1
Fazilka *India* 30°27N 74°2E 242 D6
Fazilpur *Pakistan* 29°18N 70°29E 242 E4
Fdérik *Mauritania* 22°40N 12°45W 260 D2
Feakle *Ireland* 52°56N 8°40W 166 D3
Feale ➔ *Ireland* 52°27N 9°37W 166 D2
Fear, C. *U.S.A.* 33°50N 77°58W 315 E16
Feather ➔ *U.S.A.* 38°47N 121°36W 304 G3
Feather Falls *U.S.A.* 39°36N 121°16W 306 F5
Featherston *N.Z.* 41°6S 175°20E 284 H4
Featherstone *Zimbabwe* 18°42S 30°55E 269 F3
Fécamp *France* 49°45N 0°22E 172 C7
Feda *Norway* 58°17N 6°50E 164 F3
Fedala = Mohammedia *Morocco* 33°44N 7°21W 260 B3
Federación *Argentina* 31°0S 57°55W 334 C4
Federal Capital Terr. □ *Nigeria* 9°0N 7°10E 263 D6
Federal Way *U.S.A.* 47°18N 122°19W 306 C4
Fedeshküh *Iran* 28°49N 53°50E 247 D7
FedEx Stadium *U.S.A.* 38°54N 76°51W 143 B4
Fedje *Norway* 60°47N 4°43E 164 D1
Fedorovka *Kazakhstan* 53°37N 62°42E 216 B6

Fefan I. *Pac. Oc.* 7°21N 151°51E **287** T18
Fehérgyarmat *Hungary* 47°58N 22°30E **182** C7
Fehmarn *Germany* 54°27N 11°7E **178** A7
Fehmarn Belt *Europe* 54°35N 11°20E **163** K5
Fehmarn Belt = Fehmarn Bælt *Europe* 54°35N 11°20E **163** K5
Fei Xian *China* 35°18N 117°59E **227** G9
Feicheng *China* 36°14N 116°45E **226** F9
Feidong *China* 32°0N 117°35E **229** B11
Feijó *Brazil* 8°9S 70°21W **330** B3
Feilding *N.Z.* 40°13S 175°35E **284** G4
Feira de Santana *Brazil* 12°15S 38°57W **333** D4
Feirân, W. → *Egypt* 28°39N 33°12E **251** K4
Feirâni, G. *Egypt* 28°31N 34°19E **251** K5
Feiring *Norway* 60°30N 11°10E **164** D8
Feixi *China* 31°43N 117°59E **229** B11
Feixiang *China* 36°30N 114°45E **226** F8
Fejaj, Chott el *Tunisia* 33°52N 9°14E **258** B1
Fejér □ *Hungary* 47°9N 18°30E **182** C3
Fejø *Denmark* 54°55N 11°30E **163** K5
Feke *Turkey* 37°48N 35°56E **212** D6
Fekete → *Hungary* 45°47N 18°15E **182** E3
Felanitx *Spain* 39°28N 3°9E **206** B4
Felda *U.S.A.* 26°34N 81°26W **317** J8
Feldbach *Austria* 46°57N 15°52E **180** E8
Feldberg *Baden-W., Germany* 47°52N 8°0E **179** H3
Feldberg *Mecklenburg-Vorpommern, Germany* 53°20N 13°25E **178** B9
Feldkirch *Austria* 47°15N 9°37E **180** D2
Feldkirchen *Austria* 46°44N 14°6E **180** E7
Feldkirchen *Oberbayern, Germany* 48°8N 11°43E **131** B3
Feldmoching *Germany* 48°14N 11°32E **131** A2
Félicité *Seychelles* 4°19S 55°52E **272** c
Felicity *U.S.A.* 38°51N 84°6W **311** F12
Felidhoo *Maldives* 3°29N 73°32E **272** d
Felidu Atoll *Maldives* 3°29N 73°29E **272** d
Felipe Carrillo Puerto *Mexico* 19°38N 88°3W **319** D7
Felixburg *Zimbabwe* 19°29S 30°51E **271** A5
Felixlândia *Brazil* 18°47S 44°55W **333** E3
Felixstowe *U.K.* 51°58N 1°23E **169** F9
Felletin *France* 45°53N 2°11E **174** C6
Fellingsbro *Sweden* 59°26N 15°37E **162** E9
Fellsmere *U.S.A.* 27°46N 80°36W **317** H9
Felshtin = Gvardeyskoye *Ukraine* 45°7N 34°1E **189** K8
Felsőgalla = Tatabánya *Hungary* 47°32N 18°25E **182** C3
Feltham *U.K.* 51°26N 0°24W **125** B1
Felton *U.S.A.* 37°3N 122°4W **306** H4
Feltre *Italy* 46°1N 11°54E **199** B8
Femer Bælt = Fehmarn Bælt *Europe* 54°35N 11°20E **163** K5
Femø *Denmark* 54°58N 11°35E **163** K5
Femunden *Norway* 62°10N 11°53E **164** B8
Femundsmarka △ *Norway* 62°18N 12°6E **164** B9
Fen He → *China* 35°36N 110°42E **226** G6
Fenchih *Taiwan* 23°30N 120°40E **225** C2
Fene *Spain* 43°27N 8°9W **194** B2
Fenelon Falls *Canada* 44°32N 78°45W **312** B6
Fener Burnu *Turkey* 41°1N 28°56E **122** C1
Fener Burnu *Turkey* 36°58N 27°18E **205** E9
Fenerbahçe *Turkey* 40°58N 29°2E **122** C2
Feneroa *Ethiopia* 13°5N 39°3E **257** E4
Feng Xian *Jiangsu, China* 34°43N 116°35E **226** G9
Feng Xian *Shaanxi, China* 33°54N 106°40E **226** H4
Fengari *Greece* 40°25N 25°32E **203** F9
Fengcheng *Jiangxi, China* 28°12N 115°48E **229** C10
Fengcheng *Liaoning, China* 40°28N 124°5E **224** B2
Fengdu *China* 29°55N 107°48E **228** C6
Fengfeng *China* 36°28N 114°8E **226** F8
Fenggang *China* 27°57N 107°47E **228** D6
Fenghua *China* 29°40N 121°25E **229** C13
Fenghuang *China* 27°57N 109°29E **228** D7
Fengjie *China* 31°3N 109°31E **228** B7
Fengkai *China* 23°24N 111°30E **229** F8
Fengkang *Taiwan* 22°12N 120°41E **225** D2
Fengle *China* 31°29N 112°29E **229** B9
Fenglin *Taiwan* 23°45N 121°26E **225** C3
Fengning *China* 41°10N 116°33E **226** D9
Fengpin *Taiwan* 23°36N 121°31E **225** C3
Fengqing *China* 24°38N 99°55E **228** E2
Fengqiu *China* 35°2N 114°25E **226** G8
Fengrun *China* 39°48N 118°8E **227** E10
Fengshan *Guangxi Zhuangzu, China* 24°39N 109°15E **228** E7
Fengshan *Guangxi Zhuangzu, China* 24°31N 107°3E **228** E6
Fengshan *Taiwan* 22°38N 120°21E **225** D2
Fengshun *China* 23°46N 116°10E **229** F11
Fengtai *Anhui, China* 32°50N 116°40E **229** A11
Fengtai *Beijing, China* 39°49N 116°14E **226** C1
Fengtai Stadium *China* 39°51N 116°15E **114** B1
Fengtongzhai △ *China* 30°32N 102°54E **228** B4
Fengxiang *China* 34°29N 107°25E **226** G4
Fengxin *China* 28°41N 115°18E **229** C10
Fengyang *China* 32°51N 117°29E **227** H9
Fengyi *China* 25°37N 100°20E **228** E3
Fengyüan *Taiwan* 24°15N 120°35E **225** B2
Fengzhen *China* 40°25N 113°2E **226** D7
Feni Is. *Papua N. G.* 4°0S 153°40E **286** C7
Fenino *Russia* 55°43N 37°56E **129** B5
Fennimore *U.S.A.* 42°59N 90°39W **310** B6
Fenny *Bangla.* 22°55N 91°32E **241** D3
Feno, C. de *France* 41°58N 8°33E **175** G12
Fenoarivo *Fianarantsoa, Madag.* 21°43S 46°24E **272** C2
Fenoarivo *Fianarantsoa, Madag.* 20°52S 46°53E **272** C2
Fenoarivo Afovoany *Madag.* 18°26S 46°34E **272** B2
Fenoarivo Atsinanana *Madag.* 17°22S 49°25E **272** B2
Fens, The *U.K.* 52°38N 0°2W **168** E7
Fensmark *Denmark* 55°17N 11°48E **163** J5
Fenton *U.S.A.* 42°48N 83°42W **311** B13
Fenxi *China* 36°40N 111°31E **226** F6
Fenyang *China* 37°18N 111°48E **226** F6
Fenyi *China* 27°45N 114°47E **229** D10
Fenyuan *Taiwan* 24°1N 120°37E **225** B2
Feodosiya *Ukraine* 45°2N 35°16E **189** K8
Fer, C. de *Algeria* 37°3N 7°10E **261** A6
Fera *Solomon Is.* 8°6S 159°37E **287** M10
Ferbane *Ireland* 53°16N 7°50W **166** C4
Ferdows *Iran* 33°58N 58°2E **247** C8
Fère-Champenoise *France* 48°45N 3°59E **173** D10
Fère-en-Tardenois *France* 49°10N 3°30E **173** C10
Ferencváros *Hungary* 47°29N 19°5E **117** B2
Ferentino *Italy* 41°42N 13°15E **199** G10
Feres *Greece* 40°53N 26°10E **203** F10
Ferfer *Somali Rep.* 5°4N 45°9E **267** C6
Fergana = Farghona *Uzbekistan* 40°23N 71°19E **217** D8
Fergana Range *Asia* 41°0N 73°50E **217** D8
Fergus *Canada* 43°43N 80°24W **312** C4
Fergus Falls *U.S.A.* 46°17N 96°4W **308** B5
Ferguson *U.S.A.* 38°44N 90°18W **310** F6
Fergusson I. *Papua N. G.* 9°30S 150°45E **286** E6
Fériana *Tunisia* 34°59N 8°33E **258** B1
Feričanci *Croatia* 45°32N 18°0E **182** E2
Ferihegy, Budapest ✕ (BUD) *Hungary* 47°26N 19°14E **117** B3
Ferizaj = Uroševac *Kosovo* 42°23N 21°10E **202** D5
Ferkane *Algeria* 34°37N 7°26E **261** B6
Ferkéssédougou *Ivory C.* 9°35N 5°6W **262** D3
Ferlach *Austria* 46°32N 14°18E **180** E7
Ferland *Canada* 50°19N 88°27W **298** B2
Ferlo, Vallée du *Senegal* 15°15N 14°15W **262** B2
Ferlo-Nord △ *Senegal* 15°43N 14°0W **262** B2
Ferlo-Sud △ *Senegal* 15°43N 14°0W **262** B2
Fermanagh □ *U.K.* 54°21N 7°40W **166** B4
Fermo *Italy* 43°9N 13°43E **199** E10
Fermont *Canada* 52°47N 67°5W **299** B6
Fermoselle *Spain* 41°19N 6°27W **194** D4
Fermoy *Ireland* 52°9N 8°16W **166** D3
Fern Creek *U.S.A.* 38°9N 85°36W **311** G11
Fern Gully *Jamaica* 18°22N 77°5W **320** a
Fernán Núñez *Spain* 37°40N 4°44W **195** H6
Fernández *Argentina* 27°55S 63°50W **334** B3
Fernandina, I. *Ecuador* 0°25S 91°30W **330** a
Fernandina Beach *U.S.A.* 30°40N 81°27W **316** E8
Fernando de Noronha *Brazil* 4°0S 33°10W **152** G8
Fernando Póo = Bioko *Eq. Guin.* 3°30N 8°40E **263** E6
Fernandópolis *Brazil* 20°16S 50°14W **333** F1
Ferndale *Ont., Canada* 44°58N 81°17W **312** B3
Ferndale *Gauteng, S. Africa* 26°5S 28°0E **123** A2
Ferndale *Wash., U.S.A.* 48°51N 122°36W **306** B4
Fernie *Canada* 49°30N 115°5W **296** D5
Fernlees *Australia* 23°51S 148°7E **280** C4
Fernley *U.S.A.* 39°36N 119°15W **304** G4
Fernwood *U.S.A.* 43°16N 73°38W **313** C11
Feroke *India* 11°9N 75°46E **245** J2
Feroz Shah Kotla Cricket Stadium *Delhi, India* **120** b3
Ferozepore = Firozpur *India* 30°55N 74°40E **242** D6
Ferrandina *Italy* 40°29N 16°27E **201** B9
Ferrara *Italy* 44°50N 11°35E **199** D8
Ferrato, C. *Italy* 39°18N 9°38E **200** C2
Ferré, C. *Martinique* 14°27N 60°49W **322** j
Ferreira do Alentejo *Portugal* 38°4N 8°6W **195** G2
Ferreiros Gomes *Brazil* 0°48N 51°8W **332** A1
Ferreñafe *Peru* 6°42S 79°50W **330** B2
Ferrerias *Spain* 39°59N 4°1E **206** B5
Ferret, C. *France* 44°38N 1°15W **174** D2
Ferrette *France* 47°30N 7°20E **173** E14
Ferriday *U.S.A.* 31°38N 91°33W **314** F9
Ferriere *Italy* 44°40N 9°30E **198** D6
Ferrières *France* 48°5N 2°48E **173** D9
Ferro, Capo *Italy* 41°9N 9°31E **200** A2
Ferrol *Spain* 43°29N 8°15W **194** B2
Ferrol, Pen. de *Peru* 9°10S 78°35W **330** B2
Ferron *U.S.A.* 39°5N 111°8W **304** G8
Ferros *Brazil* 19°14S 43°2W **333** E3
Ferrutx, C. de *Spain* 39°47N 3°21E **206** B4
Ferry Pass *U.S.A.* 30°31N 87°13W **317** E2
Ferryland *Canada* 47°2N 52°53W **299** C9
Ferrysburg *U.S.A.* 43°5N 86°13W **311** A10
Ferryville = Menzel-Bourguiba *Tunisia* 37°9N 9°49E **258** A1
Fertile *U.S.A.* 47°32N 96°17W **308** B5
Fertő-Hanság △ *Hungary* 47°25N 16°50E **182** C1
Fertőszentmiklós *Hungary* 47°35N 16°53E **182** C1
Fès *Morocco* 34°0N 5°0W **260** B4
Fès □ *Morocco* 34°0N 5°0W **260** B4
Feshi *Dem. Rep. of the Congo* 6°8S 18°10E **265** D3
Fessenden *U.S.A.* 47°39N 99°38W **308** B4
Festenberg = Twardogóra *Poland* 51°23N 17°28E **185** G4
Festøya *Norway* 62°22N 6°19E **164** B3
Festus *U.S.A.* 38°13N 90°24W **310** F6
Feté Bowé *Senegal* 14°56N 13°30W **262** C2
Fetești *Romania* 44°22N 27°51E **183** F12
Fethiye *Turkey* 36°36N 29°6E **205** E11
Fethiye Körfezi *Turkey* 36°40N 28°50E **205** E10
Fetlar *U.K.* 60°36N 0°52W **167** A8
Fetsund *Norway* 59°56N 11°10E **164** E8
Feuilles → *Canada* 58°47N 70°4W **295** F17
Feurs *France* 45°45N 4°13E **175** C8
Fevik *Norway* 58°22N 8°39E **164** F5
Fevzipaşa *Turkey* 37°6N 36°37E **250** D7
Feyzābād *Badākhshān, Afghan.* 37°7N 70°33E **240** A3
Feyzābād *Fāryāb, Afghan.* 36°17N 64°52E **240** A2
Fez = Fès *Morocco* 34°0N 5°0W **260** B4
Fezzan *Libya* 27°0N 13°0E **258** C2
Fia *Congo* 3°25S 14°49E **264** C2
Fiambalá *Argentina* 27°45S 67°37W **334** B2
Fianarantsoa *Madag.* 21°26S 47°5E **272** C2
Fianarantsoa □ *Madag.* 22°30S 47°0E **272** B2
Fianga *Cameroon* 9°55N 15°9E **259** G3
Fiche *Ethiopia* 9°50N 38°46E **257** F4
Fichtelgebirge *Germany* 50°2N 11°55E **179** E7
Fichtelgebirge △ *Germany* 50°8N 12°0E **179** E8
Fichtenau *Germany* 52°27N 13°42E **115** B5
Ficksburg *S. Africa* 28°51S 27°53E **271** C4
Fidenza *Italy* 44°52N 10°3E **198** D7
Fiditi *Nigeria* 7°45N 3°53E **263** D5
Fidjeland *Norway* 58°57N 6°56E **164** F3
Field → *Australia* 23°48S 138°0E **280** C2
Field I. *Australia* 12°5S 132°23E **278** B5
Field Museum of Natural History *Chicago, U.S.A.* **119** e2
Fields Corner *U.S.A.* 42°18N 71°3W **116** B2
Fieni *Romania* 45°8N 25°25E **183** E10
Fier *Albania* 40°43N 19°33E **202** F3
Fiera Camp *Italy* 45°28N 9°9E **129** B1
Fierzë *Albania* 42°15N 20°1E **202** D4
Fife □ *U.K.* 56°16N 3°1W **167** E5
Fife △ *U.K.* 56°15N 3°15W **167** E5
Fife Ness *U.K.* 56°17N 2°35W **167** E6
Fifth Cataract *Sudan* 18°22N 33°50E **256** D3
Fig Tree *St. Kitts & Nevis* 17°8N 62°35W **322** d
Figari *France* 41°29N 9°7E **175** G13
Figeac *France* 44°37N 2°2E **174** D6
Figeholm *Sweden* 57°22N 16°33E **163** G10
Figino *Italy* 45°29N 9°4E **129** B1
Figline Valdarno *Italy* 43°37N 11°28E **199** E8
Figtree *Zimbabwe* 20°22S 28°20E **269** G2
Figueira = Governador Valadares *Brazil* 18°15S 41°57W **333** E3
Figueira Castelo Rodrigo *Portugal* 40°57N 6°58W **194** E4
Figueira da Foz *Portugal* 40°7N 8°54W **194** E2
Figueiró dos Vinhos *Portugal* 39°55N 8°16W **194** F2
Figueres *Spain* 42°18N 2°58E **196** C7
Figuig *Morocco* 32°5N 1°11W **261** B4
Figuig □ *Morocco* 32°50N 2°15W **260** B5
Fihaonana *Madag.* 18°36S 47°12E **272** B2
Fiherenana *Madag.* 18°29S 48°24E **272** B2
Fiherenana → *Madag.* 23°19S 43°37E **272** C1
Fiji ■ *Pac. Oc.* 17°20S 179°0E **287** A2
Fijir *Iraq* 33°21N 44°21E **113** A2
Fik *Ethiopia* 8°10N 42°19E **257** F5
Fika *Nigeria* 11°15N 11°13E **263** C7
Filabres, Sierra de los *Spain* 37°13N 2°20W **195** H8
Filabusi *Zimbabwe* 20°34S 29°20E **271** B4
Filadelfia *Bolivia* 11°20S 68°46W **330** C4
Filadélfia *Brazil* 7°21S 47°30W **332** C2
Filadelfia *Athina, Greece* 38°2N 23°43E **112** A2
Filadelfia *Italy* 38°47N 16°17E **201** D9
Filadelfia *Paraguay* 22°21S 60°2W **334** A3
Fil'akovo *Slovak Rep.* 48°17N 19°50E **181** C12
Filchner Ice Shelf *Antarctica* 79°0S 40°0W **151** D1
Filefjell *Norway* 61°8N 8°10E **164** C5
Filey *U.K.* 54°12N 0°18W **168** C7
Filey B. *U.K.* 54°12N 0°15W **168** C7
Filfla *Malta* 35°47N 14°24E **206** F1
Fili-Mazilovo *Russia* 55°44N 37°29E **129** B2
Filiaşi *Romania* 44°32N 23°31E **183** F8
Filiates *Greece* 39°38N 20°16E **206** B10
Filiatra *Greece* 37°9N 21°35E **204** D3
Filicudi *Italy* 38°35N 14°33E **201** D7
Filim *Oman* 20°37N 58°12E **249** B7
Filingué *Niger* 14°21N 3°22E **263** C5
Filiouri = Lissos → *Greece* 41°15N 25°40E **203** E9
Filipada *Greece* 39°12N 20°53E **204** B2
Filipstad *Sweden* 59°43N 14°9E **162** E8
Filisur *Switz.* 46°41N 9°40E **179** J5
Fillmore *Calif., U.S.A.* 34°24N 118°55W **307** L8
Fillmore *Utah, U.S.A.* 38°58N 112°20W **304** G7
Filothei *Greece* 38°2N 23°46E **112** A2
Filotio *Greece* 37°3N 25°30E **205** D7
Filottrano *Italy* 43°26N 13°21E **199** E10
Filtu *Ethiopia* 5°8N 40°35E **257** F5
Fimbul Ice Shelf *S. Ocean* 69°30S 1°0W **151** C2
Fimi → *Dem. Rep. of the Congo* 3°1S 16°58E **264** C3
Fina △ *Mali* 13°15N 8°46W **262** C3
Finale Emilia *Italy* 44°50N 11°18E **199** D8
Finale Ligure *Italy* 44°10N 8°20E **198** D5
Finalmarina = Finale Lígure *Italy* 44°10N 8°20E **198** D5
Fiñana *Spain* 37°10N 2°50W **195** H8
Financial District *San Francisco, U.S.A.* **136** b3
Finch *Canada* 45°11N 75°7W **313** A9
Finch Hatton *Australia* 20°25S 148°39E **280** b
Finchaa, L. *Ethiopia* 9°35N 37°20E **266** C4
Finchley *U.K.* 51°36N 0°11W **125** A2
Findhorn → *U.K.* 57°38N 3°38W **167** D5
Findıklı *Turkey* 41°16N 41°9E **213** B9
Findlay *U.S.A.* 41°2N 83°39W **311** C13
Fine *U.S.A.* 44°14N 75°8W **313** B9
Fine Art, Museum of = Kunsthistorischesmuseum *Vienna, Austria* **142** b1
Fine Arts, Museum of *U.S.A.* 42°20N 71°5W **116** A2
Finger L. *Canada* 53°33N 93°30W **298** B1
Finger Lakes *U.S.A.* 42°40N 76°30W **313** D8
Finglas *Ireland* 53°23N 6°19W **120** A2
Fingoè *Mozam.* 15°55S 31°50E **269** F3
Finike *Turkey* 36°21N 30°10E **205** E12
Finike Körfezi *Turkey* 36°17N 30°16E **205** E12
Finiq *Albania* 39°54N 20°3E **202** G4
Finistère □ *France* 48°20N 4°0W **172** D3
Finisterre = Fisterra *Spain* 42°54N 9°16W **194** C1
Finisterre, C. = Fisterra, C. *Spain* 42°50N 9°19W **194** C1
Finisterre Ra. *Papua N. G.* 6°0S 146°30E **286** D4
Finke *Australia* 25°34S 134°35E **280** D1
Finke Gorge △ *Australia* 24°8S 132°49E **278** D5
Finland ■ *Europe* 63°0N 27°0E **160** E22
Finland, G. of *Europe* 60°0N 26°0E **188** C3
Finlay → *Canada* 57°0N 125°10W **296** B3
Finley *N.S.W., Australia* 35°38S 145°35E **283** C6
Finley *N. Dak., U.S.A.* 47°31N 97°50W **308** B5
Finn → *Ireland* 54°51N 7°28W **166** B4
Finnerödja *Sweden* 58°57N 14°24E **163** F8
Finnigan, Mt. *Australia* 15°49S 145°17E **280** B4
Finniss, C. *Australia* 33°8S 134°51E **281** E1
Finnmark *Norway* 69°37N 23°57E **160** B20
Finnsnes *Norway* 69°14N 18°0E **160** B18
Finsbury *U.K.* 51°31N 0°6W **125** A3
Finsbury Park *U.K.* 51°34N 0°6W **125** A3
Finschhafen *Papua N. G.* 6°33S 147°50E **286** D4
Finse *Norway* 60°36N 7°30E **164** D4
Finspång *Sweden* 58°43N 15°47E **163** F9
Finsteraarhorn *Switz.* 46°31N 8°10E **179** J4
Finsterwalde *Germany* 51°37N 13°42E **178** D9
Fiora → *Italy* 42°20N 11°34E **199** F8
Fiordland △ *N.Z.* 45°46S 167°0E **285** F2
Fiorenzuola d'Arda *Italy* 44°56N 9°55E **198** D6
Fiorito *Argentina* 34°42S 58°26W **117** C2
Fiq *Syria* 32°46N 35°41E **250** F6
Firat = Furāt, Nahr al → *Asia* 31°0N 47°25E **246** D5
Fire Island △ *U.S.A.* 40°38N 73°8W **313** F11
Firebag → *Canada* 57°45N 111°21W **297** B6
Firebaugh *U.S.A.* 36°52N 120°27W **306** J6
Firedrake L. *Canada* 61°25N 104°30W **297** A8
Firenze *Italy* 43°46N 11°15E **199** E8
Firenze Amerigo Vespucci ✕ (FLR) *Italy* 43°49N 11°13E **199** E8
Firenze Pisa ✕ (PSA) *Italy* 43°40N 10°22E **198** E7
Firenzuola *Italy* 44°7N 11°23E **199** D8
Firhouse *Ireland* 53°17N 6°20W **120** B2
Firk, Sha'ib → *Iraq* 30°59N 44°34E **246** D5
Firkachi *Niger* 15°40N 14°20E **259** E2
Firmi *France* 44°33N 2°19E **174** D6
Firminy *France* 45°23N 4°18E **175** C8
Firozabad *India* 27°10N 78°25E **243** F8
Firozpur *India* 30°55N 74°40E **242** D6
Firozpur-Jhirka *India* 27°48N 76°57E **242** F7
Fīrūzābād *Iran* 28°52N 52°35E **247** D7
Fīrūzkūh *Iran* 35°50N 52°50E **247** C7
Firvale *Canada* 52°27N 126°13W **296** C3
Fischerhäuser *Germany* 48°14N 11°41E **131** A3
Fish → *Namibia* 28°7S 17°10E **270** C2
Fish → *Northern Cape, S. Africa* 31°30S 20°16E **270** D3
Fish River Canyon *Namibia* 27°40S 17°35E **270** C2
Fisheating Cr. → *U.S.A.* 26°57N 81°7W **317** J8
Fisher B. *Canada* 51°35N 97°13W **297** C9
Fisher Island *U.S.A.* 25°45N 80°8W **128** D2
Fishermans Bend *Australia* 37°49S 144°55E **128** A1
Fisherman's Wharf *San Francisco, U.S.A.* **136** a1
Fishers I. *U.S.A.* 41°15N 72°0W **313** E13
Fisherville *Canada* 43°46N 79°28W **141** A2
Fishguard *U.K.* 52°0N 4°58W **169** E3
Fishing L. *Canada* 52°10N 95°24W **297** C9
Fishkill *U.S.A.* 41°32N 73°54W **313** E11
Fiskardo *Greece* 38°28N 20°35E **207** C2
Fiskenæsset = Qeqertarsuatsiaat *Greenland* 63°5N 50°45W **154** E5
Fisksätra *Sweden* 59°17N 18°13E **139** B3
Fismes *France* 49°20N 3°40E **173** C10
Fisterra *Spain* 42°54N 9°16W **194** C1
Fisterra, C. *Spain* 42°50N 9°19W **194** C1
Fitchburg *Mass., U.S.A.* 42°35N 71°48W **313** D13
Fitchburg *Wis., U.S.A.* 42°58N 89°28W **310** B7
Fitjar *Iceland* 64°28N 21°18W **155** C3
Fitjar *Hordaland, Norway* 59°55N 5°17E **164** E2
Fitri, L. *Chad* 12°50N 17°28E **259** F3
Fitz Roy *Argentina* 47°0S 67°0W **336** C3
Fitz Roy, Cerro *Argentina* 49°17S 73°5W **336** C2
Fitzgerald *Alta., Canada* 59°51N 111°36W **296** B6
Fitzgerald *U.S.A.* 31°43N 83°15W **316** D6
Fitzgerald River △ *Australia* 33°53S 119°55E **279** F3
Fitzmaurice → *Australia* 14°45S 130°5E **278** B5
Fitzroy → *Queens., Australia* 23°32S 150°52E **280** C5
Fitzroy → *W. Austral., Australia* 17°31S 123°35E **278** C3
Fitzroy Crossing *Australia* 18°9S 125°38E **278** C4
Fitzroy Gardens *Australia* 37°48S 144°58E **128** A1
Fitzwilliam I. *Canada* 45°30N 81°45W **312** A3
Fiuggi *Italy* 41°48N 13°13E **199** G10
Fiume = Rijeka *Croatia* 45°20N 14°21E **199** C11
Fiumicino, Roma ✕ (FCO) *Italy* 41°48N 12°15E **199** G9
Five Cowrie Cr. → *Nigeria* 6°26N 3°24E **124** B2
Five Dock *Australia* 33°52S 151°8E **139** B1
Five Island Harbour *Antigua & B.* 17°6N 61°54W **322** b
Five Points *U.S.A.* 36°26N 120°6W **306** J6
Fivizzano *Italy* 44°14N 10°8E **198** D7
Fizi *Dem. Rep. of the Congo* 4°17S 28°55E **268** C2
Fjæra *Norway* 59°52N 6°22E **164** E3
Fjærland *Norway* 61°24N 6°43E **164** C3
Fjærlandsfjorden *Norway* 61°17N 6°40E **164** C3
Fjällbacka *Sweden* 58°36N 11°17E **163** F5
Fjällnäs *Sweden* 62°36N 12°11E **162** B6
Fjärdhundra *Sweden* 59°47N 16°56E **162** E10
Fjellerup *Denmark* 56°29N 10°34E **163** H4
Fjellstrand *Norway* 59°47N 10°36E **133** B2
Fjerritslev *Denmark* 57°5N 9°15E **163** G3
Fjugesta *Sweden* 59°11N 14°52E **162** E8
Fkih ben Salah *Morocco* 32°32N 6°45W **260** B3
Flå *Norway* 60°25N 9°28E **164** D6
Flacq Plain *Mauritius* 20°13S 57°43E **272** e
Flagler Beach *U.S.A.* 29°29N 81°8W **317** F8
Flagstaff *U.S.A.* 35°12N 111°39W **305** J8
Flagstaff B. *St. Helena* 15°54S 5°41W **153** h
Flagstaff L. *U.S.A.* 45°12N 70°18W **313** A14
Flaherty I. *Canada* 56°15N 79°15W **298** A4
Flåm *Norway* 60°50N 7°7E **164** D4
Flamands *St.-Martin* 17°55N 62°51W **322** a
Flambeau → *U.S.A.* 45°18N 91°14W **308** C8
Flamborough Hd. *U.K.* 54°7N 0°5W **168** C7
Flamengo *Brazil* 22°56S 43°11W **135** B1
Flamengos *Azores* 38°33N 28°39W **153** d1
Fläming *Germany* 52°6N 12°23E **178** C8
Flaming Gorge △ *U.S.A.* 41°10N 109°25W **304** F9
Flaming Gorge Res. *U.S.A.* 41°10N 109°25W **304** F9
Flamingo *Fla., U.S.A.* 28°22N 81°22W **133** B2
Flamingo *Fla., U.S.A.* 25°8N 80°57W **317** K9
Flamingo, Teluk *Indonesia* 5°30S 138°0E **231** F9
Flaminio *Italy* 41°55N 12°28E **136** B1
Flanagan *U.S.A.* 40°53N 88°52W **311** D8
Flanagin Town *Trin. & Tob.* 10°25N 61°19W **323** t
Flanders = Flandre *Europe* 50°50N 2°30E **173** B9
Flandre *Europe* 50°50N 2°30E **173** B9
Flandre-Occidentale = West-Vlaanderen □ *Belgium* 51°0N 3°0E **170** D2
Flandre-Orientale = Oost-Vlaanderen □ *Belgium* 51°5N 3°50E **170** C3
Flandreau *U.S.A.* 44°3N 96°36W **308** C5
Flanigan *U.S.A.* 40°10N 119°53W **306** E7
Flannan Is. *U.K.* 58°9N 7°52W **167** C1
Flåsjön *Sweden* 64°5N 15°40E **160** D16
Flaskebekk *Norway* 59°51N 10°39E **133** A2
Flat *U.S.A.* 62°28N 158°1W **303** E8
Flat → *N.W.T., Canada* 61°33N 125°18W **296** A3
Flat → *Mich., U.S.A.* 42°56N 85°20W **311** B11
Flat Pt. *N.Z.* 41°14S 175°57E **284** H4
Flat Rock *U.S.A.* 42°6N 83°17W **311** B13
Flatbush *U.S.A.* 40°39N 73°56W **132** C2
Flateby *Norway* 59°50N 11°10E **164** E8
Flaten *Sweden* 59°15N 18°9E **139** B2
Flatey *Iceland* 66°10N 17°52W **155** A9
Flateyri *Iceland* 66°3N 23°31W **155** A3
Flathead L. *U.S.A.* 47°51N 114°8W **304** C6
Flatiron Building *New York, U.S.A.* **132** d2
Flatlands *U.S.A.* 40°37N 73°56W **132** C2
Flatow = Złotów *Poland* 53°22N 17°2E **184** E4
Flatrock → *U.S.A.* 39°12N 85°56W **311** F10
Flattery, C. *Queens., Australia* 14°58S 145°21E **280** A4
Flattery, C. *Wash., U.S.A.* 48°23N 124°29W **306** B2
Flatts Village *Bermuda* 32°18N 64°43W **153** a
Flatwoods *U.S.A.* 38°31N 82°43W **309** F12
Flecha Pt. *Phil.* 7°22N 123°24E **233** H4
Flechas Pt. *Phil.* 10°22N 119°34E **233** F2
Fleet Center *Boston, U.S.A.* **116** a2
Fleetwood *Lancs., U.K.* 53°55N 3°1W **168** D4
Fleetwood *Pa., U.S.A.* 40°27N 75°49W **313** F9
Flekke *Norway* 61°19N 5°20E **164** C2
Flekkefjord *Norway* 58°18N 6°39E **164** F3
Flemingsburg *U.S.A.* 38°25N 83°45W **311** F13
Flemington *U.S.A.* 41°7N 77°28W **312** E7
Flemington Racecourse *Australia* 37°47S 144°54E **128** A1
Flemish Cap *Atl. Oc.* 47°0N 45°0W **152** B7
Flen *Sweden* 59°4N 16°35E **162** E10
Flensburg *Germany* 54°47N 9°27E **178** A5
Flers *France* 48°47N 0°33W **172** D6
Flesberg *Norway* 59°51N 9°27E **164** E6
Flesherton *Canada* 44°16N 80°33W **312** B4
Flesko, Tanjung *Indonesia* 0°29N 124°30E **231** D6
Fletcher = Aurora *U.S.A.* 39°43N 104°49W **304** G11
Fleurance *France* 43°52N 0°40E **174** E4
Fleurier *Switz.* 46°54N 6°35E **179** J2
Fleurieu Pen. *Australia* 35°40S 138°5E **282** C3
Flevoland □ *Neths.* 52°30N 5°30E **170** B5
Flin Flon *Canada* 54°46N 101°53W **297** C8
Flinders → *Australia* 17°36S 140°36E **280** B3
Flinders B. *Australia* 34°19S 115°19E **279** F2
Flinders Chase △ *Australia* 35°50S 136°42E **282** C2
Flinders Group *Australia* 14°11S 144°15E **280** A3
Flinders I. *S. Austral., Australia* 33°44S 134°41E **281** E1
Flinders I. *Tas., Australia* 40°0S 148°0E **281** G4
Flinders Ranges *Australia* 31°30S 138°30E **282** A3
Flinders Ranges △ *Australia* 31°30S 138°40E **282** A3
Flinders Reefs *Australia* 17°37S 148°31E **280** B4
Flint *Flints., U.K.* 53°15N 3°8W **168** D4
Flint *Mich., U.S.A.* 43°1N 83°41W **311** A13
Flint → *U.S.A.* 30°57N 84°34W **316** E5
Flint I. *Kiribati* 11°26S 151°48W **289** f
Flint Pk. *U.S.A.* 34°9N 118°11W **126** B3
Flintshire □ *U.K.* 53°17N 3°17W **168** D4
Flipper Pt. *Wake I.* 19°18N 166°37E **302** b
Flisa *Norway* 60°37N 12°0E **164** D9
Flisa → *Norway* 60°37N 12°6E **164** D9
Fliseryd *Sweden* 57°6N 16°15E **163** G10
Flix *Spain* 41°14N 0°32E **196** D5
Flixecourt *France* 50°1N 2°5E **173** B9
Floby *Sweden* 58°8N 13°20E **163** F7
Floda *Sweden* 57°49N 12°22E **163** G6
Flodden *U.K.* 55°37N 2°8W **168** B5
Flogny-la-Chapelle *France* 47°57N 3°57E **173** E10
Floodplains △ *Sri Lanka* 8°10N 81°10E **245** K5
Floodwood *U.S.A.* 46°56N 92°55W **308** B7
Flora *Apayao, Phil.* 18°14N 121°5E **232** B3
Flora *Ill., U.S.A.* 38°40N 88°29W **310** F8
Flora *Ind., U.S.A.* 40°33N 86°31W **311** D10
Florac *France* 44°20N 3°37E **174** D7
Florahome *U.S.A.* 29°44N 81°54W **316** F8
Floral City *U.S.A.* 28°45N 82°17W **317** G7
Florala *U.S.A.* 31°0N 86°20W **315** F11
Florânia *Brazil* 6°8S 36°49W **332** C4
Floreana, I. = Santa María, I. *Ecuador* 1°17S 90°26W **330** a
Florence = Firenze *Italy* 43°46N 11°15E **199** E8
Florence *Ala., U.S.A.* 34°48N 87°41W **315** D11
Florence *Ariz., U.S.A.* 33°2N 111°23W **305** K8
Florence *Calif., U.S.A.* 33°57N 118°13W **126** C3
Florence *Colo., U.S.A.* 38°23N 105°8W **304** G11
Florence *Oreg., U.S.A.* 43°58N 124°7W **304** D1
Florence *S.C., U.S.A.* 34°12N 79°46W **315** D15
Florence, L. *Australia* 28°53S 138°9E **281** D2
Florence Bay = Chitimba *Malawi* 10°35S 34°13E **269** E3
Florence Bloom Bird Sanctuary △ *S. Africa* 26°7S 28°0E **123** A2
Florencia *Colombia* 1°36N 75°36W **328** C2
Florennes *Belgium* 50°15N 4°35E **170** D4
Florensac *France* 43°23N 3°28E **174** E7
Florentia *S. Africa* 26°16S 28°8E **123** B2
Florenville *Belgium* 49°40N 5°19E **170** E5
Flores *Florânia Brazil* 6°8S 36°49W **332** C4
Flores = Timon *Brazil* 5°8S 42°52W **332** C3
Flores *B. Aires, Argentina* 34°38S 58°27W **117** B2
Flores *Azores* 39°26N 31°13W **153** d2
Flores *Brazil* 7°51S 37°59W **332** C4
Flores *Guatemala* 16°59N 89°50W **320** C2
Flores *Indonesia* 8°35S 121°0E **235** D5
Flores, Mercado de *Mexico* 19°19N 99°5W **128** C2
Flores I. *Canada* 49°20N 126°10W **296** D3
Flores Sea *Indonesia* 6°30S 120°0E **231** F6
Floresta *B. Aires, Argentina* 34°37S 58°27W **117** B2
Floresta *Brazil* 8°40S 37°26W **332** C4
Florești *Moldova* 47°53N 28°17E **183** C13
Floresville *U.S.A.* 29°8N 98°10W **314** G5
Floriano *Brazil* 6°50S 43°0W **332** C3
Florianópolis *Brazil* 27°30S 48°30W **335** B6
Florida *B. Aires, Argentina* 34°31S 58°28W **117** B2
Florida *Cuba* 21°32N 78°14W **320** B4
Florida *Puerto Rico* 18°22N 66°34W **321** b
Florida *Gauteng, S. Africa* 26°10S 27°55E **123** B1
Florida *Uruguay* 34°7S 56°10W **335** C4
Florida □ *U.S.A.* 28°0N 82°0W **315** G14
Florida, Straits of *U.S.A.* 25°0N 80°0W **320** B4
Florida B. *U.S.A.* 25°0N 80°45W **320** B3
Florida City *U.S.A.* 25°27N 80°29W **317** K9
Florida Is. *Solomon Is.* 9°55S 160°15E **287** M11
Florida Keys *U.S.A.* 24°40N 81°0W **317** L8
Floridablanca *Phil.* 14°59N 120°31E **232** D3
Florídia *Italy* 37°5N 15°9E **201** E8
Floridsdorf *Austria* 48°15N 16°26E **142** A2
Florin *U.S.A.* 38°30N 121°24W **306** G5
Florina *Greece* 40°48N 21°26E **202** F5
Florina □ *Greece* 40°45N 21°20E **202** F5
Florissant *U.S.A.* 38°47N 90°19W **310** F6
Florø *Norway* 61°35N 5°1E **164** C2
Flotte, C. de *N. Cal.* 21°10S 167°25E **288** d
Flower Station *Canada* 45°10N 76°41W **313** A8
Flowerpot I. *Canada* 45°18N 81°38W **312** A3
Floydada *U.S.A.* 33°59N 101°20W **314** E4
Fludir *Iceland* 64°7N 20°6W **155** C6
Flugumyri *Iceland* 65°34N 19°19W **155** B7
Fluk *Indonesia* 1°42S 127°44E **231** E7
Flúmen → *Spain* 41°43N 0°9W **196** D4
Flumendosa → *Italy* 39°26N 9°37E **200** C2
Fluminimaggiore *Italy* 39°26N 8°30E **200** C1
Flushing = Vlissingen *Neths.* 51°26N 3°34E **170** C3
Flushing *Mich., U.S.A.* 43°4N 83°51W **311** A13
Flushing *N.Y., U.S.A.* 40°45N 73°49W **132** B3
Flushing Meadows Corona Park *U.S.A.* 40°44N 73°50W **132** B2
Fluvià → *Spain* 42°12N 3°7E **196** C8
Fly → *Papua N. G.* 8°25S 143°0E **286** E2
Flying Fish, C. *Antarctica* 72°6S 102°29W **151** D15
Flysta *Sweden* 59°22N 17°54E **139** A1
Fo Tan *China* 22°23N 114°11E **122** A2
Foa *Tonga* 19°45S 174°18W **287** P13
Foam Lake *Canada* 51°40N 103°32W **297** C8
Foča *Bos.-H.* 43°31N 18°47E **202** C2
Foça *Turkey* 38°39N 26°46E **205** C8
Fochabers *U.K.* 57°37N 3°6W **167** D5
Focşani *Romania* 45°41N 27°15E **183** E12
Fodé *C.A.R.* 5°29N 23°18E **264** A4
Fodécontéa *Guinea* 10°50N 14°22W **262** C2
Fogang *China* 23°52N 113°30E **229** F9
Foggaret el Arab *Algeria* 27°13N 2°49E **261** C5
Foggaret ez Zoua *Algeria* 27°20N 2°53E **261** C5
Fóggia *Italy* 41°27N 15°34E **201** A8
Foggy Bottom *U.S.A.* 38°54N 77°3W **143** B3
Foglia → *Italy* 43°55N 12°54E **199** E9
Fogo *Nfld. & L., Canada* 49°43N 54°17W **299** C9
Fogo *C. Verde Is.* 15°5N 24°20W **153** j
Fogo I. *Canada* 49°40N 54°5W **299** C9
Fohnsdorf *Austria* 47°12N 14°40E **180** D7
Föhr *Germany* 54°43N 8°30E **178** A4
Föhrenhain *Austria* 48°19N 16°26E **142** A2
Foia *Portugal* 37°19N 8°37W **195** H2
Foix *France* 42°58N 1°38E **174** F5
Fojnica *Bos.-H.* 43°59N 17°51E **182** G2
Fokida □ *Greece* 38°30N 22°15E **204** C4
Fokino *Russia* 53°30N 34°22E **188** F8
Fokku *Nigeria* 11°36N 4°32E **263** C5
Foksetugu *Norway* 62°7N 9°17E **164** B6
Folda *Nord-Trøndelag, Norway* 64°32N 10°30E **160** D14
Folda *Nordland, Norway* 67°38N 14°50E **160** C16
Földeák *Hungary* 46°19N 20°30E **182** D5
Folegandros *Greece* 36°40N 24°55E **204** E6
Foley *Botswana* 21°34S 27°21E **270** B4
Foley *Ala., U.S.A.* 30°24N 87°41W **315** F11
Foley *Fla., U.S.A.* 30°4N 83°32W **316** E6
Foleyet *Canada* 48°15N 82°25W **298** C3
Folgefonna *Norway* 60°3N 6°23E **164** D3
Folgefonna △ *Norway* 60°5N 6°15E **164** D3
Foligno *Italy* 42°57N 12°42E **199** F9
Folkestad *Norway* 62°7N 6°1E **164** B3
Folkestone *U.K.* 51°5N 1°12E **169** F9
Folkestone Underwater Park *Barbados* 13°11N 59°38W **323** r
Folkston *U.S.A.* 30°50N 82°0W **316** E7
Folla → *Norway* 62°7N 10°37E **164** B7
Follansbee *U.S.A.* 40°19N 80°35W **312** F4
Folldal *Norway* 62°8N 10°0E **164** B6
Folle Anse, Pte. de *Guadeloupe* 15°56N 61°19W **322** e
Follebu *Norway* 61°13N 10°16E **164** C7
Follónica *Italy* 42°55N 10°45E **198** F7
Follónica, G. di *Italy* 42°54N 10°43E **198** F7
Folsom L. *U.S.A.* 38°42N 121°9W **306** G5
Folteşti *Romania* 45°45N 28°3E **183** E13
Fomboni *Comoros Is.* 12°18S 43°46E **272** a
Fomm ir-Rih Bay *Malta* 35°54N 14°20E **206** D1
Fond-du-Lac *Sask., Canada* 59°19N 107°12W **297** B7
Fond du Lac *Wis., U.S.A.* 43°47N 88°27W **308** D9
Fond-du-Lac → *Canada* 59°17N 106°0W **297** B7
Fond Rousseau *Martinique* 14°38N 61°6W **322** j
Fond St. Jacques *St. Lucia* 13°50N 61°1W **323** m
Fonda *Iowa, U.S.A.* 42°35N 94°51W **310** B2
Fonda *N.Y., U.S.A.* 42°57N 74°22W **313** D10
Fondi *Italy* 41°21N 13°25E **200** A6
Fonds-St-Denis *Martinique* 14°44N 61°8W **322** j
Fonfría *Spain* 41°37N 6°9W **194** D4
Fongafale *Tuvalu* 8°31S 179°13E **287** D14
Fongen *Norway* 63°11N 11°38E **164** A8
Fonni *Italy* 40°7N 9°15E **200** B2
Fonsagrada = A Fonsagrada *Spain* 43°8N 7°4W **194** B3
Fonseca, G. de *Cent. Amer.* 13°10N 87°40W **320** D2
Font-Romeu-Odeillo-Via *France* 42°31N 2°3E **174** F5
Fontaine-Française *France* 47°32N 5°21E **173** E12
Fontainebleau *Seine-et-Marne, France* 48°24N 2°40E **173** D9
Fontainebleau *Gauteng, S. Africa* 26°6S 27°57E **123** A1
Fontana *U.S.A.* 34°6N 117°26W **307** L9
Fontana, L. *Argentina* 44°55S 71°30W **336** B2
Fontas → *Canada* 58°14N 121°48W **296** B4
Fonte Boa *Brazil* 2°33S 66°0W **328** D4
Fontem *Cameroon* 5°32N 9°52E **263** D6
Fontenay-aux-Roses *France* 48°47N 2°17E **134** B2
Fontenay-le-Comte *France* 46°28N 0°48W **174** B3
Fontenay-le-Fleury *France* 48°48N 2°2E **134** B1
Fontenay-sous-Bois *France* 48°51N 2°28E **134** A3
Fontenelle Res. *U.S.A.* 42°1N 110°3W **304** E8
Fontur *Iceland* 66°23N 14°32W **155** A12
Fonuafo'ou *Tonga* 20°19S 175°25W **287** Q13
Fonuakula *Cook Is.* 19°2S 169°55W **289** g
Fonualei *Tonga* 18°1S 174°19W **287** P13
Fonyód *Hungary* 46°44N 17°33E **182** D2
Foochow = Fuzhou *China* 26°5N 119°16E **229** D12
Foots Cray *U.K.* 51°24N 0°7E **125** B4
Footscray *Australia* 37°48S 144°56E **128** A1
Foping *China* 33°41N 108°0E **226** H5
Foraker, Mt. *U.S.A.* 62°58N 151°24W **303** E10
Forari *Vanuatu* 17°40S 168°31E **287** G6
Forbach *France* 49°10N 6°52E **173** C13
Forbes *Australia* 33°22S 148°5E **283** B8
Forbesganj *India* 26°17N 87°18E **243** F12
Forbidden City = Imperial Palace Museum *Beijing, China* **114** b3
Forcados *Nigeria* 5°26N 5°26E **263** D6
Forcados → *Nigeria* 5°25N 5°19E **263** D6
Forcalquier *France* 43°58N 5°47E **175** E9
Forchheim *Germany* 49°43N 11°2E **179** F7
Ford City *Calif., U.S.A.* 35°9N 119°27W **307** K7
Ford City *Pa., U.S.A.* 40°46N 79°32W **312** F5
Ford d'Or B. *St. Lucia* 13°56N 60°54W **323** m
Ford I. *U.S.A.* 21°22N 157°58W **302** K14
Førde → *Norway* 62°57N 10°46E **164** B7
Førde *Hordaland, Norway* 59°36N 5°27E **164** E2
Førde *Rogaland, Norway* 59°26N 5°23E **164** E2
Førde *Sogn og Fjordane, Norway* 61°27N 5°53E **164** C2
Førdefjorden *Norway* 61°29N 5°18E **164** C2
Fords Bridge *Australia* 29°41S 145°29E **281** D4
Ford's Theater *Washington, D.C., U.S.A.* **143** b2
Fordyce *U.S.A.* 33°49N 92°25W **314** E8
Forécariah *Guinea* 9°28N 13°10W **262** D2
Forel, Mt. *Greenland* 66°52N 36°55W **154** D7
Foremost *Canada* 49°26N 111°34W **296** D6
Foreshore *Cape Town, S. Africa* **118** a3
Forest *Belgium* 50°49N 4°20E **116** B1
Forest *Ont., Canada* 43°6N 82°0W **312** C3
Forest *Miss., U.S.A.* 32°22N 89°29W **315** E10
Forest Acres *U.S.A.* 34°1N 80°58W **316** A9
Forest City *Iowa, U.S.A.* 43°16N 93°39W **308** D7
Forest City *N.C., U.S.A.* 35°20N 81°52W **315** D14
Forest City *Pa., U.S.A.* 41°39N 75°28W **313** E9
Forest Gate *U.K.* 51°32N 0°1E **125** A4
Forest Grove *U.S.A.* 45°31N 123°7W **306** E3
Forest Heights *U.S.A.* 38°48N 77°0W **143** C3
Forest Hill *Ont., Canada* 43°41N 79°25W **141** A2
Forest Hill *London, U.K.* 51°26N 0°2W **125** B3
Forest Hills *U.S.A.* 40°42N 73°51W **132** B2
Forest Park *Ga., U.S.A.* 33°37N 84°22W **316** B5
Forest Park *Ill., U.S.A.* 41°51N 87°47W **119** B2
Forest Park *N.Y., U.S.A.* 40°42N 73°51W **132** B2
Forest Park *Ohio, U.S.A.* 39°17N 84°30W **311** E12
Forest View *U.S.A.* 41°48N 87°47W **119** C2
Forestburg *Canada* 52°35N 112°1W **296** C6
Foreste Casentinesi-Monte Falterona-Campigna △ *Italy* 43°50N 11°48E **199** E8
Foresthill *U.S.A.* 39°1N 120°49W **306** F6
Forestier Pen. *Australia* 43°0S 148°0E **281** G4
Forestville *Qué., Canada* 48°48N 69°2W **299** C6
Forestville *Calif., U.S.A.* 38°28N 122°54W **306** G4
Forestville *Md., U.S.A.* 38°50N 76°52W **143** B4
Forestville *N.Y., U.S.A.* 42°28N 79°10W **312** D5
Forêt d'Orient △ *France* 48°16N 4°25E **173** D11
Forêt du Day △ *Djibouti* 11°56N 42°40E **267** B5
Forez, Mts. du *France* 45°40N 3°50E **174** C7
Forfar *U.K.* 56°39N 2°53W **167** E6
Forillon △ *Canada* 48°46N 64°12W **299** C7
Forks *U.S.A.* 47°57N 124°23W **306** C2
Forks, The = Merritt *Canada* 50°10N 120°45W **296** C4
Forksville *U.S.A.* 41°29N 76°35W **313** E8
Forlì *Italy* 44°13N 12°3E **199** D9
Forman *U.S.A.* 46°7N 97°38W **308** B5
Formazza *Italy* 46°22N 8°26E **198** B5
Formby Pt. *U.K.* 53°33N 3°6W **168** D4
Formentera *Spain* 38°43N 1°27E **206** D1
Formentor, C. de *Spain* 39°58N 3°13E **206** B4
Formentor, Pen. de *Spain* 39°56N 3°11E **206** B4
Former Yugoslav Republic of Macedonia = Macedonia ■ *Europe* 41°53N 21°40E **202** E5
Fórmia *Italy* 41°15N 13°37E **200** A6
Formiga *Brazil* 20°27S 45°25W **333** F2
Formigine *Italy* 44°37N 10°51E **198** D7
Formosa = Taiwan ■ *Asia* 23°30N 121°0E **225** C3
Formosa *Argentina* 26°15S 58°10W **334** B4
Formosa *Brazil* 15°32S 47°20W **333** E2
Formosa □ *Argentina* 25°0S 60°0W **334** B4
Formosa, Serra *Brazil* 12°0S 55°0W **331** C7
Formosa B. = Ungwana B. *Kenya* 2°45S 40°20E **268** C5
Formosa do Rio Prêto *Brazil* 11°2S 45°3W **332** D2
Formosa Strait = Taiwan Strait *Asia* 24°40N 120°0E **229** E12
Formoso → *Brazil* 10°34S 49°56W **333** D2
Fornebu *Norway* 59°53N 10°36E **133** A2
Fornells *Spain* 40°3N 4°7E **206** A5
Fornos de Algodres *Portugal* 40°38N 7°32W **194** E3
Fornovo di Taro *Italy* 44°42N 10°6E **198** D7
Foro Romano *Rome, Italy* **136** c3
Forollhogna △ *Norway* 62°39N 10°41E **164** B7
Føroyar ☑ *Atl. Oc.* 62°0N 7°0W **160** F9
Forres *U.K.* 57°37N 3°37W **167** D5
Forrest *Vic., Australia* 38°33S 143°47E **282** E5
Forrest *W. Austral., Australia* 30°51S 128°6E **279** F4
Forrest, Mt. *Australia* 24°48S 127°45E **279** D4
Forrest City *U.S.A.* 35°1N 90°47W **315** D9
Forreston *U.S.A.* 42°8N 89°35W **310** B7
Fors *Sweden* 60°14N 16°20E **162** D10
Forsand *Norway* 58°54N 6°5E **164** F3
Forsayth *Australia* 18°33S 143°34E **280** B3
Forserum *Sweden* 57°42N 14°30E **163** G8
Forshaga *Sweden* 59°33N 13°29E **162** E7
Förslöv *Sweden* 56°21N 12°48E **163** H6
Forsmo *Sweden* 63°16N 17°11E **162** A11
Forssa *Finland* 60°49N 23°38E **165** D9
Forst *Germany* 51°45N 14°37E **178** D10
Forstenried *Germany* 48°5N 11°29E **131** B1

Forstenrieder Park Germany 48°3N 11°27E **131** B1
Forster Australia 32°12S 152°31E **283** B10
Forsvik Sweden 58°35N 14°26E **163** F8
Forsyth Ga., U.S.A. 33°2N 83°56W **316** B6
Forsyth Mont., U.S.A. 46°16N 106°41W **304** C10
Forsyth I. N.Z. 40°58S 174°5E **285** A9
Fort Mumbai, India **130** c2
Fort Abbas Pakistan 29°12N 72°52E **242** E5
Fort Albany Canada 52°15N 81°35W **298** B3
Fort-Aleksandrovsky = Fort Shevchenko
   Kazakhstan 44°35N 50°23E **191** H10
Fort Archambault = Sarh
   Chad 9°5N 18°23E **259** G3
Fort Assiniboine Canada 54°20N 114°45W **296** C6
Fort Atkinson U.S.A. 42°56N 88°50W **311** B8
Fort Augustus U.K. 57°9N 4°42W **167** D4
Fort Bay Saba 17°37N 63°15W **322** a
Fort Bayard = Zhanjiang
   China 21°15N 110°20E **229** G8
Fort Beaufort S. Africa 32°46S 26°40E **270** D4
Fort Benton U.S.A. 47°49N 110°40W **304** C8
Fort Bragg U.S.A. 39°26N 123°48W **304** G2
Fort Bridger U.S.A. 41°19N 110°23W **304** F8
Fort Canning Park Singapore **138** b2
Fort Caroline U.S.A. 30°23N 81°30W **316** E8
Fort Charles Jamaica 17°55N 76°50W **320** a
Fort Charlotte St. Lucia 13°59N 61°0W **323** m
Fort Chipewyan Canada 58°42N 111°8W **297** B6
Fort Clatsop = Lewis and Clark △
   U.S.A. 46°8N 123°53W **306** D3
Fort Collins U.S.A. 40°35N 105°5W **304** F11
Fort-Coulonge Canada 45°50N 76°45W **298** C4
Fort Covington U.S.A. 44°59N 74°29W **313** D10
Fort Dauphin = Taolanaro
   Madag. 25°2S 47°0E **272** D2
Fort Davis Ala., U.S.A. 32°15N 85°43W **316** C4
Fort Davis Tex., U.S.A. 30°35N 103°54W **314** F4
Fort-de-France Martinique 14°36N 61°2W **322** j
Fort de France, B. de
   Martinique 14°34N 61°4W **322** j
Fort de Kock = Bukittinggi
   Indonesia 0°20S 100°20E **234** C2
Fort de Polignac = Illizi
   Algeria 26°31N 8°32E **261** C6
Fort de Possel = Possel
   C.A.R. 5°5N 19°10E **264** A3
Fort Defiance U.S.A. 35°45N 109°5W **305** J9
Fort Dodge U.S.A. 42°30N 94°11W **310** B2
Fort Drum U.S.A. 27°32N 80°48W **317** H9
Fort Dupont Park U.S.A. 38°52N 76°56W **314** b
Fort Edward U.S.A. 43°16N 73°35W **313** C11
Fort Erie Canada 42°54N 78°56W **298** D4
Fort Fairfield U.S.A. 46°46N 67°50W **309** B20
Fort Flatters = Bordj Omar Driss
   Algeria 28°10N 6°40E **261** C6
Fort Foote Village U.S.A. 38°46N 77°1W **143** C3
Fort-Foureau = Kousseri
   Cameroon 12°0N 14°55E **259** F2
Fort Frances Canada 48°36N 93°24W **297** D10
Fort Franklin = Déline
   Canada 65°11N 123°25W **294** D7
Fort Frederica U.S.A. 31°13N 81°23W **316** D4
Fort Gaines U.S.A. 31°36N 85°3W **316** D4
Fort Garland U.S.A. 37°26N 105°26W **305** H11
Fort George = Chisasibi
   Canada 53°50N 79°0W **298** B4
Fort George = Prince George
   Canada 53°55N 122°50W **296** C4
Fort George Grenada 12°3N 61°45W **323** q
Fort Good Hope Canada 66°14N 128°40W **294** D6
Fort Gouraud = Fdérik
   Mauritania 22°40N 12°45W **260** D2
Fort Hancock U.S.A. 31°18N 105°51W **314** F2
Fort Hertz = Putao Burma 27°28N 97°30E **241** B6
Fort Hill = Chitipa Malawi 9°41S 33°19E **266** B3
Fort Hope = Eabametoong
   Canada 51°30N 88°0W **298** B2
Fort Irwin U.S.A. 35°16N 116°41W **307** K10
Fort Jameson = Chipata
   Zambia 13°38S 32°28E **269** E3
Fort Jeudy, Pt. of Grenada 11°59N 61°42W **323** q
Fort Johnston = Mangoche
   Malawi 14°25S 35°16E **269** E4
Fort Kent U.S.A. 47°15N 68°36W **309** B19
Fort Klamath U.S.A. 42°42N 122°0W **304** D3
Fort Lamy = Ndjamena
   Chad 12°10N 15°0E **259** F2
Fort-Laperrine = Tamanrasset
   Algeria 22°50N 5°30E **261** D6
Fort Laramie U.S.A. 42°13N 104°31W **304** E11
Fort Lauderdale U.S.A. 26°7N 80°8W **317** J9
Fort Lee U.S.A. 40°51N 73°58W **132** A2
Fort Liard Canada 60°14N 123°30W **296** B4
Fort Liberté Haiti 19°42N 71°51W **321** C5
Fort Lupton U.S.A. 40°5N 104°49W **304** F11
Fort MacKay Canada 57°12N 111°41W **296** B6
Fort Macleod Canada 49°45N 113°30W **296** D6
Fort MacMahon = El Homr
   Algeria 29°43N 1°45E **261** C5
Fort McMurray Canada 56°44N 111°7W **296** B6
Fort McPherson Canada 67°30N 134°55W **294** D5
Fort Madison U.S.A. 40°38N 91°27W **310** D5
Fort Manning = Mchinji
   Malawi 13°47S 32°58E **269** E3
Fort Marlborough
   Indonesia 3°48S 102°15E **234** C2
Fort Mason Center San Francisco, U.S.A. **136** a1
Fort Matanzas U.S.A. 29°43N 81°14W **316** F8
Fort Meade U.S.A. 27°45N 81°48W **317** H8
Fort Mitchell U.S.A. 32°20N 85°1W **316** C4
Fort Morgan U.S.A. 40°15N 103°48W **304** F12
Fort Myers U.S.A. 26°39N 81°52W **317** J8
Fort Myers Beach U.S.A. 26°27N 81°57W **317** J8
Fort Myers Villas U.S.A. 26°32N 81°52W **317** J8
Fort Napoléon Guadeloupe 15°52N 61°35W **322** e
Fort Nelson Canada 58°50N 122°44W **296** B4
Fort Nelson → Canada 59°32N 124°0W **296** B4
Fort Norman = Tulita
   Canada 64°57N 125°30W **294** E6
Fort Ogden U.S.A. 27°5N 81°57W **317** H8
Fort Payne U.S.A. 34°26N 85°43W **315** D12
Fort Peck U.S.A. 48°1N 106°27W **304** B10
Fort Peck Dam U.S.A. 48°0N 106°26W **304** C10
Fort Peck L. U.S.A. 48°0N 106°26W **304** C10
Fort Pierce U.S.A. 27°27N 80°20W **317** H9
Fort Pierre U.S.A. 44°21N 100°22W **310** C4
Fort Pierre Bordes = Ti-n-Zaouatene
   Algeria 19°55N 2°55E **261** E5
Fort. Plain U.S.A. 42°56N 74°37W **313** D10
Fort Portal Uganda 0°40N 30°20E **266** D3
Fort Providence Canada 61°3N 117°40W **296** A5
Fort Pulaski U.S.A. 32°2N 80°54W **316** C5
Fort Qu'Appelle Canada 50°45N 103°50W **297** C8
Fort Recovery U.S.A. 40°25N 84°47W **311** D12
Fort Resolution Canada 61°10N 113°40W **296** A6
Fort Rixon Zimbabwe 20°2S 29°17E **269** G2
Fort Rosebery = Mansa
   Zambia 11°13S 28°55E **267** E2
Fort Ross U.S.A. 38°32N 123°13W **306** G3
Fort-Rousset = Owando
   Congo 0°29S 15°55E **264** C3
Fort Rupert = Waskaganish
   Canada 51°30N 78°40W **298** B4

Fort St. James Canada 54°30N 124°10W **296** C4
Fort St. John Canada 56°15N 120°50W **296** B4
Fort Sandeman = Zhob
   Pakistan 31°20N 69°31E **242** D3
Fort Saskatchewan
   Canada 53°40N 113°15W **296** C6
Fort Scott U.S.A. 37°50N 94°42W **310** G7
Fort Severn Canada 56°0N 87°40W **298** A2
Fort Shevchenko
   Kazakhstan 44°35N 50°23E **191** H10
Fort Simpson Canada 61°45N 121°15W **296** B4
Fort Smith Alta., Canada 60°0N 111°51W **296** B6
Fort Smith Ark., U.S.A. 35°23N 94°25W **314** D7
Fort Stockton U.S.A. 30°53N 102°53W **314** F3
Fort Sumner U.S.A. 34°28N 104°15W **305** J11
Fort Thomas U.S.A. 39°4N 84°26W **311** E12
Fort Thompson U.S.A. 44°3N 99°26W **308** C4
Fort Trinquet = Bîr Mogreïn
   Mauritania 25°10N 11°25W **260** C2
Fort Union △ U.S.A. 35°54N 105°1W **305** J11
Fort Uritskogo = Fort Shevchenko
   Kazakhstan 44°35N 50°23E **191** H10
Fort Valley U.S.A. 32°33N 83°53W **316** C6
Fort Vermilion Canada 58°24N 116°0W **296** B5
Fort Walton Beach
   U.S.A. 30°25N 86°36W **317** E3
Fort Ware Canada 57°26N 125°41W **296** B3
Fort Wayne U.S.A. 41°4N 85°9W **311** C11
Fort White U.S.A. 29°55N 82°43W **316** F7
Fort William U.K. 56°49N 5°7W **167** E3
Fort Worth U.S.A. 32°43N 97°19W **314** E6
Fort Yates U.S.A. 46°5N 100°38W **308** B3
Fort Yukon U.S.A. 66°34N 145°16W **303** C11
Fortaleza = Pedra Azul
   Brazil 16°2S 41°17W **333** E3
Fortaleza Bolivia 12°6S 66°49W **330** C4
Fortaleza Brazil 3°45S 38°35W **332** B4
Forteau Canada 51°28N 56°58W **299** B8
Fortescue → Australia 21°0S 116°4E **278** D2
Fortescue River Roadhouse
   Australia 21°17S 116°8E **278** D2
Forth → U.K. 56°9N 3°50W **167** E5
Forth, Firth of U.K. 56°5N 2°55W **167** E5
Forth Rail Bridge U.K. 56°0N 3°23W **121** A1
Forth Road Bridge U.K. 56°0N 3°24W **121** A1
Forthassa Rharbia Algeria 32°52N 1°18E **261** B4
Fortín General Pando
   Paraguay 19°45S 59°47W **331** D6
Fortín Madrejón
   Paraguay 20°45S 59°52W **331** E6
Fortín Teniente Primero Ramiro
   Espínola Paraguay 21°27S 61°30W **331** E5
Fortín Uno Argentina 38°50S 65°18W **336** A3
Fortore → Italy 41°55N 15°17E **199** G12
Fortrose N.Z. 46°38S 168°45E **285** G3
Fortrose Highl., U.K. 57°35N 4°9W **167** D4
Fortuna Spain 38°11N 1°7W **197** G3
Fortuna Calif., U.S.A. 40°36N 124°9W **304** F1
Fortuna N. Dak., U.S.A. 48°55N 103°47W **308** A2
Fortuna Ledge = Marshall
   U.S.A. 61°53N 162°5W **303** F7
Fortune Canada 47°4N 55°50W **299** C8
Fortune B. Canada 47°30N 55°22W **299** C8
Forûr Iran 26°17N 54°32E **247** E7
Fos-sur-Mer France 43°26N 4°56E **175** E8
Fosen Norway 63°50N 10°20E **160** E14
Foshan China 23°6N 113°9E **121** B2
Fosnavåg Norway 62°22N 5°38E **164** B2
Foso Ghana 5°43N 1°15W **263** D4
Foss Iceland 63°51N 17°52W **155** D9
Fossano Italy 44°33N 7°43E **198** D4
Fossil U.S.A. 45°0N 120°9W **304** D3
Fossil Butte △ U.S.A. 41°50N 110°27W **304** F8
Fossombrone Italy 43°41N 12°48E **199** E9
Fossvellir Iceland 65°27N 14°37W **155** B12
Foster Vic., Australia 38°40S 146°15E **283** E7
Foster Qué., Canada 45°17N 72°30W **313** A12
Foster Ky., U.S.A. 38°48N 84°13W **311** F12
Foster → Canada 55°47N 105°49W **297** B7
Foster Village U.S.A. 21°21N 157°55W **302** K14
Fosters Ra. Australia 21°35S 133°48E **280** C1
Fostoria U.S.A. 41°10N 83°25W **311** C13
Fót Hungary 47°35N 19°11E **117** A3
Fotadrevo Madag. 24°3S 45°1E **272** C2
Fougamou France 47°53N 11°0E **264** C2
Fougères France 48°21N 1°14W **172** D5
Foul Pt. Sri Lanka 8°35N 81°18E **245** K5
Foula U.K. 60°10N 2°5W **167** A6
Foul Roads Trin. & Tob. 10°41N 61°33W **323** d
Fourchambault France 47°2N 3°3E **173** E10
Fourchue, Île St.-Martin 17°37N 62°53E **322** c
Fouriesburg S. Africa 28°38S 28°14E **270** C4
Fourmies France 50°1N 4°2E **173** B11
Fourna Greece 39°3N 21°52E **204** B3
Fournaise, Piton de la
   Réunion 21°14S 55°43E **272** f
Fourni Greece 37°36N 26°32E **205** D8
Fourqueux France 48°53N 2°3E **144** b
Fours France 46°50N 3°42E **173** F10
Fous, Pte. de Dominica 15°12N 61°20W **323** k
Fousinshan = Fuxin
   Canada 64°57N 125°30W **294** E6
Fouta Djallon Guinea 11°20N 12°10W **262** C2
Foux, Cap-à- Haiti 19°43N 73°27W **321** C5
Foveaux Str. N.Z. 46°42S 168°10E **285** G3
Fowler Calif., U.S.A. 36°38N 119°41W **306** J7
Fowler Colo., U.S.A. 38°8N 104°2W **304** G11
Fowler, Pt. Australia 32°2S 132°32E **279** F5
Fowlers B. Australia 31°59S 132°34E **279** F5
Fowlerville U.S.A. 42°40N 84°4W **311** B12
Fox → Canada 56°3N 93°18W **297** B10
Fox Creek Canada 54°24N 116°48W **296** C5
Fox Is. U.S.A. 53°0N 168°0W **303** D3
Fox Lake Alta., Canada 58°28N 114°31W **296** B6
Fox Lake Ill., U.S.A. 42°24N 88°11W **311** B8
Fox Studios Australia 33°55S 151°13E **139** B2
Fox Valley Canada 50°30N 109°25W **297** C7
Foxboro Ont., Canada 44°14N 77°26W **312** B7
Foxboro Mass., U.S.A. 42°4N 71°16W **313** D13
Foxdale Australia 20°22S 148°35E **282** b
Foxe Basin Canada 66°0N 77°0W **295** D16
Foxe Chan. Canada 65°0N 80°0W **295** E16
Foxe Pen. Canada 65°0N 76°0W **295** E16

Foxen Sweden 59°25N 11°55E **162** E5
Foxford Ireland 53°59N 9°7W **166** C2
Foxrock Ireland 53°17N 6°11W **128** E2
Foxton N.Z. 40°29S 175°18E **284** E4
Foyle, Lough U.K. 55°7N 7°4W **166** A4
Foynes Ireland 52°37N 9°7W **166** D2
Foz Spain 43°33N 7°20W **194** B3
Foz do Copeá Brazil 3°52S 63°19W **329** D5
Foz do Cunene Angola 17°15S 11°48E **265** F2
Foz do Gregório Brazil 6°47S 70°44W **330** B3
Foz do Iguaçu Brazil 25°30S 54°30W **335** B5
Foz do Mamoriá Brazil 2°27S 66°52W **329** D5
Frackville U.S.A. 40°47N 76°14W **313** F8
Fraga Spain 41°32N 0°21E **196** D5
Fraile Muerto Uruguay 32°31S 54°32W **335** C5
Framingham U.S.A. 42°18N 71°24W **313** D13
Framnes Iceland 66°1N 20°0W **155** C4
Frampol Poland 50°41N 22°40E **185** H9
Franca Brazil 20°33S 47°30W **333** F2
Francavilla al Mare Italy 42°25N 14°17E **199** F11
Francavilla Fontana
   Italy 40°32N 17°35E **201** B10
France ■ Europe 47°0N 3°0E **171** C5
Frances Australia 36°41S 140°55E **282** C3
Frances → Canada 60°16N 129°10W **296** A3
Frances L. Canada 61°23N 129°30W **296** A3
Franceville Gabon 1°40S 13°32E **264** C2
Franche-Comté □ France 46°50N 5°55E **173** F12
Francis Case, L. U.S.A. 43°4N 98°34W **308** D4
Francisco Beltrão Brazil 26°5S 53°4W **335** B5
Francisco de Orellana
   Ecuador 0°28S 76°58W **328** D2
Francisco Ignacio Madero Coahuila,
   Mexico 25°48N 103°18W **318** B4
Francisco Ignacio Madero Durango,
   Mexico 24°26N 104°18W **318** C4
Francisco Ignacio Madero, Presa
   Mexico 28°10N 105°37W **318** B3
Francisco Sá Brazil 16°28S 43°30W **333** E3
Francistown Botswana 21°7S 27°33E **271** B4
Francofonte Italy 37°14N 14°53E **201** E7
François Canada 47°35N 56°45W **299** C8
François, B. du Martinique 14°38N 60°54W **322** j
François L. Canada 54°0N 125°30W **296** C3
Francois Peron △
   Australia 25°42S 113°33E **279** E1
Franconia U.S.A. 38°47N 77°7W **143** C3
Frans Pk. U.S.A. 43°58N 109°20W **304** E9
Franeker Neths. 53°12N 5°33E **170** A5
Frank Hann △ Australia 32°52S 120°19E **279** F3
Frank Lloyd Wright Home
   U.S.A. 41°53N 87°47W **119** B2
Frankel U.S.A. 1°18N 103°55E **138** B3
Frankenberg Germany 51°3N 8°48E **178** D4
Frankenhöhe → Germany 49°19N 10°20E **181** F6
Frankenstein = Ząbkowice Śląskie
   Poland 50°35N 16°50E **185** H3
Frankenthal Germany 50°20N 11°30E **179** E7
Frankenwald Germany 50°15N 11°30E **179** E7
Frankfield Jamaica 18°8N 77°22W **320** a
Frankford Ont., Canada 44°12N 77°36W **312** B7
Frankford Mo., U.S.A. 39°29N 91°19W **310** E5
Frankfort Free State,
   S. Africa 27°17S 28°30E **271** C4
Frankfort Ind., U.S.A. 40°17N 86°31W **311** D10
Frankfort Kans., U.S.A. 39°42N 96°25W **308** F5
Frankfort Ky., U.S.A. 38°12N 84°52W **311** F12
Frankfort Ohio, U.S.A. 39°24N 83°11W **311** E13
Frankfort Brandenburg,
   Germany 52°20N 14°32E **178** C10
Frankfurt Hessen, Germany 50°7N 8°41E **178** E4
Frankfurt ✕ (FRA) Germany 50°1N 8°34E **179** E4
Fränkische Alb Germany 49°10N 11°23E **181** F7
Fränkische Rezat →
   Germany 49°11N 11°1E **179** F7
Fränkische Saale →
   Germany 50°3N 9°42E **179** E5
Fränkische Schweiz
   Germany 49°50N 11°16E **179** F7
Fränkische Schweiz-Veldensteiner
   Forst △ Germany 49°45N 11°22E **179** F7
Frankland → Australia 35°0S 116°48E **279** G2
Franklin Ga., U.S.A. 33°17N 85°6W **316** B4
Franklin Ind., U.S.A. 39°29N 86°3W **311** E10
Franklin Ky., U.S.A. 36°43N 86°35W **308** G10
Franklin Mass., U.S.A. 42°5N 71°24W **313** D13
Franklin N.H., U.S.A. 43°27N 71°39W **313** C13
Franklin N.Y., U.S.A. 42°20N 75°9W **313** D9
Franklin Nebr., U.S.A. 40°6N 98°57W **308** E4
Franklin Ohio, U.S.A. 39°34N 84°18W **311** E12
Franklin Pa., U.S.A. 41°24N 79°50W **312** E5
Franklin Tenn., U.S.A. 35°55N 86°52W **315** D11
Franklin W. Va., U.S.A. 38°39N 79°20W **309** F14
Franklin, Pt. U.S.A. 70°55N 158°48W **303** A8
Franklin B. Canada 69°45N 126°0W **294** D6
Franklin D. Roosevelt L.
   U.S.A. 48°18N 118°9W **304** B4
Franklin-Gordon Wild Rivers △
   Australia 42°18S 145°51E **281** G4
Franklin Harb. Australia 33°42S 136°55E **282** B2
Franklin I. Antarctica 76°10S 168°30E **151** D11
Franklin I. Ont., Canada 45°24N 80°20W **312** A4
Franklin L. U.S.A. 40°25N 115°22W **304** F6
Franklin Mts. N.W.T.,
   Canada 65°0N 125°0W **294** D6
Franklin Mts. N.Z. 44°55S 167°45E **285** F2
Franklin Park Ill., U.S.A. 41°55N 87°52W **119** B2
Franklin Park Mass.,
   U.S.A. 42°18N 71°5W **116** B2
Franklin Park Va., U.S.A. 43°25N 64°4E **175** E4
Franklin Res. N.S., Canada 34°5N 118°24W **126** B2
Franklin Str. Canada 72°0N 96°0W **294** C12
Franklinton U.S.A. 30°51N 90°9W **315** F9
Franklinville U.S.A. 42°20N 78°27W **312** D6
Franklyn Mt. U.S.A. 38°45S 172°42E **285** C7
Franklin Australia 38°8S 145°8E **283** B6
Frankston Australia 37°53N 17°50E **162** B3
Fränö Sweden 62°30N 17°50E **162** B3
Fransfontein Namibia 20°12S 15°1E **270** B2
Fränsta Sweden 62°30N 16°11E **162** B3
Frantsa Iosifa, Zemlya
   Russia 82°0N 55°0E **214** A6
Franz Canada 48°25N 84°30W **298** C3
Franz Josef Land = Frantsa Iosifa,
   Zemlya Russia 82°0N 55°0E **214** A6
Franz Josef Strauss ✕ (MUC)
   Germany 48°21N 11°47E **181** G7
Franzburg Germany 54°11N 12°55E **178** A8
Frascati Italy 41°48N 12°41E **199** G9
Fraser → B.C., Canada 49°7N 123°11W **306** A3
Fraser → Nfld. & L.,
   Canada 56°39N 62°10W **299** A7
Fraser, Mt. Australia 25°35S 118°20E **279** E2
Fraser I. Australia 25°15S 153°10E **281** D5
Fraser Lake Canada 54°0N 124°50W **296** C4
Fraserburg S. Africa 31°55S 21°30E **270** D3
Fraserburgh U.K. 57°42N 2°1W **167** D6
Fraserdale Canada 49°55N 81°37W **298** C3

Fraserpet = Kushalnagar
   India 12°14N 75°57E **245** H2
Frasertown N.Z. 38°58S 177°28E **284** E6
Fraserville = Rivière-du-Loup
   Canada 47°50N 69°30W **299** C6
Frashër Albania 40°23N 20°30E **202** F4
Frasne France 46°50N 6°10E **173** F13
Frătești Romania 43°58N 25°58E **183** G10
Frauenfeld Switz. 47°34N 8°54E **179** H4
Fresco → Brazil 7°15S 51°30W **331** B7
Fresco Ivory C. 5°3N 5°31W **262** D3
Fresco Brazil 7°15S 51°30W **331** B7
Fresh Pond U.S.A. 42°22N 71°8W **116** B2
Freshfield, C. Antarctica 68°25S 151°10E **151** C10
Fresnay-sur-Sarthe France 48°17N 0°1E **172** D7
Fresnes France 48°45N 2°18E **134** B2
Fresnillo Mexico 23°10N 102°53W **318** C4
Fresno U.S.A. 36°44N 119°47W **306** J7
Fresno Res. U.S.A. 48°36N 109°57W **304** B9
Fresvik Norway 61°4N 6°55E **164** C3
Frewsburg U.S.A. 42°3N 79°10W **312** D5
Frew → Australia 20°0S 135°38E **280** C2
Frewena Australia 19°25S 135°25E **280** C2
Frias Argentina 28°40S 65°5W **334** B2
Fribourg Switz. 46°49N 7°9E **179** J3
Fribourg □ Switz. 46°40N 7°0E **179** J3
Frick Collection New York, U.S.A. **132** b3
Fridafors Sweden 56°26N 14°39E **163** H8
Friday Harbor U.S.A. 48°32N 123°1W **306** B3
Friedberg Bayern, Germany 48°21N 10°59E **179** G6
Friedberg Hessen, Germany 50°19N 8°45E **179** E4
Friedeberg = Mirsk
   Poland 50°58N 15°23E **185** H2
Friedeberg in Neumark = Strzelce
   Krajeńskie Poland 52°52N 15°33E **185** F2
Friedenau Germany 52°28N 13°22E **115** B3
Friedens U.S.A. 40°3N 78°59W **312** F6
Friedland = Mieroszów
   Poland 50°40N 16°11E **185** H3
Friedland Germany 53°40N 13°33E **178** B9
Friedrichsfelde Germany 52°29N 13°33E **115** B4
Friedrichshafen Germany 47°39N 9°30E **179** H5
Friedrichshagen Germany 52°27N 13°37E **115** B4
Friedrichshain Germany 52°31N 13°27E **115** A3
Friedrichskoog Germany 54°1N 8°53E **178** A4
Friedrichslust Germany 52°35N 13°10E **115** A2
Friedrichstadt Germany 54°23N 9°6E **178** A5
Friendly Is. = Tonga ■
   Pac. Oc. 19°50S 174°30W **287** T13
Friendship U.S.A. 42°12N 78°8W **312** D6
Friesack Germany 52°44N 12°34E **178** C8
Friesland □ Neths. 53°5N 5°50E **170** A5
Friesoythe Germany 53°1N 7°51E **178** B3
Frigate Seychelles 4°35S 55°56E **272** c
Frigate Bay
   St. Kitts & Nevis 17°16N 62°41W **322** d
Frigate I. Grenada 12°25N 61°29W **323** q
Friggesund Sweden 61°54N 16°33E **162** C10
Frillesås Sweden 57°20N 12°12E **163** H6
Frihetsli Norway 68°48N 19°51E **160** B3
Frinnaryd Sweden 57°55N 14°50E **163** G8
Frio → U.S.A. 28°26N 98°11W **314** G5
Frio, C. Brazil 22°50S 41°50W **335** B7
Friona U.S.A. 34°38N 102°43W **314** D3
Friol Spain 43°2N 7°47W **194** B3
Frisches Haff = Zalew Wiślany
   Poland 54°20N 19°50E **184** D6
Fristad Sweden 57°50N 13°0E **163** G6
Fritch U.S.A. 35°38N 101°36W **314** D4
Fritsla Sweden 57°33N 12°47E **163** G6
Fritzlar Germany 51°7N 9°16E **178** D5
Friuli-Vénezia Giulia □
   Italy 46°0N 13°0E **199** B9
Frobisher B. Canada 62°30N 66°0W **295** E18
Frobisher Bay = Iqaluit
   Canada 63°44N 68°31W **295** E18
Frobisher L. Canada 56°20N 108°15W **297** B7
Frohavet Norway 64°0N 9°30E **160** E13
Frohnbruck = Veselí nad Lužnicí
   Czech Rep. 49°12N 14°43E **180** B7
Frohnleiten Austria 47°16N 15°19E **180** E8
Frolovo Russia 49°45N 43°40E **190** F6
Frombork Poland 54°21N 19°41E **184** D6
Frome U.K. 51°14N 2°19W **169** F5
Frome → U.K. 50°41N 2°6W **169** G5
Frome, L. Australia 30°45S 139°45E **282** A3
Frome Downs Australia 31°13S 139°45E **282** A3
Frómista Spain 42°16N 4°25W **194** C6
Front Range U.S.A. 40°25N 105°45W **301** G18
Front Royal U.S.A. 38°55N 78°12W **309** F14
Fronteira Portugal 39°3N 7°39W **195** F3
Fronteiras Brazil 7°5S 40°37W **332** C3
Frontenac △ Canada 44°32N 76°30W **313** B8
Frontera Tabasco, Mexico 18°32N 92°38W **319** D6
Frontera Mexico 30°56N 109°31E **318** A3
Frontignan France 43°27N 3°45E **174** E7
Frontón, I. Peru 12°5S 77°11W **124** b3
Frosinone Italy 41°38N 13°19E **200** A6
Frostburg U.S.A. 39°39N 78°56W **309** F14
Frostisen Norway 68°14N 17°10E **160** B17
Frostproof U.S.A. 27°45N 81°31W **317** H8
Frouard France 48°47N 6°8E **173** D13
Frøya Norway 63°43N 8°40E **160** E13
Fruges France 50°30N 2°8E **173** B9
Fruithurst U.S.A. 33°43N 85°26W **316** B4
Fruitland Park U.S.A. 28°51N 81°54W **317** G8
Frumoasa Romania 46°28N 25°48E **183** E10
Frunze = Bishkek
   Kyrgyzstan 42°54N 74°46E **218** C8
Frunze Russia 55°47N 37°13W **124** d
Fruzivka Ukraine 47°20N 29°45E **183** C14
Frutal Brazil 20°0S 49°0W **333** F2
Frutigen Switz. 46°35N 7°38E **179** J3
Frýdek-Místek Czech Rep. 49°40N 18°20E **181** B11
Frýdlant Czech Rep. 50°56N 15°9E **185** H2
Fryeburg U.S.A. 44°1N 70°59W **313** B14
Fryvaldov = Jeseník
   Czech Rep. 50°0N 17°8E **181** A10
Fthiótida □ Greece 38°50N 22°25E **204** B4
Fu Jiang → China 30°0N 106°16E **228** C6
Fu Xian = Wafangdian
   China 39°38N 121°58E **227** E11

Fu Xian China 36°0N 109°20E **226** G5
Fua Mulaku Maldives 0°17S 73°26E **272** d
Fu'an China 27°11N 119°36E **229** D12
Fubian China 31°7N 102°22E **228** B4
Fucécchio Italy 43°44N 10°48E **198** E7
Fucheng China 37°50N 116°10E **226** F9
Fuchou = Fuzhou China 26°5N 119°16E **229** D12
Fuchū Hiroshima, Japan 34°34N 133°14E **222** C5
Fuchū Tōkyō, Japan 35°40N 139°29E **140** A1
Fuchuan China 24°50N 111°5E **229** E8
Fuchun Jiang → China 30°5N 120°5E **229** B13
Fúcino, Piana del Italy 42°1N 13°31E **199** F10
Fuding China 27°20N 120°12E **229** D13
Fuencaliente Canary Is. 28°28N 17°50W **153** e1
Fuencaliente Spain 38°25N 4°18W **195** G6
Fuencaliente, Pta.
   Canary Is. 28°27N 17°51W **153** e1
Fuencarral Spain 40°29N 3°42W **127** B1
Fuengirola Spain 36°32N 4°41W **195** H6
Fuenlabrada Spain 40°17N 3°48W **127** C1
Fuensalida Spain 40°3N 4°12W **194** E6
Fuente-Álamo Spain 38°44N 1°24W **197** G3
Fuente Álamo de Murcia
   Spain 37°42N 1°6W **197** H3
Fuente de Cantos Spain 38°15N 6°18W **195** G4
Fuente del Maestre Spain 38°31N 6°28W **195** G4
Fuente el Fresno Spain 39°14N 3°46W **195** F7
Fuente Obejuna Spain 38°15N 5°25W **195** G5
Fuente Palmera Spain 37°42N 5°6W **195** H5
Fuentes de Andalucía
   Spain 37°28N 5°20W **195** H5
Fuentes de Ebro Spain 41°31N 0°38W **196** D4
Fuentes de León Spain 38°5N 6°32W **195** G4
Fuentes de Oñoro Spain 40°33N 6°52W **194** E4
Fuentesaúco Spain 41°15N 5°30W **194** D5
Fuerte → Mexico 25°54N 109°22W **318** B3
Fuerte Olimpo Paraguay 21°0S 57°51W **334** A4
Fuerteventura Canary Is. 28°30N 14°0W **153** e2
Fuerteventura ✕ (FUE)
   Canary Is. 28°24N 13°52W **153** e2
Fufeng China 34°22N 108°0E **226** G5
Fuga I. Phil. 18°52N 121°20E **232** B3
Fughmah Yemen 16°9N 49°26E **249** C5
Fugong China 27°3N 98°47E **228** D2
Fugou China 34°3N 114°25E **226** G8
Fugu China 39°2N 111°3E **226** E6
Fuhai China 47°2N 87°25E **217** C11
Fuḥaymī Iraq 34°16N 42°10E **213** E10
Fuhlsbüttel, Hamburg ✕ (HAM)
   Germany 53°35N 9°59E **178** B5
Fuhsien = Fu Xian China 36°0N 109°20E **226** G5
Fuhsing Changhua, Taiwan 24°3N 120°25E **225** B2
Fuhsing Kaohsiung,
   Taiwan 23°13N 120°48E **225** C2
Fuhsing Taoyüan, Taiwan 24°49N 121°21E **225** B3
Fuji-Hakone-Izu △
   Japan 35°15N 138°45E **223** B10
Fuji-San Japan 35°22N 138°44E **223** B10
Fuji-Yoshida Japan 35°30N 138°46E **223** B10
Fujian □ China 26°0N 118°0E **229** E12
Fujieda Japan 34°52N 138°16E **223** C10
Fujin China 47°16N 132°1E **219** B15
Fujinomiya Japan 35°10N 138°40E **223** B10
Fujioka Japan 36°15N 139°5E **223** A11
Fujisawa Japan 35°22N 139°29E **223** B11
Fujiyama, Mt. = Fuji-San
   Japan 35°22N 138°44E **223** B10
Fukagawa Hokkaidō,
   Japan 43°43N 142°2E **220** C11
Fukagawa Tōkyō, Japan 35°39N 139°48E **140** B3
Fukang China 44°10N 87°59E **217** D11
Fukaya Japan 36°12N 139°12E **223** A11
Fukiage Japan 31°27N 130°17E **222** F2
Fukiage Imperial Garden Tokyo, Japan **140** a4
Fukien = Fujian □ China 26°0N 118°0E **229** E12
Fukuchiyama Japan 35°19N 135°9E **223** B7
Fukue-Shima Japan 32°40N 128°45E **221** H4
Fukuei Chiao Taiwan 25°17N 121°32E **225** A8
Fukui Japan 36°5N 136°10E **223** A8
Fukui □ Japan 33°46N 136°12E **223** B8
Fukuma Japan 33°46N 130°28E **222** D2
Fukuoka Japan 33°39N 130°21E **222** D2
Fukuoka □ Japan 33°30N 131°0E **222** D2
Fukuoka Int. ✕ (FUK)
   Japan 33°34N 130°28E **222** D2
Fukuroi Japan 34°45N 137°55E **223** C9
Fukushima Fukushima,
   Japan 37°44N 140°28E **220** F10
Fukushima Ōsaka, Japan 34°41N 135°28E **133** A1
Fukushima □ Japan 37°30N 140°15E **220** F10
Fukuyama Japan 34°35N 133°20E **222** C6
Fulacunda Guinea-Biss. 11°44N 15°3W **262** C1
Fulaga Fiji 19°8S 178°33W **287** B3
Fulan → Sweden 61°18N 13°4E **162** C7
Fulda U.S.A. 50°32N 9°40E **178** E5
Fulda → Germany 51°25N 9°39E **178** D5
Fulford = North Miami Beach
   U.S.A. 25°55N 80°9W **128** A2
Fulford Harbour Canada 48°47N 123°27W **306** B3
Fulham U.K. 51°28N 0°12W **125** B2
Fuli Taiwan 23°11N 121°14E **225** C2
Fuliang China 29°23N 117°14E **229** C11
Fuling China 29°39N 107°17E **228** C6
Fullarton Trin. & Tob. 10°5N 61°54W **323** l
Fullerton Calif., U.S.A. 33°53N 117°56W **307** M9
Fullerton Nebr., U.S.A. 41°22N 97°58W **308** E5
Fulongquan China 44°20N 124°42E **227** B13
Fülöpszállás Hungary 46°49N 19°15E **182** D4
Fulton Ill., U.S.A. 41°52N 90°11W **310** C6
Fulton Ind., U.S.A. 40°57N 86°16W **311** D10
Fulton Mo., U.S.A. 38°52N 91°57W **310** F5
Fulton N.Y., U.S.A. 43°19N 76°25W **313** C8
Fulufjället Sweden 61°32N 12°41E **162** C6
Fumay France 49°58N 4°40E **173** C11
Fumel France 44°30N 0°58E **174** D4
Fumin China 25°10N 102°29E **228** E4
Funabashi Japan 35°45N 140°0E **223** B12
Funabori Japan 35°41N 139°52E **140** A4
Funafuti = Fongafale
   Tuvalu 8°31S 179°13E **277** B14
Funafuti Pac. Oc. 8°31S 179°13E **277** B14
Funäsdalen Sweden 62°33N 12°32E **162** B6
Funchal Madeira 32°38N 16°54W **153** c
Funchal ✕ (FNC) Madeira 32°41N 16°46W **153** c
Fundación Colombia 10°31N 74°11W **328** A3
Fundão Portugal 40°8N 7°30W **194** E3
Fundão, I. do Brazil 19°55S 40°24W **124** c
Fundong Cameroon 6°15N 10°16E **264** A2
Fundu Moldovei
   Romania 47°32N 25°24E **183** C10
Fundulea Romania 44°28N 26°31E **183** F11
Fundy, B. of Canada 45°0N 66°0W **299** D6
Funing Hebei, China 39°53N 119°12E **227** E10
Funing Jiangsu, China 33°45N 119°50E **227** H10
Funing Yunnan, China 23°35N 105°45E **228** F5
Funiu Shan China 33°30N 112°20E **226** H7
Funsi Ghana 10°21N 1°54W **262** C4

Funtua *Nigeria* 11°30N 7°18E **263** C6
Fuping *Hebei, China* 38°48N 114°12E **226** E8
Fuping *Shaanxi, China* 34°42N 109°10E **226** G5
Fuqing *China* 25°41N 119°21E **229** E12
Fuquan *China* 26°40N 107°27E **228** D6
Furano *Japan* 43°21N 142°23E **220** C11
Furāt, Nahr al → *Asia* 31°0N 47°25E **246** D5
Fureso *Denmark* 55°47N 12°25E **118** A2
Fūrg *Iran* 28°18N 55°13E **247** D7
Furkating *India* 26°28N 93°59E **241** B4
Furman *U.S.A.* 32°41N 81°11W **316** C8
Furmanov *Russia* 57°10N 41°9E **190** B5
Furnas *Azores* 37°46N 25°19W **153** d3
Furnás *Spain* 39°3N 1°32E **206** C2
Furnas, Represa de *Brazil* 20°50S 45°30W **333** F2
Furneaux Group *Australia* 40°10S 147°50E **281** G4
Furqlus *Syria* 34°36N 37°8E **250** D8
Fürstenau *Germany* 52°31N 7°40E **178** C3
Fürstenberg = Eisenhüttenstadt *Germany* 52°9N 14°38E **178** C10
Fürstenberg *Germany* 53°10N 13°8E **178** B9
Fürstenfeld *Austria* 47°3N 16°3E **180** D9
Fürstenfeldbruck *Germany* 48°11N 11°15E **179** G7
Fürstenwalde *Germany* 52°22N 14°3E **178** C10
Fürth *Mittelfranken, Germany* 49°28N 10°59E **179** F6
Fürth *Oberbayern, Germany* 48°2N 11°35E **131** B2
Furth im Wald *Germany* 49°18N 12°50E **179** F8
Furtwangen *Germany* 48°2N 8°12E **179** G4
Furudal *Sweden* 61°10N 15°11E **162** C9
Furukawa *Gifu, Japan* 36°14N 137°11E **223** A9
Furukawa *Miyagi, Japan* 38°34N 140°58E **220** E10
Furulund *Sweden* 55°46N 13°6E **163** J7
Furuvik *Sweden* 61°38N 17°20E **162** D11
Fury and Hecla Str. *Canada* 69°56N 84°0W **295** D15
Fusagasugá *Colombia* 4°21N 74°22W **328** C3
Fuscaldo *Italy* 39°25N 16°2E **201** C9
Fushan *Shandong, China* 37°30N 121°15E **227** F11
Fushan *Shanxi, China* 35°58N 111°51E **226** G6
Fushë Arrëz *Albania* 42°4N 20°2E **202** D4
Fushe Kosove = Kosovo Polje *Kosovo* 42°40N 21°5E **202** D5
Fushë Krujë *Albania* 41°29N 19°43E **202** E3
Fushun *Liaoning, China* 41°50N 123°56E **224** B1
Fushun *Sichuan, China* 29°13N 104°52E **228** C5
Fusong *China* 42°20N 127°15E **224** A3
Füssen *Germany* 47°34N 10°42E **179** H6
Fusui *China* 22°40N 107°56E **228** F6
Futago-tamagawaen *Japan* 35°36N 139°39E **140** B2
Futago-Yama *Japan* 33°35N 131°36E **222** D3
Futian *China* 22°32N 114°4E **219** a
Futiga *Amer. Samoa* 14°21S 170°45W **302** f
Futog *Serbia* 45°15N 19°42E **182** E4
Futrono *Chile* 40°8S 72°24W **336** B2
Futtsu *Japan* 35°13N 139°49E **223** B11
Fuwa *Egypt* 31°12N 30°33E **256** H7
Fuxian Hu *China* 24°30N 102°53E **228** E4
Fuxin *China* 42°5N 121°48E **227** C11
Fuxing Dao *China* 31°16N 121°33E **138** B2
Fuxing Park *China* 31°13N 121°27E **138** B1
Fuxinglu *China* 39°52N 116°16E **114** B1
Fuyang *Anhui, China* 33°0N 115°48E **226** H8
Fuyang *Zhejiang, China* 30°5N 119°57E **229** B12
Fuyang He → *China* 38°12N 117°0E **226** E9
Fuying Dao *China* 26°34N 120°9E **229** D13
Fuyong *China* 22°40N 113°49E **219** a
Fuyot Springs △ *Phil.* 17°1N 121°58E **232** C3
Fuyu *Heilongjiang, China* 47°49N 124°27E **219** B13
Fuyu *Jilin, China* 45°12N 124°43E **227** B13
Fuyuan *China* 25°40N 104°16E **228** E5
Fuyun *China* 47°0N 89°28E **217** C11
Füzesgyarmat *Hungary* 47°6N 21°14E **182** C6
Fuzhou = Linchuan *China* 27°57N 116°15E **229** D11
Fuzhou *China* 26°5N 119°16E **229** D12
Füzuli *Azerbaijan* 39°36N 47°8E **213** C12
Fyn *Denmark* 55°20N 10°30E **163** J4
Fyne, L. *U.K.* 55°59N 5°23W **167** F3
Fynshav *Denmark* 54°59N 9°59E **163** K3
Fyresdal *Norway* 59°11N 8°5E **164** E5
Fyresvatn *Norway* 59°6N 8°10E **164** E5
Fyzabad = Faizabad *India* 26°45N 82°10E **243** F10
Fyzabad *Trin. & Tob.* 10°14N 61°33W **323** t

G

G. Ross Lord Park *Canada* 43°47N 79°28W **141** A2
Ga *Ghana* 9°47N 2°30W **262** D4
Ga-eun *S. Korea* 36°38N 128°5E **224** D4
Gaafu Alifu Atoll *Maldives* 4°45N 73°26E **272** d
Gaalkacyo *Somali Rep.* 6°30N 47°30E **267** C6
Gaanda *Nigeria* 10°10N 12°27E **263** C7
Gabaldon *Phil.* 15°37N 121°20E **232** D3
Gabas → *France* 43°46N 0°42W **174** E3
Gabba *Australia* 9°45S 142°38E **280** a
Gabela *Angola* 11°0S 14°24E **265** E2
Gaberones = Gaborone *Botswana* 24°45S 25°57E **270** B4
Gabès *Tunisia* 33°53N 10°2E **258** B2
Gabès □ *Tunisia* 33°35N 9°30E **261** B6
Gabès, G. de *Tunisia* 34°0N 10°30E **258** B2
Gabgaba, W. → *Egypt* 22°10N 33°5E **256** C3
Gabia *Dem. Rep. of the Congo* 4°37S 17°14E **265** C3
Gabia la Grande *Spain* 37°8N 3°40W **195** H7
Gąbin *Poland* 52°23N 19°41E **185** F6
Gablonz = Jablonec nad Nisou *Czech Rep.* 50°43N 15°10E **180** A8
Gabon ■ *Africa* 0°10S 10°0E **264** C2
Gabon → *Gabon* 0°25N 9°20E **264** B1
Gaborone *Botswana* 24°45S 25°57E **270** B4
Gabrat Sai'd *Sudan* 16°6N 31°50E **266** A3
Gabriels *U.S.A.* 44°26N 74°12W **313** B10
Gābrīk *Iran* 25°44N 58°28E **247** E8
Gabro *Ethiopia* 6°18N 43°16E **267** C5
Gabrovo *Bulgaria* 42°52N 25°19E **203** D9
Gabú = Nova Lamego *Guinea-Biss.* 12°19N 14°11W **262** C2
Gacé *France* 48°49N 0°20E **172** D7
Gāch Sār *Iran* 36°7N 51°19E **247** B6
Gachsārān *Iran* 30°15N 50°45E **247** D6
Gacko *Bos.-H.* 43°10N 18°33E **202** C2
Gad Hinglaj *India* 16°14N 74°21E **245** F2
Gadag *India* 15°30N 75°45E **245** G2
Gadaisu *Papua N. G.* 10°22S 149°46E **286** F5
Gadamai *Sudan* 17°11N 36°10E **257** D4
Gadap *Pakistan* 25°5N 67°28E **242** G2
Gadarwara *India* 22°50N 78°50E **243** H8
Gadebusch *Germany* 53°42N 11°7E **178** B7
Gadein *Sudan* 8°10N 28°45E **257** F2
Gadhada *India* 22°0N 71°35E **242** J4
Gadis → *Indonesia* 1°2N 98°55E **234** B1
Gádor, Sierra de *Spain* 36°57N 2°45W **195** J8
Gadra *Pakistan* 25°40N 70°38E **242** G4
Gadsden *Ala., U.S.A.* 34°1N 86°1W **316** A3
Gadsden *S.C., U.S.A.* 33°51N 80°46W **316** B9
Gadwal *India* 16°10N 77°50E **245** F3
Gadyach = Hadyach *Ukraine* 50°21N 34°0E **189** G8
Gadzi *C.A.R.* 4°47N 16°42E **264** B3
Gaebong *S. Korea* 37°29N 126°52E **137** C1
Găeşti *Romania* 44°48N 25°19E **183** F10
Gaeta *Italy* 41°12N 13°35E **200** A6
Gaeta, G. di *Italy* 41°6N 13°30E **200** A6
Gaffney *U.S.A.* 35°5N 81°39W **315** D14
Gafsa *Tunisia* 34°24N 8°43E **258** B1
Gafsa □ *Tunisia* 34°30N 8°48E **261** B6
Gagarawa *Nigeria* 12°25N 9°32E **263** C6
Gagaria *India* 25°43N 70°46E **242** G4
Gagarin *Russia* 55°38N 35°0E **188** E8
Găgăuzia □ *Moldova* 46°10N 28°40E **183** D13
Gage Park *U.S.A.* 41°47N 87°42W **119** C2
Gaggenau *Germany* 48°48N 8°18E **179** G4
Gaghamni *Sudan* 11°41N 28°19E **257** E2
Gagil-Tomil, I. *Pac. Oc.* 9°31N 138°12E **287** R16
Gagino *Russia* 55°15N 45°1E **190** C7
Gagliano del Capo *Italy* 39°50N 18°22E **201** C11
Gagnef *Sweden* 60°36N 15°52E **162** D9
Gagnoa *Ivory C.* 6°56N 5°16W **262** D3
Gagnon *Canada* 51°50N 68°5W **299** B6
Gagnon, L. *Canada* 62°3N 110°27W **297** A6
Gagny *France* 48°53N 2°32E **134** A4
Gago Coutinho *São Tomé & Principe* 0°1S 6°32E **265** a
Gagra *Georgia* 43°20N 40°10E **191** J5
Gahini *Rwanda* 1°50S 30°30E **268** C3
Gahmar *India* 25°27N 83°49E **243** G10
Gai Xian = Gaizhou *China* 40°22N 122°20E **224** B1
Gaibanda *Bangla.* 25°20N 89°36E **241** C2
Gaidouronisi *Greece* 34°53N 25°41E **207** F6
Gail *U.S.A.* 32°46N 101°27W **314** E4
Gail → *Austria* 46°36N 13°53E **180** E6
Gaillac *France* 43°54N 1°54E **174** E5
Gaillard Cut *Panama* 9°3N 79°40W **320** c
Gaillimh = Galway *Ireland* 53°17N 9°3W **166** C2
Gaillon *France* 49°10N 1°20E **172** C8
Gaimán *Argentina* 43°10S 65°25W **336** B3
Gaines *U.S.A.* 41°46N 77°35W **312** E7
Gainesville *Fla., U.S.A.* 29°40N 82°20W **317** F7
Gainesville *Ga., U.S.A.* 34°18N 83°50W **315** D13
Gainesville *Mo., U.S.A.* 36°36N 92°26W **308** G7
Gainesville *Tex., U.S.A.* 33°38N 97°8W **314** E6
Gainsborough *U.K.* 53°24N 0°46W **168** D7
Gairdner, L. *Australia* 31°30S 136°0E **282** A2
Gairloch *U.K.* 57°43N 5°41W **167** D3
Gairloch, L. *U.K.* 57°43N 5°45W **167** D3
Gaizhou *China* 40°22N 122°20E **224** B1
Gaj *Croatia* 45°28N 17°3E **182** E2
Gaj → *Pakistan* 26°26N 67°21E **242** F2
Gajendragarh *India* 15°44N 75°59E **245** G2
Gakona *U.S.A.* 62°18N 145°18W **303** E11
Gakuch *Pakistan* 36°7N 73°45E **243** A5
Gal Oya △ *Sri Lanka* 7°0N 81°20E **245** L5
Gal Oya Res. *Sri Lanka* 7°5N 81°30E **245** L5
Gal Tardo *Somali Rep.* 3°34N 45°58E **267** D6
Galachipa *Bangla.* 22°8N 90°26E **241** D3
Galâla, Gebel el *Egypt* 29°21N 32°22E **256** J8
Galâla el Baharîya, G. el *Egypt* 29°22N 32°23E **251** J3
Galâla el Qiblîya, G. el *Egypt* 28°42N 32°22E **251** K3
Galán, Cerro *Argentina* 25°55S 66°52W **334** B2
Galana → *Kenya* 3°9S 40°8E **268** C5
Galangue *Angola* 13°42S 16°9E **265** E3
Galangue, Serra *Angola* 14°18S 15°52E **265** E3
Galanta *Slovak Rep.* 48°11N 17°45E **181** C10
Galapagar *Spain* 40°36N 3°58W **194** E7
Galápagos = Colón, Arch. de *Ecuador* 0°0 91°0W **330** a
Galapagos Fracture Zone *Pac. Oc.* 3°0N 110°0W **289** G17
Galapagos Rise *Pac. Oc.* 15°0S 95°0W **289** J18
Galashiels *U.K.* 55°37N 2°49W **167** F6
Galata *Turkey* 41°1N 28°58E **122** B1
Galata Tower *Turkey* 41°1N 28°59E **122** B1
Galatas *Greece* 37°30N 23°26E **204** D5
Galatea *N.Z.* 38°24S 176°45E **284** E5
Galateia *Cyprus* 35°25N 34°4E **207** E10
Galaţi *Romania* 45°27N 28°2E **183** E13
Galaţi □ *Romania* 45°45N 27°30E **183** E12
Galatia *Turkey* 39°30N 33°0E **212** C5
Galatina *Italy* 40°10N 18°10E **201** B11
Galátone *Italy* 40°9N 18°4E **201** B11
Galatsi *Greece* 38°1N 23°45E **112** A2
Galax *U.S.A.* 36°40N 80°56W **309** G13
Galaxidi *Greece* 38°22N 22°23E **204** C4
Galbin Govĭ *Mongolia* 43°0N 107°0E **226** C4
Galcaio = Gaalkacyo *Somali Rep.* 6°30N 47°30E **267** C6
Gáldar *Canary Is.* 28°9N 15°39W **153** e1
Galdhøpiggen *Norway* 61°38N 8°18E **164** C5
Galeana *Chihuahua, Mexico* 30°7N 107°38W **318** A3
Galeana *Nuevo León, Mexico* 24°50N 100°4W **318** C5
Galeão, Int. de ✕ (GIG) *Brazil* 22°49S 43°15W **135** A1
Galegu *Sudan* 12°36N 35°2E **257** E4
Galela *Indonesia* 1°50N 127°49E **231** D7
Galena *Alaska, U.S.A.* 64°44N 156°56W **303** D8
Galena *Ill., U.S.A.* 42°25N 90°26W **310** B6
Galeota Pt. *Trin. & Tob.* 10°8N 60°59W **323** t
Galera *Spain* 37°45N 2°33W **197** H2
Galera, Pta. *Chile* 39°59S 73°43W **336** A2
Galera, Pta. da *Azores* 37°42N 25°30W **153** d3
Galera Pt. *Trin. & Tob.* 10°49N 60°54W **323** t
Galesburg *Ill., U.S.A.* 40°57N 90°22W **310** D6
Galesburg *Mich., U.S.A.* 42°17N 85°26W **311** B11
Galestan △ *Iran* 37°30N 56°0E **247** B8
Galeton *U.S.A.* 41°44N 77°39W **312** E7
Galets → *Réunion* 20°56S 55°17E **272** f
Galga *Ethiopia* 6°39N 37°47E **257** F4
Galgasc *Somali Rep.* 0°11N 41°38E **267** D5
Galguduud □ *Somali Rep.* 5°0N 47°0E **267** D6
Galheirão → *Brazil* 12°23S 45°5W **333** D2
Gali *Georgia* 42°37N 41°46E **191** J5
Galicea Mare *Romania* 44°4N 23°19E **183** F8
Galich *Russia* 58°22N 42°24E **190** A6
Galiche *Bulgaria* 43°34N 23°53E **202** C7
Galicia □ *Spain* 42°43N 7°45W **194** C3
Galičica △ *Macedonia* 41°2N 20°55E **202** E4
Galien *U.S.A.* 41°48N 86°30W **311** C10
Galilee = Hagalil *Israel* 32°53N 35°18E **250** F6
Galilee, L. *Australia* 22°20S 145°50E **280** C4
Galilee, Sea of = Yam Kinneret *Israel* 32°45N 35°35E **250** F6
Galim *Cameroon* 7°6N 12°25E **263** D7
Galina Pt. *Jamaica* 18°24N 76°58W **320** a
Galinoporni *Cyprus* 35°31N 34°18E **207** E10
Galion *U.S.A.* 40°44N 82°47W **312** F2
Galion, B. du *Martinique* 14°44N 60°56W **322** j
Galite, Îs. de la *Tunisia* 37°30N 8°59E **261** A6
Galiuro Mts. *U.S.A.* 32°30N 110°20W **305** K8
Galiwinku *Australia* 12°2S 135°34E **280** A2
Gallâbât *Sudan* 12°58N 36°11E **257** E4
Gallan Hd. *U.K.* 58°15N 7°2W **167** C1
Gallarate *Italy* 45°40N 8°48E **198** C5
Gallatin *Mo., U.S.A.* 39°55N 93°58W **310** E3
Gallatin *Tenn., U.S.A.* 36°24N 86°27W **315** C11
Galle *Sri Lanka* 6°5N 80°10E **245** L5
Gállego → *Spain* 41°39N 0°51W **196** D4
Gallegos → *Argentina* 51°35S 69°0W **336** D3
Gallery of Inuit Art = Dominion Centre *Toronto, Canada* **141** b2
Galletti → *Ethiopia* 8°46N 41°10E **257** F5
Galley Hd. *Ireland* 51°32N 8°55W **166** E3
Galliate *Italy* 45°29N 8°42E **198** C5
Gallinas, Pta. *Colombia* 12°28N 71°40W **328** A3
Gallipoli = Gelibolu *Turkey* 40°28N 26°43E **203** F10
Gallipoli *Italy* 40°3N 17°58E **201** B10
Gallipolis *U.S.A.* 38°49N 82°12W **309** F12
Gällivare *Sweden* 67°9N 20°40E **160** C19
Gallneukirchen *Austria* 48°21N 14°25E **180** C7
Gällö *Sweden* 62°55N 15°13E **162** B9
Gallo, C. *Italy* 38°13N 13°19E **200** D6
Gallocanta, L. de *Spain* 40°58N 1°30W **196** E3
Galloo I. *U.S.A.* 43°55N 76°25W **313** C8
Galloway *U.K.* 55°1N 4°29W **167** F4
Galloway, Mull of *U.K.* 54°39N 4°52W **167** G4
Galloway ⌓ *U.K.* 55°3N 4°20W **167** F4
Gallup *U.S.A.* 35°32N 108°45W **305** J9
Gallur *Spain* 41°52N 1°19W **196** D3
Galma Galla *Kenya* 1°11S 40°47E **267** E5
Galong *Australia* 34°37S 148°34E **283** C8
Galool *Somali Rep.* 3°38N 43°49E **267** D5
Galoya *Sri Lanka* 8°10N 80°55E **245** K5
Galt *Calif., U.S.A.* 38°15N 121°18W **306** G5
Galt *Mo., U.S.A.* 40°8N 93°23W **310** D3
Galten *Denmark* 56°9N 9°54E **163** H3
Galtür *Austria* 46°58N 10°11E **180** E3
Galty Mts. *Ireland* 52°22N 8°10W **166** D3
Galtymore *Ireland* 52°21N 8°11W **166** D3
Galugāh *Iran* 36°43N 53°48E **247** B7
Galva *U.S.A.* 41°10N 90°3W **310** C6
Galvarino *Chile* 38°24S 72°47W **336** A2
Galve de Sorbe *Spain* 41°13N 3°10W **196** D1
Galveston *Ind., U.S.A.* 40°35N 86°11W **311** D10
Galveston *Tex., U.S.A.* 29°18N 94°48W **314** G7
Galveston B. *U.S.A.* 29°36N 94°50W **314** G7
Gálvez *Argentina* 32°0S 61°14W **334** C3
Galway *Ireland* 53°17N 9°3W **166** C2
Galway □ *Ireland* 53°22N 9°1W **166** C2
Galway B. *Ireland* 53°13N 9°10W **166** C2
Galyanovo *Russia* 55°48N 37°47E **129** B4
Gam → *Vietnam* 21°55N 105°12E **236** B5
Gamagōri *Japan* 34°50N 137°14E **223** C9
Gamaires, L. *Ethiopia* 11°32N 41°40E **257** E5
Gamawa *Nigeria* 12°10N 10°31E **263** C7
Gamay *Phil.* 12°23N 125°18E **232** E5
Gamay B. *Phil.* 12°21N 125°21E **232** E5
Gamba *Angola* 11°42S 17°14E **265** E3
Gambaga *Ghana* 10°30N 0°28W **263** C4
Gambat *Pakistan* 27°17N 68°26E **242** F3
Gambela *Ethiopia* 8°14N 34°38E **257** F3
Gambela △ *Ethiopia* 8°0N 34°0E **257** F3
Gambela Hizboch □ *Ethiopia* 8°0N 34°0E **257** F3
Gambell *U.S.A.* 63°47N 171°45W **303** E5
Gambhir → *India* 26°58N 77°27E **242** F6
Gambia ■ *W. Afr.* 13°25N 16°0W **262** C1
Gambia → *W. Afr.* 13°28N 16°34W **262** C1
Gambier *U.S.A.* 40°22N 82°23W **312** F2
Gambier, C. *Australia* 11°56S 130°57E **278** B5
Gambier, Îs. *French Polynesia* 23°8S 134°58W **289** f
Gambier Is. *Australia* 35°3S 136°30E **282** C2
Gambier Village *Bahamas* 25°4N 77°30W **153** b
Gambir *Indonesia* 6°9S 106°48E **122** A1
Gambo *C.A.R.* 4°39N 22°16E **264** B4
Gambo *Canada* 48°47N 54°13W **299** C9
Gamboa *Rio de J., Brazil* 22°53S 43°11W **135** B1
Gamboa *Panama* 9°7N 79°42W **320** c
Gamboli *Pakistan* 29°53N 68°24E **242** E3
Gamboloita *Italy* 45°26N 9°13E **129** B2
Gamboma *Congo* 1°55S 15°52E **264** C3
Gamboula *C.A.R.* 4°8N 15°9E **264** B3
Gamka → *S. Africa* 33°18S 21°39E **270** D3
Gamkab → *Namibia* 28°4S 17°54E **270** C2
Gamla Stan *Stockholm, Sweden* **139** c2
Gamlakarleby = Kokkola *Finland* 63°50N 23°8E **160** E20
Gamleby *Sweden* 57°54N 16°24E **163** G10
Gammelbyen *Norway* 59°54N 10°46E **133** A3
Gammon → *Canada* 51°24N 95°44W **297** C9
Gammon Ranges △ *Australia* 30°38S 139°8E **281** E2
Gamo-Gofa *Ethiopia* 5°40N 36°40E **257** F4
Gamoda-Saki *Japan* 33°50N 134°45E **222** D6
Gamou *Niger* 14°20N 9°55E **263** B6
Gampaha *Sri Lanka* 7°5N 79°59E **245** L4
Gampo *S. Korea* 35°48N 129°31E **224** E4
Gampola *Sri Lanka* 7°10N 80°34E **245** L5
Gamtoos → *S. Africa* 33°58S 25°1E **270** D4
Gan *France* 43°12N 0°27W **174** E3
Gan Gan *Argentina* 42°30S 68°10W **336** B3
Gan Goriama, Mts. *Cameroon* 7°44N 12°45E **263** D7
Gan Jiang → *China* 29°15N 116°0E **229** C11
Ganado *U.S.A.* 35°43N 109°33W **305** J9
Ganānita *Sudan* 18°22N 33°50E **256** D3
Gananoque *Canada* 44°20N 76°10W **313** B8
Ganassi *Phil.* 7°49N 124°6E **233** H5
Ganāveh *Iran* 29°35N 50°35E **247** D6
Gäncä *Azerbaijan* 40°45N 46°20E **191** K8
Gancheng *China* 18°51N 108°37E **236** C7
Gand = Gent *Belgium* 51°2N 3°42E **170** C3
Ganda *Angola* 13°3S 14°35E **265** E2
Gandajika *Dem. Rep. of the Congo* 6°46S 23°58E **265** D4
Gandak → *India* 25°39N 85°13E **243** G11
Gandava *Pakistan* 28°32N 67°32E **242** E2
Gander *Canada* 48°58N 54°35W **299** C9
Gander L. *Canada* 48°58N 54°35W **299** C9
Ganderkesee *Germany* 53°2N 8°32E **178** B4
Ganderowe Falls *Zimbabwe* 17°20S 29°10E **269** F2
Gandesa *Spain* 41°3N 0°26E **196** D5
Gandhi Sagar *India* 24°40N 75°40E **242** G6
Gandhinagar *India* 23°15N 72°45E **242** H5
Gandi *Nigeria* 12°55N 5°49E **263** C6
Gandia *Spain* 38°58N 0°9W **197** G4
Gandino *Italy* 45°49N 9°54E **198** C6
Gando, Pta. *Canary Is.* 27°55N 15°22W **153** e1
Gandole *Nigeria* 8°28N 11°35E **263** D7
Gandou *Congo* 2°25N 17°25E **264** B3
Gandu *Brazil* 13°45S 39°30W **333** D4
Gâneb *Mauritania* 18°29N 10°8W **262** B2
Ganedidalem = Gani *Indonesia* 0°48S 128°14E **231** E7
Ganga → *India* 23°20N 90°30E **243** H14
Ganga Sagar *India* 21°38N 88°5E **243** J13
Gangafani *Mali* 14°20N 2°20W **262** C4
Gangakher *India* 18°57N 76°45E **244** E3
Gangan → *India* 28°38N 78°58E **243** E8
Ganganagar *India* 29°56N 73°56E **242** E5
Gangapur *Maharashtra, India* 19°41N 75°1E **244** E2
Gangapur *Raj., India* 26°32N 76°49E **242** F7
Gangara *Niger* 14°35N 8°29E **259** F1
Gangaw *Burma* 22°5N 94°5E **241** D5
Gangaw Taungdan *Burma* 24°55N 96°35E **241** C6
Gangawati *India* 15°30N 76°36E **245** G3
Gangdisê Shan *China* 31°20N 81°0E **243** D9
Gangdong *S. Korea* 37°30N 127°5E **137** B2
Ganges = Ganga → *India* 23°20N 90°30E **243** H14
Ganges *Canada* 48°51N 123°31W **296** D4
Ganges *Hérault, France* 43°56N 3°42E **174** E7
Ganges, Mouths of the *India* 21°30N 90°0E **241** E3
Ganggyeong *S. Korea* 36°10N 127°0E **224** D3
Gånghester *Sweden* 57°42N 13°1E **163** G7
Ganghwa *S. Korea* 37°45N 126°30E **224** D3
Gangi *Italy* 37°48N 14°12E **201** E7
Gângiova *Romania* 43°54N 23°50E **183** G8
Gangnam *S. Korea* 37°30N 126°59E **137** B1
Gangneung *S. Korea* 37°45N 128°54E **224** D4
Gangoh *India* 29°46N 77°18E **242** E7
Gangotri *India* 30°50N 79°10E **243** D8
Gangotri △ *India* 30°50N 79°10E **243** D8
Gangseo *S. Korea* 37°32N 126°51E **137** B1
Gangseong *S. Korea* 38°24N 128°30E **224** C4
Gangtok *India* 27°20N 88°37E **241** B2
Gangtou *China* 23°12N 113°8E **121** A1
Gangu *China* 34°40N 105°15E **226** G3
Gangwa *Dem. Rep. of the Congo* 3°30S 20°54E **264** C4
Gangwei *China* 23°4N 113°11E **121** B2
Gangwon-do □ *S. Korea* 37°45N 128°15E **224** D4
Gangyao *China* 44°12N 126°37E **227** B14
Gani *Indonesia* 0°48S 128°14E **231** E7
Ganj *India* 27°45N 78°57E **243** F8
Ganjam *India* 19°23N 85°4E **244** E7
Ganjiakou *China* 39°54N 116°16E **114** B1
Ganluo *China* 28°58N 102°59E **228** C4
Ganmain *Australia* 34°47S 147°1E **283** C7
Ganna *Sudan* 7°30N 28°2E **266** C2
Gannat *France* 46°7N 3°11E **173** F10
Gannett Peak *U.S.A.* 43°11N 109°39W **304** E9
Ganquan *China* 36°20N 109°20E **226** F5
Gänserdorf *Austria* 48°20N 16°43E **181** C9
Ganshoren *Belgium* 50°52N 4°18E **116** A1
Ganshui *China* 28°40N 106°40E **228** C6
Gansu □ *China* 36°0N 104°0E **226** G3
Ganta *Liberia* 7°15N 8°59W **262** D3
Gantheaume, C. *Australia* 36°4S 137°32E **282** D2
Gantheaume B. *Australia* 27°40S 114°10E **279** E1
Gants Hill *U.K.* 51°34N 0°4E **125** A4
Gantsevichi = Hantsavichy *Belarus* 52°49N 26°30E **177** B14
Gantung *Indonesia* 2°58S 108°9E **235** C3
Ganye *Nigeria* 8°25N 12°4E **263** D7
Ganyem = Genyem *Indonesia* 2°46S 140°12E **231** E10
Ganyu *China* 34°50N 119°8E **227** G10
Ganyushkino *Kazakhstan* 46°35N 49°20E **191** G9
Ganzhou *China* 25°51N 114°56E **229** E10
Gao *Mali* 16°15N 0°5W **263** B4
Gao Xian *China* 28°21N 104°32E **228** C5
Gao'an *China* 28°26N 115°17E **229** C10
Gaobeidian *China* 39°19N 115°51E **226** E8
Gaocheng *China* 38°2N 114°49E **226** E8
Gaochun *China* 31°20N 118°49E **229** B12
Gaohebu *China* 30°43N 116°49E **229** B11
Gaokeng *China* 27°40N 113°58E **229** D9
Gaolan Dao *China* 21°55N 113°10E **229** G9
Gaoligong Shan *China* 24°45N 98°45E **228** E2
Gaomi *China* 36°20N 119°42E **227** F10
Gaoping *China* 35°45N 112°55E **226** G7
Gaoqiao *China* 31°21N 121°34E **138** A2
Gaotang *China* 36°50N 116°15E **226** F9
Gaoua *Burkina Faso* 10°20N 3°8W **262** C4
Gaoual *Guinea* 11°45N 13°25W **262** C2
Gaoxiong = Kaohsiung *Taiwan* 22°35N 120°16E **225** D2
Gaoyang *China* 38°40N 115°45E **226** E8
Gaoyao *China* 23°3N 112°27E **229** F9
Gaoyou *China* 32°47N 119°26E **229** A12
Gaoyou Hu *China* 32°45N 119°20E **227** H10
Gaoyuan *China* 37°8N 117°58E **227** F9
Gaozhou *China* 21°58N 110°50E **229** G8
Gap *France* 44°33N 6°5E **175** D10
Gapan *Phil.* 15°19N 120°57E **232** D3
Gapat → *India* 24°30N 82°28E **243** G10
Gapuwiyak *Australia* 12°25S 135°43E **280** A2
Gar *China* 32°10N 79°58E **218** E4
Gara, L. *Ireland* 53°57N 8°26W **166** C3
Garāb *Iran* 33°27N 47°16E **213** F12
Garabogazköl Aylagy *Turkmenistan* 41°0N 53°30E **187** F9
Garacad *Somali Rep.* 6°57N 49°24E **267** C6
Garachico *Canary Is.* 28°22N 16°46W **153** e1
Garachiné *Panama* 8°0N 78°12W **320** E4
Garafia *Canary Is.* 28°48N 17°57W **153** e1
Garagum *Turkmenistan* 39°30N 60°0E **247** B8
Garah *Australia* 29°5S 149°38E **281** D4
Garaina *Papua N. G.* 7°53S 147°8E **286** D4
Garajonay *Canary Is.* 28°7N 17°14W **153** e1
Garamba △ *Dem. Rep. of the Congo* 4°10N 29°40E **268** B2
Garango *Burkina Faso* 11°48N 0°34W **262** C4
Garanhuns *Brazil* 8°50S 36°30W **332** C4
Garapan *N. Marianas* 15°12N 145°43E **302** e
Garautha *India* 25°34N 79°18E **243** G8
Garawa ✪ *Australia* 16°43S 136°51E **280** B2
Garawe *Liberia* 4°35N 8°0W **262** E3
Garba Harre = Garbahaarrey *Somali Rep.* 3°19N 42°13E **267** D5
Garba Tula *Kenya* 0°30N 38°32E **268** B4
Garbagnate Milanese *Italy* 45°34N 9°4E **129** A1
Garbagududu *Ethiopia* 6°12N 43°50E **267** C5
Garbahaarrey *Somali Rep.* 3°19N 42°13E **267** D5
Garbatella *Italy* 41°51N 12°30E **136** B2
Garberville *U.S.A.* 40°6N 123°48W **304** F2
Garbiyang *India* 30°8N 80°54E **243** D9
Garbsen *Germany* 52°26N 9°31E **178** C5
Garça *Brazil* 22°14S 49°37W **333** F2
Garças → *Mato Grosso, Brazil* 15°54S 52°16W **331** D7
Garças → *Pernambuco, Brazil* 8°43S 39°41W **332** C4
Garches *France* 48°50N 2°11E **134** A2
Garching *Germany* 48°14N 11°39E **131** A3
Garchitorena *Phil.* 13°52N 123°40E **232** E4
Garcia Hernandez *Phil.* 9°37N 124°18E **233** G5
Garcias *Brazil* 20°34S 52°13W **331** E7
Gard □ *France* 44°2N 4°10E **175** D8
Gard → *France* 43°51N 4°37E **175** E8
Garda, L. di *Italy* 45°40N 10°41E **198** C7
Gardabani *Georgia* 41°27N 45°5E **191** K7
Gardanne *France* 43°27N 5°27E **175** E9
Gårdby *Sweden* 56°36N 16°38E **163** H10
Garde L. *Canada* 62°50N 106°13W **297** A7
Gardelegen *Germany* 52°32N 11°24E **178** C7
Garden City *El Qâhira, Egypt* 30°2N 31°14E **117** A2
Garden City *Ga., U.S.A.* 32°6N 81°9W **316** C8
Garden City *Kans., U.S.A.* 37°58N 100°53W **308** G3
Garden City *Mo., U.S.A.* 38°34N 94°12W **310** F2
Garden City *Tex., U.S.A.* 31°52N 101°29W **314** F4
Garden Grove *U.S.A.* 33°47N 117°55W **307** M9
Garden Reach *India* 22°33N 88°15E **124** B1
Gardens of Stone △ *Australia* 33°14S 150°11E **283** B9
Garder *Norway* 59°45N 10°38E **133** B2
Gardēz *Afghan.* 33°37N 69°9E **242** C3
Garðabær *Iceland* 64°5N 21°55W **155** C5
Garðskagi *Iceland* 64°5N 22°43W **155** C4
Garður *Iceland* 66°4N 16°46W **155** A10
Gardiki *Greece* 38°50N 21°55E **204** C3
Gardiner *Maine, U.S.A.* 44°14N 69°47W **309** C19
Gardiner *Mont., U.S.A.* 45°2N 110°22W **304** D8
Gardiners I. *U.S.A.* 41°6N 72°6W **313** E12
Gardner *Fla., U.S.A.* 27°21N 81°48W **317** H8
Gardner *Ill., U.S.A.* 41°12N 88°17W **311** C8
Gardner *Mass., U.S.A.* 42°34N 71°59W **313** D13
Gardner Canal *Canada* 53°27N 128°8W **296** C3
Gardner Pinnacles *U.S.A.* 25°0N 167°55W **302** F10
Gardnerville *U.S.A.* 38°56N 119°45W **306** G7
Gardno, Jezioro *Poland* 54°40N 17°7E **184** D4
Gardo = Qardho *Somali Rep.* 9°30N 49°6E **267** C6
Gardone Val Trómpia *Italy* 45°41N 10°11E **198** C7
Gárdony *Hungary* 47°12N 18°39E **182** C3
Gare Tigre *Fr. Guiana* 4°58N 53°9W **329** C7
Garelo I. *U.S.A.* 51°48N 178°48W **303** L3
Gares = Puente la Reina *Spain* 42°40N 1°49W **196** C3
Garešnica *Croatia* 45°36N 16°56E **199** C13
Garéssio *Italy* 44°12N 8°2E **198** D5
Garey *U.S.A.* 34°53N 120°19W **307** L6
Garfield *N.J., U.S.A.* 40°52N 74°7W **132** A1
Garfield *Wash., U.S.A.* 47°1N 117°9W **304** C5
Garfield Park *U.S.A.* 41°52N 87°42W **119** B2
Garforth *U.K.* 53°47N 1°24W **168** D6
Gargaliani *Greece* 37°4N 21°38E **204** D3
Gargan, Mt. *France* 45°37N 1°39E **174** C5
Gargano △ *Italy* 41°43N 15°52E **199** G12
Gargantua, C. *Canada* 47°36N 85°2W **309** B11
Gargareta *Greece* 37°57N 23°43E **112** B2
Gargett *Australia* 21°9S 148°47E **280** b
Gargouna *Mali* 15°56N 0°13E **263** B5
Gargždai *Lithuania* 55°43N 21°24E **184** C8
Garhchiroli *India* 20°10N 80°0E **244** D5
Garibaldi ⌓ *Canada* 49°50N 122°40W **296** D4
Garibong *S. Korea* 37°29N 126°54E **137** C1
Gariep, L. *S. Africa* 30°40S 25°40E **270** D4
Garies *S. Africa* 30°32S 17°59E **270** D2
Garig Gunak Barlu △ *Australia* 11°26S 131°58E **278** B5
Garigliano → *Italy* 41°13N 13°45E **200** A6
Garissa *Kenya* 0°25S 39°40E **268** C4
Garkida *Nigeria* 10°27N 12°36E **263** C7
Garko *Nigeria* 11°45N 8°35E **263** C6
Garland *Tex., U.S.A.* 32°54N 96°38W **314** E6
Garland *Utah, U.S.A.* 41°45N 112°10W **304** F7
Garlasco *Italy* 45°12N 8°55E **198** C5
Garliava *Lithuania* 54°49N 23°52E **184** D10
Garlin *France* 43°33N 0°16W **174** E3
Garmāb *Semnān, Iran* 35°25N 56°45E **247** C8
Garmāb *Zanjān, Iran* 35°50N 48°11E **213** E13
Garmisch-Partenkirchen *Germany* 47°30N 11°6E **179** H7
Garmo, Qullai = imeni Ismail Samani, Pik *Tajikistan* 39°0N 72°2E **217** E8
Garmsār *Iran* 35°20N 52°25E **247** C7
Garner *U.S.A.* 43°6N 93°36W **310** A3
Garnett *U.S.A.* 38°17N 95°14W **308** F6
Garnpung L. *Australia* 33°25S 143°10E **282** B5
Garo Hills *India* 25°30N 90°30E **241** C3
Garoe = Garoowe *Somali Rep.* 8°25N 48°33E **267** C6
Garonne → *France* 45°2N 0°36W **174** C3
Garonne, Canal Latéral à la *France* 44°15N 0°18E **174** D4
Garoowe *Somali Rep.* 8°25N 48°33E **267** C6
Garorimman *S. Korea* 36°54N 126°21E **224** D3
Garot *India* 24°19N 75°41E **242** G6
Garou, L. *Mali* 16°2N 2°45W **262** B4
Garoua *Cameroon* 9°19N 13°21E **263** D7
Garoua Boulaï *Cameroon* 5°53N 14°33E **264** A2
Garove I. *Papua N. G.* 4°42S 149°30E **286** C5
Garpenberg *Sweden* 60°19N 16°12E **162** D10
Garphyttan *Sweden* 59°18N 14°56E **162** E8
Garrauli *India* 25°5N 79°22E **243** G8
Garrel *Germany* 52°57N 8°1E **178** C4
Garreru *Palau* 7°19N 134°32E **288** c
Garrett *U.S.A.* 41°21N 85°8W **311** C11
Garrigues *France* 43°40N 3°55E **174** E7
Garrison *Ky., U.S.A.* 38°36N 83°10W **311** F13
Garrison *Mont., U.S.A.* 46°31N 112°49W **304** C7
Garrison *N. Dak., U.S.A.* 47°40N 101°25W **308** B3
Garrison Res. = Sakakawea, L. *U.S.A.* 47°30N 101°25W **308** B3
Garron Pt. *U.K.* 55°3N 5°59W **166** A6
Garrovillas de Alconétar *Spain* 39°40N 6°33W **195** F4
Garrucha *Spain* 37°11N 1°49W **197** H3
Garry → *U.K.* 56°44N 3°47W **167** E5
Garry, L. *Canada* 65°58N 100°18W **294** D11
Garrygala *Turkmenistan* 38°31N 56°29E **247** B8
Garsen *Kenya* 2°20S 40°5E **268** C5
Gärsnäs *Sweden* 55°32N 14°10E **163** J8
Garson L. *Canada* 56°19N 110°2W **297** B6
Garstang *U.K.* 53°55N 2°46W **168** D5
Gartempe → *France* 46°47N 0°49E **174** B4
Gartz *Germany* 53°13N 14°22E **178** B10
Garu *Ghana* 10°55N 0°11W **263** C4
Garu *India* 23°40N 84°14E **243** H11
Garub *Namibia* 26°37S 16°0E **270** C2
Garut *Indonesia* 7°14S 107°53E **235** D3
Garvanza *U.S.A.* 34°6N 118°11W **126** B3
Garvão *Portugal* 37°42N 8°21W **195** H2
Garvie Mts. *N.Z.* 45°30S 168°50E **285** F3
Garwa = Garoua *Cameroon* 9°19N 13°21E **263** D7
Garwa *India* 24°11N 83°47E **243** G10
Garwolin *Poland* 51°55N 21°38E **185** G8
Gary *U.S.A.* 41°36N 87°20W **311** C9
Garz *Germany* 54°19N 13°20E **178** A9
Garzê *China* 31°38N 100°1E **228** B3
Garzón *Colombia* 2°10N 75°40W **328** C2
Gas City *U.S.A.* 40°29N 85°37W **311** D11
Gas-San *Japan* 38°32N 140°1E **220** E10
Gasa *Bhutan* 27°55N 89°40E **241** B2
Gasan *Phil.* 13°19N 121°51E **232** E3
Gasan Kuli = Esenguly *Turkmenistan* 37°37N 53°59E **216** E4
Gascogne *France* 43°45N 0°20E **174** E4
Gascogne, G. de *Europe* 44°0N 2°0W **174** E2
Gasconade *U.S.A.* 38°40N 91°34W **310** F5
Gasconade → *U.S.A.* 38°41N 91°33W **310** F5
Gascony = Gascogne *France* 43°45N 0°20E **174** E4
Gascoyne → *Australia* 24°52S 113°37E **279** D1
Gascoyne Junction *Australia* 25°2S 115°17E **279** E2
Gascueña *Spain* 40°18N 2°31W **196** E2
Gash, Wadi → *Africa* 16°48N 35°51E **257** D4
Gash Setit ⌓ *Eritrea* 15°12N 36°58E **257** D4
Gåshaga *Sweden* 59°21N 18°13E **139** A3
Gashagar *Nigeria* 13°22N 12°47E **263** C7
Gashaka *Nigeria* 7°20N 11°29E **263** D7
Gashaka-Gumti △ *Nigeria* 7°23N 11°34E **263** D7
Gasherbrum *Pakistan* 35°40N 76°40E **243** B7
Gashua *Nigeria* 12°54N 11°0E **263** C7
Gasmata *Papua N. G.* 6°17S 150°20E **286** D6
Gasparilla I. *U.S.A.* 26°46N 82°16W **317** J7
Gasparillo *Trin. & Tob.* 10°18N 61°26W **323** t
Gasparito *Curaçao* 12°8N 68°56W **322** g
Gaspé *Canada* 48°52N 64°30W **299** C7
Gaspé, C. de *Canada* 48°48N 64°7W **299** C7
Gaspé Pen. = Gaspésie, Pén. de la *Canada* 48°45N 65°40W **299** C6
Gasper Grande *Trin. & Tob.* 10°40N 61°39W **323** t
Gaspésie, Pén. de la *Canada* 48°45N 65°40W **299** C6
Gaspésie ⌓ *Canada* 48°55N 66°10W **299** C6
Gassan *Burkina Faso* 12°49N 3°12W **262** C4
Gassen = Jasień *Poland* 51°46N 15°0E **185** G2
Gassol *Nigeria* 8°34N 10°25E **263** D7
Gasteiz = Vitoria-Gasteiz *Spain* 42°50N 2°41W **196** C2
Gaston *U.S.A.* 33°49N 81°5W **316** B8
Gastonia *U.S.A.* 35°16N 81°11W **315** D14
Gastouni *Greece* 37°51N 21°15E **204** D3
Gastouri *Greece* 39°34N 19°54E **206** B9
Gastre *Argentina* 42°20S 69°15W **336** B3
Gästrikland *Sweden* 60°45N 16°40E **162** D10
Gata, C. *Cyprus* 34°34N 33°2E **207** F9
Gata, C. de *Spain* 36°41N 2°13W **197** J2
Gata, Sierra de *Spain* 40°20N 6°45W **194** E4
Gataga → *Canada* 58°35N 126°59W **296** B3
Gătaia *Romania* 45°26N 21°30E **182** E6
Gatchina *Russia* 59°35N 30°9E **188** C6
Gatehouse of Fleet *U.K.* 54°53N 4°12W **167** G4
Gates *U.S.A.* 43°9N 77°42W **312** C7
Gates of the Arctic ⌓ *U.S.A.* 67°45N 153°15W **303** C9
Gateshead *U.K.* 54°57N 1°35W **168** C6
Gateshead I. *Canada* 70°36N 100°26W **294** C11
Gatesville *U.S.A.* 31°26N 97°45W **314** F6
Gateway ⌓ *U.S.A.* 40°38N 73°51W **132** C2
Gateway of India *India* 18°55N 72°50E **124** B2
Gaths *Zimbabwe* 20°2S 30°32E **269** G3
Gâtinais *France* 48°5N 2°40E **173** D9
Gâtine, Hauteurs de *France* 46°35N 0°45W **174** B3
Gatineau *Canada* 45°29N 75°39W **313** A9
Gatineau → *Canada* 45°27N 75°42W **298** C4
Gatineau △ *Canada* 45°40N 76°0W **298** C4
Gatow *Germany* 52°29N 13°11E **115** B1
Gattaran *Phil.* 18°4N 121°38E **232** B3
Gattinara *Italy* 45°37N 8°22E **198** C5
Gatton *Australia* 27°32S 152°17E **281** D5
Gatún, L. *Panama* 9°7N 79°56W **320** c
Gatún Dam *Panama* 9°16N 79°55W **320** c
Gatún Locks *Panama* 9°16N 79°55W **320** c
Gatwick, London ✕ (LGW) *U.K.* 51°10N 0°11W **169** F7
Gatyana *S. Africa* 32°16S 28°31E **271** D4
Gau *Fiji* 18°2S 179°18E **287** B2
Gaua *Vanuatu* 14°15S 167°30E **287** D5
Gaucín *Spain* 36°31N 5°19W **195** J5
Gauer L. *Canada* 57°0N 97°50W **297** B9
Gauhati = Guwahati *India* 26°10N 91°45E **241** B3
Gauja → *Latvia* 57°10N 24°16E **188** D3
Gaujas △ *Latvia* 57°10N 24°50E **161** H21
Gaula → *Norway* 63°21N 10°14E **164** A7
Gaupne *Norway* 61°25N 7°18E **164** C4
Gaurdak = Gowurdak *Turkmenistan* 37°50N 66°4E **217** E7
Gauri Phanta *India* 28°41N 80°36E **243** E9
Gauribidanur *India* 13°37N 77°32E **245** H3
Gaustatoppen *Norway* 59°48N 8°40E **164** E5
Gauteng □ *S. Africa* 26°0S 28°0E **271** C4
Gāv Koshī *Iran* 28°38N 57°12E **247** D8
Gavà *Spain* 41°18N 2°1W **114** B1
Gāvakān *Iran* 29°37N 53°10E **247** D7
Gavamar *Spain* 41°15N 2°1E **114** B1
Gavarnie *France* 42°44N 0°1W **174** F3
Gavāter *Iran* 25°10N 61°31E **247** E9
Gāvbandī *Iran* 27°12N 53°4E **247** E7
Gavdopoula *Greece* 34°56N 24°0E **207** F5
Gavdos *Greece* 34°50N 24°5E **207** F5
Gávea *Brazil* 22°58S 43°13W **135** B1
Gávea, Pedra da *Brazil* 22°59S 43°18W **135** B1
Gavi *Italy* 44°41N 8°49E **198** D5
Gavião *Portugal* 39°28N 7°56W **195** F3
Gaviota *U.S.A.* 34°29N 120°13W **307** L6
Gāvkhūnī, Batlāq-e *Iran* 32°6N 52°52E **247** C7
Gävle *Sweden* 60°40N 17°9E **162** D11
Gävleborgs län □ *Sweden* 61°30N 16°15E **162** C10
Gävlebukten *Sweden* 60°40N 17°20E **162** D11
Gavorrano *Italy* 42°55N 10°54E **198** F7
Gavray *France* 48°55N 1°20W **172** D5
Gavrilov Yam *Russia* 57°18N 39°49E **188** D10
Gavrio *Greece* 37°54N 24°44E **204** D6
Gawachab *Namibia* 27°4S 17°55E **270** C2
Gawai *Burma* 27°56N 97°30E **241** B6
Gawilgarh Hills *India* 21°15N 76°45E **244** D3
Gawler *Australia* 34°30S 138°42E **282** C3
Gawler Ranges *Australia* 32°30S 135°45E **282** B2
Gawu *Nigeria* 9°14N 6°52E **263** D6
Gaxun Nur *China* 42°22N 100°30E **218** C9
Gay *Russia* 51°27N 58°27E **186** D10
Gay *Ga., U.S.A.* 33°6N 84°35W **316** B5
Gaya *India* 24°47N 85°4E **243** G11
Gaya *Niger* 11°52N 3°28E **263** C5
Gaya *Nigeria* 11°57N 9°0E **263** C6
Gayasan △ *S. Korea* 35°45N 128°10E **224** E4
Gayéri *Burkina Faso* 12°39N 0°29E **263** C5
Gaylord *U.S.A.* 45°2N 84°41W **309** C11
Gayndah *Australia* 25°35S 151°32E **281** D5
Gaysin = Haysyn *Ukraine* 48°57N 29°25E **183** B14
Gayvoron = Hayvoron *Ukraine* 48°22N 29°52E **183** B14
Gaza *Gaza Strip* 31°30N 34°28E **251** G5
Gaza □ *Mozam.* 23°10S 32°45E **271** B5
Gaza Strip ■ *Asia* 31°29N 34°25E **251** G5
Gazanjyk = Bereket *Turkmenistan* 39°16N 55°32E **247** B7
Gazaoua *Niger* 13°32N 7°55E **263** C6
Gāzbor *Iran* 28°5N 58°51E **247** D8
Gazdagrét *Hungary* 47°29N 19°0E **117** B1
Gazelle Pen. *Papua N. G.* 4°40S 152°0E **286** C7
Gazi *Dem. Rep. of the Congo* 1°3N 24°30E **264** B4
Gaziantep *Turkey* 37°6N 37°23E **250** A8
Gaziantep □ *Turkey* 37°0N 37°0E **250** B8
Gazimağusa = Famagusta *Cyprus* 35°8N 33°55E **207** E9
Gaziosmanpaşa *Turkey* 41°5N 28°50E **122** B1
Gazipaşa *Turkey* 36°16N 32°18E **250** B3
Gazli *Uzbekistan* 40°8N 63°27E **216** D6
Gbadolite *Dem. Rep. of the Congo* 4°17N 21°1E **264** B4
Gbarnga *Liberia* 7°19N 9°13W **262** D3
Gboko *Nigeria* 7°17N 9°4E **263** D6
Gcoverega *Botswana* 19°8S 24°18E **270** A3
Gcuwa *S. Africa* 32°20S 28°11E **271** D4
Gdańsk *Poland* 54°22N 18°40E **184** D5
Gdańsk ✕ (GDN) *Poland* 54°22N 18°30E **184** D5
Gdańska, Zatoka *Poland* 54°30N 19°20E **184** D6
Gdingen = Gdynia *Poland* 54°35N 18°33E **184** D5
Gdov *Russia* 58°48N 27°55E **188** C4
Gdynia *Poland* 54°35N 18°33E **184** D5
Geba → *Guinea-Biss.* 11°46N 15°36W **262** C1
Gebe *Indonesia* 0°5N 129°25E **231** D7
Gebeciler *Turkey* 38°46N 30°46E **205** C12
Gebeit Mine *Sudan* 21°3N 36°29E **256** C4
Gebel Abyad *Sudan* 19°0N 28°0E **256** D2
Gebel el Ahmar *Egypt* 30°1N 31°21E **117** A3
Gebel el Muqattam *Egypt* 30°1N 31°17E **117** A2
Gebel el Tura *Egypt* 29°56N 31°15E **117** B2
Gebel Iweibid *Egypt* 30°8N 32°31E **256** H8
Gebiley *Somali Rep.* 9°42N 43°37E **267** C5
Gebze *Turkey* 40°47N 29°25E **203** F13
Gecha *Ethiopia* 7°30N 35°18E **257** F4

Gedaref *Sudan* 14°2N 35°28E **257** E4
Gedaref □ *Sudan* 14°0N 35°0E **257** E4
Gede, Tanjung *Indonesia* 6°46S 105°12E **234** D3
Gediz *Turkey* 39°1N 29°24E **205** B11
Gediz → *Turkey* 38°35N 26°48E **205** C8
Gedo *Ethiopia* 9°2N 37°25E **257** F4
Gedo □ *Somali Rep.* 2°15N 42°10E **267** D5
Gèdre *France* 42°47N 0°2E **174** F4
Gedser *Denmark* 54°35N 11°55E **163** K5
Gedung, Pulau *Malaysia* 5°17N 100°23E **237** c
Geegully Cr. → *Australia* 18°32S 123°41E **278** C3
Geel *Belgium* 51°10N 4°59E **170** C4
Geelong *Australia* 38°10S 144°22E **282** E6
Geelvink B. = Cenderwasih, Teluk *Indonesia* 3°0S 135°20E **231** E9
Geelvink Chan. *Australia* 28°30S 114°0E **279** E1
Geesthacht *Germany* 53°26N 10°22E **178** B6
Geidam *Nigeria* 12°57N 11°57E **263** C7
Geikie → *Canada* 57°45N 103°52W **297** B8
Geikie Gorge △ *Australia* 18°3S 125°41E **278** C4
Geilenkirchen *Germany* 50°57N 6°8E **178** E2
Geili *Sudan* 16°1N 32°37E **257** D3
Geilo *Norway* 60°32N 8°14E **164** D5
Geiselgasteig *Germany* 48°3N 11°33E **131** B2
Geisingen *Germany* 47°54N 8°38E **179** H4
Geislingen *Germany* 48°37N 9°50E **179** G5
Geistown *U.S.A.* 40°18N 78°52W **312** F6
Geita *Tanzania* 2°48S 32°12E **268** C3
Geitastrand *Norway* 63°22N 9°56E **164** A6
Geithus *Norway* 59°57N 9°59E **164** E6
Gejiu *China* 23°20N 103°10E **228** F4
Gel → *Sudan* 7°5N 29°10E **257** F2
Gel, Meydān-e *Iran* 29°4N 54°50E **247** D7
Gel River *Sudan* 7°5N 29°10E **257** F2
Gela *Italy* 37°4N 14°15E **201** E7
Gela, G. di *Italy* 37°0N 14°20E **201** F7
Geladi *Ethiopia* 6°59N 46°30E **267** C6
Gelahun *Liberia* 7°55N 10°28W **262** D2
Gelam *Indonesia* 2°54S 110°11E **235** C4
Gelang Patah *Malaysia* 1°27N 103°35E **237** d
Gelderland □ *Neths.* 52°5N 6°10E **170** B6
Geldern *Germany* 51°31N 6°20E **178** D2
Geldrop *Neths.* 51°25N 5°32E **170** C5
Geleen *Neths.* 50°57N 5°49E **170** D5
Gelehun *S. Leone* 8°20N 11°40W **262** D2
Gelembe *Turkey* 39°10N 27°50E **205** B9
Gelemso *Ethiopia* 8°49N 40°31E **257** F5
Gelendost *Turkey* 38°7N 31°1E **212** C4
Gelendzhik *Russia* 44°33N 38°10E **189** K10
Gelib = Jilib *Somali Rep.* 0°29N 42°46E **267** D5
Gelibolu *Turkey* 40°28N 26°43E **203** F10
Gelibolu Yarımadası *Turkey* 40°20N 26°30E **203** F10
Gelidonya Burnu *Turkey* 36°12N 30°24E **212** D4
Gellinsoor *Somali Rep.* 6°28N 46°39E **267** C6
Gelnhausen *Germany* 50°11N 9°11E **179** E5
Gelnica *Slovak Rep.* 48°51N 20°55E **181** C13
Gelsenkirchen *Germany* 51°32N 7°6E **178** D3
Gelting *Germany* 54°45N 9°53E **178** A5
Gelugur *Malaysia* 5°22N 100°18E **237** c
Gemas *Malaysia* 2°37N 102°36E **237** L4
Gembloux *Belgium* 50°34N 4°43E **170** D4
Gembu *Nigeria* 6°42N 11°10E **263** D7
Gemena *Dem. Rep. of the Congo* 3°13N 19°48E **264** B3
Gemerek *Turkey* 39°15N 36°10E **212** C7
Gemla *Sweden* 56°52N 14°39E **163** H8
Gemlik *Turkey* 40°26N 29°9E **203** F13
Gemlik Körfezi *Turkey* 40°25N 28°55E **203** F12
Gemona del Friuli *Italy* 46°16N 13°9E **199** B10
Gemsa *Egypt* 27°39N 33°35E **256** B3
Gemsbok △ *Botswana* 25°5S 21°1E **270** C3
Gemünden *Germany* 50°3N 9°42E **179** E5
Genadi *Greece* 36°2N 27°56E **206** E11
Genale → *Ethiopia* 6°2N 39°1E **257** F4
Genç *Turkey* 38°44N 40°34E **213** C9
Gençay *France* 46°23N 0°23E **174** B4
General Acha *Argentina* 37°20S 64°38W **334** D3
General Alvear *B. Aires, Argentina* 36°0S 60°0W **334** D4
General Alvear *Mendoza, Argentina* 35°0S 67°40W **334** D2
General Artigas *Paraguay* 26°52S 56°16W **334** B4
General Belgrano *Argentina* 36°35S 58°47W **334** D4
General Bernardo O'Higgins *Antarctica* 63°0S 58°3W **151** C18
General Cabrera *Argentina* 32°53S 63°52W **334** C3
General Carrera, L. *Chile* 46°35S 72°0W **336** C2
General Cepeda *Mexico* 25°21N 101°22W **318** B4
General Conesa *Argentina* 40°6S 64°25W **336** B4
General Eugenio A. Garay *Paraguay* 20°31S 62°8W **331** E5
General Germán Busch = Villa Abecia *Bolivia* 21°0S 68°18W **334** A2
General Guido *Argentina* 36°40S 57°50W **334** D4
General Juan Madariaga *Argentina* 37°0S 57°0W **334** D4
General La Madrid *Argentina* 37°17S 61°20W **334** D3
General Lorenzo Vintter *Argentina* 40°45S 64°26W **336** B4
General Luna *Phil.* 13°41N 122°10E **232** E4
General MacArthur *Phil.* 11°18N 125°28E **233** F5
General Martin Miguel de Güemes *Argentina* 24°50S 65°0W **334** A3
General Pico *Argentina* 35°45S 63°50W **334** D3
General Pinedo *Argentina* 27°15S 61°20W **334** B3
General Pinto *Argentina* 34°45S 61°50W **334** C3
General Sampaio *Brazil* 4°2S 39°29W **332** B4
General San Martín *Argentina* 34°35S 58°32W **117** B1
General Santos *Phil.* 6°5N 125°14E **233** H5
General Tinio *Phil.* 15°39N 121°10E **232** D3
General Toshevo *Bulgaria* 43°42N 28°6E **203** C12
General Treviño *Mexico* 26°14N 99°29W **319** B5
General Trías *Mexico* 28°21N 106°22W **318** B3
General Uriburu = Zárate *Argentina* 34°7S 59°0W **334** C4
General Viamonte *Argentina* 35°1S 61°3W **334** D3
General Villegas *Argentina* 35°5S 63°0W **334** D3
General Vintter, L. *Argentina* 43°55S 71°40W **336** B2
Generoso Ponce = Jaci-Paraná *Brazil* 8°15S 64°23W **331** B5
Genesee *Idaho, U.S.A.* 46°33N 116°56W **304** C5
Genesee *Pa., U.S.A.* 41°59N 77°54W **312** E7
Genesee → *U.S.A.* 43°16N 77°36W **312** C7
Geneseo *Ill., U.S.A.* 41°27N 90°9W **310** C6
Geneseo *N.Y., U.S.A.* 42°48N 77°49W **312** D7
Geneva = Genève *Switz.* 46°12N 6°9E **179** J2
Geneva *Ala., U.S.A.* 31°2N 85°52W **316** D4
Geneva *Ga., U.S.A.* 32°35N 84°33W **316** C5
Geneva *Ill., U.S.A.* 41°53N 88°18W **311** C8
Geneva *Ind., U.S.A.* 40°36N 84°58W **311** D12
Geneva *N.Y., U.S.A.* 42°52N 76°59W **312** D8
Geneva *Nebr., U.S.A.* 40°32N 97°36W **308** E5
Geneva *Ohio, U.S.A.* 41°48N 80°57W **312** E4
Geneva, L. = Léman, L. *Europe* 46°26N 6°30E **173** F13
Geneva, L. *U.S.A.* 42°38N 88°30W **311** B8
Genève *Switz.* 46°12N 6°9E **179** J2
Geng *Afghan.* 31°22N 61°28E **240** C1
Gengenbach *Germany* 48°24N 8°1E **179** G4
Gengma *China* 23°32N 99°20E **228** F2
Genichesk = Henichesk *Ukraine* 46°12N 34°50E **189** J8
Genil → *Spain* 37°42N 5°19W **195** H5
Génipa, B. de *Martinique* 14°33N 61°0W **322** j
Genisea *Greece* 41°1N 24°57E **205** A7
Genk *Belgium* 50°58N 5°32E **170** D5
Genkai-Nada *Japan* 34°0N 130°0E **222** D2
Genlis *France* 47°11N 5°12E **173** E12
Gennargentu, Mti. del *Italy* 40°1N 9°19E **200** B2
Gennes *France* 47°20N 0°17W **172** E6
Gennevilliers *France* 48°56N 2°17E **134** A2
Genoa = Génova *Italy* 44°25N 8°57E **198** D5
Genoa *Vic., Australia* 37°29S 149°35E **283** D8
Genoa *Ill., U.S.A.* 42°6N 88°42W **311** B8
Genoa *N.Y., U.S.A.* 42°40N 76°32W **313** D8
Genoa *Nebr., U.S.A.* 41°27N 97°44W **308** E5
Genoa *Nev., U.S.A.* 39°2N 119°50W **306** F7
Genoa → *Argentina* 44°55S 70°5W **336** B2
Genoa City *U.S.A.* 42°30N 88°20W **311** B8
Génova *Italy* 44°25N 8°57E **198** D5
Génova ✕ (GOA) *Italy* 44°25N 8°56E **198** D5
Génova, G. di *Italy* 44°0N 9°0E **198** E6
Genovesa, I. *Ecuador* 0°20N 89°58W **330** a
Genriyetty, Ostrov *Russia* 77°6N 156°30E **215** B16
Gent *Belgium* 51°2N 3°42E **170** C3
Genteng *Jawa Barat, Indonesia* 7°22S 106°24E **234** D3
Genteng *Jawa Timur, Indonesia* 8°22S 114°9E **231** J17
Genthin *Germany* 52°25N 12°9E **178** C8
Gentilly *Val-de-Marne, France* 48°48N 2°21E **134** B3
Gentilly *La., U.S.A.* 30°0N 90°2W **131** A2
Gentio do Ouro *Brazil* 11°25S 42°30W **332** D3
Gentofte *Denmark* 55°44N 12°32E **118** A3
Gentryville *U.S.A.* 38°6N 87°2W **311** F9
Genval *Belgium* 50°43N 4°29E **116** B2
Genyem *Indonesia* 2°46S 140°12E **231** E10
Genzano di Lucània *Italy* 40°51N 16°2E **201** B9
Genzano di Roma *Italy* 41°42N 12°41E **199** G9
Geoagiu *Romania* 45°55N 23°12E **183** E8
Geochang *S. Korea* 35°41N 127°55E **224** E3
Geogeumdo *S. Korea* 34°27N 127°10E **224** E3
Geographe B. *Australia* 33°30S 115°15E **279** F2
Geographe Chan. *Australia* 24°30S 113°0E **279** D1
Geographical Society Ø *Greenland* 72°57N 23°15W **154** C8
Geoje *S. Korea* 34°51N 128°35E **224** E4
Geojedo *S. Korea* 34°51N 128°38E **224** E4
Geokchay = Göyçay *Azerbaijan* 40°42N 47°43E **191** K8
Georga, Zemlya *Russia* 80°30N 49°0E **214** A5
George *S. Africa* 33°58S 22°29E **270** D3
George → *Canada* 58°49N 66°10W **299** A6
George, L. *N.S.W., Australia* 35°10S 149°25E **283** C8
George, L. *S. Austral., Australia* 37°25S 140°0E **282** D4
George, L. *W. Austral., Australia* 22°45S 123°40E **278** D3
George, L. *Uganda* 0°5N 30°10E **268** B3
George, L. *Fla., U.S.A.* 29°17N 81°36W **317** F8
George, L. *N.Y., U.S.A.* 43°37N 73°33W **313** C11
George Gill Ra. *Australia* 24°22S 131°45E **278** D5
George I. *Hong Kong, China* 22°13N 114°7E **122** B1
George I. *St. Helena* 15°58S 5°38W **153** h
George Pt. *Australia* 20°6S 148°36E **280** b
George River = Kangiqsualujjuaq *Canada* 58°30N 65°59W **295** F18
George Rogers Clark Nat. Memorial △ *U.S.A.* 38°41N 87°32W **311** F9
George Sound *N.Z.* 44°52S 167°25E **285** E2
George Town *Tas., Australia* 41°6S 146°49E **281** G4
George Town *Bahamas* 23°33N 75°47W **320** B4
George Town *Cayman Is.* 19°20N 81°24W **320** C3
George Town *Malaysia* 5°25N 100°20E **237** c
George V Land *Antarctica* 69°0S 148°0E **151** C10
George VI Sound *Antarctica* 71°0S 68°0W **151** D17
George West *U.S.A.* 28°20N 98°7W **314** G5
Georges River Bridge *Australia* 34°0S 151°6E **139** C1
Georgetown = Janjanbureh *Gambia* 13°30N 14°47W **262** C2
Georgetown *Ascension I.* 7°56S 14°25W **153** g
Georgetown *Queens., Australia* 18°17S 143°33E **280** B3
Georgetown *Ont., Canada* 43°40N 79°56W **312** C5
Georgetown *P.E.I., Canada* 46°13N 62°24W **299** C7
Georgetown *Guyana* 6°50N 58°12W **329** B6
Georgetown *St. Vincent* 13°16N 61°7W **323** n
Georgetown *Calif., U.S.A.* 38°54N 120°50W **306** G6
Georgetown *Colo., U.S.A.* 39°42N 105°42W **304** G11
Georgetown *D.C., U.S.A.* 38°54N 77°3W **143** B3
Georgetown *Fla., U.S.A.* 29°23N 81°38W **317** F8
Georgetown *Ga., U.S.A.* 31°53N 85°6W **316** D4
Georgetown *Ill., U.S.A.* 39°59N 87°38W **311** E9
Georgetown *Ky., U.S.A.* 38°13N 84°33W **311** F12
Georgetown *N.Y., U.S.A.* 42°46N 75°44W **313** D9
Georgetown *Ohio, U.S.A.* 38°52N 83°54W **311** F12
Georgetown *S.C., U.S.A.* 33°23N 79°17W **315** E15
Georgetown *Tex., U.S.A.* 30°38N 97°41W **314** F6
Georgia □ *U.S.A.* 32°50N 83°15W **316** C6
Georgia ■ *Asia* 42°0N 43°0E **191** J6
Georgia, Str. of *N. Amer.* 49°25N 124°0W **306** A3
Georgia Basin *S. Ocean* 50°45S 35°30W **151** B1
Georgia Dome *U.S.A.* 33°45N 84°23W **113** B2
Georgian B. *Canada* 45°15N 81°0W **312** A4
Georgian Bay Islands △ *Canada* 44°53N 79°52W **312** B5
Georgievka *Kazakhstan* 49°19N 84°34E **217** C10
Georgina → *Australia* 23°30S 139°47E **280** C2
Georgina I. *Canada* 44°22N 79°17W **312** B5
Georgioupoli *Greece* 35°20N 24°15E **207** E5
Georgiu-Dezh = Liski *Russia* 51°3N 39°30E **189** G10
Georgiyevsk *Russia* 44°12N 43°28E **191** H6
Georgsmarienhütte *Germany* 52°13N 8°3E **178** C4
Gera *Germany* 50°53N 12°4E **178** E8
Geraardsbergen *Belgium* 50°45N 3°53E **170** D3
Geraki *Greece* 37°0N 22°42E **204** D4
Geraki, Akra *Greece* 37°42N 20°59E **207** D1
Geral, Serra *Bahia, Brazil* 14°0S 41°0W **333** D3
Geral, Serra *Goiás, Brazil* 11°15S 46°30W **332** D2
Geral, Serra *Sta. Catarina, Brazil* 26°25S 50°0W **335** B6
Geral de Goiás, Serra *Brazil* 12°0S 46°0W **333** D2
Geral do Paranã, Serra *Brazil* 15°0S 47°30W **333** E2
Gerald *U.S.A.* 38°24N 91°20W **310** F5
Geraldine *N.Z.* 44°5S 171°15E **285** E6
Geraldine *Mont., U.S.A.* 47°36N 110°16W **304** C8
Geraldton = Innisfail *Australia* 17°33S 146°5E **280** B4
Geraldton *W. Austral., Australia* 28°48S 114°32E **279** E1
Geraldton *Ont., Canada* 49°44N 87°10W **298** C2
Geranium *Australia* 35°23S 140°11E **282** C4
Gérardmer *France* 48°3N 6°50E **173** D13
Gerasdorf bei Wien *Austria* 48°17N 16°28E **142** A2
Gerberau *Germany* 48°12N 11°27E **131** A1
Gercüş *Turkey* 37°34N 41°23E **213** D9
Gerdine, Mt. *U.S.A.* 61°35N 152°27W **303** F9
Gerede *Turkey* 40°45N 32°10E **212** B5
Gerês, Sierra do *Portugal* 41°48N 8°0W **194** D3
Gereshk *Afghan.* 31°47N 64°35E **240** D1
Geretsried *Germany* 47°51N 11°28E **179** H7
Gérgal *Spain* 37°7N 2°31W **197** H2
Gerik *Malaysia* 5°50N 101°15E **237** K3
Gering *U.S.A.* 41°50N 103°40W **308** E2
Geriş *Turkey* 36°57N 31°43E **250** B2
Gerlach *U.S.A.* 40°39N 119°21W **304** F4
Gerlachovský štít *Slovak Rep.* 49°11N 20°7E **181** B13
Gerli *Argentina* 34°41S 58°22W **117** C2
Gerlogubi *Ethiopia* 6°53N 45°3E **267** C6
German Bight = Deutsche Bucht *Germany* 54°15N 8°0E **178** A4
German East Africa = Tanzania ■ *Africa* 6°0S 34°0E **268** D3
German Planina *Macedonia* 42°20N 22°0E **202** D6
German South West Africa = Namibia ■ *Africa* 22°0S 18°9E **270** B2
Germania Land *Greenland* 77°5N 19°30W **154** B9
Germansen Landing *Canada* 55°43N 124°40W **296** B4
Germantown *Ohio, U.S.A.* 39°38N 84°22W **311** E12
Germantown *Tenn., U.S.A.* 35°5N 89°49W **315** D10
Germantown *Wis., U.S.A.* 43°14N 88°6W **311** A8
Germany ■ *Europe* 51°0N 10°0E **178** E6
Germencik *Turkey* 37°52N 27°37E **205** D9
Germering *Germany* 48°8N 11°22E **179** G7
Germersheim *Germany* 49°12N 8°22E **179** F4
Germī *Iran* 39°1N 48°3E **213** C13
Germiston *S. Africa* 26°13S 28°10E **271** C4
Gern *Germany* 48°10N 11°32E **131** B2
Gernene *Algeria* 21°40N 2°24E **261** D5
Gernika-Lumo *Spain* 43°19N 2°40W **196** B2
Gernsheim *Germany* 49°45N 8°30E **179** F4
Gero *Japan* 35°48N 137°14E **223** B9
Gerogery *Australia* 35°50S 147°1E **283** C7
Gerokgak *Indonesia* 8°11S 114°27E **231** J17
Gerolzhofen *Germany* 49°54N 10°21E **179** F6
Gerona = Girona *Spain* 41°58N 2°46E **196** D7
Gerona *Phil.* 15°36N 120°36E **232** D3
Geropotamos → *Greece* 35°3N 24°50E **207** E6
Gerrard *Canada* 50°30N 117°17W **296** C5
Gerringong *Australia* 34°46S 150°47E **283** C9
Gers □ *France* 43°35N 0°30E **174** E4
Gers → *France* 44°9N 0°39E **174** D4
Gersfeld *Germany* 50°27N 9°56E **178** E5
Gersoppa Falls *India* 14°12N 74°46E **245** G2
Gersthofen *Germany* 48°25N 10°53E **179** G6
Gertak Sanggul *Malaysia* 5°17N 100°12E **237** c
Gertak Sanggul, Tanjung *Malaysia* 5°16N 100°11E **237** c
Gerung *Indonesia* 8°43S 116°7E **231** K19
Géryville = El Bayadh *Algeria* 33°40N 1°1E **261** B5
Gerzat *France* 45°48N 3°8E **174** C7
Gerze *Turkey* 41°48N 35°12E **212** B6
Geseke *Germany* 51°38N 8°31E **178** D4
Geser *Indonesia* 3°50S 130°54E **231** E8
Gesira △ *Somali Rep.* 1°58N 44°59E **267** D5
Gesso → *Italy* 44°24N 7°33E **198** D4
Gestro, Wabi → *Ethiopia* 4°12N 42°2E **257** G5
Getafe *Spain* 40°18N 3°43W **127** C1
Getinge *Sweden* 56°49N 12°44E **163** H6
Getty Center, The *U.S.A.* 34°4N 118°29W **126** B2
Gettysburg *Pa., U.S.A.* 39°50N 77°14W **309** F15
Gettysburg *S. Dak., U.S.A.* 45°1N 99°57W **308** C4
Getxo *Spain* 43°21N 2°59W **196** B2
Getz Ice Shelf *Antarctica* 75°0S 130°0W **151** D14
Geumdo *S. Korea* 34°31N 127°45E **224** E3
Geumpang *Indonesia* 4°52N 96°6E **234** B1
Geunjeong *S. Korea* 37°28N 126°54E **137** C1
Geureudong, Gunung *Indonesia* 4°13N 96°42E **234** B1
Geurie *Australia* 32°22S 148°50E **283** B8
Geva Binyamin *West Bank* 31°51N 35°17E **123** A2
Gevaş *Turkey* 38°15N 43°6E **213** C10
Gévaudan *France* 44°40N 3°40E **174** D7
Gevgelija *Macedonia* 41°9N 22°30E **202** E6
Gévora → *Spain* 38°53N 6°57W **195** G4
Gevrai *India* 19°16N 75°45E **244** E2
Gewani *Ethiopia* 10°12N 40°40E **257** E5
Gex *France* 46°21N 6°3E **173** F13
Geyikli *Turkey* 39°48N 26°12E **205** B8
Geylang Serai *Singapore* 1°19N 103°53E **138** B3
Geyser *U.S.A.* 47°16N 110°30W **304** C8
Geyserville *U.S.A.* 38°42N 122°54W **306** G4
Geysir *Iceland* 64°19N 20°18W **155** C6
Geyve *Turkey* 40°30N 30°18E **212** B4
Ghâbat el Arab = Wang Kai *Sudan* 9°3N 29°23E **257** F2
Ghabeish *Sudan* 12°9N 27°21E **257** E2
Ghadāf, W. al → *Iraq* 32°56N 43°30E **213** F10
Ghadāmis *Libya* 30°11N 9°29E **258** B1
Ghadāmis □ *Libya* 30°25N 10°25E **258** B2
Ghaddūwah *Libya* 26°26N 14°19E **258** C2
Ghaggar → *India* 29°30N 74°53E **242** E6
Ghaghara → *India* 25°45N 84°40E **243** G11
Ghaghat → *Bangla.* 25°19N 89°38E **241** C2
Ghaghe *Solomon Is.* 7°24S 158°15E **287** L10
Ghagra *India* 23°17N 84°33E **243** H11
Ghagra → *India* 27°29N 81°9E **243** F9
Ghajn Tuffieha Bay *Malta* 35°56N 14°21E **206** F7
Ghajnsielem *Malta* 36°2N 14°17E **206** E7
Ghalla, Wadi el → *Sudan* 10°25N 27°32E **257** E2
Ghallamane *Mauritania* 23°15N 10°0W **260** D3
Ghallamane, Sebkhet *Mauritania* 23°41N 9°50W **260** D3
Ghamid az Zenad *Si. Arabia* 19°35N 41°24E **248** D3
Ghana ■ *W. Afr.* 8°0N 1°0W **263** D4
Ghansor *India* 22°39N 80°1E **243** H9
Ghanzi *Botswana* 21°50S 21°34E **270** B3
Gharapuri *India* 18°57N 72°57E **130** B2
Gharb = Shahrak-e Qods *Iran* 35°47N 51°22E **141** A2
Gharb *Malta* 36°4N 14°13E **206** E6
Gharb Bahr el Ghazâl □ *Sudan* 7°30N 27°30E **257** F2
Gharb Dârfûr □ *Sudan* 13°0N 23°0E **259** F4
Gharb el Istiwa'iya □ *Sudan* 5°0N 30°0E **257** G3
Gharb Kordofân □ *Sudan* 12°10N 28°0E **257** E2
Gharbîya, Es Sahrâ el *Egypt* 27°40N 26°30E **256** B2
Ghardaïa *Algeria* 32°20N 3°37E **261** B5
Ghardaïa □ *Algeria* 31°5N 3°10E **261** B5
Ghârib, G. *Egypt* 28°6N 32°54E **256** B3
Gharig *Sudan* 10°47N 27°33E **257** E2
Gharm *Tajikistan* 39°0N 70°20E **214** F8
Gharm, W. → *Oman* 19°57N 57°38E **249** C7
Gharyān *Libya* 32°10N 13°0E **258** B2
Gharyān □ *Libya* 30°35N 12°0E **258** B2
Ghāt *Libya* 24°59N 10°11E **258** C2
Ghāt □ *Libya* 25°35N 10°15E **258** C2
Ghatal *India* 22°40N 87°46E **243** H12
Ghatampur *India* 26°8N 80°13E **243** F9
Ghatgaon *India* 21°24N 85°53E **244** D7
Ghatkopar *India* 19°4N 72°54E **130** A2
Ghatprabha → *India* 16°15N 75°20E **245** F2
Ghats, Eastern *India* 14°0N 78°50E **245** H4
Ghats, Western *India* 14°0N 75°0E **245** H2
Ghatsila *India* 22°36N 86°29E **243** H12
Ghaṭṭī *Si. Arabia* 31°16N 37°31E **246** D3
Ghawdex = Gozo *Malta* 36°3N 14°15E **206** E7
Ghayl *Si. Arabia* 21°40N 46°20E **248** B4
Ghazal, Bahr el → *Chad* 13°0N 15°47E **259** F3
Ghazâl, Bahr el → *Sudan* 9°31N 30°25E **257** F3
Ghazaouet *Algeria* 35°8N 1°50W **261** A4
Ghaziabad *India* 28°42N 77°26E **242** E7
Ghazipur *Delhi, India* 28°37N 77°19E **120** B2
Ghazipur *Ut. P., India* 25°38N 83°35E **243** G10
Ghaznī *Afghan.* 33°30N 68°28E **242** C3
Ghaznī □ *Afghan.* 32°10N 68°20E **240** B3
Ghedi *Italy* 45°24N 10°16E **198** C7
Ghelari *Romania* 45°38N 22°45E **182** E7
Ghent = Gent *Belgium* 51°2N 3°42E **170** C3
Gheorghe Gheorghiu-Dej = Oneşti *Romania* 46°17N 26°47E **183** D11
Gheorgheni *Romania* 46°43N 25°41E **183** D10
Gherla *Romania* 47°2N 23°57E **183** C8
Ghidigeni *Romania* 46°3N 27°30E **183** D12
Ghilarza *Italy* 40°7N 8°50E **200** B1
Ghimeş-Făget *Romania* 46°35N 26°2E **183** D11
Ghīnah, Wādī al → *Si. Arabia* 30°27N 38°14E **246** D3
Ghirān, W. → *Si. Arabia* 20°52N 47°10E **248** B4
Ghirardelli Square *San Francisco, U.S.A.* **136** a1
Ghisonaccia *France* 42°1N 9°26E **175** F13
Ghisoni *France* 42°7N 9°12E **175** F13
Ghizar → *Pakistan* 36°15N 73°43E **243** A5
Ghizri *Pakistan* 24°49N 67°2E **123** B2
Ghizri Cr. → *Pakistan* 24°47N 67°5E **123** B2
Ghod → *India* 18°30N 74°35E **244** E2
Ghogha *India* 21°40N 72°20E **244** D1
Ghonda *India* 28°41N 77°16E **120** A2
Ghot Ogrein *Egypt* 31°10N 25°20E **256** A2
Ghotaru *India* 27°20N 70°1E **242** F4
Ghotki *Pakistan* 28°5N 69°21E **242** E3
Ghowr □ *Afghan.* 34°0N 64°20E **240** B2
Ghubbet el Bûs *Egypt* 29°35N 32°21E **251** J3
Ghughri *India* 22°39N 80°41E **243** H9
Ghugus *India* 19°58N 79°12E **244** E4
Ghulam Mohammad Barrage *Pakistan* 25°30N 68°20E **242** G3
Ghurayrah *Si. Arabia* 18°37N 42°41E **248** C3
Ghūrīān *Afghan.* 34°17N 61°25E **240** B1
Ghusuri *India* 22°37N 88°21E **124** B2
Ghuzzayil, Sabkhat *Libya* 29°30N 19°30E **258** C3
Gia Dinh *Vietnam* 10°49N 106°42E **237** G6
Gia Lai = Plei Ku *Vietnam* 13°57N 108°0E **236** F7
Gia Nghia *Vietnam* 11°58N 107°42E **237** G6
Gia Ngoc *Vietnam* 14°50N 108°58E **236** E7
Gia Vuc *Vietnam* 14°42N 108°34E **236** E7
Giali *Greece* 36°41N 27°11E **205** E9
Gialtra *Greece* 38°51N 22°59E **204** C4
Giamama = Jamaame *Somali Rep.* 0°4N 42°44E **267** D5
Gian *Phil.* 5°49N 125°12E **233** J5
Gianicolense *Italy* 41°53N 12°28E **136** B1
Gianicolo *Rome, Italy* **136** c1
Giannitsa *Greece* 40°46N 22°24E **202** F6
Giannutri *Italy* 42°15N 11°6E **198** F8
Giant Forest *U.S.A.* 36°36N 118°43W **306** J8
Giant Mts. = Krkonoše *Czech Rep.* 50°50N 15°35E **180** A8
Giant Sequoia △ *U.S.A.* 36°10N 118°35W **306** K8
Giant Wheel = Riesenrad *Austria* 48°14N 16°23E **142** A2
Giants Causeway *U.K.* 55°16N 6°29W **166** A5
Giant's Tank *Sri Lanka* 8°51N 80°2E **245** K5
Gianyar *Indonesia* 8°32S 115°20E **231** K18
Giarabub = Al Jaghbūb *Libya* 29°42N 24°38E **258** C4
Giaros *Greece* 37°32N 24°40E **204** D6
Giarre *Italy* 37°43N 15°11E **201** E8
Giaveno *Italy* 45°2N 7°21E **198** C4
Gibara *Cuba* 21°9N 76°11W **320** B4
Gibbon *U.S.A.* 40°45N 98°51W **308** E4
Gibe → *Ethiopia* 7°20N 37°36E **257** F4
Gibe I *Ethiopia* 8°7N 37°0E **257** F4
Gibe II *Ethiopia* 8°0N 37°30E **257** F4
Gibe III *Ethiopia* 7°0N 37°30E **257** F4
Gibellina Nuova *Italy* 37°47N 12°58E **200** E5
Gibeon *Namibia* 25°9S 17°43E **270** C2
Gibraleón *Spain* 37°23N 6°58W **195** H4
Gibraltar ☑ *Europe* 36°7N 5°22W **195** J5
Gibraltar, Str. of *Medit. S.* 35°55N 5°40W **195** K5
Gibraltar Pt. *Canada* 43°36N 79°23W **141** B2
Gibraltar Range △ *Australia* 29°31S 152°19E **281** D5
Gibson *U.S.A.* 33°14N 82°36W **316** B7
Gibson City *U.S.A.* 40°28N 88°22W **311** D8
Gibson Desert *Australia* 24°0S 126°0E **278** D4
Gibsonburg *U.S.A.* 41°23N 83°19W **311** C13
Gibsons *Canada* 49°24N 123°32W **296** D4
Gibsonton *U.S.A.* 27°51N 82°23W **317** H7
Gibsonville *U.S.A.* 39°46N 120°54W **306** F6
Gidami *Ethiopia* 8°59N 34°37E **266** C3
Giddalur *India* 15°20N 78°57E **245** G4
Giddings *U.S.A.* 30°11N 96°56W **314** F6
Gidea Park *U.K.* 51°35N 0°11E **125** A5
Gidole *Ethiopia* 5°40N 37°25E **257** F4
Giebnegáisi = Kebnekaise *Sweden* 67°53N 18°33E **160** C18
Gien *France* 47°40N 2°36E **173** E9
Giengen *Germany* 48°37N 10°14E **179** G6
Giesing *Germany* 48°6N 11°35E **131** B2
Giessen *Germany* 50°34N 8°41E **178** E4
Gīfān *Iran* 37°54N 57°28E **247** B8
Gifatin, Geziret *Egypt* 27°10N 33°50E **256** B3
Gifford *U.S.A.* 27°40N 80°25W **317** H9
Gifhorn *Germany* 52°30N 10°33E **178** C6
Gift Lake *Canada* 55°53N 115°49W **296** B5
Gifu *Japan* 35°30N 136°45E **223** B8
Gifu □ *Japan* 35°40N 137°0E **223** B9
Gigant *Russia* 46°28N 41°20E **191** G5
Giganta, Sa. de la *Mexico* 26°0N 111°39W **318** B2
Gigen *Bulgaria* 43°40N 24°28E **203** C8
Gigha *U.K.* 55°42N 5°44W **167** F3
Giglio *Italy* 42°20N 10°52E **198** F7
Gignac *France* 43°39N 3°32E **174** E7
Gigüela → *Spain* 39°8N 3°44W **195** F7
Gijang *S. Korea* 35°14N 129°12E **224** E4
Gijón *Spain* 43°32N 5°42W **194** B5
Gikongoro *Rwanda* 2°28S 29°34E **268** C2
Gil I. *Canada* 53°12N 129°15W **296** C3
Gila → *U.S.A.* 32°43N 114°33W **305** K6
Gila Bend *U.S.A.* 32°57N 112°43W **305** K7
Gila Bend Mts. *U.S.A.* 33°10N 113°0W **305** K7
Gila Cliff Dwellings △ *U.S.A.* 33°12N 108°16W **305** K9
Gīlān □ *Iran* 37°0N 50°0E **247** B6
Gīlān-e Gharb *Iran* 34°8N 45°55E **213** E11
Gilău *Romania* 46°45N 23°23E **183** D8
Gilbert → *Australia* 16°35S 141°15E **280** B3
Gilbert Is. *Kiribati* 1°0N 172°0E **277** A14
Gilbert River *Australia* 18°9S 142°52E **280** B3
Gilbert Seamounts *Pac. Oc.* 52°50N 150°10W **150** D18
Gilbués *Brazil* 9°50S 45°21W **332** C2
Gilead *U.S.A.* 44°24N 70°59W **313** B14
Gilf el Kebîr, Hadabat el *Egypt* 23°50N 25°50E **256** C2
Gilford I. *Canada* 50°40N 126°30W **296** C3
Gilgandra *Australia* 31°43S 148°39E **283** A8
Gilgil *Kenya* 0°30S 36°20E **268** C4
Gilgit *India* 35°50N 74°15E **243** B6
Gilgit → *Pakistan* 35°44N 74°37E **243** B6
Gilgunnia *Australia* 32°26S 146°2E **283** B7
Gili, Pulau 10°0S 115°0E **235** D5
Gili △ *Mozam.* 16°39S 38°27E **269** F4
Gilimanuk *Indonesia* 8°10S 114°26E **231** J17
Giljeva Planina *Europe* 43°9N 20°0E **202** C3
Gill Pt. *St. Helena* 15°58S 5°38W **153** h
Gillam *Canada* 56°20N 94°40W **297** B10
Gilleleje *Denmark* 56°8N 12°19E **163** H6
Gillen, L. *Australia* 26°11S 124°38E **279** E3
Gilles, L. *Australia* 32°50S 136°45E **282** B2
Gillespie *U.S.A.* 39°8N 89°49W **310** F7
Gillespies Pt. *N.Z.* 43°24S 169°49E **285** D4
Gillette *U.S.A.* 44°18N 105°30W **304** D11
Gilliat *Australia* 20°40S 141°28E **280** C3
Gillingham *U.K.* 51°23N 0°33E **169** F8
Gilman *U.S.A.* 40°46N 88°0W **311** D9
Gilman City *U.S.A.* 40°8N 93°53W **310** D3
Gilmer *U.S.A.* 32°44N 94°57W **314** E7
Gilmerton *U.K.* 55°54N 3°7W **121** B3
Gilmore, L. *Australia* 32°29S 121°37E **279** F3
Gilmour *Canada* 44°48N 77°37W **312** B7
Gilo *West Bank* 31°44N 35°11E **123** B2
Gilo → *Ethiopia* 8°10N 33°15E **257** F3
Gilort → *Romania* 44°38N 23°32E **183** F8
Gilroy *U.S.A.* 37°1N 121°34W **306** H5
Giluwe, Mt. *Papua N. G.* 6°8S 143°52E **286** D2
Gimbi *Ethiopia* 9°3N 35°42E **257** F4
Gimcheon *S. Korea* 36°11N 128°4E **224** D4
Gimhae *S. Korea* 35°14N 128°53E **224** E4
Gimhwa *S. Korea* 38°17N 127°28E **224** C3
Gimie, Mt. *St. Lucia* 13°54N 61°0W **323** m
Gimje *S. Korea* 35°48N 126°45E **224** E3
Gimli *Canada* 50°40N 97°0W **297** C9
Gimmersta *Sweden* 59°14N 18°14E **139** B3
Gimo *Sweden* 60°11N 18°12E **162** D12
Gimone → *France* 44°0N 1°6E **174** E5
Gimont *France* 43°38N 0°52E **174** E4
Gin → *Sri Lanka* 6°5N 80°7E **245** L5
Gin Gin *Australia* 25°0S 151°58E **281** D5
Ginâh *Egypt* 25°21N 30°30E **256** B3
Ginatilan *Phil.* 9°34N 123°19E **233** G4
Gineifa *Egypt* 30°12N 32°25E **256** H8
Gingee *India* 12°15N 79°25E **245** H4
Gingin *Australia* 31°22S 115°54E **279** F2
Gingindlovu *S. Africa* 29°2S 31°30E **271** C5
Gingoog *Phil.* 8°50N 125°7E **233** G5
Gingoog B. *Phil.* 8°54N 125°7E **233** G5
Ginir *Ethiopia* 7°6N 40°40E **257** F5
Ginosa *Italy* 40°35N 16°45E **201** B9
Ginowan *Japan* 26°15N 127°45E **288** a
Ginza *Tokyo, Japan* **140** b5
Ginzo de Limia = Xinzo de Limia *Spain* 42°3N 7°47W **194** C3
Giofyros → *Greece* 35°20N 25°6E **207** E6
Giohar = Jawhar *Somali Rep.* 2°48N 45°30E **267** D6
Gióia, G. di *Italy* 38°30N 15°45E **201** D8
Gióia del Colle *Italy* 40°48N 16°55E **201** B9
Gióia Táuro *Italy* 38°25N 15°54E **201** D8
Gioiosa Iónica *Italy* 38°20N 16°18E **201** D9
Gioiosa Marea *Italy* 38°10N 14°54E **201** D7
Giona, Oros *Greece* 38°38N 22°14E **204** C4
Giovi, Passo dei *Italy* 44°33N 8°57E **198** D5
Giovinazzo *Italy* 41°11N 16°40E **201** A9
Gippsland *Australia* 37°52S 147°0E **283** D7
Gir △ *India* 21°0N 71°0E **242** J4
Gir Hills *India* 21°0N 71°0E **242** J4
Girab *India* 26°2N 70°38E **242** F4
Girâfi, W. → *Egypt* 29°58N 34°39E **251** J5
Giraltovce *Slovak Rep.* 49°7N 21°32E **181** B14
Girapetra, Akra *Greece* 38°51N 20°41E **207** B2
Girard *St. Lucia* 13°59N 60°57W **323** m
Girard *Ga., U.S.A.* 33°3N 81°43W **316** B8
Girard *Ill., U.S.A.* 39°27N 89°47W **310** F7
Girard *Kans., U.S.A.* 37°31N 94°51W **308** G6
Girard *Ohio, U.S.A.* 41°9N 80°42W **312** E4
Girard *Pa., U.S.A.* 42°0N 80°19W **312** E4
Girardot *Colombia* 4°18N 74°48W **328** C3
Giraud, Pte. *Dominica* 15°20N 61°15W **323** k
Girdle Ness *U.K.* 57°9N 2°3W **167** D6
Giresun *Turkey* 40°55N 38°30E **213** B8
Giresun □ *Turkey* 40°30N 38°30E **213** B8
Girga *Egypt* 26°17N 31°55E **256** B3
Girgaum *Mumbai, India* **130** b2
Girgenti = Agrigento *Italy* 37°19N 13°34E **200** E6
Girgir, C. *Papua N. G.* 3°50S 144°35E **286** B3
Giri → *Dem. Rep. of the Congo* 0°28N 17°59E **264** B3
Giri → *India* 30°28N 77°41E **242** D7
Giridih *India* 24°10N 86°21E **243** G12
Girifalco *Italy* 38°49N 16°25E **201** D9
Girifti *Kenya* 1°59N 39°46E **268** B4
Girilambone *Australia* 31°16S 146°57E **283** A7
Girne = Kyrenia *Cyprus* 35°20N 33°20E **207** E9
Giro *Nigeria* 11°7N 4°42E **263** C5
Giromagny *France* 47°45N 6°50E **173** E13
Giron = Kiruna *Sweden* 67°52N 20°15E **160** C19
Girona *Spain* 41°58N 2°46E **196** D7
Girona □ *Spain* 42°11N 2°30E **196** C7
Gironde □ *France* 44°45N 0°30W **174** D3
Gironde → *France* 45°32N 1°7W **174** C2
Gironella *Spain* 42°2N 1°53E **196** C6
Girraween △ *Australia* 28°46S 151°54E **281** D5
Girringun △ *Australia* 18°15S 145°32E **280** B4
Giru *Australia* 19°30S 147°5E **280** B4
Girvan *U.K.* 55°14N 4°51W **167** F4
Gisborne *Vic., Australia* 37°29S 144°36E **282** D6
Gisborne *N.Z.* 38°39S 178°5E **284** E7
Gisborne □ *N.Z.* 38°30S 178°0E **284** E6
Gisenyi *Rwanda* 1°41S 29°15E **268** C2
Gislaved *Sweden* 57°19N 13°32E **163** G7
Gisors *France* 49°15N 1°47E **173** C8
Gitarama *Rwanda* 2°4S 29°45E **268** C2
Gitega *Burundi* 3°26S 29°56E **268** C2
Githio *Greece* 36°46N 22°34E **204** E4
Gitschin = Jičín *Czech Rep.* 50°25N 15°28E **180** A8
Giuba = Juba → *Somali Rep.* 1°30N 42°35E **267** D5
Giugliano in Campania *Italy* 40°56N 14°12E **201** B7
Giulianova *Italy* 42°45N 13°57E **199** F10
Giura *Greece* 39°23N 24°10E **204** B6
Giurgeni *Romania* 44°45N 27°48E **183** F12
Giurgiu *Romania* 43°52N 25°57E **183** G10
Giurgiu □ *Romania* 44°20N 26°0E **183** F10
Giurgiuleşti *Moldova* 45°29N 28°12E **183** E13
Giv'at Ram *Israel* 31°47N 35°12E **123** B2
Giv'at Ye'arim *Israel* 31°47N 35°7E **123** B1
Giv'at Ze'ev *West Bank* 31°52N 35°10E **123** A2
Give *Denmark* 55°51N 9°13E **163** J3
Givet *France* 50°8N 4°49E **173** B11
Giv'on *West Bank* 31°51N 35°10E **123** A1
Givors *France* 45°35N 4°45E **175** C8
Givry *France* 46°41N 4°46E **173** F11
Giyani *S. Africa* 23°19S 30°43E **271** B5
Giyon *Ethiopia* 8°33N 38°1E **257** F4
Giza = El Gîza *Egypt* 30°0N 31°12E **117** A2
Giza Pyramids *Egypt* 29°58N 31°9E **117** B1
Gizab *Afghan.* 33°22N 66°17E **242** C1
Gizhiga *Russia* 62°3N 160°30E **215** C17
Gizhiginskaya Guba *Russia* 61°0N 158°0E **215** C16
Gizo *Solomon Is.* 8°7S 156°50E **287** M9
Giżycko *Poland* 54°2N 21°48E **184** D8
Gizzeria *Italy* 38°59N 16°12E **201** D9
Gjakovë = Dakovica *Kosovo* 42°22N 20°26E **202** D4
Gjalicë e Lumës, Mal. *Albania* 42°2N 20°25E **202** D4
Gjegjan *Albania* 41°58N 20°3E **202** E4
Gjendesheim *Norway* 61°30N 8°48E **164** C5
Gjermundshamn *Norway* 60°40N 5°55E **164** D2
Gjersjøen *Norway* 59°47N 10°47E **133** B3
Gjerstad *Norway* 58°54N 9°1E **164** F6
Gjevilvatnet *Norway* 62°43N 9°23E **164** B6
Gjilan = Gnjilane *Kosovo* 42°28N 21°29E **202** D5
Gjirokastër *Albania* 40°7N 20°10E **202** F4
Gjoa Haven *Canada* 68°38N 95°53W **294** D12
Gjøra *Norway* 62°33N 9°4E **164** B6
Gjøvik *Norway* 60°47N 10°43E **164** D7
Gjuhës, Kep i *Albania* 40°28N 19°15E **202** F3
Glace Bay *Canada* 46°11N 59°58W **299** C8
Glacier △ *B.C., Canada* 51°15N 117°30W **296** C5
Glacier △ *Mont., U.S.A.* 48°42N 113°48W **304** B7
Glacier Bay *U.S.A.* 58°40N 136°0W **303** G14
Glacier Bay △ *U.S.A.* 58°45N 136°30W **296** B1
Glacier Peak *U.S.A.* 48°7N 121°7W **304** B3
Gladesville *Australia* 33°50S 151°8E **139** B1
Gladewater *U.S.A.* 32°33N 94°56W **314** E7
Gladsaxe *Denmark* 55°45N 12°25E **118** A2
Gladstone *Queens., Australia* 23°52S 151°16E **280** C5
Gladstone *S. Austral., Australia* 33°15S 138°22E **282** B3
Gladstone *Man., Canada* 50°13N 98°57W **297** C9
Gladstone *Ill., U.S.A.* 40°52N 90°57W **310** D6
Gladstone *Mich., U.S.A.* 45°51N 87°1W **308** C10
Gladstone *Mo., U.S.A.* 39°13N 94°35W **310** E2
Gladwin *U.S.A.* 43°59N 84°29W **309** D11
Glafsfjorden *Sweden* 59°30N 12°37E **162** E6
Glagah *Indonesia* 8°13S 114°18E **231** J17
Głagów Małapolski *Poland* 50°10N 21°56E **185** H8
Glåma = Glomma → *Norway* 59°12N 10°57E **164** E7
Gláma *Iceland* 65°48N 23°0W **155** B4
Glamis *U.S.A.* 32°55N 115°5W **307** N11
Glamoč *Bos.-H.* 44°3N 16°51E **199** D13
Glamorgan, Vale of □ *U.K.* 51°28N 3°25W **169** F4
Glåmos *Norway* 62°41N 11°25E **164** B8
Glamsbjerg *Denmark* 55°17N 10°6E **163** J4
Glanvillia *Dominica* 15°34N 61°28W **323** k
Glarus *Switz.* 47°3N 9°4E **179** H5
Glarus □ *Switz.* 47°0N 9°5E **179** J5
Glasco *Kans., U.S.A.* 39°22N 97°50W **308** F5
Glasco *N.Y., U.S.A.* 42°3N 73°57W **313** D11
Glasgow *C. of Glasg., U.K.* 55°51N 4°15W **167** F4
Glasgow *Ky., U.S.A.* 37°0N 85°55W **309** G11
Glasgow *Mo., U.S.A.* 39°14N 92°51W **310** E4
Glasgow *Mont., U.S.A.* 48°12N 106°38W **304** B10
Glasgow, City of □ *U.K.* 55°51N 4°12W **167** F4
Glasgow Int. ✕ (GLA) *U.K.* 55°51N 4°21W **167** F4
Glaslyn *Canada* 53°22N 108°21W **297** C7
Glasnevin *Ireland* 53°22N 6°15W **120** A2
Glassmanor *U.S.A.* 38°49N 77°0W **143** C4
Glasthule *Ireland* 53°17N 6°7W **120** B3
Glastonbury *U.K.* 51°9N 2°43W **169** F5
Glastonbury *Conn., U.S.A.* 41°43N 72°37W **313** E12
Glatz = Kłodzko *Poland* 50°28N 16°38E **185** H3
Glauchau *Germany* 50°49N 12°31E **178** E8
Glava *Sweden* 59°33N 12°35E **162** E6
Glavice *Croatia* 43°43N 16°41E **199** E13
Glazov *Russia* 58°9N 52°40E **190** A11
Gleichen *Canada* 50°52N 113°3W **296** C6
Gleisdorf *Austria* 47°6N 15°44E **180** D8
Gleiwitz = Gliwice *Poland* 50°22N 18°41E **185** H5
Glen *U.S.A.* 44°7N 71°11W **313** B13
Glen Affric *U.K.* 57°17N 5°1W **167** D3
Glen Afton *N.Z.* 37°37S 175°4E **284** D4
Glen Canyon *U.S.A.* 37°30N 110°40W **305** H8
Glen Canyon △ *U.S.A.* 37°15N 111°0W **305** H8
Glen Canyon Dam *U.S.A.* 36°57N 111°29W **305** H8
Glen Coe *U.K.* 56°40N 5°0W **167** E3
Glen Cove *U.S.A.* 40°51N 73°38W **313** F11
Glen Garry *U.K.* 57°3N 5°7W **167** D3
Glen Innes *Australia* 29°44S 151°44E **281** D5
Glen Iris *Australia* 37°51S 145°3E **128** B2
Glen Lyon *U.S.A.* 41°10N 76°5W **313** E8
Glen Mar Park *U.S.A.* 38°57N 77°7W **143** B3
Glen Massey *N.Z.* 37°38S 175°2E **284** D4
Glen Mor *U.K.* 57°9N 4°37W **167** D4
Glen More △ *U.K.* 57°8N 3°40W **167** D5
Glen Moriston *U.K.* 57°11N 4°52W **167** D4
Glen Robertson *Canada* 45°22N 74°30W **313** A10
Glen Rouge Park *Canada* 43°49N 79°10W **141** A4
Glen Spean *U.K.* 56°53N 4°40W **167** E4
Glen Ullin *U.S.A.* 46°49N 101°50W **308** B3
Glénan, Îs. de *France* 47°42N 4°0W **172** E3
Glenarden *U.S.A.* 38°56N 76°51W **143** B4
Glenariff △ *Ireland* 55°2N 6°10W **166** A5
Glenasmole Reservoirs *Ireland* 53°15N 6°21W **120** B1
Glenavy *N.Z.* 44°54S 171°7E **285** E6
Glenbeigh *Ireland* 52°3N 9°58W **166** D2
Glenburn *Australia* 37°27S 145°26E **283** D6
Glencoe *Ont., Canada* 42°45N 81°43W **312** D3
Glencoe *KwaZulu Natal, S. Africa* 28°11S 30°11E **271** C5
Glencoe *Ala., U.S.A.* 33°57N 85°56W **316** B4
Glencoe *Minn., U.S.A.* 44°46N 94°9W **308** C6
Glencolumbkille *Ireland* 54°43N 8°42W **166** B3
Glencorse Res. *U.K.* 55°51N 3°15W **121** B2
Glencullen *Ireland* 53°14N 6°12W **120** B2
Glendale *Ariz., U.S.A.* 33°32N 112°11W **305** K7
Glendale *Calif., U.S.A.* 34°9N 118°15W **126** B3
Glendale *Fla., U.S.A.* 30°52N 86°7W **316** E3
Glendale *Zimbabwe* 17°22S 31°5E **269** F3
Glendive *U.S.A.* 47°7N 104°43W **304** C11
Glendo *U.S.A.* 42°30N 105°2W **304** E11
Glendoo Mt. *Ireland* 53°14N 6°16W **120** B2
Glenelg *Australia* 34°58S 138°31E **282** C3
Glenelg → *Australia* 38°4S 140°59E **282** E4
Glenfield *U.S.A.* 43°43N 75°24W **313** C9
Glengad Hd. *Ireland* 55°20N 7°10W **166** A4
Glengarriff *Ireland* 51°45N 9°34W **166** E2
Glengoffe *Jamaica* 18°10N 76°53W **320** a
Glenham *N.Z.* 46°26S 168°52E **285** G3
Glenhope *N.Z.* 41°40S 172°39E **285** B7
Glenhuntly *Australia* 37°52S 145°1E **128** B2
Glenmary, Mt. *N.Z.* 43°55S 169°55E **285** D4
Glenmont *U.S.A.* 40°31N 82°6W **312** F2
Glenmorgan *Australia* 27°14S 149°42E **281** D4
Glenn *U.S.A.* 39°31N 122°1W **306** F4
Glennallen *U.S.A.* 62°7N 145°33W **303** E11
Glennamaddy *Ireland* 53°37N 8°33W **166** C3
Glenns Ferry *U.S.A.* 42°57N 115°18W **304** E6
Glennville *U.S.A.* 31°56N 81°56W **316** D8

Glenora *Canada* 44°54N 77°3W **312** B7
Glenorchy *Tas., Australia* 42°49S 147°18E **281** G4
Glenorchy *Vic., Australia* 36°55S 142°41E **282** D5
Glenorchy *N.Z.* 44°51S 168°24E **285** E3
Glenore *Australia* 17°50S 141°12E **280** B3
Glenreagh *Australia* 30°2S 153°1E **281** E5
Glenrock *U.S.A.* 42°52N 105°52W **304** E11
Glenrothes *U.K.* 56°12N 3°10W **167** E5
Glenrowan *Australia* 36°29S 146°13E **283** D7
Glens Falls *U.S.A.* 43°19N 73°39W **313** C11
Glenside *Ireland* 40°6N 75°9W **313** F9
Glenside *Pa., U.S.A.* 40°6N 75°9W **313** F9
Glenthompson *Australia* 37°38S 142°38E **282** D5
Glenties *Ireland* 54°49N 8°16W **166** B3
Glenview *U.S.A.* 38°3N 87°48W **119** A2
Glenview Countryside
 U.S.A. 42°3N 87°49W **119** A2
Glenville *U.S.A.* 38°56N 80°50W **309** F13
Glenvista *S. Africa* 26°17S 28°3E **123** B2
Glenwood *Nfld. & L.,*
 Canada 49°0N 54°58W **299** C9
Glenwood *Ark., U.S.A.* 34°20N 93°33W **314** D8
Glenwood *Ga., U.S.A.* 32°11N 82°40W **311** J4
Glenwood *Hawai'i, U.S.A.* 19°29N 155°9W **302** D6
Glenwood *Iowa, U.S.A.* 41°3N 95°45W **308** E6
Glenwood *Minn., U.S.A.* 45°39N 95°23W **308** C6
Glenwood *Wash., U.S.A.* 46°1N 121°17W **306** D5
Glenwood Springs
 U.S.A. 39°33N 107°19W **304** G10
Glettinganes *Iceland* 65°30N 13°37W **155** B13
Glidden *U.S.A.* 42°4N 94°44W **308** D2
Glifada *Greece* 37°52N 23°45E **118** D2
Glimåkra *Sweden* 56°19N 14°7E **163** H8
Glin *Ireland* 52°34N 9°17W **166** D2
Glina *Croatia* 45°20N 16°6E **199** C13
Glinojeck *Poland* 52°49N 20°21E **185** F7
Glittertind *Norway* 61°40N 8°32E **164** C5
Gliwice *Poland* 50°22N 18°41E **185** H5
Globe *U.S.A.* 33°24N 110°47W **305** K8
Glodeanu Siliştea
 Romania 44°50N 26°48E **183** F11
Glodeni *Moldova* 47°45N 27°31E **183** C12
Glödnitz *Austria* 46°53N 14°7E **180** E7
Glogau = Głogów *Poland* 51°37N 16°5E **185** G3
Gloggnitz *Austria* 47°41N 15°56E **180** D8
Głogów *Poland* 51°37N 16°5E **185** G3
Głogówek *Poland* 50°21N 17°53E **185** H4
Glomma → *Norway* 59°12N 10°57E **164** E7
Gloria *Phil.* 12°59N 121°30E **232** E3
Glorieuses, Îs. *Ind. Oc.* 11°30S 47°20E **272** d2
Glosa *Greece* 39°10N 23°45E **204** B5
Glossop *U.K.* 53°27N 1°56W **168** D6
Glostrup *Denmark* 55°39N 12°23E **118** B2
Gloucester *N.S.W.,*
 Australia 32°0S 151°59E **283** B9
Gloucester *Papua N. G.* 5°31S 148°31E **286** C5
Gloucester *Gloucs., U.K.* 51°53N 2°15W **169** F5
Gloucester *Mass., U.S.A.* 42°37N 70°40W **313** D14
Gloucester, C. *Papua N. G.* 5°26S 148°21E **286** C5
Gloucester I. *Australia* 20°0S 148°30E **280** b
Gloucester Island △
 Australia 20°12S 148°30E **280** b
Gloucester Point *U.S.A.* 37°15N 76°30W **309** G15
Gloucestershire □ *U.K.* 51°46N 2°15W **169** F5
Glover I. *Grenada* 11°59N 61°47W **323** q
Gloversville *U.S.A.* 43°3N 74°21W **313** C10
Glovertown *Canada* 48°40N 54°3W **299** C9
Gloverville = Warrenville
 U.S.A. 33°33N 81°48W **316** B8
Głowno *Poland* 51°59N 19°42E **185** G6
Głubczyce *Poland* 50°13N 17°52E **185** H4
Głubokiy *Russia* 48°35N 40°25E **191** E5
Głubokoe *Kazakhstan* 50°8N 82°18E **217** B10
Glubokoye = Hlybokaye
 Belarus 55°10N 27°45E **188** E4
Ghcholazy *Poland* 50°19N 17°24E **185** H4
Glücksburg *Germany* 54°50N 9°33E **178** A5
Glückstadt *Germany* 53°45N 9°25E **178** B5
Glukhov = Hlukhiv
 Ukraine 51°40N 33°58E **189** G7
Glusk *Belarus* 52°53N 28°41E **177** B15
Głuszyca *Poland* 50°41N 16°23E **185** H3
Glyngøre *Denmark* 56°46N 8°52E **163** H2
Gmünd *Kärnten, Austria* 46°54N 13°31E **180** E6
Gmünd *Niederösterreich,*
 Austria 48°45N 15°0E **180** C8
Gmunden *Austria* 47°55N 13°48E **180** D6
Gnali *Gabon* 2°34S 11°18E **264** C2
Gnarp *Sweden* 62°3N 17°16E **162** B11
Gnesen = Gniezno *Poland* 52°31N 17°37E **185** F4
Gnesta *Sweden* 59°3N 17°17E **162** E11
Gniew *Poland* 53°50N 18°50E **184** E5
Gniewkowo *Poland* 52°54N 18°25E **185** F5
Gniezno *Poland* 52°31N 17°37E **185** F4
Gnjilane *Kosovo* 42°28N 21°29E **202** D5
Gnoien *Germany* 53°58N 12°41E **178** B8
Gnosjö *Sweden* 57°22N 13°43E **163** G7
Gnowangerup *Australia* 33°58S 117°59E **279** F2
Go Cong *Vietnam* 10°22N 106°40E **237** G6
Gō-Gawa → *Japan* 35°2N 132°13E **222** B4
Gō-no-ura *Japan* 33°44N 129°42E **222** D1
Goa *India* 15°33N 73°59E **245** G1
Goa *Phil.* 13°42N 123°29E **232** E4
Goa □ *India* 15°33N 73°59E **245** G1
Goalen Hd. *Australia* 36°33S 150°4E **283** D9
Goalpara *India* 26°10N 90°40E **241** B3
Goaltor *India* 22°43N 87°10E **243** H12
Goaso *Ghana* 6°48N 2°30W **262** D4
Goalundo Ghat *Bangla.* 23°50N 89°47E **243** H13
Goat Fell *U.K.* 55°38N 5°11W **167** F3
Goat I. *Antigua & B.* 17°43N 61°51W **322** a
Goat Pt. *Antigua & B.* 17°44N 61°51W **322** c
Goba *Ethiopia* 7°1N 39°59E **257** F4
Goba *Mozam.* 26°15S 32°13E **271** C5
Gobabis *Namibia* 22°30S 19°0E **270** C3
Gobe *Papua N. G.* 9°4S 149°0E **286** E5
Göbel *Turkey* 40°0N 28°9E **203** F12
Gobernador Gregores
 Argentina 48°46S 70°15W **336** C2
Gobi *Asia* 44°0N 110°0E **226** C6
Gobichettipalayam *India* 11°31N 77°21E **245** J3
Gobles *U.S.A.* 42°22N 85°53W **311** B11
Gobō *Japan* 33°53N 135°10E **223** D7
Gobo *Sudan* 5°41N 31°10E **257** F2
Göçbeyli *Turkey* 39°13N 27°25E **205** B9
Gochang *S. Korea* 35°26N 126°32E **224** E3
Gochas *Namibia* 24°59S 18°55E **270** C2
God Dere *Ethiopia* 5°1N 44°1E **267** C5
Godalming *U.K.* 51°11N 0°36W **169** F7
Godavari → *India* 16°25N 82°18E **244** F6
Godavari Pt. *India* 17°0N 82°20E **244** F6
Godbout *Canada* 49°20N 67°38W **299** C6
Gode *Ethiopia* 5°53N 43°16E **267** C5
Godech *Bulgaria* 43°1N 23°4E **202** C7
Goderich *Canada* 43°45N 81°41W **312** C3
Goderville *France* 49°38N 0°22E **172** C7
Godfrey *U.S.A.* 38°58N 90°11W **310** F9
Godfrey Ra. *Australia* 24°0S 117°0E **279** D2
Goðafoss *Iceland* 65°41N 17°33W **155** B9
Godhavn = Qeqertarsuaq
 Greenland 69°15N 53°38W **154** C5
Goðafoss *Iceland* 65°41N 17°33W **155** B9

Godhra *India* 22°49N 73°40E **242** H5
Godinlabe *Somali Rep.* 5°54N 46°38E **267** C6
Godöllö *Hungary* 47°38N 19°25E **182** C4
Godoy Cruz *Argentina* 32°56S 68°52W **334** C2
Gods → *Canada* 56°22N 92°51W **298** B1
Gods L. *Canada* 54°40N 94°15W **298** B1
Gods River *Canada* 54°50N 94°5W **297** C10
Godthåb = Nuuk
 Greenland 64°10N 51°35W **154** C5
Godwin Austen = K2
 Pakistan 35°58N 76°32E **243** B7
Goeie Hoop, Kaap die = Good Hope,
 C. of S. *Africa* 34°24S 18°30E **270** D2
Goéland, L. au *Canada* 49°50N 76°48W **298** C4
Goélands, L. aux *Canada* 55°27N 64°17W **299** A7
Goeree *Neths.* 51°50N 4°0E **170** C3
Goes *Neths.* 51°30N 3°55E **170** C3
Gofca *Somali Rep.* 1°10N 43°43E **267** C5
Goffstown *U.S.A.* 43°1N 71°36W **313** C13
Gogama *Canada* 47°35N 81°43W **298** C3
Gogar *U.K.* 55°56N 3°20W **121** B2
Gogebic, L. *U.S.A.* 46°30N 89°35W **308** B9
Gogetti *Ethiopia* 8°11N 38°35E **257** F4
Gogolin *Poland* 50°30N 18°0E **185** H5
Gogonou *Benin* 10°50N 2°50E **263** C5
Gogra = Ghaghara →
 India 25°45N 84°40E **243** G11
Gogriâl *Sudan* 8°30N 28°8E **257** F2
Gogti *Ethiopia* 10°7N 42°51E **257** E5
Gohana *India* 29°8N 76°42E **242** E7
Goharganj *India* 23°1N 77°41E **242** H7
Goheung *S. Korea* 34°36N 127°17E **224** E3
Goi → *India* 22°4N 74°46E **242** H6
Goiana *Brazil* 7°33S 34°59W **333** E12
Goianésia *Brazil* 15°18S 49°7W **333** G9
Goiânia *Brazil* 16°43S 49°20W **333** G9
Goiás *Brazil* 15°55S 50°10W **333** E1
Goiás □ *Brazil* 12°10S 48°0W **332** F9
Goiatins *Brazil* 7°42S 47°10W **332** E9
Goiatuba *Brazil* 18°1S 49°23W **333** H9
Goidu Atoll *Maldives* 4°53N 72°54E **272** d
Goio-Erê *Brazil* 24°12S 53°1W **335** A5
Góis *Portugal* 40°10N 8°6W **194** E2
Gojam *Ethiopia* 10°55N 36°30E **257** E4
Gojeb, Wabi → *Ethiopia* 7°12N 36°40E **257** F4
Gojō *Japan* 34°21N 135°42E **223** C7
Gojra *Pakistan* 31°10N 72°40E **242** D5
Gokak *India* 16°11N 74°52E **245** F2
Gokarn *India* 14°33N 74°17E **245** G2
Gökçe = Sevana Lich
 Armenia 40°30N 45°20E **191** K7
Gökçeada *Turkey* 40°10N 25°50E **203** F9
Gökçedağ *Turkey* 39°33N 28°56E **205** B10
Gökçen *Turkey* 38°7N 27°53E **205** C9
Gökçeören *Turkey* 38°37N 28°3E **205** C10
Gökçeyaza *Turkey* 39°40N 27°40E **205** B9
Gökırmak → *Turkey* 41°25N 35°8E **212** B6
Gökova *Turkey* 37°8N 28°17E **205** D10
Gökova Körfezi *Turkey* 36°55N 27°50E **205** D9
Göksu → *Turkey* 36°19N 34°5E **250** B5
Göksun *Turkey* 38°2N 36°30E **212** C7
Gokteik *Burma* 22°26N 97°0E **241** D6
Göktepe *Karaman, Turkey* 36°37N 32°37E **250** B4
Göktepe *Muğla, Turkey* 37°26N 28°34E **205** D10
Göktürk *Turkey* 41°10N 28°53E **122** A1
Gokurt *Pakistan* 29°40N 67°26E **242** E2
Gokwe *Zimbabwe* 18°7S 28°58E **271** A4
Gol *Norway* 60°42N 8°55E **164** D5
Gol Gol *Australia* 34°12S 142°14E **282** C5
Gola *India* 28°3N 80°32E **243** E9
Golabari *India* 22°35N 88°20E **142** B8
Golabki *Poland* 52°12N 20°52E **142** B1
Golaghat *India* 26°30N 94°0E **241** B5
Golakganj *India* 26°8N 89°52E **241** B2
Golan Heights = Hagolan
 Syria 33°0N 35°45E **250** F6
Golańcz *Poland* 52°57N 17°18E **185** F4
Goläshkerd *Iran* 27°59N 57°16E **247** E8
Golaya Pristen = Hola Prystan
 Ukraine 46°29N 32°32E **189** J7
Gölbaşı *Adıyaman, Turkey* 37°43N 37°25E **212** D7
Gölbaşı *Ankara, Turkey* 39°47N 32°49E **212** C5
Golconda *India* 17°24N 78°23E **244** F4
Golconda *Nev., U.S.A.* 40°58N 117°30W **304** F4
Gölcük *Kocaeli, Turkey* 40°42N 29°48E **203** F13
Gölcük *Niğde, Turkey* 38°14N 34°41E **212** C6
Gold → *U.S.A.* 42°2N 77°50W **312** E7
Gold Beach *U.S.A.* 42°25N 124°25W **304** E1
Gold Coast = Ghana ■
 W. Afr. 8°0N 1°0W **263** D4
Gold Coast *Queens.,*
 Australia 28°0S 153°25E **276** F9
Gold Coast *Chicago, U.S.A.* **119** a2
Gold Coast *W. Afr.* 4°0N 1°40W **263** E4
Gold Creek *U.S.A.* 62°46N 149°41W **303** D10
Gold Hill *U.S.A.* 42°26N 123°3W **304** E2
Gold River *Canada* 49°46N 126°3W **296** D3
Goldap *Poland* 54°19N 22°18E **184** D9
Goldberg = Złotoryja
 Poland 51°8N 15°55E **185** G2
Goldberg *Germany* 53°35N 12°4E **178** B8
Golden *B.C., Canada* 51°20N 116°59W **296** C5
Golden *Ill., U.S.A.* 40°7N 91°1W **310** D5
Golden Beach *U.S.A.* 42°25N 124°25W **304** E1
Golden Buddha = Traimit
 Bangkok, Thailand **113** c2
Golden Gate *U.S.A.* 37°48N 122°29W **136** b2
Golden Gate *Canada* 37°49N 122°31W **136** A2
Golden Gate Bridge
 U.S.A. 37°49N 122°28W **136** B2
Golden Gate Highlands △
 S. Africa 28°40S 28°40E **271** C4
Golden Gate Park
 U.S.A. 37°46N 122°28W **136** B2
Golden Grove *Middlesex.,*
 Jamaica 18°19N 77°9W **320** a
Golden Grove *Surrey.,*
 Jamaica 17°55N 76°16W **320** a
Golden Hinde *Canada* 49°40N 125°44W **296** D3
Golden Horn = Haliç
 Turkey 41°1N 28°57E **122** B1
Golden Lake *Canada* 45°34N 77°21W **312** A7
Golden Rock *India* 10°45N 78°48E **245** J4
Golden Spike △ *U.S.A.* 41°37N 112°33W **304** F7
Golden Vale *Ireland* 52°33N 8°17W **166** D3
Goldendale *U.S.A.* 45°49N 120°50W **304** D3
Golders Green *U.K.* 51°34N 0°11W **125** A2
Goldfield *U.S.A.* 37°42N 117°14W **305** H5
Goldingen = Kuldīga
 Latvia 56°58N 21°59E **184** B8
Goldsand L. *Canada* 57°2N 101°8W **297** B8
Goldsboro *U.S.A.* 35°23N 77°59W **315** D16
Goldsmith *U.S.A.* 31°27N 102°37W **314** F3
Goldthwaite *U.S.A.* 31°27N 98°34W **314** F5
Golegã *Portugal* 39°3N 21°1W **194** F2
Goleniów *Poland* 53°35N 14°50E **184** E1
Goleştan □ *Iran* 37°20N 55°25E **247** B7
Golestan Palace *Iran* 35°41N 51°25E **141** A2
Golestânak *Iran* 30°36N 54°14E **247** D7
Goleta *U.S.A.* 34°27N 119°50W **307** L7
Golfito *Costa Rica* 8°41N 83°5W **320** E3
Golfo Aranci *Italy* 40°59N 9°38E **200** B2
Golfo di Orosei e del Gennargentu △
 Italy 40°9N 9°35E **200** B2
Gölgeli Dağları *Turkey* 37°10N 28°55E **205** D10

Gölhisar *Turkey* 37°8N 29°31E **205** D11
Goliad *U.S.A.* 28°40N 97°23W **314** G6
Golija *Montenegro* 43°5N 18°45E **202** C2
Golija *Serbia* 43°22N 20°15E **202** C4
Golina *Poland* 52°15N 18°4E **185** F5
Goljam Bratan = Morozov
 Bulgaria 42°30N 25°10E **203** D9
Gölköy *Turkey* 40°41N 37°37E **212** B7
Gollans Stream → *N.Z.* 41°22S 174°52E **143** B2
Gollel = Lavumisa
 Swaziland 27°20S 31°55E **271** C5
Göllersdorf *Austria* 48°29N 16°7E **180** C9
Gollnow = Goleniów
 Poland 53°35N 14°50E **184** E1
Gölmarmara *Turkey* 38°42N 27°55E **205** C9
Golmud *China* 36°25N 94°53E **218** D7
Golo → *France* 42°31N 9°32E **175** F13
Golo I. *Phil.* 13°39N 120°22E **232** E3
Gölova *Turkey* 36°48N 30°5E **205** E12
Golovin *U.S.A.* 64°33N 163°2W **303** D7
Golpâyegân *Iran* 33°27N 50°18E **247** C6
Gölpazarı *Turkey* 40°16N 30°18E **212** B4
Golra *Pakistan* 33°37N 72°56E **242** C5
Golspie *U.K.* 57°58N 3°59W **167** D5
Golub-Dobrzyń *Poland* 53°7N 19°2E **185** E6
Golubac *Serbia* 44°38N 21°38E **202** B5
Golungo Alto *Angola* 9°8S 14°46E **265** D2
Golyam Perelik *Bulgaria* 41°36N 24°33E **203** E8
Golyama Kamchiya →
 Bulgaria 43°10N 27°55E **203** C11
Golyevo *Russia* 55°48N 37°18E **129** B1
Goma *Dem. Rep. of the Congo* 1°37S 29°10E **268** C2
Gomal Pass *Pakistan* 31°56N 69°20E **242** D3
Gomantong Caves
 Malaysia 5°40N 118°6E **235** A5
Gomati → *India* 25°32N 83°11E **243** G10
Gombari
 Dem. Rep. of the Congo 2°45N 29°3E **268** B2
Gombe
 Dem. Rep. of the Congo 0°45S 17°96E **264** C3
Gombe *Nigeria* 10°19N 11°2E **263** C7
Gombe *Turkey* 36°33N 29°38E **205** E11
Gombe □ *Nigeria* 10°0N 11°10E **263** C7
Gombe → *Tanzania* 4°38S 31°40E **268** C3
Gombe Stream △ *Tanzania* 4°42S 29°37E **268** C2
Gombi *Nigeria* 10°12N 12°30E **263** C7
Gomel = Homyel *Belarus* 52°28N 31°0E **177** B16
Gomera *Canary Is.* 28°7N 17°14W **153** e1
Gómez Palacio *Mexico* 25°34N 103°30W **318** B4
Gomfi *Greece* 39°26N 21°36E **204** B3
Gomishân *Iran* 37°4N 54°6E **247** B7
Gommern *Germany* 52°4N 11°50E **178** C7
Gomogomo *Indonesia* 6°39S 134°43E **231** F8
Gomoh *India* 23°52N 86°10E **243** H12
Gomotartsi *Bulgaria* 44°6N 22°57E **202** B6
Gompa = Ganta *Liberia* 7°15N 8°59W **262** D3
Gonâbâd *Iran* 34°15N 58°45E **247** C8
Gonaïves *Haiti* 19°20N 72°42W **321** C5
Gonarezhou △ *Zimbabwe* 21°32S 31°55E **269** C3
Gonâve, G. de la *Haiti* 19°29N 72°42W **321** C5
Gonâve, Île de la *Haiti* 18°51N 73°3W **321** C5
Gonbad-e Kāvūs *Iran* 37°20N 55°25E **247** B7
Gonda *India* 27°9N 81°58E **243** F9
Gondal *India* 21°58N 70°52E **242** J4
Gonder *Ethiopia* 12°39N 37°30E **257** E4
Gondia *India* 21°23N 80°10E **244** D5
Gondola *Mozam.* 19°10S 33°37E **269** F3
Gondomar *Portugal* 41°10N 8°35W **194** D2
Gondrecourt-le-Château
 France 48°31N 5°30E **173** D12
Gönen *Balıkesir, Turkey* 40°6N 27°39E **203** F11
Gönen *Isparta, Turkey* 37°57N 30°31E **205** D12
Gönen → *Turkey* 40°6N 27°39E **203** F11
Gong Xian *China* 28°23N 104°47E **228** C5
Gong'an *China* 30°7N 112°12E **229** B9
Gongbei *China* 22°12N 113°32E **219** a
Gongchangling *China* 41°7N 123°27E **224** B1
Gongcheng *China* 24°50N 110°49E **229** E8
Gongga Shan *China* 29°40N 101°55E **228** C3
Gonggar *China* 29°23N 91°7E **218** F7
Gongguan *China* 21°48N 109°36E **229** G7
Gonghe *China* 36°18N 100°32E **218** D9
Gongju *S. Korea* 36°22N 127°7E **224** D3
Gongming *China* 22°47N 113°53E **219** a
Gongneung *S. Korea* 37°36N 127°3E **137** B2
Gongola → *Nigeria* 9°30N 12°4E **263** D7
Gongolgon *Australia* 30°21S 146°54E **281** E4
Gongshan *China* 27°43N 98°29E **228** D2
Gongtan *China* 28°55N 108°20E **228** C7
Gongzhuling *China* 43°30N 124°40E **227** C13
Goni *Greece* 39°52N 22°29E **204** B4
Goniadz *Poland* 53°30N 22°44E **184** E9
Goniri *Nigeria* 11°30N 12°15E **263** C7
Gonjo *China* 30°52N 98°17E **228** B2
Gonneux *S. Korea* 37°36N 127°3E **137** B2
Gonnesa *Italy* 39°16N 8°28E **200** C1
Gonnosfanádiga *Italy* 39°29N 8°39E **200** C1
Gono → *Japan* 35°2N 132°13E **222** B4
Gonohe *Japan* 40°32N 141°18E **220** D10
Gonzales *Calif., U.S.A.* 36°30N 121°26W **306** J5
Gonzales *Tex., U.S.A.* 29°30N 97°27W **314** G6
González *Mexico* 22°48N 98°25W **319** C5
Goobang △ *Australia* 33°0S 148°32E **283** B8
Good Hope, C. of *S. Africa* 34°24S 18°30E **270** D2
Good Hope Lake *Canada* 59°16N 129°18W **296** B3
Good Hope Plantation
 Jamaica 18°25N 77°41W **320** a
Goodenough I. *Papua N. G.* 9°20S 150°15E **286** E6
Gooderham *Canada* 44°54N 78°21W **312** B6
Goodhouse *S. Africa* 28°57S 18°13E **270** C2
Gooding *U.S.A.* 42°56N 114°43W **304** E6
Goodland *U.S.A.* 39°21N 101°43W **308** F3
Goodlow *U.S.A.* 32°35N 120°18W **306** D4
Goodmayes *U.K.* 51°33N 0°6E **125** A4
Goodnews Bay *U.S.A.* 59°7N 161°35W **303** E7
Goodooga *Australia* 29°3S 147°28E **281** D4
Goodsprings *U.S.A.* 35°49N 115°27W **307** K11
Goodwater *U.S.A.* 33°4N 86°3W **311** J2
Goodwick *U.K.* 52°0N 4°59W **169** E2
Goodwood *S. Africa* 33°55S 18°32E **118** A2
Goole *U.K.* 53°42N 0°53W **168** D7
Goolgowi *Australia* 33°58S 145°41E **283** B6
Goolwa *Australia* 35°30S 138°47E **282** C2
Goomalling *Australia* 31°15S 116°49E **279** F2
Goomeri *Australia* 26°12S 152°6E **281** D5
Goonda *Mozam.* 19°48S 33°57E **269** F3
Goondiwindi *Australia* 28°30S 150°21E **281** D5
Goongarrie *Australia* 30°3N 121°9W **279** E3
Goongarrie △ *Australia* 30°2S 121°30E **279** E3
Goonyella *Australia* 21°47S 147°58E **280** C4
Goose → *Canada* 53°20N 60°35W **299** B7
Goose Creek *U.S.A.* 32°59N 80°2W **316** B9
Goose L. *Calif., U.S.A.* 41°56N 120°26W **304** F3
Goose L. *Ill., U.S.A.* 41°56N 88°3W **131** b
Gooty *India* 15°7N 77°41E **245** G3
Gop *India* 22°5N 69°50E **242** H3
Gopalganj *Bangla.* 23°1N 89°50E **241** G2
Gopalganj *India* 26°28N 84°30E **243** F11

Göpalpur *India* 22°38N 88°26E **124** B2
Göppingen *Germany* 48°42N 9°39E **179** G5
Gor *Spain* 37°23N 2°58W **195** H8
Gora *Dolnoślaskie, Poland* 51°40N 16°31E **185** G3
Góra *Mazowieckie, Poland* 52°39N 20°6E **185** F7
Góra Kalwaria *Poland* 51°59N 21°14E **185** G8
Gorakhpur *India* 26°47N 83°23E **243** F10
Goražde *Bos.-H.* 43°38N 18°58E **182** G3
Gorbatov *Russia* 43°38N 18°58E **182** G3
Gorbea, Peña *Spain* 43°1N 2°50W **196** B2
Görce *Turkey* 38°12N 26°59E **205** C8
Gorczanski △ *Poland* 49°30N 20°10E **185** J7
Gorda, Banco *W. Indies* 15°40N 80°27W **320** D3
Gorda, Pta. *Canada* 28°45N 18°0W **153** e1
Gorda, Pta. *Nic.* 14°20N 83°10W **320** D3
Gordan B. *Australia* 11°35S 130°10E **278** B5
Gördes *Turkey* 38°54N 28°17E **205** C10
Gordon *Ga., U.S.A.* 32°54N 83°20W **316** A6
Gordon *Nebr., U.S.A.* 42°48N 102°12W **308** D2
Gordon → *Australia* 42°27N 145°30E **282** A1
Gordon, I. *Chile* 54°55S 69°30W **336** D3
Gordon Bay *Canada* 56°30N 110°25W **297** B6
Gordon L., Alta., Canada* 56°30N 110°25W **297** B6
Gordon L., N.W.T., Canada* 63°5N 113°11W **296** A6
Gordonvale *Australia* 17°5S 145°50E **280** B4
Goré *Chad* 7°59N 16°31E **259** G3
Gore *Ethiopia* 8°12N 35°32E **257** F4
Gore *N.Z.* 46°5S 168°58E **285** G3
Gore Bay *Canada* 45°57N 82°28W **298** C3
Görele *Turkey* 41°2N 39°0E **213** B8
Gorelyy → *Russia* 60°1N 30°30E **137** A3
Goreme *Turkey* 38°35N 34°52E **212** C6
Gorenki *Russia* 55°47N 37°53E **129** B5
Gorey *Ireland* 52°41N 6°18W **166** D5
Gorg *Iran* 29°29N 59°43E **247** D8
Gorgân *Iran* 36°55N 54°30E **247** B7
Gorgie *U.K.* 55°56N 3°14W **121** B2
Gorgol □ *Mauritania* 15°45N 13°0W **262** B2
Gorgona *Italy* 43°26N 9°54E **198** E6
Gorgora *Ethiopia* 12°15N 37°17E **257** E4
Gorgoram *Nigeria* 12°40N 10°45E **263** C7
Gorham *U.S.A.* 44°23N 71°10W **313** B13
Gori *Georgia* 42°0N 44°7E **191** J7
Goribidnur = Gauribidanur
 India 13°37N 77°32E **245** H3
Goriganga → *India* 29°45N 80°23E **243** E9
Gorinchem *Neths.* 51°50N 4°59E **170** C4
Gorinhatâ *Brazil* 19°15S 49°45W **333** E2
Goris *Armenia* 39°31N 46°22E **213** C12
Goritsy *Russia* 57°4N 36°43E **188** D9
Gorizia *Italy* 45°56N 13°37E **199** C10
Gorj □ *Romania* 45°0N 23°28E **202** B7
Gorki = Horki *Belarus* 54°17N 31°0E **188** E6
Gorkiy = Nizhniy Novgorod
 Russia 56°20N 44°0E **190** B7
Gorkovskoye Vdkhr. *Russia* 57°2N 43°4E **190** B6
Gorky Park *Russia* 55°43N 37°36E **129** B3
Gorleston *U.K.* 52°35N 1°44E **169** E9
Gorlice *Poland* 49°35N 21°11E **185** J8
Görlitz *Germany* 51°9N 14°58E **178** D10
Gorlovka = Horlivka
 Ukraine 48°19N 38°5E **189** H10
Gorman *U.S.A.* 32°12N 98°41W **314** E5
Gorna Djumaya = Blagoevgrad
 Bulgaria 42°2N 23°5E **202** D7
Gorna Dzhumayo = Blagoevgrad
 Bulgaria 42°2N 23°5E **202** D7
Gorna Oryakhovitsa
 Bulgaria 43°7N 25°40E **203** D9
Gornja Radgona *Slovenia* 46°40N 16°2E **199** B13
Gornja Tuzla *Bos.-H.* 44°35N 18°46E **182** F3
Gornji Grad *Slovenia* 46°20N 14°52E **199** B11
Gornji Milanovac *Serbia* 44°0N 20°29E **202** B4
Gornji Vakuf *Bos.-H.* 43°57N 17°34E **182** G2
Gorno Ablanovo *Bulgaria* 43°37N 25°43E **203** D9
Gorno-Altay □ *Russia* 51°0N 86°0E **217** D10
Gorno-Altaysk *Russia* 51°50N 86°5E **217** D10
Gorno-Badakhshan = Kühiston-
 Badakhshan □ *Tajikistan* 38°30N 73°0E **217** F8
Gornozavodsk *Russia* 46°33N 141°50E **215** E15
Gornyak *Russia* 50°59N 81°27E **217** D10
Gornyatski *Russia* 67°32N 64°3E **186** A11
Gornyatskiy *Russia* 48°18N 40°56E **191** F5
Gornyy *Primorsk, Russia* 44°57N 133°59E **220** B6
Gornyy *Saratov, Russia* 51°50N 48°30E **191** D8
Goro → *Italy* 44°53N 12°21E **199** D8
Gorodenka = Horodenka
 Ukraine 48°41N 25°29E **183** D9
Gorodets *Russia* 56°38N 43°28E **190** B6
Gorodishche = Horodyshche
 Ukraine 49°17N 31°27E **189** H6
Gorodnya = Horodnya
 Ukraine 51°55N 31°33E **189** G6
Gorodok = Haradok
 Belarus 55°30N 30°3E **188** E6
Gorodok = Horodok
 Ukraine 49°46N 23°32E **177** H2
Gorodok = Zakamensk
 Russia 50°23N 103°17E **215** D11
Gorodovikovsk *Russia* 46°5N 41°58E **191** G5
Goroka *Papua N. G.* 6°7S 145°25E **286** D3
Goroke *Australia* 36°43S 141°29E **282** C4
Gorokhov = Horokhiv
 Ukraine 50°30N 24°45E **177** H3
Gorom Gorom
 Burkina Faso 14°26N 0°14W **263** C4
Goromonzi *Zimbabwe* 17°52S 31°22E **269** F3
Gorong, Kepulauan
 Indonesia 3°59S 131°25E **231** E8
Gorongose → *Mozam.* 20°30S 34°40E **271** B5
Gorongosa *Mozam.* 18°44S 34°2E **269** F3
Gorongosa, Sa. da *Mozam.* 18°27S 34°2E **269** F3
Gorontalo *Indonesia* 0°35N 123°5E **231** D6
Gorontalo □ *Indonesia* 0°50N 122°20E **231** D6
Goronyo *Nigeria* 13°29N 5°39E **263** C6
Gorowo Iławeckie *Poland* 54°17N 20°30E **184** D7
Gorron *France* 48°25N 0°50W **172** D6
Gorror *Micronesia* 7°26N 138°4E **287** S16
Gorshechnoye *Russia* 51°33N 38°5E **190** D4
Gort *Ireland* 53°3N 8°49W **166** C3
Gortis *Greece* 35°4N 24°58E **207** E5
Görükle *Antalya, Turkey* 36°41N 30°38E **250** B4
Göynük *Bolu, Turkey* 40°24N 30°48E **212** B4
Goz Beïda *Chad* 12°10N 21°20E **259** F10
Goz Regeb *Sudan* 16°3N 35°33E **257** D4
Gozdnica *Russia* 51°28N 15°4E **185** G2
Gözneköy *Turkey* 36°58N 34°33E **250** B5
Gozo *Malta* 36°3N 14°13E **207** C1
Graaff-Reinet *S. Africa* 32°13S 24°32E **270** D3
Graben *Vienna, Austria* 48°12N 16°22E **182** b1
Grabill *U.S.A.* 41°13N 84°57W **312** E2
Grabo *Ivory C.* 4°57N 7°6W **262** E3
Grabow *Mecklenburg-Vorpommern,*
 Germany 53°17N 11°34E **178** B7
Grabów Warszawa, Poland* 52°11N 20°52E **142** C1
Grabów nad Prosną *Poland* 51°31N 18°7E **185** G5
Grabs *Switz.* 47°11N 9°26E **179** E5
Graça, Lisbon, Portugal* **126** A1
Gračac *Croatia* 44°18N 15°57E **199** D12
Gračanica *Bos.-H.* 44°43N 18°18E **182** F3
Graçay *France* 47°10N 1°50E **173** E8

Goslar *Germany* 51°54N 10°25E **178** D6
Gospel Oak *U.K.* 51°32N 0°9W **125** A3
Gospić *Croatia* 44°35N 15°23E **199** D12
Gosport *Hants., U.K.* 50°48N 1°9W **169** G6
Gosport *Ind., U.S.A.* 39°21N 86°40W **311** E10
Gossa *Norway* 62°52N 6°50E **164** B3
Gossas *Senegal* 14°29N 16°4W **262** C1
Gosse → *Australia* 19°32S 134°37E **280** B1
Gossi *Mali* 15°48N 1°20W **263** B4
Gossinga *Sudan* 8°36N 25°59E **257** F2
Gostivar *Macedonia* 41°48N 20°57E **202** E4
Gostyń *Poland* 51°50N 17°3E **185** G4
Gostynin *Poland* 52°26N 19°29E **185** F6
Gota älv → *Sweden* 57°42N 11°54E **163** H10
Göta kanal *Sweden* 58°30N 15°58E **163** F10
Götaland *Sweden* 57°30N 14°30E **163** G8
Göteborg *Sweden* 57°43N 11°59E **163** G5
Gotemba *Japan* 35°18N 138°56E **223** D10
Götene *Sweden* 58°32N 13°30E **163** F7
Gotenhafen = Gdynia
 Poland 54°35N 18°33E **184** D5
Goteşti *Moldova* 46°9N 28°10E **183** D13
Goth Goli Mar *Pakistan* 24°53N 67°1E **123** A2
Goth Sher Shah *Pakistan* 24°53N 66°59E **123** A1
Gotha *Thüringen, Germany* 50°56N 10°42E **178** E6
Gotha *Fla., U.S.A.* 28°31N 81°31W **133** A1
Gothenburg = Göteborg
 Sweden 57°43N 11°59E **163** G5
Gothenburg *U.S.A.* 40°56N 100°10W **308** E3
Gothèye *Niger* 13°52N 1°34E **263** C5
Gotland *Sweden* 57°30N 18°33E **163** G12
Gotlands län □ *Sweden* 57°15N 18°30E **163** G12
Goto Meer *Bonaire* 12°14N 68°22W **322** h
Gotō-Rettō *Japan* 32°55N 129°5E **221** H4
Gotse Delchev *Bulgaria* 41°36N 23°46E **202** E7
Gotska Sandön *Sweden* 58°24N 19°15E **163** F13
Gōtsu *Japan* 35°0N 132°14E **222** C4
Göttero, Monte *Italy* 44°29N 9°42E **198** D6
Gottesberg = Boguszów-Gorce
 Poland 50°45N 16°12E **185** H3
Göttingen *Germany* 51°31N 9°55E **178** D5
Gottsche = Kočevje
 Slovenia 45°39N 14°50E **199** C11
Gottskär *Sweden* 57°25N 12°2E **163** G6
Gottwald = Zmiyev
 Ukraine 49°39N 36°27E **189** H9
Gottwaldov = Zlín
 Czech Rep. 49°14N 17°40E **181** B10
Goubangzi *China* 41°20N 121°52E **227** D11
Gouda *Neths.* 52°1N 4°42E **170** B4
Goudiri *Senegal* 14°15N 12°45W **262** C2
Goudoumaria *Niger* 13°40N 11°10E **259** F2
Goudouras, Akra *Greece* 34°59N 26°6E **207** F7
Gouèké *Guinea* 8°2N 8°43W **262** D3
Gough I. *Atl. Oc.* 40°10S 9°45W **152** L11
Gouin, Rés. *Canada* 48°35N 74°40W **298** C5
Gouitafla *Ivory C.* 7°30N 5°53W **262** D3
Goulburn *Australia* 34°44S 149°44E **283** C8
Goulburn Is. *Australia* 11°40S 133°20E **280** A1
Goulburn River △
 Australia 32°19S 150°10E **283** B9
Goulds *U.S.A.* 25°33N 80°23W **317** K9
Goulia *Ivory C.* 10°1N 7°11W **262** C3
Goulimine *Morocco* 28°56N 10°0W **260** C3
Goulimine □ *Morocco* 29°8N 9°29W **260** C3
Goulmima *Morocco* 31°41N 4°57W **260** B4
Goundam *Mali* 15°2N 7°25W **262** B3
Gouna *Norway* 60°23N 10°31E **164** D7
Gounatolo *Solomon Is.* 8°25S 160°52E **287** M11
Goundam *Mali* 16°27N 3°40W **262** B4
Goundi *Chad* 9°22N 17°21E **259** G3
Gounou-Gaya *Chad* 9°38N 15°31E **259** G3
Goura *Greece* 37°56N 22°20E **204** D4
Gourbassi *Mali* 13°24N 11°38W **262** C2
Gourbeyre *Guadeloupe* 16°0N 61°41W **322** e
Gourdon *France* 44°44N 1°23E **174** D5
Gouré *Niger* 14°0N 10°10E **259** F2
Gourin *France* 48°8N 3°37W **172** D3
Gourits → *S. Africa* 34°21S 21°52E **270** D3
Gourma-Rharous *Mali* 16°55N 1°50W **263** B4
Gournay-en-Bray *France* 49°29N 1°44E **173** C8
Gournay-sur-Marne
 France 48°51N 2°34E **134** A4
Gourock *U.K.* 55°57N 4°49W **167** F4
Gouverneur *U.S.A.* 44°20N 75°28W **313** B9
Gouvia *Greece* 39°39N 19°50E **206** B9
Gouyave *Grenada* 12°10N 61°44W **323** q
Gouzon *France* 46°12N 2°14E **173** F9
Gove, Barragem do *Angola* 13°26S 15°53E **265** E3
Gove Peninsula *Australia* 12°17S 136°49E **280** A2
Governador, I. do *Brazil* 22°48S 43°10W **135** A1
Governador Valadares
 Brazil 18°15S 41°57W **333** E3
Governor Generoso *Phil.* 6°39N 126°5E **233** H6
Governor's Harbour
 Bahamas 25°10N 76°14W **320** B4
Governors I. *New York, U.S.A.* **132** f1
Govĭaltay □ *Mongolia* 45°30N 96°0E **217** C13
Govindgarh *India* 24°23N 81°18E **243** G9
Gowan Ra. *Australia* 25°0S 145°0E **280** D4
Gowanda *U.S.A.* 42°28N 78°56W **312** D6
Gower *U.K.* 51°35N 4°10W **169** F3
Gowers Corner *U.S.A.* 28°20N 82°30W **317** G7
Gowna, L. *Ireland* 53°51N 7°34W **166** C4
Gowrie *U.S.A.* 42°17N 94°17W **310** B2
Gowurdak *Turkmenistan* 37°34N 66°0E **217** F7
Goya *Argentina* 29°10S 59°10W **334** B4
Goyang *S. Korea* 37°39N 126°50E **224** D2
Goyave *Guadeloupe* 16°8N 61°34W **322** e
Goyaves, Grande Rivière
 à → *Guadeloupe* 16°18N 61°36W **322** e
Göyçay *Azerbaijan* 40°42N 47°45E **191** K8
Goyder Lagoon *Australia* 27°3S 138°58E **281** D2
Goyllarisquizga *Peru* 10°31S 76°24W **332** F3
Göynük *Antalya, Turkey* 36°41N 30°38E **250** B4
Göynük *Bolu, Turkey* 40°24N 30°48E **212** B4
Goz Beïda *Chad* 12°10N 21°20E **259** F10
Goz Regeb *Sudan* 16°3N 35°33E **257** D4
Gozo *Malta* 36°3N 14°13E **207** C1
Graaff-Reinet *S. Africa* 32°13S 24°32E **270** D3
Graben *Vienna, Austria* 48°12N 16°22E **182** b1
Grabill *U.S.A.* 41°13N 84°57W **312** E2
Grabo *Ivory C.* 4°57N 7°6W **262** E3

Grace, Mt. *N.Z.* 41°20S 174°55E **143** B2
Grace Cathedral *San Francisco, U.S.A.* **136** b2
Gracefield *N.Z.* 41°14S 174°55E **143** B2
Graceville *U.S.A.* 30°58N 85°31W **316** K4
Gracewood *U.S.A.* 33°22N 82°2W **316** B7
Gràcia *Spain* 41°24N 2°10E **114** A2
Gracias a Dios, C.
 Honduras 15°0N 83°10W **320** D3
Graciosa *Azores* 39°4N 28°0W **153** d1
Graciosa, I. *Canary Is.* 29°15N 13°32W **153** e2
Grad Sofiya □ *Bulgaria* 42°35N 23°20E **202** D7
Gradac *Montenegro* 43°23N 19°9E **202** C3
Gradaús *Brazil* 7°43S 51°11W **332** E8
Gradaús, Serra dos *Brazil* 8°0S 50°45W **332** C1
Gradeska Planina
 Macedonia 41°30N 22°15E **202** E6
Gradets *Bulgaria* 42°46N 26°30E **203** D10
Gradište *Slovenia* 46°37N 15°50E **199** B12
Grădiştea de Munte
 Romania 45°37N 23°13E **183** E8
Grado *Italy* 45°40N 13°23E **199** C10
Grado *Spain* 43°23N 6°4W **194** B4
Grady *U.S.A.* 34°49N 103°19W **305** J12
Graena, Lacul *Romania* 44°5N 26°10E **183** F11
Grafdorf *Iceland* 64°55N 23°16W **155** C3
Gräfelfing *Germany* 48°7N 11°25E **131** 31
Grafenau *Germany* 48°51N 13°22E **179** G9
Gräfenberg *Germany* 49°39N 11°14E **179** F7
Grafham Water *U.K.* 52°19N 0°18W **169** E7
Grafton *N.S.W., Australia* 29°38S 152°58E **281** E5
Grafton *Ill., U.S.A.* 38°58N 90°26W **310** F8
Grafton *N. Dak., U.S.A.* 48°25N 97°25W **308** A6
Grafton *W. Va., U.S.A.* 39°21N 80°2W **309** F13
Grafton Caledonia Wildlife Estate
 Trin. & Tob. 11°11N 60°47W **323** s
Grafton's Pt. *Anguilla* 18°20N 62°54W **322** a
Gragoatá *Brazil* 22°53S 43°8W **135** B2
Graham *Ont., Canada* 49°20N 90°30W **298** C1
Graham *Ga., U.S.A.* 31°50N 82°30W **316** E6
Graham *Tex., U.S.A.* 33°6N 98°35W **314** E5
Graham Bell, Ostrov = Greem-Bell,
 Ostrov 81°0N 62°0E **214** A7
Graham I., B.C., Canada* 53°40N 132°30W **296** C2
Graham I. *Nunavut,*
 Canada 77°25N 90°30W **295** B13
Graham Land *Antarctica* 65°0S 64°0W **151** C17
Grahamstown *S. Africa* 33°19S 26°31E **270** D4
Grahamsville *U.S.A.* 41°51N 74°33W **313** E10
Grahovo *Montenegro* 42°40N 18°40E **202** D3
Graïba *Tunisia* 34°30N 10°13E **258** B2
Graie, Alpi *Europe* 45°30N 7°10E **175** C11
Grain Coast *W. Afr.* 4°20N 10°0W **262** E3
Grajagan *Indonesia* 8°35S 114°13E **231** K17
Grajaú *Brazil* 5°50S 46°4W **332** D9
Grajaú → *Brazil* 3°41S 44°48W **332** D3
Grajewo *Poland* 53°39N 22°30E **184** E9
Gramada *Bulgaria* 43°49N 22°39E **202** C6
Gramat *France* 44°48N 1°43E **174** D5
Grammichele *Italy* 37°13N 14°38E **201** E7
Grámmos, Óros *Greece* 40°18N 20°47E **204** A2
Grampian *U.S.A.* 40°58N 78°37W **312** F6
Grampian Highlands = Grampian
 Mts. U.K. 56°50N 4°0W **167** E5
Grampian Mts. *U.K.* 56°50N 4°0W **167** E5
Grampians, The
 Australia 37°15S 142°20E **282** D5
Grampians △ *Australia* 37°15S 142°20E **282** D5
Gramsh *Albania* 40°52N 20°12E **202** F4
Gran *Norway* 60°23N 10°31E **164** D7
Gran → *Suriname* 4°1N 55°30W **329** C6
Gran Altiplanicie Central
 Argentina 49°0S 69°30W **336** C3
Gran Canaria *Canary Is.* 27°55N 15°35W **153** e1
Gran Chaco *S. Amer.* 25°0S 61°0W **334** B3
Gran Couva *Trin. & Tob.* 10°24N 61°22W **323** t
Gran Desierto del Pinacate △
 Mexico 31°51N 113°32W **318** A2
Gran Laguna Salada
 Argentina 44°24S 67°2W **336** B3
Gran Pajonal *Peru* 10°45S 74°30W **330** C3
Gran Paradiso *Italy* 45°33N 7°17E **198** C4
Gran Sasso d'Itália *Italy* 42°27N 13°42E **199** F10
Gran Sasso e Monti Della Laga △
 Italy 42°33N 13°22E **199** F10
Granada *Nic.* 11°58N 86°0W **320** D2
Granada *Spain* 37°10N 3°35W **195** H7
Granada *Colo., U.S.A.* 38°4N 102°19W **304** G12
Granada □ *Spain* 37°18N 3°0W **195** H7
Granadilla de Abona
 Canary Is. 28°7N 16°33W **153** e1
Granard *Ireland* 53°47N 7°30W **166** C4
Granbury *U.S.A.* 32°27N 97°47W **314** E6
Granby *Qué., Canada* 45°25N 72°45W **313** A12
Granby *Colo., U.S.A.* 40°5N 105°56W **304** F11
Grand → *Mo., Canada* 42°51N 79°34W **312** D5
Grand → *Mich., U.S.A.* 43°4N 86°15W **311** A10
Grand → *Mo., U.S.A.* 39°23N 93°7W **310** D3
Grand → *S. Dak., U.S.A.* 45°40N 100°45W **308** C3
Grand Abaque, Pte.du
 Guadeloupe 16°21N 61°0W **322** e
Grand Anse *Grenada* 12°1N 61°45W **323** q
Grand Anse B. *Grenada* 12°2N 61°45W **323** q
Grand B. *Dominica* 15°14N 61°18W **323** k
Grand Bahama I.
 Bahamas 26°40N 78°30W **320** A4
Grand Baie *Mauritius* 20°0S 57°35E **272** d
Grand Bank *Canada* 47°6N 55°48W **299** C8
Grand Banks *Atl. Oc.* 45°0N 52°0W **152** B6
Grand Bassam *Ivory C.* 5°10N 3°49W **262** D4
Grand Bassin *Réunion* 21°10S 55°32E **272** f
Grand Batanga *Cameroon* 2°50N 9°55E **264** B1
Grand Bazaar = Kapali Carsi
 Turkey 41°1N 28°58E **122** B1
Grand Bénare *Réunion* 21°5S 55°25E **272** f
Grand Bend *U.S.A.* 43°18N 81°45W **312** C3
Grand Béréby *Ivory C.* 4°38N 6°55W **262** E3
Grand Blanc *U.S.A.* 42°56N 83°36W **311** B13
Grand Bois *Haiti* 18°34N 72°3W **321** C5
Grand-Bourg *Guadeloupe* 15°53N 61°19W **322** c
Grand Canal = Da Yunhe →
 China 39°10N 117°10E **227** E9
Grand Canyon *U.S.A.* 36°3N 112°9W **305** H7
Grand Canyon △ *U.S.A.* 36°15N 112°30W **305** H7
Grand Canyon-Parashant △
 U.S.A. 36°30N 113°45W **305** H7
Grand Case *St.-Martin* 18°6N 63°4W **322** a
Grand Cayman
 Cayman Is. 19°20N 81°20W **320** C3
Grand Central Station *New York, U.S.A.* **132** c2
Grand Cess *Liberia* 4°40N 8°12W **262** E3
Grand Coulee *U.S.A.* 47°57N 119°0W **304** C4
Grand Coulee Dam
 U.S.A. 47°57N 118°59W **304** C4
Grand Cul-de-Sac Marin
 Guadeloupe 16°20N 61°35W **322** e
Grand Erg de Bilma *Niger* 18°30N 14°0E **259** E2
Grand Étang △ *Grenada* 12°5N 61°42W **323** q
Grand Falls *Canada* 47°3N 67°44W **299** C6
Grand Falls-Windsor
 Canada 48°56N 55°40W **299** C8
Grand Fond *St.-Martin* 17°53N 62°48W **322** a
Grand Forks *Canada* 49°0N 118°30W **296** D5
Grand Forks *N. Dak.,*
 U.S.A. 47°55N 97°3W **308** B6

Grand Galet Réunion 21°17S 55°38E 272 f
Grand Gaube Mauritius 20°0S 57°39E 272 e
Grand Gorge U.S.A. 42°21N 74°29W 313 D10
Grand Haven U.S.A. 43°4N 86°13W 311 A10
Grand I. Mich., U.S.A. 46°31N 86°40W 308 B10
Grand I. N.Y., U.S.A. 43°0N 78°58W 312 D6
Grand Îlet Guadeloupe 15°50N 61°35W 322 e
Grand Îlet Réunion 21°1S 55°29E 272 f
Grand Island U.S.A. 40°55N 98°21W 308 E4
Grand Isle La., U.S.A. 29°14N 90°0W 315 G9
Grand Isle Vt., U.S.A. 44°43N 73°18W 313 B11
Grand Junction Colo., U.S.A. 39°4N 108°33W 304 G9
Grand Junction Iowa, U.S.A. 42°2N 94°14W 310 B2
Grand L. N.B., Canada 45°57N 66°7W 299 C6
Grand L. Nfld. & L., Canada 49°0N 57°30W 299 C8
Grand L. Nfld. & L., Canada 53°40N 60°30W 299 B7
Grand L. La., U.S.A. 29°55N 92°47W 314 G8
Grand L. Ohio, U.S.A. 40°32N 84°25W 311 D12
Grand Lahou Ivory C. 5°10N 5°5W 262 D3
Grand Lake U.S.A. 40°15N 105°49W 304 F11
Grand Ledge U.S.A. 42°45N 84°45W 311 B12
Grand-Lieu, L. de France 47°6N 1°40W 172 E5
Grand Mal B. Grenada 12°4N 61°45W 323 q
Grand Manan I. Canada 44°45N 66°52W 299 D6
Grand Marais Mich., U.S.A. 46°40N 85°59W 309 B11
Grand Marais Minn., U.S.A. 47°45N 90°25W 298 C1
Grand Marigot B. Dominica 15°25N 61°16W 323 k
Grand-Mère Canada 46°36N 72°40W 298 C5
Grand Palace Bangkok, Thailand 113 b1
Grand Popo Benin 6°15N 1°57E 263 D5
Grand Portage U.S.A. 47°58N 89°41W 308 B9
Grand Prairie U.S.A. 32°44N 96°59W 314 E6
Grand Rapids = Wisconsin Rapids U.S.A. 44°23N 89°49W 308 C9
Grand Rapids Man., Canada 53°12N 99°19W 297 C9
Grand Rapids Mich., U.S.A. 42°58N 85°40W 311 B10
Grand Rapids Minn., U.S.A. 47°14N 93°31W 308 B7
Grand Rapids ✈ (GRR) U.S.A. 42°53N 85°31W 311 B11
Grand Récif Sud N. Cal. 22°47S 166°55E 288 d
Grand Ridge U.S.A. 30°43N 85°1W 316 E4
Grand River U.S.A. 40°49N 93°58W 310 D3
Grand River Bay Mauritius 20°9S 57°27E 272 e
Grand River South East → Mauritius 20°17S 57°46E 272 e
Grand' Rivière Martinique 14°52N 61°11W 322 j
Grand Roy Grenada 12°8N 61°45W 323 q
Grand St-Bernard, Col du Europe 45°50N 7°10E 179 K3
Grand Santi Fr. Guiana 4°20N 54°24W 329 C7
Grand Staircase-Escalante ⌓ U.S.A. 37°25N 111°33W 305 H8
Grand Teton U.S.A. 43°54N 110°50W 304 E8
Grand Teton △ U.S.A. 43°50N 110°50W 304 E8
Grand Union Canal U.K. 52°7N 0°53W 169 E7
Grandas de Salime Spain 43°13N 6°53W 194 B4
Grande → Jujuy, Argentina 24°20S 65°2W 334 A2
Grande → Mendoza, Argentina 36°52S 69°45W 334 D2
Grande → Bolivia 15°51S 64°39W 331 D5
Grande → Bahia, Brazil 11°30S 44°30W 332 D3
Grande → Minas Gerais, Brazil 20°6S 51°4W 333 F1
Grande → Venezuela 8°36N 61°39W 329 B5
Grande, B. Argentina 50°30S 68°20W 336 D3
Grande, I. Brazil 23°9S 44°14W 333 F3
Grande, Rio → N. Amer. 25°58N 97°9W 314 J6
Grande, Serra Piauí, Brazil 8°0S 45°10W 332 C2
Grande, Serra Tocantins, Brazil 11°15S 46°30W 332 D2
Grande Anse = Beauséjour Guadeloupe 16°18N 61°4W 322 e
Grande Anse Guadeloupe 16°19N 61°47W 322 e
Grande Anse Martinique 14°30N 61°5W 322 j
Grande Anse St. Lucia 14°1N 60°54W 323 m
Grande Anse Seychelles 4°18S 55°45E 272 c
Grande Baleine → Canada 55°16N 77°47W 298 A4
Grande Cache Canada 53°53N 119°8W 296 C5
Grande Casse, Pte. de la France 45°24N 6°49E 175 C10
Grande Comore Comoros Is. 11°35S 43°20E 272 a
Grande Cul de Sac B St. Lucia 13°59N 61°2W 323 m
Grande-Entrée Canada 47°30N 61°40W 299 C7
Grande Matelot Pt. Trin. & Tob. 10°49N 61°9W 323 t
Grande Place Brussels, Belgium 116 b2
Grande Prairie Canada 55°10N 118°50W 296 B5
Grande Pte. Guadeloupe 15°58N 61°37W 322 e
Grande-Rivière Qué., Canada 48°26N 64°30W 299 C7
Grande Riviere Trin. & Tob. 10°50N 61°3W 323 t
Grande Rivière, Pte. de la Guadeloupe 16°18N 61°36W 322 e
Grande Rivière Noire Mauritius 20°21S 57°21E 272 e
Grande Rivière Sud Est Mauritius 20°17S 57°46E 272 e
Grande Sertão Veredas △ Brazil 15°10S 45°40W 333 E2
Grande-Terre Guadeloupe 16°20N 61°25W 322 e
Grande Terre Mayotte 12°46S 45°7E 272 b
Grande-Vallée Canada 49°14N 65°8W 299 C6
Grande Vigie, Pte. de la Guadeloupe 16°32N 61°27W 322 e
Grandfalls U.S.A. 31°20N 102°51W 314 F3
Grândola Portugal 38°12N 8°35W 195 G2
Grandpré France 49°20N 4°50E 173 C11
Grands Causses ⌓ France 44°5N 2°58E 174 D6
Grands-Jardins ⌓ Canada 47°41N 70°51W 299 C5
Grandview Man., Canada 51°10N 100°42W 297 C8
Grandview Mo., U.S.A. 38°53N 94°32W 310 F2
Grandview Wash., U.S.A. 46°15N 119°54W 304 C4
Grandview Heights U.S.A. 39°58N 83°2W 311 E13
Grandvilliers France 49°40N 1°57E 173 C8
Graneros Chile 34°5S 70°45W 334 C1
Grange Hill Jamaica 18°18N 78°11W 320 a
Grangemouth U.K. 56°1N 3°42W 167 E5
Granger U.S.A. 41°35N 109°58W 304 F9
Grängesberg Sweden 60°6N 15°1E 162 D9
Grangeville U.S.A. 45°56N 116°7W 304 D5
Granisle Canada 54°53N 126°13W 296 C3
Granite City U.S.A. 38°42N 90°8W 310 F6
Granite Falls U.S.A. 44°49N 95°33W 308 C6
Granite L. Canada 48°8N 57°5W 299 C8
Granite Mt. U.S.A. 33°5N 116°28W 307 M10
Granite Pk. U.S.A. 45°10N 109°48W 304 D9
Graniteville S.C., U.S.A. 33°34N 81°49W 316 B8
Graniteville Vt., U.S.A. 44°8N 72°29W 313 B12
Granitola, C. Italy 37°34N 12°39E 200 E5
Granity N.Z. 41°39S 171°51E 285 B6
Granja Brazil 3°7S 40°50W 332 B3
Granja de Moreruela Spain 41°48N 5°44W 194 D5
Granja de Torrehermosa Spain 38°19N 5°35W 195 G5
Grankulla = Kauniainen Finland 60°13N 24°44E 121 B1
Gränna Sweden 58°1N 14°28E 163 F8
Granollers Spain 41°39N 2°18E 196 D7
Gransee Germany 53°1N 13°8E 178 B9
Grant Fla., U.S.A. 27°56N 80°32W 317 H9
Grant Nebr., U.S.A. 40°50N 101°43W 308 E3
Grant, Mt. U.S.A. 38°34N 118°48W 304 G4
Grant City U.S.A. 40°29N 94°25W 310 D2
Grant I. Australia 11°10S 132°52E 278 B5
Grant Park Chicago, U.S.A. 119 c2
Grant Range U.S.A. 38°30N 115°25W 304 G6
Grantham U.K. 52°55N 0°38W 168 E7
Grantley Adams Int. ✈ (BGI) Barbados 13°4N 59°29W 323 r
Granton U.K. 55°58N 3°14W 121 B2
Grantown-on-Spey U.K. 57°20N 3°36W 167 D5
Grants U.S.A. 35°9N 107°52W 305 J10
Grants Pass U.S.A. 42°26N 123°19W 304 E2
Grantsville U.S.A. 40°36N 112°28W 304 F7
Grantville U.S.A. 33°14N 84°50W 316 B5
Granville Manche, France 48°50N 1°35W 172 D5
Granville Trin. & Tob. 10°7N 61°48W 323 t
Granville Ill., U.S.A. 41°16N 89°14W 310 C7
Granville N. Dak., U.S.A. 48°16N 100°47W 308 A3
Granville N.Y., U.S.A. 43°24N 73°16W 313 C11
Granville Ohio, U.S.A. 40°4N 82°31W 312 F2
Granville L. Canada 56°18N 100°30W 297 B8
Granvin Norway 60°33N 6°45E 164 D3
Graskop S. Africa 24°56S 30°49E 271 B5
Gräsö Sweden 60°28N 18°35E 162 D12
Grass → Canada 56°3N 96°33W 297 B9
Grass Range U.S.A. 47°2N 108°48W 304 C9
Grass River ⌓ Canada 54°40N 100°50W 297 C8
Grass Valley Calif., U.S.A. 39°13N 121°4W 306 F6
Grass Valley Oreg., U.S.A. 45°22N 120°47W 304 D3
Grassano Italy 40°38N 16°17E 201 B9
Grasse France 43°38N 6°56E 175 E10
Grassflat U.S.A. 41°0N 78°6W 312 E6
Grasslands △ Canada 49°11N 107°38W 297 D7
Grassy Australia 40°3S 144°5E 281 G3
Grassy Park S. Africa 34°3S 18°30E 118 B2
Gråsten Denmark 54°55N 9°35E 163 K3
Grästorp Sweden 58°20N 12°40E 163 F6
Gratis U.S.A. 39°38N 84°32W 311 E12
Gratkorn Austria 47°8N 15°21E 180 D8
Gratosóglio Italy 45°24N 9°1E 129 B2
Gratz U.S.A. 38°28N 84°57W 311 F12
Gratzwalde Germany 52°28N 13°42E 115 B5
Graubünden □ Switz. 46°45N 9°30E 179 J5
Graudenz = Grudziądz Poland 53°30N 18°47E 184 E5
Graulhet France 43°45N 1°59E 174 E5
Graus Spain 42°11N 0°20E 196 C5
Gravberget Norway 60°53N 12°14E 164 D9
Grave, Pte. de France 45°34N 1°4W 174 C2
Gravelbourg Canada 49°50N 106°35W 297 D7
Gravelines France 51°1N 2°10E 173 A9
's-Gravenhage Neths. 52°7N 4°17E 170 B4
Gravenhurst Canada 44°52N 79°20W 312 B5
Gravesend N.S.W., Australia 29°35S 150°20E 281 D5
Gravesend Kent, U.K. 51°26N 0°22E 169 F8
Gravesend N.Y., U.S.A. 40°36N 73°56W 132 C2
Gravina in Púglia Italy 40°49N 16°25E 201 B9
Gravois, Pointe-à- Haiti 18°15N 73°56W 321 C5
Gravone → France 41°58N 8°45E 175 G12
Gray Haute-Saône, France 47°22N 5°35E 173 E12
Gray Ga., U.S.A. 33°1N 83°32W 316 B6
Grayling Alaska, U.S.A. 62°57N 160°3W 303 E7
Grayling Mich., U.S.A. 44°40N 84°43W 309 C11
Grays U.K. 51°28N 0°21E 169 F8
Grays Harbor U.S.A. 46°59N 124°1W 304 C1
Grays L. U.S.A. 43°4N 111°26W 304 E8
Grays River U.S.A. 46°21N 123°37W 306 D3
Grayville U.S.A. 38°16N 88°0W 311 F9
Grayvoron Russia 50°29N 35°41E 189 G8
Graz Austria 47°4N 15°27E 180 D8
Grazhdanka Russia 59°59N 30°24E 137 B2
Grdelica Serbia 42°55N 22°3E 202 D6
Greåker Norway 59°16N 11°12E 164 E8
Greasy L. Canada 62°55N 122°12W 296 A4
Great Abaco I. = Abaco I. Bahamas 26°25N 77°10W 320 A4
Great Artesian Basin Australia 23°0S 144°0E 280 C3
Great Australian Bight Australia 33°30S 130°0E 279 F5
Great Bacolet Bay Grenada 12°4N 61°37W 323 q
Great Bahama Bank Bahamas 23°15N 78°0W 320 B4
Great Barrier I. N.Z. 36°11S 175°25E 284 C4
Great Barrier Reef Australia 18°0S 146°50E 280 B4
Great Barrier Reef ⌓ Australia 20°0S 150°0E 280 B4
Great Barrington U.S.A. 42°12N 73°22W 313 D11
Great Basalt Wall △ Australia 19°52S 145°43E 280 B4
Great Basin U.S.A. 40°0N 117°0W 304 G5
Great Basin △ U.S.A. 38°56N 114°15W 304 G6
Great Basses Sri Lanka 6°11N 81°29E 245 L5
Great Bear → Canada 65°0N 126°0W 294 E7
Great Bear L. Canada 65°30N 120°0W 294 D8
Great Belt = Store Bælt Denmark 55°20N 11°0E 163 J4
Great Bend Kans., U.S.A. 38°22N 98°46W 308 F4
Great Bend Pa., U.S.A. 41°58N 75°45W 313 E9
Great Blasket I. Ireland 52°6N 10°32W 166 D1
Great Britain Europe 54°0N 2°15W 158 E5
Great Camanoe Br. Virgin Is. 18°30N 64°35W 321 b
Great Channel Asia 6°0N 94°0E 245 L11
Great Coco I. = Koko Kyunzu Burma 14°7N 93°22E 245 G11
Great Codroy Canada 47°51N 59°16W 299 C8
Great Divide, The = Great Dividing Ra. Australia 23°0S 146°0E 280 C4
Great Divide Basin U.S.A. 42°0N 108°0W 304 E9
Great Dividing Ra. Australia 23°0S 146°0E 280 C4
Great Driffield = Driffield U.K. 54°0N 0°26W 168 C7
Great Exuma I. Bahamas 23°30N 75°50W 320 B4
Great Falls Guyana 5°35N 61°0W 329 B5
Great Falls Mont., U.S.A. 47°30N 111°17W 304 C8
Great Falls Va., U.S.A. 38°59N 77°17W 143 B2
Great Falls Park U.S.A. 38°59N 77°14W 143 B2
Great Fish = Groot-Vis → S. Africa 33°28S 27°5E 270 D4
Great Goat I. Jamaica 17°52N 77°3W 320 a
Great Guana Cay Bahamas 24°0N 76°20W 320 B4
Great Hall of the People Beijing, China 114 c3
Great Himalayan △ India 31°30N 77°30E 242 D7
Great Inagua I. Bahamas 21°0N 73°20W 321 B5
Great Indian Desert = Thar Desert India 28°0N 72°0E 242 F5
Great Karoo S. Africa 31°55S 21°0E 270 D3
Great Khingan Mts. = Da Hinggan Ling China 48°0N 121°0E 219 B13
Great Lake Australia 41°50S 146°40E 281 G4
Great Lakes N. Amer. 46°0N 84°0W 292 E11
Great Limpopo Transfrontier △ Africa 23°0S 31°45E 271 B5
Great Malvern U.K. 52°7N 2°18W 169 E5
Great Miami → U.S.A. 39°7N 84°49W 309 F11
Great Nicobar India 7°0N 93°50E 245 L11
Great Ormes Head U.K. 53°20N 3°52W 168 D4
Great Otway △ Australia 38°50S 143°50E 282 E5
Great Ouse → U.K. 52°48N 0°21E 168 E8
Great Palm I. Australia 18°45S 146°40E 280 B4
Great Pedro Bluff Jamaica 17°51N 77°44W 320 a
Great Pee Dee → U.S.A. 33°21N 79°10W 315 E15
Great Plains N. Amer. 47°0N 105°0W 292 E9
Great Ruaha → Tanzania 7°56S 37°52E 268 D4
Great Sacandaga L. U.S.A. 43°6N 74°16W 313 C10
Great Saint Bernard Pass = Grand St-Bernard, Col du Europe 45°50N 7°10E 179 K3
Great Salt Desert = Kavīr, Dasht-e Iran 34°30N 55°0E 247 C7
Great Salt L. U.S.A. 41°15N 112°40W 304 F7
Great Salt Lake Desert U.S.A. 40°50N 113°30W 304 F7
Great Salt Plains L. U.S.A. 36°45N 98°8W 314 C5
Great Salt Pond St. Kitts & Nevis 17°14N 62°40W 322 d
Great Sand Dunes ⌓ U.S.A. 37°48N 105°45W 305 H11
Great Sand Sea Libya 29°0N 24°0E 258 C4
Great Sandy △ Australia 26°13S 153°2E 281 D5
Great Sandy Desert Australia 21°0S 124°0E 278 D3
Great Sangi = Sangihe, Pulau Indonesia 3°35N 125°30E 231 D7
Great Scarcies → S. Leone 9°0N 13°0W 262 D2
Great Sd. Bermuda 32°17N 64°51W 153 a
Great Sea Reef Fiji 16°15S 179°0E 287 A2
Great Sitkin I. U.S.A. 52°3N 176°6W 303 K3
Great Skellig Ireland 51°47N 10°33W 166 E1
Great Slave L. Canada 61°23N 115°38W 296 A5
Great Smoky Mts. △ U.S.A. 35°40N 83°40W 315 D13
Great Stour = Stour → U.K. 51°18N 1°22E 169 F9
Great Victoria Desert Australia 29°30S 126°30E 279 E4
Great Wall Antarctica 62°30S 58°0W 151 C18
Great Wall China 38°30N 109°30E 226 E5
Great Western Forum U.S.A. 33°57N 118°20W 126 C2
Great Whale River = Kuujjuarapik Canada 55°20N 77°35W 298 A4
Great Whernside U.K. 54°10N 1°58W 168 C6
Great Yarmouth U.K. 52°37N 1°44E 169 E9
Great Zab = Zāb al Kabīr → Iraq 36°1N 43°24E 213 D10
Great Zimbabwe Zimbabwe 20°16S 30°54E 269 G3
Greater Antilles W. Indies 17°40N 74°0W 321 C5
Greater London □ U.K. 51°31N 0°6W 169 F7
Greater Manchester □ U.K. 53°30N 2°15W 168 D5
Greater St. Lucia Wetlands ⌓ S. Africa 28°6S 32°27E 271 C5
Greater Sudbury = Sudbury Canada 46°30N 81°0W 298 C3
Greater Sunda Is. Indonesia 7°0S 112°0E 230 F4
Grebbestad Sweden 58°42N 11°15E 163 F5
Grebenka = Hrebenka Ukraine 50°9N 32°22E 189 G7
Greco Italy 45°30N 9°12E 129 A2
Greco, C. Cyprus 34°57N 34°5E 207 F10
Greco, Mte. Italy 41°48N 13°58E 199 G10
Gredos, Sierra de Spain 40°20N 5°0W 194 E6
Greece U.S.A. 43°13N 77°41W 312 C7
Greece ■ Europe 40°0N 23°0E 204 B3
Greeley Colo., U.S.A. 40°25N 104°42W 304 F11
Greeley Nebr., U.S.A. 41°33N 98°32W 308 E4
Greeleyville U.S.A. 33°40N 79°59W 316 B10
Greely Fd. Canada 80°30N 85°0W 295 A15
Greem-Bell, Ostrov Russia 81°0N 62°0E 214 A7
Green → Ky., U.S.A. 37°54N 87°30W 308 G10
Green → Utah, U.S.A. 38°11N 109°53W 304 G9
Green B. U.S.A. 45°0N 87°30W 308 C10
Green Bay U.S.A. 44°31N 88°0W 308 C9
Green C. Australia 37°13S 150°1E 283 D9
Green City U.S.A. 40°16N 92°57W 310 D4
Green Cove Springs U.S.A. 29°59N 81°42W 316 F8
Green I. = Lütao Taiwan 22°40N 121°30E 225 D3
Green I. Antigua & B. 17°2N 61°40W 322 b
Green I. Hong Kong, China 22°17N 114°6E 122 B1
Green I. Grenada 12°13N 61°35W 323 q
Green Is. Papua N. G. 4°35S 154°10E 286 C8
Green Island Jamaica 18°23N 78°17W 320 a
Green Island B. Phil. 10°12N 119°22E 233 F2
Green Lake Canada 54°17N 107°47W 297 C7
Green Mts. U.S.A. 43°45N 72°45W 313 C12
Green Point S. Africa 33°54S 18°25E 118 A1
Green Point Stadium S. Africa 33°54S 18°25E 118 A1
Green Pond U.S.A. 32°44N 80°37W 316 C9
Green River Papua N. G. 3°54S 141°11E 286 B1
Green River Utah, U.S.A. 38°59N 110°10W 304 G8
Green River Wyo., U.S.A. 41°32N 109°28W 304 F9
Green Valley U.S.A. 31°52N 110°56W 305 L8
Greenacres U.S.A. 26°38N 80°7W 317 J9
Greenbank U.S.A. 48°6N 122°34W 306 B4
Greenbelt U.S.A. 39°0N 76°53W 143 A4
Greenbelt Park U.S.A. 38°58N 76°53W 143 B4
Greenbush Mich., U.S.A. 44°35N 83°19W 312 B1
Greenbush Minn., U.S.A. 48°42N 96°11W 308 A5
Greencastle U.S.A. 39°38N 86°52W 311 E10
Greene Iowa, U.S.A. 42°54N 92°48W 310 B4
Greene N.Y., U.S.A. 42°20N 75°46W 313 D9
Greeneville U.S.A. 36°10N 82°50W 315 C13
Greenfield Calif., U.S.A. 36°19N 121°15W 306 J5
Greenfield Calif., U.S.A. 35°15N 119°0W 307 K8
Greenfield Ill., U.S.A. 39°21N 90°12W 310 E6
Greenfield Ind., U.S.A. 39°47N 85°46W 311 E11
Greenfield Iowa, U.S.A. 41°18N 94°28W 310 C2
Greenfield Mass., U.S.A. 42°35N 72°36W 313 D12
Greenfield Mo., U.S.A. 37°25N 93°51W 308 G7
Greenfield Ohio, U.S.A. 39°21N 83°23W 311 E13
Greenfield Park Canada 45°29N 73°28W 130 B3
Greenford U.K. 51°31N 0°21W 125 A1
Greenhill U.K. 51°34N 0°18W 125 A2
Greenhills Ireland 53°18N 6°20W 120 B1
Greenland ⧄ N. Amer. 66°0N 45°0W 154 D6
Greenland Sea Arctic 73°0N 10°0W 154 B10
Greenmarket Square Cape Town, S. Africa 118 c2
Greenock U.K. 55°57N 4°46W 167 F4
Greenore Ireland 54°2N 6°8W 166 B5
Greenore Pt. Ireland 52°14N 6°19W 166 D5
Greenough Australia 28°58S 114°43E 279 E1
Greenough → Australia 28°51S 114°38E 279 E1
Greenough Pt. Canada 44°58N 81°26W 312 B3
Greenpoint New York, U.S.A. 132 e3
Greenport U.S.A. 41°6N 72°22W 313 E12
Greensboro Fla., U.S.A. 30°34N 84°45W 316 E5
Greensboro Ga., U.S.A. 33°35N 83°11W 316 B6
Greensboro N.C., U.S.A. 36°4N 79°48W 315 C15
Greensboro Vt., U.S.A. 44°36N 72°18W 313 B12
Greensburg Ind., U.S.A. 39°20N 85°29W 311 E11
Greensburg Kans., U.S.A. 37°36N 99°18W 308 G4
Greensburg Pa., U.S.A. 40°18N 79°33W 312 F5
Greenstone = Geraldton Canada 49°44N 87°10W 298 C2
Greenstone Pt. U.K. 57°55N 5°37W 167 D3
Greentown U.S.A. 40°29N 85°58W 311 D11
Greenup U.S.A. 39°15N 88°10W 311 E8
Greenvale Australia 18°59S 145°7E 280 B4
Greenville Liberia 5°1N 9°6W 262 D3
Greenville Ala., U.S.A. 31°50N 86°38W 315 F11
Greenville Calif., U.S.A. 40°8N 120°57W 306 E6
Greenville Fla., U.S.A. 30°28N 83°38W 316 E6
Greenville Ga., U.S.A. 33°2N 84°43W 316 B5
Greenville Ill., U.S.A. 38°53N 89°25W 310 F7
Greenville Ind., U.S.A. 38°22N 85°59W 311 F11
Greenville Maine, U.S.A. 45°28N 69°35W 309 C19
Greenville Mich., U.S.A. 43°11N 85°15W 311 A11
Greenville Miss., U.S.A. 33°24N 91°4W 315 E9
Greenville Mo., U.S.A. 37°8N 90°27W 308 G8
Greenville N.C., U.S.A. 35°37N 77°23W 315 D16
Greenville N.H., U.S.A. 42°46N 71°49W 313 D13
Greenville N.Y., U.S.A. 42°25N 74°1W 313 D10
Greenville Ohio, U.S.A. 40°6N 84°38W 311 D12
Greenville Pa., U.S.A. 41°24N 80°23W 312 E4
Greenville S.C., U.S.A. 34°51N 82°24W 315 D13
Greenville Tex., U.S.A. 33°8N 96°7W 314 E6
Greenwater Lake ⌓ Canada 52°32N 103°30W 297 C8
Greenwich Conn., U.S.A. 41°2N 73°38W 313 E11
Greenwich N.Y., U.S.A. 43°5N 73°30W 313 C11
Greenwich Ohio, U.S.A. 41°2N 82°31W 312 E2
Greenwich □ U.K. 51°29N 0°1E 125 B3
Greenwich Observatory U.K. 51°28N 0°0 125 B3
Greenwich Village New York, U.S.A. 132 d1
Greenwood B.C., Canada 49°10N 118°40W 296 D5
Greenwood Ark., U.S.A. 35°13N 94°16W 314 D7
Greenwood Fla., U.S.A. 30°52N 85°10W 316 E4
Greenwood Ind., U.S.A. 39°37N 86°7W 311 E10
Greenwood Mass., U.S.A. 42°29N 71°2W 116 A2
Greenwood Miss., U.S.A. 33°31N 90°11W 315 E9
Greenwood S.C., U.S.A. 34°12N 82°10W 315 D13
Greenwood, Mt. Australia 13°48S 130°4E 278 B5
Greenwood Great House Jamaica 18°29N 77°44W 320 a
Grefsen Norway 59°56N 10°47E 133 A3
Gregbe Ivory C. 6°48N 6°43W 262 D3
Gregório → Brazil 6°50S 70°46W 330 B3
Gregory U.S.A. 43°14N 99°26W 308 D4
Gregory → Australia 17°53S 139°17E 280 B2
Gregory, L. S. Austral., Australia 28°55S 139°0E 281 D2
Gregory, L. W. Austral., Australia 20°0S 127°40E 278 D4
Gregory, L. W. Austral., Australia 25°38S 119°58E 279 E2
Gregory △ Australia 15°38S 131°15E 278 C5
Gregory Downs Australia 18°35S 138°45E 280 B2
Gregory Ra. Queens., Australia 19°30S 143°40E 280 B3
Gregory Ra. W. Austral., Australia 21°20S 121°12E 278 D3
Greifenberg = Gryfice Poland 53°55N 15°13E 184 E2
Greifenhagen = Gryfino Poland 53°16N 14°29E 185 E1
Greiffenberg = Gryfów Śląski Poland 51°2N 15°24E 185 G2
Greiffenberg Germany 53°5N 13°57E 178 B9
Greifswald Germany 54°5N 13°23E 178 A9
Greifswalder Bodden Germany 54°12N 13°35E 178 A9
Grein Austria 48°14N 14°51E 180 C7
Greiz Germany 50°39N 12°10E 178 E8
Gremikha Russia 67°59N 39°47E 186 A6
Grenaa Denmark 56°25N 10°53E 163 H4
Grenada U.S.A. 33°47N 89°49W 315 E10
Grenada ■ W. Indies 12°10N 61°40W 323 q
Grenade France 43°47N 1°17E 174 E5
Grenadier I. U.S.A. 44°3N 76°22W 313 B8
Grenadines, The St. Vincent 12°40N 61°20W 323 n
Grenchen Switz. 47°12N 7°24E 179 H3
Grenen Denmark 57°44N 10°40E 163 G4
Grenfell N.S.W., Australia 33°52S 148°8E 283 B8
Grenfell Sask., Canada 50°30N 102°56W 297 C8
Grenivík Iceland 65°57N 18°11W 155 B8
Grenjaðarstaður Iceland 65°49N 17°21W 155 B9
Grenoble France 45°12N 5°42E 175 C9
Grenville Grenada 12°7N 61°37W 323 q
Grenville, C. Australia 12°0S 143°13E 286 F2
Grenville Chan. Canada 53°40N 129°46W 296 C3
Gréoux-les-Bains France 43°45N 5°52E 175 E9
Gresham U.S.A. 45°30N 122°25W 306 E4
Gresham Park U.S.A. 33°43N 84°20W 113 B2
Gresik Indonesia 7°13S 112°38E 235 D4
Gretna Dumf. & Gall., U.K. 55°0N 3°3W 167 F5
Gretna Fla., U.S.A. 30°37N 84°40W 316 E5
Gretna La., U.S.A. 29°54N 90°3W 131 B2
Gretna City Park U.S.A. 29°54N 90°3W 131 B2
Greve Strand Denmark 55°34N 12°18E 118 B1
Greven Germany 52°6N 7°37E 178 C3
Grevena Greece 40°4N 21°25E 202 F5
Grevena □ Greece 40°2N 21°25E 202 F5
Grevenbroich Germany 51°5N 6°35E 178 D2
Grevenmacher Lux. 49°41N 6°26E 170 E6
Grevesmühlen Germany 53°52N 11°12E 178 B7
Grey → Nfld. & L., Canada 47°34N 57°6W 299 C8
Grey → N.Z. 42°27S 171°12E 285 C6
Grey, C. Australia 13°0S 136°35E 280 A2
Grey Is. Canada 50°50N 55°35W 295 G20
Grey Ra. Australia 27°0S 143°30E 281 D3
Greybull U.S.A. 44°30N 108°3W 304 D9
Greyfriars Kirk Edinburgh, U.K. 121 c3
Greymouth N.Z. 42°29S 171°13E 285 C6
Greystones Ireland 53°9N 6°5W 166 C5
Greytown N.Z. 41°5S 175°29E 284 H4
Greytown KwaZulu Natal, S. Africa 29°1S 30°36E 271 C5
Gribanovskiy Russia 51°28N 41°50E 190 E5
Gribbell I. Canada 53°23N 129°0W 296 C3
Gribës, Mal i Albania 40°17N 19°45E 202 F3
Gribingui → C.A.R. 8°33N 19°5E 264 A3
Gribingui-Bamingui ⌓ C.A.R. 7°45N 19°17E 264 A3
Gridley U.S.A. 39°22N 121°42W 306 F5
Griebeg, Ras il- Malta 35°58N 14°23E 206 F7
Griebnitzsee Germany 52°23N 13°8E 115 B1
Griekwastad S. Africa 28°49S 23°15E 270 C3
Griesheim Germany 49°51N 8°33E 179 F4
Grieskirchen Austria 48°16N 13°48E 180 C6
Griffin U.S.A. 33°15N 84°16W 316 B5
Griffin, L. U.S.A. 28°52N 81°51W 317 G8
Griffith N.S.W., Australia 34°18S 146°2E 283 C7
Griffith Ont., Canada 45°15N 77°10W 312 A7
Griffith I. Canada 44°50N 80°55W 312 B4
Griffith Park U.S.A. 34°8N 118°17W 126 B3
Griggsville U.S.A. 39°43N 90°43W 310 E6
Grignols France 44°23N 0°2W 174 D3
Grigoriopol Moldova 47°9N 29°18E 183 C14
Grimari C.A.R. 5°43N 20°6E 264 A4
Grimaylov = Hrymayliv Ukraine 49°20N 26°5E 177 D14
Grimbergen Belgium 50°56N 4°22E 116 A2
Grimes U.S.A. 39°4N 121°54W 306 F5
Grimm = Kamenskiy Russia 50°48N 45°25E 190 E7
Grimma Germany 51°14N 12°43E 178 D8
Grimmen Germany 54°7N 13°3E 178 A9
Grimsay U.K. 57°29N 7°14W 167 D1
Grimsby Ont., Canada 43°12N 79°34W 312 C5
Grimsby N.E. Lincs., U.K. 53°34N 0°5W 168 D7
Grímsey Iceland 66°33N 17°58W 155 A9
Grimshaw Canada 56°10N 117°40W 296 B5
Grimslöv Sweden 56°44N 14°34E 163 H8
Grímsstaðir Iceland 65°39N 16°7W 155 B10
Grimstad Norway 58°20N 8°35E 164 F5
Grímsvötn Iceland 64°26N 17°22W 155 C9
Grindavík Iceland 63°50N 22°26W 155 D4
Grindelwald Switz. 46°38N 8°2E 179 J4
Grindsted Denmark 55°46N 8°55E 163 J2
Grindstone I. U.S.A. 44°17N 76°27W 313 B8
Grindu Romania 44°44N 26°50E 183 F11
Grinnell U.S.A. 41°45N 92°43W 310 C4
Grinnell Pen. Canada 76°40N 95°0W 295 B13
Grintavec Slovenia 46°22N 14°32E 199 B11
Grinzing Austria 48°15N 16°20E 142 A2
Gris-Nez, C. France 50°52N 1°35E 173 B8
Grise Fiord Canada 76°25N 82°57W 295 B15
Grishino = Krasnoarmeisk Ukraine 48°18N 37°11E 189 H9
Grisolles France 43°49N 1°19E 174 E5
Grisons = Graubünden □ Switz. 46°45N 9°30E 179 J5
Grisslehamn Sweden 60°5N 18°49E 162 D12
Grmeč Planina Bos.-H. 44°43N 16°16E 199 D13
Groais I. Canada 50°55N 55°35W 299 B8
Gröbenried Germany 48°13N 11°25E 131 A1
Grobiņa Latvia 56°33N 21°10E 184 B8
Groblersdal S. Africa 25°15S 29°25E 271 C4
Grobming Austria 47°27N 13°54E 180 D6
Grochów Poland 52°15N 21°5E 142 B2
Grocka Serbia 44°40N 20°42E 202 B4
Gródek Poland 53°6N 23°40E 185 E10
Gródek Tagiellonśki = Horodok Ukraine 49°46N 23°32E 177 D12
Grodekovo = Pogranichnyy Russia 44°25N 131°24E 220 B5
Grodków Poland 50°43N 17°21E 185 H4
Grodno = Hrodna Belarus 53°42N 23°52E 184 E10
Grodzisk Poland 52°19N 21°4E 142 B2
Grodzisk Mazowiecki Poland 52°7N 20°37E 185 F7
Grodzisk Wielkopolski Poland 52°15N 16°22E 185 F3
Grodzyanka = Hrodzyanka Belarus 53°31N 28°42E 177 B15
Groenendaal Belgium 50°46N 4°26E 116 B2
Groesbeck U.S.A. 31°31N 96°32W 314 F6
Grogol Petamburin Indonesia 6°9S 106°46E 122 A1
Groix France 47°38N 3°29W 172 E3
Groix, Î. de France 47°38N 3°28W 172 E3
Grójec Poland 51°50N 20°58E 185 G7
Gronau Niedersachsen, Germany 52°5N 9°47E 178 C5
Gronau Nordrhein-Westfalen, Germany 52°12N 7°2E 178 C3
Grong Norway 64°25N 12°8E 160 D15
Grönhögen Sweden 56°16N 16°24E 163 H10
Groningen Neths. 53°15N 6°35E 170 A6
Groningen Suriname 5°48N 55°28W 329 B6
Groningen □ Neths. 53°16N 6°40E 170 A6
Grønnedal = Kangilinnguit Greenland 61°20N 47°57W 154 E6
Gronsdorf Germany 48°7N 11°42E 131 B3
Groom U.S.A. 35°12N 101°6W 314 D4
Groot → S. Africa 33°45S 24°36E 270 D3
Groot-Berg → S. Africa 32°47S 18°8E 270 D2
Groot-Brakrivier S. Africa 34°2S 22°18E 270 D3
Groot Karasberge Namibia 27°20S 18°40E 270 C2
Groot Kei → S. Africa 32°41S 28°22E 271 D4
Groot-Vis → S. Africa 33°28S 27°5E 270 D4
Grootdrink S. Africa 28°33S 21°42E 270 C3
Groote Eylandt Australia 14°0S 136°40E 280 A2
Grootfontein Namibia 19°31S 18°6E 270 A2
Grootlaagte → Africa 20°55S 21°27E 270 B3
Grootvloer → S. Africa 30°0S 20°40E 270 D3
Grorud Norway 59°57N 10°52E 133 A4
Gros C. Canada 61°59N 113°32W 296 A6
Gros Cap Guadeloupe 16°24N 61°25W 322 e
Gros Islet St. Lucia 14°5N 60°58W 323 m
Gros-Morne Martinique 14°43N 61°2W 322 j
Gros Morne △ Canada 49°40N 57°50W 299 C8
Gros Piton St. Lucia 13°49N 61°5W 323 m
Grósio Italy 46°18N 10°16E 198 B7
Grosne → France 46°42N 4°56E 173 F11
Gross-Glienicke Germany 52°28N 13°6E 115 B1
Gross-Hadern Germany 48°6N 11°29E 131 B1
Gross-Lappen Germany 48°11N 11°35E 131 A2
Gross-Meseritsch = Velké Meziříčí Czech Rep. 49°21N 16°1E 180 B9
Gross-Strehlitz = Strzelce Opolskie Poland 50°31N 18°18E 185 H5
Gross Wartenberg = Syców Poland 51°19N 17°40E 185 G4
Grossa, Pta. Spain 39°6N 1°36E 206 C2
Grosse I. U.S.A. 42°8N 83°9W 311 B13
Grosse Krampe Germany 52°23N 13°40E 115 B5
Grosse Müggelsee Germany 52°26N 13°38E 115 B4
Grosse Point U.S.A. 42°23N 82°54W 312 D2
Grosse Point Lighthouse U.S.A. 42°2N 87°41W 119 A2
Grosse Pte. Guadeloupe 16°1N 61°17W 322 e
Grossenbrode Germany 54°21N 11°4E 178 A7
Grossenhain Germany 51°17N 13°32E 178 D9
Grossenzersdorf Austria 48°12N 16°33E 142 A3
Grossenzersdorfer Arm → Austria 48°12N 16°31E 142 A3
Grosser Arber Germany 49°6N 13°8E 179 F9
Grosser Biberhaufen Austria 48°12N 16°28E 142 A2
Grosser Plöner See Germany 54°10N 10°22E 178 A6
Grosser Wannsee Germany 52°25N 13°10E 115 B2
Grosseto Italy 42°46N 11°8E 199 F8
Grossfeld-Siedlung Austria 48°16N 16°26E 142 A2
Grossgerungs Austria 48°34N 14°57E 180 C7
Grossglockner Austria 47°5N 12°40E 180 D5
Grosshesselohe Germany 48°3N 11°32E 131 B2
Grossjedlersdorf Austria 48°16N 16°23E 142 A2
Grosswardein = Oradea Romania 47°2N 21°58E 182 C6
Grossziethen Germany 52°23N 13°26E 115 B3
Groswater B. Canada 54°20N 57°40W 299 B8
Grotli Norway 62°2N 7°42E 164 B4
Groton Conn., U.S.A. 41°21N 72°5W 313 E12
Groton N.Y., U.S.A. 42°36N 76°22W 313 D8
Groton S. Dak., U.S.A. 45°27N 98°6W 308 C4
Grottáglie Italy 40°32N 17°26E 201 B10
Grottaminarda Italy 41°4N 15°2E 201 A8
Grottammare Italy 42°59N 13°52E 199 F10
Grottkau = Grodków Poland 50°43N 17°21E 185 H4
Grouard Mission Canada 55°33N 116°9W 296 B5
Grouin, Pte. du France 48°43N 1°51W 172 D5
Ground Zero New York, U.S.A. 132 e1
Groundhog → Canada 48°45N 82°58W 298 C3
Grouw Neths. 53°5N 5°51E 170 A5
Grove, The U.S.A. 42°5N 87°52W 119 A1
Grove City Fla., U.S.A. 26°56N 82°19W 317 J7
Grove City Ohio, U.S.A. 39°53N 83°6W 311 E13
Grove City Pa., U.S.A. 41°10N 80°5W 312 E4
Grove Hall U.S.A. 42°18N 71°4W 116 B2
Grove Hill U.S.A. 31°42N 87°47W 315 F11
Grove Park Hounslow, U.K. 51°28N 0°15W 125 B2
Grove Park Lewisham, U.K. 51°25N 0°1E 125 B4
Grove Park Georgia, U.S.A. 33°46N 84°26W 113 B2
Groveland Calif., U.S.A. 37°50N 120°14W 306 H6
Groveland Fla., U.S.A. 28°34N 81°51W 317 G8
Grover = Tiltonsville U.S.A. 40°10N 80°41W 312 F4
Grover Beach U.S.A. 35°7N 120°37W 307 K6
Groves U.S.A. 29°57N 93°54W 314 G8
Groveton N.H., U.S.A. 44°36N 71°31W 313 B13
Groveton Va., U.S.A. 38°46N 77°6W 143 C3
Grovetown U.S.A. 33°27N 82°12W 316 B7
Grožnjan Croatia 45°22N 13°43E 199 C10
Groznyy Russia 43°20N 45°45E 191 J7
Grua Norway 60°16N 10°40E 164 D7
Grubišno Polje Croatia 45°44N 17°12E 182 E2
Grudovo Bulgaria 42°21N 27°10E 203 D11
Grudusk Poland 53°3N 20°38E 185 E7
Grudziądz Poland 53°30N 18°47E 184 E5
Gruinard B. U.K. 57°56N 5°35W 167 D3
Gruissan France 43°8N 3°7E 174 E7
Grumo Áppula Italy 41°1N 16°42E 201 A9
Grums Sweden 59°22N 13°5E 162 E7
Grünau Germany 52°25N 13°34E 115 B4
Grünberg Germany 50°35N 8°58E 178 E4
Grünberg in Schlesien = Zielona Góra Poland 51°57N 15°31E 185 G2
Grund Iceland 65°31N 18°9W 155 B8
Gründau Germany 50°10N 9°9E 179 E5
Grundy Center U.S.A. 42°22N 92°47W 310 B4
Grunewald Germany 52°28N 13°13E 115 B2
Grungedal Norway 59°44N 7°43E 164 E4
Grünstadt Germany 49°34N 8°9E 179 F4
Grünwald Germany 48°2N 11°31E 131 B2
Grünwalder Forst Germany 48°2N 11°33E 131 B2
Gruppo di Tessa ⌓ Italy 46°47N 11°0E 198 B8
Gruvberget Sweden 61°6N 16°10E 162 C10
Gruver U.S.A. 36°16N 101°24W 314 C4
Gruyères Switz. 46°35N 7°4E 179 J3
Gruža Serbia 43°54N 20°46E 202 C4
Gryazi Russia 52°30N 39°58E 189 F10
Gryazliv = Borovichi Russia 58°25N 33°55E 188 C7
Gryazovets Russia 58°50N 40°10E 188 C11
Grybów Poland 49°36N 20°55E 185 J7
Grycksbo Sweden 60°40N 15°29E 162 D9
Gryfice Poland 53°55N 15°13E 184 E2
Gryfino Poland 53°16N 14°29E 185 E1
Gryfów Śląski Poland 51°2N 15°24E 185 G2
Grymes Hill U.S.A. 40°36N 74°6W 132 C1
Gryt Sweden 58°12N 16°48E 163 F10
Grythyttan Sweden 59°41N 14°32E 162 E8
Grytviken S. Georgia 54°19S 36°33W 152 M8
Gstaad Switz. 46°28N 7°18E 179 J3
Gua India 22°18N 85°20E 243 H11
Gua Musang Malaysia 4°53N 101°58E 237 K3
Guabún, Pta. Chile 41°48S 74°2W 336 B2
Guacanayabo, G. de Cuba 20°40N 77°20W 320 B4
Guacara Venezuela 10°14N 67°53W 328 A4
Guachípas → Argentina 25°40S 65°30W 334 B2
Guadajoz → Spain 37°50N 4°51W 195 H6
Guadalajara Jalisco, Mexico 20°40N 103°20W 318 C4
Guadalajara Spain 40°37N 3°12W 196 E1
Guadalajara □ Spain 40°47N 2°30W 196 E2
Guadalcanal Solomon Is. 9°32S 160°12E 287 M11
Guadalcanal Spain 38°5N 5°52W 195 G5
Guadalén → Spain 38°5N 3°32W 195 G7
Guadales Argentina 34°30S 67°55W 334 C2
Guadalete → Spain 36°35N 6°13W 195 J4
Guadalimar → Spain 38°5N 3°28W 195 G7
Guadalmena → Spain 38°19N 2°56W 195 G8
Guadalmez → Spain 38°46N 5°4W 195 G5
Guadalope → Spain 41°15N 0°3W 196 D4
Guadalquivir → Spain 36°47N 6°22W 195 J4
Guadalupe = Guadeloupe ⧄ W. Indies 16°20N 61°40W 322 e
Guadalupe Brazil 6°44S 43°47W 332 C3
Guadalupe Zacatecas, Mexico 22°45N 102°31W 318 C4
Guadalupe Manila, Phil. 14°34N 121°2E 127 B2
Guadalupe Spain 39°27N 5°17W 195 F5
Guadalupe Calif., U.S.A. 34°58N 120°34W 307 L6
Guadalupe → U.S.A. 28°27N 96°47W 314 G6
Guadalupe, Basilica de Mexico 19°29N 99°7W 128 B2
Guadalupe, Sierra de Spain 39°28N 5°30W 195 F5
Guadalupe Bravos Mexico 31°20N 106°10W 318 A3
Guadalupe I. Pac. Oc. 29°0N 118°50W 292 G8
Guadalupe Mts. △ U.S.A. 31°40N 104°30W 314 F2
Guadalupe Peak U.S.A. 31°50N 104°52W 314 F2
Guadalupe y Calvo Mexico 26°6N 106°58W 318 B3
Guadarrama, Sierra de Spain 41°0N 4°0W 194 E7
Guadeloupe ⧄ W. Indies 16°20N 61°40W 322 e
Guadeloupe △ Guadeloupe 16°10N 61°40W 322 e
Guadeloupe Passage W. Indies 16°50N 62°15W 322 e
Guadelupe Peru 7°15S 79°29W 330 B2
Guadiamar → Spain 36°55N 6°24W 195 J4
Guadiana → Portugal 37°14N 7°22W 195 H3
Guadiana Menor → Spain 37°56N 3°15W 195 H7
Guadiaro → Spain 36°17N 5°17W 195 J5
Guadiato → Spain 37°48N 5°5W 195 H5
Guadiela → Spain 40°22N 2°49W 196 E2
Guadix Spain 37°18N 3°11W 195 H7
Guafo, Boca del Chile 43°35S 74°0W 336 B2
Guafo, I. Chile 43°35S 74°50W 336 B2
Guaico Trin. & Tob. 10°35N 61°9W 323 t
Guainía □ Colombia 2°30N 69°0W 328 C4
Guainía → Colombia 2°1N 67°7W 328 C4
Guaíra Brazil 24°5S 54°10W 335 A5
Guaíra □ Paraguay 25°45S 56°30W 334 B4
Guaire = Gorey Ireland 52°41N 6°18W 166 D5
Guaitecas, Is. Chile 44°0S 74°30W 336 B2
Guajará-Mirim Brazil 10°50S 65°20W 331 C4
Guajira □ Colombia 11°30N 72°30W 328 A3
Guajira, Pen. de la Colombia 12°0N 72°0W 328 A3
Gualaceo Ecuador 2°54S 78°47W 328 D2
Gualán Guatemala 15°8N 89°22W 320 C2
Gualdo Tadino Italy 43°14N 12°47E 199 E9
Gualeguay Argentina 33°10S 59°14W 334 C4
Gualeguaychú Argentina 33°3S 59°31W 334 C4
Gualequay → Argentina 33°19S 59°39W 334 C4
Gualicho, Salina Argentina 40°25S 65°20W 336 B3
Gualjaina Argentina 42°45S 70°30W 336 B2
Guam ⧄ Pac. Oc. 13°27N 144°45E 302 d
Guamá → Brazil 1°29S 48°30W 332 B2
Guamblin, I. Chile 44°50S 75°0W 336 B2
Guaminí Argentina 37°1S 62°28W 334 D3
Guamote Ecuador 1°56S 78°43W 328 D2
Guampí, Sierra de Venezuela 6°0N 65°35W 329 B4
Guamúchil Mexico 25°28N 108°6W 318 B3

376 Guana I.
INDEX

Guana I. Br. Virgin Is. 18°30N 64°30W 321 b
Guanabacoa Cuba 23°8N 82°18W 320 B3
Guanabara, B. de Brazil 22°52S 43°10W 135 B1
Guanabara, Jardim Brazil 22°48S 43°11W 135 A1
Guanabara, Palácio da Brazil 22°56S 43°11W 135 B1
Guanacaste, Cordillera de Costa Rica 10°40N 85°4W 320 D2
Guanacaste △ Costa Rica 10°57N 85°30W 320 D2
Guanaceví Mexico 25°56N 105°57W 318 B3
Guanahani = San Salvador I. Bahamas 24°0N 74°40W 321 B5
Guanaja Honduras 16°30N 85°55W 320 C2
Guanajay Cuba 22°56N 82°42W 320 B3
Guanajuato Mexico 21°1N 101°15W 318 C4
Guanajuato □ Mexico 21°0N 101°0W 318 C4
Guanambi Brazil 14°13S 42°47W 333 D3
Guanapo Trin. & Tob. 10°36N 61°15W 323 t
Guanare Venezuela 8°42N 69°12W 328 B4
Guanare → Venezuela 8°13N 67°46W 328 B4
Guandacol Argentina 29°30S 68°40W 334 B2
Guandi Shan China 37°53N 111°29E 226 F6
Guane Cuba 22°10N 84°7W 320 B3
Guang'an China 30°28N 106°35E 228 B6
Guang'anmen China 39°51N 116°18E 114 B1
Guangchang China 26°50N 116°21E 229 D11
Guangde China 30°54N 119°25E 229 B12
Guangdong □ China 23°0N 113°0E 229 F9
Guangfeng China 28°20N 118°15E 229 C12
Guanghan China 30°58N 104°17E 228 B5
Guangling China 39°47N 114°22E 226 E8
Guangnan China 24°5N 105°4E 228 E5
Guangning China 23°40N 112°22E 229 F9
Guangqumen China 39°52N 116°25E 114 B2
Guangrao China 37°5N 118°25E 227 F10
Guangshui China 31°37N 114°0E 229 B9
Guangshun China 26°8N 106°21E 228 D6
Guangwu China 37°48N 105°57E 226 F3
Guangxi Zhuangzu Zizhiqu □ China 24°0N 109°0E 228 F7
Guangyuan China 32°26N 105°51E 226 H3
Guangze China 27°30N 117°12E 229 D11
Guangzhou China 23°6N 113°13E 121 B2
Guanhães Brazil 18°47S 42°57W 333 E3
Guanica Puerto Rico 17°58N 66°55W 321 b
Guanipa → Venezuela 9°56N 62°26W 329 B5
Guanling China 25°56N 105°35E 228 E5
Guannan China 34°8N 119°21E 227 G10
Guanshuo China 23°4N 113°22E 121 B3
Guanta Venezuela 10°14N 64°36W 329 A5
Guantánamo Cuba 20°10N 75°14W 321 B4
Guantánamo B. Cuba 19°59N 75°10W 321 C4
Guantao China 36°42N 115°25E 226 F8
Guanting Shuiku China 40°14N 115°35E 226 D8
Guanyang China 25°30N 111°8E 229 E8
Guanyun China 34°20N 119°18E 227 G10
Guapay = Grande → Bolivia 15°51S 64°39W 331 D5
Guapí Colombia 2°36N 77°54W 328 C2
Guápiles Costa Rica 10°10N 83°46W 320 D3
Guapo → Trin. & Tob. 10°11N 61°40W 323 t
Guapo B. Trin. & Tob. 10°12N 61°41W 323 t
Guaporé = Rondônia Brazil 10°52S 61°57W 331 C5
Guaporé Brazil 28°51S 51°54W 335 B5
Guaporé → Brazil 11°55S 65°4W 331 C4
Guaquí Bolivia 16°41S 68°54W 330 D4
Guara, Sierra de Spain 42°19N 0°15W 196 C4
Guarabira Brazil 6°51S 35°29W 332 C4
Guaracara → Trin. & Tob. 10°18N 61°28W 323 t
Guarachirá → Colombia 5°27N 70°36W 328 B3
Guaranda Ecuador 1°36S 79°0W 328 D2
Guarani = Pacajus Brazil 4°10S 38°31W 332 B4
Guarapari Brazil 20°40S 40°30W 333 F3
Guarapuava Brazil 25°20S 51°30W 333 G1
Guaratinguetá Brazil 22°49S 45°9W 335 A6
Guaratuba Brazil 25°53S 48°38W 335 B6
Guarda Portugal 40°32N 7°20W 194 E3
Guarda □ Portugal 40°40N 7°20W 194 E3
Guardafui, C. = Asir, Ras Somali Rep. 11°55N 51°10E 267 B7
Guardamar del Segura Spain 38°5N 0°39W 197 G4
Guardavalle Italy 38°30N 16°30E 201 D9
Guárdia Sanframondi Italy 41°15N 14°36E 201 A7
Guardiagrele Italy 42°11N 14°13E 199 F11
Guardo Spain 42°47N 4°50W 196 C6
Guareña Spain 38°51N 6°6W 195 G4
Guareña → Spain 41°29N 5°23W 194 D5
Guari Papua N. G. 8°3S 146°52E 286 E4
Guárico □ Venezuela 8°40N 66°35W 328 B4
Guarrojo → Colombia 4°6N 70°42W 328 C3
Guarujá Brazil 24°2S 46°25W 335 A6
Guarulhos Brazil 23°29S 46°33W 335 A6
Guasave Mexico 25°34N 108°27W 318 B3
Guascama, Pta. Colombia 2°32N 78°24W 328 C2
Guasdualito Venezuela 7°15N 70°44W 328 B3
Guasipati Venezuela 7°28N 61°54W 329 B5
Guasopa Papua N. G. 9°12S 152°56E 286 F7
Guastalla Italy 44°55N 10°39E 198 D7
Guatemala Guatemala 14°40N 90°22W 320 D1
Guatemala ■ Cent. Amer. 15°40N 90°30W 320 C1
Guatemala Basin Pac. Oc. 11°0N 95°0W 289 F18
Guatemala Trench Pac. Oc. 14°0N 95°0W 292 H10
Guatire Venezuela 10°28N 66°32W 328 A4
Guatopo △ Venezuela 10°5N 66°30W 328 A4
Guatuaro Pt. Trin. & Tob. 10°19N 60°59W 323 t
Guavi → Papua N. G. 7°48S 143°16E 286 D2
Guaviare □ Colombia 2°0N 72°30W 328 C3
Guaviare → Colombia 4°3N 67°44W 328 C4
Guaxupé Brazil 21°10S 47°5W 335 A6
Guayabero → Colombia 2°36N 72°47W 328 C3
Guayaguayare Trin. & Tob. 10°8N 61°2W 323 t
Guayaguayare B. Trin. & Tob. 10°7N 61°2W 323 t
Guayama Puerto Rico 17°59N 66°7W 321 C6
Guayaneco, Arch. Chile 47°45S 75°10W 336 C1
Guayanilla Puerto Rico 18°1N 66°47W 321 b
Guayaquil Ecuador 2°15S 79°52W 328 D2
Guayaquil Baja Calif., Mexico 29°59N 115°4W 318 B1
Guayaquil, G. de Ecuador 3°10S 81°0W 328 D1
Guayaramerín Bolivia 10°48S 65°23W 331 C4
Guayas → Ecuador 2°36S 79°52W 328 D2
Guaymas Mexico 27°56N 110°54W 318 B2
Guaynabo Puerto Rico 18°22N 66°7W 321 b
Guba Dem. Rep. of the Congo 10°38S 26°27E 269 E2
Guba Ethiopia 11°17N 35°20E 257 E4
Gûbâl, Madîq Egypt 27°30N 34°0E 256 B3
Gubam Papua N. G. 8°39S 141°53E 286 E1
Guban Somali Rep. 10°30N 44°0E 267 B5
Gubat Phil. 12°55N 124°7E 233 E6
Gubbi India 13°19N 76°56E 245 H3
Gúbbio Italy 43°21N 12°35E 199 E9
Guben Germany 51°57N 14°42E 178 D10
Gubin Poland 51°57N 14°43E 185 G1
Gubio Nigeria 12°30N 12°42E 263 C7
Gubkin Russia 51°17N 37°32E 189 G9
Gubkinskiy Russia 64°27N 76°36E 214 C8
Guča Serbia 43°46N 20°15E 202 C4
Gucheng China 32°20N 111°30E 229 A8
Gudå Norway 63°27N 11°36E 164 A8
Gudalur India 11°30N 76°29E 245 J3
Gudauta Georgia 43°7N 40°32E 191 J5
Gudbrandsdalen Norway 61°33N 10°10E 164 C7
Guddu Barrage Pakistan 28°30N 69°50E 242 E3
Gudenå → Denmark 56°29N 10°13E 163 H4
Gudermes Russia 43°24N 46°5E 191 J8
Gudhjem Denmark 55°12N 14°58E 163 J8
Gudivada India 16°30N 81°3E 245 F5
Gudiyattam India 12°57N 78°55E 245 H4
Gudö Sweden 59°12N 18°12E 139 B3
Gudur India 14°12N 79°55E 245 G4
Gudvangen Norway 60°52N 6°49E 164 D3
Guebwiller France 47°55N 7°12E 173 E14
Guecho = Getxo Spain 43°21N 2°59W 196 B2
Guékédou Guinea 8°40N 10°5W 262 D2
Guelb er Rîchât Mauritania 21°7N 11°24W 260 D2
Guéle Mendouka Cameroon 4°23N 12°55E 263 E7
Guélengdeng Chad 10°55N 15°31E 259 F3
Güell, Parque de Spain 41°24N 2°10E 114 A2
Guelma Algeria 36°25N 7°29E 261 A6
Guelma □ Algeria 36°25N 7°25E 261 A6
Guelmine = Goulimine Morocco 28°56N 10°0W 260 C3
Guelph Canada 43°35N 80°20W 312 C4
Guelta Zemmur W. Sahara 25°8N 12°22W 260 C2
Guemar Algeria 33°30N 6°49E 261 B6
Guéméné-Penfao France 47°38N 1°50W 172 E5
Guéméné-sur-Scorff France 48°4N 3°13W 172 D3
Guéné Benin 11°44N 3°16E 263 C5
Güeppí Peru 0°7S 75°15W 328 D2
Guer France 47°54N 2°8W 172 E4
Güer Aike Argentina 51°39S 69°35W 336 D3
Guera Chad 11°55N 18°12E 259 F3
Guéra □ Chad 11°30N 18°30E 259 F3
Guérande France 47°20N 2°26W 172 E4
Guerara Algeria 32°51N 4°22E 261 B5
Guercif Morocco 34°14N 3°21W 261 B4
Guéréda Chad 14°31N 22°5E 259 F4
Guéret France 46°11N 1°51E 173 F8
Guérigny France 47°6N 3°10E 173 E10
Guerneville U.S.A. 38°30N 123°0W 306 G4
Guernica = Gernika-Lumo Spain 43°19N 2°40W 196 B2
Guernsey Chan. Is., U.K. 49°26N 2°35W 169 H5
Guernsey Wyo., U.S.A. 42°16N 104°45W 304 E11
Guerrara Algeria 28°5N 0°8W 261 C4
Guerrero Mexico City, Mexico 128 a1
Guerrero □ Mexico 17°40N 100°0W 319 D5
Guerzim Algeria 29°39N 1°40W 261 C4
Guessou-Sud Benin 10°3N 2°38E 263 C5
Gueugnon France 46°36N 4°4E 173 F11
Guéyo Ivory C. 5°25N 6°5W 262 D3
Gufuðalur Iceland 65°34N 22°25W 155 B4
Guggenheim Museum New York, U.S.A. 132 b3
Gughe Ethiopia 6°12N 37°30E 257 F4
Gügher Iran 29°28N 56°27E 247 D8
Guglionesi Italy 41°55N 14°55E 199 G11
Guguan N. Marianas 17°18N 145°51E 302 a
Guhrau = Góra Poland 51°40N 16°31E 185 G3
Gui Jiang → China 23°30N 111°15E 229 F8
Guía Canary Is. 28°8N 15°38W 153 e1
Guía de Isora Canary Is. 28°12N 16°46W 153 e1
Guia Lopes da Laguna Brazil 21°26S 56°7W 335 A4
Guiana Venezuela 5°9N 63°36W 329 B5
Guiana Highlands S. Amer. 5°10N 60°40W 326 C4
Guiana I. Antigua & B. 17°6N 61°44W 322 b
Guibéroua Ivory C. 6°14N 6°10W 262 D3
Guichen B. Australia 37°10S 139°45E 282 D3
Guichi China 30°39N 117°27E 229 B11
Guider Cameroon 9°56N 13°57E 263 D7
Guidiguir Niger 13°40N 9°50E 259 F1
Guidimaka □ Mauritania 15°20N 12°0W 262 B2
Guidimouni Niger 13°42N 9°31E 259 F1
Guiding China 26°34N 107°11E 228 D6
Guidong China 26°7N 113°57E 229 D9
Guidónia-Montecélio Italy 42°1N 12°45E 199 F9
Guiers, L. de Senegal 16°10N 15°50W 262 B1
Guigang China 23°8N 109°35E 228 F7
Guiglo Ivory C. 6°45N 7°30W 262 D3
Guihulngan Phil. 10°7N 123°16E 233 F4
Guijá Mozam. 24°27S 33°0E 271 B5
Guijuelo Spain 40°33N 5°40W 194 E5
Guildford U.K. 51°14N 0°34W 169 F7
Guilford U.S.A. 41°17N 72°41W 313 E12
Guilin China 25°18N 110°15E 229 E8
Guillaume-Delisle, L. Canada 56°15N 76°17W 298 A4
Guillaumes France 44°5N 6°52E 175 D10
Guillestre France 44°39N 6°40E 175 D10
Guilvinec France 47°48N 4°17W 172 E2
Güímar Canary Is. 28°18N 16°24W 153 e1
Guimarães Brazil 2°9S 44°42W 332 B3
Guimarães Portugal 41°28N 8°24W 194 D2
Guimaras □ Phil. 10°35N 122°37E 233 F4
Guimaras Str. Phil. 10°35N 122°48E 233 F4
Guimba Phil. 15°40N 120°46E 232 D3
Guinardó Spain 41°24N 2°10E 114 A2
Guinayangan Phil. 13°54N 122°27E 232 E4
Guinda U.S.A. 38°50N 122°12W 306 G4
Guindulman Phil. 9°46N 124°29E 233 G5
Guinea Africa 8°0N 8°0E 254 F4
Guinea ■ W. Afr. 10°20N 11°30W 262 C2
Guinea, Gulf of Atl. Oc. 3°0N 2°30E 263 E5
Guinea Basin Atl. Oc. 0°0 5°0W 152 G11
Guinea-Bissau ■ Africa 12°0N 15°0W 262 C2
Güines Cuba 22°50N 82°0W 320 B3
Guingamp France 48°34N 3°10W 172 D3
Guinguinéo Senegal 14°20N 15°57W 262 C1
Guinobatan Phil. 13°11N 123°36E 232 E4
Guipavas France 48°26N 4°29W 172 D2
Guiping China 23°21N 110°2E 229 F8
Guipúzcoa □ Spain 43°12N 2°15W 196 B2
Guir Mali 18°52N 2°52W 262 B4
Guir, O. → Algeria 31°29N 2°17W 261 B4
Guiratinga Brazil 16°21S 53°45W 331 D7
Guirel Mauritania 15°30N 7°3W 262 B3
Güiria Venezuela 10°32N 62°18W 329 F8
Guiscard France 49°40N 3°1E 173 C10
Guise France 49°52N 3°35E 173 C10
Guita-Koulouba C.A.R. 5°58N 23°21E 264 A4
Guitiriz Spain 43°11N 7°50W 194 B3
Guitri Ivory C. 5°30N 5°14W 262 D3
Guiuan Phil. 11°5N 125°55E 233 F5
Guixi China 28°16N 117°15E 229 C11
Guiyang Guizhou, China 26°32N 106°40E 228 D6
Guiyang Hunan, China 25°46N 112°42E 229 E9
Guizhou □ China 27°0N 107°0E 228 D6
Gujan-Mestras France 44°38N 1°4W 174 D2
Gujar Khan Pakistan 33°16N 73°19E 242 C5
Gujarat □ India 23°20N 71°0E 242 H4
Gujiang China 27°11N 114°47E 229 D10
Gujiao China 37°54N 112°8E 226 F7
Gujranwala Pakistan 32°10N 74°12E 242 C6
Gujrat Pakistan 32°40N 74°2E 242 C6
Gukovo Russia 48°1N 39°58E 191 F5
Gulargambone Australia 31°20S 148°30E 283 A8
Gulbai Pakistan 24°52N 66°58E 123 A1
Gulbarga India 17°20N 76°50E 244 F3
Gulbene Latvia 57°8N 26°52E 188 D4
Gülchö Kyrgyzstan 40°19N 73°26E 217 D8
Guledagudda India 16°3N 75°48E 244 F2
Gülek Turkey 37°12N 34°48E 250 A5
Gulf □ Papua N. G. 8°0S 145°0E 286 D3
Gulf, The = Persian Gulf Asia 27°0N 50°0E 247 E6
Gulf Breeze U.S.A. 30°21N 87°9W 317 E2
Gulf Hammock U.S.A. 29°15N 82°43W 317 F7
Gulf Islands ⌂ U.S.A. 30°10N 87°10W 317 K2
Gulfport Fla., U.S.A. 27°44N 82°42W 317 H7
Gulfport Miss., U.S.A. 30°22N 89°6W 315 F10
Gulgong Australia 32°20S 149°49E 283 B8
Gulian China 52°56N 122°21E 219 A13
Gulin China 28°1N 105°50E 228 C5
Gulistan Pakistan 30°30N 66°35E 242 D2
Guliston Uzbekistan 40°29N 68°46E 217 D7
Gulja = Yining China 43°58N 81°10E 217 D10
Gulkana U.S.A. 62°16N 145°23W 303 E11
Gull Lake Canada 50°10N 108°29W 297 C7
Gullbrå Norway 60°50N 6°17E 164 D3
Gullbrandstorp Sweden 56°42N 12°43E 163 H6
Gullbringusýsla □ Iceland 64°0N 22°0W 155 D4
Gullfoss Iceland 64°20N 20°8W 155 C6
Gullhaug Norway 59°30N 10°15E 164 F7
Gullivan B. U.S.A. 25°45N 81°40W 317 K8
Gullspång Sweden 58°59N 14°6E 163 F8
Gullstein Norway 63°13N 8°9E 164 A5
Güllük Turkey 37°14N 27°35E 205 D9
Güllük Dağı △ Turkey 37°0N 30°30E 205 E12
Güllük Korfezi Turkey 37°12N 27°30E 205 D9
Gulma Nigeria 12°40N 4°23E 263 C5
Gulmarg India 34°3N 74°25E 243 B6
Gülnar Turkey 36°19N 33°24E 250 B4
Gulnare Australia 33°27S 138°27E 282 B3
Gülpınar Turkey 39°32N 26°7E 205 B8
Gülşehir Turkey 38°44N 34°37E 212 C6
Gülshat Kazakhstan 46°38N 74°21E 217 C8
Gulsvik Norway 60°24N 9°38E 164 D6
Gulu Uganda 2°48N 32°17E 268 B3
Gŭlŭbovo Bulgaria 42°8N 25°55E 203 D9
Gulud, J. Sudan 11°41N 29°31E 257 E2
Gulwe Tanzania 6°30S 36°25E 268 D4
Gulyaypole = Hulyaypole Ukraine 47°45N 36°21E 189 J9
Gum Lake Australia 32°42S 143°9E 282 B5
Gumaca Phil. 13°55N 122°6E 232 E4
Gumal → Pakistan 31°40N 71°50E 242 D4
Gumbaz Pakistan 30°2N 69°0E 242 D3
Gumbinnen = Gusev Russia 54°35N 22°10E 184 D9
Gumdag Turkmenistan 39°9N 54°56E 216 E4
Gumel Nigeria 12°39N 9°22E 263 C6
Gumi S. Korea 36°10N 128°12E 224 D4
Gumiel de Hizán Spain 41°46N 3°41W 194 D7
Gumla India 23°3N 84°33E 243 H11
Gumlu Australia 19°53S 147°41E 280 B4
Gumma □ Japan 36°30N 138°20E 223 A10
Gummersbach Germany 51°1N 7°34E 178 D3
Gummi Nigeria 12°4N 5°9E 263 C6
Gümüldür Turkey 38°6N 27°0E 205 C9
Gumuljina = Komotini Greece 41°9N 25°26E 203 E9
Gümüşçay Turkey 40°16N 27°17E 203 F11
Gümüşhacıköy Turkey 40°50N 35°18E 212 B6
Gümüşhane Turkey 40°30N 39°30E 213 B8
Gümüşsu Turkey 38°14N 29°1E 205 C11
Gumzai Indonesia 5°28S 134°42E 231 F8
Gun Hill Tower Barbados 13°8N 59°33W 323 f
Gun Pt. Grenada 12°32N 61°37W 323 q
Guna Amara, Ethiopia 11°43N 38°14E 266 B4
Guna Oromiya, Ethiopia 8°18N 39°52E 257 F4
Guna India 24°40N 77°19E 242 G7
Gunbalanya Australia 12°20S 133°4E 278 B5
Gundabooka △ Australia 30°30S 145°20E 281 E4
Gundagai Australia 35°3S 148°6E 283 C8
Gundarehi India 20°57N 81°17E 244 D5
Gundelfingen Germany 48°34N 10°22E 179 G6
Gundji Dem. Rep. of the Congo 2°5N 21°27E 264 B4
Gundlakamma → India 15°30N 80°15E 245 G5
Gundlupet India 11°48N 76°41E 245 J3
Gündoğmuş Turkey 36°48N 32°0E 250 B3
Gunebang Australia 33°1S 146°38E 283 B7
Güney Burdur, Turkey 37°29N 29°34E 205 D11
Güney Denizli, Turkey 38°9N 29°4E 205 C11
Güneydoğu Toroslar Turkey 38°20N 40°30E 213 C9
Gungal Australia 32°17S 150°32E 283 B9
Gungo Angola 10°58S 15°30E 265 E2
Güngören Turkey 41°1N 28°52E 122 B1
Gungu Dem. Rep. of the Congo 5°43S 19°20E 265 D3
Gunisao → Canada 53°56N 97°53W 297 C9
Gunisao L. Canada 53°33N 96°15W 297 C9
Gunjur Gambia 13°12N 16°44W 262 C1
Gunjyal Pakistan 32°20N 71°55E 242 C4
Günlüce Turkey 36°50N 28°20E 205 E10
Gunnarskog Sweden 59°49N 12°34E 162 E6
Gunnbjørn Fjeld Greenland 68°55N 29°47W 154 D8
Gunnebo Sweden 57°44N 16°32E 163 G10
Gunnedah Australia 30°59S 150°15E 283 A9
Gunnersbury U.K. 51°29N 0°17W 125 B2
Gunnewin Australia 25°59S 148°33E 281 D4
Gunningbar Cr. → Australia 31°14S 147°6E 283 A7
Gunnison Colo., U.S.A. 38°33N 106°56W 304 G10
Gunnison Utah, U.S.A. 39°9N 111°49W 304 G8
Gunnison → U.S.A. 39°4N 108°35W 304 G9
Gunsan S. Korea 35°59N 126°45E 224 E3
Guntakal India 15°11N 77°27E 245 G3
Gunter Canada 44°52N 77°32W 312 B7
Guntersville U.S.A. 34°21N 86°18W 315 D11
Guntong Malaysia 4°36N 101°3E 237 K3
Guntur India 16°23N 80°30E 245 F5
Gunung Buda △ Malaysia 4°12N 114°57E 235 B4
Gunung Ciremay △ Indonesia 6°53S 108°24E 235 D3
Gunung Gading △ Malaysia 2°2N 109°52E 235 B3
Gunung Leuser △ Indonesia 3°39N 97°32E 234 B1
Gunung Mulu △ Malaysia 4°6N 114°53E 235 B4
Gunung Palung △ Indonesia 1°9S 110°13E 235 C4
Gunungapi Indonesia 6°45S 126°30E 231 F7
Gunungsitoli Indonesia 1°15N 97°30E 234 B1
Gunungtua Indonesia 1°30N 99°37E 234 B1
Gunupur India 19°5N 83°50E 244 E6
Günz → Germany 48°27N 10°16E 179 G6
Gunza Angola 10°50S 13°50E 265 E2
Günzburg Germany 48°26N 10°17E 179 G6
Gunzenhausen Germany 49°7N 10°44E 179 F6
Guo He → China 32°59N 117°10E 227 H9
Guomao China 39°54N 116°26E 114 B2
Guoyang China 33°32N 116°12E 226 H9
Gupis Pakistan 36°15N 73°20E 243 A5
Gura Humorului Romania 47°35N 25°53E 183 C10
Gura-Teghii Romania 45°30N 26°25E 183 E11
Gurabo Puerto Rico 18°16N 65°58W 321 b
Gurag Ethiopia 8°20N 38°20E 257 F4
Gurahont Romania 46°16N 22°21E 182 D7
Gurbantüngüt Shamo China 45°8N 87°20E 217 C11
Gurdaspur India 32°5N 75°31E 242 C6
Gurdon U.S.A. 33°55N 93°9W 314 E8
Güre Balıkesir, Turkey 39°36N 26°54E 205 B8
Güre Uşak, Turkey 38°39N 29°10E 205 C11
Gurgaon India 28°27N 77°1E 242 E7
Gurgentepe Turkey 40°51N 37°50E 212 B7
Gurghiu, Munții Romania 46°41N 25°15E 183 D10
Gurgueia → Brazil 6°50S 43°24W 332 C3
Gurha India 25°12N 71°39E 242 G4
Guri, Embalse de Venezuela 7°50N 62°52W 329 B5
Gurimatu Papua N. G. 6°45S 144°45E 286 D3
Gurin Nigeria 9°5N 12°54E 263 D7
Gurinhatã Brazil 19°14S 49°48W 333 E2
Gurjaani Georgia 41°43N 45°52E 191 K7
Gurk → Austria 46°35N 14°31E 180 E7
Gurkfeld = Krško Slovenia 45°57N 15°30E 199 C12
Gurkha Nepal 28°5N 84°40E 243 E11
Gurla Mandhata = Naimona'nyi Feng Nepal 30°26N 81°18E 243 D9
Gurley Australia 29°45S 149°48E 281 D4
Gurnee U.S.A. 42°22N 87°55W 311 B9
Gurnet Point U.S.A. 42°1N 70°34W 313 D14
Guro Mozam. 17°26S 32°30E 269 F3
Gürpınar İstanbul, Turkey 40°59N 28°37E 203 F12
Gürpınar Van, Turkey 38°18N 43°25E 213 C10
Gürsu Turkey 40°13N 29°11E 203 F13
Gurué Mozam. 15°25S 36°58E 269 F4
Guruerage Ethiopia 6°23N 45°31E 267 C6
Gurun Malaysia 5°49N 100°27E 237 K3
Gürün Turkey 38°43N 37°15E 212 C7
Gurupá Brazil 1°25S 51°35W 329 D7
Gurupá, I. Grande de Brazil 1°25S 51°45W 329 D7
Gurupi Brazil 11°43S 49°4W 333 D2
Gurupi → Brazil 1°13S 46°6W 332 B2
Gurupi, Serra do Brazil 5°0S 47°50W 332 C2
Guruwe Zimbabwe 16°40S 30°42E 271 A5
Gurvan Sayhan Uul Mongolia 43°50N 104°0E 226 C3
Guryev = Atyraū Kazakhstan 47°5N 52°0E 187 E9
Guryevsk Russia 54°47N 20°38E 184 D7
Gus-Khrustalnyy Russia 55°42N 40°44E 190 C5
Gusau Nigeria 12°12N 6°40E 263 C6
Gusev Russia 54°35N 22°10E 184 D9
Gushan China 39°50N 123°35E 224 C1
Gushgy = Serhetabat Turkmenistan 35°20N 62°18E 247 C9
Gushi China 32°11N 115°41E 229 A10
Gushiago Ghana 9°55N 0°15W 263 D4
Gushikami Japan 26°7N 127°44E 288 a
Gushikawa Japan 26°21N 127°52E 288 a
Gusinje Montenegro 42°35N 19°50E 202 D3
Gusinoozersk Russia 51°16N 106°27E 215 D11
Gúspini Italy 39°32N 8°37E 200 C1
Güssing Austria 47°3N 16°20E 181 D9
Gustav Holm, Kap Greenland 66°36N 34°15W 154 D7
Gustavia St.-Martin 17°53N 62°51W 322 a
Gustavo A. Madero Mexico 19°29N 99°8W 128 B2
Gustavus U.S.A. 58°25N 135°44W 296 B1
Gustine U.S.A. 37°16N 121°0W 306 H6
Güstrow Germany 53°47N 12°10E 178 B8
Gusum Sweden 58°16N 16°30E 163 F10
Guta = Kolárovo Slovak Rep. 47°54N 18°0E 181 D10
Gütersloh Germany 51°54N 8°24E 178 D4
Gutha Australia 28°58S 115°55E 279 E2
Guthalungra Australia 19°52S 147°50E 280 B4
Guthrie Ont., Canada 44°28N 79°32W 312 B5
Guthrie Okla., U.S.A. 35°53N 97°25W 314 D6
Guthrie Tex., U.S.A. 33°37N 100°19W 314 E4
Guthrie Center U.S.A. 41°41N 94°30W 310 D2
Gutian China 26°32N 118°43E 229 D12
Gutiérrez Bolivia 19°25S 63°34W 331 D5
Guttenberg Iowa, U.S.A. 42°47N 91°6W 310 B5
Guttenberg New York, U.S.A. 132 a1
Guttentag = Dobrodzień Poland 50°45N 18°25E 185 H5
Guttstadt = Dobre Miasto Poland 53°58N 20°26E 184 E7
Gutu Zimbabwe 19°41S 31°9E 271 A5
Gutulia △ Norway 62°2N 12°11E 164 B9
Gutuyevskiy, Ostrov Russia 59°53N 30°15E 137 B1
Guwahati India 26°10N 91°45E 241 B3
Guy Fawkes River △ Australia 30°0S 152°20E 281 D5
Guy-Fayreau, Complexe Montréal, Canada 130 b2
Guyana ■ S. Amer. 5°0N 59°0W 329 C6
Guyancourt France 48°46N 2°4E 134 B1
Guyane française = French Guiana ☑ S. Amer. 4°0N 53°0W 329 C7
Guyang China 41°0N 110°5E 226 D6
Guyenne France 44°30N 0°40E 174 D4
Guymon U.S.A. 36°41N 101°29W 314 C4
Guyotville = Aïn Benian Algeria 36°48N 2°55E 261 A5
Guyra Australia 30°15S 151°40E 281 E5
Guyton U.S.A. 32°20N 81°24W 316 C8
Guyuan Hebei, China 41°37N 115°40E 226 D8
Guyuan Ningxia Huizu, China 36°0N 106°20E 226 F4
Guzar Uzbekistan 38°36N 66°15E 217 E7
Güzelbağ Turkey 36°44N 31°53E 250 B2
Güzelbahçe Turkey 38°21N 26°54E 205 C8
Güzeloluk Turkey 36°47N 34°4E 250 B5
Güzelsu Turkey 36°53N 31°51E 250 B2
Güzelyurt = Morphou Cyprus 35°12N 32°59E 207 E8
Guzhang China 28°42N 109°58E 228 C7
Guzhen China 33°22N 117°18E 227 H9
Guzmán, L. de Mexico 31°20N 107°30W 318 A3
Gvardeysk Russia 54°39N 21°5E 184 D8
Gvardeyskoye Ukraine 45°7N 34°1E 189 K8
Gvarv Norway 59°23N 9°9E 164 E6
Gwa Burma 17°36N 94°34E 241 G5
Gwaai Zimbabwe 19°15S 27°45E 269 F2
Gwaai → Zimbabwe 17°59S 26°52E 269 F2
Gwabegar Australia 30°37S 148°59E 283 A8
Gwadabawa Nigeria 13°28N 5°15E 263 C6
Gwādar Pakistan 25°10N 62°18E 240 D1
Gwagwada Nigeria 10°15N 7°15E 263 C6
Gwaii Haanas △ Canada 52°21N 131°26W 296 C2
Gwalior India 26°12N 78°10E 242 F8
Gwanak S. Korea 37°29N 126°57E 137 C1
Gwanaksan S. Korea 37°27N 126°58E 137 C1
Gwanara Nigeria 8°55N 3°9E 263 D5
Gwanda Zimbabwe 20°55S 29°0E 269 G2
Gwandu Nigeria 12°30N 4°41E 263 C5
Gwane Dem. Rep. of the Congo 4°45N 25°48E 268 B2
Gwang-yang S. Korea 34°58N 127°35E 224 E3
Gwangju S. Korea 35°9N 126°54E 224 E3
Gwangju □ S. Korea 35°10N 126°45E 224 E3
Gwanju = Gwangju S. Korea 35°9N 126°54E 224 E3
Gwaram Nigeria 10°15N 10°25E 263 C7
Gwarzo Nigeria 12°20N 8°55E 263 C6
Gwasero Nigeria 9°29N 3°30E 263 D5
Gwda → Poland 53°3N 16°44E 185 E3
Gweebarra B. Ireland 54°51N 8°23W 166 B3
Gweedore Ireland 55°3N 8°13W 166 A3
Gweru Zimbabwe 19°28S 29°45E 269 F2
Gwi Nigeria 9°0N 7°10E 263 D6
Gwinn U.S.A. 46°19N 87°27W 308 B10
Gwio Kura Nigeria 12°40N 11°2E 263 C7
Gwoza Nigeria 11°5N 13°40E 263 C7
Gwydir → Australia 29°27S 149°48E 281 D4
Gwynedd □ U.K. 52°52N 4°10W 168 E3
Gyál Hungary 47°23N 19°13E 117 B3
Gyáli-patak → Hungary 47°23N 19°7E 117 B2
Gyandzha = Gäncä Azerbaijan 40°45N 46°20E 191 K8
Gyangzê China 29°5N 89°47E 218 F6
Gyaring Hu China 34°50N 97°40E 218 E8
Gydanskiy Poluostrov Russia 70°0N 78°0E 214 C8
Gyeonggi-do □ S. Korea 36°37N 127°15E 224 D3
Gyeongju S. Korea 35°51N 129°14E 224 E4
Gyeongsan S. Korea 35°49N 128°44E 224 E4
Gyeongsangbuk-do □ S. Korea 36°20N 128°45E 224 D4
Gyeongsangnam-do □ S. Korea 35°15N 128°15E 224 E4
Gyeryongsan △ S. Korea 36°20N 127°15E 224 D3
Gyl Norway 62°57N 8°7E 164 B5
Gyldenløve Fjord Greenland 64°15N 40°30W 154 E6
Gympie Australia 26°11S 152°38E 281 D5
Gyobingauk Burma 18°13N 95°39E 241 F5
Gyōda Japan 36°10N 139°30E 223 A11
Gyodongdo S. Korea 37°47N 126°15E 224 D3
Gyomaendrőd Hungary 46°56N 20°50E 182 D5
Gyöngyös Hungary 47°48N 19°56E 182 C4
Győr Hungary 47°41N 17°40E 182 C2
Győr-Moson-Sopron □ Hungary 47°40N 17°20E 182 C2
Gypsum Pt. Canada 61°53N 114°35W 296 A6
Gypsumville Canada 51°45N 98°40W 297 C9
Gyueshevo Bulgaria 42°14N 22°28E 202 D6
Gyula Hungary 46°38N 21°17E 182 D6
Gyumri Armenia 40°47N 43°50E 191 K6
Gyzylarbat = Serdar Turkmenistan 39°4N 56°23E 247 B8
Gyzyletrek = Etrek Turkmenistan 37°36N 54°46E 247 B7
Gzhatsk = Gagarin Russia 55°38N 35°0E 188 E8
Gzira Malta 35°54N 14°29E 206 F7

H

H. Neely Henry L. U.S.A. 33°55N 86°2W 316 B3
Ha 'Arava → Israel 30°50N 35°20E 251 H6
Ha Coi Vietnam 21°26N 107°46E 228 G6
Ha Dong Vietnam 20°58N 105°46E 228 G5
Ha Giang Vietnam 22°50N 104°59E 228 F5
Ha Karmel △ Israel 32°45N 35°5E 250 F6
Ha Long = Hong Gai Vietnam 20°57N 107°5E 228 G6
Ha Long, Vinh Vietnam 20°56N 107°3E 236 B6
Ha Tien Vietnam 10°23N 104°29E 237 G5
Ha Tinh Vietnam 18°20N 105°54E 236 C5
Ha Trung Vietnam 19°58N 105°50E 236 C5
Haaga Finland 60°13N 24°53E 121 B2
Haakon VII Topp Norway 71°0N 8°20W 154 C10
Haaksbergen Neths. 52°9N 6°45E 170 B6
Ha'ano Tonga 19°41S 174°18W 287 P13
Ha'apai Group Tonga 19°47S 174°27W 287 P13
Haapiti Moorea 17°34S 149°52W 289 e
Haapsalu Estonia 58°56N 23°30E 188 C2
Haar Germany 48°6N 11°43E 131 B3
Haarby Denmark 55°13N 10°7E 163 J4
Haarlem Neths. 52°23N 4°39E 170 B4
Haas-Lilienthal House San Francisco, U.S.A. 136 b1
Haast N.Z. 43°51S 169°1E 285 D4
Haast → N.Z. 43°50S 169°2E 285 D4
Haast Pass N.Z. 44°6S 169°21E 285 E4
Haasts Bluff Australia 23°22S 132°0E 278 D5
Haasts Bluff ◎ Australia 23°39S 130°34E 278 D5
Hab → Pakistan 24°53N 66°41E 242 G3
Hab Nadi Chauki Pakistan 25°0N 66°50E 242 G2
Habahe China 48°3N 86°23E 217 C11
Ḥabarūt Yemen 17°18N 52°44E 249 C5
Habaswein Kenya 1°2N 39°30E 268 B4
Ḥabawnah, W. → Si. Arabia 17°57N 44°58E 248 C4
Habay Alta., Canada 58°50N 118°44W 296 B5
Habay Manila, Phil. 14°27N 120°56E 127 C1
Ḥabbān Yemen 14°21N 47°5E 248 D4
Ḥabbānīyah Iraq 33°17N 43°29E 213 F10
Ḥabbānīyah, Hawr al Iraq 33°17N 43°29E 213 F10
Habelschwerdt = Bystrzyca Kłodzka Poland 50°19N 16°39E 185 H3
Habibas, Îles Algeria 35°44N 1°8W 197 K3
Habichtswald ⌂ Germany 51°15N 9°15E 178 D5
Habiganj Bangla. 24°24N 91°30E 241 C3
Habirag China 42°17N 115°42E 226 C8
Habisa Sudan 15°38N 31°18E 266 A3
Habo Sweden 57°55N 14°6E 163 G8
Haboro Japan 44°22N 141°42E 220 B10
Ḥabshān U.A.E. 23°50N 53°37E 247 F7
Hachenburg Germany 50°40N 7°49E 178 E3
Hachi India 27°48N 94°2E 241 B5
Hachijō-Jima Japan 33°5N 139°45E 223 D11
Hachiman Japan 35°45N 136°57E 223 B8
Hachinohe Japan 40°30N 141°29E 220 D10
Hachiōji Japan 35°40N 139°20E 223 B11
Hacı Zeynalabdin Azerbaijan 40°37N 49°33E 191 K9
Hacıbektaş Turkey 38°56N 34°33E 212 C6
Hacılar Turkey 38°38N 35°26E 212 C6
Hack, Mt. Australia 30°45S 138°55E 282 A3
Hackås Sweden 62°56N 14°30E 162 B8
Hackbridge U.K. 51°23N 0°9W 125 B3
Hackensack U.S.A. 40°52N 74°4W 132 A1
Hackensack → U.S.A. 40°42N 74°7W 132 B1
Hackettstown U.S.A. 40°51N 74°50W 313 F10
Hackney □ U.K. 51°33N 0°3W 125 A3
Hackney Wick U.K. 51°32N 0°1W 125 A3
Häckrenmagasinet Sweden 63°15N 13°30E 162 C7
Haco Angola 10°15S 15°44E 265 E3
Hadali Pakistan 32°16N 72°11E 242 C5
Hadano Japan 35°22N 139°14E 223 B11
Hadarba, Ras Sudan 22°4N 36°51E 256 C4
Hadarom □ Israel 31°0N 35°0E 251 H6
Ḥaḍbaram Oman 17°27N 55°15E 249 C6
Ḥadd, Ra's al Oman 22°35N 59°50E 249 B7
Ḥaddā Si. Arabia 21°27N 39°34E 248 B2
Haddington U.K. 55°57N 2°47W 167 F6
Haddock U.S.A. 33°2N 83°26W 316 B6
Haddummati Atoll Maldives 2°0N 73°30E 272 d
Hadejia Nigeria 12°30N 10°5E 263 C7
Hadejia → Nigeria 12°50N 10°51E 263 C7
Ḥadera Israel 32°27N 34°55E 251 F5
Hadersleben = Haderslev Denmark 55°15N 9°30E 163 J3
Haderslev Denmark 55°15N 9°30E 163 J3
Hadgaon India 19°30N 77°40E 244 E3
Hadhramaut = Ḥaḍramawt Yemen 15°30N 49°30E 249 D5
Hadīboh Yemen 12°39N 54°2E 249 D6
Hadilik China 37°56N 86°6E 217 E11
Hadım Turkey 36°58N 32°26E 250 B3
Hadithah Si. Arabia 31°27N 37°9E 251 G8
Hadjadj, O. el → Algeria 28°18N 5°20E 261 C6
Hadjeb el Aïoun Tunisia 35°21N 9°32E 258 A1
Hadjer Kamaran Chad 12°41N 21°46E 259 F4
Hadjer-Lamis □ Chad 12°55N 16°0E 259 F3
Hadjer Mornou Chad 17°12N 23°8E 259 E4
Hadlaskar Norway 60°15N 7°9E 164 D4
Hadley B. Canada 72°31N 108°12W 294 C10
Hadong S. Korea 35°5N 127°44E 224 E3
Hadr, Warrâq el Egypt 30°5N 31°12E 117 A2
Ḥaḍramawt Yemen 15°30N 49°30E 249 D5
Ḥaḍramawt, W. → Yemen 15°10N 51°8E 249 D5
Ḥadrānīyah Iraq 35°38N 43°14E 246 C4
Hadrian's Wall U.K. 55°0N 2°30W 168 B5
Hadsten Denmark 56°19N 10°3E 163 H4
Hadsund Denmark 56°44N 10°8E 163 H4
Hadyach Ukraine 50°21N 34°0E 189 G8
Hae, Ko Thailand 7°44N 98°22E 237 a
Hægeland Norway 58°22N 7°45E 164 F4
Haeinsa S. Korea 35°45N 128°10E 224 E4
Haeju N. Korea 38°3N 125°45E 224 C2
Haeju-man N. Korea 37°54N 125°45E 224 D2
Hā'ena U.S.A. 22°14N 159°34W 302 A2
Haenam S. Korea 34°34N 126°35E 224 E3
Haenertsburg S. Africa 24°0S 29°50E 271 B4
Haerhpin = Harbin China 45°48N 126°40E 227 B14
Hafar al Bāṭin Si. Arabia 28°32N 45°52E 246 D5
Hafik Turkey 39°51N 37°23E 212 C7
Ḥafīrat al 'Aydā Si. Arabia 26°26N 39°12E 246 E3
Ḥafit Oman 23°59N 55°49E 247 F7
Hafizabad Pakistan 32°5N 73°40E 242 C5
Haflong India 25°10N 93°5E 241 C4
Hafnarfjörður Iceland 64°4N 21°57W 155 C5
Hafnir Iceland 63°56N 22°41W 155 D4
Hafslo Norway 61°19N 7°10E 164 C4
Haft Gel Iran 31°30N 49°32E 247 D6
Haga Sweden 59°21N 18°1E 139 A2
Hagalil Israel 32°53N 35°18E 250 F6
Hagari → India 15°40N 77°0E 245 G3
Hagby Sweden 56°34N 16°11E 163 H10
Hagemeister I. U.S.A. 58°39N 160°54W 303 G7
Hagen Germany 51°21N 7°27E 178 D3
Hagenbrunn Austria 48°19N 16°27E 142 A2
Hagenow Germany 53°26N 11°12E 178 B7
Hagere Hiywet Ethiopia 8°59N 37°51E 266 C4
Hagerman U.S.A. 33°7N 104°20W 305 K11
Hagerman Fossil Beds ⌂ U.S.A. 42°48N 114°57W 304 E6
Hägersten Sweden 59°18N 17°59E 139 B1
Hagerstown Ind., U.S.A. 39°55N 85°10W 311 E11
Hagerstown Md., U.S.A. 39°39N 77°43W 309 F15
Hagersville Canada 42°58N 80°3W 312 D4
Hagetmau France 43°39N 0°37W 174 E3
Hagfors Sweden 60°3N 13°45E 162 D7
Häggvik Sweden 59°26N 17°56E 139 A1
Hagi Iceland 65°28N 23°25W 155 B3
Hagi Japan 34°30N 131°22E 222 C3
Hagolan Syria 33°0N 35°45E 250 F6
Hagondange France 49°16N 6°11E 173 C13
Hágöngulón Iceland 64°35N 18°8W 155 C8
Hagonoy Bulacan, Phil. 14°50N 120°44E 232 D3
Hagonoy Manila, Phil. 14°31N 121°3E 127 B2
Hags Hd. Ireland 52°57N 9°28W 166 D2
Hague, C. de la France 49°44N 1°56W 172 C5
Hague, The = 's-Gravenhage Neths. 52°7N 4°17E 170 B4
Hague Park Canada 43°45N 79°14W 141 A3
Haguenau France 48°49N 7°47E 173 D14
Hagunía W. Sahara 27°26N 12°24W 260 C2
Hahira U.S.A. 30°59N 83°22W 316 E6
Hai Duong Vietnam 20°56N 106°19E 228 G6
Hai'an Guangdong, China 20°18N 110°11E 229 G8
Hai'an Jiangsu, China 32°37N 120°27E 229 A13
Haian Shanmo Taiwan 23°25N 121°25E 225 C3
Haicheng China 40°50N 122°45E 224 B1
Haidar Khel Afghan. 33°58N 68°38E 242 C3
Haidarâbâd = Hyderabad India 17°22N 78°29E 244 F4
Haidargarh India 26°37N 81°22E 243 F9
Haidari = Chaidari Greece 38°2N 23°38E 112 A1
Haidarpur India 28°43N 77°8E 120 A1
Haidhausen Germany 48°7N 11°36E 131 B2
Haidian China 39°59N 116°16E 114 B1
Haifa = Ḥefa Israel 32°46N 35°0E 250 F6
Haifeng China 22°58N 115°10E 229 F10
Haiger Germany 50°43N 8°12E 178 E4
Haight-Ashbury U.S.A. 37°46N 122°26W 136 B2
Haikou China 20°1N 110°16E 236 B8
Haiku-Pauwela U.S.A. 20°56N 156°19W 302 C5
Ḥā'īl Si. Arabia 27°28N 41°45E 246 E4
Ḥā'īl □ Si. Arabia 26°40N 41°40E 246 E4
Hailakandi India 24°42N 92°34E 241 C4
Hailar China 49°10N 119°38E 219 B12
Hailey U.S.A. 43°31N 114°19W 304 E6
Haileybury Canada 47°30N 79°38W 298 C4
Hailin China 44°37N 129°30E 227 B15
Hailing Dao China 21°35N 111°47E 229 G8
Hailun China 47°28N 126°50E 219 B14
Hailuoto Finland 65°3N 24°45E 160 D21
Haimen Guangdong, China 23°15N 116°38E 229 F11
Haimen Jiangsu, China 31°52N 121°10E 229 B13
Hainan □ China 19°0N 109°30E 236 C7
Hainan Dao China 19°0N 109°30E 236 C7
Hainan Str. = Qiongzhou Haixia China 20°10N 110°15E 236 B8
Hainault U.K. 51°36N 0°6E 125 A4
Hainaut □ Belgium 50°30N 4°0E 170 D4
Hainburg Austria 48°9N 16°56E 181 C9
Haines Alaska, U.S.A. 59°14N 135°26W 296 B1
Haines Oreg., U.S.A. 44°55N 117°56W 304 D5
Haines City U.S.A. 28°7N 81°38W 317 G8
Haines Junction Canada 60°45N 137°30W 296 A1
Hainfeld Austria 48°3N 15°48E 180 C8
Haining China 30°28N 120°40E 229 B13
Haiphong Vietnam 20°47N 106°41E 228 G6
Haitan Dao China 25°30N 119°45E 229 E12
Haiti ■ W. Indies 19°0N 72°30W 321 C5
Haiya Sudan 18°20N 36°21E 256 D4
Haiyan Qinghai, China 36°53N 100°59E 218 D9
Haiyan Zhejiang, China 30°28N 120°58E 229 B13
Haiyang China 36°47N 121°9E 227 F11
Haiyang Dao China 39°2N 123°10E 224 C1
Haiyuan Guangxi Zhuangzu, China 22°8N 107°35E 228 F6
Haiyuan Ningxia Huizu, China 36°35N 105°52E 226 F3
Haizhou Guangdong, China 23°5N 113°18E 121 B2
Haizhou Jiangsu, China 34°37N 119°7E 227 G10
Haizhou Wan China 34°50N 119°20E 227 G10
Haizhu Guangchang China 23°6N 113°14E 121 B2
Haj Ali Qoli, Kavīr Iran 35°55N 54°50E 247 C7
Hajar Bangar Sudan 10°40N 22°45E 259 F4
Hajdú-Bihar □ Hungary 47°30N 21°30E 182 C6
Hajdúböszörmény Hungary 47°40N 21°30E 182 C6
Hajdúdorog Hungary 47°48N 21°30E 182 C6
Hajdúhadház Hungary 47°40N 21°40E 182 C6
Hajdúnánás Hungary 47°50N 21°26E 182 C6
Hajdúsámson Hungary 47°37N 21°42E 182 C6
Hajdúszoboszló Hungary 47°27N 21°22E 182 C6
Haji Ibrahim Iraq 36°40N 44°30E 213 D11
Hājīābād Iran 33°37N 60°0E 247 C9
Hajiganj Bangla. 23°15N 90°50E 241 D3
Hajipur India 25°45N 85°13E 243 G11
Ḥajjah Yemen 15°42N 43°36E 248 D3
Ḥājjīābād Iran 28°19N 55°55E 247 D7
Ḥājjīābād-e Zarrīn Iran 33°9N 54°51E 247 C7
Hajnówka Poland 52°47N 23°35E 185 F10
Hajodo S. Korea 34°17N 126°3E 224 E3

Ḥajrah Si. Arabia 20°14N 41°3E **248** B3
Haka Burma 22°39N 93°37E **241** D4
Hakansson, Mts.
Dem. Rep. of the Congo 8°40S 25°45E **265** D5
Hakataramea N.Z. 44°43S 170°30E **285** E5
Hakkâri Turkey 37°34N 43°44E **213** D10
Hakkâri □ Turkey 37°30N 44°0E **213** D10
Hakkâri Dağları Turkey 38°2N 42°58E **213** C10
Hakken-Zan Japan 34°10N 135°54E **223** C7
Hakkōda San Japan 40°50N 141°0E **220** D10
Hakodate Japan 41°45N 140°44E **220** D10
Hakos Namibia 23°13S 16°21E **270** B2
Hakota Japan 36°5N 140°30E **223** A12
Håksberg Sweden 60°11N 15°12E **162** D9
Hakskeenpan S. Africa 26°48S 20°13E **270** C3
Haku-San Japan 36°9N 136°46E **223** A8
Haku-San △ Japan 36°15N 136°45E **223** A8
Hakuba Japan 36°42N 137°51E **223** A9
Hakui Japan 36°53N 136°47E **221** F8
Hakun Burma 26°46N 95°42E **241** B5
Hakunila Finland 60°16N 25°6E **121** B3
Hakupu Cook Is. 19°6S 169°50W **289** g
Hala Pakistan 25°43N 68°20E **240** D3
Ḥalab Syria 36°10N 37°15E **250** B8
Ḥalab □ Syria 36°10N 37°10E **250** B8
Ḥalaban Si. Arabia 23°29N 44°23E **248** B4
Ḥalabjah Iraq 35°10N 45°58E **213** E11
Halaib Sudan 22°12N 36°30E **256** C4
Halaib Triangle Africa 22°30N 35°20E **256** C4
Halandri = Chalandri
Greece 38°3N 23°48E **112** A2
Halangingie Pt. Cook Is. 19°2S 169°58W **289** g
Halasa Sudan 14°26N 30°39E **257** E3
Halásztelek Hungary 47°22N 19°0E **117** B1
Hālat 'Ammār Si. Arabia 29°10N 36°4E **246** D3
Hālawa, C. U.S.A. 21°10N 156°43W **302** B5
Hālawa Heights U.S.A. 21°23N 157°55W **302** K14
Halbā Lebanon 34°34N 36°6E **250** D7
Halberstadt Germany 51°54N 11°3E **178** D7
Halcombe N.Z. 40°8S 175°30E **284** G4
Halcon, Mt. Phil. 13°16N 121°0E **232** E3
Halde Fjäll = Haltiatunturi
Finland 69°17N 21°18E **160** B19
Halden Norway 59°9N 11°23E **164** E8
Haldensleben Germany 52°17N 11°24E **178** C7
Haldia Bangla. 22°1N 88°3E **243** H13
Haldwani India 29°31N 79°30E **243** E8
Hale U.S.A. 39°36N 93°20W **310** E3
Hale → Australia 24°56S 135°53E **280** C2
Haleakalā △ U.S.A. 20°40N 156°15W **302** C5
Hale'iwa U.S.A. 21°36N 158°6W **302** J13
Halesowen U.K. 52°27N 2°3W **169** E5
Halesworth U.K. 52°20N 1°31E **169** E9
Haleyville U.S.A. 34°14N 87°37W **315** D11
Half Assini Ghana 5°1N 2°50W **262** D4
Half Dome U.S.A. 37°44N 119°32E **306** H7
Halfa al Jadidah Sudan 15°20N 35°35E **266** A4
Halfeti Turkey 37°15N 37°52E **212** D7
Halfmoon Bay N.Z. 46°50S 168°5E **285** G3
Halfway → Canada 56°12N 121°32W **296** B4
Halfway Tree Jamaica 18°0N 76°48W **320** a
Halia India 24°50N 82°19E **243** G10
Haliburton Canada 45°3N 78°30W **312** A6
Haliç Turkey 41°1N 28°57E **122** B1
Halifax Queens., Australia 18°32S 146°22E **280** B4
Halifax N.S., Canada 44°38N 63°35W **299** D7
Halifax W. Yorks., U.K. 53°43N 1°52W **168** D6
Halifax Pa., U.S.A. 40°25N 76°55W **312** F8
Halifax B. Australia 18°50S 147°0E **280** B4
Halifax Harbour Grenada 12°6N 61°45W **323** q
Halifax I. Namibia 26°38S 15°4E **270** C2
Halik Shan China 42°20N 81°22E **217** D10
Halīl → Iran 27°40N 58°30E **247** E8
Halim Perdana Kusuma Int. ✕
(HLP) Indonesia 6°16S 106°53E **122** B2
Halimun △ Indonesia 6°42S 106°26E **234** D3
Halkett, C. U.S.A. 70°48N 152°11W **303** A9
Halki = Chalki Greece 36°17N 27°35E **205** E9
Halkida = Chalkida
Greece 38°27N 23°42E **204** C5
Halkidiki = Chalkidiki □
Greece 40°25N 23°20E **202** F7
Halkirk U.K. 58°30N 3°29W **167** C5
Hall Beach Canada 68°46N 81°12W **295** D15
Hall I. U.S.A. 60°40N 173°6W **303** F4
Hall in Tirol Austria 47°17N 11°30E **180** D4
Hall Pen. Canada 63°30N 66°0W **295** E18
Hall Pt. Australia 15°40S 124°23E **278** C3
Hallabro Sweden 56°22N 15°5E **163** H9
Halland Sweden 57°8N 12°47E **161** H15
Hallandale Beach U.S.A. 25°58N 80°8W **317** K9
Hallands län □ Sweden 57°0N 12°40E **163** H6
Hallands Väderö Sweden 56°27N 12°34E **163** H6
Hallandsås Sweden 56°22N 13°0E **163** H7
Hallāniyat, Ghubbat al
Oman 17°40N 55°45E **249** C6
Hallāniyat, Jazā'ir al
Oman 17°30N 55°58E **249** C6
Hallasan S. Korea 33°22N 126°32E **224** a
Hallasan △ S. Korea 33°20N 126°30E **224** a
Hällbybrunn Sweden 59°24N 16°25E **162** E10
Halle Belgium 50°44N 4°13E **116** B1
Halle Nordrhein-Westfalen,
Germany 52°3N 8°22E **178** C4
Halle Sachsen-Anhalt,
Germany 51°30N 11°56E **178** D7
Hällefors Sweden 59°47N 14°31E **162** E8
Hälleforsnäs Sweden 59°10N 16°30E **162** E10
Hallein Austria 47°40N 13°5E **180** D6
Hällekis Sweden 58°38N 13°27E **163** F7
Hallen Sweden 63°11N 14°4E **162** A8
Hallett Australia 33°25S 138°55E **282** B3
Hallettsville U.S.A. 29°27N 96°57W **314** G6
Halley Antarctica 75°35S 26°39W **151** D1
Hallia → India 16°55N 79°20E **244** F4
Hallim S. Korea 33°24N 126°15E **224** a
Hallingby Norway 60°7N 10°10E **164** D7
Hallingdal Norway 60°40N 9°8E **164** D6
Hallingdalselva → Norway 60°23N 9°35E **164** D6
Hallingskarvet Norway 60°36N 7°47E **164** D4
Hallingskarvet △ Norway 60°37N 7°45E **164** D4
Hallingskeid Norway 60°40N 7°17E **164** D4
Hallock U.S.A. 48°47N 96°57W **308** A5
Hallormsstaður Iceland 65°6N 14°45W **155** B12
Halls Creek Australia 18°16S 127°38E **278** C4
Halls Gap Australia 37°8S 142°34E **281** F3
Halls Lake Canada 45°7N 78°45W **312** A6
Hallsberg Sweden 59°5N 15°7E **162** E9
Hallstahammar Sweden 59°38N 16°15E **162** E10
Hallstatt Austria 47°33N 13°38E **180** D6
Hallstavik Sweden 60°5N 18°37E **162** D12
Hallstead U.S.A. 41°58N 75°45W **313** E9
Hallyeo △ S. Korea 34°45N 128°25E **224** E4
Halmahera Indonesia 0°40N 128°0E **231** D7
Halmeu Romania 47°57N 23°2E **182** C8
Halmstad Sweden 56°41N 12°52E **163** H6
Halq el Oued Tunisia 36°53N 10°18E **258** A2
Hals Denmark 57°0N 10°18E **163** H4
Halsa Norway 63°3N 8°14E **164** A5
Halsafjorden Norway 63°5N 8°10E **164** A5
Hälsingborg = Helsingborg
Sweden 56°3N 12°42E **163** H6
Hälsingland Sweden 61°40N 16°5E **162** C10
Halstead U.K. 51°57N 0°40E **169** F8
Haltdalen Norway 62°56N 11°8E **164** B8
Haltern Germany 51°44N 7°11E **178** D3
Haltiala Finland 60°16N 24°57E **121** B2
Haltiatunturi Finland 69°17N 21°18E **160** B19
Haltiavuori Finland 60°16N 24°56E **121** B2
Halton □ U.K. 53°22N 2°45W **168** D5
Haltwhistle U.K. 54°58N 2°26W **168** C5
Ḥālūl Qatar 25°40N 52°40E **247** E7
Halvad India 23°1N 71°11E **242** H4
Ḥalvān Iran 33°57N 56°15E **247** C8
Halve Dag, Pt. Curaçao 12°14N 69°7W **322** g
Ham Chad 10°1N 15°35E **259** F3
Ham Somme, France 49°45N 3°4E **173** C10
Ham London, U.K. 51°25N 0°18W **125** B2
Hamab Namibia 28°7S 19°16E **270** C2
Hamad Sudan 15°20N 33°32E **257** D3
Hamada Japan 34°56N 132°4E **222** C4
Hamadān Iran 34°52N 48°32E **213** E13
Hamadān □ Iran 35°0N 49°0E **247** C6
Hamadia Algeria 35°28N 1°57E **261** A5
Ḥamāh Syria 35°5N 36°40E **250** C7
Ḥamāh □ Syria 35°10N 37°0E **250** C8
Hamakita Japan 34°45N 137°47E **223** C9
Hamamatsu Japan 34°45N 137°45E **223** C9
Haman S. Korea 35°14N 128°28E **224** E4
Hamar Norway 60°48N 11°7E **164** D8
Hamâta, Gebel Egypt 24°17N 35°0E **246** E2
Hamatonbetsu Japan 45°10N 142°20E **220** B11
Hambantota Sri Lanka 6°10N 81°10E **245** L5
Hamber △ Canada 52°20N 118°0W **296** C5
Hamburg Hamburg,
Germany 53°33N 9°59E **178** B5
Hamburg Ark., U.S.A. 33°14N 91°48W **314** E9
Hamburg N.Y., U.S.A. 42°43N 78°50W **312** D6
Hamburg Pa., U.S.A. 40°33N 75°59W **313** F9
Hamburg □ Germany 53°30N 10°0E **178** B5
Hamburg Fuhlsbüttel ✕ (HAM)
Germany 53°35N 9°59E **178** B5
Ḥamḍ, W. al → Si. Arabia 24°55N 36°20E **246** E3
Ḥamḍah Si. Arabia 19°2N 43°36E **248** C3
Ḥamdānah Si. Arabia 19°59N 40°34E **248** C3
Hamden U.S.A. 41°23N 72°54W **313** E12
Hamdibey Turkey 39°50N 27°15E **205** B9
Häme Finland 61°38N 25°10E **160** F21
Hämeenkylä Finland 60°16N 24°48E **121** B1
Hämeenlinna Finland 61°0N 24°28E **188** B3
Hamélé Ghana 10°56N 2°45W **262** C4
Hamelin Pool Australia 26°22S 114°20E **279** E1
Hameln Germany 52°6N 9°21E **178** C5
Hamerkaz □ Israel 32°15N 34°55E **251** F5
Hamero Hadad Ethiopia 7°27N 42°14E **267** C5
Hamersley Ra. Australia 22°0S 117°45E **278** D2
Hamgyong-sanmaek
N. Korea 41°35N 129°15E **224** B4
Hamgyŏngbuk-do □
N. Korea 41°50N 129°25E **224** B4
Hamgyŏngnam-do □
N. Korea 40°0N 127°30E **224** C3
Hamhŭng N. Korea 39°54N 127°30E **224** C3
Hamhŭng-man N. Korea 39°48N 127°37E **224** C3
Hami China 42°55N 93°25E **218** C7
Hamilton = Churchill →
Canada 53°19N 60°10W **299** B7
Hamilton Vic., Australia 37°45S 142°2E **282** D5
Hamilton Bermuda 32°17N 64°47W **153** a
Hamilton Ont., Canada 43°15N 79°50W **312** C5
Hamilton N.Z. 37°47S 175°19E **284** D4
Hamilton S. Lanarks., U.K. 55°46N 4°2W **167** F4
Hamilton Ala., U.S.A. 34°9N 87°59W **315** D11
Hamilton Alaska, U.S.A. 62°54N 163°53W **303** E7
Hamilton Ga., U.S.A. 32°45N 84°53W **316** C5
Hamilton Ill., U.S.A. 40°24N 91°21W **310** D5
Hamilton Ind., U.S.A. 41°33N 84°56W **311** C12
Hamilton Mo., U.S.A. 39°45N 94°0W **310** E2
Hamilton Mont., U.S.A. 46°15N 114°10W **304** C6
Hamilton N.Y., U.S.A. 42°50N 75°33W **313** D9
Hamilton Ohio, U.S.A. 39°24N 84°34W **311** E12
Hamilton Tex., U.S.A. 31°42N 98°7W **314** F5
Hamilton → Queens.,
Australia 23°30S 139°47E **280** C2
Hamilton → S. Austral.,
Australia 26°40S 135°19E **281** D2
Hamilton City U.S.A. 39°45N 122°1W **306** F4
Hamilton I. Australia 20°21S 148°56E **280** b
Hamilton Inlet Canada 54°0N 57°30W **299** B8
Hamilton Mt. U.S.A. 43°25N 74°22W **313** C10
Hamina Finland 60°34N 27°12E **188** B4
Hamirpur H.P., India 31°41N 76°31E **242** D7
Hamirpur Ut. P., India 25°57N 80°9E **243** G9
Hamitabat Turkey 41°30N 27°17E **203** E11
Hamju N. Korea 39°51N 127°26E **224** C3
Hamlet U.S.A. 34°53N 79°42W **315** D15
Hamley Bridge Australia 34°17S 138°35E **282** C3
Hamlin = Hameln Germany 52°6N 9°21E **178** C5
Hamlin N.Y., U.S.A. 43°17N 77°55W **312** C7
Hamlin Tex., U.S.A. 32°53N 100°8W **314** E4
Hamm Germany 51°40N 7°50E **178** D3
Hammām al Alī Iraq 36°9N 43°15E **213** D10
Hammam Bouhadjar
Algeria 35°23N 0°58W **261** A4
Hammamet Tunisia 36°24N 10°38E **258** A2
Hammamet, G. de Tunisia 36°10N 10°48E **258** A2
Ḥammār, Hawr al Iraq 30°50N 47°10E **246** D5
Hammarby Sweden 59°17N 18°5E **139** B2
Hammarstrand Sweden 63°7N 16°20E **162** A10
Hamme Belgium 50°55N 4°17E **116** A1
Hammelburg Germany 50°6N 9°53E **179** E5
Hammeren Denmark 55°18N 14°47E **163** J8
Hammerfest Norway 70°39N 23°41E **160** A20
Hammersmith U.K. 51°29N 0°14W **125** B2
Hammerstein = Czarne
Poland 53°42N 16°58E **184** E3
Hammerum Denmark 56°8N 9°3E **163** H3
Hamminkeln Germany 51°43N 6°35E **178** D2
Hammond Ind., U.S.A. 41°38N 87°30W **311** C9
Hammond La., U.S.A. 30°30N 90°28W **315** F9
Hammond N.Y., U.S.A. 44°27N 75°42W **313** B9
Hammondsport U.S.A. 42°25N 77°13W **312** D7
Hammonton U.S.A. 39°39N 74°48W **309** F16
Hamoyet, Jebel Sudan 17°33N 38°2E **256** D4
Hampden N.Z. 45°18S 170°50E **285** F5
Hampshire □ U.K. 51°7N 1°23W **169** F6
Hampshire Downs U.K. 51°15N 1°10W **169** F6
Hampstead Qué., Canada 45°29N 73°38W **326** B2
Hampstead Dominica 15°36N 61°23W **323** k
Hampstead London, U.K. 51°33N 0°10W **125** A2
Hampstead Garden Suburb
U.K. 51°34N 0°11W **125** A2
Hampstead Heath U.K. 51°33N 0°10W **125** A2
Hampton N.B., Canada 45°32N 65°51W **299** C6
Hampton Ont., Canada 43°58N 78°45W **312** C6
Hampton London, U.K. 51°24N 0°21W **125** B1
Hampton Ark., U.S.A. 33°32N 92°28W **314** E8
Hampton Ga., U.S.A. 33°23N 84°17W **316** B5
Hampton Iowa, U.S.A. 42°45N 93°13W **310** D8
Hampton N.H., U.S.A. 42°57N 70°50W **313** D14
Hampton S.C., U.S.A. 32°52N 81°7W **316** C8
Hampton Va., U.S.A. 37°2N 76°21W **309** G15
Hampton Bays U.S.A. 40°53N 72°30W **313** F12
Hampton Court Palace
U.K. 51°24N 0°20W **125** B1
Hampton Springs U.S.A. 30°5N 83°40W **316** E6
Hampton Tableland
Australia 32°0S 127°0E **279** F4
Hampton Wick U.K. 51°24N 0°18W **125** B2
Hampyeong S. Korea 35°3N 126°31E **224** E3
Hampyeongman S. Korea 35°6N 126°23E **224** E3
Hamrā' Baghdād, Iraq 33°18N 44°18E **113** B1
Hamra Gävleborg, Sweden 61°39N 14°59E **162** C8
Hamra → Chad 12°52N 21°15E **259** F4
Ḥamrā, Al Ḥamādah al
Libya 29°30N 12°57E **258** C2
Hamrat esh Sheykh
Sudan 14°38N 27°55E **257** E2
Ḥamrin, Jabal Iraq 34°30N 44°30E **213** E11
Hamrun Malta 35°53N 14°29E **206** F8
Hamtik Phil. 10°42N 121°59E **233** F3
Hamur Turkey 39°37N 43°2E **213** C10
Hamyang S. Korea 35°32N 127°42E **224** E3
Hamzalar Turkey 37°7N 32°33E **250** A3
Han i Hotit Albania 42°19N 19°27E **202** D3
Han Jiang → China 23°25N 116°40E **229** F11
Han Shui → China 30°34N 114°17E **229** B10
Hāna U.S.A. 20°45N 155°59W **302** C6
Hanahan U.S.A. 32°55N 80°0W **316** C10
Hanak Si. Arabia 25°32N 37°0E **246** E3
Hanak Turkey 41°14N 42°50E **213** B10
Hanala Finland 60°20N 25°4E **121** A3
Hanalei U.S.A. 22°12N 159°30W **302** A2
Hanamaki Japan 39°23N 141°7E **220** E10
Hanamaulu U.S.A. 21°59N 159°22W **302** B2
Hanang Tanzania 4°30S 35°25E **268** C4
Hanapēpē U.S.A. 21°55N 159°35W **302** B2
Hanare Iwa Iwo Jima 24°48N 141°21E **288** b
Hanau Germany 50°7N 8°56E **179** E4
Hanauma B. U.S.A. 21°15N 157°40W **302** K14
Hanbogd = Ihbulag
Mongolia 43°11N 107°10E **226** C4
Hançalar Turkey 38°8N 29°24E **205** C11
Hâncești Moldova 46°50N 28°36E **183** D13
Hancheng China 35°31N 110°25E **226** G6
Hanchuan China 30°40N 113°50E **229** B9
Hanchung = Hanzhong
China 33°10N 107°1E **228** A6
Hancock Mich., U.S.A. 47°8N 88°35W **308** B9
Hancock N.Y., U.S.A. 41°57N 75°17W **313** E9
Hancock Vt., U.S.A. 43°55N 72°50W **313** C12
Handa Japan 34°53N 136°55E **223** C8
Handa I. U.K. 58°23N 5°11W **167** C3
Handan China 36°35N 114°28E **226** F8
Handeni Tanzania 5°25S 38°2E **268** D4
Handlová Slovak Rep. 48°45N 18°35E **181** C11
Handub Sudan 19°15N 37°16E **256** D4
Handwara India 34°21N 74°20E **243** B6
Haneda Japan 35°32N 139°44E **140** B3
Haneda, Tōkyō ✕ (HND)
Japan 35°33N 139°46E **140** B3
Hanegev Israel 30°50N 35°0E **251** H6
Hanford U.S.A. 36°20N 119°39W **306** J7
Hanford Reach △
U.S.A. 46°40N 119°30W **304** C4
Hang Chat Thailand 18°20N 99°21E **236** C2
Hang Hau China 22°19N 114°16E **122** B2
Hanga Roa Chile 27°8S 109°26W **330** b
Hangang → S. Korea 37°50N 126°30E **227** F14
Hangayn Nuruu Mongolia 47°30N 99°0E **218** B8
Hangchou = Hangzhou
China 30°18N 120°11E **229** B13
Hanger Sweden 57°6N 13°58E **163** G7
Hanggin Houqi China 40°58N 107°4E **226** D4
Hanggin Qi China 39°52N 108°50E **226** E5
Hanging Gardens Mumbai, India **130** b1
Hangkow = Wuhan
China 30°31N 114°18E **229** B10
Hangku = Hangu China 39°18N 117°53E **227** E9
Hangu China 39°18N 117°53E **227** E9
Hangzhou China 30°18N 120°11E **229** B13
Hangzhou Wan China 30°15N 120°45E **229** B13
Hanh Mongolia 51°32N 100°35E **218** A9
Hanhöhiy Uul Mongolia 49°30N 94°30E **217** C12
Hanhongor Mongolia 43°55N 104°28E **226** C3
Hani Turkey 38°24N 40°23E **213** C9
Hania = Chania Greece 35°30N 24°4E **207** E5
Ḥanīdh Si. Arabia 26°35N 48°38E **247** E6
Ḥanīsh Yemen 13°45N 42°46E **248** D3
Haniska Slovak Rep. 48°37N 21°15E **181** C14
Hanjiang China 25°26N 119°6E **229** E12
Hankinson U.S.A. 46°4N 96°54W **308** B5
Hankö Finland 59°50N 22°57E **188** C2
Hankou China 30°35N 114°30E **229** B10
Hanksville U.S.A. 38°22N 110°43W **304** G8
Hanle India 32°42N 79°4E **243** C8
Hanlon Canada 43°38N 79°39W **141** B1
Hanmer Springs N.Z. 42°32S 172°50E **285** C7
Hann → Australia 17°26S 126°17E **278** C4
Hann, Mt. Australia 15°45S 126°0E **278** C4
Hanna Alta., Canada 51°40N 111°54W **296** C6
Hanna Wyo., U.S.A. 41°52N 106°34W **304** F10
Hannah B. Canada 51°40N 80°0W **298** B4
Hannibal Mo., U.S.A. 39°42N 91°22W **310** E5
Hannibal N.Y., U.S.A. 43°19N 76°35W **313** C8
Hannik Sudan 18°12N 32°20E **256** D3
Hannover Germany 52°22N 9°46E **178** C5
Hanō Sweden 56°1N 14°50E **163** H8
Hanöbukten Sweden 55°35N 14°30E **163** J8
Hanoi Vietnam 21°5N 105°55E **228** G5
Hanover = Hannover
Germany 52°22N 9°46E **178** C5
Hanover Ont., Canada 44°9N 81°2W **312** B3
Hanover Northern Cape,
S. Africa 31°4S 24°29E **270** D3
Hanover Ind., U.S.A. 38°43N 85°28W **311** F11
Hanover N.H., U.S.A. 43°42N 72°17W **313** C12
Hanover Ohio, U.S.A. 40°4N 82°16W **312** F2
Hanover Pa., U.S.A. 39°48N 76°59W **309** F15
Hanover, I. Chile 51°0S 74°50W **336** D2
Hanpan, C. Papua N. G. 5°0S 154°35E **286** C8
Hans Lollik I.
U.S. Virgin Is. 18°24N 64°53W **321** b
Hans Meyer Ra.
Papua N. G. 4°20S 152°55E **286** C7
Hansdiha India 24°36N 87°5E **243** G12
Hanshou China 28°56N 111°50E **229** C8
Hansi H.P., India 32°27N 77°50E **242** C7
Hansi Haryana, India 29°10N 75°57E **242** E6
Hanson, L. Australia 31°0S 136°15E **282** A2
Hanstholm Denmark 57°7N 8°36E **163** G2
Hantan = Handan China 36°35N 114°28E **226** F8
Hanting China 36°46N 119°12E **227** F10
Hantsavichy Belarus 52°49N 26°30E **177** B14
Hanumangarh India 29°35N 74°19E **242** E6
Hanwell U.K. 51°30N 0°20W **125** A1
Hanworth U.K. 51°26N 0°23W **125** B1
Hanyin China 32°54N 108°28E **226** H5
Hanyū Japan 36°10N 139°32E **223** A11
Hanyuan China 29°21N 102°40E **228** C4
Hanzhong China 33°10N 107°1E **228** A6
Hanzhuang China 34°33N 117°23E **227** G9
Hao French Polynesia 18°15S 140°54W **289** f
Haora India 22°34N 88°18E **124** B1
Haouach, O. → Chad 16°45N 19°35E **259** E4
Haoxue China 30°3N 112°24E **229** B9
Haparanda Sweden 65°52N 24°8E **160** D21
Hapdeok S. Korea 36°48N 126°46E **224** D3
Hapeville U.S.A. 33°39N 84°24W **113** C2
Happy U.S.A. 34°45N 101°52W **314** D4
Happy Camp U.S.A. 41°48N 123°23W **304** F2
Happy Valley China 22°16N 114°10E **122** B2
Happy Valley-Goose Bay
Canada 53°15N 60°20W **299** B7
Hapsu N. Korea 41°13N 128°51E **224** B4
Hapur India 28°45N 77°45E **242** E7
Ḥaql Si. Arabia 29°10N 34°58E **251** J5
Haquira Peru 14°14S 72°12W **330** C3
Har Indonesia 5°16S 133°14E **231** F8
Har Adar West Bank 31°49N 35°8E **123** B1
Har-Ayrag Mongolia 45°47N 109°16E **226** B5
Har Gilo West Bank 31°43N 35°10E **123** B2
Har Homa West Bank 31°44N 35°12E **123** B2
Har Hu China 38°20N 97°38E **218** D8
Har Nof Israel 31°47N 35°11E **123** B2
Har Tsiyon Jerusalem **123** b3
Har Us Nuur Mongolia 48°0N 92°0E **217** C12
Har Yehuda Israel 31°35N 34°57E **251** G5
Ḥaraḍ Si. Arabia 24°22N 49°0E **249** A5
Ḥaraḍ Yemen 16°26N 43°5E **248** C3
Haradok Belarus 55°30N 30°3E **188** E6
Häradsbäck Sweden 56°32N 14°26E **163** H8
Harahan U.S.A. 29°56N 90°12W **131** B1
Haraiki French Polynesia 17°38S 143°27W **289** f
Haramosh Pakistan 35°50N 74°54E **243** B6
Haranomachi Japan 37°38N 140°58E **220** F10
Harare Zimbabwe 17°43S 31°2E **269** F3
Ḥarāsīs, Jiddat al Oman 19°30N 56°0E **249** C7
Harat Eritrea 16°5N 39°26E **257** D4
Harau Indonesia 0°7S 100°35E **234** C2
Haraz-Djombo Chad 14°20N 19°12E **259** F3
Harazé Chad 9°57N 20°48E **259** G4
Harbel Liberia 6°16N 10°20W **262** D2
Harbhanga India 20°38N 84°36E **244** D7
Harbin China 45°48N 126°40E **227** B14
Harbiye Turkey 36°10N 36°8E **250** B7
Harbo Sweden 60°7N 17°12E **162** D11
Harboøre Denmark 56°38N 8°10E **163** H2
Harbor Beach U.S.A. 43°51N 82°39W **312** C2
Harborcreek U.S.A. 42°9N 79°57W **312** D5
Harbour Breton Canada 47°29N 55°50W **299** C8
Harbour Deep Canada 50°25N 56°32W **299** B8
Harbour View Jamaica 17°59N 76°50W **320** a
Harburg Germany 53°27N 9°58E **178** B5
Harburger Berge △
Germany 53°26N 9°51E **178** B5
Harda India 22°27N 77°5E **242** H7
Hardangerfjorden Norway 60°5N 6°0E **164** D3
Hardangerjøkulen Norway 60°30N 7°27E **164** D4
Hardangervidda Norway 60°7N 7°20E **164** D4
Hardangervidda △ Norway 60°10N 7°25E **164** D4
Hardap △ Namibia 24°29S 17°45E **270** B2
Hardap Dam Namibia 24°32S 17°50E **270** B2
Hardeeville U.S.A. 32°17N 81°5W **316** C8
Harden Australia 34°32S 148°24E **283** C8
Hardenberg Neths. 52°34N 6°37E **170** B6
Harderwijk Neths. 52°21N 5°38E **170** B5
Hardey → Australia 22°45S 116°8E **278** D2
Hardin Ill., U.S.A. 39°10N 90°37W **310** E6
Hardin Mont., U.S.A. 45°44N 107°37W **304** D10
Harding S. Africa 30°35S 29°55E **271** D4
Harding, L. U.S.A. 32°40N 85°5W **316** C4
Harding, Ra. Australia 16°17S 124°55E **278** C3
Hardinsburg U.S.A. 37°47N 86°28W **311** G10
Hardisty Canada 52°40N 111°18W **296** C6
Hardoi India 27°26N 80°6E **243** F9
Hardwar = Haridwar India 29°58N 78°9E **242** E8
Hardwick Ga., U.S.A. 33°4N 83°14W **316** B6
Hardwick Vt., U.S.A. 44°30N 72°22W **313** B12
Hardwicke B. Australia 34°55S 137°20E **282** C2
Hardwood Lake Canada 45°12N 77°26W **312** A7
Hardy, Pen. Chile 55°30S 68°20W **336** E3
Hardy, Pte. St. Lucia 14°6N 60°56W **323** m
Hare B. Canada 51°15N 55°45W **299** B8
Hareid Norway 62°22N 6°1E **164** B3
Haren Brussels, Belgium 50°53N 4°25E **116** A2
Haren Niedersachsen,
Germany 52°47N 7°13E **178** C3
Harer Ethiopia 9°20N 42°8E **257** F5
Harerge Ethiopia 7°12N 42°0E **257** G5
Hareskovby Denmark 55°45N 12°23E **118** A2
Harestua Norway 60°11N 10°44E **164** D7
Hareto Ethiopia 9°23N 37°6E **257** F4
Harfleur France 49°30N 0°10E **172** C7
Hargeisa Somali Rep. 9°30N 44°2E **267** C5
Hargeisa △ Somali Rep. 10°0N 44°2E **267** B5
Harghita □ Romania 46°30N 25°30E **183** D10
Harghita, Munții
Romania 46°25N 25°35E **183** D10
Hargshamn Sweden 60°12N 18°30E **162** D12
Hari → Indonesia 1°16S 104°5E **234** C2
Haria Canary Is. 29°8N 13°32W **153** e2
Ḥarīb Yemen 14°56N 45°30E **248** D4
Haricha, Hamada el Mali 22°40N 3°15W **260** D4
Haridwar India 29°58N 78°9E **242** E8
Harihar India 14°32N 75°44E **245** G2
Harihari N.Z. 43°9S 170°33E **285** D5
Hārim Syria 36°14N 36°29E **250** B7
Harima, Jabal al Oman 25°58N 56°14E **247** E8
Harima-Nada Japan 34°30N 134°35E **222** C6
Haringey □ U.K. 51°34N 0°5W **125** A3
Haringhata → Bangla. 22°0N 89°58E **241** E2
Haripad India 9°14N 76°28E **245** K3
Harīr, W. al → Syria 32°44N 35°59E **250** F6
Harīrūd → Asia 37°24N 60°38E **240** A2
Härjedalen Sweden 62°22N 13°5E **162** B7
Harjusuo Finland 60°19N 25°10E **121** B3
Harlaching Germany 48°5N 11°33E **131** B2
Harlan Iowa, U.S.A. 41°39N 95°19W **308** E6
Harlan Ky., U.S.A. 36°51N 83°19W **309** G12
Hârlău Romania 47°23N 26°55E **183** C11
Harlaw Res. U.K. 55°52N 3°18W **121** B2
Harlech U.K. 52°52N 4°6W **168** E3
Harlem Ga., U.S.A. 33°25N 82°19W **316** B7
Harlem Mont., U.S.A. 48°32N 108°47W **304** B9
Harlem New York, U.S.A. **132** a3
Harlesden U.K. 51°32N 0°14W **125** A2
Hårlev Denmark 55°21N 12°14E **163** J6
Harleyville U.S.A. 33°13N 80°27W **316** B9
Harlingen Neths. 53°11N 5°25E **170** A5
Harlingen Tex., U.S.A. 26°12N 97°42W **314** H6
Harlington U.K. 51°29N 0°25W **125** B1
Harlow U.K. 51°46N 0°8E **169** F8
Harlowton U.S.A. 46°26N 109°50W **304** C9
Harmaja Finland 60°6N 24°58E **121** C2
Harmancık Turkey 39°41N 29°9E **205** B11
Harmånger Sweden 61°55N 17°20E **162** C11
Harmashatar hegy
Hungary 47°33N 19°0E **117** A2
Harmil Eritrea 16°30N 40°10E **257** D5
Harnai India 17°48N 73°6E **244** F1
Harnai Pakistan 30°6N 67°56E **242** D2
Harney, L. U.S.A. 28°45N 81°34W **317** G8
Harney Basin U.S.A. 43°0N 119°30W **304** E4
Harney L. U.S.A. 43°14N 119°8W **304** E4
Harney Peak U.S.A. 43°52N 103°32W **308** D2
Härnön Sweden 62°36N 18°0E **162** B12
Härnösand Sweden 62°38N 17°55E **162** B11
Haro Spain 42°35N 2°55W **196** C2
Harold U.S.A. 30°40N 86°53W **317** E3
Harold Pond Bahamas 25°2N 77°22W **153** b
Harolds Cross Ireland 53°19N 6°16W **120** B2
Haroldswick U.K. 60°48N 0°50W **167** A8
Háros Hungary 47°23N 19°2E **117** B1
Harp L. Canada 55°5N 61°50W **299** A7
Harpanahalli India 14°47N 76°2E **245** G3
Harper = Costa Mesa
U.S.A. 33°38N 117°55W **307** M9
Harper Liberia 4°25N 7°43W **262** E3
Harper, Mt. U.S.A. 64°14N 143°51W **303** D12
Harperrig Res. U.K. 55°50N 3°26W **121** B1
Harplinge Sweden 56°45N 12°45E **163** H6
Harrai India 22°37N 79°13E **243** H8
Harrand Pakistan 29°28N 70°3E **242** E4
Harricana → Canada 50°56N 79°32W **298** B4
Harriman U.S.A. 35°56N 84°33W **315** D12
Harrington Australia 31°52S 152°42E **283** A10
Harrington Harbour
Canada 50°31N 59°30W **299** B8
Harrington Sd. Bermuda 32°20N 64°44W **153** a
Harris Montserrat 16°44N 62°11W **323** p
Harris W. Isles, U.K. 57°50N 6°55W **167** D2
Harris, L. S. Austral.,
Australia 31°10S 135°10E **281** E2
Harris, L. Fla., U.S.A. 28°47N 81°49W **317** G8
Harris, Sd. of U.K. 57°44N 7°6W **167** D1
Harris Mts. N.Z. 44°49S 168°49E **285** E3
Harris Pt. Canada 43°6N 82°9W **312** C2
Harrisburg Ill., U.S.A. 37°44N 88°32W **311** G8
Harrisburg Nebr., U.S.A. 41°33N 103°44W **308** E2
Harrisburg Pa., U.S.A. 40°16N 76°53W **312** F8
Harrismith S. Africa 28°15S 29°8E **271** C4
Harrison Ark., U.S.A. 36°14N 93°7W **314** C8
Harrison Maine, U.S.A. 44°7N 70°39W **313** B14
Harrison Nebr., U.S.A. 42°41N 103°53W **308** D2
Harrison, C. Canada 54°55N 57°55W **299** B8
Harrison Bay U.S.A. 70°40N 151°0W **303** A10
Harrison L. Canada 49°33N 121°50W **296** D4
Harrisonburg U.S.A. 38°27N 78°52W **309** F14
Harrison's Cave Barbados 13°11N 59°34W **323** r
Harrisonville U.S.A. 38°39N 94°21W **310** F2
Harriston Canada 43°57N 80°53W **312** C4
Harrisville Mich., U.S.A. 44°39N 83°17W **312** B1
Harrisville N.Y., U.S.A. 44°9N 75°19W **313** B9
Harrisville Pa., U.S.A. 41°8N 80°0W **312** E5
Harrodsburg Ind., U.S.A. 39°1N 86°33W **311** E10
Harrodsburg Ky., U.S.A. 37°46N 84°51W **311** G12
Harrogate U.K. 54°0N 1°33W **168** C6
Harrow Vic., Australia 37°9S 141°35E **282** D4
Harrow Ont., Canada 42°2N 82°55W **312** D2
Harrow □ U.K. 51°35N 0°21W **125** A1
Harrow on the Hill U.K. 51°34N 0°21W **125** A1
Harrow School U.K. 51°34N 0°20W **125** A1
Harrow Weald U.K. 51°36N 0°20W **125** A1
Harrowsmith Canada 44°24N 76°40W **313** B8
Harry S. Truman Res.
U.S.A. 38°16N 93°24W **310** F3
Harsefeld Germany 53°27N 9°30E **178** B5
Harsewinkel Germany 51°56N 8°14E **178** D4
Harsīn Iran 34°18N 47°33E **213** E12
Hârșova Romania 44°40N 27°59E **183** F12
Harstad Norway 68°48N 16°30E **160** B17
Harsud India 22°6N 76°44E **242** H7
Hart U.S.A. 43°42N 86°22W **308** D10
Hart, L. Australia 31°10S 136°25E **282** A2
Hartbees → S. Africa 28°45S 20°32E **270** C3
Hartberg Austria 47°17N 15°58E **180** D8
Hårteigen Norway 60°11N 7°3E **164** D4
Hartford Ala., U.S.A. 31°6N 85°42W **316** D4
Hartford Conn., U.S.A. 41°46N 72°41W **313** E12
Hartford Ky., U.S.A. 37°27N 86°55W **308** G10
Hartford Mich., U.S.A. 42°13N 86°13W **311** B10
Hartford S. Dak., U.S.A. 43°38N 96°57W **308** D5
Hartford Vt., U.S.A. 43°40N 72°20W **313** C12
Hartford Wis., U.S.A. 43°19N 88°22W **308** D9
Hartford City U.S.A. 40°27N 85°22W **311** D11
Hartingsburg = Bela Bela
S. Africa 24°51S 28°19E **271** B4
Hartland N.B., Canada 46°20N 67°32W **299** C6
Hartland Wis., U.S.A. 43°6N 88°21W **311** A8
Hartland Pt. U.K. 51°1N 4°32W **169** F3
Hartlepool U.K. 54°42N 1°13W **168** C6
Hartlepool □ U.K. 54°42N 1°17W **168** C6
Hartley Bay Canada 53°25N 129°15W **296** C3
Hartmannberge Namibia 17°0S 13°0E **270** A1
Hartney Canada 49°30N 100°35W **297** D8
Hârtop Moldova 46°39N 28°40E **183** D13
Harts → S. Africa 28°24S 24°17E **270** C3
Harts Range Australia 23°6S 134°55E **280** C1
Hartselle U.S.A. 34°27N 86°56W **315** D11
Hartsfield-Atlanta Int. ✕ (ATL)
U.S.A. 33°38N 84°26W **113** C2
Hartshorne U.S.A. 34°51N 95°34W **314** D7
Hartstown U.S.A. 41°33N 80°23W **312** E4
Hartsville U.S.A. 34°23N 80°4W **315** D14
Hartswater S. Africa 27°34S 24°43E **270** C3
Hartwell U.S.A. 34°21N 82°56W **315** D13
Harumi Tokyo, Japan **140** c5
Harunabad Pakistan 29°35N 73°8E **242** E5
Harur India 12°3N 78°29E **245** H4
Hārūt → Afghan. 31°29N 61°24E **240** C1
Harvand Iran 28°25N 55°43E **247** D7
Harvard U.S.A. 42°25N 88°37W **311** B8
Harvard Univ. U.S.A. 42°22N 71°7W **116** A2
Harvey W. Austral.,
Australia 33°5S 115°54E **279** F2
Harvey Ill., U.S.A. 41°36N 87°50W **311** C9
Harvey La., U.S.A. 29°54N 90°4W **131** B2
Harvey N. Dak., U.S.A. 47°47N 99°56W **308** B4
Harwich U.K. 51°56N 1°17E **169** F9
Harwood Heights U.S.A. 41°57N 87°46W **119** B2
Haryana □ India 29°0N 76°10E **242** E7
Haryn → Belarus 52°7N 27°17E **177** B14
Harz Germany 51°38N 10°44E **178** D6
Harz △ Germany 51°40N 10°18E **178** D6
Harzgerode Germany 51°38N 11°8E **178** D7
Hasa Si. Arabia 25°50N 49°0E **247** E6
Ḥasā, W. al → Jordan 31°4N 35°29E **251** G6
Hasaheisa Sudan 14°44N 33°20E **257** E3
Ḥasanābād Eşfahan, Iran 32°8N 52°44E **247** C7
Ḥasanābād Tehrān, Iran 35°44N 51°16E **141** A1
Hasankeyf Turkey 37°42N 41°24E **213** D9
Hasanparti India 18°4N 79°32E **244** E4
Hasawinah, Jabal al Libya 28°15N 16°0E **261** C7
Ḥasb, W. → Iraq 31°45N 44°17E **246** D5
Hasbrouck Heights U.S.A. 40°51N 74°4W **132** A1
Hasdo → India 21°44N 82°44E **243** J10
Haselhorst Germany 52°33N 13°14E **115** A2
Haselünne Germany 52°40N 7°29E **178** C3
Hashima Japan 35°20N 136°40E **223** B8
Hashimoto Japan 34°19N 135°37E **223** C7
Hashtjerd Iran 35°52N 50°40E **247** C6
Hashtpur = Tālesh Iran 37°58N 48°58E **213** D13
Hashtrud Iran 37°28N 47°4E **213** D12
Hasi Nueifed W. Sahara 24°54N 14°49W **260** D2
Ḥāsik Oman 17°22N 55°17E **249** C6
Haskell U.S.A. 33°10N 99°44W **314** E5
Haskovo = Khaskovo
Bulgaria 41°56N 25°30E **203** E9
Hasköy Edirne, Turkey 41°38N 26°52E **203** E10
Hasköy İstanbul, Turkey 41°2N 28°57E **122** B1
Haslach Germany 48°16N 8°5E **179** G4
Hasle Denmark 55°11N 14°44E **163** J8
Hasle Oslo, Norway 59°46N 10°38E **133** B2
Haslemere U.K. 51°5N 0°43W **169** F7
Haslev Denmark 55°18N 11°57E **163** J5
Haslum Norway 59°55N 10°34E **133** A2
Hasparren France 43°24N 1°18W **174** E2
Hassa Turkey 36°48N 36°29E **250** B7
Hassan India 13°0N 76°5E **245** H3
Hassberge △ Germany 50°8N 10°45E **179** E6
Hassela Sweden 62°7N 16°42E **162** B10
Hasselt Belgium 50°56N 5°21E **170** D5
Hassfurt Germany 50°2N 10°30E **179** E6
Hassi bel Guebbour Algeria 28°30N 6°41E **261** C6
Hassi bou Khelala Algeria 30°17N 0°18W **261** B4
Hassi Bourarchet Algeria 27°26N 9°19E **261** C6
Hassi Djafou Algeria 30°55N 3°35E **261** B5
Hassi el Hadjar Algeria 31°28N 4°45E **261** B5
Hassi Imoulaye Algeria 29°54N 9°10E **261** C6
Hassi Inifeg Algeria 28°15N 1°30W **261** C4
Hassi Inifel Algeria 29°50N 3°41E **261** C5
Hassi Mana Algeria 28°48N 2°37W **261** C4
Hassi Marroket Algeria 30°10N 3°0E **261** B5
Hassi Mengoub Algeria 29°49N 5°26W **260** C3
Hassi Messaoud Algeria 31°51N 6°1E **261** B6
Hassi Sougoued Algeria 26°50N 9°28E **261** C6
Hassi Tartrat Algeria 30°5N 6°28E **261** B6
Hassi Zerzour Morocco 30°51N 3°56W **260** B4
Hassi Zguilma Algeria 30°19N 6°10W **260** B4
Hässleholm Sweden 56°10N 13°46E **163** H7
Hässlö Sweden 56°7N 15°28E **163** H9
Hassloch Germany 49°22N 8°16E **179** F4
Hästhagen Sweden 59°18N 18°9E **139** B2
Hästholmen Sweden 58°17N 14°38E **163** F8
Hastings Vic., Australia 38°18S 145°12E **283** E6
Hastings Barbados 13°4N 59°36W **323** r
Hastings N.Z. 39°39S 176°52E **284** F5
Hastings E. Sussex, U.K. 50°51N 0°35E **169** G8
Hastings Fla., U.S.A. 29°43N 81°31W **316** F8
Hastings Mich., U.S.A. 42°39N 85°17W **311** B11
Hastings Minn., U.S.A. 44°44N 92°51W **308** C7
Hastings Nebr., U.S.A. 40°35N 98°23W **308** E4
Hastings Ra. Australia 31°15S 152°14E **283** A10
Hästveda Sweden 56°17N 13°55E **163** H7
Hat Ukraine 48°19N 22°38E **182** B7
Hat Head △ Australia 31°3S 153°1E **283** A10
Hat Lot Vietnam 21°15N 104°7E **236** B5
Hat Yai Thailand 7°1N 100°27E **237** J3
Hataitai N.Z. 41°18S 174°48E **143** B1
Hatanbulag = Ergel
Mongolia 43°8N 109°5E **226** C5
Hatay Turkey 36°14N 36°10E **250** B7
Hatay □ Turkey 36°25N 36°15E **250** B7
Hatch U.S.A. 32°40N 107°9W **305** K10
Hatch End U.K. 51°36N 0°22W **125** A1
Hatchet L. Canada 58°36N 103°40W **297** B8
Hațeg Romania 45°36N 22°55E **182** E7
Hateruma-Shima Japan 24°3N 123°47E **221** M1
Hatfield Australia 33°54S 143°49E **282** B5
Hatgal Mongolia 50°26N 100°9E **218** A9
Hathras India 27°36N 78°6E **242** F8
Hatia Bangla. 22°30N 91°5E **241** D3
Hatia Is. Bangla. 22°30N 91°0E **241** D3
Hatiara India 22°36N 88°26E **124** B2
Ḥāṭibah, Ra's Si. Arabia 21°55N 38°57E **256** C4
Hatid India 17°17N 75°3E **244** F2
Hatillo Puerto Rico 18°29N 66°50W **321** b
Hato Bonaire 12°11N 68°17W **322** h
Hato Curaçao 12°11N 68°57W **322** g
Hato Caves Curaçao 12°11N 68°57W **322** g
Hato Corozal Colombia 6°11N 71°45W **328** B3
Hato Mayor Dom. Rep. 18°46N 69°15W **321** C6
Hatsukaichi Japan 34°22N 132°22E **222** C4
Hatta India 24°7N 79°36E **243** G8
Hatta U.A.E. 24°45N 56°4E **247** E8
Hattah Australia 34°48S 142°17E **282** C5
Hattah Kulkyne △
Australia 34°16S 142°33E **282** C5
Hatteras, C. U.S.A. 35°14N 75°32W **315** D17
Hatteras Abyssal Plain
Atl. Oc. 28°0N 72°0W **152** D4
Hattiesburg U.S.A. 31°20N 89°17W **315** F10
Hatutu French Polynesia 7°56S 140°38W **289** f
Hatvan Hungary 47°40N 19°45E **182** C4
Hau → Vietnam 9°30N 106°13E **237** H6
Haubstadt U.S.A. 38°12N 87°34W **311** F9
Haud Ethiopia 8°0N 45°0E **267** C6
Hauganes Iceland 65°56N 18°27W **155** B8
Haugastøl Norway 60°30N 7°50E **164** D4
Hauge Norway 58°20N 6°15E **164** F3
Haugesund Norway 59°23N 5°13E **164** E2
Hauhui Solomon Is. 9°10S 160°59E **287** M11
Hauhungaroa Ra. N.Z. 38°42S 175°40E **284** E4
Haukeligrend Norway 59°44N 7°33E **164** E4
Hauketo Norway 59°50N 10°48E **133** A3
Haukipudas Finland 65°12N 25°20E **160** D21
Haultain → Canada 55°51N 106°46W **297** B7
Haungpa Burma 25°29N 96°7E **241** C6
Hauraha Solomon Is. 10°46S 161°59E **287** N11
Hauraki G. N.Z. 36°35S 175°5E **284** C4
Hauroko L. N.Z. 45°59S 167°21E **285** F2
Hausruck Austria 48°6N 13°30E **180** C6
Haut Atlas Morocco 32°30N 5°0W **260** B4
Haut de la Montagne
Guadeloupe 16°26N 61°28W **322** e
Haut-Jura ⌓ France 46°23N 2°23E **173** F9
Haut-Languedoc ⌓ France 43°30N 2°43E **174** E6
Haut-Niger △ Guinea 10°20N 10°20W **262** C2
Haut-Rhin □ France 48°0N 7°15E **173** E14
Haut-Zaïre = Orientale □
Dem. Rep. of the Congo 2°20N 26°0E **268** B2
Haute-Corse □ France 42°30N 9°30E **175** F13
Haute-Garonne □ France 43°30N 1°30E **174** E5
Haute-Loire □ France 45°5N 3°50E **174** C7
Haute-Marne □ France 48°10N 5°20E **173** D12
Haute-Normandie □ France 49°20N 1°0E **172** C7
Haute-Saône □ France 47°45N 6°10E **173** E13
Haute-Savoie □ France 46°0N 6°20E **175** C10
Haute-Vienne □ France 45°50N 1°10E **174** C5
Hautes-Alpes □ France 44°42N 6°20E **175** D10
Hautes Fagnes = Hohes Venn
Belgium 50°30N 6°5E **170** D6
Hautes-Pyrénées □ France 43°0N 0°10E **174** F4
Hauteville-Lompnès France 45°58N 5°36E **175** C9
Hautmont France 50°15N 3°55E **173** B10
Hauts-de-Seine □ France 48°52N 2°15E **173** D9
Hauts Plateaux Algeria 35°0N 1°0E **261** B5
Hau'ula U.S.A. 21°37N 157°55W **302** J14
Hauz Khas India 28°33N 77°11E **120** B2
Hauzenberg Germany 48°40N 13°37E **179** G9
Havana = La Habana
Cuba 23°8N 82°22W **320** B3
Havana Fla., U.S.A. 30°37N 84°25W **316** E5
Havana Ill., U.S.A. 40°18N 90°4W **310** D6
Havant U.K. 50°51N 0°58W **169** G7
Havârna Romania 48°4N 26°43E **183** B11
Havasor = Kığzı Turkey 38°18N 43°25E **246** B4
Havasu, L. U.S.A. 34°18N 114°28W **307** L12
Havdhem Sweden 57°10N 18°20E **163** G12
Havel → Germany 52°50N 12°3E **115** A2
Havelian Pakistan 34°2N 73°10E **242** B5
Havelkanal Germany 52°36N 13°10E **115** A2
Havelock Ont., Canada 44°26N 77°53W **312** B7
Havelock N.Z. 41°17S 173°48E **285** B8
Havelock N.C., U.S.A. 34°53N 76°54W **315** D16
Havelock I. India 11°58N 93°0E **245** J11
Havelock North N.Z. 39°40S 176°53E **284** F5
Haverfordwest U.K. 51°48N 4°58W **169** F3
Haverhill Suffolk, U.K. 52°5N 0°28E **169** E8
Haverhill Fla., U.S.A. 26°42N 80°7W **317** J9
Haverhill Mass., U.S.A. 42°47N 71°5W **313** D13
Haveri India 14°53N 75°24E **245** G2
Havering □ U.K. 51°34N 0°13E **125** A5
Havering-atte-Bower U.K. 51°37N 0°11E **125** A5
Havern Sweden 62°18N 15°7E **162** B9
Haverstraw U.S.A. 41°12N 73°58W **313** E11
Håverud Sweden 58°50N 12°28E **163** F6
Havirga Mongolia 45°41N 113°5E **226** B7
Havířov Czech Rep. 49°46N 18°20E **181** B11

378 Havlíčkův Brod INDEX

Havlíčkův Brod Czech Rep. 49°36N 15°33E 180 B8
Havneby Denmark 55°5N 8°34E 163 J2
Havran Turkey 39°33N 27°6E 205 B9
Havre U.S.A. 48°33N 109°41W 304 B9
Havre-Aubert Canada 47°12N 61°56W 299 C7
Havre-St.-Pierre Canada 50°18N 63°33W 299 B7
Havsa Turkey 41°31N 26°48E 203 E10
Havza Turkey 41°0N 35°35E 212 B6
Haw → U.S.A. 35°36N 79°3W 315 D15
Hawai'i U.S.A. 19°30N 155°30W 302 D6
Hawai'i □ U.S.A. 19°30N 156°30W 302 D5
Hawai'i County U.S.A. 19°30N 155°30W 302 D6
Hawai'i Kai U.S.A. 21°16N 157°42W 302 K14
Hawai'i Volcanoes △ U.S.A. 19°25N 155°18W 302 D6
Hawaiian Is. Pac. Oc. 20°30N 156°0W 302 G12
Hawaiian Ridge Pac. Oc. 24°0N 165°0W 289 E11
Hawarden U.S.A. 43°0N 96°29W 308 D5
Hawashīyah, W. Egypt 28°31N 32°58E 251 K3
Hawea, L. N.Z. 44°28S 169°19E 285 E4
Hawea Flat N.Z. 44°40S 169°19E 285 E4
Hawera N.Z. 39°35S 174°19E 284 F3
Hawesville U.S.A. 37°54N 86°45W 311 G10
Hawi U.S.A. 20°14N 155°50W 302 C6
Hawick U.K. 55°26N 2°47W 167 F6
Hawk Junction Canada 48°5N 84°38W 298 C3
Hawk Point U.S.A. 38°58N 91°8W 310 F5
Hawkdun Ra. N.Z. 44°53S 170°5E 285 E5
Hawke B. N.Z. 39°25S 177°20E 284 F6
Hawker Australia 31°59S 138°22E 282 A3
Hawke's Bay Canada 50°36N 57°10W 299 B8
Hawke's Bay □ N.Z. 39°45S 176°35E 284 F5
Hawkesbury Canada 45°37N 74°37W 298 C5
Hawkesbury I. Canada 53°37N 129°3W 296 C3
Hawkesbury Pt. Australia 11°55S 134°5E 280 A1
Hawkinsville U.S.A. 32°17N 83°28W 316 C6
Hawks Nest Australia 32°41S 152°11E 283 B10
Hawley Minn., U.S.A. 46°53N 96°19W 308 B5
Hawley Pa., U.S.A. 41°28N 75°11W 313 E9
Haworth U.S.A. 40°57N 73°59W 132 A2
Ḥawrān, W. → Iraq 33°58N 42°34E 213 F10
Hawsh Mūssá Lebanon 33°45N 35°55E 250 E6
Hawthorne Fla., U.S.A. 29°36N 82°5W 317 F7
Hawthorne Nev., U.S.A. 38°32N 118°38W 304 G4
Hawthorne Racecourse U.S.A. 41°49N 87°44W 119 C2
Hay Australia 34°30S 144°51E 283 C6
Hay → N. Terr., Australia 24°50S 138°0E 280 C2
Hay → Alta., Canada 60°50N 116°26W 296 A5
Hay, C. Australia 14°5S 129°29E 278 B4
Hay I. Canada 44°53N 80°58W 312 B4
Hay L. Canada 58°50N 118°50W 296 B5
Hay-on-Wye U.K. 52°5N 3°8W 169 E4
Hay Point Australia 21°18S 149°17E 280 C4
Hay River Canada 60°51N 115°44W 296 A5
Hay Springs U.S.A. 42°41N 102°41W 308 D2
Haya = Tehoru Indonesia 3°23S 129°30E 231 E7
Hayachine-San Japan 39°34N 141°29E 220 E10
Hayange France 49°20N 6°2E 173 C13
Hayastan = Armenia ■ Asia 40°20N 45°0E 191 K7
Hayato Japan 31°40N 130°43E 222 F2
Haydān, W. al → Jordan 31°29N 35°34E 251 G6
Haydarlı Turkey 38°16N 30°23E 205 C12
Hayden U.S.A. 40°30N 107°16W 304 F10
Hayes Jamaica 17°52N 77°14W 320 a
Hayes Kent, U.K. 51°22N 0°0 125 B4
Hayes Middlesex, U.K. 51°30N 0°25W 125 A1
Hayes S. Dak., U.S.A. 44°23N 101°1W 308 C3
Hayes → Canada 57°3N 92°12W 298 A1
Hayes, Mt. U.S.A. 63°37N 146°43W 303 E11
Hayes Creek Australia 13°43S 131°22E 278 B5
Hayes End U.K. 51°31N 0°25W 125 A1
Hayford U.S.A. 41°45N 87°42W 119 C2
Hayle U.K. 50°11N 5°26W 169 G2
Hayling I. U.K. 50°48N 0°59W 169 G7
Haymā' Oman 19°56N 56°19E 249 C7
Hayman I. Australia 20°4S 148°53E 280 b
Haymana Turkey 39°26N 32°31E 212 C5
Haynan Yemen 15°50N 48°18E 249 D5
Haynau = Chojnów Poland 51°18N 15°58E 185 G2
Hayneville U.S.A. 32°23N 83°37W 316 C6
Hayrabolu Turkey 41°12N 27°5E 203 E11
Hays Alta., Canada 50°6N 111°48W 296 C6
Hays Kans., U.S.A. 38°53N 99°20W 308 F4
Ḥays Yemen 13°56N 43°29E 248 D3
Haysville U.S.A. 38°28N 86°55W 311 F10
Haysyn Ukraine 48°57N 29°25E 183 B14
Hayvoron Ukraine 48°22N 29°52E 183 B14
Hayward Calif., U.S.A. 37°40N 122°4W 306 H4
Hayward Wis., U.S.A. 46°1N 91°29W 308 B8
Haywards N.Z. 41°9S 174°59E 143 A2
Haywards Heath U.K. 51°0N 0°5W 169 G7
Hazafon □ Israel 32°40N 35°20E 250 F6
Hazar Turkmenistan 39°34N 53°16E 187 G9
Hazārān, Kūh-e Iran 29°35N 57°20E 247 D8
Hazard U.S.A. 37°15N 83°12W 309 G12
Hazaribag India 23°58N 85°26E 243 H11
Hazaribag Road India 24°12N 85°57E 243 G11
Hazebrouck France 50°42N 2°31E 173 B9
Hazelton B.C., Canada 55°20N 127°42W 296 B3
Hazelton N. Dak., U.S.A. 46°29N 100°17W 308 B3
Hazen U.S.A. 47°18N 101°38W 308 B3
Hazen, L. Canada 81°47N 71°1W 154 A3
Hazlehurst Ga., U.S.A. 31°52N 82°36W 316 D7
Hazlehurst Miss., U.S.A. 31°52N 90°24W 315 F9
Hazlet U.S.A. 40°25N 74°12W 313 F10
Hazleton Ind., U.S.A. 38°29N 87°33W 311 F9
Hazleton Pa., U.S.A. 40°57N 75°59W 313 F9
Hazlett, L. Australia 21°30S 128°48E 278 D4
Hazro Turkey 38°15N 40°47E 246 B4
He Xian Anhui, China 31°45N 118°20E 229 B12
He Xian Guangxi Zhuangzu, China 24°27N 111°30E 229 E8
Head of Bight Australia 31°30S 131°25E 279 F5
Headland U.S.A. 31°21N 85°21W 316 D4
Headlands Zimbabwe 18°15S 32°2E 269 F3
Healdsburg U.S.A. 38°37N 122°52W 306 G4
Healdton U.S.A. 34°14N 97°29W 314 D6
Healesville Australia 37°35S 145°30E 283 D6
Healy U.S.A. 63°52N 148°58W 303 E10
Heany Junction Zimbabwe 20°6S 28°54E 271 B4
Heanza-shima Japan 26°20N 127°57E 288 a
Heard I. Ind. Oc. 53°6S 72°36E 273 F6
Hearne U.S.A. 30°53N 96°36W 314 F6
Hearst Canada 49°40N 83°41W 298 C3
Heart → U.S.A. 46°46N 100°50W 308 B3
Heart's Content Canada 47°54N 53°27W 299 C9
Heath → Bolivia 12°31S 68°38W 330 C4
Heath, Pte. Canada 49°8N 61°40W 299 C7
Heath Mts. N.Z. 45°39S 167°9E 285 F2
Heathcote Australia 36°56S 144°45E 283 D6
Heatherwood = Edson Canada 53°35N 116°28W 296 C5
Heathfield S. Africa 34°3S 18°27E 118 B1
Heathrow, London ✕ (LHR) U.K. 51°28N 0°27W 125 B1
Heavener U.S.A. 34°53N 94°36W 314 D7
Hebbronville U.S.A. 27°18N 98°41W 314 H5
Hebe Haven China 22°21N 114°15E 122 A2
Hebei □ China 39°0N 116°0E 226 E9
Hebel Australia 28°58S 147°47E 281 D4
Heber U.S.A. 32°44N 115°32W 307 N11
Heber Springs U.S.A. 35°30N 92°2W 314 D8
Hebgen L. U.S.A. 44°52N 111°20W 304 D8
Hebi China 35°57N 114°7E 226 G8
Hebrides U.K. 57°30N 7°0W 158 D4
Hebrides, Sea of the U.K. 57°5N 7°0W 167 D2
Hebron = Al Khalīl West Bank 31°32N 35°6E 251 G6
Hebron Nfld. & L., Canada 58°5N 62°30W 295 F19
Hebron N. Dak., U.S.A. 46°54N 102°3W 308 B2
Hebron Nebr., U.S.A. 40°10N 97°35W 308 E5
Heby Sweden 59°56N 16°53E 162 E10
Hecate Str. Canada 53°10N 130°30W 296 C2
Heceta I. U.S.A. 55°46N 133°40W 296 B2
Hechi China 24°40N 108°2E 228 E7
Hechingen Germany 48°21N 8°57E 179 G4
Hechuan China 30°2N 106°12E 228 B6
Hecla U.S.A. 45°53N 98°9W 308 C4
Hecla I. Canada 51°10N 96°43W 297 C9
Hedal Norway 60°37N 9°41E 162 D3
Heddal Norway 59°36N 9°9E 164 E6
Hédé Ille-et-Vilaine, France 48°18N 1°49W 172 D5
Hede Jämtland, Sweden 62°23N 13°30E 162 B7
Hedemora Sweden 60°18N 15°58E 162 D9
Hedensted Denmark 55°46N 9°42E 163 J3
Hedesunda Sweden 60°24N 17°0E 162 D10
Hedgehope N.Z. 46°12S 168°34E 285 G3
Hedmark □ Norway 61°17N 11°40E 164 C8
Hedo Japan 26°52N 128°15E 288 a
Hedo-misaki Japan 26°52N 128°16E 288 a
Hedong China 23°5N 113°14E 121 B2
Hedrick U.S.A. 41°11N 92°19W 310 C4
He'eia U.S.A. 21°25N 157°48W 302 K14
Heel Pt. Wake I. 19°18N 166°38E 302 b
Heerde Neths. 52°24N 6°2E 170 B6
Heerenveen Neths. 52°57N 5°55E 170 B5
Heerhugowaard Neths. 52°40N 4°51E 170 B4
Heerlen Neths. 50°55N 5°58E 170 D5
Heerwegen = Polkowice Poland 51°29N 16°3E 185 G3
Ḥefa Israel 32°46N 35°0E 250 F6
Ḥefa □ Israel 32°40N 35°0E 250 F6
Hefei China 31°52N 117°18E 229 B11
Hefeng China 29°55N 109°52E 228 C7
Heflin U.S.A. 33°39N 85°35W 316 B4
Hegalig Sudan 14°36N 31°54E 257 E3
Hegang China 47°20N 130°19E 219 B15
Heggenes Norway 61°9N 9°4E 164 C6
Hegra Norway 63°27N 11°8E 164 A8
Hei Ling Chau China 22°15N 114°2E 219 a
Heiban Sudan 11°13N 30°31E 257 E3
Heichengzhen China 36°24N 106°3E 226 F4
Heidal Norway 61°45N 9°19E 164 C6
Heide Germany 54°11N 9°6E 178 A5
Heidelberg Baden-W., Germany 49°24N 8°42E 179 F4
Heidelberg Western Cape, S. Africa 34°6S 20°59E 270 D3
Heidelberg Heights Australia 37°45S 145°4E 128 A2
Heidelberg West Australia 37°43S 145°2E 128 A2
Heidelberg S. Africa 26°30S 28°21E 271 C4
Heidemühle Germany 52°29N 13°40E 115 B5
Heidenau Germany 50°57N 13°52E 178 E9
Heidenheim Germany 48°41N 10°9E 179 G6
Heideveld S. Africa 33°58S 18°32E 118 A2
Heigun-Tō Japan 33°47N 132°14E 222 D4
Heihe China 50°10N 127°30E 219 A14
Heijing China 25°22N 101°44E 228 E3
Heijō = P'yŏngyang N. Korea 39°0N 125°30E 224 C2
Heilbad Heiligenstadt Germany 51°22N 10°8E 178 D6
Heilbron S. Africa 27°16S 27°59E 271 C4
Heilbronn Germany 49°9N 9°13E 179 F5
Heiligenblut Austria 47°2N 12°51E 180 D5
Heiligenhafen Germany 54°22N 10°59E 178 A6
Heiligensee Germany 52°36N 13°13E 115 A2
Heiligenstadt Austria 48°14N 16°21E 142 A2
Heilongjiang □ China 48°0N 126°0E 219 B14
Heilprin Land Greenland 82°5N 33°0W 154 A7
Heilsberg = Lidzbark Warmiński Poland 54°7N 20°34E 184 D7
Heilunkiang = Heilongjiang □ China 48°0N 126°0E 219 B14
Heim Norway 63°26N 9°5E 164 A6
Heimaey Iceland 63°26N 20°17W 155 D6
Heimdal Norway 63°21N 10°22E 164 A7
Heineken Experience Amsterdam, Neths. 112 c2
Heinersdorf Germany 52°34N 13°26E 115 A3
Heinola Finland 61°13N 26°2E 188 B4
Heinsberg Germany 51°3N 6°5E 178 D2
Heinsun Burma 25°52N 95°35E 241 C5
Heinze Chaung Burma 14°42N 97°52E 236 E1
Heinze Kyun Burma 14°25N 97°45E 236 E1
Heirnkut Burma 25°14N 94°44E 241 C5
Heishan China 41°40N 122°5E 227 D12
Heishui Liaoning, China 42°8N 119°30E 227 C10
Heishui Sichuan, China 32°4N 103°2E 228 A4
Hejaz = Ḥijāz Si. Arabia 24°0N 40°0E 246 E3
Hejian China 38°25N 116°5E 226 E9
Hejiang China 28°43N 105°46E 228 C5
Hejin China 35°35N 110°42E 226 G6
Hejing China 42°18N 86°22E 217 D11
Hekimhan Turkey 38°50N 37°55E 212 C7
Hekinan Japan 34°52N 137°0E 223 G9
Hekla Iceland 63°56N 19°35W 155 D7
Hekou Gansu, China 36°10N 103°26E 226 F2
Hekou Guangdong, China 23°13N 112°45E 229 F9
Hekou Yunnan, China 22°30N 103°59E 228 F4
Hel Poland 54°37N 18°47E 184 D5
Helagsfjället Sweden 62°54N 12°25E 162 B6
Helan Shan China 38°30N 105°55E 226 E3
Heldenplatz Vienna, Austria 142 b1
Helden's Pt. St. Kitts & Nevis 17°25N 62°51W 322 d
Helechosa de los Montes Spain 39°22N 4°53W 195 F6
Helemano → U.S.A. 21°35N 158°7W 302 J13
Helen Atoll Palau 2°40N 132°0E 231 D8
Helena Ark., U.S.A. 34°32N 90°36W 315 D9
Helena Ga., U.S.A. 32°5N 82°55W 316 C7
Helena Mont., U.S.A. 46°36N 112°2W 304 C7
Helendale U.S.A. 34°44N 117°19W 307 L9
Hélène de Champlain, Parc △ Canada 45°31N 73°32W 130 A2
Helenelund Sweden 59°24N 17°58E 139 A1
Helensburgh N.S.W., Australia 34°11S 151°1E 283 C9
Helensburgh Argyll & Bute, U.K. 56°1N 4°43W 167 E4
Helensville N.Z. 36°41S 174°29E 284 C3
Helenvale Australia 15°43S 145°14E 280 B4
Helgasjön Sweden 56°55N 14°50E 163 H8
Helgeland Norway 66°7N 13°29E 160 C15
Helgoland Germany 54°10N 7°53E 178 A3
Helheim Gletscher Greenland 66°24N 38°12W 154 D7
Heligoland = Helgoland Germany 54°10N 7°53E 178 A3
Heligoland B. = Deutsche Bucht Germany 54°15N 8°0E 178 A4
Heliopolis = Masr el Gedida Egypt 30°5N 31°21E 117 A2
Hell Norway 63°26N 10°54E 164 A7
Hell-Bourg Réunion 21°3S 55°32E 272 f
Hell Hole Gorge △ Australia 25°31S 144°12E 280 D3
Hella Iceland 63°50N 20°24W 155 D6
Hellas = Greece ■ Europe 40°0N 23°0E 204 B3
Helleland Norway 58°33N 6°7E 164 F3
Hellersdorf Germany 52°32N 13°35E 115 A4
Hellertown U.S.A. 40°35N 75°21W 313 F9
Hellerup Denmark 55°44N 12°33E 118 A3
Hellespont = Çanakkale Boğazı Turkey 40°17N 26°32E 203 F10
Hellesylt Norway 62°6N 6°51E 164 B3
Hellevoetsluis Neths. 51°50N 4°8E 170 C4
Hellin Spain 38°31N 1°40W 197 G3
Hellissandur Iceland 64°55N 23°54W 155 C3
Hells Canyon △ U.S.A. 45°30N 117°45W 304 D5
Hells Gate Saba 17°39N 63°14W 322 a
Hell's Gate △ Kenya 0°54S 36°19E 268 C4
Hellvik Norway 58°29N 5°52E 164 F2
Helmand □ Afghan. 31°20N 64°0E 240 C2
Helmand → Afghan. 31°12N 61°34E 240 C1
Helme → Germany 51°20N 11°21E 178 D7
Helmeringhausen Namibia 25°54S 16°57E 270 C2
Helmond Neths. 51°29N 5°41E 170 C5
Helmsdale U.K. 58°7N 3°39W 167 C5
Helmsdale → U.K. 58°8N 3°43W 167 C5
Helmstedt Germany 52°12N 11°0E 178 C7
Helong China 42°40N 129°0E 224 A4
Helper U.S.A. 39°41N 110°51W 304 G8
Helsingborg Sweden 56°3N 12°42E 163 H6
Helsinge Denmark 56°2N 12°12E 163 H6
Helsingfors = Helsinki Finland 60°10N 24°55E 121 B2
Helsingør Denmark 56°2N 12°35E 163 H6
Helsinki Finland 60°10N 24°55E 121 B2
Helsinki-Vantaa ✕ (HEL) Finland 60°18N 24°58E 121 B2
Helska, Mierzeja Poland 54°45N 18°40E 184 D5
Helston U.K. 50°6N 5°17W 169 G2
Helvellyn U.K. 54°32N 3°1W 168 C4
Helwân Egypt 29°50N 31°20E 256 J7
Hemavati → India 12°30N 76°20E 245 H3
Hemel Hempstead U.K. 51°44N 0°28W 169 F7
Hemet U.S.A. 33°45N 116°58W 307 M10
Hemingford U.S.A. 42°19N 103°4W 308 D2
Hemis △ India 34°10N 77°15E 242 B7
Hemmingford Canada 45°3N 73°35W 313 A11
Hempe Dem. Rep. of the Congo 1°54N 22°42E 264 B4
Hempstead N.Y., U.S.A. 40°42N 73°37W 313 F11
Hempstead Tex., U.S.A. 30°6N 96°5W 314 F6
Hemse Sweden 57°15N 18°22E 163 G12
Hemsedal Norway 60°53N 8°30E 164 D5
Hemsön Sweden 62°42N 18°5E 162 B12
Hen Norway 60°13N 10°14E 164 D7
Hen and Chicken B. Australia 33°50S 151°7E 139 B1
Hen and Chickens Is. N.Z. 35°58S 174°45E 284 B3
Henån Sweden 58°14N 11°40E 163 F5
Henan □ China 34°0N 114°0E 226 H8
Henares → Spain 40°24N 3°30W 194 E7
Henashi-Misaki Japan 40°37N 139°51E 220 D9
Hendaye France 43°23N 1°47W 174 E2
Hendek Turkey 40°48N 30°44E 212 B4
Henderson Argentina 36°18S 61°43W 334 D3
Henderson Ga., U.S.A. 32°21N 83°47W 316 C6
Henderson Ky., U.S.A. 37°50N 87°35W 311 G9
Henderson N.C., U.S.A. 36°20N 78°25W 315 C15
Henderson N.Y., U.S.A. 43°50N 76°10W 313 C8
Henderson Nev., U.S.A. 36°2N 114°58W 124 B2
Henderson Tenn., U.S.A. 35°26N 88°38W 315 D10
Henderson Tex., U.S.A. 32°9N 94°48W 314 E7
Henderson I. Pac. Oc. 24°22S 128°19W 289 K15
Hendersonville N.C., U.S.A. 35°19N 82°28W 315 D13
Hendersonville Tenn., U.S.A. 36°18N 86°37W 315 C11
Hendījān Iran 30°14N 49°43E 247 D6
Hendon U.K. 51°35N 0°14W 125 A2
Hendorābī Iran 26°40N 53°37E 247 E7
Heng Jiang → China 28°40N 104°25E 228 C5
Heng Xian China 22°40N 109°17E 228 F7
Hengām Iran 26°38N 55°53E 249 A6
Henganofi Papua N. G. 6°15S 145°38E 286 D3
Hengcheng China 38°18N 106°28E 226 E4
Hèngch'un Taiwan 22°0N 120°44E 225 D2
Hengdaohezi China 44°52N 129°0E 227 B15
Hengduan Shan China 28°30N 98°50E 228 C2
Hengelo Neths. 52°16N 6°48E 170 B6
Henggang China 22°39N 114°12E 219 a
Hengmen China 22°33N 113°35E 219 a
Hengsha China 23°9N 113°12E 121 B2
Hengshan Hunan, China 27°16N 112°45E 229 D9
Hengshan Shaanxi, China 37°58N 109°5E 226 F5
Hengshui China 37°41N 115°40E 226 F8
Hengyang China 26°59N 112°22E 229 D9
Henichesk Ukraine 46°12N 34°50E 189 J8
Henima India 25°22N 93°36E 241 C4
Hénin-Beaumont France 50°25N 2°58E 173 B9
Hénin-Liétard = Hénin-Beaumont France 50°25N 2°58E 173 B9
Henley-on-Thames U.K. 51°32N 0°54W 169 F7
Henlopen, C. U.S.A. 38°48N 75°6W 309 F16
Henna Japan 26°19N 127°53E 288 a
Hennan Sweden 62°2N 15°54E 162 B9
Hennebont France 47°49N 3°19W 172 E3
Hennenman S. Africa 27°59S 27°1E 270 C4
Hennepin U.S.A. 41°15N 89°21W 310 C7
Hennessey U.S.A. 36°6N 97°54W 314 C6
Hennigsdorf Germany 52°38N 13°12E 115 A2
Henrietta N.Y., U.S.A. 43°4N 77°37W 312 C7
Henrietta Tex., U.S.A. 33°49N 98°12W 314 E5
Henrietta, Ostrov = Genriyetty, Ostrov Russia 77°6N 156°30E 215 B16
Henrietta Maria, C. Canada 55°9N 82°20W 298 A3
Henry U.S.A. 41°7N 89°22W 310 C7
Henry Lawrence I. India 12°9N 93°5E 245 H11
Henryetta U.S.A. 35°27N 95°59W 314 D7
Henryków Poland 52°19N 20°58E 142 B1
Henryville Canada 45°8N 73°11W 313 A11
Hensall Canada 43°26N 81°30W 312 C3
Henson Cr. → U.S.A. 38°47N 76°58W 143 C4
Henstedt-Ulzburg Germany 53°47N 10°0E 178 B6
Hentiesbaai Namibia 22°8S 14°18E 270 B1
Hentiyn Nuruu Mongolia 48°30N 108°30E 219 B10
Henttaa Finland 60°11N 24°45E 121 B1
Henty Australia 35°30S 147°3E 283 C7
Henzada Burma 17°38N 95°26E 241 G5
Hephaestia Greece 39°55N 25°14E 205 B7
Hephzibah U.S.A. 33°19N 82°4W 316 B7
Heping China 24°29N 115°0E 229 E10
Heping Park China 31°16N 121°30E 138 B2
Hepingli China 39°57N 116°23E 114 B2
Heppner U.S.A. 45°21N 119°33W 304 D4
Hepu China 21°40N 109°12E 228 G7
Hepworth Canada 44°37N 81°9W 312 B3
Heqing China 26°37N 100°11E 228 D3
Hequ China 39°20N 111°15E 226 E6
Héraðsflói Iceland 65°42N 14°12W 155 B12
Héraðsvötn → Iceland 65°45N 19°25W 155 B8
Heradsbygd Norway 60°49N 11°39E 164 D8
Heraklion = Iraklio Greece 35°20N 25°12E 207 E6
Herald Cays Australia 16°58S 149°9E 280 B4
Herand Norway 60°20N 6°22E 164 D3
Herangi Ra. N.Z. 38°33S 174°48E 284 E3
Herāt Afghan. 34°20N 62°7E 240 B1
Herāt □ Afghan. 35°0N 62°0E 240 B1
Hérault □ France 43°34N 3°15E 174 E7
Hérault → France 43°17N 3°26E 174 E7
Herbault France 47°36N 1°8E 172 E8
Herbert Canada 50°30N 107°10W 297 C7
Herbert → Australia 18°31S 146°17E 280 B4
Herbert Hoover Nat. Historic Site △ U.S.A. 41°40N 91°21W 310 C5
Herbert I. U.S.A. 52°45N 170°7W 303 K5
Herbertabad India 11°43N 92°37E 245 J11
Herberton Australia 17°20S 145°25E 280 B4
Herbertsdale S. Africa 34°1S 21°46E 270 D3
Herbertville N.Z. 40°30S 176°33E 284 G5
Herbignac France 47°27N 2°18W 172 E4
Herborn Germany 50°40N 8°18E 178 E4
Herby Poland 50°45N 18°50E 185 H5
Herceg-Novi Montenegro 42°30N 18°33E 202 D2
Hercegfalva = Mezőfalva Hungary 46°55N 18°49E 182 D3
Herchmer Canada 57°22N 94°10W 297 B10
Herculânia = Coxim Brazil 18°30S 54°55W 331 D7
Herðubreið Iceland 65°11N 16°21W 155 B10
Hereford Hereford, U.K. 52°4N 2°43W 169 E5
Hereford Tex., U.S.A. 34°49N 102°24W 314 D3
Herefordshire □ U.K. 52°8N 2°40W 169 E5
Herefoss Norway 58°32N 8°23E 164 F5
Héréhérétué French Polynesia 19°45S 144°58W 289 f
Herehogna Sweden 61°44N 12°8E 164 C9
Hereke Turkey 40°47N 29°38E 203 F13
Herekino N.Z. 35°18S 173°11E 284 B2
Herencia Spain 39°21N 3°22W 195 F7
Herentals Belgium 51°12N 4°51E 170 C4
Herford Germany 52°7N 8°39E 178 C4
Héricourt France 47°32N 6°45E 173 E13
Herington U.S.A. 38°40N 96°57W 308 F5
Heris Iran 38°14N 47°6E 213 C12
Herisau Switz. 47°22N 9°17E 179 H5
Hérisson France 46°32N 2°42E 173 F9
Herkimer U.S.A. 43°2N 74°59W 313 D10
Herlen → Asia 48°48N 117°0E 219 B12
Herlev Denmark 55°43N 12°27E 118 A2
Herlong U.S.A. 40°8N 120°8W 306 E6
Herm U.K. 49°30N 2°28W 169 H5
Hermakivka Ukraine 48°42N 26°11E 183 B11
Herman Eckstein Park S. Africa 26°9S 28°1E 123 A2
Hermana Mayor I. Phil. 15°47N 119°47E 232 D2
Hermann U.S.A. 38°42N 91°27W 310 F5
Hermannsbad = Ciechocinek Poland 52°53N 18°45E 185 F5
Hermannsburg N. Terr., Australia 23°57S 132°45E 278 D5
Hermannsburg Niedersachsen, Germany 52°50N 10°5E 178 C6
Hermannskogel Austria 48°16N 16°17E 142 A1
Hermannstadt = Sibiu Romania 45°45N 24°9E 183 E9
Hermansverk Norway 61°11N 6°52E 164 C3
Hermanus S. Africa 34°27S 19°12E 270 D2
Herment France 45°45N 2°24E 174 C6
Hermidale Australia 31°30S 146°42E 283 A7
Hermiston Edinburgh, U.K. 55°55N 3°19W 121 B2
Hermiston Oreg., U.S.A. 45°51N 119°17W 304 D4
Hermit Is. Papua N. G. 1°32S 145°5E 286 A3
Hermitage Grenada 12°27N 61°28W 323 q
Hermitage Mo., U.S.A. 37°56N 93°19W 310 G3
Hermitage and Winter Palace Russia 59°55N 30°19E 137 B2
Hermon Ont., Canada 45°6N 77°37W 312 A7
Hermon N.Y., U.S.A. 44°28N 75°14W 313 B9
Hermon, Mt. = Shaykh, J. ash Lebanon 33°25N 35°50E 250 B6
Hermosillo Mexico 29°10N 111°0W 318 B2
Hermsdorf Germany 52°37N 13°18E 115 A2
Hernád → Hungary 47°56N 21°8E 182 C6
Hernals Austria 48°13N 16°20E 142 A2
Hernandarias Paraguay 25°20S 54°40W 335 B5
Hernandez U.S.A. 36°24N 120°46W 306 J6
Hernando Argentina 32°28S 63°40W 334 C3
Hernando Fla., U.S.A. 28°54N 82°23W 317 G7
Hernando Miss., U.S.A. 34°50N 90°0W 315 D10
Hernando de Magallanes △ Chile 54°0S 72°40W 336 D2
Hernani Spain 43°16N 1°58W 196 B3
Herndon U.S.A. 40°43N 76°51W 312 F8
Herne Germany 51°32N 7°14E 170 C7
Herne Bay U.K. 51°21N 1°8E 169 F9
Herne Hill U.K. 51°27N 0°6W 125 B3
Herning Denmark 56°8N 8°58E 163 H2
Herod U.S.A. 31°42N 84°26W 316 D5
Héroes de Churubusco Mexico 19°21N 99°6W 128 B2
Heroica Caborca = Caborca Mexico 30°37N 112°6W 318 A2
Heroica Nogales = Nogales Mexico 31°19N 110°56W 318 A2
Heron Bay Canada 48°40N 86°25W 298 C2
Heron I. Australia 23°27S 151°55E 280 C5
Herons, Î. aux Canada 45°25N 73°34W 130 B2
Herradura, Pta. de la Canary Is. 28°26N 14°8W 153 e2
Herre Norway 59°6N 9°34E 164 E6
Herreid U.S.A. 45°50N 100°4W 308 C3
Herrenberg Germany 48°35N 8°52E 179 G4
Herrera Spain 37°26N 4°55W 195 H6
Herrera de Alcántara Spain 39°39N 7°25W 195 F3
Herrera de Pisuerga Spain 42°35N 4°20W 194 C6
Herrera del Duque Spain 39°10N 5°3W 195 F5
Herrestad Sweden 58°21N 11°50E 163 F5
Herrin U.S.A. 37°48N 89°2W 310 G7
Herriot Canada 56°22N 101°16W 297 B8
Herrljunga Sweden 58°5N 13°1E 163 F7
Hersbruck Germany 49°30N 11°26E 179 F7
Herschel I. Canada 69°35N 139°5W 150 C1
Hershey U.S.A. 40°17N 76°39W 313 F8
Herso = Cherso Greece 41°5N 22°47E 202 E6
Herstal Belgium 50°40N 5°38E 170 D5
Herstedoster Denmark 55°40N 12°22E 118 A2
Hertford U.K. 51°48N 0°4W 169 F7
Hertfordshire □ U.K. 51°51N 0°5W 169 F7
's-Hertogenbosch Neths. 51°42N 5°17E 170 C5
Hertsa Ukraine 48°9N 26°15E 183 B11
Herttoniemi Finland 60°12N 25°2E 121 B3
Hertzogville S. Africa 28°9S 25°30E 270 C4
Hervás Spain 40°16N 5°52W 194 E5
Hervey B. Australia 25°0S 152°52E 280 C5
Herzberg Brandenburg, Germany 51°41N 13°14E 178 D9
Herzberg Niedersachsen, Germany 51°38N 10°20E 178 D6
Herzliyya Israel 32°10N 34°50E 251 F5
Herzogenburg Austria 48°17N 15°41E 180 C8
Ḥeşār Fārs, Iran 29°52N 50°16E 247 D6
Ḥeşār Markazī, Iran 35°50N 49°12E 247 C6
Ḥeşārak Iran 35°47N 51°18E 140 A2
Hesdin France 50°21N 2°2E 173 B9
Heshan Guangdong, China 22°34N 113°4E 229 F9
Heshan Guangxi Zhuangzu, China 23°50N 108°53E 228 F7
Heshui China 35°48N 108°0E 226 G5
Heshun China 37°22N 113°32E 226 F7
Heskestad Norway 58°28N 6°22E 164 F3
Hesperia U.S.A. 34°25N 117°18W 307 L9
Hessdalen Norway 62°48N 11°10E 164 B8
Hesse = Hessen □ Germany 50°30N 9°0E 178 E4
Hessen □ Germany 50°30N 9°0E 178 E4
Hessenreuther und Manteler Wald △ Germany 49°45N 12°1E 179 F8
Hesso Australia 32°8S 137°27E 282 B2
Hesteyri Iceland 66°20N 22°53W 155 A4
Heston U.K. 51°28N 0°22W 125 B1
Hestra Sweden 57°26N 13°35E 163 G7
Hetauda Nepal 27°25N 85°2E 243 F11
Hetch Hetchy Aqueduct U.S.A. 37°29N 122°19W 306 H5
Hettinger U.S.A. 46°0N 102°42W 308 B2
Hettstedt Germany 51°39N 11°31E 178 D7
Hetzendorf Austria 48°9N 16°17E 142 B1
Heuksando S. Korea 34°40N 125°30E 224 E2
Heunghae S. Korea 36°12N 129°21E 224 D4
Heuvelton U.S.A. 44°37N 75°25W 313 B9
Hevelândia Brazil 5°12S 61°50W 329 E5
Heves Hungary 47°36N 20°17E 182 C5
Heves □ Hungary 47°50N 20°0E 182 C5
Hewitt U.S.A. 31°28N 97°12W 314 F6
Hexham U.K. 54°58N 2°4W 168 C5
Hexi Yunnan, China 24°9N 102°38E 228 E4
Hexi Zhejiang, China 27°58N 119°38E 229 D12
Hexigten Qi China 43°18N 117°30E 227 C9
Hextable U.K. 51°24N 0°10E 125 B5
Ḥeydarābād Iran 30°33N 55°38E 247 D7
Heydebreck = Kędzierzyn-Koźle Poland 50°20N 18°12E 185 H5
Heyfield Australia 37°59S 146°47E 283 D7
Heysham U.K. 54°3N 2°53W 168 C5
Heyuan China 23°39N 114°40E 229 F10
Heywood Australia 38°8S 141°37E 282 E4
Heyworth U.S.A. 40°19N 88°59W 310 D8
Heze China 35°14N 115°20E 226 G8
Hezhang China 27°8N 104°41E 228 D5
Hi-no-Misaki Japan 35°26N 132°38E 222 B4
Hi Vista U.S.A. 34°45N 117°46W 307 L9
Hialeah U.S.A. 25°51N 80°16W 128 A1
Hiawassa, L. U.S.A. 28°33N 81°28W 133 A2
Hiawatha U.S.A. 39°51N 95°32W 308 F6
Hibbing U.S.A. 47°25N 92°56W 308 B7
Hibernia Reef Australia 12°0S 123°23E 278 B3
Hibiki-Nada Japan 34°0N 130°0E 222 D2
Hickam Air Force Base U.S.A. 21°20N 157°56W 302 K14
Hickam Housing U.S.A. 21°21N 157°57W 302 K14
Hickman U.S.A. 36°34N 89°11W 308 G9
Hickory U.S.A. 35°44N 81°21W 315 D14
Hickory Hills U.S.A. 41°43N 87°49W 119 C2
Hicks, Pt. Australia 37°49S 149°17E 283 D8
Hicks Bay N.Z. 37°34S 178°21E 284 D7
Hicks L. Canada 61°25N 100°0W 297 A9
Hicksville N.Y., U.S.A. 40°46N 73°32W 313 F11
Hicksville Ohio, U.S.A. 41°18N 84°46W 311 C12
Hida Romania 47°10N 23°19E 183 C8
Hida-Gawa → Japan 35°26N 137°3E 223 B9
Hida-Sammyaku Japan 36°30N 137°40E 223 A9
Hida-Sanchi Japan 36°10N 137°0E 223 A9
Hidaka Japan 35°30N 134°44E 222 B6
Hidaka-Sammyaku Japan 42°35N 142°45E 220 C11
Hidalgo □ Mexico 20°30N 99°0W 319 C5
Hidalgo, Presa M. Mexico 26°30N 108°35W 318 B3
Hidalgo del Parral Mexico 26°56N 105°40W 318 B3
Hiddensee Germany 54°32N 13°6E 178 A9
Hidrolândia Brazil 17°0S 49°15W 333 E2
Hieflau Austria 47°36N 14°46E 180 D7
Hiekkaharju Finland 60°18N 25°2E 121 B3
Hiendelaencina Spain 41°5N 3°0W 196 D2
Hienghène N. Cal. 20°41S 164°56E 288 d
Hierro Canary Is. 27°44N 18°0W 153 e1
Hietaniemi Finland 60°10N 24°54E 121 B2
Hietzing Austria 48°10N 16°17E 142 A1
Higashi-Hiroshima Japan 34°25N 132°45E 222 C4
Higashi-Matsuyama Japan 36°2N 139°25E 223 A11
Higashi-Suidō Japan 34°0N 129°30E 222 D1
Higashiajima-San Japan 37°40N 140°10E 220 F10
Higashimurayama Japan 35°45N 139°26E 140 A1
Higashinari Japan 34°40N 135°32E 133 A2
Higashiōsaka Japan 34°39N 135°37E 223 C7
Higashisumiyoshi Japan 34°37N 135°31E 133 B2
Higashiyodogawa Japan 34°44N 135°28E 133 A1
Higbee U.S.A. 39°19N 92°31W 310 E4
Higgins U.S.A. 36°7N 100°2W 314 C4
Higgins Corner U.S.A. 39°2N 121°5W 306 F5
Higginsville U.S.A. 39°4N 93°43W 310 E3
High Bridge U.S.A. 40°40N 74°54W 313 F10
High Desert U.S.A. 43°40N 120°20W 304 E3
High Island Res. China 22°22N 114°21E 219 a
High Level Canada 58°31N 117°8W 296 B5
High Park Canada 43°38N 79°27W 141 B2
High Peak Phil. 15°29N 120°7E 232 D3
High Pk. St. Helena 15°58S 5°44W 153 h
High Point U.S.A. 35°57N 80°0W 315 D15
High Prairie Canada 55°30N 116°30W 296 B5
High River Canada 50°30N 113°50W 296 C6
High Springs U.S.A. 29°50N 82°36W 317 F7
High Tatra = Tatry Slovak Rep. 49°20N 20°0E 181 B13
High Veld Africa 27°0S 27°0E 254 J6
High Wycombe U.K. 51°37N 0°45W 169 F7
Highbank N.Z. 43°37S 171°45E 285 D6
Highbury U.K. 51°33N 0°6W 125 A3
Highgate Jamaica 18°5N 76°57W 320 a
Highgate London, U.K. 51°34N 0°8W 125 A3
Highland Ill., U.S.A. 38°44N 89°41W 310 F7
Highland Ind., U.S.A. 41°33N 87°28W 311 C9
Highland Wis., U.S.A. 43°5N 90°22W 310 A6
Highland □ U.K. 57°17N 4°21W 167 D4
Highland City U.S.A. 27°58N 81°53W 317 H8
Highland Cr. → Canada 43°46N 79°8W 141 A3
Highland Creek Canada 43°46N 79°8W 141 A3
Highland Home U.S.A. 31°57N 86°19W 316 D3
Highland Mills U.S.A. 33°17N 84°17W 316 B5
Highland Park Calif., U.S.A. 34°7N 118°13W 126 B3
Highland Park Ill., U.S.A. 42°11N 87°48W 311 B9
Highland View U.S.A. 29°50N 85°19W 316 F4
Highlands = Fort Thomas U.S.A. 39°4N 84°26W 311 E12
Highlands, The Antigua & B. 17°38N 61°47W 322 c
Highlands North S. Africa 26°8S 28°5E 123 A2
Highmore U.S.A. 44°31N 99°27W 308 C4
Highrock L. Canada 55°45N 100°30W 297 B8
Higuero, Pta. Puerto Rico 18°22N 67°16W 321 b
Higüey Dom. Rep. 18°37N 68°42W 321 C6
Hihya Egypt 30°40N 31°36E 256 H7
Hiiraan □ Somali Rep. 4°0N 45°30E 267 D6
Hiiumaa Estonia 58°50N 22°45E 188 C2
Híjar Spain 41°10N 0°27W 196 D4
Ḥijārah, Ṣaḥrā' al Iraq 30°25N 44°30E 246 D5
Ḥijāz Si. Arabia 24°0N 40°0E 246 E3
Hiji Japan 33°22N 131°32E 222 D3
Hijo = Tagum Phil. 7°33N 125°53E 233 H5
Hikari Japan 33°58N 131°58E 222 D3
Hiketa Japan 34°13N 134°24E 222 C6
Hikkaduwa Sri Lanka 6°8N 80°6E 245 L5
Hikmak, Ras el Egypt 31°15N 27°51E 256 A2
Hiko U.S.A. 37°32N 115°14W 306 H11
Hikone Japan 35°15N 136°10E 223 B8
Hikurangi Gisborne, N.Z. 37°55S 178°4E 284 E5
Hikurangi Northland, N.Z. 35°36S 174°17E 284 B3
Hikutavake Cook Is. 18°56S 169°53W 289 g
Hiland Park U.S.A. 30°12N 85°33W 316 E4
Hilawng Burma 21°23N 93°48E 241 E4
Hildburghausen Germany 50°25N 10°42E 178 E6
Hildesheim Germany 52°9N 9°56E 178 C5
Hilðarendi Iceland 63°44N 19°57W 155 D7
Hill → Australia 30°23S 115°3E 279 F2
Hill City Idaho, U.S.A. 43°18N 115°3W 304 E6
Hill City Kans., U.S.A. 39°22N 99°51W 308 F4
Hill City Minn., U.S.A. 46°59N 93°36W 308 B7
Hill City S. Dak., U.S.A. 43°56N 103°35W 308 D2
Hill Island L. Canada 60°30N 109°50W 297 A7
Hillaby, Mt. Barbados 13°12N 59°35W 323 r
Hillared Sweden 57°37N 13°10E 163 G7
Hillcrest Center U.S.A. 35°23N 118°57W 307 K8
Hillcrest Heights U.S.A. 38°49N 76°57W 143 C4
Hillegom Neths. 52°18N 4°35E 170 B4
Hillend U.K. 56°2N 3°22W 121 A1
Hillerød Denmark 55°56N 12°19E 163 J6
Hillerstorp Sweden 57°20N 13°52E 163 G7
Hilli Bangla. 25°17N 89°1E 241 C2
Hilliard U.S.A. 30°41N 81°55W 316 E8
Hillingdon □ U.K. 51°32N 0°27W 125 A1
Hillsboro = Deerfield Beach U.S.A. 26°19N 80°6W 317 J9
Hillsboro Ga., U.S.A. 33°11N 83°38W 316 B6
Hillsboro Ill., U.S.A. 39°9N 89°29W 310 F7
Hillsboro Kans., U.S.A. 38°21N 97°12W 308 F5
Hillsboro Mo., U.S.A. 38°14N 90°34W 310 F6
Hillsboro N. Dak., U.S.A. 47°26N 97°3W 308 B5
Hillsboro Ohio, U.S.A. 39°12N 83°37W 311 E13
Hillsboro Oreg., U.S.A. 45°31N 122°59W 306 E4
Hillsboro Tex., U.S.A. 32°1N 97°8W 314 E6
Hillsboro Canal U.S.A. 26°30N 80°15W 317 J9
Hillsborough Grenada 12°28N 61°28W 323 q
Hillsborough N.H., U.S.A. 43°7N 71°54W 313 C13
Hillsborough Channel Australia 20°56S 149°15E 280 b
Hillsborough Dam Trin. & Tob. 11°13N 60°40W 323 s
Hillsborough Land = Belle Glade U.S.A. 26°41N 80°40W 317 J9
Hillsdale Mich., U.S.A. 41°56N 84°38W 311 C12
Hillsdale N.Y., U.S.A. 42°11N 73°32W 313 D11
Hillsport Canada 49°27N 85°34W 298 C2
Hillston Australia 33°30S 145°31E 283 B6
Hilltonia U.S.A. 32°53N 81°40W 316 C8
Hillwood U.S.A. 38°52N 77°9W 143 B3
Hilmīya Egypt 30°6N 31°19E 117 A2
Hilo U.S.A. 19°44N 155°5W 302 D6
Hilo ✕ (ITO) U.S.A. 19°43N 155°2W 302 D6
Hilo B. U.S.A. 19°45N 155°5W 302 D6
Hilongos Phil. 10°22N 124°44E 233 F5
Hilton U.S.A. 43°17N 77°48W 312 C7
Hilton Head Island U.S.A. 32°13N 80°45W 316 C9
Hilvan Turkey 37°34N 38°58E 213 D8
Hilversum Neths. 52°14N 5°10E 170 B5
Himachal Pradesh □ India 31°30N 77°0E 242 D7
Himalaya Asia 29°0N 84°0E 243 E11
Himalchuli Nepal 28°27N 84°38E 243 E11
Himamaylan Phil. 10°6N 122°52E 233 F4
Himarë Albania 40°8N 19°43E 202 F3
Himatnagar India 23°37N 72°57E 242 H5
Hime-Jima Japan 33°43N 131°40E 222 D3
Himeji Japan 34°50N 134°40E 222 C6
Himi Japan 36°50N 136°55E 223 A8
Himmerland Denmark 56°45N 9°30E 163 H3
Ḥimş Syria 34°40N 36°45E 250 D7
Ḥimş □ Syria 34°30N 37°0E 250 D8
Hin Keng China 22°22N 114°10E 122 A2
Hinatuan Phil. 8°23N 126°20E 233 G6
Hinatuan Passage Phil. 9°45N 125°47E 233 G5
Hinche Haiti 19°9N 72°1W 321 C5
Hinchinbrook I. Australia 18°20S 146°15E 280 B4
Hinchinbrook Island △ Australia 18°14S 146°6E 280 B4
Hinckley Leics., U.K. 52°33N 1°22W 169 E6
Hinckley Minn., U.S.A. 46°1N 92°56W 308 B7
Hindaun India 26°44N 77°5E 242 F7
Hindenburg = Zabrze Poland 50°18N 18°50E 185 H5
Hindmarsh, L. Australia 36°5S 141°55E 282 D4
Hindol India 20°40N 85°10E 244 D7
Hinds N.Z. 43°59S 171°36E 285 D6
Hindsholm Denmark 55°30N 10°40E 163 J4
Hindu Bagh Pakistan 30°56N 67°50E 242 D2
Hindu Kush Asia 36°0N 71°0E 240 B3
Hindupur India 13°49N 77°32E 245 H3
Hines Creek Canada 56°20N 118°40W 296 B5
Hinesville U.S.A. 31°51N 81°36W 316 D8
Hinganghat India 20°30N 78°52E 244 D4
Hingham U.S.A. 48°33N 110°25W 304 B8
Hinghwa = Xinghua China 32°58N 119°48E 227 H10
Hingir India 21°57N 83°41E 243 J10
Hingoli India 19°41N 77°15E 244 E3
Hinigaran Phil. 10°16N 122°50E 233 F4
Hinis Turkey 39°22N 41°43E 213 C9
Hinna = Imi Ethiopia 6°28N 42°10E 257 F5
Hinna Nigeria 10°25N 11°35E 263 C7
Hinnerup Denmark 56°16N 10°4E 163 H4
Hinnøya Norway 68°35N 15°50E 160 B16
Hino Japan 35°0N 136°15E 223 C8
Hinoba-an Phil. 9°35N 122°28E 233 G4
Hinojosa del Duque Spain 38°30N 5°9W 195 G5
Hinokage Japan 32°39N 131°24E 222 E3
Hinsdale U.S.A. 42°47N 72°29W 313 D12
Hinterrhein → Switz. 46°40N 9°25E 179 J5
Hinthada = Henzada Burma 17°38N 95°26E 241 G5
Hinton Alta., Canada 53°26N 117°34W 296 C5
Hinton W. Va., U.S.A. 37°40N 80°54W 309 G13
Hinubuan = Antipolo Phil. 14°35N 121°10E 232 D3
Hinunangan Phil. 10°25N 125°12E 233 F5
Hios = Chios Greece 38°27N 26°9E 205 C8
Hirado Japan 33°22N 129°33E 222 D1
Hirado-Shima Japan 33°20N 129°30E 222 D1
Hirakata Japan 34°48N 135°38E 223 C7
Hirakud Dam India 21°32N 83°45E 244 D6
Hiran → India 23°6N 79°21E 243 H8
Hirapur India 24°22N 79°13E 243 G8
Hirara Japan 24°48N 125°17E 221 M2
Hirata Japan 35°24N 132°49E 222 B4
Hiratsuka Japan 35°19N 139°21E 223 B11
Hirekerur India 14°28N 75°23E 245 G2
Hirfanlı Barajı Turkey 39°18N 33°31E 212 C5
Hirhafok Algeria 23°49N 5°45E 261 D6
Hiromi Japan 33°13N 132°36E 222 D4
Hiroo Japan 42°17N 143°19E 220 C11
Hirosaki Japan 40°34N 140°28E 220 D10
Hiroshima Japan 34°24N 132°30E 222 C4
Hiroshima □ Japan 34°50N 133°0E 222 C5
Hiroshima-Wan Japan 34°5N 132°20E 222 C4

Hirota *Japan* 34°45N 135°20E **133** A1
Hirschberg = Jelenia Góra *Poland* 50°50N 15°45E **185** H2
Hirschstetten *Austria* 48°14N 16°27E **142** A2
Hirson *France* 49°55N 4°4E **173** C11
Hirtshals *Denmark* 57°36N 9°57E **163** G3
Hisai *Japan* 34°40N 136°28E **223** C8
Hisar *India* 29°12N 75°45E **242** E6
Hisarcık *Turkey* 39°15N 29°14E **205** B11
Hisaria *Bulgaria* 42°30N 24°44E **203** D8
Hisb, Sha'ib = Hasb, W. → *Iraq* 31°45N 44°17E **246** D5
Ḥisma *Si. Arabia* 28°30N 36°0E **251** K7
Ḥiṣn al 'Abr *Yemen* 16°8N 47°14E **248** C4
Hispaniola *W. Indies* 19°0N 71°0W **321** C5
Hīt *Iraq* 33°38N 42°49E **213** F10
Hita *Japan* 33°20N 130°58E **222** D2
Hitachi *Japan* 36°36N 140°39E **223** A12
Hitachi-Ōta *Japan* 36°30N 140°30E **223** A12
Hitchin *U.K.* 51°58N 0°16W **169** F7
Hithadhoo *Maldives* 0°36S 73°5E **272** d
Hither Green *U.K.* 51°26N 0°0 **125** B3
Hitiaa *Tahiti* 17°36S 149°18W **289** e
Hitoyoshi *Japan* 32°13N 130°45E **222** E2
Hitra *Norway* 63°30N 8°45E **164** A5
Hitzacker *Germany* 53°9N 11°2E **178** B7
Hiu *Vanuatu* 13°10S 166°35E **287** C4
Hiuchi-Nada *Japan* 34°5N 133°20E **222** C5
Hiva Oa *French Polynesia* 9°45S 139°0W **289** f
Hixon *Canada* 53°25N 122°35W **296** C4
Hiyoshi *Japan* 35°32N 139°38E **140** B2
Hiyyon, N. → *Israel* 30°25N 35°10E **251** H6
Hizma *West Bank* 31°50N 35°16E **123** B2
Hjalmar L. *Canada* 61°33N 109°25W **297** A7
Hjälmaren *Sweden* 59°18N 15°40E **162** E9
Hjältevad *Sweden* 57°38N 15°20E **163** G9
Hjalteyri *Iceland* 65°55N 18°18W **155** B8
Hjartdal *Norway* 59°37N 8°41E **164** E5
Hjelmelandsvågen *Norway* 59°14N 6°10E **164** E3
Hjelset *Norway* 62°48N 7°30E **164** B4
Hjerkinn *Norway* 62°13N 9°33E **164** B6
Hjo *Sweden* 58°22N 14°17E **163** F8
Hjørring *Denmark* 57°29N 9°59E **163** G3
Hjörsey *Iceland* 64°32N 22°21W **155** C4
Hjort Trench *S. Ocean* 58°0S 157°30E **151** B10
Hjortekær *Denmark* 55°47N 12°32E **118** A3
Hjortespring *Denmark* 55°44N 12°25E **118** A2
Hjortkvarn *Sweden* 58°54N 15°26E **163** F9
Hjukse *Norway* 59°31N 9°19E **164** E6
Hkakabo Razi *Burma* 28°25N 97°23E **228** C1
Hkakabo Razi △ *Burma* 28°0N 97°55E **241** A6
Hkamti = Singkaling Hkamti *Burma* 26°0N 95°39E **241** C5
Hko-lam *Burma* 21°7N 98°5E **241** E7
Hko-ut *Burma* 20°58N 98°2E **241** E7
Hkyenhpa *Burma* 27°43N 97°25E **241** B6
Hlaingbwe *Burma* 17°8N 97°50E **241** G6
Hlinsko *Czech Rep.* 49°45N 15°54E **180** B8
Hlobane *S. Africa* 27°42S 31°0E **271** C5
Hlohovec *Slovak Rep.* 48°26N 17°49E **181** C10
Hluboćepy *Czech Rep.* 50°2N 14°23E **135** B2
Hlučín *Czech Rep.* 49°54N 18°11E **181** B11
Hluhluwe *S. Africa* 28°1S 32°15E **271** C5
Hluhluwe △ *S. Africa* 22°10S 32°5E **271** B5
Hlukhiv *Ukraine* 51°40N 33°58E **189** G7
Hlwaze *Burma* 18°54N 96°37E **241** F6
Hlyboka *Ukraine* 48°5N 25°56E **183** B10
Hlybokaye *Belarus* 55°10N 27°45E **188** E4
Hnappadalssýsla □ *Iceland* 64°50N 22°30W **155** C4
Hnífsdalur *Iceland* 66°7N 23°8W **155** A3
Hnúšt'a *Slovak Rep.* 48°35N 19°58E **181** C12
Ho *Ghana* 6°37N 0°27E **263** D5
Ho Chi Minh City = Thanh Pho Ho Chi Minh *Vietnam* 10°58N 106°40E **237** G6
Ho Chung *China* 22°21N 114°14E **122** A2
Ho Hoa Binh *Vietnam* 20°50N 105°0E **228** G5
Ho Thac Ba *Vietnam* 21°42N 105°1E **236** A5
Ho Thuong *Vietnam* 19°32N 105°48E **236** C5
Hoa Binh *Vietnam* 20°50N 105°20E **228** G5
Hoa Hiep *Vietnam* 11°34N 105°51E **237** G5
Hoai Nhon *Vietnam* 14°28N 109°1E **236** E7
Hoang Lien △ *Vietnam* 21°30N 105°32E **236** B5
Hoang Lien Son *Vietnam* 22°0N 104°0E **228** F4
Hoanib → *Namibia* 19°27S 12°46E **270** A2
Hoare B. *Canada* 65°17N 62°30W **295** D19
Hoarusib → *Namibia* 19°3S 12°36E **270** A2
Hobart *Tas., Australia* 42°50S 147°21E **281** G4
Hobart *Ind., U.S.A.* 41°32N 87°15W **311** C9
Hobart *Okla., U.S.A.* 35°1N 99°6W **314** D5
Hobbs *U.S.A.* 32°42N 103°8W **305** K12
Hobbs Coast *Antarctica* 74°50S 131°0W **151** D14
Hobe Sound *U.S.A.* 27°4N 80°8W **317** H9
Hobo *Colombia* 2°35N 75°30W **328** C2
Hoboken *Ga., U.S.A.* 31°11N 82°8W **316** D7
Hoboken *New York, U.S.A.* **132** d1
Hobro *Denmark* 56°39N 9°46E **163** H3
Hobsons B. *Australia* 37°51S 144°55E **128** B1
Hoburgen *Sweden* 56°55N 18°7E **163** H12
Hobyo *Somali Rep.* 5°25N 48°30E **267** C6
Hocalar *Turkey* 38°36N 30°0E **205** C11
Hochbrück *Germany* 48°14N 11°37E **131** A2
Hochelaga *Canada* 45°32N 73°33W **130** A2
Hochfeld *Namibia* 21°28S 17°58E **270** B2
Hochharz △ *Germany* 51°48N 10°38E **178** D6
Hochschwab *Austria* 47°35N 15°0E **180** D8
Höchstadt *Germany* 49°42N 10°47E **179** F6
Hochtaunus △ *Germany* 50°20N 8°30E **179** E4
Hoch'uan = Hechuan *China* 30°2N 106°12E **228** B6
Hochwan = Hechuan *China* 30°2N 106°12E **228** B6
Hockenheim *Germany* 49°19N 8°32E **179** F4
Hockley = Levelland *U.S.A.* 33°35N 102°23W **314** E3
Hodaka-Dake *Japan* 36°17N 137°39E **223** A9
Hodeida = Al Ḥudaydah *Yemen* 14°50N 43°0E **248** D3
Hodgeville *Canada* 50°7N 106°58W **297** C7
Hodgkins *U.S.A.* 41°46N 87°53W **119** C1
Hodgson *Canada* 51°13N 97°36W **297** C9
Hodh El Gharbi □ *Mauritania* 16°30N 10°0W **262** B3
Hódmezővásárhely *Hungary* 46°28N 20°22E **182** D5
Hodna, Chott el *Algeria* 35°26N 4°43E **261** A6
Hodo-dan *N. Korea* 39°23N 127°32E **224** E5
Hodonín *Czech Rep.* 48°50N 17°10E **181** C10
Hœdic, Î. de *France* 47°20N 2°53W **172** E4
Hoegi *S. Korea* 37°35N 127°3E **137** B2
Hoeilaart *Belgium* 50°46N 4°28E **116** B2
Hoek van Holland *Neths.* 52°0N 4°7E **170** C4
Hoengseong *S. Korea* 37°29N 127°59E **224** F4
Hoeryong *N. Korea* 42°30N 129°45E **224** A4
Hoeyang *N. Korea* 38°43N 127°36E **224** C3
Hof *Bayern, Germany* 50°19N 11°55E **179** E7
Hof *Norður-Múlasýsla, Iceland* 65°39N 15°0W **155** B11
Hof *Suður-Múlasýsla, Iceland* 64°33N 14°40W **155** C12
Hof *Vestfold, Norway* 59°32N 10°5E **164** E7
Hofburg *Vienna, Austria* **142** b1
Hofei = Hefei *China* 31°52N 117°18E **229** B11
Hoffell *Iceland* 64°23N 15°20W **155** C11
Hoffman I. *U.S.A.* 40°34N 74°3W **132** C1
Hofgarten *Munich, Germany* **131** a3
Hofgeismar *Germany* 51°29N 9°23E **178** D5
Hofheim *Germany* 50°5N 8°26E **179** E4
Hofmeyr *S. Africa* 31°39S 25°50E **270** D4
Höfn *Iceland* 64°15N 15°13W **155** C11
Hofors *Sweden* 60°31N 16°15E **162** D10
Hofsjökull *Iceland* 64°49N 18°48W **155** C8
Hofsós *Iceland* 65°53N 19°26W **155** B7
Hōfu *Japan* 34°3N 131°34E **222** C3
Hog Harbour *Vanuatu* 15°8S 167°6E **287** E5
Hog I. = Paradise I. *Bahamas* 25°6N 77°19W **153** b
Hog I. *Grenada* 12°0N 61°44W **323** q
Hog Pt. *Antigua & B.* 17°41N 61°47W **322** c
Hogan Group *Australia* 39°13S 147°1E **281** F4
Höganäs *Sweden* 56°12N 12°33E **163** H6
Hogansville *U.S.A.* 33°10N 84°55W **316** B5
Hogarth, Mt. *Australia* 21°48S 136°58E **280** C2
Hoge Kempen △ *Belgium* 51°6N 5°35E **170** C5
Høgeloft *Norway* 61°3N 8°12E **164** C5
Hogenakai Falls *India* 12°6N 77°50E **245** H3
Hoggar = Ahaggar *Algeria* 23°0N 6°30E **261** D6
Högsäter *Sweden* 58°38N 12°5E **163** F6
Högsby *Sweden* 57°10N 16°1E **163** G10
Högsjö *Sweden* 59°4N 15°44E **162** E9
Hogsty Reef *Bahamas* 21°41N 73°48W **321** B5
Hoh → *U.S.A.* 47°45N 124°29W **306** C2
Hoh Xil Shan *China* 36°30N 89°0E **218** D6
Hohd ech Chargui □ *Mauritania* 19°0N 7°15W **260** E3
Hohe Acht *Germany* 50°22N 7°0E **179** E3
Hohe Tauern *Austria* 47°11N 12°40E **180** D5
Hohe Tauern △ *Austria* 47°5N 12°20E **180** D5
Hohenau *Austria* 48°36N 16°55E **181** C9
Hohenbrunn *Germany* 48°2N 11°42E **131** B3
Hohenelbe = Vrchlabí *Czech Rep.* 50°38N 15°37E **180** A8
Hohenems *Austria* 47°22N 9°42E **180** D2
Hohenloher Ebene *Germany* 49°14N 9°36E **179** F5
Hohenmauth = Vysoké Mýto *Czech Rep.* 49°58N 16°10E **181** B9
Hohensalza = Inowrocław *Poland* 52°50N 18°12E **185** F5
Hohensalzburg = Lunino *Russia* 53°38N 45°18E **190** D7
Hohenschönhausen *Germany* 52°33N 13°30E **115** A4
Hohenstadt = Zábřeh *Czech Rep.* 49°53N 16°52E **181** B9
Hohenstein = Olsztynek *Poland* 53°34N 20°19E **184** E7
Hohenwald *U.S.A.* 35°33N 87°33W **315** D11
Hohenwestedt *Germany* 54°5N 9°40E **178** A5
Hoher Rhön = Rhön *Germany* 50°24N 9°58E **178** E5
Hoher Vogelsberg △ *Germany* 51°45N 9°35E **178** D5
Hohes Venn *Belgium* 50°30N 6°5E **170** D6
Hohes Venn-Eifel △ *Europe* 50°30N 6°10E **178** E2
Hohhot *China* 40°52N 111°40E **226** D6
Hohoe *Ghana* 7°8N 0°32E **263** D5
Hoi An *Vietnam* 15°30N 108°19E **236** E7
Hoi Xuan *Vietnam* 20°25N 105°9E **228** G5
Hoihow = Haikou *China* 20°1N 110°16E **236** B8
Hoisington *U.S.A.* 38°31N 98°47W **308** F4
Hojai *India* 26°0N 92°54E **241** B4
Hojambaz *Turkmenistan* 38°7N 65°0E **216** E6
Højer *Denmark* 54°58N 8°42E **163** K2
Hōjō *Japan* 33°58N 132°46E **222** D4
Hok *Sweden* 57°31N 14°16E **163** G8
Hoka = Hegang *China* 47°20N 130°19E **219** B15
Hökensås *Sweden* 58°0N 14°5E **163** G8
Hökerum *Sweden* 57°51N 13°16E **163** G7
Hokianga Harbour *N.Z.* 35°31S 173°22E **284** B2
Hokitika *N.Z.* 42°42S 171°0E **285** C6
Hokkaidō □ *Japan* 43°30N 143°0E **220** C11
Hokksund *Norway* 59°48N 9°54E **164** E6
Hol-Hol *Djibouti* 11°20N 42°50E **257** E5
Hola *Kenya* 1°29S 40°2E **268** B4
Hola Prystan *Ukraine* 46°29N 32°32E **189** J7
Holakas *Greece* 35°57N 27°53E **206** F11
Holalkere *India* 14°2N 76°11E **245** G3
Holar *Iceland* 65°44N 19°8W **155** B7
Holargos = Cholargos *Greece* 37°59N 23°48E **112** B2
Holbæk *Denmark* 55°43N 11°43E **163** J5
Holborn *London, U.K.* **125** a4
Holbrook *N.S.W., Australia* 35°42S 147°18E **283** C7
Holbrook *Ariz., U.S.A.* 34°54N 110°10W **305** J8
Holcomb *U.S.A.* 42°54N 77°25W **312** D7
Holden *Mo., U.S.A.* 38°43N 94°0W **310** F3
Holden *Utah, U.S.A.* 39°6N 112°16W **304** G7
Holden, L. *U.S.A.* 28°30N 81°23W **133** B2
Holdenville *U.S.A.* 35°5N 96°24W **314** D6
Holdich *Argentina* 45°57S 68°13W **336** C3
Holdrege *U.S.A.* 40°26N 99°23W **308** E4
Hole-Narsipur *India* 12°48N 76°16E **245** H3
Holešov *Czech Rep.* 49°20N 17°35E **181** B10
Holešovice *Czech Rep.* 50°6N 14°28E **135** B2
Holetown *Barbados* 13°11N 59°38W **323** r
Holgate *U.S.A.* 41°15N 84°8W **311** C12
Holguín *Cuba* 20°50N 76°20W **320** B4
Holíč *Slovak Rep.* 48°49N 17°10E **181** C10
Holice *Czech Rep.* 50°5N 16°0E **180** A8
Holiday *U.S.A.* 28°11N 82°44W **317** G7
Höljes *Sweden* 60°50N 12°35E **162** D6
Holladay *U.S.A.* 40°39N 111°49W **304** F7
Hollabrunn *Austria* 48°34N 16°5E **180** C9
Hollams Bird I. *Namibia* 24°40S 14°30E **270** B1
Holland = Netherlands ■ *Europe* 52°0N 5°30E **170** C5
Holland *Mich., U.S.A.* 42°47N 86°7W **311** D10
Holland *N.Y., U.S.A.* 42°38N 78°32W **312** D6
Holland B. *Jamaica* 17°57N 76°13W **320** a
Holland Centre *Canada* 44°23N 80°47W **312** B4
Holland Patent *U.S.A.* 43°14N 75°15W **313** C9
Holland Tunnel *New York, U.S.A.* **132** d1
Holland Village *Singapore* 1°18N 103°47E **138** B2
Hollandale *U.S.A.* 33°10N 90°51W **315** E9
Hollandia = Jayapura *Indonesia* 2°28S 140°38E **231** E10
Holley *U.S.A.* 43°14N 78°2W **312** C6
Hollfeld *Germany* 49°56N 11°18E **179** F7
Hollidaysburg *U.S.A.* 40°26N 78°24W **312** F6
Hollins *U.S.A.* 34°41N 99°55W **314** D5
Hollis Reservoir *Trin. & Tob.* 10°40N 61°10W **323** t
Hollister *Calif., U.S.A.* 36°51N 121°24W **306** J5
Hollister *Idaho, U.S.A.* 42°21N 114°35W **304** E6
Höllriegelskreuth *Germany* 48°2N 11°30E **131** B1
Höllviken *Sweden* 55°26N 12°58E **163** J6
Höllviksnäs = Höllviken *Sweden* 55°26N 12°58E **163** J6
Holly *U.S.A.* 42°48N 83°38W **311** B13
Holly Hill *Fla., U.S.A.* 29°16N 81°3W **317** F8
Holly Hill *S.C., U.S.A.* 33°19N 80°25W **316** B9
Holly Springs *Ga., U.S.A.* 34°10N 84°30W **316** A5
Holly Springs *Miss., U.S.A.* 34°46N 89°27W **315** D10
Hollywood *Calif., U.S.A.* 34°5N 118°19W **126** B3
Hollywood *Fla., U.S.A.* 26°0N 80°8W **317** J9
Hollywood Bowl *U.S.A.* 34°7N 118°20W **126** B2
Holman *Canada* 70°44N 117°44W **294** C8
Hólmavík *Iceland* 65°42N 21°40W **155** B5
Holmen *Oppland, Norway* 60°40N 10°22E **164** D7
Holmen *Wis., U.S.A.* 43°58N 91°15W **308** D8
Holmenkollen *Norway* 59°57N 10°41E **133** A3
Holmes Beach *U.S.A.* 27°31N 82°43W **317** H7
Holmes Cr. → *U.S.A.* 30°30N 85°50W **316** E4
Holmes Reefs *Australia* 16°27S 148°0E **280** B4
Holmes Run Acres *U.S.A.* 38°51N 77°13W **143** B2
Holmestrand *Norway* 59°31N 10°14E **164** E7
Holmgård *Sweden* 59°14N 18°0E **139** B1
Holmlia *Norway* 59°49N 10°46E **133** B3
Holmsjö *Sweden* 56°25N 15°32E **163** H9
Holmsjön *Västernorrland, Sweden* 62°41N 16°33E **162** B10
Holmsjön *Västernorrland, Sweden* 62°26N 15°20E **162** B9
Holmsland Klit *Denmark* 56°0N 8°5E **163** J2
Holmsund *Sweden* 63°41N 20°20E **160** E19
Holocaust Memorial *Israel* 31°47N 35°11E **123** B2
Holocaust Memorial Park *Boston, U.S.A.* **116** b2
Holod *Romania* 46°49N 22°8E **182** D7
Holon *Israel* 32°0N 34°46E **251** G5
Holopaw *U.S.A.* 28°8N 81°5W **317** G8
Holovne *Ukraine* 51°20N 24°5E **185** G11
Holøydal *Norway* 62°12N 11°27E **164** B8
Holozubyntsi *Ukraine* 48°50N 26°55E **183** B11
Holroyd → *Australia* 14°10S 141°36E **280** A3
Holstebro *Denmark* 56°22N 8°37E **163** H2
Holsteinische Schweiz △ *Germany* 54°8N 10°30E **178** A6
Holsteinsborg = Sisimiut *Greenland* 66°40N 53°30W **154** D5
Holsworthy *U.K.* 50°48N 4°22W **169** G3
Holt *Iceland* 63°33N 19°48W **155** D7
Holt *Fla., U.S.A.* 30°43N 86°45W **317** E3
Holt *Mich., U.S.A.* 42°39N 84°31W **311** B12
Holton *Nfld. & L., Canada* 54°31N 57°12W **299** B8
Holton *Kans., U.S.A.* 39°28N 95°44W **308** F6
Holts Summit *U.S.A.* 38°38N 92°7W **310** F4
Holtville *U.S.A.* 32°49N 115°23W **307** N11
Holualoa *U.S.A.* 19°37N 155°57W **302** D6
Holum *Norway* 58°6N 7°32E **164** F4
Holwerd *Neths.* 53°22N 5°54E **170** A5
Holy Cross *U.S.A.* 62°12N 159°46W **303** E8
Holy I. *Anglesey, U.K.* 53°17N 4°37W **168** D3
Holy I. *Northumberland, U.K.* 55°40N 1°47W **168** B6
Holyhead *U.K.* 53°18N 4°38W **168** D3
Holyoke *Colo., U.S.A.* 40°35N 102°18W **304** F12
Holyoke *Mass., U.S.A.* 42°12N 72°37W **313** D12
Holyrood *Canada* 47°27N 53°8W **299** C9
Holyrood House, Palace of *U.K.* 55°57N 3°10W **121** B3
Holysloot *Neths.* 52°25N 5°2E **112** A3
Holzkirchen *Germany* 47°52N 11°42E **179** H7
Holzminden *Germany* 51°50N 9°28E **178** D5
Homa Bay *Kenya* 0°36S 34°30E **268** C3
Homalin *Burma* 24°55N 95°0E **241** C5
Homand *Iran* 32°28N 59°37E **247** C8
Homathko → *Canada* 51°0N 124°56W **296** C4
Homberg *Germany* 51°2N 9°25E **178** D5
Hombori *Mali* 15°20N 1°38W **263** B4
Hombori Tondo *Mali* 15°16N 1°40W **263** B4
Homburg *Germany* 49°28N 7°18E **179** F3
Home B. *Canada* 68°40N 67°10W **295** D18
Home Hill *Australia* 19°43S 147°25E **280** B4
Home Reef *Tonga* 18°59S 174°47W **287** P13
Homedale *U.S.A.* 43°37N 116°56W **304** E5
Homei *Taiwan* 24°7N 120°29E **225** B2
Homeland *U.S.A.* 30°51N 82°1W **316** E7
Homer *Alaska, U.S.A.* 59°39N 151°33W **303** G10
Homer *Ill., U.S.A.* 40°4N 87°57W **311** D9
Homer *La., U.S.A.* 32°48N 93°4W **314** E8
Homer *Mich., U.S.A.* 42°9N 84°49W **311** B12
Homer *N.Y., U.S.A.* 42°38N 76°10W **313** D8
Homer City *U.S.A.* 40°32N 79°10W **312** F5
Homert △ *Germany* 51°15N 8°0E **178** D4
Homerton *U.K.* 51°32N 0°2W **125** A3
Homerville *U.S.A.* 31°2N 82°45W **316** D7
Homestead *Queens., Australia* 20°20S 145°40E **280** C4
Homestead *Fla., U.S.A.* 25°28N 80°29W **317** K9
Homestead △ *U.S.A.* 40°17N 96°50W **308** E5
Hometown *U.S.A.* 41°44N 87°42W **119** C2
Homewood *U.S.A.* 41°34N 87°40W **311** C9
Hommelvik *Norway* 63°25N 10°48E **164** A7
Hommersåk *Norway* 58°56N 5°50E **164** F2
Homnabad *India* 17°45N 77°11E **244** F3
Homoine *Mozam.* 23°55S 35°8E **271** B6
Homoljske Planina *Serbia* 44°10N 21°45E **202** B5
Homonhon I. *Phil.* 10°44N 125°43E **233** F5
Homorod *Romania* 46°5N 25°15E **183** D10
Homosassa Springs *U.S.A.* 28°48N 82°35W **317** G7
Homs = Al Khums *Libya* 32°40N 14°17E **258** B2
Homs = Ḥimş *Syria* 34°40N 36°45E **250** D7
Homyel *Belarus* 52°28N 31°0E **177** B16
Homyel □ *Belarus* 52°40N 30°10E **189** F6
Hon Chong *Vietnam* 10°25N 104°30E **237** G5
Hon Hai *Vietnam* 10°0N 109°0E **237** H7
Hon Me *Vietnam* 19°23N 105°56E **236** C5
Honan = Henan □ *China* 34°0N 114°0E **226** H8
Hōnanchō *Japan* 35°40N 139°39E **140** A2
Hōnaunau *U.S.A.* 19°26N 155°55W **302** D6
Honavar *India* 14°17N 74°27E **245** G2
Honaz *Turkey* 37°46N 29°18E **205** D11
Honbetsu *Japan* 43°7N 143°37E **220** C11
Honcho *Japan* 35°40N 139°41E **140** A3
Honcut *U.S.A.* 39°20N 121°32W **306** F5
Honda *Colombia* 5°12N 74°45W **328** B3
Honda, Bahia *Cuba* 22°54N 83°10W **320** B3
Honda B. *Phil.* 9°53N 118°49E **233** G2
Hondarribia *Spain* 43°22N 1°47W **196** B3
Hondeklipbaai *S. Africa* 30°19S 17°17E **270** D2
Honden *Japan* 35°43N 139°50E **140** A4
Hondo *Japan* 32°27N 130°12E **222** E2
Hondo *Tex., U.S.A.* 29°21N 99°9W **314** G5
Hondo → *Belize* 18°25N 88°21W **319** D7
Hondo, Rio → *Calif., U.S.A.* 34°2N 118°15W **126** B4
Honduras ■ *Cent. Amer.* 14°40N 86°30W **320** D2
Honduras, G. de *Caribbean* 16°50N 87°0W **320** C2
Hønefoss *Norway* 60°10N 10°18E **164** D7
Honesdale *U.S.A.* 41°34N 75°16W **313** E9
Honey Harbour *Canada* 44°52N 79°49W **312** B5
Honey L. *U.S.A.* 40°15N 120°19W **306** E6
Honfleur *France* 49°25N 0°13E **172** C7
Høng *Denmark* 55°31N 11°18E **163** J5
Hong → *Vietnam* 20°16N 106°34E **236** B5
Hong Gai *Vietnam* 20°57N 107°5E **228** G6
Hong He → *China* 32°25N 115°35E **226** H8
Hong Hu *China* 29°54N 113°24E **229** C9
Hong Kong *China* 22°17N 114°11E **122** B1
Hong Kong □ *China* 22°11N 114°14E **229** F10
Hong Kong, Univ. of *China* 22°16N 114°8E **122** B1
Hong Kong I. *China* 22°16N 114°12E **122** B1
Hong Kong Int. ✈ (HKG) *China* 22°19N 113°57E **219** a
Hong Kong Park *Hong Kong, China* **122** c1
Honga *Angola* 15°9S 15°12E **265** F3
Hong'an *China* 31°20N 114°40E **229** B10
Hongcheon *S. Korea* 37°44N 127°53E **224** D3
Hongdo *S. Korea* 34°41N 125°12E **224** E2
Honghai Wan *China* 22°40N 115°0E **229** F10
Honghe *China* 23°25N 102°25E **228** F4
Honghu *China* 29°50N 113°30E **229** C9
Hongje *S. Korea* 37°35N 126°56E **137** B1
Hongjiang *China* 27°7N 109°59E **228** D7
Hongjimun Tunnel *S. Korea* 37°37N 126°58E **137** B1
Hongkou *China* 31°16N 121°29E **138** B1
Hongliu He → *China* 38°0N 109°50E **226** F5
Hongor *Mongolia* 45°45N 112°50E **226** B7
Hongqiao *China* 31°11N 121°22E **138** B1
Hongseong *S. Korea* 36°37N 126°38E **224** D3
Hongshan *China* 36°38N 117°58E **227** F9
Hongshui He → *China* 23°48N 109°30E **228** F7
Hongtong *China* 36°16N 111°40E **226** F6
Honguedo, Détroit d' *Canada* 49°15N 64°0W **299** C7
Hongwon *N. Korea* 40°0N 127°56E **224** C3
Hongya *China* 29°57N 103°22E **228** C4
Hongyuan *China* 32°51N 102°40E **228** A4
Hongze Hu *China* 33°15N 118°35E **227** H10
Honiara *Solomon Is.* 9°27S 159°57E **287** M10
Honiton *U.K.* 50°47N 3°11W **169** G4
Honjō *Akita, Japan* 39°23N 140°3E **220** E10
Honjō *Gumma, Japan* 36°14N 139°11E **223** A11
Honjyo *Japan* 35°41N 139°48E **140** A3
Honkawane *Japan* 35°5N 138°5E **223** B10
Honkorâb, Ras *Egypt* 24°35N 35°10E **256** C4
Honnali *India* 14°15N 75°40E **245** G2
Honningsvåg *Norway* 70°59N 25°59E **160** A21
Hönö *Sweden* 57°41N 11°39E **163** G5
Honoka'a *U.S.A.* 20°5N 155°28W **302** C6
Honokai Hale *U.S.A.* 21°20N 158°6W **302** K13
Honolulu *U.S.A.* 21°19N 157°52W **302** K14
Honolulu District *U.S.A.* 21°19N 157°46W **302** K14
Honolulu Int. ✈ (HNL) *U.S.A.* 21°19N 157°55W **302** K14
Honomu *U.S.A.* 19°52N 155°7W **302** D6
Honoré Mercier, Pont *Canada* 45°24N 73°39W **130** B1
Honouliuli *U.S.A.* 21°22N 158°2W **302** K13
Honow *Germany* 52°32N 13°38E **115** A4
Honshū *Japan* 36°0N 138°0E **223** A8
Hontoria del Pinar *Spain* 41°50N 3°10W **196** D1
Honu'apo B. *U.S.A.* 19°5N 155°33W **302** D6
Hood, I. = Española, I. *Ecuador* 1°23S 89°39W **330** a
Hood, Mt. *U.S.A.* 45°23N 121°42W **304** D3
Hood, Pt. *Australia* 34°23S 119°34E **279** F2
Hood Pt. *Papua N. G.* 10°4S 147°45E **286** F4
Hood River *U.S.A.* 45°43N 121°31W **304** D3
Hoodsport *U.S.A.* 47°24N 123°9W **306** C3
Hoofddorp *Neths.* 52°18N 4°41E **170** B4
Hooge *Germany* 54°34N 8°33E **178** A4
Hoogeveen *Neths.* 52°44N 6°28E **170** B6
Hoogezand-Sappemeer *Neths.* 53°9N 6°45E **170** A6
Hooghly = Hugli → *India* 21°56N 88°4E **243** J13
Hooghly-Chinsura = Chunchura *India* 22°53N 88°27E **243** H13
Hook *U.K.* 51°22N 0°17W **125** B2
Hook Hd. *Ireland* 52°7N 6°56W **166** D5
Hook I. *Australia* 20°4S 149°0E **280** b
Hook of Holland = Hoek van Holland *Neths.* 52°0N 4°7E **170** C4
Hooker *U.S.A.* 36°52N 101°13W **314** C4
Hooker Creek = Lajamanu *Australia* 18°23S 130°38E **278** C5
Hooker Creek © *Australia* 18°6S 130°23E **278** C5
Ho'olehua *U.S.A.* 21°10N 157°5W **302** B4
Hoonah *U.S.A.* 58°7N 135°27W **296** B1
Hoop *Bonaire* 12°7N 68°17W **322** h
Hooper Bay *U.S.A.* 61°32N 166°6W **303** F6
Hoopeston *U.S.A.* 40°28N 87°40W **311** D9
Hoopstad *S. Africa* 27°50S 25°55E **270** C4
Höör *Sweden* 55°56N 13°33E **163** J7
Hoorn *Neths.* 52°38N 5°4E **170** B5
Hoover *U.S.A.* 33°24N 86°49W **315** E11
Hoover Dam *U.S.A.* 36°1N 114°44W **307** K12
Hooversville *U.S.A.* 40°9N 78°55W **312** F6
Hop Bottom *U.S.A.* 41°42N 75°46W **313** E9
Hopa *Turkey* 41°28N 41°30E **213** B9
Hope *B.C., Canada* 49°25N 121°25W **296** D4
Hope *Ariz., U.S.A.* 33°43N 113°42W **307** M13
Hope *Ark., U.S.A.* 33°40N 93°36W **314** E8
Hope *Ind., U.S.A.* 39°18N 85°46W **311** E11
Hope, L. *S. Austral., Australia* 28°24S 139°18E **281** D2
Hope, L. *W. Austral., Australia* 32°35S 120°15E **279** F3
Hope, Pt. *U.S.A.* 68°21N 166°47W **303** B6
Hope Bay *Jamaica* 18°12N 76°34W **320** a
Hope I. *Canada* 44°55N 80°11W **312** B4
Hope Town *Bahamas* 26°35N 76°57W **320** A4
Hope Vale *Australia* 15°16S 145°20E **280** B4
Hope Vale © *Australia* 15°8S 145°15E **280** B4
Hopedale *Nfld. & L., Canada* 55°28N 60°13W **299** A7
Hopedale *Mass., U.S.A.* 42°8N 71°33W **313** D13
Hopefield *S. Africa* 33°3S 18°22E **270** D2
Hopei = Hebei □ *China* 39°0N 116°0E **226** E9
Hopelchén *Mexico* 19°46N 89°51W **319** D7
Hopetoun *Vic., Australia* 35°42S 142°22E **282** C5
Hopetoun *W. Austral., Australia* 33°57S 120°7E **279** F3
Hopetown *S. Africa* 29°34S 24°3E **270** C3
Hopewell *U.S.A.* 37°18N 77°17W **309** G15
Hopfgarten *Austria* 47°27N 12°10E **180** D5
Hopin *Burma* 24°58N 96°30E **241** C6
Hoping *Changhua, Taiwan* 24°10N 120°56E **225** B2
Hoping *T'aitung, Taiwan* 24°21N 121°20E **225** B3
Hopkins *U.S.A.* 40°33N 94°49W **310** D2
Hopkins, L. *Australia* 24°15S 128°35E **278** D4
Hopkinsville *U.S.A.* 36°52N 87°29W **308** G10
Hopland *U.S.A.* 38°58N 123°7W **306** G3
Hopong *Burma* 20°47N 97°11E **241** E6
Hopwood's Ferry = Echuca *Australia* 36°10S 144°45E **283** D6
Hoque *Angola* 14°40S 13°50E **265** E2
Hoquiam *U.S.A.* 46°59N 123°53W **306** D3
Hora Hoverla *Ukraine* 48°7N 24°41E **183** B9
Hora Sfakion = Chora Sfakion *Greece* 35°15N 24°9E **207** E5
Hōrai *Japan* 34°58N 137°32E **223** C9
Horana *Sri Lanka* 6°43N 80°4E **245** L5
Horasan *Turkey* 40°3N 42°11E **213** B10
Horažďovice *Czech Rep.* 49°19N 13°42E **180** B6
Horb *Germany* 48°26N 8°47E **179** G4
Hörby *Sweden* 55°51N 13°40E **163** J7
Horcajo de Santiago *Spain* 39°50N 3°1W **196** F1
Hordabø *Norway* 60°42N 4°54E **164** D1
Hordaland □ *Norway* 60°25N 6°15E **164** D3
Hordern Hills *Australia* 20°15S 130°0E **278** D5
Horezu *Romania* 45°6N 24°0E **183** E9
Horgen *Switz.* 47°15N 8°35E **179** H4
Horgoš *Serbia* 46°10N 20°0E **182** D4
Hořice *Czech Rep.* 50°21N 15°39E **180** A8
Horikiri *Japan* 35°44N 139°50E **140** A4
Horinchove *Ukraine* 48°16N 23°26E **183** B8
Horinger *China* 40°28N 111°48E **226** D6
Horizontina *Brazil* 27°37S 54°19W **335** B5
Horki *Belarus* 54°17N 30°59E **188** E6
Horlick Mts. *Antarctica* 84°0S 102°0W **151** E15
Horlivka *Ukraine* 48°19N 38°5E **189** H10
Hormak *Iran* 29°58N 60°51E **247** D9
Hormigueros *Puerto Rico* 18°8N 67°8W **321** b
Hormoz *Iran* 27°35N 55°0E **247** E7
Hormoz, Jaz.-ye *Iran* 27°8N 56°28E **247** E8
Hormozgān □ *Iran* 27°30N 56°0E **247** E8
Hormuz, Küh-e *Iran* 27°27N 55°10E **247** E7
Hormuz, Str. of *The Gulf* 26°30N 56°30E **247** E8
Horn *Austria* 48°39N 15°40E **180** C8
Horn *Iceland* 66°28N 22°28W **155** A4
Horn *Sweden* 57°54N 15°51E **163** G9
Horn → *Canada* 61°30N 118°1W **296** A5
Horn, Cape = Hornos, C. de *Chile* 55°50S 67°30W **336** E3
Horn, Is. *Wall. & F. Is.* 14°16S 178°6W **277** C15
Horn Head *Ireland* 55°14N 8°0W **166** A3
Horn I. *Australia* 10°37S 142°17E **286** F2
Horn Plateau *Canada* 62°15N 119°15W **296** A5
Horn Pond *U.S.A.* 42°28N 71°9W **116** A1
Hornachuelos *Spain* 37°50N 5°14W **195** H5
Hornavan *Sweden* 66°15N 17°30E **160** C17
Hornbeck *U.S.A.* 31°20N 93°24W **314** F8
Hornbrook *U.S.A.* 41°55N 122°33W **304** F2
Hornburg *Germany* 52°2N 10°37E **178** C6
Hornby *N.Z.* 43°33S 172°33E **285** D7
Horncastle *U.K.* 53°13N 0°7W **168** D7
Hornchurch *U.K.* 51°33N 0°14E **125** A5
Horndal *Sweden* 60°18N 16°23E **162** D10
Hornell *U.S.A.* 42°20N 77°40W **312** D7
Hornell L. *Canada* 62°20N 119°25W **296** A5
Hornepayne *Canada* 49°14N 84°48W **298** C3
Horni *Czech Rep.* 50°2N 14°33E **135** B3
Horní Planá *Czech Rep.* 48°46N 14°2E **180** C7
Horní Počernice *Czech Rep.* 50°6N 14°36E **135** B3
Hornindal *Norway* 61°58N 6°30E **164** C3
Hornings Mills *Canada* 44°9N 80°12W **312** B4
Hornitos *U.S.A.* 37°30N 120°14W **306** H6
Hornopirén △ *Chile* 41°58S 72°17W **336** B2
Hornos, C. de *Chile* 55°50S 67°30W **336** E3
Hornos Is. *Papua N. G.* 2°12S 147°45E **286** B4
Hornoy-le-Bourg *France* 49°50N 1°54E **173** C8
Hornsby *Australia* 33°42S 151°2E **283** B9
Hornsea *U.K.* 53°55N 0°11W **168** D7
Hornsey *U.K.* 51°35N 0°7W **125** A3
Hornsjø *Norway* 61°19N 10°38E **164** C7
Hornslandet *Sweden* 61°35N 17°37E **162** C11
Hörnum *Germany* 54°45N 8°17E **178** A4
Horobetsu = Noboribetsu *Japan* 42°24N 141°6E **220** C10
Horodenka *Ukraine* 48°41N 25°29E **183** B10
Horodnya *Ukraine* 51°55N 31°33E **189** G6
Horodok *Khmelnytskyy, Ukraine* 49°10N 26°34E **177** D14
Horodok *Lviv, Ukraine* 49°46N 23°32E **177** D12
Horodyshche *Ukraine* 49°17N 31°27E **189** H6
Horokhiv *Ukraine* 50°30N 24°45E **177** C13
Horoměřice *Czech Rep.* 50°8N 14°20E **135** B1
Horovice *Czech Rep.* 49°48N 13°53E **180** B6
Horqin Youyi Qianqi *China* 46°5N 122°3E **227** A12
Horqin Zuoyi Zhongqi *China* 44°8N 123°18E **227** B12
Horqueta *Paraguay* 23°15S 56°55W **334** A4
Horred *Sweden* 57°22N 12°28E **163** G6
Horse Cr. → *U.S.A.* 41°57N 103°58W **304** F12
Horse I. *Canada* 53°20N 99°6W **297** C9
Horse Is. *Canada* 50°15N 55°50W **299** B8
Horsefly L. *Canada* 52°25N 121°0W **296** C4
Horseheads *U.S.A.* 42°10N 76°49W **312** D8
Horsens *Denmark* 55°52N 9°51E **163** J3
Horseshoe Bend △ *U.S.A.* 32°59N 85°44W **316** C4
Horseshoe Lake *Canada* 45°17N 79°51W **312** A5
Horsham *Vic., Australia* 36°44S 142°13E **282** D5
Horsham *W. Susx., U.K.* 51°4N 0°20W **169** F7
Horšovský Týn *Czech Rep.* 49°31N 12°58E **180** B5
Horta *Azores* 38°32N 28°38W **153** d1
Hortaleza *Spain* 40°28N 3°38W **127** B2
Horten *Norway* 59°25N 10°32E **164** E7
Hortense *U.S.A.* 31°20N 81°57W **316** D8
Horti *India* 17°7N 75°47E **244** F2
Hortobágy → *Hungary* 47°30N 21°6E **182** C6
Hortobágyi △ *Hungary* 47°36N 21°10E **182** C6
Horton *Kans., U.S.A.* 39°40N 95°32W **308** F6
Horton *Mo., U.S.A.* 37°58N 94°22W **310** G2
Horton → *Canada* 69°56N 126°52W **294** C7
Hortus Botanicus *Amsterdam, Neths.* **112** b3
Horwood L. *Canada* 48°5N 82°20W **298** C3
Hosaina *Ethiopia* 7°30N 37°47E **257** F4
Hosapete = Hospet *India* 15°15N 76°20E **245** G3
Hosdrug = Kanhangad *India* 12°21N 74°58E **245** H2
Hosdurga *India* 13°49N 76°17E **245** H3
Hosenofu *Libya* 23°41N 21°4E **258** D4
Ḥoseynābād *Khuzestān, Iran* 32°45N 48°20E **247** C6
Ḥoseynābād *Kordestān, Iran* 35°33N 47°8E **213** E12
Hosford *U.S.A.* 30°23N 84°48W **316** E5
Ḥōsh 'Īsa *Egypt* 30°55N 30°17E **256** H7
Hoshangabad *India* 22°45N 77°45E **242** H7
Hoshiarpur *India* 31°30N 75°58E **242** D6
Hoskins *Papua N. G.* 5°29S 150°27E **286** C6
Hoskote *India* 13°4N 77°48E **245** H3
Hosoyama *Japan* 35°36N 139°31E **140** B2
Hospet *India* 15°15N 76°20E **245** G3
Hostafranchs *Spain* 41°21N 2°8E **114** A1
Hoste, I. *Chile* 55°0S 69°0W **336** E3
Hostens *France* 44°30N 0°40W **174** D3
Hostivař *Czech Rep.* 50°3N 14°31E **135** B3
Hosur *India* 12°43N 77°49E **245** H3
Hot *Thailand* 18°8N 98°29E **236** C2
Hot Creek Range *U.S.A.* 38°40N 116°20W **304** G5
Hot Springs = Truth or Consequences *U.S.A.* 33°8N 107°15W **305** K10
Hot Springs *Ark., U.S.A.* 34°31N 93°3W **314** D8
Hot Springs *S. Dak., U.S.A.* 43°26N 103°29W **308** D2
Hot Springs △ *U.S.A.* 34°31N 93°3W **314** D8
Hotagen *Sweden* 63°59N 14°12E **160** E16
Hotan *China* 37°25N 79°55E **217** E9
Hotan He → *China* 40°22N 80°56E **217** D10
Hotazel *S. Africa* 27°17S 22°58E **270** C3
Hotchkiss *U.S.A.* 38°48N 107°43W **304** G10
Hôtel des Invalides *Paris, France* **134** c2
Hotham, C. *Australia* 12°2S 131°18E **278** B5
Hoting *Sweden* 64°8N 16°15E **160** D17
Hotolisht *Albania* 41°10N 20°25E **202** E4
Hotspur Seamount *Atl. Oc.* 17°55S 35°55W **152** H8
Hotte, Massif de la *Haiti* 18°30N 73°45W **321** C5
Hottentotsbaai *Namibia* 26°8S 14°59E **270** C1
Hou Hai *China* 22°32N 113°56E **219** a
Houailou *N. Cal.* 21°17S 165°38E **288** d
Houat, Î. de *France* 47°24N 2°58W **172** E4
Houbětin *Czech Rep.* 50°6N 14°33E **135** B3
Houdan *France* 48°48N 1°35E **173** D8
Houei Sai *Laos* 20°18N 100°26E **228** G3
Houeillès *France* 44°12N 0°2E **174** D4
Houffalize *Belgium* 50°8N 5°48E **170** D5
Houghton *Gauteng, S. Africa* 26°10S 28°3E **123** B2
Houghton *Mich., U.S.A.* 47°7N 88°34W **308** B9
Houghton *N.Y., U.S.A.* 42°25N 78°10W **312** D6
Houghton L. *U.S.A.* 44°21N 84°44W **309** C11
Houghton-le-Spring *U.K.* 54°51N 1°28W **168** C6
Houhora Heads *N.Z.* 34°49S 173°9E **284** A2
Houilles *France* 48°56N 2°11E **134** A2
Houli *Taiwan* 24°19N 120°44E **225** B2
Houlton *U.S.A.* 46°8N 67°51W **309** B20
Houlung *Taiwan* 24°37N 120°47E **225** B2
Houma *China* 35°36N 111°20E **226** G6
Houma *La., U.S.A.* 29°36N 90°43W **315** G9
Houmt Souk = Djerba *Tunisia* 33°48N 10°54E **258** B2
Houndé *Burkina Faso* 11°34N 3°31W **262** C4
Hounslow □ *U.K.* 51°28N 0°21W **125** B1
Houpi *Taiwan* 23°22N 120°21E **225** C2
Hourtin *France* 45°11N 1°4W **174** C2
Hourtin-Carcans, Étang d' *France* 45°10N 1°6W **174** C2
Housatonic → *U.S.A.* 41°10N 73°7W **313** E11
House of Nobility = Riddarhuset *Stockholm, Sweden* **139** c2
House of Parliament = Riksdagshuset *Stockholm, Sweden* **139** b2
Houses of Parliament *London, U.K.* **125** c3
Houston *B.C., Canada* 54°25N 126°39W **296** C3
Houston *Fla., U.S.A.* 30°15N 82°54W **316** E7
Houston *Mo., U.S.A.* 37°22N 91°58W **308** G8
Houston *Tex., U.S.A.* 29°45N 95°21W **314** G7
Hout = Mogwadi → *S. Africa* 23°4S 29°36E **271** B4
Hout Bay *S. Africa* 34°2S 18°23E **118** B1
Houtkraal *S. Africa* 30°23S 24°5E **270** D3
Houtman Abrolhos *Australia* 28°43S 113°48E **279** E1
Hov *Norway* 60°42N 10°20E **164** D7
Hovd = Dund-Us *Mongolia* 48°1N 91°38E **217** C12
Hovd □ *Mongolia* 48°2N 91°37E **217** C12
Hovda *Norway* 60°53N 9°11E **164** D6
Hovden *Aust-Agder, Norway* 59°33N 7°22E **164** E4
Hovden *Sogn og Fjordane, Norway* 61°41N 4°52E **164** C1
Hove *U.K.* 50°50N 0°10W **169** G7
Hove Å → *Denmark* 55°43N 12°7E **118** B2
Hovedøya *Norway* 59°53N 10°43E **133** A3
Hovedstaden □ *Denmark* 56°0N 10°0E **163** J6
Hovenweep △ *U.S.A.* 37°20N 109°0W **305** H9
Hovet *Norway* 60°38N 8°8E **164** D5
Hoveyzeh *Iran* 31°27N 48°4E **247** D6
Hovgaard Ø *Greenland* 79°55N 18°50W **154** B9
Høvik *Norway* 59°54N 10°34E **133** A2
Hovin *Norway* 59°51N 9°0E **164** E6
Hovmantorp *Sweden* 56°47N 15°7E **163** H9
Hovorčovice *Czech Rep.* 50°10N 14°31E **135** A3
Hövsgöl *Mongolia* 43°37N 109°39E **226** C5
Hövsgöl Nuur *Mongolia* 51°0N 100°30E **218** A9
Hovsta *Sweden* 59°22N 15°15E **162** E9
Howakil *Eritrea* 15°10N 40°16E **257** D5
Howar, Wadi → *Sudan* 17°30N 27°8E **257** D2
Howard *Queens., Australia* 25°16S 152°32E **281** D5
Howard *Pa., U.S.A.* 41°1N 77°40W **312** F7
Howard *S. Dak., U.S.A.* 44°1N 97°32W **308** C5
Howard Beach *U.S.A.* 40°39N 73°50W **132** C2
Howe *U.S.A.* 43°48N 113°0W **304** E7
Howe, C. *Australia* 37°30S 150°0E **283** D9
Howe, West Cape *Australia* 35°8S 117°36E **279** G2
Howe I. *Canada* 44°16N 76°17W **313** B8
Howell *U.S.A.* 42°36N 83°56W **311** B13
Howick *Qué., Canada* 45°11N 73°51W **313** A11
Howick *N.Z.* 36°54S 174°56E **284** C3
Howick *KwaZulu Natal, S. Africa* 29°28S 30°14E **271** C5
Howick Group *Australia* 14°20S 145°30E **280** A4
Howitt, L. *Australia* 27°40S 138°40E **281** D2
Howland I. *Pac. Oc.* 0°48N 176°38W **288** G10
Howlong *Australia* 35°59S 146°38E **283** C7
Howrah = Haora *India* 22°34N 88°18E **124** B1
Howth *Ireland* 53°23N 6°6W **120** A3
Howth Hd. *Ireland* 53°22N 6°4W **120** A3
Höxter *Germany* 51°46N 9°22E **178** D5
Hoxtolgay *China* 46°35N 85°59E **217** C11
Hoxton *London, U.K.* **125** a5
Hoxud *China* 42°15N 86°51E **217** D11
Hoy *U.K.* 58°50N 3°15W **167** C5
Hoya *Niedersachsen, Germany* 52°49N 9°8E **178** C5
Hōya *Tōkyō, Japan* 35°44N 139°34E **140** A2
Høyanger *Norway* 61°13N 6°4E **164** C3
Hoyerswerda *Germany* 51°26N 14°14E **178** D10
Hoylake *U.K.* 53°24N 3°10W **168** D4
Hōyo-Kaikyō *Japan* 33°20N 131°58E **222** D3
Hoyos *Spain* 40°9N 6°45W **194** E4
Hpa-an = Pa-an *Burma* 16°51N 97°40E **241** G6
Hpawlum *Burma* 27°12N 98°12E **241** B7
Hpettintha *Burma* 24°14N 95°23E **241** C5
Hpizow *Burma* 26°57N 98°24E **241** B7
Hpunan Pass *Burma* 27°30N 96°55E **241** A6
Hradčany *Czech Rep.* 50°5N 14°24E **135** B2
Hradec Králové *Czech Rep.* 50°15N 15°50E **180** A8
Hrádek *Czech Rep.* 48°46N 16°16E **181** C9
Hrafnseyri *Iceland* 65°46N 23°28W **155** B3
Hranice *Czech Rep.* 49°34N 17°45E **181** B10
Hrazdan *Armenia* 40°30N 44°46E **191** K7
Hrebenka *Ukraine* 50°9N 32°22E **189** G7
Hrífunes *Iceland* 63°38N 18°30W **155** D8
Hrísey *Iceland* 66°0N 18°23W **155** B8
Hrisoupoli = Chrisoupoli *Greece* 40°58N 24°42E **203** F8
Hrodna *Belarus* 53°42N 23°52E **184** E10
Hrodna □ *Belarus* 53°20N 24°45E **188** F3
Hrodzyanka *Belarus* 53°31N 28°42E **177** B15
Hron → *Slovak Rep.* 47°49N 18°45E **181** D11
Hrubieszów *Poland* 50°49N 23°51E **184** H10
Hrubý Jeseník *Czech Rep.* 50°5N 17°10E **181** A10
Hrvatska = Croatia ■ *Europe* 45°20N 16°0E **199** C13
Hrymayliv *Ukraine* 49°20N 26°5E **177** D14
Hrynyava *Ukraine* 47°59N 24°53E **183** C9
Hsa-paw *Burma* 19°1N 97°24E **241** F6
Hsenwi *Burma* 23°22N 97°55E **241** D6
Hsi-hkip *Burma* 20°25N 96°42E **241** E6
Hsiafu *Taiwan* 25°7N 121°17E **225** A3
Hsiamen = Xiamen *China* 24°25N 118°4E **229** E12
Hsian = Xi'an *China* 34°15N 109°0E **226** G5
Hsiangshan *Taiwan* 24°48N 120°54E **225** B2
Hsiaochinmen Tao *Taiwan* 24°26N 118°14E **225** a
Hsiaohungt'ou Hsü *Taiwan* 21°57N 121°36E **225** E3
Hsiaokang *Taiwan* 22°34N 120°20E **225** D2
Hsiatahsi *Taiwan* 22°28N 120°56E **225** D2
Hsiaying *Taiwan* 23°14N 120°15E **225** C2
Hsichih *Taiwan* 25°4N 121°39E **225** A3
Hsikang *Taiwan* 23°7N 120°12E **225** C2
Hsilo *Taiwan* 23°48N 120°27E **225** C2
Hsinche *Taiwan* 24°10N 120°50E **225** B2
Hsinch'eng *Taiwan* 24°8N 121°39E **225** B3
Hsinchu *Taiwan* 24°48N 120°58E **225** B2
Hsinchu □ *Taiwan* 24°45N 121°10E **225** B3
Hsinchuang *Kaohsiung, Taiwan* 22°34N 120°29E **225** D2
Hsinchuang *T'aipei, Taiwan* 25°2N 121°27E **225** A3
Hsinfa *Taiwan* 23°1N 120°39E **225** C2
Hsinfeng *Taiwan* 24°54N 120°59E **225** B2
Hsinhailien = Lianyungang *China* 34°40N 119°11E **227** G10
Hsinhua *Taiwan* 23°2N 120°18E **225** C2
Hsini *Taiwan* 23°41N 120°51E **225** C2

Hsinking = Changchun China 43°57N 125°17E 227 C13
Hsinpi Taiwan 22°28N 120°33E 225 D2
Hsinshih Taiwan 23°4N 120°17E 225 C2
Hsintien Taiwan 24°57N 121°32E 225 B3
Hsinwu Taiwan 24°59N 121°6E 225 B3
Hsinying Taiwan 23°21N 120°17E 225 C2
Hsinyuan Taiwan 22°32N 120°27E 225 D2
Hsipaw Burma 22°37N 97°18E 241 D6
Hsiukuluan Hsi → Taiwan 23°28N 121°30E 225 C3
Hsiushui Taiwan 24°3N 120°30E 225 B2
Hsiyu Taiwan 23°36N 119°30E 225 C1
Hsopket Burma 23°11N 98°26E 228 F2
Hsüchou = Xuzhou China 34°18N 117°10E 227 G9
Hsüeh Shan China 24°24N 121°12E 225 B3
Hsüehchia Taiwan 23°14N 120°10E 225 C2
Hsühaitsun Taiwan 22°12N 120°52E 225 D2
Htawgaw Burma 25°57N 98°23E 241 C7
Hu Xian China 34°8N 108°42E 226 G5
Hua Hin Thailand 12°34N 99°58E 236 F2
Hua Lamphong Railway Station Bangkok, Thailand 113 c2
Hua Muang Laos 20°13N 103°52E 236 B4
Hua Shan China 34°28N 110°4E 226 G6
Hua Xian Henan, China 35°30N 114°30E 226 G8
Hua Xian Shaanxi, China 34°30N 109°48E 226 G5
Hua Yü Taiwan 23°24N 119°19E 225 C1
Hua'an China 25°1N 117°32E 229 E11
Huab → Namibia 20°52S 13°25E 270 A2
Huacaya Bolivia 20°45S 63°43W 331 E5
Huachacalla Bolivia 18°45S 68°17W 330 D4
Huacheng China 24°4N 115°37E 229 E10
Huachinera Mexico 30°9N 108°55W 318 A3
Huacho Peru 11°10S 77°35W 330 C2
Huachón Peru 10°35S 76°0W 330 C2
Huade China 41°55N 113°59E 226 D7
Huadian China 43°0N 126°40E 227 C14
Huadu China 23°22N 113°12E 229 F9
Huahine, Î. French Polynesia 16°46S 150°58W 289 f
Hua Hat △ Thailand 16°52N 104°17E 236 D5
Huai He → China 33°0N 118°30E 229 A12
Huai Kha Khaeng △ Thailand 15°48N 99°7E 236 E2
Huai Nam Dang △ Thailand 19°30N 98°30E 236 C2
Huai Yot Thailand 7°45N 99°37E 237 J2
Huai'an Hebei, China 40°30N 114°20E 226 D8
Huai'an Jiangsu, China 33°30N 119°10E 227 H10
Huaibei China 34°0N 116°48E 226 G9
Huaibin China 32°32N 115°27E 229 A10
Huaicho = Puerto Acosta Bolivia 15°32S 69°15W 330 D4
Huaide = Gongzhuling China 43°30N 124°40E 227 C13
Huaidezhen China 43°48N 124°50E 227 C13
Huaihua China 27°32N 109°57E 228 D7
Huaiji China 23°55N 112°12E 229 F9
Huainan China 32°38N 116°58E 229 A11
Huaining China 30°24N 116°40E 229 B11
Huairen China 39°48N 113°20E 226 E7
Huairou China 40°20N 116°35E 226 D9
Huaiyang China 33°40N 114°52E 226 H8
Huaiyin China 33°30N 119°2E 227 H10
Huaiyuan Anhui, China 32°55N 117°10E 227 H9
Huaiyuan Guangxi Zhuangzu, China 24°31N 108°22E 228 E7
Huajuapán de León Mexico 17°48N 97°46W 319 D5
Hualālai U.S.A. 19°42N 155°52W 302 D6
Hualapai Peak U.S.A. 35°5N 113°54W 305 J7
Hualien Taiwan 23°59N 121°36E 225 C3
Hualien □ Taiwan 23°45N 121°25E 225 C3
Huallaga → Peru 5°15S 75°30W 330 B2
Huallanca Peru 8°50S 77°56W 330 B2
Huamachuco Peru 7°50S 78°5W 330 B2
Huambo Angola 12°42S 15°54E 265 E3
Huambo □ Angola 13°0S 16°0E 265 E3
Huan Jiang → China 34°28N 109°0E 226 G5
Huan Xian China 36°33N 107°7E 226 F4
Huancabamba Peru 5°10S 79°15W 330 B2
Huancane Peru 15°10S 69°44W 330 D4
Huancapi Peru 13°40S 74°0W 330 C3
Huancavelica Peru 12°50S 75°5W 330 C2
Huancavelica □ Peru 13°0S 75°0W 330 C3
Huancayo Peru 12°5S 75°12W 330 C2
Huanchaca Bolivia 20°15S 66°40W 330 E4
Huanchaca, Serranía de Bolivia 14°30S 60°39W 331 C5
Huang Hai = Yellow Sea China 35°0N 123°0E 227 G12
Huang He → China 37°55N 118°50E 227 F10
Huang Xian China 37°38N 120°30E 227 F11
Huangchuan China 32°15N 115°10E 229 A10
Huangdao China 36°0N 120°7E 227 G11
Huanggang China 30°29N 114°52E 229 B10
Huangguoshu China 26°0N 105°40E 228 E5
Huanghua China 38°22N 117°20E 227 E9
Huanghuagang China 38°20N 117°54E 227 E9
Huanghuagang Mausoleum China 23°9N 113°17E 121 B2
Huangling China 35°34N 109°15E 226 G5
Huanglong China 35°30N 109°59E 226 G5
Huanglong △ China 32°44N 103°50E 228 A4
Huanglongtan China 32°40N 110°33E 229 A8
Huangmei China 30°5N 115°56E 229 B10
Huangpi China 30°50N 114°22E 229 B10
Huangping China 26°52N 107°54E 228 D6
Huangpu China 31°14N 121°30E 138 B2
Huangpu Jiang → China 31°11N 121°29E 138 B1
Huangpu Park China 31°14N 121°29E 138 B1
Huangshan Anhui, China 30°8N 118°9E 229 B12
Huangshan Anhui, China 29°42N 118°25E 229 C12
Huangshi China 30°10N 115°3E 229 B10
Huangsongdian China 43°45N 127°25E 227 C14
Huangtugang China 39°49N 116°15E 114 C1
Huangyan China 28°38N 121°19E 229 C13
Huangyangsi China 26°33N 111°39E 229 D8
Huaning China 24°17N 102°56E 228 E4
Huanjiang China 24°50N 108°18E 228 E7
Huanren China 41°23N 125°20E 224 B2
Huanren Shuiku China 41°17N 125°34E 224 B2
Huanta Peru 12°55S 74°20W 330 C3
Huantai China 36°58N 117°56E 227 F9
Huánuco Peru 9°55S 76°15W 330 B2
Huánuco □ Peru 9°55S 76°15W 330 B2
Huanuni Bolivia 18°16S 66°51W 330 D4
Huanzo, Cordillera de Peru 14°35S 73°20W 330 C3
Huaping China 26°46N 101°25E 228 D3
Huara Chile 19°59S 69°47W 330 D4
Huaral Peru 11°32S 77°13W 330 C2
Huaraz Peru 9°30S 77°32W 330 B2
Huari Peru 9°14S 77°14W 330 B2
Huarmey Peru 10°5S 78°5W 330 C2
Huarochirí Peru 12°9S 76°15W 330 C2
Huarocondo Peru 13°26S 72°14W 330 C3
Huarong China 29°29N 112°30E 229 C9
Huascar Peru 11°59S 77°1W 124 A2
Huascarán, Nevado Peru 9°7S 77°37W 330 B2
Huasco Chile 28°30S 71°15W 334 B1
Huasco → Chile 28°27S 71°13W 334 B1
Huasna U.S.A. 35°6N 120°24W 307 K6
Huatabampo Mexico 26°50N 109°38W 318 B3
Huauchinango Mexico 20°12N 98°3W 319 C5
Huautla de Jiménez Mexico 18°8N 96°51W 319 D5
Huaxi China 26°25N 106°40E 228 D6
Huay Khwang Thailand 13°47N 100°33E 113 B2
Huayhuash, Cordillera Peru 10°30S 76°45W 330 B2
Huayin China 34°35N 110°5E 226 G6
Huaying China 30°8N 106°44E 228 B6
Huayllay Peru 11°3S 76°21W 330 C2
Huayuan China 28°37N 109°29E 228 C7
Huazhou China 21°33N 110°33E 229 G8
Hubbali = Hubli India 15°22N 75°15E 245 G2
Hubbard Iowa, U.S.A. 42°18N 93°18W 310 B3
Hubbard Ohio, U.S.A. 41°9N 80°34W 312 E4
Hubbard Tex., U.S.A. 31°51N 96°48W 314 F6
Hubbard, Mt. N. Amer. 60°19N 139°4W 303 F13
Hubbard Glacier Canada 60°18N 139°22W 294 E4
Hubbart Pt. Canada 59°21N 94°41W 297 B10
Hubei □ China 31°0N 112°0E 229 B9
Hubli India 15°22N 75°15E 245 G2
Huch'ang N. Korea 41°25N 127°2E 224 B3
Huchow = Huzhou China 30°51N 120°8E 229 B13
Hucknall U.K. 53°3N 1°13W 168 D6
Huddersfield U.K. 53°39N 1°47W 168 D6
Huddinge Sweden 59°14N 18°0E 139 B2
Hude Germany 53°7N 8°26E 178 B4
Hudi Sudan 17°43N 34°18E 256 D3
Hudiksvall Sweden 61°43N 17°10E 162 C11
Hudson Ont., Canada 50°6N 92°9W 298 B1
Hudson Fla., U.S.A. 28°22N 82°42W 317 G7
Hudson Mass., U.S.A. 42°23N 71°34W 313 D13
Hudson Mich., U.S.A. 41°51N 84°21W 311 E11
Hudson N.Y., U.S.A. 42°15N 73°46W 313 D11
Hudson Wis., U.S.A. 44°58N 92°45W 308 C7
Hudson Wyo., U.S.A. 42°54N 108°35W 304 E9
Hudson → U.S.A. 40°42N 74°2W 313 F10
Hudson, C. Antarctica 68°21S 153°45E 151 C10
Hudson, Vol. Chile 46°4S 72°55W 336 C2
Hudson Bay Nunavut, Canada 60°0N 86°0W 295 F14
Hudson Bay Sask., Canada 52°51N 102°23W 297 C8
Hudson Falls U.S.A. 43°18N 73°35W 313 C11
Hudson Mts. Antarctica 74°32S 99°20W 151 D16
Hudson Str. Canada 62°0N 70°0W 295 E18
Hudson's Hope Canada 56°0N 121°54W 296 B4
Hudsonville U.S.A. 42°52N 85°52W 311 B11
Hue Vietnam 16°30N 107°35E 236 D6
Huebra → Spain 41°2N 6°48W 194 D4
Huechuraba Chile 33°22S 70°39W 137 B1
Huedin Romania 46°52N 23°2E 182 D8
Huehuetenango Guatemala 15°20N 91°28W 320 C1
Huejúcar Mexico 22°21N 103°13W 318 C4
Huélamo Spain 40°17N 1°48W 196 E3
Huelgoat France 48°22N 3°46W 172 D3
Huelma Spain 37°39N 3°28W 195 H7
Huelva Spain 37°18N 6°57W 195 H4
Huelva □ Spain 37°40N 7°0W 195 H4
Huelva → Spain 37°27N 6°0W 195 H5
Hueneme = Port Hueneme U.S.A. 34°7N 119°12W 307 L7
Huentelauquén Chile 31°38S 71°33W 334 C1
Huércal-Overa Spain 37°23N 1°57W 197 H3
Huerquehue △ Chile 39°6S 71°42W 336 A2
Huerta, Sa. de la Argentina 31°10S 67°30W 334 C2
Huertas, C. de las Spain 38°21N 0°24W 197 G4
Huerva → Spain 41°39N 0°52W 196 D4
Huesca Spain 42°8N 0°25W 196 C4
Huesca □ Spain 42°20N 0°1E 196 C5
Huéscar Spain 37°44N 2°35W 197 H2
Hueso Ballena, Pta. Chile 33°40S 78°46W 330 c
Huetamo Mexico 18°35N 100°53W 318 D4
Huete Spain 40°10N 2°43W 196 E2
Huevos I. Trin. & Tob. 10°42N 61°43W 323 t
Huger U.S.A. 33°6N 79°48W 316 B10
Hugh → Australia 25°1S 134°1E 280 D1
Hughenden Australia 20°52S 144°10E 280 C3
Hughes Australia 30°42S 129°31E 279 F4
Hughes U.S.A. 66°3N 154°15W 303 C9
Hughesville U.S.A. 41°14N 76°44W 313 E8
Hugli → India 21°56N 88°4E 243 J13
Hugo Colo., U.S.A. 39°8N 103°28W 304 G12
Hugo Okla., U.S.A. 34°1N 95°31W 314 D7
Hugoton U.S.A. 37°11N 101°21W 308 G3
Huguang Opera Museum Beijing, China 114 c2
Huhehaote = Hohhot China 40°52N 111°40E 226 D6
Huhsi Taiwan 23°35N 119°39E 225 C1
Hui Xian = Huixian China 35°27N 113°12E 226 G7
Hui Xian China 33°50N 106°4E 226 H4
Hui'an China 25°1N 118°43E 229 E12
Hui'anbu China 37°28N 106°38E 226 F4
Huiarau Ra. N.Z. 38°45S 176°55E 284 E5
Huichang China 25°32N 115°45E 229 E10
Huichapan Mexico 20°23N 99°39W 319 C5
Huichon N. Korea 40°10N 126°16E 224 B3
Huidong Guangdong, China 22°58N 114°43E 229 F10
Huidong Sichuan, China 26°34N 102°35E 228 D4
Huifa He → China 43°0N 127°50E 227 C14
Huila Angola 15°4S 13°32E 265 F2
Huíla □ Angola 14°0S 15°0E 265 E2
Huila □ Colombia 2°30N 75°45W 328 C2
Huila, Nevado del Colombia 3°0N 76°0W 328 C2
Huilai China 23°0N 116°18E 229 F11
Huili China 26°35N 102°17E 228 D4
Huimin China 37°27N 117°28E 227 F9
Huinan China 42°40N 126°2E 224 A3
Huinca Renancó Argentina 34°51S 64°22W 334 C3
Huining China 35°38N 105°0E 226 G3
Huinong China 39°5N 106°35E 226 E4
Huiroa N.Z. 39°15S 174°30E 284 F3
Huishui China 26°7N 106°38E 228 D6
Huisne → France 47°59N 0°11E 172 E7
Huiting China 34°5N 116°5E 226 G9
Huitong China 26°51N 109°45E 228 D7
Huixian China 35°27N 113°12E 226 G7
Huixtla Mexico 15°9N 92°28W 319 D6
Huize China 26°24N 103°15E 228 D4
Huizhou China 23°0N 114°23E 229 F10
Huizingen Belgium 50°45N 4°17E 180 E1
Hukawng Valley Burma 26°30N 96°30E 241 B6
Hukeri India 16°14N 74°36E 245 F2
Hukou Jiangxi, China 29°45N 116°21E 229 C11
Huk'ou Taiwan 24°54N 121°2E 225 B3
Hukuntsi Botswana 23°58S 21°45E 270 B3
Hula Papua N. G. 10°5S 147°43E 286 F4
Ḩulayfā' Si. Arabia 25°58N 40°45E 246 E4
Huld = Ulaanjirem Mongolia 45°5N 105°30E 226 B3
Hulin China 45°48N 132°59E 219 B15
Hulin He → China 45°0N 122°10E 227 B12
Hull = Kingston upon Hull U.K. 53°45N 0°21W 168 D7
Hull Canada 45°26N 75°43W 313 A9
Hull → U.K. 53°44N 0°20W 168 D7
Hulst Neths. 51°17N 4°2E 170 C4
Hultschin = Hlučín Czech Rep. 49°54N 18°11E 181 B11
Hultsfred Sweden 57°30N 15°52E 163 G9
Huludao China 40°45N 120°50E 227 D11
Hulun = Hailar China 49°10N 119°38E 219 B12
Hulun Nur China 49°0N 117°30E 219 B12
Hulyaypole Ukraine 47°45N 36°21E 189 J9
Huma, Tanjung Malaysia 5°29N 100°16E 237 c
Humacao Puerto Rico 18°9N 65°50W 321 b
Humahuaca Argentina 23°10S 65°25W 334 A2
Humaitá = Porto Walter Brazil 8°15S 72°40W 330 B3
Humaitá Brazil 7°35S 63°1W 331 B5
Humaitá Paraguay 27°2S 58°31W 334 B4
Humansdorp S. Africa 34°2S 24°46E 270 D3
Humansville U.S.A. 37°48N 93°35W 310 G3
Humara, J. Sudan 16°16N 30°59E 257 D3
Humayun's Tomb India 28°35N 77°15E 120 B2
Humbe Angola 16°40S 14°55E 265 F2
Humbe, Serra do Angola 12°10S 15°25E 265 E2
Humber → Ont., Canada 43°47N 79°38W 141 A1
Humber → England, U.K. 53°42N 0°27W 168 D7
Humber B. Canada 43°37N 79°27W 141 B2
Humber Bay Canada 43°38N 79°29W 141 B2
Humber Bay Park Canada 43°37N 79°28W 141 B2
Humber College Canada 43°35N 79°30W 141 B1
Humber Summit Canada 43°45N 79°32W 141 A1
Humber Valley Village Canada 43°40N 79°31W 141 A1
Humberlea Canada 43°43N 79°31W 141 A1
Humberwood Park Canada 43°44N 79°37W 141 A1
Humboldt Sask., Canada 52°15N 105°9W 297 C7
Humboldt Iowa, U.S.A. 42°44N 94°13W 310 B2
Humboldt Tenn., U.S.A. 35°50N 88°55W 315 D10
Humboldt → U.S.A. 39°59N 118°36W 304 G4
Humboldt Gletscher = Sermersuaq Greenland 79°30N 62°0W 154 B4
Humboldt Mts. N.Z. 44°30S 168°15E 285 E3
Humboldt Park U.S.A. 41°54N 87°42W 119 B2
Humbolt, Mt. N. Cal. 21°53S 166°25E 288 d
Hume U.S.A. 36°48N 118°54W 306 J8
Hume, L. Australia 36°0S 147°5E 283 D7
Humen China 22°50N 113°40E 219 a
Humenné Slovak Rep. 48°55N 21°50E 181 C14
Humera Spain 40°25N 3°46W 127 B1
Humeston U.S.A. 40°52N 93°30W 310 D3
Hummelsta Sweden 59°34N 16°58E 162 E10
Hummelvika Norway 63°29N 8°19E 164 A5
Hummingbird Centre Toronto, Canada 141 b3
Hummock Hill = Whyalla Australia 33°2S 137°30E 282 B2
Humpata Angola 15°2S 13°24E 265 F2
Humphreys, Mt. U.S.A. 37°17N 118°40W 306 H8
Humphreys Peak U.S.A. 35°21N 111°41W 305 J8
Humpolec Czech Rep. 49°31N 15°20E 180 B8
Humptulips U.S.A. 47°14N 123°57W 306 C3
Humula Australia 35°30S 147°46E 283 C7
Hūn Libya 29°2N 16°0E 258 C3
Hun He → China 40°41N 122°8E 224 B1
Hun Jiang → China 40°50N 125°38E 227 D13
Húnaflói Iceland 65°50N 20°50W 155 B6
Hunan □ China 27°30N 112°0E 229 D9
Húnavatnssýsla □ Iceland 65°30N 20°25W 155 B6
Hunaydī Iraq 33°18N 44°29E 113 B2
Hunchun China 42°52N 130°28E 227 C16
Hundested Denmark 55°58N 11°52E 163 J5
Hundewali Pakistan 31°55N 72°38E 242 D5
Hundige Denmark 55°35N 12°18E 118 B1
Hundige Strand Denmark 55°35N 12°20E 118 B2
Hundorp Norway 61°33N 9°59E 164 C7
Hundred Islands △ Phil. 16°10N 120°2E 232 C3
Hundred Mile House Canada 51°38N 121°18W 296 C4
Hundvåg Norway 59°0N 5°43E 164 E2
Hunedoara Romania 45°40N 22°50E 182 E7
Hunedoara □ Romania 45°50N 22°54E 182 E7
Hunei Taiwan 22°53N 120°14E 225 D2
Hünfeld Germany 50°39N 9°46E 178 E5
Hung Hom China 22°18N 114°11E 122 B2
Hung Yen Vietnam 20°39N 106°4E 228 G6
Hunga Ha'apai Tonga 20°41S 175°7W 287 G13
Hungary ■ Europe 47°20N 19°20E 181 D12
Hungary, Plain of Europe 47°0N 20°0E 158 F10
Hungerford Australia 28°58S 144°24E 281 D3
Hŭngnam N. Korea 39°49N 127°45E 224 C3
Hungt'ou Hsü = Lan Yü Taiwan 22°4N 121°25E 225 D3
Hungund India 16°4N 76°3E 245 F3
Huni Valley Ghana 5°33N 1°56W 262 D4
Hunjiang China 41°54N 126°26E 224 B3
Hunneberg Sweden 58°18N 12°30E 163 F6
Hunnebostrand Sweden 58°27N 11°18E 163 F5
Hunsberge Namibia 27°45S 17°12E 270 C2
Hunsrück Germany 49°56N 7°27E 179 F3
Hunstanton U.K. 52°56N 0°29E 168 E8
Hunsur India 12°16N 76°16E 245 H3
Hunte → Germany 53°14N 8°28E 178 B4
Hunter N.Z. 44°36S 171°2E 285 E6
Hunter N.Y., U.S.A. 42°13N 74°13W 313 D10
Hunter → N.S.W., Australia 32°52S 151°46E 283 B9
Hunter → N.Z. 44°21S 169°27E 285 E4
Hunter, C. Solomon Is. 9°48S 159°50E 287 M10
Hunter Hills, The N.Z. 44°26S 170°46E 285 E5
Hunter I. Tas., Australia 40°30S 144°45E 281 G3
Hunter I. B.C., Canada 51°55N 128°0W 296 C3
Hunter Mts. N.Z. 45°43S 167°25E 285 F2
Hunter Ra. Australia 32°45S 150°15E 283 B9
Hunters Hill Australia 33°50S 151°9E 139 B1
Hunters Pt. U.S.A. 37°43N 122°21W 136 B2
Hunters Road Zimbabwe 19°9S 29°49E 269 F2
Hunters Valley U.S.A. 38°54N 77°17W 143 B2
Hunterville N.Z. 39°56S 175°35E 284 F4
Huntingburg U.S.A. 38°18N 86°57W 311 F10
Huntingdon Cambs., U.K. 52°20N 0°11W 169 E7
Huntingdon Pa., U.S.A. 40°30N 78°1W 312 F6
Huntington = Shelton U.S.A. 41°19N 73°5W 313 E11
Huntington Ind., U.S.A. 40°53N 85°30W 311 D11
Huntington N.Y., U.S.A. 40°52N 73°26W 313 F11
Huntington Oreg., U.S.A. 44°21N 117°16W 304 D5
Huntington Utah, U.S.A. 39°20N 110°58W 304 G8
Huntington Va., U.S.A. 38°47N 77°4W 143 C3
Huntington W. Va., U.S.A. 38°25N 82°27W 309 F12
Huntington Beach U.S.A. 33°40N 118°5W 307 M9
Huntington Park U.S.A. 33°58N 118°13W 126 C3
Huntley Jamaica 18°4N 77°35W 320 a
Huntley Ill., U.S.A. 42°10N 88°26W 311 B8
Huntly N.Z. 37°34S 175°11E 284 D4
Huntly Aberds., U.K. 57°27N 2°47W 167 D6
Huntsville Ont., Canada 45°20N 79°14W 312 A5
Huntsville Ala., U.S.A. 34°44N 86°35W 315 D11
Huntsville Mo., U.S.A. 39°26N 92°33W 310 E4
Huntsville Tex., U.S.A. 30°43N 95°33W 314 F7
Hunyani → Zimbabwe 15°57S 30°39E 269 F3
Hunyuan China 39°42N 113°42E 226 E7
Hunza → India 35°54N 74°20E 243 B6
Huo Shan China 36°26N 111°52E 226 F6
Huo Xian = Huozhou China 36°36N 111°42E 226 F6
Huocheng China 44°0N 80°48E 217 D10
Huolin Gol China 45°32N 119°38E 227 B10
Huon G. Papua N. G. 7°0S 147°30E 286 D4
Huon Pen. Papua N. G. 6°20S 147°30E 286 D4
Huong Khe Vietnam 18°13N 105°41E 236 C5
Huonville Australia 43°0S 147°5E 281 G4
Huoqiu China 32°20N 116°12E 229 A11
Huoshan China 31°25N 116°20E 229 B11
Huoshao Dao = Lütao Taiwan 22°40N 121°30E 225 D3
Huozhou China 36°36N 111°42E 226 F6
Hupeh = Hubei □ China 31°0N 112°0E 229 B9
Hūr Iran 30°50N 57°7E 247 D8
Hurand Iran 38°51N 47°22E 213 C12
Ḩuraymila Si. Arabia 25°8N 46°8E 246 E5
Hurbanovo Slovak Rep. 47°51N 18°11E 181 D11
Hurd, C. Canada 45°13N 81°44W 312 A3
Hurdiyo Somali Rep. 10°33N 51°6E 267 B7
Hure Qi China 42°45N 121°45E 227 C11
Hurezani Romania 44°49N 23°40E 183 F8
Hurghada Egypt 27°15N 33°50E 256 B3
Hurīya Iraq 33°21N 44°19E 113 A1
Hurley N. Mex., U.S.A. 32°42N 108°8W 305 K9
Hurley Wis., U.S.A. 46°27N 90°11W 308 B8
Huron Calif., U.S.A. 36°12N 120°6W 306 J6
Huron Ohio, U.S.A. 41°24N 82°33W 312 E2
Huron S. Dak., U.S.A. 44°22N 98°13W 308 C4
Huron, L. U.S.A. 44°30N 82°40W 312 B2
Huron East Canada 43°37N 81°18W 312 C3
Hurricane U.S.A. 37°11N 113°17W 305 H7
Hurso Ethiopia 9°35N 41°33E 257 F5
Hurstville Australia 33°57S 151°6E 139 B1
Hurtsboro U.S.A. 32°15N 85°25W 316 C4
Hurungwe △ Zimbabwe 16°7S 29°5E 269 F2
Hurunui → N.Z. 42°54S 173°18E 285 C8
Hurup Denmark 56°46N 8°25E 163 H2
Húsafell Iceland 64°42N 20°53W 155 C6
Husan West Bank 31°42N 35°8E 123 B1
Húsavík Iceland 66°3N 17°21W 155 A9
Husby Sweden 59°24N 17°56E 139 A1
Huşi Romania 46°41N 28°7E 183 D13
Huskisson Australia 35°2S 150°41E 283 C9
Huskvarna Sweden 57°47N 14°15E 163 G8
Huslia U.S.A. 65°41N 156°24W 303 D8
Husnes Norway 59°52N 5°45E 164 E2
Hustad Norway 62°57N 7°6E 164 B4
Hustadvika Norway 63°0N 7°0E 164 A3
Hustontown U.S.A. 40°3N 78°2W 312 F6
Hustopeče Czech Rep. 48°57N 16°43E 181 C9
Husum København, Denmark 55°42N 12°27E 118 A2
Husum Schleswig-Holstein, Germany 54°28N 9°4E 178 A5
Husum Sweden 63°21N 19°12E 162 A13
Husut = Khust Ukraine 48°10N 23°18E 183 B8
Hutanopan Indonesia 0°40N 99°42E 234 B1
Hutchinson Kans., U.S.A. 38°5N 97°56W 308 F5
Hutchinson Minn., U.S.A. 44°54N 94°22W 308 C6
Ḩūth Yemen 16°14N 43°58E 248 C3
Hutiao Xia China 27°13N 100°9E 228 D3
Hutjena Papua N. G. 5°23S 154°42E 286 C8
Hutsonville U.S.A. 39°7N 87°40W 311 E9
Hutt → N.Z. 41°14S 174°54E 143 B2
Hutte Sauvage, L. de la Canada 56°15N 64°45W 299 A7
Hütteldorf Austria 48°12N 16°15E 142 A1
Hüttenberg Austria 46°56N 14°33E 180 E7
Hüttener Berge △ Germany 54°24N 9°40E 178 A5
Hutton, Mt. Australia 25°51S 148°20E 281 D4
Huvadu Atoll Maldives 0°30N 73°15E 272 d
Hüvösvölgy Hungary 47°32N 19°0E 117 A2
Huwei Taiwan 23°42N 120°26E 225 C2
Huwei Hsü → Taiwan 23°37N 120°22E 225 C2
Huwon Secret Garden S. Korea 37°34N 126°59E 137 B1
Huwun Ethiopia 4°23N 40°6E 257 G5
Huy Belgium 50°31N 5°15E 170 D5
Huzhou China 30°51N 120°8E 229 B13
Huzurabad India 18°12N 79°25E 244 E4
Huzurnagar India 16°54N 79°53E 244 F4
Hvalpsund Denmark 56°42N 9°11E 163 H3
Hvalstad Norway 59°51N 10°27E 133 A1
Hvalstrand Norway 59°50N 10°30E 133 A2
Hvammsfjörður Iceland 65°4N 22°5W 155 B4
Hvammstangi Iceland 65°24N 20°57W 155 B6
Hvammur Mýrasýsla, Iceland 64°50N 21°21W 155 C5
Hvammur Skagafjarðarsýsla, Iceland 65°53N 19°51W 155 B7
Hvannadalshnúkur Iceland 64°1N 16°41W 155 C10
Hvanneyri Iceland 64°34N 21°36W 155 C5
Hvar Croatia 43°11N 16°28E 199 E13
Hvarski Kanal Croatia 43°15N 16°35E 199 E13
Hveragerði Iceland 64°0N 21°12W 155 C5
Hvidovre Denmark 55°38N 12°27E 118 B2
Hvítá → Iceland 64°30N 21°58W 155 C5
Hvítárvatn Iceland 64°37N 19°50W 155 C7
Hvittingfoss Norway 59°29N 10°0E 164 E7
Hvizdets Ukraine 48°35N 25°17E 183 B10
Hvolsvöllur Iceland 63°45N 20°14W 155 D6
Hwacheon-Cheosuji S. Korea 38°5N 127°50E 224 C3
Hwagok S. Korea 37°32N 126°51E 137 B1
Hwainan = Huainan China 32°38N 116°58E 229 A11
Hwaiyin = Huaiyin China 33°30N 119°2E 227 H10
Hwang Ho = Huang He → China 37°55N 118°50E 227 F10
Hwange Zimbabwe 18°18S 26°30E 269 F2
Hwange △ Zimbabwe 19°0S 26°30E 270 A4
Hwanghaebuk-do □ N. Korea 38°30N 126°25E 224 C3
Hwanghaenam-do □ N. Korea 38°15N 125°30E 224 C2
Hwangju N. Korea 38°8N 125°46E 224 C2
Hwangshih = Huangshi China 30°10N 115°3E 229 B10
Hwaseong S. Korea 37°12N 126°48E 224 D3
Hwasun S. Korea 35°3N 126°59E 224 E3
Hwekum Burma 26°7N 95°22E 241 B5
Hyaing Burma 22°39N 94°44E 241 D5
Hyannis Mass., U.S.A. 41°39N 70°17W 309 E18
Hyannis Nebr., U.S.A. 42°0N 101°46W 308 E3
Hyargas Nuur Mongolia 49°0N 93°0E 217 C12
Hyattsville U.S.A. 38°57N 76°57W 143 B4
Hybo Sweden 61°49N 16°15E 162 C10
Hydaburg U.S.A. 55°15N 132°50W 296 B2
Hyde N.Z. 45°18S 170°16E 285 F5
Hyde Park Sydney, Australia 139 b
Hyde Park Guyana 6°30N 58°16W 329 B6
Hyde Park Gauteng, S. Africa 26°8S 28°2E 123 A2
Hyde Park London, U.K. 51°30N 0°10W 125 A2
Hyde Park Calif., U.S.A. 33°58N 118°19W 126 C3
Hyde Park Ill., U.S.A. 41°47N 87°35W 119 C3
Hyde Park Mass., U.S.A. 42°15N 71°7W 116 B2
Hyde Park N.Y., U.S.A. 41°47N 73°56W 313 E11
Hyden Australia 32°24S 118°53E 279 F2
Hyder U.S.A. 55°55N 130°5W 296 B2
Hyderabad India 17°22N 78°29E 244 E4
Hyderabad Pakistan 25°23N 68°24E 242 G3
Hydra Greece 37°20N 23°28E 205 D10
Hyen Norway 61°44N 5°56E 164 C2
Hyères France 43°8N 6°9E 175 E10
Hyères, Îs. d' France 43°0N 6°20E 175 F10
Hyesan N. Korea 41°20N 128°10E 224 B4
Hyland → Canada 59°52N 128°12W 296 B3
Hylestad Norway 59°6N 7°29E 164 E4
Hyllestad Norway 61°10N 5°17E 164 C2
Hyltebruk Sweden 56°59N 13°15E 163 H7
Hyndman Peak U.S.A. 43°45N 114°8W 304 E6
Hynnekleiv Norway 58°36N 8°25E 164 F5
Hyōgo □ Japan 35°15N 134°50E 222 B6
Hyrra Banda C.A.R. 5°58N 22°1E 264 A4
Hyrum U.S.A. 41°38N 111°51W 304 F8
Hysham U.S.A. 46°18N 107°14W 304 C10
Hythe U.K. 51°4N 1°5E 169 F9
Hyūga Japan 32°25N 131°35E 222 E3
Hyvinge = Hyvinkää Finland 60°38N 24°50E 188 B3
Hyvinkää Finland 60°38N 24°50E 188 B3

I

I-n-Akhmed Mali 19°49N 0°56W 261 E4
I-n-Azaoua Illizi, Algeria 25°42N 6°54E 261 C6
I-n-Azaoua Tamanrasset, Algeria 20°46N 7°32E 261 D6
I-n-Échaï Mali 20°10N 2°5W 260 D4
I-n-Ezzane Algeria 23°29N 11°15E 261 D7
I-n-Gall Niger 16°51N 7°1E 263 B6
I-n-Kelemet Algeria 26°57N 5°47E 261 C6
I-n-Oudad Algeria 20°17N 4°38E 261 D5
I-n-Ouzzal Algeria 20°41N 2°34E 261 D5
I-n-Tadreft Niger 19°5N 6°38E 263 B6
Iabès, Erg Algeria 27°30N 2°2W 261 C4
Ialbaniţa Romania 44°57N 27°29E 182 F7
Iaco → Brazil 9°3S 68°34W 330 B4
Iacobeni Romania 47°25N 25°20E 183 C10
Iaçu Brazil 12°45S 40°13W 333 D3
Iakora Madag. 23°6S 46°40E 272 C2
Ialibu Papua N. G. 6°17S 143°59E 286 D2
Ialissos Greece 36°24N 28°10E 206 E12
Ialomiţa □ Romania 44°30N 27°30E 183 F12
Ialomiţa → Romania 44°42N 27°51E 183 F12
Ialoveni Moldova 46°56N 28°47E 183 D13
Ialpug → Moldova 45°41N 28°35E 183 E13
Iamonia L. U.S.A. 30°38N 84°14W 316 E5
Ianca Romania 45°6N 27°29E 183 E12
Iara Romania 46°31N 23°35E 183 D8
Iarda Ethiopia 11°9N 35°53E 257 E4
Iargara Moldova 46°24N 28°23E 183 D13
Iaşi Romania 47°10N 27°40E 183 C12
Iaşi □ Romania 47°20N 27°0E 183 C12
Iasmos Greece 41°8N 25°11E 203 E9
Iauaretê Colombia 0°36N 69°12W 328 C4
Ib → India 21°34N 83°48E 243 J10
Iba Phil. 15°22N 120°0E 232 D2
Ibadan Nigeria 7°22N 3°58E 263 D5
Ibagué Colombia 4°20N 75°20W 328 C2
Ibaiti Brazil 23°50S 50°10W 333 F1
Ibajay Phil. 11°49N 122°10E 233 F4
Iballë Albania 42°12N 20°2E 202 D4
Ibăneşti Botoşani, Romania 48°4N 26°22E 183 B11
Ibăneşti Mureş, Romania 46°45N 24°57E 183 D9
Ibanshe Dem. Rep. of the Congo 4°58S 21°30E 265 C4
Ibar → Serbia 43°43N 20°45E 202 C4
Ibara Japan 34°36N 133°28E 222 C5
Ibaraki Japan 36°20N 140°30E 223 A12
Ibaraki Japan 34°49N 135°34E 223 C7
Ibaraki □ Japan 36°10N 140°10E 223 A12
Ibarra Ecuador 0°21N 78°7W 328 C2
Ibb Yemen 14°2N 44°10E 248 D3
Ibba Sudan 4°49N 29°2E 257 G2
Ibba, Bahr el → Sudan 5°30N 28°55E 257 F2
Ibbenbüren Germany 52°16N 7°43E 178 C3
Ibeke Gembo Dem. Rep. of the Congo 1°24S 18°51E 264 C3
Ibembo Dem. Rep. of the Congo 2°35N 23°35E 264 B4
Ibenga → Congo 2°19N 18°9E 264 B3
Ibera, L. Argentina 28°30S 57°9W 334 B4
Iberia Peru 11°21S 69°35W 330 C4
Iberia Mo., U.S.A. 38°5N 92°18W 310 F4
Iberian Peninsula Europe 40°0N 5°0W 158 H5
Iberville Canada 45°19N 73°17W 313 A11
Iberville, Mt. d' Canada 58°50N 63°50W 295 F19
Ibese Nigeria 6°33N 3°28E 124 A2
Ibeto Nigeria 10°29N 5°8E 263 C6
Ibi Nigeria 8°15N 9°44E 263 D6
Ibi Spain 38°38N 0°34W 197 G4
Ibiá Brazil 19°30S 46°30W 333 E2
Ibiapaba, Sa. da Brazil 4°0S 41°30W 332 B3
Ibicaraí Brazil 14°51S 39°36W 333 D4
Ibicuí Brazil 14°51S 39°59W 333 D4
Ibicuí → Brazil 29°25S 56°47W 335 B4
Ibicuy Argentina 33°55S 59°10W 334 C4
Ibirapuera Brazil 23°36S 46°40W 137 B1
Ibirapuera, Parque do Brazil 23°35S 46°38W 137 B2
Ibitiara Brazil 12°39S 42°13W 333 D3
Ibiza = Eivissa Spain 38°54N 1°26E 206 D1
Ibiza ✕ (IBZ) Spain 38°53N 1°22E 197 G6
Iblei, Monti Italy 37°15N 14°45E 201 E7
Ibn Hāni', Ra's Syria 35°35N 35°43E 250 C6
Ibo Mozam. 12°22S 40°40E 269 E5
Ibonma Indonesia 3°29S 133°31E 231 E8
Ibotirama Brazil 12°13S 43°12W 333 D3
Iboundji Gabon 1°0S 11°51E 264 C2
Ibradı Turkey 37°4N 31°35E 250 A2
Ibrāhīm → Lebanon 34°4N 35°38E 250 D6
'Ibrī Oman 23°14N 56°30E 247 F8
İbriktepe Turkey 41°0N 26°30E 203 E10
Ibshawâi Egypt 29°21N 30°40E 256 J7
Ibu Indonesia 1°35N 127°33E 231 D7
Ibusuki-Sanchi Japan 35°25N 136°18E 223 B8
Ibusuki Japan 31°12N 130°40E 222 F2
Ica Peru 14°0S 75°48W 330 C2
Ica □ Peru 14°20S 75°30W 330 C2
Iça → Brazil 2°55S 67°58W 330 A4
Icabarú Venezuela 4°20N 61°45W 329 C5
Icabarú → Venezuela 4°45N 62°15W 329 C5
Icacos Trin. & Tob. 10°3N 61°54W 323 t
Icacos Pt. Trin. & Tob. 10°3N 61°57W 323 t
Içana Brazil 0°21N 67°19W 328 C4
Içana → Brazil 0°26N 67°19W 328 C4
Icaraí Brazil 22°54S 43°6W 135 B2
Icatu Brazil 2°46S 44°4W 332 B3
Icaturama = Santa Rosa de Viterbo Colombia 5°53N 72°59W 328 B3
İçel Turkey 36°51N 34°36E 250 B5
İçel □ Turkey 36°45N 34°0E 250 B5
Iceland ■ Europe 64°45N 19°0W 155 C8
Iceland Basin Atl. Oc. 61°0N 19°0W 150 C7
Icelandic Plateau Arctic 64°0N 10°0W 150 C7
İçerenköy Turkey 40°58N 29°6E 122 C2
İçeriçumra Turkey 37°34N 32°39E 212 D5
Ichalkaranji India 16°40N 74°33E 244 F2
Ich'ang = Yichang China 30°40N 111°20E 229 B8
Ichchapuram India 19°10N 84°40E 244 E7
Icheon S. Korea 37°17N 127°27E 224 D3
Ichgao Japan 35°32N 139°32E 140 B2
Ichhawar India 23°1N 77°1E 242 H7
Ichigaya Tokyo, Japan 140 a3
Ichihara Japan 35°28N 140°5E 223 B12
Ichikawa Japan 35°43N 139°54E 140 A4
Ichilo → Bolivia 15°57S 64°50W 331 D5
Ichinohe Japan 40°13N 141°17E 220 D10
Ichinomiya Gifu, Japan 35°18N 136°48E 223 B8
Ichinomiya Kumamoto, Japan 32°58N 131°5E 222 E3
Ichinoseki Japan 38°55N 141°8E 220 E10
Ichkeul △ Tunisia 37°5N 9°37E 258 A1
Ichnya Ukraine 50°52N 32°24E 189 G7
Icht Morocco 29°6N 8°54W 260 C3
Ichu Taiwan 23°20N 120°14E 225 C2
Ichun = Yichun China 47°44N 128°52E 219 B14
Ickenham U.K. 51°33N 0°26W 125 A1
Icó Brazil 6°24S 38°51W 332 C4
Icoca Angola 8°12S 16°20E 265 D3
Icod Canary Is. 28°22N 16°43W 153 e1
İçoğuz Turkmenistan 40°11N 58°24E 216 D5
Iconi Comoros Is. 12°21S 43°51E 272 a
Icoraci Brazil 1°18S 48°28W 332 B2
Icy C. U.S.A. 70°20N 161°52W 303 A7
Ida Grove U.S.A. 42°21N 95°28W 308 D6
Idaan Somali Rep. 6°10N 48°55E 267 C6
Idabel U.S.A. 33°54N 94°50W 314 E7
Idaga Hamus Ethiopia 14°13N 39°48E 257 E4
Idah Nigeria 7°5N 6°40E 263 D6
Idaho □ U.S.A. 45°0N 115°0W 304 D6
Idaho City U.S.A. 43°50N 115°50W 304 E6
Idaho Falls U.S.A. 43°30N 112°2W 304 E7
Idalia △ Australia 24°49S 144°36E 280 C3
Idanha-a-Nova Portugal 39°50N 7°15W 194 F3
Idar-Oberstein Germany 49°43N 7°16E 179 F3
Iday Niger 14°54N 11°33E 259 F2
'Idd el Ghanam Sudan 11°30N 24°19E 259 F4
Iddo Nigeria 6°28N 3°22E 124 B2
Idelès Algeria 23°50N 5°53E 261 D6
Idensalmi = Iisalmi Finland 63°32N 27°10E 160 E22
Idfû Egypt 24°55N 32°49E 256 C3
Ídhra = Hydra Greece 37°20N 23°28E 204 D5
Idi Indonesia 5°2N 97°37E 234 A1
Idi, Oros = Psiloritis, Oros Greece 35°15N 24°45E 207 E5
Idi Amin Dada, L. = Edward, L. Africa 0°25S 29°40E 268 C2
Idi-Oro Nigeria 6°31N 3°21E 124 A2
Idil Turkey 37°20N 41°53E 213 D9
Idiofa Dem. Rep. of the Congo 4°55S 19°42E 265 C3
Idjil = Fdérik Mauritania 22°40N 12°45W 260 D2
Idkerberget Sweden 60°22N 15°15E 162 D9
Idku Egypt 31°18N 30°17E 256 H7
Idku, Bahra el Egypt 31°18N 30°18E 256 H7
Idlib Syria 35°55N 36°36E 250 C7
Idlib □ Syria 35°45N 36°45E 250 C7
Idre Sweden 61°52N 12°42E 162 C6
Idria U.S.A. 36°25N 120°41W 306 J6
Idrija Slovenia 46°0N 14°5E 199 C11
Idritsa Russia 56°17N 28°53E 188 D5
Idutywa = Dutywa S. Africa 32°8S 28°18E 271 D4
Ie Shima Japan 26°43N 127°48E 288 a
Ie Suido Japan 26°42N 127°51E 288 a
Ieper Belgium 50°51N 2°53E 170 D2
Ierapetra Greece 35°1N 25°44E 207 F6
Ierissos Greece 40°22N 23°52E 202 F7
Ierissos Kolpos Greece 40°27N 23°57E 202 F7
Iernut Romania 46°27N 24°15E 183 D9
Ieshima-Shotō Japan 34°40N 134°32E 222 C6
Iesi Italy 43°31N 13°14E 199 E10
Iésolo Italy 45°32N 12°38E 199 C9
Iet Ethiopia 4°33N 43°1E 267 D5
Ifac, Penyal d' Spain 38°38N 0°5E 197 G5
'Ifāl, W. al → Si. Arabia 28°7N 35°3E 251 K6
Ifanadiana Madag. 21°19S 47°39E 272 C2
Ife Nigeria 7°30N 4°31E 263 D5
Iférouâne Niger 19°5N 8°24E 259 E1
Ifetesene Algeria 25°30N 4°33E 261 C5
Iffley Australia 18°53S 141°12E 280 B3
Ifon Nigeria 6°58N 5°40E 263 D6
Iforas, Adrar des Africa 19°40N 1°40E 261 D5
Ifould, L. Australia 30°52S 132°6E 279 F5
Ifrane Morocco 33°33N 5°7W 260 B3
Ifrane □ Morocco 33°20N 5°15W 260 B3
Ifugao □ Phil. 16°40N 121°10E 232 C3
Iga Japan 34°45N 136°10E 223 C8
Igalo Montenegro 42°28N 18°30E 202 D2
Iganga Uganda 0°37N 33°28E 268 B3
Iganmu Nigeria 6°28N 3°22E 124 B2
Igara-Paraná → Colombia 2°9S 71°47W 328 D3
Igarapava Brazil 20°3S 47°47W 333 F2
Igarapé-Açu Brazil 1°4S 47°33W 332 B2
Igarapé-Miri Brazil 1°59S 48°58W 332 B2
Igarka Russia 67°30N 86°33E 214 C9
Igatpuri India 19°40N 73°35E 244 E1
Igbetti Nigeria 8°44N 4°8E 263 D5
Igbo-Ora Nigeria 7°29N 3°15E 263 D5
Igbobi Nigeria 6°31N 3°22E 124 A2
Igboho Nigeria 8°53N 3°50E 263 D5
Igbologun Nigeria 6°24N 3°19E 124 B1
Igbor Nigeria 7°27N 8°34E 263 D6
Iğdır Turkey 39°55N 44°2E 213 C11
Igelfors Sweden 58°52N 15°41E 163 F9
Iggesund Sweden 61°39N 17°10E 162 C11
Ighil Izane = Relizane Algeria 35°44N 0°31E 261 A5
Igiugig U.S.A. 59°20N 155°55W 303 G9
Iglau = Jihlava Czech Rep. 49°28N 15°35E 180 B8
Iglésias Italy 39°19N 8°32E 200 C1
Igli Algeria 30°25N 2°19W 261 B4
Igloolik = Iglulik Canada 69°20N 81°49W 295 D15
Iglulik Canada 69°20N 81°49W 295 D15
Iglugaarjuk = Chesterfield Inlet Canada 63°30N 90°45W 294 E13
'Igma, G. el Egypt 29°10N 34°0E 251 J5
'Igma, Gebel el Egypt 28°55N 34°0E 256 B3
Ignace Canada 49°30N 91°40W 298 C1
İğneada Turkey 41°52N 27°59E 203 E11
İğneada Burnu Turkey 41°53N 28°2E 203 E12
Igny France 48°44N 2°13E 134 B2
Igoumenitsa Greece 39°32N 20°18E 206 B10
Igrim Russia 63°12N 64°30E 214 C7
Iguaçu → Brazil 25°36S 54°36W 335 B5
Iguaçu, Cat. del Brazil 25°41S 54°26W 335 B5
Iguaçu △ Brazil 25°30S 54°0W 335 B5
Iguaçu Falls = Iguaçu, Cat. del Brazil 25°41S 54°26W 335 B5
Iguala Mexico 18°21N 99°32W 319 D5
Igualada Spain 41°37N 1°37E 196 D6
Iguape Brazil 24°43S 47°33W 333 F2
Iguaratinga = São Francisco do Maranhão Brazil 6°15S 42°52W 332 C3
Iguassu = Iguaçu → Brazil 25°36S 54°36W 335 B5
Iguatu Brazil 6°20S 39°18W 332 C4
Iguazú △ Argentina 25°42S 54°22W 335 B5
Iguéla Gabon 2°0S 9°16E 264 C1
Iguéla, Lagune Gabon 1°48S 9°16E 264 C2
Iguidi, Erg Africa 27°0N 6°0W 260 C3
Igulg Phil. 17°45N 121°44E 232 C3
Igumen = Cherven Belarus 53°45N 28°28E 177 B15
Iharana Madag. 13°25S 50°0E 272 A3
Ihavandiffulu Atoll Maldives 7°0N 72°50E 272 d
Ihbulag Mongolia 43°11N 107°10E 226 C4
Iheya-Shima Japan 27°4N 127°58E 221 L3
Ihiala Nigeria 5°51N 6°55E 263 D6
Ihirene → Algeria 20°28N 4°37E 261 D5
Ihosy Madag. 22°24S 46°8E 272 C2
Ihotry, Farihy Madag. 21°56S 43°41E 272 C1
Ihu Papua N. G. 7°55S 145°24E 286 D3

Ihugh *Nigeria* 7°2N 9°0E **263** D6
Ii *Finland* 65°19N 25°22E **160** D21
Ii-Shima *Japan* 26°43N 127°47E **221** L3
Iida *Japan* 35°35N 137°50E **223** B9
Iijoki → *Finland* 65°20N 25°20E **160** D21
Iisalmi *Finland* 63°32N 27°10E **160** E22
Iiyama *Japan* 36°51N 138°22E **221** F9
Iizuka *Japan* 33°38N 130°42E **222** D2
IJ, Het → *Neths.* 52°23N 4°54E **112** A2
IJ-meer *Neths.* 52°23N 4°54E **112** A3
Ijâfene *Mauritania* 20°40N 8°0W **260** D3
Ijebu-Igbo *Nigeria* 6°56N 4°1E **263** D5
Ijebu-Ode *Nigeria* 6°47N 3°58E **263** D5
Ijesa-Tedo *Nigeria* 6°29N 3°19E **124** B1
Ijevan *Armenia* 40°52N 45°8E **191** K7
Ijill, Sebkhet *Mauritania* 22°47N 12°53W **260** D2
IJmuiden *Neths.* 52°28N 4°35E **170** B4
Ijo älv = Iijoki →
Finland 65°20N 25°20E **160** D21
Ijora *Nigeria* 6°27N 3°22E **124** B2
IJssel → *Neths.* 52°35N 5°50E **170** B5
IJsselmeer *Neths.* 52°45N 5°20E **170** B5
Ijuí *Brazil* 28°23S 53°55W **335** B5
Ijuí → *Brazil* 27°58S 55°20W **335** B4
Ijūin *Japan* 31°37N 130°24E **222** F2
Ikalamavony *Madag.* 21°9S 46°35E **272** C2
Ikali *Dem. Rep. of the Congo* 2°2S 21°4E **264** C4
Ikamatua *N.Z.* 42°16S 171°41E **285** C6
Ikang *Nigeria* 4°49N 8°30E **263** E6
Ikanga *Kenya* 1°42S 38°4E **268** C4
Ikara *Nigeria* 11°12N 8°15E **263** C6
Ikare *Nigeria* 7°32N 5°40E **263** D6
Ikaria *Greece* 37°35N 26°10E **205** D8
Ikast *Denmark* 56°8N 9°10E **163** H3
Ikebe *Japan* 35°31N 139°34E **140** B2
Ikebukuro *Japan* 35°43N 139°42E **140** A3
Ikeda *Japan* 34°1N 133°48E **222** C5
Ikegami *Japan* 35°33N 139°42E **140** B3
Ikei-shima *Japan* 26°23N 127°59E **288** a
Ikeja *Nigeria* 6°35N 3°20E **124** A2
Ikela *Dem. Rep. of the Congo* 1°6S 23°6E **264** C4
Ikélemba *Congo* 1°12N 16°38E **264** B3
Ikélemba →
Dem. Rep. of the Congo 0°7N 18°17E **264** B3
Ikengo *Dem. Rep. of the Congo* 0°8S 18°8E **264** C3
Ikere *Nigeria* 7°25N 5°19E **263** D6
Ikeuchi *Japan* 34°35N 135°32E **133** B2
Ikhtiman *Bulgaria* 42°27N 23°48E **202** D7
Iki *Japan* 33°45N 129°42E **222** D1
Iki-Kaikyō *Japan* 33°40N 129°45E **222** D1
Ikimba L. *Tanzania* 1°30S 31°20E **268** C3
Ikire *Nigeria* 7°23N 4°15E **263** D5
Ikitsuki-Shima *Japan* 33°23N 129°26E **222** D1
İkizdere *Turkey* 40°46N 40°32E **213** B9
Iko *Congo* 0°35S 16°0E **264** C3
Ikom *Nigeria* 6°0N 8°42E **263** D6
Ikoma *Japan* 34°30N 135°40E **223** C7
Ikomu
Dem. Rep. of the Congo 1°54S 19°40E **264** C3
Ikongo *Madag.* 21°52S 47°27E **272** C2
Ikopa → *Madag.* 16°45S 46°40E **272** B2
Ikorongo △ *Tanzania* 1°50S 34°53E **268** C3
Ikot Ekpene *Nigeria* 5°12N 7°40E **263** D6
Ikoyi *Nigeria* 6°27N 3°26E **124** B2
Ikparjuk = Arctic Bay
Canada 73°1N 85°7W **295** C14
Iksan *S. Korea* 35°59N 127°0E **224** E3
Ikuata *Nigeria* 6°24N 3°21E **124** B2
Ikungu *Tanzania* 1°33S 33°42E **268** C3
Ikuno *Hyōgo, Japan* 35°10N 134°48E **222** B6
Ikuno *Ōsaka, Japan* 34°40N 135°30E **133** A2
Ikuntji = Haasts Bluff
Australia 23°22S 132°0E **278** D5
Ikurun *Nigeria* 7°54N 4°40E **263** D5
Ikuta *Japan* 35°36N 139°32E **140** B2
Il-Kullana *Malta* 35°50N 14°24E **206** F7
Il-Munxar *Malta* 35°51N 14°34E **206** F8
Ila *Dem. Rep. of the Congo* 2°53S 21°7E **264** C4
Ila *Nigeria* 8°0N 4°39E **263** D5
Ila *Oslo, Norway* 59°57N 10°35E **133** A2
Ilafer *Algeria* 21°40N 1°58E **261** D5
Ilagan *Phil.* 17°7N 121°53E **232** C3
Ilaka *Madag.* 19°33S 48°52E **272** B2
Īlām *Iran* 33°36N 46°36E **213** F12
Ilam *Nepal* 26°58N 87°58E **243** F12
Īlām □ *Iran* 33°0N 47°0E **246** C5
Ilan *Taiwan* 24°45N 121°44E **225** B3
Ilan □ *Taiwan* 24°30N 121°35E **225** B3
Ilan, Mt. *Phil.* 10°26N 119°33E **233** F2
Ilanskiy *Russia* 56°14N 96°3E **215** D10
Ilaro *Nigeria* 6°53N 3°3E **263** D5
Ilatane *Niger* 16°30N 4°45E **263** B5
Ilave *Peru* 16°5S 69°40W **330** D4
Iława *Poland* 53°36N 19°34E **184** E6
Ilayangudi *India* 9°34N 78°37E **245** K4
Ile → *Kazakhstan* 45°53N 77°10E **217** C9
Île-à-la-Crosse *Canada* 55°27N 107°53W **297** B7
Île-à-la-Crosse, Lac
Canada 55°40N 107°45W **297** B7
Île-de-France □ *France* 49°0N 2°20E **173** D9
Ileanda *Romania* 47°20N 23°38E **183** C8
Ilebo *Dem. Rep. of the Congo* 4°17S 20°55E **265** C4
Ilek *Russia* 51°32N 53°21E **216** B4
Ilek → *Russia* 51°30N 53°22E **186** D9
Iler, O. → *Algeria* 20°59N 3°14E **261** D5
Ilero *Nigeria* 8°0N 3°20E **263** D5
Ilesha *Kwara, Nigeria* 8°57N 3°28E **263** D5
Ilesha *Oyo, Nigeria* 7°37N 4°40E **263** D5
Ilet = Krasnogorskiy
Russia 56°10N 48°28E **190** B9
Iletskaya = Sol Iletsk
Russia 51°10N 55°0E **186** D10
Iletsky Gorodok = Ilek
Russia 51°32N 53°21E **216** B4
Ilford *Man., Canada* 56°4N 95°35W **297** B9
Ilford *London, U.K.* 51°33N 0°4E **125** A4
Ilfracombe *Queens.,*
Australia 23°30S 144°30E **280** C3
Ilfracombe *Devon, U.K.* 51°12N 4°8W **169** F3
Ilgaz *Turkey* 40°55N 33°37E **212** B5
Ilgaz Dağları *Turkey* 41°10N 33°50E **212** B5
Ilgın *Turkey* 38°16N 31°55E **212** C4
Ilha, Pta. da *Azores* 38°25N 28°3W **153** d1
Ilha Grande *Brazil* 0°27S 65°2W **329** D4
Ilha Grande, B. da *Brazil* 23°9S 44°30W **333** F3
Ilha Grande, Represa
Brazil 23°10S 53°5W **335** A5
Ilha Grande △ *Brazil* 23°10S 53°20W **335** A5
Ílhavo *Portugal* 40°33N 8°43W **194** E2
Ilhéus *Brazil* 14°49S 39°2W **333** D4
Ili = Ile → *Kazakhstan* 45°53N 77°10E **217** C9
Ilia *Romania* 45°57N 22°40E **182** E7
Ilia □ *Greece* 37°45N 21°35E **204** D3
Iliamna *U.S.A.* 59°45N 154°55W **303** G9
Iliamna L. *U.S.A.* 59°30N 155°0W **303** G9
Ilias, Profitis *Greece* 36°17N 27°56E **206** E11
Iliç *Turkey* 39°27N 38°33E **213** C8
Ilıca *Turkey* 39°52N 27°46E **205** B9
Ilig, Ras *Somali Rep.* 7°47N 49°50E **267** C6
Iligan *Phil.* 8°12N 124°13E **233** G5
Iligan B. *Phil.* 8°25N 124°5E **233** G5
Iligan Pt. *Phil.* 18°25N 122°25E **232** B4
Ilin I. *Phil.* 12°14N 121°5E **232** E3
'Ilio Pt. *U.S.A.* 21°13N 157°16W **302** B4
Ilion *U.S.A.* 43°1N 75°2W **313** D9
Ilioupoli *Greece* 37°54N 23°47E **112** B2
Ilirska-Bistrica *Slovenia* 45°34N 14°14E **199** C11
Iliwa = Rewa → *Guyana* 3°19N 58°42W **329** C6
Iliysk = Qapshaghay
Kazakhstan 43°51N 77°14E **217** D9
Ilkal *India* 15°57N 76°8E **245** G3
Ilkenau = Olkusz *Poland* 50°18N 19°33E **185** H6
Ilkeston *U.K.* 52°58N 1°19W **168** E6
Ilkley *U.K.* 53°56N 1°48W **168** D6
Illampu = Ancohuma, Nevado
Bolivia 16°0S 68°50W **330** D4
Illana B. *Phil.* 7°35N 123°45E **233** H4
Illapel *Chile* 32°0S 71°10W **334** C1
Ille-et-Vilaine □ *France* 48°10N 1°30W **172** D5
Ille-sur-Têt *France* 42°40N 2°38E **174** F6
Illéla *Niger* 14°32N 5°20E **263** C6
Iller → *Germany* 48°23N 9°58E **179** G5
Illertissen *Germany* 48°12N 10°7E **179** G6
Illescas *Spain* 40°8N 3°51W **194** E7
Illetas *Spain* 39°32N 2°35E **206** B3
Illichivsk *Ukraine* 46°20N 30°35E **189** J6
Illiers-Combray *France* 48°18N 1°15E **172** D8
Illimani, Nevado *Bolivia* 16°30S 67°50W **330** D4
Illinois □ *U.S.A.* 40°15N 89°30W **310** D7
Illinois → *U.S.A.* 38°58N 90°28W **310** F6
Illinois at Chicago, Univ. of
U.S.A. 41°52N 87°38W **119** B3
Illinois Institute of Technology
U.S.A. 41°50N 87°37W **119** B3
Illiopolis *U.S.A.* 39°51N 89°15W **310** E7
Illium = Troy *Turkey* 39°57N 26°12E **205** B8
Illizi *Algeria* 26°31N 8°32E **261** C6
Illizi □ *Algeria* 26°50N 8°10E **261** C6
Illkirch-Graffenstaden
France 48°34N 7°42E **173** D14
Íllora *Spain* 37°17N 3°53W **195** H7
Ilm → *Germany* 51°6N 11°40E **178** D7
Ilma, L. *Australia* 29°13S 127°46E **279** E4
Ilmajoki *Finland* 62°44N 22°34E **160** E20
Ilmen, Ozero *Russia* 58°15N 31°10E **188** C6
Ilmenau = Jordanów
Poland 49°41N 19°49E **185** J6
Ilmenau = Limanowa
Poland 49°42N 20°22E **185** J7
Ilmenau *Germany* 50°41N 10°54E **178** E6
Ilnytsya *Ukraine* 48°21N 23°5E **182** B8
Ilo *Peru* 17°40S 71°20W **330** D3
Ilobu *Nigeria* 7°45N 4°25E **263** D5
Iloc I. *Phil.* 11°17N 119°40E **233** F2
Ilocos Norte □ *Phil.* 18°10N 120°45E **232** B3
Ilocos Sur □ *Phil.* 17°20N 120°35E **232** C3
Iloilo *Phil.* 10°45N 122°33E **233** F4
Iloilo □ *Phil.* 11°0N 122°40E **233** F4
Ilomantsi *Finland* 62°38N 30°57E **160** E24
Ilora *Nigeria* 7°45N 3°50E **263** D5
Ilorin *Nigeria* 8°30N 4°35E **263** D5
Ilovatka *Russia* 50°30N 45°50E **190** E7
Ilovlya *Russia* 49°15N 44°2E **191** F7
Ilovlya → *Russia* 49°14N 44°0E **191** F7
Iłowa *Poland* 51°30N 15°10E **185** G2
Ilpendam *Neths.* 52°28N 4°57E **112** A2
Ilsos → *Greece* 37°55N 23°41E **112** B2
Ilubabor *Ethiopia* 7°25N 35°0E **257** F4
Ilulissat *Greenland* 69°12N 51°10W **154** D5
Ilva Mică *Romania* 47°17N 24°40E **183** C9
Ilwaco *U.S.A.* 46°19N 124°3W **306** D2
Ilwaki *Indonesia* 7°55S 126°30E **231** F7
Ilyichevsk = Illichivsk
Ukraine 46°20N 30°35E **189** J6
Iłża *Poland* 51°10N 21°15E **185** G8
Iłżanka → *Poland* 51°14N 21°48E **185** G8
Imabari *Japan* 34°4N 133°0E **222** C5
Imagem e do Som, Museu da
Rio de J., Brazil **135** b3
Imaichi *Japan* 36°43N 139°46E **223** A11
Imaloto → *Madag.* 23°27S 45°13E **272** C2
İmamoğlu *Turkey* 37°15N 35°38E **212** D6
Iman = Dalnerechensk
Russia 45°50N 133°40E **220** B6
Imandra, Ozero *Russia* 67°30N 33°0E **160** C25
Imanombo *Madag.* 24°26S 45°49E **272** C2
Imari *Japan* 33°15N 129°52E **222** D1
Imasa *Sudan* 18°0N 36°12E **256** D4
Imathia □ *Greece* 40°30N 22°15E **202** F6
Imatra *Finland* 61°12N 28°48E **188** B5
Imbâbah *Egypt* 30°3N 31°12E **117** A2
Imbabura □ *Ecuador* 0°30N 78°45W **328** C2
Imbaimadai *Guyana* 5°44N 60°17W **329** B5
Imbonga
Dem. Rep. of the Congo 0°43S 19°44E **264** C3
Imdahane *Morocco* 32°8N 7°0W **260** B3
Iménas *Mali* 16°20N 0°40E **263** B5
imeni 26 Bakinskikh Komissarov =
Neftçala *Azerbaijan* 39°19N 49°12E **213** C13
imeni 26 Bakinskikh Komissarov
Turkmenistan 39°22N 54°10E **247** B7
imeni Dvadtsati Shesti Bakinskikh
Komissarov = Neftçala
Azerbaijan 39°19N 49°12E **213** C13
imeni Dzerzhinskogo =
Naryan-Mar *Russia* 67°42N 53°12E **186** A9
imeni Ismail Samani, Pik
Tajikistan 39°0N 72°2E **217** E8
imeni Mikoyana = Kara-Balta
Kyrgyzstan 42°50N 73°49E **217** D8
imeni Petrovskogo G.I. =
Horodyshche *Ukraine* 49°17N 31°27E **189** H6
imeni Sverdlova = Sverdlovsk
Ukraine 48°5N 39°47E **189** H10
imeni Tovarishcha Khateyevicha =
Synelnykove *Ukraine* 48°25N 35°30E **189** H8
imeni Tretyego Internatsionala =
Novoshakhtinsk
Russia 47°46N 39°58E **189** J10
Imeri, Serra *Brazil* 0°50N 65°25W **328** C4
Imerimandroso *Madag.* 17°26S 48°35E **272** B2
Imese *Dem. Rep. of the Congo* 2°6N 18°9E **264** B3
Imfolozi △ *S. Africa* 28°18S 31°50E **271** C5
Imi *Ethiopia* 6°28N 42°10E **257** F5
Imielin *Poland* 50°9N 21°0E **142** C2
Imirim *Brazil* 23°29S 46°39W **137** A2
Imishly = İmişli *Azerbaijan* 39°55N 48°4E **191** L9
İmişli *Azerbaijan* 39°55N 48°4E **191** L9
Imitek *Morocco* 29°43N 8°10W **260** C3
Imittos *Greece* 37°55N 23°45E **112** B2
Imittos, Oros *Greece* 37°53N 23°48E **112** B2
Imjado *S. Korea* 35°5N 126°5E **224** E3
Imjin-gang → *N. Korea* 37°47N 126°39E **224** D3
Imlay *U.S.A.* 40°40N 118°9W **304** F4
Imlay City *U.S.A.* 43°2N 83°5W **312** D1
Immesarci *Sudan* 15°40N 25°31E **257** D2
Immenstadt *Germany* 47°33N 10°13E **179** H6
Immingham *U.K.* 53°37N 0°13W **168** D7
Immokalee *U.S.A.* 26°25N 81°25W **317** J8
Imo □ *Nigeria* 5°30N 7°10E **263** D6
Imo → *Nigeria* 4°36N 7°35E **263** E6
Ímola *Italy* 44°20N 11°42E **198** D8
Imotski *Croatia* 43°27N 17°12E **199** E14
Impé *Congo* 2°45S 15°16E **264** C3
Imperatorskaya Gavan = Vanino
Russia 48°50N 140°5E **215** E15
Imperatriz *Amazonas, Brazil* 5°18S 67°11W **330** B4
Imperatriz *Maranhão,*
Brazil 5°30S 47°29W **332** C2
Impéria *Italy* 43°53N 8°3E **198** E5
Imperial *Sask., Canada* 51°21N 105°28W **297** C7
Imperial *Peru* 13°4S 76°21W **330** C2
Imperial *Calif., U.S.A.* 32°51N 115°34W **307** N11
Imperial *Nebr., U.S.A.* 40°31N 101°39W **308** E3
Imperial Beach *U.S.A.* 32°35N 117°6W **307** N9
Imperial Dam *U.S.A.* 32°55N 114°25W **307** N12
Imperial Palace = Paço Imperial
Rio de J., Brazil **135** a2
Imperial Palace Museum *Beijing, China* **114** b3
Imperial Res. *U.S.A.* 32°53N 114°28W **307** N12
Imperial Valley *U.S.A.* 33°0N 115°30W **307** N11
Imperieuse Reef *Australia* 17°36S 118°50E **278** C2
Impfondo *Congo* 1°40N 18°0E **264** B3
Imphal *India* 24°48N 93°56E **241** C4
Imphy *France* 46°55N 3°16E **173** F10
Impulo *Angola* 13°51S 13°39E **265** E2
Imranlı *Turkey* 39°54N 38°7E **213** C8
İmroz = Gökçeada *Turkey* 40°10N 25°50E **203** F9
İmroz *Turkey* 40°10N 25°55E **203** F9
Imst *Austria* 47°15N 10°44E **180** D3
Imuris *Mexico* 30°47N 110°52W **318** A2
Imuruan B. *Phil.* 10°40N 119°10E **233** F2
Imus *Phil.* 14°26N 120°56E **232** D3
In Aleï *Mali* 17°42N 2°30W **262** B4
In Amenas *Algeria* 28°5N 9°33E **261** C6
In Amguel *Algeria* 23°41N 5°9E **261** D6
In Atei *Algeria* 20°33N 6°4E **261** D6
In Belbel *Algeria* 27°55N 1°12E **261** C5
In Delimane *Mali* 15°52N 1°31E **263** B5
In Ghar *Algeria* 27°10N 1°59E **261** C5
In Guezzam *Algeria* 19°37N 5°52E **261** D6
In Koufi *Mali* 19°11N 1°25E **263** B5
In Salah *Algeria* 27°10N 2°32E **261** C5
In Tallak *Mali* 16°19N 3°15E **263** B5
In Tebezas *Mali* 17°49N 1°53E **263** B5
Ina *Japan* 35°50N 137°55E **223** B9
Ina *Ill., U.S.A.* 38°9N 88°54W **311** F8
Ina-Bonchi *Japan* 35°45N 137°58E **223** B9
Inabanga *Phil.* 10°2N 124°4E **233** F5
Inaccessible I. *Atl. Oc.* 37°18S 12°40W **152** K10
Inagauan *Phil.* 9°33N 118°39E **233** G2
Inagi *Japan* 35°38N 139°31E **140** B2
Inajá *Brazil* 8°54S 37°49W **332** C4
Inambari → *Peru* 12°41S 69°44W **330** C4
Inangahua *N.Z.* 41°52S 171°59E **285** B6
Inanwatan *Indonesia* 2°8S 132°10E **231** E8
Iñapari *Peru* 11°0S 69°40W **330** C4
Inarajan *Guam* 13°16N 144°45E **302** d
Inari *Finland* 68°54N 27°1E **160** B22
Inarijärvi *Finland* 69°0N 28°0E **160** B23
Inawashiro-Ko *Japan* 37°29N 140°6E **220** F10
Inazawa *Japan* 35°15N 136°47E **223** B8
Inbin *Burma* 18°6N 95°16E **241** F5
Inca *Spain* 39°43N 2°54E **206** B3
Inca de Oro *Chile* 26°45S 69°54W **334** B2
Incahuasi *Argentina* 27°2S 68°18W **334** B2
Incahuasi *Chile* 29°12S 71°5W **334** B1
İnce Burun *Turkey* 42°7N 34°56E **212** A6
İncekum Burnu *Turkey* 36°13N 33°57E **250** B4
İncesu *Turkey* 38°38N 35°11E **212** C6
Inchcolm *U.K.* 56°2N 3°18W **121** A2
Incheon *S. Korea* 37°27N 126°40E **224** D3
Inchicore *Ireland* 53°20N 6°20W **120** A1
Inchiri □ *Mauritania* 20°0N 15°0W **260** E2
Inchkeith *U.K.* 56°2N 3°8W **121** A3
Inchmickery *U.K.* 56°0N 3°16W **121** A2
Incio = A Cruz do Incio
Spain 42°39N 7°21W **194** C3
Incirano *Italy* 45°34N 9°9E **129** A1
İncirliova *Turkey* 37°50N 27°41E **205** D9
Incline Village *U.S.A.* 39°10N 119°58W **304** G4
Incomáti → *Mozam.* 25°46S 32°43E **271** C5
Incudine, Mte. *France* 41°50N 9°12E **175** G13
Inda Silase *Ethiopia* 14°10N 38°15E **257** E4
Indal *Sweden* 62°35N 17°5E **162** B11
Indalsälven → *Sweden* 62°36N 17°30E **162** B11
Indaw *Burma* 24°15N 96°5E **241** C6
Indawgyi In *Burma* 25°8N 96°20E **241** C6
Indbir *Ethiopia* 8°7N 37°52E **257** F4
Indefatigable, I. = Santa Cruz, I.
Ecuador 0°38S 90°23W **330** a
Independence *Calif.,*
U.S.A. 36°48N 118°12W **306** J8
Independence *Iowa,*
U.S.A. 42°28N 91°54W **310** B5
Independence *Kans.,*
U.S.A. 37°14N 95°42W **308** G6
Independence *Ky.,*
U.S.A. 38°57N 84°33W **311** F12
Independence *Mo., U.S.A.* 39°6N 94°25W **310** E2
Independence Avenue
Washington, D.C., U.S.A. **143** c2
Independence Fjord
Greenland 82°10N 29°0W **154** A8
Independence Mts.
U.S.A. 41°20N 116°0W **304** F5
Independência *Brazil* 5°23S 40°19W **332** C3
Independencia *Santiago,*
Chile 33°25S 70°39W **132** B2
Independencia *Lima, Peru* 11°59S 77°3W **124** A2
Independencia, I. *Peru* 14°16S 76°12W **330** C2
Independenţa *Romania* 45°25N 27°42E **183** E12
Inderbor *Kazakhstan* 48°33N 51°47E **216** C4
Index *U.S.A.* 47°50N 121°33W **306** C5
Indi *India* 17°10N 75°58E **244** F2
India ■ *Asia* 20°0N 78°0E **239** F11
India Gate *Delhi, India* **120** c2
Indialantic *U.S.A.* 28°6N 80°34W **317** G9
Indian → *U.S.A.* 27°59N 80°34W **317** G9
Indian Cabins *Canada* 59°52N 117°40W **296** B5
Indian Creek Village
U.S.A. 25°52N 80°8W **128** A2
Indian Harbour *Canada* 54°27N 57°13W **299** B8
Indian Harbour Beach
U.S.A. 28°10N 80°35W **317** G9
Indian Head *Canada* 50°30N 103°41W **297** C8
Indian L. *U.S.A.* 43°46N 74°16W **313** C10
Indian Lake *U.S.A.* 43°47N 74°16W **313** C10
Indian Ocean 5°0S 75°0E **273** E6
Indian Rocks Beach
U.S.A. 27°52N 82°51W **317** H7
Indian Springs *U.S.A.* 36°35N 115°40W **307** J11
Indian Town Pt.
Antigua & B. 17°6N 61°40W **322** b
Indian Walk *Trin. & Tob.* 10°16N 61°20W **323** t
Indiana *U.S.A.* 40°37N 79°9W **312** F5
Indiana □ *U.S.A.* 40°0N 86°0W **311** E11
Indiana Dunes △ *U.S.A.* 41°40N 87°0W **311** E10
Indianapolis *U.S.A.* 39°46N 86°9W **311** E10
Indianapolis Int. ✕ (IND)
U.S.A. 39°43N 86°17W **311** E10
Indianola *Iowa, U.S.A.* 41°22N 93°34W **310** C3
Indianola *Miss., U.S.A.* 33°27N 90°39W **315** E9
Indianópolis *Brazil* 23°35S 46°38W **137** B2
Indiantown *U.S.A.* 27°1N 80°28W **317** H9
Indiapora *Brazil* 19°57S 50°17W **333** E1
Indiga *Russia* 67°38N 49°9E **186** A8
Indigirka → *Russia* 70°48N 148°54E **215** B15
Inđija *Serbia* 45°6N 20°7E **182** E5
Indio *U.S.A.* 33°43N 116°13W **307** M10
Indira Gandhi Canal *India* 28°0N 72°0E **242** F5
Indira Gandhi Int. ✕ (DEL)
India 28°34N 77°5E **120** B1
Indira Pt. *India* 6°44N 93°49E **245** L11
Indira Sagar *India* 22°15N 76°40E **242** H7
Indispensable Str.
Solomon Is. 9°0S 160°30E **287** M11
Indo-China *Asia* 15°0N 102°0E **210** G12
Indonesia ■ *Asia* 5°0S 115°0E **235** C4
Indore *India* 22°42N 75°53E **242** H6
Indramayu *Indonesia* 6°20S 108°19E **235** D3
Indrapura = Kerinci
Indonesia 1°40S 101°15E **234** C2
Indravati → *India* 19°20N 80°20E **244** E5
Indre □ *France* 46°50N 1°39E **173** F8
Indre → *France* 47°16N 0°11E **172** E7
Indre Ålvik *Norway* 60°26N 6°26E **164** D3
Indre Arna *Norway* 60°26N 5°30E **164** D2
Indre-et-Loire □ *France* 47°20N 0°40E **172** E7
Indulkana *Australia* 26°58S 133°5E **281** D1
Indungo *Angola* 14°48S 16°17E **265** E3
Indura *Belarus* 53°26N 23°53E **184** E10
Indus → *Pakistan* 24°20N 67°47E **242** G2
Indus, Mouths of the
Pakistan 24°0N 68°0E **242** H3
Industria *S. Africa* 26°11S 27°58E **123** B1
Industrial Canal *U.S.A.* 30°4N 90°4W **131** A2
Industry *U.S.A.* 40°20N 90°36W **310** D6
İnebolu *Turkey* 41°55N 33°40E **212** B5
İnecik *Turkey* 40°56N 27°16E **203** F11
İnegöl *Turkey* 40°5N 29°31E **203** F13
Inés, Mt. *Argentina* 48°30S 69°40W **336** C3
Ineu *Romania* 46°26N 21°51E **182** D6
Inezgane *Morocco* 30°25N 9°29W **260** B3
Infanta *Phil.* 14°45N 121°39E **232** D3
Infantes = Villanueva de los
Infantes *Spain* 38°43N 3°1W **195** G7
Infiernillo, Presa del
Mexico 18°35N 101°50W **318** D4
Infiesto *Spain* 43°21N 5°21W **194** B5
Inga, Barrage d'
Dem. Rep. of the Congo 5°39S 13°39E **265** D2
Ingabu *Burma* 17°37N 95°20E **241** G5
Inganda
Dem. Rep. of the Congo 0°5S 20°57E **264** C4
Ingapirca *Ecuador* 2°38S 78°56W **328** D2
Ingaro *Sweden* 59°12N 18°45E **162** E12
Ingelstad *Sweden* 56°45N 14°56E **163** H8
Ingende
Dem. Rep. of the Congo 0°12S 18°57E **264** C3
Ingeniero Jacobacci
Argentina 41°20S 69°36W **336** B3
Ingenio *Canary Is.* 27°55N 15°26W **153** e1
Ingenio Santa Ana
Argentina 27°25S 65°40W **334** B2
Ingersoll *Canada* 43°4N 80°55W **312** C4
Ingham *Australia* 18°43S 146°10E **280** B4
Ingierstrand *Norway* 59°49N 10°46E **133** B3
Ingleborough *U.K.* 54°10N 2°22W **168** C5
Inglefield Land *Greenland* 78°30N 70°0W **154** B4
Inglewood *Queens.,*
Australia 28°25S 151°2E **281** D5
Inglewood *Vic., Australia* 36°29S 143°53E **282** D5
Inglewood *N.Z.* 39°9S 174°14E **284** F3
Inglewood *Calif., U.S.A.* 33°58N 118°21W **126** C3
Inglis *U.S.A.* 29°2N 82°40W **317** F7
Ingliston *U.K.* 55°56N 3°23W **121** B1
Ingolf Fjord *Greenland* 80°35N 17°30W **154** A9
Ingólfshöfði *Iceland* 63°48N 16°39W **155** D10
Ingolstadt *Germany* 48°46N 11°26E **179** G7
Ingomar *U.S.A.* 46°35N 107°23W **304** C10
Ingonish *Canada* 46°42N 60°18W **299** C7
Ingore *Guinea-Biss.* 12°24N 15°48W **262** C1
Ingraj Bazar *India* 24°58N 88°10E **243** G13
Ingrid Christensen Coast
Antarctica 69°30S 76°0E **151** C6
Ingul = Inhul → *Ukraine* 46°50N 32°0E **189** J7
Ingulec = Inhulec *Ukraine* 47°42N 33°14E **189** J7
Ingulets = Inhulets →
Ukraine 46°46N 32°47E **189** J7
Inguri = Enguri →
Georgia 42°27N 41°38E **191** J5
Ingushetia □ *Russia* 43°20N 44°50E **191** J7
Ingwavuma *S. Africa* 27°9S 31°59E **271** C5
Inhaca *Mozam.* 26°1S 32°57E **271** C5
Inhaca Pen. *Mozam.* 26°13S 32°55E **271** C5
Inhafenga *Mozam.* 20°36S 33°53E **271** B5
Inhambane *Mozam.* 23°54S 35°30E **271** B6
Inhambane □ *Mozam.* 22°30S 34°20E **271** B5
Inhambupe *Brazil* 11°47S 38°21W **333** D4
Inharrime *Mozam.* 24°30S 35°0E **271** B6
Inharrime → *Mozam.* 24°30S 35°0E **271** B6
Inhaúma *Brazil* 22°51S 43°17W **135** B1
Inhisar *Turkey* 40°3N 30°23E **205** A12
Inhul → *Ukraine* 46°50N 32°0E **189** J7
Inhulec *Ukraine* 47°42N 33°14E **189** J7
Inhulets → *Ukraine* 46°46N 32°47E **189** J7
Inhumas *Brazil* 16°22S 49°30W **333** E2
Iniesta *Spain* 39°27N 1°45W **197** F3
Ining = Yining *China* 43°58N 81°10E **217** D10
Inini □ *Fr. Guiana* 4°0N 53°0W **329** C7
Inírida → *Colombia* 3°55N 67°52W **328** C4
Inis = Ennis *Ireland* 52°51N 8°59W **166** D3
Inis Córthaidh = Enniscorthy
Ireland 52°30N 6°34W **166** D5
Inishbofin *Ireland* 53°37N 10°13W **166** C1
Inisheer *Ireland* 53°3N 9°32W **166** C2
Inishfree B. *Ireland* 55°4N 8°23W **166** A3
Inishkea North *Ireland* 54°9N 10°11W **166** B1
Inishkea South *Ireland* 54°7N 10°12W **166** B1
Inishmaan *Ireland* 53°5N 9°35W **166** C2
Inishmore *Ireland* 53°8N 9°45W **166** C2
Inishmurray I. *Ireland* 54°26N 8°39W **166** B3
Inishowen Pen. *Ireland* 55°14N 7°15W **166** A4
Inishshark *Ireland* 53°37N 10°16W **166** C1
Inishturk *Ireland* 53°42N 10°7W **166** C1
Inishvickillane *Ireland* 52°3N 10°37W **166** D1
Initao *Phil.* 8°56N 124°20E **233** G5
Injāna *Iraq* 34°29N 44°38E **213** E11
Injibara *Ethiopia* 10°59N 37°0E **257** E4
Injinoo ☉ *Australia* 10°56S 142°15E **280** A3
Injune *Australia* 25°53S 148°32E **281** D4
Inkisi →
Dem. Rep. of the Congo 4°46S 14°52E **265** D3
Inklin → *N. Amer.* 58°50N 133°10W **296** B2
Inland Kaikoura Ra.
N.Z. 41°59S 173°41E **285** B8
Inland Sea = Setonaikai
Japan 34°20N 133°30E **222** C5
Inle L. *Burma* 20°30N 96°58E **241** E6
Inlet *U.S.A.* 43°45N 74°48W **313** C10
Inn → *Austria* 48°35N 13°28E **180** C6
Innamincka *Australia* 27°44S 140°46E **281** D3
Innbygda *Norway* 61°19N 12°17E **164** C9
Inner Hebrides *U.K.* 57°0N 6°30W **167** E2
Inner Mongolia = Nei Mongol
Zizhiqu □ *China* 42°0N 112°0E **226** D7
Inner Port Shelter *China* 22°22N 114°17E **122** A2
Inner Sound *U.K.* 57°30N 5°55W **167** D3
Innerkip *Canada* 43°13N 80°42W **312** C4
Innes △ *Australia* 35°25S 136°53E **282** C2
Innetalling I. *Canada* 56°0N 79°0W **298** A4
Innisfail *Queens., Australia* 17°33S 146°5E **280** B4
Innisfail *Alta., Canada* 52°2N 113°57W **296** C6
Innoko Nat. Wildlife Refuge △
U.S.A. 63°20N 158°25W **303** E8
In'noshima *Japan* 34°19N 133°10E **222** C5
Innsbruck *Austria* 47°16N 11°23E **180** D4
Innviertel *Austria* 48°15N 13°15E **180** C6
Innvik *Norway* 61°51N 6°37E **164** C3
Inny → *Ireland* 53°30N 7°50W **166** C4
Ino *Japan* 33°33N 133°26E **222** D5
Inocência *Brazil* 19°47S 51°48W **333** E1
Inongo
Dem. Rep. of the Congo 1°55S 18°30E **264** C3
Inoni *Congo* 3°4S 15°39E **264** C3
İnönü *Turkey* 39°48N 30°9E **205** B12
Inoucdjouac = Inukjuak
Canada 58°25N 78°15W **295** F16
Inousses *Greece* 38°33N 26°14E **205** C8
Inowrocław *Poland* 52°50N 18°12E **185** F5
Inquisivi *Bolivia* 16°50S 67°10W **330** D4
Inscription, C. *Australia* 25°29S 112°59E **279** E1
Insein *Burma* 16°50N 96°5E **241** G6
Insjön *Sweden* 60°41N 15°6E **162** D9
Ińsko *Poland* 53°25N 15°32E **184** E2
Insterberg = Chernyakhovsk
Russia 54°36N 21°48E **184** D8
Însurăţei *Romania* 44°50N 27°40E **183** F12
Inta *Russia* 66°5N 60°8E **186** A11
Intendente Alvear
Argentina 35°12S 63°32W **334** D3
İntepe *Turkey* 40°1N 26°20E **205** A8
Interlachen *U.S.A.* 29°37N 81°53W **317** F8
Interlagos *Brazil* 23°41S 46°42W **137** C1
Interlaken *Switz.* 46°41N 7°50E **179** J3
Interlaken *N.Y., U.S.A.* 42°37N 76°44W **313** D8
International Falls *U.S.A.* 48°36N 93°25W **308** A7
Interview I. *India* 12°55N 92°43E **245** H11
Intiyaco *Argentina* 28°43S 60°5W **334** B3
Întorsura Buzăului
Romania 45°41N 26°2E **183** E11
Intramuros *Phil.* 14°35N 120°57E **127** B1
Intrepid Air and Space Museum
New York, U.S.A. **132** b1
Intutu *Peru* 3°32S 74°48W **328** D3
Inubō-Zaki *Japan* 35°42N 140°52E **223** B12
Inukjuak *Canada* 58°25N 78°15W **295** F16
Inútil, B. *Chile* 53°30S 70°15W **336** D2
Inuvik *Canada* 68°16N 133°40W **294** D5
Inuyama *Japan* 35°23N 136°56E **223** B8
Invalides *France* 48°51N 2°18E **134** A2
Inveraray *U.K.* 56°14N 5°5W **167** E3
Inverbervie *U.K.* 56°51N 2°17W **167** E6
Invercargill *N.Z.* 46°24S 168°24E **285** G3
Inverclyde □ *U.K.* 55°55N 4°49W **167** F4
Inverell *Australia* 29°45S 151°8E **281** D5
Invergordon *U.K.* 57°41N 4°10W **167** D4
Inverkeithing *U.K.* 56°2N 3°24W **121** A1
Inverleigh *Australia* 38°6S 144°3E **282** E6
Inverloch *Australia* 38°38S 145°45E **281** F4
Invermere *Canada* 50°30N 116°2W **296** C5
Inverness *N.S., Canada* 46°15N 61°19W **299** C7
Inverness *Highl., U.K.* 57°29N 4°13W **167** D4
Inverness *Ala., U.S.A.* 32°1N 85°45W **316** C4
Inverness *Fla., U.S.A.* 28°50N 82°20W **317** G7
Inverurie *U.K.* 57°17N 2°23W **167** D6
Investigator Group
Australia 34°45S 134°20E **281** E1
Investigator Ridge *Ind. Oc.* 11°30S 98°10E **273** F8
Investigator Str. *Australia* 35°30S 137°0E **282** C2
Inya *Russia* 50°28N 86°37E **217** B11
Inyanga *Zimbabwe* 18°12S 32°40E **269** F3
Inyangani *Zimbabwe* 18°5S 32°50E **269** F3
Inyantue *Zimbabwe* 18°33S 26°39E **270** A4
Inyo Mts. *U.S.A.* 36°40N 118°0W **306** J9
Inyokern *U.S.A.* 35°39N 117°49W **307** K9
Inyonga *Tanzania* 6°45S 32°5E **268** D3
Inywa *Burma* 23°56N 96°17E **241** D6
Inza *Russia* 53°55N 46°25E **190** D8
Inzersdorf *Austria* 48°8N 16°21E **142** B2
Inzhavino *Russia* 52°22N 42°30E **190** D6
Inzia →
Dem. Rep. of the Congo 3°45S 17°57E **265** C3
Iō-Jima *Japan* 30°48N 130°18E **221** J5
Ioannina *Greece* 39°42N 20°47E **204** B2
Ioannina □ *Greece* 39°39N 20°57E **204** B2
Iokea *Papua N. G.* 8°25S 146°16E **286** E4
Iola *U.S.A.* 37°55N 95°24W **308** G6
Iolani Palace *U.S.A.* 21°18N 157°51W **302** K14
Ioma *Papua N. G.* 8°19S 147°52E **286** E4
Ion Corvin *Romania* 44°7N 27°50E **183** F12
Iona *Angola* 16°54S 12°34E **265** F2
Iona *Argyll & Bute, U.K.* 56°20N 6°25W **167** E2
Iona △ *Angola* 16°47S 12°20E **265** F2
Ione *U.S.A.* 38°21N 120°56W **306** G6
Iongo *Angola* 9°11S 17°45E **265** D3
Ionia *U.S.A.* 42°59N 85°4W **311** B11
Ionian Is. = Ionioi Nisoi
Greece 38°40N 20°0E **204** C2
Ionian Sea *Medit. S.* 37°30N 17°30E **193** D7
Ionioi Nisoi *Greece* 38°40N 20°0E **204** C2
Ionioi Nisoi □ *Greece* 38°40N 20°0E **207** B2
Ios *Greece* 36°41N 25°20E **205** E7
Iowa □ *U.S.A.* 42°18N 93°30W **310** C3
Iowa → *U.S.A.* 41°10N 91°1W **310** C5
Iowa City *U.S.A.* 41°40N 91°32W **310** C5
Iowa Falls *U.S.A.* 42°31N 93°16W **310** B3
Iowa Park *U.S.A.* 33°57N 98°40W **314** E5
Ipala *Tanzania* 4°30S 32°52E **268** C3
Ipameri *Brazil* 17°44S 48°9W **333** E2
Ipanema *Minas Gerais,*
Brazil 19°47S 41°44W **333** E3
Ipanema *Rio de J., Brazil* 22°59S 43°12W **135** B1
Iparía *Peru* 9°17S 74°29W **330** B3
Ipati *Greece* 38°52N 22°14E **204** C4
Ipatinga *Brazil* 19°32S 42°30W **333** E3
Ipatovo *Russia* 45°45N 42°50E **191** H6
Ipek = Peć *Kosovo* 42°40N 20°17E **202** D4
Ipel' → *Europe* 47°48N 18°53E **181** D11
Ipiales *Colombia* 0°50N 77°37W **328** C2
Ipiaú *Brazil* 14°8S 39°44W **333** D4
Ipil *Phil.* 7°47N 122°35E **233** H4
Ipin = Yibin *China* 28°45N 104°32E **228** C5
Ipirá *Brazil* 12°10S 39°44W **333** D4
Ipiranga *Brazil* 23°35S 46°36W **137** B2
Ipiranga → *Brazil* 23°37S 46°37W **137** B2
Ipixuna *Brazil* 7°0S 71°40W **330** B3
Ipixuna → *Amazonas,*
Brazil 7°11S 71°51W **330** B3
Ipixuna → *Amazonas, Brazil* 5°45S 63°2W **331** B5
Ipoh *Malaysia* 4°35N 101°5E **237** K3
Iponri *Nigeria* 6°28N 3°22E **124** B2
Iporá *Brazil* 16°28S 51°7W **331** D7
Ipota *Vanuatu* 18°52S 169°20E **287** H7
Ippy *C.A.R.* 6°5N 21°7E **264** A4
İpsala *Turkey* 40°55N 26°23E **203** F10
Ipsario, Oros *Greece* 40°40N 24°40E **203** F8
Ipsos *Greece* 39°43N 19°48E **206** B9
Ipswich *Queens., Australia* 27°35S 152°40E **281** D5
Ipswich *Suffolk, U.K.* 52°4N 1°10E **169** E9
Ipswich *Mass., U.S.A.* 42°41N 70°50W **313** D14
Ipswich *S. Dak., U.S.A.* 45°27N 99°2W **308** C4
Ipu *Brazil* 4°23S 40°44W **332** B3
Ipueiras *Brazil* 4°33S 40°43W **332** B3
Ipuh *Indonesia* 3°0S 101°30E **234** C2
Ipupiara *Brazil* 11°49S 42°37W **333** D3
Iqaluit *Canada* 63°44N 68°31W **295** E18
Iqaluktuutiaq = Cambridge Bay
Canada 69°10N 105°0W **294** D11
Iquique *Chile* 20°19S 70°5W **330** E3
Iquitos *Peru* 3°45S 73°10W **328** D3
Ir Gannim = Bat Yam
Israel 32°2N 34°44E **251** F5
Irabu-Jima *Japan* 24°50N 125°10E **221** M2
Iracoubo *Fr. Guiana* 5°30N 53°10W **329** B7
Īrafshān *Iran* 26°42N 61°56E **247** E9
Irago-Suidō *Japan* 34°25N 137°0E **223** C8
Irahuan *Phil.* 9°48N 118°41E **233** G2
Iraklia *Cyclades, Greece* 36°50N 25°28E **205** E7
Iraklia *Serres, Greece* 41°10N 23°16E **202** E7
Iraklio *Greece* 35°20N 25°12E **207** E6
Iraklio □ *Greece* 35°10N 25°10E **207** E6
Iraklio ✕ (HER) *Greece* 35°20N 25°15E **207** E6
Iráklion = Iraklio *Greece* 35°20N 25°12E **207** E6
Irakliou, Kolpos *Greece* 35°23N 25°8E **207** E6
Irako-Zaki *Japan* 34°35N 137°1E **223** C9
Irala *Paraguay* 25°55S 54°35W **335** B5
Iran ■ *Asia* 33°0N 53°0E **247** C7
Iran, Pegunungan
Malaysia 2°20N 114°50E **235** B4
Iran Ra. = Iran, Pegunungan
Malaysia 2°20N 114°50E **235** B4
Iranamadu Tank *Sri Lanka* 9°23N 80°29E **245** K5
Īrānshahr *Iran* 27°15N 60°40E **247** E9
Irapa *Venezuela* 10°34N 62°35W **329** A5
Irapuato *Mexico* 20°41N 101°28W **318** C4
Iraq ■ *Asia* 33°0N 44°0E **213** F10
Irarrar, O. → *Mali* 20°0N 1°30E **261** E5
Irati *Brazil* 25°25S 50°38W **335** B5
Irbes saurums *Latvia* 57°45N 22°5E **184** A9
Irbid *Jordan* 32°35N 35°48E **251** F6
Irbid □ *Jordan* 32°30N 35°50E **250** F6
Irebu *Dem. Rep. of the Congo* 0°40S 17°46E **264** C3
Irecê *Brazil* 11°18S 41°52W **332** D3
Iregua → *Spain* 42°27N 2°24E **196** C7
Ireland ■ *Europe* 53°50N 7°52W **166** C4
Ireland I. *Bermuda* 32°19N 64°50W **153** a
Ireland Island *Bermuda* 32°19N 64°50W **153** a
Ireland's Eye *Ireland* 53°24N 6°4W **120** A3
Irele *Nigeria* 7°40N 5°40E **263** D6
Ireng → *Brazil* 3°33N 59°51W **329** C6
Irerrer, O. → *Algeria* 19°25N 5°47E **261** E6
Irgiz = Yrghyz *Kazakhstan* 48°37N 61°16E **216** C6
Irgiz = Yrghyz →
Kazakhstan 48°6N 62°30E **216** C6
Irgiz, Bolshaya → *Russia* 52°10N 49°10E **190** D9
Irharhar, O. → *Algeria* 28°3N 6°15E **261** C6
Irherm *Morocco* 30°7N 8°18W **260** B3
Irhil M'Goun *Morocco* 31°30N 6°28W **260** B3
Iri = Iksan *S. Korea* 35°59N 127°0E **224** E3
Irian Barat = Papua □
Indonesia 4°0S 137°0E **231** E9
Irian Jaya = Papua □
Indonesia 4°0S 137°0E **231** E9
Irian Jaya Barat □
Indonesia 2°5S 132°50E **231** E8
Iriba *Chad* 15°7N 22°15E **259** E4
Irié *Guinea* 8°15N 9°10W **262** D3
Iriga *Phil.* 13°25N 123°25E **232** E4
Iriklinskoye Vdkhr. *Russia* 52°0N 59°0E **216** B5
Iringa *Tanzania* 7°48S 35°43E **268** D4
Iringa □ *Tanzania* 7°48S 35°43E **268** D4
Irinjalakuda *India* 10°21N 76°14E **245** J3
Iriomote △ *Japan* 24°29N 123°53E **221** M1
Iriomote-Jima *Japan* 24°19N 123°48E **221** M1
Iriona *Honduras* 15°57N 85°11W **320** C2
Iriri → *Brazil* 3°52S 52°37W **329** D7
Iriri Novo → *Brazil* 8°46S 53°22W **331** B7
Irish Republic ■ *Europe* 53°50N 7°52W **166** C4
Irish Sea *Europe* 53°38N 4°48W **168** D3
Irkeshtam Pass = Erkech-Tam Pass
Asia 39°46N 74°2E **217** E8
Irkutsk *Russia* 52°18N 104°20E **218** A9
Irlıganlı *Turkey* 37°53N 29°12E **205** D11
Irma *Canada* 52°55N 111°14W **297** C6
Irō-Zaki *Japan* 34°36N 138°51E **223** C10
Irois B. *Trin. & Tob.* 10°9N 61°45W **323** t
Iroise, Mer d' *France* 48°15N 4°45W **172** D2
Iron Baron *Australia* 32°58S 137°11E **282** B2
Iron Gate = Portile de Fier
Europe 44°44N 22°30E **182** F7
Iron Knob *Australia* 32°46S 137°8E **282** B2
Iron Mountain *U.S.A.* 45°49N 88°4W **308** C9
Iron Range △ *Australia* 12°34S 143°18E **280** A3
Iron River *U.S.A.* 46°6N 88°39W **308** B9
Irondequoit *U.S.A.* 43°13N 77°35W **312** C7
Ironton *Mo., U.S.A.* 37°36N 90°38W **308** G8
Ironton *Ohio, U.S.A.* 38°32N 82°41W **309** F12
Ironwood *U.S.A.* 46°27N 90°9W **308** B8
Ironwood Forest ⌂
U.S.A. 32°32N 111°28W **305** K8
Iroquois *Canada* 44°51N 75°19W **313** B9
Iroquois → *U.S.A.* 41°5N 87°49W **311** C9
Iroquois Falls *Canada* 48°46N 80°41W **298** C3
Iroquois Point *U.S.A.* 21°19N 157°58W **302** K14
Irosin *Phil.* 12°42N 124°2E **232** E5
Irpin *Ukraine* 50°30N 30°15E **177** C16
Irqieqa, Ras I- *Malta* 35°56N 14°29E **206** F7
Irrara Cr. → *Australia* 29°35S 145°31E **281** D4
Irrawaddy □ *Burma* 17°0N 95°0E **241** G5
Irrawaddy → *Burma* 15°50N 95°6E **241** G5
Irrawaddy, Mouths of the
Burma 15°30N 95°0E **241** H5
Irricana *Canada* 51°19N 113°37W **296** C6
Irrunytju *Australia* 26°3S 128°56E **279** E4
Irshava *Ukraine* 48°19N 23°3E **182** B8
Irsina *Italy* 40°45N 16°14E **201** B9
Irtysh → *Russia* 61°4N 68°52E **214** C7
Irumu *Dem. Rep. of the Congo* 1°32N 29°53E **268** B2
Irún *Spain* 43°20N 1°52W **196** B3
Irunea = Pamplona-Iruña
Spain 42°48N 1°38W **196** C3
Irurzun *Spain* 42°55N 1°50W **196** C3
Irvine *Alta., Canada* 49°57N 110°16W **297** D6
Irvine *N. Ayrs., U.K.* 55°37N 4°41W **167** F4
Irvine *Calif., U.S.A.* 33°41N 117°46W **307** M9
Irvine *Ky., U.S.A.* 37°42N 83°58W **311** G13
Irvinestown *U.K.* 54°28N 7°39W **166** B4
Irving *U.S.A.* 32°48N 96°56W **314** E6
Irving Park *U.S.A.* 41°57N 87°42W **119** B2
Irvington *U.S.A.* 37°53N 86°17W **311** G10
Irvona *U.S.A.* 40°46N 78°33W **312** F6
Irwin → *Australia* 29°15S 114°54E **279** E1
Irwinton *U.S.A.* 32°49N 83°10W **316** C6
Irwinville *U.S.A.* 31°39N 83°23W **316** D6
Irymple *Australia* 34°14S 142°8E **282** C5
Is, Jebel *Sudan* 22°3N 35°52E **256** C4
Is-sur-Tille *France* 47°30N 5°8E **173** E12
Isa *Nigeria* 13°14N 6°24E **263** C6
Isa Khel *Pakistan* 32°41N 71°17E **242** C4
Isaac → *Australia* 22°55S 149°20E **280** C4
Isabel *Rio de J., Brazil* 22°55S 43°14W **135** B1
Isabel *S. Dak., U.S.A.* 45°24N 101°26W **308** C3
Isabel, I. *Mexico* 21°51N 105°55W **318** C3
Isabel Segunda *Puerto Rico* 18°9N 65°27W **321** b
Isabela *Basilan, Phil.* 6°40N 121°59E **233** H3
Isabela *Negros, Phil.* 10°12N 122°59E **233** F4
Isabela *Puerto Rico* 18°30N 67°2W **321** b
Isabela □ *Phil.* 17°0N 122°0E **232** C4
Isabela, Canal *Ecuador* 0°20S 90°55W **330** a
Isabela, I. *Ecuador* 0°30S 91°0W **330** a
Isabela, Cord. *Nic.* 13°30N 85°25W **320** D2
Isabella Ra. *Australia* 21°0S 121°4E **278** D3
Isaccea *Romania* 45°16N 28°28E **183** E13
Isachsen, C. *Canada* 79°20N 105°28W **295** B10
Ísafjarðardjúp *Iceland* 66°10N 23°0W **155** A3

Ísafjarðarsýsla □ *Iceland* 66°0N 23°0W **155** B3
Ísafjörður *Iceland* 66°5N 23°9W **155** A3
Isagarh *India* 24°48N 77°51E **242** G7
Isagatedo *Nigeria* 6°31N 3°19E **124** A1
Isahaya *Japan* 32°52N 130°2E **222** E2
Isaka *Dem. Rep. of the Congo* 2°33S 18°54E **264** C3
Isaka *Tanzania* 3°56S 32°59E **268** C3
Işalniţa *Romania* 44°24N 23°44E **183** F8
Isalo, Tangorombohitr' *Madag.* 22°45S 45°15E **272** C2
Isalo △ *Madag.* 22°23S 45°16E **272** C2
Isan → *India* 26°51N 80°7E **243** F9
Isana = Içana → *Brazil* 0°26N 67°19W **328** C4
Isandja *Dem. Rep. of the Congo* 2°59S 21°59E **264** C4
Isangano △ *Zambia* 11°8S 30°35E **269** E3
Isangi *Dem. Rep. of the Congo* 0°52N 24°10E **264** B4
Isanlu Makutu *Nigeria* 8°20N 5°50E **263** D6
Isar → *Bayern, Germany* 48°48N 12°57E **179** G8
Isar → *Oberbayern, Germany* 48°15N 11°41E **131** A3
Isarco → *Italy* 46°27N 11°18E **199** B8
Isaris *Greece* 37°22N 22°0E **204** D3
Isarog, Mt. *Phil.* 13°39N 123°23E **232** E4
Isawa *Japan* 35°40N 138°35E **223** B10
Iscar *Spain* 41°22N 4°32W **194** D6
Iscayachi *Bolivia* 21°31S 65°3W **331** E4
İscehisar *Turkey* 38°51N 30°45E **205** C12
Ischia *Italy* 40°44N 13°57E **200** B6
Iscuandé *Colombia* 2°28N 77°59W **328** C2
Isdell → *Australia* 16°27S 124°51E **278** C3
Ise *Japan* 34°25N 136°45E **223** C8
Ise-Shima △ *Japan* 34°25N 136°48E **223** C8
Ise-Wan *Japan* 34°43N 136°43E **223** C8
Isefjord *Denmark* 55°53N 11°50E **163** J5
Isel → *Austria* 46°50N 12°47E **181** E5
Iseo *Italy* 45°39N 10°3E **198** C7
Iseo, L. d' *Italy* 45°43N 10°4E **198** C7
Iseramagazi *Tanzania* 4°37S 32°10E **268** C3
Isère □ *France* 45°15N 5°40E **175** C9
Isère → *France* 44°59N 4°51E **175** D8
Iserlohn *Germany* 51°22N 7°41E **178** D3
Isérnia *Italy* 41°36N 14°14E **201** A7
Isesaki *Japan* 36°19N 139°12E **223** A11
Iseyin *Nigeria* 8°0N 3°36E **263** D5
Isfahan = Eşfahān *Iran* 32°39N 51°43E **247** C6
Isfjorden *Norway* 62°35N 7°49E **164** B4
Ishbīliya *Iraq* 33°21N 44°26E **113** A2
Ishëm *Albania* 41°33N 19°34E **202** E3
Ishenga Oshwe *Dem. Rep. of the Congo* 3°57S 22°33E **264** C4
Isherton *Guyana* 2°20N 59°25W **329** C6
Ishigaki *Japan* 24°26N 124°10E **221** M2
Ishigaki-Shima *Japan* 24°20N 124°10E **221** M2
Ishikari *Japan* 43°20N 141°15E **220** C10
Ishikari-Gawa → *Japan* 43°15N 141°23E **220** C10
Ishikari-Sammyaku *Japan* 43°30N 143°0E **220** C11
Ishikari-Wan *Japan* 43°25N 141°1E **220** C10
Ishikawa *Japan* 26°25N 127°49E **288** a
Ishikawa □ *Japan* 36°30N 136°30E **223** A8
Ishim *Russia* 56°10N 69°30E **214** D7
Ishim → *Russia* 57°45N 71°10E **214** D8
Ishimbay *Russia* 53°28N 56°2E **216** B5
Ishinomaki *Japan* 38°32N 141°20E **220** E10
Ishioka *Japan* 36°11N 140°16E **223** A12
Ishizuchi-Yama *Japan* 33°45N 133°6E **222** D5
Ishkashim *Tajikistan* 36°44N 71°37E **217** E8
Ishkoman *Pakistan* 36°30N 73°50E **243** A5
Ishøj Strand *Denmark* 55°36N 12°20E **118** B2
Ishpeming *U.S.A.* 46°29N 87°40W **308** B10
Ishurdi *Bangla.* 24°9N 89°3E **241** C2
Isiboro Sécure △ *Bolivia* 16°15S 65°50W **331** D4
Isigny-sur-Mer *France* 49°19N 1°6W **172** C5
Isıklar Dağı *Turkey* 40°45N 27°15E **203** F11
Işıklı *Turkey* 38°19N 29°51E **205** C11
Isil Kul *Russia* 54°55N 71°16E **217** B8
Isili *Italy* 39°44N 9°6E **200** C2
Isiolo *Kenya* 0°24N 37°33E **268** B4
Isiro *Dem. Rep. of the Congo* 2°53N 27°40E **268** B2
Isisford *Australia* 24°15S 144°21E **280** C3
İskenderun *Turkey* 36°32N 36°10E **250** B7
İskenderun Körfezi *Turkey* 36°40N 35°50E **250** B6
İskilip *Turkey* 40°45N 34°29E **212** B6
Iskitim *Russia* 54°38N 83°18E **217** B10
Iskŭr → *Bulgaria* 43°45N 24°25E **203** C8
Iskŭr, Yazovir *Bulgaria* 42°23N 23°30E **202** D7
Iskushuban *Somali Rep.* 10°18N 50°12E **267** B7
Iskut → *Canada* 56°45N 131°49W **296** B2
Isla → *U.K.* 56°32N 3°20W **167** E5
Isla Coiba △ *Panama* 7°33N 81°36W **320** E4
Isla Cristina *Spain* 37°13N 7°17W **195** H3
Isla de Salamanca △ *Colombia* 10°59N 74°40W **328** A3
Isla Gorge △ *Australia* 25°10S 149°57E **280** D4
Isla Gorgona △ *Colombia* 2°59N 78°10W **328** C2
Isla Guamblin △ *Chile* 44°50S 75°4W **336** B1
Isla Isabel △ *Mexico* 21°54N 105°58W **318** C3
Isla Magdalena △ *Chile* 44°20S 73°13W **336** B2
Isla Tiburón y San Estebán △ *Mexico* 29°0N 112°27W **318** B2
Isla Vista *U.S.A.* 34°25N 119°53W **307** L7
İslâhiye *Turkey* 37°0N 36°35E **250** B7
Islam Headworks *Pakistan* 29°49N 72°33E **242** E5
Islamabad *Pakistan* 33°40N 73°10E **242** C5
Islamgarh *Pakistan* 27°51N 70°48E **242** F4
Islamkot *Pakistan* 24°42N 70°13E **242** G4
Islamorada *U.S.A.* 24°56N 80°37W **317** L9
Islampur *Bihar, India* 25°9N 85°12E **243** G11
Islampur *Maharashtra, India* 17°2N 74°20E **244** F2
Islampur *W. Bengal, India* 26°16N 88°12E **243** F13
Island = Iceland ■ *Europe* 64°45N 19°0W **155** C8
Island B. *Phil.* 9°6N 118°10E **233** G2
Island Bay *N.Z.* 41°20S 174°46E **143** B1
Island Harbour *Anguilla* 18°12N 63°0W **322** a
Island L. *Canada* 53°47N 94°25W **297** C10
Island Lagoon *Australia* 31°30S 136°40E **282** A2
Island Park *Canada* 43°37N 79°22W **141** B2
Island Pond *U.S.A.* 44°49N 71°53W **313** B13
Islands, B. of *Nfld. & L., Canada* 49°11N 58°15W **299** C8
Islands, B. of *N.Z.* 35°15S 174°6E **284** B3
Islay *U.K.* 55°46N 6°10W **167** F2
Isle → *France* 44°55N 0°15W **174** D3
Isle aux Morts *Canada* 47°35N 59°0W **299** C8
Isle of Hope *U.S.A.* 31°58N 81°5W **316** D8
Isle of Wight □ *U.K.* 50°41N 1°17W **169** G6
Isle Royale △ *U.S.A.* 48°0N 88°55W **308** B9
Isleton *U.S.A.* 38°10N 121°37W **306** G5
Islev *Denmark* 55°41N 12°27E **118** A2
Isleworth *U.K.* 51°28N 0°19W **126** C2
Islington *Canada* 43°38N 79°30W **141** B1
Islington □ *U.K.* 51°33N 0°5W **125** A3
Islote Pt. *Trin. & Tob.* 10°4N 61°47W **323** t
Ismail = Izmayil *Ukraine* 45°22N 28°46E **183** E13
Ismâ'iliya *Egypt* 30°37N 32°18E **251** H3
Ismâ'iliya □ *Egypt* 30°35N 32°16E **251** H3
Ismâ'iliya, Tir'at el → *Egypt* 30°4N 31°16E **251** H2
Ismaning *Germany* 48°13N 11°40E **131** A3
Ismayloskiy Park *Russia* 55°46N 37°46E **129** B4
Isna *Egypt* 25°17N 32°30E **256** B3
Isoanala *Madag.* 23°50S 45°44E **272** C2
Ísola del Liri *Italy* 41°41N 13°34E **199** G10
Ísola della Scala *Italy* 45°16N 11°0E **198** C7
Ísola di Capo Rizzuto *Italy* 38°58N 17°6E **201** D10
Isolo *Nigeria* 6°31N 3°19E **124** A1
Isparta *Turkey* 37°47N 30°30E **205** D12
Isparta □ *Turkey* 38°0N 31°0E **212** D4
Ispas *Ukraine* 48°19N 25°16E **183** B10
Isperikh *Bulgaria* 43°43N 26°50E **203** C10
Íspica *Italy* 36°47N 14°55E **201** F7
İspir *Turkey* 40°28N 40°59E **213** B9
Israel ■ *Asia* 32°0N 34°50E **251** G5
Isratu *Eritrea* 16°20N 39°53E **257** D4
Issakly *Russia* 54°8N 51°32E **190** C10
Issano *Guyana* 5°49N 59°26W **329** B6
Issaouane, Erg *Algeria* 26°58N 8°42E **258** C1
Issia *Ivory C.* 6°33N 6°33W **262** D3
Issoire *France* 45°32N 3°15E **174** C7
Issoudun *France* 46°57N 1°59E **173** F8
Issy-les-Moulineaux *France* 48°49N 2°15E **134** B2
Issyk-Kul = Balykchy *Kyrgyzstan* 42°26N 76°12E **217** D9
Issyk-Kul, Ozero = Ysyk-Köl *Kyrgyzstan* 42°25N 77°15E **217** D9
Ist *Croatia* 44°17N 14°47E **199** D11
Istaihah *U.A.E.* 23°19N 54°4E **249** B6
Istállós-kő *Hungary* 48°4N 20°26E **182** B5
İstanbul *Turkey* 41°0N 28°58E **122** C1
İstanbul □ *Turkey* 41°0N 29°0E **203** E12
İstanbul ✈ (IST) *Turkey* 40°59N 28°49E **203** F12
İstanbul Boğazı *Turkey* 41°5N 29°3E **122** B2
Istaravshan = Ŭroteppa *Tajikistan* 39°55N 69°1E **217** E7
Isteren *Norway* 61°58N 11°47E **164** B8
Istiea *Greece* 38°57N 23°9E **204** C5
İstinye *Turkey* 41°6N 29°3E **122** B2
Istmina *Colombia* 5°10N 76°39W **328** B2
Isto, Mt. *U.S.A.* 69°12N 143°48W **303** B12
Istok *Kosovo* 42°45N 20°24E **202** D4
Istokpoga, L. *U.S.A.* 27°23N 81°17W **317** H8
Istra *Croatia* 45°10N 14°0E **199** C10
Istres *France* 43°31N 4°59E **175** E8
Istria = Istra *Croatia* 45°10N 14°0E **199** C10
Isugod *Phil.* 9°19N 118°5E **233** G2
Isulan *Phil.* 6°30N 124°29E **233** H5
Itá *Paraguay* 25°29S 57°21W **334** B4
Itä Hakkila *Finland* 60°17N 25°7E **121** B3
Itabaiana *Paraíba, Brazil* 7°18S 35°19W **332** C4
Itabaiana *Sergipe, Brazil* 10°41S 37°37W **332** D4
Itabaianinha *Brazil* 11°16S 37°47W **332** D4
Itaberaba *Brazil* 12°32S 40°18W **333** D3
Itaberaí *Brazil* 16°2S 49°48W **333** E2
Itabira *Brazil* 19°37S 43°13W **333** E3
Itabirito *Brazil* 20°15S 43°48W **333** F3
Itaboca *Brazil* 4°50S 62°40W **329** D5
Itabuna *Brazil* 14°48S 39°16W **333** D4
Itacajá *Brazil* 8°19S 47°46W **332** C2
Itacaunas → *Brazil* 5°21S 49°8W **332** C2
Itaewon *S. Korea* 37°32N 126°58E **137** B1
Itaguari → *Brazil* 14°11S 44°40W **333** D3
Itaguatins *Brazil* 5°47S 47°29W **332** C2
Itaim → *Brazil* 7°2S 42°2W **332** C3
Itainópolis *Brazil* 7°24S 41°31W **332** C3
Itaipú, Represa de *Brazil* 25°30S 54°30W **335** B5
Itaituba *Brazil* 4°10S 55°50W **329** D6
Itajaí *Brazil* 27°50S 48°39W **335** B6
Itajany do Sul = Rio do Sul *Brazil* 27°13S 49°37W **335** B6
Itajubá *Brazil* 22°24S 45°30W **333** F2
Itajuípe *Brazil* 14°41S 39°22W **333** D4
Itaka *Tanzania* 8°50S 32°49E **269** D3
Itako *Japan* 35°56N 140°33E **223** B12
Itala △ *S. Africa* 27°30S 31°7E **271** C5
Italy ■ *Europe* 42°0N 13°0E **192** C6
Itamaraju *Brazil* 17°4S 39°32W **333** E4
Itamarati *Brazil* 6°24S 68°15W **330** B4
Itamarandiba *Brazil* 17°57S 42°50W **333** E3
Itambacuri *Brazil* 18°1S 41°42W **333** E3
Itambé *Brazil* 15°15S 40°37W **333** E3
Itami *Japan* 34°46N 135°24E **133** A1
Itampolo *Madag.* 24°41S 43°57E **272** C1
Itanagar *India* 27°6N 93°37E **241** B4
Itandrano *Madag.* 21°47S 45°17E **272** C2
Itanhaém *Brazil* 24°11S 46°47W **333** F2
Itanhanga *Brazil* 22°59S 43°19W **135** B1
Itanhauã → *Brazil* 4°45S 63°48W **329** D5
Itanhém *Brazil* 17°9S 40°20W **333** E3
Itano *Japan* 34°7N 134°28E **222** C6
Itapaci *Brazil* 14°57S 49°34W **333** D2
Itapagé *Brazil* 3°41S 39°34W **332** B4
Itaparica = Petrolândia *Brazil* 9°5S 38°20W **332** C4
Itaparica, I. de *Brazil* 12°54S 38°42W **333** D4
Itaparica, Represa de *Brazil* 11°3S 42°47W **332** D4
Itapebi *Brazil* 15°56S 39°32W **333** E4
Itapecuru Mirim *Brazil* 3°24S 44°20W **332** B3
Itaperuna *Brazil* 21°10S 41°54W **333** F3
Itapetinga *Brazil* 15°15S 40°15W **333** E3
Itapetininga *Brazil* 23°36S 48°7W **335** A6
Itapeva *Brazil* 23°59S 48°59W **335** A6
Itapicuru → *Bahia, Brazil* 11°47S 37°32W **332** D4
Itapicuru → *Maranhão, Brazil* 2°52S 44°12W **332** B3
Itapipoca *Brazil* 3°30S 39°35W **332** B4
Itapira = Ubaitaba *Brazil* 14°18S 39°20W **333** D4
Itapiranga *Brazil* 2°45S 58°1W **329** D6
Itapiúna *Brazil* 4°33S 38°57W **332** B4
Itaporã *Brazil* 7°18S 38°0W **332** C4
Itaporanga *Paraíba, Brazil* 7°18S 38°0W **332** C4
Itaporanga *São Paulo, Brazil* 23°42S 49°29W **333** F2
Itapuá □ *Paraguay* 26°40S 55°40W **335** B4
Itapuranga *Brazil* 15°40S 49°59W **333** E2
Itaquai → *Brazil* 4°20S 70°12W **330** A3
Itaquatiara *Brazil* 2°58S 58°30W **329** D6
Itaquí *Brazil* 29°8S 56°30W **334** B4
Itararé *Brazil* 24°6S 49°23W **335** A6
Itarsi *India* 22°36N 77°51E **242** H7
Itarumã *Brazil* 18°42S 51°25W **333** E1
Itati *Argentina* 27°16S 58°15W **334** B4
Itatiaia △ *Brazil* 22°22S 44°38W **335** A7
Itatira *Brazil* 4°30S 39°37W **332** B4
Itatuba *Brazil* 5°46S 63°20W **331** B5
Itatupã *Brazil* 0°37S 51°12W **329** D7
Itaueira *Brazil* 7°36S 43°2W **332** C3
Itaueira → *Brazil* 6°41S 42°55W **332** C3
Itaúna *Brazil* 20°4S 44°34W **333** F3
Itbayat *Phil.* 20°47N 121°51E **232** A3
Itbayat I. *Phil.* 20°45N 121°50E **232** A3
Itchen → *U.K.* 50°55N 1°22W **169** G6
Itchouma *Niger* 20°14N 13°32E **261** D7
Ite *Peru* 17°55S 70°57W **330** D3
Itea *Greece* 38°25N 22°25E **204** C4
Itezhi Tezhi, L. *Zambia* 15°30S 25°30E **269** F2
Ithaca = Ithaki *Greece* 38°25N 20°40E **207** C2
Ithaca *U.S.A.* 42°27N 76°30W **313** D8
Ithaki *Greece* 38°25N 20°40E **207** C2
Ithakis, Stenon *Greece* 38°22N 20°39E **207** C2
Iti △ *Greece* 38°50N 22°15E **204** C4
Itimbiri → *Dem. Rep. of the Congo* 2°2N 22°44E **264** B4
Itinga *Brazil* 16°36S 41°47W **333** E3
Itiquira *Brazil* 17°12S 54°7W **331** D7
Itiquira → *Brazil* 17°18S 56°44W **331** D6
Itiruçu *Brazil* 13°31S 40°9W **333** D3
Itiúba *Brazil* 10°43S 39°51W **332** D4
Ityuro → *Argentina* 22°40S 63°50W **334** A3
Itkilik → *U.S.A.* 70°9N 150°56W **303** A10
Itō *Japan* 34°58N 139°5E **223** C11
Itogon *Phil.* 16°22N 120°41E **232** C3
Itoigawa *Japan* 37°2N 137°51E **221** F8
Itoko *Dem. Rep. of the Congo* 1°0S 21°48E **264** C4
Itoman *Japan* 26°7N 127°40E **288** a
Iton → *France* 49°9N 1°12E **172** C8
Itonamas → *Bolivia* 12°28S 64°24W **331** C5
Itri *Italy* 41°17N 13°32E **200** A6
Itsa *Egypt* 29°15N 30°47E **256** J7
Itsamia *Comoros Is.* 12°21S 43°52E **272** a
Itsandra *Comoros Is.* 11°40S 43°15E **272** a
Itsuki *Japan* 32°24N 130°50E **222** E2
Itsukushima Shrine *Japan* 34°15N 132°15E **222** C4
Íttiri *Italy* 40°36N 8°34E **200** B1
Ittoqqortoormiit *Greenland* 70°20N 23°0W **154** C8
Itu *Brazil* 23°17S 47°15W **335** A6
Itu *Nigeria* 5°10N 7°58E **263** D6
Itu Aba I. *S. China Sea* 10°23N 114°21E **230** B4
Ituaçu *Brazil* 13°50S 41°18W **333** D3
Ituango *Colombia* 7°4N 75°45W **328** B2
Ituí → *Brazil* 4°38S 70°19W **328** D3
Ituiutaba *Brazil* 19°0S 49°25W **333** E2
Itumbiara *Brazil* 18°20S 49°10W **333** E2
Ituna *Canada* 51°10N 103°24W **297** C8
Itunge Port *Tanzania* 9°40S 33°55E **269** D3
Ituni *Guyana* 5°28N 58°15W **329** B6
Itupiranga *Brazil* 5°9S 49°20W **332** C2
Iturama *Brazil* 19°44S 50°11W **333** E1
Iturbe *Argentina* 23°0S 65°25W **334** A2
Ituri → *Dem. Rep. of the Congo* 1°40N 27°1E **268** B2
Iturup, Ostrov *Russia* 45°0N 148°0E **215** E15
Ituverava *Brazil* 20°20S 47°47W **333** F2
Ituxi → *Brazil* 7°18S 64°51W **331** B5
Itzehoe *Germany* 53°55N 9°31E **178** B5
Iuka *U.S.A.* 34°48N 88°11W **317** D1?
Iungsdalshytta *Norway* 60°49N 7°55E **164** D4
Ivahona *Madag.* 23°27S 46°10E **272** C2
Ivaí → *Brazil* 23°18S 53°42W **335** A5
Ivalo *Finland* 68°38N 27°35E **160** B22
Ivalojoki → *Finland* 68°40N 27°40E **160** B22
Ivanava *Belarus* 52°7N 25°29E **177** B13
Ivančice *Czech Rep.* 49°6N 16°23E **181** B9
Ivane-Puste *Ukraine* 48°39N 26°10E **183** B11
Ivănești *Romania* 46°39N 27°27E **183** D12
Ivangorod = Dęblin *Poland* 51°34N 21°50E **185** G8
Ivangorod *Russia* 59°27N 28°13E **188** C5
Ivanhoe *N.S.W., Australia* 32°56S 144°20E **282** B6
Ivanhoe *Vic., Australia* 37°45S 145°3E **128** A2
Ivanhoe *Ont., Canada* 44°23N 77°28W **312** B7
Ivanhoe *Calif., U.S.A.* 36°23N 119°13W **306** J7
Ivanhoe *Minn., U.S.A.* 44°28N 96°15W **308** C5
Ivanhorod *Ukraine* 48°48N 29°50E **183** B14
Ivanić Grad *Croatia* 45°41N 16°25E **199** C13
Ivanjica *Serbia* 43°35N 20°12E **202** C4
Ivanjska *Bos.-H.* 44°55N 17°4E **182** F2
Ivankovskoye Vdkhr. *Russia* 56°37N 36°32E **188** D9
Ivano-Frankivsk *Ukraine* 48°40N 24°40E **183** B9
Ivano-Frankivsk □ *Ukraine* 48°45N 24°30E **183** B9
Ivanof Bay *U.S.A.* 55°54N 159°29W **303** J8
Ivanovo = Ivanava *Belarus* 52°7N 25°29E **177** B13
Ivanovo *Russia* 57°5N 41°0E **188** D11
Ivanovo □ *Russia* 57°10N 41°50E **190** B5
Ivanšćica *Croatia* 46°12N 16°13E **199** B13
Ivashchenkovo = Chapayevsk *Russia* 53°0N 49°40E **190** D9
Ivato *Madag.* 20°37S 47°10E **272** C2
Ivatsevichy *Belarus* 52°43N 25°21E **177** B13
Ivaylovgrad *Bulgaria* 41°32N 26°8E **203** E10
Ivdel *Russia* 60°42N 60°24E **186** B11
Ivgres = Komsomolsk *Russia* 57°2N 40°20E **188** D11
Ivindo → *Gabon* 0°9S 12°9E **264** C2
Ivinheima → *Brazil* 23°14S 53°42W **335** A5
Ivinheima *Brazil* 22°10S 53°37W **335** A5
Iviittuut *Greenland* 61°14N 48°12W **154** E6
Iviza = Eivissa *Spain* 38°54N 1°26E **206** D1
Ivohibe *Madag.* 22°31S 46°57E **272** C2
Ivolândia *Brazil* 16°34S 50°51W **333** E1
Ivory Coast *W. Afr.* 4°20N 5°0W **262** E4
Ivory Coast ■ *Africa* 7°30N 5°0W **262** D4
Ivösjön *Sweden* 56°8N 14°25E **163** H8
Ivrea *Italy* 45°28N 7°52E **198** C4
İvrindi *Turkey* 39°34N 27°30E **205** B9
Ivry-sur-Seine *France* 48°49N 2°22E **134** B3
Ivujivik *Canada* 62°24N 77°55W **295** E16
Ivvavik △ *Canada* 69°6N 139°30W **294** D4
Ivybridge *U.K.* 50°23N 3°56W **169** G4
Iwa *Japan* 36°5N 139°52E **223** A11
Iwai-Jima *Japan* 33°47N 131°58E **222** D3
Iwaizumi *Japan* 39°50N 141°45E **220** E10
Iwaki *Japan* 37°3N 140°55E **221** F10
Iwakuni *Japan* 34°15N 132°8E **222** C4
Iwami *Japan* 35°32N 134°15E **222** B6
Iwami Ginzan *Japan* 35°10N 132°30E **222** B4
Iwamizawa *Japan* 43°12N 141°46E **220** C10
Iwanai *Japan* 42°58N 140°30E **220** C10
Iwase *Japan* 36°21N 140°6E **223** A12
Iwata *Japan* 34°42N 137°51E **223** C9
Iwate □ *Japan* 39°30N 141°30E **220** E10
Iwate-San *Japan* 39°51N 141°0E **220** E10
Iwo *Nigeria* 7°39N 4°9E **263** D5
Iwo Jima *Pac. Oc.* 24°47N 141°20E **288** b
Iwŏn *N. Korea* 40°19N 128°39E **224** E8
Iwonicz-Zdrój *Poland* 49°37N 21°47E **185** J8
Iwungu *Dem. Rep. of the Congo* 5°16S 19°17E **265** D3
Ixelles *Belgium* 50°50N 4°22E **116** B2
Ixiamas *Bolivia* 13°50S 68°5W **330** C4
Ixopo *S. Africa* 30°11S 30°5E **271** D5
Ixtepec *Mexico* 16°34N 95°6W **319** D5
Ixtlán del Río *Mexico* 21°2N 104°22W **318** C4
'Iyâdh *Yemen* 14°59N 46°51E **248** D4
Iyal Bakhit *Sudan* 13°20N 28°39E **257** E2
Iyo *Japan* 33°45N 132°45E **222** D4
Iyo-Mishima *Japan* 33°58N 133°30E **222** D5
Iyo-Nada *Japan* 33°40N 132°20E **222** D4
Izabal, L. de *Guatemala* 15°30N 89°10W **320** C2
Izamal *Mexico* 20°56N 89°1W **319** C7
Izberbash *Russia* 42°35N 47°52E **191** J8
Izbica *Poland* 50°53N 23°10E **185** H10
Izbica Kujawska *Poland* 52°25N 18°40E **185** F5
Izbiceni *Romania* 43°45N 24°40E **183** G9
Izembek Nat. Wildlife Refuge △ *U.S.A.* 55°15N 162°45W **303** J7
Izena-Shima *Japan* 26°56N 127°56E **221** L3
Izgrev *Bulgaria* 43°36N 26°58E **203** C10
Izhevsk *Russia* 56°51N 53°14E **186** C9
Izhma = Sosnogorsk *Russia* 63°37N 53°51E **186** B9
Izhma → *Russia* 65°19N 52°54E **186** A9
Izki *Oman* 22°56N 57°46E **249** B7
Izmayil *Ukraine* 45°22N 28°46E **183** E13
Izmaylovo *Russia* 55°47N 37°47E **129** B4
İzmir *Turkey* 38°25N 27°8E **205** C9
İzmir □ *Turkey* 38°15N 27°40E **205** C9
İzmir Adnan Menderes ✈ (ADB) *Turkey* 38°23N 27°6E **205** C9
İzmir Körfezi *Turkey* 38°30N 26°50E **205** C8
İzmit = Kocaeli *Turkey* 40°45N 29°50E **203** F13
Iznájar *Spain* 37°15N 4°19W **195** H6
Iznalloz *Spain* 37°24N 3°30W **195** H7
İznik *Turkey* 40°23N 29°46E **212** B3
İznik Gölü *Turkey* 40°27N 29°30E **203** F13
Izobilno-Tishchenskoye = Izobil'nyy *Russia* 45°25N 41°44E **191** H5
Izobil'nyy *Russia* 45°25N 41°44E **191** H5
Izola *Slovenia* 45°32N 13°39E **199** C10
Izozog, Bañados de *Bolivia* 18°48S 62°10W **331** D5
Izra *Syria* 32°51N 36°15E **250** F7
Iztacalco *Mexico* 19°23N 99°5W **128** B2
Iztapalapa *Mexico* 19°21N 99°6W **128** B2
Iztochni Rodopi *Bulgaria* 41°45N 25°30E **203** E9
Izu-Hantō *Japan* 34°45N 139°0E **223** C11
Izu-Shotō *Japan* 34°30N 140°0E **221** G10
Izúcar de Matamoros *Mexico* 18°36N 98°28W **319** D5
Izuhara *Japan* 34°12N 129°17E **222** C1
Izumi *Kagoshima, Japan* 32°5N 130°22E **222** E2
Izumi *Ōsaka, Japan* 34°28N 135°24E **223** C7
Izumi-Sano *Japan* 34°23N 135°18E **223** C7
Izumo *Japan* 35°20N 132°46E **222** B4
Izyaslav *Ukraine* 50°5N 26°50E **177** C14
Izyum *Ukraine* 49°12N 37°19E **189** H9

J

J.F.K. Int. ✈ (JFK) *U.S.A.* 40°38N 73°47W **313** F11
J.F. Rodrigues *Brazil* 2°55S 50°20W **332** B1
J.P. Koch Fjord *Greenland* 82°45N 44°0W **154** A6
J. Strom Thurmond L. *U.S.A.* 33°40N 82°12W **316** B7
Ja-ela *Sri Lanka* 7°5N 79°53E **245** L4
Ja-eundo *S. Korea* 34°53N 126°2E **224** E3
Jaba *Ethiopia* 6°20N 35°7E **257** F4
Jaba *West Bank* 31°51N 35°16E **123** A2
Jabal al Awliya' *Sudan* 15°14N 32°29E **266** A3
Jabal at Ţā'ir *Red Sea* 15°35N 41°52E **257** D5
Jabalón → *Spain* 38°53N 4°5W **195** G6
Jabalpur *India* 23°9N 79°58E **243** H8
Jabbūl *Syria* 36°4N 37°30E **246** B3
Jabiru *Australia* 12°40S 132°53E **278** B5
Jablah *Syria* 35°20N 36°0E **250** C7
Jablanac *Croatia* 44°42N 14°56E **199** D11
Jablanica *Bos.-H.* 43°40N 17°45E **182** G2
Jablonec nad Nisou *Czech Rep.* 50°43N 15°10E **180** A8
Jablonica *Slovak Rep.* 48°37N 17°26E **181** C10
Jabłonowo Pomorskie *Poland* 53°23N 19°10E **184** E6
Jablunkov *Czech Rep.* 49°35N 18°46E **181** B11
Jaboatão *Brazil* 8°7S 35°1W **332** C4
Jabonga *Phil.* 9°20N 125°32E **233** G5
Jaboticabal *Brazil* 21°15S 48°17W **335** A6
Jabukovac *Serbia* 44°22N 22°21E **202** B6
Jaburu *Brazil* 5°30S 64°0W **331** B5
Jaca *Spain* 42°35N 0°33W **196** C4
Jacareí *Brazil* 22°53S 43°14W **135** B1
Jacaré → *Brazil* 10°3S 42°13W **332** D3
Jacareí *Brazil* 23°20S 46°0W **335** A6
Jacarèzinho *Brazil* 23°5S 49°58W **335** A6
Jaci-Paraná *Brazil* 9°15S 64°23W **331** B5
Jaciara *Brazil* 15°59S 54°57W **331** D7
Jacinto *Brazil* 16°10S 40°17W **333** E3
Jack River △ *Australia* 14°58S 144°19E **280** A3
Jackman *U.S.A.* 45°37N 70°15W **309** C18
Jacksboro *U.S.A.* 33°13N 98°10W **314** E5
Jackson *Barbados* 13°7N 59°36W **323** r
Jackson *Ala., U.S.A.* 31°31N 87°53W **315** F11
Jackson *Calif., U.S.A.* 38°21N 120°46W **306** G6
Jackson *Ga., U.S.A.* 33°20N 83°57W **316** B6
Jackson *Ky., U.S.A.* 37°33N 83°23W **309** G12
Jackson *Mich., U.S.A.* 42°15N 84°24W **311** B12
Jackson *Minn., U.S.A.* 43°37N 95°1W **308** D6
Jackson *Miss., U.S.A.* 32°18N 90°12W **315** E9
Jackson *Mo., U.S.A.* 37°23N 89°40W **308** G9
Jackson *N.H., U.S.A.* 44°10N 71°11W **313** B13
Jackson *Ohio, U.S.A.* 39°3N 82°39W **309** F12
Jackson *S.C., U.S.A.* 33°20N 81°47W **316** B8
Jackson *Tenn., U.S.A.* 35°37N 88°49W **315** D10
Jackson *Wyo., U.S.A.* 43°29N 110°46W **304** E8
Jackson, C. *N.Z.* 40°59S 174°20E **285** A9
Jackson B. *N.Z.* 43°58S 168°42E **285** D3
Jackson Center *U.S.A.* 40°27N 84°4W **311** D12
Jackson Hd. *N.Z.* 43°58S 168°37E **285** D3
Jackson Heights *U.S.A.* 40°44N 73°53W **132** B2
Jackson L. *Fla., U.S.A.* 30°30N 84°17W **316** E5
Jackson L. *Ga., U.S.A.* 33°19N 83°50W **316** B6
Jackson L. *Wyo., U.S.A.* 43°52N 110°36W **304** E8
Jackson Park *U.S.A.* 41°46N 87°34W **119** C3
Jacksons *N.Z.* 42°46S 171°32E **285** C6
Jackson's Arm *Canada* 49°52N 56°47W **299** C8
Jacksonville *Ala., U.S.A.* 33°49N 85°46W **316** B4
Jacksonville *Ark., U.S.A.* 34°52N 92°7W **314** D8
Jacksonville *Calif., U.S.A.* 37°52N 120°24W **306** H6
Jacksonville *Fla., U.S.A.* 30°20N 81°39W **316** E8
Jacksonville *Ga., U.S.A.* 31°49N 82°59W **316** D7
Jacksonville *Ill., U.S.A.* 39°44N 90°14W **310** E6
Jacksonville *N.C., U.S.A.* 34°45N 77°26W **315** D16
Jacksonville *Tex., U.S.A.* 31°58N 95°17W **314** F7
Jacksonville Beach *U.S.A.* 30°17N 81°24W **316** E8
Jacksonville Int. ✈ (JAX) *U.S.A.* 30°30N 81°41W **316** E8
Jacmel *Haiti* 18°14N 72°32W **321** C5
Jaco, Pte. *Dominica* 15°39N 61°24W **323** k
Jacob Lake *U.S.A.* 36°43N 112°13W **305** H7
Jacobabad *Pakistan* 28°20N 68°29E **242** E3
Jacobina *Brazil* 11°11S 40°30W **332** D3
Jacobshagen = Dobrzany *Poland* 53°22N 15°25E **184** E2
Jacon Javits Convention Center *New York, U.S.A.* **132** c1
Jacotet, B. *Mauritius* 20°30S 57°26E **272** e
Jacqueline Kennedy Onassis Res. *New York, U.S.A.* **132** a3
Jacques-Cartier *Canada* 45°31N 73°27W **130** A3
Jacques-Cartier, Dét. de *Canada* 50°0N 63°30W **299** C7
Jacques-Cartier, Mt. *Canada* 48°57N 66°0W **299** C6
Jacques-Cartier, Pont *Canada* 45°31N 73°32W **130** A2
Jacques-Cartier △ *Canada* 47°15N 71°33W **299** C5
Jacqueville *Ivory C.* 5°12N 4°25W **262** D4
Jacuí → *Brazil* 30°2S 51°15W **335** C5
Jacumba *U.S.A.* 32°37N 116°11W **307** N10
Jacundá → *Brazil* 1°57S 50°26W **332** B1
Jadavpur *India* 22°28N 88°22E **124** C2
Jadcherla *India* 16°46N 78°9E **244** F4
Jade *Germany* 53°20N 8°14E **178** B4
Jade Buddha Temple *China* 31°15N 121°25E **138** B1
Jade City *Canada* 59°15N 129°37W **296** B3
Jade Dragon Snow Mt. = Yulong Xueshan *China* 27°6N 100°10E **228** D3
Jade Island *Beijing, China* **114** b2
Jade Mt. = Yü Shan *Taiwan* 23°25N 120°52E **225** C2
Jadebusen *Germany* 53°29N 8°12E **178** B4
Jadotville = Likasi *Dem. Rep. of the Congo* 10°55S 26°48E **269** E2
Jadovnik *Serbia* 43°20N 19°45E **202** C3
Jadraque *Spain* 40°55N 2°55W **196** E2
Jādū *Libya* 32°0N 12°0E **258** B2
Jægersborg *Denmark* 55°45N 12°31E **118** A3
Jægersborg Dyrehave *Denmark* 55°46N 12°33E **118** A3
Jaén *Peru* 5°25S 78°40W **330** B2
Jaén *Spain* 37°44N 3°43W **195** H7
Jaén □ *Spain* 37°50N 3°30W **195** H7
Jæren *Norway* 58°42N 5°47E **164** F2
Jærens Rev *Norway* 58°45N 5°45E **164** F2
Jafarabad *India* 20°52N 71°22E **242** J4
Jaffa = Tel Aviv-Yafo *Israel* 32°4N 34°48E **251** F5
Jaffa, C. *Australia* 36°58S 139°40E **282** D3
Jaffna *Sri Lanka* 9°45N 80°2E **245** K5
Jaffrey *U.S.A.* 42°49N 72°2W **313** D12
Jagadhri *India* 30°10N 77°20E **242** D7
Jagadishpur *Bihar, India* 25°30N 84°21E **243** G11
Jagadishpur *W. Bengal, India* 22°39N 88°17E **124** B1
Jagatpur *India* 28°44N 77°13E **120** A2
Jagdalpur *India* 19°3N 82°0E **244** E6
Jagdaqi *China* 50°25N 124°7E **219** A13
Jagersfontein *S. Africa* 29°44S 25°27E **270** C4
Jaghīn → *Iran* 27°17N 57°13E **247** E8
Jagna *Phil.* 9°39N 124°22E **233** G5
Jagodina *Serbia* 44°5N 21°15E **202** B5
Jagraon *India* 30°50N 75°25E **242** D6
Jagst → *Germany* 49°14N 9°10E **179** F5
Jagtial *India* 18°50N 79°0E **244** E4
Jaguaquara *Brazil* 13°32S 39°58W **333** D4
Jaguaré, Rib. do → *Brazil* 23°32S 46°45W **137** B1
Jaguariaíva *Brazil* 24°10S 49°50W **335** A6
Jaguaribe *Brazil* 5°53S 38°37W **332** C4
Jaguaribe → *Brazil* 4°25S 37°45W **332** B4
Jaguaruana *Brazil* 4°50S 37°47W **332** B4
Jagüey Grande *Cuba* 22°35N 81°7W **320** B3
Jagungal, Mt. *Australia* 36°8S 148°22E **283** D8
Jahanabad *India* 25°13N 84°59E **243** G11
Jahangirpur *India* 28°43N 77°12E **120** A2
Jahazpur *India* 25°37N 75°17E **242** G6
Jahrom *Iran* 28°30N 53°31E **247** D7
Jaicós *Brazil* 7°21S 41°8W **332** C3
Jaigarh *India* 17°17N 73°13E **244** F1
Jaijon *India* 31°21N 76°9E **242** D7
Jailolo *Indonesia* 1°5N 127°30E **231** D7
Jailolo, Selat *Indonesia* 0°5N 129°5E **231** D7
Jaintiapur *Bangla.* 25°8N 92°7E **241** C4
Jaipur *Assam, India* 27°16N 95°24E **241** B5
Jaipur *Raj., India* 27°0N 75°50E **242** F6
Jais *India* 26°15N 81°32E **243** F9
Jaisalmer *India* 26°55N 70°54E **242** F4
Jaisinghnagar *India* 23°38N 78°34E **243** H8
Jaitaran *India* 26°12N 73°56E **242** F5
Jaithari *India* 23°14N 78°37E **243** H8
Jājarm *Iran* 36°58N 56°27E **247** B8
Jajce *Bos.-H.* 44°19N 17°17E **182** F2
Jajpur *India* 20°53N 86°22E **244** D8
Jakam → *India* 23°54N 74°13E **242** H6
Jakar Dzong *Bhutan* 27°33N 90°43E **241** B3
Jakarta *Indonesia* 6°9S 106°52E **122** A2
Jakarta, Teluk *Indonesia* 6°5S 106°50E **122** A1
Jakarta Halim Perdana Kusuma Int. ✈ (HLP) *Indonesia* 6°16S 106°53E **122** B2
Jakhal *India* 29°48N 75°50E **242** E6
Jakharrah *Libya* 29°13N 21°34E **258** C4
Jakhau *India* 23°13N 68°43E **242** H3
Jakobshavn = Ilulissat *Greenland* 69°12N 51°10W **154** D5
Jakobstad = Pietarsaari *Finland* 63°40N 22°43E **160** E20
Jakupica *Macedonia* 41°45N 21°22E **202** E5
Jal *U.S.A.* 32°7N 103°12W **305** K12
Jalaihai Pt. *Guam* 13°18N 144°46E **302** d
Jalājil *Si. Arabia* 25°40N 45°27E **246** E5
Jalal-Abad *Kyrgyzstan* 40°56N 73°0E **217** D8
Jalal-Abad □ *Kyrgyzstan* 41°30N 72°30E **217** D8
Jalālābād *Afghan.* 34°30N 70°29E **242** B4
Jalalabad *India* 27°41N 79°42E **243** F8
Jalalpur Jattan *Pakistan* 32°38N 74°11E **242** C6
Jalama *U.S.A.* 34°29N 120°29W **307** L6
Jalan Kayu *Singapore* 1°24N 103°52E **138** A3
Jalandhar = Jullundur *India* 31°20N 75°40E **242** D6
Jalapa *Guatemala* 14°39N 89°59W **320** D2
Jalapa Enríquez = Xalapa *Mexico* 19°32N 96°55W **319** D5
Jalasjärvi *Finland* 62°29N 22°47E **160** E20
Jalaun *India* 26°8N 79°25E **243** F8
Jalāzīn *Afghan.* 37°2N 64°49E **240** A2
Jaldak *Afghan.* 31°58N 66°43E **240** C2
Jaldhaka → *Bangla.* 26°16N 89°16E **241** B2
Jales *Brazil* 20°10S 50°33W **333** F1
Jalesar *India* 27°29N 78°19E **242** F8
Jaleswar *Nepal* 26°38N 85°48E **243** F11
Jalgaon *India* 21°0N 75°42E **244** D2
Jalībah *Iraq* 30°35N 46°32E **246** D5
Jalingo *Nigeria* 8°55N 11°25E **263** D7
Jalisco □ *Mexico* 20°20N 103°40W **318** D4
Jalkot *Pakistan* 35°14N 73°24E **243** B5
Jalna *India* 19°48N 75°38E **244** E2
Jalón → *Spain* 41°47N 1°4W **196** D3
Jalor *India* 25°21N 72°37E **242** G5
Jalpa *Mexico* 21°38N 102°58W **318** C4
Jalpaiguri *India* 26°32N 88°46E **241** B2
Jalpan *Mexico* 21°14N 99°29W **319** C5
Jālq *Iran* 27°35N 62°46E **240** D1
Jālū *Libya* 29°2N 21°33E **258** C4
Jaluit I. *Marshall Is.* 6°0N 169°30E **288** G8
Jalūlā *Iraq* 34°16N 45°10E **213** E11
Jamaame *Somali Rep.* 0°4N 42°44E **267** D5
Jamaari *Nigeria* 11°44N 9°53E **263** C6
Jamaica ■ *W. Indies* 18°10N 77°30W **320** a
Jamaica B. *U.S.A.* 40°36N 73°50W **132** c3
Jamaica Channel *Jamaica* 17°0N 76°0W **321** C4
Jamaica Plain *U.S.A.* 42°18N 71°6W **116** B2
Jamakpuri *India* 28°37N 77°5E **120** B1
Jamalpur *Bangla.* 24°52N 89°56E **241** C2
Jamalpur *India* 25°18N 86°28E **243** G12
Jamalpurganj *India* 23°2N 87°59E **243** H13
Jamanota *Aruba* 12°29N 69°57W **322** f
Jamanxim → *Brazil* 4°43S 56°18W **331** A6
Jamari *Brazil* 8°45S 63°27W **331** B5
Jamari → *Brazil* 8°27S 63°30W **331** B5
Jamba *Angola* 14°40S 16°2E **265** E3
Jambewangi *Indonesia* 8°17S 114°7E **231** J17
Jambi *Indonesia* 1°38S 103°30E **234** C2
Jambi □ *Indonesia* 1°30S 102°30E **234** C2
Jambongan, Pulau *Malaysia* 6°45N 117°20E **235** A5
Jambusar *India* 22°3N 72°51E **242** H5
James *U.S.A.* 32°58N 83°29W **316** C6
James → *S. Dak., U.S.A.* 42°52N 97°18W **308** D5
James → *Va., U.S.A.* 36°56N 76°27W **309** G15
James, I. = San Salvador, I. *Ecuador* 0°16S 90°42W **330** a
James B. *Canada* 54°0N 80°0W **298** B3
James I. *Gambia* 13°19N 16°21W **262** C1
James Island *U.S.A.* 32°45N 79°55W **316** C10
James Ranges *Australia* 24°10S 132°30E **278** D5
James Ross I. *Antarctica* 63°58S 57°50W **151** C18
Jamesabad *Pakistan* 25°17N 69°15E **242** G3
Jameson Land *Greenland* 71°0N 23°30W **154** C8
Jamesport *U.S.A.* 39°58N 93°48W **310** E3
Jamestown = Wawa *Canada* 47°59N 84°47W **298** C3
Jamestown *S. Austral., Australia* 33°10S 138°32E **282** B3
Jamestown *St. Helena* 15°55S 5°43W **153** h
Jamestown *Eastern Cape, S. Africa* 31°6S 26°45E **270** D4
Jamestown *Ind., U.S.A.* 39°56N 86°38W **311** E10
Jamestown *Mo., U.S.A.* 38°48N 92°30W **310** F4
Jamestown *N. Dak., U.S.A.* 46°54N 98°42W **308** B4
Jamestown *N.Y., U.S.A.* 42°6N 79°14W **312** D5
Jamestown *Ohio, U.S.A.* 39°39N 83°33W **311** E13
Jamestown *Pa., U.S.A.* 41°29N 80°27W **312** E4
Jamestown *S.C., U.S.A.* 33°17N 79°42W **316** B10
Jamīlābād *Iran* 34°24N 48°28E **247** C6
Jamira → *India* 21°35N 88°28E **243** J13
Jämjö *Sweden* 56°12N 15°49E **163** H9
Jamkhandi *India* 16°30N 75°15E **244** F2
Jamkhed *India* 18°43N 75°19E **244** E2
Jammalamadugu *India* 14°51N 78°25E **245** G4
Jammerbugten *Denmark* 57°15N 9°20E **163** G3
Jammu *India* 32°43N 74°54E **242** C6
Jammu & Kashmir □ *India* 34°25N 77°0E **243** B7
Jamnagar *India* 22°30N 70°6E **242** H4
Jamner *India* 20°45N 75°52E **244** D2
Jamni → *India* 25°13N 78°35E **243** G8
Jampur *Pakistan* 29°39N 70°40E **242** E4
Jamrud *Pakistan* 33°59N 71°24E **242** C4
Jämsä *Finland* 61°53N 25°10E **188** B3
Jamshedpur *India* 22°44N 86°12E **243** H12
Jamshīdīyeh *Iran* 35°42N 51°22E **141** A2
Jamsil *S. Korea* 37°30N 127°4E **137** B2
Jamtara *India* 23°59N 86°49E **243** H12
Jämtland *Sweden* 63°31N 14°0E **160** E16
Jämtlands län □ *Sweden* 63°0N 14°40E **162** B7
Jamuna → *Bangla.* 23°51N 89°45E **241** D2
Jamunamukh *India* 26°6N 92°44E **241** B4
Jamurki *Bangla.* 24°9N 90°2E **241** C3
Jamwon *S. Korea* 37°30N 127°0E **137** B2
Jan L. *Canada* 54°56N 102°55W **297** C8
Jan Mayen *Arctic* 71°0N 9°0W **150** B7
Janakkala *Finland* 60°54N 24°36E **188** B3
Janakpur *Nepal* 26°42N 85°55E **244** A7
Janaúba *Brazil* 15°48S 43°19W **333** E3
Janaucu, I. *Brazil* 0°30N 50°10W **332** A1
Jand *Pakistan* 33°30N 72°6E **242** C5
Jandaia *Brazil* 17°6S 50°7W **333** E1
Jandanku ✪ *Australia* 16°20S 135°45E **280** B2
Jandaq *Iran* 34°3N 54°22E **247** C7
Jandía *Canary Is.* 28°6N 14°21W **153** e2
Jandía, Pta. de *Canary Is.* 28°3N 14°31W **153** e2
Jandía △ *Canary Is.* 28°4N 14°19W **153** e2
Jandiatuba → *Brazil* 3°28S 68°42W **328** D4
Jandola *Pakistan* 32°20N 70°9E **242** C4
Jandowae *Australia* 26°45S 151°7E **281** D5
Jándula → *Spain* 38°3N 4°6W **195** G6
Jane Pk. *N.Z.* 45°15S 168°20E **285** F3
Janesville *U.S.A.* 42°41N 89°1W **310** B7
Janga *Ghana* 10°5N 1°0W **263** C4
Jangamo *Mozam.* 24°6S 35°21E **271** B6
Janghai *India* 25°33N 82°19E **243** G10
Jangheung *S. Korea* 34°41N 126°52E **224** E3
Janghowon *S. Korea* 37°7N 127°37E **224** D3
Jangoon *India* 17°44N 79°5E **244** F4
Jangsu *S. Korea* 35°38N 127°31E **224** E3
Janhtang Ga *Burma* 26°32N 96°38E **241** B6
Jani Khel *Afghan.* 32°46N 68°24E **240** B3
Janikowo *Poland* 52°45N 18°7E **185** F5
Janinà = Ioannina □ *Greece* 39°39N 20°57E **204** B2
Janiuay *Phil.* 10°58N 122°30E **233** F4
Janja *Bos.-H.* 44°40N 19°14E **182** F4
Janjanbureh *Gambia* 13°30N 14°47W **262** C2
Janjevo *Kosovo* 42°35N 21°19E **202** D5
Janjgir *India* 22°1N 82°34E **243** J10
Janjina *Croatia* 42°58N 17°25E **199** F14
Janjina *Madag.* 20°30S 45°50E **272** C2
Jankau = Jankow *Poland* 52°45N 18°7E **185** F5
Janki *Poland* 52°8N 20°52E **142** C1
Jannaale *Somali Rep.* 1°48N 44°42E **267** D5
Janos *Mexico* 30°54N 108°10W **318** A3
Jánoshalma *Hungary* 46°18N 19°21E **182** D4
Jánosháza *Hungary* 47°8N 17°12E **182** C2
Jánossomorja *Hungary* 47°47N 17°11E **182** C2
Janów *Poland* 50°44N 19°27E **185** H6
Janów Lubelski *Poland* 50°48N 22°23E **185** H9
Janów Podlaski *Poland* 52°11N 23°11E **185** F10
Janowiec Wielkopolski *Poland* 52°45N 17°30E **185** F4
Jantho *Indonesia* 5°17N 95°38E **234** A1
Januária *Brazil* 15°25S 44°25W **333** E3
Janub △ *Sudan* 6°50N 28°45E **257** F2
Janub Dârfûr □ *Sudan* 11°0N 25°0E **257** E2
Janub Kordofân □ *Sudan* 12°0N 30°0E **257** E3
Janûb Sînî □ *Egypt* 29°30N 33°50E **251** J4
Janubio *Canary Is.* 28°56N 13°50W **153** e2
Janville *France* 48°10N 1°50E **173** D8
Janwada *India* 18°0N 77°29E **244** E3
Janzé *France* 47°55N 1°28W **172** E5
Jaora *India* 23°40N 75°10E **242** H6
Japan ■ *Asia* 36°0N 136°0E **221** G8
Japan, Sea of *Asia* 40°0N 135°0E **220** E7
Japan Center *San Francisco, U.S.A.* **136** c1
Japan Trench *Pac. Oc.* 32°0N 142°0E **288** D6
Japen = Yapen *Indonesia* 1°50S 136°0E **231** E9
Japiim *Brazil* 7°37S 72°54W **330** B3
Japla *India* 24°33N 84°1E **243** G11
Japurá *Brazil* 1°48S 66°34W **328** D4
Japura *Indonesia* 0°19S 102°21E **234** C2
Japurá → *Brazil* 3°8S 65°46W **328** D4
Jaquarão *Brazil* 32°34S 53°23W **335** C5
Jaqué *Panama* 7°27N 78°8W **320** E4
Jarābulus *Syria* 36°49N 38°1E **213** D8
Jaraguá *Goiás, Brazil* 15°45S 49°20W **333** E2
Jaraguá *São Paulo, Brazil* 23°27S 46°44W **137** A1
Jaraguá, Pico de *Brazil* 23°27S 46°46W **137** A1
Jaraguari *Brazil* 20°9S 54°25W **331** E7
Jaraicejo *Spain* 39°40N 5°49W **195** F5
Jaraíz de la Vera *Spain* 40°4N 5°45W **194** E5
Jarama → *Spain* 40°24N 3°32W **194** E7
Jaramānah *Syria* 33°29N 36°21E **250** E7
Jaramillo *Argentina* 47°10S 67°7W **336** C3
Jarandilla de la Vera *Spain* 40°8N 5°39W **194** E5
Jaranwala *Pakistan* 31°15N 73°26E **242** D5
Jarash *Jordan* 32°17N 35°54E **251** F6
Jarash □ *Jordan* 32°17N 35°54E **251** F6
Jaraucu → *Brazil* 1°48S 52°22W **329** D7
Järbo *Sweden* 60°43N 16°36E **162** D10
Jarboesville = Lexington Park *U.S.A.* 38°16N 76°27W **309** F15
Jardas al 'Abīd *Libya* 32°18N 20°59E **258** B4
Jardim *Brazil* 21°28S 56°2W **334** A4
Jardim Paulista *Brazil* 23°34S 46°41W **137** B1
Jardín → *Spain* 38°50N 2°10W **197** G2
Jardín América *Argentina* 27°3S 55°14W **335** B4
Jardin Botanique *Brussels, Belgium* **116** a3
Jardine River △ *Australia* 11°9S 142°21E **280** A3
Jardines de la Reina, Arch. de los *Cuba* 20°50N 78°50W **320** B4
Jargalang *China* 43°5N 122°55E **227** C12
Jargalant = Hovd □ *Mongolia* 48°2N 91°37E **217** C12

Juli Peru 16°10S 69°25W 330 D4
Julia Cr. → Australia 20°0S 141°11E 280 C3
Julia Creek Australia 20°39S 141°44E 280 C3
Juliaca Peru 15°25S 70°10W 330 D3
Julian U.S.A. 33°4N 116°38W 307 M10
Julian, L. Canada 54°25N 77°57W 298 B4
Julian Alps = Julijske Alpe Slovenia 46°15N 14°1E 199 B11
Juliana Top = Mandala, Puncak Indonesia 4°44S 140°20E 231 E10
Julianadorp Curaçao 12°9N 68°57W 322 g
Julianatop Suriname 3°40N 56°30W 329 C6
Julianehåb = Qaqortoq Greenland 60°43N 46°0W 154 E6
Julianów Poland 52°10N 21°9E 142 B2
Jülich Germany 50°55N 6°22E 178 E2
Juliette, L. U.S.A. 33°2N 83°50W 316 B6
Julijske Alpe Slovenia 46°15N 14°1E 199 B11
Julimes Mexico 28°25N 105°27W 318 B3
Jullundur India 31°20N 75°40E 242 D6
Julu China 37°15N 115°2E 226 F8
Jumbo Zimbabwe 17°30S 30°58E 269 F3
Jumbo Pk. U.S.A. 36°12N 114°11W 307 J12
Jumentos Cays Bahamas 23°0N 75°40W 320 B4
Jumilla Spain 38°28N 1°19W 197 G3
Jumla Nepal 29°15N 82°13E 243 E10
Jumna = Yamuna → India 25°30N 81°53E 243 G9
Jumunjin S. Korea 37°55N 128°54E 224 D4
Junagadh India 21°30N 70°30E 242 J4
Junan China 35°12N 118°53E 227 G10
Juncos Puerto Rico 18°14N 65°55W 321 b
Junction Tex., U.S.A. 30°29N 99°46W 314 F5
Junction Utah, U.S.A. 38°14N 112°13W 305 G7
Junction B. Australia 11°52S 133°55E 280 A1
Junction City Ga., U.S.A. 32°36N 84°28W 316 C5
Junction City Kans., U.S.A. 39°2N 96°50W 308 F5
Junction City Oreg., U.S.A. 44°13N 123°12W 304 D2
Junction Pt. Australia 11°45S 133°50E 280 A1
Jundah Australia 24°46S 143°2E 280 C3
Jundiaí Brazil 24°30S 47°0W 335 A6
Juneau U.S.A. 58°18N 134°25W 296 B2
Junee Australia 34°53S 147°35E 283 C7
Jung S. Korea 37°33N 126°59E 137 B1
Jungar Qi China 39°49N 110°57E 226 E6
Jungbunzlau = Mladá Boleslav Czech Rep. 50°27N 14°53E 180 A7
Jungfernheide, Volkspark Germany 52°32N 13°18E 115 A2
Jungfernsee Germany 52°25N 13°6E 115 B1
Jungfrau Switz. 46°32N 7°58E 179 J3
Junggar Pendi China 44°30N 86°0E 217 D11
Jungghwa S. Korea 37°35N 127°3E 137 B2
Jungkat Indonesia 0°4N 109°13E 235 B3
Jungnang S. Korea 37°36N 127°5E 137 B2
Jungnangcheon → S. Korea 37°32N 126°55E 137 B1
Jungsdalshytta = Iungsdalshytta Norway 60°49N 7°55E 164 D4
Jungshahi Pakistan 24°52N 67°44E 242 G2
Juniata → U.S.A. 40°24N 77°1W 312 F7
Junín Argentina 34°33S 60°57W 334 C3
Junín Peru 11°12S 76°0W 330 C2
Junín □ Peru 11°30S 75°0W 330 C3
Junín, L. de Peru 11°2S 76°6W 330 C2
Junín de los Andes Argentina 39°45S 71°0W 336 A2
Juniper Green U.K. 55°54N 3°16W 121 B2
Jūniyah Lebanon 33°59N 35°38E 250 E6
Junk B. China 22°17N 114°15E 122 B2
Junlian China 28°8N 104°29E 228 C5
Junnar India 19°12N 73°58E 244 E1
Juno Beach U.S.A. 26°52N 80°3W 317 J9
Juntas Chile 28°24S 69°58W 334 B2
Juntura U.S.A. 43°45N 118°5W 304 E4
Juparanã, L. Brazil 19°16S 40°8W 333 E3
Jupiter U.S.A. 26°57N 80°6W 317 J9
Juquiá Brazil 24°19S 47°38W 333 F2
Jur, Nahr el → Sudan 8°45N 29°15E 257 F2
Jura = Jura, Mts. du Europe 46°40N 6°5E 173 F13
Jura = Schwäbische Alb Germany 48°20N 9°30E 179 G5
Jura U.K. 56°0N 5°50W 167 F3
Jura □ France 46°47N 5°45E 173 F12
Jura □ Switz. 47°20N 7°20E 179 H3
Jūra → Lithuania 55°3N 22°9E 184 G9
Jura, Mts. du Europe 46°40N 6°5E 173 F13
Jura, Sd. of U.K. 55°57N 5°45W 167 F3
Juradó Colombia 7°7N 77°46W 328 B2
Jurbarkas Lithuania 55°4N 22°46E 184 G9
Jurien Bay Australia 30°18S 115°2E 279 F2
Jurilovca Romania 44°46N 28°52E 183 F13
Jūrmala Latvia 56°58N 23°34E 184 B10
Jurong Jiangsu, China 31°57N 119°9E 229 B12
Jurong Singapore 1°19N 103°42E 138 B2
Jurong, Selat Singapore 1°17N 103°42E 138 B2
Jurong Industrial Estate Singapore 1°19N 103°40E 138 B1
Juruá Brazil 3°27S 66°3W 328 D4
Juruá → Brazil 2°37S 65°44W 328 D4
Juruena Brazil 13°0S 58°10W 331 C6
Juruena → Brazil 7°20S 58°3W 331 B6
Jurujuba, Enseada de Brazil 22°54S 43°6W 135 B2
Juruti Brazil 2°9S 56°4W 329 D6
Jūsō Japan 34°42N 135°27E 133 A1
Jussey France 47°50N 5°55E 173 E12
Justice U.S.A. 41°44N 87°49W 119 C2
Justicia Madrid, Spain 127 a3
Justo Daract Argentina 33°52S 65°12W 334 C2
Jutaí Amazonas, Brazil 2°44S 66°57W 328 D4
Jutaí Amazonas, Brazil 5°11S 68°54W 330 B4
Jutaí → Brazil 2°43S 66°57W 328 D4
Jüterbog Germany 51°59N 13°5E 178 D9
Juticalpa Honduras 14°40N 86°12W 320 D2
Jutland = Jylland Denmark 56°25N 9°30E 163 H3
Juuka Finland 63°13N 29°17E 160 E23
Juventud, I. de la Cuba 21°40N 82°40W 320 B3
Juvigny-sous-Andaine France 48°32N 0°30W 172 D6
Juwangsan △ S. Korea 36°20N 129°15E 224 D4
Jūy Zar Iran 33°50N 46°18E 213 F12
Juye China 35°22N 116°5E 226 G9
Juzennecourt France 48°10N 4°58E 173 D11
Južni Brod = Brod Macedonia 41°32N 21°17E 202 E5
Jvari Georgia 42°42N 42°4E 191 J6
Jwalahari India 28°40N 77°6E 120 B1
Jyderup Denmark 55°40N 11°25E 163 J5
Jylland Denmark 56°25N 9°30E 163 H3
Jyväskylä Finland 62°14N 25°50E 188 A3

K

K2 Pakistan 35°58N 76°32E 243 B7
Ka → Nigeria 11°40N 4°10E 263 C5
Kaa-Iya △ Bolivia 18°35S 61°40W 331 D6
Ka'a'awa U.S.A. 21°33N 157°51W 302 J14
Kaakha = Kaka Turkmenistan 37°21N 59°36E 247 B8
Ka'ala U.S.A. 21°31N 158°9W 302 J13
Kaala-Gomén N. Cal. 20°40S 164°25E 288 d
Ka'alu'alu B. U.S.A. 18°58N 155°37W 302 E6
Kaap Plateau S. Africa 28°30S 24°0E 270 C3
Kaapkruis Namibia 21°55S 13°57E 270 B1
Kaapstad = Cape Town S. Africa 33°55S 18°22E 118 A1
Kaashidhoo Atoll Maldives 4°58N 73°28E 272 d
Kaashidhoo Channel Maldives 5°1N 73°28E 272 d
Kaatan, Mt. Phil. 8°10N 124°52E 233 G5
Kaba Guinea 10°9N 11°40W 262 C2
Kabacan Phil. 7°8N 124°49E 233 H5
Kabachishche = Zelenodolsk Russia 55°55N 48°30E 190 C9
Kabaena Indonesia 5°15S 122°0E 231 F6
Kabala S. Leone 9°38N 11°37W 262 D2
Kabale Uganda 1°15S 30°0E 268 C3
Kabalo Dem. Rep. of the Congo 6°0S 27°0E 265 D5
Kabambare Dem. Rep. of the Congo 4°41S 27°39E 268 C2
Kabango Dem. Rep. of the Congo 8°35S 28°30E 269 D2
Kabanjahe Indonesia 3°6N 98°30E 234 B1
Kabankalan Phil. 9°59N 122°49E 233 G4
Kabara Fiji 18°59S 178°56W 287 B3
Kabara Mali 16°40N 2°50W 262 B4
Kabardinka Russia 44°40N 37°57E 189 K10
Kabardino-Balkaria □ Russia 43°30N 43°30E 191 J6
Kabarega Falls = Murchison Falls Uganda 2°15N 31°30E 268 B3
Kabarnet Kenya 0°30N 35°45E 268 B4
Kabasalan Phil. 7°47N 122°44E 233 H4
Kabat Indonesia 8°16S 114°19E 231 J17
Kabaty Poland 52°8N 21°4E 142 C2
Kabba Nigeria 7°50N 6°3E 263 D6
Kabbani → India 12°13N 76°54E 245 H3
Kabi Niger 13°30N 12°35E 259 F2
Kabin Buri Thailand 13°57N 101°43E 236 F3
Kabinakagami L. Canada 48°54N 84°25W 298 C3
Kabinda Dem. Rep. of the Congo 6°10S 24°29E 265 D4
Kabkabīyah Sudan 13°50N 24°0E 259 F4
Kablungu, C. Papua N. G. 6°20S 150°1E 286 D6
Kabna Sudan 19°6N 32°40E 256 D3
Kabo C.A.R. 7°35N 18°38E 264 A3
Kabompo Zambia 13°36S 24°14E 265 E4
Kabompo → Zambia 14°11S 23°11E 265 E4
Kabondo Dem. Rep. of the Congo 8°58S 25°40E 265 D5
Kabongo Dem. Rep. of the Congo 7°22S 25°33E 265 D5
Kabot Guinea 10°48N 14°57W 262 C2
Kabou Togo 9°28N 0°55E 263 D5
Kaboudia, Rass Tunisia 35°13N 11°10E 258 A2
Kabr Sudan 10°54N 26°50E 257 E2
Kabrît, G. el Egypt 29°42N 33°16E 251 J4
Kabrousse Senegal 12°25N 16°45W 262 C1
Kabubu Dem. Rep. of the Congo 9°42S 24°40E 265 D4
Kabūd Gonbad Iran 37°5N 59°45E 247 B8
Kabudar Ahang Iran 35°11N 48°43E 213 E13
Kabugao Phil. 18°2N 121°11E 232 B3
Kābul Afghan. 34°28N 69°11E 242 B3
Kābul □ Afghan. 34°30N 69°0E 240 B3
Kābul → Pakistan 33°55N 72°14E 242 C5
Kabuli Papua N. G. 2°7S 146°40E 286 B4
Kabunga Dem. Rep. of the Congo 1°38S 28°3E 268 C2
Kaburuang Indonesia 3°50N 126°30E 231 D7
Kabushiya Sudan 16°54N 33°41E 257 D3
Kabwanga Dem. Rep. of the Congo 7°2S 22°36E 265 D4
Kabwe Zambia 14°30S 28°29E 269 E2
Kabwum Papua N. G. 6°11S 147°15E 286 D4
Kačanik Kosovo 42°13N 21°12E 202 D5
Kačerginė Lithuania 54°56N 23°42E 184 D10
Kachar Kazakhstan 53°23N 62°55E 216 B6
Kachchh, Gulf of India 22°50N 69°15E 242 H3
Kachchh, Rann of India 24°0N 70°0E 242 H4
Kachchhidhana India 21°44N 78°46E 243 J8
Kachebera Zambia 13°50S 32°50E 269 E3
Kachia Nigeria 9°50N 7°55E 263 D6
Kachikau Botswana 18°8S 24°26E 270 A3
Kachin □ Burma 26°0N 97°30E 228 D1
Kachira, L. Uganda 0°40S 31°7E 268 C3
Kachīry Kazakhstan 53°10N 75°50E 217 B9
Kachisi Ethiopia 9°40N 37°50E 257 F4
Kachnara India 23°50N 75°6E 242 H6
Kachot Cambodia 11°30N 103°3E 237 G4
Kaçkar Turkey 40°45N 41°10E 213 B9
Kada Chad 19°20N 19°39E 259 E3
Kadaingti Burma 17°37N 97°32E 241 G6
Kadanai → Afghan. 31°22N 65°45E 242 D1
Kadan Kyun Burma 12°30N 98°20E 236 F2
Kadarkút Hungary 46°13N 17°39E 182 D2
Kadavu Fiji 19°0S 178°15E 287 B2
Kadavu Passage Fiji 18°45S 178°0E 287 B2
Kade Ghana 6°7N 0°56W 263 D4
Kadei → C.A.R. 3°31N 16°3E 264 B3
Kademlija = Triglav Slovenia 46°21N 13°50E 199 B10
Kadena Japan 26°22N 127°45E 288 a
Kadhimain = Al Kāẓimīyah Iraq 33°22N 44°18E 213 F11
Kadi India 23°18N 72°23E 242 H5
Kadiak I. = Kodiak I. U.S.A. 57°30N 152°45W 303 H9
Kadiana Mali 10°45N 6°30W 262 C3
Kadıköy Turkey 40°59N 29°1E 122 C2
Kadina Australia 33°55S 137°43E 282 B2
Kadınhanı Turkey 38°14N 32°13E 212 C5
Kadiolo Mali 10°35N 5°43W 262 C3
Kadipur India 26°10N 82°23E 243 F10
Kadirabad India 19°51N 75°54E 244 E2
Kadiri India 14°12N 78°13E 245 G4
Kadirli Turkey 37°23N 36°5E 212 D7
Kadiyevka = Stakhanov Ukraine 48°35N 38°40E 189 H10
Kadja, O. → Chad 12°2N 22°28E 259 F4
Kadmat I. India 11°14N 72°47E 245 J1
Kadoka U.S.A. 43°50N 101°31W 308 D3
Kadom Russia 54°37N 42°30E 190 C6
Kadoma Ōsaka, Japan 34°44N 135°35E 133 A2
Kadoma Zimbabwe 18°20S 29°52E 269 F2
Kâdugli Sudan 11°0N 29°45E 257 E2
Kaduna Nigeria 10°30N 7°21E 263 C6
Kaduna □ Nigeria 11°0N 7°30E 263 C6
Kaduna → Nigeria 8°45N 5°48E 263 D6
Kadur India 13°34N 76°1E 245 H3
Kaduy Russia 59°12N 37°9E 188 C9
Kaédi Mauritania 16°9N 13°28W 262 B2
Kaélé Cameroon 10°7N 14°27E 259 F2
Ka'ena U.S.A. 21°34N 158°14W 302 J13
Ka'ena Pt. U.S.A. 21°35N 158°17W 302 J13
Kaeng Khoi Thailand 14°35N 101°0E 236 E3
Kaeng Krachan △ Thailand 12°57N 99°23E 236 F2
Kaeng Krung △ Thailand 9°30N 98°50E 237 H2
Kaeng Tana △ Thailand 15°25N 105°32E 236 E5
Kaeo N.Z. 35°6S 173°49E 284 B2
Kaesŏng N. Korea 37°58N 126°35E 224 D3
Kaesŏng □ N. Korea 38°0N 126°37E 224 D3
Kāf Si. Arabia 31°25N 37°29E 246 D3
Kafakumba Dem. Rep. of the Congo 9°38S 23°46E 265 D4
Kafan = Kapan Armenia 39°18N 46°27E 213 C12
Kafanchan Nigeria 9°40N 8°20E 263 D6
Kafareti Nigeria 10°25N 11°12E 263 C7
Kaffrine Senegal 14°8N 15°36W 262 C1
Kafia Kingi Sudan 9°20N 24°25E 264 A4
Kafin Nigeria 9°30N 7°4E 263 D6
Kafin Madaki Nigeria 10°41N 9°46E 263 C6
Kafinda Zambia 12°32S 30°20E 269 E3
Kafr 'Aqab West Bank 31°52N 35°13E 123 A2
Kafr el Battikh Egypt 31°25N 31°44E 256 H7
Kafr el Dauwâr Egypt 31°8N 30°8E 256 H7
Kafr el Sheikh Egypt 31°15N 30°50E 251 G1
Kafr el Sheikh □ Egypt 31°15N 30°55E 251 G1
Kafr el Zaiyât Egypt 30°49N 30°48E 256 H7
Kafue Zambia 15°46S 28°9E 269 F2
Kafue △ Zambia 15°12S 25°38E 269 F2
Kafue Flats Zambia 15°40S 27°25E 269 F2
Kafulwe Zambia 9°0S 29°1E 269 D2
Kafumba Dem. Rep. of the Congo 5°23S 18°55E 265 D3
Kaga Afghan. 34°14N 70°10E 242 B4
Kaga Japan 36°16N 136°15E 223 A8
Kaga Bandoro C.A.R. 7°0N 19°10E 264 A3
Kagamil I. U.S.A. 53°0N 169°43W 303 K5
Kaganovich = Tovarkovskiy Russia 53°40N 38°14E 188 F10
Kagarko Nigeria 9°28N 7°36E 263 D6
Kagawa □ Japan 34°15N 134°0E 222 C6
Kagera □ Tanzania 2°0S 31°30E 268 C3
Kagera → Uganda 0°57S 31°47E 268 C3
Kâğıthane Turkey 41°4N 28°58E 122 B1
Kâğıthane → Turkey 41°9N 28°56E 122 B1
Kağızman Turkey 40°5N 43°10E 213 B10
Kagmar Sudan 14°24N 30°25E 257 E3
Kagologolo Indonesia 1°9S 98°37E 234 C1
Kagopal Chad 8°16N 16°23E 259 G3
Kagoro Nigeria 9°36N 8°23E 263 D6
Kagoshima Japan 31°35N 130°33E 222 F2
Kagoshima □ Japan 31°30N 130°30E 222 F2
Kagoshima-Wan Japan 31°25N 130°40E 222 F2
Kagran Austria 48°14N 16°26E 142 A2
Kagua Papua N. G. 6°26S 143°48E 286 D2
Kagul = Cahul Moldova 45°50N 28°15E 183 E13
Kahak Iran 36°6N 49°46E 247 B6
Kāhala U.S.A. 21°16N 157°47W 302 K14
Kahalu'u U.S.A. 21°27N 157°50W 302 K14
Kahama Tanzania 4°8S 32°30E 268 C3
Kahan Pakistan 29°18N 68°54E 242 E3
Kahana U.S.A. 21°34N 157°53W 302 J14
Kahana B. U.S.A. 21°35N 157°50W 302 J14
Kahana Valley State Park △ U.S.A. 21°32N 157°53W 302 J14
Kahang Malaysia 2°12N 103°32E 237 L4
Kahayan → Indonesia 3°40S 114°0E 235 C4
Kahe Tanzania 3°30S 37°25E 268 C4
Kahemba Dem. Rep. of the Congo 7°18S 18°55E 265 D3
Kaherekoau Mts. N.Z. 45°45S 167°15E 285 F2
Kahil, Djebel bou Algeria 34°26N 4°0E 261 B5
Kahnawake Canada 45°24N 73°40W 130 B1
Kahnūj Iran 27°55N 57°40E 247 E8
Kahoka U.S.A. 40°25N 91°44W 310 D5
Kaho'olawe U.S.A. 20°33N 156°37W 302 C5
Kahouanne Guadeloupe 16°15N 61°12W 322 e
Kahouanne, Îlet à Guadeloupe 16°22N 61°46W 322 e
Kahramanmaraş Turkey 37°37N 36°53E 212 D7
Kahramanmaraş □ Turkey 37°35N 36°33E 212 D7
Kâhta Turkey 37°46N 38°36E 213 D8
Kahuku U.S.A. 21°41N 157°57W 302 J14
Kahuku Pt. U.S.A. 21°43N 157°59W 302 J14
Kahul, Ozero Ukraine 45°24N 28°24E 183 E13
Kahului U.S.A. 20°54N 156°28W 302 C5
Kahului ✕ (OGG) U.S.A. 20°54N 156°26W 302 C5
Kahurangi △ N.Z. 41°10S 172°32E 285 B7
Kahurangi Pt. N.Z. 40°50S 172°10E 285 A7
Kahuta Pakistan 33°35N 73°24E 242 C5
Kahuzi-Biega △ Dem. Rep. of the Congo 1°50S 27°55E 268 C2
Kai, Kepulauan Indonesia 5°55S 132°45E 231 F8
Kai Besar Indonesia 5°35S 133°0E 231 F8
Kai Is. = Kai, Kepulauan Indonesia 5°55S 132°45E 231 F8
Kai Kecil Indonesia 5°45S 132°40E 231 F8
Kai Xian China 31°11N 108°21E 228 B7
Kaiama Nigeria 9°36N 4°1E 263 D5
Kaiapit Papua N. G. 6°18S 146°18E 286 D4
Kaiapoi N.Z. 43°24S 172°40E 285 D7
Kaidu He → China 41°46N 86°31E 218 C6
Kaieteur Falls Guyana 5°1N 59°10W 329 B6
Kaifeng China 34°48N 114°21E 226 G8
Kaihua China 29°12N 118°20E 229 C12
Kaijiang China 31°7N 107°55E 228 B6
Kaikohe N.Z. 35°25S 173°49E 284 B2
Kaikoura N.Z. 42°25S 173°43E 285 C8
Kaikoura Pen. N.Z. 42°25S 173°43E 285 C8
Kaikoura Ra. N.Z. 41°59S 173°41E 285 C8
Kailahun S. Leone 8°18N 10°39W 262 D2
Kailash = Kangrinboqe Feng China 31°0N 81°25E 243 D9
Kailashahar India 24°19N 92°0E 241 C4
Kaileuna I. Papua N. G. 8°32S 150°57E 286 E6
Kaili China 26°33N 107°59E 228 D6
Kailu China 43°38N 121°18E 227 C11
Kailua U.S.A. 21°24N 157°44W 302 K14
Kailua B. U.S.A. 21°25N 157°40W 302 K14
Kailua Kona U.S.A. 19°39N 155°59W 302 D6
Kaim → Papua N. G. 6°55S 141°33E 286 D1
Kaimaktsalan Oros = Voras Oros Greece 40°57N 21°45E 202 F5
Kaimana Indonesia 3°39S 133°45E 231 E8
Kaimanawa Mts. N.Z. 39°15S 175°56E 284 F4
Kaimata N.Z. 42°34S 171°28E 285 C6
Kaimes U.K. 55°54N 3°10W 121 B2
Kaimganj India 27°33N 79°24E 243 F8
Kaimon-Dake Japan 31°11N 130°32E 222 F2
Kaimur Hills India 24°30N 82°0E 243 G10
Kainab → Namibia 28°32S 19°34E 270 C2
Kainan Japan 34°9N 135°12E 223 C7
Kainantu Papua N. G. 6°18S 145°52E 286 D3
Kainji Dam Nigeria 9°55N 4°35E 263 D5
Kainji Lake △ Nigeria 10°5N 4°6E 263 C5
Kainji Res. Nigeria 10°1N 4°40E 263 C5
Kainsk = Samara Russia 53°8N 50°6E 190 D10
Kainuu Finland 64°30N 29°7E 160 D23
Kaipara Harbour N.Z. 36°25S 174°14E 284 C3
Kaiping China 22°23N 112°42E 229 F9
Kaipokok B. Canada 54°54N 59°47W 299 B8
Kaira India 22°45N 72°50E 242 H5
Kairana India 29°24N 77°15E 242 E7
Kairiru I. Papua N. G. 3°21S 143°34E 286 B2
Kaironi Indonesia 0°47S 133°40E 231 E8
Kairouan Tunisia 35°45N 10°5E 258 A2
Kairouan □ Tunisia 35°30N 9°46E 261 A6
Kairuku Papua N. G. 8°51S 146°35E 286 E4
Kaiser Wilhelm Kanal = Nord-Ostsee-Kanal Germany 54°12N 9°32E 178 A5
Kaiser Wilhelm Kirche Berlin, Germany 115 b2
Kaiser-Wilhelmsland = Papua □ Indonesia 4°0S 137°0E 231 E9
Kaiserebersdorf Austria 48°9N 16°26E 142 B2
Kaiserslautern Germany 49°26N 7°45E 179 F3
Kaiserstuhl Germany 48°4N 7°40E 179 G3
Kaita Japan 34°22N 132°32E 222 C4
Kaitaia N.Z. 35°8S 173°17E 284 B2
Kaitangata N.Z. 46°17S 169°51E 285 G4
Kaithal India 29°48N 76°26E 242 E7
Kaitu → Pakistan 33°10N 70°30E 242 C4
Kaivoksela Finland 60°15N 24°53E 121 B2
Kaiwi Channel U.S.A. 21°15N 157°30W 302 K14
Kaiyang China 27°4N 106°59E 228 D6
Kaiyuan Liaoning, China 42°28N 124°1E 224 A2
Kaiyuan Yunnan, China 23°40N 103°12E 228 F4
Kaiyuh Mts. U.S.A. 64°30N 158°0W 303 D8
Kajaani Finland 64°17N 27°46E 160 D22
Kajabbi Australia 20°0S 140°1E 280 C3
Kajaki Afghan. 32°18N 65°5E 242 C1
Kajana = Kajaani Finland 64°17N 27°46E 160 D22
Kajang Malaysia 2°59N 101°48E 237 L3
Kajaran Armenia 39°10N 46°7E 213 C12
Kajiado Kenya 1°53S 36°48E 268 C4
Kajo Kaji Sudan 3°58N 31°40E 257 G3
Kajok Sudan 8°19N 28°0E 257 F2
Kajuru Nigeria 10°15N 7°34E 263 C6
Kaka Sudan 10°38N 32°10E 257 E3
Kaka Turkmenistan 37°21N 59°36E 247 B8
Kakabeka Falls Canada 48°24N 89°37W 298 C2
Kakadu △ Australia 12°0S 132°3E 278 B5
Kakamas S. Africa 28°45S 20°33E 270 C3
Kakamega Kenya 0°20N 34°46E 268 B3
Kakamigahara Japan 35°28N 136°48E 223 B8
Kakana India 9°7N 92°48E 245 K11
Kakanj Bos.-H. 44°4N 18°4E 182 F3
Kakanui Mts. N.Z. 45°10S 170°30E 285 F5
Kakata Liberia 6°35N 10°20W 262 D2
Kakdwip India 21°53N 88°11E 243 J13
Kake Japan 34°36N 132°19E 222 C4
Kake Alaska, U.S.A. 56°59N 133°57W 296 B2
Kakegawa Japan 34°45N 138°1E 223 C10
Kakeroma-Jima Japan 28°8N 129°14E 221 K4
Kākhak Iran 34°9N 58°38E 247 C8
Kakhib Russia 42°28N 46°34E 191 J8
Kakhonak U.S.A. 59°26N 154°51W 303 G9
Kakhovka Ukraine 46°45N 33°30E 189 J7
Kakhovske Vdskh. Ukraine 47°5N 34°0E 189 J7
Kakinada India 16°57N 82°11E 244 F6
Kakisa Canada 60°56N 117°25W 296 A5
Kakisa → Canada 61°3N 118°10W 296 A5
Kakisa L. Canada 60°56N 117°43W 296 A5
Käkisalmi = Priozersk Russia 61°2N 30°7E 188 B6
Kakogawa Japan 34°46N 134°51E 222 C6
Kaktovik U.S.A. 70°8N 143°38W 303 A12
Kakum △ Ghana 5°24N 1°20W 263 D4
Kakuma Kenya 3°43N 34°52E 268 B3
Kakwa → Canada 54°37N 118°28W 296 C5
Kāl Gūsheh Iran 30°59N 58°12E 247 D8
Kal Sefīd Iran 34°52N 47°23E 213 E12
Kala Nigeria 12°2N 14°40E 263 C7
Kala Oya → Sri Lanka 8°20N 79°45E 245 K4
Kalaa-Kebira Tunisia 35°59N 10°32E 258 A2
Kalaallit Nunaat = Greenland ☑ N. Amer. 66°0N 45°0W 154 D6
Kalabagh Pakistan 33°0N 71°28E 242 C4
Kalabahi Indonesia 8°13S 124°31E 231 F6
Kalabak = Radomir Bulgaria 42°37N 22°59E 202 D6
Kalabakan Malaysia 4°25N 117°29E 235 B5
Kalabana Mali 14°10N 8°35W 262 C3
Kalabo Zambia 14°58S 22°40E 265 E4
Kalach Russia 50°22N 41°0E 190 E5
Kalach na Donu Russia 48°43N 43°32E 191 F6
Kalachinsk Russia 55°3N 74°33E 217 A8
Kaladan → Burma 20°20N 93°5E 241 E4
Kaladar Canada 44°37N 77°5W 312 B7
Kalae U.S.A. 18°55N 155°41W 302 E6
Kalahari Africa 24°0S 21°30E 270 B3
Kalahari Gemsbok △ S. Africa 25°30S 20°30E 270 C3
Kalaheo U.S.A. 21°56N 159°32W 302 B2
Kalaikhum Tajikistan 38°28N 70°46E 217 E8
Kalajoki Finland 64°12N 24°10E 160 D21
Kalakamati Botswana 20°40S 27°25E 271 B4
Kalakan Russia 55°15N 116°45E 215 D12
Kalakol Kenya 3°33N 35°54E 266 D4
K'alak'unlun Shank'ou = Karakoram Pass Asia 35°33N 77°50E 243 B7
Kalam Pakistan 35°34N 72°30E 243 B5
Kalama Dem. Rep. of the Congo 2°52S 28°35E 268 C2
Kalama Wash., U.S.A. 46°1N 122°51W 306 E4
Kalamaki Greece 37°52N 23°43E 112 B2
Kalamariá Greece 40°33N 22°55E 202 F6
Kalamata Greece 37°3N 22°10E 204 D4
Kalamazoo U.S.A. 42°17N 85°35W 311 B11
Kalamazoo → U.S.A. 42°40N 86°10W 311 B10
Kalamb India 18°3N 74°48E 244 E2
Kalambaka Greece 39°42N 21°39E 204 B3
Kalambo Falls Tanzania 8°37S 31°35E 269 D3
Kalamitsi Greece 38°45N 20°36E 207 B2
Kalamnuri India 19°40N 77°20E 244 E3
Kalamos Attiki, Greece 38°17N 23°52E 204 C5
Kalamos Lefkada, Greece 38°37N 20°55E 207 B2
Kalan Turkey 39°7N 39°32E 246 B3
Kalangadoo Australia 37°34S 140°41E 282 D4
Kalankalan Guinea 10°7N 8°54W 262 C3
Kalannie Australia 30°22S 117°5E 279 F2
Kalāntarī Iran 32°10N 54°8E 247 C7
Kalao Indonesia 7°21S 121°0E 231 F6
Kalaoa U.S.A. 19°43N 155°58W 302 D6
Kalaotoa Indonesia 7°20S 121°50E 231 F6
Kalapana U.S.A. 19°21N 154°59W 302 D7
Kälarne Sweden 62°59N 16°5E 162 B10
Kalasin Thailand 16°26N 103°30E 236 D4
Kalat Iran 25°29N 59°22E 247 E8
Kalat Pakistan 29°8N 66°31E 240 C2
Kalāteh Iran 36°33N 55°41E 247 B7
Kalāteh-ye Ganj Iran 27°31N 57°55E 247 E8
Kalathos Greece 36°9N 28°8E 206 E12
Kalatungan, Mt. Phil. 7°54N 124°50E 233 H5
Kalaupapa U.S.A. 21°12N 156°59W 302 B5
Kalaupapa △ U.S.A. 21°10N 156°59W 302 B5
Kalaus → Russia 45°40N 44°7E 191 H7
Kalavrita Greece 38°3N 22°8E 204 C4
Kalaw Burma 20°38N 96°34E 241 E6
Kalawao County U.S.A. 21°11N 156°58W 302 B5
Kalbā U.A.E. 25°5N 56°22E 247 E8
Kalbadevi Mumbai, India 130 b2
Kalbān Oman 20°18N 58°38E 249 B7
Kalbarri Australia 27°40S 114°10E 279 E1
Kalbarri △ Australia 27°51S 114°30E 279 E1
Kalburgi = Gulbarga India 17°20N 76°50E 244 F3
Kalce Slovenia 45°54N 14°13E 176 F8
Kaldrananes Iceland 65°45N 21°25W 158 D3
Kale Antalya, Turkey 36°14N 30°0E 205 E12
Kale Denizli, Turkey 37°27N 28°49E 205 D10
Kalecik Turkey 40°4N 33°26E 212 B5
Kalegauk Kyun Burma 15°33N 97°35E 236 E1
Kalehe Dem. Rep. of the Congo 2°6S 28°50E 268 C2
Kalema Tanzania 1°12S 31°55E 268 C3
Kalemie Dem. Rep. of the Congo 5°55S 29°9E 268 D2
Kalemyo Burma 23°11N 94°4E 241 D5
Kalety Poland 50°35N 18°52E 185 H5
Kalewa Burma 23°10N 94°15E 241 D5
Kaleybar Iran 38°47N 47°2E 213 C12
Kálfafell Iceland 63°57N 17°41W 155 D9
Kalgan = Zhangjiakou China 40°48N 114°55E 226 D8
Kalghatgi India 15°11N 74°58E 245 G2
Kalgoorlie-Boulder Australia 30°40S 121°22E 279 F3
Kalhovd Norway 60°4N 8°21E 164 D5
Kali → India 27°6N 79°55E 243 F8
Kali Sindh → India 25°32N 76°17E 242 G6
Kaliakra, Nos Bulgaria 43°21N 28°30E 203 C12
Kalianda Indonesia 5°50S 105°45E 234 D3
Kalibo Phil. 11°43N 122°22E 233 F4
Kaliganj Bangla. 22°25N 89°8E 241 D2
Kalihi U.S.A. 21°20N 157°53W 302 K14
Kalihi Valley U.S.A. 21°20N 157°52W 302 K14
Kalima Dem. Rep. of the Congo 2°33S 26°32E 268 C2
Kalimantan Indonesia 0°0 114°0E 235 C4
Kalimantan Barat □ Indonesia 0°0 110°30E 235 C4
Kalimantan Selatan □ Indonesia 2°30S 115°30E 235 C5
Kalimantan Tengah □ Indonesia 2°0S 113°30E 235 C4
Kalimantan Timur □ Indonesia 1°30N 116°30E 235 B5
Kálimnos Greece 37°0N 27°0E 205 D8
Kalimpong India 27°4N 88°35E 241 B2
Kalinadi → India 14°50N 74°7E 245 G2
Kalinga □ Phil. 17°30N 121°20E 232 C3
Kalinikinsk Russia 51°29N 44°28E 216 B2
Kalinin = Tver Russia 56°55N 35°59E 188 D8
Kaliningrad Russia 54°42N 20°32E 184 D7
Kaliningrad ✕ (KGD) Russia 54°45N 20°33E 184 D7
Kalininsk = Petrozavodsk Russia 61°41N 34°20E 188 B8
Kalininsk Russia 51°30N 44°40E 190 E7
Kalinkavichy Belarus 52°12N 29°20E 177 B15
Kalinkovichi = Kalinkavichy Belarus 52°12N 29°20E 177 B15
Kalinovik Bos.-H. 43°31N 18°25E 202 C2
Kalipetrovo Bulgaria 44°5N 27°14E 203 B11
Kalipur India 22°40N 88°17E 124 A1
Kalirachi Greece 40°40N 24°35E 203 F8
Kaliro Uganda 0°56N 33°30E 268 B3
Kalispell U.S.A. 48°12N 114°19W 304 B6
Kalisz Poland 51°45N 18°8E 185 G5
Kalisz Pomorski Poland 53°17N 15°55E 185 E2
Kalithea Greece 37°56N 23°43E 112 B2
Kaliua Tanzania 5°5S 31°48E 268 D3
Kaliveli Tank India 12°5N 79°50E 245 H4
Kalivia Thorikou Greece 37°50N 23°55E 204 D5
Kalix = Kalixälven → Sweden 65°50N 23°11E 160 D20
Kalix Sweden 65°53N 23°12E 160 D20
Kalixälven → Sweden 65°50N 23°11E 160 D20
Kalka India 30°46N 76°57E 242 D7
Kalkaji India 28°32N 77°12E 120 B2
Kalkali Ghat India 24°36N 92°20E 241 C4
Kalkan Turkey 36°15N 29°23E 205 E11
Kalkarindji Australia 17°30S 130°47E 278 C5
Kalkaska U.S.A. 44°44N 85°11W 309 C11
Kalkfeld Namibia 20°57S 16°14E 270 B2
Kalkfontein Botswana 22°4S 20°57E 270 B3
Kalkım Turkey 39°48N 27°13E 205 B9
Kalkrand Namibia 24°1S 17°35E 270 B2
Kallakkurichchi India 11°44N 79°1E 245 J4
Kållandsö Sweden 58°40N 13°5E 163 F7
Kallavesi Finland 62°58N 27°30E 160 E22
Källby Sweden 58°30N 13°8E 163 F7
Kållered Sweden 57°32N 12°4E 163 G6
Kallidaikurichi India 8°38N 77°31E 245 K3
Kallies = Kalisz Pomorski Poland 53°17N 15°55E 185 E2
Kallimasia Greece 38°18N 26°6E 205 C8
Kallinge Sweden 56°15N 15°18E 163 H9
Kallmet Albania 41°51N 19°41E 202 E3
Kallsjön Sweden 63°38N 13°0E 160 E15
Kalmalo Nigeria 13°40N 5°20E 263 C6
Kalmanstunga Iceland 64°44N 20°48W 155 D3
Kalmar Sweden 56°40N 16°20E 163 H10
Kalmar län □ Sweden 57°25N 16°15E 163 G10
Kalmar sund Sweden 56°40N 16°25E 163 H10
Kalmunai Sri Lanka 7°25N 81°49E 245 L5
Kalmykia □ Russia 46°5N 46°1E 191 G8
Kalna India 23°13N 88°25E 243 H13
Kalnai India 22°46N 83°30E 243 H10
Kalni → Bangla. 24°21N 91°13E 241 C3
Kalo Papua N. G. 10°1S 147°48E 286 F4
Kalo Nero Greece 37°20N 21°38E 204 D3
Kalocsa Hungary 46°32N 19°0E 182 D4
Kalofer Bulgaria 42°37N 24°59E 203 D8
Kalohi Channel U.S.A. 21°0N 157°0W 302 C5
Kalokhorio Cyprus 34°51N 33°2E 207 F9
Kaloko Dem. Rep. of the Congo 6°47S 25°48E 265 D5
Kaloko-Honokōhau △ U.S.A. 19°40N 156°1W 302 D5
Kalol Gujarat, India 22°37N 73°31E 242 H5
Kalol Gujarat, India 23°15N 72°33E 242 H5
Kalolimnos Greece 37°4N 27°5E 205 D9
Kalomo Zambia 17°0S 26°30E 269 F2
Kalona U.S.A. 41°29N 91°43W 310 C5
Kaloni Greece 39°14N 26°12E 205 B8
Kaloni, Kolpos Greece 39°10N 26°10E 205 B8
Kalookan = Caloocan Phil. 14°39N 120°58E 127 B1
Kalpeni I. India 10°5N 73°38E 245 J1
Kalpi India 26°8N 79°47E 243 F8
Kalpitiya Sri Lanka 8°14N 79°46E 245 K4
Kalputhi I. India 10°49N 72°10E 245 J1
Kalrayan Hills India 11°45N 78°40E 245 J4
Kalsubai India 19°35N 73°45E 244 E1
Kaltag U.S.A. 64°20N 158°43W 303 D8
Kaltern = Caldaro Italy 46°25N 11°14E 199 B8
Kaltukatjara Australia 24°52S 129°5E 279 D4
Kaltungo Nigeria 9°48N 11°19E 263 D7
Kalu Pakistan 25°5N 67°39E 242 G2
Kaluga Russia 54°35N 36°10E 188 E9
Kaluga □ Russia 54°15N 34°50E 188 E8
Kalulong, Bukit Malaysia 3°14N 114°39E 235 B4
Kalulushi Zambia 12°50S 28°3E 269 E2
Kalumburu Australia 13°55S 126°35E 278 B4
Kalumburu ◎ Australia 14°17S 126°38E 278 B4
Kalundborg Denmark 55°41N 11°5E 163 J5
Kalush Ukraine 49°3N 24°23E 177 D13
Kałuszyn Poland 52°13N 21°52E 185 F8
Kalutara Sri Lanka 6°35N 80°0E 245 L5
Kalvåg Norway 61°46N 4°51E 164 C1
Kalvarija Lithuania 54°24N 23°14E 184 D10
Kalvebod Fælled Denmark 55°35N 12°33E 118 B3
Kalveboderne Denmark 55°37N 12°31E 118 B3
Kalwakurti India 16°41N 78°30E 244 F4
Kalya Russia 60°15N 59°59E 186 B10
Kalyan Maharashtra, India 20°30N 74°3E 244 D2
Kalyan Maharashtra, India 19°15N 73°9E 244 E1
Kalyandurg India 14°33N 77°6E 245 G3
Kalyani India 17°52N 76°57E 244 F3
Kalyansingapuram India 19°30N 83°19E 244 E6
Kalyazin Russia 57°15N 37°55E 188 D9
Kam Albania 42°17N 20°18E 202 D4
Kam → Nigeria 8°15N 1°10E 263 D7
Kama Burma 19°1N 95°4E 241 F5
Kama Dem. Rep. of the Congo 3°30S 27°5E 268 C2
Kama → Russia 55°45N 52°0E 186 C9
Kama Iwa Iwo Jima 24°47N 141°17E 288 b
Kamachumu Tanzania 1°37S 31°37E 268 C3
Kamae Japan 32°48N 131°56E 222 E3
Kamaing Burma 25°26N 96°35E 241 C6
Kamaishi Japan 39°16N 141°53E 220 E10
Kamakou U.S.A. 21°7N 156°52W 302 B5
Kamakura Japan 35°19N 139°33E 223 B11
Kamalapurum India 14°35N 78°39E 245 G4
Kamalété Gabon 0°43S 11°49E 264 C2
Kamalia Pakistan 30°44N 72°42E 242 D5
Kaman India 27°39N 77°16E 242 F6
Kaman Turkey 39°22N 33°44E 212 C5
Kamana Dem. Rep. of the Congo 5°59S 24°58E 265 D4
Kamananui → U.S.A. 21°38N 158°4W 302 J13
Kamanjab Namibia 19°35S 14°51E 270 A2
Kamapanda Zambia 12°5S 24°0E 269 E1
Kamara Mali 14°38N 9°23W 262 C3
Kamarān Yemen 15°21N 42°35E 248 D3
Kamareddi India 18°19N 78°21E 244 E4
Kamarhati India 22°40N 88°23E 124 A2
Kamata Japan 35°33N 139°43E 140 B3
Kamativi Zimbabwe 18°20S 27°6E 270 A4
Kamba Dem. Rep. of the Congo 4°0S 22°22E 265 C4
Kamba Nigeria 11°50N 3°45E 263 C5
Kambalda West Australia 31°10S 121°37E 279 F3
Kambam India 9°45N 77°16E 245 K3
Kambangan, Nusa Indonesia 7°40S 108°10E 235 D3
Kambar Pakistan 27°37N 68°1E 242 F3
Kambarka Russia 56°15N 54°11E 186 C9
Kambia S. Leone 9°3N 12°53W 262 D2
Kambolé Togo 8°43N 1°39E 263 D5
Kambolé Zambia 8°47S 30°48E 269 D3
Kambos Cyprus 35°2N 32°44E 207 E8
Kambove Dem. Rep. of the Congo 10°51S 26°33E 269 E2
Kambuie Dem. Rep. of the Congo 6°59S 22°19E 265 D4
Kambwata Zambia 14°3S 23°43E 265 E4
Kamchatka, Poluostrov Russia 57°0N 160°0E 215 D17
Kamchatka Pen. = Kamchatka, Poluostrov Russia 57°0N 160°0E 215 D17
Kamchiya → Bulgaria 43°4N 27°44E 203 C11
Kame Ruins Zimbabwe 20°7S 28°25E 269 G2
Kameari Japan 35°45N 139°50E 140 A4
Kameda-Hantō Japan 41°50N 141°0E 220 D10
Kameido Japan 35°42N 139°50E 140 A4
Kamen Russia 53°50N 81°30E 217 B10
Kamen-Rybolov Russia 44°46N 132°2E 220 B5
Kamende Dem. Rep. of the Congo 6°26S 24°35E 265 D4
Kamenica Serbia 43°27N 22°27E 202 C6
Kamenica Serbia 44°25N 19°40E 202 B3
Kamenice nad Lipou Czech Rep. 49°18N 15°2E 180 B8
Kamenjak, Rt Croatia 44°47N 13°55E 199 D10
Kamenka = Kamyanka Ukraine 49°3N 32°6E 189 H7
Kamenka Kazakhstan 51°7N 50°19E 190 E10
Kamenka Arkhangelsk, Russia 65°58N 44°0E 186 A7
Kamenka Penza, Russia 53°10N 44°5E 190 D6
Kamenka Voronezh, Russia 50°47N 39°20E 189 G10
Kamenka Bugskaya = Kamyanka-Buzka Ukraine 50°8N 24°16E 177 C13
Kamenka Dneprovskaya = Kamyanka-Dniprovska Ukraine 47°29N 34°28E 189 J8
Kamenka-Shevchenkovskaya = Kamyanka-Buzka Ukraine 50°8N 24°16E 177 C13
Kamennomostskiy Russia 44°18N 40°13E 191 H5
Kameno Bulgaria 42°34N 27°18E 203 D11
Kamenolomini Russia 47°40N 40°14E 191 G5
Kamensk-Shakhtinskiy Russia 48°23N 40°20E 191 F5
Kamensk Uralskiy Russia 56°25N 62°2E 214 D7
Kamenskaya = Kamensk-Shakhtinskiy Russia 48°23N 40°20E 191 F5
Kamenskiy Russia 50°48N 45°25E 190 E7
Kamenskoye = Dniprodzerzhynsk Ukraine 48°32N 34°37E 189 H8
Kamenskoye Russia 62°45N 165°30E 215 C17
Kamenyak Bulgaria 43°24N 26°57E 203 C10
Kamenz Germany 51°15N 14°5E 178 D10
Kameoka Japan 35°0N 135°35E 223 C7
Kamet India 30°55N 79°35E 243 D8
Kameyama Japan 34°51N 136°27E 223 C8
Kami-Itabashi Japan 35°45N 139°40E 140 A3
Kami-Jima Japan 32°27N 130°20E 222 E2
Kami-Koshiki-Jima Japan 31°50N 129°52E 222 F1
Kamiagata Japan 34°40N 129°24E 222 C1
Kamiah U.S.A. 46°14N 116°2W 304 C5
Kamień Krajeński Poland 53°32N 17°32E 184 E4
Kamień Pomorski Poland 53°57N 14°43E 184 E1
Kamienna → Poland 51°6N 21°47E 185 G8
Kamienna Góra Poland 50°47N 16°2E 185 H3
Kamieńsk Poland 51°12N 19°29E 185 G6
Kamieskroon S. Africa 30°9S 17°56E 270 D2
Kamikatazawa Japan 35°39N 139°36E 140 B2
Kamilukuak L. Canada 62°22N 101°40W 297 A8
Kamin-Kashyrskyy Ukraine 51°39N 24°56E 177 C13
Kamina Dem. Rep. of the Congo 8°45S 25°0E 265 D5
Kaminak L. Canada 62°10N 95°0W 297 A10
Kaminoyama Japan 38°9N 140°17E 220 E10
Kamioka Japan 36°25N 137°15E 223 A9
Kamiros Greece 36°20N 27°56E 206 E11
Kamishak Bay U.S.A. 59°15N 153°45W 303 G9
Kamisu Japan 35°50N 140°45E 223 B12
Kamitsuruma Japan 35°30N 139°26E 140 B1
Kamitsushima Japan 34°50N 129°25E 222 C1
Kamituga Dem. Rep. of the Congo 3°2S 28°10E 268 C2
Kamla → India 25°35N 86°36E 243 G12
Kamloops Canada 50°40N 120°20W 296 C4
Kamnik Slovenia 46°14N 14°37E 199 B11
Kamo Armenia 40°21N 45°7E 191 K7
Kamo Japan 37°39N 139°3E 220 F9
Kamo N.Z. 35°42S 174°20E 284 B3
Kamoa Mts. Guyana 1°30N 59°0W 329 C6
Kamogawa Japan 35°5N 140°5E 223 B12
Kamojima Japan 34°4N 134°21E 222 C6
Kamoke Pakistan 32°4N 74°4E 242 C6
Kamo'oloa U.S.A. 21°34N 158°7W 302 J13
Kamoshida Japan 35°33N 139°31E 140 B2
Kamp → Austria 48°23N 15°42E 180 C8
Kampala Uganda 0°20N 32°30E 268 B3
Kampar Malaysia 4°18N 101°9E 237 K3
Kampar → Indonesia 0°30N 103°8E 234 B2
Kampen Neths. 52°33N 5°53E 170 B5
Kamphaeng Phet Thailand 16°28N 99°30E 236 D2
Kampinoski △ Poland 52°21N 20°40E 185 F7

Kampolombo, L. *Zambia* 11°37S 29°42E **269** E2
Kampong Cham *Cambodia* 12°0N 105°30E **237** G5
Kampong Chhnang *Cambodia* 12°20N 104°35E **237** F5
Kampong Landang *Singapore* 1°20N 103°55E **138** A3
Kampong Pengerang *Malaysia* 1°22N 104°7E **237** d
Kampong Punggai *Malaysia* 1°27N 104°18E **237** d
Kampong Saom *Cambodia* 10°38N 103°30E **237** G4
Kampong Saom, Chaak *Cambodia* 10°50N 103°32E **237** G4
Kampong Tanjong Langsat *Malaysia* 1°28N 104°1E **237** d
Kampong Tanjong Penjuru *Singapore* 1°18N 103°45E **138** B2
Kampong Telok Ramunia *Malaysia* 1°22N 104°15E **237** d
Kampot *Cambodia* 10°36N 104°10E **237** G5
Kampsville *U.S.A.* 39°18N 90°37W **310** E6
Kampti *Burkina Faso* 10°7N 3°25W **262** C4
Kampuchea = Cambodia ■ *Asia* 12°15N 105°0E **236** F5
Kampung Air Putih *Malaysia* 4°15N 103°10E **237** K4
Kampung Bali *Indonesia* 6°11S 106°48E **122** B1
Kampung Jerangau *Malaysia* 4°50N 103°10E **237** K4
Kampung Raja *Malaysia* 5°45N 102°35E **237** K4
Kampungbaru = Tolitoli *Indonesia* 1°5N 120°50E **231** D6
Kamrau, Teluk *Indonesia* 3°30S 133°36E **231** E8
Kamsack *Canada* 51°34N 101°54W **297** C8
Kamsar *Guinea* 10°40N 14°36W **262** C2
Kamskoye Ustye *Russia* 55°10N 49°20E **190** C9
Kamskoye Vdkhr. *Russia* 58°41N 56°7E **186** C10
Kamsuuma *Somali Rep.* 0°15N 42°46E **267** D5
Kamthi *India* 21°9N 79°19E **244** D4
Kamuchawie L. *Canada* 56°18N 101°59W **297** B8
Kamuela *U.S.A.* 20°1N 155°41W **302** C6
Kamui-Misaki *Japan* 43°20N 140°21E **220** C10
Kamyanets-Podilskyy *Ukraine* 48°45N 26°40E **183** B11
Kamyanka *Ukraine* 49°3N 32°6E **189** H7
Kamyanka-Buzka *Ukraine* 50°8N 24°16E **177** C13
Kamyanka-Dniprovska *Ukraine* 47°29N 34°28E **189** J8
Kamyanyets *Belarus* 52°23N 23°49E **185** F10
Kamyanyuki *Belarus* 52°32N 23°49E **185** F10
Kāmyārān *Iran* 34°47N 46°56E **213** E12
Kamyshin *Russia* 50°10N 45°24E **190** E7
Kamyzyak *Russia* 46°4N 48°10E **191** G9
Kan = Gan Jiang → *China* 29°15N 116°0E **229** C11
Kan *Burma* 22°25N 94°5E **241** D5
Kan *Sudan* 9°1N 31°47E **257** F3
Kanaaupscow → *Canada* 54°2N 76°30W **298** B4
Kanab *U.S.A.* 37°3N 112°32W **305** H7
Kanab Cr. → *U.S.A.* 36°24N 112°38W **305** H7
Kanacea *Lau Group, Fiji* 17°15S 179°6W **287** A3
Kanacea *Taveuni, Fiji* 16°59S 179°56E **287** A2
Kanaga I. *U.S.A.* 51°45N 177°22W **303** L3
Kanagawa ◻ *Japan* 35°20N 139°20E **223** B11
Kanagi *Japan* 40°54N 140°27E **220** D10
Kanairiktok → *Canada* 55°2N 60°18W **299** A7
Kanakanak *U.S.A.* 59°0N 158°32W **303** G8
Kanakapura *India* 12°33N 77°28E **245** H3
Kanalia *Greece* 39°30N 22°53E **204** B4
Kanamori *Japan* 35°31N 139°27E **140** B1
Kananga *Dem. Rep. of the Congo* 5°55S 22°18E **265** D4
Kanangra-Boyd △ *Australia* 33°57S 150°15E **283** B9
Kanash *Russia* 55°30N 47°32E **190** C8
Kanaskat *U.S.A.* 47°19N 121°54W **306** C5
Kanastraíon, Ákra = Paliouri, Akra *Greece* 39°57N 23°45E **202** G7
Kanawha → *U.S.A.* 38°50N 82°9W **309** F12
Kanazawa *Japan* 36°30N 136°38E **223** A8
Kanbalu *Burma* 23°12N 95°31E **241** D5
Kanchanaburi *Thailand* 14°2N 99°31E **236** E2
Kanchenjunga *Nepal* 27°50N 88°10E **243** F13
Kanchipuram *India* 12°52N 79°45E **245** H4
Kanchow = Ganzhou *China* 25°51N 114°56E **229** E10
Kańczuga *Poland* 49°59N 22°25E **185** J9
Kanda *Tokyo, Japan* **140** a5
Kanda Kanda *Dem. Rep. of the Congo* 6°52S 23°48E **265** D4
Kandagach = Qandyaghash *Kazakhstan* 49°28N 57°25E **187** E10
Kandaghat *India* 30°59N 77°7E **242** D7
Kandahār *Kandahār, Afghan.* 31°32N 65°43E **240** C2
Kandahar *India* 18°52N 77°12E **244** E3
Kandahār ◻ *Afghan.* 31°0N 65°0E **240** C2
Kandala *Dem. Rep. of the Congo* 6°20S 19°40E **265** D3
Kandalaksha *Russia* 67°9N 32°30E **160** C25
Kandalakshskiy Zaliv *Russia* 66°0N 35°0E **186** A6
Kandang *Indonesia* 3°3N 97°19E **234** B1
Kandangan *Indonesia* 2°50S 115°20E **235** C5
Kandanos *Greece* 35°19N 23°44E **207** E4
Kandava *Latvia* 57°2N 22°46E **184** A9
Kandavu = Kadavu *Fiji* 19°0S 178°15E **287** B2
Kandavu Passage = Kadavu Passage *Fiji* 18°45S 178°0E **287** B2
Kandep *Papua N. G.* 5°54S 143°32E **286** C2
Kandhkot *Pakistan* 28°16N 69°8E **242** E3
Kandhla *India* 29°18N 77°19E **242** E7
Kandi *Benin* 11°7N 2°55E **263** C5
Kandi *India* 23°58N 88°5E **243** H13
Kandiaro *Pakistan* 27°4N 68°13E **242** F3
Kandila *Arkadia, Greece* 37°46N 22°22E **204** D4
Kandila *Etoloakarnania, Greece* 38°42N 20°56E **207** B2
Kandilli *Turkey* 41°4N 29°3E **122** B2
Kandıra *Turkey* 41°4N 30°9E **212** B4
Kandla *India* 23°0N 70°10E **242** H4
Kandor, O. → *Chad* 17°13N 20°52E **259** E4
Kandos *Australia* 32°45S 149°58E **283** B8
Kandreho *Madag.* 17°29S 46°6E **272** B2
Kandrian *Papua N. G.* 6°14S 149°37E **286** D5
Kandy *Sri Lanka* 7°18N 80°43E **245** L5
Kane *U.S.A.* 41°40N 78°49W **312** E6
Kane Basin *Greenland* 79°1N 70°0W **154** B4
Kaneilio Pt. *U.S.A.* 21°27N 158°12W **302** K13
Kanel *Senegal* 15°30N 13°18W **262** B2
Kanem ◻ *Chad* 15°0N 16°0E **259** F3
Kāne'ohe *U.S.A.* 21°25N 157°48W **302** K14
Kāne'ohe B. *U.S.A.* 21°30N 157°50W **302** K14
Kaneohe Marine Corps Air Station *U.S.A.* 21°27N 157°46W **302** K14
Kanevskaya *Russia* 46°3N 38°57E **191** G4
Kanfanar *Croatia* 45°7N 13°50E **199** C10
Kang *Botswana* 23°41S 22°50E **270** B3
Kangaamiut *Greenland* 65°50N 53°20W **154** D5
Kangaatsiaq *Greenland* 68°18N 53°28W **154** D5
Kangaba *Mali* 11°56N 8°25W **262** C3
Kangal *Turkey* 39°14N 37°23E **212** C7
Kangān *Fārs, Iran* 27°50N 52°3E **247** E7
Kangān *Hormozgān, Iran* 25°48N 57°28E **247** E8
Kangar *Malaysia* 6°27N 100°12E **237** J3
Kangaré *Mali* 11°36N 8°4W **262** C3
Kangaroo I. *Australia* 35°45S 137°0E **282** C2
Kangaroo Mts. *Australia* 23°29S 141°51E **280** C3
Kangasala *Finland* 61°28N 24°4E **188** B3
Kangāvar *Iran* 34°40N 48°0E **213** E12
Kangding *China* 30°2N 101°57E **228** B3
Kangdong *N. Korea* 39°9N 126°5E **224** C3
Kangean, Kepulauan *Indonesia* 6°55S 115°23E **235** D5
Kangean Is. = Kangean, Kepulauan *Indonesia* 6°55S 115°23E **235** D5
Kangen → *Sudan* 6°47N 33°9E **257** F3
Kangerdlugssuak *Greenland* 68°10N 32°20W **154** D7
Kangerluarsoruseq *Greenland* 63°45N 51°27W **154** E5
Kangerluarsoruset = Kangerluarsoruseq *Greenland* 63°45N 51°27W **154** E5
Kangerlussuaq *Greenland* 66°59N 50°40W **154** D5
Kangertittivaq = Scoresby Sund *Greenland* 70°28N 21°46W **154** C8
Kanggye *N. Korea* 41°0N 126°35E **224** B3
Kanghsi *Taiwan* 23°34N 120°8E **225** C2
Kangikajik *Greenland* 70°7N 22°0W **154** C8
Kangilinnguit *Greenland* 61°20N 47°57W **154** E6
Kangiqliniq = Rankin Inlet *Canada* 62°30N 93°0W **294** E13
Kangiqsualujjuaq *Canada* 58°30N 65°59W **295** F18
Kangiqsujuaq *Canada* 61°30N 72°0W **295** E17
Kangiqtugaapik = Clyde River *Canada* 70°30N 68°30W **295** C18
Kangirsuk *Canada* 60°0N 70°0W **295** F18
Kangkar Chemaran *Malaysia* 1°34N 104°12E **237** d
Kangkar Sungai Tiram *Malaysia* 1°35N 103°55E **237** d
Kangkar Teberau *Malaysia* 1°32N 103°51E **237** d
Kango *Gabon* 0°11N 10°5E **264** B2
Kangoku Iwa *Iwo Jima* 24°48N 141°17E **288** b
Kangoya *Dem. Rep. of the Congo* 9°55S 22°48E **265** D4
Kangping *China* 42°43N 123°18E **227** C12
Kangpokpi *India* 25°8N 93°58E **241** C4
Kangra *India* 32°6N 76°16E **242** C7
Kangrinboqe Feng *China* 31°0N 81°25E **243** D9
Kangshan *Taiwan* 22°48N 120°17E **225** D2
Kangto *China* 27°50N 92°35E **241** B4
Kangtzu *Taiwan* 22°8N 120°52E **225** D2
Kangwon-do ◻ *N. Korea* 38°47N 127°35E **224** C3
Kangyidaung *Burma* 16°56N 94°54E **241** G5
Kanha △ *India* 22°15N 80°40E **243** H9
Kanhan → *India* 21°4N 79°34E **244** D4
Kanhangad *India* 12°21N 74°58E **245** H2
Kanhar → *India* 24°28N 83°8E **243** G10
Kanheri *India* 19°13N 72°50E **244** E1
Kani *Sagaing, Burma* 23°52N 95°22E **241** D5
Kani *Sagaing, Burma* 22°26N 94°51E **241** D5
Kani *Ivory C.* 8°29N 6°36W **262** D3
Kani *Japan* 35°25N 137°7E **223** B9
Kani-Keli *Mayotte* 12°57S 45°6E **272** b
Kaniama *Dem. Rep. of the Congo* 7°30S 24°12E **265** D4
Kaniapiskau = Caniapiscau → *Canada* 56°40N 69°30W **299** A6
Kaniapiskau, L. = Caniapiscau, L. *Canada* 54°10N 69°55W **299** B6
Kaniere, L. *N.Z.* 42°50S 171°10E **285** C6
Kanif *Micronesia* 9°31N 138°5E **287** R16
Kanigiri *India* 15°24N 79°31E **245** G4
Kanin, Poluostrov *Russia* 68°0N 45°0E **186** A8
Kanin Nos, Mys *Russia* 68°39N 43°32E **186** A7
Kanin Pen. = Kanin, Poluostrov *Russia* 68°0N 45°0E **186** A8
Kaninë *Albania* 40°23N 19°30E **202** F3
Kaniva *Australia* 36°22S 141°18E **282** D4
Kanjiža *Serbia* 46°3N 20°4E **182** D5
Kanjut Sar *Pakistan* 36°7N 75°25E **243** A6
Kankaanpää *Finland* 61°44N 22°50E **188** B2
Kankakee *U.S.A.* 41°7N 87°52W **311** C9
Kankakee → *U.S.A.* 41°23N 88°15W **311** C8
Kankan *Guinea* 10°23N 9°15W **262** C3
Kankendy = Xankändi *Azerbaijan* 39°52N 46°49E **213** C12
Kanker *India* 20°10N 81°40E **244** D5
Kankesanturai *Sri Lanka* 9°49N 80°2E **245** K5
Kankossa *Mauritania* 15°54N 11°31W **262** B2
Kankroli *India* 25°4N 73°53E **242** G5
Kankurgachi *India* 22°34N 88°23E **124** B2
Kanlıca *Turkey* 41°5N 29°3E **122** B2
Kanmaw Kyun *Burma* 11°40N 98°28E **237** G2
Kanmuri-Yama *Japan* 34°30N 132°4E **222** C4
Kannabe *Japan* 34°32N 133°23E **222** C5
Kannapolis *U.S.A.* 35°30N 80°37W **315** D14
Kannauj *India* 27°3N 79°56E **243** F8
Kanniyakumari *India* 8°5N 77°34E **245** K3
Kannur = Cannanore *India* 11°53N 75°27E **245** J2
Kannyakumari *India* 8°3N 77°40E **245** K3
Kano *Nigeria* 12°2N 8°30E **263** C6
Kano ◻ *Nigeria* 11°30N 8°30E **263** C6
Kanonerskiy, Ostrov *Russia* 59°53N 30°13E **137** B1
Kan'onji *Japan* 34°7N 133°39E **222** C5
Kanoroba *Ivory C.* 9°7N 6°8W **262** D3
Kanowha *U.S.A.* 42°57N 93°47W **310** B3
Kanowit *Malaysia* 2°14N 112°20E **235** B4
Kanoya *Japan* 31°25N 130°50E **222** F2
Kanpetlet *Burma* 21°10N 93°59E **241** E4
Kanpur *India* 26°28N 80°20E **243** F9
Kansai Int. ✈ (KIX) *Japan* 34°27N 135°12E **133** B2
Kansas *U.S.A.* 39°33N 87°56W **311** E9
Kansas ◻ *U.S.A.* 38°30N 99°0W **308** F4
Kansas → *U.S.A.* 39°7N 94°37W **308** F6
Kansas City *Kans., U.S.A.* 39°7N 94°38W **310** E2
Kansas City *Mo., U.S.A.* 39°6N 94°35W **310** E2
Kansas City Int. ✈ (MCI) *U.S.A.* 39°18N 94°43W **310** E2
Kansenia *Dem. Rep. of the Congo* 10°20S 26°0E **269** E2
Kansk *Russia* 56°20N 95°37E **215** D10
Kansu = Gansu ◻ *China* 36°0N 104°0E **226** G3
Kantaphor *India* 22°35N 76°34E **242** H7
Kantchari *Burkina Faso* 12°37N 1°37E **263** C5
Kantché *Niger* 13°31N 8°30E **259** F1
Kanté *Togo* 9°57N 1°3E **263** D5
Kantemirovka *Russia* 49°43N 39°55E **189** H10
Kanth = Kąty Wrocławskie *Poland* 51°2N 16°45E **185** G3
Kantharalak *Thailand* 14°39N 104°39E **236** E5
Kanthi = Contai *India* 21°54N 87°46E **243** J12
Kantishna *U.S.A.* 63°31N 150°57W **303** E10
Kantishna → *U.S.A.* 64°45N 149°58W **303** D10
Kantli → *India* 28°20N 75°30E **242** E6
Kantō ◻ *Japan* 36°15N 139°30E **223** A11
Kantō-Sanchi *Japan* 35°59N 138°50E **223** B10
Kantu-long *Burma* 19°57N 97°36E **241** F6
Kanturk *Ireland* 52°11N 8°54W **166** D3
Kanuma *Japan* 36°34N 139°42E **223** A11
Kanus *Namibia* 27°50S 18°39E **270** C2
Kanuti Nat. Wildlife Refuge ⌓ *U.S.A.* 66°25N 151°50W **303** C10
Kanye *Botswana* 24°55S 25°28E **270** B4
Kanzaki → *Japan* 34°41N 135°24E **133** A1
Kanzenze *Dem. Rep. of the Congo* 10°30S 25°12E **265** E5
Kanzi, Ras *Tanzania* 7°1S 39°33E **268** D4
Kanzoni, Chissioua *Comoros Is.* 12°23S 43°40E **272** a
Kao *Tonga* 19°40S 175°1W **287** P13
Kao Phara *Thailand* 8°3N 98°22E **237** a
Kaohsiung *Taiwan* 22°35N 120°16E **225** D2
Kaohsung ◻ *Taiwan* 23°0N 120°35E **225** D2
Kaoka *Solomon Is.* 9°42S 160°43E **287** M11
Kaokaona = Kirakira *Solomon Is.* 10°27S 161°56E **287** N11
Kaokoveld *Namibia* 19°15S 14°30E **270** A1
Kaolack *Senegal* 14°5N 16°8W **262** C1
Kaolack ◻ *Senegal* 14°0N 15°15W **262** C1
Kaolan = Lanzhou *China* 36°1N 103°52E **226** F2
Kaolo *Solomon Is.* 8°24S 159°38E **287** M10
Kaoma *Zambia* 14°47S 24°48E **265** E4
Kaoshan *China* 44°38N 124°50E **227** B13
Kaoshu *Taiwan* 22°49N 120°36E **225** D2
Kaouar *Niger* 19°5N 12°52E **259** E2
Kaoyao = Zhaoqing *China* 23°0N 112°20E **229** F9
Kapa'a *U.S.A.* 22°5N 159°19W **302** A2
Kapadvanj *India* 23°5N 73°0E **242** H5
Kapagere *Papua N. G.* 9°46S 147°42E **286** E4
Kapahulu *U.S.A.* 21°16N 157°49W **302** K14
Kapaklı *Turkey* 41°19N 27°59E **203** E11
Kapali Carsi *Turkey* 41°1N 28°58E **122** B1
Kapalua *U.S.A.* 20°59N 156°39W **302** C5
Kapan *Armenia* 39°18N 46°27E **213** C12
Kapanga *Bandundu, Dem. Rep. of the Congo* 5°4S 16°58E **265** D3
Kapanga *Katanga, Dem. Rep. of the Congo* 8°30S 22°40E **265** D4
Kapapa I. *U.S.A.* 21°29N 157°48W **302** K14
Kapatagan *Phil.* 7°52N 123°44E **233** H4
Kapchagai = Qapshaghay *Kazakhstan* 43°51N 77°14E **217** D9
Kapchagaiskoye Vdkhr. = Qapshaghay Bögeni *Kazakhstan* 43°45N 77°50E **217** D9
Kapedo *Kenya* 1°10N 36°6E **268** B4
Kapela = Velika Kapela *Croatia* 45°10N 15°5E **199** C12
Kapellerfeld *Austria* 48°18N 16°29E **142** A2
Kapellskär *Sweden* 59°44N 19°2E **162** E13
Kapelo, Akra *Greece* 36°9N 23°3E **204** E5
Kapema *Dem. Rep. of the Congo* 10°45S 28°22E **269** E2
Kapenguria *Kenya* 1°14N 35°7E **268** B4
Kapfenberg *Austria* 47°26N 15°18E **180** D8
Kapı Dağı *Turkey* 40°28N 27°50E **203** F11
Kapia *Dem. Rep. of the Congo* 4°17S 19°46E **265** C3
Kapiri Mposhi *Zambia* 13°59S 28°43E **269** E2
Kāpīsā ◻ *Afghan.* 35°0N 69°20E **240** B3
Kapiskau → *Canada* 52°47N 81°55W **298** B3
Kapit *Malaysia* 2°0N 112°55E **235** B4
Kapiti I. *N.Z.* 40°50S 174°56E **284** G3
Kapka, Massif du *Chad* 15°7N 21°45E **259** E4
Kaplan *U.S.A.* 30°0N 92°17W **314** F8
Kaplice *Czech Rep.* 48°42N 14°30E **180** C7
Kapoe *Thailand* 9°34N 98°32E **237** H2
Kapoeta *Sudan* 4°50N 33°35E **257** G3
Kapoho *U.S.A.* 19°30N 154°50W **302** D7
Kapolei *U.S.A.* 21°19N 158°5W **302** K13
Kápolnásnyék *Hungary* 47°16N 18°41E **182** C3
Kapombo *Dem. Rep. of the Congo* 10°40S 23°30E **265** E4
Kaponga *N.Z.* 39°29S 174°9E **284** F3
Kapos → *Hungary* 46°44N 18°30E **182** D3
Kaposvár *Hungary* 46°25N 17°47E **182** D2
Káposztásmegyer *Hungary* 47°35N 19°6E **117** A2
Kapotnya *Russia* 55°39N 37°48E **129** C4
Kapowsin *U.S.A.* 46°59N 122°13W **306** D4
Kapp *Norway* 60°43N 10°52E **164** D7
Käppala *Sweden* 59°21N 18°13E **139** A3
Kappeln *Germany* 54°40N 9°55E **178** A5
Kappelshamn *Sweden* 57°52N 18°47E **163** G12
Kapps *Namibia* 22°32S 17°18E **270** B2
Kaprije *Croatia* 43°42N 15°43E **199** E12
Kapsabet *Kenya* 0°12N 35°6E **268** B4
Kapsan *N. Korea* 41°4N 128°19E **224** B4
Kapsukas = Marijampolė *Lithuania* 54°33N 23°19E **184** D10
Kaptai *Bangla.* 22°21N 92°17E **241** D4
Kaptai L. *Bangla.* 22°40N 92°20E **241** D4
Kapuas → *Kalimantan Barat, Indonesia* 0°25S 109°20E **235** C3
Kapuas → *Kalimantan Tengah, Indonesia* 3°1S 114°19E **235** C4
Kapuas Hulu, Pegunungan *Malaysia* 1°30N 113°30E **235** B4
Kapuas Hulu Ra. = Kapuas Hulu, Pegunungan *Malaysia* 1°30N 113°30E **235** B4
Kapuk *Indonesia* 6°7S 106°44E **122** A1
Kapulo *Dem. Rep. of the Congo* 8°18S 29°15E **269** D2
Kapunda *Australia* 34°20S 138°56E **282** C3
Kapuni *N.Z.* 39°29S 174°8E **284** F3
Kapurthala *India* 31°23N 75°25E **242** D6
Kapuskasing *Canada* 49°25N 82°30W **298** C3
Kapuskasing → *Canada* 49°49N 82°0W **298** C3
Kapustin Yar *Russia* 48°37N 45°40E **191** F7
Kaputar, Mt. *Australia* 30°15S 150°10E **281** E5
Kaputir *Kenya* 2°5N 35°28E **268** B4
Kapuvár *Hungary* 47°36N 17°1E **182** C2
Käpylä *Finland* 60°13N 24°57E **121** B2
Kara *Russia* 69°10N 65°0E **214** C7
Karā, W. → *Si. Arabia* 20°45N 41°42E **256** C5
Kara Ada *Turkey* 36°58N 27°28E **205** E9
Kara-Balta *Kyrgyzstan* 42°50N 73°49E **217** D8
Kara Bogaz Gol, Zaliv = Garabogazköl Aylagy *Turkmenistan* 41°0N 53°30E **187** F9
Kara Burun *Turkey* 36°32N 27°58E **205** E9
Kara-Kala = Garrygala *Turkmenistan* 38°31N 56°29E **247** B8
Kara Kalpak Republic = Qoraqalpoghistan ◻ *Uzbekistan* 43°0N 58°0E **216** D5
Kara-Köl *Kyrgyzstan* 41°40N 72°43E **217** D8
Kara Kum = Garagum *Turkmenistan* 39°30N 60°0E **247** B8
Kara-Saki *Japan* 34°41N 129°30E **222** C1
Kara Sea *Russia* 75°0N 70°0E **214** B8
Karaadilli *Turkey* 38°18N 30°37E **205** C12
Karabiğa *Turkey* 40°23N 27°17E **203** F11
Karabük *Turkey* 41°12N 32°37E **212** B5
Karabük ◻ *Turkey* 41°10N 32°30E **212** B5
Karaburun *Albania* 40°25N 19°20E **202** F3
Karaburun *Turkey* 38°41N 26°28E **205** C8
Karabutak = Qarabutaq *Kazakhstan* 50°0N 60°14E **216** C6
Karacabey *Turkey* 40°12N 28°21E **203** F12
Karacakılavuz *Turkey* 41°8N 27°21E **203** E11
Karacaköy *Turkey* 41°24N 28°22E **203** E12
Karaçal Tepesi *Turkey* 36°21N 32°38E **250** B3
Karacasu *Turkey* 37°43N 28°35E **205** D10
Karachala = Qaraçala *Azerbaijan* 39°45N 48°53E **191** L9
Karachayevsk *Russia* 43°50N 41°55E **191** J5
Karachev *Russia* 53°10N 35°5E **189** F8
Karachey-Cherkessia ◻ *Russia* 43°40N 41°30E **191** J5
Karachi *Pakistan* 24°50N 67°0E **123** A2
Karachi Int. ✈ (KHI) *Pakistan* 24°53N 67°9E **123** A2
Karad *India* 17°15N 74°10E **244** F2
Karadirek *Turkey* 38°34N 30°11E **205** C12
Karaga *Ghana* 9°58N 0°28W **263** D4
Karaganda = Qaraghandy *Kazakhstan* 49°50N 73°10E **217** C8
Karagayly = Qaraghayly *Kazakhstan* 49°26N 76°0E **214** E8
Karaginskiy, Ostrov *Russia* 58°45N 164°0E **215** D17
Karagiye, Vpadina *Kazakhstan* 43°27N 51°45E **187** F9
Karagiye Depression = Karagiye, Vpadina *Kazakhstan* 43°27N 51°45E **187** F9
Karagola Road *India* 25°29N 87°23E **243** G12
Karagüney Dağları *Turkey* 40°30N 34°40E **212** B6
Karahallı *Turkey* 38°21N 29°33E **205** C11
Kárahnjúkar *Iceland* 64°57N 15°46W **155** C11
Karaikal *India* 10°59N 79°50E **245** J4
Karaikkudi *India* 10°5N 78°45E **245** J4
Karaisali *Turkey* 37°16N 35°2E **212** D6
Karaiskakis *Greece* 38°35N 21°4E **207** B3
Karaitivu I. *Sri Lanka* 9°45N 79°52E **245** K4
Karaj *Iran* 35°48N 51°0E **247** C6
Karajarri ☼ *Australia* 19°0S 122°30E **278** C3
Karak *Malaysia* 3°25N 102°2E **237** L4
Karakalpakstan = Qoraqalpoghistan ◻ *Uzbekistan* 43°0N 58°0E **216** D5
Karakaya Barajı *Turkey* 38°31N 38°23E **213** C8
Karakelong *Indonesia* 4°35N 126°50E **231** D7
Karakitang *Indonesia* 3°14N 125°28E **231** D7
Karaklis = Vanadzor *Armenia* 40°48N 44°30E **191** K7
Karakoçan *Turkey* 38°57N 40°2E **213** C9
Karakol *Kyrgyzstan* 42°30N 78°20E **217** D9
Karakoram Pass *Asia* 35°33N 77°50E **243** B7
Karakoram Ra. *Pakistan* 35°30N 77°0E **243** B7
Karakul = Qarakol *Uzbekistan* 39°32N 63°50E **216** E6
Karakul *Tajikistan* 39°2N 73°33E **217** E8
Karakul, Ozero *Tajikistan* 39°5N 73°25E **217** E8
Karakurt *Turkey* 40°10N 42°37E **213** B10
Karakuwisa *Namibia* 18°56S 19°40E **270** A2
Karal *Chad* 12°50N 14°46E **259** F2
Karalon *Russia* 57°5N 115°50E **215** D12
Karama *Jordan* 31°57N 35°35E **251** G6
Karaman *Balıkesir, Turkey* 39°39N 28°0E **205** B9
Karaman *Konya, Turkey* 37°14N 33°13E **212** D5
Karaman ◻ *Turkey* 37°5N 33°15E **250** A4
Karamanlı *Turkey* 37°23N 29°47E **205** D11
Karamay *China* 45°30N 84°58E **217** C10
Karambu *Indonesia* 3°53S 116°6E **235** C5
Karamea *N.Z.* 41°14S 172°6E **285** B7
Karamea → *N.Z.* 41°13S 172°26E **285** B7
Karamea Bight *N.Z.* 41°22S 171°40E **285** B6
Karamian *Indonesia* 5°5S 114°40E **235** D4
Karamnasa → *India* 25°31N 83°52E **243** G10
Karamürsel *Turkey* 40°41N 29°36E **203** F13
Karān *Si. Arabia* 27°43N 49°49E **247** E6
Karand *Iran* 34°16N 46°15E **213** E12
Karangana *Mali* 12°15N 5°4W **262** C3
Karanganyar *Indonesia* 7°38S 109°37E **235** D3
Karangasem = Amlapura *Indonesia* 8°27S 115°37E **231** J18
Karanja *Maharashtra, India* 21°11N 78°24E **244** D4
Karanja *Maharashtra, India* 20°29N 77°31E **244** D3
Karanjia *India* 21°47N 85°58E **243** J11
Karankasso *Burkina Faso* 10°50N 3°53W **262** C4
Karaova *Turkey* 37°5N 27°40E **205** D9
Karapınar *Turkey* 37°41N 33°30E **212** D5
Karapiro *N.Z.* 37°53S 175°32E **284** D4
Karasburg *Namibia* 28°0S 18°44E **270** C2
Karasino *Russia* 66°50N 86°50E **214** C9
Karasjok *Norway* 69°27N 25°30E **160** B21
Karasu *Turkey* 41°4N 30°46E **212** B4
Karasu → *Antalya, Turkey* 36°18N 30°10E **205** E12
Karasu → *Hatay, Turkey* 36°20N 36°20E **250** B7
Karasubazar = Bilohirsk *Ukraine* 45°3N 34°35E **189** K8
Karasuk *Russia* 53°44N 78°2E **217** B9
Karasuyama *Japan* 36°39N 140°9E **223** A12
Karataş *Adana, Turkey* 36°36N 35°21E **250** B6
Karataş *Manisa, Turkey* 38°35N 28°16E **205** C10
Karataş Burnu *Turkey* 36°31N 35°24E **250** B6
Karatau, Khrebet = Qarataū *Kazakhstan* 43°30N 69°30E **217** D7
Karatax Shan *China* 35°57N 81°0E **217** E10
Karateki Shan *China* 40°40N 77°50E **217** D9
Karativu *Sri Lanka* 8°22N 79°47E **245** K4
Karatoprak *Turkey* 37°2N 27°15E **205** D9
Karatoya → *India* 24°7N 89°36E **241** C2
Karatsu *Japan* 33°26N 129°58E **222** D1
Karaul *Russia* 70°6N 82°15E **214** B9
Karauli *India* 26°30N 77°4E **242** F7
Karavastasë, L. e *Albania* 40°55N 19°30E **202** F3
Karavia *Greece* 36°49N 23°37E **204** E5
Karavostasi *Cyprus* 35°8N 32°50E **207** E8
Karawa *Dem. Rep. of the Congo* 3°18N 20°17E **264** B4
Karawang *Indonesia* 6°30S 107°15E **235** D3
Karawanken *Europe* 46°30N 14°40E **180** E7
Karayazı *Turkey* 39°41N 42°9E **213** C10
Karazhal = Qarazhal *Kazakhstan* 48°2N 70°49E **214** E8
Karbalā' *Iraq* 32°36N 44°3E **213** F11
Karbalā' ◻ *Iraq* 32°30N 43°50E **213** F10
Kårböle *Sweden* 61°59N 15°22E **162** C9
Karcag *Hungary* 47°19N 20°57E **182** C5
Karcha → *Pakistan* 34°45N 76°10E **243** B7
Karchana *India* 25°17N 81°56E **243** G9
Karczew *Poland* 52°5N 21°15E **185** F8
Kardakata *Greece* 38°17N 20°28E **207** C1
Kardam *Bulgaria* 43°45N 28°6E **203** C12
Kardamila *Greece* 38°35N 26°5E **205** C8
Kardamili *Greece* 36°53N 22°13E **204** E4
Kardeljovo = Ploče *Croatia* 43°4N 17°26E **199** E14
Karditsa *Greece* 39°23N 21°54E **204** B3
Karditsa ◻ *Greece* 39°15N 21°50E **204** B3
Kärdla *Estonia* 59°0N 22°45E **188** C2
Kardzhali = Kŭrdzhali *Bulgaria* 41°38N 25°21E **203** E9
Kareeberge *S. Africa* 30°59S 21°50E **270** D3
Kareha → *India* 25°44N 86°21E **243** G12
Kareima *Sudan* 18°30N 31°49E **256** D3
Karelia ◻ *Russia* 65°30N 32°30E **186** A5
Karelian Republic = Karelia ◻ *Russia* 65°30N 32°30E **186** A5
Karelo-Finnish S.S.R. = Karelia ◻ *Russia* 65°30N 32°30E **186** A5
Karema *Papua N. G.* 9°12S 147°18E **286** E4
Karen = Kayin ◻ *Burma* 18°0N 97°30E **241** G6
Karenni = Kayah ◻ *Burma* 19°15N 97°15E **241** F6
Karera *India* 25°32N 78°9E **242** G8
Kārevāndar *Iran* 27°53N 60°44E **247** E9
Kargasok *Russia* 59°3N 80°53E **214** D9
Kargat *Russia* 55°10N 80°15E **214** D9
Kargi *Eastern, Kenya* 2°31N 37°34E **268** B4
Kargı *Turkey* 41°11N 34°30E **212** B6
Kargil *India* 34°32N 76°12E **243** B7
Kargopol *Russia* 61°30N 38°58E **188** B10
Kargowa *Poland* 52°5N 15°51E **185** F2
Karguéri *Niger* 13°27N 10°30E **259** F2
Karhal *India* 27°1N 78°57E **243** F8
Karia *Greece* 38°45N 20°39E **207** B2
Karia ba Mohammed *Morocco* 34°22N 5°12W **260** B3
Karīān *Iran* 26°57N 57°14E **247** E8
Karianga *Madag.* 22°25S 47°22E **272** C2
Kariba *Zimbabwe* 16°28S 28°50E **269** F2
Kariba, L. *Zimbabwe* 16°40S 28°25E **269** F2
Kariba Dam *Zimbabwe* 16°30S 28°35E **269** F2
Kariba Gorge *Zambia* 16°30S 28°50E **269** F2
Karibib *Namibia* 22°0S 15°56E **270** B2
Karies *Greece* 40°14N 24°19E **203** F8
Karijini △ *Australia* 23°8S 118°15E **278** D2
Karikari, C. *N.Z.* 34°46S 173°24E **284** A2
Karimata, Kepulauan *Indonesia* 1°25S 109°0E **235** C3
Karimata, Selat *Indonesia* 2°0S 108°40E **235** C3
Karimata Is. = Karimata, Kepulauan *Indonesia* 1°25S 109°0E **235** C3
Karimganj *India* 24°52N 92°20E **241** C4
Karimnagar *India* 18°26N 79°10E **244** E4
Karimun, Pulau *Indonesia* 1°3N 103°22E **237** d
Karimun Kecil, Pulau *Indonesia* 1°8N 103°22E **237** d
Karimunjawa, Kepulauan *Indonesia* 5°50S 110°30E **235** D4
Karin *Bari, Somali Rep.* 10°59N 49°13E **267** B6
Karin *Woqooyi Galbeed, Somali Rep.* 10°50N 45°52E **267** B6
Karistos *Greece* 38°1N 24°29E **204** C6
Karīt *Iran* 33°29N 56°55E **247** C8
Kariya *Japan* 34°58N 137°1E **223** C9
Kariyangwe *Zimbabwe* 18°0S 27°38E **271** A4
Karjala *Finland* 62°0N 30°25E **188** A5
Karjat *India* 18°33N 75°0E **244** E2
Karkal *India* 13°15N 74°56E **245** H2
Karkar *Papua N. G.* 4°32S 145°57E **286** C3
Karkar I. *Papua N. G.* 4°40S 146°0E **286** C4
Karkaralinsk = Qarqaraly *Kazakhstan* 49°26N 75°30E **217** C9
Karkh *Iraq* 33°20N 44°22E **113** A2
Karkheh → *Iran* 31°2N 47°29E **246** D5
Karkinitska Zatoka *Ukraine* 45°56N 33°0E **189** K7
Karkinitskiy Zaliv = Karkinitska Zatoka *Ukraine* 45°56N 33°0E **189** K7
Karkuk = Kirkūk *Iraq* 35°30N 44°21E **213** E11
Karkur Tohl *Egypt* 22°5N 25°5E **256** C2
Karl Liebknecht *Russia* 51°40N 35°35E **189** G8
Karl-Marx-Stadt = Chemnitz *Germany* 50°51N 12°54E **178** E8
Karla, L. = Volvi, L. *Greece* 40°40N 23°34E **202** F7
Karlantijpa North ☼ *Australia* 19°27S 133°33E **278** C5
Karlantijpa South ☼ *Australia* 20°31S 133°9E **278** D5
Karleby = Kokkola *Finland* 63°50N 23°8E **160** E20
Karlholmsbruk *Sweden* 60°31N 17°37E **162** D11
Karlin *Czech Rep.* 50°5N 14°26E **135** B2
Karlino *Poland* 54°3N 15°53E **184** D2
Karlıova *Turkey* 39°17N 41°0E **213** C9
Karlivka *Ukraine* 49°29N 35°8E **189** H8
Karlobag *Croatia* 44°32N 15°5E **199** D12
Karlovac *Croatia* 45°31N 15°36E **199** C12
Karlovarský ◻ *Czech Rep.* 50°10N 12°50E **180** A5
Karlovasi *Greece* 37°45N 26°42E **205** D8
Karlovka = Karlivka *Ukraine* 49°29N 35°8E **189** H8
Karlovo *Bulgaria* 42°38N 24°47E **203** D8
Karlovo náměstí *Prague, Czech Rep.* **135** c1
Karlovy Vary *Czech Rep.* 50°13N 12°51E **180** A5
Karlowitz = Sremski Karlovci *Serbia* 45°12N 19°56E **182** E4
Karlowitz = Velké Karlovice *Czech Rep.* 49°20N 18°17E **181** B11
Karlsbad = Karlovy Vary *Czech Rep.* 50°13N 12°51E **180** A5
Karlsborg *Sweden* 58°33N 14°33E **163** F8
Karlsburg = Alba-Iulia *Romania* 46°8N 23°39E **183** D8
Karlsena, Mys *Russia* 77°0N 67°42E **214** B7
Karlsfeld *Germany* 48°13N 11°28E **131** A1
Karlshamn *Sweden* 56°10N 14°51E **163** H8
Karlshorst *Germany* 52°29N 13°31E **115** B4
Karlshus *Norway* 59°21N 10°52E **164** E7
Karlskoga *Sweden* 59°28N 14°33E **162** E8
Karlskrona *Sweden* 56°10N 15°35E **163** H9
Karlsplatz *Munich, Germany* **131** b1
Karlsruhe *Germany* 49°0N 8°23E **179** F4
Karlstad = Karlovac *Croatia* 45°31N 15°36E **199** C12
Karlstad *Sweden* 59°23N 13°30E **162** E7
Karlstad *Minn., U.S.A.* 48°35N 96°31W **308** A5
Karlstadt *Germany* 49°57N 9°47E **179** F5
Karluk *U.S.A.* 57°34N 154°28W **303** H9
Karlův most *Prague, Czech Rep.* **135** b1
Karma *Niger* 13°38N 1°52E **263** C5
Karmala *India* 18°25N 75°12E **244** E2
Karmi'el *Israel* 32°55N 35°18E **250** F6
Karmøy *Norway* 59°15N 5°15E **164** E2
Karnak *Egypt* 25°43N 32°39E **256** B3
Karnal *India* 29°42N 77°2E **242** E7
Karnali → *Nepal* 28°45N 81°16E **243** E9
Karnaphuli Res. = Kaptai L. *Bangla.* 22°40N 92°20E **241** D4
Karnaprayag *India* 30°16N 79°15E **243** D8
Karnataka ◻ *India* 13°15N 77°0E **245** H3
Karnes City *U.S.A.* 28°53N 97°54W **314** G6
Karnische Alpen *Europe* 46°36N 13°0E **180** E6
Karnobat *Bulgaria* 42°39N 26°59E **203** D10
Kärnten ◻ *Austria* 46°52N 13°30E **180** E6
Karntner Strasse *Vienna, Austria* **142** b2
Karo *Mali* 12°16N 3°18W **262** C4
Karoi *Zimbabwe* 16°48S 29°45E **269** F2
Karol Bagh *India* 28°39N 77°11E **120** B2
Karolinenhof *Germany* 52°23N 13°38E **115** B4
Karon, Ao *Thailand* 7°51N 98°17E **237** a
Karonga *Malawi* 9°57S 33°55E **269** D3
Karoo △ *S. Africa* 32°18S 22°27E **270** D3
Karoonda *Australia* 35°1S 139°59E **282** C3
Karor *Pakistan* 31°15N 70°59E **242** D4
Karora *Sudan* 17°44N 38°15E **256** D4
Karori *N.Z.* 41°17S 174°44E **143** B1
Karosa *Indonesia* 1°48S 119°20E **235** C5
Karounga *Mali* 15°20N 7°35W **262** B3
Karousades *Greece* 39°47N 19°45E **206** B9
Karow *Germany* 52°36N 13°29E **115** A3
Karpacz *Poland* 50°46N 15°46E **185** H2
Karpasia *Cyprus* 35°32N 34°15E **207** E10
Karpathos *Greece* 35°37N 27°10E **205** F9
Karpathos, Stenon *Greece* 36°0N 27°30E **205** F9
Karpatsky △ *Ukraine* 48°20N 24°35E **183** B9
Karpenisi *Greece* 38°55N 21°40E **204** C3
Karpilovka = Aktsyabrski *Belarus* 52°38N 28°53E **177** B15
Karpinsk *Russia* 59°45N 60°1E **186** C11
Karpogory *Russia* 64°0N 44°27E **186** B7
Karpuz Burnu = Apostolos Andreas, C. *Cyprus* 35°42N 34°35E **207** E10
Karpuzlu *Turkey* 37°33N 27°51E **205** D9
Karrādah *Iraq* 33°17N 44°23E **113** B2
Karratha *Australia* 20°44S 116°52E **278** D2
Kars *Turkey* 40°40N 43°5E **213** B10
Kars ◻ *Turkey* 40°40N 43°0E **213** B10
Karsakpay *Kazakhstan* 47°55N 66°40E **217** C7
Karsha *Kazakhstan* 49°45N 51°35E **190** F10
Karshi = Qarshi *Uzbekistan* 38°53N 65°48E **217** E7
Karsiyang *India* 26°56N 88°18E **241** B2
Karsog *India* 31°23N 77°12E **242** D7
Kärsön *Sweden* 59°19N 17°54E **139** B1
Karst = Kras *Croatia* 45°35N 14°0E **199** C10
Kartal *Turkey* 40°53N 29°11E **203** F13
Kartal Dağları *Turkey* 37°4N 36°55E **250** A7
Kartala *Comoros Is.* 11°45S 43°21E **272** a
Kartaly *Russia* 53°3N 60°40E **216** B6
Kartapur *India* 31°27N 75°32E **242** D6
Karthaus *U.S.A.* 41°8N 78°9W **312** E6
Kartuzy *Poland* 54°22N 18°10E **184** D5
Karuah *Australia* 32°37S 151°56E **283** B9
Karufa *Indonesia* 3°50S 133°20E **231** E8
Karuma ⌓ *Uganda* 2°5N 32°15E **268** B3
Karumba *Australia* 17°31S 140°50E **280** B3
Karumo *Tanzania* 2°25S 32°50E **268** C3
Karumwa *Tanzania* 3°12S 32°38E **268** C3
Kārūn → *Iran* 30°26N 48°10E **247** D6
Karungu *Kenya* 0°50S 34°10E **268** C3
Karup *Denmark* 56°19N 9°10E **163** H3
Karur *India* 10°59N 78°2E **245** J4
Karviná *Czech Rep.* 49°53N 18°31E **181** B11
Karwan → *India* 27°26N 78°4E **242** F8
Karwar *India* 14°55N 74°13E **245** G2
Karwendel ⌓ *Austria* 47°25N 11°30E **180** D4
Karwi *India* 25°12N 80°57E **243** G9
Karymskoye *Russia* 51°36N 114°21E **215** D12
Kas *Sudan* 12°30N 24°17E **259** F4
Kaş *Turkey* 36°11N 29°37E **205** E11
Kasaan *U.S.A.* 55°32N 132°24W **303** J14
Kasaba *Turkey* 36°18N 29°44E **205** E11
Kasabi *Zambia* 14°52S 23°45E **265** E4
Kasache *Malawi* 13°25S 34°20E **269** E3
Kasai *Hyōgo, Japan* 34°55N 134°52E **222** C6
Kasai *Tōkyō, Japan* 35°39N 139°52E **140** B4
Kasai → *Dem. Rep. of the Congo* 3°30S 16°10E **265** C3
Kasai-Occidental ◻ *Dem. Rep. of the Congo* 6°0S 22°0E **265** D4
Kasai-Oriental ◻ *Dem. Rep. of the Congo* 5°0S 24°30E **265** D4
Kasaji *Dem. Rep. of the Congo* 10°25S 23°27E **265** E4
Kasama *Japan* 36°23N 140°16E **223** A12
Kasama *Zambia* 10°16S 31°9E **269** E3
Kasan-dong *N. Korea* 41°18N 126°55E **224** B3
Kasandra *Greece* 40°0N 23°30E **202** F7
Kasandra Kolpos *Greece* 40°5N 23°30E **202** F7
Kasandras, Akra *Greece* 39°57N 23°30E **202** G7
Kasane *Namibia* 17°34S 24°50E **270** A3
Kasanga *Tanzania* 8°30S 31°10E **269** D3
Kasangaie *Dem. Rep. of the Congo* 6°20S 22°42E **265** D4
Kasangulu *Dem. Rep. of the Congo* 4°33S 15°15E **265** C3
Kasanka △ *Zambia* 11°34S 30°15E **269** E3
Kasaoka *Japan* 34°30N 133°30E **222** C5
Kasar, Ras *Sudan* 18°2N 38°36E **256** D4
Kasaragod *India* 12°30N 74°58E **245** H2
Kasat *Burma* 15°56N 98°13E **241** G7
Kasba *Bangla.* 23°45N 91°2E **241** D3
Kasba L. *Canada* 60°20N 102°10W **297** A8
Kasba Tadla *Morocco* 32°36N 6°17W **260** B3
Kaschau = Košice *Slovak Rep.* 48°42N 21°15E **181** C14
Kaseda *Japan* 31°25N 130°19E **222** F2
Kāseh Garān *Iran* 34°5N 46°2E **246** C5
Kasempa *Zambia* 13°30S 25°44E **269** E2
Kasenga *Dem. Rep. of the Congo* 10°20S 28°45E **269** E2
Kasese *Uganda* 0°13N 30°3E **268** B3
Kasganj *India* 27°48N 78°42E **243** F8
Kashabowie *Canada* 48°40N 90°26W **298** C1
Kashaf *Iran* 35°58N 61°7E **247** C9
Kāshān *Iran* 34°5N 51°30E **247** C6
Kashechewan *Canada* 52°18N 81°37W **298** B3
Kashgān → *Iran* 33°5N 47°31E **213** F12
Kashgar = Kashi *China* 39°30N 76°2E **217** E9
Kashi *China* 39°30N 76°2E **217** E9
Kashihara *Japan* 34°27N 135°46E **223** C7
Kashiji Plain *Zambia* 13°12S 22°20E **265** E4
Kashima *Ibaraki, Japan* 35°58N 140°38E **223** B12
Kashima *Saga, Japan* 33°7N 130°6E **222** D2
Kashima-Nada *Japan* 36°0N 140°45E **223** B12
Kashimbo *Dem. Rep. of the Congo* 11°12S 26°19E **269** E2
Kashin *Russia* 57°20N 37°36E **188** D9
Kashing = Jiaxing *China* 30°49N 120°45E **229** B13
Kashipur *Orissa, India* 19°16N 83°3E **244** E6
Kashipur *Uttarakhand, India* 29°15N 79°0E **243** E8
Kashira *Russia* 54°45N 38°10E **188** E10
Kashiwa *Japan* 35°52N 139°59E **223** B11
Kashiwabara = Severo-Kurilsk *Russia* 50°40N 156°8E **215** D16
Kashiwazaki *Japan* 37°22N 138°33E **221** F9
Kashk-e Kohneh *Afghan.* 34°55N 62°30E **240** B1
Kashksaray *Iran* 38°27N 45°34E **213** C11
Kashkū'īyeh *Iran* 30°31N 55°40E **247** D7
Kāshmar *Iran* 35°16N 58°26E **247** C8
Kashmir *Asia* 34°0N 76°0E **243** C7
Kashmor *Pakistan* 28°28N 69°32E **242** E3
Kashpirovka *Russia* 53°0N 48°30E **190** D9
Kashun Noerh = Gaxun Nur *China* 42°22N 100°30E **218** C9
Kasiari *India* 22°8N 87°14E **243** H12
Kasilof *U.S.A.* 60°23N 151°18W **303** F10
Kasimov *Russia* 54°55N 41°20E **190** C5
Kasinge *Dem. Rep. of the Congo* 6°15S 26°58E **268** D2
Kasipur *India* 22°37N 88°22E **124** B2
Kasiruta *Indonesia* 0°25S 127°12E **231** E7
Kaskaskia → *U.S.A.* 37°58N 89°57W **310** G7
Kaskattama → *Canada* 57°3N 90°4W **297** B10
Kaskinen *Finland* 62°22N 21°15E **160** E19
Kaskö = Kaskinen *Finland* 62°22N 21°15E **160** E19
Kaslo *Canada* 49°55N 116°55W **296** D5
Kasmere L. *Canada* 59°34N 101°10W **297** B8
Kasongan *Indonesia* 2°0S 113°23E **235** C4
Kasongo *Dem. Rep. of the Congo* 4°30S 26°33E **268** C2
Kasongo Lunda *Dem. Rep. of the Congo* 6°35S 16°49E **265** D3
Kasos *Greece* 35°20N 26°55E **205** F8
Kasos, Stenon *Greece* 35°30N 26°30E **205** F8
Kaspi *Georgia* 41°59N 44°26E **191** K7
Kaspichan *Bulgaria* 43°18N 27°11E **203** C11
Kaspiysk *Russia* 42°52N 47°40E **191** J8
Kaspiyskiy *Russia* 45°22N 47°23E **191** H8
Kassab *Syria* 35°55N 35°59E **250** C6
Kassab ed Doleib *Sudan* 13°30N 33°35E **257** E3
Kassaba *Egypt* 22°40N 29°55E **256** C2
Kassalâ *Sudan* 15°30N 36°0E **257** D4
Kassalâ ◻ *Sudan* 15°20N 36°26E **257** D4
Kassandrino *Greece* 40°1N 23°27E **202** F7

386 Kassel INDEX

Kassel Germany 51°18N 9°26E 178 D5
Kasserine Tunisia 35°10N 8°50E 258 A1
Kasserine □ Tunisia 35°15N 9°0E 258 A1
Kassinger Sudan 18°46N 31°51E 256 D3
Kassiopi Greece 39°48N 19°53E 206 B9
Kasson U.S.A. 44°2N 92°45W 308 C7
Kastamonu Turkey 41°25N 33°43E 212 B5
Kastamonu □ Turkey 41°20N 34°0E 212 B5
Kastav Croatia 45°22N 14°20E 199 C11
Kasteli Greece 35°29N 23°38E 207 E4
Kastellet Copenhagen, Denmark 118 a3
Kastelli Greece 35°12N 25°20E 207 E6
Kastellorizo = Megisti
Greece 36°8N 29°34E 205 E11
Kastelo, Akra Greece 35°30N 27°15E 205 F9
Kasterlee Belgium 51°15N 4°59E 170 C4
Kastlösa Sweden 56°26N 16°25E 163 H10
Kastoria Greece 40°30N 21°19E 202 F5
Kastoria □ Greece 40°30N 21°15E 202 F5
Kastorias, L. Greece 40°30N 21°20E 202 F5
Kastorio Greece 37°10N 22°17E 204 D4
Kastornoye Russia 51°55N 38°2E 189 G10
Kastos Greece 38°35N 20°55E 207 B2
Kastrosikia Greece 39°6N 20°38E 207 A2
Kastrup Denmark 55°38N 12°39E 118 B3
Kastrup, København ✕ (CPH)
Denmark 55°37N 12°39E 118 B3
Kastsyukovichy Belarus 53°20N 32°4E 189 F7
Kasuga Fukuoka, Japan 33°32N 130°26E 222 D2
Kasuga Tōkyō, Japan 35°45N 139°38E 140 A2
Kasugai Japan 35°12N 136°59E 223 B8
Kasuge Japan 35°45N 139°49E 140 A3
Kasukabe Japan 35°58N 139°49E 223 B11
Kasulu Tanzania 4°37S 30°5E 268 C3
Kasumi Japan 35°38N 134°38E 222 B6
Kasumiga-Ura Japan 36°0N 140°25E 223 B12
Kasumigaseki Tokyo, Japan 140 b4
Kasumkent Russia 41°47N 48°15E 191 K9
Kasungu Malawi 13°0S 33°29E 269 E3
Kasungu △ Malawi 12°53S 33°9E 269 E3
Kasur Pakistan 31°5N 74°25E 242 D6
Kata, Ao Thailand 7°48N 98°18E 237 J2
Kata Archanes Greece 35°15N 25°10E 207 E6
Kata Tjuta Australia 25°20S 130°50E 279 E5
Kataba Zambia 16°5S 25°10E 269 F2
Katagum Nigeria 12°18N 10°21E 263 C7
Katahdin, Mt. U.S.A. 45°54N 68°56W 309 C19
Kataka = Cuttack India 20°25N 85°57E 244 D7
Katako Kombe
Dem. Rep. of the Congo 3°25S 24°20E 264 C4
Katakolo Greece 37°38N 21°19E 204 D3
Katale Tanzania 4°52S 31°7E 268 C3
Katalla U.S.A. 60°12N 144°31W 303 F11
Katamatite Australia 36°6S 145°41E 283 D6
Katanda Katanga,
Dem. Rep. of the Congo 7°52S 24°13E 265 D4
Katanda Nord-Kivu,
Dem. Rep. of the Congo 0°55S 29°21E 268 C2
Katanga □
Dem. Rep. of the Congo 8°0S 25°0E 268 D2
Katangi India 21°56N 79°50E 244 D4
Katanning Australia 33°40S 117°33E 279 F2
Katapakishi
Dem. Rep. of the Congo 8°15S 22°49E 265 D4
Katastari Greece 37°50N 20°45E 207 D2
Katavi △ Tanzania 6°51S 31°3E 268 D3
Katavi Swamp Tanzania 6°50S 31°10E 268 D3
Katchall India 7°57N 93°22E 245 L11
Katchiungo Angola 12°35S 16°13E 265 E3
Katerini Greece 40°18N 22°37E 202 F6
Katghora India 22°30N 82°33E 243 H10
Katha Burma 24°10N 96°30E 241 C6
Kathapa △ Burma 22°20N 94°30E 241 D5
Katherîna, Gebel Egypt 28°30N 33°57E 251 K4
Katherine Australia 14°27S 132°20E 278 B5
Katherine Gorge = Nitmiluk △
Australia 14°6S 132°15E 278 B5
Kathi India 21°47N 74°3E 242 J6
Kathiawar India 22°20N 71°0E 242 H4
Kathikas Cyprus 34°55N 32°25E 207 F8
Kathleen U.S.A. 28°7N 82°2W 317 G7
Kathmandu Nepal 27°45N 85°20E 243 F11
Kathua India 32°23N 75°34E 242 C6
Kati Mali 12°41N 8°4W 262 C3
Katihar India 25°34N 87°36E 243 G12
Katikati N.Z. 37°32S 175°57E 284 D4
Katima Mulilo Namibia 17°28S 24°13E 270 A3
Katimbira Malawi 12°40S 34°0E 269 E3
Katingan = Mendawai →
Indonesia 3°30S 113°0E 235 C4
Katiola Ivory C. 8°10N 5°10W 262 D3
Katipunan Phil. 8°31N 123°17E 233 G4
Katiti ◎ Australia 25°1S 131°11E 279 E5
Katla Iceland 63°36N 19°7W 155 D7
Katlabukh, Ozero Ukraine 45°28N 29°0E 183 E14
Katlanovo Macedonia 41°52N 21°40E 202 E5
Katmai △ U.S.A. 58°20N 155°0W 303 G9
Katmandu = Kathmandu
Nepal 27°45N 85°20E 243 F11
Katni = Murwara India 23°46N 80°28E 243 H9
Katni India 23°51N 80°24E 243 H9
Kato Achaia Greece 38°8N 21°33E 204 C3
Kato Chorio Greece 35°3N 25°47E 207 E6
Kato Korakiana Greece 39°42N 19°45E 206 B9
Káto Pyrgos Cyprus 35°11N 32°41E 207 E8
Katochi Greece 38°26N 21°15E 204 C3
Katol India 21°17N 78°38E 244 D4
Katompe
Dem. Rep. of the Congo 6°2S 26°23E 265 D5
Katong Singapore 1°18N 103°53E 138 B3
Katonga → Uganda 0°34N 31°50E 268 B3
Katoomba Australia 33°41S 150°19E 283 B9
Katouna Greece 38°47N 21°7E 204 C3
Katowice Poland 50°17N 19°5E 185 H6
Katrancı Dağı Turkey 37°27N 30°25E 205 D12
Katrine, L. U.K. 56°15N 4°30W 167 E4
Katrineholm Sweden 59°0N 16°12E 162 E10
Katsepe Madag. 15°45S 46°15E 272 B2
Katsina Nigeria 13°0N 7°32E 263 C6
Katsina □ Nigeria 12°30N 7°30E 263 C6
Katsina Ala Nigeria 7°10N 9°30E 263 D6
Katsina Ala → Nigeria 7°10N 9°20E 263 D6
Katsumoto Japan 33°51N 129°42E 222 D1
Katsushika Japan 35°44N 139°51E 140 A4
Katsuta Japan 36°25N 140°31E 223 A12
Katsuura Japan 35°10N 140°20E 223 B12
Katsuyama Fukui, Japan 36°3N 136°30E 223 A8
Katsuyama Okayama,
Japan 35°5N 133°41E 222 B5
Kattaqŭrghon Uzbekistan 39°55N 66°15E 217 E7
Kattavia Greece 35°57N 27°46E 206 F11
Kattegat Denmark 56°40N 11°20E 163 H5
Katthammarsvik Sweden 57°26N 18°51E 163 G12
Kattowitz = Katowice
Poland 50°17N 19°5E 185 H6
Katul, J. Sudan 14°12N 29°25E 257 E2
Katumba
Dem. Rep. of the Congo 7°40S 25°17E 265 D5
Katun → Russia 52°25N 85°1E 217 B11
Katwa India 23°30N 88°5E 243 H13
Katwijk Neths. 52°12N 4°24E 170 B4
Kąty Wrocławskie Poland 51°2N 16°45E 185 G3
Ka'ū Desert U.S.A. 19°21N 155°19W 302 D6
Kau Pai Chau China 22°12N 114°15E 122 B2
Kau-Ye Kyun Burma 11°1N 98°32E 237 G2
Kau Yi Chau China 22°17N 114°4E 122 B1
Kaua'i U.S.A. 22°3N 159°30W 302 A2
Kauai Channel U.S.A. 21°45N 158°50W 302 B3
Kauai Island Lihue Municipal ✕
(LIH) U.S.A. 21°58N 159°20W 302 B2
Kaub Germany 50°5N 7°46E 179 E3
Kaudom △ Namibia 18°45S 20°51E 270 A3
Kauehi French Polynesia 15°49S 145°10W 289 f
Kaufbeuren Germany 47°53N 10°37E 179 H6
Kaufman U.S.A. 32°35N 96°19W 314 E6
Kauhajoki Finland 62°25N 22°10E 160 E20
Kaukauna U.S.A. 44°17N 88°17W 308 C9
Kaukauveld Namibia 20°0S 20°15E 270 B3
Kaukonahua → U.S.A. 21°35N 158°7W 302 J13
Ka'ula I. U.S.A. 21°40N 160°33W 302 B1
Kaulakahi Channel
U.S.A. 22°0N 159°55W 302 B2
Kaulsdorf Germany 52°29N 13°34E 115 B4
Kaunā Pt. U.S.A. 19°2N 155°53W 302 D6
Kaunakakai U.S.A. 21°6N 157°1W 302 B4
Kaunas Lithuania 54°54N 23°54E 184 D10
Kaunas ✕ (KUN)
Lithuania 54°57N 24°3E 184 D11
Kaunchi = Yangiyul
Uzbekistan 41°0N 69°3E 217 D7
Kaunghein Burma 25°41N 95°26E 241 C5
Kaunia Bangla. 25°46N 89°26E 241 C2
Kauniainen Finland 60°13N 24°44E 121 B1
Kaunos Turkey 36°49N 28°39E 205 E10
Kaupangur Iceland 65°38N 18°2W 155 B8
Kaura Namoda Nigeria 12°37N 6°33E 263 C6
Kauru Nigeria 10°33N 8°12E 263 C6
Kautokeino Norway 69°0N 23°4E 160 B20
Kauwapur India 27°31N 82°18E 243 F10
Kavacha Russia 60°16N 169°51E 215 C17
Kavadarci Macedonia 41°26N 22°3E 202 E6
Kavajë Albania 41°11N 19°33E 202 E3
Kavak Turkey 41°4N 36°3E 212 B7
Kavak Dağı Turkey 37°10N 28°2E 205 D10
Kavaklı Turkey 41°39N 27°10E 203 E11
Kavaklıdere Turkey 37°27N 28°21E 205 D10
Kavaklii = Topolovgrad
Bulgaria 42°5N 26°20E 203 D10
Kavala Greece 40°57N 24°28E 203 F8
Kavala □ Greece 41°5N 24°30E 203 E8
Kavala Kolpos Greece 40°50N 24°25E 203 F8
Kavalerovo Russia 44°15N 135°4E 220 B7
Kavali India 14°55N 80°1E 245 G5
Kavār Iran 29°11N 52°44E 247 D7
Kavaratti India 10°34N 72°37E 245 J1
Kavaratti I. India 10°33N 72°38E 245 J1
Kavarna Bulgaria 43°26N 28°22E 203 C12
Kavava
Dem. Rep. of the Congo 8°52S 22°19E 265 D4
Kavi India 22°12N 72°38E 242 H5
Kavieng Papua N. G. 2°36S 150°51E 286 B6
Kavimba Botswana 18°2S 24°38E 270 A3
Kavīr, Dasht-e Iran 34°30N 55°0E 247 C7
Kavīr △ Iran 34°40N 52°0E 247 C7
Kavirondo G. = Winam G.
Kenya 0°20S 34°15E 268 C3
Kavkaz Russia 45°20N 36°40E 189 K9
Kävlinge Sweden 55°47N 13°9E 163 J7
Kavos Greece 39°23N 20°3E 206 C10
Kavousi Greece 35°7N 25°51E 207 E6
Kavungo Angola 11°31S 23°3E 265 E4
Kaw Fr. Guiana 4°30N 52°15W 329 C7
Kawa Sudan 13°42N 32°34E 257 E3
Kawachi-Nagano Japan 34°28N 135°31E 223 C7
Kawagama L. Canada 45°18N 78°45W 312 A6
Kawagoe Japan 35°55N 139°29E 223 B11
Kawaguchi Japan 35°52N 139°45E 223 B11
Kawah Ijen △ Indonesia 8°3S 114°14E 235 D4
Kawaihae B. U.S.A. 20°0N 155°50W 302 C6
Kawaihoa Pt. U.S.A. 21°47N 160°12W 302 B1
Kawaikini U.S.A. 22°5N 159°29W 302 A2
Kawailoa U.S.A. 21°36N 158°3W 302 J13
Kawailoa Beach U.S.A. 21°37N 158°5W 302 J13
Kawakawa N.Z. 35°23S 174°6E 284 B3
Kawambwa Zambia 9°48S 29°3E 269 D2
Kawana Zambia 13°5S 25°58E 265 E5
Kawanabe Japan 31°23N 130°24E 222 F2
Kawanoe Japan 34°1N 133°34E 222 C5
Kawardha India 22°0N 81°17E 243 J9
Kawasaki Japan 35°31N 139°43E 140 B3
Kawasi Indonesia 1°38S 127°28E 231 E7
Kawau I. N.Z. 36°25S 174°52E 284 C3
Kawawa Japan 35°31N 139°33E 140 B2
Kawawachikamach
Canada 54°48N 66°50W 299 B6
Kawęczyn Poland 52°16N 21°5E 142 B2
Kawela U.S.A. 21°42N 158°1W 302 J13
Kawerau N.Z. 38°7S 176°42E 284 E5
Kawhia N.Z. 38°4S 174°49E 284 E3
Kawhia Harbour N.Z. 38°5S 174°51E 284 E3
Kawio, Kepulauan
Indonesia 4°30N 125°30E 231 D7
Kawkareik Burma 16°33N 98°14E 241 G7
Kawlin Burma 23°47N 95°41E 241 D5
Kawthaung Burma 10°5N 98°36E 237 H2
Kawthoolei = Kayin □
Burma 18°0N 97°30E 241 G6
Kawthule = Kayin □
Burma 18°0N 97°30E 241 G6
Kawya Burma 24°50N 94°58E 241 C5
Kaxgar He → China 39°45N 78°24E 217 E9
Kaxholmen Sweden 57°51N 14°19E 163 G8
Kaya Burkina Faso 13°4N 1°10W 263 C4
Kayah □ Burma 19°15N 97°15E 241 F6
Kayak I. U.S.A. 59°56N 144°23W 303 G11
Kayalıköy Barajı Turkey 41°50N 27°5E 203 E11
Kayan Burma 16°54N 96°34E 241 G6
Kayan → Indonesia 2°55N 117°35E 235 B5
Kayan Mentarang △
Indonesia 2°25N 115°30E 235 B5
Kayankulam India 9°10N 76°33E 245 K3
Kaycee U.S.A. 43°43N 106°38W 304 E10
Kayeli Indonesia 3°20S 127°10E 231 E7
Kayenda
Dem. Rep. of the Congo 10°48S 23°6E 265 E4
Kayenta U.S.A. 36°44N 110°15W 305 H8
Kayes Congo 4°25S 11°41E 265 C2
Kayes Mali 14°25N 11°30W 262 C2
Kayes □ Mali 14°0N 11°0W 262 C2
Kayı Turkey 39°12N 30°46E 205 B12
Kayima S. Leone 8°54N 11°15W 262 D2
Kayin □ Burma 18°0N 97°30E 241 G6
Kaymakçı Turkey 38°10N 28°8E 205 C10
Kayoa Indonesia 0°1N 127°28E 231 D7
Kayomba Zambia 13°11S 24°2E 269 E1
Kayombo Zambia 13°3S 23°51E 265 E4
Kaysatskoye Russia 49°47N 46°49E 190 F8
Kayseri Turkey 38°45N 35°30E 212 C6
Kayseri □ Turkey 38°40N 36°0E 212 C7
Kaysville U.S.A. 41°2N 111°56W 304 F8
Kayts Sri Lanka 9°42N 79°51E 245 K4
Kayu Putih Indonesia 6°10S 106°53E 122 B2
Kayuagung Indonesia 3°24S 104°50E 234 C2
Kayuni Malawi 10°2S 33°51E 269 D3
Kaz Dağı Turkey 39°42N 26°50E 205 B8
Kazachye Russia 70°52N 135°58E 215 B14
Kazakhstan ■ Asia 50°0N 70°0E 217 C8
Kazan Russia 55°50N 49°10E 190 C9
Kazan → Canada 64°2N 95°29W 297 A9
Kazan-Rettō Pac. Oc. 25°0N 141°0E 288 E6
Kazancı Turkey 36°29N 32°51E 250 B3
Kazanlı Turkey 36°49N 34°43E 250 B5
Kazanlŭk Bulgaria 42°38N 25°20E 203 D9
Kazanskaya Russia 49°50N 41°10E 190 F5
Kazatin = Kozyatyn
Ukraine 49°45N 28°50E 177 D15
Kazaure Nigeria 12°42N 8°28E 263 C6
Kazbek Russia 42°42N 44°30E 191 J7
Kāzerūn Iran 29°38N 51°40E 247 D6
Kazi Magomed = Qazımämmäd
Azerbaijan 40°3N 49°0E 191 K9
Kazimierz Dolny Poland 51°19N 21°57E 185 G8
Kazimierza Wielka Poland 50°15N 20°30E 185 H7
Kazincbarcika Hungary 48°17N 20°36E 182 B5
Kazipet India 17°58N 79°30E 244 F4
Kaziranga △ India 26°40N 93°30E 241 B4
Kaziza
Dem. Rep. of the Congo 10°42S 23°52E 265 E4
Kazlų Rūda Lithuania 54°46N 23°30E 184 D10
Kazo Japan 36°7N 139°36E 223 A11
Kaztalovka Kazakhstan 49°47N 48°43E 190 F9
Kazu Burma 25°27N 97°46E 241 C6
Kazuma Pan △ Zimbabwe 18°20S 25°48E 269 F2
Kazumba
Dem. Rep. of the Congo 6°25S 22°5E 265 D4
Kazungula Zambia 17°35S 25°15E 265 F5
Kazuno Japan 40°10N 140°45E 220 D10
Kazym → Russia 63°54N 65°50E 214 C7
Kbely Czech Rep. 50°8N 14°32E 135 B3
Kcynia Poland 53°0N 17°30E 185 F4
Ke-hsi Mansam Burma 21°56N 97°50E 241 E6
Ké-Macina Mali 13°58N 5°22W 262 C3
Kea Greece 37°35N 24°22E 204 D6
Kea'au U.S.A. 19°37N 155°2W 302 D6
Keady U.K. 54°15N 6°42W 166 B5
Keahi Pt. U.S.A. 21°19N 157°59W 302 K14
Keahole Pt. U.S.A. 19°44N 156°4W 302 D5
Kealaikahiki Channel
U.S.A. 20°35N 156°50W 302 C5
Kealakekua U.S.A. 19°31N 155°55W 302 D6
Kearney Mo., U.S.A. 39°22N 94°22W 310 E2
Kearney Nebr., U.S.A. 40°42N 99°5W 308 E4
Kearney ◎ Australia 20°10S 128°4E 278 D4
Kearny U.S.A. 33°3N 110°55W 305 K8
Kearsarge, Mt. U.S.A. 43°22N 71°50W 313 C13
Keban Turkey 38°50N 38°50E 213 C8
Keban Barajı Turkey 38°41N 38°33E 213 C8
Kebara Congo 2°27S 14°25E 264 C2
Kebayoran Baru Indonesia 6°14S 106°47E 122 B1
Kebayoran Lama
Indonesia 6°13S 106°46E 122 B1
Kebbi □ Nigeria 11°35N 4°0E 263 C5
Kébémèr Senegal 15°23N 16°34W 262 B1
Kébi Ivory C. 9°18N 6°37W 262 D3
Kebi, Mayo → Cameroon 9°18N 13°33E 264 A2
Kebili Tunisia 33°47N 9°0E 258 B1
Kebili □ Tunisia 33°30N 8°50E 261 B6
Kebnekaise Sweden 67°53N 18°33E 160 C18
Kebon Jeruk Indonesia 6°11S 106°46E 122 B1
Kebri Dehar Ethiopia 6°45N 44°17E 267 C5
Kebumen Indonesia 7°42S 109°40E 235 D3
Kecel Hungary 46°31N 19°16E 182 D4
Kechika → Canada 59°41N 127°12W 296 B3
Keçiborlu Turkey 37°57N 30°18E 205 D12
Kecskemét Hungary 46°57N 19°42E 182 D4
Kedada Ethiopia 5°25N 35°58E 257 F4
Kedah □ Malaysia 5°50N 100°40E 237 K3
Kėdainiai Lithuania 55°15N 24°2E 184 C11
Kedar West Bank 31°44N 35°18E 123 B2
Kedarnath India 30°44N 79°4E 243 D8
Kedgwick Canada 47°40N 67°20W 299 C6
Kedist Ijill Mauritania 22°38N 12°33W 260 D2
Kediri Indonesia 7°51S 112°1E 235 D4
Kedja Dem. Rep. of the Congo 4°50N 19°16E 264 B3
Kédjebi Ghana 8°12N 0°25E 263 D5
Kédougou Senegal 12°35N 12°10W 262 C2
Kedoya Indonesia 6°10S 106°45E 122 B1
Kedros Oros Greece 35°11N 24°37E 207 E5
Kędzierzyn-Koźle Poland 50°20N 18°12E 185 H5
Ke'ehi Lagoon U.S.A. 21°20N 157°54W 302 K14
Keeler U.S.A. 36°29N 117°52W 306 J9
Keeley L. Canada 54°54N 108°8W 297 C7
Keeling Is. = Cocos Is.
Ind. Oc. 12°10S 96°55E 273 F8
Keelung = Chilung
Taiwan 25°3N 121°45E 225 A3
Keenapusan Phil. 6°50N 118°50E 233 H2
Keene Ont., Canada 44°15N 78°10W 312 B6
Keene Calif., U.S.A. 35°13N 118°33W 307 K8
Keene N.H., U.S.A. 42°56N 72°17W 313 D12
Keene N.Y., U.S.A. 44°16N 73°46W 313 B11
Keeper River △ Australia 15°49S 129°8E 278 C4
Keeper Hill Ireland 52°45N 8°16W 166 D3
Keepit, L. Australia 30°50S 150°30E 283 A9
Keerweer, C. Australia 14°0S 141°32E 280 A3
Keeseville U.S.A. 44°29N 73°30W 313 B11
Keetmanshoop Namibia 26°35S 18°8E 270 C2
Keewatin Canada 49°46N 94°34W 297 D10
Keewatin → Canada 56°29N 100°46W 297 B8
Kefa Ethiopia 6°55N 36°30E 257 F4
Kefalonia Greece 38°15N 20°30E 207 C2
Kefalonia □ Greece 38°15N 20°30E 207 C2
Kefalonia ✕ (EFL) Greece 38°10N 20°30E 207 C1
Kefalos Greece 36°45N 26°59E 205 E8
Kefamenanu Indonesia 9°28S 124°29E 231 F6
Kefar Sava Israel 32°11N 34°54E 251 F5
Keffi Nigeria 8°55N 7°43E 263 D6
Keffin Hausa Nigeria 12°13N 9°59E 263 C6
Keflavík Iceland 64°2N 22°35W 155 C4
Keflavík ✕ (KEF) Iceland 64°0N 22°45W 155 C4
Keffiya Ethiopia 13°54N 37°7E 257 E4
Keg River Canada 57°54N 117°55W 296 B5
Kegalla Sri Lanka 7°15N 80°21E 245 L5
Kegaska Canada 50°9N 61°18W 299 B7
Kehancha Kenya 1°11S 34°37E 268 C3
Keheili Sudan 19°25N 32°50E 256 D3
Kehena U.S.A. 19°23N 154°55W 302 D7
Kehl Germany 48°34N 7°50E 179 G3
Keibul Lamjao △ India 24°30N 93°55E 241 C4
Keighley U.K. 53°52N 1°54W 168 D6
Keijo = Seoul S. Korea 37°31N 126°58E 137 B2
Keila Estonia 59°18N 24°25E 188 C3
Keilor Australia 37°42S 144°50E 128 A1
Keilor North Australia 37°44S 144°51E 128 A1
Keimoes S. Africa 28°41S 20°59E 270 C3
Keimola Finland 60°20N 24°49E 121 A1
Keita Niger 14°46N 5°56E 263 C6
Keïta, B. → Chad 9°14N 18°21E 259 G3
Keitele Finland 63°10N 26°20E 160 E22
Keith S. Austral., Australia 36°6S 140°20E 282 D4
Keith Moray, U.K. 57°32N 2°57W 167 D6
Keithsburg U.S.A. 41°6N 90°56W 310 C6
Keiyasi Fiji 17°53S 177°46E 287 A1
Keizer U.S.A. 44°57N 123°1W 304 D2
Kejimkujik △ Canada 44°25N 65°25W 299 D6
Kejserr Franz Joseph Fd.
Greenland 73°30N 24°30W 154 C8
Kekaha U.S.A. 21°58N 159°43W 302 B2
Kekri India 26°0N 75°10E 242 G6
Keksgolm = Priozersk
Russia 61°2N 30°7E 188 B6
Kelafo Ethiopia 5°37N 44°8E 267 C5
Kelamet Eritrea 16°0N 38°30E 257 D4
Kelan China 38°43N 111°31E 226 E6
Kelang = Klang Malaysia 3°2N 101°26E 237 L3
Kelani Ganga → Sri Lanka 6°58N 79°50E 245 L4
Kelantan □ Malaysia 5°10N 102°0E 237 K3
Kelantan → Malaysia 6°13N 102°14E 237 J4
Kelapa Gading Indonesia 6°9S 106°52E 122 A2
Këlcyrë Albania 40°20N 20°12E 202 F4
Kelekçi Turkey 37°15N 29°20E 205 D11
Kelenföld Hungary 47°27N 19°2E 117 B2
Keles Turkey 39°54N 29°14E 203 G13
Keleti-főcsatorna Hungary 47°45N 21°20E 182 C6
Kelheim Germany 48°54N 11°52E 179 G7
Kelibia Tunisia 36°50N 11°3E 258 A2
Kelkit Turkey 40°7N 39°16E 213 B8
Kelkit → Turkey 40°45N 36°32E 212 B7
Kellé Congo 0°8S 14°38E 264 C2
Kellé Niger 14°16N 10°7E 263 C7
Keller U.S.A. 31°50N 81°15W 316 D8
Kellerberrin Australia 31°36S 117°38E 279 F2
Kellett, C. Canada 72°0N 126°0W 150 B1
Kelleys I. U.S.A. 41°36N 82°42W 312 E2
Kellogg U.S.A. 47°32N 116°7W 304 C5
Kells = Ceanannus Mor
Ireland 53°44N 6°53W 166 C5
Kelmė Lithuania 55°38N 22°56E 184 C9
Kelmentsi Ukraine 48°28N 26°50E 183 B11
Kélo Chad 9°10N 15°45E 259 G3
Kelokedhara Cyprus 34°48N 32°39E 207 F8
Kelowna Canada 49°50N 119°25W 296 D5
Kelsey Creek Australia 20°26S 148°31E 280 b
Kelseyville U.S.A. 38°59N 122°50W 306 G4
Kelso N.Z. 45°54S 169°15E 285 F4
Kelso Borders, U.K. 55°36N 2°26W 167 F6
Kelso Wash., U.S.A. 46°9N 122°54W 306 D4
Keluang = Kluang
Malaysia 2°3N 103°18E 237 L4
Kelvin S. Africa 26°4S 28°5E 123 A2
Kelvington Canada 52°10N 103°30W 297 C8
Kem Russia 65°0N 34°38E 186 B5
Kem → Russia 64°57N 34°41E 186 B5
Kem-Kem Morocco 30°40N 4°30W 260 B4
Kema Indonesia 1°22N 125°8E 231 D7
Kemah Turkey 39°32N 39°5E 213 C8
Kemaliye Erzincan, Turkey 39°16N 38°29E 213 C8
Kemaliye Manisa, Turkey 38°27N 28°25E 205 C10
Kemalpaşa Turkey 38°25N 27°27E 205 C9
Kemaman Malaysia 4°12N 103°18E 237 K4
Kemang Indonesia 6°15S 106°48E 122 B1
Kemano Canada 53°35N 128°0W 296 C3
Kemapyu Burma 18°49N 97°19E 241 F6
Kemasik Malaysia 4°25N 103°27E 237 K4
Kemayoran Indonesia 6°10S 106°51E 122 B2
Kembé C.A.R. 4°36N 21°54E 264 B4
Kembolcha Ethiopia 11°2N 39°42E 257 E4
Kemer Antalya, Turkey 36°36N 30°34E 205 E12
Kemer Burdur, Turkey 37°21N 30°4E 205 D12
Kemer Muğla, Turkey 36°40N 29°22E 205 E11
Kemer Barajı Turkey 37°30N 28°37E 205 D10
Kemerburgaz Turkey 41°9N 28°54E 122 B1
Kemerovo Russia 55°20N 86°5E 214 D9
Kemerovo □ Russia 55°0N 86°0E 217 B11
Ķemeru △ Latvia 56°58N 23°25E 184 B10
Kemi Finland 65°44N 24°34E 160 D21
Kemi älv = Kemijoki →
Finland 65°47N 24°32E 160 D21
Kemi träsk = Kemijärvi
Finland 66°43N 27°22E 160 C22
Kemijärvi Finland 66°43N 27°22E 160 C22
Kemijoki → Finland 65°47N 24°32E 160 D21
Kemmerer U.S.A. 41°48N 110°32W 304 F8
Kemmuna = Comino
Malta 36°1N 14°20E 206 E7
Kemp, L. U.S.A. 33°46N 99°9W 314 E5
Kemp Land Antarctica 69°0S 55°0E 151 C5
Kempas Malaysia 1°33N 103°42E 237 d
Kempen = Kępno Poland 51°18N 17°58E 185 G4
Kempsey Australia 31°1S 152°50E 283 A10
Kempt, L. Canada 47°25N 74°22W 298 C5
Kempten Germany 47°45N 10°17E 179 H6
Kempton Tas., Australia 42°31S 147°12E 281 G4
Kempton Ind., U.S.A. 40°17N 86°14W 311 D10
Kempton Park Races U.K. 51°24N 0°23W 125 B1
Kemptville Canada 45°0N 75°38W 313 B9
Ken → India 25°13N 80°27E 243 G9
Kenadsa Algeria 31°48N 2°26W 261 B4
Kenai U.S.A. 60°33N 151°16W 303 F10
Kenai Fjords △ U.S.A. 59°40N 149°50W 303 G10
Kenai Mts. U.S.A. 60°0N 150°0W 303 G10
Kenai Nat. Wildlife Refuge △
U.S.A. 60°20N 150°30W 303 F10
Kenamuke Swamp Sudan 5°55N 33°48E 257 F3
Kenansville U.S.A. 27°53N 80°59W 317 H9
Kendai India 22°45N 82°37E 243 H10
Kendal Indonesia 6°56S 110°14E 235 D4
Kendal Cumb., U.K. 54°20N 2°44W 168 C5
Kendall N.S.W.,
Australia 31°35S 152°44E 283 A10
Kendall Fla., U.S.A. 25°40N 80°19W 317 K9
Kendall → Australia 14°4S 141°35E 280 A3
Kendallville U.S.A. 41°27N 85°16W 311 C11
Kendari Indonesia 3°50S 122°30E 231 E6
Kendawangan Indonesia 2°32S 110°17E 235 C4
Kende Nigeria 11°30N 4°12E 263 C5
Kendégué Chad 10°0N 18°36E 259 F3
Kendi, Pulau Malaysia 5°13N 100°11E 237 c
Kendrapara India 20°35N 86°30E 244 D8
Këndrevicës, Maja e
Albania 40°15N 19°52E 202 F3
Kendrew S. Africa 32°32S 24°30E 270 D3
Kendrick U.S.A. 29°15N 82°10W 317 F7
Kene Thao Laos 17°44N 101°10E 236 D3
Kenedy U.S.A. 28°49N 97°51W 314 G6
Kenema S. Leone 7°50N 11°14W 262 D2
Keng Kok Laos 16°26N 105°12E 236 D5
Keng Tawng Burma 20°45N 98°18E 241 E7
Keng Tung Burma 21°18N 99°39E 236 B2
Kengani
Dem. Rep. of the Congo 2°59S 17°36E 264 C3
Kenge Dem. Rep. of the Congo 4°50S 17°4E 265 C3
Kengeja Tanzania 5°26S 39°45E 268 D4
Kenhardt S. Africa 29°19S 21°12E 270 C3
Kéniéba Mali 12°54N 11°17W 262 C2
Kenilworth S. Africa 33°59S 18°27E 118 A1
Keningau Malaysia 5°20N 116°10E 235 A5
Kenitra Morocco 34°15N 6°40W 260 B3
Kenitra □ Morocco 34°18N 6°25W 260 B3
Kenli China 37°30N 118°20E 227 F10
Kenmare Kerry, Ireland 51°53N 9°36W 166 E2
Kenmare N. Dak., U.S.A. 48°41N 102°5W 308 A2
Kenmare River Ireland 51°48N 9°51W 166 E2
Kennebago Lake U.S.A. 45°4N 70°40W 313 A14
Kennebec U.S.A. 43°54N 99°52W 308 D4
Kennebec → U.S.A. 43°45N 69°46W 309 D19
Kennebunk U.S.A. 43°23N 70°33W 313 C14
Kennedy Zimbabwe 18°52S 27°10E 270 A4
Kennedy, C. = Canaveral, C.
U.S.A. 28°27N 80°32W 317 G9
Kennedy Channel Arctic 80°50N 66°0W 154 A4
Kennedy Entrance
U.S.A. 59°1N 152°0W 303 G10
Kennedy Ra. Australia 24°45S 115°10E 279 D2
Kennedy Range △
Australia 24°34S 115°2E 279 D2
Kennedy Space Center
U.S.A. 28°40N 80°42W 317 G9
Kennedy Town China 22°16N 114°6E 122 B1
Kenner U.S.A. 29°59N 90°14W 131 A1
Kennesaw U.S.A. 34°1N 84°37W 316 A5
Kennet → U.K. 51°27N 0°57W 169 F7
Kenneth Ra. Australia 23°50S 117°8E 279 D2
Kennett U.S.A. 36°14N 90°3W 308 G8
Kennewick U.S.A. 46°12N 119°7W 304 C4
Kennington London, U.K. 125 c4
Kennisis Lake Canada 45°13N 78°36W 312 A6
Kenogami → Canada 51°6N 84°28W 298 B3
Kenora Canada 49°47N 94°29W 297 D10
Kenosha U.S.A. 42°35N 87°49W 311 B9
Kensal Green U.K. 51°32N 0°13W 125 A2
Kensal Rise London, U.K. 125 a1
Kensington N.S.W.,
Australia 33°54S 151°13E 139 B2
Kensington P.E.I., Canada 46°28N 63°34W 299 C7
Kensington Gauteng,
S. Africa 26°11S 28°6E 123 B2
Kensington London, U.K. 51°29N 0°10W 125 B2
Kensington N.Y., U.S.A. 40°38N 73°57W 132 C2
Kensington Palace U.K. 51°30N 0°11W 125 A2
Kent Ohio, U.S.A. 41°9N 81°22W 312 E3
Kent Tex., U.S.A. 31°4N 104°13W 314 F2
Kent Wash., U.S.A. 47°22N 122°14W 306 C4
Kent □ U.K. 51°12N 0°40E 169 F8
Kent Group Australia 39°30S 147°20E 281 F4
Kent Pen. Canada 68°30N 107°0W 294 D10
Kent Village U.S.A. 38°55N 76°53W 143 B4
Kentaŭ Kazakhstan 43°32N 68°36E 217 D7
K'enting △ Taiwan 21°57N 120°48E 225 E2
Kentish Town U.K. 51°32N 0°8W 125 A3
Kentland U.S.A. 40°46N 87°27W 311 D9
Kenton London, U.K. 51°34N 0°17W 125 A2
Kenton Ohio, U.S.A. 40°39N 83°37W 311 D13
Kentucky □ U.S.A. 37°0N 84°0W 309 G11
Kentucky → U.S.A. 38°41N 85°11W 311 F11
Kentucky L. U.S.A. 37°1N 88°16W 308 G9
Kentville Canada 45°6N 64°29W 299 C7
Kentwood La., U.S.A. 30°56N 90°31W 315 F9
Kentwood Mich., U.S.A. 42°52N 85°39W 311 B11
Kenwood House U.K. 51°34N 0°9W 125 A3
Kenya ■ Africa 1°0N 38°0E 268 B4
Kenya, Mt. Kenya 0°10S 37°18E 268 C4
Kenyir, Tasik Malaysia 5°1N 102°54E 237 K4
Kenzou Cameroon 4°10N 15°2E 264 B3
Keo Neua, Deo Vietnam 18°23N 105°10E 236 C5
Keokuk U.S.A. 40°24N 91°24W 310 D5
Keoladeo △ India 27°0N 77°20E 242 F7
Keonjhargarh India 21°28N 85°35E 243 J11
Keosauqua U.S.A. 40°44N 91°58W 310 D5
Keota U.S.A. 41°22N 91°57W 310 C5
Kep Cambodia 10°29N 104°19E 237 G5
Kep Vietnam 21°24N 106°16E 236 B6
Kep △ Cambodia 10°30N 104°18E 237 G5
Kepa Poland 52°13N 21°3E 142 B2
Kepala Batas Malaysia 5°31N 100°26E 237 c
Kepez Turkey 40°5N 26°24E 203 F10
Kepi Indonesia 6°32S 139°19E 231 F9
Kępice Poland 54°16N 16°51E 184 D3
Kepler Mts. N.Z. 45°25S 167°20E 285 F2
Kępno Poland 51°18N 17°58E 185 G4
Keppel Harbour Singapore 1°15N 103°49E 138 B2
Keppel Pt. Papua N. G. 10°10S 147°58E 286 F4
Kepsut Turkey 39°40N 28°9E 205 B10
Kepuhi Pt. U.S.A. 21°29N 158°14W 302 K13
Kepulauan Karimunjawa △
Indonesia 5°50S 110°25E 235 D4
Kerala □ India 11°0N 76°15E 245 J3
Keram → Papua N. G. 4°7S 144°5E 286 C3
Kerama-Rettō Japan 26°5N 127°15E 221 L3
Keramikos Athens, Greece 112 b1
Keran Pakistan 34°35N 73°59E 243 B5
Keran △ Togo 10°9N 0°41E 263 C5
Kerang Vic., Australia 35°40S 143°55E 282 C5
Kerang Indonesia 2°15S 116°3E 235 C5
Keranyo Ethiopia 5°3N 38°18E 257 F4
Kerao → Sudan 11°0N 32°41E 257 E3
Keratea Greece 37°48N 23°58E 204 D5
Keraudren, C. Australia 19°58S 119°45E 278 C2
Kerava Finland 60°25N 25°5E 188 B3
Keravat Papua N. G. 4°17S 152°2E 286 C7
Kerch Ukraine 45°20N 36°20E 189 K9
Kerchenskiy Proliv
Black Sea 45°10N 36°30E 189 K9
Kerchoual Mali 17°12N 0°20E 263 B5
Kerema Papua N. G. 7°58S 145°50E 286 D3
Kerempe Burnu Turkey 42°2N 33°20E 212 A5
Keren Eritrea 15°45N 38°28E 257 D4
Kerewan Gambia 13°29N 16°10W 262 C1
Kerguelen Ind. Oc. 49°15S 69°10E 273 J5
Kerguelen Plateau S. Ocean 55°0S 75°0E 273 K6
Keri Greece 37°40N 20°49E 207 D2
Keri Kera Sudan 12°21N 32°42E 257 E3
Kerian, Kuala Malaysia 5°10N 100°25E 237 c
Kericho Kenya 0°22S 35°15E 268 C4
Kerikeri N.Z. 35°12S 173°59E 284 B2
Kerinci Indonesia 1°40S 101°15E 234 C2
Kerinci Seblat △ Indonesia 2°30S 101°30E 234 C1
Kerintji = Kerinci
Indonesia 1°40S 101°15E 234 C2
Keriya He → China 38°30N 82°10E 217 E10
Kerkenna, Îs. Tunisia 34°48N 11°11E 258 B2
Kerki = Atamyrat
Turkmenistan 37°50N 65°12E 217 E7
Kerkini, L. Greece 41°12N 23°10E 202 E7
Kerkouane Tunisia 36°58N 11°2E 200 F4
Kerkrade Neths. 50°53N 6°4E 170 D6
Kerkyra Greece 39°38N 19°50E 206 B9
Kerkyra □ Greece 39°37N 19°50E 206 B9
Kerkyra ✕ (CFU) Greece 39°35N 19°54E 204 B1
Kerkyras, Notio Steno
Greece 39°34N 20°0E 206 B10
Kerma Sudan 19°33N 30°32E 256 D3
Kermadec Is. Pac. Oc. 30°0S 178°15W 277 G15
Kermadec Trench
Pac. Oc. 30°30S 176°0W 277 G15
Kermān Iran 30°15N 57°1E 247 D8
Kerman Calif., U.S.A. 36°43N 120°4W 306 J6
Kermān □ Iran 30°0N 57°0E 247 D8
Kermān, Bīābān-e Iran 28°45N 59°45E 247 D8
Kermānshāh Iran 34°23N 47°0E 213 E12
Kermānshāh □ Iran 34°0N 46°30E 246 C5
Kermen Bulgaria 42°30N 26°16E 203 D10
Kermine = Navoi
Uzbekistan 40°9N 65°22E 217 D7
Kermit U.S.A. 31°52N 103°6W 314 F3
Kern → U.S.A. 35°16N 119°18W 307 K7
Kernhof Austria 47°49N 15°32E 180 D8
Kernow = Cornwall □
U.K. 50°26N 4°40W 169 G3
Kernville U.S.A. 35°45N 118°26W 307 K8
Keroh Malaysia 5°43N 101°1E 237 K3
Keros Greece 36°54N 25°40E 205 E7
Kérou Benin 10°50N 2°5E 263 C5
Kérouane Guinea 9°15N 9°0W 262 D3
Kerowagi Papua N. G. 5°51S 144°51E 286 C3
Kerpen Germany 50°51N 6°41E 178 E2
Kerrera U.K. 56°24N 5°33W 167 E3
Kerrobert Canada 51°56N 109°8W 297 C7
Kerrville U.S.A. 30°3N 99°8W 314 F5
Kerry □ Ireland 52°7N 9°35W 166 D2
Kerry Hd. Ireland 52°25N 9°56W 166 D2
Kersa Ethiopia 9°28N 41°48E 257 F5
Kertosono Indonesia 7°38S 112°9E 235 D4
Kerulen = Herlen →
Asia 48°48N 117°0E 219 B12
Kervo = Kerava Finland 60°25N 25°5E 188 B3
Kerzaz Algeria 29°29N 1°37W 261 C4
Kesagami → Canada 51°40N 79°45W 298 B4
Kesagami L. Canada 50°23N 80°15W 298 B3
Keşan Turkey 40°49N 26°38E 203 F10
Kesariani Greece 37°57N 23°46E 112 B2
Kesennuma Japan 38°54N 141°35E 220 E10
Keshāvar Iran 36°50N 46°22E 213 D12
Keshit Iran 29°43N 58°17E 247 D8
Kesigi = Kosgi India 15°51N 77°16E 245 G3
Keşiş Dağ Turkey 39°47N 39°46E 213 C8
Keskal India 20°5N 81°35E 244 D5
Keskin Turkey 39°40N 33°36E 212 C5
Kestenga Russia 65°50N 31°45E 160 D24
Keswick U.K. 54°36N 3°8W 168 C4
Keszthely Hungary 46°50N 17°15E 182 D2
Ket → Russia 58°55N 81°32E 214 D9
Keta Ghana 5°49N 1°0E 263 D5
Keta Lagoon Ghana 5°55N 1°0E 263 D5
Ketapang Jawa Timur,
Indonesia 8°9S 114°23E 231 J17
Ketapang Kalimantan Barat,
Indonesia 1°55S 110°0E 235 C4
Ketchenery Russia 47°18N 44°32E 191 G7
Ketchikan U.S.A. 55°21N 131°39W 296 B2
Ketchum U.S.A. 43°41N 114°22W 304 E6
Kete Krachi Ghana 7°46N 0°1W 263 D4
Ketef, Khalîg Umm el
Egypt 23°40N 35°35E 246 F2
Keti Bandar Pakistan 24°8N 67°27E 242 G2
Kétou Benin 7°25N 2°45E 263 D5
Ketri India 28°1N 75°50E 242 E6
Kętrzyn Poland 54°7N 21°22E 184 D8
Ketta Congo 1°28N 15°54E 264 B3
Kettering Northants., U.K. 52°24N 0°43W 169 E7
Kettering Md., U.S.A. 38°53N 76°49W 143 B5
Kettering Ohio, U.S.A. 39°41N 84°10W 311 E12
Kettle → Canada 56°40N 89°34W 297 B11
Kettle Falls U.S.A. 48°37N 118°3W 304 B4
Kettle Point Canada 43°10N 82°1W 312 C2
Kettle Pt. Canada 43°13N 82°1W 312 C2
Kettleman City U.S.A. 36°1N 119°58W 306 J7
Kęty Poland 49°51N 19°16E 185 J6
Keuka L. U.S.A. 42°30N 77°9W 312 D7
Keuruu Finland 62°16N 24°41E 188 A3
Kevelaer Germany 51°36N 6°15E 178 D2
Kew Vic., Australia 37°48S 145°2E 128 A2
Kew London, U.K. 51°28N 0°17W 125 B2
Kew Gardens Ont.,
Canada 43°39N 79°18W 141 A3
Kew Gardens London, U.K. 51°28N 0°17W 125 B2
Kewanee U.S.A. 41°14N 89°56W 310 C7
Kewanna U.S.A. 41°1N 86°25W 311 C10
Kewaunee U.S.A. 44°27N 87°31W 308 C10
Keweenaw B. U.S.A. 47°0N 88°15W 308 B9
Keweenaw Pen. U.S.A. 47°15N 88°15W 308 B9
Keweenaw Pt. U.S.A. 47°25N 87°43W 308 B10
Kexholm = Priozersk Russia 61°2N 30°7E 188 B6
Key, L. Ireland 54°0N 8°15W 166 C3
Key Biscayne U.S.A. 25°41N 80°9W 128 B2
Key Colony Beach U.S.A. 24°45N 80°57W 317 L9
Key Lake Mine Canada 57°5N 105°32W 297 B7
Key Largo U.S.A. 25°5N 80°27W 317 K9
Key West U.S.A. 24°33N 81°48W 317 L8
Keyala Sudan 4°27N 32°52E 257 G3
Keynsham U.K. 51°24N 2°29W 169 F5
Keyser U.S.A. 39°26N 78°59W 309 F14
Keystone Heights U.S.A. 29°47N 82°2W 316 F7
Keytesville U.S.A. 39°26N 92°56W 310 E4
Kezhma Russia 58°59N 101°9E 215 D11
Kezi Zimbabwe 20°58S 28°32E 271 B4
Kežmarok Slovak Rep. 49°10N 20°28E 181 B13
Kgalagadi Transfrontier △
Africa 25°10S 21°0E 270 C3
Khabarovsk Russia 48°30N 135°5E 219 B16
Khabr Iran 28°51N 56°22E 247 D8
Khābūr → Syria 35°17N 40°35E 213 E9
Khachmas = Xaçmaz
Azerbaijan 41°31N 48°42E 191 K9
Khachrod India 23°25N 75°20E 242 H6
Khadari, W. el → Sudan 10°29N 27°15E 257 E2
Khadro Pakistan 26°11N 68°50E 242 F3
Khadyzhensk Russia 44°26N 39°32E 191 H4
Khadzhilyangar = Dahongliutan
China 35°45N 79°20E 243 B8
Khaga India 25°47N 81°7E 243 G9
Khagaria India 25°30N 86°32E 243 G12
Khaipur Pakistan 29°34N 72°17E 242 E5
Khair India 27°57N 77°46E 242 F7
Khairabad India 27°33N 80°47E 243 F9
Khairagarh India 21°27N 81°2E 243 J9
Khairpur Pakistan 27°32N 68°49E 242 F3
Khairpur Nathan Shah
Pakistan 27°6N 67°44E 242 F2
Khairwara India 23°58N 73°38E 242 H5
Khaisor → Pakistan 31°17N 68°59E 242 D3
Khajuri Kach Pakistan 32°4N 69°51E 242 C3
Khak Dow Afghan. 34°57N 67°16E 240 B2
Khakassia □ Russia 53°0N 90°0E 217 B12
Khakhea Botswana 24°48S 23°22E 270 B3
Khalafābād Iran 30°54N 49°24E 247 D6
Khalfūt Yemen 15°52N 52°10E 249 D6
Khalīj Iraq 33°18N 44°28E 113 B2
Khalilabad India 26°48N 83°5E 243 F10
Khalīlī Iran 27°38N 53°17E 247 E7
Khalkhāl Iran 37°37N 48°32E 213 D13
Khalkis = Chalkida
Greece 38°27N 23°42E 204 C5
Khalmer-Sede = Tazovskiy
Russia 67°30N 78°44E 214 C8
Khalmer Yu Russia 67°58N 65°1E 214 C7
Khalturin Russia 58°40N 48°50E 186 C8
Kham Keut Laos 18°15N 104°43E 236 C5
Khamaria India 23°5N 80°48E 243 H9
Khambhaliya India 22°14N 69°41E 242 H3
Khambhat India 22°23N 72°33E 242 H5
Khambhat, G. of India 20°45N 72°30E 239 E10
Khamgaon India 20°42N 76°37E 244 D3
Khamīr Iran 26°57N 55°36E 247 E7
Khamir Yemen 16°2N 44°0E 248 D3
Khamīs Mushayṭ
Si. Arabia 18°18N 42°44E 248 C3
Khammam India 17°11N 80°6E 244 F5
Khamsa Egypt 30°27N 32°23E 251 H3
Khan → Namibia 22°37S 14°56E 270 B2
Khān Abū Shāmat Syria 33°39N 36°53E 250 B5
Khān al Baghdādī Iraq 33°51N 42°32E 213 G10
Khān al Ḥammād Iraq 32°19N 44°16E 213 G11
Khān Azād Iraq 33°7N 44°22E 246 C5
Khān Mujiddah Iraq 32°21N 43°48E 246 C4
Khān Shaykhūn Syria 35°26N 36°38E 212 E7
Khan Tengri, Pik Asia 42°12N 80°10E 217 D10
Khān Yūnis Gaza Strip 31°21N 34°18E 251 G5
Khānābād Afghan. 36°45N 69°5E 240 A3
Khanai Pakistan 30°30N 67°8E 242 D2
Khānaqīn Iraq 34°23N 45°25E 213 E11
Khānaṣir Syria 35°45N 37°30E 250 C8
Khānbāghī Iran 36°10N 55°25E 247 B7
Khandallah N.Z. 41°15S 174°47E 143 B1
Khandwa India 21°49N 76°22E 244 D3
Khandyga Russia 62°42N 135°35E 215 C14
Khanewal Pakistan 30°20N 71°55E 242 D4
Khangah Dogran
Pakistan 31°50N 73°37E 242 D5
Khanh Duong Vietnam 12°44N 108°44E 236 F7

Khaniá = Chania Greece 35°30N 24°4E 207 E5
Khaniadhana India 25°1N 78°8E 242 G8
Khanka, L. Asia 45°0N 132°24E 220 B6
Khankendy = Xankändi Azerbaijan 39°52N 46°49E 213 C12
Khanna India 30°42N 76°16E 242 D7
Khanozai Pakistan 30°37N 67°19E 242 D2
Khanpur Pakistan 28°42N 70°35E 242 E4
Khansā' Iraq 33°21N 44°28E 113 A2
Khanty-Mansiysk Russia 61°0N 69°0E 214 C7
Khanzira, Ras Somali Rep. 10°52N 45°48E 267 B6
Khao Khitchakut △ Thailand 12°50N 102°10E 236 F4
Khao Laem △ Thailand 14°56N 98°31E 236 E2
Khao Laem Res. Thailand 14°50N 98°30E 236 E2
Khao Lak △ Malaysia 8°38N 98°18E 237 H2
Khao Luang △ Thailand 8°34N 99°42E 237 H2
Khao Nam Khang △ Thailand 6°32N 100°35E 237 J3
Khao Phlu Thailand 9°29N 99°59E 237 b
Khao Pu-Khao Ya △ Thailand 7°26N 99°57E 237 J2
Khao Sam Roi Yot △ Thailand 12°13N 99°57E 237 F2
Khao Sok △ Thailand 8°55N 98°38E 237 H2
Khao Yai △ Thailand 14°21N 101°29E 236 E3
Khaoen Si Nakarin △ Thailand 14°47N 99°0E 236 E2
Khapalu Pakistan 35°10N 76°20E 243 B7
Khapcheranga Russia 49°42N 112°24E 215 E12
Khaptao △ Nepal 29°20N 81°10E 243 E9
Kharabali Russia 47°25N 47°15E 187 G8
Kharagauli Georgia 42°1N 43°12E 191 J6
Kharaghoda India 23°11N 71°46E 242 H4
Kharagpur India 22°20N 87°25E 243 H12
Kharan Kalat Pakistan 28°34N 65°21E 240 C2
Kharānaq Iran 32°20N 54°45E 247 C7
Kharavli India 18°54N 72°55E 130 B2
Kharda India 18°40N 75°34E 244 E2
Khardung La India 34°20N 77°43E 243 B7
Kharg = Khārk, Jazīreh-ye Iran 29°15N 50°28E 247 D6
Khârga, El Wâhât el Egypt 25°10N 30°35E 256 B3
Khargon India 21°45N 75°40E 244 D2
Khari → India 25°54N 74°31E 242 G6
Kharian Pakistan 32°49N 73°52E 242 C5
Khariar India 20°17N 82°46E 244 D6
Kharit, Wadi el → Egypt 24°26N 33°3E 256 C3
Khārk, Jazīreh-ye Iran 29°15N 50°28E 247 D6
Kharkiv Ukraine 49°58N 36°20E 189 H9
Kharkiv □ Ukraine 48°20N 36°20E 189 H9
Kharkov = Kharkiv Ukraine 49°58N 36°20E 189 H9
Kharmanli Bulgaria 41°55N 25°55E 203 E9
Kharovsk Russia 59°56N 40°13E 188 C11
Kharsawangarh India 22°48N 85°50E 243 H11
Kharta Turkey 40°55N 29°7E 212 B3
Khartoum = El Khartûm Sudan 15°31N 32°35E 257 D3
Khartum Canada 45°15N 77°5W 312 A7
Khasan Russia 42°25N 130°40E 220 C5
Khasavyurt Russia 43°16N 46°40E 191 J8
Khāsh Iran 28°15N 61°15E 240 C1
Khâsh, Dasht-e Afghan. 31°50N 62°30E 240 C1
Khashm el Girba Sudan 14°59N 35°58E 257 E4
Khashum Sudan 12°27N 28°2E 257 E2
Khashuri Georgia 42°3N 43°35E 191 J6
Khasi Hills India 25°30N 91°30E 241 C3
Khaskovo Bulgaria 41°56N 25°30E 203 E9
Khaskovo □ Bulgaria 42°0N 25°40E 203 E9
Khatanga Russia 72°0N 102°20E 215 B11
Khatanga → Russia 72°55N 106°0E 215 B11
Khatauli India 29°17N 77°43E 242 E7
Khatlon □ Tajikistan 37°50N 69°0E 217 E7
Khatra India 22°59N 86°51E 243 H12
Khātūnābād Iran 30°1N 55°25E 247 D7
Khatyrka Russia 62°3N 175°15E 215 C18
Khavda India 23°51N 69°43E 242 H2
Khawlaf, Ra's Yemen 12°40N 54°7E 249 D6
Khawr Fakkān U.A.E. 25°21N 56°22E 247 E8
Khay' Si. Arabia 18°45N 41°24E 248 C3
Khaybar, Ḥarrat Si. Arabia 25°30N 39°45E 246 E4
Khāzimiyah Iraq 34°46N 43°37E 246 C4
Khazzān Jabal al Awliyā Sudan 15°24N 32°20E 257 D3
Khe Bo Vietnam 19°8N 104°41E 236 C5
Khe Long Vietnam 21°29N 104°46E 236 B5
Khe Sanh Vietnam 16°37N 106°45E 236 D6
Khed Maharashtra, India 17°43N 73°27E 244 F1
Khed Maharashtra, India 18°51N 73°56E 244 E1
Khed Brahma India 24°7N 73°5E 242 G5
Khefren Egypt 29°58N 31°8E 117 B1
Khekra India 28°52N 77°20E 242 E7
Khem-Beldyr = Kyzyl Russia 51°50N 94°30E 217 B12
Khemarak Phouminville = Krong Kaoh Kong Cambodia 11°37N 102°59E 237 G4
Khemisset Morocco 33°50N 6°1W 260 B3
Khemisset □ Morocco 33°40N 6°15W 260 B3
Khemmarat Thailand 16°10N 105°15E 236 D5
Khenāmān Iran 30°27N 56°29E 247 D8
Khenchela Algeria 35°28N 7°11E 261 A6
Khenchela □ Algeria 35°0N 7°0E 261 B6
Khenifra Morocco 32°58N 5°46W 260 B3
Kherrata Algeria 36°27N 5°13E 261 A6
Khersān → Iran 31°33N 50°22E 247 D6
Kherson Ukraine 46°35N 32°35E 189 J7
Kherson □ Ukraine 46°15N 33°10E 189 J7
Kheta → Russia 71°54N 102°6E 215 B11
Khewari Pakistan 26°36N 68°52E 242 F3
Khibinogorsk = Kirovsk Russia 67°32N 33°41E 186 A5
Khichripur India 28°37N 77°18E 120 B2
Khidirpur India 22°32N 88°19E 124 B1
Khilchipur India 24°2N 76°34E 242 G7
Khilok Russia 51°30N 110°45E 215 D12
Khimki Russia 55°50N 37°20E 188 E9
Khimki-Khovrino Russia 55°51N 37°31E 129 A3
Khios = Chios Greece 38°27N 26°9E 205 C8
Khirbet Batin Abu Lihyah West Bank 31°50N 35°6E 123 A1
Khirbet el-Misbah West Bank 31°53N 35°4E 123 A1
Khirbet Jub e-Rum West Bank 31°44N 35°16E 123 B2
Khirsadoh India 22°11N 78°47E 243 H8
Khiuma = Hiiumaa Estonia 58°50N 22°45E 138 C2
Khiva Uzbekistan 41°30N 60°18E 216 D6
Khlebarovo Bulgaria 43°37N 26°15E 203 C10
Khlong Khlung Thailand 16°12N 99°43E 236 D2
Khlong Lan △ Thailand 16°12N 99°13E 236 D2
Khlong Phanom △ Thailand 8°45N 98°38E 237 H2
Khlong San Thailand 13°43N 100°29E 113 B2
Khlong Toey Thailand 13°43N 100°36E 113 B2
Khmelnik Ukraine 49°33N 27°58E 177 D14
Khmelnytskyy Ukraine 49°23N 27°0E 177 D14
Khmelnytskyy □ Ukraine 49°50N 26°40E 177 D14
Khmer Rep. = Cambodia ■ Asia 12°15N 105°0E 236 F5
Khoai, Hon Vietnam 8°26N 104°50E 237 H5
Khodoriv Ukraine 49°24N 24°19E 177 D13
Khodzent = Khŭjand Tajikistan 40°17N 69°37E 217 D7
Khojak Pass Afghan. 30°51N 66°34E 242 D2
Khojayli Uzbekistan 42°29N 59°31E 216 D5
Khok Kloi Thailand 8°17N 98°19E 237 a
Khok Pho Thailand 6°43N 101°6E 237 J3
Khok Samrong Thailand 15°3N 100°43E 236 E3
Khokhropār Pakistan 25°42N 70°12E 240 D3
Kholm Afghan. 36°45N 67°40E 240 A2
Kholm Russia 57°10N 31°15E 188 D6
Kholmsk Russia 47°40N 142°5E 215 E15
Khomārlu Iran 39°6N 47°3E 213 C12
Khomas Hochland Namibia 22°40S 16°0E 270 B2
Khombole Senegal 14°43N 16°42W 262 C1
Khomeyn Iran 33°40N 50°7E 247 C6
Khomeynī Shahr Iran 32°41N 51°31E 247 C6
Khomodino Botswana 22°46S 23°52E 270 B3
Khon Kaen Thailand 16°30N 102°47E 236 D4
Khong → Cambodia 13°32N 105°58E 236 F5
Khong Sedone Laos 15°34N 105°49E 236 E5
Khonuu Russia 66°30N 143°12E 215 C15
Khoper → Russia 49°30N 42°20E 190 F6
Khor el 'Atash Sudan 13°20N 34°15E 257 E3
Khorāsān-e Janūb □ Iran 32°0N 59°0E 247 C8
Khorāsān-e Razavī □ Iran 35°0N 59°0E 247 C8
Khorāsān-e Shemālī □ Iran 37°0N 57°0E 247 B8
Khorat = Nakhon Ratchasima Thailand 14°59N 102°12E 236 E4
Khorat, Cao Nguyen Thailand 15°30N 102°50E 236 E4
Khorazm = Xorazm □ Uzbekistan 43°0N 60°0E 216 D6
Khorb el Ethel Algeria 28°30N 6°17W 260 C3
Khorel India 22°41N 88°18E 124 A1
Khorixas Namibia 20°16S 14°59E 270 B1
Khorol Ukraine 49°48N 33°15E 189 H7
Khorosovo Russia 55°46N 37°27E 129 B2
Khorramābād Khorāsān, Iran 35°6N 57°57E 247 C8
Khorramābād Lorestān, Iran 33°30N 48°25E 213 F13
Khorramdarreh Iran 36°11N 49°11E 213 D13
Khorrāmshahr Iran 30°29N 48°15E 247 D6
Khorugh Tajikistan 37°30N 71°36E 240 A3
Khosravi Iran 30°48N 51°28E 247 D6
Khosrowābād Khuzestān, Iran 30°10N 48°25E 247 D6
Khosrowābād Kordestān, Iran 35°31N 47°38E 213 E12
Khost Pakistan 30°13N 67°35E 242 D2
Khosūyeh Iran 28°32N 54°26E 247 D7
Khotan = Hotan China 37°25N 79°55E 227 F6
Khotyn Ukraine 48°31N 26°27E 183 B11
Khouribga Morocco 32°58N 6°57W 260 B3
Khouribga □ Morocco 32°56N 6°36W 260 B3
Khowai Bangla. 24°5N 91°40E 241 C3
Khowst Afghan. 33°22N 69°58E 242 C3
Khowst □ Afghan. 33°20N 70°0E 240 B3
Khoyniki Belarus 51°54N 29°55E 177 C15
Khram, Ko Thailand 12°42N 100°47E 236 F3
Khrami → Georgia 41°25N 45°0E 191 K7
Khrenovoye Russia 51°4N 40°16E 190 E5
Khromtaū Kazakhstan 50°17N 58°27E 216 B5
Khrysokhou B. Cyprus 35°6N 32°25E 207 E8
Khuan Wa Thailand 7°53N 98°17E 237 a
Khudrah, W. → Yemen 18°10N 50°20E 249 C5
Khudzhand = Khŭjand Tajikistan 40°17N 69°37E 217 D7
Khuff Si. Arabia 24°55N 44°53E 246 E5
Khūgīānī Afghan. 31°34N 66°32E 242 D2
Khuis Botswana 26°40S 21°49E 270 C3
Khuiyala India 27°9N 70°25E 242 F4
Khŭjand Tajikistan 40°17N 69°37E 217 D7
Khŭjayli = Khojayli Uzbekistan 42°29N 59°31E 216 D5
Khujner India 23°47N 76°36E 242 H7
Khukhan Thailand 14°42N 104°12E 236 E5
Khulays Si. Arabia 22°9N 39°19E 248 B2
Khulna Bangla. 22°45N 89°34E 241 D2
Khulna □ Bangla. 22°25N 89°35E 241 D2
Khulo Georgia 41°33N 42°19E 191 K6
Khumago Botswana 20°26S 24°32E 270 B3
Khumrah Si. Arabia 21°22N 39°13E 248 B2
Khunjerab △ Pakistan 36°40N 75°30E 243 A6
Khunjerab Pass = Kinjirap Daban Asia 36°40N 75°25E 240 A4
Khūnsorkh Iran 27°9N 56°7E 247 E8
Khunti India 23°5N 85°17E 243 H11
Khūr Iran 32°55N 58°18E 247 C8
Khurai India 24°3N 78°23E 242 G8
Khuraydah Yemen 15°33N 48°18E 249 D5
Khurayṣ Si. Arabia 25°6N 48°2E 247 E6
Khurda India 20°11N 85°37E 244 D7
Khureit Sudan 13°59N 26°3E 257 E2
Khurja India 28°15N 77°58E 242 E7
Khūrmāl Iraq 35°18N 46°2E 213 E12
Khurr, Wādī al Iraq 32°3N 43°52E 246 C4
Khūsf Iran 32°46N 58°53E 247 C8
Khushab Pakistan 32°20N 72°20E 242 C5
Khust Ukraine 48°10N 23°18E 183 B8
Khutse △ Botswana 23°31S 24°12E 270 B3
Khuwei Sudan 13°5N 29°14E 257 E2
Khuzdar Pakistan 27°52N 66°30E 242 F2
Khūzestān □ Iran 31°0N 49°0E 247 D6
Khvāf Iran 34°33N 60°8E 247 C9
Khvājeh Iran 38°9N 46°35E 246 B5
Khvājeh Moḥammad, Kūh-e Afghan. 36°22N 70°17E 240 A3
Khvalynsk Russia 52°30N 48°2E 190 D9
Khvānsār Iran 29°56N 54°8E 247 D7
Khvatovka Russia 52°24N 46°32E 190 D8
Khvor Iran 33°45N 55°0E 247 C7
Khvorgū Iran 27°34N 56°27E 247 E8
Khvormūj Iran 28°40N 51°30E 247 D6
Khvoy Iran 38°35N 45°0E 213 C11
Khvoynaya Russia 58°58N 34°28E 188 C8
Khwae Noi → Thailand 14°1N 99°32E 236 E2
Khyber Pass Afghan. 34°10N 71°8E 242 B4
Khyriv Ukraine 49°32N 22°50E 185 J9
Kia Fiji 16°16S 179°8E 287 A2
Kia Solomon Is. 7°32S 158°26E 287 L10
Kiabukwa Dem. Rep. of the Congo 8°40S 24°48E 265 D4
Kiadho → India 19°37N 77°40E 244 E3
Kiama N.S.W., Australia 34°40S 150°50E 283 C9
Kiama Dem. Rep. of the Congo 7°19S 17°49E 265 D3
Kiamari Pakistan 24°49N 66°58E 123 B1
Kiamba Phil. 6°2N 124°46E 233 H5
Kiambi Dem. Rep. of the Congo 7°15S 28°0E 268 D2
Kiambu Kenya 1°8S 36°50E 268 C4
Kiamusze = Jiamusi China 46°40N 130°26E 219 B15
Kian = Ji'an China 41°5N 126°10E 227 D14
Kiana U.S.A. 66°58N 160°26W 303 C7
Kiang West △ Gambia 13°25N 15°50W 262 C1
Kiangara Madag. 17°58S 47°2E 272 B2
Kiangsi = Jiangxi □ China 27°30N 116°0E 229 D11
Kiangsu = Jiangsu □ China 33°0N 120°0E 227 H11
Kiato Greece 38°1N 22°45E 204 C4
Kibæk Denmark 56°2N 8°51E 163 H2
Kibale △ Uganda 0°16N 30°18E 268 B3
Kibanga Port Uganda 0°10N 32°58E 268 B3
Kibangou Congo 3°26S 12°22E 264 C2
Kibara Tanzania 2°8S 33°30E 268 C3
Kibare, Mts. Dem. Rep. of the Congo 8°25S 27°10E 268 D2
Kibawe Phil. 7°34N 125°0E 233 H5
Kibenga Dem. Rep. of the Congo 7°56S 17°30E 265 D3
Kibira △ Burundi 3°6S 30°24E 268 C3
Kiboga Uganda 0°58N 31°45E 268 B3
Kibombo Dem. Rep. of the Congo 3°57S 25°53E 265 C5
Kibondo Tanzania 3°35S 30°45E 268 C3
Kibre Mengist Ethiopia 5°54N 38°59E 257 F4
Kıbrıs = Cyprus ■ Asia 35°0N 33°0E 207 F9
Kibumbu Burundi 3°32S 29°45E 268 C2
Kibungo Rwanda 2°10S 30°32E 268 C3
Kibuye Burundi 3°39S 29°59E 268 C2
Kibuye Rwanda 2°3S 29°21E 268 C2
Kibwesa Tanzania 6°30S 29°58E 268 D2
Kibwezi Kenya 2°27S 37°57E 268 C4
Kıcasalih Turkey 41°23N 26°48E 203 E10
Kičevo Macedonia 41°34N 20°59E 202 E4
Kichha India 28°53N 79°30E 243 E8
Kichha → India 28°41N 79°18E 243 E8
Kichmengskiy Gorodok Russia 59°59N 45°48E 186 B8
Kicking Horse Pass Canada 51°28N 116°16W 296 C5
Kid, W. → Egypt 28°9N 34°27E 251 K5
Kid I. Antigua & B. 17°42N 61°49W 322 c
Kidal Mali 18°26N 1°22E 263 B5
Kidal □ Mali 19°55N 1°5E 261 E5
Kidapawan Phil. 7°1N 125°3E 233 H5
Kidderminster U.K. 52°24N 2°15W 169 E5
Kidepo Valley △ Uganda 3°52N 33°50E 268 B3
Kidete Tanzania 6°25S 37°17E 268 D4
Kidira Senegal 14°28N 12°13W 262 C2
Kidnappers, C. N.Z. 39°38S 177°5E 284 F6
Kidsgrove U.K. 53°5N 2°14W 168 D5
Kidston Australia 18°52S 144°8E 280 B3
Kidugallo Tanzania 6°49S 38°15E 268 D4
Kidurong, Tanjong Malaysia 3°16N 113°3E 235 B4
Kiel Germany 54°19N 10°8E 178 A6
Kiel Canal = Nord-Ostsee-Kanal Germany 54°12N 9°32E 178 A5
Kiel-Kanal = Nord-Ostsee-Kanal Germany 54°12N 9°32E 178 A5
Kielce Poland 50°52N 20°42E 185 H7
Kielder Water U.K. 55°11N 2°31W 168 B5
Kieler Bucht Germany 54°35N 10°25E 178 A6
Kiembara Burkina Faso 13°15N 2°44W 262 C4
Kienge Dem. Rep. of the Congo 10°30S 27°30E 269 E2
Kierling Austria 48°18N 16°16E 142 A1
Kierlingbach → Austria 48°18N 16°19E 142 A1
Kiessé Niger 13°29N 4°1E 263 C5
Kieta Papua N. G. 6°12S 155°36E 286 D8
Kiev = Kyyiv Ukraine 50°30N 30°28E 177 C16
Kifaya Guinea 12°10N 13°4W 262 C2
Kiffa Mauritania 16°37N 11°24W 262 B2
Kifisos → Athina, Greece 37°58N 23°42E 112 B2
Kifisos → Voiotia, Greece 38°35N 23°20E 204 C5
Kifissia Greece 38°4N 23°49E 204 C5
Kifri Iraq 34°45N 45°0E 213 E11
Kigali Rwanda 1°59S 30°4E 268 C3
Kigarama Tanzania 1°1S 31°50E 268 C3
Kigelle Sudan 8°40N 34°2E 257 F3
Kigezi △ Uganda 0°34S 29°55E 268 C2
Kiğı Turkey 39°18N 40°21E 213 C9
Kigoma □ Tanzania 5°0S 30°0E 268 D3
Kigoma-Ujiji Tanzania 4°55S 29°36E 268 C2
Kigomasha, Ras Tanzania 4°58S 38°58E 268 C4
Kigosi △ Tanzania 4°10S 31°45E 268 C3
Kığzı Turkey 38°18N 43°25E 246 B4
Kīhei U.S.A. 20°47N 156°28W 302 D5
Kihikihi N.Z. 38°2S 175°22E 284 E4
Kihnu Estonia 58°9N 24°1E 188 C3
Kīholo B. U.S.A. 19°50N 155°55W 302 D6
Kii-Hantō Japan 34°0N 135°45E 223 D7
Kii-Nagashima Japan 34°12N 136°20E 223 D8
Kii-Sanchi Japan 34°20N 136°0E 223 D8
Kii-Suidō Japan 33°40N 134°45E 222 D6
Kiira Dam Uganda 0°25N 33°0E 268 B3
Kiire Japan 31°22N 130°33E 222 F2
Kijik U.S.A. 60°20N 154°20W 303 F9
Kikaiga-Shima Japan 28°19N 129°59E 221 K4
Kikiak = Rigolet Canada 54°10N 58°23W 299 B8
Kikinda Serbia 45°50N 20°30E 182 E5
Kikládhes = Cyclades Greece 37°0N 24°30E 204 E6
Kikoira Australia 33°39S 146°40E 283 B7
Kikombo Bandundu, Dem. Rep. of the Congo 5°37S 18°50E 265 D3
Kikombo Bandundu, Dem. Rep. of the Congo 5°49S 17°45E 265 D3
Kikongo Dem. Rep. of the Congo 4°16S 17°17E 265 C3
Kikori Papua N. G. 7°25S 144°15E 286 D3
Kikori → Papua N. G. 7°38S 144°20E 286 D3
Kikuchi Japan 32°59N 130°47E 222 E2
Kikuna Japan 35°30N 139°37E 140 B2
Kikwit Dem. Rep. of the Congo 5°0S 18°45E 265 D3
Kil Sweden 59°30N 13°20E 162 E7
Kilafors Sweden 61°14N 16°36E 162 C10
Kilakkarai India 9°12N 78°47E 245 K4
Kilar India 33°6N 76°25E 242 C7
Kīlauea U.S.A. 22°13N 159°25W 302 A2
Kīlauea Caldera U.S.A. 19°25N 155°17W 302 D6
Kilbarrack Ireland 53°23N 6°9W 120 A2
Kilbeggan Ireland 53°22N 7°30W 166 C4
Kilbirnie N.Z. 41°19S 174°48E 143 B1
Kilbrannan Sd. U.K. 55°37N 5°26W 167 F3
Kilbuck Mts. U.S.A. 60°36N 159°53W 303 F8
Kilburn U.K. 51°32N 0°11W 125 A2
Kilchu N. Korea 40°57N 129°25E 224 D4
Kilcoy Australia 26°59S 152°30E 281 D5
Kildare Ireland 53°9N 6°55W 166 C5
Kildare □ Ireland 53°10N 6°50W 166 C5
Kildinstroy Russia 68°48N 33°6E 160 B25
Kileikli Sudan 11°25N 25°31E 257 E2
Kilembe Dem. Rep. of the Congo 5°42S 19°55E 265 D3
Kilen Norway 59°20N 8°49E 164 E5
Kilfinnane Ireland 52°21N 8°28W 166 D3
Kilgarvan Ireland 51°54N 9°27W 166 E2
Kilgore U.S.A. 32°23N 94°53W 314 E7
Kilgoris Kenya 1°0S 34°53E 268 C3
Kilibo Benin 8°32N 2°38E 263 D5
Kilifi Kenya 3°40S 39°48E 268 C4
Kilimanjaro Tanzania 3°7S 37°20E 268 C4
Kilimanjaro □ Tanzania 4°0S 38°0E 268 C4
Kilimanjaro △ Tanzania 3°2S 37°19E 268 C4
Kilimli Turkey 41°28N 31°50E 212 B4
Kilinailau Is. Papua N. G. 4°45S 155°20E 286 C8
Kilindini Kenya 4°4S 39°40E 268 C4
Kilis Turkey 36°42N 37°6E 250 B8
Kilis □ Turkey 36°50N 37°10E 212 D7
Kiliya Ukraine 45°28N 29°16E 183 E14
Kilkee Ireland 52°41N 9°39W 166 D2
Kilkeel U.K. 54°4N 6°0W 166 B5
Kilkenny Ireland 52°39N 7°15W 166 D4
Kilkenny □ Ireland 52°35N 7°15W 166 D4
Kilkieran B. Ireland 53°20N 9°41W 166 C2
Kilkis Greece 40°58N 22°57E 202 F6
Kilkis □ Greece 41°5N 22°50E 202 E6
Killakee Ireland 53°15N 6°19W 120 B2
Killala Ireland 54°13N 9°12W 166 B2
Killala B. Ireland 54°16N 9°8W 166 B2
Killaloe Ont., Canada 45°33N 77°25W 312 A7
Killaloe Clare, Ireland 52°48N 8°28W 166 D3
Killarney Queens., Australia 28°20S 152°18E 281 D5
Killarney Man., Canada 49°10N 99°40W 297 D9
Killarney Kerry, Ireland 52°4N 9°30W 166 D2
Killarney, L. Bahamas 25°3N 77°27W 153 b
Killarney △ Ireland 52°0N 9°33W 166 D2
Killary Harbour Ireland 53°38N 9°52W 166 C2
Killdeer U.S.A. 47°22N 102°45W 308 B2
Killeberg Sweden 56°29N 14°5E 163 H8
Killeen U.S.A. 31°7N 97°44W 314 F6
Killester Ireland 53°22N 6°11W 120 A2
Killin U.K. 56°28N 4°19W 167 E4
Killiney Ireland 53°15N 6°7W 120 B3
Killiney B. Ireland 53°16N 6°5W 120 B3
Killington Pk. U.S.A. 43°36N 72°49W 313 C12
Killini = Kyllini Greece 37°55N 21°8E 207 D3
Killini Greece 37°54N 22°25E 204 D4
Killorglin Ireland 52°6N 9°47W 166 D2
Killybegs Ireland 54°38N 8°26W 166 B3
Kilmacud Ireland 53°17N 6°13W 120 B2
Kilmainham Ireland 53°20N 6°17W 120 A2
Kilmainham Gaol Ireland 53°21N 6°19W 120 A2
Kilmarnock U.K. 55°37N 4°29W 167 F4
Kilmashogue Mt. Ireland 53°15N 6°15W 120 B2
Kilmez Russia 56°58N 50°55E 190 B10
Kilmez → Russia 56°58N 50°28E 190 B10
Kilmore Vic., Australia 37°25S 144°53E 283 D6
Kilmore Dublin, Ireland 53°23N 6°13W 120 A2
Kilmore Quay Ireland 52°10N 6°36W 166 D5
Kilnamanagh Ireland 53°18N 6°22W 120 B1
Kilo Finland 60°13N 24°47E 121 B1
Kilokri India 28°34N 77°15E 120 B2
Kilómetro 1082 = Joaquín V. González Argentina 25°10S 64°0W 334 B3
Kilondo Tanzania 9°45S 34°20E 269 D3
Kilosa Tanzania 6°48S 37°0E 268 D4
Kilrush Ireland 52°38N 9°29W 166 D2
Kiltan I. India 11°29N 73°0E 245 J1
Kiltiernan Ireland 53°15N 6°11W 120 B2
Kilwa Kisiwani Tanzania 8°58S 39°32E 269 D4
Kilwa Kivinje Tanzania 8°45S 39°25E 269 D4
Kilwa Masoko Tanzania 8°55S 39°30E 269 D4
Kilwinning U.K. 55°39N 4°43W 167 F4
Kim U.S.A. 37°15N 103°21W 305 H12
Kim → Cameroon 5°28N 11°7E 263 D7
Kimaam Indonesia 7°58S 138°53E 231 F9
Kimamba Tanzania 6°45S 37°10E 268 D4
Kimba Australia 33°8S 136°23E 282 B2
Kimball Nebr., U.S.A. 41°14N 103°40W 308 E2
Kimball S. Dak., U.S.A. 43°45N 98°57W 308 D4
Kimbanda Dem. Rep. of the Congo 4°16S 18°30E 265 C3
Kimbe Papua N. G. 5°33S 150°11E 286 C6
Kimbe B. Papua N. G. 5°15S 150°30E 286 C6
Kimberley W. Austral., Australia 16°20S 127°0E 278 C4
Kimberley B.C., Canada 49°40N 115°59W 296 D5
Kimberley Ont., Canada 44°23N 80°32W 312 B4
Kimberley Northern Cape, S. Africa 28°43S 24°46E 270 C3
Kimberly U.S.A. 42°32N 114°22W 304 E6
Kimbongo Dem. Rep. of the Congo 6°8S 18°1E 265 D3
Kimch'aek N. Korea 40°40N 129°10E 224 B4
Kimhae = Gimhae S. Korea 35°14N 128°53E 224 E4
Kimhwa N. Korea 38°25N 127°36E 224 C3
Kimi Greece 38°38N 24°6E 204 C6
Kimitsu Japan 35°19N 139°54E 223 B11
Kimjŏngsugŭp N. Korea 41°24N 127°45E 224 B3
Kimmage Ireland 53°18N 6°17W 120 B2
Kimmirut Canada 62°50N 69°50W 295 E18
Kimolos Greece 36°48N 24°37E 204 E6
Kimongo Congo 4°27S 12°53E 265 C2
Kimovsk Moskva, Russia 55°21N 37°28E 188 E9
Kimovsk Tula, Russia 54°0N 38°29E 188 E10
Kimpangu Dem. Rep. of the Congo 5°52S 15°3E 265 D3
Kimparana Mali 12°48N 5°0W 262 C4
Kimpese Congo 5°33S 14°26E 265 D2
Kimpese Dem. Rep. of the Congo 5°35S 14°26E 265 D2
Kimry Russia 56°55N 37°15E 188 D9
Kimstad Sweden 58°35N 15°58E 163 F9
Kimvula Dem. Rep. of the Congo 5°44S 15°58E 265 D3
Kin Burma 22°46N 94°42E 241 D5
Kin-u Burma 22°46N 95°37E 241 D5
Kin-wan Japan 26°23N 127°55E 288 a
Kinabalan, Mt. Phil. 8°12N 125°26E 233 G5
Kinabalu, Gunung Malaysia 6°3N 116°14E 235 A5
Kinabalu △ Malaysia 6°0N 116°30E 235 A5
Kinango Kenya 4°8S 39°19E 268 C4
Kinard U.S.A. 30°16N 85°15W 316 E4
Kinaros Greece 36°59N 26°15E 205 E8
Kinaskan L. Canada 57°38N 130°8W 296 B2
Kinbasket L. Canada 52°0N 118°10W 296 C5
Kincaid Canada 49°40N 107°0W 297 D7
Kincardine Canada 44°10N 81°40W 312 B3
Kinchafoonee Cr. → U.S.A. 31°38N 84°10W 316 D5
Kinchega △ Australia 32°27S 142°15E 282 B5
Kincolith Canada 55°0N 129°57W 296 C3
Kinda Kasai-Or., Dem. Rep. of the Congo 9°18S 25°4E 265 D5
Kinda Katanga, Dem. Rep. of the Congo 4°47S 21°48E 265 C4
Kindambi Dem. Rep. of the Congo 5°6S 18°14E 265 D4
Kindberg Austria 47°30N 15°27E 180 D8
Kinde U.S.A. 43°56N 83°0W 312 C2
Kindele Dem. Rep. of the Congo 8°39S 24°10E 265 D4
Kinder Scout U.K. 53°24N 1°52W 168 D6
Kinderhook U.S.A. 39°42N 91°10W 310 E5
Kindersley Canada 51°30N 109°10W 297 C7
Kindi Iraq 33°18N 44°22E 113 B2
Kindia Guinea 10°0N 12°52W 262 D2
Kindongo Dem. Rep. of the Congo 3°58S 17°30E 264 C3
Kindu Dem. Rep. of the Congo 2°55S 25°50E 264 C5
Kinel Russia 53°15N 50°40E 190 D10
Kineshma Russia 57°30N 42°5E 190 B6
Kinesi Tanzania 1°25S 33°50E 268 C3
King, L. Australia 33°10S 119°35E 279 F2
King, Mt. Australia 25°10S 147°30E 280 D4
King Christian I. Canada 77°48N 101°40W 295 B11
King City Calif., U.S.A. 36°13N 121°8W 306 J5
King City Mo., U.S.A. 40°3N 94°31W 310 D2
King Cove U.S.A. 55°3N 162°19W 303 J7
King Cr. → Australia 24°35S 139°30E 280 C2
King Edward → Australia 14°14S 126°35E 278 B4
King Edward Point S. Georgia 54°17S 36°30W 151 B1
King Frederick VI Land = Kong Frederik VI.s Kyst Greenland 63°0N 43°0W 154 E6
King George B. Falk. Is. 51°30S 60°30W 153 f
King George I. Antarctica 60°0S 60°0W 151 C18
King George Is. Canada 57°20N 80°30W 295 F15
King George Sd. Australia 35°5S 118°0E 279 G2
King George VI Falls Guyana 5°42N 61°5W 329 B5
King I. = Kadan Kyun Burma 12°30N 98°20E 236 F2
King I. Tas., Australia 39°50S 144°0E 281 F3
King I. B.C., Canada 52°10N 127°40W 296 C3
King Khalid Military City = Madinat al Malik Khālid al Askarīyah Si. Arabia 27°54N 45°31E 246 E5
King Leopold Ranges Australia 17°30S 125°45E 278 C4
King of Prussia U.S.A. 40°5N 75°23W 313 F9
King Salmon U.S.A. 58°42N 156°40W 303 G8
King Sd. Australia 16°50S 123°20E 278 C3
King Sejong Antarctica 62°30S 58°0W 151 C18
King William I. Canada 69°10N 97°25W 294 D12
King William's Town S. Africa 32°51S 27°22E 270 D4
Kingaok = Bathurst Inlet Canada 66°50N 108°1W 294 D10
Kingaroy Australia 26°32S 151°51E 281 D5
Kingdom City U.S.A. 38°56N 91°56W 310 F5
Kingfisher U.S.A. 35°52N 97°56W 314 D6
Kinghorn U.K. 56°5N 3°10W 121 A2
Kingirbān Iraq 34°40N 44°54E 246 C5
Kingisepp = Kuressaare Estonia 58°15N 22°30E 188 C2
Kingisepp Russia 59°25N 28°40E 188 C5
Kingking = Pantukan Phil. 7°9N 125°54E 233 H5
Kinglake △ Australia 37°30S 145°22E 283 D6
Kingman Ariz., U.S.A. 35°12N 114°4W 307 K12
Kingman Ind., U.S.A. 39°58N 87°18W 311 E9
Kingman Kans., U.S.A. 37°39N 98°7W 308 G4
Kingoonya Australia 30°55S 135°19E 281 E2
Kingri Pakistan 30°27N 69°49E 242 D3
Kings → U.S.A. 36°3N 119°50W 306 J7
Kings Canyon Australia 24°15S 131°34E 278 D5
Kings Canyon △ U.S.A. 36°50N 118°40W 306 J8
Kings County = Offaly □ Ireland 53°15N 7°30W 166 C4
Kings Cross Sydney, Australia 139 c3
King's Cross London, U.K. 125 a4
Kings Domain Australia 37°49S 144°58E 128 A1
Kings Forest = Kongelunden Denmark 55°34N 12°34E 118 B3
King's Lynn U.K. 52°45N 0°24E 168 E8
Kings Park N.Y., U.S.A. 40°53N 73°16W 313 F11
Kings Park Va., U.S.A. 38°48N 77°17W 143 C2
Kings Park West U.S.A. 38°48N 77°18W 143 C2
Kings Peak U.S.A. 40°46N 110°23W 304 F8
King's Trough Atl. Oc. 43°48N 22°0W 152 B9
Kingsbridge U.K. 50°17N 3°47W 169 G4
Kingsburg U.S.A. 36°31N 119°33W 306 J7
Kingsbury Vic., Australia 37°43S 145°2E 128 A2
Kingsbury London, U.K. 51°34N 0°15W 125 A2
Kingscote Australia 35°40S 137°38E 282 C2
Kingscourt Ireland 53°55N 6°48W 166 C5
Kingsford N.S.W., Australia 33°56S 151°14E 139 B2
Kingsford Mich., U.S.A. 45°48N 88°4W 308 C9
Kingsford Smith, Sydney ✕ (SYD) Australia 33°57S 151°11E 139 B2
Kingsland U.S.A. 30°48N 81°41W 316 E8
Kingsport U.S.A. 36°33N 82°33W 315 C13
Kingston Ont., Canada 44°14N 76°30W 313 B8
Kingston Jamaica 18°0N 76°50W 320 a
Kingston N.Z. 45°20S 168°43E 285 F3
Kingston N.H., U.S.A. 42°56N 71°3W 313 D13
Kingston N.Y., U.S.A. 41°56N 73°59W 313 E11
Kingston Pa., U.S.A. 41°16N 75°54W 313 E9
Kingston R.I., U.S.A. 41°29N 71°30W 313 E13
Kingston Pk. U.S.A. 35°44N 115°55W 307 K11
Kingston South East Australia 36°51S 139°55E 282 D3
Kingston upon Hull U.K. 53°45N 0°21W 168 D7
Kingston upon Hull □ U.K. 53°45N 0°21W 168 D7
Kingston-upon-Thames □ U.K. 51°24N 0°17W 125 B2
Kingston Vale U.K. 51°25N 0°25W 125 B2
Kingstown = Dún Laoghaire Ireland 53°17N 6°8W 120 B3
Kingstown N.S.W., Australia 30°29S 151°6E 283 A9
Kingstown St. Vincent 13°10N 61°10W 323 n
Kingstree U.S.A. 33°40N 79°50W 316 B10
Kingsville Ont., Canada 42°2N 82°45W 312 D2
Kingsville Tex., U.S.A. 27°31N 97°52W 314 H6
Kingsway Canada 43°38N 79°32W 141 B1
Kingtechen = Jingdezhen China 29°20N 117°11E 229 C11
Kingunda Dem. Rep. of the Congo 6°36S 16°58E 265 D3
Kingussie U.K. 57°6N 4°2W 167 D4
Kingwood U.S.A. 30°2N 95°16W 314 F7
Kinhwa = Jinhua China 29°8N 119°38E 229 C12
Kınık Antalya, Turkey 36°20N 29°20E 205 E11
Kınık İzmir, Turkey 39°6N 27°24E 205 B9
Kinistino Canada 52°57N 105°2W 297 C7
Kinjirap Daban Asia 36°40N 75°25E 240 A4
Kinkala Congo 4°18S 14°49E 265 C2
Kinki □ Japan 33°45N 136°0E 223 D8
Kinkony, Farihin' Madag. 16°8S 45°50E 272 B2
Kinleith N.Z. 38°20S 175°56E 284 E4
Kinlochleven U.K. 56°43N 5°0W 167 E4
Kinmount Canada 44°48N 78°45W 312 B6
Kinmundy U.S.A. 38°46N 88°51W 311 F8
Kinn Norway 61°34N 4°45E 164 C1
Kinna Sweden 57°32N 12°42E 163 G6
Kinnairds Hd. U.K. 57°43N 2°1W 167 D6
Kinnared Sweden 57°2N 13°7E 163 G7
Kinnarp Sweden 58°5N 13°32E 163 F7
Kinneviken Sweden 58°35N 13°15E 163 F7
Kinngait Canada 64°14N 76°32W 295 E16
Kino Nuevo Mexico 28°52N 112°3W 318 B2
Kinogitan Phil. 9°0N 124°48E 233 G5
Kinoje → Canada 52°8N 81°25W 298 B3
Kinokawa Japan 34°15N 135°20E 223 C7
Kinomoto Japan 35°30N 136°13E 223 B8
Kinoni Uganda 0°41S 30°28E 268 C3
Kinoosao Canada 57°5N 102°1W 297 B8
Kinross U.K. 56°13N 3°25W 167 E5
Kinsale Cork, Ireland 51°42N 8°31W 166 E3
Kinsale Montserrat 16°41N 62°13W 323 p
Kinsale, Old Hd. of Ireland 51°37N 8°33W 166 E3
Kinsaley Ireland 53°24N 6°11W 120 A2
Kinsarvik Norway 60°22N 6°43E 164 D3
Kinsha = Chang Jiang → China 31°48N 121°10E 229 B13
Kinshasa Dem. Rep. of the Congo 4°20S 15°15E 265 C3
Kinsley U.S.A. 37°55N 99°25W 308 G4
Kinsman U.S.A. 41°26N 80°35W 312 E4
Kinston Ala., U.S.A. 31°13N 86°10W 316 D3
Kinston N.C., U.S.A. 35°16N 77°35W 315 D16
Kintamani Indonesia 8°14S 115°19E 231 J18
Kintampo Ghana 8°5N 1°41W 263 D4
Kintap Indonesia 3°51S 115°13E 235 C5
Kintore U.K. 57°14N 2°20W 167 D6
Kintore Ra. Australia 23°15S 128°47E 278 D4
Kintshua Dem. Rep. of the Congo 4°27S 19°38E 265 C3
Kintyre U.K. 55°30N 5°35W 167 F3
Kintyre, Mull of U.K. 55°17N 5°47W 167 F3
Kinu-Gawa → Japan 35°36N 139°57E 223 B11
Kinushseo → Canada 55°15N 83°45W 298 A3
Kinuso Canada 55°20N 115°25W 296 B5
Kinvarra Ireland 53°8N 8°56W 166 C3
Kinwat India 19°38N 78°12E 244 E4
Kinyangiri Tanzania 4°25S 34°37E 268 C3
Kinyeti Sudan 3°57N 32°54E 257 G3
Kinzia Dem. Rep. of the Congo 3°36S 18°26E 264 C3
Kinzig → Germany 48°36N 7°49E 179 G3
Kinzua U.S.A. 41°52N 78°58W 312 E6
Kioni Greece 38°27N 20°41E 207 C2
Kiosk Canada 46°6N 78°53W 298 C4
Kiowa Kans., U.S.A. 37°1N 98°29W 308 G4
Kiowa Okla., U.S.A. 34°43N 95°54W 314 D7
Kipahigan L. Canada 55°20N 101°55W 297 B8
Kipanga Tanzania 6°15S 35°20E 268 D4
Kipapa → U.S.A. 21°24N 158°1W 302 K13
Kiparissia Greece 37°15N 21°40E 204 D3
Kiparissiakos Kolpos Greece 37°25N 21°25E 204 D3
Kipawa, L. Canada 46°50N 79°0W 298 C4
Kipembawe Tanzania 7°38S 33°27E 268 D3
Kipengere Ra. Tanzania 9°12S 34°15E 269 D3
Kipili Tanzania 7°28S 30°32E 268 D3
Kipini Kenya 2°30S 40°32E 268 C5
Kipling Canada 50°6N 102°38W 297 C8
Kipling Heights Canada 43°43N 79°34W 141 A1
Kipnuk U.S.A. 59°56N 164°3W 303 G6
Kippure Ireland 53°11N 6°21W 166 C5
Kipseli Athens, Greece 112 a3
Kipushi Dem. Rep. of the Congo 11°48S 27°12E 269 E2
Kira Panagia Greece 39°17N 24°4E 204 B6
Kirakira Solomon Is. 10°27S 161°56E 287 N11
Kirandul India 18°33N 81°10E 244 E5
Kirane Mali 15°20N 10°20W 262 B2
Kiranomena Madag. 18°17S 46°2E 272 B2
Kiraz Turkey 38°14N 28°13E 205 C10
Kirazlı Turkey 40°2N 26°41E 203 F10
Kirchhain Germany 50°47N 8°56E 178 E4
Kirchheim Germany 48°39N 9°27E 179 G5
Kirchheimbolanden Germany 49°40N 8°0E 179 F3
Kirchschlag Austria 47°30N 16°19E 181 D9
Kirchstockbach Germany 48°1N 11°40E 131 B3
Kirchtrudering Germany 48°7N 11°40E 131 B3
Kirdâsa Egypt 30°2N 31°6E 251 H2
Kirdimi Chad 18°11N 18°31E 259 E3
Kireç Turkey 39°33N 28°22E 205 B10
Kirensk Russia 57°50N 107°55E 215 D11
Kirghiz Range Asia 42°40N 73°40E 217 D8
Kirghizia = Kyrgyzstan ■ Asia 42°0N 75°0E 217 D9
Kirgiz-Kulak = Chirchiq Uzbekistan 41°29N 69°35E 217 D7
Kirgiziya Steppe Eurasia 50°0N 55°0E 187 E10
Kiri Dem. Rep. of the Congo 1°29S 19°0E 264 C3
Kiri Buru India 22°0N 85°0E 244 D7
Kiribati ■ Pac. Oc. 3°0S 180°0E 277 A15
Kırıkhan Turkey 36°31N 36°21E 250 B7
Kirikiri Nigeria 6°26N 3°18E 124 B1
Kırıkkale Turkey 39°51N 33°32E 212 C5
Kirikopuni N.Z. 35°50S 174°1E 284 B3
Kirillov Russia 59°49N 38°24E 188 C10
Kirin = Jilin China 43°44N 126°30E 227 C14
Kirindi Oya → Sri Lanka 6°15N 81°20E 245 L5
Kirinyaga = Kenya, Mt. Kenya 0°10S 37°18E 268 C4
Kirirom △ Cambodia 11°18N 104°5E 237 G5
Kirishi Russia 59°28N 32°0E 188 C7
Kirishima Yaku △ Japan 31°24N 130°50E 221 J5
Kirishima-Yama Japan 31°58N 130°55E 222 F2
Kiritimati Kiribati 1°58N 157°27W 289 G12
Kiriwina I. Papua N. G. 8°40S 151°6E 286 E6
Kirka Turkey 39°17N 30°33E 205 B12
Kırkağaç Turkey 39°8N 27°40E 205 B9
Kirkby U.K. 53°30N 2°54W 168 D5
Kirkby-in-Ashfield U.K. 53°6N 1°14W 168 D6
Kirkby Lonsdale U.K. 54°12N 2°36W 168 C5
Kirkby Stephen U.K. 54°29N 2°21W 168 C5
Kirkcaldy U.K. 56°7N 3°9W 167 E5
Kirkcudbright U.K. 54°50N 4°2W 167 G4
Kirke Værløse Denmark 55°47N 12°19E 118 A1
Kirkehamn Norway 58°14N 6°31E 164 F3
Kirkenær Norway 60°27N 12°3E 164 D9
Kirkenes Norway 69°40N 30°5E 160 B24
Kirkfield Canada 44°34N 78°59W 312 B6
Kirkhill U.K. 55°50N 3°13W 121 B2
Kirkintilloch U.K. 55°56N 4°8W 167 F4
Kirkjubæjarklaustur Iceland 63°47N 18°4W 155 D8
Kirkkonummi Finland 60°8N 24°26E 188 B3
Kirkland Ill., U.S.A. 42°6N 88°51W 311 B8
Kirkland Wash., U.S.A. 47°40N 122°12W 306 C4
Kirkland Lake Canada 48°9N 80°2W 298 C3
Kırklareli Turkey 41°44N 27°15E 203 E11
Kırklareli □ Turkey 41°45N 27°15E 203 E11
Kirklin U.S.A. 40°12N 86°22W 311 D10
Kirkliston U.K. 55°57N 3°24W 121 B1
Kirkliston Ra. N.Z. 44°25S 170°34E 285 E5
Kirknewton U.K. 55°53N 3°25W 121 B1
Kirknitz = Cerknica Slovenia 45°48N 14°21E 199 C11
Kirksville U.S.A. 40°12N 92°35W 310 D4
Kirkūk Iraq 35°30N 44°21E 213 E11
Kirkwall U.K. 58°59N 2°58W 167 C6
Kirkwood Eastern Cape, S. Africa 33°22S 25°15E 270 D4
Kirkwood Mo., U.S.A. 38°35N 90°24W 310 F6
Kirlampudi India 17°12N 82°12E 244 F6
Kirmasti = Mustafakemalpaşa Turkey 40°2N 28°24E 203 F12
Kirn Germany 49°47N 7°26E 179 F3
Kirobası Turkey 36°43N 33°52E 250 B4
Kirov Kaluga, Russia 54°3N 34°20E 188 E8
Kirov Kirov, Russia 58°35N 49°40E 186 C8
Kirov Palace of Culture Russia 59°55N 30°16E 137 B1
Kirovabad = Gäncä Azerbaijan 40°45N 46°20E 191 K8
Kirovakan = Vanadzor Armenia 40°48N 44°30E 191 K7
Kirovo = Kirovohrad Ukraine 48°35N 32°20E 189 H7
Kirovograd = Kirovohrad Ukraine 48°35N 32°20E 189 H7
Kirovohrad Ukraine 48°35N 32°20E 189 H7
Kirovohrad □ Ukraine 48°30N 31°30E 189 H6
Kirovsk Russia 67°32N 33°41E 186 A5
Kirovskiy = Balpyq Bī Kazakhstan 44°52N 78°12E 217 D9
Kirovskiy Astrakhan, Russia 45°51N 48°11E 191 H9
Kirovskiy Kamchatka, Russia 54°27N 155°42E 215 D16
Kirovskiy Primorsk, Russia 45°7N 133°30E 220 B6
Kirriemuir U.K. 56°41N 3°1W 167 E5
Kirsanov Russia 52°35N 42°40E 190 D6
Kırşehir Turkey 39°14N 34°5E 212 C6
Kirtachi Niger 12°52N 2°30E 263 C5
Kīrteh Afghan. 32°15N 63°0E 240 B1

Kirthar △ *Pakistan* 25°45N 67°30E **242** F2
Kirthar Range *Pakistan* 27°0N 67°0E **242** F2
Kirtland *U.S.A.* 36°44N 108°21W **305** H9
Kiruna *Sweden* 67°52N 20°15E **160** C19
Kirundu *Dem. Rep. of the Congo* 0°50S 25°35E **264** C5
Kirya *Russia* 55°8N 46°55E **190** C8
Kiryat Anavim *Israel* 31°49N 35°6E **123** B1
Kiryat Ha Yovel *Israel* 31°46N 35°10E **123** B1
Kiryū *Japan* 36°24N 139°20E **223** A11
Kisa *Sweden* 58°0N 15°39E **163** G9
Kisaga *Tanzania* 4°30S 34°23E **268** C3
Kisalföld *Hungary* 47°30N 17°0E **182** C2
Kisambo *Dem. Rep. of the Congo* 6°25S 18°14E **265** D3
Kisandji *Dem. Rep. of the Congo* 6°18S 19°16E **265** D3
Kisanga *Dem. Rep. of the Congo* 2°30N 26°35E **268** B2
Kisangani *Dem. Rep. of the Congo* 0°35N 25°15E **268** B2
Kisantu *Dem. Rep. of the Congo* 5°7S 15°5E **265** D3
Kisar *Indonesia* 8°5S 127°10E **231** F7
Kisaran *Indonesia* 3°0N 99°37E **234** B1
Kisarawe *Tanzania* 6°53S 39°0E **268** D4
Kisarazu *Japan* 35°23N 139°55E **223** B11
Kisbér *Hungary* 47°30N 18°2E **182** C3
Kiselevsk *Russia* 54°5N 86°39E **217** B11
Kish = Qeys *Iran* 26°32N 53°58E **249** A6
Kishanganga → *Pakistan* 34°18N 73°28E **243** B5
Kishanganj *India* 26°3N 88°14E **241** B2
Kishangarh *Raj., India* 26°34N 74°52E **242** F6
Kishangarh *Raj., India* 27°50N 70°30E **242** F4
Kishb, Ḩarrat al *Si. Arabia* 22°30N 40°15E **248** B3
Kishi *Nigeria* 9°1N 3°52E **263** D5
Kishinev = Chişinău *Moldova* 47°2N 28°50E **183** C13
Kishiwada *Japan* 34°28N 135°22E **223** C7
Kishkareny = Lazo *Moldova* 47°33N 28°2E **183** C13
Kishkeneköl *Kazakhstan* 53°38N 72°20E **217** B8
Kishorganj *Bangla.* 24°26N 90°40E **241** C3
Kishtwar *India* 33°20N 75°48E **242** C6
Kishwaukee → *U.S.A.* 42°12N 89°8W **310** B7
Kisielice *Poland* 53°36N 19°16E **184** E6
Kisigo ⌓ *Tanzania* 6°27S 34°17E **268** D3
Kisii *Kenya* 0°40S 34°45E **268** C3
Kisiju *Tanzania* 7°23S 39°19E **268** D4
Kısıklı *Turkey* 41°1N 29°2E **122** B2
Kisir *Turkey* 41°0N 43°5E **213** B10
Kisizi *Uganda* 1°0S 29°58E **268** C2
Kiska I. *U.S.A.* 51°59N 177°30E **303** L2
Kiskomárom = Zalakomár *Hungary* 46°33N 17°10E **182** D2
Kiskörei-víztároló *Hungary* 47°31N 20°36E **182** C5
Kiskőrös *Hungary* 46°37N 19°20E **182** D4
Kiskundorozsma *Hungary* 46°16N 20°5E **182** D5
Kiskunfélegyháza *Hungary* 46°42N 19°53E **182** D4
Kiskunhalas *Hungary* 46°28N 19°37E **182** D4
Kiskunmajsa *Hungary* 46°30N 19°48E **182** D4
Kiskunsági △ *Hungary* 46°39N 19°30E **182** D4
Kislovodsk *Russia* 43°50N 42°45E **191** J6
Kismaayo *Somali Rep.* 0°22S 42°32E **267** E5
Kismayu △ *Somali Rep.* 1°25N 41°30E **267** D5
Kiso-Gawa → *Japan* 35°20N 136°45E **223** B8
Kiso-Sammyaku *Japan* 35°45N 137°45E **223** B9
Kisofukushima *Japan* 35°52N 137°43E **223** B9
Kisoro *Uganda* 1°17S 29°48E **268** C2
Kispest *Hungary* 47°27N 19°8E **117** B2
Kissamos = Kasteli *Greece* 35°29N 23°38E **207** E4
Kissamos, Kolpos *Greece* 35°30N 23°38E **207** E4
Kissidougou *Guinea* 9°5N 10°5W **262** D2
Kissimmee *U.S.A.* 28°18N 81°24W **317** G8
Kissimmee → *U.S.A.* 27°9N 80°52W **317** H8
Kissimmee, L. *U.S.A.* 27°55N 81°17W **317** H8
Kississing L. *Canada* 55°10N 101°20W **297** B8
Kissónerga *Cyprus* 34°49N 32°24E **207** F8
Kissu, J. *Sudan* 21°37N 25°10E **256** C2
Kista *Sweden* 59°24N 17°57E **139** A1
Kistanje *Croatia* 43°58N 15°55E **199** E12
Kistna = Krishna → *India* 15°57N 80°59E **245** G5
Kisújszállás *Hungary* 47°12N 20°50E **182** C5
Kisuki *Japan* 35°17N 132°54E **222** B4
Kisumu *Kenya* 0°3S 34°45E **268** C3
Kisvárda *Hungary* 48°14N 22°4E **182** B7
Kiswani *Tanzania* 4°5S 37°57E **268** C4
Kiswere *Tanzania* 9°27S 39°30E **269** D4
Kit Carson *U.S.A.* 38°46N 102°48W **304** G12
Kita *Ōsaka, Japan* 34°41N 135°30E **133** A2
Kita *Tōkyō, Japan* 35°44N 139°44E **140** A3
Kita *Mali* 13°5N 9°25W **262** C3
Kita-Ura *Japan* 36°0N 140°34E **223** B12
Kitaa □ *Greenland* 70°0N 47°0W **154** C6
Kitaibaraki *Japan* 36°50N 140°45E **221** F10
Kitakami *Japan* 39°20N 141°10E **220** E10
Kitakami-Gawa → *Japan* 38°25N 141°19E **220** E10
Kitakami-Sammyaku *Japan* 39°30N 141°30E **220** E10
Kitakata *Japan* 37°39N 139°52E **220** F9
Kitakyūshū *Japan* 33°50N 130°50E **222** D2
Kitale *Kenya* 1°0N 35°0E **268** B4
Kitami *Japan* 43°48N 143°54E **220** C11
Kitami-Sammyaku *Japan* 44°22N 142°43E **220** B11
Kitangiri, L. *Tanzania* 4°5S 34°20E **268** C3
Kitanglad △ *Phil.* 8°57N 124°21E **233** G5
Kitano Hana *Iwo Jima* 24°49N 141°20E **288** b
Kitano-Kaikyō *Japan* 34°17N 134°58E **222** C6
Kitaotao *Phil.* 7°40N 125°1E **233** H5
Kitava I. *Papua N. G.* 8°40S 151°20E **286** E6
Kitaya *Tanzania* 10°38S 40°8E **269** E5
Kitazawa *Japan* 35°39N 139°40E **140** B3
Kitcharao *Phil.* 9°27N 125°36E **233** G5
Kitchener *Canada* 43°27N 80°29W **312** C4
Kitee *Finland* 62°5N 30°8E **188** A6
Kitega = Gitega *Burundi* 3°26S 29°56E **268** C2
Kitengo *Dem. Rep. of the Congo* 7°26S 24°8E **265** D4
Kitgum *Uganda* 3°17N 32°52E **268** B3
Kíthira = Kythira *Greece* 36°8N 23°0E **204** E5
Kithnos *Greece* 37°26N 24°27E **204** D6
Kiti *Cyprus* 34°50N 33°34E **207** F9
Kiti, C. *Cyprus* 34°48N 33°36E **207** F9
Kitimat *Canada* 54°3N 128°38W **296** C3
Kitinen → *Finland* 67°14N 27°27E **160** C22
Kitiyab *Sudan* 17°13N 33°35E **257** D3
Kitombe *Dem. Rep. of the Congo* 5°22S 18°59E **265** D3
Kitridge Pt. *Barbados* 13°9N 59°25W **323** r
Kitros *Greece* 40°22N 22°34E **202** F6
Kitsman *Ukraine* 48°26N 25°46E **183** B10
Kitsuki *Japan* 33°25N 131°37E **222** D3
Kittakittaooloo, L. *Australia* 28°3S 138°14E **281** D2
Kittanning *U.S.A.* 40°49N 79°31W **312** F5
Kittatinny Mt. *U.S.A.* 41°19N 74°39W **313** F10
Kittery *U.S.A.* 43°5N 70°45W **313** C14
Kittilä *Finland* 67°40N 24°51E **160** C21
Kitui *Kenya* 1°17S 38°0E **268** C4
Kitwanga *Canada* 55°6N 128°4W **296** B3
Kitwe *Zambia* 12°54S 28°13E **269** E2
Kityang = Jieyang *China* 23°35N 116°21E **229** F11
Kitzbühel *Austria* 47°27N 12°24E **180** D5
Kitzbühler Alpen *Austria* 47°20N 12°20E **180** D5
Kitzingen *Germany* 49°44N 10°9E **179** F6
Kiu Tsiu *China* 22°22N 114°17E **122** A2
Kiukiang = Jiujiang *China* 29°42N 115°58E **229** C10
Kiunga *Papua N. G.* 6°7S 141°18E **286** D1
Kiunga Marine ⌓ *Kenya* 2°1S 41°14E **268** C5
Kivalina *U.S.A.* 67°44N 164°33W **303** C6
Kivarli *India* 24°33N 72°46E **242** G5
Kivertsi *Ukraine* 50°50N 25°28E **177** C13
Kividhes *Cyprus* 34°46N 32°51E **207** F8
Kivik *Sweden* 55°41N 14°13E **163** J8
Kivistö *Finland* 60°18N 24°50E **121** B2
Kivotos *Greece* 40°13N 21°26E **202** F5
Kivu, L. *Dem. Rep. of the Congo* 1°48S 29°0E **268** C2
Kiwai I. *Papua N. G.* 8°35S 143°30E **286** E2
Kiwirrkurra *Australia* 22°49S 127°45E **278** D4
Kiwirrkurra ✪ *Australia* 22°49S 127°45E **278** D4
Kiyev = Kyyiv *Ukraine* 50°30N 30°28E **177** C16
Kiyevskoye Vdkhr. = Kyyivske Vdskh. *Ukraine* 51°0N 30°25E **177** C16
Kıyıköy *Turkey* 41°38N 28°5E **203** E12
Kizel *Russia* 59°3N 57°40E **186** C10
Kizhi, Ostrov *Russia* 65°12N 35°28E **188** B8
Kiziba-Baluba ⌓ *Congo* 11°50S 28°0E **269** E2
Kiziguru *Rwanda* 1°46S 30°23E **268** C3
Kızıl Adalar *Turkey* 40°52N 29°5E **203** F13
Kızıl Dağ *Turkey* 36°19N 35°57E **250** B6
Kızıl Irmak → *Turkey* 41°44N 35°58E **212** B6
Kizil Jilga *China* 35°26N 78°50E **243** B8
Kizil Yurt *Russia* 43°13N 46°54E **191** J8
Kızılcabölük *Turkey* 37°37N 29°1E **205** D11
Kızılcadağ *Turkey* 37°1N 29°58E **205** D11
Kızılcahamam *Turkey* 40°30N 32°30E **212** B5
Kızıldağ △ *Turkey* 38°5N 31°20E **246** B1
Kızılhisar *Turkey* 37°32N 29°17E **212** D3
Kızılırmak *Turkey* 40°21N 33°59E **212** B5
Kızılkaya *Turkey* 37°18N 30°27E **205** D12
Kızılören *Turkey* 38°15N 30°10E **205** C12
Kızıltepe *Turkey* 37°12N 40°35E **213** D9
Kızıltoprak *Turkey* 40°58N 29°3E **122** C2
Kizimkazi *Tanzania* 6°28S 39°30E **268** D4
Kizlyar *Russia* 43°51N 46°40E **191** J8
Kizuri *Japan* 34°38N 135°34E **133** B2
Kizyl-Arvat = Serdar *Turkmenistan* 39°4N 56°23E **247** B8
Kjellerup *Denmark* 56°17N 9°25E **163** H3
Kjellmyra *Norway* 60°39N 12°1E **164** D9
Kjelsås *Norway* 59°57N 10°47E **133** A3
Kjølen *Norway* 62°3N 8°45E **164** C5
Kjölur *Iceland* 64°50N 19°25W **155** C7
Kjósarsýsla □ *Iceland* 64°15N 21°30W **155** C5
Kladanj *Bos.-H.* 44°14N 18°42E **182** F3
Kladnica *Serbia* 43°23N 20°2E **202** C4
Kladno *Czech Rep.* 50°10N 14°7E **180** A7
Kladovo *Serbia* 44°36N 22°33E **202** B6
Kladow *Germany* 52°27N 13°9E **115** B1
Klæbu *Norway* 63°18N 10°29E **164** A7
Klaeng *Thailand* 12°47N 101°39E **236** F3
Klagan *Malaysia* 5°58N 117°27E **235** A5
Klagenfurt *Austria* 46°38N 14°20E **180** E7
Klaipėda *Lithuania* 55°43N 21°10E **184** C8
Klaipėda □ *Lithuania* 55°43N 21°7E **184** C8
Klaksvík *Færoe Is.* 62°14N 6°35W **160** E9
Klamath → *U.S.A.* 41°33N 124°5W **304** F1
Klamath Falls *U.S.A.* 42°13N 121°46W **304** E3
Klamath Mts. *U.S.A.* 41°50N 123°20W **304** F2
Klamono *Indonesia* 1°8S 131°30E **231** E8
Klampenborg *Denmark* 55°46N 12°35E **118** A3
Klampo *Indonesia* 0°7N 116°58E **235** B5
Klang *Malaysia* 3°2N 101°26E **237** L3
Klangklang *Burma* 22°41N 93°26E **241** D4
Klanjec *Croatia* 46°3N 15°45E **199** B12
Klappan → *Canada* 58°0N 129°43W **296** B3
Klara = Trysilelva → *Norway* 61°2N 12°35E **164** C9
Klarälven → *Sweden* 59°23N 13°32E **162** E7
Klässbol *Sweden* 59°33N 12°45E **162** E6
Klaten *Indonesia* 7°43S 110°36E **235** D4
Klatovy *Czech Rep.* 49°23N 13°18E **180** B6
Klausenburg = Cluj-Napoca *Romania* 46°47N 23°38E **183** D8
Klawer *S. Africa* 31°44S 18°36E **270** D2
Klawock *U.S.A.* 55°33N 133°6W **303** J14
Klazienaveen *Neths.* 52°44N 7°0E **170** B6
Klé *Mali* 12°0N 6°28W **262** C3
Klečany *Czech Rep.* 50°10N 14°24E **135** A2
Kłecko *Poland* 52°38N 17°25E **185** F4
Kleczew *Poland* 52°22N 18°9E **185** F5
Kledering *Austria* 48°8N 16°26E **142** B2
Kleena Kleene *Canada* 52°0N 124°59W **296** C4
Klein Bonaire *Bonaire* 12°9N 68°18W **322** h
Klein Jukskei → *S. Africa* 26°6S 27°57E **123** A1
Klein-Karas *Namibia* 27°33S 18°7E **270** C2
Klein-Schlatten = Zlatna *Romania* 46°8N 23°11E **183** D8
Kleinbegin *S. Africa* 28°54S 21°40E **270** C3
Kleinmachnow *Germany* 52°24N 13°14E **115** B2
Kleinschönebeck *Germany* 52°29N 13°42E **115** B5
Klekovača *Bos.-H.* 44°25N 16°32E **199** D13
Klembivka *Ukraine* 48°23N 28°25E **183** B13
Klemetsrud *Norway* 59°50N 10°51E **133** A4
Klender *Indonesia* 6°12S 106°54E **122** A2
Klenoec *Macedonia* 41°32N 20°49E **202** E4
Klenovec *Slovak Rep.* 48°36N 19°54E **181** C12
Klerksdorp *S. Africa* 26°53S 26°38E **270** C4
Kleszczele *Poland* 52°35N 23°19E **185** F10
Kletnya *Russia* 53°23N 33°12E **188** F7
Kletsk = Klyetsk *Belarus* 53°5N 26°45E **177** B14
Kletskiy *Russia* 49°16N 43°11E **191** F6
Kleve *Germany* 51°47N 6°7E **178** D2
Kličany *Czech Rep.* 50°11N 14°25E **135** A2
Klickitat *U.S.A.* 45°49N 121°9W **304** D3
Klickitat → *U.S.A.* 45°42N 121°17W **306** E5
Klidhes *Cyprus* 35°42N 34°36E **207** E10
Klimovichi *Belarus* 53°36N 32°0E **188** F6
Klin *Russia* 56°20N 36°48E **188** D9
Klina *Kosovo* 42°37N 20°35E **202** D4
Klinaklini → *Canada* 51°21N 125°40W **296** C3
Klintehamn *Sweden* 57°24N 18°12E **163** G12
Klintsy *Russia* 52°50N 32°10E **189** F7
Klip → *S. Africa* 27°3S 29°3E **271** C4
Klipdale *S. Africa* 34°19S 19°57E **270** D2
Klippan *Sweden* 56°8N 13°10E **163** H7
Klipplaat *S. Africa* 33°1S 24°22E **270** D3
Klipriviersberg Nature Reserve *S. Africa* 26°16S 28°2E **123** B2
Klishkivtsi *Ukraine* 48°26N 26°16E **183** B11
Klisura *Bulgaria* 42°40N 24°28E **203** D8
Kljajićevo *Serbia* 45°45N 19°17E **182** E4
Ključ *Bos.-H.* 44°32N 16°48E **199** D13
Kłobuck *Poland* 50°55N 18°55E **185** H5
Klockestrand *Sweden* 62°53N 17°55E **162** B11
Kłodawa *Poland* 52°15N 18°55E **185** F5
Kłodzko *Poland* 50°28N 16°38E **185** H3
Kløfta *Norway* 60°4N 11°10E **164** D8
Klondike *Canada* 64°0N 139°26W **294** E4
Klondike Goldrush ⌓ *U.S.A.* 59°27N 135°19W **303** G14
Klong Wang Chao △ *Thailand* 16°20N 99°9E **236** D2
Klos *Albania* 41°28N 20°10E **202** E4
Klosterneuburg *Austria* 48°18N 16°19E **142** A1
Klosters *Switz.* 46°52N 9°52E **179** J5
Klötze *Germany* 52°37N 11°10E **178** C7
Klouto *Togo* 6°57N 0°44E **263** D5
Klövsjö *Sweden* 62°32N 14°11E **162** B8
Kluane △ *Canada* 60°45N 139°30W **296** A1
Kluane L. *Canada* 61°15N 138°40W **294** E4
Kluang *Malaysia* 2°3N 103°18E **237** L4
Kluczbork *Poland* 50°58N 18°12E **185** H5
Klukhori = Karachayevsk *Russia* 43°50N 41°55E **191** J5
Klukwan *U.S.A.* 59°24N 135°54W **296** B1
Klungkung *Indonesia* 8°32S 115°24E **231** K18
Klyetsk *Belarus* 53°5N 26°45E **177** B14
Klyuchevskaya, Gora *Russia* 55°50N 160°30E **215** D17
Klyuchi *Russia* 56°18N 160°51E **215** D17
Knaben *Norway* 58°40N 7°4E **164** F4
Knappavellir *Iceland* 63°54N 16°36W **155** D10
Knäred *Sweden* 56°31N 13°19E **163** H7
Knaresborough *U.K.* 54°1N 1°28W **168** C6
Knarvik *Norway* 60°32N 5°19E **164** D2
Knee L. *Man., Canada* 55°3N 94°45W **298** A1
Knee L. *Sask., Canada* 55°51N 107°0W **297** B7
Kneïss, Îs. *Tunisia* 34°22N 10°18E **258** B2
Knesset *Jerusalem* **123** b1
Knezha *Bulgaria* 43°30N 24°5E **203** C8
Knight I. *U.S.A.* 60°21N 147°45W **303** F11
Knight Inlet *Canada* 50°45N 125°40W **296** C3
Knighton *U.K.* 52°21N 3°3W **169** E4
Knights Ferry *U.S.A.* 37°50N 120°40W **306** H6
Knights Landing *U.S.A.* 38°48N 121°43W **306** G5
Knightsbridge *London, U.K.* **125** c2
Knightstown *U.S.A.* 39°48N 85°32W **311** E11
Knin *Croatia* 44°3N 16°17E **199** D13
Knislinge *Sweden* 56°12N 14°5E **163** H8
Knittelfeld *Austria* 47°13N 14°51E **180** D7
Knivsta *Sweden* 59°43N 17°48E **162** E11
Knjaževac *Serbia* 43°35N 22°18E **202** C6
Knob, C. *Australia* 34°32S 119°16E **279** F2
Knob Lake = Kawawachikamach *Canada* 54°48N 66°50W **299** B6
Knob Noster *U.S.A.* 38°46N 93°33W **310** F3
Knock *Ireland* 53°48N 8°55W **166** C3
Knockmealdown Mts. *Ireland* 52°14N 7°56W **166** D4
Knokke-Heist *Belgium* 51°21N 3°17E **170** C3
Knossos *Greece* 35°16N 25°10E **207** E6
Knowlton *Canada* 45°13N 72°31W **313** A12
Knox *U.S.A.* 41°18N 86°37W **311** C10
Knox Coast *Antarctica* 66°30S 108°0E **151** C8
Knoxville *Ga., U.S.A.* 32°47N 83°59W **316** C6
Knoxville *Ill., U.S.A.* 40°55N 90°17W **310** D6
Knoxville *Iowa, U.S.A.* 41°19N 93°6W **310** C4
Knoxville *Pa., U.S.A.* 41°57N 77°27W **312** E7
Knoxville *Tenn., U.S.A.* 35°58N 83°55W **315** D13
Knud Rasmussen Land *Greenland* 78°0N 60°0W **154** B4
Knysna *S. Africa* 34°2S 23°2E **270** D3
Knyszyn *Poland* 53°20N 22°56E **184** E9
Ko Kha *Thailand* 18°11N 99°24E **236** C2
Kō-Saki *Japan* 34°5N 129°13E **222** C1
Ko Tarutao △ *Thailand* 6°31N 99°26E **237** J2
Ko Yao *Thailand* 8°7N 98°35E **237** a
Koartac = Quaqtaq *Canada* 60°55N 69°40W **295** E18
Koba *Aru, Indonesia* 6°37S 134°37E **231** F8
Koba *Bangka, Indonesia* 2°26S 106°14E **234** C3
Kőbánya *Hungary* 47°28N 19°9E **117** B2
Kobarid *Slovenia* 46°15N 13°30E **199** B10
Kobayashi *Japan* 31°56N 130°59E **222** F2
Kobbegem *Belgium* 50°55N 4°15E **116** A1
Kobdo = Hovd □ *Mongolia* 48°2N 91°37E **217** C12
Kōbe *Japan* 34°41N 135°13E **223** C7
Kobelyaky *Ukraine* 49°11N 34°9E **189** H8
København *Denmark* 55°40N 12°26E **118** A2
København ✈ **(CPH)** *Denmark* 55°37N 12°39E **118** B3
Kobenni *Mauritania* 15°58N 9°24W **262** B3
Kōbi-Sho *Japan* 25°56N 123°41E **221** M1
Koblenz *Germany* 50°21N 7°36E **179** E3
Kobo *Dem. Rep. of the Congo* 4°54S 17°9E **265** C3
Kobo *Ethiopia* 12°2N 39°56E **257** E4
Kobryn *Belarus* 52°15N 24°22E **177** B13
Kobuchizawa *Japan* 35°52N 138°19E **223** B10
Kobuk *U.S.A.* 66°55N 156°52W **303** C8
Kobuk → *U.S.A.* 66°54N 160°38W **303** C7
Kobuk Valley △ *U.S.A.* 67°0N 160°0W **303** C7
Kobuleti *Georgia* 41°55N 41°45E **191** K5
Kobyletska Polyana *Ukraine* 48°3N 24°4E **183** B9
Kobylin *Poland* 51°43N 17°12E **185** G4
Kobylisy *Czech Rep.* 50°7N 14°26E **135** B2
Kobyłka *Poland* 52°20N 21°10E **142** A3
Kobylkino *Russia* 54°8N 43°56E **190** C6
Koca → *Turkey* 40°8N 27°57E **203** F11
Kocabaş *Turkey* 37°49N 29°20E **205** D11
Kocaeli *Turkey* 40°45N 29°50E **203** F13
Kocaeli □ *Turkey* 40°45N 29°55E **203** F13
Kočane *Serbia* 43°12N 21°52E **202** C5
Kočani *Macedonia* 41°55N 22°25E **202** E6
Koçarlı *Turkey* 37°45N 27°43E **205** D9
Koceljevo *Serbia* 44°28N 19°50E **202** B3
Kočevje *Slovenia* 45°39N 14°50E **199** C11
Kocgiri = Zara *Turkey* 39°58N 37°43E **212** C7
Koch Bihar *India* 26°22N 89°29E **241** B2
Kochas *India* 25°15N 83°56E **243** G10
Kocher → *Germany* 49°13N 9°12E **179** F5
Kochi = Cochin *India* 9°58N 76°20E **245** K3
Kōchi *Japan* 33°30N 133°35E **222** D5
Kōchi □ *Japan* 33°40N 133°30E **222** D5
Kochiu = Gejiu *China* 23°20N 103°10E **228** F4
Kochkor *Kyrgyzstan* 42°13N 75°46E **217** D9
Kochubey *Russia* 44°23N 46°32E **191** H8
Kock *Poland* 51°38N 22°27E **185** G9
Kodaira *Japan* 35°43N 139°28E **140** A1
Kodala *India* 19°38N 84°57E **244** E7
Kodanaka *Japan* 35°34N 139°37E **140** B2
Kodarma *India* 24°28N 85°36E **243** G11
Koddiyar B. *Sri Lanka* 8°33N 81°15E **245** K5
Kode *Sweden* 57°57N 11°51E **163** G5
Kodenmacho *Tokyo, Japan* **140** a5
Kodi *Dem. Rep. of the Congo* 3°34S 22°12E **264** C4
Kodi *Indonesia* 9°33S 119°0E **278** A2
Kodiak *U.S.A.* 57°47N 152°24W **303** H9
Kodiak I. *U.S.A.* 57°30N 152°45W **303** H9
Kodikkarai = Point Calimere *India* 10°17N 79°49E **245** J4
Kodinar *India* 20°46N 70°46E **242** J4
Kodinsk *Russia* 58°40N 99°10E **215** D10
Kodlipet *India* 12°48N 75°53E **245** H2
Kodok *Sudan* 9°53N 32°7E **257** F3
Kodori → *Georgia* 42°47N 41°10E **191** J5
Kodoro *Dem. Rep. of the Congo* 1°16N 20°6E **264** B4
Kodungallur = Cranganore *India* 10°13N 76°13E **245** J3
Kodyma *Ukraine* 48°6N 29°7E **183** B14
Koedoesberge *S. Africa* 32°40S 20°11E **270** D3
Koekelberg *Belgium* 50°52N 4°20E **116** A1
Koes *Namibia* 26°0S 19°15E **270** C2
Kofarnihon *Tajikistan* 38°33N 69°1E **217** E7
Kofçaz *Turkey* 41°58N 27°12E **203** E11
Koffiefontein *S. Africa* 29°30S 25°0E **270** C4
Kofiau *Indonesia* 1°11S 129°50E **231** E7
Köflach *Austria* 47°4N 15°5E **180** D8
Koforidua *Ghana* 6°3N 0°17W **263** D4
Kōfu *Japan* 35°40N 138°30E **223** B10
Koga *Japan* 33°45N 130°25E **222** D2
Koga *Japan* 36°11N 139°43E **223** A11
Kogaluc → *Canada* 56°12N 61°44W **299** A7
Koganei *Japan* 35°42N 139°31E **140** A2
Kogarah *Australia* 33°57S 151°8E **139** B1
Køge *Denmark* 55°27N 12°11E **163** J6
Køge Bugt *Denmark* 55°34N 12°24E **163** J6
Kogi □ *Nigeria* 7°45N 6°45E **263** D6
Kogin Baba *Nigeria* 7°55N 11°35E **263** D7
Kogo *Eq. Guin.* 1°5N 9°42E **264** B1
Kogon *Uzbekistan* 39°43N 64°33E **216** E6
Koh-i-Khurd *Afghan.* 33°30N 65°59E **242** C1
Koh-i-Maran *Pakistan* 29°18N 66°50E **242** E2
Koh Ker *Cambodia* 13°47N 104°32E **236** F5
Koh Wai *Thailand* 11°54N 102°25E **237** H4
Kohala Mts. *U.S.A.* 20°5N 155°45W **302** C6
Kohat *Pakistan* 33°40N 71°29E **242** C4
Kohima *India* 25°35N 94°10E **241** C5
Kohkīlūyeh va Būyer Aḩmadi □ *Iran* 31°30N 50°30E **247** D6
Kohler Ra. *Antarctica* 77°0S 110°0W **151** D15
Kohlfurt = Węgliniec *Poland* 51°18N 15°10E **185** G2
Kohlu *Pakistan* 29°54N 69°15E **242** E3
Kohtla-Järve *Estonia* 59°20N 27°20E **188** C4
Kohukohu *N.Z.* 35°22S 173°38E **284** B2
Kohylnyk → *Ukraine* 45°49N 29°40E **183** E14
Koi Sanjaq *Iraq* 36°5N 44°38E **213** D11
Koidu *S. Leone* 8°38N 10°59W **262** D2
Koihoa *India* 8°12N 93°29E **245** K11
Koilkuntla *India* 15°14N 78°19E **245** G4
Koillismaa *Finland* 65°44N 28°36E **160** D23
Koimbani *Comoros Is.* 11°37S 43°21E **272** a
Koin *N. Korea* 40°28N 126°18E **224** B3
Koinare *Bulgaria* 43°21N 24°8E **203** C8
Koindu *S. Leone* 8°26N 10°19W **262** D2
Koivisto = Primorsk *Russia* 60°22N 28°37E **188** B5
Koivupää *Finland* 60°18N 24°53E **121** B2
Koja *Indonesia* 6°8S 106°52E **122** A2
Koja Utara *Indonesia* 6°5S 106°53E **122** A2
Kojetín *Czech Rep.* 49°21N 17°20E **181** B10
Kojŏ *N. Korea* 38°58N 127°58E **224** C3
Kojonup *Australia* 33°48S 117°10E **279** F2
Kojūr *Iran* 36°23N 51°43E **247** B6
Kokand = Qŭqon *Uzbekistan* 40°31N 70°56E **217** D8
Kokas *Indonesia* 2°42S 132°26E **231** E8
Kokava *Slovak Rep.* 48°35N 19°50E **181** C12
Kokcha → *Afghan.* 37°9N 69°24E **240** A3
Kokchetav = Kökshetaū *Kazakhstan* 53°20N 69°25E **217** B7
Köke'e State Park ⌓ *U.S.A.* 22°6N 159°40W **302** A2
Kokemäenjoki → *Finland* 61°32N 21°44E **188** B1
Kokerite *Guyana* 7°12N 59°35W **329** B6
Kokhav Ya'akov *West Bank* 31°53N 35°14E **123** A2
Kokhma *Russia* 56°57N 41°8E **190** B5
Koki *Senegal* 15°30N 15°59W **262** B1
Kokiu = Gejiu *China* 23°20N 103°10E **228** F4
Kokkilai *Sri Lanka* 9°0N 80°57E **245** K5
Kokkina *Cyprus* 35°11N 32°36E **207** E8
Kokkola *Finland* 63°50N 23°8E **160** E20
Koko *Nigeria* 11°28N 4°29E **263** C5
Koko Head *U.S.A.* 21°16N 157°43W **302** K14
Koko Kyunzu *Burma* 14°7N 93°22E **245** G11
Kokobunji *Japan* 35°42N 139°27E **140** A1
Kokobunji-Temple *Japan* 35°44N 139°55E **140** A4
Kokoda *Papua N. G.* 8°54S 147°47E **286** E4
Kokologo *Burkina Faso* 12°11N 1°53W **262** C4
Kokolopozo *Ivory C.* 5°8N 6°5W **262** D3
Kokomo *U.S.A.* 40°29N 86°8W **311** D10
Kokopo *Papua N. G.* 4°22S 152°19E **286** C7
Kokoro *Niger* 14°12N 0°55E **263** C5
Koksan *N. Korea* 38°46N 126°40E **224** C3
Kökshetaū *Kazakhstan* 53°20N 69°25E **217** B7
Koksoak → *Canada* 58°30N 68°10W **295** F18
Kokstad *S. Africa* 30°32S 29°29E **271** D4
Köktal *Kazakhstan* 44°8N 79°48E **217** D9
Kokubu *Japan* 31°44N 130°46E **222** F2
Kokyar *China* 37°23N 77°10E **217** E9
Kola *Indonesia* 5°35S 134°30E **231** F8
Kola *Russia* 68°45N 33°8E **160** B25
Kola Pen. = Kolskiy Poluostrov *Russia* 67°30N 38°0E **186** A6
Kolachel *India* 8°10N 77°15E **245** K3
Kolachi → *Pakistan* 27°8N 67°2E **242** F2
Kolahoi *India* 34°12N 75°22E **243** B6
Kolahun *Liberia* 8°15N 10°4W **262** D2
Kolaka *Indonesia* 4°3S 121°46E **231** E6
Kolar *India* 13°12N 78°15E **245** H4
Kolar Gold Fields *India* 12°58N 78°16E **245** H4
Kolarängen *Sweden* 59°16N 18°10E **139** B3
Kolaras *India* 25°14N 77°36E **242** G6
Kolari *Finland* 67°20N 23°48E **160** C20
Kolarovgrad = Shumen *Bulgaria* 43°18N 26°55E **203** C10
Kolárovo *Slovak Rep.* 47°54N 18°0E **181** D10
Kolašin *Montenegro* 42°50N 19°31E **202** D3
Kolayat *India* 27°50N 72°50E **242** F5
Kolbäck *Sweden* 59°34N 16°15E **162** E10
Kolbäcksån → *Sweden* 59°36N 16°16E **162** E10
Kolbeinsstaðir *Iceland* 64°59N 22°16W **155** C4
Kolberg = Kołobrzeg *Poland* 54°10N 15°35E **184** D2
Kolbermoor *Germany* 47°51N 12°4E **179** H8
Kolbio *Kenya* 1°8S 41°12E **267** E5
Kolbotn *Norway* 59°48N 10°48E **133** B3
Kolbu *Norway* 60°39N 10°45E **164** D7
Kolbuszowa *Poland* 50°15N 21°46E **185** H8
Kolchugino = Leninsk-Kuznetskiy *Russia* 54°44N 86°10E **217** B11
Kolchugino *Russia* 56°17N 39°22E **188** D10
Kolda *Senegal* 12°55N 14°57W **262** C2
Kolda □ *Senegal* 13°5N 14°50W **262** C2
Koldegi *Sudan* 12°3N 30°16E **257** E3
Kolding *Denmark* 55°30N 9°29E **163** J3
Kole *Dem. Rep. of the Congo* 3°16S 22°42E **264** C4
Koléa *Algeria* 36°38N 2°46E **261** A5
Kolepom = Dolak, Pulau *Indonesia* 8°0S 138°30E **231** F9
Kolguyev, Ostrov *Russia* 69°20N 48°30E **186** A8
Kolhapur *India* 16°43N 74°15E **244** F2
Kolia *Ivory C.* 9°46N 6°28W **262** D3
Koliganek *U.S.A.* 59°48N 157°25W **303** G8
Kolimbia *Greece* 36°15N 28°10E **206** E12
Kolín *Czech Rep.* 50°2N 15°9E **180** A8
Kolind *Denmark* 56°21N 10°34E **163** H4
Kolkas rags *Latvia* 57°46N 22°37E **184** A9
Kolkata *India* 22°34N 88°21E **124** B2
Kolkata Dum Dum Int. ✈ **(CCU)** *India* 22°38N 88°26E **124** B2
Kolkata Maidan *India* 22°33N 88°21E **124** B1
Kollam = Quilon *India* 8°50N 76°38E **245** K3
Kölleda *Germany* 51°11N 11°15E **178** D7
Kollegal *India* 12°9N 77°9E **245** H3
Kolleru L. *India* 16°40N 81°10E **244** F5
Kollum *Neths.* 53°17N 6°10E **170** A6
Kolmanskop *Namibia* 26°45S 15°14E **270** C2
Köln *Germany* 50°56N 6°57E **178** E2
Kolno *Poland* 53°25N 21°56E **184** E8
Koło *Warszawa, Poland* 52°14N 20°56E **142** B1
Koło *Wielkopolskie, Poland* 52°14N 18°40E **185** F5
Kołobrzeg *Poland* 54°10N 15°35E **184** D2
Kolochava *Ukraine* 48°26N 23°41E **183** B8
Kologi *Sudan* 10°51N 30°58E **257** E3
Kolokani *Mali* 13°35N 7°45W **262** C3
Kolokinthou *Greece* 38°0N 23°42E **112** B2
Koloko *Burkina Faso* 11°5N 5°19W **262** C3
Kololo *Ethiopia* 7°29N 41°58E **257** F5
Kolombangara *Solomon Is.* 8°0S 157°5E **287** M9
Kolomna *Russia* 55°8N 38°45E **188** E10
Kolomyagi *Russia* 60°0N 30°19E **137** A1
Kolomyya *Ukraine* 48°31N 25°2E **183** B10
Kolondiéba *Mali* 11°5N 6°54W **262** C3
Kolonodale *Indonesia* 2°0S 121°19E **231** E6
Kolonos *Greece* 37°59N 23°43E **112** B2
Kolonowskie *Poland* 50°39N 18°22E **185** H5
Kolosib *India* 24°15N 92°45E **241** C4
Kolpashevo *Russia* 58°20N 83°5E **214** D9
Kolpino *Russia* 59°44N 30°39E **188** C6
Kolpny *Russia* 52°17N 37°1E **189** F9
Kolsås *Norway* 59°55N 10°30E **133** A2
Kolskiy Poluostrov *Russia* 67°30N 38°0E **186** A6
Kolskiy Zaliv *Russia* 69°23N 34°0E **160** B26
Kolsva *Sweden* 59°36N 15°51E **162** E9
Kolubara → *Serbia* 44°35N 20°15E **202** B4
Kolumadulu Atoll *Maldives* 2°22N 73°7E **272** d
Koluszki *Poland* 51°45N 19°46E **185** G6
Kolwezi *Dem. Rep. of the Congo* 10°40S 25°25E **269** E2
Kolyma → *Russia* 69°30N 161°0E **215** C17
Kolymskoye Nagorye *Russia* 63°0N 157°0E **215** C16
Kôm Hamâda *Egypt* 30°46N 30°41E **256** H7
Kôm Ombo *Egypt* 24°25N 32°52E **256** C3
Komadugu Gana → *Nigeria* 13°5N 12°24E **263** C7
Komae *Japan* 35°37N 139°34E **140** B2
Komagane *Japan* 35°44N 137°58E **223** B9
Komagome *Japan* 35°43N 139°45E **140** A3
Komaki *Japan* 35°17N 136°55E **223** B8
Komandorskiye Is. = Komandorskiye Ostrova *Russia* 55°0N 167°0E **215** D17
Komandorskiye Ostrova *Russia* 55°0N 167°0E **215** D17
Komárno *Slovak Rep.* 47°49N 18°5E **181** D11
Komarnyky *Ukraine* 48°59N 23°3E **182** B8
Komárom *Hungary* 47°43N 18°7E **182** C3
Komárom-Esztergom □ *Hungary* 47°35N 18°20E **182** C3
Komáromújváros = Komárom *Hungary* 47°43N 18°7E **182** C3
Komatipoort *S. Africa* 25°25S 31°55E **271** C5
Komatou Yialou *Cyprus* 35°25N 34°8E **207** E10
Komatsu *Japan* 36°25N 136°30E **223** A8
Komatsushima *Japan* 34°0N 134°35E **222** D6
Komavangard = Sobinka *Russia* 56°0N 40°0E **188** E11
Komazawa *Japan* 35°37N 139°40E **140** B3
Komba *Dem. Rep. of the Congo* 2°52N 24°3E **264** B4
Kombissiri *Burkina Faso* 12°4N 1°20W **263** C4
Kombo *Gabon* 0°20S 12°22E **264** C2
Kombong *India* 28°7N 94°51E **241** A5
Kombori *Burkina Faso* 13°26N 3°56W **262** C4
Komboti *Greece* 39°6N 21°5E **204** B3
Kome Channel *Uganda* 0°10S 32°35E **268** C3
Komebail Lagoon *Palau* 7°25N 134°25E **288** c
Komen *Slovenia* 45°49N 13°45E **199** C10
Komenda *Ghana* 5°4N 1°28W **263** D4
Komi *Cyprus* 35°24N 34°0E **207** E10
Komi □ *Russia* 64°0N 55°0E **186** B10
Kominter = Novoshakhtinsk *Russia* 47°46N 39°58E **189** J10
Komintern = Marhanets *Ukraine* 47°40N 34°40E **189** J8
Komiža *Croatia* 43°3N 16°11E **199** E13
Komló *Hungary* 46°15N 18°16E **182** D3
Kommamur Canal *India* 16°0N 80°25E **245** G5
Kommunarsk = Alchevsk *Ukraine* 48°30N 38°45E **189** H10
Kommunizma, Pik = imeni Ismail Samani, Pik *Tajikistan* 39°0N 72°2E **217** E8
Komodo *Indonesia* 8°37S 119°20E **235** D5
Komodo △ *Indonesia* 8°36S 119°34E **235** D5
Komono *Congo* 3°10S 13°20E **264** C2
Komoran, Pulau *Indonesia* 8°18S 138°45E **231** F9
Komoro *Japan* 36°19N 138°26E **223** A10
Komotau = Chomutov *Czech Rep.* 50°28N 13°23E **180** A6
Komotini *Greece* 41°9N 25°26E **203** E9
Komovi *Montenegro* 42°41N 19°39E **202** D3
Kompasberg *S. Africa* 31°45S 24°32E **270** D3
Kompong Chhnang = Kampong Chhnang *Cambodia* 12°20N 104°35E **237** F5
Kompong Chikreng *Cambodia* 13°5N 104°18E **236** F5
Kompong Kleang *Cambodia* 13°6N 104°8E **236** F5
Kompong Luong *Cambodia* 11°49N 104°48E **237** G5
Kompong Pranak *Cambodia* 13°35N 104°55E **236** F5
Kompong Som = Kampong Saom *Cambodia* 10°38N 103°30E **237** G4
Kompong Som, Chhung = Kampong Saom, Chaak *Cambodia* 10°50N 103°32E **237** G4
Kompong Speu *Cambodia* 11°26N 104°32E **237** G5
Kompong Sralau *Cambodia* 14°5N 105°46E **236** E5
Kompong Thom *Cambodia* 12°35N 104°51E **236** F5
Kompong Trabeck *Cambodia* 13°6N 105°14E **236** F5
Kompong Trach *Cambodia* 11°25N 105°48E **237** G5
Kompong Tralach *Cambodia* 11°54N 104°47E **237** G5
Komrat = Comrat *Moldova* 46°18N 28°40E **183** D13
Komsberg *S. Africa* 32°40S 20°45E **270** D3
Komsomolets = Qarabalyq *Kazakhstan* 53°45N 62°2E **216** B6
Komsomolets, Ostrov *Russia* 80°30N 95°0E **215** A10
Komsomolsk *Russia* 57°2N 40°20E **188** D11
Komsomolsk-na-Amur *Russia* 50°30N 137°0E **219** A16
Komsomolskiy *Russia* 54°27N 45°33E **190** C7
Komsomolskoe *Kazakhstan* 50°25N 60°5E **216** B6
Komsomolsky = Chirchiq *Uzbekistan* 41°29N 69°35E **217** D7
Kömür Burnu *Turkey* 38°39N 26°12E **205** C8
Kon Ka Kinh △ *Vietnam* 14°19N 107°23E **236** E6
Kon Tum *Vietnam* 14°24N 108°0E **236** E7
Kon Tum, Plateau du *Vietnam* 14°30N 108°30E **236** E7
Kona *W. Bengal, India* 22°37N 88°18E **124** B1
Kona *Mali* 14°57N 3°53W **262** C4
Kona *Nigeria* 8°57N 11°21E **263** D7
Kona ✈ **(KOA)** *U.S.A.* 19°44N 156°3W **302** D5
Könähuanui *U.S.A.* 21°21N 157°47W **302** K14
Konakovo *Russia* 56°40N 36°51E **188** D9
Konala *Finland* 60°14N 24°52E **121** B2
Konar □ *Afghan.* 34°30N 71°3E **240** B3
Konarak *India* 19°54N 86°7E **244** E8
Konārak *Iran* 25°21N 60°23E **249** A8
Konārī *Iran* 28°13N 51°36E **247** D6
Konch *India* 26°0N 79°10E **243** G8
Kondagaon *India* 19°35N 81°35E **244** E5
Konde *Tanzania* 4°57S 39°45E **268** C4
Kondias *Greece* 39°49N 25°10E **205** B7
Kondinin *Australia* 32°34S 118°8E **279** F2
Kondli *India* 28°36N 77°19E **120** B2
Kondo *Dem. Rep. of the Congo* 5°35S 13°0E **265** D2
Kondoa *Tanzania* 4°55S 35°50E **268** C4
Kondopoga *Russia* 62°12N 34°17E **188** A8
Kondratyevo *Russia* 57°22N 98°15E **215** D10
Kondrovo *Russia* 54°48N 35°56E **188** E8
Konduga *Nigeria* 11°35N 13°26E **263** C7
Kondukur *India* 15°12N 79°57E **245** G4
Kondūz *Afghan.* 36°50N 68°50E **240** A3
Kondūz □ *Afghan.* 36°50N 68°50E **240** A3
Koné *Cameroon* 8°50N 13°17E **259** G2
Koné *N. Cal.* 21°4S 164°52E **288** d
Köneürgench *Turkmenistan* 42°19N 59°10E **216** D5
Konevo *Russia* 62°8N 39°20E **188** A10
Kong = Khong → *Cambodia* 13°32N 105°58E **236** F5
Kong *Ivory C.* 8°54N 4°36W **262** D4
Kong, Koh *Cambodia* 11°20N 103°0E **237** G4
Kong Christian IX.s Land *Greenland* 68°0N 36°0W **154** D7
Kong Christian X.s Land *Greenland* 74°0N 29°0W **154** C8
Kong Frederik IX.s Land *Greenland* 67°0N 52°0W **154** D5
Kong Frederik VI.s Kyst *Greenland* 63°0N 43°0W **154** E6
Kong Frederik VIII.s Land *Greenland* 78°30N 26°0W **154** B8
Kong Karls Land *Svalbard* 79°0N 28°0E **154** B13
Kong Oscar Fjord *Greenland* 72°20N 24°0W **154** C8
Kongauru I. *Palau* 7°3N 134°16E **288** c
Kongbo *C.A.R.* 4°44N 21°23E **264** B4
Kongeå → *Denmark* 55°23N 8°39E **163** J2
Kongelunden *Denmark* 55°34N 12°34E **118** B3
Kongens Lyngby *Denmark* 55°46N 12°30E **118** A3
Kongerslev *Denmark* 56°54N 10°6E **163** H4
Kongkemul *Indonesia* 1°52N 116°10E **235** B5
Konglu *Burma* 27°13N 97°57E **241** B6
Kongmoon = Jiangmen *China* 22°32N 113°0E **229** F9
Kongo *Finland* 60°20N 24°47E **121** A1
Kongola *Namibia* 17°45S 23°20E **270** A3
Kongolo *Kasai-Or., Dem. Rep. of the Congo* 5°26S 24°49E **265** D4
Kongolo *Katanga, Dem. Rep. of the Congo* 5°22S 27°0E **268** D2
Kongor *Sudan* 7°1N 31°27E **257** F3
Kongossambougou ⌓ *Mali* 14°0N 8°30W **262** C3
Kongoulou *Cameroon* 2°59N 11°7E **264** B2
Kongoussi *Burkina Faso* 13°19N 1°32W **263** C4
Kongsberg *Norway* 59°39N 9°39E **164** E6
Kongsvinger *Norway* 60°12N 12°2E **164** D9
Kongur Shan *China* 38°34N 75°18E **217** E9
Kongwa *Tanzania* 6°11S 36°26E **268** D4
Koni *Dem. Rep. of the Congo* 10°40S 27°11E **269** E2
Koniakari *Mali* 14°35N 10°50W **262** C2
Koniecpol *Poland* 50°46N 19°40E **185** H6
Königgrätz = Hradec Králové *Czech Rep.* 50°15N 15°50E **180** A8
Königs Wusterhausen *Germany* 52°19N 13°38E **178** C9
Königsberg = Chojna *Poland* 52°58N 14°25E **185** F1
Königsberg = Kaliningrad *Russia* 54°42N 20°32E **184** D7
Königsbrunn *Germany* 48°16N 10°54E **179** G6
Königshütte = Chorzów *Poland* 50°18N 18°57E **185** H5
Königslutter *Germany* 52°15N 10°49E **178** C6
Konin *Poland* 52°12N 18°15E **185** F5
Königinhof an der Elbe = Dvůr Králové nad Labem *Czech Rep.* 50°27N 15°50E **180** A8
Koninklijk Paleis *Amsterdam, Neths.* **112** a2
Konispol *Albania* 39°42N 20°10E **206** B10
Konitsa *Greece* 40°5N 20°48E **204** A2
Konjic *Bos.-H.* 43°42N 17°58E **182** G2
Konkiep *Namibia* 26°49S 17°15E **270** C2
Konkō *Japan* 34°33N 133°36E **222** C4
Konkouré → *Guinea* 9°50N 13°42W **262** D2
Konnagar *India* 22°42N 88°21E **124** A2
Könnern *Germany* 51°41N 11°47E **178** D7
Konnur *India* 16°14N 74°49E **245** F2
Kono *S. Leone* 8°30N 11°5W **262** D2
Konogogo *Papua N. G.* 3°29S 152°10E **286** B7
Konohana *Japan* 34°40N 135°26E **133** A1
Konongo *Ghana* 6°40N 1°15W **263** D4
Konos *Papua N. G.* 3°10S 151°44E **286** B6
Konosha *Russia* 61°0N 40°5E **188** B11
Kōnosu *Japan* 36°3N 139°31E **223** A11
Konotop *Ukraine* 51°12N 33°7E **189** G7
Konqi He → *China* 41°0N 86°0E **217** D11
Konradshof = Skawina *Poland* 49°59N 19°50E **185** J6
Konradshöhe *Germany* 52°35N 13°13E **115** A2
Konrei *Palau* 7°43N 134°36E **288** c
Konsankoro *Guinea* 9°2N 9°0W **262** D3
Końskie *Poland* 51°15N 20°23E **185** G7
Konsmo *Norway* 58°16N 7°23E **164** F4
Konstadt = Wołczyn *Poland* 51°1N 18°3E **185** G5
Konstancin-Jeziorna *Poland* 52°5N 21°7E **185** F8
Konstantinograd = Krasnohrad *Ukraine* 49°27N 35°27E **189** H8
Konstantinovka = Kostyantynivka *Ukraine* 48°32N 37°39E **189** H9
Konstantinovsk *Russia* 47°33N 41°10E **191** G5
Konstantynów Łódźki *Poland* 51°45N 19°20E **185** G6
Konstanz *Germany* 47°40N 9°10E **179** H5
Kont *Iran* 26°55N 61°50E **247** E9
Konta *India* 17°48N 81°23E **244** F5
Kontagora *Nigeria* 10°23N 5°27E **263** C6
Kontcha *Cameroon* 7°59N 12°15E **263** D7
Kontiolahti *Finland* 62°46N 29°50E **160** E23
Kontokali *Greece* 39°38N 19°51E **206** B9
Konya *Turkey* 37°52N 32°35E **212** D5
Konya □ *Turkey* 37°46N 32°20E **250** A3
Konya Ovası *Turkey* 38°9N 33°5E **212** C5
Konyin *Burma* 22°58N 94°42E **241** D5
Konz *Germany* 49°42N 6°34E **179** F2
Konza *Kenya* 1°45S 37°7E **268** C4
Koo-wee-rup *Australia* 38°13S 145°28E **283** E6
Koocanusa, L. *Canada* 49°20N 115°15W **304** B6
Kookynie *Australia* 29°17S 121°22E **279** E3
Ko'olau Range *U.S.A.* 21°35N 157°50W **302** J14
Ko'olauloa District *U.S.A.* 21°35N 157°55W **302** J14
Ko'olaupoko District *U.S.A.* 21°25N 157°50W **302** K14
Kō'Ōlina *U.S.A.* 21°19N 158°7W **302** K13
Koolyanobbing *Australia* 30°48S 119°36E **279** F2
Koondrook *Australia* 35°33S 144°8E **282** C6
Koonibba *Australia* 31°54S 133°25E **281** E1
Koorawatha *Australia* 34°2S 148°33E **283** C8
Koorda *Australia* 30°48S 117°35E **279** F2

Kooskia U.S.A. 46°9N 115°59W 304 C6
Kootenay → U.S.A. 49°19N 117°39W 296 D5
Kootenay △ Canada 51°0N 116°0W 296 C5
Kootenay L. Canada 49°45N 116°50W 304 B5
Kootingal Australia 31°3S 151°4E 283 A9
Kopanina Czech Rep. 50°3N 14°17E 135 B1
Kopaonik △ Serbia 43°10N 20°50E 244 C4
Kopaonik ⌂ Serbia 43°20N 20°50E 202 C4
Kopargaon India 19°51N 74°28E 244 E2
Koparkhairna India 19°6N 72°59E 130 A2
Kópasker Iceland 66°18N 16°27W 155 A10
Kópavogur Iceland 64°6N 21°55W 155 C5
Kopayhorod Ukraine 48°52N 27°53E 183 B12
Köpenick Germany 52°26N 13°35E 115 B4
Koper Slovenia 45°31N 13°44E 199 C10
Kopervik Norway 59°17N 5°17E 164 E2
Kopet Dagh Asia 38°0N 58°0E 247 B8
Kopeysk Russia 55°7N 61°37E 216 A6
Kopi Australia 33°24S 135°40E 281 E2
Köping Sweden 59°31N 16°3E 162 E10
Köpingsvik Sweden 56°53N 16°43E 163 H10
Koplik Albania 42°15N 19°25E 202 D3
Köpmanholmen Sweden 63°10N 18°35E 162 A12
Koppa India 13°33N 75°21E 245 H2
Koppal India 15°23N 76°5E 245 G3
Koppang Norway 61°34N 11°3E 164 C8
Kopparberg Sweden 59°52N 15°0E 162 E9
Koppeh Dägh = Kopet Dagh
  Asia 38°0N 58°0E 247 B8
Kopperå Norway 63°24N 11°50E 164 A8
Koppies S. Africa 27°20S 27°30E 271 C4
Koppom Sweden 59°43N 12°10E 162 E6
Koprivlen Bulgaria 41°31N 23°53E 202 E7
Koprivnica Croatia 46°12N 16°45E 199 B13
Kopřivnice Czech Rep. 49°36N 18°9E 181 B11
Koprivshtitsa Bulgaria 42°40N 24°19E 203 D8
Köprü → Turkey 36°48N 31°11E 250 B2
Köprübaşı Turkey 38°43N 28°23E 205 C10
Köprülü Turkey 36°43N 32°5E 250 B3
Köprülü △ Turkey 37°20N 31°5E 246 B1
Kopychyntsi Ukraine 49°7N 25°58E 177 D13
Kor Aban Somali Rep. 3°58N 42°44E 267 D5
Kora ⌂ Kenya 0°14S 38°44E 268 C4
Koraa Shiir Somali Rep. 3°16N 46°16E 267 D6
Korab Macedonia 41°44N 20°40E 202 E4
Korahe Ethiopia 6°39N 44°5E 267 C5
Koral India 21°50N 73°12E 242 J5
Korangal India 17°6N 77°38E 244 E3
Korangi Pakistan 24°47N 67°8E 123 B2
Koraput India 18°50N 82°40E 244 E6
Korarou, L. Mali 15°45N 3°15W 262 B4
Korba India 22°20N 82°45E 243 H10
Korbach Germany 51°16N 8°52E 178 D4
Korbu, Gunung Malaysia 4°41N 101°18E 237 K3
Korçë Albania 40°37N 20°50E 202 F4
Korčula Croatia 42°56N 16°57E 199 F13
Korčulanski Kanal
  Croatia 43°3N 16°40E 199 E13
Kord Küy Iran 36°48N 54°7E 247 B7
Kord Sheykh Iran 28°31N 52°53E 247 D7
Kordestän = Kurdistan
  Asia 37°20N 43°30E 213 D10
Kordestän □ Iran 36°0N 47°0E 246 C5
Kordie Burkina Faso 12°36N 2°22W 262 C4
Koré Mayroua Niger 13°18N 3°55E 263 C5
Korea, North ■ Asia 40°0N 127°0E 227 E14
Korea, South ■ Asia 36°0N 128°0E 227 G15
Korea Bay Korea 39°0N 124°0E 224 C2
Korea Strait Asia 34°0N 129°30E 227 H15
Koregaon India 17°40N 74°10E 244 F2
Korem Ethiopia 12°30N 39°32E 257 E4
Koremasa Japan 35°39N 139°29E 140 B1
Korenevo Kursk, Russia 51°27N 34°55E 189 G8
Korenevo Moskva, Russia 55°40N 38°0E 129 B6
Korenica = Titova Korenica
  Croatia 44°45N 15°41E 199 D12
Korenovsk Russia 45°30N 39°22E 191 H4
Korets Ukraine 50°40N 27°5E 177 C14
Korfantów Poland 50°29N 17°36E 185 H4
Korgan Turkey 40°44N 37°13E 212 B7
Korgus Sudan 19°16N 33°29E 256 D3
Korhogo Ivory C. 9°29N 5°28W 262 D4
Koribundu S. Leone 7°41N 11°46W 262 D2
Koridalos Greece 37°59N 23°39E 112 B1
Korienzé Mali 15°22N 3°50W 262 B4
Korinthia □ Greece 37°50N 22°35E 204 C4
Korinthiakos Kolpos
  Greece 38°16N 22°30E 204 C4
Korinthos Greece 37°56N 22°55E 204 D4
Korioumé Mali 16°35N 3°0W 262 B4
Korissia, L. Greece 39°27N 19°53E 206 D9
Korithi Greece 37°55N 20°42E 207 D2
Kōriyama Japan 37°24N 140°23E 220 F10
Korkino Russia 54°54N 61°23E 216 B6
Korkuteli Turkey 37°4N 30°13E 205 D12
Korla China 41°45N 86°4E 217 D11
Kormakiti, C. Cyprus 35°23N 32°56E 207 E8
Körmend Hungary 47°5N 16°35E 182 C1
Kormor Iraq 35°8N 44°50E 213 E11
Kornat Croatia 43°50N 15°20E 199 E12
Kornat △ Croatia 43°48N 15°12E 199 E12
Korneshty = Corneşti
  Moldova 47°21N 28°1E 183 C13
Korneuburg Austria 48°20N 16°20E 181 C9
Kórnik Poland 52°15N 17°5E 185 F4
Kornsjø Norway 58°57N 11°39E 164 F8
Koro Fiji 17°19S 179°23E 287 A2
Koro Ivory C. 8°32N 7°30W 262 D3
Koro Mali 14°1N 2°58W 262 C4
Koro Sea Fiji 17°30S 179°45W 287 A3
Koro Toro Chad 16°5N 18°30E 253 C9
Koroba Papua N. G. 5°44S 142°47E 286 C2
Korobkovo = Gubkin
  Russia 51°17N 37°32E 189 G9
Korocha Russia 50°54N 37°19E 189 G9
Köroğlu Dağları Turkey 40°38N 33°0E 212 B5
Korogwe Tanzania 5°5S 38°25E 268 D4
Koroit Australia 38°18S 142°24E 282 E5
Korokoro N.Z. 41°14S 174°52E 143 B2
Korokoro Stream →
  N.Z. 41°14S 174°52E 143 B2
Koroleve Ukraine 48°9N 23°8E 183 B8
Korolevu Fiji 18°12S 177°46E 287 B1
Koromiri Cook Is. 21°15S 159°43W 289 h
Korona U.S.A. 29°25N 81°12W 317 F8
Koronadal Phil. 6°12N 124°51E 233 H6
Korong Vale Australia 36°22S 143°45E 282 D5
Koroni Greece 36°48N 21°57E 204 E3
Koronia, L. Greece 40°47N 23°10E 202 F7
Koronowo Poland 53°19N 17°55E 185 E4
Koropelé C.A.R. 4°44N 17°11E 264 A3
Koropets Ukraine 48°56N 25°10E 183 B10
Koror Palau 7°20N 134°28E 288 c
Körös → Hungary 46°43N 20°12E 182 D5
Körös Maros ⌂ Hungary 46°53N 21°3E 182 D6
Kőröstarcsa Hungary 46°53N 21°3E 182 D6
Korosten Ukraine 50°54N 28°36E 183 C13
Korostyshev Ukraine 50°19N 29°4E 177 C15
Korotoyak Russia 51°1N 39°2E 189 G10
Korovou Fiji 17°47S 178°32E 287 A2
Koroyanitu △ Fiji 17°40S 177°35E 287 A1

Korraraika, Helodranon' i
  Madag. 17°45S 43°57E 272 B1
Korror I. Palau 7°20N 134°29E 288 c
Korsakov Russia 46°36N 142°42E 215 E15
Korsberga Sweden 57°19N 15°7E 163 G9
Korshiv Ukraine 48°39N 25°1E 183 B10
Korshunovo Russia 58°37N 110°10E 215 D12
Korsør Denmark 55°20N 11°9E 163 J5
Korsun Shevchenkovskiy
  Ukraine 49°26N 31°16E 189 H6
Korsze Poland 54°11N 21°9E 184 D8
Korti Sudan 18°6N 31°33E 256 D3
Kortrijk Belgium 50°50N 3°17E 170 D3
Korucu Turkey 39°28N 27°22E 205 B9
Korumburra Australia 38°26S 145°50E 283 E6
Korup △ Cameroon 5°15N 9°2E 264 A1
Korwai India 24°7N 78°5E 242 G8
Koryakskiy Nagorye
  Russia 61°0N 171°0E 215 C18
Koryazhma Russia 61°16N 47°7E 216 B8
Koryŏng S. Korea 35°44N 128°15E 226 G3
Koryukivka Ukraine 51°46N 32°16E 189 G7
Kos Greece 36°50N 27°15E 205 E9
Kosa Ethiopia 7°50N 36°50E 257 F4
Kosa Russia 34°42N 137°32E 223 C9
Kosan N. Korea 38°52N 127°25E 224 C3
Kosaya Gora Russia 54°10N 37°30E 188 D9
Kościan Poland 52°5N 16°40E 185 F3
Kościerzyna Poland 54°8N 17°59E 184 D4
Kosciusko U.S.A. 33°4N 89°35W 315 E10
Kosciuszko, Mt.
  Australia 36°27S 148°16E 283 D8
Kosciuszko △ Australia 36°30S 148°20E 283 D8
Kösely → Hungary 47°25N 21°5E 182 C6
Kosgi Andhra Pradesh, India 16°58N 77°43E 244 F3
Kosgi Andhra Pradesh, India 15°51N 77°16E 245 G3
Kosha Sudan 20°50N 30°30E 256 C3
Koshava Bulgaria 44°4N 23°2E 202 B7
Kōshi Japan 32°53N 130°48E 222 E2
Koshigaya Japan 35°54N 139°49E 223 J3
Koshiki-Kaikyo Japan 31°30N 130°0E 222 F1
Koshiki-Rettō Japan 31°45N 129°49E 222 F1
Koshim = Kazakhstan 49°20N 50°30E 190 F10
Koshkonong L. U.S.A. 42°52N 88°58W 311 B8
Koshoku Japan 36°38N 138°6E 223 A10
Kosi → India 27°48N 77°29E 242 F7
Kosi → India 28°41N 78°57E 243 E8
Košice Slovak Rep. 48°42N 21°15E 181 C14
Košický □ Slovak Rep. 48°45N 21°0E 181 C14
Kosino Russia 55°43N 37°50E 129 B5
Kosiv Ukraine 48°19N 25°6E 183 B10
Kosjerić Serbia 44°0N 19°55E 202 B3
Kŏsŏng Korea 37°50N 128°3E 224 C3
Koskinou Greece 36°23N 28°13E 206 E12
Koslan Russia 63°34N 49°14E 186 B8
Koślin = Koszalin Poland 54°11N 16°8E 184 D3
Kosmach Ukraine 48°20N 24°50E 183 B9
Kosmonde N. Korea 38°40N 128°22E 224 C4
Kosovo ■ Europe 42°30N 21°0E 202 D4
Kosovo Polje Kosovo 42°40N 21°5E 202 D5
Kosovska Kamenica
  Kosovo 42°35N 21°35E 202 D5
Kosovska Mitrovica
  Kosovo 42°54N 20°52E 202 D4
Kossou, L. de Ivory C. 6°59N 5°31W 262 D3
Kosta Sweden 56°50N 15°24E 163 H9
Kostajnica Croatia 45°17N 16°30E 199 C13
Kostanjevica Slovenia 45°51N 15°27E 199 C12
Kostenets = Pernik
  Bulgaria 42°35N 23°2E 202 D7
Kostenets Bulgaria 42°15N 23°52E 202 D7
Koster S. Africa 25°52S 26°54E 270 C4
Kôstî Sudan 13°8N 32°43E 257 E3
Kostinbrod Bulgaria 42°49N 23°13E 202 D7
Kostolac Serbia 44°37N 21°15E 202 B5
Kostopil Ukraine 50°51N 26°22E 177 C14
Kostroma Russia 57°50N 40°58E 188 D11
Kostroma □ Russia 58°10N 42°50E 190 A6
Kostromskoye Vdkhr.
  Russia 57°52N 40°49E 188 D11
Kostrzhivka Ukraine 48°39N 25°43E 183 B10
Kostrzyn Lubuskie, Poland 52°35N 14°39E 185 F1
Kostrzyn Wielkopolskie,
  Poland 52°24N 17°14E 185 F4
Kostyantynivka Ukraine 48°32N 37°39E 189 H10
Kostyukovichi = Kastsyukovichy
  Belarus 53°20N 32°4E 189 F7
Kosugi Japan 35°34N 139°6E 140 B2
Koszalin Poland 54°11N 16°8E 184 D3
Kőszeg Hungary 47°23N 16°33E 182 C1
Kot Addu Pakistan 30°30N 71°0E 242 D4
Kot Kapura India 30°35N 74°50E 242 D6
Kot Moman Pakistan 32°13N 73°0E 242 C5
Kot Sultan Pakistan 30°46N 70°56E 242 D4
Kota India 25°14N 75°49E 242 G6
Kota Jakarta, Indonesia 6°7S 106°48E 122 A1
Kota Barrage India 25°6N 75°51E 242 G6
Kota Belud Malaysia 6°21N 116°26E 235 A5
Kota Bharu Malaysia 6°7N 102°14E 237 J4
Kota Kinabalu Malaysia 6°0N 116°4E 235 A5
Kota Tinggi Malaysia 1°44N 103°53E 237 M4
Kotaagung Indonesia 5°38S 104°29E 234 D2
Kotabaru Kalimantan Barat,
  Indonesia 0°49S 111°31E 235 C4
Kotabaru Kalimantan Selatan,
  Indonesia 3°20S 116°20E 235 C5
Kotabaru Sumatera Barat,
  Indonesia 1°5S 101°43E 234 C2
Kotabesi Indonesia 2°24S 112°58E 235 C4
Kotabumi Indonesia 4°49S 104°54E 234 C2
Kotajawa Indonesia 5°37S 104°19E 234 D2
Kotamobagu Indonesia 0°57N 124°31E 231 D6
Kotapad India 19°9N 82°21E 244 E6
Kotaparh Indonesia 1°53N 109°52E 237 M3
Kotawaringin Indonesia 2°28S 111°27E 235 C4
Kotchandpur Bangla. 23°24N 89°1E 241 D2
Kotcho L. Canada 59°7N 121°12W 296 B4
Kotdwara India 29°45N 78°32E 243 E8
Kotel Bulgaria 42°52N 26°26E 203 D10
Kotelnich Russia 58°22N 48°24E 190 A9
Kotelnikovo Russia 47°38N 43°8E 191 G6
Kotelnyy, Ostrov Russia 75°10N 139°0E 215 B14
Koti C.A.R. (?)
Kotgudem India 17°30N 80°40E 244 F5
Kotha India 27°43N 95°10E (?)
Kothagudem India 17°30N 80°40E 244 F5
Kothapet India 19°21N 79°28E 244 E4
Kothari → India 25°20N 75°4E 242 G6
Köthen Germany 51°44N 11°59E 178 D7
Kothi Mad. P., India 24°45N 80°40E 243 G9
Kothi Chhattisgarh, India 23°24N 80°40E 243 G9
Kotiro Pakistan 26°17N 67°13E 242 F2
Kotka Finland 60°28N 26°58E 188 B4
Kotlas Russia 61°17N 46°43E 186 B8
Kotlenska Planina
  Bulgaria 42°56N 26°30E 203 D10
Kotli Pakistan 33°30N 73°55E 242 C5
Kotlik U.S.A. 63°2N 163°33W 303 D7
Kotma India 23°12N 81°58E 243 H9
Kötö Japan 35°40N 139°48E 140 B2
Kotohira Japan 34°11N 133°49E 222 C5
Koton-Karifi Nigeria 7°58N 6°48E 263 D6
Kotonkoro Nigeria 11°3N 5°58E 263 C6
Kotor Montenegro 42°25N 18°47E 202 D2
Kotor Varoš Bos.-H. 44°38N 17°22E 182 F2
Kotoriba Croatia 46°23N 16°48E 199 B13

Kotovo Russia 50°22N 44°45E 190 E7
Kotovsk Russia 52°36N 41°32E 190 D5
Kotovsk Ukraine 47°45N 29°35E 177 E15
Kotputli India 27°43N 76°12E 242 F7
Kotri Pakistan 25°22N 68°22E 242 G3
Kotri → India 19°15N 80°35E 244 E5
Kotronas Greece 36°38N 22°29E 204 E4
Kotrung India 22°41N 88°20E 124 A2
Kötschach-Mauthen
  Austria 46°41N 13°1E 180 E6
Kottayam India 9°35N 76°33E 245 K3
Kotto C.A.R. 4°14N 22°2E 264 B4
Kotto → C.A.R. 4°14N 22°2E 264 B4
Kottur India 10°34N 76°56E 245 J3
Kotturu India 14°45N 76°10E 245 G3
Kotu Group Tonga 20°0S 174°45W 287 Q13
Kotuy → Russia 71°54N 102°6E 215 B11
Kotuzhanny Ukraine 48°48N 27°42E 183 B12
Kotzebue Russia 66°53N 162°39W 303 C7
Kotzebue Sound U.S.A. 66°20N 163°0W 303 C7
Kotzenau = Chocianów
  Poland 51°27N 15°55E 185 G2
Kouango C.A.R. 5°0N 20°10E 264 B4
Kouchibouguac △ Canada 46°50N 65°0W 299 C6
Koudougou Burkina Faso 12°10N 2°20W 262 C4
Koufey Niger 13°57N 7°56E 259 F1
Koufonisi Iraklio, Greece 34°56N 26°8E 207 F7
Koufonisi Notio Aigaio,
  Greece 36°57N 25°35E 205 E7
Kougaberge S. Africa 33°48S 23°50E 270 D3
Kø'ouhu Taiwan 23°35N 120°11E 225 C2
Kouibli Ivory C. 7°15N 7°14W 262 D3
Kouilou → Congo 4°10S 12°5E 265 C2
Koukdjuak → Canada 66°43N 73°0W 293 C12
Kouki C.A.R. 7°22N 17°3E 264 A3
Koukourou, Mt. Comoros Is. 12°18S 43°41E 272 a
Koukourou → C.A.R. 7°12N 20°2E 264 A4
Koula Guinea 11°23N 24°4E 203 D8
Koula Moutou Gabon 1°15S 12°25E 264 C2
Koulen = Kulen
  Cambodia 13°50N 104°40E 236 F5
Koulikoro Mali 12°40N 7°50W 262 C3
Koulikoro □ Mali 12°40N 7°45W 262 C3
Kouloura Greece 39°42N 19°54E 206 B9
Koumac N. Cal. 20°33S 164°17E 288 d
Koumala Australia 21°38S 149°15E 280 C4
Koumameveng Gabon 0°11N 11°51E 264 B2
Koumankou Mali 11°58N 6°6W 262 C3
Koumbia Burkina Faso 11°10N 3°50W 262 C4
Koumbia Guinea 11°48N 13°29W 262 C2
Koumboum Guinea 10°25N 13°0W 262 C2
Koumpenntoum Senegal 13°59N 14°34W 262 C2
Koumra Chad 8°50N 17°35E 259 G3
Koun-Fao Ivory C. 7°30N 3°15W 262 D4
Koundara Guinea 12°29N 13°18W 262 C2
Koundé C.A.R. 6°7N 14°38E 264 A2
Koungheul Senegal 14°0N 14°50W 262 C2
Koungou Mayotte 12°43S 45°12E 272 b
Koungoulou Congo 3°31S 13°20E 264 C2
Kountze U.S.A. 30°22N 94°19W 314 F7
Koupéla Burkina Faso 12°11N 0°21W 263 C4
Kouponia Greece 38°37N 23°47E 112 B2
Kourémalé Mali 11°59N 8°42E 262 C3
Kouri-shima Japan 26°42N 128°1E 288 a
Kouris → Cyprus 34°38N 32°54E 207 F8
Kourizo, P. de Chad 22°28N 15°27E 258 D3
Kourou Fr. Guiana 5°9N 52°39W 329 B7
Kourouba Mali 12°10N 10°57W 262 C2
Koûroudjél Mauritania 16°12N 11°30W 262 B2
Kouroukoto Mali 12°35N 10°5W 262 C2
Kouroussa Guinea 11°35N 10°50W 262 C2
Kourouninkoto Mali 13°52N 9°35W 262 C3
Kouroussa Guinea 10°45N 9°45W 262 C3
Koussanar Senegal 14°53N 14°50W 262 C2
Koussané Mali 14°53N 11°14W 262 C2
Koussane Senegal 14°10N 12°22W 262 C2
Kousséri Cameroon 12°0N 14°55E 259 F2
Koutiala Mali 12°25N 5°23W 262 C3
Kouto Ivory C. 9°53N 6°25W 262 D3
Kouts U.S.A. 41°19N 87°2W 311 C9
Kouvé Togo 6°25N 1°25E 263 D5
Kouvola Finland 60°52N 26°43E 188 B4
Kouyi Congo 2°29S 12°25E 264 C2
Kouyou → Congo 0°44S 16°38E 264 C3
Kovačica Serbia 45°5N 20°38E 182 E5
Kovdor Russia 67°34N 30°24E 160 C24
Kovel Ukraine 51°11N 24°38E 177 C13
Kovilpatti India 9°10N 77°50E 245 K3
Kovin Serbia 44°44N 20°59E 182 F5
Kovno = Kaunas
  Lithuania 54°54N 23°54E 184 D10
Kovrov Russia 56°25N 41°25E 190 B5
Kovur Andhra Pradesh, India 17°3N 81°39E 244 E5
Kovur Andhra Pradesh, India 14°30N 80°1E 245 G5
Kowal Poland 52°32N 19°7E 185 F6
Kowalewo Pomorskie
  Poland 53°10N 18°52E 185 E5
Kowanyama Australia 15°29S 141°44E 280 B3
Kowanyama ○ Australia 15°20S 141°47E 280 B3
Kowli'an Afghan. 37°39N 65°56E 248 B2
Kowloon China 22°19N 114°11E 122 B1
Kowloon Park Hong Kong, China 122 a2
Kowloon Peak China 22°20N 114°13E 122 A2
Kowloon Res. China 22°21N 114°9E 122 A1
Kowloon Tong China 22°20N 114°10E 122 A2
Kowŏn N. Korea 39°26N 127°14E 224 D3
Kōyama Japan 31°20N 130°56E 222 F2
Koyampattur = Coimbatore
  India 11°2N 76°59E 245 J3
Köyceğiz Turkey 36°57N 28°40E 205 E10
Köyceğiz Gölü Turkey 36°50N 28°37E 205 E10
Köytendag Turkmenistan 37°30N 66°11E 248 A2
Koyuk U.S.A. 64°56N 161°9W 303 D7
Koyukuk U.S.A. 64°55N 157°32W 303 D8
Koyukuk → U.S.A. 64°55N 157°32W 303 D8
Koyukuk Nat. Wildlife Refuge ⌂
  U.S.A. 66°35N 156°30W 303 D8
Koyulhisar Turkey 40°20N 37°52E 212 B7
Koyunyeri Turkey 40°50N 26°26E 203 F10
Koza = Okinawa Japan 26°19N 127°46E 288 a
Kozak Turkey 39°15N 27°6E 205 B9
Kozaklı Turkey 39°13N 34°49E 212 C6
Kozan Turkey 37°26N 35°50E 212 D6
Kozani Greece 40°19N 21°47E 202 F5
Kozani □ Greece 40°18N 21°45E 202 F5
Kozara Bos.-H. 45°0N 17°0E 182 F1
Kozara △ Bos.-H. 45°0N 17°0E 182 F1
Kozarac Bos.-H. 44°58N 16°48E 199 D13
Kozelets Ukraine 50°50N 31°18E 189 G6
Kozelsk Russia 54°2N 35°48E 188 D8
Kozhikode = Calicut India 11°15N 75°43E 245 J2
Kozhva Russia 65°43N 57°0E 186 A11
Koziegłowy Poland 50°37N 19°8E 185 H6
Kozienice Poland 51°35N 21°34E 185 G8
Kozje Slovenia 46°5N 15°35E 199 B12
Kozloduy Bulgaria 43°45N 23°42E 202 C7
Kozlov = Michurinsk
  Russia 52°58N 40°27E 190 D5
Kozlovets Bulgaria 43°30N 25°20E 203 C9
Kozlovka Russia 55°51N 48°16E 190 B8
Kozlu Turkey 41°26N 31°45E 212 B4
Koźmin Poland 51°48N 17°27E 185 G4
Kozmodemyansk Russia 56°20N 46°36E 190 B8

Kōzu-Shima Japan 34°13N 139°10E 223 C11
Kożuchów Poland 51°45N 15°31E 185 G2
Kozyatyn Ukraine 49°45N 28°50E 177 D15
Kozyrevsk Russia 56°3N 159°51E 215 D16
Kpabia Ghana 9°10N 0°20W 263 D4
Kpalimé Togo 6°57N 0°44E 263 D5
Kpandae Ghana 8°30N 0°5W 263 D4
Kpessi Togo 8°4N 1°16E 263 D5
Kra, Isthmus of = Kra, Kho Khot
  Thailand 10°15N 99°30E 237 G2
Kra, Kho Khot Thailand 10°15N 99°30E 237 G2
Kra Buri Thailand 10°22N 98°46E 237 G2
Kraai → S. Africa 30°40S 26°45E 270 D4
Kraainem Belgium 50°52N 4°28E 116 A2
Krabi Thailand 8°4N 98°55E 237 H2
Kracheh = Kratie
  Cambodia 12°32N 106°10E 236 F6
Kragan Indonesia 6°43S 111°38E 235 D4
Kragerø Norway 58°52N 9°25E 164 F6
Kragujevac Serbia 44°2N 20°56E 202 B4
Krailling Germany 48°5N 11°25E 131 B1
Krainburg = Kranj
  Slovenia 46°16N 14°22E 199 B11
Krajenka Poland 53°18N 16°59E 185 E3
Krakatau = Rakata, Pulau
  Indonesia 6°10S 105°20E 234 D3
Krakatoa = Rakata, Pulau
  Indonesia 6°10S 105°20E 234 D3
Krakau = Kraków Poland 50°4N 19°57E 185 H6
Krakor Cambodia 12°32N 104°12E 236 F5
Kraków Poland 50°4N 19°57E 185 H6
Kraków ✈ (KRK) Poland 50°5N 19°52E 185 H6
Kraksaan Indonesia 7°43S 113°23E 235 D4
Kralanh Cambodia 13°35N 103°25E 236 F4
Kralendijk Bonaire 12°9N 68°16W 322 h
Kraljeviča Croatia 45°16N 14°36E 199 C11
Kraljevo Serbia 43°44N 20°41E 202 C4
Královéhradecký □
  Czech Rep. 50°25N 15°50E 180 A8
Kralovský Chlmec
  Slovak Rep. 48°27N 22°0E 181 C14
Kralupy nad Vltavou
  Czech Rep. 50°13N 14°20E 180 A7
Kramatorsk Ukraine 48°50N 37°30E 189 H10
Kramfors Sweden 62°55N 17°48E 162 B11
Kramis, C. Algeria 36°26N 0°45E 261 A5
Krampnitz Germany 52°27N 13°3E 115 B1
Krampnitzsee Germany 52°27N 13°3E 115 B1
Krania Greece 39°53N 21°18E 202 G5
Krania Elasonas Greece 39°57N 22°2E 204 B4
Kranidi Greece 37°20N 23°10E 204 D5
Kranj Slovenia 46°16N 14°22E 199 B11
Kranji, Sungei →
  Singapore 1°26N 103°44E 138 A2
Kranji Industrial Estate
  Singapore 1°26N 103°43E 138 A2
Kranjska Gora Slovenia 46°29N 13°48E 199 B10
Krankskop S. Africa 28°0S 30°47E 271 C5
Kranz = Zelenogradsk
  Russia 54°53N 20°29E 184 D7
Krapina Croatia 46°10N 15°52E 199 B12
Krapina → Croatia 45°50N 15°50E 199 C12
Krapkowice Poland 50°29N 17°56E 185 H4
Kras Croatia 45°35N 14°0E 199 C10
Krasavino Russia 60°58N 46°29E 186 B8
Kraskino Russia 42°44N 130°48E 220 C5
Krasków Russia 55°39N 37°25E 129 C5
Kraslava Latvia 55°54N 27°10E 188 E4
Kraslice Czech Rep. 50°19N 12°31E 180 A5
Krasnaya Gorbatka
  Russia 55°52N 41°45E 190 C5
Krasnaya Polyana Russia 43°40N 40°13E 191 J5
Krasnaya Sloboda =
  Krasnoslobodsk Russia 48°42N 44°33E 191 F7
Krasne Ukraine 46°7N 29°15E 183 D14
Krasni Okny Ukraine 47°32N 29°27E 183 C14
Krasnik Poland 50°55N 22°15E 185 H9
Krasno-Presnenskaya
  Russia 55°45N 37°32E 129 B3
Krasnoarmeisk = Tayynsha
  Kazakhstan 53°50N 69°45E 218 F7
Krasnoarmeysk Russia 51°0N 45°42E 190 E7
Krasnoarmeysk Russia 50°10N 42°12E 191 G6
Krasnoarmeysky Rudnik =
  Dobropole Poland 50°33N 23°12E 185 H10
Krasnobród Poland 50°33N 23°12E 185 H10
Krasnodar Russia 45°5N 39°0E 191 H4
Krasnodar □ Russia 45°0N 39°0E 191 H4
Krasnodarskoye Vdkhr.
  Russia 45°1N 39°32E 191 H4
Krasnodon Ukraine 48°14N 39°44E 189 H11
Krasnogorsk Russia 55°49N 37°18E 129 B3
Krasnograd = Krasnohrad
  Ukraine 49°27N 35°27E 189 H8
Krasnogvardeysk = Gatchina
  Russia 59°35N 30°9E 188 C6
Krasnogvardeyskoye
  Russia 45°52N 41°33E 191 H5
Krasnohrad Ukraine 49°27N 35°27E 189 H8
Krasnokamensk Russia 50°3N 118°0E 215 D12
Krasnokamsk Russia 58°4N 55°48E 186 C10
Krasnokutsk Ukraine 50°10N 34°50E 189 G8
Krasnoperekopsk Ukraine 46°0N 33°54E 189 J7
Krasnorechenskiy
  Russia 44°41N 135°14E 220 B7
Krasnoselkup Russia 65°20N 82°10E 214 C9
Krasnoslobodsk Mordvinia,
  Russia 54°25N 43°45E 190 C6
Krasnoslobodsk Volgograd,
  Russia 48°42N 44°33E 191 F7
Krasnoturinsk Russia 59°46N 60°12E 186 C11
Krasnoufimsk Russia 56°36N 57°38E 186 C10
Krasnouralsk Russia 58°21N 60°3E 186 C11
Krasnovishersk Russia 60°23N 57°3E 186 B10
Krasnovodsk = Türkmenbashi
  Turkmenistan 40°5N 53°5E 247 A7
Krasnoyarsk Russia 56°8N 93°0E 214 D10
Krasnoyarskoye Vdkhr.
  Russia 54°31N 91°56E 214 D9
Krasnoye = Krasnyy
  Russia 54°25N 31°30E 188 E6
Krasnoye = Ulan Erge
  Russia 46°16N 44°46E 191 H7
Krasnyy Russia 54°25N 31°30E 188 E6
Krasnyy Kholm Russia 58°10N 37°10E 188 C9
Krasnyy Kut Russia 50°50N 47°0E 190 E8
Krasnyy Liman Ukraine 48°58N 37°50E 189 H10
Krasnyy Luch Ukraine 48°13N 39°0E 189 H11

Kruger △ S. Africa 24°50S 26°10E 271 B4
Krugersdorp S. Africa 26°5S 27°46E 271 C4
Krui Indonesia 5°10S 103°55E 234 D2
Kruisfontein S. Africa 33°59S 24°43E 270 D3
Krujë Albania 41°32N 19°46E 202 E3
Krulevshchina = Krulyewshchyna
  Belarus 55°5N 27°45E 188 E4
Krulyewshchyna Belarus 55°5N 27°45E 188 E4
Krumbach Germany 48°13N 10°22E 179 G6
Krumë Albania 42°14N 20°28E 202 D4
Krummau = Český Krumlov
  Czech Rep. 48°43N 14°21E 180 C7
Krumme Lanke Germany 52°27N 13°14E 115 B2
Krummensee Germany 52°35N 13°41E 115 A5
Krummhübel = Karpacz
  Poland 50°46N 15°46E 185 H2
Krumovgrad Bulgaria 41°29N 25°38E 203 E9
Krung Thep = Bangkok
  Thailand 13°45N 100°35E 113 B2
Krupanj Serbia 44°25N 19°22E 202 B3
Krupina Slovak Rep. 48°22N 19°5E 181 C12
Krupinica → Slovak Rep. 48°4N 18°55E 181 C11
Krupki Belarus 54°19N 29°8E 177 A15
Krusboda Sweden 59°13N 18°14E 139 B3
Krusenstern, C. U.S.A. 67°8N 163°45W 303 C7
Kruševac Serbia 43°35N 21°28E 202 C5
Kruševo Macedonia 41°23N 21°19E 202 E5
Krushchyov = Svitlovodsk
  Ukraine 49°2N 33°13E 189 H7
Krushelnyksya Ukraine 49°7N 23°29E 185 J10
Kruszwica Poland 52°40N 18°20E 185 F5
Krychaw Belarus 53°40N 31°41E 177 B16
Krylatskoye Russia 55°44N 37°23E 129 B2
Krymsk Russia 54°50N 38°0E 189 K10
Krymskiy Poluostrov = Krymskyy
  Pivostriv Ukraine 45°0N 34°0E 189 K8
Krymskyy Pivostriv Ukraine 45°0N 34°0E 189 K8
Krynica Poland 49°25N 20°57E 185 J7
Krynica Morska Poland 54°23N 19°28E 184 D6
Krynki Poland 53°17N 23°43E 185 E10
Krynychne Ukraine 45°32N 28°40E 183 E13
Kryvyy Rih Ukraine 47°51N 33°20E 189 J7
Kryzhopil Ukraine 48°23N 28°53E 183 B13
Krzemienice = Kremenets
  Ukraine 50°8N 25°43E 177 C13
Krzepice Poland 50°58N 18°50E 185 H5
Krzeszów Poland 50°24N 22°21E 185 H9
Krzna → Poland 52°8N 23°32E 185 F10
Krzywiń Poland 51°58N 16°50E 185 G3
Krzyż Wielkopolski Poland 52°51N 16°0E 185 F3
Ksabi Morocco 32°51N 4°13W 260 B4
Ksar Chellala Algeria 35°13N 2°19E 261 A5
Ksar el Boukhari Algeria 35°51N 2°52E 261 A5
Ksar el Kebir Morocco 35°0N 6°0W 260 B3
Ksar es Souk = Er Rachidia
  Morocco 31°58N 4°20W 260 B4
Ksar Rhilane Tunisia 33°0N 9°39E 258 B1
Ksiąz Wielkopolski Poland 52°4N 17°14E 185 F4
Ksour, Mts. des Algeria 32°45N 0°30W 261 B4
Kstovo Russia 56°12N 44°13E 190 B7
Ku, W. el → Sudan 13°37N 25°15E 257 E2
Ku-Ring-Gai Chase ⌂
  Australia 33°39S 151°14E 283 B9
Ku Tree Res. U.S.A. 21°30N 157°59W 302 D4
Kuah Malaysia 6°19N 99°51E 237 J2
Kuala Indonesia 2°55N 105°47E 234 B3
Kuala Belait Malaysia 4°35N 114°11E 235 B4
Kuala Berang Malaysia 5°5N 103°1E 237 K4
Kuala Dungun = Dungun
  Malaysia 4°45N 103°25E 237 K4
Kuala Kangsar Malaysia 4°46N 100°56E 237 K3
Kuala Kelawang Malaysia 2°56N 102°5E 237 L4
Kuala Kerai Malaysia 5°30N 102°12E 237 K4
Kuala Kubu Bharu
  Malaysia 3°34N 101°39E 237 L3
Kuala Lipis Malaysia 4°10N 102°3E 237 K4
Kuala Lumpur Malaysia 3°9N 101°41E 237 L3
Kuala Nerang Malaysia 6°16N 100°37E 237 J3
Kuala Pilah Malaysia 2°45N 102°15E 237 L4
Kuala Rompin Malaysia 2°49N 103°29E 237 L4
Kuala Selangor Malaysia 3°20N 101°15E 237 L3
Kuala Sepetang Malaysia 4°49N 100°28E 237 K3
Kuala Terengganu
  Malaysia 5°20N 103°8E 237 K4
Kualajelai Indonesia 2°58S 110°46E 235 C4
Kualakapuas Indonesia 1°10S 113°50E 235 C4
Kualapembuang Indonesia 3°14S 112°38E 235 C4
Kualasimpang Indonesia 4°17N 98°3E 234 B1
Kualau'u U.S.A. 21°9N 157°2W 302 B4
Kualatungkal Indonesia 0°49S 103°28E 234 C2
Kualoa Pt. U.S.A. 21°31N 157°50W 302 J14
Kuamut Malaysia 5°13N 117°30E 235 A5
Kuan Shan Taiwan 23°14N 120°54E 225 a
Kuanao Taiwan 24°31N 118°24E 225 a
Kuandang Indonesia 0°56N 123°1E 231 D6
Kuandian China 40°37N 124°30E 227 D13
Kuangchou = Guangzhou
  China 23°6N 113°13E 121 B2
Kuangfu Taiwan 23°40N 121°25E 225 C2
Kuanhsi Taiwan 24°48N 121°11E 225 C2
Kuanmiao Taiwan 22°58N 120°19E 225 D2
Kuantan Malaysia 3°49N 103°20E 237 L4
Kuanyin Ilan, Taiwan 24°23N 121°46E 225 B3
Kuanyin Taoyüan, Taiwan 25°2N 121°4E 225 B3
Kuapá Pond U.S.A. 21°17N 157°42W 302 K14
Kuapá Balinsasayao △
  Phil. 9°21N 123°13E 233 F5
Kuba = Quba Azerbaijan 41°21N 48°32E 191 K9
Kubadh △ Malaysia 1°35N 110°9E 235 B4
Kuban → Russia 45°20N 37°30E 189 K9
Kuban Depression =
  Prikubanskaya Nizmennost
  Russia 45°39N 38°33E 191 H4
Kubaysah Iraq 33°35N 42°37E 213 G10
Kubenskoye, Ozero
  Russia 59°40N 39°25E 188 C10
Kuberle = Krasnoarmeyskiy
  Russia 50°10N 42°12E 191 G6
Kubokawa Japan 33°12N 133°8E 222 D5
Kubor, Mt. Papua N. G. 6°10S 144°44E 286 D3
Kubrat Bulgaria 43°49N 26°31E 203 C10
Kubu Indonesia 8°16S 115°35E 231 J18
Kubumesaai Indonesia 2°10N 114°16E 235 B4
Kubutambahan Indonesia 8°5S 115°10E 231 J18
Kucar, Tanjung
  Indonesia 8°39S 114°34E 231 K18
Kučevo Serbia 44°30N 21°40E 202 B5
Kuchaman India 27°13N 74°47E 242 F6
Kuchaveli Sri Lanka 8°49N 81°6E 245 K5
Kuchinda India 21°44N 84°21E 243 J11
Kuchino-eruba-Jima
  Japan 30°28N 130°12E 221 J5
Kuchino-Shima Japan 29°57N 129°55E 221 K4
Kuchinotsu Japan 32°36N 130°11E 222 E2
Kuchl Austria 47°37N 13°10E 180 D6
Kūchnay Darvīshān
  Afghan. 30°59N 64°10E 240 C2
Kuchurhan → Ukraine 46°39N 30°57E 183 D14
Kucing = Kuching
  Malaysia 1°33N 110°25E 235 B4

Kuçovë Albania 40°47N 19°57E 202 F3
Küçükbahçe Turkey 38°33N 26°24E 205 C8
Küçükköy Balıkesir, Turkey 39°16N 26°42E 205 B8
Küçükköy İstanbul, Turkey 41°3N 28°52E 122 B1
Küçükkuyu Turkey 39°32N 26°36E 205 B8
Küçükmenderes → Turkey 37°57N 27°16E 205 D9
Küçüksu Turkey 41°5N 29°5E 122 B2
Kud → Pakistan 26°5N 66°20E 242 F2
Kuda India 23°10N 71°15E 242 H4
Kuda Indonesia 1°1N 112°58E 235 B4
Kudahuvadhoo Maldives 2°40N 72°54E 272 d
Kudahuvadhoo Channel Maldives 2°40N 73°0E 272 d
Kudaka-shima Japan 26°9N 127°53E 288 a
Kudal India 16°2N 73°41E 245 F1
Kudalier → India 18°35N 79°48E 244 E4
Kudamatsu Japan 34°0N 131°52E 222 D3
Kudankita Tokyo, Japan 140 a3
Kudarebe Aruba 12°37N 70°4W 322 f
Kudat Malaysia 6°55N 116°55E 235 A5
Kudirkos Naumiestis Lithuania 54°46N 22°53E 184 D9
Kudowa-Zdrój Poland 50°27N 16°15E 185 H3
Kudremukh India 13°15N 75°20E 245 H2
Kudrovo Russia 59°54N 30°30E 137 B3
Kudus Indonesia 6°48S 110°51E 235 D4
Kudymkar Russia 59°1N 54°39E 186 C9
Kueishan Tao Taiwan 24°51N 121°57E 225 B3
Kueiyang = Guiyang China 26°32N 106°40E 228 D6
Kufra Oasis = Al Kufrah Libya 24°17N 23°15E 258 D4
Kufstein Austria 47°35N 12°11E 180 D5
Kugaaruk = Pelly Bay Canada 68°38N 89°50W 295 D14
Kugluktuk Canada 67°50N 115°5W 294 D8
Kugong I. Canada 56°18N 79°50W 298 A4
Kūh Dasht Iran 33°32N 47°36E 213 F12
Kūh-e Jebāl Bārez Iran 29°0N 58°0E 247 D8
Kūh-e Sorkh Iran 35°30N 58°45E 247 C8
Kūhak Iran 27°12N 63°10E 240 D1
Kuhan Pakistan 28°19N 67°14E 242 E2
Kūhbonān Iran 31°23N 56°19E 247 D8
Kūhestak Iran 26°47N 57°2E 247 E8
Kūhestān Afghan. 34°39N 61°12E 240 B1
Kūhīn Iran 36°22N 49°40E 247 B6
Kūhīrī Iran 26°55N 61°2E 247 E9
Kūhiston-Badakhshon □ Tajikistan 38°30N 73°0E 217 E8
Kuhmo Finland 64°7N 29°31E 160 D23
Kuhn Chae △ Thailand 19°8N 99°24E 236 C2
Kuhnsdorf Austria 46°37N 14°38E 180 E7
Kūhpāyeh Eşfahan, Iran 32°44N 52°20E 247 C7
Kūhpāyeh Kermān, Iran 30°35N 57°15E 247 D8
Kūhrān, Kūh-e Iran 26°46N 58°12E 247 E8
Kui Buri Thailand 12°3N 99°52E 237 F2
Kuiburi △ Thailand 12°10N 99°37E 237 F2
Kuichong China 22°38N 114°25E 219 a
Kuiseb → Namibia 22°59S 14°31E 270 B1
Kuito Angola 12°22S 16°55E 265 E3
Kuiu I. U.S.A. 57°45N 134°10W 296 B2
Kujang N. Korea 39°57N 126°1E 224 C3
Kujawsko-Pomorskie □ Poland 53°20N 18°30E 184 E5
Kuji Japan 40°11N 141°46E 220 D10
Kujū-San Japan 33°5N 131°15E 222 D3
Kukarka = Sovetsk Russia 57°38N 48°53E 190 B9
Kukava Ukraine 48°37N 27°43E 183 B12
Kukavica Serbia 42°48N 21°57E 202 D5
Kukawa Nigeria 12°58N 13°27E 263 C7
Kuk'eng Taiwan 23°38N 120°33E 225 C2
Kukës Albania 42°5N 20°27E 202 D4
Kuki Japan 36°4N 139°40E 223 A11
Kukipi Papua N. G. 8°10S 146°6E 286 E4
Kukmor Russia 56°11N 50°54E 190 B10
Kükong = Shaoguan China 24°48N 113°35E 229 E9
Kuku Pt. Wake I. 19°18N 166°34E 302 b
Kukuan Taiwan 24°17N 121°2E 225 B3
Kukuihaele U.S.A. 20°5N 155°35W 302 C6
Kukup Malaysia 1°20N 103°27E 237 d
Kukup, Pulau Malaysia 1°18N 103°25E 237 d
Kukvidze Russia 50°40N 43°0E 190 E6
Kula Bulgaria 43°52N 22°36E 202 C6
Kula Serbia 45°37N 19°32E 182 E4
Kula Turkey 38°32N 28°40E 205 C10
Kula Gulf Solomon Is. 8°5S 157°18E 287 M9
K'ula Kangri Asia 28°14N 90°36E 241 A3
K'ula Shan Bhutan 28°14N 90°36E 218 F7
Kulachi Pakistan 31°56N 70°27E 242 D4
Kulai Malaysia 1°44N 103°35E 237 M4
Kulal, Mt. Kenya 2°43N 36°56E 266 D4
Kulaly, Ostrov = Kulaly Aral Kazakhstan 45°0N 50°5E 191 H10
Kulaly Aral Kazakhstan 45°0N 50°5E 191 H10
Kulasekarappattinam India 8°20N 78°5E 245 K4
Kulassein I. Phil. 6°25N 120°41E 233 H3
Kulaura Bangla. 24°32N 92°3E 241 C4
Kulautuva Lithuania 54°56N 23°36E 184 D10
Kuldīga Latvia 56°58N 21°59E 184 B8
Kuldīga □ Latvia 56°55N 22°0E 184 B8
Kuldja = Yining China 43°58N 81°10E 217 D10
Kuldu Sudan 12°50N 28°30E 257 E2
Kulebaki Russia 55°22N 42°25E 190 C6
Kulen Cambodia 13°50N 104°40E 236 F5
Kulen Vakuf Bos.-H. 44°35N 16°2E 199 D13
Kulgam India 33°36N 75°2E 243 C6
Kulgera Australia 25°50S 133°18E 280 D1
Kulhudhuffushi Maldives 6°37N 73°3E 272 d
Kulim Malaysia 5°22N 100°34E 237 K3
Kulin Australia 32°40S 118°2E 279 F2
Kulittalai India 10°55N 78°25E 245 J4
Kulkayu = Hartley Bay Canada 53°25N 129°15W 296 C3
Kullen Sweden 56°18N 12°26E 163 H6
Kullu India 31°58N 77°6E 242 D7
Kulmbach Germany 50°6N 11°26E 179 E7
Kŭlob Tajikistan 37°55N 69°50E 217 E7
Kulosaari Finland 60°11N 25°0E 121 B3
Kulp Turkey 38°29N 41°2E 213 C9
Kulpawn → Ghana 10°20N 1°5W 263 D4
Kulsary = Qulsary Kazakhstan 46°59N 54°1E 187 E9
Kulti India 23°43N 86°50E 243 H12
Kulu Turkey 39°5N 33°4E 212 C5
Kulumadau Papua N. G. 9°3S 152°43E 286 E7
Kulunda Russia 52°35N 78°57E 217 B9
Kulundinskoye, Ozero Russia 53°0N 79°36E 217 B9
Kulungar Afghan. 34°0N 69°2E 242 C3
Kūlvand Iran 31°21N 54°35E 247 D7
Kulwin Australia 35°2S 142°42E 282 C5
Kulyab = Kŭlob Tajikistan 37°55N 69°50E 217 E7
Kuma Japan 33°39N 132°54E 222 D4
Kuma → Russia 44°55N 47°0E 191 H8
Kumafşarı Turkey 37°19N 29°32E 205 D11
Kumaganum Nigeria 13°8N 10°38E 263 C7
Kumagaya Japan 36°9N 139°22E 223 A11
Kumai Indonesia 2°44S 111°43E 235 C4
Kumai, Teluk Indonesia 3°0S 111°43E 235 C4
Kumalar Dağı Turkey 38°15N 30°20E 205 C12
Kumamba, Kepulauan Indonesia 1°36S 138°45E 231 E9
Kumamoto Japan 32°45N 130°45E 222 E2
Kumamoto □ Japan 32°55N 130°55E 222 E2
Kumano Japan 33°54N 136°5E 223 D8
Kumano-Nada Japan 33°47N 136°20E 223 D8
Kumanovo Macedonia 42°9N 21°42E 202 D5
Kumar → Afghan. 34°30N 70°28E 240 B3
Kumara N.Z. 42°37S 171°12E 285 C6
Kumarina Roadhouse Australia 24°41S 119°32E 279 D2
Kumarkhali Bangla. 23°51N 89°15E 241 D2
Kumasi Ghana 6°41N 1°38W 262 D4
Kumba Cameroon 4°36N 9°24E 263 E6
Kumbağ Turkey 40°51N 27°27E 203 F11
Kumbakonam India 10°58N 79°25E 245 J4
Kumbarilla Australia 27°15S 150°55E 281 D5
Kumbatine △ Australia 31°8S 152°35E 283 A10
Kumbhraj India 24°22N 77°3E 242 G7
Kumbia Australia 26°41S 151°39E 281 D5
Kumbo Cameroon 6°15N 10°36E 263 D7
Kumbukkan Oya → Sri Lanka 6°35N 81°40E 245 L5
Kŭmch'on N. Korea 38°10N 126°29E 224 C3
Kumdah Si. Arabia 20°23N 45°5E 248 B4
Kume-Shima Japan 26°20N 126°47E 221 L3
Kumeny Russia 58°10N 49°47E 190 A9
Kumertau Russia 52°45N 55°57E 186 D10
Kumharsain India 31°19N 77°27E 242 D7
Kumi Uganda 1°30N 33°58E 268 B3
Kumkale Turkey 39°59N 26°11E 203 G10
Kumla Örebro, Sweden 59°8N 15°10E 162 E9
Kumla Stockholm, Sweden 59°13N 18°11E 139 B3
Kumlu Turkey 36°21N 36°27E 250 B7
Kumluca Turkey 36°22N 30°20E 205 E12
Kummerower See Germany 53°49N 12°51E 178 B8
Kumo Nigeria 10°1N 11°12E 263 C7
Kumo älv = Kokemäenjoki → Finland 61°32N 21°44E 188 B1
Kumon Bum Burma 26°30N 97°15E 241 B6
Kumotori-Yama Japan 35°51N 138°57E 223 B10
Kumta India 14°29N 74°25E 245 G2
Kumtag Shamo China 39°40N 92°0E 218 D7
Kumukahi, C. U.S.A. 19°31N 154°49W 302 D7
Kumusi → Papua N. G. 8°16S 148°13E 286 E5
Kumylzhenskaya Russia 49°51N 42°38E 190 F6
Kunágota Hungary 46°26N 21°3E 182 D6
Kunak Malaysia 4°41N 118°15E 235 B5
Kunashir, Ostrov Russia 44°0N 146°0E 215 E15
Kunchaung Burma 23°50N 96°35E 241 D6
Kunda Estonia 59°30N 26°34E 188 C4
Kunda India 25°43N 81°31E 243 G9
Kundar → Pakistan 31°56N 69°19E 242 D3
Kundelungu △ Dem. Rep. of the Congo 10°30S 27°40E 269 E2
Kundelungu Ouest △ Dem. Rep. of the Congo 9°55S 27°17E 269 D2
Kundian Pakistan 32°27N 71°28E 242 C4
Kundiawa Papua N. G. 6°2S 145°1E 286 D3
Kundla India 21°21N 71°25E 242 J4
Kundur Indonesia 0°45N 103°25E 234 B2
Kung, Ao Thailand 8°5N 98°24E 237 a
Kunga → Bangla. 21°46N 89°30E 241 E2
Kungälv Sweden 57°53N 11°59E 163 G5
Kungens kurva Sweden 59°15N 17°53E 139 B1
Kunghit I. Canada 52°6N 131°3W 296 C2
Kungkuan Taiwan 24°35N 120°44E 225 B2
Kungliao Taiwan 25°1N 121°54E 225 A3
Kungliga Slottet Stockholm, Sweden 139 b2
Kungrad = Qŭnghirot Uzbekistan 43°2N 58°50E 216 D5
Kungsängen Sweden 59°29N 17°45E 162 E11
Kungsbacka Sweden 57°30N 12°5E 163 G6
Kungsgården Sweden 60°37N 16°35E 162 D10
Kungshamn Sweden 58°22N 11°15E 163 F5
Kungshatt Sweden 59°17N 17°53E 139 B1
Kungsholmen Sweden 59°20N 18°2E 139 A2
Kungsör Sweden 59°25N 16°5E 162 E10
Kungssuliao Taiwan 24°37N 120°45E 225 B2
Kungu Dem. Rep. of the Congo 2°47N 19°12E 264 B3
Kungur Russia 57°25N 56°57E 186 C10
Kungurri Australia 21°4S 148°45E 280 b
Kungyangon Burma 16°27N 96°20E 241 G6
Kunhar → Pakistan 34°20N 73°30E 243 B5
Kunhegyes Hungary 47°22N 20°36E 182 C5
Kunia U.S.A. 21°28N 158°4W 302 K13
Kunigami Japan 26°46N 128°12E 288 a
Kunimi-Dake Japan 32°33N 131°1E 222 E3
Kuningan Jakarta, Indonesia 6°13S 106°49E 122 B1
Kuningan Jawa Barat, Indonesia 6°59S 108°29E 235 D3
Kunisaki Japan 33°33N 131°45E 222 D3
Kunitachi Japan 35°41N 139°27E 140 A1
Kunjirap Daban Pakistan 36°52N 75°27E 240 A4
Kunlara Australia 34°54S 139°55E 282 C3
Kunlong Burma 23°20N 98°50E 228 F2
Kunlun Shan Asia 36°0N 86°30E 217 E11
Kunlun Shankou China 35°38N 94°4E 218 D7
Kunmadaras Hungary 47°28N 20°45E 182 C5
Kunming China 25°1N 102°41E 228 E4
Kunming Hu China 39°59N 116°13E 114 B1
Kunmunya ✪ Australia 15°26S 124°42E 278 C3
Kunnamkulam India 10°38N 76°7E 245 J3
Kunów Poland 50°57N 21°17E 185 H8
Kunratice Czech Rep. 50°0N 14°28E 135 B2
Kunshan China 31°22N 120°58E 229 B13
Kunsthistorischesmuseum Vienna, Austria 142 b1
Kunszentmárton Hungary 46°50N 20°20E 182 D5
Kunszentmiklós Hungary 47°2N 19°8E 182 C4
Kuntaur Senegal 13°40N 14°48W 262 C2
Kuntsevo Russia 55°43N 37°23E 129 B2
Kunua Papua N. G. 5°46S 154°43E 286 C8
Kununurra Australia 15°40S 128°50E 278 C4
Kunwari → India 26°26N 79°11E 243 F8
Kunya-Urgench = Köneürgench Turkmenistan 42°19N 59°10E 216 D5
Künzelsau Germany 49°17N 9°42E 179 F5
Kunzulu Dem. Rep. of the Congo 3°28S 16°12E 264 C3
Kuohsing Taiwan 24°2N 120°51E 225 B2
Kuopio Finland 62°53N 27°35E 160 E22
Kupa → Croatia 45°28N 16°24E 199 C13
Kupang Indonesia 10°19S 123°39E 231 F6
Kupchino Russia 59°50N 30°23E 137 B2
Kupiano Papua N. G. 10°4S 148°14E 286 F5
Küpikipiki'ö Pt. U.S.A. 21°15N 157°47W 302 K14
Kupino Russia 54°21N 77°16E 217 B9
Kupreanof I. U.S.A. 56°50N 133°30W 296 B2
Kupres Bos.-H. 43°56N 17°15E 182 G2
Kupyansk Ukraine 49°52N 37°35E 189 H9
Kupyansk-Uzlovoi Ukraine 49°40N 37°43E 189 H9
Kuqa China 41°35N 82°30E 217 D10
Kür → Azerbaijan 39°29N 49°15E 213 C13
Kur → Bhutan 26°50N 91°0E 241 B3
Kür Dili Azerbaijan 39°3N 49°13E 213 C13
Kura = Kür → Azerbaijan 39°29N 49°15E 213 C13
Kurahashi-Jima Japan 34°8N 132°31E 222 C4
Kuramo Waters Nigeria 6°25N 3°26E 124 B2
Kuranda Australia 16°48S 145°35E 280 B4
Kuranga India 22°4N 69°10E 242 H3
Kurashiki Japan 34°40N 133°50E 222 C5
Kurayn Si. Arabia 27°39N 49°50E 247 E6
Kurayoshi Japan 35°26N 133°50E 222 B5
Kurbağalı → Turkey 40°58N 29°1E 122 C2
Kŭrchatov Kazakhstan 50°45N 78°32E 217 B9
Kürdämir Azerbaijan 40°25N 48°3E 191 K9
Kurdistan Asia 37°20N 43°30E 213 D10
Kurduvadi India 18°8N 75°29E 244 E2
Kŭrdzhali Bulgaria 41°38N 25°21E 203 E9
Kŭrdzhali □ Bulgaria 41°38N 25°21E 203 E9
Kure Japan 34°14N 132°32E 222 C4
Küre Turkey 41°48N 33°43E 212 B5
Küre Dağları Turkey 41°50N 34°10E 212 B6
Kure I. U.S.A. 28°25N 178°25W 302 F8
Kuressaare Estonia 58°15N 22°30E 188 C2
Kurgan Russia 55°26N 65°18E 216 A7
Kurgan-Tyube = Qŭrghonteppa Tajikistan 37°50N 68°47E 217 E7
Kurganinsk Russia 44°54N 40°34E 191 H5
Kurgannaya = Kurganinsk Russia 44°54N 40°34E 191 H5
Kuri India 26°37N 70°43E 242 F4
Kuria Maria Is. = Hallāniyat, Jazā'ir al Oman 17°30N 55°58E 249 C6
Kurichchi India 11°36N 77°35E 245 J3
Kuridala Australia 21°16S 140°29E 280 C3
Kurigram Bangla. 25°49N 89°39E 241 C2
Kurihara Japan 35°45N 139°34E 140 A2
Kurikka Finland 62°36N 22°24E 160 E20
Kuril Basin Pac. Oc. 47°0N 150°0E 150 E15
Kuril Is. = Kurilskiye Ostrova Russia 45°0N 150°0E 215 E16
Kuril-Kamchatka Trench Pac. Oc. 44°0N 153°0E 288 C7
Kurilsk Russia 45°14N 147°53E 215 E15
Kurilskiye Ostrova Russia 45°0N 150°0E 215 E16
Kurino Japan 31°57N 130°43E 222 F2
Kurinskaya Kosa = Kür Dili Azerbaijan 39°3N 49°13E 213 C13
Kurisches Haff = Kurshskiy Zaliv Russia 55°9N 21°6E 184 C8
Kürkçü Turkey 36°34N 33°39E 250 B4
Kurkheda India 20°37N 80°12E 244 D5
Kurkur Egypt 23°50N 32°0E 256 C3
Kurla India 19°4N 72°52E 130 A2
Kurlkuta ✪ Australia 24°0S 127°5E 278 D4
Kurlovskiy Russia 55°25N 40°40E 190 C5
Kurmuk Sudan 10°33N 34°21E 257 E3
Kurmuri India 19°4N 72°53E 130 A2
Kurnool India 15°45N 78°0E 245 G4
Kuro-Shima Kagoshima, Japan 30°50N 129°57E 221 J4
Kuro-Shima Okinawa, Japan 24°14N 124°1E 221 M2
Kurobe-Gawe → Japan 36°55N 137°25E 223 A9
Kurogi Japan 33°12N 130°40E 222 D2
Kuror, J. Sudan 20°27N 31°30E 256 C3
Kurow N.Z. 44°44S 170°29E 285 E5
Kurów Poland 51°23N 22°12E 185 G9
Kurrajong Australia 33°33S 150°42E 283 B9
Kurram → Pakistan 32°36N 71°20E 242 C4
Kurri Kurri Australia 32°50S 151°28E 283 B9
Kurrimine Australia 17°47S 146°6E 280 B4
Kursavka Russia 44°29N 42°32E 191 H6
Kurse Korhi India 20°14N 80°46E 244 D5
Kurseong = Karsiyang India 26°56N 88°18E 241 B2
Kürshim Kazakhstan 48°34N 83°39E 217 C10
Kurshskaya Kosa ⌂ Russia 55°7N 20°45E 184 C7
Kurshskiy Zaliv Russia 55°9N 21°6E 184 C8
Kuršių Nerijos △ Lithuania 55°30N 21°6E 184 C8
Kursk Russia 51°42N 36°11E 189 G9
Kursk □ Russia 51°50N 36°10E 189 G9
Kursu = Salla Finland 66°50N 28°49E 160 C23
Kuršumlija Serbia 43°9N 21°19E 202 C5
Kuršumlijska Banja Serbia 43°3N 21°11E 202 C5
Kurşunlu Bursa, Turkey 40°3N 29°40E 203 F13
Kurşunlu Çankırı, Turkey 40°51N 33°15E 212 B5
Kurtalan Turkey 37°56N 41°44E 213 D9
Kurtbey Turkey 41°9N 26°35E 203 E10
Kurtistown U.S.A. 19°36N 155°4W 302 D6
Kuru Sudan 7°43N 26°31E 257 F2
Kuru, Bahr el → Sudan 8°10N 26°50E 257 F2
Kurucaşile Turkey 41°49N 32°42E 212 B5
Kuruçay Turkey 39°39N 38°29E 246 B3
Kurukshetra = Thanesar India 30°1N 76°52E 242 D7
Kuruktag China 41°0N 89°0E 217 D11
Kuruman S. Africa 27°28S 23°28E 270 C3
Kuruman → S. Africa 26°56S 20°39E 270 C3
Kurume Fukuoka, Japan 33°15N 130°30E 222 D2
Kurume Tōkyō, Japan 35°45N 139°31E 140 A2
Kurun → Sudan 5°30N 34°17E 257 F3
Kurunegala Sri Lanka 7°30N 80°23E 245 L5
Kurupukari Guyana 4°43N 58°37W 329 C6
Kurya Russia 61°42N 57°9E 186 B10
Kuryanovo Russia 55°39N 37°42E 129 C4
Kus Gölü Turkey 40°10N 27°55E 203 F11
Kuşadası Turkey 37°52N 27°15E 212 D2
Kuşadası Körfezı Turkey 37°56N 27°0E 205 D8
Kusamba Indonesia 8°34S 115°27E 231 K18
Kusatsu Gumma, Japan 36°37N 138°36E 223 A10
Kusatsu Shiga, Japan 34°58N 135°57E 223 C7
Kusawa L. Canada 60°20N 136°13W 296 A1
Kusel Germany 49°32N 7°24E 179 F3
Kushaka Nigeria 10°32N 6°48E 263 C6
Kushalgarh India 23°10N 74°27E 242 H6
Kushalnagar India 12°14N 75°57E 245 H2
Kushchevskaya Russia 46°33N 39°35E 191 G4
Kusheriki Nigeria 10°33N 6°28E 263 C6
Kushikino Japan 31°44N 130°16E 222 F2
Kushima Japan 31°29N 131°14E 222 F3
Kushimoto Japan 33°28N 135°47E 223 D7
Kushiro Japan 43°0N 144°25E 220 C12
Kushiro-Gawa → Japan 42°59N 144°23E 220 C12
Kushiro Shitsugen △ Japan 43°9N 144°26E 220 C12
Kūshk Iran 28°46N 56°51E 247 D8
Kushka = Serhetabat Turkmenistan 35°20N 62°18E 247 C9
Kushmurun = Qusmuryn Kazakhstan 52°27N 64°36E 216 B6
Kushnytsya Ukraine 48°27N 23°15E 183 B8
Kushol India 33°40N 76°36E 243 C7
Kushtia Bangla. 23°55N 89°5E 241 D2
Kushva Russia 58°18N 59°45E 186 C10
Kuskan Turkey 36°29N 33°17E 250 B4
Kuskokwim → U.S.A. 60°5N 162°25W 303 F7
Kuskokwim B. U.S.A. 59°45N 162°25W 303 G7
Kuskokwim Mts. U.S.A. 62°30N 156°0W 303 E9
Kuskovo Russia 55°44N 37°48E 129 B4
Kusmi India 23°17N 83°55E 243 H10
Kusŏng N. Korea 39°59N 125°15E 224 C2
Kussharo-Ko Japan 43°38N 144°21E 220 C12
Kustanay = Qostanay Kazakhstan 53°10N 63°35E 216 B6
Küstenje = Constanţa Romania 44°14N 28°38E 183 F13
Kustia India 22°31N 88°23E 124 B2
Küstrin = Kostrzyn Poland 52°35N 14°39E 185 F1
Kusu Japan 33°16N 131°9E 222 D3
Kut, Ko Thailand 11°40N 102°35E 237 G4
Kuta Indonesia 8°43S 115°11E 231 K18
Kutacane Indonesia 3°50N 97°50E 234 B1
Kütahya Turkey 39°30N 30°2E 205 B12
Kütahya □ Turkey 39°10N 29°30E 205 B11
Kutai △ Indonesia 0°23N 117°16E 235 B5
Kutaisi Georgia 42°19N 42°40E 191 J6
Kutaraja = Banda Aceh Indonesia 5°35N 95°20E 234 A1
Kutch, Gulf of = Kachchh, Gulf of India 22°50N 69°15E 242 H3
Kutch, Rann of = Kachchh, Rann of India 24°0N 70°0E 242 H4
Kutina Croatia 45°29N 16°48E 199 C13
Kutiyana India 21°36N 70°2E 242 J4
Kutjevo Croatia 45°23N 17°55E 182 E2
Kutkai Burma 23°27N 97°56E 241 D6
Kutkashen Azerbaijan 40°58N 47°47E 191 K8
Kutná Hora Czech Rep. 49°57N 15°16E 180 B8
Kutno Poland 52°15N 19°23E 185 F6
Kutru India 19°5N 80°46E 244 E5
Kutse Botswana 21°7S 22°16E 270 B3
Kutsino Russia 55°44N 37°55E 129 B5
Kuttabul Australia 21°1S 148°54E 280 b
Kutu Dem. Rep. of the Congo 2°40S 18°11E 264 C3
Kutu Moke Dem. Rep. of the Congo 3°12S 17°21E 264 C3
Kutum Sudan 14°10N 24°40E 257 E1
Kúty Slovak Rep. 48°40N 17°3E 181 C10
Kuty Ukraine 48°16N 25°11E 183 B10
Kuujjuaq Canada 58°6N 68°15W 295 F18
Kuujjuarapik Canada 55°20N 77°35W 298 A4
Kuusamo Finland 65°57N 29°8E 160 D23
Kuusankoski Finland 60°55N 26°38E 188 B4
Kuvango Angola 14°28S 16°20E 265 E3
Kuvshinovo Russia 57°2N 34°11E 188 D8
Kuwait = Al Kuwayt Kuwait 29°30N 48°0E 246 D5
Kuwait ■ Asia 29°30N 47°30E 246 D5
Kuwana Japan 35°5N 136°43E 223 B8
Kuwana → India 26°25N 83°15E 243 F10
Kuwol-san N. Korea 38°30N 125°15E 224 C2
Kuybyshev = Samara Russia 53°8N 50°6E 190 D10
Kuybyshev Russia 55°27N 78°19E 214 D8
Kuybyshevka-Vostochnaya = Belogorsk Russia 51°0N 128°20E 215 D13
Kuybyshevo Ukraine 47°25N 36°40E 189 J9
Kuybyshevskoye Vdkhr. Russia 55°2N 49°30E 190 C9
Kuye He → China 38°23N 110°46E 226 E6
Kūyeh Iran 38°45N 47°57E 246 B5
Kuyto, Ozero Russia 65°6N 31°20E 160 D24
Kuytun China 44°25N 85°0E 217 D11
Kuyucak Turkey 37°55N 28°28E 205 D10
Kuyumba Russia 60°58N 96°59E 215 C10
Kuzey Anadolu Dağları Turkey 41°0N 36°45E 212 B7
Kuzguncuk Turkey 41°2N 29°2E 122 B2
Kuzhitturai India 8°18N 77°11E 245 K3
Kuzitrin → U.S.A. 65°10N 165°25W 303 D6
Kuzmin Serbia 45°2N 19°25E 182 E4
Kuznetsk Russia 53°12N 46°40E 190 D8
Kuznetsovo = Konakovo Russia 56°40N 36°51E 188 D9
Kuzomen Russia 66°22N 36°50E 186 A6
Kuzucubelen Turkey 36°51N 34°27E 250 B5
Kuzyminki Russia 55°42N 37°46E 129 B4
Kvænangen Norway 70°5N 21°15E 160 A19
Kværndrup Denmark 55°10N 10°31E 163 J4
Kvaløya Norway 69°40N 18°30E 160 B18
Kvam Norway 61°40N 9°42E 164 C6
Kvänum Sweden 58°18N 13°11E 163 F7
Kvareli = Qvareli Georgia 41°57N 45°47E 191 K7
Kvarner Croatia 44°50N 14°10E 199 D11
Kvarnerič Croatia 44°43N 14°37E 199 D11
Kvås Norway 58°16N 7°14E 164 F4
Kvernaland Norway 58°47N 5°45E 164 F2
Kvichak B. U.S.A. 58°48N 157°30W 303 G8
Kvicksund Sweden 59°27N 16°19E 162 E10
Kvikne Norway 62°35N 10°16E 164 B7
Kvillsfors Sweden 57°24N 15°29E 163 G9
Kvina → Norway 58°19N 6°55E 164 F3
Kvinlog Norway 58°31N 6°55E 164 F3
Kvirily = Zestaponi Georgia 42°6N 43°0E 191 J6
Kvismare kanal Sweden 59°11N 15°35E 162 E9
Kvissleby Sweden 62°18N 17°22E 162 B11
Kviteseid Norway 59°24N 8°29E 164 E5
Kvitøya Svalbard 80°8N 32°35E 154 A14
Kwabhaca S. Africa 30°51S 29°0E 271 D4
Kwai = Khwae Noi → Thailand 14°1N 99°32E 236 E2
Kwai Chung China 22°22N 114°7E 122 A1
Kwajalein Marshall Is. 9°5N 167°20E 288 G8
Kwakhanai Botswana 21°39S 21°16E 270 B3
Kwakoegron Suriname 5°12N 55°25W 329 B6
Kwale Coast, Kenya 4°15S 39°31E 268 C4
Kwale Nigeria 5°46N 6°26E 263 D6
Kwamalasamutu Suriname 2°20N 56°47W 329 C6
KwaMashu S. Africa 29°45S 30°58E 271 C5
Kwamouth Dem. Rep. of the Congo 3°9S 16°12E 264 C3
Kwando → Africa 18°27S 23°32E 265 F4
Kwangchow = Guangzhou China 23°6N 113°13E 121 B2
Kwangdaeri N. Korea 40°34N 127°33E 227 D14
Kwango → Dem. Rep. of the Congo 3°14S 17°22E 264 C3
Kwangsi-Chuang = Guangxi Zhuangzu Zizhiqu □ China 24°0N 109°0E 228 F7
Kwangtung = Guangdong □ China 23°0N 113°0E 229 F9
Kwara □ Nigeria 8°45N 4°30E 263 D6
Kwataboahegan → Canada 51°9N 80°50W 298 B3
Kwatisore Indonesia 3°18S 134°50E 231 E8
KwaZulu Natal □ S. Africa 29°0S 30°0E 271 C5
Kweichow = Guizhou □ China 27°0N 107°0E 228 D6
Kweilin = Guilin China 25°18N 110°15E 229 E8
Kweisui = Hohhot China 40°52N 111°40E 226 D6
Kweiyang = Guiyang China 26°32N 106°40E 228 D6
Kwekwe Zimbabwe 18°58S 29°48E 269 F2
Kwenge → Dem. Rep. of the Congo 4°50S 18°44E 265 C3
Kwethluk U.S.A. 60°49N 161°26W 303 F7
Kwidzyn Poland 53°44N 18°55E 184 E5
Kwigillingok U.S.A. 59°51N 163°8W 303 G7
Kwiha Ethiopia 13°29N 39°32E 257 E4
Kwikila Papua N. G. 9°49S 147°38E 286 E4
Kwilu → Dem. Rep. of the Congo 3°22S 17°22E 265 C3
Kwinana Australia 32°15S 115°47E 279 F2
Kwinbet Burma 16°20N 94°14E 241 G5
Kwisa → Poland 51°34N 15°24E 185 G2
Kwoka Indonesia 0°31S 132°27E 231 E8
Kwolla Nigeria 9°0N 9°15E 263 D6
Kwun Tong China 22°19N 114°13E 122 B2
Kya-in-Seikkyi Burma 16°2N 98°8E 241 G7
Kyabé Chad 9°30N 19°0E 259 G3
Kyabra Cr. → Australia 25°36S 142°55E 281 D3
Kyabram Australia 36°19S 145°4E 283 D6
Kyaikkami Burma 16°4N 97°34E 241 G6
Kyaiklat Burma 16°25N 95°40E 241 G5
Kyaikmaraw Burma 16°23N 97°44E 241 G6
Kyaikthin Burma 23°32N 95°40E 241 D5
Kyaikto Burma 17°20N 97°3E 236 D1
Kyaing Tong = Keng Tung Burma 21°18N 99°39E 236 B2
Kyakhta Russia 50°30N 106°25E 215 D11
Kyambura ⌂ Uganda 0°7S 30°9E 268 C3
Kyan-zaki Japan 26°5N 127°39E 288 a
Kyancutta Australia 33°8S 135°33E 281 E2
Kyangin Burma 18°20N 95°20E 241 F5
Kyaukhnyat Burma 18°15N 97°31E 241 F6
Kyaukki Burma 18°27N 96°56E 241 F6
Kyaukkyi Burma 18°15N 94°29E 241 F5
Kyaukme Burma 22°32N 97°2E 241 D6
Kyaukpadaung Burma 20°52N 95°8E 241 E5
Kyaukpyu Burma 19°28N 93°30E 241 F4
Kyaukse Burma 21°36N 96°10E 241 E6
Kyauktaga Burma 18°10N 96°37E 241 F6
Kyauktan Burma 16°38N 96°19E 241 G6
Kyauktaw Burma 20°51N 92°59E 241 E4
Kyaunggon Burma 17°6N 95°11E 241 G5
Kyawkku Burma 21°48N 96°56E 241 E6
Kybartai Lithuania 54°39N 22°45E 184 D9
Kyburz U.S.A. 38°47N 120°18W 306 G6
Kyeintali Burma 18°0N 94°29E 241 G5
Kyelang India 32°35N 77°2E 242 C7
Kyenjojo Uganda 0°40N 30°37E 268 B3
Kyidaunggan Burma 19°53N 96°12E 241 F6
Kyje Czech Rep. 50°6N 14°33E 135 B3
Kyjov Czech Rep. 49°1N 17°7E 181 B10
Kyle Canada 50°50N 108°2W 297 C7
Kyle Dam Zimbabwe 20°15S 31°0E 269 G3
Kyle of Lochalsh U.K. 57°17N 5°44W 167 D3
Kyll → Germany 49°48N 6°41E 179 F2
Kyllburg Germany 50°2N 6°34E 179 E2
Kyllini Greece 37°55N 21°8E 207 D3
Kyllini, Akra Greece 37°57N 21°8E 207 D3
Kymijoki → Finland 60°30N 26°55E 188 B4
Kymmene älv = Kymijoki → Finland 60°30N 26°55E 188 B4
Kyneton Australia 37°10S 144°29E 282 D6
Kynuna Australia 21°37S 141°55E 280 C3
Kyō-ga-Saki Japan 35°45N 135°15E 223 B7
Kyoga, L. Uganda 1°35N 33°0E 268 B3
Kyogle Australia 28°40S 153°0E 281 D5
Kyom → Sudan 8°58N 28°13E 257 F2
Kyŏngju = Gyeongju S. Korea 35°51N 129°14E 224 E4
Kyŏngsŏng N. Korea 41°35N 129°36E 224 B4
Kyōto Japan 35°0N 135°45E 223 C7
Kyōto □ Japan 35°15N 135°45E 223 B7
Kyparissovouno Cyprus 35°19N 33°10E 207 E9
Kyperounda Cyprus 34°56N 32°58E 207 F8
Kypros = Cyprus ■ Asia 35°0N 33°0E 207 F9
Kyrenia Cyprus 35°20N 33°20E 207 E9
Kyrgyzstan ■ Asia 42°0N 75°0E 217 D9
Kyritz Germany 52°56N 12°24E 178 C8
Kyrkhult Sweden 56°22N 14°34E 163 H8
Kyrksæterøra Norway 63°18N 9°5E 164 A6
Kyrnasivka Ukraine 48°35N 28°58E 183 B13
Kyrnychky Ukraine 45°42N 29°4E 183 E14
Kyro älv = Kyrönjoki → Finland 63°14N 21°45E 160 E19
Kyrönjoki → Finland 63°14N 21°45E 160 E19
Kystatyam Russia 67°20N 123°10E 215 C13
Kysucké Nové Mesto Slovak Rep. 49°18N 18°47E 181 B11
Kytay, Ozero Ukraine 45°40N 29°13E 183 E14
Kythira Greece 36°8N 23°0E 204 E5
Kythréa Cyprus 35°15N 33°29E 207 E9
Kyu-hkok Burma 24°4N 98°4E 241 C7
Kyūhōji Japan 34°38N 135°33E 133 B2
Kyunhla Burma 23°25N 95°15E 241 D5
Kyuquot Sound Canada 50°2N 127°22W 296 D3
Kyurdamir = Kürdämir Azerbaijan 40°25N 48°3E 191 K9
Kyūshū Japan 33°0N 131°0E 222 E3
Kyūshū □ Japan 33°0N 131°0E 222 E3
Kyushu-Palau Ridge Pac. Oc. 20°0N 136°0E 288 E5
Kyūshū-Sanchi Japan 32°35N 131°17E 222 E3
Kyūshū Trench Japan 31°35N 134°10E 222 F6
Kyustendil Bulgaria 42°16N 22°41E 202 D6
Kyustendil □ Bulgaria 42°16N 22°41E 202 D6
Kyusyur Russia 70°19N 127°30E 215 B13
Kywong Australia 34°58S 146°44E 283 C7
Kyyiv Ukraine 50°30N 30°28E 177 C16
Kyyiv □ Ukraine 50°5N 30°45E 189 G6
Kyyivske Vdskh. Ukraine 51°0N 30°25E 177 C16
Kyzyl Russia 51°50N 94°30E 217 B12
Kyzyl-Adyr Kyrgyzstan 42°39N 71°35E 217 D8
Kyzyl-Burun = Siyäzän Azerbaijan 41°3N 49°10E 191 K9
Kyzyl-Khoto = Kyzyl Russia 51°50N 94°30E 217 B12
Kyzyl Kum Asia 42°0N 65°0E 238 A9
Kyzyl Kum Uzbekistan 42°30N 65°0E 217 D7
Kyzyl Kyya Kyrgyzstan 40°16N 72°8E 217 D8
Kyzyl Orda = Qyzylorda Kazakhstan 44°48N 65°28E 217 D7
Kyzyl-Suu Kyrgyzstan 42°20N 78°0E 217 D9

L

La Albuera Spain 38°45N 6°49W 195 G4
La Alcarria Spain 40°31N 2°45W 196 E2
La Almarcha Spain 39°41N 2°24W 196 F2
La Almunia de Doña Godina Spain 41°29N 1°23W 196 D3
La Amistad △ Cent. Amer. 9°28N 83°18W 320 E3
La Asunción Venezuela 11°2N 63°53W 329 A5
La Baie Canada 48°19N 70°53W 299 C5
La Banda Argentina 27°45S 64°10W 334 B3
La Bañeza Spain 42°17N 5°54W 194 C5
La Barca Mexico 20°17N 102°34W 318 C4
La Barceloneta Spain 41°22N 2°11E 114 A2
La Barge U.S.A. 42°16N 110°12W 304 E8
La Barra Nic. 12°54N 83°33W 320 D3
La Bastide-Puylaurent France 44°35N 3°55E 174 D7
La Baule France 47°17N 2°24W 172 E4
La Belle Fla., U.S.A. 26°46N 81°26W 317 J8
La Belle Mo., U.S.A. 40°7N 91°55W 310 D5
La Biche → Canada 59°57N 123°50W 296 B4
La Biche, L. Canada 54°50N 112°3W 296 C6
La Bisbal d'Empordà Spain 41°58N 3°2E 196 D8
La Blanca Chile 33°30S 70°40W 137 C2
La Boca Argentina 34°38S 58°22W 117 B2
La Brea Peru 4°40S 81°7W 330 A1
La Brea Trin. & Tob. 10°15N 61°37W 323 t
La Brède France 44°41N 0°32W 174 D3
La Bresse France 48°2N 6°53E 173 D13
La Bretèche France 48°51N 2°1E 134 A1
La Bureba Spain 42°36N 3°24W 194 C7
La Cal → Bolivia 17°27S 58°15W 331 D6
La Calera Chile 32°50S 71°10W 334 C1
La Calle = El Kala Algeria 36°53N 8°26E 261 A6
La Campana △ Chile 32°58S 71°14W 334 C1
La Campiña Lima, Peru 12°11S 77°0W 124 C2
La Campiña Spain 37°45N 4°45W 195 H6
La Canal = Sa Canal Spain 38°51N 1°23E 206 D1
La Cañiza = A Cañiza Spain 42°13N 8°16W 194 C2
La Canourgue France 44°26N 3°13E 174 D7
La Capelle France 49°59N 3°50E 173 C10
La Carlota Argentina 33°30S 63°20W 334 C3
La Carlota Phil. 10°25N 122°55E 233 F4
La Carlota Spain 37°40N 4°56W 195 H6
La Carolina Spain 38°17N 3°38W 195 G7
La Castellana Phil. 10°20N 123°3E 233 F4
La Cavalerie France 44°1N 3°10E 174 D7
La Ceiba Honduras 15°40N 86°50W 320 C2
La Ceiba Venezuela 9°28N 71°4W 328 C3
La Celle-St-Cloud France 48°50N 2°9E 134 A1
La Chaise-Dieu France 45°18N 3°42E 174 C7
La Chapelle d'Angillon France 47°21N 2°25E 173 E9
La Chapelle-St-Luc France 48°20N 4°3E 173 D11
La Chapelle-sur-Erdre France 47°18N 1°34W 172 E5
La Charité-sur-Loire France 47°10N 3°1E 173 E10
La Chartre-sur-le-Loir France 47°44N 0°34E 172 E7
La Châtaigneraie France 46°39N 0°44W 174 B3
La Châtre France 46°35N 2°0E 173 F9
La Chaux → Mauritius 20°23S 57°41E 272 e
La Chaux-de-Fonds Switz. 47°7N 6°50E 179 H2
La Chorrera Colombia 0°44S 73°1W 328 D3
La Chorrera Panama 8°53N 79°47W 320 c
La Ciotat France 43°10N 5°37E 175 E9
La Cisterna Chile 33°32S 70°39W 137 C2
La Ciudadela Mexico City, Mexico 128 c2
La Clayette France 46°17N 4°19E 173 F11
La Cocha Argentina 27°50S 65°40W 334 B2
La Concepción = Ri-Aba Eq. Guin. 3°28N 8°40E 263 E6
La Concepción Panama 8°31N 82°37W 320 E3
La Concepción Venezuela 10°30N 71°50W 328 A3
La Concordia Mexico 16°5N 92°38W 319 D6
La Constitución, Plaza de = Zócalo Mexico City, Mexico 128 b3
La Coruña = A Coruña Spain 43°20N 8°25W 194 B2
La Côte-St-André France 45°24N 5°15E 175 C9
La Courneuve France 48°55N 2°22E 134 A3
La Courtine France 45°41N 2°15E 174 C6
La Crau Bouches-du-Rhône, France 43°32N 4°40E 175 E8
La Crau Var, France 43°9N 6°4E 175 E10
La Crescent U.S.A. 43°50N 91°18W 308 D8
La Crete Canada 58°11N 116°24W 296 B5
La Crosse Fla., U.S.A. 29°51N 82°24W 316 F7
La Crosse Kans., U.S.A. 38°32N 99°18W 308 F4
La Crosse Wis., U.S.A. 43°48N 91°15W 308 D8
La Cruz Costa Rica 11°4N 85°39W 320 D2
La Cruz Sinaloa, Mexico 23°55N 106°54W 318 C3
La Cumbre, Volcán Ecuador 0°21S 91°32W 330 a
La Dehesa Chile 33°21S 70°33W 137 B2
La Désirade Guadeloupe 16°18N 61°3W 322 e
La Digue Seychelles 4°20S 55°51E 272 c
La Dorada Colombia 5°30N 74°40W 328 B3
La Encantada Peru 12°13S 77°1W 124 C2
La Esperanza Argentina 40°26S 68°32W 336 B3
La Esperanza Cuba 22°46N 83°44W 320 B3
La Esperanza Honduras 14°15N 88°10W 320 D2
La Estación Spain 40°27N 3°48W 127 B1
La Estrada = A Estrada Spain 42°43N 8°27W 194 C2
La Falaise, Gorges de Martinique 14°49N 61°10W 322 j
La Faouët France 48°2N 3°30W 172 D3
La Fayette U.S.A. 34°42N 85°17W 315 D12
La Fé Cuba 22°2N 84°15W 320 B3
La Fère France 49°39N 3°21E 173 C10
La Ferté-Bernard France 48°10N 0°40E 172 D7
La Ferté-Gaucher France 48°47N 3°19E 173 D10
La Ferté-Macé France 48°35N 0°22W 172 D6
La Ferté-St-Aubin France 47°42N 1°57E 173 E8
La Ferté-sous-Jouarre France 48°56N 3°8E 173 D10
La Ferté-Vidame France 48°37N 0°53E 172 D7
La Flèche France 47°42N 0°4W 172 E6
La Floresta Spain 41°26N 2°3E 114 A1
La Florida Chile 33°33S 70°34W 137 C2
La Foa N. Cal. 21°43S 165°50E 288 d
La Follette U.S.A. 36°23N 84°7W 315 C12
La Fontaine U.S.A. 40°40N 85°43W 311 D11
La Fortuna Spain 40°21N 3°46W 127 B1
La França Spain 41°22N 2°9E 114 A1
La Fregeneda Spain 40°58N 6°54W 194 E4
La Fría Venezuela 8°13N 72°15W 328 B3
La Fuente de San Esteban Spain 40°49N 6°15W 194 E4
La Gacilly France 47°45N 2°8W 172 E4
La Garenne-Colombes France 48°54N 2°15E 134 A2
La Gi Vietnam 10°40N 107°45E 237 G6
La Gineta Spain 39°8N 2°1W 197 F2
La Giustiniana Italy 41°59N 12°24E 136 B1
La Glória Colombia 8°37N 73°48W 328 B3
La Goulette = Halq el Oued Tunisia 36°53N 10°18E 258 A2
La Gran Sabana Venezuela 5°30N 61°30W 329 B5
La Grand'Combe France 44°13N 4°2E 175 D8
La Grande U.S.A. 45°20N 118°5W 304 D4
La Grande → Canada 53°50N 79°0W 298 B5
La Grande 3, Rés. Canada 53°40N 75°10W 298 B4
La Grande 4, Rés. Canada 54°0N 73°15W 298 B5
La Grande-Motte France 43°23N 4°5E 175 E8
La Grange Calif., U.S.A. 37°42N 120°27W 306 H6
La Grange Ga., U.S.A. 33°2N 85°2W 316 B4
La Grange Ill., U.S.A. 41°48N 87°53W 119 C1
La Grange Ky., U.S.A. 38°24N 85°22W 311 F11
La Grange Mo., U.S.A. 40°3N 91°35W 310 D5
La Grange Tex., U.S.A. 29°54N 96°52W 314 G6
La Grange Park U.S.A. 41°49N 87°51W 119 C1
La Granja Chile 33°31S 70°38W 137 C2
La Grave France 45°3N 6°18E 175 C10
La Grita Venezuela 8°8N 71°59W 328 B3
La Guaira Venezuela 10°36N 66°56W 328 A4
La Guardia = A Guarda Spain 41°56N 8°52W 194 D2
La Guardia, New York ✈ (LGA) U.S.A. 40°46N 73°52W 132 B2
La Gudiña = A Gudiña Spain 42°4N 7°8W 194 C3
La Güera Mauritania 20°51N 17°0W 260 D1
La Guerche-de-Bretagne France 47°57N 1°16W 172 E5
La Guerche-sur-l'Aubois France 46°58N 2°56E 173 F9
La Habana Cuba 23°8N 82°22W 320 B3
La Harpe U.S.A. 40°35N 90°58W 310 D6
La Haute Vallée de Chevreuse ⌂ France 48°35N 1°58E 173 D8
La Haye-du-Puits France 49°17N 1°33W 172 C5
La Horqueta Venezuela 7°55N 60°20W 329 B5
La Horra Spain 41°44N 3°53W 194 D7
La Hulpe Belgium 50°43N 4°30E 116 B2
La Independencia Mexico 16°15N 92°1W 319 D6
La Isabela Dom. Rep. 19°58N 71°2W 321 C5
La Jonquera Spain 42°25N 2°53E 196 C7
La Joya Peru 16°43S 71°52W 330 D3
La Junta U.S.A. 37°59N 103°33W 304 H12
La Laguna Canary Is. 28°28N 16°18W 153 e1
La Lézarde → Martinique 14°35N 61°1W 322 j
La Libertad = Puerto Libertad Mexico 29°55N 112°43W 318 B2
La Libertad Guatemala 16°47N 90°7W 320 C1
La Libertad □ Peru 8°0S 78°30W 330 B2
La Ligua Chile 32°30S 71°16W 334 C1

La Línea de la Concepción Spain 36°15N 5°23W 195 J5
La Llacuna Spain 41°24N 2°12E 114 A2
La Loche Canada 56°29N 109°26W 297 B7
La Loma Mexico 19°31N 99°11W 128 A1
La Londe-les-Maures France 43°8N 6°14E 175 E10
La Lora Spain 42°45N 4°0W 194 C7
La Loupe France 48°29N 1°0E 172 D8
La Louvière Belgium 50°27N 4°10E 170 D4
La Lucila Argentina 34°30S 58°29W 117 B2
La Lune Trin. & Tob. 10°3N 61°22W 323 t
La Machine France 46°54N 3°27E 173 F10
La Maddalena Italy 41°13N 9°24E 200 A2
La Maladrerie France 48°54N 2°1E 134 A1
La Malbaie Canada 47°40N 70°10W 299 C5
La Malinche △ Mexico 19°15N 98°3W 319 D5
La Mancha Spain 39°10N 2°54W 197 F2
La Manche → Martinique 14°33N 61°0W 322 j
La Mariña Spain 43°30N 7°40W 194 B3
La Martre, L. Canada 63°15N 117°55W 296 A5
La Merced Peru 11°3S 75°19W 330 C2
La Mesa Baja Calif., Mexico 32°30N 116°57W 307 N10
La Mesa Calif., U.S.A. 32°46N 117°1W 307 N9
La Mesilla U.S.A. 32°16N 106°48W 305 K10
La Milla, Cerro Peru 12°2S 77°5W 124 B2
La Misión Mexico 32°6N 116°53W 318 A1
La Moille U.S.A. 41°32N 89°17W 310 C7
La Moine → U.S.A. 39°59N 90°31W 310 E6
La Monachina Italy 41°53N 12°21E 136 B1
La Montagne Réunion 20°53S 55°26E 272 f
La Monte U.S.A. 38°46N 93°26W 310 F3
La Moraleja Spain 40°30N 3°38W 127 A2
La Mothe-Achard France 46°37N 1°40W 172 F5
La Motte-Chalançon France 44°30N 5°21E 175 D9
La Motte-du-Caire France 44°20N 6°3E 175 D10
La Motte-Servolex France 45°35N 5°53E 175 C9
La Moure U.S.A. 46°21N 98°18W 308 B4
La Moustique → Guadeloupe 16°10N 61°34W 322 e
La Muela Spain 41°36N 1°7W 196 D3
La Mure France 44°55N 5°48E 175 D9
La Negra Chile 23°46S 70°18W 334 A1
La Nopalera Mexico 19°18N 99°5W 128 C2
La Oliva Canary Is. 28°36N 13°57W 153 e2
La Oraya Peru 11°32S 75°54W 330 C2
La Orotava Canary Is. 28°22N 16°31W 153 e1
La Oroya Peru 11°32S 75°54W 330 C2
La Pacaudière France 46°11N 3°52E 173 F10
La Pagerie Martinique 14°32N 61°3W 322 j
La Palma Canary Is. 28°40N 17°50W 153 e1
La Palma Panama 8°15N 78°0W 320 E4
La Palma del Condado Spain 37°21N 6°38W 195 H4
La Paloma Chile 30°35S 71°0W 334 C1
La Pampa □ Argentina 36°50S 66°0W 334 D2
La Paragua Venezuela 6°50N 63°20W 329 B5
La Pastora Trin. & Tob. 10°42N 61°19W 323 t
La Paternal Argentina 34°35S 58°26W 117 B2
La Paya △ Colombia 0°0 75°5W 328 C2
La Paz Entre Ríos, Argentina 30°50S 59°45W 334 C4
La Paz San Luis, Argentina 33°30S 67°20W 334 C2
La Paz Bolivia 16°20S 68°10W 330 D4
La Paz Honduras 14°20N 87°47W 320 D2
La Paz Baja Calif. S., Mexico 24°10N 110°18W 318 C2
La Paz Abra, Phil. 17°40N 120°41E 232 C3
La Paz Tarlac, Phil. 15°26N 120°45E 232 D3
La Paz □ Bolivia 15°30S 68°0W 330 D4
La Paz Centro Nic. 12°20N 86°41W 320 D2
La Pedrera Colombia 1°18S 69°43W 328 D4
La Pérade Canada 46°35N 72°12W 299 C5
La Perla Chihuahua, Mexico 28°18N 104°32W 318 B4
La Perla Lima, Peru 12°4S 77°7W 124 B2
La Perouse Australia 33°59S 151°14E 139 B2
La Perouse, Bahía Chile 27°5S 109°18W 330 b
La Perouse Str. Asia 45°40N 142°0E 220 B11
La Pesca Mexico 23°46N 97°47W 319 C5
La Piedad Mexico 20°21N 102°0W 318 C4
La Pine U.S.A. 43°40N 121°30W 304 E3
La Pisana Italy 41°51N 12°23E 136 B1
La Plaine Dominica 15°20N 61°15W 323 k
La Plaine des Cafres Réunion 21°13S 55°33E 272 f
La Plaine des Palmistes Réunion 21°7S 55°38E 272 f
La Plata Argentina 35°0S 57°55W 334 C4
La Plata Colombia 2°23N 75°53W 328 C2
La Plata Mo., U.S.A. 40°2N 92°29W 310 D4
La Plata, L. Argentina 44°55S 71°50W 336 B2
La Pobla de Lillet Spain 42°16N 1°59E 196 C6
La Pobla de Segur Spain 42°15N 0°58E 196 C5
La Pocatière Canada 47°22N 70°2W 299 C5
La Pola de Gordón Spain 42°51N 5°41W 194 C5
La Porta France 42°25N 9°21E 175 F13
La Porte U.S.A. 29°40N 95°1W 314 G7
La Porte City U.S.A. 42°19N 92°12W 310 B4
La Possession Réunion 20°55S 55°21E 272 f
La Prairie Canada 45°25N 73°29W 130 B3
La Presanella Italy 46°13N 10°40E 198 B7
La Puebla = Sa Pobla Spain 39°46N 3°1E 206 B4
La Puebla de Cazalla Spain 37°10N 5°20W 195 H5
La Puebla de los Infantes Spain 37°47N 5°24W 195 H5
La Puebla de Montalbán Spain 39°52N 4°22W 194 F6
La Puebla del Río Spain 37°16N 6°3W 195 H4
La Puerta de Segura Spain 38°22N 2°45W 195 G8
La Punta Peru 12°4S 77°10W 124 B1
La Puntigala Spain 41°27N 2°13E 114 A2
La Purísima Mexico 26°10N 112°4W 318 B2
La Push U.S.A. 47°55N 124°38W 306 C2
La Queue-en-Brie France 48°47N 2°34E 134 B4
La Quiaca Argentina 22°5S 65°35W 334 A2
La Reina Chile 33°26S 70°33W 137 B2
La Réole France 44°35N 0°1W 174 D3
La Republica, Plaza de Mexico City, Mexico 128 b1
La Restinga Canary Is. 27°38N 17°59W 153 e1
La Ribera Spain 41°21N 2°4E 114 A1
La Rioja Argentina 29°20S 67°0W 334 B2
La Rioja □ Argentina 29°30S 67°0W 334 B2
La Rioja □ Spain 42°20N 2°20W 196 C2
La Rivière des Pluies Réunion 20°54S 55°31E 272 f
La Robla Spain 42°50N 5°41W 194 C5
La Roche N. Cal. 21°26S 168°2E 288 d
La Roche-Bernard France 47°31N 2°19W 172 E4
La Roche-Canillac France 45°12N 1°57E 174 C5
La Roche-en-Ardenne Belgium 50°11N 5°35E 170 D5
La Roche-sur-Foron France 46°4N 6°19E 173 F13
La Roche-sur-Yon France 46°40N 1°25W 172 F5
La Rochefoucauld France 45°44N 0°24E 174 C4
La Rochelle France 46°10N 1°9W 174 B2
La Roda Spain 39°13N 2°15W 197 F2
La Roda de Andalucía Spain 37°12N 4°46W 195 H6
La Romaine Canada 50°13N 60°40W 299 B7
La Romana Dom. Rep. 18°27N 68°57W 321 C6
La Ronge Canada 55°5N 105°20W 297 B7
La Rue U.S.A. 40°35N 83°23W 311 D13
La Rumorosa Mexico 32°34N 116°6W 307 N10
La Sabina = Sa Savina Spain 38°44N 1°25E 206 D1
La Sagra Spain 37°57N 2°35W 197 H2
La Sagrera Spain 41°25N 2°11E 114 A2
La Salada Argentina 34°43S 58°28W 117 C2
La Saline Réunion 21°4S 55°16E 272 f
La Salle U.S.A. 41°20N 89°6W 310 C7
La Sanabria Spain 42°0N 6°30W 194 C4
La Santa Canary Is. 29°5N 13°40W 153 e2
La Sarre Canada 48°45N 79°15W 298 C4
La Scala Italy 45°28N 9°11E 129 B2
La Scie Canada 49°57N 55°36W 299 C8
La Selva Spain 42°0N 2°45E 196 C7
La Selva Beach U.S.A. 36°56N 121°51W 306 J5
La Selva del Camp Spain 41°13N 1°8E 196 D6
La Serena Chile 29°55S 71°10W 334 B1
La Serena Spain 38°45N 5°40W 195 G5
La Seu d'Urgell Spain 42°22N 1°23E 196 C6
La Seyne-sur-Mer France 43°7N 5°52E 175 E9
La Sila Italy 39°15N 16°35E 201 C9
La Solana Spain 38°59N 3°14W 195 G7
La Soufrière St. Vincent 13°20N 61°11W 323 n
La Souterraine France 46°15N 1°30E 173 F8
La Spézia Italy 44°7N 9°50E 198 D6
La Storta Italy 41°59N 12°20E 136 A1
La Suze-sur-Sarthe France 47°53N 0°2E 172 E7
La Tagua Colombia 0°3N 74°40W 328 C3
La Taxonera Spain 41°25N 2°10E 114 A2
La Teste-de-Buch France 44°37N 1°8W 174 D2
La Tortuga Venezuela 11°0N 65°22W 321 D6
La Tour-du-Pin France 45°33N 5°27E 175 C9
La Tranche-sur-Mer France 46°20N 1°27W 172 F5
La Tremblade France 45°46N 1°8W 174 C2
La Trinidad Phil. 16°28N 120°35E 232 C3
La Trinité Martinique 14°45N 60°58W 322 j
La Tuque Canada 47°30N 72°50W 298 C5
La Unión Chile 40°10S 73°0W 336 B2
La Unión Colombia 1°35N 77°5W 328 C2
La Unión El Salv. 13°20N 87°50W 320 D2
La Unión Guerrero, Mexico 17°58N 101°49W 318 D4
La Unión Peru 9°43S 76°45W 330 B2
La Unión Spain 37°38N 0°53W 197 H4
La Union □ Phil. 16°30N 120°25E 232 C3
La Urbana Venezuela 7°8N 66°56W 328 B4
La Vache B. Trin. & Tob. 10°45N 61°29W 323 t
La Vache Pt. Trin. & Tob. 10°47N 61°28W 323 t
La Vall d'Uixó Spain 39°49N 0°15W 196 F4
La Vecilla Spain 42°51N 5°27W 194 C5
La Vega Dom. Rep. 19°20N 70°30W 321 C5
La Vega Peru 10°41S 77°44W 330 C2
La Vela de Coro Venezuela 11°27N 69°34W 328 A4
La Veleta Spain 37°1N 3°22W 195 H7
La Venta Mexico 18°5N 94°3W 319 D6
La Venturosa Colombia 6°8N 68°48W 328 B4
La Vergne U.S.A. 36°1N 86°35W 315 C11
La Veronica Trin. & Tob. 10°42N 61°21W 323 t
La Victoria Lima, Peru 12°3S 77°2W 124 B2
La Victoria Venezuela 10°14N 67°20W 328 A4
La Villa Joiosa = Villajoyosa Spain 38°30N 0°12W 197 G4
La Voulte-sur-Rhône France 44°48N 4°46E 175 D8
Laa an der Thaya Austria 48°43N 16°23E 181 C9
Laaber, Grosse → Germany 48°55N 12°30E 179 G8
Laage Germany 53°55N 12°21E 178 B8
Laajalahti Finland 60°11N 24°48E 121 B1
Laajasalo Finland 60°10N 25°1E 121 B3
Laaksolahti Finland 60°14N 24°45E 121 B1
Laas Dawaco Somali Rep. 10°28N 49°0E 267 B6
Laascaanood = Las Anod Somali Rep. 8°26N 47°19E 267 C6
Laasqoray Somali Rep. 11°10N 48°20E 267 B6
Laatzen Germany 52°19N 9°48E 178 C5
Lä'au Pt. U.S.A. 21°6N 157°19W 302 B4
Laba → Russia 45°11N 39°42E 191 H4
Labagou National Forest Park China 40°1N 116°22E 114 A2
Laban Burma 25°52N 96°40E 241 C6
Labasa Fiji 16°30S 179°27E 287 A2
Labason Phil. 8°4N 122°31E 233 G4
Labastide-Murat France 44°39N 1°33E 174 D5
Labastide-Rouairoux France 43°28N 2°39E 174 E6
Labbézenga Mali 15°2N 0°48E 263 B5
Labdah = Leptis Magna Libya 32°40N 14°12E 258 B2
Labe = Elbe → Europe 53°50N 9°0E 178 B4
Labé Guinea 11°24N 12°16W 262 C2
Laberge, L. Canada 61°11N 135°12W 296 A1
Labes = Łobez Poland 53°38N 15°39E 184 E2
Labian, Tanjong Malaysia 5°9N 119°13E 235 A5
Labiau = Polessk Russia 54°50N 21°8E 184 D8
Labig Pt. = Iligan Pt. Phil. 18°25N 122°25E 232 B4
Labin Croatia 45°5N 14°8E 199 C11
Labinsk Russia 44°40N 40°48E 191 H5
Labis Malaysia 2°22N 103°2E 237 L4
Łabiszyn Poland 52°57N 17°54E 185 F4
Lablâba, W. el → Egypt 30°1N 31°19E 117 A2
Labo Phil. 14°9N 122°51E 232 D4
Laboe Germany 54°24N 10°13E 178 A6
Laborec → Slovak Rep. 48°37N 21°58E 181 C14
Laborie St. Lucia 13°45N 61°2W 323 m
Labouheyre France 44°13N 0°55W 174 D3
Laboulaye Argentina 34°10S 63°30W 334 C3
Labrador Canada 53°20N 61°0W 299 B7
Labrador City Canada 52°57N 66°55W 299 B6
Labrador Sea Atl. Oc. 57°0N 54°0W 295 F21
Lábrea Brazil 7°15S 64°51W 331 B5
Labruguière France 43°31N 2°16E 174 E6
Labuan □ Malaysia 5°20N 115°12E 235 A5
Labuan, Pulau Malaysia 5°21N 115°13E 235 A5
Labuha Indonesia 0°30S 127°30E 231 E7
Labuhan Indonesia 6°22S 105°50E 234 D3
Labuhanbajo Indonesia 8°28S 119°54E 235 D5
Labuhanbilik Indonesia 2°31N 100°10E 237 L3
Labuk, Telok Malaysia 6°10N 117°50E 235 A5
Labutta Burma 16°9N 94°46E 241 G5
Labyrinth, L. Australia 30°40S 135°11E 281 E2
Labytnangi Russia 66°39N 66°21E 186 A12
Laç Albania 41°38N 19°43E 202 E3
Lac □ Chad 13°30N 14°30E 259 F2
Lac Bay Bonaire 12°6N 68°13W 322 h
Lac-Bouchette Canada 48°16N 72°11W 299 C5
Lac Édouard Canada 47°40N 72°16W 298 C5
Lac La Biche Canada 54°45N 111°58W 296 C6
Lac la Martre = Wha Ti Canada 63°8N 117°16W 294 E8
Lac La Ronge ⌓ Canada 55°9N 104°41W 297 B7
Lac-Mégantic Canada 45°35N 70°53W 299 C5
Lac Thien Vietnam 12°25N 108°11E 236 F7
Lacanau France 44°58N 1°5W 174 D2
Lacanau, Étang de France 44°58N 1°7W 174 D2
Lacantún → Mexico 16°36N 90°39W 319 D6
Lácara → Spain 38°55N 6°25W 195 G4
Lacaune France 43°43N 2°40E 174 E6
Lacaune, Mts. de France 43°43N 2°50E 174 E6
Laccadive Is. = Lakshadweep Is. India 10°0N 72°30E 245 J1
Lacepede B. Australia 36°40S 139°40E 282 D3
Lacepede Is. Australia 16°55S 122°0E 278 C3
Lacerdónia Mozam. 18°3S 35°35E 269 F4
Lacey U.S.A. 47°7N 122°49W 306 C4
Lachania Greece 35°58N 27°54E 206 F11
Lachay, Pta. Peru 11°17S 77°44W 330 C2
Lachen India 27°46N 88°36E 241 B2
Lachhmangarh India 27°50N 75°4E 242 F6
Lachi Pakistan 33°25N 71°20E 242 C4
Lachia Taiwan 22°43N 120°53E 225 D2
Lachine Canada 45°26N 73°42W 130 B1
Lachine, Canal de Canada 45°26N 73°38W 130 B2
Lachlan → Australia 34°22S 143°55E 282 C5
Lachoc Peru 12°50S 75°6W 330 C2
Lachute Canada 45°39N 74°21W 298 C5
Lackagh Hills Ireland 54°16N 8°10W 166 B3
Lackawanna U.S.A. 42°50N 78°50W 312 D6
Lackawaxen U.S.A. 41°29N 74°59W 313 E10
Lacolle Canada 45°5N 73°22W 313 A11
Lacombe Canada 52°30N 113°44W 296 C6
Lacon U.S.A. 41°2N 89°24W 310 C7
Lacona Iowa, U.S.A. 41°12N 93°23W 310 C3
Lacona N.Y., U.S.A. 43°39N 76°10W 313 C8
Láconi Italy 39°54N 9°4E 200 C2
Laconia U.S.A. 43°32N 71°28W 313 C13
Lacoochee U.S.A. 28°28N 82°11W 317 G7
Lacq France 43°25N 0°35W 174 E3
Lacre Punt Bonaire 12°1N 68°14W 322 h
Lad Phrao Thailand 13°47N 100°35E 113 B2
Ladakh Ra. India 34°0N 78°0E 243 C8
Ladário Brazil 19°1S 57°35W 331 D6
Ladd U.S.A. 41°23N 89°13W 310 C7
Laddonia U.S.A. 39°15N 91°39W 310 E5
Lądek-Zdrój Poland 50°21N 16°53E 185 H3
Ladera Heights U.S.A. 33°59N 118°22W 126 C2
Lâdik Turkey 40°57N 35°58E 212 B6
Ladismith S. Africa 33°28S 21°15E 270 D3
Ladíspoli Italy 41°56N 12°5E 199 G9
Lādīz Iran 28°55N 61°15E 247 D9
Ladnun India 27°38N 74°25E 242 F6
Ladoga, L. = Ladozhskoye Ozero Russia 61°15N 30°30E 188 B6
Ladonas → Greece 37°40N 21°50E 204 D3
Ladozhskoye Ozero Russia 61°15N 30°30E 188 B6
Ladrillero, G. Chile 49°20S 75°35W 336 C1
Ladson U.S.A. 32°59N 80°6W 316 C9
Ladushkin Russia 54°34N 20°10E 184 D7
Ládvi Czech Rep. 50°8N 14°27E 135 B2
Łady Poland 52°8N 20°57E 142 C1
Lady Elliott I. Australia 24°7S 152°42E 280 C5
Lady Frere S. Africa 31°42S 27°14E 270 D4
Lady Grey S. Africa 30°43S 27°13E 270 D4
Lady Lake U.S.A. 28°55N 81°55W 317 G8
Ladybrand S. Africa 29°9S 27°29E 270 C4
Ladysmith B.C., Canada 49°0N 123°49W 306 B3
Ladysmith KwaZulu Natal, S. Africa 28°32S 29°46E 271 C4
Ladysmith Wis., U.S.A. 45°28N 91°12W 308 C8
Ladyznyn Ukraine 48°40N 29°15E 183 B14
Lae Papua N. G. 6°40S 147°2E 286 D4
Lae 'o Kealaikahiki U.S.A. 20°32N 156°42W 302 C5
Laem Hin Khom Thailand 9°25N 99°56E 237 b
Laem Khat Thailand 8°6N 98°26E 237 a
Laem Nga Thailand 7°55N 98°27E 237 a
Laem Ngop Thailand 12°10N 102°26E 237 F4
Laem Phan Wa Thailand 7°47N 98°25E 237 a
Laem Pho Thailand 6°55N 101°19E 237 J3
Laem Phrom Thep Thailand 7°45N 98°19E 237 a
Laem Riang Thailand 8°7N 98°27E 237 a
Laem Sam Rong Thailand 9°35N 100°4E 237 b
Laem Son Thailand 7°59N 98°16E 237 a
Laem Son △ Thailand 9°29N 98°24E 237 H2
Laem Yamu Thailand 7°59N 98°26E 237 a
Lærdalsøyri Norway 61°6N 7°28E 164 C4
Laerma Greece 36°9N 27°57E 206 E11
Læsø Denmark 57°15N 11°5E 163 G5
Læsø Rende Denmark 57°20N 10°45E 163 G4
Lafayette Ala., U.S.A. 32°54N 85°24W 316 C4
Lafayette Ind., U.S.A. 40°25N 86°54W 311 D10
Lafayette La., U.S.A. 30°14N 92°1W 314 F8
Lafayette Tenn., U.S.A. 36°31N 86°2W 315 C11
Lafayette Park San Francisco, U.S.A. 136 b1
Lafayette Square New Orleans, U.S.A. 131 b2
Laferte → Canada 61°53N 117°44W 296 A5
Lafia Nigeria 8°30N 8°34E 263 D6
Lafiagi Nigeria 8°52N 5°20E 263 D6
Lafkos Greece 39°9N 23°14E 204 B5
Lafleche Canada 49°45N 106°40W 297 D7
Lafon Sudan 5°5N 32°29E 257 F3
Lafontaine Montréal, Canada 130 a1
Lafontaine, Parc Canada 45°33N 73°34W 130 A2
Laful India 7°10N 93°52E 245 L11
Lagaip → Papua N. G. 5°4S 142°52E 286 C2
Lagan = Kaspiyskiy Russia 45°22N 47°23E 191 H8
Lagan Sweden 56°56N 13°58E 163 H7
Lagan → Sweden 56°30N 12°58E 163 H6
Lagan → Antrim, U.K. 54°36N 5°55W 166 B6
Lagana, Kolpas Greece 37°42N 20°53E 207 D2
Laganas Greece 37°44N 20°53E 207 D2
Lagangilang Phil. 17°37N 120°44E 232 C3
Lagarfljót → Iceland 65°40N 14°18W 155 B12
Lagarto Brazil 10°54S 37°41W 332 D4
Lagawe Phil. 16°49N 121°6E 232 C3
Lagdo Cameroon 9°3N 13°44E 259 G2
Lagdo, L. de Cameroon 8°40N 14°0E 264 A2
Lage Germany 51°59N 8°48E 178 D4
Lågen → Oppland, Norway 61°8N 10°25E 164 C7
Lågen → Vestfold, Norway 59°3N 10°3E 164 E7
Lägerdorf Germany 53°53N 9°34E 178 B5
Lages Brazil 27°48S 50°20W 335 B5
Laggan = Lake Louise Canada 51°30N 116°10W 296 C5
Lagh Badana △ Somali Rep. 1°16S 41°49E 267 E5
Laghmān □ Afghan. 34°20N 70°0E 240 B3
Laghouat Algeria 33°50N 2°59E 261 B5
Laghouat □ Algeria 33°35N 2°40E 261 B5
Lagnieu France 45°55N 5°20E 175 C9
Lagny-sur-Marne France 48°52N 2°44E 173 D9
Lago = Niassa □ Mozam. 13°30S 36°0E 269 E4
Lago Italy 39°10N 16°9E 201 C9
Lago Agrio Ecuador 0°5N 76°52W 328 C2
Lago de Sanabria y Entorno ⌓ Spain 42°9N 6°45W 194 C4
Lago Posadas Argentina 47°30S 71°40W 336 C2
Lago Puela △ Argentina 42°30S 71°55W 336 B2
Lago Ranco Chile 40°19S 72°30W 336 B2
Lagoa Azores 37°45N 25°20W 153 d3
Lagoa Rio de J., Brazil 22°58S 43°11W 135 B1
Lagôa Portugal 37°8N 8°27W 195 H2
Lagoa do Peixe △ Brazil 31°12S 50°55W 335 C5
Lagoa Vermelha Brazil 28°13S 51°32W 335 B5
Lagoaça Portugal 41°11N 6°44W 194 D4
Lagodekhi Georgia 41°50N 46°22E 191 K8
Lagona = Laguna Beach U.S.A. 33°33N 117°47W 307 M9
Lagónegro Italy 40°8N 15°45E 201 B8
Lagonoy G. Phil. 13°35N 123°50E 232 E4
Lagos Angola 16°3S 16°35E 265 F3
Lagos Greece 41°1N 25°6E 203 E9
Lagos Nigeria 6°25N 3°27E 124 B2
Lagos Portugal 37°5N 8°41W 195 H2
Lagos □ Nigeria 6°28N 3°25E 263 D5
Lagos de Moreno Mexico 21°21N 101°55W 318 C4
Lagos Harbour Nigeria 6°26N 3°23E 124 B2
Lagos-Ikeja ✈ (LOS) Nigeria 6°34N 3°19E 124 A1
Lagos Island Nigeria 6°26N 3°23E 124 B2
Lagos Lagoon Nigeria 6°30N 3°28E 124 B2
Lagrange = Bidyadanga Australia 18°45S 121°43E 278 C3
Lagrange U.S.A. 41°39N 85°25W 311 C11
Lagrange B. Australia 18°38S 121°42E 278 C3
Laguardia Spain 42°33N 2°35W 196 C2
Laguépie France 44°8N 1°57E 174 D5
Lagún Curaçao 12°19N 69°10W 322 g
Laguna = Padilla Bolivia 19°19S 64°20W 331 D5
Laguna Brazil 28°30S 48°50W 335 B6
Laguna N. Mex., U.S.A. 35°2N 107°25W 305 J10
Laguna □ Phil. 14°10N 121°20E 232 D3
Laguna, Sa. de la Mexico 23°35N 109°55W 318 C3
Laguna Beach U.S.A. 33°33N 117°47W 307 M9
Laguna Blanca △ Argentina 39°0S 70°5W 336 A2
Laguna de B. Phil. 14°29N 121°6E 127 C2
Laguna de Duera Spain 41°35N 4°43W 194 D6
Laguna de Lachuá △ Guatemala 15°55N 90°40W 320 C1
Laguna de Tacarigua △ Venezuela 10°59N 64°7W 328 A4
Laguna del Laja △ Chile 37°27S 71°20W 334 D1
Laguna del Tigre △ Guatemala 17°32N 90°56W 320 C1
Laguna Limpia Argentina 26°32S 59°45W 334 B4
Laguna San Rafael △ Chile 46°54S 73°31W 336 C2
Lagunas Chile 21°0S 69°45W 334 A2
Lagunas Peru 5°10S 75°35W 330 B2
Lagunas de Chacahua △ Mexico 16°0N 97°43W 319 D5
Lagunas de Montebello △ Mexico 16°4N 91°42W 319 D6
Lagunas de Ruidera ⌓ Spain 38°57N 2°52W 197 G2
Lagunillas Bolivia 19°38S 63°43W 331 D5
Lahad Datu Malaysia 5°0N 118°20E 235 A5
Lahad Datu, Telok Malaysia 4°50N 118°20E 235 B5
Lahaina U.S.A. 20°53N 156°41W 302 C5
Lahan Sai Thailand 14°25N 102°52E 236 E4
Lahanam Laos 16°16N 105°16E 236 D5
Lahar India 26°12N 78°57E 243 F8
Laharpur India 27°43N 80°56E 243 F9
Lahat Indonesia 3°45S 103°30E 234 C2
Lahe Burma 26°20N 95°26E 241 B5
Lahewa Indonesia 1°22N 97°12E 234 B1
Laḥij Yemen 13°4N 44°53E 248 D4
Lāhījān Iran 37°10N 50°6E 247 B6
Lahilahi Pt. U.S.A. 21°28N 158°13W 302 K13
Lähn = Wleń Poland 51°2N 15°39E 185 G2
Lahn → Germany 50°19N 7°37E 179 E3
Lahnstein Germany 50°19N 7°37E 179 E3
Laholm Sweden 56°30N 13°2E 163 H7
Laholmsbukten Sweden 56°30N 12°45E 163 H6
Lahore Pakistan 31°32N 74°22E 242 D6
Lahpongsel Burma 27°7N 98°25E 241 B7
Lahr Germany 48°20N 7°53E 179 G3
Lahri Pakistan 29°11N 68°13E 242 E3
Lāhrūd Iran 38°30N 47°52E 213 C12
Lahti Finland 60°58N 25°40E 188 B3
Lahtis = Lahti Finland 60°58N 25°40E 188 B3
Lahugala Kitulana △ Sri Lanka 6°50N 81°40E 245 L5
Laï Chad 9°25N 16°18E 259 G3
Lai Chau Vietnam 22°5N 103°3E 228 F4
Lai-hka Burma 21°16N 97°40E 241 E6
Laiagam Papua N. G. 5°33S 143°30E 286 C2
Lai'an China 32°28N 118°30E 229 A12
Laibach = Ljubljana Slovenia 46°4N 14°33E 199 B11
Laibin China 23°42N 109°14E 228 F7
Lä'ie U.S.A. 21°39N 157°56W 302 J14
Laifeng China 29°27N 109°20E 228 C7
L'Aigle France 48°46N 0°38E 172 D7
Laignes France 47°50N 4°20E 173 E11
L'Aiguillon-sur-Mer France 46°20N 1°18W 174 B2
Laila = Layla Si. Arabia 22°10N 46°40E 248 B4
Laim Germany 48°7N 11°30E 131 B2
Lainate Italy 45°34N 9°1E 129 A1
Laingsburg S. Africa 33°9S 20°52E 270 D3
Lainioälven → Sweden 67°35N 22°40E 160 C20
Lainz Austria 48°10N 16°16E 142 B1
Lairg U.K. 58°2N 4°24W 167 C4
Laïri, B. de Chad 12°28N 16°45E 259 F3
Lais Indonesia 3°31S 102°3E 234 C2
Lais Phil. 6°20N 125°39E 233 H5
Laisamis Kenya 1°36N 37°48E 268 B4
Laissac France 44°23N 2°50E 174 D6
Láives Italy 46°26N 11°20E 199 B8
Laiwu China 36°15N 117°40E 227 F9
Laixi China 36°50N 120°31E 227 F11
Laiyang China 36°59N 120°45E 227 F11
Laiyuan China 39°20N 114°40E 226 E8
Laizhou China 37°8N 119°57E 227 F10
Laizhou Wan China 37°30N 119°30E 227 F10
Laja → Mexico 20°55N 100°46W 318 C4
Lajamanu Australia 18°23S 130°38E 278 C5
Lajeado = Guiratinga Brazil 16°21S 53°45W 331 D7
Lajedo Azores 39°23N 31°15W 153 d2
Lajere Nigeria 12°10N 11°25E 263 C7
Lajes Azores 38°46N 27°6W 153 d1
Lajes Rio Grande do N., Brazil 5°41S 36°14W 332 C4
Lajes das Flores Azores 39°23N 31°10W 153 d2
Lajes do Pico Azores 38°23N 28°16W 153 d1
Lajinha Brazil 20°9S 41°37W 333 F3
Lajkovac Serbia 44°27N 20°14E 202 B4
Lajosmizse Hungary 47°3N 19°32E 182 C4
Lak Sao Laos 18°11N 104°59E 236 C5
Lakaband Pakistan 31°2N 69°15E 242 D3
Lakamané Mali 14°35N 9°44W 262 C3
Lakatoro Vanuatu 16°6S 167°25E 287 F5
Lake U.S.A. 44°33N 110°24W 304 D8
Lake Alfred U.S.A. 28°6N 81°44W 317 G8
Lake Alpine U.S.A. 38°29N 120°0W 306 G7
Lake Andes U.S.A. 43°9N 98°32W 308 D4
Lake Arthur U.S.A. 30°5N 92°41W 314 F8
Lake Bindegolly △ Australia 28°0S 144°12E 281 D3
Lake Boga Australia 35°26S 143°38E 282 C5
Lake Buena Vista U.S.A. 28°23N 81°32W 133 B1
Lake Butig △ Phil. 7°45N 124°16E 233 H5
Lake Butler U.S.A. 30°1N 82°21W 316 E7
Lake Cain Hills U.S.A. 28°29N 81°28W 133 B2
Lake Cargelligo Australia 33°15S 146°22E 283 B7
Lake Charles U.S.A. 30°14N 93°13W 314 F8
Lake City Colo., U.S.A. 38°2N 107°19W 304 G10
Lake City Fla., U.S.A. 30°11N 82°38W 316 E7
Lake City Iowa, U.S.A. 42°16N 94°44W 310 B2
Lake City Mich., U.S.A. 44°20N 85°13W 309 C11
Lake City Minn., U.S.A. 44°27N 92°16W 308 C7
Lake City Pa., U.S.A. 42°1N 80°21W 312 D4
Lake City S.C., U.S.A. 33°52N 79°45W 316 B10
Lake Clark △ U.S.A. 61°0N 154°0W 303 F9
Lake Clarke Shores U.S.A. 26°39N 80°5W 317 J9
Lake Coleridge N.Z. 43°17S 171°30E 285 D6
Lake Cowichan Canada 48°49N 124°3W 296 D4
Lake District △ U.K. 54°30N 3°21W 168 C4
Lake Eildon △ Australia 37°10S 145°56E 283 D6
Lake Elsinore U.S.A. 33°38N 117°20W 307 M9
Lake Eyre △ Australia 28°40S 137°31E 281 D2
Lake Fairfax Park U.S.A. 38°57N 77°19W 143 B2
Lake Forest U.S.A. 42°15N 87°50W 311 B9
Lake Gairdner △ Australia 31°41S 135°51E 281 E2
Lake Geneva U.S.A. 42°36N 88°26W 311 B8
Lake George U.S.A. 43°26N 73°43W 313 C11
Lake Grace Australia 33°7S 118°28E 279 F2
Lake Gregory ◎ Australia 20°12S 127°27E 278 D4
Lake Harbor U.S.A. 26°42N 80°48W 317 J9
Lake Harbour = Kimmirut Canada 62°50N 69°50W 295 E18
Lake Havasu City U.S.A. 34°27N 114°22W 307 L12
Lake Helen U.S.A. 28°59N 81°14W 317 G8
Lake Hughes U.S.A. 34°41N 118°26W 307 L8
Lake Isabella U.S.A. 35°38N 118°28W 307 K8
Lake Jackson U.S.A. 29°3N 95°27W 314 G7
Lake King Australia 33°5S 119°45E 279 F2
Lake Kopiago Papua N. G. 5°23S 142°31E 286 C2
Lake Kutubu Papua N. G. 6°20S 143°18E 286 D2
Lake Lenore Canada 52°24N 104°59W 297 C8
Lake Louise Canada 51°30N 116°10W 296 C5
Lake Mackay ◎ Australia 21°48S 129°46E 278 D4
Lake Mburo △ Uganda 0°33S 30°56E 268 C3
Lake Mead ⌓ U.S.A. 36°30N 114°22W 307 K12
Lake Meredith ⌓ U.S.A. 35°50N 101°50W 314 D4
Lake Mills Iowa, U.S.A. 43°25N 93°32W 308 D7
Lake Mills Wis., U.S.A. 43°5N 88°55W 311 A8
Lake Murray Papua N. G. 6°48S 141°29E 286 D1
Lake Nakura △ Kenya 0°21S 36°8E 268 C4
Lake Odessa U.S.A. 42°47N 85°8W 311 B11
Lake Orion U.S.A. 42°47N 83°14W 311 B13
Lake Park Fla., U.S.A. 26°48N 80°3W 317 J9
Lake Park Ga., U.S.A. 30°41N 83°11W 316 E6
Lake Placid Fla., U.S.A. 27°18N 81°22W 317 H8
Lake Placid N.Y., U.S.A. 44°17N 73°59W 313 B11
Lake Pleasant U.S.A. 43°28N 74°25W 313 C10
Lake Point Tower Chicago, U.S.A. 119 b3
Lake Providence U.S.A. 32°48N 91°10W 314 E9
Lake Pukaki N.Z. 44°11S 170°8E 285 E5
Lake Roosevelt ⌓ U.S.A. 48°5N 118°14W 304 B4
Lake St. Peter Canada 45°18N 78°2W 312 A6
Lake Shore Drive Chicago, U.S.A. 119 a2
Lake Shore Park Chicago, U.S.A. 119 a2
Lake Superior ⌓ Canada 47°45N 84°45W 298 C3
Lake Tekapo N.Z. 44°0S 170°30E 285 E5
Lake Torrens △ Australia 30°55S 137°40E 281 E2
Lake View U.S.A. 42°18N 95°3W 310 B1
Lake Villa U.S.A. 42°25N 88°5W 311 B8
Lake Village U.S.A. 33°20N 91°17W 314 E9
Lake Wales U.S.A. 27°54N 81°35W 317 H8
Lake Worth U.S.A. 26°37N 80°3W 317 J9
Lake Zurich U.S.A. 42°12N 88°5W 311 B8
Lakeba Fiji 18°13S 178°47W 287 B3
Lakeba Passage Fiji 18°0S 178°45W 287 B3
Lakefield Canada 44°25N 78°16W 312 B6
Lakefield △ Australia 15°24S 144°26E 280 B3
Lakehurst U.S.A. 40°1N 74°19W 313 F10
Lakeland Queens., Australia 15°49S 144°57E 280 B3
Lakeland Fla., U.S.A. 28°3N 81°57W 317 G8
Lakeland Ga., U.S.A. 31°2N 83°4W 316 D6
Lakemba = Lakeba Fiji 18°13S 178°47W 287 B3
Lakemba Australia 33°55S 151°5E 139 B1
Lakepa Cook Is. 18°59S 169°48W 289 g
Lakeport Calif., U.S.A. 39°3N 122°55W 306 F4
Lakeport Mich., U.S.A. 43°7N 82°30W 312 C2
Lakes Entrance Australia 37°50S 148°0E 283 D8
Lakeside Gauteng, S. Africa 26°5S 28°8E 123 A2
Lakeside Western Cape, S. Africa 34°5S 18°27E 118 B1
Lakeside Calif., U.S.A. 32°52N 116°55W 307 N10
Lakeside Nebr., U.S.A. 42°3N 102°26W 308 D2
Lakeside Center Chicago, U.S.A. 119 f3
Lakeview Ill., U.S.A. 41°56N 87°38W 119 B3
Lakeview La., U.S.A. 30°0N 90°6W 131 A2
Lakeview Oreg., U.S.A. 42°11N 120°21W 304 E3
Lakeville U.S.A. 44°39N 93°14W 308 C7
Lakewood Colo., U.S.A. 39°42N 105°4W 304 G11
Lakewood N.J., U.S.A. 40°6N 74°13W 313 F10
Lakewood N.Y., U.S.A. 42°6N 79°19W 312 D5
Lakewood Ohio, U.S.A. 41°28N 81°47W 312 E3
Lakewood Wash., U.S.A. 47°11N 122°32W 306 C4
Lakewood Park Fla., U.S.A. 27°33N 80°24W 317 H9
Lakewood Park Georgia, U.S.A. 33°43N 84°24W 113 B2
Lakha India 26°9N 70°54E 242 F4
Lakhimpur India 27°57N 80°46E 243 F9
Lakhipur Assam, India 24°48N 93°0E 241 C4
Lakhipur Assam, India 26°2N 90°18E 241 B3
Lakhisarai India 25°11N 86°5E 243 G12
Lakhnadon India 22°36N 79°36E 243 H8
Lakhnau = Lucknow India 26°50N 81°0E 243 F9
Lakhonpheng Laos 15°54N 105°34E 236 E5
Lakhpat India 23°48N 68°47E 242 H3
Lakhtinskiy Russia 59°59N 30°9E 137 B1
Lakhtinskiy Razliv, Oz. Russia 59°59N 30°12E 137 B1
Läki Azerbaijan 40°34N 47°22E 191 K8
Laki Iceland 64°4N 18°14W 155 C8
Lakin U.S.A. 37°57N 101°15W 308 G3
Lakitusaki → Canada 54°21N 82°25W 298 B3
Lakka Greece 39°17N 20°9E 206 C10
Lakki Greece 35°24N 23°57E 207 E4
Lakki Pakistan 32°36N 70°55E 242 C4
Lakonia □ Greece 36°55N 22°30E 204 E4
Lakonikos Kolpos Greece 36°40N 22°40E 204 E4
Lakor Indonesia 8°15S 128°17E 231 F7
Lakota Ivory C. 5°50N 5°30W 262 D3
Lakota N. Dak., U.S.A. 48°2N 98°21W 308 A4
Laksar India 29°46N 78°3E 242 E8
Laksefjorden Norway 70°45N 26°50E 160 A22
Lakselv Norway 70°2N 25°0E 160 A21
Laksettipet India 18°52N 79°13E 244 E4
Lakshadweep □ India 10°0N 72°30E 245 J1
Lakshadweep Is. India 10°0N 72°30E 245 J1
Laksham Bangla. 23°14N 91°8E 241 D3
Lakshimpur Bangla. 22°58N 90°50E 241 D3
Lakshmanpur Chhattisgarh, India 22°58N 83°3E 243 H10
Lakshmanpur W. Bengal, India 22°38N 88°16E 124 B1
Lakshmeshwar India 15°9N 75°28E 245 G2
Lakshmikantapur India 22°5N 88°20E 243 H13
Laksi Thailand 13°53N 100°35E 113 A2
Lakuramau Papua N. G. 2°54S 151°15E 286 B6
Lal-lo Phil. 18°12N 121°40E 232 B3
Lal Qila Delhi, India 120 a3
Lala Dem. Rep. of the Congo 4°10S 20°30E 265 C4
Lala Phil. 7°59N 123°46E 233 H4
Lala Musa Pakistan 32°40N 73°57E 242 C5
Lalaghat India 24°30N 92°40E 241 C4
Lalago Tanzania 3°28S 33°58E 268 C3
Lalang → Indonesia 2°24S 104°39E 234 C2
Lalapanzi Zimbabwe 19°20S 30°15E 269 F3
Lalapaşa Turkey 41°49N 26°44E 203 E10
Lalara Gabon 0°19N 11°32E 264 B2
Lalbenque France 44°19N 1°34E 174 D5
Lalbert Australia 35°38S 143°20E 282 C5
L'Albufera Spain 39°20N 0°27W 197 F4
L'Alcora Spain 40°5N 0°14W 196 E4
L'Alfàs del Pi Spain 38°35N 0°5W 197 G4
Lalganj India 25°52N 85°13E 243 G11
Lalgola India 24°25N 88°15E 243 G13
Lālī Iran 32°21N 49°6E 247 C6
Lalibela Ethiopia 12°3N 39°0E 257 E4
Lalin Heilongjiang, China 45°12N 127°0E 227 B14
Lalín Spain 42°40N 8°5W 194 C2
Lalin He → China 45°32N 125°40E 227 B13
Lalinde France 44°50N 0°44E 174 D4
Lalitapur Nepal 27°40N 85°20E 243 F11
Lalitpur India 24°42N 78°28E 243 G8
Lalkua India 29°5N 79°31E 243 E8
Lalm Norway 61°50N 9°17E 164 C6
Lalsot India 26°34N 76°20E 242 F7
Lam Nam Nan △ Thailand 17°55N 100°28E 236 D3
Lam Pao Res. Thailand 16°50N 103°15E 236 D4
Lam Tin China 22°18N 114°14E 122 B2
Lama Kara Togo 9°30N 1°15E 263 D5
Lamae Thailand 9°51N 99°5E 237 H2
Lamag Malaysia 5°29N 117°49E 235 A5
Lamaing Burma 15°25N 97°53E 236 E1
Lamaipum Burma 25°40N 97°57E 241 C6
Lamap Vanuatu 16°26S 167°43E 287 F5
Lamar Colo., U.S.A. 38°5N 102°37W 304 G12
Lamar Mo., U.S.A. 37°30N 94°16W 308 G6
Lamarque Argentina 39°24S 65°40W 336 A3
Lamas Peru 6°28S 76°31W 330 B2
Lamastre France 44°59N 4°35E 175 D8
Lamayuru India 34°25N 76°56E 243 B7
Lambach Austria 48°6N 13°51E 180 C6
Lamballe France 48°29N 2°31W 172 D4
Lambaréné Gabon 0°41S 10°12E 264 C2
Lambasa = Labasa Fiji 16°30S 179°27E 287 A2
Lambay I. Ireland 53°29N 6°1W 166 C5
Lambayeque □ Peru 6°45S 80°0W 330 B2
Lambert Norway 59°52N 10°48E 133 A3
Lambert, C. Papua N. G. 4°11S 151°31E 286 C6
Lambert-St. Louis Int. ✈ (STL) U.S.A. 38°45N 90°22W 310 F6
Lambert's Bay S. Africa 32°5S 18°17E 270 D2
Lambertville U.S.A. 41°46N 83°35W 311 C13
Lambesc France 43°39N 5°16E 175 E9
Lambèse = Tazoult Algeria 35°29N 6°11E 261 A6
Lambeth Canada 42°54N 81°18W 312 D3
Lambeth □ U.K. 51°28N 0°6W 125 B3
Lambi Solomon Is. 9°22S 159°39E 287 M10
Lambia Greece 37°52N 21°53E 204 D3
Lambir Hills △ Malaysia 4°12N 114°1E 235 B4
Lambomakondro Madag. 22°41S 44°44E 272 C1
Lambon Papua N. G. 4°45S 152°48E 286 C7
Lambrate Italy 45°28N 9°16E 129 B2
Lambro → Italy 45°8N 9°32E 198 C6
Lambro, Parco Italy 45°29N 9°14E 129 B2
Lambton Mills Canada 43°39N 79°30W 141 B1
Lambu Papua N. G. 3°18S 151°43E 286 B6
Lambunao Phil. 11°3N 122°29E 233 F4
Lamé Chad 9°15N 14°32E 259 G2
Lame Nigeria 10°30N 9°20E 263 C6
Lame Deer U.S.A. 45°37N 106°40W 304 D10
Lamego Portugal 41°5N 7°52W 194 D3
Lamentin Guadeloupe 16°16N 61°38W 322 e
Lamèque Canada 47°45N 64°38W 299 C7
Lameroo Australia 35°19S 140°33E 282 C4
Lamesa U.S.A. 32°44N 101°58W 314 E4
Lamia Greece 38°55N 22°26E 204 C4
Lamigan Pt. Phil. 6°48N 126°21E 233 H6
Lamine → U.S.A. 38°59N 92°51W 310 F4
Lamington △ Australia 28°13S 153°12E 281 D5
Lamitan Phil. 6°39N 122°8E 233 H4
Lamlam, Mt. Guam 13°22N 144°41E 302 d
Lamma I. China 22°12N 114°7E 122 B1
Lammermuir Hills U.K. 55°50N 2°40W 167 F6
Lammeulo Indonesia 5°14N 95°56E 234 A1
Lammhult Sweden 57°10N 14°35E 163 G8
Lamoille → U.S.A. 44°38N 73°13W 313 B11
Lamon B. Phil. 14°30N 122°20E 232 D4
Lamongan Indonesia 7°7S 112°25E 235 D4
Lamoni U.S.A. 40°37N 93°56W 310 D3
Lamont Alta., Canada 53°46N 112°50W 296 C6
Lamont Calif., U.S.A. 35°15N 118°55W 307 K8
Lamont Fla., U.S.A. 30°23N 83°49W 316 E6
Lamont Iowa, U.S.A. 42°36N 91°39W 310 B5
Lamont Wyo., U.S.A. 42°13N 107°29W 304 E10
Lamotte-Beuvron France 47°36N 2°2E 173 E9
Lampa Peru 15°22S 70°22W 330 D3
Lampang Thailand 18°16N 99°32E 236 C2
Lampasas U.S.A. 31°4N 98°11W 314 F5
Lampazos de Naranjo Mexico 27°1N 100°31W 318 B4
Lampedusa Medit. S. 35°36N 12°40E 261 A7
Lampertheim Germany 49°35N 8°27E 179 F4
Lampeter U.K. 52°7N 4°4W 169 E3
Lamphun Thailand 18°40N 99°2E 236 C2
Lampione Medit. S. 35°33N 12°20E 258 A2
Lampman Canada 49°25N 102°50W 297 D8
Lamprechtshausen Austria 48°0N 12°58E 180 D5
Lampung □ Indonesia 5°30S 104°30E 234 D2
Lampung, Teluk Indonesia 5°40S 105°20E 234 D3
Lamta India 22°8N 80°7E 243 H9
Lamu Burma 19°14N 94°10E 241 F5
Lamu Coast, Kenya 2°16S 40°55E 268 C5
Lamud Peru 6°10S 77°57W 330 B2
Lamy U.S.A. 35°29N 105°53W 305 J11
Lan Xian China 38°15N 111°35E 226 E6
Lan Yü Taiwan 22°4N 121°25E 225 D3
Läna'i U.S.A. 20°50N 156°55W 302 C5
Läna'i City U.S.A. 20°50N 156°55W 302 C5
Läna'ihale U.S.A. 20°49N 156°53W 302 C5
Lanak La China 34°27N 79°32E 243 B8
Lanak'o Shank'ou = Lanak La China 34°27N 79°32E 243 B8
Lanao, L. Phil. 7°52N 124°15E 233 H5
Lanao del Norte □ Phil. 8°0N 124°10E 233 H5
Lanao del Sur □ Phil. 7°40N 124°15E 233 H5
Lanark Ont., Canada 45°1N 76°22W 313 A8
Lanark S. Lanarks., U.K. 55°40N 3°47W 167 F5
Lanark Ill., U.S.A. 42°6N 89°50W 310 B7
Lanbi Kyun Burma 10°50N 98°20E 237 G2
Lancang China 22°36N 99°58E 228 F2
Lancang Jiang → China 21°40N 101°10E 228 G3
Lancashire □ U.K. 53°50N 2°48W 168 D5
Lancaster Ont., Canada 45°10N 74°30W 313 A10
Lancaster Lancs., U.K. 54°3N 2°48W 168 C5
Lancaster Calif., U.S.A. 34°42N 118°8W 307 L8
Lancaster Ky., U.S.A. 37°37N 84°35W 309 G11
Lancaster Mo., U.S.A. 40°31N 92°32W 310 D4
Lancaster N.H., U.S.A. 44°29N 71°34W 313 B13
Lancaster Ohio, U.S.A. 39°43N 82°36W 309 F12
Lancaster Pa., U.S.A. 40°2N 76°19W 313 F8
Lancaster S.C., U.S.A. 34°43N 80°46W 315 D14
Lancaster Wis., U.S.A. 42°51N 90°43W 310 B6
Lancaster, Récif = Neilson, Récif Pac. Oc. 27°1S 146°2W 289 f
Lancaster Sd. Canada 74°13N 84°0W 295 C15
Lancelin Australia 31°0S 115°18E 279 F2
Lanchow = Lanzhou China 36°1N 103°52E 226 F2
Lanchyn Ukraine 48°33N 24°45E 183 B9
Lanciano Italy 42°14N 14°23E 199 F11
Lanco Chile 39°24S 72°46W 336 A2
Lancones Peru 4°30S 80°30W 330 A1
Lancun China 36°25N 120°10E 227 F11
Łańcut Poland 50°10N 22°13E 185 H9

Land Between the Lakes △
  U.S.A. 36°25N 88°0W 315 C11
Landau Bayern, Germany 48°40N 12°41E 179 G8
Landau Rhld.-Pfz., Germany 49°12N 8°6E 179 F4
Landay Afghan. 30°31N 63°47E 240 C1
Lander U.S.A. 42°50N 108°44W 304 E9
Lander → Australia 22°0S 132°0E 278 D5
Landerneau France 48°28N 4°17W 172 D2
Landeryd Sweden 57°7N 13°15E 163 G7
Landes France 44°0N 1°0W 174 D2
Landes □ France 43°57N 0°48W 174 E3
Landes de Gascogne △
  France 44°23N 0°50W 174 D3
Landeshut = Kamienna Góra
  Poland 50°47N 16°2E 185 H3
Landete Spain 39°56N 1°25W 196 F3
Landfall I. India 13°40N 93°2E 245 H11
Landi Kotal Pakistan 34°7N 71°6E 242 B4
Landianchang China 39°56N 116°17E 114 B1
Landisburg U.S.A. 40°21N 77°19W 312 F7
Landivisiau France 48°31N 4°6W 172 D2
Landmannalaugar Iceland 63°59N 19°4W 155 D7
Landover Hills U.S.A. 38°56N 76°54W 143 B4
Landquart Switz. 46°58N 9°32E 179 J5
Landrecies France 50°7N 3°40E 173 B10
Land's End U.K. 50°4N 5°44W 169 G2
Landsberg = Górowo Iławeckie
  Poland 54°17N 20°30E 184 D7
Landsberg Germany 48°21N 10°53E 179 G6
Landsberg an der Warthe = Gorzów
  Wielkopolski Poland 52°43N 15°15E 185 F2
Landsberg in Oberschlesien =
  Gorzów Śląski Poland 51°3N 18°22E 185 G5
Landsborough Cr. →
  Australia 22°28S 144°35E 280 C3
Landsbro Sweden 57°24N 14°56E 163 G8
Landshut Germany 48°34N 12°8E 179 G8
Landskrona Sweden 55°53N 12°50E 163 J6
Landsmeer Neths. 52°26N 4°55E 112 A2
Landstrasse Austria 48°12N 16°23E 142 A2
Landstuhl Germany 49°24N 7°33E 179 F3
Landvetter Sweden 57°41N 12°17E 163 G6
Landwehr kanal Germany 52°29N 13°24E 115 B3
Lane U.S.A. 33°32N 79°53W 316 B10
Lane Cove Australia 33°48S 151°9E 139 A1
Lane Cove Nat. Park △
  Australia 33°47S 151°8E 139 A1
Lanesboro U.S.A. 41°57N 75°34W 313 E9
Lanester France 47°46N 3°22W 172 E3
Lanett U.S.A. 32°52N 85°12W 316 C4
Lang Shan China 41°0N 106°30E 226 D4
Lang Son Vietnam 21°52N 106°42E 228 G6
Lang Suan Thailand 9°57N 99°4E 237 H2
Langå Midtjylland, Denmark 56°23N 9°54E 163 H3
Langa Western Cape,
  S. Africa 33°57S 18°31E 118 A2
La'nga Co China 30°45N 81°15E 243 D9
Langa-Langa
  Dem. Rep. of the Congo 3°50S 15°59E 264 C3
Langadás Greece 40°46N 23°6E 202 F7
Langadia Greece 37°43N 22°1E 204 D4
Långan → Sweden 63°19N 14°44E 162 A8
Langano, L. Ethiopia 7°36N 38°43E 257 F4
Langanes Iceland 66°20N 14°53W 155 A12
Langar Afghan. 37°2N 73°47E 240 A4
Langar Iran 35°23N 60°25E 247 C9
Langarūd Iran 37°11N 50°8E 247 B6
Långås Sweden 56°58N 12°26E 163 H6
Langatabbetje Suriname 4°59N 54°28W 329 C7
Langdai China 26°6N 105°21E 228 D5
Langdon U.S.A. 48°45N 98°22W 308 A4
Länge Jan = Ölands södra udde
  Sweden 56°12N 16°23E 163 H10
Langeac France 45°7N 3°29E 174 C7
Langeais France 47°20N 0°24E 172 E7
Langeb Baraka → Sudan 17°28N 36°50E 256 D4
Langeberg S. Africa 33°55S 21°0E 270 D3
Langeberge S. Africa 28°15S 22°33E 270 C3
Langeland Denmark 54°56N 10°48E 163 K4
Langen Hessen, Germany 49°59N 8°40E 179 F4
Langen Niedersachsen,
  Germany 53°36N 8°37E 178 B4
Langenbielau = Bielawa
  Poland 50°43N 16°37E 185 H3
Langenburg Canada 50°51N 101°43W 297 C3
Langeneß Germany 54°38N 8°36E 178 A4
Langenlois Austria 48°29N 15°40E 180 C8
Langenzersdorf Austria 48°18N 16°21E 142 A2
Langeoog Germany 53°43N 7°30E 178 B3
Langer See Germany 52°24N 13°37E 115 B4
Langeskov Denmark 55°22N 10°35E 163 J4
Langesund Norway 59°0N 9°45E 164 F4
Langevåg Norway 62°26N 6°13E 164 B3
Langfang China 39°30N 116°41E 226 E9
Langgapayung Indonesia 1°43N 99°58E 236 D1
Länghem Sweden 57°36N 13°14E 163 G7
Langhirano Italy 44°37N 10°16E 198 D7
Langholm U.K. 55°9N 3°0W 167 F5
Langjökull Iceland 64°39N 20°12W 155 C6
Langkawi, Pulau Malaysia 6°30N 99°45E 237 J2
Langklip S. Africa 28°12S 20°20E 270 C3
Langkon Malaysia 6°30N 116°40E 235 A5
Langley B.C., Canada 49°7N 122°39W 306 A4
Langley Va., U.S.A. 38°57N 77°11W 143 B2
Langley Park U.S.A. 38°59N 76°59W 143 B4
Langnau Switz. 46°56N 7°47E 179 J3
Langogne France 44°43N 3°50E 174 D7
Langon France 44°33N 0°16W 174 D3
Langøya Norway 68°45N 14°50E 160 B16
Langreo Spain 43°18N 5°40W 194 B5
Langres France 47°52N 5°20E 173 E12
Langres, Plateau de France 47°45N 5°3E 173 E12
Langsa Indonesia 4°30N 97°57E 234 B1
Långsele Sweden 63°12N 17°4E 162 A11
Långshyttan Sweden 60°27N 16°2E 162 D10
Langtang → Nepal 28°10N 85°30E 243 E11
Langtao Burma 27°15N 97°40E 241 B6
Langting India 25°31N 93°7E 241 C4
Langtou China 40°1N 124°19E 227 D13
Langtry U.S.A. 29°49N 101°34W 314 C3
Langu Thailand 6°53N 99°47E 237 J2
Langue de Barbarie △
  Senegal 14°54N 16°30W 262 C1
Languedoc France 43°58N 3°55E 174 E7
Languedoc-Roussillon □
  France 43°58N 3°0E 174 E6
Langwald Germany 48°10N 11°25E 131 A1
Langwang China 31°38N 110°37E 229 B9
Langxi China 31°10N 119°12E 229 B12
Langzhong China 31°38N 105°58E 228 B5
Lanham U.S.A. 38°59N 76°51W 143 B4
Lanigan Canada 51°51N 105°2W 297 C7
Lanikai U.S.A. 21°23N 157°42W 302 K14
Lanín △ Argentina 40°0S 71°58W 336 B2
Lanjigarh India 19°43N 83°23E 244 E6
Lankao China 34°48N 114°50E 226 G8
Länkäran Azerbaijan 38°48N 48°52E 213 C13
Lankwitz Germany 52°25N 13°21E 115 B3
Lanmeur France 48°39N 3°43E 172 D2
Lannemezan France 43°8N 0°23E 174 E4
Lannilis France 48°35N 4°32W 172 D1

Lannion France 48°46N 3°29W 172 D3
L'Annonciation Canada 46°25N 74°55W 298 C5
L'Annunziatella Italy 41°49N 12°33E 186 H3
Lanouaille France 45°24N 1°9E 174 C5
Lanping China 26°28N 99°15E 228 D2
Lansang △ Thailand 16°45N 99°0E 236 D2
Lansdale U.S.A. 40°14N 75°17W 313 F9
Lansdowne N.S.W.,
  Australia 31°48S 152°30E 283 A10
Lansdowne Ont., Canada 44°24N 76°1W 313 B8
Lansdowne India 29°50N 78°41E 243 E8
Lansdowne Western Cape,
  S. Africa 33°59S 18°30E 118 A2
Lansdowne House = Neskantaga
  Canada 52°14N 87°53W 298 B2
L'Anse U.S.A. 46°45N 88°27W 308 B9
L'Anse à l'Âne Martinique 14°32N 61°4W 322 j
L'Anse au Loup Canada 51°32N 56°50W 299 B8
L'Anse aux Epines Grenada 11°59N 61°45W 323 q
L'Anse aux Meadows
  Canada 51°36N 55°32W 299 B8
L'Anse la Raye St. Lucia 13°55N 61°3W 323 m
L'Anse Mitan Martinique 14°32N 61°3W 322 j
Lansford U.S.A. 40°50N 75°53W 313 F9
Lanshan China 25°24N 112°10E 229 E9
Lanshantou China 35°5N 119°20E 227 G10
Länsi-Turunmaa Finland 60°18N 22°18E 188 B2
Lansing Ont., Canada 43°45N 79°24W 141 A2
Lansing Mich., U.S.A. 42°44N 84°33W 311 B12
Lanslebourg-Mont-Cenis
  France 45°17N 6°52E 175 C10
Lanta, Ko Thailand 7°35N 99°3E 237 J2
Lantana U.S.A. 26°35N 80°3W 317 J9
Lantau I. China 22°15N 113°56E 219 a
Lantewa Nigeria 12°16N 11°44E 263 C7
Lantian China 34°11N 109°20E 226 G5
Lanus Argentina 34°42S 58°23W 117 C2
Lanusei Italy 39°52N 9°34E 200 D2
Lanuza Phil. 9°14N 126°4E 233 G6
Lanxi China 29°13N 119°28E 229 C12
Lanyang Hsi → Taiwan 24°43N 121°49E 225 B3
Lanyù Taiwan 22°2N 121°33E 225 D3
Lanzarote Canary Is. 29°0N 13°40W 153 e2
Lanzarote ✕ (ACE)
  Canary Is. 28°57N 13°40W 153 e2
Lanzhou China 36°1N 103°52E 226 F2
Lanzo Torinese Italy 45°16N 7°28E 198 C4
Lao → Italy 39°47N 15°48E 201 C8
Lao Bao Laos 16°35N 106°30E 239 F17
Lao Cai Vietnam 22°30N 103°57E 228 F4
Laoag Phil. 18°7N 120°34E 232 B3
Laoang Phil. 12°32N 125°8E 232 E5
Laoha He → China 43°25N 120°35E 227 C11
Laohekou China 32°22N 111°38E 229 A9
Laois □ Ireland 52°57N 7°36W 166 D4
Laon France 49°33N 3°35E 173 C10
Laona U.S.A. 45°34N 88°40W 308 C9
Laonung Hsi → Taiwan 22°47N 120°27E 225 D2
Laos ■ Asia 17°45N 105°0E 236 D5
Lapa Paraná, Brazil 25°46S 49°44W 335 B6
Lapa Rio de J., Brazil 22°54S 43°10W 135 B1
Lapac I. Phil. 5°32N 120°47E 233 J3
Lapai Nigeria 9°2N 6°55E 263 C6
Lapalisse France 46°15N 3°38E 173 F10
Laparan I. Phil. 5°57N 120°0E 233 J2
Lapeer U.S.A. 43°3N 83°19W 311 A13
Lapeyrade France 44°1N 0°33W 174 D3
Lapithos Cyprus 35°21N 33°11E 207 E9
Lapland = Lappland
  Europe 68°7N 24°0E 160 B21
LaPorte Ind., U.S.A. 41°36N 86°43W 311 C10
Laporte Pa., U.S.A. 41°25N 76°30W 313 E8
Lapovo Serbia 44°10N 21°2E 202 B5
Lappeenranta Finland 61°3N 28°12E 188 B5
Lappland Europe 68°7N 24°0E 160 B21
Lappo = Lapua Finland 62°58N 23°0E 160 E20
Laprida Argentina 37°34S 60°45W 334 D4
Lâpseki Turkey 40°20N 26°41E 203 F10
Laptev Sea Russia 76°0N 125°0E 215 B13
Lapu-Lapu Phil. 10°20N 123°55E 233 F4
Lapua Finland 62°58N 23°0E 160 E20
Lapuş → Romania 47°25N 23°40E 183 C8
Lapuş, Munţii Romania 47°20N 23°50E 183 C8
Lapuşna Moldova 46°53N 28°25E 183 D13
Lapy Poland 52°59N 22°52E 185 F9
Laqiya Arba'in Sudan 20°1N 28°1E 256 C2
Laqiya Umran Sudan 19°55N 28°18E 256 D2
L'Aquila Italy 42°22N 13°22E 199 F10
Lär Iran 27°40N 54°14E 247 E7
Lara Australia 38°2S 144°26E 282 E6
Lara □ Venezuela 10°10N 69°50E 328 A5
Larabanga Ghana 9°16N 1°56W 262 D4
Laragne-Montéglin France 44°18N 5°49E 175 D9
Lārak Iran 26°31N 56°21E 249 A7
Laramie U.S.A. 41°19N 105°35W 304 F11
Laramie Mts. U.S.A. 42°0N 105°30W 304 F11
Laranjal do Jari Brazil 0°51S 52°32W 329 D7
Laranjeiras Brazil 22°55S 43°10W 135 B1
Laranjeiras do Sul Brazil 25°23S 52°23W 335 B5
Larantuka Indonesia 8°21S 122°55E 234 F6
Larat Indonesia 7°0S 132°0E 231 F8
L'Arbresle France 45°50N 4°36E 175 C8
Lärbro Sweden 57°47N 18°50E 163 G12
Lårdal Norway 59°25N 8°10E 164 F4
Larde Mozam. 16°28S 39°43E 269 F4
Larder Lake Canada 48°5N 79°40W 298 C4
Lardos Greece 36°6N 28°1E 206 G12
Lardos, Akra = Lindos, Akra
  Greece 36°4N 28°10E 206 G12
Lardos, Ormos Greece 36°4N 28°2E 206 G12
Lare Kenya 0°20N 37°56E 268 C4
Laredo U.S.A. 39°39N 93°30W 310 E7
Laredo Tex., U.S.A. 27°30N 99°30W 314 H5
Laredo Sd. Canada 52°30N 128°53W 306 C3
Larena Phil. 9°15N 123°35E 233 G4
Lares Puerto Rico 18°18N 66°53W 321 b
Large I. Grenada 12°24N 61°33W 323 q
Largeau Chad 17°44N 14°18E 175 D8
L'Argentière-la-Bessée
  France 44°47N 6°33E 175 D10
Largo U.S.A. 27°54N 82°47W 317 H7
Largo, Key U.S.A. 25°15N 80°19W 317 K9
Largs U.K. 55°47N 4°52W 167 F4
Lari Italy 43°34N 10°35E 198 E7
Lariang Indonesia 1°26S 119°17E 235 C5
Larimore U.S.A. 47°54N 97°38W 308 B6
Larino Italy 41°48N 14°54E 199 G11
Larisa Italy 39°36N 22°27E 204 B4
Larisis Station Athens, Greece 112 A1
Larissa = Larisa Greece 39°36N 22°27E 204 B4
Larissos □ Greece 39°36N 22°27E 204 B4
Larkana Pakistan 27°32N 68°18E 242 F3
Larkins = South Miami
  U.S.A. 25°42N 80°17W 128 B1
Larnaca Cyprus 34°55N 33°38E 207 E9
Larnaca ✕ (LCA) Cyprus 34°55N 33°38E 207 F9
Larnaca Bay Cyprus 34°53N 33°45E 207 F9
Larnare, Pte. Martinique 14°47N 61°13W 322 j

Larose U.S.A. 29°34N 90°23W 315 G9
Larose, Pte. Martinique 14°39N 60°53W 322 j
Larrimah Australia 15°35S 133°12E 278 C5
Larsen Bay U.S.A. 57°32N 153°59W 303 H9
Larsen Ice Shelf Antarctica 67°0S 62°0W 151 C17
Laruns France 43°0N 0°26W 174 F3
Larvik Norway 59°4N 10°2E 164 F7
Larzac, Causse du France 43°50N 3°17E 174 E7
La Sabana
  Argentina 27°50S 59°55W 334 B4
Las Alpujarras Spain 36°55N 3°20W 197 J1
Las Animas U.S.A. 38°4N 103°13W 304 G12
Las Anod Somali Rep. 8°26N 47°19E 267 C6
Las Arenas Spain 43°17N 4°50W 194 B6
Las Batuecas → Spain 40°32N 6°5W 194 E4
Las Bonitas Venezuela 7°52N 65°40W 328 B4
Las Brenãs Argentina 27°5S 61°7W 334 B3
Las Cabezas de San Juan
  Spain 36°57N 5°58W 195 J5
Las Chimeneas Mexico 32°8N 116°5W 307 N10
Las Coloradas Argentina 39°34S 70°36W 336 A2
Las Cruces U.S.A. 32°19N 106°47W 305 K10
Las Flores Argentina 36°10S 59°7W 334 D4
Las Gabias = Gabia la Grande
  Spain 37°8N 3°40W 195 H7
Las Heras Mendoza,
  Argentina 32°51S 68°49W 334 C2
Las Heras Santa Cruz,
  Argentina 46°33S 68°57W 336 C3
Las Hermosas △ Colombia 3°45N 75°51W 328 C2
Las Horquetas Argentina 48°14S 71°11W 336 C2
Las Kabacki Poland 52°7N 21°2E 142 C2
Las Khoreh = Laasqoray
  Somali Rep. 11°10N 48°20E 267 B6
Las Lajas Argentina 38°30S 70°25W 336 A2
Las Lomas Peru 4°40S 80°10W 330 A1
Las Lomitas Argentina 24°43S 60°35W 334 A3
Las Marismas Spain 37°5N 6°20W 195 H4
Las Mercedes Venezuela 9°7N 66°24W 328 B4
Las Minas Spain 38°20N 1°41W 197 G3
Las Navas de la Concepción
  Spain 37°56N 5°30W 195 H5
Las Navas del Marqués
  Spain 40°36N 4°20W 194 E6
Las Nieves Phil. 8°46N 125°34E 233 G5
Las Orquídeas △ Colombia 6°36N 76°16W 328 B2
Las Palmas Argentina 27°8S 58°45W 334 B4
Las Palmas Canary Is. 28°7N 15°26W 153 e1
Las Palmas → Mexico 32°31N 116°58W 307 N10
Las Palmas ✕ (LPA)
  Canary Is. 27°55N 15°25W 153 e1
Las Pedroñas Spain 39°26N 2°40W 197 F2
Las Piedras Puerto Rico 18°11N 65°52W 321 b
Las Piedras Uruguay 34°44S 56°14W 335 C4
Las Pinas Phil. 14°29N 120°58E 127 C1
Las Pipinas Argentina 35°30S 57°19W 334 D4
Las Plumas Argentina 43°40S 67°15W 336 B3
Las Rejas Chile 33°27S 70°42W 137 B1
Las Rosas Argentina 32°30S 61°35W 334 C3
Las Rozas Spain 40°29N 3°52W 194 E7
Las Tablas Panama 7°49N 80°14W 320 E3
Las Toscas Argentina 28°21S 59°18W 334 B4
Las Truchas Mexico 17°57N 102°13W 318 D4
Las Tunas Cuba 20°58N 76°59W 320 B4
Las Varillas Argentina 31°50S 62°50W 334 C3
Las Vegas N. Mex.,
  U.S.A. 35°36N 105°13W 305 J11
Las Vegas Nev., U.S.A. 36°10N 115°8W 124 A2
Las Vegas McCarran Int. ✕ (LAS)
  U.S.A. 36°5N 115°9W 124 B2
Lasa = Lhasa China 29°25N 90°58E 218 F7
LaSalle Canada 45°26N 73°38W 130 B2
LaSalle Street Chicago, U.S.A. 119 a1
Lasanga I. Papua N. G. 7°25S 147°15E 286 D4
Lasarte-Oria Spain 43°16N 2°1W 196 B2
Lascano Uruguay 33°35S 54°12W 335 C5
Lascelles Australia 35°34S 142°34E 282 C5
Lasek Bielański Poland 52°17N 20°57E 142 B1
Lasek Na Kole Poland 52°15N 20°56E 142 B1
Lasek-le Joveyn Afghan. 31°45N 61°30E 240 C1
Lashburn Canada 53°10N 109°40W 297 C7
Lashio Burma 22°56N 97°45E 241 D6
Lashkar India 26°10N 78°10E 242 F8
Lashkar Gāh Afghan. 31°35N 64°21E 240 C2
Lasin Poland 53°30N 19°2E 184 E6
Lasithi Greece 35°11N 25°31E 207 E6
Lasithi □ Greece 35°5N 25°50E 207 E6
Låsjærd Iran 35°24N 53°4E 247 C7
Lask Poland 51°34N 19°8E 185 G6
Laskarzew Poland 51°48N 21°36E 185 G8
Laško Slovenia 46°10N 15°16E 198 B12
Lassance Brazil 17°54S 44°34W 333 E3
Lassay-les-Châteaux
  France 48°27N 0°30W 172 D6
Lassen Pk. U.S.A. 40°29N 121°30W 304 F3
Lassen Volcanic △
  U.S.A. 40°30N 121°20W 304 F3
Lassongo Angola 12°5S 22°46E 265 E4
Last Mountain L. Canada 51°5N 105°14W 297 C7
Lastchance Cr. → U.S.A. 40°2N 121°15W 306 E5
Lastoursville Gabon 0°55S 12°38E 264 E2
Lastovo Croatia 42°46N 16°55E 199 F13
Lastovski Kanal Croatia 42°50N 17°0W 199 F13
Lat Yao Thailand 15°45N 99°48E 236 E2
Lata Mt. Amer. Samoa 14°14S 169°27W 302 f
Latacunga Ecuador 0°50S 78°35W 328 D2
Latakia = Al Lādhiqīyah
  Syria 35°30N 35°45E 250 C6
Latchford Canada 47°20N 79°50W 298 C4
Late Tonga 18°48S 174°39W 287 P13
Latehar India 23°45N 84°30E 243 H10
Laterza Italy 40°38N 16°48E 201 B9
Latham Australia 29°44S 116°20E 279 E2
Lathen Germany 52°52N 7°19E 178 C3
Lathi India 27°43N 71°23E 242 G4
Lathi Vanuatu 14°57S 167°8E 287 D5
Lathrop U.S.A. 37°33N 94°20W 310 E2
Lathrop Wells U.S.A. 36°39N 116°24W 307 J10
Latiano Italy 40°33N 17°43E 201 B10
Latin, Quartier Montréal, Canada 130 B2
Latina Italy 41°28N 12°52E 200 A5
Latina Madrid, Spain 40°24N 3°44W 127 B1
Latium = Lazio □ Italy 42°10N 12°30E 199 C10
Laton U.S.A. 36°26N 119°41W 124 C2
Latorytsya → Slovak Rep. 48°28N 21°50E 181 C14
Latouche Treville, C.
  Australia 18°27S 121°49E 278 C3
Latouma Niger 22°10N 14°50E 259 D2
Látrar Iceland 66°24N 23°9W 155 A3
Latrobe Tas., Australia 41°14S 146°30E 281 G4
Latrobe U.S.A. 40°19N 79°23W 312 F5
Latrónico Italy 40°5N 16°1E 201 B9
Latur India 18°25N 76°40E 244 E3
Latvia ■ Europe 56°50N 24°0E 188 D2
Latviak Phil. 8°11N 117°33W 307 N10
Lau Nigeria 9°11N 11°19E 263 C7
Lau Basin Pac. Oc. 20°0S 177°0W 277 E15
Lau Fau Shan China 22°28N 113°55E 219 a
Lau Group Fiji 17°0S 178°30W 287 K14
Lau Ridge Pac. Oc. 20°0S 178°30W 287 M14
Lauban = Lubań Poland 51°5N 15°15E 185 G2
Lauca → Bolivia 19°9S 68°10W 330 D4

Lauchhammer Germany 51°29N 13°47E 178 D9
Lauda-Königshofen
  Germany 49°33N 9°42E 179 F5
Laudal Norway 58°15N 7°30E 164 F4
Laudat Dominica 15°20N 61°21W 323 k
Lauenbrug = Lębork
  Poland 54°33N 17°46E 184 D4
Lauenburg Germany 53°22N 10°33E 178 B6
Lauenburgische Seen □
  Germany 53°38N 10°45E 178 B6
Lauf Germany 49°30N 11°16E 179 F7
Laufás Iceland 65°53N 18°4W 155 B5
Laugar Iceland 65°15N 21°48W 155 B5
Laugarás Iceland 64°7N 20°30E 155 C5
Laugarbakki Iceland 65°20N 20°55W 155 B5
Laugarvatn Iceland 64°13N 20°44W 155 C5
Lauge Koch Kyst
  Greenland 75°45N 57°45W 295 B20
Laughlin U.S.A. 35°10N 114°34W 305 J6
Laujar de Andarax Spain 37°0N 2°54W 197 H2
Laukaa Finland 62°24N 25°56E 160 E21
Laulau, Bahia N. Marianas 15°8N 145°45E 302 e
Launceston Tas., Australia 41°24S 147°8E 281 G4
Launceston Corn., U.K. 50°38N 4°22W 169 G3
Laune → Ireland 52°7N 9°47W 166 D2
Launglon Bok Burma 13°50N 97°54E 236 F1
Laupheim Germany 48°14N 9°52E 179 G5
Laura Queens., Australia 15°32S 144°32E 280 B3
Laura S. Austral.,
  Australia 33°10S 138°18E 282 B3
Laureana di Borrello Italy 38°30N 16°5E 201 D9
Laurel Fla., U.S.A. 27°8N 82°27W 317 H7
Laurel Ind., U.S.A. 39°30N 85°11W 311 E11
Laurel Miss., U.S.A. 31°41N 89°8W 315 F10
Laurel Mont., U.S.A. 45°40N 108°46W 304 D9
Laurel Bay U.S.A. 32°27N 80°47W 316 C9
Laurel Hill U.S.A. 40°14N 79°6W 312 F5
Laurencekirk U.K. 56°50N 2°28W 167 E6
Laurens Iowa, U.S.A. 42°51N 94°52W 308 D2
Laurens S.C., U.S.A. 34°30N 82°1W 315 D13
Laurentian Plateau Canada 52°0N 70°0W 299 B6
Lauria Italy 40°2N 15°50E 201 B8
Laurie L. Canada 56°35N 101°57W 297 B8
Laurinburg U.S.A. 34°47N 79°28W 315 D15
Laurium U.S.A. 47°14N 88°27W 308 B9
Lausanne Switz. 46°32N 6°38E 179 J2
Laut Indonesia 4°45N 108°0E 235 B3
Laut, Pulau Indonesia 3°40S 116°10E 235 C5
Laut Kecil, Kepulauan
  Indonesia 4°45S 115°40E 235 C5
Lautaro Chile 38°31S 72°27W 336 A2
Lauterbach Germany 50°37N 9°24E 178 E5
Lauterecken Germany 49°38N 7°35E 179 F3
Lautoka Fiji 17°37S 177°27E 287 A1
L'Autre Bord Guadeloupe 16°20N 61°20W 322 e
Lauttasaari Finland 60°9N 24°53E 121 C2
Lauwe Belgium 50°44N 3°15E 174 B1
Lauzon Canada 46°50N 71°10W 131 B5
Lava → Russia 54°37N 21°14E 184 D8
Lava Beds △ U.S.A. 41°40N 121°30W 304 F3
Lavagh More Ireland 54°46N 8°6W 166 B3
Lavagna Italy 44°18N 9°22E 198 D6
Laval France 48°4N 0°48W 172 D6
Laval-des-Rapides Canada 45°33N 73°42W 130 A1
Lavalle Argentina 28°15S 65°15W 334 B2
Lāvān Iran 26°48N 53°22E 247 F7
Lavanggu Solomon Is. 11°36S 160°16E 287 N11
Lavant Canada 45°3N 76°42W 313 A8
Lavardac France 44°12N 0°20E 174 D4
Lavau France 43°40N 1°49E 174 E5
Lavelanet France 42°57N 1°51E 174 F5
Lavello Italy 41°3N 15°48E 201 A8
L'Avery, C. Papua N. G. 5°33S 155°4E 286 C8
Lavers Hill Australia 38°40S 143°25E 282 E5
Laverton Australia 28°44S 122°29E 279 E3
Lavik Norway 61°6N 5°25E 164 C2
Lavis Italy 46°8N 11°7E 198 B8
Lavizān Iran 35°47N 51°30E 141 A2
Lavos Portugal 40°6N 8°49W 194 E2
Lavras Brazil 21°20S 45°0W 333 F3
Lavre Portugal 38°46N 8°22W 195 G2
Lavrio Greece 37°40N 24°4E 207 D6
Lavris Greece 35°25N 24°40E 207 D6
Lavumisa Swaziland 27°0S 31°55E 271 C5
Lavushi Manda △ Zambia 12°46S 31°0E 269 E3
Lawa → Phil. 11°5N 125°41E 233 H5
Lawa-an Phil. 11°5N 125°3E 233 F5
Lawaki Fiji 17°40S 178°35E 287 A2
Lawas Malaysia 4°55N 115°25E 235 B5
Lawdar Yemen 13°53N 45°52E 248 E4
Lawele Indonesia 5°13S 122°57E 231 F6
Lawit Indonesia 1°23N 112°55E 234 B4
Lawksawk Burma 21°15N 96°52E 241 D7
Lawn Hill = Boodjamulla △
  Australia 18°15S 138°6E 280 C2
Lawndale U.S.A. 41°50N 87°42W 119 B2
Lawne L. U.S.A. 28°36N 81°26W 128 A2
Lawqah Si. Arabia 29°49N 42°45E 246 D4
Lawra Ghana 10°39N 2°51W 262 C4
Lawrence N.Z. 45°55S 169°41E 285 F4
Lawrence Ind., U.S.A. 39°50N 86°2W 311 E10
Lawrence Kans., U.S.A. 38°58N 95°14W 308 F2
Lawrence Mass., U.S.A. 42°43N 71°10W 313 D13
Lawrence Heights Canada 43°43N 79°27W 141 A2
Lawrenceburg U.S.A.
Lawrenceburg Ky., U.S.A. 38°2N 84°53W 311 G12
Lawrenceburg Tenn.,
  U.S.A. 35°14N 87°20W 315 D11
Lawrenceville Ga., U.S.A. 33°57N 83°59W 316 B6
Lawrenceville Ill., U.S.A. 38°44N 87°41W 311 F9
Lawrenceville Pa., U.S.A. 41°59N 77°8W 312 E7
Laws U.S.A. 37°24N 118°20W 306 H8
Lawson U.S.A. 39°26N 94°12W 308 G12
Lawtey U.S.A. 30°3N 82°5W 316 D6
Lawton Mich., U.S.A. 42°10N 85°50W 311 B11
Lawton Okla., U.S.A. 34°37N 98°25W 314 D5
Lawu Indonesia 7°40S 111°13E 235 D4
Lawz, J. al Si. Arabia 28°39N 35°18E 246 E2
Laxå Sweden 58°59N 14°37E 163 F8
Laxamýri Iceland 65°56N 17°24W 155 B9
Laxford, L. U.K. 58°24N 5°6W 167 C3
Laxou France 48°41N 6°8E 173 D13
Lay → France 46°18N 1°1W 172 F5
Layari → Pakistan 24°52N 66°58E 123 A1
Laylá Si. Arabia 22°10N 46°40E 248 B4
Laylán Iraq 35°18N 44°31E 246 C5
Layon → France 47°20N 0°45W 172 E6
Laysan I. Pac. Oc. 25°30N 167°0W 287 M10
Layton U.S.A. 41°4N 111°58W 304 E7
Laytonville U.S.A. 39°41N 123°29W 306 G2
Lazarato Greece 38°47N 20°48E 204 C3
Lazarev Russia 52°13N 141°30E 215 D15
Lazarev Sea S. Ocean 67°30S 51°0E 151 C2
Lazarevac Serbia 44°23N 20°17E 202 B4
Lazarevskoye Russia 43°55N 39°21E 191 H4
Lazarivo Madag. 23°54S 44°59E 272 C1

Lázaro Cárdenas Mexico 17°55N 102°11W 318 D4
Lazdijai Lithuania 54°14N 23°31E 184 D10
Lazhuglung China 34°52N 81°24E 217 F10
Lazi Phil. 9°8N 123°38E 233 G4
Lazienki Palace Warsaw, Poland 142 c3
Lazio □ Italy 42°10N 12°30E 199 F9
Lazo Moldova 47°33N 28°2E 183 C13
Lazo Russia 43°25N 133°55E 220 C6
Lbishchensk = Chapaev
  Kazakhstan 50°25N 51°10E 190 E10
Leba Poland 54°45N 17°32E 184 D4
Leba → Poland 54°46N 17°32E 184 D4
Lebach Germany 49°25N 6°54E 179 F2
Lebak Phil. 6°32N 124°5E 233 H5
Lebam U.S.A. 46°34N 123°33W 306 D3
Lebango Congo 0°39N 14°21E 264 B2
Lebango → Congo 0°2N 14°52E 264 B2
Lebanon Ind., U.S.A. 40°3N 86°28W 311 D10
Lebanon Ill., U.S.A. 38°36N 89°49W 311 F8
Lebanon Kans., U.S.A. 39°49N 98°33W 308 F4
Lebanon Ky., U.S.A. 37°34N 85°15W 309 G11
Lebanon Mo., U.S.A. 37°41N 92°40W 310 G6
Lebanon N.H., U.S.A. 43°39N 72°15W 313 C12
Lebanon Ohio, U.S.A. 39°26N 84°13W 311 G12
Lebanon Pa., U.S.A. 40°20N 76°26W 313 F8
Lebanon Tenn., U.S.A. 36°12N 86°18W 315 C11
Lebanon ■ Asia 34°0N 36°0E 250 C7
Lebanon Junction
  U.S.A. 37°50N 85°44W 311 G11
Lebap □ Turkmenistan 40°0N 63°0E 216 C6
Lebedyan Russia 53°0N 39°10E 189 F10
Lebel-sur-Quévillon
  Canada 49°3N 76°59W 298 C4
Leblon Brazil 22°59S 43°14W 135 B1
Lebo Dem. Rep. of the Congo 4°30N 23°58E 264 B4
Lebomboberge S. Africa 24°30S 32°0E 271 B5
Lebork Poland 54°33N 17°46E 184 D4
Lebowakgomo S. Africa 24°12S 29°30E 271 B4
Lebrija Spain 36°53N 6°5W 195 J4
Lebsko, Jezioro Poland 54°40N 17°25E 184 D4
Lebu Chile 37°40N 73°47W 334 D1
Leca da Palmeira Portugal 41°12N 8°42W 194 D2
Lecce Italy 40°23N 18°11E 201 B11
Lecco Italy 45°51N 9°23E 198 C6
Lecco, L. di Italy 45°51N 9°25E 198 C6
Lécera Spain 41°13N 0°43W 196 D4
Lech Austria 47°13N 10°9E 180 D3
Lech → Germany 48°43N 10°56E 179 G6
Lechang China 25°10N 113°20E 229 E9
Lechena Greece 37°57N 21°16E 204 D3
Lechtaler Alpen Austria 47°15N 10°30E 180 D3
Lecontes Mills U.S.A. 41°5N 78°17W 312 E6
Lectoure France 43°56N 0°38E 174 E4
Łęczna Poland 51°18N 22°53E 185 G9
Łęczyca Poland 52°5N 19°15E 185 F6
Ledang, Gunung Malaysia 2°22N 102°37E 237 L4
Ledesma Spain 41°6N 5°59W 194 D5
Lediba Dem. Rep. of the Congo 3°1S 16°34E 264 C3
Ledong China 18°41N 109°5E 236 C7
Leduc Canada 53°15N 113°30W 296 C6
Lee → U.K. 51°53N 8°56W 166 E3
Lee Fla., U.S.A. 30°25N 83°18W 316 E6
Lee Mass., U.S.A. 42°19N 73°15W 313 D11
Lee → Ireland 51°53N 8°56W 166 E3
Lee Vining U.S.A. 37°58N 119°7W 306 H7
Leech L. U.S.A. 47°10N 94°24W 308 B3
Leechburg U.S.A. 40°37N 79°36W 312 F5
Leeds U.K. 53°48N 1°33W 168 D6
Leeds Ala., U.S.A. 33°33N 86°33W 315 C11
Leek Neths. 53°10N 6°24E 178 A6
Leek Staffs., U.K. 53°7N 2°1W 168 D5
Leeman Australia 29°57S 114°58E 279 E1
Leeming U.S.A. 41°22N 91°89W 312 E6
Leer Germany 53°13N 7°26E 178 B3
Lee's Summit U.S.A. 38°55N 94°23W 310 F2
Leesburg Fla., U.S.A. 28°49N 81°53W 317 G8
Leesburg Ohio, U.S.A. 39°21N 83°33W 311 E13
Leeston N.Z. 43°45S 172°19E 285 F7
Leesville U.S.A. 31°8N 93°16W 314 F7
Leeton Australia 34°33S 146°23E 283 C7
Leetonia U.S.A. 40°53N 80°45W 312 F4
Leeu Gamka S. Africa 32°47S 21°59E 270 D3
Leeuwarden Neths. 53°15N 5°48E 178 A6
Leeuwin, C. Australia 34°20S 115°9E 279 F2
Leeward Is. Atl. Oc. 16°30N 63°30W 323 C7
Lefini → Congo 2°55S 16°20E 264 C3
Léfini Congo 2°55S 15°20E 264 C3
Lefka Cyprus 35°6N 32°51E 207 D8
Lefkada Greece 38°40N 20°43E 204 C3
Lefkimis, Akra Greece 39°29N 20°4E 206 C10
Lefkosa Ukraine 35°18N 33°44E 207 D9
Lefroy Canada 44°16N 79°34W 312 B5
Lefroy, L. Australia 31°21S 121°40E 279 F3
Leg → Poland 50°42N 21°50E 185 H8
Leganés Spain 40°19N 3°45W 127 C1
Legazpi Phil. 13°10N 123°45E 232 E4
Lège-Cap-Ferret France 44°48N 1°9W 174 D2
Legendre I. Australia 20°22S 116°55E 278 D2
Leghorn = Livorno Italy 43°33N 10°19E 198 E7
Legian Indonesia 8°42S 115°10E 231 K18
Legionowo Poland 52°25N 20°50E 185 F7
Legnago Italy 45°11N 11°18E 198 C8
Legnano Italy 45°36N 8°53E 198 C5
Legnica Poland 51°12N 16°10E 185 G3
Legrad Croatia 46°17N 16°51E 199 B13
Leh India 34°9N 77°35E 243 B7
Lehigh Acres U.S.A. 26°36N 81°39W 317 J8
Lehighton U.S.A. 40°50N 75°43W 313 F9
Lehliu Romania 44°29N 26°50E 183 F11
Lehua → Sudan 7°7N 33°5E 257 F3
Lehrte Germany 52°22N 9°58E 178 C5
Lehtsaari Finland 60°10N 24°51E 121 B2
Lehututu Botswana 23°54S 21°55E 270 B3
Lei Shui → China 26°55N 112°35E 229 E9
Leiah Pakistan 30°58N 70°58E 242 D4
Leião Portugal 38°43N 9°17W 126 A1
Leibnitz Austria 46°47N 15°34E 180 E8
Leibo China 28°11N 103°34E 228 C4
Leicester U.K. 52°38N 1°8W 169 E6
Leicester City □ U.K. 52°38N 1°9W 169 E6
Leicester Square London, U.K. 125 b3
Leicestershire □ U.K. 52°41N 1°17W 169 E6
Leichhardt → Australia 17°35S 139°48E 280 B2
Leichhardt Australia 33°53S 151°9E 139 E6
Leichhardt Ra. Australia 20°46S 147°40E 280 C4
Leie → Belgium 51°2N 3°45E 174 B1
Leigh → U.K. 51°31N 0°1E 169 F8
Leigh Australia 38°18S 144°30E 282 E6
Leigh Creek Australia 30°38S 138°26E 282 A3

Leikang *Norway* 62°15N 5°47E **164** B2
Leikanger *Sogn og Fjordane, Norway* 62°8N 5°18E **164** B2
Leikanger *Sogn og Fjordane, Norway* 61°10N 6°51E **164** C3
Leiktho *Burma* 19°13N 96°35E **241** F6
Leimen *Germany* 49°21N 8°41E **179** F4
Leimus *Nic.* 14°40N 84°3W **320** D3
Leine → *Germany* 52°43N 9°36E **178** C5
Leinefelde *Germany* 51°23N 10°19E **178** D6
Leinster *Australia* 27°51S 120°36E **279** E3
Leinster □ *Ireland* 53°3N 7°8W **166** C4
Leinster, Mt. *Ireland* 52°37N 6°46W **166** D5
Leipalingis *Lithuania* 54°5N 23°51E **184** D10
Leipe = Lipno *Poland* 52°49N 19°15E **185** F6
Leipzig *Germany* 51°18N 12°22E **178** D8
Leira *Norway* 60°58N 9°17E **164** D6
Leiria *Portugal* 39°46N 8°53W **194** F2
Leiria □ *Portugal* 39°46N 8°53W **194** F2
Leirvassbu *Norway* 61°33N 8°13E **164** C5
Leirvik *Norway* 59°47N 5°28E **164** E2
Leishan *China* 26°15N 108°20E **228** D7
Leisler, Mt. *Australia* 23°23S 129°20E **278** D4
Leisure City *U.S.A.* 25°30N 80°26W **317** K9
Leith *U.K.* 55°59N 3°11W **121** B3
Leith Hill *U.K.* 51°11N 0°22W **169** F7
Leitha → *Europe* 47°50N 17°15E **181** D10
Leitir Ceanainn = Letterkenny *Ireland* 54°57N 7°45W **166** B4
Leitrim *Ireland* 54°0N 8°5W **166** B3
Leitrim □ *Ireland* 54°8N 8°0W **166** B4
Leitza *Spain* 43°5N 1°55W **196** B3
Leiyang *China* 26°27N 112°45E **229** D9
Leizhou *China* 20°52N 110°8E **229** G8
Leizhou Bandao *China* 21°0N 110°0E **228** G7
Leizhou Wan *China* 20°50N 110°20E **229** G8
Lek → *Neths.* 51°54N 4°35E **170** C4
Leka *Norway* 65°5N 11°35E **160** D14
Lekani *Greece* 41°10N 24°35E **203** E8
Lekbibaj *Albania* 42°17N 19°56E **202** D3
Lekeitio *Spain* 43°20N 2°32W **196** B2
Lékéti, Mt. *Congo* 2°34S 14°17E **264** C2
Lekki *Nigeria* 6°26N 3°28E **124** B2
Lekki Lagoon *Nigeria* 6°30N 4°7E **263** D5
Léko *Mali* 13°37N 9°2W **262** C3
Lékoli-Pandaka ⌓ *Congo* 0°41N 14°50E **264** B2
Lékoni *Gabon* 1°35S 14°14E **264** C2
Lékoni → *Gabon* 1°11S 13°16E **264** C2
Lekoui *Burkina Faso* 12°37N 3°40W **262** C4
Leksand *Sweden* 60°44N 15°1E **162** D9
Leksura = Lentekhi *Georgia* 42°47N 42°45E **191** J6
Leland *Mich., U.S.A.* 45°1N 85°45W **309** C11
Leland *Miss., U.S.A.* 33°24N 90°54W **315** E9
Lelång *Sweden* 59°10N 12°5E **162** E6
Lelepa *Vanuatu* 17°35S 168°11E **287** G6
Leleque *Argentina* 42°28S 71°0W **336** B2
Leli *Solomon Is.* 8°42S 161°4E **287** M11
Leling *China* 37°44N 117°13E **227** F9
Lélouma *Guinea* 11°11N 12°56W **262** C2
Lelu *Burma* 19°4N 95°30E **241** F5
Lelydorp *Suriname* 5°42N 55°14W **329** B6
Lelystad *Neths.* 52°30N 5°25E **170** B5
Lem *Denmark* 56°1N 8°24E **163** H2
Lema *Nigeria* 12°58N 4°13E **263** C5
Lema Shilindi *Ethiopia* 4°50N 42°6E **257** G5
Léman, L. *Europe* 46°26N 6°30E **173** F13
Lemankoa *Papua N. G.* 5°3S 154°34E **286** C8
Lembar *Indonesia* 8°45S 116°4E **231** K19
Lemberg = Lviv *Ukraine* 49°50N 24°0E **177** D13
Lembongan, Nusa *Indonesia* 8°40S 115°27E **231** K18
Lembuak *Indonesia* 8°36S 116°11E **231** K19
Leme *Brazil* 22°58S 43°10W **135** B1
Lemera *Dem. Rep. of the Congo* 3°0S 28°55E **268** C2
Lemery *Phil.* 13°51N 120°56E **232** E3
Lemfu *Dem. Rep. of the Congo* 5°18S 15°13E **265** D3
Lemhi Ra. *U.S.A.* 44°0N 113°0W **304** D7
Lemmer *Neths.* 52°51N 5°43E **170** B5
Lemmon *U.S.A.* 45°57N 102°10W **308** C2
Lemon Grove *U.S.A.* 32°44N 117°1W **307** N9
Lemoore *U.S.A.* 36°18N 119°46W **306** J7
Lemotol B. *Micronesia* 7°21N 151°35E **287** T17
Lemoyne *Canada* 45°29N 73°29W **130** B3
Lempdes *France* 45°22N 3°17E **174** C7
Lemsid *W. Sahara* 26°33N 13°51W **260** C2
Lemukutan *Indonesia* 0°45N 108°43E **235** B3
Lemvig *Denmark* 56°33N 8°20E **163** H2
Lemyethna *Burma* 17°36N 95°9E **241** G5
Lena *U.S.A.* 42°23N 89°49W **310** B7
Lena → *Russia* 72°52N 126°40E **215** B13
Lenadoon Pt. *Ireland* 54°18N 9°3W **166** B2
Lenakel *Vanuatu* 19°38S 169°16E **287** J7
Lenart *Slovenia* 46°36N 15°48E **199** B12
Lenartovce *Slovak Rep.* 48°18N 20°19E **181** C13
Lencloître *France* 46°50N 0°20E **172** F7
Lençóis *Brazil* 12°35S 41°24W **333** D3
Lençóis Maranhenses △ *Brazil* 2°30S 43°0W **332** B3
Lendava *Slovenia* 46°35N 16°25E **199** B13
Lendinara *Italy* 45°5N 11°36E **199** C8
Lenger *Kazakhstan* 42°12N 69°54E **217** D7
Lengerich *Germany* 52°11N 7°52E **178** C3
Lenggong *Malaysia* 5°6N 100°58E **237** K3
Lenggries *Germany* 47°41N 11°35E **179** H7
Léngoué *Congo* 1°15N 15°38E **264** B3
Lengshuijiang *China* 27°40N 111°26E **229** D8
Lengshuitan *China* 26°27N 111°35E **229** D8
Lengua de Vaca, Pta. *Chile* 30°14S 71°38W **334** C1
Lengwe △ *Malawi* 16°14S 34°45E **269** F3
Lengwethen = Lunino *Russia* 53°38N 45°18E **190** D7
Lengyeltóti *Hungary* 46°40N 17°40E **182** D2
Lengyeltótihács = Lengyeltóti *Hungary* 46°40N 17°40E **182** D2
Lenhovda *Sweden* 57°0N 15°16E **163** G9
Lenin *Russia* 55°43N 37°34E **129** B3
Lenin Mausoleum *Moscow, Russia* **129** b2
Lenina, Kanal → *Russia* 43°44N 45°17E **191** J7
Leninabad = Khŭjand *Tajikistan* 40°17N 69°37E **217** D7
Leninakan = Gyumri *Armenia* 40°47N 43°50E **191** K6
Lenine *Ukraine* 45°17N 35°46E **189** K8
Leningrad = Sankt-Peterburg *Russia* 59°55N 30°20E **137** B1
Leningrad □ *Russia* 59°40N 32°0E **188** C7
Lenino = Leninsk-Kuznetskiy *Russia* 54°44N 86°10E **217** B11
Lenino *Russia* 55°38N 37°39E **129** C3
Leninogorsk *Kazakhstan* 50°20N 83°30E **217** B10
Leninogorsk *Russia* 54°36N 52°30E **216** B4
Leninsk = Petrodvorets *Russia* 59°52N 29°54E **188** C5
Leninsk *Russia* 48°40N 45°15E **191** F7
Leninsk-Kuznetskiy *Russia* 54°44N 86°10E **217** B11
Leninsk-Turkmensky = Türkmenabat *Turkmenistan* 39°6N 63°34E **247** B9
Leninskiye Gory *Russia* 55°41N 37°32E **129** B3
Leninskoye *Russia* 58°23N 47°3E **190** A8
Lenk *Switz.* 46°27N 7°28E **179** J3
Lenkoran = Länkäran *Azerbaijan* 38°48N 48°52E **213** C13
Lenmalu *Indonesia* 1°45S 130°15E **231** E8
Lennartsfors *Sweden* 59°20N 11°55E **162** E5
Lenne → *Germany* 51°25N 7°29E **178** D3
Lennestadt *Germany* 51°8N 8°2E **178** D4
Lennox *Calif., U.S.A.* 33°56N 118°20W **126** C2
Lennox *S. Dak., U.S.A.* 43°21N 96°53W **308** D5
Lennox, I. *Chile* 55°18S 66°50W **336** E3
Lennoxville *Canada* 45°22N 71°51W **313** A13
Leno *Italy* 45°22N 10°13E **198** C7
Lenoir *U.S.A.* 35°55N 81°32W **315** D14
Lenoir City *U.S.A.* 35°48N 84°16W **315** D12
Lenore L. *Canada* 52°30N 104°59W **297** C8
Lenox *Ga., U.S.A.* 31°16N 83°28W **316** D6
Lenox *Iowa, U.S.A.* 40°53N 94°34W **310** D2
Lenox *Mass., U.S.A.* 42°22N 73°17W **313** D11
Lens *France* 50°26N 2°50E **173** B9
Lensahn *Germany* 54°13N 10°53E **178** A6
Lensk *Russia* 60°48N 114°55E **215** C12
Lensvik *Norway* 63°31N 9°48E **164** A6
Lentas *Greece* 34°56N 24°56E **207** F5
Lentekhi *Georgia* 42°47N 42°45E **191** J6
Lenti *Hungary* 46°37N 16°33E **182** D1
Lentini *Italy* 37°17N 15°0E **201** E8
Lentschütz = Łęczyca *Poland* 52°5N 19°15E **185** F6
Lenwood *U.S.A.* 34°53N 117°7W **307** L9
Lenya *Burma* 11°33N 98°57E **237** G2
Lenzen *Germany* 53°5N 11°29E **178** B7
Léo *Burkina Faso* 11°3N 2°2W **262** C4
Leoben *Austria* 47°22N 15°5E **180** D8
Leobschütz = Głubczyce *Poland* 50°13N 17°52E **185** H4
Leodhas = Lewis *U.K.* 58°9N 6°40W **167** C2
Leola *U.S.A.* 45°43N 98°56W **308** C4
Leominster *Hereford, U.K.* 52°14N 2°43W **169** E5
Leominster *Mass., U.S.A.* 42°32N 71°46W **313** D13
León = Cotopaxi □ *Ecuador* 0°5S 78°55W **328** D2
León *Landes, France* 43°53N 1°18W **174** E2
León *Guanajuato, Mexico* 21°6N 101°41W **318** C4
León *Nic.* 12°27N 86°51W **320** D2
León *Spain* 42°38N 5°34W **194** C5
Leon *Iowa, U.S.A.* 40°44N 93°45W **310** D3
León □ *Spain* 42°40N 5°55W **194** C5
Leon → *U.S.A.* 31°14N 97°28W **314** F6
León, Montes de *Spain* 42°30N 6°18W **194** C4
Leonardo da Vinci, Roma ✈ **(FCO)** *Italy* 41°48N 12°15E **199** G9
Leonardtown *U.S.A.* 38°17N 76°38W **309** F15
Leonardville *Namibia* 23°29S 18°49E **270** B2
Leonberg *Germany* 48°48N 9°1E **179** G5
Leonding *Austria* 48°16N 14°15E **180** C7
Leone *Amer. Samoa* 14°23S 170°48W **302** f
Leonessa *Italy* 42°34N 12°58E **199** F9
Leonforte *Italy* 37°38N 14°23E **201** E7
Leongatha *Australia* 38°30S 145°58E **283** E6
Leonia *Fla., U.S.A.* 30°55N 86°1W **316** E3
Leonia *N.J., U.S.A.* 40°51N 73°59W **132** A2
Leonidio *Greece* 37°9N 22°52E **204** D4
Leonora *Australia* 28°49S 121°19E **279** E3
Leopardstown *Ireland* 53°16N 6°11W **120** B2
Leopold II, L. = Mai-Ndombe, L. *Dem. Rep. of the Congo* 2°0S 18°20E **264** C3
Leopoldau *Austria* 48°15N 16°26E **142** A2
Leopoldina = Aruanã *Brazil* 14°54S 51°10W **333** D1
Leopoldina = Parnamirim *Brazil* 8°5S 39°34W **332** C4
Leopoldina *Brazil* 21°28S 42°40W **333** F3
Leopoldo Bulhões *Brazil* 16°37S 48°46W **333** E2
Leopoldsburg *Belgium* 51°7N 5°13E **170** C5
Leopoldsdorf *Austria* 48°7N 16°23E **142** B2
Leopoldstadt *Austria* 48°13N 16°22E **142** A2
Leopoldville = Kinshasa *Dem. Rep. of the Congo* 4°20S 15°15E **265** C3
Leoti *U.S.A.* 38°29N 101°21W **308** F3
Leova *Moldova* 46°28N 28°15E **183** D13
Leoville *Canada* 53°39N 107°33W **297** C7
Lepar *Indonesia* 2°57S 106°49E **234** C3
Lepe *Spain* 37°15N 7°12W **195** H3
Lepel = Lyepyel *Belarus* 54°50N 28°40E **188** E5
Lepenou *Greece* 38°42N 21°17E **204** C3
Leping *China* 28°47N 117°7E **229** C11
Lépo, L. do *Angola* 17°0S 19°0E **265** F3
Lepontine, Alpi *Italy* 46°22N 8°27E **198** B5
Leportovo *Russia* 55°46N 37°43E **129** B4
Leposavić *Kosovo* 43°6N 20°48E **202** C4
Leppävaara *Finland* 60°13N 24°49E **121** B1
Leppävirta *Finland* 62°29N 27°46E **160** E22
Lepsény *Hungary* 47°0N 18°15E **182** D3
Leptis Magna *Libya* 32°40N 14°12E **258** B2
Lequeitio = Lekeitio *Spain* 43°20N 2°32W **196** B2
Lercara Friddi *Italy* 37°45N 13°36E **200** E6
Léré *C.A.R.* 6°46N 17°25E **264** A3
Léré *Chad* 9°39N 14°13E **259** G2
Léré *Mali* 15°45N 4°55W **262** B4
Lere *Bauchi, Nigeria* 9°43N 9°18E **263** D6
Lere *Kaduna, Nigeria* 10°23N 8°35E **263** C6
Leribe *Lesotho* 28°51S 28°3E **271** C4
Lérici *Italy* 44°4N 9°55E **198** D6
Lérida = Lleida *Spain* 41°37N 0°39E **196** D5
Lérins, Îs. de *France* 43°31N 7°3E **175** E11
Lerma *Spain* 42°0N 3°47W **194** C7
Leros *Greece* 37°10N 26°50E **205** D8
Lérouville *France* 48°44N 5°30E **173** D12
Lerum *Sweden* 57°46N 12°16E **163** G6
Lerwick *U.K.* 60°9N 1°9W **167** A7
Les *Romania* 46°58N 21°50E **182** D6
Les Abrets *France* 45°32N 5°35E **175** C9
Les Abymes *Guadeloupe* 16°17N 61°32W **322** e
Les Andelys *France* 49°15N 1°25E **172** C8
Les Anses-d'Arlets *Martinique* 14°28N 61°6W **322** j
Les Avirons *Réunion* 21°14S 55°20E **272** f
Les Borges Blanques *Spain* 41°31N 0°52E **196** D5
Les Cayes *Haiti* 18°15N 73°46W **321** C5
Les Coteaux *Canada* 45°15N 74°13W **313** A10
Les Escoumins *Canada* 48°21N 69°24W **299** C6
Les Essarts *France* 46°47N 1°12W **172** F5
Les Grands Fonds *Guadeloupe* 16°16N 61°26W **322** e
Les Herbiers *France* 46°52N 1°1W **172** F5
Les Lilas *France* 48°52N 2°25E **134** A3
Les Loges-en-Josas *France* 48°45N 2°8E **134** B1
Les Mangles *Guadeloupe* 16°23N 61°27W **322** e
Les Minquiers, Plateau des *Chan. Is.* 48°58N 2°8W **172** D4
Les Moroubas *C.A.R.* 6°11N 20°13E **264** A4
Les Pavillons-sous-Bois *France* 48°54N 2°30E **134** A4
Les Pieux *France* 49°30N 1°48W **172** C5
Les Ponts-de-Cé *France* 47°25N 0°30W **172** E6
Les Riceys *France* 47°59N 4°22E **173** E11
Les Sables-d'Olonne *France* 46°30N 1°45W **174** B2
Les Tantes *Grenada* 12°19N 61°33W **323** q
Les Trois-Bassins *Réunion* 21°5S 55°18E **272** f
Les Trois-Îlets *Martinique* 14°32N 61°2W **322** j
Les Vans *France* 44°25N 4°7E **175** D8
Lesbos *Greece* 39°10N 26°20E **205** B8
L'Escala *Spain* 42°7N 3°8E **196** C8
L'Escalier *Mauritius* 20°28S 57°36E **272** e
Leschnitz = Leśnica *Poland* 50°26N 18°11E **185** H5
Leshan *China* 29°33N 103°41E **228** C4
Leshukonskoye *Russia* 64°54N 45°46E **186** B8
Leshwe ⌓ *Dem. Rep. of the Congo* 12°45S 29°30E **269** E2
Lésigny *France* 48°44N 2°37E **134** B4
Lésina *Italy* 41°52N 15°21E **199** G12
Lésina, L. di *Italy* 41°53N 15°26E **199** G12
Lesjaskog *Norway* 62°14N 8°22E **164** B5
Lesjaverk *Norway* 62°12N 8°34E **164** B5
Lesjöfors *Sweden* 59°58N 14°11E **162** E8
Leskhimstroy = Syeverodonetsk *Ukraine* 48°58N 38°35E **189** H10
Lesko *Poland* 49°30N 22°23E **185** J9
Leskov I. *Antarctica* 56°0S 28°0W **151** B1
Leskovac *Serbia* 43°0N 21°58E **202** C5
Leskovik *Albania* 40°10N 20°34E **202** F4
Leslau = Włocławek *Poland* 52°40N 19°3E **185** F6
Leslie *Ga., U.S.A.* 31°57N 84°5W **316** D5
Leslie *Mich., U.S.A.* 42°27N 84°26W **311** B12
Leśna *Poland* 51°1N 15°15E **185** G2
Lesneven *France* 48°35N 4°20W **172** D2
Leśnica *Poland* 50°26N 18°11E **185** H5
Lešnica *Serbia* 44°39N 19°20E **202** B3
Lesnoi = Umba *Russia* 66°42N 34°11E **186** A5
Lesnoye *Russia* 58°15N 35°18E **188** C8
Lesnozavodskaya *Russia* 59°51N 30°29E **137** B2
Lesopilnoye *Russia* 46°44N 134°20E **220** A7
Lesotho ■ *Africa* 29°40S 28°0E **271** C4
Lesozavodsk *Russia* 45°30N 133°29E **220** B6
Lesparre-Médoc *France* 45°18N 0°57W **174** C3
L'Espluga de Francolí *Spain* 41°24N 1°7E **196** D6
Lessay *France* 49°14N 1°30W **172** C5
Lesse → *Belgium* 50°15N 4°54E **170** D4
Lesse et Lomme ⌓ *Belgium* 50°8N 5°9E **170** D5
Lessebo *Sweden* 56°45N 15°16E **163** H9
Lesser Antilles *W. Indies* 15°0N 61°0W **321** D7
Lesser Slave L. *Canada* 55°30N 115°25W **296** B5
Lesser Sunda Is. *Indonesia* 8°0S 120°0E **235** D5
Lessines *Belgium* 50°42N 3°50E **170** D3
Lester B. Pearson Int., Toronto ✈ **(YYZ)** *Canada* 43°46N 79°35W **141** A1
L'Esterre *Grenada* 12°28N 61°29W **323** q
Lestershire = Johnson City *U.S.A.* 42°7N 75°58W **313** D9
Lestock *Canada* 51°19N 103°59W **297** C8
Lesuer I. *Australia* 13°50S 127°17E **278** B4
Lesueur △ *Australia* 30°11S 115°10E **279** F2
Lesung *Indonesia* 0°42N 114°42E **235** B4
Lésvos = Lesbos *Greece* 39°10N 26°20E **205** B8
Leszno *Poland* 51°50N 16°30E **185** G3
Letaba *S. Africa* 23°59S 31°50E **271** B5
Letälven → *Sweden* 59°5N 14°20E **162** E8
L'Étang-la-Ville *France* 48°52N 2°4E **134** A1
L'Étang-Salé *Réunion* 21°15S 55°23E **272** f
Létavértes *Hungary* 47°23N 21°55E **182** C6
Letchworth *U.K.* 51°59N 0°13W **169** F7
Letea, Ostrov *Romania* 45°18N 29°20E **183** E14
Lethbridge *Canada* 49°45N 112°45W **296** D6
Lethem *Guyana* 3°20N 59°50W **329** C6
Leti, Kepulauan *Indonesia* 8°10S 128°0E **231** F7
Leti Is. = Leti, Kepulauan *Indonesia* 8°10S 128°0E **231** F7
Letiahau → *Botswana* 21°16S 24°0E **270** B3
Leticia *Colombia* 4°9S 70°0W **328** D4
Leting *China* 39°23N 118°55E **227** E10
Letjiesbos *S. Africa* 32°34S 22°16E **270** D3
Letlhakane *Botswana* 21°27S 25°30E **270** B4
Letlhakeng *Botswana* 24°0S 24°59E **270** B3
Letná *Prague, Czech Rep.* **135** a2
Letňany *Czech Rep.* 50°8N 14°30E **135** B3
Letopolis = Ausîm *Egypt* 30°7N 31°8E **117** A1
Letpadan *Burma* 17°45N 95°45E **241** G5
Letpan *Burma* 19°28N 94°10E **241** F5
Letsôk-aw Kyun *Burma* 11°30N 98°25E **237** G2
Letterkenny *Ireland* 54°57N 7°45W **166** B4
Leu *Romania* 44°10N 24°0E **183** F9
Léua *Angola* 11°34S 20°32E **265** E4
Leucadia *U.S.A.* 33°4N 117°18W **307** M9
Leucate *France* 42°56N 3°3E **174** F7
Leucate, Étang de *France* 42°50N 3°0E **174** F7
Leuchars *U.K.* 56°24N 2°53W **167** E6
Leuk *Switz.* 46°19N 7°37E **179** J3
Leușeni *Moldova* 46°49N 28°12E **183** D13
Leuser, Gunung *Indonesia* 3°46N 97°12E **234** B1
Leusoalii *Amer. Samoa* 14°14S 169°25W **302** f
Leutkirch *Germany* 47°49N 10°1E **179** H6
Leutschau = Levoča *Slovak Rep.* 49°2N 20°35E **181** B13
Leuven *Belgium* 50°52N 4°42E **170** D4
Leuze-en-Hainaut *Belgium* 50°36N 3°37E **170** D3
Lev Tolstoy *Russia* 53°13N 39°29E **188** F10
Levallois-Perret *France* 48°53N 2°16E **134** A2
Levan *Albania* 40°40N 19°28E **202** F3
Levanger *Norway* 63°45N 11°19E **160** E14
Levant, Î. du *France* 43°3N 6°28E **175** E10
Lévanto *Italy* 44°10N 9°38E **198** D6
Lévanzo *Italy* 38°0N 12°20E **200** D5
Leveld *Norway* 60°44N 8°33E **164** D5
Levelland *U.S.A.* 33°35N 102°23W **314** E3
Levelock *U.S.A.* 59°7N 156°51W **303** G8
Leven *U.K.* 56°12N 3°0W **167** E6
Leven, L. *U.K.* 56°12N 3°22W **167** E5
Leven, Toraka *Madag.* 12°30S 47°45E **272** A2
Levent *Turkey* 41°5N 29°0E **122** B2
Leveque C. *Australia* 16°20S 123°0E **278** C3
Levera △ *Grenada* 12°13N 61°38W **323** q
Leverano *Italy* 40°17N 18°0E **201** B10
Leverger = Santo Antônio do Leverger *Brazil* 15°52S 56°5W **331** D6
Leverkusen *Germany* 51°1N 7°1E **178** D3
Levice *Slovak Rep.* 48°13N 18°35E **181** C11
Lévico Terme *Italy* 46°0N 11°18E **199** C8
Levie *France* 41°40N 9°7E **175** G13
Levier *France* 46°58N 6°8E **173** F13
Levin *N.Z.* 40°37S 175°18E **284** G4
Lévis *Canada* 46°48N 71°9W **299** C5
Levis, L. *Canada* 62°37N 117°58W **296** A5
Levitha *Greece* 37°0N 26°28E **205** D8
Levittown *N.Y., U.S.A.* 40°44N 73°31W **313** F11
Levittown *Pa., U.S.A.* 40°9N 74°51W **313** F10
Levka *Bulgaria* 41°52N 26°15E **203** E10
Levka Oros *Greece* 35°18N 24°3E **207** E5
Levkada □ *Greece* 38°45N 20°40E **207** B2
Levkás = Lefkada *Greece* 38°40N 20°43E **207** B2
Levkôsia = Nicosia *Cyprus* 35°10N 33°25E **207** E9
Levoča *Slovak Rep.* 49°2N 20°35E **181** B13
Levroux *France* 46°59N 1°38E **173** F8
Levski *Bulgaria* 43°21N 25°10E **203** C9
Levskigrad = Karlovo *Bulgaria* 42°38N 24°47E **203** D8
Levuka *Fiji* 17°34S 179°0E **287** A2
Lewe *Burma* 19°38N 96°7E **241** F6
Lewes *E. Sussex, U.K.* 50°52N 0°1E **169** G8
Lewes *Del., U.S.A.* 38°46N 75°9W **309** F16
Lewin Brzeski *Poland* 50°45N 17°37E **185** H4
Lewis *U.K.* 58°9N 6°40W **167** C2
Lewis *U.S.A.* 45°51N 122°48W **306** E4
Lewis, Butt of *U.K.* 58°31N 6°16W **167** C2
Lewis and Clark ⌓ *U.S.A.* 46°8N 123°53W **306** D3
Lewis Pass *N.Z.* 42°31S 172°11E **285** C7
Lewis Ra. *Australia* 20°3S 128°50E **278** D4
Lewis Range *U.S.A.* 48°5N 113°5W **304** B7
Lewis Run *U.S.A.* 41°52N 78°40W **312** E6
Lewisburg *Ohio, U.S.A.* 39°51N 84°33W **311** E12
Lewisburg *Pa., U.S.A.* 40°58N 76°54W **312** F8
Lewisburg *Tenn., U.S.A.* 35°27N 86°48W **315** D11
Lewisburg *W. Va., U.S.A.* 37°48N 80°27W **309** G13
Lewisdale *U.S.A.* 38°58N 76°59W **143** B4
Lewisham □ *U.K.* 51°27N 0°1W **125** B3
Lewisport *U.S.A.* 37°56N 86°54W **311** G10
Lewisporte *Canada* 49°15N 55°3W **299** C8
Lewiston *Idaho, U.S.A.* 46°25N 117°1W **304** C5
Lewiston *Maine, U.S.A.* 44°6N 70°13W **309** C18
Lewiston *N.Y., U.S.A.* 43°11N 79°3W **312** C5
Lewistown *Ill., U.S.A.* 40°24N 90°9W **310** D6
Lewistown *Mo., U.S.A.* 40°5N 91°49W **310** D5
Lewistown *Mont., U.S.A.* 47°4N 109°26W **304** C9
Lewistown *Pa., U.S.A.* 40°36N 77°34W **312** F7
Lexington *Ga., U.S.A.* 33°52N 83°7W **316** B6
Lexington *Ill., U.S.A.* 40°39N 88°47W **311** D8
Lexington *Ky., U.S.A.* 38°3N 84°30W **311** F12
Lexington *Mass., U.S.A.* 42°25N 71°12W **116** A1
Lexington *Mich., U.S.A.* 43°16N 82°32W **312** C2
Lexington *Mo., U.S.A.* 39°11N 93°52W **310** E3
Lexington *N.C., U.S.A.* 35°49N 80°15W **315** D14
Lexington *N.Y., U.S.A.* 42°15N 74°22W **313** D10
Lexington *Nebr., U.S.A.* 40°47N 99°45W **308** E4
Lexington *Ohio, U.S.A.* 40°41N 82°35W **312** F2
Lexington *S.C., U.S.A.* 33°59N 81°11W **316** B8
Lexington *Tenn., U.S.A.* 35°39N 88°24W **315** D10
Lexington *Va., U.S.A.* 37°47N 79°27W **309** G14
Lexington Park *U.S.A.* 38°16N 76°27W **309** F15
Leyburn *U.K.* 54°19N 1°48W **168** C6
Leye *China* 24°48N 106°29E **228** E6
Leyeh *Taiwan* 23°28N 120°42E **225** C2
Leyland *U.K.* 53°42N 2°43W **168** D5
Leyre → *France* 44°39N 1°1W **174** D2
Leyte *Phil.* 10°30N 125°0E **233** F5
Leyte □ *Phil.* 11°0N 125°0E **233** F5
Leyte Gulf *Phil.* 10°50N 125°25E **233** F5
Leyton *U.K.* 51°33N 0°1W **125** A3
Leytonstone *U.K.* 51°34N 0°0 **125** A4
Leżajsk *Poland* 50°16N 22°25E **185** H9
Lezay *France* 46°15N 0°1W **174** B3
Lezhë *Albania* 41°47N 19°39E **202** E3
Lezhi *China* 30°19N 104°58E **228** B5
Lézignan-Corbières *France* 43°13N 2°43E **174** E6
Lezoux *France* 45°49N 3°21E **174** C7
Lgov *Russia* 51°42N 35°16E **189** G8
Lhasa *China* 29°25N 90°58E **218** F7
L'Haÿ-les-Roses *France* 48°46N 2°20E **134** B3
Lhazê *China* 29°5N 87°38E **218** F6
L'Hermite, I. *Chile* 55°50S 68°0W **336** E3
Lhokkruet *Indonesia* 4°55N 95°24E **234** B1
Lhokseumawe *Indonesia* 5°10N 97°10E **234** A1
Lhoksukon *Indonesia* 5°2N 97°19E **234** A1
L'Hospitalet de Llobregat *Spain* 41°21N 2°6E **114** A1
Lhotka *Czech Rep.* 50°1N 14°26E **135** B2
Lhuntsi Dzong *Bhutan* 27°39N 91°10E **241** B3
Lhut, W. → *Somali Rep.* 10°17N 50°9E **267** B7
Li *Thailand* 17°48N 98°57E **236** D2
Li Jiang → *China* 24°40N 110°40E **229** E8
Li Jiang △ *China* 24°38N 110°38E **229** E8
Li Shan *China* 35°30N 111°56E **226** G6
Li Shui → *China* 29°24N 112°1E **229** C9
Li Xian *Gansu, China* 34°10N 105°5E **226** G3
Li Xian *Hebei, China* 38°30N 115°35E **226** E8
Li Xian *Hunan, China* 29°36N 111°42E **229** C8
Lia-Moya *C.A.R.* 6°54N 16°17E **264** A3
Liadi *Greece* 36°50N 26°11E **205** E8
Liamuiga, Mt. *St. Kitts & Nevis* 17°22N 62°48W **322** d
Lian *Phil.* 14°3N 120°39E **232** D3
Liancheng *China* 25°42N 116°40E **229** E11
Liancourt Rocks = Tokdo *Asia* 37°15N 131°52E **221** F5
Liang Tao *Taiwan* 26°23N 128°28E **225** b
Lianga *Phil.* 8°38N 126°6E **233** G6
Lianga B. *Phil.* 8°37N 126°12E **233** G6
Liangcheng *Nei Monggol Zizhiqu, China* 40°28N 112°25E **226** D7
Liangcheng *Shandong, China* 35°32N 119°37E **227** G10
Liangdang *China* 33°56N 106°18E **226** H4
Lianghe *China* 24°50N 98°20E **228** E2
Lianghekou *China* 29°11N 108°44E **228** C7
Liangping *China* 30°38N 107°47E **228** B6
Liangpran *Indonesia* 1°4N 114°23E **235** B4
Liangshui He → *China* 39°48N 116°35E **114** B2
Lianhua *China* 27°3N 113°54E **229** D9
Lianhua Chi *China* 39°52N 116°16E **114** B1
Lianhua He → *China* 39°52N 116°13E **114** B1
Lianhua Shan *China* 23°40N 115°48E **229** F10
Lianjiang *Fujian, China* 26°12N 119°27E **229** D12
Lianjiang *Guangdong, China* 21°40N 110°20E **229** G8
Lianping *China* 24°26N 114°30E **229** E10
Lianshan *China* 24°38N 112°8E **229** E9
Lianshanguan *China* 40°53N 123°43E **224** B1
Lianshui *China* 33°42N 119°20E **227** H10
Lianyuan *China* 27°40N 111°38E **229** D8
Lianyungang *China* 34°40N 119°11E **227** G10
Lianzhou *China* 24°51N 112°22E **229** E9
Liao He → *China* 41°0N 121°50E **227** D11
Liaocheng *China* 36°28N 115°58E **226** F8
Liaodong Bandao *China* 40°0N 122°30E **227** E12
Liaodong Wan *China* 40°20N 121°10E **227** D11
Liaoning □ *China* 41°40N 122°30E **224** B1
Liaotung, G. of = Liaodong Wan *China* 40°20N 121°10E **227** D11
Liaoyang *China* 41°15N 122°58E **224** B1
Liaoyuan *China* 42°58N 125°2E **227** C13
Liaozhong *China* 41°23N 122°50E **224** B1
Liapades *Greece* 39°42N 19°40E **206** B9
Liard → *Canada* 61°51N 121°18W **296** A4
Liard River *Canada* 59°25N 126°5W **296** B3
Liari *Pakistan* 25°37N 66°30E **242** G2
Liat *Indonesia* 2°53S 107°5E **234** C3
Libano *Colombia* 4°55N 75°4W **328** C2
Libau = Liepāja *Latvia* 56°30N 21°0E **184** B8
Libby *U.S.A.* 48°23N 115°33W **304** B6
Libčice nad Vltavou *Czech Rep.* 50°11N 14°22E **135** A2
Libeň *Czech Rep.* 50°6N 14°27E **135** B2
Libenge *Dem. Rep. of the Congo* 3°40N 18°55E **264** B3
Liberal *U.S.A.* 37°3N 100°55W **308** G3
Liberdade *Acre, Brazil* 10°5S 70°20W **330** C3
Liberdade *São Paulo, Brazil* 23°33S 46°37W **137** B2
Liberdade → *Brazil* 9°40S 52°17W **331** B7
Liberdade, Avenida da *Lisbon, Portugal* **126** b1
Liberec *Czech Rep.* 50°47N 15°7E **180** A8
Liberecký □ *Czech Rep.* 50°45N 15°0E **180** A8
Liberia *Costa Rica* 10°40N 85°30W **320** D2
Liberia ■ *W. Afr.* 6°30N 9°30W **262** D3
Libertad *Antique, Phil.* 11°46N 121°55E **233** F3
Libertad *Venezuela* 8°20N 69°37W **328** B4
Libertador □ *Chile* 34°15S 70°45W **334** C1
Liberton *U.K.* 55°54N 3°9W **121** B3
Liberty *Ind., U.S.A.* 39°38N 84°56W **311** E12
Liberty *Mo., U.S.A.* 39°15N 94°25W **310** E2
Liberty *N.Y., U.S.A.* 41°48N 74°45W **313** E10
Liberty *Pa., U.S.A.* 41°34N 77°6W **312** E7
Liberty *Tex., U.S.A.* 30°3N 94°48W **314** F7
Liberty Center *U.S.A.* 41°27N 84°1W **311** C11
Liberty I. *U.S.A.* 40°41N 74°2W **132** B1
Liberty-Newark Int. ✈ **(EWR)** *U.S.A.* 40°42N 74°10W **313** F10
Liberty Osaka Museum *Japan* 34°38N 135°29E **133** B1
Liberty State Park ⌓ *U.S.A.* 40°42N 74°2W **132** B1
Libertyville *U.S.A.* 42°18N 87°57W **311** B9
Libeznice *Czech Rep.* 50°11N 14°29E **135** A2
Libiąż *Poland* 50°7N 19°21E **185** H6
Libîbi *Angola* 14°42S 17°44E **265** E3
Lîbîya, Sahrâ' *Africa* 25°0N 25°0E **258** C4
Libjo *Phil.* 10°12N 125°32E **233** F5
Libmanan *Phil.* 13°42N 123°4E **232** E4
Libo *China* 25°22N 107°53E **228** E6
Libobo, Tanjung *Indonesia* 0°54S 128°28E **231** E7
Libode *S. Africa* 31°33S 29°2E **271** D4
Libohovë *Albania* 40°3N 20°10E **202** F4
Liboi *Kenya* 0°24N 40°57E **267** D5
Libona *Phil.* 8°20N 124°44E **233** G5
Libonda *Zambia* 14°28S 23°12E **265** E4
Libong, Ko *Thailand* 7°15N 99°23E **237** J2
Libourne *France* 44°55N 0°14W **174** D3
Libramont *Belgium* 49°55N 5°23E **170** E5
Library of Congress *Washington, D.C., U.S.A.* **143** b3
Librazhd *Albania* 41°12N 20°22E **202** E4
Libreville *Gabon* 0°25N 9°26E **264** B1
Libro Pt. *Phil.* 11°25N 119°28E **233** F2
Libuš *Czech Rep.* 50°0N 14°27E **135** B2
Libya ■ *N. Afr.* 27°0N 17°0E **258** C3
Libyan Desert = Lîbîya, Sahrâ' *Africa* 25°0N 25°0E **258** C4
Libyan Plateau = Ed Déffa *Egypt* 30°40N 26°30E **256** A2
Licantén *Chile* 35°55S 72°0W **334** D1
Licata *Italy* 37°6N 13°56E **200** E6
Lice *Turkey* 38°27N 40°39E **213** C9
Licheng *China* 36°28N 113°20E **226** F7
Lichfield *U.K.* 52°41N 1°49W **169** E6
Lichia *Taiwan* 22°47N 121°3E **225** D3
Lichiao *China* 23°3N 113°18E **121** B2
Lichinga *Mozam.* 13°13S 35°11E **269** E4
Lichtenburg *Berlin, Germany* 52°31N 13°30E **115** A4
Lichtenburg *North West, S. Africa* 26°8S 26°8E **270** C4
Lichtenfels *Germany* 50°8N 11°4E **179** E7
Lichterfelde *Germany* 52°25N 13°19E **115** B2
Lichuan *Hubei, China* 30°18N 108°57E **228** B7
Lichuan *Jiangxi, China* 27°18N 116°55E **229** D11
Licking → *U.S.A.* 39°6N 84°30W **311** F11
Licosa, Punta *Italy* 40°15N 14°54E **201** B7
Licungo → *Mozam.* 17°40S 37°15E **269** F4
Lida *Belarus* 53°53N 25°15E **177** B13
Liden *Sweden* 62°42N 16°48E **162** B10
Lidhult *Sweden* 56°50N 13°27E **163** H7
Lidingö *Sweden* 59°21N 18°8E **139** A2
Lidköping *Sweden* 58°31N 13°7E **163** F7
Lido *Italy* 45°25N 12°22E **199** C9
Lido *Niger* 12°54N 3°44E **263** C5
Lido di Roma = Ostia, Lido di *Italy* 41°43N 12°17E **199** G9
Lidoriki *Greece* 38°32N 22°12E **204** C4
Lidzbark *Poland* 53°15N 19°49E **185** E6
Lidzbark Warmiński *Poland* 54°7N 20°34E **184** D7
Liebenthal = Lubomierz *Poland* 51°1N 15°31E **185** G2
Liebenwalde *Germany* 52°52N 13°24E **178** C9
Lieberose *Germany* 51°59N 14°17E **178** D10
Liebig, Mt. *Australia* 23°18S 131°22E **278** D5
Liebling *Romania* 45°36N 21°20E **182** E6
Liechtenstein ■ *Europe* 47°8N 9°35E **179** H5
Liège *Belgium* 50°38N 5°35E **170** D5
Liège □ *Belgium* 50°32N 5°35E **170** D5
Liegnitz = Legnica *Poland* 51°12N 16°10E **185** G3
Lieksa *Finland* 63°18N 30°2E **160** E24
Lienart *Dem. Rep. of the Congo* 3°3N 25°31E **268** B2
Lienyünchiangshih = Lianyungang *China* 34°40N 119°11E **227** G10
Lienz *Austria* 46°50N 12°46E **180** E5
Liepāja *Latvia* 56°30N 21°0E **184** B8
Liepāja □ *Latvia* 56°30N 21°0E **184** B8
Liepājas ezers *Latvia* 56°27N 21°3E **184** B8
Lier *Belgium* 51°7N 4°34E **170** C4
Liernais *France* 47°13N 4°16E **173** E11
Lieshi Lingyuan *China* 23°7N 113°16E **121** B2
Liesing *Austria* 48°8N 16°17E **142** B2
Liesing → *Austria* 48°8N 16°28E **142** B2
Liești *Romania* 45°38N 27°34E **183** E12
Lietuva = Lithuania ■ *Europe* 55°30N 24°0E **188** E2
Liévin *France* 50°24N 2°47E **173** B9
Lièvre → *Canada* 45°31N 75°26W **298** C4
Liezen *Austria* 47°34N 14°15E **180** D7
Liffey → *Ireland* 53°21N 6°13W **166** C5
Lifford *Ireland* 54°51N 7°29W **166** B4
Liffré *France* 48°12N 1°30W **172** D5
Lifjell *Norway* 59°27N 8°45E **164** E5
Lifou, Î. *N. Cal.* 20°53S 167°13E **288** d
Lifudzin *Russia* 44°21N 134°58E **220** B7
Lifuka *Tonga* 19°48S 174°21W **287** P13
Ligao *Phil.* 13°14N 123°32E **232** E4
Ligasa *Dem. Rep. of the Congo* 0°44N 23°49E **264** B4
Lighthouse Point *U.S.A.* 26°15N 80°7W **317** J9
Lighthouse Pt. *U.S.A.* 29°54N 84°21W **316** F5
Lightning Ridge *Australia* 29°22S 148°0E **281** D4
Lignano Sabbiadoro *Italy* 45°42N 13°9E **199** C10
Ligny-en-Barrois *France* 48°36N 5°20E **173** D12
Ligonha → *Mozam.* 16°54S 39°9E **269** F4
Ligonier *Ind., U.S.A.* 41°28N 85°35W **311** C11
Ligonier *Pa., U.S.A.* 40°15N 79°14W **312** F5
Ligourio *Greece* 37°37N 23°4E **204** D5
Ligovo *Russia* 59°49N 30°10E **137** C1
Ligueil *France* 47°2N 0°49E **172** E7
Liguria □ *Italy* 44°30N 8°50E **198** D5
Ligurian Sea *Medit. S.* 43°20N 9°0E **198** E5
Lihir Group *Papua N. G.* 3°0S 152°35E **286** B7
Lihir I. *Papua N. G.* 3°5S 152°35E **286** B7
Lihou Reefs and Cays *Australia* 17°25S 151°40E **280** B5
Lihu'e *U.S.A.* 21°59N 159°23W **302** B2
Lihué Calel △ *Argentina* 38°0S 65°10W **334** D2
Lijiang *China* 26°55N 100°20E **228** D3
Lijiang *Norway* 59°56N 10°36E **133** B2
Lik → *Laos* 18°31N 102°30E **236** C4
Likala *Dem. Rep. of the Congo* 0°9N 19°12E **264** B3
Likang *Taiwan* 22°47N 120°29E **225** D2
Likasi *Dem. Rep. of the Congo* 10°55S 26°48E **269** E2
Likati *Dem. Rep. of the Congo* 3°20N 24°0E **264** B4
Likati → *Dem. Rep. of the Congo* 2°53N 24°3E **264** B4
Likenäs *Sweden* 60°37N 13°3E **162** D7
Likete *Dem. Rep. of the Congo* 0°48S 21°31E **264** C4
Likhaya = Likhovskoy *Russia* 48°10N 40°10E **191** F5
Likhoborka → *Russia* 55°50N 37°37E **129** A3
Likhoslavl *Russia* 57°12N 35°30E **188** D8
Likhovskoy *Russia* 48°10N 40°10E **191** F5
Likhvin = Chekalin *Russia* 54°10N 36°10E **188** E9
Likimi *Dem. Rep. of the Congo* 2°44N 20°47E **264** B4
Likita *Dem. Rep. of the Congo* 4°15N 23°36E **264** B4
Liknes *Norway* 58°19N 6°59E **164** F3
Likokou *Gabon* 0°12S 12°48E **264** C2
Likoma I. *Malawi* 12°3S 34°45E **269** E3
Likouala → *Congo* 0°2N 14°53E **264** C3
Likouala aux Herbes → *Congo* 0°52S 17°8E **264** C3
Liku *Cook Is.* 19°2S 168°47W **289** g
Likumburu *Tanzania* 9°43S 35°8E **269** D4
Lilanga *Dem. Rep. of the Congo* 0°34S 23°56E **264** C4
L'Île-Bouchard *France* 47°7N 0°26E **172** E7
L'Île-Rousse *France* 42°38N 8°57E **175** F12
Lilenga *Dem. Rep. of the Congo* 1°4N 22°26E **264** B4
Liling *China* 27°42N 113°29E **229** D9
Lilla Edet *Sweden* 58°9N 12°8E **163** F6
Lilla Värtan *Sweden* 59°20N 18°11E **139** A3
Lille *France* 50°38N 3°3E **173** B10
Lille Bælt *Denmark* 55°20N 9°45E **163** J3
Lille Værløse *Denmark* 55°47N 12°22E **118** A2
Lillebonne *France* 49°30N 0°32E **172** C7
Lillehammer *Norway* 61°8N 10°30E **164** C7
Lillesand *Norway* 58°15N 8°23E **164** F5
Lillestrøm *Norway* 59°58N 11°5E **164** E8
Lillhärdal *Sweden* 61°51N 14°5E **162** C8
Lillian Pt. *Australia* 27°40S 126°6E **279** E4
Lillo *Spain* 39°45N 3°20W **194** F7
Lillooet *Canada* 50°44N 121°57W **296** C4
Lillooet → *Canada* 49°15N 121°57W **296** D4
Lilongwe *Malawi* 14°0S 33°48E **269** E3
Liloy *Phil.* 8°4N 122°39E **233** G4
Liluah *India* 22°37N 88°19E **124** B1
Lim → *Europe* 43°45N 19°15E **202** C3
Lim Chu Kang *Singapore* 1°26N 103°43E **138** A2
Lima *Brazil* 4°36S 63°40W **329** D5
Lima *Indonesia* 3°39S 127°58E **231** E7
Lima *Peru* 12°3S 77°2W **124** B2
Lima *Ill., U.S.A.* 40°11N 91°23W **310** D5
Lima *Mont., U.S.A.* 44°38N 112°36W **304** D7
Lima *N.Y., U.S.A.* 42°54N 77°36W **312** D7
Lima *Ohio, U.S.A.* 40°44N 84°6W **311** D12
Lima □ *Peru* 12°3S 77°2W **330** C2
Lima → *Portugal* 41°41N 8°50W **194** D2
Lima Jorge Chavez, Int. ✈ **(LIM)** *Peru* 12°2S 77°8W **124** B2
Liman = Krasnyy Liman *Ukraine* 48°58N 37°50E **189** H9
Liman *Russia* 45°45N 47°12E **191** H8
Limanowa *Poland* 49°42N 20°22E **185** J7
Limassol *Cyprus* 34°42N 33°1E **207** F9
Limavady *U.K.* 55°3N 6°56W **166** A5
Limay → *Argentina* 39°0S 68°0W **336** A3
Limay Mahuida *Argentina* 37°10S 66°45W **334** D2
Limbach-Oberfrohna *Germany* 50°52N 12°43E **178** E8
Limbang *Malaysia* 4°42N 115°6E **235** B5
Limbara, Mte. *Italy* 40°51N 9°10E **200** B2
Limbaži *Latvia* 57°31N 24°42E **188** D3
Limbdi *India* 22°34N 71°51E **242** H4
Limbe *Cameroon* 4°1N 9°10E **263** E6
Limbiate *Italy* 45°35N 9°7E **129** A1
Limbueta *Angola* 12°30S 18°42E **265** E3
Limbuhan = Pio V. Corpuz *Phil.* 11°55N 124°2E **233** F5
Limburg *Germany* 50°22N 8°4E **179** E4
Limburg □ *Belgium* 51°2N 5°25E **170** C5
Limburg □ *Neths.* 51°20N 5°55E **170** C5
Lime Village *U.S.A.* 61°21N 155°28W **303** F9
Limedsforsen *Sweden* 60°52N 13°25E **162** D7
Limehouse *U.K.* 51°30N 0°1W **125** A3
Limeil-Brévannes *France* 48°44N 2°29E **134** B3
Limeira = Joaçaba *Brazil* 27°5S 51°31W **335** B5
Limeira *Brazil* 22°35S 47°28W **335** A6
Limenaria *Greece* 40°38N 24°32E **203** F8
Limenas Chersonisou *Greece* 35°18N 25°21E **207** E6
Limerick *Limerick, Ireland* 52°40N 8°37W **166** D3
Limerick *Maine, U.S.A.* 43°41N 70°48W **313** C14
Limerick □ *Ireland* 52°30N 8°50W **166** D3
Limestone *U.S.A.* 42°2N 78°38W **312** D6
Limestone → *Canada* 56°31N 94°7W **297** B10
Limestone Hill = Lackawanna *U.S.A.* 42°50N 78°50W **312** D6
Limfjorden *Denmark* 56°55N 9°0E **163** H3
Limia = Lima → *Portugal* 41°41N 8°50W **194** D2
Limingen *Norway* 64°48N 13°35E **160** D15
Limmared *Sweden* 57°34N 13°20E **163** G7
Limmen ◎ *Australia* 15°15S 135°30E **280** B2
Limmen Bight *Australia* 14°40S 135°35E **280** A2
Limmen Bight → *Australia* 15°7S 135°44E **280** B2
Limni *Greece* 38°43N 23°18E **204** C5
Limnos *Greece* 39°50N 25°5E **205** B7
Limoeiro *Brazil* 7°52S 35°27W **332** C4
Limoeiro do Norte *Brazil* 5°5S 38°0W **332** C4
Limoges *Ont., Canada* 45°20N 75°16W **313** A9
Limoges *Haute-Vienne, France* 45°50N 1°15E **174** C5
Limón *Costa Rica* 10°0N 83°2W **320** E3
Limon *Colo., U.S.A.* 39°16N 103°41W **304** G12
Limone Piemonte *Italy* 44°12N 7°34E **198** D4
Limonlu *Turkey* 36°34N 34°15E **250** B5
Limousin □ *France* 45°30N 1°30E **174** C5
Limousin, Plateaux du *France* 45°45N 1°15E **174** C5
Limoux *France* 43°4N 2°12E **174** E6
Limpopo □ *S. Africa* 24°5S 29°0E **271** B4
Limpopo → *Africa* 25°5S 33°30E **271** C5
Limuru *Kenya* 1°2S 36°35E **268** C4
Lin Xian *China* 37°57N 110°58E **226** F6
Lin'an *China* 30°15N 119°42E **229** B12
Linao Pt. *Phil.* 6°46N 123°58E **233** H4
Linapacan *Phil.* 11°30N 119°52E **233** F2
Linapacan I. *Phil.* 11°27N 119°49E **233** F2
Linapacan Str. *Phil.* 11°37N 119°56E **233** F2
Linares *Chile* 35°50S 71°40W **334** D1
Linares *Colombia* 1°23N 77°31W **328** C2
Linares *Nuevo León, Mexico* 24°52N 99°34W **319** C5
Linares *Spain* 38°10N 3°40W **195** G7
Linaria *Greece* 38°52N 24°31E **204** C6
Linaro, Capo *Italy* 42°2N 11°50E **199** F8
Linas Mte. *Italy* 39°25N 8°38E **200** C1
Linate, Milano ✈ **(LIN)** *Italy* 45°27N 9°16E **129** B2
Linbropark *S. Africa* 26°5S 28°7E **123** A2
Lincang *China* 23°58N 100°1E **228** F3
Lincheng *China* 37°25N 114°30E **226** F8
Linchuan *China* 27°57N 116°15E **229** D11
Lincoln = Beamsville *Canada* 43°12N 79°28W **312** C5
Lincoln *Argentina* 34°55S 61°30W **334** C3
Lincoln *N.Z.* 43°38S 172°30E **285** D7
Lincoln *Lincs., U.K.* 53°14N 0°32W **168** D7
Lincoln *Calif., U.S.A.* 38°54N 121°17W **306** G5
Lincoln *Ill., U.S.A.* 40°9N 89°22W **310** D7
Lincoln *Kans., U.S.A.* 39°3N 98°9W **308** F4
Lincoln *Maine, U.S.A.* 45°22N 68°30W **309** C19
Lincoln *N.H., U.S.A.* 44°3N 71°40W **313** B13
Lincoln *N. Mex., U.S.A.* 33°30N 105°23W **305** K11
Lincoln *Nebr., U.S.A.* 40°49N 96°41W **308** E5
Lincoln Boyhood ⌓ *U.S.A.* 38°7N 86°59W **311** F10
Lincoln Center for Performing Arts *New York, U.S.A.* **132** b2
Lincoln City *U.S.A.* 44°57N 124°1W **304** D1
Lincoln Hav = Lincoln Sea *Arctic* 84°0N 55°0W **154** A5

Lincoln Heights U.S.A. 34°4N 118°12W 126 B3
Lincoln Memorial U.S.A. 38°52N 77°4W 143 B3
Lincoln Park Calif., U.S.A. 37°47N 122°30W 136 B1
Lincoln Park Ga., U.S.A. 32°52N 84°20W 316 C5
Lincoln Park Ill., U.S.A. 41°57N 87°38W 119 B3
Lincoln Park Mich., U.S.A. 42°15N 83°11W 311 B13
Lincoln Park N.J., U.S.A. 40°55N 74°18W 132 B1
Lincoln Park Zoo U.S.A. 41°55N 87°38W 119 B3
Lincoln Sea Arctic 84°0N 55°0W 154 A5
Lincoln Tunnel New York, U.S.A. 132 c1
Lincolnshire □ U.K. 53°14N 0°32W 168 D7
Lincolnshire Wolds U.K. 53°26N 0°13W 168 D7
Lincolnton Ga., U.S.A. 33°48N 82°29W 316 B7
Lincolnton N.C., U.S.A. 35°29N 81°16W 315 D14
Lincolnwood U.S.A. 42°1N 87°43W 119 A2
Lind U.S.A. 46°58N 118°37W 304 C4
Linda U.S.A. 39°8N 121°34W 306 F5
Linda-a-Pastora Portugal 38°42N 9°15W 126 A1
Lindale U.S.A. 34°11N 85°11W 316 A4
Lindås Norway 60°44N 5°9E 164 D2
Lindau Germany 47°33N 9°42E 179 H5
Lindeman I. Australia 20°27S 149°3E 280 b
Lindeman Islands △ Australia 20°28S 149°5E 280 b
Linden = Gladstone U.S.A. 39°13N 94°35W 310 E2
Linden Guyana 6°0N 58°10W 329 B6
Linden Wellington, N.Z. 41°10S 174°50E 143 A1
Linden Gauteng, S. Africa 26°8S 28°0E 123 A2
Linden Ala., U.S.A. 32°18N 87°48W 315 E11
Linden Calif., U.S.A. 38°1N 121°5W 306 G5
Linden Ind., U.S.A. 40°11N 86°54W 311 D10
Linden Mich., U.S.A. 42°49N 83°47W 311 B13
Linden Tex., U.S.A. 33°1N 94°22W 314 E7
Lindenberg Germany 52°36N 13°31E 115 A4
Lindenhurst U.S.A. 40°41N 73°23W 313 F11
Lindenow Fjord Greenland 60°30N 43°25W 154 E6
Lindesberg Sweden 59°36N 15°15E 162 E9
Lindesnes Norway 57°58N 7°3E 164 G4
Lindi Tanzania 9°58S 39°38E 269 D4
Lindi □ Tanzania 9°40S 38°30E 269 D4
Lindi → Dem. Rep. of the Congo 0°33N 25°5E 268 B2
Lindley U.S.A. 42°1N 77°8W 312 D7
Lindö Sweden 58°37N 16°15E 163 F10
Lindome Sweden 57°35N 12°5E 163 G6
Lindos Greece 36°6N 28°4E 206 E12
Lindos, Akra Greece 36°4N 28°10E 206 E12
Lindoso Portugal 41°52N 8°11W 194 D2
Lindow Germany 52°58N 12°59E 178 C8
Lindøya Norway 59°53N 10°42E 133 A3
Lindsay Ont., Canada 44°22N 78°43W 312 B6
Lindsay Calif., U.S.A. 36°12N 119°5W 306 J7
Lindsay Okla., U.S.A. 34°50N 97°38W 314 D6
Lindsborg U.S.A. 38°35N 97°40W 308 F5
Lindsdal Sweden 56°44N 16°18E 163 H10
Line Islands Pac. Oc. 7°0N 160°0W 289 H12
Linesville U.S.A. 41°39N 80°26W 312 E4
Lineville Ala., U.S.A. 33°19N 85°45W 316 B4
Lineville Iowa, U.S.A. 40°35N 93°32W 310 D3
Linfen China 36°3N 111°30E 226 F6
Ling Xian Hunan, China 26°29N 113°48E 229 D9
Ling Xian Shandong, China 37°22N 116°30E 226 F9
Lingal India 16°17N 78°31E 245 F4
Linganamakki Res. India 14°6N 74°52E 245 G2
Lingao China 19°56N 109°42E 236 C7
Lingayen Phil. 16°1N 120°14E 232 C3
Lingayen G. Phil. 16°10N 120°15E 232 C3
Lingbao China 34°31N 110°51E 226 G6
Lingbi China 33°33N 117°33E 227 H9
Lingbo Sweden 61°3N 16°41E 162 C10
Lingchuan Guangxi Zhuangzu, China 25°26N 110°21E 229 E8
Lingchuan Shanxi, China 35°45N 113°12E 226 G7
Lingding Yang China 22°25N 113°44E 219 a
Lingen Germany 52°31N 7°19E 178 C3
Lingga Indonesia 0°12S 104°37E 234 C2
Lingga, Kepulauan Indonesia 0°10S 104°30E 234 C2
Lingga Arch. = Lingga, Kepulauan Indonesia 0°10S 104°30E 234 C2
Linghed Sweden 60°48N 15°55E 162 D9
Linghem Sweden 58°26N 15°47E 163 F9
Lingig Phil. 8°2N 126°24E 233 G6
Lingle U.S.A. 42°8N 104°21W 304 E11
Lingomo Dem. Rep. of the Congo 0°38N 22°3E 264 B4
Lingqiu China 39°28N 114°22E 226 E8
Lingshan China 22°25N 109°18E 228 F7
Lingshi China 36°48N 111°48E 226 F6
Lingshou China 38°20N 114°20E 226 E8
Lingshui China 18°27N 110°0E 236 C8
Lingsugur India 16°10N 76°31E 245 F3
Lingtai China 35°0N 107°40E 226 G4
Linguère Senegal 15°25N 15°5W 262 B1
Lingui China 25°12N 110°2E 229 E8
Lingunda Dem. Rep. of the Congo 0°49N 21°8E 264 C3
Lingwu China 38°6N 106°20E 226 E4
Lingyuan China 41°10N 119°15E 227 D10
Lingyun China 25°2N 106°35E 228 E6
Linhai China 28°50N 121°8E 229 C13
Linhares Brazil 19°25S 40°4W 333 E3
Linhe China 40°48N 107°20E 226 D4
Liniers Argentina 34°39S 58°30W 117 B1
Linjiang China 41°50N 127°0E 224 B3
Linkebeek Belgium 50°46N 4°20E 116 B2
Linköping Sweden 58°28N 15°36E 163 F9
Linkou China 45°15N 130°18E 227 B16
Linksfield S. Africa 26°9S 28°6E 123 A2
Linli China 29°27N 111°30E 229 C8
Linlithgow = West Lothian □ U.K. 55°54N 3°36W 167 F5
Linmeyer S. Africa 26°15S 28°4E 123 B2
Linn U.S.A. 38°29N 91°51W 310 F5
Linna Finland 60°20N 24°50E 121 A2
Linnei Taiwan 23°45N 120°36E 225 C2
Linneus U.S.A. 39°53N 93°11W 310 E3
Linnhe, L. U.K. 56°36N 5°25W 167 E3
Linosa Medit. S. 35°51N 12°50E 258 A2
Linpien Taiwan 22°26N 120°30E 225 D2
Linqi China 35°45N 113°52E 226 G7
Linqing China 36°50N 115°42E 226 F8
Linqu China 36°25N 118°30E 227 F10
Linquan China 33°5N 115°17E 229 A10
Lins Brazil 21°40S 49°44W 335 A6
Linshu China 34°53N 118°38E 227 G10
Linshui China 30°21N 106°57E 228 B6
Linsia = Linxia China 35°36N 103°10E 218 D9
Linstead Jamaica 18°8N 77°2W 320 a
Linta → Madag. 25°2S 44°5E 272 D1
Lintao China 35°26N 103°58E 226 G2
Linth → Switz. 47°7N 9°7E 179 H5
Linthal Switz. 46°54N 9°0E 179 J5
Linton Ind., U.S.A. 39°2N 87°10W 311 F9
Linton N. Dak., U.S.A. 46°16N 100°14W 308 B3
Lintong China 34°20N 109°10E 226 G5
Lintuvaara Finland 60°14N 24°49E 121 B1
Linwood Canada 43°35N 80°43W 312 C4
Linwu China 25°19N 112°31E 229 E9
Linxi Hebei, China 39°42N 118°26E 227 E10
Linxi Liaoning, China 43°36N 118°2E 227 C10
Linxia China 35°36N 103°10E 218 D9
Linxiang China 29°28N 113°23E 229 C9
Linyanti → Africa 17°50S 25°5E 270 A4
Linyi Shandong, China 37°13N 116°54E 226 F9
Linyi Shandong, China 35°5N 118°21E 227 G10
Linying China 33°48N 113°56E 226 H7
Linyuan Taiwan 22°30N 120°23E 225 D2
Linz Austria 48°18N 14°18E 180 C7
Linz Rhld-Pfz., Germany 50°34N 7°17E 178 E3
Linzhenzhen China 36°30N 109°59E 226 F5
Linzhou China 36°4N 113°49E 226 F7
Linzi China 36°50N 118°20E 227 F10
Lioko Équateur, Dem. Rep. of the Congo 0°2N 22°4E 264 B4
Lioko Orientale, Dem. Rep. of the Congo 1°25N 23°7E 264 B4
Liomseter Norway 61°15N 9°35E 164 C6
Lion, G. du France 43°10N 4°0E 174 E7
Lion Rock Country Park ⌂ China 22°21N 114°11E 122 A2
Lionárisso Cyprus 35°28N 34°8E 207 E10
Lionel Town Jamaica 17°50N 77°15W 320 a
Lioni Italy 40°52N 15°11E 201 B8
Lions, G. of = Lion, G. du France 43°10N 4°0E 174 E7
Lion's Den Zimbabwe 17°15S 30°5E 269 F3
Lion's Head Ont., Canada 44°58N 81°15W 312 B3
Lion's Head Western Cape, S. Africa 33°56S 18°23E 118 A1
Liouesso Congo 1°2N 15°43E 264 B3
Lioumi Greece 38°0N 23°40E 112 B2
Liozno = Lyozna Belarus 55°0N 30°50E 188 E6
Lipa Phil. 13°57N 121°10E 232 E3
Lipali Mozam. 15°50S 35°50E 269 F4
Lipany Slovak Rep. 49°9N 20°58E 181 B13
Lípari Italy 38°26N 14°58E 201 D7
Lípari, I. Italy 38°29N 14°56E 201 D7
Lípari, Is. = Eólie, Ís. Italy 38°30N 14°57E 201 D7
Lipatkain Indonesia 0°1N 101°12E 234 B2
Lipcani Moldova 48°14N 26°48E 183 B11
Liperi Finland 62°31N 29°24E 160 E23
Lipetsk Russia 52°37N 39°35E 189 F10
Lipetsk □ Russia 52°50N 38°50E 190 D4
Lipiany Poland 53°2N 14°58E 185 E1
Liping China 26°15N 109°7E 228 D7
Lipisi Greece 37°19N 26°50E 205 D8
Lipjan = Lipljan Kosovo 42°31N 21°7E 202 D5
Lipkany = Lipcani Moldova 48°14N 26°48E 183 B11
Lipljan Kosovo 42°31N 21°7E 202 D5
Lipník nad Bečvou Czech Rep. 49°32N 17°36E 181 B10
Lipno Poland 52°49N 19°15E 185 F6
Lipova Romania 46°8N 21°42E 182 D6
Lipovets Ukraine 49°12N 29°1E 177 D15
Lippe → Germany 51°39N 6°36E 178 D2
Lippehne = Lipiany Poland 53°2N 14°58E 185 E1
Lippstadt Germany 51°41N 8°22E 178 D4
Lipscomb U.S.A. 36°14N 100°16W 314 C4
Lipsk Poland 53°44N 23°24E 184 E10
Lipsko Poland 51°9N 21°40E 185 G8
Liptovský Hrádok Slovak Rep. 49°2N 19°44E 181 B12
Liptovský Milkuláš Slovak Rep. 49°6N 19°35E 181 B12
Liptrap, C. Australia 38°50S 145°55E 283 E6
Lipu China 24°30N 110°22E 229 E8
Lira Uganda 2°17N 32°57E 268 B3
Liranga Congo 0°43S 17°32E 264 C3
Liri → Italy 41°25N 13°52E 200 A6
Liria = Lliria Spain 39°37N 0°35W 197 F4
Līsakovsk Kazakhstan 52°33N 62°37E 216 B6
Lisala Dem. Rep. of the Congo 2°12N 21°38E 264 B4
Lisboa Portugal 38°42N 9°8W 126 A2
Lisboa □ Portugal 39°0N 9°12W 195 F1
Lisboa ✈ (LIS) Portugal 38°46N 9°8W 126 A2
Lisbon = Lisboa Portugal 38°42N 9°8W 126 A2
Lisbon N. Dak., U.S.A. 46°27N 97°41W 308 B5
Lisbon N.H., U.S.A. 44°13N 71°55W 313 B13
Lisbon N.Y., U.S.A. 44°43N 75°19W 313 B9
Lisbon Ohio, U.S.A. 40°46N 80°46W 312 F4
Lisbon Falls U.S.A. 44°0N 70°4W 309 D18
Lisburn U.K. 54°31N 6°3W 166 B5
Lisburn, C. Vanuatu 15°39S 166°46E 287 E4
Lisburne, C. U.S.A. 68°53N 166°13W 303 B6
Liscannor B. Ireland 52°55N 9°24W 166 D2
Liscia → Italy 41°11N 9°9E 200 A2
Lisdoonvarna Ireland 53°2N 9°18W 166 C2
Lishan Taiwan 24°16N 121°14E 225 B3
Lishe Jiang → China 24°15N 101°35E 228 E3
Lishi China 37°31N 111°8E 226 F6
Lishu China 43°20N 124°18E 227 C13
Lishui Guangdong, China 23°12N 113°9E 121 A1
Lishui Jiangsu, China 31°38N 119°2E 229 B12
Lishui Zhejiang, China 28°28N 119°54E 229 C12
Lisianski I. U.S.A. 26°2N 174°0W 302 F9
Lisichansk = Lysychansk Ukraine 48°55N 38°30E 189 H10
Lisieux France 49°10N 0°12E 172 C7
Liski Russia 51°3N 39°30E 189 G10
L'Isle-Jourdain Gers, France 43°36N 1°5E 174 E5
L'Isle-Jourdain Vienne, France 46°13N 0°31E 174 B4
L'Isle-sur-la-Sorgue France 43°54N 5°2E 175 E9
Lisle-sur-Tarn France 43°52N 1°49E 174 E5
Lismore N.S.W., Australia 28°44S 153°21E 281 D5
Lismore Waterford, Ireland 52°8N 7°55W 166 D4
Lissa = Leszno Poland 51°50N 16°30E 185 G3
Lissos → Greece 41°15N 25°40E 203 E9
Lista Norway 58°7N 6°39E 164 F3
Lister, Mt. Antarctica 78°0S 162°0E 151 D11
Lister og Mandals = Vest-Agder □ Norway 58°30N 7°15E 164 F4
Liston Australia 28°39S 152°6E 281 D5
Listowel Ont., Canada 43°44N 80°58W 312 C4
Listowel Kerry, Ireland 52°27N 9°29W 166 D2
Lit Sweden 63°19N 14°51E 162 A8
Lit-et-Mixe France 44°2N 1°15W 174 D2
Litang Guangxi Zhuangzu, China 23°12N 109°8E 228 F7
Litang Sichuan, China 30°1N 100°17E 228 B3
Litang Malaysia 5°27N 118°31E 235 A5
Litang Qu → China 28°4N 101°32E 228 C3
Litani → Lebanon 33°20N 35°15E 250 E6
Litchfield Vic., Australia 36°18S 142°52E 282 D5
Litchfield Calif., U.S.A. 40°24N 120°23W 306 E6
Litchfield Conn., U.S.A. 41°45N 73°11W 313 E11
Litchfield Ill., U.S.A. 39°11N 89°39W 310 E7
Litchfield Minn., U.S.A. 45°8N 94°32W 308 C6
Litchfield △ Australia 13°14S 131°1E 278 B5
Liteni Romania 47°32N 26°32E 183 C11
Lithakia Greece 37°43N 20°50E 207 D2
Lithgow Australia 33°25S 150°8E 283 B9
Lithino, Akra Greece 34°55N 24°44E 207 F5
Lithuania ■ Europe 55°30N 24°0E 188 E2
Litija Slovenia 46°3N 14°50E 199 B11
Lititz U.S.A. 40°9N 76°18W 313 F8
Litochoro Greece 40°8N 22°34E 202 F6
Litoko Dem. Rep. of the Congo 1°13S 24°47E 264 C4
Litoměřice Czech Rep. 50°33N 14°10E 180 A7
Litomyšl Czech Rep. 49°52N 16°20E 181 B9
Litschau Austria 48°58N 15°4E 180 C8
Little Abaco Bahamas 26°50N 77°30W 320 A4
Little Andaman I. India 10°45N 92°30E 245 J11
Little Aral Sea = Northern Aral Sea Kazakhstan 46°20N 60°30E 216 C6
Little B. N.S.W., Australia 33°58S 151°15E 139 B2
Little B. Montserrat 16°43N 62°11W 323 p
Little Barrier I. N.Z. 36°12S 175°8E 284 C4
Little Basses Sri Lanka 6°24N 81°43E 245 L5
Little Belt Mts. U.S.A. 46°40N 110°45W 304 C8
Little Bighorn Battlefield ⌂ U.S.A. 45°34N 107°25W 304 D10
Little Blue → U.S.A. 39°42N 96°41W 308 F5
Little Buffalo → Canada 61°0N 113°46W 296 A6
Little Calumet → U.S.A. 41°39N 87°34W 119 D3
Little Cayman Cayman Is. 19°41N 80°3W 320 C3
Little Churchill → Canada 57°30N 95°22W 297 B9
Little Coco I. Burma 14°0N 93°13E 245 H11
Little Colorado → U.S.A. 36°12N 111°48W 305 H8
Little Current Canada 45°55N 82°0W 298 C3
Little Current → Canada 50°57N 84°36W 298 B3
Little Desert △ Australia 37°25S 141°30E 282 D4
Little Diomede I. U.S.A. 65°45N 168°56W 303 D5
Little Falls Minn., U.S.A. 45°59N 94°22W 308 C6
Little Falls N.Y., U.S.A. 43°3N 74°51W 313 C10
Little Ferry U.S.A. 40°50N 74°2W 132 A1
Little Fork → U.S.A. 48°31N 93°35W 308 A7
Little Grand Rapids Canada 52°0N 95°29W 297 C9
Little Humboldt → U.S.A. 41°1N 117°43W 304 F5
Little Inagua I. Bahamas 21°40N 73°50W 321 B5
Little Italy New York, U.S.A. 132 e2
Little Karoo S. Africa 33°45S 21°0E 270 D3
Little Khingan Mts. = Xiao Hinggan Ling China 49°0N 127°0E 219 B14
Little Lake U.S.A. 35°56N 117°55W 307 K9
Little Lake Conway U.S.A. 28°29N 81°21W 133 B2
Little Laut Is. = Laut Kecil, Kepulauan Indonesia 4°45S 115°40E 235 C5
Little London Jamaica 18°15N 78°13W 320 a
Little Mecatina = Petit-Mécatina → Canada 50°40N 59°30W 299 B8
Little Mermaid = Den Lille Havfrue Copenhagen, Denmark 118 a3
Little Minch U.K. 57°35N 6°45W 167 D2
Little Missouri → U.S.A. 47°36N 102°25W 308 B2
Little Nicobar India 7°20N 93°40E 245 L11
Little Ouse → U.K. 52°22N 1°12E 169 E9
Little Rann India 23°25N 71°25E 242 H4
Little Red → U.S.A. 35°11N 91°27W 314 D9
Little Red School House Nature Center U.S.A. 41°42N 87°51W 119 C1
Little River N.Z. 43°45S 172°49E 285 D7
Little Rock U.S.A. 34°45N 92°17W 314 D8
Little Rouge → Canada 43°45N 79°11W 141 A4
Little Ruaha → Tanzania 7°57S 37°53E 268 D4
Little Sable Pt. U.S.A. 43°38N 86°33W 308 D10
Little Scarcies → S. Leone 8°50N 13°10W 262 D2
Little Sioux → U.S.A. 41°48N 96°4W 308 E5
Little Sitkin I. U.S.A. 51°57N 178°31E 303 L2
Little Smoky → Canada 54°44N 117°11W 296 C5
Little Snake → U.S.A. 40°27N 108°26W 304 F9
Little Sound Bermuda 32°15N 64°50W 153 a
Little Tokyo Los Angeles, U.S.A. 127 c2
Little Valley U.S.A. 42°15N 78°48W 312 D6
Little Wabash → U.S.A. 37°55N 88°5W 311 G8
Little White → U.S.A. 43°40N 100°40W 308 D3
Little York U.S.A. 41°1N 90°45W 310 C6
Little Zab = Zāb aş Şaghīr → Iraq 35°17N 43°29E 213 E10
Littlefield U.S.A. 33°55N 102°20W 314 E3
Littlehampton U.K. 50°49N 0°32W 169 G7
Littleton U.S.A. 44°18N 71°46W 313 B13
Littoral □ Cameroon 4°0N 10°0E 263 E7
Littoria = Latina Italy 41°28N 12°52E 200 A5
Litunga Angola 13°19S 16°48E 265 E3
Litvinov Czech Rep. 50°36N 13°37E 180 A6
Liu He → Jilin, China 42°46N 126°13E 224 A3
Liu He → Liaoning, China 40°55N 121°35E 227 D11
Liu Jiang → China 23°55N 109°30E 228 F7
Liuba China 33°38N 106°55E 228 A6
Liucheng China 24°38N 109°14E 228 E7
Liuchia Taiwan 23°13N 120°21E 225 C2
Liuch'iu Taiwan 22°21N 120°23E 225 D2
Liuch'iu Yü Taiwan 22°21N 120°22E 225 D2
Liugou China 40°57N 118°15E 227 D10
Liuhang China 31°21N 121°21E 138 A1
Liuhe China 42°17N 125°43E 224 A2
Liuheng Dao China 29°40N 122°5E 229 C14
Liujiang China 24°26N 109°11E 228 E7
Liukang Tenggaja = Sabalana, Kepulauan Indonesia 6°45S 118°50E 231 F5
Liuli Tanzania 11°3S 34°38E 269 E3
Liupan Shan China 35°39N 106°12E 226 G4
Liupanshui China 26°38N 104°48E 228 D5
Liurong Temple China 23°8N 113°15E 121 B2
Liuwa Plain Zambia 14°20S 22°30E 265 E4
Liuwa Plain △ Zambia 14°45S 22°35E 265 E4
Liuyang China 28°10N 113°37E 229 C9
Liuying Taiwan 23°17N 120°18E 225 C2
Liuzhou China 24°22N 109°22E 228 E7
Liuzhuang China 33°12N 120°18E 227 H11
Livada Romania 47°52N 23°5E 182 C8
Livadero Greece 40°2N 21°57E 202 F5
Livadhia Cyprus 34°57N 33°38E 207 F9
Livadhje Albania 39°47N 20°7E 206 B10
Livadi Greece 40°8N 22°9E 204 A4
Livadia Greece 38°27N 22°54E 204 C4
Livarot France 48°58N 0°9E 172 D7
Live Oak Calif., U.S.A. 39°17N 121°40W 306 F5
Live Oak Fla., U.S.A. 30°18N 82°59W 316 E7
Live Oak Manor U.S.A. 29°57N 90°14W 131 B1
Lively Canada 46°26N 81°9W 309 B13
Livengood U.S.A. 65°32N 148°33W 303 D10
Liveras Cyprus 35°23N 32°57E 207 E8
Livermore U.S.A. 37°41N 121°47W 306 H5
Livermore, Mt. U.S.A. 30°38N 104°11W 314 F2
Livermore Falls U.S.A. 44°29N 70°11W 309 C18
Liverpool N.S.W., Australia 33°54S 150°58E 283 B9
Liverpool N.S., Canada 44°5N 64°41W 299 D7
Liverpool Mersey., U.K. 53°25N 3°0W 168 D4
Liverpool N.Y., U.S.A. 43°6N 76°13W 313 C8
Liverpool Bay U.K. 53°30N 3°20W 168 D4
Liverpool Plains Australia 31°15S 150°15E 283 A9
Liverpool Ra. Australia 31°50S 150°30E 283 A9
Liverpool Street London, U.K. 125 a5
Livigno Italy 46°35N 10°10E 198 B7
Livingston Guatemala 15°50N 88°50W 320 C2
Livingston W. Loth., U.K. 55°54N 3°30W 167 F5
Livingston Ala., U.S.A. 32°35N 88°11W 315 E10
Livingston Calif., U.S.A. 37°23N 120°43W 306 H6
Livingston Mont., U.S.A. 45°40N 110°34W 304 D8
Livingston S.C., U.S.A. 33°38N 81°7W 315 E14
Livingston Tenn., U.S.A. 36°23N 85°19W 315 C12
Livingston Tex., U.S.A. 30°43N 94°56W 314 F7
Livingston Wis., U.S.A. 42°54N 90°26W 310 B6
Livingston, L. U.S.A. 30°50N 95°10W 314 F7
Livingston Manor U.S.A. 41°54N 74°50W 313 E10
Livingstone Zambia 17°46S 25°52E 269 F2
Livingstone △ Australia 35°22S 147°22E 283 C7
Livingstone Mts. N.Z. 45°15S 168°9E 285 F3
Livingstone Mts. Tanzania 9°40S 34°20E 269 D3
Livingstonia Malawi 10°38S 34°5E 269 E3
Livno Bos.-H. 43°50N 17°1E 182 G2
Livny Russia 52°30N 37°30E 189 F9
Livonia Mich., U.S.A. 42°23N 83°23W 311 B13
Livonia N.Y., U.S.A. 42°49N 77°40W 312 D7
Livorno Italy 43°33N 10°19E 198 E7
Livradois-Forez ⌂ France 44°0N 3°0E 174 E7
Livramento = Nossa Senhora do Livramento Brazil 15°48S 56°22W 331 D6
Livramento Brazil 30°55S 55°30W 335 C4
Livramento do Brumado Brazil 13°39S 41°50W 333 D3
Livron-sur-Drôme France 44°46N 4°51E 175 D8
Livry-Gargan France 48°55N 2°31E 134 A4
Livyntsi Ukraine 48°25N 26°37E 183 B11
Liwale Tanzania 9°48S 37°58E 269 D4
Liwan China 23°3N 113°13E 121 B2
Liwiec → Poland 52°36N 21°34E 185 F8
Liwonde Malaysia 15°4S 35°13E 269 F4
Liwonde △ Malawi 14°48S 35°20E 269 E4
Lixi China 26°23N 101°59E 228 D3
Lixian China 31°23N 103°13E 228 B4
Lixin China 33°8N 116°13E 229 A11
Lixouri Greece 38°12N 20°26E 207 C2
Liyang China 31°26N 119°28E 229 B12
Lizard → Trin. & Tob. 10°9N 61°1W 323 t
Lizard I. Australia 14°42S 145°30E 280 A4
Lizard Pt. U.K. 49°57N 5°13W 169 H2
Lizarda Brazil 9°36S 46°41W 332 C2
Lizarra = Estella Spain 42°40N 2°2W 196 C2
Lizella U.S.A. 32°48N 83°49W 316 C6
Lizzano Italy 40°23N 17°27E 201 B10
Ljan Norway 59°50N 10°46E 133 A3
Ljig Serbia 44°13N 20°18E 202 B4
Ljøra → Norway 61°24N 12°35E 164 C9
Ljørdalen Norway 61°23N 12°41E 164 C9
Ljosland Norway 58°47N 7°22E 164 F4
Ljubija Bos.-H. 44°55N 16°35E 199 D13
Ljubinje Bos.-H. 42°58N 18°5E 202 D2
Ljubišnja Europe 43°18N 19°6E 202 C3
Ljubljana Slovenia 46°4N 14°33E 199 B11
Ljubljana ✈ (LJU) Slovenia 46°14N 14°33E 199 B11
Ljubno Slovenia 46°25N 14°46E 199 B11
Ljubovija Serbia 44°11N 19°22E 202 B3
Ljugarn Sweden 57°20N 18°43E 163 G12
Ljung Sweden 57°59N 13°3E 163 G7
Ljungan → Sweden 62°18N 17°23E 162 B11
Ljungaverk Sweden 62°30N 16°5E 162 B10
Ljungby Sweden 56°49N 13°55E 163 H7
Ljungbyholm Sweden 56°39N 16°5E 163 H10
Ljungdalen Sweden 62°51N 12°47E 162 B6
Ljungsbro Sweden 58°31N 15°30E 163 F9
Ljungskile Sweden 58°14N 11°55E 163 F5
Ljusdal Sweden 61°46N 16°3E 162 C10
Ljusfallshammar Sweden 58°48N 15°30E 163 F9
Ljusnan → Sweden 61°12N 17°8E 162 C11
Ljusne Sweden 61°13N 17°7E 162 C11
Ljusterö Sweden 59°31N 18°37E 162 E12
Ljustorp Sweden 62°38N 17°19E 162 B11
Ljutomer Slovenia 46°31N 16°11E 199 B13
Llagostera Spain 41°50N 2°54E 196 D7
Llamellín Peru 9°0S 76°54W 330 B2
Llancanelo, Salina Argentina 35°40S 69°8W 334 D2
Llandeilo U.K. 51°53N 3°59W 169 F4
Llandovery U.K. 51°59N 3°48W 169 F4
Llandrindod Wells U.K. 52°14N 3°22W 169 E4
Llandudno U.K. 53°19N 3°50W 168 D4
Llanelli U.K. 51°41N 4°10W 169 F3
Llanes Spain 43°25N 4°50W 194 B6
Llanganates △ Ecuador 0°51S 72°20W 328 D3
Llangollen U.K. 52°58N 3°11W 168 E4
Llanidloes U.K. 52°27N 3°31W 169 E4
Llano U.S.A. 30°45N 98°41W 314 F5
Llano → U.S.A. 30°39N 98°26W 314 F5
Llano de Can Gineu Spain 41°27N 2°10E 114 A2
Llano Estacado U.S.A. 33°30N 103°0W 314 E3
Llanos S. Amer. 5°0N 71°35W 326 C3
Llanos de Challe △ Chile 28°8S 71°1W 334 B1
Llanquihue, L. Chile 41°10S 72°50W 336 B1
Llanwrtyd Wells U.K. 52°7N 3°38W 169 E4
Llata Peru 9°25S 76°47W 330 B2
Llebeig, C. des Spain 39°33N 2°18E 206 B3
Lleida Spain 41°37N 0°39E 196 D5
Lleida □ Spain 42°6N 1°0E 196 C6
Llentrisca, C. Spain 38°52N 1°15E 206 D1
Llera de Canales Mexico 23°19N 99°1W 319 C5
Llerena Spain 38°17N 6°0W 195 G5
Llevant, Sa. de Spain 39°35N 3°17E 206 B4
Lleyn Peninsula U.K. 52°51N 4°36W 168 E3
Llica Bolivia 19°52S 68°16W 330 D4
Llico Chile 34°46S 72°5W 334 C1
Lliria Spain 39°37N 0°35W 197 F4
Llívia Spain 42°28N 1°59E 174 F5
Llobregat → Spain 41°19N 2°5E 196 D7
Llodio Spain 43°9N 2°58W 196 B2
Llorente Phil. 11°25N 125°33E 233 F5
Lloret de Mar Spain 41°41N 2°53E 196 D7
Lloseta Spain 39°43N 2°52E 206 B3
Lloyd B. Australia 12°45S 143°27E 280 A3
Lloyd L. Canada 57°22N 108°57W 297 B7
Lloydminster Canada 53°17N 110°0W 297 C7
Llubí Spain 39°42N 3°0E 206 B4
Llucena del Cid Spain 40°9N 0°17W 196 E4
Llucmajor Spain 39°29N 2°53E 206 B3
Lluidas Vale Jamaica 18°6N 77°5W 320 a
Llullaillaco, Volcán S. Amer. 24°43S 68°30W 334 A2
Llullaillaco △ Chile 24°50S 68°51W 334 A2
Lo → Vietnam 21°18N 105°25E 236 B5
Lo Aranguiz Chile 33°23S 70°40W 137 B2
Lo Boza Chile 33°23S 70°43W 137 B1
Lo Chau China 22°11N 114°15E 122 B2
Lo Chau Pak Mai China 22°11N 114°14E 122 B2
Lo Espejo Chile 33°31S 70°42W 137 C1
Lo Hermida Chile 33°28S 70°33W 137 B2
Lo Prado Chile 33°26S 70°42W 137 B1
Lo So Shing China 22°12N 114°7E 122 B1
Lo Wai China 22°22N 114°8E 122 A1
Loa U.S.A. 38°24N 111°39W 304 G8
Loa → Chile 21°26S 70°41W 334 A1
Loagan Bunut △ Malaysia 3°32N 114°40E 235 B4
Loaita I. S. China Sea 10°41N 114°25E 230 B4
Loakulu Indonesia 0°31S 117°1E 235 C5
Loange → Dem. Rep. of the Congo 4°17S 20°2E 265 C4
Loango Congo 4°38S 11°50E 265 C2
Loanhead U.K. 55°53N 3°9W 121 B3
Loano Italy 44°8N 8°15E 198 D5
Loay Phil. 9°36N 124°1E 233 G5
Lobamba Swaziland 26°28S 31°12E 271 C5
Lobatse Botswana 25°12S 25°40E 270 C4
Lobau Wien, Austria 48°10N 16°31E 142 A3
Löbau Sachsen, Germany 51°5N 14°40E 178 D10
Lobaye → C.A.R. 3°41N 18°35E 264 B3
Loben = Lubliniec Poland 50°43N 18°45E 185 H5
Lobenstein Germany 50°25N 11°39E 178 E7
Lobería Argentina 38°10S 58°40W 334 D4
Löberöd Sweden 55°47N 13°31E 163 J7
Łobez Poland 53°38N 15°39E 184 E2
Lobito Angola 12°18S 13°35E 265 E2
Lobo Phil. 13°39N 121°13E 232 E3
Lobo → Ivory C. 6°2N 6°45W 262 D3
Lobos Argentina 35°10S 59°0W 334 D4
Lobos, I. Mexico 27°20N 110°36W 318 B2
Lobos, I. de Canary Is. 28°45N 13°50W 153 e2
Lobos, Pt. U.S.A. 37°46N 122°30W 136 B1
Lobos de Afuera, Islas Peru 6°57S 80°42W 330 B1
Lobos de Tierra, I. Peru 6°27S 80°52W 330 B1
Łobżenica Poland 53°18N 17°15E 185 E4
Loc Binh Vietnam 21°46N 106°54E 236 B6
Loc Ninh Vietnam 11°50N 106°34E 237 G6
Locarno Switz. 46°10N 8°47E 179 J4
Loch Baghasdail = Lochboisdale U.K. 57°9N 7°20W 167 D1
Loch Garman = Wexford Ireland 52°20N 6°28W 166 D5
Loch Lomond and the Trossachs △ U.K. 56°10N 4°40W 167 E4
Loch Nam Madadh = Lochmaddy U.K. 57°36N 7°10W 167 D1
Lochaber U.K. 56°59N 5°1W 167 E3
Locham Germany 48°7N 11°26E 131 B1
Locharbriggs U.K. 55°7N 3°35W 167 F5
Lochboisdale U.K. 57°9N 7°20W 167 D1
Loche, L. La Canada 56°30N 109°30W 297 B7
Lochem Neths. 52°9N 6°26E 170 B6
Loches France 47°7N 1°0E 172 E7
Lochgilphead U.K. 56°2N 5°26W 167 E3
Lochino Russia 55°41N 37°17E 129 B1
Lochinvar △ Zambia 15°55S 27°15E 269 F2
Lochinver U.K. 58°9N 5°14W 167 C3
Lochkov Czech Rep. 50°0N 14°21E 135 B2
Lochloosa L. U.S.A. 29°30N 82°7W 317 F7
Lochmaddy U.K. 57°36N 7°10W 167 D1
Lochnagar Queens., Australia 23°33S 145°38E 280 C4
Lochnagar Aberds., U.K. 56°57N 3°15W 167 E5
Łochów Poland 52°33N 21°42E 185 F8
Lochy, L. U.K. 57°0N 4°53W 167 E4
Lock Australia 33°34S 135°46E 281 E2
Lock Haven U.S.A. 41°8N 77°28W 312 E7
Lockeford U.S.A. 38°10N 121°9W 306 G5
Lockeport Canada 43°47N 65°4W 299 D6
Lockerbie U.K. 55°7N 3°21W 167 F5
Lockhart N.S.W., Australia 35°14S 146°40E 283 C7
Lockhart Tex., U.S.A. 29°53N 97°40W 314 G6
Lockhart, L. Australia 33°15S 119°3E 279 F2
Lockhart River Australia 12°58S 143°30E 280 A3
Lockhart River ✪ Australia 12°47S 143°20E 280 A3
Lockhausen Germany 48°10N 11°24E 131 A1
Lockney U.S.A. 34°7N 101°27W 314 D4
Lockport Ill., U.S.A. 41°35N 88°3W 311 C8
Lockport N.Y., U.S.A. 43°10N 78°42W 312 C6
Locminé France 47°54N 2°51W 172 E4
Locri Italy 38°14N 16°16E 201 D9
Locronan France 48°7N 4°15W 172 D2
Locust Cr. → U.S.A. 39°40N 93°17W 310 E3
Locust Grove U.S.A. 33°21N 84°7W 316 B5
Lod Israel 31°57N 34°54E 251 G5
Lodalskåpa Norway 61°47N 7°13E 164 C4
Lodeinoye Pole Russia 60°44N 33°33E 188 B7
Lodève France 43°44N 3°19E 174 E7
Lodge Bay Canada 52°14N 55°51W 299 B8
Lodge Grass U.S.A. 45°19N 107°22W 304 D10
Lodhran Pakistan 29°32N 71°30E 242 E4
Lodi Italy 45°19N 9°30E 198 C6
Lodi Calif., U.S.A. 38°8N 121°16W 306 G5
Lodi N.J., U.S.A. 40°52N 74°5W 132 A1
Lodi Ohio, U.S.A. 41°2N 82°1W 312 E3
Lodi Estate India 28°36N 77°15E 120 B2
Lodja Dem. Rep. of the Congo 3°30S 23°23E 264 C4
Lodosa Spain 42°25N 2°4W 196 C2
Lödöse Sweden 58°2N 12°9E 163 F6
Lodwar Kenya 3°7N 35°36E 268 B4
Łódź Poland 51°45N 19°27E 185 G6
Łódzkie □ Poland 51°30N 19°30E 185 G6
Loei Thailand 17°29N 101°35E 236 D3
Loengo Dem. Rep. of the Congo 4°48S 26°30E 265 C5
Loeriesfontein S. Africa 31°0S 19°26E 270 D2
Lofa → Liberia 6°35N 11°8W 263 D2
Lofa Mano △ Liberia 7°55N 10°25W 262 D2
Lofer Austria 47°35N 12°41E 180 D5
Lofoten Norway 68°30N 13°59E 160 B16
Lofsdalen Sweden 62°10N 13°20E 162 B7
Lofsen → Sweden 62°7N 13°57E 162 B7
Loftahammar Sweden 57°54N 16°41E 163 G10
Loga Niger 13°40N 3°15E 263 C5
Logan Iowa, U.S.A. 41°39N 95°47W 308 E6
Logan Ohio, U.S.A. 39°32N 82°25W 309 F12
Logan Utah, U.S.A. 41°44N 111°50W 304 F8
Logan W. Va., U.S.A. 37°51N 81°59W 309 G13
Logan, Mt. Canada 60°34N 140°23W 294 E3
Logan Int., Boston ✈ (BOS) U.S.A. 42°22N 71°1W 116 A2
Logan Martin L. U.S.A. 33°26N 86°20W 316 B3
Logan Square U.S.A. 41°55N 87°42W 119 B2
Logandale U.S.A. 36°36N 114°29W 307 J12
Logansport Ind., U.S.A. 40°45N 86°22W 311 D10
Logansport La., U.S.A. 31°58N 94°0W 314 F8
Logirim Sudan 4°43N 33°14E 257 G3
Lognes-Émerainville ✈ (XLG) France 48°49N 2°37E 134 B4
Logo Sudan 5°20N 30°18E 257 F3
Logone → Chad 12°6N 15°2E 259 F3
Logone Gana Chad 11°36N 15°4E 259 F3
Logone Occidental □ Chad 8°30N 16°0E 259 G3
Logone Occidental → Chad 8°50N 16°0E 259 G3
Logone Oriental □ Chad 8°30N 16°30E 259 G3
Logone Orientale → Chad 9°7N 16°26E 259 G3
Logroño Spain 42°28N 2°27W 196 C2
Logrosán Spain 39°20N 5°32W 195 F5
Løgstør Denmark 56°58N 9°14E 163 H3
Logtak L. India 24°33N 93°50E 241 C4
Løgumkloster Denmark 55°4N 8°57E 163 J2
Loh Vanuatu 13°21S 166°38E 287 C4
Lohals Denmark 55°8N 10°55E 163 J4
Lohardaga India 23°27N 84°45E 243 H11
Loharia India 23°45N 74°14E 242 H6
Loharu India 28°27N 75°49E 242 E6
Lohja Finland 60°12N 24°5E 188 B3
Löhme Germany 52°37N 13°40E 115 A5
Löhne Germany 52°11N 8°40E 178 C4
Loho = Luohe China 33°32N 114°2E 226 H8
Lohr Germany 49°59N 9°35E 179 F5
Lohri Wah → Pakistan 27°27N 67°37E 242 F2
Loi-kaw Burma 19°40N 97°17E 241 F6
Loi-lem Burma 20°52N 97°28E 241 E6
Loimaa Finland 60°50N 23°5E 188 B2
Loir → France 47°33N 0°32W 172 E6
Loir-et-Cher □ France 47°40N 1°20E 172 E8
Loire □ France 45°40N 4°5E 175 C8
Loire → France 47°16N 2°10W 172 E4
Loire Anjou Touraine ⌂ France 47°14N 0°5W 172 E6
Loire-Atlantique □ France 47°25N 1°40W 172 E5
Loire Inférieure = Loire-Atlantique □ France 47°25N 1°40W 172 E5
Loiret □ France 47°55N 2°30E 173 E9
Loitz Germany 53°58N 13°8E 178 B9
Loja Ecuador 3°59S 79°16W 330 A2
Loja Spain 37°10N 4°10W 195 H6
Loja □ Ecuador 4°0S 79°13W 328 D2
Loje → Angola 7°49S 13°6E 265 D2
Loji = Kawasi Indonesia 1°38S 127°28E 231 E7
Lojo = Lohja Finland 60°12N 24°5E 188 B3
Løjt Kirkeby Denmark 55°7N 9°26E 163 J3
Lojung China 24°27N 109°36E 228 E7
Loka Dem. Rep. of the Congo 0°22N 18°2E 264 B3
Loka Sudan 4°13N 31°0E 257 G3
Lokako Dem. Rep. of the Congo 0°57S 18°55E 264 C4
Lokandu Dem. Rep. of the Congo 2°30S 25°45E 264 C5
Lokaw Dem. Rep. of the Congo 2°40S 20°12E 264 C4
Løken Norway 59°48N 11°29E 164 E8
Lokeren Belgium 51°6N 3°59E 170 C3
Lokgwabe Botswana 24°10S 21°50E 270 B3
Lokhvytsya Ukraine 50°25N 33°18E 189 G7
Lokichar Kenya 2°23N 35°39E 268 B4
Lokichokio Kenya 4°19N 34°13E 268 B3
Lokitaung Kenya 4°12N 35°48E 268 B4
Lokkan tekojärvi Finland 67°55N 27°35E 160 C22
Løkken Denmark 57°22N 9°41E 163 G3
Løkken Sør-Trøndelag, Norway 63°9N 9°41E 164 A6
Loknya Russia 56°49N 30°4E 188 D6
Loko C.A.R. 3°38N 18°2E 264 B3
Loko Nigeria 8°1N 7°53E 263 D6
Lokoja Nigeria 7°47N 6°45E 263 D6
Lokolama Dem. Rep. of the Congo 2°35S 19°50E 264 C3
Lokolenge Dem. Rep. of the Congo 1°12N 22°38E 264 B4
Lokolo → Dem. Rep. of the Congo 1°43S 18°23E 264 C3
Lokot Russia 52°34N 34°36E 189 F8
Loktak L. = Logtak L. India 24°33N 93°50E 241 C4
Lokuru Solomon Is. 8°20S 157°0E 287 M9
Lol Sudan 6°26N 29°37E 257 F2
Lol → Sudan 9°13N 26°30E 257 F2
Lola Angola 14°19S 13°37E 265 E2
Lola Guinea 7°52N 8°29W 262 D3
Lola, Mt. U.S.A. 39°26N 120°22W 306 F6
Lolgorien Kenya 1°14S 34°48E 268 C3
Lolibai, Gebel Sudan 3°50N 33°0E 257 G3
Lolimi Sudan 4°35N 34°0E 257 G3
Loliondo Tanzania 2°2S 35°39E 268 C4
Lolland Denmark 54°45N 11°30E 163 K5
Lollar Germany 50°37N 8°43E 178 E4
Lolo U.S.A. 46°45N 114°5W 304 C6
Lolo → Eq. Guin. 1°36N 9°37E 264 B1
Lolo → Gabon 0°18S 12°18E 264 C2
Lolobau I. Papua N. G. 4°55S 151°10E 286 C6
Lolodorf Cameroon 3°16N 10°49E 263 E7
Lolokhet Pakistan 24°54N 67°2E 123 A2
Loloma Zambia 13°24S 24°21E 265 E4
Loltong Vanuatu 15°32S 168°10E 287 E6
Lom Bulgaria 43°48N 23°12E 202 C7
Lom Oppland, Norway 61°50N 8°34E 164 C5
Lom → Bulgaria 43°45N 23°15E 202 C7
Lom → Cameroon 5°20N 13°24E 264 A2
Lom Kao Thailand 16°53N 101°14E 236 D3
Lom Sak Thailand 16°47N 101°15E 236 D3
Loma U.S.A. 47°56N 110°30W 304 C8
Loma Linda U.S.A. 34°3N 117°16W 307 L9
Loma Mansa S. Leone 9°13N 11°7W 262 D2
Loma Mts. S. Leone 9°10N 11°7W 262 D2
Lomako → Dem. Rep. of the Congo 0°50N 20°50E 264 B4
Lomaloma Fiji 17°17S 178°59W 287 A3
Lomami → Dem. Rep. of the Congo 0°46N 24°16E 264 B4
Lomas Chapultepec Mexico 19°25N 99°12W 128 B1
Lomas de San Angel Inn Mexico 19°20N 99°13W 128 B1
Lomas de Zamora Argentina 34°45S 58°24W 334 C4
Lombadina Australia 16°31S 122°54E 278 C3
Lombard U.S.A. 41°53N 88°1W 311 C8
Lombárdia □ Italy 45°40N 9°30E 198 C6
Lombardy = Lombárdia □ Italy 45°40N 9°30E 198 C6
Lombardy East S. Africa 26°6S 28°7E 123 A2
Lombe Angola 9°27S 16°13E 265 D3
Lombez France 43°29N 0°55E 174 E4
Lomblen Indonesia 8°30S 123°32E 231 F6
Lombok Indonesia 8°45S 116°30E 235 D5
Lombok, Selat Indonesia 8°30S 115°50E 231 K18
Lomé Togo 6°9N 1°20E 263 D5
Lomela Dem. Rep. of the Congo 2°19S 23°15E 264 C4
Lomela → Dem. Rep. of the Congo 0°15S 20°40E 264 C4
Lomianki Poland 52°21N 20°54E 142 A1
Lomié Cameroon 3°13N 13°38E 264 B2
Lomma Sweden 55°43N 13°6E 163 J7
Lommel Belgium 51°14N 5°19E 170 C5
Lomond Canada 50°24N 112°36W 296 C6
Lomond, L. U.K. 56°8N 4°38W 167 E4
Lomonosov Ridge Arctic 88°0N 140°0E 150 A
Lomphat Cambodia 13°30N 106°59E 236 F6
Lompobatang Indonesia 5°24S 119°56E 231 F5
Lompoc U.S.A. 34°38N 120°28W 307 L6
Lomseggje Norway 61°49N 8°21E 164 C5
Lomus Reforma Mexico 19°24N 99°14W 128 B1
Łomża Poland 53°10N 22°2E 185 E9
Lon, Ko Thailand 7°47N 98°23E 237 a
Lonavale India 18°46N 73°29E 244 E1
Loncoche Chile 39°20S 72°50W 336 A2
Loncopué Argentina 38°4S 70°37W 336 A2
Londa India 15°30N 74°30E 245 G2
Londiani Kenya 0°10S 35°33E 268 C4
Londinières France 49°50N 1°25E 172 C8
London Ont., Canada 42°59N 81°15W 312 D3
London London, U.K. 51°30N 0°3W 125 B3
London Ky., U.S.A. 37°8N 84°5W 309 G11
London Ohio, U.S.A. 39°53N 83°27W 311 E13
London, Greater □ U.K. 51°36N 0°5W 169 F7
London Avenue Canal U.S.A. 30°3N 90°6W 131 A2
London Bridge Grenada 12°15N 61°35W 323 q
London Bridge London, U.K. 125 b5
London City ✈ (LCY) U.K. 51°30N 0°3E 125 A4
London Gatwick ✈ (LGW) U.K. 51°10N 0°11W 169 F7
London Heathrow ✈ (LHR) U.K. 51°28N 0°27W 125 B1
London Mills U.S.A. 40°43N 90°11W 310 D6
London Stansted ✈ (STN) U.K. 51°54N 0°14E 169 F8
London Zoo U.K. 51°31N 0°9W 125 A3
Londonderry U.K. 55°0N 7°20W 166 B4
Londonderry □ U.K. 55°0N 7°20W 166 B4
Londonderry, C. Australia 13°45S 126°55E 278 B4
Londonderry, I. Chile 55°0S 71°0W 336 E2
Londrina Brazil 23°18S 51°10W 335 A5
Londuimbale Angola 12°15S 15°19E 265 E3
Lone Pine U.S.A. 36°36N 118°4W 306 J8
Lonely Mine Zimbabwe 19°30S 28°49E 271 A4
Long, Î. Martinique 14°36N 60°51W 322 j
Long Akah Malaysia 3°19N 114°47E 235 B4
Long B. N.S.W., Australia 33°59S 151°15E 139 B2
Long B. Cornwall, Jamaica 18°20N 78°20W 320 a
Long B. S.C., U.S.A. 33°35N 78°45W 315 E15

Long Beach _Calif.,_
  _U.S.A._ 33°46N 118°11W **307 M8**
Long Beach _N.Y., U.S.A._ 40°35N 73°39W **313 F11**
Long Beach _Wash., U.S.A._ 46°21N 124°3W **306 D2**
Long Branch _Ont., Canada_ 43°33N 79°31W **141 B1**
Long Branch _N.J., U.S.A._ 40°18N 74°0W **313 F10**
Long Brook _→ U.S.A._ 38°49N 77°5W **143 C2**
Long Cay _Bahamas_ 25°6N 77°22W **153 b**
Long Creek _U.S.A._ 44°43N 119°6W **304 D4**
Long Ditton _U.K._ 51°22N 0°19W **125 B2**
Long Eaton _U.K._ 52°53N 1°15W **168 E6**
Long I. _Antigua & B._ 17°8N 61°45W **322 b**
Long I. _Queens., Australia_ 20°22S 148°51E **280 b**
Long I. _Bahamas_ 23°20N 75°10W **321 B4**
Long I. _Nunavut, Canada_ 54°50N 79°20W **298 B4**
Long I. _Cork, Ireland_ 51°30N 9°34W **166 E2**
Long I. _Papua N. G._ 5°20S 147°5E **286 C4**
Long I. _N.Y., U.S.A._ 40°45N 73°30W **313 F11**
Long Island City _U.S.A._ 40°45N 73°56W **132 B2**
Long Island Sd. _U.S.A._ 41°10N 73°0W **313 E12**
Long L. _Ont., Canada_ 49°30N 86°50W **298 C2**
Long L. _N.Y., U.S.A._ 44°0N 74°23W **313 C10**
Long Lake _U.S.A._ 43°58N 74°25W **313 C10**
Long Mountain _Mauritius_ 20°8S 57°33E **272 e**
Long Point _Canada_ 42°34N 80°25W **312 D4**
Long Point B. _Canada_ 42°40N 80°10W **312 D4**
Long Prairie _U.S.A._ 45°59N 94°52W **306 B8**
Long Prairie _→ U.S.A._ 46°5N 94°36W **308 B6**
Long Pt. _Bahamas_ 25°1N 77°20W **153 b**
Long Pt. _Ont., Canada_ 42°35N 80°2W **312 D4**
Long Pt. _Ont., Canada_ 43°56N 76°53W **313 C8**
Long Pt. _Otago, N.Z._ 46°34S 169°36E **285 G4**
Long Range Mts. _Canada_ 49°30N 57°30W **299 C8**
Long Reef _Australia_ 14°1S 125°48E **278 B4**
Long Sault _Canada_ 45°2N 74°53W **313 A10**
Long Str. = Longa, Proliv
  Russia 70°0N 175°0E **215 C18**
Long Street _Cape Town, S. Africa_ **118 c2**
Long Thanh _Vietnam_ 10°47N 106°57E **237 G6**
Long Xian _China_ 34°55N 106°55E **226 G4**
Long Xuyen _Vietnam_ 10°19N 105°28E **237 G5**
Longa _U.S.A._ 14°42S 18°32E **265 E3**
Longa _Greece_ 36°53N 21°55E **204 E3**
Longa _→ Angola_ 10°14S 13°29E **265 D2**
Longa, Proliv _Russia_ 70°0N 175°0E **215 C18**
Longa Mavinga _→ Angola_ 16°20S 20°15E **265 D4**
Longagung _Indonesia_ 2°16N 115°16E **235 B5**
Long'an _China_ 23°10N 107°40E **228 F6**
Longana _Vanuatu_ 15°18S 168°0E **287 E5**
Longarone _Italy_ 46°16N 12°18E **199 B9**
Longbenton _U.K._ 55°1N 1°31W **168 B6**
Longberang _Indonesia_ 3°43N 116°7E **235 B5**
Longbia _Indonesia_ 2°37N 116°42E **235 B5**
Longboat Key _U.S.A._ 27°23N 82°39W **317 H7**
Longboh _Indonesia_ 0°52N 115°1E **235 D5**
Longburn _N.Z._ 40°33N 175°35E **284 G4**
Longchamp, Hippodrome de
  France 48°51N 2°13E **134 A2**
Longchang _China_ 29°18N 105°15E **228 C5**
Longchuan _Guangdong,_
  China 24°5N 115°17E **229 E10**
Longchuan _Yunnan, China_ 24°23N 97°58E **228 E1**
Longde _China_ 35°30N 106°20E **226 G4**
Longdenville _Trin. & Tob._ 10°31N 61°23W **323 t**
Longeau _France_ 47°47N 5°20E **173 E12**
Longford _Tas., Australia_ 41°32S 147°3E **281 G4**
Longford _Longf., Ireland_ 53°43N 7°49W **166 C4**
Longford _→ Ireland_ 53°42N 7°45W **166 C4**
Longgang Shan _China_ 42°19N 126°30E **224 A3**
Longhai _China_ 24°25N 117°46E **229 E11**
Longhua _Guangdong, China_ 22°39N 114°0E **219 a**
Longhua _Hebei, China_ 41°18N 117°45E **227 D9**
Longhua Pagoda _China_ 31°10N 121°26E **138 B1**
Longhua Park _China_ 31°10N 121°26E **138 B1**
Longhui _China_ 27°7N 111°2E **229 D8**
Longido _Tanzania_ 2°43S 36°42E **268 C4**
Longiram _Indonesia_ 0°5S 115°45E **235 D5**
Longjela _Indonesia_ 2°28N 115°0E **235 B5**
Longjing _China_ 42°46N 129°27E **227 C15**
Longjohn Slough _U.S.A._ 41°42N 87°52W **119 C1**
Longkou _Jiangxi, China_ 26°8N 115°10E **229 D10**
Longkou _Shandong,_
  China 37°40N 120°18E **227 F11**
Longli _China_ 26°25N 106°58E **228 D6**
Longlin _China_ 24°47N 105°20E **228 E5**
Longling _China_ 24°37N 98°39E **228 E2**
Longmeadow _U.S.A._ 42°3N 72°34W **313 D12**
Longmen _China_ 23°40N 114°18E **229 F10**
Longmen Shiku _China_ 34°34N 112°10E **226 G7**
Longming _China_ 22°59N 107°7E **228 F6**
Longmont _U.S.A._ 40°10N 105°6W **304 F11**
Longnan _China_ 24°55N 114°47E **229 E10**
Longnawan _Indonesia_ 1°51N 114°55E **235 B4**
Longnan _China_ 27°9N 116°37E **201 C9**
Longoni, B. de _Mayotte_ 12°41S 45°8E **272 b**
Longonot _△ Kenya_ 0°55S 36°28E **266 C4**
Longos _Greece_ 39°16N 20°7E **206 C10**
Longquan _China_ 28°7N 119°10E **229 C12**
Longreach _Australia_ 23°28S 144°14E **280 C3**
Longshan _China_ 29°29N 109°25E **228 C7**
Longsheng _China_ 25°48N 110°0E **229 E8**
Longtan Dam _China_ 25°5N 107°0E **228 E6**
Longtan Hu _China_ 39°51N 116°24E **114 B2**
Longué-Jumelles _France_ 47°22N 0°8W **172 E6**
Longue-Pointe _Canada_ 45°35N 73°31W **130 A2**
Longueau _France_ 49°52N 2°21E **173 C9**
Longueuil _Canada_ 45°31N 73°29W **130 A3**
Longuy _Cameroon_ 3°5N 9°58E **264 B1**
Longuyon _France_ 49°27N 5°35E **173 C12**
Longvic _France_ 47°17N 5°4E **173 E12**
Longview _Tex., U.S.A._ 32°30N 94°44W **314 E7**
Longview _Wash., U.S.A._ 46°8N 122°57W **306 D4**
Longwood _St. Helena_ 15°57S 5°41W **153 h**
Longwood _Fla., U.S.A._ 28°42N 81°21W **317 G8**
Longwy _France_ 49°30N 5°46E **173 C12**
Longxi _China_ 34°53N 104°40E **226 G3**
Longxue Dao _China_ 22°41N 113°38E **219 a**
Longyan _China_ 25°10N 117°0E **229 E11**
Longyearbyen _Svalbard_ 78°13N 15°40E **150 B8**
Longyou _China_ 29°1N 119°8E **229 C12**
Longzhou _China_ 22°22N 106°50E **228 F6**
Loni _India_ 28°45N 77°17E **120 A2**
Lonigo _Italy_ 45°23N 11°23E **199 C8**
Löningen _Germany_ 52°44N 7°46E **178 C3**
Lonja _→ Croatia_ 45°22N 16°40E **199 C13**
Lonkala
  Dem. Rep. of the Congo 4°37S 23°14E **265 C4**
Lonkin _Burma_ 25°39N 96°22E **234 D1**
Lonoke _U.S.A._ 34°47N 91°54W **314 D9**
Lonquimay _Chile_ 38°26S 71°14W **336 A2**
Lons-le-Saunier _France_ 46°40N 5°31E **173 F12**
Lönsboda _Sweden_ 56°24N 14°20E **163 H8**
Lønset _Norway_ 62°46N 7°24E **164 B4**
Lonton _Burma_ 25°6N 96°17E **241 C6**
Looc _Phil._ 12°15N 121°50E **233 D6**
Looe _U.K._ 50°22N 4°28W **169 E3**
Loogootee _U.S.A._ 38°41N 86°55W **311 F10**
Lookout, C. _Canada_ 55°18N 83°56W **298 A3**
Lookout, C., N.C., U.S.A. 34°35N 76°32W **315 H7**
Loolmalasin _Tanzania_ 3°0S 35°53E **268 C4**
Loon _→ Alta., Canada_ 57°8N 115°3W **296 B5**
Loon _→ Man., Canada_ 52°30N 101°59W **297 B8**
Loon Lake _Canada_ 54°2N 109°10W **297 B7**
Loongana _Australia_ 30°52S 127°5E **279 F4**
Loop, The _Chicago, U.S.A._ **119 c1**

Loop Hd. _Ireland_ 52°34N 9°56W **166 D2**
Lop _China_ 37°3N 80°11E **217 E10**
Lop Nor = Lop Nur _China_ 40°20N 90°10E **217 D12**
Lop Nur _China_ 40°20N 90°10E **217 D12**
Lopare _Bos.-H._ 44°39N 18°46E **182 F3**
Lopatin _Russia_ 43°50N 47°35E **191 J8**
Lopatina, Gora _Russia_ 50°47N 143°10E **215 D15**
Lopatino = Volzhsk
  Russia 55°57N 48°23E **190 C9**
Lopatka, Mys _Russia_ 50°52N 156°40E **215 D16**
Lopaye _Sudan_ 6°37N 33°40E **257 F3**
Lopburi _Thailand_ 14°48N 100°37E **236 E3**
Lopé-Okanda _△ Gabon_ 0°45S 11°54E **264 C2**
Lopevi _Vanuatu_ 16°30S 168°21E **287 F6**
Lopez _Phil._ 13°53N 122°15E **232 E4**
Lopez _Pa., U.S.A._ 41°27N 76°20W **313 E8**
Lopez, C. _Gabon_ 0°47S 8°40E **264 C1**
López de Filippis = Mariscal
  Estigarribia _Paraguay_ 22°3S 60°40W **334 A3**
Lopinot _Trin. & Tob._ 10°41N 61°19W **323 t**
Lopori _→
  Dem. Rep. of the Congo_ 1°14N 19°49E **264 B3**
Lopphavet _Norway_ 70°27N 21°15E **160 A19**
Lora _Norway_ 62°8N 8°45E **164 B5**
Lora _→ Afghan._ 31°35N 66°32E **240 C2**
Lora = Oppland, Norway 62°8N 8°42E **164 B5**
Lora, Hāmūn-i- _Pakistan_ 29°38N 64°58E **240 C2**
Lora Cr. _→ Australia_ 28°10S 135°22E **281 D2**
Lora del Rio _Spain_ 37°39N 5°33W **195 H5**
Lorain _U.S.A._ 41°28N 82°11W **312 E2**
Loraine _U.S.A._ 40°9N 91°13W **310 D5**
Loralai _Pakistan_ 30°20N 68°41E **242 D3**
Lorca _Spain_ 37°41N 1°42W **197 H3**
Lord Howe I. _Pac. Oc._ 31°33S 159°6E **287 G8**
Lord Howe Rise _Pac. Oc._ 30°0S 162°30E **277 H12**
Lord Howe Seamount Chain
  Pac. Oc. 28°0S 159°0E **277 F10**
Lord Loughborough I.
  Burma 10°25N 97°54E **237 G1**
Lord's Cricket Ground
  _U.K._ 51°31N 0°10W **125 A2**
Lordsburg _U.S.A._ 32°21N 108°43W **305 K9**
Lorengau _Papua N. G._ 2°1S 147°15E **286 B4**
Lorestān □ _Iran_ 33°30N 48°40E **247 C6**
Loreto _Bolivia_ 15°13S 64°40W **331 D5**
Loreto _Brazil_ 7°5S 45°10W **332 C2**
Loreto Marche, _Italy_ 43°26N 13°36E **199 E10**
Loreto _Piemonte, Italy_ 45°29N 9°12E **129 B2**
Loreto _Baja Calif. S.,_
  Mexico 26°0N 111°21W **318 B2**
Loreto _Surigao N., Phil._ 10°21N 125°34E **233 F5**
Loreto □ _Peru_ 5°0S 75°0W **328 E3**
Lorgues _France_ 43°28N 6°22E **175 E10**
Lorhosso _Burkina Faso_ 10°17N 3°38W **264 C4**
Lorian Swamp _Kenya_ 0°40N 39°35E **267 D4**
Lorica _Colombia_ 9°14N 75°49W **328 B2**
Lorient _Morbihan, France_ 47°45N 3°23W **172 E3**
Lorient _St.-Martin_ 17°54N 62°49W **322 a**
Lorignac _France_ 41°8N 94°3W **310 C2**
Lőrinci _Hungary_ 47°44N 19°41E **182 C4**
Lormi _India_ 22°17N 81°41E **243 H9**
Lorn, Firth of _U.K._ 56°26N 5°10W **167 E3**
Lorne _Australia_ 38°33S 143°59E **282 E5**
Loronyo _Sudan_ 4°38N 32°28E **257 G3**
Lorovouno _Cyprus_ 35°8N 32°36E **207 E8**
Lörrach _Germany_ 47°36N 7°40E **179 C13**
Lorraine _→ Baker
  U.S.A._ 46°22N 104°17W **304 C11**
Lorraine □ _France_ 48°53N 6°0E **173 D13**
Lorraine △ _France_ 48°55N 5°50E **173 D12**
Los _Sweden_ 61°45N 15°10E **162 C9**
Los, Îles de _Guinea_ 9°30N 13°50W **262 D2**
Los Alamos _Calif., U.S.A._ 34°44N 120°17W **307 L6**
Los Alamos _N. Mex.,_
  _U.S.A._ 35°53N 106°19W **305 J10**
Los Alcornocales △ _Spain_ 36°21N 5°32W **195 J5**
Los Alerces △ _Argentina_ 42°55S 71°55W **336 B2**
Los Altos _Chile_ 22°33N 122°7W **306 H4**
Los Andes _Chile_ 32°50S 70°40W **334 C1**
Los Angeles _Chile_ 37°28S 72°23W **334 D1**
Los Angeles _Calif., U.S.A._ 34°4N 118°15W **126 B3**
Los Angeles, Bahia de
  Mexico 28°56N 113°34W **318 B2**
Los Angeles Aqueduct
  _U.S.A._ 35°22N 118°5W **307 K9**
Los Angeles Int. ✈ (LAX)
  _U.S.A._ 33°57N 118°25W **126 C2**
Los Antiguos _Argentina_ 46°35S 71°40W **336 C2**
Los Banos _U.S.A._ 37°4N 120°51W **306 H6**
Los Barrios _Spain_ 36°11N 5°30W **195 J5**
Los Blancos _Argentina_ 23°40S 62°30W **334 A3**
Los Cardones △ _Argentina_ 25°8S 65°55W **334 B2**
Los Cerrillos ✈ (ULC)
  Chile 33°29S 70°42W **137 B1**
Los Chiles _Costa Rica_ 11°2N 84°43W **320 D3**
Los Corrales de Buelna
  Spain 43°15N 4°5W **194 B6**
Los Cristianos _Canary Is._ 28°3N 16°42W **153 e1**
Los Gallardos _Spain_ 37°18N 1°57W **197 H3**
Los Gallos Pt. _Trin. & Tob._ 10°5N 61°55W **323 t**
Los Gatos _U.S.A._ 37°14N 121°59W **306 H5**
Los Glaciares △ _Argentina_ 50°0S 73°55W **336 C2**
Los Haïtises △ _Dom. Rep._ 19°4N 69°36W **321 C6**
Los Hermanos Is.
  Venezuela 11°45N 64°25W **321 D7**
Los Huemules _Chile_ 46°10S 73°23W **336 C2**
Los Islotes _Canary Is._ 29°4N 13°44W **153 e2**
Los Katíos △ _Colombia_ 7°50N 77°10W **320 B2**
Los Lagos _Chile_ 39°51S 72°50W **336 A2**
Los Llanos de Aridane
  Canary Is. 28°38N 17°54W **153 e1**
Los Loros _Chile_ 27°50S 70°6W **334 B1**
Los Lunas _U.S.A._ 34°48N 106°44W **305 J10**
Los Menucos _Argentina_ 40°50S 68°50W **336 B3**
Los Mochis _Mexico_ 25°45N 108°57W **318 B3**
Los Monegros _Spain_ 41°29N 0°13W **196 D4**
Los Monos _Argentina_ 46°1S 69°36W **336 C3**
Los Muermos _Chile_ 41°24S 73°29W **336 B2**
Los Nevados △ _Colombia_ 4°41N 75°21W **328 C3**
Los Nietos _Spain_ 37°39N 0°47W **197 H4**
Los Nietos _Calif., U.S.A._ 33°57N 118°4W **126 C4**
Los Olivos _Lima, Peru_ 11°57S 77°39W **320 a**
Los Olivos _Calif., U.S.A._ 34°40N 120°7W **307 L6**
Los Palacios _Cuba_ 22°35N 83°15W **320 B3**
Los Palacios y Villafranca
  Spain 37°10N 5°56W **195 H5**
Los Queñes _Chile_ 35°1S 70°48W **334 D1**
Los Remedios ✈ _Mexico_ 19°28N 99°11W **318 d2**
Los Reyes _Mexico_ 19°21N 99°6W **128 B2**
Los Reyes de Salgado
  Mexico 19°35N 102°29W **318 D4**
Los Ríos □ _Ecuador_ 1°30S 79°25W **328 D2**
Los Roques Is. _Venezuela_ 11°50N 66°45W **321 D6**
Los Santos de Maimona
  Spain 38°27N 6°22W **195 G4**
Los Teques _Venezuela_ 10°21N 67°2W **328 A5**
Los Testigos, Is. _Venezuela_ 11°23N 63°6W **329 A5**
Los Vilos _Chile_ 32°10S 71°30W **334 C1**
Los Yébenes _Spain_ 39°36N 3°55W **195 F7**
Loš,
  Dem. Rep. of the Congo 6°6S 20°37E **265 C4**
Low, L. _Canada_ 52°29N 76°17W **298 B4**
Low B. _Antigua & B._ 17°39N 61°51W **322 b**
Low Pt. _Australia_ 32°25S 127°25E **279 F4**

Løsning _Denmark_ 55°48N 9°42E **163 J3**
Losombo
  Dem. Rep. of the Congo 1°2N 19°4E **264 B3**
Lossiemouth _U.K._ 57°42N 3°17W **167 D5**
Lossnen _Sweden_ 62°26N 14°36E **162 B6**
Lostwithiel _U.K._ 50°24N 4°41W **169 G3**
Losuia _Papua N. G._ 8°30S 151°4E **286 D7**
Lot □ _France_ 44°39N 1°40E **174 D5**
Lot _→ France_ 44°18N 0°20E **174 D4**
Lot-et-Garonne □ _France_ 44°22N 0°30E **174 D4**
Lota _Chile_ 37°5S 73°10W **334 D1**
Lotagipi Swamp _Sudan_ 4°36N 34°55E **257 G3**
Løten _Norway_ 60°51N 11°21E **164 D8**
Lotfābād _Iran_ 37°32N 59°20E **247 B8**
Lothair _S. Africa_ 26°22S 30°27E **271 C5**
Loto
  Dem. Rep. of the Congo 2°48S 22°3E **264 C4**
Lotoi _→
  Dem. Rep. of the Congo_ 1°35S 18°30E **264 C3**
Lotorp _Sweden_ 58°44N 15°50E **163 F9**
Lötschbergtunnel _Switz._ 46°26N 7°43E **179 J3**
Lotta _→ Europe_ 68°42N 31°6E **160 B24**
Löttorp _Sweden_ 57°10N 17°0E **163 H11**
Lotung _Taiwan_ 24°41N 121°46E **225 B3**
Lotus River _S. Africa_ 34°4S 18°31E **118 B2**
Lotus Temple _India_ 28°33N 77°15E **120 B2**
Lötzen = Giżycko _Poland_ 54°2N 21°48E **184 D8**
Lou I. _Papua N. G._ 2°22S 147°22E **286 B4**
Loubière _Dominica_ 15°16N 61°23W **323 k**
Loubomo _Congo_ 4°9S 12°47E **264 C2**
Loudéac _France_ 48°11N 2°47W **172 D4**
Loudi _China_ 27°42N 111°59E **229 D8**
Loudima _Congo_ 4°6S 13°5E **264 C2**
Loudonville _U.S.A._ 40°38N 82°14W **312 F2**
Loudun _France_ 47°3N 0°5E **172 E7**
Loue _→ France_ 47°1N 5°28E **173 E12**
Louga _Senegal_ 15°45N 16°5W **262 B1**
Louga _△ Senegal_ 15°20N 15°35W **262 B1**
Loughborough _U.K._ 52°47N 1°11W **168 E6**
Lougheed I. _Canada_ 77°26N 105°6W **295 B10**
Loughlinstown _Ireland_ 53°15N 6°7W **120 B3**
Loughman _U.S.A._ 28°14N 81°34W **317 G8**
Loughrea _Ireland_ 53°12N 8°33W **166 C3**
Loughros More B. _Ireland_ 54°48N 8°32W **166 B3**
Louhans _France_ 46°38N 5°12E **173 F12**
Louis Armstrong New Orleans
  Int. ✈ (MSY) _U.S.A._ 30°0N 90°15W **131 A1**
Louis Armstrong Park
  New Orleans, U.S.A. **131 a2**
Louis-Gentil = Youssoufia
  Morocco 32°16N 8°31W **260 B3**
Louis Trichardt _S. Africa_ 23°1S 29°43E **271 B4**
Louis XIV, Pte. _Canada_ 54°37N 79°45W **298 B4**
Louisa _U.S.A._ 38°7N 82°36W **309 F12**
Louisbourg _Canada_ 45°55N 60°0W **299 C8**
Louisburg _U.S.A._ 38°37N 94°41W **310 F2**
Louisburgh _Ireland_ 53°46N 9°49W **166 C2**
Louise, I. _Canada_ 28°28N 81°32W **133 B1**
Louise I. _Canada_ 52°55N 131°50W **296 C2**
Louiseville _Canada_ 46°20N 72°56W **298 C5**
Louisiade Arch.
  Papua N. G. 11°10S 153°0E **286 F7**
Louisiana _U.S.A._ 39°27N 91°3W **310 E6**
Louisiana □ _U.S.A._ 30°50N 92°0W **314 F9**
Louisiana Superdome
  New Orleans, U.S.A. **131 b1**
Louisville _U.S.A._ 31°47N 85°33W **316 D4**
Louisville _Ga., U.S.A._ 33°0N 82°25W **316 B7**
Louisville _Ill., U.S.A._ 38°46N 88°30W **311 F11**
Louisville _Ky., U.S.A._ 38°15N 85°46W **311 F11**
Louisville _Miss., U.S.A._ 33°7N 89°3W **315 E10**
Louisville _Ohio, U.S.A._ 40°50N 81°16W **312 F3**
Louisville Ridge _Pac. Oc._ 31°0S 172°30W **288 L10**
Loukoléla _Congo_ 1°4S 17°0E **264 C3**
Loukouo _Congo_ 3°38S 14°39E **264 C2**
Loulay _France_ 46°3N 0°30W **174 B3**
Loulé _Portugal_ 37°9N 8°0W **195 H3**
Loulouni _Mali_ 10°54N 5°36E **262 C3**
Loum _Cameroon_ 4°42N 9°44E **264 B1**
Loup _→ Czech Rep._ 50°20N 13°48E **180 A6**
Loup City _U.S.A._ 41°17N 98°58W **308 E4**
Loups Marins, Lacs des
  Canada 56°30N 73°45W **298 A5**
Lourdes _Canada_ 43°6N 0°3W **174 E3**
Lourdes-de-Blanc-Sablon
  Canada 51°24N 57°12W **299 B8**
Lourenço _Brazil_ 2°30N 51°40W **329 C7**
Lourenço Marques = Maputo
  Mozam. 25°58S 32°32E **271 C5**
Loures _Portugal_ 38°49N 9°10W **126 A1**
Lourinhã _Portugal_ 39°14N 9°17W **195 F1**
Louros _Greece_ 39°3N 20°47E **207 E2**
Louroujina _Cyprus_ 35°0N 33°28E **207 F9**
Lousã _Portugal_ 40°7N 8°14W **194 E2**
Louth _Burkina Faso_ 13°0N 3°10W **262 C4**
Louth _N.S.W., Australia_ 30°30S 145°8E **283 A6**
Louth _Louth, Ireland_ 53°58N 6°32W **166 C5**
Louth □ _Ireland_ 53°56N 6°34W **166 C5**
Louth B. _Australia_ 34°33S 135°56E **282 C1**
Loutra Edipsou _Greece_ 38°54N 23°2E **204 C5**
Loutra Kyllinis _Greece_ 37°52N 21°17E **207 D3**
Loutraki _Greece_ 37°58N 22°57E **204 D4**
Loutropoli Thermis _Greece_ 39°11N 26°29E **205 B8**
Louvain = Leuven _Belgium_ 50°52N 4°42E **170 D4**
Louvale _U.S.A._ 32°10N 84°50W **316 D5**
Louveciennes _France_ 48°51N 2°8E **134 A1**
Louviers _France_ 49°12N 1°10E **172 C8**
Louvre, Musée du _Paris, France_ **134 b4**
Louvre, Palais du _Paris, France_ **134 b4**
Louwsburg _S. Africa_ 27°37S 31°7E **271 C5**
Lovat _→ Russia_ 58°14N 31°28E **188 C6**
Lovćen _Montenegro_ 42°23N 18°51E **202 D2**
Lovćen △ _Montenegro_ 42°20N 18°50E **202 D2**
Lovech _Bulgaria_ 43°8N 24°42E **203 D8**
Lovech □ _Bulgaria_ 43°0N 24°45E **203 D8**
Loveland _Colo., U.S.A._ 40°24N 105°5W **304 E11**
Loveland _Ohio, U.S.A._ 39°16N 84°16W **311 E12**
Lovell _U.S.A._ 44°50N 108°24W **304 D9**
Lovelock _U.S.A._ 40°11N 118°28W **304 F4**
Lovere _Italy_ 45°49N 10°4E **198 C7**
Lovers Leap _Jamaica_ 17°52N 77°39W **320 a**
Lovers Park _U.S.A._ 42°19N 89°3W **310 D9**
Loviisa _Finland_ 60°28N 26°12E **188 B4**
Lovilia _U.S.A._ 41°8N 92°55W **310 C4**
Lovina _Indonesia_ 8°9S 115°1E **237 K18**
Loving _U.S.A._ 32°17N 104°6W **305 K11**
Lovington _Ill., U.S.A._ 39°43N 88°38W **311 E8**
Lovisa = Loviisa _Finland_ 32°57N 103°21W **305 K12**
  _U.S.A._ 60°28N 26°12E **188 B4**
Lovosice _Czech Rep._ 50°30N 14°2E **180 A7**
Lovran _Croatia_ 45°18N 14°15E **199 C11**
Lovrin _Romania_ 45°58N 20°48E **182 E5**
Lövstabukten _Sweden_ 60°25N 17°53E **162 D11**
Lövstakken _Sweden_ 55°52N 13°54E **163 J7**
Lovua _Lunda Norte, Angola_ 7°19S 20°12E **268 D4**
Lóvua _Moxico, Angola_ 11°33S 23°33E **265 E4**
Lóvua _→
  Dem. Rep. of the Congo_ 6°6S 20°37E **265 C4**

Low Tatra = Nízké Tatry
  Slovak Rep. 48°55N 19°30E **181 C12**
Lowa
  Dem. Rep. of the Congo 1°24S 25°51E **268 C2**
Lowa _→
  Dem. Rep. of the Congo_ 1°24S 25°51E **268 C2**
Lowden _U.S.A._ 41°52N 90°56W **310 C6**
Lowell _Ind., U.S.A._ 41°18N 87°25W **311 C8**
Lowell _Mass., U.S.A._ 42°38N 71°19W **313 D13**
Lowell _Mich., U.S.A._ 42°56N 85°20W **311 A11**
Lowellville _U.S.A._ 41°2N 80°32W **312 E4**
Löwen = Lewin Brzeski
  Poland 50°45N 17°37E **185 H4**
Löwen _→ Namibia_ 26°51S 18°17E **270 C2**
Löwenberg = Lwówek Śląski
  Poland 51°49N 17°42E **185 G6**
Lower Alkali L. _U.S.A._ 41°16N 120°2W **304 F3**
Lower Arrow L. _Canada_ 49°40N 118°5W **296 D5**
Lower Austria = Niederösterreich □
  Austria 48°35N 15°40E **180 C8**
Lower California = Baja California
  Mexico 31°10N 115°12W **318 A1**
Lower East Side _New York, U.S.A._ **132 e2**
Lower Glenelg △ _Australia_ 38°4S 141°41E **282 E4**
Lower Hutt _N.Z._ 41°10S 174°55E **143 B2**
Lower Kalskag _U.S.A._ 61°31N 160°23W **316 C7**
Lower Lake _U.S.A._ 38°55N 122°37W **306 G4**
Lower Manhattan _New York, U.S.A._ **132 f1**
Lower Manitou L. _Canada_ 49°15N 93°0W **297 D10**
Lower Manzanilla
  Trin. & Tob. 10°31N 61°3W **323 t**
Lower New York B. = Lower B.
  _U.S.A._ 40°32N 74°5W **132 C1**
Lower Paia _U.S.A._ 20°55N 156°23W **302 C5**
Lower Post _Canada_ 59°58N 128°30W **296 B3**
Lower Red L. _U.S.A._ 47°58N 95°0W **308 B6**
Lower Saxony = Niedersachsen □
  Germany 52°50N 9°0E **178 C4**
Lower Shing Mun Res.
  China 22°22N 114°9E **122 A1**
Lower Tunguska = Tunguska,
  Nizhnyaya _→ Russia_ 65°48N 88°4E **215 C9**
Lower Zambezi △ _Zambia_ 15°25S 29°40E **269 F2**
Lowestoft _U.K._ 52°29N 1°45E **169 E9**
Lowgar □ _Afghan._ 34°0N 69°0E **240 B3**
Łowicz _Poland_ 52°6N 19°55E **185 F6**
Lowly, Pt. _Australia_ 33°3S 137°46E **282 B2**
Lowry Bay _N.Z._ 41°15S 174°55E **143 B2**
Lowry City _U.S.A._ 38°8N 93°44W **310 F3**
Lowther I. _Canada_ 74°33N 97°30W **295 C12**
Lowville _U.S.A._ 43°47N 75°29W **313 C9**
Loxton _S. Austral.,
  Australia_ 34°28S 140°31E **282 C4**
Loxton _Northern Cape,
  S. Africa_ 31°30S 22°22E **270 D3**
Loyalton _U.S.A._ 39°41N 120°14W **306 F6**
Loyalty, Is. = Loyauté, Îs.
  N. Cal. 20°50S 166°30E **288 d**
Loyang = Luoyang
  China 34°40N 112°26E **226 G7**
Loyauté, Îs. _N. Cal._ 20°50S 166°30E **288 d**
Loyev = Loyew _Belarus_ 51°56N 30°46E **177 C16**
Loyew _Belarus_ 51°56N 30°46E **177 C16**
Loyola Univ. _U.S.A._ 42°0N 87°39W **119 B3**
Loyoro _Uganda_ 3°22N 34°14E **268 B3**
Lož _Slovenia_ 45°43N 14°30E **199 C11**
Lozère □ _France_ 44°35N 3°30E **174 D7**
Loznica _Serbia_ 44°32N 19°12E **202 B3**
Lozova _Ukraine_ 49°0N 36°28E **189 H9**
Lualaltuma ☆ _Australia_ 23°57S 132°25E **278 D5**
Lü Shan _China_ 29°39N 115°58E **229 C11**
Lü Xun, Tomb of _China_ 31°17N 121°29E **138 B1**
Lu Wo _China_ 22°33N 114°6E **219 a**
Lü Xun Museum _Beijing, China_ **114 b1**
Lü Xun Park _China_ 31°17N 121°28E **138 B1**
Lua _→
  Dem. Rep. of the Congo_ 2°46N 18°26E **264 B3**
Lua Makiki _U.S.A._ 20°33N 156°37W **302 C5**
Luachimo _Angola_ 7°23S 20°48E **265 D4**
Luacono _Angola_ 11°15S 21°37E **265 E4**
Luajan _→ India_ 24°44N 85°1E **243 G11**
Lualaba _→
  Dem. Rep. of the Congo_ 0°26N 25°20E **268 B2**
Luama _→
  Dem. Rep. of the Congo_ 4°17S 20°2E **265 C4**
Luambe △ _Zambia_ 12°30S 32°15E **269 E3**
Luampa _Zambia_ 15°4S 24°20E **269 F1**
Lu'an _China_ 31°45N 116°29E **229 B11**
Luan Chau _Vietnam_ 21°38N 103°24E **228 B4**
Luan He _→ China_ 39°20N 119°5E **227 E10**
Luan Xian _China_ 39°40N 118°40E **227 E10**
Luancheng _Guangxi Zhuangzu,
  China_ 22°48N 108°55E **228 F7**
Luancheng _Hebei, China_ 37°53N 114°40E **226 F8**
Luanco _Spain_ 43°37N 5°48W **194 B5**
Luanda _Angola_ 8°50S 13°15E **265 D2**
Luando _→ Angola_ 10°21S 16°27E **265 E3**
Luando △ _Angola_ 11°35S 30°15E **269 E3**
Luang, Doi _Thailand_ 18°30N 101°15E **238 C3**
Luang, Thale _Thailand_ 7°30N 100°15E **237 J3**
Luang Nam Tha _Laos_ 20°58N 101°30E **228 G3**
Luang Prabang _Laos_ 19°52N 102°10E **228 H4**
Luangwa _Zambia_ 15°35S 30°16E **269 F3**
Luangwa _→ Zambia_ 14°25S 30°25E **269 E3**
Luangwa Valley _Zambia_ 13°30S 31°30E **269 E3**
Luangwe = Loange _→
  Dem. Rep. of the Congo_ 4°17S 20°2E **265 C4**
Luanne _China_ 40°55N 117°40E **227 D9**
Luanping _China_ 40°53N 117°23E **227 D9**
Luanshya _Zambia_ 13°3S 28°28E **269 E2**
Luapula □ _Zambia_ 11°0S 29°0E **269 E2**
Luapula _→ Africa_ 9°26S 28°33E **269 D2**
Luar, Danau _Indonesia_ 0°35S 111°5E **235 B4**
Luarca _Spain_ 43°32N 6°32W **194 B4**

Lübben _Germany_ 51°56N 13°54E **178 D9**
Lübbenau _Germany_ 51°52N 13°57E **178 D9**
Lübbock _U.S.A._ 33°35N 101°51W **314 E4**
Lübeck _Germany_ 53°52N 10°40E **178 B6**
Lübecker Bucht _Germany_ 54°3N 10°54E **178 A6**
Lubefu
  Dem. Rep. of the Congo 4°47S 24°27E **265 C4**
Lubefu _→
  Dem. Rep. of the Congo_ 4°10S 23°0E **265 C4**
Lubelskie □ _Poland_ 51°0N 22°30E **185 G9**
Lubień = Lubin _Poland_ 51°24N 16°11E **185 G3**
Löwen = Lewin Brzeski
  Poland 50°45N 17°37E **185 H4**

Lüfeng _Yunnan, China_ 25°0N 102°5E **228 E4**
Lufico _Angola_ 6°24S 13°23E **265 D2**
Lufira _→
  Dem. Rep. of the Congo_ 9°30S 27°0E **269 D2**
Lufkin _U.S.A._ 31°21N 94°44W **314 F7**
Lufupa _→
  Dem. Rep. of the Congo_ 10°37S 24°56E **265 E4**
Luga _Russia_ 58°40N 29°55E **188 C5**
Luga _→ Russia_ 59°40N 28°18E **188 C5**
Lugano _Switz._ 46°1N 8°57E **179 J4**
Lugano, L. di _Switz._ 46°0N 9°0E **198 C6**
Lugansk = Luhansk
  Ukraine 48°38N 39°15E **189 H10**
Luganville _Vanuatu_ 15°27S 167°10E **287 E5**
Lugard's Falls _Kenya_ 3°6S 38°41E **268 C4**
Lugela _→ Mozam._ 11°25S 38°33E **269 E4**
Lugenda _→ Mozam._ 11°25S 38°33E **269 E4**
Lugh = Luug _Somali Rep._ 3°48N 42°34E **267 D5**
Lugnaquillia _Ireland_ 52°58N 6°28W **166 D5**
Lugnvik _Sweden_ 62°56N 17°55E **162 B11**
Lugo _Italy_ 44°25N 11°54E **199 D8**
Lugo _Spain_ 43°2N 7°35W **194 B3**
Lugo □ _Spain_ 43°0N 7°30W **194 C3**
Lugoj _Romania_ 45°42N 21°57E **182 E6**
Lugovoy = Qulan
  Kazakhstan 42°55N 72°43E **214 E8**
Lugus I. _Phil._ 5°41N 120°50E **233 J3**
Luhansk _Ukraine_ 48°38N 39°15E **189 H10**
Luhansk □ _Ukraine_ 49°10N 38°45E **189 H10**
Luhe _China_ 32°19N 118°50E **229 A12**
Luhe _→ Germany_ 53°23N 10°13E **178 B6**
Luhit _→ India_ 27°48N 95°28E **241 D10**
Luhu _China_ 23°9N 113°16E **121 B2**
Luhuo _China_ 31°21N 100°48E **228 B3**
Lui → _Angola_ 8°21S 17°33E **265 D3**
Lui _→ Zambia_ 16°18S 23°17E **265 F4**
Luia _Angola_ 8°10S 21°52E **265 D4**
Luiana _Angola_ 8°32S 21°47E **265 D4**
Luiana _→ Angola_ 17°24S 23°3E **265 F4**
Luiana △ _Angola_ 16°55S 22°20E **265 F4**
Luichow = Liuzhou
  China 24°22N 109°22E **228 E7**
Luichow Pen. = Leizhou Bandao
  China 21°0N 110°0E **228 G7**
Luikui _Taiwan_ 23°0N 120°38E **225 D2**
Luilaka _→
  Dem. Rep. of the Congo_ 0°52S 20°12E **264 C4**
Luimneach = Limerick
  Ireland 52°40N 8°37W **166 D3**
Luing _U.K._ 56°14N 5°39W **167 E3**
Luino _Italy_ 45°59N 8°44E **198 C5**
Luís Correia _Brazil_ 3°0S 41°35W **332 B3**
Luís Gonçalves _Brazil_ 5°37S 50°25W **332 C1**
Luitpold Coast _Antarctica_ 78°30S 32°0W **151 D1**
Luiza _Dem. Rep. of the Congo_ 7°40S 22°30E **265 D4**
Luizi _Dem. Rep. of the Congo_ 6°0S 27°25E **268 D2**
Luján _Argentina_ 34°45S 59°5W **334 C4**
Lujiang _China_ 31°20N 117°15E **229 B11**
Lukala
  Dem. Rep. of the Congo 5°31S 14°32E **265 D2**
Lukang _Taiwan_ 24°1N 120°22E **225 B2**
Lukanga Swamp _Zambia_ 14°30S 27°40E **269 E2**
Lukavac _Bos.-H._ 44°33N 18°32E **182 F3**
Lukenie _→
  Dem. Rep. of the Congo_ 3°0S 18°50E **264 C3**
Lŭki _Bulgaria_ 41°50N 24°43E **203 E8**
Lukk _Libya_ 32°1N 24°46E **258 B4**
Lukolela _Equateur,
  Dem. Rep. of the Congo_ 1°10S 17°12E **264 C3**
Lukolela _Kasai-Or.,
  Dem. Rep. of the Congo_ 5°23S 24°32E **268 D1**
Lukosi _Zimbabwe_ 18°30S 26°30E **269 F2**
Lukovë _Albania_ 39°59N 19°54E **202 G3**
Lukovit _Bulgaria_ 43°13N 24°11E **203 D8**
Łuków _Poland_ 51°55N 22°23E **185 G9**
Lukoyanov _Russia_ 55°2N 44°29E **190 C7**
Lukseflfjell _Norway_ 59°23N 9°34E **164 E6**
Luku _Taiwan_ 23°44N 120°45E **225 D2**
Lukulu _Zambia_ 14°35S 23°25E **269 E1**
Lukuni
  Dem. Rep. of the Congo 36°2N 121°33W **306 J5**
Lula _U.S.A._ 34°27N 90°29W **315 E9**
Lul'kusuzi △ _Zambia_ 12°43S 32°35E **269 E3**
Lulang Shan _China_ 38°0N 111°0E **226 F6**
Luleå _Sweden_ 65°35N 22°10E **160 D20**
Luleälven _→ Sweden_ 65°35N 22°10E **160 D20**
Luleburgaz _Turkey_ 41°23N 27°22E **203 E11**
Luliang _China_ 25°0N 103°40E **228 E4**
Lulima
  Dem. Rep. of the Congo 4°12S 25°36E **268 C2**
Luling _U.S.A._ 29°41N 97°39W **314 G6**
Lulong _China_ 39°53N 118°51E **227 E10**
Lulonga _→
  Dem. Rep. of the Congo_ 1°0N 18°10E **264 B3**
Lulu _→
  Dem. Rep. of the Congo_ 1°18N 23°42E **264 B4**
Lulua _→
  Dem. Rep. of the Congo_ 4°30S 20°30E **265 C4**
Luluabaurg = Kananga
  Dem. Rep. of the Congo 5°55S 22°18E **265 D4**
Luma _Amer. Samoa_ 14°16S 169°33W **302 f**
Lumai _Angola_ 13°13S 21°25E **265 E4**
Lumajang _Indonesia_ 8°8S 113°13E **235 D4**
Lumaku, Gunong
  Malaysia 4°52N 115°38E **235 B5**
Lumär _Iran_ 33°33N 46°49E **213 F12**
Lumbala = Lumbala N'guimbo
  Angola 12°39S 22°35E **265 E4**
Lumbala Kaquengue
  Angola 12°39S 22°34E **265 E4**
Lumbala N'guimbo
  Angola 14°18S 21°18E **265 E4**
Lumber _→ Zambia_ 16°44S 23°41E **265 F4**
Lumber City _U.S.A._ 31°56N 82°41W **316 D7**
Lumberton _U.S.A._ 34°37N 79°0W **315 D15**
Lumbis _Indonesia_ 4°18N 116°15E **235 B5**
Lumbo _Mozam._ 15°0S 40°40E **269 F5**
Lumbres _France_ 50°42N 2°5E **173 B9**
Lumding _India_ 25°46N 93°10E **241 E4**
Lumi _Papua N. G._ 3°30S 142°2E **286 B3**
Lumiar _Portugal_ 38°46N 9°10W **126 A1**
Lumphng _U.S.A._ 38°57N 83°0W **312 F2**
Lumsden _Sask., Canada_ 50°39N 104°52W **297 C8**
Lumsden _N.Z._ 45°44S 168°27E **285 F3**
Lumut _Malaysia_ 4°13N 100°37E **237 K3**
Lumut, Tanjung _Indonesia_ 3°50S 105°58E **234 C2**
Luna _India_ 23°43N 69°16E **242 H3**
Luna _Apayao, Phil._ 18°18N 121°21E **232 B3**
Luna _Ilocos Norte, Phil._ 18°18N 120°42E **232 B3**
Lunavada _India_ 23°8N 73°37E **242 H5**
Lunca _Romania_ 47°22N 25°1E **186 B2**
Lunca Corbului _Romania_ 44°42N 24°42E **183 E9**
Lund _Sweden_ 55°44N 13°12E **163 J6**
Lunda Norte □ _Angola_ 8°20S 18°50E **265 D4**
Lunda Sul □ _Angola_ 10°0S 25°50E **265 E4**
Lundazi _Zambia_ 12°20S 33°7E **269 E3**
Lunde _Norway_ 63°6N 10°19E **164 A7**
Lundazi _Zambia_ 12°20S 33°7E **269 E3**
Lunde _Sweden_ 62°53N 17°51E **162 B11**
Lundenburg = Břeclav
  Czech Rep. 48°46N 16°53E **181 C9**
Lunderskov _Denmark_ 55°29N 9°19E **163 J3**

Lundi → Zimbabwe 21°43S 32°34E 269 G3
Lundtofte Denmark 55°47N 12°32E 118 A3
Lundu Malaysia 1°40N 109°50E 235 B3
Lundy U.K. 51°10N 4°41W 169 F3
Lune → U.K. 54°0N 2°51W 168 C5
Lüneburg Germany 53°15N 10°24E 178 B6
Lüneburg Heath = Lüneburger Heide Germany 53°10N 10°12E 178 B6
Lüneburger Heide Germany 53°10N 10°12E 178 B6
Lunel France 43°39N 4°9E 175 E8
Lünen Germany 51°37N 7°32E 178 D3
Lunenburg Canada 44°22N 64°18W 299 D7
Lunéville France 48°36N 6°30E 173 D13
Lung Mei China 22°23N 114°15E 122 A2
Lunga Dem. Rep. of the Congo 5°46S 12°14E 265 C4
Lunga → Zambia 14°34S 26°25E 269 E2
Lunga Lunga Kenya 4°33S 39°7E 268 C4
Lungchin Taiwan 24°12N 120°31E 225 B2
Lunge Angola 12°13S 16°7E 265 E3
Lungga Solomon Is. 9°25S 160°3E 287 M11
Lungi S. Leone 8°40N 13°17W 262 D1
Lunglei India 22°55N 92°45E 241 D4
Lungngo Burma 21°57N 93°36E 241 E4
Lung'tan Taiwan 24°52N 121°12E 225 B3
Lungwebungu → Zambia 14°19S 23°14E 265 E4
Luni India 26°0N 73°6E 242 G5
Luni → India 24°41N 71°14E 242 G4
Luninets = Luninyets Belarus 52°15N 26°50E 177 B14
Luning U.S.A. 38°30N 118°11W 304 G4
Lunino Russia 53°38N 45°18E 190 D7
Luninyets Belarus 52°15N 26°50E 177 B14
Lunkaransar India 28°29N 73°44E 242 E5
Lunner Norway 60°19N 10°35E 164 D7
Lunpei Taiwan 24°45N 120°21E 225 C2
Lunsar S. Leone 8°41N 12°32W 262 D2
Lunsemfwa → Zambia 14°54S 30°12E 269 E3
Lunsemfwa Falls Zambia 14°30S 29°6E 269 E2
Luntai China 41°46N 84°14E 217 D10
Luo He → China 34°35N 110°20E 226 G6
Luocheng China 24°48N 108°53E 228 E7
Luochuan China 35°45N 109°26E 226 G5
Luoci China 25°19N 102°18E 228 E4
Luodian China 25°24N 106°43E 228 E6
Luoding China 22°45N 111°40E 229 F8
Luofu Dem. Rep. of the Congo 0°10S 29°15E 268 C2
Luohe China 33°32N 114°2E 226 H8
Luojiang Guangdong, China 23°5N 113°17E 121 B2
Luojiang Sichuan, China 31°18N 104°33E 228 B5
Luonan China 34°5N 110°10E 226 G6
Luoning China 34°35N 111°40E 226 G6
Luoshan China 32°13N 114°30E 229 A10
Luotian China 30°46N 115°22E 229 B10
Luoxiao Shan China 26°30N 114°1E 229 D10
Luoyang China 34°40N 112°26E 226 G7
Luoyuan China 26°28N 119°30E 229 D12
Luozi Dem. Rep. of the Congo 4°54S 14°0E 265 C2
Luozigou China 43°42N 130°18E 227 C16
Lupeni Romania 45°21N 23°13E 183 E8
Lupilichi Mozam. 11°47S 35°13E 269 E4
Lupire Angola 14°36S 19°29E 265 E3
Lupków Poland 49°15N 22°4E 185 J9
Lupoing China 24°53N 104°21E 228 E5
Lupon Phil. 6°54N 126°0E 233 H6
Luputa Dem. Rep. of the Congo 7°7S 23°43E 265 D4
Luqa Malta 35°52N 14°29E 206 F7
Luquan Hebei, China 38°4N 114°17E 226 E8
Luquan Yunnan, China 25°35N 102°25E 228 E4
Luque Paraguay 25°19S 57°25W 334 B4
Luquembo Angola 10°44S 17°43E 265 D3
Luquillo Puerto Rico 18°23N 65°43W 321 b
Luquillo, Sierra de Puerto Rico 18°20N 65°47W 321 b
Lúras Italy 40°56N 9°10E 200 B2
Luray U.S.A. 38°40N 78°28W 309 F14
Lure France 47°40N 6°30E 173 E13
Luremo Angola 8°30S 17°50E 265 D3
Lurgan U.K. 54°28N 6°19W 166 B5
Luribay Bolivia 17°6S 67°39W 330 D4
Lurín Peru 12°17S 76°52W 330 C2
Lúrio Mozam. 13°32S 40°30E 269 E5
Lusaka Zambia 15°28S 28°16E 269 F2
Lusaka □ Zambia 15°30S 29°0E 269 F2
Lusambo Dem. Rep. of the Congo 4°58S 23°28E 265 C4
Lusancay Is. and Reefs Papua N. G. 8°30S 150°30E 286 E6
Lusangaye Dem. Rep. of the Congo 4°54S 26°0E 265 C5
Luseland Canada 52°5N 109°24W 297 C7
Lusenga Plain △ Zambia 9°22S 29°14E 269 D2
Lusengo Dem. Rep. of the Congo 1°47N 19°31E 264 B3
Lushan Henan, China 33°45N 112°55E 226 H7
Lushan Sichuan, China 30°12N 102°52E 228 B4
Lushan △ China 29°33N 115°58E 229 C10
Lushi China 34°3N 111°3E 226 G6
Lushnjë Albania 40°55N 19°41E 202 F3
Lushoto Tanzania 4°47S 38°20E 268 C4
Lushui China 25°58N 98°44E 228 E2
Lüshuihe China 42°31N 127°47E 224 A3
Lüshun China 38°45N 121°15E 227 E11
Lusignan France 46°26N 0°8E 174 B4
Lusigny-sur-Barse France 48°16N 4°15E 173 D11
Lusiye Zambia 15°30S 23°57E 265 F4
Lusk U.S.A. 42°46N 104°27W 304 E11
Lussac-les-Châteaux France 46°24N 0°43E 174 B4
Lustenau Austria 47°26N 9°39E 180 D2
Lustheim Germany 48°14N 11°34E 131 A2
Lustrafjorden Norway 61°23N 7°25E 164 C4
Lūt, Dasht-e Iran 31°30N 58°0E 247 D8
Luta = Dalian China 38°50N 121°40E 227 E11
Lütao Taiwan 22°40N 121°30E 225 D3
Lutembo Angola 13°26S 21°16E 265 E4
Lutherstadt Wittenberg Germany 51°53N 12°39E 178 D8
Luthersville U.S.A. 33°13N 84°45W 316 B5
Luti Solomon Is. 7°14S 157°0E 287 L9
Luton U.K. 51°53N 0°24W 169 F7
Luton □ U.K. 51°53N 0°24W 169 F7
Lutong Malaysia 4°28N 114°0E 235 B4
Lutsel K'e Canada 62°24N 110°44W 297 A6
Lutshima → Dem. Rep. of the Congo 5°22S 18°59E 265 D3
Lutsk Ukraine 50°50N 25°15E 177 C13
Luttenberg = Ljutomer Slovenia 46°31N 16°11E 199 B13
Lutto = Lotta → Europe 68°42N 31°6E 160 B24
Lutuai Angola 12°41S 20°7E 265 E4
Lutz U.S.A. 28°9N 82°28W 317 G7
Lützow Holmbukta Antarctica 69°10S 37°30E 151 C4
Lutzputs S. Africa 28°3S 20°40E 270 C3
Luuk Phil. 5°58N 121°18E 233 J3
Luuq Somali Rep. 3°48N 42°34E 257 D5
Luverne Ala., U.S.A. 31°43N 86°16W 316 D3
Luverne Minn., U.S.A. 43°39N 96°13W 308 D5
Luvo Angola 5°51S 14°5E 265 D2
Luvua Dem. Rep. of the Congo 8°48S 25°17E 265 D5
Luvua → Dem. Rep. of the Congo 6°50S 27°30E 268 D2
Luvuvhu → S. Africa 22°25S 31°18E 271 B5
Luwan China 31°12N 121°27E 138 B1
Luwegu → Tanzania 8°31S 37°23E 269 D4
Luwero Uganda 0°50N 32°28E 268 B3
Luwuk Indonesia 0°56S 122°47E 231 E6
Luxembourg Lux. 49°37N 6°9E 170 E6
Luxembourg □ Belgium 49°58N 5°30E 170 E5
Luxembourg ■ Europe 49°45N 6°0E 170 E5
Luxembourg ✈ (LUX) Lux. 49°37N 6°10E 170 E6
Luxembourg, Palais du Paris, France 134 c4
Luxemburg U.S.A. 42°36N 91°5W 310 B5
Luxeuil-les-Bains France 47°49N 6°24E 173 E13
Luxi Hunan, China 28°20N 110°7E 229 C8
Luxi Yunnan, China 24°40N 103°55E 228 E4
Luxi Yunnan, China 24°27N 98°36E 228 E2
Luxian China 29°9N 105°24E 228 C5
Luxor = El Uqsur Egypt 25°41N 32°38E 256 B3
Luy-de-Béarn → France 43°39N 0°48W 174 E3
Luy-de-France → France 43°39N 0°48W 174 E3
Luyeh Hualien, Taiwan 23°35N 121°32E 225 C3
Luyeh T'aitung, Taiwan 22°55N 121°8E 225 D3
Luyi China 33°50N 115°35E 226 H8
Luz Azores 39°1N 28°0W 153 d1
Luz-St-Sauveur France 42°53N 0°0 174 F4
Luza Russia 60°39N 47°10E 186 B8
Luzern Switz. 47°3N 8°18E 179 H4
Luzern □ Switz. 47°2N 7°55E 179 H3
Luzhai China 24°29N 109°42E 228 E7
Luzhany Ukraine 48°22N 25°47E 183 B10
Luzhi China 26°21N 105°16E 228 D5
Luzhniki Sports Centre Russia 55°43N 37°31E 129 B3
Luzhou China 28°52N 105°20E 228 C5
Luziânia Brazil 16°20S 48°0W 333 E2
Luzilândia Brazil 3°28S 42°22W 332 B3
Lužnice → Czech Rep. 49°14N 14°23E 180 B7
Luzon Phil. 16°0N 121°0E 232 C3
Luzon Strait Asia 21°0N 120°40E 229 G13
Luzy France 46°47N 3°58E 173 F10
Luzzi Italy 39°27N 16°17E 201 C9
Lviv Ukraine 49°50N 24°0E 177 D13
Lviv □ Ukraine 49°30N 23°45E 177 D12
Lvov = Lviv Ukraine 49°50N 24°0E 177 D13
Lwówek Poland 52°28N 16°10E 185 F3
Lwówek Śląski Poland 51°7N 15°38E 185 G2
Lyakhavichy Belarus 53°2N 26°32E 177 B14
Lyakhovskiye, Ostrova Russia 73°40N 141°0E 215 B15
Lyaki = Läki Azerbaijan 40°34N 47°22E 191 K8
Lyal I. Canada 44°57N 81°24W 312 B3
Lyall Mt. N.Z. 45°16S 167°32E 285 F2
Lyallpur = Faisalabad Pakistan 31°30N 73°5E 242 D5
Lyaskovets Bulgaria 43°6N 25°44E 203 C9
Lyasnaya → Belarus 52°9N 23°31E 185 F10
Lybster U.K. 58°18N 3°15W 167 C5
Lycabettus Athens, Greece 112 b3
Lycaonia Turkey 38°0N 33°0E 212 D5
Lychen Germany 53°12N 13°18E 178 B9
Lychkova Russia 57°55N 32°24E 188 D7
Lycia Turkey 36°30N 29°30E 205 E11
Lyck = Ełk Poland 53°50N 22°21E 184 E9
Lyckebyån → Sweden 56°12N 15°39E 163 H9
Lycksele Sweden 64°38N 18°40E 160 D18
Lycosura Greece 37°20N 22°3E 204 D4
Lydda = Lod Israel 31°57N 34°54E 251 D3
Lyddan I. Antarctica 74°0S 21°0W 151 D2
Lydenburg S. Africa 25°10S 30°29E 271 C5
Lydia Turkey 38°48N 28°19E 205 C10
Łydynia → Poland 52°43N 20°26E 185 F7
Lyell N.Z. 41°48S 172°4E 285 B7
Lyell I. Canada 52°40N 131°35W 296 C2
Lyepyel Belarus 54°50N 28°40E 188 E5
Lyford Cay Bahamas 25°2N 77°33W 153 b
Lygnern Sweden 57°30N 12°15E 163 G6
Lykavittos Hill = Lycabettus Athens, Greece 112 b3
Lykens U.S.A. 40°34N 76°42W 313 F8
Lyman Ukraine 45°41N 29°45E 183 E14
Lyman Wyo., U.S.A. 41°20N 110°18W 304 F8
Lymanske Ukraine 46°40N 29°58E 183 D14
Lyme B. U.K. 50°42N 2°53W 169 G4
Lyme Regis U.K. 50°43N 2°57W 169 G5
Lymington U.K. 50°45N 1°32W 169 G6
Łyna → Poland 54°37N 21°14E 184 D8
Lynchburg Ohio, U.S.A. 39°15N 83°48W 311 E13
Lynchburg S.C., U.S.A. 34°3N 80°4W 316 A9
Lynchburg Va., U.S.A. 37°25N 79°9W 309 G14
Lynd → Australia 16°28S 143°18E 280 B3
Lynd Ra. Australia 25°30S 149°20E 281 D4
Lynden Ont., Canada 43°14N 80°9W 312 C4
Lynden Wash., U.S.A. 48°57N 122°27W 306 B4
Lyndhurst S. Austral., Australia 30°15S 138°18E 281 E2
Lyndhurst N.J., U.S.A. 40°49N 74°7W 132 B1
Lyndon → Australia 23°29S 114°6E 279 D1
Lyndonville N.Y., U.S.A. 43°20N 78°23W 312 C6
Lyndonville Vt., U.S.A. 44°31N 72°1W 313 B12
Lyngdal Buskerud, Norway 59°54N 9°32E 164 E6
Lyngdal Vest-Agder, Norway 58°8N 7°7E 164 F4
Lyngen Norway 69°45N 20°30E 160 B19
Lyngør Norway 58°38N 9°8E 164 F6
Lynher Reef Australia 15°27S 121°55E 278 C3
Lynn Ind., U.S.A. 40°3N 84°56W 311 D12
Lynn Mass., U.S.A. 42°28N 70°57W 313 D14
Lynn Canal U.S.A. 58°50N 135°15W 303 G14
Lynn Haven U.S.A. 30°15N 85°39W 316 E4
Lynn Lake Canada 56°51N 101°3W 297 B8
Lynn Woods Res. U.S.A. 42°29N 71°0W 116 A2
Lynne U.S.A. 29°12N 81°55W 317 F8
Lynnville U.S.A. 38°12N 87°18W 311 F9
Lynnwood U.S.A. 47°49N 122°18W 306 C4
Lynton U.K. 51°13N 3°50W 169 F4
Lyntupy Belarus 55°4N 26°23E 188 E4
Lynx L. Canada 62°25N 106°15W 297 A7
Lyon France 45°46N 4°50E 175 C8
Lyon, Gare de Paris, France 134 c5
Lyon St-Exupery ✈ (LYS) France 45°44N 5°2E 175 C9
Lyonnais France 45°45N 4°15E 175 C8
Lyons = Lyon France 45°46N 4°50E 175 C8
Lyons Ga., U.S.A. 32°12N 82°19W 316 C7
Lyons Ill., U.S.A. 41°48N 87°49W 119 C2
Lyons Kans., U.S.A. 38°21N 98°12W 308 F4
Lyons N.Y., U.S.A. 43°5N 77°0W 312 C8
Lyons → Australia 25°2S 115°9E 279 E2
Lyons Falls U.S.A. 43°37N 75°22W 313 C9
Lyozna Belarus 55°0N 30°50E 188 E6
Lyra Reef Papua N. G. 1°50S 153°35E 286 A7
Lys = Leie → Belgium 51°2N 3°45E 170 C3
Lysá nad Labem Czech Rep. 50°11N 14°51E 180 A7
Lysaker Norway 59°54N 10°38E 133 A2
Lysakerselva → Norway 59°54N 10°38E 133 A2
Lysebotn Norway 59°3N 6°37E 164 E3
Lysefjorden Norway 59°0N 6°23E 164 E3
Lysekil Sweden 58°17N 11°26E 163 F5
Lysi Cyprus 35°6N 33°41E 207 E9
Lyskovo Russia 56°0N 45°3E 190 B7
Lysolaje Czech Rep. 50°8N 14°22E 135 B2
Lystrup Denmark 56°14N 10°14E 163 H4
Lysva Russia 58°7N 57°49E 186 C10
Lysvik Sweden 60°1N 13°9E 162 D7
Lysychansk Ukraine 48°55N 38°30E 189 H10
Lytham St. Anne's U.K. 53°45N 3°0W 168 D4
Lyttelton N.Z. 43°35S 172°44E 285 D7
Lytton Canada 50°13N 121°31W 296 C4
Lyuban Russia 59°16N 31°18E 188 C6
Lyubertsy Russia 55°40N 37°51E 129 B5
Lyubim Russia 58°20N 40°39E 188 C11
Lyubimets Bulgaria 41°50N 26°5E 203 E10
Lyuboml Ukraine 51°11N 24°4E 185 G11
Lyubotyn Ukraine 50°0N 36°0E 189 H8
Lyubytino Russia 58°50N 33°16E 188 C7
Lyudinovo Russia 53°52N 34°28E 188 F8

M

M.R. Stefanik, Bratislava ✈ (BTS) Slovak Rep. 48°11N 17°9E 181 C10
Ma → Vietnam 19°47N 105°56E 228 H5
Ma, O. el → Algeria 27°45N 7°52W 260 C3
Ma Nam Wat China 22°21N 114°16E 122 A2
Ma On Shan Country Park ⌂ China 22°22N 114°14E 122 A2
Ma'adaba Jordan 31°43N 35°47E 251 H6
Maafushi Maldives 3°59N 73°27E 272 d
Ma'ale Adumim West Bank 31°49N 35°17E 123 B2
Ma'ale Ha Khamisha Israel 31°49N 35°7E 123 B1
Ma'ale Mikhmas West Bank 31°52N 35°18E 123 A2
Maamba Zambia 17°17S 26°28E 270 A4
Ma'ān Jordan 30°12N 35°44E 251 H6
Ma'ān □ Jordan 30°0N 36°0E 251 J7
Maana'oba Solomon Is. 8°17S 160°50E 287 M11
Maanselkä Finland 63°52N 28°32E 160 E23
Ma'anshan China 31°44N 118°29E 229 B12
Maantiekylä Finland 60°20N 25°0E 121 A3
Maarianhamina = Mariehamn Finland 60°5N 19°55E 161 F18
Maarifa Iraq 33°15N 44°21E 113 B2
Maarmorilik Greenland 71°3N 51°0W 154 C5
Ma'arrat an Nu'mān Syria 35°43N 36°43E 250 C7
Maas → Neths. 51°45N 4°32E 170 C4
Maaseik Belgium 51°6N 5°45E 170 C5
Maasim Phil. 5°52N 125°0E 233 J5
Maasin Phil. 10°8N 124°50E 233 F5
Maastricht Neths. 50°50N 5°40E 170 D5
Maasupa Solomon Is. 9°16S 161°17E 287 M11
Maave Mozam. 21°4S 34°47E 271 B5
Mababe Depression Botswana 18°50S 24°15E 270 A3
Mabaia Angola 7°12S 14°2E 265 D2
Mabalane Mozam. 23°37S 32°31E 271 B5
Mabanga Dem. Rep. of the Congo 1°30N 19°6E 264 B3
Ma'bar Yemen 14°48N 44°17E 248 D4
Mabaruma Guyana 8°10N 59°50W 329 B6
Mabato Pt. Phil. 14°29N 121°3E 127 C2
Mabein Burma 23°29N 96°37E 241 D6
Mabel, L. U.S.A. 28°25N 81°32W 133 B1
Mabel L. Canada 50°35N 118°43W 296 C5
Mabenga Dem. Rep. of the Congo 3°39S 18°40E 264 C3
Mabenge Dem. Rep. of the Congo 4°15N 24°12E 264 B4
Maberly Canada 44°50N 76°32W 313 B8
Mabesi, L. S. Leone 7°10N 11°42W 262 D2
Mabian China 28°47N 103°37E 228 C4
Mabil Ethiopia 10°26N 36°52E 257 E4
Mabinay Phil. 9°48N 122°54E 233 G4
Mabirou Congo 1°3S 15°42E 264 C3
Mablethorpe U.K. 53°20N 0°15E 168 D8
Mableton U.S.A. 33°49N 84°35W 316 B5
Mably France 46°5N 4°4E 173 F11
Maboma Dem. Rep. of the Congo 2°30N 28°10E 268 B2
Mabonto S. Leone 8°53N 11°50W 262 D2
Maboukou Congo 3°39S 12°31E 264 C2
Mabouya I. Grenada 12°29N 61°30W 323 q
Mabroûk Mali 19°29N 1°15W 261 E4
Mabrous Niger 21°14N 13°35E 259 D2
Mabuasehube ⌂ Botswana 25°5S 21°10E 270 C3
Mabudis Phil. 20°55N 121°55E 232 A3
Mabuiag Australia 9°57S 142°11E 280 a
Mac Bac Vietnam 9°46N 106°7E 237 H6
Macachín Argentina 37°10S 63°43W 334 D3
Macaco, Morro do Brazil 22°56S 43°6W 135 B2
Macaé Brazil 22°20S 41°43W 333 F3
Macael Spain 37°20N 2°18W 197 H2
Macaíba Brazil 5°51S 35°21W 332 C4
Macajalar B. Phil. 8°55N 124°39E 233 G5
Macajuba Brazil 12°9S 40°22W 333 D3
McAlester U.S.A. 34°56N 95°46W 314 D7
McAllen U.S.A. 26°12N 98°14W 314 H5
McAlpin U.S.A. 30°8N 82°57W 316 E7
McAlpine L. Canada 66°32N 102°45W 294 D11
Macamic Canada 48°45N 79°0W 298 C4
Macao = Macau China 22°12N 113°33E 229 F9
Macão Portugal 39°35N 7°59W 195 F3
Macapá Brazil 0°5N 51°4W 329 C7
Macaque, Morne Dominica 15°20N 61°20W 323 k
Macará Ecuador 4°23S 79°57W 328 D2
Macarani Brazil 15°33S 40°24W 333 E3
Macarena, Serranía de la Colombia 2°45N 73°55W 328 C3
Macareo, Caño → Venezuela 9°47N 61°36W 329 B5
Macarthur Australia 38°5S 142°0E 282 E5
McArthur → Australia 15°54S 136°40E 280 B2
McArthur, Port Australia 16°4S 136°23E 280 B2
Macas Ecuador 2°19S 78°7W 328 D2
Macate Peru 8°48S 78°7W 330 B2
Macau Brazil 5°15S 36°40W 332 C4
Macau China 22°12N 113°33E 229 F9
Macaúbas Brazil 13°2S 42°42W 333 D3
Macauley I. Pac. Oc. 30°12S 178°28W 277 G15
Macaya → Colombia 0°59N 72°20W 328 C3
McBride Canada 53°20N 120°19W 296 C4
McCall U.S.A. 44°55N 116°6W 304 D5
McCamey U.S.A. 31°8N 102°14W 314 F3
McCammon U.S.A. 42°39N 112°12W 304 E7
McCarran Int., Las Vegas ✈ (LAS) U.S.A. 36°5N 115°9W 124 B2
McCarthy U.S.A. 61°26N 142°56W 303 F12
McCauley I. Canada 53°40N 130°15W 296 C2
McCleary U.S.A. 47°3N 123°16W 306 C3
Macclenny U.S.A. 30°17N 82°7W 316 E7
Macclesfield U.K. 53°15N 2°8W 168 D5
M'Clintock Chan. Canada 72°0N 102°0W 294 C11
McClintock Ra. Australia 18°44S 127°38E 278 C4
McCloud U.S.A. 41°15N 122°8W 304 F2
McCluer I. Australia 11°5S 133°0E 278 B5
McClure U.S.A. 40°42N 77°19W 312 F7
McClure, L. U.S.A. 37°35N 120°16W 306 H6
M'Clure Str. Canada 75°0N 119°0W 295 C8
McClusky U.S.A. 47°29N 100°27W 308 B3
McComb U.S.A. 31°15N 90°27W 315 F9
McCook Ill., U.S.A. 41°47N 87°49W 119 C2
McCook Nebr., U.S.A. 40°12N 100°38W 308 E3
McCormick U.S.A. 33°55N 82°17W 316 B7
McCreary Canada 50°47N 99°29W 297 C9
McCullough Mt. U.S.A. 35°35N 115°13W 307 K11
McCusker → Canada 55°32N 108°39W 297 B7
McDavid U.S.A. 30°52N 87°19W 317 E2
McDermitt U.S.A. 41°59N 117°43W 304 F5
McDonald U.S.A. 40°22N 80°14W 312 F4
Macdonald, L. Australia 23°30S 129°0E 278 D4
Macdonald, Mt. Vanuatu 17°36S 168°23E 287 G6
McDonald Is. Ind. Oc. 53°0S 73°0E 273 K6
MacDonnell Ranges Australia 23°40S 133°0E 278 D5
McDonough U.S.A. 33°27N 84°9W 316 B5
McDougalls Well Australia 31°8S 141°15E 282 A4
MacDowell L. Canada 52°15N 92°45W 298 B1
Macduff U.K. 57°40N 2°31W 167 D6
Maceda Spain 42°16N 7°39W 194 C3
Macedonia U.S.A. 41°19N 81°31W 312 E3
Macedonia ■ Europe 41°53N 21°40E 202 E5
Maceió Brazil 9°40S 35°41W 332 C4
Maceira Portugal 39°41N 8°55W 194 F2
Macenta Guinea 8°35N 9°32W 262 D3
Macerata Italy 43°18N 13°27E 199 E10
McFarland U.S.A. 35°41N 119°14W 307 K7
McFarlane → Canada 59°12N 107°58W 297 B7
Macfarlane, L. Australia 32°0S 136°40E 282 B2
McGehee U.S.A. 33°38N 91°24W 314 E9
McGill U.S.A. 39°23N 114°47W 304 G6
McGill Univ. Montréal, Canada 130 b1
Macgillycuddy's Reeks Ireland 51°58N 9°45W 166 E2
McGrath U.S.A. 62°58N 155°36W 303 E9
McGraw U.S.A. 42°36N 76°8W 313 D8
McGregor U.S.A. 43°1N 91°11W 310 A5
McGregor Ra. Australia 27°0S 142°45E 281 D3
McGuire, Mt. Australia 20°18S 148°23E 280 b
Mach Pakistan 29°50N 67°20E 242 E2
Māch Kowr Iran 25°48N 61°28E 247 E9
Machacalis Brazil 17°5S 40°45W 333 E3
Machado = Jiparaná → Brazil 8°3S 62°52W 331 B5
Machagai Argentina 26°56S 60°2W 334 B3
Machakos Kenya 1°30S 37°15E 268 C4
Machala Ecuador 3°20S 79°57W 328 D2
Machalilla △ Ecuador 1°24S 80°42W 328 D1
Machanga Mozam. 20°59S 35°0E 271 B6
Machattie, L. Australia 24°50S 139°48E 280 C2
Machault France 49°21N 4°29E 173 C11
Machava Mozam. 25°54S 32°28E 271 C5
Machecoul France 47°0N 1°49W 172 F5
Macheke Zimbabwe 18°5S 31°51E 271 A5
Machelen Belgium 50°55N 4°26E 116 A2
Macheng China 31°12N 115°2E 229 B10
McHenry U.S.A. 42°21N 88°16W 311 B8
Macherado Greece 37°46N 20°49E 207 D2
Macherla India 16°29N 79°26E 244 F4
Machero Spain 39°21N 4°20W 195 F6
Machgaon India 20°5N 86°17E 244 D8
Machhu → India 23°6N 70°46E 242 H4
Machiara △ Pakistan 34°40N 73°30E 242 B5
Machias Maine, U.S.A. 44°43N 67°28W 309 C20
Machias N.Y., U.S.A. 42°25N 78°29W 312 D6
Machichi → Canada 57°3N 92°6W 297 B10
Machico Madeira 32°43N 16°44W 153 c
Machida Japan 35°32N 139°26E 140 B1
Machilipatnam India 16°12N 81°8E 245 F5
Machiques Venezuela 10°4N 72°34W 328 A3
Machu Picchu Peru 13°8S 72°30W 330 C3
Machynlleth U.K. 52°35N 3°50W 169 E4
Macia Mozam. 25°2S 33°8E 271 C5
Macias Nguema Biyoga = Bioko Eq. Guin. 3°30N 8°40E 263 E6
Maciejowice Poland 51°36N 21°26E 185 G8
McIlwraith Ra. Australia 13°50S 143°20E 280 A3
Măcin Romania 45°16N 28°8E 183 E13
Macina Mali 14°50N 5°0W 262 C4
McInnes L. Canada 52°13N 93°45W 297 C10
McIntosh U.S.A. 45°55N 101°21W 308 C3
McIntosh L. Canada 55°45N 105°0W 297 B8
Macintosh Ra. Australia 27°39S 125°32E 279 E4
Macintyre → Australia 28°37S 150°47E 281 D5
Maciołki Poland 52°19N 21°9E 142 B2
Macizo Galaico Spain 42°30N 7°30W 194 C3
Maçka Turkey 40°49N 39°36E 213 B8
Mackay Queens., Australia 21°8S 149°11E 280 K7
Mackay Idaho, U.S.A. 43°55N 113°37W 304 E7
MacKay → Canada 57°10N 111°38W 296 B6
Mackay, L. Australia 22°30S 129°0E 278 D4
McKay Ra. Australia 23°0S 122°30E 278 D3
McKean Kiribati 3°36S 174°8W 277 A16
McKeesport U.S.A. 40°20N 79°51W 312 F5
McKellar Canada 45°30N 79°55W 312 A5
McKenna U.S.A. 46°56N 122°33W 306 D4
Mackenzie Canada 55°20N 123°5W 296 B4
McKenzie U.S.A. 36°8N 88°31W 315 C10
Mackenzie → Queens., Australia 23°38S 149°46E 280 C4
Mackenzie → N.W.T., Canada 69°10N 134°20W 294 D5
McKenzie → U.S.A. 44°7N 123°6W 304 D2
Mackenzie Bay Canada 69°0N 137°30W 292 C6
Mackenzie City = Linden Guyana 6°0N 58°10W 329 B6
Mackenzie King I. Canada 77°45N 111°0W 295 B9
Mackenzie Mts. Canada 64°0N 130°0W 292 C6
Mackenzie Plains N.Z. 44°10S 170°25E 285 E5
McKerrow, L. N.Z. 44°25S 168°5E 285 E3
McKerrow, Mt. N.Z. 41°19S 174°58E 143 B2
Mackheim = Maków Mazowiecki Poland 52°52N 21°6E 185 F8
Mackinac, Straits of U.S.A. 45°50N 84°40W 301 F23
Mackinaw U.S.A. 40°32N 89°21W 310 D7
Mackinaw → U.S.A. 40°33N 89°44W 310 D7
Mackinaw City U.S.A. 45°47N 84°44W 309 C11
McKinlay Australia 21°16S 141°18E 280 C3
McKinlay → Australia 20°50S 141°28E 280 C3
McKinley, Mt. U.S.A. 63°4N 151°0W 303 E10
McKinley Park Alaska, U.S.A. 63°44N 148°55W 303 E10
McKinley Park Ill., U.S.A. 41°49N 87°40W 119 C2
McKinley Sea Arctic 82°0N 0°0 154 A11
McKinney U.S.A. 33°12N 96°37W 314 E6
Mackinnon Road Kenya 3°40S 39°1E 268 C4
McKittrick Calif., U.S.A. 35°18N 119°37W 307 K7
McKittrick Mo., U.S.A. 38°44N 91°27W 310 F5
Macklin Canada 52°20N 109°56W 297 C7
Macksville Australia 30°40S 152°56E 283 A10
McLaren Vale Australia 35°13S 138°31E 282 C3
McLaughlin U.S.A. 45°49N 100°49W 308 C3
Maclean Australia 29°26S 153°16E 281 D5
McLean Ill., U.S.A. 40°19N 89°10W 310 D7
McLean Tex., U.S.A. 35°14N 100°36W 314 D4
McLean Va., U.S.A. 38°56N 77°10W 132 B1
McLeansboro U.S.A. 38°6N 88°32W 311 F8
Maclear S. Africa 31°2S 28°23E 271 D4
Maclear, C. Malawi 13°58S 34°49E 269 E3
Macleay → Australia 30°56S 153°0E 283 A10
McLennan Canada 55°42N 116°50W 296 B5
MacLeod = Fort Macleod Canada 49°45N 113°30W 296 D6
McLeod → Canada 54°9N 115°44W 296 C5
MacLeod, L. Australia 24°9S 113°47E 279 D1
MacLeod B. Canada 62°53N 110°0W 297 A7
MacLeod Lake Canada 54°58N 123°0W 296 C4
McLoughlin, Mt. U.S.A. 42°27N 122°19W 304 E2
MacMahon = Aïn Touta Algeria 35°26N 5°54E 261 A6
McMechen U.S.A. 39°57N 80°44W 312 G4
McMinnville Oreg., U.S.A. 45°13N 123°12W 304 D2
McMinnville Tenn., U.S.A. 35°41N 85°46W 315 D12
McMurdo Antarctica 77°51S 166°37E 151 D11
McMurdo Sd. Antarctica 77°0S 170°0E 151 D11
McMurray = Fort McMurray Canada 56°44N 111°7W 296 B6
McMurray U.S.A. 48°19N 122°14W 306 B4
Maco Phil. 7°20N 125°50E 233 H5
Maçobere Mozam. 21°13S 32°47E 269 G3
Macocola Angola 6°47S 16°8E 265 D3
Macodoene Mozam. 23°32S 35°5E 271 B6
Macolo Angola 7°5S 16°42E 265 D3
Macomb U.S.A. 40°27N 90°40W 310 D6
Macomer Italy 40°16N 8°47E 200 B1
Mâcon Saône-et-Loire, France 46°19N 4°50E 173 F11
Macon Ga., U.S.A. 32°51N 83°38W 316 C6
Macon Ill., U.S.A. 39°43N 89°0W 310 E8
Macon Miss., U.S.A. 33°7N 88°34W 315 E10
Macon Mo., U.S.A. 39°44N 92°28W 310 E4
Macondo Angola 12°37S 23°46E 265 E4
Macopocho → Chile 33°24S 70°40W 137 B1
Macossa Mozam. 17°55S 33°56E 269 F3
Macou → Dominica 15°25N 61°27W 323 k
Macou, Pte. Guadeloupe 16°21N 61°31W 322 e
Macouba Martinique 14°52N 61°9W 322 j
Macoun L. Canada 56°32N 103°40W 297 B8
Macoupin Cr. → U.S.A. 39°11N 90°38W 310 E6
Macovane Mozam. 21°30S 35°2E 271 B6
McPherson = Kapuskasing Canada 49°25N 82°30W 298 C3
McPherson U.S.A. 38°22N 97°40W 308 F5
McPherson Pk. U.S.A. 34°53N 119°53W 307 L7
McPherson Ra. Australia 28°15S 153°15E 281 D5
Macquarie → Australia 30°7S 147°24E 283 A7
Macquarie Harbour Australia 42°15S 145°23E 281 G4
Macquarie I. Pac. Oc. 54°36S 158°55E 288 N7
Macquarie Ridge S. Ocean 57°0S 159°0E 151 B10
Macqueripe B. Trin. & Tob. 10°44N 61°37W 323 t
McRae U.S.A. 32°4N 82°54W 316 C7
MacRitchie Res. Singapore 1°20N 103°49E 138 A2
MacRobertson Land Antarctica 71°0S 64°0E 151 D6
Macrohon Phil. 10°4N 124°56E 233 F5
Macroom Ireland 51°54N 8°57W 166 E3
MacTier Canada 45°8N 79°47W 312 A5
Macubela Mozam. 16°53S 37°49E 269 F4
Macugnaga Italy 45°58N 7°58E 198 C4
Macuira △ Colombia 12°9N 71°21W 328 A3
Macuje Colombia 0°24N 73°10W 328 C3
Macul Chile 33°30S 70°35W 137 C2
Macumba → Australia 27°52S 137°12E 281 D2
Macuro Venezuela 10°42N 61°55W 329 F9
Macusani Peru 14°4S 70°29W 330 C3
Macuse Mozam. 17°45S 37°10E 269 F4
Macuspana Mexico 17°46N 92°36W 319 D6
Macusse Angola 17°48S 20°23E 265 F4
Mada → Nigeria 7°59N 7°55E 263 D6
Ma'dabā □ Jordan 31°43N 35°47E 251 G6
Madadeni S. Africa 27°43S 30°3E 271 C5
Madadi Chad 18°28N 20°45E 259 E4
Madagali Nigeria 10°56N 13°33E 263 C7
Madagascar ■ Africa 20°0S 47°0E 272 B2
Madagoi → Somali Rep. 0°49N 42°58E 267 D5
Madā'in Sālih Si. Arabia 26°46N 37°57E 246 E3
Madakasira India 13°56N 77°16E 245 H3
Madalena Azores 38°32N 28°32W 153 d1
Madama Niger 22°0N 13°40E 259 D2
Madame, I. Canada 45°30N 60°58W 299 C7
Madame Tussaud's London, U.K. 125 a3
Madan Bulgaria 41°30N 24°57E 203 E8
Madanapalle India 13°33N 78°28E 245 H4
Madang Papua N. G. 5°12S 145°49E 286 C3
Madang □ Papua N. G. 5°0S 145°30E 286 C3
Madaoua Niger 14°5N 6°27E 263 C6
Madara Nigeria 11°45N 10°35E 263 C7
Madaripur Bangla. 23°19N 90°15E 241 D3
Madau I. Papua N. G. 8°58S 152°28E 286 E7
Madauk Burma 17°56N 96°52E 241 G6
Madawaska Canada 45°30N 78°0W 312 A7
Madawaska → Canada 45°27N 76°21W 312 A7
Madaxmaroodi Somali Rep. 2°39N 44°36E 267 D5
Madaya Burma 22°12N 96°10E 241 D6
Madbar Sudan 6°17N 30°45E 257 F3
Maddalena Italy 41°16N 9°23E 200 A2
Maddaloni Italy 41°2N 14°23E 201 A7
Maddela Phil. 16°21N 121°41E 232 C3
Maddur India 12°36N 77°4E 245 H3
Madeira Atl. Oc. 32°50N 17°0W 153 c
Madeira Ohio, U.S.A. 39°11N 84°21W 311 E12
Madeira → Brazil 3°22S 58°45W 329 D6
Madeleine, Îs. de la Canada 47°30N 61°40W 299 C7
Maden Turkey 38°23N 39°40E 213 C8
Madera Chihuahua, Mexico 29°12N 108°7W 318 B3
Madera Calif., U.S.A. 36°57N 120°3W 306 J6
Madera Pa., U.S.A. 40°49N 78°26W 312 F6
Madgaon India 15°12N 73°58E 245 G1
Madha India 18°0N 75°30E 244 F2
Madhavpur India 21°15N 69°58E 242 J3
Madhepura India 26°11N 86°23E 243 F12
Madhira India 16°55N 80°22E 244 F5
Madhubani India 26°21N 86°7E 243 F12
Madhugiri India 13°40N 77°12E 245 H3
Madhumati → Bangla. 22°53N 89°52E 241 D2
Madhupur Bangla. 24°37N 90°2E 241 C3
Madhupur India 24°16N 86°39E 243 G12
Madhya Pradesh □ India 22°50N 78°0E 242 J8
Madhyamgram India 22°41N 88°26E 124 B2
Madidi → Bolivia 12°32S 66°52W 330 C4
Madikeri India 12°30N 75°45E 245 H2
Madikwe ⌂ S. Africa 27°38S 32°15E 271 C5
Madill U.S.A. 34°6N 96°46W 314 D6
Madimba Angola 6°36S 14°23E 265 D2
Madimba Dem. Rep. of the Congo 4°58S 15°5E 265 C3
Madín Mexico, Mexico 19°32N 99°16W 128 A1
Ma'din Syria 35°45N 39°36E 213 E8
Madín, L. Mexico 19°31N 99°16W 128 A1
Madina Mali 13°25N 8°50W 262 C3
Madīnat Al Manṣūr Iraq 33°18N 44°20E 113 B2
Madinani Ivory C. 9°37N 6°57W 262 D3
Madīnat al Malik Khālid al Askarīyah Si. Arabia 27°54N 45°31E 246 E5
Madīnat ash Sha'b Yemen 12°50N 45°0E 248 D4
Madīnat ath Thawrah Syria 35°50N 38°32E 213 E8
Madînet Nasr Egypt 30°4N 31°18E 117 A2
Madingo Congo 4°5S 11°24E 264 C2
Madingou Congo 4°10S 13°33E 264 C2
Madîq Gûbâl Egypt 27°47N 33°55E 251 L4
Madîq Tîrân Egypt 27°55N 34°30E 251 L5
Madirovalo Madag. 16°26S 46°32E 272 B2
Madison Calif., U.S.A. 38°41N 121°59W 306 G5
Madison Fla., U.S.A. 30°28N 83°25W 316 E6
Madison Ga., U.S.A. 33°36N 83°28W 316 B6
Madison Ind., U.S.A. 38°44N 85°23W 311 F11
Madison Mo., U.S.A. 39°28N 92°13W 310 E4
Madison Nebr., U.S.A. 41°50N 97°27W 308 E5
Madison Ohio, U.S.A. 41°46N 81°3W 312 E3
Madison S. Dak., U.S.A. 44°0N 97°7W 308 C5
Madison Wis., U.S.A. 43°4N 89°24W 310 A7
Madison → U.S.A. 45°56N 111°31W 304 D8
Madison Avenue New York, U.S.A. 132 c2
Madison Heights U.S.A. 37°25N 79°8W 309 G14
Madison Square New York, U.S.A. 132 d2
Madison Square Garden New York, U.S.A. 132 c2
Madisonville Ky., U.S.A. 37°20N 87°30W 308 G10
Madisonville Tex., U.S.A. 30°57N 95°55W 314 F7
Madista Botswana 21°15S 25°6E 270 B4
Madiun Indonesia 7°38S 111°32E 235 D4
Madjingo Gabon 1°20N 14°4E 264 B2
Mado Gashi Kenya 0°44N 39°10E 268 B4
Madoc Canada 44°30N 77°28W 312 B7
Madoi China 34°46N 98°18E 218 E8
Madon → France 48°36N 6°6E 173 D13
Madona Latvia 56°53N 26°5E 188 D4
Madonie Italy 37°50N 13°50E 200 E6
Madonna di Campiglio Italy 46°14N 10°49E 198 B7
Madra Dağı Turkey 39°23N 27°12E 205 B9
Madrakah, Ra's al Oman 19°0N 57°50E 249 C7
Madras = Chennai India 13°8N 80°19E 245 H5
Madras = Tamil Nadu □ India 11°0N 77°0E 245 J3
Madras U.S.A. 44°38N 121°8W 304 D3
Madre, L. U.S.A. 25°15N 97°30W 314 J6
Madre, Sierra Phil. 17°0N 122°0E 232 C4
Madre de Dios □ Peru 12°0S 70°15W 330 C3
Madre de Dios → Bolivia 10°59S 66°8W 330 C4
Madre de Dios, I. Chile 50°20S 75°10W 336 D1
Madre del Sur, Sierra Mexico 17°30N 100°0W 319 D5
Madre Occidental, Sierra Mexico 27°0N 107°0W 318 B3
Madre Oriental, Sierra Mexico 25°0N 100°0W 318 C5
Madri India 24°16N 73°32E 242 G5
Madrid Spain 40°24N 3°42W 127 B1
Madrid Ala., U.S.A. 31°2N 85°24W 316 D4
Madrid Iowa, U.S.A. 41°53N 93°49W 310 C3
Madrid N.Y., U.S.A. 44°45N 75°8W 313 B9
Madrid □ Spain 40°30N 3°45W 194 E7
Madrid Barajas ✈ (MAD) Spain 40°26N 3°34W 127 B2
Madridejos Spain 39°28N 3°33W 195 F7
Madrigal de las Altas Torres Spain 41°5N 5°0W 194 D6
Madrona Spain 41°27N 2°1E 114 A1
Madrona, Sierra Spain 38°27N 4°16W 195 G6
Madroñera Spain 39°26N 5°42W 195 F5
Madrusah Libya 24°48N 14°32E 258 D2
Madu Sudan 14°37N 26°4E 257 E2
Madula Dem. Rep. of the Congo 0°27N 25°22E 264 B5
Maduo Dem. Rep. of the Congo 1°24S 20°44E 264 C4
Madura W. Austral., Australia 31°55S 127°0E 279 F4
Madura Indonesia 7°30S 114°0E 231 G15
Madura, Selat Indonesia 7°30S 113°20E 235 D4
Madura Oya △ Sri Lanka 7°20N 81°10E 245 L5
Madurai India 9°55N 78°10E 245 K4
Madurantakam India 12°30N 79°50E 245 H4
Madzhalis Russia 42°9N 47°47E 191 J8
Mae Chan Thailand 20°9N 99°52E 236 B2
Mae Charim △ Thailand 18°17N 100°59E 236 C3
Mae Hong Son Thailand 19°16N 97°56E 236 C2
Mae Khlong → Thailand 13°24N 100°0E 236 F3
Mae Moei △ Thailand 17°26N 98°7E 236 D2
Mae Phang △ Thailand 19°7N 99°13E 236 C2
Mae Phrik Thailand 17°27N 99°7E 236 D2
Mae Ping △ Thailand 17°37N 98°51E 236 D2
Mae Ramat Thailand 16°58N 98°31E 236 D2
Mae Rim Thailand 18°54N 98°57E 236 C2
Mae Sai Thailand 20°20N 99°55E 236 B2
Mae Sot Thailand 16°43N 98°34E 236 D2
Mae Suai Thailand 19°39N 99°33E 228 H2
Mae Tha Thailand 18°28N 99°8E 236 C2
Mae Tup Res. Thailand 17°52N 98°45E 236 D2
Mae Wa △ Thailand 17°23N 99°16E 236 D2
Mae Wong △ Thailand 15°54N 99°12E 236 E2
Mae Yom △ Thailand 18°43N 100°15E 236 C3
Maebaru Japan 33°33N 130°12E 222 D2
Maebashi Japan 36°24N 139°4E 223 A11
Maella Spain 41°8N 0°7E 196 D5
Maelpaeg L. Canada 48°20N 56°30W 299 C8
Maesawa Japan 35°44N 139°31E 140 A2
Maesteg U.K. 51°36N 3°40W 169 F4
Maestra, Sierra Cuba 20°15N 77°0W 320 B4
Maestre de Campo I. Phil. 12°56N 121°42E 232 E3
Maetambe, Mt. Solomon Is. 7°3S 157°1E 287 L9
Maevatanana Madag. 16°56S 46°49E 272 B2
Maéwo Vanuatu 15°10S 168°10E 287 E6
Mafadi S. Africa 29°12S 29°21E 271 C4
Mafate, Cirque de Réunion 21°3S 55°25E 272 f
Mafeking = Mafikeng S. Africa 25°50S 25°38E 270 C4
Mafeking Canada 52°40N 101°10W 297 C8
Maféré Ivory C. 5°30N 3°2W 262 D4
Mafeteng Lesotho 29°51S 27°15E 270 C4
Maffra Australia 37°53S 146°58E 283 D7
Mafia I. Tanzania 7°45S 39°50E 268 D4
Mafikeng S. Africa 25°50S 25°38E 270 C4
Mafra Brazil 26°10S 49°55W 335 B6
Mafra Portugal 38°55N 9°20W 195 G1
Mafungabusi Plateau Zimbabwe 18°30S 29°8E 269 F2
Magadan Russia 59°38N 150°50E 215 D16
Magadi India 12°58N 77°14E 245 H3
Magadi Rift Valley, Kenya 1°54S 36°19E 268 C4
Magadi, L. Kenya 1°54S 36°19E 268 C4
Magaliesburg S. Africa 26°0S 27°32E 271 C4
Magallanes = Punta Arenas Chile 53°10S 71°0W 336 D2
Magallanes Phil. 12°50N 123°50E 232 E4
Magallanes □ Chile 52°0S 72°0W 336 D2
Magallanes, Estrecho de Chile 52°30S 75°0W 336 D2
Magaluf Spain 39°29N 2°32E 206 B3
Magangué Colombia 9°14N 74°45W 328 B3
Maganoy Phil. 6°51N 124°31E 233 H5
Magaria Niger 13°4N 9°5E 259 F1
Magarida Papua N. G. 10°18S 149°20E 286 F5
Magburaka S. Leone 8°47N 12°0W 262 D2
Magdagachi Russia 53°25N 125°48E 215 D13
Magdalen Is. = Madeleine, Îs. de la Canada 47°30N 61°40W 299 C7
Magdalena Argentina 35°5S 57°30W 334 D4
Magdalena Bolivia 13°13S 63°57W 331 C5
Magdalena Lima, Peru 12°5S 77°5W 124 B2
Magdalena N. Mex., U.S.A. 34°7N 107°15W 305 J10
Magdalena □ Colombia 10°0N 74°0W 328 B3
Magdalena → Colombia 11°6N 74°51W 328 A3
Magdalena → Mexico 30°40N 112°25W 318 A2
Magdalena, B. Mexico 24°35N 112°0W 318 C2
Magdalena, I. Chile 44°40S 73°0W 336 B2
Magdalena, I. Mexico 24°40N 112°15W 318 C2
Magdalena, Llano de Mexico 25°0N 111°25W 318 C2
Magdalena Contreras Mexico 19°20N 99°13W 128 C1

Magdalena de Kino
  Mexico 30°38N 110°57W **318** A2
Magdeburg *Germany* 52°7N 11°38E **178** C7
Magdelaine Cays
  Australia 16°33S 150°18E **280** B5
Magdub *Sudan* 13°42N 25°5E **257** D2
Magee *U.S.A.* 31°52N 89°44W **315** F10
Magelang *Indonesia* 7°29S 110°13E **235** D4
Magellan's Str. = Magallanes,
  Estrecho de *Chile* 52°30S 75°0W **336** D2
Magenta *Italy* 45°28N 8°53E **198** C5
Magenta, L. *Australia* 33°30S 119°2E **279** F2
Magerøya *Norway* 71°3N 25°40E **160** A21
Maggea *Australia* 34°28S 140°2E **282** C4
Maggia ◻ *Switz.* 46°18N 8°36E **179** J4
Maggiorasca, Mte. *Italy* 44°33N 9°29E **198** D6
Maggiore, Lago *Italy* 45°57N 8°39E **198** C5
Maggotty *Jamaica* 18°9N 77°46W **320** a
Maghâgha *Egypt* 28°38N 30°50E **256** B3
Maghama *Mauritania* 15°32N 12°57W **262** B2
Magherafelt *U.K.* 54°45N 6°37W **166** B5
Maghnia *Algeria* 34°50N 1°43W **261** B4
Maghreb *N. Afr.* 32°0N 4°0W **254** C3
Maginu *Japan* 35°34N 139°34E **140** B2
Magione *Italy* 43°10N 12°12E **199** E9
Magistralnyy *Russia* 56°16N 107°36E **215** D11
Maglaj *Bos.-H.* 44°33N 18°7E **182** F3
Magliana in Toscana
  Italy 42°36N 11°17E **199** F8
Máglie *Italy* 40°7N 18°18E **201** B11
Magnac-Laval *France* 46°13N 1°11E **174** B5
Magnetic Pole (North)
  Arctic 82°42N 114°24W **150** A1
Magnetic Pole (South)
  Antarctica 64°8S 138°8E **151** C9
Magnisía ◻ *Greece* 39°15N 23°0E **204** B5
Magnitogorsk *Russia* 53°27N 59°4E **186** D10
Magnolia *Ark., U.S.A.* 33°16N 93°14W **314** E8
Magnolia *Miss., U.S.A.* 31°9N 90°28W **315** F9
Magnor *Norway* 59°56N 12°15E **164** E9
Magny-en-Vexin *France* 49°9N 1°47E **173** C8
Magny-les-Hameaux *France* 48°44N 2°3E **134** B1
Mago *Fiji* 17°26S 179°8W **287** A3
Mago △ *Ethiopia* 5°40N 36°18E **257** F4
Magog *Canada* 45°18N 72°9W **313** A12
Magoro *Uganda* 1°45N 34°12E **268** B3
Magosa = Famagusta
  Cyprus 35°8N 33°55E **207** E9
Magoye *Zambia* 16°1S 27°30E **269** F2
Magpet *Phil.* 7°6N 125°6E **233** H5
Magpie, L. *Canada* 51°0N 64°41W **299** B7
Magrath *Canada* 49°25N 112°50W **296** D6
Magre → *Spain* 39°11N 0°25E **197** F4
Magrur, Wadi → *Sudan* 16°5N 26°30E **257** D2
Magsingal *Phil.* 17°41N 120°25E **232** C3
Magta Lahjar *Mauritania* 17°28N 13°17W **262** B2
Magu *Tanzania* 2°30S 33°30E **268** C3
Maguan *China* 23°0N 104°21E **228** F5
Maguarinho, C. *Brazil* 0°15S 48°30W **332** B2
Magude *Mozam.* 25°2S 32°40E **271** C5
Maguindanao ◻ *Phil.* 7°5N 124°40E **233** H5
Magurski, b. *Poland* 49°30N 21°30E **185** J8
Magwe *Burma* 20°10N 95°0E **241** E5
Magwe *Sudan* 4°8N 32°17E **257** G3
Magwe ◻ *Burma* 20°0N 95°0E **241** F5
Magyarország = Hungary ■
  Europe 47°20N 19°20E **181** D12
Maha Oya *Sri Lanka* 7°31N 81°22E **245** L5
Maha Sarakham
  Thailand 16°12N 103°16E **236** D4
Mahābād *Iran* 36°50N 45°45E **213** D11
Mahabaleshwar *India* 17°58N 73°43E **244** F1
Mahabharat Lekh *Nepal* 28°30N 82°0E **243** E10
Mahabo *Madag.* 20°23S 44°40E **272** C7
Mahad *India* 18°6N 73°29E **244** E1
Mahaddayweyne
  Somali Rep. 2°58N 45°32E **267** D6
Mahadeo Hills *India* 22°20N 78°30E **243** H8
Mahadeopur *India* 18°48N 80°0E **244** E5
Mahaffey *U.S.A.* 40°53N 78°44W **312** F6
Mahagi
  Dem. Rep. of the Congo 2°20N 31°0E **268** B3
Mahagnao Volcano △
  Phil. 10°52N 124°51E **233** F6
Mahaicony *Guyana* 6°36N 57°48W **329** B6
Mahajamba → *Madag.* 15°33S 47°8E **272** B2
Mahajamba, Helodranon' i
  Madag. 15°24S 47°5E **272** B2
Mahajan *India* 28°48N 73°56E **242** E5
Mahajanga *Madag.* 15°40S 46°25E **272** B2
Mahajanga ◻ *Madag.* 17°0S 47°0E **272** B2
Mahajilo → *Madag.* 19°42S 45°22E **272** B2
Mahakam → *Indonesia* 0°35S 117°17E **235** C5
Mahalapye *Botswana* 23°1S 26°51E **270** A4
Mahalaxmi *Mumbai, India* 130 a1
Mahalchhar *Bangla.* 22°55N 92°2E **241** D4
Mahale Mts. *Tanzania* 6°20S 30°0E **268** D3
Mahale Mts. △ *Tanzania* 6°10S 29°50E **268** D3
Mahallāt *Iran* 33°55N 50°30E **247** C6
Māhān *Iran* 30°5N 57°18E **247** D8
Mahan → *India* 23°30N 82°50E **243** H10
Mahanadi → *India* 20°20N 86°25E **244** D8
Mahananda → *India* 25°12N 87°52E **243** G12
Mahanoro *Madag.* 19°54S 48°48E **272** B2
Mahanoy City *U.S.A.* 40°49N 76°9W **313** F8
Mahaplag *Phil.* 10°35N 124°57E **233** F5
Maharashtra ◻ *India* 20°30N 75°30E **244** D2
Maharès *Tunisia* 34°32N 10°29E **258** B2
Maharivo → *Madag.* 20°26S 44°10E **272** C7
Mahasamund *India* 21°5N 82°23E **243** J9
Mahasham, W. → *Egypt* 30°15N 34°10E **251** H5
Mahasoa *Madag.* 22°33S 45°41E **272** C2
Mahasolo *Madag.* 19°7S 46°22E **272** B2
Mahattat ash Shīdīyah
  Jordan 29°55N 35°55E **251** J6
Mahattat 'Unayzah
  Jordan 30°30N 35°47E **251** H6
Mahaut *Dominica* 15°21N 61°24W **323** k
Mahaut *Guadeloupe* 16°4N 61°34W **322** e
Mahavavy → *Madag.* 15°57S 45°54E **272** B2
Mahaweli Ganga →
  Sri Lanka 8°27N 81°13E **245** K5
Mahaxay *Laos* 17°22N 105°12E **236** D5
Mahbubabad *India* 17°42N 80°2E **244** F5
Mahbubnagar *India* 16°45N 77°59E **244** F3
Mahd adh Dhahab
  Si. Arabia 23°30N 40°52E **248** B3
Mahda *U.A.E.* 25°20N 56°15E **247** E8
Maḩdah *Oman* 24°24N 55°59E **247** E7
Mahdia *Guyana* 5°13N 59°9W **329** B6
Mahdia *Tunisia* 35°28N 11°0E **258** B2
Mahdia ◻ *Tunisia* 35°20N 10°50E **261** A7
Mahe *Jammu & Kashmir,*
  India 33°10N 78°32E **243** C8
Mahé *Pondicherry, India* 11°42N 75°34E **245** J2
Mahé *Seychelles* 5°0S 55°30E **272** c
Mahé ✈ (SEZ) *Seychelles* 4°40S 55°31E **272** c

Mahébourg *Mauritius* 20°24S 57°42E **272** e
Mahendra Giri *India* 8°20N 77°30E **245** K3
Mahendragani *India* 25°20N 89°45E **241** C7
Mahendragarh *India* 28°17N 76°14E **242** E7
Mahendranagar *Nepal* 28°55N 80°20E **243** E9
Maheno *N.Z.* 45°10S 170°50E **285** F5
Mahesana *India* 23°39N 72°26E **242** H5
Maheshtala *India* 22°29N 88°15E **124** C1
Maheshwar *India* 22°11N 75°35E **242** H6
Mahgawan *India* 26°29N 78°37E **243** F8
Mahi → *India* 22°15N 72°55E **242** H5
Mahia Pen. *N.Z.* 39°9S 177°55E **284** C7
Mahiabadhoo *Maldives* 3°47N 72°58E **272** d
Mahighe *Solomon Is.* 8°30S 159°58E **287** M10
Mahilyow *Belarus* 53°55N 30°18E **177** B16
Mahilyow ◻ *Belarus* 54°0N 30°50E **188** E6
Mahim *Maharashtra, India* 19°2N 72°50E **130** A2
Mahim *Maharashtra, India* 19°39N 72°44E **244** E1
Mahim B. *India* 19°2N 72°49E **130** A1
Mahina *Tahiti* 17°30S 149°27W **289** e
Mahiriya *Morocco* 34°0N 3°16W **261** B4
Mahlaing *Burma* 21°6N 95°39E **241** F5
Mahlsdorf *Germany* 52°30N 13°37E **115** A4
Mahmud Kot *Pakistan* 30°16N 71°0E **242** D4
Mahmudia *Romania* 45°5N 29°5E **183** E14
Mahmudiye *Turkey* 39°48N 30°15E **205** B12
Mahmutbey *Turkey* 41°3N 28°49E **203** E12
Mahmutlar *Turkey* 36°29N 32°25E **250** B3
Mähneshän *Iran* 36°44N 47°39E **213** D12
Mahnomen *U.S.A.* 47°19N 95°58W **308** B6
Maho *Sri Lanka* 7°49N 80°16E **245** L5
Mahoba *India* 25°15N 79°55E **243** G8
Mahomet *U.S.A.* 40°12N 88°24W **311** D8
Mahón = Maó *Spain* 39°53N 4°16E **206** B5
Mahon, Menorca ✈ (MAH)
  Spain 39°50N 4°16E **196** F9
Mahone Bay *Canada* 44°27N 64°23W **299** D7
Mahongo → *Namibia* 18°0S 23°15E **270** B3
Mahopac *U.S.A.* 41°22N 73°45W **313** E11
Mahoua *Chad* 11°49N 18°26E **259** F3
Mahrauli *India* 28°31N 77°10E **120** B2
Mährisch-Budwitz = Moravské
  Budějovice *Czech Rep.* 49°4N 15°49E **180** B8
Mährisch-Schönberg = Šumperk
  Czech Rep. 49°59N 16°59E **181** B9
Mährisch-Trübau = Moravská
  Třebová *Czech Rep.* 49°45N 16°40E **181** B9
Mahul *India* 19°0N 72°53E **130** A2
Mahuta *Nigeria* 11°32N 4°58E **263** C5
Mahuva *India* 21°5N 71°48E **242** J4
Mahya Dağı *Turkey* 41°47N 27°36E **203** E11
Mai-Ndombe, L.
  Dem. Rep. of the Congo 2°0S 18°20E **264** C3
Mai Thon, Ko *Thailand* 7°29S 98°28E **237** a
Maia *Amer. Samoa* 14°13S 169°25W **302** g
Maia *Azores* 36°56N 25°1W **153** d4
Maia *Portugal* 41°14N 8°37W **194** D2
Maials *Spain* 41°22N 0°30E **196** D5
Maicao *Colombia* 11°23N 72°13W **328** A3
Maîche *France* 47°16N 6°48E **173** E13
Maicurú → *Brazil* 6°30S 61°43W **329** A8
Maicuru → *Brazil* 2°14S 54°17W **329** D7
Máida *Italy* 38°51N 16°22E **201** D9
Maida Vale *London, U.K.* 125 a1
Maidan Khula *Afghan.* 33°36N 69°50E **242** C3
Maidenhead *U.K.* 51°31N 0°42W **169** F7
Maidstone *Vic., Australia* 37°47S 144°52E **128** A1
Maidstone *Sask., Canada* 53°5N 109°20W **297** C7
Maidstone *Kent, U.K.* 51°16N 0°32E **169** F8
Maiduguri *Nigeria* 12°0N 13°20E **263** C7
Maienfeld *Italy* 42°5N 14°59E **199** F11
Mäieruş *Romania* 45°53N 25°31E **183** E10
Maigatari *Nigeria* 12°46N 9°27E **263** C6
Maigh Nuad = Maynooth
  Ireland 53°23N 6°34W **166** C5
Maignelay Montigny
  France 49°32N 2°30E **173** C9
Maigo *Phil.* 8°10N 123°57E **233** G4
Maigualida, Sierra
  Venezuela 5°30N 65°10W **329** B4
Maigudo *Ethiopia* 7°30N 37°8E **257** F4
Maihar *India* 24°16N 80°45E **243** G9
Maihara *Japan* 35°19N 136°17E **140** B4
Maikala Ra. *India* 22°0N 81°0E **244** D5
Maiko △
  Dem. Rep. of the Congo 0°30S 27°50E **268** C2
Mailani *India* 28°17N 80°21E **243** E9
Mä'ili *U.S.A.* 21°25N 158°11W **302** K13
Mä'ili Pt. *U.S.A.* 21°24N 158°11W **302** K13
Maillezais *France* 46°22N 0°44W **174** B3
Mailsi *Pakistan* 29°48N 72°15E **242** E5
Maimbung *Phil.* 5°56N 121°2E **233** J3
Main → *Bayern, Germany* 50°0N 8°18E **179** F4
Main *U.K.* 54°48N 6°18E **166** B5
Main Channel *Canada* 45°21N 81°45W **312** A3
Main Range △ *Australia* 28°11S 152°27E **281** D5
Main Ridge *Trin. & Tob.* 11°16N 60°40W **323** s
Mainburg *Germany* 48°38N 11°47E **179** G7
Maindargi *India* 17°28N 76°14E **244** F3
Maine *France* 48°20N 0°15W **172** D6
Maine □ *Ireland* 52°9N 9°45E **166** D2
Maine □ *U.S.A.* 45°20N 69°0W **309** C19
Maine, G. of *U.S.A.* 43°0N 68°30W **309** D18
Maine-et-Loire □ *France* 47°31N 0°30W **172** E6
Maine-Soroa *Niger* 13°13N 12°2E **263** C7
Maingkaing *Burma* 24°48N 95°16E **241** D6
Maingkwan *Burma* 26°15N 96°37E **241** B6
Mainistir an Corann = Midleton
  Ireland 51°55N 8°10W **166** E3
Mainit *Phil.* 9°32N 125°32E **233** G5
Mainit, L. *Phil.* 9°31N 125°30E **233** G5
Mainland *Orkney, U.K.* 58°59N 3°8W **167** C5
Mainland *Shet., U.K.* 60°15N 1°22W **167** A7
Mainpuri *India* 27°18N 79°4E **243** F8
Maintal *Germany* 50°9N 8°48E **179** E4
Maintenon *France* 48°35N 1°35E **173** D8
Maintirano *Madag.* 18°3S 44°1E **272** B7
Mainz *Germany* 50°1N 8°14E **179** F4
Maio *C. Verde Is.* 15°10N 23°10W **153** j
Maipú *Argentina* 36°52S 57°52W **334** D4
Maipú *Santiago, Chile* 33°30S 70°45W **337** C2
Maiquetía *Venezuela* 10°36N 66°57W **328** A4
Maira → *Italy* 44°49N 7°38E **198** D4
Mairabari *India* 26°30N 92°22E **241** B4
Mairipotaba *Brazil* 17°18S 49°28W **333** G2
Maisí *Cuba* 20°17N 74°9W **321** B5
Maisi, Pta. de *Cuba* 20°10N 74°10W **321** B5
Maiskhal I. *Bangla.* 21°31N 91°56E **241** E7
Maison Coloniale
  Guadeloupe 16°18N 61°16W **322** e
Maisonnette, Parc
  Canada 45°32N 73°33W **130** A2
Maisons-Alfort *France* 48°48N 2°26E **134** B3
Maisons-Laffitte *France* 48°57N 2°9E **134** A1
Maissouneuve *Canada* 45°32N 73°33W **130** A2
Maitland *N.S.W.,*
  Australia 32°33S 151°36E **283** B5
Maitland *S. Austral.,*
  Australia 34°23S 137°40E **282** C2
Maitland *Western Cape,*
  S. Africa 33°55S 18°29E **118** A1

Maitland → *Canada* 43°45N 81°43W **312** C3
Maitland, Banjaran
  Malaysia 4°55N 116°37E **235** B5
Maitri *Antarctica* 70°0S 3°0W **151** D3
Maitum *Phil.* 6°2N 124°30E **233** H5
Maiyema *Nigeria* 12°5N 4°25E **263** C5
Maiyuan *China* 25°34N 117°28E **229** E11
Maíz, Is. del *Nic.* 12°15N 83°4W **320** D3
Maizuru *Japan* 35°25N 135°22E **223** B7
Majagual *Colombia* 8°33N 74°38W **328** B3
Majalengka *Indonesia* 6°50S 108°13E **235** D3
Majanji *Uganda* 0°16N 34°0E **268** B3
Majari → *Brazil* 3°29N 60°58W **329** C5
Majene *Indonesia* 3°38S 118°57E **235** D5
Majes → *Peru* 16°40S 72°44W **330** D3
Majete △ *Malawi* 15°54S 34°24E **269** G3
Majevica *Bos.-H.* 44°45N 18°50E **182** F3
Maji *Ethiopia* 6°12N 35°30E **257** F4
Majiang *China* 26°28N 107°32E **228** D6
Majorca = Mallorca *Spain* 39°30N 3°0E **206** B4
Majors Creek *Australia* 35°33S 149°45E **283** C8
Majuria *Brazil* 3°0S 64°55W **331** B5
Majuro *Marshall Is.* 7°9N 171°12E **288** G9
Mak, Ko *Thailand* 11°49N 102°29E **237** G4
Mâkaha *Hawai'i, U.S.A.* 21°29N 158°13W **302** K13
Makaha *Zimbabwe* 17°20S 32°39E **271** A5
Mâkaha Pt. *U.S.A.* 21°41N 157°56W **302** J14
Makak *Cameroon* 3°36N 11°0E **263** D7
Makaka *Congo* 3°45S 13°39E **264** C2
Makakilo City *U.S.A.* 21°22N 158°5W **302** K13
Makakou *Gabon* 0°15S 12°12E **264** C2
Makalamabedi *Botswana* 20°19S 23°51E **270** B3
Makale *Indonesia* 3°6S 119°51E **235** C5
Makalu *Asia* 27°55N 87°8E **243** F12
Makalu-Barun △ *Nepal* 27°45N 87°10E **243** F12
Makamba *Burundi* 4°8S 29°49E **268** C2
Makapu'u Pt. *U.S.A.* 21°19N 157°39W **302** K14
Makarewa Junction *N.Z.* 46°20S 168°21E **285** G3
Makari *Cameroon* 12°35N 10°27E **259** F2
Makarikari = Makgadikgadi Salt
  Pans *Botswana* 20°40S 25°45E **270** B4
Makarov Basin *Arctic* 87°0N 150°0W **150** A
Makarovo *Russia* 57°40N 107°45E **215** D11
Makarska *Croatia* 43°20N 17°2E **198** E14
Makaryev *Russia* 57°52N 43°50E **190** B6
Makasar *Indonesia* 6°17S 106°52E **122** A2
Makasar, Selat *Indonesia* 5°10S 119°20E **235** C5
Makassar, Selat *Indonesia* 1°0S 118°20E **235** C5
Makassar, Str. of = Makassar, Selat
  Indonesia 1°0S 118°20E **235** C5
Makat = Maqat
  Kazakhstan 47°39N 53°19E **187** E9
Makati *Phil.* 14°33N 121°2E **127** B2
Makaw
  Dem. Rep. of the Congo 3°29S 18°20E **264** C3
Makawao *U.S.A.* 20°52N 156°17W **302** C5
Makaya
  Dem. Rep. of the Congo 3°21S 18°1E **264** C3
Makedonija = Macedonia ■
  Europe 41°53N 21°40E **202** E5
Makefu *Cook Is.* 18°59S 169°55W **334** D2
Makemo *French Polynesia* 16°35S 143°40W **289** f
Makeni *S. Leone* 8°55N 12°5W **262** D2
Makeyevka = Makiyivka
  Ukraine 48°0N 38°0E **189** H9
Makgadikgadi △
  Botswana 20°27S 24°47E **270** B3
Makgadikgadi Salt Pans
  Botswana 20°40S 25°45E **270** B4
Makhachkala *Russia* 43°0N 47°30E **191** J8
Makhado = Louis Trichardt
  S. Africa 23°1S 29°43E **271** B4
Makham, Ao *Thailand* 7°51N 98°25E **237** a
Makharadze = Ozurgeti
  Georgia 41°55N 42°2E **191** K5
Makhfar al Buşayyah *Iraq* 30°0N 46°10E **246** D5
Makhmūr *Iraq* 35°46N 43°35E **246** C4
Makhtal *India* 16°30N 77°31E **245** E3
Makhyah, W. → *Yemen* 17°40N 49°1E **249** G5
Makian *Indonesia* 0°20N 127°20E **231** D7
Makina *Solomon Is.* 9°50S 160°50E **287** M11
Makindu *Kenya* 2°18S 37°50E **268** C4
Mäkiniitty *Finland* 60°20N 24°58E **121** A2
Makinsk *Kazakhstan* 52°37N 70°26E **217** B8
Makira = San Cristóbal
  Solomon Is. 10°30S 161°0E **287** N11
Makiyivka *Ukraine* 48°0N 38°0E **189** H9
Makkah *Si. Arabia* 21°30N 39°54E **248** B2
Makkah □ *Si. Arabia* 21°30N 42°30E **248** B3
Makkovik *Canada* 55°10N 59°10W **299** A8
Makó *Hungary* 46°14N 20°33E **182** D5
Mako *Senegal* 12°52N 12°22W **262** B2
Makogai *Fiji* 17°28S 179°0E **287** A2
Makok *Gabon* 0°1S 9°35E **264** C1
Makokou *Gabon* 0°40N 12°50E **264** B2
Makongo
  Dem. Rep. of the Congo 3°25N 26°17E **268** B2
Makoro
  Dem. Rep. of the Congo 3°10N 29°59E **268** B2
Makoua *Congo* 0°5S 15°50E **264** C3
Maków Mazowiecki
  Poland 52°52N 21°6E **185** F8
Maków Podhalański
  Poland 49°43N 19°45E **185** J6
Makra *Greece* 36°15N 25°54E **205** E7
Makrai *India* 22°2N 77°0E **242** H7
Makran *Asia* 26°13N 61°30E **240** D1
Makran Coast Range
  Pakistan 25°40N 64°0E **240** D2
Makrana *India* 27°2N 74°46E **242** F6
Makrany *Belarus* 51°48N 24°17E **185** G11
Makri *India* 19°46N 81°55E **244** E5
Makrigialos *Greece* 35°2N 25°59E **205** E8
Makthar *Tunisia* 35°48N 9°12E **258** A1
Mākū *Iran* 39°15N 44°31E **213** D11
Mākūra *U.S.A.* 21°32N 158°13W **302** J13
Maku Military Reservation
  U.S.A. 21°32N 158°14W **302** J13
Makum *India* 27°30N 95°23E **241** B5
Makumbi
  Dem. Rep. of the Congo 5°50S 20°43E **265** D4
Makunda *Botswana* 22°30S 20°7E **270** B3
Makung *Taiwan* 23°34N 119°34E **225** D5
Makungo *Somali Rep.* 0°49N 42°35E **268** B5
Makurazaki *Japan* 31°15N 130°20E **223** J5
Makurdi *Nigeria* 7°43N 8°35E **263** D6
Makushin Volcano △
  U.S.A. 53°53N 166°55W **303** K6
Makūyeh *Iran* 28°7N 53°9E **247** D7
Makwassie *S. Africa* 27°17S 26°0E **270** D4
Makwiro *Zimbabwe* 17°58S 30°25E **271** A5
Mal *India* 26°51N 88°45E **244** B7
Mâl *Mauritania* 17°0N 14°0W **262** a
Mal B. *Ireland* 52°50N 9°30W **166** D2
Mala = Mallow *Ireland* 52°8N 8°39W **166** D3
Mala *Peru* 12°40S 76°33W **330** C2
Mala ◻ *Australia* 21°39S 130°45E **278** D5

Mala, Pta. *Panama* 7°28N 80°2W **320** E3
Mala Belozërka *Ukraine* 47°12N 34°56E **189** J8
Malá Fatra △ *Slovak Rep.* 49°10N 19°0E **181** B12
Mala Panew → *Poland* 50°43N 17°54E **185** H4
Malá Strana *Czech Rep.* 50°4N 14°24E **135** B2
Mala Vyska *Ukraine* 48°39N 31°36E **189** H6
Malabang *Phil.* 7°36N 124°3E **233** H5
Malabar *N.S.W., Australia* 33°58S 151°14E **139** B2
Malabar *Fla., U.S.A.* 28°0N 80°34W **317** H9
Malabar Coast *India* 11°0N 75°0E **245** J2
Malabar Hill *India* 18°57N 72°48E **130** B1
Malabar Pt. *India* 18°56N 72°48E **130** B1
Malabo = Rey Malabo
  Eq. Guin. 3°45N 8°50E **263** E6
Malabrigo = Puerto Chicama
  Peru 7°45S 79°20W **330** B2
Malabrigo Pt. *Phil.* 13°36N 121°15E **232** E3
Malabu *Nigeria* 9°32N 12°48E **263** D7
Malabungan *Phil.* 9°3N 117°38E **233** G1
Malacañang Palace *Phil.* 14°35N 120°59E **127** B1
Malacca, Straits of *Indonesia* 3°0N 101°0E **237** L3
Malacky *Slovak Rep.* 48°27N 17°0E **181** C10
Malad City *U.S.A.* 42°12N 112°15W **304** E7
Malad → *U.S.A.* 42°39N 90°39E **186** 9E
Maladzyechna *Belarus* 54°20N 26°50E **177** A14
Málaga *Colombia* 6°42N 72°44W **328** B3
Málaga *Spain* 36°43N 4°23W **195** A6
Málaga □ *Spain* 36°38N 4°58W **195** A6
Malagarasi *Tanzania* 5°5S 30°50E **268** D3
Malagarasi → *Tanzania* 5°12S 29°47E **268** D2
Malagasy Rep. = Madagascar ■
  Africa 20°0S 47°0E **272** B2
Malagón *Spain* 39°11N 3°52W **195** F7
Malaĥide *Ireland* 53°26N 6°9W **166** C5
Malaimbandy *Madag.* 20°20S 45°36E **272** C2
Malaita *Solomon Is.* 9°0S 161°0E **287** M11
Malakal *Sudan* 9°33N 31°40E **257** G3
Malakal Harb. *Palau* 7°19N 134°27E **288** c
Malakanagiri *India* 18°21N 81°54E **244** E5
Malakand *Pakistan* 34°40N 71°55E **242** B4
Malakhovka *Russia* 55°39N 38°0E **129** C6
Malakoff *France* 48°49N 2°18E **134** B2
Malakwal *Pakistan* 32°34N 73°13E **242** C5
Malalaua *Papua N. G.* 8°4S 146°10E **286** E4
Malam *Chad* 11°27N 20°59E **259** F4
Malamala *Indonesia* 3°21S 120°55E **231** E6
Malang *Indonesia* 7°59S 112°45E **235** D4
Malanga *Mozam.* 13°28S 36°7E **269** E4
Malangas *Phil.* 7°37N 123°1E **233** H4
Malanje □ *Angola* 9°36S 16°17E **265** D3
Malanje *Angola* 9°36S 16°17E **265** D3
Malanje □ *Norway* 69°24N 18°37E **160** B18
Malanut B. *Phil.* 9°15N 117°59E **233** G1
Malapatan *Phil.* 5°59N 125°18E **233** H6
Mälaren *Sweden* 59°30N 17°10E **162** E11
Malargüe *Argentina* 35°32S 69°30W **334** D2
Mälarhöjaen *Sweden* 59°18N 17°58E **139** B1
Malartic *Canada* 48°9N 78°9W **298** C4
Malaryta *Belarus* 51°50N 24°3E **185** G11
Malasiqui *Phil.* 15°55N 120°22E **232** D3
Malaspina Glacier
  U.S.A. 59°50N 140°30W **303** G12
Malatya *Turkey* 38°25N 38°20E **213** C8
Malatya □ *Turkey* 38°15N 38°0E **212** C7
Malawali, Pulau *Malaysia* 7°3N 117°18E **235** A5
Malawi ■ *Africa* 11°55S 34°0E **269** E3
Malawi, L. *Africa* 12°30S 34°30E **269** E3
Malay Pen. *Asia* 7°25N 100°0E **237** J3
Malaya Belozërka = Mala Belozërka
  Ukraine 47°12N 34°56E **189** J8
Malaya Neva *Russia* 59°56N 30°16E **137** B1
Malaya Okhta *Russia* 59°55N 30°25E **137** B2
Malaya Vishera *Russia* 58°55N 32°25E **188** C7
Malay Quarter *Cape Town, S. Africa* 118 C2
Malaybalay *Phil.* 8°5N 125°7E **233** G5
Mäläyer *Iran* 34°19N 48°51E **213** E13
Malaysia ■ *Asia* 5°0N 110°0E **237** K4
Malazgirt *Turkey* 39°10N 42°33E **213** C10
Malbaza *Niger* 13°59N 5°38E **263** C6
Malbon *Australia* 21°5S 140°17E **280** D2
Malbooma *Australia* 30°41S 134°11E **281** E1
Malbork *Poland* 54°3N 19°1E **184** D6
Malca Dube *Ethiopia* 6°47N 42°4E **267** C5
Malcésine *Italy* 45°46N 10°48E **198** C7
Malchin *Germany* 53°44N 12°44E **178** B8
Malchow *Germany* 53°28N 12°25E **178** B8
Malchow *Berlin, Germany* 52°34N 13°29E **115** A3
Malchow *Mecklenburg-Vorpommern,*
  Germany 53°28N 12°25E **178** B8
Malcolm *Australia* 28°51S 121°25E **279** F3
Malcolm, Pt. *Australia* 33°48S 123°45E **279** F3
Malczyce *Poland* 51°14N 16°29E **185** H3
Maldah *India* 25°2N 88°9E **243** G13
Maldegem *Belgium* 51°14N 3°26E **170** C3
Malden *London, U.K.* 51°23N 0°15W **125** b2
Malden *Mass., U.S.A.* 42°26N 71°3W **116** b2
Malden *Mo., U.S.A.* 36°34N 89°57W **308** G9
Malden I. *Kiribati* 4°3S 155°1W **289** H12
Maldives ■ *Ind. Oc.* 5°0N 73°0E **272** d
Maldon *Vic., Australia* 37°0S 144°6E **282** D6
Maldon *Essex, U.K.* 51°44N 0°42E **169** F8
Maldonado *Uruguay* 34°59S 55°0W **335** C5
Maldonado, Pta. *Mexico* 16°20N 98°33W **319** D5
Malé *Maldives* 4°0N 73°28E **272** d
Malé *Italy* 46°21N 10°55E **198** B7
Malé ✈ (MLE) *Maldives* 4°11N 73°28E **272** d
Malé Atoll *Maldives* 4°45N 73°15E **272** d
Malé Karpaty *Slovak Rep.* 48°30N 17°20E **181** C10
Maleas, Akra *Greece* 36°28N 23°7E **204** E5
Malebo, Pool *Africa* 4°17S 15°20E **264** C3
Malegaon *India* 20°30N 74°38E **244** D2
Malei *Mozam.* 17°12S 36°58E **269** F4
Maleizen *Belgium* 50°45N 4°31E **116** B3
Malek *Sudan* 6°4N 31°36E **257** G3
Malek Kandi *Iran* 37°9N 46°6E **213** D12
Malela *Bas-Congo,*
  Dem. Rep. of the Congo 5°59S 12°37E **265** D2
Malela *Maniema,*
  Indonesia 4°22S 26°8E **265** C5
Malema *Mozam.* 14°57S 37°20E **269** E4
Maleme *Greece* 35°31N 23°49E **205** D6
Malendok I. *Papua N. G.* 3°28S 153°13E **286** B7
Malerkotla *India* 30°32N 75°58E **242** D6
Malés *Greece* 35°6N 25°35E **205** E8
Malesherbes *France* 48°15N 2°24E **173** D9
Malestroit *France* 47°49N 2°25E **172** E4
Maleševska Planina
  Europe 41°38N 23°7E **202** E7
Malešice *Czech Rep.* 50°5N 14°29E **135** B3
Malha *India* 16°1N 88°45E **244** 4E
Malheur → *U.S.A.* 44°4N 116°59W **304** D5
Malheur L. *U.S.A.* 43°20N 118°48W **304** E4
Malheur L. *U.S.A.* 43°20N 118°48W **304** E4

Malha *Sudan* 15°8N 25°10E **257** D2
Malhada *Brazil* 14°21S 43°47W **333** D3
Malhargarh *India* 24°17N 74°59E **242** G6
Malheur I. *U.S.A.* 44°4N 116°59W **304** D5
Malheur L. *U.S.A.* 43°20N 118°48W **304** E4
Mali *Guinea* 12°10N 12°20E **262** C2
Mali ■ *Africa* 17°0N 3°0W **262** B4
Mali → *Burma* 25°42N 97°30E **241** C6
Mali Kanal *Serbia* 45°36N 19°24E **182** E4
Mali Kyun *Burma* 13°0N 98°20E **236** F2
Malia *Greece* 35°17N 25°32E **207** E6
Malia, Kolpos *Greece* 35°19N 25°37E **207** E6
Maliao *Taiwan* 23°48N 120°13E **225** C2
Malibu *U.S.A.* 34°2N 118°41W **307** L8
Maligaya = Gloria *Phil.* 12°59N 121°30E **232** E3
Maliku = Minicoy I. *India* 8°17N 73°2E **245** K1
Maliku *Indonesia* 0°39S 123°16E **231** E6
Malili *Indonesia* 2°42S 121°6E **231** E6
Mälilla *Sweden* 57°23N 15°48E **163** G9
Malimba, Mts.
  Dem. Rep. of the Congo 7°30S 29°30E **268** D2
Malin Hd. *Ireland* 55°23N 7°23W **166** A4
Malin Pen. *Ireland* 55°20N 7°17W **166** A4
Malindang, Mt. *Phil.* 8°13N 123°38E **233** G4
Malindi *Kenya* 3°12S 40°5E **268** C5
Malindi Marine △ *Kenya* 3°15S 40°7E **268** C5
Malines = Mechelen
  Belgium 51°2N 4°29E **170** C4
Malino *Indonesia* 1°0N 121°0E **231** D6
Malinyi *Tanzania* 8°56S 36°0E **269** D4
Malipo *China* 23°7N 104°42E **228** F5
Maliq *Albania* 40°45N 20°48E **202** F4
Malir → *Pakistan* 24°49N 67°1E **242** G2
Malita *Phil.* 6°19N 125°39E **233** H5
Maliwun *Burma* 10°17N 98°40E **237** G2
Maliya *India* 23°5N 70°46E **242** H4
Maljenik *Serbia* 43°54N 21°43E **202** C5
Malkapur *India* 20°53N 76°12E **244** D3
Malkara *Turkey* 40°53N 26°53E **203** F10
Malkhangiri = Malakanagiri
  India 18°21N 81°54E **244** E5
Malkinia Górna *Poland* 52°42N 22°5E **185** F9
Malko Tŭrnovo *Bulgaria* 41°59N 27°31E **203** E11
Mall, The *Washington, D.C., U.S.A.* 143 B2
Mallacoota *Australia* 37°40S 149°40E **283** D8
Mallacoota Inlet
  Australia 37°34S 149°40E **283** D8
Mallaig *U.K.* 57°0N 5°50W **167** D3
Mallala *Australia* 34°26S 138°30E **282** C3
Mallaoua *Niger* 13°2N 9°36E **263** C6
Mallard *U.S.A.* 42°56N 94°41W **310** B2
Mallawan *India* 27°4N 80°12E **243** F9
Mallawi *Egypt* 27°44N 30°44E **256** B3
Mallee Cliffs △ *Australia* 34°16S 142°32E **282** C5
Mallemort *France* 43°43N 5°11E **175** E9
Mallemort *U.K.* 55°52N 3°59W **121** B2
Mallet Creek *U.S.A.* 41°9N 81°55W **312** E3
Mallina *Australia* 20°53S 118°2E **278** D2
Mallorca *Spain* 39°30N 3°0E **206** B4
Mallorytown *Canada* 44°29N 75°53W **313** B9
Mallow *Ireland* 52°8N 8°39W **166** D3
Malmbäck *Sweden* 57°34N 14°28E **163** G8
Malmberget *Sweden* 67°11N 20°40E **160** C19
Malmédy *Belgium* 50°25N 6°2E **170** D6
Malmesbury *S. Africa* 33°28S 18°41E **270** D2
Malmi *Finland* 60°15N 24°59E **121** B2
Malmivaara = Malmberget
  Sweden 67°11N 20°40E **160** C19
Malmköping *Sweden* 59°8N 16°44E **162** E10
Malmö *Sweden* 55°36N 12°59E **163** J6
Malmslätt *Sweden* 58°27N 15°33E **163** F9
Malmyzh *Russia* 56°31N 50°41E **190** B10
Malnaş *Romania* 46°2N 25°49E **183** D10
Malo *Vanuatu* 15°40S 167°11E **287** E5
Malo Konare *Bulgaria* 42°12N 24°24E **203** D8
Maloarkhangelsk *Russia* 52°28N 36°30E **189** F9
Maloca *Brazil* 0°43N 55°57W **329** C6
Malolos *Phil.* 14°50N 120°49E **232** D3
Malombe L. *Malawi* 14°40S 35°15E **269** E4
Malomir *Bulgaria* 42°16N 26°32E **203** D10
Malone *U.S.A.* 30°57N 85°10W **316** F3
Malone *N.Y., U.S.A.* 44°51N 74°18W **313** B10
Malong *China* 25°24N 103°34E **228** E4
Malonga
  Dem. Rep. of the Congo 10°24S 23°10E **265** E4
Malopolskie □ *Poland* 49°50N 20°0E **185** J7
Malorad *Bulgaria* 43°28N 23°41E **202** C7
Malorita = Malaryta
  Belarus 51°50N 24°3E **185** G11
Maloya *Norway* 61°57N 5°6E **164** C2
Maloyaroslavets *Russia* 55°5N 36°30E **188** D9
Malpartida de Cáceres
  Spain 39°26N 6°30W **195** F4
Malpaso *Canary Is.* 27°43N 18°3W **153** e1
Malpaso, Presa = Netzahualcóyotl,
  Presa *Mexico* 17°8N 93°35W **319** D6
Malpelo, I. de *Colombia* 4°3N 81°35W **289** G19
Malpica de Bergantiños
  Spain 43°19N 8°50W **194** B2
Malprabha → *India* 16°20N 76°5E **245** E2
Malpur *India* 23°21N 73°27E **242** H5
Malpura *India* 26°17N 75°23E **242** F6
Mals = Málles Venosta
  Italy 46°41N 10°32E **198** B7
Malsiras *India* 17°54N 75°5E **244** F2
Malta *Brazil* 6°54S 37°31W **332** C4
Malta *Idaho, U.S.A.* 42°18N 113°22W **304** F7
Malta *Mont., U.S.A.* 48°21N 107°52W **304** B10
Malta ■ *Europe* 35°55N 14°26E **201** J8
Malta ✈ (MLA) *Malta* 35°51N 14°27E **201** J8
Maltaĥöhe *Namibia* 24°55S 17°0E **270** B2
Maltepe *Turkey* 40°55N 29°8E **203** F13
Malton *Ont., Canada* 43°42N 79°38W **141** A1
Malton *N. Yorks., U.S.A.* 54°8N 0°49W **168** C7
Malu'u *Solomon Is.* 8°20S 160°39E **287** M11
Maludam = Malaysia* 1°39N 111°21E **235** B4
Malulu *Sudan* 14°15N 32°53E **257** E3
Malumfashi *Nigeria* 11°48N 7°39E **263** C6
Malundo *Angola* 14°51S 22°0E **265** E4
Maluso *Phil.* 6°33N 121°53E **233** H4
Malvan *India* 16°2N 73°30E **245** G1
Malvern *U.S.A.* 34°22N 92°49E **314** H8
Malvern *U.K.* 52°2N 2°19W **169** E5

398 Manawatu INDEX

Manawatu → *N.Z.* 40°28S 175°12E **284** G4
Manawatu-Wanganui □ *N.Z.* 39°50S 175°30E **284** F4
Manay *Phil.* 7°17N 126°33E **233** H6
Manbij *Syria* 36°31N 37°57E **212** D7
Mancha Real *Spain* 37°48N 3°39W **195** H7
Manche □ *France* 49°10N 1°20W **172** C5
Manchegorsk *Russia* 67°54N 32°58E **214** C4
Manchester *Gt. Man., U.K.* 53°29N 2°12W **168** D5
Manchester *Calif., U.S.A.* 38°58N 123°41W **306** G3
Manchester *Conn., U.S.A.* 41°47N 72°31W **313** E12
Manchester *Ga., U.S.A.* 32°51N 84°37W **316** C5
Manchester *Iowa, U.S.A.* 42°29N 91°27W **310** B5
Manchester *Ky., U.S.A.* 37°9N 83°46W **309** G12
Manchester *Mich., U.S.A.* 42°9N 84°2W **311** B12
Manchester *N.H., U.S.A.* 42°59N 71°28W **313** D13
Manchester *N.Y., U.S.A.* 42°56N 77°16W **312** D7
Manchester *Ohio, U.S.A.* 38°41N 83°36W **311** F13
Manchester *Pa., U.S.A.* 40°4N 76°43W **313** F8
Manchester *Tenn., U.S.A.* 35°29N 86°5W **315** D11
Manchester *Vt., U.S.A.* 43°10N 73°5W **313** C11
Manchester Int. ✕ **(MAN)** *U.K.* 53°21N 2°17W **168** D5
Manchester L. *Canada* 61°28N 107°29W **297** A7
Manchhar L. *Pakistan* 26°25N 67°39E **242** F2
Manchineel Bay *Grenada* 12°26N 61°29W **323** q
Manchou *Taiwan* 22°1N 120°50E **225** D2
Manchuria = Dongbei *China* 45°0N 125°0E **227** D13
Manchurian Plain *China* 47°0N 124°0E **210** D14
Manciano *Italy* 42°35N 11°31E **199** F8
Mancifa *Ethiopia* 6°53N 41°50E **257** F5
Máncora *Peru* 4°9S 81°1W **330** A1
Mand → *India* 21°42N 83°15E **243** J10
Mand → *Iran* 28°20N 52°30E **247** D7
Manda *Ludewe, Tanzania* 10°30S 34°40E **269** E3
Manda *Mbeya, Tanzania* 7°58S 32°29E **268** D3
Manda *Mbeya, Tanzania* 8°30S 32°49E **269** D3
Manda △ *Chad* 9°45N 17°52E **259** G3
Mandabé *Madag.* 21°0S 44°55E **272** C1
Mandaguari *Brazil* 23°32S 51°42W **335** A5
Mandah = Töhöm *Mongolia* 44°27N 108°2E **226** B5
Mandal *Norway* 58°2N 7°25E **164** F4
Mandala, Puncak *Indonesia* 4°44S 140°20E **231** E10
Mandalay *Burma* 22°0N 96°4E **241** E6
Mandalay □ *Burma* 22°0N 96°5E **241** E5
Mandale = Mandalay *Burma* 22°0N 96°4E **241** E6
Mandalgarh *India* 25°12N 75°6E **242** G6
Mandalgovĭ *Mongolia* 45°45N 106°10E **226** B4
Mandalī *Iraq* 33°43N 45°28E **213** F11
Mandalselva → *Norway* 58°2N 7°28E **164** F4
Mandaluyong *Phil.* 14°35N 121°1E **127** B2
Mandan *U.S.A.* 46°50N 100°54W **308** B3
Mandaoli *India* 28°37N 77°17E **120** B2
Mandaon *Phil.* 12°13N 123°17E **232** E4
Mandaqui → *Brazil* 23°30S 46°40W **137** A2
Mandar, Teluk *Indonesia* 3°32S 119°21E **235** C5
Mandara Mts. *Nigeria* 10°40N 13°40E **259** F2
Mándas *Italy* 39°40N 9°8E **200** C2
Mandasor = Mandsaur *India* 24°3N 75°8E **242** G6
Mandaue *Phil.* 10°20N 123°56E **233** F4
Mandelieu-la-Napoule *France* 43°34N 6°57E **175** E10
Mandera *Kenya* 3°55N 41°53E **268** B5
Mandeville *Jamaica* 18°2N 77°31W **320** a
Mandi *India* 31°39N 76°58E **242** D7
Mandi Burewala *Pakistan* 30°9N 72°41E **242** E5
Mandi Dabwali *India* 29°58N 74°42E **242** E6
Mandiana *Guinea* 10°37N 8°39W **262** C3
Mandigos = Manica *Mozam.* 18°58S 32°59E **271** A5
Mandimba *Mozam.* 14°20S 35°40E **269** E4
Mandioli *Indonesia* 0°40S 127°20E **231** E7
Mandioré, L. *S. Amer.* 18°8S 57°33W **331** D6
Mandla *India* 22°39N 80°30E **243** H9
Mandø *Denmark* 55°18N 8°33E **163** J2
Mandoli *India* 28°41N 77°18E **120** A2
Mandorah *Australia* 12°32S 130°42E **278** B5
Mandoto *Madag.* 19°34S 46°17E **272** B2
Mandoudi *Greece* 38°48N 23°29E **204** C5
Mandoul *Chad* 9°40N 15°30E **259** G3
Mandra *Greece* 38°4N 23°30E **204** C5
Mandra *Pakistan* 33°23N 73°12E **242** C5
Mandraki *Greece* 36°36N 27°11E **205** E9
Mandrare → *Madag.* 25°10S 46°30E **272** D2
Mandritsara *Madag.* 15°50S 48°49E **272** B2
Mandronarivo *Madag.* 21°7S 45°38E **272** C2
Mandsaur *India* 24°3N 75°8E **242** G6
Mandurah *Australia* 32°36S 115°48E **279** F2
Mandúria *Italy* 40°24N 17°38E **201** B10
Mandvi *Gujarat, India* 22°51N 69°22E **242** H3
Mandvi *Maharashtra, India* 18°56N 72°50E **130** B2
Mandya *India* 12°30N 77°0E **245** H3
Mandzai *Pakistan* 30°55N 67°6E **242** D2
Mané *Burkina Faso* 12°59N 1°21W **263** C4
Maneh *Iran* 37°39N 57°7E **247** B8
Manenberg *S. Africa* 33°58S 18°33E **118** A2
Manengouba, Mts. *Cameroon* 5°0N 9°50E **263** E6
Maner → *India* 18°30N 79°40E **244** E4
Manera *Madag.* 22°55S 44°20E **272** C1
Manèrbio *Italy* 45°21N 10°8E **198** C7
Maneroo Cr. → *Australia* 23°21S 143°53E **280** C3
Manfalût *Egypt* 27°20N 30°52E **256** B3
Manfred *Australia* 33°19S 143°45E **282** B5
Manfredónia *Italy* 41°38N 15°55E **199** G12
Manfredónia, G. di *Italy* 41°35N 16°5E **199** G13
Mang Kung Uk *China* 22°18N 114°16E **122** B2
Mang-won *S. Korea* 37°33N 126°55E **137** B1
Manga *Brazil* 14°46S 43°56W **333** D3
Manga *Burkina Faso* 11°40N 1°4W **263** C4
Manga *Congo* 0°13S 16°5E **264** C3
Manga *Niger* 15°0N 14°0E **259** F2
Mangabeiras, Chapada das *Brazil* 10°0S 46°30W **332** D2
Mangai *Dem. Rep. of the Congo* 4°2S 19°32E **265** C3
Mangaia *Cook Is.* 21°55S 157°55W **289** K12
Mangakino *N.Z.* 38°22S 175°47E **284** E4
Mangal *Phil.* 6°25N 121°58E **233** H3
Mangalagiri *India* 16°26N 80°36E **245** F5
Mangaldai *India* 26°26N 92°2E **241** B4
Mangaldan *Phil.* 16°4N 120°24E **232** C3
Mangalia *Romania* 43°50N 28°35E **183** G13
Mangalmé *Chad* 12°26N 19°37E **259** F3
Mangalore *India* 12°55N 74°47E **245** H2
Mangaluru = Mangalore *India* 12°55N 74°47E **245** H2
Mangalvedha *India* 17°31N 75°28E **244** F2
Mangan *India* 27°31N 88°32E **241** B2
Mangaon *India* 18°15N 73°20E **244** E1
Mangawan *India* 24°41N 81°33E **243** G9
Mangaweka *N.Z.* 39°48S 175°47E **284** F4
Mangaweka, Mt. *N.Z.* 39°49S 176°5E **284** F5
Mange *Dem. Rep. of the Congo* 0°54N 20°30E **264** B4
Manger *Norway* 60°38N 5°3E **164** D2
Manggar *Indonesia* 2°50S 108°10E **235** C3
Manggawitu *Indonesia* 4°8S 133°32E **231** E8
Mangghystaū *Kazakhstan* 43°40N 51°13E **216** D4
Mangghystaū □ *Kazakhstan* 45°0N 53°0E **216** D4
Mangghystaū Tübegi *Kazakhstan* 44°30N 52°30E **216** D4
Manggis *Indonesia* 8°29S 115°31E **231** J18
Mangin Taungdan *Burma* 24°15N 95°45E **241** C5
Mangindrano *Madag.* 14°17S 48°58E **272** A2
Mangkalihat, Tanjung *Indonesia* 1°2N 118°59E **235** B5
Mangkururrpa ✪ *Australia* 20°35S 129°43E **278** D4
Mangla *Pakistan* 33°7N 73°39E **242** C5
Mangla Dam *Pakistan* 33°9N 73°44E **243** C5
Manglares, C. *Colombia* 1°36N 79°2W **328** C2
Manglaur *India* 29°44N 77°49E **242** E7
Manglisi *Georgia* 41°41N 44°22E **191** K7
Mangnai *China* 37°52N 91°43E **218** D7
Mangnai Zhen *China* 38°24N 90°14E **217** E12
Mango *Togo* 10°20N 0°30E **263** C5
Mango *Tonga* 20°17S 174°29W **287** Q13
Mangoche *Malawi* 14°25S 35°16E **269** E4
Mangoky → *Madag.* 21°29S 43°41E **272** C1
Mangole *Indonesia* 1°50S 125°55E **231** E6
Mangolpuri *India* 28°41N 77°6E **120** A1
Mangombe *Dem. Rep. of the Congo* 1°20S 26°48E **268** C2
Mangonui *N.Z.* 35°1S 173°32E **284** B2
Mangoro → *Madag.* 20°0S 48°45E **272** C2
Mangrol *Mad. P., India* 21°7N 70°7E **242** J4
Mangrol *Raj., India* 25°20N 76°31E **242** G6
Mangrul Pir *India* 20°19N 77°21E **244** D3
Manguaba = Pilar *Brazil* 9°36S 35°56W **332** C4
Mangualde *Portugal* 40°38N 7°48W **194** E3
Mangueigne *Chad* 10°30N 21°15E **259** F4
Mangueira, L. da *Brazil* 33°0S 52°50W **335** C5
Manguéni, Hamada *Niger* 22°35N 12°40E **258** D2
Manguinhos ✕ *Brazil* 22°52S 43°14W **135** B1
Mangum *U.S.A.* 34°53N 99°30W **314** D5
Mangungu *Dem. Rep. of the Congo* 5°16S 19°36E **265** D3
Manguri *Australia* 28°58S 134°22E **281** A1
Mangyshlak, Poluostrov = Mangghystaū Tübegi *Kazakhstan* 44°30N 52°30E **216** D4
Manhattan *Kans., U.S.A.* 39°11N 96°35W **308** F5
Manhattan *New York, U.S.A.* **132** d2
Manhattan Beach *U.S.A.* 40°34N 73°56W **132** C2
Manhattan Bridge *New York, U.S.A.* **132** f2
Manhatten *U.S.A.* 41°26N 87°59W **311** C9
Manhiça *Mozam.* 25°23S 32°49E **271** C5
Manhuaçu *Brazil* 20°15S 42°2W **333** F3
Manhumirim *Brazil* 20°22S 41°57W **333** F3
Mani *Colombia* 4°49N 72°17W **328** C3
Mani *China* 34°52N 87°11E **218** E6
Mania → *Madag.* 19°42S 45°22E **272** B2
Maniago *Italy* 46°10N 12°43E **199** B9
Manica *Mozam.* 18°58S 32°59E **271** A5
Manica □ *Mozam.* 19°10S 33°45E **271** A5
Manicahan *Phil.* 7°1N 122°12E **233** H4
Manicaland □ *Zimbabwe* 19°0S 32°30E **269** F3
Manicoré *Brazil* 5°48S 61°16W **331** B5
Manicoré → *Brazil* 5°51S 61°19W **331** B5
Manicouagan → *Canada* 49°30N 68°30W **299** C6
Manicouagan, Rés. *Canada* 51°5N 68°40W **299** B6
Maniema □ *Dem. Rep. of the Congo* 3°0S 26°0E **268** C2
Manīfah *Si. Arabia* 27°44N 49°0E **247** E6
Manifold, C. *Australia* 22°41S 150°50E **280** C5
Maniganggo *China* 31°56N 99°10E **228** B2
Manigotagan *Canada* 51°6N 96°18W **297** C9
Manigotagan → *Canada* 51°7N 96°20W **297** C9
Manihari *India* 25°21N 87°38E **243** G12
Manihi *French Polynesia* 14°24S 145°56W **289** f
Manihiki *Cook Is.* 10°24S 161°1W **289** J11
Manihiki Plateau *Pac. Oc.* 11°0S 164°0W **289** J11
Maniitsoq *Greenland* 65°26N 52°55W **154** D5
Manika, Plateau de la *Dem. Rep. of the Congo* 10°0S 25°5E **269** E2
Manikchhari *Bangla.* 22°51N 91°50E **241** D3
Manikganj *Bangla.* 23°52N 90°0E **241** D3
Manikpur *India* 25°4N 81°7E **243** G9
Manila *Phil.* 14°35N 120°58E **127** B1
Manila *Utah, U.S.A.* 40°59N 109°43W **304** F9
Manila B. *Phil.* 14°40N 120°35E **232** D3
Manila Ninoy Aquino Int. ✕ **(MNL)** *Phil.* 14°31N 121°0E **127** B2
Manildra *Australia* 33°11S 148°41E **283** B8
Manilla *Australia* 30°45S 150°43E **283** A9
Manimpé *Mali* 14°11N 5°28W **262** C3
Maningrida *Australia* 12°3S 134°13E **280** A1
Maninian *Ivory C.* 10°3N 7°52W **262** C3
Maninjau, Danau *Indonesia* 0°19S 100°11E **234** C2
Manipur □ *India* 25°0N 94°0E **241** C5
Manipur → *Burma* 23°45N 94°20E **241** D5
Manisa *Turkey* 38°38N 27°30E **205** C9
Manisa □ *Turkey* 38°40N 28°0E **205** C9
Manistee *U.S.A.* 44°15N 86°19W **308** C10
Manistee → *U.S.A.* 44°15N 86°21W **308** C10
Manistique *U.S.A.* 45°57N 86°15W **308** C10
Manito *U.S.A.* 40°26N 89°47W **310** D7
Manitoba □ *Canada* 53°30N 97°0W **297** B9
Manitoba, L. *Canada* 51°0N 98°45W **297** C9
Manitou *Canada* 49°15N 98°32W **297** D9
Manitou, L. *Canada* 50°55N 65°17W **299** B6
Manitou Beach *U.S.A.* 41°58N 84°19W **311** C12
Manitou Is. *U.S.A.* 45°8N 86°0W **308** C10
Manitou L. *Canada* 52°43N 109°43W **297** C7
Manitou Springs *U.S.A.* 38°52N 104°55W **304** G11
Manitoulin I. *Canada* 45°40N 82°30W **298** C3
Manitouwadge *Canada* 49°8N 85°48W **298** C2
Manitowoc *U.S.A.* 44°5N 87°40W **308** C10
Manitsauá-Missu → *Brazil* 10°58S 53°20W **331** C7
Maniyachi *India* 8°51N 77°55E **245** K3
Manizales *Colombia* 5°5N 75°32W **328** B2
Manja *Madag.* 21°26S 44°20E **272** C1
Manjacaze *Mozam.* 24°45S 34°0E **271** B5
Manjakandriana *Madag.* 18°55S 47°47E **272** B2
Manjeri *India* 11°7N 76°11E **245** J3
Manjhand *Pakistan* 25°50N 68°10E **242** G3
Manjiang *China* 41°56N 127°35E **224** B3
Manjil *Iran* 36°46N 49°30E **247** B6
Manjimup *Australia* 34°15S 116°6E **279** F2
Manjlegaon *India* 19°9N 76°14E **244** E3
Manjo *Cameroon* 4°50N 9°49E **264** B1
Manjra → *India* 18°49N 77°52E **244** E3
Mankato *Kans., U.S.A.* 39°47N 98°13W **308** F4
Mankato *Minn., U.S.A.* 44°10N 94°0W **308** C6
Mankayan *Phil.* 16°52N 120°47E **232** C3
Mankayane *Swaziland* 26°40S 31°4E **271** C5
Mankera *Pakistan* 31°23N 71°26E **242** D4
Mankim *Cameroon* 5°1N 12°0E **263** D7
Mankkaa *Finland* 60°11N 24°47E **121** B1
Mankono *Ivory C.* 8°1N 6°10W **262** D3
Mankota *Canada* 49°25N 107°5W **297** D7
Mankulam *Sri Lanka* 9°8N 80°26E **245** K5
Manlay = Üydzin *Mongolia* 44°9N 107°0E **226** B4
Manleluag △ *Phil.* 15°4N 120°17E **232** D3
Manley Hot Springs *U.S.A.* 65°0N 150°38W **303** D10
Manlleu *Spain* 42°2N 2°17E **196** C7
Manly *Australia* 33°47S 151°17E **139** A2
Manmad *India* 20°18N 74°28E **244** D2
Mann, L. *U.S.A.* 28°32N 81°35W **133** A2
Mann Ranges *Australia* 26°6S 130°5E **279** E5
Manna *Indonesia* 4°25S 102°55E **234** C2
Mannahill *Australia* 32°25S 140°0E **282** B4
Mannar *Sri Lanka* 9°1N 79°54E **245** K4
Mannar, G. of *Asia* 8°30N 79°0E **245** K4
Mannar I. *Sri Lanka* 9°5N 79°45E **245** K4
Mannargudi *India* 10°45N 79°51E **245** J4
Mannheim *Germany* 49°29N 8°29E **179** F4
Manning *Alta., Canada* 56°53N 117°39W **296** B5
Manning *Oreg., U.S.A.* 45°45N 123°13W **306** E3
Manning *S.C., U.S.A.* 33°42N 80°13W **316** B9
Manning → *Australia* 31°52S 152°43E **283** A10
Manning Str. *Solomon Is.* 7°30S 158°0E **287** L10
Mann's Chinese Theatre *U.S.A.* 34°6N 118°20W **126** B2
Mannswörth *Austria* 48°8N 16°30E **142** B3
Mannu → *Italy* 39°16N 9°0E **200** C2
Mannu, C. *Italy* 40°3N 8°21E **200** B1
Mannum *Australia* 34°50S 139°20E **282** C3
Mano *S. Leone* 8°3N 12°2W **262** D2
Mano → *Liberia* 6°56N 11°30W **262** D2
Mano River *Liberia* 7°20N 11°6W **262** D2
Manoa *Bolivia* 9°40S 65°27W **331** B4
Manoharpur *India* 22°23N 85°12E **243** H11
Manokotak *U.S.A.* 58°58N 159°3W **303** G8
Manokwari *Indonesia* 0°54S 134°0E **231** E8
Manolada *Greece* 38°4N 21°21E **204** C3
Manolo Fortich *Phil.* 8°28N 124°50E **233** G5
Manombo *Madag.* 22°57S 43°28E **272** C1
Manono *Dem. Rep. of the Congo* 7°15S 27°25E **268** D2
Manono *Samoa* 13°50S 172°5W **287** V19
Manoppello *Italy* 42°15N 14°3E **199** F11
Manor Park *Wellington, N.Z.* 41°10S 174°59E **143** A2
Manor Park *London, U.K.* 51°32N 0°1E **125** A4
Manora *Pakistan* 24°47N 66°58E **123** B1
Manora Pt. *Pakistan* 24°47N 66°58E **123** B1
Manorhamilton *Ireland* 54°18N 8°9W **166** B3
Manosque *France* 43°49N 5°47E **175** E9
Manotick *Canada* 45°13N 75°41W **313** A9
Manouane → *Canada* 49°30N 71°10W **299** C5
Manouane, L. *Canada* 50°45N 70°45W **299** B5
Manovo-Gounda Saint Floris △ *C.A.R.* 9°30N 21°25E **264** A4
Manp'o *N. Korea* 41°6N 126°24E **224** B3
Manpojin = Manp'o *N. Korea* 41°6N 126°24E **224** B3
Manpur *Chhattisgarh, India* 23°17N 83°35E **243** H10
Manpur *Chhattisgarh, India* 20°22N 80°43E **244** D5
Manpur *Mad. P., India* 22°26N 75°37E **242** H6
Manquehue, Cerro *Chile* 33°21S 70°35W **137** B2
Manra *Kiribati* 4°27S 171°15W **277** A16
Manresa *Spain* 41°48N 1°50E **196** D6
Mansa *Gujarat, India* 23°27N 72°45E **242** H5
Mansa *Punjab, India* 30°0N 75°27E **242** E6
Mansa *Zambia* 11°13S 28°55E **269** E2
Mansa Konko *Gambia* 13°28N 15°33W **262** C1
Mansalay *Phil.* 12°31N 121°26E **232** E3
Månsåsen *Sweden* 63°5N 14°18E **162** A8
Mansehra *Pakistan* 34°20N 73°15E **242** B5
Mansel I. *Canada* 62°0N 80°0W **295** E15
Mansfield *Vic., Australia* 37°4S 146°6E **283** D7
Mansfield *Notts., U.K.* 53°9N 1°11W **168** D6
Mansfield *Ga., U.S.A.* 33°31N 83°44W **316** B6
Mansfield *La., U.S.A.* 32°2N 93°43W **314** E8
Mansfield *Mass., U.S.A.* 42°2N 71°13W **313** D13
Mansfield *Ohio, U.S.A.* 40°45N 82°31W **312** F2
Mansfield *Pa., U.S.A.* 41°48N 77°5W **312** E7
Mansfield *Tex., U.S.A.* 32°33N 97°8W **314** E6
Mansfield, Mt. *U.S.A.* 44°33N 72°49W **313** B12
Mansi *Burma* 24°48N 95°52E **241** C5
Mansidão *Brazil* 10°43S 44°2W **332** D3
Mansilla de las Mulas *Spain* 42°30N 5°25W **194** C5
Mansle *France* 45°52N 0°12E **174** C4
Manso → *Brazil* 13°50S 47°0W **333** D2
Mansôa *Guinea-Biss.* 12°0N 15°20W **262** C1
Manson *U.S.A.* 42°32N 94°32W **310** B2
Manson Creek *Canada* 55°37N 124°32W **296** B4
Mansoura *Algeria* 36°1N 4°31E **261** A5
Manta *Ecuador* 1°0S 80°40W **328** D1
Manta, B. de *Ecuador* 0°54S 80°44W **328** D1
Mantadia △ *Madag.* 18°54S 48°21E **272** B2
Mantalingajan, Mt. *Phil.* 8°55N 117°45E **233** G1
Mantantale *Dem. Rep. of the Congo* 2°10S 20°11E **264** C4
Mantare *Tanzania* 2°42S 33°13E **268** C3
Mantaro → *Peru* 12°16S 73°57W **330** C3
Manteca *U.S.A.* 37°48N 121°13W **306** H5
Mantecal *Venezuela* 7°34N 69°17W **328** B4
Mantena *Brazil* 18°47S 40°59W **333** E3
Manteno *U.S.A.* 41°15N 87°50W **311** C9
Manteo *U.S.A.* 35°55N 75°40W **315** D17
Mantes-la-Jolie *France* 48°58N 1°41E **173** D8
Mantha *India* 19°40N 76°23E **244** E3
Manthani *India* 18°40N 79°35E **244** E4
Manti *U.S.A.* 39°16N 111°38W **304** G8
Mantiqueira, Serra da *Brazil* 22°0S 44°0W **333** F3
Manton *U.S.A.* 44°25N 85°24W **309** C11
Mantorp *Sweden* 58°21N 15°20E **163** F9
Mántova *Italy* 45°9N 10°48E **198** C7
Mänttä Vilppula *Finland* 62°3N 24°40E **188** A3
Mantua = Mántova *Italy* 45°9N 10°48E **198** C7
Mantung *Australia* 34°35S 140°3E **282** C4
Manturovo *Russia* 58°23N 44°45E **190** A7
Manu *Peru* 12°10S 70°51W **330** C3
Manú → *Peru* 12°16S 70°55W **330** C3
Manu'a Is. *Amer. Samoa* 14°13S 169°35W **287** W21
Manuel Alves → *Brazil* 11°19S 48°28W **333** D2
Manuel Alves Grande → *Brazil* 7°27S 47°35W **332** C2
Manuel Urbano *Brazil* 8°53S 69°18W **330** B4
Manui *Indonesia* 3°35S 123°5E **231** E6
Manukan *Phil.* 8°32N 123°5E **233** G4
Manukau *N.Z.* 37°0S 174°52E **284** D3
Manukau Harbour *N.Z.* 37°3S 174°45E **284** D3
Manunui *N.Z.* 38°54S 175°21E **284** E4
Manuoha *N.Z.* 38°39S 177°7E **284** E6
Manuripi → *Bolivia* 11°6S 67°36W **330** C4
Manus □ *Papua N. G.* 2°0S 147°0E **286** B4
Manus I. *Papua N. G.* 2°0S 147°0E **286** B4
Manvi *India* 15°57N 76°59E **245** G3
Manwath *India* 19°19N 76°32E **244** E3
Many *U.S.A.* 31°34N 93°29W **314** F8
Manyallaluk ✪ *Australia* 14°16S 132°49E **278** B5
Manyani *Kenya* 3°5S 38°30E **268** C4
Manyara, L. *Tanzania* 3°40S 35°50E **268** C4
Manyara △ *Tanzania* 3°35S 35°50E **268** C4
Manyas *Turkey* 40°2N 27°59E **203** F11
Manyas Gölü = Kus Gölü *Turkey* 40°10N 27°55E **203** F11
Manyava *Ukraine* 48°39N 24°21E **183** B9
Manych → *Russia* 47°15N 40°0E **191** G5
Manych-Gudilo, Ozero *Russia* 46°24N 42°38E **191** G6
Manyonga → *Tanzania* 4°10S 34°15E **268** C3
Manyoni *Tanzania* 5°45S 34°55E **268** D3
Manzai *Pakistan* 32°12N 70°15E **242** C4
Manzala, Bahra el *Egypt* 31°10N 31°56E **256** H7
Manzanar △ *U.S.A.* 36°44N 118°9W **306** J7
Manzanares *Spain* 39°2N 3°22W **195** F7
Manzanares, Canal de *Spain* 40°19N 3°38W **127** C2
Manzaneda *Spain* 42°12N 7°15W **194** C3
Manzanilla Pt. *Trin. & Tob.* 10°31N 61°1W **323** t
Manzanillo *Cuba* 20°20N 77°31W **320** B4
Manzanillo *Colima, Mexico* 19°3N 104°20W **318** D4
Manzanillo, Pta. *Panama* 9°30N 79°40W **320** E4
Manzano Mts. *U.S.A.* 34°40N 106°20W **305** J10
Manzarīyeh *Iran* 34°53N 50°50E **247** C6
Manzhouli *China* 49°35N 117°25E **219** B12
Manzini *Swaziland* 26°30S 31°25E **271** C5
Manzur Vadisi △ *Turkey* 39°10N 39°30E **246** B3
Mao *Chad* 14°4N 15°19E **259** F3
Maó *Spain* 39°53N 4°16E **206** B5
Mao Mausoleum *Beijing, China* **114** c3
Maoka = Kholmsk *Russia* 47°40N 142°5E **215** E15
Maoke, Pegunungan *Indonesia* 3°40S 137°30E **231** E9
Maolin *China* 43°58N 123°30E **227** C12
Maoming *China* 21°50N 110°54E **229** G8
Maopi T'ou *China* 21°56N 120°43E **225** E2
Maouri, Dallol → *Niger* 12°5N 3°32E **263** C5
Maoxian *China* 31°41N 103°49E **228** B4
Maoxing *China* 45°28N 124°40E **227** B13
Map *Micronesia* 9°35N 138°10E **287** R16
Mapalma *Dem. Rep. of the Congo* 2°3N 24°30E **264** B4
Mapam Yumco *China* 30°45N 81°28E **243** D9
Mapastepec *Mexico* 15°26N 92°54W **319** D6
Mapfongui *Gabon* 1°15S 12°59E **264** C2
Maphrao, Ko *Thailand* 7°56N 98°26E **237** a
Mapia, Kepulauan *Indonesia* 0°50N 134°20E **231** D8
Mapimí *Mexico* 25°49N 103°51W **318** B4
Mapimí, Bolsón de *Mexico* 27°0N 104°15W **318** B4
Maping *China* 31°34N 113°32E **229** B9
Mapinga *Tanzania* 6°40S 39°12E **268** D4
Mapinhane *Mozam.* 22°20S 35°0E **271** B6
Mapire *Venezuela* 7°45N 64°42W **329** B5
Maple → *U.S.A.* 42°59N 84°57W **311** B12
Maple Creek *Canada* 49°55N 109°29W **297** D7
Maple Valley *U.S.A.* 47°25N 122°3W **306** C4
Mapleton *U.S.A.* 44°2N 123°52W **304** D2
Mapo *S. Korea* 37°32N 126°56E **137** B1
Mapoon ✪ *Australia* 11°44S 142°8E **280** A3
Mapourika, L. *N.Z.* 43°16S 170°12E **285** D5
Maprik *Papua N. G.* 3°44S 143°3E **286** B2
Mapuca *India* 15°36N 73°46E **245** G1
Mapuera → *Brazil* 1°5S 57°2W **329** D6
Mapulanguene *Mozam.* 24°29S 32°6E **271** B5
Mapungubwe △ *S. Africa* 22°12S 29°22E **271** B4
Maputo *Mozam.* 25°58S 32°32E **271** C5
Maputo □ *Mozam.* 26°0S 32°25E **271** C5
Maputo, B. de *Mozam.* 25°50S 32°45E **271** C5
Maputo △ *Mozam.* 26°23S 32°48E **271** C5
Maqanshy *Kazakhstan* 46°47N 82°1E **217** C10
Maqat *Kazakhstan* 47°39N 53°19E **187** E9
Maqên *China* 34°24N 100°6E **218** E8
Maqên Gangri *China* 34°55N 99°18E **218** E8
Maqiaohe *China* 44°40N 130°30E **227** B16
Maqnā *Si. Arabia* 28°25N 34°50E **251** K5
Maqran, W. → *Si. Arabia* 20°55N 47°12E **248** B4
Maqteïr *Mauritania* 21°50N 11°40W **260** D2
Maqu *China* 33°52N 101°42E **218** E9
Maquan He = Brahmaputra → *Asia* 23°40N 90°35E **241** D3
Maqueda *Spain* 40°4N 4°22W **194** E6
Maqueda Channel *Phil.* 13°42N 124°1E **232** E5
Maquela do Zombo *Angola* 6°0S 15°15E **265** D3
Maquinchao *Argentina* 41°15S 68°50W **336** B3
Maquoketa *U.S.A.* 42°4N 90°40W **310** B6
Mar *Canada* 44°49N 81°12W **312** B3
Mar, Serra do *Brazil* 25°30S 49°0W **335** B6
Mar Chiquita, L. *Argentina* 30°40S 62°50W **334** C3
Mar del Plata *Argentina* 38°0S 57°30W **334** D4
Mar Menor *Spain* 37°40N 0°45W **197** H4
Mar Vista *U.S.A.* 34°0N 118°25W **126** B2
Mara *Guyana* 6°0N 57°36W **329** B6
Mara *India* 28°11N 94°14E **241** A5
Mara *Tanzania* 1°30S 34°32E **268** C3
Mara □ *Tanzania* 1°45S 34°20E **268** C3
Maraã *Brazil* 1°52S 65°25W **328** D4
Maraa *Tahiti* 17°46S 149°34W **289** e
Marabá *Brazil* 5°20S 49°5W **332** C2
Marabahan *Indonesia* 3°0S 114°45E **235** C4
Maraboon, L. *Australia* 23°41S 148°0E **280** C4
Maracá, I. de *Brazil* 2°10N 50°30W **329** C7
Maracaibo *Venezuela* 10°40N 71°37W **328** A3
Maracaibo, L. de *Venezuela* 9°40N 71°30W **328** B3
Maracaju *Brazil* 21°38S 55°9W **335** A4
Maracajú, Serra de *Brazil* 20°57S 55°1W **331** E6
Maracanã *Pará, Brazil* 0°46S 47°27W **332** B2
Maracanã *Rio de J., Brazil* 22°54S 43°13W **135** B1
Maracanaú *Brazil* 3°52S 38°38W **332** B4
Maracás *Brazil* 13°26S 40°18W **333** D3
Maracas *Trin. & Tob.* 10°41N 61°24W **323** t
Maracas → *Trin. & Tob.* 10°34N 61°25W **323** t
Maracas B. *Trin. & Tob.* 10°46N 61°26W **323** t
Maracas Bay Village *Trin. & Tob.* 10°46N 61°28W **323** t
Maracas Falls *Trin. & Tob.* 10°44N 61°24W **323** t
Maracay *Venezuela* 10°15N 67°28W **328** A4
Maracena *Spain* 37°12N 3°38W **195** H7
Marādah *Libya* 29°15N 19°15E **258** C3
Maradi *Niger* 13°29N 7°20E **263** C6
Maradi □ *Niger* 14°15N 7°15E **263** C6
Marāgheh *Iran* 37°30N 46°12E **213** D12
Maragogipe *Brazil* 12°46S 38°55W **333** D4
Marāh *Si. Arabia* 25°0N 45°35E **246** E5
Marahoue △ *Ivory C.* 7°0N 6°7W **262** D3
Marais du Cotentin et du Bessin △ *France* 49°10N 1°30W **172** C5
Marais Poitevin, Val de Sèvre et Vendée △ *France* 46°18N 0°35W **174** B3
Maraisburg = Hofmeyr *S. Africa* 31°39S 25°50E **270** D4
Marajó, B. de *Brazil* 1°0S 48°30W **332** B2
Marajó, I. de *Brazil* 1°0S 49°30W **332** B2
Marākand *Iran* 38°51N 45°16E **246** B5
Marakele △ *S. Africa* 24°30S 25°30E **271** B4
Maralal *Kenya* 1°0N 36°38E **268** B4
Maralinga *Australia* 30°13S 131°32E **279** F5
Maralinga Tjarutja ✪ *Australia* 29°30S 131°0E **279** E5
Maram *India* 25°25N 94°6E **241** C5
Marama *Australia* 35°10S 140°10E **282** C4
Maramag *Phil.* 7°46N 125°0E **233** H5
Maramaraereğlisi *Turkey* 40°57N 27°57E **203** F11
Maramasike *Solomon Is.* 9°30S 161°25E **287** M11
Marambio *Antarctica* 64°0S 56°0W **151** C18
Maramureş □ *Romania* 47°45N 24°0E **183** C9
Maran *Malaysia* 3°35N 102°45E **237** L4
Marana *U.S.A.* 32°27N 111°13W **305** K8
Maranboy *Australia* 14°40S 132°39E **278** B5
Maranchón *Spain* 41°6N 2°15W **196** D2
Marand *Iran* 38°30N 45°45E **213** C11
Marandochori *Greece* 38°38N 20°39E **207** B2
Marang *Malaysia* 5°12N 103°13E **237** K4
Maranguape *Brazil* 3°55S 38°50W **332** B4
Maranhão = São Luís *Brazil* 2°39S 44°15W **332** B3
Maranhão □ *Brazil* 5°0S 46°0W **332** C2
Marano, L. di *Italy* 45°44N 13°10E **199** C10
Maranoa → *Australia* 27°50S 148°37E **281** A4
Marañón → *Peru* 4°30S 73°35W **330** A3
Marão *Mozam.* 24°18S 34°2E **271** B5
Maraoli *India* 19°2N 72°53E **130** A2
Marapi → *Brazil* 0°37N 55°58W **329** C6
Marari *Brazil* 5°43S 67°47W **330** B4
Maraş = Kahramanmaraş *Turkey* 37°37N 36°53E **212** D7
Mărăşeşti *Romania* 45°52N 27°14E **183** E12
Maratea *Italy* 39°59N 15°43E **201** C8
Marateca *Portugal* 38°34N 8°40W **195** G2
Marathasa *Cyprus* 34°59N 32°51E **207** F8
Marathia, Akra *Greece* 37°39N 20°50E **207** D2
Marathokambos *Greece* 37°43N 26°42E **205** D8
Marathon *Queens., Australia* 20°51S 143°32E **280** C3
Marathon *Ont., Canada* 48°44N 86°23W **298** C2
Marathon *Fla., U.S.A.* 24°43N 81°5W **317** L8
Marathon *N.Y., U.S.A.* 42°27N 76°2W **313** D8
Marathon *Tex., U.S.A.* 30°12N 103°15W **314** F3
Marathonas *Greece* 38°11N 23°58E **204** C5
Marathóvouno *Cyprus* 35°13N 33°37E **207** E9
Maratua *Indonesia* 2°10N 118°35E **235** B5
Maraú *Brazil* 14°6S 39°0W **333** D4
Marau *Indonesia* 2°9S 110°42E **235** C4
Marau *Solomon Is.* 10°31S 161°31E **287** N11
Maraval *Trin. & Tob.* 10°42N 61°31W **323** t
Maraval → *Trin. & Tob.* 10°39N 61°32W **323** t
Maravari *Solomon Is.* 7°50S 156°42E **287** L9
Maravatío *Mexico* 19°54N 100°27W **318** D4
Marawi City *Phil.* 8°0N 124°21E **233** G5
Marāwih *U.A.E.* 24°18N 53°18E **247** E7
Marazliyivka *Ukraine* 46°8N 30°3E **183** D15
Marbella *Spain* 36°30N 4°57W **195** J6
Marble Bar *Australia* 21°9S 119°44E **278** D2
Marble Falls *U.S.A.* 30°35N 98°16W **314** F5
Marblehead *Mass., U.S.A.* 42°29N 70°51W **313** D14
Marblehead *Ohio, U.S.A.* 41°32N 82°44W **312** E2
Mårbu *Norway* 60°11N 8°9E **164** D5
Marburg = Maribor *Slovenia* 46°36N 15°40E **199** B12
Marburg *Germany* 50°47N 8°46E **178** E4
Marca, Pta. do *Angola* 16°31S 11°43E **265** F2
Marcal → *Hungary* 47°41N 17°40E **182** C2
Marcali *Hungary* 46°35N 17°25E **182** D2
Marcapata *Peru* 13°31S 70°52W **330** C3
Marcaria *Italy* 45°7N 10°32E **198** C7
Mărcăuţi *Moldova* 48°20N 27°14E **183** B12
Marcelin *Poland* 52°19N 20°59E **142** B1
Marceline *U.S.A.* 39°43N 92°57W **310** E4
March *U.K.* 52°33N 0°5E **169** E8
Marchal *Dem. Rep. of the Congo* 5°16S 14°58E **265** D2
Marchand = Rommani *Morocco* 33°31N 6°40W **260** B3
Marche *France* 46°5N 1°20E **174** B5
Marche □ *Italy* 43°30N 13°15E **199** E10
Marché Bonsecours *Montréal, Canada* **130** b3
Marche-en-Famenne *Belgium* 50°14N 5°19E **170** D5
Marchena *Spain* 37°18N 5°23W **195** H5
Marchena, Canal de *Ecuador* 0°19N 90°12W **330** a
Marchena, I. *Ecuador* 0°19N 90°29W **330** a
Marches = Marche □ *Italy* 43°30N 13°15E **199** E10
Marchesale △ *Italy* 38°32N 16°13E **201** D9
Marciana Marina *Italy* 42°48N 10°12E **198** F7
Marcianise *Italy* 41°2N 14°17E **201** A7
Marcigny *France* 46°17N 4°2E **173** F11
Marcillat-en-Combraille *France* 46°12N 2°38E **173** F9
Marck *France* 50°57N 1°57E **173** B8
Marckolsheim *France* 48°10N 7°30E **173** D14
Marco Island *U.S.A.* 25°58N 81°44W **317** K8
Marco Rondon *Brazil* 12°0S 60°56W **331** C5
Marcona *Peru* 15°10S 75°10W **330** D3
Marcos Juárez *Argentina* 32°42S 62°5W **334** C3
Mărculeşti *Moldova* 47°52N 28°14E **183** C13
Marcus Baker, Mt. *U.S.A.* 61°26N 147°45W **303** F11
Marcus I. = Minami-Tori-Shima *Pac. Oc.* 24°20N 153°58E **288** E7
Marcy, Mt. *U.S.A.* 44°7N 73°56W **313** B11
Mardan *Pakistan* 34°20N 72°0E **242** B5
Mardarivka *Ukraine* 47°32N 29°44E **183** C14
Mardie *Australia* 21°12S 115°59E **278** D2
Mardin *Turkey* 37°20N 40°43E **213** D9
Mårdsjö *Sweden* 63°18N 15°35E **162** A9
Maré, Î. *N. Cal.* 21°30S 168°0E **277** E12
Marécchia → *Italy* 44°4N 12°34E **199** D9
Marechal Deodoro *Brazil* 9°43S 35°54W **332** C4
Marechal Floriano = Piranhas *Brazil* 9°27S 37°46W **332** C4
Maree, L. *U.K.* 57°40N 5°26W **167** D3
Mareeba *Australia* 16°59S 145°28E **280** B4
Mareeg *Somali Rep.* 3°46N 47°18E **267** D6
Mareetsane *S. Africa* 26°9S 25°25E **270** C4
Mareil-Marly *France* 48°52N 2°4E **134** A1
Maremma *Italy* 42°30N 11°30E **199** F8
Maremma △ *Italy* 42°35N 11°8E **198** F8
Maréna *Kayes, Mali* 14°36N 10°45W **262** C2
Maréna *Koulikoro, Mali* 13°55N 7°20W **262** C3
Marengo *Ind., U.S.A.* 38°22N 86°21W **311** F10
Marengo *Iowa, U.S.A.* 41°48N 92°4W **310** C4
Marennes *France* 45°49N 1°7W **174** C2
Marerano *Madag.* 21°23S 44°52E **272** C1
Marettimo *Italy* 37°58N 12°4E **200** E5
Mareuil *France* 45°26N 0°29E **174** C4
Marfa *U.S.A.* 30°19N 104°1W **314** F2
Marganets = Marhanets *Ukraine* 47°40N 34°40E **189** J8
Margao = Madgaon *India* 15°12N 73°58E **245** G1
Margaret → *Australia* 18°9S 125°41E **278** C4
Margaret Bay *Canada* 51°20N 127°35W **296** C3
Margaret L. *Canada* 58°56N 115°25W **296** B5
Margaret River *Australia* 33°57S 115°4E **279** F2
Margareten *Austria* 48°11N 16°21E **142** A2
Margarita, I. de *Venezuela* 11°0N 64°0W **329** A5
Margariti *Greece* 39°22N 20°26E **204** B2
Margaritovo *Russia* 43°25N 134°45E **220** C7
Margate *KwaZulu Natal, S. Africa* 30°50S 30°20E **271** D5
Margate *Kent, U.K.* 51°23N 1°23E **169** F9
Margate *Fla., U.S.A.* 26°15N 80°12W **317** J9
Margeride, Mts. de la *France* 44°43N 3°38E **174** D7
Marggrabowa = Olecko *Poland* 54°2N 22°31E **184** D9
Margherita *India* 27°16N 95°40E **241** B5
Margherita di Savóia *Italy* 41°22N 16°9E **201** A9
Margherita Pk. *Uganda* 0°22N 29°51E **268** B2
Marghilon *Uzbekistan* 40°27N 71°42E **217** D8
Marghita *Romania* 47°22N 22°22E **182** C7
Margonin *Poland* 52°58N 17°5E **185** F4
Margosatubig *Phil.* 7°34N 123°10E **233** H4
Mārgow, Dasht-e *Afghan.* 30°40N 62°30E **240** C1
Marguerite *Canada* 52°30N 122°25W **296** C4
Marhanets *Ukraine* 47°40N 34°40E **189** J8
Marhoum *Algeria* 34°27N 0°11W **261** B4
Mari *Papua N. G.* 9°11S 141°42E **286** E1
Mārī *Syria* 36°29N 37°10E **250** B8
Mari El □ *Russia* 56°30N 48°0E **190** B8
Mari Indus *Pakistan* 32°57N 71°34E **242** C4
Mari Republic = Mari El □ *Russia* 56°30N 48°0E **190** B8
Maria *Austria* 48°11N 16°21E **142** A2
Maria, Îs. *French Polynesia* 21°48S 154°41W **289** f
Maria, Sa. de *Spain* 37°39N 2°14W **197** H2
Maria Aurora *Phil.* 15°48N 121°28E **232** D3
Maria de la Salut *Spain* 39°40N 3°5E **206** B4
Maria Elena *Chile* 22°18S 69°40W **334** A2
Maria Grande *Argentina* 31°45S 59°55W **334** C4
Maria I. *N. Terr., Australia* 14°52S 135°45E **280** A2
Maria I. *Tas., Australia* 42°35S 148°0E **281** G4
Maria Is. *St. Lucia* 13°44N 60°56W **323** m
Maria Island △ *Australia* 42°38S 148°5E **281** G4
Maria Pereira = Mombaça *Brazil* 5°43S 39°45W **332** C4
Maria Theresiopel = Subotica *Serbia* 46°6N 19°39E **182** D4
Maria van Diemen, C. *N.Z.* 34°29S 172°40E **284** A1
Mariager *Denmark* 56°40N 9°59E **163** H3
Mariager Fjord *Denmark* 56°42N 10°19E **163** H4
Mariahilferstrasse *Vienna, Austria* **142** b1
Mariakani *Kenya* 3°50S 39°27E **268** C4
Mariala △ *Australia* 25°57S 145°2E **281** D4
Marian *Australia* 21°9S 148°57E **280** b
Marian L. *Canada* 63°0N 116°15W **296** A5
Mariana Islands *N. Marianas* 15°15N 145°48E **302** a
Mariana Trench *Pac. Oc.* 13°0N 145°0E **302** a
Mariani *India* 26°39N 94°19E **241** B5
Marianica, Cord. = Morena, Sierra *Spain* 38°20N 4°0W **195** G7
Marianna *Ark., U.S.A.* 34°46N 90°46W **315** D9
Marianna *Fla., U.S.A.* 30°46N 85°14W **316** E4
Mariannelund *Sweden* 57°37N 15°35E **163** G9
Mariánské Lázně *Czech Rep.* 49°58N 12°41E **180** B5
Marias → *U.S.A.* 47°56N 110°30W **304** C8
Marías, Is. *Mexico* 21°25N 106°28W **318** C3
Mariato, Punta *Panama* 7°12N 80°52W **320** E3
Mariazell *Austria* 47°47N 15°19E **180** D8
Ma'rib *Yemen* 15°25N 45°21E **248** D4
Maribo *Denmark* 54°48N 11°30E **163** K5
Maribor *Slovenia* 46°36N 15°40E **199** B12
Maricaban I. *Phil.* 13°39N 120°53E **232** E3
Maricao *Puerto Rico* 18°11N 66°59W **321** b
Marico → *Africa* 23°35S 26°57E **270** B4
Maricopa *Ariz., U.S.A.* 33°4N 112°3W **305** K7
Maricopa *Calif., U.S.A.* 35°4N 119°24W **307** K7
Maridalen *Norway* 59°59N 10°45E **133** A3
Maridalsvatnet *Norway* 59°59N 10°46E **133** A3
Maridī *Sudan* 4°55N 29°25E **257** G2
Maridī, Wadi → *Sudan* 6°15N 29°21E **257** F2
Marié → *Brazil* 0°27S 66°26W **328** D4
Marie Byrd Land *Antarctica* 79°30S 125°0W **151** D14
Marie-Galante *Guadeloupe* 15°56N 61°16W **322** e
Marie-Galante, Canal de *Guadeloupe* 16°0N 61°25W **322** e
Mariecourt = Kangiqsujuaq *Canada* 61°30N 72°0W **295** E17
Mariefred *Sweden* 59°15N 17°12E **162** E11
Mariehamn *Finland* 60°5N 19°55E **161** F18
Marieholm *Sweden* 55°53N 13°10E **163** J7
Mariembourg *Belgium* 50°6N 4°31E **170** D4
Marienbad = Mariánské Lázně *Czech Rep.* 49°58N 12°41E **180** B5
Marienberg *Germany* 50°39N 13°9E **178** E9
Marienburg = Malbork *Poland* 54°3N 19°1E **184** D6
Mariendorf *Germany* 52°26N 13°23E **115** B3
Marienfelde *Germany* 52°24N 13°23E **115** B3
Marienplatz *Munich, Germany* **131** b2
Mariental *Namibia* 24°36S 18°0E **270** B2
Marienville *U.S.A.* 41°28N 79°8W **312** E5
Mariestad *Sweden* 58°43N 13°50E **163** F7
Marietta *Ga., U.S.A.* 33°57N 84°33W **316** B5
Marietta *Ohio, U.S.A.* 39°25N 81°27W **309** F13
Marieville *Canada* 45°26N 73°10W **313** A11
Mariga → *Nigeria* 9°40N 5°55E **263** C6
Marignane *France* 43°25N 5°13E **175** E9
Marigot *Dominica* 15°33N 61°18W **323** k
Marigot *Guadeloupe* 16°5N 61°46W **322** e
Marigot *St.-Martin* 18°4N 63°5W **322** a
Marigot Bay *St. Lucia* 13°58N 61°1W **323** m
Marihatag *Phil.* 8°48N 126°18E **233** G6
Mariinsk *Russia* 56°10N 87°20E **214** D9
Mariinsk Water = Volgo-Baltiyskiy Kanal *Russia* 60°0N 38°0E **188** B9
Mariinskiy Posad *Russia* 56°10N 47°45E **190** B8
Marijampolė *Lithuania* 54°33N 23°19E **184** D10
Marijampolė □ *Lithuania* 54°34N 23°21E **184** D10
Marikina *Phil.* 14°37N 121°5E **127** B2
Marikina → *Phil.* 14°33N 121°3E **127** B2
Marília *Brazil* 22°13S 50°0W **335** A6
Marimba *Angola* 8°28S 17°8E **265** D3
Marín *Spain* 42°23N 8°42W **194** C2
Marin, Cul-de-Sac du *Martinique* 14°27N 60°53W **322** j
Marin City *U.S.A.* 37°52N 122°30W **136** A1
Marin Pen. *U.S.A.* 37°50N 122°30W **136** A1
Marina *U.S.A.* 36°41N 121°48W **306** J5
Marina del Rey *U.S.A.* 33°58N 118°27W **126** C2
Marinduque *Phil.* 13°25N 122°0E **231** B6
Marinduque □ *Phil.* 13°18N 122°0E **232** E4
Marine City *U.S.A.* 42°43N 82°30W **312** D2
Marine Drive *Mumbai, India* **130** b1
Marineland *U.S.A.* 29°40N 81°13W **316** F8
Marineo *Italy* 37°57N 13°25E **200** E6
Marinette *U.S.A.* 45°6N 87°38W **308** C10
Maringá *Brazil* 23°26S 52°2W **335** A5
Maringa → *Dem. Rep. of the Congo* 1°14N 19°48E **264** B3
Marinha Grande *Portugal* 39°45N 8°56W **194** F2
Marinho dos Abrolhos △ *Brazil* 17°50S 39°0W **333** E4
Marino *Dublin, Ireland* 53°22N 6°14W **120** A2
Marino *Italy* 41°46N 12°39E **199** G9
Marion *Ala., U.S.A.* 32°38N 87°19W **315** E11
Marion *Ill., U.S.A.* 37°44N 88°56W **310** G8
Marion *Ind., U.S.A.* 40°32N 85°40W **311** D11
Marion *Iowa, U.S.A.* 42°2N 91°36W **310** B5
Marion *Kans., U.S.A.* 38°21N 97°1W **308** F5
Marion *N.C., U.S.A.* 35°41N 82°1W **315** D13
Marion *Ohio, U.S.A.* 40°35N 83°8W **311** D13
Marion *S.C., U.S.A.* 34°11N 79°24W **315** D15
Marion *Va., U.S.A.* 36°50N 81°31W **309** G13
Marion, L. *U.S.A.* 33°28N 80°10W **316** B9
Marion Bay *Australia* 35°12S 136°59E **282** C2
Marion I. *Ind. Oc.* 47°0S 38°0E **273** J2
Maripa *Venezuela* 7°26N 65°9W **329** B4
Maripasoula *Fr. Guiana* 3°40N 54°4W **329** C7
Maripipi I. *Phil.* 11°47N 124°19E **233** F5
Mariposa *U.S.A.* 37°29N 119°58W **306** H7
Mariscal Estigarribia *Paraguay* 22°3S 60°40W **334** A3
Marisco, Ponta do *Brazil* 23°1S 43°18W **135** C1
Maritime Alps = Maritimes, Alpes *Europe* 44°10N 7°10E **175** D11
Maritimes, Alpes *Europe* 44°10N 7°10E **175** D11
Maritsa = Evros → *Greece* 41°40N 26°34E **203** F10
Maritsa *Greece* 36°22N 28°8E **206** E12

Mayesville *U.S.A.* 34°0N 80°12W **316** A9
Mayfair *Gauteng, S. Africa* 26°11S 28°0E **123** B2
Mayfair *London, U.K.* **125** b3
Mayfield *Ky., U.S.A.* 36°44N 88°38W **308** G9
Mayfield *N.Y., U.S.A.* 43°6N 74°16W **313** C10
Mayhill *U.S.A.* 32°53N 105°29W **305** K11
Mayiladuthurai *India* 11°3N 79°42E **245** J4
Maykop *Russia* 44°35N 40°10E **191** H5
Mayma *Russia* 52°3N 85°55E **217** B11
Maymyo *Burma* 22°2N 96°28E **236** A1
Maynard *Mass., U.S.A.* 42°26N 71°27W **313** D13
Maynard *Wash., U.S.A.* 47°59N 122°55W **306** C4
Maynard Hills *Australia* 28°28S 119°49E **279** E2
Mayne → *Australia* 23°40S 141°55E **280** C3
Maynooth *Ont., Canada* 45°13N 77°56W **312** A7
Maynooth *Kildare, Ireland* 53°23N 6°34W **166** C5
Mayo *Yukon, Canada* 63°38N 135°57W **294** E4
Mayo *Trin. & Tob.* 10°21N 61°23W **323** t
Mayo *Fla., U.S.A.* 30°3N 83°10W **316** E6
Mayo □ *Ireland* 53°53N 9°3W **166** C2
Mayo → *Argentina* 45°45S 69°45W **336** C3
Mayo → *Peru* 6°38S 76°15W **330** B2
Mayo B. *Phil.* 6°56N 126°22E **233** H6
Mayo Daga *Nigeria* 6°59N 11°25E **263** D7
Mayo Faran *Nigeria* 8°57N 12°4E **263** D7
Mayo-Kébbi Est □ *Chad* 10°20N 15°30E **259** F3
Mayo-Kébbi Ouest □ *Chad* 9°40N 17°50E **259** G3
Mayoko *Congo* 2°18S 12°49E **264** C2
Mayoko *Dem. Rep. of the Congo* 1°6S 23°50E **264** C4
Mayon Volcano *Phil.* 13°15N 123°41E **232** E4
Mayor Buratovich *Argentina* 39°15S 62°37W **336** A4
Mayor I. *N.Z.* 37°16S 176°17E **284** D5
Mayor Pablo Lagerenza *Paraguay* 19°55S 60°47W **331** D5
Mayorga *Spain* 42°10N 5°16W **194** C5
Mayotte ◪ *Ind. Oc.* 12°50S 45°10E **272** b
Mayoyao *Phil.* 16°59N 121°14E **232** C3
Mayqayyng *Kazakhstan* 51°27N 75°47E **217** B9
Mayraira Pt. *Phil.* 18°39N 120°51E **232** B3
Mayreau *St. Vincent* 12°39N 61°23W **323** n
Maysān □ *Iraq* 31°55N 47°15E **246** D5
Mayskiy *Russia* 43°47N 44°2E **191** J7
Maysville *Ky., U.S.A.* 38°39N 83°46W **311** F13
Maysville *Mo., U.S.A.* 39°53N 94°22W **310** E2
Maytiguid I. *Phil.* 11°3N 119°36E **233** F2
Mayu *Indonesia* 1°30N 126°30E **231** D7
Mayumba *Gabon* 3°25S 10°39E **264** C2
Mayuram = Mayiladuthurai *India* 11°3N 79°42E **245** J4
Mayville *N. Dak., U.S.A.* 47°30N 97°20W **308** B5
Mayville *N.Y., U.S.A.* 42°15N 79°30W **312** D5
Maywood *Calif., U.S.A.* 33°59N 118°12W **126** C3
Maywood *Ill., U.S.A.* 41°52N 87°51W **119** B1
Maywood *N.J., U.S.A.* 40°53N 74°3W **132** A1
Maywood Park Race Track *U.S.A.* 41°54N 87°50W **119** B1
Mazabuka *Zambia* 15°52S 27°44E **269** F2
Mazagán = El Jadida *Morocco* 33°11N 8°17W **260** B3
Mazagão *Brazil* 0°7S 51°16W **329** D7
Mazagaon *Mumbai, India* **130** a2
Mazamet *France* 43°30N 2°20E **174** E6
Mazán *Peru* 3°30S 73°0W **328** D3
Māzandarān □ *Iran* 36°30N 52°0E **247** B7
Mazapil *Mexico* 24°39N 101°34W **318** C4
Mazar *China* 36°32N 77°1E **217** E9
Mazar, O. → *Algeria* 31°50N 1°36E **261** B5
Mazār-e Sharīf *Afghan.* 36°41N 67°0E **240** A2
Mazara del Vallo *Italy* 37°39N 12°35E **200** E5
Mazarredo *Argentina* 47°10S 66°50W **336** C3
Mazarrón *Spain* 37°38N 1°19W **197** H3
Mazarrón, G. de *Spain* 37°27N 1°19W **197** H3
Mazaruni → *Guyana* 6°25N 58°35W **329** B6
Mazatán *Mexico* 29°0N 110°8W **318** B2
Mazatenango *Guatemala* 14°35N 91°30W **320** D1
Mazatlán *Mexico* 23°13N 106°25W **318** C3
Mažeikiai *Lithuania* 56°20N 22°20E **184** B9
Mazhafa, J. *Si. Arabia* 28°52N 35°5E **251** K6
Māzhān *Iran* 32°30N 59°0E **247** C8
Mazıdağı *Turkey* 37°28N 40°29E **213** D9
Mazīnān *Iran* 36°19N 56°56E **247** B8
Mazo Cruz *Peru* 16°45S 69°44W **330** D4
Mazoe *Mozam.* 16°42S 33°7E **269** F3
Mazoe → *Mozam.* 16°20S 33°30E **269** F3
Mazomanie *U.S.A.* 43°11N 89°48W **310** A7
Mazon *U.S.A.* 41°14N 88°25W **311** C8
Mazowe *Zimbabwe* 17°28S 30°58E **269** F3
Mazowieckie □ *Poland* 52°40N 21°0E **185** F8
Mazrûb *Sudan* 14°0N 29°20E **257** E2
Mazurski, Pojezierze *Poland* 53°50N 21°0E **184** E7
Mazyr *Belarus* 51°59N 29°15E **177** B15
Mba *Fiji* 17°33S 177°41E **287** A1
Mbaba *Senegal* 14°59N 16°44W **262** C1
Mbabane *Swaziland* 26°18S 31°6E **271** C5
Mbaéré → *C.A.R.* 3°47N 17°31E **264** B3
Mbagne *Mauritania* 16°6N 14°47W **262** B2
M'bahiakro *Ivory C.* 7°33N 4°19W **262** D4
Mbaïki *C.A.R.* 3°53N 18°1E **264** B3
Mbakana, Mt. de *Cameroon* 7°57N 15°6E **264** A3
Mbala *Zambia* 8°46S 31°24E **269** D3
Mbalabala *Zimbabwe* 20°27S 29°3E **271** B4
Mbalam *Cameroon* 2°13N 13°49E **264** B2
Mbale *Uganda* 1°8N 34°12E **268** B3
Mbali → *C.A.R.* 4°27N 18°20E **264** B3
Mbalmayo *Cameroon* 3°33N 11°33E **263** E7
Mbam → *Cameroon* 4°24N 11°17E **263** E7
Mbamba Bay *Tanzania* 11°13S 34°49E **269** E3
Mbandaka *Dem. Rep. of the Congo* 0°1N 18°18E **264** B3
Mbandjok *Cameroon* 4°27N 11°54E **264** B2
Mbanga *Cameroon* 4°30N 9°33E **263** E6
Mbanika *Solomon Is.* 9°3S 159°13E **287** M10
M'Banio, Lagune *Gabon* 3°35S 11°0E **264** C2
Mbanza Congo *Angola* 6°18S 14°16E **265** D2
Mbanza Ngungu *Dem. Rep. of the Congo* 5°12S 14°53E **265** D2
Mbarangandu *Tanzania* 10°11S 36°48E **269** D4
Mbarara *Uganda* 0°35S 30°40E **268** C3
Mbari → *C.A.R.* 4°34N 22°43E **264** B4
Mbatto *Ivory C.* 6°28N 4°22W **262** D4
Mbava *Solomon Is.* 7°47S 156°33E **287** L9
Mbé *Congo* 3°14S 15°50E **264** C3
Mbe *Eq. Guin.* 1°47N 9°56E **264** B1
Mbengga = Beqa *Fiji* 18°23S 178°8E **287** B2
Mbengué *Gabon* 2°2S 11°7E **264** C2
Mbengui *Gabon* 2°3S 10°4E **264** C2
Mbéni *Comoros Is.* 11°30S 43°22E **272** a
Mbenkuru → *Tanzania* 9°25S 39°50E **269** D4
Mbéré → *Cameroon* 7°45N 15°36E **264** A3
Mberengwa *Zimbabwe* 20°29S 29°57E **269** G2
Mberengwa, Mt. *Zimbabwe* 20°37S 29°55E **269** G2
Mberubu *Nigeria* 6°10N 7°38E **263** D6
Mbesuma *Zambia* 10°0S 32°2E **269** E3
Mbeya *Tanzania* 8°54S 33°29E **269** D3
Mbeya □ *Tanzania* 8°15S 33°30E **268** D3
Mbhashe → *S. Africa* 32°15S 28°54E **271** D4
Mbigou *Gabon* 1°53S 11°56E **264** C2
M'bili *Sudan* 7°35N 28°15E **257** F2
Mbinga *Tanzania* 10°50S 35°0E **269** E4
Mbini = Río Muni □ *Eq. Guin.* 1°30N 10°0E **264** B2
Mbini *Eq. Guin.* 1°35N 9°37E **264** B1
Mbizi *Zimbabwe* 21°23S 31°1E **269** G3
Mboi *Dem. Rep. of the Congo* 6°57S 21°54E **265** D4
Mboki *C.A.R.* 5°19N 25°58E **257** F2
Mbokonimbeti *Solomon Is.* 8°57S 160°7E **287** M11
Mboli *Dem. Rep. of the Congo* 4°8N 23°9E **264** B4
Mbomo *Congo* 0°25N 14°42E **264** B2
M'bonge *Cameroon* 4°33N 9°5E **263** E6
Mboro *Senegal* 15°9N 16°54W **262** B1
Mboua *Cameroon* 4°25N 14°16E **264** A2
Mbouda *Cameroon* 5°38N 10°15E **264** A2
M'boukou, L. de *Cameroon* 6°23N 12°50E **263** D7
Mboune *Senegal* 14°42N 13°34W **262** C2
Mbouoma *Congo* 0°52S 15°4E **264** C3
Mbour *Senegal* 14°22N 16°54W **262** C1
Mbout *Mauritania* 16°1N 12°38W **262** B2
Mbrés *C.A.R.* 6°40N 19°48E **264** A3
M'Bridge → *Angola* 7°12S 12°51E **265** D2
Mbuji-Mayi *Dem. Rep. of the Congo* 6°9S 23°40E **265** D4
Mbulu *Tanzania* 3°45S 35°30E **268** C4
Mbuma *Dem. Rep. of the Congo* 3°32N 24°50E **264** B4
Mbuma *Solomon Is.* 8°59S 160°46E **287** M11
Mburucuyá *Argentina* 28°1S 58°14W **334** B4
Mburucuyá △ *Argentina* 28°1S 58°12W **334** B4
M'bwat *Cameroon* 6°29N 10°45E **264** A2
Mcherrah *Algeria* 27°0N 4°30W **260** C4
Mchinga *Tanzania* 9°44S 39°45E **269** D4
Mchinji *Malawi* 13°47S 32°58E **269** E3
Mdantsane *S. Africa* 32°56S 27°46E **271** D4
Mdennah *Mauritania* 24°37N 6°0W **260** D3
Me'a She' Arim *Jerusalem* **123** a2
Mead, L. *U.S.A.* 36°0N 114°44W **307** J12
Meade = Atqasuk → *U.S.A.* 70°52N 155°55W **303** A9
Meade *U.S.A.* 37°17N 100°20W **308** G3
Meade River = Atqasuk *U.S.A.* 70°28N 157°24W **303** A8
Meadow Lake *Canada* 54°10N 108°26W **297** C7
Meadow Lake ⌓ *Canada* 54°27N 109°0W **297** C7
Meadow Valley Wash → *U.S.A.* 36°40N 114°34W **307** J12
Meadowbank Park *Australia* 33°49S 151°6E **139** A1
Meadville *Mo., U.S.A.* 39°47N 93°18W **310** E3
Meadville *Pa., U.S.A.* 41°39N 80°9W **312** E4
Meaford *Canada* 44°36N 80°35W **312** B4
Meakan Dake *Japan* 45°15N 144°0E **220** C11
Mealhada *Portugal* 40°22N 8°27W **194** E2
Mealy Mts. *Canada* 53°10N 58°0W **299** B8
Meander River *Canada* 59°2N 117°42W **296** B5
Meares, C. *U.S.A.* 45°37N 124°0W **304** D1
Mearim → *Brazil* 3°4S 44°35W **332** B3
Meath □ *Ireland* 53°40N 6°57W **166** C5
Meath Park *Canada* 53°27N 105°22W **297** C7
Meaulne *France* 46°36N 2°36E **173** F9
Meaux *France* 48°58N 2°50E **173** D9
Mebechi-Gawa → *Japan* 40°31N 141°31E **220** D10
Mebonden *Norway* 63°13N 11°2E **164** A8
Mebulu, Tanjung *Indonesia* 8°50S 115°5E **231** K18
Mecanhelas *Mozam.* 15°12S 35°54E **269** F4
Mecaya → *Colombia* 0°29N 75°11W **328** C2
Mecca = Makkah *Si. Arabia* 21°30N 39°54E **248** B2
Mecca *U.S.A.* 33°34N 116°5W **307** M10
Mechanicsburg *Ohio, U.S.A.* 40°4N 83°33W **311** D13
Mechanicsburg *Pa., U.S.A.* 40°13N 77°1W **312** F8
Mechanicsville *U.S.A.* 41°54N 91°16W **310** C5
Mechanicville *U.S.A.* 42°54N 73°41W **313** D11
Mechara *Ethiopia* 8°36N 40°20E **257** F5
Mechelen *Belgium* 51°2N 4°29E **170** C4
Mecheria *Algeria* 33°35N 0°18W **261** B4
Mechernich *Germany* 50°35N 6°39E **178** E2
Mechetinskaya *Russia* 46°45N 40°32E **191** G5
Mechol *Micronesia* 9°37N 138°9E **287** R16
Měcholupy *Czech Rep.* 50°3N 14°32E **135** B3
Mechra Bel Ksiri *Morocco* 34°34N 5°57W **260** B3
Mechra Benâbbou *Morocco* 32°39N 7°48W **260** B3
Měčice *Czech Rep.* 50°11N 14°31E **135** A3
Mecidiye *Turkey* 40°38N 26°32E **203** F10
Mecidiyeköy *Turkey* 41°4N 29°0E **122** B2
Mecitözü *Turkey* 40°32N 35°17E **212** B6
Mecklenburg *Germany* 53°33N 11°40E **176** B7
Mecklenburg-Vorpommern □ *Germany* 53°45N 12°15E **178** B8
Mecklenburger Bucht *Germany* 54°20N 11°40E **178** A7
Meconta *Mozam.* 14°59S 39°50E **269** E4
Mecsek *Hungary* 46°10N 18°18E **182** D3
Mecubúri *Mozam.* 14°39S 38°54E **269** E4
Mecubúri → *Mozam.* 14°10S 40°30E **269** E5
Mecúfi *Mozam.* 13°20S 40°32E **269** E5
Meda *Portugal* 40°57N 7°18W **194** E3
Medak *India* 18°1N 78°15E **244** E4
Medan *Indonesia* 3°40N 98°38E **234** B1
Medang *Indonesia* 8°9S 117°22E **235** D5
Médanos *Argentina* 38°50S 62°42W **336** A4
Médanos de Coro △ *Venezuela* 11°35N 69°44W **328** A4
Medanosa, Pta. *Argentina* 48°8S 66°0W **336** C3
Medart *U.S.A.* 30°5N 84°23W **316** E5
Medaryville *U.S.A.* 41°5N 86°55W **311** C10
Medawachchiya *Sri Lanka* 8°30N 80°30E **245** K5
Medchal *India* 17°37N 78°29E **244** F4
Mede *Italy* 45°6N 8°44E **198** C5
Médéa *Algeria* 36°12N 2°50E **261** A5
Médéa □ *Algeria* 35°0N 3°0E **261** B5
Mededa *Bos.-H.* 43°44N 19°10E **182** G4
Médégué *Gabon* 0°37N 10°8E **264** B2
Medeiros Neto *Brazil* 17°20S 40°14W **333** E3
Medellín *Colombia* 6°15N 75°35W **328** B2
Medelpad *Sweden* 62°33N 16°30E **162** B10
Medemblik *Neths.* 52°46N 5°8E **170** B5
Médenine *Tunisia* 33°21N 10°30E **258** B2
Médenine □ *Tunisia* 32°20N 10°0E **261** B7
Mederdra *Mauritania* 17°0N 15°38W **262** B1
Medford *Mass., U.S.A.* 42°25N 71°7W **116** A2
Medford *Oreg., U.S.A.* 42°19N 122°52W **304** E2
Medford *Wis., U.S.A.* 45°9N 90°20W **308** C8
Medgidia *Romania* 44°15N 28°19E **183** F13
Medi *Sudan* 5°4N 30°42E **257** F3
Media Agua *Argentina* 31°58S 68°25W **334** C2
Media Luna *Argentina* 34°45S 66°44W **334** C2
Medianeira *Brazil* 25°17S 54°5W **335** B5
Mediapolis *U.S.A.* 41°0N 91°10W **310** D5
Mediaş *Romania* 46°9N 24°22E **183** D9
Medicilândia *Brazil* 3°33S 53°8W **329** D7
Medicina *Italy* 44°28N 11°38E **199** D8
Medicine Bow *U.S.A.* 41°54N 106°12W **304** F10
Medicine Bow Mts. *U.S.A.* 40°40N 106°0W **304** F10
Medicine Bow Pk. *U.S.A.* 41°21N 106°19W **304** F10
Medicine Hat *Canada* 50°0N 110°45W **297** D6
Medicine Lake *U.S.A.* 48°30N 104°30W **304** B11
Medicine Lodge *U.S.A.* 37°17N 98°35W **308** G4
Medina = Al Madīnah *Si. Arabia* 24°35N 39°52E **246** E3
Medina *Brazil* 16°15S 41°29W **333** E3
Medina *Colombia* 4°30N 73°21W **328** C3
Medina *Mis. Or., Phil.* 8°55N 125°0E **233** G5
Medina *N. Dak., U.S.A.* 46°54N 99°18W **308** B4
Medina *N.Y., U.S.A.* 43°13N 78°23W **312** C6
Medina *Ohio, U.S.A.* 41°8N 81°52W **312** E3
Medina → *U.S.A.* 29°16N 98°29W **314** G5
Medina de Pomar *Spain* 42°56N 3°29W **194** C7
Medina de Rioseco *Spain* 41°53N 5°3W **194** D5
Medina del Campo *Spain* 41°18N 4°55W **194** D6
Médina Gounas *Senegal* 13°8N 13°45W **262** C2
Medina L. *U.S.A.* 29°32N 98°56W **314** G5
Medina Sidonia *Spain* 36°28N 5°57W **195** J5
Medinaceli *Spain* 41°12N 2°30W **196** D2
Medinipur *India* 22°25N 87°21E **243** H12
Mediodia *Spain* 40°22N 3°39W **127** B2
Mediterranean Sea *Europe* 35°0N 15°0E **193** D7
Medjerda, O. → *Tunisia* 37°7N 10°13E **258** A2
Mednogorsk *Russia* 51°24N 57°37E **216** B5
Medny = Mednogorsk *Russia* 51°24N 57°37E **216** B5
Médoc *France* 45°10N 0°50W **174** C3
Medora *U.S.A.* 38°49N 86°10W **311** F10
Médouneu *Gabon* 0°57N 10°47E **264** B2
Medulin *Croatia* 44°49N 13°55E **199** D10
Medveđa *Serbia* 42°50N 21°32E **202** D5
Medvedevo *Russia* 56°37N 47°47E **190** B8
Medveditsa → *Tver, Russia* 57°5N 37°30E **188** D9
Medveditsa → *Volgograd, Russia* 49°35N 42°41E **190** F6
Medvedok *Russia* 57°20N 50°1E **190** B10
Medvezhi, Ostrava *Russia* 71°0N 161°0E **215** B17
Medvezhiy Ozyora *Russia* 55°52N 37°59E **129** A5
Medvezhye = Krasnogvardeyskoye *Russia* 45°52N 41°33E **191** H5
Medvezhyegorsk *Russia* 63°0N 34°25E **186** B5
Medway □ *U.K.* 51°25N 0°32E **169** F8
Medway → *U.K.* 51°27N 0°46E **169** F8
Medzev *Slovak Rep.* 48°43N 20°55E **181** C13
Medzilaborce *Slovak Rep.* 49°17N 21°52E **181** B14
Medžitlija *Macedonia* 40°56N 21°26E **202** F5
Meekatharra *Australia* 26°32S 118°29E **279** E2
Meeker *U.S.A.* 40°2N 107°55W **304** F10
Meeniyan *Australia* 38°35S 146°3E **283** E7
Meersburg *Germany* 47°41N 9°16E **179** H5
Meerut *India* 29°1N 77°42E **242** E7
Meeteetse *U.S.A.* 44°9N 108°52W **304** D9
Mega *Ethiopia* 3°57N 38°19E **257** G4
Mega *Indonesia* 4°0S 101°2E **234** C2
Megalo *Ethiopia* 6°51N 40°47E **267** C5
Megalo Chorio *Greece* 36°27N 27°24E **205** E9
Megalonisos *Greece* 38°0N 24°15E **204** D6
Megalopoli *Greece* 37°25N 22°7E **204** D4
Meganisi *Greece* 38°38N 20°46E **207** B2
Megara *Greece* 37°58N 23°22E **204** D5
Megasini *India* 21°38N 86°21E **243** J12
Megdovas = Tavropos → *Greece* 39°10N 21°45E **204** B3
Megève *France* 45°51N 6°37E **175** C10
Meghalaya □ *India* 25°50N 91°0E **241** C3
Meghezez *Ethiopia* 9°18N 39°26E **257** F4
Meghna → *Bangla.* 22°50N 90°50E **241** D3
Megion *Russia* 61°3N 76°6E **214** C8
Mégiscane, L. *Canada* 48°35N 75°55W **298** C4
Megiste *Greece* 36°8N 29°35E **205** E11
Megisti *Greece* 36°8N 29°34E **205** E11
Megra *Russia* 60°11N 37°14E **188** B9
Meguro *Japan* 35°37N 139°42E **140** B3
Meguro → *Japan* 35°37N 139°45E **140** B3
Mehadia *Romania* 44°56N 22°23E **182** F7
Mehaïguene, O. → *Algeria* 32°15N 2°59E **261** B5
Meharry, Mt. *Australia* 22°59S 118°35E **278** D2
Mehedeby *Sweden* 60°27N 17°25E **162** D11
Mehedinţi □ *Romania* 44°40N 22°45E **182** F7
Meheisa *Sudan* 19°38N 32°57E **256** D3
Mehekar *India* 20°9N 76°34E **244** D3
Méhétia *French Polynesia* 17°52S 148°3W **289** f
Mehlville *U.S.A.* 38°31N 90°19W **308** F8
Mehndawal *India* 26°58N 83°5E **243** F10
Mehpalpur *India* 28°32N 77°7E **120** B1
Mehr Jān *Iran* 33°50N 55°6E **247** C7
Mehrābād *Iran* 36°53N 47°55E **213** D12
Mehrābād ✈ **(THR)** *Iran* 35°41N 51°18E **141** A1
Mehrabān *Iran* 38°4N 47°7E **213** C12
Mehram Nagar *India* 28°34N 77°8E **120** B1
Mehrān *Iran* 33°7N 46°10E **213** F12
Mehrān → *Iran* 26°45N 55°26E **247** E7
Mehrgarh *Pakistan* 29°30N 67°30E **242** E2
Mehrīz *Iran* 31°35N 54°28E **247** D7
Mehrow *Germany* 52°34N 13°37E **115** A4
Mehun-sur-Yèvre *France* 47°10N 2°13E **173** E9
Mei Jiang → *China* 24°25N 116°35E **229** E11
Mei Lanfang, Pantheon of *Beijing, China* **114** a2
Mei Xian *China* 34°18N 107°55E **226** G4
Meia Ponte → *Brazil* 18°32S 49°36W **333** E2
Meicheng *China* 29°29N 119°16E **229** C12
Meichengzhen *China* 28°9N 111°40E **229** C8
Meichuan *China* 30°8N 115°31E **229** B10
Meidling *Austria* 48°10N 16°20E **142** A2
Meidougou *Cameroon* 6°25N 14°13E **264** A2
Méier *Brazil* 22°52S 43°15W **135** B1
Meiganga *Cameroon* 6°30N 14°25E **264** A2
Meighen I. *Canada* 80°0N 99°30W **295** B12
Meigs *U.S.A.* 31°4N 84°6W **316** D5
Meigu *China* 28°16N 103°20E **228** C4
Meihekou *China* 42°32N 125°40E **224** A2
Meiji Shrine *Tokyo, Japan* **140** b1
Meiktila *Burma* 20°53N 95°54E **241** E5
Meili Xue Shan *China* 28°30N 98°39E **228** C2
Meinerzhagen *Germany* 51°6N 7°38E **178** D3
Meiningen *Germany* 50°34N 10°25E **178** E6
Meinung *Taiwan* 22°54N 120°32E **225** D2
Meio → *Brazil* 13°36S 44°7W **333** D3
Meira, Serra de *Spain* 43°15N 7°15W **194** B3
Meiringen *Switz.* 46°43N 8°12E **179** J4
Meise *Belgium* 50°56N 4°20E **116** A1
Meishan *Sichuan, China* 30°3N 103°23E **228** B4
Meishan *Taiwan* 23°35N 120°33E **225** C2
Meissen *Germany* 51°9N 13°29E **178** D9
Meissner *Germany* 51°14N 9°50E **178** D5
Meissner-Kaufunger Wald ⌓ *Germany* 51°16N 9°45E **178** D5
Meitan *China* 27°45N 107°29E **228** D6
Meizhou *China* 24°16N 116°6E **229** E11
Meja *India* 25°9N 82°7E **243** G10
Mejillones *Chile* 23°10S 70°30W **334** A1
Mejiro *Japan* 35°43N 139°43E **140** A3
Mékambo *Gabon* 1°2N 13°50E **264** B2
Mekdela *Ethiopia* 11°24N 39°10E **257** E4
Mekele *Ethiopia* 13°33N 39°30E **257** E4
Mekerghene, Sebkra *Algeria* 26°21N 1°30E **261** C5
Mékhé *Senegal* 15°7N 16°38W **262** B1
Mekhomiya = Razlog *Bulgaria* 41°53N 23°28E **202** E7
Mekhtar *Pakistan* 30°30N 69°15E **240** C3
Meknès *Morocco* 33°57N 5°33W **260** B3
Meknès □ *Morocco* 33°3N 5°35W **260** B3
Meko *Nigeria* 7°27N 2°52E **263** D5
Mekong → *Asia* 9°30N 106°15E **237** H6
Mekongga *Indonesia* 3°39S 121°15E **231** E6
Mekoryuk *U.S.A.* 60°23N 166°11W **303** F6
Mekrou → *Benin* 12°25N 2°50E **263** C5
Mekvari = Kür → *Azerbaijan* 39°29N 49°15E **213** C13
Mel *Italy* 46°4N 12°5E **199** B9
Melagiri Hills *India* 12°20N 77°30E **245** H3
Melah, Oued el → *Algeria* 32°20N 2°28E **261** B5
Melaka *Malaysia* 2°15N 102°15E **237** L4
Melaka □ *Malaysia* 2°15N 102°15E **237** L4
Melambes *Greece* 35°8N 24°40E **207** E5
Melanesia *Pac. Oc.* 4°0S 155°0E **277** A10
Melanesian Basin *Pac. Oc.* 0°5N 160°35E **288** G8
Melapalaiyam *India* 8°39N 77°44E **245** K3
Melawi → *Indonesia* 0°5N 111°29E **235** B4
Melaya *Indonesia* 8°17S 114°30E **231** J17
Melbourne *Vic., Australia* 37°48S 144°58E **128** A1
Melbourne *Fla., U.S.A.* 28°5N 80°37W **317** G9
Melbourne *Iowa, U.S.A.* 41°57N 93°6W **310** C3
Melbourne ✈ **(MEL)** *Australia* 37°40S 144°50E **128** A1
Melcher-Dallas *U.S.A.* 41°14N 93°15W **310** C3
Melchor Múzquiz *Mexico* 27°53N 101°31W **318** B4
Melchor Ocampo *Mexico* 24°51N 101°39W **318** C4
Meldal *Norway* 63°3N 9°44E **164** A6
Méldola *Italy* 44°7N 12°5E **199** D9
Meldorf *Germany* 54°5N 9°5E **178** A5
Mélé *C.A.R.* 9°46N 21°33E **264** A4
Mele B. *Vanuatu* 17°44S 168°14E **287** G6
Meleden *Somali Rep.* 10°25N 49°51E **267** B6
Melegnano *Italy* 45°21N 9°19E **198** C6
Meleizem *Mauritania* 22°19N 11°24W **260** D2
Melekeok *Palau* 7°27N 134°38E **288** c
Melekess = Dimitrovgrad *Russia* 54°14N 49°39E **190** C9
Melenci *Serbia* 45°32N 20°20E **182** E5
Melenki *Russia* 55°20N 41°37E **190** C5
Meleuz *Russia* 52°58N 55°55E **216** B5
Mélèzes → *Canada* 57°40N 69°29W **298** A5
Melfi *Chad* 11°0N 17°59E **259** F3
Melfi *Italy* 41°0N 15°39E **201** B8
Melfort *Sask., Canada* 52°50N 104°37W **297** C8
Melfort *Zimbabwe* 18°0S 31°25E **269** F3
Melgaço *Portugal* 42°7N 8°15W **194** C2
Melgar de Fernamental *Spain* 42°27N 4°17W **194** C6
Melgraseyri *Iceland* 66°1N 22°27W **155** A4
Melhus *Norway* 63°17N 10°18E **164** A7
Melide *Spain* 42°55N 8°1W **194** C2
Meligales *Greece* 37°15N 21°59E **204** D3
Melilla *N. Afr.* 35°21N 2°57W **261** A4
Melilli *Italy* 37°11N 15°7E **201** E8
Melintang, Danau *Indonesia* 0°18S 116°20E **235** C5
Melipilla *Chile* 33°42S 71°15W **334** C1
Melissa *Canada* 45°24N 79°14W **312** A5
Melissa, Akra *Greece* 35°6N 24°33E **207** E5
Melissa Oros *Greece* 37°32N 26°4E **205** D8
Melissani Cave *Greece* 38°15N 20°38E **207** C2
Melita *Canada* 49°15N 101°0W **297** D8
Mélito di Porto Salvo *Italy* 37°55N 15°47E **201** E8
Melitopol *Ukraine* 46°50N 35°22E **189** J8
Melk *Austria* 48°13N 15°20E **180** C8
Melkki *Finland* 60°8N 24°53E **121** C2
Mellan Fryken *Sweden* 59°45N 13°10E **162** E7
Mellansel *Sweden* 63°26N 18°19E **160** E18
Mellbystrand *Sweden* 56°30N 12°56E **163** H6
Melle *Deux-Sèvres, France* 46°14N 0°10W **174** B3
Melle *Niedersachsen, Germany* 52°12N 8°20E **178** C4
Mellègue, O. → *Tunisia* 36°36N 9°14E **258** A1
Mellen *U.S.A.* 46°20N 90°40W **308** B8
Mellerud *Sweden* 58°41N 12°28E **163** F6
Mellette *U.S.A.* 45°9N 98°30W **308** C4
Mellid = Melide *Spain* 42°55N 8°1W **194** C2
Mellieha *Malta* 35°57N 14°22E **206** F7
Mellieha Bay *Malta* 35°59N 14°22E **206** F7
Mellit *Sudan* 14°7N 25°34E **257** E2
Mellizo Sur, Cerro *Chile* 48°33S 73°10W **336** C2
Mellrichstadt *Germany* 50°25N 10°17E **178** E6
Mellunkylä *Finland* 60°14N 25°5E **121** B3
Mellunmäki *Finland* 60°14N 25°6E **121** B3
Melnik *Bulgaria* 41°30N 23°25E **202** E7
Mělník *Czech Rep.* 50°22N 14°23E **180** A7
Melnytsya Podilska *Ukraine* 48°37N 26°10E **183** B11
Melo *Uruguay* 32°20S 54°10W **335** C5
Melolo *Indonesia* 9°53S 120°40E **231** F6
Melouprey *Cambodia* 13°48N 105°16E **236** F5
Melrhir, Chott *Algeria* 34°13N 6°30E **261** B6
Melrose *N.S.W., Australia* 32°42S 146°57E **283** B7
Melrose *Borders, U.K.* 55°36N 2°43W **167** F6
Melrose *Mass., U.S.A.* 42°27N 71°2W **116** A2
Melrose *Minn., U.S.A.* 45°40N 94°49W **308** C6
Melrose *N. Mex., U.S.A.* 34°26N 103°38W **305** J12
Melrose *N.Y., U.S.A.* 40°49N 73°55W **132** B2
Melrose Park *U.S.A.* 41°53N 87°50W **119** B1
Melsbroek *Belgium* 50°55N 4°29E **116** A2
Melsisi *Vanuatu* 15°46S 168°10E **287** E6
Melstone *U.S.A.* 46°36N 107°52W **304** C10
Melsungen *Germany* 51°7N 9°32E **178** D5
Melton *Australia* 37°41S 144°35E **282** D6
Melton Mowbray *U.K.* 52°47N 0°54W **168** E7
Melun *France* 48°32N 2°39E **173** D9
Melur *India* 10°2N 78°23E **245** J4
Melut *Sudan* 10°30N 32°13E **257** E3
Melville *Sask., Canada* 50°55N 102°50W **297** C8
Melville *Gauteng, S. Africa* 26°11S 28°1E **123** B2
Melville, C. *Queens., Australia* 14°11S 144°30E **280** A3
Melville, C. *Phil.* 7°49N 117°0E **233** H1
Melville, L. *Canada* 53°30N 60°0W **299** B8
Melville B. *N. Terr., Australia* 12°0S 136°45E **280** A2
Melville B. *Greenland* 75°30N 63°0W **154** B4
Melville I. *N. Terr., Australia* 11°30S 131°0E **278** B5
Melville I. *Canada* 75°30N 112°0W **295** B9
Melville Pen. *Canada* 68°0N 84°0W **295** D15
Melvin, Lough *Ireland* 54°26N 8°10W **166** B3
Mélykút *Hungary* 46°11N 19°25E **182** D4
Memaliaj *Albania* 40°25N 19°56E **202** F3
Memba *Mozam.* 14°11S 40°30E **269** E5
Membalong *Indonesia* 3°9S 107°37E **235** C3
Memboro *Indonesia* 9°30S 119°30E **278** A2
Membrilla *Spain* 38°59N 3°21W **195** G7
Memel = Klaipėda *Lithuania* 55°43N 21°10E **184** C8
Memel *S. Africa* 27°38S 29°36E **271** C4
Memmingen *Germany* 47°58N 10°10E **179** H6
Mempawah *Indonesia* 0°30N 109°5E **235** B3
Memphis *Egypt* 29°52N 31°12E **256** J7
Memphis *Mich., U.S.A.* 42°54N 82°46W **312** D2
Memphis *Mo., U.S.A.* 40°28N 92°10W **310** D4
Memphis *Tenn., U.S.A.* 35°8N 90°2W **315** D9
Memphis *Tex., U.S.A.* 34°44N 100°33W **314** D4
Memphrémagog, L. *N. Amer.* 45°8N 72°17W **313** B12
Mena *Ukraine* 51°31N 32°13E **189** G7
Mena *Ark., U.S.A.* 34°35N 94°15W **314** D7
Mena → *Ethiopia* 5°40N 40°50E **257** F5
Menado = Manado *Indonesia* 1°29N 124°51E **231** D6
Menai Strait *U.K.* 53°11N 4°13W **168** D3
Ménaka *Mali* 15°59N 2°18E **263** B5
Menan = Chao Phraya → *Thailand* 13°40N 100°31E **236** F3
Menarandra → *Madag.* 25°17S 44°30E **272** D1
Menard *U.S.A.* 30°55N 99°47W **314** F5
Menard Fracture Zone *Pac. Oc.* 43°0S 97°0W **289** M18
Menate *Indonesia* 0°12S 113°3E **235** C4
Menawashei *Sudan* 12°41N 24°59E **257** E1
Mendaña Fracture Zone *Pac. Oc.* 16°0S 91°0W **289** J18
Mendawai → *Indonesia* 3°30S 113°0E **235** C4
Mende *France* 44°31N 3°30E **174** D7
Mendebo Mts. *Ethiopia* 7°0N 39°22E **257** F4
Mendeleyev Ridge *Arctic* 80°0N 178°0W **150** B17
Menden *Germany* 51°26N 7°47E **178** D3
Mendenhall, C. *U.S.A.* 59°45N 166°10W **303** G6
Menderes *Turkey* 38°14N 27°8E **205** C9
Mendhar *India* 33°35N 74°10E **243** C6
Mendi *Ethiopia* 9°47N 35°4E **257** F4
Mendi *Papua N. G.* 6°11S 143°39E **286** D2
Mendip Hills *U.K.* 51°17N 2°40W **169** F5
Mendocino *U.S.A.* 39°19N 123°48W **304** G2
Mendocino, C. *U.S.A.* 40°26N 124°25W **304** F1
Mendocino Fracture Zone *Pac. Oc.* 40°0N 142°0W **289** D13
Mendol *Indonesia* 0°36N 103°13E **234** B2
Mendon *U.S.A.* 42°0N 85°27W **311** B11
Mendooran *Australia* 31°50S 149°6E **283** A8
Mendota *Calif., U.S.A.* 36°45N 120°23W **306** J6
Mendota *Ill., U.S.A.* 41°33N 89°7W **310** C7
Mendoyo *Indonesia* 8°23S 114°42E **231** J17
Mendoza *Argentina* 32°50S 68°52W **334** C2
Mendoza □ *Argentina* 33°0S 69°0W **334** C2
Mene Grande *Venezuela* 9°49N 70°56W **328** B3
Menemen *Turkey* 38°34N 27°3E **205** C9
Menen *Belgium* 50°47N 3°7E **170** D3
Menéndez, L. *Argentina* 42°40S 71°51W **336** B2
Menfi *Italy* 37°36N 12°58E **200** E5
Mengcheng *China* 33°12N 116°36E **226** H9
Mengdingjie *China* 23°31N 98°58E **228** F2
Mengeš *Slovenia* 46°10N 14°35E **199** B11
Menggala *Indonesia* 4°30S 105°15E **234** C3
Menghai *China* 21°49N 100°55E **228** G3
Mengíbar *Spain* 37°58N 3°48W **195** H7
Mengjin *China* 34°55N 112°45E **226** G7
Mengla *China* 21°20N 101°25E **228** G3
Menglian *China* 22°21N 99°27E **228** F2
Mengong *Cameroon* 2°56N 11°25E **264** B2
Mengshan *China* 24°14N 110°55E **229** E8
Mengyin *China* 35°40N 117°58E **227** G9
Mengzhe *China* 22°2N 100°15E **228** F3
Mengzi *China* 23°20N 103°22E **228** F4
Menihek *Canada* 54°28N 56°36W **299** B6
Menihek L. *Canada* 54°0N 67°0W **299** B6
Menin = Menen *Belgium* 50°47N 3°7E **170** D3
Menindee *Australia* 32°20S 142°25E **282** B5
Menindee L. *Australia* 32°20S 142°25E **282** B5
Meningie *Australia* 35°50S 139°18E **282** C3
Menjangan, Pulau *Indonesia* 8°7S 114°31E **231** J17
Menkrour *Algeria* 26°27N 8°9E **261** C6
Menlo Park *U.S.A.* 37°27N 122°12W **306** H4
Menngen ❂ *Australia* 15°21S 131°16E **278** C5
Menominee *U.S.A.* 45°6N 87°37W **308** C10
Menominee → *U.S.A.* 45°6N 87°35W **308** C10
Menomonee Falls *U.S.A.* 43°10N 88°7W **311** A8
Menomonie *U.S.A.* 44°53N 91°55W **308** C8
Menongue *Angola* 14°48S 17°52E **265** E3
Menorca *Spain* 40°0N 4°0E **206** B5
Menorca ✈ **(MAH)** *Spain* 39°50N 4°16E **196** F9
Mentakab *Malaysia* 3°29N 102°21E **237** L4
Mentasta Lake *U.S.A.* 62°55N 143°45W **303** E12
Mentawai, Kepulauan *Indonesia* 2°0S 99°0E **234** C1
Mentawai, Selat *Indonesia* 1°45S 100°0E **234** C2
Menteng *Indonesia* 6°11S 106°49E **122** B1
Menton *France* 43°50N 7°29E **175** E11
Mentone *U.S.A.* 41°10N 86°2W **311** C10
Mentor *U.S.A.* 41°40N 81°21W **312** E3
Menyamya *Papua N. G.* 7°10S 145°59E **286** D3
Menyapa *Indonesia* 1°4N 116°4E **235** B5
Menzel-Bourguiba *Tunisia* 37°9N 9°49E **258** A1
Menzel-Chaker *Tunisia* 35°0N 10°26E **258** B2
Menzel-Temime *Tunisia* 36°46N 11°0E **258** A2
Menzelinsk *Russia* 55°47N 53°11E **186** C9
Menzies *Australia* 29°40S 121°2E **279** E3
Meob B. *Namibia* 24°25S 14°34E **270** B1
Me'ona *Israel* 33°1N 35°15E **250** E6
Meoqui *Mexico* 28°17N 105°29W **318** B3
Mepaco *Mozam.* 15°57S 30°48E **269** F3
Meppel *Neths.* 52°42N 6°12E **170** B6
Meppen *Germany* 52°42N 7°17E **178** C3
Mequinenza *Spain* 41°22N 0°17E **196** D5
Mequinenza, Embalse de *Spain* 41°25N 0°15E **196** D5
Mequon *U.S.A.* 43°14N 87°59W **311** A9
Mer *France* 47°42N 1°30E **172** E8
Merai *Papua N. G.* 4°52S 152°19E **286** C7
Merak *Indonesia* 6°10N 106°26E **231** F12
Meråker *Norway* 63°25N 11°46E **164** A8
Meramangye, L. *Australia* 28°25S 132°13E **279** E5
Meramec → *U.S.A.* 38°24N 90°21W **310** F6
Meran = Merano *Italy* 46°40N 11°9E **199** B8
Merano *Italy* 46°40N 11°9E **199** B8
Mérantaise → *France* 48°42N 2°8E **134** B1
Merapi *Indonesia* 7°32S 110°26E **235** D4
Merate *Italy* 45°42N 9°25E **198** C6
Meratus, Pegunungan *Indonesia* 2°45S 115°40E **235** C5
Merauke *Indonesia* 8°29S 140°24E **231** F10
Merbein *Australia* 34°10S 142°2E **282** C5
Merca = Marka *Somali Rep.* 1°48N 44°50E **267** D5
Mercamadrid *Spain* 40°21N 3°39W **127** B2
Mercantour △ *France* 44°16N 6°43E **175** D10
Mercato Saraceno *Italy* 43°57N 12°12E **199** E9
Merced *U.S.A.* 37°18N 120°29W **306** H6
Merced → *U.S.A.* 37°21N 120°59W **306** H6
Merced, L. *U.S.A.* 37°43N 122°29W **136** B2
Merced Pk. *U.S.A.* 37°36N 119°24W **306** H7
Mercedes *B. Aires, Argentina* 34°40S 59°30W **334** C4
Mercedes *Corrientes, Argentina* 29°10S 58°5W **334** B4
Mercedes *San Luis, Argentina* 33°40S 65°21W **334** C2
Mercedes *Camarines N., Phil.* 14°7N 123°1E **232** D4
Mercedes *Uruguay* 33°12S 58°0W **334** C4
Merceditas *Chile* 28°20S 70°35W **334** B1
Mercer *N.Z.* 37°16S 175°5E **284** D4
Mercer *Mo., U.S.A.* 40°31N 93°32W **310** D3
Mercer *Pa., U.S.A.* 41°14N 80°15W **312** E4
Mercer Island *U.S.A.* 47°34N 122°13W **306** C4
Merchandise Mart *Chicago, U.S.A.* **119** b1
Mercier *Bolivia* 10°42S 68°5W **330** C4
Mercury *U.S.A.* 36°40N 115°59W **307** J11
Mercury B. *N.Z.* 36°48S 175°45E **284** C4
Mercury Is. *N.Z.* 36°37S 175°52E **284** C4
Mercy, C. *Canada* 65°0N 63°30W **295** E19
Merdrignac *France* 48°11N 2°27W **172** D4
Mere *U.K.* 51°6N 2°16W **169** F5
Mere Lava *Vanuatu* 14°25S 168°3E **287** D6
Merebuk, Gunung *Indonesia* 8°13S 114°39E **231** J17
Meredale *S. Africa* 26°16S 27°58E **123** B1
Meredith *Australia* 37°49S 144°5E **282** D6
Meredith, C. *Falk. Is.* 52°15S 60°40W **153** f
Meredith, L. *U.S.A.* 35°43N 101°33W **314** D4
Meredosia *U.S.A.* 39°50N 90°34W **310** E6
Merefa *Ukraine* 49°48N 36°3E **189** H9
Merei *Romania* 45°7N 26°43E **183** E11
Merga = Nukheila *Sudan* 19°1N 26°21E **256** D2
Mergui *Burma* 12°26N 98°34E **236** F2
Mergui Arch. = Myeik Kyunzu *Burma* 11°30N 97°30E **237** G1
Meribah *Australia* 34°43S 140°51E **282** C4
Méribel-les-Allues *France* 45°25N 6°34E **175** C10
Meriç *Turkey* 41°11N 26°25E **203** E10
Meriç → *Turkey* 40°52N 26°12E **203** F10
Mérida *Yucatán, Mexico* 20°58N 89°37W **319** C7
Merida *Phil.* 10°55N 124°32E **233** F5
Mérida *Spain* 38°55N 6°25W **195** G4
Mérida *Venezuela* 8°24N 71°8W **328** B3
Mérida □ *Venezuela* 8°30N 71°10W **328** B3
Mérida, Cord. de *Venezuela* 9°0N 71°0W **328** B3
Meriden *W. Mids., U.K.* 52°26N 1°38W **169** E6
Meriden *Conn., U.S.A.* 41°32N 72°48W **313** E12
Meridian *Calif., U.S.A.* 39°9N 121°55W **306** F5
Meridian *Ga., U.S.A.* 31°27N 81°23W **316** D8
Meridian *Idaho, U.S.A.* 43°37N 116°24W **304** E5
Meridian *Miss., U.S.A.* 32°22N 88°42W **315** E10
Mérignac *France* 44°51N 0°39W **174** D3
Merimbula *Australia* 36°53S 149°54E **283** D8
Merin Gubai *Somali Rep.* 1°26N 44°20E **267** D5
Merinda *Australia* 20°2S 148°11E **280** C4
Mering *Germany* 48°16N 10°59E **179** G6
Meringa *Nigeria* 10°44N 12°9E **263** C7
Meringur *Australia* 34°20S 141°19E **282** C4
Merir *Palau* 4°10N 132°30E **231** D8
Merirumã *Brazil* 1°15N 54°50W **329** C7
Merizo *Guam* 13°16N 144°40E **302** d
Merkel *U.S.A.* 32°28N 100°1W **314** E4
Merlimau, Pulau *Singapore* 1°17N 103°42E **138** B2
Mermaid Reef *Australia* 17°6S 119°36E **278** C2
Mero *Dominica* 15°25N 61°26W **323** k
Meroe *India* 7°33N 93°33E **245** L11
Merowe *Sudan* 18°29N 31°46E **256** D3
Merowe Dam *Sudan* 18°35N 31°56E **256** D3
Merredin *Australia* 31°28S 118°18E **279** F2
Merri Cr. → *Australia* 37°47S 144°59E **128** A1
Merrick *U.K.* 55°8N 4°28W **167** F4
Merrickville *Canada* 44°55N 75°50W **313** B9
Merrill *Oreg., U.S.A.* 42°1N 121°36W **304** E3
Merrill *Wis., U.S.A.* 45°11N 89°41W **308** C9
Merrillville *U.S.A.* 41°29N 87°20W **311** C9
Merrimack → *U.S.A.* 42°49N 70°49W **313** D14
Merriman *U.S.A.* 42°55N 101°42W **308** D3
Merrion *Ireland* 53°19N 6°12W **120** B2
Merrionette Park *U.S.A.* 41°41N 87°40W **119** C2
Merritt *Canada* 50°10N 120°45W **296** C4
Merritt Island *U.S.A.* 28°21N 80°42W **317** G9
Merriwa *Australia* 32°6S 150°22E **283** B9
Merriwagga *Australia* 33°47S 145°43E **283** B6
Merry I. *Canada* 55°29N 77°31W **298** A4
Merrygoen *Australia* 31°51S 149°12E **283** A8
Merryville *U.S.A.* 30°45N 93°33W **314** F8
Mersa Fatma *Eritrea* 14°57N 40°17E **257** E5
Mersch *Lux.* 49°44N 6°7E **170** E6
Merse → *Italy* 43°5N 11°22E **199** E8
Mersea I. *U.K.* 51°47N 0°58E **169** F8
Merseburg *Germany* 51°22N 11°59E **178** D7
Mersey → *U.K.* 53°25N 3°1W **168** D4
Merseyside □ *U.K.* 53°31N 3°2W **168** D4
Mersin = İçel *Turkey* 36°51N 34°36E **250** B5
Mersing *Malaysia* 2°25N 103°50E **237** L4
Merta *India* 26°39N 74°4E **242** F6
Merta Road *India* 26°43N 73°55E **242** F5
Merthyr Tydfil *U.K.* 51°45N 3°22W **169** F4
Merthyr Tydfil □ *U.K.* 51°46N 3°21W **169** F4
Merti *Kenya* 1°4N 38°40E **268** B4
Mértola *Portugal* 37°40N 7°40W **195** H3
Merton □ *U.K.* 51°25N 0°11W **125** B2
Mertzon *U.S.A.* 31°16N 100°49W **314** F4
Méru *Oise, France* 49°13N 2°8E **173** C9
Meru *Eastern, Kenya* 0°3N 37°40E **268** B4
Meru *Tanzania* 3°15S 36°46E **268** C4
Meru △ *Kenya* 0°5N 38°10E **268** B4
Meru Betiri △ *Indonesia* 8°27S 113°51E **235** D4
Merv = Mary *Turkmenistan* 37°40N 61°50E **247** B9
Merville *France* 50°38N 2°38E **173** B9
Méry-sur-Seine *France* 48°31N 3°54E **173** D10
Merzifon *Turkey* 40°53N 35°32E **212** B6
Merzig *Germany* 49°26N 6°38E **179** F2
Merzouga, Erg Tin *Algeria* 24°0N 11°4E **261** D7
Mesa *U.S.A.* 33°25N 111°50W **305** K8
Mesa Verde △ *U.S.A.* 37°11N 108°29W **305** H9
Mesach Mellet *Libya* 24°30N 11°30E **258** D2
Mesada *Israel* 31°20N 35°19E **251** G6
Mesagne *Italy* 40°34N 17°48E **201** B10
Mesanagros *Greece* 36°1N 27°49E **206** E11
Mesaoría *Cyprus* 35°12N 33°14E **207** E9
Meschede *Germany* 51°20N 8°18E **178** D4
Mescit *Turkey* 40°21N 41°11E **213** B9
Mesemvriya = Nesebŭr *Bulgaria* 42°41N 27°46E **203** D11
Mesfinto *Ethiopia* 13°20N 37°22E **257** E4
Mesgarābād *Iran* 35°27N 51°30E **141** B3
Mesgouez, L. *Canada* 51°20N 75°0W **298** B5
Meshcherskiy *Russia* 55°40N 37°23E **129** B2
Meshchovsk *Russia* 54°22N 35°17E **188** E8
Meshed = Mashhad *Iran* 36°20N 59°35E **247** B8
Meshgīn Shahr *Iran* 38°30N 47°45E **213** C12
Meshkede-Ser = Bābol Sar *Iran* 36°45N 52°45E **247** B7
Meshoppen *U.S.A.* 41°36N 76°3W **313** E8
Meshra er Req *Sudan* 8°25N 29°18E **257** F2
Mesilinka → *Canada* 56°6N 124°30W **296** B4
Meslay-du-Maine *France* 47°58N 0°33W **172** E6
Mesocco *Switz.* 46°23N 9°12E **179** J5
Mesologi *Greece* 38°21N 21°28E **204** C3
Mesongi *Greece* 39°29N 19°56E **206** C9
Mesopotamia = Al Jazirah *Iraq* 33°30N 44°0E **213** E10
Mesopotamia *U.S.A.* 41°27N 80°57W **312** E4
Mesopotamo *Greece* 39°14N 20°32E **204** B2
Mesoraca *Italy* 39°5N 16°48E **201** C9
Mésou Volímais = Volimes *Greece* 37°52N 20°39E **207** D2
Mesquite *U.S.A.* 36°48N 114°4W **305** H6
Messaad *Algeria* 34°8N 3°30E **261** B5
Messac *France* 47°49N 1°50W **172** E5
Messalo → *Mozam.* 12°25S 39°15E **269** E4
Messaména *Cameroon* 3°48N 12°49E **264** B2
Messara, Kolpos *Greece* 35°6N 24°47E **207** E5
Messe *Austria* 48°13N 16°24E **142** A2
Messier, Canal *Chile* 48°20S 74°33W **336** C2
Messina = Musina *S. Africa* 22°20S 30°5E **271** B5
Messina *Italy* 38°11N 15°34E **201** D8
Messina, Str. di *Italy* 38°15N 15°35E **201** D8
Messini *Greece* 37°4N 22°1E **204** D4
Messinia □ *Greece* 37°10N 22°0E **204** D3
Messiniakos Kolpos *Greece* 36°45N 22°5E **204** E4
Messkirch *Germany* 47°59N 9°7E **179** H5
Messlingen *Sweden* 62°40N 12°50E **162** B6
Mesta = Nestos → *Europe* 40°54N 24°49E **203** E8
Mesta, Akra *Greece* 38°16N 25°53E **205** C7
Mestanza *Spain* 38°35N 4°4W **195** G6
Mestersvig *Greenland* 72°10N 23°40W **154** C8
Mestre *Italy* 45°29N 12°15E **199** C9

Mestre, Espigão *Brazil* 12°30S 46°10W **333** D2
Mesudiye *Turkey* 40°28N 37°46E **212** B7
Meta *U.S.A.* 38°19N 92°10W **310** F4
Meta □ *Colombia* 3°30N 73°0W **328** C3
Meta → *S. Amer.* 6°12N 67°28W **328** B4
Meta Incognita Pen. *Canada* 62°45N 68°30W **295** E18
Metabetchouan *Canada* 48°26N 71°52W **299** C5
Metairie *U.S.A.* 29°59N 90°9W **131** A2
Metalici, Munţii *Romania* 46°15N 22°50E **182** D7
Metaline Falls *U.S.A.* 48°52N 117°22W **304** B5
Metallifere, Colline *Italy* 43°10N 11°0E **198** E8
Metamora *U.S.A.* 40°47N 89°22W **310** D7
Metán *Argentina* 25°30S 65°0W **334** B3
Metangula *Mozam.* 12°40S 34°50E **269** E3
Metanópoli *Italy* 45°24N 9°15E **129** B2
Metauro → *Italy* 43°50N 13°3E **199** E10
Metcalf *U.S.A.* 30°43N 83°59W **316** E6
Metcalfe *Canada* 45°14N 75°28W **313** A9
Metema *Ethiopia* 12°58N 36°12E **257** E4
Metengobalame *Mozam.* 14°49S 34°30E **269** E3
Methana *Greece* 37°35N 23°23E **204** D5
Methoni *Greece* 36°49N 21°42E **204** E3
Methven *N.Z.* 43°38S 171°40E **285** D6
Metil *Mozam.* 16°24S 39°0E **269** F4
Metkovets *Bulgaria* 43°37N 23°10E **202** C7
Metković *Croatia* 43°6N 17°39E **199** E14
Metlakatla *U.S.A.* 55°8N 131°35W **303** J15
Metlaoui *Tunisia* 34°24N 8°24E **258** B1
Metlik *Papua N. G.* 4°46S 152°55E **286** C7
Metlika *Slovenia* 45°40N 15°20E **199** C12
Metlili Chaamba *Algeria* 32°16N 3°38E **261** B5
Metro *Indonesia* 5°5S 105°20E **234** D3
Metro-Dade Cultural Centre *U.S.A.* 25°46N 80°12W **128** B2
Metro Toronto Zoo *Canada* 43°48N 79°10W **141** A3
Metropolis *U.S.A.* 37°9N 88°44W **308** G9
Metropolitan Museum of Art *New York, U.S.A.* **132** b3
Metropolitana □ *Chile* 33°30S 70°50W **334** C1
Metsovo *Greece* 39°48N 21°12E **204** B3
Metter *U.S.A.* 32°24N 82°3W **316** C7
Mettuppalaiyam *India* 11°18N 76°59E **245** J3
Mettur *India* 11°48N 77°47E **245** J3
Metu *Ethiopia* 8°18N 35°35E **257** F4
Metz *France* 49°8N 6°10E **173** C13
Metzingen *Germany* 48°31N 9°17E **179** G5
Meudon *France* 48°48N 2°14E **134** B2
Meulaboh *Indonesia* 4°11N 96°3E **234** B1
Meung-sur-Loire *France* 47°50N 1°40E **173** E8
Meureudu *Indonesia* 5°19N 96°10E **234** A1
Meurthe → *France* 48°47N 6°9E **173** D13
Meurthe-et-Moselle □ *France* 48°52N 6°0E **173** D13
Meuse □ *France* 49°8N 5°25E **173** C12
Meuse → *Europe* 50°45N 5°41E **170** D5
Meuselwitz *Germany* 51°2N 12°17E **178** D8
Mewatpok, Mt. *Malaysia* 5°40N 117°0E **235** A5
Mevaseret Tsiyon *Israel* 31°48N 35°9E **123** B1
Mevo Beitar *Israel* 31°43N 35°6E **123** B1
Mexia *U.S.A.* 31°41N 96°29W **314** F6
Mexiana, I. *Brazil* 0°0 49°30W **332** B2
Mexicali *Mexico* 32°40N 115°30W **307** N11
Mexican Plateau *Mexico* 25°0N 104°0W **292** G9
Mexican Water *U.S.A.* 36°57N 109°32W **305** H9
México *Distrito Federal, Mexico* 19°24N 99°9W **128** B2
Mexico *Maine, U.S.A.* 44°34N 70°33W **313** B14
Mexico *Mo., U.S.A.* 39°10N 91°53W **310** E5
Mexico *N.Y., U.S.A.* 43°28N 76°14W **313** C8
México □ *Mexico* 19°20N 99°30W **319** D5
Mexico ■ *Cent. Amer.* 25°0N 105°0W **318** C4
México, Ciudad de *Mexico* 19°24N 99°9W **128** B2
Mexico, G. of *Cent. Amer.* 25°0N 90°0W **319** C7
Mexico B. *U.S.A.* 43°35N 76°20W **313** C8
Mexico Beach *U.S.A.* 29°57N 85°25W **316** F4
Mexico City Int. ✕ (MEX) *Mexico* 19°25N 99°5W **128** B2
Meydān-e Naftūn *Iran* 31°56N 49°18E **247** D6
Meydani, Ra's-e *Iran* 25°24N 59°6E **247** E8
Meyenburg *Germany* 53°18N 12°14E **178** B8
Meyers Chuck *U.S.A.* 55°45N 132°15W **296** B2
Meyersdal *S. Africa* 26°17S 28°5E **123** B2
Meymac *France* 45°32N 2°10E **174** C6
Meymaneh *Afghan.* 35°53N 64°38E **240** B2
Meyo *Cameroon* 2°50N 11°1E **264** B2
Meyrueis *France* 44°12N 3°27E **174** D7
Meyssac *France* 45°3N 1°40E **174** C5
Meyzieu *France* 45°46N 4°59E **175** C8
Mezdra *Bulgaria* 43°12N 23°42E **202** C7
Mèze *France* 43°27N 3°36E **174** E7
Mezen *Russia* 65°50N 44°20E **186** A7
Mezen → *Russia* 65°44N 44°22E **186** A7
Mézenc, Mt. *France* 44°54N 4°11E **175** D8
Mezeş, Munţii *Romania* 47°5N 23°5E **182** C8
Mezha → *Russia* 55°44N 31°33E **188** E6
Mezhdurechensk *Russia* 53°41N 88°3E **217** B11
Mezhdurechenskiy *Russia* 59°36N 65°56E **214** D7
Mezhdurechye = Shali *Russia* 43°9N 45°55E **191** J7
Mezhevaya Utka = Sinegorskiy *Russia* 47°55N 40°52E **191** G5
Mézidon-Canon *France* 49°5N 0°1W **172** C6
Mézières-en-Brenne *France* 46°49N 1°13E **174** B5
Mézilhac *France* 44°49N 4°21E **175** D8
Mézin *France* 44°4N 0°16E **174** D4
Mezitli *Turkey* 36°45N 34°29E **250** B5
Mezőberény *Hungary* 46°49N 21°3E **182** D6
Mezőfalva *Hungary* 46°55N 18°49E **182** D3
Mezőhegyes *Hungary* 46°19N 20°49E **182** D5
Mezőkovácsháza *Hungary* 46°25N 20°57E **182** D5
Mezőkövesd *Hungary* 47°49N 20°35E **182** C5
Mézos *France* 44°5N 1°10W **174** D2
Mezőtúr *Hungary* 47°1N 20°41E **182** C5
Mezquital *Mexico* 23°29N 104°23W **318** C4
Mezzate *Italy* 45°26N 9°17E **129** B2
Mezzolombardo *Italy* 46°13N 11°5E **198** B8
Mfolozi → *S. Africa* 28°25S 32°26E **271** C5
Mgarr *Malta* 35°55N 14°22E **206** F7
Mgarr *Gozo, Malta* 36°2N 14°18E **206** E7
Mgeta *Tanzania* 8°22S 36°6E **269** D4
Mglin *Russia* 53°2N 32°50E **189** F7
Mhamid *Morocco* 29°49N 5°43W **260** C3
Mhlaba Hills *Zimbabwe* 18°30S 30°30E **269** F3
Mhow *India* 22°33N 75°50E **244** H6
Mi-Shima *Japan* 34°46N 131°9E **222** C3
Miadong *S. Korea* 37°36N 127°0E **137** B2
Miagao *Phil.* 10°39N 122°14E **233** F4
Miahuatlán *Mexico* 16°20N 96°36W **319** D5
Miajadas *Spain* 39°9N 5°54W **195** F5
Miami *Fla., U.S.A.* 25°46N 80°11W **128** B2
Miami *Okla., U.S.A.* 36°53N 94°53W **314** C7
Miami *Tex., U.S.A.* 35°42N 100°38W **314** D4
Miami Beach *U.S.A.* 25°47N 80°7W **128** B2
Miami Canal *U.S.A.* 25°45N 80°12W **128** A1
Miami Int. ✕ (MIA) *U.S.A.* 25°48N 80°17W **128** B1
Miami Shores *U.S.A.* 25°51N 80°11W **128** A2
Miami Springs *U.S.A.* 25°49N 80°17W **128** B1
Miamisburg *U.S.A.* 39°38N 84°17W **311** E12
Mian Xian *China* 33°10N 106°32E **228** A6
Mianchi *China* 34°48N 111°48E **226** G6
Miāndarreh *Iran* 35°37N 53°39E **247** C7
Mīāndowāb *Iran* 37°0N 46°5E **213** D12
Miandrivazo *Madag.* 19°31S 45°29E **272** B2
Mīāneh *Iran* 37°30N 47°40E **213** D12
Mianning *China* 28°32N 102°9E **228** C4
Mianwali *Pakistan* 32°38N 71°28E **242** C4
Mianyang *China* 31°22N 104°47E **228** B5
Mianzhu *China* 31°22N 104°7E **228** B5
Miao Ling *China* 26°5N 107°30E **228** D6
Miaodao Qundao *China* 38°10N 120°45E **227** E11
Miaoli *Taiwan* 24°37N 120°49E **225** B2
Miaoli □ *Taiwan* 24°30N 120°55E **225** B2
Miarinarivo *Antananarivo, Madag.* 18°57S 46°55E **272** B2
Miarinarivo *Toamasina, Madag.* 16°38S 48°15E **272** B2
Miariravaratra *Madag.* 20°13S 47°31E **272** C2
Miass *Russia* 54°59N 60°6E **186** D11
Miasteczko Krajeńskie *Poland* 53°7N 17°1E **185** E4
Miastko *Poland* 54°0N 16°58E **184** E3
Miasto *Poland* 52°15N 21°0E **142** B2
Mica *S. Africa* 24°10S 30°48E **271** B5
Micanopy *U.S.A.* 29°30N 82°17W **317** F7
Micăsasa *Romania* 46°7N 24°7E **183** D9
Micco *U.S.A.* 27°53N 80°30W **317** H9
Miccosukee *U.S.A.* 30°36N 84°3W **316** E5
Miccosukee, L. *U.S.A.* 30°33N 83°53W **316** E6
Michael, Mt. *Papua N. G.* 6°27S 145°22E **286** D3
Michalovce *Slovak Rep.* 48°47N 21°58E **181** C14
Michałowice *Poland* 52°10N 20°52E **142** B1
Michigan □ *U.S.A.* 44°0N 85°0W **309** C11
Michigan, L. *U.S.A.* 44°0N 87°0W **311** B9
Michigan Avenue *Chicago, U.S.A.* **119** b2
Michigan Center *U.S.A.* 42°14N 84°20W **311** B12
Michigan City *U.S.A.* 41°43N 86°54W **311** C10
Michika *Nigeria* 10°36N 13°23E **263** C7
Michipicoten I. *Canada* 47°40N 85°40W **298** C2
Michle *Czech Rep.* 50°3N 14°28E **135** B2
Michoacán □ *Mexico* 19°10N 101°50W **318** D4
Michurin *Bulgaria* 42°9N 27°51E **203** D11
Michurinsk *Russia* 52°58N 40°27E **190** D5
Miconje *Angola* 4°26S 12°48E **265** C2
Micoud *St. Lucia* 13°49N 60°54W **323** m
Micronesia *Pac. Oc.* 11°0N 160°0E **288** G7
Micronesia, Federated States of ■ *Pac. Oc.* 9°0N 150°0E **288** G7
Mid-Atlantic Ridge *Atl. Oc.* 0°0 20°0W **152** J10
Mid-City *Calif., U.S.A.* 34°4N 118°20W **126** B2
Mid City *La., U.S.A.* 29°58N 90°6W **131** B2
Mid-Indian Ocean Basin *Ind. Oc.* 10°0S 80°0E **273** F7
Mid-Indian Ridge *Ind. Oc.* 30°0S 75°0E **273** H6
Mid-Pacific Seamounts *Pac. Oc.* 18°0N 177°0W **288** F10
Midai *Indonesia* 3°0N 107°47E **235** B3
Midale *Canada* 49°25N 103°20W **297** D8
Middelburg *Neths.* 51°30N 3°36E **170** C3
Middelburg *Eastern Cape, S. Africa* 31°30S 25°0E **270** D4
Middelburg *Mpumalanga, S. Africa* 25°49S 29°28E **271** C4
Middelfart *Denmark* 55°30N 9°43E **163** J3
Middelpos *S. Africa* 31°55S 20°13E **270** D3
Middelwit *S. Africa* 24°51S 27°3E **270** B4
Middle → *U.S.A.* 41°26N 93°30W **310** C3
Middle Alkali L. *U.S.A.* 41°27N 120°5W **304** F3
Middle America Trench = Guatemala Trench *Pac. Oc.* 14°0N 95°0W **292** H10
Middle Andaman I. *India* 12°30N 92°50E **245** H11
Middle Bass I. *U.S.A.* 41°41N 82°48W **312** E2
Middle East *Asia* 35°0N 40°0E **210** E5
Middle Fork Feather → *U.S.A.* 38°33N 121°30W **306** F5
Middle Ground *Midway Is.* 28°14N 177°24W **302** c
Middle Harbour *Australia* 33°47S 151°14E **139** A2
Middle Hd. *Australia* 33°49S 151°16E **139** A2
Middle I. *Australia* 34°6S 123°11E **279** F3
Middle Island *St. Kitts & Nevis* 17°20N 62°48W **322** d
Middle Loup → *U.S.A.* 41°17N 98°24W **308** E4
Middle Park *Australia* 37°50S 144°57E **128** B1
Middle Raccoon → *U.S.A.* 41°35N 93°35W **310** C3
Middle Village *U.S.A.* 40°43N 73°52W **132** B2
Middleboro *U.S.A.* 41°54N 70°55W **313** E14
Middleburg *Fla., U.S.A.* 30°4N 81°52W **316** E8
Middleburg *Pa., U.S.A.* 40°47N 77°3W **312** F7
Middleburgh *U.S.A.* 42°36N 74°20W **313** D10
Middlebury *Ind., U.S.A.* 41°41N 85°42W **311** C11
Middlebury *Vt., U.S.A.* 44°1N 73°10W **313** B11
Middlefield *U.S.A.* 41°27N 81°4W **312** E3
Middlemarch *N.Z.* 45°30S 170°9E **285** F5
Middlemount *Australia* 22°50S 148°40E **280** C4
Middleport *N.Y., U.S.A.* 43°13N 78°29W **312** C6
Middleport *Ohio, U.S.A.* 39°0N 82°3W **309** F12
Middlesboro *U.S.A.* 36°36N 83°43W **309** G12
Middlesbrough *U.K.* 54°35N 1°13W **168** C6
Middlesbrough □ *U.K.* 54°28N 1°13W **168** C6
Middlesex *Belize* 17°2N 88°31W **320** C2
Middlesex *N.J., U.S.A.* 40°36N 74°30W **313** F10
Middlesex *N.Y., U.S.A.* 42°42N 77°16W **312** D7
Middlesex □ *Jamaica* 18°10N 77°5W **320** a
Middlesex Fells Reservation *U.S.A.* 42°27N 71°6W **116** A2
Middleton *Queens., Australia* 22°22S 141°32E **280** C3
Middleton *N.S., Canada* 44°57N 65°4W **299** D6
Middleton *Wis., U.S.A.* 43°6N 89°30W **310** A7
Middleton Cr. → *Australia* 22°35S 141°51E **280** C3
Middleton I. *U.S.A.* 59°26N 146°20W **303** G11
Middletown *Armagh, U.K.* 54°17N 6°51W **166** B5
Middletown *Calif., U.S.A.* 38°45N 122°37W **306** G4
Middletown *Conn., U.S.A.* 41°34N 72°39W **313** E12
Middletown *Ky., U.S.A.* 38°14N 85°32W **311** F11
Middletown *N.Y., U.S.A.* 41°27N 74°25W **313** E10
Middletown *Ohio, U.S.A.* 39°31N 84°24W **311** E12
Middletown *Pa., U.S.A.* 40°12N 76°44W **313** F8
Middleville *U.S.A.* 42°43N 85°28W **311** B11
Midelt *Morocco* 32°46N 4°44W **260** B4
Midge Point *Australia* 20°39S 148°43E **280** b
Midhirst *N.Z.* 39°17S 174°18E **284** F3
Miðsandur *Iceland* 64°24N 21°28W **155** C5
Midhurst *Ont., Canada* 44°26N 79°43W **312** B5
Midhurst *W. Susx., U.K.* 50°59N 0°44W **169** G7
Midi, Canal du → *France* 43°45N 1°21E **174** E5
Midi, Gare du *Brussels, Belgium* **116** c1
Midi d'Ossau, Pic du *France* 42°50N 0°26W **174** F3
Midi-Pyrénées □ *France* 43°55N 1°45E **174** E5
Midland *W. Austral., Australia* 31°54S 116°1E **279** F2
Midland *Ont., Canada* 44°45N 79°50W **312** B5
Midland *Calif., U.S.A.* 33°52N 114°48W **307** M12
Midland *Mich., U.S.A.* 43°37N 84°14W **309** D11
Midland *Pa., U.S.A.* 40°39N 80°27W **312** F4
Midland *Tex., U.S.A.* 32°0N 102°3W **314** E3
Midland Beach *U.S.A.* 40°34N 74°6W **132** C1
Midlands □ *Zimbabwe* 19°40S 29°0E **269** F2
Midleton *Ireland* 51°55N 8°10W **166** E3
Midlothian □ *U.K.* 55°51N 3°5W **167** F5
Midnapore = Medinipur *India* 22°25N 87°21E **243** H12
Midongy, Tangorombohitr' i *Madag.* 23°30S 47°0E **272** C2
Midongy Atsimo *Madag.* 23°35S 47°1E **272** C2
Midori *Japan* 36°30N 139°15E **223** A11
Midou → *France* 43°54N 0°30W **174** E3
Midouze → *France* 43°48N 0°51W **174** E3
Midsayap *Phil.* 7°12N 124°32E **233** H5
Midsund *Norway* 62°41N 6°40E **164** B3
Midtgulen *Norway* 61°44N 5°11E **164** C2
Midtjylland □ *Denmark* 56°30N 9°0E **163** H2
Midu *China* 25°18N 100°30E **228** E3
Midville *U.S.A.* 32°49N 82°14W **316** C7
Midway *Ala., U.S.A.* 32°5N 85°31W **316** C4
Midway *Fla., U.S.A.* 30°30N 84°27W **316** E5
Midway Is. *Pac. Oc.* 28°13N 177°22W **302** c
Midway Wells *U.S.A.* 32°41N 115°7W **307** N11
Midwest *U.S.A.* 42°0N 90°0W **301** G22
Midwest *Wyo., U.S.A.* 43°25N 106°16W **304** E10
Midwest City *U.S.A.* 35°27N 97°24W **314** D6
Midwood *U.S.A.* 40°37N 73°57W **132** C2
Midyat *Turkey* 37°25N 41°23E **213** D9
Midžor *Bulgaria* 43°24N 22°40E **202** C6
Mie *Japan* 32°58N 131°35E **222** E3
Mie □ *Japan* 34°30N 136°10E **223** C8
Miechów *Poland* 50°21N 20°5E **185** H7
Miedwie, Jezioro *Poland* 53°17N 14°54E **185** E1
Miedzeszyn *Poland* 52°10N 21°11E **142** B3
Międzybórz *Poland* 51°25N 17°34E **185** G4
Międzychód *Poland* 52°35N 15°53E **185** F2
Międzylesie *Dolnośląskie, Poland* 50°8N 16°40E **185** H3
Międzylesie *Warszawa, Poland* 52°12N 21°10E **142** B3
Międzyrzec Podlaski *Poland* 51°58N 22°45E **185** G9
Międzyrzecz *Poland* 52°26N 15°35E **185** F2
Międzyzdroje *Poland* 53°56N 14°26E **184** E1
Miejska Górka *Poland* 51°39N 16°58E **185** G3
Miélan *France* 43°27N 0°19E **174** E4
Mielau = Mława *Poland* 53°9N 20°25E **185** E7
Mielec *Poland* 50°15N 21°25E **185** H8
Mienga *Angola* 17°12S 19°48E **265** F3
Miercurea-Ciuc *Romania* 46°21N 25°48E **183** D10
Miercurea Sibiului *Romania* 45°53N 23°48E **183** E8
Mieres *Spain* 43°18N 5°48W **194** B5
Mieroszów *Poland* 50°40N 16°11E **185** H3
Mies = Stříbro *Czech Rep.* 49°44N 13°0E **180** A6
Mieso *Ethiopia* 9°15N 40°43E **257** F5
Miessaari *Finland* 60°8N 24°47E **121** C1
Mieszkowice *Poland* 52°47N 14°30E **185** F1
Mifflintown *U.S.A.* 40°34N 77°24W **312** F7
Mifraz Ḥefa *Israel* 32°52N 35°0E **250** F6
Migang Shan *China* 35°32N 106°13E **226** G4
Migennes *France* 47°58N 3°31E **173** E10
Migliarino *Italy* 44°46N 11°56E **199** D8
Migliarino-San Rossore-Massaciuccoli △ *Italy* 43°44N 10°20E **198** E7
Migori *Kenya* 1°4S 34°28E **268** C3
Miguasha △ *Canada* 48°5N 66°19W **299** C6
Miguel Alemán, Presa *Mexico* 18°15N 96°32W **319** D5
Miguel Alves *Brazil* 4°11S 42°55W **332** B3
Miguel Calmon *Brazil* 11°26S 40°36W **332** D3
Miguel Hidalgo *Mexico* 19°25N 99°12W **128** B1
Migueltura *Spain* 38°58N 3°53W **195** G7
Mihăileni *Romania* 47°58N 26°9E **183** C11
Mihăileşti *Romania* 44°20N 25°54E **183** F10
Mihailovca *Moldova* 46°33N 28°56E **183** D13
Mihalgazi *Turkey* 40°2N 30°34E **205** A12
Mihaliççık *Turkey* 39°53N 31°30E **212** C4
Mihara *Japan* 34°24N 133°5E **222** C5
Mihara-Yama *Japan* 34°43N 139°23E **223** C11
Miheşu de Cîmpie *Romania* 46°41N 24°9E **183** D9
Mijas *Spain* 36°36N 4°40W **195** J6
Mikawa-Wan *Japan* 34°44N 137°13E **223** C9
Mikese *Tanzania* 6°48S 37°55E **268** D4
Mikha-Tskhakaya = Senaki *Georgia* 42°15N 42°1E **191** J6
Mikhailovka = Mykhaylivka *Ukraine* 47°12N 35°15E **189** J8
Mikhaylov *Russia* 54°14N 39°0E **188** E10
Mikhaylovgrad = Montana *Bulgaria* 43°27N 23°16E **202** C7
Mikhaylovka = Kimovsk *Russia* 54°0N 38°29E **188** E10
Mikhaylovka *Russia* 50°3N 43°5E **190** E6
Mikhelysona *Russia* 55°42N 37°52E **129** B5
Mikhnevo *Russia* 55°4N 37°59E **188** E9
Miki *Hyōgo, Japan* 34°48N 134°59E **222** C6
Miki *Kagawa, Japan* 34°12N 134°7E **222** C6
Mikines *Greece* 37°43N 22°46E **204** D4
Mikir Hills *India* 26°10N 93°30E **241** B4
Mikkeli *Finland* 61°43N 27°15E **188** B4
Mikkwa → *Canada* 58°25N 114°46W **296** B6
Mikniya *Sudan* 17°0N 33°45E **257** D3
Mikołajki *Poland* 53°49N 21°37E **184** E8
Míkonos = Mykonos *Greece* 37°30N 25°25E **205** D7
Mikope *Dem. Rep. of the Congo* 4°58S 20°43E **265** C4
Mikoyan-Shakhar = Karachayevsk *Russia* 43°50N 41°55E **191** J5
Mikri Prespa, L. *Greece* 40°47N 21°3E **202** F5
Mikro Derio *Greece* 41°19N 26°6E **203** E10
Mikstat *Poland* 51°32N 17°59E **185** G4
Mikulov *Czech Rep.* 48°48N 16°39E **181** C9
Mikumi *Tanzania* 7°26S 37°0E **268** D4
Mikumi △ *Tanzania* 7°35S 37°15E **268** D4
Mikun *Russia* 62°20N 50°0E **186** B9
Mikuni *Japan* 36°13N 136°9E **223** A8
Mikuni-Tōge *Japan* 36°50N 138°50E **223** A10
Mikura-Jima *Japan* 33°52N 139°36E **223** D11
Mila *Algeria* 36°27N 6°16E **261** A6
Mila □ *Algeria* 36°25N 6°10E **261** A6
Milaca *U.S.A.* 45°45N 93°39W **308** C7
Miladummadulu Atoll *Maldives* 5°50N 73°30E **272** d
Milagro *Ecuador* 2°11S 79°36W **328** D2
Milagros *Phil.* 12°13N 123°30E **232** E4
Milan = Milano *Italy* 45°28N 9°10E **129** B1
Milan *Ga., U.S.A.* 32°1N 83°4W **316** C6
Milan *Ill., U.S.A.* 41°27N 90°34W **310** C6
Milan *Mich., U.S.A.* 42°5N 83°41W **311** B13
Milan *Mo., U.S.A.* 40°12N 93°7W **310** D3
Milan *Tenn., U.S.A.* 35°55N 88°46W **315** D10
Miland *Norway* 59°54N 8°45E **164** E5
Milando *Angola* 8°45S 17°36E **265** D3
Milando △ *Angola* 8°45S 17°10E **265** D3
Milanese, Parco Regionale △ *Italy* 45°35N 9°5E **129** A1
Milang *Australia* 35°24S 138°58E **282** C3
Milange *Mozam.* 16°3S 35°45E **269** F4
Milano *Italy* 45°28N 9°10E **129** B1
Milano Due *Italy* 45°24N 9°15E **129** B2
Milano Linate ✕ (LIN) *Italy* 45°27N 9°16E **129** B2
Milano San Felice *Italy* 45°28N 9°18E **129** B2
Milanoa *Madag.* 13°35S 49°47E **272** A2
Milâs *Turkey* 37°20N 27°50E **205** D9
Milatos *Greece* 35°18N 25°34E **207** E6
Milazzo *Italy* 38°13N 15°15E **201** D8
Milbank *U.S.A.* 45°13N 96°38W **308** C5
Milbanke Sd. *Canada* 52°19N 128°33W **296** C3
Milbertshofen *Germany* 48°10N 11°34E **131** A2
Milden *Canada* 51°29N 107°32W **297** C7
Mildenhall *U.K.* 52°21N 0°32E **169** E8
Mildmay *Canada* 44°3N 81°7W **312** B3
Mildura *Australia* 34°13S 142°9E **282** C5
Mile *China* 24°28N 103°20E **228** E4
Mile and a Quarter *Barbados* 13°16N 59°37W **323** r
Miles *Australia* 26°40S 150°9E **281** D5
Miles City *U.S.A.* 46°25N 105°51W **304** C11
Mileşti *Moldova* 47°13N 28°3E **183** C13
Milestone *Canada* 49°59N 104°31W **297** D8
Mileto *Italy* 38°36N 16°4E **201** D9
Miletto, Mte. *Italy* 41°27N 14°22E **201** A7
Miletus *Turkey* 37°30N 27°18E **205** D9
Milevsko *Czech Rep.* 49°27N 14°21E **180** B7
Milford *Calif., U.S.A.* 40°10N 120°22W **306** E6
Milford *Conn., U.S.A.* 41°14N 73°3W **313** E11
Milford *Del., U.S.A.* 38°55N 75°26W **309** F16
Milford *Ill., U.S.A.* 40°38N 87°42W **311** D9
Milford *Mass., U.S.A.* 42°8N 71°31W **313** D13
Milford *Mich., U.S.A.* 42°35N 83°36W **311** B13
Milford *N.H., U.S.A.* 42°50N 71°39W **313** D13
Milford *N.Y., U.S.A.* 42°35N 74°56W **313** D10
Milford *Pa., U.S.A.* 41°19N 74°48W **313** E10
Milford *Utah, U.S.A.* 38°24N 113°1W **304** G7
Milford Haven *U.K.* 51°42N 5°7W **169** F2
Milford Sd. *N.Z.* 44°41S 167°47E **285** E2
Milḥ, Baḥr al = Razāzah, Buḥayrat ar *Iraq* 32°40N 43°35E **213** F10
Miliana *Aïn Salah, Algeria* 27°20N 2°32E **261** C5
Miliana *Médéa, Algeria* 36°20N 2°15E **261** A5
Milicz *Poland* 51°31N 17°19E **185** G4
Milies *Greece* 39°20N 23°9E **204** B5
Milikapiti *Australia* 11°26S 130°40E **278** B5
Mililani Town *U.S.A.* 21°28N 158°1W **302** K13
Miling *Australia* 30°30S 116°17E **279** F2
Militello in Val di Catánia *Italy* 37°16N 14°48E **201** E7
Militsch = Milicz *Poland* 51°31N 17°19E **185** G4
Milk, Wadi el → *Sudan* 17°55N 30°20E **256** D3
Milk River *Canada* 49°10N 112°5W **296** D6
Milk River Spa *Jamaica* 17°50N 77°22W **320** a
Mill → *U.S.A.* 42°57N 83°23W **312** D1
Mill Hill *U.K.* 51°37N 0°14W **125** A2
Mill I. *Antarctica* 66°0S 101°30E **151** C8
Mill I. *Nunavut, Canada* 63°58N 77°47W **295** E16
Mill Shoals *U.S.A.* 38°15N 88°21W **311** F8
Mill Valley *U.S.A.* 37°54N 122°32W **306** H4
Millárs → *Spain* 39°55N 0°1W **196** F4
Millau *France* 44°8N 3°4E **174** D7
Millbridge *Canada* 44°41N 77°36W **312** B7
Millbrook *Ont., Canada* 44°10N 78°29W **312** B6
Millbrook *Ala., U.S.A.* 32°29N 86°22W **315** E11
Millbrook *N.Y., U.S.A.* 41°47N 73°42W **313** E11
Mille Lacs, L. des *Canada* 48°45N 90°35W **298** C1
Mille Lacs L. *U.S.A.* 46°15N 93°39W **308** B7
Milledgeville *Ga., U.S.A.* 33°5N 83°14W **316** B6
Milledgeville *Ill., U.S.A.* 41°58N 89°46W **310** C7
Millen *U.S.A.* 32°48N 81°57W **316** C8
Millennium Dome *U.K.* 51°30N 0°0 **125** A4
Millennium I. = Caroline I. *Kiribati* 9°58S 150°13W **289** H12
Millennium Park *Chicago, U.S.A.* **119** c2
Miller *U.S.A.* 44°31N 98°59W **308** C4
Miller Lake *Canada* 45°6N 81°26W **312** A3
Miller Meadow *U.S.A.* 41°51N 87°49W **119** B2
Millerhill *U.K.* 55°55N 3°5W **121** B3
Millerovo *Russia* 48°57N 40°28E **191** F5
Miller's Flat *N.Z.* 45°39S 169°23E **285** F4
Millers Point *Sydney, Australia* **139** a1
Millersburg *Ind., U.S.A.* 41°32N 85°42W **311** C11
Millersburg *Ohio, U.S.A.* 40°33N 81°55W **312** F3
Millersburg *Pa., U.S.A.* 40°32N 76°58W **312** F8
Millerton *N.Z.* 41°39S 171°54E **285** B6
Millerton *N.Y., U.S.A.* 41°57N 73°31W **313** E11
Millerton L. *U.S.A.* 37°1N 119°41W **306** J7
Millet *St. Lucia* 13°55N 60°59W **323** m
Millevaches, Plateau de *France* 45°45N 2°0E **174** C6
Millheim *U.S.A.* 40°54N 77°29W **312** F7
Millicent *Australia* 37°34S 140°21E **282** D4
Milligan *U.S.A.* 30°45N 86°38W **317** E3
Millington *U.S.A.* 35°20N 89°53W **315** D10
Millinocket *U.S.A.* 45°39N 68°43W **309** C19
Millmerran *Australia* 27°53S 151°16E **281** D5
Millom *U.K.* 54°13N 3°16W **168** C4
Mills L. *Canada* 61°30N 118°20W **296** A5
Millsboro *U.S.A.* 40°0N 80°0W **312** G5
Millstream Chichester △ *Australia* 21°35S 117°6E **278** D2
Millstreet *Ireland* 52°4N 9°4W **166** D2
Millthorpe *Australia* 33°26S 149°12E **283** B8
Milltown *Ireland* 53°19N 6°14W **120** B2
Milltown Malbay *Ireland* 52°52N 9°24W **166** D2
Millville *N.J., U.S.A.* 39°24N 75°2W **309** F16
Millville *Pa., U.S.A.* 41°7N 76°32W **313** E8
Millwood *U.S.A.* 38°52N 76°52W **143** B4
Millwood L. *U.S.A.* 33°42N 93°58W **314** E8
Milna *Croatia* 43°20N 16°28E **199** E13
Milne → *Australia* 21°10S 137°33E **280** C2
Milne Bay □ *Papua N. G.* 10°0S 152°30E **286** E7
Milne Land *Greenland* 70°40N 26°30W **154** C8
Milnerton *S. Africa* 33°53S 18°29E **118** A1
Milo *U.S.A.* 45°15N 68°59W **309** C19
Milo → *Guinea* 8°52N 9°0W **262** D3
Milolii *U.S.A.* 19°11N 155°55W **302** D6
Milon, Akra *Greece* 36°15N 28°11E **206** E12
Milon-la-Chapelle *France* 48°43N 2°3E **134** B1
Milos *Greece* 36°44N 24°25E **204** E6
Miłosław *Poland* 52°12N 17°32E **185** F4
Milot *Albania* 41°41N 19°43E **202** E3
Milparinka *Australia* 29°46S 141°57E **281** D3
Milpitas *U.S.A.* 37°26N 121°55W **306** H5
Milroy *U.S.A.* 39°30N 85°28W **311** E11
Miltenberg *Germany* 49°41N 9°16E **179** F5
Milton *N.S.W., Australia* 35°20S 150°27E **283** C9
Milton *N.S., Canada* 44°4N 64°45W **299** D7
Milton *Ont., Canada* 43°31N 79°53W **312** C5
Milton *N.Z.* 46°7S 169°59E **285** G4
Milton *Calif., U.S.A.* 38°3N 120°51W **306** G6
Milton *Fla., U.S.A.* 30°38N 87°3W **317** E2
Milton *Iowa, U.S.A.* 40°41N 92°10W **310** D4
Milton *Mass., U.S.A.* 42°14N 71°2W **116** B2
Milton *Pa., U.S.A.* 41°1N 76°51W **312** F8
Milton *Vt., U.S.A.* 44°38N 73°7W **313** B11
Milton *Wis., U.S.A.* 42°47N 88°56W **311** B8
Milton Bridge *U.K.* 55°51N 3°11W **121** B2
Milton-Freewater *U.S.A.* 45°56N 118°23W **304** D4
Milton Keynes *U.K.* 52°1N 0°44W **169** E7
Milton Keynes □ *U.K.* 52°1N 0°44W **169** E7
Milton Park *Montréal, Canada* **130** b1
Miltou *Chad* 10°14N 17°26E **259** F3
Miluo *China* 29°0N 112°59E **229** C9
Milverton *Canada* 43°34N 80°55W **312** C4
Milwaukee *U.S.A.* 43°2N 87°54W **311** A9
Milwaukee Deep *Atl. Oc.* 19°50N 68°0W **321** C6
Milwaukie *U.S.A.* 45°26N 122°38W **306** E4
Mim *Ghana* 6°57N 2°33W **262** D4
Mimico *Canada* 43°36N 79°29W **141** B2
Mimico Creek → *Canada* 43°38N 79°28W **141** B1
Mimili *Australia* 27°0S 132°42E **279** E5
Mimizan *France* 44°12N 1°13W **174** D2
Mimoň *Czech Rep.* 50°38N 14°43E **180** A7
Mimongo *Gabon* 1°11S 11°36E **264** C2
Mimoso *Brazil* 15°10S 48°5W **333** E2
Mims *U.S.A.* 28°40N 80°51W **317** G9
Min Jiang → *Fujian, China* 26°0N 119°35E **229** E12
Min Jiang → *Sichuan, China* 28°45N 104°40E **228** C5
Min Xian *China* 34°25N 104°5E **226** G3
Mīnā' Jabal 'Alī *U.A.E.* 25°2N 55°8E **247** E7
Mina Pirquitas *Argentina* 22°40S 66°30W **334** A2
Mīnā Su'ud *Si. Arabia* 28°45N 48°28E **247** D6
Mīnā'al Aḥmadī *Kuwait* 29°5N 48°10E **247** D6
Minago → *Canada* 54°33N 98°59W **297** C9
Minakami *Japan* 36°49N 138°59E **223** A10
Minaki *Canada* 49°59N 94°40W **297** D10
Minakuchi *Japan* 34°58N 136°10E **223** C8
Minalungao △ *Phil.* 15°2N 121°8E **232** D3
Minamata *Japan* 32°10N 130°30E **222** E2
Minami *Japan* 34°40N 135°30E **133** A2
Minami-Arapusa △ *Japan* 35°30N 138°9E **223** B10
Minami-Tori-Shima *Pac. Oc.* 24°20N 153°58E **288** E7
Minamitsunashima *Japan* 35°32N 139°37E **140** B2
Minas *Indonesia* 0°50N 101°26E **234** B2
Minas *Uruguay* 34°20S 55°10W **335** C4
Minas, Sierra de las *Guatemala* 15°9N 89°31W **320** C2
Minas Basin *Canada* 45°20N 64°12W **299** C7
Minas de Riotinto *Spain* 37°42N 6°35W **195** H4
Minas Gerais □ *Brazil* 18°50S 46°0W **333** E2
Minas Novas *Brazil* 17°15S 42°36W **333** E3
Minatitlán *Mexico* 17°59N 94°31W **319** D6
Minato *Ōsaka, Japan* 34°39N 135°25E **133** B1
Minato *Tokyo, Japan* **140** c3
Minbu *Burma* 20°10N 94°52E **241** E5
Minbya *Burma* 20°22N 93°16E **241** E4
Minchinabad *Pakistan* 30°10N 73°34E **242** D5
Mincio → *Italy* 45°4N 10°59E **198** C7
Minčol *Slovak Rep.* 49°15N 20°58E **181** B13
Mindanao *Phil.* 8°0N 125°0E **233** H5
Mindanao Sea = Bohol Sea *Phil.* 9°0N 124°0E **233** G5
Mindanao Trench *Pac. Oc.* 12°0N 126°6E **232** E5
Mindel → *Germany* 48°31N 10°23E **179** G6
Mindelheim *Germany* 48°2N 10°29E **179** G6
Mindelo *C. Verde Is.* 16°24N 25°0W **153** j
Minden *Ont., Canada* 44°55N 78°43W **312** B6
Minden *Nordrhein-Westfalen, Germany* 52°17N 8°55E **178** C4
Minden *La., U.S.A.* 32°37N 93°17W **314** E8
Minden *Nev., U.S.A.* 38°57N 119°46W **306** G7
Mindibungu = Billiluna *Australia* 19°37S 127°41E **278** C4
Mindiptana *Indonesia* 5°55S 140°22E **231** F10
Mindon *Burma* 19°21N 94°44E **241** F5
Mindona L. *Australia* 33°6S 142°6E **282** B5
Mindoro *Phil.* 13°0N 121°0E **232** E3
Mindoro Occidental □ *Phil.* 13°0N 120°55E **232** E3
Mindoro Oriental □ *Phil.* 13°0N 121°5E **232** E3
Mindoro Str. *Phil.* 12°30N 120°30E **232** E3
Mindouli *Congo* 4°12S 14°28E **265** C2
Mindourou *Cameroon* 3°29N 13°26E **264** B2
Mine *Japan* 34°12N 131°7E **222** C3
Minehead *U.K.* 51°12N 3°29W **169** F4
Mineiros *Brazil* 17°34S 52°34W **331** D7
Mineola *N.Y., U.S.A.* 40°44N 73°38W **313** F11
Mineola *Tex., U.S.A.* 32°40N 95°29W **314** E7
Mineral Bath *Jamaica* 17°58N 76°22W **320** a
Mineral King *U.S.A.* 36°27N 118°36W **306** J8
Mineral Point *U.S.A.* 42°52N 90°11W **310** B6
Mineral Wells *U.S.A.* 32°48N 98°7W **314** E5
Mineralnyye Vody *Russia* 44°15N 43°8E **191** H6
Miners Bay *Canada* 44°49N 78°46W **312** B6
Minersville *U.S.A.* 40°41N 76°16W **313** F8
Minerva *N.Y., U.S.A.* 43°47N 73°59W **313** C11
Minerva *Ohio, U.S.A.* 40°44N 81°6W **312** F3
Minervino Murge *Italy* 41°5N 16°5E **201** A9
Minetto *U.S.A.* 43°24N 76°28W **313** C8
Minfeng *China* 37°4N 82°46E **217** E10
Ming-Kush *Kyrgyzstan* 41°40N 74°28E **217** D8
Mingäçevir *Azerbaijan* 40°45N 47°0E **191** K8
Mingäçevir Su Anbarı *Azerbaijan* 40°57N 46°50E **191** K8
Mingala *C.A.R.* 5°6N 21°49E **264** A4
Mingan *Canada* 50°20N 64°0W **299** B7
Mingary *Australia* 32°8S 140°45E **282** B4
Mingchien *Taiwan* 23°50N 120°42E **225** C2
Mingechaur = Mingäçevir *Azerbaijan* 40°45N 47°0E **191** K8
Mingechaurskoye Vdkhr. = Mingäçevir Su Anbarı *Azerbaijan* 40°57N 46°50E **191** K8
Mingela *Australia* 19°52S 146°38E **280** B4
Mingenew *Australia* 29°12S 115°21E **279** E2
Mingera Cr. → *Australia* 20°38S 137°45E **280** C2
Minggang *China* 32°24N 114°3E **229** A10
Mingguang *China* 32°46N 117°59E **229** A11
Mingin *Burma* 22°50N 94°30E **241** D5
Mingir *Moldova* 46°40N 28°20E **183** D13
Minglanilla *Spain* 39°34N 1°38W **197** F3
Minglun *China* 25°10N 108°21E **228** E7
Mingo *Congo* 1°55S 15°1E **264** C3
Mingo Junction *U.S.A.* 40°19N 80°37W **312** F4
Mingora *Pakistan* 34°48N 72°22E **243** B5
Mingorría *Spain* 40°45N 4°40W **194** E6
Mingshan *China* 30°6N 103°10E **228** B4
Mingteke Daban = Mintaka Pass *Pakistan* 37°0N 74°58E **243** A6
Mingxi *China* 26°18N 117°12E **229** D11
Mingyuegue *China* 43°2N 128°50E **227** C15
Minhe *China* 36°9N 102°45E **218** D9
Minhla *Magwe, Burma* 19°58N 95°3E **241** F5
Minhla *Pegu, Burma* 17°59N 95°43E **241** G5
Minho = Miño → *Spain* 41°52N 8°40W **194** D2
Minhou *China* 26°0N 119°15E **229** E12
Minhsiung *Taiwan* 23°33N 120°35E **225** C2
Miničevo *Serbia* 43°42N 22°18E **182** G7
Minicoy I. *India* 8°17N 73°2E **245** K1
Minidoka *U.S.A.* 42°45N 113°29W **304** E7
Minier *U.S.A.* 40°26N 89°19W **310** D7
Minigwal, L. *Australia* 29°31S 123°14E **279** E3
Minilya → *Australia* 23°45S 114°0E **279** D1
Minilya Roadhouse *Australia* 23°55S 114°0E **279** D1
Mininera *Australia* 37°37S 142°58E **282** D5
Minipi L. *Canada* 52°25N 60°45W **299** B7
Minj *Papua N. G.* 5°54S 144°37E **286** D3
Minjilang *Australia* 11°8S 132°33E **278** B5
Mink L. *Canada* 61°54N 117°40W **296** A5
Minkammen *Sudan* 6°3N 31°32E **257** F3
Minkebé *Gabon* 1°45N 12°45E **264** B2
Minlaton *Australia* 34°45S 137°35E **282** C2
Minna *Nigeria* 9°37N 6°30E **263** D6
Minna-shima *Japan* 26°39N 127°49E **288** a
Minneapolis *Kans., U.S.A.* 39°8N 97°42W **308** F5
Minneapolis *Minn., U.S.A.* 44°57N 93°16W **308** C8
Minnedosa *Canada* 50°14N 99°50W **297** C9
Minnesota □ *U.S.A.* 46°0N 94°15W **308** B6
Minnesota → *U.S.A.* 44°54N 93°9W **308** C7
Minnesund *Norway* 60°23N 11°14E **164** D8
Minnewaukan *U.S.A.* 48°4N 99°15W **308** A4
Minnipa *Australia* 32°51S 135°9E **281** E2
Minnitaki L. *Canada* 49°57N 92°10W **298** C1
Mino *Japan* 35°32N 136°55E **223** B8
Miño *Spain* 43°21N 8°12W **194** B2
Miño → *Spain* 41°52N 8°40W **194** D2
Mino-Kamo *Japan* 35°23N 137°2E **223** B9
Mino-Mikawa-Kōgen *Japan* 35°10N 137°20E **223** B9
Minoa *Greece* 35°6N 25°45E **205** F7
Minobu *Japan* 35°22N 138°26E **223** B10
Minobu-Sanchi *Japan* 35°14N 138°20E **223** B10
Minonk *U.S.A.* 40°54N 89°2W **310** D7
Minooka *U.S.A.* 41°27N 88°16W **311** C8
Minorca = Menorca *Spain* 40°0N 4°0E **206** B5
Minore *Australia* 32°14S 148°27E **283** B8
Minot *U.S.A.* 48°14N 101°18W **308** A3
Minqin *China* 38°38N 103°20E **226** E2
Minqing *China* 26°15N 118°50E **229** D12
Minsen *Germany* 53°41N 7°58E **178** B3
Minshât el Bekkârî *Egypt* 30°0N 31°8E **117** A1
Minsk *Belarus* 53°52N 27°30E **177** B14
Minsk □ *Belarus* 53°15N 27°30E **188** F4
Mińsk Mazowiecki *Poland* 52°10N 21°33E **185** F8
Minster *U.S.A.* 40°24N 84°23W **311** D12
Mintabie *Australia* 27°15S 133°7E **281** D1
Mintaka Pass *Pakistan* 37°0N 74°58E **243** A6
Minthami *Burma* 23°55N 94°16E **241** D5
Minto *N.B., Canada* 46°5N 66°5W **299** C6
Minto *Alaska, U.S.A.* 64°53N 149°10W **303** D10
Minto, L. *Canada* 57°13N 75°0W **298** A5
Minton *Canada* 49°10N 104°35W **297** D8
Mintom *Gabon* 0°27N 12°16E **264** B2
Minturn *U.S.A.* 39°35N 106°26W **304** G10
Minturno *Italy* 41°15N 13°45E **200** A6
Minudasht *Iran* 37°17N 56°7E **247** B8
Minûf *Egypt* 30°26N 30°52E **256** H7
Minusinsk *Russia* 53°43N 91°20E **217** B12
Minutang *India* 28°15N 96°30E **241** A6
Minvoul *Gabon* 2°9N 12°8E **264** B2
Minwakh *Yemen* 16°48N 48°6E **249** C5
Minya el Qamh *Egypt* 30°31N 31°21E **256** H7
Minya Konka = Gongga Shan *China* 29°40N 101°55E **228** C3
Minyip *Australia* 36°29S 142°36E **282** D5
Minzhong *China* 22°37N 113°30E **219** a
Mionica *Bos.-H.* 44°51N 18°29E **182** F3
Mionica *Serbia* 44°14N 20°6E **202** B4
Miquan *China* 43°58N 87°42E **217** D11
Miquelon *Qué., Canada* 49°25N 76°27W **298** C4
Miquelon *St.-P. & M.* 47°8N 56°22W **299** C8
Mir *Niger* 14°5N 11°59E **259** F2
Mīr Kūh *Iran* 26°22N 58°55E **247** E8
Mīr Shahdād *Iran* 26°15N 58°29E **247** E8
Mira *Italy* 45°26N 12°8E **199** C9
Mira *Portugal* 40°26N 8°44W **194** E2
Mira → *Colombia* 1°36N 79°1W **328** C2
Mira → *Portugal* 37°43N 8°47W **195** H2
Mira por vos Cay *Bahamas* 22°9N 74°30W **321** B5
Mīrābād *Afghan.* 30°25N 61°50E **240** C1
Mirabella Eclano *Italy* 41°2N 14°59E **201** A7
Mirabello, Kolpos *Greece* 35°10N 25°50E **207** E6
Miracema do Norte *Brazil* 9°33S 48°24W **332** C2
Mirador *Brazil* 6°22S 44°22W **332** C3
Mirador-Río Azul △ *Guatemala* 17°45N 89°50W **320** C1
Miraflores = Rovira *Colombia* 4°15N 75°20W **328** C2
Miraflores *Colombia* 1°25N 72°13W **328** C3
Miraflores *Lima, Peru* 12°7S 77°2W **124** B2
Miraflores, L. *Panama* 9°1N 79°36W **320** c
Miraflores Locks *Panama* 9°0N 79°36W **320** c
Miraj *India* 16°50N 74°45E **244** F2
Miram Shah *Pakistan* 33°0N 70°2E **242** C4
Miramar *Argentina* 38°15S 57°50W **334** D4
Miramar *Mozam.* 23°50S 35°35E **271** B6
Miramar *N.Z.* 41°18S 174°49E **143** B1
Miramas *France* 43°33N 4°59E **175** E8
Mirambeau *France* 45°23N 0°35W **174** C3
Miramichi *Canada* 47°2N 65°28W **299** C6
Miramichi B. *Canada* 47°15N 65°0W **299** C7
Miramont-de-Guyenne *France* 44°37N 0°21E **174** D4
Miranda *Brazil* 20°10S 56°15W **331** E6
Miranda □ *Venezuela* 10°15N 66°25W **328** A4
Miranda → *Brazil* 19°25S 57°20W **331** D6
Miranda de Ebro *Spain* 42°41N 2°57W **196** C2
Miranda do Corvo *Portugal* 40°6N 8°20W **194** E2
Miranda do Douro *Portugal* 41°30N 6°16W **194** D4
Mirande *France* 43°31N 0°25E **174** E4
Mirandela *Portugal* 41°32N 7°10W **194** D3
Mirándola *Italy* 44°53N 11°4E **198** D8
Mirandópolis *Brazil* 21°9S 51°6W **335** A5
Mirango *Malawi* 13°32S 34°58E **269** E3
Mirani *Australia* 21°8S 148°53E **280** b
Mirano *Italy* 45°30N 12°7E **199** C9
Miras *Albania* 40°30N 20°56E **202** F4
Mirassol *Brazil* 20°46S 49°28W **335** A6
Mirbāţ *Oman* 17°0N 54°45E **249** C6
Mirboo North *Australia* 38°24S 146°10E **283** E7
Mirear *Egypt* 23°15N 35°41E **256** C4
Mirebeau *France* 46°49N 0°10E **172** F7
Mirebeau-sur-Bèze *France* 47°25N 5°20E **173** E12
Mirecourt *France* 48°20N 6°10E **173** D13
Mirgorod = Myrhorod *Ukraine* 49°58N 33°37E **189** H7
Miri *Malaysia* 4°23N 113°59E **235** B4
Mirialguda *India* 16°52N 79°35E **244** F4
Miriam Vale *Australia* 24°20S 151°33E **280** C5
Miribel *France* 45°50N 4°57E **173** G11
Mirigama *Sri Lanka* 7°15N 80°8E **245** L5
Mirim, L. *S. Amer.* 32°45S 52°50W **335** C5
Mirimire *Venezuela* 11°10N 68°43W **328** A4
Miringoni *Comoros Is.* 12°17S 43°38E **272** a
Miriti *Brazil* 6°15S 59°0W **331** B6
Miriuwung Gajerrong ◎ *Australia* 15°0S 128°45E **278** C4
Mīrjāveh *Iran* 29°1N 61°30E **247** D9
Mirny *Antarctica* 66°50S 92°30E **151** C14
Mirnyy *Russia* 62°33N 113°53E **215** C12
Miroč *Serbia* 44°32N 22°16E **202** B6
Mirokhan *Pakistan* 27°46N 68°6E **242** F3
Mirond L. *Canada* 55°6N 102°47W **297** B8
Mirosławiec *Poland* 53°20N 16°5E **184** E3
Mirpur *Pakistan* 33°32N 73°56E **243** C5
Mirpur Batoro *Pakistan* 24°44N 68°16E **242** G3
Mirpur Bibiwari *Pakistan* 28°33N 67°44E **242** E2
Mirpur Khas *Pakistan* 25°30N 69°0E **242** G3
Mirpur Sakro *Pakistan* 24°33N 67°41E **242** G2
Mirria *Niger* 13°43N 9°7E **259** F1
Mirrool *Australia* 34°19S 147°10E **283** C7
Mirs Bay = Tai Pang Wan *China* 22°33N 114°24E **219** a
Mirsale *Somali Rep.* 5°57N 47°59E **267** C6
Mirsk *Poland* 50°58N 15°23E **185** H2
Mirtağ *Turkey* 38°23N 41°56E **246** B4
Mirtoo Sea *Greece* 37°0N 23°20E **204** D5
Mirtou, Kolpos *Greece* 38°20N 20°27E **207** C1
Miryang *S. Korea* 35°31N 128°44E **224** E4
Mirzaani *Georgia* 41°24N 46°5E **191** K8
Mirzachul = Gulistan *Uzbekistan* 40°29N 68°46E **217** D7
Mirzapur *India* 25°10N 82°34E **243** G10

Mirzapur-cum-Vindhyachal =
Mirzapur *India* 25°10N 82°34E **243** G10
Mirzoyan = Taraz
Kazakhstan 42°54N 71°22E **217** D8
Misaki *Japan* 34°18N 135°09E **223** G4
Misamis = Ozamiz *Phil.* 8°15N 123°50E **233** G4
Misamis Occidental □
Phil. 8°20N 123°42E **233** G4
Misamis Oriental □ *Phil.* 8°45N 125°0E **233** G5
Misawa *Japan* 40°41N 141°24E **220** D10
Miscou I. *Canada* 47°57N 64°31W **299** C7
Misdroy = Międzyzdroje
Poland 53°56N 14°26E **184** E1
Misericordia = Itaporanga
Brazil 7°18S 38°0W **332** C4
Misericordia, Sa. da
Brazil 22°51S 43°17W **135** B1
Misha *India* 7°59N 93°20E **245** L10
Mish'āb, Ra's al *Si. Arabia* 28°15N 48°43E **247** D6
Mishagua → *Peru* 11°12S 72°58W **330** C3
Mishamo *Tanzania* 5°41S 30°41E **268** D3
Mishan *China* 45°37N 131°48E **220** B5
Mishawaka *U.S.A.* 41°40N 86°11W **314** E2
Mishbih, Gebel *Egypt* 22°38N 34°44E **256** C3
Mishima *Japan* 35°10N 138°52E **223** B10
Mishmi Hills *India* 29°0N 96°0E **241** A4
Mishō *Japan* 32°57N 132°35E **222** E4
Misima I. *Papua N. G.* 10°40S 152°45E **286** F7
Misión *Mexico* 32°6N 116°53W **307** N10
Misión Fagnano
Argentina 54°32S 67°17W **336** D3
Misiones □ *Argentina* 27°0S 55°0W **335** B5
Misiones □ *Paraguay* 27°0S 56°0W **334** B4
Miskah *Si. Arabia* 24°49N 42°56E **246** E4
Miski, E. → *Chad* 20°0N 17°55E **259** E3
Miskitos, Cayos *Nic.* 14°26N 82°50W **320** D3
Miskolc *Hungary* 48°7N 20°50E **182** B5
Misoke *Dem. Rep. of the Congo* 0°42S 28°2E **268** C2
Misool *Indonesia* 1°52S 130°10E **231** E8
Misr = Egypt ■ *Africa* 28°0N 31°0E **256** B3
Miṣrātah *Libya* 32°24N 15°3E **258** B3
Miṣrātah □ *Libya* 33°0N 17°0E **258** B3
Missanabie *Canada* 48°20N 84°6W **298** C3
Missão Catrimani *Brazil* 2°48N 62°18W **329** C5
Missão Velha *Brazil* 7°15S 39°10W **332** C4
Missinaibi → *Canada* 50°43N 81°29W **298** B3
Missinaibi L. *Canada* 48°23N 83°40W **298** C3
Mission *B.C., Canada* 49°10N 122°15W **296** D4
Mission *Calif., U.S.A.* 34°18N 122°25W **136** B2
Mission *S. Dak., U.S.A.* 43°18N 100°39W **308** D3
Mission *Tex., U.S.A.* 26°13N 98°20W **314** H5
Mission Beach *Australia* 17°53S 146°6E **280** B4
Mission Viejo *U.S.A.* 33°36N 117°40W **307** M9
Missirah *Senegal* 13°40N 16°30W **262** C1
Missisa L. *Canada* 52°20N 85°7W **298** B2
Missisicabi → *Canada* 51°14N 79°31W **298** B4
Mississagi → *Canada* 46°15N 83°9W **298** C3
Mississauga *Canada* 43°32N 79°35W **141** D3
Mississinewa L. *U.S.A.* 40°42N 85°52W **311** D10
Mississippi □ *U.S.A.* 33°0N 90°0W **315** E10
Mississippi → *U.S.A.* 29°9N 89°15W **310** E5
Mississippi L. *Canada* 45°5N 76°10W **313** A8
Mississippi River Delta
U.S.A. 29°10N 89°15W **315** G10
Mississippi Sd. *U.S.A.* 30°20N 89°0W **315** F10
Missoula *U.S.A.* 46°52N 114°1W **304** C6
Missour *Morocco* 33°3N 4°0W **260** B4
Missouri □ *U.S.A.* 38°25N 92°30W **310** F8
Missouri → *U.S.A.* 38°49N 90°7W **310** F6
Missouri City *U.S.A.* 29°37N 95°32W **314** G7
Missouri Valley *U.S.A.* 41°34N 95°53W **308** E6
Mist *U.S.A.* 45°59N 123°15W **306** E3
Mistassibi → *Canada* 48°53N 72°13W **299** B5
Mistassini *Canada* 48°53N 72°12W **299** C5
Mistassini, L. *Canada* 48°42N 72°20W **299** C5
Mistastin L. *Canada* 55°57N 63°30W **299** A7
Mistelbach *Austria* 48°34N 16°34E **181** C9
Misterbianco *Italy* 37°31N 15°1E **201** E8
Misteriosa Bank
W. Indies 18°50N 83°50W **320** C3
Misti, Volcán *Peru* 16°18S 71°24W **330** D3
Mistinibi, L. *Canada* 55°56N 64°17W **299** A7
Mistissini *Canada* 48°53N 72°12W **299** C5
Mistretta *Italy* 37°56N 14°22E **201** E7
Misty Fjords Nat. Monument △
U.S.A. 55°40N 130°40W **303** J15
Misty L. *Canada* 58°53N 101°40W **297** B8
Misugi *Japan* 34°31N 136°16E **223** C8
Misumi *Japan* 32°37N 130°27E **222** E2
Misurata = Miṣrātah *Libya* 32°24N 15°3E **258** B3
Mît Ghamr *Egypt* 30°42N 31°12E **256** H7
Mitaka *Japan* 35°41N 139°34E **160** A2
Mitande *Mozam.* 14°6S 35°58E **269** E4
Mitatib *Sudan* 15°59N 36°12E **257** D4
Mitau = Jelgava *Latvia* 56°41N 23°49E **184** B10
Mitava = Jelgava *Latvia* 56°41N 23°49E **184** B10
Mitcham *U.K.* 51°23N 0°10W **125** B2
Mitcham Common *U.K.* 51°23N 0°9W **125** B2
Mitchell
Australia 26°29S 147°58E **281** D4
Mitchell *Ont., Canada* 43°28N 81°12W **312** C3
Mitchell *Ga., U.S.A.* 33°13N 82°42W **317** E4
Mitchell *Ind., U.S.A.* 38°44N 86°28W **311** F10
Mitchell *Nebr., U.S.A.* 41°57N 103°49W **308** E2
Mitchell *Oreg., U.S.A.* 44°34N 120°9W **304** D3
Mitchell *S. Dak., U.S.A.* 43°43N 98°2W **308** D5
Mitchell → *Australia* 15°12S 141°35E **280** B3
Mitchell, Mt. *U.S.A.* 35°46N 82°16W **315** D13
Mitchell-Alice Rivers △
Australia 15°28S 142°5E **280** B3
Mitchell Museum of the American
Indian *U.S.A.* 42°4N 87°43W **119** A2
Mitchell Ra. *Australia* 12°49S 135°36E **280** A2
Mitchell River △
Australia 37°37S 147°22E **283** D7
Mitchell's Plain *S. Africa* 34°4S 18°35E **168** E2
Mitchelstown *Ireland* 52°15N 8°16W **166** D3
Mitha Tiwana *Pakistan* 32°13N 72°6E **242** C5
Mithi *Pakistan* 24°44N 69°48E **242** G3
Mithimna *Greece* 39°20N 26°12E **205** B8
Mithrao *Pakistan* 27°28N 69°40E **242** F3
Mitiamo *Australia* 36°12S 144°15E **283** C3
Mitikas *Etolokarnania,
Greece* 38°40N 21°5E **207** B2
Mitilíni *Greece* 39°6N 26°35E **205** B9
Mitilinii *Greece* 37°42N 26°56E **205** D8
Mitino *Russia* 55°51N 37°20E **129** A2
Mitla Pass = Mamarr Mitlā
Egypt 30°2N 32°54E **251** H3
Mito *Japan* 36°20N 140°30E **223** A12
Mitra, Mt. *Eq. Guin.* 1°23N 9°19E **264** B1
Mitre, Mt. *N.Z.* 40°50S 175°30E **284** G4
Mitrofanovka *Russia* 49°58N 39°18E **189** H10
Mitrovica = Kosovska Mitrovica
Kosovo 42°54N 20°52E **202** D4
Mitrowitz = Sremska Mitrovica
Serbia 44°59N 19°38E **182** F4
Mitsamiouli *Comoros Is.* 11°20S 43°16E **272** a
Mitsinjo *Madag.* 16°1S 45°52E **272** B2
Mitsiwa *Eritrea* 15°35N 39°25E **257** D4
Mitsiwa Channel *Eritrea* 15°30N 40°0E **257** D5

Mitsoudjé *Comoros Is.* 11°48S 43°16E **272** a
Mitsukaidō *Japan* 36°1N 139°59E **223** A11
Mitsushima *Japan* 34°15N 129°20E **222** C1
Mittagong *Australia* 34°28S 150°29E **283** C9
Mitte *Germany* 52°32N 13°24E **115** A3
Mittel Isarkanal →
Germany 48°12N 11°40E **131** A3
Mittel Schreiberhau = Szklarska
Poreba *Poland* 50°50N 15°33E **185** H2
Mittelberg *Austria* 47°20N 10°10E **180** D3
Mittelfranken □ *Germany* 49°25N 10°40E **179** F6
Mittellandkanal →
Germany 52°20N 8°28E **178** C4
Mittelwalde = Międzylesie
Poland 50°8N 16°40E **185** H3
Mittenwalde *Germany* 52°15N 13°31E **178** C9
Mittersill *Austria* 47°16N 12°29E **180** D5
Mittimatalik = Pond Inlet
Canada 72°40N 77°0W **295** C16
Mittweida *Germany* 50°59N 12°59E **178** E8
Mitú *Colombia* 1°15N 70°13W **328** C3
Mituas *Colombia* 3°52N 68°49W **328** C4
Mitumba *Tanzania* 7°8S 31°2E **268** D3
Mitumba, Mts.
Dem. Rep. of the Congo 7°0S 27°30E **268** D2
Mitwaba
Dem. Rep. of the Congo 8°2S 27°17E **269** D2
Mityana *Uganda* 0°23N 32°2E **268** B3
Mitzic *Gabon* 0°45N 11°40E **264** D2
Miura *Japan* 35°12N 139°40E **223** B11
Mixcoac *Mexico* 19°23N 99°11W **128** B1
Mixteco → *Mexico* 18°11N 98°30W **319** D5
Miyagi □ *Japan* 38°15N 140°45E **220** E10
Miyah, W. el → *Egypt* 25°0N 33°23E **256** C3
Miyah, W. el → *Syria* 34°44N 39°57E **246** C3
Miyake-jima *Japan* 34°5N 139°30E **223** C11
Miyako *Japan* 39°40N 141°59E **220** E10
Miyako-jima *Japan* 24°45N 125°20E **221** M2
Miyako-Rettō *Japan* 24°24N 125°0E **221** M2
Miyakonojō *Japan* 31°40N 131°5E **222** E3
Miyako *Japan* 31°40N 47°26E **213** E12
Miyani *India* 21°50N 69°26E **242** J3
Miyanojō *Japan* 31°54N 130°27E **222** F2
Miyanoura-Dake *Japan* 30°20N 130°31E **221** J5
Miyata *Japan* 33°49N 130°42E **222** D2
Miyazaki *Japan* 31°56N 131°30E **222** F3
Miyazaki □ *Japan* 32°30N 131°30E **222** E3
Miyazu *Japan* 35°35N 135°10E **223** B7
Miyet, Bahr el = Dead Sea
Asia 31°30N 35°30E **251** G6
Miyi *China* 26°47N 102°9E **228** D4
Miyun *China* 40°28N 116°50E **226** D4
Miyun Shuiku *China* 40°30N 117°0E **227** D9
Mizan Teferi *Ethiopia* 6°57N 35°30E **257** F4
Mizdah *Libya* 31°30N 13°0E **258** B2
Mizdah □ *Libya* 31°26N 12°59E **258** B2
Mizen Hd. *Cork, Ireland* 51°27N 9°50W **166** E2
Mizen Hd. *Wicklow, Ireland* 52°51N 6°4W **166** C5
Mizhhirya *Ukraine* 48°32N 23°30E **183** B8
Mizhi *China* 37°47N 110°12E **226** F5
Mizil *Romania* 44°59N 26°29E **183** F11
Mizo Hills = Mizoram □
India 23°30N 92°40E **241** D4
Mizonokuchi *Japan* 35°35N 139°34E **140** B2
Mizoram □ *India* 23°30N 92°40E **241** D4
Mizpe Ramon *Israel* 30°34N 34°49E **251** H5
Mizue *Japan* 35°31N 139°54E **140** A4
Mizuho *Antarctica* 70°30S 41°0E **151** D5
Mizuho *Japan* 35°36N 135°17E **223** B7
Mizunami *Japan* 35°22N 137°15E **223** B9
Mizusawa *Japan* 39°8N 141°8E **220** E10
Mjällby *Sweden* 56°3N 14°40E **163** H8
Mjöbäck *Sweden* 57°28N 12°53E **163** H6
Mjölby *Sweden* 58°20N 15°10E **163** F9
Mjörn *Sweden* 57°59N 12°25E **163** H6
Mjøsa *Norway* 60°48N 10°20E **163** E6
Mjøsa *Norway* 60°40N 11°0E **163** E6
Mkata *Tanzania* 5°45S 38°20E **268** D4
Mkhaya △ *Swaziland* 26°34S 31°45E **271** C5
Mkhuze △ *S. Africa* 29°27S 29°30E **271** C4
Mkokotoni *Tanzania* 5°55S 39°15E **268** D4
Mkomazi *Tanzania* 4°40S 38°7E **268** C4
Mkomazi → *S. Africa* 30°12S 30°50E **271** D5
Mkomazi △ *Tanzania* 4°4S 38°2E **268** C4
Mkulwe *Tanzania* 8°37S 32°20E **268** D3
Mkumbi, Ras *Tanzania* 7°38S 39°55E **268** D4
Mkushi *Zambia* 14°25S 29°15E **269** E2
Mkushi River *Zambia* 13°32S 29°45E **269** E2
Mkuze *S. Africa* 27°10S 32°0E **271** C5
Mladá Boleslav *Czech Rep.* 50°27N 14°53E **180** A7
Mladenovac *Serbia* 44°28N 20°44E **202** B5
Mlala Hills *Tanzania* 6°50S 31°40E **268** D3
M'lang *Phil.* 6°56N 124°52E **233** H5
Mlange = Mulanje, Mt.
Malawi 16°2S 35°33E **269** F4
Mlava → *Serbia* 44°45N 21°13E **202** B5
Mława *Poland* 53°9N 20°25E **185** B7
Mlawula △ *Swaziland* 26°12S 32°2E **271** C5
Mlinište *Bos.-H.* 44°15N 16°50E **199** D13
Mljet *Croatia* 42°43N 17°30E **199** F14
Mljet △ *Croatia* 42°45N 17°34E **199** F14
Mljetski Kanal *Croatia* 42°48N 17°35E **199** F14
Mlociny *Poland* 52°19N 20°57E **142** B3
Mlociny *Poland* 52°18N 21°3E **142** B4
Mlynary *Poland* 54°12N 19°46E **184** D6
Mmabatho *S. Africa* 25°49S 25°30E **270** C4
Mme *Cameroon* 6°18N 10°14E **263** D7
Mnevniki *Russia* 55°45N 37°28E **129** B2
Mnichovo Hradiště
Czech Rep. 50°32N 14°59E **180** A7
Mo *Hordaland, Norway* 60°49N 5°48E **164** D2
Mo *More og Romsdal, Norway* 63°40N 8°59E **164** A5
Mo *Telemark, Norway* 59°28N 7°50E **164** E4
Mo i Rana *Norway* 66°15N 14°7E **160** C16
Moa *Australia* 10°11S 142°16E **280** a
Moa *Cuba* 20°40N 74°56W **321** B4
Moa *Indonesia* 8°0S 128°0E **231** F7
Moa → *S. Leone* 6°59N 11°36W **262** D2
Moab *U.S.A.* 38°35N 109°33W **304** G9
Moabi *Gabon* 2°24S 10°59E **264** E2
Moala *Fiji* 18°36S 179°53E **287** B2
Moama *Australia* 36°7S 144°46E **283** C3
Moamba *Mozam.* 25°36S 32°15E **271** C5
Moapa *U.S.A.* 36°40N 114°37W **307** J12
Moate *Ireland* 53°24N 7°44W **166** C4
Moba *Dem. Rep. of the Congo* 7°0S 29°48E **268** D2
Moba *Lagos, Nigeria* 6°26N 3°28E **124** D2
Mobara *Japan* 35°25N 140°18E **223** B12
Mobārakābād *Iran* 28°24N 53°20E **247** D7
Mobaye *C.A.R.* 4°25N 21°5E **264** B4
Mobayi
Dem. Rep. of the Congo 4°15N 21°8E **264** B4
Moberly *U.S.A.* 39°25N 92°26W **310** F8
Moberly Lake *Canada* 55°50N 121°44W **296** B4
Mobile *U.S.A.* 30°41N 88°3W **315** F11
Mobile B. *U.S.A.* 30°30N 88°0W **315** F11
Mobridge *U.S.A.* 45°32N 100°26W **308** C4

Mobutu Sese Seko, L. = Albert, L.
Africa 1°30N 31°0E **268** B3
Moc Chau *Vietnam* 20°50N 104°38E **236** B5
Moc Hoa *Vietnam* 10°46N 105°56E **237** G5
Moca *Puerto Rico* 18°24N 67°10W **321** b
Mocabe Kasari
Dem. Rep. of the Congo 9°58S 26°12E **269** D2
Mocajuba *Brazil* 2°35S 49°30W **332** B2
Moçambique = Mozambique ■
Africa 19°0S 35°0E **269** F4
Moçambique *Mozam.* 15°3S 40°42E **269** F5
Moçâmedes = Namibe
Angola 15°7S 12°11E **265** F2
Mocanaqua *U.S.A.* 41°9N 76°8W **313** E8
Mocapra → *Venezuela* 7°56N 66°46W **328** B4
Mocha, Morro de *Angola* 12°28S 15°11E **265** E3
Moce *Fiji* 18°40S 178°29W **287** B3
Mocha = Al Mukhā
Yemen 13°18N 43°15E **248** D3
Mocha, I. *Chile* 38°22S 73°56W **336** A2
Mochos *Greece* 35°16N 25°27E **207** E6
Mochudi *Botswana* 24°27S 26°7E **270** B4
Mocimboa da Praia
Mozam. 11°25S 40°20E **269** E5
Mociu *Romania* 46°46N 24°3E **183** D9
Möckeln *Sweden* 56°40N 14°15E **163** H8
Mockfjärd *Sweden* 60°30N 14°57E **162** D8
Moclips *U.S.A.* 47°14N 124°13W **306** C2
Mocoa *Colombia* 1°15N 76°45W **328** C2
Mococa *Brazil* 21°28S 47°0W **335** A6
Mocorito *Mexico* 25°29N 107°55W **318** B3
Moctezuma *Mexico* 29°48N 109°42W **318** B3
Moctezuma → *Mexico* 21°59N 98°34W **319** C5
Mocuba *Mozam.* 16°54S 36°57E **269** F4
Mocúzari, Presa *Mexico* 27°10N 109°10W **318** B3
Moda *Burma* 24°22N 96°24E **241** A6
Modane *France* 45°12N 6°40E **175** C10
Modasa *India* 23°30N 73°21E **242** H5
Modder → *S. Africa* 29°2S 24°37E **270** C3
Modderfontein = Niekerkshoop
S. Africa 29°32S 22°51E **270** C3
Modderrivier *S. Africa* 26°5S 28°10E **123** A2
Modderrivier *S. Africa* 29°2N 24°38E **270** C3
Módena *Italy* 44°40N 10°55E **198** D7
Modena *Utah, U.S.A.* 37°48N 113°56W **305** H7
Modesto *U.S.A.* 37°39N 121°0W **306** H6
Modigliana *Italy* 44°9N 11°48E **199** D8
Modimolle *S. Africa* 24°42S 28°22E **271** A4
Modjamboli
Dem. Rep. of the Congo 2°28N 22°6E **264** B4
Mödling *Austria* 48°5N 16°17E **181** C9
Modo *Sudan* 5°31N 30°33E **257** F3
Modoc *U.S.A.* 33°44N 82°13W **317** E4
Modra *Slovak Rep.* 48°19N 17°20E **181** C10
Modřany *Czech Rep.* 50°0N 14°24E **135** B2
Modriča *Bos.-H.* 44°57N 18°17E **182** F3
Moe *Australia* 38°12S 146°19E **283** D6
Moebase *Mozam.* 17°3S 38°41E **269** F4
Moëlan-sur-Mer *France* 47°49N 3°38W **172** E3
Moelv *Norway* 60°56N 10°43E **164** D7
Moen I. = Weno *Pac. Oc.* 7°27N 151°52E **287** T18
Moengo *Suriname* 5°45N 54°20W **329** B7
Moerbeke *Belgium* 7°56N 66°46W **328** B4
Moga *India* 30°48N 75°8E **242** D6
Mogadiscio = Muqdisho
Somali Rep. 2°2N 45°25E **267** D6
Mogador = Essaouira
Morocco 31°32N 9°42W **260** B3
Mogadouro *Portugal* 41°22N 6°47W **194** D4
Mogami-Gawa → *Japan* 38°45N 140°0E **220** E10
Mogán *Canary Is.* 27°53N 15°43W **153** e1
Mogandjo
Dem. Rep. of the Congo 1°23N 24°15E **264** B4
Mogaung *Burma* 25°20N 97°0E **241** G6
Møgeltønder *Denmark* 54°57N 8°48E **163** J2
Mogente = Moixent *Spain* 38°50N 0°45W **197** G4
Mogho *Ethiopia* 4°54N 40°16E **257** F5
Mogi-Guaçu → *Brazil* 20°53S 48°10W **335** A6
Mogi das Cruzes *Brazil* 23°31S 46°11W **335** A6
Mogi-Mirim *Brazil* 22°29S 47°0W **335** A6
Mogielnica *Poland* 51°42N 20°41E **185** G7
Mogige *Ethiopia* 5°24N 36°14E **257** F4
Mogilev = Mahilyow
Belarus 53°55N 30°18E **177** B16
Mogilev-Podolskiy = Mohyliv-
Podilskyy *Ukraine* 48°26N 27°48E **183** D12
Mogilno *Poland* 52°39N 17°55E **185** F4
Mogincual *Mozam.* 15°35S 40°25E **269** F5
Mogliano Véneto *Italy* 45°33N 12°14E **199** C9
Mogocha *Russia* 53°40N 119°50E **215** D12
Mogoditshane *Botswana* 24°37S 25°57E **270** B4
Mogok *Burma* 23°0N 96°40E **241** D6
Mogollon Rim *U.S.A.* 34°10N 110°50W **305** J8
Mógoro *Italy* 39°41N 8°47E **200** C1
Mograt *Sudan* 19°28N 33°16E **256** D3
Mogroum *Chad* 11°6N 15°25E **259** F3
Moguer *Spain* 37°15N 6°52W **195** H4
Mogumber *Australia* 31°2S 116°3E **279** F2
Mogwadi → *S. Africa* 23°4S 29°36E **271** A4
Mogwase *S. Africa* 25°29N 27°6W **271** B4
Mogyoród *Hungary* 47°35N 19°14E **117** A3
Mohács *Hungary* 45°58N 18°41E **182** F3
Mohaka → *N.Z.* 39°7S 177°12E **284** F6
Mohala *India* 20°35N 80°44E **244** D5
Mohales Hoek *Lesotho* 30°7S 27°26E **270** D4
Mohali *Congo* 0°15N 15°29E **264** B3
Mohall *U.S.A.* 48°46N 101°31W **308** A4
Mohammadābād *Iran* 37°52N 59°5E **247** B8
Mohammedia *Morocco* 35°30N 9°36E **258** B1
Mohammedia *Morocco* 33°44N 7°21W **260** B3
Mohammerah = Khorramshahr
Iran 30°29N 48°15E **247** D6
Mohana *India* 19°27N 84°24E **244** D7
Mohana → *India* 24°43N 85°0E **243** G11
Mohanganj *Bangla.* 24°54N 90°59E **241** D3
Mohanlalganj *India* 26°41N 80°58E **243** F9
Mohave, L. *U.S.A.* 35°12N 114°34W **307** K12
Mohawk → *U.S.A.* 42°47N 73°41W **313** D11
Moheda *Sweden* 57°1N 14°35E **163** H8
Mohéli *Comoros Is.* 12°20S 43°40E **272** a
Mohéli × (NWA)
Comoros Is. 12°19S 43°47E **272** a
Mohenjodaro *Pakistan* 27°19N 68°7E **242** F3
Moher, Cliffs of *Ireland* 52°58N 9°27W **166** D2
Mohican, C. *U.S.A.* 60°12N 167°25W **303** F6
Mohicanville Res. *U.S.A.* 40°45N 82°9W **312** F2
Möhne → *Germany* 51°29N 7°57E **178** D3
Mohns Ridge *Arctic* 72°30N 5°0E **150** B7
Mohnyin *Burma* 24°47N 96°22E **241** G6
Mohoro *Tanzania* 8°6S 39°8E **268** D4
Mohsenābād *Iran* 36°40N 59°35E **247** B8
Mohyliv-Podilskyy
Ukraine 48°26N 27°48E **183** D12
Moi *Norway* 58°27N 6°32E **164** F3
Moia *Sudan* 5°3N 28°2E **257** F2
Moidart, L. *U.K.* 56°47N 5°52W **167** E3
Moinești *Romania* 46°28N 26°31E **183** D11
Moinho Velho, Cor. →
Brazil 23°35S 46°35W **137** B2
Moira → *Canada* 44°21N 77°24W **312** B7

Moirang *India* 24°30N 93°46E **241** C4
Moirans *France* 45°20N 5°33E **175** C9
Moirans-en-Montagne
France 46°26N 5°43E **173** F12
Moisakula *Estonia* 58°3N 25°12E **188** C3
Moisie *Canada* 50°12N 66°1W **299** B6
Moisie → *Canada* 50°14N 66°5W **299** B6
Moissac *France* 44°7N 1°5E **174** C5
Moïssala *Chad* 8°21N 17°46E **259** G3
Moita *Portugal* 38°38N 8°58E **195** G2
Moixent *Spain* 38°50N 0°45W **197** G4
Möja *Sweden* 59°26N 18°55E **163** D12
Mojácar *Spain* 37°6N 1°55W **197** H3
Mojados *Spain* 41°26N 4°40W **194** D6
Mojave *U.S.A.* 35°3N 118°10W **307** K8
Mojave △ *U.S.A.* 35°0N 116°30W **307** L10
Mojave Desert *U.S.A.* 35°0N 116°30W **307** K11
Moji-Guaçu *Brazil* 20°53S 48°10W **335** A6
Moji-Guaçu → *Brazil* 20°53S 48°10W **335** A6
Mojiang *China* 23°37N 101°35E **228** D3
Mojjo → *Ethiopia* 7°55N 42°0E **257** F5
Mojkovac *Montenegro* 42°58N 19°35E **202** D3
Mojo *Bolivia* 21°48S 65°33W **334** A2
Mojo *Ethiopia* 8°35N 39°5E **257** F4
Mojokerto *Indonesia* 7°28S 112°26E **235** D4
Mojos, Llanos de *Bolivia* 15°10S 65°0W **331** D5
Moju *Brazil* 1°53S 48°46W **332** B2
Moju → *Brazil* 1°40S 48°25W **332** B2
Mok, S. Korea *S. Korea* 37°32N 126°52E **137** G5
Moka *Mauritius* 20°13S 57°29E **272** e
Mokai *N.Z.* 38°32S 175°56E **284** F4
Mokala △ *S. Africa* 29°10S 24°10E **270** C3
Mokameh
Dem. Rep. of the Congo 12°25S 28°20E **269** E2
Mokameh *India* 25°24N 85°55E **243** G11
Mokane *U.S.A.* 38°41N 91°53W **310** F8
Mokapu Peninsula
U.S.A. 21°25N 157°45W **302** K14
Mokau *N.Z.* 38°42S 174°39E **284** E3
Mokau → *N.Z.* 38°35S 174°35E **284** E3
Mokelumne → *U.S.A.* 38°13N 121°28W **306** G5
Mokelumne Hill *U.S.A.* 38°18N 120°43W **306** G6
Mokhotlong *Lesotho* 29°22S 29°2E **271** C4
Mokihinui *N.Z.* 41°33S 171°58E **285** B6
Möklinta *Sweden* 60°4N 16°33E **162** D10
Mokoan, L. *Australia* 36°25S 146°5E **283** D7
Mokokchung *India* 26°15N 94°30E **241** B5
Mōkōlea Rock *U.S.A.* 21°27N 157°44W **302** K14
Mokolo *Cameroon* 10°35N 13°54E **259** F2
Mokolo →
Dem. Rep. of the Congo 1°55N 18°6E **264** B3
Mokolo → *S. Africa* 23°14S 27°43E **271** B4
Mokombe
Dem. Rep. of the Congo 0°14S 23°48E **264** C4
Mokopane *S. Africa* 24°10S 28°55E **271** A4
Mokotów *Poland* 52°12N 21°0E **142** B2
Mokpo *S. Korea* 34°50N 126°25E **229** C7
Mokra Gora *Europe* 42°50N 20°30E **202** D4
Mokronog *Slovenia* 45°57N 15°9E **199** C12
Moksha → *Russia* 54°45N 41°53E **190** C6
Mokshan *Russia* 53°25N 44°35E **190** D7
Mokuauia I. *U.S.A.* 21°40N 157°56W **302** J14
Mokulē'ia *U.S.A.* 21°35N 158°9W **302** L13
Mokulua Is. *U.S.A.* 21°24N 157°42W **302** K14
Mokumanu *U.S.A.* 21°28N 157°43W **302** K14
Mokwa *Nigeria* 9°19N 5°0E **263** D6
Mol *Belgium* 51°11N 5°5E **170** C5
Mola di Bari *Italy* 41°4N 17°5E **201** A10
Molai *Greece* 36°49N 22°56E **204** E4
Molakalmuru *India* 14°55N 76°50E **245** G3
Molale *Ethiopia* 10°10N 39°41E **257** E4
Molaly *Kazakhstan* 45°27N 78°18E **217** C9
Molanda
Dem. Rep. of the Congo 2°2N 22°5E **264** B4
Molara *Italy* 40°52N 9°43E **200** B2
Molat *Croatia* 44°15N 14°50E **199** D11
Molave *Phil.* 8°5N 123°30E **233** G4
Molchanova *Russia* 57°40N 83°50E **214** D9
Mold *U.K.* 53°9N 3°8W **168** D4
Moldava nad Bodvou
Slovak Rep. 48°38N 21°0E **181** C14
Moldavia = Moldova ■
Europe 47°0N 28°0E **183** C13
Moldavia *Romania* 46°30N 27°0E **183** D12
Molde *Norway* 62°45N 7°9E **164** A4
Moldova ■ *Europe* 47°0N 28°0E **183** C13
Moldova → *Romania* 46°38N 27°0E **183** C12
Moldova Nouă *Romania* 44°45N 21°41E **182** F6
Moldoveanu, Vf. *Romania* 45°36N 24°45E **183** F9
Moldoveanu *Romania* 47°41N 25°32E **183** C10
Mole → *U.K.* 51°24N 0°21W **125** C2
Mole △ *Ghana* 9°43N 1°44W **263** D4
Molegbwe
Dem. Rep. of the Congo 4°12N 20°53E **264** B4
Molekolole *Botswana* 24°28S 25°28E **270** B4
Molepolole *Botswana* 24°28S 25°28E **270** B4
Molesworth *N.Z.* 42°5S 173°16E **285** C6
Molfetta *Italy* 41°12N 16°36E **201** A9
Molì'i Pond *U.S.A.* 21°31N 157°51W **302** J14
Molina de Aragón *Spain* 40°46N 1°52W **196** D3
Molina de Segura *Spain* 38°3N 1°12W **197** G3
Moline *U.S.A.* 41°30N 90°31W **310** D8
Molinella *Italy* 44°37N 11°40E **199** D8
Molino de Rosas *Mexico* 19°21N 99°14W **128** B1
Molinos *Argentina* 25°28S 66°15W **334** B2
Moliro
Dem. Rep. of the Congo 8°12S 30°30E **268** D3
Moliterno *Italy* 40°14N 15°52E **201** B8
Molkom *Sweden* 59°37N 13°44E **162** D7
Mölle *Sweden* 56°17N 12°31E **163** H6
Molledo *Spain* 43°8N 4°6E **194** A7
Mollendo *Peru* 17°0S 72°0W **330** D3
Mollerin, L. *Australia* 30°30S 117°35E **279** F2
Mollerussa *Spain* 41°37N 0°54E **196** D6
Mollina *Spain* 37°8N 4°38W **195** H6
Mollins de Rey *Spain* 41°24N 2°1E **114** A1
Mölln *Germany* 53°37N 10°41E **178** B6
Mölltorp *Sweden* 58°30N 14°26E **163** F8
Mölndal *Sweden* 57°40N 12°3E **163** H6
Mölnlycke *Sweden* 57°40N 12°3E **163** H6
Molo *Burma* 23°22N 96°53E **241** D6
Molo *Kenya* 0°15S 35°44E **268** C4
Molochansk *Ukraine* 47°15N 35°35E **191** B8
Molochnoye, Ozero
Ukraine 46°30N 35°20E **189** J8
Molodechno = Maladzyechna
Belarus 54°20N 26°50E **177** A13
Molodezhnaya *Antarctica* 67°40S 45°51E **151** C5
Molodovoe *Ukraine* 51°38N 29°29E **183** D14
Moloka'i *U.S.A.* 21°8N 157°0W **302** B6
Molokai Fracture Zone
Pac. Oc. 28°0N 125°0W **289** C10
Molokini I. *U.S.A.* 20°38N 156°30W **302** C5
Molong *Australia* 33°5S 148°54E **283** B8
Molopo → *Africa* 28°30S 20°12E **270** C2
Molos *Greece* 38°47N 22°37E **204** C4
Molotov = Perm *Russia* 58°0N 56°10E **186** C10
Molotov, Mys = Arkticheskiy, Mys
Russia 81°10N 95°0E **215** A10
Molotovsk = Nolinsk
Russia 57°28N 49°57E **190** B9

Molotovsk = Severodvinsk
Russia 64°27N 39°58E **186** B6
Molotovskoye =
Krasnogvardeyskoye
Russia 45°52N 41°33E **191** H5
Moloundou *Cameroon* 2°8N 15°15E **264** B3
Molowaie
Dem. Rep. of the Congo 5°47S 23°18E **265** D4
Molsheim *France* 48°33N 7°29E **173** D14
Molson L. *Canada* 54°22N 96°40W **297** C9
Molteno *S. Africa* 31°22S 26°22E **270** E4
Molu *Indonesia* 6°45S 131°40E **231** F8
Molucca Sea *Indonesia* 0°0 125°0E **231** E6
Moluccas = Maluku
Indonesia 1°0S 127°0E **231** E7
Molundu *Phil.* 7°57N 124°23E **233** H5
Moma *Dem. Rep. of the Congo* 1°35S 23°52E **264** C4
Moma *Mozam.* 16°47S 39°4E **269** F4
Momba *Australia* 30°58S 143°30E **282** B5
Mombaça *Brazil* 5°43S 39°45W **332** C4
Mombango
Dem. Rep. of the Congo 1°45N 24°26E **264** B4
Mombasa *Kenya* 4°3S 39°40E **268** C4
Mombetsu *Japan* 44°21N 143°22E **220** B11
Mombil *Burma* 27°46N 98°6E **241** B7
Momboyo →
Dem. Rep. of the Congo 0°16S 19°0E **264** C3
Mombuey *Spain* 42°3N 6°20W **194** C4
Momchilgrad *Bulgaria* 41°33N 25°23E **203** E9
Momence *U.S.A.* 41°10N 87°40W **311** C9
Momi *Dem. Rep. of the Congo* 1°42S 27°0E **268** C2
Momote *Papua N. G.* 2°4S 147°27E **286** B4
Mompoq Pass. *Phil.* 13°34N 122°12E **232** E4
Mompós *Colombia* 9°14N 74°26W **328** B3
Møn *Denmark* 54°57N 12°20E **163** K6
Mon □ *Burma* 16°0N 97°30E **241** G6
Mon → *Burma* 16°0N 97°30E **241** G6
Mona, Canal de la = Mona Passage
W. Indies 18°30N 67°45W **321** C6
Mona, Isla *Puerto Rico* 18°5N 67°54W **321** C6
Mona, Pta. *Costa Rica* 9°37N 82°36W **320** E3
Mona Passage *W. Indies* 18°30N 67°45W **321** C6
Monaca *U.S.A.* 40°41N 80°17W **312** F4
Monadhliath Mts. *U.K.* 57°10N 4°4W **167** D8
Monadnock, Mt. *U.S.A.* 42°52N 72°7W **313** D12
Monagas □ *Venezuela* 9°20N 63°0W **329** B5
Monaghan *Ireland* 54°15N 6°57W **166** B5
Monaghan □ *Ireland* 54°11N 6°56W **166** B5
Monahans *U.S.A.* 31°36N 102°54W **314** F3
Monapo *Mozam.* 14°56S 40°19E **269** F5
Monar, L. *U.K.* 57°26N 5°8W **167** D7
Monaragala *Sri Lanka* 6°52N 81°2E **245** L5
Monarch Mt. *Canada* 51°55N 125°57W **296** C3
Monashee Mts. *Canada* 51°0N 118°43W **296** C5
Monasterevin *Ireland* 53°8N 7°4W **166** C4
Monastir = Bitola
Macedonia 41°1N 21°20E **202** E5
Monastir *Tunisia* 35°50N 10°49E **258** A2
Monastir □ *Tunisia* 35°37N 10°54E **261** A7
Monbetsu *Japan* 42°30N 142°10E **220** C11
Moncalieri *Italy* 45°0N 7°41E **198** D4
Moncalvo *Italy* 45°3N 8°16E **198** D5
Moncarapacho *Portugal* 37°5N 7°46W **195** H3
Moncayo, Sierra del *Spain* 41°48N 1°50W **196** D3
Moncha-Guba = Monchegorsk
Russia 67°54N 32°58E **160** C25
Monchegorsk *Russia* 67°54N 32°58E **160** C25
Mönchengladbach
Germany 51°11N 6°27E **178** D2
Monchique *Portugal* 37°19N 8°38W **195** H2
Moncks Corner *U.S.A.* 33°12N 80°1W **316** E5
Monclova *Mexico* 26°54N 101°25W **318** B4
Moncontour *France* 48°22N 2°38W **172** D4
Moncton *Canada* 46°7N 64°51W **299** C7
Mondariz *Spain* 42°14N 8°27W **194** C2
Mondego → *Portugal* 40°9N 8°54W **194** E2
Mondego, C. *Portugal* 40°11N 8°54W **194** E2
Mondeodo *Indonesia* 3°34S 122°9E **231** E6
Mondeor *S. Africa* 26°16S 28°2E **123** B2
Mondeville *France* 49°10N 0°18W **172** C6
Mondo *Chad* 13°47N 15°32E **259** F3
Mondolfo *Italy* 43°45N 13°8E **199** E10
Mondoñedo *Spain* 43°25N 7°23W **194** B3
Mondovi *Italy* 44°23N 7°49E **198** D4
Mondragó *Spain* 39°21N 3°12E **206** B4
Mondragon = Arrasate
Spain 43°4N 2°30W **196** B2
Mondragone *Italy* 41°7N 13°53E **200** A6
Mondrain I. *Australia* 34°9S 122°14E **279** F3
Moneague *Jamaica* 18°16N 77°7W **320** a
Moneron, Ostrov
Russia 46°15N 141°16E **220** A10
Monessen *U.S.A.* 40°9N 79°54W **312** F5
Monesterio *Spain* 38°6N 6°15W **195** G4
Monestier-de-Clermont
France 44°55N 5°38E **175** D9
Monett *U.S.A.* 36°55N 93°55W **308** F7
Moneymore *U.K.* 54°41N 6°40W **166** B5
Monfalcone *Italy* 45°49N 13°32E **199** C10
Monflanquin *France* 44°32N 0°47E **174** D4
Monforte *Portugal* 39°6N 7°25W **195** F3
Monforte de Lemos *Spain* 42°31N 7°33W **194** C3
Mong Hpayak *Burma* 20°52N 99°55E **236** B2
Mong Hsat *Burma* 20°31N 99°51E **236** B2
Mong Hsu *Burma* 21°54N 98°30E **241** G7
Mong Hta *Burma* 19°50N 98°35E **241** H7
Mong Kok *China* 22°19N 114°10E **122** B2
Mong Kung *Burma* 21°35N 97°35E **241** H7
Mong Kyawt *Burma* 19°56N 98°45E **241** H7
Mong Long *Burma* 22°7N 96°41E **241** H7
Mong Nai *Burma* 20°32N 97°46E **241** J7
Mong Pan *Burma* 20°17N 98°45E **241** J7
Mong Ping *Burma* 21°22N 99°2E **241** J7
Mong Ton *Burma* 20°17N 98°45E **241** J7
Mong Wa *Burma* 21°26N 100°27E **241** J8
Mong Yai *Burma* 22°21N 98°3E **241** H7
Mong Yang *Burma* 21°54N 99°39E **241** H7
Mong Yu *Burma* 23°30N 97°42E **241** H7
Mongala →
Dem. Rep. of the Congo 1°53N 19°46E **264** B3
Mongalla *Sudan* 5°8N 31°42E **257** F3
Mongandjo
Dem. Rep. of the Congo 1°53N 19°46E **264** B3
Mongar *Bhutan* 27°17N 91°15E **243** F13
Mongers, L. *Australia* 29°25S 117°5E **279** E2
Mongga *Solomon Is.* 7°52S 157°0E **287** a
Monghyr = Munger
India 25°23N 86°30E **243** G12
Mongibello = Etna *Italy* 37°50N 14°55E **201** E7

Mongla *Bangla.* 22°8N 89°35E **241** D8
Mongmong *Guam* 13°28N 144°45E **302** d
Mongngaw *Burma* 22°47N 96°59E **241** D6
Mongo *Chad* 12°14N 18°43E **259** F3
Mongo *Eq. Guin.* 1°52N 10°10E **264** B2
Mongo → *S. Leone* 9°35N 12°10W **262** D2
Mongolia ■ *Asia* 47°0N 103°0E **218** D9
Mongomo *Eq. Guin.* 1°38N 11°19E **264** D2
Mongonu *Nigeria* 13°32S 43°50E **269** C2
Mongororo *Chad* 12°3N 22°26E **259** F4
Mongstad *Norway* 60°49N 5°2E **164** D2
Mongu *Zambia* 15°16S 23°12E **265** F4
Môngua *Angola* 16°43S 15°20E **265** D3
Moniac *U.S.A.* 30°31N 82°14W **316** F7
Monifieth *U.K.* 56°30N 2°48W **167** E6
Monistrol-sur-Loire *France* 45°17N 4°11E **175** C8
Monkayo *Phil.* 7°57N 126°5E **233** H6
Monkey Bay *Malawi* 14°7S 35°1E **269** E4
Monkey Mia *Australia* 25°48S 113°43E **279** E1
Monkey River *Belize* 16°22N 88°29W **320** C2
Monkey Town *Trin. & Tob.* 10°12N 61°25W **323** t
Mońki *Poland* 53°23N 22°48E **184** E9
Monkland *Canada* 45°11N 74°52W **313** A10
Monkoto
Dem. Rep. of the Congo 1°38S 20°35E **264** C4
Monkstown *Ireland* 53°18N 6°10W **120** B3
Monkton *Canada* 43°35N 81°5W **312** C3
Monmouth *Monmouths.□
U.K.* 51°48N 2°42W **169** F5
Monmouth *Ill., U.S.A.* 40°55N 90°39W **310** D7
Monmouth *Oreg., U.S.A.* 44°51N 123°14W **304** D2
Monmouthshire □ *U.K.* 51°48N 2°54W **169** F5
Monnickendam *Neths.* 52°28N 5°2E **112** A3
Mono *Solomon Is.* 7°20S 155°35E **287** L8
Mono → *Togo* 6°17N 1°51E **263** D5
Mono, Pta. *Nic.* 12°0N 83°30W **320** D3
Mono L. *U.S.A.* 38°1N 119°1W **306** H7
Monolith *U.S.A.* 35°7N 118°22W **307** K8
Monólithos *Greece* 36°7N 27°45E **206** C1
Monon *U.S.A.* 40°52N 86°53W **311** D10
Monona *Iowa, U.S.A.* 43°3N 91°23W **310** A8
Monona *Wis., U.S.A.* 43°4N 89°20W **310** A7
Monongahela *U.S.A.* 40°12N 79°56W **312** F5
Monópoli *Italy* 40°57N 17°18E **201** B10
Monor *Hungary* 47°21N 19°27E **182** C4
Monos I. *Trin. & Tob.* 10°42N 61°44W **323** t
Monóvar *Spain* 38°28N 0°53W **197** G4
Monowai *N.Z.* 45°53S 167°31E **285** F2
Monowai, L. *N.Z.* 45°53S 167°25E **285** F2
Monqoumba *C.A.R.* 3°33N 18°40E **264** B3
Monreal del Campo *Spain* 40°47N 1°20W **196** D3
Monreale *Italy* 38°5N 13°17E **200** D6
Monroe *Ga., U.S.A.* 33°47N 83°43W **316** B6
Monroe *Iowa, U.S.A.* 41°31N 93°6W **310** C7
Monroe *La., U.S.A.* 32°30N 92°7W **314** E8
Monroe *Mich., U.S.A.* 41°55N 83°24W **311** C14
Monroe *N.C., U.S.A.* 34°59N 80°33W **315** D14
Monroe *N.Y., U.S.A.* 41°20N 74°11W **313** E10
Monroe *Ohio, U.S.A.* 39°27N 84°22W **311** E12
Monroe *Utah, U.S.A.* 38°38N 112°7W **304** G7
Monroe *Wash., U.S.A.* 47°51N 121°58W **306** C5
Monroe, L. *U.S.A.* 28°50N 81°19W **317** G5
Monroe City *U.S.A.* 39°39N 91°44W **310** F8
Monroe City *Mo., U.S.A.* 39°39N 91°44W **310** F8
Monroeton *U.S.A.* 41°43N 76°29W **313** E8
Monroeville *Ala., U.S.A.* 31°31N 87°20W **315** F11
Monroeville *Pa., U.S.A.* 40°26N 79°45W **312** F5
Monrovia *Liberia* 6°18N 10°47W **262** D2
Monrovia *Calif., U.S.A.* 34°9N 118°1W **126** B4
Mons *Belgium* 50°27N 3°58E **170** D3
Møns Klint *Denmark* 54°57N 12°33E **163** K6
Monsanto *Portugal* 38°44N 9°12W **126** A1
Monsanto, Parque Florestal de
Portugal 38°43N 9°11W **126** A1
Monsaraz *Portugal* 38°28N 7°22W **195** G3
Monse *Indonesia* 4°7S 123°15E **231** E6
Monsefú *Peru* 6°52S 79°52W **330** B2
Monségur *France* 44°38N 0°4E **174** D4
Mönsterås *Sweden* 57°3N 16°26E **163** H10
Mont-de-Marsan *France* 43°54N 0°31W **174** E3
Mont-Dore *N. Cal.* 22°16S 166°34E **288** d
Mont Fouari △ *Congo* 2°52S 11°32E **264** C2
Mont-Joli *Canada* 48°37N 68°10W **299** C6
Mont-Laurier *Canada* 46°35N 75°30W **298** C4
Mont-Louis *Canada* 49°15N 65°44W **299** C6
Mont Peko △ *Ivory C.* 7°0N 7°15E **262** D3
Mont-roig del Camp *Spain* 41°5N 0°58E **196** D6
Mont-Royal *Canada* 45°30N 73°38W **130** A2
Mont-Royal, Parc *Canada* 45°30N 73°35W **130** A2
Mont-St-Michel, Le *France* 48°40N 1°30W **172** D5
Mont Sangbé △ *Ivory C.* 8°0N 7°10W **262** D3
Mont-Tremblant
Canada 46°30N 74°30W **298** C5
Montabaur *Germany* 50°26N 7°50E **178** E3
Montagnac = Remchi
Algeria 35°2N 1°26W **261** A4
Montagnac *France* 43°29N 3°28E **174** E7
Montagnana *Italy* 45°14N 11°29E **199** C8
Montagne Blanche
Mauritius 20°16S 57°39E **272** e
Montagne d'Ambre △
Madag. 12°35S 49°8E **272** A2
Montagne de Reims △
France 49°8N 4°0E **173** C11
Montagu *S. Africa* 33°45S 20°8E **270** D3
Montagu I. *Antarctica* 58°25S 26°20W **151** B1
Montague *Canada* 46°10N 62°39W **299** C7
Montague *Calif., U.S.A.* 41°45N 114°48W **318** A2
Montague, I. *Mexico* 31°45N 114°48W **318** A2
Montague I. *Alaska,
U.S.A.* 60°0N 147°30W **303** G11
Montague Ra. *Australia* 27°15S 119°30E **279** E2
Montague Sd. *Australia* 14°28S 125°20E **278** B4
Montaigu *France* 46°59N 1°18W **172** F5
Montalbán *Spain* 40°50N 0°45W **196** E4
Montalbano Iónico *Italy* 40°17N 16°34E **201** B9
Montalbo *Spain* 39°53N 2°42W **196** F2
Montalcino *Italy* 43°3N 11°29E **198** E8
Montalegre *Portugal* 41°49N 7°47W **194** D3
Montalto *Italy* 38°50N 16°7E **201** C9
Montalto di Castro *Italy* 42°21N 11°37E **199** F8
Montalto Uffugo *Italy* 39°24N 16°9E **201** C9
Montalvo *U.S.A.* 34°15N 119°12W **307** L7
Montana *Bulgaria* 43°27N 23°16E **202** C7
Montaña *Peru* 6°0S 73°0W **330** B2
Montana □ *U.S.A.* 47°0N 110°0W **304** C8
Montaña Clara, I.
Canary Is. 29°17N 13°33W **153** e2
Montana de Montjuich
Spain 41°21N 2°9E **114** A1
Montañas de Málaga △
Spain 36°48N 4°32W **195** J6
Montánchez *Spain* 39°15N 6°8W **195** F4
Montañas do Tumucumaque
Brazil 2°5N 53°0W **329** C7

Montañita Colombia 1°22N 75°28W 328 C2
Montargil Portugal 39°5N 8°10W 195 F2
Montargis France 47°59N 2°43E 173 E9
Montauban France 44°2N 1°21E 174 D5
Montauk U.S.A. 41°3N 71°57W 313 E13
Montauk Pt. U.S.A. 41°4N 71°51W 313 E13
Montbard France 47°38N 4°20E 173 E11
Montbarrey France 47°1N 5°39E 173 E12
Montbéliard France 47°31N 6°48E 173 E13
Montblanc Spain 41°23N 1°4E 196 D6
Montbrison France 45°36N 4°3E 175 C8
Montcada i Reixac Spain 41°29N 2°12W 114 A2
Montcalm, Pic de France 42°40N 1°25E 174 F5
Montceau-les-Mines France 46°40N 4°23E 173 F11
Montcenis France 46°47N 4°23E 175 B8
Montclair U.S.A. 40°49N 74°12W 313 F10
Montcornet France 49°40N 4°1E 173 C11
Montcuq France 44°21N 1°13E 174 D5
Montdidier France 49°38N 2°35E 173 C9
Monte Albán Mexico 17°2N 96°46W 319 D5
Monte Alegre Brazil 2°0S 54°0W 329 D7
Monte Alegre de Goiás Brazil 13°14S 47°10W 333 D2
Monte Alegre de Minas Brazil 18°52S 48°52W 333 E2
Monte Alegre do Piauí Brazil 9°46S 45°18W 332 C2
Monte Azul Brazil 15°9S 42°53W 333 E3
Monte-Carlo Monaco 43°44N 7°25E 175 E11
Monte Carmelo Brazil 18°43S 47°29W 333 E2
Monte Caseros Argentina 30°10S 57°50W 334 C4
Monte Chingolo Argentina 34°43S 58°22W 117 C2
Monte Comán Argentina 34°40S 67°53W 334 C2
Monte Cristi Dom. Rep. 19°52N 71°39W 321 C5
Monte Cucco △ Italy 43°22N 12°43E 199 E9
Monte Dinero Argentina 52°18S 68°33W 336 D3
Monte Dourado Brazil 0°52S 52°31W 329 D7
Monte Lindo ➝ Paraguay 23°56S 57°12W 334 A4
Monte Palatino Rome, Italy 136 c3
Monte Pascoal △ Brazil 16°51S 39°21W 333 E4
Monte Patria Chile 30°42S 70°58W 334 C1
Monte Quemado Argentina 25°53S 62°41W 334 B3
Monte Redondo Portugal 39°53N 8°50W 194 F2
Monte Rio U.S.A. 38°28N 123°0W 306 G4
Monte San Giovanni Campano Italy 41°38N 13°31E 200 A6
Monte San Giuliano = Érice Italy 38°2N 12°35E 200 D5
Monte San Savino Italy 43°20N 11°43E 199 E8
Monte Sant' Ángelo Italy 41°42N 15°59E 199 G12
Monte Santu, C. di Italy 40°5N 9°44E 200 B2
Monte Sibillini △ Italy 42°55N 13°15E 199 F10
Monte Subasio △ Italy 43°5N 12°40E 199 E9
Monte Vista U.S.A. 37°35N 106°9W 305 H10
Monteagudo Argentina 27°14S 54°8W 335 B5
Monteagudo Bolivia 19°49S 63°59W 331 D5
Montealegre del Castillo Spain 38°48N 1°17W 197 G3
Montebello Qué., Canada 45°40N 74°55W 298 C5
Montebello Guadeloupe 16°10N 61°36W 322 e
Montebello Calif., U.S.A. 34°1N 118°8W 126 B4
Montebello Iónico Italy 37°59N 15°45E 201 E8
Montebello Is. Australia 20°30S 115°45E 278 D2
Montebelluna Italy 45°47N 12°3E 199 C9
Montebourg France 49°30N 1°20W 172 C5
Montecarlo Argentina 26°34S 54°47W 335 B5
Montecastrilli Italy 42°39N 12°29E 199 F9
Montecatini Terme Italy 43°53N 10°46E 198 E7
Montecito U.S.A. 34°26N 119°40W 307 L7
Montecristi Ecuador 1°0S 80°40W 328 D1
Montecristo Italy 42°20N 10°19E 198 F7
Montefalco Italy 42°54N 12°39E 199 F9
Montefiascone Italy 42°32N 12°2E 199 F9
Montefrío Spain 37°20N 4°0W 195 H7
Montegiórgio Italy 43°6N 13°33E 199 E10
Montego B. Jamaica 18°28N 77°56W 320 a
Montego Bay Jamaica 18°28N 77°55W 320 a
Montehermoso Spain 40°5N 6°21W 194 E4
Monteiro Brazil 7°48S 37°2W 332 C4
Montejicar Spain 37°33N 3°30W 195 H7
Montelbaanstoren Amsterdam, Neths. 112 b3
Monteleone di Calabria = Vibo Valéntia Italy 38°40N 16°6E 201 D9
Montelíbano Colombia 8°5N 75°29W 328 B2
Montélimar France 44°33N 4°45E 175 D8
Montella Italy 40°51N 15°1E 201 B8
Montellano Spain 36°59N 5°29W 195 J5
Montello U.S.A. 43°48N 89°20W 308 D9
Montemayor, Meseta de Argentina 44°20S 66°10W 336 B3
Montemor Portugal 38°49N 9°12W 126 A1
Montemor-o-Novo Portugal 38°40N 8°12W 195 G2
Montemor-o-Velho Portugal 40°11N 8°40W 194 E2
Montemorelos Mexico 25°12N 99°49W 319 B5
Montendre France 45°16N 0°26W 174 C3
Montenegro Brazil 29°39S 51°29W 335 B5
Montenegro ■ Europe 42°40N 19°20E 202 D3
Montenero di Bisáccia Italy 41°57N 14°47E 199 G11
Montepuez Mozam. 13°8S 38°59E 269 E4
Montepuez ➝ Mozam. 12°32S 40°27E 269 E5
Montepulciano Italy 43°5N 11°47E 199 E8
Montereale Italy 42°31N 13°15E 199 F10
Montereau-Faut-Yonne France 48°22N 2°57E 173 D9
Monterey Calif., U.S.A. 36°37N 121°55W 306 J5
Monterey Ind., U.S.A. 41°11N 86°30W 311 C10
Monterey B. U.S.A. 36°45N 122°0W 306 J5
Monterey Hills U.S.A. 34°6N 118°10W 126 B3
Monterey Park U.S.A. 34°3N 118°7W 126 B4
Montería Colombia 8°46N 75°53W 328 B2
Montero Bolivia 17°20S 63°15W 331 D5
Monteros Argentina 27°11S 65°30W 334 B2
Monterotondo Italy 42°3N 12°37E 199 F9
Monterrey Mexico 25°40N 100°19W 318 B4
Montes Altos Brazil 5°50S 47°4W 332 C2
Montes Azules △ Mexico 16°21N 91°3W 319 D6
Montes Claros Brazil 16°30S 43°50W 333 E3
Montesano U.S.A. 46°59N 123°36W 306 D3
Montesano sulla Marcellana Italy 40°16N 15°42E 201 B8
Montesárchio Italy 41°4N 14°38E 201 A7
Montescaglioso Italy 40°33N 16°40E 201 B9
Montesilvano Italy 42°29N 14°8E 199 F11
Montesinho △ Portugal 41°54N 6°52W 194 D4
Montespaccato Italy 41°54N 12°23E 136 B1
Montesson France 48°54N 2°8E 134 A1
Montevarchi Italy 43°31N 11°34E 199 E8
Monteverde Nuovo Italy 41°52N 12°26E 136 B1
Montevideo Uruguay 34°50S 56°11W 335 C4
Montevideo Minn., U.S.A. 44°57N 95°43W 308 C6
Montezuma Ga., U.S.A. 32°18N 84°2W 316 C5
Montezuma Ind., U.S.A. 39°48N 87°22W 311 E9
Montezuma Iowa, U.S.A. 41°35N 92°32W 310 C4
Montezuma Castle △ U.S.A. 34°39N 111°45W 305 J8
Montfaucon France 47°6N 1°7W 172 E5
Montfaucon-d'Argonne France 49°16N 5°8E 173 C12
Montfaucon-en-Velay France 45°11N 4°20E 175 C8
Montfermeil France 48°54N 2°33E 134 A4
Montfort-le-Gesnois France 48°3N 0°25E 172 D7
Montfort-sur-Meu France 48°9N 1°58W 172 D5
Montfragüe △ Spain 39°48N 5°52W 194 F5
Montgenèvre France 44°56N 6°43E 175 D10
Montgomery = Sahiwal Pakistan 30°45N 73°8E 242 D5
Montgomery Powys, U.K. 52°34N 3°8W 169 E4
Montgomery Ala., U.S.A. 32°23N 86°19W 316 C3
Montgomery Ill., U.S.A. 41°44N 88°21W 311 C8
Montgomery Pa., U.S.A. 41°10N 76°53W 312 E8
Montgomery W. Va., U.S.A. 38°11N 81°19W 309 F13
Montgomery City U.S.A. 38°59N 91°30W 310 F5
Montguyon France 45°12N 0°12W 174 C3
Monthermé France 49°52N 4°42E 173 C11
Monthey Switz. 46°15N 6°56E 179 J2
Monthois France 49°19N 4°43E 173 C11
Monti Italy 40°49N 9°19E 200 B2
Monti Lucrétili △ Italy 42°5N 12°50E 199 F9
Monti Picentini △ Italy 40°45N 15°2E 201 B8
Monti Simbruini △ Italy 41°55N 13°13E 199 G10
Monticelli d'Ongina Italy 45°5N 9°56E 198 C6
Monticello Ark., U.S.A. 33°38N 91°47W 314 E9
Monticello Fla., U.S.A. 30°33N 83°52W 316 E6
Monticello Ga., U.S.A. 33°18N 83°40W 316 B6
Monticello Ill., U.S.A. 40°1N 88°34W 311 D8
Monticello Ind., U.S.A. 40°45N 86°46W 311 D10
Monticello Iowa, U.S.A. 42°15N 91°12W 310 B5
Monticello Ky., U.S.A. 36°50N 84°51W 309 G11
Monticello Minn., U.S.A. 45°18N 93°48W 308 C7
Monticello Miss., U.S.A. 31°33N 90°7W 315 F9
Monticello Mo., U.S.A. 40°7N 91°43W 310 D5
Monticello N.Y., U.S.A. 41°39N 74°42W 313 E10
Monticello Utah, U.S.A. 37°52N 109°21W 305 H9
Montichiari Italy 45°25N 10°23E 198 C7
Montier-en-Der France 48°30N 4°45E 173 D11
Montignac France 45°4N 1°10E 174 C5
Montigny-le-Bretonneux France 48°46N 2°1E 134 B1
Montigny-les-Metz France 49°7N 6°10E 173 C13
Montigny-sur-Aube France 47°57N 4°45E 173 E11
Montijo Portugal 38°41N 8°54W 195 G2
Montijo Spain 38°52N 6°39W 195 G4
Montilla Spain 37°36N 4°40W 195 H6
Montivilliers France 49°33N 0°12E 172 C7
Montjay-la-Tour France 48°54N 2°40E 134 A4
Montjuïc Spain 41°22N 2°10E 114 A2
Montjuïc, Parc de Barcelona, Spain 114 c1
Montluçon France 46°22N 2°36E 173 F9
Montmagny Canada 46°58N 70°34W 299 C5
Montmarault France 46°19N 2°57E 173 F9
Montmartre Canada 50°14N 103°27W 297 C8
Montmédy France 49°30N 5°20E 173 C12
Montmélian France 45°30N 6°4E 175 C10
Montmirail France 48°51N 3°30E 173 D10
Montmoreau-St-Cybard France 45°23N 0°8E 174 C4
Montmorillon France 46°26N 0°50E 174 B4
Montmort-Lucy France 48°55N 3°49E 173 D10
Monto Australia 24°52S 151°6E 280 C5
Montoire-sur-le-Loir France 47°45N 0°52E 172 E7
Montongbuwoh Indonesia 8°33S 116°4E 231 K19
Montório al Vomano Italy 42°35N 13°38E 199 F10
Montoro Spain 38°1N 4°27W 195 G6
Montour Falls U.S.A. 42°21N 76°51W 312 D8
Montoursville U.S.A. 41°15N 76°55W 312 E8
Montparnasse, Gare France 48°50N 2°19E 134 A2
Montpelier Idaho, U.S.A. 42°19N 111°18W 304 E8
Montpelier Ind., U.S.A. 40°33N 85°17W 311 D11
Montpelier Ohio, U.S.A. 41°35N 84°37W 311 C12
Montpelier Vt., U.S.A. 44°16N 72°35W 313 B12
Montpellier France 43°37N 3°52E 174 E7
Montpezat-de-Quercy France 44°15N 1°30E 174 D5
Montpon-Ménestérol France 45°0N 0°11E 174 D4
Montréal Qué., Canada 45°30N 73°33W 130 A2
Montréal Aude, France 43°13N 2°8E 174 E6
Montréal Gers, France 43°56N 0°11E 174 E4
Montreal ➝ Canada 47°14N 84°39W 298 C3
Montréal, Î. de Canada 45°30N 73°40W 130 A2
Montréal, Univ. de Canada 45°29N 73°37W 130 B2
Montréal Est Canada 45°37N 73°31W 130 A2
Montréal L. Canada 54°20N 105°45W 297 C7
Montreal Lake Canada 54°3N 105°46W 297 C7
Montréal-Nord Canada 45°36N 73°36W 130 A2
Montréal-Ouest Canada 45°27N 73°39W 130 B1
Montréal Trudeau Int. ✕ (YUL) Canada 45°28N 73°44W 130 B1
Montredon-Labessonnié France 43°45N 2°18E 174 E6
Montréjeau France 43°6N 0°35E 174 E4
Montrésor France 47°10N 1°10E 172 E8
Montret France 46°40N 5°7E 173 F12
Montreuil Pas-de-Calais, France 50°27N 1°45E 173 B8
Montreuil Seine-St-Denis, France 48°51N 2°27E 134 A3
Montreuil-Bellay France 47°8N 0°9W 172 E6
Montreux Switz. 46°26N 6°55E 179 J2
Montrevel-en-Bresse France 46°21N 5°8E 173 F12
Montrichard France 47°20N 1°10E 172 E8
Montrose Angus, U.K. 56°44N 2°27W 167 E6
Montrose Colo., U.S.A. 38°29N 107°53W 304 G10
Montrose Pa., U.S.A. 41°50N 75°53W 313 E9
Montrose, L. U.S.A. 38°18N 93°50W 310 F3
Montrouge France 48°48N 2°18E 134 B2
Monts, Pte. des Canada 49°20N 67°12W 299 C6
Montsalvy France 44°41N 2°30E 174 D6
Montsant, Serra de Spain 41°17N 1°0E 196 D6
Montsauche-les-Settons France 47°13N 4°2E 173 E11
Montsec, Serra del Spain 42°0N 0°45E 196 C5
Montseny △ Spain 41°43N 2°22W 196 D7
Montserrat B. Aires, Argentina 34°37S 58°24W 117 B2
Montserrat Spain 41°36N 1°49E 196 D6
Montserrat ☑ W. Indies 16°40N 62°10W 323 p
Montserrat & Tobago Hills Trin. & Tob. 10°23N 61°21W 323 t
Montuenga Spain 41°3N 4°38W 194 D6
Montuiri Spain 39°34N 2°59E 206 B3
Montvert-les-Bas Réunion 21°19S 55°32E 272 f
Monveda Dem. Rep. of the Congo 2°52N 21°30E 264 B4
Monyo Burma 17°59N 95°30E 241 G5
Monywa Burma 22°7N 95°11E 241 D5
Monza Italy 45°35N 9°16E 129 A2
Monze Zambia 16°17S 27°29E 269 F2
Monze, C. Pakistan 24°47N 66°37E 242 G2
Monzón Spain 41°52N 0°10E 196 D5
Monzoro Italy 45°27N 9°2E 129 B1
Moóca Brazil 23°33S 46°35W 137 B2
Moodyville = North Vancouver Canada 49°19N 123°4W 306 A3
Mooers U.S.A. 44°58N 73°35W 313 B11
Mooi ➝ S. Africa 28°45S 30°34E 271 C5
Mooi River S. Africa 29°13S 29°50E 271 C4
Mo'oka Japan 36°26N 140°1E 223 A12
Mookgophong = Mookgopong S. Africa 24°31S 28°44E 271 B4
Mookgopong S. Africa 24°31S 28°44E 271 B4
Moomba Australia 28°6S 140°12E 281 A3
Moonachie U.S.A. 40°50N 74°2W 132 B1
Moonah ➝ Australia 22°3S 138°33E 280 C2
Moonda, L. Australia 25°52S 140°25E 280 D3
Moonee Ponds Australia 37°45S 144°53E 128 A1
Moonee Valley Racecourse Australia 37°45S 144°55E 128 A1
Moonie Australia 27°46S 150°20E 281 D5
Moonie ➝ Australia 29°19S 148°43E 281 D4
Moonta Australia 34°6S 137°32E 282 C2
Moora Australia 30°37S 115°58E 279 F2
Moorcroft U.S.A. 44°16N 104°57W 304 D11
Moore ➝ Australia 31°22S 115°30E 279 F2
Moore, L. Australia 29°50S 117°35E 279 E2
Moore Falls Canada 44°48N 78°48W 312 B6
Moore Haven U.S.A. 26°50N 81°6W 317 J8
Moore Park Australia 24°43S 152°17E 280 C5
Moore Res. U.S.A. 44°20N 71°53W 313 B13
Moore River △ Australia 31°7S 115°39E 279 F2
Moorea French Polynesia 17°30S 149°50W 289 e
Moorefield U.S.A. 39°4N 78°58W 309 F14
Mooresville U.S.A. 39°37N 86°22W 311 E10
Moorfoot Hills U.K. 55°44N 3°8W 167 F5
Moorhead U.S.A. 46°53N 96°45W 308 B5
Moorland U.S.A. 42°26N 94°18W 310 B2
Moormerland Germany 53°20N 7°20E 178 B3
Moornanyah L. Australia 33°15S 143°42E 282 B5
Mooroopna Australia 36°25S 145°22E 283 D6
Moorpark U.S.A. 34°17N 118°53W 307 L8
Moorreesburg S. Africa 33°6S 18°38E 270 D2
Moorrinya △ Australia 21°42S 144°58E 280 C3
Moosach Germany 48°10N 11°30E 131 A2
Moosburg Germany 48°27N 11°56E 179 G7
Moose ➝ Ont., Canada 51°20N 80°25W 298 B3
Moose ➝ U.S.A. 43°38N 75°24W 313 C9
Moose Creek Canada 45°15N 74°58W 313 A10
Moose Factory Canada 51°16N 80°32W 298 B3
Moose Jaw Canada 50°24N 105°30W 297 C7
Moose Jaw ➝ Canada 50°34N 105°18W 297 C7
Moose Lake Man., Canada 53°46N 100°8W 297 C8
Moose Lake Minn., U.S.A. 46°27N 92°46W 308 B7
Moose Mountain △ Canada 49°48N 102°25W 297 D8
Moose Pass U.S.A. 60°29N 149°22W 303 F10
Moosehead L. U.S.A. 45°38N 69°40W 309 C19
Mooselookmeguntic L. U.S.A. 44°55N 70°49W 313 B14
Moosilauke, Mt. U.S.A. 44°3N 71°40W 313 B13
Moosomin Canada 50°9N 101°40W 297 C8
Moosonee Canada 51°17N 80°39W 298 B3
Moosup U.S.A. 41°43N 71°53W 313 E13
Mootwingee △ Australia 31°10S 142°30E 282 A5
Mopane S. Africa 22°37S 29°52E 271 B4
Mopeia Velha Mozam. 17°30S 35°40E 269 F4
Mopipi Botswana 21°6S 24°55E 270 B3
Mopoi C.A.R. 5°6N 26°54E 268 A2
Mopti Mali 14°30N 4°0W 262 C4
Mopti ☐ Mali 14°40N 4°0W 262 C4
Moqatta Sudan 14°38N 35°50E 257 E4
Moqor Afghan. 32°50N 67°42E 242 C2
Moquegua Peru 17°15S 70°46W 330 D3
Moquegua ☐ Peru 16°50S 70°55W 330 D3
Mór Hungary 47°25N 18°12E 182 C3
Mora Cameroon 11°2N 14°7E 259 F2
Mora Maharashtra, India 18°54N 72°55E 130 B2
Móra Portugal 38°55N 8°10W 195 G2
Mora Spain 39°41N 3°46W 195 F7
Mora Sweden 61°2N 14°38E 162 C8
Mora Minn., U.S.A. 45°53N 93°18W 308 C7
Mora N. Mex., U.S.A. 35°58N 105°20W 305 J11
Mora de Rubielos Spain 40°15N 0°45W 196 E4
Móra d'Ebre Spain 41°6N 0°38E 196 D5
Móra la Nova Spain 41°7N 0°39E 196 D5
Morača ➝ Montenegro 42°20N 19°9E 202 D3
Morada Nova Brazil 5°7S 38°23W 332 C4
Morada Nova de Minas Brazil 18°37S 45°22W 333 E2
Moradabad India 28°50N 78°50E 243 E8
Morafenobe Madag. 17°50S 44°53E 272 B1
Morąg Poland 53°55N 19°56E 184 E6
Moral de Calatrava Spain 38°51N 3°33W 195 G7
Moraleda, Canal Chile 44°30S 73°30W 336 B2
Moraleja Spain 40°6N 6°43W 194 E4
Morales Bolivar, Colombia 8°16N 73°51W 328 B3
Morales Cauca, Colombia 2°45N 76°38W 328 C2
Moramanga Madag. 18°56S 48°12E 272 B2
Moran Kans., U.S.A. 37°55N 95°10W 308 G6
Moran Wyo., U.S.A. 43°50N 110°31W 304 E8
Moranbah Australia 22°1S 148°6E 280 C4
Morané French Polynesia 23°10S 137°7W 289 f
Morang = Biratnagar Nepal 26°27N 87°17E 243 F12
Moranhat India 27°10N 94°50E 241 B5
Morano Cálabro Italy 39°50N 16°8E 201 C9
Morant Bay Jamaica 17°53N 76°25W 320 a
Morant Cays Jamaica 17°22N 76°0W 320 C4
Morant Pt. Jamaica 17°55N 76°12W 320 a
Morar India 26°14N 78°14E 242 F8
Morar, L. U.K. 56°57N 5°40W 167 E3
Moratalaz Spain 40°24N 3°39W 127 B2
Moratalla Spain 38°14N 1°49W 197 G3
Moratuwa Sri Lanka 6°45N 79°55E 245 L4
Morava ➝ Slovak Rep. 48°10N 16°59E 181 C9
Moravia Iowa, U.S.A. 40°53N 92°49W 310 D4
Moravia N.Y., U.S.A. 42°43N 76°25W 313 D8
Moravian Hts. = Českomoravská Vrchovina Czech Rep. 49°30N 15°40E 180 B8
Moravica ➝ Serbia 43°52N 20°8E 202 C4
Moraviţa Romania 45°17N 21°14E 182 E6
Moravská Třebová Czech Rep. 49°45N 16°40E 181 B9
Moravské Budějovice Czech Rep. 49°4N 15°49E 180 B8
Morawa Australia 29°13S 116°0E 279 E2
Morawhanna Guyana 8°30N 59°40W 329 B6
Moray ☐ U.K. 57°31N 3°18W 167 D5
Moray Firth U.K. 57°40N 3°52W 167 D5
Morbach Germany 49°48N 7°6E 179 F3
Morbegno Italy 46°8N 9°34E 198 B6
Morbi India 22°50N 70°42E 242 H4
Morbihan ☐ France 47°55N 2°50W 172 E4
Mörby Sweden 59°23N 18°3E 134 B2
Mörbylånga Sweden 56°32N 16°22E 163 H10
Morcenx France 44°3N 0°55W 174 D3
Morcone Italy 41°20N 14°40E 201 A7
Mordelles France 48°5N 1°52W 172 D5
Morden Man., Canada 49°15N 98°10W 297 D9
Morden London, U.K. 51°24N 0°13W 125 B2
Mordoğan Turkey 38°30N 26°37E 205 C8
Mordovian Republic = Mordvinia ☐ Russia 54°20N 44°30E 190 C7
Mordovo Russia 52°6N 40°50E 190 D5
Mordvinia ☐ Russia 54°20N 44°30E 190 C7
Mordy Poland 52°13N 22°31E 185 F9
Møre og Romsdal ☐ Norway 62°30N 8°0E 164 B4
Moreau ➝ U.S.A. 45°18N 100°43W 308 C3
Morebeng S. Africa 23°30S 29°55E 271 B4
Morecambe U.K. 54°5N 2°52W 168 C5
Morecambe B. U.K. 54°7N 3°0W 168 C5
Moree Australia 29°28S 149°54E 281 D4
Morée ➝ France 48°57N 2°25E 134 A3
Morehead Papua N. G. 8°41S 141°41E 286 E1
Morehead Ky., U.S.A. 38°11N 83°26W 311 F12
Morehead City U.S.A. 34°43N 76°43W 315 D16
Morel ➝ India 26°13N 76°36E 242 F7
Moreland U.S.A. 33°17N 84°46W 316 B5
Morelia Mexico 19°42N 101°7W 318 D4
Morella Queens., Australia 23°0S 143°52E 280 C3
Morella Spain 40°35N 0°5W 196 E4
Morelos Mexico 26°42N 107°40W 318 B3
Morelos ☐ Mexico 18°45N 99°0W 319 D5
Moremi △ Botswana 19°18S 23°10E 270 A3
Morena India 26°30N 78°4E 242 F8
Morena, Sierra Spain 38°20N 4°0W 195 G7
Morenci U.S.A. 41°43N 84°13W 311 C12
Moreni Romania 44°59N 25°36E 183 F10
Moreno Bolivia 11°9S 66°15W 330 C4
Moreno Valley U.S.A. 33°56N 117°14W 307 M10
Moreru ➝ Brazil 10°10S 59°10W 331 C6
Moresby I. Canada 52°30N 131°40W 296 C2
Morestel France 45°40N 5°28E 175 C9
Moreton I. Australia 27°10S 153°25E 281 D5
Moreton Island △ Australia 27°2S 153°24E 281 D5
Moreuil France 49°46N 2°30E 173 C9
Morez France 46°31N 6°2E 173 F13
Morgan S. Austral., Australia 34°2S 139°35E 282 C3
Morgan Ga., U.S.A. 31°32N 84°36W 316 D5
Morgan Utah, U.S.A. 41°2N 111°41W 304 F8
Morgan City U.S.A. 29°42N 91°12W 314 G9
Morgan Hill U.S.A. 37°8N 121°39W 306 H5
Morgan Park U.S.A. 41°41N 87°38W 119 C3
Morganfield U.S.A. 37°41N 87°55W 308 G10
Morganton U.S.A. 35°45N 81°41W 315 D14
Morgantown Ind., U.S.A. 39°22N 86°16W 311 E10
Morgantown W. Va., U.S.A. 39°38N 79°57W 309 F14
Morgenzon S. Africa 26°45S 29°36E 271 C4
Morges Switz. 46°31N 6°29E 179 J2
Morghak Iran 29°7N 57°54E 247 D8
Morgongåva Sweden 59°57N 16°58E 162 E10
Morhange France 48°55N 6°38E 173 D13
Morhar ➝ India 25°29N 85°11E 243 G11
Mori China 43°49N 90°11E 217 D12
Mori Italy 45°51N 10°59E 198 C7
Mori Japan 42°6N 140°35E 220 C10
Moriah Trin. & Tob. 11°15N 60°43W 323 s
Moriarty U.S.A. 34°59N 106°3W 305 J10
Moribaya Guinea 9°53N 9°32W 262 D3
Morice L. Canada 53°50N 127°40W 296 C3
Morichal Largo ➝ Venezuela 9°27N 62°25W 329 B5
Morichal Viejo Colombia 2°13N 70°2W 328 C3
Moriguchi Japan 34°43N 135°34E 133 A2
Moriki Nigeria 12°52N 6°30E 263 C6
Morinville Canada 53°49N 113°41W 296 C6
Morioka Japan 39°45N 141°8E 220 E10
Moris Mexico 28°10N 108°32W 318 B3
Morisset Australia 33°6S 151°30E 283 B9
Morivione Italy 45°26N 9°12E 129 B2
Moriyama Japan 35°4N 135°59E 223 B7
Morlaàs France 43°21N 0°18W 174 E3
Morlaix France 48°36N 3°52W 172 D3
Mörlunda Sweden 57°19N 15°52E 163 G9
Mormanno Italy 39°53N 15°59E 201 C8
Mormant France 48°37N 2°52E 173 D9
Morne-à-l'Eau Guadeloupe 16°20N 61°27W 322 e
Morne des Esses Martinique 14°44N 61°1W 322 j
Morne Diablotins Dominica 15°30N 61°24W 323 k
Morne Fendue Grenada 12°12N 61°38W 323 q
Morne Raquette Dominica 15°27N 61°27W 323 k
Morne Trois Pitons △ Dominica 15°22N 61°20W 323 k
Morningside Gauteng, S. Africa 26°4S 28°3E 123 A2
Morningside Edinburgh, U.K. 55°56N 3°12W 121 B2
Morningside Md., U.S.A. 38°49N 76°53W 143 C4
Morningside Park Ont., Canada 43°47N 79°12W 141 A3
Morningside Park Fla., U.S.A. 28°26N 81°24W 133 B2
Mornington Australia 38°15S 145°5E 283 E6
Mornington, I. Chile 49°50S 75°30W 336 C1
Mornington I. Australia 16°30S 139°30E 280 B2
Mornington Peninsula △ Australia 38°28S 144°53E 283 E6
Mornos ➝ Greece 38°25N 21°50E 204 C3
Moro Pakistan 26°40N 68°0E 242 F2
Moro Sudan 10°50N 30°9E 257 E3
Moro ➝ Pakistan 29°42N 67°22E 242 E2
Moro G. Phil. 6°30N 123°0E 233 H4
Morobe Papua N. G. 7°49S 147°38E 286 D4
Morobe ☐ Papua N. G. 7°0S 147°0E 286 D4
Morocco U.S.A. 40°57N 87°27W 311 D9
Morocco ■ N. Afr. 32°0N 5°50W 260 B3
Morococha Peru 11°40S 76°5W 330 C2
Morogoro Tanzania 6°50S 37°40E 268 D4
Morogoro ☐ Tanzania 8°0S 37°0E 268 D4
Moroleón Mexico 20°8N 101°12W 318 C4
Morombe Madag. 21°45S 43°22E 272 C1
Moron = Morong Phil. 14°41N 120°16E 232 D3
Morón Argentina 34°39S 58°37W 334 C4
Morón Cuba 22°8N 78°39W 320 B4
Mörön Mongolia 49°38N 100°9E 218 B9
Morón de Almazán Spain 41°29N 2°27W 196 D2
Morón de la Frontera Spain 37°6N 5°28W 195 H5
Morona ➝ Peru 4°40S 77°10W 328 D2
Morona-Santiago ☐ Ecuador 2°30S 78°0W 328 D2
Morondava Madag. 20°17S 44°17E 272 C1
Morondo Ivory C. 8°57N 6°47W 262 D3
Morong Phil. 14°41N 120°16E 232 D3
Morongo Valley U.S.A. 34°3N 116°37W 307 L10
Moroni Comoros Is. 11°40S 43°16E 272 a
Moroni Utah, U.S.A. 39°32N 111°35W 304 G8
Moroni Iconi ✕ (YVA) Comoros Is. 11°32S 43°15E 272 a
Moronou Ivory C. 6°16N 4°59W 262 D4
Morotai Indonesia 2°10N 128°30E 231 D7
Moroto Uganda 2°28N 34°42E 268 B3
Moroto, Mt. Uganda 2°30N 34°43E 268 B3
Morozov Bulgaria 42°30N 25°10E 203 D9
Morozovsk Russia 48°25N 41°50E 191 F5
Morpeth Ont., Canada 42°23N 81°50W 312 D3
Morpeth Northumberland, U.K. 55°10N 1°41W 168 B6
Morphou Cyprus 35°12N 32°59E 207 E8
Morphou Bay Cyprus 35°15N 32°50E 207 D8
Morrelganj Bangla. 22°28N 89°51E 241 D2
Morrilton U.S.A. 35°9N 92°44W 314 D8
Morrinhos Ceará, Brazil 3°14S 40°7W 332 B3
Morrinhos Minas Gerais, Brazil 17°45S 49°10W 333 E2
Morrinsville N.Z. 37°40S 175°32E 284 D4
Morris Man., Canada 49°25N 97°22W 297 D9
Morris Ill., U.S.A. 41°22N 88°26W 311 C8
Morris Minn., U.S.A. 45°35N 95°55W 308 C6
Morris N.Y., U.S.A. 42°33N 75°15W 313 D9
Morris Pa., U.S.A. 41°35N 77°17W 312 E7
Morris, Mt. Australia 26°9S 131°4E 279 E5
Morris Jesup, Kap Greenland 83°40N 34°0W 154 A7
Morrisburg Canada 44°55N 75°7W 313 B9
Morrison U.S.A. 41°49N 89°58W 310 C7
Morrisonville U.S.A. 39°25N 89°27W 310 E7
Morristown Ariz., U.S.A. 33°51N 112°37W 305 K7
Morristown Ind., U.S.A. 39°40N 85°42W 311 E11
Morristown N.J., U.S.A. 40°48N 74°29W 313 F10
Morristown N.Y., U.S.A. 44°35N 75°39W 313 B9
Morristown Tenn., U.S.A. 36°13N 83°18W 315 C13
Morrisville N.Y., U.S.A. 42°53N 75°35W 313 D9
Morrisville Pa., U.S.A. 40°13N 74°47W 313 F10
Morrisville Vt., U.S.A. 44°34N 72°36W 313 B12
Morro, Pta. Chile 27°6S 71°0W 334 B1
Morro Bay U.S.A. 35°22N 120°51W 306 K6
Morro Chico Chile 52°2S 71°26W 336 D2
Morro del Jable Canary Is. 28°3N 14°23W 153 e2
Morro do Chapéu Brazil 11°33S 41°9W 333 D3
Morro Grande = Barão de Cocais Brazil 19°56S 43°28W 333 E3
Morro Jable, Pta. de Canary Is. 28°2N 14°20W 153 e2
Morro Solar, Cerro Peru 12°11S 77°1W 124 C2
Morrocoy △ Venezuela 10°48N 68°13W 328 A4
Morros Brazil 2°52S 44°3W 332 B3
Morrosquillo, G. de Colombia 9°35N 75°40W 320 E4
Morrow U.S.A. 39°21N 84°8W 311 E12
Mörrum Sweden 56°12N 14°45E 163 H8
Morrumbene Mozam. 23°31S 35°16E 271 B6
Mörrumsån ➝ Sweden 56°10N 14°45E 163 H8
Mors Denmark 56°50N 8°45E 163 H2
Morshansk Russia 53°28N 41°50E 190 D5
Morsi India 21°21N 78°0E 244 D4
Mörsil Sweden 63°19N 13°40E 162 A7
Mortagne ➝ France 48°33N 6°27E 173 D13
Mortagne-au-Perche France 48°31N 0°33E 172 D7
Mortagne-sur-Gironde France 45°28N 0°47W 174 C3
Mortagne-sur-Sèvre France 47°0N 0°59W 172 F6
Mortain France 48°40N 0°57W 172 D6
Mortara Italy 45°15N 8°44E 198 C5
Morteau France 47°3N 6°35E 173 E13
Morteros Argentina 30°50S 62°0W 334 C3
Mortes, R. das ➝ Brazil 11°45S 50°44W 333 D1
Mortlach Canada 50°27N 106°4W 297 C7
Mortlake N.S.W., Australia 33°50S 151°6E 139 B1
Mortlake Vic., Australia 38°5S 142°50E 282 E5
Mortlake London, U.K. 51°27N 0°15W 125 B2
Morton Ill., U.S.A. 40°37N 89°28W 310 D7
Morton Tex., U.S.A. 33°44N 102°46W 314 E3
Morton Wash., U.S.A. 46°34N 122°17W 306 D4
Morton △ Australia 35°0S 150°12E 283 C9
Morton Grove U.S.A. 42°2N 87°46W 119 A2
Moruga Trin. & Tob. 10°4N 61°16W 323 t
Moruga ➝ Trin. & Tob. 10°5N 61°16W 323 t
Morumbi Brazil 23°35S 46°42W 137 B1
Morundah Australia 34°57S 146°19E 283 C7
Morung Sudan 10°32N 31°3E 266 B3
Moruya Australia 35°58S 150°3E 283 C9
Morvan France 47°5N 4°3E 173 E11
Morvan △ France 47°12N 4°3E 173 E11
Morvant Trin. & Tob. 10°40N 61°29W 323 t
Morven Queens., Australia 26°22S 147°5E 281 D4
Morven N.Z. 44°50S 171°6E 285 E6
Morven Ga., U.S.A. 30°57N 83°30W 316 E6
Morvern U.K. 56°38N 5°44W 167 E3
Morwell Australia 38°10S 146°22E 283 E7
Morwell △ Australia 38°14S 146°23E 283 E7
Moryń Poland 52°51N 14°22E 185 F1
Morzhovets, Ostrov Russia 66°44N 42°35E 186 A7
Morzine France 46°11N 6°42E 173 F13
Mosakahiken = Moose Lake Canada 53°46N 100°8W 297 C8
Mosalsk Russia 54°30N 34°55E 188 E8
Mosbach Germany 49°21N 9°9E 179 F5
Mosby Norway 58°12N 7°55E 164 F4
Moscavide Portugal 38°47N 9°6W 126 A2
Mošćenice Croatia 45°17N 14°16E 199 C11
Moschato Greece 37°55N 23°40E 112 B2
Mosciano Sant' Ángelo Italy 42°42N 13°52E 199 F10
Moscone Convention Center San Francisco, U.S.A. 136 c2
Moscos Is. Burma 14°0N 97°30E 236 F1
Moscow = Moskva Russia 55°45N 37°37E 129 B3
Moscow Idaho, U.S.A. 46°44N 117°0W 304 C5
Moscow Mich., U.S.A. 42°3N 84°30W 311 B12
Moscow Pa., U.S.A. 41°20N 75°31W 313 E9
Moscow Mills U.S.A. 38°57N 90°55W 310 F6
Mosel ➝ Europe 50°22N 7°36E 173 B14
Moselle = Mosel ➝ Europe 50°22N 7°36E 173 B14
Moselle ☐ France 48°59N 6°33E 173 D13
Moses Lake U.S.A. 47°8N 119°17W 304 C4
Mosgiel N.Z. 45°53S 170°21E 285 F5
Moshaweng ➝ S. Africa 26°35S 22°50E 270 C3
Moshchnyy, Ostrav Russia 60°1N 27°50E 188 B4
Moshi Tanzania 3°22S 37°18E 268 C4
Moshi ➝ Nigeria 9°18N 4°38E 263 D5
Moshupa Botswana 24°46S 25°29E 270 B4
Mosina Poland 52°15N 16°50E 185 F3
Mosite Dem. Rep. of the Congo 0°53N 23°40E 264 B4
Mosjøen Norway 65°51N 13°12E 160 D15
Moskenesøya Norway 67°58N 13°0E 160 C15
Moskenstraumen Norway 67°47N 12°45E 160 C15
Moskog Norway 61°26N 6°0E 164 C2
Moskva Russia 55°45N 37°37E 129 B3
Moskva ☐ Russia 56°20N 37°20E 188 D9
Moskva ➝ Russia 55°5N 38°51E 188 E10
Moskvoretskiy Russia 55°42N 37°37E 129 B3
Moslavačka Gora Croatia 45°40N 16°37E 199 C13
Mosman Australia 33°49S 151°15E 139 B2
Moso Vanuatu 17°30S 168°15E 287 G6
Mosomane Botswana 24°2S 26°19E 270 B4
Mosonmagyaróvár Hungary 47°52N 17°18E 182 C2
Mošorin Serbia 45°19N 20°4E 182 E5
Mospyne Ukraine 47°52N 38°0E 189 J9
Mosqueiro Brazil 1°10S 48°28W 332 B2
Mosquera Colombia 2°35N 78°24W 328 C2
Mosquero U.S.A. 35°47N 103°58W 305 J12
Mosqueruela Spain 40°21N 0°27W 196 E4
Mosquitia Honduras 15°20N 84°10W 320 C3
Mosquito Coast = Mosquitia Honduras 15°20N 84°10W 320 C3
Mosquito Creek L. U.S.A. 41°18N 80°46W 312 E4
Mosquito L. Canada 62°35N 103°20W 297 A8
Mosquitos, G. de los Panama 9°15N 81°10W 320 E3
Moss Norway 59°27N 10°40E 164 E7
Moss Vale Australia 34°32S 150°25E 283 C9
Mossaka Congo 1°15S 16°45E 264 C3
Mossâmedes Brazil 16°7S 50°11W 333 E1
Mossbank Canada 49°56N 105°56W 297 D7
Mossburn N.Z. 45°41S 168°15E 285 F3
Mosselbaai S. Africa 34°11S 22°8E 270 D3
Mossendjo Congo 2°55S 12°42E 264 C2
Mossfellsbær Iceland 64°10N 21°45W 155 C5
Mossgiel Australia 33°15S 144°5E 282 B6
Mössingen Germany 48°24N 9°4E 179 G5
Mossman Australia 16°21S 145°15E 280 B4
Mossoró Brazil 5°10S 37°15W 332 C4
Mossuril Mozam. 14°58S 40°42E 269 E5
Mossy Head U.S.A. 30°45N 86°19W 317 E3
Mossy Point Australia 35°50S 150°11E 283 C9
Most Czech Rep. 50°31N 13°38E 180 A6
Mosta Malta 35°55N 14°26E 206 F7
Mostaganem Algeria 35°54N 0°5E 261 A5
Mostaganem ☐ Algeria 35°40N 0°5E 261 A5
Mostar Bos.-H. 43°22N 17°50E 182 G2
Mostardas Brazil 31°2S 50°51W 335 C5
Mostefa, Rass Tunisia 36°55N 11°3E 258 A2
Mosteiros Azores 37°53N 25°49W 153 d3
Mosterhamn Norway 59°42N 5°21E 164 E2
Mostiska = Mostyska Ukraine 49°48N 23°4E 185 J10
Móstoles Spain 40°19N 3°53W 194 E7
Mosty = Masty Belarus 53°27N 24°38E 177 B13
Mostyska Ukraine 49°48N 23°4E 185 J10
Mosul = Al Mawşil Iraq 36°15N 43°5E 213 D10
Møsvatnet Norway 59°52N 8°5E 164 E5
Mota Ethiopia 11°5N 37°52E 257 E4
Mota Vanuatu 13°49S 167°42E 287 C5
Mota del Cuervo Spain 39°30N 2°52W 197 F2
Mota del Marqués Spain 41°38N 5°11W 194 D5
Mota Lava Vanuatu 13°40S 167°40E 287 C5
Motaba Congo 2°6N 18°2E 264 B3
Motagua ➝ Guatemala 15°44N 88°14W 320 C2
Motala Sweden 58°32N 15°1E 163 F9
Motaze Mozam. 24°48S 32°52E 271 B5
Moţca Romania 47°15N 26°37E 183 C11
Motegi Japan 36°32N 140°11E 223 A12
Moth India 25°43N 78°57E 243 G8
Motherwell U.K. 55°47N 3°58W 167 F5
Moti Bagh India 28°33N 77°10E 120 B2
Motihari India 26°30N 84°55E 243 F11
Motilla del Palancar Spain 39°34N 1°55W 197 F3
Motiti I. N.Z. 37°38S 176°25E 284 D5
Motnik Slovenia 46°14N 14°54E 199 B11
Motobu Japan 26°39N 127°53E 288 a
Motocurunya Venezuela 4°24N 64°5W 329 C5
Motol Czech Rep. 50°3N 14°21E 135 B2
Motovun Croatia 45°20N 13°50E 199 C10
Motozintla de Mendoza Mexico 15°22N 92°14W 319 D6
Motril Spain 36°31N 3°37W 195 J7
Motru Romania 44°48N 22°59E 182 F7
Motru ➝ Romania 44°32N 23°31E 183 F8
Motsa Israel 31°47N 35°9E 123 B2
Motsa Ilit Israel 31°48N 35°9E 123 B1
Motspur Park U.K. 51°23N 0°14W 125 B2
Mott U.S.A. 46°23N 102°20W 308 B2
Mottingham U.K. 51°26N 0°1E 125 B4
Möttling = Metlika Slovenia 45°40N 15°20E 199 C12
Móttola Italy 40°38N 17°2E 201 B10
Motu ➝ N.Z. 37°52S 177°36E 284 D6
Motu Nui Chile 27°12S 109°28W 330 b
Motu Tapu Cook Is. 21°14S 159°43W 289 h
Motuba Dem. Rep. of the Congo 2°20N 18°34E 264 B3
Motueka N.Z. 41°7S 173°1E 285 B8
Motueka ➝ N.Z. 41°5S 173°1E 285 B8
Motul Mexico 21°6N 89°17W 319 C7
Motupena Pt. Papua N. G. 6°30S 155°10E 286 D8
Mou N. Cal. 21°5S 167°26E 288 d
Mouanda Gabon 1°28S 13°7E 264 C2
Mouchalagane ➝ Canada 50°56N 68°41W 299 B6
Mouchoir Bank W. Indies 20°57N 70°47W 321 B5
Mouding China 25°20N 101°28E 228 E3
Moudjeria Mauritania 17°50N 12°28W 262 B2
Moudon Switz. 46°40N 6°49E 179 J2
Moudros Greece 39°50N 25°18E 205 B7
Mougoundou Congo 2°40S 12°41E 264 C2
Mouhoun = Black Volta ➝ Africa 8°41N 1°33W 262 D4
Mouila Gabon 1°50S 11°0E 264 C2
Mouka C.A.R. 7°16N 21°52E 264 A4
Moukalaba △ Gabon 2°50S 10°35E 264 C2
Moukambo Gabon 3°55S 11°38E 264 C2
Moul Niger 15°5N 13°11E 259 F2
Moulamein Australia 35°3S 144°1E 282 C6
Moule à Chique, C. St. Lucia 13°43N 60°57W 323 m
Moulhoulé Djibouti 11°58N 42°58E 267 B5
Mouliana Greece 35°10N 25°59E 207 E6
Moulin Rouge Paris, France 134 a3
Moulins France 46°35N 3°19E 173 F10
Moulmein Burma 16°30N 97°40E 241 G6
Moulmeingyun Burma 16°23N 95°16E 241 G5
Moulouya, O. ➝ Morocco 35°5N 2°25W 261 A4
Moulton U.S.A. 40°41N 92°41W 310 D4
Moultrie U.S.A. 31°11N 83°47W 316 D6
Moultrie, L. U.S.A. 33°20N 80°5W 316 B9
Mounana Gabon 1°18S 13°12E 264 C2
Mound City Mo., U.S.A. 40°7N 95°14W 308 E6
Mound City S. Dak., U.S.A. 45°44N 100°4W 308 C3
Moundou Chad 8°40N 16°10E 259 G3
Moundsville U.S.A. 39°55N 80°44W 312 G4
Mounembé Congo 3°20S 12°32E 264 C2
Moung Cambodia 12°46N 103°27E 236 F4
Moungoudi Congo 2°45S 11°46E 264 C2
Mount Airy U.S.A. 36°31N 80°37W 315 C14
Mount Albert Canada 44°8N 79°19W 312 B5
Mount Apo △ Phil. 7°0N 125°10E 233 H5
Mount Arayat △ Phil. 15°39N 120°44E 232 D3
Mount Aspiring △ N.Z. 44°19S 168°47E 285 E3
Mount Ayliff = Maxesibeni S. Africa 30°49S 29°23E 271 D4
Mount Ayr U.S.A. 40°43N 94°14W 310 D2
Mount Barker S. Austral., Australia 35°5S 138°52E 282 C3
Mount Barker W. Austral., Australia 34°38S 117°40E 279 F2
Mount Barnett Roadhouse Australia 16°39S 125°57E 278 C4
Mount Beauty Australia 36°47S 147°10E 283 D7
Mount Bellew Bridge Ireland 53°28N 8°31W 166 C3
Mount Brydges Canada 42°54N 81°29W 312 D3
Mount Buffalo △ Australia 36°43S 146°46E 283 D7
Mount Burr Australia 37°34S 140°26E 282 D4
Mount Carmel = Ha Karmel △ Israel 32°45N 35°5E 250 F6
Mount Carmel Ill., U.S.A. 38°25N 87°46W 311 F9
Mount Carmel Pa., U.S.A. 40°47N 76°26W 313 F8
Mount Carroll U.S.A. 42°6N 89°59W 310 B7
Mount Clemens U.S.A. 42°35N 82°53W 312 D2
Mount Cook N.Z. 43°44S 170°5E 285 D5
Mount Cook △ N.Z. 43°35S 170°15E 285 D5
Mount Coolon Australia 21°25S 147°25E 280 C4
Mount Darwin Zimbabwe 16°47S 31°38E 269 F3
Mount Dennis Canada 43°40N 79°28W 141 A2
Mount Desert I. U.S.A. 44°21N 68°20W 309 C19
Mount Dora U.S.A. 28°48N 81°38W 317 G8
Mount Ebenezer Australia 25°6S 132°34E 279 E5
Mount Eccles △ Australia 38°5S 141°54E 282 E4
Mount Eden U.S.A. 38°3N 85°9W 311 F11
Mount Edziza △ Canada 57°30N 130°45W 296 B2
Mount Elgon △ E. Afr. 1°4N 34°42E 268 B3
Mount Field △ Australia 42°39S 146°35E 281 G4
Mount Fletcher S. Africa 30°40S 28°30E 271 D4

Mount Forest *Canada* 43°59N 80°43W **312** C4
Mount Frankland △ *Australia* 31°47S 116°37E **279** F2
Mount Frederick ☼ *Australia* 19°39S 129°18E **278** C4
Mount Frere = Kwabhaca *S. Africa* 30°51S 29°0E **271** D4
Mount Gambier *Australia* 37°50S 140°46E **282** D4
Mount Garnet *Australia* 17°37S 145°6E **280** B4
Mount Greenwood *U.S.A.* 41°42N 87°42W **119** C2
Mount Hagen *Papua N. G.* 5°52S 144°16E **286** C3
Mount Hamiguitan △ *Phil.* 6°44N 126°10E **233** H6
Mount Holly *U.S.A.* 39°59N 74°47W **313** G10
Mount Holly Springs *U.S.A.* 40°7N 77°12W **312** F7
Mount Hood Memorial Park ⌓ *U.S.A.* 42°26N 71°1W **116** A2
Mount Hope *N.S.W., Australia* 32°51S 145°51E **283** B6
Mount Hope *S. Austral., Australia* 34°7S 135°23E **281** E2
Mount Horeb *U.S.A.* 43°1N 89°44W **310** B7
Mount Iglit-Mount Baco △ *Phil.* 12°45N 121°8E **232** E3
Mount Isa *Australia* 20°42S 139°26E **280** C2
Mount Isarog △ *Phil.* 13°38N 123°24E **232** E4
Mount James ☼ *Australia* 24°51S 116°54E **279** D2
Mount Jewett *U.S.A.* 41°44N 78°39W **312** E6
Mount Ka'ala Nat. Area Reserve ⌓ *U.S.A.* 21°31N 158°7W **302** J13
Mount Kaputar △ *Australia* 30°16S 150°10E **281** E5
Mount Kenya △ *Kenya* 0°7S 37°21E **268** C4
Mount Kisco *U.S.A.* 41°12N 73°44W **313** E11
Mount Laguna *U.S.A.* 32°52N 116°25W **307** N10
Mount Larcom *Australia* 23°48S 150°59E **280** C5
Mount Lofty Ranges *Australia* 34°35S 139°5E **282** C3
Mount McKinley = Denali △ *U.S.A.* 63°30N 152°0W **303** E10
Mount Magnet *Australia* 28°2S 117°47E **279** E2
Mount Malindang △ *Phil.* 8°17N 123°32E **233** G4
Mount Manara *Australia* 32°29S 143°58E **282** B5
Mount Maunganui *N.Z.* 37°40S 176°14E **284** D5
Mount Merrion *Ireland* 53°18N 6°12W **120** B2
Mount Molloy *Australia* 16°42S 145°20E **280** B4
Mount Morgan *Australia* 23°40S 150°25E **280** C5
Mount Morris *Mich., U.S.A.* 43°7N 83°42W **311** A13
Mount Morris *N.Y., U.S.A.* 42°44N 77°52W **312** D7
Mount Olive *U.S.A.* 39°4N 89°44W **310** E7
Mount Olivet *U.S.A.* 38°32N 84°2W **311** F12
Mount Olympus *U.S.A.* 34°7N 118°21W **126** B2
Mount Orab *U.S.A.* 39°2N 83°55W **311** E13
Mount Pearl *Canada* 47°31N 52°47W **299** C9
Mount Penn *U.S.A.* 40°20N 75°54W **313** F9
Mount Perry *Australia* 25°13S 151°42E **281** D5
Mount Pleasant *Iowa, U.S.A.* 40°58N 91°33W **310** D5
Mount Pleasant *Mich., U.S.A.* 43°36N 84°46W **309** D11
Mount Pleasant *Pa., U.S.A.* 40°9N 79°33W **312** F5
Mount Pleasant *S.C., U.S.A.* 32°47N 79°52W **316** C10
Mount Pleasant *Tenn., U.S.A.* 35°32N 87°12W **315** D11
Mount Pleasant *Tex., U.S.A.* 33°9N 94°58W **314** E7
Mount Pleasant *Utah, U.S.A.* 39°33N 111°27W **304** G8
Mount Pocono *U.S.A.* 41°7N 75°22W **313** E9
Mount Pulaski *U.S.A.* 40°1N 89°17W **310** D7
Mount Pulog △ *Phil.* 16°35N 120°57E **232** C3
Mount Rainier *U.S.A.* 38°56N 76°57W **143** B4
Mount Rainier △ *U.S.A.* 46°55N 121°50W **306** D5
Mount Remarkable △ *Australia* 32°47S 138°3E **282** B3
Mount Revelstoke △ *Canada* 51°5N 118°30W **296** C5
Mount Robson ⌓ *Canada* 53°0N 119°0W **296** C5
Mount St. Helens ⌓ *U.S.A.* 46°14N 122°11W **306** D4
Mount Selinda *Zimbabwe* 20°24S 32°43E **271** B5
Mount Shasta *U.S.A.* 41°19N 122°19W **304** F2
Mount Signal *U.S.A.* 32°39N 115°37W **307** N11
Mount Somers *N.Z.* 43°45S 171°27E **285** D6
Mount Sterling *Ill., U.S.A.* 39°59N 90°45W **310** E6
Mount Sterling *Ky., U.S.A.* 38°4N 83°56W **311** F13
Mount Sterling *Ohio, U.S.A.* 39°43N 83°16W **311** E13
Mount Surprise *Australia* 18°10S 144°17E **280** B3
Mount Union *U.S.A.* 40°23N 77°53W **312** F7
Mount Upton *U.S.A.* 42°26N 75°23W **313** D9
Mount Vernon *Ga., U.S.A.* 32°11N 82°36W **316** C7
Mount Vernon *Ill., U.S.A.* 38°19N 88°55W **308** F9
Mount Vernon *Ind., U.S.A.* 37°56N 87°54W **308** G10
Mount Vernon *Iowa, U.S.A.* 41°55N 91°23W **310** C5
Mount Vernon *N.Y., U.S.A.* 40°54N 73°49W **132** A3
Mount Vernon *Ohio, U.S.A.* 40°23N 82°29W **312** F2
Mount Vernon *Wash., U.S.A.* 48°25N 122°20W **306** B4
Mount Vernon Square *Washington, D.C., U.S.A.* **143** a2
Mount Victor *Australia* 32°11S 139°44E **282** B3
Mount Washington *U.S.A.* 39°5N 84°24W **311** F11
Mount Wellington *N.Z.* 36°55S 174°52E **284** C3
Mount William △ *Australia* 40°56S 148°14E **281** G4
Mount Wynne *St. Vincent* 13°14N 61°16W **323** n
Mount Zion = Har Tsiyon *Jerusalem* **123** b3
Mount Zion *U.S.A.* 39°46N 88°53W **311** E8
Mounta, Akra *Greece* 38°3N 20°47E **207** C2
Mountain □ *Phil.* 17°20N 121°10E **232** C3
Mountain Ash *U.K.* 51°40N 3°23W **169** F4
Mountain Center *U.S.A.* 33°42N 116°44W **307** M10
Mountain City *Nev., U.S.A.* 41°50N 115°58W **304** F6
Mountain City *Tenn., U.S.A.* 36°29N 81°48W **315** C14
Mountain Dale *U.S.A.* 41°41N 74°32W **313** E10
Mountain Grove *U.S.A.* 37°8N 92°16W **308** G7
Mountain Home *Ark., U.S.A.* 36°20N 92°23W **314** C8
Mountain Home *Idaho, U.S.A.* 43°8N 115°41W **304** E6
Mountain Iron *U.S.A.* 47°32N 92°37W **308** B7
Mountain Pass *U.S.A.* 35°29N 115°35W **307** K11
Mountain View *Ark., U.S.A.* 35°52N 92°7W **314** D8
Mountain View *Calif., U.S.A.* 37°23N 122°5W **306** H4
Mountain View *Hawai'i, U.S.A.* 19°33N 155°7W **302** D6
Mountain Village *U.S.A.* 62°5N 163°43W **303** E7
Mountain Zebra △ *S. Africa* 32°14S 25°27E **270** D4
Mountainair *U.S.A.* 34°31N 106°15W **305** J10
Mountlake Terrace *U.S.A.* 47°47N 122°18W **306** C4
Mountmellick *Ireland* 53°7N 7°20W **166** C4
Mountrath *Ireland* 53°0N 7°28W **166** D4
Moura *Queens., Australia* 24°35S 149°58E **280** C4
Moura *Brazil* 1°32S 61°38W **329** D5
Moura *Portugal* 38°7N 7°30W **195** G3
Mourão *Portugal* 38°22N 7°22W **195** G3
Mourdi, Dépression du *Chad* 18°10N 23°0E **259** E4
Mourdiah *Mali* 14°35N 7°25W **262** C3
Mourenx *France* 43°22N 0°38W **174** E3
Mouri *Ghana* 5°6N 1°14W **263** D4
Mourilyan *Australia* 17°35S 146°3E **280** B4
Mourmelon-le-Grand *France* 49°8N 4°22E **173** C11
Mourne → *U.K.* 54°52N 7°26W **166** B4
Mourne Mts. *U.K.* 54°10N 6°0W **166** B5
Mournies *Greece* 35°29N 24°1E **207** E5
Mouscron *Belgium* 50°45N 3°12E **170** D3
Mousgougou *Chad* 10°47N 16°9E **259** F3
Moussa 'Ali *Djibouti* 12°27N 42°24E **267** B5
Moussoro *Chad* 13°41N 16°35E **259** F3
Moustique, Morne *Guadeloupe* 16°7N 61°44W **322** e
Mouthe *France* 46°44N 6°12E **173** F13
Moutier *Switz.* 47°16N 7°21E **179** H3
Moûtiers *France* 45°29N 6°32E **175** C10
Moutong *Indonesia* 0°28N 121°13E **231** D6
Mouy *France* 49°18N 2°20E **173** C9
Mouydir, Monts du *Algeria* 25°30N 4°10E **261** C5
Mouyondzi *Congo* 4°1S 13°59E **264** C2
Mouzaki *Greece* 39°25N 21°37E **204** B3
Mouzarak *Chad* 13°17N 15°58E **259** F3
Mouzon *France* 49°36N 5°3E **173** C12
Movas *Mexico* 28°10N 109°25W **318** B3
Moville *Ireland* 55°11N 7°3W **166** A4
Mowandjum *Australia* 17°22S 123°40E **278** C3
Moweaqua *U.S.A.* 39°38N 89°1W **310** E7
Moxico □ *Angola* 12°0S 20°30E **265** E4
Moxotó → *Brazil* 9°19S 38°14W **332** C4
Moy → *Ireland* 54°8N 9°8W **166** B2
Moya *Comoros Is.* 12°18S 44°18E **272** a
Moyale *Ethiopia* 3°34N 39°5E **266** D4
Moyale *Kenya* 3°30N 39°4E **257** G4
Moyamba *S. Leone* 8°4N 12°30W **262** D2
Moyen Atlas *Morocco* 33°0N 5°0W **260** B4
Moyen-Chari □ *Chad* 9°0N 18°0E **259** G3
Moyo *Indonesia* 8°10S 117°40E **235** D5
Moyobamba *Peru* 6°0S 77°0W **330** B2
Moyowosi ⌓ *Tanzania* 3°50S 31°0E **268** C3
Moyto *Chad* 12°35N 16°33E **259** F3
Moyu *China* 37°15N 79°44E **217** E9
Moyyero → *Russia* 68°44N 103°42E **215** C11
Moyynqum *Zhambyl, Kazakhstan* 44°17N 72°57E **217** D8
Moyynqum *Zhambyl, Kazakhstan* 44°12N 71°0E **217** D8
Moyynty *Kazakhstan* 47°10N 73°18E **217** C8
Mozambique = Moçambique *Mozam.* 15°3S 40°42E **269** F5
Mozambique ■ *Africa* 19°0S 35°0E **269** F4
Mozambique Basin *Ind. Oc.* 30°0S 40°0E **273** G2
Mozambique Chan. *Africa* 17°30S 42°30E **271** A7
Mozarthaus *Vienna, Austria* **142** b2
Mozdok *Russia* 43°45N 44°48E **191** J7
Mozdūrān *Iran* 36°9N 60°35E **247** B9
Mozhaysk *Russia* 55°30N 36°2E **188** E9
Mozhga *Russia* 56°26N 52°15E **190** B11
Mozhnābād *Iran* 34°7N 60°6E **247** C9
Mozirje *Slovenia* 46°22N 14°58E **199** B11
Mozyr = Mazyr *Belarus* 51°59N 29°15E **177** B15
Mpanda *Tanzania* 6°23S 31°1E **268** D3
Mpé *Congo* 2°58S 14°38E **264** C2
Mpese *Dem. Rep. of the Congo* 5°16S 15°30E **265** D3
Mpésoba *Mali* 12°31N 5°39W **262** C3
Mphoeng *Zimbabwe* 21°10S 27°51E **269** G2
Mpika *Zambia* 11°51S 31°25E **269** E3
Mpoko → *C.A.R.* 4°19N 18°33E **264** B3
Mpouya *Congo* 2°38S 16°13E **264** C3
Mpulungu *Zambia* 8°51S 31°5E **269** D3
Mpumalanga *S. Africa* 29°50S 30°33E **271** C5
Mpumalanga □ *S. Africa* 26°0S 30°0E **271** C5
Mpwapwa *Tanzania* 6°23S 36°30E **268** D4
Mqabba *Malta* 35°51N 14°28E **206** F7
Mqanduli *S. Africa* 31°49S 28°45E **271** D4
Mqinvartsveri = Kazbek *Russia* 42°42N 44°30E **191** J7
Mrągowo *Poland* 53°52N 21°18E **184** E8
M'ramani *Comoros Is.* 12°20S 44°31E **272** a
Mramor *Serbia* 43°20N 21°45E **202** C5
Mrauk-u = Myohaung *Burma* 20°35N 93°11E **241** E4
Mrimina *Morocco* 29°50N 7°9W **260** C3
Mrkonjić Grad *Bos.-H.* 44°26N 17°4E **182** F2
Mrkopalj *Croatia* 45°21N 14°52E **199** C11
Mrocza *Poland* 53°16N 17°35E **185** E4
Msaken *Tunisia* 35°49N 10°33E **258** A2
Msambansovu *Zimbabwe* 15°50S 30°3E **269** F3
Msida *Malta* 35°54N 14°29E **206** F7
M'sila *Algeria* 35°46N 4°30E **261** A5
M'sila □ *Algeria* 35°20N 4°20E **261** A5
Msoro *Zambia* 13°35S 31°50E **269** E3
Msta → *Russia* 58°25N 31°20E **188** C6
Mstislavl = Mstsislaw *Belarus* 54°0N 31°50E **177** A16
Mstsislaw *Belarus* 54°0N 31°50E **177** A16
Mszana Dolna *Poland* 49°41N 20°5E **185** J7
Mszczonów *Poland* 51°58N 20°33E **185** G7
Mtama *Tanzania* 10°17S 39°21E **269** E4
Mtamvuna = Mthamvuna → *S. Africa* 31°6S 30°12E **271** D5
Mthamvuna → *S. Africa* 31°6S 30°12E **271** D5
Mthatha *S. Africa* 31°36S 28°49E **271** D4
Mtilikwe → *Zimbabwe* 21°9S 31°30E **269** G3
Mtima *Congo* 3°49S 12°7E **264** C2
Mtirala △ *Georgia* 41°50N 42°2E **191** K6
Mtito Andei *Kenya* 2°41S 38°10E **268** C4
Mtsamboro *Mayotte* 12°42S 45°4E **272** b
Mtsamboro, Î. *Mayotte* 12°38S 45°2E **272** b
Mtsangamouji *Mayotte* 12°45S 45°5E **272** b
Mtsapéré *Mayotte* 12°46S 45°11E **272** b
Mtsensk *Russia* 53°17N 36°36E **188** F9
Mtskheta *Georgia* 41°52N 44°45E **191** K7
Mtubatuba *S. Africa* 28°30S 32°8E **271** C5
Mtwalume *S. Africa* 30°30S 30°38E **271** D5
Mtwara-Mikindani *Tanzania* 10°20S 40°20E **269** E5
Mu → *Burma* 21°56N 95°38E **241** E5
Mu Gia, Deo *Vietnam* 17°40N 105°47E **236** D5
Mu Ko Chang △ *Thailand* 11°59N 102°22E **237** G4
Mu Ko Surin *Thailand* 9°30N 97°55E **237** H1
Mu Us Shamo *China* 39°0N 109°0E **226** E5
Muacandala *Angola* 10°2S 19°40E **265** E3
Muan *S. Korea* 34°59N 126°28E **224** E3
Muaná *Brazil* 1°25S 49°15W **332** B2
Muanda *Dem. Rep. of the Congo* 6°0S 12°20E **265** D2
Muang Beng *Laos* 20°23N 101°46E **228** G3
Muang Chiang Rai = Chiang Rai *Thailand* 19°52N 99°50E **228** H2
Muang Et *Laos* 20°49N 104°1E **236** B5
Muang Hiam *Laos* 20°5N 103°22E **236** B4
Muang Hongsa *Laos* 19°43N 101°20E **236** C3
Muang Houn *Laos* 20°8N 101°23E **228** G3
Muang Kau *Laos* 15°6N 105°47E **236** E5
Muang Khao *Laos* 19°38N 103°32E **236** C4
Muang Khong *Laos* 14°7N 105°51E **236** E5
Muang Khoua *Laos* 21°5N 102°31E **228** G4
Muang Liap *Laos* 18°29N 101°40E **236** C3
Muang Mai *Thailand* 8°5N 98°21E **237** a
Muang May *Laos* 14°49N 106°56E **236** E6
Muang Na Mo *Laos* 21°3N 101°49E **228** G3
Muang Ngeun *Laos* 20°36N 101°3E **228** G3
Muang Ngoi *Laos* 20°43N 102°41E **228** G4
Muang Nong *Laos* 16°22N 106°30E **236** D6
Muang Ou Neua *Laos* 22°18N 101°48E **228** F3
Muang Ou Tay *Laos* 22°7N 101°48E **228** F3
Muang Pak Beng *Laos* 19°54N 101°8E **228** H3
Muang Phalane *Laos* 16°39N 105°34E **236** D5
Muang Phiang *Laos* 19°6N 101°32E **236** C3
Muang Phine *Laos* 16°32N 106°2E **236** D6
Muang Saiapoun *Laos* 18°24N 101°31E **236** C3
Muang Sing *Laos* 21°11N 101°9E **228** G3
Muang Son *Laos* 20°27N 103°19E **236** B4
Muang Soui *Laos* 19°33N 102°52E **236** C4
Muang Va *Laos* 21°53N 102°19E **228** G4
Muang Va *Laos* 18°18N 101°20E **236** C3
Muang Xai *Laos* 20°42N 101°59E **228** G3
Muang Xamteu *Laos* 19°59N 104°38E **236** C5
Muangai *Angola* 12°32S 19°55E **265** E3
Muar *Malaysia* 2°3N 102°34E **237** L4
Muara Takus *Indonesia* 0°20N 100°39E **234** B2
Muaraaman *Indonesia* 3°7S 102°12E **234** C2
Muarabadak *Indonesia* 0°20S 117°26E **235** C5
Muarabeliti *Indonesia* 3°15S 103°1E **234** C2
Muarabungo *Indonesia* 1°28S 102°52E **234** C2
Muaradua *Indonesia* 4°31S 104°4E **234** C2
Muaraenim *Indonesia* 3°40S 103°50E **234** C2
Muarajambi *Indonesia* 1°28S 103°40E **234** C2
Muarajuloi *Indonesia* 0°12S 114°3E **235** C4
Muarakaman *Indonesia* 0°2S 116°45E **235** C5
Muararupit *Indonesia* 2°43S 102°54E **234** C2
Muarasabak *Indonesia* 1°7S 103°51E **234** C2
Muarasiberut *Indonesia* 1°35S 99°12E **234** C1
Muaratebo *Indonesia* 1°30S 102°26E **234** C2
Muaratembesi *Indonesia* 1°42S 103°8E **234** C2
Muarateweh *Indonesia* 0°58S 114°52E **235** C4
Muarawahau *Indonesia* 1°1N 116°52E **235** B5
Mubarakpur *India* 26°6N 83°18E **243** F10
Mubarraz = Al Mubarraz *Si. Arabia* 25°30N 49°40E **247** E6
Mubende *Uganda* 0°33N 31°22E **268** B3
Mubi *Nigeria* 10°18N 13°16E **263** C7
Mucaba, Sa. de *Angola* 7°12S 15°0E **265** D3
Mucajá *Brazil* 3°57S 57°32W **329** D6
Mucajaí → *Brazil* 2°25N 60°52W **329** C5
Mucajaí, Serra do *Brazil* 2°23N 61°10W **329** C5
Mucari *Angola* 9°30S 16°54E **265** D3
Muchachos, Roque de los *Canary Is.* 28°44N 17°52W **153** e1
Mücheln *Germany* 51°17N 11°47E **178** D7
Muchinga Mts. *Zambia* 11°30S 31°30E **269** E3
Muchkapskiy *Russia* 51°52N 42°28E **190** E6
Muchuan *China* 28°57N 103°55E **228** C5
Muck *U.K.* 56°50N 6°15W **167** E2
Muckadilla *Australia* 26°35S 148°23E **281** D4
Muckalee Cr. → *U.S.A.* 31°38N 84°9W **316** D5
Muckaty ☼ *Australia* 18°37S 133°52E **280** B1
Muckle Flugga *U.K.* 60°51N 0°54W **167** A8
Muco → *Colombia* 4°15N 70°21W **328** C3
Mucoma *Angola* 15°18S 13°39E **265** F2
Muconda *Angola* 10°31S 21°15E **265** E4
Mucope *Angola* 16°24S 14°52E **265** F2
Mucugê *Brazil* 13°0S 41°23W **333** D3
Mucuim → *Brazil* 6°33S 64°18W **331** B5
Mucur *Turkey* 39°3N 34°22E **212** C6
Mucura *Brazil* 2°31S 62°43W **329** D5
Mucuri *Brazil* 18°0S 39°36W **333** E4
Mucurici *Brazil* 18°6S 40°31W **333** E3
Mucusso *Angola* 18°1S 21°25E **265** F4
Mucusso ⌓ *Angola* 17°27S 21°0E **265** F4
Mucussueje *Angola* 11°1S 21°56E **265** E4
Muda *Canary Is.* 28°34N 13°57W **153** e2
Mudanjiang *China* 44°38N 129°30E **227** B15
Mudanya *Turkey* 40°25N 28°50E **203** F12
Muddebihal *India* 16°20N 76°8E **245** F3
Muddy Cr. → *U.S.A.* 38°24N 110°42W **304** G8
Mudgee *Australia* 32°32S 149°31E **283** B8
Mudhol *Andhra Pradesh, India* 18°58N 77°55E **244** E3
Mudhol *Karnataka, India* 16°21N 75°17E **245** F2
Mudiata *Dem. Rep. of the Congo* 7°15S 22°1E **265** D4
Mudigere *India* 13°8N 75°38E **245** H2
Mudjatik → *Canada* 56°1N 107°36W **297** B7
Mudon *Burma* 16°15N 97°44E **241** G6
Mudug □ *Somali Rep.* 7°0N 48°0E **267** C6
Mudukulattur *India* 9°21N 78°31E **245** K4
Mudumu △ *Namibia* 18°5S 23°29E **270** A3
Mudurnu *Turkey* 40°27N 31°12E **212** B4
Muecate *Mozam.* 14°55S 39°40E **269** E4
Mueda *Mozam.* 11°36S 39°28E **269** E4
Mueller Ranges *Australia* 18°18S 126°46E **278** C4
Muende *Mozam.* 14°28S 33°0E **269** E3
Muerto, Mar *Mexico* 16°10N 94°10W **319** D6
Mufu Shan *China* 29°20N 114°30E **229** C10
Mufulira *Zambia* 12°32S 28°15E **269** E2
Mufuma *Angola* 9°12S 16°29E **265** D3
Mufumbiro Range *Africa* 1°25S 29°30E **268** C2
Mugardos *Spain* 43°27N 8°15W **194** B2
Muge → *Portugal* 39°8N 8°44W **195** F2
Müggelberge *Germany* 52°25N 13°37E **115** B4
Müggelheim *Germany* 52°24N 13°40E **115** B5
Múggia *Italy* 45°36N 13°46E **199** C10
Muggiò *Italy* 45°35N 9°13E **129** A2
Mughal Gardens *Delhi, India* **120** c1
Mughal Sarai *India* 25°18N 83°7E **243** G10
Mughalzhar Taūy *Kazakhstan* 49°0N 58°40E **216** C5
Mughayrā' *Si. Arabia* 29°17N 37°41E **246** D3
Mugi *Japan* 33°40N 134°25E **222** D6
Mugia = Muxía *Spain* 43°3N 9°10W **194** B1
Mugila, Mts. *Dem. Rep. of the Congo* 7°0S 28°50E **268** D2
Muginga *Angola* 8°21S 17°36E **265** D3
Muğla *Turkey* 37°15N 28°22E **205** D10
Muğla □ *Turkey* 37°15N 28°0E **205** D10
Muglad *Sudan* 11°1N 27°50E **257** E2
Mŭglizh *Bulgaria* 42°37N 25°32E **203** D9
Mugodzhary = Mughalzhar Taūy *Kazakhstan* 49°0N 58°40E **216** C5
Mugu *Nepal* 29°45N 82°30E **243** E10
Muhagiriya *Sudan* 12°0N 25°38E **259** F5
Muhala *Congo* 5°40S 28°43E **268** D2
Muhammad, Râs *Egypt* 27°44N 34°16E **251** L5
Muhammad Qol *Sudan* 20°53N 37°9E **256** C4
Muhammadabad *India* 26°4N 83°25E **243** F10
Muḩayriqah *Si. Arabia* 23°59N 45°4E **248** B4
Muhesi → *Tanzania* 7°0S 35°20E **268** D4
Mühlacker *Germany* 48°57N 8°51E **179** G4
Mühldorf *Germany* 48°14N 12°32E **179** G8
Mühleiten *Austria* 48°10N 16°33E **142** A3
Mühlenfliess → *Germany* 52°32N 13°42E **115** A5
Mühlhausen = Milevsko *Czech Rep.* 49°27N 14°21E **180** B7
Mühlhausen *Germany* 51°12N 10°27E **178** D6
Mühlig Hofmann fjell *Antarctica* 72°30S 5°0E **151** D3
Mühlviertel *Austria* 48°30N 14°10E **180** C7
Muhoro *Kenya* 1°1S 34°7E **266** E3
Muhos *Finland* 64°47N 25°59E **160** D21
Muḩradah *Syria* 35°15N 36°35E **250** C7
Muhu *Estonia* 58°36N 23°11E **188** C2
Muhutwe *Tanzania* 1°35S 31°45E **268** C3
Mui Wo *China* 22°16N 113°59E **219** a
Muiden *Neths.* 52°20N 5°4E **112** A3
Muie *Angola* 14°23S 20°25E **265** E4
Muika *Japan* 37°5N 138°50E **221** F9
Muine Bheag *Ireland* 52°42N 6°58W **166** D5
Muineachán = Monaghan *Ireland* 54°15N 6°57W **166** B5
Muir, L. *Australia* 34°30S 116°40E **279** F2
Muir of Ord *U.K.* 57°32N 4°28W **167** D4
Muisné *Ecuador* 0°36N 80°2W **328** C1
Muizenberg *S. Africa* 34°5S 18°27E **118** B1
Mujahidpur *India* 28°33N 77°14E **120** B2
Mujeres, I. *Mexico* 21°13N 86°43W **320** B2
Mujnak = Muynak *Uzbekistan* 43°44N 59°10E **216** D5
Mujuí dos Campos *Brazil* 2°35S 54°41W **329** D7
Muka, Tanjung *Malaysia* 5°28N 100°11E **237** c
Mukacheve *Ukraine* 48°27N 22°45E **182** B7
Mukachevo = Mukacheve *Ukraine* 48°27N 22°45E **182** B7
Mukah *Malaysia* 2°55N 112°5E **235** B4
Mukandpur *India* 28°44N 77°11E **120** A2
Mukandwara *India* 24°49N 75°59E **242** G6
Mukawa *Papua N. G.* 9°38S 149°59E **286** E5
Mukawwa, Geziret *Egypt* 23°55N 35°53E **246** F2
Mukawwar *Sudan* 20°50N 37°17E **256** C4
Mukaylah *Si. Arabia* 19°16N 41°48E **248** C3
Mukdahan *Thailand* 16°32N 104°43E **236** D5
Mukdahan △ *Thailand* 16°26N 104°45E **236** D5
Mukden = Shenyang *China* 41°48N 123°27E **224** B1
Mukerian *India* 31°57N 75°37E **242** D6
Mukhavyets → *Belarus* 52°5N 23°39E **185** F10
Mukher *India* 18°42N 77°22E **244** E3
Mukhmas *West Bank* 31°52N 35°17E **123** A2
Mukhtolovo *Russia* 55°29N 43°15E **190** C6
Mukhtuya = Lensk *Russia* 60°48N 114°55E **215** C12
Mukinbudin *Australia* 30°55S 118°5E **279** F2
Mukishi *Kasai-Occ., Dem. Rep. of the Congo* 5°39S 21°3E **265** D4
Mukishi *Katanga, Dem. Rep. of the Congo* 8°30S 24°44E **265** D4
Muko *Japan* 34°55N 135°40E **223** C7
Muko → *Japan* 34°48N 135°22E **133** A1
Muko Phetra △ *Thailand* 6°57N 99°33E **237** J2
Mukojima *Japan* 35°43N 139°49E **140** A3
Mukomuko *Indonesia* 2°30S 101°10E **234** C2
Mukomwenze *Dem. Rep. of the Congo* 6°49S 27°15E **268** D2
Mukono *Uganda* 0°21N 32°45E **268** B3
Muktsar *India* 30°30N 74°30E **242** D6
Mukur = Moqor *Afghan.* 32°50N 67°42E **242** C2
Mukutuwa → *Canada* 53°10N 97°24W **297** C9
Mukwela *Zambia* 17°0S 26°40E **269** F2
Mukwonago *U.S.A.* 42°52N 88°20W **311** B8
Mul *India* 20°4N 79°40E **244** D4
Mula *Spain* 38°3N 1°33W **197** G3
Mula → *India* 18°34N 74°21E **244** E2
Mula → *Pakistan* 27°57N 67°36E **242** F2
Mulaku Atoll *Maldives* 3°0N 73°30E **272** d
Mulamba *Dem. Rep. of the Congo* 6°21S 21°13E **265** D4
Mulanay *Phil.* 13°31N 122°24E **232** E4
Mulange *Dem. Rep. of the Congo* 3°40S 27°10E **268** C2
Mulanje, Mt. *Malawi* 16°2S 35°33E **269** F4
Mulatre, Pte. *Dominica* 15°17N 61°15W **323** k
Mulatupo Sasardi *Panama* 8°57N 77°45W **328** B2
Mulbagal *India* 13°10N 78°24E **245** H4
Mulbarton *S. Africa* 26°17S 28°3E **123** B2
Mulberry *U.S.A.* 27°54N 81°59W **317** H8
Mulberry Grove *U.S.A.* 38°56N 89°16W **310** F7
Mulchatna → *U.S.A.* 59°40N 157°7W **303** G8
Mulchén *Chile* 37°45S 72°20W **334** D1
Mulde → *Germany* 51°53N 12°15E **178** D8
Muldraugh *U.S.A.* 37°56N 85°59W **311** G11
Mule Creek Junction *U.S.A.* 43°23N 104°13W **304** E11
Muleba *Tanzania* 1°50S 31°37E **268** C3
Mulegé *Mexico* 26°53N 111°59W **318** B2
Muleshoe *U.S.A.* 34°13N 102°43W **314** D3
Muletta, Gara *Ethiopia* 9°15N 41°44E **257** F5
Mulgrave *Canada* 45°38N 61°31W **299** C7
Mulgrave I. = Badu *Australia* 10°7S 142°11E **280** a
Mulhacén *Spain* 37°4N 3°20W **195** H7
Mülheim *Germany* 51°25N 6°54E **178** D2
Mulhouse *France* 47°40N 7°20E **173** E14
Muli *Sichuan, China* 27°52N 101°8E **228** D3
Muli *Maldives* 2°55N 73°34E **272** d
Mulifanua *Samoa* 13°50S 171°59W **287** V20
Muling *China* 44°35N 130°10E **227** B16
Mulki *India* 13°6N 74°48E **245** H2
Mull *U.K.* 56°25N 5°56W **167** E3
Mull, Sound of *U.K.* 56°30N 5°50W **167** E3
Mullach Íde = Malahide *Ireland* 53°26N 6°9W **120** A3
Mullaittivu *Sri Lanka* 9°15N 80°49E **245** K5
Mullen *U.S.A.* 42°3N 101°1W **308** D3
Mullengudgery *Australia* 31°43S 147°23E **281** B4
Mullens *U.S.A.* 37°35N 81°23W **309** G13
Muller, Pegunungan *Indonesia* 0°30N 113°30E **235** B4
Muller Ra. *Papua N. G.* 5°35S 142°20E **286** C2
Mullet Pen. *Ireland* 54°13N 10°2W **166** B1
Mulletbaai *St.-Maarten* 18°4N 63°7W **322** a
Mullewa *Australia* 28°29S 115°30E **279** E2
Müllheim *Germany* 47°47N 7°36E **179** H3
Mulligan → *Australia* 25°0S 139°0E **280** D2
Mullingar *Ireland* 53°31N 7°21W **166** C4
Mullins *U.S.A.* 34°12N 79°15W **315** D15
Mullsjö *Sweden* 57°56N 13°55E **163** G7
Mullumbimby *Australia* 28°30S 153°30E **281** D5
Mulobezi *Zambia* 16°45S 25°7E **269** F2
Mulondo *Angola* 15°41S 15°12E **265** F3
Mulonga Plain *Zambia* 16°20S 22°40E **265** F4
Mulroy B. *Ireland* 55°15N 7°46W **166** A4
Mulshi L. *India* 18°30N 73°48E **244** E1
Multai *India* 21°50N 78°21E **244** D4
Multan *Pakistan* 30°15N 71°36E **242** D4
Mulu, Gunung *Malaysia* 4°3N 114°56E **235** B4
Mulug *India* 18°11N 79°57E **244** E4
Mulumbe, Mts. *Dem. Rep. of the Congo* 8°40S 27°30E **269** D2
Mulundu *Dem. Rep. of the Congo* 6°40S 20°33E **265** D4
Mulungushi Dam *Zambia* 14°48S 28°48E **269** E2
Mulurulu L. *Australia* 33°15S 143°20E **282** B5
Mulvane *U.S.A.* 37°29N 97°15W **308** G5
Mulwad *Sudan* 18°45N 30°39E **256** D3
Mulwala *Australia* 35°59S 146°0E **283** C7
Mulwala, L. *Australia* 35°59S 146°1E **281** C4
Muma *Dem. Rep. of the Congo* 3°25N 23°21E **264** B4
Mumbai *India* 18°56N 72°50E **130** B2
Mumbai Chhatrapati Shivaji Int. ✈ (BOM) *India* 19°5N 72°51E **130** A2
Mumbai Harbour *India* 18°58N 72°55E **130** B2
Mumbeji *Zambia* 13°51S 23°39E **265** E4
Mumbondo *Angola* 10°9S 14°15E **265** E2
Mumbwa *Zambia* 15°0S 27°0E **269** F2
Mumeng *Papua N. G.* 7°1S 146°37E **286** D4
Mumias *Kenya* 0°20N 34°29E **268** C4
Mummel Gulf △ *Australia* 31°17S 151°51E **283** A9
Mumra *Russia* 45°45N 47°41E **191** H8
Mun → *Thailand* 15°19N 105°30E **236** E5
Mun-gyeong *S. Korea* 36°35N 128°12E **224** D4
Muna *Indonesia* 5°0S 122°30E **231** F6
Munabao *India* 25°45N 70°17E **242** G4
Munakata *Japan* 33°48N 130°38E **222** D2
Munamagi *Estonia* 57°43N 27°4E **188** D4
Muncan *Indonesia* 8°34S 115°11E **231** K18
Muncar *Indonesia* 8°26S 114°20E **231** J17
Munch-museum *Norway* 59°55N 10°46E **133** A3
Münchberg *Germany* 50°11N 11°47E **179** E7
Müncheberg *Germany* 52°30N 14°9E **178** C10
Münchehofe *Germany* 52°29N 13°40E **115** B5
München *Germany* 48°8N 11°34E **131** B2
München Franz Josef Strauss Int. ✈ (MUC) *Germany* 48°21N 11°47E **131** A2
Munchen-Gladbach = Mönchengladbach *Germany* 51°11N 6°27E **178** D2
Munchique △ *Colombia* 2°44N 77°1W **328** C2
Muncho Lake *Canada* 59°0N 125°50W **296** B3
Munch'ŏn *N. Korea* 39°14N 127°19E **224** C3
Muncie *U.S.A.* 40°12N 85°23W **311** D11
Muncoonie L. West *Australia* 25°12S 138°40E **280** D2
Munda *Solomon Is.* 8°20S 157°16E **287** M9
Mundabbera *Australia* 25°36S 151°18E **281** D5
Mundakayam *India* 9°30N 76°50E **245** K3
Mundal *Sri Lanka* 7°48N 79°48E **245** L4
Munday *U.S.A.* 33°27N 99°38W **314** E5
Mundelein *U.S.A.* 42°16N 88°0W **311** B8
Mundemba *Cameroon* 4°57N 8°52E **264** B1
Münden *Germany* 51°25N 9°38E **178** D5
Münden ⌓ *Germany* 51°28N 9°42E **178** D5
Mundiwindi *Australia* 23°47S 120°9E **278** D3
Mundo → *Spain* 38°30N 2°15W **197** G2
Mundo Novo *Brazil* 11°50S 40°29W **333** D3
Mundo Nuevo *Trin. & Tob.* 10°28N 61°15W **323** t
Mundra *India* 22°54N 69°48E **242** H3
Mundrabilla *Australia* 31°52S 127°51E **279** F4
Munenga *Angola* 10°2S 14°41E **265** E2
Munera *Spain* 39°2N 2°29W **197** F2
Muneru → *India* 16°45N 80°3E **244** F5
Mungallala *Australia* 26°28S 147°34E **281** D4
Mungallala Cr. → *Australia* 28°53S 147°5E **281** D4
Mungana *Australia* 17°8S 144°27E **280** B3
Mungaoli *India* 24°24N 78°7E **242** G8
Mungari *Mozam.* 17°12S 33°30E **269** F3
Mungbere *Dem. Rep. of the Congo* 2°36N 28°28E **268** B2
Mungeli *India* 22°4N 81°41E **243** H9
Munger *India* 25°23N 86°30E **243** G12
Mungerannie *Australia* 28°1S 138°39E **281** A2
Mungilli ☼ *Australia* 25°14S 124°17E **279** E3
Mungkan Kandju △ *Australia* 13°35S 142°52E **280** A3
Mungkarta ☼ *Australia* 20°22S 134°2E **280** C1
Mungo *Angola* 11°49S 16°16E **265** E3
Mungo, L. *Australia* 33°45S 143°0E **282** B5
Mungo △ *Australia* 33°44S 143°6E **282** B5
Munhango *Angola* 12°10S 18°38E **265** E3
Munhango → *Angola* 11°17S 19°44E **265** E4
Munich = München *Germany* 48°8N 11°34E **131** B2
Munirabad *India* 15°20N 76°20E **245** F3
Munising *U.S.A.* 46°25N 86°40W **308** B10
Munka-Ljungby *Sweden* 56°16N 12°58E **163** H6
Munkebo *Denmark* 55°27N 10°34E **163** J4
Munkedal *Sweden* 58°28N 11°40E **163** F5
Munkfors *Sweden* 59°47N 13°30E **162** E7
Munkkiniemi *Finland* 60°11N 24°52E **121** B2
Munku-Sardyk *Russia* 51°45N 100°20E **215** D11
Münnerstadt *Germany* 50°14N 10°12E **179** E6
Munnsville *U.S.A.* 42°58N 75°35W **313** D9
Munoz *Phil.* 15°43N 120°54E **232** D3
Muñoz Gamero, Pen. *Chile* 52°30S 73°5W **336** D2
Munro *Argentina* 34°31S 58°31W **117** B1
Munroe L. *Canada* 59°13N 98°35W **297** B9
Munsan *S. Korea* 37°51N 126°48E **224** D3
Munshiganj *Bangla.* 23°33N 90°32E **241** D3
Munson *U.S.A.* 30°52N 86°52W **317** E3
Munster *Haut-Rhin, France* 48°2N 7°8E **173** D14
Münster *Niedersachsen, Germany* 52°58N 10°5E **178** C6
Münster *Nordrhein-Westfalen, Germany* 51°58N 7°37E **178** D3
Munster □ *Ireland* 52°18N 8°44W **166** D3
Münsterberg = Ziębice *Poland* 50°37N 17°2E **185** H4
Muntadgin *Australia* 31°45S 118°33E **279** F2
Muntele Mare, Vf. *Romania* 46°30N 23°12E **183** D8
Muntinlupa *Phil.* 14°23N 121°2E **127** C2
Muntok *Indonesia* 2°5S 105°10E **234** C3
Munzur Dağları *Turkey* 39°30N 39°10E **213** C8
Muong Nhie *Vietnam* 22°12N 102°28E **228** F4
Muong Sen *Vietnam* 19°24N 104°8E **236** C5
Muong Te *Vietnam* 22°24N 102°49E **228** F4
Muong Xia *Vietnam* 20°19N 104°50E **236** B5
Muonio *Finland* 67°57N 23°40E **160** C20
Muonio älv = Muonionjoki → *Finland* 67°11N 23°34E **160** C20
Muonioälven = Muonionjoki → *Finland* 67°11N 23°34E **160** C20
Muonionjoki → *Finland* 67°11N 23°34E **160** C20
Mupa *Angola* 16°5S 15°50E **265** F3
Mupa → *Mozam.* 18°58S 35°54E **269** F4
Mupa △ *Angola* 15°55S 15°35E **265** F3
Muping *China* 37°22N 121°36E **227** F11
Mupoi *Sudan* 5°28N 27°40E **257** F2
Muqaddam, Wadi → *Sudan* 18°4N 31°30E **256** D3
Muqdisho *Somali Rep.* 2°2N 45°25E **267** D6
Muqshin, W. → *Oman* 19°44N 55°14E **249** C6
Muquequete *Angola* 14°50S 14°16E **265** E2
Mur → *Austria* 46°18N 16°52E **181** E9
Mûr-de-Bretagne *France* 48°12N 3°0W **172** D4
Muradiye *Manisa, Turkey* 38°39N 27°21E **205** C9
Muradiye *Van, Turkey* 39°0N 43°44E **213** C10
Murai Res. *Singapore* 1°23N 103°40E **138** A2
Murakami *Japan* 38°14N 139°29E **220** E9
Muralag = Prince of Wales I. *Australia* 10°40S 142°10E **286** F2
Murallón, Cerro *Chile* 49°48S 73°30W **336** C2
Muranda *Rwanda* 1°52S 29°20E **268** C2
Murang'a *Kenya* 0°45S 37°9E **268** C4
Muranów *Poland* 52°14N 20°58E **142** B1
Murashi *Russia* 59°30N 49°0E **186** C8
Murat *France* 45°7N 2°53E **174** C6
Murat → *Turkey* 38°46N 40°0E **213** C9
Murat Bay = Ceduna *Australia* 32°7S 133°46E **281** E1
Murat Dağı *Turkey* 38°55N 29°43E **205** C11
Muratlı *Turkey* 41°10N 27°29E **203** E11
Murato *France* 42°35N 9°20E **175** F13
Murau *Austria* 47°6N 14°10E **180** D7
Murava *Belarus* 52°39N 24°15E **185** F11
Muravera *Italy* 39°25N 9°34E **200** C2
Muravyevo = Mažeikiai *Lithuania* 56°20N 22°20E **184** B9
Muravyovsky = Korsakov *Russia* 46°36N 142°42E **215** E15
Murayama *Japan* 38°30N 140°25E **220** E10
Murça *Portugal* 41°24N 7°28W **194** D3
Murcaayo *Somali Rep.* 11°41N 50°34E **267** B7
Murchison *N.Z.* 41°49S 172°21E **285** B7
Murchison → *Australia* 27°45S 114°0E **279** E1
Murchison, Mt. *Antarctica* 73°25S 166°20E **151** D11
Murchison, Mt. *N.Z.* 43°0S 171°22E **285** D6
Murchison Falls *Uganda* 2°15N 31°30E **268** B3
Murchison Falls △ *Uganda* 2°17N 31°48E **268** B3
Murchison Mts. *N.Z.* 45°13S 167°23E **285** F2
Murchison Ra. *Australia* 20°0S 134°10E **280** C1
Murchison Rapids *Malawi* 15°55S 34°35E **269** F3
Murchison Roadhouse *Australia* 27°39S 116°14E **279** E2
Murcia *Spain* 38°5N 1°10W **197** G3
Murcia □ *Spain* 37°50N 1°30W **197** H3
Murdo *U.S.A.* 43°53N 100°43W **308** D3
Murdoch Pt. *Australia* 14°37S 144°55E **280** A3
Mürefte *Turkey* 40°40N 27°14E **203** F11
Mureş □ *Romania* 46°45N 24°40E **183** D9
Mureş → *Romania* 46°15N 20°13E **182** D5
Mureşul = Mureş → *Romania* 46°15N 20°13E **182** D5
Muret *France* 43°30N 1°20E **174** E5
Murewa *Zimbabwe* 17°39S 31°47E **271** A5
Murfreesboro *N.C., U.S.A.* 36°27N 77°6W **315** C16
Murfreesboro *Tenn., U.S.A.* 35°51N 86°24W **315** D11
Murgap *Tajikistan* 38°10N 74°2E **217** E8
Murgap → *Turkmenistan* 38°18N 61°12E **247** B9
Murgenella *Australia* 11°34S 132°56E **278** B5
Murgeni *Romania* 46°12N 28°1E **183** D13
Murgha Kibzai *Pakistan* 30°44N 69°25E **242** D3
Murghob = Murgap *Tajikistan* 38°10N 74°2E **217** E8
Murgon *Australia* 26°15S 151°54E **281** D5
Muri *Cook Is.* 21°15S 159°43W **289** h
Muri *India* 23°22N 85°52E **243** H11
Muria *Indonesia* 6°36S 110°53E **235** D4
Muriaé *Brazil* 21°8S 42°23W **333** F3
Murias de Paredes *Spain* 42°52N 6°11W **194** C4
Murici *Brazil* 9°19S 35°56W **332** C4
Muriége *Angola* 9°58S 21°11E **265** D4
Muriel Mine *Zimbabwe* 17°14S 30°40E **269** F3
Murila *Angola* 10°44S 20°20E **265** E4
Murino *Russia* 59°59N 30°29E **137** B2
Müritz *Germany* 53°25N 12°42E **178** B8
Müritz △ *Germany* 53°22N 12°55E **178** B8
Muriwai Beach *N.Z.* 36°50S 174°26E **284** C3
Murkong Selek *India* 27°44N 95°18E **241** B5
Murliganj *India* 25°54N 86°59E **243** G12
Murmansk *Russia* 68°57N 33°10E **160** B25
Murmashi *Russia* 68°47N 32°42E **160** B25
Murnau *Germany* 47°40N 11°12E **179** H7
Muro *Haute-Corse, France* 42°34N 8°54E **175** F12
Muro *Spain* 39°44N 3°3E **206** B4
Muro, C. de *France* 41°44N 8°37E **175** G12
Muro de Alcoy *Spain* 38°46N 0°26W **197** G4
Muro Lucano *Italy* 40°45N 15°29E **201** B8
Murom *Russia* 55°35N 42°3E **190** C6
Muroran *Japan* 42°25N 141°0E **220** C10
Muros *Spain* 42°45N 9°5W **194** C1
Muros e Noya, Ría de → *Spain* 42°45N 9°0W **194** C1
Muroto *Japan* 33°18N 134°9E **222** D6
Muroto-Misaki *Japan* 33°15N 134°10E **222** D6
Murovani Kurylivtsi *Ukraine* 48°44N 27°31E **183** B12
Murowana Goślina *Poland* 52°35N 17°0E **185** F3
Murphy *U.S.A.* 43°13N 116°33W **304** E5
Murphys *U.S.A.* 38°8N 120°28W **306** G6
Murphy's Station = Sunnyvale *U.S.A.* 37°23N 122°2W **306** H4
Murphysboro *U.S.A.* 37°46N 89°20W **310** G7
Murrat *Sudan* 18°51N 29°33E **256** D2
Murrat Wells *Sudan* 21°3N 32°55E **256** C3
Murray *Queens., Australia* 9°56S 144°2E **280** a
Murray *Iowa, U.S.A.* 41°3N 93°57W **310** C3
Murray *Ky., U.S.A.* 36°37N 88°19W **308** G9
Murray *Utah, U.S.A.* 40°40N 111°53W **304** F8
Murray → *Australia* 35°20S 139°22E **282** C3
Murray, L. *Papua N. G.* 7°0S 141°35E **286** D1
Murray, L. *S.C., U.S.A.* 34°3N 81°13W **316** A8
Murray Bridge *Australia* 35°6S 139°14E **282** C3
Murray Fracture Zone *Pac. Oc.* 35°0N 130°0W **289** D14
Murray Harbour *Canada* 46°0N 62°28W **299** C7
Murray River △ *Australia* 34°23S 140°32E **281** E3
Murray-Sunset △ *Australia* 34°45S 141°30E **282** C4
Murrayfield *U.K.* 55°57N 3°15W **121** B2
Murraysburg *S. Africa* 31°58S 23°47E **270** D3
Murrayville *U.S.A.* 39°35N 90°15W **310** E6
Murree *Pakistan* 33°56N 73°28E **242** C5
Murrieta *U.S.A.* 33°33N 117°13W **307** M9
Murro di Porco, Capo *Italy* 37°0N 15°20E **201** F8
Murrumbateman *Australia* 34°58S 149°0E **283** C8
Murrumbidgee → *Australia* 34°43S 143°12E **282** C5
Murrumburrah *Australia* 34°32S 148°22E **283** C8
Murrurundi *Australia* 31°42S 150°51E **283** A9
Murshid *Sudan* 21°40N 31°10E **256** C3
Murshidabad *India* 24°11N 88°19E **243** G13
Murska Sobota *Slovenia* 46°39N 16°12E **199** B13
Murtala Mohammed International ✈ (LOS) *Nigeria* 6°34N 3°19E **124** A1
Murtazapur *India* 20°40N 77°25E **244** D3
Murtle L. *Canada* 52°8N 119°38W **296** C5
Murtoa *Australia* 36°35S 142°28E **282** D5
Murtosa *Portugal* 40°44N 8°40W **194** E2
Muru → *Brazil* 8°9S 70°45W **330** B3
Murud *India* 18°19N 72°58E **244** E1
Murung → *Indonesia* 0°12N 114°3E **235** B4
Murungu *Tanzania* 4°12S 31°10E **268** C3
Murupara *N.Z.* 38°28S 176°42E **284** E5
Mururoa *French Polynesia* 21°52S 138°55W **289** f
Murwara *India* 23°46N 80°28E **243** H9
Murwillumbah *Australia* 28°18S 153°27E **281** D5
Mürz → *Austria* 47°30N 15°25E **180** D8
Mürzzuschlag *Austria* 47°36N 15°41E **180** D8
Mus *India* 9°14N 92°47E **245** K11
Muş *Turkey* 38°45N 41°30E **213** C9
Muş □ *Turkey* 38°45N 41°30E **213** C9
Musa *Dem. Rep. of the Congo* 2°40N 19°18E **264** B3
Musa → *Papua N. G.* 9°3S 148°55E **286** E5
Mûsa, Gebel *Egypt* 28°33N 33°59E **251** K4
Musa Khel *Pakistan* 30°59N 69°52E **242** D3
Mūsa Qal'eh *Afghan.* 32°20N 64°50E **240** B2
Musabeyli *Turkey* 36°53N 36°55E **250** B7

Musadi
Dem. Rep. of the Congo 2°31S 22°50E 264 C4
Musafirkhana India 26°22N 81°48E 243 F9
Musala Bulgaria 42°13N 23°37E 202 D7
Musala Indonesia 1°41N 98°28E 234 B1
Musan N. Korea 42°12N 129°12E 224 A4
Musandam, Ra's Oman 26°20N 56°20E 249 A7
Musangu
Dem. Rep. of the Congo 10°28S 23°55E 265 E4
Musasa Tanzania 3°25S 31°30E 268 C3
Musashino Japan 35°42N 139°33E 140 A2
Musay'īd Qatar 25°0N 51°33E 247 E6
Musaymīr Yemen 13°27N 44°37E 248 D4
Muscat = Masqat Oman 23°37N 58°36E 249 B7
Muscat & Oman = Oman ■
Asia 23°0N 58°0E 249 B7
Muscatatuck → U.S.A. 38°46N 86°10W 311 F10
Muscatine U.S.A. 41°25N 91°3W 310 C5
Muschu I. Papua N. G. 3°25S 143°35E 286 B2
Muscle Shoals U.S.A. 34°45N 87°40W 315 D11
Muscoda U.S.A. 43°11N 90°27W 310 A6
Musengezi = Unsengedsi →
Zimbabwe 15°43S 31°14E 269 F3
Museu Nacional Brazil 22°59S 43°13W 135 B1
Museumquartier Vienna, Austria 142 c1
Musgrave Harbour
Canada 49°27N 53°58W 299 C9
Musgrave Ranges Australia 26°0S 132°0E 279 E5
Mushie
Dem. Rep. of the Congo 2°56S 16°55E 264 C3
Mushima Zambia 14°10S 24°56E 265 E4
Mushin Nigeria 6°31N 3°21E 124 A2
Musi → India 16°41N 79°40E 244 F4
Musi → Indonesia 2°20S 104°56E 234 C2
Musiektheater Amsterdam, Neths. 112 b3
Musina S. Africa 22°20S 30°5E 271 B5
Musiri India 10°56N 78°27E 245 J4
Muskeg → Canada 60°20N 123°20W 296 A4
Muskego U.S.A. 42°55N 88°8W 311 B8
Muskegon U.S.A. 43°14N 86°16W 311 A10
Muskegon → U.S.A. 43°14N 86°21W 308 D10
Muskegon Heights
U.S.A. 43°12N 86°16W 311 A10
Muskogee U.S.A. 35°45N 95°22W 314 D7
Muskoka, L. Canada 45°0N 79°25W 312 B5
Muskoka Falls Canada 44°59N 79°17W 312 B5
Muskwa → Canada 58°47N 122°48W 296 B4
Muslim Mindanao □ Phil. 8°0N 123°0E 233 H3
Muslim Quarter Jerusalem 123 a3
Muslīmiyah Syria 36°19N 37°12E 246 B3
Musmar Sudan 18°13N 35°40E 256 D4
Musocco Italy 45°29N 9°8E 129 B1
Musofu Zambia 13°30S 29°0E 269 E2
Musoma Tanzania 1°30S 33°48E 268 C3
Musquaro, L. Canada 50°38N 61°5W 299 B7
Musquodoboit Harbour
Canada 44°50N 63°9W 299 D7
Mussau I. Papua N. G. 1°30S 149°40E 286 A5
Musselburgh U.K. 55°57N 3°2W 167 F5
Musselshell → U.S.A. 47°21N 107°57W 304 C10
Mussende Angola 10°32S 16°5E 265 E3
Musserra Angola 7°37S 13°2E 265 D2
Mussidan France 45°2N 0°22E 174 C4
Mussolinea di Sardegna = Arboréa
Italy 39°46N 8°35E 200 C1
Mussolo Angola 9°59S 17°19E 265 D3
Mussomeli Italy 37°35N 13°45E 200 E6
Mussoorie India 30°27N 78°6E 242 D8
Mussuco Angola 17°2S 19°3E 265 F3
Mustafakemalpaşa
Turkey 40°2N 28°24E 203 F12
Mustahil Ethiopia 5°16N 44°45E 267 C5
Mustang Nepal 29°10N 83°55E 243 E10
Mustansirīya Iraq 33°22N 44°24E 113 A2
Musters, L. Argentina 45°20S 69°25W 336 C3
Mustique I. St. Vincent 12°52N 61°11W 323 n
Musturud Egypt 30°8N 31°17E 117 A2
Musudan N. Korea 40°50N 129°43E 224 B4
Muswell Hill U.K. 51°35N 0°8W 125 A3
Muswellbrook Australia 32°16S 150°56E 283 B9
Muszyna Poland 49°22N 20°55E 185 J7
Mût Egypt 25°28N 28°58E 256 B2
Mut Turkey 36°40N 33°28E 250 B4
Mutalau Cook Is. 18°56S 169°50W 289 g
Mutanabi Iraq 33°19N 44°21E 113 B2
Mutanda
Dem. Rep. of the Congo 5°17S 16°34E 265 D3
Mutanda Mozam. 21°0S 33°34E 271 B5
Mutanda Zambia 12°24S 26°13E 269 E2
Mutankiang = Mudanjiang
China 44°38N 129°30E 227 B15
Mutanshe Taiwan 22°9N 120°48E 225 D2
Mutare Zimbabwe 18°58S 32°38E 269 F3
Mutawintji △ Australia 31°10S 142°30E 281 E3
Mutha Kenya 1°48S 38°26E 268 C4
Muthana Iraq 33°19N 44°27E 113 B2
Muting Indonesia 7°23S 140°20E 231 F10
Mutki = Mirtağ Turkey 38°23N 41°56E 246 B4
Mutoko Zimbabwe 17°24S 32°13E 271 A5
Mutomo Kenya 1°51S 38°12E 268 C4
Mutoray Russia 60°56N 101°0E 215 C11
Mutoto
Dem. Rep. of the Congo 5°42S 22°42E 265 D4
Mutoxo Angola 12°17S 21°40E 265 E4
Mutsamudu Comoros Is. 12°10S 44°25E 272 a
Mutshatsha
Dem. Rep. of the Congo 10°35S 24°20E 265 E4
Mutsu Japan 41°5N 140°55E 220 D10
Mutsu-Wan Japan 41°5N 140°55E 220 D10
Muttaburra Australia 22°38S 144°29E 280 C3
Muttalip Turkey 39°50N 30°32E 205 B12
Mutton I. Ireland 52°49N 9°32W 166 D2
Muttra = Mathura India 27°30N 77°40E 242 F7
Muttukuru India 14°16N 80°6E 245 G5
Mutuáli Mozam. 14°55S 37°0E 269 E4
Mutum Biyu Nigeria 8°40N 10°50E 263 D7
Mutumba Burundi 3°25S 29°21E 268 C2
Mutunópolis Brazil 13°40S 49°15W 333 F2
Mutur Sri Lanka 8°27N 81°16E 245 K5
Muweilih Egypt 30°42N 34°19E 251 H5
Muxaluando Angola 8°8S 14°18E 265 D2
Muxia Spain 43°3N 9°10W 194 B1
Muxima Angola 9°33S 13°58E 265 D2
Muy Muy Nic. 12°39N 85°36W 320 D2
Muyinga Burundi 3°14S 30°33E 268 C3
Muynak Uzbekistan 43°44N 59°10E 216 D5
Muyunkum, Peski = Moyynqum
Kazakhstan 44°12N 71°0E 217 D8
Muz Tag China 36°25N 87°25E 217 E11
Muzaffarabad Pakistan 34°25N 73°30E 243 B5
Muzaffargarh Pakistan 30°5N 71°14E 242 D4
Muzaffarnagar India 29°26N 77°40E 242 E7
Muzaffarpur India 26°7N 85°23E 243 F11
Muzafirpur Pakistan 30°58N 69°9E 242 D3
Muzeze Angola 15°3S 17°43E 265 F3
Muzhi Russia 65°25N 64°40E 186 A11
Muzillac France 47°35N 2°30W 172 E4
Muzon, C. U.S.A. 54°40N 132°42W 303 J14
Muztagh-Ata China 38°17N 75°7E 217 E9
Muztor = Toktogul
Kyrgyzstan 41°50N 72°50E 217 D8
Muzūra Egypt 28°53N 30°48E 256 J7
Mvadhi-Ousyé Gabon 1°13N 13°12E 264 B2
Mvam Gabon 0°13S 9°39E 264 C1
Mvangan Cameroon 2°17N 11°43E 264 B2
Mvôlô Sudan 6°2N 29°53E 257 F2
Mvuma Zimbabwe 19°16S 30°30E 269 F3
Mvurwi Zimbabwe 17°0S 30°57E 269 F3
Mwabvi △ Malawi 16°42S 35°0E 269 F3
Mwadi-Kalumbu
Dem. Rep. of the Congo 7°53S 18°43E 265 D3
Mwadui Tanzania 3°26S 33°32E 268 C3
Mwali = Mohéli Comoros Is. 12°20S 43°40E 272 a
Mwambo Tanzania 10°30S 40°22E 269 E5
Mwandi Zambia 17°30S 24°51E 269 F1
Mwanza Katanga,
Dem. Rep. of the Congo 7°55S 26°43E 265 D5
Mwanza Tanzania 2°30S 32°58E 268 C3
Mwanza Zambia 16°58S 24°28E 265 F4
Mwanza □ Tanzania 2°0S 33°0E 268 C3
Mwaya Tanzania 9°32S 33°55E 269 D3
Mweelrea Ireland 53°39N 9°49W 166 C2
Mweka
Dem. Rep. of the Congo 4°50S 21°34E 265 C4
Mwendjila
Dem. Rep. of the Congo 7°12S 18°51E 265 D3
Mwene-Ditu
Dem. Rep. of the Congo 6°35S 22°27E 265 D4
Mwenezi Zimbabwe 21°15S 30°48E 269 G3
Mwenezi → Mozam. 22°40S 31°50E 269 G3
Mwenga
Dem. Rep. of the Congo 3°1S 28°28E 268 C2
Mweru, L. Zambia 9°0S 28°40E 269 D2
Mweru Wantipa △ Zambia 8°39S 29°25E 269 D2
Mwetshi
Dem. Rep. of the Congo 4°50S 22°38E 265 C4
Mweza Range Zimbabwe 21°0S 30°0E 269 G3
Mwilambwe
Dem. Rep. of the Congo 8°7S 25°5E 265 D5
Mwimbi Tanzania 8°38S 31°39E 269 D3
Mwingi Kenya 0°56S 38°4E 268 C4
Mwinilunga Zambia 11°43S 24°25E 265 E4
My Son Vietnam 15°48N 108°7E 236 E7
My Tho Vietnam 10°29N 106°23E 237 G6
Mya, O. → Algeria 30°46N 4°54E 261 B5
Myajlar India 26°15N 70°20E 242 F4
Myakinino Russia 55°48N 37°22E 129 B2
Myakka → U.S.A. 26°56N 82°11W 317 J7
Myall Lakes △ Australia 32°25S 152°30E 283 B10
Myanaung Burma 18°18N 95°22E 241 F5
Myanmar = Burma ■ Asia 21°0N 96°30E 241 E6
Myaungmya Burma 16°30N 94°40E 241 G5
Mycenæ = Mikines
Greece 37°43N 22°46E 204 D4
Myebon Burma 20°3N 93°22E 241 E4
Myedna Belarus 51°52N 23°42E 185 G10
Myeik = Mergui Burma 12°26N 98°34E 236 F2
Myeik Kyunzu Burma 11°30N 97°30E 237 G1
Myerstown U.S.A. 40°22N 76°19W 313 F8
Myingyan Burma 21°30N 95°20E 241 E5
Myitkyina Burma 25°24N 97°26E 241 C6
Myitson Burma 23°16N 96°34E 241 D6
Myitta Burma 21°25N 96°8E 241 E6
Myittha → Burma 23°12N 94°17E 241 D5
Myjava Slovak Rep. 48°41N 17°37E 181 C10
Mykerinos Egypt 29°58N 31°8E 117 B1
Mykhaylivka Ukraine 47°12N 35°15E 189 J8
Mykines Færoe Is. 62°7N 7°35W 160 E9
Myking Norway 60°41N 5°19E 164 D2
Mykolayiv Ukraine 46°58N 32°0E 189 J7
Mykolayiv □ Ukraine 47°20N 31°50E 189 J6
Mykonos Greece 37°30N 25°25E 205 D7
Mylius Erichsen Land
Greenland 81°30N 27°0W 154 A8
Myllypuro Finland 60°13N 25°3E 121 B3
Mymensingh Bangla. 24°45N 90°24E 241 C3
Mynydd Du U.K. 51°52N 3°50W 169 F4
Myo-gyi Burma 21°27N 96°22E 241 E6
Myohaung Burma 20°35N 93°11E 241 E4
Myohla Burma 19°16N 95°25E 241 F5
Myotha Burma 21°41N 95°43E 241 E5
Myothit Kachin, Burma 24°24N 97°24E 241 C6
Myothit Magwe, Burma 20°12N 95°27E 241 E5
Myrasýsla □ Iceland 64°45N 21°30W 155 C5
Mýrdalsjökull Iceland 63°40N 19°6W 155 D7
Myrhorod Ukraine 49°58N 33°37E 189 H7
Mýri Iceland 65°23N 17°23W 155 B9
Myrtle Beach U.S.A. 33°42N 78°53W 315 E15
Myrtle Creek U.S.A. 43°1N 123°17W 304 E2
Myrtle Grove U.S.A. 30°23N 87°17W 317 E2
Myrtle Point U.S.A. 43°4N 124°8W 304 E1
Myrtleford Australia 36°34S 146°44E 283 D7
Myrtou Cyprus 35°18N 33°4E 207 E9
Myrviken Sweden 62°58N 14°20E 162 B8
Mysen Norway 59°33N 11°20E 164 E8
Mysia Turkey 39°50N 27°0E 203 G11
Myślenice Poland 49°51N 19°57E 185 J6
Myślibórz Poland 52°55N 14°50E 185 F1
Mysłowice Poland 50°15N 19°12E 185 H6
Mysłowitz = Mysłowice
Poland 50°15N 19°12E 185 H6
Mysore = Karnataka □
India 13°15N 77°0E 245 H3
Mysore India 12°17N 76°41E 245 H3
Mystic Conn., U.S.A. 41°21N 71°58W 313 E13
Mystic Iowa, U.S.A. 40°47N 92°57W 310 D4
Mystic → U.S.A. 42°22N 71°3W 116 A2
Mysuru = Mysore India 12°17N 76°41E 245 H3
Myszków Poland 50°45N 19°22E 185 H6
Myszyniec Poland 53°23N 21°21E 184 E8
Mytishchi Russia 55°50N 37°50E 188 E9
Mývatn Iceland 65°36N 17°0W 155 B10
M'zab, Oued → Algeria 32°15N 5°0E 261 B6
Mže → Czech Rep. 49°46N 13°24E 180 B6
Mzimba Malawi 11°55S 33°39E 269 E3
Mzimkulu → S. Africa 30°44S 30°28E 271 D5
Mzimvubu → S. Africa 31°38S 29°33E 271 D4
Mzuzu Malawi 11°30S 33°55E 269 E3

N

Na Clocha Liatha = Greystones
Ireland 53°9N 6°5W 166 C5
Na Haeo △ Thailand 17°31N 100°58E 236 D3
Na Hearadh = Harris U.K. 57°50N 6°55W 167 D2
Na-lang Burma 22°42N 97°33E 241 D6
Na Noi Thailand 18°19N 100°43E 236 C3
Na Phao Laos 17°35N 105°44E 236 D5
Na Sam Vietnam 22°3N 106°37E 228 F6
Na Thon Thailand 9°32N 99°56E 237 b
Naab → Germany 49°1N 12°2E 179 F8
Na'ālehu U.S.A. 19°4N 155°35W 302 D6
Na'am Sudan 9°42N 28°27E 257 F2
Na'am → Sudan 6°48N 29°57E 257 F2
Naama Algeria 33°16N 0°19E 261 B5
Naama □ Algeria 33°15N 0°45E 261 B5
Naantali Finland 60°29N 22°2E 188 B1
Naas Ireland 53°12N 6°40W 166 C5
Nababeep S. Africa 29°36S 17°46E 270 C2
Nabadwip = Navadwip
India 23°34N 88°20E 243 H13
Nabari Japan 34°37N 136°5E 223 C8
Nabawa Australia 28°30S 114°48E 279 E1
Nabberu, L. Australia 25°50S 120°30E 279 E3
Nabburg Germany 49°27N 12°11E 179 F8
Naberezhnyye Chelny
Russia 55°42N 52°19E 190 C11
Nabesna U.S.A. 62°22N 143°0W 303 E12
Nabeul Tunisia 36°30N 10°44E 258 A2
Nabeul □ Tunisia 36°30N 10°40E 261 A7
Nabha India 30°26N 76°14E 242 D7
Nabī Sâlih Egypt 28°37N 33°59E 251 K4
Nabīd Iran 29°40N 57°38E 247 D8
Nabire Indonesia 3°15S 135°26E 231 E9
Nabisar Pakistan 25°8N 69°40E 242 G3
Nabisipi → Canada 50°14N 62°13W 299 B7
Nabiswera Uganda 1°27N 32°15E 268 B3
Nāblus = Nābulus
West Bank 32°14N 35°15E 251 F6
Naboomspruit S. Africa 24°32S 28°40E 271 B4
Nabou Burkina Faso 11°25N 2°50W 262 C4
Nabouwalu Fiji 17°0S 178°45E 287 A2
Nabq Egypt 28°5N 34°25E 251 K5
Nabua Phil. 13°24N 123°22E 232 E4
Nābulus West Bank 32°14N 35°15E 251 F6
Nabunturan Phil. 7°35N 125°58E 233 H5
Nacala Mozam. 14°32S 40°34E 269 E5
Nacaome Honduras 13°31N 87°30W 320 D2
Nacaroa Mozam. 14°22S 39°56E 269 E4
Naches U.S.A. 46°44N 120°42W 304 C3
Naches → U.S.A. 46°38N 120°31W 306 D6
Nachicapau, L. Canada 56°40N 68°5W 299 A6
Nachikatsuura Japan 33°33N 135°58E 223 D7
Nachingwea Tanzania 10°23S 38°49E 269 E4
Nachna India 27°34N 71°41E 242 F4
Náchod Czech Rep. 50°25N 16°8E 180 A9
Nachuge India 10°47N 92°21E 245 J11
Nacimiento, L. U.S.A. 35°46N 120°53W 306 K6
Nacka Sweden 59°19N 18°10E 139 B3
Nackara Australia 32°48S 139°12E 282 B3
Naco Mexico 31°19N 109°56W 318 A3
Nacogdoches U.S.A. 31°36N 94°39W 314 F7
Nácori Chico Mexico 29°40N 108°57W 318 B3
Nacozari de García
Mexico 30°25N 109°38W 318 A3
Nacula Fiji 16°54S 177°27E 287 A1
Nada = Danzhou China 19°31N 109°33E 236 C7
Nådendal = Naantali
Finland 60°29N 22°2E 188 B1
Nadezhdinsky = Serov
Russia 59°29N 60°35E 186 C11
Nadi Fiji 17°42S 177°20E 287 A1
Nadi Sudan 18°40N 33°41E 256 D3
Nadiad India 22°41N 72°56E 242 H5
Nădlac Romania 46°10N 20°50E 182 D5
Nador Morocco 35°14N 2°58W 261 A4
Nadur Malta 35°54N 14°22E 206 F7
Nadur Gozo, Malta 36°2N 14°18E 206 E7
Nadūshan Iran 32°2N 53°35E 247 C7
Nadvirna Ukraine 48°37N 24°30E 183 B9
Nadvoitsy Russia 63°52N 34°14E 186 B5
Nadvornaya = Nadvirna
Ukraine 48°37N 24°30E 183 B9
Nadym Russia 65°35N 72°42E 214 C8
Nadym → Russia 66°12N 72°0E 214 C8
Naenae N.Z. 41°12S 174°57E 133 B1
Nærbø Norway 58°40N 5°39E 164 F2
Næsnes Norway 59°45N 10°27E 133 B1
Næstved Denmark 55°13N 11°44E 163 J5
Nafada Nigeria 11°8N 11°20E 263 C7
Nafpaktos Greece 38°24N 21°50E 204 C3
Nafplio Greece 37°33N 22°50E 204 D4
Naft-e Safīd Iran 31°40N 49°17E 247 D6
Naftan Pt. N. Marianas 15°5N 145°45E 302 e
Naftshahr Iran 34°0N 45°30E 213 E11
Nafud Desert = An Nafūd
Si. Arabia 28°15N 41°0E 246 D4
Nafūsah, Jabal Libya 32°12N 12°30E 258 B2
Nag Hammâdi Egypt 26°2N 32°18E 256 B3
Naga Japan 26°34N 127°43E 288 a
Naga Camarines S., Phil. 13°38N 123°15E 232 E4
Naga Cebu, Phil. 10°13N 123°45E 233 F4
Naga Zamboanga del S.,
Phil. 7°46N 122°45E 233 H4
Naga, Kreb en Africa 24°12N 6°0W 260 D3
Naga Hills = Nagaland □
India 26°0N 94°30E 241 C5
Naga-Shima Kagoshima,
Japan 32°10N 130°9E 222 E2
Naga-Shima Yamaguchi,
Japan 33°49N 132°5E 222 D4
Nagagami Canada 50°23N 84°20W 298 B3
Nagahama Ehime, Japan 33°36N 132°29E 222 D4
Nagahama Shiga, Japan 35°23N 136°16E 223 B8
Nagai Japan 38°6N 140°2E 220 E10
Nagai I. U.S.A. 55°5N 160°0W 303 J8
Nagaland □ India 26°0N 94°30E 241 C5
Nagambie Australia 36°47S 145°10E 283 D6
Nagano Japan 36°40N 138°10E 223 A10
Nagano □ Japan 36°15N 138°0E 223 A10
Nagaoka Japan 37°27N 138°51E 221 F9
Nagaon = Nowgong India 26°20N 92°50E 241 B4
Nagappattinam India 10°46N 79°51E 245 J4
Nagar → Bangla. 24°27N 89°12E 241 C2
Nagar Karnul India 16°29N 78°20E 245 F4
Nagar Parkar Pakistan 24°28N 70°46E 242 G4
Nagara-Gawa → Japan 35°40N 136°43E 223 B8
Nagaram India 18°21N 80°26E 244 E5
Nagarhole △ India 12°0N 76°10E 245 J3
Nagari Hills India 13°3N 79°45E 245 H4
Nagarjuna Sagar India 16°30N 79°13E 245 F4
Nagasaki Japan 32°47N 129°50E 222 E1
Nagasaki □ Japan 32°50N 129°40E 222 E1
Nagato Japan 34°19N 131°5E 222 C3
Nagatsuta Japan 35°32N 139°31E 140 B2
Nagaur India 27°15N 73°45E 242 F5
Nagayo Japan 32°48N 129°52E 222 E1
Nagbhir India 20°34N 79°55E 244 D4
Nagda India 23°27N 75°25E 242 H6
Nagercoil India 8°12N 77°26E 245 K3
Nagina India 29°30N 78°30E 243 E8
Nagīneh Iran 34°20N 57°15E 247 C8
Naginimara India 26°49N 94°54E 241 B5
Nagir Pakistan 36°12N 74°42E 243 A6
Naglarby Sweden 60°25N 15°34E 162 D9
Nagles Mts. Ireland 52°8N 8°30W 166 D3
Nago-wan Japan 26°34N 127°57E 288 a
Nagod India 24°34N 80°36E 243 G9
Nagold Germany 48°32N 8°43E 179 G4
Nagold → Germany 48°52N 8°42E 179 G4
Nagoorin Australia 24°17S 151°15E 280 C5
Nagorno-Karabakh □
Azerbaijan 39°55N 46°45E 213 C12
Nagornyy Russia 55°58N 124°57E 215 D13
Nagoya Indonesia 1°15N 104°5E 234 B2
Nagoya Japan 35°10N 136°50E 223 B8
Nagoya ✗ (NGO) Japan 35°14N 136°57E 223 B8
Nagpartian = Burgos
Phil. 18°31N 120°39E 232 B3
Nagpur India 21°8N 79°10E 244 D4
Nagqu China 31°29N 92°3E 218 E7
Nags Head St. Kitts & Nevis 17°13N 62°38W 322 d
Nagua Dom. Rep. 19°23N 69°50W 321 C6
Naguabo Puerto Rico 18°13N 65°44W 321 d
Nagurunguru ✪
Australia 16°45S 129°45E 278 C4
Nagyatád Hungary 46°14N 17°22E 182 D2
Nagyecsed Hungary 47°53N 22°24E 182 C7
Nagykálló Hungary 47°53N 21°51E 182 C6
Nagykanizsa Hungary 46°28N 17°0E 182 D2
Nagykáta Hungary 47°25N 19°45E 182 C4
Nagykőrös Hungary 47°5N 19°48E 182 C4
Nagyszombat = Trnava
Slovak Rep. 48°23N 17°35E 181 C10
Nagytétény Hungary 47°23N 18°59E 117 B1
Nagyvárad = Oradea
Romania 47°2N 21°58E 182 C6
Naha Japan 26°13N 127°42E 288 a
Nahabuan Indonesia 0°49N 114°4E 235 B4
Nahalin West Bank 31°41N 35°7E 123 B1
Nahan India 30°33N 77°18E 242 D7
Nahanni △ Canada 61°36N 125°41W 296 A4
Nahanni Butte Canada 61°2N 123°31W 296 A4
Nahargarh Mad. P., India 24°10N 75°14E 242 G6
Nahargarh Raj., India 24°55N 76°50E 242 G7
Nahariyya Israel 33°1N 35°5E 250 F6
Nahāvand Iran 34°10N 48°22E 213 E13
Nahe → Germany 49°58N 7°54E 179 F3
Nahirne Ukraine 45°26N 28°27E 183 E13
Nahîya, W. → Egypt 28°55N 31°0E 256 B3
Nahuel Huapi, L. Argentina 41°0S 71°32W 336 B2
Nahuel Huapi △ Argentina 41°3S 71°59W 336 B2
Nahuelbuta △ Chile 37°44S 72°57W 334 D1
Nahunta U.S.A. 31°12N 81°59W 316 D8
Nai Yong Thailand 8°14N 98°22E 237 a
Naic Phil. 14°19N 120°46E 232 D3
Naicá Mexico 27°53N 105°31W 318 B3
Naicam Canada 52°30N 104°30W 297 C8
Naifaru Maldives 5°26N 73°20E 272 d
Naikoon △ Canada 53°55N 131°55W 296 C2
Naikul India 21°20N 84°58E 244 D7
Naila Germany 50°19N 11°42E 179 E7
Naimisharanya India 27°21N 80°30E 243 F9
Naimona'nyi Feng Nepal 30°26N 81°18E 243 D9
Nain Nfld. & L., Canada 56°34N 61°40W 299 A7
Nā'īn Iran 32°54N 53°0E 247 C7
Nain Jamaica 17°57N 77°38W 320 a
Naini Tal India 29°30N 79°30E 243 E8
Nainpur India 22°30N 80°10E 243 H9
Naintré France 46°46N 0°29E 172 F7
Nainwa India 25°46N 75°51E 242 G6
Naipu Romania 44°12N 25°47E 183 F10
Nairai Fiji 17°49S 179°15E 287 A2
Nairn U.K. 57°35N 3°53W 167 D5
Nairobi Kenya 1°17S 36°48E 268 C4
Nairobi △ Kenya 1°22S 36°50E 268 C4
Naissaar Estonia 59°34N 24°29E 188 C3
Naita, Mt. Ethiopia 5°30N 35°18E 257 F4
Naitaba Fiji 17°0S 179°16W 287 A3
Naivasha Kenya 0°40S 36°30E 268 C4
Naivasha, L. Kenya 0°48S 36°20E 268 C4
Najac France 44°14N 1°58E 174 D5
Najaf = An Najaf Iraq 32°3N 44°15E 213 G11
Najafābād Iran 32°40N 51°15E 247 C6
Najafgarh Drain → India 28°39N 77°4E 120 B1
Najd Si. Arabia 26°30N 42°0E 248 A3
Nájera Spain 42°26N 2°48W 196 C2
Najerilla → Spain 42°32N 2°48W 196 C2
Najibabad India 29°40N 78°20E 242 E8
Najin N. Korea 42°12N 130°15E 224 A5
Najmah Si. Arabia 26°42N 50°6E 247 E6
Najrān Si. Arabia 17°34N 44°18E 248 C4
Najrān □ Si. Arabia 18°30N 45°50E 248 C4
Naju S. Korea 35°3N 126°43E 224 E3
Naka Japan 36°30N 140°35E 223 A12
Naka-Gawa → Japan 36°20N 140°36E 223 A12
Nakadōri-Shima Japan 32°57N 129°4E 221 H4
Nakagusuku-wan Japan 26°14N 127°53E 288 a
Nakahara Japan 35°33N 139°37E 140 B2
Nakał = Nakło nad Notecią
Poland 53°9N 17°38E 185 E4
Nakalagba
Dem. Rep. of the Congo 2°50N 27°58E 268 B2
Nakalele Pt. U.S.A. 21°2N 156°35W 302 B5
Nakama Japan 33°56N 130°43E 222 D2
Nakambé = White Volta →
Ghana 9°10N 1°15W 263 D4
Nakaminato Japan 36°21N 140°36E 223 A12
Nakamura Japan 32°59N 132°56E 222 E4
Nakanai Mts. Papua N. G. 5°40S 151°0E 286 C6
Nakano Nagano, Japan 36°45N 138°22E 223 A10
Nakano Tōkyō, Japan 35°42N 139°39E 140 A2
Nakano-Shima Japan 29°51N 129°52E 221 K4
Nakanojō Japan 36°35N 138°51E 223 A10
Nakashibetsu Japan 43°33N 144°59E 220 C12
Nakatsu Japan 33°34N 131°15E 222 D3
Nakatsugawa Japan 35°29N 137°30E 223 B9
Nakfa Eritrea 16°40N 38°32E 257 D4
Nakfa △ Eritrea 17°28N 38°55E 257 D4
Nakha Yai, Ko Thailand 8°3N 98°28E 237 a
Nakhichevan = Naxçıvan
Azerbaijan 39°12N 45°15E 213 C11
Nakhichevan Rep. = Naxçıvan □
Azerbaijan 39°25N 45°26E 213 C11
Nakhl Egypt 29°55N 33°43E 251 J4
Nakhl-e Taqī Iran 27°28N 52°36E 247 E7
Nakhodka Russia 42°53N 132°54E 220 C6
Nakhon Nayok Thailand 14°12N 101°13E 236 E3
Nakhon Pathom Thailand 13°49N 100°3E 236 F3
Nakhon Phanom
Thailand 17°23N 104°43E 236 D5
Nakhon Ratchasima
Thailand 14°59N 102°12E 236 E4
Nakhon Sawan Thailand 15°35N 100°10E 236 E3
Nakhon Si Thammarat
Thailand 8°29N 100°0E 237 H3
Nakhon Thai Thailand 17°5N 100°44E 236 D3
Nakhtarana India 23°20N 69°15E 242 H3
Nakijin Japan 26°40N 127°58E 288 a
Nakina Canada 50°10N 86°40W 298 B2
Nakło nad Notecią Poland 53°9N 17°38E 185 E4
Naknek U.S.A. 58°44N 157°1W 303 G8
Nako Burkina Faso 10°40N 3°4W 262 C4
Nakodar India 31°8N 75°31E 242 D6
Nakskov Denmark 54°50N 11°8E 163 K5
Naktong → S. Korea 35°7N 128°57E 227 G15
Nakuru Kenya 0°15S 36°4E 268 C4
Nakuru, L. Kenya 0°23S 36°5E 268 C4
Nakusp Canada 50°20N 117°45W 296 C5
Nal Pakistan 27°40N 66°12E 242 F2
Nal → Pakistan 25°20N 65°30E 242 G1
Nalázi Mozam. 24°3S 33°20E 271 B5
Nalchik Russia 43°30N 43°33E 191 J6
Nałęczów Poland 51°17N 22°9E 185 G9
Nalerigu Ghana 10°35N 0°25W 263 C4
Nalgonda India 17°6N 79°15E 244 F4
Nalhati India 24°17N 87°52E 243 G12
Naliya India 23°16N 68°50E 242 H3
Nallamalai Hills India 15°30N 78°50E 245 G4
Nallıhan Turkey 40°11N 31°20E 212 B4
Nalolo Zambia 15°33S 23°7E 265 F4
Nalón → Spain 43°32N 6°4W 194 B4
Nalong Burma 24°44N 97°28E 241 C6
Nalubaale Dam Uganda 0°30N 33°5E 268 B3
Nalumasortoq Greenland 60°23N 44°28W 154 E6
Nālūt Libya 31°54N 11°0E 258 B2
Nālūt □ Libya 31°52N 10°58E 258 B2
Nam Can Vietnam 8°46N 104°59E 237 H5
Nam-ch'on N. Korea 38°15N 126°26E 224 C3
Nam Co China 30°30N 90°45E 218 E7
Nam Dinh Vietnam 20°25N 106°5E 228 G6
Nam Du, Quan Dao
Vietnam 9°41N 104°21E 237 H5
Nam Hke → Burma 25°34N 95°41E 228 G2
Nam Loi → Burma 21°3N 98°27E 228 G3
Nam Nao △ Thailand 16°44N 101°32E 236 D3
Nam Ngum Res. Laos 18°35N 102°34E 236 C4
Nam-Phan Vietnam 10°30N 106°0E 237 G6
Nam Phong Thailand 16°42N 102°52E 236 D4
Nam Theun Res. Laos 17°51N 105°3E 236 D5
Nam Tok Thailand 14°21N 99°4E 236 E2
Nam Un Res. Thailand 17°13N 103°44E 236 D4
Namachire Angola 11°26S 22°43E 265 E4
Namacunde Angola 17°18S 15°50E 265 F3
Namacurra Mozam. 17°30S 36°50E 271 A6
Namadgi △ Australia 35°42S 149°0E 283 C8
Namai B. Palau 7°31N 134°38E 288 c
Namak, Daryācheh-ye
Iran 34°30N 52°0E 247 C7
Namak, Kavir-e Iran 34°30N 57°30E 247 C8
Namakkal India 11°13N 78°13E 245 J4
Namakzār, Daryācheh-ye
Iran 34°0N 60°30E 240 B1
Namaland Namibia 26°0S 17°0E 270 B2
Namanga Kenya 2°33S 36°47E 268 C4
Namangan Uzbekistan 41°0N 71°40E 217 D8
Namangan □ Uzbekistan 41°0N 71°15E 217 D8
Namapa Mozam. 13°43S 39°50E 269 E4
Namaqua △ S. Africa 30°0S 17°30E 270 D2
Namaqualand S. Africa 30°0S 17°25E 270 D2
Namasagali Uganda 1°2N 33°0E 268 B3
Namatanai Papua N. G. 3°40S 152°29E 286 B7
Namber Indonesia 1°2S 134°49E 231 E8
Nambour Australia 26°32S 152°58E 281 D5
Nambouwalu = Nabouwalu
Fiji 17°0S 178°45E 287 A2
Nambuangongo Angola 8°1S 14°12E 265 D2
Nambucca Heads
Australia 30°37S 153°0E 283 A10
Nambung △ Australia 30°30S 115°5E 279 F2
Namcha Barwa China 29°40N 95°10E 218 F8
Namche Bazar Nepal 27°51N 86°47E 243 F12
Namchonjŏm = Nam-ch'on
N. Korea 38°15N 126°26E 224 C3
Namdapha △ India 27°30N 96°50E 241 B6
Namecunda Mozam. 14°54S 37°37E 269 E4
Nameh Indonesia 2°34N 116°21E 235 B5
Namen = Namur Belgium 50°27N 4°52E 170 D4
Namenalala Fiji 17°8S 179°9E 287 A2
Nameponda Mozam. 15°50S 39°50E 269 F4
Nameri △ India 26°55N 92°55E 241 B4
Namerikawa Japan 36°46N 137°20E 223 A9
Náměšť nad Oslavou
Czech Rep. 49°12N 16°10E 181 B9
Námestovo Slovak Rep. 49°24N 19°25E 181 B12
Nametil Mozam. 15°40S 39°21E 269 F4
Namew L. Canada 54°14N 101°56W 297 C8
Namgia India 31°48N 78°40E 243 D8
Namhkam Burma 23°50N 97°41E 228 E1
Namho Burma 22°4N 99°1E 228 F2
Namhsan Burma 22°48N 97°2E 241 D6
Namialo Mozam. 14°55S 39°59E 269 E4
Namib Desert Namibia 22°30S 15°0E 270 B2
Namib-Naukluft ⌓
Namibia 24°40S 15°16E 270 B2
Namibe Angola 15°7S 12°11E 265 F2
Namibe □ Angola 16°35S 12°30E 265 F2
Namibe ⌓ Angola 16°35S 12°20E 265 F2
Namibia ■ Africa 22°0S 18°9E 270 B2
Namibia Abyssal Plain
Atl. Oc. 30°0S 5°30E 152 J12
Namibwoestyn = Namib Desert
Namibia 22°30S 15°0E 270 B2
Namīn Iran 38°25N 48°30E 213 C13
Namjeju S. Korea 33°14N 126°33E 224 a
Namlan Burma 22°15N 97°24E 241 D6
Namlea Indonesia 3°18S 127°5E 231 E7
Namoi → Australia 30°12S 149°30E 283 A8
Namous, O. en → Algeria 31°0N 0°15W 261 B4
Nampa U.S.A. 43°34N 116°34W 304 E5
Nampala Mali 15°20N 5°30W 262 B3
Namp'o N. Korea 38°52N 125°10E 224 C2
Namp'o □ N. Korea 38°52N 125°25E 224 C2
Nampō-Shotō Japan 32°0N 140°0E 221 J10
Nampula Mozam. 15°6S 39°15E 269 F4
Namrole Indonesia 3°46S 126°46E 231 E7
Namsan Park S. Korea 37°32N 126°59E 137 B1
Namsang Burma 20°53N 97°43E 241 E6
Namse Shankou China 30°0N 82°25E 243 E10
Namsen → Norway 64°28N 11°37E 160 D14
Namslau = Namysłów
Poland 51°6N 17°42E 185 G4
Namsos Norway 64°29N 11°30E 160 D14
Namtok Chat Trakan △
Thailand 17°17N 100°40E 236 D3
Namtok Huay Yang △
Thailand 11°35N 99°30E 237 G2
Namtok Mae Surin △
Thailand 18°55N 98°2E 236 C2
Namtok Ngao △ Thailand 9°58N 98°46E 237 H2
Namtok Phlew △
Thailand 12°32N 102°13E 236 F4
Namtok Yong △ Thailand 8°15N 98°45E 237 H2
Namtsy Russia 62°43N 129°37E 215 C13
Namtu Burma 23°5N 97°28E 241 D6
Namtumbo Tanzania 10°30S 36°4E 269 E4
Namu Canada 51°52N 127°50W 296 C3
Namuka-i-Lau Fiji 18°53S 178°37W 287 B3
Namukulu Cook Is. 18°57S 169°54W 289 g
Namumea Tuvalu 5°41S 176°9E 277 B14
Namur Belgium 50°27N 4°52E 170 D4
Namur □ Belgium 50°17N 5°0E 170 D4
Namuruputh Kenya 4°34N 35°57E 268 B4
Namutoni Namibia 18°49S 16°55E 270 A2
Namwala Zambia 15°44S 26°30E 269 F2
Namwon Jeju-do, S. Korea 33°16N 126°43E 224 a
Namwon Jeollabuk-do,
S. Korea 35°23N 127°23E 224 E3
Namyang N. Korea 42°57N 129°52E 224 A4
Namyangju S. Korea 37°38N 127°12E 224 D3
Namyeong S. Korea 37°32N 126°57E 137 B1
Namysłów Poland 51°6N 17°42E 185 G4
Nan Thailand 18°48N 100°46E 236 C3
Nan → Thailand 15°42N 100°9E 236 E3
Nan-ch'ang = Nanchang
China 28°42N 115°55E 229 C10
Nan Ling China 25°0N 112°30E 229 E8
Nan Xian China 29°20N 112°22E 229 C9
Nana C.A.R. 5°0N 15°50E 264 A3
Nana Romania 44°17N 26°34E 183 F11
Nana-Barya △ C.A.R. 7°40N 17°29E 264 A3
Nana Kru Liberia 4°55N 8°45W 262 E3
Nanaimo Canada 49°10N 124°0W 296 D4
Nānākuli U.S.A. 21°24N 158°9W 302 K13
Nanam N. Korea 41°44N 129°40E 224 B4
Nan'an China 24°59N 118°21E 229 E12
Nanango Australia 26°40S 152°0E 281 D5
Nan'ao Guangdong, China 23°28N 117°5E 229 F11
Nan'ao Japan 37°0N 137°0E 221 F8
Nanao Taiwan 24°28N 121°48E 225 B3
Nanbiancun China 23°4N 113°1E 121 B1
Nanbu China 31°18N 106°3E 228 B6
Nanchang China 28°42N 115°55E 229 C10
Nanchang He → China 39°58N 116°14E 114 B1
Nancheng China 27°33N 116°35E 229 D11
Nanching = Nanjing
China 32°2N 118°47E 229 A12
Nanchong China 30°43N 106°2E 228 B6
Nanchuan China 29°9N 107°6E 228 C6
Nanchung = Nanchong
China 30°43N 106°2E 228 B6
Nancowry India 7°59N 93°32E 245 L11
Nancy France 48°42N 6°12E 173 D13
Nanda Devi India 30°23N 79°59E 243 D8
Nanda Devi △ India 30°30N 79°50E 243 D8
Nanda Kot India 30°17N 80°5E 243 D9
Nandan Guangxi Zhuangzu,
China 24°58N 107°29E 228 E6
Nandan Japan 34°10N 134°42E 222 C6
Nandang China 23°6N 113°12E 121 B2
Nanded India 19°10N 77°20E 244 E3
Nandewar Ra. Australia 30°15S 150°35E 281 E5
Nandgaon India 20°19N 74°39E 244 D2
Nandi = Nadi Fiji 17°42S 177°20E 287 A1
Nandi Zimbabwe 20°58S 31°44E 269 G3
Nandigama India 16°47N 80°18E 244 F5
Nandigram India 22°1N 87°58E 243 H12
Nandikotkur India 15°52N 78°18E 245 G4
Nandura India 20°52N 76°25E 244 D3
Nandurbar India 21°20N 74°15E 244 D2
Nandyal India 15°30N 78°30E 245 G4
Nanfeng Guangdong,
China 23°45N 111°47E 229 F8
Nanfeng Jiangxi, China 27°12N 116°28E 229 D11
Nang Rong Thailand 14°38N 102°48E 236 E4
Nanga-Eboko Cameroon 4°41N 12°22E 263 E7
Nanga Parbat Pakistan 35°10N 74°35E 243 B6
Nangade Mozam. 11°5S 39°36E 269 E4
Nangal Dewat India 28°33N 77°5E 120 B1
Nangalao I. Phil. 11°26N 120°10E 233 F3
Nangamau Indonesia 0°6S 111°55E 235 C4
Nangamentebah Indonesia 0°33N 112°46E 235 B4
Nangapinoh Indonesia 0°20S 111°44E 235 C4
Nangar △ Australia 33°23S 148°3E 283 B8
Nangarhār □ Afghan. 34°20N 70°0E 240 B3
Nangatayap Indonesia 1°32S 110°34E 235 C4
Nangbéto, L. de Togo 7°26N 1°25E 262 D5
Nangeya Mts. Uganda 3°30N 33°30E 268 B3
Nangis France 48°33N 3°1E 173 D10
Nangnim-sanmaek
N. Korea 40°13N 126°51E 224 B3
Nangong China 37°23N 115°22E 226 F8
Nangtud, Mt. Phil. 11°17N 122°11E 233 F4
Nanguneri India 8°29N 77°40E 245 K3
Nangwarry Australia 37°33S 140°48E 282 D4
Nanhua Yunnan, China 25°13N 101°21E 228 E3
Nanhua Taiwan 23°2N 120°28E 225 C2
Nanhuang China 36°58N 121°48E 227 F11
Nanhui China 31°5N 121°44E 229 B13
Nanhunan Shan Taiwan 24°21N 121°26E 225 B3
Nanisivik Canada 73°2N 84°33W 295 C15
Naniwa Japan 34°39N 135°29E 133 B1
Nanjangud India 12°6N 76°43E 245 H3
Nanji Shan China 27°27N 121°4E 229 D13
Nanjian China 25°2N 100°25E 228 E3
Nanjiang China 32°28N 106°51E 228 A6
Nanjing Fujian, China 24°25N 117°20E 229 E11
Nanjing Jiangsu, China 32°2N 118°47E 229 A12
Nanjirinji Tanzania 9°41S 39°5E 269 D4
Nankana Sahib Pakistan 31°27N 73°38E 242 D5
Nankang Jiangxi, China 25°40N 114°45E 229 E10
Nankang Taiwan 25°3N 121°35E 225 A3
Nanking = Nanjing
China 32°2N 118°47E 229 A12
Nankoku Japan 33°39N 133°44E 222 D5
Nanlang China 22°30N 113°32E 219 a
Nanliao Taiwan 24°50N 120°55E 225 B2
Nanling China 30°55N 118°20E 229 B12
Nannial India 19°4N 79°38E 244 E4
Nanning China 22°48N 108°20E 228 F7
Nannup Australia 33°59S 115°48E 279 F2
Nanole India 19°0N 72°55E 130 A2
Nanortalik Greenland 60°10N 45°17W 154 E6
Nanpan Jiang → China 25°10N 106°5E 228 E6
Nanpara India 27°52N 81°33E 243 F9
Nanping Fujian, China 26°38N 118°10E 229 D12
Nanping Henan, China 29°55N 112°3E 229 C9
Nanpu Bridge China 31°12N 121°30E 138 B2
Nanri Dao China 25°15N 119°25E 229 E12
Nansei-Shotō = Ryūkyū-Rettō
Japan 26°0N 126°0E 221 M3
Nansen Basin Arctic 84°0N 50°0E 150 A10
Nansen Land Greenland 83°0N 43°0W 154 A6
Nansen Sd. Canada 81°0N 91°0W 295 A13
Nansha China 22°45N 113°34E 219 a
Nanshan China 18°19N 109°10E 236 C7
Nanshan I. S. China Sea 10°45N 115°49E 230 B5
Nanshi China 31°12N 121°29E 138 B1
Nansio Tanzania 2°3S 33°4E 268 C3
Nant France 44°1N 3°18E 174 D7
Nantawarrinna ✪
Australia 30°49S 138°58E 281 B2
Nanterre France 48°53N 2°12E 134 A2
Nantes France 47°12N 1°33W 172 E5
Nantiat France 46°1N 1°11E 174 B5
Nanticoke U.S.A. 41°12N 76°0W 313 E8
Nanton Canada 50°21N 113°46W 296 C6
Nanton Pt. Antigua & B. 17°0N 61°45W 322 b
Nantong China 32°1N 120°52E 229 A13
Nantou China 22°32N 113°55E 219 a
Nant'ou Taiwan 23°55N 120°41E 225 C2
Nant'ou □ Taiwan 23°50N 121°0E 225 C3
Nantua France 46°10N 5°35E 173 F12
Nantucket U.S.A. 41°17N 70°6W 309 E18
Nantucket I. U.S.A. 41°16N 70°5W 309 E18
Nantulo Mozam. 12°32S 38°45E 269 E4
Nantung = Nantong
China 32°1N 120°52E 229 A13
Nantwich U.K. 53°4N 2°31W 168 D5
Nanty Glo U.S.A. 40°28N 78°50W 312 F6
Nantzu Taiwan 22°44N 120°19E 225 D2
Nanuku Passage Fiji 16°45S 179°15W 287 A3
Nanumanga Pac. Oc. 6°18S 176°20E 277 B14
Nanuque Brazil 17°50S 40°21W 333 E3
Nanusa, Kepulauan
Indonesia 4°45N 127°1E 231 D7
Nanutarra Roadhouse
Australia 22°32S 115°30E 278 D2
Nanwan Taiwan 21°57N 120°46E 225 E2
Nanxi China 28°54N 104°59E 228 C5
Nanxiong China 25°6N 114°15E 229 E10
Nanyang China 33°11N 112°30E 226 H7
Nanyi Hu China 31°5N 119°0E 229 B12
Nanyuan China 39°47N 116°24E 226 E9
Nanyuki Kenya 0°2N 37°4E 268 B4
Nanzhang China 31°45N 111°50E 229 B8
Nanzhao China 33°30N 112°20E 226 H7
Nao, C. de la Spain 38°44N 0°14E 197 G5
Naococane, L. Canada 52°50N 70°45W 299 B5
Naogaon Bangla. 24°52N 88°52E 241 C2
Naoné Vanuatu 15°0S 168°8E 287 E6
Naoussa Cyclades, Greece 37°7N 25°14E 205 D7
Naoussa Imathia, Greece 40°42N 22°9E 202 F6
Naozhou Dao China 20°55N 110°20E 229 G8
Napa U.S.A. 38°18N 122°17W 306 G4
Napa → U.S.A. 38°10N 122°19W 306 G4
Napaimiut U.S.A. 61°33N 158°42W 303 F8
Napakiak U.S.A. 60°42N 161°57W 303 F7
Nāpali Coast U.S.A. 22°11N 159°39W 302 A2
Napanee Canada 44°15N 77°0W 312 B8
Napanoch U.S.A. 41°44N 74°22W 313 E10
Napaskiak U.S.A. 60°43N 161°55W 303 F7
Nape Laos 18°18N 105°6E 236 C5
Nape Pass = Keo Neua, Deo
Vietnam 18°23N 105°10E 236 C5
Naperville U.S.A. 41°46N 88°9W 311 C8
Napier N.Z. 39°30S 176°56E 284 F5
Napier Broome B.
Australia 14°2S 126°37E 278 B4

Napier Mole *Pakistan* 24°49N 66°58E **123** B1
Napier Pen. *Australia* 12°4S 135°43E **280** A2
Napierville *Canada* 45°11N 73°25W **313** A11
Napili-Honokowai *U.S.A.* 20°58N 156°39W **302** C5
Naples = Nápoli *Italy* 40°50N 14°15E **201** B7
Naples *U.S.A.* 26°8N 81°48W **317** J8
Naples Park *U.S.A.* 26°17N 81°46W **317** J8
Napo *China* 23°22N 105°50E **228** F5
Napo □ *Ecuador* 0°30S 77°0W **328** D2
Napo → *Peru* 3°20S 72°40W **328** D3
Napoleon *N. Dak., U.S.A.* 46°30N 99°46W **308** B4
Napoleon *Ohio, U.S.A.* 41°23N 84°8W **311** C12
Napoleon's Tomb *St. Helena* 15°56S 5°42W **153** h
Nápoli *Italy* 40°50N 14°15E **201** B7
Nápoli, G. di *Italy* 40°43N 14°10E **201** B7
Nápoli Capodichino ✈ (NAP) *Italy* 40°53N 14°16E **201** B7
Napopo *Dem. Rep. of the Congo* 4°15N 28°0E **268** B2
Nappanee *U.S.A.* 41°27N 86°0W **311** C11
Napperby *Australia* 33°9S 138°7E **282** B3
Naqadeh *Iran* 36°57N 45°23E **213** D11
Naqb, Ra's an *Jordan* 29°48N 35°44E **251** J6
Naqqāsh *Iran* 35°40N 49°6E **247** C6
När *Sweden* 57°15N 18°35E **163** G10
Nara *Japan* 34°40N 135°49E **223** C7
Nara *Mali* 15°10N 7°20W **262** B3
Nara □ *Japan* 34°30N 136°0E **223** C8
Nara Canal *Pakistan* 24°30N 69°20E **242** G3
Nara Visa *U.S.A.* 35°37N 103°6W **305** J12
Naracoorte *Australia* 36°58S 140°45E **282** D4
Naradhan *Australia* 33°34S 146°17E **283** B7
Naraina *India* 28°36N 77°8E **120** B1
Naraini *India* 25°11N 80°29E **243** G9
Naranjos *Mexico* 21°21N 97°41W **319** C5
Narasannapeta *India* 18°25N 84°3E **244** E7
Narasapur *India* 16°26N 81°40E **245** F5
Narasaropet *India* 16°14N 80°4E **245** F5
Narathiwat *Thailand* 6°30N 101°48E **237** J3
Narayanapatnam *India* 18°53N 83°10E **244** E6
Narayangadh = Bharatpur *Nepal* 27°34N 84°10E **243** F11
Narayanganj *Bangla.* 23°40N 90°33E **241** D3
Narayanpet *India* 16°45N 77°30E **244** F3
Narbada = Narmada → *India* 21°38N 72°36E **242** J5
Narberth *U.K.* 51°47N 4°44W **169** F3
Narbonne *France* 43°11N 3°0E **174** E7
Narborough, I. = Fernandina, I. *Ecuador* 0°25S 91°30W **330** a
Narbuvoll *Norway* 62°21N 11°27E **164** B8
Narcea → *Spain* 43°33N 6°44W **194** B4
Narcondam I. *India* 13°20N 94°16E **245** H12
Nardīn *Iran* 37°3N 55°59E **247** B7
Nardò *Italy* 40°11N 18°2E **201** B11
Narembeen *Australia* 32°7S 118°24E **279** F2
Narendranagar *India* 30°10N 78°18E **242** D8
Nares Abyssal Plain *Atl. Oc.* 22°0N 67°0W **152** D5
Nares Str. *Arctic* 80°0N 70°0W **154** B3
Naretha *Australia* 31°0S 124°45E **279** F3
Narew → *Poland* 52°26N 20°41E **185** F7
Nari → *Pakistan* 28°0N 67°40E **242** F2
Nariman Point *Mumbai, India* **130** c1
Nariman Pt. *India* 18°55N 72°49E **130** B1
Narin *Afghan.* 36°5N 69°0E **240** A3
Narindra, Helodranon' i *Madag.* 14°55S 47°30E **272** A2
Narino □ *Colombia* 1°30N 78°0W **328** C2
Narita *Japan* 35°47N 140°19E **223** B12
Narita, Tōkyō ✈ (NRT) *Japan* 35°45N 140°25E **223** B12
Nariva □ *Trin. & Tob.* 10°22N 61°10W **323** t
Nariva → *Trin. & Tob.* 10°24N 61°14W **323** t
Nariva Swamp *Trin. & Tob.* 10°26N 61°4W **323** t
Närke *Sweden* 59°10N 15°0E **162** E8
Narmada → *India* 21°38N 72°36E **242** J5
Narmada Canal *India* 22°20N 73°45E **244** C1
Nārmak *Iran* 35°42N 51°28E **141** A2
Narman *Turkey* 40°26N 41°57E **213** B9
Narnaul *India* 28°5N 76°11E **242** E7
Narni *Italy* 42°30N 12°30E **199** F9
Naro *Ghana* 10°22N 2°27W **262** C4
Naro Fominsk *Russia* 55°23N 36°43E **188** E9
Narodnaya *Russia* 65°5N 59°58E **186** A10
Narok *Kenya* 1°55S 35°52E **268** C4
Narón *Spain* 43°32N 8°9W **194** B2
Narooma *Australia* 36°14S 150°4E **283** D9
Narowal *Pakistan* 32°6N 74°52E **242** C6
Narrabri *Australia* 30°19S 149°46E **281** E4
Narran → *Australia* 28°37S 148°12E **281** D4
Narrandera *Australia* 34°42S 146°31E **283** C7
Narrogin *Australia* 32°58S 117°14E **279** F2
Narromine *Australia* 32°12S 148°12E **283** B8
Narrow Hills ⌓ *Canada* 54°0N 104°37W **297** C8
Narrows, The *St. Kitts & Nevis* 17°12N 62°40W **322** d
Narsampet *India* 17°57N 79°58E **244** F4
Narsaq *Greenland* 60°57N 46°4W **154** E6
Narsimhapur *India* 22°54N 79°14E **243** H8
Narsinghgarh *India* 23°45N 76°40E **242** H7
Narsinghpur *India* 20°28N 85°5E **244** D7
Narsipatnam *India* 17°40N 82°37E **244** F6
Nartes, L. e *Albania* 40°32N 19°25E **202** F3
Nartkala *Russia* 43°33N 43°51E **191** J6
Naruo *Japan* 34°43N 135°22E **133** A1
Naruto *Kantō, Japan* 34°11N 134°37E **222** C6
Narutō *Shikoku, Japan* 35°36N 140°25E **223** B12
Naruto-Kaikyō *Japan* 34°14N 134°39E **222** C6
Narva *Estonia* 59°23N 28°12E **188** C5
Narva → *Russia* 59°27N 28°2E **188** C4
Narva Bay = Narva Laht *Estonia* 59°35N 27°35E **161** G22
Narva Laht *Estonia* 59°35N 27°35E **161** G22
Narvacan *Phil.* 17°25N 120°28E **232** C3
Narvik *Norway* 68°28N 17°26E **160** B17
Narvskoye Vdkhr. *Russia* 59°18N 28°14E **188** C5
Narwana *India* 29°39N 76°6E **242** E7
Narwiański △ *Poland* 52°5N 22°53E **185** F9
Narwinbi ✪ *Australia* 16°7S 136°17E **280** B2
Naryan-Mar *Russia* 67°42N 53°12E **186** A9
Narym *Russia* 59°0N 81°30E **214** D9
Naryn *Kyrgyzstan* 41°26N 75°58E **217** D9
Naryn □ *Kyrgyzstan* 41°26N 75°58E **217** D9
Naryn → *Uzbekistan* 40°52N 71°36E **217** D8
Naryn Qum *Kazakhstan* 47°30N 49°0E **191** G9
Nasa *Norway* 66°29N 15°23E **160** C16
Nasau *Fiji* 17°19S 179°27E **287** A2
Năsăud *Romania* 47°19N 24°29E **183** C9
Nasawa *Vanuatu* 15°12S 168°9E **287** E6
Naşb, W. → *Egypt* 28°29N 34°31E **251** K5
Näsby *Sweden* 59°25N 18°5E **139** A2
Näsbypark *Sweden* 59°25N 18°5E **139** A2
Nasca *Peru* 14°50S 74°57W **330** C3
Nasca Ridge *Pac. Oc.* 20°0S 80°0W **289** K19
Naseby *N.Z.* 45°1S 170°10E **285** F5
Naselle *U.S.A.* 46°22N 123°49W **306** D3
Naser, Buheirat en *Egypt* 23°0N 32°30E **256** C3
Nashik = Nasik *India* 19°58N 73°50E **244** E1
Nashua *Iowa, U.S.A.* 42°57N 92°32W **310** B4
Nashua *Mont., U.S.A.* 48°8N 106°22W **304** B10
Nashua *N.H., U.S.A.* 42°45N 71°28W **313** D13
Nashville *Ark., U.S.A.* 33°57N 93°51W **314** E8
Nashville *Ga., U.S.A.* 31°12N 83°15W **316** D6
Nashville *Ill., U.S.A.* 38°21N 89°23W **310** F7
Nashville *Ind., U.S.A.* 39°12N 86°15W **311** E10
Nashville *Mich., U.S.A.* 42°36N 85°5W **311** B11
Nashville *Tenn., U.S.A.* 36°10N 86°47W **315** C11
Našice *Croatia* 45°32N 18°4E **182** E3
Nasielsk *Poland* 52°35N 20°50E **185** F7
Nasik *India* 19°58N 73°50E **244** E1
Nasipit *Phil.* 8°57N 125°19E **233** G5
Nasir *Sudan* 8°36N 33°4E **257** F3
Nasirabad = Mymensingh *Bangla.* 24°45N 90°24E **241** C3
Nasirabad *India* 26°15N 74°45E **242** F6
Nasirabad *Pakistan* 28°23N 68°24E **242** E3
Nasiri = Ahvāz *Iran* 31°20N 48°40E **247** D6
Nasiriyah = An Nāşirīyah *Iraq* 31°0N 46°15E **246** D5
Naskaupi → *Canada* 53°47N 60°51W **299** B7
Naso *Italy* 38°7N 14°47E **201** D7
Naso Pt. *Phil.* 10°25N 121°57E **233** F3
Naşrābād *Iran* 34°8N 51°26E **247** C6
Naşriān-e Pā'īn *Iran* 32°52N 46°52E **246** C5
Nass → *Canada* 55°0N 129°40W **296** C3
Nassarawa *Nigeria* 8°32N 7°41E **263** D6
Nassarawa □ *Nigeria* 8°30N 8°20E **263** D6
Nassau *Bahamas* 25°5N 77°20W **153** b
Nassau *N.Y., U.S.A.* 42°31N 73°37W **313** D11
Nassau, B. *Chile* 55°20S 68°0W **336** E3
Nassau Int. ✈ (NAS) *Bahamas* 25°3N 77°28W **153** b
Nasser, L. = Naser, Buheirat en *Egypt* 23°0N 32°30E **256** C3
Nasser City = Kôm Ombo *Egypt* 24°25N 32°52E **256** C3
Nassian *Ivory C.* 8°28N 3°28W **262** D4
Nässjö *Sweden* 57°39N 14°42E **163** G8
Nastapoka → *Canada* 56°55N 76°33W **298** A4
Nastapoka, Is. *Canada* 56°55N 76°50W **298** A4
Nasugbu *Phil.* 14°5N 120°38E **232** D3
Näsum *Sweden* 56°10N 14°29E **163** H8
Näsviken *Sweden* 61°46N 16°52E **162** C10
Nata *Botswana* 20°12S 26°12E **270** B4
Nata → *Botswana* 20°14S 26°10E **270** B4
Natagaima *Colombia* 3°37N 75°6W **328** C2
Natal *Brazil* 5°47S 35°13W **332** C4
Natal *Indonesia* 0°35N 99°7E **234** B1
Natal Drakensberg ⌓ *S. Africa* 29°27S 29°30E **271** C4
Natalinci *Serbia* 44°15N 20°49E **182** F5
Naţanz *Iran* 33°30N 51°55E **247** C6
Natashquan *Canada* 50°14N 61°46W **299** B7
Natashquan → *Canada* 50°7N 61°50W **299** B7
Natchez *U.S.A.* 31°34N 91°24W **314** F9
Natchitoches *U.S.A.* 31°46N 93°5W **314** F8
Natewa B. *Fiji* 16°35S 179°40E **287** A2
Nathalia *Australia* 36°1S 145°13E **283** D6
Nathan Philips Square *Toronto, Canada* **141** b2
Nathan Road *Hong Kong, China* **122** a2
Nathdwara *India* 24°55N 73°50E **242** G5
Nathu La *China* 27°24N 88°49E **241** B2
Nati, Pta. *Spain* 40°3N 3°50E **206** A4
Natimuk *Australia* 36°42S 142°0E **282** D5
Nation → *Canada* 55°30N 123°32W **296** B4
National Arboretum *U.S.A.* 38°54N 76°59W **143** B3
National Art Gallery *Beijing, China* **114** b2
National Capital District □ *Papua N. G.* 9°25S 147°10E **286** E4
National City *U.S.A.* 32°40N 117°5W **307** N9
National Grand Theatre *Beijing, China* **114** c2
National Place *Washington, D.C., U.S.A.* **143** b2
National Zoological Park *U.S.A.* 38°55N 77°4W **143** B3
Nationals Park *U.S.A.* 38°53N 77°1W **143** B3
Natitingou *Benin* 10°20N 1°26E **263** C5
Natividad, I. *Mexico* 27°52N 115°11W **318** B1
Natividade *Brazil* 11°43S 47°47W **333** D2
Nativity, Basilica of *West Bank* 31°42N 33°12E **123** B2
Natkyizin *Burma* 14°57N 97°59E **236** E1
Natmauk *Burma* 20°20N 95°24E **241** E5
Natogyi *Burma* 21°25N 95°39E **241** E5
Natolin *Poland* 52°8N 21°4E **142** C2
Natonin *Phil.* 17°6N 121°18E **232** C3
Natron, L. *Tanzania* 2°20S 36°0E **268** C4
Natrona Heights *U.S.A.* 40°37N 79°44W **312** F5
Natrûn, W. el → *Egypt* 30°25N 30°13E **256** H7
Nattai △ *Australia* 34°12S 150°22E **283** C9
Nättraby *Sweden* 56°13N 15°31E **163** H9
Natukanaoka Pan *Namibia* 18°40S 15°45E **270** A2
Natuna Besar, Kepulauan *Indonesia* 4°0N 108°15E **235** B3
Natuna Is. = Natuna Besar, Kepulauan *Indonesia* 4°0N 108°15E **235** B3
Natuna Selatan, Kepulauan *Indonesia* 2°45N 109°0E **235** B3
Natural Bridge *U.S.A.* 44°5N 75°30W **313** B9
Natural Bridges ⌓ *U.S.A.* 37°36N 110°0W **305** H9
Naturaliste, C. *Tas., Australia* 40°50S 148°15E **281** G4
Naturaliste, C. *W. Austral., Australia* 33°32S 115°0E **279** F2
Naturaliste Plateau *Ind. Oc.* 34°0S 112°0E **276** G1
Nau Qala *Afghan.* 34°5N 68°5E **242** B3
Naucalpan de Juárez *Mexico* 19°28N 99°14W **128** B1
Naucelle *France* 44°13N 2°20E **174** D6
Nauders *Austria* 46°54N 10°30E **180** E3
Nauen *Germany* 52°36N 12°52E **178** C8
Naugard = Nowogard *Poland* 53°41N 15°10E **184** E2
Naugatuck *U.S.A.* 41°30N 73°3W **313** E11
Naujaat = Repulse Bay *Canada* 66°30N 86°30W **295** D14
Naujan *Phil.* 13°20N 121°18E **232** E3
Naujan Lake △ *Phil.* 13°9N 121°20E **232** E3
Naujoji Akmenė *Lithuania* 56°19N 22°54E **184** B9
Naulila *Angola* 17°13S 14°39E **265** F2
Naumburg *Germany* 51°9N 11°47E **178** D7
Naumburg am Queis = Nowogrodziec *Poland* 51°12N 15°24E **185** G2
Naupada *Andhra Pradesh, India* 18°34N 84°18E **244** E7
Naupada *Maharashtra, India* 19°3N 72°50E **130** A2
Nā'ūr *Jordan* 31°53N 35°50E **251** G6
Nauru ■ *Pac. Oc.* 1°0S 166°0E **288** H8
Naushahra = Nowshera *Pakistan* 34°0N 72°0E **240** B4
Naushahro *Pakistan* 26°50N 68°7E **242** F3
Naushon I. *U.S.A.* 41°29N 70°45W **313** E14
Nausori *Fiji* 18°2S 178°32E **287** B2
Naustdal *Norway* 61°31N 5°43E **164** C2
Nauta *Peru* 4°31S 73°35W **328** D3
Nautanwa *India* 27°20N 83°25E **243** F10
Naute ⌓ *Namibia* 26°55S 17°57E **270** C2
Nautla *Mexico* 20°13N 96°47W **319** C5
Nauvoo *U.S.A.* 40°33N 91°23W **310** D5
Nava *Coahuila, Mexico* 28°25N 100°45W **318** B4
Nava *Spain* 43°21N 5°31W **194** B5
Nava del Rey *Spain* 41°22N 5°6W **194** D5
Navadwip *India* 23°34N 88°20E **243** H13
Navahermosa *Spain* 39°41N 4°28W **195** F6
Navahrudak *Belarus* 53°40N 25°50E **177** B13
Navai *Fiji* 17°36S 177°57E **287** A1
Navajo Res. *U.S.A.* 36°48N 107°36W **305** H10
Naval *Phil.* 11°34N 124°23E **233** F5
Navalcarnero *Spain* 40°17N 4°5W **194** E6
Navalgund *India* 15°34N 75°22E **245** G2
Navalmoral de la Mata *Spain* 39°52N 5°33W **194** F5
Navalvillar de Pela *Spain* 39°9N 5°24W **195** F5
Navan = An Uaimh *Ireland* 53°39N 6°41W **166** C5
Navanagar = Jamnagar *India* 22°30N 70°6E **242** H4
Navapolatsk *Belarus* 55°32N 28°37E **188** E5
Navarin, Mys *Russia* 62°15N 179°5E **215** C18
Navarino, I. *Chile* 55°0S 67°40W **336** E3
Navarra □ *Spain* 42°40N 1°40W **196** C3
Navarre *Fla., U.S.A.* 30°24N 86°52W **317** E3
Navarre *Ohio, U.S.A.* 40°43N 81°31W **312** F3
Navarro → *U.S.A.* 39°11N 123°45W **306** F3
Navas de San Juan *Spain* 38°30N 3°19W **195** G7
Navasota *U.S.A.* 30°23N 96°5W **314** F6
Navassa I. *W. Indies* 18°30N 75°0W **321** C5
Nävekvarn *Sweden* 58°38N 16°49E **163** F10
Naver → *U.K.* 58°32N 4°14W **167** C4
Navet *Trin. & Tob.* 10°21N 61°10W **323** t
Navet → *Trin. & Tob.* 10°24N 61°5W **323** t
Navet Res. *Trin. & Tob.* 10°24N 61°15W **323** t
Navi Mumbai *India* 19°5N 73°0E **130** A2
Navia *Spain* 43°35N 6°42W **194** B4
Navia → *Spain* 43°15N 6°50W **194** B4
Navia de Suarna = A Pobre *Spain* 42°58N 7°3W **194** C3
Navibandar *India* 21°26N 69°48E **242** J3
Navidad *Chile* 33°57S 71°50W **334** C1
Navidad Bank *W. Indies* 20°0N 68°58W **321** B6
Navíglio di Pavia *Italy* 45°24N 9°9E **129** B1
Navíglio Grande *Italy* 45°25N 9°5E **129** B1
Naviraí *Brazil* 23°8S 54°13W **335** A5
Naviti *Fiji* 17°7S 177°15E **287** A1
Navlakhi *India* 22°58N 70°28E **242** H4
Navlya *Russia* 52°53N 34°30E **189** F8
Năvodari *Romania* 44°19N 28°36E **183** F13
Navoi *Uzbekistan* 40°9N 65°22E **217** D7
Navojoa *Mexico* 27°6N 109°26W **318** B3
Navolato *Mexico* 24°47N 107°42W **318** C3
Navona, Piazza *Rome, Italy* **136** b2
Navotas *Phil.* 14°39N 120°56E **127** B1
Navrongo *Ghana* 10°51N 1°3W **263** C4
Navsari *India* 20°57N 72°59E **244** D1
Navua *Fiji* 18°12S 178°11E **287** B2
Navy Pier *Chicago, U.S.A.* **119** b3
Nawa Kot *Pakistan* 28°21N 71°24E **242** E4
Nawab Khan *Pakistan* 30°17N 69°12E **242** D3
Nawabganj *Bangla.* 24°35N 88°14E **241** C2
Nawabganj *Ut. P., India* 26°56N 81°14E **243** F9
Nawabganj *Ut. P., India* 28°32N 79°40E **243** E8
Nawabshah *Pakistan* 26°15N 68°25E **242** F3
Nawada *India* 24°50N 85°33E **243** G11
Nāwah *Afghan.* 32°19N 67°53E **240** B2
Nawakot *Nepal* 27°55N 85°10E **243** F11
Nawalgarh *India* 27°50N 75°15E **242** F6
Nawanshahr *India* 32°33N 74°48E **243** C6
Nawapara *India* 20°46N 82°33E **244** D6
Nawar, Dasht-i- *Afghan.* 33°52N 68°0E **242** C3
Nawāsīf, Ḩarrat *Si. Arabia* 21°20N 42°10E **248** B3
Nawi *Sudan* 18°32N 30°50E **256** D3
Nawng Hpa *Burma* 22°30N 98°30E **241** D7
Nawoiy = Navoi *Uzbekistan* 40°9N 65°22E **217** D7
Nawş, Ra's *Oman* 17°15N 55°16E **249** C6
Naxçıvan *Azerbaijan* 39°12N 45°15E **213** C11
Naxçıvan □ *Azerbaijan* 39°25N 45°26E **213** C11
Naxos *Greece* 37°8N 25°25E **205** D7
Naxxar *Malta* 35°55N 14°27E **206** F7
Nay *France* 43°10N 0°18W **174** E3
Nay, Mui *Vietnam* 12°54N 109°26E **236** F7
Nāy Band *Būshehr, Iran* 27°20N 52°40E **247** E7
Nāy Band *Khorāsān, Iran* 32°20N 57°34E **247** C8
Naya → *Colombia* 3°13N 77°22W **328** C2
Nayagarh *India* 20°8N 85°6E **244** D7
Nayakhan *Russia* 61°56N 159°0E **215** C16
Nayarit □ *Mexico* 22°0N 105°0W **318** C4
Nayé *Senegal* 14°28N 12°12W **262** C2
Nayong *China* 26°50N 105°20E **228** D5
Nayoro *Japan* 44°21N 142°28E **220** B11
Naypyidaw *Burma* 19°44N 96°12E **236** C1
Nayudupeta *India* 13°54N 79°54E **245** H4
Nayyāl, W. → *Si. Arabia* 28°35N 39°4E **246** D3
Nazal Hikmat Beg *Iraq* 33°23N 44°25E **113** A2
Nazar Kahrizi *Iran* 37°20N 46°45E **213** D12
Nazaré *Bahia, Brazil* 13°2S 39°0W **333** D4
Nazaré *Pará, Brazil* 6°25S 52°29W **331** B7
Nazaré *Tocantins, Brazil* 6°23S 47°40W **332** C2
Nazaré *Portugal* 39°36N 9°4W **195** F1
Nazareth = Nazerat *Israel* 32°42N 35°17E **250** F6
Nazareth *U.S.A.* 40°44N 75°19W **313** F9
Nazarovo *Russia* 57°2N 90°40E **215** D10
Nazas *Mexico* 25°14N 104°8W **318** B4
Nazas → *Mexico* 25°12N 104°12W **318** B4
Nazca = Nasca *Peru* 14°50S 74°57W **330** C3
Naze *Japan* 28°22N 129°27E **221** K4
Naze, The *U.K.* 51°53N 1°18E **169** F9
Nazerat *Israel* 32°42N 35°17E **250** F6
Nāzīk *Iran* 39°1N 45°4E **213** C11
Nazilli *Turkey* 37°55N 28°15E **205** D10
Nazimabad *Pakistan* 24°54N 67°1E **123** A2
Nazinon = Red Volta → *Africa* 10°34N 0°30W **263** C4
Nazir Hat *Bangla.* 22°35N 91°49E **241** D3
Nazko *Canada* 53°1N 123°37W **296** C4
Nazko → *Canada* 53°7N 123°34W **296** C4
Nazlet el Simmân *Egypt* 29°59N 31°9E **117** B1
Nāzlu *Iran* 37°41N 45°0E **213** D11
Nazret *Ethiopia* 8°32N 39°22E **257** F4
Ncama *Eq. Guin.* 1°55N 10°56E **264** B2
Nchanga *Zambia* 12°30S 27°49E **269** E2
Ncheu *Malawi* 14°50S 34°47E **269** E3
Ncue *Eq. Guin.* 2°1N 10°28E **264** B2
Ndala *Tanzania* 4°45S 33°15E **268** C3
Ndalatando *Angola* 9°12S 14°48E **265** D2
Ndali *Benin* 9°50N 2°46E **263** D5
Ndareda *Tanzania* 4°12S 35°30E **268** C4
Ndélé *C.A.R.* 8°25N 20°36E **264** A4
Ndendé *Gabon* 2°22S 11°23E **264** C2
Ndiael ⌓ *Senegal* 16°15N 16°0W **262** B1
Ndikinimeki *Cameroon* 4°46N 10°50E **263** E7
Ndim *Cameroon* 5°10N 10°41E **264** A2
Ndindi *Gabon* 3°46S 11°9E **264** C2
N'Dioum *Senegal* 16°31N 14°39W **262** B2
Ndjamena *Chad* 12°10N 15°0E **259** F3
Ndjolé *Gabon* 0°10S 10°45E **264** C2
Ndogo, Lagune *Gabon* 2°35S 10°0E **264** C2
Ndok *Cameroon* 7°57N 14°42E **264** A2
Ndoki-Nouabalé ⌓ *Congo* 2°32N 16°32E **264** B3
Ndola *Zambia* 13°0S 28°34E **269** E2
Ndomo ⌓ *S. Africa* 26°52S 32°15E **271** C5
Ndoto Mts. *Kenya* 2°0N 37°0E **268** B4
Ndoua, C. *N. Cal.* 22°24S 166°56E **288** d
Ndouba *Congo* 0°9S 14°4E **264** C2
Ndoukou *C.A.R.* 4°33N 20°39E **264** B4
Nduguti *Tanzania* 4°18S 34°41E **268** C3
Nea → *Norway* 63°15N 11°0E **164** A8
Nea Alexandria *Greece* 37°52N 23°46E **112** B2
Nea Alikarnassos *Greece* 35°18N 25°13E **205** F7
Nea Anchialos *Greece* 39°16N 22°49E **204** B4
Nea Epidavros *Greece* 37°40N 23°7E **204** D5
Nea Ionia *Athina, Greece* 38°3N 23°45E **112** A2
Nea Ionia *Magnisia, Greece* 39°21N 22°56E **204** B4
Nea Kalikratia *Greece* 40°21N 23°3E **202** F7
Nea Liosia *Greece* 38°3N 23°43E **112** A2
Nea Makri *Greece* 38°5N 23°59E **204** C5
Nea Moudania *Greece* 40°15N 23°17E **202** F7
Nea Peramos *Attiki, Greece* 38°0N 23°26E **204** C5
Nea Peramos *Kavala, Greece* 40°50N 24°18E **203** F8
Nea Samsounda *Greece* 39°5N 20°45E **207** A2
Nea Smirni *Greece* 37°54N 23°43E **112** B2
Nea Visa *Greece* 41°34N 26°33E **203** E10
Nea Zichni *Greece* 41°2N 23°49E **202** E7
Neagari *Japan* 36°26N 136°25E **223** A8
Neagh, Lough *U.K.* 54°37N 6°25W **166** B5
Neah Bay *U.S.A.* 48°22N 124°37W **306** B2
Neale, L. *Australia* 24°15S 130°0E **278** D5
Neales → *Australia* 28°8S 136°47E **281** D2
Neamati *India* 26°50N 94°20E **241** B5
Neamţ □ *Romania* 47°0N 26°20E **183** C11
Neapoli *Athens, Greece* **112** a3
Neapoli *Kozani, Greece* 40°20N 21°24E **202** F5
Neapoli *Kriti, Greece* 35°15N 25°37E **207** E6
Neapoli *Lakonia, Greece* 36°27N 23°8E **204** E5
Near Is. *U.S.A.* 52°30N 174°0E **303** K1
Near North *Chicago, U.S.A.* **119** b1
Neath *U.K.* 51°39N 3°48W **169** F4
Neath Port Talbot □ *U.K.* 51°42N 3°45W **169** F4
Nebbi *Uganda* 2°28N 31°6E **268** B3
Nebbou *Burkina Faso* 11°9N 1°51W **263** C4
Nebelat el Hagana *Sudan* 13°13N 29°2E **257** E2
Nebine Cr. → *Australia* 29°27S 146°56E **281** D4
Nebitdag = Balkanabat *Turkmenistan* 39°30N 54°22E **247** B7
Nebka *Algeria* 27°28N 3°12W **260** C4
Neblina, Pico da *Brazil* 0°48N 66°0W **328** C4
Nebo *Australia* 21°42S 148°42E **280** C4
Nebolchy *Russia* 59°8N 33°18E **188** C7
Nebraska □ *U.S.A.* 41°30N 99°30W **308** E4
Nebraska City *U.S.A.* 40°41N 95°52W **308** E6
Nébrodi, Monti *Italy* 37°54N 14°35E **201** E7
Nebušice *Czech Rep.* 50°6N 14°19E **135** B1
Necedah *U.S.A.* 44°2N 90°4W **308** C8
Nechako → *Canada* 53°55N 122°42W **296** C4
Neches → *U.S.A.* 29°58N 93°51W **314** G8
Nechisar △ *Ethiopia* 5°58N 37°55E **257** F4
Neckar → *Germany* 49°27N 8°29E **179** F4
Neckartal-Odenwald ⌓ *Germany* 49°30N 9°5E **179** F5
Necker I. *U.S.A.* 23°35N 164°42W **302** G11
Necochea *Argentina* 38°30S 58°50W **334** D4
Nectar Brook *Australia* 32°43S 137°57E **282** B2
Neda *Spain* 43°30N 8°9W **194** B2
Neda → *Greece* 37°25N 21°45E **204** D3
Nedalshytta *Norway* 62°59N 12°3E **164** B9
Nedelino *Bulgaria* 41°27N 25°3E **203** E9
Nedelišće *Croatia* 46°23N 16°22E **199** B13
Nederhorst *Neths.* 52°16N 5°3E **112** B3
Nederland = Netherlands ■ *Europe* 52°0N 5°30E **170** C5
Nedlitz *Germany* 52°25N 13°3E **115** B1
Nedoboyivtsi *Ukraine* 48°26N 26°21E **183** B11
Nedreberg *Norway* 60°59N 11°41E **164** D8
Nedroma *Algeria* 35°1N 1°45W **261** A4
Nedstrand *Norway* 59°21N 5°49E **164** E2
Nee Soon *Singapore* 1°24N 103°49E **138** A2
Needham *U.S.A.* 42°17N 71°14W **116** B1
Needham Heights *U.S.A.* 42°17N 71°14W **116** B1
Needles *B.C., Canada* 49°53N 118°7W **296** D5
Needles *Calif., U.S.A.* 34°51N 114°37W **307** L12
Needles, The *U.K.* 50°39N 1°35W **169** G6
Needles Pt. *N.Z.* 36°3S 175°25E **284** C4
Neembucú □ *Paraguay* 27°0S 58°0W **334** B4
Neemuch = Nimach *India* 24°30N 74°56E **242** G6
Neenah *U.S.A.* 44°11N 88°28W **308** C9
Neepawa *Canada* 50°15N 99°30W **297** C9
Neeses *U.S.A.* 33°33N 81°7W **316** B8
Nefta *Tunisia* 33°53N 7°50E **258** B1
Neftçala *Azerbaijan* 39°19N 49°12E **213** C13
Neftechala = Neftçala *Azerbaijan* 39°19N 49°12E **213** C13
Neftegorsk *Krasnodar, Russia* 44°25N 39°45E **191** H4
Neftegorsk *Sakhalin, Russia* 53°1N 142°58E **215** D15
Neftekumsk *Russia* 44°46N 44°50E **191** H7
Nefteyugansk *Russia* 61°5N 72°42E **214** C8
Nefyn *U.K.* 52°56N 4°31W **168** E3
Négala *Mali* 12°52N 8°30W **262** C3
Negapatam = Nagappattinam *India* 10°46N 79°51E **245** J4
Negara *Indonesia* 8°22S 114°37E **231** J17
Negaunee *U.S.A.* 46°30N 87°36W **308** B10
Negele *Oromiya, Ethiopia* 5°20N 39°36E **257** F4
Negele *Oromiya, Ethiopia* 7°21N 38°42E **266** C4
Negeri Sembilan □ *Malaysia* 2°45N 102°10E **237** L4
Negev Desert = Hanegev *Israel* 30°50N 35°0E **251** H6
Negoiul, Vf. *Romania* 45°38N 24°35E **183** E9
Negombo *Sri Lanka* 7°12N 79°50E **245** L4
Negotin *Serbia* 44°16N 22°37E **202** B6
Negotino *Macedonia* 41°29N 22°7E **202** E6
Negra, Peña *Spain* 42°11N 6°30W **194** C4
Negra, Pta. *Mauritania* 22°54N 16°18W **260** D1
Negra, Pta. *Peru* 6°6S 81°10W **330** B1
Negra Pt. *Phil.* 18°40N 120°50E **232** B3
Negra Pt. *Trin. & Tob.* 10°4N 61°23W **323** t
Negrais, C. = Maudin Sun *Burma* 16°0N 94°30E **241** G5
Nègres, Pte. des *Martinique* 14°35N 61°5W **322** j
Negreşti *Romania* 46°50N 27°30E **183** D12
Negreşti-Oaş *Romania* 47°52N 23°26E **183** C8
Negril *Jamaica* 18°22N 78°20W **320** a
Négrine *Algeria* 34°30N 7°30E **261** B6
Negro → *Argentina* 41°2S 62°47W **336** B4
Negro → *Bolivia* 14°11S 63°7W **331** C5
Negro → *Brazil* 3°0S 60°0W **329** D6
Negro → *Uruguay* 33°24S 58°22W **334** C4
Negro, C. = Tarf, Ras *Morocco* 35°40N 5°11W **260** A3
Negros *Phil.* 9°30N 122°40E **233** G4
Negros Occidental □ *Phil.* 10°0N 122°55E **233** F4
Negros Oriental □ *Phil.* 9°45N 123°0E **233** G4
Negru Vodă *Romania* 43°47N 28°21E **183** G13
Neguac *Canada* 47°15N 65°5W **299** C6
Nehalem → *U.S.A.* 45°40N 123°56W **306** E3
Nehāvand *Iran* 35°56N 49°31E **247** C6
Nehbandān *Iran* 31°35N 60°5E **247** D9
Nehe *China* 48°29N 124°50E **219** B13
Nehoiu *Romania* 45°24N 26°20E **183** E11
Nei Mongol Zizhiqu □ *China* 42°0N 112°0E **226** D7
Neiafu *Tonga* 18°39S 173°59W **287** P14
Neidenburg = Nidzica *Poland* 53°25N 20°28E **185** E7
Neiges, Piton des *Réunion* 21°5S 55°29E **272** f
Neijiang *China* 29°35N 104°55E **228** C5
Neikiang = Neijiang *China* 29°35N 104°55E **228** C5
Neilingding Dao *China* 22°25N 113°48E **219** a
Neill I. *India* 11°50N 93°3E **245** J11
Neillsville *U.S.A.* 44°34N 90°36W **308** C8
Neilson, Récif *Pac. Oc.* 27°1S 146°2W **289** f
Neilton *U.S.A.* 47°25N 123°53W **304** C2
Neipu *Taiwan* 22°37N 120°33E **225** D2
Neiqiu *China* 37°15N 114°30E **226** F8
Neisse = Nysa → *Europe* 52°4N 14°46E **178** C10
Neiva *Colombia* 2°56N 75°18W **328** C2
Neiwan *Taiwan* 24°42N 121°10E **225** B3
Neixiang *China* 33°10N 111°52E **226** H6
Nejanilini L. *Canada* 59°33N 97°48W **297** B9
Nejd = Najd *Si. Arabia* 26°30N 42°0E **248** A3
Nejo *Ethiopia* 9°30N 35°28E **257** F4
Nekā *Iran* 36°39N 53°19E **247** B7
Nekemte *Ethiopia* 9°4N 36°30E **257** F4
Nêkheb *Egypt* 25°10N 32°48E **256** B3
Nekrasovka *Russia* 55°41N 37°55E **129** B5
Neksø *Denmark* 55°4N 15°8E **163** J9
Nelamangala *India* 13°6N 77°24E **245** H3
Nelas *Portugal* 40°32N 7°52W **194** E3
Nelaug *Norway* 58°39N 8°40E **164** F5
Nelia *Australia* 20°39S 142°12E **280** C3
Nelidovo *Russia* 56°13N 32°49E **188** D7
Neligh *U.S.A.* 42°8N 98°2W **308** D4
Nelkan *Russia* 57°40N 136°4E **215** D14
Nellikuppam *India* 11°46N 79°43E **245** J4
Nellis Air Force Base ✈ (LSV) *U.S.A.* 36°14N 115°2W **124** A2
Nellore *India* 14°27N 79°59E **245** G4
Nelson *B.C., Canada* 49°30N 117°20W **296** D5
Nelson *N.Z.* 41°18S 173°16E **285** B8
Nelson *Lancs., U.K.* 53°50N 2°13W **168** D5
Nelson *Ariz., U.S.A.* 35°31N 113°19W **305** J7
Nelson *Nev., U.S.A.* 35°42N 114°49W **307** K12
Nelson □ *N.Z.* 41°20S 173°20E **285** B8
Nelson → *Canada* 54°33N 98°2W **297** C9
Nelson, C. *Vic., Australia* 38°26S 141°32E **282** E4
Nelson, C. *Papua N. G.* 9°0S 149°20E **286** E5
Nelson, Estrecho *Chile* 51°30S 75°0W **336** D2
Nelson Bay *Australia* 32°43S 152°9E **283** B10
Nelson Forks *Canada* 59°30N 124°0W **296** B4
Nelson House *Canada* 55°47N 98°51W **297** B9
Nelson L. *Canada* 55°48N 100°7W **297** B8
Nelson Lakes △ *N.Z.* 41°55S 172°44E **285** B7
Nelson's Dockyard *Antigua & B.* 17°1N 61°46W **322** b
Nelspoort *S. Africa* 32°7S 23°0E **270** D3
Nelspruit *S. Africa* 25°29S 30°59E **271** C5
Néma *Mauritania* 16°40N 7°15W **262** B3
Neman = Nemunas → *Lithuania* 55°25N 21°10E **184** C8
Neman *Russia* 55°2N 22°2E **184** C9
N'ematābād *Iran* 35°38N 51°21E **141** B2
Nembe *Nigeria* 4°32N 6°24E **263** E6
Nembrala *Indonesia* 10°53S 122°50E **278** B3
Nemchinovka *Russia* 55°42N 37°19E **129** B1
Nemea *Greece* 37°49N 22°40E **204** D4
Nemecký Brod = Havlíčkův Brod *Czech Rep.* 49°36N 15°33E **180** B8
Nemeiben L. *Canada* 55°20N 105°20W **297** B7
Nemërçkë, Mal *Albania* 40°15N 20°15E **202** F4
Nemira, Vf. *Romania* 46°17N 26°19E **183** D11
Nemiscau *Canada* 51°18N 76°54W **298** B4
Nemiscau, L. *Canada* 51°25N 76°40W **298** B4
Nemours = Ghazaouet *Algeria* 35°8N 1°50W **261** A4
Nemours *France* 48°16N 2°40E **173** D9
Nemrut Daği △ *Turkey* 38°0N 38°55E **213** C8
Nemšová *Slovak Rep.* 48°58N 18°7E **181** C11
Nemunas → *Lithuania* 55°25N 21°10E **184** C8
Nemuro *Japan* 43°20N 145°35E **220** C12
Nemuro-Kaikyō *Japan* 43°30N 145°30E **220** C12
Nemyriv *Ukraine* 50°7N 23°27E **185** H10
Nen Jiang → *China* 45°28N 124°30E **227** B13
Nenagh *Ireland* 52°52N 8°11W **166** D3
Nenana *U.S.A.* 64°34N 149°5W **303** D10
Nenasi *Malaysia* 3°9N 103°23E **237** L4
Nendo *Pac. Oc.* 10°45S 165°54E **277** C12
Nene → *U.K.* 52°49N 0°11E **169** E8
Nengkao Shan *Taiwan* 23°58N 121°16E **225** C3
Nengonengo *French Polynesia* 18°47S 141°48W **289** f
Nenita *Greece* 38°14N 26°6E **205** C8
Nenjiang *China* 49°10N 125°10E **219** B14
Neno *Malawi* 15°25S 34°40E **269** F3
Neo Chori *Greece* 38°25N 21°17E **204** C3
Neochori *Greece* 39°4N 21°0E **204** B2
Neodesha *U.S.A.* 37°25N 95°41W **308** G6
Neoga *U.S.A.* 39°19N 88°27W **311** E8
Neon Petritsi *Greece* 41°16N 23°15E **202** E7
Neópolis *Brazil* 10°18S 36°35W **332** D4
Neora Valley △ *India* 27°0N 88°45E **241** B2
Neosho *U.S.A.* 36°52N 94°22W **308** G6
Neosho → *U.S.A.* 36°48N 95°18W **314** C7
Nepal ■ *Asia* 28°0N 84°30E **243** F11
Nepalganj *Nepal* 28°5N 81°40E **243** E9
Nepalganj Road *India* 28°1N 81°41E **243** E9
Nepean B. *Australia* 35°42S 137°37E **282** C2
Nephi *U.S.A.* 39°43N 111°50W **304** G8
Nephin *Ireland* 54°1N 9°22W **166** B2
Nephin Beg Range *Ireland* 54°0N 9°40W **166** C2
Nepi *Italy* 42°14N 12°21E **199** F9
Nepomuk *Czech Rep.* 49°29N 13°35E **180** B6
Neppel = Moses Lake *U.S.A.* 47°8N 119°17W **304** C4
Neptune *U.S.A.* 40°13N 74°2W **313** F10
Neptune Is. *Australia* 35°17S 136°10E **282** C2
Neqāb *Iran* 36°42N 57°25E **247** B8
Nera → *Italy* 42°26N 12°24E **199** F9
Nera → *Romania* 44°48N 21°25E **182** F6
Nérac *France* 44°8N 0°21E **174** D4
Nerang *Australia* 27°58S 153°20E **281** D5
Nerastro, Sarīr *Libya* 24°20N 20°37E **258** D4
Neratovice *Czech Rep.* 50°16N 14°31E **180** A7
Nerchinsk *Russia* 52°0N 116°39E **215** D12
Nereju *Romania* 45°43N 26°43E **183** E11
Nerekhta *Russia* 57°26N 40°38E **188** D11
Neresnytsya *Ukraine* 48°7N 23°46E **183** B8
Néret, L. *Canada* 54°45N 70°44W **299** B5
Neretvanski Kanal *Croatia* 43°7N 17°10E **199** E14
Nerima *Japan* 35°44N 139°40E **140** A3
Neringa *Lithuania* 55°20N 21°5E **184** C8
Neris → *Lithuania* 55°8N 24°16E **188** E3
Nerja *Spain* 36°43N 3°55W **195** J7
Nerl → *Russia* 56°11N 40°34E **188** D11
Nerpio *Spain* 38°11N 2°16W **197** G2
Nerva *Spain* 37°42N 6°30W **195** H4
Nervi *Italy* 44°23N 9°2E **198** D6
Neryungri *Russia* 57°38N 124°28E **215** D13
Nes *Iceland* 65°53N 17°24W **155** B9
Nes *Buskerud, Norway* 60°34N 9°59E **164** D6
Nesbyen *Norway* 60°34N 9°8E **164** D6
Nescopeck *U.S.A.* 41°3N 76°12W **313** E8
Nesebŭr *Bulgaria* 42°41N 27°46E **203** D11
Neset *Norway* 61°53N 10°7E **164** C7
Nesflaten *Norway* 59°38N 6°48E **164** E3
Nesjahverfi *Iceland* 64°20N 15°15W **155** C11
Neskantaga *Canada* 52°14N 87°53W **298** B2
Neskaupstaður *Iceland* 65°9N 13°42W **155** B13
Nesland *Norway* 59°31N 7°59E **164** E4
Neslandsvatn *Norway* 58°57N 9°10E **164** F6
Nesodden *Norway* 59°48N 10°41E **133** B3
Nesoddtangen *Norway* 59°48N 10°40E **133** A3
Nesøya *Norway* 59°52N 10°31E **133** A2
Ness, L. *U.K.* 57°15N 4°32W **167** D4
Ness City *U.S.A.* 38°27N 99°54W **308** F4
Nesterov = Zhovkva *Ukraine* 50°4N 23°58E **177** C12
Nesterov *Russia* 54°38N 22°41E **184** D9
Nestorio *Greece* 40°24N 21°5E **202** F5
Nestos → *Europe* 40°54N 24°49E **203** E8
Nesttun *Norway* 60°19N 5°20E **164** D2
Nesvady *Slovak Rep.* 47°56N 18°7E **181** D11
Nesvizh = Nyasvizh *Belarus* 53°14N 26°38E **177** B14
Netanya *Israel* 32°20N 34°51E **251** F5
Netarhat *India* 23°29N 84°16E **243** H11
Nete → *Belgium* 51°7N 4°14E **170** C4
Netherdale *Australia* 21°10S 148°33E **280** b
Netherlands ■ *Europe* 52°0N 5°30E **170** C5
Netherlands Antilles = ABC Islands *W. Indies* 12°15N 69°0W **321** D6
Netherlands East Indies = Indonesia ■ *Asia* 5°0S 115°0E **235** C4
Netherlands Guiana = Suriname ■ *S. Amer.* 4°0N 56°0W **329** C6
Neto → *Italy* 39°12N 17°9E **201** C10
Netrakona *Bangla.* 24°53N 90°47E **241** C3
Netrang *India* 21°39N 73°21E **242** J5
Nettancourt *France* 48°51N 4°57E **173** D11
Nettetal *Germany* 51°19N 6°12E **178** D2
Nettilling L. *Canada* 66°30N 71°0W **295** D17
Nettuno *Italy* 41°27N 12°39E **200** A5
Netzahualcóyotl, Presa *Mexico* 17°8N 93°35W **319** D6
Neu Aubing *Germany* 48°8N 11°25E **131** B1
Neu-Bentschen = Zbąszynek *Poland* 52°16N 15°51E **185** F2
Neu Buch *Germany* 52°37N 13°31E **115** A4
Neu Buchhorst *Germany* 52°24N 13°44E **115** B5
Neu Fahrland *Germany* 52°26N 13°3E **115** B1
Neu-Isenburg *Germany* 50°3N 8°42E **179** E4
Neu-Langenburg = Tukuyu *Tanzania* 9°17S 33°35E **269** D3
Neu Lindenberg *Germany* 52°36N 13°33E **115** A4
Neu-Mecklenberg = New Ireland *Papua N. G.* 3°20S 151°50E **286** B6
Neu Pommern = New Britain *Papua N. G.* 5°50S 150°20E **286** C6
Neu-Sandec = Nowy Sącz *Poland* 49°40N 20°41E **185** J7
Neu Sandez = Nowy Sącz *Poland* 49°40N 20°41E **185** J7
Neu-Ulm *Germany* 48°22N 10°0E **179** G6
Neubiberg *Germany* 48°4N 11°40E **131** B3
Neubrandenburg *Germany* 53°33N 13°15E **178** B9
Neubukow *Germany* 54°2N 11°39E **178** A7
Neuburg *Germany* 48°44N 11°11E **179** G7
Neuchâtel *Switz.* 47°0N 6°55E **179** J2
Neuchâtel □ *Switz.* 47°0N 6°55E **179** J2
Neuchâtel, Lac de *Switz.* 46°53N 6°50E **179** J2
Neudau *Austria* 47°11N 16°6E **180** D9
Neuenberg an der Elbe = Nymburk *Czech Rep.* 50°10N 15°1E **180** A8
Neuenhagen *Germany* 52°32N 13°38E **115** A4
Neuenhaus *Germany* 52°30N 6°58E **178** C2
Neuessling *Austria* 48°15N 16°32E **142** A3
Neuf-Brisach *France* 48°1N 7°30E **173** D14
Neufahrn *Bayern, Germany* 48°41N 12°11E **179** G8
Neufahrn *Bayern, Germany* 48°18N 11°40E **179** G7
Neufchâteau *Belgium* 49°50N 5°25E **170** E5
Neufchâteau *Vosges, France* 48°21N 5°40E **173** D12
Neufchâtel-en-Bray *France* 49°44N 1°26E **172** C8
Neufchâtel-sur-Aisne *France* 49°26N 4°1E **173** C11
Neuhaus = Jindřichův Hradec *Czech Rep.* 49°10N 15°2E **180** B8
Neuhaus *Germany* 53°17N 10°56E **178** B6
Neuhäusel = Nové Zámky *Slovak Rep.* 48°2N 18°8E **181** C11
Neuhausen *Germany* 48°9N 11°32E **131** B2
Neuherberg *Germany* 48°13N 11°35E **131** A2
Neuhönow *Germany* 52°34N 13°44E **115** A5
Neuillé-Pont-Pierre *France* 47°33N 0°33E **172** E7
Neuilly-Plaisance *France* 48°51N 2°30E **134** A4
Neuilly-St-Front *France* 49°10N 3°15E **173** C10
Neuilly-sur-Marne *France* 48°51N 2°31E **134** A4
Neuilly-sur-Seine *France* 48°53N 2°15E **134** A2
Neukagran *Austria* 48°14N 16°27E **142** A2
Neukalen *Germany* 53°49N 12°46E **178** B8
Neukettenhof *Austria* 48°7N 16°28E **142** B2
Neukölln *Germany* 52°28N 13°25E **115** B3
Neumarkt = Nowy Targ *Poland* 49°29N 20°2E **185** J7
Neumarkt = Środa Śląska *Poland* 51°10N 16°36E **185** G3
Neumarkt *Germany* 49°26N 11°27E **179** F7
Neumarktl = Tržič *Slovenia* 46°22N 14°18E **199** B11
Neumayer *Antarctica* 71°0S 68°30W **151** D17
Neumittelwalde = Międzybórz *Poland* 51°25N 17°34E **185** G4
Neumünster *Germany* 54°4N 9°58E **178** A5
Neung-sur-Beuvron *France* 47°30N 1°50E **173** E8
Neunkirchen *Austria* 47°43N 16°4E **180** D9
Neunkirchen *Saarland, Germany* 49°20N 7°9E **179** F3
Neuperlach *Germany* 48°6N 11°37E **131** B2
Neuquén *Argentina* 38°55S 68°0W **336** A3
Neuquén □ *Argentina* 38°0S 69°50W **334** D2
Neuquén → *Argentina* 38°59S 68°0W **336** A3
Neuried *Germany* 48°5N 11°27E **131** B1
Neuruppin *Germany* 52°55N 12°48E **178** C8
Neusalz an der Oder = Nowa Sól *Poland* 51°48N 15°44E **185** G2
Neusäss *Germany* 48°24N 10°50E **179** G6
Neusatz = Novi Sad *Serbia* 45°18N 19°52E **182** E4
Neuse → *U.S.A.* 35°6N 76°29W **315** D16
Neusiedl *Austria* 47°57N 16°50E **181** D9
Neusiedler See *Austria* 47°50N 16°47E **181** D9
Neusiedler See-Seewinkel △ *Austria* 47°50N 16°45E **181** D9
Neusohl = Banská Bystrica *Slovak Rep.* 48°46N 19°14E **181** C12
Neuss *Germany* 51°11N 6°42E **178** D2
Neussargues-Moissac *France* 45°9N 3°0E **174** C7
Neustadt = Lwówek *Poland* 52°28N 16°10E **185** F3
Neustadt = Prudnik *Poland* 50°20N 17°38E **185** H4
Neustadt = Wejherowo *Poland* 54°35N 18°12E **184** D5
Neustadt *Bayern, Germany* 49°44N 12°10E **179** F8
Neustadt *Bayern, Germany* 48°48N 11°46E **179** G7
Neustadt *Bayern, Germany* 49°34N 10°37E **179** F6
Neustadt *Bayern, Germany* 50°19N 11°7E **179** E7
Neustadt *Brandenburg, Germany* 52°50N 12°27E **178** C8
Neustadt *Hessen, Germany* 50°51N 9°9E **178** E5
Neustadt *Niedersachsen, Germany* 52°30N 9°30E **178** C5
Neustadt *Rhld-Pfz., Germany* 49°21N 8°10E **179** F4
Neustadt *Sachsen, Germany* 51°2N 14°12E **178** D10
Neustadt *Schleswig-Holstein, Germany* 54°6N 10°49E **178** A6
Neustadt *Thüringen, Germany* 50°45N 11°43E **178** E7
Neustädtel = Nowe Miasteczko *Poland* 51°42N 15°42E **185** G2
Neustädtl = Novo Mesto *Slovenia* 45°47N 15°12E **199** C12

Neustettin = Szczecinek
Poland 53°43N 16°41E 184 E3
Neustift am Walde Austria 48°14N 16°17E 142 A1
Neustrelitz Germany 53°21N 13°4E 178 B9
Neusüssenbrunn Austria 48°16N 16°29E 142 A2
Neutitschein = Nový Jičín
Czech Rep. 49°30N 18°2E 181 B11
Neuvic France 45°23N 2°16E 174 C6
Neuville-sur-Saône France 45°52N 4°51E 175 C8
Neuvy-le-Roi France 47°36N 0°36E 172 E7
Neuvy-St-Sépulchre France 46°35N 1°48E 173 F8
Neuvy-sur-Barangeon
France 47°20N 2°15E 173 E9
Neuwaldegg Austria 48°14N 16°17E 142 A1
Neuwedell = Drawno
Poland 53°13N 15°46E 185 E2
Neuwerk Germany 53°55N 8°30E 178 B4
Neuwied Germany 50°26N 7°29E 178 E3
Neva ➜ Russia 59°56N 30°20E 188 C6
Nevada Iowa, U.S.A. 42°1N 93°27W 310 B3
Nevada Mo., U.S.A. 37°51N 94°22W 310 G2
Nevada □ U.S.A. 39°0N 117°0W 304 G5
Nevada City U.S.A. 39°16N 121°1W 306 F6
Nevado, Cerro Argentina 35°30S 68°32W 334 D2
Nevado de Colima = Volcán de
Colima △ Mexico 19°30N 103°40W 318 D4
Nevado de Tres Cruces △
Chile 27°13S 69°5W 334 B2
Nevado del Huila △
Colombia 3°5N 75°58W 328 C2
Nevasa India 19°34N 75°0E 244 E2
Neve, Sa. da Angola 13°43S 13°10E 265 E2
Neve Ya'akov West Bank 31°50N 35°14E 123 A2
Nevel Russia 56°0N 29°55E 188 D5
Nevelsk Russia 46°40N 141°51E 215 E15
Nevers France 47°0N 3°9E 173 F10
Nevertire Australia 31°50S 147°44E 283 A7
Neves Brazil 22°51S 43°5W 135 B2
Nevesinje Bos.-H. 43°14N 18°6E 202 C2
Neville Canada 49°58N 107°39W 297 D7
Nevinnomyssk Russia 44°40N 42°0E 191 H6
Nevis St. Kitts & Nevis 17°0N 62°30W 322 d
Nevis Pk. St. Kitts & Nevis 17°9N 62°34W 322 d
Nevlunghavn Norway 58°58N 9°53E 164 F6
Nevoso, Mte. = Snežnik
Slovenia 45°36N 14°35E 199 C11
Nevrokop = Gotse Delchev
Bulgaria 41°36N 23°46E 202 E7
Nevşehir Turkey 38°33N 34°40E 212 C6
Nevşehir □ Turkey 38°50N 34°40E 212 C6
Nevskoye Russia 54°32N 22°39E 184 D9
Nevyansk Russia 57°30N 60°13E 186 C11
New ➜ Guyana 3°20N 57°37W 329 C6
New ➜ W. Va., U.S.A. 38°10N 81°12W 309 F13
New Aiyansh Canada 55°12N 129°4W 296 B3
New Albany Ind., U.S.A. 38°18N 85°49W 311 F11
New Albany Miss., U.S.A. 34°29N 89°0W 315 D10
New Albany Pa., U.S.A. 41°36N 76°27W 313 E8
New Amsterdam Guyana 6°15N 57°36W 329 B6
New Athens U.S.A. 38°19N 89°53W 310 F7
New Baghdād Iraq 33°18N 44°28E 113 B2
New Baltimore U.S.A. 42°41N 82°44W 312 D2
New Barakpur India 22°40N 88°26E 124 A2
New Barbadoes = Hackensack
U.S.A. 40°52N 74°4W 132 A1
New Bedford U.S.A. 41°38N 70°56W 313 E14
New Berlin = North Canton
U.S.A. 40°53N 81°24W 312 F3
New Berlin Ill., U.S.A. 39°44N 89°55W 310 E7
New Berlin N.Y., U.S.A. 42°37N 75°20W 313 D9
New Berlin Pa., U.S.A. 40°50N 76°57W 312 F8
New Berlin Wis., U.S.A. 42°59N 88°6W 311 B8
New Bern U.S.A. 35°7N 77°3W 315 D16
New Bethlehem U.S.A. 41°0N 79°20W 312 F5
New Bight Bahamas 24°19N 75°24W 321 B4
New Bloomfield U.S.A. 40°25N 77°11W 312 F7
New Boston U.S.A. 33°28N 94°25W 314 E7
New Braunfels U.S.A. 29°42N 98°8W 314 G5
New Brighton N.Z. 43°29S 172°43E 285 D7
New Brighton N.Y., U.S.A. 40°38N 74°5W 132 C1
New Brighton Pa., U.S.A. 40°42N 80°19W 312 F4
New Britain Papua N. G. 5°50S 150°20E 286 C6
New Britain Conn.,
U.S.A. 41°40N 72°47W 313 E12
New Britain Trench Pac. Oc. 6°0S 153°0E 276 J3
New Brockton U.S.A. 31°23N 85°56W 316 D4
New Brookland = West Columbia
U.S.A. 33°59N 81°4W 316 B8
New Brunswick U.S.A. 40°30N 74°27W 313 F10
New Brunswick □
Canada 46°50N 66°30W 299 C6
New Buffalo U.S.A. 41°47N 86°45W 311 C10
New Bussa Nigeria 9°53N 4°31E 263 D5
New Caledonia ☑ Pac. Oc. 21°0S 165°0E 288 d
New Caledonia Trough
Pac. Oc. 30°0S 165°0E 288 L8
New Canada S. Africa 26°12S 27°56E 123 B1
New Canada Dam
S. Africa 26°12S 27°56E 123 B1
New Carlisle Ind., U.S.A. 41°45N 86°32W 311 C10
New Carlisle Ohio, U.S.A. 39°56N 84°2W 311 E12
New Carrollton U.S.A. 38°58N 76°53W 144 B3
New Castile = Castilla-La Mancha □
Spain 39°30N 3°30W 195 F7
New Castle Ind., U.S.A. 39°55N 85°22W 311 E11
New Castle Ky., U.S.A. 38°26N 85°10W 311 F11
New Castle Pa., U.S.A. 41°0N 80°21W 312 F4
New City U.S.A. 41°9N 73°59W 313 E11
New Concord U.S.A. 39°59N 81°54W 312 G3
New Cross U.K. 51°28N 0°1W 125 B3
New Cumberland U.S.A. 40°30N 80°36W 312 F4
New Cuyama U.S.A. 34°57N 119°38W 307 L7
New Delhi India 28°36N 77°11E 120 B2
New Denver Canada 50°0N 117°25W 296 D5
New Don Pedro Res.
U.S.A. 37°43N 120°24W 306 H6
New Dorp U.S.A. 40°34N 74°7W 132 C1
New Dorp Beach U.S.A. 40°33N 74°6W 132 C1
New Ellenton U.S.A. 33°28N 81°41W 316 B8
New England U.S.A. 43°0N 71°0W 301 G25
New England N. Dak.,
U.S.A. 46°32N 102°52W 308 B2
New England △
Australia 30°25S 152°30E 283 A10
New England Aquarium Boston, U.S.A. 116 b3
New England Ra.
Australia 30°20S 151°45E 281 E5
New England Seamounts
Atl. Oc. 38°0N 63°0W 152 C5
New Forest △ U.K. 50°53N 1°34W 169 G6
New Franklin U.S.A. 39°1N 92°44W 310 E4
New Galloway U.K. 55°5N 4°9W 167 F4
New Georgia Is.
Solomon Is. 8°15S 157°30E 287 M9
New Georgia Sound
Solomon Is. 8°0S 158°20E 287 L9
New Glarus U.S.A. 42°49N 89°38W 310 B7
New Glasgow Canada 45°35N 62°36W 299 C7
New Grant Trin. & Tob. 10°17N 61°19W 323 t
New Guinea Oceania 4°0S 136°0E 276 B7
New Halfa = Halfa al Jadidah
Sudan 15°20N 35°35E 266 A4
New Hamburg Canada 43°23N 80°42W 312 C4
New Hampshire □
U.S.A. 44°0N 71°30W 313 C13
New Hampton U.S.A. 43°3N 92°19W 310 A4
New Hanover Papua N. G. 2°30S 150°10E 286 B6
New Hanover KwaZulu Natal,
S. Africa 29°22S 30°31E 271 C5
New Harmony U.S.A. 38°8N 87°56W 311 F9
New Hartford U.S.A. 43°4N 75°18W 313 C9
New Haven Conn.,
U.S.A. 41°18N 72°55W 313 E12
New Haven Ill., U.S.A. 37°55N 88°8W 311 G8
New Haven Ind., U.S.A. 41°4N 85°1W 311 C11
New Haven Mich., U.S.A. 42°44N 82°48W 312 D2
New Haven Mo., U.S.A. 38°37N 91°13W 310 F5
New Haven N.Y., U.S.A. 43°28N 76°18W 313 C8
New Hazelton Canada 55°20N 127°30W 296 B3
New Hebrides = Vanuatu ■
Pac. Oc. 15°0S 168°0E 287 E6
New Holland U.S.A. 40°6N 76°5W 313 F8
New Iberia U.S.A. 30°1N 91°49W 314 F9
New Ireland Papua N. G. 3°20S 151°50E 286 B6
New Ireland □ Papua N. G. 3°0S 151°30E 286 B6
New Jersey □ U.S.A. 40°0N 74°30W 309 F16
New Kensington U.S.A. 40°34N 79°46W 312 F5
New Lexington U.S.A. 39°43N 82°13W 309 F12
New Liskeard Canada 47°31N 79°41W 298 C4
New London Conn.,
U.S.A. 41°22N 72°6W 313 E12
New London Iowa, U.S.A. 40°55N 91°24W 310 D5
New London Mo., U.S.A. 39°35N 91°24W 310 E5
New London Ohio, U.S.A. 41°5N 82°24W 312 E2
New London Wis., U.S.A. 44°23N 88°45W 308 C9
New Madrid U.S.A. 36°36N 89°32W 308 G9
New Malden U.K. 51°24N 0°15W 125 B2
New Martinsville U.S.A. 39°39N 80°52W 309 F13
New Meadows U.S.A. 44°58N 116°18W 304 D5
New Melones L. U.S.A. 37°57N 120°31W 306 H6
New Mexico □ U.S.A. 34°30N 106°0W 305 J11
New Miami U.S.A. 39°26N 84°32W 311 E12
New Milford Conn.,
U.S.A. 41°35N 73°25W 313 E11
New Milford N.Y., U.S.A. 40°56N 74°0W 132 A1
New Milford Pa., U.S.A. 41°52N 75°44W 313 E9
New Moore I. Ind. Oc. 21°37N 89°10E 241 E2
New Mumbai = Navi Mumbai
India 19°5N 73°0E 130 A2
New Norcia Australia 30°57S 116°13E 279 F2
New Norfolk Australia 42°46S 147°2E 281 G4
New Orleans U.S.A. 29°57N 90°4W 131 B2
New Orleans Int. ✈ (MSY)
U.S.A. 30°0N 90°15W 131 A1
New Palestine U.S.A. 39°45N 85°52W 311 E11
New Paris U.S.A. 39°51N 84°48W 311 E12
New Pekin U.S.A. 38°30N 86°0W 311 F10
New Philadelphia U.S.A. 40°30N 81°27W 312 F3
New Plymouth N.Z. 39°4S 174°5E 284 F3
New Plymouth Idaho,
U.S.A. 43°58N 116°49W 304 E5
New Pomerania = New Britain
Papua N. G. 5°50S 150°20E 286 C6
New Port Richey U.S.A. 28°16N 82°43W 317 G7
New Providence Bahamas 25°25N 78°35W 153 b
New Quay U.K. 52°13N 4°21W 169 E3
New Radnor U.K. 52°15N 3°9W 169 E4
New Richmond Qué.,
Canada 48°15N 65°45W 299 C6
New Richmond Ohio,
U.S.A. 38°57N 84°17W 311 F12
New Richmond Wis.,
U.S.A. 45°7N 92°32W 308 C7
New River Gorge ⌂
U.S.A. 37°53N 81°5W 309 G13
New Roads U.S.A. 30°42N 91°26W 314 F9
New Rochelle U.S.A. 40°55N 73°46W 313 F11
New Rockford U.S.A. 47°41N 99°8W 308 B4
New Romney U.K. 50°59N 0°57E 169 G8
New Ross Ireland 52°23N 6°57W 166 D5
New Salem U.S.A. 46°51N 101°25W 308 B3
New Scone = Scone U.K. 56°25N 3°24W 167 E5
New Sharon U.S.A. 41°28N 92°39W 310 C4
New Siberian I. = Novaya Sibir,
Ostrov Russia 75°10N 150°0E 215 B16
New Siberian Is. = Novosibirskiye
Ostrova Russia 75°0N 142°0E 215 B15
New Smyrna Beach U.S.A. 29°1N 80°56W 317 F9
New South Wales □
Australia 33°0S 146°0E 283 B7
New Stuyahok U.S.A. 59°29N 157°20W 303 G8
New Tecumseth = Alliston
Canada 44°9N 79°52W 312 B5
New Territories China 22°23N 114°10E 122 A1
New Toronto Canada 43°35N 79°30W 141 B1
New Town = Nowe Miasto
Warsaw, Poland 142 a2
New Town Edinburgh, U.K. 121 a2
New Town N. Dak.,
U.S.A. 47°59N 102°30W 308 B2
New Tredegar U.K. 51°44N 3°16W 169 F4
New Ulm U.S.A. 44°19N 94°28W 308 C6
New Utrecht U.S.A. 40°36N 73°59W 132 C2
New Vienna U.S.A. 39°19N 83°42W 311 E13
New Washington Phil. 11°39N 122°26E 233 F4
New Waterford Canada 46°13N 60°4W 299 C7
New Westminster
Canada 49°13N 122°55W 306 A4
New York U.S.A. 40°43N 74°0W 132 B3
New York □ U.S.A. 43°0N 75°0W 313 D9
New York Avenue
Washington, D.C., U.S.A. 143 a2
New York J.F. Kennedy Int. ✈ (JFK)
U.S.A. 40°38N 73°47W 313 F11
New York La Guardia ✈ (LGA)
U.S.A. 40°46N 73°52W 132 B2
New York University New York, U.S.A. 132 d2
New Zealand ■ Oceania 40°0S 176°0E 284 G5
Newaj ➜ India 24°24N 76°49E 242 G7
Newala Tanzania 10°58S 39°18E 269 E4
Newark Del., U.S.A. 39°41N 75°46W 309 F16
Newark N.J., U.S.A. 40°44N 74°10W 313 F10
Newark N.Y., U.S.A. 43°3N 77°6W 312 C7
Newark Ohio, U.S.A. 40°3N 82°24W 312 F2
Newark B. U.S.A. 40°40N 74°8W 132 B1
Newark Liberty Int. ✈ (EWR)
U.S.A. 40°42N 74°10W 313 F10
Newark-on-Trent U.K. 53°5N 0°48W 168 D7
Newark Valley U.S.A. 42°14N 76°11W 313 D8
Newbattle U.K. 55°53N 3°4W 121 B3
Newberg U.S.A. 45°18N 122°58W 304 D2
Newberry Fla., U.S.A. 29°39N 82°37W 317 F7
Newberry Mich., U.S.A. 46°21N 85°30W 309 B11
Newberry S.C., U.S.A. 34°17N 81°37W 315 D14
Newberry Springs
U.S.A. 34°50N 116°41W 307 L10
Newboro L. Canada 44°38N 76°20W 313 B8
Newbridge = Droichead Nua
Ireland 53°11N 6°48W 166 C5
Newburg U.S.A. 37°55N 91°54W 310 G5
Newburgh Ont., Canada 44°19N 76°52W 312 B8
Newburgh Ind., U.S.A. 37°57N 87°24W 311 G9
Newburgh N.Y., U.S.A. 41°30N 74°1W 313 E10
Newbury W. Berkshire,
U.K. 51°24N 1°20W 169 F6
Newbury N.H., U.S.A. 43°19N 72°3W 313 B12
Newbury Vt., U.S.A. 44°5N 72°4W 313 B12
Newbury Park U.K. 51°34N 0°5E 125 A4
Newburyport U.S.A. 42°49N 70°53W 313 D14
Newcastle N.S.W.,
Australia 33°0S 151°46E 283 B9
Newcastle N.B., Canada 47°1N 65°38W 299 C6
Newcastle Ont., Canada 43°55N 78°35W 298 D4
Newcastle St. Kitts & Nevis 17°14N 62°42W 322 d
Newcastle KwaZulu Natal,
S. Africa 27°45S 29°58E 271 C4
Newcastle Down, U.K. 54°13N 5°54W 166 B6
Newcastle Calif., U.S.A. 38°53N 121°8W 306 G5
Newcastle Wyo., U.S.A. 43°50N 104°11W 304 E11
Newcastle Emlyn U.K. 52°2N 4°28W 169 E3
Newcastle Ra. Australia 15°45S 130°15E 278 C5
Newcastle-under-Lyme
U.K. 53°1N 2°14W 168 D5
Newcastle-upon-Tyne
U.K. 54°58N 1°36W 168 C6
Newcastle Waters
Australia 17°30S 133°28E 280 B1
Newcastle West Ireland 52°27N 9°3W 166 D2
Newcomb U.S.A. 43°58N 74°10W 313 C10
Newcomerstown U.S.A. 40°16N 81°36W 312 F3
Newcraighall U.K. 55°56N 3°5W 121 B3
Newdegate Australia 33°6S 119°0E 279 F2
Newell Queens., Australia 16°20S 145°16E 280 B4
Newell Iowa, U.S.A. 42°36N 95°0W 310 B1
Newell S. Dak., U.S.A. 44°43N 103°25W 308 C2
Newenham, C. U.S.A. 58°39N 162°11W 303 G7
Newfane U.S.A. 43°17N 78°43W 312 C6
Newfield U.S.A. 42°18N 76°33W 313 D8
Newfound L. U.S.A. 43°40N 71°47W 313 C13
Newfoundland Canada 49°0N 55°0W 299 C8
Newfoundland Pa.,
U.S.A. 41°18N 75°19W 313 E9
Newfoundland & Labrador □
Canada 53°0N 58°0W 299 B8
Newhalen U.S.A. 59°43N 154°54W 303 G9
Newham □ U.K. 51°31N 0°3E 125 A4
Newhaven E. Sussex, U.K. 50°47N 0°3E 169 G8
Newhaven Edinburgh, U.K. 55°59N 3°11W 121 B2
Newington Edinburgh, U.K. 55°56N 3°10W 121 B2
Newington London, U.K. 125 c5
Newington Ga., U.S.A. 32°35N 81°30W 316 C8
Newkirk U.S.A. 36°53N 97°3W 314 C6
Newlands Wellington,
N.Z. 41°13S 174°49E 143 B1
Newlands Gauteng,
S. Africa 26°10S 27°57E 123 B1
Newlyn U.K. 50°6N 5°34W 169 G2
Newman W. Austral.,
Australia 23°18S 119°45E 278 D2
Newman Calif., U.S.A. 37°19N 121°1W 306 H5
Newman Ill., U.S.A. 39°48N 87°59W 311 E9
Newmarket Ont., Canada 44°3N 79°28W 312 B5
Newmarket Cork, Ireland 52°13N 9°0W 166 D2
Newmarket Jamaica 18°9N 77°55W 320 a
Newmarket Suffolk, U.K. 52°15N 0°25E 169 E8
Newmarket N.H., U.S.A. 43°5N 70°56W 313 C14
Newnan U.S.A. 33°23N 84°48W 316 B5
Newport = Nieuwpoort
Curaçao 12°3N 68°49W 322 g
Newport Vic., Australia 37°50S 144°51E 128 B1
Newport Mayo, Ireland 53°53N 9°33W 166 C2
Newport I. of W., U.K. 50°42N 1°17W 169 G6
Newport Newport, U.K. 51°35N 3°0W 169 F5
Newport Ark., U.S.A. 35°37N 91°16W 314 D9
Newport Fla., U.S.A. 30°11N 84°10W 316 E5
Newport Ind., U.S.A. 39°53N 87°25W 311 E9
Newport Ky., U.S.A. 39°5N 84°29W 311 E12
Newport N.H., U.S.A. 43°22N 72°10W 313 C12
Newport N.Y., U.S.A. 43°11N 75°1W 313 C9
Newport Oreg., U.S.A. 44°39N 124°3W 304 D1
Newport Pa., U.S.A. 40°29N 77°8W 312 F7
Newport R.I., U.S.A. 41°29N 71°19W 313 E13
Newport Tenn., U.S.A. 35°58N 83°11W 315 D13
Newport Vt., U.S.A. 44°56N 72°13W 313 B12
Newport Wash., U.S.A. 48°11N 117°3W 304 B5
Newport □ U.K. 51°33N 3°1W 169 F4
Newport Beach U.S.A. 33°37N 117°56W 307 M9
Newport News U.S.A. 36°58N 76°25W 309 G15
Newport Pagnell U.K. 52°5N 0°43W 169 E7
Newquay U.K. 50°25N 5°6W 169 G2
Newry U.K. 54°11N 6°21W 166 B5
Newry Islands △ Australia 20°51S 148°56E 280 b
Newtok U.S.A. 60°56N 164°38W 303 F6
Newton Ga., U.S.A. 31°19N 84°20W 316 D5
Newton Ill., U.S.A. 38°59N 88°10W 311 F8
Newton Iowa, U.S.A. 41°42N 93°3W 310 C3
Newton Kans., U.S.A. 38°3N 97°21W 308 F5
Newton Mass., U.S.A. 42°21N 71°12W 116 B1
Newton Miss., U.S.A. 32°19N 89°10W 315 E10
Newton N.C., U.S.A. 35°40N 81°13W 315 D14
Newton N.J., U.S.A. 41°3N 74°45W 313 E10
Newton Tex., U.S.A. 30°51N 93°46W 314 F8
Newton Abbot U.K. 50°32N 3°37W 169 G4
Newton Aycliffe U.K. 54°37N 1°34W 168 C6
Newton Falls N.Y.,
U.S.A. 44°12N 74°59W 313 B10
Newton Falls Ohio, U.S.A. 41°11N 80°59W 312 E4
Newton L. U.S.A. 38°55N 88°15W 311 F8
Newton Stewart U.K. 54°57N 4°30W 167 G4
Newton Terrace Barbados 13°4N 59°32W 323 r
Newtonbrook Canada 43°47N 79°24W 141 A2
Newtongrange U.K. 55°53N 3°3W 121 B3
Newtonmore U.K. 57°4N 4°8W 167 D4
Newtontoppen Svalbard 79°0N 17°30E 154 B12
Newtonville U.S.A. 42°20N 71°11W 116 A1
Newtown N.S.W.,
Australia 33°54S 151°11E 139 B2
Newtown Powys, U.K. 52°31N 3°19W 169 E4
Newtown Ill., U.S.A. 40°13N 87°9W 311 D9
Newtown Mo., U.S.A. 40°22N 93°20W 310 D3
Newtownabbey U.K. 54°40N 5°56W 166 B6
Newtownards U.K. 54°36N 5°42W 166 B6
Newtownbarry = Bunclody
Ireland 52°39N 6°40W 166 D5
Newtownstewart U.K. 54°43N 7°23W 166 B4
Newville U.S.A. 40°10N 77°24W 312 F7
Nexon France 45°41N 1°11E 174 C5
Neya Russia 58°21N 43°49E 190 A6
Neyrīz Iran 29°15N 54°19E 247 D7
Neyshābūr Iran 36°10N 58°50E 247 B8
Neyveli India 11°32N 79°29E 245 J4
Neyyattinkara India 8°26N 77°5E 245 K3
Nezametny = Aldan
Russia 58°40N 125°30E 215 D13
Nezhin = Nizhyn Ukraine 51°5N 31°55E 189 G6
Nezperce U.S.A. 46°14N 116°14W 304 C5
Nezvysko Ukraine 48°46N 25°15E 183 B10
Ngaanyatjarra ◎
Australia 22°40S 127°0E 278 D4
Ngabang Indonesia 0°23N 109°55E 235 B3
Ngabe Congo 3°12S 16°12E 264 C3
Ngabordamlu, Tanjung
Indonesia 6°56S 134°11E 231 F8
N'Gage Angola 7°46S 15°15E 265 D3
Ngaio N.Z. 41°15S 174°46E 143 B1
Ngaiphaipi Burma 22°14N 93°15E 241 D4
Ngala Nigeria 12°20N 14°11E 263 C7
Ngaliwurru Nungali ◎
Australia 15°42S 130°4E 278 C5
Ngalurrtju ◎ Australia 22°44S 132°5E 278 D5
Ngama Chad 11°45N 17°6E 259 F3
Ngambé Centre, Cameroon 5°48N 11°29E 263 D7
Ngambé Littoral, Cameroon 4°21N 10°40E 263 E7
Ngami Depression
Botswana 20°30S 22°46E 270 B3
Ngamo Zimbabwe 19°3S 27°32E 269 F2
Ngamring China 29°14N 87°10E 218 F6
Nganbéto, L. de Togo 7°26N 1°25E 263 D5
Ngangala Sudan 4°42N 31°55E 257 G3
Nganglong Kangri China 33°0N 81°0E 243 C9
Ngao Thailand 18°46N 99°59E 236 C2
Ngaoundéré Cameroon 7°15N 13°35E 264 A2
Ngapali Burma 18°26N 94°19E 241 F5
Ngapara N.Z. 44°57S 170°46E 285 E5
Ngape Burma 20°2N 94°28E 241 E5
Ngara Tanzania 2°29S 30°40E 268 C3
Ngardmau Palau 7°37N 134°34E 288 c
Ngardmau B. Palau 7°38N 134°34E 288 c
Ngardololok Palau 7°0N 134°14E 288 c
Ngaregur Palau 7°45N 134°37E 288 c
Ngarluma ◎ Australia 21°30S 118°30E 278 D2
Ngaruawahia N.Z. 37°42S 175°11E 284 D4
Ngaruroro ➜ N.Z. 39°34S 176°55E 284 F5
Ngatangiia Cook Is. 21°14S 159°43W 289 h
Ngatapa N.Z. 38°32S 177°45E 284 E6
Ngathainggyaung Burma 17°24N 95°5E 241 G5
Ngau Chi Wan China 22°20N 114°12E 122 A2
Ngau Tau Kok China 22°19N 114°12E 122 B2
Ngauranga N.Z. 41°15S 174°49E 143 B1
Ngauruhoe, Mt. N.Z. 39°13S 175°45E 284 F4
Ngawi Indonesia 7°24S 111°26E 235 D4
Ngcobo S. Africa 31°37S 28°0E 271 D4
Ngele Dem. Rep. of the Congo 0°30S 20°22E 264 C4
Ngelebok Cameroon 4°16N 14°3E 264 B2
Ngeregong Palau 7°6N 134°21E 288 c
Ngergoi Palau 7°5N 134°15E 288 c
Ngeru Uganda 0°27N 33°10E 268 B3
Ngesebus I. Palau 7°3N 134°15E 288 c
Nggatokae Solomon Is. 8°45S 158°15E 287 M10
Nggela Pile Solomon Is. 9°5S 160°20E 287 M11
Nggela Sule Solomon Is. 9°2S 160°12E 287 M11
Nghia Lo Vietnam 21°33N 104°28E 228 G5
Ngidinga
Dem. Rep. of the Congo 5°37S 15°17E 265 D3
Ngo Congo 2°29S 15°45E 264 C3
Ngoap Cameroon 4°9N 12°51E 264 B2
Ngobasangel Palau 7°16N 134°19E 288 c
Ngoboli Sudan 4°57N 32°37E 257 G3
N'Gola Angola 14°10S 14°30E 265 E2
Ngoma Malawi 13°8S 33°45E 269 E3
Ngomahura Zimbabwe 20°26S 30°43E 269 G3
Ngomba Tanzania 8°20S 32°53E 269 D3
Ngomeni, Ras Kenya 2°59S 40°14E 268 C5
Ngong Kenya 1°22S 36°39E 268 C4
Ngong Shuen Chau China 22°19N 114°8E 122 B1
Ngongotaha N.Z. 38°5S 176°12E 284 E5
Ngonye Falls Zambia 16°40S 23°25E 265 F4
Ngop Sudan 6°17N 30°9E 257 F3
Ngoring Hu China 34°55N 97°5E 218 E8
Ngorkou Mali 15°40N 3°41W 262 B4
Ngorongoro Tanzania 3°11S 35°32E 268 C4
Ngorongoro ⌂ Tanzania 2°40S 35°30E 268 C4
Ngoto C.A.R. 3°59N 17°19E 264 B3
Ngouo, Dj. C.A.R. 7°55N 24°38E 264 A4
Ngoura Chad 12°44N 16°21E 259 F3
Ngouri Chad 13°38N 15°22E 259 F3
Ngourti Niger 15°19N 13°12E 259 E2
Ngoussou Gabon 3°0S 11°7E 264 C2
Ngozi Burundi 2°54S 29°50E 268 C2
Ngua Kok Wan China 22°21N 114°5E 122 A1
Ngudu Tanzania 2°58S 33°25E 268 C3
Nguigmi Niger 14°20N 13°20E 259 F2
Nguila Cameroon 4°41N 11°43E 263 E7
Nguiu Australia 11°46S 130°38E 278 B5
Ngukurr Australia 14°44S 134°44E 280 A1
Ngum ➜ Laos 18°31N 102°32E 236 C4
Nguna Vanuatu 17°26S 168°22E 287 G6
Ngundu Zimbabwe 18°11S 31°15E 269 F3
Ngunga Tanzania 3°37S 33°37E 268 C3
Nguru Nigeria 12°56N 10°29E 263 C7
Nguru Mts. Tanzania 6°0S 37°30E 268 D4
Ngusi Malawi 14°0S 34°50E 269 E3
Nguyen Binh Vietnam 22°39N 105°56E 228 F5
Ngwedaung Burma 19°31N 97°9E 241 F6
Nha Bang Vietnam 10°37N 105°0E 237 G5
Nha Trang Vietnam 12°16N 109°10E 237 F7
Nhacoongo Mozam. 24°18S 35°14E 271 B6
Nhamaabué Mozam. 17°25S 35°5E 269 F4
Nhambiquara Brazil 12°50S 59°49W 331 C6
Nhamundá Brazil 2°14S 56°43W 329 D6
Nhamundá ➜ Brazil 2°12S 56°41W 329 D6
Nhangulaze, L. Mozam. 24°0S 34°30E 271 B5
Nharêa Angola 11°38S 16°58E 265 E3
Nharnuwangga, Wajarri and
Ngarlawangga ◎
Australia 24°50S 118°0E 279 D2
Nhava Sheva India 18°58N 72°55E 130 B2
Nhecolândia Brazil 19°17S 56°58W 331 D6
Nhill Australia 36°18S 141°40E 282 D4
Nho Quan Vietnam 20°18N 105°45E 228 G5
Nhulunbuy Australia 12°10S 137°20E 280 A2
Nhundo Angola 14°25S 21°23E 265 E4
Nia-nia
Dem. Rep. of the Congo 1°30N 27°40E 268 B2
Niafounké Mali 16°0N 4°5W 262 B4
Niagara Falls Ont., Canada 43°7N 79°5W 312 C5
Niagara Falls N.Y., U.S.A. 43°5N 79°4W 312 C6
Niagara-on-the-Lake
Canada 43°15N 79°4W 312 C5
Niah Malaysia 3°58N 113°46E 235 B4
Nialaha'u Pt. Solomon Is. 9°47S 161°34E 287 M11
Niamey Niger 13°27N 2°6E 263 C5
Niamtougou Togo 9°46N 1°6E 263 D5
Niandan-Koro Guinea 11°5N 9°15W 262 C3
Nianforando Guinea 9°37N 10°36W 262 D2
Niangara
Dem. Rep. of the Congo 3°42N 27°50E 268 B2
Niangay, L. Mali 15°50N 3°0W 262 B4
Niangbo Ivory C. 8°49N 5°10W 262 D3
Niangoloko Burkina Faso 10°15N 4°55W 262 C4
Niangua ➜ U.S.A. 38°58N 92°48W 310 G4
Niantic U.S.A. 41°20N 72°11W 313 E12
Niari Congo 4°9S 14°9E 264 C2
Niaro Sudan 10°38N 31°31E 257 E3
Nias Indonesia 1°0N 97°30E 234 B1
Niassa □ Mozam. 13°30S 36°0E 269 E4
Niassa ⌂ Mozam. 12°4S 36°57E 269 E4
Niāvarān Iran 35°47N 51°29E 141 A2
Nibāk Si. Arabia 24°25N 50°50E 247 E7
Nibe Denmark 56°59N 9°38E 163 H3
Nibra India 22°36N 88°15E 124 B1
Nicaragua ■ Cent. Amer. 11°40N 85°30W 320 D2
Nicaragua, L. de Nic. 12°0N 85°30W 320 D2
Nicastro Italy 38°59N 16°19E 201 D9
Nice France 43°42N 7°14E 175 E11
Nice-Côte-d'Azur ✈ (NCE)
France 43°41N 7°12E 175 E11
Niceville U.S.A. 30°31N 86°30W 317 E3
Nichicun, L. Canada 53°5N 71°0W 299 B5
Nichinan Japan 31°38N 131°23E 222 F3
Nicholás, Canal W. Indies 23°30N 80°5W 320 B3
Nicholasville U.S.A. 37°53N 84°34W 311 G12
Nicholls U.S.A. 31°31N 82°38W 316 D7
Nichols U.S.A. 42°1N 76°22W 313 D8
Nicholson W. Austral.,
Australia 18°2S 128°54E 278 C4
Nicholson Pa., U.S.A. 41°37N 75°47W 313 E9
Nicholson ➜ Australia 17°31S 139°36E 280 B2
Nicholson L. Canada 62°40N 102°40W 297 A8
Nicholson Ra. Australia 27°15S 116°45E 279 E2
Nicholville U.S.A. 44°41N 74°39W 313 B10
Nickerie ➜ Suriname 5°58N 57°0W 329 B6
Nico Pérez = José Batlle y Ordóñez
Uruguay 33°20S 55°10W 335 C4
Nicobar Is. Ind. Oc. 8°0N 93°30E 245 L11
Nicola Canada 50°12N 120°40W 296 C4
Nicolls Town Bahamas 25°8N 78°0W 320 A4
Nicosia Cyprus 35°10N 33°25E 207 E12
Nicosia Italy 37°45N 14°24E 201 E7
Nicótera Italy 38°33N 15°56E 201 D8
Nicoya Costa Rica 10°9N 85°27W 320 D2
Nicoya, G. de Costa Rica 10°0N 85°0W 320 E3
Nicoya, Pen. de Costa Rica 9°45N 85°40W 320 E2
Nictheroy = Niterói Brazil 22°53S 43°7W 135 B2
Nida Lithuania 55°20N 21°4E 184 C8
Nidāl Iraq 33°19N 44°25E 113 B2
Nidaros = Trondheim
Norway 63°36N 10°25E 164 A7
Nidd ➜ U.K. 53°59N 1°23W 168 D6
Nidda Germany 50°23N 9°1E 179 E5
Nidda ➜ Germany 50°17N 8°48E 179 E4
Niddrie Vic., Australia 37°44S 144°51E 128 A1
Niddrie Edinburgh, U.K. 55°56N 3°7W 121 B3
Nidri Greece 38°43N 20°42E 207 C8
Nidwalden □ Switz. 46°50N 8°25E 179 J4
Nidzica Poland 53°25N 20°28E 185 E7
Niebüll Germany 54°46N 8°48E 178 A4
Nied ➜ Germany 49°23N 6°40E 173 C13
Nieder Neuendorf
Germany 52°36N 13°12E 115 A2
Niederaula Germany 50°47N 9°36E 178 E5
Niederbayern □ Germany 48°40N 12°50E 179 G8
Niederbronn-les-Bains
France 48°57N 7°39E 173 D14
Niedere Tauern Austria 47°20N 14°0E 180 D7
Niederlausitz Germany 51°42N 13°59E 178 D9
Niederösterreich □
Austria 48°25N 15°40E 180 C8
Niedersachsen □ Germany 52°50N 9°0E 178 C4
Niedersächsisches Wattenmeer △
Germany 53°45N 7°30E 178 B3
Niederschöneweide
Germany 52°27N 13°30E 115 B3
Niederschönhausen
Germany 52°35N 13°25E 115 A3
Niefang Eq. Guin. 1°50N 10°14E 264 B2
Niekerkshoop S. Africa 29°19S 22°51E 270 C3
Niellé Ivory C. 10°5N 5°38W 262 C3
Niellim Chad 9°42N 17°49E 259 G3
Niem C.A.R. 6°12N 15°14E 264 A3
Niemba
Dem. Rep. of the Congo 5°58S 28°24E 268 D2
Niemen = Nemunas ➜
Lithuania 55°25N 21°10E 184 C8
Niemeyer Brazil 22°59S 43°16W 135 B1
Niemodlin Poland 50°38N 17°38E 185 H4
Niemur Australia 35°17S 144°9E 282 C6
Nienburg Germany 52°39N 9°13E 178 C5
Niepołomice Poland 50°3N 20°13E 185 H7
Niers ➜ Germany 51°43N 5°57E 178 D1
Niesky Germany 51°17N 14°49E 178 D10
Nieszawa Poland 52°52N 18°50E 185 F5
Nieu Bethesda S. Africa 31°51S 24°34E 270 D3
Nieuw Amsterdam
Suriname 5°53N 55°5W 329 B6
Nieuw Nickerie Suriname 6°0N 56°59W 329 B6
Nieuwe Kerk Amsterdam, Neths. 112 a2
Nieuwendam Neths. 52°23N 4°57E 112 A2
Nieuwoudtville S. Africa 31°23S 19°7E 270 D2
Nieuwpoort Belgium 51°8N 2°45E 170 C2
Nieuwpoort Curaçao 12°3N 68°49W 322 g
Nieves, Pico de las
Canary Is. 27°57N 15°35W 153 e1
Nièvre □ France 47°10N 3°40E 173 E10
Nif Micronesia 9°28N 138°4E 287 S16
Niga Mali 13°38N 5°27W 262 C3
Niğde Turkey 37°58N 34°40E 212 D6
Niğde □ Turkey 38°0N 34°30E 212 D6
Nigel S. Africa 26°27S 28°25E 271 C4
Niger □ Nigeria 10°0N 5°30E 263 D6
Niger ■ W. Afr. 17°30N 10°0E 259 E2
Niger ➜ W. Afr. 5°33N 6°33E 263 D6
Niger Delta Africa 5°0N 6°0E 263 E6
Nigeria ■ W. Afr. 8°30N 8°0E 263 D6
Nighasin India 28°14N 80°52E 243 E9
Nightcaps N.Z. 45°57S 168°2E 285 F3
Nightmute U.S.A. 60°29N 164°44W 303 F6
Nigrita Greece 40°56N 23°29E 202 F7
Nihoa U.S.A. 23°6N 161°58W 302 G11
Nihon = Japan ■ Asia 36°0N 136°0E 221 G8
Nihonbashi Tokyo, Japan 140 b5
Nii-Jima Japan 34°20N 139°15E 223 C11
Niigata Japan 37°58N 139°0E 220 F9
Niigata □ Japan 37°15N 138°45E 221 F9
Niihama Japan 33°55N 133°16E 222 D5
Ni'ihau U.S.A. 21°54N 160°9W 302 B1
Niimi Japan 34°59N 133°28E 222 C5
Niipperi Finland 60°18N 24°45E 121 B1
Niislel Khureheh = Ulaanbaatar
Mongolia 47°55N 106°53E 218 B10
Niitsu Japan 37°48N 139°7E 220 F9
Nij Laluk India 27°7N 93°56E 241 B4
Nijar Spain 36°53N 2°15W 197 J2
Nijil Jordan 30°32N 35°33E 251 H6
Nijkerk Neths. 52°13N 5°30E 170 B5
Nijmegen Neths. 51°50N 5°52E 170 C5
Nijverdal Neths. 52°22N 6°28E 170 B6
Nīk Pey Iran 36°50N 48°10E 213 D13
Nikao Cook Is. 21°12S 159°48W 289 h
Nikawaratiya Sri Lanka 7°45N 80°7E 245 L5
Nike Nigeria 6°26N 7°29E 263 D6
Nikea Greece 37°57N 23°38E 112 B1
Nikel Russia 69°24N 30°13E 160 B24
Nikiboko Bonaire 12°9N 68°16W 322 h
Nikiniki Indonesia 9°49S 124°30E 278 A3
Nikisiani Greece 40°57N 24°9E 203 F8
Nikiski U.S.A. 61°41N 151°18W 303 F10
Nikiti Greece 40°13N 23°43E 202 F7
Nikitinskiye promysly = Kirovskiy
Russia 45°51N 48°11E 191 H9
Nikki Benin 9°58N 3°12E 263 D5
Nikkō Japan 36°45N 139°35E 223 A11
Nikkō △ Japan 36°56N 139°37E 221 F9
Nikolai U.S.A. 62°58N 154°10W 303 E9
Nikolainkaupunki = Vaasa
Finland 63°6N 21°38E 160 E19
Nikolaistad = Vaasa
Finland 63°6N 21°38E 160 E19
Nikolassee Germany 52°25N 13°12E 115 B2
Nikolayev = Mykolayiv
Ukraine 46°58N 32°0E 189 J7
Nikolayevsk Russia 50°0N 45°35E 190 E7
Nikolayevsk-na-Amur
Russia 53°8N 140°44E 215 D15
Nikolsburg = Mikulov
Czech Rep. 48°48N 16°39E 181 C9
Nikolsk Russia 59°30N 45°28E 190 C5
Nikolsk-Ussuriysky = Ussuriysk
Russia 43°48N 131°59E 220 B5
Nikolskaya Pestravka = Nikolsk
Russia 53°49N 46°4E 190 D8
Nikolski U.S.A. 52°56N 168°52W 303 K5
Nikolskiy Russia 55°49N 37°29E 129 B2
Nikolskoye = Ussuriysk
Russia 43°48N 131°59E 220 C5
Nikolskoye Russia 55°12N 166°0E 215 D17
Nikolsky Khutor = Sursk
Russia 53°3N 45°40E 190 D7
Nikolyskoye Russia 55°46N 37°53E 129 B5
Nikopol Bulgaria 43°43N 24°54E 203 C8
Nikopol Ukraine 47°35N 34°25E 189 J8
Nikopolis Greece 39°5N 20°43E 207 A2
Niksar Turkey 40°31N 37°2E 212 B7
Nīkshahr Iran 26°15N 60°10E 247 E9
Nikšić Montenegro 42°50N 18°57E 202 D2
Nikulino Russia 55°40N 37°25E 129 B2
Nikumaroro Kiribati 4°40S 174°32W 277 A16
Nikunau Kiribati 1°22S 176°28E 277 A14
Nîl, Nahr en ➜ Africa 30°10N 31°6E 256 H7
Nîl el Abyad ➜ Sudan 15°38N 32°31E 257 D3
Nîl el Azraq ➜ Sudan 15°38N 32°31E 257 D3
Nila Indonesia 6°44S 129°31E 231 F7
Nilakkottai India 10°10N 77°52E 245 J3
Niland U.S.A. 33°14N 115°31W 307 M11
Nilanga India 18°6N 76°46E 244 E3
Nile = Nîl, Nahr en ➜
Africa 30°10N 31°6E 256 H7
Nile Delta Egypt 31°40N 31°0E 256 H7
Niles Ill., U.S.A. 42°1N 87°48W 119 A2
Niles Mich., U.S.A. 41°50N 86°15W 311 C10
Niles Ohio, U.S.A. 41°11N 80°46W 312 E4
Niles Center = Skokie
U.S.A. 42°2N 87°43W 119 A2
Nileshwar India 12°15N 75°6E 245 H2
Nilgiri Hills India 11°30N 76°30E 245 J3
Nilo Peçanha Brazil 13°37S 39°6W 333 D4
Nilsebu Norway 59°11N 6°39E 164 E3
Nilüfer ➜ Turkey 40°18N 28°27E 203 F12
Nim Ka Thana India 27°44N 75°48E 242 F6
Nimach India 24°30N 74°56E 242 G6
Nimba, Mts. Africa 7°37N 8°25W 262 D3
Nimbahera India 24°37N 74°45E 242 G6
Nîmes France 43°50N 4°23E 175 E8
Nimfaíon, Ákra = Pines, Ákra
Greece 40°5N 24°20E 203 F8
Nimmitabel Australia 36°29S 149°15E 283 D8
Nīmrūz □ Afghan. 30°0N 62°0E 240 C1
Nimta India 22°40N 88°24E 124 A2
Nimule Sudan 3°32N 32°3E 257 G3
Nimule △ Sudan 3°38N 32°3E 257 G3
Nin Croatia 44°16N 15°12E 199 D12
Nīnawá Iraq 36°25N 43°10E 213 D10
Nīnawá □ Iraq 36°15N 43°0E 246 B4
Ninda Angola 14°47S 21°24E 265 E4
Nindigully Australia 28°21S 148°50E 281 D4
Nine Degree Channel India 9°0N 73°0E 245 K1
Ninepin Group China 22°16N 114°21E 219 a
Ninety Mile Beach N.Z. 34°48S 173°0E 284 A2
Ninety Mile Beach, The
Australia 38°15S 147°24E 283 E7
Ninety Six U.S.A. 34°11N 82°1W 316 A7
Ninetyeast Ridge Ind. Oc. 1°0S 90°0E 273 E7
Nineveh = Nīnawá Iraq 36°25N 43°10E 213 D10
Ning Xian China 35°30N 107°58E 226 G4
Ningaloo Marine △
Australia 22°23S 113°32E 278 D1
Ning'an China 44°22N 129°20E 227 B15
Ningbo China 29°51N 121°28E 229 C13
Ningcheng China 41°32N 119°53E 227 D10
Ningde China 26°38N 119°23E 229 D12
Ningdu China 26°25N 115°59E 229 D10
Ningerum Papua N. G. 5°41S 141°8E 286 C1
Ninggang China 26°42N 113°55E 229 D9
Ningguo China 30°35N 119°0E 229 B12
Ninghai China 29°15N 121°27E 229 C13
Ninghua China 26°14N 116°45E 229 D11
Ningi Nigeria 10°55N 9°30E 263 C6
Ningjin China 37°35N 114°57E 226 F8
Ningjing Shan China 31°0N 98°20E 228 C2
Ninglang China 27°20N 100°55E 228 D3
Ningling China 34°25N 115°22E 226 G8
Ningming China 22°8N 107°4E 228 F6
Ningnan China 27°5N 102°36E 228 D4
Ningpo = Ningbo China 29°51N 121°28E 229 C13
Ningqiang China 32°47N 106°15E 226 H4
Ningshan China 33°21N 108°21E 228 A7
Ningsia Hui A.R. = Ningxia Huizu
Zizhiqu □ China 38°0N 106°0E 226 F4
Ningwu China 39°0N 112°18E 226 E7
Ningxia Huizu Zizhiqu □
China 38°0N 106°0E 226 F4
Ningxiang China 28°15N 112°30E 229 C9
Ningyang China 35°47N 116°45E 226 G9
Ningyuan China 25°37N 111°57E 229 E8
Ninh Binh Vietnam 20°15N 105°55E 228 G5
Ninh Giang Vietnam 20°44N 106°24E 236 B6
Ninh Hoa Vietnam 12°30N 109°7E 236 F7
Ninh Ma Vietnam 12°48N 109°21E 236 F7
Nini-Suhien △ Ghana 5°20N 2°34W 262 D4
Ninigo Group Papua N. G. 1°22S 144°17E 286 A3
Ninove Belgium 50°51N 4°2E 170 D4
Ninoy Aquino Int. ✈ (MNL)
Phil. 14°31N 121°0E 127 B2
Nioaque Brazil 21°5S 55°50W 335 A4
Niobrara U.S.A. 42°45N 98°2W 308 D4
Niobrara ➜ U.S.A. 42°46N 98°3W 308 D4
Nioki Dem. Rep. of the Congo 2°47S 17°40E 264 C3
Niokolo-Koba △ Senegal 13°3N 13°2W 262 C2
Niono Mali 14°15N 6°0W 262 C3
Nionsamoridougou Guinea 8°45N 8°50W 262 D3
Nioro du Rip Senegal 13°40N 15°50W 262 C1
Nioro du Sahel Mali 15°15N 9°30W 262 B3
Niort France 46°19N 0°29W 174 B3
Nioumachoua Comoros Is. 12°21S 43°42E 272 a
Nipa Papua N. G. 6°9S 143°29E 286 D2
Nipani India 16°20N 74°25E 245 F2
Nipawin Canada 53°20N 104°0W 297 C8
Nipfjället Sweden 61°59N 12°50E 162 C6
Nipigon Canada 49°0N 88°17W 298 C2
Nipigon, L. Canada 49°50N 88°30W 298 C2
Nipishish L. Canada 54°12N 60°45W 299 B7
Nipissing, L. Canada 46°20N 80°0W 298 C4
Nipomo U.S.A. 35°3N 120°29W 307 K6
Nippa Japan 35°31N 139°36E 140 B2
Nippon = Japan ■ Asia 36°0N 136°0E 221 G8
Nipponi Japan 35°43N 139°45E 140 A3
Nipton U.S.A. 35°28N 115°16W 307 K11
Niquelândia Brazil 14°33S 48°23W 333 D2
Nīr Iran 38°2N 47°59E 213 C12
Nira ➜ India 17°58N 75°8E 244 F2
Nirasaki Japan 35°42N 138°27E 223 B10
Nirayama Japan 35°2N 138°52E 223 B10
Nirmal India 19°3N 78°20E 244 E4
Nirmali India 26°20N 86°35E 243 F12
Niš Serbia 43°19N 21°58E 202 C5
Nisa = Nysa ➜ Europe 52°4N 14°46E 178 C10
Nisa Portugal 39°30N 7°41W 195 F3
Niṣāb Si. Arabia 29°11N 44°43E 246 D5
Niṣāb Yemen 14°25N 46°29E 248 D4
Nišava ➜ Serbia 43°20N 21°46E 202 C5
Niscemi Italy 37°9N 14°23E 201 E7
Nishi Japan 35°26N 139°38E 133 A1
Nishi-Sonogi-Hantō
Japan 32°55N 129°45E 222 E1
Nishi-Tosa Japan 33°13N 132°46E 222 D4
Nishinari Japan 34°37N 135°28E 133 B1
Nishinomiya Japan 34°45N 135°20E 133 A1
Nishino'omote Japan 30°43N 130°59E 221 J5
Nishio Japan 34°52N 137°3E 223 C9
Nishiwaki Japan 34°59N 134°58E 222 C6
Nishiyodogawa Japan 34°41N 135°24E 133 A1

Nisibin = Nusaybin *Turkey* 37°3N 41°10E **213** D9
Niška Banja *Serbia* 43°18N 22°1E **202** C6
Niskibi → *Canada* 56°29N 88°9W **298** A2
Nisko *Poland* 50°35N 22°7E **185** H9
Nisporeni *Moldova* 47°4N 28°10E **188** D3
Nisqually → *U.S.A.* 47°7N 122°42W **306** C4
Nissaki *Greece* 39°43N 19°52E **206** B9
Nissan → *Sweden* 56°40N 12°51E **163** H6
Nissedal *Norway* 59°10N 8°30E **164** E3
Nisser *Norway* 59°7N 8°28E **164** E3
Nissiros *Greece* 36°35N 27°12E **205** D9
Nissum Bredning *Denmark* 56°40N 8°20E **163** H2
Nissum Fjord *Denmark* 56°20N 8°11E **163** H2
Nistru = Dnister →
　Europe 46°18N 30°17E **177** E16
Nisutlin → *Canada* 60°14N 132°34W **296** A2
Nitchequon *Canada* 53°10N 70°58W **299** B5
Niterói *Brazil* 22°53S 43°7W **135** B2
Nith → *Ont., Canada* 43°12N 80°23W **312** C4
Nith → *Dumf. & Gall., U.K.* 55°14N 3°33W **167** F5
Nitmiluk △ *Australia* 14°6S 132°15E **280** B5
Nitra *Slovak Rep.* 48°19N 18°4E **181** C11
Nitra → *Slovak Rep.* 47°46N 18°10E **181** D11
Nitriansky □ *Slovak Rep.* 48°10N 18°30E **181** C11
Nittenau *Germany* 49°12N 12°16E **179** F8
Niu Valley *U.S.A.* 21°19N 157°44W **302** K14
Niua Group *Tonga* 15°57S 173°45W **277** D16
Niuafo'ou *Tonga* 15°30S 175°58W **277** D15
Niuatoputapu *Tonga* 15°57S 173°54W **277** D15
Niue ☑ *Pac. Oc.* 19°2S 169°54W **289** g
Niulakita *Pac. Oc.* 10°45S 179°30E **277** E14
Niulan Jiang → *China* 27°30N 103°5E **228** D4
Niulantsun *Taiwan* 25°1N 121°2E **225** A3
Niur *Indonesia* 0°26S 103°30E **234** C2
Niut *Indonesia* 0°55N 109°54E **235** B4
Niutao *Pac. Oc.* 6°7S 177°18E **277** E14
Niutou Shan *China* 29°5N 121°59E **223** C13
Niuzhuang *China* 40°58N 122°28E **224** B1
Nivala *Finland* 63°56N 24°57E **160** E21
Nivelles *Belgium* 50°35N 4°20E **170** D4
Nivernais *France* 47°15N 3°30E **173** E10
Niverville *Canada* 49°36N 97°3W **297** D9
Niwas *India* 23°3N 80°26E **243** H9
Nixa *U.S.A.* 37°3N 93°18W **308** G7
Nixon *U.S.A.* 29°16N 97°46W **314** G6
Nizam Sagar *India* 18°10N 77°58E **244** E3
Nizamabad *India* 18°45N 78°7E **244** E4
Nizamghat *India* 28°20N 95°45E **241** A5
Nizhne Kolymsk *Russia* 68°34N 160°55E **215** C17
Nizhne-Gorskiy = Nyzhnohirskyy
　Ukraine 45°27N 34°38E **189** K8
Nizhnekamsk *Russia* 55°38N 51°49E **190** C10
Nizhneudinsk *Russia* 54°54N 99°3E **215** D10
Nizhnevartovsk *Russia* 60°56N 76°38E **214** C8
Nizhniy Bestyakh
　Russia 61°57N 129°54E **215** C13
Nizhniy Chir *Russia* 48°22N 43°5E **191** F6
Nizhniy Lomov *Russia* 53°34N 43°38E **190** D6
Nizhniy Novgorod *Russia* 56°20N 44°0E **190** B7
Nizhniy Novgorod □
　Russia 56°30N 44°20E **190** B7
Nizhniy Tagil *Russia* 57°55N 59°57E **186** C10
Nizhnie Kresty = Cherskiy
　Russia 68°45N 161°18E **215** C17
Nizina Mazowiecka *Poland* 52°30N 21°0E **185** F8
Nizip *Turkey* 37°5N 37°50E **212** D7
Nízké Tatry *Slovak Rep.* 48°55N 19°30E **181** C12
Nízké Tatry △
　Slovak Rep. 48°55N 19°37E **181** C12
Nízký Jeseník *Czech Rep.* 49°50N 17°30E **181** B10
Nizwá *Oman* 22°56N 57°32E **249** B7
Nizza Monferrato *Italy* 44°46N 8°21E **198** D5
Njakwa *Malawi* 11°1S 33°56E **269** E3
Njarðvík *Iceland* 64°0N 22°33W **155** D4
Njazidja = Grande Comore
　Comoros Is. 11°35S 43°20E **272** a
Njegoš *Montenegro* 42°53N 18°45E **202** D2
Njinjo *Tanzania* 8°48S 38°54E **269** D4
Njoko → *Zambia* 17°8S 24°4E **265** F4
Njombe *Tanzania* 9°20S 34°50E **269** D3
Njombe → *Tanzania* 6°56S 35°6E **268** D4
Njurundabommen
　Sweden 62°15N 17°25E **162** B11
Nkambe *Cameroon* 6°35N 10°40E **263** D7
Nkana *Zambia* 12°50S 28°8E **269** E2
Nkandla *S. Africa* 28°37S 31°5E **271** D5
Nkawkaw *Ghana* 6°36N 0°49W **263** D4
Nkayi *Congo* 4°9S 13°1E **264** C2
Nkayi *Zimbabwe* 19°41S 29°20E **269** F2
Nkhotakota *Malawi* 12°56S 34°15E **269** E3
Nkhotakota □ *Malawi* 12°50S 34°0E **269** E3
Nkolabona *Gabon* 1°14N 11°43E **264** B2
Nkomi, Lagune *Gabon* 1°35S 9°17E **264** C1
Nkondwe *Tanzania* 5°51S 30°51E **268** D3
Nkone *Dem. Rep. of the Congo* 1°2S 22°20E **264** C4
Nkongsamba *Cameroon* 4°55N 9°55E **263** E6
Nkoteng *Cameroon* 4°31N 12°2E **264** B2
Nkunga
　Dem. Rep. of the Congo 4°41S 18°34E **265** C3
Nkurenkuru *Namibia* 17°42S 18°32E **270** A2
Nkwanta *Ghana* 6°10N 0°10W **262** D4
Nmai → *Burma* 25°30N 97°25E **228** F2
Noakhali *Bangla.* 22°48N 91°10E **241** D3
Noatak *U.S.A.* 67°34N 162°58W **303** C7
Noatak △ *U.S.A.* 68°10N 160°0W **303** B8
Nob Hill *San Francisco, U.S.A.* **136** B1
Nobel *Canada* 45°25N 80°6W **312** A4
Nobeoka *Japan* 32°36N 131°41E **222** E3
Noble *U.S.A.* 38°42N 88°14W **311** F8
Noblejas *Spain* 39°58N 3°26W **194** F7
Noblesville *U.S.A.* 40°3N 86°1W **311** E11
Noboribetsu *Japan* 42°24N 141°6E **220** C10
Nocatee *U.S.A.* 27°10N 81°53W **317** H8
Noccundra *Australia* 27°50S 142°36E **281** D3
Noce → *Italy* 46°9N 11°4E **198** B8
Nocera Inferiore *Italy* 40°44N 14°38E **201** B7
Nocera Umbra *Italy* 43°8N 12°47E **199** C10
Noci *Italy* 40°48N 17°7E **201** B10
Nockeby *Sweden* 59°19N 17°56E **139** B1
Nocona *U.S.A.* 33°47N 97°44W **314** E6
Nocrich *Romania* 45°55N 24°26E **183** E9
Noda *Japan* 35°56N 139°52E **223** B11
Nodeland *Norway* 58°8N 7°51E **164** F4
Noel Kempff Mercado △
　Bolivia 14°9S 60°49W **331** C5
Noel Park *U.K.* **125** A3
Nogal Valley = Nugaaleed, Dooxo
　Somali Rep. 8°35N 48°35E **267** C6
Nogales *Sonora, Mexico* 31°21N 110°56W **318** A2
Nogales *Ariz., U.S.A.* 31°21N 110°56W **305** L8
Nogaro *France* 43°45N 0°2W **174** E3
Nogat → *Poland* 54°17N 19°17E **184** D6
Nõgata *Japan* 33°48N 130°44E **222** D2
Nogatino *Russia* 55°37N 37°41E **129** B4
Noggerup *Australia* 33°32S 116°5E **277** F2
Noginsk *Moskva, Russia* 55°50N 38°25E **188** E10
Noginsk *Tunguska, Russia* 64°30N 90°50E **215** C10

Nogliki *Russia* 51°50N 143°10E **215** D15
Nogoa → *Australia* 23°40S 147°55E **280** C4
Nogoyá *Argentina* 32°24S 59°48W **334** C4
Nógrád □ *Hungary* 48°0N 19°30E **182** C4
Noguera Pallaresa →
　Spain 41°55N 0°55E **196** D5
Noguera Ribagorçana →
　Spain 41°40N 0°43E **196** D5
Nohar *India* 29°11N 74°49E **242** E6
Nohfelden *Germany* 49°35N 7°7E **179** F3
Nohili Pt. *U.S.A.* 22°4N 159°47W **302** A2
Nohta *India* 23°40N 79°34E **243** H8
Nohwa *S. Korea* 34°10N 126°34E **224** E3
Nohwado *S. Korea* 34°12N 126°35E **224** E3
Noia *Spain* 42°48N 8°53W **194** C2
Noichi *Japan* 33°33N 133°42E **222** D5
Noida *India* 28°36N 77°19E **242** E7
Noioupos *Papua N. G.* 2°25S 150°7E **286** B6
Noire, Montagne *France* 43°28N 2°20E **174** E6
Noires, Mts. *France* 48°11N 3°40W **172** D3
Noirétable *France* 45°48N 3°46E **174** E7
Noirmoutier, Î. de *France* 46°58N 2°10W **172** F4
Noirmoutier-en-l'Île *France* 46°59N 2°18W **172** F4
Noiseau *France* 48°46N 2°32E **134** B4
Noisiel *France* 48°51N 2°37E **134** A4
Noisy-le-Grand *France* 48°50N 2°33E **134** A4
Noisy-le-Roi *France* 48°50N 2°3E **134** A1
Noisy-le-Sec *France* 48°53N 2°27E **134** A3
Nojane *Botswana* 23°15S 20°14E **270** B3
Nojima-Zaki *Japan* 34°54N 139°53E **223** C11
Nok Kundi *Pakistan* 28°50N 62°45E **240** C1
Nok Ta Phao, Ko *Thailand* 9°23N 99°40E **237** b
Nokaneng *Botswana* 19°40S 22°17E **270** A3
Nokia *Finland* 61°30N 23°30E **163** B8
Nokkala *Finland* 60°8N 24°45E **121** C1
Nokkeushi = Kitami
　Japan 43°48N 143°54E **220** C11
Nokomis *Sask., Canada* 51°35N 105°0W **297** C7
Nokomis *Fla., U.S.A.* 27°7N 82°27W **317** H7
Nokomis *Ill., U.S.A.* 39°18N 89°18W **310** F7
Nokomis L. *Canada* 57°0N 103°0W **297** B8
Nokou *Chad* 14°35N 14°47E **263** F8
Nokuku *Vanuatu* 14°54S 166°35E **287** D4
Nola *C.A.R.* 3°35N 16°4E **264** B3
Nola *Italy* 40°55N 14°33E **201** B7
Nolay *France* 46°58N 4°35E **173** F11
Noli, C. di *Italy* 44°12N 8°25E **198** D5
Nolinsk *Russia* 57°28N 49°57E **190** B9
Noma *U.S.A.* 30°59N 85°37W **316** E4
Noma Omuramba →
　Namibia 18°52S 20°53E **270** A3
Noma-Saki *Japan* 31°25N 130°7E **222** E2
Nomad *Papua N. G.* 6°19S 142°13E **286** D2
Nombre de Dios *Panama* 9°34N 79°28W **320** E4
Nome *U.S.A.* 64°30N 165°25W **303** D6
Nomentano *Italy* 41°55N 12°30E **136** B3
Nomgon *Mongolia* 42°50N 105°8E **226** C3
Nomo-Zaki *Japan* 32°35N 129°44E **222** E1
Nomonas *Micronesia* 7°24N 151°53E **287** T18
Nomuka *Tonga* 20°17S 174°48W **287** Q13
Nomuka Group *Tonga* 20°20S 174°48W **287** Q13
Nonacho L. *Canada* 61°42N 109°40W **297** A7
Nonakashinden *Japan* 35°44N 139°30E **140** A2
Nonancourt *France* 48°47N 1°11E **172** D8
Nonda *Australia* 20°40S 142°28E **280** C3
Nondalton *U.S.A.* 60°0N 154°51W **303** F9
None *Italy* 44°56N 7°32E **198** D4
Nong Chang *Thailand* 15°23N 99°51E **236** E2
Nong Han Res. *Thailand* 17°11N 104°9E **236** D4
Nong Het *Laos* 19°29N 103°59E **236** C4
Nong Khai *Thailand* 17°50N 102°46E **236** D4
Nong'an *China* 44°25N 125°5E **227** B13
Nongjrong *India* 25°29N 92°6E **241** C4
Nongminyundong Jiangxiuso
　China 23°7N 113°15E **121** B2
Nongoma *S. Africa* 27°58S 31°35E **271** C5
Nongsa *Indonesia* 1°11N 104°8E **237** d
Nongstoin *India* 25°31N 91°16E **241** C3
Nonhyeon *S. Korea* 37°30N 127°1E **137** B2
Nono *Ethiopia* 8°32N 37°26E **266** C4
Nonoava *Mexico* 27°28N 106°44W **318** B3
Nonoc I. *Phil.* 9°51N 125°37E **233** G5
Nonoichi *Japan* 36°35N 136°35E **223** A8
Nonsan *S. Korea* 36°12N 127°5E **224** D3
Nonsuch B. *Antigua & B.* 17°6N 61°42W **322** b
Nonthaburi *Thailand* 13°50N 100°29E **113** A1
Nontron *France* 45°31N 0°40E **174** C4
Nonza *France* 42°47N 9°21E **175** F13
Noon Gun *Cape Town, S. Africa* **118** b1
Noonamah *Australia* 12°40S 131°4E **278** B5
Noondie, L. *Australia* 28°30S 119°30E **279** E2
Noonkanbah ◎ *Australia* 18°30S 124°50E **278** C3
Noord *Aruba* 12°34N 70°1W **322** f
Noord Brabant □ *Neths.* 51°40N 5°0E **170** C5
Noord Holland □ *Neths.* 52°30N 4°45E **170** C5
Noord Salina *Bonaire* 12°11N 68°16W **322** h
Noordbeveland *Neths.* 51°35N 3°50E **170** C3
Noordenveld *Neths.* 53°8N 6°28E **170** A6
Noordgessig *S. Africa* 26°13S 27°58E **123** B1
Noordkaap *Aruba* 12°34N 70°1W **322** f
Noordoostpolder *Neths.* 52°45N 5°45E **170** B5
Noordpunt *Bonaire* 12°18N 68°23W **322** h
Noordpunt *Curaçao* 12°24N 69°10W **322** g
Noordwijk *Neths.* 52°14N 4°26E **170** B4
Noorvik *U.S.A.* 66°50N 161°3W **303** C7
Noosa Heads *Australia* 26°25S 153°6E **281** D5
Nootka I. *Canada* 49°32N 126°42W **296** D3
Nopiming ○ *Canada* 50°30N 95°37W **297** C9
Nóqui *Angola* 5°55S 13°30E **265** D2
Nor-Bayzset = Kamo
　Armenia 40°21N 45°7E **191** K7
Nora *Eritrea* 16°6N 40°4E **257** D5
Nora *Sweden* 59°32N 15°2E **162** E9
Nora Springs *U.S.A.* 43°9N 93°0W **310** A4
Norala *Phil.* 6°32N 124°40E **233** H5
Noralee *Canada* 53°59N 126°26W **296** C3
Noranda = Rouyn-Noranda
　Canada 48°20N 79°0W **298** C4
Norberg *Sweden* 60°4N 15°56E **162** D9
Norborne *U.S.A.* 39°18N 93°40W **310** E3
Nórcia *Italy* 42°48N 13°5E **199** C10
Norco *U.S.A.* 33°56N 117°33W **307** M9
Norcross *U.S.A.* 33°56N 84°13W **316** B5
Nord □ *Cameroon* 8°30N 14°0E **263** D7
Nord □ *France* 50°15N 3°30E **173** B10
Nord, Gare du *Paris, France* **134** a4
Nord, Pt. *Comoros Is.* 11°22S 43°19E **272** a
Nord-Kivu □
　Dem. Rep. of the Congo 1°0S 29°0E **268** C2
Nord-og-Østgrønland △
　Greenland 75°0N 30°0W **154** C7
Nord-Ostsee-Kanal =
　Germany 54°12N 9°32E **178** A5
Nord-Ouest □ *Cameroon* 6°20N 10°30E **263** D7
Nord-Pas-de-Calais □
　France 50°30N 2°50E **173** B9
Nordagutu *Norway* 59°25N 9°20E **164** E6
Nordaustlandet *Svalbard* 79°14N 23°0E **160** B9
Nordberg *Norway* 61°54N 8°10E **164** C5
Nordborg *Denmark* 55°5N 9°50E **163** J3
Nordby *Denmark* 55°27N 8°24E **163** J2
Norddeich *Germany* 53°36N 7°9E **178** B3
Nordegg *Canada* 52°29N 116°5E **296** C5
Norden *Germany* 53°35N 7°12E **178** B3

Nordenham *Germany* 53°30N 8°30E **178** B4
Nordenskjöld Sea = Laptev Sea
　Russia 76°0N 125°0E **215** B13
Norderhov *Norway* 60°7N 10°17E **164** D7
Norderney *Germany* 53°42N 7°9E **178** B3
Norderstedt *Germany* 53°42N 10°1E **178** B6
Nordfjord *Norway* 61°55N 5°30E **164** C2
Nordfjordeid *Norway* 61°54N 6°0E **164** C2
Nordfriesische Inseln =
　U.S.A. 37°30N 121°47W **306** C5
North Bennington
　U.S.A. 42°56N 73°15W **313** D11
North Bergen *U.S.A.* 40°48N 74°0W **132** B1
North Berwick *E. Loth.,*
　U.K. 56°4N 2°42W **167** E6
North Berwick *Maine,*
　U.S.A. 43°18N 70°44W **313** C14
North Borneo = Sabah □
　Malaysia 6°0N 117°0E **235** A5
North Breakers
　Midway Is. **153** b
North Brother I. *India* 10°59N 92°40E **245** J11
North Bruce *Canada* 44°22N 81°26W **312** B3
North Bull I. *Ireland* 53°22N 6°9W **120** A3
North C. *N.B., Canada* 47°5N 64°0W **299** C7
North C. *N.Z.* 34°23S 173°4E **284** A2
North C. *Papua N. G.* 2°32S 150°50E **286** B6
North Canadian →
　U.S.A. 35°22N 95°37W **314** D7
North Canton *U.S.A.* 40°53N 81°24W **312** F3
North Cape = Nordkapp
　Norway 71°10N 25°50E **160** A21
North Caribou L. *Canada* 52°50N 90°40W **298** B2
North Carolina □ *U.S.A.* 35°30N 80°0W **315** D15
North Cascades △
　U.S.A. 48°45N 121°10W **304** B3
North Cay *Bahamas* 25°6N 77°26W **153** b
North Channel *Ont., Canada* 46°0N 83°0W **298** C3
North Channel *U.K.* 55°13N 5°52W **167** F3
North Charleston *U.S.A.* 32°53N 79°58W **316** C10
North Cheam *U.K.* 51°22N 0°11W **125** B2
North Chicago *U.S.A.* 42°19N 87°51W **311** B9
North College Hill
　U.S.A. 39°13N 84°33W **311** E12
North Collins *U.S.A.* 42°35N 78°56W **312** D6
North Comino Channel
　Malta 36°1N 14°20E **206** E7
North Cotabato □ *Phil.* 7°10N 125°0E **233** H5
North Cray *U.K.* 51°25N 0°8E **125** B4
North Creek *U.S.A.* 43°42N 73°59W **313** C11
North Dakota □ *U.S.A.* 47°30N 100°15W **308** B3
North Decatur *U.S.A.* 33°48N 84°17W **118** B3
North Downs *U.K.* 51°19N 0°21E **169** F8
North Druid Hills *U.S.A.* 33°49N 84°17W **118** B3
North East *U.S.A.* 42°13N 79°50W **312** D5
North East B. *Ascension I.* 7°55S 14°21W **153** g
North East Frontier Agency =
　Arunachal Pradesh □
　India 28°0N 95°0E **241** B5
North East Lincolnshire □
　U.K. 53°34N 0°2W **168** D7
North Eastern □ *Kenya* 1°30N 40°0E **268** B5
North End *Boston, U.S.A.* **116** A3
North Esk → *Angus, U.K.* 56°46N 2°24W **167** E6
North Esk → *Midloth., U.K.* 55°54N 3°4W **121** B2
North Fabius → *U.S.A.* 39°54N 91°30W **310** E5
North Foreland *U.K.* 51°22N 1°28E **169** F9
North Fork *U.S.A.* 37°14N 119°21W **306** H7
North Fork, Salt →
　U.S.A. 39°26N 91°53W **310** E5
North Fork American →
　U.S.A. 38°57N 120°59W **306** G5
North Fork Edisto →
　U.S.A. 33°16N 80°54W **316** D9
North Fork Feather →
　U.S.A. 39°29N 121°30W **306** F5
North Fork Grand →
　U.S.A. 45°47N 102°16W **308** C2
North Fork Red →
　U.S.A. 34°24N 99°14W **314** D5
North Fort Myers *U.S.A.* 26°41N 81°53W **317** J8
North Frisian Is. = Nordfriesische
　Inseln *Germany* 54°40N 8°20E **178** A4
North Gower *Canada* 45°8N 75°43W **313** A9
North Greenfield = West Allis
　U.S.A. 43°1N 88°0W **311** B8
North Gyle *U.K.* 55°57N 3°19W **121** B2
North Hackensack *U.S.A.* 40°54N 74°2W **132** A1
North Harbor *Phil.* 14°37N 120°57E **127** B1
North Hd. *N.S.W.,*
　Australia 25°4S 122°30E **279** E3
North Hd. *W. Austral.,*
　Australia 30°14S 114°59E **279** F1
North Henik L. *Canada* 61°45N 97°40W **297** A9
North Highlands *U.S.A.* 38°40N 121°23W **306** G5
North Hollywood *U.S.A.* 34°9N 118°22W **126** B2
North Horr *Kenya* 3°20N 37°8E **268** B4
North I. *India* 10°8N 72°20E **245** J7
North I. *Kenya* 4°5N 36°5E **268** B4
North I. *N.Z.* 38°0S 175°0E **284** C4
North I. *Seychelles* 4°25S 55°13E **272** a
North Judson *U.S.A.* 41°13N 86°46W **311** C10
North Kingsville *U.S.A.* 41°54N 80°42W **312** E4
North Kitui ○ *Kenya* 0°35S 38°29E **268** C4
North Knife → *Canada* 58°53N 94°45W **297** B10
North Koel → *India* 24°45N 83°50E **243** G10
North Korea ■ *Asia* 40°0N 127°0E **227** E14
North L. *Australia* 32°30S 143°5E **282** B5
North Lakhimpur *India* 27°14N 94°7E **241** B5
North Lanarkshire □ *U.K.* 55°52N 3°56W **167** F5
North Las Vegas *U.S.A.* 36°12N 115°7W **124** A1
North Las Vegas ✈ (VGT)
　U.S.A. 36°12N 115°11W **124** A1
North Lexington *U.S.A.* 37°17N 114°4W **116** A1
North Liberty *U.S.A.* 41°32N 86°26W **311** C10
North Lincolnshire □
　U.K. 53°36N 0°30W **168** D7
North Little Rock *U.S.A.* 34°45N 92°16W **314** D8
North Loup → *U.S.A.* 41°17N 98°24W **308** E4
North Luangwa △ *Zambia* 11°49S 32°9E **269** E3
North Magnetic Pole
　Arctic 82°42N 114°24W **150** A1
North Malé Atoll *Maldives* 4°25N 73°30E **272** d
North Malosmadulu Atoll
　Maldives 5°30N 72°50E **272** d
North Manchester *U.S.A.* 41°0N 85°46W **311** C11
North Mankato *U.S.A.* 44°10N 94°2W **308** C6
North Minch *U.K.* 58°5N 5°55W **167** C3
North Moose L. *Canada* 54°4N 100°12W **297** C8
North Myrtle Beach
　U.S.A. 33°48N 78°41W **316** D11
North Nahanni →
　Canada 62°15N 123°20W **296** A4
North Naples *U.S.A.* 26°12N 81°48W **317** J8
North Nazimabad *Pakistan* 24°55N 67°2E **123** A2
North New River Canal
　U.S.A. 26°30N 80°30W **317** J9

Northern Virginia Regional Park △
　U.S.A. 38°55N 77°6W **143** B3
Northfield *Minn., U.S.A.* 44°27N 93°9W **308** C7
Northfield *Vt., U.S.A.* 44°9N 72°40W **313** B12
Northgate *Canada* 49°0N 102°16W **297** D8
Northlake *U.S.A.* 41°54N 87°53W **119** B1
Northland □ *N.Z.* 35°30S 173°30E **284** B3
Northmount *Canada* 43°46N 79°23W **141** A2
Northolt *U.K.* 51°32N 0°22W **125** A1
Northome *U.S.A.* 47°52N 94°17W **308** B6
Northport *Ala., U.S.A.* 33°14N 87°35W **315** E11
Northport *Wash., U.S.A.* 48°55N 117°48W **304** B5
Northumberland □, *C.*
　Australia 38°5S 140°40E **282** A4
Northumberland Heath
　U.K. 51°28N 0°10E **125** B3
Northumberland Is.
　Australia 21°30S 149°50E **280** C4
Northumberland Str.
　Canada 46°20N 64°0W **299** C7
Northville *Ont., Canada* 43°10N 81°34W **312** C3
Northville *N.Y., U.S.A.* 43°13N 74°11W **313** C10
Northway *Canada* 52°58N 141°56W **303** E12
Northwest Atlantic Mid-Ocean
　Canyon *Atl. Oc.* 50°0N 48°0W **152** A7
Northwest Pacific Basin
　Pac. Oc. 32°0N 165°0E **288** D8
Northwest Providence Channel
　W. Indies 26°0N 78°0W **320** A4
Northwest Pt. *Bahamas* 25°4N 77°31W **153** b
Northwest Territories □
　Canada 63°0N 118°0W **294** E8
Northwestern Hawaiian Is. Marine
　Nat. Monument =
　Papahānaumokuākea Marine
　Nat. Monument
　U.S.A. 25°25N 170°35W **302** F9
Northwestern Station
　U.S.A. 41°52N 87°38W **119** B3
Northwestern Univ.
　U.S.A. 42°3N 87°40W **119** A2
Northwich *U.K.* 53°15N 2°31W **168** D5
Northwood *London, U.K.* 51°36N 0°25W **125** A1
Northwood *Iowa, U.S.A.* 43°27N 93°13W **310** A4
Northwood *N. Dak.,*
　U.S.A. 47°44N 97°34W **308** B5
Norton *Kans., U.S.A.* 39°50N 99°53W **308** F4
Norton *Zimbabwe* 17°52S 30°40E **269** F3
Norton B. *U.S.A.* 64°45N 161°15W **303** D7
Norton Sd. *U.S.A.* 63°50N 164°0W **303** E7
Norton Shores *U.S.A.* 43°10N 86°16W **311** A10
Nortorf *Germany* 54°10N 9°50E **178** A5
Norwalk *Calif., U.S.A.* 33°54N 118°4W **307** M8
Norwalk *Conn., U.S.A.* 41°7N 73°22W **313** E11
Norwalk *Iowa, U.S.A.* 41°29N 93°41W **310** C3
Norwalk *Ohio, U.S.A.* 41°15N 82°37W **312** E2
Norway *Maine, U.S.A.* 44°13N 70°32W **309** C18
Norway *Mich., U.S.A.* 45°47N 87°55W **308** C1
Norway ■ *Europe* 63°0N 11°0E **160** E14
Norway House *Canada* 53°59N 97°50W **297** C9
Norwegian B. *Canada* 77°30N 90°0W **295** B14
Norwegian Basin *Atl. Oc.* 68°0N 2°0W **150** C7
Norwegian Sea *Atl. Oc.* 66°0N 1°0E **158** B6
Norwich *U.K.* 52°38N 1°18E **169** E9
Norwich *Conn., U.S.A.* 41°31N 72°5W **313** E12
Norwich *N.Y., U.S.A.* 42°32N 75°32W **313** D9
Norwood *Canada* 44°23N 77°59W **312** B7
Norwood *Gauteng, S. Africa* 26°9S 28°4E **123** A2
Norwood *N.Y., U.S.A.* 44°45N 75°0W **313** B10
Norwood *Ohio, U.S.A.* 39°9N 84°27W **311** E12
Norwood Park *U.S.A.* 41°59N 87°48W **119** B2
Noryangjin *S. Korea* 37°31N 126°56E **137** B2
Nosappu-Misaki *Japan* 45°26N 141°39E **220** C12
Noshaq *Pakistan* 36°24N 71°49E **240** A3
Noshiro *Japan* 40°12N 140°0E **220** D10
Nosivka *Ukraine* 50°50N 31°37E **189** K6
Nosok *Russia* 70°10N 82°20E **221** B9
Nosovka = Nosivka
　Ukraine 50°50N 31°37E **189** K6
Noṣratābād *Iran* 29°55N 60°0E **247** D8
Noss Hd. *U.K.* 58°28N 3°3W **167** C5
Nossa Senhora da Glória
　Brazil 10°14S 37°25W **332** D4
Nossa Senhora das Dores
　Brazil 10°29S 37°13W **332** D4
Nossa Senhora de Candelária
　Rio de J., Brazil **135** a2
Nossa Senhora do Livramento
　Brazil 15°48S 56°22W **331** D6
Nossa Senhora do Ó
　Brazil 23°30S 46°41W **137** B1
Nossa Senhora do Socorro
　Brazil 10°52S 37°7W **332** D4
Nossebro *Sweden* 58°12N 12°43E **163** F6
Nossegem *Belgium* 50°53N 4°30E **116** A3
Nossombougou *Mali* 13°25N 7°55W **262** C3
Nosy Bé *Madag.* 13°25S 48°15E **272** A2
Nosy Boraha *Madag.* 16°50S 49°55E **272** B3
Nosy Lava *Madag.* 14°33S 47°36E **272** A2
Nosy Mitsio *Madag.* 12°54S 48°36E **272** A2
Nosy Varika *Madag.* 20°35S 48°32E **272** C2
Notasulga *U.S.A.* 32°34N 85°41W **316** C4
Noteć → *Poland* 52°44N 15°26E **185** F2
Notikewin → *Canada* 57°2N 117°38W **296** B5
Notio Aigaio □ *Greece* 36°52N 25°34E **205** E7
Notios Evvoikos Kolpos
　Greece 38°20N 24°0E **205** E6
Noto *Italy* 36°53N 15°4E **201** F8
Noto, G. di *Italy* 36°50N 15°10E **201** F8
Noto-Hantō *Japan* 37°15N 136°40E **221** F8
Notodden *Norway* 59°35N 9°17E **164** E6

Notre Dame *Paris, France* **134** c4
Notre-Dame, Basilique
　Montréal, Canada **130** c3
Notre-Dame, Bois *France* 48°45N 2°34E **134** B4
Notre-Dame-de-Grace
　Canada 45°28N 73°38W **130** B2
Notre-Dame-de-Koartac = Quaqtaq
　Canada 60°55N 69°40W **295** E18
Notre-Dame-des-Bois
　Canada 45°24N 71°4W **313** A13
Notre-Dame-d'Ivugivic = Ivujivik
　Canada 62°24N 77°55W **295** E16
Notre-Dame-du-Nord
　Canada 47°36N 79°30W **298** C4
Notsé *Togo* 7°0N 1°17E **263** D5
Nottawasaga B. *Canada* 44°35N 80°15W **312** B4
Nottaway → *Canada* 51°22N 78°55W **298** B4
Notting Hill *London, U.K.* **125** b1
Nottingham *Canada* 51°28N 0°6W **168** E6
Nottingham, City of □
　U.K. 52°58N 1°10W **168** E6
Nottingham I. *Canada* 63°20N 77°55W **295** E16
Nottinghamshire □ *U.K.* 53°10N 1°3W **168** D6
Notwane → *Botswana* 23°35S 26°58E **270** B4
Nouâdhibou *Mauritania* 20°54N 17°0W **260** D2

Nouâdhibou, Dakhlet Mauritania 20°55N 16°52W 260 D1
Nouâdhibou, Râs Mauritania 20°50N 17°0W 260 D1
Nouakchott Mauritania 18°9N 15°58W 262 B1
Nouâmghâr Mauritania 19°20N 16°20W 262 B1
Nouméa N. Cal. 22°17S 166°30E 288 d
Nouna Burkina Faso 12°45N 3°52W 262 C4
Noupoort S. Africa 31°10S 24°57E 270 D3
Nouveau Comptoir = Wemindji Canada 53°0N 78°49W 298 B4
Nouvelle Amsterdam, Î. Ind. Oc. 38°30S 77°30E 273 H6
Nouvelle-Calédonie = New Caledonia ☑ Pac. Oc. 21°0S 165°0E 288 d
Nouvelle France Mauritius 20°22S 57°33E 272 e
Nouzonville France 49°48N 4°44E 173 C11
Nová Baňa Slovak Rep. 48°28N 18°39E 181 C11
Nová Bystřice Czech Rep. 49°2N 15°8E 180 B8
Nova Cruz Brazil 6°28S 35°25W 332 C4
Nova Era Brazil 19°45S 43°3W 333 E3
Nova Esperança Brazil 23°8S 52°24W 335 A5
Nova Fontesvila = Vila Machado Mozam. 19°15S 34°14E 269 F3
Nova-Freixo = Cuamba Mozam. 14°45S 36°22E 269 E4
Nova Friburgo Brazil 22°16S 42°30W 333 F3
Nova Gaia = Cambundi-Catembo Angola 10°10S 17°35E 265 E3
Nova Gorica Slovenia 45°57N 13°39E 199 C10
Nova Gradiška Croatia 45°17N 17°28E 182 E2
Nova Granada Brazil 20°30S 49°20W 333 F2
Nova Iguaçu Brazil 22°45S 43°28W 333 F3
Nova Iorque Brazil 7°0S 44°5W 332 C3
Nova Kakhovka Ukraine 46°42N 33°27E 189 J7
Nova Lamego Guinea-Biss. 12°19N 14°11W 262 C2
Nova Lisboa = Huambo Angola 12°42S 15°54E 265 E3
Nova Lusitânia Mozam. 19°50S 34°34E 269 F3
Nova Mambone Mozam. 21°0S 35°3E 271 B6
Nova Milanese Italy 45°35N 9°12E 129 A2
Nova Odesa Ukraine 47°19N 31°47E 189 J6
Nova Olinda do Norte Brazil 3°45S 59°3W 329 D6
Nová Paka Czech Rep. 50°29N 15°30E 180 A8
Nova Pavova Serbia 44°56N 20°14E 182 F5
Nova Ponte Brazil 19°8S 47°41W 333 E2
Nova Russas Brazil 4°42S 40°34W 332 B3
Nova Scotia ☐ Canada 45°10N 63°0W 299 C7
Nova Siri Italy 40°10N 16°35E 201 B9
Nova Sofala Mozam. 20°7S 34°42E 271 B5
Nova Ushytsya Ukraine 48°50N 27°17E 183 B12
Nova Varoš Serbia 43°29N 19°48E 202 C3
Nova Venécia Brazil 18°45S 40°24W 333 E3
Nova Vida Brazil 10°11S 62°47W 331 C5
Nova Zagora Bulgaria 42°32N 26°1E 203 D10
Novaci Macedonia 41°5N 21°29E 202 E5
Novaci Romania 45°10N 23°42E 183 E8
Novafeltria Italy 43°53N 12°17E 199 E9
Novannenskiy = Novoannenskiy Russia 50°32N 42°39E 190 E6
Novar Canada 45°27N 79°15W 312 A5
Novara Italy 45°28N 8°38E 198 C5
Novate Milanese Italy 45°30N 9°8E 129 A1
Novato U.S.A. 38°6N 122°35W 306 G4
Novaya Aleksandriya = Puławy Poland 51°23N 21°59E 185 G8
Novaya Bukhara = Kogon Uzbekistan 39°43N 64°33E 216 E6
Novaya Derevnya Russia 60°0N 30°19E 137 A1
Novaya Kakhovka = Nova Kakhovka Ukraine 46°42N 33°27E 189 J7
Novaya Kazanka = Zhangaqala Kazakhstan 48°56N 49°36E 191 F9
Novaya Ladoga Russia 60°7N 32°16E 188 B7
Novaya Lyalya Russia 59°4N 60°45E 186 C11
Novaya Pismyanka = Leninogorsk Kazakhstan 50°20N 83°30E 217 B10
Novaya Sibir, Ostrov Russia 75°10N 150°0E 215 B16
Novaya Zemlya Russia 75°0N 56°0E 214 B6
Nové Město Praha, Czech Rep. 50°4N 14°25E 135 B2
Nové Město Slovak Rep. 48°45N 17°50E 181 C10
Nové Město na Moravě Czech Rep. 49°34N 16°5E 180 B9
Nové Město nad Metují Czech Rep. 50°20N 16°10E 181 A9
Nové Zámky Slovak Rep. 48°2N 18°8E 181 C11
Novelda Spain 38°24N 0°45W 197 G4
Novellara Italy 44°51N 10°44E 198 D7
Novelty U.S.A. 40°1N 92°12W 310 D4
Noventa Vicentina Italy 45°17N 11°32E 199 C8
Novgorod Russia 58°30N 31°25E 188 C6
Novgorod ☐ Russia 58°50N 32°30E 188 C7
Novgorod-Severskiy = Novhorod-Siverskyy Ukraine 52°2N 33°10E 189 G7
Novgradets = Suvorovo Bulgaria 43°20N 27°35E 203 C11
Novhorod-Siverskyy Ukraine 52°2N 33°10E 189 G7
Novi Bečej Serbia 45°36N 20°10E 182 E5
Novi Iskar Bulgaria 42°48N 23°21E 202 D7
Novi Kneževac Serbia 46°4N 20°8E 182 D5
Novi Ligure Italy 44°46N 8°47E 198 D5
Novi Pazar Bulgaria 43°25N 27°15E 203 C11
Novi Pazar Serbia 43°12N 20°28E 202 C4
Novi Sad Serbia 45°18N 19°52E 182 E4
Novi Slankamen Serbia 45°8N 20°15E 182 E5
Novi Travnik Bos.-H. 44°10N 17°40E 182 F2
Novi Vinodolski Croatia 45°10N 14°48E 199 C11
Novigrad Istra, Croatia 45°19N 13°33E 199 C10
Novigrad Zadar, Croatia 44°10N 15°32E 199 D12
Novigradsko More Croatia 44°12N 15°33E 199 D12
Novinger U.S.A. 40°14N 92°43W 310 D4
Novo Acôrdo Brazil 10°10S 46°48W 332 D2
Novo Airão Brazil 2°40S 60°59W 329 D5
Novo Aripuanã Brazil 5°8S 60°22W 329 E5
Novo Cruzeiro Brazil 17°29S 41°53W 333 E3
Novo Hamburgo Brazil 29°37S 51°7W 335 B5
Novo Horizonte Brazil 21°25S 49°10W 333 F2
Novo Ivanivka Ukraine 45°30N 29°25E 183 E14
Novo-Mariinsk = Anadyr Russia 64°35N 177°20E 215 C18
Novo Mesto Slovenia 45°47N 15°12E 199 C12
Novo Miloševo Serbia 45°42N 20°20E 182 E5
Novo Nikolaevsk = Novosibirsk Russia 55°0N 83°5E 217 B10
Novo Paraiso Brazil 1°17N 60°28W 329 C5
Novo-Starobinsk = Salihorsk Belarus 52°51N 27°27E 177 B14
Novo Urgench = Urganch Uzbekistan 41°40N 60°41E 216 D6
Novoaleksandrovsk = Zarasai Lithuania 55°40N 26°20E 188 E4
Novoaleksandrovsk Russia 45°29N 41°17E 191 H5
Novoaleksandrovskaya = Novoaleksandrovsk Russia 45°29N 41°17E 191 H5
Novoaleksandrovskoye Russia 59°50N 30°31E 137 B2
Novoaltaysk Russia 53°30N 84°0E 217 B10
Novoannenskiy Russia 50°32N 42°39E 190 E6
Novoazovsk Ukraine 47°15N 38°4E 189 J10
Novocheboksarsk Russia 56°5N 47°27E 190 B8
Novocherkassk Russia 47°27N 40°15E 191 G5
Novodevichye Russia 53°37N 48°50E 190 D9
Novodvinsk Russia 64°25N 40°42E 186 B7
Novogireyevo Russia 55°45N 37°46E 129 B4
Novogrudok = Navahrudak Belarus 53°40N 25°50E 177 B13
Novohrad-Volynskyy Ukraine 50°34N 27°35E 177 C14
Novoivanovskoye Russia 55°42N 37°21E 129 B1
Novokachalinsk Russia 45°5N 132°0E 220 B5
Novokazalinsk = Zhangaqazaly Kazakhstan 45°48N 62°6E 216 C6
Novokhopersk Russia 51°5N 41°39E 190 E5
Novokiyevskoye = Kraskino Russia 42°44N 130°48E 220 C5
Novokuybyshevsk Russia 53°7N 49°58E 190 D9
Novokuznetsk Russia 53°45N 87°10E 217 B11
Novolazarevskaya Antarctica 71°0S 12°0E 151 D3
Novolyalinsky = Novaya Lyalya Russia 59°4N 60°45E 186 C11
Novomoskovsk Russia 54°5N 38°15E 188 E10
Novomoskovsk Ukraine 48°33N 35°17E 189 H8
Novomyrhorod Ukraine 48°45N 31°33E 189 H6
Novonikolayevka = Novoazovsk Ukraine 47°15N 38°4E 189 J10
Novonikolyskoye Russia 55°50N 37°14E 129 A1
Novopolotsk = Navapolatsk Belarus 55°32N 28°37E 188 E5
Novorossiysk Russia 44°43N 37°46E 189 K9
Novorybnoye Russia 72°50N 105°50E 215 B11
Novorzhev Russia 57°3N 29°25E 188 D5
Novosaratovka Russia 59°50N 30°32E 137 B3
Novosej Albania 41°56N 20°35E 202 E4
Novoselytsya Ukraine 48°14N 26°15E 183 B11
Novoshakhtinsk Russia 47°46N 39°58E 189 J10
Novosibirsk Russia 55°0N 83°5E 217 B10
Novosibirskiye Ostrova Russia 75°0N 142°0E 215 B15
Novosibirskiye Vdkhr. Russia 54°35N 82°35E 217 B10
Novosil Russia 52°59N 37°2E 189 F9
Novosokolniki Russia 56°20N 30°2E 188 D6
Novotitarovskaya Russia 45°17N 39°2E 191 H4
Novotroitsk Russia 51°10N 58°15E 186 D10
Novotroitskoye = Tôle Bī Kazakhstan 43°42N 73°46E 217 D8
Novoukrayinka Ukraine 48°25N 31°30E 189 H6
Novoulyanovsk Russia 54°8N 48°24E 190 C9
Novouzensk Russia 50°32N 48°17E 190 E9
Novovolynsk Ukraine 50°45N 24°4E 185 H11
Novovoronezhskiy Russia 51°19N 39°13E 189 G10
Novoyavoriske Ukraine 49°53N 23°33E 185 J10
Novozybkov Russia 52°30N 32°0E 189 F6
Novska Croatia 45°19N 17°0E 199 C14
Nový Bor Czech Rep. 50°46N 14°35E 180 A7
Novy Bug = Novyy Buh Ukraine 47°34N 32°29E 189 J7
Nový Bydžov Czech Rep. 50°14N 15°29E 180 A8
Novy Dvor Belarus 52°50N 24°21E 185 F11
Nowy Dwór Mazowiecki Poland 52°26N 20°44E 185 F7
Nový Jičín Czech Rep. 49°30N 18°2E 181 B11
Novy Margelan = Farghona Uzbekistan 40°23N 71°19E 217 D8
Novyy Afon Georgia 43°7N 40°50E 191 J5
Novyy Bor Russia 66°43N 52°19E 186 A9
Novyy Buh Ukraine 47°34N 32°29E 189 J7
Novyy Oskol Russia 50°44N 37°55E 189 G9
Novyy Port Russia 67°40N 72°30E 214 C8
Novyy Urengoy Russia 65°48N 76°52E 214 C8
Nowa Deba Poland 50°26N 21°41E 185 H8
Nowa Nowa Australia 37°44S 148°3E 283 D8
Nowa Ruda Poland 50°35N 16°30E 185 H3
Nowa Sarzyna Poland 50°21N 22°21E 185 H9
Nowa Sól Poland 51°48N 15°44E 185 G2
Nowata U.S.A. 36°42N 95°38W 314 C7
Nowbarān Iran 35°8N 49°42E 247 C6
Nowe Poland 53°41N 18°44E 184 E5
Nowe-Babice Poland 52°15N 20°51E 142 B1
Nowe Miasteczko Poland 51°42N 15°42E 185 G2
Nowe Miasto Mazowieckie, Poland 51°38N 20°34E 185 G7
Nowe Miasto Warsaw, Poland 142 a2
Nowe Miasto Lubawskie Poland 53°27N 19°33E 184 E6
Nowe Skalmierzyce Poland 51°43N 18°0E 185 G4
Nowe Warpno Poland 53°42N 14°18E 184 E1
Nowendoc Australia 31°32S 151°44E 283 A9
Nowendoc △ Australia 31°33S 151°45E 283 A9
Nowghāb Iran 33°53N 59°4E 247 C8
Nowgong Assam, India 26°20N 92°50E 241 B4
Nowgong Mad. P., India 25°4N 79°27E 243 G8
Nowitna Nat. Wildlife Refuge ⌂ U.S.A. 64°40N 154°16W 303 D9
Nowogard Poland 53°41N 15°10E 184 E2
Nowogród Poland 53°14N 21°53E 185 E8
Nowogród Bobrzanski Poland 51°48N 15°15E 185 G2
Nowogrodziec Poland 51°12N 15°24E 185 G2
Noworadomsk = Radomsko Poland 51°5N 19°28E 185 G6
Nowra Australia 34°53S 150°35E 283 C9
Nowrangapur India 19°14N 82°33E 244 E6
Nowshāk = Noshaq Pakistan 36°24N 71°49E 240 A3
Nowshera Pakistan 34°0N 72°0E 240 B4
Nowy Dwór Gdański Poland 54°13N 19°7E 184 D6
Nowy Sącz Poland 49°40N 20°41E 185 J7
Nowy Staw Poland 54°13N 19°2E 184 D6
Nowy Targ Poland 49°29N 20°2E 185 J7
Nowy Tomyśl Poland 52°19N 16°10E 185 F3
Nowy Wiśnicz Poland 49°55N 20°28E 185 J7
Noxen U.S.A. 41°25N 76°4W 313 E8
Noyabr'sk Russia 64°34N 76°21E 214 C8
Noyant France 47°30N 0°6E 172 E7
Noyers France 47°40N 4°0E 173 E10
Nöykkiö Finland 60°10N 24°42E 121 B1
Noyon France 49°34N 2°59E 173 C9
Noyon Mongolia 43°2N 102°4E 226 C2
Nozay France 47°34N 1°38W 172 E5
Nqutu S. Africa 28°13S 30°32E 271 C5
Nsa Congo 2°22S 15°19E 264 C3
Nsa, O. en → Algeria 32°28N 5°24E 261 B6
Nsa, Plateau de Congo 2°26S 15°20E 264 C3
Nsanje Malawi 16°55S 35°12E 269 F4
Nsawam Ghana 5°50N 0°24W 263 D4
Nseluka Zambia 9°58S 31°16E 269 D3
Nsok Eq. Guin. 1°10N 11°19E 264 B2
Nsomba Zambia 10°45S 29°51E 269 E2
Nsontin Dem. Rep. of the Congo 3°7S 17°56E 264 C3
Nsopzup Burma 25°51N 97°30E 241 C6
Nsukka Nigeria 6°51N 7°29E 263 D6
Ntaria ◎ Australia 24°0S 132°41E 278 D5
Ntem → Cameroon 2°21N 9°49E 264 B2
Ntingui, Mt. Comoros Is. 12°12S 44°25E 272 a
Ntoum Gabon 0°22N 9°47E 264 B1
N'Tsama Congo 0°53S 14°44E 264 C2
Ntsaouéni Comoros Is. 11°27S 43°15E 272 a
Ntsoudjini Comoros Is. 11°39S 43°15E 272 a
Ntui Cameroon 4°27N 11°38E 263 E7
Ntungamo Uganda 0°56S 30°17E 268 C3
Nu Jiang → China 29°58N 97°25E 228 E2
Nu Shan China 26°0N 99°20E 228 E2
Nuakata I. Papua N. G. 10°17S 151°2E 286 F6
Nuba Mts. = Nubah, Jibalan Sudan 12°0N 31°0E 257 E3
Nubah, Jibalan Sudan 12°0N 31°0E 257 E3
Nubia Africa 21°0N 32°0E 254 D7
Nubian Desert = Nûbîya, Es Sahrâ en Sudan 21°30N 33°30E 256 C3
Nûbîya, Es Sahrâ en Sudan 21°30N 33°30E 256 C3
Nubl Syria 36°22N 36°59E 250 B7
Nubledo Spain 43°31N 5°52W 194 B5
Nuboai Indonesia 2°10S 136°30E 231 E9
Nubra → India 34°35N 77°35E 243 B7
Nucet Romania 46°28N 22°35E 182 D7
Nueces → U.S.A. 27°51N 97°30W 314 H6
Nueltin L. Canada 60°30N 99°30W 297 A9
Nuestra Señora del Rosario de Caá-Cati Argentina 27°45S 57°36W 334 B4
Nueva, I. Chile 55°13S 66°30W 336 E3
Nueva Antioquia Colombia 6°5N 69°26W 328 B4
Nueva Atzacoalco Mexico 19°29N 99°4W 128 B2
Nueva Carteya Spain 37°35N 4°28W 195 H6
Nueva Ciudad Guerrero Mexico 26°34N 99°12W 319 B5
Nueva Ecija ☐ Phil. 15°35N 121°0E 232 D3
Nueva Esparta ☐ Venezuela 11°0N 64°0W 329 A5
Nueva Gerona Cuba 21°53N 82°49W 320 B3
Nueva Imperial Chile 38°45S 72°58W 336 A2
Nueva Loja = Lago Agrio Ecuador 0°5N 76°52W 328 C2
Nueva Palmira Uruguay 33°52S 58°20W 334 C4
Nueva Pompeya Argentina 34°40S 58°25W 117 C2
Nueva Rosita Mexico 27°57N 101°13W 318 B4
Nueva San Salvador El Salv. 13°40N 89°18W 320 D2
Nueva Tabarca Spain 38°17N 0°30W 197 G4
Nueva Tenochtitlán Mexico 19°27N 99°5W 128 B2
Nueva Vizcaya ☐ Phil. 16°20N 121°20E 232 C3
Nuéve de Julio Argentina 35°30S 61°0W 334 D3
Nuevitas Cuba 21°30N 77°20W 320 B4
Nuevo, G. Argentina 43°0S 64°30W 336 B4
Nuevo Casas Grandes Mexico 30°25N 107°55W 318 A3
Nuevo Laredo Mexico 27°30N 99°31W 319 B5
Nuevo León ☐ Mexico 25°20N 100°0W 318 C5
Nuevo Mundo, Cerro Bolivia 21°55S 66°53W 330 E4
Nuevo Rocafuerte Ecuador 0°55S 75°27W 328 D2
Nugaal ☐ Somali Rep. 8°10N 49°0E 267 C6
Nugaal → Somali Rep. 8°0N 49°47E 267 C6
Nugaaleed, Dooxo Somali Rep. 8°35N 48°35E 267 C6
Nugget Pt. N.Z. 46°27S 169°50E 285 G4
Nugrus, Gebel Egypt 24°47N 34°35E 256 C3
Nuguria Is. Papua N. G. 3°20S 154°45E 286 B8
Nuhaka N.Z. 39°3S 177°45E 284 F6
Nui Pac. Oc. 7°15S 177°10E 277 B14
Nuijala Finland 60°12N 24°46E 121 B1
Nuits-St-Georges France 47°10N 4°56E 173 E11
Nukey Bluff Australia 32°26S 135°29E 281 E2
Nukha = Şaki Azerbaijan 41°10N 47°5E 191 K8
Nukhayb Iraq 32°4N 42°3E 213 F10
Nukheila Sudan 19°1N 26°21E 256 D2
Nukiki Solomon Is. 6°46S 156°35E 287 L9
Nuku Papua N. G. 3°41S 142°28E 286 B2
Nuku Hiva French Polynesia 8°54S 140°6W 289 f
Nuku'alofa Tonga 21°10S 175°12W 287 Q13
Nukuhu Papua N. G. 5°34S 149°22E 286 C5
Nukulaelae Tuvalu 9°23S 179°52E 277 B14
Nukunonu Pac. Oc. 9°12S 171°54W 277 B16
Nukus Uzbekistan 42°27N 59°41E 216 D5
Nulato U.S.A. 64°43N 158°6W 303 D8
Nules Spain 39°51N 0°9W 196 F4
Nullagine Australia 21°53S 120°7E 278 D3
Nullagine → Australia 21°20S 120°20E 278 D3
Nullarbor Australia 31°28S 130°55E 279 F5
Nullarbor △ Australia 32°39S 130°0E 279 F2
Nullarbor Plain Australia 31°10S 129°0E 279 F4
Numabukuro Japan 35°43N 139°39E 140 A2
Numalla, L. Australia 28°43S 144°20E 281 D3
Numan Nigeria 9°29N 12°3E 263 D7
Numanuma Papua N. G. 9°41S 150°55E 286 E6
Numata Japan 36°45N 139°4E 223 A11
Numatinna → Sudan 7°38N 27°20E 257 F2
Numaykoos Lake ⌂ Canada 57°52N 95°58W 297 B9
Numazu Japan 35°7N 138°51E 223 B10
Numbulwar Australia 14°15S 135°45E 280 A2
Numedal Norway 60°6N 9°6E 164 D6
Numfoor Indonesia 1°0S 134°50E 231 E8
Numurkah Australia 36°5S 145°26E 283 D6
Nunaksaluk I. Canada 55°49N 60°20W 299 A7
Nunap Isua Greenland 59°48N 43°55W 154 F6
Nunavik Greenland 71°50N 54°25W 154 C5
Nunavut ☐ Canada 66°0N 85°0W 295 D15
Nunda U.S.A. 42°35N 77°56W 312 D7
Nuneaton U.K. 52°32N 1°27W 169 E6
Nuñez Argentina 34°32S 58°27W 117 B2
Nungarin Australia 31°12S 118°6E 279 F2
Nungo Mozam. 13°23S 37°43E 269 E4
Nungwe Tanzania 2°48S 32°2E 268 C3
Nunhead U.K. 51°27N 0°3W 125 B3
Nunivak I. U.S.A. 60°10N 166°30W 303 F6
Nunkun India 33°57N 76°2E 243 C7
Ñuñoa Chile 33°27S 70°35W 137 B2
Nunukan Indonesia 4°4N 117°40E 235 B5
Nùoro Italy 40°20N 9°20E 200 B2
Núpur Iceland 65°56N 23°36W 155 B3
Nuqayy, Jabal Libya 23°11N 19°30E 258 D3
Nuqūb Yemen 14°59N 45°48E 248 D4
Nuquí Colombia 5°42N 77°17W 328 B2
Nūr Iran 36°33N 52°1E 247 B7
Nur Dağı Turkey 36°54N 35°39E 250 B6
Nur Dağları Turkey 36°50N 36°32E 250 B7
Nura → Kazakhstan 50°30N 69°59E 217 B7
Nūrābād Hormozgān, Iran 27°47N 57°12E 247 E8
Nūrābād Lorestān, Iran 34°4N 47°58E 213 E12
Nurabad Uzbekistan 39°36N 66°17E 217 E7
Nure → Italy 45°3N 9°49E 198 C6
Nuremberg = Nürnberg Germany 49°27N 11°3E 179 F7
Nuri Sonora, Mexico 28°5N 109°22W 318 B3
Nuri Sudan 18°29N 31°59E 256 D3
Nuriootpa Australia 34°27S 139°0E 282 C3
Nuristān ☐ Afghan. 35°20N 71°0E 217 E8
Nurlat Russia 54°29N 50°45E 190 C10
Nurmes Finland 63°33N 29°10E 160 E23
Nürnberg Germany 49°27N 11°3E 179 F7
Nurpur Pakistan 31°53N 71°54E 242 D4
Nurra, La Italy 40°45N 8°15E 200 B1
Nurran, L. = Terewah, L. Australia 29°52S 147°35E 281 D4
Nurrari Lakes Australia 29°1S 130°5E 279 E5
Nurri Italy 39°43N 9°14E 200 C2
Nürtingen Germany 48°37N 9°19E 179 G5
Nurzec → Poland 52°37N 22°25E 185 F9
Nus Italy 45°45N 7°28E 198 C4
Nusa Dua Indonesia 8°48S 115°14E 231 K18
Nusa Tenggara Barat ☐ Indonesia 8°50S 117°30E 235 D5
Nusa Tenggara Timur ☐ Indonesia 9°30S 122°0E 231 F6
Nusaybin Turkey 37°3N 41°10E 213 D9
Nuşayrīyah, J. an Syria 35°20N 36°13E 250 C7
Nushki Pakistan 29°35N 66°0E 242 E2
Nusle Czech Rep. 50°3N 14°26E 135 B2
Nussdorf Austria 48°15N 16°21E 142 A2
Nuuk Greenland 64°10N 51°35W 154 E5
Nuupere, Pte. Moorea 17°36S 149°47W 289 e
Nuussuaq Greenland 74°8N 57°3W 154 C5
Nu'uuli Amer. Samoa 14°19S 170°42W 302 f
Nuwakot Nepal 28°10N 83°55E 243 E10
Nuwara Eliya Sri Lanka 6°58N 80°48E 245 L5
Nuwaybʻī, W. an → Si. Arabia 29°18N 34°57E 251 J5
Nuweiba' Egypt 28°59N 34°39E 251 K5
Nuwerus S. Africa 31°8S 18°24E 270 D2
Nuweveldberge S. Africa 32°10S 21°45E 270 D3
Nuyts, Pt. Australia 35°4S 116°38E 279 G2
Nuyts Arch. Australia 32°35S 133°20E 281 E1
N'Vinda Angola 13°8S 19°2E 265 E3
Nxai Pan △ Botswana 19°50S 24°46E 270 A3
Nxaunxau Botswana 18°57S 21°4E 270 A3
Nyaake Liberia 4°52N 7°37W 262 E3
Nyabessan Cameroon 2°28N 10°24E 264 B2
Nyabing Australia 33°33S 118°9E 279 F2
Nyack U.S.A. 41°5N 73°55W 313 E11
Nyagan Russia 62°30N 65°38E 214 C7
Nyah West Australia 35°16S 143°21E 282 C5
Nyahanga Tanzania 2°20S 33°37E 268 C3
Nyahua Tanzania 5°25S 33°23E 268 D3
Nyahururu Kenya 0°2N 36°27E 268 B4
Nyainqêntanglha Shan China 30°0N 90°0E 218 F7
Nyakanazi Tanzania 3°2S 31°10E 268 C3
Nyakrom Ghana 5°40N 0°50W 263 D4
Nyâlâ Sudan 12°2N 24°58E 257 E1
Nyalam China 28°32N 86°4E 218 F6
Nyamandhlovu Zimbabwe 19°55S 28°16E 269 F2
Nyambiti Tanzania 2°48S 33°27E 268 C3
Nyamira Kenya 0°36S 34°52E 268 B4
Nyamlell Sudan 9°7N 26°59E 257 F2
Nyamwaga Tanzania 1°27S 34°33E 268 C3
Nyandekwa Tanzania 3°57S 32°32E 268 C3
Nyanding → Sudan 8°40N 32°41E 257 F3
Nyandoma Russia 61°40N 40°12E 188 B11
Nyanga Congo 2°52S 11°57E 264 C2
Nyanga Western Cape, S. Africa 33°59S 18°35E 118 A2
Nyanga → Gabon 2°58S 10°15E 264 C2
Nyanga △ Zimbabwe 18°17S 32°46E 269 F3
Nyangana Namibia 18°0S 20°40E 270 A3
Nyanguge Tanzania 2°30S 33°12E 268 C3
Nyanji Zambia 14°25S 31°46E 269 E3
Nyankpala Ghana 9°21N 0°58W 263 D4
Nyanza Rwanda 2°20S 29°42E 268 C2
Nyanza ☐ Kenya 0°10S 34°15E 268 C3
Nyanza-Lac Burundi 4°21S 29°36E 268 C2
Nyaponges Sudan 5°5N 33°45E 257 F3
Nyasa, L. = Malawi, L. Africa 12°30S 34°30E 269 E3
Nyasaland = Malawi ■ Africa 11°55S 34°0E 269 E3
Nyasvizh Belarus 53°14N 26°38E 177 B14
Nyaunglebin Burma 17°52N 96°42E 241 G6
Nyazepetrovsk Russia 56°3N 59°36E 186 C10
Nyazura Zimbabwe 18°40S 32°16E 269 F3
Nyazwidzi → Zimbabwe 20°0S 31°17E 269 G3
Nybergsund Norway 61°15N 12°19E 164 C9
Nyborg Denmark 55°18N 10°47E 163 J4
Nybro Sweden 56°44N 15°55E 163 H9
Nyda Russia 66°40N 72°58E 214 C8
Nyeboe Land Greenland 82°0N 57°0W 154 A5
Nyengo Swamp Zambia 14°51S 22°7E 265 E4
Nyeri Kenya 0°23S 36°56E 268 C4
Nyerol Sudan 8°41N 32°1E 257 F3
Nyhammar Sweden 60°17N 14°58E 162 D8
Nyika △ Malawi 10°30S 33°53E 269 E3
Nyimba Zambia 14°33S 30°50E 269 E3
Nyinahin Ghana 6°43N 2°3W 262 D4
Nyingchi China 29°32N 94°25E 218 F7
Nyíradony Hungary 47°41N 21°55E 182 C6
Nyírbátor Hungary 47°49N 22°9E 182 C7
Nyíregyháza Hungary 47°58N 21°47E 182 C6
Nyiru, Mt. Kenya 2°8N 36°50E 268 B4
Nykarleby = Uusikaarlepyy Finland 63°32N 22°31E 160 E20
Nykirke Norway 60°54N 10°19E 164 D7
Nykøbing Nordjylland, Denmark 56°48N 8°51E 163 H2
Nykøbing Sjælland, Denmark 54°56N 11°52E 163 K5
Nykøbing Sjælland, Denmark 55°55N 11°40E 163 J5
Nyköping Sweden 58°45N 17°1E 163 F11
Nykroppa Sweden 59°37N 14°18E 162 E8
Nykvarn Sweden 59°11N 17°25E 162 E11
Nyland Sweden 63°1N 17°45E 162 A11
Nylstroom = Modimolle S. Africa 24°42S 28°22E 271 B4
Nymagee Australia 32°7S 146°20E 283 B7
Nymboida △ Australia 29°38S 152°26E 281 D5
Nymburk Czech Rep. 50°10N 15°1E 180 A8
Nymphenburg Germany 48°9N 11°30E 131 B2
Nymphenburg, Schloss Germany 48°9N 11°30E 131 B2
Nynäshamn Sweden 58°54N 17°57E 163 F11
Nyngan Australia 31°30S 147°8E 283 A7
Nyoma Rap India 33°10N 78°40E 243 C8
Nyoman = Nemunas → Lithuania 55°25N 21°10E 184 C8
Nyon Switz. 46°23N 6°14E 179 J2
Nyong → Cameroon 3°17N 9°54E 263 E6
Nyons France 44°22N 5°10E 175 D9
Nyou Burkina Faso 12°42N 2°1W 263 C4
Nýrsko Czech Rep. 49°18N 13°9E 180 B6
Nysa Poland 50°30N 17°22E 185 H4
Nysa → Europe 52°4N 14°46E 178 C10
Nysa Kłodzka → Poland 50°49N 17°40E 185 H4
Nysæter Norway 62°2N 8°20E 164 B5
Nysäter Sweden 59°17N 12°47E 162 E6
Nyslott = Savonlinna Finland 61°52N 28°53E 188 B5
Nyssa U.S.A. 43°53N 117°0W 304 E5
Nystad = Uusikaupunki Finland 60°47N 21°25E 188 B1
Nysted Denmark 54°40N 11°44E 163 K5
Nyunzu Dem. Rep. of the Congo 5°57S 27°58E 268 D2
Nyurba Russia 63°17N 118°28E 215 C12
Nyzhankovychi Ukraine 49°40N 22°52E 185 J9
Nyzhnohirskyy Ukraine 45°27N 34°38E 189 K8
Nyzhny Vorota Ukraine 48°46N 23°6E 182 B8
Nzébéla Guinea 8°9N 9°3W 262 D3
Nzega Tanzania 4°10S 33°12E 268 C3
Nzérékoré Guinea 7°49N 8°48W 262 D3
Nzeto Angola 7°10S 12°52E 265 D2
Nzilo, Chutes de Dem. Rep. of the Congo 10°18S 25°27E 265 E5
Nzilo, L. Dem. Rep. of the Congo 10°35S 25°39E 265 E5
N'zo → Ivory C. 6°15N 7°3W 262 D3
N'zo △ Ivory C. 6°15N 7°15W 262 D3
Nzubuka Tanzania 4°45S 32°50E 268 C3
Nzwani = Anjouan Comoros Is. 12°15S 44°20E 272 a

O

O Barco Spain 42°23N 6°58W 194 C4
O Carballiño Spain 42°26N 8°5W 194 C2
O Corgo Spain 42°56N 7°25W 194 C3
O Le Pupū Pu'e △ Samoa 13°59S 171°44W 287 V20
O Pino Spain 42°56N 8°20W 194 C2
O Porriño Spain 42°10N 8°37W 194 C2
Ō-Shima Hokkaidō, Japan 41°30N 139°22E 220 D9
Ō-Shima Nagasaki, Japan 33°29N 129°33E 222 D1
Ō-Shima Shizuoka, Japan 34°44N 139°24E 223 C11
O.R. Tambo Int. ✕ (JNB) S. Africa 27°7S 29°16E 123 A2
Oa, Mull of U.K. 55°35N 6°20W 167 F2
Oacoma U.S.A. 43°48N 99°24W 308 D4
Oahe, L. U.S.A. 44°27N 100°24W 308 C3
Oahe Dam U.S.A. 44°27N 100°24W 308 C3
O'ahu U.S.A. 21°28N 157°58W 302 K14
Oak Creek U.S.A. 42°52N 87°55W 311 B9
Oak Grove U.S.A. 33°50N 84°18W 113 A3
Oak Harbor U.S.A. 48°18N 122°39W 306 B4
Oak Hill Fla., U.S.A. 28°52N 80°51W 317 G9
Oak Hill Mass., U.S.A. 42°18N 71°10W 116 B1
Oak Hill W. Va., U.S.A. 37°59N 81°9W 309 G13
Oak Island U.S.A. 33°55N 78°10W 315 E15
Oak Lawn U.S.A. 41°42N 87°45W 119 C2
Oak Park Ga., U.S.A. 32°22N 82°19W 316 C7
Oak Park Ill., U.S.A. 41°52N 87°47W 119 B2
Oak Ridge U.S.A. 36°1N 84°16W 315 C12
Oak Street Beach Chicago, U.S.A. 119 a2
Oak View Calif., U.S.A. 34°24N 119°18W 307 L7
Oak View Md., U.S.A. 39°1N 76°58W 143 A4
Oakan-Dake Japan 43°27N 144°10E 220 C12
Oakbank Australia 33°4S 140°33E 282 B4
Oakdale Calif., U.S.A. 37°46N 120°51W 306 H6
Oakdale Georgia, U.S.A. 33°51N 84°30W 113 A2
Oakdale La., U.S.A. 30°49N 92°40W 314 F8
Oakes U.S.A. 46°8N 98°6W 308 B4
Oakesdale U.S.A. 47°8N 117°15W 304 C5
Oakey Australia 27°25S 151°43E 281 D5
Oakfield Ga., U.S.A. 31°47N 83°58W 316 D6
Oakfield N.Y., U.S.A. 43°4N 78°16W 312 C6
Oakford U.S.A. 40°6N 89°58W 310 D7
Oakham U.K. 52°40N 0°43W 169 E7
Oakhurst U.S.A. 37°19N 119°40W 306 H7
Oakland Calif., U.S.A. 37°48N 122°18W 136 B3
Oakland Ill., U.S.A. 39°39N 88°2W 311 E8
Oakland Md., U.S.A. 38°53N 76°54W 143 B4
Oakland Pa., U.S.A. 41°57N 75°36W 313 E9
Oakland City U.S.A. 38°20N 87°21W 311 F9
Oakland Park U.S.A. 26°10N 80°7W 317 J9
Oaklands Australia 35°34S 146°10E 283 C7
Oaklawn U.S.A. 38°46N 76°56W 143 C4
Oakleigh Australia 37°54S 145°5E 128 B2
Oakley Idaho, U.S.A. 42°15N 113°53W 304 E7
Oakley Kans., U.S.A. 39°8N 100°51W 308 F3
Oakover → Australia 21°0S 120°40E 278 D3
Oakridge U.S.A. 43°45N 122°28W 304 E2
Oaks, The Australia 34°3S 150°34E 283 C9
Oakton U.S.A. 38°52N 77°18W 143 B2
Oaktown U.S.A. 38°52N 87°27W 311 F9
Oakville Ont., Canada 43°27N 79°41W 312 C5
Oakville Wash., U.S.A. 46°51N 123°14W 306 D3
Oakwood U.S.A. 41°6N 84°23W 311 C12
Oakwood Beach U.S.A. 40°33N 74°7W 132 C1
Oamaru N.Z. 45°5S 170°59E 285 F5
Ōamishirasato Japan 35°31N 140°18E 223 B12
Oancea Romania 45°21N 27°42E 183 E12
Oarai Japan 36°21N 140°34E 223 A12
Oasi Faunistica di Vendicari ⌂ Italy 36°49N 15°6E 201 F8
Oasis Calif., U.S.A. 37°29N 117°55W 306 H9
Oasis Calif., U.S.A. 33°28N 116°6W 307 M10
Oates Land Antarctica 69°0S 160°0E 151 C11
Oatley Australia 33°59S 151°4E 139 B1
Oatman U.S.A. 35°1N 114°19W 307 K12
Oaxaca Mexico 17°3N 96°43W 319 D5
Oaxaca ☐ Mexico 17°0N 96°30W 319 D5
Ob → Russia 66°45N 69°30E 214 C7
Oba Canada 49°4N 84°7W 298 C3
Obala Cameroon 4°9N 11°32E 263 E7
Obalende Nigeria 6°26N 3°25E 124 B2
Obama Fukui, Japan 35°30N 135°45E 223 B7
Obama Nagasaki, Japan 32°43N 130°13E 222 E2
Oban Nigeria 5°17N 8°33E 263 D6
Oban Argyll & Bute, U.K. 56°25N 5°29W 167 E3
Oba's Palace Nigeria 6°26N 3°22E 124 B2
Obbia = Hobyo Somali Rep. 5°25N 48°30E 267 C6
Obdorsk = Salekhard Russia 66°30N 66°35E 214 C7
Oberá Argentina 27°21S 55°2W 335 B4
Oberammergau Germany 47°36N 11°4E 179 H7
Oberasbach Germany 49°25N 10°57E 179 F6
Oberbayern ☐ Germany 48°5N 11°50E 179 G7
Oberburg = Gornji Grad Slovenia 46°20N 14°52E 199 B11
Oberdonau = Oberösterreich ☐ Austria 48°10N 14°0E 180 C7
Oberdrauburg Austria 46°44N 12°58E 180 E5
Obere Donau ⌂ Germany 48°5N 9°0E 179 G5
Oberer Bayerischer Wald ⌂ Germany 49°15N 12°40E 179 F8
Oberföhring Germany 48°10N 11°37E 131 B2
Oberfranken ☐ Germany 50°10N 11°20E 179 E7
Oberglogau = Głogówek Poland 50°21N 17°53E 185 H4
Oberhaching Germany 48°1N 11°35E 131 C2
Oberhausen Germany 51°28N 6°51E 178 D2
Oberkirch Germany 48°31N 8°4E 179 G4
Oberlaa Austria 48°8N 16°24E 142 B2
Oberlaibach = Vrhnika Slovenia 45°58N 14°15E 199 C11
Oberlausitz Germany 51°16N 14°18E 178 D10
Oberlin Kans., U.S.A. 39°49N 100°32W 308 F3
Oberlin La., U.S.A. 30°37N 92°46W 314 F8
Oberlin Ohio, U.S.A. 41°18N 82°13W 312 E2
Oberlisse Austria 48°17N 16°26E 142 A2
Obermenzing Germany 48°10N 11°28E 131 A1
Obermoos Schwaige Germany 48°14N 11°27E 131 A1
Obernai France 48°28N 7°30E 173 D14
Oberndorf Germany 48°17N 8°34E 179 G4
Obernigk = Oborniki Śląskie Poland 51°17N 16°53E 185 G3
Oberon Australia 33°45S 149°52E 283 B8
Oberösterreich ☐ Austria 48°10N 14°0E 180 C7
Oberpfalz ☐ Germany 49°20N 12°10E 179 F8
Oberpfälzer Wald Germany 49°30N 12°30E 179 F8
Oberpfälzer Wald ⌂ Germany 49°40N 12°20E 179 F8
Oberschleissheim Germany 48°15N 11°33E 131 A2
Oberschöneweide Germany 52°27N 13°31E 115 B4
Oberstdorf Germany 47°24N 10°15E 179 H6
Oberting Gabon 0°22S 9°46E 264 C1
Obertyn Ukraine 48°42N 25°10E 183 B10
Oberursel Germany 50°11N 8°35E 179 E4
Oberwart Austria 47°17N 16°12E 181 D9
Obi, Kepulauan Indonesia 1°23S 127°45E 231 E7
Obiaruku Nigeria 5°51N 6°9E 263 D6
Óbidos Brazil 1°50S 55°30W 329 D6
Óbidos Portugal 39°19N 9°10W 195 F1
Obihiro Japan 42°56N 143°12E 220 C11
Obilatu Indonesia 1°25S 127°20E 231 E7
Obilnoye Russia 47°32N 44°30E 191 G7
Obing Germany 48°0N 12°24E 179 G8
Objat France 45°16N 1°24E 174 C5
Oblong U.S.A. 39°0N 87°55W 311 F9
Obluchye Russia 49°1N 131°4E 215 E14
Obninsk Russia 55°8N 36°37E 188 E9
Obo C.A.R. 5°20N 26°32E 264 A5
Obock Djibouti 12°0N 43°20E 257 E5
Obodivka Ukraine 48°24N 29°15E 183 B14
Oborniki Poland 52°39N 16°50E 185 F3
Oborniki Śląskie Poland 51°17N 16°53E 185 G3
Obouya Congo 0°56S 15°43E 264 C3
Oboyan Russia 51°15N 36°21E 189 G9
Obozerskaya = Obozerskiy Russia 63°34N 40°21E 186 B7
Obozerskiy Russia 63°34N 40°21E 186 B7
Obrenovac Serbia 44°40N 20°11E 202 B4
O'Brien U.S.A. 30°2N 82°57W 316 E7
Obrovac Croatia 44°11N 15°41E 199 D12
Obruk Turkey 38°7N 33°12E 212 C5
Obrzycko Poland 52°42N 16°32E 185 F3
Observatory Sydney, Australia 139 a1
Observatory Gauteng, S. Africa 26°10S 28°4E 123 B2
Observatory Inlet Canada 55°10N 129°54W 296 B3
Obshchi Syrt Russia 52°0N 53°0E 158 E16
Obskaya Guba Russia 69°0N 73°0E 214 C8
Obu Japan 35°0N 136°58E 223 B8
Obuasi Ghana 6°17N 1°40W 263 D4
Obubra Nigeria 6°8N 8°20E 263 D6
Óbuda Hungary 47°33N 19°2E 117 A2
Obudu Nigeria 6°38N 9°5E 263 D6
Obukhovo Russia 59°53N 30°22E 137 B2
Obura Papua N. G. 6°33S 145°58E 286 D3
Obvodnyy Kanal Russia 59°54N 30°20E 137 B1
Obwalden ☐ Switz. 46°55N 8°15E 179 J4
Obzor Bulgaria 42°50N 27°52E 203 D11
Ocala U.S.A. 29°11N 82°8W 317 F7
Ocamo → Venezuela 2°48N 65°14W 329 C4
Ocampo Chihuahua, Mexico 28°11N 108°23W 318 B3
Ocampo Tamaulipas, Mexico 22°50N 99°20W 319 C5
Ocaña Colombia 8°15N 73°20W 328 B3
Ocaña Spain 39°55N 3°30W 194 F7
Occidental, Cordillera Colombia 5°0N 76°0W 328 C2
Occidental, Cordillera Peru 14°0S 74°0W 330 C3
Occidental, Grand Erg Algeria 30°20N 1°0E 261 B5
Ocean City Md., U.S.A. 38°20N 75°5W 309 F16
Ocean City N.J., U.S.A. 39°17N 74°35W 309 F16
Ocean City Wash., U.S.A. 47°4N 124°10W 306 C2
Ocean Falls Canada 52°18N 127°48W 296 C3
Ocean I. = Banaba Kiribati 0°45S 169°50E 288 H8
Ocean Park Hong Kong, China 22°13N 114°10E 122 B2
Ocean Park Wash., U.S.A. 46°30N 124°3W 306 D2
Oceano U.S.A. 35°6N 120°37W 307 K6
Oceanport U.S.A. 40°19N 74°3W 313 F10
Oceanside U.S.A. 33°12N 117°23W 307 M9
Ochagavía Spain 42°55N 1°5W 196 C3
Ochakiv Ukraine 46°37N 31°33E 189 J6
Ochakovo Russia 55°41N 37°26E 129 B2
Ochamchira Georgia 42°46N 41°32E 191 J5
Ochi, Oros Greece 38°5N 24°25E 204 C6
Ochiai Japan 35°1N 133°45E 222 B5
Ochil Hills U.K. 56°14N 3°40W 167 E5
Ochlocknee U.S.A. 30°58N 84°3W 316 E5
Ochlockonee → U.S.A. 29°59N 84°26W 316 F5
Ocho Rios Jamaica 18°24N 77°6W 320 a
Ochopee U.S.A. 25°54N 81°18W 317 K8
Ochota Poland 52°13N 20°58E 142 B1
Ochsenfurt Germany 49°40N 10°4E 179 F6
Ochsenhausen Germany 48°4N 9°57E 179 G5
Ockelbo Sweden 60°54N 16°45E 162 D10
Ocmulgee → U.S.A. 31°58N 82°33W 316 D7
Ocmulgee ⌂ U.S.A. 32°49N 83°37W 316 C6
Ocna Mureş Romania 46°23N 23°55E 183 D8
Ocna Sibiului Romania 45°52N 24°2E 183 E9
Ocnele Mari Romania 45°8N 24°18E 183 E9
Ocniţa Moldova 48°25N 27°30E 183 B12
Ocoee U.S.A. 28°34N 81°32W 133 A1
Ocoña Peru 16°26S 73°8W 330 D3
Ocoña → Peru 16°28S 73°8W 330 D3
Oconee → U.S.A. 31°58N 82°33W 316 D7
Oconee, L. U.S.A. 33°28N 83°15W 316 B6
O'Connell Street Dublin, Ireland 120 b2
Oconomowoc U.S.A. 43°7N 88°30W 311 A8
Oconto U.S.A. 44°53N 87°52W 308 C10
Oconto Falls U.S.A. 44°52N 88°9W 308 C9
Ocosingo Mexico 16°53N 92°6W 319 D6
Ocotal Nic. 13°41N 86°31W 320 D2
Ocotlán Jalisco, Mexico 20°21N 102°46W 318 C4
Ocotlán Oaxaca, Mexico 16°48N 96°40W 319 D5
Ocreza → Portugal 39°32N 7°50W 195 F3
Öcsa Hungary 47°17N 19°15E 182 C4
Octeville France 49°38N 1°40W 172 C5
Ocumare del Tuy Venezuela 10°7N 66°46W 328 A4
Ocurí Bolivia 18°45S 65°50W 331 D4
Ocussi = Pante Macassar E. Timor 9°30S 123°58E 231 F6
Oda Ghana 5°50N 0°51W 263 D4
Ōda Shimane, Japan 35°11N 132°30E 222 B4
Oda, J. Sudan 20°21N 36°39E 256 C4
Ódáðahraun Iceland 65°5N 17°0W 155 B9
Ŏdaejin N. Korea 41°34N 129°40E 224 B4
Odaesan △ S. Korea 37°40N 128°30E 224 D4
Ödåkra Sweden 56°7N 12°45E 163 H6
Ödana Japan 35°33N 139°35E 140 B2
Odate Japan 40°16N 140°34E 220 D10
Odawara Japan 35°20N 139°6E 223 B11
Odda Norway 60°3N 6°35E 164 D3
Odder = Xuddur Somali Rep. 4°11N 43°52E 267 D5
Odder Denmark 55°58N 10°10E 163 J4
Odei → Canada 56°6N 96°54W 297 B9
Odell U.S.A. 41°0N 88°31W 311 C8
Odemira Portugal 37°35N 8°40W 195 H2
Ödemiş Turkey 38°15N 28°0E 205 C9
Öden-Stockach Germany 48°5N 11°41E 131 B3
Ödenburg = Sopron Hungary 47°45N 16°32E 182 C1
Odendaalsrus S. Africa 27°48S 26°45E 270 C4
Odensbacken Sweden 59°10N 15°32E 162 E9
Odense Denmark 55°22N 10°23E 163 J4
Odenwald = Neckartal-Odenwald ⌂ Germany 49°30N 9°5E 179 F5
Odenwald Germany 49°35N 9°0E 179 F5
Oder → Europe 53°33N 14°38E 178 B10
Oder-Havel Kanal Germany 52°52N 14°2E 178 C10
Oderzo Italy 45°47N 12°29E 199 C9
Odesa Ukraine 46°30N 30°45E 189 J6
Odesa ☐ Ukraine 47°20N 29°55E 189 J5
Ödeshög Sweden 58°14N 14°39E 163 F8

Odessa = Odesa Ukraine 46°30N 30°45E 189 J6
Odessa Ont., Canada 44°17N 76°43W 313 B8
Odessa Mo., U.S.A. 39°0N 93°57W 310 F3
Odessa Tex., U.S.A. 31°52N 102°23W 314 F3
Odessa Wash., U.S.A. 47°20N 118°41W 304 C4
Odiakwe Botswana 20°12S 25°17E 270 B4
Odiel → Spain 37°10N 6°55W 195 H4
Odienné Ivory C. 9°30N 7°34W 262 D3
Odilampi Finland 60°18N 24°45E 121 B1
Odimba Gabon 2°2S 9°33E 264 C2
Odintsovo Russia 55°40N 37°16E 129 B1
Odiongan Phil. 12°24N 121°59E 232 E3
Odivelas Portugal 38°47N 9°10W 126 A1
Odobeşti Romania 45°43N 27°4E 183 E12
Odolanów Poland 51°34N 17°40E 185 G4
Odolany Poland 52°13N 20°55E 142 B1
O'Donnell U.S.A. 32°58N 101°50W 314 E4
O'Donnell Pt. Canada 45°5N 80°5W 312 A4
Odorheiu Secuiesc Romania 46°21N 25°21E 183 D10
Odoyevo Russia 53°56N 36°42E 188 F9
Odra = Oder → Europe 53°33N 14°38E 178 B10
Odra → Spain 42°14N 4°17W 194 C6
Odum U.S.A. 31°40N 82°2W 316 D7
Odžaci Serbia 45°30N 19°17E 182 E4
Odžak Bos.-H. 45°3N 18°18E 182 E3
Odzala Congo 0°37N 14°37E 264 B2
Odzala △ Congo 0°55N 14°55E 264 B2
Odzi Zimbabwe 19°0S 32°20E 271 A5
Odzi → Zimbabwe 19°45S 32°23E 271 A5
Oebisfelde Germany 52°27N 10°57E 178 C6
Oedong S. Korea 35°42N 129°14E 224 E4
Oeiras Brazil 7°0S 42°8W 332 C3
Oeiras Portugal 38°41N 9°18W 126 A1
Oeiras do Para Brazil 1°58S 49°51W 329 D8
Oelrichs U.S.A. 43°11N 103°14W 308 D2
Oels in Schlesien = Oleśnica Poland 51°13N 17°22E 185 G4
Oelsnitz Germany 50°24N 12°10E 179 E8
Oelwein U.S.A. 42°41N 91°55W 310 B5
Oenarodo S. Korea 34°26N 127°30E 224 E3
Oeno I. Pac. Oc. 24°0S 131°0W 289 K14
Oenpelli = Gunbalanya Australia 12°20S 133°4E 278 B5
Oetz Austria 47°13N 10°53E 180 D3
Of Turkey 40°59N 40°23E 213 B9
O'Fallon U.S.A. 38°49N 90°42W 310 F6
Ofanto → Italy 41°22N 16°13E 201 A9
Offa Nigeria 8°13N 4°42E 263 D5
Offaly □ Ireland 53°15N 7°30W 166 C4
Offenbach Germany 50°6N 8°44E 179 E4
Offenburg Germany 48°28N 7°56E 179 G3
Officer Cr. → Australia 27°46S 132°30E 279 E5
Offida Italy 42°56N 13°41E 199 F10
Offoué → Gabon 0°4S 11°44E 264 C2
Ofidousa Greece 36°33N 26°8E 205 E8
Ofin Nigeria 6°32N 3°30E 124 A3
Ofolanga Tonga 19°38S 174°27W 287 P13
Ofotfjorden Norway 68°27N 17°0E 160 B17
Ofte Norway 59°30N 8°12E 164 E5
Ofu Amer. Samoa 14°11S 169°41W 302 g
Ōfunato Japan 39°4N 141°43E 220 E10
Oga Japan 39°55N 139°50E 220 E9
Oga-Hantō Japan 39°58N 139°47E 220 E9
Ogaden Ethiopia 7°30N 45°30E 267 C6
Ōgaki Japan 35°21N 136°37E 223 B8
Ogallala U.S.A. 41°8N 101°43W 308 E3
Ogan → Indonesia 3°1S 104°44E 234 C2
Ogasawara Gunto Pac. Oc. 27°0N 142°0E 211 F16
Ogawa Japan 35°44N 139°28E 140 A1
Ogbomosho Nigeria 8°1N 4°11E 263 D5
Ogden Iowa, U.S.A. 42°2N 94°2W 310 B2
Ogden Utah, U.S.A. 41°13N 111°58W 304 F8
Ogden Park U.S.A. 41°46N 87°39W 119 C2
Ogden Slip Chicago, U.S.A. 119 b3
Ogdensburg U.S.A. 44°42N 75°30W 313 B9
Ogea Driki Fiji 19°12S 178°27W 287 B3
Ogea Levu Fiji 19°8S 178°24W 287 B3
Ogeechee → U.S.A. 31°50N 81°3W 316 D8
Ogi Japan 33°20N 130°15E 222 D2
Ogikubo Japan 35°42N 139°37E 140 A2
Ogilby U.S.A. 32°49N 114°50W 307 N12
Oglat Beraber Algeria 30°15N 3°34W 260 B4
Oglat el Khnâchich Mali 21°51N 3°58W 260 D4
Oglesby U.S.A. 41°18N 89°4W 310 C7
Oglethorpe U.S.A. 32°18N 84°4W 316 C5
Óglio → Italy 45°2N 10°39E 198 C7
Óglio Nord ⌓ Italy 45°22N 9°54E 198 C6
Óglio Sud ⌓ Italy 45°7N 10°24E 198 C7
Ogmore Australia 22°37S 149°35E 280 C4
Ognon → France 47°16N 5°28E 173 E12
Ogogoro Nigeria 6°25N 3°24E 124 B2
Ogoja Nigeria 6°38N 8°39E 263 D6
Ogoki Canada 51°38N 85°58W 298 B2
Ogoki → Canada 51°38N 85°57W 298 B2
Ogoki L. Canada 50°50N 87°10W 298 B2
Ogoki Res. Canada 50°45N 88°15W 298 B2
Ogooué → Gabon 1°0S 9°0E 264 C1
Ogōri Japan 34°6N 131°24E 222 C3
Ogōri Japan 33°25N 130°30E 222 D2
Ogosta → Bulgaria 43°48N 23°55E 202 C7
Ogou → Togo 7°50N 1°19E 263 D5
Ogoueïleten Nmâdi Mauritania 19°46N 11°1W 260 E2
Ogowe = Ogooué → Gabon 1°0S 9°0E 264 C1
Ogoyo Nigeria 6°25N 3°29E 124 B2
Ogr = Sharafa Sudan 11°59N 27°7E 257 E2
Ograźden Macedonia 41°30N 22°50E 202 E6
Ogre Latvia 56°49N 24°36E 188 D3
Ogrein Sudan 17°55N 34°50E 256 D3
Ogudu Nigeria 6°34N 3°24E 124 A2
Ogulin Croatia 45°16N 15°16E 199 C12
Ogun □ Nigeria 7°0N 3°0E 263 D5
Oguni Japan 33°11N 131°8E 222 D3
Ögur Iceland 66°2N 22°44W 155 A4
Ogurja Ada Turkmenistan 38°55N 53°2E 247 B7
Oguta Nigeria 5°44N 6°44E 263 D6
Oğuzeli Turkey 36°57N 37°30E 250 B8
Ogwashi-Uku Nigeria 6°15N 6°30E 263 D6
Ogwe Nigeria 5°0N 7°14E 263 E6
Ohai N.Z. 45°55S 168°0E 285 F3
Ohakune N.Z. 39°24S 175°24E 284 F4
Ohanet Algeria 28°44N 8°46E 261 C6
Ōhara Japan 35°15N 140°23E 223 B12
O'Hare Int., Chicago ✈ (ORD) U.S.A. 41°59N 87°54W 119 B1
Ohariu Stream → N.Z. 41°12S 174°47E 143 B1
Ohata Japan 41°24N 141°10E 220 D10
Ohatchee U.S.A. 33°47N 86°0W 316 B4
Ohau, L. N.Z. 44°15S 169°53E 285 E4
Ohaupo N.Z. 37°56S 175°20E 284 D4
O'Higgins, C. Chile 27°5S 109°15W 330 b
O'Higgins, Parque Chile 33°27S 70°40W 137 B2
O'Higgins, Pta. Chile 33°41S 79°0W 330 c
Ohio □ U.S.A. 40°15N 82°45W 312 F2
Ohio → U.S.A. 36°59N 89°8W 311 G8
Ohio City U.S.A. 40°46N 84°37W 311 D12
Ohiwa Harbour N.Z. 37°59S 177°10E 284 D6
Ohlau = Oława Poland 50°57N 17°20E 185 H4
Ohře → Czech Rep. 50°30N 14°10E 180 A7
Ohre → Sachsen-Anhalt, Germany 52°18N 11°46E 178 C7
Ohrid Macedonia 41°8N 20°52E 202 E4
Ohridsko Jezero Macedonia 41°8N 20°52E 202 E4
Ohrigstad S. Africa 24°39S 30°36E 271 B5
Öhringen Germany 49°12N 9°31E 179 F5
Ohura N.Z. 38°51S 174°59E 284 E3
Oi Qu → China 28°37N 98°16E 228 C2
Oiapoque Brazil 3°50N 51°50W 329 C7
Oiapoque → S. Amer. 4°8N 51°40W 329 C7
Oikou China 38°35N 117°42E 227 E9
Oil City U.S.A. 41°26N 79°42W 312 E5
Oil Springs Canada 42°47N 82°7W 312 D2
Oildale U.S.A. 35°25N 119°1W 307 K7
Ōimachi Japan 35°35N 139°43E 140 B3
Oinousa = Inousses Greece 38°33N 26°14E 205 C8
Oise □ France 49°28N 2°30E 173 C9
Oise → France 49°0N 2°4E 173 C9
Oistins Barbados 13°4N 59°33W 323 r
Ōita Japan 33°14N 131°36E 222 D3
Ōita □ Japan 33°15N 131°30E 222 D3
Ojai U.S.A. 34°27N 119°15W 307 L7
Ojcowski △ Poland 50°15N 19°50E 185 H6
Ojhar India 20°6N 73°56E 244 D1
Ojinaga Mexico 29°34N 104°25W 318 B4
Ojiya Japan 37°18N 138°48E 221 F9
Ojo Caliente Mexico 21°53N 102°15W 318 C4
Ojo de Liebre, L. Mexico 27°45N 114°15W 318 B2
Ojos del Salado, Cerro Argentina 27°0S 68°40W 334 B2
Ojota Nigeria 6°35N 3°23E 124 A2
Oka Nigeria 7°9N 3°38E 263 D5
Oka → Russia 56°20N 43°59E 190 B7
Okaba Indonesia 8°6S 139°42E 231 F9
Okahandja Namibia 22°0S 16°59E 270 B2
Okahukura N.Z. 38°48S 175°14E 284 E4
Okaihau N.Z. 35°19S 173°47E 284 B2
Okalataka Congo 0°18S 14°54E 264 C2
Okanagan L. Canada 50°0N 119°30W 296 D5
Okandja Gabon 0°35S 13°45E 264 C2
Okano → Gabon 0°5S 10°57E 264 C2
Okanogan U.S.A. 48°22N 119°35W 304 B4
Okanogan → U.S.A. 48°6N 119°44W 304 B4
Okanogan Range N. Amer. 49°0N 119°55W 296 D5
Okány Hungary 46°52N 21°21E 182 D6
Okapa Papua N. G. 6°38S 145°39E 286 D3
Okapi △ Dem. Rep. of the Congo 2°30N 27°20E 268 B2
Okaputa Namibia 20°5S 17°0E 270 B2
Okara Pakistan 30°50N 73°31E 242 D5
Okarito N.Z. 43°15S 170°9E 285 D5
Okato N.Z. 39°12S 173°53E 284 F2
Okau Micronesia 9°32N 138°6E 287 R16
Okaukuejo Namibia 19°10S 16°0E 270 A2
Okavango Delta Botswana 18°45S 22°45E 270 A3
Okavango Swamp = Okavango Delta Botswana 18°45S 22°45E 270 A3
Ōkawa Japan 33°9N 130°21E 222 D2
Okawville U.S.A. 38°26N 89°33W 310 F7
Okaya Japan 36°5N 138°10E 223 A10
Okayama Japan 34°40N 133°54E 222 C5
Okayama □ Japan 35°0N 133°50E 222 C5
Okazaki Japan 34°57N 137°10E 223 C9
Oke-Iho Nigeria 8°1N 3°18E 263 D5
Oke-Ira Nigeria 6°29N 3°22E 124 B2
Okęcie Poland 52°11N 20°56E 142 B1
Okęcie, Warszawa ✈ (WAW) Poland 52°9N 20°59E 142 B1
Okeechobee U.S.A. 27°15N 80°50W 317 H9
Okeechobee, L. U.S.A. 27°0N 80°50W 317 J9
Okefenokee ⌓ U.S.A. 30°45N 82°18W 316 E7
Okefenokee Swamp U.S.A. 30°40N 82°20W 316 E7
Okehampton U.K. 50°44N 4°0W 169 G4
Okemos U.S.A. 42°43N 84°26W 311 B12
Okene Nigeria 7°32N 6°11E 263 D6
Okeogbe Nigeria 6°24N 3°23E 124 B2
Oker → Germany 52°32N 10°22E 178 C6
Okha Gujarat, India 22°27N 69°4E 242 H3
Okha Russia 53°40N 143°0E 215 D15
Okhla India 28°33N 77°16E 120 B2
Okhotsk Russia 59°20N 143°10E 215 D15
Okhotsk, Sea of Asia 55°0N 145°0E 215 D15
Okhotskiy Perevoz Russia 61°52N 135°35E 215 C14
Okhta → Russia 59°56N 30°25E 137 B2
Okhtyrka Ukraine 50°25N 35°0E 189 G8
Oki-no-Shima Japan 32°44N 132°33E 222 E4
Oki-Shotō Japan 36°5N 133°15E 222 A5
Okiep S. Africa 29°39S 17°53E 270 C2
Okigwi Nigeria 5°52N 7°20E 263 D6
Okija Nigeria 5°54N 6°55E 263 D6
Okinawa Japan 26°19N 127°46E 288 a
Okinawa □ Japan 26°40N 128°0E 288 a
Okinawa-Guntō Japan 26°40N 128°0E 221 L4
Okinawa-Jima Japan 26°32N 128°0E 221 L4
Okino-erabu-Shima Japan 27°21N 128°33E 221 L4
Okitipupa Nigeria 6°31N 4°50E 263 D5
Okkervil → Russia 59°56N 30°30E 137 B2
Oklahoma □ U.S.A. 35°20N 97°30W 314 D6
Oklahoma City U.S.A. 35°30N 97°30W 314 D6
Oklawaha → U.S.A. 29°28N 81°41W 317 F8
Okmulgee U.S.A. 35°37N 95°58W 314 D7
Oknitsa = Ocniţa Moldova 48°25N 27°30E 183 B12
Oko, W. → Sudan 21°15N 35°56E 256 C4
Okolo Uganda 2°37N 31°8E 268 B3
Okolona Ky., U.S.A. 38°8N 85°41W 311 F11
Okolona Miss., U.S.A. 34°0N 88°45W 315 E10
Okombahe Namibia 21°23S 15°22E 270 B2
Okonek Poland 53°32N 16°51E 184 E3
Okotoks Canada 50°43N 113°58W 296 C6
Okoyo Congo 1°28S 15°0E 264 C3
Okrika Nigeria 4°40N 7°10E 263 E6
Okrzeszyn Poland 52°8N 21°8E 142 C2
Oksapmin Papua N. G. 5°17S 142°15E 286 C2
Øksendalsøra Norway 62°42N 8°27E 164 B5
Oksovskiy Russia 62°33N 39°57E 186 B6
Oksval Norway 59°51N 10°40E 133 A3
Oktwin Burma 18°49N 96°26E 241 F6
Oktyabrsk = Qandyaghash Kazakhstan 49°28N 57°25E 187 E10
Oktyabrsk Russia 53°11N 48°40E 190 D9
Oktyabrskiy = Aktsyabrski Belarus 52°38N 28°53E 177 B15
Oktyabrskiy Bashkortostan, Russia 54°28N 53°28E 186 D9
Oktyabrskiy Kamchatka, Russia 52°39N 156°14E 215 D16
Oktyabrskiy Moskva, Russia 55°41N 37°35E 129 B3
Oktyabrskiy Rostov, Russia 47°30N 40°4E 191 G5
Oktyabrskoy Revolyutsii, Ostrov Russia 79°30N 97°0E 215 B10
Oktyabrskoye = Zhovtneve Ukraine 46°54N 32°3E 189 J7
Okubo Tokyo, Japan 140 a2
Ōkuchi Japan 32°4N 130°37E 222 E2
Okulovka Russia 58°25N 33°19E 188 C7
Ōkura Japan 35°35N 139°27E 140 B1
Okuru N.Z. 43°55S 168°55E 285 D3
Okushiri-Tō Japan 42°15N 139°30E 220 C9
Okuta Nigeria 9°14N 3°12E 263 D5
Okwa → Botswana 22°30S 23°0E 270 B3
Ola Russia 59°35N 151°17E 215 D16
Ola Ark., U.S.A. 35°2N 93°13W 314 D8
Ólafsfjörður Iceland 66°4N 18°39W 155 A8
Ólafsvík Iceland 64°53N 23°43W 155 C3
Olaine Latvia 56°48N 23°59E 184 B10
Olancha U.S.A. 36°17N 118°1W 307 J8
Olancha Pk. U.S.A. 36°16N 118°7W 307 J8
Olanchito Honduras 15°30N 86°30W 320 C2
Öland Sweden 56°45N 16°38E 163 H10
Ölands norra udde Sweden 57°22N 17°5E 163 G11
Ölands södra udde Sweden 56°12N 16°23E 163 H10
Olanta U.S.A. 33°56N 79°56W 316 B10
Olar U.S.A. 33°11N 81°11W 316 B8
Olargues France 43°34N 2°53E 174 E6
Olari Finland 60°10N 24°44E 121 B1
Olaria Brazil 22°50S 43°16W 135 B1
Olary Australia 32°18S 140°19E 282 B4
Olascoaga Argentina 35°15S 60°39W 334 D3
Olathe U.S.A. 38°53N 94°49W 308 F6
Olavarría Argentina 36°55S 60°20W 334 D3
Oława Poland 50°57N 17°20E 185 H4
Olbernhau Germany 50°40N 13°19E 178 E9
Ólbia Italy 40°55N 9°31E 200 B2
Ólbia, G. di Italy 40°55N 9°39E 200 B2
Olching Germany 48°12N 11°21E 179 G7
Olcott U.S.A. 43°20N 78°42W 312 C6
Old Admiralty Russia 59°55N 30°20E 137 B1
Old Bahama Chan. = Bahama, Canal Viejo de W. Indies 22°10N 77°30W 320 B4
Old Baldy Pk. = San Antonio, Mt. U.S.A. 34°17N 117°38W 307 L9
Old Bar Australia 31°58S 152°35E 283 A10
Old Bridge U.S.A. 40°25N 74°22W 313 F10
Old Castile = Castilla y Leon □ Spain 42°0N 5°0W 194 D6
Old City Shanghai, China 31°13N 121°29E 138 B1
Old City Delhi, India 120 a3
Old City Jerusalem 123 b3
Old Crow Canada 67°30N 139°55W 294 D4
Old Dale U.S.A. 34°8N 115°47W 307 L11
Old Forge N.Y., U.S.A. 43°43N 74°58W 313 C10
Old Forge Pa., U.S.A. 41°22N 75°45W 313 E9
Old Fort = Purana Qila Delhi, India 120 c3
Old Fort B. Bahamas 25°3N 77°32W 153 b
Old Fort Pt. Montserrat 16°40N 62°11W 323 p
Old Fort York Canada 43°39N 79°24W 141 B2
Old Harbor Alaska, U.S.A. 57°12N 153°18W 303 H9
Old Harbor Mass., U.S.A. 42°19N 71°1W 116 B2
Old Harbour Jamaica 17°56N 77°7W 320 a
Old Harbour Bay Jamaica 17°54N 77°6W 320 a
Old Ironside Boston, U.S.A. 116 a3
Old Mapoon ☼ Australia 11°5S 142°22E 280 A3
Old Panamao Phil. 5°59N 121°13E 233 J3
Old Perlican Canada 48°5N 53°1W 299 C9
Old Road Bluff Antigua & B. 16°59N 61°50W 322 b
Old Road Town St. Kitts & Nevis 17°17N 62°47W 322 d
Old Roundhouse Toronto, Canada 141 c2
Old Shinyanga Tanzania 3°33S 33°27E 268 C3
Old Speck Mt. U.S.A. 44°34N 70°57W 313 B14
Old Town = Stare Miasto Warsaw, Poland 142 a2
Old Town Edinburgh, U.K. 121 a2
Old Town Fla., U.S.A. 29°36N 82°59W 317 F7
Old Town Ill., U.S.A. 41°54N 87°37W 119 B3
Old Town Maine, U.S.A. 44°56N 68°39W 309 C19
Old Town Hall = Altes Rathaus Munich, Germany 131 b3
Old Town Square Warsaw, Poland 142 a2
Old Washington U.S.A. 40°2N 81°27W 312 F3
Old Wives L. Canada 50°5N 106°0W 297 C7
Oldbawn Ireland 53°17N 6°21W 120 B1
Oldbury U.K. 51°38N 2°33W 169 F5
Oldcastle Ireland 53°46N 7°10W 166 C4
Oldeani Tanzania 3°22S 35°35E 268 C4
Olden Norway 61°49N 6°49E 164 C3
Oldenburg Niedersachsen, Germany 53°9N 8°13E 178 B4
Oldenburg Schleswig-Holstein, Germany 54°17N 10°52E 178 A6
Oldenzaal Neths. 52°19N 6°53E 170 B6
Oldham U.K. 53°33N 2°7W 168 D5
Oldman → Canada 49°57N 111°42W 296 D6
Oldmeldrum U.K. 57°20N 2°19W 167 D6
Olds Canada 51°50N 114°10W 296 C6
Oldsmar U.S.A. 28°2N 82°39W 317 G7
Olduvai Gorge Tanzania 2°57S 35°23E 268 C4
Öldziyt Mongolia 44°40N 109°1E 226 B5
Ole Rømer Land Greenland 74°10N 24°30W 154 C8
Olean U.S.A. 42°5N 78°26W 312 D6
Oleby Sweden 60°8N 13°2E 162 D7
Olecko Poland 54°2N 22°31E 184 D9
Oléggio Italy 45°36N 8°38E 198 C5
Oleiros Portugal 39°56N 7°56W 194 F3
Oleiros Spain 43°20N 8°19W 194 B2
Olekma → Russia 60°22N 120°42E 215 C13
Olekminsk Russia 60°25N 120°30E 215 C13
Oleksandrivka Ukraine 48°55N 32°20E 189 H7
Oleksandriya Kirovohrad, Ukraine 48°42N 33°3E 189 H7
Oleksandriya Rivne, Ukraine 50°37N 26°19E 177 C14
Olema U.S.A. 38°3N 122°47W 306 G4
Ølen Norway 59°36N 5°48E 164 E2
Olenegorsk Russia 68°9N 33°18E 160 B25
Olenek Russia 68°28N 112°18E 215 C12
Olenek → Russia 73°0N 120°10E 215 B13
Olenino Russia 56°15N 33°30E 188 D7
Olenya = Olenegorsk Russia 68°9N 33°18E 160 B25
Oléron, Î. d' France 45°55N 1°15W 174 C2
Olesk Ukraine 51°6N 24°11E 185 G11
Oleśnica Poland 51°13N 17°22E 185 G4
Olesno Poland 50°51N 18°26E 185 H5
Olevsk Ukraine 51°12N 27°39E 177 C14
Olga, L. Canada 49°47N 77°15W 298 C4
Olgas, The = Kata Tjuta Australia 25°20S 130°50E 279 E5
Olgino Russia 60°0N 30°10E 137 A1
Ölgiy Mongolia 48°56N 89°57E 217 C11
Ølgod Denmark 55°49N 8°36E 163 J2
Olhão Portugal 37°3N 7°48W 195 H3
Olhopil Ukraine 48°12N 29°30E 183 B14
Olhovatka Russia 54°30N 22°18E 184 D9
Olib Croatia 44°23N 14°44E 199 D11
Oliena Italy 40°16N 9°24E 200 B2
Oliete Spain 41°1N 0°41W 196 D4
Olifants = Elefantes → Africa 24°10S 32°40E 271 B5
Olifants → Namibia 25°30S 19°30E 270 B2
Olifantshoek S. Africa 27°57S 22°42E 270 C3
Olimbos Greece 35°44N 27°11E 205 F9
Ólimbos, Óros = Olymbos Oros Greece 40°6N 22°23E 202 F6
Olímpia Brazil 20°44S 48°54W 335 A6
Olimpico, Estadio Mexico 19°20N 99°11W 128 C1
Olimpos-Beydaglari △ Turkey 36°36N 30°30E 205 E12
Olin U.S.A. 42°0N 91°9W 310 B5
Olinda Brazil 8°1S 34°51W 332 C5
Olite Spain 42°29N 1°40W 196 C3
Oliva Argentina 32°0S 63°38W 334 C3
Oliva Spain 38°58N 0°9W 197 G4
Oliva, Punta del Spain 43°37N 5°28W 194 B5
Oliva de la Frontera Spain 38°17N 6°54W 195 G4
Olivais Portugal 38°45N 9°7W 126 A2
Olivar de los Padres Mexico 19°21N 99°14W 128 B1
Olivar del Conde Mexico 19°22N 99°12W 128 B1
Olivares, Cerro los Argentina 30°18S 69°55W 334 C2
Olivares de Júcar Spain 39°46N 2°20W 196 F2
Olive Branch U.S.A. 34°57N 89°49W 315 D10
Olive Hill U.S.A. 38°18N 83°13W 311 F13
Olive Park Chicago, U.S.A. 119 b3
Olivehurst U.S.A. 39°6N 121°34W 306 F5
Oliveira Brazil 20°39S 44°50W 333 F3
Oliveira de Azeméis Portugal 40°49N 8°29W 194 E2
Oliveira do Douro Portugal 41°5N 8°2W 194 D2
Oliveira dos Brejinhos Brazil 12°19S 42°54W 333 D3
Olivenza Spain 38°41N 7°9W 195 G3
Oliver Canada 49°13N 119°37W 296 D5
Oliver L. Canada 56°56N 103°22W 297 B8
Olives, Mt. of West Bank 31°46N 35°15E 123 B2
Olivet Loiret, France 47°51N 1°55E 173 E8
Olivet Mich., U.S.A. 42°27N 84°56W 311 B12
Olivia, L. U.S.A. 28°31N 81°31W 133 A1
Olivine Ra. N.Z. 44°15S 168°30E 285 E3
Olivos Argentina 34°30S 58°28W 117 B2
Olkhovka Russia 49°48N 44°32E 190 F7
Olkusz Poland 50°18N 19°33E 185 H6
Ollachea Peru 13°49S 70°29W 330 C3
Ollagüe Chile 21°15S 68°10W 334 A2
Ollombo Congo 1°18S 15°53E 264 C3
Olloua Congo 0°54S 14°34E 264 C2
Olmaliq Uzbekistan 40°50N 69°35E 217 D7
Olmedo Spain 41°20N 4°43W 194 D6
Olmeto France 41°43N 8°55E 175 G12
Olmos Peru 5°59S 79°46W 330 B2
Olmütz = Olomouc Czech Rep. 49°38N 17°12E 181 B10
Olney Ill., U.S.A. 38°44N 88°5W 311 F8
Olney Tex., U.S.A. 33°22N 98°45W 314 E5
Olofström Sweden 56°17N 14°32E 163 H8
Oloitokitok Kenya 2°56S 37°30E 268 C4
Ololi Congo 0°15S 14°36E 264 C2
Oloma Cameroon 3°29N 11°19E 263 E7
Olomane → Canada 50°14N 60°37W 299 B7
Olomouc Czech Rep. 49°38N 17°12E 181 B10
Olomoucký □ Czech Rep. 49°45N 17°5E 181 B10
Olona → Italy 45°29N 9°6E 129 B1
Olonets Russia 61°0N 32°54E 188 B7
Olongapo Phil. 14°50N 120°18E 232 D3
Olonne-sur-Mer France 46°32N 1°47W 174 B2
Oloron, Gave d' → France 43°33N 1°5W 174 E2
Oloron-Ste-Marie France 43°11N 0°38W 174 E3
Olosega Amer. Samoa 14°10S 169°37W 302 g
Olosenga = Swains I. Amer. Samoa 11°11S 171°4W 289 J11
Olot Spain 42°11N 2°30E 196 C7
Olovo Bos.-H. 44°8N 18°35E 182 F3
Olovyannaya Russia 50°58N 115°35E 215 D12
Oloy → Russia 66°29N 159°29E 215 C16
Olsberg Germany 51°21N 8°31E 178 D4
Olshammar Sweden 58°45N 14°48E 163 F8
Olshanka Ukraine 48°16N 30°58E 189 H6
Olshany Ukraine 50°3N 35°53E 189 G8
Olsztyn Poland 53°48N 20°29E 184 E7
Olsztynek Poland 53°34N 20°19E 184 E7
Olt □ Romania 44°20N 24°30E 183 F9
Olt → Romania 43°43N 24°51E 183 G9
Oltedal Norway 58°49N 6°2E 164 F3
Olten Switz. 47°21N 7°53E 179 H3
Olteniţa Romania 44°7N 26°42E 183 F11
Olton U.S.A. 34°11N 102°8W 314 D3
Oltu Turkey 40°35N 41°58E 213 B9
Oluan Pi Taiwan 21°53N 120°51E 225 E2
Oluanpi Taiwan 21°54N 120°51E 225 E2
Olula del Rio Spain 37°21N 2°18W 197 H2
Olur Turkey 40°49N 42°8E 213 B10
Olustee U.S.A. 30°12N 82°26W 316 E7
Olutanga Phil. 7°26N 122°54E 233 H4
Olutanga I. Phil. 7°22N 122°52E 233 H4
Olvega Spain 41°47N 2°0W 196 D2
Olvera Spain 36°55N 5°18W 195 J5
Olymbos Cyprus 35°21N 33°45E 207 E9
Olymbos Oros Greece 40°6N 22°23E 202 F6
Olympia Greece 37°39N 21°39E 204 D3
Olympia London, U.K. 125 c1
Olympia Wash., U.S.A. 47°3N 122°53W 306 D4
Olympia, L. U.S.A. 28°34N 81°31W 133 A1
Olympic △ U.S.A. 47°45N 123°43W 306 C3
Olympic Dam Australia 30°30S 136°55E 282 A2
Olympic Green China 39°59N 116°23E 114 B2
Olympic Mts. U.S.A. 47°55N 123°45W 306 C3
Olympic Stadium = Turner Field U.S.A. 33°44N 84°23W 113 B2
Olympic Stadium Beijing, China 39°59N 116°23E 114 B2
Olympic Stadium Helsinki, Finland 60°11N 24°55E 121 B2
Olympique, Stade Canada 45°33N 73°33W 130 A2
Olympus Cyprus 34°56N 32°52E 207 F8
Olympus, Mt. = Olymbos Oros Greece 40°6N 22°23E 202 F6
Olympus, Mt. = Uludağ Turkey 40°4N 29°13E 203 F13
Olympus, Mt. U.S.A. 47°48N 123°43W 306 C3
Olyphant U.S.A. 41°27N 75°36W 313 E9
Olyutorskiy, Mys Russia 59°55N 170°27E 215 D18
Om → Russia 54°59N 73°22E 217 B8
Om Hajer Eritrea 14°20N 36°41E 257 E4
Om Koi Thailand 17°48N 98°22E 236 D2
Ōma Japan 41°45N 141°5E 220 D10
Ōmachi Japan 36°30N 137°50E 223 A9
Omae-Zaki Japan 34°36N 138°14E 223 C10
Ōmagari Japan 39°27N 140°29E 220 E10
Omagh U.K. 54°36N 7°19W 166 B4
Omagh □ U.K. 54°35N 7°15W 166 B4
Omaha U.S.A. 41°17N 95°58W 308 E6
Omak U.S.A. 48°25N 119°31W 304 B4
Omalos Greece 35°19N 23°55E 207 E4
Omalur India 11°44N 78°4E 245 J4
Oman ■ Asia 23°0N 58°0E 249 B7
Oman, G. of Asia 24°30N 58°30E 247 E8
Omapere N.Z. 35°37S 173°25E 284 B2
Omar Combon Somali Rep. 3°10N 45°47E 267 D6
Omaruru Namibia 21°26S 16°0E 270 B2
Omaruru → Namibia 22°7S 14°15E 270 B1
Omate Peru 16°45S 71°0W 330 D3
Ombai, Selat Indonesia 8°30S 124°50E 231 F6
Omboué Gabon 1°35S 9°15E 264 C1
Ombrone → Italy 42°42N 11°5E 198 F8
Omchi Chad 21°22N 17°53E 259 D3
Omdurmân Sudan 15°40N 32°28E 257 D3
Ōme Japan 35°47N 139°15E 223 B11
Omega U.S.A. 31°21N 83°36W 316 D6
Omegna Italy 45°53N 8°24E 198 C5
Omemee Canada 44°18N 78°33W 312 B6
Omeo Australia 37°6S 147°36E 283 D7
Omeonga Dem. Rep. of the Congo 3°40S 24°22E 264 C4
Ometepe, I. de Nic. 11°32N 85°35W 320 D2
Ometepec Mexico 16°41N 98°25W 319 D5
Ōmi-Shima Ehime, Japan 34°15N 133°0E 222 C5
Ōmi-Shima Yamaguchi, Japan 34°25N 131°9E 222 C3
Omihachiman Japan 35°7N 136°3E 223 B8
Omin Micronesia 9°36N 138°9E 287 R16
Ominato Japan 41°17N 141°10E 220 D10
Omineca → Canada 56°3N 124°16W 296 B4
Omineca Mts. Canada 56°30N 125°30W 296 B3
Omiš Croatia 43°28N 16°40E 199 E13
Omišalj Croatia 45°13N 14°32E 199 C11
Omitara Namibia 22°16S 18°2E 270 B2
Ōmiya = Saitama Japan 35°54N 139°38E 223 B11
Ommaney, C. U.S.A. 56°10N 134°40W 303 H14
Omme Å → Denmark 55°56N 8°32E 163 J2
Ommen Neths. 52°31N 6°26E 170 B6
Ömnögovĭ □ Mongolia 43°15N 104°0E 226 C3
Omo → Ethiopia 6°25N 36°10E 257 F4
Omo △ Ethiopia 5°54N 35°55E 257 F4
Omo Valley Ethiopia 5°7N 36°0E 257 F4
Omodeo, L. Italy 40°8N 8°56E 200 B1
Omodhos Cyprus 34°51N 32°48E 207 F8
Omoï Congo 2°56S 13°13E 264 C2
Omoko Nigeria 5°19N 6°40E 263 D6
Omolon → Russia 68°42N 158°36E 215 C16
Omona Solomon Is. 7°30S 158°43E 287 L10
Omonia Square Athens, Greece 112 b1
Omono-Gawa → Japan 39°46N 140°3E 220 E10
Ōmori Japan 35°34N 139°43E 140 B3
Ompha Canada 45°0N 76°50W 313 B8
Omsk Russia 55°0N 73°12E 217 B8
Omsukchan Russia 62°32N 155°48E 215 C16
Ōmu Japan 44°34N 142°58E 220 B11
Omul, Vf. Romania 45°27N 25°29E 183 E10
Omulew → Poland 53°5N 21°33E 185 E8
Ōmura Japan 32°56N 129°57E 222 E1
Ōmura-Wan Japan 32°57N 129°52E 222 E1
Omuramba Omatako → Namibia 17°45S 20°25E 270 A2
Omuramba Ovambo → Namibia 18°45S 16°59E 270 A2
Omurtag Bulgaria 43°8N 26°26E 203 C10
Ōmuta Japan 33°5N 130°26E 222 D2
On-ma-thi Burma 22°17N 96°41E 241 D6
On-Take Japan 31°35N 130°39E 222 F2
Oña Spain 42°43N 3°25W 194 C7
Ona Fla., U.S.A. 27°29N 81°55W 317 H8
Ona Dikonde Dem. Rep. of the Congo 3°51S 24°11E 264 C4
Onaga U.S.A. 39°29N 96°10W 308 F5
Onalaska U.S.A. 43°53N 91°14W 308 D8
Onancock U.S.A. 37°43N 75°45W 309 G16
Onang Indonesia 3°2S 118°49E 235 C5
Onangue, L. Gabon 0°57S 10°4E 264 C1
Onaping L. Canada 47°3N 81°30W 298 C3
Onarga U.S.A. 40°43N 88°1W 311 D8
Oñati Spain 43°3N 2°25W 196 B2
Onavas Mexico 28°31N 109°35W 318 B3
Onawa U.S.A. 42°2N 96°6W 308 D5
Oncócua Angola 16°30S 13°25E 265 F2
Onda Spain 39°55N 0°17W 196 F4
Ondangwa Namibia 17°57S 16°4E 270 A2
Ondarroa Spain 43°19N 2°25W 196 B2
Ondas → Brazil 12°8S 44°55W 333 D3
Ondava → Slovak Rep. 48°27N 21°48E 181 C14
Ondjiva Angola 16°48S 15°50E 265 F3
Ondo Japan 34°11N 132°32E 222 C4
Ondo Nigeria 7°4N 4°47E 263 D5
Ondo □ Nigeria 6°45N 5°0E 263 D6
Öndörhaan Mongolia 47°19N 110°39E 219 B11
Öndverðarnes Iceland 64°52N 24°0W 155 C2
One and a Half Degree Channel Maldives 1°30N 73°20E 272 d
One Arm Point Australia 16°26S 123°3E 278 C3
One Arm Point ☼ Australia 16°31S 122°53E 278 C3
One Tree Australia 34°11S 144°43E 281 E3
Oneata Fiji 18°26S 178°25W 287 B3
Oneco U.S.A. 27°25N 82°31W 317 H7
Onega Russia 64°0N 38°10E 186 B6
Onega → Russia 63°58N 38°2E 186 B6
Onega, G. of = Onezhskaya Guba Russia 64°24N 36°38E 186 B6
Onega, L. = Onezhskoye Ozero Russia 61°44N 35°22E 188 B8
Onehunga N.Z. 36°55S 174°48E 284 C3
Oneida Ill., U.S.A. 41°4N 90°13W 310 C6
Oneida N.Y., U.S.A. 43°6N 75°39W 313 C9
Oneida L. U.S.A. 43°12N 75°54W 313 C9
O'Neill U.S.A. 42°27N 98°39W 308 D4
Onekotan, Ostrov Russia 49°25N 154°45E 215 E16
Onema Dem. Rep. of the Congo 4°35S 24°30E 265 C4
Oneonta U.S.A. 42°27N 75°4W 313 D9
Onerahi N.Z. 35°45S 174°22E 284 B3
Oneroa Cook Is. 21°15S 159°43W 289 h
Oneşti Romania 46°17N 26°47E 183 D11
Onezhskaya Guba Russia 64°24N 36°38E 186 B6
Onezhskoye Ozero Russia 61°44N 35°22E 188 B8
Ongarue N.Z. 38°42S 175°19E 284 E4
Ongea Levu = Ogea Levu Fiji 19°8S 178°24W 287 B3
Ongers → S. Africa 31°4S 23°13E 270 D3
Ongerup Australia 33°58S 118°28E 279 F2
Ongi Mongolia 45°27N 103°54E 226 B2
Ongjin N. Korea 37°56N 125°21E 224 D2
Ongkharak Thailand 14°8N 101°1E 236 E3
Ongniud Qi China 43°0N 118°38E 227 C10
Ongoka Dem. Rep. of the Congo 1°20S 26°0E 268 C2
Ongole India 15°33N 80°2E 245 G5
Ongon = Havirga Mongolia 45°41N 113°5E 226 B7
Ongouendjo Gabon 1°23S 9°5E 264 C1
Ongoujou Comoros Is. 12°18S 44°30E 272 a
Ongtüstik Qazaqstan □ Kazakhstan 43°0N 68°0E 217 D7
Oni Georgia 42°33N 43°26E 191 J6
Onida U.S.A. 44°42N 100°4W 308 C3
Onilahy → Madag. 23°34S 43°45E 272 C1
Onima Bonaire 12°15N 68°19W 322 h
Onisigun Nigeria 6°35N 3°24E 124 A2
Onitsha Nigeria 6°6N 6°42E 263 D6
Onna Japan 26°29N 127°51E 288 a
Ono Fiji 18°55S 178°29E 287 B2
Ono Fukui, Japan 35°59N 136°29E 223 B8
Ono Hyōgo, Japan 34°51N 134°56E 222 C6
Onoda Japan 33°59N 131°11E 222 C3
Onohara Japan 34°5N 133°40E 222 C5
Onoke, L. N.Z. 41°22S 175°8E 284 H4
Onomichi Japan 34°25N 133°12E 222 C5
Onotoa Kiribati 1°52S 175°34E 277 A14
Ons, I. de Spain 42°23N 8°55W 194 C2
Onsala Sweden 57°26N 12°0E 163 G6
Onslow Australia 21°40S 115°12E 278 D2
Onslow B. U.S.A. 34°20N 77°15W 315 D16
Ontake-San Japan 35°53N 137°29E 223 B9
Ontar Vanuatu 14°17S 167°27E 287 D5
Ontario Calif., U.S.A. 34°4N 117°39W 307 L9
Ontario Oreg., U.S.A. 44°2N 116°58W 304 D5
Ontario □ Canada 48°0N 83°0W 298 B2
Ontario, L. N. Amer. 43°20N 78°0W 312 C7
Ontario Science Centre Canada 43°43N 79°20W 141 A2
Ontinyent Spain 38°50N 0°35W 197 G4
Ontonagon U.S.A. 46°52N 89°19W 308 B9
Ontong Java Plateau Pac. Oc. 1°0N 157°0E 277 A10
Ontur Spain 38°38N 1°29W 197 G3
Onverwacht Suriname 5°35N 55°11W 329 B6
Onyx U.S.A. 35°41N 118°14W 307 K8
Oodaaq Greenland 83°40N 30°40W 154 A8
Oodnadatta Australia 27°33S 135°30E 281 D2
Oodweyne Somali Rep. 9°25N 45°4E 267 C6
'Ō'ōkala U.S.A. 20°1N 155°17W 302 C6
Ōokayama Japan 35°36N 139°40E 140 B3
Ooku = Ōma Japan 41°45N 141°5E 220 D10
Ooldea Australia 30°27S 131°50E 279 F5
Oombulgurri Australia 15°15S 127°45E 278 C4
Oombulgurri ☼ Australia 15°10S 127°50E 278 C4
Oorindi Australia 20°40S 141°1E 280 C3
Oost-Vlaanderen □ Belgium 51°5N 3°50E 170 C3
Oostende Belgium 51°15N 2°54E 170 C2
Oosterhout Neths. 51°39N 4°47E 170 C4
Oosterschelde → Neths. 51°33N 4°0E 170 C4
Oosterwolde Neths. 53°0N 6°17E 170 B6
Oostpunt Curaçao 12°2N 68°44W 322 g
Oostzaan Tuindorp Neths. 52°25N 4°54E 112 A2
Ootacamund = Udagamandalam India 11°30N 76°44E 245 J3
Ootha Australia 33°6S 147°29E 283 B7
Ootsa L. Canada 53°50N 126°2W 296 C3
Ooty = Udagamandalam India 11°30N 76°44E 245 J3
Op Luang △ Thailand 18°12N 98°32E 236 C2
Opa-Locka U.S.A. 25°54N 80°15W 128 A1
Opa-Locka ✈ (OPF) U.S.A. 25°54N 80°16W 128 A1
Opacz Poland 52°10N 20°53E 142 B1
Opaka Bulgaria 43°28N 26°10E 203 C10
Opala Dem. Rep. of the Congo 0°40S 24°20E 264 C4
Opalenica Poland 52°18N 16°24E 185 F3
Opan Bulgaria 42°13N 25°41E 203 D9
Opanake Sri Lanka 6°35N 80°40E 245 L5
Opapa N.Z. 39°47S 176°42E 284 F5
Opasatika Canada 49°30N 82°50W 298 C3
Opasquia ⌓ Canada 53°33N 93°5W 298 B1
Opatija Croatia 45°21N 14°17E 199 C11
Opatów Poland 50°50N 21°27E 185 H8
Opava Czech Rep. 49°57N 17°58E 181 B10
Opelika U.S.A. 32°39N 85°23W 316 C4
Opelousas U.S.A. 30°32N 92°5W 314 F8
Opémisca, L. Canada 49°56N 74°52W 298 C5
Opheim U.S.A. 48°51N 106°24W 304 B10
Ophir U.S.A. 63°10N 156°31W 303 E8
Ophirton S. Africa 26°13S 28°1E 123 B2
Ophthalmia Ra. Australia 23°15S 119°30E 278 D2
Opi Nigeria 6°36N 7°28E 263 D6
Opihikao U.S.A. 19°26N 154°53W 302 D7
Opinaca → Canada 52°15N 78°2W 298 B4
Opinaca, Rés. Canada 52°39N 76°20W 298 B4
Opinnagau → Canada 54°12N 82°25W 298 B3
Opiscotéo, L. Canada 53°10N 68°10W 299 B6
Opobo Nigeria 4°35N 7°34E 263 E6
Opochka Russia 56°42N 28°45E 188 D5
Opoczno Poland 51°22N 20°18E 185 G7
Opol Phil. 8°31N 124°34E 233 G5
Opole Poland 50°42N 17°58E 185 H4
Opole Lubelskie Poland 51°9N 21°58E 185 G8
Opolskie □ Poland 50°30N 18°0E 185 H5
Opon = Lapu-Lapu Phil. 10°20N 123°55E 233 F4
Oponono L. Namibia 18°8S 15°45E 270 A2
Opornyy Kazakhstan 46°11N 54°25E 216 C4
Oporto = Porto Portugal 41°8N 8°40W 194 D2
Opotiki N.Z. 38°1S 177°19E 284 E6
Opp U.S.A. 31°17N 86°16W 316 D3
Oppdal Norway 62°35N 9°41E 164 B6
Oppegård Norway 59°45N 10°49E 133 B3
Oppeln = Opole Poland 50°42N 17°58E 185 H4
Oppem Belgium 50°56N 4°18E 116 A1
Óppido Mamertina Italy 38°16N 15°59E 201 D8
Oppland □ Norway 61°15N 9°40E 164 C6
Opportunity U.S.A. 47°39N 117°15W 304 C5
Oppsal Norway 59°53N 10°50E 133 A4
Oprişor Romania 44°17N 23°5E 182 F8
Oprtalj Croatia 45°23N 13°50E 199 C10
Opua N.Z. 35°19S 174°9E 284 B3
Opunake N.Z. 39°26S 173°52E 284 F2
Opuwo Namibia 18°3S 13°45E 270 A1
Opuzen Croatia 43°1N 17°34E 199 E14
Oquawka U.S.A. 40°56N 90°57W 310 D6
Or → Kazakhstan 51°11N 58°32E 216 B5
Ora Cyprus 34°51N 33°12E 207 F9
Ora Israel 31°45N 35°9E 123 B1
Oracabessa Jamaica 18°24N 76°57W 320 a
Oracle U.S.A. 32°37N 110°46W 305 K8
Oracuzar Peru 4°42S 78°6W 328 D2
Oradea Romania 47°2N 21°58E 182 C6
Oradell U.S.A. 40°57N 74°2W 132 A1
Oradell Res. U.S.A. 40°57N 74°1W 132 A1
Öræfajökull Iceland 64°2N 16°39W 155 C10
Orahovac Kosovo 42°24N 20°40E 202 D4
Orahovica Croatia 45°35N 17°52E 182 E2
Orai India 25°58N 79°30E 243 G8
Oraison France 43°55N 5°55E 175 E9
Oral = Zhayyq → Kazakhstan 47°0N 51°48E 187 E9
Oral Kazakhstan 51°20N 51°20E 190 E10
Oran Algeria 35°45N 0°39W 261 A4
Oran □ Algeria 35°0N 0°45W 261 B4
Orange N.S.W., Australia 33°15S 149°7E 283 B8
Orange Vaucluse, France 44°8N 4°47E 175 D8
Orange Calif., U.S.A. 33°47N 117°51W 307 M9
Orange Mass., U.S.A. 42°35N 72°19W 313 D12
Orange Tex., U.S.A. 30°6N 93°44W 314 F8
Orange Va., U.S.A. 38°15N 78°7W 309 F14
Orange → S. Africa 28°41S 16°28E 270 C2
Orange, C. Brazil 4°20N 51°30W 329 C7
Orange Bowl Stadium U.S.A. 25°46N 80°14W 128 B2
Orange City U.S.A. 28°57N 81°18W 317 G8
Orange Cove U.S.A. 36°38N 119°19W 306 J7
Orange Free State = Free State □ S. Africa 28°30S 27°0E 270 C4
Orange Grove U.S.A. 27°58N 97°56W 314 H6
Orange Hill Barbados 13°12N 59°36W 323 r
Orange Hill Jamaica 18°16N 77°59W 320 a
Orange Hill St. Vincent 13°19N 61°7W 323 n
Orange L. U.S.A. 29°25N 82°13W 317 F7
Orange Park U.S.A. 30°10N 81°42W 316 E8
Orange River Colony = Free State □ S. Africa 28°30S 27°0E 270 C4
Orange Walk Belize 18°6N 88°33W 319 D7
Orangeburg U.S.A. 33°30N 80°52W 316 B9
Orangeville Ont., Canada 43°55N 80°5W 312 C4
Orangeville Ill., U.S.A. 42°28N 89°39W 310 B7
Orangi Pakistan 24°54N 67°0E 123 A2
Orango Guinea-Biss. 11°5N 16°0W 262 C1
Orani Phil. 14°49N 120°32E 232 D3
Oranienburg Germany 52°45N 13°14E 178 C9
Oranje = Orange → S. Africa 28°41S 16°28E 270 C2
Oranjemund Namibia 28°38S 16°29E 270 C2
Oranjerivier S. Africa 29°40S 24°12E 270 C3
Oranjestad Aruba 12°32N 70°2W 322 f
Oranjestad St. Eustatius 17°28N 62°59W 322 a
Orap Vanuatu 15°58S 167°20E 287 E5
Oras Phil. 12°9N 125°28E 232 E5

Orašje Bos.-H. 45°11N 18°42E 182 E3
Orăştie Romania 45°50N 23°10E 183 E8
Orava → Slovak Rep. 49°9N 19°8E 181 B12
Orava, Vodna nádrž
Slovak Rep. 49°25N 19°35E 181 B12
Oraviţa Romania 45°2N 21°43E 182 E6
Orawia N.Z. 46°1S 167°50E 285 G2
Orb → France 43°15N 3°18E 174 E7
Orba → Italy 44°53N 8°37E 198 D5
Ørbæk Denmark 55°17N 10°39E 163 J4
Orbe Switz. 46°43N 6°32E 179 J2
Orbec France 49°1N 0°23E 172 C7
Orbetello Italy 42°27N 11°13E 199 F8
Órbigo → Spain 42°5N 5°42W 194 C5
Orbisonia U.S.A. 40°15N 77°54W 312 F7
Orbost Australia 37°40S 148°29E 283 D8
Örbyhus Sweden 60°15N 17°43E 162 D11
Orcadas Antarctica 60°44S 44°37W 151 C18
Orcas I. U.S.A. 48°42N 122°56W 306 B4
Orce Spain 37°44N 2°28W 197 H2
Orce → Spain 37°44N 2°28W 197 H2
Orchard City U.S.A. 38°50N 107°58W 304 G10
Orchard Homes U.S.A. 46°55N 114°4W 304 C6
Orchard Road Singapore 138 a1
Orchid I. = Lan Yü
Taiwan 22°4N 121°25E 225 D3
Orchies France 50°28N 3°14E 173 B10
Orchila, I. Venezuela 11°48N 66°10W 321 D6
Orchilla, Pta. Canary Is. 27°42N 18°10W 153 e1
Órcia → Italy 42°58N 11°21E 199 F8
Orco → Italy 45°10N 7°52E 198 C4
Orcopampa Peru 15°20S 72°23W 330 D3
Orcutt U.S.A. 34°52N 120°27W 307 L6
Ord U.S.A. 41°36N 98°56W 308 E4
Ord → Australia 15°33S 128°15E 278 C4
Ord, Mt. Australia 17°20S 125°34E 278 C4
Ord Mts. U.S.A. 34°39N 116°45W 307 L10
Ordenes = Ordes Spain 43°5N 8°29W 194 B2
Orderville U.S.A. 37°17N 112°38W 305 H7
Ordes Spain 43°5N 8°29W 194 B2
Ordesa y Monte Perido △
Spain 42°40N 0°10W 196 C4
Ording = St-Peter-Ording
Germany 54°20N 8°36E 178 A4
Ordos = Mu Us Shamo
China 39°0N 109°0E 226 E5
Ordrup Denmark 55°45N 12°34E 118 A3
Ordu Turkey 40°55N 37°53E 212 B7
Ordu □ Turkey 41°0N 37°50E 212 B7
Ordubad Azerbaijan 38°54N 46°1E 213 C12
Orduña Álava, Spain 42°58N 2°58W 196 C2
Orduña Granada, Spain 37°20N 3°30W 195 H7
Ordway U.S.A. 38°13N 103°46W 304 G12
Ordzhonikidze = Denisovka
Kazakhstan 52°27N 61°39E 216 B6
Ordzhonikidze = Vladikavkaz
Russia 43°0N 44°35E 191 J7
Ordzhonikidze = Yenakiyeve
Ukraine 48°15N 38°15E 189 H10
Ordzhonikidze Ukraine 47°39N 34°3E 189 J8
Ore Dem. Rep. of the Congo 3°17N 29°30E 268 B2
Ore Mts. = Erzgebirge
Germany 50°27N 12°55E 178 E8
Orealla Guyana 5°15N 57°23W 329 B6
Orebić Croatia 43°0N 17°11E 199 F14
Örebro Sweden 59°20N 15°18E 162 E9
Örebro län □ Sweden 59°27N 15°0E 162 E8
Orecchiella ⌂ Italy 44°16N 10°22E 198 D7
Orech Czech Rep. 50°1N 14°17E 135 B1
Oregon Ill., U.S.A. 42°1N 89°20W 310 B7
Oregon Ohio, U.S.A. 41°38N 83°25W 311 C13
Oregon Wis., U.S.A. 42°56N 89°23W 310 B7
Oregon □ U.S.A. 44°0N 121°0W 304 E3
Oregon City U.S.A. 45°21N 122°36W 306 E4
Oregon Dunes ⌂ U.S.A. 43°40N 124°10W 304 E1
Öregrund Sweden 60°21N 18°30E 162 D12
Öregrundsgrepen
Sweden 60°25N 18°15E 162 D12
Oregun Nigeria 6°35N 3°22E 124 A2
Orekhov = Orikhiv
Ukraine 47°30N 35°48E 189 J8
Orekhovo-Zuyevo Russia 55°50N 38°55E 188 E10
Orel Russia 52°57N 36°3E 189 F9
Orel □ Russia 52°30N 36°40E 189 F9
Orellana □ Ecuador 0°45S 76°25W 328 D2
Orellana, Canal de Spain 39°2N 6°0W 195 F5
Orellana, Embalse de Spain 39°5N 5°10W 195 F5
Orellana la Vieja Spain 39°1N 5°32W 195 F5
Orem U.S.A. 40°19N 111°42W 304 F8
Ören Turkey 37°3N 27°57E 205 D9
Orenburg Russia 51°45N 55°6E 186 D10
Örencik Turkey 39°16N 29°33E 205 B11
Orense = Ourense Spain 42°19N 7°55W 194 C3
Orepuki N.Z. 46°19S 167°46E 285 G2
Ørestad Denmark 55°38N 12°35E 118 B3
Orestes Pereyra Mexico 26°30N 105°39W 318 B3
Orestiada Greece 41°30N 26°33E 203 E10
Øresund Europe 55°45N 12°40E 163 J6
Oretana, Cordillera = Toledo,
Montes de Spain 39°33N 4°20W 195 F6
Oreti → N.Z. 46°28S 168°14E 285 G3
Orfanos Kolpos Greece 40°33N 24°0E 202 F7
Orford Ness U.K. 52°5N 1°35E 169 E9
Organ Pipe Cactus ⌂
U.S.A. 32°0N 112°52W 305 K7
Organos, Pta. de los
Canary Is. 28°12N 17°17W 153 e1
Organyà Spain 42°13N 1°20E 196 C6
Orgaz Spain 39°39N 3°53W 195 F7
Ørgenvika Norway 60°17N 9°42E 164 D6
Orgeyev = Orhei
Moldova 47°24N 28°50E 183 C13
Orgūn Afghan. 32°55N 69°12E 240 B3
Orhaneli Turkey 39°54N 28°59E 203 G12
Orhaneli → Turkey 39°50N 28°55E 203 G12
Orhangazi Turkey 40°29N 29°18E 203 F13
Orhei Moldova 47°24N 28°50E 183 C13
Orhon Gol → Mongolia 50°21N 106°0E 218 A10
Oria Italy 40°30N 17°38E 201 B10
Orida Niger 21°20N 12°15E 261 D7
Orient Heights U.S.A. 42°23N 70°59W 116 A3
Oriental, Cordillera Bolivia 17°0S 66°0W 331 D4
Oriental, Cordillera Colombia 6°0N 73°0W 328 B3
Oriental, Grand Erg Algeria 30°0N 6°30E 261 C6
Orientale □
Dem. Rep. of the Congo 2°20N 26°0E 268 B2
Oriente Argentina 38°44S 60°37W 334 D3
Orihuela Spain 38°7N 0°55W 197 G4
Orihuela del Tremedal
Spain 40°33N 1°39W 196 E3
Orikhiv Ukraine 47°30N 35°48E 189 J8
Orikum Albania 40°20N 19°26E 202 F3
Oril → Ukraine 48°40N 34°39E 189 H8
Orillia Canada 44°40N 79°24W 312 B5
Orinduik Guyana 4°40N 60°3W 329 C5
Orinoco → Venezuela 9°15N 61°30W 329 B5
Orinoco, Delta del
Venezuela 9°0N 61°30W 329 B5
Orion Canada 49°27N 110°49W 297 D6
Orion Ala., U.S.A. 31°58N 86°0W 316 D4
Orion Ill., U.S.A. 41°21N 90°23W 310 C6
Oriskany U.S.A. 43°10N 75°20W 313 C9
Orissa □ India 20°0N 84°0E 244 E7
Orissaare Estonia 58°34N 23°5E 188 C2
Oristano Italy 39°54N 8°36E 200 C1
Oristano, G. di Italy 39°50N 8°29E 200 C1
Orituco → Venezuela 8°45N 67°27W 328 B4
Oriximina Brazil 1°45S 55°52W 329 D6
Orizaba Mexico 18°51N 97°6W 319 D5
Orizaba, Pico de Mexico 18°58N 97°15W 319 D5
Orizare Bulgaria 42°44N 27°39E 203 D11
Orizona Brazil 17°3S 48°18W 333 E2
Ørje Norway 59°29N 11°39E 164 E8
Orjen Bos.-H. 42°35N 18°34E 202 D2
Orjiva Spain 36°53N 3°24W 195 J7
Orkanger Norway 63°18N 9°52E 164 A6
Örkelljunga Sweden 56°17N 13°17E 163 H7
Örken Sweden 57°6N 15°1E 163 G9
Örkény Hungary 47°9N 19°26E 182 C4
Orkhaniye = Botevgrad
Bulgaria 42°55N 23°47E 202 D7
Orkla → Norway 63°18N 9°51E 164 A6
Orkney S. Africa 26°58S 26°40E 270 C4
Orkney □ U.K. 59°2N 3°13W 167 B5
Orkney Is. U.K. 59°0N 3°0W 167 B6
Orland Calif., U.S.A. 39°45N 122°12W 306 F4
Orland Ind., U.S.A. 41°47N 85°12W 311 C11
Orland Park U.S.A. 41°38N 87°52W 311 C8
Orlando U.S.A. 28°32N 81°22W 133 A2
Orlando, C. d' Italy 38°10N 14°43E 201 D7
Orlando Dam S. Africa 26°15S 27°55E 123 B1
Orlando East S. Africa 26°14S 27°55E 123 B1
Orlando Executive ✈ (ORL)
U.S.A. 28°32N 81°20W 133 A2
Orlando Int. ✈ (MCO)
U.S.A. 28°26N 81°19W 133 B3
Orléanais France 48°0N 2°0E 173 E9
Orléans France 47°54N 1°52E 173 E8
Orleans Ind., U.S.A. 38°40N 86°27W 311 F10
Orleans Vt., U.S.A. 44°49N 72°12W 313 B12
Orléans, Î. d' Canada 46°54N 70°58W 299 C5
Orléansville = Ech Chéliff
Algeria 36°10N 1°20E 261 A5
Orlice → Czech Rep. 50°13N 15°50E 180 A8
Orlivka Ukraine 45°19N 28°27E 183 E13
Orlov = Khalturin Russia 58°40N 48°50E 186 C8
Orlov Slovak Rep. 49°17N 20°51E 181 B13
Orlov Gay Russia 50°56N 48°19E 190 E9
Orlová Czech Rep. 49°51N 18°26E 181 B11
Orlovat Serbia 45°14N 20°33E 182 E5
Orlovista U.S.A. 28°32N 81°27W 133 A2
Orlovo Russia 55°38N 37°22E 129 C2
Orly France 48°45N 2°23E 134 B3
Orly, Paris ✈ (ORY) France 48°44N 2°23E 134 B3
Ormara Pakistan 25°16N 64°33E 240 D2
Ormea Italy 44°9N 7°54E 198 D4
Ormesson-sur-Marne
France 48°47N 2°32E 134 B4
Ormilia Greece 40°16N 23°39E 202 F7
Ormoc Phil. 11°0N 124°37E 233 F5
Ormond Vic., Australia 37°54S 145°1E 128 B2
Ormond N.Z. 38°33S 177°56E 284 E6
Ormond Beach U.S.A. 29°17N 81°3W 317 F8
Ormond-by-the-Sea
U.S.A. 29°21N 81°4W 317 F8
Ormondville N.Z. 40°5S 176°19E 284 G5
Ormøya Norway 59°52N 10°45E 133 A3
Ormož Slovenia 46°25N 16°10E 199 B13
Ormskirk U.K. 53°35N 2°54W 168 D5
Ormstown Canada 45°8N 74°0W 313 A11
Ormtjernkampen △
Norway 61°12N 9°48E 164 C6
Ornans France 47°7N 6°10E 173 E13
Orne □ France 48°40N 0°5E 172 D7
Orne → France 49°18N 0°15W 172 C6
Orneta Poland 54°8N 20°9E 184 D7
Ornö Sweden 59°4N 18°24E 162 E12
Örnsköldsvik Sweden 63°17N 18°40E 162 A12
Oro N. Korea 40°1N 127°27E 224 B3
Oro → Mexico 25°35N 105°2W 318 B3
Oro Grande U.S.A. 34°36N 117°20W 307 L9
Oro Valley U.S.A. 32°26N 110°58W 305 K8
Orobie, Alpi Italy 46°7N 10°0E 198 B6
Orobie Bergamasche ⌂
Italy 46°0N 9°45E 198 C6
Orobie Valtellinesi ⌂ Italy 46°5N 9°45E 198 B6
Orocué Colombia 4°48N 71°20W 328 C3
Orodara Burkina Faso 11°0N 4°55W 262 C4
Orodo Nigeria 5°34N 7°4E 263 D6
Orofino U.S.A. 46°29N 116°15W 304 C5
Orohena, Mt. Tahiti 17°37S 149°28W 289 e
Orol Dengizi = Aral Sea
Asia 44°30N 60°0E 216 C5
Oromiya □ Ethiopia 7°0N 40°0E 257 F5
Oromocto Canada 45°54N 66°29W 299 C6
Oron Nigeria 4°48N 8°14E 263 E6
Orona Kiribati 4°31S 172°11W 277 A16
Orongo Chile 27°11S 109°47W 330 b
Orono Ont., Canada 43°59N 78°37W 312 C6
Orono Maine, U.S.A. 44°53N 68°40W 309 C19
Oronsay U.K. 56°1N 6°15W 167 E2
Oropesa Spain 39°57N 5°10W 194 F5
Oropuche → Trin. & Tob. 10°36N 61°6W 323 t
Oropuche Lagoon
Trin. & Tob. 10°14N 61°31W 323 t
Oroquieta Phil. 8°32N 123°44E 233 G4
Orós Brazil 6°15S 38°55W 332 C4
Orosei Italy 40°23N 9°42E 200 B2
Orosei, G. di Italy 40°15N 9°44E 200 B2
Orosháza Hungary 46°32N 20°42E 182 D5
Oroszlány Hungary 47°29N 18°19E 182 C3
Orote Pen. Guam 13°26N 144°38E 302 d
Orotukan Russia 62°16N 151°42E 215 C16
Oroville Calif., U.S.A. 39°31N 121°33W 306 F5
Oroville Wash., U.S.A. 48°56N 119°26W 304 B4
Oroville, L. U.S.A. 39°33N 121°29W 306 F5
Orpington U.K. 51°22N 0°6E 125 B4
Orrefors Sweden 56°50N 15°45E 163 H9
Orrick U.S.A. 39°13N 94°7W 310 E2
Orroroo Australia 32°43S 138°38E 282 B3
Orrviken Sweden 63°6N 14°26E 162 A8
Orrville U.S.A. 40°50N 81°46W 312 F3
Orsa Sweden 61°7N 14°37E 162 C8
Orsara di Púglia Italy 41°17N 15°16E 201 A8
Orsasjön Sweden 61°7N 14°37E 162 C8
Orsay, Musée d' Paris, France 134 b3
Orsha Belarus 54°30N 30°25E 188 E6
Örsjö Sweden 56°42N 15°45E 163 H9
Orsk Russia 51°12N 58°34E 216 B5
Orşova Romania 44°41N 22°25E 182 F7
Ørsta Norway 62°13N 6°8E 164 B3
Ørsted Denmark 56°30N 10°20E 163 H4
Örsundsbro Sweden 59°44N 17°18E 162 E11
Országos Levéltár Budapest, Hungary 117 b1
Orta Turkey 40°38N 33°6E 212 B5
Orta, L. d' Italy 45°49N 8°24E 198 C5
Orta Nova Italy 41°19N 15°42E 201 A8
Ortaca Turkey 36°49N 28°45E 205 E10
Ortakent Turkey 37°5N 27°21E 205 D9
Ortaklar Turkey 37°53N 27°30E 205 D9
Ortaköy Çorum, Turkey 40°16N 35°15E 212 B6
Ortaköy Istanbul, Turkey 41°3N 29°1E 122 B2
Ortaköy Niğde, Turkey 38°44N 34°3E 212 C5
Orte Italy 42°27N 12°23E 199 F9
Ortegal, C. Spain 43°43N 7°52W 194 B3
Orteguaza → Colombia 0°43N 75°16W 328 C2
Ortelsburg = Szczytno
Poland 53°33N 21°0E 184 E7
Orthez France 43°29N 0°48W 174 E3
Ortica Italy 45°28N 9°16E 129 B2
Ortigueira Spain 43°40N 7°50W 194 B3
Orting U.S.A. 47°6N 122°12W 306 C4
Ortisei Italy 46°34N 11°40E 199 B8
Ortles Italy 46°31N 10°33E 198 B7
Ortnevik Norway 61°6N 6°7E 164 C3
Ortoire → Trin. & Tob. 10°20N 61°0W 323 t
Ortón → Bolivia 10°50S 67°0W 330 C4
Ortona Italy 42°21N 14°24E 199 F11
Ortonville U.S.A. 45°19N 96°27W 308 C5
Oruba Nigeria 6°34N 3°24E 124 A2
Orukuizu Palau 7°10N 134°25E 288 c
Orūmīyeh Iran 37°40N 45°0E 213 D11
Orūmīyeh, Daryācheh-ye
Iran 37°50N 45°30E 213 D11
Orune Italy 40°24N 9°22E 200 B2
Oruro Bolivia 18°0S 67°9W 330 D4
Oruro □ Bolivia 18°40S 67°30W 330 D4
Orust Sweden 58°10N 11°40E 163 F5
Oruzgān □ Afghan. 33°0N 66°0E 240 B2
Orvault France 47°17N 1°38W 172 E5
Orvieto Italy 42°43N 12°7E 199 F9
Orwell N.Y., U.S.A. 43°35N 75°50W 313 C9
Orwell Ohio, U.S.A. 41°32N 80°52W 312 E4
Orwell → U.K. 51°59N 1°18E 169 F9
Orwigsburg U.S.A. 40°38N 76°6W 313 F8
Oryakhovo Bulgaria 43°40N 23°57E 202 C7
Orynyn Ukraine 48°46N 26°24E 183 B11
Oryol = Orel Russia 52°57N 36°3E 189 F9
Orzinuovi Italy 45°24N 9°55E 198 C6
Orzyc → Poland 52°46N 21°14E 185 F8
Orzysz Poland 53°50N 21°58E 184 E8
Os Norway 62°30N 11°14E 164 B8
Osa Russia 57°17N 55°26E 186 C10
Osa → Poland 53°33N 18°46E 184 E5
Osa, Pen. de Costa Rica 8°0N 84°0W 320 E3
Osage U.S.A. 43°17N 92°49W 308 D7
Osage → U.S.A. 38°36N 91°57W 310 F5
Osage City U.S.A. 38°38N 95°50W 308 F6
Ōsaka Japan 34°42N 135°30E 133 B2
Ōsaka □ Japan 34°30N 135°30E 223 C7
Ōsaka Castle Japan 34°41N 135°30E 133 A2
Ōsaka Harbour Japan 34°38N 135°25E 133 B1
Ōsaka Itami Int. ✈ (ITM)
Japan 34°46N 135°26E 133 A1
Ōsaka Kansai Int. ✈ (KIX)
Japan 34°27N 135°12E 133 B2
Ōsaka-Wan Japan 34°30N 135°18E 223 C7
Osakarovka Kazakhstan 50°33N 72°34E 217 B8
Ōsaki Kagoshima, Japan 31°25N 131°2E 222 F3
Ōsaki Tōkyō, Japan 35°36N 139°42E 140 B3
Osan S. Korea 37°11N 127°4E 224 D3
Osasco Brazil 23°31S 46°46W 137 B1
Osawatomie U.S.A. 38°31N 94°57W 308 F6
Osborn Plateau Ind. Oc. 14°45S 87°0E 273 F7
Osborne U.S.A. 39°26N 98°42W 308 F4
Osby Sweden 56°23N 13°59E 163 H7
Osceola Ark., U.S.A. 35°42N 89°58W 315 D10
Osceola Iowa, U.S.A. 41°2N 93°46W 310 C3
Osceola Mo., U.S.A. 38°3N 93°42W 310 F3
Oschatz Germany 51°17N 13°6E 178 D9
Oschersleben Germany 52°2N 11°14E 178 C7
Öschiri Italy 40°43N 9°6E 200 B2
Oscoda U.S.A. 44°26N 83°20W 312 B1
Osdorf Germany 52°24N 13°20E 115 B3
Osdorp Neths. 52°22N 4°47E 112 A1
Osečina Serbia 44°23N 19°34E 202 B3
Ösel = Saaremaa Estonia 58°30N 22°30E 188 C2
Osensjøen Norway 61°13N 11°50E 164 C8
Osery Russia 54°52N 38°28E 188 E10
Osgood U.S.A. 39°8N 85°18W 311 E11
Osgoode Canada 45°8N 75°36W 313 A9
Osgoode Hall Toronto, Canada 141 b2
Osh Kyrgyzstan 40°37N 72°49E 217 D8
Osh □ Kyrgyzstan 40°0N 73°0E 217 E8
Oshawa Canada 43°50N 78°50W 312 C6
Oshigambo Namibia 17°45S 16°5E 270 A2
Oshika-Hantō Japan 38°20N 141°30E 220 E10
Oshivelo Namibia 18°37S 17°10E 270 A2
Oshkosh Nebr., U.S.A. 41°24N 102°21W 308 E2
Oshkosh Wis., U.S.A. 44°1N 88°33W 308 C9
Oshmyany = Ashmyany
Belarus 54°26N 25°52E 177 A13
Oshnovīyeh Iran 37°2N 45°6E 213 D11
Oshodi Nigeria 6°33N 3°21E 124 A2
Oshogbo Nigeria 7°48N 4°37E 263 D5
Oshtorīnān Iran 34°1N 48°38E 213 E13
Oshwe
Dem. Rep. of the Congo 3°25S 19°28E 264 C3
Osi Nigeria 8°8N 5°14E 263 D6
Osieczna Poland 51°55N 16°40E 185 G3
Osijek Croatia 45°34N 18°41E 182 E3
Ósilo Italy 40°45N 8°40E 200 B1
Ósimo Italy 43°28N 13°30E 199 E10
Osintorf Belarus 54°40N 30°39E 188 E6
Osipenko = Berdyansk
Ukraine 46°45N 36°50E 189 J9
Osipovichi = Asipovichy
Belarus 53°19N 28°33E 177 B15
Osiyan India 26°43N 72°55E 242 F5
Osizweni S. Africa 27°49S 30°7E 271 C5
Oskaloosa U.S.A. 41°18N 92°39W 310 C4
Oskarshamn Sweden 57°15N 16°27E 163 G10
Oskarström Sweden 56°48N 12°58E 163 H6
Oskélanéo Canada 48°5N 75°15W 298 C4
Öskemen Kazakhstan 50°0N 82°36E 217 C10
Oskol → Ukraine 49°6N 37°25E 189 H9
Osku Iran 37°54N 46°8E 213 D12
Oslo Norway 59°54N 10°43E 133 A3
Oslo □ Norway 59°54N 10°43E 164 D7
Oslo ✈ (OSL) Norway 60°11N 11°5E 164 D8
Oslob Phil. 9°31N 123°26E 233 G4
Oslofjorden Norway 59°20N 10°35E 164 E7
Osmanabad India 18°5N 76°10E 244 E3
Osmancık Turkey 40°58N 34°47E 212 B6
Osmaniye Turkey 37°5N 36°10E 250 A7
Osmanlı Turkey 41°35N 26°51E 203 E10
Osmannagar India 18°32N 79°20E 244 E4
Ösmo Sweden 58°58N 17°55E 162 F11
Osnabrück Germany 52°17N 8°3E 178 C4
Ośno Lubuskie Poland 52°28N 14°51E 185 F1
Osoblaha Czech Rep. 50°17N 17°44E 181 A10
Osogovska Planina
Macedonia 42°10N 22°30E 202 D6
Osone Japan 35°31N 139°37E 140 B2
Osor Italy 44°42N 14°24E 199 D11
Osório Brazil 29°53S 50°17W 335 B5
Osório da Fonseca Brazil 3°52S 58°14W 329 D6
Osorno Chile 40°25S 73°0W 336 B2
Osorno Spain 42°24N 4°22W 194 C6
Osorno □ Chile 40°34S 73°9W 336 B2
Osorno, Vol. Chile 41°0S 72°30W 336 B2
Osorun Nigeria 6°33N 3°29E 124 A2
Osoyoos Canada 49°0N 119°30W 296 D5
Osøyro Norway 60°9N 5°30E 164 D2
Óspakseyri Iceland 65°27N 21°6W 160 D3
Ospiate Italy 45°32N 9°6E 129 A1
Ospika → Canada 56°20N 124°0W 296 B4
Osprey U.S.A. 27°12N 82°29W 317 H7
Osprey Reef Australia 13°52S 146°36E 280 A4
Oss Neths. 51°46N 5°32E 170 C5
Ossa, Mt. Australia 41°52S 146°3E 281 G4
Ossa, Oros Greece 39°47N 22°42E 204 B4
Ossa de Montiel Spain 38°58N 2°45W 197 G2
Ossabaw I. U.S.A. 31°50N 81°5W 316 D8
Ossabaw Sd. U.S.A. 31°50N 81°6W 316 D8
Osse → Lot-et-Garonne,
France 44°7N 0°17E 174 D4
Osse → Nigeria 6°10N 5°20E 263 D6
Ossersee = Zarasai
Lithuania 55°40N 26°20E 188 E4
Ossi Italy 40°40N 8°35E 200 B1
Ossining U.S.A. 41°10N 73°55W 313 E11
Ossipee U.S.A. 43°41N 71°7W 313 C13
Ossokmanuan L. Canada 53°25N 65°0W 299 B7
Ossora Russia 59°20N 163°13E 215 D17
Ostankino Russia 55°49N 37°37E 129 B3
Ostashkov Russia 57°4N 33°2E 188 D7
Östavall Sweden 62°26N 15°29E 162 B9
Østby Norway 61°15N 12°33E 164 C9
Oste → Germany 53°49N 9°2E 178 B5
Ostenburg = Pultusk
Poland 52°43N 21°6E 185 F8
Ostend = Oostende
Belgium 51°15N 2°54E 170 C2
Ostend N.Z. 36°48S 175°2E 284 C4
Oster Ukraine 50°57N 30°53E 177 C16
Österbotten = Pohjanmaa
Finland 62°58N 22°50E 160 E20
Østerbro Copenhagen, Denmark 118 a1
Osterburg Sachsen-Anhalt,
Germany 52°47N 11°45E 178 C7
Osterburg Pa., U.S.A. 40°16N 78°31W 312 F6
Österburken Germany 49°25N 9°26E 179 F5
Österbybruk Sweden 60°13N 17°55E 162 D11
Österbymo Sweden 57°49N 15°15E 163 G9
Österdalälven → Sweden 60°30N 15°7E 162 C7
Østerdalen Norway 61°40N 10°50E 162 C4
Österfärnebo Sweden 60°19N 16°48E 162 D10
Österforse Sweden 63°9N 17°3E 162 A11
Östergötlands län □
Sweden 58°35N 15°45E 163 F9
Osterholz-Scharmbeck
Germany 53°13N 8°47E 178 B4
Østerild Denmark 57°2N 8°51E 163 G2
Osterley U.K. 51°28N 0°21W 125 B1
Osterley Park U.K. 51°29N 0°21W 125 B1
Östermalm Stockholm, Sweden 139 a3
Östermyra = Seinäjoki
Finland 62°40N 22°51E 160 E20
Osterode Germany 51°43N 10°15E 178 D6
Osterode in Ostpreussen = Ostróda
Poland 53°42N 19°58E 184 E6
Österreich = Austria ■
Europe 47°0N 14°0E 180 E7
Österreich ober der Ems =
Oberösterreich □
Austria 48°10N 14°0E 180 C7
Österskär Sweden 59°26N 18°16E 139 A3
Östersund Sweden 63°10N 14°38E 162 A8
Östervåla Sweden 60°11N 17°11E 162 D11
Østfold □ Norway 59°25N 11°25E 164 E8
Ostfriesische Inseln
Germany 53°42N 7°0E 178 B3
Ostfriesland Germany 53°20N 7°30E 178 B3
Østgrønland = Tunu □
Greenland 75°0N 30°0W 154 C7
Östhammar Sweden 60°16N 18°22E 162 D12
Óstia, Lido di Italy 41°43N 12°17E 199 G9
Óstia Malpasso Italy 41°47N 12°26E 136 C1
Ostiense Italy 41°51N 12°29E 136 B1
Ostíglia Italy 45°4N 11°8E 199 C8
Östmark Sweden 60°17N 12°45E 162 D6
Østmarkkapellet Norway 59°52N 10°51E 133 A4
Ostøya Norway 59°52N 10°34E 133 A2
Östra Husby Sweden 58°35N 16°33E 163 F10
Ostrava Czech Rep. 49°51N 18°18E 181 B11
Ostravský □ Czech Rep. 49°55N 17°58E 181 B10
Østre Aker Norway 59°54N 10°49E 133 A3
Ostróda Poland 53°42N 19°58E 184 E6
Ostrogozhsk Russia 50°55N 39°7E 189 G10
Ostroh Ukraine 50°20N 26°30E 177 C14
Ostrołęka Poland 53°4N 21°32E 185 E8
Ostrov Bulgaria 43°40N 24°9E 203 C8
Ostrov Czech Rep. 50°18N 12°57E 180 A5
Ostrov Romania 44°6N 27°24E 183 F12
Ostrov Russia 57°25N 28°20E 188 D5
Ostrów Lubelski Poland 51°29N 22°51E 185 G9
Ostrów Mazowiecka
Poland 52°50N 21°51E 185 F8
Ostrów Wielkopolski
Poland 51°36N 17°44E 185 G4
Ostrowiec-Świętokrzyski
Poland 50°55N 21°22E 185 H8
Ostrowo = Ostrów Wielkopolski
Poland 51°36N 17°44E 185 G4
Ostrožac Bos.-H. 43°43N 17°49E 182 G2
Ostrzeszów Poland 51°25N 17°52E 185 G4
Ostseebad Kühlungsborn
Germany 54°8N 11°44E 178 A7
Oststirol □ Austria 46°50N 12°30E 180 E5
Ostuni Italy 40°44N 17°35E 201 B10
Ostyako-Vogulsk =
Khanty-Mansiysk Russia 61°0N 69°0E 214 C7
Osum → Albania 40°40N 20°10E 202 F4
Osŭm → Bulgaria 43°40N 24°50E 203 C8
Ōsumi-Hantō Japan 31°20N 130°55E 222 F2
Ōsumi-Kaikyō Japan 30°55N 131°0E 221 J5
Ōsumi-Shotō Japan 30°30N 130°0E 221 J5
Osun □ Nigeria 7°30N 4°30E 263 D5
Osuna Spain 37°14N 5°8W 195 H5
Oswegatchie → U.S.A. 44°42N 75°30W 313 B9
Oswego U.S.A. 43°27N 76°31W 313 C8
Oswego → U.S.A. 43°27N 76°30W 313 C8
Oswestry U.K. 52°52N 3°3W 168 E4
Oświęcim Poland 50°2N 19°11E 185 H6
Ōta Fukui, Japan 35°57N 136°3E 223 B8
Ōta Gumma, Japan 36°18N 139°22E 223 A11
Ōta Tōkyō, Japan 35°34N 139°41E 140 B3
Ōta-Gawa → Japan 34°21N 132°18E 222 C4
Otaci Moldova 48°27N 27°47E 183 B12
Otago □ N.Z. 45°15S 170°0E 285 F4
Otago Harbour N.Z. 45°47S 170°42E 285 F5
Otago Pen. N.Z. 45°48S 170°39E 285 F5
Otaheite B. Trin. & Tob. 10°15N 61°30W 323 t
Otahuhu N.Z. 36°56S 174°51E 284 C3
Ōtake Japan 34°12N 132°13E 222 C4
Otaki Japan 35°17N 140°15E 223 B12
Otaki N.Z. 40°45S 175°10E 284 G4
Otane N.Z. 39°54S 176°39E 284 F5
Otaniemi Finland 60°11N 24°49E 121 B1
Otari Open Air Museum
N.Z. 41°16S 174°46E 143 B1
Otaru Japan 43°10N 141°0E 220 C10
Otaru-Wan = Ishikari-Wan
Japan 43°25N 141°1E 220 C10
Otautau N.Z. 46°9S 168°1E 285 G3
Otava → Czech Rep. 49°26N 14°12E 180 B7
Otavalo Ecuador 0°13N 78°20W 328 C2
Otavi Namibia 19°40S 17°24E 270 A2
Otawara Japan 36°50N 140°5E 221 F10
Otchinjau Angola 16°30S 13°56E 265 F2
Otego U.S.A. 42°23N 75°10W 313 D9
Oteiza = Marihatag Phil. 8°48N 126°18E 233 G6
Otelec Romania 45°36N 20°50E 182 E5
Otelnuk, L. Canada 56°9N 68°12W 299 A6
Oţelu Roşu Romania 45°32N 22°22E 182 E7
Otero de Rey = Outeiro de Rei
Spain 43°6N 7°36W 194 B3
Othello U.S.A. 46°50N 119°10W 304 C4
Othoni Greece 39°52N 19°22E 206 B9
Othris, Oros Greece 39°2N 22°37E 204 B4
Oti → Africa 7°48N 0°8E 263 D5
Oti ⌂ Togo 10°40N 0°35E 263 C5
Otira N.Z. 42°49S 171°35E 285 C6
Otira Gorge N.Z. 42°53S 171°33E 285 C6
Otish, Mts. Canada 52°22N 70°30W 299 B5
Otjiwarongo Namibia 20°30S 16°33E 270 B2
Otmuchów Poland 50°28N 17°10E 185 H4
Oto Tolu Group Tonga 20°21S 174°32W 287 Q13
Otočac Croatia 44°53N 15°12E 199 D12
Otoineppu Japan 44°44N 142°16E 220 B11
Otok Croatia 43°42N 16°44E 199 E13
Otomavi = Korsakov
Russia 46°36N 142°42E 215 E15
Oton Phil. 10°42N 122°29E 233 F4
Otopeni, Bucureşti ✈ (OTP)
Romania 44°30N 26°11E 183 F11
Otorohanga N.Z. 38°12S 175°14E 284 E4
Otoskwin → Canada 52°13N 88°6W 298 B2
Ōtoyo Japan 33°43N 133°45E 222 D5
Otpor = Zabaykalsk
Russia 49°40N 117°25E 215 E12
Otra → Norway 58°9N 8°1E 164 F5
Otradnyy Russia 53°22N 51°21E 190 D10
Otranto Italy 40°9N 18°28E 201 B11
Otranto, C. d' Italy 40°7N 18°30E 201 B11
Otranto, Str. of Italy 40°15N 18°40E 201 B11
Otrobanda Curaçao 12°7N 68°57W 322 g
Otrokovice Czech Rep. 49°12N 17°32E 181 B10
Otse S. Africa 25°2S 25°45E 270 C4
Otsego U.S.A. 42°27N 85°42W 311 B11
Otsego L. U.S.A. 42°45N 74°53W 313 D10
Ōtsu Japan 35°0N 135°50E 223 C7
Otsuka Japan 35°43N 139°44E 140 A3
Ōtsuki Japan 35°36N 138°57E 223 B10
Otta Norway 61°46N 9°32E 164 C6
Otta → Norway 61°46N 9°31E 164 C6
Ottakring Austria 48°12N 16°18E 142 A1
Ottapalam India 10°46N 76°23E 245 J3
Ottávia Italy 41°57N 12°24E 136 B1
Ottawa = Outaouais →
Canada 45°27N 74°8W 298 C5
Ottawa Ont., Canada 45°26N 75°42W 313 A9
Ottawa Ill., U.S.A. 41°21N 88°51W 311 C8
Ottawa Kans., U.S.A. 38°37N 95°16W 308 F6
Ottawa Ohio, U.S.A. 41°1N 84°3W 311 C12
Ottawa Is. Canada 59°35N 80°10W 295 F15
Ottélé Cameroon 3°38N 11°19E 263 E7
Ottensheim Austria 48°21N 14°12E 180 C7
Otter Cr. → U.S.A. 44°13N 73°17W 313 B11
Otter Creek U.S.A. 29°19N 82°46W 317 F7
Otter Lake Canada 45°17N 79°56W 312 A5
Otterbäcken Sweden 58°57N 14°3E 163 F8
Otterbein U.S.A. 40°29N 87°6W 311 D9
Otterndorf Germany 53°48N 8°53E 178 B4
Otterøya Norway 62°45N 6°50E 164 B3
Otterup Denmark 55°30N 10°22E 163 J4
Otterville Ont., Canada 42°55N 80°36W 312 D4
Otterville Mo., U.S.A. 38°42N 93°0W 310 F4
Ottery S. Africa 34°1S 18°32E 118 B2
Ottery St. Mary U.K. 50°44N 3°17W 169 G4
Ottilien Reef Papua N. G. 4°33S 148°49E 286 C5
Ottmachau = Otmuchów
Poland 50°28N 17°10E 185 H4
Otto Beit Bridge Zimbabwe 15°59S 28°56E 269 F2
Ottobrunn Germany 48°3N 11°40E 131 B3
Ottosdal S. Africa 26°46S 25°59E 270 C4
Ottoville U.S.A. 40°57N 84°22W 311 D12
Ottumwa U.S.A. 41°1N 92°25W 310 D4
Otukpa Nigeria 7°9N 7°41E 263 D6
Otuquis △ Bolivia 19°45S 58°44W 331 D6
Oturkpo Nigeria 7°16N 8°8E 263 D6
Otvazhnoye = Zhigulevsk
Russia 53°28N 49°30E 190 D9
Otvazhny = Zhigulevsk
Russia 53°28N 49°30E 190 D9
Otway, B. Chile 53°30S 74°0W 336 D2
Otway, C. Australia 38°52S 143°30E 282 E5
Otway, Seno de Chile 53°0S 71°30W 336 D2
Otway △ Australia 38°47S 143°34E 282 E5
Otwock Poland 52°5N 21°20E 185 F8
Otyniya Ukraine 48°44N 24°51E 183 B9
Ötztaler Ache → Austria 47°14N 10°50E 180 D3
Ötztaler Alpen Austria 46°56N 11°0E 180 E3
Ou → Laos 20°4N 102°13E 236 B4
Ou-Sammyaku Japan 39°20N 140°35E 220 E10
Ouachita → U.S.A. 31°38N 91°49W 314 F9
Ouachita, L. U.S.A. 34°34N 93°12W 314 D8
Ouachita Mts. U.S.A. 34°30N 94°30W 314 D7
Ouadâne Mauritania 20°50N 11°40W 260 D2
Ouadda C.A.R. 8°15N 22°20E 264 A4
Ouaddaï □ Chad 13°0N 21°0E 259 F4
Ouagadougou
Burkina Faso 12°25N 1°30W 263 C4
Ouahigouya Burkina Faso 13°31N 2°25W 262 C4
Ouahran = Oran Algeria 35°45N 0°39W 261 A4
Oualâta Mauritania 17°20N 6°55W 262 B3
Ouallah Comoros Is. 12°19S 43°39E 272 a
Ouallam Niger 14°23N 2°10E 263 C5
Ouallene Algeria 24°41N 1°11E 261 D5
Ouanary Fr. Guiana 4°13N 51°40W 329 C7
Ouanda Djallé C.A.R. 8°55N 22°53E 264 A4
Ouandago C.A.R. 7°13N 18°50E 264 A3
Ouandja C.A.R. 8°28N 23°17E 264 A4
Ouandjia, Bahr → C.A.R. 9°35N 21°43E 264 A4
Ouandjia-Vakaga ⌂ C.A.R. 9°2N 22°18E 264 A4
Ouangani Mayotte 12°50S 45°8E 272 b
Ouango C.A.R. 4°19N 22°30E 264 B4
Ouani Comoros Is. 12°9S 44°18E 272 a
Ouantonou C.A.R. 7°19N 15°18E 264 A3
Ouarâne Mauritania 21°0N 10°30W 260 D2
Ouargaye Burkina Faso 11°40N 0°5E 263 C5
Ouargla Algeria 31°59N 5°16E 261 B6
Ouargla □ Algeria 30°30N 6°10E 261 B6
Ouarkoye Burkina Faso 12°5N 3°40W 262 C4
Ouarkziz, Jebel Algeria 28°50N 8°0W 260 C3
Ouarra → C.A.R. 5°5N 24°26E 264 A4
Ouarzazate Morocco 30°55N 6°50W 260 B3
Ouarzazate □ Morocco 30°45N 6°30W 260 B3
Ouassouas Mali 16°10N 1°23E 263 B5
Ouatagouna Mali 15°11N 0°43E 263 B5
Ouatere C.A.R. 5°30N 19°8E 264 A3
Oubangi →
Dem. Rep. of the Congo 0°30S 17°50E 264 C3
Oubarakai, O. → Algeria 27°20N 9°0E 261 C6
Ouche → France 47°6N 5°16E 173 E12
Oud Zuid Amsterdam, Neths. 112 c1
Ouddorp Neths. 51°50N 3°57E 170 C3
Oude Kerk Amsterdam, Neths. 112 a2
Oude Rijn → Neths. 52°12N 4°24E 170 B4
Oudeïka Mali 17°30N 1°40W 263 B4
Oudenaarde Belgium 50°50N 3°37E 170 D3
Ouderkerk Neths. 52°18N 4°55E 112 B2
Oudon → France 47°41N 0°53W 172 E6
Oudtshoorn S. Africa 33°35S 22°14E 270 D3
Oued Zem Morocco 32°52N 6°34W 260 B3
Ouégoa N. Cal. 20°20S 164°26E 288 d
Oueita Chad 17°47N 20°39E 259 E4
Ouella Niger 14°48N 3°38E 263 C5
Ouellé Ivory C. 7°26N 4°1W 262 D4
Ouémé → Benin 6°30N 2°30E 263 D5
Ouenza Algeria 35°57N 8°4E 261 A6
Ouessa Burkina Faso 11°4N 2°47W 262 C4
Ouessant, Î. d' France 48°28N 5°6W 172 D1
Ouesso Congo 1°37N 16°5E 264 B3
Ouest □ Cameroon 5°30N 10°30E 263 D7
Ouest, Pte. de l' Canada 49°52N 64°40W 299 C7
Ouezzane Morocco 34°51N 5°35W 260 B3
Ougarou Burkina Faso 12°10N 0°58E 263 C5
Oughter, L. Ireland 54°1N 7°28W 166 B4
Oughterard Ireland 53°26N 9°18W 166 C2
Ouham → C.A.R. 6°35N 15°12E 264 A3
Ouhan → Chad 9°18N 18°14E 259 G3
Ouidah Benin 6°25N 2°0E 263 D5
Ouidi Niger 14°10N 13°0E 259 F2
Ouissongo Angola 7°40S 15°41E 265 E3
Ouistreham France 49°17N 0°18W 172 C6
Oujda Morocco 34°41N 1°55W 261 B4
Oujda □ Morocco 33°18N 2°24W 260 B4
Oujeft Mauritania 20°2N 13°0W 260 D2
Oulad-Teïma Morocco 30°24N 9°12W 260 B3
Oulainen Finland 64°17N 24°47E 160 D21
Ould Yenjé Mauritania 15°38N 12°16W 262 B2
Ouled Djellal Algeria 34°28N 5°2E 261 B6
Ouled Naïl, Mts. des
Algeria 34°30N 3°30E 261 B5
Ouli Cameroon 5°12N 14°33E 264 A2
Oullins France 45°43N 4°49E 175 C8
Oulmès Morocco 33°17N 6°0W 260 B3
Oulou, Bahr → C.A.R. 9°48N 21°32E 264 A4
Oulu Finland 65°1N 25°29E 160 D21
Oulujärvi Finland 64°25N 27°15E 160 D22
Oulujoki → Finland 65°1N 25°30E 160 D21
Oulunkylä Finland 60°13N 24°58E 121 B2
Oulx Italy 45°2N 6°50E 198 C3
Oum Chalouba Chad 15°48N 20°46E 259 E4
Oum-el-Bouaghi Algeria 35°55N 7°6E 261 A6
Oum-el-Bouaghi □ Algeria 35°50N 7°5E 261 A6
Oum el Ksi Algeria 29°4N 6°59W 260 C3
Oum-er-Rbia, O. →
Morocco 33°19N 8°21W 260 B3
Oum Hadjer Chad 13°18N 19°41E 259 F3
Oum Hadjer, O. → Chad 16°38N 20°14E 259 E4
Oumé Ivory C. 6°21N 5°27W 262 D3
Oumm ed Droûs Guebli, Sebkhet
Mauritania 24°3N 11°45W 260 D2
Oumm ed Droûs Telli, Sebkhet
Mauritania 24°20N 11°30W 260 D2
Ounane, Dj. Algeria 25°4N 7°19E 261 C6
Ounasjoki → Finland 66°31N 25°40E 160 C21
Ounguati Namibia 22°0S 15°46E 270 B2
Ounianga Kébir Chad 19°4N 20°29E 259 E4
Ounianga Sérir Chad 18°54N 20°51E 259 E4
Ounissoui Niger 17°34N 12°13E 259 E2
Our → Lux. 49°55N 6°5E 170 E6
Oura, Akra Greece 38°10N 26°2E 205 C8
Oura-wan Japan 26°32N 128°4E 288 a
Ouranoupoli Greece 40°20N 23°59E 202 F7
Ourârene Niger 19°30N 7°10E 263 B6
Ourari, Tarso Chad 21°27N 17°27E 259 D3
Ouray U.S.A. 38°1N 107°40W 305 G10
Ourcq → France 49°1N 3°1E 173 C10
Ourcq, Canal de l' France 48°54N 2°28E 134 A3
Ourém Brazil 1°33S 47°6W 332 B2
Ourense Spain 42°19N 7°55W 194 C3
Ourense □ Spain 42°15N 7°51W 194 C3
Ouricuri Brazil 7°53S 40°5W 332 C3
Ourinhos Brazil 23°0S 49°54W 335 A6
Ourique Portugal 37°38N 8°16W 195 H2
Ouro Fino Brazil 22°16S 46°25W 335 A6
Ouro-Ndia Mali 15°8N 4°35W 262 B4
Ouro Prêto Brazil 20°20S 43°30W 333 F3
Ouro Prêto do Oeste
Brazil 10°40S 62°18W 331 C5
Ouro Sogui Senegal 15°36N 13°19W 262 B2
Oursi Burkina Faso 14°41N 0°27W 263 C4
Ourthe → Belgium 50°29N 5°35E 170 D5
Ouse → E. Sussex, U.K. 50°47N 0°4E 169 G8
Ouse → N. Yorks., U.K. 53°44N 0°55W 168 D7
Oust France 42°52N 1°13E 174 F5
Oust → France 47°35N 2°6W 172 E4
Outamba-Kilimi △
S. Leone 9°50N 12°40W 262 D2
Outaouais → Canada 45°27N 74°8W 298 C5
Outardes → Canada 49°24N 69°30W 299 C6
Outat Oulad el Haj
Morocco 33°22N 3°42W 261 B4
Outeiro de Rei Spain 43°6N 7°36W 194 B3
Outer Hebrides U.K. 57°30N 7°40W 167 D1
Outer Mission U.S.A. 37°43N 122°26W 136 B2
Outes = A Serra de Outes
Spain 42°52N 8°55W 194 C2
Outjo Namibia 20°5S 16°7E 270 B2
Outlook Canada 51°30N 107°0W 297 C7
Outokumpu Finland 62°43N 29°1E 160 E23
Outreau France 50°40N 1°36E 173 B8
Outremont Canada 45°31N 73°36W 130 A2
Ouvéa, Î. N. Cal. 20°35S 166°35E 288 d
Ouvèze → France 43°59N 4°51E 175 E8
Ouyen Australia 35°1S 142°22E 282 C5
Ouzinkie U.S.A. 57°56N 152°30W 303 H9
Ouzouer-le-Marché France 47°54N 1°32E 173 E8
Ovacık Turkey 36°11N 33°40E 250 B4
Ovada Italy 44°38N 8°38E 198 D5
Ovahe Chile 27°5S 109°19W 330 b
Ovalau Fiji 17°40S 178°48E 287 A2
Ovalle Chile 30°33S 71°18W 334 C1
Ovamboland Namibia 18°30S 16°0E 270 A2
Ovan Gabon 0°19N 12°10E 264 B2
Ovanåker Sweden 61°22N 15°53E 162 C9
Ovar Portugal 40°51N 8°40W 194 E2
Ovau Solomon Is. 6°40S 156°8E 287 L9
Overath Germany 50°56N 7°17E 178 E3
Overflakkee Neths. 51°44N 4°10E 170 C4
Overijse Belgium 50°47N 4°32E 116 B3
Overijssel □ Neths. 52°25N 6°35E 170 B6
Overland U.S.A. 38°42N 90°21W 310 F6
Overland Park U.S.A. 38°58N 94°40W 308 F6
Overlander Roadhouse
Australia 26°19S 114°28E 279 E1
Overton U.S.A. 36°33N 114°27W 307 J12
Övertorneå Sweden 66°23N 23°38E 160 C20
Överum Sweden 58°0N 16°20E 163 F10
Ovid Mich., U.S.A. 43°1N 84°22W 311 A12
Ovid N.Y., U.S.A. 42°41N 76°49W 313 D8
Ovidiopol Ukraine 46°15N 30°30E 189 J6
Ovidiu Romania 44°16N 28°34E 183 F13
Oviedo Spain 43°25N 5°50W 194 B5
Oviedo Fla., U.S.A. 28°40N 81°13W 317 G8
Oviksfjällen Sweden 63°0N 13°49E 162 A7
Ovišrags Latvia 57°33N 21°44E 184 A8
Ovoot Mongolia 45°21N 113°45E 226 B7
Övör Hangay □ Mongolia 45°0N 102°30E 226 B2
Ovoro Nigeria 5°26N 7°16E 263 D6
Øvre Årdal Norway 61°19N 7°48E 164 C4
Övre Fryken Sweden 60°0N 13°7E 162 E7
Øvre Rendal Norway 61°54N 11°4E 164 C8
Øvre Rindal Norway 63°6N 9°10E 164 A6
Øvre Sirdal Norway 58°48N 6°43E 164 F3
Ovruch Ukraine 51°25N 28°45E 177 C15
Owaka N.Z. 46°27S 169°40E 285 G4
Owambo = Ovamboland
Namibia 18°30S 16°0E 270 A2
Owando Congo 0°29S 15°55E 264 C3
Owariasahi Japan 35°10N 137°5E 223 B9
Owasco L. U.S.A. 42°50N 76°31W 313 D8
Owase Japan 34°7N 136°12E 223 C8
Owatonna U.S.A. 44°5N 93°14W 308 C7
Owbeh Afghan. 34°28N 63°10E 240 B1
Owego U.S.A. 42°6N 76°16W 313 D8

Owen Australia 34°15S 138°32E 282 C3
Owen, Mt. N.Z. 41°35S 172°33E 285 B7
Owen Falls Dam = Nalubaale Dam Uganda 0°30N 33°5E 268 B3
Owen Sound Canada 44°35N 80°55W 312 B4
Owen Stanley Ra. Papua N. G. 8°30S 147°0E 286 E4
Owendo Gabon 0°17N 9°30E 264 B1
Oweniny → Ireland 54°8N 9°34W 166 B2
Owens → U.S.A. 36°32N 117°59W 306 J9
Owens L. U.S.A. 36°26N 117°57W 307 J9
Owensboro U.S.A. 37°46N 87°7W 311 G9
Owensville Ind., U.S.A. 38°16N 87°41W 311 F9
Owensville Mo., U.S.A. 38°21N 91°30W 310 F5
Owenteik Guyana 4°27N 59°35W 329 C6
Owenton U.S.A. 38°32N 84°50W 311 F12
Owerri Nigeria 5°29N 7°0E 263 D6
Owhango N.Z. 39°0S 175°23E 284 F4
Owhiro Bay N.Z. 41°21S 174°45E 143 C1
Owingsville U.S.A. 38°9N 83°46W 311 F13
Owl → Canada 57°51N 92°44W 297 B10
Owo Nigeria 7°10N 5°39E 263 D6
Oworonsoki Nigeria 6°32N 3°24E 124 A2
Owosso U.S.A. 43°0N 84°10W 311 B12
Owyhee U.S.A. 41°57N 116°6W 304 F5
Owyhee → U.S.A. 43°49N 117°2W 304 E5
Owyhee, L. U.S.A. 43°38N 117°14W 304 E5
Ox Mts. = Slieve Gamph Ireland 54°6N 9°0W 166 B3
Oxapampa Peru 10°33S 75°26W 330 C2
Öxarfjörður Iceland 66°15N 16°45W 155 A10
Oxbow Canada 49°14N 102°10W 297 D8
Oxelösund Sweden 58°43N 17°5E 163 F11
Oxford N.Z. 43°18S 172°11E 285 D7
Oxford Oxon., U.K. 51°46N 1°15W 169 F6
Oxford Ala., U.S.A. 33°36N 85°51W 316 B4
Oxford Iowa, U.S.A. 41°43N 91°47W 310 C5
Oxford Mass., U.S.A. 42°7N 71°52W 313 D13
Oxford Mich., U.S.A. 42°49N 83°16W 311 B13
Oxford Miss., U.S.A. 34°22N 89°31W 315 D10
Oxford N.C., U.S.A. 36°19N 78°35W 315 C15
Oxford N.Y., U.S.A. 42°27N 75°36W 313 D9
Oxford Ohio, U.S.A. 39°31N 84°45W 311 E12
Oxford L. Canada 54°51N 95°37W 297 C9
Oxford Street London, U.K. 125 b3
Oxfordshire □ U.K. 51°48N 1°16W 169 F6
Oxgangs U.K. 55°54N 3°13W 121 B2
Oxia Greece 38°18N 21°6E 207 C3
Oxie Sweden 55°33N 13°6E 163 J7
Oxilithos Greece 38°35N 24°7E 204 C6
Oxley Australia 34°11S 144°6E 282 C6
Oxley Wild Rivers △ Australia 30°57S 152°12E 283 A10
Oxnard U.S.A. 34°12N 119°11W 307 L7
Oxon Hill U.S.A. 38°48N 76°59W 143 C4
Oxsjövålen Sweden 62°34N 13°57E 162 B7
Oxus = Amudarya → Uzbekistan 43°58N 59°34E 216 D5
Oya Malaysia 2°55N 111°55E 235 B4
Oyabe Japan 36°47N 136°56E 223 A8
Oyama Japan 36°18N 139°48E 223 A11
Oyambre ⌓ Spain 43°22N 4°21W 194 B6
Oyapock → Fr. Guiana 4°8N 51°40W 329 C7
Øye Norway 58°16N 6°49E 164 F3
Oyem Gabon 1°34N 11°31E 264 B2
Oyen Canada 51°22N 110°28W 297 C6
Øyer Norway 61°16N 10°25E 164 C7
Øyeren Norway 59°50N 11°15E 164 E8
Oykel → U.K. 57°56N 4°26W 167 D4
Oymyakon Russia 63°25N 142°44E 215 C15
Oyo Congo 0°0 15°51E 264 C3
Oyo Nigeria 7°46N 3°56E 263 D5
Oyo Sudan 21°58N 36°10E 256 C4
Oyo □ Nigeria 8°15N 3°30E 263 D5
Oyodo Japan 34°42N 135°29E 133 A1
Oyón Peru 10°37S 76°47W 330 C2
Oyonnax France 46°16N 5°40E 173 F12
Oyrot = Gorno-Altay □ Russia 51°0N 86°0E 217 B11
Oyrot-Tura = Gorno-Altaysk Russia 51°50N 86°5E 217 B11
Øyslebø Norway 58°9N 7°34E 164 F4
Oyster Bay U.S.A. 40°52N 73°32W 313 F11
Oyster Harbour = Ladysmith Canada 49°0N 123°49W 306 B3
Oyster Rock India 18°54N 72°49E 130 B1
Oyster Rocks Pakistan 24°48N 66°59E 123 B2
Øystese Norway 60°22N 6°9E 164 D3
Ōyūbari Japan 43°1N 142°5E 220 C11
Oyyl → Kazakhstan 49°4N 54°40E 216 C4
Özalp Turkey 38°39N 43°59E 213 C10
Ozamiz Phil. 8°15N 123°50E 233 G4
Ozar = Ojhar India 20°6N 73°56E 244 D1
Ozark Ala., U.S.A. 31°28N 85°39W 316 D4
Ozark Ark., U.S.A. 35°29N 93°50W 314 D8
Ozark Mo., U.S.A. 37°1N 93°12W 308 G7
Ozark Plateau U.S.A. 37°20N 91°40W 308 G8
Ozarks, L. of the U.S.A. 38°12N 92°38W 310 F4
Ożarów Poland 50°53N 21°40E 185 H8
Ózd Hungary 48°14N 20°15E 182 B5
Ozernovskiy Russia 51°30N 156°31E 215 D16
Ozernoye Russia 51°46N 51°28E 190 E10
Ozero Svityaz Ukraine 51°30N 23°50E 185 G10
Ozersk Russia 54°25N 22°0E 184 D8
Ozette, L. U.S.A. 48°6N 124°38W 306 B2
Ozieri Italy 40°35N 9°0E 200 B2
Ozimek Poland 50°41N 18°11E 185 H5
Ozinki Russia 51°12N 49°44E 190 E9
Ozoir-la-Ferrière France 48°46N 2°40E 134 B4
Ozona U.S.A. 30°43N 101°12W 314 F4
Ozone Park U.S.A. 40°40N 73°50W 132 B2
Ozorków Poland 51°57N 19°16E 185 G6
Ozren Bos.-H. 43°55N 18°29E 182 G3
Ōzu Ehime, Japan 33°30N 132°33E 222 D4
Ōzu Kumamoto, Japan 32°52N 130°52E 222 E2
Ozuluama Mexico 21°40N 97°51W 319 C5
Ozun Romania 45°47N 25°50E 183 E10
Ozurgeti Georgia 41°55N 42°0E 191 K5

P

Pa Burkina Faso 11°33N 3°19W 262 C4
Pa-an Burma 16°51N 97°40E 241 G6
Pa Mong Dam Thailand 18°0N 102°22E 236 D4
Pa Sak → Thailand 15°30N 101°0E 236 E3
Paama Vanuatu 16°28S 168°14E 287 F6
Paamiut Greenland 62°0N 49°43W 154 E6
Paar → Germany 48°46N 11°36E 179 G7
Paarl S. Africa 33°45S 18°56E 270 D2
Pa'auilo U.S.A. 20°2N 155°22W 302 C6
Pab Hills Pakistan 26°30N 66°45E 242 F2
Pabbay U.K. 57°46N 7°14W 167 D1
Pabean Indonesia 6°49S 115°19E 235 D5
Pabianice Poland 51°40N 19°20E 185 G6
Pabna Bangla. 24°1N 89°18E 241 C2
Pabo Uganda 3°1N 32°10E 268 B3
Pacaás Novos, Serra dos Brazil 10°45S 64°15W 331 C5
Pacaás Novos △ Brazil 11°0S 63°0W 331 C5
Pacaipampa Peru 5°35S 79°39W 330 B2
Pacaja → Brazil 1°56S 50°50W 332 B1
Pacajus Brazil 4°10S 38°31W 332 B4
Pacaraima, Sa. S. Amer. 4°0N 62°30W 329 C5
Pacarán Peru 12°50S 76°3W 330 C2
Pacaraos Peru 11°12S 76°42W 330 C2
Pacasmayo Peru 7°20S 79°35W 330 B2
Pace U.S.A. 30°36N 87°10W 317 E2
Paceco Italy 37°59N 12°33E 200 E5
Pachacamac Peru 12°14S 77°53W 330 C2
Pachang Hsi → Taiwan 23°20N 120°7E 225 C2
Pachao Yü Taiwan 23°22N 119°29E 225 C1
Pachia Greece 36°17N 25°50E 205 E7
Pachino Italy 36°43N 15°5E 201 F8
Pachitea → Peru 8°46S 74°33W 330 B3
Pachiza Peru 7°16S 76°46W 330 B2
Pachmarhi India 22°28N 78°26E 243 H8
Pachnai India 26°57N 92°19E 241 B4
Pachnes Greece 35°16N 24°4E 207 E5
Pacho Colombia 5°8N 74°10W 328 B3
Pachora India 20°38N 75°29E 244 D2
Pachpadra India 25°58N 72°10E 242 G5
Pachuca Mexico 20°7N 98°44W 319 C5
Pacific U.S.A. 38°29N 90°45W 310 F6
Pacific Antarctic Ridge Pac. Oc. 43°0S 115°0W 151 B13
Pacific City = Huntington Beach U.S.A. 33°40N 118°5W 307 M9
Pacific Grove U.S.A. 36°38N 121°56W 306 J5
Pacific Heights U.S.A. 37°47N 122°26W 136 B2
Pacific Manor U.S.A. 37°38N 122°27W 136 C2
Pacific Ocean 10°0N 140°0W 289 G14
Pacific Palisades Calif., U.S.A. 34°2N 118°32W 126 B1
Pacific Palisades Hawai'i, U.S.A. 21°25N 157°58W 302 K14
Pacific Rim △ Canada 48°40N 124°45W 306 B2
Pacifica U.S.A. 37°37N 122°27W 136 C2
Pacitan Indonesia 8°12S 111°7E 235 D4
Packsaddle Australia 30°36S 141°58E 282 A4
Packwood U.S.A. 46°36N 121°40W 306 D5
Paco Phil. 14°35N 120°59E 127 B1
Paco de Arcos Portugal 38°41N 9°17W 126 A1
Paço Imperial Rio de J., Brazil 135 a2
Pacov Czech Rep. 49°27N 15°0E 180 B8
Pacoval Brazil 2°40S 54°11W 329 D7
Pacuí → Brazil 16°46S 45°1W 333 E2
Pacy-sur-Eure France 49°1N 1°23E 172 C8
Padaido, Kepulauan Indonesia 1°15S 136°30E 231 E9
Padali = Amursk Russia 50°14N 136°54E 215 D14
Padampur India 20°59N 83°4E 244 D6
Padang Kalimantan Barat, Indonesia 1°39S 108°55E 235 C3
Padang Riau, Indonesia 1°30N 102°30E 237 M4
Padang Sumatera Barat, Indonesia 1°0S 100°20E 234 C2
Padang Endau Malaysia 2°40N 103°38E 237 L4
Padang Lawas Indonesia 1°40N 99°56E 234 B1
Padangpanjang Indonesia 0°40S 100°20E 234 C2
Padangsidempuan Indonesia 1°30N 99°15E 234 B1
Padangtikar Indonesia 0°44S 109°15E 235 C3
Padatchaung Burma 19°46N 94°48E 241 F5
Padauari → Brazil 0°15S 64°5W 329 D5
Padaung Burma 18°43N 95°9E 241 F5
Padborg Denmark 54°49N 9°21E 163 K3
Padcaya Bolivia 21°52S 64°48W 331 E5
Paddington N.S.W., Australia 33°53S 151°14E 139 B2
Paddington London, U.K. 125 b2
Paddle Prairie Canada 57°57N 117°29W 296 B5
Paderborn Germany 51°42N 8°45E 178 D4
Paderno Italy 45°33N 9°9E 129 A1
Paderoo India 18°5N 82°40E 244 E6
Padeş, Vf. Romania 45°40N 22°22E 182 E7
Padilla Bolivia 19°19S 64°20W 331 D5
Padina Romania 44°50N 27°8E 183 F12
Padma India 24°12N 85°22E 243 G11
Padma → Bangla. 23°22N 90°32E 241 D3
Pádova Italy 45°25N 11°53E 199 C8
Padra India 22°15N 73°7E 242 H5
Padrão, Pta. Angola 6°5S 12°20E 265 D2
Padrauna India 26°54N 83°59E 243 F10
Padre I. U.S.A. 27°10N 97°25W 314 H6
Padre Island ⌓ U.S.A. 27°0N 97°25W 314 H6
Padrón Spain 42°41N 8°39W 194 C2
Padstow U.K. 50°33N 4°58W 169 G3
Padthaway Australia 36°36S 140°31E 282 D4
Padua = Pádova Italy 45°25N 11°53E 199 C8
Paducah Ky., U.S.A. 37°5N 88°37W 308 G9
Paducah Tex., U.S.A. 34°1N 100°18W 314 D4
Padukka Sri Lanka 6°50N 80°5E 245 L5
Padul Spain 37°1N 3°38W 195 H7
Padwa India 18°27N 82°47E 244 E6
Paea Tahiti 17°41S 149°35W 289 e
Paekakariki N.Z. 40°59S 174°58E 284 G3
Paektu-san N. Korea 41°59N 128°4E 224 B4
Paengaroa N.Z. 37°49S 176°29E 284 D5
Paeroa N.Z. 37°23S 175°41E 284 D4
Paesana Italy 44°41N 7°16E 198 D4
Paete Phil. 14°23N 121°29E 232 D3
Pafúri Mozam. 22°28S 31°17E 271 B5
Pag Croatia 44°25N 15°3E 199 D12
Paga Gabon 0°45S 10°21E 264 C2
Paga Ghana 11°1N 1°8W 263 C4
Pagadian Phil. 7°55N 123°30E 233 H4
Pagai Selatan, Pulau Indonesia 3°0S 100°15E 234 C2
Pagai Utara, Pulau Indonesia 2°35S 100°0E 234 C2
Pagalu = Annobón Atl. Oc. 1°25S 5°36E 255 G4
Pagalungan Phil. 7°4N 124°41E 233 H5
Pagan Burma 21°10N 94°52E 241 E5
Pagan N. Marianas 18°7N 145°46E 302 a
Pagara India 24°22N 80°1E 243 G9
Pagaralam Indonesia 4°1S 103°16E 234 C2
Pagastikos Kolpos Greece 39°15N 23°0E 204 B5
Pagatan Indonesia 3°33S 115°59E 235 C5
Page U.S.A. 36°57N 111°27W 305 H8
Pagėgiai Lithuania 55°9N 21°54E 184 C8
Pagei Papua N. G. 3°2S 141°10E 286 B1
Paget, Mt. S. Georgia 54°26S 36°31W 326 H6
Paget I. India 13°26N 92°50E 245 H11
Pagewood Australia 33°56S 151°14E 139 B2
Pago B. Guam 13°25N 144°47E 302 d
Pago Pago Amer. Samoa 14°16S 170°43W 302 f
Pago Pago Harbor Amer. Samoa 14°17S 170°40W 302 f
Pagosa Springs U.S.A. 37°16N 107°1W 305 H10
Pagote India 18°53N 72°59E 130 B2
Pagri China 27°45N 89°10E 218 F6
Pagsanjan Phil. 14°16N 121°27E 232 D3
Pagua B. Dominica 15°32N 61°17W 323 k
Pagudpud Phil. 18°34N 120°47E 232 B3
Pagwa River Canada 50°2N 85°14W 298 B2
Pagwi Papua N. G. 4°4S 143°2E 286 C2
Pāhala U.S.A. 19°12N 155°29W 302 D6
Pahang □ Malaysia 3°30N 102°45E 237 L4
Pahang → Malaysia 3°30N 103°9E 237 L4
Paharpur Bangla. 24°51N 88°44E 241 C2
Pahia Pt. N.Z. 46°20S 167°41E 285 G2
Pahiatua N.Z. 40°27S 175°50E 284 G4
Pāhoa U.S.A. 19°30N 154°57W 302 D7
Pahokee U.S.A. 26°50N 80°40W 317 J9
Pahrump U.S.A. 36°12N 115°59W 307 J11
Pahute Mesa U.S.A. 37°20N 116°45W 306 H10
Pai Thailand 19°19N 98°27E 236 C2
Pai, I. do Brazil 22°59S 43°5W 135 B2
Paia U.S.A. 20°54N 156°22W 302 C5
Paichuan Liehtao Taiwan 25°58N 119°57E 225 b
Paicines U.S.A. 36°44N 121°17W 306 J5
Paide Estonia 58°53N 25°33E 188 C3
Paignton U.K. 50°26N 3°35W 169 G4
Paihia N.Z. 35°17S 174°6E 284 B3
Paiho Taiwan 23°21N 120°25E 225 C2
Paiján Peru 7°42S 79°20W 330 B2
Päijänne Finland 61°30N 25°30E 188 B3
Pailani India 25°45N 80°26E 243 G9
Pailin Cambodia 12°46N 102°36E 236 F4
Pailolo Channel U.S.A. 21°0N 156°40W 302 B5
Paimpol France 48°48N 3°4W 172 D3
Painan Indonesia 1°21S 100°34E 234 C2
Paine Grande, Cerro Chile 50°59S 73°4W 336 D2
Painesville U.S.A. 41°43N 81°15W 312 E3
Paint Hills = Wemindji Canada 53°0N 78°49W 298 B4
Paint L. Canada 55°28N 97°57W 297 B9
Painted Desert U.S.A. 36°0N 111°0W 305 H8
Paintsville U.S.A. 37°49N 82°48W 309 G12
País Vasco □ Spain 42°50N 2°45W 196 C2
Paisha Taiwan 23°40N 119°35E 225 C1
Paisley Ont., Canada 44°18N 81°16W 312 B3
Paisley Renf., U.K. 55°50N 4°25W 167 F4
Paisley Oreg., U.S.A. 42°42N 120°32W 304 E3
Païta N. Cal. 22°8S 166°22E 288 d
Paita Peru 5°11S 81°9W 330 B1
Paithan India 19°29N 75°23E 244 E2
Paiva → Portugal 41°4N 8°16W 194 D2
Paizhou China 30°12N 113°55E 229 B9
Paja, Cerro Ecuador 1°17S 90°26W 330 a
Pájara Canary Is. 28°21N 14°6W 153 e2
Pajares Spain 43°1N 5°46W 194 B5
Pajares, Puerto de Spain 42°58N 5°46W 194 C5
Pajarito Colombia 5°17N 72°43W 328 B3
Pajęczno Poland 51°10N 19°0E 185 G5
Paju S. Korea 37°45N 126°46E 224 D3
Pak Kok China 22°14N 114°7E 122 B1
Pak Kong China 22°22N 114°15E 122 A2
Pak Lay Laos 18°15N 101°27E 236 C3
Pak Ou Laos 20°3N 102°12E 236 B4
Pak Phanang Thailand 8°21N 100°12E 237 H3
Pak Sane Laos 18°22N 103°39E 236 C4
Pak Song Laos 15°11N 106°14E 236 E6
Pak Suang Laos 19°58N 102°15E 228 H4
Pak Tam Chung China 22°24N 114°19E 219 a
Pak Thong Chai Thailand 14°43N 102°1E 236 E4
Pakala India 13°29N 79°8E 245 H4
Pakaraima Mts. Guyana 6°0N 60°0W 329 B6
Pakaur India 24°38N 87°51E 243 G12
Pakch'ŏn N. Korea 39°44N 125°35E 224 C2
Pakenham Vic., Australia 38°6S 145°30E 283 E6
Pakenham Ont., Canada 45°18N 76°18W 313 A8
Pakhoi = Beihai China 21°28N 109°6E 228 G7
Pakhuis S. Africa 32°9S 19°5E 270 D2
Pakila Finland 60°15N 24°55E 121 B2
Pakistan ■ Asia 30°0N 70°0E 242 E4
Pakkading Laos 18°19N 103°59E 236 C4
Paklay = Sayaboury Laos 19°15N 101°45E 236 C3
Paklenica △ Croatia 44°20N 15°39E 199 D12
Pakokku Burma 21°20N 95°0E 241 E5
Pakość Poland 52°48N 18°6E 185 F5
Pakowki L. Canada 49°20N 111°0W 297 D6
Pakpattan Pakistan 30°25N 73°27E 242 D5
Pakrac Croatia 45°27N 17°12E 182 E2
Pakruojis Lithuania 55°58N 23°52E 184 C10
Paks Hungary 46°38N 18°55E 182 D3
Paktīā □ Afghan. 33°30N 69°15E 240 B3
Paktīkā □ Afghan. 32°30N 69°0E 240 B3
Paku, Tanjung Indonesia 3°6S 106°31E 234 C3
Pakwach Uganda 2°28N 31°27E 268 B3
Pakxe Laos 15°5N 105°52E 236 E5
Pal Lahara India 21°27N 85°11E 243 J11
Pala Chad 9°25N 15°5E 259 G3
Pala Dem. Rep. of the Congo 6°45S 29°30E 268 D2
Pala Calif., U.S.A. 33°22N 117°5W 307 M9
Palabek Uganda 3°22N 32°33E 268 B3
Palacio Real Madrid, Spain 127 b1
Palacios U.S.A. 28°42N 96°13W 314 G6
Palafrugell Spain 41°55N 3°10E 196 D8
Palagiano Italy 40°35N 17°2E 201 B10
Palagonía Italy 37°19N 14°45E 201 E7
Palagruža Croatia 42°24N 16°15E 199 F13
Palais Royal Brussels, Belgium 116 b3
Palaiseau France 48°42N 2°14E 134 B2
Palakkad = Palghat India 10°46N 76°42E 245 J3
Palakol India 16°31N 81°46E 245 F5
Palalankwe India 10°52N 92°29E 245 J11
Palam India 19°0N 77°0E 244 E3
Palamas Greece 39°26N 22°4E 204 B4
Palamós Spain 41°50N 3°10E 196 D8
Palampur India 32°10N 76°30E 242 C7
Palamut Turkey 38°59N 27°41E 205 C9
Palana Tas., Australia 39°45S 147°55E 281 F4
Palana Russia 59°10N 159°59E 215 D16
Palanan Phil. 17°8N 122°29E 232 C4
Palanan B. Phil. 17°9N 122°27E 232 C4
Palanan Pt. Phil. 17°17N 122°30E 232 C4
Palandri Pakistan 33°42N 73°40E 243 C5
Palanga Lithuania 55°58N 21°3E 184 C8
Palanganene Dem. Rep. of the Congo 6°32S 18°52E 265 D3
Palangkaraya Indonesia 2°16S 113°56E 235 C4
Palani India 10°30N 77°30E 245 J3
Palani Hills India 10°14N 77°33E 245 J3
Palanpur India 24°10N 72°25E 242 G5
Palaoa Pt. U.S.A. 20°44N 156°58W 302 C5
Palapag Phil. 12°33N 125°7E 232 E5
Palapye Botswana 22°30S 27°7E 270 B4
Palar → India 12°27N 80°13E 245 H5
Palas Pakistan 35°4N 73°14E 243 B5
Palas de Rei Spain 42°52N 7°52W 194 C3
Palasan I. Phil. 14°51N 122°2E 232 D4
Palasponga India 21°47N 85°34E 243 J11
Palatine U.S.A. 42°7N 88°3W 311 B8
Palatka Russia 60°6N 150°54E 215 C16
Palatka Fla., U.S.A. 29°39N 81°38W 316 F8
Palau Italy 41°11N 9°23E 200 A2
Palau ■ Palau 7°30N 134°30E 288 c
Palaui I. Phil. 18°32N 122°8E 232 B4
Palauk Burma 13°10N 98°40E 236 F2
Palaw Burma 12°58N 98°39E 236 F2
Palawan Phil. 9°30N 118°30E 233 G2
Palawan □ Phil. 10°0N 119°0E 233 G2
Palawan Passage Phil. 10°0N 118°0E 233 G2
Palayan Phil. 15°36N 121°8E 232 D3
Palayankottai India 8°45N 77°45E 245 K3
Palazzo, Pte. France 42°28N 8°30E 175 F12
Palazzo San Gervásio Italy 40°56N 15°59E 201 B8
Palazzolo Italy 45°34N 9°9E 129 A1
Palazzolo Acréide Italy 37°4N 14°54E 201 E7
Palca Chile 19°7S 69°9W 330 D4
Paldiski Estonia 59°23N 24°9E 188 C3
Pale Bos.-H. 43°50N 18°38E 182 G3
Palekastro Greece 35°12N 26°15E 207 E7
Palel India 24°27N 94°2E 241 C5
Paleleh Indonesia 1°10N 121°50E 231 D6
Palembang Indonesia 3°0S 104°50E 234 C2
Palena → Chile 43°50S 73°50W 336 B2
Palena, L. Chile 43°55S 71°40W 336 B2
Palencia Spain 42°1N 4°34W 194 C6
Palencia □ Spain 42°31N 4°33W 194 C6
Paleng Taiwan 24°41N 121°23E 225 B3
Palenque Mexico 17°29N 92°1W 319 D6
Paleo Faliro Greece 37°53N 23°42E 112 B2
Paleochora Greece 35°16N 23°39E 207 E4
Paleokastritsa Greece 39°40N 19°41E 206 B9
Paleometokho Cyprus 35°7N 33°11E 207 E9
Paleopoli Greece 37°49N 24°50E 204 D6
Palermo B. Aires, Argentina 34°35S 58°24W 117 B2
Palermo Colombia 2°54N 75°26W 328 C2
Palermo Italy 38°7N 13°22E 200 D6
Palermo Calif., U.S.A. 39°26N 121°33W 304 G3
Palermo ✈ (PMO) Italy 38°11N 13°5E 200 D6
Paleros Greece 38°47N 20°53E 207 B2
Palestina = Jordânia Brazil 15°55S 40°11W 333 E3
Palestine Asia 32°0N 35°0E 251 G6
Palestine Ill., U.S.A. 39°0N 87°37W 311 F9
Palestine Tex., U.S.A. 31°46N 95°38W 314 F7
Palestrina Italy 41°50N 12°53E 199 G9
Paletwa Burma 21°10N 92°50E 241 E4
Palghat India 10°46N 76°42E 245 J3
Palgrave, Mt. Australia 23°22S 115°58E 278 D2
Palhais Portugal 38°37N 9°2W 126 B2
Pali India 25°50N 73°20E 242 G5
Pali Taiwan 25°8N 121°23E 225 A3
Pali-Aike △ Chile 52°6S 69°44W 336 D3
Palikea U.S.A. 21°26N 158°6W 302 K13
Palikir Micronesia 6°55N 158°9E 288 G7
Palimbang Phil. 6°12N 124°12E 233 H5
Palin, Mt. Malaysia 6°10N 117°10E 235 A5
Palinuro Italy 40°2N 15°17E 201 B8
Palinuro, C. Italy 40°2N 15°16E 201 B8
Paliouri, Akra Greece 39°57N 23°45E 202 G7
Palisades Park U.S.A. 40°50N 74°1W 132 A1
Palisades Res. U.S.A. 43°20N 111°12W 304 E8
Palisadoes, The Jamaica 17°57N 76°48W 320 a
Paliseul Belgium 49°54N 5°8E 170 E5
Palitana India 21°32N 71°49E 242 J4
Palizada Mexico 18°15N 92°5W 319 D6
Palk Bay Asia 9°30N 79°15E 245 K4
Palk Strait Asia 10°0N 79°45E 245 K4
Palkānah Iraq 35°49N 44°26E 246 C5
Palkonda India 18°36N 83°48E 244 E6
Palkonda Ra. India 13°50N 79°20E 245 H4
Palkot India 22°53N 84°39E 243 H11
Palla Road = Dinokwe Botswana 23°29S 26°37E 270 B4
Pallanza = Verbánia Italy 45°56N 8°33E 198 C5
Pallarenda Australia 19°12S 146°46E 280 B4
Pallasovka Russia 50°4N 47°0E 190 E8
Palleru → India 16°45N 80°2E 244 F5
Pallës, Bishti i Albania 41°24N 19°24E 202 E3
Pallinup → Australia 34°27S 118°50E 279 F2
Pallisa Uganda 1°12N 33°43E 268 B3
Palliser, C. N.Z. 41°37S 175°14E 284 H4
Palliser, Îs. French Polynesia 15°30S 146°30W 289 f
Palliser B. N.Z. 41°26S 175°5E 284 H4
Pallu India 28°59N 74°14E 242 E6
Palm Bay U.S.A. 28°2N 80°35W 317 G9
Palm Beach Aruba 12°34N 70°2W 322 f
Palm Beach Fla., U.S.A. 26°43N 80°2W 317 J9
Palm Coast U.S.A. 29°35N 81°12W 317 F8
Palm Desert U.S.A. 33°43N 116°22W 307 M10
Palm-Grove △ Australia 24°57S 149°21E 280 C4
Palm Harbor U.S.A. 28°5N 82°46W 317 G7
Palm Is. Australia 18°40S 146°35E 280 B4
Palm Springs U.S.A. 33°50N 116°33W 307 M10
Palm Valley U.S.A. 30°11N 81°23W 316 E8
Palma = Paraná Brazil 12°30S 47°48W 333 D2
Palma Mozam. 10°46S 40°29E 269 E5
Palma → Brazil 12°33S 47°52W 333 D2
Palma, B. de Spain 39°30N 2°39E 206 B3
Palma de Mallorca Spain 39°35N 2°39E 206 B3
Palma de Mallorca ✈ (PMI) Spain 39°34N 2°43E 197 F7
Palma del Río Spain 37°43N 5°17W 195 H5
Palma di Montechiaro Italy 37°11N 13°46E 200 E6
Palma Nova = Palmanova Spain 39°32N 2°34E 206 B3
Palma Soriano Cuba 20°15N 76°0W 320 B4
Palmaner India 13°12N 78°45E 245 H4
Palmanova Spain 39°32N 2°34E 206 B3
Palmares Brazil 8°41S 35°28W 332 C4
Palmarito Venezuela 7°37N 70°10W 328 B3
Palmarola Italy 40°56N 12°51E 200 B5
Palmas Paraná, Brazil 26°29S 52°0W 335 B5
Palmas Tocantins, Brazil 10°13S 48°16W 332 D2
Palmas, C. Liberia 4°27N 7°46W 262 E3
Pálmas, G. di Italy 39°0N 8°30E 200 D1
Palmas de Monte Alto Brazil 14°16S 43°10W 333 D3
Palmdale Calif., U.S.A. 34°35N 118°7W 307 L8
Palmdale Fla., U.S.A. 26°57N 81°19W 317 J8
Palmeira Brazil 25°25S 50°0W 333 G2
Palmeira das Missões Brazil 27°55S 53°17W 335 B5
Palmeira dos Índios Brazil 9°25S 36°37W 332 C4
Palmeirais Brazil 6°0S 43°0W 332 C3
Palmeiras Brazil 12°31S 41°34W 333 D3
Palmeiras → Brazil 12°22S 47°8W 333 D2
Palmeirinhas, Pta. das Angola 9°2S 12°57E 265 D2
Palmela Portugal 38°32N 8°57W 195 G2
Palmelo Brazil 17°20S 48°27W 333 E2
Palmer Antarctica 64°35S 65°0W 151 C17
Palmer Alaska, U.S.A. 61°36N 149°7W 303 F10
Palmer → Australia 16°0S 142°26E 280 B3
Palmer Arch. Antarctica 64°15S 65°0W 151 C17
Palmer Lake U.S.A. 39°7N 104°55W 304 G11
Palmer Land Antarctica 73°0S 63°0W 151 D18
Palmer Park U.S.A. 38°55N 76°52W 143 B4
Palmerston = Darwin Australia 12°25S 130°51E 278 B5
Palmerston N. Terr., Australia 12°31S 130°59E 278 B5
Palmerston Ont., Canada 43°50N 80°51W 312 C4
Palmerston Dublin, Ireland 53°20N 6°22W 120 A1
Palmerston N.Z. 45°29S 170°43E 285 F5
Palmerston North N.Z. 40°21S 175°39E 284 G4
Palmerton U.S.A. 40°48N 75°37W 313 F9
Palmetto Fla., U.S.A. 27°31N 82°34W 317 H7
Palmetto Ga., U.S.A. 33°31N 84°40W 316 B5
Palmetto Pt. Antigua & B. 17°37N 61°51W 322 c
Palmetto Pt. St. Kitts & Nevis 17°18N 62°46W 322 d
Palmi Italy 38°21N 15°51E 201 D8
Palmira Argentina 32°59S 68°34W 334 C2
Palmira Colombia 3°32N 76°16W 328 C2
Palms U.S.A. 34°1N 118°24W 126 B2
Palmyra = Tudmur Syria 34°36N 38°15E 213 E8
Palmyra Ill., U.S.A. 39°26N 90°0W 310 E7
Palmyra Mo., U.S.A. 39°48N 91°32W 310 E5
Palmyra N.J., U.S.A. 40°0N 75°1W 313 F9
Palmyra N.Y., U.S.A. 43°5N 77°18W 312 C7
Palmyra Pa., U.S.A. 40°18N 76°36W 313 F8
Palmyra Wis., U.S.A. 42°52N 88°36W 311 B8
Palmyra Is. Pac. Oc. 5°52N 162°5W 289 G11
Palmyras = Santos Dumont Brazil 22°55S 43°10W 333 F3
Palmyras Pt. India 20°46N 87°1E 244 D8
Palo Phil. 11°10N 124°59E 233 F5
Palo Alto U.S.A. 37°27N 122°10W 306 H4
Palo Seco Trin. & Tob. 10°4N 61°36W 323 t
Palo Verde U.S.A. 33°26N 114°44W 307 M12
Palo Verde △ Costa Rica 10°21N 85°21W 320 D2
Paloh Indonesia 1°43N 109°18E 235 B3
Paloheinä Finland 60°15N 24°56E 121 B2
Paloich Sudan 10°28N 32°32E 257 E3
Palomar Mt. U.S.A. 33°22N 116°50W 307 M10
Palomeras Spain 40°22N 3°39W 127 B2
Palompon Phil. 11°3N 124°23E 233 F5
Palopo Indonesia 3°0S 120°16E 231 E6
Palos, C. de Spain 37°38N 0°40W 197 H4
Palos de la Frontera Spain 37°14N 6°53W 195 H4
Palos Heights U.S.A. 41°39N 87°47W 119 D2
Palos Hills U.S.A. 41°42N 87°49W 119 C2
Palos Hills Forest U.S.A. 41°40N 87°52W 119 C1
Palos Park U.S.A. 41°40N 87°50W 119 C1
Palos Verdes, Pt. U.S.A. 33°46N 118°25W 307 M8
Palos Verdes Estates U.S.A. 33°48N 118°23W 307 M8
Palpa Peru 14°30S 75°15W 330 C2
Palpara India 22°38N 88°22E 124 B2
Pålsboda Sweden 59°3N 15°22E 162 E9
Palu Indonesia 1°0S 119°52E 235 C5
Palu Turkey 38°45N 40°0E 213 C9
Paluan Phil. 13°26N 120°29E 232 E3
Paluke Liberia 5°2N 8°5W 262 D3
Paluma Ra. Australia 19°9S 146°22E 280 B4
Paluzza Italy 46°32N 13°1E 199 B10
Palwal India 28°8N 77°19E 242 E7
Pama Burkina Faso 11°19N 0°44E 263 C5
Pama → C.A.R. 4°23N 18°43E 264 B3
Pama ⌓ Burkina Faso 11°27N 0°40E 263 C5
Pamandzi Mayotte 12°47S 45°16E 272 b
Pamanukan Indonesia 6°16S 107°49E 235 D3
Pamban I. India 9°15N 79°20E 245 K4
Pamekasan Indonesia 7°10S 113°28E 235 D4
Pamenang Indonesia 8°24S 116°6E 231 J19
Pameungpeuk Indonesia 7°37S 107°43E 235 D3
Pamiers France 43°7N 1°39E 174 E5
Pamir Tajikistan 37°40N 73°0E 217 E8
Pamirsky Post = Murgap Tajikistan 38°10N 74°2E 217 E8
Pamlico → U.S.A. 35°20N 76°28W 315 D16
Pamlico Sd. U.S.A. 35°20N 76°0W 315 D17
Pampa U.S.A. 35°32N 100°58W 314 D4
Pampa de Agma Argentina 43°45S 69°40W 336 B3
Pampa de las Salinas Argentina 32°1S 66°58W 334 C2
Pampa Grande Bolivia 18°5S 64°6W 331 D5
Pampa Hermosa Peru 7°7S 75°4W 330 B2
Pampanga □ Phil. 15°4N 120°40E 232 D3
Pampanua Indonesia 4°16S 120°8E 231 E6
Pampas Argentina 35°0S 63°0W 334 D3
Pampas Peru 12°20S 74°50W 330 C3
Pampas → Peru 13°24S 73°12W 330 C3
Pamphylia Turkey 37°0N 31°20E 250 B2
Pamplemousses Mauritius 20°6S 57°34E 272 e
Pamplona Colombia 7°23N 72°39W 328 B3
Pamplona Phil. 18°31N 121°20E 232 B3
Pamplona-Iruña Spain 42°48N 1°38W 196 C3
Pampoenpoort S. Africa 31°3S 22°40E 270 D3
Pamuk → Turkey 37°2N 34°49E 250 A5
Pamukçu Turkey 39°30N 27°54E 205 B9
Pamukkale Turkey 37°55N 29°8E 205 D11
Pan de Azúcar Chile 24°5S 68°10W 334 A2
Pan de Azúcar △ Chile 26°0S 70°40W 334 B1
Pan Xian China 25°46N 104°38E 228 E5
Pana U.S.A. 39°23N 89°5W 310 E7
Panabo Phil. 7°19N 125°42E 233 H5
Panaca U.S.A. 37°47N 114°23W 305 H6
Panacea U.S.A. 30°2N 84°23W 316 E5
Panagyurishte Bulgaria 42°30N 24°15E 203 D8
Panaitan Indonesia 6°36S 105°12E 234 D3
Panajam Indonesia 1°15S 116°46E 235 C5
Panaji India 15°25N 73°50E 245 G1
Panamá Panama 9°0N 79°25W 320 c
Panama Sri Lanka 6°45N 81°48E 245 L5
Panama ■ Cent. Amer. 8°48N 79°55W 320 E4
Panamá, G. de Panama 8°4N 79°20W 320 E4
Panama, Isthmus of Cent. Amer. 9°0N 79°0W 292 J12
Panama Basin Pac. Oc. 5°0N 83°30W 289 G19
Panama Canal Panama 9°10N 79°37W 320 c
Panama City U.S.A. 30°10N 85°40W 316 E4
Panama City Beach U.S.A. 30°11N 85°48W 316 E4
Panamint Range U.S.A. 36°20N 117°20W 307 J9
Panamint Springs U.S.A. 36°20N 117°28W 307 J9
Panão Peru 9°55S 75°55W 330 B2
Panaon I. Phil. 9°50N 125°13E 233 G5
Panare Thailand 6°51N 101°30E 237 J3
Panarea Italy 38°38N 15°4E 201 D8
Panaro → Italy 44°55N 11°25E 199 D8
Panay Phil. 11°10N 122°30E 233 F4
Panay G. Phil. 11°0N 122°30E 233 F4
Pančevo Serbia 44°52N 20°41E 182 F5
Panch'iao Taiwan 25°1N 121°27E 225 A3
Panchur India 22°32N 88°16E 124 B1
Panciu Romania 45°54N 27°8E 183 E12
Pancol Phil. 10°52N 119°25E 233 F2
Pancorbo, Desfiladero Spain 42°32N 3°5W 194 C7
Pâncota Romania 46°20N 21°45E 182 D6
Panda Mozam. 24°2S 34°45E 271 B5
Pandacan Phil. 14°35N 121°0E 127 B2
Pandan Malaysia 1°32N 103°46E 237 d
Pandan Antique, Phil. 11°45N 122°10E 233 F4
Pandan Catanduanes, Phil. 14°3N 124°10E 232 D5
Pandan, Selat Singapore 1°15N 103°44E 138 B2
Pandan B. Phil. 11°43N 122°0E 233 F4
Pandan Res. Singapore 1°18N 103°44E 138 B2
Pandan Tampoi = Tampoi Malaysia 1°30N 103°39E 237 d
Pandanan I. Phil. 8°17N 117°13E 233 G1
Pandegelang Indonesia 6°25S 106°5E 234 D3
Pandhana India 21°42N 76°13E 242 J7
Pandharkawada India 20°1N 78°32E 244 D4
Pandharpur India 17°41N 75°20E 244 F2
Pandhurna India 21°36N 78°35E 244 D4
Pando Uruguay 34°44S 56°0W 335 C4
Pando □ Bolivia 11°20S 67°40W 330 C4
Pando, L. = Hope, L. Australia 28°24S 139°18E 281 D2
Pandokratoras Greece 39°45N 19°50E 206 B9
Pandora Costa Rica 9°43N 83°3W 320 E3
Pandrup Denmark 57°14N 9°40E 163 G3
Pandu Dem. Rep. of the Congo 4°59N 19°16E 264 B3
Panepistimio Athens, Greece 112 b2
Panevéggio-Pale di San Martino ⌓ Italy 46°14N 11°46E 199 B8
Panevėžys Lithuania 55°42N 24°25E 188 E3
Panfilov = Zharkent Kazakhstan 44°10N 80°0E 217 D10
Panfilovo Russia 50°25N 42°46E 190 E6
Pang Sida △ Thailand 14°5N 102°17E 236 E4
Panga Dem. Rep. of the Congo 1°52N 26°18E 268 B2
Pangaíon Óros Greece 40°50N 24°0E 203 F8
Pangala Congo 3°16S 14°34E 264 C2
Pangalanes, Canal des = Ampangalana, Lakandranon' Madag. 22°48S 47°50E 272 C2
Pangandaran Indonesia 7°40S 108°39E 235 D3
Pangandaran △ Indonesia 7°43S 108°42E 235 D3
Pangani Tanzania 5°25S 38°58E 268 D4
Pangani → Tanzania 5°26S 38°58E 268 D4
Pangantocan Phil. 7°50N 124°49E 233 H5
Pangar Djeréme ⌓ Cameroon 5°50N 13°10E 263 D7
Pangasinan □ Phil. 15°55N 120°20E 232 D3
Pangfou = Bengbu China 32°58N 117°20E 227 H9
Pangga, Tanjung Indonesia 8°54S 116°2E 231 K19
Pangil Dem. Rep. of the Congo 3°10S 26°35E 268 C2
Pangjiabu China 40°38N 115°26E 226 D8
Pangkah, Tanjung Indonesia 6°51S 112°33E 235 D4
Pangkai Burma 22°49N 98°39E 228 F2
Pangkajene Indonesia 4°46S 119°34E 235 C5
Pangkalanbrandan Indonesia 4°1N 98°20E 234 B1
Pangkalanbuun Indonesia 2°41S 111°37E 235 C4
Pangkalansusu Indonesia 4°2N 98°13E 234 B1
Pangkalpinang Indonesia 2°10S 106°10E 234 C3
Pangkoh Indonesia 3°5S 114°8E 235 C4
Pangkor, Pulau Malaysia 4°13N 100°34E 237 K3
Panglao Phil. 9°35N 123°45E 233 G4
Panglao I. Phil. 9°35N 123°48E 233 G4
Pangniqtuuq = Pangnirtung Canada 66°8N 65°43W 295 D18
Pangnirtung Canada 66°8N 65°43W 295 D18
Pango Alucuem Angola 8°43S 14°33E 265 D2
Pangody Russia 65°52N 74°27E 214 C8
Pangong Tso = Bangong Co China 33°45N 78°43E 243 C8
Pangrati Greece 37°56N 23°45E 112 B2
Pangsau Pass Burma 27°15N 96°10E 241 B6
Pangsua, Sungei → Singapore 1°25N 103°45E 138 A2
Pangtara Burma 20°57N 96°40E 241 E6
Panguipulli Chile 39°38S 72°20W 336 A2
Panguitch U.S.A. 37°50N 112°26W 305 H7
Panguna Papua N. G. 6°21S 155°25E 286 D8
Pangururan Indonesia 2°37N 98°42E 234 B1
Pangutaran Phil. 6°18N 120°35E 233 H3
Pangutaran Group Phil. 6°18N 120°34E 233 H3
Panhala India 16°49N 74°7E 244 F2
Panhandle U.S.A. 35°21N 101°23W 314 D4
Pani Mines India 22°29N 73°50E 242 H5
Pania-Mutombo Dem. Rep. of the Congo 5°11S 23°51E 265 D4
Pānī'au U.S.A. 21°56N 160°5W 302 B1
Panié, Mt. N. Cal. 20°36S 164°46E 288 d
Panihati India 22°41N 88°22E 124 A2
Panikota I. India 20°46N 71°21E 242 J4
Panipat India 29°25N 77°2E 242 E7
Paniqui Phil. 15°40N 120°34E 232 D3
Panitan Phil. 11°28N 122°46E 233 F4
Panj = Pyandzh → Asia 37°6N 68°20E 240 A2
Panjab Afghan. 34°23N 67°1E 240 B2
Panjakent = Pendzhikent Tajikistan 39°29N 67°37E 217 E7
Panjal Range = Pir Panjal Range India 32°30N 76°50E 242 C7
Panjang Kepulauan Riau, Indonesia 4°15N 108°12E 235 B3
Panjang Lampung, Indonesia 5°25S 105°20E 234 D3
Panjang, Bukit Singapore 1°22N 103°45E 138 A2
Panjgur Pakistan 27°0N 64°5E 240 D2
Panjhra → India 21°13N 74°57E 244 D2
Panjim = Panaji India 15°25N 73°50E 245 G1
Panjin China 41°3N 122°2E 227 D12
Panjnad → Pakistan 28°57N 70°30E 242 E4
Panjnad Barrage Pakistan 29°22N 71°15E 242 E4
Panjsher □ Afghan. 35°50N 69°45E 240 B3
Panjwai Afghan. 31°26N 65°27E 242 D1
Panke → Germany 52°31N 13°22E 115 A3
Pankow Germany 52°34N 13°23E 115 A3
Pankshin Nigeria 9°16N 9°25E 263 D6
Panmunjŏm N. Korea 37°59N 126°38E 224 D3
Panna India 24°40N 80°15E 243 G9
Panna △ India 24°40N 80°0E 243 G8
Panna Hills India 24°40N 81°15E 243 G9
Pannawonica Australia 21°39S 116°19E 278 D2
Panngi Vanuatu 15°58S 168°12E 287 E6
Pano Akil Pakistan 27°51N 69°7E 242 F3
Pano Lefkara Cyprus 34°53N 33°20E 207 F9
Pano Panayia Cyprus 34°55N 32°38E 207 F8
Panopah Indonesia 1°55S 111°10E 235 C4
Panora U.S.A. 41°42N 94°22W 310 C2
Panorama Brazil 21°21S 51°51W 335 A5
Panormos Greece 35°25N 24°41E 207 E5
Panruti India 11°46N 79°35E 245 J4
Pansemal India 21°39N 74°42E 242 J6
Panshan = Panjin China 41°3N 122°2E 227 D12
Panshi China 42°58N 126°5E 227 C14
Pantabangan L. Phil. 15°50N 121°9E 232 D3
Pantanal Matogrossense △ Brazil 17°35S 57°27W 331 D6
Pantanaw Burma 16°59N 95°28E 241 G5
Pantanos de Centla ⌓ Mexico 18°25N 92°25W 319 D6
Pantar Indonesia 8°28S 124°10E 231 F6
Pante Macassar E. Timor 9°30S 123°58E 231 F6
Pantelleria Italy 36°50N 11°57E 200 F4
Panthéon Paris, France 134 c4
Pantheon Rome, Italy 136 b2
Panthersville U.S.A. 33°43N 84°16W 113 B3
Panti Indonesia 0°22N 100°3E 234 B2
Pantin France 48°53N 2°24E 134 A3
Pantin Sakan Burma 18°38N 97°33E 241 F6
Pantitlán Mexico 19°24N 99°4W 128 B2
Pantoja Peru 0°58S 75°10W 328 D2
Pantón Spain 42°31N 7°37W 194 C3
Pantukan Phil. 7°9N 125°54E 233 H5
Panu Dem. Rep. of the Congo 3°50S 19°10E 264 C3
Pánuco Mexico 22°3N 98°10W 319 C5
Panuitan I. Phil. 19°26N 121°30E 232 B3
Panukulan Phil. 14°56N 121°49E 232 D3
Panvel India 18°59N 73°4E 244 E1
Panyabungan Indonesia 0°51N 99°33E 234 B1
Panyam Nigeria 9°27N 9°8E 263 D6
Panyu = Guangzhou China 23°6N 113°13E 121 B2
Panyu Guangdong, China 23°1N 113°21E 121 B2
Panyu Guangdong, China 22°51N 113°20E 229 F9
Panzhihua China 26°33N 101°44E 228 D3
Panzi Dem. Rep. of the Congo 7°17S 18°1E 265 D3
Pao → Anzoátegui, Venezuela 8°6N 64°17W 329 B5
Pao → Apure, Venezuela 8°33N 68°1W 328 B4
Paoay Phil. 18°3N 120°30E 232 B3
Paochi = Baoji China 34°20N 107°5E 226 G4
Paoki = Baoji China 34°20N 107°5E 226 G4
Páola Italy 39°21N 16°2E 201 C9
Paola Malta 35°52N 14°30E 206 F8
Paola Kans., U.S.A. 38°35N 94°53W 308 F6
Paoli U.S.A. 38°33N 86°28W 311 F10
Paonia U.S.A. 38°52N 107°36W 304 G10
Paopao Moorea 17°30S 149°49W 289 e
Paoting = Baoding China 38°50N 115°28E 226 E8
Paot'ou = Baotou China 40°32N 110°2E 226 D6
Paoua C.A.R. 7°9N 16°20E 264 A3
Pápa Hungary 47°22N 17°30E 182 C2
Päpä Hawai'i, U.S.A. 19°13N 155°52W 302 D6
Papa Stour U.K. 60°20N 1°42W 167 A7
Papa Westray U.K. 59°20N 2°55W 167 B6
Päpa'aloa U.S.A. 19°59N 155°13W 302 D6

Papagayo → Mexico 16°46N 99°43W 319 D5
Papagayo, G. de Costa Rica 10°30N 85°50W 320 D2
Papagni → India 15°35N 77°45E 245 G3
Papahānaumokuākea Marine Nat. Monument U.S.A. 25°25N 170°35W 302 F9
Papaïchton Fr. Guiana 3°48N 54°10W 329 C7
Pāpa'ikou U.S.A. 19°47N 155°6W 302 D6
Papakura N.Z. 37°4S 174°59E 284 D3
Papantla Mexico 20°27N 97°19W 319 C5
Papar Malaysia 5°45N 116°0E 235 A5
Papara Tahiti 17°43S 149°31W 289 e
Paparangi N.Z. 41°12S 174°48E 143 B1
Paparoa N.Z. 36°6S 174°16E 284 C3
Paparoa △ N.Z. 42°7S 171°26E 285 C6
Paparoa Ra. N.Z. 42°5S 171°35E 285 C6
Papas, Akra Greece 38°13N 21°20E 204 C3
Papatoetoe N.Z. 36°59S 174°51E 284 C3
Papatura Solomon Is. 7°32S 158°47E 287 L10
Papeete Tahiti 17°32S 149°34W 289 e
Papenburg Germany 53°5N 7°23E 178 B3
Papenoo Tahiti 17°30S 149°25W 289 e
Papenoo → Tahiti 17°30S 149°25W 289 e
Papetoai Moorea 17°29S 149°52W 289 e
Paphlagonia Turkey 41°30N 33°0E 212 B5
Paphos Cyprus 34°46N 32°25E 207 F8
Paphos ✕ (PFO) Cyprus 34°43N 32°30E 207 F8
Papien Chiang = Da → Vietnam 21°15N 105°20E 228 G5
Papikio Oros Greece 41°15N 25°13E 203 E9
Papiol Spain 41°25N 2°1E 114 A1
Paposo Chile 25°0S 70°30W 334 B1
Papoutsa Cyprus 34°54N 33°4E 207 F9
Papua □ Indonesia 4°0S 137°0E 231 E9
Papua, G. of Papua N. G. 9°0S 144°50E 286 E3
Papua New Guinea ■ Oceania 8°0S 145°0E 286 E3
Papudo Chile 32°29S 71°27W 334 C1
Papuk Croatia 45°30N 17°30E 182 E2
Papun Burma 18°2N 97°30E 241 F6
Papunya Australia 23°15S 131°54E 278 D5
Pará = Belém Brazil 1°20S 48°30W 332 B2
Pará □ Brazil 3°20S 52°0W 331 A7
Paraburdoo Australia 23°14S 117°32E 278 D2
Paracale Phil. 14°17N 122°48E 232 D4
Paracas, Pen. de Peru 13°53S 76°20W 330 C2
Paracatu Brazil 17°10S 46°50W 333 E2
Paracatu → Brazil 16°30S 45°4W 333 E2
Paracel Is. S. China Sea 15°50N 112°0E 230 A4
Parachilna Australia 31°10S 138°21E 282 A3
Parachinar Pakistan 33°55N 70°5E 242 C4
Paraćin Serbia 43°54N 21°27E 202 C5
Paracuru Brazil 3°24S 39°4W 332 B4
Parada, Punta Peru 15°22S 75°11W 330 D2
Paradas Spain 37°18N 5°29W 195 H5
Paradela Spain 42°44N 7°37W 194 C3
Paradera Aruba 12°32N 70°0W 322 f
Paradip India 20°15N 86°35E 244 D8
Paradise Calif., U.S.A. 39°46N 121°37W 306 F5
Paradise Nev., U.S.A. 36°5N 115°8W 124 B2
Paradise → Canada 53°27N 57°19W 299 B8
Paradise Hill Canada 53°32N 109°28W 297 C7
Paradise I. Bahamas 25°6N 77°19W 153 b
Paradise River Canada 53°27N 57°17W 299 B8
Paradise Valley U.S.A. 41°30N 117°32W 304 F5
Paradisi Greece 36°18N 28°7E 206 E12
Parado Indonesia 8°42S 118°30E 231 F5
Paragould U.S.A. 36°3N 90°29W 315 C9
Paragua = Palawan Phil. 9°30N 118°30E 233 G2
Paraguá → Bolivia 13°34S 61°53W 331 C5
Paragua → Venezuela 6°55N 62°55W 329 B5
Paraguaçu = Paraguaçu Paulista Brazil 22°22S 50°35W 335 A5
Paraguaçú → Brazil 12°45S 38°54W 333 D4
Paraguaçu Paulista Brazil 22°22S 50°35W 335 A5
Paraguaipoa Venezuela 11°21N 71°57W 328 A3
Paraguaná, Pen. de Venezuela 12°0N 70°0W 328 A4
Paraguari Paraguay 25°36S 57°0W 334 B4
Paraguarí □ Paraguay 26°0S 57°10W 334 B4
Paraguay ■ S. Amer. 23°0S 57°0W 334 A4
Paraguay → Paraguay 27°18S 58°38W 334 B4
Paraíba = João Pessoa Brazil 7°10S 34°52W 332 C5
Paraíba □ Brazil 7°0S 36°0W 332 C4
Paraíba do Sul → Brazil 21°37S 41°3W 333 F3
Paraiso Brazil 19°3S 52°59W 331 D7
Paraíso Tabasco, Mexico 18°24N 93°14W 319 D6
Paraiso Panama 9°3N 79°38W 320 c
Parak Iran 27°38N 52°25E 247 E7
Parakhino Paddubye Russia 58°26N 33°10E 188 C7
Parakou Benin 9°25N 2°40E 263 D5
Parakylia Australia 30°24S 136°25E 282 A2
Paralimni Cyprus 35°2N 33°58E 207 E9
Paralio Astros Greece 37°25N 22°45E 204 D4
Paralkote India 19°47N 80°41E 244 E5
Param I. Micronesia 7°21N 151°47E 287 T18
Parama I. Papua N. G. 9°0S 143°25E 286 E2
Paramaribo Suriname 5°50N 55°10W 329 B6
Parambu Brazil 6°13S 40°43W 332 C3
Paramillo, Cerro Colombia 7°4N 75°55W 328 B2
Paramillo △ Colombia 7°37N 76°13W 328 B2
Paramirim Brazil 13°26S 42°15W 333 D3
Paramirim → Brazil 11°34S 43°18W 333 D3
Paramithia Greece 39°30N 20°35E 204 B2
Paramonga Peru 10°40S 77°50W 330 C2
Paramount Studios U.S.A. 34°5N 118°19W 126 B3
Paramus U.S.A. 40°56N 74°2W 132 A1
Paramushir, Ostrov Russia 50°24N 156°0E 215 D16
Paran → Israel 30°20N 35°10E 251 H6
Paraná Argentina 31°45S 60°30W 334 C3
Paranã Brazil 12°30S 47°48W 333 D2
Paraná □ Brazil 24°30S 51°0W 335 A5
Paraná → Argentina 33°43S 59°15W 334 C4
Paranã → Brazil 12°30S 48°14W 333 D2
Paranaguá Brazil 25°30S 48°30W 335 B6
Paranaíba Brazil 19°40S 51°11W 331 D7
Paranaíba → Brazil 20°6S 51°4W 333 F1
Paranapanema → Brazil 22°40S 53°9W 335 A5
Paranapiacaba, Serra do Brazil 24°31S 48°35W 335 A6
Paranaque Phil. 14°30N 120°59E 127 B1
Paranas Phil. 11°42N 125°2E 233 F5
Paranavaí Brazil 23°4S 52°56W 335 A5
Parang Maguindanao, Phil. 7°23N 124°16E 233 H5
Parang Sulu, Phil. 5°55N 120°54E 233 J3
Parangippettai India 11°30N 79°38E 245 J4
Parângul Mare, Vf. Romania 45°20N 23°37E 183 E8
Paranthan Sri Lanka 9°26N 80°24E 245 K5
Paraoa French Polynesia 19°9S 140°43W 289 f
Paraparaumu N.Z. 40°57S 175°3E 284 G4
Parapetí → Bolivia 18°58S 62°21W 331 D5
Paraspori, Akra Greece 35°55N 27°15E 205 F9
Paratinga Brazil 12°40S 43°10W 333 D3
Paratoo Australia 32°42S 139°20E 282 B3
Paraúna Brazil 16°55S 50°26W 333 E1
Paray-le-Monial France 46°27N 4°7E 173 F11
Paray-Vieille-Poste France 48°42N 2°20E 134 B3
Parbati → Mad. P., India 25°50N 76°30E 242 G7
Parbati → Raj., India 26°54N 77°53E 242 F7
Parbatipur Bangla. 25°39N 88°55E 241 C2
Parbhani India 19°8N 76°52E 244 E3
Parchim Germany 53°26N 11°52E 178 B7
Parchwitz = Prochowice Poland 51°17N 16°20E 185 G3
Parco = Sinclair U.S.A. 41°47N 107°7W 304 F10
Parczew Poland 51°40N 22°52E 185 G9
Pardes Hanna-Karkur Israel 32°28N 34°57E 251 F5
Pardilla Spain 41°33N 3°43W 194 D7
Pardisān Nature Park Iran 35°44N 51°22E 141 A2
Pardo → Bahia, Brazil 15°40S 39°0W 333 E4
Pardo → Mato Grosso, Brazil 21°46S 52°9W 335 A5
Pardo → Minas Gerais, Brazil 15°48S 44°48W 333 E3
Pardo → São Paulo, Brazil 20°10S 48°38W 333 F2
Pardoo Roadhouse Australia 20°6S 119°3E 278 D2
Pardubice Czech Rep. 50°3N 15°45E 180 A8
Pardubický □ Czech Rep. 49°50N 16°0E 180 B8
Pardubitz = Pardubice Czech Rep. 50°3N 15°45E 180 A8
Pare Indonesia 7°43S 112°12E 231 G15
Pare Mts. Tanzania 4°0S 37°45E 268 C4
Parecis, Serra dos Brazil 13°0S 60°0W 331 C6
Paredes de Nava Spain 42°9N 4°42W 194 C6
Parel India 18°59N 72°49E 130 B1
Parelhas Brazil 6°41S 36°39W 332 C4
Paren Russia 62°30N 163°15E 215 C17
Parenda India 18°16N 75°28E 244 E2
Parengarenga Harbour N.Z. 34°31S 173°0E 284 A2
Parent Canada 47°55N 74°35W 298 C5
Parent, L. Canada 48°31N 77°1W 298 C4
Parentis-en-Born France 44°21N 1°4W 174 D2
Parepare Indonesia 4°0S 119°40E 235 C5
Parfino Russia 57°59N 31°34E 188 D6
Parga Greece 39°15N 20°29E 204 B2
Pargas = Länsi-Turunmaa Finland 60°18N 22°18E 188 B2
Pargi India 17°11N 77°53E 244 E3
Pargo, Pta. do Madeira 32°49N 17°17W 153 c
Parguera Puerto Rico 17°59N 67°3W 321 b
Parham Canada 44°39N 76°43W 313 B8
Pari Brazil 23°32S 46°36W 137 B2
Paria → U.S.A. 36°52N 111°36W 305 H8
Paria, G. de Venezuela 10°20N 62°0W 323 t
Paria, Pen. de Venezuela 10°50N 62°30W 329 A5
Pariaguán Venezuela 8°51N 64°34W 329 B5
Pariaman Indonesia 0°47S 100°11E 234 C2
Paricatuba Brazil 4°26S 61°53W 329 D5
Paricutín, Cerro Mexico 19°28N 102°15W 318 D4
Parigi Indonesia 0°50S 120°5E 231 E6
Parika Guyana 6°50N 58°20W 329 B6
Parikia Greece 37°6N 25°11E 205 D7
Parikkala Finland 61°33N 29°31E 188 B5
Parima, Serra Brazil 2°30N 64°0W 329 C5
Parinari Peru 4°35S 74°25W 330 A3
Pariñas, Pta. Peru 4°30S 82°0W 330 A1
Parincea Romania 46°27N 27°9E 183 D12
Paringa Australia 34°10S 140°46E 282 C4
Parintins Brazil 2°40S 56°50W 329 D6
Parioli Italy 41°55N 12°29E 136 B1
Paripatit Kyun Burma 14°52N 93°41E 245 G11
Paris Ont., Canada 43°12N 80°25W 312 C4
Paris France 48°53N 2°20E 134 A3
Paris Idaho, U.S.A. 42°14N 111°24W 304 E8
Paris Ill., U.S.A. 39°36N 87°42W 311 E9
Paris Ky., U.S.A. 38°13N 84°15W 311 F12
Paris Mo., U.S.A. 39°29N 92°0W 310 E5
Paris Tenn., U.S.A. 36°18N 88°19W 315 C10
Paris Tex., U.S.A. 33°40N 95°33W 314 E7
Paris, Ville de □ France 48°50N 2°20E 173 D9
Paris Charles de Gaulle ✕ (CDG) France 49°0N 2°32E 173 D9
Paris Orly ✕ (ORY) France 48°44N 2°23E 134 B3
Parish U.S.A. 43°25N 76°8W 313 C8
Parishville U.S.A. 44°38N 74°49W 313 B10
Pariti Indonesia 10°1S 123°45E 278 B3
Parje India 18°54N 72°57E 130 B2
Park U.S.A. 48°45N 122°18W 306 B4
Park City U.S.A. 37°48N 97°20W 308 G5
Pärk-e Āzādegān Iran 35°37N 51°28E 141 B2
Pärk-e Mellat Iran 35°47N 51°24E 141 A2
Park Falls U.S.A. 45°56N 90°27W 308 C8
Park Forest U.S.A. 41°29N 87°40W 311 C9
Park Head Canada 44°36N 81°9W 312 B3
Park Hills U.S.A. 37°51N 90°51W 310 G6
Park Range U.S.A. 40°41N 106°41W 304 F10
Park Rapids U.S.A. 46°55N 95°4W 308 B6
Park Ridge U.S.A. 42°2N 87°51W 119 A1
Park River U.S.A. 48°24N 97°45W 308 A5
Park Royal U.K. 51°31N 0°16W 125 A2
Park Rynie S. Africa 30°25S 30°45E 271 D5
Parkā Bandar Iran 25°55N 59°35E 247 E8
Parkal India 18°12N 79°43E 244 E4
Parkān = Štúrovo Slovak Rep. 47°48N 18°41E 181 D11
Parkano Finland 62°1N 23°0E 188 A2
Parkchester U.S.A. 40°49N 73°50W 132 B2
Parkdale Canada 43°38N 79°25W 141 B2
Parkent Uzbekistan 41°18N 69°40E 217 D7
Parker Ariz., U.S.A. 34°9N 114°17W 307 L12
Parker Pa., U.S.A. 41°5N 79°41W 312 E5
Parker Center Los Angeles, U.S.A. 127 b2
Parker Dam U.S.A. 34°18N 114°8W 307 L12
Parkersburg Iowa, U.S.A. 42°35N 92°47W 310 B4
Parkersburg W. Va., U.S.A. 39°16N 81°34W 309 F13
Parkes Australia 33°9S 148°11E 283 B8
Parkfield U.S.A. 35°54N 120°26W 306 K6
Parkhill Canada 43°15N 81°38W 312 C3
Parkhurst S. Africa 26°8S 28°1E 123 A2
Parkland U.S.A. 47°9N 122°26W 306 C4
Parklawn U.S.A. 38°50N 77°7W 143 B3
Parkmore S. Africa 26°5S 28°2E 123 A2
Parkside U.S.A. 37°44N 122°29W 136 B2
Parkston U.S.A. 43°24N 97°59W 308 D5
Parksville Canada 49°20N 124°21W 296 D4
Parktown S. Africa 26°10S 28°2E 123 B2
Parkview S. Africa 26°9S 28°1E 123 A2
Parkville U.S.A. 40°38N 73°57W 132 C2
Parkway U.S.A. 38°32N 121°26W 306 G5
Parkwood Gauteng, S. Africa 26°9S 28°2E 123 A2
Parkwood Western Cape, S. Africa 34°2S 18°30E 118 B1
Parla Spain 40°14N 3°46W 194 E7
Parlakimidi India 18°45N 84°5E 244 E7
Parlatuvier Trin. & Tob. 11°18N 60°39W 323 s
Parli India 18°50N 76°35E 244 E3
Parliament Budapest, Hungary 117 b2
Pârlita Moldova 47°19N 27°52E 183 C12
Parma Italy 44°48N 10°20E 198 D7
Parma Idaho, U.S.A. 43°47N 116°57W 304 E5
Parma Ohio, U.S.A. 41°24N 81°43W 312 E3
Parma → Italy 44°56N 10°26E 198 D7
Parnaguá Brazil 10°10S 44°38W 332 D3
Parnaíba Brazil 2°54S 41°47W 332 B3
Parnaíba → Brazil 3°0S 41°50W 332 B3
Parnamirim Pernambuco, Brazil 8°5S 39°34W 332 C4
Parnamirim Rio Grande do N., Brazil 5°55S 35°15W 332 C4
Parnarama Brazil 5°31S 43°6W 332 C3
Parnassos Greece 38°35N 22°30E 204 C4
Parnassus N.Z. 42°42S 173°23E 285 C8
Parndana Australia 35°48S 137°12E 282 C2
Parner India 19°0N 74°26E 244 E2
Parnitha Greece 38°14N 23°45E 204 C5
Parnitha △ Greece 38°12N 23°44E 204 C5
Parnonas Oros Greece 37°15N 22°45E 204 D4
Pärnu Estonia 58°28N 24°33E 188 C3
Paro Dzong Bhutan 27°32N 89°53E 241 B2
Parola India 20°47N 75°7E 244 D2
Paroo → Australia 31°28S 143°32E 282 A5
Paros Greece 37°5N 25°12E 205 D7
Parow S. Africa 33°53S 18°37E 118 A2
Parowan U.S.A. 37°51N 112°50W 305 H7
Parpaillon France 44°30N 6°40E 175 D10
Parque Chacabuco Argentina 34°39S 58°26W 117 B2
Parque Patricios Argentina 34°39S 58°23W 117 B2
Parral Chile 36°10S 71°52W 334 D1
Parramatta Australia 33°48S 151°1E 283 B9
Parramatta → Australia 33°49S 151°3E 139 A1
Parras Mexico 25°25N 102°11W 318 B4
Parrett → U.K. 51°12N 3°1W 169 F4
Parris I. U.S.A. 32°20N 80°41W 316 C9
Parrish U.S.A. 27°35N 82°26W 317 H7
Parrott U.S.A. 31°54N 84°31W 316 D5
Parrsboro Canada 45°30N 64°25W 299 C7
Parry Channel Canada 74°15N 94°0W 295 C13
Parry I. Canada 45°18N 80°10W 312 A4
Parry Is. Canada 77°0N 110°0W 295 B10
Parry Sound Canada 45°20N 80°0W 312 A5
Parsābād Iran 39°39N 47°50E 213 C12
Parsaloi Kenya 1°16N 36°51E 268 B4
Parsberg Germany 49°10N 11°43E 179 F7
Parsęta → Poland 54°11N 15°34E 184 D2
Parsnip → Canada 55°10N 123°2W 296 B4
Parsons U.S.A. 37°20N 95°16W 308 G6
Parsons Ra. Australia 13°30S 135°15E 280 A2
Partabpur India 20°0N 80°42E 244 E5
Partanna Italy 37°43N 12°53E 200 E5
Partenio △ Italy 40°56N 14°38E 201 B7
Parthenay France 46°38N 0°16W 172 F6
Parthenon Athens, Greece 112 c2
Partinico Italy 38°3N 13°7E 200 D6
Partizansk Russia 43°8N 133°9E 215 E14
Partizánske Slovak Rep. 48°38N 18°23E 181 C11
Partridge I. Canada 55°59N 87°37W 298 A2
Partry Mts. Ireland 53°40N 9°28W 166 C2
Partur India 19°40N 76°14E 244 E3
Paru → Brazil 1°33S 52°38W 329 D7
Parú → Venezuela 4°20N 66°27W 328 C4
Paru de Oeste → Brazil 1°30N 56°0W 329 C6
Parucito → Venezuela 5°18N 65°59W 328 B4
Parur India 10°13N 76°14E 245 J3
Paruro Peru 13°45S 71°50W 330 C3
Parvān □ Afghan. 35°0N 69°0E 240 B3
Parvatipuram India 18°50N 83°25E 244 E6
Parvatsar India 26°52N 74°49E 242 F6
Påryd Sweden 56°34N 15°55E 163 H9
Parys S. Africa 26°52S 27°29E 270 C4
Pas, Pta. des Spain 38°46N 1°26E 206 D1
Pas, The Canada 53°45N 101°15W 297 C8
Pas-de-Calais □ France 50°30N 2°10E 173 B9
Paşabahçe Turkey 41°6N 29°5E 122 B2
Pasada Spain 43°23N 5°40W 194 B5
Pasadena Nfld. & L., Canada 49°1N 57°36W 299 C8
Pasadena Calif., U.S.A. 34°9N 118°8W 126 B4
Pasadena Tex., U.S.A. 29°43N 95°13W 314 G7
Pasaje Ecuador 3°23S 79°50W 328 D2
Pasaje → Argentina 25°39S 63°56W 334 B3
Paşalimanı Turkey 40°29N 27°36E 203 F11
Pasar Indonesia 8°27S 114°54E 231 J17
Pasar Minggu Indonesia 6°16S 106°49E 122 B1
Pasarkuok Indonesia 1°27S 100°36E 234 C2
Pasarsibuhuan Indonesia 1°3N 99°43E 234 B1
Pasay Phil. 14°32N 120°59E 127 B1
Pascagoula U.S.A. 30°21N 88°33W 315 F10
Pascagoula → U.S.A. 30°23N 88°37W 315 F10
Paşcani Romania 47°14N 26°45E 183 C11
Pasco U.S.A. 46°14N 119°6W 304 C4
Pasco □ Peru 10°40S 75°0W 330 C3
Pasco I. Australia 20°57S 115°20E 278 D2
Pascoag U.S.A. 41°57N 71°42W 313 E13
Pascoe Vale Australia 37°43S 144°55E 128 A1
Pascua, I. de Chile 27°7S 109°23W 330 b
Paseo de la Reforma Mexico City, Mexico 128 b2
Pasewalk Germany 53°30N 13°58E 178 B9
Pasfield L. Canada 58°24N 105°20W 297 B7
Pasha → Russia 60°29N 32°55E 188 B7
Pashmakli = Smolyan Bulgaria 41°36N 24°38E 203 E8
Pasig Phil. 14°33N 121°4E 127 B2
Pasig → Phil. 14°31N 121°6E 127 B2
Pasighat India 28°4N 95°21E 241 A5
Pasila Finland 60°12N 24°56E 121 B2
Pasing Germany 48°8N 11°28E 131 B1
Pasinler Turkey 39°59N 41°41E 213 C9
Pasir Mas Malaysia 6°2N 102°8E 237 J4
Pasir Panjang Singapore 1°18N 103°46E 138 B2
Pasir Putih Malaysia 5°50N 102°24E 237 K4
Pasir Ris Singapore 1°22N 103°56E 138 A3
Pasirian Indonesia 8°13S 113°8E 235 D4
Pasirkuning = Dabo Indonesia 0°30S 104°33E 234 C2
Pasirpengarayan Indonesia 0°51N 100°16E 234 B2
Påskallavik Sweden 57°10N 16°26E 163 G10
Paskūh Iran 27°34N 61°39E 247 E9
Pasłęk Poland 54°3N 19°41E 184 D6
Pasłęka → Poland 54°26N 19°46E 184 D6
Pasley, C. Australia 33°52S 123°35E 279 F3
Pašman Croatia 43°58N 15°20E 199 E12
Pasmore → Australia 31°5S 139°49E 282 A3
Pasni Pakistan 25°15N 63°27E 240 D1
Paso Bravo △ Paraguay 22°32S 57°5W 334 A4
Paso Cantinela Mexico 32°33N 115°47W 307 N11
Paso de Indios Argentina 43°55S 69°0W 336 B3
Paso de los Indios Argentina 38°32S 69°25W 336 A3
Paso de los Libres Argentina 29°44S 57°10W 334 B4
Paso de los Toros Uruguay 32°45S 56°30W 334 C4
Paso Flores Argentina 40°35S 70°38W 336 B2
Paso Robles U.S.A. 35°38N 120°41W 306 K6
Pasorapa Bolivia 18°16S 64°37W 331 D5
Paspébiac Canada 48°3N 65°17W 299 C6
Pasrur Pakistan 32°16N 74°43E 242 C6
Passage East Ireland 52°14N 7°0W 166 D5
Passage West Ireland 51°52N 8°21W 166 E3
Passaic U.S.A. 40°51N 74°7W 132 A1
Passaic → U.S.A. 40°42N 74°10W 132 B1
Passam Papua N. G. 3°41S 143°38E 286 B2
Passau Germany 48°34N 13°28E 179 G9
Passenheim = Pasym Poland 53°48N 20°49E 184 E7
Passero, C. Italy 36°41N 15°10E 201 F8
Passi Phil. 11°6N 122°38E 233 F4
Passirana Italy 45°32N 9°2E 129 A1
Passo Fundo Brazil 28°10S 52°20W 335 B5
Passos Brazil 20°45S 46°37W 333 F2
Passow Germany 53°8N 14°6E 178 B10
Passy France 45°55N 6°41E 175 C10
Pastavy Belarus 55°4N 26°50E 188 E4
Pastaza □ Ecuador 2°0S 77°0W 328 D2
Pastaza → Peru 4°50S 76°52W 328 D2
Pasto Colombia 1°13N 77°17W 328 C2
Pastol B. U.S.A. 63°7N 163°15W 303 E7
Pastos Bons Brazil 6°36S 44°5W 332 C3
Pastrana Spain 40°27N 2°53W 196 E2
Pasuquin Phil. 18°20N 120°37E 232 B3
Pasuruan Indonesia 7°40S 112°44E 235 D4
Pasym Poland 53°48N 20°49E 184 E7
Pásztó Hungary 47°52N 19°43E 182 C4
Pata Phil. 5°51N 121°10E 233 J3
Pata I. Phil. 5°49N 121°10E 233 J3
Patagonia Argentina 45°0S 69°0W 336 C3
Patagonia Ariz., U.S.A. 31°33N 110°45W 305 L8
Patambar Iran 29°45N 60°17E 247 D9
Patan = Lalitapur Nepal 27°40N 85°20E 243 F11
Patan = Somnath India 20°53N 70°22E 242 J4
Patan Gujarat, India 23°54N 72°14E 242 H5
Patan Maharashtra, India 17°22N 73°57E 244 F1
Patani Indonesia 0°20N 128°50E 231 D7
Pătârlagele Romania 45°19N 26°21E 183 E11
Pataudi India 28°18N 76°48E 242 E7
Patchewollock Australia 35°22S 142°12E 282 C5
Patchogue U.S.A. 40°46N 73°1W 313 F11
Pate Coast, Kenya 2°10S 41°0E 268 C5
Pate Taiwan 24°56N 121°17E 225 B3
Patea N.Z. 39°45S 174°30E 284 F3
Pategi Nigeria 8°50N 5°45E 263 D6
Patel Nagar India 28°39N 77°10E 120 B1
Patensie S. Africa 33°46S 24°49E 270 D3
Paterna Spain 39°30N 0°26W 197 F4
Paternion Austria 46°43N 13°38E 180 E6
Paternò Italy 37°34N 14°54E 201 E7
Pateros Manila, Phil. 14°32N 121°3E 127 B2
Pateros Wash., U.S.A. 48°3N 119°54W 304 B4
Paterson N.S.W., Australia 32°35S 151°36E 283 B9
Paterson N.J., U.S.A. 40°54N 74°9W 313 F10
Paterson Inlet N.Z. 46°56S 168°12E 285 G3
Paterson Ra. Australia 21°45S 122°10E 278 D3
Pathankot India 32°18N 75°45E 242 C6
Pathardi India 19°10N 75°11E 244 E2
Patharghata Bangla. 22°2N 89°58E 241 D2
Pathein = Bassein Burma 16°45N 94°30E 241 G5
Pathfinder Res. U.S.A. 42°28N 106°51W 304 E10
Pathiu Thailand 10°42N 99°19E 237 G2
Pathri India 19°15N 76°27E 244 E3
Pathum Thani Thailand 14°1N 100°32E 236 E3
Pathumwan Thailand 13°44N 100°31E 113 B2
Pati Indonesia 6°45S 111°1E 235 D4
Pati Pt. Guam 13°35N 144°57E 302 d
Patía Colombia 2°4N 77°4W 328 C2
Patía → Colombia 2°13N 78°40W 328 C2
Patiala Punjab, India 30°23N 76°26E 242 D7
Patiala Ut. P., India 27°43N 79°1E 243 F8
Patine Kouka Senegal 12°45N 13°45W 262 C2
Patipukur India 22°36N 88°24E 124 B2
Patisia Greece 38°2N 23°45E 112 A2
Patitiri Greece 39°8N 23°50E 204 B5
Patkai Bum India 27°0N 95°30E 241 B5
Patmos Greece 37°21N 26°36E 205 D8
Patna India 25°35N 85°12E 243 G11
Patnagarh India 20°43N 83°9E 244 D6
Patnanongan I. Phil. 14°48N 122°11E 232 D4
Patnongon Phil. 10°55N 122°0E 233 F4
Patnos Turkey 39°13N 42°51E 213 C10
Pato Branco Brazil 26°13S 52°40W 335 B5
Patoka L. U.S.A. 38°20N 86°40W 311 F10
Patong, Ao Thailand 7°54N 98°17E 237 a
Patonga Uganda 2°45N 33°15E 268 B3
Patos Albania 40°42N 19°38E 202 F3
Patos Brazil 6°55S 37°16W 332 C4
Patos, L. dos Brazil 31°20S 51°0W 335 C5
Patos, Río de los → Argentina 31°18S 69°25W 334 C2
Patos de Minas Brazil 18°35S 46°32W 333 E2
Patquía Argentina 30°2S 66°55W 334 C2
Patra Greece 38°14N 21°47E 204 C3
Patraikos Kolpos Greece 38°17N 21°30E 204 C3
Patras = Patra Greece 38°14N 21°47E 204 C3
Patreksfjörður Iceland 65°35N 24°0W 155 B2
Patriarsheye = Donskoy Russia 53°55N 38°15E 188 F10
Patricio Lynch, I. Chile 48°35S 75°30W 336 C1
Patriot Hills Antarctica 82°20S 81°25W 151 E16
Patrocínio Brazil 18°57S 47°0W 333 E2
Pattada Italy 40°35N 9°6E 200 B2
Pattallassang Indonesia 5°26S 119°26E 235 D5
Pattani Thailand 6°48N 101°15E 237 J3
Pattaya Thailand 12°52N 100°55E 236 F3
Patten U.S.A. 46°0N 68°38W 309 B19
Patterson Calif., U.S.A. 37°28N 121°8W 306 H5
Patterson Ga., U.S.A. 31°23N 82°8W 316 D7
Patterson La., U.S.A. 29°42N 91°18W 314 G9
Patterson, Mt. U.S.A. 38°29N 119°20W 306 G7
Patteson, Passage Vanuatu 15°26S 168°12E 287 E6
Patti Punjab, India 31°17N 74°54E 242 D6
Patti Ut. P., India 25°55N 82°12E 243 G10
Patti Italy 38°8N 14°58E 201 D7
Pattoki Pakistan 31°5N 73°52E 242 D5
Patton = Monroeville U.S.A. 40°26N 79°45W 312 F5
Patton U.S.A. 40°38N 78°39W 312 F6
Pattonsburg U.S.A. 40°3N 94°8W 310 D2
Pattukkattai India 10°25N 79°20E 245 J4
Patu Brazil 6°6S 37°38W 332 C4
Patuakhali Bangla. 22°20N 90°25E 241 D3
Patuanak Canada 55°55N 107°43W 297 B7
Patuca → Honduras 15°50N 84°18W 320 C3
Patuca, Punta Honduras 15°49N 84°14W 320 C3
Patuca △ Honduras 14°30N 85°30W 320 D2
Pătulele Romania 44°21N 22°47E 182 F7
Patur India 20°27N 76°56E 244 D3
Patvinsuo △ Finland 63°7N 30°45E 160 E24
Pátzcuaro Mexico 19°31N 101°38W 318 D4
Pau France 43°19N 0°25W 174 E3
Pau, Gave de → France 43°33N 1°12W 174 E2
Pau d' Arco Brazil 7°30S 49°22W 332 C2
Pau dos Ferros Brazil 6°7S 38°10W 332 C4
Pauanui N.Z. 37°1S 175°52E 284 D4
Paucartambo Peru 13°19S 71°35W 330 C3
Paudash Canada 44°59N 77°58W 312 B7
Pauillac France 45°11N 0°46W 174 C3
Pauini Brazil 7°40S 66°58W 330 B4
Pauini → Brazil 1°42S 62°50W 329 D5
Pauk Burma 21°27N 94°30E 241 E5
Paukkaung Burma 18°54N 95°33E 241 F5
Pauktaw Burma 20°11N 93°4E 241 E4
Paul I. Canada 56°30N 61°20W 299 A7
Paul Isnard Fr. Guiana 4°47N 54°1W 329 C7
Paul Revere Park Boston, U.S.A. 116 a2
Paul Smiths U.S.A. 44°26N 74°15W 313 B10
Paulatuk Canada 69°25N 124°0W 294 D7
Paulding U.S.A. 41°8N 84°35W 311 C12
Paulding Bay S. Ocean 66°0S 118°0E 151 C8
Paulhan France 43°33N 3°28E 174 E7
Paulis = Isiro Dem. Rep. of the Congo 2°53N 27°40E 268 B2
Paulista = Paulistana Brazil 8°9S 41°9W 332 C3
Paulista Brazil 7°57S 34°53W 332 C5
Paulistana Brazil 8°9S 41°9W 332 C3
Paulström Sweden 57°28N 15°31E 163 G9
Paulo Afonso Brazil 9°21S 38°15W 332 C4
Paulo de Faria Brazil 20°2S 49°24W 333 F2
Paulo E. Virginia, Gruta Brazil 22°56S 43°16W 135 B1
Paulpietersburg S. Africa 27°23S 30°50E 271 C5
Pauls Valley U.S.A. 34°44N 97°13W 314 D6
Paulshof Germany 52°34N 13°42E 115 A5
Pauma Valley U.S.A. 33°16N 116°58W 307 M10
Paung Burma 16°37N 94°28E 241 G5
Paungde Burma 18°29N 95°30E 241 F5
Pauni India 20°48N 79°40E 244 D4
Pauri India 30°9N 78°47E 243 D8
Pausa Peru 15°16S 73°22W 330 D3
Pauto → Colombia 5°9N 70°55W 328 B3
Pavagada India 14°6N 77°16E 245 G3
Pāveh Iran 35°3N 46°22E 213 E12
Pavelets Russia 53°49N 39°14E 188 F10
Pavia Italy 45°7N 9°8E 198 C6
Pavilion U.S.A. 42°52N 78°1W 312 D6
Pavilly France 49°34N 0°57E 172 C7
Pāvilosta Latvia 56°53N 21°14E 184 B8
Pavlikeni Bulgaria 43°14N 25°20E 203 C9
Pavlodar Kazakhstan 52°33N 77°0E 217 B9
Pavlograd = Pavlohrad Ukraine 48°30N 35°52E 189 H8
Pavlohrad Ukraine 48°30N 35°52E 189 H8
Pavlovo Russia 55°58N 43°5E 190 C6
Pavlovsk Russia 50°26N 40°5E 190 G5
Pavlovskaya Russia 46°17N 39°47E 191 G4
Pavlovskiy-Posad Russia 55°47N 38°42E 188 E10
Pavo U.S.A. 30°58N 83°45W 316 E6
Pavshino Russia 55°49N 37°20E 129 B1
Pavullo nel Frignano Italy 44°20N 10°50E 198 D7
Pavuvu Solomon Is. 9°4S 159°8E 287 M10
Paw Paw Ill., U.S.A. 41°41N 88°59W 310 C8
Paw Paw Mich., U.S.A. 42°13N 85°53W 311 B11
Pawahku Burma 26°11N 98°40E 241 B7
Pawai, Pulau Singapore 1°11N 103°44E 237 d
Pawan → Indonesia 1°55S 110°0E 235 C4
Pawayan India 28°4N 80°6E 243 E9
Pawhuska U.S.A. 36°40N 96°20W 314 C6
Pawling U.S.A. 41°34N 73°36W 313 E11
Pawnee Ill., U.S.A. 39°36N 89°35W 310 E7
Pawnee Okla., U.S.A. 36°20N 96°48W 314 C6
Pawnee City U.S.A. 40°7N 96°9W 308 E5
Pawtucket U.S.A. 41°53N 71°23W 313 E13
Paxi Greece 39°14N 20°12E 206 C10
Paximadia Greece 35°0N 24°35E 207 F6
Paxson U.S.A. 63°2N 145°30W 303 E11
Paxton U.S.A. 40°27N 88°6W 311 D8
Paya Lebar Singapore 1°21N 103°52E 138 A3
Payagyi Burma 17°29N 96°32E 241 G6
Payakumbuh Indonesia 0°20S 100°35E 234 C2
Payapa = General Tinio Phil. 15°39N 121°10E 232 D3
Payas = Yakacık Turkey 36°46N 36°11E 250 F7
Payerne Switz. 46°49N 6°56E 179 J2
Payette U.S.A. 44°5N 116°56W 304 D5
Paymogo Spain 37°44N 7°21W 195 H3
Payne U.S.A. 41°5N 84°44W 311 C11
Payne Bay = Kangirsuk Canada 60°0N 70°0W 295 F18
Payne L. Canada 59°30N 74°30W 295 F17
Payne Pt. Ascension I. 7°57S 14°25W 153 g
Paynes Find Australia 29°15S 117°42E 279 E2
Paynesville Liberia 6°20N 10°45W 262 D2
Paynesville Minn., U.S.A. 45°23N 94°43W 308 C6
Payo Obispo = Chetumal Mexico 18°30N 88°20W 319 D7
Pays de la Loire □ France 47°45N 0°25W 172 E6
Paysandú Uruguay 32°19S 58°8W 334 C4
Payson Ariz., U.S.A. 34°14N 111°20W 305 J8
Payson Utah, U.S.A. 40°3N 111°44W 304 F8
Paz → Guatemala 13°44N 90°10W 320 D1
Paz, B. de la Mexico 24°9N 110°25W 318 C2
Pāzanān Iran 30°35N 49°59E 247 D6
Pazar Turkey 41°10N 40°50E 213 B9
Pazarcık Turkey 37°30N 37°17E 212 D7
Pazardzhik Bulgaria 42°12N 24°20E 203 D8
Pazardzhik □ Bulgaria 42°12N 24°20E 203 D8
Pazarköy Turkey 39°51N 27°24E 205 B9
Pazarlar Turkey 39°0N 29°7E 205 C11
Pazaryeri Turkey 40°0N 29°56E 205 B11
Pazaryolu Turkey 40°21N 40°47E 213 B9
Pazin Croatia 45°14N 13°56E 199 C10
Pazña Bolivia 18°36S 66°55W 330 D4
Pčinja → Macedonia 41°50N 21°45E 202 E5
Pe Ell U.S.A. 46°34N 123°18W 306 D3
Pea → U.S.A. 31°1N 85°51W 316 D4
Peabody U.S.A. 42°31N 70°56W 313 D14
Peace → Alta., Canada 59°0N 111°25W 296 B6
Peace → Fla., U.S.A. 26°56N 82°6W 317 J7
Peace Point Canada 59°7N 112°27W 296 B6
Peace River Canada 56°15N 117°18W 296 B5
Peach Springs U.S.A. 35°32N 113°25W 305 J7
Peachland Canada 49°47N 119°45W 296 D5
Peachtree City U.S.A. 33°25N 84°35W 316 B4
Peacock Pt. Wake I. 19°16N 166°37E 302 b
Peak, The = Kinder Scout U.K. 53°24N 1°52W 168 D6
Peak, The Ascension I. 7°57S 14°20W 153 g
Peak Charles △ Australia 32°42S 121°10E 279 F3
Peak District △ U.K. 53°24N 1°46W 168 D6
Peak Hill Australia 32°47S 148°11E 283 B8
Peak Ra. Australia 22°50S 148°20E 280 C4
Peake Australia 35°25S 139°55E 282 C3
Peake Cr. → Australia 28°2S 136°7E 281 D2
Peakhurst Australia 33°57S 151°3E 139 B1
Peal de Becerro Spain 37°55N 3°7W 195 H7
Peale, Mt. U.S.A. 38°26N 109°14W 304 G9
Peale I. Wake I. 19°18N 166°37E 302 b
Peania Greece 37°56N 23°50E 112 B3
Pearblossom U.S.A. 34°30N 117°55W 307 L9
Pearce U.S.A. 31°54N 109°49W 305 L9
Pearl → U.S.A. 30°11N 89°32W 315 F10
Pearl and Hermes Reef U.S.A. 27°55N 175°45W 302 F8
Pearl Banks Sri Lanka 8°45N 79°45E 245 K4
Pearl City U.S.A. 21°24N 157°59W 302 K14
Pearl Harbor U.S.A. 21°21N 157°57W 302 K14
Pearl Harbor Nat. Wildlife Refuge ⌂ U.S.A. 21°23N 157°59W 302 K14
Pearl River = Zhu Jiang → China 22°45N 113°37E 229 F9
Pearl River U.S.A. 41°4N 74°2W 313 E10
Pearl River Bridge China 22°15N 113°48E 219 a
Pearls Grenada 12°9N 61°37W 323 q
Pearls Rock Grenada 12°9N 61°36W 323 q
Pearsall U.S.A. 28°54N 99°6W 314 G5
Pearson U.S.A. 31°18N 82°51W 316 D7
Pearson Int. Toronto ✕ (YYZ) Canada 43°46N 79°35W 141 A1
Peary Land Greenland 82°40N 33°0W 154 A7
Pease → U.S.A. 34°12N 99°2W 314 D5
Peawanuck Canada 55°15N 85°12W 298 A2
Pebane Mozam. 17°10S 38°8E 269 F4
Pebas Peru 3°10S 71°46W 328 D3
Pebble, I. Falk. Is. 51°20S 59°40W 152 A1
Pebble Beach U.S.A. 36°34N 121°57W 306 J5
Peć Kosovo 42°40N 20°17E 202 D4
Peçanha Brazil 18°33S 42°34W 333 E3
Pecatonica U.S.A. 42°19N 89°22W 310 B7
Pecatonica → U.S.A. 42°26N 89°12W 310 B7
Péccioli Italy 43°33N 10°43E 198 E7
Pechea Romania 45°36N 27°49E 183 E12
Pechenga Russia 69°29N 31°4E 160 B24
Pechenizhyn Ukraine 48°30N 24°48E 183 B9
Pechiguera, Pta. Canary Is. 28°51N 13°53W 153 e2
Pechnezhskoye Vdkhr. Ukraine 50°5N 36°54E 189 G9
Pechora Russia 65°10N 57°11E 186 A10
Pechora → Russia 68°13N 54°15E 186 A9
Pechorskaya Guba Russia 68°40N 54°0E 186 A9
Pechory Russia 57°48N 27°40E 188 D4
Pecica Romania 46°10N 21°3E 182 D6
Pecka Serbia 44°18N 19°33E 202 B3
Peckham U.K. 51°28N 0°3W 125 B3
Pécora, C. Italy 39°27N 8°23E 200 C1
Pecos N. Mex., U.S.A. 35°35N 105°41W 305 J11
Pecos Tex., U.S.A. 31°26N 103°30W 314 F3
Pecos → U.S.A. 29°42N 101°22W 314 G4
Pécs Hungary 46°5N 18°15E 182 D3
Pedasí Panama 7°32N 80°2W 320 E3
Pedda Bellala India 19°4N 78°49E 244 E4
Peddapalli India 18°40N 79°24E 244 E4
Peddapuram India 17°6N 82°8E 244 F6
Pedder, L. Australia 42°55S 146°10E 281 G4
Peddie S. Africa 33°14S 27°7E 271 D4
Pedernales Dom. Rep. 18°2N 71°44W 321 C5
Pedernales Ecuador 0°5N 80°3W 328 C1
Pederstrup Denmark 55°44N 12°20E 118 A2
Pedieos → Cyprus 35°10N 33°54E 207 E9
Pedirka Desert Australia 26°47S 134°11E 281 A1
Pedra Azul Brazil 16°2S 41°17W 333 E3
Pedra Branca Brazil 0°51N 51°58W 329 C7
Pedra Grande, Recifes de Brazil 17°45S 38°58W 333 E4
Pedra Lume C. Verde Is. 16°40N 22°52W 153 j
Pedralbes Spain 41°23N 2°7E 114 A1
Pedras Negras Brazil 12°51S 62°54W 331 C5
Pedras Tinhosas, I. São Tomé & Principe 1°22N 7°17E 265 a
Pedregal de San Angel, Jardines del Mexico 19°19N 99°12W 128 C1
Pedreguer Spain 38°48N 0°3E 197 G5
Pedreiras Brazil 4°32S 44°40W 332 B3
Pedro Afonso Brazil 9°0S 48°10W 332 C2
Pedro Bank W. Indies 17°5N 78°20W 320 C4
Pedro Bay U.S.A. 59°47N 154°7W 303 G9
Pedro Cays Jamaica 17°5N 77°48W 320 C4
Pedro Chico Colombia 1°4N 70°25W 328 C3
Pedro de Valdivia Chile 22°55S 69°38W 334 A2
Pedro Dorado Colombia 1°0N 70°14W 328 C3
Pedro Juan Caballero Paraguay 22°30S 55°40W 335 A4
Pedro Miguel Locks Panama 9°1N 79°36W 320 c
Pedro Muñoz Spain 39°25N 2°56W 195 F8
Pedro Pt. = North West Pt. Jamaica 18°27N 78°13W 320 a
Pedrógão Grande Portugal 39°55N 8°9W 194 F2
Pee Dee = Great Pee Dee → U.S.A. 33°21N 79°10W 315 E15
Peebinga Australia 34°52S 140°57E 282 C4
Peebles Borders, U.K. 55°40N 3°11W 167 F5
Peebles Ohio, U.S.A. 38°57N 83°24W 311 F13
Peekskill U.S.A. 41°17N 73°55W 313 E11
Peel I. of Man 54°13N 4°40W 168 C3
Peel → N.S.W., Australia 30°50S 150°29E 283 A9
Peel → N.W.T., Canada 67°0N 135°0W 294 D5
Peel Sd. Canada 73°0N 96°0W 294 C12
Peene → Germany 54°9N 13°46E 178 A9
Peera Peera Poolanna L. Australia 26°30S 138°0E 281 D2
Peerless Lake Canada 56°37N 114°40W 296 B6
Peers Canada 53°40N 116°0W 296 C5
Peery L. Australia 30°45S 143°35E 282 A5
Pegasus Bay N.Z. 43°20S 173°10E 285 D8
Peggau Austria 47°12N 15°21E 180 D8
Pegnitz Germany 49°44N 11°31E 179 F7
Pegnitz → Germany 49°30N 10°59E 179 F6
Pego Spain 38°51N 0°8W 197 G4
Pegu Burma 17°20N 96°29E 241 G6
Pegu □ Burma 17°30N 96°30E 241 G6
Pegu Yoma Burma 19°0N 96°0E 241 F6
Peguera Spain 39°32N 2°26E 206 B3
Pehčevo Macedonia 41°41N 22°55E 202 E6
Pehlivanköy Turkey 41°20N 26°55E 203 E10
Pehuajó Argentina 35°45S 62°0W 334 D3
Pei Xian China 34°44N 116°55E 226 G9
Peian = Bei'an China 48°10N 126°20E 219 B14
Peihai = Beihai China 21°28N 109°6E 228 G7
Peikang Taiwan 23°34N 120°18E 225 C2
Peikang Hsi → Taiwan 24°2N 120°50E 225 B2
Peikant'ang Taiwan 26°13N 120°0E 225 b
Peimen Taiwan 23°16N 120°7E 225 C2
Peinan Taiwan 22°47N 121°7E 225 D3
Peinan Hsi → Taiwan 22°46N 121°10E 225 D3
Peinanchu Shan Taiwan 23°23N 120°52E 225 C2
Peine Chile 23°45S 68°8W 334 A2
Peine Niedersachsen, Germany 52°19N 10°14E 178 C6
Peip'ing = Beijing China 39°53N 116°21E 114 B1
Peipu Taiwan 24°2N 121°36E 225 B3
Peipus, L. = Chudskoye, Ozero Russia 58°13N 27°30E 188 C4
Peissenberg Germany 47°48N 11°4E 179 H7
Peitawu Shan Taiwan 22°38N 120°46E 225 D2
Peitou Changhua, Taiwan 23°52N 120°30E 225 C2
Peitou T'aipei, Taiwan 25°11N 121°27E 225 A3
Peitun Taiwan 24°10N 120°41E 225 B2
Peitz Germany 51°51N 14°24E 178 D10
Peixe Brazil 12°0S 48°40W 333 D2
Peixe → Brazil 21°31S 51°58W 333 F1
Peixoto de Azeredo → Brazil 10°6S 55°31W 331 C6
Pejantan, Pulau Indonesia 0°7N 107°13E 234 B3
Peje = Peć Kosovo 42°40N 20°17E 202 D4
Pek → Serbia 44°45N 21°29E 202 B5
Pekalongan Indonesia 6°53S 109°40E 235 D3
Pekan Malaysia 3°30N 103°25E 237 L4
Pekan Nenas Malaysia 1°31N 103°31E 237 d
Pekanbaru Indonesia 0°30N 101°15E 234 B2
Pekhorka → Russia 55°37N 38°2E 129 C6
Pekhra-Pokrovskoye Russia 55°50N 37°56E 129 A5
Pekhra-Yakovlevskaya Russia 55°47N 37°57E 129 B5
Pekin U.S.A. 40°35N 89°40W 310 D7
Peking = Beijing China 39°53N 116°21E 114 B1
Pekutatan Indonesia 8°25S 114°49E 231 J17
Pela Greece 40°46N 22°23E 202 F6
Pelabuhan Ratu, Teluk Indonesia 7°5S 106°30E 234 D3
Pelabuhanratu Indonesia 7°0S 106°32E 234 D3
Pélagos = Kira Panagia Greece 39°17N 24°4E 204 B6
Pelaihari Indonesia 3°55S 114°45E 235 C4
Pelat, Mt. France 44°16N 6°42E 175 D10
Pelcowizna Poland 52°17N 21°0E 142 B2
Pelczyce Poland 53°3N 15°16E 184 E2
Peleaga, Vf. Romania 45°22N 22°55E 182 E7
Pelechuco Bolivia 14°48S 69°4W 330 C4
Pelée, Mt. Martinique 14°48N 61°10W 322 j
Pelee, Pt. Canada 41°54N 82°30W 298 D3
Pelee I. Canada 41°47N 82°40W 312 E2
Pelejo Peru 6°10S 75°49W 330 B2
Pelekech Kenya 3°52N 35°8E 268 B4
Peleliu I. Palau 7°1N 134°15E 288 c

Peleng *Indonesia* 1°20S 123°30E **231** E6
Pelenge *Dem. Rep. of the Congo* 2°44S 22°39E **264** C4
Pelentong *Malaysia* 1°32N 103°49E **237** d
Pélézi *Ivory C.* 7°17N 6°54W **262** D3
Pelham *U.S.A.* 31°8N 84°9W **316** D5
Pelhřimov *Czech Rep.* 49°24N 15°12E **180** B8
Pelican *U.S.A.* 57°58N 136°14W **296** B1
Pelican L. *Canada* 52°28N 100°20W **297** C8
Pelican Narrows *Canada* 55°10N 102°56W **297** B8
Pelion *U.S.A.* 33°46N 81°15W **316** B8
Pelister △ *Macedonia* 41°0N 21°10E **202** F5
Pelješac *Croatia* 42°55N 17°25E **199** F14
Pelkosenniemi *Finland* 67°6N 27°28E **160** C22
Pell City *U.S.A.* 33°35N 86°17W **316** B3
Pella *Northern Cape, S. Africa* 29°1S 19°6E **270** C2
Pella *Iowa, U.S.A.* 41°25N 92°55W **310** C4
Pella □ *Greece* 40°52N 22°0E **202** F6
Pello *Finland* 66°47N 23°59E **160** C20
Pellworm *Germany* 54°31N 8°39E **178** A4
Pelly → *Canada* 62°47N 137°19W **296** A1
Pelly Bay *Canada* 68°38N 89°50W **295** D14
Peloponnesos □ *Greece* 37°10N 22°0E **204** D4
Peloponnisos Station *Athens, Greece* **112** a1
Peloritani, Monti *Italy* 38°3N 15°20E **201** D8
Pelorus → *N.Z.* 41°16S 173°45E **285** B8
Pelorus Sd. *N.Z.* 40°59S 173°59E **285** A8
Pelotas *Brazil* 31°42S 52°23W **335** C5
Pelotas → *Brazil* 27°28S 51°55W **335** B5
Pelovo *Bulgaria* 43°26N 24°17E **203** C8
Pelplin *Poland* 53°55N 18°42E **184** E5
Pelvoux, Massif du *France* 44°52N 6°20E **175** D10
Pemalang *Indonesia* 6°53S 109°23E **235** D3
Pemanggil, Pulau *Malaysia* 2°37N 104°21E **237** L5
Pematangsiantar *Indonesia* 2°57N 99°5E **234** B1
Pemba *Mozam.* 12°58S 40°30E **269** E5
Pemba *Zambia* 16°30S 27°28E **269** F2
Pemba Channel *Tanzania* 5°0S 39°37E **268** D4
Pemba I. *Tanzania* 5°0S 39°45E **268** D4
Pemberton *W. Austral., Australia* 34°30S 116°0E **279** F2
Pemberton *B.C., Canada* 50°25N 122°50W **296** C4
Pembina → *Canada* 54°45N 114°17W **296** C6
Pembroke *Ont., Canada* 45°50N 77°7W **298** C4
Pembroke *Trin. & Tob.* 11°13N 60°37W **323** s
Pembroke *Pembs., U.K.* 51°41N 4°55W **169** F3
Pembroke *Ga., U.S.A.* 32°8N 81°37W **316** C8
Pembroke Pines *U.S.A.* 26°0N 80°13W **317** J9
Pembrokeshire □ *U.K.* 51°52N 4°56W **169** F3
Pembrokeshire Coast △ *U.K.* 51°50N 5°2W **169** F2
Pembuang → *Indonesia* 3°24S 112°33E **235** C4
Pen *India* 18°45N 73°5E **244** E1
Pen-y-Ghent *U.K.* 54°10N 2°14W **168** C5
Peña, Sierra de la *Spain* 42°32N 0°45W **196** C4
Peña de Francia, Sierra de la *Spain* 40°32N 6°10W **194** E4
Penafiel *Portugal* 41°12N 8°17W **194** D2
Peñafiel *Spain* 41°35N 4°7W **194** D6
Peñaflor *Spain* 37°43N 5°21W **195** H5
Penal *Trin. & Tob.* 10°9N 61°29W **323** t
Peñalara *Spain* 40°51N 3°57W **194** E7
Peñalolén *Chile* 33°28S 70°32W **137** B2
Penalva *Brazil* 3°18S 45°10W **332** B2
Penamacôr *Portugal* 40°10N 7°10W **194** E3
Penang = Pinang *Malaysia* 5°25N 100°15E **237** c
Penápolis *Brazil* 21°30S 50°0W **335** A6
Peñaranda de Bracamonte *Spain* 40°53N 5°13W **194** E5
Peñarroya *Spain* 40°25N 0°40W **196** E4
Peñarroya-Pueblonuevo *Spain* 38°19N 5°16W **195** G5
Penarth *U.K.* 51°26N 3°11W **169** F4
Peñas, C. de *Spain* 43°42N 5°52W **194** B5
Peñas, G. de *Chile* 47°0S 75°0W **336** C2
Peñas, Pta. *Venezuela* 11°17N 62°0W **329** A5
Peñas de San Pedro *Spain* 38°44N 2°0W **197** G3
Peñas del Chache *Canary Is.* 29°6N 13°33W **153** e2
Peñausende *Spain* 41°17N 5°52W **194** D5
Pencarrow Hd. *N.Z.* 41°22S 174°51E **143** C2
Pench → *India* 21°17N 79°10E **244** D4
Pench △ *India* 21°45N 79°20E **243** J8
Pench'i = Benxi *China* 41°20N 123°48E **224** B1
Pend Oreille → *U.S.A.* 49°4N 117°37W **304** B5
Pend Oreille, L. *U.S.A.* 48°10N 116°21W **304** B5
Pendalofos *Greece* 40°14N 21°12E **202** F5
Pendé → *C.A.R.* 7°55N 16°36E **264** A3
Pendembu *Eastern, S. Leone* 8°10N 10°42W **262** D2
Pendembu *Northern, S. Leone* 9°7N 11°14W **262** D2
Pendências *Brazil* 5°15S 36°43W **332** C4
Pender B. *Australia* 16°45S 122°42E **278** C3
Pendik *Turkey* 40°53N 29°13E **203** F13
Pendjari → *Benin* 10°55N 0°50E **263** C5
Pendjari △ *Benin* 11°15N 1°32E **263** C5
Pendleton *Ind., U.S.A.* 40°0N 85°45W **311** E11
Pendleton *Oreg., U.S.A.* 45°40N 118°47W **304** D4
Pendopo *Indonesia* 3°16S 103°52E **234** C2
Pendra *India* 22°46N 81°57E **243** H9
Pendzhikent *Tajikistan* 39°29N 67°37E **217** E7
Penebangan *Indonesia* 1°13S 109°15E **235** C3
Peneda-Gerês △ *Portugal* 41°57N 8°15W **194** D2
Penedo *Brazil* 10°15S 36°36W **332** D4
Penelokan *Indonesia* 8°17S 115°22E **231** J18
Penetanguishene *Canada* 44°50N 79°55W **312** B5
Penfield *U.S.A.* 41°13N 78°35W **312** E6
Peng Chau *China* 22°17N 114°2E **219** a
Peng Siang → *Singapore* 1°24N 103°43E **138** A2
Peng'an *China* 31°2N 106°22E **228** B6
Penganga → *India* 19°53N 79°9E **244** E4
Penge *Kasai-Or., Dem. Rep. of the Congo* 5°30S 24°33E **265** D4
Penge *Sud-Kivu, Dem. Rep. of the Congo* 4°27S 28°25E **268** C2
Penge *London, U.K.* 51°24N 0°3W **125** B3
P'enghu □ *Taiwan* 23°30N 119°30E **225** C1
P'enghu Ch'üntou *Taiwan* 23°34N 119°30E **225** C1
P'enghu Tao *Taiwan* 23°34N 119°37E **225** C1
Penglai *China* 37°48N 120°42E **227** F11
Pengshan *China* 30°14N 103°58E **228** B4
Pengshui *China* 29°17N 108°12E **228** C7
Penguin *Australia* 41°8S 146°6E **281** G4
Pengxi *China* 30°44N 105°45E **228** B5
Pengze *China* 29°52N 116°32E **229** C11
Pengzhou *China* 31°4N 103°32E **228** B4
Penha *Brazil* 22°49S 43°17W **135** A1
Penhalonga *Zimbabwe* 18°52S 32°40E **269** F3
Peniche *Portugal* 39°19N 9°22W **195** F1
Penicuik *U.K.* 55°50N 3°13W **121** B2
Penida, Nusa *Indonesia* 8°45S 115°30E **231** K18
Peninnes, Alpes = Pennine, Alpi *Alps* 46°4N 7°30E **179** J3
Peninsular Malaysia □ *Malaysia* 4°0N 102°0E **237** L4
Peñíscola *Spain* 40°22N 0°24E **196** E5
Penitente, Serra do *Brazil* 8°45S 46°20W **332** C2
Penjaringan *Indonesia* 6°7S 106°48E **122** A1
Pēnjwīn *Iraq* 35°37N 45°56E **213** E11
Penki = Benxi *China* 41°20N 123°48E **224** B1
Penkridge *U.K.* 52°44N 2°6W **168** E5
Penmarch *France* 47°49N 4°21W **172** E2
Penmarch, Pte. de *France* 47°48N 4°22W **172** E2
Penn = Penn Hills *U.S.A.* 40°28N 79°52W **312** F5
Penn Hills *U.S.A.* 40°28N 79°52W **312** F5
Penn Station *New York, U.S.A.* **132** c2
Penn Yan *U.S.A.* 42°40N 77°3W **312** D7
Penna, Punta della *Italy* 42°10N 14°43E **199** F11
Pennant *Canada* 50°32N 108°14W **297** C7
Penne *Italy* 42°27N 13°55E **199** F10
Penner → *India* 14°35N 80°10E **245** G5
Penneshaw *Australia* 35°44S 137°56E **282** C2
Pennine, Alpi *Alps* 46°4N 7°30E **179** J3
Pennines *U.K.* 54°45N 2°27W **168** C5
Pennington *U.S.A.* 39°15N 121°47W **306** F5
Pennington → *Nigeria* 4°45N 5°35E **263** E6
Pennino, Mte. *Italy* 43°6N 12°53E **199** E9
Pennsburg *U.S.A.* 40°23N 75°29W **313** F9
Pennsylvania □ *U.S.A.* 40°45N 77°30W **309** E15
Pennsylvania Avenue *Washington, D.C., U.S.A.* **143** b2
Pennville *U.S.A.* 40°30N 85°9W **311** D11
Penny *Canada* 53°51N 121°20W **296** C4
Peno *Russia* 57°2N 32°49E **188** D7
Penobscot → *U.S.A.* 44°30N 68°48W **309** C19
Penobscot B. *U.S.A.* 44°35N 68°50W **309** C19
Penola *Australia* 37°25S 140°48E **282** D4
Penong *Australia* 31°56S 133°1E **279** F5
Penonomé *Panama* 8°31N 80°21W **320** E3
Penot, Mt. *Vanuatu* 16°20S 167°31E **287** F5
Penrhyn *Cook Is.* 9°0S 158°0W **289** H12
Penrith *N.S.W., Australia* 33°43S 150°38E **283** B9
Penrith *Cumb., U.K.* 54°40N 2°45W **168** C5
Penryn *U.K.* 50°9N 5°7W **169** G2
Pensacola *U.S.A.* 30°25N 87°13W **317** E2
Pensacola B. *U.S.A.* 30°25N 87°5W **317** E2
Pensacola Mts. *Antarctica* 84°0S 40°0W **151** E1
Pense *Canada* 50°25N 104°59W **297** C8
Penshurst *Australia* 37°49S 142°20E **282** D5
Pensiangan *Malaysia* 4°33N 116°19E **235** B5
Pentagon *U.S.A.* 38°53N 77°3W **143** B3
Pentecost = Pentecôte *Vanuatu* 15°42S 168°10E **287** E6
Pentecostes *Brazil* 3°48S 39°17W **332** B4
Pentecôte *Vanuatu* 15°42S 168°10E **287** E6
Penticton *Canada* 49°30N 119°38W **296** D5
Pentland *Australia* 20°32S 145°25E **280** C4
Pentland Firth *U.K.* 58°43N 3°10W **167** C5
Pentland Hills *U.K.* 55°48N 3°25W **167** F5
Pentland Hills ⌂ *U.K.* 55°50N 3°20W **167** F5
Penukonda *India* 14°5N 77°38E **245** G3
Penyagino *Russia* 55°50N 37°20E **129** A2
Penza *Russia* 53°15N 45°5E **190** D7
Penza □ *Russia* 52°50N 44°50E **190** D7
Penzance *U.K.* 50°7N 5°33W **169** G2
Penzberg *Germany* 47°45N 11°22E **179** H7
Penzhino *Russia* 63°30N 167°55E **215** C17
Penzhinskaya Guba *Russia* 61°30N 163°0E **215** C17
Penzing *Austria* 48°11N 16°18E **142** A1
Penzlin *Germany* 53°30N 13°5E **178** B9
People's Park *China* 31°13N 121°28E **138** B1
People's Square *China* 31°13N 121°28E **138** B1
Peoria *Ariz., U.S.A.* 33°43N 112°14W **305** K7
Peoria *Ill., U.S.A.* 40°42N 89°36W **310** D7
Peoria Heights *U.S.A.* 40°45N 89°35W **310** D7
Peotone *U.S.A.* 41°20N 87°48W **311** C9
Pepacton Res. *U.S.A.* 42°5N 74°58W **313** D10
Pepani → *S. Africa* 25°49S 22°47E **270** C3
Pepeekeo *U.S.A.* 19°51N 155°6W **302** D6
Pepel *S. Leone* 8°40N 13°5W **262** D2
Peqin *Albania* 41°3N 19°44E **202** E3
Pera Hd. *Australia* 12°55S 141°37E **280** A3
Perabumulih *Indonesia* 3°27S 104°15E **234** C2
Perachora *Greece* 38°2N 22°56E **204** C4
Perachori *Greece* 38°21N 20°43E **207** C2
Perak □ *Malaysia* 5°0N 101°0E **237** K3
Perak → *Malaysia* 4°0N 100°50E **237** K3
Perales del Alfambra *Spain* 40°38N 1°0W **196** E4
Perales del Puerto *Spain* 40°10N 6°40W **194** E4
Perales del Rio *Spain* 40°18N 3°38W **127** C2
Perama *Kerkyra, Greece* 39°34N 19°54E **206** B9
Perama *Kriti, Greece* 35°20N 24°40E **207** E5
Perancak *Indonesia* 8°24S 114°37E **231** J17
Peräpohjola *Finland* 66°16N 26°10E **160** C22
Perast *Montenegro* 42°31N 18°47E **202** D2
Peratia *Greece* 38°49N 20°45E **207** B2
Peravillo *Mexico City, Mexico* **128** a3
Percé *Canada* 48°31N 64°13W **299** C7
Perche *France* 48°31N 1°1E **172** D8
Perche, Collines du *France* 48°30N 0°40E **171** B4
Perche ⌂ *France* 48°24N 0°46E **172** D7
Perchtoldsdorf *Austria* 48°7N 16°17E **142** B1
Percival Lakes *Australia* 21°25S 125°0E **278** D4
Percy *Manche, France* 48°55N 1°11W **172** D5
Percy *Ill., U.S.A.* 38°5N 89°41W **310** F7
Percy Is. *Australia* 21°39S 150°16E **280** C5
Perdido → *Argentina* 42°55S 67°0W **336** B3
Perdido, Mte. *Spain* 42°40N 0°5E **196** C5
Perdizes *Brazil* 23°32S 46°39W **137** B2
Perdu, Mt. = Perdido, Mte. *Spain* 42°40N 0°5E **196** C5
Perechyn *Ukraine* 48°44N 22°28E **182** B7
Peredelkino *Russia* 55°38N 37°20E **129** C2
Perehinske *Ukraine* 48°49N 24°11E **183** B9
Pereira *Colombia* 4°49N 75°43W **328** C2
Perelazovskiy *Russia* 49°8N 42°35E **191** F6
Peremul Par *India* 11°10N 72°4E **245** J1
Peremyshl = Przemyśl *Poland* 49°50N 22°45E **185** J9
Perené → *Peru* 11°9S 74°14W **330** C3
Perenjori *Australia* 29°26S 116°16E **279** E2
Peresecina *Moldova* 47°16N 28°46E **183** C13
Pereslavl-Zalesskiy *Russia* 56°45N 38°50E **188** D10
Peretu *Romania* 44°3N 25°5E **183** F10
Pereyaslav-Khmelnytskyy *Ukraine* 50°3N 31°28E **189** G6
Pereyma *Ukraine* 48°4N 29°30E **183** B14
Pérez, I. *Mexico* 22°24N 89°42W **319** C7
Perg *Austria* 48°15N 14°38E **180** C7
Pergamino *Argentina* 33°52S 60°30W **334** C3
Pergamon Museum *Berlin, Germany* **115** a4
Pergau → *Malaysia* 5°23N 102°2E **237** K3
Perge *Turkey* 37°3N 30°56E **250** A1
Pérgine Valsugana *Italy* 46°4N 11°14E **199** B8
Pérgola *Italy* 43°34N 12°50E **199** E9
Perham *U.S.A.* 46°36N 95°34W **308** B6
Perhentian, Kepulauan *Malaysia* 5°54N 102°42E **237** K4
Peri → *Turkey* 38°53N 39°52E **213** C8
Periam *Romania* 46°2N 20°52E **182** D5
Péribonka → *Canada* 48°45N 72°5W **299** C5
Péribonka, L. *Canada* 50°1N 71°10W **299** B5
Péribonka, La Centrale de *Canada* 49°30N 71°10W **299** C5
Perico *Argentina* 24°20S 65°5W **334** A2
Pericos *Mexico* 25°3N 107°42W **318** B3
Périers *France* 49°11N 1°25W **172** C5
Périgord *France* 45°0N 0°40E **174** D4
Périgord-Limousin ⌂ *France* 45°40N 0°50E **174** C4
Périgueux *France* 45°10N 0°42E **174** C4
Perijá, Sierra de *Colombia* 9°30N 73°3W **328** B3
Perijá △ *Venezuela* 9°30N 72°55W **328** B3
Peringat *Malaysia* 6°2N 102°17E **237** J4
Perisher Valley *Australia* 36°27S 148°25E **283** D8
Peristera *Greece* 39°15N 23°58E **204** B5
Peristeri *Greece* 38°1N 23°42E **112** A2
Peristerona → *Cyprus* 35°8N 33°5E **207** E9
Perito Moreno *Argentina* 46°36S 70°56W **336** C2
Perito Moreno △ *Argentina* 47°49S 72°17W **336** C2
Peritoró *Brazil* 4°20S 44°18W **332** B3
Perivale *U.K.* 51°31N 0°18W **125** A2
Perivol = Dragovishtitsa *Bulgaria* 42°22N 22°39E **202** D6
Periyakulam *India* 10°5N 77°30E **245** J3
Periyar → *India* 10°15N 76°10E **245** J3
Periyar, L. *India* 9°25N 77°10E **245** K3
Periyar △ *India* 9°25N 77°10E **245** K3
Perk *Belgium* 50°56N 4°30E **116** A2
Perkasie *U.S.A.* 40°22N 75°18W **313** F9
Perković *Croatia* 43°41N 16°10E **199** E13
Perlach *Germany* 48°5N 11°37E **131** B2
Perlacher Forst *Germany* 48°4N 11°34E **131** B2
Perlas, Arch. de las *Panama* 8°41N 79°7W **320** E4
Perlas, Punta de *Nic.* 12°30N 83°30W **320** D3
Perleberg *Germany* 53°5N 11°52E **178** B7
Perlez *Serbia* 45°11N 20°22E **182** E5
Perlis □ *Malaysia* 6°30N 100°15E **237** J2
Perm *Russia* 58°0N 56°10E **186** C10
Përmet *Albania* 40°15N 20°21E **202** F4
Permskoye = Komsomolsk-na-Amur *Russia* 50°30N 137°0E **219** A16
Pernambuco = Recife *Brazil* 8°0S 35°0W **332** C5
Pernambuco □ *Brazil* 8°0S 37°0W **332** C4
Pernambuco Abyssal Plain *Atl. Oc.* 5°0S 24°0W **152** G9
Pernatty Lagoon *Australia* 31°30S 137°12E **282** A2
Pernik *Bulgaria* 42°35N 23°2E **202** D7
Pernik □ *Bulgaria* 42°35N 23°2E **202** D7
Pernov = Pärnu *Estonia* 58°28N 24°33E **188** C3
Pero *Italy* 45°30N 9°5E **129** A1
Peron Is. *Australia* 13°9S 130°4E **278** B5
Peron Pen. *Australia* 26°0S 113°10E **279** E1
Péronne *France* 49°55N 2°57E **173** C9
Peropok, Bukit *Singapore* 1°19N 103°42E **138** B2
Perosa Argentina *Italy* 44°58N 7°10E **198** D4
Perovo *Russia* 55°44N 37°45E **129** B4
Perovsk = Qyzylorda *Kazakhstan* 44°48N 65°28E **217** D7
Perow *Canada* 54°35N 126°10W **296** C3
Perparim = Pogradec *Albania* 40°54N 20°37E **202** F4
Perpignan *France* 42°42N 2°53E **174** F6
Perrégaux = Mohammadia *Algeria* 35°33N 0°3E **261** A5
Perrine *U.S.A.* 25°36N 80°21W **317** K9
Perris *U.S.A.* 33°47N 117°14W **307** M9
Perros-Guirec *France* 48°49N 3°28W **172** D3
Perry *Fla., U.S.A.* 30°7N 83°35W **316** E6
Perry *Ga., U.S.A.* 32°28N 83°44W **316** C6
Perry *Iowa, U.S.A.* 41°51N 94°6W **310** C2
Perry *Mich., U.S.A.* 42°50N 84°13W **311** B12
Perry *Mo., U.S.A.* 39°26N 91°40W **310** E5
Perry *N.Y., U.S.A.* 42°42N 78°0W **312** D7
Perry *Okla., U.S.A.* 36°17N 97°14W **314** C6
Perrysburg *U.S.A.* 41°34N 83°38W **311** C13
Perryton *U.S.A.* 36°24N 100°48W **314** C4
Perryville *Alaska, U.S.A.* 55°55N 159°9W **303** J8
Perryville *Mo., U.S.A.* 37°43N 89°52W **310** G7
Persan *France* 49°9N 2°16E **173** C9
Persberg *Sweden* 59°47N 14°15E **162** E8
Perşembe *Turkey* 41°5N 37°46E **212** B7
Persepolis *Iran* 29°55N 52°50E **247** D7
Perseverancia *Bolivia* 14°44S 62°48W **331** C5
Pershing Square *Los Angeles, U.S.A.* **127** c1
Pershotravensk *Ukraine* 50°13N 27°40E **177** C14
Pershotravnevoye = Pershotravensk *Ukraine* 50°13N 27°40E **177** C14
Persia = Iran ■ *Asia* 33°0N 53°0E **247** C7
Persian Gulf *Asia* 27°0N 50°0E **247** E6
Perstorp *Sweden* 56°10N 13°25E **163** H7
Pertek *Turkey* 38°51N 39°19E **213** C8
Perth *W. Austral., Australia* 31°57S 115°52E **279** F2
Perth *Ont., Canada* 44°55N 76°15W **313** B8
Perth *Perth & Kinr., U.K.* 56°24N 3°26W **167** E5
Perth & Kinross □ *U.K.* 56°45N 3°55W **167** E5
Perth Amboy *U.S.A.* 40°30N 74°15W **313** F10
Perth-Andover *Canada* 46°44N 67°42W **299** C6
Pertuis *France* 43°42N 5°30E **175** E9
Pertusato, C. *France* 41°21N 9°11E **175** G13
Pertusella *Italy* 45°35N 9°3E **129** A1
Peru *Ill., U.S.A.* 41°20N 89°8W **310** C7
Peru *Ind., U.S.A.* 40°45N 86°4W **311** D10
Peru *N.Y., U.S.A.* 44°35N 73°32W **313** B11
Peru ■ *S. Amer.* 4°0S 75°0W **328** D3
Peru Basin *Pac. Oc.* 20°0S 95°0W **289** J18
Peru-Chile Trench *Pac. Oc.* 20°0S 72°0W **326** E3
Perúgia *Italy* 43°7N 12°23E **199** E9
Perušić *Croatia* 44°40N 15°22E **199** D12
Peruvian Vale *St. Vincent* 13°13N 61°12W **323** n
Pervomaysk *Russia* 54°56N 43°58E **190** C6
Pervomaysk *Ukraine* 48°10N 30°46E **189** H6
Pervomayskīy *Kazakhstan* 50°16N 82°0E **217** B10
Pervouralsk *Russia* 56°59N 59°59E **186** C10
Pervouralsky = Pervouralsk *Russia* 56°59N 59°59E **186** C10
Pesada *Greece* 38°7N 20°35E **207** C2
Pesagot *West Bank* 31°54N 35°13E **123** A2
Pesanggrahag, Kali → *Indonesia* 6°10S 106°44E **122** B1
Pésaro *Italy* 43°54N 12°55E **199** E9
Pescadores = P'enghu Ch'üntou *Taiwan* 23°34N 119°30E **225** C1
Pescara *Italy* 42°28N 14°13E **199** F11
Pescara → *Italy* 42°28N 14°13E **199** F11
Peschanokopskoye *Russia* 46°14N 41°4E **191** G5
Peschanoye = Yashkul *Russia* 46°11N 45°21E **191** G7
Peschiera Borromeo *Italy* 45°26N 9°19E **129** B2
Péscia *Italy* 43°54N 10°41E **198** E7
Pescina *Italy* 42°2N 13°39E **199** F10
Pesek, Pulau *Singapore* 1°17N 103°41E **138** B2
Peshawar *Pakistan* 34°2N 71°37E **242** B4
Peshkopi *Albania* 41°41N 20°25E **202** E4
Peshtera *Bulgaria* 42°2N 24°18E **203** D8
Peshtigo *U.S.A.* 45°3N 87°45W **308** C10
Peski *Russia* 51°14N 42°29E **190** E6
Peski *Turkmenistan* 38°11N 62°59E **216** E6
Pêso da Régua *Portugal* 41°10N 7°47W **194** D3
Pesochnya = Kirov *Russia* 54°3N 34°20E **188** E8
Pesqueira *Brazil* 8°20S 36°42W **332** C4
Pessac *France* 44°48N 0°37W **174** D3
Pest *Hungary* 47°29N 19°4E **117** B2
Pest □ *Hungary* 47°29N 19°5E **182** C4
Pesterzsébet *Hungary* 47°26N 19°6E **117** B2
Pesthidegkút *Hungary* 47°33N 18°57E **117** A1
Pestimre *Hungary* 47°24N 19°11E **117** B3
Pestlörinc *Hungary* 47°26N 19°11E **117** B3
Pestovo = Zavolzhye *Russia* 56°37N 43°26E **190** B6
Pestovo *Russia* 58°33N 35°42E **188** C8
Pestravka *Russia* 52°28N 49°57E **190** D9
Pestújhely *Hungary* 47°32N 19°7E **117** A2
Petah Tiqwa *Israel* 32°6N 34°53E **251** F5
Petalas *Greece* 38°25N 21°5E **207** C3
Petalidi *Greece* 36°57N 21°55E **204** E3
Petaling Jaya *Malaysia* 3°4N 101°42E **237** L3
Petaloudes *Greece* 36°18N 28°5E **206** E12
Petaluma *U.S.A.* 38°14N 122°39W **306** G4
Pétange *Lux.* 49°33N 5°55E **170** E5
Petaro *Pakistan* 25°31N 68°18E **242** G3
Petas *Helsinki, Finland* 60°15N 24°50E **121** B2
Petas *Greece* 39°10N 21°2E **204** B3
Petatlán *Mexico* 17°31N 101°16W **318** D4
Petauke *Zambia* 14°14S 31°20E **269** E3
Petawawa *Canada* 45°54N 77°17W **298** C4
Petén Itzá, L. *Guatemala* 16°58N 89°50W **320** C2
Peter I. *Br. Virgin Is.* 18°22N 64°35W **321** b
Peter I. Øy *Antarctica* 69°0S 91°0W **151** C16
Peter Pond L. *Canada* 55°55N 108°44W **297** B7
Peterbell *Canada* 48°36N 83°21W **298** C3
Peterborough *S. Austral., Australia* 32°58S 138°51E **282** B3
Peterborough *Ont., Canada* 44°20N 78°20W **312** B6
Peterborough *Peterborough, U.K.* 52°35N 0°15W **169** E7
Peterborough *N.H., U.S.A.* 42°53N 71°57W **313** D13
Peterborough □ *U.K.* 52°35N 0°15W **169** E7
Peterculter *U.K.* 57°6N 2°16W **167** D6
Peterhead *U.K.* 57°31N 1°48W **167** D7
Peterhof = Petrodvorets *Russia* 59°52N 29°54E **188** C5
Peterlee *U.K.* 54°47N 1°20W **168** C6
Petermann ◎ *Australia* 24°58S 130°0E **279** E4
Petermann Bjerg *Greenland* 73°7N 28°25W **154** C8
Petermann Gletscher *Greenland* 80°30N 60°0W **154** A4
Petermann Ranges *Australia* 26°0S 130°30E **279** E5
Peter's Mine *Guyana* 6°14N 59°20W **329** B6
Petersburg = Peterborough *Australia* 32°58S 138°51E **282** B3
Petersburg *Alaska, U.S.A.* 56°48N 132°58W **303** H14
Petersburg *Ill., U.S.A.* 40°1N 89°51W **310** D7
Petersburg *Ind., U.S.A.* 38°30N 87°17W **311** F9
Petersburg *Mich., U.S.A.* 41°54N 83°43W **311** C13
Petersburg *Pa., U.S.A.* 40°34N 78°3W **312** F6
Petersburg *Va., U.S.A.* 37°14N 77°24W **309** G15
Petersburg *W. Va., U.S.A.* 39°1N 79°5W **309** F14
Petersfield *U.K.* 51°1N 0°56W **169** F7
Petershagen *Germany* 52°23N 8°58E **178** C4
Petília Policastro *Italy* 39°7N 16°48E **201** C9
Petit Batanga *Cameroon* 3°15N 9°54E **264** B1
Petit-Bourg *Guadeloupe* 16°11N 61°37W **322** e
Petit-Canal *Guadeloupe* 16°25N 61°31W **322** e
Petit Cul-de-Sac Marin *Guadeloupe* 16°12N 61°33W **322** e
Petit Dominique *Grenada* 12°30N 61°24W **323** q
Petit Goâve *Haiti* 18°27N 72°51W **321** C5
Petit Lac Manicouagan *Canada* 51°25N 67°40W **299** B6
Petit Loango ⌂ *Gabon* 2°20S 9°40E **264** C1
Petit-Mécatina → *Canada* 50°40N 59°30W **299** B8
Petit-Mécatina, Î. du *Canada* 50°30N 59°25W **299** B8
Petit Piton *St. Lucia* 13°51N 61°5W **323** m
Petit Raffray *Mauritius* 20°0S 57°36E **272** e
Petit-Saguenay *Canada* 48°15N 70°4W **299** C5
Petit Saint Bernard, Col du *Italy* 45°40N 6°52E **175** C10
Petit Saut, Barrage de *Fr. Guiana* 5°0N 53°10W **248** B7
Petit Soufrière B. *Dominica* 15°23N 61°15W **323** k
Petitcodiac *Canada* 45°57N 65°11W **299** C6
Petite Anse *Martinique* 14°28N 61°4W **322** j
Petite-Île *Réunion* 21°20S 55°35E **272** f
Petite Martinique *Grenada* 12°31N 61°23W **323** q
Petite Rivière *Mauritius* 20°11S 57°26E **272** e
Petite Savane *Dominica* 15°15N 61°17W **323** k
Petite Terre = Pamandzi *Mayotte* 12°47S 45°16E **272** b
Petite Terre, Îles de la *Guadeloupe* 16°13N 61°9W **322** e
Petites-Anses *Guadeloupe* 15°51N 61°38W **322** e
Petitjean = Sidi Kacem *Morocco* 34°12N 5°42W **260** B3
Petitot → *Canada* 60°14N 123°29W **296** A4
Petitsikapau L. *Canada* 54°37N 66°25W **299** B6
Petlad *India* 22°30N 72°45E **242** H5
Peto *Mexico* 20°8N 88°55W **319** C7
Petone *N.Z.* 41°13S 174°53E **143** B2
Petorca *Chile* 32°15S 70°56W **334** C1
Petoskey *U.S.A.* 45°22N 84°57W **309** C11
Petra *Jordan* 30°20N 35°22E **251** H6
Petra *Spain* 39°37N 3°6E **206** B4
Petra, Ostrov *Russia* 76°15N 118°30E **215** B12
Petra Velikogo, Zaliv *Russia* 42°40N 132°0E **220** C6
Petre, Pt. *Canada* 43°50N 77°9W **312** C7
Petrel = Petrer *Spain* 38°30N 0°46W **197** G4
Petrella, Monte *Italy* 41°18N 13°40E **200** A6
Petrer *Spain* 38°30N 0°46W **197** G4
Petreto-Bicchisano *France* 41°47N 8°58E **175** G12
Petrich *Bulgaria* 41°24N 23°13E **202** E7
Petrified Forest △ *U.S.A.* 35°0N 109°30W **305** J9
Petrijanec *Croatia* 46°23N 16°17E **199** B13
Petrikov = Pyetrikaw *Belarus* 52°11N 28°29E **177** B15
Petrila *Romania* 45°29N 23°29E **183** E8
Petrinja *Croatia* 45°28N 16°18E **199** C13
Petrodvorets *Russia* 59°52N 29°54E **188** C5
Petrograd = Sankt-Peterburg *Russia* 59°55N 30°20E **137** B1
Petrogradskaya Storona *Russia* 59°56N 30°20E **137** B2
Petrolândia *Brazil* 9°5S 38°20W **332** C4
Petrolia *Canada* 42°54N 82°9W **312** D2
Petrolina *Brazil* 9°24S 40°30W **332** C3
Petromaryevka = Pervomaysk *Ukraine* 48°10N 30°46E **189** H6
Petropavl *Kazakhstan* 54°53N 69°13E **217** B7
Petropavlovsk = Petropavl *Kazakhstan* 54°53N 69°13E **217** B7
Petropavlovsk-Kamchatskiy *Russia* 53°3N 158°43E **215** D16
Petropavlovskiy = Akhtubinsk *Russia* 48°13N 46°7E **191** F8
Petropavlovsky = Severouralsk *Russia* 60°9N 59°57E **186** B10
Petrópolis *Brazil* 22°33S 43°9W **333** F3
Petroşani *Romania* 45°28N 23°20E **183** E8
Petroupoli *Greece* 38°3N 23°40E **112** A2
Petrova Gora *Croatia* 45°15N 15°45E **199** C12
Petrovac *Montenegro* 42°13N 18°57E **202** D2
Petrovac *Serbia* 44°22N 21°26E **202** B5
Petrovaradin *Serbia* 45°16N 19°55E **182** E4
Petrovgrad = Zrenjanin *Serbia* 45°22N 20°23E **182** E5
Petrovice *Czech Rep.* 50°2N 14°33E **135** B3
Petrovsk *Russia* 52°22N 45°19E **190** D7
Petrovsk-Port = Makhachkala *Russia* 43°0N 47°30E **191** J8
Petrovsk-Zabaykalskiy *Russia* 51°20N 108°55E **215** D11
Petrovskaya *Russia* 45°25N 37°58E **189** K9
Petrovskiy Park *Russia* 55°47N 37°34E **129** B3
Petrovsko-Razumovskoye *Russia* 55°49N 37°34E **129** B3
Petrovskoye = Svetlograd *Russia* 45°25N 42°58E **191** H6
Petrovsky Zavod = Petrovsk-Zabaykalskiy *Russia* 51°20N 108°55E **215** D11
Petrozavodsk *Russia* 61°41N 34°20E **188** B8
Petrus Steyn *S. Africa* 27°38S 28°8E **271** C4
Petrusburg *S. Africa* 29°4S 25°26E **270** C4
Petsamo = Pechenga *Russia* 69°29N 31°4E **160** B24
Pettycur *U.K.* 56°4N 3°10W **121** A2
Petukhovo *Russia* 55°6N 67°58E **217** A7
Petuna = Fuyu *China* 45°12N 124°43E **227** B13
Petzeck *Austria* 46°57N 12°48E **180** E5
Peumo *Chile* 34°21S 71°12W **334** C1
Peureulak *Indonesia* 4°48N 97°45E **234** B1
Peusangan → *Indonesia* 5°16N 96°51E **234** A1
Peutie *Belgium* 50°56N 4°27E **116** A2
Pevek *Russia* 69°41N 171°19E **215** C18
Pevely *U.S.A.* 38°17N 90°24W **310** F6
Peveragno *Italy* 44°20N 7°37E **198** D4
Peyrehorade *France* 43°34N 1°7W **174** E2
Peyruis *France* 44°1N 5°56E **175** D9
Pézenas *France* 43°28N 3°24E **174** E7
Pezinok *Slovak Rep.* 48°17N 17°17E **181** C10
Pfaffenhofen *Germany* 48°31N 11°31E **179** G7
Pfälzerwald ⌂ *Germany* 49°18N 9°55E **179** F5
Pfarrkirchen *Germany* 48°25N 12°56E **179** G8
Pfaueninsel *Germany* 52°26N 13°7E **115** B1
Pfeffenhausen *Germany* 48°39N 11°58E **179** G7
Pforzheim *Germany* 48°52N 8°41E **179** G4
Pfullendorf *Germany* 47°55N 9°15E **179** H5
Pfungstadt *Germany* 49°48N 8°35E **179** F4
Pha Taem △ *Thailand* 15°32N 105°30E **236** E5
Phaestos *Greece* 35°2N 24°50E **207** E5
Phagwara *India* 31°10N 75°40E **242** D6
Phala *Botswana* 23°45S 26°50E **270** B4
Phalaborwa *S. Africa* 23°57S 31°7E **271** B5
Phalera = Phulera *India* 26°52N 75°16E **242** F6
Phalodi *India* 27°12N 72°24E **242** F5
Phalsbourg *France* 48°46N 7°15E **173** D14
Phaltan *India* 17°59N 74°26E **244** F2
Phaluai, Ko *Thailand* 9°32N 99°41E **237** b
Phan *Thailand* 19°28N 99°43E **236** C2
Phan Rang-Thap Cham *Vietnam* 11°34N 109°0E **237** G7
Phan Ri Cua *Vietnam* 11°16N 108°40E **237** G7
Phan Si Pan *Vietnam* 22°18N 103°46E **236** A4
Phan Thiet *Vietnam* 11°1N 108°9E **237** G7
Phan Thiet, Vinh *Vietnam* 10°53N 108°5E **237** G7
Phanae *Greece* 38°8N 25°57E **205** C7
Phanat Nikhom *Thailand* 13°27N 101°11E **236** F3
Phangan, Ko *Thailand* 9°45N 100°0E **237** H3
Phangnga *Thailand* 8°28N 98°30E **237** H2
Phangnga, Ao *Thailand* 8°16N 98°33E **237** a
Phanom Sarakham *Thailand* 13°45N 101°21E **236** F3
Phaphund *India* 26°36N 79°28E **243** F8
Pharenda *India* 27°5N 83°17E **243** F10
Pharr *U.S.A.* 26°12N 98°11W **314** H5
Phatthalung *Thailand* 7°39N 100°6E **237** J3
Phaya Thai *Thailand* 13°45N 100°37E **113** B2
Phayam, Ko *Thailand* 9°44N 98°25E **237** H2
Phayao *Thailand* 19°11N 99°55E **236** C2
Phelps *U.S.A.* 42°58N 77°3W **312** D7
Phelps L. *Canada* 59°15N 103°15W **297** B8
Phenix City *U.S.A.* 32°28N 85°0W **315** E12
Phet Buri = Phetchaburi *Thailand* 13°1N 99°55E **236** F2
Phetchabun *Thailand* 16°25N 101°8E **236** D3
Phetchabun, Thiu Khao *Thailand* 16°0N 101°20E **236** E3
Phetchaburi *Thailand* 13°1N 99°55E **236** F2
Phi Phi, Ko *Thailand* 7°45N 98°46E **237** J2
Phiafay *Laos* 14°48N 106°0E **236** E6
Phibun Mangsahan *Thailand* 15°14N 105°14E **236** E5
Phichai *Thailand* 17°22N 100°10E **236** D3
Phichit *Thailand* 16°26N 100°22E **236** D3
Phihai *Pakistan* 24°50N 67°8E **123** A2
Philadelphia *Miss., U.S.A.* 32°46N 89°7W **315** E10
Philadelphia *N.Y., U.S.A.* 44°9N 75°43W **313** B9
Philadelphia *Pa., U.S.A.* 39°57N 75°9W **313** G9
Philip *U.S.A.* 44°2N 101°40W **308** C3
Philip Smith Mts. *U.S.A.* 68°0N 148°0W **303** C10
Philipi *Greece* 41°1N 24°16E **203** E8
Philippeville = Skikda *Algeria* 36°50N 6°58E **261** A6
Philippeville *Belgium* 50°12N 4°33E **170** D4
Philippi *U.S.A.* 39°9N 80°3W **309** F13
Philippi L. *Australia* 24°20S 138°55E **280** C2
Philippine Basin *Pac. Oc.* 17°0N 132°0E **288** F5
Philippine Sea *Pac. Oc.* 18°0N 125°0E **288** F4
Philippine Trench = Mindanao Trench *Pac. Oc.* 12°0N 126°6E **232** E5
Philippines ■ *Asia* 12°0N 123°0E **232** E4
Philippolis *S. Africa* 30°15S 25°16E **270** D4
Philippopolis = Plovdiv *Bulgaria* 42°8N 24°44E **203** D8
Philipsburg *Qué., Canada* 45°2N 73°5W **313** A11
Philipsburg *St.-Maarten* 18°3N 63°5W **322** a
Philipsburg *Mont., U.S.A.* 46°20N 113°18W **304** C7
Philipsburg *Pa., U.S.A.* 40°54N 78°13W **312** F6
Philipstown = Daingean *Ireland* 53°18N 7°17W **166** C4
Philipstown *S. Africa* 30°28S 24°30E **270** D3
Phillip B. *Australia* 33°58S 151°14E **139** B2
Phillip I. *Australia* 38°30S 145°12E **283** E6
Phillips *U.S.A.* 45°42N 90°24W **308** C8
Phillipsburg *Ga., U.S.A.* 31°25N 83°30W **316** D6
Phillipsburg *Kans., U.S.A.* 39°45N 99°19W **308** F4
Phillipsburg *N.J., U.S.A.* 40°42N 75°12W **313** F9
Philmont *U.S.A.* 42°15N 73°39W **313** D11
Philomath *Ga., U.S.A.* 33°44N 82°59W **316** B7
Philomath *Oreg., U.S.A.* 44°32N 123°22W **304** D2
Phimai *Thailand* 15°13N 102°30E **236** E4
Phitsanulok *Thailand* 16°50N 100°12E **236** D3
Phnom Kulen △ *Cambodia* 13°38N 104°15E **236** F5
Phnom Penh *Cambodia* 11°33N 104°55E **237** G5
Phnum Penh = Phnom Penh *Cambodia* 11°33N 104°55E **237** G5
Phoenicia *U.S.A.* 42°5N 74°14W **313** D10
Phoenix *Mauritius* 20°17S 57°30E **272** e
Phoenix *Ariz., U.S.A.* 33°26N 112°4W **305** K7
Phoenix *N.Y., U.S.A.* 43°14N 76°18W **313** C8
Phoenix Is. *Kiribati* 3°30S 172°0W **277** A16
Phoenix Park *Ireland* 53°21N 6°20W **120** A2
Phoenixville *U.S.A.* 40°8N 75°31W **313** F9
Phon *Thailand* 15°49N 102°36E **236** E4
Phong → *Thailand* 16°23N 102°56E **236** D4
Phong Nha -Ke Bang △ *Vietnam* 17°30N 106°10E **236** D6
Phong Saly *Laos* 21°42N 102°9E **228** G4
Phong Tho *Vietnam* 22°32N 103°21E **236** A4
Phonhong *Laos* 18°30N 102°25E **236** C4
Phonsavan *Laos* 19°27N 103°10E **236** C4
Phonum *Thailand* 8°49N 98°48E **237** H2
Phosphate Hill *Australia* 21°53S 139°58E **280** C2
Photharam *Thailand* 13°41N 99°51E **236** F2
Phra Kaeo *Bangkok, Thailand* **113** b1
Phra Khanong *Thailand* 13°40N 100°36E **113** B2
Phra Nakhon *Thailand* 13°45N 100°30E **113** B2
Phra Nakhon Si Ayutthaya *Thailand* 14°25N 100°30E **236** E3
Phra Pradaeng *Thailand* 13°39N 100°33E **113** C2
Phra Thong, Ko *Thailand* 9°5N 98°17E **237** H2
Phrae *Thailand* 18°7N 100°9E **236** C3
Phranakhon *Thailand* 13°44N 100°29E **113** B1
Phrom Phiram *Thailand* 17°2N 100°12E **236** D3
Phrygia *Turkey* 38°40N 30°0E **212** C4
Phu Bia *Laos* 19°10N 103°0E **236** C4
Phu Chong-Na Yoi △ *Thailand* 14°25N 105°30E **236** E5
Phu Hin Rong Kla △ *Thailand* 17°0N 100°59E **236** D3
Phu Kao -Phu Phan Kham △ *Thailand* 16°53N 102°31E **236** D4
Phu Kradung △ *Thailand* 17°2N 101°44E **236** D3
Phu Loi *Laos* 20°14N 103°14E **236** B4
Phu Luang △ *Thailand* 17°15N 101°29E **236** D3
Phu Ly *Vietnam* 20°35N 105°50E **228** G5
Phu My *Vietnam* 14°15N 109°5E **236** E7
Phu Pha Man △ *Thailand* 16°44N 101°50E **236** D3
Phu Phan △ *Thailand* 17°0N 103°56E **236** D4
Phu Quoc, Dao *Vietnam* 10°20N 104°0E **237** G4
Phu Sa Dok Bua △ *Thailand* 16°11N 104°45E **236** D5
Phu Sang △ *Thailand* 19°35N 100°19E **236** C3
Phu Tho *Vietnam* 21°24N 105°13E **228** G5
Phu Wiang △ *Thailand* 16°39N 102°23E **236** D4
Phuc Yen *Vietnam* 21°16N 105°45E **228** G5
Phuket *Thailand* 7°53N 98°24E **237** a
Phuket, Ko *Thailand* 8°0N 98°22E **237** a
Phul *India* 30°19N 75°14E **242** D6
Phulad *India* 25°38N 73°49E **242** G5
Phulbani *India* 20°28N 84°14E **244** D7
Phulbari *India* 25°55N 90°2E **241** C3
Phulchari *Bangla.* 25°11N 89°37E **241** C2
Phulera *India* 26°52N 75°16E **242** F6
Phulpur *India* 25°31N 82°49E **243** G10
Phunphin *Thailand* 9°7N 99°12E **237** H2
Phuntsholing *Bhutan* 26°51N 89°23E **243** F13
Phuphrabat *Thailand* 17°40N 102°45E **236** D4
Phuthaditjhaba *S. Africa* 28°29S 28°48E **271** C4
Pia ◎ *Australia* 27°7S 116°23E **279** E2
Piaçabuçu *Brazil* 10°24S 36°25W **332** D4
Piacenza *Italy* 45°1N 9°40E **198** C6
Piai, Tanjung *Malaysia* 1°17N 103°30E **237** d
Piako → *N.Z.* 37°12S 175°30E **284** D4
Pian Cr. → *Australia* 30°2S 148°12E **281** E4
Pian-Upe ⌂ *Uganda* 1°44N 34°20E **268** B3
Piana *France* 42°15N 8°34E **175** F12
Pianella *Italy* 42°24N 14°2E **199** F11
Piangil *Australia* 35°5S 143°20E **282** C5
Pianosa *Puglia, Italy* 42°12N 15°44E **199** F12
Pianosa *Toscana, Italy* 42°35N 10°5E **198** F7
Piao'ertun *China* 41°50N 123°47E **227** D12
Piapot *Canada* 49°59N 109°8W **297** D7
Piarco *Trin. & Tob.* 10°35N 61°20W **323** t
Piarco Int. ✕ (POS) *Trin. & Tob.* 10°36N 61°20W **323** t
Pias *Portugal* 38°1N 7°29W **195** G3
Piaseczno *Poland* 52°5N 21°2E **185** F8
Piaski *Poland* 51°8N 22°52E **185** G9
Piastów *Poland* 52°12N 20°48E **185** F7
Piatã *Brazil* 13°9S 41°48W **333** D3
Piatra *Romania* 43°51N 25°9E **183** G10
Piatra Craiului △ *Romania* 45°30N 25°12E **183** E10
Piatra Neamţ *Romania* 46°56N 26°21E **183** D11
Piatra Olt *Romania* 44°22N 24°16E **183** F9
Piauí □ *Brazil* 7°0S 43°0W **332** C3
Piauí → *Brazil* 6°38S 42°42W **332** C3
Piave → *Italy* 45°32N 12°44E **199** C9
Piazza Ármerina *Italy* 37°21N 14°20E **201** E7
Pibor → *Sudan* 7°35N 33°0E **257** F3
Pibor Post *Sudan* 6°47N 33°3E **257** F3
Pica *Chile* 20°35S 69°25W **330** E4
Picardie □ *France* 49°50N 3°0E **173** C10
Picardie, Plaine de *France* 50°0N 2°0E **173** C9
Picardy = Picardie □ *France* 49°50N 3°0E **173** C10
Picasso, Museu *Barcelona, Spain* **114** c2
Picayune *U.S.A.* 30°32N 89°41W **315** F10
Piccadilly *London, U.K.* **125** b3
Picerno *Italy* 40°38N 15°38E **201** B8
Pichhor *India* 25°58N 78°20E **243** G8
Pichilemu *Chile* 34°22S 72°0W **334** C1
Pichincha, □ *Ecuador* 0°10S 78°40W **328** D2
Pichor *India* 25°11N 78°11E **242** G8
Pickerel L. *Canada* 48°40N 91°25W **298** C1
Pickering *U.K.* 54°15N 0°46W **168** C7
Pickering, Vale of *U.K.* 54°14N 0°45W **168** C7
Pickle Lake *Canada* 51°30N 90°12W **298** B1
Pickwick L. *U.S.A.* 35°4N 88°15W **315** D10
Pico *Azores* 38°28N 28°20W **153** d1
Pico, Ponta do *Azores* 38°28N 28°25W **153** d1
Pico Bonito △ *Honduras* 15°34N 86°48W **320** C2
Pico da Neblina △ *Brazil* 0°19N 66°28W **328** C4
Pico Rivera *U.S.A.* 33°59N 118°5W **126** C4
Pico Truncado *Argentina* 46°40S 68°0W **336** C3
Picos = Colinas *Brazil* 6°0S 44°10W **332** C3
Picos *Brazil* 7°5S 41°28W **332** C3
Picos de Europa △ *Spain* 43°14N 4°59W **194** B6
Picota *Peru* 6°54S 76°24W **330** B2
Picton *N.S.W., Australia* 34°12S 150°34E **283** C9
Picton *Ont., Canada* 44°1N 77°9W **312** B7
Picton *N.Z.* 41°18S 174°3E **285** B9
Picton, I. *Chile* 55°2S 66°57W **336** E3
Pictou *Canada* 45°41N 62°42W **299** C7
Picture Butte *Canada* 49°55N 112°45W **296** D6
Pictured Rocks ⌂ *U.S.A.* 46°30N 86°30W **308** B10
Picuí *Brazil* 6°31S 36°21W **332** C4
Picún Leufú *Argentina* 39°30S 69°5W **336** A3
Pidbuzh *Ukraine* 49°19N 23°14E **185** J10
Pidurutalagala *Sri Lanka* 7°10N 80°50E **245** L5
Piechowice *Poland* 50°51N 15°36E **185** H2
Piedade *Rio de J., Brazil* 22°52S 43°18W **135** B1
Piedade *Lisboa, Portugal* 38°49N 9°16W **126** A1
Piedade, Cova da *Portugal* 38°40N 9°8W **126** A2
Piedecuesta *Colombia* 6°59N 73°3W **328** B3
Piedimonte Matese *Italy* 41°22N 14°22E **201** A7
Piedmont = Piemonte □ *Italy* 45°0N 8°0E **198** D5
Piedmont *Ala., U.S.A.* 33°55N 85°37W **316** B4
Piedmont *S.C., U.S.A.* 34°42N 82°28W **292** F11
Piedmont Park *U.S.A.* 33°47N 84°22W **113** B2
Piedra → *Spain* 41°18N 1°47W **196** D3
Piedra del Águila *Argentina* 40°2S 70°4W **336** B2
Piedra del Águila, Embalse *Argentina* 40°15S 70°4W **336** B2
Piedra Lais *Venezuela* 3°10N 65°50W **328** C4
Piedrabuena *Spain* 39°0N 4°10W **195** G6
Piedrahita *Spain* 40°28N 5°23W **194** E5
Piedralaves *Spain* 40°19N 4°42W **194** E6
Piedras, R. de las → *Peru* 12°30S 69°15W **330** C4
Piedras Blancas *Spain* 43°33N 5°58W **194** B5
Piedras Negras *Mexico* 28°42N 100°31W **318** B4
Piedras Pt. *Phil.* 10°11N 118°48E **233** F2
Piekar = Piekary Śląskie *Poland* 50°24N 18°57E **185** H5
Piekary Śląskie *Poland* 50°24N 18°57E **185** H5
Pieksämäki *Finland* 62°18N 27°10E **188** A4
Pielinen *Finland* 63°15N 29°40E **160** E23
Piemonte □ *Italy* 45°0N 8°0E **198** D5
Pienaarsrivier *S. Africa* 25°15S 28°18E **271** C4

Pieniężno *Poland* 54°14N 20°8E 184 D7
Pieninský △ *Europe* 49°25N 20°28E 181 B13
Pieńsk *Poland* 51°16N 15°2E 185 G2
Piercefield *U.S.A.* 44°13N 74°35W 313 B10
Pierceland *Canada* 54°20N 109°46W 297 C7
Pieria ☐ *Greece* 40°13N 22°25E 202 F6
Pierpont *U.S.A.* 41°45N 80°34W 312 E4
Pierre *U.S.A.* 44°22N 100°21W 308 C3
Pierre-Buffière *France* 45°41N 1°22E 174 C5
Pierre-de-Bresse *France* 46°54N 5°13E 173 F12
Pierre Elliott Trudeau ✕ (YUL) *Canada* 45°28N 73°44W 130 B1
Pierrefonds *Canada* 45°29N 73°51W 313 A11
Pierrefontaine-les-Varans *France* 47°14N 6°32E 173 E13
Pierrefort *France* 44°55N 2°50E 174 D6
Pierrelatte *France* 44°23N 4°43E 175 D8
Pierson *U.S.A.* 29°14N 81°28W 317 F8
Piešťany *Slovak Rep.* 48°38N 17°55E 181 C10
Piesting ➔ *Austria* 48°6N 16°40E 181 C9
Pieszyce *Poland* 50°43N 16°33E 185 H3
Piet Retief *S. Africa* 27°1S 30°50E 271 C5
Pietarsaari *Finland* 63°40N 22°43E 160 E20
Pieter Both *Mauritius* 20°11S 57°32E 272 e
Pietermaritzburg *S. Africa* 29°35S 30°25E 271 C5
Pietersburg = Polokwane *S. Africa* 23°54S 29°25E 271 B4
Pietragalla *Italy* 40°45N 15°53E 201 B8
Pietralata *Italy* 41°55N 12°33E 136 B2
Pietrasanta *Italy* 43°57N 10°14E 198 E7
Pietroşiţa *Romania* 45°11N 25°26E 183 E10
Pietrosul, Vf. *Maramureş, Romania* 47°35N 24°43E 183 C9
Pietrosul, Vf. *Suceava, Romania* 47°12N 25°18E 183 C10
Pieve di Cadore *Italy* 46°26N 12°22E 199 B9
Pieve di Teco *Italy* 44°3N 7°56E 198 D4
Pievepélago *Italy* 44°12N 10°37E 198 D7
Pigadítsa *Greece* 39°59N 21°23E 202 G5
Pigeon *Guadeloupe* 16°9N 61°46W 322 e
Pigeon I. *India* 14°2N 74°20E 245 G2
Pigeon I. *St. Lucia* 14°6N 60°58W 323 m
Pigeon L. *Canada* 44°27N 78°30W 312 B6
Piges *Greece* 39°17N 21°25E 204 B3
Piggott *U.S.A.* 36°23N 90°11W 315 C9
Pigna *Italy* 43°56N 7°40E 198 E4
Pigüe *Argentina* 37°36S 62°25W 334 D3
Piha *N.Z.* 36°57S 174°28E 284 C3
Pihani *India* 27°36N 80°15E 243 F9
Pihlajamäki *Finland* 60°14N 24°58E 121 B2
Pihlajasaari *Finland* 60°8N 24°55E 121 C2
Pihlajavesi *Finland* 61°45N 28°45E 188 B5
Pijijiapan *Mexico* 15°42N 93°14W 319 D6
Pikalevo *Russia* 59°37N 34°9E 188 C8
Pikangikum *Canada* 51°49N 94°0W 297 C10
Pikes Peak *U.S.A.* 38°50N 105°3W 304 G11
Piketberg *S. Africa* 32°55S 18°40E 270 D2
Pikeville *U.S.A.* 37°29N 82°31W 309 G12
Pikit *Phil.* 7°4N 124°41E 233 H5
Pikou *China* 39°18N 122°22E 227 E12
Pikounda *Congo* 0°30N 16°44E 264 B3
Pikwitonei *Canada* 55°35N 97°9W 297 B9
Piła *Poland* 53°10N 16°48E 185 E3
Pila *Spain* 38°16N 1°11W 197 G3
Pilanesberg △ *S. Africa* 25°15S 27°4E 270 C4
Pilani *India* 28°22N 75°33E 242 E6
Pilar *Brazil* 9°36S 35°56W 332 C4
Pilar *Paraguay* 26°50S 58°20W 334 B4
Pilar *Capiz, Phil.* 11°29N 123°0E 233 F4
Pilar *Sorsogon, Phil.* 12°56N 123°40E 232 E4
Pilar de la Horadada *Spain* 37°52N 0°47W 197 H4
Pilares *Brazil* 22°52S 43°18W 135 B1
Pilas Group *Phil.* 6°45N 121°35E 233 H3
Pilat ⌓ *France* 45°20N 4°30E 175 C8
Piława *Poland* 51°57N 21°32E 185 G8
Pilaya ➔ *Bolivia* 20°55S 64°4W 331 E5
Pilbara *Australia* 21°15S 118°16E 278 D2
Pilcomaya ➔ *Paraguay* 25°21S 57°42W 334 B4
Pílea *Greece* 40°32N 22°59E 202 F6
Pilgrim's Rest *S. Africa* 24°55S 30°44E 271 B5
Pilgrimstad *Sweden* 62°57N 15°2E 162 B9
Pili *Greece* 36°50N 27°15E 205 E9
Pili *Phil.* 13°33N 123°19E 232 E4
Pilibhit *India* 28°40N 79°50E 243 E8
Pilica ➔ *Poland* 51°52N 21°17E 185 G8
Pilio, Oros *Greece* 39°27N 23°3E 204 B5
Pilipinas = Philippines ■ *Asia* 12°0N 123°0E 232 E4
Pilis *Hungary* 47°17N 19°35E 182 C4
Pilisvörösvár *Hungary* 47°38N 18°56E 182 C3
Pilkhawa *India* 28°43N 77°42E 242 E7
Pillar B. *Ascension I.* 7°59S 14°21W 153 g
Pillaro *Ecuador* 1°10S 78°32W 328 D2
Pillau = Baltiysk *Russia* 54°41N 19°58E 184 D6
Pilliga *Australia* 30°21S 148°54E 281 E4
Pilos *Greece* 36°55N 21°42E 204 E3
Pilot Grove *U.S.A.* 38°53N 92°55W 310 F4
Pilot Mound *Canada* 49°15N 98°54W 297 D9
Pilot Point *Alaska, U.S.A.* 57°34N 157°35W 303 H8
Pilot Point *Tex., U.S.A.* 33°24N 96°58W 314 E6
Pilot Rock *U.S.A.* 45°29N 118°50W 304 D4
Pilot Station *U.S.A.* 61°56N 162°53W 303 F7
Pilote ➔ *Martinique* 14°28N 60°55W 322 j
Pilsen = Pilzno *Poland* 49°58N 21°16E 185 J8
Pilsen = Plzeň *Czech Rep.* 49°45N 13°22E 180 B6
Pilštanj *Slovenia* 46°8N 15°39E 199 B12
Piltene *Latvia* 57°13N 21°40E 184 A8
Pilton *U.K.* 55°58N 3°13W 121 B2
Pilzno *Poland* 49°58N 21°16E 185 J8
Pima *U.S.A.* 32°54N 109°50W 305 K9
Pimba *Australia* 31°18S 136°46E 282 A2
Pimenta Bueno *Brazil* 11°35S 61°10W 331 C5
Pimenteiras *Brazil* 13°40S 60°58W 331 C5
Pimentel *Peru* 6°45S 79°55W 330 B2
Pimlico *London, U.K.* 125 c3
Pimmit Hills *U.S.A.* 38°54N 77°12W 143 B2
Pimpri Chinchwad *India* 18°37N 73°47E 244 E1
Pimu *Dem. Rep. of the Congo* 1°42N 20°58E 264 B4
Pin Valley △ *India* 31°50N 77°50E 242 D7
Pina de Ebro *Spain* 41°29N 0°33W 196 D4
Pinamalayan *Phil.* 13°2N 121°29E 232 E3
Pinang *Malaysia* 5°25N 100°15E 237 c
Pinang ☐ *Malaysia* 5°20N 100°20E 237 K3
Pinar, C. des *Spain* 39°53N 3°12E 206 B4
Pinar del Río *Cuba* 22°26N 83°40W 320 B3
Pınarbaşı *Çanakkale, Turkey* 39°53N 26°15E 205 B8
Pınarbaşı *Kayseri, Turkey* 38°43N 36°23E 212 C7
Pınarhisar *Turkey* 41°37N 27°30E 203 E11
Pinatubo, Mt. *Phil.* 15°8N 120°21E 232 D3
Pinawa *Canada* 50°9N 95°50W 297 C9
Pincehely *Hungary* 46°41N 18°27E 182 D3
Pinchang *China* 31°36N 107°3E 228 B6
Pincher Creek *Canada* 49°30N 113°57W 296 D6
Pinchi L. *Canada* 54°38N 124°30W 296 C4
Pinckard *U.S.A.* 31°19N 85°33W 316 D4
Pinckneyville *U.S.A.* 38°5N 89°23W 310 F7
Pińczów *Poland* 50°32N 20°32E 185 H7
Pind Dadan Khan *Pakistan* 32°36N 73°7E 217 F8
Pindar *Australia* 28°30S 115°47E 279 E2
Pindaré ➔ *Brazil* 3°17S 44°47W 332 B3
Pindaré-Mirim *Brazil* 3°37S 45°21W 332 B2
Pindera Downs ✿ *Australia* 29°24S 142°37E 281 A3
Pindi Gheb *Pakistan* 33°14N 72°21E 242 C5
Pindiga *Nigeria* 9°58N 10°53E 263 D7
Pindobal *Brazil* 3°16S 48°25W 332 B2
Pindos △ *Greece* 39°52N 21°11E 204 B3
Pindos Oros *Greece* 40°0N 21°0E 204 B3
Pindus Mts. = Pindos Oros *Greece* 40°0N 21°0E 204 B3
Pine ➔ *B.C., Canada* 56°8N 120°43W 296 B4
Pine ➔ *Sask., Canada* 58°50N 105°38W 297 B7
Pine Bluff *U.S.A.* 34°13N 92°1W 314 D8
Pine Bluffs *U.S.A.* 41°11N 104°4W 304 F11
Pine Castle *U.S.A.* 28°28N 81°22W 133 B2
Pine City *U.S.A.* 45°50N 92°59W 308 C7
Pine Cr. ➔ *U.S.A.* 41°10N 77°16W 312 E7
Pine Creek *Australia* 13°50S 131°50E 278 B5
Pine Falls *Canada* 50°34N 96°11W 297 C9
Pine Flat L. *U.S.A.* 36°50N 119°20W 306 J7
Pine Grove *Ont., Canada* 43°47N 79°34W 141 A1
Pine Grove *Pa., U.S.A.* 40°33N 76°23W 313 F8
Pine Hill *Australia* 23°38S 146°57E 280 C4
Pine Hills *U.S.A.* 28°33N 81°27W 133 A2
Pine I. *U.S.A.* 26°36N 82°7W 317 J7
Pine Island Glacier *Antarctica* 76°0S 100°0W 151 D15
Pine Level *U.S.A.* 32°4N 86°4W 316 C3
Pine Mountain *U.S.A.* 32°49N 84°51W 316 C5
Pine Pass *Canada* 55°25N 122°42W 296 B4
Pine Point *Canada* 60°50N 114°28W 296 A6
Pine Ridge *N.S.W., Australia* 31°30S 150°28E 283 A9
Pine Ridge *S. Dak., U.S.A.* 43°2N 102°33W 308 D2
Pine River *Man., Canada* 51°45N 100°30W 297 C8
Pine River *Minn., U.S.A.* 46°43N 94°24W 308 B6
Pine Valley *U.S.A.* 32°50N 116°32W 307 N10
Pinecrest *U.S.A.* 38°12N 120°1W 306 G6
Pineda de Mar *Spain* 41°37N 2°42E 196 D7
Pinedale *Calif., U.S.A.* 36°50N 119°48W 306 J7
Pinedale *Wyo., U.S.A.* 42°52N 109°52W 304 E9
Pinega ➔ *Russia* 64°30N 44°19E 186 B8
Pinehouse L. *Canada* 55°32N 106°35W 297 B7
Pineimuta ➔ *Canada* 52°8N 88°33W 298 B1
Pinellas Park *U.S.A.* 27°50N 82°41W 317 H7
Pinerolo *Italy* 44°53N 7°21E 198 D4
Pines, Akra *Greece* 40°5N 24°20E 203 F8
Pineto *Italy* 42°36N 14°4E 199 F11
Pinetop-Lakeside *U.S.A.* 34°9N 109°58W 305 J9
Pinetown *S. Africa* 29°48S 30°54E 271 C5
Pinetta *U.S.A.* 30°36N 83°21W 316 E6
Pineview *U.S.A.* 32°7N 83°30W 316 C6
Pineville *La., U.S.A.* 31°19N 92°26W 314 F8
Pineville *S.C., U.S.A.* 33°26N 80°1W 316 B9
Pinewood *U.S.A.* 33°44N 80°27W 316 B9
Pinewood Park *U.S.A.* 25°52N 80°13W 128 A2
Piney *France* 48°22N 4°21E 173 D11
Piney Run ➔ *U.S.A.* 38°58N 77°14W 143 B2
Ping ➔ *Thailand* 15°42N 100°9E 236 E3
Pingaring *Australia* 32°40S 118°32E 279 F2
Pingba *China* 26°23N 106°12E 228 D6
Pingbian *China* 23°0N 103°45E 228 F4
Pingchuan *China* 27°35N 101°55E 228 D3
Pingding *China* 37°47N 113°38E 226 F7
Pingdingshan *China* 33°43N 113°27E 226 H7
Pingdu *China* 36°42N 119°59E 227 F10
Pingelly *Australia* 32°32S 117°5E 279 F2
Pingguo *China* 23°19N 107°36E 228 F6
Pinghe *China* 24°17N 117°21E 229 E11
Pinghu *China* 30°40N 121°2E 229 B13
Pingjiang *China* 28°45N 113°36E 229 C9
Pingle *China* 24°40N 110°40E 229 E8
Pingli *China* 32°27N 109°22E 228 A7
Pingliang *China* 35°35N 106°31E 226 G4
Pinglin *Taiwan* 24°56N 121°42E 225 B3
Pinglu *China* 39°31N 112°30E 226 E7
Pingluo *China* 38°52N 106°30E 226 E4
Pingnan *Fujian, China* 26°55N 119°0E 229 D12
Pingnan *Guangxi Zhuangzu, China* 23°33N 110°22E 229 F8
Pingo *Gabon* 1°19S 10°55E 264 C2
Pingquan *China* 41°1N 118°37E 227 D10
Pingrup *Australia* 33°32S 118°29E 279 F2
Pingshan *China* 28°39N 104°3E 228 C5
Pingtan *China* 25°31N 119°47E 229 E12
Pingtang *China* 25°49N 107°17E 228 E6
P'ingtung *Taiwan* 22°38N 120°30E 225 D2
P'ingtung ☐ *Taiwan* 22°30N 120°40E 225 D2
Pingwu *China* 32°25N 104°30E 226 H3
Pingxiang *Guangxi Zhuangzu, China* 22°6N 106°46E 228 F6
Pingxiang *Jiangxi, China* 27°43N 113°48E 229 D9
Pingyao *China* 37°12N 112°10E 226 F7
Pingyi *China* 35°30N 117°35E 227 G9
Pingyin *China* 36°20N 116°25E 226 F9
Pingyuan *Guangdong, China* 24°37N 115°57E 229 E10
Pingyuan *Shandong, China* 37°10N 116°22E 226 F9
Pingyuanjie *China* 23°45N 103°48E 228 F4
Pingzhou *China* 23°1N 113°11E 121 B2
Pinhal Novo *Portugal* 38°38N 8°55W 195 G2
Pinheiro = Icoraci *Brazil* 1°18S 48°28W 332 B2
Pinheiro *Brazil* 2°31S 45°5W 332 B2
Pinheiro Machado *Brazil* 31°34S 53°23W 335 C5
Pinheiros ➔ *Brazil* 23°37S 46°44W 137 B1
Pinhel *Portugal* 40°50N 7°1W 194 E3
Pinhuá ➔ *Brazil* 6°21S 65°0W 331 B5
Pini *Indonesia* 0°10N 98°40E 234 B1
Piniós ➔ *Ilia, Greece* 37°48N 21°20E 204 D3
Piniós ➔ *Trikala, Greece* 39°55N 22°41E 204 B4
Pinjarra *Australia* 32°37S 115°52E 279 F2
Pinjrapur *Pakistan* 24°53N 67°4E 123 A2
Pink Beach *Bonaire* 12°5N 68°17W 322 h
Pink Mountain *Canada* 57°3N 122°52W 296 B4
Pinkafeld *Austria* 47°22N 16°9E 181 D9
Pinlaung *Burma* 20°8N 96°47E 241 E6
Pinlebu *Burma* 24°5N 95°22E 241 C5
Pinnacle Is. = Senkaku-Shotō *E. China Sea* 25°45N 123°30E 221 M1
Pinnacles ⌓ *U.S.A.* 36°25N 121°12W 306 J5
Pinnaroo *Australia* 35°17S 140°53E 282 C4
Pinneberg *Germany* 53°40N 9°48E 178 B5
Pinner *U.K.* 51°35N 0°22W 125 A1
Pinner Green *U.K.* 51°35N 0°23W 125 A1
Pino Hachado, Paso *S. Amer.* 38°39S 70°54W 336 A2
Pinon Hills *U.S.A.* 34°26N 117°39W 307 L9
Pinos *Mexico* 22°18N 101°34W 318 C4
Pinos, Mt. *U.S.A.* 34°49N 119°8W 307 L7
Pinos Pt. *U.S.A.* 36°38N 121°57W 305 H3
Pinos Puente *Spain* 37°15N 3°45W 195 H7
Pinrang *Indonesia* 3°46S 119°41E 235 C5
Pins, Î. des *N. Cal.* 22°37S 167°30E 288 d
Pins, Pte. aux *Canada* 42°15N 81°51W 312 D3
Pinsk *Belarus* 52°10N 26°1E 177 B14
Pinta, Canal de *Ecuador* 0°27N 90°38W 330 a
Pinta, I. *Ecuador* 0°35N 90°44W 330 a
Pintados *Chile* 20°35S 69°40W 330 E4
Pintuyan *Phil.* 9°57N 125°15E 233 G5
Pinukpuk *Phil.* 17°35N 121°22E 232 C3
Pinyang *China* 27°42N 120°31E 229 D13
Pinyug *Russia* 60°5N 48°0E 186 B8
Pio Duran *Phil.* 13°2N 123°25E 232 E4
Pio V. Corpuz *Phil.* 11°55N 124°2E 233 F5
Pio XII *Brazil* 3°53S 45°17W 332 B2
Pioche *U.S.A.* 37°56N 114°27W 305 H6
Pioltello *Italy* 45°30N 9°19E 129 A2
Piombino *Italy* 42°55N 10°32E 198 F7
Piombino, Canale di *Italy* 42°53N 10°30E 198 F7
Pioner, Ostrov *Russia* 79°50N 92°0E 215 B10
Pionerskiy *Russia* 54°56N 20°14E 184 D7
Pionki *Poland* 51°29N 21°28E 185 G8
Piopiotaki = Milford Sd. *N.Z.* 44°41S 167°47E 285 E2
Piorini ➔ *Brazil* 3°23S 63°30W 329 D5
Piorini, L. *Brazil* 3°15S 62°35W 329 D5
Piotrków Trybunalski *Poland* 51°23N 19°43E 185 G6
Piove di Sacco *Italy* 45°18N 12°2E 199 C9
Pīp *Iran* 26°45N 60°10E 247 E9
Pipar *India* 26°25N 73°31E 242 F5
Pipar Road *India* 26°27N 73°27E 242 F5
Piparia *Mad. P., India* 22°45N 78°23E 242 H8
Piparia *Mad. P., India* 21°49N 77°37E 242 J7
Piparo *Trin. & Tob.* 10°20N 61°20W 323 t
Pipas *Angola* 14°57S 12°11E 265 E2
Piperi *Greece* 39°20N 24°19E 204 B6
Piperno = Priverno *Italy* 41°28N 13°11E 200 A6
Pipestone *U.S.A.* 44°0N 96°19W 308 D5
Pipestone ➔ *Canada* 52°53N 89°23W 298 B2
Pipestone Cr. ➔ *Canada* 49°38N 100°15W 297 D8
Pipinui Pt. *N.Z.* 41°10S 174°44E 143 A1
Pipiriki *N.Z.* 39°28S 175°5E 284 F4
Piplan *Pakistan* 32°17N 71°21E 242 C4
Piploda *India* 23°37N 74°56E 242 H6
Pipmuacan, Rés. *Canada* 49°45N 70°30W 299 C5
Pippingarra *Australia* 20°27S 118°42E 278 D2
Pipriac *France* 47°59N 1°58W 172 E5
Piqua *U.S.A.* 40°9N 84°15W 311 D12
Piquet Carneiro *Brazil* 5°48S 39°25W 332 C4
Piquiri ➔ *Brazil* 24°3S 54°14W 335 A5
Pir Panjal Range *India* 32°30N 76°50E 242 C7
Pīr Sohrāb *Iran* 25°44N 60°54E 247 E9
Pira *Benin* 8°28N 1°48E 263 D5
Piracanjuba *Brazil* 17°18S 49°1W 333 E2
Piracicaba *Brazil* 22°45S 47°40W 335 A6
Piracuruca *Brazil* 3°50S 41°50W 332 B3
Pirae *Tahiti* 17°31S 149°32W 289 e
Piræus = Pireas *Greece* 37°57N 23°42E 112 B1
Piraiévs = Pireas *Greece* 37°57N 23°42E 112 B1
Pirajuçara ➔ *Brazil* 23°33S 46°42W 137 B1
Pirajuí *Brazil* 21°59S 49°29W 335 A6
Piram I. *India* 21°36N 72°21E 242 J5
Piran *Slovenia* 45°31N 13°33E 199 C10
Pirané *Argentina* 25°42S 59°6W 334 B4
Piranhas *Brazil* 9°27S 37°46W 332 C4
Pirano = Piran *Slovenia* 45°31N 13°33E 199 C10
Pīrānshahr *Iran* 36°41N 45°8E 213 D11
Pirapemas *Brazil* 3°43S 44°14W 332 B3
Pirapora *Brazil* 17°20S 44°56W 333 E3
Pirara *Guyana* 3°37N 59°40W 329 C6
Pirawa *India* 24°10N 76°2E 242 G7
Piray ➔ *Bolivia* 16°32S 63°45W 331 D5
Pirdop *Bulgaria* 42°40N 24°10E 203 D8
Pireas *Greece* 37°57N 23°42E 112 B1
Pires do Rio *Brazil* 17°18S 48°17W 333 E2
Pirganj *Bangla.* 25°51N 88°24E 241 C2
Pirgi *Greece* 38°13N 25°59E 205 C7
Pirgos *Ilia, Greece* 37°40N 21°27E 204 D3
Pirgos *Kriti, Greece* 35°0N 25°9E 207 E6
Pirgovo *Bulgaria* 43°44N 25°43E 203 C9
Piribebuy *Paraguay* 25°26S 57°2W 334 B4
Pirimapun *Indonesia* 6°20S 138°24E 231 F9
Pirin △ *Bulgaria* 41°48N 23°22E 202 E7
Pirin Planina *Bulgaria* 41°40N 23°30E 202 E7
Pirinçi *Turkey* 41°10N 28°52E 122 B1
Pirineos = Pyrénées *Europe* 42°45N 0°18E 174 F4
Piripiri *Brazil* 4°15S 41°46W 332 B3
Piritu *Venezuela* 9°23N 69°12W 328 B4
Pirituba *Brazil* 23°29S 46°44W 137 A1
Pirkkola *Finland* 60°14N 24°55E 121 B2
Pirlangimpi *Australia* 11°24S 130°26E 278 B5
Pirmasens *Germany* 49°12N 7°36E 179 F3
Pirna *Germany* 50°57N 13°56E 178 E9
Pirojpur *Bangla.* 22°35N 90°1E 241 D3
Pirot *Serbia* 43°9N 22°33E 202 C6
Piru *Indonesia* 3°4S 128°12E 231 E7
Piru *Calif., U.S.A.* 34°25N 118°48W 307 L8
Piryatin = Pyryatyn *Ukraine* 50°15N 32°25E 189 G7
Pisa *Italy* 43°43N 10°23E 198 E7
Pisa ➔ *Poland* 53°14N 21°52E 185 E8
Pisa, Firenze ✕ (PSA) *Italy* 43°40N 10°22E 198 E7
Pisa Ra. *N.Z.* 44°52S 169°12E 285 E4
Pisac *Peru* 13°25S 71°50W 330 C3
Pisagne *Italy* 45°45N 10°10E 198 C7
Pisagua *Chile* 19°40S 70°15W 330 D3
Pisarovina *Croatia* 45°35N 15°50E 199 C12
Pisau, Tanjong *Malaysia* 6°4N 117°59E 235 A5
Pisba △ *Colombia* 5°54N 72°39W 328 B3
Pisco *Peru* 13°50S 76°12W 330 C2
Piscu *Romania* 45°30N 27°43E 183 E12
Písek *Czech Rep.* 49°19N 14°10E 180 B7
Pisgat O'mer *West Bank* 31°49N 35°14E 123 B2
Pisgat Ze'ev *West Bank* 31°49N 35°14E 123 B2
Pishan *China* 37°30N 78°33E 217 E9
Pishcha *Ukraine* 51°35N 23°50E 185 G10
Pishchanka *Ukraine* 48°12N 28°54E 183 B13
Pīshīn *Iran* 26°6N 61°47E 247 E9
Pishin *Pakistan* 30°35N 67°0E 242 D2
Pishin Lora ➔ *Pakistan* 29°9N 64°5E 242 E1
Pishpek = Bishkek *Kyrgyzstan* 42°54N 74°46E 218 C3
Pisidia *Turkey* 37°30N 31°40E 212 D4
Pising *Indonesia* 5°8S 121°53E 235 D6
Pisinoe, Pte. *Guadeloupe* 15°59N 61°13W 322 e
Pismo Beach *U.S.A.* 35°9N 120°38W 307 K6
Písnice *Czech Rep.* 49°59N 14°28E 135 C2
Piso, L. *Liberia* 6°50N 11°15W 262 D2
Pissila *Burkina Faso* 13°7N 0°50W 263 C4
Pissis, Cerro *Argentina* 27°45S 68°48W 334 B2
Pissos *France* 44°19N 0°49W 174 D3
Pissouri *Cyprus* 34°40N 32°42E 207 E8
Pisticci *Italy* 40°23N 16°33E 201 B9
Pistóia *Italy* 43°55N 10°54E 198 E7
Pistol B. *Canada* 62°25N 92°37W 297 A10
Pisuerga ➔ *Spain* 41°33N 4°52W 194 D6
Pisz *Poland* 53°38N 21°49E 184 E8
Pit ➔ *U.S.A.* 40°47N 122°6W 304 F2
Pita *Guinea* 11°5N 12°15W 262 C2
Pitalito *Colombia* 1°51N 76°2W 328 C2
Pitampura *India* 28°41N 77°7E 120 A1
Pitanga *Brazil* 24°46S 51°44W 333 F1
Pitangui *Brazil* 19°40S 44°54W 333 E3
Pitarpunga L. *Australia* 34°24S 143°30E 282 C5
Pitcairn I. *Pac. Oc.* 25°5S 130°5W 289 K14
Pitch Pt. *Trin. & Tob.* 10°16N 61°37W 323 t
Piteå *Sweden* 65°20N 21°25E 160 D19
Piteälven ➔ *Sweden* 65°20N 21°25E 160 D19
Piterka *Russia* 50°41N 47°29E 190 E8
Pitești *Romania* 44°52N 24°54E 183 F9
Pithapuram *India* 17°10N 82°15E 244 F6
Pithara *Australia* 30°20S 116°35E 279 F2
Pithio *Greece* 41°24N 26°40E 203 E10
Pithiviers *France* 48°10N 2°13E 173 D9
Pithora *India* 21°16N 82°31E 244 D6
Pithoragarh *India* 29°35N 80°13E 243 E9
Pithoro *Pakistan* 25°31N 69°23E 242 G3
Piti *Guam* 13°28N 144°41E 302 d
Pitigliano *Italy* 42°38N 11°40E 199 F8
Pitkäjärvi *Finland* 60°15N 24°45E 121 B1
Pitkyaranta *Russia* 61°34N 31°37E 188 B6
Pitlochry *U.K.* 56°42N 3°44W 167 E5
Pitnak = Drujba *Uzbekistan* 41°13N 61°18E 216 D6
Pitoa *Cameroon* 9°23N 13°32E 264 A2
Pitogo *Phil.* 13°47N 122°5E 232 E4
Piton, Pte. du *Guadeloupe* 16°30N 61°26W 322 e
Piton de la Petite Rivière Noire *Mauritius* 20°24S 57°23E 272 e
Pitons, Anses des *St. Lucia* 13°49N 61°4W 323 m
Pitou *Taiwan* 23°53N 120°27E 225 C2
Pitou Chiao *Taiwan* 25°8N 121°55E 225 A3
Pitrufquén *Chile* 38°59S 72°39W 336 A2
Pitrzyk = Byczyna *Poland* 51°7N 18°12E 185 G5
Pitsilia *Cyprus* 34°55N 33°0E 207 E9
Pitt, Pta. *Ecuador* 0°43S 89°14W 330 a
Pitt I. *B.C., Canada* 53°30N 129°50W 296 C3
Pitt I. *N.Z.* 44°15S 176°15W 285 a
Pitti I. *India* 10°50N 72°38E 245 J1
Pittsburg *Calif., U.S.A.* 38°2N 121°53W 306 G5
Pittsburg *Kans., U.S.A.* 37°25N 94°42W 308 G6
Pittsburg *Tex., U.S.A.* 33°0N 94°59W 314 E7
Pittsburgh *U.S.A.* 40°26N 79°58W 312 F5
Pittsfield *Ill., U.S.A.* 39°36N 90°49W 310 E6
Pittsfield *Maine, U.S.A.* 44°47N 69°23W 309 C19
Pittsfield *Mass., U.S.A.* 42°27N 73°15W 313 D11
Pittsfield *N.H., U.S.A.* 43°18N 71°20W 313 C13
Pittston *U.S.A.* 41°19N 75°47W 313 E9
Pittsview *U.S.A.* 32°11N 85°10W 316 C4
Pittsworth *Australia* 27°41S 151°37E 281 D5
Pituri ➔ *Australia* 22°35S 138°30E 280 C2
Pium *Brazil* 10°27S 49°11W 332 D2
Piumafua Mt. *Amer. Samoa* 14°11S 169°37W 302 f
Piumhi *Brazil* 20°28S 45°58W 333 F2
Piura *Peru* 5°15S 80°38W 330 B1
Piura ☐ *Peru* 5°10S 80°0W 330 B2
Piva ➔ *Montenegro* 43°20N 18°50E 202 C2
Pivijay *Colombia* 10°28N 74°37W 328 A3
Piwniczna *Poland* 49°27N 20°42E 185 J7
Pixian *China* 30°48N 103°52E 228 B4
Pixley *U.S.A.* 35°58N 119°18W 306 K7
Pizarra *Spain* 36°36N 4°42W 195 J6
Pizarro *Colombia* 4°58N 77°22W 328 C2
Pizhou = Pei Xian *China* 34°44N 116°55E 226 G9
Pizhou *China* 34°18N 117°57E 227 G9
Pizzo *Italy* 38°44N 16°10E 201 D9
Placentia *Canada* 47°20N 54°0W 299 C9
Placentia B. *Canada* 47°0N 54°40W 299 C9
Placer *Masbate, Phil.* 11°52N 123°55E 233 F4
Placer *Surigao N., Phil.* 9°36N 125°38E 233 G5
Placerville *U.S.A.* 38°44N 120°48W 306 G6
Placetas *Cuba* 22°15N 79°44W 320 B4
Plácido de Castro *Brazil* 10°20S 67°11W 330 C4
Plačkovica *Macedonia* 41°45N 22°30E 202 E6
Plaine des Jarres *Laos* 19°27N 103°10E 236 C4
Plaine Magnien *Mauritius* 20°25S 57°39E 272 e
Plaines des Papayes *Mauritius* 20°3S 57°34E 272 e
Plainfield *Ill., U.S.A.* 41°37N 88°12W 311 C8
Plainfield *Ind., U.S.A.* 39°42N 86°24W 311 E10
Plainfield *N.J., U.S.A.* 40°37N 74°25W 313 F10
Plainfield *Ohio, U.S.A.* 40°13N 81°43W 312 F3
Plainfield *Vt., U.S.A.* 44°17N 72°26W 313 B12
Plains *Ga., U.S.A.* 32°2N 84°24W 316 C5
Plains *Mont., U.S.A.* 47°28N 114°53W 304 C6
Plains *Tex., U.S.A.* 33°11N 102°50W 314 E3
Plainview *Nebr., U.S.A.* 42°21N 97°47W 308 D5
Plainview *Tex., U.S.A.* 34°11N 101°43W 314 D4
Plainwell *U.S.A.* 42°27N 85°38W 311 B11
Plaisance *France* 43°36N 0°3E 174 E4
Plaistow *U.S.A.* 42°50N 71°6W 313 D13
Plaju *Indonesia* 2°58S 104°49E 234 C2
Plaka *Greece* 40°0N 25°24E 205 B7
Plaka, Akra *Greece* 35°11N 26°19E 207 E7
Plakenska Planina *Macedonia* 41°14N 21°2E 202 E5
Plampang *Indonesia* 8°47S 117°46E 235 D5
Planá *Czech Rep.* 49°50N 12°44E 180 B5
Plana Cays *Bahamas* 22°38N 73°30W 321 B5
Planada *U.S.A.* 37°16N 120°19W 306 H6
Planchón *Peru* 12°14S 69°11W 330 C4
Plancoët *France* 48°32N 2°13W 172 D4
Plandište *Serbia* 45°16N 21°10E 182 E6
Planegg *Germany* 48°6N 11°25E 131 B1
Planeta Rica *Colombia* 8°25N 75°36W 328 B2
Plano *U.S.A.* 33°1N 96°42W 314 E6
Plant City *U.S.A.* 28°1N 82°7W 317 G7
Plantation *U.S.A.* 26°7N 80°14W 317 J9
Plaquemine *U.S.A.* 30°17N 91°14W 314 F9
Plasencia *Spain* 40°3N 6°8W 194 E4
Plaški *Croatia* 45°4N 15°22E 199 C12
Plassen *Norway* 61°9N 12°30E 164 C9
Plast *Russia* 54°22N 60°50E 216 B6
Plaster City *U.S.A.* 32°47N 115°51W 307 N11
Plaster Rock *Canada* 46°53N 67°22W 299 C6
Plastun *Russia* 44°45N 136°19E 220 B8
Plasy *Czech Rep.* 49°56N 13°24E 180 B6
Plata, Río de la ➔ *S. Amer.* 34°45S 57°30W 334 C4
Plátani ➔ *Italy* 37°23N 13°16E 200 E6
Platanos *Greece* 35°28N 23°33E 207 D5
Plataria *Greece* 39°27N 20°16E 206 C10
Plateau ☐ *Nigeria* 8°30N 9°0E 263 D6
Plateau d'Ipassa ⌓ *Gabon* 0°26N 12°40E 264 B2
Plathe = Płoty *Poland* 53°48N 15°18E 184 E2
Platinum *U.S.A.* 59°1N 161°49W 303 G7
Plato *Colombia* 9°47N 74°47W 328 B3
Platte *U.S.A.* 43°23N 98°51W 308 D4
Platte ➔ *Mo., U.S.A.* 39°16N 94°50W 310 E2
Platte ➔ *Nebr., U.S.A.* 41°4N 95°53W 308 E6
Platte City *U.S.A.* 39°22N 94°47W 310 E2
Platteville *U.S.A.* 42°44N 90°29W 310 B6
Plattling *Germany* 48°46N 12°53E 179 G8
Plattsburg *U.S.A.* 39°34N 94°27W 310 E2
Plattsburgh *U.S.A.* 44°42N 73°28W 313 B11
Plattsmouth *U.S.A.* 41°1N 95°53W 308 E6
Plau *Germany* 53°27N 12°15E 178 B8
Plauen *Germany* 50°30N 12°8E 178 E8
Plauer See *Germany* 53°28N 12°17E 178 B8
Plav *Montenegro* 42°38N 19°57E 202 D3
Plavinas *Latvia* 56°35N 25°46E 188 D3
Plavnica *Montenegro* 42°20N 19°13E 202 D3
Plavno *Croatia* 44°9N 16°10E 199 D13
Plavsk *Russia* 53°40N 37°18E 188 F9
Playa Blanca Sur *Canary Is.* 28°51N 13°50W 153 e2
Playa de las Americas *Canary Is.* 28°5N 16°43W 153 e1
Playa de Mogán *Canary Is.* 27°48N 15°47W 153 e1
Playa del Carmen *Mexico* 20°37N 87°4W 319 C7
Playa del Inglés *Canary Is.* 27°45N 15°33W 153 e1
Playa Esmerelda *Canary Is.* 28°8N 14°16W 153 e2
Playas *Ecuador* 2°38S 80°23W 328 D1
Playgreen L. *Canada* 54°0N 98°15W 297 C9
Plaza Mayor *Madrid, Spain* 127 b2
Pleasant Bay *Canada* 46°51N 60°48W 299 C7
Pleasant Hill *Calif., U.S.A.* 37°57N 122°4W 306 H4
Pleasant Hill *Ill., U.S.A.* 39°27N 90°52W 310 E6
Pleasant Hill *Mo., U.S.A.* 38°47N 94°16W 310 F2
Pleasant Mount *U.S.A.* 41°44N 75°26W 313 E9
Pleasant Point *N.Z.* 44°16S 171°9E 285 E3
Pleasant Prairie *U.S.A.* 42°33N 87°56W 311 B9
Pleasanton *Calif., U.S.A.* 37°39N 121°52W 306 H5
Pleasanton *Tex., U.S.A.* 28°58N 98°29W 314 G5
Pleasantville *Iowa, U.S.A.* 41°23N 93°18W 310 C3
Pleasantville *N.J., U.S.A.* 39°24N 74°32W 309 F16
Pleasantville *Pa., U.S.A.* 41°35N 79°34W 312 E5
Pleasure Island *U.S.A.* 28°21N 81°31W 133 B1
Pleasure Ridge Park *U.S.A.* 38°9N 85°50W 311 F11
Pléaux *France* 45°8N 2°13E 174 C6
Plei Ku *Vietnam* 13°57N 108°0E 236 F7
Plélan-le-Grand *France* 48°0N 2°7W 172 D4
Pléneuf-Val-André *France* 48°35N 2°32W 172 D4
Plenita *Romania* 44°14N 23°10E 183 F8
Plenty ➔ *Australia* 23°25S 136°31E 280 C2
Plenty, B. of *N.Z.* 37°45S 177°0E 284 D6
Plentywood *U.S.A.* 48°47N 104°34W 304 B11
Plérin *France* 48°32N 2°46W 172 D4
Plesetsk *Russia* 62°43N 40°20E 186 B7
Pleskau = Pskov *Russia* 57°50N 28°25E 188 D5
Plessisville *Canada* 46°14N 71°47W 299 C5
Plestin-les-Grèves *France* 48°40N 3°39W 172 D3
Pleszew *Poland* 51°53N 17°47E 185 G4
Pleternica *Croatia* 45°17N 17°48E 182 E2
Plétipi, L. *Canada* 51°44N 70°6W 299 B5
Pleven *Bulgaria* 43°26N 24°37E 203 C8
Pleven ☐ *Bulgaria* 43°26N 24°37E 203 C8
Plevlja *Montenegro* 43°21N 19°21E 202 C3
Plevna *Canada* 44°58N 76°59W 312 B8
Plitvička Jezera △ *Croatia* 44°54N 15°35E 199 D12
Plješevica *Croatia* 44°45N 15°45E 199 D12
Ploaghe *Italy* 40°40N 8°45E 200 B1
Ploče *Croatia* 43°4N 17°26E 199 E14
Płock *Poland* 52°32N 19°40E 185 F6
Plöckenpass *Italy* 46°37N 12°57E 199 B9
Plöckenstein *Germany* 48°46N 13°51E 179 G9
Ploemeur *France* 47°44N 3°26W 172 E3
Ploërmel *France* 47°55N 2°26W 172 E4
Plöhnen = Płońsk *Poland* 52°37N 20°21E 185 F7
Ploiești *Romania* 44°57N 26°5E 183 F11
Plomari *Greece* 38°59N 26°22E 205 C8
Plombières-les-Bains *France* 47°58N 6°27E 173 E13
Plomin *Croatia* 45°8N 14°10E 199 C11
Plön *Germany* 54°9N 10°24E 178 A6
Plonge, Lac la *Canada* 55°8N 107°20W 297 B7
Płońsk *Poland* 52°37N 20°21E 185 F7
Plopeni *Romania* 45°4N 25°59E 183 E10
Plopișului, Munţii *Romania* 47°5N 22°30E 182 C7
Płotsk = Płock *Poland* 52°32N 19°40E 185 F6
Płoty *Poland* 53°48N 15°18E 184 E2
Plouaret *France* 48°37N 3°28W 172 D3
Plouay *France* 47°55N 3°21W 172 E3
Ploučnice ➔ *Czech Rep.* 50°46N 14°13E 180 A7
Ploudalmézeau *France* 48°34N 4°41W 172 D2
Plouescat *France* 48°39N 4°10W 172 D2
Plougasnou *France* 48°42N 3°49W 172 D3
Plougastel-Daoulas *France* 48°22N 4°17W 172 D2
Plouguerneau *France* 48°36N 4°30W 172 D2
Plouha *France* 48°41N 2°57W 172 D4
Plouhinec *France* 48°0N 4°29W 172 E2
Plovdiv *Bulgaria* 42°8N 24°44E 203 D8
Plovdiv ☐ *Bulgaria* 42°15N 24°30E 203 D8
Plover Cove Res. *China* 22°28N 114°15E 219 a
Pluies, R. des ➔ *Réunion* 20°52S 55°31E 272 f
Plum *U.S.A.* 40°29N 79°47W 312 F5
Plum I. *U.S.A.* 41°11N 72°12W 313 E12
Plumas *U.S.A.* 39°45N 120°4W 306 F6
Plummer *U.S.A.* 47°20N 116°53W 304 C5
Plumridge Lakes *Australia* 29°26S 125°16E 279 E4
Plumstead *Western Cape, S. Africa* 34°1S 18°28E 118 B1
Plumstead *London, U.K.* 51°29N 0°5E 125 B4
Plumtree *Zimbabwe* 20°27S 27°55E 269 G2
Plungė *Lithuania* 55°53N 21°59E 184 C8
Pluvigner *France* 47°46N 3°1W 172 E3
Plužine *Montenegro* 43°8N 18°51E 202 C2
Plymouth *Montserrat* 16°41N 62°12W 323 p
Plymouth *Trin. & Tob.* 11°14N 60°48W 323 s
Plymouth *U.K.* 50°22N 4°10W 169 G3
Plymouth *Calif., U.S.A.* 38°29N 120°51W 306 G6
Plymouth *Ill., U.S.A.* 40°18N 90°58W 310 D6
Plymouth *Ind., U.S.A.* 41°21N 86°19W 311 C10
Plymouth *Mass., U.S.A.* 41°57N 70°40W 313 E14
Plymouth *N.C., U.S.A.* 35°52N 76°43W 315 D16
Plymouth *N.H., U.S.A.* 43°46N 71°41W 313 C13
Plymouth *Pa., U.S.A.* 41°14N 75°57W 313 E9
Plymouth *Wis., U.S.A.* 43°45N 87°59W 308 D10
Plympton-Wyoming = Wyoming *Canada* 42°57N 82°7W 312 D2
Plynlimon = Pumlumon Fawr *U.K.* 52°28N 3°46W 169 E4
Plyusa *Russia* 58°28N 29°27E 188 C5
Plyusa ➔ *Russia* 59°4N 28°6E 188 C5
Plyushchevo *Russia* 55°44N 37°45E 129 B4
Plzeň *Czech Rep.* 49°45N 13°22E 180 B6
Plzeňský ☐ *Czech Rep.* 49°35N 13°0E 180 B6
Pmere Nyente ✿ *Australia* 24°15S 136°10E 280 C2
Pniewy *Poland* 52°31N 16°16E 185 F3
Pnika *Athens, Greece* 112 c1
Pô *Burkina Faso* 11°14N 1°5W 263 C4
Po ➔ *Italy* 44°57N 12°4E 199 D9
Po, Foci del *Italy* 44°55N 12°30E 199 D9
Pô △ *Burkina Faso* 11°25N 1°5W 263 C4
Po Hai = Bo Hai *China* 39°0N 119°0E 227 E10
Po Toi *China* 22°10N 114°16E 122 B2
Po Toi O *China* 22°16N 114°17E 122 B2
Poasco *Italy* 45°24N 9°16E 129 B2
Pobé *Benin* 7°0N 2°56E 263 D5
Pobé *Burkina Faso* 13°53N 1°42W 263 C4
Pobeda *Russia* 65°12N 146°12E 215 C15
Pobedy, Pik *Kyrgyzstan* 42°0N 79°58E 217 D9
Pobiedziska *Poland* 52°29N 17°11E 185 F4
Pobladura del Valle *Spain* 42°6N 5°44W 194 C5
Pobra de Trives *Spain* 42°20N 7°10W 194 C3
Pocahontas *Ark., U.S.A.* 36°16N 90°58W 310 G6
Pocahontas *Ill., U.S.A.* 38°50N 89°33W 310 F7
Pocahontas *Iowa, U.S.A.* 42°44N 94°40W 310 B2
Pocatello *U.S.A.* 42°52N 112°27W 304 E7
Počátky *Czech Rep.* 49°15N 15°14E 180 B8
Pocheon *S. Korea* 37°53N 127°13E 224 D3
Pochep *Russia* 52°58N 33°29E 189 F7
Pochinki *Russia* 54°41N 44°59E 190 C7
Pochinok *Russia* 54°28N 32°29E 188 E7
Pöchlarn *Austria* 48°12N 15°12E 180 C8
Poci *Venezuela* 5°57N 61°29W 329 B5
Pocinhos *Brazil* 7°4S 36°3W 332 C4
Pocking *Germany* 48°23N 13°19E 179 G9
Pocklington Reef *Papua N. G.* 10°51S 155°44E 286 F8
Poções *Brazil* 14°31S 40°21W 333 D3
Pocomoke City *U.S.A.* 38°5N 75°34W 309 F16
Poconé *Brazil* 16°15S 56°37W 331 D6
Poços de Caldas *Brazil* 21°50S 46°33W 335 A6
Podbaba *Czech Rep.* 50°7N 14°23E 135 B2
Podbořany *Czech Rep.* 50°14N 13°25E 180 A6
Poddębice *Poland* 51°54N 18°58E 185 G5
Poděbrady *Czech Rep.* 50°9N 15°8E 180 A8
Podensac *France* 44°40N 0°22W 174 D3
Podenzano *Italy* 44°57N 9°41E 198 D6
Podgorač *Croatia* 45°27N 18°13E 182 E3
Podgorica *Montenegro* 42°30N 19°19E 202 D3
Podgorie *Albania* 40°49N 20°48E 202 F4
Podile *India* 15°37N 79°37E 245 G4
Podilska Vysochyna *Ukraine* 49°0N 28°0E 183 B13
Podkarpackie ☐ *Poland* 50°0N 22°10E 185 H9
Podkova *Bulgaria* 41°24N 25°24E 203 E9
Podlapača *Croatia* 44°37N 15°47E 199 D12
Podlaskie ☐ *Poland* 53°10N 23°0E 185 E10
Podocarpus △ *Ecuador* 4°13S 79°2W 328 D2
Podoleni *Romania* 46°46N 26°39E 183 D11
Podolí *Czech Rep.* 50°2N 14°25E 135 B2
Podolínec *Slovak Rep.* 49°16N 20°31E 181 B13
Podolsk *Russia* 55°25N 37°30E 188 E9
Podor *Senegal* 16°40N 15°2W 262 B1
Podporozhye *Russia* 60°55N 34°2E 188 B8
Podu Iloaiei *Romania* 47°13N 27°16E 183 C12
Podu Turcului *Romania* 46°11N 27°25E 183 D12
Podujevo *Kosovo* 42°54N 21°10E 202 D5
Poduskino *Russia* 55°43N 37°15E 129 B1
Podyjí △ *Czech Rep.* 48°51N 15°57E 180 C8
Poechos *Peru* 4°41S 80°34W 328 D1
Poel *Germany* 54°0N 11°25E 178 B6
Pofadder *S. Africa* 29°10S 19°22E 270 C2
Poggiardo *Italy* 40°3N 18°23E 201 B11
Poggibonsi *Italy* 43°28N 11°9E 198 E8
Póggio Mirteto *Italy* 42°16N 12°41E 199 F9
Pogoanele *Romania* 44°55N 27°0E 183 F12
Pogorzela *Poland* 51°50N 17°12E 185 G4
Pogoso *Dem. Rep. of the Congo* 6°46S 17°12E 265 D3
Pogradec *Albania* 40°54N 20°37E 202 F4
Pogranichnyy *Russia* 44°25N 131°24E 220 B5
Poh *Indonesia* 0°46S 122°51E 231 E6
Pohang *S. Korea* 36°1N 129°23E 224 D4
Pohick Creek ➔ *U.S.A.* 38°48N 77°15W 143 C2
Pohjanmaa *Finland* 62°58N 22°50E 160 E20
Pohjois-Pirkkala = Nokia *Finland* 61°30N 23°30E 188 B2
Pohnpei *Micronesia* 6°55N 158°10E 288 G7
Pohořelá *Slovak Rep.* 48°50N 20°2E 181 C13
Pohořelice *Czech Rep.* 48°59N 16°31E 181 C9
Pohorje *Slovenia* 46°30N 15°20E 199 B12
Pohri *India* 25°32N 77°22E 242 G6
Pōhue B. *U.S.A.* 19°0N 155°48W 302 E6
Poi *Solomon Is.* 10°9S 161°42E 287 N11
Poiana Mare *Romania* 43°57N 23°5E 182 G8
Poiana Ruscăi, Munţii *Romania* 45°45N 22°25E 182 E7
Poiana Stampei *Romania* 47°19N 25°8E 183 C10
Poie *Dem. Rep. of the Congo* 2°50S 23°14E 264 C4
Poike, Peninsula *Chile* 27°6S 109°15W 330 b
Poindimié *N. Cal.* 20°56S 165°20E 288 d
Poinsett, C. *Antarctica* 65°42S 113°18E 151 C8
Point Arena *U.S.A.* 38°55N 123°41W 306 G3
Point Baker *U.S.A.* 56°21N 133°37W 296 B2
Point Calimere *India* 10°17N 79°49E 245 J4
Point Fortin *Trin. & Tob.* 10°10N 61°42W 323 t
Point Hope *U.S.A.* 68°21N 166°47W 303 B6
Point L. *Canada* 65°15N 113°4W 294 D9
Point Lay *U.S.A.* 69°46N 163°3W 303 B7
Point Lisas *Trin. & Tob.* 10°24N 61°29W 323 t
Point Pedro *Sri Lanka* 9°50N 80°15E 245 K5
Point Pelee △ *Canada* 41°57N 82°31W 312 E2
Point Pleasant *N.J., U.S.A.* 40°5N 74°4W 313 F10
Point Pleasant *W. Va., U.S.A.* 38°51N 82°8W 309 F12
Point Reyes ⌓ *U.S.A.* 38°10N 122°55W 306 G2
Point Salines Int. ✕ (GND) *Grenada* 12°0N 61°46W 323 q
Pointe-à-Pierre *Trin. & Tob.* 10°19N 61°28W 323 t
Pointe-à-Pitre *Guadeloupe* 16°10N 61°32W 322 e
Pointe-au-Pic = La Malbaie *Canada* 47°40N 70°10W 299 C5
Pointe-Aux-Trembles *Canada* 45°38N 73°30W 130 A2
Pointe-Claire *Canada* 45°26N 73°50W 313 A11
Pointe-Gatineau *Canada* 45°27N 75°41W 313 A9
Pointe Michel *Dominica* 15°15N 61°23W 323 k
Pointe-Noire *Congo* 4°48S 11°53E 265 C2
Pointe-Noire *Guadeloupe* 16°14N 61°47W 322 e
Poio *Spain* 42°28N 8°41W 194 C2
Poipet *Cambodia* 13°39N 102°33E 236 F4
Poirino *Italy* 44°56N 7°48E 198 D4
Poisonbush Ra. *Australia* 22°30S 121°30E 278 D3
Poissonnier Pt. *Australia* 19°57S 119°10E 278 C2
Poissy *France* 48°55N 2°2E 134 A1
Poitiers *France* 46°35N 0°20E 172 F7
Poitou *France* 46°40N 0°10W 174 B3
Poitou-Charentes ☐ *France* 46°10N 0°15E 174 B4
Poix-de-Picardie *France* 49°47N 1°58E 173 C8
Poix-Terron *France* 49°38N 4°38E 173 C11
Pojoaque *U.S.A.* 35°54N 106°1W 305 J10
Pok Fu Lam *China* 22°16N 114°7E 122 B1
Pōka'ī B. *U.S.A.* 21°27N 158°12W 302 K13
Pokaran *India* 27°0N 71°50E 242 F4
Pokataroo *Australia* 29°30S 148°36E 281 D4
Pokcheong *S. Korea* 37°28N 127°8E 137 C2
Pokhara *Nepal* 28°14N 83°58E 243 E10
Pokhvistnevo *Russia* 53°36N 52°10E 190 D11
Pokigron *Suriname* 4°30N 55°22W 329 C6
Poko *Dem. Rep. of the Congo* 3°7N 26°52E 268 B2
Poko *Sudan* 5°41N 31°55E 257 F3
Pokrov *Russia* 55°55N 39°7E 188 E10
Pokrovka = Kyzyl-Suu *Kyrgyzstan* 42°20N 78°0E 217 D9
Pokrovsk = Engels *Russia* 51°28N 46°6E 190 E8
Pokrovsk *Russia* 61°29N 129°0E 215 C13
Pokrovsko-Sresnevo *Russia* 55°48N 37°27E 129 B2
Pokrovskoy = Priazovskoye *Ukraine* 46°44N 35°40E 189 J8
Pokrovskoye *Russia* 47°25N 38°54E 189 J10
Pol-e Dokhtar *Iran* 33°9N 47°42E 213 F12
Pol-e Khomri *Afghan.* 35°56N 68°42E 240 B3
Pol-e Zahāb *Iran* 34°27N 45°51E 213 E11
Pola = Istra *Croatia* 45°10N 14°0E 199 C10
Pola = Pula *Croatia* 44°54N 13°57E 199 D10
Pola *Russia* 57°55N 32°0E 188 D7
Pola de Allande *Spain* 43°16N 6°37W 194 B4
Pola de Lena *Spain* 43°10N 5°49W 194 B5
Pola de Siero *Spain* 43°24N 5°39W 194 B5
Pola de Somiedo *Spain* 43°5N 6°15W 194 B4
Pola I. *Amer. Samoa* 14°14S 170°40W 302 f
Polacca *U.S.A.* 35°50N 110°23W 305 J8
Polan *Iran* 25°30N 61°10E 247 E9
Pol'ana *Slovak Rep.* 48°38N 19°29E 181 C12
Poland *U.S.A.* 43°13N 75°3W 313 C9
Poland ■ *Europe* 52°0N 20°0E 185 G3
Polanica-Zdrój *Poland* 50°24N 16°32E 185 H3
Połaniec *Poland* 50°26N 21°12E 185 H8
Polanów *Poland* 54°7N 16°41E 184 D3
Polar Bear ⌓ *Canada* 55°0N 83°45W 298 A2
Polatlı *Turkey* 39°36N 32°9E 212 C5
Polatsk *Belarus* 55°30N 28°50E 188 E5
Polavaram *India* 17°15N 81°38E 244 F5
Polcura *Chile* 37°17S 71°43W 334 D1
Połczyn-Zdrój *Poland* 53°47N 16°5E 184 E3
Poldasht *Iran* 39°20N 45°4E 213 C11
Poleski △ *Poland* 51°29N 23°5E 185 G10
Polessk *Russia* 54°50N 21°8E 184 D8
Polesye = Pripet Marshes *Europe* 52°10N 27°10E 177 B15
Polevskoy *Russia* 56°26N 60°11E 186 C11
Polewali *Indonesia* 3°25S 119°20E 235 C5
Polgar *Hungary* 47°54N 21°6E 182 C6
Poli *Cameroon* 8°34N 13°15E 263 C7

Policastro, G. di Italy 40°0N 15°35E 201 C8
Police Poland 53°33N 14°33E 184 E1
Police, Pte. Seychelles 4°51S 55°32E 272 c
Polichnitos Greece 39°6N 26°10E 205 B8
Polička Czech Rep. 49°43N 16°15E 181 B9
Policoro Italy 40°13N 16°41E 201 B9
Poliegos Greece 36°45N 24°38E 204 E6
Poligiros Greece 40°23N 23°25E 202 F7
Polignano a Mare Italy 41°0N 17°13E 201 A9
Poligny France 46°50N 5°42E 173 F12
Polillo Phil. 14°43N 121°56E 232 D3
Polillo Is. Phil. 14°56N 122°0E 232 D4
Polillo Str. Phil. 14°44N 121°51E 232 D3
Polis Cyprus 35°2N 32°26E 207 E8
Polístena Italy 38°24N 16°4E 201 D9
Pölitz = Police Poland 53°33N 14°33E 184 E1
Polk U.S.A. 41°22N 79°56W 312 E5
Polkowice Poland 51°29N 16°3E 185 G3
Polkwitz = Polkowice Poland 51°29N 16°3E 185 G3
Polla Italy 40°31N 15°29E 201 B8
Pollachi India 10°35N 77°0E 245 J3
Pollença Spain 39°54N 3°1E 206 B4
Pollença, B. de Spain 39°53N 3°8E 206 B4
Pollfoss Norway 61°58N 7°54E 164 C4
Póllica Italy 40°11N 15°3E 201 B8
Pollino, Mte. Italy 39°55N 16°11E 201 C9
Pollino △ Italy 40°0N 16°12E 201 C9
Polna Russia 58°31N 28°5E 188 C5
Polnovat Russia 63°50N 65°54E 214 C7
Polo Ill., U.S.A. 41°59N 89°35W 310 C7
Polo Mo., U.S.A. 39°33N 94°3W 310 E2
Pology Ukraine 47°29N 36°15E 189 J9
Polokwane S. Africa 23°54S 29°25E 271 B4
Polokwane → S. Africa 22°25S 30°5E 271 B5
Polomolok Phil. 6°13N 125°3E 233 H5
Polonnaruwa Sri Lanka 7°56N 81°0E 245 L5
Polonne Ukraine 50°6N 27°30E 177 C14
Polonnoye = Polonne Ukraine 50°6N 27°30E 177 C14
Polski Trŭmbesh Bulgaria 43°20N 25°38E 203 C9
Polsko Kosovo Bulgaria 43°23N 25°38E 203 C9
Polson U.S.A. 47°41N 114°9W 304 C6
Poltár Slovak Rep. 48°26N 19°48E 181 C12
Poltava Ukraine 49°35N 34°35E 189 H8
Poltava ☐ Ukraine 50°15N 33°15E 189 G7
Polton U.K. 55°52N 3°7W 121 B3
Poltoratsk = Ashgabat Turkmenistan 38°0N 57°50E 247 B8
Põltsamaa Estonia 58°39N 25°58E 188 C3
Polunochnoye Russia 60°52N 60°25E 214 C7
Polur India 12°32N 79°11E 245 H4
Põlva Estonia 58°3N 27°3E 188 C4
Polvoranca, Parque de Spain 40°19N 3°48W 127 C1
Polyana Ukraine 48°38N 22°58E 182 B7
Polyarny Russia 69°8N 33°20E 160 B25
Polyarnyye Zori Russia 67°22N 32°30E 160 C25
Polynesia Pac. Oc. 10°0S 162°0W 289 F11
Polynesian Cultural Center U.S.A. 21°38N 157°55W 302 J14
Polynésie française = French Polynesia ⊠ Pac. Oc. 20°0S 145°0W 289 f
Polyustrovo Russia 59°57N 30°25E 137 B2
Pomabamba = Azurduy Bolivia 19°59S 64°29W 331 D5
Pomabamba Peru 8°50S 77°28W 330 B2
Pomarance Italy 43°18N 10°52E 198 E7
Pombal Brazil 6°45S 37°50W 332 C4
Pombal Portugal 39°55N 8°40W 194 F2
Pombia Greece 35°0N 24°51E 207 F5
Pombos, B. dos Angola 11°40S 13°47E 265 E2
Pomene Mozam. 22°53S 35°33E 271 B6
Pomeroy Ohio, U.S.A. 39°2N 82°2W 309 F12
Pomeroy Wash., U.S.A. 46°28N 117°36W 304 C5
Pomézia Italy 41°40N 12°30E 200 A5
Pomichna Ukraine 48°13N 31°36E 189 H6
Pomio Papua N. G. 5°32S 151°33E 286 C6
Pomme de Terre L. U.S.A. 37°54N 93°19W 310 G3
Pomme Rose Grenada 12°3N 61°39W 323 q
Pomona Queens., Australia 26°22S 152°52E 281 D5
Pomona Calif., U.S.A. 34°4N 117°45W 307 L9
Pomona Park U.S.A. 29°30N 81°36W 317 F8
Pomorie Bulgaria 42°32N 27°41E 203 D11
Pomorskie ☐ Poland 54°30N 18°0E 184 D5
Pomorskie, Pojezierze Poland 53°40N 16°37E 184 E3
Pomos Cyprus 35°9N 32°33E 207 E8
Pomos, C. Cyprus 35°10N 32°33E 207 E8
Pompano Beach U.S.A. 26°14N 80°7W 317 J9
Pompei Italy 40°45N 14°30E 201 B7
Pompey France 48°46N 6°6E 173 D13
Pompeys Pillar U.S.A. 45°59N 107°57W 304 D10
Pompeys Pillar ⌂ U.S.A. 46°0N 108°0W 304 D10
Pompidou, Centre Paris, France 134 b4
Pomprap Thailand 13°44N 100°30E 113 B2
Pompton Lakes U.S.A. 41°0N 74°17W 313 F10
Ponape = Pohnpei Micronesia 6°55N 158°10E 288 G7
Ponask L. Canada 54°0N 92°41W 298 B1
Ponca U.S.A. 42°34N 96°43W 308 D5
Ponca City U.S.A. 36°42N 97°5W 314 C6
Ponce Puerto Rico 18°1N 66°37W 321 C6
Ponce de Leon U.S.A. 30°44N 85°56W 316 E4
Ponce de Leon B. U.S.A. 25°15N 81°10W 317 K8
Ponchatoula U.S.A. 30°26N 90°26W 315 F9
Poncheville, L. Canada 50°10N 76°55W 298 B4
Pond U.S.A. 35°43N 119°20W 307 K7
Pond Inlet Canada 72°40N 77°0W 295 C16
Pondicherry = Puducherry India 11°59N 79°50E 245 J4
Pondo Papua N. G. 4°33S 151°38E 286 C6
Pondok Gede Indonesia 6°20S 106°55E 122 A2
Pondok Indah Indonesia 6°16S 106°46E 122 B1
Ponds, I. of Canada 53°27N 55°52W 299 B8
Ponérihouen N. Cal. 21°5S 165°24E 288 d
Ponferrada Spain 42°32N 6°35W 194 C4
Pongo, Wadi → Sudan 8°42N 27°40E 257 F2
Poniatowa Poland 51°11N 22°3E 185 G9
Poniec Poland 51°48N 16°50E 185 G3
Ponikva Slovenia 46°16N 15°26E 199 B12
Ponizovkino = Krasnyy Profintern Russia 57°45N 40°27E 188 D11
Ponnaiyar → India 11°50N 79°45E 245 J4
Ponnani India 10°45N 75°59E 245 J2
Ponneri India 13°20N 80°15E 245 H5
Ponnuru India 16°5N 80°34E 245 F5
Ponoka Canada 52°42N 113°40W 296 C6
Ponorogo Indonesia 7°52S 111°27E 235 D4
Ponot Phil. 8°25N 123°0E 233 G4
Ponoy Russia 67°0N 41°13E 186 A7
Ponoy → Russia 66°59N 41°17E 186 A7
Pons = Ponts Spain 41°55N 1°12E 196 D6
Pons France 45°35N 0°34W 174 C3
Ponsul → Portugal 39°40N 7°31W 194 F3
Pont-à-Mousson France 48°54N 6°1E 173 D13
Pont-Audemer France 49°21N 0°30E 172 C7
Pont-Aven France 47°51N 3°47W 172 E3
Pont Canavese Italy 45°25N 7°36E 198 C4
Pont Casse Dominica 15°22N 61°21W 323 k
Pont-d'Ain France 46°3N 5°21E 173 F12
Pont-de-Roide France 47°23N 6°45E 173 E13
Pont-de-Salars France 44°18N 2°44E 174 D6
Pont-de-Vaux France 46°26N 4°56E 173 F11
Pont-de-Veyle France 46°17N 4°53E 173 F11
Pont-du-Château France 45°47N 3°15E 173 G10
Pont-l'Abbé France 47°52N 4°15W 172 E2
Pont-l'Évêque France 49°18N 0°11E 172 C7
Pont-St-Esprit France 44°16N 4°40E 175 D8
Pont-St-Martin Italy 45°36N 7°48E 198 C4
Pont-Ste-Maxence France 49°18N 2°36E 173 C9
Pont-sur-Yonne France 48°18N 3°10E 173 D10
Pont-Viau Canada 45°35N 73°41W 130 A1
Ponta de Pedras Brazil 1°23S 48°52W 332 B2
Ponta Delgada Flores, Azores 39°31N 31°13W 153 d2
Ponta Delgada São Miguel, Azores 37°44N 25°40W 153 d3
Ponta Delgada ✈ (PDL) Azores 37°44N 25°41W 153 d3
Ponta do Sol Madeira 32°42N 17°7W 153 c
Ponta Grossa Brazil 25°7S 50°10W 335 B5
Ponta Porã Brazil 22°20S 55°35W 335 A4
Pontacq France 43°11N 0°8W 174 E3
Pontailler-sur-Saône France 47°13N 5°25E 173 E12
Pontal → Brazil 9°8S 40°12W 332 C3
Pontalina Brazil 17°31S 49°27W 333 E2
Pontarlier France 46°54N 6°20E 173 F13
Pontassieve Italy 43°46N 11°26E 199 E8
Pontault-Combault France 48°47N 2°36E 134 B4
Pontaumur France 45°52N 2°40E 174 C6
Pontcharra France 45°26N 6°1E 175 C10
Pontchartrain, L. U.S.A. 30°5N 90°5W 315 F9
Pontchâteau France 47°25N 2°5W 172 E4
Ponte Alta, Serra do Brazil 19°42S 47°40W 333 E2
Ponte Alta do Norte Brazil 10°45S 47°34W 332 D2
Ponte Branca Brazil 16°27S 52°40W 331 D7
Ponte da Barca Portugal 41°48N 8°25W 194 D2
Ponte de Sor Portugal 39°17N 8°1W 195 F2
Ponte dell'Ólio Italy 44°52N 9°39E 198 D6
Ponte di Legno Italy 46°16N 10°31E 198 B7
Ponte do Lima Portugal 41°46N 8°35W 194 D2
Ponte do Pungué Mozam. 19°30S 34°33E 269 F3
Ponte-Leccia France 42°28N 9°13E 175 F13
Ponte nelle Alpi Italy 46°11N 12°16E 199 B9
Ponte Nova Brazil 20°25S 42°54W 333 F3
Ponte Vedra Beach U.S.A. 30°15N 81°23W 316 E8
Ponteareas Spain 42°10N 8°28W 194 C2
Pontebba Italy 46°30N 13°18E 199 B10
Ponteceso Spain 43°15N 8°54W 194 B2
Pontecorvo Italy 41°27N 13°40E 200 A6
Pontedeume Spain 43°24N 8°10W 194 B2
Ponteix Canada 49°46N 107°29W 297 D7
Pontes e Lacerda Brazil 15°12S 59°22W 331 D6
Pontevedra Capiz, Phil. 11°29N 122°50E 233 F4
Pontevedra Neg. Occ., Phil. 10°22N 122°52E 233 F4
Pontevedra Spain 42°26N 8°40W 194 C2
Pontevedra ☐ Spain 42°25N 8°39W 194 C2
Pontevedra, R. de → Spain 42°22N 8°45W 194 C2
Pontevico Italy 45°16N 10°5E 198 C7
Pontiac Ill., U.S.A. 40°53N 88°38W 311 D8
Pontiac Mich., U.S.A. 42°38N 83°18W 311 B13
Pontian Kechil Malaysia 1°29N 103°23E 237 d
Pontianak Indonesia 0°3S 109°15E 235 C3
Pontine Is. = Ponziane, Ísole Italy 40°55N 12°57E 200 B5
Pontine Mts. = Kuzey Anadolu Dağları Turkey 41°0N 36°45E 212 B7
Pontinha Portugal 38°45N 9°11W 126 A1
Pontínia Italy 41°25N 13°2E 200 A6
Pontivy France 48°5N 2°58W 172 D4
Pontoise France 49°3N 2°5E 173 C9
Ponton → Canada 58°27N 116°11W 296 B5
Pontorson France 48°34N 1°30W 172 D5
Pontrémoli Italy 44°22N 9°53E 198 D6
Pontrieux France 48°42N 3°10W 172 D3
Ponts Spain 41°55N 1°12E 196 D6
Pontypool Ont., Canada 44°6N 78°38W 312 B6
Pontypool Torf., U.K. 51°42N 3°2W 169 F4
Ponza Italy 40°54N 12°58E 200 B5
Ponziane, Ísole Italy 40°55N 12°57E 200 B5
Poochera Australia 32°43S 134°51E 281 E1
Poole Trin. & Tob. 10°17N 61°14W 323 t
Poole Poole, U.K. 50°43N 1°59W 169 G6
Poole ☐ U.K. 50°43N 1°59W 169 G6
Poole → Trin. & Tob. 10°15N 61°5W 323 t
Pooler U.S.A. 32°7N 81°15W 316 C8
Poona = Pune India 18°29N 73°57E 244 E1
Poonamallee India 13°3N 80°10E 245 H5
Pooncarie Australia 33°22S 142°31E 282 B5
Poopelloe L. Australia 31°40S 144°0E 282 A6
Poopó Bolivia 18°23S 66°59W 330 D4
Poopó, L. de Bolivia 18°30S 67°35W 330 D4
Poor Knights Is. N.Z. 35°29S 174°43E 284 B3
Poorman U.S.A. 64°5N 155°33W 303 D9
Popa Gabon 1°35S 12°32E 264 C2
Popa, Mt. Burma 20°55N 95°15E 241 E5
Popayán Colombia 2°27N 76°36W 328 C2
Poperinge Belgium 50°51N 2°42E 170 D2
Popiltah L. Australia 33°10S 141°42E 282 B4
Popina Bulgaria 44°7N 26°57E 203 B10
Popio L. Australia 33°10S 141°52E 282 B4
Poplar London, U.K. 51°30N 0°0 125 A3
Poplar Mont., U.S.A. 48°7N 105°12W 304 B11
Poplar → Canada 53°0N 97°19W 297 C9
Poplar Bluff U.S.A. 36°46N 90°24W 308 G8
Poplar Head = Dothan U.S.A. 31°13N 85°24W 316 D4
Poplarville U.S.A. 30°51N 89°32W 315 F10
Popocatépetl, Volcán Mexico 19°2N 98°38W 319 D5
Popokabaka Dem. Rep. of the Congo 5°41S 16°40E 265 D3
Pópoli Italy 42°10N 13°50E 199 F10
Popolo Dem. Rep. of the Congo 2°22N 21°8E 264 B4
Popolo, Porta del Rome, Italy 136 a2
Popomanaseu, Mt. Solomon Is. 9°40S 160°1E 287 M11
Popondetta Papua N. G. 8°48S 148°17E 286 E5
Popovača Croatia 45°30N 16°41E 199 C13
Popovo Bulgaria 43°21N 26°18E 203 C10
Poppberg Germany 49°26N 11°37E 179 F7
Poppi Italy 43°43N 11°46E 199 E8
Poppintree Ireland 53°23N 6°17W 120 A2
Poprad Slovak Rep. 49°3N 20°18E 181 B13
Poprad → Slovak Rep. 49°38N 20°42E 181 B13
Poradaha Bangla. 23°51N 89°1E 241 D2
Porali → Pakistan 25°58N 66°26E 242 G2
Porangaba Brazil 8°48S 70°36W 330 B3
Porangahau N.Z. 40°17S 176°37E 284 G5
Porangatu Brazil 13°26S 49°10W 333 D2
Porbandar India 21°44N 69°43E 242 J3
Porce → Colombia 7°28N 74°53W 328 B3
Porcher I. Canada 53°50N 130°30W 296 C2
Porco Bolivia 19°50S 65°59W 331 D4
Porcos → Brazil 12°42S 45°7W 333 D2
Porcuna Spain 37°52N 4°11W 195 H6
Porcupine → Sask., Canada 59°11N 104°46W 297 B8
Porcupine → Alaska, U.S.A. 66°34N 145°19W 303 C11
Porcupine Abyssal Plain Atl. Oc. 48°0N 8°0W 152 B10
Porcupine Gorge △ Australia 20°22S 144°26E 280 C3
Pordenone Italy 45°57N 12°39E 199 C9
Pordim Bulgaria 43°23N 24°51E 203 C8
Pore Colombia 5°43N 72°0W 328 B3
Poreč Croatia 45°14N 13°36E 199 C10
Porecatu Brazil 22°43S 51°24W 333 F1
Porechye = Demidov Russia 55°16N 31°30E 188 E6
Poretskoye Russia 55°9N 46°21E 190 C8
Porgera Papua N. G. 5°28S 143°12E 286 C2
Pori Finland 61°29N 21°48E 188 B1
Pori Greece 35°58N 23°13E 204 F5
Porirua N.Z. 41°8S 174°52E 143 A2
Porirua East N.Z. 41°8S 174°52E 143 A2
Porkhov Russia 57°45N 29°38E 188 D5
Porlamar Venezuela 10°57N 63°51W 329 A5
Porlezza Italy 46°2N 9°7E 198 B6
Porma → Spain 42°49N 5°28W 194 C5
Pormpuraaw Australia 14°59S 141°26E 280 A3
Pormpuraaw ☼ Australia 14°55S 141°47E 280 A3
Pornic France 47°7N 2°5W 172 E4
Poronaysk Russia 49°13N 143°0E 219 B17
Poros Attiki, Greece 37°30N 23°30E 204 D5
Poros Kefalonia, Greece 38°9N 20°47E 207 C2
Poros Lefkada, Greece 38°38N 20°43E 207 B2
Poroshiri-Dake Japan 42°41N 142°52E 220 C11
Poroszló Hungary 47°39N 20°40E 182 C5
Poroto Mts. Tanzania 9°0S 33°30E 269 D3
Porpoise B. Antarctica 66°0S 127°0E 151 C9
Porpoise Pt. Ascension I. 7°54S 14°21W 153 g
Porquerolles, Î. de France 43°0N 6°13E 175 F10
Porrentruy Switz. 47°25N 7°6E 179 H3
Porreres Spain 39°31N 3°2E 206 B4
Porsangerfjorden Norway 70°40N 25°40E 160 A21
Porsgrunn Norway 59°10N 9°40E 164 E6
Port Adelaide Australia 34°50S 138°30E 282 C3
Port Alberni Canada 49°14N 124°50W 296 D4
Port Albert Australia 38°42S 146°42E 283 E7
Port Alexander U.S.A. 56°15N 134°38W 303 H14
Port Alfred S. Africa 33°36S 26°55E 270 D4
Port Alice Canada 50°20N 127°25W 296 C3
Port Allegany U.S.A. 41°48N 78°17W 312 E6
Port Allen U.S.A. 30°27N 91°12W 314 F9
Port Alma Queens., Australia 23°38S 150°53E 280 C5
Port Alma Ont., Canada 42°10N 82°14W 312 D2
Port Angeles U.S.A. 48°7N 123°27W 306 B3
Port Antonio Jamaica 18°10N 76°26W 320 a
Port Aransas U.S.A. 27°50N 97°4W 314 H6
Port Arthur Tas., Australia 43°7S 147°50E 281 G4
Port Arthur Tex., U.S.A. 29°54N 93°56W 314 G8
Port au Choix Canada 50°43N 57°22W 299 B8
Port au Port B. Canada 48°40N 58°50W 299 C8
Port-au-Prince Haiti 18°40N 72°20W 321 C5
Port Augusta Australia 32°30S 137°50E 282 B2
Port Austin U.S.A. 44°3N 83°1W 312 B2
Port Authority Bus Terminal New York, U.S.A. 132 c2
Port-aux-Français Kerguelen 49°21S 70°13E 273 J6
Port Bell Uganda 0°18N 32°35E 268 B3
Port Bergé Vaovao Madag. 15°33S 47°40E 272 B2
Port Blair India 11°40N 92°45E 245 J11
Port Blandford Canada 48°20N 54°10W 299 C9
Port Botany Australia 33°58S 151°13E 139 B2
Port-Bouët Ivory C. 5°16N 3°57W 262 D4
Port Bradshaw Australia 12°30S 137°20E 280 A2
Port Broughton Australia 33°37S 137°56E 282 B2
Port Bruce Canada 42°39N 81°0W 312 D4
Port Burwell Canada 42°40N 80°48W 312 D4
Port Byron U.S.A. 41°36N 90°20W 310 C6
Port Campbell Vic., Australia 38°37S 143°1E 282 E5
Port Campbell India 11°56N 92°37E 245 J11
Port Campbell △ Australia 38°8S 143°6E 282 E5
Port Canning India 22°23N 88°40E 243 H13
Port Carling Canada 45°7N 79°35W 312 A5
Port-Cartier Canada 50°2N 66°50W 299 B6
Port Chalmers N.Z. 45°49S 170°30E 285 F5
Port Charles N.Z. 36°33S 175°30E 284 C4
Port Charlotte U.S.A. 26°59N 82°6W 317 J7
Port Chester U.S.A. 41°0N 73°40W 313 F11
Port Clements Canada 53°40N 132°10W 296 C2
Port Clinton U.S.A. 41°31N 82°56W 311 C14
Port Colborne Canada 42°50N 79°10W 312 D5
Port Coquitlam Canada 49°15N 122°45W 306 A4
Port Cornwallis India 13°17N 93°5E 245 H11
Port Credit Canada 43°33N 79°35W 312 C5
Port-Cros △ France 43°0N 6°24E 175 F10
Port Curtis Australia 23°57S 151°20E 280 C5
Port d'Alcúdia Spain 39°50N 3°7E 206 B4
Port Dalhousie Canada 43°13N 79°16W 312 C5
Port d'Andratx Spain 39°32N 2°23E 206 B3
Port Darwin N. Terr., Australia 12°24S 130°45E 278 B5
Port Darwin Falk. Is. 51°50S 59°0W 153 f
Port Davey Australia 43°16S 145°55E 281 G4
Port-de-Bouc France 43°24N 4°59E 175 E8
Port-de-Paix Haiti 19°50N 72°50W 321 C5
Port de Pollença Spain 39°54N 3°4E 206 B4
Port de Sóller Spain 39°48N 2°42E 206 B3
Port Dickson Malaysia 2°30N 101°49E 237 L3
Port Douglas Australia 16°30S 145°30E 280 B4
Port Dover Canada 42°47N 80°12W 312 D4
Port Edward Canada 54°12N 130°10W 296 C2
Port Elgin Canada 44°25N 81°25W 312 B3
Port Elizabeth S. Africa 33°58S 25°40E 270 D4
Port Ellen U.K. 55°38N 6°11W 167 F2
Port Elliot Australia 35°32S 138°41E 282 C3
Port-en-Bessin-Huppain France 49°21N 0°45W 172 C6
Port Erin I. of Man 54°5N 4°45W 168 C3
Port Essington Australia 11°15S 132°10E 278 B5
Port Etienne = Nouâdhibou Mauritania 20°54N 17°0W 260 D1
Port Ewen U.S.A. 41°54N 73°59W 313 E11
Port Fairy Australia 38°22S 142°12E 282 E5
Port Fitzroy N.Z. 36°8S 175°20E 284 C4
Port Florence = Kisumu Kenya 0°3S 34°45E 268 C3
Port Fouâd = Bûr Fuad Egypt 31°15N 32°20E 256 H8
Port Francqui = Ilebo Dem. Rep. of the Congo 4°17S 20°55E 265 C4
Port Gamble U.S.A. 47°51N 122°34W 306 C4
Port-Gentil Gabon 0°40S 8°50E 264 C1
Port Germein Australia 33°1S 138°1E 281 E2
Port Ghalib Egypt 25°20N 34°50E 246 E2
Port Gibson U.S.A. 31°58N 90°59W 314 F9
Port Glasgow U.K. 55°56N 4°41W 167 F4
Port-Gueydon = Azeffoun Algeria 36°51N 4°26E 261 A5
Port Harcourt Nigeria 4°40N 7°10E 263 E6
Port Hardy Canada 50°41N 127°30W 296 C3
Port Harrison = Inukjuak Canada 58°25N 78°15W 295 F16
Port Hawkesbury Canada 45°36N 61°22W 299 C7
Port Hedland Australia 20°25S 118°35E 278 D2
Port Heiden U.S.A. 56°55N 158°41W 303 H8
Port Henry U.S.A. 44°3N 73°28W 313 B11
Port Herald = Nsanje Malawi 16°55S 35°12E 269 F4
Port Hood Canada 46°0N 61°32W 299 C7
Port Hope Ont., Canada 43°56N 78°20W 312 C6
Port Hope Mich., U.S.A. 43°57N 82°43W 312 C2
Port Hope Simpson Canada 52°33N 56°18W 299 B8
Port Hueneme U.S.A. 34°7N 119°12W 307 L7
Port Huron U.S.A. 42°58N 82°26W 312 D2
Port Iliç Azerbaijan 38°53N 48°47E 213 C13
Port Jefferson U.S.A. 40°57N 73°3W 313 F11
Port Jervis U.S.A. 41°22N 74°41W 313 E10
Port-Joinville France 46°45N 2°23W 172 F4
Port Katon Russia 46°52N 38°46E 189 J10
Port Kembla Australia 34°52S 150°49E 283 C9
Port Kenny Australia 33°10S 134°41E 281 E1
Port-la-Nouvelle France 43°1N 3°3E 174 E7
Port Lairge = Waterford Ireland 52°15N 7°8W 166 D4
Port Laoise Ireland 53°2N 7°18W 166 C4
Port Lavaca U.S.A. 28°37N 96°38W 314 G6
Port Leyden U.S.A. 43°35N 75°21W 313 C9
Port Lincoln Australia 34°42S 135°52E 282 C1
Port Lions U.S.A. 57°52N 152°53W 303 H9
Port Loko S. Leone 8°48N 12°46W 262 D2
Port Louis Morbihan, France 47°42N 3°22W 172 E3
Port-Louis Guadeloupe 16°28N 61°32W 322 e
Port Louis Mauritius 20°10S 57°30E 272 e
Port Lyautey = Kenitra Morocco 34°15N 6°40W 260 B3
Port MacDonnell Australia 38°5S 140°48E 282 E4
Port McNeill Canada 50°35N 127°6W 296 C3
Port Macquarie Australia 31°25S 152°25E 283 A10
Port Maria Jamaica 18°22N 76°54W 320 a
Port Mathurin Rodrigues 19°41S 63°25E 273 F5
Port Matilda U.S.A. 40°48N 78°3W 312 F6
Port Mayaca U.S.A. 26°59N 80°36W 317 J9
Port McNicoll Canada 44°44N 79°48W 312 B5
Port Mearnóg = Portmarnock Ireland 53°26N 6°8W 120 A3
Port Melbourne Australia 37°50S 144°54E 128 B1
Port Mellon Canada 49°32N 123°31W 296 D4
Port-Menier Canada 49°51N 64°15W 299 C7
Port Moller U.S.A. 55°59N 160°34W 303 J7
Port Moody Canada 49°17N 122°51W 306 A4
Port Morant Jamaica 17°54N 76°19W 320 a
Port Moresby Papua N. G. 9°24S 147°8E 286 E4
Port Mourant Guyana 6°15N 57°20W 329 B6
Port Musgrave Australia 11°55S 141°50E 280 A3
Port Narevin Vanuatu 18°45S 169°10E 287 H7
Port-Navalo France 47°34N 2°54W 172 E4
Port Neches U.S.A. 30°0N 93°59W 314 G8
Port Nicholson N.Z. 41°20S 174°52E 143 B2
Port Nolloth S. Africa 29°17S 16°52E 270 C2
Port Nouveau-Québec = Kangiqsualujjuaq Canada 58°30N 65°59W 295 F18
Port of Climax Canada 49°10N 108°20W 297 D7
Port of Coronach Canada 49°7N 105°31W 297 D7
Port of Spain Trin. & Tob. 10°40N 61°31W 323 t
Port Olry Vanuatu 15°1S 167°4E 287 E5
Port Orange U.S.A. 29°9N 80°59W 317 F9
Port Orchard U.S.A. 47°32N 122°38W 306 C4
Port Orford U.S.A. 42°45N 124°30W 304 E1
Port Pegasus N.Z. 47°12S 167°41E 285 H2
Port Perry Canada 44°6N 78°56W 312 B6
Port Phillip B. Australia 38°10S 144°50E 283 E6
Port Pirie Australia 33°10S 138°1E 282 B3
Port Renfrew Canada 48°30N 124°20W 306 B2
Port Richmond U.S.A. 40°38N 74°7W 132 C1
Port Roper Australia 14°45S 135°25E 280 A2
Port Rowan Canada 42°40N 80°30W 312 D4
Port Royal Jamaica 17°56N 76°51W 320 a
Port Royal Sd. U.S.A. 32°15N 80°40W 316 C9
Port Safaga = Bûr Safâga Egypt 26°43N 33°57E 246 E2
Port Said = Bûr Sa'îd Egypt 31°16N 32°18E 256 H8
Port St. Joe U.S.A. 29°49N 85°18W 316 F4
Port St. John U.S.A. 28°29N 80°47W 317 G9
Port St. Johns = Umzimvubu S. Africa 31°38S 29°33E 271 D4
Port-St-Louis-du-Rhône France 43°23N 4°49E 175 E8
Port St. Lucie U.S.A. 27°18N 80°21W 317 H9
Port-Ste-Marie France 44°15N 0°25E 174 D4
Port Salerno U.S.A. 27°9N 80°12W 317 H9
Port Sanilac U.S.A. 43°26N 82°33W 312 C2
Port Severn Canada 44°48N 79°43W 312 B5
Port Shelter China 22°20N 114°17E 122 A2
Port Shepstone S. Africa 30°44S 30°28E 271 D5
Port Simpson Canada 54°30N 130°20W 296 C2
Port Stanley = Stanley Falk. Is. 51°40S 59°51W 153 f
Port Stanley Canada 42°40N 81°10W 312 D3
Port Sudan = Bûr Sûdân Sudan 19°32N 37°9E 256 D4
Port Sulphur U.S.A. 29°29N 89°42W 315 G10
Port-sur-Saône France 47°42N 6°2E 173 E13
Port Talbot U.K. 51°35N 3°47W 169 F4
Port Taufiq = Bûr Taufiq Egypt 29°54N 32°32E 256 J8
Port Townsend U.S.A. 48°7N 122°45W 306 B4
Port Union Canada 43°47N 79°7W 141 A4
Port-Vato Vanuatu 16°20S 168°1E 287 F6
Port-Vendres France 42°32N 3°8E 174 F7
Port Victoria Australia 34°30S 137°29E 282 C2
Port Vila Vanuatu 17°45S 168°18E 287 G6
Port Vladimir Russia 69°25N 33°6E 160 B25
Port Wakefield Australia 34°12S 138°10E 282 C3
Port Washington U.S.A. 43°23N 87°53W 308 D10
Port Weld = Kuala Sepetang Malaysia 4°49N 100°28E 237 K3
Port Wentworth U.S.A. 32°9N 81°10W 316 C8
Porta Orientalis Romania 45°6N 22°18E 177 F12
Portachuelo Bolivia 17°10S 63°20W 331 D5
Portacloy Ireland 54°20N 9°46W 166 B2
Portadown U.K. 54°25N 6°27W 166 B5
Portaferry U.K. 54°23N 5°33W 166 B6
Portage Ind., U.S.A. 41°34N 87°11W 311 C10
Portage Mich., U.S.A. 42°12N 85°35W 311 B11
Portage Pa., U.S.A. 40°23N 78°41W 312 F6
Portage Wis., U.S.A. 43°33N 89°28W 308 D9
Portage → U.S.A. 41°31N 83°5W 311 C14
Portage la Prairie Canada 49°58N 98°18W 297 D9
Portage Park U.S.A. 41°56N 87°45W 119 B2
Portageville U.S.A. 36°26N 89°42W 308 G9
Portal U.S.A. 32°33N 81°56W 316 C8
Portal de la Pau, Plaza Barcelona, Spain 114 c2
Portalegre Portugal 39°19N 7°25W 195 F3
Portalegre ☐ Portugal 39°20N 7°40W 195 F3
Portales U.S.A. 34°11N 103°20W 305 J12
Portarlington Ireland 53°9N 7°14W 166 C4
Portbou Spain 42°25N 3°9E 196 C8
Porteira Brazil 1°5S 57°4W 329 D6
Porteirinha Brazil 15°44S 43°2W 333 E3
Portel Brazil 1°57S 50°49W 332 B1
Portel Portugal 38°19N 7°41W 195 G3
Portela, Lisboa ✈ (LIS) Portugal 38°46N 9°8W 126 A2
Porter U.S.A. 41°36N 87°4W 311 C9
Porter, L. U.S.A. 28°30N 81°19W 133 A3
Porter L. N.W.T., Canada 61°41N 108°5W 297 A7
Porter L. Sask., Canada 56°20N 107°20W 297 B7
Porterville Western Cape, S. Africa 33°0S 19°0E 270 D2
Porterville Calif., U.S.A. 36°4N 119°1W 306 J8
Portes-lès-Valence France 44°52N 4°54E 175 D8
Porthcawl U.K. 51°29N 3°42W 169 F4
Porthill U.S.A. 48°59N 116°30W 304 B5
Porthmadog U.K. 52°55N 4°8W 168 E3
Portile de Fier Europe 44°44N 22°30E 182 F7
Portimão Portugal 37°8N 8°32W 195 H2
Portishead U.K. 51°29N 2°46W 169 F5
Portiţei, Gura Romania 44°41N 29°0E 183 F14
Portknockie U.K. 57°42N 2°51W 167 D6
Portland N.S.W., Australia 33°20S 150°0E 283 B9
Portland Vic., Australia 38°20S 141°35E 282 E4
Portland Ont., Canada 44°42N 76°12W 313 B8
Portland Conn., U.S.A. 41°34N 72°38W 313 E12
Portland Fla., U.S.A. 30°31N 86°12W 316 E3
Portland Ind., U.S.A. 40°26N 84°59W 311 D12
Portland Maine, U.S.A. 43°39N 70°16W 309 D18
Portland Mich., U.S.A. 42°52N 84°54W 311 B12
Portland Oreg., U.S.A. 45°32N 122°37W 306 E4
Portland Pa., U.S.A. 40°55N 75°6W 313 F9
Portland Tex., U.S.A. 27°53N 97°20W 314 H6
Portland, I. of U.K. 50°33N 2°26W 169 G5
Portland, Récif French Polynesia 23°42S 134°30W 289 f
Portland B. Australia 38°15S 141°45E 282 E4
Portland Bight Jamaica 17°52N 77°5W 320 a
Portland Bill U.K. 50°31N 2°28W 169 G5
Portland Canal U.S.A. 55°56N 130°0W 296 B2
Portland I. N.Z. 39°20S 177°51E 284 F6
Portland Int. ✈ (PDX) U.S.A. 45°35N 122°36W 306 E4
Portland Pt. Ascension I. 7°59S 14°25W 153 g
Portland Pt. Jamaica 17°42N 77°11W 320 a
Portmadoc = Porthmadog U.K. 52°55N 4°8W 168 E3
Portmarnock Ireland 53°26N 6°8W 120 A3
Portmore Jamaica 17°53N 76°53W 320 a
Porto Brazil 3°54S 42°42W 332 B3
Porto Corse-du-Sud, France 42°16N 8°42E 175 F12
Porto Portugal 41°8N 8°40W 194 D2
Porto ☐ Portugal 41°8N 8°20W 194 D2
Porto, G. de France 42°17N 8°34E 175 F12
Porto Acre Brazil 9°34S 67°31W 330 B4
Pôrto Alegre = Luzilândia Brazil 3°28S 42°22W 332 B3
Pôrto Alegre Pará, Brazil 4°22S 52°44W 329 D7
Pôrto Alegre Rio Grande do S., Brazil 30°5S 51°10W 335 C5
Porto Alegre São Tomé & Príncipe 0°2N 6°32E 265 a
Porto Amboim = Gunza Angola 10°50S 13°50E 265 E2
Porto Amélia = Pemba Mozam. 12°58S 40°30E 269 E5
Porto Azzurro Italy 42°46N 10°24E 198 F7
Porto Brandão Portugal 38°40N 9°12W 126 A1
Pôrto Cajueiro Brazil 11°3S 55°53W 331 C6
Porto Colom Spain 39°26N 3°15E 206 B4
Porto Cristo Spain 39°33N 3°20E 206 B4
Pôrto da Fôlha Brazil 9°55S 37°17W 332 C4
Porto de Moz Brazil 1°41S 52°13W 329 D7
Porto de Pedras Brazil 9°10S 35°17W 332 C4
Pôrto des Meinacos Brazil 12°33S 53°7W 331 C7
Pôrto dos Gaúchos Brazil 11°32S 57°16W 331 C6
Porto Empédocle Italy 37°17N 13°32E 200 E6
Porto Esperança Brazil 19°37S 57°29W 331 D6
Porto Espirdão Brazil 15°51S 58°28W 331 D6
Porto Formoso Azores 37°49N 25°25W 153 d3
Porto Franco Brazil 6°20S 47°24W 332 C2
Porto Grande Brazil 0°42N 51°24W 329 C7
Porto Inglês C. Verde Is. 15°21N 23°10W 153 j
Porto Jofre Brazil 17°20S 56°48W 331 D6
Porto Lengone = Porto Azzurro Italy 42°46N 10°24E 198 F7
Porto Maurizio = Impéria Italy 43°53N 8°3E 198 E5
Porto Mendes Brazil 24°30S 54°15W 335 A5
Porto Moniz Madeira 32°52N 17°11W 153 c
Porto Murtinho Brazil 21°45S 57°55W 331 E6
Porto Nacional Brazil 10°40S 48°30W 332 D2
Porto-Novo Benin 6°23N 2°42E 263 D5
Pôrto Novo Rio de J., Brazil 22°50S 43°7W 135 A2
Porto Novo Cr. → Nigeria 6°25N 3°22E 124 B2
Porto Primavera, Represa Brazil 22°10S 52°45W 335 A5
Porto San Giórgio Italy 43°11N 13°48E 199 E10
Porto Sant' Elpídio Italy 43°15N 13°43E 199 E10
Porto Santana Brazil 0°3S 51°11W 329 D7
Porto Santo, I. de Madeira 33°45N 16°25W 260 B1
Porto Santo Stéfano Italy 42°26N 11°7E 198 F8
Porto São José Brazil 22°43S 53°10W 335 A5
Porto Seguro = Guadalupe Brazil 6°44S 43°47W 332 C3
Porto Seguro Brazil 16°26S 39°5W 333 E4
Porto Tolle Italy 44°56N 12°22E 199 D9
Porto Tórres Italy 40°50N 8°24E 200 B1
Porto União Brazil 26°10S 51°10W 335 B5
Porto-Vecchio France 41°35N 9°16E 175 G13
Pôrto Velho Brazil 8°46S 63°54W 331 B5
Porto Walter Brazil 8°15S 72°40W 330 B3
Portobello U.K. 55°57N 3°7W 121 B3
Portobelo Panama 9°35N 79°42W 320 E4
Portoferráio Italy 42°48N 10°20E 198 F7
Portogruaro Italy 45°47N 12°50E 199 C9
Portola U.S.A. 39°49N 120°28W 306 F6
Portomaggiore Italy 44°42N 11°48E 199 D8
Portopetro Spain 39°22N 3°13E 206 B4
Portør Norway 58°48N 9°28E 164 F6
Portoscuso Italy 39°12N 8°24E 200 C1
Portovénere Italy 44°3N 9°51E 198 D6
Portoviejo Ecuador 1°7S 80°28W 328 D1
Portpatrick U.K. 54°51N 5°7W 167 G3
Portree U.K. 57°25N 6°12W 167 D2
Portrero U.S.A. 37°46N 122°25W 136 B3
Portrush U.K. 55°12N 6°40W 166 A5
Portsmouth Dominica 15°34N 61°27W 323 k
Portsmouth Portsmouth, U.K. 50°48N 1°6W 169 G6
Portsmouth N.H., U.S.A. 43°5N 70°45W 313 C14
Portsmouth Ohio, U.S.A. 38°44N 82°57W 309 F12
Portsmouth R.I., U.S.A. 41°36N 71°15W 313 E13
Portsmouth Va., U.S.A. 36°58N 76°23W 309 G15
Portsmouth ☐ U.K. 50°48N 1°6W 169 G6
Portsoy U.K. 57°41N 2°41W 167 D6
Portstewart U.K. 55°11N 6°43W 166 A5
Porttipahdan tekojärvi Finland 68°5N 26°40E 160 B22
Portugal ■ Europe 40°0N 8°0W 194 F3
Portugalete Spain 43°19N 3°4W 196 B1
Portuguesa ☐ Venezuela 9°10N 69°15W 328 B4
Portuguese East Africa = Mozambique ■ Africa 19°0S 35°0E 269 F4
Portuguese Guinea = Guinea-Bissau ■ Africa 12°0N 15°0W 262 C2
Portuguese Timor = East Timor ■ Asia 8°50S 126°0E 231 F7
Portuguese West Africa = Angola ■ Africa 12°0S 18°0E 265 E3
Portumna Ireland 53°6N 8°14W 166 C3
Portville U.S.A. 42°3N 78°20W 312 D6
Poruma Australia 10°2S 143°4E 280 a
Porus Jamaica 18°2N 77°25W 320 a
Porvenir Bolivia 11°10S 68°50W 330 C4
Porvenir Chile 53°10S 70°16W 336 D2
Porvoo Finland 60°24N 25°40E 188 B3
Porzuna Spain 39°9N 4°9W 195 F6
Pos Chiquito Aruba 12°27N 69°57W 322 f
Posada Italy 40°38N 9°43E 200 B2
Posada → Italy 40°39N 9°45E 200 B2
Posadas Argentina 27°30S 55°50W 335 B4
Posadas Spain 37°47N 5°11W 195 H5
Poschiavo Switz. 46°19N 10°4E 179 J6
Posen = Poznań Poland 52°25N 16°55E 185 F3
Posets Spain 42°39N 0°25E 196 C5
Poseyville U.S.A. 38°10N 87°47W 311 F9
Poshan = Boshan China 36°28N 117°49E 227 F9
Posht-e Badam Iran 33°2N 55°23E 247 C7
Posidium Greece 35°30N 27°10E 205 F9
Poso Indonesia 1°20S 120°55E 231 E6
Poso, Danau Indonesia 1°52S 120°35E 231 E6
Posoegroenoe Suriname 4°23N 55°43W 329 C6
Posof Turkey 41°30N 42°43E 213 B10
Pospelikha Russia 51°57N 81°46E 217 B10
Posse Brazil 14°4S 46°18W 333 D2
Possedimenti Italiani dell'Egeo = Dodecanese Greece 36°35N 27°0E 205 E8
Possel C.A.R. 5°5N 19°10E 264 A3
Possession I. Antarctica 72°4S 172°0E 151 D11
Pössneck Germany 50°42N 11°35E 178 E7
Possum Kingdom L. U.S.A. 32°52N 98°26W 314 E5
Post U.S.A. 33°12N 101°23W 314 E4
Post Falls U.S.A. 47°43N 116°57W 304 C5
Postavy = Pastavy Belarus 55°4N 26°50E 188 E4
Poste, R. du Mauritius 20°29S 57°36E 272 e
Poste de Flacq Mauritius 20°9S 57°43E 272 e
Poste de Flacq → Mauritius 20°9S 57°44E 272 e
Poste-de-la-Baleine = Kuujjuarapik Canada 55°20N 77°35W 298 A4
Postmasburg S. Africa 28°18S 23°5E 270 C3
Postojna Slovenia 45°46N 14°12E 199 C11
Poston U.S.A. 34°0N 114°24W 307 M12
Postumia = Postojna Slovenia 45°46N 14°12E 199 C11
Postville Nfld. & L., Canada 54°54N 59°47W 299 B8
Postville Iowa, U.S.A. 43°5N 91°34W 310 A5
Posyet Russia 42°39N 130°48E 220 C5
Potamos Antikythira, Greece 35°52N 23°15E 204 F5
Potamos Kythira, Greece 36°15N 22°58E 204 E4
Potchefstroom S. Africa 26°41S 27°7E 270 C4
Potcoava Romania 44°30N 24°39E 183 F9
Poté Brazil 17°49S 41°49W 333 E3
Poteau U.S.A. 35°3N 94°37W 314 D7
Poteet U.S.A. 29°2N 98°35W 314 G5
Potenza Italy 40°38N 15°48E 201 B8
Potenza → Italy 43°25N 13°40E 199 E10
Potenza Picena Italy 43°22N 13°37E 199 E10
Poteriteri, L. N.Z. 46°5S 167°10E 285 G2
Potgietersrus = Mokopane S. Africa 24°10S 28°55E 271 B4
Poti Georgia 42°10N 41°38E 191 J5
Potiraguá Brazil 15°36S 39°53W 333 E4
Potiskum Nigeria 11°39N 11°2E 263 C7
Potlogi Romania 44°34N 25°34E 183 F10
Potomac U.S.A. 38°59N 77°13W 143 A2
Potomac → U.S.A. 38°0N 76°23W 309 F14
Potomac Park Washington, D.C., U.S.A. 143 c1
Potosí Bolivia 19°38S 65°50W 331 D4
Potosi Mo., U.S.A. 37°56N 90°47W 310 G6
Potosí ☐ Bolivia 20°31S 67°0W 330 E4
Potosi Mt. U.S.A. 35°57N 115°29W 307 K11
Pototan Phil. 10°54N 122°38E 233 F4
Potrerillos Chile 26°30S 69°30W 334 B2
Potrero Pt. U.S.A. 37°45N 122°22W 136 B2
Potsdam Brandenburg, Germany 52°23N 13°3E 115 B1
Potsdam N.Y., U.S.A. 44°40N 74°59W 313 B10
Potsdamer Platz Berlin, Germany 115 b3
Pottangi India 18°34N 82°58E 244 E6
Pottenstein Germany 49°46N 11°24E 179 F7
Potters Village Antigua & B. 17°5N 61°49W 322 b
Pottersville U.S.A. 43°43N 73°50W 313 C11
Pottery Hill = Abû Ballas Egypt 24°26N 27°36E 256 C2
Pottstown U.S.A. 40°15N 75°39W 313 F9
Pottsville U.S.A. 40°41N 76°12W 313 F8
Pottuvil Sri Lanka 6°55N 81°50E 245 L5
Potzham Germany 48°1N 11°36E 131 B2
Pötzleinsdorf Austria 48°14N 16°17E 142 A1
P'otzu Taiwan 23°28N 120°15E 225 C2
Pouancé France 47°44N 1°10W 172 E5
Pouce Coupé Canada 55°40N 120°10W 296 B4
Pouébo N. Cal. 20°24S 164°36E 288 d
Poughkeepsie U.S.A. 41°42N 73°56W 313 E11
Pouilly-sur-Loire France 47°17N 2°57E 173 E9
Poulan U.S.A. 31°31N 83°47W 316 D6
Poulaphouca Res. Ireland 53°8N 6°30W 166 C5
Poulata Greece 38°14N 20°36E 207 C2
Poulsbo U.S.A. 47°44N 122°38W 306 C4
Poultney U.S.A. 43°31N 73°14W 313 C11
Poulton-le-Fylde U.K. 53°51N 2°58W 168 D5
Poum N. Cal. 20°14S 164°2E 288 d
Pounga-Nganda Gabon 2°58S 10°51E 264 C2
Pouso Alegre Mato Grosso, Brazil 11°46S 57°16W 331 C6
Pouso Alegre Minas Gerais, Brazil 22°14S 45°57W 335 A6
Pouso Alto = Piracanjuba Brazil 17°18S 49°1W 333 E2
Pout Senegal 14°45N 17°0W 262 C1
Pouthisat Cambodia 12°34N 103°50E 236 F4
Pouytenga Burkina Faso 12°15N 0°25W 263 C4
Pouzauges France 46°47N 0°50W 172 F6
Pova de Santa Iria Portugal 38°51N 9°4W 195 G1
Považská Bystrica Slovak Rep. 49°8N 18°27E 181 B11
Povenets Russia 62°50N 34°50E 186 B5
Poverty B. N.Z. 38°43S 178°2E 284 E7
Povlen Serbia 44°9N 19°44E 202 B3
Póvoa de Lanhosa Portugal 41°33N 8°15W 194 D2
Póvoa de Santo Adriao Portugal 38°47N 9°9W 126 A2
Póvoa de Varzim Portugal 41°25N 8°46W 194 D2
Povoação Azores 37°45N 25°15W 153 d3
Povorino Russia 51°12N 42°5E 190 E6
Povorotnyy, Mys Russia 42°40N 133°2E 220 C6
Povungnituk = Puvirnituq Canada 60°2N 77°10W 295 E16
Powassan Canada 46°5N 79°25W 298 C4
Poway U.S.A. 32°58N 117°2W 307 N9
Powązki Poland 52°15N 20°58E 142 B1
Powder → U.S.A. 45°45N 105°26W 304 C11
Powder River U.S.A. 43°2N 106°59W 304 E10
Powder Springs U.S.A. 33°52N 84°41W 316 B5
Powell U.S.A. 44°45N 108°46W 304 D9
Powell, L. U.S.A. 36°57N 111°29W 305 H8
Powell River Canada 49°50N 124°35W 296 D4
Powelton U.S.A. 33°26N 82°52W 316 B7
Power House = Drayton Valley Canada 53°12N 114°58W 296 C6
Powers U.S.A. 45°41N 87°32W 308 C10
Powiśle Poland 52°14N 21°1E 142 B2
Pownal U.S.A. 42°45N 73°14W 313 D11
Powsin Poland 52°8N 21°6E 142 C2
Powsinek Poland 52°9N 21°6E 142 C2
Powys ☐ U.K. 52°20N 3°20W 169 E4
Poxoréo Brazil 15°50S 54°23W 331 D7
Poya N. Cal. 21°19S 165°7E 288 d
Poyan Res. Singapore 1°22N 103°40E 138 A2
Poyang Hu China 29°5N 116°20E 229 C11
Poyarkovo Russia 49°36N 128°41E 215 E13

Poysdorf *Austria* 48°40N 16°37E **181** C9
Poza de la Sal *Spain* 42°35N 3°31W **194** C7
Poza Rica *Mexico* 20°33N 97°27W **319** C5
Pozantı *Turkey* 37°25N 34°50E **212** D6
Požarevac *Serbia* 44°35N 21°18E **202** B5
Pozazal, Puerto *Spain* 42°56N 4°10W **194** C6
Požega *Croatia* 45°20N 17°40E **182** E2
Požega *Serbia* 43°53N 20°2E **202** C4
Poznań *Poland* 52°25N 16°55E **185** F3
Poznań ✈ (POZ) *Poland* 52°26N 16°45E **185** F3
Pozo *U.S.A.* 35°20N 120°24W **307** K6
Pozo Alcón *Spain* 37°42N 2°56W **195** H8
Pozo Almonte *Chile* 20°10S 69°50W **330** E4
Pozo Colorado *Paraguay* 23°30S 58°45W **334** A4
Pozoblanco *Spain* 38°23N 4°51W **195** G6
Pozorrubio *Phil.* 16°7N 120°33E **232** C3
Pozuelo de Alarcón *Spain* 40°24N 3°53W **127** B1
Pozuzo *Peru* 10°5S 75°35W **330** C2
Pozzallo *Italy* 36°43N 14°51E **201** F7
Pozzomaggiore *Italy* 40°24N 8°39E **200** B1
Pozzuoli *Italy* 40°49N 14°7E **201** B7
Pra → *Ghana* 5°1N 1°37W **263** D4
Prabuty *Poland* 53°47N 19°15E **184** E6
Prača *Bos.-H.* 43°47N 18°43E **182** G3
Prachatice *Czech Rep.* 49°1N 14°0E **180** B6
Prachin Buri *Thailand* 14°0N 101°25E **236** F3
Prachuap Khirikhan *Thailand* 11°49N 99°48E **237** G2
Pradelles *France* 44°46N 3°52E **174** D7
Pradera *Colombia* 3°25N 76°15W **328** C2
Prades *France* 42°38N 2°23E **174** F6
Prado *Brazil* 17°20S 39°13W **333** E4
Prado, Museo del *Madrid, Spain* **127** b3
Prado Churubusco *Mexico* 19°20N 99°8W **128** B2
Prado del Rey *Spain* 36°48N 5°33W **195** J5
Præstø *Denmark* 55°8N 12°2E **163** J6
Praga *Poland* 52°15N 21°2E **142** B2
Pragersko *Slovenia* 46°27N 15°42E **199** B12
Prague = Praha *Czech Rep.* 50°4N 14°25E **135** B2
Praha *Czech Rep.* 50°4N 14°25E **135** B2
Praha ✈ (PRG) *Czech Rep.* 50°6N 14°16E **135** B1
Prahecq *France* 46°19N 0°26W **174** B3
Prahita → *India* 19°0N 79°55E **244** E4
Prahova □ *Romania* 45°10N 26°0E **183** E10
Prahova → *Romania* 44°50N 25°50E **183** F10
Prahovo *Serbia* 44°18N 22°39E **202** B6
Praia *Azores* 39°3N 27°58W **153** d1
Praia *C. Verde Is.* 15°2N 23°34W **153** j
Praia a Mare *Italy* 39°50N 15°45E **201** C8
Praia da Vitória *Azores* 38°44N 27°4W **153** d1
Praia do Norte *Azores* 38°36N 28°46W **153** d1
Praia Grande *Brazil* 24°0S 46°24W **333** F2
Praid *Romania* 46°32N 25°10E **183** D10
Prainha *Azores* 38°27N 28°12W **153** d1
Prainha *Pará, Brazil* 1°45S 53°30W **329** D7
Prainha Nova *Brazil* 7°10S 60°30W **331** B5
Praires, R. des → *Canada* 45°38N 73°36W **130** A2
Prairie *Australia* 20°50S 144°35E **280** C3
Prairie City *U.S.A.* 44°28N 118°43W **304** D4
Prairie Dog Town Fork Red → *U.S.A.* 34°34N 99°58W **314** D5
Prairie du Chien *U.S.A.* 43°3N 91°9W **310** A5
Prairie du Rocher *U.S.A.* 38°5N 90°6W **310** F6
Prairie Village *U.S.A.* 38°58N 94°38W **310** F2
Prairies, L. of the *Canada* 51°16N 101°32W **297** C8
Pramanda *Greece* 39°32N 21°8E **204** B3
Prambanan △ *Indonesia* 7°45S 110°28E **231** G14
Prampram *Ghana* 5°43N 0°8E **263** D5
Pran Buri *Thailand* 12°23N 99°55E **236** F2
Pranbanan *Indonesia* 7°48S 110°15E **235** D4
Prándarjökull *Iceland* 64°40N 14°55W **155** C12
Prang *Ghana* 8°1N 0°56W **263** D4
Prapat *Indonesia* 2°41N 98°58E **234** B1
Praslin *St. Lucia* 13°52N 60°54W **323** m
Praslin *Seychelles* 4°18S 55°45E **272** c
Prasonisi, Akra *Greece* 35°42N 27°46E **206** F11
Prassberg = Mozirje *Slovenia* 46°22N 14°58E **199** B11
Praszka *Poland* 51°5N 18°31E **185** G5
Prata *Brazil* 19°25S 48°54W **333** E2
Pratabpur *India* 23°28N 83°15E **243** H10
Pratapgarh *Raj., India* 24°2N 74°40E **242** G6
Pratapgarh *Ut. P., India* 25°56N 81°59E **243** G9
Pratas I. = Dongsha Dao *S. China Sea* 20°45N 116°43E **229** G11
Prater *Austria* 48°12N 16°25E **142** A2
Prato *Italy* 43°53N 11°6E **198** E8
Prátola Peligna *Italy* 42°6N 13°52E **199** F10
Prats-de-Mollo-la-Preste *France* 42°25N 2°27E **174** F6
Pratt *U.S.A.* 37°39N 98°44W **308** G4
Prattville *U.S.A.* 32°28N 86°29W **315** E11
Praust = Pruszcz Gdański *Poland* 54°17N 18°40E **184** D5
Pravara → *India* 19°35N 74°45E **244** E2
Pravdinsk *Kaliningrad, Russia* 54°27N 21°1E **184** D8
Pravdinsk *Nizhniy Novgorod, Russia* 56°29N 43°28E **190** B6
Pravets *Bulgaria* 42°53N 23°55E **202** D7
Pravia *Spain* 43°30N 6°12W **194** B4
Praya *Indonesia* 8°39S 116°17E **235** D5
Prayag = Allahabad *India* 25°25N 81°58E **243** G9
Pré-en-Pail *France* 48°28N 0°12W **172** D6
Preah Vihear *Cambodia* 14°23N 104°41E **236** E5
Preau *Trin. & Tob.* 10°12N 61°19W **323** t
Preble *U.S.A.* 42°44N 76°8W **313** D8
Prêcheur *Martinique* 14°48N 61°13W **322** j
Precipice △ *Australia* 25°18S 150°5E **281** D5
Precordillera *Argentina* 30°0S 69°1W **334** C2
Precotto *Italy* 45°30N 9°13E **129** A2
Predáppio *Italy* 44°6N 11°59E **199** D8
Predazzo *Italy* 46°19N 11°36E **199** B8
Predeal *Romania* 45°30N 25°34E **183** E10
Predejane *Serbia* 42°51N 22°9E **202** D6
Preeceville *Canada* 51°57N 102°40W **297** C8
Preetz *Germany* 54°14N 10°18E **178** A6
Pregolya → *Russia* 54°41N 20°22E **184** D7
Pregrada *Croatia* 46°11N 15°45E **199** B12
Preiļi *Latvia* 56°18N 26°43E **188** D4
Preko *Croatia* 44°7N 15°10E **199** D12
Prelog *Croatia* 46°18N 16°32E **199** B13
Premer *Australia* 31°29S 149°56E **283** A8
Prémery *France* 47°10N 3°18E **173** E10
Premià de Mar *Spain* 41°29N 2°22E **196** D7
Premont *U.S.A.* 27°22N 98°7W **314** H5
Premuda *Croatia* 44°20N 14°36E **199** D11
Prenestino Labicano *Italy* 41°53N 12°33E **136** B2
Prentice *U.S.A.* 45°33N 90°17W **308** C8
Prenzlau *Germany* 53°19N 13°50E **178** B9
Prenzlauerberg *Germany* 52°32N 13°24E **115** A3
Preobrazheniye *Russia* 42°54N 133°54E **220** C6
Preparis I. = Pariparit Kyun *Burma* 14°52N 93°41E **245** G11
Preparis North Channel *Ind. Oc.* 15°27N 94°5E **245** G11
Preparis South Channel *Ind. Oc.* 14°33N 93°30E **245** G11
Přerov *Czech Rep.* 49°28N 17°27E **181** B10
Prescott *Ont., Canada* 44°45N 75°30W **313** B9
Prescott *Ariz., U.S.A.* 34°33N 112°28W **305** J7
Prescott *Ark., U.S.A.* 33°48N 93°23W **314** E8
Prescott Valley *U.S.A.* 34°40N 112°18W **305** J7
Preservation Inlet *N.Z.* 46°8S 166°35E **285** G1
Preševo *Serbia* 42°19N 21°39E **202** D5
Presho *U.S.A.* 43°54N 100°3W **308** D3
Presicce *Italy* 39°54N 18°16E **201** C11
Presidencia de la Plaza *Argentina* 27°0S 59°50W **334** B4
Presidencia Roque Saenz Peña *Argentina* 26°45S 60°30W **334** B3
Président-Thiers, Récif *French Polynesia* 24°30S 146°0W **289** f
Presidente Dutra *Brazil* 5°15S 44°30W **332** C3
Presidente Epitácio *Brazil* 21°56S 52°6W **333** F1
Presidente Figueiredo *Brazil* 1°57S 60°2W **329** D5
Presidente Hayes □ *Paraguay* 24°0S 59°0W **334** A4
Presidente Juán Perón = Chaco □ *Argentina* 26°30S 61°0W **334** B3
Presidente Médici *Brazil* 11°17S 61°55W **331** C5
Presidente Prudente *Brazil* 22°5S 51°25W **335** A5
Presidente Vargas = Nova Era *Brazil* 19°45S 43°3W **333** E3
Presidio *Mexico* 29°29N 104°23W **318** B4
Presidio *Tex., U.S.A.* 29°34N 104°22W **314** G2
Preslav *Bulgaria* 43°10N 26°52E **203** C10
Preslavska Planina *Bulgaria* 43°10N 26°45E **203** C10
Prešov *Slovak Rep.* 49°0N 21°15E **181** B14
Prešovský □ *Slovak Rep.* 49°10N 21°0E **181** B13
Prespa *Bulgaria* 41°44N 24°55E **203** E8
Prespa, L. = Prespansko Jezero *Macedonia* 40°55N 21°0E **202** F5
Prespa △ *Greece* 40°48N 21°4E **202** F5
Prespansko Jezero *Macedonia* 40°55N 21°0E **202** F5
Presque I. *U.S.A.* 42°10N 80°6W **312** D4
Presque Isle *U.S.A.* 46°41N 68°1W **309** B19
Pressburg = Bratislava *Slovak Rep.* 48°10N 17°7E **181** C10
Prestatyn *U.K.* 53°20N 3°24W **168** D4
Prestea *Ghana* 5°22N 2°7W **262** D4
Presteigne *U.K.* 52°17N 3°0W **169** E5
Přeštice *Czech Rep.* 49°34N 13°20E **180** B6
Presto *Bolivia* 18°55S 64°56W **331** D5
Preston *Vic., Australia* 37°44S 145°0E **128** A1
Preston *Ont., Canada* 43°23N 80°21W **312** C4
Preston *Lancs., U.K.* 53°46N 2°42W **168** D5
Preston *Ga., U.S.A.* 32°4N 84°32W **316** C5
Preston *Idaho, U.S.A.* 42°6N 111°53W **304** E8
Preston *Iowa, U.S.A.* 42°3N 90°24W **310** B6
Preston *Minn., U.S.A.* 43°40N 92°5W **308** D7
Preston *Mo., U.S.A.* 37°56N 93°13W **310** G3
Preston, C. *Australia* 20°51S 116°12E **278** D2
Prestonsburg *U.S.A.* 37°40N 82°47W **309** G12
Prestranda *Norway* 59°6N 9°4E **162** E3
Prestwick *U.K.* 55°29N 4°37W **167** F4
Prêto → *Amazonas, Brazil* 0°8S 64°6W **329** D5
Prêto → *Bahia, Brazil* 11°21S 43°52W **332** D3
Prêto do Igapó-Açu → *Brazil* 4°26S 59°48W **329** D6
Pretoria *S. Africa* 25°44S 28°12E **271** C4
Pretos Forros, Sa. dos *Brazil* 22°54S 43°17W **135** B1
Preuilly-sur-Claise *France* 46°51N 0°56E **172** F7
Preussisch-Eylau = Bagrationovsk *Russia* 54°23N 20°39E **184** D7
Preussisch Friedland = Debrzno *Poland* 53°31N 17°14E **184** E4
Preussisch Holland = Pasłęk *Poland* 54°3N 19°41E **184** D6
Preussisch-Stargard = Starogard Gdański *Poland* 53°59N 18°30E **184** E5
Preveza *Greece* 38°57N 20°45E **207** B2
Preveza □ *Greece* 39°10N 20°40E **204** B2
Preveza-Lefkada ✈ (PVK) *Greece* 38°57N 20°45E **207** B2
Préville *Canada* 45°28N 73°29W **130** B3
Prey Veng *Cambodia* 11°35N 105°29E **237** G5
Přezletice *Czech Rep.* 50°9N 14°34E **135** B3
Priazovskoye *Ukraine* 46°44N 35°40E **189** J8
Pribalkhash = Balqash *Kazakhstan* 46°50N 74°50E **214** E8
Pribilof Is. *U.S.A.* 57°0N 170°0W **303** H5
Priboj *Serbia* 43°35N 19°32E **202** C3
Příbram *Czech Rep.* 49°41N 14°2E **180** B7
Price *U.S.A.* 39°36N 110°49W **304** G8
Price, C. *India* 13°34N 93°3E **245** H11
Price I. *Canada* 52°23N 128°41W **296** C3
Prichard *U.S.A.* 30°44N 88°5W **315** F10
Prickly Pear Cays *Anguilla* 18°16N 63°11W **322** a
Prickly Pt. *Grenada* 11°59N 61°45W **323** q
Priego *Spain* 40°26N 2°21W **196** E2
Priego de Córdoba *Spain* 37°27N 4°12W **195** H6
Priekule *Latvia* 56°26N 21°35E **184** B8
Priekule *Lithuania* 55°33N 21°19E **184** C8
Prien *Germany* 47°51N 12°20E **179** H8
Prienai *Lithuania* 54°38N 23°57E **184** D10
Prieska *S. Africa* 29°40S 22°42E **270** C3
Priest L. *U.S.A.* 48°35N 116°52W **304** B5
Priest River *U.S.A.* 48°11N 116°55W **304** B5
Priest Valley *U.S.A.* 36°10N 120°39W **306** J6
Prieto Diaz *Phil.* 13°2N 124°12E **232** E5
Prievidza *Slovak Rep.* 48°46N 18°36E **181** C11
Prignitz *Germany* 53°6N 11°45E **178** B7
Prijedor *Bos.-H.* 44°58N 16°41E **199** D13
Prijepolje *Serbia* 43°27N 19°40E **202** C3
Prikaspiyskaya Nizmennost = Caspian Depression *Eurasia* 47°0N 48°0E **191** G9
Prikro *Ivory C.* 7°40N 3°59W **262** D4
Prikubanskaya Nizmennost *Russia* 45°39N 38°33E **191** H4
Prilep *Macedonia* 41°21N 21°32E **202** E5
Priluki = Pryluky *Ukraine* 50°30N 32°24E **189** G7
Prima Porta *Italy* 42°0N 12°30E **136** B1
Primavalle *Italy* 41°55N 12°25E **136** B1
Prime Seal I. *Australia* 40°3S 147°43E **281** G4
Primeira Cruz *Brazil* 2°30S 43°26W **332** B3
Primkenau = Przemków *Poland* 51°31N 15°48E **185** G2
Primo Tapia *Mexico* 32°16N 116°54W **307** N10
Primorsk *Kaliningrad, Russia* 54°44N 20°0E **184** D6
Primorsk *St. Petersburg, Russia* 60°22N 28°37E **188** B5
Primorskiy Kray □ *Russia* 45°0N 135°0E **220** B7
Primorsko *Bulgaria* 42°15N 27°44E **203** D11
Primorsko-Akhtarsk *Russia* 46°2N 38°10E **189** J10
Primrose *S. Africa* 26°11S 28°9E **123** B2
Primrose L. *Canada* 54°55N 109°45W **297** C7
Prince Albert *Sask., Canada* 53°15N 105°50W **297** C7
Prince Albert *Western Cape, S. Africa* 33°12S 22°2E **270** D3
Prince Albert △ *Canada* 54°0N 106°25W **297** C7
Prince Albert Mts. *Antarctica* 76°0S 161°30E **151** D11
Prince Albert Pen. *Canada* 72°30N 116°0W **294** C8
Prince Albert Sd. *Canada* 70°25N 115°0W **294** C9
Prince Alfred, C. *Canada* 74°20N 124°40W **150** B1
Prince Charles I. *Canada* 67°47N 76°12W **295** D16
Prince Charles Mts. *Antarctica* 72°0S 67°0E **151** D6
Prince Edward Fracture Zone *Ind. Oc.* 46°0S 35°0E **151** A4
Prince Edward I. □ *Canada* 46°20N 63°20W **299** C7
Prince Edward Is. *Ind. Oc.* 46°35S 38°0E **273** J2
Prince George *Canada* 53°55N 122°50W **296** C4
Prince of Wales, C. *U.S.A.* 65°36N 168°5W **303** D5
Prince of Wales I. *Queens., Australia* 10°40S 142°10E **286** F2
Prince of Wales I. *Nunavut, Canada* 73°0N 99°0W **294** C12
Prince of Wales I. *Alaska, U.S.A.* 55°47N 132°50W **303** J14
Prince of Wales Icefield *Canada* 78°15N 79°0W **295** B16
Prince of Wales Str. *Canada* 73°0N 117°0W **294** C8
Prince Patrick I. *Canada* 77°0N 120°0W **295** B8
Prince Regent Inlet *Canada* 73°0N 90°0W **295** C14
Prince Rupert *Canada* 54°20N 130°20W **296** C2
Prince Rupert B. *Dominica* 15°34N 61°29W **323** k
Prince Rupert Bluff Pt. *Dominica* 15°35N 61°29W **323** k
Prince William Sd. *U.S.A.* 60°40N 147°0W **303** F11
Princes Street *Edinburgh, U.K.* **121** b2
Princes Town *Trin. & Tob.* 10°16N 61°23W **323** t
Princesa Isabel *Brazil* 7°44S 38°0W **332** C4
Princess Charlotte B. *Australia* 14°25S 144°0E **280** A3
Princess Elizabeth Trough *S. Ocean* 64°10S 83°0E **151** C7
Princess May Ranges *Australia* 15°30S 125°30E **278** C4
Princess Royal I. *Canada* 53°0N 128°40W **296** C3
Princeton *B.C., Canada* 49°27N 120°30W **296** D4
Princeton *Calif., U.S.A.* 39°24N 122°1W **306** F4
Princeton *Ill., U.S.A.* 41°23N 89°28W **310** C7
Princeton *Ind., U.S.A.* 38°21N 87°34W **311** F9
Princeton *Ky., U.S.A.* 37°7N 87°53W **308** G10
Princeton *Mo., U.S.A.* 40°24N 93°35W **310** D3
Princeton *N.J., U.S.A.* 40°21N 74°39W **313** F10
Princeton *W. Va., U.S.A.* 37°22N 81°6W **309** G13
Princeville *Hawai'i, U.S.A.* 22°13N 159°29W **302** A2
Princeville *Ill., U.S.A.* 40°56N 89°46W **310** D7
Príncipe *São Tomé & Príncipe* 1°37N 7°25E **265** a
Principe da Beira *Brazil* 12°20S 64°30W **331** C5
Prineville *U.S.A.* 44°18N 120°51W **304** D3
Pringles Bay *Dominica* 15°21N 61°25W **323** k
Pringsewu *Indonesia* 5°24S 104°55E **234** D2
Prins Christian Sund *Greenland* 60°4N 43°10W **154** E6
Prins Harald Kyst *Antarctica* 70°0S 35°1E **151** D4
Prins Karls Forland *Svalbard* 78°30N 11°0E **154** B12
Prinsesse Astrid Kyst *Antarctica* 70°45S 12°30E **151** D3
Prinsesse Ragnhild Kyst *Antarctica* 70°15S 27°30E **151** D4
Printer's Row *Chicago, U.S.A.* **119** d2
Prinzapolca *Nic.* 13°20N 83°35W **320** D3
Prior, C. *Spain* 43°34N 8°17W **194** B2
Priozersk *Russia* 61°2N 30°7E **188** B6
Pripet = Prypyat → *Europe* 51°20N 30°15E **177** C16
Pripet Marshes *Europe* 52°10N 27°10E **177** B15
Pripyat Marshes = Pripet Marshes *Europe* 52°10N 27°10E **177** B15
Pripyats = Prypyat → *Europe* 51°20N 30°15E **177** C16
Prishib = Leninsk *Russia* 48°40N 45°15E **191** F7
Prishtine = Priština *Kosovo* 42°40N 21°13E **202** D5
Prislop, Pasul *Romania* 47°37N 24°48E **183** C9
Pristen *Russia* 51°15N 36°44E **189** G9
Priština *Kosovo* 42°40N 21°13E **202** D5
Pritzwalk *Germany* 53°9N 12°10E **178** B8
Privas *France* 44°45N 4°37E **175** D8
Priverno *Italy* 41°28N 13°11E **200** A6
Privolzhsk *Russia* 57°23N 41°16E **190** B5
Privolzhskaya Vozvyshennost *Russia* 51°0N 46°0E **190** E7
Privolzhskiy *Russia* 51°25N 46°3E **190** E8
Privolzhskiy □ *Russia* 56°0N 50°0E **190** D9
Privolzhye *Russia* 52°52N 48°33E **190** D9
Priyutnoye *Russia* 46°12N 43°40E **191** G6
Prizren *Kosovo* 42°13N 20°45E **202** D4
Prizzi *Italy* 37°43N 13°26E **200** E6
Prnjavor *Bos.-H.* 44°52N 17°43E **182** F2
Probolinggo *Indonesia* 7°46S 113°13E **235** D4
Prochowice *Poland* 51°17N 16°20E **185** G3
Proctor *U.S.A.* 43°40N 73°2W **313** C11
Proddatur *India* 14°45N 78°30E **245** G4
Prodhromos *Cyprus* 34°57N 32°50E **207** F8
Proença-a-Nova *Portugal* 39°45N 7°54W **194** F3
Profilia *Greece* 36°5N 27°51E **206** E11
Profondeville *Belgium* 50°23N 4°52E **170** D4
Progreso *Coahuila, Mexico* 27°28N 100°59W **318** B4
Progreso *Yucatán, Mexico* 21°20N 89°40W **319** C7
Progreso Nacional *Mexico* 19°30N 99°9W **128** A2
Progress *Antarctica* 66°22S 76°22E **151** C12
Progress *Russia* 49°45N 129°37E **215** E13
Prokhladnyy *Russia* 43°50N 44°2E **191** J7
Prokletije *Albania* 42°30N 19°45E **202** D3
Prokopyevsk *Russia* 54°0N 86°45E **217** B11
Prokuplje *Serbia* 43°16N 21°36E **202** C5
Proletarsk *Russia* 46°42N 41°50E **191** G5
Proletarskaya = Proletarsk *Russia* 46°42N 41°50E **191** G5
Prome *Burma* 18°49N 95°13E **241** F5
Promise City *U.S.A.* 40°45N 93°9W **310** D3
Promzino = Surskoye *Russia* 54°30N 46°44E **190** C8
Prophet → *Canada* 58°48N 122°40W **296** B4
Prophet River *Canada* 58°6N 122°43W **296** B4
Prophetstown *U.S.A.* 41°40N 89°56W **310** C7
Propriá *Brazil* 10°13S 36°51W **332** D4
Propriano *France* 41°41N 8°52E **175** G12
Prosek *Czech Rep.* 50°7N 14°30E **135** B3
Proserpine *Australia* 20°21S 148°36E **280** b
Proskurov = Khmelnytskyy *Ukraine* 49°23N 27°0E **177** D14
Prosna → *Poland* 52°6N 17°44E **185** F4
Prospect *N.Y., U.S.A.* 43°18N 75°9W **313** C9
Prospect *Ohio, U.S.A.* 40°27N 83°11W **311** D13
Prospect Hill Park *U.S.A.* 42°23N 71°13W **116** A1
Prosperidad *Phil.* 8°34N 125°52E **233** G5
Prosperity *U.S.A.* 30°51N 85°56W **316** E4
Prosperous B. *St. Helena* 15°56S 5°39W **153** h
Prosser *U.S.A.* 46°12N 119°46W **304** C4
Prossnitz = Prostějov *Czech Rep.* 49°30N 17°9E **181** B10
Prostějov *Czech Rep.* 49°30N 17°9E **181** B10
Prostki *Poland* 53°42N 22°25E **184** E9
Proston *Australia* 26°8S 151°32E **281** D5
Proszowice *Poland* 50°13N 20°16E **185** H7
Proti *Greece* 37°5N 21°32E **204** D3
Provadiya *Bulgaria* 43°12N 27°30E **203** C11
Provence *France* 43°40N 5°46E **175** E9
Provence-Alpes-Côte d'Azur □ *France* 44°0N 6°15E **175** D10
Providence *Seychelles* 9°14S 51°2E **273** E4
Providence *Ky., U.S.A.* 37°24N 87°46W **308** G10
Providence *R.I., U.S.A.* 41°49N 71°24W **313** E13
Providence, C. *N.Z.* 45°59S 166°29E **285** F1
Providence Bay *Canada* 45°41N 82°15W **298** C3
Providence Mts. *U.S.A.* 35°10N 115°15W **307** K11
Providencia *Chile* 33°25S 70°36W **137** B2
Providencia, I. de *Colombia* 13°25N 81°26W **320** D3
Provideniya *Russia* 64°23N 173°18W **215** C19
Provincetown *U.S.A.* 42°3N 70°11W **309** D18
Provins *France* 48°33N 3°15E **173** D10
Provo *U.S.A.* 40°14N 111°39W **304** F8
Provost *Canada* 52°25N 110°20W **297** C6
Prozor *Bos.-H.* 43°50N 17°34E **182** G2
Prrenjas *Albania* 41°4N 20°32E **202** E4
Prudential Building *Chicago, U.S.A.* **119** c2
Prudentópolis *Brazil* 25°12S 50°57W **333** G1
Prudhoe Bay *U.S.A.* 70°18N 148°22W **303** A10
Prudhoe I. *Australia* 21°19S 149°41E **280** C4
Prud'homme *Canada* 52°20N 105°54W **297** C7
Prudnik *Poland* 50°20N 17°38E **185** H4
Průhonice *Czech Rep.* 50°0N 14°33E **135** C3
Prüm *Germany* 50°12N 6°25E **179** E2
Prundu *Romania* 44°6N 26°14E **183** F11
Pruszcz Gdański *Poland* 54°17N 18°40E **184** D5
Pruszków *Poland* 52°9N 20°49E **185** F7
Prut → *Romania* 45°28N 28°10E **183** E13
Pruzhany *Belarus* 52°33N 24°28E **177** B13
Prvič *Croatia* 44°55N 14°47E **199** D11
Prydz B. *Antarctica* 69°0S 74°0E **151** C6
Pryluky *Ukraine* 50°30N 32°24E **189** G7
Prymorske *Ukraine* 46°48N 36°20E **189** J9
Pryor *U.S.A.* 36°19N 95°19W **314** C7
Prypyat → *Europe* 51°20N 30°15E **177** C16
Przasnysz *Poland* 53°2N 20°54E **185** E7
Przedbórz *Poland* 51°6N 19°53E **185** G6
Przedecz *Poland* 52°20N 18°53E **185** F5
Przemków *Poland* 51°31N 15°48E **185** G2
Przemyśl *Poland* 49°50N 22°45E **185** J9
Przeworsk *Poland* 50°6N 22°32E **185** H9
Przewóz *Poland* 51°28N 14°57E **185** G1
Przhevalsk = Karakol *Kyrgyzstan* 42°30N 78°20E **217** D9
Przysucha *Poland* 51°22N 20°38E **185** G7
Psachna *Greece* 38°34N 23°35E **204** C5
Psara *Greece* 38°37N 25°38E **205** C7
Psathoura *Greece* 39°30N 24°12E **204** B6
Pserimos *Greece* 36°56N 27°8E **205** E9
Psichiko *Greece* 38°1N 23°46E **112** A2
Psiloritis, Oros *Greece* 35°15N 24°45E **207** E5
Psira *Greece* 35°12N 25°52E **207** E6
Pskov *Russia* 57°50N 28°25E **188** D5
Pskov □ *Russia* 57°20N 29°0E **188** D5
Pskovskoye, Ozero *Russia* 58°0N 27°58E **188** D5
Psol → *Ukraine* 49°10N 33°37E **189** H7
Psunj *Croatia* 45°25N 17°19E **182** E2
Pteleos *Greece* 39°3N 22°57E **204** B4
Ptich = Ptsich → *Belarus* 52°9N 28°52E **177** B15
Ptichia = Vidos *Greece* 39°38N 19°55E **206** B9
Ptolemaida *Greece* 40°30N 21°43E **202** F5
Ptsich → *Belarus* 52°9N 28°52E **177** B15
Ptuj *Slovenia* 46°28N 15°50E **199** B12
Ptujska Gora *Slovenia* 46°23N 15°47E **199** B12
Pu Xian *China* 36°24N 111°6E **226** F6
Pua *Thailand* 19°11N 100°55E **236** C3
Pua'ena Pt. *U.S.A.* 21°36N 158°6W **302** J13
Puán *Argentina* 37°30S 62°45W **334** D3
Pu'an *Guizhou, China* 25°46N 104°57E **228** E5
Pu'apu'a *Samoa* 13°34S 172°9W **287** V19
Pubei *China* 22°16N 109°31E **228** F7
Pucacuro → *Peru* 3°20S 74°58W **328** D3
Pucallpa *Peru* 8°25S 74°30W **330** B3
Pucará *Bolivia* 18°43S 64°11W **331** D5
Pucará *Cajamarca, Peru* 6°0S 79°7W **330** B2
Pucará *Puno, Peru* 15°5S 70°24W **330** D3
Pucarani *Bolivia* 16°23S 68°30W **330** D4
Pucheng *China* 27°59N 118°31E **229** D12
Pucheni *Romania* 45°12N 25°17E **183** E10
Puchheim *Germany* 48°9N 11°21E **179** G7
Puch'on = Bucheon *S. Korea* 37°28N 126°45E **224** D3
Púchov *Slovak Rep.* 49°8N 18°20E **181** B11
Pucio Pt. *Phil.* 11°46N 121°51E **233** F3
Pucioasa *Romania* 45°5N 25°25E **183** E10
Pučišća *Croatia* 43°22N 16°43E **199** E13
Puck *Poland* 54°45N 18°23E **184** D5
Pucka, Zatoka *Poland* 54°30N 18°40E **184** D5
Puçol *Spain* 39°37N 0°18W **197** F4
Pudasjärvi *Finland* 65°23N 26°53E **160** D22
Puding *China* 26°18N 105°44E **228** D5
Pudong New Area *China* 31°13N 121°30E **138** B2
Pudozh *Russia* 61°48N 36°32E **188** B9
Pudu = Suizhou *China* 31°42N 113°24E **229** B9
Puducherry *India* 11°59N 79°50E **245** J4
Pudukkottai *India* 10°28N 78°47E **245** J4
Pue *Cook Is.* 21°12S 159°45W **289** h
Puebla *Mexico* 19°3N 98°12W **319** D5
Puebla □ *Mexico* 18°50N 98°0W **319** D5
Puebla de Alcocer *Spain* 38°59N 5°14W **195** G5
Puebla de Don Fadrique *Spain* 37°58N 2°25W **197** H2
Puebla de Don Rodrigo *Spain* 39°5N 4°37W **195** F6
Puebla de Guzmán *Spain* 37°37N 7°15W **195** H3
Puebla de la Calzada *Spain* 38°54N 6°37W **195** G4
Puebla de Sanabria *Spain* 42°4N 6°38W **194** C4
Puebla de Trives = Pobra de Trives *Spain* 42°20N 7°10W **194** C3
Pueblo *U.S.A.* 38°16N 104°37W **304** G11
Pueblo Libre *Peru* 12°5S 77°4W **124** B2
Pueblo Nuevo *Barcelona, Spain* 41°23N 2°11E **114** A2
Pueblo Nuevo *Madrid, Spain* 40°25N 3°37W **127** B2
Puelches *Argentina* 38°5S 65°51W **334** D2
Puelén *Argentina* 37°32S 67°38W **334** D2
Puente Alto *Chile* 33°32S 70°35W **334** C1
Puente-Genil *Spain* 37°22N 4°47W **195** H6
Puente la Reina *Spain* 42°40N 1°49W **196** C3
Puente San Miguel *Spain* 43°21N 4°5W **194** B6
Puenteareas = Ponteareas *Spain* 42°10N 8°28W **194** C2
Puentedeume = Pontedeume *Spain* 43°24N 8°10W **194** B2
Puentes de Garcia Rodriguez = As Pontes de García Rodríguez *Spain* 43°27N 7°50W **194** B3
Pu'er *China* 23°0N 101°15E **228** F3
Puerca, Pta. *Puerto Rico* 18°13N 65°36W **321** b
Puerco → *U.S.A.* 34°22N 107°50W **305** J10
Puerta del Sol, Plaza *Madrid, Spain* **127** b2
Puerto Acosta *Bolivia* 15°32S 69°15W **330** D4
Puerto Aisén *Chile* 45°27S 73°0W **336** C2
Puerto Ángel *Mexico* 15°40N 96°29W **319** D5
Puerto Arista *Mexico* 15°56N 93°48W **319** D6
Puerto Armuelles *Panama* 8°20N 82°51W **320** E3
Puerto Asis *Colombia* 0°30N 76°30W **328** C2
Puerto Ayacucho *Venezuela* 5°40N 67°35W **328** B4
Puerto Ayora *Ecuador* 0°45S 90°19W **330** a
Puerto Baquerizo Moreno *Ecuador* 0°54S 89°36W **330** a
Puerto Barrios *Guatemala* 15°40N 88°32W **320** C2
Puerto Bermejo *Argentina* 26°55S 58°34W **334** B4
Puerto Bermúdez *Peru* 10°20S 74°58W **330** C3
Puerto Bolívar *Ecuador* 3°19S 79°55W **328** D2
Puerto Cabello *Venezuela* 10°28N 68°1W **328** A4
Puerto Cabezas *Nic.* 14°0N 83°30W **320** D3
Puerto Cabo Gracias á Dios *Nic.* 15°0N 83°10W **320** D3
Puerto Capaz = El Jebha *Morocco* 35°11N 4°43W **260** A4
Puerto Carreño *Colombia* 6°12N 67°22W **328** B4
Puerto Castilla *Honduras* 16°0N 86°0W **320** C2
Puerto Chicama *Peru* 7°45S 79°20W **330** B2
Puerto Cisnes *Chile* 44°45S 72°42W **336** B2
Puerto Coig *Argentina* 50°54S 69°15W **336** D3
Puerto Cortés *Honduras* 15°51N 88°0W **320** C2
Puerto Cumarebo *Venezuela* 11°29N 69°30W **328** A4
Puerto de Alcudia = Port d'Alcúdia *Spain* 39°50N 3°7E **206** B4
Puerto de Cabras = Puerto del Rosario *Canary Is.* 28°30N 13°52W **153** e2
Puerto de Cabrera *Spain* 39°8N 2°56E **206** B3
Puerto de Gran Tarajal *Canary Is.* 28°13N 14°1W **153** e2
Puerto de la Cruz *Canary Is.* 28°24N 16°32W **153** e1
Puerto de los Angeles ⌓ *Mexico* 23°39N 105°45W **318** C3
Puerto de Mazarrón *Spain* 37°34N 1°15W **197** H3
Puerto de Pozo Negro *Canary Is.* 28°19N 13°55W **153** e2
Puerto de Sóller = Port de Sóller *Spain* 39°48N 2°42E **206** B3
Puerto de Somosierra *Spain* 41°9N 3°35W **194** D7
Puerto del Carmen *Canary Is.* 28°55N 13°38W **153** e2
Puerto del Rosario *Canary Is.* 28°30N 13°52W **153** e2
Puerto Deseado *Argentina* 47°55S 66°0W **336** C3
Puerto Escondido *Mexico* 15°50N 97°3W **319** D5
Puerto Gaitán *Colombia* 4°19N 72°4W **328** C3
Puerto Galera *Phil.* 13°30N 120°57E **232** E3
Puerto Guaraní *Paraguay* 21°18S 57°55W **331** E6
Puerto Heath *Bolivia* 12°34S 68°39W **330** C4
Puerto Huitoto *Colombia* 0°18N 74°3W **328** C3
Puerto Inca *Peru* 9°22S 74°54W **330** B3
Puerto Inírida *Colombia* 3°53N 67°52W **328** C4
Puerto Juárez *Mexico* 21°11N 86°49W **319** C7
Puerto La Cruz *Venezuela* 10°13N 64°38W **329** A5
Puerto Leguízamo *Colombia* 0°12S 74°46W **328** D3
Puerto Lempira *Honduras* 15°16N 83°46W **320** C3
Puerto Libertad *Mexico* 29°55N 112°43W **318** B2
Puerto Limón *Colombia* 3°23N 73°30W **328** C3
Puerto Lobos *Argentina* 42°0S 65°3W **336** B3
Puerto López *Colombia* 4°5N 72°58W **328** C3
Puerto Lumbreras *Spain* 37°34N 1°48W **197** H3
Puerto Madero *Argentina* 34°37S 58°21W **117** B2
Puerto Madryn *Argentina* 42°48S 65°4W **336** B3
Puerto Maldonado *Peru* 12°30S 69°10W **330** C4
Puerto Manatí *Cuba* 21°22N 76°50W **320** B4
Puerto Mariti *Colombia* 1°10S 69°59W **328** D4
Puerto Mercedes *Colombia* 1°11N 72°53W **328** C3
Puerto Mexico = Coatzacoalcos *Mexico* 18°7N 94°25W **319** D6
Puerto Miraña *Colombia* 1°20S 70°19W **328** D3
Puerto Montt *Chile* 41°28S 73°0W **336** B2
Puerto Morazán *Nic.* 12°51N 87°11W **320** D2
Puerto Morelos *Mexico* 20°50N 86°52W **319** C7
Puerto Nariño *Colombia* 4°56N 67°48W **328** C4
Puerto Natales *Chile* 51°45S 72°15W **336** D2
Puerto Nuevo *Colombia* 5°53N 69°56W **328** B4
Puerto Ordaz *Venezuela* 8°16N 62°44W **329** B5
Puerto Oscuro *Chile* 31°24S 71°35W **334** C1
Puerto Padre *Cuba* 21°13N 76°35W **320** B4
Puerto Páez *Venezuela* 6°13N 67°28W **328** B4
Puerto Peñasco *Mexico* 31°20N 113°33W **318** A2
Puerto Pinasco *Paraguay* 22°36S 57°50W **334** A4
Puerto Pirámides *Argentina* 42°35S 64°20W **336** B4
Puerto Piritu *Venezuela* 10°4N 65°3W **329** A4
Puerto Plata *Dom. Rep.* 19°48N 70°45W **321** C5
Puerto Pollensa = Port de Pollença *Spain* 39°54N 3°4E **206** B4
Puerto Portillo *Peru* 9°45S 72°42W **330** B3
Puerto Princesa *Phil.* 9°46N 118°45E **233** G2
Puerto Princesa Subterranean River △ *Phil.* 10°10N 118°55E **233** F2
Puerto Quepos *Costa Rica* 9°29N 84°6W **320** E3
Puerto Real *Spain* 36°33N 6°12W **195** J4
Puerto Rico *Bolivia* 11°5S 67°38W **330** C4
Puerto Rico *Canary Is.* 27°47N 15°42W **153** e1
Puerto Rico ☑ *W. Indies* 18°15N 66°45W **321** C6
Puerto Rico Trench *Atl. Oc.* 19°50N 66°0W **321** C6
Puerto Rondón *Colombia* 6°17N 71°6W **328** B3
Puerto Saavedra *Chile* 38°47S 73°24W **336** A2
Puerto San Julián *Argentina* 49°15S 67°45W **336** C3
Puerto Santa Cruz *Argentina* 50°0S 68°32W **336** D3
Puerto Sastre *Paraguay* 22°2S 57°55W **334** A4
Puerto Serrano *Spain* 36°56N 5°33W **195** J5
Puerto Siles *Bolivia* 12°48S 65°5W **331** C4
Puerto Suárez *Bolivia* 18°58S 57°52W **331** D6
Puerto Supe *Peru* 11°0S 77°30W **330** C2
Puerto Tejada *Colombia* 3°14N 76°24W **328** C2
Puerto Umbría *Colombia* 0°52N 76°33W **328** C2
Puerto Vallarta *Mexico* 20°37N 105°15W **318** C3
Puerto Varas *Chile* 41°19S 72°59W **336** B2
Puerto Velasco Ibarra *Ecuador* 1°17S 90°29W **330** a
Puerto Villamil *Ecuador* 0°56S 91°1W **330** a
Puerto Villazón *Bolivia* 13°32S 61°57W **331** C5
Puerto Wilches *Colombia* 7°21N 73°54W **328** B3
Puerto Williams *Chile* 54°56S 67°37W **336** D3
Puertollano *Spain* 38°43N 4°7W **195** G6
Puesto Cunambo *Peru* 2°10S 76°0W **328** D2
Pueu *Tahiti* 17°44S 149°13W **289** e
Pueyrredón, L. *Argentina* 47°20S 72°0W **336** C2
Púez Odle ⌓ *Italy* 46°37N 11°48E **199** B8
Puffin I. *Ireland* 51°50N 10°24W **166** E1
Pugachev *Russia* 52°0N 48°49E **190** D9
Pugal *India* 28°30N 72°48E **242** E5
Puge *Sichuan, China* 27°20N 102°31E **228** D4
Puge *Tanzania* 4°45S 33°11E **268** C3
Puget Sound *U.S.A.* 47°50N 122°30W **304** C2
Puget-Théniers *France* 43°58N 6°53E **175** E10
Púglia □ *Italy* 41°15N 16°15E **201** A9
Pugŏdong *N. Korea* 42°5N 130°0E **224** A5
Pugu *Tanzania* 6°55S 39°4E **268** D4
Pūgūnzī *Iran* 25°49N 59°10E **247** E8
Puha *N.Z.* 38°30S 177°50E **284** E6
Puhuangyu *China* 39°50N 116°22E **114** B2
Pui *Romania* 45°30N 23°4E **182** E8
Puica *Peru* 15°0S 72°33W **330** D3
Puieşti *Romania* 46°25N 27°33E **183** D12
Puig Major *Spain* 39°48N 2°47E **206** B3
Puigcerdà *Spain* 42°24N 1°50E **196** C6
Puigmal *Spain* 42°23N 2°7E **196** C7
Puigpunyent *Spain* 39°38N 2°32E **206** B3
Puijiang *China* 30°14N 103°30E **228** B4
Puisaye, Collines de la *France* 47°37N 3°20E **173** E10
Puiseaux *France* 48°11N 2°30E **173** D9
Puistola *Finland* 60°16N 25°2E **121** B3
Pujehun *S. Leone* 7°23N 11°45W **262** D2
Pujiang *China* 29°29N 119°54E **229** C12
Pujilí *Ecuador* 0°57S 78°41W **328** D2
Pujols *France* 44°48N 0°2W **174** D3
Pujon *Indonesia* 1°19S 114°19E **235** C4
Pujon-ho *N. Korea* 40°35N 127°35E **224** B3
Puka Puka *French Polynesia* 14°49S 138°48W **289** f
Puka Ruha *French Polynesia* 18°20S 137°2W **289** f
Pukaki, L. *N.Z.* 44°4S 170°1E **285** E5
Pukalani *U.S.A.* 20°51N 156°20W **302** C5
Pukapuka *Cook Is.* 10°53S 165°49W **289** J11
Pukaskwa △ *Canada* 48°20N 86°0W **298** C2
Pukatawagan *Canada* 55°45N 101°20W **297** B8
Pukchin *N. Korea* 40°12N 125°45E **224** B2
Pukch'ŏng *N. Korea* 40°14N 128°10E **224** B4
Pukë *Albania* 42°2N 19°53E **202** D3
Pukearuhe *N.Z.* 38°55S 174°31E **284** E3
Pukekohe *N.Z.* 37°12S 174°55E **284** D3
Puketeraki Ra. *N.Z.* 42°58S 172°13E **285** C7
Puketoi Ra. *N.Z.* 40°30S 176°5E **284** G5
Pukeuri *N.Z.* 45°4S 171°2E **285** F6
Pukhrayan *India* 26°14N 79°51E **243** F8
Pukinmäki *Finland* 60°15N 24°57E **121** B2
Puksubaek-san *N. Korea* 40°42N 127°45E **224** B3
Pula *Croatia* 44°54N 13°57E **199** D10
Pula *Italy* 39°1N 9°0E **200** C1
Pulacayo *Bolivia* 20°25S 66°41W **330** E4
Pulandian *China* 39°25N 121°58E **227** E11
Pulanduta Pt. *Phil.* 11°54N 123°9E **233** F4
Pulangpisau *Indonesia* 2°46S 114°13E **235** C4
Pulaski *N.Y., U.S.A.* 43°34N 76°8W **313** C8
Pulaski *Tenn., U.S.A.* 35°12N 87°2W **315** D11
Pulaski *Va., U.S.A.* 37°3N 80°47W **309** G13
Pulau → *Indonesia* 5°50S 138°15E **231** F9
Pulau Gili *Indonesia* 8°21S 116°1E **231** J19
Pulau Miangas *Indonesia* 5°35N 126°34E **233** J6
Puławy *Poland* 51°23N 21°59E **185** G8
Pulga *U.S.A.* 39°48N 121°29W **306** F5
Pulgaon *India* 20°44N 78°21E **244** D4
Puli *Taiwan* 23°58N 120°57E **225** C2
Pulicat *India* 13°25N 80°19E **245** H5
Pulicat L. *India* 13°40N 80°15E **245** H5
Pulivendla *India* 14°25N 78°14E **245** G4
Puliyangudi *India* 9°11N 77°24E **245** K3
Pulkovo Int. ✈ (LED) *Russia* 59°48N 30°18E **137** C1
Pullach *Germany* 48°3N 11°31E **131** B1
Pullman *U.S.A.* 46°44N 117°10W **304** C5
Pullman Historic District *U.S.A.* 41°41N 87°36W **119** C3
Pulo Gadung *Indonesia* 6°11S 106°54E **122** B2
Pulog, Mt. *Phil.* 16°40N 120°50E **232** C3
Pułtusk *Poland* 52°43N 21°6E **185** F8
Pülümür *Turkey* 39°30N 39°51E **213** C8
Pumlumon Fawr *U.K.* 52°28N 3°46W **169** E4
Puna *Bolivia* 19°45S 65°28W **331** D4
Puná, I. *Ecuador* 2°55S 80°5W **328** D1
Punaauia *Tahiti* 17°37S 149°34W **289** e
Pūnak *Iran* 35°46N 51°20E **141** A2
Punakha Dzong *Bhutan* 27°42N 89°52E **241** B2
Punalur *India* 9°0N 76°56E **245** K3
Punalu'u *U.S.A.* 21°35N 157°53W **302** J14
Punasar *India* 27°6N 73°6E **242** F5
Punata *Bolivia* 17°32S 65°50W **331** D4
Punch *India* 33°48N 74°4E **243** C6
Punch → *Pakistan* 33°12N 73°40E **242** C5
Punchbowl *Australia* 33°55S 151°3E **139** B1
Punda *Curaçao* 12°6N 68°55W **322** g
Punda Maria *S. Africa* 22°40S 31°5E **271** B5
Punde *India* 18°53N 72°57E **130** B2
Pune *India* 18°29N 73°57E **244** E1
Punggol *Singapore* 1°23N 103°54E **138** A3
Punggol, Sungei → *Singapore* 1°24N 103°54E **138** A3
Punggol Pt. *Singapore* 1°24N 103°54E **138** A3
Pungo Andongo *Angola* 9°44S 15°35E **265** D3
P'ungsan *N. Korea* 40°50N 128°9E **224** B4
Pungsan *S. Korea* 36°34N 128°34E **224** D4
Pungue, Ponte de *Mozam.* 19°0S 34°0E **269** F3
Puning *China* 23°20N 116°12E **229** F11
Punjab □ *India* 31°0N 76°0E **242** D7
Punjab □ *Pakistan* 32°0N 72°30E **242** E6
Punjabi Bagh *India* 28°40N 77°6E **120** A1
Puno *Peru* 15°55S 70°3W **330** D3
Puno □ *Peru* 15°0S 70°0W **330** C3
Punpun → *India* 25°31N 85°18E **243** G11
Punta, Cerro de *Puerto Rico* 18°10N 66°37W **321** b
Punta Alta *Argentina* 38°53S 62°4W **336** A4
Punta Arenas *Chile* 53°10S 71°0W **336** D2
Punta Cardón *Venezuela* 11°38N 70°14W **328** A3
Punta Coles *Peru* 17°43S 71°23W **330** D3
Punta de Bombón *Peru* 17°10S 71°48W **330** D3
Punta del Díaz *Chile* 28°0S 70°45W **334** B1
Punta del Hidalgo *Canary Is.* 28°33N 16°19W **153** e1
Punta Delgado *Argentina* 42°43S 63°38W **336** B4
Punta Gorda *Belize* 16°10N 88°45W **320** C2
Punta Gorda *Fla., U.S.A.* 26°56N 82°3W **317** J7
Punta Prieta *Mexico* 28°58N 114°17W **318** B2
Punta Prima *Spain* 39°48N 4°16E **206** B5
Punta Umbría *Spain* 37°10N 6°56W **195** H4
Puntarenas *Costa Rica* 10°0N 84°50W **320** E3
Puntland *Somali Rep.* 8°0N 49°0E **267** C6
Punto Fijo *Venezuela* 11°50N 70°13W **328** A3
Punxsutawney *U.S.A.* 40°57N 78°59W **312** F6
Punyu = Guangzhou *China* 23°6N 113°13E **121** B2
Puotila *Finland* 60°13N 25°6E **121** B3
Pupuan *Indonesia* 8°19S 115°0E **231** J18
Pūpūkea *U.S.A.* 21°40N 158°3W **302** J13
Puqi *China* 29°40N 113°50E **229** C9
Puquio *Peru* 14°45S 74°10W **330** C3
Pur → *Russia* 67°31N 77°55E **214** C8
Puracé, Vol. *Colombia* 2°21N 76°23W **328** C2
Puracé △ *Colombia* 2°10N 76°21W **328** C2
Puračić *Bos.-H.* 44°33N 18°28E **182** F3
Puralia = Puruliya *India* 23°17N 86°24E **243** H12
Purana Qila *Delhi, India* **120** c3
Puranpur *India* 28°31N 80°9E **243** E9
Purari → *Papua N. G.* 7°49S 145°0E **286** D3
Purbalingga *Indonesia* 7°23S 109°21E **235** D3
Purbeck, Isle of *U.K.* 50°39N 1°59W **169** G5
Purcell *U.S.A.* 35°1N 97°22W **314** D6
Purcell Mts. *Canada* 49°55N 116°15W **296** D5
Purdy *Canada* 45°19N 77°44W **312** A7
Puri *India* 19°50N 85°58E **244** E7
Purificación *Colombia* 3°51N 74°55W **328** C3
Purmerend *Neths.* 52°32N 4°58E **170** B4
Purna → *India* 19°6N 77°2E **244** E3
Purnia *India* 25°45N 87°31E **243** G12
Purnululu △ *Australia* 17°20S 128°20E **278** C4
Pursat = Pouthisat *Cambodia* 12°34N 103°50E **236** F4
Purukcahu *Indonesia* 0°35S 114°35E **235** C4
Puruliya *India* 23°17N 86°24E **243** H12
Purus → *Brazil* 3°42S 61°28W **329** D5
Purutu I. *Papua N. G.* 8°24S 143°27E **286** E2
Puruvesi *Finland* 61°50N 29°30E **188** B5
Purvis *U.S.A.* 31°9N 89°25W **315** F10
Pŭrvomay *Bulgaria* 42°8N 25°17E **203** D9
Purwa *India* 26°28N 80°47E **243** F9
Purwakarta *Indonesia* 6°35S 107°29E **235** D3
Purwo, Tanjung *Indonesia* 8°44S 114°21E **231** K18
Purwodadi *Indonesia* 7°7S 110°55E **235** D4
Purwokerto *Indonesia* 7°25S 109°14E **235** D3
Purworejo *Indonesia* 7°43S 110°2E **235** D4
Puryŏng *N. Korea* 42°5N 129°43E **224** A4
Pus → *India* 19°55N 77°55E **244** E3

Pusa India 25°59N 85°41E 243 G11
Pusad India 19°56N 77°36E 244 E3
Pusan = Busan S. Korea 35°5N 129°0E 224 E4
Pushkin Russia 59°45N 30°25E 188 C6
Pushkino Moskva, Russia 56°2N 37°49E 188 D9
Pushkino Saratov, Russia 51°16N 47°0E 190 E8
Püspökladány Hungary 47°19N 21°6E 182 C6
Pustoshka Russia 56°20N 29°30E 188 D5
Puszczykowo Poland 52°18N 16°49E 185 F3
Put-in-Bay U.S.A. 41°39N 82°49W 312 E2
Putahow L. Canada 59°54N 100°40W 297 B8
Putai Taiwan 23°23N 120°9E 225 C2
Putao Burma 27°28N 97°30E 241 B6
Putaruru N.Z. 38°2S 175°50E 284 E4
Putatan Malaysia 5°53N 116°3E 235 A5
Putbus Germany 54°22N 13°28E 178 A9
Puteaux France 48°53N 2°14E 134 A2
Puteran Indonesia 7°5S 114°0E 235 D4
Putian China 25°23N 119°0E 229 E12
Putignano Italy 40°51N 17°7E 201 B10
Putilkovo Russia 55°51N 37°22E 129 A2
Putina Peru 14°55S 69°55W 330 C4
Puting, Tanjung Indonesia 3°31S 111°46E 235 C4
Putlitz Germany 53°15N 12°2E 178 B8
Putna Romania 47°50N 25°33E 183 C10
Putna → Romania 45°42N 27°26E 183 E12
Putnam U.S.A. 41°55N 71°55W 313 E13
Putney London, U.K. 51°27N 0°13W 125 B2
Putney Ga., U.S.A. 31°29N 84°8W 316 D5
Putnok Hungary 48°18N 20°26E 182 B5
Putorana, Gory Russia 69°0N 95°0E 215 C10
Putorino N.Z. 39°4S 176°58E 284 F5
Putrajaya Malaysia 2°55N 101°40E 237 L3
Putre Chile 18°12S 69°35W 330 D4
Puttalam Sri Lanka 8°1N 79°55E 245 K5
Puttalam Lagoon Sri Lanka 8°15N 79°45E 245 K4
Puttegga Norway 62°13N 7°42E 164 B4
Puttgarden Germany 54°30N 11°10E 178 A7
Püttlingen Germany 49°17N 6°53E 179 F2
Puttur Andhra Pradesh, India 13°27N 79°33E 245 H4
Puttur Karnataka, India 12°46N 75°12E 245 H2
Putty Australia 32°57S 150°42E 283 B9
Putumayo → S. Amer. 3°7S 67°58W 328 D4
Putuo Shanghai, China 31°15N 121°24E 138 B1
Putuo Zhejiang, China 29°56N 122°20E 229 C14
Putussibau Indonesia 0°50N 112°56E 235 B4
Pututahi N.Z. 38°39S 177°53E 284 E6
Putxet Spain 41°24N 2°8E 114 A1
Putyla Ukraine 48°0N 25°5E 183 B10
Pu'uanahulu U.S.A. 19°49N 155°51W 302 D6
Pu'uhonua o Hōnaunau ⌓ U.S.A. 19°25N 155°54W 302 D6
Pu'uka'aumakua U.S.A. 21°30N 157°54W 302 J14
Pu'ukeahiakahoe U.S.A. 21°23N 157°49W 302 K14
Pu'ukoholā Heiau ⌓ U.S.A. 20°1N 155°49W 302 C6
P'u'ula'ula U.S.A. 20°42N 156°15W 302 C5
Pu'u'oke'oke'o U.S.A. 19°13N 155°44W 302 D6
Pu'uwai U.S.A. 21°54N 160°12W 302 B1
Puvirnituq Canada 60°2N 77°10W 295 E16
Puxi China 31°12N 121°30E 138 B1
Puy-de-Dôme France 45°46N 2°57E 174 C6
Puy-de-Dôme □ France 45°40N 3°5E 174 C7
Puy-l'Évêque France 44°31N 1°9E 174 D5
Puyallup U.S.A. 47°12N 122°18W 306 C4
Puyang China 35°40N 115°1E 226 G8
Puyehue Chile 40°40S 72°37W 336 B2
Puyehue △ Chile 40°27S 72°6W 336 B2
Puylaurens France 43°35N 2°0E 174 E6
Puyo Ecuador 1°28S 77°59W 328 D2
Puysegur Pt. N.Z. 46°9S 166°37E 285 G1
Pūzeh Rīg Iran 27°20N 58°40E 247 E8
Puzhaykove Ukraine 48°7N 29°50E 183 B14
Pwani □ Tanzania 7°0S 39°0E 268 D4
Pweto Dem. Rep. of the Congo 8°25S 28°51E 269 D2
Pwinbyu Burma 20°23N 94°40E 241 E5
Pwllheli U.K. 52°53N 4°25W 168 E3
Pyana → Russia 55°43N 46°1E 190 C8
Pyandzh = Dusti Tajikistan 37°20N 68°40E 217 E7
Pyandzh → Asia 37°6N 68°20E 240 A2
Pyaozero, Ozero Russia 66°5N 30°58E 160 C24
Pyapon Burma 16°20N 95°40E 241 G5
Pyasina → Russia 73°30N 87°0E 215 B9
Pyatigorsk Russia 44°2N 43°6E 191 H6
Pyatykhatky Ukraine 48°28N 33°38E 189 H7
Pyawbwe Burma 20°35N 96°4E 241 E6
Pyaye Burma 19°12N 95°10E 241 F5
Pydhuni Mumbai, India 130 b2
Pydna Greece 40°20N 22°34E 202 F6
Pyè = Prome Burma 18°49N 95°13E 241 F5
Pyeonghae S. Korea 36°43N 129°26E 224 D4
Pyeongtaek S. Korea 37°1N 127°4E 224 D3
Pyetrikaw Belarus 52°11N 28°29E 177 B15
Pyhäjoki Finland 64°28N 24°14E 160 D21
Pyinbauk Burma 19°10N 95°12E 241 F5
Pyingaing Burma 23°9N 94°50E 241 D5
Pyinkayaing Burma 15°58N 94°24E 241 H5
Pyinmana Burma 19°45N 96°12E 241 F6
Pyinyaung Burma 20°49N 96°25E 241 E6
Pyla Cyprus 35°1N 33°41E 250 C4
Pyla, C. Cyprus 34°56N 33°51E 207 F9
Pymatuning Res. U.S.A. 41°30N 80°28W 312 E4
Pyŏktong N. Korea 40°50N 125°50E 224 B2
P'yŏnganbuk-do □ N. Korea 40°0N 125°15E 224 C2
P'yŏngannam-do □ N. Korea 39°30N 126°24E 224 C3
Pyŏnggang N. Korea 38°24N 127°17E 224 C3
P'yŏngsong N. Korea 39°14N 125°52E 224 C2
P'yŏngyang N. Korea 39°0N 125°30E 224 C2
P'yŏngyang □ N. Korea 39°4N 125°50E 224 C2
Pyote U.S.A. 31°32N 103°8W 314 F3
Pyramid L. U.S.A. 40°1N 119°35W 304 F4
Pyramid Pk. U.S.A. 36°25N 116°37W 307 J10
Pyramid Pt. Ascension I. 7°55S 14°24W 153 g
Pyramids Egypt 29°58N 31°9E 117 B1
Pyrénées Europe 42°45N 0°18E 174 F4
Pyrénées △ France 42°52N 0°10W 174 F3
Pyrénées-Atlantiques □ France 43°10N 0°50W 174 E3
Pyrénées-Orientales □ France 42°35N 2°26E 174 F6
Pyry Poland 52°8N 21°0E 142 C1
Pyryatyn Ukraine 50°15N 32°25E 189 G7
Pyrzyce Poland 53°10N 14°55E 185 E1
Pyskowice Poland 50°24N 18°38E 185 H5
Pytalovo Russia 57°5N 27°55E 188 D4
Pyttegga = Puttegga Norway 62°13N 7°42E 164 B4
Pyu Burma 18°30N 96°28E 241 F6
Pyzdry Poland 52°11N 17°42E 185 F4

Q

Qaanaaq Greenland 77°30N 69°10W 154 B4
Qabanbay Kazakhstan 45°50N 80°37E 217 C10
Qabirri → Azerbaijan 41°3N 46°17E 191 K8
Qabr Hūd Yemen 16°9N 49°34E 249 C5
Qachasnek S. Africa 30°6S 28°42E 271 D4
Qādisiyah, Buhayrat al Iraq 34°20N 42°12E 213 E10
Qādub Yemen 12°37N 53°57E 249 D6
Qa'el Jafr Jordan 30°20N 36°25E 251 H7
Qa'emābād Iran 31°44N 60°2E 247 D9
Qā'emshahr Iran 36°30N 52°53E 247 B7
Qagan Nur Jilin, China 45°15N 124°18E 227 B13
Qagan Nur Nei Monggol Zizhiqu, China 43°30N 114°55E 226 C8
Qahar Youyi Zhongqi China 41°12N 112°40E 226 D7
Qahremānshahr = Kermānshāh Iran 34°23N 47°0E 213 E12
Qaidam Pendi China 37°0N 95°0E 218 D8
Qaiyara Iraq 35°48N 43°17E 213 E10
Qajarīyeh Iran 31°1N 48°22E 247 D6
Qala Malta 36°2N 14°19E 206 E7
Qala, Ras il Malta 36°2N 14°20E 206 E7
Qala-i-Jadid = Spīn Būldak Afghan. 31°1N 66°25E 242 D2
Qala Point = Qala, Ras il Malta 36°2N 14°20E 206 E7
Qala Viala Pakistan 30°49N 67°17E 242 D2
Qala Yangi Afghan. 34°20N 66°30E 242 B2
Qalācheh Afghan. 35°30N 67°43E 240 B2
Qalaikhum = Kalaikhum Tajikistan 38°28N 70°46E 217 E8
Qalandiya West Bank 31°52N 35°12E 123 A2
Qalansīyah Yemen 12°41N 53°29E 249 D6
Qal'at al Akhḑar Si. Arabia 28°4N 37°9E 251 K8
Qal'at Bīshah Si. Arabia 20°0N 42°36E 248 C3
Qal'at Dīzah Iraq 36°11N 45°7E 213 D11
Qalāt-i-Ghilzai Afghan. 32°15N 66°58E 240 B2
Qal'at Şāliḩ Iraq 31°31N 47°16E 246 D5
Qal'at Sukkar Iraq 31°51N 46°5E 213 G12
Qal'eh Morghī Iran 35°38N 51°22E 141 B2
Qal'eh-ye Bost Afghan. 31°30N 64°21E 240 C2
Qal'eh-ye Now Afghan. 35°0N 63°5E 240 B1
Qal'eh-ye Panjeh Afghan. 37°0N 72°35E 240 A4
Qal'eh-ye Sarkari Afghan. 35°54N 67°17E 240 B2
Qal'eh-ye Valī Afghan. 35°46N 63°45E 240 B1
Qalyûb Egypt 30°12N 31°11E 251 H2
Qalyûbîya □ Egypt 30°18N 31°18E 251 H2
Qamani'tuaq = Baker Lake Canada 64°20N 96°3W 294 E12
Qamar, Ghubbat al Yemen 16°20N 52°30E 249 C6
Qamar, Jabal al Oman 16°48N 53°15E 249 C6
Qamdo China 31°15N 97°6E 228 B1
Qamea Fiji 16°45S 179°45W 287 A3
Qamīnis Libya 31°40N 20°1E 258 B4
Qammieh Point Malta 35°58N 14°19E 206 F7
Qamruddin Karez Pakistan 31°45N 68°20E 242 D3
Qanâ el Ismâ'ilîya Egypt 30°7N 31°17E 117 A2
Qandahār = Kandahār Afghan. 31°32N 65°43E 240 C2
Qandahār = Kandahār □ Afghan. 31°0N 65°0E 240 C2
Qandala Somali Rep. 11°30N 49°58E 267 B6
Qandyaghash Kazakhstan 49°28N 57°25E 187 E10
Qapān Iran 37°40N 55°47E 247 B7
Qapqal China 43°48N 81°5E 217 D10
Qapshaghay Kazakhstan 43°51N 77°14E 217 D9
Qapshaghay Bögeni Kazakhstan 43°45N 77°50E 217 D9
Qaqortoq Greenland 60°43N 46°0W 154 E6
Qâra Egypt 29°38N 26°30E 256 B2
Qarā', Jabal al Oman 17°15N 54°15E 249 C6
Qara Dāgh Iraq 35°18N 45°18E 213 E11
Qara Qash → China 35°0N 78°30E 243 B8
Qarabalyq Kazakhstan 53°45N 62°2E 216 B6
Qarabutaq Kazakhstan 50°0N 60°14E 216 C6
Qaraçala Azerbaijan 39°45N 48°53E 191 L9
Qaraghandy Kazakhstan 49°50N 73°10E 217 C8
Qaraghayly Kazakhstan 49°26N 76°0E 214 E8
Qārah Si. Arabia 29°55N 40°3E 246 D4
Qarah Āghāj Iran 37°8N 46°58E 213 D12
Qarakol Uzbekistan 39°32N 63°50E 216 E6
Qaraoba Kazakhstan 47°6N 56°15E 216 C5
Qaraqīya Oyysy Kazakhstan 43°27N 51°45E 216 D4
Qaraqosh Iraq 36°16N 43°22E 213 D10
Qarataū Ongtüstik Qazaqstan, Kazakhstan 43°30N 69°30E 217 D7
Qarataū Zhambyl, Kazakhstan 43°10N 70°28E 217 D8
Qarāvol Afghan. 37°14N 68°46E 240 A3
Qarazhal Kazakhstan 48°2N 70°49E 214 E8
Qardho Somali Rep. 9°30N 49°6E 267 C6
Qardud Sudan 10°20N 29°56E 257 E2
Qareh → Iran 39°25N 47°22E 213 C12
Qareh Tekān Iran 36°38N 49°29E 247 B6
Qarnein U.A.E. 24°56N 52°52E 247 E7
Qarqan He → China 39°30N 88°30E 217 E11
Qarqaraly Kazakhstan 49°26N 75°30E 217 C9
Qarqin Afghan. 37°24N 66°4E 240 A2
Qarrasa Sudan 14°38N 32°5E 257 E3
Qarshi Uzbekistan 38°53N 65°48E 217 E7
Qartabā Lebanon 34°4N 35°50E 250 D6
Qārūh Kuwait 28°49N 48°46E 247 D6
Qaryat al Gharab Iraq 31°27N 44°48E 246 D5
Qaryat al 'Ulyā Si. Arabia 27°33N 47°42E 246 E5
Qarynzharyq Oyysy Kazakhstan 42°55N 54°25E 216 D4
Qaşbah, Râs al Si. Arabia 28°2N 34°38E 251 K5
Qāsemābād Iran 35°46N 51°30E 141 A3
Qashqadaryo □ Uzbekistan 38°35N 66°0E 217 E7
Qasigiannguit Greenland 68°50N 51°18W 154 D5
Qasr 'Amra Jordan 31°48N 36°35E 246 D3
Qaşr Bū Hadi Libya 31°1N 16°45E 258 B3
Qasr-e Fīrūzeh Iran 35°29N 51°31E 141 B3
Qaşr-e Qand Iran 26°15N 60°45E 247 E9
Qaşr-e Shīrīn Iran 34°31N 45°35E 213 E11
Qasr Farâfra Egypt 27°0N 28°1E 256 B2
Qaşr Larocu Libya 26°32N 13°19E 258 C2
Qasuittuq = Resolute Canada 74°42N 94°54W 295 C13
Qa'ţabah Yemen 13°51N 44°42E 248 D4
Qatanā Syria 33°26N 36°4E 250 E7
Qaţānan, Ra's Yemen 12°21N 53°33E 249 D6
Qatane West Bank 31°50N 35°6E 123 B1
Qatar ■ Asia 25°30N 51°15E 247 E6
Qatlīsh Iran 37°50N 57°19E 247 B8
Qattâra Egypt 30°12N 27°3E 256 A2
Qattâra, Munkhafed el Egypt 29°30N 27°30E 256 B2
Qattâra Depression = Qattâra, Munkhafed el Egypt 29°30N 27°30E 256 B2
Qawām al Ḩamzah = Al Ḩamzah Iraq 31°43N 44°58E 246 D5
Qawra Point Malta 35°58N 14°26E 206 F7
Qāyen Iran 33°40N 59°10E 247 C8
Qaynar Kazakhstan 49°12N 77°22E 217 C9
Qazaly Kazakhstan 45°45N 62°6E 216 C6
Qazaqstan = Kazakhstan ■ Asia 50°0N 70°0E 217 C8
Qazaqtyng Usaqshogylyghy Kazakhstan 50°0N 72°0E 217 C8
Qazax Azerbaijan 41°5N 45°21E 191 K7
Qazımämmäd Azerbaijan 40°3N 49°0E 191 K9
Qazvīn Iran 36°15N 50°0E 247 B6
Qazvīn □ Iran 36°20N 50°0E 247 B6
Qazyghurt Kazakhstan 41°45N 69°23E 217 D7
Qeisari = Caesarea Israel 32°30N 34°53E 251 F5
Qeissan Sudan 11°4N 34°40E 257 E3
Qena Egypt 26°10N 32°43E 256 B3
Qena, W. → Egypt 26°12N 32°44E 256 B3
Qeqertarsuaq Greenland 69°45N 53°30W 154 D5
Qeqertarsuaq Greenland 69°15N 53°38W 154 D5
Qeqertarsuatsiaat Greenland 63°5N 50°45W 154 E5
Qeshlāq Iran 34°55N 46°28E 213 E12
Qeshm Iran 26°55N 56°10E 247 E8
Qeydār Iran 36°6N 48°35E 213 D13
Qeys Iran 26°32N 53°58E 249 A6
Qezel Owzen → Iran 36°45N 49°22E 247 B6
Qezi'ot Israel 30°52N 34°26E 251 H5
Qi Xian China 34°40N 114°48E 226 G8
Qian Gorlos China 45°5N 124°42E 227 B13
Qian Hai China 22°32N 113°54E 219 a
Qian Xian China 34°31N 108°15E 226 G5
Qian'an China 40°0N 118°41E 227 E10
Qiancheng China 27°12N 109°50E 228 D7
Qianjiang Guangxi Zhuangzu, China 23°38N 108°58E 228 F7
Qianjiang Hubei, China 30°24N 112°55E 229 B9
Qianjiang Sichuan, China 29°33N 108°47E 228 C7
Qianjin China 47°34N 133°4E 219 B15
Qianmen China 39°51N 116°21E 114 B2
Qianshan Anhui, China 30°37N 116°35E 229 B11
Qianshan Guangdong, China 22°15N 113°31E 219 a
Qianwei China 29°13N 103°56E 228 C4
Qianxi China 27°3N 106°3E 228 D6
Qianyang Hunan, China 27°18N 110°10E 229 D8
Qianyang Shaanxi, China 34°40N 107°8E 226 G4
Qianyang Zhejiang, China 30°11N 119°25E 229 B12
Qi'ao China 22°25N 113°39E 219 a
Qi'ao Dao China 22°25N 113°38E 219 a
Qiaocun China 39°56N 112°55E 226 E7
Qiaojia China 26°56N 102°58E 228 D4
Qichun China 30°18N 115°25E 229 B10
Qidong Hunan, China 26°49N 112°7E 229 D9
Qidong Jiangsu, China 31°48N 121°38E 229 B13
Qiemo China 38°8N 85°32E 217 E11
Qijiang China 28°57N 106°35E 228 C6
Qijiaojing China 43°28N 91°36E 217 D12
Qikiqtarjuaq Canada 67°33N 63°0W 295 D19
Qila Saifullāh Pakistan 30°45N 68°17E 242 D3
Qilian Shan China 38°30N 96°0E 218 D8
Qimen China 29°50N 117°42E 229 C11
Qin He → China 35°1N 113°22E 226 G7
Qin Jiang → Guangxi Zhuangzu, China 21°53N 108°35E 228 F7
Qin Jiang → Jiangxi, China 26°15N 115°55E 229 D10
Qin Ling = Qinling Shandi China 33°50N 108°10E 226 H5
Qināb, W. → Yemen 17°55N 49°59E 249 C5
Qin'an China 34°48N 105°40E 226 G3
Qing Xian China 38°35N 116°45E 226 E9
Qingcheng China 37°15N 117°40E 227 F9
Qingcheng Shan China 30°58N 103°31E 228 B4
Qingchuan China 32°36N 105°9E 226 H3
Qingdao China 36°5N 120°20E 227 F11
Qingfeng China 35°52N 115°8E 226 G8
Qinghai □ China 36°0N 98°0E 218 D8
Qinghai Hu China 36°40N 100°10E 218 D9
Qinghe China 46°37N 90°25E 217 C12
Qinghecheng China 41°28N 124°15E 224 B2
Qinghemen China 41°48N 121°25E 227 D11
Qinghuayuan China 39°59N 116°19E 114 B1
Qingjian China 37°8N 110°8E 226 F6
Qingjiang = Huaiyin China 33°30N 119°2E 227 H10
Qingliu China 26°11N 116°48E 229 D11
Qinglong China 25°49N 105°12E 228 E5
Qingningsi China 31°16N 121°33E 138 B2
Qingping China 26°39N 107°47E 228 D6
Qingpu China 31°10N 121°6E 229 B13
Qingshui China 34°48N 106°8E 226 G4
Qingshuihe China 39°55N 111°35E 226 E6
Qingtian China 28°12N 120°15E 229 C13
Qingtongxia China 38°2N 106°3E 226 E4
Qingtongxia Shuiku China 37°50N 105°58E 226 F3
Qingxi China 27°8N 108°43E 228 D7
Qingxu China 37°34N 112°22E 226 F7
Qingyang Anhui, China 30°38N 117°50E 229 B11
Qingyang Gansu, China 36°2N 107°55E 226 F4
Qingyi Jiang → China 29°32N 103°44E 228 C4
Qingyuan Guangdong, China 23°40N 112°59E 229 F9
Qingyuan Liaoning, China 42°10N 124°55E 224 A2
Qingyuan Zhejiang, China 27°36N 119°3E 229 D12
Qingyun China 37°45N 117°20E 227 F9
Qingzhen China 26°31N 106°25E 228 D6
Qinhuangdao China 39°56N 119°30E 227 E10
Qinling Shandi China 33°50N 108°10E 226 H5
Qinshui China 35°40N 112°8E 226 G7
Qinyang = Jiyuan China 35°7N 112°57E 226 G7
Qinyang China 35°5N 112°56E 226 G7
Qinyuan China 36°29N 112°20E 226 F7
Qinzhou China 21°58N 108°38E 228 G7
Qionghai China 19°15N 110°26E 236 C8
Qionglai China 30°25N 103°31E 228 B4
Qionglai Shan China 31°0N 102°30E 228 B4
Qiongshan China 19°51N 110°26E 236 C8
Qiongzhou Haixia China 20°10N 110°15E 236 B8
Qiqihar China 47°26N 124°0E 219 B13
Qira China 37°0N 80°48E 217 E10
Qiraîya, W. → Egypt 30°27N 34°0E 251 H5
Qiryat Ata Israel 32°47N 35°6E 250 F6
Qiryat Gat Israel 31°32N 34°46E 251 G5
Qiryat Mal'akhi Israel 31°44N 34°44E 251 G5
Qiryat Shemona Israel 33°13N 35°35E 250 E6
Qiryat Yam Israel 32°51N 35°4E 250 F6
Qirzah, W. → Libya 30°56N 14°31E 258 B2
Qishan China 34°25N 107°38E 226 G4
Qishn Yemen 15°26N 51°40E 249 D5
Qitai China 44°2N 89°35E 217 D11
Qitaihe China 45°48N 130°51E 220 B5
Qitbīt, W. → Oman 19°15N 54°23E 249 C6
Qiubei China 24°2N 104°12E 228 E5
Qixia China 37°17N 120°52E 227 F11
Qiyang China 26°35N 111°50E 229 D8
Qızılağac Körfäzi Azerbaijan 39°9N 49°0E 213 C13
Qobda Kazakhstan 50°55N 54°31E 216 B4
Qojūr Iran 36°12N 47°55E 246 B5
Qolhak Iran 35°45N 51°26E 141 A2
Qom Iran 34°40N 51°0E 247 C6
Qom □ Iran 34°40N 51°0E 247 C6
Qomolangma Feng = Everest, Mt. Nepal 28°5N 86°58E 243 E12
Qomsheh Iran 32°0N 51°55E 247 D6
Qondūz = Kondūz Afghan. 36°50N 68°50E 240 A3
Qondūz → Afghan. 37°0N 68°16E 240 A3
Qong Muztag China 35°42N 82°22E 217 E10
Qoqek = Tacheng China 46°40N 82°58E 217 C10
Qoqon = Qŭqon Uzbekistan 40°31N 70°56E 217 D8
Qoraqalpoghistan □ Uzbekistan 43°0N 58°0E 216 D5
Qormi Malta 35°53N 14°28E 206 F7
Qorveh Iran 35°10N 47°48E 213 E12
Qosshaghyl Kazakhstan 46°40N 54°0E 187 E9
Qostanay Kazakhstan 53°10N 63°35E 216 B6
Qotanqaraghay Kazakhstan 49°10N 85°36E 217 C11
Qoţūr Iran 38°28N 44°25E 213 C11
Qoz Salsilgo C.A.R. 10°45N 22°54E 264 A4
Qrejten Point Malta 35°57N 14°27E 206 F7
Qu Jiang → China 30°1N 106°24E 228 B6
Qu Xian China 30°48N 106°58E 228 B6
Quabbin Res. U.S.A. 42°20N 72°20W 313 D12
Quadraro Italy 41°51N 12°33E 136 B2
Quaid-i-Azam Pakistan 24°50N 66°59E 123 A1
Quairading Australia 32°0S 117°21E 279 F2
Quakenbrück Germany 52°41N 7°57E 178 C3
Quakertown U.S.A. 40°26N 75°21W 313 F9
Qualicum Beach Canada 49°22N 124°26W 296 D4
Quambatook Australia 35°49S 143°34E 282 C5
Quambone Australia 30°57S 147°53E 283 A7
Quamby Australia 20°22S 140°17E 280 C3
Quan Long = Ca Mau Vietnam 9°7N 105°8E 237 H5
Quanah U.S.A. 34°18N 99°44W 314 D5
Quandialla Australia 34°1S 147°47E 283 C7
Quang Ngai Vietnam 15°13N 108°58E 236 E7
Quang Tri Vietnam 16°45N 107°13E 236 D6
Quang Yen Vietnam 20°56N 106°52E 228 G6
Quannan China 24°45N 114°33E 229 E10
Quantock Hills U.K. 51°8N 3°10W 169 F4
Quanyang China 42°21N 127°32E 227 C14
Quanzhou Fujian, China 24°55N 118°34E 229 E12
Quanzhou Guangxi Zhuangzu, China 25°57N 111°5E 229 E8
Qu'Appelle → Canada 50°33N 103°53W 297 C8
Quaqtaq Canada 60°55N 69°40W 295 E18
Quaraí Brazil 30°15S 56°20W 334 C4
Quarré-les-Tombes France 47°21N 4°0E 173 E11
Quarteira Portugal 37°4N 8°6W 195 H2
Quarter, The Anguilla 18°13N 63°3W 322 a
Quartier D'Orléans St.-Martin 18°5N 63°2W 322 a
Quartier Militaire Mauritius 20°14S 57°35E 272 e
Quartiere Zingone Italy 45°25N 9°3E 129 B1
Quartu Sant'Élena Italy 39°15N 9°10E 200 C2
Quartzsite U.S.A. 33°40N 114°13W 307 M12
Quatre, I. à St. Vincent 12°59N 61°15W 323 n
Quatre Bornes Mauritius 20°15S 57°28E 272 e
Quatsino Sd. Canada 50°25N 127°58W 296 C3
Quba Azerbaijan 41°21N 48°32E 191 K9
Qubeiba West Bank 31°50N 35°8E 123 A1
Qūchān Iran 37°10N 58°27E 247 B8
Quds Iraq 33°23N 44°24E 113 A2
Queanbeyan Australia 35°17S 149°14E 283 C8
Québec Canada 46°52N 71°13W 299 C5
Québec □ Canada 48°0N 74°0W 299 C6
Quebo Guinea-Biss. 11°20N 14°56W 262 C2
Quebrada del Condorito △ Argentina 31°49S 64°40W 334 C3
Quebradillas Puerto Rico 18°29N 66°56W 321 b
Quedlinburg Germany 51°47N 11°8E 178 D7
Queen Alexandra Ra. Antarctica 85°0S 170°0E 151 E11
Queen Charlotte B. Falk. Is. 51°50S 60°40W 153 f
Queen Charlotte City Canada 53°15N 132°2W 296 C2
Queen Charlotte Is. Canada 53°20N 132°10W 296 C2
Queen Charlotte Sd. B.C., Canada 51°0N 128°0W 296 C3
Queen Charlotte Sd. N.Z. 41°10S 174°15E 285 B9
Queen Charlotte Strait Canada 50°45N 127°10W 296 C3
Queen City U.S.A. 40°25N 92°34W 310 D4
Queen Elizabeth △ Uganda 0°0 30°0E 268 C3
Queen Elizabeth ⌓ U.K. 56°7N 4°30W 167 E4
Queen Elizabeth Is. Canada 76°0N 95°0W 295 B13
Queen Elizabeth Nat. Park = Ruwenzori △ Uganda 0°20N 30°0E 268 B2
Queen Mary Land Antarctica 70°0S 95°0E 151 D7
Queen Mary Res. U.K. 51°24N 0°27W 125 B1
Queen Maud G. Canada 68°15N 102°30W 294 D11
Queen Maud Land = Dronning Maud Land Antarctica 72°30S 12°0E 151 D3
Queen Maud Mts. Antarctica 86°0S 160°0W 151 E13
Queen Street Edinburgh, U.K. 121 a1
Queen Victoria Market Australia 37°47S 144°57W 128 A1
Queens Channel Australia 15°0S 129°30E 278 C4
Queens-Midtown Tunnel New York, U.S.A. 132 d2
Queen's Quay Terminal Toronto, Canada 141 c2
Queensboro Bridge New York, U.S.A. 132 c3
Queensbury U.K. 51°35N 0°16W 125 A2
Queenscliff Australia 38°16S 144°39E 282 E6
Queenscliffe Australia 33°47S 151°17E 139 A2
Queensferry U.K. 55°59N 3°23W 121 B1
Queensland U.S.A. 31°46N 83°14W 316 D6
Queensland □ Australia 22°0S 142°0E 280 C3
Queensland Plateau Pac. Oc. 17°0S 150°0E 276 D8
Queenstown = Cóbh Ireland 51°51N 8°17W 166 E3
Queenstown Tas., Australia 42°4S 145°35E 281 G4
Queenstown N.Z. 45°1S 168°40E 285 F3
Queenstown Singapore 1°18N 103°48E 138 B2
Queenstown Eastern Cape, S. Africa 31°52S 26°52E 270 D4
Queets U.S.A. 47°32N 124°19W 306 C2
Queguay Grande → Uruguay 32°9S 58°9W 334 C4
Queimada, Pta. da Azores 38°23N 28°14W 153 d1
Queimadas Brazil 11°0S 39°38W 332 D4
Queiros, C. Vanuatu 14°55S 167°1E 287 D5
Quela Angola 9°10S 16°56E 265 D3
Quelimane Mozam. 17°53S 36°58E 269 F4
Quellerina S. Africa 26°9S 27°56E 123 A1
Quellón Chile 43°7S 73°37W 336 B2
Quelo Angola 6°29S 12°36E 265 D2
Quelpart = Jeju-do S. Korea 33°29N 126°34E 224 a
Queluz Portugal 38°45N 9°14W 126 A1
Quemado N. Mex., U.S.A. 34°20N 108°30W 305 J9
Quemado Tex., U.S.A. 28°56N 100°37W 314 G4
Quemoy = Chinmen Taiwan 24°26N 118°19E 225 a
Quemú-Quemú Argentina 36°3S 63°36W 334 D3
Quepem India 15°13N 74°3E 245 G2
Quequén Argentina 38°30S 58°30W 334 D4
Querco Peru 13°50S 74°52W 330 C3
Querétaro Mexico 20°36N 100°23W 318 C4
Querétaro □ Mexico 21°0N 99°55W 318 C5
Querfurt Germany 51°23N 11°35E 178 D7
Quérigut France 42°42N 2°6E 174 F6
Querqueville France 49°40N 1°42W 172 C5
Quesada Spain 37°51N 3°4W 195 H7
Queshan China 32°55N 114°2E 229 A10
Quesnel Canada 53°0N 122°30W 296 C4
Quesnel → Canada 52°58N 122°29W 296 C4
Quesnel L. Canada 52°30N 121°20W 296 C4
Questa U.S.A. 36°42N 105°36W 305 H11
Questembert France 47°40N 2°28W 172 E4
Quetena Bolivia 22°10S 67°25W 330 E4
Quetico ⌓ Canada 48°30N 91°45W 298 C1
Quetrequile Argentina 41°33S 69°22W 336 B3
Quetta Pakistan 30°15N 66°55E 242 D2
Queulat △ Chile 44°29S 72°24W 336 B2
Quevedo Ecuador 1°2S 79°29W 328 D2
Queyras ⌓ France 44°45N 6°50E 175 D10
Quezaltenango Guatemala 14°50N 91°30W 320 D1
Quezon Phil. 9°15N 117°59E 233 G1
Quezon □ Phil. 14°40N 121°30E 232 D3
Quezon △ Phil. 14°0N 121°55E 232 D3
Quezon City Phil. 14°37N 121°2E 127 B2
Qufār Si. Arabia 27°26N 41°37E 246 E4
Qufu China 35°35N 116°59E 226 G9
Qui Nhon Vietnam 13°40N 109°13E 236 F7
Quibala Angola 10°46S 14°59E 265 E2
Quibaxe Angola 8°24S 14°27E 265 D2
Quibdó Colombia 5°42N 76°40W 328 B2
Quiberon France 47°29N 3°9W 172 E3
Quiberon, Presqu'île de France 47°30N 3°8W 172 E3
Quiçama △ Angola 9°41S 13°35E 265 D2
Quickborn Germany 53°42N 9°52E 178 B5
Quiet L. Canada 61°5N 133°5W 296 A2
Quiindy Paraguay 25°58S 57°14W 334 B4
Quilá Mexico 24°23N 107°13W 318 C3
Quilán, C. Chile 43°15S 74°30W 336 B2
Quilcene U.S.A. 47°49N 122°53W 306 C4
Quilenda Angola 10°39S 14°23E 265 E2
Quilengues Angola 14°12S 14°12E 265 E2
Quilicura Chile 33°22S 70°43W 137 B1
Quilimarí Chile 32°5S 71°30W 334 C1
Quilino Argentina 30°14S 64°29W 334 C3
Quill, The St. Eustatius 17°28N 62°57W 322 a
Quillabamba Peru 12°50S 72°50W 330 C3
Quillacollo Bolivia 17°26S 66°17W 330 D4
Quillagua Chile 21°40S 69°40W 334 A2
Quillan France 42°53N 2°10E 174 F6
Quillota Chile 32°54S 71°16W 334 C1
Quilmes Argentina 34°43S 58°15W 334 C4
Quilon India 8°50N 76°38E 245 K3
Quilpie Australia 26°35S 144°11E 281 D3
Quilpué Chile 33°5S 71°33W 334 C1
Quilua Mozam. 16°17S 39°54E 269 F4
Quimbele Angola 6°17S 16°41E 265 D3
Quimbo Angola 14°4S 16°11E 265 E3
Quimbonge Angola 8°36S 18°30E 265 D3
Quime Bolivia 17°2S 67°15W 330 D4
Quimilí Argentina 27°40S 62°30W 334 B3
Quimper France 48°0N 4°9W 172 E2
Quimperlé France 47°53N 3°33W 172 E3
Quinam B. Trin. & Tob. 10°4N 61°30W 323 t
Quinault → U.S.A. 47°21N 124°18W 306 C2
Quince Mil Peru 13°15S 70°40W 330 C3
Quincy Calif., U.S.A. 39°56N 120°57W 306 F6
Quincy Fla., U.S.A. 30°35N 84°34W 316 E5
Quincy Ill., U.S.A. 39°56N 91°23W 310 E5
Quincy Mass., U.S.A. 42°14N 71°0W 116 B2
Quincy Mich., U.S.A. 41°57N 84°53W 311 C12
Quincy Wash., U.S.A. 47°14N 119°51W 304 C4
Quincy B. U.S.A. 42°16N 70°59W 116 B3
Quines Argentina 32°13S 65°48W 334 C2
Quinga Mozam. 15°49S 40°15E 269 F5
Quingey France 47°7N 5°52E 173 E12
Quingombe Angola 6°38S 13°1E 265 D2
Quinhagak U.S.A. 59°45N 161°54W 303 G7
Quinhámel Guinea-Biss. 11°53N 15°51W 262 C1
Quiniluban Group Phil. 11°27N 120°48E 233 F3
Quinta Normal Chile 33°26S 70°42W 137 B1
Quintana de la Serena Spain 38°45N 5°40W 195 G5
Quintana Roo □ Mexico 19°40N 88°30W 319 D7
Quintanar de la Orden Spain 39°36N 3°5W 195 F7
Quintanar de la Sierra Spain 41°57N 2°55W 196 D2
Quintanar del Rey Spain 39°21N 1°56W 197 F3
Quintero Chile 32°45S 71°30W 334 C1
Quintin France 48°26N 2°56W 172 D4
Quinto Spain 41°25N 0°32W 196 D4
Quinto de Stampi Italy 45°24N 9°10E 129 B2
Quinto Romano Italy 45°28N 9°7E 129 B1
Quinzáu Angola 6°51S 12°44E 265 D2
Quípar → Spain 38°15N 1°40W 197 G3
Quipeio Angola 12°27S 15°30E 265 E3
Quirihue Chile 36°15S 72°35W 334 D1
Quirima Angola 10°47S 18°6E 265 E3
Quirimbas △ Mozam. 12°30S 40°15E 269 E5
Quirimbo Angola 10°36S 14°12E 265 E2
Quirinale Italy 41°53N 12°29E 136 B1
Quirinale, Palazzo dei Rome, Italy 136 b3
Quirindi Australia 31°28S 150°40E 283 A9
Quirino □ Phil. 16°15N 121°40E 232 C3
Quirinópolis Brazil 18°32S 50°30W 333 E1
Quiroga Spain 42°28N 7°18W 194 C3
Quiruvilca Peru 8°1S 78°19W 330 B2
Quissac France 43°55N 4°0E 175 E8
Quissanga Mozam. 12°24S 40°28E 269 E5
Quissico Mozam. 24°42S 34°44E 271 B5
Quitapa Angola 10°20S 18°19E 265 E3
Quitilipi Argentina 26°50S 60°13W 334 B3
Quitman U.S.A. 30°47N 83°34W 316 E6
Quito Ecuador 0°15S 78°35W 328 D2
Quitralco △ Chile 45°43S 73°25W 336 C2
Quixadá Brazil 4°55S 39°0W 332 B4
Quixaxe Mozam. 15°17S 40°4E 269 F5
Quixeramobim Brazil 5°12S 39°17W 332 C4
Quixico Angola 7°59S 14°25E 265 D2
Quixinge Angola 9°52S 14°23E 265 D2
Quizenga Angola 9°21S 15°28E 265 D3
Qujing China 25°32N 103°41E 228 E4
Qulan Kazakhstan 42°55N 72°43E 214 E8
Qul'ân, Jazâ'ir Egypt 24°22N 35°31E 246 E2
Qulsary Kazakhstan 46°59N 54°1E 187 E9
Qumbu S. Africa 31°10S 28°48E 271 D4
Qunayyin, Sabkhat al Libya 30°10N 21°0E 258 B4
Qŭnghirot Uzbekistan 43°2N 58°50E 216 D5
Qu'nyido China 31°15N 98°6E 228 B2
Quoin I. Australia 14°54S 129°32E 278 B4
Quoin Pt. S. Africa 34°46S 19°37E 270 D2
Quorn Australia 32°25S 138°5E 282 B3
Qŭqon Uzbekistan 40°31N 70°56E 217 D8
Qurein Sudan 13°30N 34°50E 257 E3
Qŭrghonteppa Tajikistan 37°50N 68°47E 217 E7
Qurimbas Mozam. 12°20S 40°10E 269 E5
Qurnat as Sawdā' Lebanon 34°18N 36°6E 250 D7
Quryq Kazakhstan 43°12N 51°39E 216 D4
Qûs Egypt 25°55N 32°50E 256 B3
Qusar Azerbaijan 41°25N 48°26E 191 K9
Quşaybā' Si. Arabia 26°53N 43°35E 246 E4
Qusaybah Iraq 34°24N 40°59E 213 E9
Quşay'ir Yemen 14°55N 50°20E 249 D5
Quseir Egypt 26°7N 34°16E 246 E2
Qūshchī Iran 37°59N 45°3E 213 D11
Qusmuryn Kazakhstan 52°27N 64°36E 216 B6
Qusmuryn Köli Kazakhstan 52°41N 64°48E 216 B6
Qutang Gorge = Qutang Xia China 31°0N 109°40E 228 B7
Qutang Xia China 31°0N 109°40E 228 B7
Quthing Lesotho 30°25S 27°36E 271 D4
Qūţīābād Iran 35°47N 48°30E 213 E13
Quttinirpaaq △ Canada 82°13N 72°13W 295 A17
Quwayq → Syria 36°20N 37°10E 250 B8
Quweisna Egypt 30°34N 31°9E 251 H2
Quwo China 35°38N 111°25E 226 G6
Quyang China 38°35N 114°40E 226 E8
Quynh Nhai Vietnam 21°49N 103°33E 236 B4
Quyon Canada 45°31N 76°14W 313 A8
Quzhou China 28°57N 118°54E 229 C12
Quzi China 36°20N 107°20E 226 F4
Qvareli Georgia 41°57N 45°47E 191 K7
Qytet Stalin = Kuçovë Albania 40°47N 19°57E 202 F3
Qyzylorda Kazakhstan 44°48N 65°28E 217 D7
Qyzylorda □ Kazakhstan 45°0N 65°0E 216 D6
Qyzylzhar Kazakhstan 48°17N 69°38E 217 C7

R

R.F.K. Memorial Stadium U.S.A. 38°52N 76°58W 143 B4
Ra, Ko Thailand 9°13N 98°16E 237 H2
Raab Austria 48°21N 13°39E 180 C6
Raahe Finland 64°40N 24°28E 160 D21
Raalte Neths. 52°23N 6°16E 170 B6
Ra'ananna Israel 32°10N 34°52E 251 F5
Raas Indonesia 7°8S 114°33E 235 D4
Raasay U.K. 57°25N 6°4W 167 D2
Raasay, Sd. of U.K. 57°30N 6°8W 167 D2
Raasdorf Austria 48°14N 16°33E 142 A3
Raasepori Finland 60°0N 23°26E 188 B2
Rab Croatia 44°45N 14°45E 199 D11
Raba Indonesia 8°36S 118°55E 235 D5
Rába → Hungary 47°38N 17°38E 182 C2
Raba → Poland 50°8N 20°30E 185 H7
Rabaçal → Portugal 41°30N 7°12W 194 D3
Rabah Nigeria 13°5N 5°30E 263 C6
Rabai Kenya 3°50S 39°31E 268 C4
Rabak Sudan 13°9N 32°44E 257 E3
Rabaraba Papua N. G. 9°58S 149°49E 286 E5
Rabastens France 43°50N 1°43E 174 E5
Rabastens-de-Bigorre France 43°23N 0°9E 174 E4
Rabat = Victoria Malta 36°3N 14°14E 206 E6
Rabat Malta 35°53N 14°24E 206 F7
Rabat Morocco 34°2N 6°48W 260 B3
Rabat □ Morocco 34°10N 6°45W 260 B3
Rabaul Papua N. G. 4°24S 152°18E 286 C7
Rabbit Flat Australia 20°11S 130°1E 278 D5
Rabbit Lake Mine Canada 58°4N 104°5W 297 B8
Rabi Fiji 16°30S 179°59W 287 A3
Rābigh Si. Arabia 22°50N 39°5E 248 B2
Rabka Poland 49°37N 19°59E 185 J6
Râbniţa Moldova 47°45N 29°0E 183 C14
Rābor Iran 29°17N 56°55E 247 D8
Rabwah = Chenab Nagar Pakistan 31°45N 72°55E 242 D5
Rabyānah Libya 24°15N 22°0E 258 D4
Rača Serbia 44°14N 21°0E 202 B4
Răcăciuni Romania 46°20N 26°59E 183 D11
Răcăşdia Romania 44°59N 21°36E 182 F6
Racconigi Italy 44°46N 7°46E 198 D4
Raccoon → U.S.A. 41°35N 93°37W 310 C3
Raccoon Cr. → U.S.A. 39°47N 87°23W 311 E9
Race, C. Canada 46°40N 53°5W 299 C9
Race Course Jamaica 17°51N 77°20W 320 a
Race Pond U.S.A. 31°1N 82°8W 316 D7
Rach Gia Vietnam 10°5N 105°5E 237 G5
Rach Soi Vietnam 9°57N 105°7E 237 H5
Racha Noi, Ko Thailand 7°30N 98°19E 237 J2
Racha Yai, Ko Thailand 7°36N 98°21E 237 J2
Rachid Mauritania 18°45N 11°35W 262 B2
Raciąż Poland 52°46N 20°10E 185 F7
Racibórz Poland 50°7N 18°18E 185 H5
Racichy Belarus 53°44N 23°42E 184 E10
Racine U.S.A. 42°44N 87°47W 311 B9
Račisdorf = Rača Serbia 44°14N 21°0E 202 B4
Rackerby U.S.A. 39°26N 121°22W 306 F5
Råda Sweden 60°0N 13°36E 162 E7
Radama, Nosy Madag. 14°0S 47°47E 272 A2
Radama, Saikanosy Madag. 14°16S 47°53E 272 A2
Radan Serbia 42°59N 21°29E 202 D5
Rădăuţi Romania 47°50N 25°59E 183 C10
Rădăuţi-Prut Romania 48°14N 26°48E 183 B11
Radbuza → Czech Rep. 49°45N 13°22E 180 B6
Radcliff U.S.A. 37°51N 85°57W 311 G11
Radcliffe College U.S.A. 42°22N 71°7W 116 A2
Radeberg Germany 51°7N 13°53E 178 D9
Radebeul Germany 51°6N 13°39E 178 D9
Radeče Slovenia 46°5N 15°14E 199 B12
Radekhiv Ukraine 50°25N 24°32E 177 C13
Radekhov = Radekhiv Ukraine 50°25N 24°32E 177 C13
Radenthein Austria 46°48N 13°43E 180 E6
Radew → Poland 54°2N 15°52E 184 D2
Radford U.S.A. 37°8N 80°34W 309 G13
Radhanpur India 23°50N 71°38E 242 H4
Rådhus Oslo, Norway 133 b1
Radhwa, Jabal Si. Arabia 24°34N 38°18E 246 E3
Radika → Macedonia 41°38N 20°37E 202 E4
Radisson Qué., Canada 53°47N 77°37W 298 B4
Radisson Sask., Canada 52°30N 107°20W 297 C7
Radium Hot Springs Canada 50°35N 116°2W 296 C5
Radlice Czech Rep. 50°3N 14°23E 135 B2
Radlje ob Dravi Slovenia 46°38N 15°13E 199 B12
Radmannsdorf = Radovljica Slovenia 46°22N 14°12E 199 B11
Radnevo Bulgaria 42°17N 25°58E 203 D9
Radnice Czech Rep. 49°51N 13°35E 180 B6
Radnor Forest U.K. 52°17N 3°10W 169 E4
Radolfzell Germany 47°39N 8°59E 179 H4
Radom Poland 51°23N 21°12E 185 G8
Radom △ Sudan 9°20N 23°50E 264 A4
Radomir Bulgaria 42°37N 22°59E 202 D6
Radomka → Poland 51°43N 21°28E 185 G8
Radomsko Poland 51°5N 19°28E 185 G6
Radomyshl Ukraine 50°30N 29°12E 177 C15
Radomyśl Wielki Poland 50°14N 21°15E 185 H8
Radość Poland 52°11N 21°11E 142 B3
Radoszyce Poland 51°4N 20°15E 185 G7
Radotin Czech Rep. 49°59N 14°21E 135 C2
Radoviš Macedonia 41°38N 22°28E 202 E6
Radovljica Slovenia 46°22N 14°12E 199 B11
Radstadt Austria 47°24N 13°28E 180 D6
Radstock, C. Australia 33°12S 134°20E 281 E1
Răducăneni Romania 46°58N 27°54E 183 D12
Raduša Macedonia 42°7N 21°15E 202 D5
Raduzhnyy Russia 62°5N 77°28E 214 C8
Radvanichy Belarus 52°1N 24°0E 185 F11
Radviliškis Lithuania 55°49N 23°33E 184 C10
Radville Canada 49°30N 104°15W 297 D8
Raḑwá, J. Si. Arabia 24°34N 38°18E 256 C4
Radymno Poland 49°59N 22°52E 185 J9
Radzanów Poland 52°56N 20°8E 185 F7
Radziejów Poland 52°40N 18°30E 185 F5
Radzyń Chełmiński Poland 53°23N 18°55E 184 E5
Radzyń Podlaski Poland 51°47N 22°37E 185 G9
Rae Canada 62°50N 116°3W 296 A5
Rae Bareli India 26°18N 81°20E 243 F9
Rae Isthmus Canada 66°40N 87°30W 295 D14
Raeren Belgium 50°41N 6°7E 170 D6
Raeside, L. Australia 29°20S 122°0E 279 E3
Raetihi N.Z. 39°25S 175°17E 284 F4
Rafaela Argentina 31°10S 61°30W 334 C3
Rafah Gaza Strip 31°18N 34°14E 251 G5
Rafai C.A.R. 4°59N 23°58E 264 B4
Rafat West Bank 31°52N 35°11E 123 A2

Raffadali *Italy* 37°24N 13°32E **200** E6
Raffili *Sudan* 6°50N 28°0E **257** F2
Raffles Hotel *Singapore* **138** b3
Raffles Park *Singapore* 1°19N 103°48E **138** B2
Rafḥā *Si. Arabia* 29°35N 43°35E **246** D4
Rafina *Greece* 38°2N 24°0E **204** C6
Rafsanjān *Iran* 30°30N 56°5E **247** D8
Raft Pt. *Australia* 16°4S 124°26E **278** C3
Râgâ *Sudan* 8°28N 25°41E **257** F2
Raga → *Sudan* 8°41N 25°52E **257** F2
Ragachow *Belarus* 53°8N 30°5E **177** B16
Ragag *Sudan* 10°59N 24°40E **257** E1
Ragang, Mt. *Phil.* 7°43N 124°32E **233** H5
Ragay *Phil.* 13°49N 122°47E **232** E4
Ragay G. *Phil.* 13°30N 122°45E **232** E4
Ragged, Mt. *Australia* 33°27S 123°25E **279** F3
Rāgh *Afghan.* 37°32N 70°27E **240** A3
Raghunathpalli *India* 22°14N 84°48E **243** H11
Raghunathpur *India* 23°33N 86°40E **243** H12
Raglan *N.Z.* 37°55S 174°55E **284** D3
Raglan Harbour *N.Z.* 37°47S 174°50E **284** D3
Ragland *U.S.A.* 33°45N 86°9W **316** B3
Ragnit = Neman *Russia* 55°2N 22°2E **184** C9
Raguda, Ghubbet
Somali Rep. 10°43N 46°22E **267** B6
Ragusa = Dubrovnik
Croatia 42°39N 18°6E **202** D2
Ragusa *Italy* 36°55N 14°44E **201** F7
Raha *Indonesia* 4°55S 123°0E **231** E6
Rahad, Nahr ed → *Sudan* 14°28N 33°31E **257** E3
Rahad al Bardī *Sudan* 11°20N 23°40E **259** F4
Rahaeng = Tak *Thailand* 16°52N 99°8E **236** D2
Rahat, Ḥarrat *Si. Arabia* 23°0N 40°5E **256** C5
Rahatgarh *India* 23°47N 78°22E **243** H8
Rahden *Germany* 52°26N 8°36E **178** C4
Raheb, Ras ir- *Malta* 35°54N 14°20E **206** F7
Raheita *Eritrea* 12°46N 43°4E **257** E5
Raheng = Tak *Thailand* 16°52N 99°8E **236** D2
Raheny *Ireland* 53°22N 6°10W **120** A3
Rahimyar Khan *Pakistan* 28°30N 70°25E **242** E4
Rāhjerd *Iran* 34°22N 50°22E **247** C6
Rahnsdorf *Germany* 52°25N 13°41E **115** B5
Rahole △ *Kenya* 0°5N 38°57E **268** B4
Råholt *Norway* 60°16N 11°11E **164** D8
Rahon *India* 31°3N 76°7E **242** D7
Rahotu *N.Z.* 39°20S 173°49E **284** F2
Rahovec = Orahovac
Kosovo 42°24N 20°40E **202** D4
Rahuri *India* 19°23N 74°39E **244** E2
Rai, Hon *Vietnam* 9°48N 104°38E **237** H5
Raiatéa, Î. *French Polynesia* 16°50S 151°25W **289** f
Raichur *India* 16°10N 77°20E **245** F3
Raiford *U.S.A.* 30°4N 82°14W **316** E7
Raiganj *India* 25°37N 88°10E **243** G13
Raigarh *India* 21°56N 83°25E **244** D6
Raighar *India* 19°51N 82°6E **244** E6
Raijua *Indonesia* 10°37S 121°36E **231** F6
Raikot *India* 30°41N 75°42E **242** D6
Railton *Australia* 41°25S 146°28E **281** G4
Rainbow Bridge △ *U.S.A.* 37°5N 110°58W **305** H8
Rainbow City *U.S.A.* 33°57N 86°5W **316** B3
Rainbow Lake *Canada* 58°30N 119°23W **296** B5
Rainier *U.S.A.* 46°53N 122°41W **306** D4
Rainier, Mt. *U.S.A.* 46°52N 121°46W **306** D5
Rainy L. *Canada* 48°42N 93°10W **297** D10
Rainy River *Canada* 48°43N 94°29W **297** D10
Raippaluoto *Finland* 63°13N 21°14E **160** E19
Raipur *India* 21°17N 81°45E **244** D5
Rairakhol *India* 21°4N 84°21E **244** D7
Ra'is *Si. Arabia* 23°33N 38°43E **256** C4
Raisen *India* 23°20N 77°48E **242** H8
Raisio *Finland* 60°28N 22°11E **188** B2
Raivavae *French Polynesia* 23°52S 147°40W **289** f
Raj Ghat *Delhi, India* **120** b3
Raj Nandgaon *India* 21°5N 81°5E **244** D5
Raj Nilgiri *India* 21°28N 86°46E **243** J12
Raja, Ujung *Indonesia* 3°40N 96°25E **234** B1
Raja Ampat, Kepulauan
Indonesia 0°30S 130°0E **231** E8
Rajah Sikatuna △ *Phil.* 9°40N 124°20E **233** G5
Rajahmundry *India* 17°1N 81°48E **244** F5
Rajaji △ *India* 30°10N 78°20E **242** D8
Rajakylä *Finland* 60°15N 25°5E **121** B3
Rajampet *India* 14°11N 79°10E **245** G4
Rajang → *Malaysia* 2°30N 112°0E **235** B4
Rajang Mangroves △
Malaysia 2°6N 111°16E **235** B4
Rajanpur *Pakistan* 29°6N 70°19E **242** E4
Rajapalaiyam *India* 9°25N 77°35E **245** K3
Rajapur *India* 16°40N 73°31E **244** F1
Rajasthan □ *India* 26°45N 73°30E **242** F5
Rajasthan Canal = Indira Gandhi Canal *India* 28°0N 72°0E **242** F5
Rajauri *India* 33°25N 74°21E **243** C6
Rajbari *Bangla.* 23°47N 89°41E **241** D2
Rajendranagar *India* 17°18N 78°27E **244** F4
Rajgarh *Mad. P., India* 24°2N 76°45E **242** G7
Rajgarh *Raj., India* 27°14N 76°38E **242** F7
Rajgarh *Raj., India* 28°40N 75°25E **242** E6
Rajghat Dam *India* 24°45N 78°20E **244** B4
Rajgir *India* 25°2N 85°25E **243** G11
Rajgród *Poland* 53°42N 22°42E **184** E9
Rajim *India* 20°58N 81°53E **244** D5
Rajkot *India* 22°15N 70°56E **242** H4
Rajmahal Hills *India* 24°30N 87°30E **243** G12
Rajpath *Delhi, India* **120** c2
Rajpipla *India* 21°50N 73°30E **244** D1
Rajpur *India* 22°18N 74°21E **242** H6
Rajpura *Delhi, India* 28°41N 77°12E **120** A2
Rajpura *Punjab, India* 30°25N 76°32E **242** D7
Rajputana = Rajasthan □
India 26°45N 73°30E **242** F5
Rajsamand = Kankroli
India 25°4N 73°53E **242** G5
Rajshahi *Bangla.* 24°22N 88°39E **241** C2
Rajshahi □ *Bangla.* 25°0N 89°0E **241** C2
Rājū *Syria* 36°40N 36°40E **250** B7
Rajula *India* 21°3N 71°26E **242** J4
Rajur *India* 20°7N 78°55E **244** D4
Rajura *India* 19°47N 79°22E **244** E4
Rakaia *N.Z.* 43°45S 172°1E **285** D7
Rakaia → *N.Z.* 43°36S 172°15E **285** D7
Rakan, Ra's *Qatar* 26°10N 51°20E **247** E6
Rakaposhi *Pakistan* 36°10N 74°25E **243** A6
Rakata, Pulau *Indonesia* 6°10S 105°20E **234** D3
Rakbah, Sahl *Si. Arabia* 22°15N 41°0E **256** C5
Rakhiv *Ukraine* 48°3N 24°12E **183** B9
Rakhni *Pakistan* 30°4N 69°56E **242** D3
Rakhni → *Pakistan* 29°31N 69°36E **242** E3
Rakhny-Lisovi *Ukraine* 48°47N 28°29E **183** B13
Rakhyūt *Oman* 16°44N 53°20E **249** C6
Rakiraki *Fiji* 17°22S 178°11E **287** A2
Rakitnoye *Russia* 45°36N 134°17E **220** B7
Rakitovo *Bulgaria* 41°59N 24°5E **203** E8
Rakiura = Stewart I.
N.Z. 46°58S 167°54E **285** G2
Rakkestad *Norway* 59°25N 11°21E **164** E8
Rakoniewice *Poland* 52°10N 16°16E **185** F3
Rakops *Botswana* 21°1S 24°28E **270** B3
Rákos-patak → *Hungary* 47°29N 19°12E **117** B3
Rákoshegy *Hungary* 47°27N 19°14E **117** B3
Rákoskeresztúr *Hungary* 47°29N 19°15E **117** B3
Rákoskert *Hungary* 47°28N 19°18E **117** B3
Rákosliget *Hungary* 47°29N 19°16E **117** B3
Rákospalota *Hungary* 47°34N 19°7E **117** B2
Rákosszentmihály
Hungary 47°31N 19°8E **117** A2
Rakovica *Croatia* 44°59N 15°38E **199** D12
Rakovník *Czech Rep.* 50°6N 13°42E **180** A6
Rakovski *Bulgaria* 42°21N 24°57E **203** D8
Raków *Poland* 52°11N 20°56E **142** B1
Rakshan → *Pakistan* 27°10N 63°25E **240** D1
Rakvere *Estonia* 59°20N 26°25E **188** C4
Raleigh *Fla., U.S.A.* 29°25N 82°32W **317** F7
Raleigh *N.C., U.S.A.* 35°47N 78°39W **315** D15
Ralik Chain *Pac. Oc.* 8°0N 168°0E **288** G8
Ralja *Serbia* 44°33N 20°34E **202** B4
Rälla *Sweden* 56°40N 16°30E **163** H10
Ralls *U.S.A.* 33°41N 101°24W **314** E4
Ralston *U.S.A.* 41°30N 76°57W **312** E8
Ram *West Bank* 31°51N 35°14E **123** A2
Ram → *Canada* 62°1N 123°41W **296** A4
Rām Allāh *West Bank* 31°55N 35°10E **123** A2
Rama *Nic.* 12°9N 84°15W **320** D3
Ramacca *Italy* 37°23N 14°42E **201** E7
Ramachandrapuram *India* 16°50N 82°4E **244** F6
Ramadān *Iraq* 33°19N 44°20E **113** B2
Ramagiri Udayagiri *India* 19°5N 84°18E **244** E7
Ramagundam *India* 18°55N 79°15E **244** E4
Ramakona *India* 21°43N 78°50E **243** J8
Ramakrishna Puram
India 28°32N 77°10E **120** B1
Ramales de la Victoria
Spain 43°15N 3°28W **194** B7
Ramalho, Serra do *Brazil* 13°45S 44°0W **333** D3
Rāmallāh = Rām Allāh
West Bank 31°55N 35°10E **123** A2
Raman *Thailand* 6°29N 101°18E **237** J3
Ramanathapuram *India* 9°25N 78°55E **245** K4
Ramanathpur *India* 22°41N 88°14E **124** A1
Ramanujganj *India* 23°48N 83°42E **243** H10
Ramas C. *India* 15°5N 73°55E **245** G1
Ramat Allon *West Bank* 31°49N 35°12E **123** B2
Ramat Eshkol *West Bank* 31°48N 35°13E **123** B2
Ramat Gan *Israel* 32°4N 34°48E **251** F5
Ramat Razi'el *Israel* 31°46N 35°4E **123** B1
Ramat Shafet *West Bank* 31°48N 35°12E **123** B2
Ramatlhabama *S. Africa* 25°37S 25°33E **270** C4
Ramban *India* 33°14N 75°12E **243** C6
Rambervillers *France* 48°20N 6°38E **173** D13
Rambi = Rabi *Fiji* 16°30S 179°59W **287** A3
Rambipuji *Indonesia* 8°12S 113°37E **235** D4
Rambla, La *Barcelona, Spain* **114** b2
Rambler Channel *China* 22°21N 114°6E **122** A1
Rambouillet *France* 48°39N 1°50E **173** D8
Rambrai *India* 25°40N 91°19E **241** C3
Rambutyo I. *Papua N. G.* 2°18S 147°49E **286** B4
Ramdurg *India* 15°58N 75°22E **245** G2
Rame Hd. *Australia* 37°47S 149°30E **283** D8
Ramechhap *Nepal* 27°25N 86°10E **243** F12
Ramenki *Russia* 55°41N 37°28E **129** B2
Ramenskoye *Russia* 55°32N 38°15E **188** E10
Ramer *U.S.A.* 32°3N 86°13W **316** C3
Ramersdorf *Germany* 48°6N 11°35E **131** B2
Rameses Station *Egypt* 30°3N 31°15E **117** A2
Rameswaram *India* 9°17N 79°18E **245** K4
Ramganga → *India* 27°5N 79°58E **243** F8
Ramgarh *Bangla.* 22°59N 91°44E **241** D3
Ramgarh *Jharkhand, India* 23°40N 85°35E **243** H11
Ramgarh *Raj., India* 27°16N 75°14E **242** F6
Ramgarh *Raj., India* 27°30N 70°36E **242** F4
Rāmhormoz *Iran* 31°15N 49°35E **247** D6
Ramīān *Iran* 37°3N 55°16E **247** B7
Ramingining *Australia* 12°19S 135°3E **280** A2
Ramla *Israel* 31°55N 34°52E **251** G5
Ramlat Zalṭan *Libya* 28°30N 19°30E **258** C3
Ramlu *Eritrea* 13°32N 41°40E **257** E5
Ramm = Rum *Jordan* 29°39N 35°26E **251** J6
Râmna → *Romania* 45°36N 27°3E **183** E12
Ramnad = Ramanathapuram
India 9°25N 78°55E **245** K4
Ramnagar *Jammu & Kashmir,*
India 32°47N 75°18E **243** C6
Ramnagar *Uttarakhand,*
India 29°24N 79°7E **243** E8
Ramnäs *Sweden* 59°46N 16°12E **162** E10
Râmnicu Sărat *Romania* 45°26N 27°3E **183** E12
Râmnicu Vâlcea *Romania* 45°9N 24°21E **183** E9
Ramnous *Greece* 38°12N 24°3E **204** C6
Ramon *Isabela, Phil.* 16°50N 121°31E **232** C3
Ramon *Russia* 51°55N 39°21E **189** G10
Ramona *U.S.A.* 33°2N 116°52W **307** M10
Ramonville-St-Agne
France 43°33N 1°28E **174** E5
Ramore *Canada* 48°30N 80°25W **298** C3
Ramos *Brazil* 22°50S 43°14W **135** B1
Ramos → *Nigeria* 5°8N 5°22E **263** D6
Ramos I. *Phil.* 8°6N 117°1E **233** G1
Ramos Mejía *Argentina* 34°39S 58°33W **117** B1
Ramot *West Bank* 31°48N 35°13E **123** B2
Ramotswa *Botswana* 24°50S 25°52E **270** B4
Rampanalgas *Trin. & Tob.* 10°44N 60°59W **323** t
Rampart *U.S.A.* 65°30N 150°10W **303** D10
Rampur *H.P., India* 31°26N 77°43E **242** D7
Rampur *Mad. P., India* 23°25N 73°53E **242** H5
Rampur *Orissa, India* 21°48N 83°58E **244** D6
Rampur *Ut. P., India* 28°44N 77°18E **120** A2
Rampur *Ut. P., India* 28°50N 79°5E **243** E8
Rampur Hat *India* 24°10N 87°50E **243** G12
Rampura *India* 24°30N 75°27E **242** G6
Ramrama Tola *India* 21°52N 79°55E **243** J8
Ramree I. *Burma* 19°0N 93°40E **241** F5
Rāmsar *Iran* 36°53N 50°41E **247** B6
Ramsey *I. of Man* 54°20N 4°22W **168** C3
Ramsey *Ill., U.S.A.* 39°8N 89°7W **310** F7
Ramsey *N.J., U.S.A.* 41°4N 74°9W **313** E10
Ramsey L. *Canada* 47°13N 82°15W **298** C3
Ramsgate *N.S.W.,*
Australia 33°58S 151°8E **139** B1
Ramsgate *Kent, U.K.* 51°20N 1°25E **169** F9
Ramshai *India* 26°44N 88°51E **241** B2
Ramsjö *Sweden* 62°11N 15°37E **162** B9
Ramstein *Germany* 49°27N 7°32E **179** F3
Ramtek *India* 21°20N 79°15E **244** D4
Ramu *Kenya* 3°55N 41°10E **268** B5
Ramu → *Papua N. G.* 4°0S 144°41E **286** C3
Ramvik *Sweden* 62°49N 17°51E **162** B11
Ramville, Î. = Chancel, Î.
Martinique 14°41N 60°53W **322** j
Rana Pratap Sagar Dam
India 24°58N 75°38E **242** G6
Ranaghat *India* 23°15N 88°35E **243** H13
Ranahu *Pakistan* 25°55N 69°45E **242** G3
Ranai *Indonesia* 3°55N 108°22E **235** B3
Ranau *Malaysia* 6°2N 116°40E **235** A5
Ranau, Danau *Indonesia* 4°49S 103°55E **234** C2
Rancagua *Chile* 34°10S 70°50W **334** C1
Rance → *France* 48°34N 1°59W **172** D5
Rancharia *Brazil* 22°15S 50°55W **333** F1
Rancheria → *Canada* 60°13N 129°7W **296** A3
Ranchester *U.S.A.* 44°54N 107°10W **304** D10
Ranchi *India* 23°19N 85°27E **243** H11
Rancho Cordova *U.S.A.* 38°36N 121°18W **306** G5
Rancho Cucamonga
U.S.A. 34°10N 117°30W **307** L9
Rancho Park *U.S.A.* 34°3N 118°26W **126** B2
Ranco, L. *Chile* 40°15S 72°25W **336** B2
Rand *Australia* 35°33S 146°32E **283** C7
Rand ✈ (QRA) *S. Africa* 26°14S 28°8E **123** B2
Randaberg *Norway* 59°1N 5°36E **164** E2
Randabygda *Norway* 61°51N 6°20E **164** C3
Randalls I. *U.S.A.* 40°47N 73°55W **132** B2
Randalstown *U.K.* 54°45N 6°19W **166** B5
Randan *France* 46°2N 3°21E **173** F10
Randazzo *Italy* 37°53N 14°57E **201** E7
Randburg *S. Africa* 26°5S 27°57E **123** A1
Rander *India* 21°14N 72°47E **244** D1
Randers *Denmark* 56°29N 10°1E **163** H4
Randers Fjord *Denmark* 56°37N 10°20E **163** H4
Randfontein *S. Africa* 26°8S 27°45E **271** C4
Randhart *S. Africa* 26°16S 28°7E **123** B2
Randle *U.S.A.* 46°32N 121°57W **306** D5
Randolph *Mass., U.S.A.* 42°10N 71°2W **313** D13
Randolph *N.Y., U.S.A.* 42°10N 78°59W **312** D6
Randolph *Utah, U.S.A.* 41°40N 111°11W **304** F8
Randolph *Vt., U.S.A.* 43°55N 72°40W **313** C12
Randpark Ridge *S. Africa* 26°6S 27°58E **123** A1
Randsburg *U.S.A.* 35°22N 117°39W **307** K9
Randsfjorden *Norway* 60°25N 10°24E **164** D7
Randsverk *Norway* 61°44N 9°3E **164** C6
Randwick *Australia* 33°54S 151°14E **139** B2
Råneälven → *Sweden* 65°50N 22°20E **160** D20
Ranelagh *Ireland* 53°20N 6°15W **120** A2
Ranenburg = Chaplygin
Russia 53°15N 40°0E **188** F11
Ranfurly *N.Z.* 45°7S 170°6E **285** F5
Rangae *Thailand* 6°19N 101°44E **237** J3
Rangamati *Bangla.* 22°38N 92°12E **241** D4
Rangapara *India* 26°49N 92°39E **241** B4
Rangárvallasýsla □
Iceland 63°55N 20°0W **155** D7
Rangataua *N.Z.* 39°26S 175°28E **284** F4
Rangaunu B. *N.Z.* 34°51S 173°15E **284** A2
Range, The *Zimbabwe* 19°2S 31°2E **269** F3
Rangeley *U.S.A.* 44°58N 70°39W **313** B14
Rangeley L. *U.S.A.* 44°55N 70°43W **313** B14
Rangely *U.S.A.* 40°5N 108°48W **304** F9
Ranger *U.S.A.* 32°28N 98°41W **314** E5
Rangia *India* 26°28N 91°38E **241** B3
Rangiora *N.Z.* 43°19S 172°36E **285** D7
Rangiroa *French Polynesia* 15°10S 147°35W **289** f
Rangitaiki *N.Z.* 38°52S 176°24E **284** E5
Rangitaiki → *N.Z.* 37°54S 176°49E **284** D5
Rangitata → *N.Z.* 43°45S 171°15E **285** D6
Rangitikei → *N.Z.* 40°17S 175°15E **284** G4
Rangitoto ke te tonga = D'Urville I.
N.Z. 40°50S 173°55E **285** A8
Rangitoto Ra. *N.Z.* 38°25S 175°35E **284** E4
Rangkasbitung *Indonesia* 6°21S 106°15E **234** D3
Rangoon *Burma* 16°45N 96°20E **241** G6
Rangoon □ *Burma* 17°0N 96°10E **241** G6
Rangpur *Bangla.* 25°42N 89°22E **241** C2
Rangpuri *India* 28°32N 77°8E **120** B1
Rangsang *Indonesia* 1°20N 103°5E **237** M4
Rangwe *Kenya* 0°36S 34°35E **266** E3
Ranibennur *India* 14°35N 75°30E **245** G2
Raniganj *India* 27°3N 82°13E **243** F9
Ranikhet *India* 29°39N 79°25E **243** E8
Ranippettai *India* 12°56N 79°23E **245** H4
Raniwara *India* 24°50N 72°10E **242** G5
Rāniyah *Iraq* 36°15N 44°53E **213** D11
Ranka *India* 23°59N 83°47E **243** H10
Ranken → *Australia* 20°31S 137°36E **280** C2
Rankin *Ill., U.S.A.* 40°28N 87°54W **311** D9
Rankin *Tex., U.S.A.* 31°13N 101°56W **314** F4
Rankin Inlet *Canada* 62°30N 93°0W **294** E13
Rankins Springs
Australia 33°49S 146°14E **283** B7
Rankovicevo = Kraljevo
Serbia 43°44N 20°41E **202** C4
Rankweil *Austria* 47°17N 9°39E **180** D2
Rannersdorf *Austria* 48°7N 16°27E **142** B2
Rannoch, L. *U.K.* 56°41N 4°20W **167** E4
Rannoch Moor *U.K.* 56°38N 4°48W **167** E4
Rano Kau *Chile* 27°11S 109°26W **330** b
Rano Raraku, Volcán
Chile 27°7S 109°17W **330** b
Ranobe *Madag.* 17°10S 44°8E **272** B1
Ranobe, Helodranon' i
Madag. 23°3S 43°33E **272** C1
Ranohira *Madag.* 22°29S 45°24E **272** C2
Ranomafana *Toamasina,*
Madag. 18°57S 48°50E **272** B2
Ranomafana *Toliara,*
Madag. 24°34S 47°0E **272** C2
Ranomafana △ *Madag.* 21°16S 47°25E **272** C2
Ranomena *Madag.* 23°25S 47°17E **272** C2
Ranon *Vanuatu* 16°8S 168°7E **287** F6
Ranong *Thailand* 9°56N 98°40E **237** H2
Ranongga *Solomon Is.* 8°5S 156°35E **287** M9
Ranotsara Nord *Madag.* 22°48S 46°36E **272** C2
Ranpur *India* 20°5N 85°20E **244** D7
Rānsa *Iran* 33°39N 48°18E **247** C6
Ransbèche *Belgium* 50°56N 4°27E **116** B2
Ransdorp *Neths.* 52°24N 5°0E **112** A2
Ransiki *Indonesia* 1°30S 134°10E **231** E8
Ransom *U.S.A.* 41°9N 88°39W **311** C8
Rantabe *Madag.* 15°42S 49°39E **272** B2
Rantau *Indonesia* 2°56S 115°9E **235** C5
Rantau Abang *Malaysia* 4°52N 103°24E **237** K4
Rantaupanjang *Kalimantan Tengah,*
Indonesia 1°22S 112°4E **235** C4
Rantaupanjang *Kalimantan Timur,*
Indonesia 2°9N 117°25E **235** B5
Rantauprapat *Indonesia* 2°15N 99°50E **234** B1
Rantaupulut *Indonesia* 1°55S 112°12E **235** C4
Rantemario *Indonesia* 3°15S 119°57E **231** E5
Ranthambore △ *India* 26°10N 76°30E **242** F7
Rantoul *U.S.A.* 40°19N 88°9W **310** D8
Ranum *Denmark* 56°54N 9°14E **163** H3
Ranvad *India* 18°53N 72°55E **130** B2
Ranyah, W. → *Si. Arabia* 21°18N 43°20E **248** B3
Raohe *China* 46°47N 134°0E **220** A7
Raon l'Étape *France* 48°24N 6°50E **173** D13
Raoping *China* 23°42N 117°1E **229** F11
Raoui, Erg er *Algeria* 29°0N 2°0W **261** C4
Raoul I. *Pac. Oc.* 29°16S 177°54W **277** F15
Raoyang *China* 38°15N 115°45E **226** E8
Rap, Ko *Thailand* 9°19N 99°58E **237** b
Rapa *French Polynesia* 27°35S 144°20W **289** f
Rapa Nui = Pascua, I. de
Chile 27°7S 109°23W **330** b
Rapallo *Italy* 44°21N 9°14E **198** D6
Rapar *India* 23°34N 70°38E **242** H4
Rāpch *Iran* 25°40N 59°15E **247** E8
Rapel, Lago *Chile* 34°20S 71°14W **334** C1
Raper, C. *Canada* 69°44N 67°6W **295** D18
Rapid City *U.S.A.* 44°5N 103°14W **308** C2
Rapid River *U.S.A.* 45°55N 86°58W **308** C10
Rapla *Estonia* 59°1N 24°52E **188** C3
Raposo *Portugal* 38°40N 9°11W **126** A1
Rapti → *India* 26°18N 83°41E **243** F10
Rapu Rapu I. *Phil.* 13°12N 124°9E **232** E5
Raqaba ez Zarqa → *Sudan* 9°14N 29°44E **257** F2
Rāqūbah *Libya* 28°58N 19°2E **258** C3
Raquette → *U.S.A.* 45°0N 74°42W **313** B10
Raquette Lake *U.S.A.* 43°49N 74°40W **313** C10
Rara △ *Nepal* 29°30N 82°10E **243** E10
Raraka *French Polynesia* 16°10S 144°54W **289** f
Raroia *French Polynesia* 16°1S 142°27W **289** f
Rarotonga *Cook Is.* 21°30S 160°0W **289** h
Ras Abu Soma *Egypt* 26°51N 33°58E **256** B3
Ra's al 'Ayn *Syria* 36°45N 40°12E **213** D9
Ras al Hadd *Oman* 22°30N 59°50E **249** B7
Ra's al Khaymah *U.A.E.* 25°50N 55°59E **247** E7
Ra's aṭ Tīb *Tunisia* 37°1N 11°2E **258** A2
Ras el Ma *Algeria* 34°26N 0°50W **261** B4
Râs el Mâ *Mali* 16°35N 4°30W **262** B4
Râs el Oued *Algeria* 35°57N 5°2E **261** A6
Rās Ghārib *Egypt* 28°6N 33°18E **256** B3
Rās Kōh *Pakistan* 28°43N 64°55E **240** C2
Ra's Lānūf *Libya* 30°46N 18°11E **258** B3
Râs Muhammad △ *Egypt* 27°45N 34°16E **256** B3
Ra's Shamrah *Syria* 35°35N 35°45E **250** C6
Râs Sudr *Egypt* 29°40N 32°42E **256** B3
Rasa, Pta. *Argentina* 36°20S 56°41W **334** D4
Rasa, Punta *Argentina* 40°50S 62°15W **336** B4
Rasa I. *Phil.* 9°13N 118°26E **233** G2
Rasca, Pta. de la
Canary Is. 27°59N 16°41W **153** e1
Râşcani *Moldova* 47°58N 27°33E **183** C12
Rasdhoo *Maldives* 4°17N 72°58E **272** d
Rasdu Atoll *Maldives* 4°18N 72°58E **272** d
Raseiniai *Lithuania* 55°25N 23°5E **184** C10
Rashad *Sudan* 11°55N 31°0E **257** E3
Rashîd *Egypt* 31°21N 30°22E **256** H7
Rashîd, Masabb *Egypt* 31°22N 30°17E **256** H7
Rashin = Najin *N. Korea* 42°12N 130°15E **224** A5
Rashmi *India* 25°4N 74°22E **242** G6
Rasht *Iran* 37°20N 49°40E **213** D13
Rashtrapati Bhawan *Delhi, India* **120** c1
Rasi Salai *Thailand* 15°20N 104°9E **236** E5
Rasipuram *India* 11°30N 78°15E **245** J4
Raška *Serbia* 43°19N 20°39E **202** C4
Râsnov *Romania* 45°35N 25°27E **183** E10
Rason L. *Australia* 28°45S 124°25E **279** E3
Raşova *Romania* 44°15N 27°55E **183** F12
Rasovo *Bulgaria* 43°42N 23°17E **202** C7
Rasra *India* 25°50N 83°50E **243** G10
Rasskazovo *Russia* 55°38N 37°20E **129** C2
Rasskazovo *Russia* 52°35N 41°50E **190** D5
Rast *Romania* 43°53N 23°16E **183** G8
Rastaala *Finland* 60°15N 24°47E **121** B1
Rastatt *Germany* 48°50N 8°11E **179** G4
Rastede *Germany* 53°15N 8°12E **178** B4
Rastenburg = Kętrzyn
Poland 54°7N 21°22E **184** D8
Rastila *Finland* 60°12N 25°7E **121** B3
Răstolița *Romania* 46°59N 24°58E **183** D9
Rastyapino = Dzerzhinsk
Russia 56°14N 43°30E **190** B6
Rasul *Pakistan* 32°42N 73°34E **242** C5
Raszków *Poland* 51°43N 17°40E **185** G4
Raszyn *Poland* 52°9N 20°54E **142** C1
Rat → *Canada* 49°35N 97°10W **297** D9
Rat Buri = Ratchaburi
Thailand 13°30N 99°54E **236** F2
Rat I. *St. Lucia* 14°2N 60°58W **323** m
Rat I. *Alaska, U.S.A.* 51°48N 178°15E **303** L2
Rat Islands *U.S.A.* 52°0N 178°0E **303** L2
Rat L. *Canada* 56°10N 99°40W **297** B9
Ratak Chain *Pac. Oc.* 1°0N 170°0E **288** G8
Rätan *Sweden* 62°29N 14°33E **162** B8
Ratangarh *India* 28°5N 74°35E **242** E6
Raṭāwī *Iraq* 30°38N 47°13E **246** D5
Ratcatchers L. *Australia* 32°30S 143°12E **282** B5
Ratchaburi *Thailand* 13°30N 99°54E **236** F2
Rath *India* 25°36N 79°37E **243** G8
Rath Luirc *Ireland* 52°21N 8°40W **166** D3
Rathangan *Ireland* 53°13N 7°1W **166** C4
Rathbun L. *U.S.A.* 40°54N 93°5W **310** D4
Rathdrum *Ireland* 52°56N 6°14W **166** D5
Rathedaung *Burma* 20°29N 92°45E **241** E4
Rathenow *Germany* 52°37N 12°19E **178** C8
Rathfarnham *Ireland* 53°18N 6°16W **120** B2
Rathkeale *Ireland* 52°32N 8°56W **166** D3
Rathlin I. *U.K.* 55°18N 6°14W **166** A5
Rathmelton *Ireland* 55°2N 7°38W **166** A4
Ratho *U.K.* 55°55N 3°23W **121** B1
Ratho Station *U.K.* 55°56N 3°23W **121** B1
Ratibor = Racibórz *Poland* 50°7N 18°18E **185** H5
Rätikon *Austria* 47°0N 9°55E **180** D2
Ratingen *Germany* 51°18N 6°52E **178** D2
Ratlam *India* 23°20N 75°0E **242** H6
Ratmanova Ostrov
Russia 65°46N 169°6W **300** B6
Ratnagiri *India* 16°57N 73°18E **244** F1
Ratnapura *Sri Lanka* 6°40N 80°20E **245** L5
Rato *Portugal* 38°43N 9°8W **126** A2
Ratodero *Pakistan* 27°48N 68°18E **242** F3
Raton *U.S.A.* 36°54N 104°24W **305** H11
Ratsch = Radeče
Slovenia 46°5N 15°14E **199** B12
Rattaphum *Thailand* 7°8N 100°16E **237** J3
Ratten *Austria* 47°28N 15°44E **180** D8
Rattray Hd. *U.K.* 57°38N 1°50W **167** D7
Rättvik *Sweden* 60°52N 15°7E **162** D9
Ratz, Mt. *Canada* 57°23N 132°12W **296** B2
Ratzeburg *Germany* 53°40N 10°46E **178** B6
Raub *Malaysia* 3°47N 101°52E **237** L3
Rauch *Argentina* 36°45S 59°5W **334** D4
Raudales *Mexico* 17°27N 93°39W **319** D6
Raudeberg *Norway* 61°59N 5°7E **164** C2
Raufarhöfn *Iceland* 66°27N 15°57W **155** A11
Raufoss *Norway* 60°44N 10°37E **164** D7
Raukumara *N.Z.* 38°5S 177°55E **284** E6
Raukumara Ra. *N.Z.* 38°5S 177°55E **284** E6
Raul Soares *Brazil* 20°5S 42°22W **333** F3
Rauma *Finland* 61°10N 21°30E **188** B1
Rauma → *Norway* 62°34N 7°43E **164** B4
Raumo = Rauma *Finland* 61°10N 21°30E **188** B1
Raung, Gunung *Indonesia* 8°8S 114°3E **231** J17
Raurkela *India* 22°14N 84°50E **243** H11
Rausu-Dake *Japan* 44°4N 145°7E **220** B12
Răut → *Moldova* 47°15N 29°9E **183** C14
Rava-Ruska *Ukraine* 50°15N 23°42E **185** H10
Rava Russkaya = Rava-Ruska
Ukraine 50°15N 23°42E **185** H10
Ravahere *French Polynesia* 18°14S 142°9W **289** f
Ravalli *U.S.A.* 47°17N 114°11W **304** C6
Ravānsar *Iran* 34°43N 46°40E **213** E12
Ravanusa *Italy* 37°16N 13°58E **200** E6
Rāvar *Iran* 31°20N 56°51E **247** D8
Ravelston *U.K.* 55°57N 3°14W **121** B2
Ravena *U.S.A.* 42°28N 73°49W **313** D11
Ravenel *U.S.A.* 32°46N 80°15W **316** C9
Ravenna *Italy* 44°25N 12°12E **199** D9
Ravenna *Ky., U.S.A.* 37°41N 83°57W **311** G13
Ravenna *Nebr., U.S.A.* 41°1N 98°55W **308** E4
Ravenna *Ohio, U.S.A.* 41°9N 81°15W **312** E3
Ravensburg *Germany* 47°46N 9°36E **179** H5
Ravenshoe *Australia* 17°37S 145°29E **280** B4
Ravensthorpe *Australia* 33°35S 120°2E **279** F3
Ravenswood *Queens.,*
Australia 20°6S 146°54E **280** C4
Ravenswood *W. Va.,*
U.S.A. 38°57N 81°46W **309** F13
Ravensworth *Australia* 32°26S 151°4E **283** B9
Ravenwood *U.S.A.* 40°22N 94°41W **310** D2
Raver *India* 21°15N 76°2E **244** D3
Ravi → *Pakistan* 30°35N 71°49E **242** D4
Ravine Chaude *Guadeloupe* 16°14N 61°40W **322** e
Ravna Gora *Croatia* 45°24N 14°50E **199** C11
Ravna Reka *Serbia* 44°1N 21°35E **202** B5
Ravne na Koroškem
Slovenia 46°36N 14°59E **199** B11
Rawa Mazowiecka
Poland 51°46N 20°12E **185** G7
Rawaki *Kiribati* 3°43S 170°43W **277** A16
Rawalpindi *Pakistan* 33°38N 73°8E **242** C5
Rawamangun *Indonesia* 6°11S 106°52E **122** B2
Rawang *Malaysia* 3°20N 101°35E **237** L3
Rawene *N.Z.* 35°25S 173°32E **284** B2
Rawi, Ko *Thailand* 6°33N 99°14E **237** J2
Rawicz *Poland* 51°36N 16°52E **185** G3
Rawitsch = Rawicz
Poland 51°36N 16°52E **185** G3
Rawka → *Poland* 52°9N 20°8E **185** F7
Rawlinna *Australia* 30°58S 125°28E **279** F4
Rawlins *U.S.A.* 41°47N 107°14W **304** F10
Rawlinson Ra. *Australia* 24°40S 128°30E **279** D4
Rawson *Argentina* 43°15S 65°5W **336** B3
Raxaul *India* 26°59N 84°51E **243** F11
Ray *U.S.A.* 48°21N 103°10W **308** A2
Ray, C. *Canada* 47°33N 59°15W **299** C8
Ray City *U.S.A.* 31°5N 83°11W **316** D6
Ray Mts. *U.S.A.* 66°0N 152°0W **303** D10
Raya Ring, Ko *Thailand* 8°18N 98°29E **237** a
Rayachoti *India* 14°4N 78°50E **245** G4
Rayadurg *India* 14°40N 76°50E **245** G3
Rayagada *India* 19°15N 83°20E **244** E6
Raychikhinsk *Russia* 49°46N 129°25E **215** E13
Rāyen *Iran* 29°34N 57°26E **247** D8
Rayle *U.S.A.* 33°48N 82°54W **316** B7
Rayleigh *U.K.* 51°36N 0°37E **169** F8
Raymond *Alta., Canada* 49°30N 112°35W **296** D6
Raymond *Calif., U.S.A.* 37°13N 119°54W **306** H7
Raymond *Ill., U.S.A.* 39°19N 89°34W **310** E7
Raymond *N.H., U.S.A.* 43°2N 71°11W **313** C13
Raymond *Wash., U.S.A.* 46°41N 123°44W **306** D3
Raymond Terrace
Australia 32°45S 151°44E **283** B9
Raymondville *U.S.A.* 26°29N 97°47W **314** H6
Raymore *Canada* 51°25N 104°31W **297** C8
Rayners Lane *U.K.* 51°34N 0°23W **125** A1
Raynes Park *U.K.* 51°24N 0°12W **125** B2
Rayón *Mexico* 29°43N 110°35W **318** B2
Rayong *Thailand* 12°40N 101°20E **236** F3
Raypur *India* 22°28N 88°22E **124** C2
Raystown L. *U.S.A.* 40°25N 78°5W **312** F6
Raytown *U.S.A.* 39°1N 94°28W **310** E2
Rayville *U.S.A.* 32°29N 91°46W **314** E9
Raz, Pte. du *France* 48°2N 4°47W **172** D2
Razan *Iran* 35°23N 49°2E **213** E13
Ražana *Serbia* 44°6N 19°55E **202** B3
Ražanj *Serbia* 43°40N 21°31E **202** C5
Razāzah, Buḥayrat ar
Iraq 32°40N 43°35E **213** F10
Razazah, L. = Razāzah, Buḥayrat ar
Iraq 32°40N 43°35E **213** F10
Razdelna *Bulgaria* 43°13N 27°41E **203** C11
Razdel'naya = Rozdilna
Ukraine 46°50N 30°2E **183** D15
Razdolnoye *Russia* 43°30N 131°52E **220** C5
Razdolnoye *Ukraine* 45°46N 33°29E **189** K7
Razdory *Russia* 55°44N 37°17E **129** B1
Razeh *Iran* 32°47N 48°9E **247** C6
Razgrad *Bulgaria* 43°33N 26°34E **203** C10
Razgrad □ *Bulgaria* 43°33N 26°34E **203** C10
Razim, Lacul *Romania* 44°50N 29°0E **183** F14
Razlog *Bulgaria* 41°53N 23°28E **202** E7
Razmak *Pakistan* 32°45N 69°50E **242** C3
Re, Cu Lao *Vietnam* 15°22N 109°8E **236** E7
Ré, Î. de *France* 46°12N 1°30W **174** B2
Reach Falls *Jamaica* 18°2N 76°18W **320** a
Reading *U.K.* 51°27N 0°58W **169** F7
Reading *Mich., U.S.A.* 41°50N 84°45W **311** C12
Reading *Ohio, U.S.A.* 39°13N 84°26W **311** E12
Reading *Pa., U.S.A.* 40°20N 75°56W **313** F9
Reading □ *U.K.* 51°27N 0°58W **169** F7
Real, Cordillera *Bolivia* 17°0S 67°10W **330** D4
Real Felipe, Fuerte *Peru* 12°4S 77°9W **128** B1
Realejo Alto *Canary Is.* 28°22N 16°34W **153** e1
Realicó *Argentina* 35°0S 64°15W **334** D3
Réalmont *France* 43°48N 2°10E **174** E6
Ream *Cambodia* 10°34N 103°39E **237** G4
Ream △ *Cambodia* 10°30N 103°45E **237** G4
Reams, L. *U.S.A.* 28°26N 81°34W **133** B1
Réao *French Polynesia* 18°31S 136°23W **289** f
Reay Forest *U.K.* 58°22N 4°55W **167** C4
Rebais *France* 48°50N 3°10E **173** D10
Rebecca, L. *Australia* 30°0S 122°15E **279** F3
Rebi *Indonesia* 6°23S 134°7E **231** F8
Rebiana *Libya* 24°12N 22°10E **258** D4
Rebiana, Sahrâ' *Libya* 24°30N 21°0E **258** D4
Reboly *Russia* 63°49N 30°47E **160** E24
Rebun-Tō *Japan* 45°23N 141°2E **220** B10
Recanati *Italy* 43°24N 13°32E **199** E10
Recaş *Romania* 45°46N 21°30E **182** E6
Recco *Italy* 44°22N 9°9E **198** D6
Recherche, Arch. of the
Australia 34°15S 122°50E **279** F3
Rechna Doab *Pakistan* 31°35N 73°30E **242** D5
Rechytsa *Belarus* 52°21N 30°24E **177** B16
Recife *Brazil* 8°0S 35°0W **332** C5
Recife *Seychelles* 4°36S 55°42E **272** c
Recklinghausen *Germany* 51°37N 7°12E **170** C7
Reclining Buddha = Wat Pho
Bangkok, Thailand **113** b1
Recoleta *B. Aires,*
Argentina 34°36S 58°24W **117** B2
Recoleta *Santiago, Chile* 33°25S 70°40W **137** B2
Reconquista *Argentina* 29°10S 59°45W **334** B4
Recreio *Brazil* 8°0S 58°25W **331** B6
Recreo *Argentina* 29°25S 65°10W **334** B2
Recuay *Peru* 9°43S 77°28W **330** B2
Recz *Poland* 53°16N 15°31E **185** E2
Red = Hong → *Vietnam* 20°16N 106°34E **236** B5
Red → *U.S.A.* 31°1N 91°45W **314** F9
Red Bank *U.S.A.* 40°21N 74°5W **313** F10
Red Bay *Canada* 51°44N 56°25W **299** B8
Red Bluff *U.S.A.* 40°11N 122°15W **304** F2
Red Bluff Res. *U.S.A.* 31°54N 103°55W **305** L12
Red Bud *U.S.A.* 38°13N 89°59W **310** F7
Red Cliffs *Australia* 34°19S 142°11E **282** C5
Red Cloud *U.S.A.* 40°5N 98°32W **308** E4
Red Creek *U.S.A.* 43°14N 76°45W **313** C8
Red Deer *Canada* 52°20N 113°50W **296** C6
Red Deer → *Alta., Canada* 50°58N 110°0W **297** C7
Red Deer → *Man.,*
Canada 52°53N 101°1W **297** C8
Red Deer L. *Canada* 52°55N 101°20W **297** C8
Red Devil *U.S.A.* 61°46N 157°19W **303** E8
Red Fort = Lal Qila *Delhi, India* **120** a3
Red Hook *U.S.A.* 41°55N 73°53W **313** E11
Red Indian L. *Canada* 48°35N 57°0W **299** C8
Red L. *Canada* 51°3N 93°49W **297** C10
Red Lake *Canada* 51°3N 93°49W **297** C10
Red Lake Falls *U.S.A.* 47°53N 96°16W **308** B5
Red Lake Road *Canada* 49°59N 93°25W **297** C10
Red Lodge *U.S.A.* 45°11N 109°15W **304** D9
Red Mountain *U.S.A.* 35°37N 117°38W **307** K9
Red Oak *U.S.A.* 41°1N 95°14W **308** E6
Red River of the North →
N. Amer. 49°0N 97°15W **308** A5
Red Rock *Canada* 48°55N 88°15W **298** C2
Red Rock, L. *U.S.A.* 41°22N 92°59W **310** C3
Red Rocks Pt. *Australia* 32°13S 127°32E **279** F4
Red Sea *Asia* 25°0N 36°0E **238** E3
Red Slate Mt. *U.S.A.* 37°31N 118°52W **306** H8
Red Square *Moscow, Russia* **129** b2
Red Sucker L. *Canada* 54°9N 93°40W **298** B1
Red Tower Pass = Turnu Roşu, P.
Romania 45°33N 24°17E **183** E9
Red Volta → *Africa* 10°34N 0°30W **263** C4
Red Wing *U.S.A.* 44°34N 92°31W **308** C7
Reda *Poland* 54°40N 18°19E **184** D5
Redang, Pulau *Malaysia* 5°49N 103°2E **237** K4
Redange *Lux.* 49°46N 5°52E **170** E5
Redbridge □ *U.K.* 51°35N 0°7E **125** A4
Redcar *U.K.* 54°37N 1°4W **168** C6
Redcar & Cleveland □ *U.K.* 54°29N 1°0W **168** C7
Redcliff *Canada* 50°10N 110°50W **304** A8
Redcliffe *Australia* 27°12S 153°6E **281** D5
Redcliffe, Mt. *Australia* 28°30S 121°30E **279** E3
Reddersburg *S. Africa* 29°41S 26°10E **270** C4
Reddick *Fla., U.S.A.* 29°22N 82°12W **317** F7
Reddick *Ill., U.S.A.* 41°6N 88°15W **311** C8
Redding *Calif., U.S.A.* 40°35N 122°24W **304** F2
Redding *Iowa, U.S.A.* 40°36N 94°23W **310** D2
Redditch *U.K.* 52°18N 1°55W **169** E6
Redenção *Brazil* 4°13S 38°43W **332** B4
Redfern *Australia* 33°54S 151°12E **139** B2
Redfield *U.S.A.* 44°53N 98°31W **308** C4
Redford *U.S.A.* 44°38N 73°48W **313** B11
Redhead *Trin. & Tob.* 10°44N 60°58W **323** t
Redkey *U.S.A.* 40°21N 85°9W **311** D11
Redkino *Russia* 56°39N 36°16E **188** D9
Redlands *U.S.A.* 34°4N 117°11W **307** M9
Redmond *Oreg., U.S.A.* 44°17N 121°11W **304** D3
Redmond *Wash., U.S.A.* 47°40N 122°7W **306** C4
Redon *France* 47°40N 2°6W **172** E4
Redonda *Antigua & B.* 16°58N 62°19W **321** C7
Redonda, Pta. *Chile* 27°10S 109°22W **330** b
Redondela *Spain* 42°15N 8°38W **194** C2
Redondo *Portugal* 38°39N 7°37W **195** G3
Redondo Beach *U.S.A.* 33°50N 118°23W **307** M8
Redoubt Volcano *U.S.A.* 60°29N 152°45W **303** F9
Redpath Sugar Museum
Toronto, Canada **141** c3
Redruth *U.K.* 50°14N 5°14W **169** G2
Redvers *Canada* 49°35N 101°40W **297** D8
Redwater *Canada* 53°55N 113°6W **296** C6
Redwood *Wellington, N.Z.* 41°11S 174°49E **143** B1
Redwood *N.Y., U.S.A.* 44°18N 75°48W **313** B9
Redwood △ *U.S.A.* 41°40N 124°5W **304** F1
Redwood City *U.S.A.* 37°30N 122°15W **306** H4
Redwood Falls *U.S.A.* 44°32N 95°7W **308** C6
Ree, L. *Ireland* 53°35N 8°0W **166** C3
Reed City *U.S.A.* 43°53N 85°31W **309** D11
Reed L. *Canada* 54°38N 100°30W **297** C8
Reedley *U.S.A.* 36°36N 119°27W **306** J7
Reedsburg *U.S.A.* 43°32N 90°0W **308** D8
Reedsport *U.S.A.* 43°42N 124°6W **304** E1
Reedsville *U.S.A.* 40°39N 77°35W **312** F7
Reedy Creek *Australia* 36°58S 140°2E **282** D4
Reef Is. *Pac. Oc.* 10°15S 166°10E **277** C12
Reefton *N.Z.* 42°6S 171°51E **285** C6
Rees *Germany* 51°46N 6°24E **178** D2
Reese → *U.S.A.* 40°48N 117°4W **304** F5
Reetz = Recz *Poland* 53°16N 15°31E **185** E2
Refahiye *Turkey* 39°54N 38°47E **213** C8
Reflecting Pool *Washington, D.C., U.S.A.* **143** b1
Refshaleøen *Denmark* 55°41N 12°36E **118** A3
Reftele *Sweden* 57°11N 13°35E **163** G7
Refugio *U.S.A.* 28°18N 97°17W **314** G6
Rega → *Poland* 54°10N 15°18E **184** D2
Regalbuto *Italy* 37°39N 14°38E **201** E7
Regana, C. de *Spain* 39°25N 2°43E **206** B3
Regen *Germany* 48°58N 13°8E **179** G9
Regen → *Germany* 49°1N 12°6E **179** F8
Regeneração *Brazil* 6°15S 42°41W **332** C3
Regensburg *Germany* 49°1N 12°6E **179** F8
Regenstauf *Germany* 49°7N 12°8E **179** F8
Regents Park *Gauteng,*
S. Africa 26°14S 28°3E **123** B2
Regent's Park *London, U.K.* **125** a2
Regenwalde = Resko
Poland 53°47N 15°25E **184** E2
Reggâne = Zaouiet Reggâne
Algeria 26°32N 0°3E **261** C5
Reggello *Italy* 43°41N 11°32E **199** E8
Réggio di Calábria *Italy* 38°6N 15°39E **201** D8
Réggio nell'Emília *Italy* 44°43N 10°36E **198** D7
Reghin *Romania* 46°46N 24°42E **183** D9
Regina *Sask., Canada* 50°27N 104°35W **297** C8
Regina *Fr. Guiana* 4°19N 52°8W **329** C7
Regina Beach *Canada* 50°47N 105°0W **297** C8
Register *U.S.A.* 32°22N 81°53W **316** C8
Registro *Brazil* 24°29S 47°49W **335** A6
Rego Park *U.S.A.* 40°43N 73°51W **132** B2
Reguengos de Monsaraz
Portugal 38°25N 7°32W **195** G3
Rehar → *India* 23°55N 82°40E **243** H10
Rehli *India* 23°38N 79°5E **243** H8
Rehoboth *Namibia* 23°15S 17°4E **270** B2
Rehovot *Israel* 31°54N 34°48E **251** G5
Reïbell = Ksar Chellala
Algeria 35°13N 2°19E **261** A5
Reichenau = Rychnov nad Kněžnou
Czech Rep. 50°10N 16°17E **181** A9
Reichenbach = Dzierżoniów
Poland 50°45N 16°39E **185** H3
Reichenbach *Germany* 50°37N 12°17E **178** E8
Reichenberg = Liberec
Czech Rep. 50°47N 15°7E **180** A8
Reichshof = Rzeszów
Poland 50°5N 21°58E **185** H8
Reichstag *Berlin, Germany* **115** a3
Reid *Australia* 30°49S 128°26E **279** F4
Reidsville *Ga., U.S.A.* 32°6N 82°7W **316** C7
Reidsville *N.C., U.S.A.* 36°21N 79°40W **315** C15
Reifnig = Ribnica
Slovenia 45°45N 14°45E **199** C11
Reigate *U.K.* 51°14N 0°12W **169** F7
Reillo *Spain* 39°54N 1°53W **196** F3
Reims *France* 49°15N 4°1E **173** C11
Reina Adelaida, Arch.
Chile 52°20S 74°0W **336** D2
Reina Beatrix Int. ✈ **(AUA)**
Aruba 12°30N 70°1W **322** f
Reina Sofía, Centro de Arte
Madrid, Spain **127** c3
Reina Sofia, Tenerife ✈ **(TFS)**
Canary Is. 28°3N 16°33W **153** e1
Reinbeck *U.S.A.* 42°19N 92°36W **310** B4
Reinbek *Germany* 53°30N 10°16E **178** B6
Reindeer → *Canada* 55°36N 103°11W **297** B8
Reindeer I. *Canada* 52°30N 98°0W **297** C9
Reindeer L. *Canada* 57°15N 102°15W **297** B8
Reinga, C. *N.Z.* 34°25S 172°43E **284** A1
Reinheimen △ *Norway* 62°10N 7°45E **164** B4
Reinickendorf *Germany* 52°34N 13°22E **115** A3
Reinosa *Spain* 43°2N 4°15W **194** B6
Reinsvoll *Norway* 60°40N 10°38E **164** D7
Reitan *Norway* 62°49N 11°22E **164** B8
Reitz *S. Africa* 27°48S 28°29E **271** C4
Reivilo *S. Africa* 27°36S 24°8E **270** C3
Rejaf *Sudan* 4°45N 31°35E **257** G3
Rejmyre *Sweden* 58°50N 15°55E **163** F9
Rejowiec Fabryczny
Poland 51°5N 23°17E **185** G10
Reka → *Slovenia* 45°40N 14°0E **199** C11
Rekohu = Chatham I.
N.Z. 43°50S 176°20W **285** a
Rekola *Finland* 60°19N 25°4E **121** B3
Rekovac *Serbia* 43°51N 21°3E **202** C5
Reliance *Canada* 63°0N 109°20W **297** A7
Relizane *Algeria* 35°44N 0°31E **261** A5

Relizane □ *Algeria* 35°45N 0°55E **261** A5
Remad, Oued → *Algeria* 33°28N 1°20W **261** B4
Rémalard *France* 48°26N 0°47E **172** D7
Remanso *Brazil* 9°41S 42°4W **332** C3
Remarkable, Mt. *Australia* 32°48S 138°10E **282** B3
Remarkables, The *N.Z.* 45°10S 168°50E **285** F3
Rembang *Indonesia* 6°42S 111°21E **235** D4
Rembau *Malaysia* 2°35N 102°6E **234** B2
Rembert *U.S.A.* 34°6N 80°32W **316** A9
Rembertów *Poland* 52°15N 21°9E **142** B2
Rembrandthuis *Amsterdam, Neths.* **112** b3
Rembrandtpark *Neths.* 52°22N 4°51E **112** A2
Rembrandtplein *Amsterdam, Neths.* **112** b2
Remchi *Algeria* 35°2N 1°26W **261** A4
Remedios *Colombia* 7°2N 74°41W **328** B3
Remedios *Panama* 8°15N 81°50W **320** E3
Remedios de Escalada *Argentina* 34°43S 58°24W **117** C2
Remeshk *Iran* 26°55N 58°50E **247** E8
Remetea *Romania* 46°45N 25°29E **183** D10
Remich *Lux.* 49°32N 6°22E **170** E6
Remington *U.S.A.* 40°46N 87°9W **311** D9
Rémire *Fr. Guiana* 4°53N 52°17W **329** C7
Remiremont *France* 48°2N 6°36E **173** D13
Remo *Ethiopia* 6°48N 41°20E **257** F3
Rémola, Estany del *Spain* 41°16N 2°4E **114** B1
Remontnoye *Russia* 46°34N 43°37E **191** G6
Remoulins *France* 43°55N 4°35E **175** E8
Rempang *Indonesia* 0°51N 104°10E **234** B2
Rempart → *Mauritius* 20°19S 57°22E **272** e
Remparts → *Réunion* 21°22S 55°37E **272** f
Remscheid *Germany* 51°11N 7°12E **170** C7
Ren Xian *China* 37°8N 114°40E **226** F8
Rena *Norway* 61°8N 11°20E **164** C8
Rena → *Norway* 61°8N 11°23E **164** C8
Renascença *Brazil* 3°50S 66°21W **328** D4
Renca *Chile* 33°24S 70°42W **137** B1
Rend Lake *U.S.A.* 38°2N 88°58W **310** F8
Rendang *Indonesia* 8°26S 115°25E **231** J18
Rende *Italy* 39°20N 16°11E **201** C9
Rendezvous *Barbados* 13°4N 59°35W **323** r
Rendina *Greece* 39°4N 21°58E **204** B3
Rendova *Solomon Is.* 8°33S 157°17E **287** M9
Rendsburg *Germany* 54°17N 9°39E **178** A5
Renfrew *Canada* 45°30N 76°40W **313** A8
Renfrewshire □ *U.K.* 55°49N 4°38W **167** F4
Renfroe *U.S.A.* 32°14N 84°43W **316** C5
Rengat *Indonesia* 0°30S 102°45E **234** C2
Rengo *Chile* 34°24S 70°50W **334** C1
Renhua *China* 25°5N 113°40E **229** E9
Renhuai *China* 27°48N 106°24E **228** D6
Reni = Taranagar *India* 28°43N 74°50E **242** E6
Reni *Ukraine* 45°28N 28°15E **183** E13
Renigunta *India* 13°38N 79°30E **245** H4
Renk *Sudan* 11°50N 32°50E **257** E3
Renland *Greenland* 71°10N 26°30W **154** C8
Renmark *Australia* 34°11S 140°43E **282** C4
Rennebu *Norway* 62°52N 9°49E **164** B6
Rennell *Solomon Is.* 11°40S 160°10E **287** N11
Rennell Sd. *Canada* 53°23N 132°35W **296** C2
Rennemoulin *France* 48°50N 2°2E **134** A1
Renner Springs *Australia* 18°20S 133°47E **280** B1
Rennes *France* 48°7N 1°41W **172** D5
Rennick Glacier *Antarctica* 70°30S 161°45E **151** D11
Rennie L. *Canada* 61°32N 105°35W **297** A7
Reno *U.S.A.* 39°31N 119°48W **306** F7
Reno → *Italy* 44°38N 12°16E **199** D9
Renovo *U.S.A.* 41°20N 77°45W **312** E7
Renqiu *China* 38°43N 116°5E **226** E9
Rens *Denmark* 54°54N 9°5E **163** K3
Renshou *China* 29°59N 104°9E **228** C5
Rensselaer *Ind., U.S.A.* 40°57N 87°9W **311** D9
Rensselaer *N.Y., U.S.A.* 42°38N 73°45W **313** D11
Renton *U.S.A.* 47°28N 122°12W **306** C4
Renukoot *India* 24°12N 83°2E **243** G10
Renwick *N.Z.* 41°30S 173°51E **285** B8
Renwick Gallery *Washington, D.C., U.S.A.* **143** a1
Réo *Burkina Faso* 12°28N 2°35W **262** C4
Reocín = Puente San Miguel *Spain* 43°21N 4°5W **194** B6
Reotipur *India* 25°33N 83°45E **243** G10
Repalle *India* 16°2N 80°45E **245** F5
Répcelak *Hungary* 47°24N 17°1E **182** C2
Řeporyje *Czech Rep.* 50°1N 14°18E **135** B1
Reppen = Rzepin *Poland* 52°20N 14°49E **185** F1
Republic *Mo., U.S.A.* 37°7N 93°29W **308** G7
Republic *Wash., U.S.A.* 48°39N 118°44W **304** B4
Republican → *U.S.A.* 39°4N 96°48W **308** F5
Republiek *Suriname* 5°30N 55°13W **329** B6
République, Place de la *Paris, France* **134** b5
Repulse B. *Australia* 20°35S 148°46E **280** b
Repulse Bay *Nunavut, Canada* 66°30N 86°30W **295** D14
Repulse Bay *Hong Kong, China* 22°13N 114°10E **122** B2
Repy *Czech Rep.* 50°4N 14°17E **135** B1
Requena *Peru* 5°5S 73°52W **330** B3
Requena *Spain* 39°30N 1°4W **197** F3
Requin Bay *Grenada* 12°2N 61°39W **323** q
Réquista *France* 44°1N 2°32E **174** D6
Reşadiye *Muğla, Turkey* 36°45N 27°39E **205** E9
Reşadiye *Tokat, Turkey* 40°23N 37°20E **212** B7
Reşadiye Yarımadası *Turkey* 36°40N 27°45E **205** E9
Resava *Serbia* 44°4N 21°31E **202** B5
Resen *Macedonia* 41°5N 21°0E **202** E5
Reserve *U.S.A.* 33°43N 108°45W **305** K9
Resht = Rasht *Iran* 37°20N 49°40E **213** D13
Residenz *Germany* 48°8N 11°34E **131** B2
Residenzmuseum *Munich, Germany* **131** b3
Resistencia *Argentina* 27°30S 59°0W **334** B4
Reşiţa *Romania* 45°18N 21°53E **182** E6
Resko *Poland* 53°47N 15°25E **184** E2
Reso = Raisio *Finland* 60°28N 22°11E **188** B2
Resolute *Canada* 74°42N 94°54W **295** C13
Resolution I. *Nunavut, Canada* 61°30N 65°0W **295** E19
Resolution I. *N.Z.* 45°40S 166°40E **285** F1
Resplandes *Brazil* 6°17S 45°13W **332** C2
Resplendor *Brazil* 19°20S 41°15W **333** E3
Ressano Garcia *Mozam.* 25°25S 32°0E **271** C5
Restinga de Jurubatiba △ *Brazil* 22°5S 41°20W **333** F3
Reston *Man., Canada* 49°33N 101°6W **297** D8
Reston *Va., U.S.A.* 38°57N 77°20W **143** B2
Resulayn = Ceylanpınar *Turkey* 36°50N 40°2E **213** D9
Reszel *Poland* 54°4N 21°10E **184** D8
Retalhuleu *Guatemala* 14°33N 91°46W **320** D1
Retenue, L. de *Dem. Rep. of the Congo* 11°0S 27°0E **269** E2
Retezat, Munţii *Romania* 45°25N 23°0E **182** E8
Retezat △ *Romania* 45°23N 22°56E **182** E7
Retford *U.K.* 53°19N 0°56W **167** D8
Rethel *France* 49°30N 4°20E **173** C11
Rethem *Germany* 52°47N 9°22E **178** C5
Rethimno *Greece* 35°18N 24°30E **207** E5
Rethimno □ *Greece* 35°23N 24°28E **207** E5
Reti *Pakistan* 28°5N 69°48E **242** E3
Retiche, Alpi *Switz.* 46°30N 10°0E **179** E5
Retiers *France* 47°55N 1°23W **172** E5
Retiro *B. Aires, Argentina* 34°35S 58°23W **117** B2
Retiro *Madrid, Spain* 40°24N 3°40W **127** B1
Retiro, Puerto *Argentina* 34°36S 58°21W **117** B2
Retortillo *Spain* 40°48N 6°21W **194** E4
Retournac *France* 45°12N 4°2E **175** C8
Retreat *S. Africa* 34°4S 18°28E **118** B1
Rétság *Hungary* 47°58N 19°10E **182** C4
Réunion ☒ *Ind. Oc.* 21°0S 56°0E **272** f
Reus *Spain* 41°10N 1°5E **196** D6
Reusam *Indonesia* 2°11N 96°38E **234** B1
Reuterstadt Stavenhagen *Germany* 53°42N 12°54E **178** B8
Reutlingen *Germany* 48°29N 9°12E **179** G5
Reutov *Russia* 55°45N 37°50E **129** B5
Reutte *Austria* 47°29N 10°42E **180** D3
Reval = Tallinn *Estonia* 59°22N 24°48E **186** C3
Revda *Russia* 56°48N 59°57E **186** C10
Réveillon → *France* 48°42N 2°30E **134** B4
Revel = Tallinn *Estonia* 59°22N 24°48E **186** C3
Revel *France* 43°28N 2°1E **174** E6
Revelganj *India* 25°50N 84°40E **243** G11
Revelstoke *Canada* 51°0N 118°10W **296** C5
Reventazón *Peru* 6°10S 80°58W **330** B1
Revere *U.S.A.* 42°25N 71°0W **116** A2
Revere House *Boston, U.S.A.* **116** b3
Revigny-sur-Ornain *France* 48°49N 4°59E **173** D11
Revillagigedo, Is. de *Pac. Oc.* 18°40N 112°0W **318** D2
Revin *France* 49°55N 4°39E **173** C11
Revúca *Slovak Rep.* 48°41N 20°7E **181** C13
Revuè → *Mozam.* 19°50S 34°0E **269** F3
Rewa *India* 24°33N 81°25E **243** G9
Rewa → *Guyana* 3°19N 58°42W **329** C6
Rewari *India* 28°15N 76°40E **242** E7
Rexburg *U.S.A.* 43°49N 111°47W **304** E8
Rexdale *Canada* 43°43N 79°35W **141** A1
Rey *Iran* 35°35N 51°25E **247** C6
Rey, I. del *Panama* 8°20N 78°30W **320** E4
Rey, L. del *Mexico* 27°1N 103°26W **318** B4
Rey, Mayo → *Cameroon* 8°47N 14°7E **264** A2
Rey, Rio-del- → *Cameroon* 4°31N 8°45E **264** B1
Rey Bouba *Cameroon* 8°40N 14°15E **264** A2
Rey Malabo *Eq. Guin.* 3°45N 8°50E **263** E6
Reyðarfjörður *Iceland* 65°2N 14°13W **155** B12
Reyes *Bolivia* 14°19S 67°23W **330** C4
Reyes, Pt. *U.S.A.* 38°0N 123°0W **306** H3
Reyhanlı *Turkey* 36°16N 36°35E **250** B7
Reykhólar *Iceland* 65°27N 22°12W **155** B4
Reykholt *Árnessýsla, Iceland* 64°40N 21°18W **155** C5
Reykholt *Borgarfjarðarsýsla, Iceland* 64°10N 20°25W **155** C6
Reykjahlið *Iceland* 65°40N 16°55W **155** B10
Reykjanes *Iceland* 63°48N 22°40W **155** D4
Reykjanes Ridge *Atl. Oc.* 59°0N 31°0W **152** A8
Reykjavík *Iceland* 64°10N 21°57W **155** C5
Reykjavík Keflavík ✕ (KEF) *Iceland* 64°0N 22°45W **155** C4
Reynolds *Ga., U.S.A.* 32°33N 84°6W **316** C5
Reynolds *Ill., U.S.A.* 41°20N 90°40W **310** C6
Reynolds Ra. *Australia* 22°30S 133°0E **278** D5
Reynoldsville *Ga., U.S.A.* 30°51N 84°47W **316** E5
Reynoldsville *Pa., U.S.A.* 41°6N 78°53W **312** E6
Reynosa *Mexico* 26°7N 98°18W **319** B5
Reynosa Tamaulipas *Mexico* 19°30N 99°10W **128** A1
Reza'iyeh = Orūmīyeh *Iran* 37°40N 45°0E **213** D11
Reza'iyeh, L. = Orūmīyeh, Daryācheh-ye *Iran* 37°50N 45°30E **213** D11
Rēzekne *Latvia* 56°30N 27°17E **188** D4
Rezhitsa = Rēzekne *Latvia* 56°30N 27°17E **188** D4
Rezina *Moldova* 47°45N 28°58E **183** C13
Rezovo *Bulgaria* 42°0N 28°0E **203** D12
Rezvān *Iran* 27°34N 56°6E **247** E8
Rezvānshahr *Iran* 37°32N 49°7E **213** D13
Rgotina *Serbia* 44°1N 22°17E **202** B6
Rharbi, Zahrez *Algeria* 34°50N 2°55E **261** B5
Rharis, O. → *Algeria* 26°0N 5°4E **261** C6
Rhayader *U.K.* 52°18N 3°29W **169** E4
Rheda-Wiedenbrück *Germany* 51°50N 8°20E **178** D4
Rhede *Germany* 51°50N 6°24E **178** D2
Rhein → *Europe* 51°52N 6°2E **170** C6
Rhein-Main-Donau-Kanal *Germany* 49°1N 11°27E **179** F7
Rhein-Ruhr, Düsseldorf ✕ (DUS) *Germany* 51°17N 6°46E **178** D2
Rhein-Taunus △ *Germany* 50°10N 8°10E **179** E4
Rhein-Westerwald △ *Germany* 50°32N 7°20E **178** E3
Rheinbach *Germany* 50°38N 6°57E **178** E2
Rheine *Germany* 52°17N 7°26E **178** C3
Rheinfelden *Germany* 47°33N 7°47E **179** H3
Rheinhessen-Pfalz □ *Germany* 49°20N 8°0E **179** F3
Rheinland-Pfalz □ *Germany* 50°0N 7°0E **179** E2
Rheinsberg *Germany* 53°6N 12°54E **178** B8
Rheris, Oued → *Morocco* 30°50N 4°34W **260** B4
Rhin = Rhein → *Europe* 51°52N 6°2E **170** C6
Rhine = Rhein → *Europe* 51°52N 6°2E **170** C6
Rhine *U.S.A.* 31°59N 83°12W **316** D6
Rhinebeck *U.S.A.* 41°56N 73°55W **313** E11
Rhineland-Palatinate = Rheinland-Pfalz □ *Germany* 50°0N 7°0E **179** E2
Rhinelander *U.S.A.* 45°38N 89°25W **308** C9
Rhinns Pt. *U.K.* 55°40N 6°29W **167** F2
Rhino Camp *Uganda* 3°0N 31°22E **268** B3
Rhir, Cap *Morocco* 30°38N 9°54W **260** B3
Rho *Italy* 45°31N 9°2E **129** A1
Rhode Island □ *U.S.A.* 41°40N 71°30W **313** E13
Rhodes *N.S.W., Australia* 33°49S 151°6E **139** A1
Rhodes *Greece* 36°15N 28°10E **206** E12
Rhodes ✕ (RHO) *Greece* 36°23N 28°12E **205** E10
Rhodesia = Zimbabwe ■ *Africa* 19°0S 30°0E **269** F3
Rhodon *France* 48°42N 2°3E **134** B1
Rhodon → *France* 48°42N 2°4E **134** B1
Rhodope Mts. = Rhodopi Planina *Bulgaria* 41°40N 24°20E **203** E8
Rhodopi Planina *Bulgaria* 41°40N 24°20E **203** E8
Rhön *Germany* 50°24N 9°58E **178** E5
Rhondda *U.K.* 51°39N 3°31W **169** F4
Rhondda Cynon Taff □ *U.K.* 51°42N 3°27W **169** F4
Rhône □ *France* 45°54N 4°35E **175** C8
Rhône → *France* 43°28N 4°42E **175** E8
Rhône-Alpes □ *France* 45°40N 6°0E **175** C9
Rhum *U.K.* 57°0N 6°20W **167** E2
Rhyl *U.K.* 53°20N 3°29W **168** D4
Ri-Aba *Eq. Guin.* 3°28N 8°40E **263** E6
Ria Formosa △ *Portugal* 37°1N 7°48W **195** H3
Riachão *Brazil* 7°20S 46°37W **332** C2
Riacho de Santana *Brazil* 13°37S 42°57W **333** D3
Rialma *Brazil* 15°18S 49°34W **333** E2
Rialto Towers *Australia* 37°49S 144°57E **128** A1
Riam *Indonesia* 1°49S 111°54E **235** C4
Riang *India* 27°31N 92°56E **241** F18
Riangnom *Sudan* 9°55N 30°1E **257** F3
Riaño *Spain* 42°59N 4°59W **194** C6
Rians *France* 43°37N 5°44E **175** E9
Riansáres → *Spain* 39°32N 3°18W **195** F7
Riasi *India* 33°10N 74°50E **243** C6
Riau □ *Indonesia* 0°0 102°35E **234** B2
Riau, Kepulauan □ *Indonesia* 0°30N 104°20E **234** B2
Riau Arch. = Riau, Kepulauan □ *Indonesia* 0°30N 104°20E **234** B2
Riaza *Spain* 41°18N 3°30W **194** D7
Riaza → *Spain* 41°42N 3°55W **194** D7
Riba de Saelices *Spain* 40°55N 2°17W **196** E2
Riba-roja de Túria *Spain* 39°33N 0°34W **197** F4
Ribadavia *Spain* 42°17N 8°8W **194** C2
Ribadeo *Spain* 43°35N 7°5W **194** B3
Ribadesella *Spain* 43°30N 5°7W **194** B5
Ribado *Nigeria* 9°16N 12°47E **263** D7
Ribao *Cameroon* 6°32N 11°30E **263** D7
Ribas = Ribes de Freser *Spain* 42°19N 2°15E **196** C7
Ribas do Rio Pardo *Brazil* 20°27S 53°46W **331** E7
Ribauè *Mozam.* 14°57S 38°17E **269** E4
Ribble → *U.K.* 53°52N 2°25W **168** D5
Ribe *Denmark* 55°19N 8°44E **163** J2
Ribeauvillé *France* 48°10N 7°20E **173** D14
Ribécourt-Dreslincourt *France* 49°30N 2°55E **173** C9
Ribeira = Santa Uxía de Ribeira *Spain* 42°36N 8°58W **194** C2
Ribeira *Brazil* 22°49S 43°10W **135** A1
Ribeira Brava *Madeira* 32°41N 17°4W **153** c
Ribeira do Pombal *Brazil* 10°50S 38°32W **332** D4
Ribeira Grande *Azores* 37°49N 25°31W **153** d3
Ribeira Grande *C. Verde Is.* 17°0N 25°4W **153** j
Ribeirão *Brazil* 8°31S 35°23W **332** C4
Ribeirão Prêto *Brazil* 21°10S 47°50W **335** A6
Ribeiro Gonçalves *Brazil* 7°32S 45°14W **332** C2
Ribemont *France* 49°47N 3°27E **173** C10
Ribera *Italy* 37°30N 13°16E **200** E6
Ribérac *France* 45°15N 0°20E **174** C4
Riberalta *Bolivia* 11°0S 66°0W **331** C4
Ribes de Freser *Spain* 42°19N 2°15E **196** C7
Ribnica *Slovenia* 45°45N 14°45E **199** C11
Ribnitz-Damgarten *Germany* 54°15N 12°27E **178** A8
Ričany *Czech Rep.* 50°0N 14°40E **180** B7
Riccarda, Estany de la *Spain* 41°17N 2°6E **114** B1
Riccarton *N.Z.* 43°32S 172°37E **285** D7
Riccia *Italy* 41°30N 14°50E **201** A7
Riccione *Italy* 43°59N 12°39E **199** E9
Rice *U.S.A.* 34°5N 114°51W **307** L12
Rice L. *Canada* 44°12N 78°10W **312** B6
Rice Lake *U.S.A.* 45°30N 91°44W **308** C8
Riceboro *U.S.A.* 31°44N 81°26W **316** D8
Rich *Morocco* 32°16N 4°30W **260** B4
Rich, C. *Canada* 44°43N 80°38W **312** B4
Richard Toll *Senegal* 16°25N 15°42W **262** B1
Richards Bay *S. Africa* 28°48S 32°6E **271** C5
Richardson → *Canada* 58°25N 111°14W **297** B6
Richardson Lakes *U.S.A.* 44°46N 70°58W **309** C18
Richardson Mts. *N.Z.* 44°49S 168°34E **285** E3
Richardson Springs *U.S.A.* 39°51N 121°46W **306** F5
Riche, C. *Australia* 34°36S 118°47E **279** F2
Richelieu *France* 47°1N 0°20E **172** E7
Richey *U.S.A.* 47°39N 105°4W **304** C11
Richfield *U.S.A.* 38°46N 112°5W **304** G7
Richfield Springs *U.S.A.* 42°51N 74°59W **313** D10
Richford *U.S.A.* 45°0N 72°40W **313** B12
Richibucto *Canada* 46°42N 64°54W **299** C7
Richland *Ga., U.S.A.* 32°5N 84°40W **316** C5
Richland *Iowa, U.S.A.* 41°13N 92°0W **310** C5
Richland *Mo., U.S.A.* 37°51N 92°26W **310** G4
Richland *Wash., U.S.A.* 46°17N 119°18W **304** C4
Richland Center *U.S.A.* 43°21N 90°23W **308** D8
Richlands *U.S.A.* 37°6N 81°48W **309** G13
Richmond *N.S.W., Australia* 33°35S 150°42E **283** B9
Richmond *Queens., Australia* 20°43S 143°8E **280** C3
Richmond *Vic., Australia* 37°48S 145°0E **128** A2
Richmond *Nelson-Marlborough, N.Z.* 41°20S 173°12E **285** B8
Richmond *N. Yorks., U.K.* 54°25N 1°43W **168** C6
Richmond *Calif., U.S.A.* 37°46N 122°27W **136** B2
Richmond *Calif., U.S.A.* 37°56N 122°21W **306** H4
Richmond *Ind., U.S.A.* 39°50N 84°53W **311** E12
Richmond *Ky., U.S.A.* 37°45N 84°18W **311** G12
Richmond *Mich., U.S.A.* 42°49N 82°45W **312** D2
Richmond *Mo., U.S.A.* 39°17N 93°58W **310** E3
Richmond *Tex., U.S.A.* 29°35N 95°46W **314** G7
Richmond *Utah, U.S.A.* 41°56N 111°48W **304** F8
Richmond *Va., U.S.A.* 37°33N 77°27W **309** G15
Richmond *Vt., U.S.A.* 44°24N 72°59W **313** B12
Richmond, Mt. *N.Z.* 41°32S 173°22E **285** B8
Richmond Hill *Ont., Canada* 43°52N 79°27W **312** C5
Richmond Hill *Ga., U.S.A.* 31°56N 81°18W **316** D8
Richmond Hill *N.Y., U.S.A.* 40°41N 73°51W **132** B2
Richmond Park *U.K.* 51°26N 0°16W **125** B2
Richmond Peak *St. Vincent* 13°17N 61°13W **323** n
Richmond Ra. *N.S.W., Australia* 29°0S 152°45E **281** D5
Richmond Ra. *N.Z.* 41°32S 173°22E **285** B8
Richmond-upon-Thames □ *U.K.* 51°27N 0°17W **125** B2
Richmondville *U.S.A.* 42°38N 74°33W **313** D10
Richtersveld △ *S. Africa* 28°15S 17°10E **270** C2
Richville *U.S.A.* 44°25N 75°23W **313** B9
Richwood *Ohio, U.S.A.* 40°26N 83°18W **311** D13
Richwood *W. Va., U.S.A.* 38°14N 80°32W **309** F13
Ricla *Spain* 41°31N 1°24W **196** D3
Ricupe *Angola* 14°37S 21°25E **265** E4
Ridā' *Yemen* 14°25N 44°50E **248** D4
Riddarholmen *Stockholm, Sweden* **139** c1
Riddarhuset *Stockholm, Sweden* **139** c2
Ridder = Leninogorsk *Kazakhstan* 50°20N 83°30E **217** B10
Riddlesburg *U.S.A.* 40°9N 78°15W **312** F6
Ridge, The *India* 28°37N 77°10E **120** B2
Ridge Farm *U.S.A.* 39°54N 87°39W **311** E9
Ridge Spring *U.S.A.* 33°51N 81°40W **316** B8
Ridgecrest *U.S.A.* 35°38N 117°40W **307** K9
Ridgefield *Conn., U.S.A.* 41°17N 73°30W **313** E11
Ridgefield *N.J., U.S.A.* 40°49N 74°0W **132** B1
Ridgefield *Wash., U.S.A.* 45°49N 122°45W **306** E4
Ridgefield Park *U.S.A.* 40°52N 74°1W **132** A1
Ridgeland *Miss., U.S.A.* 32°26N 90°8W **315** E9
Ridgeland *S.C., U.S.A.* 32°29N 80°59W **316** C9
Ridgetown *Canada* 42°26N 81°52W **312** D3
Ridgeville *Ind., U.S.A.* 40°18N 85°2W **311** D11
Ridgeville *S.C., U.S.A.* 33°6N 80°19W **316** B9
Ridgewood *N.J., U.S.A.* 40°59N 74°7W **313** F10
Ridgewood *N.Y., U.S.A.* 40°42N 73°53W **132** B2
Ridgway *Ill., U.S.A.* 37°48N 88°16W **311** G8
Ridgway *Pa., U.S.A.* 41°25N 78°44W **312** E6
Riding Mountain △ *Canada* 50°50N 100°0W **297** C9
Ridley, Mt. *Australia* 33°12S 122°7E **279** F3
Riebeek-Oos *S. Africa* 33°10S 26°10E **270** D4
Ried *Austria* 48°14N 13°30E **180** C6
Riedlingen *Germany* 48°9N 9°28E **179** G5
Riedstadt *Germany* 49°45N 8°30E **179** F4
Riem *Germany* 48°8N 11°41E **131** B3
Rienza → *Italy* 46°49N 11°47E **199** B8
Riesa *Germany* 51°17N 13°17E **178** D9
Riesco, I. *Chile* 52°55S 72°40W **336** D2
Riesenburg = Prabuty *Poland* 53°47N 19°15E **184** E6
Riesenrad *Austria* 48°14N 16°23E **142** A2
Riesi *Italy* 37°17N 14°5E **201** E7
Riet → *S. Africa* 29°0S 23°54E **270** C3
Rietavas *Lithuania* 55°44N 21°56E **184** C8
Rietbron *S. Africa* 32°54S 23°10E **270** D3
Rietfontein *Namibia* 21°58S 20°58E **270** B3
Rieti *Italy* 42°24N 12°51E **199** F9
Rieupeyroux *France* 44°19N 2°12E **174** D6
Riez *France* 43°49N 6°6E **175** E10
Rif = Er Rif *Morocco* 35°1N 4°1W **261** A4
Rif *Iceland* 64°56N 23°49W **155** C3
Riffe L. *U.S.A.* 46°32N 122°26W **306** D4
Rifle *U.S.A.* 39°32N 107°47W **304** G10
Rifstangi *Iceland* 66°32N 16°12W **155** A10
Rift Valley *Africa* 7°0N 30°0E **254** G7
Rift Valley □ *Kenya* 0°20N 36°0E **268** B4
Rig Rig *Chad* 14°13N 14°25E **259** F2
Riga *India* 28°26N 95°2E **241** A5
Rīga *Latvia* 56°53N 24°8E **184** B11
Rīga ✕ (RIX) *Latvia* 56°54N 23°59E **184** B10
Riga, G. of *Latvia* 57°40N 23°45E **184** A10
Rigacikun *Nigeria* 10°40N 7°28E **263** C6
Rīgān *Iran* 28°37N 58°58E **247** D8
Rīgas Jūras Līcis = Riga, G. of *Latvia* 57°40N 23°45E **184** A10
Rigaud *Canada* 45°29N 74°18W **313** A10
Rigby *U.S.A.* 43°40N 111°55W **304** E8
Rīgestān *Afghan.* 30°15N 65°0E **240** C2
Riggins *U.S.A.* 45°25N 116°19W **304** D5
Rignac *France* 44°25N 2°16E **174** D6
Rigolet *Canada* 54°10N 58°23W **299** B8
Rigu *Ghana* 9°59N 0°48W **263** D4
Rihand Dam *India* 24°9N 83°2E **243** G10
Riihimäki *Finland* 60°45N 24°48E **188** B3
Riiser-Larsen-halvøya *Antarctica* 68°0S 35°0E **151** C4
Riiser-Larsen Ice Shelf *S. Ocean* 74°0S 19°0W **151** D2
Riiser-Larsen Sea *S. Ocean* 67°30S 22°0E **151** C4
Rijau *Nigeria* 11°8N 5°17E **263** C6
Rijeka *Croatia* 45°20N 14°21E **199** C11
Rijeka Crnojevića *Montenegro* 42°24N 19°1E **202** D3
Rijksmuseum *Amsterdam, Neths.* **112** c1
Rijssen *Neths.* 52°19N 6°31E **170** B6
Rika → *Ukraine* 48°11N 23°16E **183** B8
Rikā', W. ar → *Si. Arabia* 22°25N 44°50E **248** B4
Rike *Ethiopia* 10°50N 39°53E **257** E4
Rikers I. *U.S.A.* 40°47N 73°53W **132** B2
Riksdagshuset *Stockholm, Sweden* **139** b2
Rikuchū-Kaigan △ *Japan* 39°20N 142°0E **220** E11
Rikuzentakada *Japan* 39°0N 141°40E **220** E10
Rila *Bulgaria* 42°7N 23°7E **202** D7
Rila Planina *Bulgaria* 42°10N 23°20E **202** D7
Riley *U.S.A.* 43°32N 119°28W **304** E4
Rima → *Nigeria* 13°4N 5°10E **263** C6
Rimac *Peru* 12°2S 77°2W **124** B2
Rimah, Wadi ar → *Si. Arabia* 26°5N 41°30E **246** E4
Rimatara *French Polynesia* 22°38S 152°51W **289** f
Rimau, Pulau *Malaysia* 5°15N 100°16E **237** c
Rimavská Sobota *Slovak Rep.* 48°22N 20°2E **181** C13
Rimbey *Canada* 52°35N 114°15W **296** C6
Rimbo *Sweden* 59°44N 18°21E **162** E12
Rimé, O. → *Chad* 14°2N 18°3E **259** F3
Rimersburg *U.S.A.* 41°3N 79°30W **312** E5
Rimforsa *Sweden* 58°6N 15°43E **163** F9
Rímini *Italy* 44°3N 12°33E **199** D9
Rimouski *Canada* 48°27N 68°30W **299** C6
Rimrock *U.S.A.* 46°40N 121°7W **306** D5
Rinca *Indonesia* 8°45S 119°35E **235** F5
Rincon *Bonaire* 12°14N 68°20W **322** h
Rincon *Puerto Rico* 18°20N 67°15W **321** b
Rincon *Ga., U.S.A.* 32°18N 81°14W **316** C8
Rincón de la Victoria *Spain* 36°43N 4°18W **195** J6
Rincón de Romos *Mexico* 22°14N 102°18W **318** C4
Rincon Falls *Trin. & Tob.* 10°46N 61°24W **323** t
Rinconada *Argentina* 22°26S 66°10W **334** A2
Rind → *India* 25°53N 80°33E **243** G9
Rindal *Norway* 63°9N 9°13E **164** A6
Ringarum *Sweden* 58°21N 16°26E **163** F10
Ringas *India* 27°21N 75°34E **242** F6
Ringdove *Vanuatu* 16°40S 168°10E **287** F6
Ringe *Denmark* 55°13N 10°28E **163** J4
Ringebu *Norway* 61°32N 10°7E **164** C7
Ringgi *Solomon Is.* 8°55S 157°10E **287** M9
Ringgold Is. *Fiji* 16°15S 179°25W **287** A3
Ringim *Nigeria* 12°13N 9°10E **263** C6
Ringkøbing *Denmark* 56°5N 8°15E **163** H2
Ringkøbing Fjord *Denmark* 56°0N 8°15E **163** H2
Ringoma *Angola* 12°25S 17°32E **265** E3
Ringsaker *Norway* 60°54N 10°45E **164** D7
Ringsend *Ireland* 53°20N 6°12W **120** A2
Ringsjön *Sweden* 55°55N 13°30E **163** J7
Ringsted *Denmark* 55°25N 11°46E **163** J5
Ringvassøya *Norway* 69°56N 19°15E **160** B18
Ringwood *U.S.A.* 41°7N 74°15W **313** E10
Rinia *Greece* 37°23N 25°13E **205** D7
Rinjani, Gunung *Indonesia* 8°24S 116°28E **235** D5
Rinjani △ *Indonesia* 8°26S 116°23E **235** D5
Rinkeby *Sweden* 59°23N 17°55E **139** A1
Rinteln *Germany* 52°10N 9°8E **178** C5
Rio, Punta del *Spain* 36°49N 2°24W **197** J2
Rio Bonito = Caiapônia *Brazil* 16°57S 51°49W **331** D7
Rio Branco = Arcoverde *Brazil* 8°25S 37°4W **332** C4
Rio Branco = Paratinga *Brazil* 12°40S 43°10W **333** D3
Rio Branco = Roraima □ *Brazil* 2°0N 61°30W **329** C5
Rio Branco *Brazil* 9°58S 67°49W **330** B4
Rio Branco *Uruguay* 32°40S 53°40W **335** C5
Rio Bravo *Mexico* 25°59N 98°6W **319** B5
Rio Bravo △ *N. Amer.* 29°2N 102°45W **318** B4
Rio Bravo del Norte → *Mexico* 25°57N 97°9W **319** B5
Rio Brilhante *Brazil* 21°48S 54°33W **335** A5
Rio Bueno *Chile* 40°19S 72°58W **336** B2
Rio Bueno *Jamaica* 18°28N 77°28W **320** a
Rio Caribe *Venezuela* 10°42N 63°7W **329** A5
Rio Chico *Venezuela* 10°19N 65°59W **328** A4
Rio Claro *Brazil* 22°19S 47°35W **335** A6
Rio Claro *Trin. & Tob.* 10°20N 61°25W **323** t
Rio Cobre → *Jamaica* 17°59N 76°52W **320** a
Rio Colorado *Argentina* 39°0S 64°0W **336** A4
Rio Comprido *Brazil* 22°55S 43°13W **135** B1
Rio Cuarto *Argentina* 33°10S 64°25W **334** C3
Rio das Pedras *Mozam.* 23°8S 35°28E **271** B6
Rio de Contas *Brazil* 13°36S 41°48W **333** D3
Rio de Janeiro *Brazil* 22°54S 43°12W **135** B1
Rio de Janeiro □ *Brazil* 22°50S 43°0W **333** F3
Rio de Janeiro Galeão ✕ (GIG) *Brazil* 22°49S 43°15W **135** A1
Rio de Mouro *Portugal* 38°46N 9°15W **126** A1
Rio de Oro, B. de *W. Sahara* 23°45N 15°50W **260** D1
Rio do Prado *Brazil* 16°35S 40°34W **333** E3
Rio do Sul *Brazil* 27°13S 49°37W **335** B6
Rio Dulce △ *Guatemala* 15°43N 88°50W **320** C2
Rio Gallegos *Argentina* 51°35S 69°15W **336** D3
Rio Grande *Argentina* 53°50S 67°45W **336** D3
Rio Grande *Bolivia* 20°51S 67°17W **330** E4
Rio Grande *Brazil* 32°0S 52°20W **335** C5
Rio Grande *Zacatecas, Mexico* 23°50N 103°2W **318** C4
Rio Grande *Puerto Rico* 18°23N 65°50W **321** b
Rio Grande → *N. Amer.* 25°58N 97°9W **314** J6
Rio Grande City *U.S.A.* 26°23N 98°49W **314** H5
Rio Grande de Santiago → *Mexico* 21°36N 105°26W **318** C3
Rio Grande do Norte □ *Brazil* 5°40S 36°0W **332** C4
Rio Grande do Sul □ *Brazil* 30°0S 53°0W **335** C5
Rio Grande Rise *Atl. Oc.* 31°0S 35°0W **152** K8
Rio Hato *Panama* 8°22N 80°10W **320** E3
Rio Lagartos *Mexico* 21°36N 88°10W **319** C7
Rio Largo *Brazil* 9°28S 35°50W **332** C4
Rio Maior *Portugal* 39°19N 8°57W **195** F2
Rio Marina *Italy* 42°49N 10°25E **198** F7
Rio Mayo *Argentina* 45°40S 70°15W **336** C2
Rio Mulatos *Bolivia* 19°40S 66°50W **330** D4
Rio Muni □ *Eq. Guin.* 1°30N 10°0E **264** B2
Rio Negro *Brazil* 26°0S 49°55W **335** B6
Rio Negro *Chile* 40°47S 73°14W **336** B2
Rio Negro, Pantanal do *Brazil* 19°0S 56°0W **331** D6
Rio Novo = Ipiaú *Brazil* 14°8S 39°44W **333** D4
Rio Pardo = Ribas do Rio Pardo *Brazil* 20°27S 53°46W **331** E7
Rio Pardo *Brazil* 30°0S 52°30W **335** C5
Rio Pico *Argentina* 44°0S 70°22W **336** B2
Rio Pilcomayo △ *Argentina* 25°5S 58°5W **334** B4
Rio Platano △ *Honduras* 15°45N 85°0W **320** C2
Rio Prêto = Santa Rita de Cássia *Brazil* 11°0S 44°32W **332** D3
Rio Preto da Eva *Brazil* 2°46S 59°41W **329** D6
Rio Rancho *U.S.A.* 35°14N 106°41W **305** J10
Rio Real *Brazil* 11°28S 37°56W **333** D4
Rio Seco = Villa de María *Argentina* 29°55S 63°43W **334** B3
Rio Segundo *Argentina* 31°40S 63°59W **334** C3
Rio Simpson △ *Chile* 45°27S 73°30W **336** C2
Rio Tercero *Argentina* 32°15S 64°8W **334** C3
Rio Tinto *Brazil* 6°48S 35°5W **332** C4
Rio Tinto *Portugal* 41°11N 8°34W **194** D2
Rio Tuba *Phil.* 8°31N 117°26E **233** G1
Rio Turbio *Argentina* 51°32S 72°18W **336** D2
Rio Verde *Brazil* 17°50S 51°0W **333** E1
Rio Verde *San Luis Potosí, Mexico* 21°56N 99°59W **319** C5
Rio Verde de Mato Grosso *Brazil* 18°56S 54°52W **331** D7
Rio Viejo △ *Venezuela* 7°15N 71°20W **328** B3
Rio Vista *U.S.A.* 38°10N 121°42W **306** G5
Riobamba *Ecuador* 1°50S 78°45W **328** D2
Riohacha *Colombia* 11°33N 72°55W **328** A3
Rioja *Peru* 6°11S 77°5W **330** B2
Riom *France* 45°54N 3°7E **174** C7
Riom-ès-Montagnes *France* 45°17N 2°39E **174** C6
Rion-des-Landes *France* 43°55N 0°56W **174** E3
Rionegro *Antioquia, Colombia* 6°9N 75°22W **328** B2
Rionegro *Santander, Colombia* 7°15N 73°9W **328** B3
Rionero in Vúlture *Italy* 40°55N 15°40E **201** B8
Rioni → *Georgia* 42°14N 41°44E **191** J5
Riós *Spain* 41°58N 7°16W **194** D3
Riosinho → *Brazil* 7°7S 51°39W **331** B7
Riosucio *Caldas, Colombia* 5°30N 75°40W **328** B2
Riosucio *Choco, Colombia* 7°27N 77°7W **328** B2
Riou L. *Canada* 59°7N 106°25W **297** B7
Rioz *France* 47°26N 6°5E **173** E13
Riozinho → *Brazil* 2°55S 67°7W **328** D4
Ripatransone *Italy* 42°59N 13°46E **199** F10
Ripley *Ont., Canada* 44°4N 81°35W **312** B3
Ripley *Calif., U.S.A.* 33°32N 114°39W **307** M12
Ripley *N.Y., U.S.A.* 42°16N 79°43W **312** D5
Ripley *Ohio, U.S.A.* 38°45N 83°51W **311** F13
Ripley *Tenn., U.S.A.* 35°45N 89°32W **315** D10
Ripley *W. Va., U.S.A.* 38°49N 81°43W **309** F13
Ripoll *Spain* 42°15N 2°13E **196** C7
Ripollet *Spain* 41°26N 2°10E **114** A1
Ripon *N. Yorks., U.K.* 54°9N 1°31W **168** C6
Ripon *Calif., U.S.A.* 37°44N 121°7W **306** H5
Ripon *Wis., U.S.A.* 43°51N 88°50W **308** D9
Riposto *Italy* 37°44N 15°12E **201** E8
Rippin = Rypin *Poland* 53°3N 19°25E **185** E6
Ris *Norway* 59°56N 10°41E **133** A3
Risan *Montenegro* 42°32N 18°42E **202** D2
Risaralda □ *Colombia* 5°0N 76°10W **328** C2
Risby *Denmark* 55°41N 12°19E **118** A1
Riscle *France* 43°39N 0°5W **174** E3
Rishā', W. ar → *Si. Arabia* 25°33N 44°5E **246** E5
Rishiri-Rebun-Sarobetsu △ *Japan* 45°26N 141°30E **220** B10
Rishiri-Tō *Japan* 45°11N 141°15E **220** B10
Rishon le Ziyyon *Israel* 31°58N 34°48E **251** G5
Rishra *India* 22°42N 88°20E **124** A2
Rising Sun *U.S.A.* 38°57N 84°51W **311** F12
Risle → *France* 49°26N 0°23E **172** C7
Risnjak △ *Croatia* 45°25N 14°36E **199** C11
Rison *U.S.A.* 33°58N 92°11W **314** E8
Risør *Norway* 58°43N 9°13E **164** F6
Rissani *Morocco* 31°18N 4°12W **260** B4
Rita Blanca Cr. → *U.S.A.* 35°40N 102°29W **314** D3
Ritchie *U.S.A.* 38°52N 76°51W **143** B4
Ritchie's Arch. *India* 12°14N 93°10E **245** H11
Rithala *India* 28°43N 77°6E **120** A1
Riti *Nigeria* 7°57N 9°41E **263** D6
Ritidian Pt. *Guam* 13°39N 144°51E **302** d
Ritter, Mt. *U.S.A.* 37°41N 119°12W **306** H7
Rittman *U.S.A.* 40°58N 81°47W **312** F3
Ritzville *U.S.A.* 47°8N 118°23W **304** C4
Riu *India* 28°19N 95°3E **241** A5
Riva del Garda *Italy* 45°53N 10°50E **198** C7
Riva Ligure *Italy* 43°50N 7°50E **198** E4
Rivadavia *B. Aires, Argentina* 35°29S 62°59W **334** D3
Rivadavia *Mendoza, Argentina* 33°13S 68°30W **334** C2
Rivadavia *Salta, Argentina* 24°5S 62°54W **334** A3
Rivadavia *Chile* 29°57S 70°35W **334** B1
Rivarolo Canavese *Italy* 45°19N 7°43E **198** C4
Rivas *Nic.* 11°30N 85°50W **320** D2
Rivash *Iran* 35°28N 58°26E **247** C8
Rive-de-Gier *France* 45°32N 4°37E **175** C8
Rive Sud, Canal de la *Canada* 45°24N 73°31W **130** B2
River Cess *Liberia* 5°30N 9°32W **262** D3
River Edge *U.S.A.* 40°56N 74°1W **132** A1
River Estate & Waterwheel *Trin. & Tob.* 10°41N 61°33W **323** t
River Forest *U.S.A.* 41°53N 87°49W **119** B2
River Grove *U.S.A.* 41°55N 87°50W **119** B1
River Jordan *Canada* 48°26N 124°3W **306** B2
River North *Chicago, U.S.A.* **119** b1
River Ridge *U.S.A.* 29°57N 90°12W **131** B1
Rivera *Argentina* 37°12S 63°14W **334** D3
Rivera *Uruguay* 31°0S 55°50W **335** C4
Riverbank *U.S.A.* 37°44N 120°56W **306** H6
Riverdale *Calif., U.S.A.* 36°26N 119°52W **306** J7
Riverdale *Ga., U.S.A.* 33°34N 84°25W **316** B5
Riverdale *Md., U.S.A.* 38°57N 76°54W **143** B4
Riverdale *N.Y., U.S.A.* 40°59N 74°17W **132** A2
Riverdale Park *Canada* 43°40N 79°21W **141** A2
Riverhead *U.S.A.* 40°55N 72°40W **313** F12
Riverhurst *Canada* 50°55N 106°50W **297** C7
Riverlea *S. Africa* 26°12S 27°58E **123** B1
Rivers *Canada* 50°2N 100°14W **297** C8
Rivers □ *Nigeria* 4°30N 7°10E **263** E6
Rivers Inlet *Canada* 51°42N 127°15W **296** C3
Riversdale *Ont., Canada* 44°5N 81°20W **312** B3
Riversdale *N.Z.* 45°54S 168°44E **285** F3
Riversdale *Western Cape, S. Africa* 34°7S 21°15E **270** D3
Riverside *Calif., U.S.A.* 33°59N 117°22W **307** M9
Riverside *Ill., U.S.A.* 41°49N 87°49W **119** C2
Riverton *S. Austral., Australia* 34°10S 138°46E **282** C3
Riverton *Man., Canada* 51°1N 97°0W **297** C9
Riverton *N.Z.* 46°21S 168°0E **285** G3
Riverton *Ill., U.S.A.* 39°51N 89°33W **310** E7
Riverton *Wyo., U.S.A.* 43°2N 108°23W **304** E9
Riverview *Fla., U.S.A.* 27°52N 82°20W **317** H7
Riverview *Fla., U.S.A.* 30°32N 87°12W **317** E2
Riverwood *Australia* 33°57S 151°3E **139** B1
Rives *France* 45°21N 5°31E **175** C9
Rivesaltes *France* 42°47N 2°50E **174** F6
Riviera *U.S.A.* 35°4N 114°35W **307** K12
Riviera Beach *U.S.A.* 26°47N 80°3W **317** J9
Riviera di Levante *Italy* 44°15N 9°30E **198** D6
Riviera di Ponente *Italy* 44°10N 8°20E **198** D5
Rivière à Goyave, Pte. de la *Guadeloupe* 16°8N 61°33W **322** e
Rivière-au-Renard *Canada* 48°59N 64°23W **299** C7
Rivière des Anguilles *Mauritius* 20°29S 57°33E **272** e
Rivière-des-Prairies *Canada* 45°38N 73°34W **130** A2
Rivière-du-Loup *Canada* 47°50N 69°30W **299** C6
Rivière du Rempart *Mauritius* 20°6S 57°41E **272** e
Rivière-Pentecôte *Canada* 49°57N 67°1W **299** C6
Rivière-Pilote *Martinique* 14°26N 60°53W **322** j
Rivière St-Paul *Canada* 51°28N 57°45W **299** B8
Rivière-Salée *Martinique* 14°31N 61°0W **322** j
Rivne *Odesa, Ukraine* 46°1N 29°10E **183** D14
Rivne *Rivne, Ukraine* 50°40N 26°10E **177** C14
Rivne □ *Ukraine* 51°15N 26°30E **177** C14
Rívoli *Italy* 45°3N 7°31E **198** C4
Rivoli B. *Australia* 37°32S 140°3E **282** D4
Riwaka *N.Z.* 41°5S 172°59E **285** B7
Rixensart *Belgium* 50°43N 4°32E **116** B3
Rixheim *France* 47°40N 7°24E **173** E14
Riyadh = Ar Riyāḍ *Si. Arabia* 24°41N 46°42E **246** E5
Riyadh al Khabrā' *Si. Arabia* 26°2N 43°33E **246** E4
Riza *Greece* 40°31N 23°15E **202** F7
Rizal *Cagayan, Phil.* 17°51N 121°21E **232** C3
Rizal *Nueva Ecija, Phil.* 15°43N 121°6E **232** D3
Rizal *Zamboanga del N., Phil.* 8°35N 123°26E **233** G4
Rizal Park *Phil.* 14°35N 120°58E **127** B1
Rizal Stadium *Phil.* 14°34N 120°59E **127** B1
Rize *Turkey* 41°0N 40°30E **213** B9
Rize □ *Turkey* 41°0N 40°30E **213** B9
Rizhao *China* 35°25N 119°30E **227** G10
Rizokarpaso *Cyprus* 35°36N 34°23E **207** E10
Rizzuto, C. *Italy* 38°53N 17°5E **201** D10
Rjukan *Norway* 59°54N 8°33E **164** E5
Rjuven *Norway* 59°9N 7°8E **164** E4
Rkîz, L. *Mauritania* 16°50N 15°23W **262** B1
Ro *Greece* 36°9N 29°33E **205** E11
Roa *Dem. Rep. of the Congo* 3°49N 24°56E **264** B4
Roa *Oppland, Norway* 60°17N 10°37E **164** D7
Røa *Oslo, Norway* 59°57N 10°39E **133** A2
Roa *Spain* 41°41N 3°56W **194** D7
Roachdale *U.S.A.* 39°51N 86°48W **311** E10
Road Town *Br. Virgin Is.* 18°27N 64°37W **321** C7
Roan Plateau *U.S.A.* 39°20N 109°20W **304** G9
Roanne *France* 46°3N 4°4E **173** F11
Roanoke *Ala., U.S.A.* 33°9N 85°22W **316** B4
Roanoke *Ind., U.S.A.* 40°58N 85°22W **311** D11
Roanoke *Va., U.S.A.* 37°16N 79°56W **309** G14
Roanoke → *U.S.A.* 35°57N 76°42W **315** D16
Roanoke I. *U.S.A.* 35°53N 75°39W **315** D17
Roanoke Rapids *U.S.A.* 36°28N 77°40W **315** C16
Roatán *Honduras* 16°18N 86°35W **320** C2
Rob Roy *Solomon Is.* 7°23S 157°36E **287** L9
Robāt *Iran* 34°16N 46°47E **213** E12
Robāt Sang *Iran* 35°35N 59°10E **247** C8
Robāţkarīm *Iran* 35°25N 50°59E **247** C6
Robben I. *S. Africa* 33°46S 18°22E **270** D2
Robbins *U.S.A.* 41°38N 87°42W **119** D2
Robbins I. *Australia* 40°42S 145°0E **281** G4
Róbbio *Italy* 45°17N 8°35E **198** C5
Robe *Australia* 37°11S 139°45E **282** D3
Robe → *Australia* 21°42S 116°15E **278** D2
Röbel *Germany* 53°22N 12°35E **178** B8
Robert, Havre du *Martinique* 14°40N 60°55W **322** j
Robert Bourassa, Rés. *Canada* 53°40N 76°55W **298** B4
Robert Lee *U.S.A.* 31°54N 100°29W **314** F4
Roberta *U.S.A.* 32°43N 84°1W **316** C5
Roberts *U.S.A.* 40°37N 88°11W **311** D8
Roberts, Mt. *Trin. & Tob.* 10°47N 61°10W **323** t
Roberts, Mt. *Alaska, U.S.A.* 60°2N 166°16W **303** F6
Robertsdale *U.S.A.* 40°11N 78°6W **312** F6
Robertsganj *India* 24°44N 83°4E **243** G10
Robertsham *S. Africa* 26°15S 28°1E **123** B2
Robertson *S. Africa* 33°46S 19°50E **270** D2
Robertson I. *Antarctica* 65°15S 59°30W **151** C18
Robertson Ra. *Australia* 23°15S 121°0E **278** D3
Robertsport *Liberia* 6°45N 11°26W **262** D2
Robertstown *Australia* 33°58S 139°5E **282** B3
Roberval *Canada* 48°32N 72°15W **299** C5
Robeson Chan. *N. Amer.* 82°0N 61°30W **154** A4
Robesonia *U.S.A.* 40°21N 76°8W **313** F8
Robi *Ethiopia* 7°52N 39°38E **257** F4
Robinson *U.S.A.* 39°0N 87°44W **311** F9
Robinson → *Australia* 16°3S 137°16E **280** B2
Robinson Crusoe I. *Pac. Oc.* 33°38S 78°52W **330** c
Robinson Ra. *Australia* 25°40S 119°0E **279** E2
Robinvale *Australia* 34°40S 142°45E **282** C5
Robledo *Spain* 38°46N 2°26W **197** G2
Roblin *Canada* 51°14N 101°21W **297** C8
Roboré *Bolivia* 18°10S 59°45W **331** D6
Robson, Mt. *Canada* 53°10N 119°10W **296** C5
Robstown *U.S.A.* 27°47N 97°40W **314** H6
Roca, C. da *Portugal* 38°40N 9°31W **195** G1
Roca Partida, I. *Mexico* 19°1N 112°2W **318** D2
Rocamadour *France* 44°48N 1°37E **174** D5
Rocca San Casciano *Italy* 44°3N 11°50E **199** D8
Roccadaspide *Italy* 40°25N 15°1E **201** B8
Roccastrada *Italy* 43°0N 11°10E **199** F8
Roccella Iònica *Italy* 38°19N 16°24E **201** D9
Rocciamelone, Monte = Roche Melon *Italy* 45°12N 7°5E **175** C11
Rocha *Uruguay* 34°30S 54°25W **335** C5
Rochdale *U.K.* 53°38N 2°9W **168** D6
Roche Melon *Italy* 45°12N 7°5E **175** C11
Rochechouart *France* 45°50N 0°49E **174** C4

Rochedo *Brazil* 19°57S 54°52W **331** D7
Rochefort *Belgium* 50°9N 5°12E **170** D5
Rochefort *Charente-Maritime, France* 45°56N 0°57W **174** C3
Rochefort-en-Terre *France* 47°42N 2°22W **172** E4
Rochelle *Ga., U.S.A.* 31°57N 83°27W **316** D6
Rochelle *Ill., U.S.A.* 41°56N 89°4W **310** C7
Rochelle Park *U.S.A.* 40°54N 74°4W **132** A1
Rocher River *Canada* 61°23N 112°44W **296** A6
Roches, R. des → *Réunion* 21°0S 55°42E **272** f
Roche's Bluff *Montserrat* 16°42N 62°9W **323** p
Roches Noires *Mauritius* 20°6S 57°42E **272** e
Rocheservière *France* 46°57N 1°30W **172** F5
Rochester *Vic., Australia* 36°22S 144°41E **282** D6
Rochester *Medway, U.K.* 51°23N 0°31E **169** F8
Rochester *Ind., U.S.A.* 41°4N 86°13W **311** C10
Rochester *Minn., U.S.A.* 44°1N 92°28W **308** C7
Rochester *N.H., U.S.A.* 43°18N 70°59W **313** C14
Rochester *N.Y., U.S.A.* 43°10N 77°37W **312** C7
Rochester Hills *U.S.A.* 42°41N 83°8W **311** B13
Rociu *Romania* 44°43N 25°2E **183** F10
Rock → *Yukon, Canada* 60°7N 127°7W **296** A3
Rock → *Ill., U.S.A.* 41°29N 90°37W **310** C6
Rock, The *Australia* 35°15S 147°2E **283** C7
Rock Cr. → *U.S.A.* 38°54N 77°3W **143** B3
Rock Creek *U.S.A.* 41°40N 80°52W **312** E4
Rock Creek Park *U.S.A.* 38°56N 77°2W **143** B3
Rock Falls *U.S.A.* 41°47N 89°41W **310** C7
Rock Flat *Australia* 36°21S 149°13E **283** D8
Rock Hall *Barbados* 13°11N 59°36W **323** r
Rock Hill *U.S.A.* 34°56N 81°1W **315** D14
Rock Island *U.S.A.* 41°30N 90°34W **310** C6
Rock Port *U.S.A.* 40°25N 95°31W **308** E6
Rock Pt. *N.Z.* 41°8S 174°47E **143** A1
Rock Rapids *U.S.A.* 43°26N 96°10W **308** D5
Rock Sound *Bahamas* 24°54N 76°12W **320** B4
Rock Springs *Mont., U.S.A.* 46°49N 106°15W **304** C10
Rock Springs *Wyo., U.S.A.* 41°35N 109°14W **304** F9
Rock Valley *U.S.A.* 43°12N 96°18W **308** D5
Rockall *Atl. Oc.* 57°37N 13°42W **158** D3
Rockall Trough *Atl. Oc.* 57°0N 12°0W **152** A10
Rockaway Beach *U.S.A.* 40°34N 73°49W **132** C3
Rockaway Pt. *U.S.A.* 40°33N 73°54W **132** C2
Rockdale *N.S.W., Australia* 33°57S 151°8E **139** B1
Rockdale *Tex., U.S.A.* 30°39N 97°0W **314** F6
Rockdale *Wash., U.S.A.* 47°22N 121°28W **306** C5
Rockeby = Mungkan Kandju △ *Australia* 13°35S 142°52E **280** A3
Rockefeller Center *New York, U.S.A.* **132** c2
Rockefeller Plateau *Antarctica* 76°0S 130°0W **151** E14
Rockford *Ala., U.S.A.* 32°53N 86°13W **316** C3
Rockford *Ill., U.S.A.* 42°16N 89°6W **310** B7
Rockford *Iowa, U.S.A.* 43°3N 92°57W **310** A4
Rockford *Mich., U.S.A.* 43°7N 85°34W **311** A11
Rockford *Ohio, U.S.A.* 40°41N 84°39W **311** D12
Rockglen *Canada* 49°11N 105°57W **297** D7
Rockhampton *Australia* 23°22S 150°32E **280** C5
Rockingham *W. Austral., Australia* 32°15S 115°38E **279** F2
Rockingham *N.C., U.S.A.* 34°57N 79°46W **315** D15
Rockingham *Vt., U.S.A.* 43°11N 72°29W **313** C12
Rockingham B. *Australia* 18°5S 146°10E **280** B4
Rocklake *U.S.A.* 48°47N 99°15W **308** A4
Rockland *Ont., Canada* 45°33N 75°17W **313** A9
Rockland *Idaho, U.S.A.* 42°34N 112°53W **304** E7
Rockland *Maine, U.S.A.* 44°6N 69°7W **309** C19
Rockland *Mich., U.S.A.* 46°44N 89°11W **308** B9
Rocklands Bird Sanctuary *Jamaica* 18°24N 77°55W **320** a
Rocklands Reservoir *Australia* 37°15S 142°5E **282** D5
Rockledge *U.S.A.* 28°20N 80°43W **317** G9
Rocklin *U.S.A.* 38°48N 121°14W **306** G5
Rockly B. *Trin. & Tob.* 11°9N 60°46W **323** s
Rockmart *U.S.A.* 34°0N 85°3W **315** D12
Rockport *Ind., U.S.A.* 37°53N 87°3W **311** G9
Rockport *Mass., U.S.A.* 42°39N 70°37W **313** D14
Rockport *Tex., U.S.A.* 28°2N 97°3W **314** G6
Rocksprings *U.S.A.* 30°1N 100°13W **314** F4
Rockstone *Guyana* 5°59N 58°33W **329** B6
Rockville *Conn., U.S.A.* 41°52N 72°28W **313** E12
Rockville *Ind., U.S.A.* 39°46N 87°14W **311** E9
Rockville *Md., U.S.A.* 39°5N 77°9W **309** F15
Rockwall *U.S.A.* 32°56N 96°28W **314** E6
Rockwell City *U.S.A.* 42°24N 94°38W **310** B2
Rockwood *Ont., Canada* 43°37N 80°8W **312** C4
Rockwood *Maine, U.S.A.* 45°41N 69°45W **309** C19
Rockwood *Tenn., U.S.A.* 35°52N 84°41W **315** D12
Rocky Ford *U.S.A.* 38°3N 103°43W **304** G12
Rocky Fork L. *U.S.A.* 39°11N 83°26W **311** E13
Rocky Gully *Australia* 34°30S 116°57E **279** F2
Rocky Harbour *Canada* 49°36N 57°55W **299** C8
Rocky Island L. *Canada* 46°55N 83°0W **298** C3
Rocky Lane *Canada* 58°31N 116°22W **296** B5
Rocky Mount *U.S.A.* 35°57N 77°48W **315** D16
Rocky Mountain △ *U.S.A.* 40°25N 105°45W **304** F11
Rocky Mountain House *Canada* 52°22N 114°55W **296** C6
Rocky Mts. *N. Amer.* 49°0N 115°0W **304** B6
Rocky Point *Namibia* 19°3S 12°30E **270** A2
Rocky Run → *U.S.A.* 38°58N 77°14W **143** B2
Rocroi *France* 49°55N 4°30E **173** C11
Rod *Pakistan* 28°10N 63°5E **240** C1
Roda = Stadtroda *Germany* 50°52N 11°44E **178** E7
Roda *Greece* 39°48N 19°46E **206** B9
Roda, Gezîret el *Egypt* 30°1N 31°13E **117** A2
Roda I. = Roda, Gezîret el *Egypt* 30°1N 31°13E **117** A2
Rodaon *Austria* 48°8N 16°16E **142** B1
Rødberg *Norway* 60°17N 8°56E **164** D5
Rødby *Denmark* 54°41N 11°23E **163** K5
Rødbyhavn *Denmark* 54°39N 11°22E **163** K5
Roddickton *Canada* 50°51N 56°8W **299** B8
Rødding *Denmark* 55°23N 9°3E **163** J3
Rödeby *Sweden* 56°15N 15°37E **163** H9
Rødekro *Denmark* 55°4N 9°20E **163** J3
Rodenkirchen *Germany* 53°23N 8°26E **178** B4
Rodez *France* 44°21N 2°33E **174** D6
Ródhos = Rhodes *Greece* 36°15N 28°10E **206** E12
Rodi Gargánico *Italy* 41°55N 15°53E **199** G12
Rodia *Greece* 35°22N 25°1E **207** E6
Rodina *Kazakhstan* 52°10N 66°53E **217** B8
Rodna *Romania* 47°25N 24°50E **183** C9
Rodna ◎ *Australia* 23°45S 132°4E **278** D5
Rodnei, Munţii *Romania* 47°35N 24°35E **183** C9
Rodney *Canada* 42°34N 81°41W **312** D3
Rodney, C. *N.Z.* 36°17S 174°50E **284** C3
Rodney B. *St. Lucia* 14°5N 60°58W **323** m
Rodniki *Russia* 57°7N 41°47E **190** B5
Rodolivos *Greece* 40°55N 24°0E **202** F7
Rodonit, Kepi i *Albania* 41°35N 19°27E **202** E3
Rodopi □ *Greece* 41°5N 25°30E **203** E9
Rodopos *Greece* 35°34N 23°45E **207** E4
Rødovre *Denmark* 55°40N 12°26E **118** A2
Rodrigo de Freitas, L. *Brazil* 22°58S 43°12W **135** B1
Rodrigues *Ind. Oc.* 19°45S 63°20E **273** F5
Roe → *U.K.* 55°6N 6°59W **166** A5
Roebling *U.S.A.* 40°7N 74°47W **313** F10
Roebourne *Australia* 20°44S 117°9E **278** D2
Roebuck B. *Australia* 18°5S 122°20E **278** C3
Roebuck Roadhouse *Australia* 17°59S 122°36E **278** C3
Roehampton *U.K.* 51°27N 0°15W **125** B2
Roermond *Neths.* 51°12N 6°0E **170** C6
Roes Welcome Sd. *Canada* 65°0N 87°0W **295** E14
Roeselare *Belgium* 50°57N 3°7E **170** D3
Rogachev = Ragachow *Belarus* 53°8N 30°5E **177** B16
Rogačica *Serbia* 44°4N 19°40E **202** B3
Rogagua, L. *Bolivia* 13°43S 66°50W **330** C4
Rogaland □ *Norway* 59°12N 6°20E **164** E3
Rogaška Slatina *Slovenia* 46°15N 15°42E **199** B12
Rogatec *Slovenia* 46°15N 15°46E **199** B12
Rogatica *Bos.-H.* 43°47N 19°0E **182** G4
Rogatyn *Ukraine* 49°24N 24°36E **177** D13
Rogen *Sweden* 62°20N 12°20E **162** B6
Rogers *U.S.A.* 36°20N 94°7W **314** C7
Rogers Centre *Toronto, Canada* **141** c1
Rogers City *U.S.A.* 45°25N 83°49W **309** C12
Rogers Park *U.S.A.* 42°0N 87°40W **119** A3
Rogersville *Canada* 46°44N 65°26W **299** C6
Roggan → *Canada* 54°24N 79°25W **298** B4
Roggan L. *Canada* 54°8N 77°50W **298** B4
Roggeveen Basin *Pac. Oc.* 31°30S 95°30W **289** L18
Roggeveldberge *S. Africa* 32°10S 20°10E **270** D3
Roggiano Gravina *Italy* 39°37N 16°9E **201** C9
Rogliano *Haute-Corse, France* 42°57N 9°30E **175** F13
Rogliano *Italy* 39°10N 16°19E **201** C9
Rogoaguado, L. *Bolivia* 13°0S 65°30W **331** C4
Rogojampi *Indonesia* 8°19S 114°17E **231** J17
Rogoźno *Poland* 52°45N 16°59E **185** F3
Rogue → *U.S.A.* 42°26N 124°26W **304** E1
Roha *India* 18°26N 73°7E **244** E1
Rohan *France* 48°4N 2°45W **172** D4
Rohnert Park *U.S.A.* 38°16N 122°40W **306** G4
Rohri *Pakistan* 27°45N 68°51E **242** F3
Rohri Canal *Pakistan* 26°15N 68°27E **242** F3
Rohtak *India* 28°55N 76°43E **242** E7
Rohtsch-Sauerbrunn = Rogaška Slatina *Slovenia* 46°15N 15°42E **199** B12
Roi Et *Thailand* 16°4N 103°40E **236** D4
Roi-Georges, Îs. du *French Polynesia* 14°32S 145°8W **289** f
Roihuvuori *Finland* 60°11N 25°2E **121** B3
Roissy-en-Brie *France* 48°48N 2°39E **134** B4
Roja *Latvia* 57°29N 22°43E **184** A9
Rojas *Argentina* 34°10S 60°45W **334** C3
Rojište *Romania* 44°4N 23°56E **183** F8
Rojo, C. *Mexico* 21°33N 97°20W **319** C5
Rokan → *Indonesia* 2°0N 100°50E **234** B2
Rokel → *S. Leone* 8°30N 12°48W **262** D2
Rokin *Amsterdam, Neths.* **112** b2
Rokiškis *Lithuania* 55°55N 25°35E **188** E3
Rokitno *Russia* 50°57N 35°56E **189** G8
Rokycany *Czech Rep.* 49°43N 13°35E **180** B6
Rokytka → *Czech Rep.* 50°6N 14°27E **135** B3
Rolândia *Brazil* 23°18S 51°23W **335** A5
Røldal *Norway* 59°47N 6°50E **164** E3
Rolfe *U.S.A.* 42°49N 94°31W **310** B2
Rolla *Mo., U.S.A.* 37°57N 91°46W **310** G5
Rolla *N. Dak., U.S.A.* 48°52N 99°37W **308** A4
Rolleston *Queens., Australia* 24°28S 148°35E **280** C4
Rolleston *N.Z.* 43°35S 172°24E **285** D7
Rolling Fork → *U.S.A.* 37°55N 85°50W **311** G11
Rollingstone *Australia* 19°2S 146°24E **280** B4
Rom *Vest-Agder, Norway* 58°8N 7°5E **164** F4
Rom *Sudan* 9°54N 32°16E **257** F3
Roma *Queens., Australia* 26°32S 148°49E **281** D4
Roma *Italy* 41°54N 12°28E **136** B1
Roma *Sweden* 57°32N 18°26E **163** G12
Roma Fiumicino ✈ (FCO) *Italy* 41°48N 12°15E **199** G9
Roma-Los Saenz *U.S.A.* 26°24N 99°1W **314** H5
Roma Urbe ✈ *Italy* 41°57N 12°30E **136** B2
Római-Fürdő *Hungary* 47°34N 19°4E **117** A2
Roman, C. *U.S.A.* 33°0N 79°22W **315** E15
Romaine → *Canada* 50°18N 63°47W **299** B7
Romainville *France* 48°52N 2°26E **134** A3
Roman *Bulgaria* 43°8N 23°57E **202** C7
Roman *Romania* 46°57N 26°55E **183** D11
Roman Forum = Foro Romano *Rome, Italy* **136** c3
Roman-Kosh, Gora *Ukraine* 44°37N 34°15E **189** K8
Romanche → *France* 45°5N 5°43E **175** C9
Romang *Indonesia* 7°30S 127°20E **231** F7
Români *Egypt* 30°59N 32°38E **251** H3
Romania ■ *Europe* 46°0N 25°0E **183** D10
Romanija *Bos.-H.* 43°50N 18°45E **182** G3
Romano, C. *U.S.A.* 25°51N 81°41W **317** K8
Romano, Cayo *Cuba* 22°0N 77°30W **320** B4
Romano Banco *Italy* 45°25N 9°6E **129** B1
Romanov-Borisoglebsk = Tutayev *Russia* 57°53N 39°32E **188** D10
Romanovka = Basarabeasca *Moldova* 46°21N 28°58E **183** D13
Romanovna-Murmane = Murmansk *Russia* 68°57N 33°10E **160** B25
Romanovsk = Kropotkin *Russia* 45°28N 40°28E **191** H5
Romanovskiy Khutor = Kropotkin *Russia* 45°28N 40°28E **191** H5
Romans-sur-Isère *France* 45°3N 5°3E **175** C9
Romanshorn *Switz.* 47°33N 9°22E **179** H5
Romanzof C. *U.S.A.* 61°49N 166°6W **303** F6
Romashkovo *Russia* 55°43N 37°19E **129** B1
Rombari *Sudan* 4°33N 31°2E **257** G3
Romblon *Phil.* 12°33N 122°17E **232** E4
Romblon □ *Phil.* 12°30N 122°15E **232** E4
Romblon Pass. *Phil.* 12°27N 122°12E **232** E4
Rome = Roma *Italy* 41°54N 12°28E **136** B1
Rome *Ga., U.S.A.* 34°15N 85°10W **315** D12
Rome *N.Y., U.S.A.* 43°13N 75°27W **313** C9
Rome *Pa., U.S.A.* 41°51N 76°21W **313** E8
Romema *Israel* 31°48N 35°12E **123** B2
Romeoville *U.S.A.* 41°39N 88°3W **311** C8
Rometta *Italy* 38°10N 15°25E **201** D8
Romford *U.K.* 51°34N 0°11E **125** A5
Romilly-sur-Seine *France* 48°31N 3°44E **173** D10
Romitan *Uzbekistan* 39°56N 64°23E **216** E6
Rommani *Morocco* 33°31N 6°40W **260** B3
Romney *U.S.A.* 39°21N 78°45W **309** F14
Romney Marsh *U.K.* 51°2N 0°54E **169** F8
Romny *Ukraine* 50°48N 33°28E **189** G7
Rømø *Denmark* 55°10N 8°30E **163** J2
Romodan *Ukraine* 49°55N 33°15E **189** G7
Romodanovo *Russia* 54°26N 45°23E **190** C7
Romont *Switz.* 46°42N 6°54E **179** J2
Romorantin-Lanthenay *France* 47°21N 1°45E **173** E8
Rompin → *Malaysia* 2°49N 103°29E **237** L4
Romsdalen *Norway* 62°25N 7°52E **164** B4
Romsdalsfjorden *Norway* 62°38N 7°20E **164** B4
Romsey *U.K.* 51°0N 1°29W **169** G6
Ron *India* 15°40N 75°44E **245** G2
Ron *Vietnam* 17°53N 106°27E **236** D6
Rona *U.K.* 57°34N 5°59W **167** D3
Ronald Reagan Nat. Washington ✈ (DCA) *U.S.A.* 38°51N 77°2W **143** B3
Ronan *U.S.A.* 47°32N 114°6W **304** C6
Roncador, Cayos *Colombia* 13°32N 80°4W **320** D3
Roncador, Serra do *Brazil* 12°30S 52°30W **333** D1
Ronciglione *Italy* 42°17N 12°13E **199** F9
Ronco → *Italy* 44°24N 12°12E **199** D9
Ronda *Spain* 36°46N 5°12W **195** J5
Ronda, Serranía de *Spain* 36°44N 5°3W **195** J5
Rondane *Norway* 61°57N 9°50E **164** C6
Rondane △ *Norway* 61°55N 9°44E **164** C6
Ronde, Pt. *Dominica* 15°33N 61°29W **323** k
Ronde I. *Grenada* 12°29N 61°36W **323** q
Rondebosch *S. Africa* 33°58S 18°28E **118** A1
Rondón *Colombia* 6°17N 71°6W **328** B3
Rondônia *Brazil* 10°52S 61°57W **331** C5
Rondônia □ *Brazil* 11°0S 63°0W **331** C5
Rondonópolis *Brazil* 16°28S 54°38W **331** D7
Rondslottet *Norway* 61°55N 9°45E **164** C6
Rondu *Pakistan* 35°32N 75°10E **243** B6
Rong, Koh *Cambodia* 10°45N 103°15E **237** G4
Rong Jiang → *China* 24°35N 109°20E **228** E7
Rong Xian *China* 22°50N 110°31E **229** F8
Rong'an *China* 25°14N 109°22E **228** E7
Rongchang *China* 29°20N 105°32E **228** C5
Rongcheng *China* 37°9N 122°23E **227** F12
Ronge, L. la *Canada* 55°6N 105°17W **297** B7
Rongjiang *China* 25°57N 108°28E **228** E7
Rongotea *N.Z.* 40°19S 175°25E **284** G4
Rongshui *China* 25°5N 109°12E **228** E7
Rongxian *China* 29°23N 104°22E **228** C5
Rønne *Denmark* 55°6N 14°43E **163** J8
Ronne Ice Shelf *Antarctica* 77°30S 60°0W **151** D18
Ronneby *Sweden* 56°12N 15°17E **163** H9
Ronnebyån → *Sweden* 56°11N 15°18E **163** H9
Rönneshytta *Sweden* 58°56N 15°2E **163** F9
Ronsard, C. *Australia* 24°46S 113°10E **279** D1
Ronse *Belgium* 50°45N 3°35E **170** D3
Ronuro → *Brazil* 11°56S 53°33W **331** C7
Roodepoort *S. Africa* 26°11S 27°54E **271** C4
Roodhouse *U.S.A.* 39°29N 90°24W **310** E6
Roof Butte *U.S.A.* 36°28N 109°5W **305** H9
Rooiboklaagte → *Namibia* 20°50S 21°0E **270** B3
Rooniu, Mt. *Tahiti* 17°49S 149°12W **289** e
Roopville *U.S.A.* 33°27N 85°8W **316** B4
Roorkee *India* 29°52N 77°59E **242** E7
Roosendaal *Neths.* 51°32N 4°29E **170** C4
Roosevelt *U.S.A.* 40°18N 109°59W **304** F9
Roosevelt → *Brazil* 7°35S 60°20W **331** B5
Roosevelt, Mt. *Canada* 58°26N 125°20W **296** B3
Roosevelt I. *Antarctica* 79°30S 162°0W **151** D12
Roosevelt Island *New York, U.S.A.* **132** c3
Ropczyce *Poland* 50°4N 21°38E **185** H8
Roper → *Australia* 14°43S 135°27E **280** A2
Roper Bar *Australia* 14°43S 134°44E **280** A1
Roper River = St. Vidgeon's ◎ *Australia* 14°47S 134°53E **280** A1
Roppongi *Tokyo, Japan* **140** c3
Roque Pérez *Argentina* 35°25S 59°24W **334** D4
Roquefort *France* 44°2N 0°20W **174** D3
Roquemaure *France* 44°3N 4°48E **175** D8
Roquetas de Mar *Spain* 36°46N 2°36W **197** J2
Roquetes *Spain* 40°50N 0°30E **196** E5
Roquevaire *France* 43°20N 5°36E **175** E9
Roraima □ *Brazil* 2°0N 61°30W **329** C5
Roraima, Mt. *Venezuela* 5°10N 60°40W **329** B5
Røros *Norway* 62°35N 11°23E **164** B8
Rorschach *Switz.* 47°28N 9°28E **179** H5
Ros Comáin = Roscommon *Ireland* 53°38N 8°11W **166** C3
Rosa *Zambia* 9°33S 31°15E **269** D3
Rosa, C. *Algeria* 37°0N 8°16E **261** A6
Rosa, C. *Galápagos Is., Ecuador* 1°4S 91°10W **330** a
Rosa, Monte *Europe* 45°57N 7°53E **198** C4
Rosais, Pta. dos *Azores* 38°45N 28°19W **153** d1
Rosal de la Frontera *Spain* 37°59N 7°13W **195** H3
Rosales *Phil.* 15°54N 120°38E **232** D3
Rosalia *U.S.A.* 47°14N 117°22W **304** C5
Rosalie *Dominica* 15°22N 61°16W **323** k
Rosalie → *Dominica* 15°22N 61°15W **323** k
Rosalind Bank *W. Indies* 16°30N 80°30W **320** C3
Rosamond *U.S.A.* 34°52N 118°10W **307** L8
Rosans *France* 44°24N 5°29E **175** D9
Rosario *Argentina* 33°0S 60°40W **334** C3
Rosário *Maranhão, Brazil* 3°0S 44°15W **332** B3
Rosario *Baja Calif., Mexico* 30°0N 115°50W **318** B1
Rosario *Sinaloa, Mexico* 22°58N 105°53W **318** C3
Rosario *Paraguay* 24°30S 57°35W **334** A4
Rosario *Agusan del S., Phil.* 8°24N 125°59E **233** G5
Rosario *Batangas, Phil.* 13°50N 121°12E **232** E3
Rosario, Villa del *Venezuela* 10°19N 72°19W **328** A3
Rosario de la Frontera *Argentina* 25°50S 65°0W **334** B3
Rosario de Lerma *Argentina* 24°59S 65°35W **334** A2
Rosario del Tala *Argentina* 32°20S 59°10W **334** C4
Rosário do Sul *Brazil* 30°15S 54°55W **335** C5
Rosário Oeste *Brazil* 14°50S 56°25W **331** C6
Rosarito *Mexico* 32°20N 117°2W **307** N9
Rosarno *Italy* 38°29N 15°58E **201** D8
Rosas = Roses *Spain* 42°19N 3°10E **196** C8
Roscoe *Mo., U.S.A.* 37°58N 93°48W **310** G3
Roscoe *N.Y., U.S.A.* 41°56N 74°55W **313** E10
Roscoff *France* 48°44N 3°58W **172** D3
Roscommon *Ireland* 53°38N 8°11W **166** C3
Roscommon □ *Ireland* 53°49N 8°23W **166** C3
Roscrea *Ireland* 52°57N 7°49W **166** D4
Rose → *Australia* 14°16S 135°45E **280** A2
Rose, L. *Bahamas* 21°0N 73°30W **321** B5
Rose, L. *Fla., U.S.A.* 28°32N 81°30W **133** A1
Rose Belle *Mauritius* 20°24S 57°36E **272** e
Rose Blanche *Canada* 47°38N 58°45W **299** C8
Rose Bowl *U.S.A.* 34°9N 118°10W **126** B4
Rose Hall Great House *Jamaica* 18°31N 77°49W **320** a
Rose Hill = Port Mourant *Guyana* 6°15N 57°20W **329** B6
Rose Hill *Mauritius* 20°14S 57°27E **272** e
Rose Hill *Va., U.S.A.* 38°47N 77°6W **143** C3
Rose Pt. *Canada* 54°11N 131°39W **296** C2
Rose Rock *Grenada* 12°24N 61°28W **323** q
Rose Valley *Canada* 52°19N 103°49W **297** C8
Roseau *Dominica* 15°17N 61°24W **323** k
Roseau *Minn., U.S.A.* 48°51N 95°46W **308** A6
Rosebank *Gauteng, S. Africa* 26°8S 28°2E **123** a2
Rosebank *N.Y., U.S.A.* 40°36N 74°4W **132** C1
Rosebery *N.S.W., Australia* 33°55S 151°12E **139** B2
Rosebery *Tas., Australia* 41°46S 145°33E **281** G4
Rosebud *Vic., Australia* 38°21S 144°54E **282** E6
Rosebud *S. Dak., U.S.A.* 43°14N 100°51W **308** D3
Rosebud *Tex., U.S.A.* 31°4N 96°59W **314** F6
Roseburg *U.S.A.* 43°13N 123°20W **304** E2
Rosedal La Candelaria *Mexico* 19°20N 99°10W **128** B2
Rosedale *U.S.A.* 33°51N 91°2W **316** B1
Rosehearty *U.K.* 57°42N 2°7W **167** D6
Roseires Res. *Sudan* 11°51N 34°23E **266** B3
Roseland *Calif., U.S.A.* 38°25N 122°43W **306** G4
Roseland *Ill., U.S.A.* 41°42N 87°37W **119** C3
Rosemary *Canada* 50°46N 112°5W **296** C6
Rosemead *U.S.A.* 34°4N 118°4W **126** B4
Rosemont *Qué., Canada* 45°34N 73°33W **130** A2
Rosemont *Ill., U.S.A.* 41°59N 87°53W **119** B1
Rosenberg = Olesno *Poland* 50°51N 18°26E **185** H5
Rosenberg = Susz *Poland* 53°44N 19°20E **184** E6
Rosenberg *U.S.A.* 29°34N 95°49W **314** G7
Rosenberg Slot *Copenhagen, Denmark* **118** b2
Rosendaël *France* 51°3N 2°24E **173** A9
Rosendal *Norway* 59°59N 6°0E **164** E3
Rosendale *U.S.A.* 40°4N 94°51W **310** D2
Rosenheim *Germany* 47°51N 12°7E **179** H8
Rosenthal *Germany* 52°35N 13°22E **115** A3
Roses *Spain* 42°19N 3°10E **196** C8
Roses, G. de *Spain* 42°10N 3°15E **196** C8
Roseto degli Abruzzi *Italy* 42°41N 14°1E **199** F11
Rosetown *Canada* 51°35N 107°59W **297** C7
Rosetta = Rashîd *Egypt* 31°21N 30°22E **256** H7
Rosettenville *S. Africa* 26°15S 28°3E **123** B2
Roseville *Calif., U.S.A.* 38°45N 121°17W **306** G5
Roseville *Ill., U.S.A.* 40°44N 90°40W **310** D6
Roseville *Mich., U.S.A.* 42°30N 82°56W **312** D2
Roseville *Pa., U.S.A.* 41°51N 76°57W **313** E8
Rosewell *U.K.* 55°51N 3°8W **121** B3
Rosewood *Australia* 27°38S 152°36E **281** D5
Rosherville Dam *S. Africa* 26°13S 28°6E **123** B2
Roshkhvār *Iran* 34°58N 59°37E **247** C8
Rosières-en-Santerre *France* 49°49N 2°42E **173** C9
Rosignano Marittimo *Italy* 43°24N 10°28E **198** E7
Rosignol *Guyana* 6°15N 57°30W **329** B6
Roşiori de Vede *Romania* 44°9N 25°0E **183** F10
Rositsa *Bulgaria* 43°57N 27°57E **203** C11
Rositsa → *Bulgaria* 43°10N 25°30E **203** C9
Rösjön *Sweden* 59°26N 18°0E **139** A2
Roskilde *Denmark* 55°38N 12°3E **163** J6
Roskovec *Albania* 40°44N 19°43E **202** F3
Roslags-Näsby *Sweden* 59°25N 18°2E **139** A2
Roslavl *Russia* 53°57N 32°55E **188** F7
Roslin *U.K.* 55°51N 3°11W **121** B3
Roslindale *U.S.A.* 42°17N 71°7W **116** B2
Rosmaninhal *Portugal* 39°44N 7°5W **194** F3
Rosmead *S. Africa* 31°29S 25°8E **270** D4
Røsnæs *Denmark* 55°44N 10°55E **163** J4
Rosny-sous-Bois *France* 48°52N 2°30E **134** A4
Rosolini *Italy* 36°49N 14°57E **201** F7
Rosporden *France* 47°57N 3°50W **172** E3
Ross *Tas., Australia* 42°2S 147°30E **281** G4
Ross *N.Z.* 42°53S 170°49E **285** C5
Ross Béthio *Mauritania* 16°15N 16°8W **262** B1
Ross Dependency *Antarctica* 76°0S 170°0W **151** D12
Ross I. *Antarctica* 77°30S 168°0E **151** D11
Ross Ice Shelf *Antarctica* 80°0S 180°0E **151** E12
Ross L. *U.S.A.* 48°44N 121°4W **304** B3
Ross Mhic Thriúin = New Ross *Ireland* 52°23N 6°57W **166** D5
Ross-on-Wye *U.K.* 51°54N 2°34W **169** F5
Ross River *N. Terr., Australia* 23°44S 134°30E **280** C1
Ross River *Yukon, Canada* 62°30N 131°30W **296** A2
Ross Sea *Antarctica* 74°0S 178°0E **151** D11
Rossall Pt. *U.K.* 53°55N 3°3W **168** D4
Rossan Pt. *Ireland* 54°42N 8°47W **166** B3
Rossano *Italy* 39°36N 16°39E **201** C9
Rossburn *Canada* 50°40N 100°49W **297** C8
Rosseau *Canada* 45°16N 79°39W **312** A5
Rosseau, L. *Canada* 45°10N 79°35W **312** A5
Rössel = Reszel *Poland* 54°4N 21°10E **184** D8
Rossel I. *Papua N. G.* 11°21S 154°9E **286** F8
Rosses, The *Ireland* 55°2N 8°20W **166** A3
Rossford *U.S.A.* 41°36N 83°34W **311** C13
Rossignol, L. *Canada* 52°43N 73°40W **298** B5
Rossignol L. *Canada* 44°12N 65°10W **299** D6
Rossiya = Russia ■ *Eurasia* 62°0N 105°0E **215** C11
Rosskreppfjorden *Norway* 59°4N 7°10E **164** E4
Rossland *Canada* 49°6N 117°50W **296** D5
Rosslare *Ireland* 52°17N 6°24W **166** D5
Rosslare Harbour *Ireland* 52°15N 6°20W **166** D5
Rosslau *Germany* 51°52N 12°15E **178** D8
Rosslyn *U.S.A.* 38°53N 77°4W **143** B3
Rossmore *Canada* 44°8N 77°23W **312** B7
Rosso *Mauritania* 16°40N 15°45W **262** B1
Rosso, C. *France* 42°13N 8°32E **175** F12
Rossosh *Russia* 50°15N 39°28E **189** G10
Rossvatnet *Norway* 65°45N 14°5E **160** D16
Rossville *Ill., U.S.A.* 40°23N 87°40W **311** D9
Rossville *Ind., U.S.A.* 40°25N 86°36W **311** D10
Røst *Norway* 67°32N 12°10E **160** C15
Rostāq *Afghan.* 37°7N 69°49E **240** A3
Rosthern *Canada* 52°40N 106°20W **297** C7
Rostock *Germany* 54°5N 12°8E **178** A8
Rostov *Don, Russia* 47°15N 39°45E **189** J10
Rostov *Yaroslavl, Russia* 57°14N 39°25E **188** D10
Rostov □ *Russia* 48°50N 41°10E **191** F5
Rostrenen *France* 48°14N 3°21W **172** D3
Roswell *Ga., U.S.A.* 34°2N 84°22W **316** A5
Roswell *N. Mex., U.S.A.* 33°24N 104°32W **305** K11
Rosyth *U.K.* 56°2N 3°25W **121** A1
Rot-Front = Dobropole *Ukraine* 48°25N 37°2E **189** H9
Rota *N. Marianas* 14°9N 145°12E **302** a
Rota *Spain* 36°37N 6°20W **195** J4
Rotan *U.S.A.* 32°51N 100°28W **314** E4
Rotenburg *Hessen, Germany* 50°59N 9°44E **178** E5
Rotenburg *Niedersachsen, Germany* 53°6N 9°25E **178** B5
Roth *Germany* 49°15N 11°5E **179** F7
Rothaargebirge *Germany* 51°2N 8°13E **178** D4
Rothaargebirge △ *Germany* 51°0N 8°15E **178** E4
Rothenburg ob der Tauber *Germany* 49°23N 10°11E **179** F6
Rother → *U.K.* 50°59N 0°45E **169** G8
Rothera *Antarctica* 67°34S 68°8W **151** C17
Rotherham *U.K.* 53°26N 1°20W **168** D6
Rotherhithe *U.K.* 51°29N 0°2W **125** B3
Rothes *U.K.* 57°32N 3°13W **167** D5
Rothesay *N.B., Canada* 45°23N 66°0W **299** C6
Rothesay *Argyll & Bute, U.K.* 55°50N 5°3W **167** F3
Rothneusiedl *Austria* 48°8N 16°23E **142** B2
Rothschmaige *Germany* 48°14N 11°27E **131** A1
Roti *Indonesia* 10°50S 123°0E **231** F6
Rotja, Pta. *Spain* 38°38N 1°35E **206** D2
Rotnes *Norway* 60°3N 10°51E **164** D7
Roto *Australia* 33°0S 145°30E **283** B6
Rotoaira, L. *N.Z.* 39°3S 175°45E **284** F4
Rotoehu, L. *N.Z.* 38°1S 176°32E **284** E5
Rotoiti, L. *Bay of Plenty, N.Z.* 38°2S 176°26E **284** E5
Rotoiti, L. *W. Coast, N.Z.* 41°51S 172°49E **285** B7
Rotoma, L. *N.Z.* 38°2S 176°35E **284** E5
Rotondo, Mte. *France* 42°14N 9°8E **175** F13
Rotoroa, L. *N.Z.* 41°55S 172°39E **285** B7
Rotorua *N.Z.* 38°9S 176°16E **284** E5
Rotorua, L. *N.Z.* 38°5S 176°18E **284** E5
Rott → *Germany* 48°27N 13°25E **179** G9
Rottenburg *Germany* 48°28N 8°55E **179** G4
Rottenmann *Austria* 47°31N 14°22E **180** D7
Rotterdam *Neths.* 51°55N 4°30E **170** C4
Rotterdam *N.Y., U.S.A.* 42°48N 74°1W **313** D10
Rottne *Sweden* 57°1N 14°54E **163** G8
Rottnest I. *Australia* 32°0S 115°27E **279** F2
Rottumeroog *Neths.* 53°33N 6°34E **170** A6
Rottweil *Germany* 48°9N 8°37E **179** G4
Rotuma *Fiji* 12°25S 177°5E **277** C14
Roubaix *France* 50°40N 3°10E **173** B10
Rouche Island *St. Lucia* 13°57N 60°52W **323** m
Roudnice nad Labem *Czech Rep.* 50°25N 14°15E **180** A7
Rouen *France* 49°27N 1°4E **172** C8
Rouergue *France* 44°15N 2°0E **174** D5
Rouge Hill *Canada* 43°48N 79°6W **141** A3
Rough Ridge *N.Z.* 45°10S 169°55E **285** F4
Rouillac *France* 45°47N 0°4W **174** C3
Rouissat *Algeria* 31°55N 5°20E **261** B6
Rouleau *Canada* 50°10N 104°56W **297** C8
Roulers = Roeselare *Belgium* 50°57N 3°7E **170** D3
Roulpmaulpma ◎ *Australia* 23°52S 133°0E **278** D5
Round Hill *Jamaica* 17°50N 77°23W **320** a
Round Hill *St. Kitts & Nevis* 17°11N 62°36W **322** d
Round I. *China* 22°13N 114°11E **122** B2
Round Mountain *U.S.A.* 38°43N 117°4W **304** G5
Round Mt. *Australia* 30°26S 152°16E **283** A10
Round Rock *U.S.A.* 30°31N 97°41W **314** F6
Roundhouse Park *Toronto, Canada* **141** c2
Roundup *U.S.A.* 46°27N 108°33W **304** C9
Roura *Fr. Guiana* 4°44N 52°20W **329** C7
Rousay *U.K.* 59°10N 3°2W **167** B5
Rouses Point *U.S.A.* 44°59N 73°22W **313** B11
Rouseville *U.S.A.* 41°28N 79°42W **312** E5
Rousse = Ruse *Bulgaria* 43°48N 25°59E **203** C9
Roussenski Lom △ *Bulgaria* 43°40N 26°10E **203** C10
Roussillac Swamp *Trin. & Tob.* 10°14N 61°35W **323** t
Roussillon *Isère, France* 45°24N 4°49E **175** C8
Roussillon *Pyrénées-Or., France* 42°30N 2°35E **174** F6
Rouxville *S. Africa* 30°25S 26°50E **270** D4
Rouyn-Noranda *Canada* 48°20N 79°0W **298** C4
Rovaniemi *Finland* 66°29N 25°41E **160** C21
Rovato *Italy* 45°34N 10°0E **198** C7
Rovenki *Ukraine* 48°5N 39°21E **189** H10
Rovereto *Italy* 45°53N 11°3E **198** C8
Roverud *Norway* 60°15N 12°3E **164** D9
Rovigno = Rovinj *Croatia* 45°5N 13°40E **199** C10
Rovigo *Italy* 45°4N 11°47E **199** C8
Rovinj *Croatia* 45°5N 13°40E **199** C10
Rovira *Colombia* 4°15N 75°20W **328** C2
Rovno = Rivne *Ukraine* 50°40N 26°10E **177** C14
Rovnoye *Russia* 50°52N 46°3E **190** E8
Rovuma = Ruvuma → *Tanzania* 10°29S 40°28E **269** E5
Row'ān *Iran* 35°8N 48°51E **247** C6
Rowena *Australia* 29°48S 148°55E **281** D4
Rowley I. *Canada* 69°6N 77°52W **295** D16
Rowley Shoals *Australia* 17°30S 119°0E **278** C2
Roxa *Guinea-Biss.* 11°15N 15°45W **262** C1
Roxas *Capiz, Phil.* 11°36N 122°49E **233** F4
Roxas *Isabela, Phil.* 17°8N 121°36E **232** C3
Roxas *Mind. Or., Phil.* 12°35N 121°31E **232** E3
Roxas *Palawan, Phil.* 10°20N 119°21E **233** F2
Roxboro *U.S.A.* 36°24N 78°59W **315** C15
Roxborough *Trin. & Tob.* 11°15N 60°35W **323** s
Roxburgh *N.Z.* 45°33S 169°19E **285** F4
Roxbury *Mass., U.S.A.* 42°19N 71°5W **116** B2
Roxbury *N.Y., U.S.A.* 42°17N 74°33W **313** D10
Roxbury *Pa., U.S.A.* 40°6N 77°39W **312** F7
Roxby Downs *Australia* 30°43S 136°46E **281** E2
Roxen *Sweden* 58°30N 15°40E **163** F9
Roxeth *U.K.* 51°33N 0°20W **125** A1
Roy *Mont., U.S.A.* 47°20N 108°58W **304** C9
Roy *N. Mex., U.S.A.* 35°57N 104°12W **305** J11
Roy *Utah, U.S.A.* 41°10N 112°2W **304** F7
Roy Thomson Hall *Toronto, Canada* **141** b2
Royal △ *Australia* 34°5S 151°5E **283** C9
Royal Bardia △ *Nepal* 28°20N 81°20E **243** E9
Royal Botanic Gardens *Sydney, Australia* **139** b2
Royal Botanic Gardens *Edinburgh, U.K.* 55°58N 3°12W **121** B2
Royal Canal *Ireland* 53°30N 7°13W **166** C4
Royal Center *U.S.A.* 40°52N 86°30W **311** D10
Royal Chitawan △ *Nepal* 26°30N 84°30E **243** F11
Royal Geographical Society Is. *Canada* 68°56N 100°15W **294** D11
Royal Leamington Spa *U.K.* 52°18N 1°31W **169** E6
Royal Manas △ *Bhutan* 26°45N 90°50E **241** B3
Royal Natal △ *S. Africa* 28°43S 28°51E **271** C4
Royal Oak *U.S.A.* 42°30N 83°9W **311** B13
Royal Observatory *U.K.* 55°55N 3°12W **121** B2
Royal Palace = Koninklijk Paleis *Amsterdam, Neths.* **112** a2
Royal Palace = Kungliga Slottet *Stockholm, Sweden* **139** b2
Royal Palace = Palacio Real *Madrid, Spain* **127** b1
Royal Palace = Palais Royal *Brussels, Belgium* **116** b3
Royal Palace = Slottet *Oslo, Norway* **133** a1
Royal Palm Beach *U.S.A.* 26°42N 80°14W **317** J9
Royal Park *Australia* 37°46S 144°57E **128** A1
Royal Tunbridge Wells *U.K.* 51°7N 0°16E **169** F8
Royal Turf Club *Bangkok, Thailand* **113** b2
Royale, Isle *U.S.A.* 48°0N 88°54W **308** B9
Royalla *Australia* 35°30S 149°9E **283** C8
Royan *France* 45°37N 1°2W **174** C2
Roye *France* 49°42N 2°48E **173** C9
Röylä *Finland* 60°18N 24°42E **121** B1
Royston *U.K.* 52°3N 0°0 **169** E7
Rožaj *Montenegro* 42°50N 20°11E **202** D4
Różan *Poland* 52°52N 21°25E **185** F8
Rozas, Portilleros de las *Spain* 40°29N 3°49W **127** B1
Rozay-en-Brie *France* 48°41N 2°58E **173** D9
Rozdilna *Ukraine* 46°50N 30°2E **183** D16
Rozhnyativ *Ukraine* 48°56N 24°9E **183** B9
Rozhyshche *Ukraine* 50°54N 25°15E **177** C13
Rožmitál pod Třemšínem *Czech Rep.* 49°36N 13°53E **180** B6
Rožňava *Slovak Rep.* 48°37N 20°35E **181** C13
Rozogi *Poland* 53°28N 21°19E **184** E8
Rozoy-sur-Serre *France* 49°40N 4°8E **173** C11
Roztoczański △ *Poland* 50°37N 23°0E **185** H10
Roztoky *Czech Rep.* 50°9N 14°23E **135** B2
Rozzano *Italy* 45°22N 9°10E **129** B1
Rrëshen *Albania* 41°47N 19°49E **202** E3
Rrogozhine *Albania* 41°4N 19°50E **202** E3
Rtanj *Serbia* 43°45N 21°50E **202** C5
Rtishchevo *Russia* 52°18N 43°46E **190** D6
Rúa = A Rúa *Spain* 42°24N 7°6W **194** C3
Ruacaná *Namibia* 17°27S 14°21E **265** F2
Ruaha △ *Tanzania* 7°41S 34°30E **268** D3
Ruahine Ra. *N.Z.* 39°55S 176°2E **284** F5
Ruamahanga → *N.Z.* 41°24S 175°8E **284** H4
Ruapehu *N.Z.* 39°17S 175°35E **284** F4
Ruapuke I. *N.Z.* 46°46S 168°31E **285** G3
Ruâq, W. → *Egypt* 30°0N 33°49E **251** J4
Ruatoria *N.Z.* 37°55S 178°20E **284** D7
Ruawai *N.Z.* 36°8S 173°59E **284** C2
Rub' al Khālī *Si. Arabia* 19°0N 48°0E **249** D5
Rubeho Mts. *Tanzania* 6°50S 36°25E **268** D4
Rubezhnoye = Rubizhne *Ukraine* 49°6N 38°25E **189** H10
Rubh a' Mhail *U.K.* 55°56N 6°8W **167** F2
Rubha Hunish *U.K.* 57°42N 6°20W **167** D2
Rubha Robhanais = Lewis, Butt of *U.K.* 58°31N 6°16W **167** C2
Rubí *Spain* 41°29N 2°2E **196** D7
Rubi → *Dem. Rep. of the Congo* 2°48N 23°54E **264** B4
Rubí → *Barcelona, Spain* 41°26N 2°1E **114** A1
Rubiataba *Brazil* 15°8S 49°48W **333** E2
Rubicon → *U.S.A.* 38°53N 121°4W **306** G5
Rubicone → *Italy* 44°8N 12°28E **199** D9
Rubik *Albania* 41°46N 19°47E **202** E3
Rubinéia *Brazil* 20°13S 51°2W **333** F1
Rubino *Ivory C.* 6°4N 4°18W **262** D4
Rubio *Venezuela* 7°43N 72°22W **328** B3
Rubizhne *Ukraine* 49°6N 38°25E **189** H10
Rublovo *Russia* 55°47N 37°21E **129** B2
Rubondo △ *Tanzania* 2°18S 31°58E **268** C3
Rubtsovsk *Russia* 51°30N 81°10E **217** B10
Ruby *U.S.A.* 64°45N 155°30W **303** D9
Ruby Beach = Jacksonville Beach *U.S.A.* 30°17N 81°24W **316** E8
Ruby L. *U.S.A.* 40°10N 115°28W **304** F6
Ruby Mts. *U.S.A.* 40°30N 115°20W **304** F6
Rubyvale *Australia* 23°25S 147°42E **280** C4
Rucheng *China* 25°33N 113°38E **229** E9
Ruciane-Nida *Poland* 53°40N 21°32E **184** E8
Rūd Sar *Iran* 37°8N 50°18E **247** B6
Ruda *Sweden* 57°6N 16°7E **163** G10
Ruda Śląska *Poland* 50°16N 18°50E **185** H5
Rudall *Australia* 33°43S 136°17E **282** B2
Rudall → *Australia* 22°34S 122°13E **278** D3
Rudall River △ *Australia* 22°38S 122°30E **278** D3
Rūdbār *Afghan.* 30°9N 62°36E **240** C1
Rudbar *Iran* 36°48N 49°23E **247** B6
Rüdersdorf *Germany* 52°27N 13°47E **178** C9
Rudewa *Tanzania* 10°7S 34°40E **269** E3
Rudkøbing *Denmark* 54°56N 10°41E **163** K4
Rudky *Ukraine* 49°38N 23°29E **185** J10
Rudna *Poland* 51°30N 16°17E **185** G3
Rudnevka → *Russia* 55°43N 37°56E **129** B5
Rudnik *Bulgaria* 42°36N 27°30E **203** D11
Rudnik *Poland* 50°26N 22°15E **185** H9
Rudnik *Serbia* 44°7N 20°35E **202** B4
Rudnya *Russia* 54°55N 31°7E **188** E6
Rudnytsa *Ukraine* 48°16N 28°54E **183** B13
Rudnyy *Kazakhstan* 52°57N 63°7E **216** B6
Rudo *Bos.-H.* 43°41N 19°23E **182** G4
Rudolfa, Ostrov *Russia* 81°45N 58°30E **214** A6
Rudolfsheim *Austria* 48°12N 16°20E **142** A2
Rudolfshöhe *Germany* 52°37N 13°44E **115** A5
Rudolstadt *Germany* 50°44N 11°19E **178** E7
Rudong *China* 32°20N 121°12E **229** A13
Rudow *Germany* 52°24N 13°29E **115** B3
Rudozem *Bulgaria* 41°29N 24°51E **203** E8
Rudyard *U.S.A.* 46°14N 84°36W **309** B11
Rue *France* 50°15N 1°40E **173** B8
Rueil-Malmaison *France* 48°52N 2°11E **134** A2
Ruenya → *Africa* 16°24S 33°48E **269** F3
Rufa'a *Sudan* 14°44N 33°22E **257** E3
Ruffin *U.S.A.* 33°0N 80°49W **316** B9
Ruffling Pt. *Br. Virgin Is.* 18°44N 64°27W **321** b
Rufiji → *Tanzania* 7°50S 39°15E **268** D4
Rufino *Argentina* 34°20S 62°50W **334** C3
Rufisque *Senegal* 14°40N 17°15W **262** C1
Rufunsa *Zambia* 15°4S 29°34E **269** F2
Rugao *China* 32°23N 120°31E **229** A13
Rugby *Warks., U.K.* 52°23N 1°16W **169** E6
Rugby *N. Dak., U.S.A.* 48°22N 100°0W **308** A4
Rügen *Germany* 54°22N 13°24E **178** A9
Rügen △ *Germany* 54°25N 13°25E **178** A9
Rugles *France* 48°50N 0°40E **172** D7
Ruhea *Bangla.* 26°10N 88°25E **241** B2
Ruhengeri *Rwanda* 1°30S 29°36E **268** C2
Ruhla *Germany* 50°54N 10°23E **178** E6
Ruhland *Germany* 51°27N 13°51E **178** D9
Ruhnu *Estonia* 57°48N 23°15E **184** A10
Ruhr → *Germany* 51°27N 6°43E **178** D2
Ruhuhu → *Tanzania* 10°31S 34°34E **269** E3
Rui Barbosa *Brazil* 12°18S 40°27W **333** D3
Rui'an *China* 27°47N 120°40E **229** D13
Ruichang *China* 29°40N 115°39E **229** C10
Ruidoso *U.S.A.* 33°20N 105°41W **305** K11
Ruijin *China* 25°48N 116°0E **229** E10
Ruili *China* 24°1N 97°43E **228** E1
Ruisbroek *Belgium* 50°47N 4°18E **116** B1
Ruislip *U.K.* 51°34N 0°24W **125** A1
Ruivo, Pico *Madeira* 32°45N 16°56W **153** c
Ruj *Bulgaria* 42°52N 22°34E **202** D6
Rujen *Macedonia* 42°9N 22°30E **202** D6
Rujm Tal'at al Jamā'ah *Jordan* 30°24N 35°30E **251** H6
Ruk *Pakistan* 27°50N 68°42E **242** F3
Rukan-sho *Japan* 26°6N 127°32E **288** a
Rukhla *Pakistan* 32°27N 71°57E **242** C4
Rukwa □ *Tanzania* 7°0S 31°30E **268** D3
Rukwa, L. *Tanzania* 8°0S 32°20E **268** D3
Rulenge *Burundi* 2°43S 30°37E **268** C3
Rulhieres, C. *Australia* 13°56S 127°22E **278** B4
Rum = Rhum *U.K.* 57°0N 6°20W **167** E2
Rum *Jordan* 29°39N 35°26E **251** J6
Rum Cay *Bahamas* 23°40N 74°58W **321** B5
Rum Jungle *Australia* 13°0S 130°59E **278** B5
Ruma *Serbia* 45°0N 19°50E **182** E4
Ruma △ *Kenya* 0°39S 34°18E **268** C3
Rumāḩ *Si. Arabia* 25°29N 47°10E **246** E5
Rumah Kulit *Malaysia* 2°9N 114°15E **235** B4
Rumania = Romania ■ *Europe* 46°0N 25°0E **183** D10
Rumaylah *Iraq* 30°47N 47°37E **246** D5
Rumaylah, 'Urūq ar *Si. Arabia* 22°0N 48°30E **249** B5
Rumbêk *Sudan* 6°54N 29°37E **257** F2
Rumburk *Czech Rep.* 50°57N 14°32E **180** A7
Rumelihisarı *Turkey* 41°4N 29°3E **124** A3
Rumford *U.S.A.* 44°33N 70°33W **313** B14
Rumia *Poland* 54°37N 18°25E **184** D5
Rumilly *France* 45°53N 5°56E **175** C9
Rummelsburg = Miastko *Poland* 54°0N 16°58E **184** E3
Rumoi *Japan* 43°56N 141°39E **220** C10
Rumonge *Burundi* 3°59S 29°26E **268** C2
Rumphi *Malawi* 11°1S 33°52E **269** E3
Rumson *U.S.A.* 40°23N 74°0W **313** F11
Rumung *Micronesia* 9°37N 138°9E **287** R16
Rumuruti *Kenya* 0°17N 36°32E **268** B4
Rumyantsevo *Russia* 55°38N 37°25E **129** C2
Runan *China* 33°0N 114°30E **226** H8
Runanga *N.Z.* 42°25S 171°15E **285** C6
Runaway, C. *N.Z.* 37°32S 177°59E **284** D6
Runaway B. *Antigua & B.* 17°9N 61°51W **322** b
Runaway Bay *Jamaica* 18°27N 77°20W **320** a
Runcorn *U.K.* 53°21N 2°44W **168** D5
Rundu *Namibia* 17°52S 19°43E **270** A2
Rungis *France* 48°44N 2°20E **134** B3
Rungwa *Tanzania* 6°55S 33°32E **268** D3
Rungwa → *Tanzania* 7°36S 31°50E **268** D3
Rungwa △ *Tanzania* 6°53S 34°2E **268** D3
Rungwe *Tanzania* 9°11S 33°32E **269** D3
Rungwe, Mt. *Tanzania* 9°8S 33°40E **268** D3
Runka *Nigeria* 12°28N 7°20E **263** C6
Runn *Sweden* 60°30N 15°40E **162** D9
Runton Ra. *Australia* 23°31S 123°6E **278** D3
Runu *Micronesia* 9°35N 138°8E **287** R16
Ruo Shui → *China* 41°0N 100°16E **218** C9
Ruokolahti *Finland* 61°17N 28°50E **188** B5
Ruoqiang *China* 38°55N 88°10E **217** E11

422 Rupa INDEX

Rupa India 27°15N 92°21E 241 B4
Rupar India 31°2N 76°38E 242 D7
Rupat Indonesia 1°45N 101°40E 234 B2
Rupea Romania 46°2N 25°13E 183 D10
Rupen → India 23°28N 71°31E 242 H4
Rupert U.S.A. 42°37N 113°41W 304 E7
Rupert → Canada 51°29N 78°45W 298 B4
Rupert B. Canada 51°35N 79°0W 298 B4
Rupert House = Waskaganish Canada 51°30N 78°40W 298 B4
Rupsa India 21°37N 87°1E 243 J12
Rupununi → Guyana 4°3N 58°35W 329 C6
Rur → Germany 51°11N 5°59E 178 D1
Rurópolis Brazil 4°3S 54°59W 329 D7
Rurrenabaque Bolivia 14°30S 67°32W 330 C4
Rurutu French Polynesia 22°26S 151°20W 289 f
Rus → Spain 39°30N 2°30W 197 F2
Rusāfa Iraq 33°21N 44°23E 113 A2
Rusambo Zimbabwe 16°30S 32°4E 269 F3
Rusape Zimbabwe 18°35S 32°8E 269 F3
Ruschuk = Ruse Bulgaria 43°48N 25°59E 203 C9
Ruse Bulgaria 43°48N 25°59E 203 C9
Ruse □ Bulgaria 43°35N 25°40E 203 C9
Ruşeţu Romania 44°57N 27°14E 183 F12
Rush Ireland 53°31N 6°6W 166 C5
Rush Green U.K. 51°33N 0°10E 125 A5
Rushan China 36°56N 121°30E 227 F11
Rushden U.K. 52°18N 0°35W 169 E7
Rushikulya → India 19°23N 85°5E 244 E7
Rushmore, Mt. U.S.A. 43°53N 103°28W 308 D2
Rushville Ill., U.S.A. 40°7N 90°34W 310 D6
Rushville Ind., U.S.A. 39°37N 85°27W 311 E11
Rushville Nebr., U.S.A. 42°43N 102°28W 308 D2
Rushworth Australia 36°32S 145°1E 283 D6
Ruskin U.S.A. 27°43N 82°26W 317 H7
Russa India 22°29N 88°21E 124 C2
Russas Brazil 4°55S 37°50W 332 B4
Russell Man., Canada 50°50N 101°20W 297 C8
Russell N.Z. 35°16S 174°10E 284 B3
Russell Fla., U.S.A. 30°3N 81°45W 316 E8
Russell Kans., U.S.A. 38°54N 98°52W 308 F4
Russell N.Y., U.S.A. 44°27N 75°9W 313 B9
Russell Pa., U.S.A. 41°56N 79°8W 312 E5
Russell Cave ⌂ U.S.A. 34°59N 85°49W 315 D12
Russell Is. Solomon Is. 9°4S 159°12E 287 M10
Russell L. Man., Canada 56°15N 101°30W 297 B8
Russell L. N.W.T., Canada 63°5N 115°44W 296 A5
Russellkonda India 19°57N 84°42E 244 E7
Russells Point U.S.A. 40°28N 83°54W 311 D13
Russellville Ala., U.S.A. 34°30N 87°44W 315 D11
Russellville Ark., U.S.A. 35°17N 93°8W 314 D8
Russellville Ky., U.S.A. 36°51N 86°53W 308 G10
Rüsselsheim Germany 49°59N 8°23E 179 F4
Russi Italy 44°22N 12°2E 199 D9
Russia ■ Eurasia 62°0N 105°0E 215 C11
Russian → U.S.A. 38°27N 123°8W 306 G3
Russian Hill San Francisco, U.S.A. 136 a1
Russian Mission U.S.A. 61°47N 161°19W 303 F7
Russiaville U.S.A. 40°25N 86°16W 311 D10
Rust Austria 47°49N 16°42E 181 D9
Rustam Shahr Pakistan 26°58N 66°6E 242 F2
Rustavi Georgia 41°30N 45°0E 191 K7
Rustenburg S. Africa 25°41S 27°14E 270 C4
Ruston U.S.A. 32°32N 92°38W 314 E8
Rutana Burundi 3°55S 30°0E 268 C3
Rute Spain 37°19N 4°23W 195 H6
Ruteng Indonesia 8°35S 120°30E 231 F6
Rutenga Zimbabwe 21°15S 30°44E 269 G3
Ruth U.S.A. 43°42N 82°45W 312 C2
Rutherford Calif., U.S.A. 38°26N 122°24W 306 G4
Rutherford N.J., U.S.A. 40°49N 74°6W 132 B1
Rutherglen Australia 36°5S 146°29E 283 D7
Rutland U.S.A. 43°37N 72°58W 313 C12
Rutland □ U.K. 52°38N 0°40W 169 E7
Rutland I. India 11°25N 92°10E 245 J11
Rutland Water U.K. 52°39N 0°38W 169 E7
Rutledalen Norway 61°4N 5°10E 164 F2
Rutledge U.S.A. 33°38N 83°37W 316 B6
Rutledge → Canada 61°4N 112°0W 297 A6
Rutledge L. Canada 61°33N 110°47W 297 A6
Rutog China 33°27N 79°42E 217 F9
Rutqa, W. → Syria 34°30N 41°3E 213 E9
Rutshuru Dem. Rep. of the Congo 1°13S 29°25E 268 C2
Ruvo di Púglia Italy 41°7N 16°29E 201 A9
Ruvu Tanzania 6°49S 38°43E 268 D4
Ruvu → Tanzania 6°23S 38°52E 268 D4
Ruvuba △ Burundi 3°3S 29°33E 268 C2
Ruvuma □ Tanzania 10°20S 36°0E 269 E4
Ruvuma → Tanzania 10°29S 40°28E 269 E5
Ruwais U.A.E. 24°5N 52°50E 247 E7
Ruwenzori Africa 0°30N 29°55E 268 B2
Ruwenzori △ Uganda 0°20N 30°0E 268 B2
Ruya → Zimbabwe 16°27S 32°5E 271 A5
Ruyang China 34°9N 112°27E 226 G7
Ruyigi Burundi 3°29S 30°15E 268 C3
Ruyuan China 24°46N 113°16E 229 E9
Ruzaevka Kazakhstan 52°49N 66°56E 217 B7
Ruzayevka Russia 54°4N 45°0E 190 C7
Rūzhevo Konare Bulgaria 42°23N 24°46E 203 D8
Ruzhou China 34°11N 112°52E 226 G7
Ružomberok Slovak Rep. 49°3N 19°17E 181 B12
Ruzyně Czech Rep. 50°5N 14°17E 135 B1
Ruzyne, Praha ✕ (PRG) Czech Rep. 50°6N 14°16E 135 B1
Rwanda ■ Africa 2°0S 30°0E 268 C3
Ryakhovo Bulgaria 43°58N 26°18E 203 C10
Ryan, L. U.K. 55°0N 5°2W 167 G3
Ryazan Russia 54°40N 39°40E 188 E10
Ryazan □ Russia 54°5N 39°30E 190 C4
Ryazhsk Russia 53°45N 40°3E 188 F11
Rybachiy Russia 55°10N 20°50E 184 C7
Rybachiy Poluostrov Russia 69°43N 32°0E 160 B25
Rybachye = Balykchy Kyrgyzstan 42°26N 76°12E 217 D9
Rybatskaya Russia 59°59N 30°29E 137 B2
Rybinsk Russia 58°5N 38°50E 188 C10
Rybinskoye Vdkhr. Russia 58°30N 38°25E 188 C10
Rybnik Poland 50°6N 18°32E 185 H5
Rybnitsa = Râbniţa Moldova 47°45N 29°0E 183 C14
Rybnoye Russia 54°45N 39°30E 188 E10
Rychnov nad Kněžnou Czech Rep. 50°10N 16°17E 181 A9
Rychwał Poland 52°4N 18°10E 185 F5
Rycroft Canada 55°45N 118°40W 296 B5
Ryd Sweden 56°27N 14°42E 163 H8
Rydaholm Sweden 56°59N 14°18E 163 H8
Rydboholm Sweden 59°26N 18°12E 139 A3
Ryde N.S.W., Australia 33°48S 151°6E 139 A1
Ryde I. of W., U.K. 50°43N 1°9W 169 G6
Ryderwood U.S.A. 46°23N 123°3W 306 D3
Rydzyna Poland 51°47N 16°39E 185 G3
Rye U.K. 50°57N 0°45E 169 G8
Rye → U.K. 54°11N 0°44W 168 C7
Rye Bay U.K. 50°52N 0°49E 169 G8
Rye Patch Res. U.S.A. 40°28N 118°19W 304 F4
Ryegate U.S.A. 46°18N 109°15W 304 C9
Ryerson University Toronto, Canada 141 a3
Ryfylke Norway 59°25N 6°25E 164 E3
Rykene Norway 58°24N 8°37E 164 F5
Ryki Poland 51°38N 21°56E 185 G8
Rykovo = Yenakiyeve Ukraine 48°15N 38°15E 189 H10
Ryley Canada 53°17N 112°26W 296 C6
Rylsk Russia 51°36N 34°43E 189 G8
Rylstone Australia 32°46S 149°58E 283 B8
Rymanów Poland 49°35N 21°51E 185 J8
Ryn Poland 53°57N 21°34E 184 E8
Ryn Peski = Naryn Qum Kazakhstan 47°30N 49°0E 191 G9
Ryogoku Japan 35°40N 139°48E 140 A3
Ryōhaku-Sanchi Japan 36°9N 136°49E 223 A8
Ryojun = Lüshun China 38°45N 121°15E 227 E11
Ryōtsu Japan 38°5N 138°26E 220 E9
Rypin Poland 53°3N 19°25E 185 E6
Ryssby Sweden 56°52N 14°10E 163 H8
Rysy Europe 49°10N 20°4E 181 B13
Ryūgasaki Japan 35°54N 140°11E 223 B12
Ryukyu Is. = Ryūkyū-Rettō Japan 26°0N 126°0E 221 M3
Ryūkyū-Rettō Japan 26°0N 126°0E 221 M3
Ryūō Japan 35°42N 138°30E 223 B10
Rzepin Poland 52°20N 14°49E 185 F1
Rzeszów Poland 50°5N 21°58E 185 H8
Rzhev Russia 56°20N 34°20E 188 D8
Rzhevka Russia 59°59N 30°31E 137 B3

S

Sa Cabaneta Spain 39°37N 2°45E 206 B3
Sa Canal Spain 38°51N 1°23E 206 D1
Sa Conillera Spain 38°59N 1°13E 206 D1
Sa Dec Vietnam 10°20N 105°46E 237 G5
Sa Dragonera Spain 39°35N 2°19E 206 B3
Sa Kaeo Thailand 13°49N 102°4E 236 F4
Sa-koi Burma 19°54N 97°3E 241 F6
Sa Mesquida Spain 39°55N 4°16E 206 B5
Sa Pa Vietnam 22°20N 103°47E 236 A4
Sa Pobla Spain 39°46N 3°1E 206 B4
Sa Savina Spain 38°44N 1°25E 206 D1
Sa'a Solomon Is. 9°43S 161°35E 287 M11
Sa'ādatābād Fārs, Iran 30°10N 53°5E 247 D7
Sa'ādatābād Hormozgān, Iran 28°3N 55°53E 247 D7
Sa'ādatābād Kermān, Iran 29°40N 55°51E 247 D7
Sa'ādatābād Tehrān, Iran 35°47N 51°22E 141 A2
Saadūn Iraq 33°19N 44°25E 113 B2
Saale → Germany 51°56N 11°54E 178 D7
Saaler Bodden Germany 54°20N 12°27E 178 A8
Saalfeld Germany 50°38N 11°21E 178 E7
Saalfelden Austria 47°25N 12°51E 180 D5
Saane → Switz. 47°8N 7°10E 179 H3
Saanich Canada 48°29N 123°26W 306 B3
Saar → Europe 49°41N 6°32E 170 E6
Saar-Hunsrück ⌂ Germany 49°30N 6°50E 179 F2
Saar in Mähren = Žďár nad Sázavou Czech Rep. 49°34N 15°57E 180 B8
Saarbrücken Germany 49°14N 6°59E 179 F2
Saarburg Germany 49°36N 6°32E 179 F2
Saaremaa Estonia 58°30N 22°30E 188 C2
Saarijärvi Finland 62°43N 25°16E 160 E21
Saarland □ Germany 49°20N 7°0E 179 F2
Saarlautern = Saarlouis Germany 49°18N 6°45E 179 F2
Saarlouis Germany 49°18N 6°45E 179 F2
Saatlı Azerbaijan 39°55N 48°22E 213 C13
Saavedra Argentina 34°33S 58°29W 117 B2
Saaz = Žatec Czech Rep. 50°20N 13°32E 180 A6
Sab 'Ābar Syria 33°46N 37°41E 212 F7
Saba W. Indies 17°38N 63°14W 322 a
Šabac Serbia 44°48N 19°42E 202 B3
Sabadell Spain 41°28N 2°7E 196 D7
Sabae Japan 35°57N 136°11E 223 B8
Sabah □ Malaysia 6°0N 117°0E 235 A5
Şabāḩ, Wadi → Si. Arabia 23°50N 48°30E 249 B5
Sabak Bernam Malaysia 3°46N 100°58E 237 L3
Sabalān, Kūhhā-ye Iran 38°15N 47°45E 213 C12
Sabalana, Kepulauan Indonesia 6°45S 118°50E 231 F5
Sabalana, Kepuluauan Indonesia 6°45S 118°49E 235 D5
Sabana, Arch. de Cuba 23°0N 80°0W 320 B3
Sábana de la Mar Dom. Rep. 19°7N 69°24W 321 C6
Sabana Grande Puerto Rico 18°5N 66°58W 321 b
Sabana Westpunt = Westpunt Curaçao 12°22N 69°10W 322 g
Sabanalarga Colombia 10°38N 74°55W 328 A3
Sabaneta Pt. N. Marianas 15°17N 145°49E 302 e
Sabang Indonesia 5°50N 95°15E 234 A1
Şabanözü Turkey 40°28N 33°16E 212 B5
Săbăoani Romania 47°1N 26°51E 183 C11
Sabari → India 17°35N 81°16E 244 F5
Sabarmati → India 22°18N 72°22E 242 H5
Sab'atayn, Ramlat as Yemen 15°30N 46°10E 248 D4
Sabattis U.S.A. 44°6N 74°40W 313 B10
Sabáudia Italy 41°18N 13°1E 200 A6
Sabaya Bolivia 19°1S 68°23W 330 D4
Şabāyā, Jaza'ir Si. Arabia 18°35N 41°3E 248 C3
Saberania Indonesia 2°5S 138°18E 231 E9
Sabhā Libya 27°9N 14°29E 258 C2
Sabi → India 28°29N 76°44E 242 E7
Sabi Game Reserve = Kruger △ S. Africa 24°50S 26°10E 271 B4
Sabidana, J. Sudan 18°4N 36°50E 256 D4
Sabie S. Africa 25°10S 30°48E 271 C5
Sabina U.S.A. 39°29N 83°38W 311 E13
Sabinal Chihuahua, Mexico 30°57N 107°30W 318 A3
Sabinal Tex., U.S.A. 29°19N 99°28W 314 G5
Sabiñánigo Spain 42°31N 0°22W 196 C4
Sabinas Mexico 27°51N 101°7W 318 B4
Sabinas → Mexico 27°37N 100°42W 318 B4
Sabinas Hidalgo Mexico 26°30N 100°10W 318 B4
Sabine → U.S.A. 29°59N 93°47W 314 G8
Sabine L. U.S.A. 29°53N 93°51W 314 G8
Sabine Pass U.S.A. 29°44N 93°54W 314 G8
Sabinópolis Brazil 18°40S 43°6W 333 E3
Sabinov Slovak Rep. 49°6N 21°5E 181 B14
Sabirabad Azerbaijan 40°5N 48°30E 191 K9
Sabka Chad 19°15N 16°35E 259 E3
Sablayan Phil. 12°50N 120°50E 232 E3
Sable Canada 55°30N 68°21W 299 A6
Sable, C. N.S., Canada 43°29N 65°38W 299 D6
Sable, C. Fla., U.S.A. 25°9N 81°8W 317 K8
Sable I. N.S., Canada 44°0N 60°0W 299 D8
Sable I. Papua N. G. 3°38S 154°42E 286 B8
Sablé-sur-Sarthe France 47°50N 0°20W 172 E6
Saboeiro Brazil 6°32S 39°54W 332 C4
Saboli India 28°42N 77°18E 120 A2
Sabonkafi Niger 14°40N 8°45E 259 F1
Sabor → Portugal 41°10N 7°7W 194 D3
Sabou Burkina Faso 12°1N 2°15W 262 C4
Şabrātah Libya 32°47N 12°29E 258 B2
Sabres France 44°9N 0°43W 174 D3
Sabrina Coast Antarctica 68°0S 120°0E 151 C9
Sabtang I. Phil. 20°19N 121°52E 232 A3
Sabugal Portugal 40°20N 7°5W 194 E3
Sabugo Portugal 38°49N 9°17W 126 A1
Sabula U.S.A. 42°4N 90°10W 310 B6
Sabulubek Indonesia 1°36S 98°40E 234 C1
Sabuncu Turkey 39°33N 30°12E 205 B12
Şabyā Si. Arabia 17°9N 42°37E 248 C3
Sabzevār Iran 36°15N 57°40E 247 B8
Sabzi Mand India 28°40N 77°12E 120 A2
Sabzvārān = Jiroft Iran 28°45N 57°50E 247 D8
Sac City U.S.A. 42°25N 95°0W 310 B2
Sacaolo Angola 12°58S 22°28E 265 E4
Sacatengo Angola 13°16S 21°20E 265 E4
Sacavém Portugal 38°47N 9°5W 126 A2
Sacedón Spain 40°29N 2°41W 196 E2
Săcele Romania 45°37N 25°41E 183 E10
Sacheon S. Korea 35°0N 128°6E 224 E4
Sachigo → Canada 55°6N 88°58W 298 A2
Sachigo, L. Canada 53°50N 92°12W 298 B1
Sachimbo Angola 9°14S 20°16E 265 D4
Sachin India 21°5N 72°53E 244 D1
Sachkhere Georgia 42°25N 43°28E 191 J6
Sachsen □ Germany 50°55N 13°10E 178 E9
Sachsen-Anhalt □ Germany 52°0N 12°0E 178 D7
Sächsische Schweiz △ Germany 50°55N 14°10E 178 E10
Sacile Italy 45°57N 12°30E 199 C9
Sackets Harbor U.S.A. 43°57N 76°7W 313 C8
Sackville Canada 45°54N 64°22W 299 C7
Saclay France 48°43N 2°10E 134 B2
Saclay, Étang de France 48°44N 2°9E 134 B1
Saco Maine, U.S.A. 43°30N 70°27W 313 C14
Saco Mont., U.S.A. 48°28N 107°21W 304 B10
Sacol I. Phil. 6°58N 122°13E 233 H4
Sacomã Brazil 23°36S 46°35W 137 B2
Sacramento = Itatupã Brazil 0°37S 51°12W 329 D7
Sacramento Brazil 19°53S 47°27W 333 E2
Sacramento Calif., U.S.A. 38°35N 121°29W 306 G5
Sacramento → U.S.A. 38°3N 121°56W 306 G5
Sacramento Mts. U.S.A. 32°30N 105°30W 305 K11
Sacramento Valley U.S.A. 39°30N 122°0W 306 G5
Sacratif, C. Spain 36°42N 3°28W 195 J7
Sacré Cœur Paris, France 134 a4
Sacrow Germany 52°25N 13°6E 115 B1
Sacrower See Germany 52°26N 13°6E 115 B1
Săcueni Romania 47°20N 22°5E 182 C7
Sada Mayotte 12°51S 45°6E 272 b
Sada Spain 43°22N 8°15W 194 B2
Sada-Misaki Japan 33°20N 132°5E 222 D4
Sada-Misaki-Hantō Japan 33°22N 132°1E 222 D4
Sádaba Spain 42°19N 1°12W 196 C3
Sadabad India 27°27N 78°3E 242 F8
Şa'dah Yemen 16°15N 43°37E 248 D3
Sadang S. Korea 37°29N 126°58E 137 C1
Sadani Tanzania 5°58S 38°35E 268 D4
Sadani △ Tanzania 6°3S 38°47E 268 D4
Sadao Thailand 6°38N 100°26E 237 J3
Sadar Bazar Delhi, India 120 a1
Sadaseopet India 17°38N 77°59E 244 F3
Sadd el Aali Egypt 23°54N 32°54E 256 C3
Saddle → U.S.A. 40°51N 74°6W 132 A1
Saddle Brook U.S.A. 40°53N 74°5W 132 A1
Saddle Hill St. Kitts & Nevis 17°7N 62°33W 322 d
Saddle Mt. U.S.A. 45°58N 123°41W 306 E3
Saddle Pk. India 13°9N 93°1E 245 H11
Saddle Pt. St. Helena 15°57S 5°38W 153 h
Sade Nigeria 11°22N 10°45E 263 C7
Şadḩ Oman 17°3N 55°4E 249 D6
Sadhoowa Trin. & Tob. 10°8N 61°27W 323 t
Sadimi Dem. Rep. of the Congo 9°25S 23°32E 265 D4
Sadiola Mali 13°50N 11°40W 262 C2
Sadiya India 27°50N 95°40E 241 B5
Sa'dīyah, Hawr as Iraq 32°15N 46°30E 213 F12
Sadlers St. Kitts & Nevis 17°24N 62°47W 322 d
Sado Japan 38°0N 138°25E 220 F9
Sado → Portugal 38°29N 8°55W 195 G2
Sadon Russia 42°52N 43°58E 191 J6
Sadovoye Russia 47°47N 44°31E 191 G7
Sadowara Japan 32°2N 131°26E 222 E3
Sadr Pakistan 24°51N 67°2E 123 A2
Sadr City Iraq 33°23N 44°27E 113 B2
Sadra India 23°21N 72°43E 242 H5
Sadri India 25°11N 73°26E 242 G5
Sadyba Poland 52°11N 21°3E 142 B2
Sæbøvik Norway 59°47N 5°40E 164 E2
Sæby Denmark 57°21N 10°30E 163 G4
Saegertown U.S.A. 41°43N 80°9W 312 E4
Saelices Spain 39°55N 2°49W 196 F2
Sætre Norway 59°41N 10°33E 164 E7
Sævareid Norway 60°11N 5°46E 164 D2
Safaalan Turkey 41°26N 28°6E 203 E12
Şafājah Si. Arabia 26°25N 39°0E 246 E3
Šafárikovo = Tornal'a Slovak Rep. 48°25N 20°20E 181 C13
Safata B. Samoa 14°0S 171°50W 287 W20
Safdar Jang's Tomb India 28°35N 77°12E 120 B2
Safed Koh Afghan. 34°0N 70°0E 240 B3
Säffle Sweden 59°8N 12°55E 162 E6
Safford U.S.A. 32°50N 109°43W 305 K9
Saffron Walden U.K. 52°1N 0°16E 169 E8
Safi Morocco 32°18N 9°20W 260 B3
Safi □ Morocco 32°10N 8°50W 260 B3
Safia Papua N. G. 9°35S 148°38E 286 E5
Safia, Hamada Mali 23°10N 4°15W 260 D4
Şafīābād Iran 36°45N 57°58E 247 B8
Safid Dasht Iran 33°27N 48°11E 247 C6
Safīd Kūh Afghan. 34°45N 63°0E 240 B1
Safid Rūd → Iran 37°23N 50°11E 247 B6
Safipur India 26°44N 80°21E 243 F9
Şāfītā Syria 34°48N 36°7E 250 D7
Safonovo Russia 55°4N 33°16E 188 E7
Safranbolu Turkey 41°15N 32°41E 212 B5
Saft el Laban Egypt 30°1N 31°10E 117 A2
Saft Rashîn Egypt 28°58N 30°55E 256 J7
Şafwān Iraq 30°7N 47°43E 246 D5
Sag Harbor U.S.A. 41°0N 72°18W 313 F12
Sag Sag Papua N. G. 5°32S 148°23E 286 C5
Saga Kōchi, Japan 33°5N 133°6E 222 D5
Saga Saga, Japan 33°15N 130°16E 222 D2
Saga □ Japan 33°15N 130°20E 222 D2
Sagae Japan 38°22N 140°17E 220 E10
Sagaing Burma 21°52N 95°59E 241 E5
Sagaing □ Burma 23°55N 95°56E 241 D5
Sagala Mali 14°9N 6°38W 262 C3
Sagami-Nada Japan 34°58N 139°30E 223 C11
Sagami-Wan Japan 35°15N 139°25E 223 B11
Sagamihara Japan 35°33N 139°25E 223 B11
Sagamore U.S.A. 40°46N 79°14W 312 F5
Sagan = Żagań Poland 51°39N 15°22E 185 G2
Saganaga L. Canada 48°14N 90°52W 308 A8
Saganashkee Slough U.S.A. 41°41N 87°53W 119 C1
Saganoseki Japan 33°15N 131°53E 222 D3
Saganthit Kyun Burma 11°56N 98°29E 237 G2
Sagar Karnataka, India 16°38N 76°48E 244 F3
Sagar Karnataka, India 14°14N 75°6E 245 G2
Sagar Mad. P., India 23°50N 78°44E 243 H8
Sagara Japan 34°41N 138°12E 223 C10
Sagara, L. Tanzania 5°20S 31°0E 268 D3
Sagarejo Georgia 41°44N 45°19E 191 K7
Sagarmatha = Everest, Mt. Nepal 28°5N 86°58E 243 E12
Sagarmatha △ Nepal 27°55N 86°45E 243 F12
Sagavanirktok → U.S.A. 70°19N 147°53W 303 A11
Sagay Phil. 10°57N 123°25E 232 F4
Sagene Norway 59°55N 10°46E 133 A3
Saghîr, El Bahr el → Egypt 31°28N 31°54E 251 G2
Sagiada Greece 39°38N 20°12E 206 B10
Saginaw U.S.A. 43°26N 83°56W 309 D12
Saginaw B. U.S.A. 43°50N 83°40W 309 D12
Sagleipie Liberia 7°0N 8°52W 262 D3
Saglouc = Salluit Canada 62°14N 75°38W 295 E16
Sagone France 42°7N 8°42E 175 F12
Sagone, G. de France 42°4N 8°40E 175 F12
Sagrada Familia, Templo de Barcelona, Spain 114 a2
Sagres Portugal 37°0N 8°58W 195 J2
Sagu Burma 20°13N 94°46E 241 E5
Sagua la Grande Cuba 22°50N 80°10W 320 B3
Saguache U.S.A. 38°5N 106°8W 304 G10
Saguaro △ U.S.A. 32°12N 110°38W 305 K8
Saguenay → Canada 48°22N 71°0W 299 C5
Saguia el Hamra → W. Sahara 27°24N 13°43W 260 C2
Sagunt Spain 39°42N 0°18W 196 F4
Sagunto = Sagunt Spain 39°42N 0°18W 196 F4
Sagvåg Norway 59°46N 5°25E 164 E2
Sagwara India 23°41N 74°1E 242 H6
Sahaba Sudan 18°57N 30°25E 256 D3
Sahagún Colombia 8°57N 75°27W 328 B2
Sahagún Spain 42°18N 5°2W 194 C5
Saḩam al Jawlān Syria 32°45N 35°55E 250 F6
Sahamandrevo Madag. 23°15S 45°35E 272 C2
Sahand, Kūh-e Iran 37°44N 46°27E 213 D12
Sahar, Mumbai ✕ (BOM) India 19°5N 72°51E 130 A2
Sahara Africa 23°0N 5°0E 254 D4
Saḩara, G. Egypt 28°2N 34°8E 251 K5
Saharan Atlas = Saharien, Atlas Algeria 33°30N 1°0E 261 B5
Saharan Seamounts Atl. Oc. 25°30N 19°50W 152 D10
Saharanpur India 29°58N 77°33E 242 E7
Saharien, Atlas Algeria 33°30N 1°0E 261 B5
Saharsa India 25°53N 86°36E 243 G12
Sahasinaka Madag. 21°49S 47°49E 272 C2
Sahaswan India 28°5N 78°45E 243 E8
Saheira, W. el → Egypt 30°5N 33°25E 251 H4
Sahel Africa 16°0N 5°0E 254 E3
Sahel, Canal du Mali 14°20N 6°0W 262 C3
Sahibganj India 25°12N 87°40E 243 G12
Şāḩilīyah Iraq 33°43N 42°42E 213 F10
Sahiwal Pakistan 30°45N 73°8E 242 D5
Şaḩneh Iran 34°29N 47°41E 213 E12
Sahrawi = Western Sahara ■ Africa 25°0N 13°0W 260 D2
Sahuaripa Mexico 29°3N 109°14W 318 B3
Sahuarita U.S.A. 31°57N 110°58W 305 L8
Sahuayo de Díaz Mexico 20°4N 102°43W 318 C4
Šahy Slovak Rep. 48°4N 18°55E 181 C11
Sai → India 25°39N 82°47E 243 G10
Sai Buri Thailand 6°43N 101°45E 237 J3
Saï-Cinza Brazil 6°17S 57°42W 331 B6
Sai Kung China 22°23N 114°16E 122 A2
Sai Thong △ Thailand 15°56N 101°10E 236 E3
Sai Wan Ho China 22°17N 114°12E 122 B2
Sai Ying Pun China 22°17N 114°8E 122 B1
Sai Yok △ Thailand 14°25N 98°40E 236 E2
Saibai I. Australia 9°25S 142°40E 280 a
Sa'id Bundâs Sudan 8°24N 24°48E 259 G4
Saïda Algeria 34°50N 0°11E 261 B5
Saïda □ Algeria 34°40N 0°20E 261 B5
Sa'īdābād = Sīrjān Iran 29°30N 55°45E 247 D7
Sa'īdābād Iran 36°8N 54°11E 247 B7
Saidaiji Japan 34°39N 134°2E 222 C6
Saïdia Morocco 35°5N 2°14W 261 A4
Sa'īdīyeh Iran 36°20N 48°55E 247 B6
Saidor Papua N. G. 5°40S 146°29E 286 C4
Saidpur Bangla. 25°48N 89°0E 241 C2
Saidpur India 25°33N 83°11E 243 G10
Saidu Sharif Pakistan 34°43N 72°24E 243 B5
Saignes France 45°20N 2°31E 174 C6
Saigō Japan 36°12N 133°20E 222 A5
Saigon = Thanh Pho Ho Chi Minh Vietnam 10°58N 106°40E 237 G6
Saijō Japan 33°55N 133°11E 222 D5
Saikai △ Japan 33°12N 129°36E 222 D1
Saikanosy Masoala Madag. 15°45S 50°10E 272 B3
Saikhoa Ghat India 27°50N 95°40E 241 B5
Saiki Japan 32°58N 131°51E 222 E3
Sailana India 23°28N 74°55E 242 H6
Saillans France 44°42N 5°12E 175 D9
Sailolof Indonesia 1°15S 130°46E 231 E8
Sailu India 19°28N 76°28E 244 E3
Saimaa Finland 61°15N 28°15E 188 B5
Saimbeyli Turkey 37°59N 36°6E 212 D7
Saimen = Saimaa Finland 61°15N 28°15E 188 B5
Şa'in Dezh Iran 36°40N 46°25E 213 D12
St. Abb's Head U.K. 55°55N 2°8W 167 F6
St-Affrique France 43°57N 2°53E 174 E6
St-Agrève France 45°0N 4°23E 175 C8
St-Aignan France 47°16N 1°22E 172 E8
St. Alban's Nfld. & L., Canada 47°51N 55°50W 299 C8
St. Albans Herts., U.K. 51°45N 0°19W 169 F7
St. Albans Vt., U.S.A. 44°49N 73°5W 313 B11
St. Albans W. Va., U.S.A. 38°23N 81°50W 309 F13
St. Alban's Head U.K. 50°34N 2°4W 169 G5
St. Albert Canada 53°37N 113°32W 296 C6
St-Amand-en-Puisaye France 47°32N 3°5E 173 E10
St-Amand-les-Eaux France 50°27N 3°25E 173 B10
St-Amand-Montrond France 46°43N 2°30E 173 F9
St-Amarin France 47°54N 7°2E 173 E14
St-Amour France 46°26N 5°21E 173 F12
St-André Montréal, Canada 130 c1
St-André Réunion 20°57S 55°39E 272 f
St-André-de-Cubzac France 44°59N 0°26W 174 D3
St-André-les-Alpes France 43°58N 6°30E 175 E10
St. Andrew □ Trin. & Tob. 10°35N 61°10W 323 t
St. Andrew Sd. U.S.A. 30°58N 81°25W 316 E8
St. Andrew's Nfld. & L., Canada 47°45N 59°15W 299 C8
St. Andrews N.Z. 44°33S 171°10E 285 E6
St. Andrews Fife, U.K. 56°20N 2°47W 167 E6
St. Andrews S.C., U.S.A. 32°47N 80°0W 316 C9
St-Anicet Canada 45°8N 74°22W 313 A10
St. Anne U.S.A. 41°1N 87°43W 311 C9
St. Annes Canada 49°40N 96°39W 297 D9
St. Anns B. Canada 46°22N 60°25W 299 C7
St. Ann's Bay Jamaica 18°26N 77°12W 320 a
St. Anthony Nfld. & L., Canada 51°22N 55°35W 299 B8
St. Anthony Idaho, U.S.A. 43°58N 111°41W 304 E8
St-Antoine Canada 46°22N 64°45W 299 C7
St-Antonin-Noble-Val France 44°10N 1°45E 174 D5
St. Arnaud = El Eulma Algeria 36°9N 5°42E 261 A6
St. Arnaud Australia 36°40S 143°16E 282 D5
St. Arnaud Ra. N.Z. 42°1S 172°53E 285 C7
St-Astier France 45°8N 0°31E 174 C4
St-Aubin France 48°44N 2°8E 134 B1
St-Aubin-du-Cormier France 48°15N 1°26W 172 D5
St-Augustin Canada 51°13N 58°38W 299 B8
St-Augustin → Canada 51°16N 58°40W 299 B8
St. Augustine U.S.A. 29°54N 81°19W 316 F8
St. Augustine Beach U.S.A. 29°51N 81°16W 316 F8
St-Aulaye France 45°12N 0°9E 174 C4
St. Austell U.K. 50°20N 4°47W 169 G3
St-Avold France 49°6N 6°43E 173 C13
St. Barbe Canada 51°12N 56°46W 299 B8
St-Barthélemy W. Indies 17°50N 62°50W 322 a
St-Barthélemy Channel St.-Martin 18°0N 63°0W 322 a
St. Basil's Cathedral Moscow, Russia 129 b3
St. Bathans N.Z. 44°53S 169°50E 285 E4
St. Bathan's, Mt. N.Z. 44°45S 169°45E 285 E4
St-Béat France 42°55N 0°41E 174 F4
St. Bees Hd. U.K. 54°31N 3°38W 168 C4
St. Bees I. Australia 20°56S 149°26E 280 b
St-Benoît Réunion 21°2S 55°43E 272 f
St-Benoît-du-Sault France 46°26N 1°24E 174 B5
St-Bonnet-en-Champsaur France 44°40N 6°5E 175 D10
St-Brevin-les-Pins France 47°14N 2°10W 172 E4
St-Brice-en-Coglès France 48°25N 1°22W 172 D5
St. Bride's Canada 46°56N 54°10W 299 C9
St. Brides B. U.K. 51°49N 5°9W 169 F2
St-Brieuc France 48°30N 2°46W 172 D4
St-Calais France 47°55N 0°45E 172 E7
St-Cast-le-Guildo France 48°37N 2°18W 172 D4
St. Catharines Canada 43°10N 79°15W 312 C5
St. Catherine, Mt. Grenada 12°10N 61°40W 323 q
St. Catherine Pt. Bermuda 32°23N 64°40W 153 a
St. Catherines I. U.S.A. 31°40N 81°10W 316 D8
St. Catherine's Monastery Egypt 28°34N 33°58E 251 K4
St. Catherine's Pt. U.K. 50°34N 1°18W 169 G6
St-Céré France 44°51N 1°54E 174 D5
St-Cergue Switz. 46°27N 6°10E 179 J2
St-Cernin France 45°5N 2°25E 174 C6
St-Chamond France 45°28N 4°31E 175 C8
St. Charles Ill., U.S.A. 41°54N 88°19W 311 C8
St. Charles Md., U.S.A. 38°36N 76°56W 309 F15
St. Charles Mo., U.S.A. 38°47N 90°29W 310 F6
St. Charles Va., U.S.A. 36°48N 83°4W 309 G12
St-Chély-d'Apcher France 44°48N 3°17E 174 D7
St-Chinian France 43°25N 2°56E 174 E6
St. Christopher = St. Kitts W. Indies 17°20N 62°40W 322 d
St. Christopher-Nevis = St. Kitts & Nevis ■ W. Indies 17°20N 62°40W 322 d
St-Ciers-sur-Gironde France 45°17N 0°37W 174 C3
St. Clair Ga., U.S.A. 33°9N 82°13W 316 B7
St. Clair Mich., U.S.A. 42°50N 82°30W 312 D2
St. Clair Mo., U.S.A. 38°21N 90°59W 310 F6
St. Clair Pa., U.S.A. 40°43N 76°12W 313 F8
St. Clair → U.S.A. 42°38N 82°31W 312 D2
St. Clair, L. S. Austral., Australia 37°20S 139°55E 282 D3
St. Clair, L. N. Amer. 42°27N 82°39W 312 D2
St. Clair Shores U.S.A. 42°30N 82°53W 311 B14
St. Clairsville U.S.A. 40°5N 80°54W 312 F4
St-Claud France 45°54N 0°28E 174 C4
St. Claude Canada 49°40N 98°20W 297 D9
St-Claude Jura, France 46°22N 5°52E 173 F12
St-Claude Guadeloupe 16°3N 61°42W 322 e
St. Clears U.K. 51°49N 4°31W 169 F3
St-Clet Canada 45°21N 74°13W 313 A10
St-Cloud France 48°50N 2°12E 134 A2
St. Cloud Fla., U.S.A. 28°15N 81°17W 317 G8
St. Cloud Minn., U.S.A. 45°34N 94°10W 308 C6
St. Cricq, C. Australia 25°17S 113°6E 279 E1
St. Croix U.S. Virgin Is. 17°45N 64°45W 321 C7
St. Croix → U.S.A. 44°45N 92°48W 308 C7
St. Croix Falls U.S.A. 45°24N 92°38W 308 C7
St-Cyprien France 42°37N 3°2E 174 F7
St-Cyr-l'École France 48°47N 2°4E 134 B1
St-Cyr-l'École ✕ France 48°48N 2°4E 134 B1
St-Cyr-sur-Mer France 43°11N 5°43E 175 E9
St. David U.S.A. 40°30N 90°3W 310 D6
St. David □ Trin. & Tob. 10°47N 61°3W 323 t
St. David's Nfld. & L., Canada 48°12N 58°52W 299 C8
St. David's Grenada 12°2N 61°40W 323 q
St. David's Pembs., U.K. 51°53N 5°16W 169 F2
St. David's Head U.K. 51°54N 5°19W 169 F2
St. David's I. Bermuda 32°21N 64°39W 153 a
St-Denis = Sig Algeria 35°32N 0°12W 261 A4
St-Denis Seine-St-Denis, France 48°56N 2°20E 134 A3
St-Denis Réunion 20°52S 55°27E 272 f
St-Denis → Réunion 20°52S 55°27E 272 f
St-Denis ✕ (RUN) Réunion 20°53S 55°32E 272 f
St-Dié France 48°17N 6°56E 173 D13
St-Dizier France 48°38N 4°56E 173 D11
St-Égrève France 45°14N 5°41E 175 C9
St. Elias, Mt. U.S.A. 60°18N 140°56W 303 F12
St. Elias Mts. N. Amer. 60°33N 139°28W 296 A1
St-Élie Fr. Guiana 4°49N 53°17W 329 C7
St. Elmo U.S.A. 39°2N 88°51W 311 E8
St-Éloy-les-Mines France 46°10N 2°51E 173 F9
St-Émilion France 44°53N 0°9W 174 D3
St-Étienne France 45°27N 4°22E 175 C8
St-Étienne → Réunion 21°17S 55°25E 272 f
St-Étienne-de-Tinée France 44°16N 6°56E 175 D10
St-Étienne-du-Rouvray France 49°23N 1°6E 172 C8
St. Eugène Canada 45°30N 74°28W 313 A10
St. Eustatius W. Indies 17°20N 63°0W 322 a
St-Exupery, Lyon ✕ (LYS) France 45°44N 5°2E 175 C9
St-Fargeau France 47°39N 3°4E 173 E10
St-Félicien Canada 48°40N 72°25W 298 C5
St. Ferdinand = Florissant U.S.A. 38°47N 90°19W 310 F6
St-Florent France 42°41N 9°18E 175 F13
St-Florent, G. de France 42°47N 9°12E 175 F13
St-Florent-sur-Cher France 46°59N 2°15E 173 F9
St-Florentin France 48°0N 3°45E 173 E10
St-Flour France 45°2N 3°6E 174 C7
St. Francis U.S.A. 39°47N 101°48W 308 F3
St. Francis → U.S.A. 34°38N 90°36W 315 D9
St. Francis, C. S. Africa 34°14S 24°49E 270 D3
St. Francisville Ill., U.S.A. 38°36N 87°39W 311 F9
St. Francisville La., U.S.A. 30°47N 91°23W 314 F9
St-François Guadeloupe 16°16N 61°18W 322 e
St-François, L. Canada 45°10N 74°22W 313 A10
St-Fulgent France 46°50N 1°10W 172 F5
St-Gabriel Canada 46°17N 73°24W 298 C5
St. Gallen = Sankt Gallen Switz. 47°26N 9°22E 179 H5
St-Galmier France 45°35N 4°19E 173 G11
St-Gaudens France 43°6N 0°44E 174 E4
St-Gaultier France 46°39N 1°26E 172 F8
St-Gengoux-le-National France 46°37N 4°40E 173 F11
St-Geniez-d'Olt France 44°27N 2°58E 174 D6
St. George Queens., Australia 28°1S 148°30E 281 D4
St. George Bermuda 32°24N 64°40W 153 a
St. George N.B., Canada 45°11N 66°50W 299 C6
St. George Ont., Canada 43°15N 80°15W 312 C4
St. George Ga., U.S.A. 30°31N 82°2W 316 E7
St. George S.C., U.S.A. 33°11N 80°35W 316 B9
St. George Utah, U.S.A. 37°6N 113°35W 305 H7
St. George □ Trin. & Tob. 10°40N 61°25W 323 t
St. George, C. Nfld. & L., Canada 48°30N 59°16W 299 C8
St. George, C. Papua N. G. 4°49S 152°53E 286 C7
St. George, C. Fla., U.S.A. 29°40N 85°5W 316 F4
St. George I. Alaska, U.S.A. 56°35N 169°35W 303 H5
St. George I. Fla., U.S.A. 29°35N 84°55W 316 F5
St. George Ra. Australia 18°40S 125°0E 278 C4
St. George's Canada 48°26N 58°31W 299 C8
St-Georges Qué., Canada 46°8N 70°40W 299 C5
St-Georges Fr. Guiana 3°53N 51°50W 329 C7
St. George's Grenada 12°5N 61°43W 323 q
St. George's B. Canada 48°24N 58°53W 299 C8
St. Georges Basin N.S.W., Australia 35°7S 150°36E 283 C9
St. Georges Basin W. Austral., Australia 15°23S 125°2E 278 C4
St. George's Channel Europe 52°0N 6°0W 166 E6
St. George's Channel India 7°15N 93°43E 245 L11
St. George's Channel Papua N. G. 4°10S 152°20E 286 C7
St. Georges Harbour Bermuda 32°33N 64°42W 153 a
St. Georges Hd. Australia 35°12S 150°42E 283 C9
St. Georges I. Bermuda 32°23N 64°40W 153 a
St-Georges-lès-Baillargeaux France 46°41N 0°22E 174 B4
St-Germain, Forêt de France 48°57N 2°5E 134 A1
St-Germain-de-Calberte France 44°13N 3°48E 174 D7
St-Germain-en-Laye France 48°53N 2°4E 134 A1
St-Germain-Lembron France 45°27N 3°14E 174 C7
St-Gervais-d'Auvergne France 46°4N 2°50E 173 F9
St-Gervais-les-Bains France 45°53N 6°42E 175 C10
St-Gildas, Pte. de France 47°8N 2°14W 172 E4
St. Giles Cathedral Edinburgh, U.K. 121 b2
St-Gilles Brussels, Belgium 50°49N 4°20E 116 B2
St-Gilles Gard, France 43°40N 4°26E 175 E8
St-Gilles Réunion 21°2S 55°14E 272 f
St-Gilles-les-Hauts Réunion 21°2S 55°15E 272 f
St-Girons Ariège, France 42°59N 1°8E 174 F5
St-Girons Landes, France 43°56N 1°18W 174 E2
St. Gotthard P. = San Gottardo, P. del Switz. 46°33N 8°33E 179 J4
St. Helena Atl. Oc. 15°58S 5°42W 153 h
St. Helena Calif., U.S.A. 38°30N 122°28W 304 G2
St. Helena, Mt. U.S.A. 38°40N 122°36W 306 G4
St. Helena B. S. Africa 32°40S 18°10E 270 D2
St. Helena Sd. U.S.A. 32°15N 80°25W 316 C9
St. Helens Tas., Australia 41°20S 148°15E 281 G4
St. Helens Mersey., U.K. 53°27N 2°44W 168 D5
St. Helens Oreg., U.S.A. 45°52N 122°48W 306 E4
St. Helens, Mt. U.S.A. 46°12N 122°12W 306 D4
St. Helier Chan. Is., U.K. 49°10N 2°7W 169 H5
St. Helier London, U.K. 51°23N 0°11W 125 B2
St-Herblain France 47°13N 1°40W 172 E5
St-Hilaire-du-Harcouët France 48°35N 1°5W 172 D5
St-Hippolyte France 47°19N 6°50E 173 E13
St-Hippolyte-du-Fort France 43°58N 3°52E 174 E7
St-Honoré-les-Bains France 46°54N 3°50E 173 F10
St-Hubert Belgium 50°2N 5°23E 170 D5
St-Hubert Qué., Canada 45°29N 73°25W 130 B3
St. Hubert, Galeries Royales Brussels, Belgium 116 b2
St-Hyacinthe Canada 45°40N 72°58W 298 C5
St. Ignace U.S.A. 45°52N 84°44W 309 C11
St. Ignace I. Canada 48°45N 88°0W 298 C2
St. Ignatius U.S.A. 47°19N 114°6W 304 C6
St-Imier Switz. 47°9N 6°58E 179 H2
St. Isaac's Cathedral Russia 59°55N 30°19E 137 B1
St. Ives Cambs., U.K. 52°20N 0°4W 169 E7
St. Ives Corn., U.K. 50°12N 5°30W 169 G2
St-Jacques Montréal, Canada 130 a2
St-Jacques → Canada 45°26N 73°29W 130 B3
St-James France 48°31N 1°20W 172 D5
St. James Minn., U.S.A. 43°59N 94°38W 308 D6
St. James Mo., U.S.A. 38°0N 91°37W 310 G5
St. James Cathedral Toronto, Canada 141 b3
St. James's London, U.K. 125 b3
St-Jean St.-Martin 17°53N 62°50W 322 a
St-Jean → Canada 50°17N 64°20W 299 B7
St-Jean, L. Canada 48°40N 72°0W 299 C5
St-Jean Baptiste Montréal, Canada 130 a1
St-Jean-d'Angély France 45°57N 0°31W 174 C3
St-Jean-de-Braye France 47°53N 1°58E 173 E8
St-Jean-de-Luz France 43°23N 1°39W 174 E2
St-Jean-de-Maurienne France 45°16N 6°21E 175 C10
St-Jean-de-Monts France 46°47N 2°4W 172 F4
St-Jean-du-Gard France 44°7N 3°52E 174 D7
St-Jean-en-Royans France 45°1N 5°18E 175 C9
St-Jean-Pied-de-Port France 43°10N 1°14W 174 E2
St-Jean-Port-Joli Canada 47°15N 70°13W 299 C5
St-Jean-sur-Richelieu Canada 45°20N 73°20W 313 A11
St-Jérôme Canada 45°47N 74°0W 298 C5
St. Joe U.S.A. 41°19N 84°54W 311 C12
St. John N.B., Canada 45°20N 66°8W 299 C6
St. John Kans., U.S.A. 38°0N 98°46W 308 F4
St. John → Liberia 6°40N 9°10W 262 D2
St. John → N. Amer. 45°12N 66°5W 309 C20
St. John, C. Canada 50°0N 55°32W 299 C8
St. John I. U.S. Virgin Is. 18°20N 64°42W 321 e
St. John's Antigua & B. 17°6N 61°51W 322 b
St. John's Nfld. & L., Canada 47°35N 52°40W 299 C9
St. Johns Montserrat 16°46N 62°11W 322 h
St. Johns Ariz., U.S.A. 34°30N 109°22W 305 J9
St. Johns Mich., U.S.A. 43°0N 84°33W 311 B12
St. Johns → U.S.A. 30°24N 81°24W 316 E8
St. John's Cathedral Hong Kong, China 122 c1
St. John's Pt. Ireland 54°34N 8°27W 166 B3
St. Johnsbury U.S.A. 44°25N 72°1W 313 B12
St. Johnston Village Antigua & B. 17°7N 61°50W 322 b
St. Johnsville U.S.A. 43°0N 74°43W 313 C10
St-Joost-Ten-Node Belgium 50°51N 4°21E 116 A2
St. Joseph Ont., Canada 43°24N 81°42W 312 C3
St. Joseph Dominica 15°24N 61°26W 323 k
St-Joseph Martinique 14°39N 61°4W 322 j
St-Joseph Réunion 21°22S 55°37E 272 f
St. Joseph Mayaro, Trin. & Tob. 10°18N 60°59W 323 t
St. Joseph St. George, Trin. & Tob. 10°40N 61°25W 323 t
St. Joseph Ill., U.S.A. 40°7N 88°2W 311 D8
St. Joseph La., U.S.A. 31°55N 91°14W 314 F9
St. Joseph Mich., U.S.A. 42°6N 86°29W 311 B10
St. Joseph Mo., U.S.A. 39°46N 94°50W 310 E2
St. Joseph → U.S.A. 42°7N 86°29W 311 B10
St. Joseph, I. Canada 46°12N 83°58W 298 C3
St. Joseph, L. Canada 51°10N 90°35W 298 B1
St. Joseph Pt. U.S.A. 29°52N 85°24W 316 F4
St-Juéry France 43°57N 2°12E 174 E6
St. Julian's Malta 35°55N 14°29E 206 F7
St-Julien-Chapteuil France 45°2N 4°4E 175 C8
St-Julien-de-Vouvantes France 47°38N 1°13W 172 E5

St-Julien-en-Genevois
  France 46°9N 6°5E **173** F13
St-Junien France 45°53S 0°55E **174** C4
St-Just-en-Chaussée France 49°30N 2°25E **173** C9
St-Just-en-Chevalet France 45°55N 3°50E **174** C7
St. Kilda Vic., Australia 37°51S 144°58E **128** B1
St. Kilda N.Z. 45°53S 170°31E **285** F5
St. Kilda W. Isles, U.K. 57°49N 8°34W **165** C2
St. Kitts N.Z. 17°20N 62°40W **322** d
St. Kitts & Nevis ■
  W. Indies 17°20N 62°40W **322** d
St-Lambert Qué., Canada 45°30N 73°29W **130** A3
St-Lambert Yvelines, France 48°43N 2°1E **138** B1
St. Laurent 50°25N 97°58W **297** C9
St. Laurent Canada 45°30N 73°43W **130** A1
St-Laurent-de-la-Salanque
  France 42°46N 2°59E **174** F6
St. Lawrence Queens.,
  Australia 22°16S 149°31E **280** C4
St. Lawrence Nfld. & L.,
  Canada 46°54N 55°23W **299** C8
St. Lawrence → Canada 49°30N 66°00W **299** C6
St. Lawrence, Gulf of
  Canada 48°25N 62°00W **299** C7
St. Lawrence I. U.S.A. 63°30N 170°30W **303** E5
St. Lawrence Islands △
  Canada 44°27N 75°52W **313** B9
St. Lawrence Market Toronto, Canada **141** b3
St-Lazare, Gare Paris, France **134** a3
St. Léonard Canada 47°12N 67°58W **299** C6
St. Léonard Canada 45°35N 73°34W **130** A2
St-Léonard-de-Noblat
  France 45°49N 1°29E **174** C5
St-Leu Réunion 21°9S 55°18E **272** f
St. Lewis → Canada 52°26N 56°11W **299** B8
St-Lô France 49°7N 1°5W **172** C5
St-Louis Montréal, Canada **130** b2
St-Louis Haut-Rhin, France 47°30N 7°34E **173** E14
St-Louis Guadeloupe 15°56N 61°19W **322** e
St-Louis Réunion 21°16S 55°25E **272** f
St. Louis Senegal 16°8N 16°27W **262** B1
St. Louis Mo., U.S.A. 38°37N 90°11W **310** F6
St-Louis ∇ Senegal 16°20N 15°00W **262** B1
St. Louis → U.S.A. 46°44N 92°9W **308** B7
St. Louis Lambert Int. ✈ (STL)
  U.S.A. 38°45N 90°22W **310** F6
St-Loup-sur-Semouse
  France 47°53N 6°16E **173** E13
St-Luc Canada 45°22N 73°18W **313** A11
St. Lucia ■ W. Indies 14°0N 60°57W **323** m
St. Lucia, L. S. Africa 28°5S 32°30E **271** C5
St. Lucia Channel
  W. Indies 14°15N 61°0W **321** D7
St. Lucie U.S.A. 27°29N 80°20W **317** H9
St. Lucie Canal U.S.A. 27°10N 80°18W **317** H9
St. Maarten ∇ W. Indies 18°0N 63°5W **322** a
St. Magelungen Sweden 59°13N 18°4E **139** B2
St. Magnus B. U.K. 60°25N 1°35W **167** A7
St-Maixent-l'École France 46°24N 0°12W **174** B3
St-Malo France 48°39N 2°1W **172** D4
St-Malo, G. de France 48°50N 2°30W **172** D4
St-Mandé France 48°50N 2°24E **134** A3
St-Mandrier-sur-Mer France 43°4N 5°57E **175** E9
St-Marc Haiti 19°10N 72°41W **321** C5
St-Marcellin France 45°9N 5°20E **175** C9
St-Marcouf, Îs. France 49°30N 1°10W **172** C5
St. Margaret's Ireland 53°25N 6°18W **120** A2
St. Maries U.S.A. 47°19N 116°35W **304** C5
St. Mark B. Grenada 12°11N 61°42W **323** q
St. Marks U.S.A. 30°9N 84°12W **316** E5
St-Martin ∇ W. Indies 18°0N 63°0W **322** a
St-Martin, Bois France 48°48N 2°35E **134** B4
St. Martin, C. Martinique 14°52N 61°14W **322** j
St. Martin, L. Canada 51°40N 98°30W **297** C9
St-Martin-de-Crau France 43°38N 4°48E **175** E8
St-Martin-de-Ré France 46°12N 1°21W **174** B2
St-Martin-d'Hères France 45°10N 5°45E **175** C9
St-Martin-Vésubie France 44°4N 7°15E **175** D11
St. Martin's I. Bangla. 20°36N 92°20E **241** E4
St-Martory France 43°9N 0°56E **174** E4
St. Mary U.S.A. 37°53N 89°57W **310** G7
St. Mary, Mt. Papua N. G. 8°8S 147°2E **286** E4
St. Mary Cray U.K. 51°23N 0°7E **125** B4
St. Mary Is. U.S.A. 13°20N 74°35E **245** H2
St. Mary Pk. Australia 31°32S 138°34E **282** A3
St. Marys Tas., Australia 41°35S 148°11E **281** G4
St. Marys Ont., Canada 43°20N 81°10W **312** C3
St. Mary's Trin. & Tob. 10°14N 61°33W **323** t
St. Mary's Corn., U.K. 49°55N 6°18W **169** H1
St. Mary's Orkney, U.K. 58°54N 2°54W **167** C6
St. Mary's Alaska, U.S.A. 62°4N 163°10W **303** C7
St. Marys Ga., U.S.A. 30°44N 81°33W **316** E8
St. Marys Ohio, U.S.A. 40°33N 84°24W **311** D12
St. Marys Pa., U.S.A. 41°26N 78°34W **312** E6
St. Marys → U.S.A. 30°43N 81°27W **316** E8
St. Mary's, C. Canada 46°50N 54°12W **299** C9
St. Mary's, B. Canada 46°50N 53°50W **299** C9
St. Mary's Bay Canada 44°25N 66°10W **299** D6
St. Mary's Cathedral
  San Francisco, U.S.A. **136** c1
St-Mathieu, Pte. France 48°20N 4°45W **172** D2
St. Matthew I. U.S.A. 60°24N 172°42W **303** F4
St. Matthews S.C., U.S.A. 33°40N 80°46W **316** D7
St. Matthews Ky., U.S.A. 38°15N 85°39W **311** F11
St. Matthews, I. = Zadetkyi Kyun
  Burma 10°0N 98°25E **237** G2
St. Matthias Group
  Papua N. G. 1°30S 150°0E **286** A6
St-Maur-des-Fossés France 48°48N 2°29E **134** B3
St-Maurice France 48°49N 2°24E **134** B4
St-Maurice → Canada 46°21N 72°31W **298** C5
St. Mawes U.K. 50°10N 5°2W **169** G2
St-Maximin-la-Ste-Baume
  France 43°27N 5°52E **175** E9
St-Médard-en-Jalles
  France 44°53N 0°43W **174** D3
St-Méen-le-Grand France 48°11N 2°12W **172** D4
St. Meinrad U.S.A. 38°10N 86°49W **311** F10
St. Michael U.S.A. 63°29N 162°2W **303** E7
St. Michael's Cathedral Toronto, Canada **141** a3
St-Michel Canada 45°34N 73°37W **130** A2
St-Mihiel France 48°54N 5°33E **172** C7
St-Nazaire France 47°17N 2°12W **172** E4
St. Neots U.K. 52°14N 0°15W **169** E7
St-Nicolas-de-Port France 48°38N 6°18E **173** D13
St. Niklaas Belgium 51°10N 4°8E **170** C4
St. Nikolaus-Kirchen
  Czech Rep. 50°5N 14°23E **135** B2
St-Omer France 50°45N 2°15E **173** B9
St-Ouen France 48°56N 2°20E **134** A3
St-Palais-sur-Mer France 45°38N 1°8W **174** C2
St-Pamphile Canada 46°58N 69°48W **299** C6
St. Pancras International London, U.K. **125** a4
St-Pardoux-la-Rivière
  France 45°29N 0°45E **174** C4
St. Paris U.S.A. 40°8N 83°58W **311** D13
St-Pascal Canada 47°32N 69°48W **299** C6
St. Patrick △ Trin. & Tob. 10°10N 61°35W **323** s
St. Patricks Barbados 13°6N 59°30W **323** r

St. Patrick's Cathedral Dublin, Ireland **120** c1
St. Patrick's Cathedral New York, U.S.A. **132** C2
St. Patrick's Church Toronto, Canada **141** a1
St-Paul Canada 54°0N 111°17W **296** C6
St-Paul Alpes-de-Haute-Provence,
  France 44°31N 6°45E **175** D10
St-Paul Réunion 20°59S 55°17E **272** f
St. Paul Alaska, U.S.A. 57°7N 170°17W **303** H5
St. Paul Ind., U.S.A. 39°26N 85°38W **311** E11
St. Paul Minn., U.S.A. 44°56N 93°5W **308** C7
St. Paul Nebr., U.S.A. 41°13N 98°27W **308** E4
St. Paul → Canada 51°27N 57°42W **299** B8
St. Paul → Liberia 6°25N 10°48E **262** D2
St. Paul, Î. Ind. Oc. 38°55S 77°34E **273** H6
St-Paul-de-Fenouillet
  France 42°48N 2°30E **174** F6
St. Paul I. N.S.A. 47°12N 60°9W **299** C7
St. Paul I. Alaska, U.S.A. 57°10N 170°15W **303** H5
St-Paul-lès-Dax France 43°44N 1°3W **174** E2
St. Paul's Bay Malta 35°57N 14°24E **206** F7
St. Paul's Cathedral London, U.K. **125** b4
St. Paul's Cray U.K. 51°23N 0°6E **125** B4
St-Péray France 44°57N 4°50E **175** D8
St. Pete Beach U.S.A. 27°43N 82°44W **317** H7
St. Peter U.S.A. 44°20N 93°57W **308** C7
St. Peter & St. Paul San Francisco, U.S.A. **136** a2
St-Peter-Ording Germany 54°20N 8°36E **178** A4
St. Peter Port U.K. 49°26N 2°33W **169** H5
St. Peters N.S.W.,
  Australia 33°55S 151°11E **139** B2
St. Peters N.S., Canada 45°40N 60°53W **299** C7
St. Peters P.E.I., Canada 46°25N 62°35W **299** C7
St. Peters Montserrat 16°43N 62°13W **323** p
St. Peters Mo., U.S.A. 38°46N 90°37W **310** F6
St. Peter's Square = San Pietro,
  Piazza Rome. Italy **136** b1
St. Petersburg = Sankt-Peterburg
  Russia 59°55N 30°20E **137** B1
St. Petersburg U.S.A. 27°46N 82°40W **317** H7
St. Petersburg Pulkovo Int. ✈ (LED)
  Russia 59°48N 30°18E **137** C1
St-Philbert-de-Grand-Lieu
  France 47°2N 1°39W **172** E5
St-Philippe Réunion 21°21S 55°44E **272** f
St-Pie Canada 45°30N 72°54W **313** A12
St-Pierre Qué., Canada 45°27N 73°38W **130** B2
St-Pierre Martinique 14°45N 61°10W **322** j
St-Pierre Mauritius 20°13S 57°31E **272** e
St-Pierre Réunion 21°19S 55°28E **272** f
St-Pierre St-P. & M. 46°46N 56°12W **299** C8
St-Pierre Seychelles 9°20S 46°0E **273** E3
St-Pierre, L. Canada 46°12N 72°52W **298** C5
St-Pierre, Rade de
  Martinique 14°44N 61°11W **322** j
St-Pierre-de-la-Pointe-aux-
  Esquimaux = Havre-St-Pierre
  Canada 50°18N 63°33W **299** B7
St-Pierre-d'Oléron France 45°57N 1°19W **174** C2
St-Pierre-en-Port France 49°48N 0°30E **172** C7
St-Pierre-et-Miquelon ∇
  N. Amer. 46°55N 56°10W **299** C8
St-Pierre-le-Moûtier France 46°47N 3°7E **173** F10
St-Pierre-sur-Dives France 49°2N 0°1W **172** C6
St-Pieters Leew Belgium 50°47N 4°16E **116** B1
St-Pol-de-Léon France 48°41N 4°0W **172** D3
St-Pol-sur-Mer France 51°1N 2°20E **173** A9
St-Pol-sur-Ternoise France 50°23N 2°20E **173** B9
St-Pons France 43°30N 2°45E **174** E6
St-Pourçain-sur-Sioule
  France 46°18N 3°18E **173** F10
St-Priest France 45°42N 4°57E **175** C8
St-Quay-Portrieux France 48°39N 2°51W **172** D4
St-Quentin N.B., Canada 47°30N 67°23W **299** C6
St-Quentin Aisne, France 49°50N 3°16E **173** C10
St-Quentin, Étang de France 48°47N 2°0E **134** B1
St-Rambert-d'Albon
  France 45°17N 4°49E **175** C8
St-Raphaël France 43°25N 6°46E **175** E10
St. Regis U.S.A. 47°18N 115°6W **304** C6
St. Regis Falls U.S.A. 44°40N 74°32W **313** B10
St-Renan France 48°26N 4°37W **172** D2
St. Robert U.S.A. 37°50N 92°11W **310** G4
St-Saëns France 49°41N 1°16E **172** C8
St-Savin France 46°34N 0°53E **174** B4
St-Savinien France 45°53N 0°42W **174** C3
St. Sebastien, Tanjon' i
  Madag. 12°26S 48°44E **272** A2
St-Seine-l'Abbaye France 47°26N 4°47E **173** E11
St-Sernin-sur-Rance
  France 43°54N 2°35E **174** E6
St-Sever France 43°45N 0°35W **174** E3
St-Siméon Canada 47°51N 69°54W **299** C6
St. Simons I. U.S.A. 31°12N 81°15W **316** D8
St. Simons Island U.S.A. 31°9N 81°22W **315** F14
St. Stephen N.B., Canada 45°16N 67°17W **299** D6
St. Stephen S.C., U.S.A. 33°24N 79°55W **316** B10
St. Stephen's Basilica Budapest, Hungary **117** b2
St. Stephen's Cathedral =
  Stephansdom Vienna, Austria **142** b2
St. Stephen's Green Dublin, Ireland **120** c3
St-Stevens-Woluwe
  Belgium 50°52N 4°26E **116** A2
St-Sulpice France 43°46N 1°41E **174** E5
St-Sulpice-Laurière France 46°3N 1°29E **174** B5
St-Sulpice-les-Feuilles
  France 46°19N 1°21E **174** B5
St-Syprien = St-Cyprien
  France 42°37N 3°2E **174** F7
St. Teresa U.S.A. 29°55N 84°27W **316** F5
St-Thégonnec France 48°31N 3°57W **172** D3
St. Thomas = Charlotte Amalie
  U.S. Virgin Is. 18°21N 64°56W **321** C7
St. Thomas Canada 42°45N 81°10W **312** D3
St. Thomas Bay Malta 35°51N 14°34E **206** F8
St. Thomas I.
  U.S. Virgin Is. 18°20N 64°55W **321** C7
St-Tite Canada 46°45N 72°34W **298** C5
St-Tropez France 43°17N 6°38E **175** E10
St-Troud = St. Truiden
  Belgium 50°48N 5°10E **170** D5
St. Truiden Belgium 50°48N 5°10E **170** D5
St-Vaast-la-Hougue
  France 49°35N 1°17W **172** C5
St-Valéry-en-Caux France 49°52N 0°43E **172** C7
St-Valéry-sur-Somme
  France 50°11N 1°38E **173** B8
St-Vallier France 46°38N 4°23E **173** F11
St-Vallier-de-Thiey France 43°42N 6°51E **175** D10
St-Varent France 46°53N 0°13W **172** F6
St-Vaury France 46°12N 1°29E **174** B5
St. Vidgeon's ◎ Australia 14°47S 134°53E **280** A1
St. Vincent = São Vicente
  C. Verde Is. 17°0N 25°0W **153** j
St. Vincent Italy 45°45N 7°39E **198** C4
St. Vincent W. Australia 35°0S 138°0E **282** C3
St. Vincent, G. Australia 35°0S 138°0E **282** C3
St. Vincent & the Grenadines ■
  W. Indies 13°0N 61°10W **323** h
St-Vincent-de-Paul
  Canada 45°36N 73°39W **130** A2
St-Vincent-de-Tyrosse
  France 43°39N 1°19W **174** E2
St. Vincent I. U.S.A. 29°36N 85°3W **317** F4
St. Vincent Passage
  W. Indies 13°30N 61°0W **321** D7

St-Vith Belgium 50°17N 6°9E **170** D6
St-Vivien-de-Médoc France 45°25N 1°2W **174** C2
St. Walburg Canada 53°39N 109°12W **297** D7
St. Xavier Univ. U.S.A. 41°42N 87°42W **119** C2
St-Yrieix-la-Perche France 45°31N 1°12E **174** C5
Saintala India 20°26N 83°20E **244** D6
St-Adresse France 49°31N 0°5E **172** C7
Ste-Agathe-des-Monts
  Canada 46°3N 74°17W **298** C5
Ste-Anne Guadeloupe 16°13N 61°24W **322** e
Ste-Anne Martinique 14°25N 60°54W **322** j
Ste-Anne Réunion 21°4S 55°45E **272** f
Ste-Anne Seychelles 4°36S 55°31E **273** b
Ste-Anne, L. Canada 50°0N 67°42W **299** B6
Ste-Anne-des-Monts
  Canada 49°8N 66°30W **299** C6
Ste-Catherine Canada 45°24N 73°34W **130** B2
Ste-Croix Switz. 46°49N 6°34E **179** J2
Ste-Enimie France 44°22N 3°26E **174** D7
Ste-Foy-la-Grande France 44°50N 0°13E **174** D4
Ste-Hélène, Î. Canada 45°31N 73°32W **130** a2
Ste-Hermine France 46°32N 1°4W **174** B2
Ste-Livrade-sur-Lot France 44°24N 0°36E **174** D4
Ste-Luce Martinique 14°28N 60°55W **322** j
Ste. Madeleine Trin. & Tob. 10°16N 61°26W **323** t
Ste-Marguerite Guadeloupe 16°23N 61°24W **322** e
Ste-Marguerite → Canada 50°9N 66°36W **299** B6
Ste-Marie Canada 46°26N 71°0W **299** C5
Ste. Marie Gabon 3°48S 11°1E **264** C2
Ste. Marie Canada 16°6N 61°33W **322** e
Ste-Marie Martinique 14°48N 61°1W **322** j
Ste-Marie Réunion 20°53S 55°33E **272** f
Ste-Marie, Ile = Nosy Boraha
  Madag. 16°50S 49°55E **272** B2
Ste-Marie-aux-Mines
  France 48°15N 7°12E **173** D14
Ste-Marthe Guadeloupe 16°15N 61°15W **322** e
Ste-Maure-de-Touraine
  France 47°7N 0°37E **172** E7
Ste-Maxime France 43°19N 6°39E **175** E10
Ste-Menehould France 49°5N 4°54E **173** C11
Ste-Mère-Église France 49°24N 1°19W **172** C5
Ste-Rose Guadeloupe 16°20N 61°45W **322** e
Ste-Rose Réunion 21°8S 55°45E **272** f
Ste. Rose du Lac Canada 51°4N 99°30W **297** C9
Ste-Savine France 48°18N 4°3E **173** D11
Ste-Sigolène France 45°15N 4°14E **175** C8
Ste-Suzanne Réunion 20°54S 55°36E **272** f
Saintes France 45°45N 0°37W **174** C3
Saintes, Canal des
  Guadeloupe 15°55N 61°40W **322** b
Saintes, Îs. des Guadeloupe 15°50N 61°35W **322** e
Stes-Maries-de-la-Mer
  France 43°26N 4°26E **175** E8
Saintfield U.K. 54°28N 5°49W **166** B6
Saintonge France 45°40N 0°50W **174** C3
Saipan N. Marianas 15°12N 145°45E **302** e
Saipan Channel
  N. Marianas 15°15N 145°41E **302** e
Sairang India 23°50N 92°45E **241** D4
Sairecábur, Cerro Bolivia 22°43S 67°54W **334** A2
Saitama Japan 35°54N 139°38E **223** A11
Saitama □ Japan 36°25N 139°30E **223** A11
Saiteli = Kadınhanı
  Turkey 38°14N 32°13E **212** C5
Saiți Moldova 46°30N 29°24E **183** D14
Saiwai → Australia 38°5S 147°6E **283** E7
Saiyid Pakistan 33°7N 73°2E **242** C5
Saja → Spain 43°10N 4°9W **196** B6
Sajama Bolivia 18°7S 69°0W **330** D4
Sajama, Nevado Bolivia 18°6S 68°54W **330** D4
Sajan Serbia 45°50N 20°20E **182** E5
Sajó → Hungary 48°12N 21°7E **182** C6
Sajószentpéter Hungary 48°12N 20°44E **182** B5
Sajum India 33°20N 79°0E **243** C8
Sak → S. Africa 30°52S 20°25E **270** D3
Saka Kenya 0°9S 39°20E **268** B4
Saka Kalat Pakistan 27°3N 65°3E **240** D2
Sakaba Nigeria 11°4N 5°35E **263** C6
Sakai Japan 34°34N 135°27E **133** B1
Sakai Harbour Japan 34°36N 133°50E **222** C5
Sakaide Japan 34°19N 133°50E **222** C5
Sakaiminato Japan 35°38N 133°11E **222** B5
Sakâkah Si. Arabia 30°0N 40°8E **246** D4
Sakakawea, L. U.S.A. 47°30N 101°25W **308** B3
Sakami → Canada 53°40N 76°40W **298** B4
Sakami, L. Canada 53°15N 77°0W **298** B4
Sâkâne, 'Erg i-n Mali 20°30N 1°30W **260** D4
Sakania
  Dem. Rep. of the Congo 12°43S 28°30E **269** E2
Sakar I. Papua N. G. 5°25S 148°9E **286** C6
Sakaraha Madag. 22°55S 44°32E **272** C1
Sakartvelo = Georgia ■
  Asia 42°0N 43°0E **191** J6
Sakarya Turkey 40°48N 30°25E **212** B4
Sakarya □ Turkey 40°45N 30°25E **212** B4
Sakarya → Turkey 41°7N 30°39E **212** B4
Sakashima-Guntō Japan 24°46N 124°0E **221** M2
Sakassou Ivory C. 7°29N 5°19W **262** D3
Sakata Japan 38°55N 139°50E **220** E9
Sakawa Japan 33°28N 133°11E **222** D5
Sakchu N. Korea 40°23N 125°2E **224** B2
Sakeny → Madag. 20°0S 45°25E **272** C2
Sakété Benin 6°40N 2°45E **263** D5
Sakha □ Russia 66°0N 130°0E **215** C14
Sakhalin Russia 51°0N 143°0E **215** D15
Sakhalinskiy Zaliv Russia 54°0N 141°0E **215** D15
Sakhi Gopal India 19°58N 85°50E **244** E7
Şaki Azerbaijan 41°10N 47°0E **191** K8
Šakiai Lithuania 54°59N 23°2E **184** D10
Sakiz-Adasi = Chios Greece 38°27N 26°9E **205** C8
Sakmara → Russia 51°46N 55°1E **216** B5
Sakoli India 21°5N 79°59E **244** D4
Sakon Nakhon Thailand 17°10N 104°9E **238** D5
Sakra, Pulau Singapore 1°15N 103°41E **138** B2
Sakrand Pakistan 26°10N 68°15E **242** F3
Sakri Maharashtra, India 26°13N 86°5E **243** F12
Sakri Maharashtra, India 21°2N 74°20E **244** D2
Sakrivier S. Africa 30°54S 20°28E **270** D3
Sakskøbing Denmark 54°49N 11°39E **163** J6
Sakti India 22°2N 82°58E **243** H10
Sakuma Japan 35°3N 137°49E **223** B9
Sakura Japan 35°43N 140°14E **223** B11
Sakurai Japan 34°30N 135°51E **223** C7
Sakurajima = On-Take
  Japan 31°35N 130°39E **222** F2
Saky Ukraine 45°9N 33°34E **189** K7
Sal → S. Africa 47°31N 40°45E **191** G5
Sal Rei C. Verde Is. 16°11N 22°53W **153** j
Sala Eritrea 16°11N 22°53W **153** j
Sala, O. → Chad 17°0N 20°0E **264** B2
Sala Consilina Italy 40°23N 15°36E **201** B8
Sala y Gómez Pac. Oc. 26°28S 105°28W **289** K17
Sala y Gómez Ridge
  Pac. Oc. 25°0S 99°0W **289** K18
Salaberry-de-Valleyfield
  Canada 45°15N 74°8W **313** A10

Salacgrīva Latvia 57°45N 24°21E **184** A11
Salada, L. Mexico 32°20N 115°40W **305** K6
Saladas Argentina 28°15S 58°40W **334** B4
Saladillo Argentina 35°40S 59°55W **334** D4
Salado → B. Aires.
  Argentina 35°44S 57°22W **334** D4
Salado → La Pampa,
  Argentina 37°30S 67°0W **336** A3
Salado → Rio Negro,
  Argentina 41°34S 65°3W **336** B3
Salado → Santa Fe,
  Argentina 31°40S 60°41W **334** C3
Salado → Tamaulipas,
  Mexico 26°52N 99°19W **314** H5
Salaga Ghana 8°31N 0°31E **263** D4
Sālah Syria 32°40N 36°45E **250** F7
Salāh ad Dīn □ Iraq 34°35N 43°35E **246** C4
Salahin Somali Rep. 2°57N 46°26E **267** D6
Sâlaj □ Romania 47°15N 23°0E **182** B8
Salakos Greece 36°17N 27°57E **206** E11
Salal Chad 14°48N 17°12E **259** F3
Salala Liberia 6°42N 10°7W **262** D2
Salala Sudan 21°17N 36°16E **256** C4
Salālah Oman 16°56N 53°59E **249** C6
Salam Iraq 33°20N 44°20E **113** A2
Salamanca Chile 31°46S 70°59W **334** C1
Salamanca Madrid, Spain 40°25N 3°41W **127** B1
Salamanca Salamanca,
  Spain 40°58N 5°39W **194** E5
Salamanca N.Y., U.S.A. 42°10N 78°43W **312** D6
Salamanca U.S.A. 40°57N 5°40W **194** E5
Salamanca □ Spain 40°57N 5°40W **194** E5
Salamat □ Chad 10°30N 20°30E **259** G4
Salamat, Bahr → Chad 9°20N 18°0E **259** G3
Salamatābād Iran 35°39N 47°50E **246** C5
Salamina Colombia 5°25N 75°29W **328** B2
Salamina Greece 37°56N 23°30E **204** D5
Salamis Cyprus 35°11N 33°54E **207** E19
Salamonie L. U.S.A. 40°46N 85°37W **311** D11
Salmān Pak Iraq 33°6N 44°34E **213** G11
Salmannsdorf Austria 48°14N 16°14E **142** A1
Salmās Iran 38°11N 44°47E **213** C11
Salmedina Spain 40°18N 3°35W **127** C2
Salmerón Spain 40°33N 2°29W **196** E2
Salmo Canada 49°10N 117°20W **296** D5
Salmon U.S.A. 45°11N 113°54W **304** D7
Salmon → B.C., Canada 54°3N 122°40W **296** C4
Salmon → Idaho, U.S.A. 45°51N 116°47W **304** D5
Salmon Arm Canada 50°40N 119°15W **296** C5
Salmon Gums Australia 32°59S 121°38E **279** F3
Salmon Pt. Canada 43°52N 77°15W **312** C7
Salmon River Mts.
  U.S.A. 44°50N 115°30W **304** D6
Salmon River Res. U.S.A. 43°32N 75°55W **313** C9
Salo Finland 60°22N 23°10E **188** B2
Salò Italy 45°36N 10°31E **198** C7
Salobreña Spain 36°44N 3°35W **195** D1
Salome U.S.A. 33°47N 113°37W **307** M13
Salomea Poland 52°11N 20°55E **142** B1
Salomon, C. Martinique 14°30N 61°6W **322** j
Salon India 26°2N 81°27E **243** F9
Salon-de-Provence France 43°39N 5°6E **175** E8
Salonga →
  Dem. Rep. of the Congo 0°10S 19°50E **264** C4
Salonga-Nord △
  Dem. Rep. of the Congo 1°55S 21°45E **264** C4
Salonga-Sud △
  Dem. Rep. of the Congo 2°25S 21°0E **264** C4
Salonica = Thessaloniki
  Greece 40°38N 22°58E **202** F6
Salonta Romania 46°49N 21°42E **182** D6
Salop = Shropshire □
  U.K. 52°36N 2°45W **169** E5
Salor → Spain 39°39N 7°3W **195** F3
Salou Spain 41°4N 1°10E **196** D6
Salou, C. de Spain 41°3N 1°10E **196** D6
Saloum → Senegal 13°50N 16°45W **262** C1
Salpausselkä Finland 61°0N 26°15E **188** B4
Salsacate Argentina 31°20S 65°5W **334** C2
Salses France 42°50N 2°55E **174** F6
Salsette I. India 19°2N 72°53E **130** A2
Salsk Russia 46°28N 41°30E **191** G5
Salso → Italy 37°6N 13°57E **200** D6
Salsomaggiore Terme Italy 44°49N 9°59E **198** D6
Salt Spain 41°58N 2°46E **196** D7
Salt → Alta., Canada 60°0N 112°25W **296** B6
Salt → Ariz., U.S.A. 33°23N 112°19W **305** K7
Salt → Mo., U.S.A. 39°29N 91°4W **310** F5
Salt Cay Bahamas 25°6N 77°18W **153** b
Salt Flats = Witte Pan
  Bonaire 12°3N 68°17W **322** h
Salt Fork Red → U.S.A. 34°27N 99°21W **314** B5
Salt L. N.S.W., Australia 30°6S 142°8E **281** E3
Salt L. Hawai'i, U.S.A. 21°21N 157°55W **302** K14
Salt Lake City = Bidhan Nagar
  India 22°35N 88°27E **244** H4
Salt Lake City U.S.A. 40°45N 111°53W **304** F8
Salt Range Pakistan 32°30N 72°25E **242** C5
Salt River S. Africa 34°6S 18°28E **118** A1
Salt Springs U.S.A. 29°21N 81°44W **317** F8
Salt Water L. India 22°33N 88°26E **244** H4
Salta Argentina 24°57S 65°25W **334** A2
Salta □ Argentina 24°48S 65°30W **334** A2
Saltaire U.K. 53°50N 1°47W **168** D6
Saltara Italy 43°45N 12°55E **199** E9
Saltash U.K. 50°24N 4°14W **169** G3
Saltburn by the Sea U.K. 54°35N 0°58W **168** C7
Saltcoats U.K. 55°38N 4°47W **167** F4
Saltee Is. Ireland 52°7N 6°37W **166** E6
Saltfjellet Norway 66°40N 15°15E **160** C16
Saltfjorden Norway 67°15N 14°10E **160** C16
Saltholm Denmark 55°38N 12°43E **163** J6
Salthólmavík Iceland 65°24N 21°57W **155** D3
Saltillo Mexico 25°25N 101°0W **318** B4
Salto Argentina 34°20S 60°15W **334** C3
Salto Uruguay 31°27S 57°50W **334** C4
Salto → Italy 42°26N 12°41E **199** F9
Salto da Divisa Brazil 16°0S 39°57W **333** E6
Salto del Guaíra Paraguay 24°3S 54°17W **335** A5
Salton City U.S.A. 33°18N 115°57W **307** M11
Salton Sea U.S.A. 33°15N 115°45W **307** M11
Saltpond Ghana 5°15N 1°3W **263** D4
Saltrød Norway 58°30N 8°49E **164** F5
Saltsjö-Duvnäs Sweden 59°18N 18°12E **162** B2
Saltykovka Russia 55°45N 37°54E **129** B5
Saltville U.S.A. 36°53N 81°46W **316** B6
Saluda → U.S.A. 34°1N 81°4W **316** D7
Saluda → U.S.A. 34°1N 81°4W **315** G12
Saluq, Kūh-e Iran 36°59N 58°12E **247** B8
Salūm Egypt 31°31N 25°7E **256** A2
Salūm, Khalīg el Egypt 31°30N 25°9E **256** A2
Salur India 18°27N 83°18E **244** E6
Salut, Is. du Fr. Guiana 5°15N 52°35W **329** B7
Saluzzo Italy 44°39N 7°29E **198** D4
Salvación B. Chile 50°50S 75°10W **336** G1
Salvador Brazil 13°0S 38°30W **333** E6
Salvador Sask., Canada 52°10N 109°32W **297** C7
Salvador, L. U.S.A. 29°43N 90°15W **314** E9
Salvador, L. ■ Cent. Amer. 13°50N 89°0W **320** D2
Salvaterra de Magos
  Portugal 39°1N 8°47W **195** F2
Salviac France 44°41N 1°16E **174** D5
Salvisa U.S.A. 37°54N 84°51W **311** G11
Sálvora, I. de Spain 42°28N 9°0W **194** C2
Salween → Burma 16°31N 97°37E **241** G6
Salyan Azerbaijan 39°33N 48°59E **213** C13

Salīya I. Grenada 12°26N 61°28W **323** q
Salza → Austria 47°40N 14°43E **180** D7
Salzach → Austria 48°12N 12°56E **180** D5
Salzburg Austria 47°48N 13°2E **180** D6
Salzburg □ Austria 47°15N 13°0E **180** D6
Salzburgen = Château-Salins
  France 48°50N 6°32E **173** D13
Salzgitter Germany 52°9N 10°19E **178** B6
Salzkotten Germany 51°40N 8°37E **178** D4
Salzwedel Germany 52°52N 11°10E **178** C7
Sam India 26°50N 70°31E **242** F4
Sam Neua Laos 20°29N 104°5E **228** G5
Sam Ngao Thailand 17°18N 99°0E **236** D2
Sam Rayburn Res. U.S.A. 31°4N 94°5W **314** F7
Sam Son Vietnam 19°44N 105°54E **236** C5
Sam Teu Laos 19°59N 104°38E **236** C5
Sama de Langreo = Langreo
  Spain 43°18N 5°40W **194** B5
Samacevda Angola 13°35S 16°6E **267** E3
Samad Oman 22°48N 58°9E **249** E7
Samagaltay Russia 50°36N 95°3E **217** B13
Samā'il Oman 23°40N 57°50E **249** E7
Samal I. Phil. 7°3N 125°42E **233** H5
Samal I. Phil. 7°3N 125°44E **233** H5
Samales Group Phil. 6°0N 122°0E **233** J3
Samalkot India 17°3N 82°13E **244** F6
Samālūṭ Egypt 28°20N 30°42E **256** C6
Samana India 30°10N 76°13E **242** D7
Samana Cay Bahamas 23°3N 73°45W **321** B5
Samandağ Turkey 36°5N 35°59E **250** B6
Samandıra Turkey 40°59N 29°13E **203** F13
Samanga Tanzania 8°20S 39°13E **269** D4
Samangān □ Afghan. 36°15N 68°3E **240** A3
Samangwa
  Dem. Rep. of the Congo 4°23S 24°10E **265** C4
Samani Japan 42°7N 142°56E **220** C11
Samanli Dağları Turkey 40°32N 29°10E **203** G13
Samannûd Egypt 30°57N 31°14E **251** H2
Samar Phil. 12°0N 125°0E **233** F5
Samar Sea Phil. 11°50N 125°0E **233** F5
Samara Russia 53°8N 50°6E **190** D10
Samara → Russia 53°10N 50°4E **190** D10
Samara → Ukraine 48°28N 35°7E **189** H8
Samarai Papua N. G. 10°39S 150°41E **286** F6
Samaria = Shōmrōn
  West Bank 32°15N 35°13E **251** F6
Samaria West Bank 32°17N 35°12E **251** F6
Samaria △ Greece 35°17N 23°58E **207** E4
Samariá Indonesia 0°36S 117°9E **235** C5
Samariapo Venezuela 5°15N 67°48W **328** B4
Samarinda Indonesia 0°30S 117°9E **235** C5
Samarkand = Samarqand
  Uzbekistan 39°40N 66°55E **217** E7
Samarkandsky = Temirtau
  Kazakhstan 50°5N 72°56E **217** B8
Samarqand Uzbekistan 39°40N 66°55E **217** E7
Samarqand □ Uzbekistan 39°35N 66°55E **217** E7
Sāmarrā' Iraq 34°12N 43°52E **213** E10
Samastipur India 25°50N 85°50E **243** G11
Samatya Turkey 40°59N 28°55E **122** C1
Samaúma Brazil 7°50S 60°2W **331** B5
Şamaxı Azerbaijan 40°38N 48°37E **191** K9
Samba Équateur,
  Dem. Rep. of the Congo 0°13N 21°25E **264** B4
Samba Maniema,
  Dem. Rep. of the Congo 4°38S 26°22E **265** C5
Samba Jammu & Kashmir,
  India 32°32N 75°10E **243** C6
Samba Caju Angola 8°46S 15°24E **265** D3
Sambaíba Brazil 7°8S 45°21W **332** C4
Sambalpur India 21°28N 84°4E **244** D7
Sambar, Tanjung
  Indonesia 2°59S 110°19E **235** C4
Sambas Indonesia 1°20N 109°20E **235** B3
Sambava Madag. 14°16S 50°10E **272** A3
Sambawizi Zimbabwe 18°24S 26°13E **269** F2
Sambhajinagar = Aurangabad
  India 19°50N 75°23E **244** E2
Sambhal India 28°35N 78°37E **243** E8
Sambhar India 26°52N 75°6E **242** F6
Sambhar L. India 26°55N 75°12E **242** F6
Sambiase Italy 38°58N 16°17E **201** D9
Sambir Ukraine 49°30N 23°10E **185** J10
Sambo Angola 13°3S 16°9E **265** E3
Sambo Indonesia 3°22S 118°52E **235** C5
Sambor Cambodia 12°46N 106°0E **238** F6
Sambor Prei Kuk
  Cambodia 12°46N 105°58E **238** F5
Samborombón, B.
  Argentina 36°5S 57°20W **334** D4
Sambuca di Sicilia Italy 37°39N 13°7E **200** E6
Samburu □ Kenya 0°37N 37°31E **268** B4
Samch'ok S. Korea 37°30N 129°10E **224** D4
Same Tanzania 4°2S 37°38E **268** C4
Samer France 50°38N 1°44E **173** B8
Samfya Zambia 11°22S 29°31E **267** E5
Samhān, Jabal Oman 17°12N 54°55E **249** D6
Sami Greece 38°15N 20°39E **207** C2
Samka Burma 20°9N 96°57E **241** E6
Şämkir Azerbaijan 40°50N 46°0E **191** K8
Şamlı Turkey 39°48N 27°51E **205** B9
Sammanturai Sri Lanka 7°36N 81°39E **245** L5
Samnah Si. Arabia 25°10N 37°15E **246** E3
Samnū Libya 27°15N 14°55E **258** C2
Samo Alto Chile 30°22S 71°0W **334** C1
Samoa ■ Pac. Oc. 14°0S 172°0W **287** V20
Samoa Is. Pac. Oc. 14°0S 171°0W **287** V20
Samobor Croatia 45°47N 15°44E **199** C12
Samoëns France 46°5N 6°45E **173** F13
Samokov Bulgaria 42°18N 23°35E **202** D7
Samorín Slovak Rep. 48°2N 17°19E **181** C10
Samorogouin
  Burkina Faso 11°21N 4°57W **262** C4
Samos Greece 37°45N 26°50E **205** D8
Samos Spain 42°44N 7°20W **194** C3
Samoš Serbia 45°13N 20°46E **182** E5
Samothráki = Mathráki
  Greece 39°48N 19°31E **206** B9
Samovlovka Russia 51°32N 43°43E **190** E6
Sampa Ghana 8°10N 2°40W **262** D4
Sampacho Argentina 33°20S 64°50W **334** C3
Sampaloc Phil. 14°36N 120°59E **127** B1
Sampang Indonesia 7°11S 113°13E **235** D4
Sampéyre Italy 44°34N 7°11E **198** D4
Samphanthawong
  Thailand 13°44N 100°31E **113** B2
Sampit Indonesia 2°34S 113°0E **235** C3
Sampit → Indonesia 2°44S 112°5E **235** C3
Sampit, Teluk Indonesia 3°5S 113°3E **235** C3
Sampun Papua N. G. 4°15S 152°20E **286** C6
Samrong Cambodia 14°15N 103°30E **238** E4
Samsø Denmark 55°50N 10°35E **163** J4
Samsun U.S.A. 31°7N 86°3W **316** F2

Samsun *Turkey* 41°15N 36°22E **212** B7
Samsun □ *Turkey* 41°10N 36°10E **212** B7
Samtah *Si. Arabia* 16°36N 42°56E **248** C3
Samtredia *Georgia* 42°7N 42°24E **191** J6
Samuel Smith Park *Canada* 43°35N 79°30W **141** B1
Samui, Ko *Thailand* 9°30N 100°0E **237** b
Samur → *Russia* 41°53N 48°32E **191** K9
Samurskiy Khrebet *Russia* 41°55N 47°11E **191** K8
Samusole *Dem. Rep. of the Congo* 10°2S 24°0E **265** E4
Samut Prakan *Thailand* 13°40N 100°36E **113** B2
Samut Sakhon *Thailand* 13°32N 100°17E **236** F3
Samut Songkhram *Thailand* 13°24N 100°1E **236** F3
Samwari *Pakistan* 28°30N 66°46E **242** E2
San *Mali* 13°15N 4°57W **262** C4
San → *Cambodia* 13°32N 105°57E **236** F5
San → *Poland* 50°45N 21°51E **185** H8
San Adrián *Spain* 42°20N 1°56W **196** C3
San Adrián, C. de *Spain* 43°21N 8°50W **194** B2
San Agustín *Colombia* 1°53N 76°16W **328** C2
San Agustin *Romblon, Phil.* 12°34N 122°6E **232** E4
San Agustin, C. *Phil.* 6°20N 126°13E **233** H6
San Agustín de Valle Fértil *Argentina* 30°35S 67°30W **334** C2
San Ambrosio *Pac. Oc.* 26°28S 79°53W **326** F3
San Andreas *U.S.A.* 38°12N 120°41W **306** G6
San Andres *Catanduanes, Phil.* 13°36N 124°6E **232** E5
San Andres *Romblon, Phil.* 13°19N 122°41E **232** E4
San Andres *Romblon, Phil.* 12°31N 122°2E **232** E4
San Andrés *Barcelona, Spain* 41°26N 2°11E **114** A2
San Andrés, I. de *Caribbean* 12°42N 81°46W **320** D3
San Andrês del Rabanedo *Spain* 42°37N 5°36W **194** C5
San Andres Mts. *U.S.A.* 33°0N 106°30W **305** K10
San Andres Pt. *Phil.* 13°34N 121°52E **232** E3
San Andrés Tuxtla *Mexico* 18°27N 95°13W **319** D5
San Angel *Mexico* 19°20N 99°11W **128** B1
San Angelo *U.S.A.* 31°28N 100°26W **314** F4
San Anselmo *U.S.A.* 37°59N 122°34W **306** H4
San Antonio *Belize* 16°15N 89°2W **320** C2
San Antonio *Chile* 33°40S 71°40W **334** C1
San Antonio *Phil.* 14°57N 120°5E **232** D3
San Antonio *N. Mex., U.S.A.* 33°55N 106°52W **305** K10
San Antonio *Tex., U.S.A.* 29°25N 98°29W **314** G5
San Antonio *Venezuela* 3°30N 66°44W **328** C4
San Antonio → *U.S.A.* 28°30N 96°54W **314** G6
San Antonio, C. *Argentina* 36°15S 56°40W **334** D4
San Antonio, C. de *Cuba* 21°50N 84°57W **320** B3
San Antonio, C. de *Spain* 38°48N 0°12E **197** G5
San Antonio, Mt. *U.S.A.* 34°17N 117°38W **307** L9
San Antonio B. *Phil.* 8°38N 117°35E **233** G1
San Antonio de los Baños *Cuba* 22°54N 82°31W **320** B3
San Antonio de los Cobres *Argentina* 24°10S 66°17W **334** A2
San Antonio Oeste *Argentina* 40°40S 65°0W **336** B4
San Arcángelo *Italy* 40°14N 16°14E **201** B9
San Ardo *U.S.A.* 36°1N 120°54W **306** J6
San Augustín *Canary Is.* 27°47N 15°32W **153** e1
San Augustine *U.S.A.* 31°32N 94°7W **314** F7
San Bartolomé *Canary Is.* 28°59N 13°37W **153** e2
San Bartolomé de Tirajana *Canary Is.* 27°54N 15°34W **153** e1
San Bartolomeo in Galdo *Italy* 41°24N 15°1E **201** A8
San Basilio *Italy* 41°56N 12°35E **136** B2
San Benedetto del Tronto *Italy* 42°57N 13°53E **199** F10
San Benedetto Po *Italy* 45°2N 10°55E **198** C7
San Benedicto, I. *Mexico* 19°18N 110°49W **318** D2
San Benito *U.S.A.* 26°8N 97°38W **314** H6
San Benito → *U.S.A.* 36°53N 121°34W **306** J5
San Benito Mt. *U.S.A.* 36°22N 120°37W **306** J6
San Bernardino *U.S.A.* 34°7N 117°19W **307** L9
San Bernardino Mts. *U.S.A.* 34°10N 116°45W **307** L10
San Bernardino Str. *Phil.* 12°30N 124°10E **232** E5
San Bernardo *Chile* 33°40S 70°50W **334** C1
San Bernardo, I. de *Colombia* 9°45N 75°50W **328** B2
San-Beyse = Choybalsan *Mongolia* 48°4N 114°30E **219** B11
San Blas *Mexico* 26°5N 108°46W **318** B3
San Blas, Arch. de *Panama* 9°50N 78°31W **320** E4
San Blas, C. *U.S.A.* 29°40N 85°21W **316** F4
San Bonifacio *Italy* 45°24N 11°16E **199** C8
San Borja *Bolivia* 14°50S 66°52W **330** C4
San Borja *Lima, Peru* 12°6S 76°59W **124** B3
San Bóvio *Italy* 45°27N 9°18E **129** B2
San Bruno, Pt. *U.S.A.* 37°39N 122°24W **136** C2
San Bruno Mountain State Park ⌂ *U.S.A.* 37°41N 122°26W **136** B2
San Buenaventura = Ventura *U.S.A.* 34°17N 119°18W **307** L7
San Buenaventura *Bolivia* 14°28S 67°35W **330** C4
San Buenaventura *Coahuila, Mexico* 27°5N 101°32W **318** B4
San Carlos = Butuku-Luba *Eq. Guin.* 3°29N 8°33E **263** E6
San Carlos = Sant Carles *Spain* 39°3N 1°34E **206** C2
San Carlos *Argentina* 33°50S 69°0W **334** C2
San Carlos *Bolivia* 17°24S 63°45W **331** D5
San Carlos *Chile* 36°10S 72°0W **334** D1
San Carlos *Baja Calif. S., Mexico* 24°47N 112°7W **318** C2
San Carlos *Coahuila, Mexico* 29°1N 100°51W **318** B4
San Carlos *Nic.* 11°12N 84°50W **320** D3
San Carlos *Neg. Occ., Phil.* 10°29N 123°25E **233** F4
San Carlos *Pangasinan, Phil.* 15°55N 120°20E **232** D3
San Carlos *Uruguay* 34°46S 54°58W **335** C5
San Carlos *Ariz., U.S.A.* 33°21N 110°27W **305** K8
San Carlos *Amazonas, Venezuela* 1°55N 67°4W **328** C4
San Carlos *Cojedes, Venezuela* 9°40N 68°36W **328** B4
San Carlos de Bariloche *Argentina* 41°10S 71°25W **336** B2
San Carlos de Bolívar *Argentina* 36°15S 61°6W **334** D3
San Carlos de la Rápita = Sant Carles de la Ràpita *Spain* 40°37N 0°35E **196** E5
San Carlos de Río Negro *Venezuela* 1°55N 67°4W **328** C4
San Carlos del Zulia *Venezuela* 9°1N 71°55W **328** B3
San Carlos L. *U.S.A.* 33°11N 110°32W **305** K8
San Carlos Park *U.S.A.* 26°28N 81°49W **317** J8
San Cataldo *Italy* 37°29N 13°59E **200** E6
San Celoni = Sant Celoni *Spain* 41°42N 2°30E **196** D7
San Clemente *Chile* 35°30S 71°29W **334** D1
San Clemente *Spain* 39°24N 2°25W **197** F2
San Clemente *Calif., U.S.A.* 33°26N 117°37W **307** M9
San Clemente I. *U.S.A.* 32°53N 118°29W **307** N8
San Cristóbal = Es Migjorn Gran *Spain* 39°57N 4°3E **206** B5
San Cristóbal *B. Aires, Argentina* 34°38S 58°23W **117** B2
San Cristóbal *Santa Fe, Argentina* 30°20S 61°10W **334** C3
San Cristóbal *Colombia* 2°18S 73°2W **328** D3
San Cristóbal *Dom. Rep.* 18°25N 70°6W **321** C5
San Cristóbal *Solomon Is.* 10°30S 161°0E **287** N11
San Cristobal *Madrid, Spain* 40°25N 3°35W **127** B2
San Cristóbal *Venezuela* 7°46N 72°14W **328** B3
San Cristóbal, Cerro *Chile* 33°25S 70°38W **137** B2
San Cristóbal, I. *Ecuador* 0°50S 89°26W **330** a
San Cristóbal, Virgen del *Chile* 33°25S 70°38W **137** B2
San Cristóbal de las Casas *Mexico* 16°45N 92°38W **319** D6
San Cristoforo *Italy* 45°26N 9°9E **129** B1
San Damiano d'Asti *Italy* 44°50N 8°4E **198** D5
San Daniele del Friuli *Italy* 46°9N 13°1E **199** B10
San Diego *Calif., U.S.A.* 32°42N 117°9W **307** N9
San Diego *Tex., U.S.A.* 27°46N 98°14W **314** H5
San Diego, C. *Argentina* 54°40S 65°10W **336** D3
San Diego de la Unión *Mexico* 21°28N 100°52W **318** C4
San Diego Int. ✈ (SAN) *U.S.A.* 32°44N 117°11W **307** N9
San Dimitri, Ras *Malta* 36°4N 14°11E **206** E6
San Dimitri Point = San Dimitri, Ras *Malta* 36°4N 14°11E **206** E6
San Donà di Piave *Italy* 45°38N 12°34E **199** C9
San Donato Milanese *Italy* 45°24N 9°16E **129** B2
Sân el Hagar *Egypt* 30°58N 31°52E **251** H2
San Estanislao *Paraguay* 24°39S 56°26W **334** A4
San Esteban △ *Venezuela* 10°24N 67°58W **328** A4
San Esteban de Gormaz *Spain* 41°34N 3°13W **196** D1
San Eugenio = Artigas *Uruguay* 30°20S 56°30W **334** C4
San Felice Circeo *Italy* 41°14N 13°5E **200** A6
San Felice sul Panaro *Italy* 44°50N 11°8E **199** D8
San Felipe *Chile* 32°43S 70°42W **334** C1
San Felipe *Colombia* 1°55N 67°6W **328** C4
San Felipe *Baja Calif., Mexico* 31°1N 114°52W **318** A2
San Felipe *Phil.* 15°4N 120°4E **232** D3
San Felipe *Venezuela* 10°20N 68°44W **328** A4
San Felipe → *U.S.A.* 33°10N 115°49W **307** M11
San Félix *Chile* 28°56S 70°28W **334** B1
San Félix *Pac. Oc.* 26°23S 80°0W **326** F2
San Fernando = Sant Ferran *Spain* 38°42N 1°28E **206** D1
San Fernando *Chile* 34°30S 71°0W **334** C1
San Fernando *Tamaulipas, Mexico* 24°51N 98°10W **319** C5
San Fernando *Cebu, Phil.* 10°10N 123°42E **233** F4
San Fernando *La Union, Phil.* 16°40N 120°23E **232** C3
San Fernando *Pampanga, Phil.* 15°5N 120°37E **232** D3
San Fernando *Romblon, Phil.* 12°18N 122°36E **232** E4
San Fernando *Cádiz, Spain* 36°28N 6°17W **195** J4
San Fernando *Trin. & Tob.* 10°16N 61°28W **323** t
San Fernando *Calif., U.S.A.* 34°17N 118°26W **307** L8
San Fernando de Apure *Venezuela* 7°54N 67°15W **328** B4
San Fernando de Atabapo *Venezuela* 4°3N 67°42W **328** C4
San Fernando di Púglia *Italy* 41°18N 16°5E **201** A9
San Francique = Erin *Trin. & Tob.* 10°5N 61°39W **323** t
San Francisco *Córdoba, Argentina* 31°30S 62°5W **334** C3
San Francisco *Bolivia* 15°16S 65°31W **331** D4
San Francisco *Peru* 12°36S 73°49W **330** C3
San Francisco *Agusan del S., Phil.* 8°30N 125°56E **233** G5
San Francisco *Cebu, Phil.* 10°39N 124°23E **233** F5
San Francisco *Quezon, Phil.* 13°21N 122°31E **232** E4
San Francisco *S. Leyte, Phil.* 10°4N 125°9E **233** F5
San Francisco *Calif., U.S.A.* 37°46N 122°23W **136** B2
San Francisco → *U.S.A.* 32°59N 109°22W **305** K9
San Francisco, C. de *Colombia* 6°18N 77°29W **328** B2
San Francisco, Paso de *S. Amer.* 27°0S 68°0W **334** B2
San Francisco B. *U.S.A.* 37°39N 122°14W **136** B3
San Francisco Culhuacán *Mexico* 19°19N 99°8W **128** C2
San Francisco de Macorís *Dom. Rep.* 19°19N 70°15W **321** C5
San Francisco del Monte de Oro *Argentina* 32°36S 66°8W **334** C2
San Francisco del Oro *Mexico* 26°52N 105°51W **318** B3
San Francisco Int. ✈ (SFO) *U.S.A.* 37°37N 122°22W **306** H4
San Francisco Javier = Sant Francesc de Formentera *Spain* 38°42N 1°26E **206** D1
San Fratello *Italy* 38°1N 14°36E **201** D7
San Fruttuoso *Italy* 45°34N 9°14E **129** A2
San Gabriel *Chile* 33°47S 70°15W **334** C1
San Gabriel *Ecuador* 0°36N 77°49W **328** C2
San Gabriel *Calif., U.S.A.* 34°5N 118°5W **126** B4
San Gabriel → *U.S.A.* 33°58N 118°5W **126** C4
San Gabriel Chilac *Mexico* 18°19N 97°21W **319** D5
San Gabriel Mts. *U.S.A.* 34°17N 117°38W **307** L9
San Gavino Monreale *Italy* 39°33N 8°47E **200** C1
San German *Puerto Rico* 18°4N 67°4W **321** b
San Gil *Colombia* 6°33N 73°8W **328** B3
San Giljan = St. Julian's *Malta* 35°55N 14°29E **206** F7
San Gimignano *Italy* 43°28N 11°2E **198** E8
San Giórgio di Nogaro *Italy* 45°50N 13°13E **199** C10
San Giórgio Iónico *Italy* 40°27N 17°23E **201** B10
San Giovanni Bianco *Italy* 45°52N 9°39E **198** C6
San Giovanni in Fiore *Italy* 39°15N 16°42E **201** C9
San Giovanni in Persiceto *Italy* 44°38N 11°11E **199** D8
San Giovanni Rotondo *Italy* 41°42N 15°44E **199** G12
San Giovanni Valdarno *Italy* 43°34N 11°32E **199** E8
San Giuliano Milanese *Italy* 45°24N 9°17E **129** B2
San Giuliano Terme *Italy* 43°46N 10°26E **198** E7
San Gorgonio Mt. *U.S.A.* 34°6N 116°50W **307** L10
San Gottardo, P. del *Switz.* 46°33N 8°33E **179** J4
San Gregorio *Uruguay* 32°37S 55°40W **335** C4
San Gregorio *Calif., U.S.A.* 37°20N 122°23W **306** H4
San Guillermo △ *Argentina* 27°50S 69°45W **334** B2
San Guiseppe Jato *Italy* 37°57N 13°11E **200** E6
San Ignacio *Belize* 17°10N 89°5W **320** C2
San Ignacio *Beni, Bolivia* 14°53S 65°36W **331** C4
San Ignacio *Santa Cruz, Bolivia* 16°20S 60°55W **331** D5
San Ignacio *Baja Calif. S., Mexico* 27°27N 112°51W **318** B2
San Ignacio *Paraguay* 26°52S 57°3W **334** B4
San Ignacio *Peru* 5°8S 78°59W **330** B2
San Ignacio, L. *Mexico* 26°54N 113°13W **318** B2
San Ildefonso *Phil.* 15°4N 120°56E **232** D3
San Ildefonso, C. *Phil.* 16°0N 122°1E **232** C4
San Ildefonso Pen. *Phil.* 16°9N 122°25E **232** C4
San Isidro *Argentina* 34°29S 58°31W **334** C4
San Isidro *Lima, Peru* 12°5S 77°2W **124** B2
San Isidro *Phil.* 6°50N 126°5E **233** H6
San Isidro de Potot = Burgos *Phil.* 16°4N 119°52E **232** C2
San Jacinto *Colombia* 9°50N 75°8W **328** B2
San Jacinto *Phil.* 12°34N 123°44E **232** E4
San Jacinto *Calif., U.S.A.* 33°47N 116°57W **307** M10
San Jaime = Sant Jaume *Spain* 39°54N 4°4E **206** B5
San Javier *Misiones, Argentina* 27°55S 55°5W **335** B4
San Javier *Santa Fe, Argentina* 30°40S 59°55W **334** C4
San Javier *Beni, Bolivia* 14°34S 64°42W **331** C5
San Javier *Santa Cruz, Bolivia* 16°18S 62°30W **331** D5
San Javier *Chile* 35°40S 71°45W **334** D1
San Javier *Spain* 37°49N 0°50W **197** H4
San Jerónimo Lidice *Mexico* 19°19N 99°14W **128** C1
San Jerónimo Taviche *Mexico* 16°44N 96°35W **319** D5
San Joaquín *Bolivia* 13°4S 64°49W **331** C5
San Joaquín *Santiago, Chile* 33°29S 70°35W **137** B2
San Joaquin *Phil.* 10°35N 122°8E **233** F4
San Joaquin *Calif., U.S.A.* 36°36N 120°11W **306** J6
San Joaquín → *Bolivia* 13°8S 63°41W **331** C5
San Joaquin → *Calif., U.S.A.* 38°4N 121°51W **306** G5
San Joaquín, Cerro *Ecuador* 0°53S 89°30W **330** a
San Joaquin Valley *U.S.A.* 37°20N 121°0W **306** J6
San Jon *U.S.A.* 35°6N 103°20W **305** J12
San Jordi = Sant Jordi *Spain* 39°33N 2°46E **206** B3
San Jorge *Argentina* 31°54S 61°50W **334** C3
San Jorge *Solomon Is.* 8°28S 159°38E **287** M10
San Jorge, B. *Mexico* 31°20N 113°20W **318** A2
San Jorge, G. *Argentina* 46°0S 66°0W **336** C3
San José = San Josep *Spain* 38°55N 1°18E **206** D1
San José *Argentina* 32°12S 58°15W **334** C4
San José *Costa Rica* 9°55N 84°2W **320** E3
San José *Guatemala* 14°0N 90°50W **320** D1
San Jose *N. Marianas* 14°58N 145°37E **302** e
San Jose *Mind. Occ., Phil.* 12°27N 121°4E **232** E3
San Jose *Nueva Ecija, Phil.* 15°45N 120°55E **232** D3
San Jose *Calif., U.S.A.* 37°20N 121°53W **306** H5
San Jose *Ill., U.S.A.* 40°18N 89°36W **310** D7
San Jose *N. Mex., U.S.A.* 35°24N 105°28W **305** J11
San Jose → *U.S.A.* 34°25N 106°45W **305** J10
San José, Golfo *Argentina* 42°20S 64°18W **336** B4
San José, I. *Mexico* 25°0N 110°38W **318** C2
San Jose de Buenavista *Phil.* 10°45N 121°56E **233** F3
San José de Chiquitos *Bolivia* 17°53S 60°50W **331** D5
San José de Feliciano *Argentina* 30°26S 58°46W **334** C4
San José de Guanipa *Venezuela* 8°53N 64°9W **329** B5
San José de Jáchal *Argentina* 30°15S 68°46W **334** C2
San José de Mayo *Uruguay* 34°27S 56°40W **334** C4
San José de Ocuné *Colombia* 4°15N 70°20W **328** C3
San José de Uchapiamonas *Bolivia* 14°13S 68°5W **330** C4
San José del Cabo *Mexico* 23°3N 109°41W **318** C3
San José del Guaviare *Colombia* 2°35N 72°38W **328** C3
San Jose del Monte *Phil.* 14°49N 121°3E **232** D3
San José do Anauá *Brazil* 0°58N 61°22W **329** C5
San José Río Hondo *Mexico* 19°26N 99°14W **128** B1
San Josep *Spain* 38°55N 1°18E **206** D1
San Juan *Argentina* 31°30S 68°30W **334** C2
San Juan *Antioquia, Colombia* 8°46N 76°32W **328** B2
San Juan *Curaçao* 12°15N 69°6W **322** g
San Juan *Ica, Peru* 15°22S 75°7W **330** D2
San Juan *Batangas, Phil.* 13°50N 121°24E **232** E3
San Juan *S. Leyte, Phil.* 10°16N 125°10E **233** F5
San Juan *Puerto Rico* 18°28N 66°7W **321** C6
San Juan *Trin. & Tob.* 10°39N 61°29W **323** t
San Juan □ *Argentina* 31°9S 69°0W **334** C2
San Juan → *Argentina* 32°20S 67°25W **334** C2
San Juan → *Bolivia* 21°2S 65°19W **331** E4
San Juan → *Colombia* 4°3N 77°27W **328** C2
San Juan → *Nic.* 10°56N 83°42W **320** D3
San Juan → *Manila, Phil.* 14°35N 121°0E **127** B2
San Juan → *Utah, U.S.A.* 37°16N 110°26W **305** H8
San Juan → *Venezuela* 10°14N 62°38W **329** A5
San Juan, C. *Argentina* 54°44S 63°44W **336** D4
San Juan, C. *Eq. Guin.* 1°5N 9°20E **264** B1
San Juan Bautista = Sant Joan de Labritja *Spain* 39°5N 1°31E **206** C2
San Juan Bautista = Villahermosa *Mexico* 17°59N 92°55W **319** D6
San Juan Bautista *Chile* 33°37S 78°50W **330** c
San Juan Bautista *Paraguay* 26°37S 57°6W **334** B4
San Juan Bautista *Calif., U.S.A.* 36°51N 121°32W **306** J5
San Juan Capistrano *U.S.A.* 33°30N 117°40W **307** M9
San Juan Cr. → *U.S.A.* 35°40N 120°22W **306** J5
San Juan de Aragón *Mexico* 19°28N 99°4W **128** B2
San Juan de Aragón, Parque *Mexico* 19°27N 99°4W **128** B2
San Juan de Guadelupe *Mexico* 24°38N 102°44W **318** C4
San Juan de Guía, Cabo de *Colombia* 11°21N 73°59W **328** A3
San Juan de la Costa *Mexico* 24°20N 110°41W **318** C2
San Juan de los Lagos *Mexico* 21°15N 102°18W **318** C4
San Juan de los Morros *Venezuela* 9°55N 67°21W **328** B4
San Juan de Lurigancho *Peru* 11°59S 77°0W **124** A2
San Juan de Manapiare *Venezuela* 5°15N 66°5W **328** B4
San Juan de Villa Hermosa = Villahermosa *Mexico* 17°59N 92°55W **319** D6
San Juan del Cèsar *Colombia* 10°46N 73°1W **328** A3
San Juan del Monte *Phil.* 14°36N 121°1E **127** B2
San Juan del Norte *Nic.* 10°58N 83°40W **320** D3
San Juan del Norte, B. de *Nic.* 11°0N 83°40W **320** D3
San Juan del Río *Mexico* 20°23N 100°0W **319** C5
San Juan del Sur *Nic.* 11°20N 85°51W **320** D2
San Juan I. *U.S.A.* 48°32N 123°5W **306** B3
San Juan Island ⌂ *U.S.A.* 48°35N 123°8W **306** B4
San Juan Ixtacala *Mexico* 19°31N 99°10W **128** A1
San Juan Mts. *U.S.A.* 37°30N 107°0W **305** H10
San Julián *Phil.* 11°45N 125°27E **233** F5
San Just, Sierra de *Spain* 40°45N 0°49W **196** E4
San Just Desvern *Spain* 41°22N 2°4E **114** A1
San Justo *B. Aires, Argentina* 34°40S 58°33W **117** C1
San Justo *Santa Fe, Argentina* 30°47S 60°30W **334** C3
San Kamphaeng *Thailand* 18°45N 99°8E **236** C2
San Lázaro, C. *Mexico* 24°50N 112°18W **318** C2
San Leandro *U.S.A.* 37°42N 122°9W **306** H4
San Leonardo de Yagüe *Spain* 41°51N 3°5W **196** D1
San Lorenzo = Sant Llorenç des Cardassar *Spain* 39°37N 3°17E **206** B4
San Lorenzo *Argentina* 32°45S 60°45W **334** C3
San Lorenzo *Beni, Bolivia* 15°22S 65°48W **331** D4
San Lorenzo *Tarija, Bolivia* 21°26S 64°47W **331** E5
San Lorenzo *Ecuador* 1°15N 78°50W **328** C2
San Lorenzo *Paraguay* 25°20S 57°32W **334** B4
San Lorenzo → *Mexico* 24°15N 107°24W **318** C3
San Lorenzo, I. *Baja Calif., Mexico* 28°38N 112°51W **318** B2
San Lorenzo, I. *Peru* 12°7S 77°15W **330** C2
San Lorenzo, Mte. *Argentina* 47°40S 72°20W **336** C2
San Lorenzo de la Parrilla *Spain* 39°51N 2°22W **196** F2
San Lorenzo de Morunys = Sant Llorenç de Morunys *Spain* 42°8N 1°35E **196** C6
San Lorenzo Tezonco *Mexico* 19°19N 99°3W **128** C2
San Lucas = Cabo San Lucas *Mexico* 22°53N 109°54W **318** C3
San Lucas *Bolivia* 20°5S 65°7W **331** E4
San Lucas *Baja Calif. S., Mexico* 27°10N 112°14W **318** B2
San Lucas *Calif., U.S.A.* 36°8N 121°1W **306** J5
San Lucas, C. *Mexico* 22°52N 109°53W **318** C3
San Lúcido *Italy* 39°18N 16°3E **201** C9
San Luis = Entre Ríos *Bolivia* 21°30S 64°25W **334** A3
San Luis = Sevilla *Colombia* 4°16N 75°57W **328** C2
San Luis *Argentina* 33°20S 66°20W **334** C2
San Luis *Pinar del Río, Cuba* 22°17N 83°46W **320** B3
San Luis *Guatemala* 16°14N 89°27W **320** C2
San Luis *Lima, Peru* 12°4S 77°0W **124** B2
San Luis *Ariz., U.S.A.* 32°29N 114°47W **305** K6
San Luis *Colo., U.S.A.* 37°12N 105°25W **305** H11
San Luis □ *Argentina* 34°0S 66°0W **334** C2
San Luis, I. *Mexico* 29°58N 114°26W **318** B2
San Luis, L. de *Bolivia* 13°45S 64°0W **331** C5
San Luis, Sierra de *Argentina* 32°30S 66°10W **334** C2
San Luis de la Paz *Mexico* 21°18N 100°31W **318** C4
San Luis Obispo *U.S.A.* 35°17N 120°40W **307** K6
San Luis Potosí *Mexico* 22°9N 100°59W **318** C4
San Luis Potosí □ *Mexico* 23°0N 101°0W **318** C4
San Luis Res. *U.S.A.* 37°4N 121°5W **306** H5
San Luis Río Colorado *Mexico* 32°29N 114°58W **318** A2
San Manuel *Phil.* 16°4N 120°40E **232** C3
San Manuel *Ariz., U.S.A.* 32°36N 110°38W **305** K8
San Marco, C. *Italy* 39°51N 8°26E **200** C1
San Marco Argentano *Italy* 39°33N 16°7E **201** C9
San Marco in Lámis *Italy* 41°43N 15°38E **199** G12
San Marcos *Colombia* 8°39N 75°8W **328** B2
San Marcos *Guatemala* 14°59N 91°52W **320** D1
San Marcos *Calif., U.S.A.* 33°9N 117°10W **307** M9
San Marcos *Tex., U.S.A.* 29°53N 97°56W **314** G6
San Marcos, I. *Mexico* 27°13N 112°6W **318** B2
San Mariano *Phil.* 17°0N 122°2E **232** C4
San Marino *San Marino* 43°55N 12°30E **199** E9
San Marino *Calif., U.S.A.* 34°7N 118°5W **126** B4
San Marino ■ *Europe* 43°56N 12°25E **199** E9
San Martín = Tarapoto *Peru* 6°30S 76°20W **330** B2
San Martín *Antarctica* 68°11S 67°0W **151** C17
San Martín *Argentina* 33°5S 68°28W **334** C2
San Martín *Colombia* 3°42N 73°42W **328** C3
San Martín *Barcelona, Spain* 41°24N 2°11E **114** A2
San Martín □ *Peru* 7°0S 76°50W **330** B2
San Martín → *Bolivia* 13°8S 63°43W **331** C5
San Martín, L. *Argentina* 48°50S 72°50W **336** C2
San Martín de la Vega *Spain* 40°13N 3°34W **194** E7
San Martín de los Andes *Argentina* 40°10S 71°20W **336** B2
San Martín de Porras *Peru* 12°1S 77°5W **124** B2
San Martín de Valdeiglesias *Spain* 40°21N 4°24W **194** E6
San Mateo = Sant Mateu *Baleares, Spain* 39°3N 1°23E **206** C1
San Mateo = Sant Mateu *Valencia, Spain* 40°28N 0°10E **196** E5
San Mateo *Isabela, Phil.* 16°54N 121°33E **232** C3
San Mateo *Calif., U.S.A.* 37°34N 122°19W **306** H4
San Mateo Tlaltenango *Mexico* 19°20N 99°16W **128** B1
San Matías *Bolivia* 16°25S 58°20W **331** D6
San Matías, G. *Argentina* 41°30S 64°0W **336** B4
San Miguel = Linapacan *Phil.* 11°30N 119°52E **233** F2
San Miguel = Sant Miquel *Spain* 39°3N 1°26E **206** C1
San Miguel = Sarrat *Phil.* 18°9N 120°39E **232** B3
San Miguel *Bolivia* 16°42S 61°1W **331** C5
San Miguel *Santiago, Chile* 33°29S 70°39W **137** B2
San Miguel *El Salv.* 13°30N 88°12W **320** D2
San Miguel *Panama* 8°27N 78°55W **320** E4
San Miguel *Lima, Peru* 12°5S 77°6W **124** B2
San Miguel *Bulacan, Phil.* 15°9N 120°59E **232** D3
San Miguel *Palawan, Phil.* 11°30N 119°51E **233** F2
San Miguel *Surigao S., Phil.* 9°3N 125°59E **233** G6
San Miguel *Calif., U.S.A.* 35°45N 120°42W **306** K6
San Miguel → *Bolivia* 13°52S 63°56W **331** C5
San Miguel → *Ecuador* 0°25N 76°30W **328** C2
San Miguel, Golfo de *Panama* 8°22N 78°17W **328** B2
San Miguel B. *Phil.* 13°51N 123°11E **232** E4
San Miguel de Huachi *Bolivia* 15°40S 67°15W **330** D4
San Miguel de Tucumán *Argentina* 26°50S 65°20W **334** B2
San Miguel del Monte *Argentina* 35°23S 58°50W **334** D4
San Miguel I. *U.S.A.* 34°2N 120°23W **307** L6
San Miguel Is. *Phil.* 7°45N 118°28E **233** H2
San Miniato *Italy* 43°41N 10°51E **198** E7
San Narciso *Phil.* 13°34N 122°34E **232** E4
San Nicolas = Sint Nicolaas *Curaçao* 12°17N 69°8W **322** g
San Nicolás *B. Aires, Argentina* 34°36S 58°22W **117** B2
San Nicolás *Canary Is.* 27°58N 15°47W **153** e1
San Nicolas *Phil.* 18°10N 120°36E **232** B3
San Nicolás de los Arroyos *Argentina* 33°25S 60°10W **334** C3
San Nicolas I. *U.S.A.* 33°15N 119°30W **307** M7
San Onofre *Colombia* 9°44N 75°32W **328** B2
San Onofre *Calif., U.S.A.* 33°22N 117°34W **307** M9
San Onófrio *Italy* 41°57N 12°33E **136** B1
San Pablo *Bolivia* 21°43S 66°38W **334** A2
San Pablo *Isabela, Phil.* 17°27N 121°48E **232** C3
San Pablo *Laguna, Phil.* 14°11N 121°31E **232** D3
San Pablo *Calif., U.S.A.* 37°58N 122°21W **306** H4
San Pablo de Manta = Manta *Ecuador* 1°0S 80°40W **328** D1
San Pàolo di Civitate *Italy* 41°44N 15°15E **199** G12
San Pascual *Phil.* 13°8N 122°59E **232** E4
San Pedro *B. Aires, Argentina* 33°40S 59°40W **334** C4
San Pedro *Misiones, Argentina* 26°30S 54°10W **335** B5
San Pedro *Chile* 33°54S 71°28W **334** C1
San Pedro *Colombia* 4°56N 71°53W **328** C3
San Pedro *Ivory C.* 4°50N 6°33W **262** E3
San Pedro *Baja Calif. S., Mexico* 23°55N 110°17W **318** C2
San Pedro *Peru* 14°49S 74°5W **330** C3
San Pedro □ *Paraguay* 24°0S 57°0W **334** A4
San Pedro → *Chihuahua, Mexico* 28°20N 106°10W **318** B3
San Pedro → *Nayarit, Mexico* 21°45N 105°30W **318** C3
San Pedro → *Ariz., U.S.A.* 32°59N 110°47W **305** K8
San Pedro, Pta. *Chile* 25°30S 70°38W **334** B1
San Pedro, Sierra de *Spain* 39°18N 6°40W **195** F4
San Pedro B. *Phil.* 11°10N 125°6E **233** F5
San Pedro Channel *U.S.A.* 33°30N 118°25W **307** M8
San Pedro de Arimena *Colombia* 4°37N 71°42W **328** C3
San Pedro de Atacama *Chile* 22°55S 68°15W **334** A2
San Pedro de Jujuy *Argentina* 24°12S 64°55W **334** A3
San Pedro de las Colonias *Mexico* 25°45N 102°59W **318** B4
San Pedro de Lloc *Peru* 7°15S 79°28W **330** B2
San Pedro de Macorís *Dom. Rep.* 18°30N 69°18W **321** C6
San Pedro del Norte *Nic.* 13°4N 84°33W **320** D3
San Pedro del Paraná *Paraguay* 26°43S 56°13W **334** B4
San Pedro del Pinatar *Spain* 37°50N 0°50W **197** H4
San Pedro Mártir *Spain* 41°23N 2°6E **114** A1
San Pedro Mártir, Sierra *Mexico* 31°0N 115°30W **318** A1
San Pedro Mártir △ *Mexico* 31°0N 115°21W **318** A1
San Pedro Ocampo = Melchor Ocampo *Mexico* 24°51N 101°39W **318** C4
San Pedro Pochutla *Mexico* 15°44N 96°28W **319** D5
San Pedro Sula *Honduras* 15°30N 88°0W **320** C2
San Pedro Tututepec *Mexico* 16°9N 97°38W **319** D5
San Pedro Zacatenco *Mexico* 19°30N 99°6W **128** A2
San Pietro *Italy* 39°8N 8°17E **200** C1
San Pietro, Piazza *Rome, Italy* **136** b1
San Pietro Vernótico *Italy* 40°29N 18°0E **201** B11
San Po Kong *China* 22°20N 114°11E **122** A2
San Rafael *Argentina* 34°40S 68°21W **334** C2
San Rafael *Bolivia* 16°45S 60°34W **331** D5
San Rafael *Trin. & Tob.* 10°34N 61°16W **323** t
San Rafael *Calif., U.S.A.* 37°58N 122°32W **306** H4
San Rafael *N. Mex., U.S.A.* 35°7N 107°53W **305** J10
San Rafael *Venezuela* 10°58N 71°46W **328** A3
San Rafael Champa *Mexico* 19°27N 99°15W **128** B1
San Rafael Hills *U.S.A.* 34°10N 118°12W **126** A3
San Rafael Mt. *U.S.A.* 34°41N 119°52W **307** L7
San Rafael Mts. *U.S.A.* 34°40N 119°50W **307** L7
San Ramón *Bolivia* 13°17S 64°43W **331** C5
San Ramón de la Nueva Orán *Argentina* 23°10S 64°20W **334** A3
San Remo *Italy* 43°49N 7°46E **198** E4
San Román, C. *Venezuela* 12°12N 70°0W **328** A4
San Roque *Argentina* 28°25S 58°45W **334** B4
San Roque *Manila, Phil.* 14°37N 121°5E **127** B2
San Roque *N. Samar, Phil.* 12°37N 124°52E **232** E5
San Roque *Spain* 36°17N 5°21W **195** J5
San Rosendo *Chile* 37°16S 72°43W **334** D1
San Saba *U.S.A.* 31°12N 98°43W **314** F5
San Salvador *El Salv.* 13°40N 89°10W **320** D2
San Salvador, Canal de *Ecuador* 0°25S 90°30W **330** a
San Salvador, I. *Ecuador* 0°16S 90°42W **330** a
San Salvador de Jujuy *Argentina* 24°10S 64°48W **334** A3
San Salvador I. *Bahamas* 24°0N 74°40W **321** B5
San Salvo *Italy* 42°3N 14°44E **199** F11
San Sebastián = Donostia-San Sebastián *Spain* 43°17N 1°58W **196** B3
San Sebastián *Argentina* 53°10S 68°30W **336** D3
San Sebastián *Puerto Rico* 18°20N 66°59W **321** b
San Sebastián de la Gomera *Canary Is.* 28°5N 17°7W **153** e1
San Serra = Son Serra *Spain* 39°43N 3°13E **206** B4
San Serverino Marche *Italy* 43°13N 13°10E **199** E10
San Severo *Italy* 41°41N 15°23E **199** G12
San Simeon *U.S.A.* 35°39N 121°11W **306** K5
San Simon *U.S.A.* 32°16N 109°14W **305** K9
San Siro *Italy* 45°28N 9°7E **129** B1
San Souci *Australia* 33°59S 151°8E **139** B1
San Stéfano di Cadore *Italy* 46°34N 12°33E **199** B9
San Stino di Livenza *Italy* 45°44N 12°41E **199** C9
San Telmo = Sant Elm *Spain* 39°35N 2°21E **206** B3
San Telmo *B. Aires, Argentina* 34°37S 58°23W **117** B2
San Telmo *Baja Calif., Mexico* 30°58N 116°6W **318** A1
San Teodoro *Phil.* 13°26N 121°1E **232** E3
San Tiburcio *Mexico* 24°8N 101°32W **318** C4
San Valentin, Mte. *Chile* 46°30S 73°30W **336** C2
San Vicenç dels Horts *Spain* 41°23N 2°0E **114** A1
San Vicente de Alcántara *Spain* 39°22N 7°8W **195** F3
San Vicente de Cañete *Peru* 13°8S 76°30W **330** C2
San Vicente de la Barquera *Spain* 43°23N 4°29W **194** B6
San Vicente del Caguán *Colombia* 2°7N 74°46W **328** C3
San Vincenzo *Italy* 43°6N 10°32E **198** E7
San Vito *Costa Rica* 8°50N 82°58W **320** E3
San Vito *Italy* 39°26N 9°32E **200** C2
San Vito, C. *Italy* 38°11N 12°41E **200** D5
San Vito al Tagliamento *Italy* 45°54N 12°52E **199** C9
San Vito Chietino *Italy* 42°18N 14°27E **199** F11
San Vito dei Normanni *Italy* 40°39N 17°42E **201** B10
San Yanaro *Colombia* 2°47N 69°42W **328** C4
Saña *Peru* 6°54S 79°36W **330** B2
Sana' *Yemen* 15°27N 44°12E **248** D4
Sana → *Bos.-H.* 45°3N 16°23E **199** C13
Sanaag □ *Somali Rep.* 10°30N 48°0E **267** B6
Sanaba *Burkina Faso* 12°25N 3°47W **262** C4
Sanae IV *Antarctica* 70°20S 9°0W **151** D2
Şanāfir *Si. Arabia* 27°56N 34°42E **251** L5
Sanaga → *Cameroon* 3°35N 9°38E **263** E6
Sanak I. *U.S.A.* 54°25N 162°40W **303** J7
Sanaloa, Presa *Mexico* 24°50N 107°20W **318** C3
Sanām *Si. Arabia* 23°40N 44°45E **248** B4
Sanana *Indonesia* 2°4S 125°58E **231** E7
Sanand *India* 22°59N 72°25E **242** H5
Sanandaj *Iran* 35°18N 47°1E **213** E12
Sanandita *Bolivia* 21°40S 63°45W **334** A3
Sanaroa I. *Papua N. G.* 9°37S 151°0E **286** E6
Sanary-sur-Mer *France* 43°7N 5°49E **175** E9
Sanāw *Yemen* 17°50N 51°5E **249** C5
Sanawad *India* 22°11N 76°5E **242** H7
Sanbancho *Tokyo, Japan* **140** a3
Sanbe-San *Japan* 35°6N 132°38E **222** B4
Sancellas = Sencelles *Spain* 39°39N 2°54E **206** B3
Sancergues *France* 47°10N 2°54E **173** E9
Sancerre *France* 47°20N 2°50E **173** E9
Sancerrois, Collines du *France* 47°20N 2°40E **173** E9
Sancha He → *China* 26°48N 106°7E **228** D6
Sanchahe *China* 44°50N 126°2E **227** B14
Sánchez *Dom. Rep.* 19°15N 69°36W **321** C6
Sanchez Mira *Phil.* 18°34N 121°14E **232** B3
Sanchih *Taiwan* 25°15N 121°30E **225** A3
Sanchor *India* 24°45N 71°55E **242** G4
Sanch'ung *Taiwan* 25°4N 121°30E **225** A3
Sanco Pt. *Phil.* 8°15N 126°27E **233** G6
Sancoins *France* 46°47N 2°55E **173** F9
Sancti Spíritus *Cuba* 21°52N 79°33W **320** B4
Sancy, Puy de *France* 45°32N 2°50E **174** C6
Sand = Polokwane → *S. Africa* 22°25S 30°5E **271** B5
Sand *Norway* 59°29N 6°16E **164** E3
Sand Bank B. *St. Kitts & Nevis* 17°15N 62°38W **322** d
Sand Cr. → *U.S.A.* 39°3N 85°51W **311** E11
Sand Hills *Guyana* 6°27N 58°19W **329** B6
Sand Hills *Nebr., U.S.A.* 42°10N 101°30W **308** D3
Sand I. *Midway Is.* 28°12N 177°23W **302** c
Sand I. *Hawai'i, U.S.A.* 21°19N 157°53W **302** K14
Sand Islet *Midway Is.* 28°16N 177°22W **302** c
Sand Lakes ⌂ *Canada* 57°51N 98°32W **297** B9
Sand Point *U.S.A.* 55°20N 160°30W **303** J7
Sand Springs *U.S.A.* 36°9N 96°7W **314** C6
Sanda *Japan* 34°53N 135°14E **223** C7
Sandai *Indonesia* 1°15S 110°31E **235** C4
Sandakan *Malaysia* 5°53N 118°4E **235** A5
Sandalwood *Australia* 34°55S 140°9E **282** C4
Sandan = Sambor *Cambodia* 12°46N 106°0E **236** F6
Sandane *Norway* 61°46N 6°13E **164** C3
Sandanski *Bulgaria* 41°35N 23°16E **202** E7
Sandaré *Mali* 14°40N 10°15W **262** C2
Sandared *Sweden* 57°43N 12°47E **163** G6
Sandarne *Sweden* 61°16N 17°9E **162** C11
Sanday *U.K.* 59°16N 2°31W **167** B6
Sande *Møre og Romsdal, Norway* 62°15N 5°27E **164** B2
Sande *Sogn og Fjordane, Norway* 61°20N 5°47E **164** C2
Sande *Vestfold, Norway* 59°36N 10°12E **162** E4
Sandefjord *Norway* 59°10N 10°15E **164** E7
Sandeid *Norway* 59°33N 5°52E **164** E2
Sanders *Ariz., U.S.A.* 35°13N 109°20W **305** J9
Sanders *Ky., U.S.A.* 38°40N 84°56W **311** F12
Sanderson *Fla., U.S.A.* 30°15N 82°16W **316** E7
Sanderson *Tex., U.S.A.* 30°9N 102°24W **314** F3
Sandersville *U.S.A.* 32°59N 82°48W **316** C7
Sandfire Roadhouse *Australia* 19°45S 121°15E **278** C3
Sandfloegga *Norway* 59°58N 7°10E **164** E4
Sandfly L. *Canada* 55°43N 106°6W **297** B7
Sandfontein *Namibia* 23°48S 19°1E **270** B2
Sandhammaren *Sweden* 55°23N 14°14E **163** J8
Sandheads, The *India* 21°10N 88°20E **241** E2
Sandgerði *Iceland* 64°3N 22°42W **155** C4
Sandia *Peru* 14°10S 69°30W **330** C4
Sandıklı *Turkey* 38°28N 30°17E **205** C12
Sandila *India* 27°5N 80°31E **243** F9
Sandilands *Bahamas* 25°3N 77°19W **153** b
Sanding *Indonesia* 3°28S 100°40E **234** C2
Sanding, Selat *Indonesia* 3°24S 100°34E **234** C2
Sandnes *Aust-Agder, Norway* 58°53N 7°45E **164** F4
Sandnes *Rogaland, Norway* 58°50N 5°45E **164** F2
Sandnessjøen *Norway* 66°2N 12°38E **160** C15
Sandoa *Dem. Rep. of the Congo* 9°41S 23°0E **265** D4
Sandomierz *Poland* 50°40N 21°43E **185** H8
Sândominic *Romania* 46°35N 25°47E **183** D10
Sandona *Colombia* 1°17N 77°28W **328** C2
Sandongo *Angola* 15°30S 21°28E **265** F4
Sandoval *U.S.A.* 38°37N 89°7W **310** F7
Sandover → *Australia* 21°43S 136°32E **280** C2
Sandoway = Thandwe *Burma* 18°20N 94°30E **241** F5
Sandown *S. Africa* 26°5S 28°4E **123** A2
Sandown Park Races *U.K.* 51°22N 0°21W **125** B1
Sandoy *Færoe Is.* 61°52N 6°46W **160** F9
Sandpoint *U.S.A.* 48°17N 116°33W **304** B5
Sandray *U.K.* 56°53N 7°31W **167** E1
Sandringham *U.K.* 52°51N 0°31E **168** E8
Sandstone *Australia* 27°59S 119°16E **279** E2
Sandton *S. Africa* 26°5S 28°4E **123** A2
Sandu *China* 26°0N 107°52E **228** E6
Sandumba *Angola* 13°45S 17°34E **265** E3
Sandur *India* 15°6N 76°33E **245** F3
Sandusky *Mich., U.S.A.* 43°25N 82°50W **312** C2
Sandusky *Ohio, U.S.A.* 41°27N 82°42W **312** E2
Sandusky → *U.S.A.* 41°27N 83°0W **311** C14
Sandveld *Namibia* 21°25S 20°0E **270** B3
Sandvig *Denmark* 55°18N 14°47E **163** J8
Sandvika *Norway* 59°54N 10°31E **133** A2
Sandviken *Sweden* 60°38N 16°46E **162** D10
Sandwich *U.S.A.* 41°39N 88°37W **311** C8
Sandwich, C. *Australia* 18°14S 146°18E **280** B4
Sandwich B. *Nfld. & L., Canada* 53°40N 57°15W **299** B8
Sandwich B. *Namibia* 23°25S 14°20E **270** B1
Sandwip I. *Bangla.* 22°30N 91°27E **241** D3
Sandy *Oreg., U.S.A.* 45°24N 122°16W **306** E4
Sandy *Pa., U.S.A.* 41°6N 78°46W **312** E6
Sandy *Utah, U.S.A.* 40°32N 111°50W **304** F8
Sandy B. *St. Helena* 16°0S 5°43W **153** h
Sandy Bay *Canada* 55°31N 102°19W **297** B8
Sandy Bight *Australia* 33°50S 123°20E **279** F3
Sandy C. *Queens., Australia* 24°42S 153°15E **280** C5

Sandy C. Tas., Australia 41°25S 144°45E 281 G3
Sandy Cay Bahamas 23°13N 75°18W 321 B4
Sandy Cr. → N.S.W., Australia 31°54S 145°18E 281 B4
Sandy Cr. → Wyo., U.S.A. 41°51N 109°47W 304 F9
Sandy Creek U.S.A. 43°38N 76°5W 313 C8
Sandy Ground Village Anguilla 18°12N 63°6W 322 a
Sandy Hill Bay Anguilla 18°13N 63°1W 322 a
Sandy I. Anguilla 18°13N 63°7W 322 a
Sandy I. Grenada 12°29N 61°29W 323 q
Sandy I. Grenada 12°13N 61°35W 323 q
Sandy L. Canada 53°2N 93°0W 298 B1
Sandy Lake Canada 53°0N 93°15W 298 B1
Sandy Point India 10°32N 92°22E 245 J11
Sandy Point Town St. Kitts & Nevis 17°22N 62°51W 322 d
Sandy Springs U.S.A. 33°56N 84°23W 316 B5
Sandy Valley U.S.A. 35°49N 115°38W 307 K11
Sandyford Ireland 53°17N 6°13W 120 B2
Sandymount Ireland 53°20N 6°13W 120 B2
Sånfjället △ Sweden 62°17N 13°35E 162 B7
Sanford Fla., U.S.A. 28°48N 81°16W 317 G8
Sanford Maine, U.S.A. 43°27N 70°47W 313 C14
Sanford N.C., U.S.A. 35°29N 79°10W 315 D15
Sanford → Australia 27°22S 115°53E 279 E2
Sanford, Mt. U.S.A. 62°13N 144°8W 303 E11
Sang-i-Masha Afghan. 33°8N 67°27E 242 C2
Sanga Angola 11°9S 15°21E 265 E3
Sanga Mozam. 12°22S 35°21E 269 E4
Sanga → Congo 1°5S 17°0E 264 C3
Sangaie Dem. Rep. of the Congo 6°48S 22°46E 265 D4
Sangamner India 19°37N 74°15E 244 E2
Sangamon → U.S.A. 40°1N 90°26W 310 D6
Sangān Iran 34°23N 60°15E 247 C9
Sanganeb Atoll △ Sudan 19°33N 37°11E 256 D4
Sangar Afghan. 32°56N 65°30E 242 C1
Sangar Russia 64°2N 127°31E 215 C13
Sangar Sarai Afghan. 34°27N 70°35E 242 B4
Sangareddi India 17°38N 78°7E 244 F4
Sangaredi Guinea 11°7N 13°52W 262 C2
Sangarh → Pakistan 30°43N 70°44E 242 D4
Sangasanga Indonesia 0°36S 117°13E 235 C5
Sangasso Mali 12°5N 5°35W 262 C3
Sangatte France 50°56N 1°44E 173 B8
Sangāw Iraq 35°17N 45°10E 213 E11
Sangay Ecuador 2°0S 78°20W 328 D2
Sangay △ Ecuador 2°15S 78°26W 328 D2
Sangbé Cameroon 6°3N 12°28E 264 A2
Sangchris L. U.S.A. 39°39N 89°29W 310 E7
Sangdong S. Korea 37°7N 128°49E 224 D4
Sange Dem. Rep. of the Congo 6°58S 28°21E 268 D2
Sangeang Indonesia 8°12S 119°6E 235 D5
Sangenjaya Japan 35°37N 139°39E 140 B2
Sângeorz-Băi Romania 47°22N 24°41E 183 C9
Sanger U.S.A. 36°42N 119°33W 306 J7
Sângera Moldova 46°55N 28°58E 183 D13
Sangerhausen Germany 51°28N 11°18E 178 D7
Sanggan He → China 38°12N 117°15E 226 E9
Sanggau Kalimantan Barat, Indonesia 0°5N 110°30E 235 B4
Sanggau Kalimantan Barat, Indonesia 1°7N 109°36E 235 B3
Sanggye S. Korea 37°38N 127°3E 137 B2
Sanghar Pakistan 26°2N 68°57E 242 F3
Sangihe, Kepulauan Indonesia 3°0N 125°30E 231 D7
Sangihe, Pulau Indonesia 3°35N 125°30E 231 D7
Sangiran Indonesia 7°25S 110°55E 235 D4
Sangiran △ Indonesia 7°27S 110°50E 231 G14
Sangju S. Korea 36°25N 128°10E 224 D4
Sangkapura Indonesia 5°52S 112°40E 235 D4
Sangkha Thailand 14°37N 103°52E 236 E4
Sangkhla Buri Thailand 14°57N 98°28E 236 E2
Sangkulirang Indonesia 0°59N 117°58E 235 B5
Sangla Pakistan 31°43N 73°23E 242 D5
Sangley Pt. Phil. 14°29N 120°54E 127 C1
Sangli India 16°55N 74°33E 244 F2
Sangmélima Cameroon 2°57N 12°1E 263 E7
Sango Angola 9°51S 15°44E 265 D2
Sango Zimbabwe 18°44S 31°44E 269 F3
Sangod India 24°55N 76°17E 242 G7
Sangole India 17°26N 75°12E 244 F2
Sangorodok = Ust-Vorkuta Russia 67°24N 64°0E 186 A11
Sangpang Bum Burma 26°30N 95°50E 241 B5
Sangre de Cristo Mts. U.S.A. 37°30N 105°20W 305 H11
Sangre Grande Trin. & Tob. 10°35N 61°8W 323 t
Sangro → Italy 42°14N 14°32E 199 F11
Sangrur India 30°14N 75°50E 242 D6
Sangudo Canada 53°50N 114°54W 296 C6
Sangue → Brazil 11°1S 58°39W 331 C6
Sangüesa Spain 42°37N 1°17W 196 C3
Sanguinaires, Îs. France 41°51N 8°36E 175 G12
Sangzhi China 29°25N 110°12E 229 C8
Sanhala Ivory C. 10°3N 6°51W 262 C3
Sanhsia Taiwan 24°56N 121°22E 225 B3
Sanhsien Hualien, Taiwan 23°8N 121°25E 225 C3
Sanhsien T'aitung, Taiwan 23°24N 121°19E 225 C3
Sanhsing Taiwan 24°40N 121°36E 225 B3
Sani Taiwan 24°24N 120°46E 225 B2
Sanibel U.S.A. 26°27N 82°1W 317 J7
Sanibel I. U.S.A. 26°26N 82°6W 317 J7
Sanikluaq Canada 56°32N 79°14W 298 A4
Sanin-Kaigan △ Japan 35°39N 134°37E 222 B6
Sanirajak = Hall Beach Canada 68°46N 81°12W 295 D15
Sanjawi Pakistan 30°17N 68°21E 242 D3
Sanje Uganda 0°49S 31°30E 268 C3
Sanjiang China 25°48N 109°37E 228 E7
Sanjo Japan 37°37N 138°57E 220 F9
Sankarankovil India 9°10N 77°35E 245 K3
Sankeshwar India 16°23N 74°32E 245 F2
Sankh → India 22°15N 84°48E 243 H11
Sankosh → India 26°24N 89°47E 241 B2
Sankrail India 22°33N 88°13E 124 B1
Sankt Andrä Austria 46°46N 14°50E 180 E7
Sankt Anton Austria 47°8N 10°16E 179 H6
Sankt Augustin Germany 50°45N 7°10E 178 E3
Sankt Blasien Germany 47°47N 8°7E 179 H4
Sankt Gallen Switz. 47°26N 9°22E 179 H5
Sankt Gallen □ Switz. 47°25N 9°22E 179 H5
Sankt Goar Germany 50°12N 7°43E 179 E3
Sankt Ingbert Germany 49°16N 7°6E 179 F3
Sankt Johann im Pongau Austria 47°22N 13°12E 180 D6
Sankt Johann in Tirol Austria 47°30N 12°25E 180 D5
Sankt Marein = Smarje Slovenia 46°15N 15°34E 199 B12
Sankt Michel = Mikkeli Finland 61°43N 27°15E 188 B4
Sankt Moritz Switz. 46°30N 9°51E 179 J5
Sankt-Peterburg Russia 59°55N 30°20E 137 B1
Sankt Pölten Austria 48°12N 15°38E 180 C8
Sankt Ulrich = Ortisei Italy 46°34N 11°40E 199 B8
Sankt Valentin Austria 48°11N 14°33E 180 C7
Sankt Veit Austria 48°11N 16°16E 142 A1
Sankt Veit an der Glan Austria 46°47N 14°22E 180 E7
Sankt Wendel Germany 49°27N 7°9E 179 F3
Sankt Wolfgang Austria 47°43N 13°27E 180 D6
Sankuru → Dem. Rep. of the Congo 4°17S 20°25E 265 C4
Sanlihe China 39°53N 116°18E 114 B1
Sanlintang China 31°9N 121°29E 138 C1
Sanliurfa Turkey 37°12N 38°50E 213 D8
Sanliurfa □ Turkey 37°0N 39°0E 213 D8
Sanlúcar de Barrameda Spain 36°46N 6°21W 195 J4
Sanluri Italy 39°34N 8°54E 200 C1
Sânmartin Romania 46°19N 25°58E 183 D10
Sanmen China 29°5N 121°35E 229 C13
Sanmenxia China 34°47N 111°12E 226 G6
Sanming China 26°15N 117°40E 229 D11
Sannan Japan 35°2N 135°1E 223 B7
Sannat Malta 36°1N 14°15E 206 E6
Sannicandro Gargánico Italy 41°50N 15°34E 199 G12
Sânnicolau Mare Romania 46°5N 20°39E 182 D5
Sannieshof S. Africa 26°30S 25°47E 270 C4
Sannīn, J. Lebanon 33°57N 35°52E 250 E6
Sanniquellie Liberia 7°19N 8°38W 262 D3
Sannûr Egypt 28°58N 31°3E 251 K2
Sannûr, W. → Egypt 28°59N 31°3E 251 K2
Sano Japan 36°19N 139°35E 223 A11
Sanok Poland 49°35N 22°10E 185 J9
Sanqingshan △ China 28°50N 118°5E 229 C12
Sanquhar U.K. 55°22N 3°54W 167 F5
Sanquianga △ Colombia 2°33N 78°14W 328 C2
Sans Spain 41°22N 2°7E 114 A1
Sans Souci St. Vincent 13°13N 61°7W 323 n
Sans Souci Trin. & Tob. 10°50N 61°0W 323 t
Sansanding Mali 13°48N 6°0W 262 C3
Sansané Niger 13°50N 1°36E 263 C5
Sansepolcro Italy 43°34N 12°8E 199 E9
Sansha China 26°58N 120°12E 229 D13
Sanshui China 23°10N 112°56E 229 F9
Sanski Most Bos.-H. 44°46N 16°40E 199 D13
Sanssouci Germany 52°23N 13°2E 115 B1
Sansui China 26°58N 108°39E 228 D7
Sant Agusti Barcelona, Spain 114 c2
Sant Ambrogio, Basilica di Italy 45°27N 9°10E 129 B2
Sant Antoni de Portmany Spain 38°59N 1°19E 206 D1
Sant Boi de Llobregat Spain 41°20N 2°2E 114 A1
Sant Carles Spain 39°3N 1°34E 206 C2
Sant Carles de la Ràpita Spain 40°37N 0°35E 196 E5
Sant Celoni Spain 41°42N 2°30E 196 D7
Sant Cugat Spain 41°28N 2°5E 114 A1
Sant Elm Spain 39°35N 2°21E 206 B3
Sant Feliu de Guíxols Spain 41°45N 3°1E 196 D8
Sant Feliu de Llobregat Spain 41°22N 2°2E 114 A1
Sant Ferran Spain 38°42N 1°28E 206 D1
Sant Francesc de Formentera Spain 38°42N 1°26E 206 D1
Sant Jaume Spain 39°54N 4°4E 206 B5
Sant Joan Spain 39°36N 3°4E 206 B4
Sant Joan d'Alacant Spain 38°24N 0°26W 197 G4
Sant Joan de Labritja Spain 39°5N 1°31E 206 C2
Sant Joan Despi Spain 41°22N 2°2E 114 A1
Sant Jordi Ibiza, Spain 38°53N 1°24E 206 D1
Sant Jordi Mallorca, Spain 39°33N 2°46E 206 B3
Sant Jordi, G. de Spain 40°53N 1°2E 196 E6
Sant Llorenç de Morunys Spain 42°8N 1°35E 196 C6
Sant Llorenç del Munt y l'Obac ⌂ Spain 41°39N 1°55W 196 D3
Sant Llorenç des Cardassar Spain 39°37N 3°17E 206 B4
Sant Maria del Mar Barcelona, Spain 114 b3
Sant Mateu Baleares, Spain 39°3N 1°23E 206 C1
Sant Mateu Valencia, Spain 40°28N 0°10E 196 E5
Sant Miquel Spain 39°3N 1°26E 206 C1
Sant Pau del Camp Barcelona, Spain 114 c2
Sant Salvador Spain 39°27N 3°11E 206 B4
Sant Vicent del Raspeig Spain 38°24N 0°31W 197 G4
Santa Peru 8°59S 78°40W 330 B2
Sant' Ágata Militello Italy 38°2N 14°8E 201 D7
Santa Agnés Spain 39°3N 1°21E 206 C1
Santa Ana Beni, Bolivia 13°50S 65°40W 331 C4
Santa Ana La Paz, Bolivia 15°31S 67°30W 330 D4
Santa Ana Santa Cruz, Bolivia 18°43S 58°44W 331 D6
Santa Ana Santa Cruz, Bolivia 16°37S 60°43W 331 D5
Santa Ana Ecuador 1°16S 80°20W 328 D1
Santa Ana El Salv. 14°0N 89°31W 320 D2
Santa Ana Guam 13°32N 145°46E 302 d
Santa Ana Sonora, Mexico 30°33N 111°7W 318 A2
Santa Ana Cagayan, Phil. 18°28N 122°20E 232 B4
Santa Ana Manila, Phil. 14°34N 121°0E 127 B2
Santa Ana Solomon Is. 10°50S 162°30E 287 N12
Santa Ana Calif., U.S.A. 33°46N 117°52W 307 M9
Santa Ana → Venezuela 9°30N 71°57W 328 B3
Sant' Ángelo Lodigiano Italy 45°14N 9°25E 198 C6
Santa Anita Park U.S.A. 34°8N 118°5W 126 B4
Sant' Antioco Italy 39°4N 8°27E 200 C1
Santa Bárbara Santa Maria, Azores 36°59N 25°4W 153 d4
Santa Bárbara Terciera, Azores 38°41N 27°20W 153 d1
Santa Bárbara Chile 37°40S 72°1W 334 D1
Santa Bárbara Colombia 5°53N 75°35W 328 B2
Santa Barbara Curaçao 12°5N 68°51W 322 g
Santa Bárbara Honduras 14°53N 88°14W 320 D2
Santa Bárbara Chihuahua, Mexico 26°48N 105°49W 318 B3
Santa Barbara Phil. 10°50N 122°32E 233 F4
Santa Barbara Spain 40°42N 0°29E 196 E5
Santa Barbara Calif., U.S.A. 34°25N 119°42W 307 L7
Santa Bárbara Amazonas, Venezuela 3°57N 67°6W 328 C4
Santa Bárbara Barinas, Venezuela 7°47N 71°10W 328 B3
Santa Bárbara, Mt. Spain 37°23N 2°50W 197 H2
Santa Bárbara, Serra de Azores 38°44N 27°19W 153 d1
Santa Barbara Channel U.S.A. 34°15N 120°0W 307 L7
Santa Barbara I. U.S.A. 33°29N 119°2W 307 M7
Santa Catalina Colombia 10°36N 75°17W 328 A2
Santa Catalina Neg. Or., Phil. 9°20N 122°52E 233 G4
Santa Catalina Solomon Is. 10°53S 162°29E 287 N12
Santa Catalina, Gulf of U.S.A. 33°10N 117°50W 307 N9
Santa Catalina, I. Mexico 25°40N 110°47W 318 B2
Santa Catalina I. U.S.A. 33°23N 118°25W 307 M8
Santa Catarina □ Brazil 27°25S 48°30W 335 B6
Santa Catarina, I. de Brazil 27°30S 48°40W 335 B6
Santa Caterina di Pittinuri Italy 40°6N 8°27E 200 B1
Santa Caterina Villarmosa Italy 37°35N 14°2E 201 E7
Santa Cecília Brazil 26°56S 50°18W 335 B5
Santa Clara Cuba 22°20N 80°0W 320 B4
Santa Clara Calif., U.S.A. 37°21N 121°57W 306 H5
Santa Clara N.Y., U.S.A. 44°38N 74°27W 313 B10
Santa Clara Utah, U.S.A. 37°8N 113°39W 305 H7
Santa Clara, I. Chile 33°42S 79°0W 330 c
Santa Clara de Olimar Uruguay 32°50S 54°54W 335 C5
Santa Clara Valley U.S.A. 36°50N 121°30W 306 J5
Santa Clarita U.S.A. 34°24N 118°33W 307 L8
Santa Clotilde Peru 2°33S 73°45W 328 D3
Santa Coloma de Farners Spain 41°50N 2°39E 196 D7
Santa Coloma de Gramenet Spain 41°27N 2°13E 114 A2
Santa Comba Spain 43°2N 8°49W 194 B2
Santa Croce Camerina Italy 36°50N 14°31E 201 F7
Santa Croce di Magliano Italy 41°42N 14°59E 199 G11
Santa Cruz Aruba 12°30N 69°59W 322 f
Santa Cruz Bolivia 17°43S 63°10W 331 D5
Santa Cruz Brazil 6°13S 36°1W 332 C4
Santa Cruz Chile 34°38S 71°27W 334 C1
Santa Cruz Costa Rica 10°15N 85°35W 320 D2
Santa Cruz Curaçao 12°18N 69°7W 322 g
Santa Cruz Maharashtra, India 19°4N 72°51E 130 A1
Santa Cruz Jamaica 18°3N 77°43W 320 a
Santa Cruz Madeira 32°42N 16°46W 153 c
Santa Cruz Peru 5°40S 75°56W 330 B2
Santa Cruz Davao del S., Phil. 6°50N 125°25E 233 H5
Santa Cruz Laguna, Phil. 14°20N 121°24E 232 D3
Santa Cruz Manila, Phil. 14°36N 120°58E 127 B1
Santa Cruz Marinduque, Phil. 13°28N 122°2E 232 E4
Santa Cruz Mind. Occ., Phil. 13°4N 120°43E 232 E3
Santa Cruz Zambales, Phil. 15°46N 119°55E 232 D2
Santa Cruz Calif., U.S.A. 36°58N 122°1W 306 J4
Santa Cruz Venezuela 8°3N 64°27W 329 B5
Santa Cruz □ Argentina 49°0S 70°0W 336 C3
Santa Cruz □ Bolivia 17°43S 63°10W 331 D5
Santa Cruz → Argentina 50°10S 68°20W 336 D3
Santa Cruz, B. Curaçao 12°18N 69°10W 322 g
Santa Cruz, I. Ecuador 0°38S 90°23W 330 a
Santa Cruz, I. de Brazil 22°51S 43°7W 135 B2
Santa Cruz Cabrália Brazil 16°17S 39°2W 333 E4
Santa Cruz da Graciosa Azores 39°5N 28°1W 153 d1
Santa Cruz das Flores Azores 39°27N 31°7W 153 d2
Santa Cruz de Bravo = Felipe Carrillo Puerto Mexico 19°38N 88°3W 319 D7
Santa Cruz de la Palma Canary Is. 28°41N 17°46W 153 e1
Santa Cruz de la Palma ✕ (SPC) Canary Is. 28°40N 17°45W 153 e1
Santa Cruz de Mudela Spain 38°39N 3°28W 195 G7
Santa Cruz de Olorde Spain 41°25N 2°3E 114 A1
Santa Cruz de Tenerife Canary Is. 28°28N 16°15W 153 e1
Santa Cruz del Norte Cuba 23°9N 81°55W 320 B3
Santa Cruz del Retamar Spain 40°8N 4°14W 194 E6
Santa Cruz del Sur Cuba 20°44N 78°0W 320 B4
Santa Cruz do Rio Pardo Brazil 22°54S 49°37W 335 A6
Santa Cruz do Sul Brazil 29°42S 52°25W 335 B5
Santa Cruz I. U.S.A. 34°1N 119°43W 307 M7
Santa Cruz Is. Solomon Is. 10°30S 166°0E 277 C12
Santa Cruz la Vieja △ Bolivia 17°55S 60°50W 331 D5
Santa Cruz Mts. Jamaica 17°58N 77°43W 320 a
Santa Domingo, Cay Bahamas 21°25N 75°15W 320 B4
Santa Efigênia Brazil 23°32S 46°38W 137 B2
Sant' Egidio alla Vibrata Italy 42°49N 13°42E 199 F10
Santa Elena Argentina 30°58S 59°47W 334 C4
Santa Elena Ecuador 2°16S 80°52W 328 D1
Santa Elena Camarines N., Phil. 14°12N 122°24E 232 D4
Santa Elena Manila, Phil. 14°38N 121°5E 127 B2
Santa Elena, C. Costa Rica 10°54N 85°56W 320 D2
Santa Elena del Gomero Chile 33°28S 70°45W 137 B1
Sant' Eufémia, G. di Italy 38°51N 16°4E 201 D9
Santa Eulalia Spain 41°25N 2°10E 114 A2
Santa Eulària des Riu Spain 38°59N 1°32E 206 D2
Santa Fé Argentina 31°35S 60°41W 334 C3
Santa Fe Nueva Vizcaya, Phil. 16°10N 120°57E 232 C3
Santa Fe Romblon, Phil. 12°10N 122°0E 232 E4
Santa Fe Spain 37°11N 3°43W 195 H7
Santa Fe N. Mex., U.S.A. 35°41N 105°57W 305 J11
Santa Fé □ Argentina 31°50S 60°55W 334 C3
Santa Fé, Canal de Ecuador 0°48S 89°55W 330 a
Santa Fé, I. Ecuador 0°49S 90°5W 330 a
Santa Fé do Sul Brazil 20°13S 50°56W 333 F1
Santa Fe Springs U.S.A. 33°56N 118°3W 126 C4
Santa Filomena Brazil 9°6S 45°50W 332 C2
Santa Fiora Italy 42°50N 11°35E 199 F8
Santa Gertrudis Spain 39°0N 1°26E 206 C1
Santa Giustina Italy 46°10N 12°5E 199 B9
Santa Helena Brazil 2°14S 45°18W 332 B2
Santa Helena de Goiás Brazil 17°53S 50°35W 333 E1
Santa Inês Bahia, Brazil 13°17S 39°48W 333 D4
Santa Inês Maranhão, Brazil 3°39S 45°20W 332 B2
Santa Inés Extremadura, Spain 38°32N 5°37W 195 G5
Santa Inés, I. Chile 54°0S 73°0W 336 D2
Santa Iria da Azóia Portugal 38°49N 9°5W 126 A2
Santa Isabel = Rey Malabo Eq. Guin. 3°45N 8°50E 263 E6
Santa Isabel Argentina 36°10S 66°54W 334 D2
Santa Isabel Puerto Rico 17°58N 66°24W 321 b
Santa Isabel Solomon Is. 8°0S 159°0E 287 M10
Santa Isabel do Araguaia Brazil 6°7S 48°19W 332 C2
Santa Isabel do Morro Brazil 11°34S 50°40W 333 D1
Santa Isabel do Río Negro Brazil 0°24S 65°2W 329 D4
Santa Julia Chile 33°30S 70°35W 137 C2
Santa Lucía Corrientes, Argentina 28°58S 59°5W 334 B4
Santa Lucía San Juan, Argentina 31°30S 68°30W 334 C2
Santa Lucía Canary Is. 27°55N 15°32W 153 e1
Santa Lucia Phil. 17°7N 120°27E 232 C3
Santa Lucía Spain 37°35N 0°58W 197 H4
Santa Lucía Uruguay 34°27S 56°24W 334 C4
Santa Lucia Range U.S.A. 36°0N 121°20W 306 K5
Santa Luzia Brazil 16°20S 48°0W 333 E2
Santa Luzia Brazil 19°47S 43°52W 333 E3
Santa Luzia C. Verde Is. 16°50N 24°35W 153 j
Santa Margalida Spain 39°42N 3°6E 206 B4
Santa Margarita Argentina 38°28S 61°35W 334 D3
Santa Margarita Calif., U.S.A. 35°23N 120°37W 306 K6
Santa Margarita → U.S.A. 33°13N 117°23W 307 M9
Santa Margarita, I. Mexico 24°27N 111°50W 318 C2
Santa Margherita Italy 38°58N 8°58E 200 D1
Santa Margherita Ligure Italy 44°20N 9°11E 198 D6
Santa María Argentina 26°40S 66°0W 334 B2
Santa Maria Azores 36°58N 25°6W 153 d4
Santa Maria Brazil 29°40S 53°48W 335 B5
Santa Maria C. Verde Is. 16°31N 22°53W 153 j
Santa María Mexico City, Mexico 128 a1
Santa Maria Ilocos S., Phil. 17°22N 120°29E 232 C3
Santa Maria Isabela, Phil. 17°28N 121°45E 232 C3
Santa Maria Calif., U.S.A. 34°57N 120°26W 307 L6
Santa María → Mexico 31°0N 107°14W 318 A3
Santa María, B. de Mexico 25°4N 108°6W 318 B3
Santa Maria, C. de Portugal 36°58N 7°53W 195 J3
Santa María, I. Ecuador 1°17S 90°26W 330 a
Santa Maria Cápua Vétere Italy 41°5N 14°15E 201 A7
Santa Maria da Feira Portugal 40°55N 8°35W 194 E2
Santa Maria da Vitória Brazil 13°24S 44°12W 333 D3
Santa María de Ipire Venezuela 8°49N 65°19W 329 B4
Santa Maria del Camí Spain 39°38N 2°47E 206 B3
Santa Maria di Léuca, C. Italy 39°47N 18°22E 201 C11
Santa Maria do Boiaçu Brazil 0°25S 61°48W 329 D5
Santa Maria do Suaçuí Brazil 18°12S 42°25W 333 E3
Santa Maria dos Marmelos Brazil 6°7S 61°51W 331 B5
Santa María la Real de Nieva Spain 41°4N 4°24W 194 D6
Santa Marinella Italy 42°2N 11°52E 199 F8
Santa Marta Colombia 11°15N 74°13W 328 A3
Santa Marta, Sierra Nevada de Colombia 10°55N 73°50W 328 A3
Santa Marta de Tormes Spain 40°57N 5°38W 194 E5
Santa Marta Grande, C. Brazil 28°43S 48°50W 335 B6
Santa Marta Ortigueira, Ría de Spain 43°44N 7°45W 194 B3
Santa Martabaai = Sint Marthabaai Curaçao 12°17N 69°8W 322 g
Santa Maura = Lefkada Greece 38°40N 20°43E 207 B2
Santa Monica U.S.A. 34°1N 118°29W 126 B2
Santa Monica Mts. U.S.A. 34°6N 118°29W 126 B2
Santa Monica Mts. ⌂ U.S.A. 34°4N 118°44W 307 L8
Santa Olalla Spain 40°2N 4°25W 194 E6
Santa Olalla del Cala Spain 37°54N 6°14W 195 H4
Santa Paula U.S.A. 34°21N 119°4W 307 L7
Santa Pola Spain 38°13N 0°35W 197 G4
Santa Ponça Spain 39°30N 2°28E 206 B3
Santa Quitéria Brazil 4°20S 40°10W 332 B3
Santa Rita = Itumbiara Brazil 18°20S 49°10W 333 E2
Santa Rita Amazonas, Brazil 3°29S 69°19W 328 D4
Santa Rita Paraíba, Brazil 7°8S 34°58W 332 C5
Santa Rita Colombia 4°53N 68°24W 328 C4
Santa Rita Guam 13°23N 144°40E 302 d
Santa Rita Samar, Phil. 11°27N 124°56E 233 F5
Santa Rita Zulia, Venezuela 10°32N 71°32W 328 A3
Santa Rita de Cássia Brazil 11°0S 44°32W 332 D3
Santa Rita do Araguaia = Guiratinga Brazil 16°21S 53°45W 331 D7
Santa Rita do Araguaia Brazil 17°20S 53°12W 331 D7
Santa Rosa = Bella Unión Uruguay 30°15S 57°40W 334 C4
Santa Rosa La Pampa, Argentina 36°40S 64°17W 334 D3
Santa Rosa San Luis, Argentina 32°21S 65°10W 334 C2
Santa Rosa Beni, Bolivia 14°10S 66°53W 330 C4
Santa Rosa Pando, Bolivia 10°36S 67°20W 330 C4
Santa Rosa Santa Cruz, Bolivia 17°7S 63°35W 331 D5
Santa Rosa Brazil 27°52S 54°29W 335 B5
Santa Rosa Colombia 3°32N 69°48W 328 C4
Santa Rosa Curaçao 12°7N 68°53W 322 g
Santa Rosa El Oro, Ecuador 3°27S 79°58W 328 D2
Santa Rosa Galápagos Is., Ecuador 0°40S 90°25W 330 a
Santa Rosa Puno, Peru 14°30S 70°50W 330 C3
Santa Rosa San Martin, Peru 6°41S 76°37W 330 B2
Santa Rosa Phil. 15°25N 120°57E 232 D3
Santa Rosa Calif., U.S.A. 38°26N 122°43W 306 G4
Santa Rosa N. Mex., U.S.A. 34°57N 104°41W 305 J11
Santa Rosa Amazonas, Venezuela 1°29N 66°55W 328 C4
Santa Rosa, Mt. Guam 13°32N 144°55E 302 d
Santa Rosa and San Jacinto Mts. ⌂ U.S.A. 33°28N 116°20W 307 M10
Santa Rosa Beach U.S.A. 30°22N 86°14W 316 E3
Santa Rosa de Amanadona Venezuela 1°29N 66°55W 328 C4
Santa Rosa de Cabal Colombia 4°52N 75°38W 328 C2
Santa Rosa de Copán Honduras 14°47N 88°46W 320 D2
Santa Rosa de la Roca Bolivia 16°3S 61°34W 331 D5
Santa Rosa de Locobe Chile 33°25S 70°33W 137 B2
Santa Rosa de Osos Colombia 6°39N 75°28W 328 B2
Santa Rosa de Río Primero Argentina 31°8S 63°20W 334 C3
Santa Rosa de Viterbo Colombia 5°53N 72°59W 328 B3
Santa Rosa del Palmar Bolivia 16°54S 62°24W 331 D5
Santa Rosa I. Calif., U.S.A. 33°58N 120°6W 307 M6
Santa Rosa I. Fla., U.S.A. 30°20N 86°50W 317 E3
Santa Rosa Range U.S.A. 41°45N 117°40W 304 F5
Santa Rosalía Mexico 27°19N 112°17W 318 B2
Santa Sylvina Argentina 27°50S 61°10W 334 B3
Santa Tecla = Nueva San Salvador El Salv. 13°40N 89°18W 320 D2
Santa Teresa Argentina 33°25S 60°47W 334 C3
Santa Teresa N. Terr., Australia 24°8S 134°22E 280 C1
Santa Teresa Brazil 19°55S 40°36W 333 E3
Santa Teresa Tamaulipas, Mexico 25°17N 97°51W 319 B5
Santa Teresa Venezuela 4°43N 61°4W 329 C5
Santa Teresa △ Uruguay 33°57S 53°31W 335 C5
Santa Teresa de la Ovalle Chile 33°22S 70°44W 137 B1
Santa Teresa di Riva Italy 37°57N 15°22E 201 E8
Santa Teresa Gallura Italy 41°14N 9°11E 200 A2
Santa Teresinha Brazil 10°28S 50°31W 332 D1
Santa Teresita Argentina 36°32S 56°41W 334 D4
Santa Uxía de Ribeira Spain 42°36N 8°58W 194 C2
Santa Vitória Brazil 18°50S 50°8W 333 E1
Santa Vitória do Palmar Brazil 33°32S 53°25W 335 C5
Santa Ynez → U.S.A. 34°41N 120°36W 307 L6
Santa Ynez Mts. U.S.A. 34°30N 120°0W 307 L6
Santa Ysabel U.S.A. 33°7N 116°40W 307 M10
Santadi Italy 39°5N 8°43E 200 C1
Santaella Spain 37°34N 4°51W 195 H6
Santahamina Finland 60°8N 25°2E 121 C3
Santahar Bangla. 24°48N 88°59E 241 C2
Santai China 31°5N 104°58E 228 B5
Santaluz Brazil 11°15S 39°22W 332 D4
Santan Indonesia 0°3S 117°28E 235 C5
Santana = Uruaçu Brazil 14°30S 49°10W 333 D2
Santana Bahia, Brazil 13°2S 44°5W 333 D3
Santana São Paulo, Brazil 23°29S 46°36W 137 A2
Santana Madeira 32°48N 16°52W 153 c
Sântana Romania 46°20N 21°30E 182 D6
Santana, Coxilha de Brazil 30°50S 55°35W 335 C4
Santana do Ipanema Brazil 9°22S 37°14W 332 C4
Santana do Livramento Brazil 30°55S 55°30W 335 C4
Santana do Paranaíba = Paranaíba Brazil 19°40S 51°11W 331 D7
Santander Colombia 3°1N 76°28W 328 C2
Santander Phil. 9°25N 123°20E 233 G4
Santander Spain 43°27N 3°51W 194 B7
Santander □ Colombia 7°0N 73°15W 328 B3
Santander Jiménez Mexico 24°13N 98°28W 319 C5
Sant'Angelo, Castel Rome, Italy 136 b1
Santanilla, Is. Honduras 17°22N 83°57W 320 C3
Santanyí Spain 39°20N 3°5E 206 B4
Santaquin U.S.A. 39°59N 111°47W 304 G8
Santarcángelo di Romagna Italy 44°4N 12°26E 199 D9
Santarém Brazil 2°25S 54°42W 329 D7
Santarém Portugal 39°12N 8°42W 195 F2
Santarém □ Portugal 39°10N 8°40W 195 F2
Santaren Channel W. Indies 24°0N 79°30W 320 B4
Santee U.S.A. 32°50N 116°58W 307 N10
Santee → U.S.A. 33°7N 79°17W 315 E15
Santeny France 48°43N 2°34E 134 B4
Santéramo in Colle Italy 40°49N 16°45E 201 B9
Santerno → Italy 44°34N 11°58E 199 D8
Santhià Italy 45°22N 8°10E 198 C5
Santi Taiwan 22°43N 120°39E 225 D2
Santi-Quaranta = Sarandë Albania 39°52N 19°55E 206 B9
Santiago = Río Grande de Santiago → Mexico 21°36N 105°26W 318 C3
Santiago = São Tiago C. Verde Is. 15°0N 23°40W 153 j
Santiago Brazil 29°11S 54°52W 335 B5
Santiago Canary Is. 28°2N 17°12W 153 e1
Santiago Chile 33°26S 70°40W 137 B2
Santiago Panama 8°0N 81°0W 320 E3
Santiago Peru 14°11S 75°43W 330 C2
Santiago Ilocos S., Phil. 17°18N 120°27E 232 C3
Santiago Isabela, Phil. 16°41N 121°33E 232 C3
Santiago → Peru 4°27S 77°38W 328 D2
Santiago, C. Chile 50°46S 75°27W 336 D1
Santiago, I. = San Salvador, I. Ecuador 0°16S 90°42W 330 a
Santiago, Punta de Eq. Guin. 3°12N 8°40E 263 E6
Santiago, Sierra de Bolivia 18°25S 59°25W 331 D6
Santiago Benítez ✕ (SCL) Chile 33°33S 70°42W 137 B1
Santiago de Chiquitos Bolivia 18°19S 59°34W 331 D6
Santiago de Chuco Peru 8°9S 78°11W 330 B2
Santiago de Compostela Spain 42°52N 8°37W 194 C2
Santiago de Cuba Cuba 20°0N 75°49W 320 C4
Santiago de los Caballeros Dom. Rep. 19°30N 70°40W 321 C5
Santiago de Surco Peru 12°9S 77°0W 124 B2
Santiago del Estero Argentina 27°50S 64°15W 334 B3
Santiago del Estero □ Argentina 27°40S 63°15W 334 B3
Santiago del Teide Canary Is. 28°17N 16°48W 153 e1
Santiago do Boqueirão = Santiago Brazil 29°11S 54°52W 335 B5
Santiago do Cacém Portugal 38°1N 8°42W 195 G2
Santiago I. Phil. 16°23N 119°56E 232 C2
Santiago Ixcuintla Mexico 21°49N 105°13W 318 C3
Santiago Jamiltepec Mexico 16°17N 97°49W 319 D5
Santiago Papasquiaro Mexico 25°3N 105°25W 318 C3
Santiago Pinotepa Nacional Mexico 16°19N 98°1W 319 D5
Santiaguillo, L. de Mexico 24°48N 104°48W 318 C4
Santialing Taiwan 25°5N 121°51E 225 A3
Santiao Chiao Taiwan 25°1N 122°0E 225 A3
Santiaolun Taiwan 23°39N 120°9E 225 C2
Santiguila Mali 12°42N 7°25W 262 C3
Santillana del Mar Spain 43°24N 4°6W 194 B6
Santisteban del Puerto Spain 38°17N 3°15W 195 G7
Santo → Peru 8°56S 78°37W 330 B2
Santo Amaro Bahia, Brazil 12°30S 38°43W 333 D4
Santo Amaro São Paulo, Brazil 23°39S 46°42W 137 B1
Santo Amaro Lisboa, Portugal 38°42N 9°11W 126 A1
Santo Anastácio Brazil 21°58S 51°39W 335 A5
Santo André Brazil 23°39S 46°29W 335 A6
Santo André Lisboa, Portugal 38°38N 9°3W 126 B2
Santo Ângelo Brazil 28°15S 54°15W 335 B5
Santo Antão C. Verde Is. 16°52N 25°10W 153 j
Santo Antão do Tojal Portugal 38°49N 9°9W 126 A2
Santo Antônia São Tomé & Príncipe 1°37N 7°27E 265 a
Santo Antônio Brazil 2°24S 60°58W 329 D5
Santo Antônio, Qta. de Portugal 38°39N 9°15W 126 B1
Santo Antônio da Cachoeira = Itaguatins Brazil 5°47S 47°29W 332 C2
Santo Antônio de Jesus Brazil 12°58S 39°16W 333 D4
Santo Antônio do Abaixo = Santo Antônio do Leverger Brazil 15°52S 56°5W 331 D6
Santo Antônio do Içá Brazil 3°5S 67°57W 328 D4
Santo Antônio do Leverger Brazil 15°52S 56°5W 331 D6
Santo Corazón Bolivia 18°0S 58°45W 331 D6
Santo Domingo Dom. Rep. 18°30N 69°59W 321 C6
Santo Domingo Baja Calif., Mexico 30°43N 116°2W 318 A1
Santo Domingo Baja Calif. S., Mexico 25°29N 111°55W 318 B2
Santo Domingo Nic. 12°14N 84°59W 320 D3
Santo Domingo de la Calzada Spain 42°26N 2°57W 196 C2
Santo Domingo de los Colorados Ecuador 0°15S 79°9W 328 D2
Santo Domingo Pueblo U.S.A. 35°31N 106°22W 305 J10
Santo Nino I. Phil. 11°54N 124°26E 233 F5
Santo Stéfano di Camastro Italy 38°1N 14°22E 201 D7
Santo Tirso Portugal 41°21N 8°28W 194 D2
Santo Tomás Galápagos Is., Ecuador 0°51S 91°2W 330 a
Santo Tomás Baja Calif., Mexico 31°33N 116°24W 318 A1
Santo Tomás Peru 14°26S 72°8W 330 C3
Santo Tomas Phil. 7°32N 125°37E 233 H5
Santo Tomas, Univ. of Phil. 14°36N 120°59E 127 B1
Santo Tomás, Volcán Ecuador 0°48S 91°7W 330 a
Santo Tomé Argentina 28°40S 56°5W 335 B4
Santo Tomé de Guayana = Ciudad Guayana Venezuela 8°0N 62°30W 329 B5
Santomera Spain 38°4N 1°3W 197 G3
Santoña Spain 43°29N 3°27W 194 B7
Santorini Greece 36°23N 25°27E 205 E7
Santos Brazil 24°0S 46°20W 335 A6
Santos, Sierra de los Spain 38°7N 5°12W 195 G5
Santos Dumont Brazil 22°55S 43°10W 333 F3
Santos Dumont ✕ (SDU) Brazil 22°54S 43°9W 135 B2
Santoshpur India 22°31N 88°16E 124 B1
Santragachi India 22°35N 88°17E 124 B1
Santry Ireland 53°24N 6°15W 120 A2
Santuario de Aves Laguna Colorada △ Bolivia 22°10S 67°45W 334 A2
Sanur Indonesia 8°41S 115°15E 231 K18
Sanwan Taiwan 24°39N 120°57E 225 B2
Sanwer India 22°59N 75°50E 242 H6
Sanxenxo Spain 42°24N 8°49W 194 C2
Sanxia Shuiku China 30°3N 107°58E 228 B6
Sanxiang China 22°21N 113°25E 219 a
Sanya China 18°14N 109°29E 236 C7
San'yō Japan 34°2N 131°5E 222 C3
Sanyuan China 34°35N 108°58E 226 G5
Sanyuanli China 23°8N 113°14E 121 B2
Sanyuki-Sammyaku Japan 34°5N 134°0E 222 C6
Sanza Pombo Angola 7°18S 15°56E 265 D3
São Bartolomeu de Messines Portugal 37°15N 8°17W 195 H2
São Benedito = Beneditinos Brazil 5°27S 42°22W 332 C3
São Benedito Brazil 4°3S 40°53W 332 B3
São Benedito → Brazil 9°11S 57°2W 331 B6
São Bento Brazil 2°42S 44°50W 332 B3
São Bento do Norte Brazil 5°4S 36°2W 332 C4
São Bernardo do Campo Brazil 23°45S 46°34W 333 F2
São Borja Brazil 28°39S 56°0W 335 B4
São Brás de Alportel Portugal 37°8N 7°37W 195 H3
São Braz, C. de Angola 9°58S 13°19E 265 D2
São Caetano do Sul Brazil 23°37S 46°34W 137 B2
São Caitano Brazil 8°21S 36°6W 332 C4
São Carlos Brazil 22°0S 47°50W 335 A6
São Conrado Brazil 23°55S 43°17W 135 B1
São Cristóvão Rio de J., Brazil 22°53S 43°13W 135 B1
São Cristóvão Sergipe, Brazil 11°1S 37°15W 332 D4
São Domingo do Capim Brazil 1°41S 47°47W 332 B2
São Domingos Brazil 13°25S 46°19W 333 D2
São Domingos Guinea-Biss. 12°19N 16°13W 262 C1
São Domingos da Boa Vista = São Domingo do Capim Brazil 1°41S 47°47W 332 B2
São Domingos do Maranhão Brazil 5°42S 44°22W 332 C3
São Felipe = Içana Brazil 0°21N 67°19W 328 C4
São Felippe = Eirunepé Brazil 6°35S 69°53W 330 B4
São Félix Brazil 11°36S 50°39W 333 D1
São Félix do Xingu Brazil 6°38S 51°59W 331 B7
São Filipe C. Verde Is. 15°2N 24°30W 153 j
São Francisco = Itapagé Brazil 3°41S 39°34W 332 B4
São Francisco Brazil 16°0S 44°50W 333 E3
São Francisco → Brazil 10°30S 36°24W 332 D4
São Francisco do Maranhão Brazil 6°15S 42°52W 332 C3
São Francisco do Sul Brazil 26°15S 48°36W 335 B6
São Francisco Penitência Rio de J., Brazil 135 b1
São Gabriel Brazil 30°20S 54°20W 335 C5
São Gabriel da Cachoeira Brazil 0°8S 67°5W 328 D4
São Gabriel da Palha Brazil 18°47S 40°39W 333 E3
São Gonçalo = Araripina Brazil 7°33S 40°34W 332 C3
São Gonçalo Brazil 22°48S 43°5W 333 F3
São Gotardo Brazil 19°19S 46°3W 333 E2
São Hill Tanzania 8°20S 35°12E 269 D4
São João Guinea-Biss. 11°32N 15°25W 262 C1
São João da Baliza Brazil 0°52N 59°52W 329 C6
São João da Barra Brazil 21°38S 41°3W 333 F3
São João da Boa Vista Brazil 22°0S 46°52W 335 A6
São João da Madeira Portugal 40°54N 8°30W 194 E2
São João da Pesqueira Portugal 41°8N 7°24W 194 D3
São João da Ponte Brazil 15°56S 44°1W 333 E3
São João de Meriti Brazil 22°48S 43°21W 135 A1
São João de Montenegro = Montenegro Brazil 29°39S 51°29W 335 B5
São João del Rei Brazil 21°8S 44°15W 333 F3
São João do Araguaia Brazil 5°23S 48°46W 332 C2
São João do Paraíso Brazil 15°19S 42°1W 333 E3
São João do Piauí Brazil 8°21S 42°15W 332 C3
São João do Sul Angola 15°46S 12°0E 265 F2
São João dos Patos Brazil 6°30S 43°42W 332 C3
São Joaquim Amazonas, Brazil 0°1S 67°16W 328 D4
São Joaquim Sta. Catarina, Brazil 28°18S 49°56W 335 B6
São Joaquim △ Brazil 28°12S 49°37W 335 B6

São Joaquim da Barra *Brazil* 20°35S 47°53W **333** F2
São Jorge *Azores* 38°38N 28°3W **153** d1
São Jorge, Canal de *Azores* 38°30N 28°0W **153** d1
São Jorge, Castelo de *Portugal* 38°42N 9°8W **126** A2
São Jorge, Pta. de *Azores* 38°42N 27°3W **153** d1
São Jorge, Pta. de *Madeira* 32°50N 16°53W **153** c
São José *Brazil* 27°38S 48°39W **335** B5
São José, B. de *Brazil* 2°38S 44°4W **332** B3
São José da Lagoa = Nova Era *Brazil* 19°45S 43°3W **333** E3
São José da Laje *Brazil* 9°1S 36°3W **332** C4
São José de Mipibu *Brazil* 6°5S 35°15W **332** C4
São José de Ribamar *Brazil* 2°33S 44°3W **332** B3
São José de Tocantins = Niquelândia *Brazil* 14°33S 48°23W **333** D2
São José do Norte *Brazil* 32°1S 52°3W **335** C5
São José do Peixe *Brazil* 7°24S 42°34W **332** C3
São José do Rio Preto *Brazil* 20°50S 49°20W **335** A6
São José dos Campos *Brazil* 23°7S 45°52W **335** A6
São José dos Cocais = Nossa Senhora do Livramento *Brazil* 15°48S 56°22W **331** D6
São José dos Matões = Parnarama *Brazil* 5°31S 43°6W **332** C3
São Juliao do Tojal *Portugal* 38°49N 9°8W **126** A2
São Leopoldo *Brazil* 29°50S 51°10W **335** B5
São Lourenço *Brazil* 22°7S 45°3W **333** F2
São Lourenço → *Brazil* 17°53S 57°27W **331** D6
São Lourenço, Pantanal do *Brazil* 17°30S 56°20W **331** D6
São Lourenço, Pta. de *Madeira* 32°44N 16°39W **153** c
São Lourenço do Sul *Brazil* 31°22S 51°58W **335** C5
São Luís *Brazil* 2°39S 44°15W **332** B3
São Luís do Curu *Brazil* 3°40S 39°14W **332** B4
São Luís do Tapajós *Brazil* 4°25S 56°12W **329** D6
São Luís Gonzaga = Ipixuna *Brazil* 7°0S 71°40W **330** B3
São Luís Gonzaga *Brazil* 28°25S 55°0W **335** B5
São Marcos → *Brazil* 18°15S 47°37W **333** E2
São Marcos, B. de *Brazil* 2°0S 44°0W **332** B3
São Martinho da Cortiça *Portugal* 40°18N 8°8W **194** E2
São Mateus *Azores* 38°26N 28°27W **153** d1
São Mateus *Brazil* 18°44S 39°50W **333** E4
São Mateus → *Brazil* 18°35S 39°44W **333** E4
São Mateus do Sul *Brazil* 25°52S 50°23W **335** B5
São Miguel *Azores* 37°47N 25°30W **153** d3
São Miguel do Araguaia *Brazil* 13°19S 50°13W **333** D1
São Miguel do Guamá *Brazil* 1°37S 47°29W **332** B2
São Miguel do Oeste *Brazil* 26°45S 53°34W **335** B5
São Miguel dos Campos *Brazil* 9°47S 36°5W **332** C4
São Nicolau *C. Verde Is.* 16°20N 24°20W **153** j
São Nicolau → *Angola* 14°16S 12°22E **265** E2
São Nicolau → *Brazil* 5°45S 42°2W **332** C3
São Paulo *Atl. Oc.* 0°56N 29°22W **152** F9
São Paulo *Brazil* 23°32S 46°38W **137** B2
São Paulo □ *Brazil* 22°0S 49°0W **335** A6
São Paulo Congonhas ✈ **(CGH)** *Brazil* 23°38S 46°39W **137** B2
São Paulo de Olivença *Brazil* 3°27S 68°48W **328** D4
São Pedro *Atl. Oc.* 0°56N 29°22W **152** F9
São Pedro do Sul *Portugal* 40°46N 8°4W **194** E2
São Rafael *Brazil* 5°47S 36°55W **332** C4
São Raimundo das Mangabeiras *Brazil* 7°1S 45°29W **332** C2
São Raimundo Nonato *Brazil* 9°1S 42°42W **332** C3
São Romão *Brazil* 16°22S 45°4W **333** E2
São Roque *Madeira* 32°46N 16°48W **153** c
São Roque, C. de *Brazil* 5°30S 35°16W **332** C4
São Roque do Pico *Azores* 38°31N 28°19W **153** d1
São Salvador do Congo = Mbanza Congo *Angola* 6°18S 14°16E **265** D2
São Sebastião *Azores* 38°39N 27°6W **153** d1
São Sebastião, I. de *Brazil* 23°50S 45°18W **335** A6
São Sebastião do Paraíso *Brazil* 20°54S 46°59W **335** A6
São Simão *Brazil* 18°56S 50°30W **333** E1
São Teotónio *Portugal* 37°30N 8°42W **195** H2
São Tiago *C. Verde Is.* 15°0N 23°40W **153** j
São Tomé *Brazil* 5°58S 36°4W **332** C4
São Tomé *São Tomé & Príncipe* 0°10N 6°39E **265** a
São Tomé, C. de *Brazil* 22°0S 40°59W **333** F3
São Tomé, Pico de *São Tomé & Príncipe* 0°16N 6°33E **265** a
São Tomé & Príncipe ■ *Africa* 0°12N 6°39E **265** a
São Vicente = Araguatins *Brazil* 5°38S 48°7W **332** C2
São Vicente *Brazil* 23°57S 46°23W **335** A6
São Vicente *C. Verde Is.* 17°0N 25°0W **153** j
São Vicente *Madeira* 32°48N 17°3W **153** c
São Vicente, C. de *Portugal* 37°0N 9°0W **195** H1
Saona, I. *Dom. Rep.* 18°10N 68°40W **321** C6
Saône → *France* 45°44N 4°50E **173** G11
Saône-et-Loire □ *France* 46°30N 4°50E **173** F11
Saonek *Indonesia* 0°22S 130°55E **231** E8
Saoura, O. → *Algeria* 29°0N 0°55W **261** C4
Sapa *India* 22°30N 88°15E **124** B1
Sapam, Ao *Thailand* 8°0N 98°26E **237** a
Sapanca *Turkey* 40°41N 30°16E **212** B4
Sapanjang *Indonesia* 7°10S 115°50E **235** D5
Sapão → *Brazil* 11°1S 45°32W **332** D2
Saparua *Indonesia* 3°33S 128°40E **231** E7
Sapateiro, Cor. do → *Brazil* 23°35S 46°41W **137** B1
Sapé *Brazil* 7°6S 35°13W **332** C4
Sape *Indonesia* 8°34S 118°59E **235** D5
Sape, Teluk *Indonesia* 8°32S 119°4E **235** D5
Sapele *Nigeria* 5°50N 5°40E **263** D6
Sapelo I. *U.S.A.* 31°25N 81°12W **316** D8
Sapelo Sound *U.S.A.* 31°30N 81°10W **316** D8
Sapes *Greece* 41°2N 25°43E **203** E9
Şaphane *Turkey* 39°1N 29°13E **205** B11
Sapi ⌓ *Zimbabwe* 15°48S 29°42E **269** F2
Sapienza *Greece* 36°45N 21°43E **204** E3
Sapindji *Dem. Rep. of the Congo* 9°39S 23°12E **265** D4
Sapo △ *Liberia* 5°15N 8°30W **262** D3
Sapone *Burkina Faso* 12°3N 1°35W **263** C4
Saposoa *Peru* 6°55S 76°45W **330** B2
Sapotskina *Belarus* 53°49N 23°40E **184** E10
Sapouy *Burkina Faso* 11°34N 1°44W **263** C4
Sapozhok *Russia* 53°59N 40°41E **190** D5
Sapphire *Australia* 23°28S 147°43E **280** C4
Sappho *U.S.A.* 48°4N 124°16W **306** B2
Sapporo *Japan* 43°0N 141°21E **220** C10
Sapri *Italy* 40°4N 15°38E **201** B8
Sapu *Angola* 12°28S 19°26E **265** E3
Sapudi *Indonesia* 7°6S 114°20E **235** D4
Sapulpa *U.S.A.* 35°59N 96°5W **314** D6
Sapulut *Malaysia* 4°42N 116°28E **235** B5
Saqqez *Iran* 36°15N 46°20E **213** D12
Sar Dasht *Āzarbāyjān-e Gharbī, Iran* 36°9N 45°28E **213** D11
Sar Dasht *Khuzestān, Iran* 32°32N 48°52E **247** C6
Sar-e Pol *Afghan.* 36°10N 66°0E **240** A2
Sar-e Pol □ *Afghan.* 36°20N 65°50E **240** A2
Sar Gachīneh = Yāsūj *Iran* 30°31N 51°31E **247** D6
Sar Passage *Palau* 7°12N 134°22E **288** c
Sar Planina *Macedonia* 42°0N 21°0E **202** E4
Sara *Burkina Faso* 11°40N 3°53W **262** C4
Sara *Niger* 20°46N 12°35E **259** D2
Sara *Phil.* 11°16N 123°1E **233** F4
Šara △ *Serbia* 42°12N 21°0E **202** D5
Sara Buri = Saraburi *Thailand* 14°30N 100°55E **236** E3
Sarāb *Iran* 37°55N 47°40E **213** D12
Sarābādī *Iraq* 33°1N 44°48E **246** C5
Sarabît el Khâdim *Egypt* 29°2N 33°25E **251** J4
Sarābleh *Iran* 33°44N 46°34E **213** F12
Saraburi *Thailand* 14°30N 100°55E **236** E3
Saradiya *India* 21°34N 70°2E **242** J4
Saraféré *Mali* 15°50N 3°40W **262** B4
Saragossa = Zaragoza *Spain* 41°39N 0°53W **196** D4
Saraguro *Ecuador* 3°35S 79°16W **328** D2
Sarahs *Turkmenistan* 36°32N 61°13E **247** B9
Sarai Naurang *Pakistan* 32°50N 70°47E **242** C4
Saraikela *India* 22°42N 85°56E **243** H11
Saraipali *India* 21°20N 82°59E **244** D6
Saraiu *Romania* 44°43N 28°10E **183** F13
Sarajevo *Bos.-H.* 43°52N 18°26E **182** G3
Sarakhs = Sarahs *Turkmenistan* 36°32N 61°13E **247** B9
Sarakhs *Iran* 36°32N 61°9E **216** E6
Saramacca → *Suriname* 5°50N 55°55W **329** B6
Saramati *Burma* 25°44N 95°2E **241** C5
Saran, Gunung *Indonesia* 0°30S 111°25E **235** C4
Saranac *U.S.A.* 42°56N 85°13W **311** B11
Saranac Lake *U.S.A.* 44°20N 74°10W **313** B10
Saranac Lakes *U.S.A.* 44°20N 74°28W **313** B10
Saranda *Tanzania* 5°45S 34°59E **268** D3
Sarandë *Albania* 39°52N 19°55E **206** B9
Sarandi *Argentina* 34°40S 58°20W **117** C2
Sarandí del Yí *Uruguay* 33°18S 55°38W **335** C4
Sarandí Grande *Uruguay* 33°44S 56°20W **334** C4
Sarangani □ *Phil.* 5°45N 125°20E **233** J5
Sarangani B. *Phil.* 6°0N 125°13E **233** J5
Sarangani I. *Phil.* 5°26N 125°28E **233** J5
Sarangani Is. *Phil.* 5°25N 125°25E **233** J5
Sarangarh *India* 21°30N 83°5E **244** D6
Saranovo = Septemvri *Bulgaria* 42°13N 24°6E **203** D8
Saransk *Russia* 54°10N 45°10E **190** C7
Sarapul *Russia* 56°28N 53°48E **186** C9
Sarāqib *Syria* 35°52N 36°47E **250** C7
Sarar Plain = Bannaanka Saraar *Somali Rep.* 9°25N 46°17E **267** C6
Sarasota *U.S.A.* 27°20N 82°32W **317** H7
Saraswati → *India* 22°46N 88°15E **124** A1
Sarata *Ukraine* 46°1N 29°40E **183** D14
Sarata → *Ukraine* 45°51N 29°41E **183** E14
Saratoga *Calif., U.S.A.* 37°16N 122°2W **306** H4
Saratoga *Wyo., U.S.A.* 41°27N 106°49W **304** F10
Saratoga ⌓ *U.S.A.* 43°0N 73°38W **313** D11
Saratoga L. *U.S.A.* 43°1N 73°44W **313** C11
Saratoga Springs *U.S.A.* 43°5N 73°47W **313** C11
Saratok *Malaysia* 1°55N 111°17E **235** B4
Saratov *Russia* 51°30N 46°2E **190** E7
Saratov □ *Russia* 51°50N 46°20E **190** E8
Sarāvān *Iran* 27°25N 62°15E **247** E9
Saravane *Laos* 15°43N 106°25E **236** E6
Sarawak □ *Malaysia* 2°0N 113°0E **235** B4
Saray *Tekirdağ, Turkey* 41°26N 27°55E **203** E11
Saray *Van, Turkey* 38°38N 44°9E **213** C11
Saraya *Senegal* 12°50N 11°45W **262** C2
Saraycık *Turkey* 39°1N 29°49E **205** B11
Sarayköy *Turkey* 37°55N 28°54E **205** D10
Saraylar *Turkey* 40°39N 27°40E **203** F11
Sarayönü *Turkey* 38°16N 32°24E **212** C5
Sarbāz *Iran* 26°38N 61°19E **247** E9
Sarbīsheh *Iran* 32°30N 59°40E **247** C8
Sárbogárd *Hungary* 46°50N 18°40E **182** D3
Sarca → *Italy* 45°52N 10°52E **198** C7
Sarcelles *France* 49°1N 2°23E **173** D9
Sarda → *India* 27°21N 81°23E **243** F9
Sardalas *Libya* 25°50N 10°34E **258** C2
Sardar Sarovar Dam *India* 21°50N 73°50E **244** D1
Sardarshahr *India* 28°30N 74°29E **242** E6
Sardegna □ *Italy* 40°0N 9°0E **200** B1
Sardhana *India* 29°9N 77°39E **242** E7
Sardina, Pta. *Canary Is.* 28°9N 15°44W **153** e1
Sardinata *Colombia* 8°5N 72°48W **328** B3
Sardinia = Sardegna □ *Italy* 40°0N 9°0E **200** B1
Sardinia *U.S.A.* 39°0N 83°49W **311** F13
Sardis *Turkey* 38°28N 27°58E **205** C10
Sardis *Ga., U.S.A.* 32°58N 81°46W **316** C8
Sārdūīyeh = Dar Mazār *Iran* 29°14N 57°20E **247** D8
Sarecky potok → *Czech Rep.* 50°7N 14°23E **135** B2
Saren *Indonesia* 8°26S 115°34E **231** J18
S'Arenal *Spain* 39°30N 2°45E **206** B3
Sarentino *Italy* 46°38N 11°21E **199** B8
Saréyamou *Mali* 16°7N 3°10W **262** B4
Sargasso Sea *Atl. Oc.* 27°0N 72°0W **292** G13
Sargent *U.S.A.* 33°26N 84°52W **316** B5
Sargodha *Pakistan* 32°10N 72°40E **242** C5
Sarh *Chad* 9°5N 18°23E **259** G3
Sarhala *Ivory C.* 8°22N 6°8W **262** D3
Sarhro, Jebel *Morocco* 31°6N 5°0W **260** B4
Sārī *Iran* 36°30N 53°4E **247** B7
Sari d'Orcino *France* 42°3N 8°49E **175** F12
Saria *Greece* 35°54N 27°17E **205** F9
Saria *India* 21°38N 83°22E **243** J10
Sariab *Pakistan* 30°6N 66°59E **242** D2
Sarıbeyler *Turkey* 39°24N 27°35E **205** B9
Saricumbe *Angola* 12°12S 19°46E **265** E3
Sarigan *N. Marianas* 16°43N 145°47E **302** a
Sarıgöl *Turkey* 38°14N 28°41E **212** C3
Sarıkamiş *Turkey* 40°22N 42°35E **213** B10
Sarıkaya *Turkey* 39°29N 35°22E **212** C6
Sarikei *Malaysia* 2°8N 111°30E **235** B4
Sarıköy *Turkey* 40°12N 27°37E **203** F11
Sarila *India* 25°46N 79°41E **243** G8
Sarimbun *Singapore* 1°24N 103°40E **138** A2
Sarimbun Res. *Singapore* 1°25N 103°41E **138** A2
Sarina *Australia* 21°22S 149°13E **280** C4
Sariñena *Spain* 41°47N 0°10W **196** D4
Sarinleey *Somali Rep.* 2°22N 42°17E **267** D5
Sarıoğlan *Turkey* 39°5N 35°59E **212** C6
Sariri *Papua N. G.* 9°11S 148°35E **286** E5
Sarita *U.S.A.* 27°13N 97°47W **314** H6
Sarıveliler *Turkey* 36°41N 32°37E **250** B3
Sariwŏn *N. Korea* 38°31N 125°46E **224** C2
Sariyar Barajı *Turkey* 40°2N 31°33E **212** B4
Sarıyer *Turkey* 41°10N 29°3E **122** A2
Sarız *Turkey* 38°28N 36°30E **212** C7
Sarju → *India* 27°21N 81°23E **243** F9
Sark *U.K.* 49°25N 2°22W **169** H5
Sarkad *Hungary* 46°47N 21°23E **182** D6
Sarkari Tala *India* 27°39N 70°52E **242** F4
Şarkışla *Turkey* 39°21N 36°25E **212** C7
Şarköy *Turkey* 40°36N 27°6E **203** F11
Sarlat-la-Canéda *France* 44°54N 1°13E **174** D5
Sărmăşag *Romania* 47°21N 22°50E **182** C7
Sărmaşu *Romania* 46°45N 24°13E **183** D9
Sarmi *Indonesia* 1°49S 138°44E **231** E9
Sarmiento *Argentina* 45°35S 69°5W **336** C3
Sarmizegetusa *Romania* 45°31N 22°47E **182** E7
Särna *Sweden* 61°41N 13°8E **162** C7
Sarnano *Italy* 43°2N 13°18E **199** E10
Sarnen *Switz.* 46°53N 8°13E **179** J4
Sarnia *Canada* 42°58N 82°23W **312** D2
Sarno *Italy* 40°49N 14°37E **201** B7
Sarnthein = Sarentino *Italy* 46°38N 11°21E **199** B8
Särö *Sweden* 57°31N 11°57E **163** G5
Sarolangun *Indonesia* 2°19S 102°42E **234** C2
Saronikos Kolpos *Greece* 37°45N 23°45E **204** D5
Saronno *Italy* 45°38N 9°2E **198** C6
Saros Körfezi *Turkey* 40°30N 26°15E **203** F10
Sárospatak *Hungary* 48°18N 21°33E **182** B6
Sarowbī *Afghan.* 34°36N 69°44E **240** B3
Sarpsborg *Norway* 59°16N 11°7E **164** E8
Sarqan *Kazakhstan* 45°24N 79°55E **217** C9
Sarracín *Spain* 42°15N 3°45W **194** C7
Sarralbe *France* 49°0N 7°1E **173** D14
Sarrat *Phil.* 18°9N 120°39E **232** B3
Sarre = Saar → *Europe* 49°41N 6°32E **170** E6
Sarre *Italy* 45°40N 7°15E **198** C4
Sarre-Union *France* 48°57N 7°4E **173** D14
Sarrebourg *France* 48°43N 7°3E **173** D14
Sarreguemines *France* 49°5N 7°4E **173** C14
Sarriá *Barcelona, Spain* 41°22N 2°8E **114** A1
Sarria *Galicia, Spain* 42°49N 7°29W **194** C3
Sarrión *Spain* 40°9N 0°49W **196** E4
Sarro *Mali* 13°40N 5°15W **262** C3
Sarsing *Iraq* 37°2N 43°20E **213** D10
Sarstedt *Germany* 52°14N 9°52E **178** C5
Sarsuna *India* 22°28N 88°17E **124** C1
Sartène *France* 41°38N 8°58E **175** G12
Sarthe □ *France* 48°10N 0°10E **172** D7
Sarthe → *France* 47°33N 0°31W **172** E6
Sartilly *France* 48°45N 1°28W **172** D5
Sartrouville *France* 48°56N 2°10E **134** A2
Saruhanlı *Turkey* 38°44N 27°36E **205** C9
Sărulești *Romania* 44°25N 26°39E **183** F11
Saruna → *Pakistan* 26°31N 67°7E **242** F2
Sarupeta *India* 26°30N 91°5E **241** B3
Särur *Azerbaijan* 39°22N 45°5E **213** C11
Saruwaged Ra. *Papua N. G.* 6°13S 146°45E **286** D4
Sárvár *Hungary* 47°15N 16°56E **182** C1
Sarvar *India* 26°4N 75°0E **242** F6
Sarvestān *Iran* 29°20N 53°10E **247** D7
Särvfjället *Sweden* 62°42N 13°30E **162** B7
Sárviz → *Hungary* 46°24N 18°41E **182** D3
Sary-Tash *Kyrgyzstan* 39°44N 73°15E **217** E8
Sarych, Mys *Ukraine* 44°25N 33°45E **189** K7
Saryesik-Atyraū Qumy *Kazakhstan* 45°30N 76°0E **217** C9
Sarykamyshskoye, Ozero = Saryqamysh Köli *Turkmenistan* 41°56N 57°25E **216** D5
Sarykemer *Kazakhstan* 43°0N 71°30E **217** D8
Sarykenggir → *Kazakhstan* 48°22N 67°59E **217** C7
Saryköl *Kazakhstan* 53°20N 65°12E **216** B7
Sarykolskiy Khrebet *Tajikistan* 38°30N 74°30E **217** E8
Saryözek *Kazakhstan* 44°22N 77°59E **217** D9
Saryqamysh Köli *Turkmenistan* 41°56N 57°25E **216** D5
Saryshaghan *Kazakhstan* 46°12N 73°38E **217** C8
Sarysū → *Kazakhstan* 45°12N 66°36E **217** C7
Sarzana *Italy* 44°7N 9°58E **198** D6
Sarzeau *France* 47°31N 2°48W **172** E4
Sasabeneh *Ethiopia* 7°59N 44°43E **267** C5
Sasad *Hungary* 47°28N 19°0E **117** B2
Sasamungga *Solomon Is.* 7°0S 156°50E **287** L9
Sasan Gir *India* 21°10N 70°36E **242** J4
Sasaram *India* 24°57N 84°5E **243** G11
Sasari, Mt. *Solomon Is.* 8°10S 159°30E **287** M10
Sasayama *Japan* 35°4N 135°13E **223** B7
Sasebo *Japan* 33°10N 129°43E **222** D1
Saser Kangri *India* 34°50N 77°50E **243** B7
Sashalom *Hungary* 47°30N 19°10E **117** A3
Saska *Poland* 52°14N 21°3E **142** B2
Saskatchewan □ *Canada* 54°40N 106°0W **297** C7
Saskatchewan → *Canada* 53°37N 100°40W **297** C8
Saskatoon *Canada* 52°10N 106°38W **297** C7
Saskylakh *Russia* 71°55N 114°1E **215** B12
Sasolburg *S. Africa* 26°46S 27°49E **271** C4
Sason *Turkey* 38°19N 41°24E **213** C9
Sasovo *Russia* 54°25N 41°55E **190** C5
Sassandra *Ivory C.* 4°55N 6°8W **262** E3
Sassandra → *Ivory C.* 4°58N 6°5W **262** E3
Sássari *Italy* 40°43N 8°34E **200** B1
Sassie *Australia* 10°2S 142°51E **280** a
Sassnitz *Germany* 54°29N 13°39E **178** A9
Sasso Marconi *Italy* 44°24N 11°15E **199** D8
Sassocorvaro *Italy* 43°47N 12°30E **199** E9
Sassoferrato *Italy* 43°26N 12°51E **199** E9
Sassuolo *Italy* 44°33N 10°47E **198** D7
Sástago *Spain* 41°19N 0°21W **196** D4
Sastamala *Finland* 61°20N 22°54E **188** B2
Sastown *Liberia* 4°45N 8°27W **262** E3
Sasvad *India* 18°20N 74°2E **244** E2
Sasyk, Ozero *Ukraine* 45°45N 29°40E **183** E14
Sasyqköl *Kazakhstan* 46°35N 81°0E **217** C10
Sata-Misaki *Japan* 31°0N 130°40E **222** F2
Satadougou *Mali* 12°25N 11°25W **262** C2
Satakunda = Satakunta *Finland* 61°45N 23°0E **160** F20
Satakunta *Finland* 61°45N 23°0E **160** F20
Satalice *Czech Rep.* 50°7N 14°34E **135** B3
Satama-Soukoura *Ivory C.* 7°55N 4°27W **262** D4
Satara *India* 17°44N 73°58E **244** F1
Satara *S. Africa* 24°29S 31°47E **271** B5
Sätbaev *Kazakhstan* 48°10N 67°31E **217** C7
Satbarwa *India* 23°55N 84°16E **243** H11
Satellite Beach *U.S.A.* 28°10N 80°36W **317** G9
Säter *Sweden* 60°21N 15°45E **162** D9
Satevó *Mexico* 27°57N 106°7W **318** B3
Satgachi *India* 22°37N 88°25E **124** B2
Satilla → *U.S.A.* 30°59N 81°29W **316** E8
Satipo *Peru* 11°15S 74°25W **330** C3
Satka *Russia* 55°3N 59°1E **186** C10
Satkania *Bangla.* 22°4N 92°3E **241** D4
Satkhira *Bangla.* 22°43N 89°8E **241** D2
Satmala Hills *Andhra Pradesh, India* 19°45N 78°45E **244** E4
Satmala Hills *Maharashtra, India* 20°15N 74°40E **244** D2
Satna *India* 24°35N 80°50E **243** G9
Šator *Bos.-H.* 44°11N 16°37E **199** D13
Sátoraljaújhely *Hungary* 48°25N 21°41E **182** B6
Satpukur *India* 22°37N 88°24E **124** B2
Satpura △ *India* 22°40N 78°15E **242** H8
Satpura Ra. *India* 21°25N 76°10E **244** D3
Sätra *Sweden* 59°17N 17°54E **139** B1
Satrup *Germany* 54°41N 9°36E **178** A5
Satsuma-Hantō *Japan* 31°25N 130°25E **222** F2
Satsuna-Shotō *Japan* 30°0N 130°0E **221** K5
Sattahip *Thailand* 12°41N 100°54E **236** F3
Sattenapalle *India* 16°25N 80°6E **245** F5
Sattru Phai *Bangkok, Thailand* **113** b2
Satu Mare *Romania* 47°46N 22°55E **182** C7
Satu Mare □ *Romania* 47°45N 23°0E **182** C8
Satui *Indonesia* 3°50S 115°27E **235** C5
Satun *Thailand* 6°43N 100°2E **237** J3
Satupa'itea *Samoa* 13°45S 172°18W **287** V19
Saturnina → *Brazil* 12°15S 58°10W **331** C6
Sauce = Juan L. Lacaze *Uruguay* 34°26S 57°25W **334** C4
Sauce *Argentina* 30°5S 58°46W **334** C4
Sauceda *Mexico* 25°46N 101°19W **318** B4
Saucillo *Mexico* 28°1N 105°17W **318** B3
Sauda *Norway* 59°40N 6°20E **164** E3
Saudasjøen *Norway* 59°38N 6°17E **164** E3
Saúde *Bahia, Brazil* 10°56S 40°24W **332** D3
Saúde *São Paulo, Brazil* 23°36S 46°37W **137** B2
Sauðarkrókur *Iceland* 65°45N 19°40W **155** B7
Saudi Arabia ■ *Asia* 26°0N 44°0E **246** B3
Sauerland *Germany* 51°12N 7°59E **176** C4
Saugatuck *U.S.A.* 42°40N 86°12W **311** B10
Saugeen → *Canada* 44°30N 81°22W **312** B3
Saugerties *U.S.A.* 42°5N 73°57W **313** D11
Saugues *France* 44°58N 3°32E **174** D7
Saugus *Calif., U.S.A.* 34°25N 118°32W **307** L8
Saugus *Mass., U.S.A.* 42°28N 71°0W **116** A2
Saugus → *U.S.A.* 42°27N 70°58W **116** A2
Saujbulagh = Mahābād *Iran* 36°50N 45°45E **213** D11
Saujon *France* 45°41N 0°55W **174** C3
Sauk Centre *U.S.A.* 45°44N 94°57W **308** C6
Sauk City *U.S.A.* 43°17N 89°43W **310** A7
Sauk Rapids *U.S.A.* 45°35N 94°10W **308** C6
Saül *Fr. Guiana* 3°37N 53°12W **329** C7
Sauland *Norway* 59°37N 8°56E **164** E5
Saulgau *Germany* 48°1N 9°29E **179** G5
Saulieu *France* 47°17N 4°14E **173** E11
Sault *France* 44°6N 5°24E **175** D9
Sault-au-Récollet *Canada* 45°35N 73°39W **130** A2
Sault Ste. Marie *Ont., Canada* 46°30N 84°20W **298** C3
Sault Ste. Marie *Mich., U.S.A.* 46°30N 84°21W **309** B11
Saūmalkol *Kazakhstan* 53°17N 68°6E **217** B7
Saumlaki *Indonesia* 7°55S 131°20E **231** F8
Saumur *France* 47°15N 0°5W **172** E6
Saundatti *India* 15°47N 75°7E **245** G2
Saunders, C. *N.Z.* 45°53S 170°45E **285** F5
Saunders I. *Antarctica* 57°48S 26°28W **151** B1
Saunders Pt. *Australia* 27°52S 125°38E **279** E4
Saunemin *U.S.A.* 40°54N 88°24W **311** D8
Saupite *Angola* 13°54S 17°43E **265** E3
Saurbær *Borgarfjarðarsýsla, Iceland* 64°24N 21°35W **155** C5
Saurbær *Eyjafjarðarsýsla, Iceland* 65°27N 18°13W **155** B8
Sauri *Nigeria* 11°42N 6°44E **263** C6
Saurimo *Angola* 9°40S 20°12E **265** D4
Sausalito *U.S.A.* 37°51N 122°29W **136** A2
Sautatá *Colombia* 7°50N 77°4W **328** B2
Sauteurs *Grenada* 12°14N 61°38W **323** q
Sauveterre-de-Béarn *France* 43°24N 0°57W **174** E3
Sauzé-Vaussais *France* 46°8N 0°8E **174** B4
Savá *Honduras* 15°32N 86°15W **320** C2
Sava *Italy* 40°24N 17°33E **201** B10
Sava → *Serbia* 44°50N 20°26E **182** F5
Savage *U.S.A.* 47°27N 104°21W **304** C11
Savage I. = Niue ⊠ *Pac. Oc.* 19°2S 169°54W **289** g
Savage River *Australia* 41°31S 145°14E **281** G4
Savai'i *Samoa* 13°28S 172°24W **287** V19
Savalou *Benin* 7°57N 1°58E **263** D5
Savane *Mozam.* 19°37S 35°8E **269** F4
Savaneta *Aruba* 12°27N 69°56W **322** f
Savanna *U.S.A.* 42°5N 90°8W **310** B6
Savanna-la-Mar *Jamaica* 18°10N 78°10W **320** a
Savannah *Ga., U.S.A.* 32°5N 81°6W **316** C8
Savannah *Mo., U.S.A.* 39°56N 94°50W **310** E2
Savannah *Tenn., U.S.A.* 35°14N 88°15W **315** D10
Savannah → *U.S.A.* 32°2N 80°53W **316** C9
Savannah Beach = Tybee Island *U.S.A.* 32°1N 80°51W **316** C9
Savannakhet *Laos* 16°30N 104°49E **236** D5
Savanne, Piton *Mauritius* 20°26S 57°29E **272** e
Savannes B. *St. Lucia* 13°45N 60°56W **323** m
Savant L. *Canada* 50°16N 90°44W **298** B1
Savant Lake *Canada* 50°14N 90°40W **298** B1
Savantvadi *India* 15°55N 73°54E **245** G1
Savanur *India* 14°59N 75°21E **245** G2
Savarkundla = Kundla *India* 21°21N 71°25E **242** J4
Săvârşin *Romania* 46°1N 22°14E **182** D7
Savaştepe *Turkey* 39°22N 27°42E **205** B9
Savda *India* 21°9N 75°56E **244** D2
Savé *Benin* 8°2N 2°29E **263** D5
Save → *Haute-Garonne, France* 43°47N 1°17E **174** E5
Save → *Mozam.* 21°16S 34°0E **271** B5
Sāveh *Iran* 35°2N 50°20E **247** C6
Savelugu *Ghana* 9°38N 0°54W **263** D4
Savenay *France* 47°20N 1°55W **172** E5
Săveni *Romania* 47°57N 26°52E **183** C11
Saverdun *France* 43°14N 1°34E **174** E5
Saverne *France* 48°43N 7°20E **173** D14
Savigliano *Italy* 44°38N 7°40E **198** D4
Savigny-sur-Braye *France* 47°53N 0°49E **172** E7
Sávio → *Italy* 44°19N 12°20E **199** D9
Šavnik *Montenegro* 42°59N 19°10E **202** D3
Savo *Finland* 62°45N 27°30E **160** E22
Savo *Solomon Is.* 9°8S 159°48E **287** M10
Savoie □ *France* 45°26N 6°25E **175** C10
Savolax = Savo *Finland* 62°45N 27°30E **160** E22
Savona *Italy* 44°17N 8°30E **198** D5
Savona *N.Y., U.S.A.* 42°17N 77°13W **312** D7
Savonet *Curaçao* 12°21N 69°7W **322** g
Savonlinna *Finland* 61°52N 28°53E **188** B5
Savoonga *U.S.A.* 63°42N 170°29W **303** E5
Savoy = Savoie □ *France* 45°26N 6°25E **175** C10
Şavşat *Turkey* 41°15N 42°20E **213** B10
Sävsjö *Sweden* 57°20N 14°40E **163** G8
Savur *Turkey* 37°34N 40°53E **246** B4
Savusavu *Fiji* 16°34S 179°15E **287** A2
Savusavu B. *Fiji* 16°45S 179°15E **287** A2
Sawah Besar *Indonesia* 6°8S 106°49E **122** A1
Sawahlunto *Indonesia* 0°40S 100°52E **234** C2
Sawai *Indonesia* 3°0S 129°5E **231** E7
Sawai Madhopur *India* 26°0N 76°25E **242** G7
Sawaleke *Fiji* 17°59S 179°18E **287** A2
Sawang Daen Din *Thailand* 17°28N 103°28E **236** D4
Sawankhalok *Thailand* 17°19N 99°50E **236** D2
Sawara *Japan* 35°55N 140°30E **223** B12
Sawatch Range *U.S.A.* 39°0N 106°30W **304** G10
Sawdā', Jabal as *Libya* 28°51N 15°12E **258** C3
Sawel Mt. *U.K.* 54°50N 7°2W **166** B4
Sawfajjin, W. → *Libya* 31°41N 14°44E **258** B2
Sawi *Thailand* 10°14N 99°5E **237** G2
Sawla *Ghana* 9°17N 2°25W **262** D4
Sawmills *Zimbabwe* 19°30S 28°2E **269** F2
Şawqirah *Oman* 18°7N 56°32E **249** C7
Şawqirah, Ghubbat *Oman* 18°35N 57°0E **249** C7
Sawtell *Australia* 30°19S 153°6E **283** A10
Sawtelle *U.S.A.* 34°2N 118°27W **126** B2
Sawtooth ⌓ *U.S.A.* 44°0N 114°50W **304** D6
Sawtooth Range *U.S.A.* 44°3N 114°58W **304** D6
Sawu *Indonesia* 10°35S 121°50E **231** F6
Sawu Sea *Indonesia* 9°30S 121°50E **231** F6
Saxby → *Australia* 18°25S 140°53E **280** B3
Saxmundham *U.K.* 52°13N 1°30E **169** E9
Saxony = Sachsen □ *Germany* 50°55N 13°10E **178** E9
Saxony, Lower = Niedersachsen □ *Germany* 52°50N 9°0E **178** C4
Saxton *U.S.A.* 40°13N 78°15W **312** F6
Say *Mali* 13°50N 4°57W **262** C4
Say *Niger* 13°8N 2°22E **263** C5
Saya *Nigeria* 9°30N 3°18E **263** D5
Sayabec *Canada* 48°35N 67°41W **299** C6
Sayaboury *Laos* 19°15N 101°45E **236** C3
Sayán *Peru* 11°8S 77°12W **330** C2
Sayan, Vostochnyy *Russia* 54°0N 96°0E **215** D10
Sayan, Zapadnyy *Russia* 52°30N 94°0E **217** B12
Sayanogorsk *Russia* 53°5N 91°23E **215** D10
Saydā *Lebanon* 33°35N 35°25E **250** E6
Sayghān *Afghan.* 35°10N 67°55E **240** B2
Sayhandulaan = Öldziyt *Mongolia* 44°40N 109°1E **226** B5
Sayhūt *Yemen* 15°12N 51°10E **249** D5
Saykhin *Kazakhstan* 48°50N 46°47E **191** F8
Saylac *Somali Rep.* 11°21N 43°30E **267** B5
Saylorville L. *U.S.A.* 41°48N 93°46W **310** C3
Saynshand = Buyant-Uhaa *Mongolia* 44°55N 110°11E **226** B6
Sayō *Japan* 34°59N 134°22E **222** C6
Sayre *Okla., U.S.A.* 35°18N 99°38W **314** D5
Sayre *Pa., U.S.A.* 41°59N 76°32W **313** E8
Sayreville *U.S.A.* 40°28N 74°22W **313** F10
Sayula *Mexico* 19°52N 103°36W **318** D4
Sayward *Canada* 50°21N 125°55W **296** C3
Saywūn *Yemen* 15°56N 48°47E **249** D5
Saza *Japan* 33°14N 129°39E **222** D1
Sazanit *Albania* 40°30N 19°20E **202** F3
Sázava → *Czech Rep.* 49°53N 14°24E **180** B7
Sazin *Pakistan* 35°35N 73°30E **243** B5
Sazlika → *Bulgaria* 41°59N 25°50E **203** E9
Sbeïtla *Tunisia* 35°12N 9°7E **258** A1
Scaër *France* 48°2N 3°42W **172** D3
Scafell Pike *U.K.* 54°27N 3°14W **168** C4
Scald Law *U.K.* 55°50N 3°17W **121** B2
Scalea *Italy* 39°49N 15°47E **201** C8
Scalloway *U.K.* 60°9N 1°17W **167** A7
Scalpay *U.K.* 57°18N 6°0W **167** D3
Scammon Bay *U.S.A.* 61°51N 165°35W **303** F6
Scandia *Canada* 50°20N 112°2W **296** C6
Scandiano *Italy* 44°36N 10°43E **198** D7
Scandicci *Italy* 43°45N 11°11E **199** E8
Scandinavia *Europe* 64°0N 12°0E **160** E15
Scansano *Italy* 42°41N 11°20E **199** F8
Scapa Flow *U.K.* 58°53N 3°3W **167** C5
Scappoose *U.S.A.* 45°45N 122°53W **306** E4
Scarámia, Capo *Italy* 36°47N 14°29E **201** F7
Scarba *U.K.* 56°11N 5°43W **167** E3
Scarborough *Ont., Canada* 43°44N 79°14W **141** A3
Scarborough *Trin. & Tob.* 11°11N 60°42W **323** s
Scarborough *N. Yorks., U.K.* 54°17N 0°24W **168** C7
Scarborough Bluffs *Canada* 43°42N 79°14W **141** A3
Scarborough Shoal *S. China Sea* 15°0N 117°50E **232** D1
Scargill *N.Z.* 42°56S 172°58E **285** C7
Scariff I. *Ireland* 51°44N 10°15W **166** E1
Scarp *U.K.* 58°1N 7°8W **167** C1
Scarpanto = Karpathos *Greece* 35°37N 27°10E **205** F9
Scarpe-Escaut ⌓ *France* 50°26N 3°23E **173** B10
Scarsdale *Australia* 37°41S 143°39E **282** D5
Sceaux *France* 48°46N 2°17E **134** B2
Scebeli = Shabeelle → *Somali Rep.* 2°0N 44°0E **267** D5
Šćedro *Croatia* 43°6N 16°43E **199** E13
Scenery, Mt. *Saba* 17°38N 63°14W **322** a
Schaal See *Germany* 53°36N 10°55E **178** B6
Schaalsee ⌓ *Germany* 53°40N 10°59E **178** B6
Schaerbeek *Belgium* 50°52N 4°22E **116** A2
Schaffhausen *Switz.* 47°42N 8°39E **179** H4
Schagen *Neths.* 52°49N 4°48E **170** B4
Schaghticoke *U.S.A.* 42°54N 73°35W **313** D11
Schärding *Austria* 48°27N 13°27E **180** C6
Scharfenberg *Germany* 52°35N 13°15E **115** A2
Scharfenwiese = Ostrołęka *Poland* 53°4N 21°32E **185** E8
Scharhörn *Germany* 53°57N 8°24E **178** B4
Schässburg = Sighişoara *Romania* 46°12N 24°50E **183** D9
Scheessel *Germany* 53°10N 9°29E **178** B5
Schefferville *Canada* 54°48N 66°50W **299** B6
Scheibbs *Austria* 48°1N 15°9E **180** C8
Scheidt = Schelde → *Belgium* 51°15N 4°16E **170** C4
Schelde → *Belgium* 51°15N 4°16E **170** C4
Schell City *U.S.A.* 38°1N 94°7W **310** F2
Schell Creek Ra. *U.S.A.* 39°25N 114°40W **304** G6
Schellsburg *U.S.A.* 40°3N 78°39W **312** F6
Schemnitz = Banská Štiavnica *Slovak Rep.* 48°25N 18°55E **181** C11
Schenectady *U.S.A.* 42°49N 73°57W **313** D11
Schenevus *U.S.A.* 42°33N 74°50W **313** D10
Scherfede *Germany* 51°32N 9°2E **178** D5
Schesslitz *Germany* 49°58N 11°1E **179** F7
Schiedam *Neths.* 51°55N 4°25E **170** C4
Schieratz = Sieradz *Poland* 51°37N 18°41E **185** G5
Schiermonnikoog *Neths.* 53°30N 6°15E **170** A6
Schiller Park *U.S.A.* 41°56N 87°52W **119** B1
Schiller Woods *U.S.A.* 41°57N 87°51W **119** B1
Schiltigheim *France* 48°35N 7°45E **173** D14
Schinousa *Greece* 36°53N 25°31E **205** E7
Schio *Italy* 45°43N 11°21E **199** C8
Schiphol, Amsterdam ✈ **(AMS)** *Neths.* 52°18N 4°45E **112** B1
Schippenbeil = Sępopol *Poland* 54°16N 21°2E **184** D8
Schivelbein = Świdwin *Poland* 53°47N 15°49E **184** E2
Schlachtensee *Germany* 52°26N 13°13E **115** B2
Schladming *Austria* 47°23N 13°41E **180** D6
Schlanders = Silandro *Italy* 46°38N 10°46E **198** B7
Schlawa = Sława *Poland* 51°52N 16°2E **185** G3
Schlei → *Germany* 54°40N 10°0E **178** A5
Schleiden *Germany* 50°31N 6°28E **178** E2
Schleinitz Ra. *Papua N. G.* 3°0S 151°30E **286** B6
Schleiz *Germany* 50°35N 11°49E **178** E7
Schlesiersee = Sława *Poland* 51°52N 16°2E **185** G3
Schleswig *Germany* 54°31N 9°34E **178** A5
Schleswig-Holstein □ *Germany* 54°30N 9°30E **178** A5
Schlettstadt = Sélestat *France* 48°16N 7°26E **173** D14
Schlichtingsheim = Szlichtyngowa *Poland* 51°42N 16°15E **185** G3
Schlochau = Człuchów *Poland* 53°41N 17°22E **184** E4
Schloppe = Człopa *Poland* 53°6N 16°6E **185** E3
Schlossgarten *Germany* 52°31N 13°18E **115** A2
Schlüchtern *Germany* 50°20N 9°32E **179** E5
Schmalkalden *Germany* 50°44N 10°26E **178** E6
Schmargendorf *Germany* 52°28N 13°17E **115** B2
Schmölln *Germany* 50°54N 12°19E **178** E8
Schneeberg *Austria* 47°47N 15°48E **180** D8
Schneeberg *Sachsen, Germany* 50°35N 12°38E **178** E8
Schneidemühl = Piła *Poland* 53°10N 16°48E **185** E3
Schneider *U.S.A.* 41°13N 87°28W **311** C9
Schneverdingen *Germany* 53°7N 9°48E **178** B5
Schœlcher *Martinique* 14°36N 61°7W **322** j
Schofield Barracks *U.S.A.* 21°29N 158°7W **302** K13
Schoharie *U.S.A.* 42°40N 74°19W **313** D10
Schoharie Cr. → *U.S.A.* 42°57N 74°18W **313** D10
Scholls *U.S.A.* 45°24N 122°56W **306** E4
Schönau = Swierzawa *Poland* 51°1N 15°54E **185** G2
Schönberg *Mecklenburg-Vorpommern, Germany* 53°52N 10°56E **178** B6
Schönberg *Schleswig-Holstein, Germany* 54°23N 10°21E **178** A6
Schönblick *Germany* 52°27N 13°43E **115** B5
Schönbrunn *Austria* 48°10N 16°19E **142** A1
Schönbuch ⌓ *Germany* 48°35N 9°2E **179** G5
Schönebeck *Germany* 52°2N 11°44E **178** C7
Schöneberg *Germany* 52°28N 13°20E **115** B3
Schönefeld *Germany* 52°22N 13°33E **115** B4
Schöneiche *Germany* 52°28N 13°41E **115** B5
Schöngau *Germany* 47°47N 10°53E **179** H6
Schöningen *Germany* 52°8N 10°56E **178** C6
Schönlanke = Trzcianka *Poland* 53°3N 16°25E **185** E3
Schönstein = Šoštanj *Slovenia* 46°23N 15°4E **199** B12
Schönwalde *Germany* 52°37N 13°7E **115** A1
Schoolcraft *U.S.A.* 42°7N 85°38W **311** B11
Schopfheim *Germany* 47°38N 7°50E **179** H3
Schorndorf *Germany* 48°47N 9°32E **179** G5
Schortens *Germany* 53°31N 7°56E **178** B3
Schotschekloof *Cape Town, S. Africa* **118** b1
Schottegat *Curaçao* 12°7N 68°55W **322** g
Schouten I. *Australia* 42°20S 148°20E **281** G4
Schouten Is. = Supiori *Indonesia* 1°0S 136°0E **231** E9
Schouten Is. *Papua N. G.* 3°30S 144°30E **286** B3
Schouwen *Neths.* 51°43N 3°45E **170** C3
Schramberg *Germany* 48°13N 8°22E **179** G4
Schrankogel *Austria* 47°3N 11°7E **180** D4
Schreiber *Canada* 48°45N 87°20W **298** C2
Schrems *Austria* 48°47N 15°4E **180** C8
Schrobenhausen *Germany* 48°34N 11°16E **179** G7
Schroffenstein *Namibia* 27°11S 18°42E **270** C2
Schroon Lake *U.S.A.* 43°50N 73°46W **313** C11
Schröttersberg = Płock *Poland* 52°32N 19°40E **185** F6
Schruns *Austria* 47°5N 9°56E **180** D2
Schuchye = Shchūchīnsk *Kazakhstan* 52°56N 70°12E **217** B8
Schuler *Canada* 50°20N 110°6W **297** C6
Schulzendorf *Germany* 52°36N 13°16E **115** A2
Schumacher *Canada* 48°30N 81°16W **298** C3
Schurz *U.S.A.* 38°57N 118°49W **304** G4
Schuyler *U.S.A.* 41°27N 97°4W **308** E5
Schuylerville *U.S.A.* 43°6N 73°35W **313** C11
Schuylkill → *U.S.A.* 39°53N 75°12W **313** G9
Schuylkill Haven *U.S.A.* 40°37N 76°11W **313** F8
Schwabach *Germany* 49°19N 11°2E **179** F7
Schwaben □ *Germany* 48°15N 10°30E **179** G6
Schwabing *Germany* 48°10N 11°35E **131** B2
Schwäbisch-Fränkischer Wald ⌓ *Germany* 49°0N 9°30E **179** G5
Schwäbisch Gmünd *Germany* 48°48N 9°47E **179** G5
Schwäbisch Hall *Germany* 49°6N 9°44E **179** F5
Schwäbische Alb *Germany* 48°20N 9°30E **179** G5
Schwabmünchen *Germany* 48°10N 10°46E **179** G6
Schwalmstadt *Germany* 50°55N 9°10E **178** E5
Schwandorf *Germany* 49°20N 12°7E **179** F8
Schwanebeck *Germany* 52°37N 13°32E **115** A4
Schwanenwerder *Germany* 52°26N 13°10E **115** B2
Schwaner, Pegunungan *Indonesia* 1°0S 112°30E **235** C4
Schwanewede *Germany* 53°14N 8°35E **178** B4
Schwarmstedt *Germany* 52°39N 9°38E **178** C5
Schwarze Elster → *Germany* 51°48N 12°50E **178** D8
Schwarzenberg *Germany* 50°32N 12°47E **178** E8
Schwarzlackenau *Austria* 48°16N 16°23E **142** A2
Schwarzrand *Namibia* 25°37S 16°50E **270** C2
Schwarzwald *Germany* 48°30N 8°20E **179** G4
Schwatka Mts. *U.S.A.* 67°20N 156°30W **303** C8
Schwaz *Austria* 47°20N 11°44E **180** D4
Schwechat *Austria* 48°8N 16°28E **142** B2
Schwechat, Wien ✈ **(VIE)** *Austria* 48°7N 16°35E **142** B3
Schwedt *Germany* 53°3N 14°16E **178** B10
Schweidnitz = Świdnica *Poland* 50°50N 16°30E **185** H3
Schweinfurt *Germany* 50°3N 10°14E **179** E6
Schweiz = Switzerland ■ *Europe* 46°30N 8°0E **179** J4
Schweizer-Reneke *S. Africa* 27°11S 25°18E **270** C4
Schwenningen = Villingen-Schwenningen *Germany* 48°3N 8°26E **179** G4
Schwerin = Skwierzyna *Poland* 52°33N 15°30E **185** F2
Schwerin *Germany* 53°36N 11°22E **178** B7
Schweriner See *Germany* 53°43N 11°28E **178** B7
Schwetzingen *Germany* 49°23N 8°35E **179** F4
Schwiebus = Świebodzin *Poland* 52°15N 15°31E **185** F2
Schwyz *Switz.* 47°2N 8°39E **179** H4
Schwyz □ *Switz.* 47°2N 8°39E **179** H4
Sciacca *Italy* 37°31N 13°3E **200** E6
Scicli *Italy* 36°47N 14°42E **201** F7
Science and Industry, Museum of *U.S.A.* 41°47N 87°34W **119** C3
Sciliar ⌓ *Italy* 46°28N 11°35E **199** B8
Scilla *Italy* 38°15N 15°43E **201** D8
Scilly, Isles of *U.K.* 49°56N 6°22W **169** H1
Ścinawa *Poland* 51°25N 16°26E **185** G3
Scione *Greece* 39°57N 23°36E **202** G7
Scioto → *U.S.A.* 38°44N 83°1W **311** D13
Scitrek Museum *U.S.A.* 33°46N 84°22W **113** B2
Scituate *U.S.A.* 42°12N 70°44W **313** D14
Scobey *U.S.A.* 48°47N 105°25W **304** B11
Scone *N.S.W., Australia* 32°5S 150°52E **283** B9
Scone *Perth & Kinr., U.K.* 56°25N 3°24W **167** E5
Scopus, Mt. *West Bank* 31°48N 35°14E **123** B2
Scordia *Italy* 37°18N 14°51E **201** E7
Scoresby Sund *Greenland* 70°28N 21°46W **154** C8
Scoresbysund = Ittoqqortoormiit *Greenland* 70°20N 23°0W **154** C8
Scorniceşti *Romania* 44°34N 24°33E **183** F9
Scotia *Calif., U.S.A.* 40°29N 124°6W **304** F1
Scotia *N.Y., U.S.A.* 42°50N 73°58W **313** D11
Scotia Sea *Antarctica* 56°5S 56°0W **151** B18
Scotland *Canada* 43°1N 80°22W **312** C4
Scotland □ *U.K.* 57°0N 4°0W **167** E5
Scott *Antarctica* 77°50S 166°45E **151** D11
Scott, C. *Australia* 13°30S 129°49E **278** B4
Scott Circle *Washington, D.C., U.S.A.* **143** a1
Scott City *U.S.A.* 38°29N 100°54W **308** F3
Scott Glacier *Antarctica* 66°15S 100°5E **151** C8
Scott I. *Antarctica* 67°0S 179°0E **151** C11
Scott Is. *Canada* 50°48N 128°40W **296** C3
Scott L. *Canada* 59°55N 106°18W **297** B7
Scott Monument *Edinburgh, U.K.* **121** b2
Scott Reef *Australia* 14°0S 121°50E **278** B3

Scottburgh S. Africa 30°15S 30°47E 271 D5
Scottdale Georgia, U.S.A. 33°47N 84°16W 113 B3
Scottdale Pa., U.S.A. 40°6N 79°35W 312 F5
Scottish Borders □ U.K. 55°35N 2°50W 167 F6
Scotts Head N.S.W., Australia 30°45S 153°0E 283 A10
Scotts Head Dominica 15°13N 61°23W 323 k
Scotts Head Village Dominica 15°12N 61°22W 323 k
Scotts Valley U.S.A. 37°3N 122°1W 306 H4
Scottsbluff U.S.A. 41°52N 103°40W 308 E2
Scottsboro U.S.A. 34°40N 86°2W 315 D11
Scottsburg U.S.A. 38°41N 85°47W 311 F11
Scottsdale Tas., Australia 41°9S 147°31E 281 G4
Scottsdale Ariz., U.S.A. 33°40N 111°53W 305 K8
Scottsville Ky., U.S.A. 36°45N 86°11W 308 G10
Scottsville N.Y., U.S.A. 43°2N 77°47W 312 C7
Scottville U.S.A. 43°58N 86°17W 308 D10
Scranton U.S.A. 41°25N 75°40W 313 E9
Screven U.S.A. 31°29N 82°1W 316 D7
Scrub I. Anguilla 18°19N 62°55W 322 a
Scugog, L. Canada 44°10N 78°55W 312 B6
Sculeni Moldova 47°20N 27°37E 183 C12
Scunthorpe U.K. 53°36N 0°39W 168 D7
Scuol Schuls Switz. 46°48N 10°17E 179 J6
Scutari = Shkodër Albania 42°4N 19°32E 202 D3
Scutari = Üsküdar Turkey 41°1N 29°0E 122 B2
Sea Is. U.S.A. 31°30N 81°7W 315 F14
Sea Lake Australia 35°28S 142°55E 282 C5
Sea Point S. Africa 34°5S 18°23E 118 A1
Seabra = Tarauacá Brazil 8°6S 70°48W 330 B3
Seabra Brazil 12°25S 41°46W 333 D3
Seabrook U.S.A. 38°58N 76°49W 143 B5
Seabrook, L. Australia 30°55S 119°40E 279 F2
Seacliff U.S.A. 37°47N 122°28W 136 B2
Seaford E. Sussex, U.K. 50°47N 0°7E 169 G8
Seaford Del., U.S.A. 38°39N 75°37W 309 F16
Seaforth N.S.W., Australia 33°48S 151°15E 139 A2
Seaforth Queens., Australia 20°55S 148°57E 280 b
Seaforth Ont., Canada 43°35N 81°25W 312 C3
Seaforth, L. U.K. 57°52N 6°36W 167 D2
Seagate U.S.A. 40°34N 74°0W 132 C1
Seagraves U.S.A. 32°57N 102°34W 314 E3
Seaham U.K. 54°50N 1°20W 168 C6
Seal → Canada 59°4N 94°48W 297 B10
Seal I. Anguilla 18°16N 63°9W 322 a
Seal L. Canada 54°20N 61°30W 299 B7
Seale U.S.A. 32°18N 85°10W 316 C4
Sealy U.S.A. 29°47N 96°9W 314 G6
Seaman U.S.A. 38°57N 83°34W 311 F13
Searchlight U.S.A. 35°28N 114°55W 307 K12
Searcy U.S.A. 35°15N 91°44W 314 D9
Searles L. U.S.A. 35°44N 117°21W 307 K9
Sears Tower Chicago, U.S.A. 119 c1
Seascale U.K. 54°24N 3°29W 168 C4
Seaside Calif., U.S.A. 36°37N 121°50W 306 J5
Seaside Oreg., U.S.A. 46°0N 123°56W 306 E3
Seaspray Australia 38°25S 147°15E 283 E7
Seat Pleasant U.S.A. 38°53N 76°53W 143 B4
Seattle U.S.A. 47°36N 122°19W 306 C4
Seattle-Tacoma Int. ✈ (SEA) U.S.A. 47°27N 122°18W 306 C4
Seaview N.Z. 41°15S 174°54E 143 B2
Seaward Kaikoura Ra. N.Z. 42°10S 173°44E 285 C8
SeaWorld U.S.A. 28°24N 81°28W 133 B2
Seba Indonesia 10°29S 121°50E 278 B3
Sebago L. U.S.A. 43°52N 70°34W 313 C14
Sebago Lake U.S.A. 43°51N 70°34W 313 C14
Sebakung Indonesia 1°37S 116°25E 235 C5
Sebangau △ Indonesia 2°34S 113°38E 235 C4
Sebangka Indonesia 0°7N 104°36E 234 B2
Sebastian U.S.A. 27°49N 80°28W 317 H9
Sebastián Vizcaíno, B. Mexico 28°0N 114°30W 318 B2
Sebastopol = Sevastopol Ukraine 44°35N 33°30E 189 K7
Sebastopol U.S.A. 38°24N 122°49W 306 G4
Sebatik Asia 4°10N 117°45E 235 B5
Sebba Burkina Faso 13°35N 0°32E 263 C5
Sebderat Eritrea 15°26N 36°42E 257 D4
Sebdou Algeria 34°38N 1°19W 261 B4
Sébé → Gabon 1°2S 13°6E 264 C2
Sébékoro Mali 12°58N 9°0W 262 C3
Seben Turkey 40°24N 31°34E 212 B4
Šeberov Czech Rep. 50°0N 14°30E 135 B3
Sebeş Romania 45°58N 23°34E 183 E8
Sebeşului, Munţii Romania 45°36N 23°40E 183 E8
Sebewaing U.S.A. 43°44N 83°27W 309 D12
Sebezh Russia 56°14N 28°22E 188 D5
Sebha = Sabhā Libya 27°9N 14°29E 258 C2
Sébi Mali 15°50N 4°12W 262 B4
Şebinkarahisar Turkey 40°22N 38°28E 213 B8
Sebiş Romania 46°23N 22°13E 182 D7
Seblat Indonesia 3°14S 101°38E 234 C2
Sebnitz Germany 50°58N 14°15E 178 E10
Sebou, Oued → Morocco 34°16N 6°40W 260 B3
Sebring Fla., U.S.A. 27°30N 81°27W 317 H8
Sebring Ohio, U.S.A. 40°55N 81°2W 312 F3
Sebringville Canada 43°24N 81°4W 312 C3
Sebta = Ceuta N. Afr. 35°52N 5°18W 260 A3
Sebuku Indonesia 3°30S 116°25E 235 C5
Sebuku, Teluk Indonesia 4°0N 118°10E 235 B5
Sečanj Serbia 45°25N 20°47E 182 E5
Secaucus U.S.A. 40°47N 74°3W 132 B1
Secchia → Italy 45°4N 11°0E 198 C8
Sechelt Canada 49°25N 123°42W 296 D4
Sechura Peru 5°39S 80°50W 330 B1
Sechura, Desierto de Peru 6°0S 80°30W 330 B1
Seclin France 50°33N 3°2E 173 B10
Second World War Memorial Washington, D.C., U.S.A. 143 b1
Secondigny France 46°37N 0°26W 172 F6
Sečovce Slovak Rep. 48°42N 21°40E 181 C14
Secretary I. N.Z. 45°15S 166°56E 285 F1
Secunderabad India 17°28N 78°30E 244 F4
Sécure → Bolivia 15°10S 64°52W 331 D5
Security U.S.A. 38°45N 104°45W 304 G11
Sedalia U.S.A. 38°42N 93°14W 310 F3
Sedam India 17°11N 77°17E 244 E3
Sedan S. Austral., Australia 34°34S 139°19E 282 C3
Sedan Ardennes, France 49°43N 4°57E 173 C11
Sedan Kans., U.S.A. 37°8N 96°11W 308 G5
Sedano Spain 42°43N 3°49W 194 C7
Sedaw Burma 22°19N 96°19E 241 D6
Sedbergh U.K. 54°20N 2°31W 168 C5
Seddinsee Germany 52°23N 13°41E 115 B5
Seddon N.Z. 41°40S 174°7E 285 B9
Seddonville N.Z. 41°33S 172°1E 285 B7
Sedé Boqér Israel 30°52N 34°47E 251 H5
Sedeh Fārs, Iran 30°45N 52°11E 247 D7
Sedeh Khorāsān, Iran 33°20N 59°14E 247 C8
Séderon France 44°12N 5°32E 175 D9
Sederot Israel 31°32N 34°37E 251 G5
Sédhiou Senegal 12°44N 15°30W 262 C1
Sedico Italy 46°8N 12°6E 199 B9
Sedlčany Czech Rep. 49°40N 14°25E 180 B7
Sedley Canada 50°10N 104°0W 297 C8
Sedom Israel 31°5N 35°20E 251 G6
Sedona U.S.A. 34°52N 111°46W 305 J8
Sedova, Pik Russia 73°29N 54°58E 214 B6
Sedrata Algeria 36°7N 7°31E 261 A6
Sedro-Woolley U.S.A. 48°30N 122°14W 306 B4
Šeduva Lithuania 55°45N 23°45E 184 C10
Sędziszów Poland 50°35N 20°4E 185 H7
Sędziszów Małapolski Poland 50°5N 21°45E 185 H8
Seebad Ahlbeck Germany 53°56N 14°10E 178 B10
Seeberg Germany 52°33N 13°41E 115 A5
Seeburg = Jeziorany Poland 53°58N 20°46E 184 E7
Seeburg Germany 52°30N 13°7E 115 A1
Seefeld Germany 52°37N 13°40E 115 A5
Seefeld in Tirol Austria 47°19N 11°13E 180 D4
Seegefeld Germany 52°33N 13°5E 115 A1
Seehausen Germany 52°54N 11°45E 178 C7
Seeheim Namibia 26°50S 17°45E 270 C2
Seeheim-Jugenheim Germany 49°49N 8°40E 179 F4
Seehof Germany 52°24N 13°17E 115 B2
Seeis Namibia 22°29S 17°39E 270 B2
Seekoei → S. Africa 30°18S 25°1E 270 D4
Seeley's Bay Canada 44°29N 76°14W 313 B8
Seelow Germany 52°32N 14°23E 178 C10
Sées France 48°38N 0°10E 172 D7
Seesen Germany 51°54N 10°10E 178 D6
Seevetal Germany 53°26N 10°1E 178 B6
Seewinkel = Neusiedler See-Seewinkel △ Austria 47°50N 16°45E 181 D9
Şefaatli Turkey 39°30N 34°45E 212 C6
Seferihisar Turkey 38°10N 26°50E 205 C8
Séféto Mali 14°8N 9°49W 262 C3
Sefophe Botswana 22°11S 27°58E 271 B4
Sefrou Morocco 33°52N 4°52W 260 B4
Sefrou □ Morocco 33°49N 4°49W 260 B4
Sefton N.Z. 43°15S 172°41E 285 D7
Sefuri-San Japan 33°28N 130°18E 222 D2
Sefwi Bekwai Ghana 6°10N 2°25W 262 D4
Seg-ozero Russia 63°20N 33°46E 186 B5
Segag Ethiopia 7°39N 42°50E 267 C5
Segamat Malaysia 2°30N 102°50E 237 L4
Şegarcea Romania 44°6N 23°43E 183 F8
Ségbana Benin 10°55N 3°42E 263 C5
Segbwema S. Leone 8°0N 11°0W 262 D2
Segeltorp Sweden 59°16N 17°56E 139 B1
Segersta Sweden 61°16N 16°39E 162 C10
Segesta Italy 37°56N 12°50E 200 E5
Seget Indonesia 1°24S 130°58E 231 E8
Segewold = Sigulda Latvia 57°10N 24°55E 188 D3
Segezha Russia 63°44N 34°19E 186 B5
Seggueur, O. → Algeria 32°14N 1°48E 261 B5
Seghe Solomon Is. 8°32S 157°54E 287 M9
Segmon Sweden 59°17N 13°3E 162 E7
Segonzac France 45°36N 0°14W 174 C3
Segorbe Spain 39°50N 0°30W 196 F4
Ségou Mali 13°30N 6°16W 262 C3
Ségou □ Mali 14°0N 6°0W 262 C3
Segovia = Coco → Cent. Amer. 15°0N 83°8W 320 D3
Segovia Colombia 7°7N 74°42W 328 B3
Segovia Spain 40°57N 4°10W 194 E6
Segovia □ Spain 40°55N 4°10W 194 E6
Segrate Italy 45°29N 9°17E 129 B2
Segré France 47°40N 0°52W 172 E6
Segre → Spain 41°40N 0°43E 196 D5
Seguam I. U.S.A. 52°19N 172°30W 303 K4
Seguam Pass U.S.A. 52°0N 172°30W 303 K4
Séguédine Niger 20°9N 12°55E 259 D2
Séguéla Ivory C. 7°55N 6°40W 262 D3
Séguélon Ivory C. 9°13N 7°7W 262 D3
Séguénéga Burkina Faso 13°25N 1°58W 263 C4
Seguin U.S.A. 29°34N 97°58W 314 G6
Segundo → Argentina 30°53S 62°44W 334 C3
Segura → Spain 38°3N 0°44W 197 G4
Segura, Sierra de Spain 38°5N 2°45W 197 G2
Seguro Italy 45°28N 9°3E 129 B1
Seh Konj, Kūh-e Iran 30°6N 57°30E 247 D8
Seh Qal'eh Iran 33°40N 58°24E 247 C8
Sehitwa Botswana 20°30S 22°30E 270 B3
Sehlabathebe △ Lesotho 29°53S 29°7E 271 C4
Sehore India 23°10N 77°5E 242 H7
Sehulea Papua N. G. 9°58S 151°10E 286 E6
Sehwan Pakistan 26°28N 67°53E 242 F2
Şeica Mare Romania 46°1N 24°7E 183 D9
Seikan Tunnel Japan 41°28N 140°10E 220 D10
Seikpyu Burma 20°54N 94°48E 241 E5
Seil U.K. 56°18N 5°38W 167 E3
Seiland Norway 70°25N 23°15E 160 A20
Seilhac France 45°22N 1°43E 174 C5
Seiling U.S.A. 36°9N 98°56W 314 C5
Seille → Moselle, France 49°7N 6°11E 173 C13
Seille → Saône-et-Loire, France 46°31N 4°57E 173 F11
Sein, Î. de France 48°2N 4°52W 172 D2
Seinäjoki Finland 62°40N 22°51E 160 E20
Seine → France 49°26N 0°26E 172 C7
Seine, B. de la France 49°40N 0°40W 172 C6
Seine-et-Marne □ France 48°45N 3°0E 173 D10
Seine-Inférieure = Seine-Maritime □ France 49°40N 1°0E 172 C7
Seine-Maritime □ France 49°40N 1°0E 172 C7
Seine-St-Denis □ France 48°58N 2°24E 173 D9
Seini Romania 47°44N 23°21E 183 C8
Seirijai Lithuania 54°14N 23°49E 184 D10
Seis de Septiembre = Moron Argentina 34°39S 58°37W 334 C4
Seistan = Sīstān Asia 30°50N 61°0E 247 D9
Seistan, Daryācheh-ye = Sīstan, Daryācheh-ye Iran 31°0N 61°0E 247 D9
Seitler = Nyzhnohirskyy Ukraine 45°27N 34°38E 189 K8
Seixal Portugal 38°38N 9°5W 126 B2
Sejerø Denmark 55°54N 11°9E 163 J5
Sejerø Bugt Denmark 55°53N 11°15E 163 J5
Sejny Poland 54°6N 23°21E 184 D10
Seka Ethiopia 8°10N 36°52E 257 F4
Sekadau Indonesia 0°1N 110°54E 235 C4
Sekayu Indonesia 2°51S 103°51E 234 C2
Seke Tanzania 3°20S 33°31E 268 C3
Seke-Banza Dem. Rep. of the Congo 5°20S 13°16E 265 D2
Sekenke Tanzania 4°18S 34°11E 268 C3
Sekhira Tunisia 34°20N 10°5E 258 B2
Seki Japan 35°29N 136°55E 223 B8
Seki Turkey 36°48N 29°33E 205 E11
Sekigahara Japan 35°22N 136°28E 223 B8
Sekondi-Takoradi Ghana 4°58N 1°45W 262 E4
Sekota Ethiopia 12°40N 39°2E 257 E4
Sekseüil Kazakhstan 47°5N 61°9E 216 C6
Seksna Russia 59°13N 38°30E 188 C10
Sekudai Malaysia 1°32N 103°39E 237 d
Sekuma Botswana 24°36S 23°50E 270 B3
Selah U.S.A. 46°39N 120°32W 304 C3
Selama Malaysia 5°12N 100°42E 237 K3
Selangor □ Malaysia 3°10N 101°30E 237 L3
Selárgius Italy 39°16N 9°10E 200 C2
Selaru Indonesia 8°9S 131°0E 231 F8
Selatan, Selat Malaysia 5°15N 100°20E 237 c
Selatpanjang Indonesia 1°0N 102°43E 234 B2
Selawik U.S.A. 66°36N 160°0W 303 C8
Selawik L. U.S.A. 66°30N 160°45W 303 C7
Selawik Nat. Wildlife Refuge ⌓ U.S.A. 66°35N 159°10W 303 C8
Selb Germany 50°10N 12°7E 179 E8
Selbusjøen Norway 63°15N 10°50E 164 A7
Selby Gauteng, S. Africa 26°12S 28°2E 123 B2
Selby N. Yorks., U.K. 53°47N 1°5W 168 D6
Selby S. Dak., U.S.A. 45°31N 100°2W 308 C3
Selca Croatia 43°20N 16°50E 199 E13
Selçuk Turkey 37°56N 27°22E 205 D9
Selden U.S.A. 39°33N 100°34W 308 F3
Seldovia U.S.A. 59°26N 151°43W 303 G10
Sele → Italy 40°29N 14°56E 201 B7
Selebi-Phikwe Botswana 21°58S 27°48E 271 B4
Selemdzha → Russia 51°42N 128°53E 215 D13
Selendi Manisa, Turkey 38°43N 28°50E 205 C10
Selendi Manisa, Turkey 38°46N 27°53E 205 C9
Selenga = Selenge Mörön → Asia 52°16N 106°16E 218 A10
Selenge Dem. Rep. of the Congo 1°58S 18°11E 264 C3
Selenge Mörön → Asia 52°16N 106°16E 218 A10
Selenicë Albania 40°33N 19°39E 202 F3
Selenter See Germany 54°18N 10°26E 178 A6
Sélestat France 48°16N 7°26E 173 D14
Seletan, Tanjung Indonesia 4°10S 114°40E 235 C4
Seletar, Pulau Singapore 1°26N 103°51E 138 A3
Seletar Hills Singapore 1°23N 103°52E 138 A3
Seletar Res. Singapore 1°24N 103°48E 138 A2
Selevac Serbia 44°28N 20°52E 202 B4
Selfoss Iceland 63°56N 21°0W 155 D6
Selhurst U.K. 51°23N 0°5W 125 B3
Sélibabi Mauritania 15°10N 12°15W 262 B2
Seliger, Ozero Russia 57°15N 33°0E 188 D7
Seligman U.S.A. 35°20N 112°53W 305 J7
Şelim Turkey 40°30N 42°46E 213 B10
Selîma Sudan 21°22N 29°19E 256 C2
Selimiye Turkey 37°24N 27°40E 205 D9
Selinda Spillway → Botswana 18°35S 23°10E 270 A3
Sélingué, L. de Mali 11°37N 8°14W 262 C3
Selinsgrove U.S.A. 40°48N 76°52W 312 F8
Selizharovo Russia 56°51N 33°27E 188 D7
Selje Norway 62°3N 5°22E 164 B2
Seljord Norway 59°30N 8°40E 164 E5
Selkirk Man., Canada 50°10N 96°55W 297 C9
Selkirk Ont., Canada 42°49N 79°56W 312 D5
Selkirk Borders, U.K. 55°33N 2°50W 167 F6
Selkirk I. = Horse I. Canada 53°20N 99°6W 297 C9
Selkirk Mts. Canada 51°15N 117°40W 294 G8
Sellafield U.K. 54°25N 3°29W 168 C4
Sellama Sudan 12°51N 29°46E 257 E2
Sellia Greece 35°12N 24°23E 207 E5
Sellières France 46°50N 5°32E 173 F12
Sells U.S.A. 31°55N 111°53W 305 L8
Sellye Hungary 45°52N 17°51E 182 E2
Selma Ala., U.S.A. 32°25N 87°1W 315 E11
Selma Calif., U.S.A. 36°34N 119°37W 306 J7
Selma N.C., U.S.A. 35°32N 78°17W 315 D15
Selmer U.S.A. 35°10N 88°36W 315 D10
Selong Indonesia 8°39S 116°32E 235 D5
Selongey France 47°36N 5°11E 173 E12
Selouane Morocco 35°7N 2°57W 261 A4
Selous ⌓ Tanzania 8°37S 37°42E 269 D4
Selowandoma Falls Zimbabwe 21°15S 31°50E 269 G3
Selpele Indonesia 0°1S 130°5E 231 E8
Selsey Bill U.K. 50°43N 0°47W 169 G7
Seltso Russia 53°22N 34°4E 188 F8
Seltz France 48°54N 8°4E 173 D15
Selu Indonesia 7°32S 130°55E 231 F8
Sélune → France 48°38N 1°22W 172 D5
Selva = La Selva del Camp Spain 41°13N 1°8E 196 D6
Selva Argentina 29°50S 62°0W 334 B3
Selva Mallorca, Spain 39°46N 2°54E 206 B3
Selva Lancandona = Montes Azules ⌓ Mexico 16°21N 91°3W 319 D6
Selvagens, Ilhas Madeira 30°5N 15°55W 260 B1
Selvas Brazil 6°30S 67°0W 330 B4
Selwyn L. Canada 60°0N 104°30W 297 B8
Selwyn Mts. Canada 63°0N 130°0W 294 E5
Selwyn Passage Vanuatu 16°3S 168°12E 287 F6
Selwyn Ra. Australia 21°10S 140°0E 280 C3
Selyatyn Ukraine 47°50N 25°12E 183 C10
Sem Norway 59°14N 10°17E 164 E7
Sem Kolodezey = Lenine Ukraine 45°17N 35°46E 189 K8
Semadrek = Samothraki Greece 40°28N 25°28E 203 F9
Seman → Albania 40°47N 19°30E 202 F3
Semangka, Teluk Indonesia 5°36S 104°42E 234 D2
Semarang Indonesia 7°0S 110°26E 235 D4
Semarapura = Klungkung Indonesia 8°32S 115°24E 231 K18
Sematan Malaysia 1°48N 109°46E 235 B3
Semayang, Danau Indonesia 0°14S 116°28E 235 C5
Sembabule Uganda 0°4S 31°25E 268 C3
Sembawang Singapore 1°27N 103°50E 138 A2
Sembé Congo 1°39N 14°36E 264 B2
Sembilang △ Indonesia 1°59S 104°34E 234 C2
Sembung Indonesia 8°28S 115°11E 231 J18
Şemdinli Turkey 37°18N 44°35E 213 D11
Sémé Senegal 15°4N 13°41W 262 B2
Semeih Sudan 12°43N 30°53E 257 E3
Semendua Dem. Rep. of the Congo 3°10S 18°6E 264 C3
Semenivka Chernihiv, Ukraine 52°8N 32°36E 189 F7
Semenivka Kremenchuk, Ukraine 49°37N 33°10E 189 H7
Semenov Russia 56°43N 44°30E 190 B7
Semeru Indonesia 8°4S 112°55E 235 D4
Semey Kazakhstan 50°30N 80°10E 217 B10
Semichi Is. U.S.A. 52°42N 174°0E 303 K1
Semikarakorskiy Russia 47°31N 40°48E 191 G5
Semiluki Russia 51°41N 39°2E 189 G10
Seminoe Res. U.S.A. 42°9N 106°55W 304 E10
Seminole Fla., U.S.A. 27°50N 82°47W 317 H7
Seminole Okla., U.S.A. 35°14N 96°41W 314 D6
Seminole Tex., U.S.A. 32°43N 102°39W 314 E3
Seminole, L. U.S.A. 30°43N 84°52W 316 E5
Seminole Draw → U.S.A. 32°27N 102°20W 314 E3
Semipalatinsk = Semey Kazakhstan 50°30N 80°10E 217 B10
Semirara I. Phil. 12°4N 121°23E 232 E3
Semirara Is. Phil. 12°0N 121°20E 233 F3
Semisopochnoi I. U.S.A. 51°55N 179°36E 303 L2
Semitau Indonesia 0°29N 111°57E 235 B4
Semliki △ Uganda 0°49N 30°4E 268 B3
Semlin = Zemun Serbia 44°51N 20°25E 202 B4
Semmelweis Museum Budapest, Hungary 117 c2
Semmering P. Austria 47°41N 15°45E 180 D8
Semnān Iran 35°40N 53°23E 247 C7
Semnān □ Iran 36°0N 54°0E 247 C7
Sempang Mengayou, Tanjong Malaysia 7°0N 116°40E 235 A5
Semporna Malaysia 4°30N 118°33E 235 B5
Semuda Indonesia 2°51S 112°58E 235 C4
Semur-en-Auxois France 47°30N 4°20E 173 E11
Semyonovka = Arsenev Russia 44°10N 133°15E 220 B6
Semyonovskoye = Bereznik Russia 62°51N 42°40E 186 B7
Sen → Cambodia 12°32N 104°28E 236 F5
Sena Bolivia 11°32S 67°11W 330 C4
Senā Iran 28°27N 51°36E 247 D6
Sena Mozam. 17°25S 35°0E 269 F4
Sena → Bolivia 11°31S 67°11W 330 C4
Sena Madureira Brazil 9°5S 68°45W 330 B4
Senachwine L. U.S.A. 41°10N 89°18W 310 C7
Senador José Porfírio Brazil 2°35S 51°55W 329 D7
Senador Pompeu Brazil 5°40S 39°20W 332 C4
Senago Italy 45°34N 9°7E 129 A1
Senaja Malaysia 6°45N 117°3E 235 A5
Senaki Georgia 42°15N 42°1E 191 J6
Senang, Pulau Singapore 1°11N 103°52E 237 d
Senanga Zambia 16°7S 23°16E 265 F4
Senatobia U.S.A. 34°37N 89°58W 315 D10
Sencelles Spain 39°39N 2°54E 206 B3
Sendafa Ethiopia 9°11N 39°3E 257 F4
Sendai Kagoshima, Japan 31°50N 130°20E 222 F2
Sendai Miyagi, Japan 38°15N 140°53E 220 E10
Sendai-Wan Japan 38°15N 141°0E 220 E10
Senden Bayern, Germany 48°19N 10°4E 179 G6
Senden Nordrhein-Westfalen, Germany 51°52N 7°22E 178 D3
Sendhwa India 21°41N 75°6E 242 J6
Sendling Germany 48°7N 11°31E 131 B2
Sendlinger Tor Platz Munich, Germany 131 c1
Sendurjana India 21°32N 78°17E 244 D4
Sene → Ghana 7°30N 0°33W 263 D4
Senec Slovak Rep. 48°12N 17°23E 181 C10
Seneca Ill., U.S.A. 41°19N 88°37W 311 C8
Seneca S.C., U.S.A. 34°41N 82°57W 315 D13
Seneca Falls U.S.A. 42°55N 76°48W 313 D8
Seneca L. U.S.A. 42°40N 76°54W 312 D8
Senecaville L. U.S.A. 39°55N 81°25W 312 G3
Senegal ■ W. Afr. 14°30N 14°30W 262 C2
Sénégal → W. Afr. 15°48N 16°32W 262 B1
Senegambia Africa 12°45N 12°0W 254 E2
Senegambia & Niger = Mali ■ Africa 17°0N 3°0W 262 B4
Senekal S. Africa 28°20S 27°36E 271 C4
Senftenberg Germany 51°32N 14°0E 178 D10
Senga Hill Zambia 9°19S 31°11E 269 D3
Senge Khambab = Indus → Pakistan 24°20N 67°47E 242 G2
Sengerema Tanzania 2°42S 32°35E 268 C3
Sengeti Indonesia 1°28S 103°31E 234 C2
Senggigi Indonesia 8°29S 116°2E 231 J19
Sengiley Russia 53°58N 48°46E 190 D9
Sengua → Zimbabwe 17°7S 28°5E 269 F2
Senguerr → Argentina 45°35S 68°50W 336 C3
Senhor-do-Bonfim Brazil 10°30S 40°10W 332 D3
Senica Slovak Rep. 48°41N 17°25E 181 C10
Senigállia Italy 43°43N 13°13E 199 E10
Seniku Burma 25°32N 97°48E 241 C6
Senio → Italy 44°35N 12°15E 199 D9
Senirkent Turkey 38°6N 30°33E 205 C12
Senise Italy 40°9N 16°17E 201 B9
Senj Croatia 45°0N 14°58E 199 D11
Senja Norway 69°25N 17°30E 160 B17
Senju Japan 35°44N 139°48E 140 A3
Senkaku-Shotō E. China Sea 25°45N 123°30E 221 M1
Senlis France 49°13N 2°35E 173 C9
Senmonorom Cambodia 12°27N 107°12E 236 F6
Sennâr Sudan 13°30N 33°35E 257 E3
Sennâr □ Sudan 13°0N 34°0E 257 E3
Senneterre Canada 48°25N 77°15W 298 C4
Senno Belarus 54°45N 29°43E 188 E5
Sénnori Italy 40°47N 8°35E 200 B1
Seno Laos 16°35N 104°50E 236 D5
Senoia U.S.A. 33°18N 84°33W 316 B5
Senonches France 48°34N 1°2E 172 D8
Senorbì Italy 39°32N 9°8E 200 C2
Senožeče Slovenia 45°43N 14°3E 199 C11
Senqu = Orange → S. Africa 28°41S 16°28E 270 C2
Senriyama Japan 34°47N 135°30E 133 A2
Sens France 48°11N 3°15E 173 D10
Senta Serbia 45°55N 20°3E 182 E5
Sentarum, Danau Indonesia 0°51N 112°6E 235 B4
Sentery = Lubao Dem. Rep. of the Congo 5°17S 25°42E 265 D5
Sentinel U.S.A. 32°52N 113°13W 305 K7
Šentjur Slovenia 46°14N 15°24E 199 B12
Sentosa Singapore 1°16N 103°50E 138 B2
Sentry Hill St.-Maarten 18°2N 63°4W 322 a
Senwabarana S. Africa 23°17S 29°7E 271 B4
Senya Beraku Ghana 5°28N 0°31W 263 D4
Seo de Urgel = La Seu d'Urgell Spain 42°22N 1°23E 196 C6
Seobinggo S. Korea 37°31N 126°58E 137 B1
Seocho S. Korea 37°28N 127°0E 137 C1
Seodaemun S. Korea 37°34N 126°55E 137 B1
Seogwipo S. Korea 33°13N 126°34E 224 a
Seohara India 29°15N 78°33E 243 E8
Seokguram Grotto S. Korea 35°45N 129°18E 224 E4
Seokkwan S. Korea 37°35N 127°2E 137 B2
Seonath → India 21°44N 82°28E 243 J10
Seondha India 26°9N 78°48E 243 F8
Seongbuk S. Korea 37°35N 127°0E 137 B2
Seongdong S. Korea 37°33N 127°3E 137 B2
Seongmodo S. Korea 37°41N 126°19E 224 D3
Seongnam S. Korea 37°26N 127°8E 224 D3
Seongsu S. Korea 37°32N 127°2E 137 B2
Seoni India 22°5N 79°30E 243 H8
Seoni Malwa India 22°27N 77°28E 242 H8
Seonsan S. Korea 36°14N 128°17E 224 D4
Seonyudo S. Korea 35°49N 126°24E 224 E3
Seoraksan S. Korea 38°7N 128°27E 224 C4
Seoraksan △ S. Korea 38°10N 128°25E 224 C4
Seoriuarayan India 21°45N 82°34E 244 D6
Seosan S. Korea 36°47N 126°27E 224 D3
Seoul S. Korea 37°31N 126°58E 137 B2
Seoul Nat. Univ. S. Korea 37°28N 126°57E 137 C1
Seoul Tower S. Korea 37°32N 126°59E 137 B1
Separation Pt. N.Z. 40°47S 172°59E 285 A7
Sepasu Indonesia 0°43N 117°34E 235 B5
Sepatini → Brazil 7°36S 65°24W 330 B4
Sepi Solomon Is. 8°31S 159°52E 287 M10
Sepīdān Iran 30°20N 52°5E 247 D7
Sepik → Papua N. G. 3°49S 144°30E 286 B3
Sepo-ri N. Korea 38°57N 127°25E 224 C3
Sepolia Greece 38°1N 23°42E 112 A2
Sępólno Krajeńskie Poland 53°26N 17°30E 184 E4
Sepone Laos 16°45N 106°13E 236 D6
Sępopol Poland 54°16N 21°2E 184 D8
Sept-Îles Canada 50°13N 66°22W 299 B6
Septemvri Bulgaria 42°13N 24°6E 203 D8
Sepúlveda Spain 41°18N 3°45W 194 D7
Sepulveda Dam Rec. Area ⌓ U.S.A. 34°10N 118°28W 126 A2
Sequeros Spain 40°31N 6°2W 194 E4
Sequim U.S.A. 48°5N 123°6W 306 B3
Sequoia △ U.S.A. 36°30N 118°30W 306 J8
Serafimovich Russia 49°36N 42°43E 190 F6
Seraing Belgium 50°35N 5°32E 170 D5
Serakhis → Cyprus 35°13N 32°55E 207 E8
Seram Indonesia 3°10S 129°0E 231 E7
Seram Sea Indonesia 2°30S 128°30E 231 E7
Serampore = Shrirampur India 22°44N 88°21E 243 H13
Seranantsara Madag. 18°30S 49°5E 272 B2
Serang Indonesia 6°8S 106°10E 234 D3
Serangoon Singapore 1°23N 103°54E 138 A3
Serangoon, Pulau Singapore 1°23N 103°55E 138 A3
Serangoon, Sungei → Singapore 1°23N 103°55E 138 A3
Serangoon Harbour Singapore 1°23N 103°57E 138 A3
Serasan Indonesia 2°29N 109°4E 235 B3
Serasan, Selat Indonesia 2°20N 109°0E 235 B3
Seravezza Italy 43°59N 10°13E 198 E7
Seraya, Pulau Singapore 1°16N 103°43E 138 B2
Serbâl, G. Egypt 28°40N 33°39E 251 K4
Şerbettar Turkey 41°27N 26°46E 203 E10
Serbia ■ Europe 43°20N 20°0E 202 C4
Şercaia Romania 45°49N 25°9E 183 E10
Serdar Turkmenistan 39°4N 56°23E 247 B8
Serdo Ethiopia 11°56N 41°14E 257 E5
Serdobol = Sortavala Russia 61°42N 30°41E 188 B6
Serdobsk Russia 52°28N 44°10E 190 D7
Serebryanka Russia 55°44N 37°53E 129 B5
Serebryanka → Russia 55°47N 37°44E 129 B4
Serebryansk Kazakhstan 49°41N 83°17E 217 C10
Sered' Slovak Rep. 48°17N 17°44E 181 C10
Sereda = Furmanov Russia 57°10N 41°9E 190 B5
Seredka Russia 58°12N 28°10E 188 C5
Serednye Ukraine 48°32N 22°30E 182 B7
Şereflikoçhisar Turkey 38°56N 33°32E 212 C5
Seregno Italy 45°39N 9°12E 198 C6
Seremban Malaysia 2°43N 101°53E 237 L3
Serengeti △ Tanzania 2°11S 35°0E 268 C3
Serengeti Plain Tanzania 2°40S 35°0E 268 C4
Serenje Zambia 13°14S 30°15E 269 E3
Seret → Ukraine 48°37N 25°52E 183 B10
Sereth = Siret → Romania 45°24N 28°1E 183 E12
Sergach Russia 55°30N 45°30E 190 C7
Sergeevka Kazakhstan 53°52N 67°24E 217 B7
Sergen Turkey 41°41N 27°42E 203 E11
Sergeya Kirova, Ostrova Russia 77°30N 89°0E 215 B10
Sergino Russia 62°25N 65°12E 214 C7
Sergiopol = Ayaköz Kazakhstan 48°10N 80°10E 217 C10
Sergipe □ Brazil 10°30S 37°30W 332 D4
Sergiyev Posad Russia 56°20N 38°10E 188 D10
Sergo = Stakhanov Ukraine 48°35N 38°40E 189 H10
Serhetabat Turkmenistan 35°20N 62°18E 247 C9
Seria Brunei 4°37N 114°23E 235 B4
Serian Malaysia 1°10N 110°31E 235 B4
Seriate Italy 45°41N 9°43E 198 C6
Seribu △ Indonesia 5°32S 106°33E 234 D3
Seribudolok Indonesia 2°55N 98°37E 234 B1
Sericho Kenya 1°5N 39°5E 268 B4
Sérifontaine France 49°20N 1°45E 173 C8
Serifos Greece 37°9N 24°30E 204 D6
Sérignan France 43°17N 3°17E 174 E7
Sérigny → Canada 56°47N 66°0W 299 A6
Serik Turkey 36°55N 31°7E 250 B2
Seringapatam Reef Australia 13°38S 122°5E 278 B3
Serinhisar Turkey 37°36N 29°18E 205 D11
Seririt Indonesia 8°12S 114°56E 231 J17
Serishābād Iran 35°14N 47°36E 213 E12
Serkout Algeria 23°56N 6°47E 261 D6
Sermaize-les-Bains France 48°47N 4°54E 173 D11
Sermata Indonesia 8°15S 128°50E 231 F7
Sermersuaq Greenland 79°30N 62°0W 154 B4
Sérmide Italy 45°0N 11°18E 199 D8
Sernovodsk Russia 53°58N 51°16E 190 D10
Sernur Russia 56°52N 49°2E 190 B9
Serock Poland 52°31N 21°4E 185 F8
Seroe Colorado Aruba 12°25N 69°52W 322 f
Serón Spain 37°20N 2°29W 197 H2
Seròs Spain 41°27N 0°24E 196 D5
Serouenout Algeria 24°18N 7°25E 261 D6
Serov Russia 59°29N 60°35E 186 C11
Serowe Botswana 22°25S 26°43E 270 B4
Serpa Portugal 37°57N 7°38W 195 H3
Serpeddí, Punta Italy 39°22N 9°18E 200 C2
Serpentara Italy 39°8N 9°36E 200 C2
Serpentine Lakes Australia 28°30S 129°10E 279 E4
Serpent's Mouth = Sierpe, Bocas de la Venezuela 10°0N 61°30W 329 G9
Serpis → Spain 38°59N 0°9W 197 G4
Serpneve Ukraine 46°18N 29°1E 183 D14
Serpukhov Russia 54°55N 37°28E 188 E9
Serra Brazil 20°7S 40°18W 333 F3
Serra da Bocaina △ Brazil 23°0S 44°40W 333 F3
Serra da Canastra △ Brazil 20°3S 46°50W 333 F2
Serra da Capivara △ Brazil 8°42S 42°15W 332 C3
Serra da Estrela ⌓ Portugal 40°27N 7°33W 194 E3
Serra das Confusões △ Brazil 8°50S 43°50W 332 C3
Serra de Mesa, Barragem de Brazil 14°30S 49°10W 333 D2
Serra do Cipó △ Brazil 19°14S 43°23W 333 E3
Serra do Divisor △ Brazil 8°3S 73°29W 330 B3
Serra do Navio Brazil 0°59N 52°3W 329 C7
Serra do Salitre Brazil 19°6S 46°41W 333 E2
Serra dos Orgãos △ Brazil 22°25S 43°8W 333 F3
Serra San Bruno Italy 38°35N 16°20E 201 D9
Serra Talhada Brazil 7°59S 38°18W 332 C4
Serradilla Spain 39°50N 6°9W 194 F4
Serramanna Italy 39°25N 8°55E 200 C1
Serramonte U.S.A. 37°39N 122°28W 136 C2
Serranía de la Neblina △ Venezuela 1°5N 65°51W 328 C4
Serranía San Luís △ Paraguay 22°35S 57°22W 334 A4
Serranía San Rafael △ Paraguay 26°30S 56°0W 335 B4
Serranilla Bank W. Indies 15°50N 80°0W 320 C4
Serranópolis Brazil 18°16S 52°0W 331 D7
Serras d'Aire e Candeeiros ⌓ Portugal 39°31N 8°48W 195 F2
Serrat, C. Tunisia 37°14N 9°10E 261 A6
Serravalle Scrívia Italy 44°43N 8°51E 198 D5
Serre-Ponçon, L. de France 44°22N 6°20E 175 D10
Serres Hautes-Alpes, France 44°26N 5°43E 175 D9
Serres Greece 41°5N 23°31E 202 E7
Serres □ Greece 41°5N 23°37E 202 E7
Serrezuela Argentina 30°40S 65°20W 334 C2
Serrinha Brazil 11°39S 39°0W 333 D4
Serrita Brazil 7°56S 39°19W 332 C4
Sersale Italy 39°1N 16°43E 201 C9
Sertã Portugal 39°48N 8°6W 194 F2
Sertânia Brazil 8°5S 37°20W 332 C4
Sertanópolis Brazil 23°4S 51°2W 335 A5
Sêrtar China 32°20N 100°41E 228 A3
Serua Indonesia 6°18S 130°1E 231 F8
Serui Indonesia 1°53S 136°10E 231 E9
Serule Botswana 21°57S 27°20E 270 B4
Serutu Indonesia 1°42S 108°45E 235 C3
Servia Greece 40°11N 22°0E 202 F6
Serzedelo Portugal 41°24N 8°14W 194 D2
Ses Salines Spain 39°21N 3°3E 206 B4
Sesayap → Indonesia 3°36N 117°15E 235 B5
Sese Is. Uganda 0°20S 32°20E 268 C3
Seseko-shima Japan 26°39N 127°52E 288 a
Sesepe Indonesia 1°30S 127°59E 231 E7
Sesfontein Namibia 19°7S 13°39E 270 A1
Sesheke Zambia 17°29S 24°13E 270 A3
Sésia → Italy 45°5N 8°37E 198 C5
Sesimbra Portugal 38°28N 9°6W 195 G1
S'Espalmador Spain 38°47N 1°26E 206 D1
S'Espardell Spain 38°48N 1°29E 206 D1
Sessa Angola 13°56S 20°38E 265 E4
Sessa Aurunca Italy 41°14N 13°56E 200 A6
Sesser U.S.A. 38°5N 89°1W 310 F7
S'Estanyol Spain 39°22N 2°54E 206 B3
Sestao Spain 43°18N 3°0W 196 B2
Sesto Calende Italy 45°44N 8°37E 198 C5
Sesto San Giovanni Italy 45°31N 9°13E 129 A2
Sesto Ulteriano Italy 45°24N 9°16E 129 B2
Sestri Levante Italy 44°16N 9°24E 198 D6
Sestriere Italy 44°57N 6°53E 198 D3
Sestroretsk Russia 60°5N 29°58E 188 B6
Sestrunj Croatia 44°10N 15°0E 199 D11
Sestu Italy 39°18N 9°5E 200 C2
Setagaya Japan 35°37N 139°36E 140 B2
Setaka Japan 33°9N 130°28E 222 D2
Setana Japan 42°26N 139°51E 220 C9
Sète France 43°25N 3°42E 174 E7
Sete Cidades △ Brazil 4°0S 41°37W 332 B3
Sete Lagoas Brazil 19°27S 44°16W 333 E3
Seter Norway 59°52N 10°47E 133 A3
Setesdalsheiene = Suldalsheiene Norway 59°28N 7°10E 164 E3
Setia Budi Indonesia 6°12S 106°49E 122 B1
Sétif Algeria 36°9N 5°26E 261 A6
Sétif □ Algeria 36°10N 5°0E 261 A6
Setit → Sudan 14°20N 35°50E 257 E4
Seto Japan 35°14N 137°6E 223 B9
Setonaikai Japan 34°20N 133°30E 222 C5
Setonaikai △ Japan 34°15N 133°15E 222 C5
Setsan Burma 16°3N 95°23E 241 G5
Settat Morocco 33°0N 7°40W 260 B3
Settat □ Morocco 33°5N 7°25W 260 B3
Setté-Cama Gabon 2°32S 9°45E 264 C1
Settebagni Italy 42°0N 12°31E 136 A2
Settecamini Italy 41°57N 12°38E 136 B2
Séttimo Milanese Italy 45°28N 9°3E 129 B1
Séttimo Torinese Italy 45°9N 7°46E 198 C4
Setting L. Canada 55°0N 98°38W 297 C9
Settle U.K. 54°5N 2°16W 168 C5
Settlement Wake I. 19°18N 166°38E 302 b
Settlement, The Br. Virgin Is. 18°43N 64°22W 321 b
Settlers S. Africa 25°2S 28°30E 271 C4
Settsu Japan 34°47N 135°33E 133 A2
Setúbal Portugal 38°30N 8°58W 195 G2
Setúbal □ Portugal 38°25N 8°35W 195 G2
Setúbal, B. de Portugal 38°40N 8°56W 195 G2
Setuny → Russia 55°43N 37°21E 129 B2
Seugne → France 45°42N 0°32W 174 C3
Seul, Lac Canada 50°20N 92°30W 298 B1
Seulimeum Indonesia 5°27N 95°15E 234 A1
Seurre France 47°0N 5°8E 173 F12
Seutula Finland 60°20N 24°52E 121 A2
Sevan Armenia 40°33N 44°56E 191 K7
Sevan, Ozero = Sevana Lich Armenia 40°30N 45°20E 191 K7
Sevana Lich Armenia 40°30N 45°20E 191 K7
Sevastopol Ukraine 44°35N 33°30E 189 K7
Seven Corners U.S.A. 38°53N 77°9W 143 B3
Seven Islands = Sept-Îles Canada 50°13N 66°22W 299 B6
Seven Kings U.K. 51°33N 0°5E 125 A4
Seven Sisters Canada 54°56N 128°10W 296 C3
Seventeenth Street Canal U.S.A. 30°3N 90°7W 131 A2
Sever → Spain 39°40N 7°32W 195 F3
Sévérac-le-Château France 44°20N 3°5E 174 D7
Severn → Ont., Canada 56°2N 87°36W 298 A2
Severn → U.K. 51°35N 2°40W 169 F5
Severnaya Zemlya Russia 79°0N 100°0E 215 B11
Severnyye Uvaly Russia 60°0N 50°0E 186 C8
Severo-Kurilsk Russia 50°40N 156°8E 215 D16
Severo-Yeniseyskiy Russia 60°22N 93°1E 215 C10
Severo-Zapadnyy □ Russia 65°0N 40°0E 214 C4
Severobaykalsk Russia 55°39N 109°19E 215 D11
Severočeský □ Czech Rep. 50°30N 14°0E 180 A7
Severodonetsk = Syeverodonetsk Ukraine 48°58N 38°35E 189 H10
Severodvinsk Russia 64°27N 39°58E 186 B6
Severomoravský □ Czech Rep. 49°38N 17°40E 181 B10
Severomorsk Russia 69°5N 33°27E 160 B25
Severouralsk Russia 60°9N 59°57E 186 B10
Seversk Russia 56°36N 84°49E 214 D9
Sévesco → Italy 45°35N 9°9E 129 A1
Sevier → U.S.A. 39°4N 113°6W 304 G7
Sevier Desert U.S.A. 39°40N 112°45W 304 G7
Sevier L. U.S.A. 38°54N 113°9W 304 G7
Sevilla Colombia 4°16N 75°57W 328 C2
Sevilla Spain 37°23N 5°58W 195 H5
Sevilla □ Spain 37°25N 5°30W 195 H5
Seville = Sevilla Spain 37°23N 5°58W 195 H5
Seville Fla., U.S.A. 29°19N 81°30W 317 F8
Seville Ga., U.S.A. 31°58N 83°36W 316 D6
Sevlievo Bulgaria 43°2N 25°6E 203 C9
Sevnica Slovenia 46°2N 15°19E 199 B12
Sevran France 48°56N 2°31E 134 A4
Sèvre-Nantaise → France 47°12N 1°33W 172 E5
Sèvre-Niortaise → France 46°28N 0°50W 174 B3
Sevsk Russia 52°10N 34°30E 189 F8
Sewa → S. Leone 7°20N 12°10W 262 D2
Sewani India 28°58N 75°39E 242 E6
Seward Alaska, U.S.A. 60°7N 149°27W 303 F10
Seward Nebr., U.S.A. 40°55N 97°6W 308 E5
Seward Pa., U.S.A. 40°25N 79°1W 312 F5
Seward Peninsula U.S.A. 65°30N 166°0W 303 D6
Sewell Chile 34°10S 70°23W 334 C1
Sewer Indonesia 5°53S 134°40E 231 F8
Sewickley U.S.A. 40°32N 80°12W 312 F4
Sewri India 18°59N 72°50E 130 B2
Sexsmith Canada 55°21N 118°47W 296 B5
Seychelles ■ Ind. Oc. 5°0S 56°0E 272 c
Seyðisfjörður Iceland 65°16N 13°57W 155 B13
Seydişehir Turkey 37°25N 31°51E 212 D4
Seydvān Iran 38°34N 45°2E 213 C11
Seyhan → Turkey 36°43N 34°53E 250 B5
Seyhan Barajı Turkey 37°2N 35°18E 212 D6
Seyitgazi Turkey 39°27N 30°43E 205 B12
Seyitömer Turkey 39°34N 29°52E 205 B11
Seym → Ukraine 51°27N 32°34E 189 G7
Seymen Turkey 41°6N 27°57E 203 E11
Seymour Vic., Australia 37°2S 145°10E 283 D6
Seymour Eastern Cape, S. Africa 32°33S 26°46E 271 D4
Seymour Conn., U.S.A. 41°24N 73°4W 313 E11
Seymour Ind., U.S.A. 38°58N 85°53W 311 F11
Seymour Tex., U.S.A. 33°35N 99°16W 314 E5
Seyne France 44°21N 6°22E 175 D10
Seyssel France 45°57N 5°50E 175 C9
Sežana Slovenia 45°43N 13°41E 199 C10
Sézanne France 48°40N 3°40E 173 D10
Sezze Italy 41°30N 13°3E 200 A6
Sfântu Gheorghe Covasna, Romania 45°52N 25°48E 183 E10
Sfântu Gheorghe Tulcea, Romania 44°53N 29°36E 183 F14
Sfântu Gheorghe, Braţul → Romania 44°51N 29°36E 183 F14
Sfax Tunisia 34°49N 10°48E 258 B2

Sfax □ *Tunisia* 34°40N 10°20E **261** B7
Sforzesso, Castello *Italy* 45°28N 9°10E **129** B2
Sha Kok Mei *China* 22°23N 114°14E **122** A2
Sha Tau Kok *China* 22°33N 114°13E **219** a
Sha Tin *China* 22°23N 114°12E **122** A2
Sha Xi → *China* 26°35N 118°0E **229** D12
Sha Xian *China* 26°23N 117°45E **229** D11
Shaanxi □ *China* 35°0N 109°0E **226** G5
Sha'ar Binyamin
　West Bank 31°52N 35°16E **123** A2
Shaba = Katanga □
　Dem. Rep. of the Congo 8°0S 25°0E **268** D2
Shaba △ *Kenya* 0°38N 37°48E **268** B4
Shabeellaha Dhexe □
　Somali Rep. 3°0N 46°0E **267** D6
Shabeellaha Hoose □
　Somali Rep. 1°0N 44°0E **267** D5
Shabeelle → *Somali Rep.* 2°0N 44°0E **267** D6
Shabestar *Iran* 38°11N 45°41E **213** C11
Shabla *Bulgaria* 43°31N 28°32E **203** C12
Shabogamo L. *Canada* 53°15N 66°30W **299** B6
Shabrāmant *Egypt* 29°56N 31°11E **117** B2
Shabunda
　Dem. Rep. of the Congo 2°40S 27°16E **268** C2
Shabwah *Yemen* 15°22N 47°1E **248** D4
Shache *China* 38°20N 77°10E **217** E9
Shackleton Fracture Zone
　S. Ocean 60°0S 60°0W **151** B18
Shackleton Ice Shelf
　Antarctica 66°0S 100°0E **151** C8
Shackleton Inlet
　Antarctica 83°0S 160°0E **151** E11
Shādegān *Iran* 30°40N 48°38E **247** D6
Shadi *Jiangxi, China* 26°7N 114°47E **229** D10
Shadi *Jammu & Kashmir,*
　India 33°24N 77°14E **243** C7
Shadrinsk *Russia* 56°5N 63°32E **214** D7
Shady Dale *U.S.A.* 33°24N 83°36W **316** B6
Shady Grove *U.S.A.* 30°17N 83°38W **316** E6
Shadyside *U.S.A.* 39°58N 80°45W **312** G4
Shafer, L. *U.S.A.* 40°46N 86°46W **311** D10
Shaffa *Nigeria* 10°30N 12°6E **263** C7
Shafter *U.S.A.* 35°30N 119°16W **307** K7
Shaftesbury *U.K.* 51°0N 2°11W **169** F5
Shaftsbury *U.S.A.* 43°0N 73°11W **313** D11
Shag Pt. *N.Z.* 45°29S 170°52E **285** F5
Shag Rocks *Atl. Oc.* 53°0S 41°0W **152** M7
Shagamu *Nigeria* 6°51N 3°39E **263** D5
Shageluk *U.S.A.* 62°41N 159°34W **303** E8
Shagram *Pakistan* 36°24N 72°20E **243** A5
Shah Alam *Malaysia* 3°5N 101°32E **237** L3
Shah Alizai *Pakistan* 29°25N 66°33E **242** E2
Shah Bunder *Pakistan* 24°13N 67°56E **242** G2
Shah Juy *Afghan.* 32°31N 67°25E **240** B2
Shah Mosque *Iran* 32°39N 51°52E **141** A2
Shahabad *Karnataka, India* 17°10N 76°54E **244** F3
Shahabad *Punjab, India* 30°10N 76°55E **242** D7
Shahabad *Raj., India* 25°15N 77°11E **242** G7
Shahabad *Ut. P., India* 27°36N 79°56E **243** F8
Shahada *India* 21°33N 74°30E **244** D2
Shahadpur *Pakistan* 25°55N 68°35E **242** G3
Shahapur *India* 15°50N 74°4E **245** G2
Shahbā' *Syria* 32°52N 36°38E **250** F7
Shahbazpur 1. *Bangla.* 22°30N 90°45E **241** D3
Shahdād *Iran* 30°30N 57°40E **247** D8
Shahdād, Namakzār-e
　Iran 30°20N 58°20E **247** D8
Shahdadkot *Pakistan* 27°50N 67°55E **242** F2
Shahdara *India* 28°40N 77°18E **120** A2
Shahdol *India* 23°19N 81°26E **243** H9
Shahe *Guangdong, China* 23°9N 113°9E **121** B2
Shahe *Hebei, China* 37°0N 114°32E **226** F8
Shahganj *India* 26°3N 82°44E **243** F10
Shahgarh *India* 27°15N 69°50E **242** F3
Shaḥḥāt *Libya* 32°48N 21°54E **258** B4
Shahīdān *Afghan.* 36°42N 67°49E **240** A2
Shahjahanpur *India* 27°54N 79°57E **243** F8
Shahpur = Salmās *Iran* 38°11N 44°47E **213** C11
Shahpur *Karnataka, India* 16°40N 76°48E **244** F3
Shahpur *Mad. P., India* 22°12N 77°58E **242** H7
Shahpur *Baluchistan,*
　Pakistan 28°46N 68°27E **242** E3
Shahpur *Punjab, Pakistan* 32°17N 72°26E **242** C5
Shahpur Chakar *Pakistan* 26°9N 68°39E **242** F3
Shahpura *Mad. P., India* 23°10N 80°45E **243** H9
Shahpura *Raj., India* 25°38N 74°56E **242** G6
Shahr-e Bābak *Iran* 30°7N 55°9E **247** D7
Shahr-e Kord *Iran* 32°15N 50°55E **247** C6
Shahr-e Rey *Iran* 35°36N 51°25E **141** B1
Shahrak-e Golshahr *Iran* 35°36N 51°18E **141** B1
Shahrak-e Qods *Iran* 35°47N 51°12E **141** A2
Shahrakht *Iran* 33°38N 60°16E **247** C9
Shahrezā = Qomsheh *Iran* 32°0N 51°55E **247** D6
Shahrig *Pakistan* 30°15N 67°40E **242** D2
Shahrisabz *Uzbekistan* 39°33N 66°50E **217** F7
Shāhrūd = Emāmrūd *Iran* 36°30N 55°0E **247** B7
Shahukou *China* 40°20N 112°18E **226** D7
Shaikh Aomar *Iraq* 33°20N 44°23E **113** A2
Shaikhabad *Afghan.* 34°2N 68°45E **242** B3
Shajapur *India* 23°27N 76°21E **242** H7
Shajing *China* 22°44N 113°48E **219** a
Shajuwan *Taiwan* 23°13N 121°23E **225** C3
Shakargarh *Pakistan* 32°17N 75°10E **242** C6
Shakawe *Botswana* 18°28S 21°49E **270** A3
Shakenge
　Dem. Rep. of the Congo 6°14S 18°41E **265** D3
Shaker Heights *U.S.A.* 41°28N 81°32W **312** E3
Shakhtersk *Russia* 49°10N 142°8E **215** E15
Shakhtīnsk *Kazakhstan* 49°42N 72°37E **217** C8
Shakhty *Russia* 47°40N 40°16E **191** G5
Shakhtyorskoye = Pershotravensk
　Ukraine 50°13N 27°40E **177** C14
Shakhunya *Russia* 57°40N 46°46E **190** B8
Shaki *Nigeria* 8°41N 3°21E **263** D5
Shākir *Egypt* 27°30N 33°59E **256** B3
Shakotan-Hantō *Japan* 43°10N 140°30E **220** C10
Shaksam Valley *Asia* 36°0N 76°20E **243** A7
Shaktoolik *U.S.A.* 64°20N 161°9W **303** D7
Shakurbasti *India* 28°41N 77°6E **120** A1
Shala, L. *Ethiopia* 7°30N 38°30E **257** F4
Shalkar Köli *Kazakhstan* 50°35N 51°47E **190** E10
Shalkiya *Kazakhstan* 42°36N 68°21E **124** B2
Shallow Lake *Canada* 44°36N 81°5W **312** B3
Shalqar *Kazakhstan* 47°48N 59°39E **216** C5
Shalqar Köli *Kazakhstan* 50°33N 51°40E **216** B6
Shalskiy *Russia* 61°48N 35°58E **188** B8
Shalu *Taiwan* 24°14N 120°34E **225** B2
Shaluli Shan *China* 30°40N 99°55E **228** B2
Shām *Iran* 26°39N 57°21E **247** E8
Shām, Bādiyat ash *Asia* 32°0N 40°0E **246** C3
Shām, J. ash *Oman* 23°10N 57°5E **249** B7
Sham Shui Po *China* 22°19N 114°9E **122** B2
Shamāl Bahr el Ghazal □
　Sudan 8°0N 27°30E **257** F2
Shamāl Dârfûr □ *Sudan* 15°0N 25°0E **257** E2
Shamāl Kordofân □ *Sudan* 15°0N 30°0E **257** E2
Shamāl Sīnî □ *Egypt* 30°30N 33°30E **251** H4
Shamapur *India* 28°44N 77°0E **120** A2
Shamattawa *Canada* 55°51N 92°5W **298** A1
Shamattawa → *Canada* 55°1N 85°23W **298** A2
Shambe *Sudan* 7°8N 30°46E **257** F3
Shambe △ *Sudan* 6°57N 30°55E **257** F3
Shambu *Ethiopia* 9°32N 37°3E **257** F4
Shamgong Dzong *Bhutan* 27°13N 90°35E **241** B8

Shamian *China* 23°6N 113°13E **121** B2
Shamīl *Iran* 27°30N 56°55E **247** E8
Shamkhor = Şämkir
　Azerbaijan 40°50N 46°0E **191** K8
Shāmkūh *Iran* 35°47N 57°50E **247** C8
Shamli *India* 29°32N 77°18E **242** E7
Shammar, Jabal *Si. Arabia* 27°40N 41°0E **246** E4
Shamo = Gobi *Asia* 44°0N 110°0E **226** C6
Shamo, L. *Ethiopia* 5°45N 37°30E **257** F4
Shamokin *U.S.A.* 40°47N 76°34W **313** F8
Shamrock, Ont., Canada 51°3N 106°35W **314** A4
Shamrock *Tex., U.S.A.* 35°13N 100°15W **314** D4
Shamva *Zimbabwe* 17°20S 31°32E **269** B5
Shan □ *Burma* 21°30N 98°30E **241** E7
Shan Mei *China* 22°24N 114°10E **122** A2
Shan Shan *China* 42°52N 90°10E **217** D12
Shan Xian *China* 34°50N 116°5E **226** G9
Shana = Kurilsk *Russia* 45°14N 147°53E **215** E15
Shanan → *Ethiopia* 8°0N 40°20E **257** F5
Shanchengzhen *China* 42°37N 125°22E **226** C12
Shancheng *China* 34°31N 115°26E **229** B10
Shāndak *Iran* 28°28N 60°27E **247** D9
Shandan *China* 38°45N 101°15E **218** D9
Shandon *U.S.A.* 35°39N 120°23W **306** K6
Shandong □ *China* 36°0N 118°0E **227** G10
Shandong Bandao *China* 37°0N 121°0E **227** F11
Shandur Pass *Pakistan* 36°4N 72°31E **243** A5
Shang Xian = Shangzhou
　China 33°50N 109°58E **226** H5
Shangalowe
　Dem. Rep. of the Congo 10°50S 26°30E **269** E2
Shangani *Zimbabwe* 19°41S 29°20E **271** A4
Shangani → *Zimbabwe* 18°41S 27°10E **269** B4
Shangbancheng *China* 40°50N 118°1E **227** D10
Shangcheng *China* 31°47N 115°26E **229** B10
Shangchuan Dao *China* 21°40N 112°50E **229** G9
Shangdu *China* 41°30N 113°30E **226** D7
Shanggao *China* 28°17N 114°55E **229** C10
Shanghai *China* 31°11N 121°26E **138** B2
Shanghai Hongqiao ✈ (SHA)
　China 31°12N 121°20E **138** B1
Shanghai Pudong ✈ (PVG)
　China 31°9N 121°47E **138** B2
Shanghai Shi □ *China* 31°0N 121°30E **229** B13
Shanghang *China* 25°2N 116°23E **229** E11
Shanghe *China* 37°20N 117°10E **227** F9
Shangjiao = Shangrao
　China 28°25N 117°59E **229** C11
Shanglin *China* 23°27N 108°33E **228** F7
Shangnan *China* 33°32N 110°50E **226** H6
Shangqiu *China* 34°26N 115°36E **226** G8
Shangrao *China* 28°25N 117°59E **229** C11
Shangri-La = Zhongdian
　China 27°48N 99°42E **228** D2
Shangshui *China* 33°42N 114°35E **226** H8
Shangsi *China* 22°8N 107°58E **228** F6
Shangyi *China* 41°4N 113°57E **226** D7
Shangyou *China* 25°48N 114°32E **229** E10
Shangyu *China* 30°0N 120°52E **229** B13
Shangzhi *China* 45°22N 127°56E **227** B14
Shangzhou *China* 33°50N 109°58E **226** H5
Shanhetun *China* 44°33N 127°15E **227** B14
Shanhua Tan *Taiwan* 23°12N 120°23E **225** C2
Shanhua *Taiwan* 23°8N 120°17E **225** C2
Shani *Nigeria* 10°14N 12°2E **263** C7
Shānidar *Iraq* 36°48N 44°14E **113** A3
Shankill *Ireland* 53°14N 6°7W **120** B3
Shanklin *U.K.* 50°38N 1°11W **169** G6
Shanlin *Taiwan* 23°0N 120°32E **225** C2
Shannon *N.Z.* 40°33S 175°25E **284** D4
Shannon → *Ireland* 52°35N 9°30W **166** D2
Shannon ✈ (SNN) *Ireland* 52°42N 8°57W **166** D3
Shannon, Mouth of the
　Ireland 52°30N 9°55W **166** D2
Shannon △ *Australia* 34°35S 116°25E **279** F2
Shannon Ø *Greenland* 75°10N 18°30W **159** B10
Shannonbridge *Ireland* 53°17N 8°3W **166** C3
Shannontown *U.S.A.* 33°53N 80°21W **316** B9
Shanshan *Taiwan* 23°6N 120°21E **225** C2
Shansi = Shanxi □ *China* 37°0N 112°0E **226** F7
Shantar, Ostrov Bolshoy
　Russia 55°9N 137°40E **215** D14
Shantipur *India* 23°17N 88°25E **243** H13
Shantou *China* 23°18N 116°40E **229** F11
Shantung = Shandong □
　China 36°0N 118°0E **227** G10
Shanwei *China* 22°48N 115°22E **229** F10
Shanxi □ *China* 37°0N 112°0E **226** F7
Shanyang *China* 39°25N 112°56E **226** E7
Shanyin *China* 39°25N 112°56E **226** E7
Shaodong *China* 27°15N 111°43E **229** D8
Shaoguan *China* 24°48N 113°35E **229** E9
Shaohing = Shaoxing
　China 30°0N 120°35E **229** C13
Shaoshan *China* 27°55N 112°33E **229** D9
Shaowu *China* 27°22N 117°28E **229** D11
Shaoxing *China* 30°0N 120°35E **229** C13
Shaoyang *Hunan, China* 26°59N 111°20E **229** D8
Shaoyang *Hunan, China* 27°14N 111°25E **229** D8
Shap *U.K.* 54°32N 2°40W **168** C5
Shapinsay *U.K.* 59°3N 2°51W **167** B6
Shaqlāwah *Iraq* 36°23N 44°20E **113** B5
Shaqq el Gi'eifer → *Sudan* 15°16N 26°0E **257** D2
Shaqra' *Si. Arabia* 25°15N 45°16E **246** E5
Shaqrā' *Yemen* 13°22N 45°44E **248** D4
Shar *Kazakhstan* 49°35N 81°2E **217** C10
Sharafa *Sudan* 11°59N 27°7E **257** E2
Sharafkhāneh *Iran* 38°11N 45°3E **213** C11
Sharashova *Belarus* 52°34N 24°12E **185** F11
Sharavati → *India* 14°20N 74°25E **245** G2
Sharbaqty *Kazakhstan* 51°23N 78°17E **217** B9
Sharbot Lake *Canada* 44°46N 76°41W **313** B8
Shardara, Step *Kazakhstan* 42°26N 68°0E **217** D7
Sharhorod *Ukraine* 48°45N 28°5E **183** B13
Shari *Japan* 43°55N 144°40E **220** C12
Shariff Aguak = Maganoy
　Phil. 6°51N 124°31E **233** H5
Shariff Kabunsuan □ *Phil.* 7°5N 124°5E **233** H5
Sharjah = Ash Shāriqah
　U.A.E. 25°23N 55°26E **247** E7
Shark B. *Australia* 25°30S 113°32E **279** E1
Shark Bay △ *Australia* 25°30S 113°37E **279** E1
Sharm el Sheikh *Egypt* 27°53N 34°18E **251** E5
Sharon, Ont. *Canada* 44°6N 79°26W **312** B5
Sharon *Mass., U.S.A.* 42°7N 71°11W **313** D13
Sharon *Pa., U.S.A.* 41°14N 80°31W **312** E4
Sharon Springs *Kans.,*
　U.S.A. 38°54N 101°45W **308** F3
Sharon Springs *N.Y.,*
　U.S.A. 42°48N 74°37W **313** D10
Sharonville *U.S.A.* 39°16N 84°25W **311** E12
Sharp I. *China* 22°21N 114°17E **122** A2
Sharp Pk. *Phil.* 5°58N 125°31E **233** J5
Sharpe L. *Canada* 54°24N 93°40W **298** B1
Sharpes *U.S.A.* 28°26N 80°45W **316** G6
Sharpel Istiwa'iya □ *Sudan* 5°0N 33°0E **257** G3
Sharpsville *U.S.A.* 41°15N 80°29W **312** E4
Sharq el Istiwa'iya □ *Sudan* 5°0N 33°0E **257** G3
Sharqī, Al Jabal ash
　Lebanon 33°40N 36°10E **250** B5
Sharqīya □ *Egypt* 30°30N 31°0E **256** B2
Sharya *Russia* 58°22N 45°20E **190** A7
Shasha *Ethiopia* 6°29N 35°59E **257** F4
Shashemene *Ethiopia* 7°13N 38°33E **257** F4

Shashi *Botswana* 21°15S 27°27E **271** B4
Shashi → *Africa* 21°14S 29°20E **269** C2
Shashi → *China* 30°25N 112°14E **229** B9
Shasta, Mt. *U.S.A.* 41°25N 122°12W **304** F2
Shasta L. *U.S.A.* 40°43N 122°25W **304** F2
Shastrinagar *India* 14°39N 32°6E **257** E3
Shatawi *Sudan* 14°39N 32°6E **257** E3
Shāṭi', Wādī ash → *Libya* 27°30N 15°0E **258** C3
Shatilki = Svyetlahorsk
　Belarus 52°38N 29°46E **177** B15
Shatsk *Russia* 54°5N 41°55E **190** C5
Shatsk *Ukraine* 51°25N 23°55E **185** G10
Shatsky Rise *Pac. Oc.* 34°0N 157°0E **288** D7
Shatskiy □ *Ukraine* 51°30N 23°52E **185** G10
Shatt al Arab *Asia* 29°57N 48°34E **247** D6
Shatura *Russia* 55°33N 39°21E **188** E10
Shaturtof = Shatura
　Russia 55°33N 39°21E **188** E10
Shau Kei Wan *China* 22°16N 114°13E **122** B2
Shaumyani = Shulaveri
　Georgia 41°22N 44°45E **191** K7
Shaunavon *Canada* 49°35N 108°25W **297** D7
Shaver L. *U.S.A.* 37°9N 119°18W **306** H7
Shavli = Šiauliai
　Lithuania 55°56N 23°15E **184** C10
Shaw → *Australia* 20°21S 119°17E **278** D2
Shaw I. *Australia* 20°30S 149°2E **280** b
Shawanaga *Canada* 45°31N 80°17W **312** A4
Shawangunk Mts.
　U.S.A. 41°35N 74°30W **313** E10
Shawano *U.S.A.* 44°47N 88°36W **308** C9
Shawinigan *Canada* 46°35N 72°50W **298** C5
Shawmari, J. ash *Jordan* 30°35N 36°35E **251** H7
Shawnee *Kans., U.S.A.* 32°29N 81°25W **316** C8
Shawnee *Kans., U.S.A.* 39°1N 94°43W **310** G2
Shawnee *Okla., U.S.A.* 35°20N 96°55W **314** D6
Shawocun *China* 39°53N 116°13E **114** B1
Shay Gap *Australia* 20°30S 120°10E **278** D3
Shayang *China* 30°42N 112°29E **229** B9
Shaybārā *Si. Arabia* 25°26N 36°47E **246** E3
Shayib el Banat, Gebel
　Egypt 26°59N 33°29E **256** B3
Shaykh, J. ash *Lebanon* 33°25N 35°50E **250** E6
Shaykh Miskin *Syria* 32°49N 36°9E **250** F7
Shaykh Sa'd *Iraq* 32°34N 46°17E **213** F12
Shaykh 'Uthmān *Yemen* 12°52N 44°59E **248** D4
Shaytansky Zavod = Pervouralsk
　Russia 56°59N 59°59E **186** C10
Shchekino *Russia* 54°1N 37°34E **188** E9
Shcherbakov = Rybinsk
　Russia 58°5N 38°50E **188** C10
Shchigry *Russia* 51°55N 36°58E **189** G9
Shchors *Ukraine* 51°48N 31°56E **189** G9
Shchuchinsk *Kazakhstan* 52°56N 70°12E **217** B8
She Xian *Anhui, China* 29°50N 118°25E **229** C12
She Xian *Hebei, China* 36°30N 113°40E **226** F7
Shea *Guyana* 2°48N 59°4W **329** C6
Shebekino *Russia* 50°28N 36°54E **189** G9
Shebele = Shabeelle →
　Somali Rep. 2°0N 44°0E **267** D6
Shebele *Ethiopia* 8°8N 42°40E **267** C5
Sheberghān *Afghan.* 36°40N 65°45E **240** A2
Sheboygan *U.S.A.* 43°46N 87°45W **308** D10
Shebshi Mts. *Nigeria* 8°30N 12°0E **263** D7
Shedd Aquarium *Chicago, U.S.A.* ... **119** e3
Shediac *Canada* 46°14N 64°32W **299** C7
Sheelin, L. *Ireland* 53°48N 7°20W **166** C4
Sheen, L. *Ireland* 52°4N 9°30W **166** E2
Sheenjek → *U.S.A.* 66°45N 144°33W **303** C11
Sheep Haven *Ireland* 55°11N 7°52W **166** A4
Sheep Range *U.S.A.* 36°35N 115°15W **307** J11
Sheepshead Bay *U.S.A.* 40°35S 73°55W **132** C2
Sheerness *U.K.* 51°26N 0°47E **169** F8
Sheet Harbour *Canada* 44°56N 62°31W **299** D7
Sheffield *N.Z.* 43°23S 172°1E **285** D7
Sheffield *S. Yorks., U.K.* 53°23N 1°28W **168** D6
Sheffield *Ala., U.S.A.* 34°46N 87°41W **315** D1
Sheffield *Ill., U.S.A.* 41°21N 89°44W **310** D7
Sheffield *Iowa, U.S.A.* 42°54N 93°13W **310** B8
Sheffield *Mass., U.S.A.* 42°5N 73°21W **313** D11
Sheffield *Pa., U.S.A.* 41°42N 79°3W **312** E5
Shegaon *India* 20°48N 76°47E **244** D3
Sheho *Canada* 51°35N 103°13W **295** C8
Shehojele *Ethiopia* 10°40N 35°9E **257** E4
Shehong *China* 30°54N 105°12E **228** B5
Sheheun → *Argentina* 49°35S 69°34W **336** G3
Shei-Pa △ *Taiwan* 24°36N 121°22E **225** B3
Shei Shan *Taiwan* 24°34N 121°51E **225** B3
Sheikh, W. el → *Egypt* 28°41N 33°41E **251** K4
Sheikh Zayed Canal *Egypt* 22°36N 30°55E **256** C3
Sheikhpura *India* 25°9N 85°53E **243** G11
Shek Hasan *Ethiopia* 12°5N 35°58E **257** E4
Shek O *China* 22°13N 114°15E **122** B2
Shekhupura *Pakistan* 31°42N 73°58E **242** D5
Sheki = Şäki *Azerbaijan* 41°10N 47°5E **191** K8
Shekki = Zhongshan
　China 22°26N 113°20E **229** F9
Shekou *China* 22°30N 113°55E **219** a
Shelbina *U.S.A.* 39°47N 92°2W **310** F6
Shelburne *N.S., Canada* 43°47N 65°20W **299** D6
Shelburne *Ont., Canada* 44°4N 80°15W **312** B4
Shelburne *Vt., U.S.A.* 44°23N 73°14W **313** B11
Shelburne B. *Australia* 11°50S 142°50E **280** A3
Shelburne Falls *U.S.A.* 42°36N 72°45W **313** D12
Shelby *Mich., U.S.A.* 43°37N 86°22W **308** D10
Shelby *Miss., U.S.A.* 33°57N 90°46W **315** D9
Shelby *Mont., U.S.A.* 48°30N 111°51W **304** B8
Shelby *N.C., U.S.A.* 35°17N 81°32W **317** D4
Shelby *Ohio, U.S.A.* 40°53N 82°40W **312** F2
Shelbyville *Ill., U.S.A.* 39°24N 88°48W **311** F8
Shelbyville *Ind., U.S.A.* 39°31N 85°47W **311** F11
Shelbyville *Ky., U.S.A.* 38°13N 85°14W **311** F11
Shelbyville *Mo., U.S.A.* 39°48N 92°2W **310** F6
Shelbyville *Tenn., U.S.A.* 35°29N 86°28W **315** D1
Shelbyville, L. *U.S.A.* 39°26N 88°46W **311** F8
Sheldon *Ill., U.S.A.* 40°46N 87°34W **311** D9
Sheldon *Iowa, U.S.A.* 43°11N 95°51W **308** D6
Sheldon *Mo., U.S.A.* 37°40N 94°18W **310** G3
Sheldon *S.C., U.S.A.* 32°35N 80°49W **316** D9
Sheldon Point *U.S.A.* 62°32N 164°52W **303** E6
Sheldrake *Canada* 50°20N 64°51W **299** B7
Shelek *Kazakhstan* 43°36N 78°17E **217** D9
Shelengo, Khawr →
　Sudan 10°33N 28°40E **257** E2
Shelikhova, Zaliv *Russia* 59°30N 157°0E **215** D16
Shelikof Strait *U.S.A.* 57°30N 155°0W **303** F9
Shell Beach = Huntington Beach
　U.S.A. 33°40N 117°59W **307** M9
Shell Lakes *Australia* 29°20S 127°30E **279** E4
Shellbrook *Canada* 53°13N 106°24W **295** C7
Shellharbour *Australia* 34°31S 150°51E **283** C5
Shellman *U.S.A.* 31°46N 84°37W **316** D1
Shellsburg *U.S.A.* 42°6N 91°52W **310** B8
Shelon → *Russia* 58°10N 30°30E **188** C6
Shelter Bay = Port-Cartier
　Canada 50°2N 66°50W **299** B6
Shelter I. *Hong Kong,*
　China 22°19N 114°17E **122** B2
Shelter I. *N.Y., U.S.A.* 41°4N 72°20W **313** E12
Shelton *Conn., U.S.A.* 41°19N 73°5W **313** E11

Shelton *Wash., U.S.A.* 47°13N 123°6W **306** C3
Shemakha = Şamaxı
　Azerbaijan 40°38N 48°37E **191** K9
Shemonaïkha
　Kazakhstan 50°37N 81°54E **217** B10
Shēmri *Albania* 42°4N 20°13E **202** D4
Shemsi *Sudan* 19°2N 29°57E **256** D2
She Xian *China* 36°15N 115°40E **226** F8
Shenandoah *Iowa, U.S.A.* 40°46N 95°22W **308** E6
Shenandoah *Pa., U.S.A.* 40°49N 76°12W **313** F8
Shenandoah *Va., U.S.A.* 38°29N 78°37W **309** F14
Shenandoah → *U.S.A.* 39°19N 77°44W **309** F15
Shenandoah △ *U.S.A.* 38°35N 78°22W **309** F14
Shenchi *China* 39°8N 112°10E **226** E7
Shencottah *India* 8°59N 77°18E **245** K3
Shendam *Nigeria* 8°49N 9°30E **263** D6
Shendi *Sudan* 16°46N 33°22E **257** D3
Shendurni *India* 20°39N 75°36E **244** D2
Shenge *S. Leone* 7°54N 12°55W **262** D2
Shengfang *China* 39°3N 116°42E **228** E9
Shěnggǐn *Albania* 41°17N 20°10E **202** E4
Shěngjin *Albania* 41°50N 19°33E **202** E3
Shengzhou *China* 29°35N 120°50E **229** C13
Shenjingzi *China* 44°40N 124°30E **227** B13
Shenkang *Taiwan* 24°9N 120°39E **225** B2
Shenmu *China* 38°50N 110°29E **226** E6
Shennongjia *China* 31°43N 110°44E **229** B8
Shensi = Shaanxi □ *China* 35°0N 109°0E **226** G5
Shenyang *China* 41°48N 123°27E **226** D12
Shenzhen *China* 22°32N 114°5E **229** F10
Shenzhen ✈ (SZX) *China* 22°41N 113°49E **219** a
Shenzhen Shuiku *China* 22°34N 114°8E **219** a
Sheo *India* 26°11N 71°15E **242** F4
Sheopur Kalan *India* 25°40N 76°40E **242** G7
Shepetivka *Ukraine* 50°10N 27°10E **177** C14
Shepherd Is. *Vanuatu* 16°55S 168°36E **287** F6
Shepherds Bush *U.K.* 51°30N 0°13W **125** A2
Shepherdsville *U.S.A.* 37°59N 85°43W **311** G11
Shepparton *Australia* 36°23S 145°26E **283** D6
Shepperton *U.K.* 51°23N 0°26W **125** B1
Sheppey, I. of *U.K.* 51°25N 0°48E **169** F8
Shepton Mallet *U.K.* 51°11N 2°33W **169** F5
Sheqi *China* 33°12N 112°57E **226** H7
Sher Khan Qala *Afghan.* 29°53N 66°13E **242** D2
Sher Qila *Afghan.* 36°7N 74°2E **243** A6
Sherab *Sudan* 10°44N 24°41E **257** E1
Sherabad *Uzbekistan* 37°40N 67°1E **217** F7
Sherborne *U.K.* 50°57N 2°31W **169** G5
Sherbro → *S. Leone* 7°45N 12°55W **262** D2
Sherbro I. *S. Leone* 7°30N 12°40W **262** D2
Sherbrooke *N.S., Canada* 45°8N 61°59W **299** C7
Sherbrooke *Qué., Canada* 45°28N 71°57W **313** A13
Sherburne *U.S.A.* 42°41N 75°30W **313** D9
Sherburne Reef *Papua N. G.* 3°20S 148°0E **286** B5
Sherda *Chad* 20°7N 16°46E **259** D3
Shereik *Sudan* 18°44N 33°47E **256** D3
Shergaon *India* 27°7N 92°16E **241** B7
Shergarh *India* 26°20N 72°18E **242** F5
Sherghati *India* 24°34N 84°47E **243** G11
Sheridan *Ark., U.S.A.* 34°19N 92°24W **314** D8
Sheridan *Ill., U.S.A.* 41°32N 88°41W **311** D8
Sheridan *Ind., U.S.A.* 40°8N 86°13W **311** D10
Sheridan *Wyo., U.S.A.* 44°48N 106°58W **304** D10
Sheringham *U.K.* 52°56N 1°13E **168** E9
Sherkot *India* 29°22N 78°35E **243** E8
Sherlovaya Gora *Russia* 50°34N 116°15E **215** D12
Sherman *N.Y., U.S.A.* 42°9N 79°35W **312** D5
Sherman *Tex., U.S.A.* 33°38N 96°36W **314** E6
Sherman Oaks *U.S.A.* 34°8N 118°29E **136** B3
Sherman Park *U.S.A.* 41°47N 87°39W **119** C2
Sherpur *Bangla.* 25°0N 90°0E **241** C3
Sherpur *India* 32°34N 83°47E **243** G10
Sherridon *Canada* 55°8N 101°5W **297** B8
Sherriffs *St. Kitts & Nevis* 17°10N 62°32W **322** d
Shertallai *India* 9°42N 76°20E **245** K3
Sherwood *U.S.A.* 41°17N 84°33W **311** C12
Sherwood, L. *U.S.A.* 28°33N 81°19W **133** A2
Sherwood Forest *U.K.* 53°11N 1°7W **168** D6
Sherwood Park *Canada* 53°31N 113°19W **296** D6
Sheslay → *Canada* 58°48N 132°5W **296** B2
Shet Bandar *India* 18°57N 72°55E **130** B2
Shethanei L. *Canada* 58°48N 97°50W **297** B9
Shetland □ *U.K.* 60°30N 1°30W **167** A7
Shetland Is. *U.K.* 60°30N 1°30W **167** A7
Shetou *Taiwan* 23°53N 120°35E **225** C2
Shetpe *Kazakhstan* 44°10N 52°7E **216** E6
Shetrunji → *India* 21°19N 72°7E **242** J5
Sheung Fa Shan *China* 22°23N 114°5E **122** A1
Sheung Lau Wan *China* 22°16N 114°16E **122** B2
Sheung Shui *China* 22°30N 114°7E **219** a
Sheung Wan *China* 22°16N 114°9E **122** B2
Sheva *India* 18°56N 72°57E **130** B2
Sheva Nhava *India* 18°57N 72°57E **130** B2
Shevaroy Hills *India* 11°58N 78°12E **245** J4
Shevchenkovo = Dolynska
　Ukraine 48°6N 32°46E **189** H7
Shevchenkovo *Ukraine* 45°30N 29°30E **183** E14
Shevgaon *India* 19°21N 75°14E **244** E2
Shevisheh *Iran* 35°21N 46°40E **213** E12
Shewa *Ethiopia* 9°33N 38°10E **257** F4
Shewa Gimira *Ethiopia* 7°4N 35°51E **257** F4
Shey-Phoksundo △
　Nepal 29°30N 82°45E **243** E10
Sheyang *China* 33°48N 120°29E **227** H11
Sheyenne → *U.S.A.* 47°2N 96°50W **308** B5
Shiashkotan, Ostrov
　Russia 48°49N 154°6E **215** E16
Shiba *Tokyo, Japan* ... **140** C1
Shibām *Yemen* 15°59N 48°36E **249** D5
Shibata *Japan* 37°57N 139°20E **222** F9
Shibecha *Japan* 43°17N 144°36E **220** C12
Shibetsu *Japan* 43°30N 145°10E **220** C12
Shibetsu *Japan* 44°10N 142°23E **220** B11
Shibin el Kôm *Egypt* 30°31N 30°55E **256** H7
Shibin el Qanâtir *Egypt* 30°19N 31°19E **256** H7
Shibing *China* 27°2N 108°7E **228** D7
Shibogama L. *Canada* 53°35N 88°15W **298** B2
Shibpur *India* 22°34N 88°19E **124** B1
Shibukawa *Japan* 36°29N 139°0E **223** A11
Shibushi *Japan* 31°25N 131°8E **222** F3
Shibushi-Wan *Japan* 31°24N 131°8E **222** F3
Shibuya *Tokyo, Japan* ... **140** c1
Shicheng *China* 26°22N 116°20E **229** E11
Shicheng Dao *China* 39°31N 122°59E **226** E11
Shickshock Mts. = Chic-Chocs, Mts.
　Canada 48°55N 66°0W **299** C6
Shidad *Si. Arabia* 21°19N 40°3E **248** B3
Shidao *China* 36°50N 122°25E **227** F12
Shiderti → *Kazakhstan* 51°20N 74°50E **217** B8
Shidian *China* 24°40N 99°5E **228** E2
Shido *Japan* 34°19N 134°10E **222** G6
Shiel, L. *U.K.* 56°48N 5°34W **167** E3
Shield, C. *Australia* 13°20S 136°20E **280** A2
Shieli *Kazakhstan* 44°20N 66°15E **216** E7
Shifang *China* 31°8N 104°10E **228** B5
Shiga □ *Japan* 35°20N 136°0E **223** G8
Shiga *Japan* 36°57N 137°31E **222** F5
Shigaib *Sudan* 15°5N 23°35E **259** E11
Shiganyurt *Kazakhstan* 50°2N 66°59W **299** B6
Shihchiachuangi = Shijiazhuang
　China 38°2N 114°28E **226** E8
Shihezi *China* 44°15N 86°2E **217** D11

Shīrvān *Iran* 37°30N 57°50E **247** B8
Shirwa, L. = Chilwa, L.
　Malawi 15°15S 35°40E **269** F4
Shishaldin Volcano
　U.S.A. 54°5N 163°58W **303** J7
Shishi *China* 24°44N 118°37E **229** E12
Shishmaref *U.S.A.* 66°15N 166°4W **303** C6
Shishou *China* 29°38N 112°22E **229** C9
Shitai *China* 30°12N 117°25E **229** B11
Shitennoji Temple *Japan* 34°39N 135°31E **133** B2
Shithâthah *Iraq* 32°34N 43°28E **213** G10
Shivamogga = Shimoga
　India 13°57N 75°32E **245** H2
Shivpuri *India* 25°26N 77°42E **242** G7
Shiwela = Ixmiquilpan *Mexico* ...
Shiweitang *China* 23°6N 113°12E **121** B2
Shixian *China* 43°5N 129°50E **227** C15
Shixing *China* 24°46N 114°5E **229** E10
Shiyan *Guangdong, China* 22°42N 113°56E **219** a
Shiyan *Hubei, China* 32°35N 110°45E **229** A8
Shiyan Shuiku *China* 22°42N 113°54E **219** a
Shiyata *Egypt* 29°25N 25°7E **256** B2
Shizhu *China* 29°58N 108°7E **228** C7
Shizong *China* 24°50N 104°0E **228** E5
Shizuishan *China* 39°15N 106°50E **226** E4
Shizuoka *Japan* 34°57N 138°24E **223** C10
Shizuoka □ *Japan* 35°─N 138°40E **223** B10
Shkhara *Georgia* 43°0N 43°8E **213** A10
Shklov = Shklow *Belarus* 54°16N 30°15E **177** A16
Shklov *Belarus* 54°16N 30°15E **177** A16
Shkodër *Albania* 42°4N 19°32E **202** D3
Shkodra = Shkodër
　Albania 42°4N 19°32E **202** D3
Shkumbini → *Albania* 41°2N 19°31E **202** E3
Shmidta, Ostrov *Russia* 81°0N 91°0E **215** A10
Shō-Gawa → *Japan* 36°47N 137°4E **222** F5
Shoal Cr. → *U.S.A.* 39°44N 93°32W **310** E3
Shoal L. *Canada* 49°33S 95°1W **297** D9
Shoal Lake *Canada* 50°30N 100°35W **297** C8
Shoalhaven → *Australia* 34°54S 150°42E **283** C5
Shoals *U.S.A.* 38°40N 86°47W **311** F10
Shōbara *Japan* 34°51N 133°1E **222** C5
Shōdo-Shima *Japan* 34°30N 134°15E **222** C6
Shogunle *Nigeria* 6°34N 3°20E **124** A2
Sholapur = Solapur *India* 17°43N 75°56E **244** F2
Sholomu *Nigeria* 6°32N 3°22E **124** A2
Shōmrōn *West Bank* 32°15N 35°13E **251** F6
Shonian Harb. *Palau* 7°10N 134°23E **288** c
Shonzhy *Kazakhstan* 43°32N 79°28E **217** D9
Shooters Hill *U.K.* 51°28N 0°4E **125** B4
Shoranur *India* 10°46N 76°19E **245** J3
Shorapur *India* 16°31N 76°48E **245** F3
Shoreditch *London, U.K.* ... **125** a5
Shoreham *U.S.A.* 43°53N 73°18W **313** C11
Shorewood *U.S.A.* 43°5N 87°53W **311** A9
Shori → *Pakistan* 28°29N 69°44E **242** E3
Shorkot Road *Pakistan* 30°50N 72°0E **242** D4
Shorter *U.S.A.* 32°24N 85°57W **316** C4
Shortland I. *Solomon Is.* 31°34N 85°6W **316** D4
Shortland Is. *Solomon Is.* 7°0S 155°45E **287** L8
Shortland *U.K.* 51°23N 0°0E **125** B4
Shortt's I. *India* 20°47N 87°4E **244** D8
Shoshone *Calif., U.S.A.* 35°58N 116°16W **307** K10
Shoshone *Idaho, U.S.A.* 42°56N 114°25W **304** E6
Shoshone L. *U.S.A.* 44°22N 110°43W **304** D8
Shoshone Mts. *U.S.A.* 39°20N 117°25W **304** G5
Shoshong *Botswana* 22°56S 26°31E **270** B4
Shoshoni *U.S.A.* 43°14N 108°7W **304** E9
Shostka *Ukraine* 51°57N 33°32E **189** G8
Shot *Iran* 39°12N 44°49E **213** C11
Shotor Khūn *Afghan.* 34°19N 64°56E **240** B2
Shotover → *N.Z.* 44°59S 168°41E **285** E3
Shou Xian *China* 32°37N 116°42E **229** A11
Shouchang *China* 26°18N 119°12E **229** C12
Shouchia *Taiwan* 22°14N 120°35E **225** C2
Shoufeng *Taiwan* 23°52N 121°30E **225** C3
Shouguang *China* 37°52N 118°45E **227** F10
Shouning *China* 27°27N 119°31E **229** D12
Shouyang *China* 37°54N 113°8E **226** F7
Show Low *U.S.A.* 34°15N 110°2W **305** J9
Showa *Japan* 35°36N 138°29E **223** B10
Showak *Sudan* 14°23N 35°52E **257** E4
Shpola *Ukraine* 49°1N 31°30E **189** H6
Shpykiv *Ukraine* 48°47N 28°34E **183** B13
Shqipëria = Albania ■
　Europe 41°0N 20°0E **202** E4
Shreveport *U.S.A.* 32°31N 93°45W **314** E8
Shrewsbury *U.K.* 52°43N 2°45W **169** E5
Shri Mohangarh *India* 27°17N 71°18E **242** F4
Shrigonda *India* 18°37N 74°41E **244** E2
Shrirampur *India* 22°44N 88°21E **243** H13
Shropshire □ *U.K.* 52°36N 2°45W **169** E5
Shterpce = Štrpce *Kosovo* 42°14N 21°1E **202** D5
Shū *Kazakhstan* 43°36N 73°42E **217** D8
Shū → *Kazakhstan* 45°0N 67°44E **217** E7
Shu'afat *West Bank* 31°49N 35°14E **123** B2
Shuangcheng *China* 45°20N 126°15E **227** B14
Shuangfeng *China* 27°29N 112°16E **229** D9
Shuanggou *China* 34°2N 117°30E **227** G9
Shuangjiang *China* 23°28N 99°46E **228** F2
Shuangliao *China* 43°29N 123°30E **227** C13
Shuangshanzi *China* 40°20N 119°8E **227** D10
Shuangyashan *China* 46°28N 131°5E **227** B15
Shu'b, Ra's *Yemen* 12°36N 53°26E **249** E5
Shubarqudyq *Kazakhstan* 49°36N 56°34E **216** C5
Shubarshi *Kazakhstan* 48°55N 57°11E **216** C5
Shubrā *Egypt* 30°5N 31°11E **117** A2
Shubrā el Kheima *Egypt* 30°10N 31°10E **117** A2
Shubrā Khit *Egypt* 31°2N 30°42E **256** H7
Shugozero *Russia* 59°45N 34°10E **188** C8
Shuguri Falls *Tanzania* 8°33S 37°22E **269** D4
Shubayr → *Yemen* 14°41N 49°23E **249** D5
Shuiding = Huocheng
　China 44°0N 80°48E **217** D10
Shuiji *China* 27°33N 118°20E **229** D11
Shuikou *China* 23°10N 113°10E **121** A2
Shuili *Taiwan* 23°49N 120°51E **225** C2
Shuilian *Taiwan* 23°47N 121°18E **225** C3
Shuiliao *Taiwan* 22°23N 120°35E **225** C2
Shujalpur *India* 23°18N 76°46E **242** H7
Shukpa Kunzang *India* 34°28N 78°22E **243** B8
Shulan *China* 44°28N 127°0E **227** B14
Shulaveri *Georgia* 41°22N 44°45E **191** K7
Shule *China* 39°25N 76°3E **217** E9
Shule He → *China* 40°20N 92°50E **218** C7
Shullsburg *U.S.A.* 42°35N 90°13W **310** B8
Shumagin Is. *U.S.A.* 55°7N 160°30W **303** J8
Shumen *Bulgaria* 43°18N 26°55E **203** C10
Shumerlya *Russia* 55°30N 46°25E **190** C8
Shumikha *Russia* 55°10N 63°15E **214** D7
Shunan *Japan* 34°3N 131°50E **222** G5
Shunchang *China* 26°54N 117°48E **229** D11
Shunde *China* 22°42N 113°14E **229** F9
Shungnak *Kazakhstan* 46°45N 69°30E **216** D7
Shungnak *U.S.A.* 66°52N 157°9W **303** C8
Shuo Xian = Shuozhou
　China 39°20N 112°33E **226** E7

Shuozhou China 39°20N 112°33E 226 E7
Shūr → Fārs, Iran 28°30N 55°0E 247 D7
Shūr → Kermān, Iran 30°52N 57°37E 247 D8
Shūr → Yazd, Iran 31°45N 55°15E 247 D7
Shūr Āb Iran 34°23N 51°11E 247 C6
Shūr Gaz Iran 29°10N 59°20E 247 D8
Shūrāb Iran 33°43N 56°29E 247 C8
Shuri Japan 26°13N 127°43E 288 a
Shūrjestān Iran 31°24N 52°25E 247 D7
Shurkhua Burma 22°15N 93°38E 241 D4
Shurugwi Zimbabwe 19°40S 30°0E 269 F3
Shūsf Iran 31°50N 60°5E 247 D9
Shūsh Iran 32°11N 48°15E 213 F13
Shushenskoye Russia 53°19N 91°56E 217 B12
Shūshtar Iran 32°0N 48°50E 247 D6
Shuswap L. Canada 50°55N 119°3W 296 C5
Shute Harbour △ Australia 20°17S 148°47E 280 b
Shuya Russia 56°50N 41°28E 190 B5
Shuyak I. U.S.A. 58°31N 152°30W 303 G9
Shuyang China 34°10N 118°42E 227 G10
Shuzenji Japan 34°58N 138°56E 223 C10
Shūzū Iran 29°52N 54°30E 247 D7
Shwangliao = Liaoyuan China 42°58N 125°2E 227 C13
Shwebo Burma 22°30N 95°45E 241 D5
Shwegu Burma 24°15N 96°26E 241 C6
Shwegun Burma 17°9N 97°39E 241 G6
Shwegyin Burma 17°55N 96°53E 241 G6
Shweli → Burma 23°45N 96°45E 241 D6
Shwenyaung Burma 20°46N 96°57E 241 E6
Shyamnagar India 13°21N 92°57E 245 H11
Shyghanaq Kazakhstan 45°6N 73°59E 217 C8
Shyghys Qazaqstan □ Kazakhstan 48°30N 82°0E 217 D10
Shymkent Kazakhstan 42°18N 69°36E 217 D7
Shyok India 34°13N 78°12E 243 B8
Shyok → Pakistan 35°13N 75°53E 243 B6
Shyroke Odesa, Ukraine 45°59N 30°5E 183 E15
Shyroke Ternopil, Ukraine 48°13N 23°6E 182 B8
Si Kiang = Xi Jiang → China 22°5N 113°20E 229 F9
Si Lanna △ Thailand 19°17N 99°12E 236 C2
Si Nakarin Res. Thailand 14°35N 99°0E 236 E2
Si-ngan = Xi'an China 34°15N 109°0E 226 G5
Si Phangnga Thailand 9°8N 98°29E 237 H2
Si Prachan Thailand 14°37N 100°9E 236 E3
Si Racha Thailand 13°10N 100°48E 236 F3
Si Sa Ket Thailand 15°8N 104°23E 236 E5
Siachen Glacier Asia 35°20N 77°30E 243 B7
Sīah Chashmeh Iran 39°3N 44°25E 213 C11
Siahaf → Pakistan 29°3N 68°57E 242 E3
Siahan Range Pakistan 27°30N 64°40E 240 D2
Siak → Indonesia 1°13N 102°9E 234 B2
Siak Sri Indrapura Indonesia 0°51N 102°0E 234 B2
Sialkot Pakistan 32°32N 74°30E 242 C6
Sialsuk India 23°24N 92°45E 241 D4
Sialum Papua N. G. 6°5S 147°36E 286 D4
Siam = Thailand ■ Asia 16°0N 102°0E 236 E4
Sian = Xi'an China 34°15N 109°0E 226 G5
Sian Ka'an ⌂ Mexico 19°35N 87°40W 319 D7
Siangtan = Xiangtan China 27°51N 112°54E 229 D9
Sianów Poland 54°13N 16°18E 184 D3
Siantan Indonesia 3°10N 106°15E 234 B3
Siàpo → Venezuela 2°7N 66°28W 328 C4
Sīāreh Iran 28°5N 60°14E 247 D9
Siargao I. Phil. 9°52N 126°3E 233 G6
Siasi Phil. 5°34N 120°50E 233 J3
Siasi I. Phil. 5°33N 120°51E 233 J3
Siassi Papua N. G. 5°40S 147°51E 286 C4
Siatista Greece 40°15N 21°33E 202 F5
Siaton Phil. 9°4N 123°2E 233 G4
Siau Indonesia 2°50N 125°25E 231 D7
Šiauliai Lithuania 55°56N 23°15E 184 C10
Šiauliai □ Lithuania 55°56N 23°19E 184 C10
Siavonga Zambia 16°33S 28°42E 271 A4
Siazan = Siyäzän Azerbaijan 41°3N 49°10E 191 K9
Sibâi, Gebel el Egypt 25°45N 34°10E 246 E2
Sibang Gabon 0°25N 9°31E 264 B1
Sibang Bali, Indonesia 8°34S 115°13E 231 K18
Sibay Russia 52°42N 58°39E 186 D10
Sibay I. Phil. 11°51N 121°29E 233 F3
Sibayi, L. S. Africa 27°20S 32°45E 271 C5
Sibdu Sudan 10°57N 26°17E 257 E2
Šibenik Croatia 43°48N 15°54E 199 E12
Siberia = Sibirskiy □ Russia 58°0N 90°0E 215 D10
Siberia Russia 60°0N 100°0E 150 D13
Siberië Curaçao 12°14N 69°3W 322 g
Siberut Indonesia 1°30S 99°0E 234 C1
Siberut, Selat Indonesia 0°42S 98°35E 234 C1
Siberut △ Indonesia 1°17S 98°45E 234 C1
Sibi Pakistan 29°30N 67°54E 242 E2
Sibigo Indonesia 2°50N 95°54E 234 B1
Sibiloi △ Kenya 4°0N 36°20E 268 B4
Sibirskiy □ Russia 58°0N 90°0E 215 D10
Sibirtsevo Russia 44°12N 132°26E 220 B5
Sibiti Congo 3°38S 13°19E 264 C2
Sibiu Romania 45°45N 24°9E 183 E9
Sibiu □ Romania 45°50N 24°15E 183 E9
Sibium Mts. Papua N. G. 9°19S 148°25E 286 E5
Sibley Ill., U.S.A. 40°35N 88°23W 311 D8
Sibley Iowa, U.S.A. 43°24N 95°45W 308 D6
Sibo Sweden 61°13N 16°37E 162 C10
Sibolga Indonesia 1°42N 98°45E 234 B1
Siborongborong Indonesia 2°13N 98°58E 237 L2
Sibsagar India 27°0N 94°36E 241 B5
Sibu Malaysia 2°18N 111°49E 235 B4
Sibuco Phil. 7°20N 122°10E 233 H4
Sibuguey B. Phil. 7°50N 122°45E 233 H4
Sibut C.A.R. 5°46N 19°10E 264 A3
Sibutu Phil. 4°45N 119°30E 235 B5
Sibutu Group Phil. 4°45N 119°20E 233 J2
Sibutu I. Phil. 4°47N 119°29E 233 J2
Sibutu Passage E. Indies 4°50N 120°0E 233 J3
Sibuyan I. Phil. 12°25N 122°40E 232 E4
Sibuyan Sea Phil. 12°30N 122°20E 232 E4
Sic Romania 46°56N 23°53E 183 D8
Sicamous Canada 50°49N 119°0W 296 C5
Sicapoo, Mt. Phil. 18°1N 120°56E 232 B3
Sicasica Bolivia 17°22S 67°45W 330 D4
Siccus → Australia 31°55S 139°17E 282 A3
Sichelberg = Sierpc Poland 52°55N 19°43E 185 F6
Sichon Thailand 9°0N 99°54E 237 H2
Sichuan □ China 30°30N 103°0E 228 B5
Sichuan Pendi China 31°0N 105°0E 228 B5
Sicilia Italy 37°30N 14°30E 201 E7
Sicily = Sicilia Italy 37°30N 14°30E 201 E7
Sicily, Str. of Medit. S. 37°35N 11°56E 200 E4
Sico → Honduras 15°58N 84°58W 320 C3
Sicuani Peru 14°21S 71°10W 330 C3
Šid Serbia 45°8N 19°14E 182 E4
Sidamo Ethiopia 5°0N 37°50E 257 G4
Sidaouet Niger 18°34N 8°3E 259 E1
Sidari Greece 39°47N 19°41E 206 B9
Sidcup U.K. 51°25N 0°6E 125 B4
Siddapur India 14°20N 74°53E 245 G2
Siddhapur India 23°56N 72°25E 242 H5
Siddipet India 18°5N 78°51E 244 E4
Side Turkey 36°45N 31°23E 250 B2
Sidensjö Sweden 63°18N 18°17E 162 A12
Sidéradougou Burkina Faso 10°42N 4°12W 262 C4
Siderno Italy 38°16N 16°18E 201 D9
Sideros, Akra Greece 35°19N 26°19E 207 E7
Sidhauli India 27°17N 80°50E 243 F9
Sidhi India 24°25N 81°53E 243 G9
Sîdi Abd el Rahmân Egypt 30°55N 29°44E 256 A2
Sîdi Barrâni Egypt 31°38N 25°58E 256 A2
Sidi-bel-Abbès Algeria 35°13N 0°39W 261 A4
Sidi-bel-Abbès □ Algeria 34°50N 0°30W 261 B4
Sidi Bennour Morocco 32°40N 8°25W 260 B3
Sidi Bou Zid Tunisia 35°1N 9°16E 258 B1
Sidi Bou Zid □ Tunisia 35°0N 9°30E 258 B1
Sidi Boubekeur Algeria 35°1N 0°4E 261 A5
Sîdi Haneish Egypt 31°10N 27°35E 256 A2
Sidi Ifni Morocco 29°29N 10°12W 260 C2
Sidi Kacem Morocco 34°12N 5°42W 260 B3
Sîdi Omar Egypt 31°24N 24°57E 256 A1
Sidi Slimane Morocco 34°16N 5°56W 260 B3
Sidi Smaïl Morocco 32°50N 8°31W 260 B3
Sīdī 'Uzayz Libya 31°41N 24°55E 258 B4
Sidikalang Indonesia 2°45N 98°19E 237 L2
Sidimo Somali Rep. 2°27N 41°58E 267 D5
Siding No 14 = Ponoka Canada 52°42N 113°40W 296 C6
Sidirokastro Greece 41°13N 23°24E 202 E7
Sidlaw Hills U.K. 56°32N 3°2W 167 E5
Sidley, Mt. Antarctica 77°2S 126°2W 151 D14
Sidmouth U.K. 50°40N 3°15W 169 G4
Sidmouth, C. Australia 13°25S 143°36E 280 A3
Sidney B.C., Canada 48°39N 123°24W 306 B3
Sidney Mont., U.S.A. 47°43N 104°9W 304 C11
Sidney N.Y., U.S.A. 42°19N 75°24W 313 D9
Sidney Nebr., U.S.A. 41°8N 102°59W 308 E2
Sidney Ohio, U.S.A. 40°17N 84°9W 311 D12
Sidney Lanier, L. U.S.A. 34°10N 84°4W 316 A5
Sido Mali 11°37N 7°29W 262 C3
Sidoarjo Indonesia 7°27S 112°43E 235 D4
Sidoktaya Burma 20°27N 94°15E 241 E5
Sidon = Saydā Lebanon 33°35N 35°25E 250 E6
Sidra, G. of = Surt, Khalīj Libya 31°40N 18°30E 258 B3
Sidrolândia Brazil 20°55S 54°58W 331 E7
Siebenhirten Austria 48°8N 16°17E 142 B1
Siedlce Poland 52°10N 22°20E 185 F9
Siedlung Germany 52°35N 13°7E 115 A1
Sieg → Germany 50°46N 7°6E 178 E3
Siegburg Germany 50°47N 7°12E 178 E3
Siegen Germany 50°51N 8°0E 178 E4
Siekierki Poland 52°12N 21°4E 142 B2
Sielce Poland 52°12N 21°2E 142 B2
Siem Pang Cambodia 14°7N 106°23E 236 E6
Siem Reap = Siemreab Cambodia 13°20N 103°52E 236 F4
Siemensstadt Germany 52°32N 13°16E 115 A2
Siemiatycze Poland 52°27N 22°53E 185 F9
Siemreab Cambodia 13°20N 103°52E 236 F4
Siena Italy 43°19N 11°21E 199 E8
Sieniawa Poland 50°11N 22°38E 185 H9
Sienyang = Xianyang China 34°20N 108°40E 226 G5
Sieradz Poland 51°37N 18°41E 185 G5
Sieraków Poland 52°39N 16°2E 185 F3
Sierck-les-Bains France 49°26N 6°20E 173 C13
Sierning Austria 48°2N 14°18E 180 C7
Sierpc Poland 52°55N 19°43E 185 F6
Sierpe, Bocas de la Venezuela 10°0N 61°30W 329 G9
Sierra Blanca U.S.A. 31°11N 105°22W 314 F2
Sierra Blanca Peak U.S.A. 33°23N 105°49W 305 K11
Sierra City U.S.A. 39°34N 120°38W 306 F6
Sierra Colorada Argentina 40°35S 67°50W 336 B3
Sierra de Agalta △ Honduras 15°1N 85°48W 320 C2
Sierra de Aracena y Picas de Aroche ⌂ Spain 37°53N 6°41W 195 H4
Sierra de Bahoruco △ Dom. Rep. 18°10N 71°25W 321 C5
Sierra de Baza ⌂ Spain 37°20N 2°48W 197 H2
Sierra de Castril ⌂ Spain 37°54N 2°50W 197 H2
Sierra de Espuña ⌂ Spain 37°50N 1°31W 197 H3
Sierra de Grazalema ⌂ Spain 36°31N 5°28W 195 J5
Sierra de Gredos ⌂ Spain 40°17N 5°17W 194 E5
Sierra de Hornachuelos ⌂ Spain 37°56N 5°14W 195 H5
Sierra de Huétor ⌂ Spain 37°14N 3°30W 195 H7
Sierra de la Culata △ Venezuela 8°48N 70°56W 328 B3
Sierra de la Macarena △ Colombia 11°19N 74°1W 328 A3
Sierra de las Nieves ⌂ Spain 36°42N 5°0W 195 J6
Sierra de las Quijadas △ Argentina 32°29S 67°5W 334 C2
Sierra de María-Los Vélez ⌂ Spain 37°41N 2°10W 197 H2
Sierra de San Luis △ Venezuela 11°11N 69°33W 328 A4
Sierra de San Pedro Mártir △ Mexico 31°10N 115°30W 318 A1
Sierra de Yeguas Spain 37°7N 4°52W 195 H6
Sierra del São Mamede ⌂ Portugal 39°17N 7°18W 195 F3
Sierra Gorda Chile 22°50S 69°15W 334 A2
Sierra Grande Argentina 41°36S 65°22W 336 B3
Sierra Leone ■ W. Afr. 9°0N 12°0W 262 D2
Sierra Leone Basin Atl. Oc. 5°0N 17°0W 152 F10
Sierra Leone Rise Atl. Oc. 7°0N 22°0W 152 F9
Sierra Madre Mexico 16°0N 93°0W 319 D6
Sierra Madre Calif., U.S.A. 34°9N 118°3W 126 B4
Sierra Madre Occidental Mexico 27°0N 107°0W 318 B3
Sierra Madre Oriental Mexico 25°0N 100°0W 318 C5
Sierra Mágina ⌂ Spain 37°44N 3°28W 195 H7
Sierra Mojada Mexico 27°18N 103°41W 318 B4
Sierra Nevada Spain 37°3N 3°15W 195 H7
Sierra Nevada Calif., U.S.A. 39°0N 120°30W 306 H8
Sierra Nevada ⌂ Spain 37°4N 3°7W 195 H7
Sierra Norte de Sevilla ⌂ Spain 37°55N 5°46W 195 H5
Sierra Subbéticas ⌂ Spain 37°26N 4°18W 195 H6
Sierra Vista U.S.A. 31°33N 110°18W 305 L8
Sierras de Cardeña y Montoro ⌂ Spain 38°13N 4°15W 195 G6
Sierras de Cazorla, Segura y las Villas ⌂ Spain 37°0N 2°45W 197 J2
Sierraville U.S.A. 39°36N 120°22W 306 F6
Sierre Switz. 46°17N 7°31E 179 J3
Sievering Austria 48°15N 16°20E 142 A2
Sifani Ethiopia 12°18N 40°19E 257 E5
Sifié Ivory C. 8°0N 7°5W 262 D3
Sifnos Greece 37°0N 24°45E 204 E6
Sifton Canada 51°21N 100°8W 297 C8
Sifton Pass Canada 57°52N 126°15W 296 B3
Sig Algeria 35°32N 0°12W 261 A4
Sigaboy = Governor Generoso Phil. 6°39N 126°5E 233 H6
Sigatoka Fiji 18°8S 177°32E 287 B1
Sigdal Norway 60°3N 9°38E 164 D6
Sigean France 43°2N 2°58E 174 E6
Siggiewi Malta 35°51N 14°26E 206 F7
Sighetu-Marmației Romania 47°57N 23°52E 183 C8
Sighișoara Romania 46°12N 24°50E 183 D9
Sighthill U.K. 55°56N 3°17W 121 B2
Sigira Yemen 12°37N 54°20E 249 D6
Sigiriya Sri Lanka 7°57N 80°45E 245 L5
Sigli Indonesia 5°25N 96°0E 234 A1
Siglufjörður Iceland 66°12N 18°55W 155 A8
Siglunes Iceland 66°12N 18°50W 155 A8
Sigmaringen Germany 48°5N 9°12E 179 G5
Signa Italy 43°45N 11°10E 198 E8
Signakhi = Tsnori Georgia 41°40N 45°57E 191 K7
Signal de Botrang Belgium 50°29N 6°4E 170 D6
Signal Hill S. Africa 34°5S 18°24E 118 A1
Signal Pk. U.S.A. 33°20N 114°2W 307 M12
Signy I. Antarctica 60°43S 45°36W 151 C18
Signy-l'Abbaye France 49°40N 4°25E 173 C11
Sigourney U.S.A. 41°20N 92°12W 310 C4
Sigsbee U.S.A. 31°16N 83°52W 316 D6
Sigsbee Deep Caribbean 25°0N 92°0W 152 D1
Sígsig Ecuador 3°0S 78°50W 328 D2
Sigtuna Sweden 59°36N 17°44E 162 E11
Sigüenza Spain 41°3N 2°40W 196 D2
Siguiri Guinea 11°31N 9°10W 262 C3
Sigulda Latvia 57°10N 24°55E 188 D3
Siguniangshan China 31°15N 103°10E 228 B4
Sihanoukville = Kampong Saom Cambodia 10°38N 103°30E 237 G4
Sihawa India 20°19N 81°55E 244 D5
Siheung Gyeonggi-do, S. Korea 37°25N 126°47E 224 D3
Siheung Seoul, S. Korea 37°28N 126°54E 137 C1
Sihong China 33°27N 118°16E 227 H10
Sihora India 23°29N 80°6E 243 H9
Sihuas Peru 8°40S 77°40W 330 B2
Sihui China 23°20N 112°40E 229 F9
Siikajoki → Finland 64°50N 24°43E 160 D21
Siilinjärvi Finland 63°4N 27°39E 160 E22
Siirt Turkey 37°57N 41°55E 213 D9
Siirt □ Turkey 37°55N 41°55E 213 D9
Sijarira Ra. = Chizarira Zimbabwe 17°36S 27°45E 269 F2
Sijungjung Indonesia 0°42S 100°58E 234 C2
Sika India 22°26N 69°47E 242 H3
Sikanni Chief → Canada 57°47N 122°15W 296 B4
Sikao Thailand 7°34N 99°21E 237 J2
Sikar India 27°33N 75°10E 242 F6
Sikasso Mali 11°18N 5°35W 262 C3
Sikasso □ Mali 10°55N 7°0W 262 C3
Sikátorpuszta Hungary 47°34N 19°10E 117 A3
Sikelenge Zambia 14°53S 24°14E 265 E4
Sikeston U.S.A. 36°53N 89°35W 308 G9
Sikhote Alin, Khrebet Russia 45°0N 136°0E 220 B8
Sikhote Alin Ra. = Sikhote Alin, Khrebet Russia 45°0N 136°0E 220 B8
Sikia Greece 40°2N 23°56E 202 F7
Sikinos Greece 36°40N 25°8E 205 E7
Sikkim □ India 27°50N 88°30E 241 B2
Siklós Hungary 45°50N 18°19E 182 E3
Sil → Spain 42°27N 7°43W 194 C3
Silacayoapan Mexico 17°30N 98°9W 319 D5
Šilalė Lithuania 55°28N 22°12E 184 C9
Silampur India 28°39N 77°16E 120 B2
Silandro Italy 46°38N 10°46E 198 B7
Silang Phil. 14°14N 120°58E 232 D3
Silawad India 21°54N 74°54E 242 J6
Silay Phil. 10°47N 122°58E 233 F4
Silba Croatia 44°24N 14°41E 199 D11
Silchar India 24°49N 92°48E 241 C4
Sildegapet Norway 62°5N 5°0E 164 B2
Şile Turkey 41°10N 29°37E 203 E13
Silent Valley △ India 11°10N 76°20E 245 J3
Siler City U.S.A. 35°44N 79°28W 315 D15
Sileru → India 17°49N 81°24E 244 F5
Silesia = Śląsk Poland 51°0N 16°30E 176 C9
Silet Algeria 22°44N 4°37E 261 D5
Siletitengiz Köli Kazakhstan 53°20N 73°10E 217 B8
Silgarhi Doti Nepal 29°15N 81°0E 243 E9
Silghat India 26°35N 93°0E 241 B4
Silhouette Seychelles 4°29S 55°12E 272 c
Sili Burkina Faso 11°37N 2°30W 262 C4
Siliana Tunisia 36°5N 9°22E 261 A6
Siliana □ Tunisia 36°0N 9°20E 261 A6
Silifke Turkey 36°22N 33°58E 250 B4
Siliguri = Shiliguri India 26°45N 88°25E 241 B2
Silil Somali Rep. 11°0N 43°26E 267 B5
Siling Co China 31°50N 89°20E 218 E6
Silistea Nouă Romania 44°23N 25°1E 183 F10
Silistra Bulgaria 44°6N 27°19E 203 B11
Silistra □ Bulgaria 44°6N 27°19E 203 B11
Silivri Turkey 41°4N 28°14E 203 E12
Siljan Telemark, Norway 59°18N 9°42E 164 E6
Siljan Sweden 60°55N 14°45E 162 D8
Siljansnäs Sweden 60°47N 14°52E 162 D8
Silkeborg Denmark 56°10N 9°32E 163 H3
Silkwood Australia 17°45S 146°2E 280 B4
Silla Spain 39°22N 0°25W 197 F4
Sillajhuay, Cordillera Chile 19°46S 68°40W 330 D4
Sillamäe Estonia 59°24N 27°45E 188 C4
Sillé-le-Guillaume France 48°10N 0°8W 172 D6
Silleda Spain 42°42N 8°14W 194 C2
Sillein = Žilina Slovak Rep. 49°12N 18°42E 181 B11
Sillim S. Korea 37°28N 126°56E 137 C1
Sillod India 20°18N 75°39E 244 D2
Silloth U.K. 54°52N 3°23W 168 C4
Sillustani Peru 15°50S 70°7W 330 D3
Silo Greece 41°10N 25°53E 203 E9
Siloam Springs U.S.A. 36°11N 94°32W 314 C7
Silopi Turkey 37°15N 42°27E 213 D10
Silsbee U.S.A. 30°21N 94°11W 314 F7
Siltou Chad 16°46N 15°33E 259 E3
Siluko Nigeria 6°35N 5°10E 263 D6
Šilutė Lithuania 55°21N 21°33E 184 C8
Silva Porto = Kuito Angola 12°22S 16°55E 265 E3
Silvan Turkey 38°7N 41°2E 213 C9
Silvani India 23°18N 78°25E 243 H8
Silvassa India 20°16N 73°1E 244 D1
Silver, L. U.S.A. 28°35N 81°23W 133 A2
Silver Bank W. Indies 20°30N 69°45W 321 B6
Silver Bank Passage W. Indies 20°0N 70°0W 321 B5
Silver City U.S.A. 32°46N 108°17W 305 K9
Silver Cr. → U.S.A. 43°16N 119°13W 304 E4
Silver Creek U.S.A. 42°33N 79°10W 312 D5
Silver Grove U.S.A. 39°2N 84°23W 311 E12
Silver Hill Montserrat 16°49N 62°11W 323 p
Silver Hill Md., U.S.A. 38°49N 76°55W 143 C4
Silver L. U.S.A. 38°39N 120°6W 306 G6
Silver Lake Calif., U.S.A. 34°5N 118°15W 126 B3
Silver Lake Calif., U.S.A. 35°21N 116°7W 307 K10
Silver Lake Ind., U.S.A. 41°4N 85°53W 311 C11
Silver Lake Oreg., U.S.A. 43°8N 121°3W 304 E3
Silver Lake Wis., U.S.A. 42°33N 88°13W 311 B8
Silver Spring U.S.A. 38°59N 77°2W 143 A3
Silver Springs U.S.A. 29°13N 82°3W 317 F7
Silverdalen Sweden 57°32N 15°45E 163 G9
Silvermine Mts. Ireland 52°47N 8°15W 166 D3
Silvermine Nature Reserve S. Africa 34°6S 18°27E 118 B1
Silverton N.S.W., Australia 31°52S 141°10E 282 A4
Silverton Colo., U.S.A. 37°49N 107°40W 305 H10
Silverton Tex., U.S.A. 34°28N 101°19W 314 D4
Silves Brazil 2°54S 58°27W 329 D6
Silves Portugal 37°11N 8°26W 195 H2
Silvi Marina Italy 42°34N 14°5E 199 F11
Silvia Colombia 2°37N 76°21W 328 C2
Silvies → U.S.A. 43°34N 119°2W 304 E4
Silvolantekojärvi Finland 60°17N 24°54E 121 B2
Silvrettahorn Switz. 46°50N 10°6E 198 B7
Silwa Bahari Egypt 24°45N 32°55E 256 C3
Silz Austria 47°16N 10°56E 180 D3
Sim, C. Morocco 31°26N 9°51W 260 B3
Simakumba Zambia 14°12S 23°16E 265 E4
Simaltala India 24°43N 86°33E 243 G12
Simaluguri India 26°55N 94°46E 241 B5
Sim'ān, J. Syria 36°25N 36°53E 250 B7
Simanggang = Bandar Sri Aman Malaysia 1°15N 111°32E 235 B4
Simao China 22°47N 101°5E 228 F3
Simão Dias Brazil 10°44S 37°49W 332 D4
Simara I. Phil. 12°48N 122°3E 232 E4
Simard, L. Canada 47°40N 78°40W 298 C4
Şimareh → Iran 33°9N 47°41E 213 F12
Simav Turkey 39°4N 28°58E 205 B10
Simav → Turkey 40°23N 28°31E 203 F12
Simav Dağları Turkey 39°10N 28°30E 205 B10
Simba Dem. Rep. of the Congo 0°38N 22°59E 264 B4
Simba Tanzania 2°10S 37°36E 268 C4
Simbach Germany 48°16N 13°2E 179 G9
Simberi I. Papua N. G. 2°38S 152°0E 286 B7
Simbirsk = Ulyanovsk Russia 54°20N 48°25E 190 C9
Simbo Solomon Is. 8°16S 156°33E 287 M9
Simbo Tanzania 4°51S 29°41E 268 C2
Simcoe Canada 42°50N 80°23W 312 D4
Simcoe, L. Canada 44°25N 79°20W 312 B5
Simdega India 22°37N 84°31E 243 H11
Simei Singapore 1°20N 103°47E 138 A3
Simeonovgrad Bulgaria 42°1N 25°50E 203 D9
Simeria Romania 45°51N 23°1E 182 E8
Simeto → Italy 37°24N 15°6E 201 E8
Simeulue Indonesia 2°45N 95°45E 234 B1
Simferopol Ukraine 44°55N 34°3E 189 K8
Simi Greece 36°35N 27°50E 205 E9
Simi Valley U.S.A. 34°16N 118°47W 307 L8
Simien Mts. △ Ethiopia 13°19N 38°0E 257 E4
Simikot Nepal 30°0N 81°50E 243 E9
Similajau △ Malaysia 3°27N 113°15E 235 B4
Simineh → Iran 36°59N 45°54E 213 D11
Simití Colombia 7°58N 73°57W 328 B3
Simitli Bulgaria 41°52N 23°7E 202 E7
Simla = Shimla India 31°2N 77°9E 242 D7
Simla India 22°35N 88°22E 124 B2
Simlångsdalen Sweden 56°43N 13°6E 163 H7
Şimleu-Silvaniei Romania 47°17N 22°50E 182 C7
Simlipal △ India 21°45N 86°30E 243 J12
Simmering Austria 48°10N 16°24E 142 A2
Simmering Heide Austria 48°10N 16°26E 142 A2
Simmern Germany 49°58N 7°30E 179 F3
Simmie Canada 49°56N 108°6W 297 D7
Simmler U.S.A. 35°21N 119°59W 307 K7
Simnas Lithuania 54°24N 23°39E 184 D10
Simo älv = Simojoki → Finland 65°35N 25°1E 160 D21
Simões Brazil 7°36S 40°49W 332 C3
Simojoki → Finland 65°35N 25°1E 160 D21
Simojovel Mexico 17°12N 92°38W 319 D6
Simonette → Canada 55°9N 118°15W 296 B5
Simonière, Plaine de la Guadeloupe 16°16N 61°19W 322 e
Simonkylä Finland 60°18N 25°1E 121 B3
Šimonovany = Partizánske Slovak Rep. 48°38N 18°23E 181 C11
Simonstown S. Africa 34°14S 18°26E 270 D2
Simontornya Hungary 46°45N 18°33E 182 D3
Simpang Indonesia 1°16S 104°4E 234 C2
Simpang Empat Malaysia 5°27N 100°29E 237 c
Simpangkiri → Indonesia 2°50N 97°40E 234 B1
Simplício Mendes Brazil 7°51S 41°54W 332 C3
Simplonpass Switz. 46°15N 8°3E 179 J4
Simplontunnel Switz. 46°15N 8°7E 179 J4
Simpson, Mt. Papua N. G. 10°2S 149°34E 286 F5
Simpson Bay Lagoon St.-Martin 18°3N 63°6W 322 a
Simpson Desert Australia 25°0S 137°0E 280 D2
Simpson Desert △ Australia 24°59S 138°21E 280 C2
Simpson Pen. Canada 68°34N 88°45W 295 D14
Simrishamn Sweden 55°33N 14°22E 163 J8
Simsbury U.S.A. 41°53N 72°48W 313 E12
Simsonbaai St.-Maarten 18°2N 63°7W 322 a
Simuk Indonesia 0°4S 97°52E 234 C1
Simunjan Malaysia 1°25N 110°45E 235 B4
Simunul Phil. 4°54N 119°51E 233 J2
Simushir, Ostrov Russia 46°50N 152°30E 215 E16
Sin Cowe I. S. China Sea 9°53N 114°19E 230 C4
Sin-do N. Korea 39°52N 124°14E 224 C2
Sina → India 17°30N 75°55E 244 F2
Sina Dhago Somali Rep. 5°50N 47°0E 267 C6
Sinabang Indonesia 2°30N 96°24E 234 B1
Sinai = Es Sînâ' Egypt 29°0N 34°0E 246 D2
Sinai, Mt. = Mûsa, Gebel Egypt 28°33N 33°59E 251 K4
Sinai, Mt. Grenada 12°4N 61°42W 323 q
Sinai Peninsula Egypt 29°30N 34°0E 251 J5
Sinaia Romania 45°21N 25°38E 183 E10
Sinait Phil. 17°52N 120°27E 232 C3
Sinako, Mt. Phil. 7°30N 125°17E 233 H5
Sinaloa □ Mexico 25°0N 107°30W 318 C3
Sinaloa de Leyva Mexico 25°50N 108°14W 318 B3
Sinalunga Italy 43°12N 11°44E 199 E8
Sinan China 27°56N 108°13E 228 D7
Sînandrei Romania 45°52N 21°13E 182 E6
Sinarades Greece 39°34N 19°51E 206 B9
Sīnāwan Libya 31°0N 10°37E 258 B2
Sinbaungwe Burma 19°43N 95°10E 241 F5
Sinbo Burma 24°46N 97°3E 241 C6
Sincan Turkey 40°0N 32°36E 212 B5
Sincanlı Turkey 38°45N 30°15E 205 C12
Sincé Colombia 9°15N 75°9W 328 B2
Sincelejo Colombia 9°18N 75°24W 328 B2
Sinch'ang N. Korea 40°7N 128°28E 224 B4
Sincheorwon S. Korea 38°8N 127°18E 224 C3
Sinch'ŏn N. Korea 38°17N 125°21E 224 C2
Sinchon Seoul, S. Korea 37°34N 126°57E 137 B1
Sinclair U.S.A. 41°47N 107°7W 304 F10
Sinclair, L. U.S.A. 33°8N 83°12W 316 B6
Sinclair Mills Canada 54°5N 121°40W 296 C4
Sinclair's B. U.K. 58°31N 3°5W 167 C5
Sinclairville U.S.A. 42°16N 79°16W 312 D5
Sind = Sindh □ Pakistan 26°0N 69°0E 242 G3
Sind → Jammu & Kashmir, India 34°18N 74°45E 243 B6
Sind → Mad. P., India 26°26N 79°13E 243 F8
Sind Sagar Doab Pakistan 32°0N 71°30E 242 D4
Sindal Denmark 57°28N 10°10E 163 G4
Sindang S. Korea 37°35N 127°2E 137 B2
Sindangan Phil. 8°10N 123°5E 233 G4
Sindangan B. Phil. 8°11N 122°50E 233 G4
Sindangbarang Indonesia 7°27S 107°1E 234 D3
Sindara Gabon 1°7S 10°41E 264 C2
Sinde Zambia 17°28S 25°51E 269 F2
Sindelfingen Germany 48°42N 9°0E 179 G4
Sindewahi India 20°17N 79°39E 244 D4
Sindgi India 16°55N 76°14E 244 F3
Sindh = Indus → Pakistan 24°20N 67°47E 242 G2
Sindh □ Pakistan 26°0N 69°0E 242 G3
Sindhnur India 15°47N 76°46E 245 F3
Sindi India 20°48N 78°52E 244 D4
Sındırgı Turkey 39°13N 28°10E 205 B10
Sindou Burkina Faso 10°35N 5°4W 262 C3
Sindri India 23°45N 86°42E 243 H12
Sine → Senegal 14°10N 16°28W 262 C1
Sinegorskiy Russia 47°55N 40°52E 191 G5
Sinekli Turkey 41°14N 28°12E 203 E12
Sinelnikovo = Synelnykove Ukraine 48°25N 35°30E 189 H8
Sinendé Benin 10°20N 2°22E 263 C5
Sines Portugal 37°56N 8°51W 195 H2
Sines, C. de Portugal 37°58N 8°53W 195 H2
Sineu Spain 39°38N 3°1E 206 B4
Sinewit, Mt. Papua N. G. 4°44S 152°2E 286 C7
Sinfra Ivory C. 6°35N 5°56W 262 D3
Sing Buri Thailand 14°53N 100°25E 236 E3
Sing Sing = Ossining U.S.A. 41°10N 73°55W 313 E11
Singa Sudan 13°10N 33°57E 257 E3
Singako Chad 9°50N 19°24E 259 G3
Singalila △ India 27°10N 88°5E 241 B2
Singanallur India 11°2N 77°1E 245 J3
Singapore ■ Asia 1°17N 103°51E 138 B3
Singapore, Straits of Asia 1°15N 104°0E 237 d
Singapore, Univ. of Singapore 1°19N 103°49E 138 B2
Singapore Changi ✈ (SIN) Singapore 1°23N 103°59E 138 A3
Singaraja Indonesia 8°7S 115°6E 231 J18
Singatoka = Sigatoka Fiji 18°8S 177°32E 287 B1
Singen Germany 47°45N 8°50E 179 H4
Singida Tanzania 4°49S 34°48E 268 C3
Singida □ Tanzania 6°0S 34°30E 268 D3
Singkaling Hkamti Burma 26°0N 95°39E 241 C5
Singkang Indonesia 4°8S 120°1E 231 E6
Singkarak, Danau Indonesia 0°36S 100°32E 234 C2
Singkawang Indonesia 1°0N 108°57E 235 B3
Singkep Indonesia 0°30S 104°25E 234 C2
Singkil Indonesia 2°17N 97°49E 237 L1
Singkuang Indonesia 1°3N 98°55E 237 L2
Singleton Australia 32°33S 151°10E 283 B9
Singleton, Mt. N. Terr., Australia 22°0S 130°46E 278 D5
Singleton, Mt. W. Austral., Australia 29°27S 117°15E 279 E2
Singö Sweden 60°12N 18°45E 162 D12
Singoli India 25°0N 75°22E 242 G6
Singora = Songkhla Thailand 7°13N 100°37E 237 J3
Singri India 26°36N 92°29E 241 B4
Singsås Norway 62°56N 10°37E 164 B7
Singu Burma 22°33N 96°0E 241 D6
Sinhgarh India 18°22N 73°45E 244 E1
Sinhŭng Hamgyŏngnam-do, N. Korea 40°11N 127°34E 224 B3
Sinhŭng Hamgyŏngnam-do, N. Korea 41°8N 127°31E 224 B3
Sinicka → Russia 55°52N 37°18E 129 A1
Siniloan Phil. 14°25N 121°27E 232 D3
Sining = Xining China 36°34N 101°40E 218 D9
Siniscóla Italy 40°34N 9°41E 200 B2
Sinj Croatia 43°42N 16°39E 199 E13
Sinjai Indonesia 5°7S 120°20E 231 F6
Sinjajevina Montenegro 42°57N 19°22E 202 D3
Sinjār Iraq 36°19N 41°52E 213 D9
Sinjār Syria 35°35N 37°0E 250 C8
Sinjār, Jabal Iraq 36°23N 41°47E 213 D9
Sinkat Sudan 18°55N 36°49E 256 D4
Sinki, Selat Singapore 1°15N 103°42E 138 B2
Sinkiang = Xinjiang Uygur Zizhiqu □ China 42°0N 86°0E 217 D11
Sinko Guinea 8°53N 8°16W 262 D3
Sinlumkaba Burma 24°16N 97°31E 241 C6
Sinmak N. Korea 38°25N 126°14E 224 C3
Sinmi-do N. Korea 39°33N 124°53E 224 C2
Sínnai Italy 39°18N 9°13E 200 C2
Sinnar India 19°48N 74°0E 244 E2
Sinni → Italy 40°8N 16°41E 201 B9
Sinnuris Egypt 29°26N 30°31E 256 J7
Sinoie, Lacul Romania 44°35N 28°50E 183 F13
Sinop Turkey 42°1N 35°11E 212 A6
Sinop □ Turkey 42°0N 35°0E 212 B6
Sinor India 21°55N 73°20E 242 J5
Sinp'o N. Korea 40°0N 128°13E 224 C4
Sinsa S. Korea 37°31N 127°0E 137 B2
Sinsang N. Korea 39°38N 127°24E 224 C3
Sinsheim Germany 49°15N 8°52E 179 F4
Sinsiang = Xinxiang China 35°18N 113°50E 226 G7
Sinsk Russia 61°8N 126°48E 215 C13
Sint Annabaai Curaçao 12°6N 68°55W 322 g
Sint Christoffelberg Curaçao 12°20N 69°8W 322 g
Sint-Genesius-Rode Belgium 50°45N 4°22E 116 B2
Sint Jorisbaai Curaçao 12°7N 68°48W 322 g
Sint Marie, K. Curaçao 12°11N 69°3W 322 g
Sint Marthabaai Curaçao 12°17N 69°8W 322 g
Sint Michiel Curaçao 12°8N 69°0W 322 g
Sint Nicolaas Aruba 12°27N 69°54W 322 f
Sint Nicolaas Curaçao 12°17N 69°8W 322 g
Sint Willibrordus Curaçao 12°12N 69°4W 322 g
Sintang Indonesia 0°5N 111°35E 235 B4
Sinton U.S.A. 28°2N 97°31W 314 G6
Sintra Portugal 38°47N 9°25W 195 G1
Sintra-Cascais ⌂ Portugal 38°50N 9°25W 195 G1
Sinŭiju N. Korea 40°5N 124°24E 224 B2
Sinujif Somali Rep. 8°33N 48°59E 267 C6
Sinyukha → Ukraine 48°3N 30°51E 189 H6
Sinzig Germany 50°32N 7°14E 178 E3
Sio → Hungary 46°20N 18°53E 182 D3
Siocon Phil. 7°40N 122°10E 233 H4
Siófok Hungary 46°54N 18°3E 182 D3
Sioma Zambia 16°40S 23°32E 265 F4
Sioma Ngwezi △ Zambia 17°14S 23°26E 265 F4
Sion Maharashtra, India 19°3N 72°52E 130 A2
Sion Switz. 46°14N 7°20E 179 J3
Sion Mills U.K. 54°48N 7°29W 166 B4
Sionainn = Shannon → Ireland 52°35N 9°30W 166 D2
Sioux Center U.S.A. 43°5N 96°11W 308 D5
Sioux City U.S.A. 42°30N 96°24W 308 D5
Sioux Falls U.S.A. 43°33N 96°44W 308 D5
Sioux Lookout Canada 50°10N 91°50W 298 B1
Sioux Narrows Canada 49°25N 94°10W 297 D10
Sipadan Malaysia 4°6N 118°38E 235 B5
Sipalay Phil. 9°45N 122°24E 233 G4
Šipan Croatia 42°45N 17°52E 202 D1
Sipang, Tanjong Malaysia 1°48N 110°20E 235 B4
Siparia Trin. & Tob. 10°8N 61°31W 323 t
Sipil Daği △ Turkey 38°35N 27°30E 205 C9
Siping China 43°8N 124°21E 227 C13
Sipitang Malaysia 5°5N 115°33E 235 A5
Sipiwesk L. Canada 55°5N 97°35W 297 B9
Siple Antarctica 75°0S 74°0W 151 D7
Sipocot Phil. 13°46N 122°58E 232 E4
Šipovo Bos.-H. 44°16N 17°6E 182 F2
Sipra → India 23°55N 75°28E 242 H6
Sipson U.K. 51°29N 0°26W 125 B1
Sipsongpanna = Xishuangbanna China 22°5N 101°1E 228 F3
Sipur India 21°11N 85°9E 244 D7
Sipura Indonesia 2°18S 99°40E 234 C1
Sipura, Selat Indonesia 2°27S 99°54E 234 C1
Siqeil Egypt 30°7N 31°10E 117 A1
Siqueira Campos Brazil 23°42S 49°50W 333 F2
Siquia → Nic. 12°10N 84°20W 320 D3
Siquijor Phil. 9°12N 123°35E 233 G4
Siquijor □ Phil. 9°11N 123°35E 233 G4
Siquirres Costa Rica 10°6N 83°30W 320 D3
Siquisique Venezuela 10°34N 69°42W 328 A4
Şīr Abu Nu'ayr U.A.E. 25°20N 54°20E 247 E7
Şīr Banī Yās U.A.E. 24°19N 52°37E 247 E7
Sir Edward Pellew Group Australia 15°40S 137°10E 280 B2
Sir Graham Moore Is. Australia 13°53S 126°34E 278 B4
Sir James MacBrien, Mt. Canada 62°7N 127°41W 294 E6
Sira India 13°41N 76°49E 245 H3
Sira Vest-Agder, Norway 58°24N 6°40E 164 F3
Sira → Norway 58°23N 6°34E 164 F3
Siracusa Italy 37°4N 15°17E 201 E8
Sirajganj Bangla. 24°25N 89°47E 241 C2
Sirakoro Mali 12°41N 9°14W 262 C3
Şiran Turkey 40°11N 39°7E 213 B8
Sirasso Ivory C. 9°16N 6°6W 262 D3
Sirathu India 25°39N 81°19E 243 G9
Siraway Phil. 7°34N 122°8E 233 H4
Sirdalsvatnet Norway 58°34N 6°43E 164 F3
Sīrdān Iran 36°39N 49°12E 213 D13
Sirdaryo □ Uzbekistan 40°30N 68°45E 217 D7
Sire Ethiopia 6°55N 35°36E 257 F4
Siren U.S.A. 45°47N 92°24W 308 C7
Sirente-Velino ⌂ Italy 42°10N 13°32E 199 F10
Sirer Spain 38°56N 1°22E 206 D1
Siret Romania 47°55N 26°5E 183 C11
Siret → Romania 45°24N 28°1E 183 E12
Sirevåg Norway 58°30N 5°48E 164 F2
Sirghāyā Syria 33°51N 36°8E 250 E7
Şiria Romania 46°16N 21°38E 182 D6
Sirik, Tanjong Malaysia 2°47N 111°15E 235 B4
Sirikit Res. Thailand 17°45N 100°34E 236 C3
Sirinat △ Thailand 8°6N 98°17E 237 a
Sirino, Mte. Italy 40°7N 15°50E 201 B8
Sīrjān Iran 29°30N 55°45E 247 D7
Sirkali = Sirkazhi India 11°15N 79°41E 245 J4
Sirkazhi India 11°15N 79°41E 245 J4
Sirmans U.S.A. 30°21N 83°39W 316 E6
Sirmaur India 24°51N 81°23E 243 G9
Sirmilik △ Canada 72°50N 80°35W 295 C15
Sirna Greece 36°22N 26°42E 205 E8
Şirnak Turkey 37°32N 42°28E 213 D10
Sirohi India 24°52N 72°53E 242 G5
Sirombu Indonesia 0°57N 97°25E 234 B1
Sironj India 24°5N 77°39E 242 G7
Síros = Ermoupoli Greece 37°28N 24°57E 204 D6
Siroz = Serres Greece 41°5N 23°31E 202 E7
Sirpur India 19°29N 79°36E 244 E4
Sirr, Nafud as Si. Arabia 25°33N 44°35E 246 E5
Sirrayn Si. Arabia 19°38N 40°36E 248 C3
Sirretta Pk. U.S.A. 35°56N 118°19W 307 K8
Sīrrī Iran 25°55N 54°32E 247 E7
Sirsa India 29°33N 75°4E 242 E6
Sirsa → India 26°51N 79°4E 243 F8
Sirsi India 14°40N 74°49E 245 G2
Sirsilla India 18°23N 78°50E 244 E4
Siruela Spain 38°58N 5°3W 195 G5
Siruguppa India 15°38N 76°54E 245 F3
Sirur India 18°50N 74°23E 244 E2
Sirvān → Iran 35°4N 46°50E 213 E12
Sisak Croatia 45°30N 16°21E 199 C13
Sisante Spain 39°25N 2°12W 197 F2
Sisargas, Is. Spain 43°21N 8°50W 194 B2
Sishen S. Africa 27°47S 22°59E 270 C3
Sishui China 35°42N 117°18E 227 G9
Sisian Armenia 39°31N 46°1E 213 C12
Sisiga Solomon Is. 7°54S 159°10E 287 L10
Sisimiut Greenland 66°40N 53°30W 154 D5
Sisipuk L. Canada 55°45N 101°50W 297 B8
Şişli Turkey 41°3N 28°58E 122 B1
Sisophon Cambodia 13°38N 102°59E 236 F4
Sissano Papua N. G. 3°0S 142°3E 286 B2
Sisseton U.S.A. 45°40N 97°3W 308 C5
Sisson = Mount Shasta U.S.A. 41°19N 122°19W 304 F2
Sissonne France 49°34N 3°51E 173 C10
Sīstān Asia 30°50N 61°0E 247 D9
Sīstan, Daryācheh-ye Iran 31°0N 61°0E 247 D9
Sīstān va Balūchestān □ Iran 27°0N 62°0E 247 E9
Sisteron France 44°12N 5°57E 175 D9
Sisters U.S.A. 44°18N 121°33W 304 D3
Sisters, The Grenada 12°18N 61°36W 323 q
Sisters, The Seychelles 4°16S 55°52E 272 c
Sisters Pk. Ascension I. 7°56S 14°22W 153 g
Sisters Rocks Trin. & Tob. 11°20N 60°39W 323 s
Siswa Bazar India 27°9N 83°46E 243 F10
Sitakili Mali 13°7N 11°14W 262 C2
Sitakunda Bangla. 22°37N 91°39E 241 D3
Sitamarhi India 26°37N 85°30E 243 F11
Sitampiky Madag. 16°41S 46°6E 272 B2
Sitangkai Phil. 4°40N 119°24E 233 J2
Sitapur India 27°38N 80°45E 243 F9
Siteki Swaziland 26°32S 31°58E 271 C5
Sitges Spain 41°17N 1°47E 196 D6
Sithonia Greece 40°0N 23°45E 202 F7
Sitia Greece 35°13N 26°6E 207 E7
Sitia ✈ (JSH) Greece 35°15N 26°5E 207 E7
Sítio da Abadia Brazil 14°48S 46°16W 333 D2
Sitito-Ozima Ridge Pac. Oc. 23°0N 143°0E 288 E6
Sitka U.S.A. 57°3N 135°20W 296 B1
Sitka ⌂ U.S.A. 57°3N 135°19W 303 H14
Sitkinak I. U.S.A. 56°33N 154°10W 303 H9
Sitoti Botswana 23°15S 23°40E 270 B3
Sitra Egypt 28°40N 26°53E 256 B2
Sittang Myit → Burma 17°20N 96°45E 241 G6
Sittard Neths. 51°0N 5°52E 170 C5
Sittaung Burma 24°10N 94°35E 241 C5
Sittensen Germany 53°17N 9°32E 178 B5
Sittingbourne U.K. 51°21N 0°45E 169 F8
Sittona Eritrea 14°25N 37°23E 257 E4
Sittoung = Sittang Myit → Burma 17°20N 96°45E 241 G6
Sittwe Burma 20°18N 92°45E 241 E4
Situbondo Indonesia 7°42S 113°56E 235 D4
Siufaalete Pt. Amer. Samoa 14°17S 169°29W 302 f
Siulagi Pt. Amer. Samoa 14°13S 169°30W 302 g
Si'umu Samoa 14°1S 171°48W 287 W20
Siuna Nic. 13°37N 84°45W 320 D3
Siuri India 23°50N 87°34E 243 H12
Siutghiol, Lacul Romania 44°15N 28°35E 183 F13
Sivaganga India 9°50N 78°28E 245 K4
Sivagiri India 9°16N 77°26E 245 K3
Sivakasi India 9°24N 77°47E 245 K3
Sīvand Iran 30°5N 52°55E 247 D7
Sivas Turkey 39°43N 36°58E 212 C7
Sivas □ Turkey 39°45N 37°0E 212 C7
Sivasamudram India 12°16N 77°10E 245 H3
Sivaslı Turkey 38°31N 29°42E 205 C11
Siverek Turkey 37°50N 39°19E 213 D8
Sivomaskinskiy Russia 66°40N 62°35E 186 A11
Sivota Greece 39°24N 20°13E 206 C10
Sivrihisar Turkey 39°30N 31°35E 212 C4
Sivros Greece 38°40N 20°39E 207 B2
Sîwa Egypt 29°11N 25°31E 256 B2
Sîwa, El Wâhât es Egypt 29°10N 25°30E 256 B2
Siwa Oasis = Sîwa, El Wâhât es Egypt 29°10N 25°30E 256 B2

Siwalik Range Nepal 28°0N 83°0E 243 F10
Siwan India 26°13N 84°21E 243 F11
Siwana India 25°38N 72°25E 242 G5
Six Cross Roads Barbados 13°7N 59°28W 323 r
Sixian China 33°30N 117°50E 227 H9
Sixmilebridge Ireland 52°44N 8°46W 166 D3
Sixth Cataract Sudan 16°20N 32°42E 257 D3
Siyabuswa S. Africa 25°7S 29°3E 271 C4
Siyah Kuh, Kavīr-e Iran 32°55N 53°55E 247 C7
Siyāl, Jazā'ir Egypt 22°49N 36°12E 256 C4
Siyang China 33°42N 118°40E 227 H10
Siyäzän Azerbaijan 41°3N 49°10E 191 K9
Siziwang Qi China 41°25N 111°40E 226 D6
Sjælland Denmark 55°30N 11°30E 163 J5
Sjælland □ Denmark 55°30N 11°30E 163 J5
Sjællands Odde Denmark 55°58N 11°24E 163 J5
Sjenica Serbia 43°16N 20°0E 202 C3
Sjoa Norway 61°41N 9°33E 164 C6
Sjöbo Sweden 55°37N 13°45E 163 J7
Sjøholt Norway 62°27N 6°52E 164 B3
Sjølisand Norway 61°29N 11°18E 164 C8
Sjötofta Sweden 57°22N 13°17E 163 G7
Sjötorp Sweden 58°50N 14°0E 163 F8
Sjumen = Shumen
Bulgaria 43°18N 26°55E 203 C10
Sjuntorp Sweden 58°12N 12°13E 163 F6
Skåbu Norway 61°32N 9°24E 164 C6
Skadarsko Jezero Europe 42°10N 19°20E 202 D3
Skadarsko Jezero △
Montenegro 42°10N 19°20E 202 D3
Skadovsk Ukraine 46°17N 32°52E 189 J7
Skælskør Denmark 55°15N 11°18E 163 J5
Skærbæk Denmark 55°9N 8°45E 163 J2
Skaftafell Iceland 64°1N 17°0W 155 C9
Skaftafell △ Iceland 64°9N 16°50W 155 C9
Skagafjarðarsýsla □
Iceland 65°30N 19°0W 155 B7
Skagafjörður Iceland 65°54N 19°35W 155 B7
Skagastølstindane Norway 61°28N 7°52E 164 C4
Skagaströnd Iceland 65°50N 20°19W 155 B6
Skagatá Iceland 66°7N 20°6W 155 A6
Skagen Denmark 57°43N 10°35E 163 G4
Skagern Sweden 59°0N 14°20E 162 E8
Skagerrak Denmark 57°30N 9°0E 163 G2
Skagit → U.S.A. 48°23N 122°22W 306 B4
Skagway U.S.A. 59°28N 135°19W 303 G14
Skala Greece 38°5N 20°47E 207 C2
Skala nad Zbruczem = Skala-Podilska Ukraine 48°50N 26°15E 183 B11
Skala-Podilska Ukraine 48°50N 26°15E 183 B11
Skalat Ukraine 49°23N 25°55E 177 D13
Skálavík Iceland 66°11N 23°29W 155 A3
Skalbmierz Poland 50°20N 20°25E 185 H7
Skälderviken Sweden 56°22N 12°30E 163 H6
Skålevik Norway 58°5N 8°1E 164 F5
Skalica Slovak Rep. 48°50N 17°15E 181 C10
Skallingen Denmark 55°32N 8°13E 163 J2
Skalni Dol = Kamenyak
Bulgaria 43°24N 26°57E 203 C10
Skanderborg Denmark 56°2N 9°55E 163 H3
Skåne Sweden 55°59N 13°30E 163 J7
Skåne län □ Sweden 56°15N 14°0E 163 H7
Skaneateles U.S.A. 42°57N 76°26W 313 D8
Skaneateles L. U.S.A. 42°51N 76°22W 313 D8
Skånevik Norway 59°43N 5°53E 164 E2
Skänninge Sweden 58°24N 15°5E 163 F9
Skanör med Falsterbo
Sweden 55°24N 12°50E 163 J6
Skansen Sweden 59°19N 18°7E 139 B2
Skantzoura Greece 39°5N 24°6E 204 B6
Skara Sweden 58°25N 13°30E 163 F7
Skärblacka Sweden 58°35N 15°54E 163 F9
Skarð Iceland 65°17N 22°19W 155 B4
Skardu Pakistan 35°20N 75°44E 243 B6
Skare Hordaland, Norway 59°55N 6°36E 164 E3
Skåre Sweden 59°26N 13°26E 162 E7
Skärhamn Sweden 57°59N 11°34E 163 G5
Skärholmen Sweden 59°16N 17°53E 139 B1
Skarnes Norway 60°15N 11°41E 164 D8
Skärpäng Sweden 59°26N 18°0E 139 A2
Skarpnäck Sweden 59°16N 18°7E 139 B2
Skarszewy Poland 54°4N 18°25E 184 D5
Skaryszew Poland 51°19N 21°15E 185 G8
Skaryszewski, Park Poland 52°15N 21°3E 142 B2
Skarżysko-Kamienna
Poland 51°7N 20°52E 185 G7
Skattkärr Sweden 59°25N 13°40E 162 E7
Skattungbyn Sweden 61°10N 14°56E 162 C8
Skawina Poland 49°59N 19°50E 185 J6
Skebobruk Sweden 59°58N 18°36E 162 E12
Skee Sweden 58°56N 11°19E 163 F5
Skeena → Canada 54°9N 130°5W 296 C2
Skeena Mts. Canada 56°40N 128°30W 296 B3
Skegness U.K. 53°9N 0°20E 168 D8
Skei Norway 61°34N 6°28E 164 C3
Skeiðarársandur Iceland 63°54N 17°14W 155 D9
Skeiðflötur Iceland 63°26N 19°11W 155 D7
Skeldon = Corriverton
Guyana 5°55N 57°20W 329 B6
Skeleton Coast ⌓ Namibia 20°0S 13°20E 270 B1
Skellefteå Sweden 64°45N 20°50E 160 D19
Skellefteälven → Sweden 64°45N 21°10E 160 D19
Skelleftehamn Sweden 64°40N 21°9E 160 D19
Skellig Michael = Great Skellig
Ireland 51°47N 10°33W 166 E1
Skender Vakuf Bos.-H. 44°29N 17°22E 182 F2
Skenderaj = Srbica
Kosovo 42°45N 20°47E 202 D4
Skeppsholmen Stockholm, Sweden 139 c3
Skerries, The U.K. 53°25N 4°36W 168 D3
Skhidnytsya Ukraine 49°13N 23°20E 185 J10
Skhiza Greece 36°41N 21°40E 204 E3
Ski Norway 59°43N 10°52E 164 E7
Skiathos Greece 39°12N 23°30E 204 B5
Skibbereen Ireland 51°33N 9°16W 166 E2
Skiddaw U.K. 54°39N 3°9W 168 C4
Skidegate Canada 53°15N 132°1W 296 C2
Skidra Greece 40°46N 22°10E 202 F6
Skien Norway 59°12N 9°35E 164 E6
Skierniewice Poland 51°58N 20°10E 185 G7
Skihist, Mt. Canada 50°12N 121°54W 296 C4
Skikda Algeria 36°50N 6°58E 261 A6
Skikda □ Algeria 36°45N 6°50E 261 A6
Skillet Fork → U.S.A. 38°5N 88°5W 311 F8
Skillingaryd Sweden 57°27N 14°5E 163 G8
Skillinge Sweden 55°30N 14°16E 163 J8
Skilloura Cyprus 35°14N 33°10E 207 D12
Skinari, Akra Greece 37°56N 20°42E 207 D2
Skinnastaðir Iceland 66°4N 16°27W 155 A10
Skinnskatteberg Sweden 59°50N 15°42E 162 E9
Skipton Vic., Australia 37°39S 143°40E 282 D5
Skipton N. Yorks., U.K. 53°58N 2°3W 168 D5
Skiptvet Norway 59°28N 11°11E 164 E8
Skiring, C. Senegal 12°26N 16°46W 262 C1
Skirmish Pt. Australia 11°59S 134°17E 280 A1
Skiropoula Greece 38°50N 24°21E 204 C6
Skiros Greece 38°55N 24°34E 204 C6
Skivarp Sweden 55°26N 13°34E 163 J7
Skive Denmark 56°33N 9°2E 163 H3
Skjærhalden Norway 59°2N 11°2E 164 E8
Skjálfandafljót → Iceland 65°59N 17°25W 155 B9
Skjálfandi Iceland 66°5N 17°30W 155 A9
Skjeberg Norway 59°12N 11°12E 164 E8
Skjern Denmark 55°57N 8°30E 163 J2
Skjold Norway 59°31N 5°34E 164 E2
Skjolden Norway 61°29N 7°36E 164 C4
Skjöldólfsstaðir Iceland 65°19N 15°7W 155 B11
Skjønhaug Norway 59°39N 11°19E 164 E8
Skobelev = Farghona
Uzbekistan 40°23N 71°19E 217 D8
Skoczów Poland 49°49N 18°45E 185 J5
Skodje Norway 62°30N 6°43E 164 B3
Škofja Loka Slovenia 46°9N 14°19E 199 B11
Skógar Iceland 63°32N 19°28W 155 D7
Skógarnes Iceland 64°46N 22°34W 155 C4
Skoghall Sweden 59°20N 13°30E 162 E7
Skogstorp Sweden 59°19N 16°29E 162 E10
Skoki Poland 52°40N 17°11E 185 F4
Skokie U.S.A. 42°2N 87°43W 119 A2
Skokie → U.S.A. 42°3N 87°46W 119 A2
Skokie Heritage Museum
U.S.A. 42°2N 87°44W 119 A2
Skollfjell Norway 59°50N 10°40E 133 A3
Skole Ukraine 49°3N 23°30E 177 D12
Skollenborg Norway 59°38N 9°43E 164 E6
Sköndal Sweden 59°15N 18°6E 139 B2
Skopelos Greece 39°9N 23°47E 204 B5
Skopi Greece 35°11N 26°2E 207 E7
Skopin Russia 53°55N 39°32E 188 F10
Skopje Macedonia 42°1N 21°26E 202 D5
Skopje ✈ (SKP) Macedonia 41°59N 21°29E 202 E5
Skoppum Norway 59°23N 10°26E 164 E7
Skórcz Poland 53°47N 18°30E 184 E5
Skørping Denmark 56°50N 9°53E 163 H3
Skotfoss Norway 59°12N 9°30E 164 E6
Skotterud Norway 60°0N 12°7E 164 D9
Skövde Sweden 58°24N 13°50E 163 F7
Skovlunde Denmark 55°42N 12°25E 118 A2
Skovorodino Russia 54°0N 124°0E 215 D13
Skovshoved Denmark 55°45N 12°35E 118 A3
Skowhegan U.S.A. 44°46N 69°43W 309 C19
Skradin Croatia 43°52N 15°53E 199 E12
Skrea Sweden 56°53N 12°34E 163 H6
Skreia Norway 60°40N 10°56E 164 D7
Skrim Norway 59°31N 9°38E 164 E6
Skrunda Latvia 56°41N 22°1E 184 B9
Skudeneshavn Norway 59°10N 5°10E 164 E2
Skuleskogen △ Sweden 63°6N 18°30E 162 A12
Skull Ireland 51°32N 9°34W 166 E2
Skultorp Sweden 58°24N 13°51E 163 F7
Skultuna Sweden 59°43N 16°25E 162 E10
Skunk → U.S.A. 40°42N 91°7W 310 D5
Skuodas Lithuania 56°16N 21°33E 184 B8
Skuru Sweden 59°18N 18°12E 139 B3
Skurup Sweden 55°28N 13°30E 163 J7
Skutskär Sweden 60°37N 17°25E 162 D11
Skútustaðir Iceland 65°34N 17°2W 155 B9
Skvyra Ukraine 49°44N 29°40E 177 D15
Skwierzyna Poland 52°33N 15°30E 185 F2
Sky Dome = Rogers Centre
Toronto, Canada 141 c1
Sky Lake U.S.A. 28°27N 81°23W 133 B2
Skye U.K. 57°15N 6°10W 167 D2
Skykomish U.S.A. 47°42N 121°22W 304 C3
Skyland U.S.A. 33°53N 84°19W 113 A3
Skyring, Seno Chile 52°35S 72°0W 336 D3
Skyros = Skiros Greece 38°55N 24°34E 204 C6
Skyttorp Sweden 60°5N 17°44E 162 D11
Slade Green U.K. 51°27N 0°11E 125 B5
Slade Point Australia 21°4S 149°13E 280 b
Slade Pt. Australia 21°5S 149°13E 280 b
Slættaratindur Færoe Is. 62°18N 7°1W 160 E9
Slagelse Denmark 55°23N 11°19E 163 J5
Slamet Indonesia 7°16S 109°8E 235 D3
Slane Ireland 53°42N 6°33W 166 C5
Slaney → Ireland 52°26N 6°33W 166 D5
Slangberge S. Africa 31°32S 20°48E 270 D3
Slănic Romania 45°14N 25°58E 183 E10
Slano Croatia 42°48N 17°53E 202 D1
Slantsy Russia 59°7N 28°5E 188 C5
Slaný Czech Rep. 50°13N 14°6E 180 A7
Śląsk Poland 51°0N 16°30E 176 C9
Śląskie □ Poland 50°30N 19°0E 185 H6
Slåtbaken Sweden 58°25N 16°45E 163 F10
Slate Is. Canada 48°40N 87°0W 298 C2
Slater U.S.A. 39°13N 93°4W 310 E3
Slatina Croatia 45°42N 17°45E 182 E2
Slatina Romania 44°28N 24°22E 183 F9
Slatina Timiş Romania 45°15N 22°17E 182 E7
Slatington U.S.A. 40°45N 75°37W 313 F9
Slaton U.S.A. 33°26N 101°39W 314 E4
Slave → Canada 61°18N 113°39W 296 A6
Slave Coast W. Afr. 6°0N 2°30E 263 D5
Slave Lake Canada 55°17N 114°43W 296 B6
Slave Pt. Canada 61°11N 115°56W 296 A5
Slavgorod Russia 53°1N 78°37E 217 B9
Slavinja Serbia 43°9N 22°50E 202 C6
Slavkov u Brna Czech Rep. 49°10N 16°52E 181 B9
Slavkovský Les ⌓
Czech Rep. 50°5N 12°44E 180 A5
Slavonija Europe 45°20N 17°40E 182 E2
Slavonski Brod Croatia 45°11N 18°1E 182 E3
Slavsk Russia 55°3N 21°41E 184 C8
Slavske Ukraine 48°51N 23°27E 183 B8
Slavskoye Russia 54°30N 20°27E 184 D7
Slavuta Ukraine 50°15N 27°2E 177 C14
Slavyanka Russia 42°53N 131°21E 220 C5
Slavyanovo Bulgaria 43°28N 24°52E 203 C8
Slavyansk = Slovyansk
Ukraine 48°55N 37°36E 189 H9
Slavyansk-na-Kubani
Russia 45°15N 38°11E 189 K10
Sława Poland 51°52N 16°2E 185 G3
Slawharad Belarus 53°27N 31°0E 177 B16
Sławno Poland 54°20N 16°41E 184 D3
Sławoborze Poland 53°55N 15°42E 184 E2
Sleaford U.K. 53°0N 0°24W 168 D7
Sleaford B. Australia 34°55S 135°45E 281 E2
Sleat, Sd. of U.K. 57°5N 5°47W 167 D3
Sleðbrjótur Iceland 65°34N 14°30W 155 B12
Sleeper Is. Canada 58°30N 81°0W 295 F15
Sleeping Bear Dunes ⌓
U.S.A. 44°50N 86°5W 308 C10
Sleepy Eye U.S.A. 44°18N 94°43W 308 C6
Sleetmute U.S.A. 61°42N 157°10W 303 F8
Slemon L. Canada 63°13N 116°4W 296 A5
Slependen Norway 59°52N 10°30E 133 A2
Ślesin Poland 52°22N 18°14E 185 F5
Slide Mt. U.S.A. 42°0N 74°25W 313 E10
Slidell U.S.A. 30°17N 89°47W 315 F10
Slidre Norway 61°5N 8°58E 164 C5
Sliema Malta 35°55N 14°30E 206 F8
Slieve Aughty Ireland 53°4N 8°30W 166 C3
Slieve Bloom Ireland 53°4N 7°40W 166 C4
Slieve Donard U.K. 54°11N 5°55W 166 B6
Slieve Gamph Ireland 54°6N 9°0W 166 B3
Slieve Gullion U.K. 54°7N 6°26W 166 B5
Slieve League Ireland 54°40N 8°42W 166 B3
Slieve Mish Ireland 52°12N 9°50W 166 D2
Slievenamon Ireland 52°25N 7°34W 166 D4
Sligeach = Sligo Ireland 54°16N 8°28W 166 B3
Sligo Sligo, Ireland 54°16N 8°28W 166 B3
Sligo Pa., U.S.A. 41°6N 79°29W 312 E5
Sligo □ Ireland 54°8N 8°42W 166 B3
Sligo B. Ireland 54°18N 8°40W 166 B3
Slipi Indonesia 6°11S 106°47E 122 B1
Slippery Rock U.S.A. 41°4N 80°3W 312 E4
Slite Sweden 57°42N 18°48E 163 G12
Slīteres ⌓ Latvia 57°41N 22°21E 184 A9
Sliven Bulgaria 42°42N 26°19E 203 D10
Sliven □ Bulgaria 42°42N 26°19E 203 D10
Slivenec Czech Rep. 50°1N 14°21E 135 B2
Slivnitsa Bulgaria 42°50N 23°2E 202 D7
Sljeme Croatia 45°57N 15°58E 199 C12
Sloan U.S.A. 35°57N 115°13W 307 K11
Sloansville U.S.A. 42°45N 74°22W 313 D10
Slobidka Ukraine 47°54N 29°21E 183 C14
Slobodskoy Russia 58°40N 50°6E 186 C9
Slobozia Moldova 46°45N 29°42E 183 D14
Slobozia Argeş, Romania 44°30N 25°14E 183 F10
Slobozia Ialomiţa,
Romania 44°34N 27°23E 183 F12
Slocan Canada 49°48N 117°28W 296 D5
Slocomb U.S.A. 31°7N 85°36W 316 D4
Slomikhino = Zhalpaqtal
Kazakhstan 49°42N 49°25E 190 F9
Słomniki Poland 50°16N 20°4E 185 H7
Slonim Belarus 53°4N 25°19E 177 B13
Slot, The = New Georgia Sound
Solomon Is. 8°0S 158°20E 287 L9
Sloten Neths. 52°21N 4°48E 112 A1
Sloterdijk Neths. 52°23N 4°51E 112 A1
Sloterpark Neths. 52°22N 4°49E 112 A1
Slottet Oslo, Norway 133 a1
Slough U.K. 51°30N 0°36W 169 F7
Slough □ U.K. 51°30N 0°36W 169 F7
Sloughhouse U.S.A. 38°26N 121°12W 306 G5
Slovak Rep. ■ Europe 48°30N 20°0E 181 C13
Slovakia = Slovak Rep. ■
Europe 48°30N 20°0E 181 C13
Slovakian Ore Mts. = Slovenské
Rudohorie Slovak Rep. 48°45N 20°0E 181 C12
Slovenia ■ Europe 45°58N 14°30E 199 C11
Slovenija = Slovenia ■
Europe 45°58N 14°30E 199 C11
Slovenj Gradec Slovenia 46°31N 15°5E 199 B12
Slovenska = Slovak Rep. ■
Europe 48°30N 20°0E 181 C13
Slovenska Bistrica
Slovenia 46°24N 15°35E 199 B12
Slovenské Konjice
Slovenia 46°20N 15°28E 199 B12
Slovenské Rudohorie
Slovak Rep. 48°45N 20°0E 181 C12
Slovenský Raj △
Slovak Rep. 48°53N 20°25E 181 C13
Slovyansk Ukraine 48°55N 37°36E 189 H9
Słowiński △ Poland 54°43N 17°26E 184 D4
Słubice Poland 52°22N 14°35E 185 F1
Sluch → Ukraine 51°37N 26°38E 177 C14
Sluhy Czech Rep. 50°11N 14°33E 135 A3
Sluis Neths. 51°18N 3°23E 170 C3
Slŭnchev Bryag Bulgaria 42°40N 27°41E 203 D11
Slunj Croatia 45°6N 15°33E 199 C12
Słupca Poland 52°15N 17°52E 185 F4
Słupia → Poland 54°35N 16°51E 184 D3
Słupsk Poland 54°30N 17°3E 184 D4
Slurry S. Africa 25°49S 25°42E 270 C4
Slutsk = Pavlovsk Russia 50°26N 40°5E 190 E5
Slutsk Belarus 53°2N 27°31E 177 B14
Slużew Poland 52°10N 21°0E 142 B2
Slużewiec Poland 52°10N 21°0E 142 B2
Slyne Hd. Ireland 53°25N 10°10W 166 C1
Slyudyanka Russia 51°40N 103°40E 215 D11
Smaalenene = Østfold □
Norway 59°25N 11°25E 164 E8
Småland Sweden 57°15N 15°25E 163 G9
Smålandsfarvandet
Denmark 55°10N 11°20E 163 J5
Smålandsstenar Sweden 57°10N 13°25E 163 G7
Smaldeel = Theunissen
S. Africa 28°26S 26°43E 270 C4
Smalltree L. Canada 61°0N 105°0W 297 A8
Smallwood Res. Canada 54°5N 64°30W 299 B7
Smara W. Sahara 26°48N 11°41W 260 C2
Smarhon Belarus 54°20N 26°24E 177 A14
Smarje Slovenia 46°15N 15°34E 199 B12
Smartt Syndicate Dam
S. Africa 30°45S 23°10E 270 D3
Smartville U.S.A. 39°13N 121°18W 306 F5
Smeaton Canada 53°30N 104°49W 297 C8
Smedby Sweden 56°41N 16°13E 163 H10
Smederevo Serbia 44°40N 20°57E 202 B4
Smederevska Palanka
Serbia 44°22N 20°58E 202 B4
Smedjebacken Sweden 60°8N 15°25E 162 D9
Smela = Smila Ukraine 49°15N 31°58E 189 H6
Smerwick Harbour
Ireland 52°12N 10°23W 166 D1
Smethport U.S.A. 41°49N 78°27W 312 E6
Smíchov Czech Rep. 50°4N 14°23E 135 B2
Smidovich Russia 48°36N 133°49E 215 E14
Śmigiel Poland 52°1N 16°32E 185 F3
Smila Ukraine 49°15N 31°58E 189 H6
Smilyan Bulgaria 41°29N 24°46E 203 E8
Smith Canada 55°10N 114°0W 296 B6
Smith B. U.S.A. 70°30N 154°20W 303 A9
Smith Center U.S.A. 39°47N 98°47W 308 F4
Smith Forest Preserve
U.S.A. 41°59N 87°45W 119 B2
Smith I. Nunavut, Canada 60°45N 78°25W 295 E16
Smith I. India 13°20N 93°4E 245 H11
Smith Islands △ Australia 20°40S 149°9E 280 b
Smith River ⌓ U.S.A. 41°55N 124°0W 304 F2
Smith Sd. N. Amer. 78°25N 74°0W 154 B3
Smithburne → Australia 17°3S 140°57E 280 B3
Smithers Canada 54°45N 127°10W 296 C3
Smithfield Free State,
S. Africa 30°9S 26°30E 271 D4
Smithfield N.C., U.S.A. 35°31N 78°21W 315 D15
Smithfield Utah, U.S.A. 41°50N 111°50W 304 F8
Smiths U.S.A. 32°32N 85°6W 316 C4
Smiths Falls Canada 44°55N 76°0W 313 B9
Smithsonian Institution
Washington, D.C., U.S.A. 143 b2
Smithton Australia 40°53S 145°6E 281 G4
Smithville Ont., Canada 43°6N 79°33W 312 C5
Smithville Ga., U.S.A. 31°54N 84°15W 316 D5
Smithville Mo., U.S.A. 39°23N 94°35W 310 E2
Smithville Tex., U.S.A. 30°1N 97°10W 314 F6
Smoke Creek Desert
U.S.A. 40°30N 119°40W 304 F4
Smoky → Canada 56°10N 117°21W 296 B5
Smoky Bay Australia 32°22S 134°13E 281 E1
Smoky Hill → U.S.A. 39°4N 96°48W 308 F5
Smoky Hills U.S.A. 39°15N 99°30W 308 F4
Smoky Lake Canada 54°10N 112°30W 296 C6
Smøla Norway 63°23N 8°3E 164 A5
Smolensk Russia 54°45N 32°5E 188 E7
Smolensk □ Russia 55°20N 33°0E 188 E7
Smolikas, Oros Greece 40°9N 20°58E 202 F4
Smolník Slovak Rep. 48°43N 20°44E 181 C13
Smolny Russia 59°56N 30°25E 137 B2
Smolny Cathedral Russia 59°56N 30°24E 137 B2
Smolyan Bulgaria 41°36N 24°38E 203 E8
Smolyan □ Bulgaria 41°36N 24°38E 203 E8
Smooth Rock Falls
Canada 49°17N 81°37W 298 C3
Smoothstone L. Canada 54°40N 106°50W 297 C7
Smorgon = Smarhon
Belarus 54°20N 26°24E 177 A14
Smotrych Ukraine 48°57N 26°33E 183 B11
Smotrych → Ukraine 48°34N 26°39E 183 B11
Smulţi Romania 45°57N 27°44E 183 E12
Smyadovo Bulgaria 43°2N 27°1E 203 C11
Smygehamn Sweden 55°21N 13°22E 163 J7
Smygehuk Sweden 55°20N 13°20E 163 J7
Smyrna = İzmir Turkey 38°25N 27°8E 205 C9
Smyrna Del., U.S.A. 39°18N 75°36W 309 F16
Smyrna Ga., U.S.A. 33°53N 84°31W 316 B5
Snæfell Iceland 64°48N 15°34W 155 C11
Snaefell I. of Man 54°16N 4°27W 168 C3
Snæfellsjökull Iceland 64°49N 23°46W 155 C3
Snæfellsnessýsla □ Iceland 65°0N 23°0W 155 C3
Snake → U.S.A. 46°12N 119°2W 304 C4
Snake Creek Canal
U.S.A. 25°57N 80°19W 128 A2
Snake I. Australia 38°47S 146°33E 283 E7
Snake Pt. Anguilla 18°17N 62°58W 322 a
Snake Range U.S.A. 39°0N 114°20W 304 G6
Snake River Plain U.S.A. 42°50N 114°0W 304 E7
Snakeden Branch →
U.S.A. 38°55N 77°18W 143 B1
Snarøya Norway 59°52N 10°33E 133 A2
Snasahögarna Sweden 63°13N 12°21E 162 A6
Snåsavatnet Norway 64°12N 12°0E 160 D15
Snättringe Sweden 59°15N 17°58E 139 B1
Snedsted Denmark 56°55N 8°32E 163 H2
Sneek Neths. 53°2N 5°40E 170 A5
Sneem Ireland 51°50N 9°54W 166 E2
Sneeuberge S. Africa 31°46S 24°20E 270 D3
Snegurovka = Tetiyev
Ukraine 49°22N 29°38E 177 D15
Snejbjerg Denmark 56°8N 8°54E 163 H2
Snelling Calif., U.S.A. 37°31N 120°26W 306 H6
Snelling S.C., U.S.A. 33°15N 81°27W 316 B8
Snells Beach N.Z. 36°25S 174°44E 284 C3
Snezhnoye Ukraine 48°0N 38°58E 189 H10
Sněžka Europe 50°41N 15°50E 185 A8
Snežnik Slovenia 45°36N 14°35E 199 C11
Śniadowo Poland 53°2N 22°0E 185 E8
Sniardwy, Jezioro Poland 53°48N 21°50E 184 E8
Śnieżka Europe 50°44N 15°44E 180 A8
Snigirevka = Snihurivka
Ukraine 47°2N 32°49E 189 J7
Snihurivka Ukraine 47°2N 32°49E 189 J7
Snillfjord Norway 63°24N 9°30E 164 A6
Snina Slovak Rep. 48°58N 22°9E 181 C15
Snizort, L. U.K. 57°33N 6°28W 167 D2
Snøhetta Norway 62°19N 9°16E 164 B6
Snohomish U.S.A. 47°55N 122°6W 306 C4
Snønuten Norway 59°31N 6°52E 164 E3
Snoqualmie Pass U.S.A. 47°25N 121°25W 306 C5
Snoul Cambodia 12°4N 106°26E 237 F6
Snover U.S.A. 43°27N 82°58W 312 C2
Snovsk = Shchors
Ukraine 51°48N 31°56E 189 G6
Snow Hill U.S.A. 38°11N 75°24W 309 F16
Snow Lake Canada 54°52N 100°3W 297 C8
Snow Mt. Calif., U.S.A. 39°23N 122°45W 306 F4
Snow Mt. Maine, U.S.A. 45°18N 70°48W 313 A14
Snow Shoe U.S.A. 41°2N 77°57W 312 E7
Snowbird L. Canada 60°45N 103°0W 297 A8
Snowdon U.K. 53°4N 4°5W 168 D3
Snowdonia △ U.K. 53°7N 3°59W 168 D4
Snowdoun U.S.A. 32°15N 86°18W 316 C3
Snowdrift = Łutsel K'e
Canada 62°24N 110°44W 297 A6
Snowdrift → Canada 62°24N 110°44W 297 A6
Snowflake U.S.A. 34°30N 110°5W 305 J8
Snowshoe Pk. U.S.A. 48°13N 115°41W 304 B6
Snowtown Australia 33°46S 138°14E 282 B3
Snowville U.S.A. 41°58N 112°43W 304 F7
Snowy → Australia 37°46S 148°30E 283 D8
Snowy Mt. U.S.A. 43°42N 74°23W 313 C10
Snowy Mts. Australia 36°30S 148°20E 283 D8
Snowy River △ Australia 37°15S 147°29E 283 D7
Snug Corner Bahamas 22°33N 73°52W 321 B5
Snug Harbour Canada 45°22N 80°17W 312 A4
Snyatyn Ukraine 48°27N 25°38E 183 B10
Snyder Okla., U.S.A. 34°40N 98°57W 314 D5
Snyder Tex., U.S.A. 32°44N 100°55W 314 E4
Soacha Colombia 4°35N 74°13W 328 C3
Soahanina Madag. 18°42S 44°13E 272 B1
Soalala Madag. 16°6S 45°20E 272 B2
Soaloka Madag. 18°32S 45°15E 272 B2
Soamanonga Madag. 23°52S 44°47E 272 C1
Soan → Pakistan 33°1N 71°44E 242 C4
Soanierana-Ivongo
Madag. 16°55S 49°35E 272 B2
Soanindraniny Madag. 19°54S 47°14E 272 B2
Şoarş Romania 45°56N 24°55E 183 E9
Soavina Madag. 20°23S 46°56E 272 C2
Soavinandriana Madag. 19°9S 46°45E 272 B2
Soba Nigeria 10°58N 8°4E 263 C6
Sobaeksan △ S. Korea 36°58N 128°25E 224 D4
Sobat, Nahr → Sudan 9°22N 31°33E 257 F3
Soběslav Czech Rep. 49°16N 14°45E 180 B7
Sobhapur India 22°47N 78°17E 242 H8
Sobinka Russia 56°0N 40°0E 188 E11
Sobo-Yama Japan 32°51N 131°22E 222 E3
Søborg Denmark 55°43N 12°29E 118 A2
Sobótka Poland 50°54N 16°44E 185 H3
Sobra Croatia 42°44N 17°34E 199 F14
Sobradinho, Represa de
Brazil 9°30S 42°0W 332 C3
Sobral Brazil 3°50S 40°20W 332 B3
Sobrance Slovak Rep. 48°45N 22°11E 181 C15
Sobreda Portugal 38°39N 9°11W 126 B1
Sobreira Formosa Portugal 39°46N 7°51W 194 F3
Soc Giang Vietnam 22°54N 106°1E 228 F6
Soc Trang Vietnam 9°37N 105°50E 237 H5
Soča → Europe 46°20N 13°40E 180 E6
Socastee U.S.A. 33°41N 78°59W 315 E15
Soccsksargen □ Phil. 6°30N 125°0E 233 J5
Sochaczew Poland 52°15N 20°13E 185 F7
Soch'e = Shache China 38°20N 77°10E 217 E9
Sochi Russia 43°35N 39°40E 191 J4
Sochos Greece 40°48N 23°22E 202 F7
Social Circle U.S.A. 33°39N 83°43W 316 B6
Société, Îs. de la
French Polynesia 17°0S 151°0W 289 f
Society Hill U.S.A. 32°26N 85°27W 316 C4
Society Is. = Société, Îs. de la
French Polynesia 17°0S 151°0W 289 f
Socompa, Portezuelo de
Chile 24°27S 68°18W 334 A2
Socorro = Fronteiras Brazil 7°5S 40°37W 332 C3
Socorro Colombia 6°29N 73°16W 328 B3
Socorro Phil. 9°37N 125°58E 233 G5
Socorro N. Mex., U.S.A. 34°4N 106°54W 305 J10
Socorro Tex., U.S.A. 31°39N 106°18W 314 F1
Socorro, I. Mexico 18°45N 110°58W 318 D2
Socotra Yemen 12°30N 54°0E 249 D6
Socovos Spain 38°20N 1°58W 197 G3
Socuéllamos Spain 39°16N 2°47W 197 F2
Soda L. U.S.A. 35°10N 116°4W 305 J5
Soda Plains India 35°30N 79°0E 243 B8
Soda Springs U.S.A. 42°39N 111°36W 304 E8
Sodankylä Finland 67°29N 26°40E 160 C22
Soddy-Daisy U.S.A. 35°17N 85°10W 316 A4
Söderala Sweden 61°17N 16°55E 162 C10
Söderåsen △ Sweden 56°2N 13°13E 163 H7
Söderbärke Sweden 60°5N 15°33E 162 D9
Söderby Sweden 59°24N 18°12E 139 A3
Söderfors Sweden 60°23N 17°25E 162 D11
Söderhamn Sweden 61°18N 17°10E 162 C11
Söderköping Sweden 58°31N 16°20E 163 F10
Södermalm Sweden 59°18N 18°4E 139 B2
Södermanland Sweden 58°56N 16°55E 161 G17
Södermanlands län □
Sweden 59°10N 16°30E 162 E10
Södertälje Sweden 59°12N 17°39E 162 E11
Sodiri Sudan 14°27N 29°0E 257 E2
Sodo Ethiopia 7°0N 37°41E 257 F4
Sodpur India 22°42N 88°24E 124 A2
Södra Finnskoga Sweden 60°42N 12°34E 162 D6
Södra Sandby Sweden 55°43N 13°21E 163 J7
Södra Ulvön Sweden 62°59N 18°38E 162 B12
Södra Vi Sweden 57°45N 15°45E 163 G9
Sodražica Slovenia 45°45N 14°39E 199 C11
Sodus U.S.A. 43°14N 77°4W 312 C7
Sodwana Bay △ S. Africa 27°35S 32°43E 271 C5
Soe Indonesia 9°52S 124°17E 278 A3
Soekmekaar = Morebeng
S. Africa 23°30S 29°55E 271 B4
Soest Nordrhein-Westfalen,
Germany 51°34N 8°7E 178 D4
Soest Neths. 52°9N 5°19E 170 B5
Soeurs, Î. des Canada 45°27N 73°32W 130 B2
Sofades Greece 39°20N 22°4E 204 B4
Sofaïa Guadeloupe 16°17N 61°43W 322 e
Sofala □ Mozam. 19°30S 34°30E 271 A5
Sofara Mali 13°59N 4°9W 262 C4
Sofia = Sofiya Bulgaria 42°45N 23°20E 202 D7
Sofia → Madag. 15°27S 47°23E 272 B2
Sofievka Ukraine 48°6N 33°55E 189 H7
Sofiko Greece 37°47N 23°3E 204 D5
Sofiya Bulgaria 42°45N 23°20E 202 D7
Sofiya □ Bulgaria 42°15N 23°20E 202 D7
Sofiya ✈ (SOF) Bulgaria 42°46N 23°28E 202 D7
Sofrana Greece 36°5N 26°24E 205 E8
Sōfu-Gan Japan 29°49N 140°21E 221 K10
Sogakofe Ghana 6°2N 0°39E 263 D5
Sogamoso Colombia 5°43N 72°56W 328 B3
Sogār Iran 25°53N 58°6E 247 E8
Sögel Germany 52°50N 7°31E 178 C3
Sogeri Papua N. G. 9°26S 147°35E 286 E4
Sogn og Fjordane □
Norway 61°40N 6°45E 164 C3
Sogndalsfjøra Norway 61°14N 7°5E 164 C4
Søgne Norway 58°5N 7°48E 164 F4
Sognefjorden Norway 61°10N 5°50E 164 C2
Sognsvatn Norway 59°58N 10°43E 133 A3
Sogod Phil. 10°28N 124°59E 233 F5
Söğüt Bilecik, Turkey 40°2N 30°11E 205 A12
Söğüt Burdur, Turkey 37°2N 29°50E 205 D11
Söğüt Dağı Turkey 37°50N 29°55E 205 D11
Söğütköy Turkey 36°40N 28°8E 205 E10
Soh Iran 33°26N 51°27E 247 C6
Sohâg Egypt 26°33N 31°43E 256 B3
Sohagpur India 22°42N 78°12E 242 H8
Sohano Papua N. G. 5°22S 154°37E 286 C8
Sohela India 21°18N 83°24E 244 D6
Soheuksando S. Korea 34°4N 125°7E 224 E2
Sohm Abyssal Plain Atl. Oc. 36°0N 55°0W 152 C6
Soho London, U.K. 125 b3
Soho New York, U.S.A. 132 e1
Sohoton △ Phil. 11°22N 125°6E 233 F5
Soignes, Forêt de Belgium 50°47N 4°25E 116 B2
Soignies Belgium 50°35N 4°5E 170 D4
Soin Burkina Faso 12°47N 3°50W 262 C4
Soira Eritrea 14°45N 39°30E 257 E4
Soissons France 49°25N 3°19E 173 C10
Sōja Japan 34°40N 133°45E 222 C5
Sojat India 25°55N 73°45E 242 G5
Sok → Russia 53°24N 50°8E 190 D10
Sok Kwu Wan China 22°12N 114°7E 122 B1
Sokal Ukraine 50°31N 24°15E 177 C13
Sokcho S. Korea 38°12N 128°36E 224 C4
Söke Turkey 37°48N 27°28E 205 D9
Sokelo
Dem. Rep. of the Congo 9°55S 24°36E 265 D4
Sokhumi Georgia 43°0N 41°0E 191 J5
Sokki, Oued In → Algeria 29°30N 3°42E 261 C5
Sokna Norway 60°16N 9°50E 164 D6
Soknedal Norway 62°57N 10°13E 164 B7
Soko Banja Serbia 43°40N 21°51E 202 C5
Soko Is. China 22°10N 113°54E 219 a
Sokodé Togo 9°0N 1°11E 263 D5
Sokol Russia 59°30N 40°5E 188 C11
Sokolac Bos.-H. 43°56N 18°48E 182 G3
Sokółka Poland 53°25N 23°30E 184 E10
Sokolniki Russia 55°47N 37°40E 129 B4
Sokolniki Park Russia 55°48N 37°40E 129 B4
Sokolo Ségou, Mali 14°53N 6°8W 262 C3
Sokolo Sikasso, Mali 10°52N 6°59W 262 C3
Sokolov Czech Rep. 50°12N 12°40E 180 A5
Sokołów Poland 52°9N 20°51E 142 C1
Sokołów Małpolski Poland 50°12N 22°7E 185 H9
Sokołów Podlaski Poland 52°25N 22°15E 185 F9
Sokoły Poland 52°59N 22°42E 185 F9
Sokoto Nigeria 13°2N 5°16E 263 C6
Sokoto □ Nigeria 12°30N 6°0E 263 C6
Sokoto → Nigeria 11°20N 4°10E 263 C5
Sokyrnytsya Ukraine 48°7N 23°23E 183 B8
Sokyryany Ukraine 48°27N 27°25E 183 B12
Sol Iletsk Russia 51°10N 55°0E 186 D10
Sola Rogaland, Norway 58°53N 5°36E 164 F2
Sola Vanuatu 13°51S 167°33E 287 C5
Sola → Poland 50°4N 19°15E 185 H6
Solai Kenya 0°2N 36°12E 268 B4
Solalinden Germany 48°5N 11°42E 131 B3
Solan India 30°55N 77°7E 242 D7
Solana Phil. 17°39N 121°41E 232 C3
Solana Beach U.S.A. 32°58N 117°16W 307 N9
Solander I. N.Z. 46°34S 166°54E 285 G1
Solano Phil. 16°31N 121°15E 232 C3
Solapur India 17°43N 75°56E 244 F2
Solca Romania 47°40N 25°50E 183 C10
Solda Gölü Turkey 37°33N 29°42E 205 D11
Soldăneşti Moldova 47°49N 28°48E 183 C13
Soldeu Andorra 42°35N 1°40E 196 C6
Soldier Field Chicago, U.S.A. 119 e3
Soldier Pt. Antigua & B. 17°2N 61°41W 322 b
Soldin = Myślibórz Poland 52°55N 14°50E 185 F1
Soldotna U.S.A. 60°29N 151°3W 303 F10
Soléa Cyprus 35°5N 33°4E 207 E9
Solec Kujawski Poland 53°5N 18°14E 185 E5
Solédad Colombia 10°55N 74°46W 328 A3
Soledad Calif., U.S.A. 36°26N 121°20W 306 J5
Soledad Venezuela 8°10N 63°34W 329 B5
Solen Norway 61°53N 11°31E 164 C8
Solent, The U.K. 50°45N 1°25W 169 G6
Solenzara France 41°53N 9°23E 175 G13
Solesmes France 50°10N 3°30E 173 B10
Solfonntaggen Norway 60°2N 6°57E 164 D3
Solhan Turkey 38°57N 41°3E 213 C9
Solheim Norway 60°53N 5°27E 164 D2
Soligalich Russia 59°5N 42°10E 186 C7
Soligorsk = Salihorsk
Belarus 52°51N 27°27E 177 B14
Solihull U.K. 52°26N 1°47W 169 E6
Solikamsk Russia 59°38N 56°50E 186 C10
Solila Madag. 21°25S 46°37E 272 C2
Solimões = Amazonas →
S. Amer. 0°5S 50°0W 329 D8
Solin Croatia 43°33N 16°30E 199 E13
Solingen Germany 51°10N 7°5E 178 D3
Söll Austria 47°30N 12°11E 179 H8
Sollebrunn Sweden 58°8N 12°32E 163 F6
Sollefteå Sweden 63°12N 17°20E 162 A11
Sollentuna Sweden 59°25N 17°56E 139 A1
Sóller Spain 39°46N 2°43E 206 B3
Sollerön Sweden 60°55N 14°37E 162 D8
Solling Germany 51°42N 9°38E 178 D5
Solling-Vogler ⌓ Germany 51°45N 9°32E 178 D5
Solln Germany 48°4N 11°31E 131 B2
Sollsvika Norway 60°26N 4°58E 164 D1
Solna Sweden 59°21N 17°59E 139 A1
Solnechnogorsk Russia 56°10N 36°57E 188 D9
Solntsevo Russia 55°39N 37°24E 129 C2
Solo → Indonesia 6°47S 112°22E 231 G15
Solofra Italy 40°50N 14°51E 201 B7
Sologne France 47°40N 1°45E 173 E8
Solok Indonesia 0°45S 100°40E 234 C2
Sololá Guatemala 14°49N 91°10W 320 D1
Sololo Kenya 3°33N 38°39E 268 B4
Solomon, N. Fork →
U.S.A. 39°29N 98°26W 308 F4
Solomon, S. Fork →
U.S.A. 39°25N 99°12W 308 F4
Solomon Is. Papua N. G. 6°0S 155°0E 286 D8
Solomon Is. ■ Pac. Oc. 6°0S 155°0E 287 L8
Solomon Rise Pac. Oc. 1°0N 157°0E 288 G7
Solomon Sea Papua N. G. 7°0S 150°0E 286 D6
Solon China 46°32N 121°10E 219 B13
Solon Springs U.S.A. 46°22N 91°49W 308 B8
Solonópole Brazil 5°44S 39°1W 332 C4
Solor Indonesia 8°27S 123°0E 231 F6
Solotcha Russia 54°48N 39°53E 188 E10
Solothurn Switz. 47°13N 7°32E 179 H3
Solothurn □ Switz. 47°18N 7°40E 179 H3
Solotvyn Ukraine 48°42N 24°25E 183 B9
Solsona Phil. 18°5N 120°46E 232 B3
Solsona Spain 42°0N 1°31E 196 C6
Solt Hungary 46°45N 19°1E 182 D4
Šolta Croatia 43°24N 16°15E 199 E13
Solţānābād Khorāsān, Iran 34°13N 59°58E 247 C8
Solţānābād Khorāsān, Iran 36°29N 58°5E 247 B8
Soltau Germany 52°59N 9°50E 178 C5
Soltsy Russia 58°10N 30°30E 188 C6
Soltüstik Qazaqstan □
Kazakhstan 54°0N 70°0E 217 B8
Solund Norway 61°5N 4°50E 164 C1
Solunska Glava Macedonia 41°44N 21°31E 202 E5
Solvang U.S.A. 34°36N 120°8W 307 L6
Solvay U.S.A. 43°3N 76°13W 313 C8
Sölvesborg Sweden 56°5N 14°35E 163 H8
Solvychegodsk Russia 61°21N 46°56E 186 B8
Solway Firth U.K. 54°49N 3°35W 168 C4
Solwezi Zambia 12°11S 26°21E 269 E2
Sōma Japan 37°40N 140°50E 220 F10
Soma Turkey 39°10N 27°35E 205 B9
Somabhula Zimbabwe 19°42S 29°40E 271 A4
Somali = Sumale □ Ethiopia 7°0N 45°0E 267 C6
Somali Pen. Africa 7°0N 46°0E 254 F8
Somali Rep. ■ Africa 7°0N 47°0E 267 C6
Somalia = Somali Rep. ■
Africa 7°0N 47°0E 267 C6
Somaliland □ Somali Rep. 9°0N 46°0E 267 C6
Sombe Dzong Bhutan 27°13N 89°8E 241 B2
Sombernon France 47°20N 4°40E 173 E11
Sombo Angola 8°42S 20°59E 265 D4
Sombor Serbia 45°46N 19°9E 182 E4
Sombra Canada 42°43N 82°29W 312 D2
Sombrerete Mexico 23°38N 103°39W 318 C4
Sombrero Anguilla 18°37N 63°30W 321 C7
Sombrero Channel India 7°41N 93°35E 245 L11
Şomcuta Mare Romania 47°31N 23°28E 183 C8
Somdari India 25°47N 72°38E 242 G5
Someido ⌓ Spain 43°5N 6°11W 194 B4
Somers U.S.A. 48°5N 114°13W 304 B6
Somerset Bermuda 32°17N 64°52W 153 a
Somerset Ky., U.S.A. 37°5N 84°36W 309 G11
Somerset Mass., U.S.A. 41°47N 71°8W 313 E13
Somerset Md., U.S.A. 38°57N 77°5W 143 B3
Somerset Pa., U.S.A. 40°1N 79°5W 312 F5
Somerset □ U.K. 51°9N 3°0W 169 F5
Somerset East S. Africa 32°42S 25°35E 270 D4
Somerset I. Bermuda 32°17N 64°52W 153 a
Somerset I. Nunavut,
Canada 73°30N 93°0W 294 C13
Somerset West S. Africa 34°8S 18°50E 270 D2
Somersworth U.S.A. 43°16N 70°52W 313 C14
Somerton U.S.A. 32°36N 114°43W 305 K6
Somerville Mass., U.S.A. 42°22N 71°5W 116 A2
Somerville N.J., U.S.A. 40°35N 74°38W 313 F10
Someş → Romania 47°49N 22°43E 182 C7
Somes I. N.Z. 41°15S 174°52E 143 B2
Someşul Mare → Romania 47°9N 23°55E 183 C8
Somme □ France 49°57N 2°20E 173 C9
Somme → France 50°11N 1°38E 173 B8
Somme, B. de la France 50°14N 1°33E 172 B8
Sommen Jönköping, Sweden 58°12N 14°58E 163 F8
Sommen Östergötland,
Sweden 58°0N 15°15E 163 F9
Sommepy-Tahure France 49°15N 4°31E 173 C11
Sömmerda Germany 51°9N 11°7E 178 D7
Sommerfeld = Lubsko
Poland 51°45N 14°57E 185 G1
Sommesous France 48°44N 4°12E 173 D11
Sommières France 43°47N 4°6E 175 E8
Somnath India 20°53N 70°22E 242 J4
Somogy □ Hungary 46°19N 17°30E 182 D2
Somogyszob Hungary 46°18N 17°20E 182 D2
Somosomo Fiji 16°47S 179°58W 287 A3
Somosomo Str. Fiji 16°0S 180°0E 287 A3
Somoto Nic. 13°28N 86°37W 320 D2
Sompolno Poland 52°26N 18°30E 185 F5
Somport, Tunnel de Spain 42°48N 0°31W 196 C4
Somuncurá, Meseta de
Argentina 41°30S 67°0W 336 B3
Somvarpet India 12°36N 75°52E 245 H2
Son Norway 59°32N 10°42E 164 E7
Son → India 25°42N 84°52E 243 G11
Son Ha Vietnam 15°3N 108°34E 236 E7
Son La Vietnam 21°20N 103°50E 228 G4
Son Morrell Spain 39°44N 3°20E 206 B4
Son Rapinya Spain 39°35N 2°37E 206 B3
Son Sardina Spain 39°37N 2°40E 206 B3
Son Serra Spain 39°43N 3°13E 206 B4
Son Servera Spain 39°37N 3°21E 206 B4
Son Tay Vietnam 21°8N 105°30E 228 G5
Son Tinh Vietnam 15°10N 108°40E 236 E7
Soná Panama 8°0N 81°20W 320 E3
Sonamarg India 34°18N 75°21E 243 B6
Sonamukhi India 23°18N 87°27E 243 H12
Sonamura India 23°29N 91°15E 241 D3
Sonar → India 24°24N 79°56E 243 G8
Sonari India 18°54N 72°59E 130 B2
Sŏnch'ŏn N. Korea 39°48N 124°55E 224 C2
Sondags → S. Africa 33°44S 25°51E 270 D4
Sondalo Italy 46°20N 10°19E 198 B7
Søndeled Norway 58°47N 9°3E 164 F6
Sønder Felding Denmark 55°57N 8°47E 163 J2
Sønder Omme Denmark 55°50N 8°54E 163 J2
Sønderborg Denmark 54°55N 9°49E 163 K3
Sondershausen Germany 51°22N 10°51E 178 D6
Sønderso Denmark 55°46N 12°21E 118 A2
Søndre Bergenhaus = Hordaland □
Norway 60°25N 6°15E 164 D3
Søndre Strømfjord = Kangerlussuaq
Greenland 66°59N 50°40W 154 D5
Søndre Trøndhjem =
Sør-Trøndelag □ Norway 63°0N 11°0E 164 A7
Sondrio Italy 46°10N 9°52E 198 B6
Sondur → India 20°40N 82°1E 244 D6
Sone Mozam. 17°23S 34°55E 269 F3

Sonepur India 20°55N 83°50E 244 D6
Sonfim Brazil 6°0S 67°52W 330 B4
Song Nigeria 9°49N 12°39E 263 D7
Song Thailand 18°28N 100°11E 236 C3
Song Cau Vietnam 13°27N 109°18E 236 F7
Song-Köl Kyrgyzstan 41°50N 75°12E 217 D9
Song Ma Vietnam 20°56N 103°53E 228 G4
Song Qingling, Former Residence of Beijing, China 114 a2
Song Xian China 34°12N 112°8E 226 G7
Songadh India 21°9N 73°33E 244 D1
Songan Indonesia 8°13S 115°24E 231 J18
Songavatnet Norway 59°52N 7°32E 164 E4
Songea Tanzania 10°40S 35°40E 269 E4
Songeons France 49°32N 1°50E 173 C8
Sŏnggan N. Korea 40°47N 126°34E 224 B3
Songgang China 22°46N 113°50E 219 a
Songhua Hu China 43°35N 126°50E 227 C14
Songhua Jiang → China 47°45N 132°30E 219 B15
Songimvelo ⌓ S. Africa 25°50S 31°2E 271 C5
Songjiang Jilin, China 42°34N 128°20E 224 A4
Songjiang Shanghai, China 31°1N 121°12E 229 B13
Songjianghe China 42°10N 127°29E 224 A3
Sŏngjin = Kimch'aek N. Korea 40°40N 129°10E 224 B4
Songkan China 28°35N 106°52E 228 C6
Songkhla Thailand 7°13N 100°37E 237 J3
Songming China 25°12N 103°2E 228 E4
Songnim N. Korea 38°45N 125°39E 224 C2
Songnisan △ S. Korea 36°28N 127°45E 224 D3
Songo Angola 7°22S 14°51E 265 D2
Songo Mozam. 15°34S 32°38E 271 A5
Songololo = Mbanza Ngungu Dem. Rep. of the Congo 5°12S 14°53E 265 D2
Songololo Dem. Rep. of the Congo 5°42S 14°2E 265 D2
Songpa S. Korea 37°30N 127°7E 137 B2
Songpan China 32°40N 103°30E 228 A4
Songtao China 28°11N 109°10E 228 C7
Songwe Dem. Rep. of the Congo 3°20S 26°16E 268 C2
Songwe → Africa 9°44S 33°58E 269 D3
Songxi China 27°31N 118°44E 229 D12
Songzi China 30°12N 111°45E 229 B8
Sonhat India 23°29N 82°31E 243 H10
Sonid Youqi China 42°45N 112°48E 226 C7
Sonid Zuoqi China 43°50N 113°42E 226 C7
Sonipat India 29°0N 77°5E 242 E7
Sonkach India 22°59N 76°21E 242 H7
Sonkovo Russia 57°50N 37°5E 188 D9
Sonmiani Pakistan 25°25N 66°40E 242 G2
Sonmiani B. Pakistan 25°15N 66°30E 242 G2
Sonnino Italy 41°25N 13°14E 200 A6
Sono → Minas Gerais, Brazil 17°2S 45°32W 333 E2
Sono → Tocantins, Brazil 9°58S 48°11W 332 C2
Sonobe Japan 35°6N 135°28E 223 B7
Sonoma U.S.A. 38°18N 122°28W 306 G4
Sonora Calif., U.S.A. 37°59N 120°23W 306 H6
Sonora Tex., U.S.A. 30°34N 100°39W 314 F4
Sonora □ Mexico 29°20N 110°40W 318 B2
Sonora → Mexico 29°5N 110°55W 318 B2
Sonoran Desert U.S.A. 33°40N 113°30W 307 L12
Sonoyta Mexico 31°51N 112°50W 318 A2
Sonqor Iran 34°47N 47°36E 213 E12
Sonseca Spain 39°42N 3°57W 195 F7
Sonsón Colombia 5°43N 75°18W 328 B2
Sonsonate El Salv. 13°43N 89°44W 320 D2
Sonstorp Sweden 58°44N 15°38E 163 F9
Sonthofen Germany 47°30N 10°16E 179 H6
Sony Picture Studio U.S.A. 34°1N 118°4W 126 B2
Soochow = Suzhou China 31°19N 120°38E 229 B13
Sooke Canada 48°13N 123°43W 306 B3
Sool □ Somali Rep. 8°40N 47°30E 267 C6
Soomaaliya = Somali Rep. ■ Africa 7°0N 47°0E 267 C6
Sop Hao Laos 20°33N 104°27E 228 G5
Sop Prap Thailand 17°53N 99°20E 236 D2
Sopachuy Bolivia 19°29S 64°31W 331 D5
Sopchoppy U.S.A. 30°4N 84°29W 316 E5
Sopelana Spain 43°23N 2°58W 196 B2
Soperton U.S.A. 32°23N 82°35W 316 C7
Sopi Indonesia 2°34N 128°28E 231 D7
Sopo, Nahr → Sudan 8°40N 26°30E 257 F2
Sopot Bulgaria 42°39N 24°45E 203 D8
Sopot Poland 54°27N 18°31E 184 D5
Sopot Serbia 44°29N 20°36E 202 B4
Sopotnica Macedonia 41°18N 21°13E 202 E5
Sopron Hungary 47°45N 16°32E 182 C1
Sopur India 34°18N 74°27E 243 B6
Sør-Rondane Antarctica 72°0S 25°0E 151 D4
Sør-Trøndelag □ Norway 63°0N 11°0E 164 A7
Sora Italy 41°43N 13°37E 199 G10
Sorab India 14°23N 75°6E 245 G2
Sorada India 19°45N 84°26E 244 E7
Sorah Pakistan 27°13N 68°56E 242 F3
Soråker Sweden 62°30N 17°32E 162 B11
Sorang Kazakhstan 49°46N 72°51E 217 C8
Sorano Italy 42°41N 11°43E 199 F8
Soraon India 25°37N 81°51E 243 G9
Sorata Bolivia 15°50S 68°40W 330 D4
Sorbas Spain 37°6N 2°7W 197 H2
Sörbygden Sweden 62°48N 16°12E 162 B10
Sord = Swords Ireland 53°28N 6°13W 120 A2
Sordellen Sweden 61°48N 16°43E 162 C10
Sore France 44°18N 0°35W 174 D3
Søre Osa → Norway 61°18N 11°46E 164 C8
Sorel-Tracy Canada 46°0N 73°10W 298 C5
Soresina Italy 45°17N 9°51E 198 C6
Sørfjorden Norway 60°20N 6°37E 164 D3
Sörforsa Sweden 61°43N 16°58E 162 C10
Sórgono Italy 40°1N 9°6E 200 B2
Sorgues France 44°1N 4°53E 175 D8
Sorgun Turkey 39°46N 35°11E 212 C6
Sorgun → Turkey 36°36N 34°20E 250 B5
Sori Papua N. G. 1°58S 146°42E 286 A4
Soria Spain 41°43N 2°32W 196 D2
Soria □ Spain 41°46N 2°28W 196 D2
Soriano Uruguay 33°24S 58°19W 334 C4
Soriano nel Cimino Italy 42°25N 12°14E 199 F9
Sorkh, Kuh-e Iran 35°40N 58°30E 247 C8
Sorø Denmark 55°26N 11°32E 163 J5
Soro Guinea 10°9N 9°48W 262 C3
Soroca Moldova 48°8N 28°12E 183 B13
Sorocaba Brazil 23°31S 47°27W 335 A6
Sorochinsk Russia 52°26N 53°10E 186 D9
Soroka = Belomorsk Russia 64°35N 34°54E 186 B5
Soroki = Soroca Moldova 48°8N 28°12E 183 B13
Sorokino = Krasnodon Ukraine 48°17N 39°44E 189 H10
Soroksár Hungary 47°24N 19°7E 117 B2
Soroksari Duna → Hungary 47°25N 19°5E 117 B2
Sorong Indonesia 0°55S 131°15E 231 E8
Soroni Greece 36°21N 28°1E 206 E12
Soroti Uganda 1°43N 33°35E 268 B3
Sørøya Norway 70°40N 22°30E 160 A20
Sørøyane Norway 62°25N 5°32E 164 B2
Sørøysundet Norway 70°25N 23°0E 160 A20
Sorraia → Portugal 38°55N 8°53W 195 G2
Sorrell Australia 42°47S 147°34E 281 G4
Sorrento Italy 40°37N 14°22E 201 B7
Sorsele Sweden 65°31N 17°30E 160 D17
Sörsjön Sweden 61°24N 13°5E 162 C7
Sorso Italy 40°48N 8°34E 200 B1
Sorsogon Phil. 13°0N 124°0E 232 E5
Sorsogon □ Phil. 12°50N 123°55E 232 E4
Sortavala Russia 61°42N 30°41E 188 B6
Sortino Italy 37°9N 15°2E 201 E8
Sortland Norway 68°42N 15°25E 160 B16
Sortot Sudan 19°30N 30°28E 256 D3
Sørum Norway 60°30N 10°17E 164 D7
Sorvizhi Russia 57°52N 48°32E 190 B9
Sos del Rey Católico Spain 42°30N 1°13W 196 C3
Soscumica, L. Canada 50°15N 77°27W 298 B4
Sösdala Sweden 56°2N 13°41E 163 H7
Sosenka → Russia 55°46N 37°42E 129 B4
Sosna → Russia 52°42N 38°55E 189 F10
Sosnogorsk Russia 63°37N 53°51E 186 B9
Sosnovka Kirov, Russia 56°17N 51°17E 190 B10
Sosnovka St. Petersburg, Russia 60°0N 30°22E 137 B2
Sosnovka Tambov, Russia 53°13N 41°24E 190 D5
Sosnovyy Bor Russia 59°55N 29°6E 188 C5
Sosnowiec Poland 50°20N 19°10E 185 H6
Sosnowitz = Sosnowiec Poland 50°20N 19°10E 185 H6
Soso C.A.R. 3°55N 15°30E 264 B3
Sospel France 43°52N 7°27E 175 E11
Sossus Vlei Namibia 24°40S 15°23E 270 B2
Šoštanj Slovenia 46°23N 15°4E 199 B12
Sŏsura N. Korea 42°16N 130°36E 224 A5
Sot → India 27°27N 79°37E 243 F8
Sotasæter Norway 61°49N 7°43E 164 C4
Sotavento C. Verde Is. 15°0N 25°0W 153 j
Sotik Kenya 0°41S 35°7E 268 C4
Sotkamo Finland 64°8N 28°23E 160 D23
Soto Curaçao 12°16N 69°6W 322 g
Soto del Barco Spain 43°32N 6°4W 194 B4
Soto la Marina Mexico 23°46N 98°13W 319 C5
Soto la Marina → Mexico 23°45N 97°45W 319 C5
Soto y Amío Spain 42°46N 5°53W 194 C5
Sotouboua Togo 8°34N 0°59E 263 D5
Sotrondio Spain 43°17N 5°36W 194 B5
Sotuf, Adrar W. Sahara 21°42N 15°36W 260 D1
Sotuta Mexico 20°36N 89°1W 319 C7
Souanké Congo 2°10N 14°3E 264 B2
Soubré Ivory C. 5°50N 6°35W 262 D3
Souda Greece 35°29N 24°4E 207 E5
Soudas, Ormos Greece 35°25N 24°10E 207 E5
Souderton U.S.A. 40°19N 75°19W 313 F9
Soufflay Congo 2°1N 14°54E 264 B2
Soufli Greece 41°12N 26°18E 203 E10
Soufrière Dominica 15°13N 61°22W 323 k
Soufrière Guadeloupe 16°5N 61°40W 322 e
Soufrière St. Lucia 13°51N 61°3W 323 m
Soufrière Bay Dominica 15°13N 61°22W 323 k
Soufrière Bay St. Lucia 13°51N 61°4W 323 m
Soufrière Hills Volcano Montserrat 16°43N 62°10W 323 p
Souillac Lot, France 44°53N 1°29E 174 D5
Souillac Mauritius 20°31S 57°31E 272 e
Souilly France 49°3N 5°17E 173 C12
Souk-Ahras Algeria 36°23N 7°57E 261 A6
Souk-Ahras □ Algeria 36°10N 7°55E 261 A6
Souk el Arba du Rharb Morocco 34°43N 5°59W 260 B3
Soukhouma Laos 14°38N 105°48E 236 E5
Sŏul = Seoul S. Korea 37°31N 126°58E 137 B2
Soulac-sur-Mer France 45°30N 1°7W 174 C2
Soulougou Burkina Faso 13°1N 0°25E 263 C5
Soultz-sous-Forêts France 48°57N 7°52E 173 D14
Sound, The = Øresund Europe 55°45N 12°40E 163 J6
Sound, The U.K. 50°20N 4°10W 169 G3
Sound I. India 12°58N 92°59E 245 H11
Soundview U.S.A. 40°49N 73°53W 132 B2
Sounio, Akra Greece 37°37N 24°1E 206 D6
Sour el Ghozlane Algeria 36°10N 3°45E 261 A5
Sources, Mt. aux Lesotho 28°45S 28°50E 271 C4
Soure Brazil 0°35S 48°30W 332 B2
Soure Portugal 40°4N 8°38W 194 E2
Souris Man., Canada 49°40N 100°20W 297 D8
Souris P.E.I., Canada 46°21N 62°15W 299 C7
Souris → N. Amer. 49°40N 99°34W 308 A4
Souriya → Africa 12°45N 3°25W 262 C4
Sourpi Greece 39°6N 22°54E 204 E4
Sous, O. → Morocco 30°27N 9°31W 260 B3
Sous le Vent, Is. French Polynesia 16°30S 155°30W 289 f
Sous le Vent, Région Réunion 21°12S 55°20E 272 f
Sousa-Massa △ Morocco 31°26N 9°35W 260 B3
Sousa Brazil 6°45S 38°10W 332 C4
Sousel Brazil 2°38S 52°29W 332 B1
Sousel Portugal 38°57N 7°40W 195 G3
Sousse Tunisia 35°50N 10°38E 258 A2
Sousse □ Tunisia 35°40N 10°30E 261 A7
Soustons France 43°45N 1°19W 174 E2
Sout → S. Africa 31°35S 18°24E 270 D2
South Africa ■ Africa 32°0S 23°0E 270 D3
South America 10°0S 60°0W 326 E5
South Andaman India 11°45N 92°10E 245 J11
South Aulatsivik I. Canada 56°45N 61°30W 299 A7
South Australia □ Australia 32°0S 139°0E 282 B3
South Australian Basin Ind. Oc. 38°0S 126°0E 288 L4
South Ayrshire □ U.K. 55°18N 4°41W 167 F4
South Baldy Pk. U.S.A. 34°6N 107°11W 305 J10
South Bass I. U.S.A. 41°39N 82°49W 312 E2
South Bay U.S.A. 26°40N 80°43W 317 J9
South Beach Bahamas 25°1N 77°20W 153 b
South Beach N.Y., U.S.A. 40°35N 74°4W 132 C1
South Beach Harbor San Francisco, U.S.A. 136 c3
South Beloit U.S.A. 42°29N 89°2W 310 B7
South Bend Ind., U.S.A. 41°41N 86°15W 311 C10
South Bend Wash., U.S.A. 46°40N 123°48W 306 D3
South Bend Park U.S.A. 33°42N 84°23W 113 B2
South Boston Mass., U.S.A. 42°20N 71°2W 116 A2
South Boston Va., U.S.A. 36°42N 78°54W 309 G14
South Branch Canada 47°55N 59°2W 299 C8
South Branch Chicago River → Chicago, U.S.A. 119 d1
South Brook Canada 49°26N 56°5W 299 C8
South Brother I. India 10°56N 92°37E 245 J11
South Bruny I. Australia 43°20S 147°15E 281 G4
South C. = Kalae U.S.A. 18°55N 155°41W 302 E6
South Carolina □ U.S.A. 34°0N 81°0W 315 E14
South Channel Phil. 14°13N 120°37E 232 D3
South Charleston U.S.A. 38°22N 81°44W 309 F13
South China Sea Asia 10°0N 113°0E 230 C4
South Comino Channel Malta 36°0N 14°20E 206 F7
South Congaree U.S.A. 33°53N 81°9W 316 B8
South Cotabato □ Phil. 6°0N 125°0E 233 J5
South Cumberland Is. △ Australia 20°42S 149°11E 280 b
South Dakota □ U.S.A. 44°15N 100°0W 308 C4
South Dayton U.S.A. 42°21N 79°3W 312 D5
South Daytona U.S.A. 29°10N 81°0W 317 F8
South Decatur U.S.A. 33°44N 84°16W 113 B3
South Deerfield U.S.A. 42°29N 72°37W 313 D12
South Deering U.S.A. 41°42N 87°33W 119 C3
South Downs U.K. 50°52N 0°25W 169 G7
South Downs △ U.K. 50°50N 0°50W 169 G7
South East B. Ascension I. 7°57S 14°18W 153 g
South East C. Australia 43°40S 146°50E 281 G4
South East Forest △ Australia 37°0S 149°30E 283 D8
South East Is. Australia 34°17S 123°30E 279 F3
South El Monte U.S.A. 34°3N 118°2W 126 B4
South Elgin U.S.A. 42°0N 88°18W 311 C8
South Esk → U.K. 56°43N 2°31W 167 E6
South Fiji Basin Pac. Oc. 26°0S 175°0E 288 K9
South Foreland U.K. 51°8N 1°24E 169 F9
South Fork American → U.S.A. 38°57N 120°59W 306 G5
South Fork Edisto → U.S.A. 33°16N 80°54W 316 B9
South Fork Feather → U.S.A. 39°17N 121°36W 306 F5
South Fork Grand → U.S.A. 45°43N 102°17W 308 C2
South Fork Licking → U.S.A. 38°40N 84°18W 311 F12
South Fork Milk → U.S.A. 48°4N 106°19W 304 B10
South Fork Republican → U.S.A. 40°3N 101°31W 308 E3
South Gate U.S.A. 33°56N 118°12W 126 C3
South Georgia Antarctica 54°30S 37°0W 151 B1
South Gloucestershire □ U.K. 51°32N 2°28W 169 F5
South Grand → U.S.A. 38°17N 93°25W 310 F3
South Hadley U.S.A. 42°16N 72°35W 313 D12
South Harbor Phil. 14°34N 120°58E 127 B1
South Harrow U.K. 51°33N 0°21W 125 A1
South Haven U.S.A. 42°24N 86°16W 311 B10
South Hd. Australia 33°50S 151°16E 139 B2
South Henik L. Canada 61°30N 97°20W 297 A9
South Hill Village Anguilla 18°11N 63°5W 322 a
South Hills S. Africa 26°14S 28°5E 123 B2
South Horr Kenya 2°12N 36°56E 268 B4
South I. India 10°3N 72°17E 245 J1
South I. Eastern, Kenya 2°35N 36°35E 268 B4
South I. N.Z. 44°0S 170°0E 285 E5
South Indian Lake Canada 56°47N 98°56W 297 B9
South Invercargill N.Z. 46°26S 168°23E 285 G3
South Island △ Kenya 2°39N 36°35E 268 B4
South Kensington London, U.K. 125 c2
South Kitui △ Kenya 1°48S 38°46E 268 C4
South Knife → Canada 58°55N 94°37W 297 B10
South Koel → India 22°32N 85°14E 243 H11
South Korea ■ Asia 36°0N 128°0E 227 G15
South Lake Tahoe U.S.A. 38°57N 119°59W 306 G6
South Lanarkshire □ U.K. 55°37N 3°53W 167 F5
South Lawn U.S.A. 38°47N 77°0W 143 C3
South Loop Chicago, U.S.A. 119 f2
South Loup → U.S.A. 41°4N 98°39W 308 E4
South Luangwa △ Zambia 13°0S 31°20E 269 E3
South Lyon U.S.A. 42°28N 83°39W 311 B13
South Magnetic Pole Antarctica 64°8S 138°8E 151 C9
South Malé Atoll Maldives 4°0N 73°25E 272 d
South Malosmadulu Atoll Maldives 5°12N 73°0E 272 d
South Miami U.S.A. 25°42N 80°17W 128 B1
South Milwaukee U.S.A. 42°55N 87°52W 311 B9
South Molton U.K. 51°1N 3°51W 169 F4
South Monroe U.S.A. 41°54N 83°26W 311 C13
South Moose L. Canada 53°49N 100°1W 297 C8
South Nahanni → Canada 61°3N 123°21W 296 A4
South Nation → Canada 45°34N 75°6W 313 A9
South Natuna Is. = Natuna Selatan, Kepulauan Indonesia 2°45N 109°0E 235 B3
South Negril Pt. Jamaica 18°16N 78°22W 320 a
South New Hebrides Trench Pac. Oc. 22°30S 170°0E 277 E13
South Newport U.S.A. 31°38N 81°24W 316 D8
South Nilandu Atoll Maldives 2°52N 72°57E 272 d
South Norwood U.K. 51°23N 0°3W 125 B3
South of Market San Francisco, U.S.A. 136 c2
South Orkney Is. Antarctica 63°0S 45°0W 151 C18
South Ossetia □ Georgia 42°21N 44°2E 191 J7
South Otselic U.S.A. 42°38N 75°46W 313 D9
South Ozone Park U.S.A. 40°41N 73°49W 132 B3
South Pagai, I. = Pagai Selatan, Pulau Indonesia 3°0S 100°15E 234 C2
South Paris U.S.A. 44°14N 70°31W 313 B14
South Pasadena U.S.A. 34°7N 118°8W 126 B4
South Pekin U.S.A. 40°30N 89°39W 310 D7
South Pittsburg U.S.A. 35°1N 85°42W 315 D12
South Platte → U.S.A. 41°7N 100°42W 308 E3
South Pole Antarctica 90°0S 0°0 151 E
South Ponte Vedra Beach U.S.A. 30°3N 81°20W 316 E8
South Porcupine Canada 48°30N 81°12W 298 C3
South Portland U.S.A. 43°38N 70°15W 309 D18
South Pt. Ascension I. 8°0S 14°24W 153 g
South Pt. Barbados 13°2N 59°32W 323 r
South Pt. Mich., U.S.A. 44°52N 83°19W 312 B1
South Res. U.S.A. 42°26N 71°6W 116 A2
South River Ont., Canada 45°52N 79°23W 298 C4
South River N.J., U.S.A. 40°27N 74°23W 313 F10
South Ronaldsay U.K. 58°48N 2°58W 167 C6
South Ruislip U.K. 51°33N 0°24W 125 A1
South Rukuru Malaysia 10°44S 34°14E 269 E3
South San Francisco U.S.A. 37°38N 122°26W 136 C2
South San Gabriel U.S.A. 34°3N 118°6W 126 B4
South Sandwich Is. Antarctica 57°0S 27°0W 151 B1
South Sandwich Trench Atl. Oc. 56°0S 24°0W 151 B1
South Saskatchewan → Canada 53°15N 105°5W 297 C7
South Seal → Canada 58°48N 98°8W 297 B9
South Sentinel I. India 10°59N 92°14E 245 J11
South Shetland Is. Antarctica 62°0S 59°0W 151 C18
South Shields U.K. 55°0N 1°25W 168 C6
South Shore U.S.A. 41°45N 87°34W 119 C3
South Sioux City U.S.A. 42°28N 96°24W 308 D5
South Sister U.S.A. 44°4N 121°51W 304 D3
South Solomon Trench Pac. Oc. 11°0S 164°30E 277 C11
South Soufrière Hills Montserrat 16°41N 62°10W 323 p
South Street Boston, U.S.A. 116 c2
South Talpatti = New Moore I. Ind. Oc. 21°37N 89°10E 241 E2
South Taranaki Bight N.Z. 39°40S 174°5E 284 F3
South Tasman Rise S. Ocean 48°0S 146°0E 151 A10
South Thompson → Canada 50°40N 120°20W 296 C4
South Twin I. Canada 53°7N 79°52W 298 B4
South Tyne → U.K. 54°59N 2°8W 168 C5
South Ubian Phil. 5°11N 120°30E 233 J3
South Uist U.K. 57°20N 7°15W 167 D1
South Valley U.S.A. 35°1N 106°41W 305 J10
South Venice U.S.A. 27°3N 82°25W 317 H7
South Verde I. Phil. 10°4N 119°13E 233 F2
South Wayne U.S.A. 42°34N 89°53W 310 B7
South Wellesley Is. Australia 16°58S 139°17E 280 B2
South West Africa = Namibia ■ Africa 22°0S 18°9E 270 B2
South West B. Ascension I. 7°58S 14°25W 153 g
South West B. Bahamas 25°0N 77°32W 153 b
South West C. Tas., Australia 43°34S 146°3E 281 G4
South West C. N.Z. 47°17S 167°28E 285 H2
South West Pt. Papua N. G. 2°14S 146°34E 286 B4
South West Pt. St. Helena 15°59S 5°48W 153 h
South West Rocks Australia 30°52S 153°3E 283 A10
South Whitley U.S.A. 41°5N 85°38W 311 C11
South Williamsport U.S.A. 41°13N 77°0W 312 E8
South Yemen = Yemen ■ Asia 15°0N 44°0E 248 D4
South Yorkshire □ U.K. 53°27N 1°36W 168 D6
Southall U.K. 51°30N 0°22W 125 A1
Southampton Ont., Canada 44°30N 81°25W 312 B3
Southampton Southampton, U.K. 50°54N 1°23W 169 G6
Southampton N.Y., U.S.A. 40°53N 72°23W 313 F12
Southampton □ U.K. 50°54N 1°23W 169 G6
Southampton I. Canada 64°30N 84°0W 295 E15
Southaven U.S.A. 34°59N 90°0W 315 D9
Southbank Canada 54°2N 125°46W 296 C3
Southborough U.K. 51°23N 0°3E 125 B4
Southbridge N.Z. 43°48S 172°16E 285 D7
Southbridge Mass., U.S.A. 42°5N 72°2W 313 D12
Southeast C. U.S.A. 62°56N 169°39W 303 E5
Southeast Indian Ridge Ind. Oc. 43°0S 80°0E 273 J10
Southend Sask., Canada 56°19N 103°22W 297 B8
Southend London, U.K. 51°25N 0°0 125 B3
Southend-on-Sea U.K. 51°32N 0°44E 169 F8
Southend-on-Sea □ U.K. 51°32N 0°44E 169 F8
Southern = Janub □ Sudan 6°50N 28°45E 257 F2
Southern = Yedebub Biheroch Bihereseboch na Hizboch □ Ethiopia 12°0N 36°0E 257 F4
Southern = Yuzhnyy □ Russia 44°0N 40°0E 191 H6
Southern □ Malawi 15°0S 35°0E 269 F4
Southern □ S. Leone 8°0N 12°30W 262 D2
Southern □ Zambia 16°20S 26°20E 269 F2
Southern Alps N.Z. 43°41S 170°11E 285 D5
Southern California, Univ. of U.S.A. 34°1N 118°17W 126 B3
Southern Cross Australia 31°12S 119°15E 279 F2
Southern Highlands □ Papua N. G. 6°15S 143°25E 286 D2
Southern Indian L. Canada 57°10N 98°30W 297 B9
Southern Lau Group Fiji 18°40S 178°40W 287 B3
Southern Leyte □ Phil. 10°30N 125°10E 233 F5
Southern Ocean Antarctica 62°0S 60°0E 151 C6
Southern Pines U.S.A. 35°11N 79°24W 315 D15
Southern Rhodesia = Zimbabwe ■ Africa 19°0S 30°0E 269 F3
Southern Uplands U.K. 55°28N 3°52W 167 F5
Southfield U.S.A. 42°28N 83°15W 311 B13
Southfields U.K. 51°26N 0°11W 125 B2
Southington U.S.A. 41°36N 72°53W 313 E12
Southland □ N.Z. 45°30S 168°0E 285 F3
Southold U.S.A. 41°4N 72°26W 313 E12
Southport Queens., Australia 27°58S 153°25E 281 D5
Southport Mersey., U.K. 53°39N 3°0W 168 D4
Southport Fla., U.S.A. 30°17N 85°38W 316 E4
Southport La., U.S.A. 29°57N 90°8W 131 B2
Southport N.Y., U.S.A. 42°3N 76°49W 312 D8
Southwark □ U.K. 51°29N 0°6W 125 B3
Southwest △ Australia 43°8S 146°5E 281 G4
Southwest Museum U.S.A. 34°6N 118°13W 126 B3
Southwest Pacific Basin Pac. Oc. 40°0S 140°0W 277 G17
Southwest Pt. U.S. Virgin Is. 17°40N 64°55W 321 b
Southwold U.K. 52°20N 1°41E 169 E9
Southwood △ Australia 27°48S 150°8E 281 D5
Soutpansberg S. Africa 23°0S 29°30E 271 B4
Souvigny France 46°33N 3°10E 173 F10
Søvang Denmark 55°34N 12°37E 118 B3
Sovata Romania 46°35N 25°3E 183 D10
Soverato Italy 38°41N 16°33E 201 D9
Sovetsk Kaliningrad, Russia 55°6N 21°50E 184 C8
Sovetsk Kirov, Russia 57°38N 48°53E 190 B9
Sovetskaya Gavan Russia 48°58N 140°18E 215 E15
Sovetskoye = Zelenokumsk Russia 44°24N 44°0E 191 H6
Sovicille Italy 43°17N 11°13E 199 E8
Søvik Norway 62°33N 6°17E 164 B3
Soweto S. Africa 26°14S 27°52E 123 B1
Sowhānak Iran 35°48N 51°31E 141 A3
Sowma'eh Sarā Iran 37°17N 49°18E 213 D13
Soya Japan 35°44N 139°55E 140 A4
Sōya-Kaikyō = La Perouse Str. Asia 45°40N 142°0E 220 B11
Sōya-Misaki Japan 45°30N 141°55E 220 B10
Soyangho S. Korea 37°57N 127°54E 224 D3
Soyaux France 45°39N 0°12E 174 C4
Søyland Norway 58°41N 5°36E 164 F2
Soyo Angola 6°13S 12°20E 265 D2
Sozaq Kazakhstan 44°8N 68°28E 217 D7
Sozh → Belarus 51°57N 30°48E 177 B16
Sozopol Bulgaria 42°23N 27°42E 203 D11
Spa Belgium 50°29N 5°53E 170 D5
Spaans Lagoen Aruba 12°28N 69°58W 322 f
Spaanse Water Curaçao 12°4N 68°51W 322 g
Spaccaforno = Íspica Italy 36°47N 14°55E 201 F7
Spain ■ Europe 39°0N 4°0W 192 D3
Spalato = Split Croatia 43°31N 16°26E 199 E13
Spalding S. Austral., Australia 33°30S 138°37E 282 B3
Spalding Lincs., U.K. 52°48N 0°9W 168 E7
Spanaway U.S.A. 47°6N 122°26W 306 C4
Spandau Germany 52°33N 13°9E 115 A1
Spånga Sweden 59°23N 17°53E 139 A1
Spangler U.S.A. 40°39N 78°48W 312 F6
Spanische Reitschule Vienna, Austria 142 b1
Spanish Canada 46°12N 82°20W 298 C3
Spanish Fork U.S.A. 40°7N 111°39W 304 F8
Spanish Monastery U.S.A. 25°55N 80°11W 128 A2
Spanish Pt. Antigua & B. 17°33N 61°44W 322 c
Spanish Pt. Bermuda 32°18N 64°49W 153 a
Spanish Riding School = Spanische Reitschule Vienna, Austria 142 b1
Spanish Town Br. Virgin Is. 17°43N 64°26W 321 b
Spanish Town Jamaica 18°0N 76°57W 320 a
Sparks Ga., U.S.A. 31°11N 83°26W 316 D6
Sparks Nev., U.S.A. 39°32N 119°45W 306 F7
Sparreholm Sweden 59°4N 16°49E 162 E10
Sparrow Bay Grenada 12°30N 61°27W 323 q
Sparta = Sparti Greece 37°5N 22°25E 204 D4
Sparta Ga., U.S.A. 33°17N 82°58W 316 B7
Sparta Ill., U.S.A. 38°8N 89°42W 310 F7
Sparta Mich., U.S.A. 43°10N 85°42W 311 A11
Sparta N.J., U.S.A. 41°2N 74°38W 313 E10
Sparta Wis., U.S.A. 43°56N 90°49W 308 D8
Spartanburg U.S.A. 34°56N 81°57W 315 D14
Spartel, C. Morocco 35°47N 5°56W 260 A3
Sparti Greece 37°5N 22°25E 204 D4
Spartivento, C. Calabria, Italy 37°55N 16°4E 201 E9
Spartivento, C. Sard., Italy 38°53N 8°50E 200 D1
Spartochori Greece 38°40N 20°46E 207 B2
Sparwood Canada 49°44N 114°53W 296 D6
Spas-Demensk Russia 54°20N 34°0E 188 E7
Spas-Klepiki Russia 55°10N 40°10E 188 E11
Spassk = Bednodemyanovsk Russia 53°55N 43°15E 190 D6
Spassk Dalniy Russia 44°40N 132°48E 220 B6
Spassk-Ryazanskiy Russia 54°24N 40°25E 188 E11
Spatha, Akra Greece 35°42N 23°43E 207 E4
Spatsizi → Canada 57°42N 128°7W 296 B3
Spatsizi Plateau Wilderness ⌓ Canada 57°40N 128°0W 296 B3
Spean → U.K. 56°55N 4°59W 167 E4
Spearfish U.S.A. 44°30N 103°52W 308 C2
Spearman U.S.A. 36°12N 101°12W 314 C4
Spectacle I. U.S.A. 42°19N 70°59W 116 A3
Speculator U.S.A. 43°30N 74°22W 313 C10
Speed Australia 35°21S 142°27E 282 C5
Speedway U.S.A. 39°48N 86°16W 310 F10
Speery I. St. Helena 16°1S 5°46W 153 h
Speia Moldova 46°59N 29°19E 183 D14
Speicher-See Germany 48°12N 11°42E 131 A3
Speightstown Barbados 13°15N 59°39W 323 r
Speising Austria 48°10N 16°17E 142 B1
Speke Gulf Tanzania 2°20S 32°50E 268 C3
Spello Italy 42°59N 12°40E 199 F9
Spence Bay = Taloyoak Canada 69°32N 93°32W 294 D13
Spencer Idaho, U.S.A. 44°22N 112°11W 304 D7
Spencer Ind., U.S.A. 39°17N 86°46W 311 E10
Spencer Iowa, U.S.A. 43°9N 95°9W 308 D6
Spencer N.Y., U.S.A. 42°13N 76°30W 313 D8
Spencer Nebr., U.S.A. 42°53N 98°43W 308 D4
Spencer, C. Australia 35°20S 136°53E 282 C2
Spencer B. Namibia 25°30S 14°47E 270 C1
Spencer G. Australia 34°0S 137°20E 282 C2
Spencerville Ont., Canada 44°51N 75°33W 313 B9
Spencerville Ohio, U.S.A. 40°43N 84°21W 311 D12
Spences Bridge Canada 50°25N 121°20W 296 C4
Spennymoor U.K. 54°42N 1°36W 168 C6
Spenser Mts. N.Z. 42°15S 172°45E 285 C7
Spentrup Denmark 56°33N 10°2E 163 H4
Sperchios → Greece 38°57N 22°3E 204 C4
Sperrillen Norway 60°28N 10°3E 164 D7
Sperrin Mts. U.K. 54°50N 7°0W 166 B5
Spessart Germany 49°56N 9°18E 179 F5
Spetalen Norway 59°18N 10°45E 164 E7
Spetses Greece 37°15N 23°10E 204 D5
Spey → U.K. 57°40N 3°6W 167 D5
Speyer Germany 49°29N 8°25E 179 F4
Speyside Trin. & Tob. 11°17N 60°32W 323 s
Spezand Pakistan 29°59N 67°0E 242 E2
Spezzano Albanese Italy 39°40N 16°19E 201 C9
Sphinx Egypt 29°58N 31°8E 117 B1
Spickard U.S.A. 40°14N 93°36W 310 D3
Spiddle Ireland 53°15N 9°18W 166 C2
Spiekeroog Germany 53°46N 7°42E 178 B3
Spiez Switz. 46°40N 7°40E 179 J3
Spili Greece 35°13N 24°31E 207 E5
Spilimbergo Italy 46°7N 12°54E 199 B9
Spīn Būldak Afghan. 31°1N 66°25E 242 D2
Spinaceto Italy 41°47N 12°27E 136 C1
Spinalonga Greece 35°18N 25°44E 207 E6
Spinazzola Italy 40°58N 16°5E 201 B9
Spineni Romania 44°43N 24°37E 183 F9
Spinifex ⌓ Australia 28°30S 128°30E 279 E4
Spirding = Sniardwy, Jezioro Poland 53°48N 21°50E 184 E8
Spirit Lake U.S.A. 46°15N 122°9W 306 D4
Spirit River Canada 55°45N 118°50W 296 B5
Spiritwood Canada 53°24N 107°33W 297 C7
Spišská Nová Ves Slovak Rep. 48°58N 20°34E 181 C13
Spišské Podhradie Slovak Rep. 49°0N 20°48E 181 B13
Spit Junction Australia 33°49S 151°14E 139 A2
Spital Austria 47°42N 14°18E 180 D7
Spithead U.K. 50°45N 1°10W 169 G6
Spittal an der Drau Austria 46°48N 13°31E 180 E6
Spitzbergen = Svalbard Arctic 78°0N 17°0E 154 B12
Spjelkavik Norway 62°28N 6°22E 164 B3
Split Croatia 43°31N 16°26E 199 E13
Split ✈ (SPU) Croatia 43°33N 16°15E 199 E13
Split L. Canada 56°8N 96°15W 297 B9
Split Lake Canada 56°8N 96°15W 297 B9
Splitski Kanal Croatia 43°31N 16°20E 199 E13
Splügenpass Switz. 46°30N 9°20E 179 J5
Spofford U.S.A. 29°10N 100°25W 314 G4
Spokane U.S.A. 47°40N 117°24W 304 C5
Spoleto Italy 42°44N 12°44E 199 F9
Sponvika Norway 59°7N 11°15E 164 E8
Spoon → U.S.A. 40°19N 90°4W 310 D6
Spooner U.S.A. 45°50N 91°53W 308 C8
Spořilov Czech Rep. 50°2N 14°29E 135 B3
Sporyy Navolok, Mys Russia 75°50N 68°40E 214 B7
Spot Pond U.S.A. 42°26N 71°4W 116 A2
Spotswood Australia 37°50S 144°52E 128 B1
Sprague U.S.A. 47°18N 117°59W 304 C5
Spratly I. S. China Sea 8°38N 111°55E 230 C4
Spratly Is. S. China Sea 8°20N 112°0E 230 C4
Spray U.S.A. 44°50N 119°48W 304 D4
Spreča → Bos.-H. 44°44N 18°6E 182 F3
Spree → Germany 52°32N 13°12E 178 C9
Spreewald Germany 51°58N 13°51E 178 D9
Spremberg Germany 51°34N 14°22E 178 D10
Sprengisandur Iceland 64°52N 18°7W 155 C8
Spring City U.S.A. 40°11N 75°33W 313 F9
Spring Cr. → U.S.A. 30°54N 84°45W 316 E5
Spring Creek U.S.A. 40°44N 115°35W 304 F6
Spring Garden Guyana 6°59N 58°31W 329 B6
Spring Garden Calif., U.S.A. 39°52N 120°47W 306 F6
Spring Green U.S.A. 43°11N 90°4W 310 A6
Spring Hill Ala., U.S.A. 31°42N 85°58W 316 D4
Spring Hill Fla., U.S.A. 28°27N 82°41W 317 G7
Spring Mts. U.S.A. 36°0N 115°45W 307 J11
Spring Valley Calif., U.S.A. 32°44N 116°59W 307 N10
Spring Valley Ill., U.S.A. 41°20N 89°12W 310 C7
Spring Valley Nev., U.S.A. 36°6N 115°14W 124 B1
Springbok S. Africa 29°42S 17°54E 270 C2
Springboro U.S.A. 41°48N 80°22W 312 E4
Springdale Nfld. & L., Canada 49°30N 56°6W 299 C8
Springdale Ark., U.S.A. 36°11N 94°8W 314 C7
Springdale Ohio, U.S.A. 39°17N 84°29W 311 E12
Springe Germany 52°13N 9°33E 178 C5
Springeberg Germany 52°26N 13°43E 115 B5
Springer U.S.A. 36°22N 104°36W 305 H11
Springerville U.S.A. 34°8N 109°17W 305 J9
Springfield Ont., Canada 42°50N 80°56W 312 D4
Springfield Dominica 15°21N 61°23W 323 k
Springfield N.Z. 43°19S 171°56E 285 D6
Springfield Colo., U.S.A. 37°24N 102°37W 305 H12
Springfield Fla., U.S.A. 30°10N 85°37W 316 E4
Springfield Ga., U.S.A. 32°22N 81°18W 316 C8
Springfield Ill., U.S.A. 39°48N 89°39W 310 E7
Springfield Ky., U.S.A. 37°41N 85°13W 311 G11
Springfield Mass., U.S.A. 42°6N 72°35W 313 D12
Springfield Mo., U.S.A. 37°13N 93°17W 308 G7
Springfield Ohio, U.S.A. 39°55N 83°49W 311 E13
Springfield Oreg., U.S.A. 44°3N 123°1W 304 D2
Springfield S.C., U.S.A. 33°30N 81°17W 316 B8
Springfield Tenn., U.S.A. 36°31N 86°53W 315 C11
Springfield Va., U.S.A. 38°46N 77°10W 143 C2
Springfield Vt., U.S.A. 43°18N 72°29W 313 C12
Springfield, L. U.S.A. 39°46N 89°36W 310 E7
Springfontein S. Africa 30°15S 25°40E 270 D4
Springhill Canada 45°40N 64°4W 299 C7
Springhill La., U.S.A. 33°0N 93°28W 314 E8
Springhouse Canada 51°56N 122°7W 296 C4
Springs S. Africa 26°13S 28°25E 271 C4
Springsure Australia 24°8S 148°6E 280 C4
Springvale Ga., U.S.A. 31°50N 84°53W 316 D5
Springvale Maine, U.S.A. 43°28N 70°48W 313 C14
Springville Calif., U.S.A. 36°8N 118°49W 306 J8
Springville Iowa, U.S.A. 42°3N 91°27W 310 B5
Springville N.Y., U.S.A. 42°31N 78°40W 312 D6
Springville Utah, U.S.A. 40°10N 111°37W 304 F8
Springwater U.S.A. 42°38N 77°35W 312 D7
Sprottau = Szprotawa Poland 51°33N 15°35E 185 G2
Spruce-Creek U.S.A. 40°36N 78°9W 312 F6
Spruce Knob-Seneca Rocks ⌓ U.S.A. 38°50N 79°30W 309 F14
Spruce Mt. U.S.A. 44°12N 72°19W 313 B12
Sprucedale Canada 45°29N 79°28W 312 A5
Spur U.S.A. 33°28N 100°52W 314 E4
Spurn Hd. U.K. 53°35N 0°8E 168 D8
Spuž Montenegro 42°32N 19°10E 202 D3
Spuzzum Canada 49°37N 121°23W 296 D4
Spydeberg Norway 59°36N 11°5E 164 E8
Squam L. U.S.A. 43°45N 71°32W 313 C13
Squamish Canada 49°45N 123°10W 296 D4
Squantum U.S.A. 42°17N 71°0W 116 B2
Square Islands Canada 52°47N 55°47W 299 B8
Squillace, G. di Italy 38°45N 16°50E 201 D9
Squinzano Italy 40°26N 18°2E 201 B11
Squires, Mt. Australia 26°14S 127°28E 279 E4
Sragen Indonesia 7°26S 111°2E 235 D4
Srbac Bos.-H. 45°7N 17°30E 182 E2
Srbica Kosovo 42°45N 20°47E 202 D4
Srbija = Serbia ■ Europe 43°20N 20°0E 202 C4
Srbobran Serbia 45°32N 19°48E 182 E4
Sre Ambel Cambodia 11°8N 103°46E 237 G4
Sre Khtum Cambodia 12°10N 106°52E 237 F6
Sre Umbell = Sre Ambel Cambodia 11°8N 103°46E 237 G4
Srebrenica Bos.-H. 44°6N 19°18E 182 F4
Sredinnyy Khrebet Russia 57°0N 160°0E 215 D17
Sredinnyy Ra. = Sredinnyy Khrebet Russia 57°0N 160°0E 215 D17
Središče Slovenia 46°24N 16°17E 199 B13
Sredna Gora Bulgaria 42°40N 24°20E 203 D8
Srednaya Rogatka Russia 59°49N 30°22E 137 C2
Srednekolymsk Russia 67°27N 153°40E 215 C16
Sredni Rodopi Bulgaria 41°40N 24°45E 203 E8
Srednogorie Bulgaria 42°43N 24°10E 203 D8
Śrem Poland 52°6N 17°2E 185 F4
Sremska Mitrovica Serbia 44°59N 19°38E 182 F4
Sremski Karlovci Serbia 45°12N 19°56E 182 E4
Srepok → Cambodia 13°33N 106°16E 236 F6
Sretensk Russia 52°10N 117°40E 215 D12
Sri Aman = Bandar Sri Aman Malaysia 1°15N 111°32E 235 B4
Sri Kalahasti India 13°45N 79°44E 245 H4
Sri Lanka ■ Asia 7°30N 80°50E 245 L5
Sriharikota I. India 13°40N 80°20E 245 H5
Srikakulam India 18°14N 83°58E 244 E6
Srinagar India 34°5N 74°50E 243 B6
Sripur Bangla. 24°14N 90°30E 241 C3
Srivardhan India 18°4N 73°3E 244 E1
Srivilliputtur India 9°31N 77°40E 245 K3
Środa Śląska Poland 51°10N 16°36E 185 G3
Środa Wielkopolski Poland 52°15N 17°19E 185 F4
Śródmieście Poland 52°13N 21°0E 142 B2
Srono Indonesia 8°24S 114°16E 231 J17
Srpska Crnja Serbia 45°38N 20°44E 182 E5
Srpski Itebej Serbia 45°35N 20°44E 182 E5
Srungavarapukota India 18°7N 83°10E 244 E6
Ssese Is. = Sese Is. Uganda 0°20S 32°20E 268 C3
Ssuhu Taiwan 23°38N 120°13E 225 C2
Staaken Germany 52°31N 13°8E 115 A1
Staaten → Australia 16°24S 141°17E 280 B3
Staaten River △ Australia 16°15S 142°40E 280 B3
Stabekk Norway 59°54N 10°36E 133 A2
Staberhuk Germany 54°23N 11°18E 178 A7
Stade Germany 53°35N 9°29E 178 B5
Staðarfell Iceland 65°7N 22°12W 155 B4
Staðarhólskirkja Iceland 65°23N 21°58W 155 B5
Staðastaður Iceland 64°49N 23°1W 155 C3
Stadhavet Norway 62°13N 5°0E 164 B2
Stadhiou Athens, Greece 112 c3
Stadhuis Amsterdam, Neths. 112 b3
Staður Húnavatnssýsla, Iceland 65°9N 21°3W 155 B5
Staður Ísafjarðarsýsla, Iceland 66°15N 22°50W 155 A4
Stadlandet Norway 62°10N 5°10E 164 B2
Stadlau Austria 48°13N 16°27E 142 A2
Stadshuset Stockholm, Sweden 139 b1
Stadskanaal Neths. 53°4N 6°55E 170 A6
Stadsschouwburg Amsterdam, Neths. 112 c1
Stadtallendorf Germany 50°48N 9°1E 178 E5
Stadthagen Germany 52°19N 9°13E 178 C5
Stadtlohn Germany 51°59N 6°55E 178 D2
Stadtroda Germany 50°52N 11°44E 178 E7
Stafafell Iceland 64°25N 14°52W 155 C12
Staffa U.K. 56°27N 6°21W 167 E2
Staffanstorp Sweden 55°39N 13°13E 163 J7
Stafford Staffs., U.K. 52°49N 2°7W 168 E5
Stafford Kans., U.S.A. 37°58N 98°36W 308 G4
Stafford, L. U.S.A. 29°20N 82°29W 317 F7
Stafford Springs U.S.A. 41°57N 72°18W 313 E12
Staffordshire □ U.K. 52°53N 2°10W 168 E5
Stagnone Italy 37°53N 12°26E 200 E5
Stagnone di Marsala ⌓ Italy 37°52N 12°26E 200 E5
Staines U.K. 51°26N 0°29W 169 F7
Stains France 48°57N 2°22E 134 A3
Stainz Austria 46°53N 15°17E 180 E8
Stakhanov Ukraine 48°35N 38°40E 189 H10
Stalać Serbia 43°43N 21°28E 202 C5
Stalin = Kuçovë Albania 40°47N 19°57E 202 F3
Stalin = Varna Bulgaria 43°13N 27°56E 203 C11
Stalin Pk. = Gerlachovský štít Slovak Rep. 49°11N 20°7E 181 B13
Stalin Pk. = imeni Ismail Samani, Pik Tajikistan 39°0N 72°2E 217 E8
Stalin Pk. = Musala Bulgaria 42°13N 23°37E 202 D7

Stalinabad = Dushanbe Tajikistan 38°33N 68°48E 217 E7
Stalingrad = Volgograd Russia 48°40N 44°25E 191 F7
Staliniri = Tskhinvali Georgia 42°14N 44°1E 191 J7
Stalinogorsk = Novomoskovsk Russia 54°5N 38°15E 188 E10
Stalinogrod = Katowice Poland 50°17N 19°5E 185 H6
Stalinsk = Novokuznetsk Russia 53°45N 87°10E 217 B11
Stalinstadt = Eisenhüttenstadt Germany 52°9N 14°38E 178 C10
Stallarholmen Sweden 59°22N 17°12E 162 E11
Stålldalen Sweden 59°56N 14°56E 162 E8
Stalowa Wola Poland 50°34N 22°3E 185 H9
Stalybridge U.K. 53°28N 2°3W 168 D5
Stamford Queens., Australia 21°15S 143°46E 280 C3
Stamford Lincs., U.K. 52°39N 0°29W 169 E7
Stamford Conn., U.S.A. 41°3N 73°32W 313 E11
Stamford N.Y., U.S.A. 42°25N 74°38W 313 D10
Stamford Tex., U.S.A. 32°57N 99°48W 314 E5
Stamford Hill U.K. 51°34N 0°4W 125 A3
Stammersdorf Austria 48°18N 16°24E 142 A2
Stamnes Norway 60°40N 5°45E 164 D2
Stamping Ground U.S.A. 38°16N 84°41W 311 F12
Stampriet Namibia 24°20S 18°28E 270 B2
Stamps U.S.A. 33°22N 93°30W 314 E8
Stanberry U.S.A. 40°13N 94°35W 310 D2
Stančevo = Kalipetrovo Bulgaria 44°5N 27°14E 203 B11
Standerton S. Africa 26°55S 29°7E 271 C4
Standish U.S.A. 43°59N 83°57W 309 D12
Stanford S. Africa 34°26S 19°29E 270 D2
Stanford Mont., U.S.A. 47°9N 110°13W 304 C8
Stånga Sweden 57°17N 18°29E 163 G12
Stange Norway 60°43N 11°5E 164 D8
Stanger S. Africa 29°27S 31°14E 271 C5
Stängselåsen = Salpausselkä Finland 61°3N 26°15E 188 B4
Stangvik Norway 62°55N 8°28E 164 B5
Stanhope Vic., Australia 36°27S 144°59E 283 D6
Stanhope Iowa, U.S.A. 42°17N 93°48W 310 B3
Stanimaka = Asenovgrad Bulgaria 42°1N 24°51E 203 D8
Stanišić Serbia 45°56N 19°10E 182 E4
Stanislaus ➔ U.S.A. 37°40N 121°14W 306 H5
Stanislav = Ivano-Frankivsk Ukraine 48°40N 24°40E 183 B9
Stanisławów = Ivano-Frankivsk Ukraine 48°40N 24°40E 183 B9
Stanisławów Poland 52°18N 21°33E 185 F8
Stanley Tas., Australia 40°46S 145°19E 281 G4
Stanley Hong Kong, China 22°13N 114°12E 122 B2
Stanley Falk. Is. 51°40S 59°51W 153 f
Stanley Durham, U.K. 54°53N 1°41W 168 C6
Stanley Idaho, U.S.A. 44°13N 114°56W 304 D6
Stanley N. Dak., U.S.A. 48°19N 102°23W 308 A2
Stanley N.Y., U.S.A. 42°48N 77°6W 312 D7
Stanley Falls = Boyoma, Chutes Dem. Rep. of the Congo 0°35N 25°23E 264 B5
Stanley Mission Canada 55°25N 104°33W 297 B8
Stanley Pen. China 22°12N 114°12E 122 B2
Stanley Pool = Malebo, Pool Africa 4°17S 15°20E 265 C3
Stanley Res. India 11°50N 77°40E 245 J3
Stanleyville = Kisangani Dem. Rep. of the Congo 0°35N 25°15E 268 B2
Stanmore U.K. 51°37N 0°18W 125 A2
Stannards U.S.A. 42°5N 77°55W 312 D7
Stanovoy Khrebet Russia 55°0N 130°0E 215 D14
Stanovoy Ra. = Stanovoy Khrebet Russia 55°0N 130°0E 215 D14
Stansmore Ra. Australia 21°23S 128°33E 278 D4
Stansted, London ✈ (STN) U.K. 51°54N 0°14E 169 F8
Stanthorpe Australia 28°36S 151°59E 281 D5
Stanton Ky., U.S.A. 37°54N 83°52W 311 G13
Stanton Tex., U.S.A. 32°8N 101°48W 314 E4
Stanwood U.S.A. 48°15N 122°23W 306 B4
Staples Ont., Canada 42°10N 82°35W 312 D2
Staples Minn., U.S.A. 46°21N 94°48W 308 B6
Stapleton N.Y., U.S.A. 40°36N 74°5W 132 C1
Stapleton Nebr., U.S.A. 41°29N 100°31W 308 E3
Stąporków Poland 51°9N 20°31E 185 G7
Star City Canada 52°50N 104°20W 297 C8
Star Ferry Hong Kong, China 122 a2
Star Harbour Solomon Is. 10°47S 162°19E 287 N12
Star Lake U.S.A. 44°10N 75°2W 313 B9
Stará Ďala = Hurbanovo Slovak Rep. 47°51N 18°11E 181 D11
Stará L'ubovňa Slovak Rep. 49°18N 20°42E 181 B13
Stara Moravica Serbia 45°50N 19°30E 182 E4
Stara Pazova Serbia 44°58N 20°10E 182 F5
Stara Planina Bulgaria 43°15N 23°0E 202 C7
Stara Sil Ukraine 49°29N 22°58E 185 J9
Stará Turá Slovak Rep. 48°47N 17°42E 181 C10
Stara Ushytsya Ukraine 48°35N 27°8E 183 B12
Stara Zagora Bulgaria 42°26N 25°39E 203 D9
Stara Zagora ☐ Bulgaria 42°26N 25°39E 203 D9
Starachowice Poland 51°3N 21°2E 185 G8
Staraya Derevnya Russia 59°58N 30°15E 137 B1
Staraya Russa Russia 57°58N 31°23E 188 D6
Starbuck I. Kiribati 5°37S 155°55W 289 H12
Starchiojd Romania 45°19N 26°11E 183 E11
Starcke △ Australia 14°56S 145°2E 280 A4
Staré Město Czech Rep. 50°5N 14°25E 135 B2
Stare Miasto Warsaw, Poland 142 a2
Stargard in Pommern = Stargard Szczeciński Poland 53°20N 15°0E 184 E2
Stargard Szczeciński Poland 53°20N 15°0E 184 E2
Stårheim Norway 61°56N 5°40E 164 C2
Stari Bar Montenegro 42°7N 19°10E 202 D3
Stari Bečej = Bečej Serbia 45°36N 20°3E 182 E5
Stari Trg Slovenia 45°29N 15°7E 199 C12
Staritsa Russia 56°33N 34°55E 188 D8
Starke U.S.A. 29°57N 82°7W 316 F7
Starke, L. U.S.A. 28°34N 81°32W 133 A1
Starkville U.S.A. 33°28N 88°49W 315 E10
Starnberg Germany 48°0N 11°21E 179 H7
Starnberger See Germany 47°54N 11°19E 179 H7
Starobilsk Ukraine 49°16N 39°0E 189 H10
Starodub Russia 52°30N 32°50E 189 F7
Starogard Gdański Poland 53°59N 18°30E 184 E5
Starokonstantinov = Starokonstyantyniv Ukraine 49°48N 27°10E 177 D14
Starokonstyantyniv Ukraine 49°48N 27°10E 177 D14
Starokozache Ukraine 46°20N 29°59E 183 D14
Starominskaya Russia 46°33N 39°0E 191 G4
Staroshcherbinovskaya Russia 46°40N 38°53E 191 G4
Starrs Mill U.S.A. 33°19N 84°31W 316 B5
Start Pt. U.K. 50°13N 3°39W 169 G4
Stary Sącz Poland 49°33N 20°35E 185 J7
Staryy Biryuzyak Russia 44°46N 46°50E 191 H8
Staryy Chartoriysk Ukraine 51°15N 25°54E 177 C13
Staryy Krym Ukraine 45°3N 35°8E 189 K8
Staryy Margilan = Marghilon Uzbekistan 40°27N 71°42E 217 D8
Staryy Oskol Russia 51°19N 37°55E 189 G9
Staryy Sambir Ukraine 49°27N 22°59E 185 J9
Stassfurt Germany 51°51N 11°35E 178 D7
Staszów Poland 50°33N 21°10E 185 H8
State Center U.S.A. 42°1N 93°10W 310 B3
State College U.S.A. 40°48N 77°52W 312 F7
Stateline U.S.A. 38°57N 119°56W 306 G7
Staten, I. = Estados, I. de Los Argentina 54°40S 64°30W 336 D4
Staten I. U.S.A. 40°35N 74°9W 313 F10
Staten Island Zoo U.S.A. 40°38N 74°6W 132 C1
Staten Islands Ferry Terminal U.S.A. 40°38N 74°4W 132 C1
Statenice Czech Rep. 50°9N 14°19E 135 B1
Statenville U.S.A. 30°42N 83°2W 316 E6
Statesboro U.S.A. 32°27N 81°47W 316 C8
Statesville U.S.A. 35°47N 80°53W 315 D14
Statham U.S.A. 33°58N 83°35W 316 B6
Stathelle Norway 59°3N 9°41E 164 E6
Statia = St. Eustatius W. Indies 17°20N 63°0W 322 a
Statue Square Hong Kong, China 122 c1
Stauffer U.S.A. 34°45N 119°3W 307 L7
Staunton Ill., U.S.A. 39°1N 89°47W 310 F7
Staunton Va., U.S.A. 38°9N 79°4W 309 F14
Stavanger = Rogaland ☐ Norway 59°12N 6°20E 164 E3
Stavanger Norway 58°57N 5°40E 164 F2
Stavelot Belgium 50°23N 5°55E 170 D5
Stavern Norway 59°0N 10°1E 164 F7
Stavoren Neths. 52°53N 5°22E 170 B5
Stavropol Russia 45°5N 42°0E 191 H6
Stavropol ☐ Russia 47°20N 42°50E 191 G6
Stavros Cyprus 35°1N 32°38E 207 E8
Stavros Ithaki, Greece 38°27N 20°39E 207 C2
Stavros Kriti, Greece 35°12N 24°45E 207 E5
Stavros Thessaloniki, Greece 40°39N 23°43E 202 F7
Stavros, Akra Greece 35°26N 24°58E 207 E5
Stavroupoli Greece 41°12N 24°45E 203 E8
Stawell Australia 37°5S 142°47E 282 D5
Stawell ➔ Australia 20°20S 142°55E 280 C3
Stawiski Poland 53°22N 22°9E 184 E9
Stawiszyn Poland 51°56N 18°4E 185 G5
Stayner Canada 44°25N 80°5W 312 B4
Stayton U.S.A. 44°48N 122°48W 304 D2
Steamboat Springs U.S.A. 40°29N 106°50W 304 F10
Stean Norway 59°16N 8°33E 164 E5
Stebbins U.S.A. 63°31N 162°17W 303 E7
Steblevë Albania 41°23N 20°33E 202 E4
Stedelijk Museum Neths. 52°21N 4°52E 112 A2
Steele Ala., U.S.A. 33°56N 86°12W 316 B3
Steele N. Dak., U.S.A. 46°51N 99°55W 308 B4
Steele Creek Australia 37°44S 144°52E 128 A1
Steelton U.S.A. 40°14N 76°50W 312 F8
Steelville U.S.A. 37°58N 91°22W 310 G5
Steen River Canada 59°40N 117°12W 296 B5
Steenkool = Bintuni Indonesia 2°7S 133°32E 231 E8
Steenokkerzeel Belgium 50°55N 4°31E 116 A2
Steens Mt. U.S.A. 42°35N 118°40W 304 E4
Steenstrup Gletscher Greenland 75°15N 57°0W 154 B5
Steenwijk Neths. 52°47N 6°7E 170 B6
Steep Pt. Australia 26°8S 113°8E 279 E1
Steep Rock Canada 51°30N 98°48W 297 C9
Steer, L. U.S.A. 28°31N 81°30W 133 A2
Ştefan Vodă Moldova 46°27N 29°42E 183 D14
Ştefănesti Romania 47°44N 27°15E 183 C12
Stefanie △ Ethiopia 4°55N 36°55E 257 G4
Stefanie L. = Chew Bahir Ethiopia 4°40N 36°50E 257 G4
Stefansson Bay Antarctica 67°20S 59°8E 151 C5
Stefansson I. Canada 73°20N 105°45W 295 C10
Stege Denmark 54°59N 12°18E 163 K6
Stegi = Siteki Swaziland 26°32S 31°58E 271 C5
Steglitz Germany 52°27N 13°19E 115 B2
Stegman = Artesia U.S.A. 32°51N 104°24W 305 K11
Ştei Romania 46°32N 22°27E 182 D7
Steiermark ☐ Austria 47°26N 15°0E 180 D8
Steigerwald Germany 49°44N 10°26E 179 F6
Steigerwald ⌓ Germany 49°50N 10°30E 179 F6
Steilacoom U.S.A. 47°10N 122°36W 306 C4
Steilrandberge Namibia 17°45S 13°20E 270 A1
Stein = Kamnik Slovenia 46°14N 14°37E 199 B11
Steinbach Canada 49°32N 96°40W 297 D9
Steinfurt Germany 52°9N 7°20E 178 C3
Steinhatchee U.S.A. 29°40N 83°23W 316 F6
Steinhausen Namibia 21°49S 18°20E 270 B2
Steinheim Germany 51°51N 9°5E 178 D5
Steinhuder Meer Germany 52°29N 9°21E 178 C5
Steinhuder Meer ⌓ Germany 52°30N 9°16E 178 C5
Steinkjer Norway 64°1N 11°31E 160 D14
Steinkopf S. Africa 29°18S 17°43E 270 C2
Steinshamn Norway 62°47N 6°28E 164 B3
Steinwald ⌓ Germany 49°55N 12°8E 179 F8
Stellarton Canada 45°32N 62°30W 299 C7
Stellenbosch S. Africa 33°58S 18°50E 270 D2
Stelvio, Paso dello Italy 46°32N 10°27E 198 B7
Stenay France 49°29N 5°12E 173 C12
Stendal Germany 52°36N 11°53E 178 C7
Stende Latvia 57°11N 22°33E 184 A9
Stenen Koraal Curaçao 12°10N 68°56W 322 g
Stenhamra Sweden 59°20N 17°41E 162 E11
Stenshuvud △ Sweden 55°39N 14°15E 163 J8
Stenstorp Sweden 58°17N 13°45E 163 F7
Stenungsund Sweden 58°6N 11°50E 163 F5
Steornabhaigh = Stornoway U.K. 58°13N 6°23W 167 C2
Stepanakert = Xankändi Azerbaijan 39°52N 46°49E 213 C12
Stepanavan Armenia 41°1N 44°23E 191 K7
Stepaside Ireland 53°15N 6°12W 120 B2
Stephansdom Vienna, Austria 142 b2
Stephens, C. N.Z. 40°42S 173°58E 285 A8
Stephens Creek Australia 31°50S 141°30E 282 A4
Stephens I. B.C., Canada 54°10N 130°45W 296 C2
Stephens I. N.Z. 40°40S 174°1E 285 A9
Stephens L. Canada 56°32N 95°0W 297 B9
Stephenville Nfld. & L., Canada 48°31N 58°35W 299 C8
Stephenville Tex., U.S.A. 32°13N 98°12W 314 E5
Stepney U.K. 51°30N 0°3W 125 A3
Stepnica Poland 53°38N 14°36E 184 E1
Stepnogorsk Kazakhstan 52°21N 71°53E 217 B8
Stepnoi = Elista Russia 46°16N 44°14E 191 G7
Steppe Asia 50°0N 50°0E 210 C7
Steps Pt. Amer. Samoa 14°23S 170°45W 302 f
Sterea Ellas ☐ Greece 38°50N 23°0E 204 C4
Sterkstroom S. Africa 31°32S 26°32E 270 D4
Sterling Alaska, U.S.A. 60°32N 150°46W 303 F10
Sterling Colo., U.S.A. 40°37N 103°13W 304 F12
Sterling Ga., U.S.A. 31°16N 81°34W 316 D8
Sterling Ill., U.S.A. 41°48N 89°42W 310 C7
Sterling Kans., U.S.A. 38°13N 98°12W 308 F4
Sterling City U.S.A. 31°51N 101°0W 314 F4
Sterling Heights U.S.A. 42°35N 83°2W 311 B13
Sterling Park U.S.A. 37°41N 122°27W 136 B2
Sterling Run U.S.A. 41°25N 78°12W 312 E6
Sterlitamak Russia 53°40N 56°0E 186 D10
Sternberg Germany 53°42N 11°50E 178 B7
Šternberk Czech Rep. 49°45N 17°15E 181 B10
Sternes Greece 35°30N 24°9E 207 E5
Sterzing = Vipiteno Italy 46°54N 11°26E 199 B8
Stettin = Szczecin Poland 53°27N 14°27E 184 E1
Stettiner Haff Germany 53°47N 14°15E 178 B10
Stettler Canada 52°19N 112°40W 296 C6
Steubenville U.S.A. 40°22N 80°37W 312 F4
Stevenage U.K. 51°55N 0°13W 169 F7
Stevens Point U.S.A. 44°31N 89°34W 308 C9
Stevens Pottery U.S.A. 32°57N 83°17W 316 C6
Stevens Village U.S.A. 66°1N 149°6W 303 C10
Stevenson U.S.A. 45°42N 121°53W 306 E5
Stevenson ➔ Australia 27°6S 135°33E 281 D2
Stevenson L. Canada 53°55N 96°0W 297 C9
Stevensville U.S.A. 46°30N 114°5W 304 C6
Stevns Klint Denmark 55°17N 12°28E 163 J6
Steward U.S.A. 41°51N 89°1W 310 C7
Stewardson U.S.A. 39°16N 88°38W 311 E8
Stewart B.C., Canada 55°56N 129°57W 296 B3
Stewart Ga., U.S.A. 33°25N 83°52W 316 B6
Stewart Nev., U.S.A. 39°5N 119°46W 306 F7
Stewart ➔ Canada 63°19N 139°26W 294 E4
Stewart, C. Australia 11°57S 134°56E 280 A1
Stewart, I. Chile 54°50S 71°15W 336 D2
Stewart I. N.Z. 46°58S 167°54E 285 G2
Stewarts Point U.S.A. 38°39N 123°24W 306 G3
Stewartsville U.S.A. 39°45N 94°30W 310 E2
Stewartville U.S.A. 43°51N 92°29W 308 D7
Stewiacke Canada 45°9N 63°22W 299 C7
Steynsburg S. Africa 31°15S 25°49E 270 D4
Steyr Austria 48°3N 14°25E 180 C7
Steyr ➔ Austria 48°3N 14°25E 180 C7
Steytlerville S. Africa 33°17S 24°19E 270 D3
Stia Italy 43°48N 11°42E 199 E8
Sticklinge udde Sweden 59°23N 18°6E 139 A2
Stickney U.S.A. 41°49N 87°46W 119 C2
Stigler U.S.A. 35°15N 95°8W 314 D7
Stigliano Italy 40°24N 16°14E 201 B9
Stigtomta Sweden 58°47N 16°48E 163 F10
Stikine ➔ Canada 56°40N 132°30W 296 B2
Stilfontein S. Africa 26°51S 26°50E 270 C4
Stilida Greece 38°55N 22°47E 204 C4
Stillmore U.S.A. 32°27N 82°13W 316 C7
Stillorgan Ireland 53°17N 6°11W 120 B2
Stillwater N.Y., U.S.A. 42°55N 73°41W 313 D11
Stillwater Okla., U.S.A. 36°7N 97°4W 314 C6
Stillwater Range U.S.A. 39°50N 118°5W 304 G4
Stillwater Res. U.S.A. 43°54N 75°3W 313 C9
Stilo, Pta. Italy 38°25N 16°35E 201 D9
Stilwell U.S.A. 35°49N 94°38W 314 D7
Stînga Nistrului ☐ Moldova 47°20N 29°15E 183 C14
Štip Macedonia 41°42N 22°10E 202 E6
Stira Greece 38°9N 24°14E 204 C6
Stirling Ont., Canada 44°18N 77°33W 312 B7
Stirling N.Z. 46°14S 169°49E 285 G4
Stirling Stirling, U.K. 56°8N 3°57W 167 E5
Stirling ☐ U.K. 56°12N 4°18W 167 E4
Stirling Ra. Australia 34°23S 118°0E 279 F2
Stirling Range △ Australia 34°26S 118°20E 279 F2
Stittsville Canada 45°15N 75°55W 313 A9
Stjernøya Norway 70°20N 22°40E 160 A20
Stjørdalshalsen Norway 63°29N 10°51E 164 A7
Stock Island U.S.A. 24°32N 81°34W 317 L8
Stocka Sweden 61°53N 17°20E 162 C11
Stockach Germany 47°50N 9°1E 179 H5
Stockaryd Sweden 57°19N 14°36E 163 G8
Stockbridge Ga., U.S.A. 33°33N 84°14W 316 B5
Stockbridge Mich., U.S.A. 42°27N 84°11W 311 B12
Stockerau Austria 48°24N 16°12E 181 C9
Stockholm Sweden 59°19N 18°4E 139 B2
Stockholm Arlanda ✈ (ARN) Sweden 59°41N 17°56E 139 A1
Stockholms län ☐ Sweden 59°30N 18°20E 162 E12
Stockport U.K. 53°25N 2°9W 168 D5
Stocksbridge U.K. 53°29N 1°35W 168 D6
Stocksund Sweden 59°23N 18°3E 139 A2
Stockton Calif., U.S.A. 37°58N 121°17W 306 H5
Stockton Ill., U.S.A. 42°21N 90°1W 310 B6
Stockton Kans., U.S.A. 39°26N 99°16W 308 F4
Stockton Mo., U.S.A. 37°42N 93°48W 310 G3
Stockton-on-Tees U.K. 54°35N 1°19W 168 C6
Stockton-on-Tees ☐ U.K. 54°35N 1°19W 168 C6
Stockton Plateau U.S.A. 30°30N 102°30W 314 F3
Stoczek Łukowski Poland 51°58N 21°58E 185 G8
Stöde Sweden 62°28N 16°35E 162 B10
Stöðvarfjörður Iceland 64°49N 13°52W 155 C13
Stodůlky Czech Rep. 50°3N 14°19E 135 B1
Stoeng Treng Cambodia 13°31N 105°58E 236 F5
Stoer, Pt. of U.K. 58°16N 5°23W 167 C3
Stogovo Macedonia 41°31N 20°38E 202 E4
Stoholm Denmark 56°30N 9°8E 163 H3
Stoke N.Z. 41°19S 173°14E 285 B8
Stoke Newington U.K. 51°33N 0°4W 125 A3
Stoke-on-Trent U.K. 53°1N 2°11W 168 D5
Stoke-on-Trent ☐ U.K. 53°1N 2°11W 168 D5
Stokes △ Australia 33°45S 121°11E 279 F3
Stokes Bay Canada 45°0N 81°28W 312 B3
Stokes Pt. Australia 40°10S 143°56E 281 G3
Stokes Ra. Australia 15°50S 130°50E 278 C5
Stokes Valley N.Z. 41°10S 174°59E 143 B2
Stokkseyri Iceland 63°50N 21°2W 155 D5
Stokksnes Iceland 64°14N 14°58W 155 C12
Stokmarknes Norway 68°34N 14°54E 160 B16
Stolac Bos.-H. 43°5N 17°59E 202 C1
Stolberg Germany 50°47N 6°13E 178 E2
Stolbovoy, Ostrov Russia 74°44N 135°14E 215 B14
Stolbtsy = Stowbtsy Belarus 53°30N 26°43E 177 B14
Stolin Belarus 51°53N 26°50E 177 C14
Stöllet Sweden 60°26N 13°15E 162 D7
Stolnici Romania 44°31N 24°48E 183 F9
Stolp = Słupsk Poland 54°30N 17°3E 184 D4
Stolpmünde = Ustka Poland 54°35N 16°55E 184 D3
Stomio Greece 35°21N 23°32E 207 E4
Ston Croatia 42°51N 17°43E 199 F14
Stone U.K. 52°55N 2°9W 168 E5
Stone Canyon Res. U.S.A. 34°6N 118°27W 126 B2
Stone Mountain U.S.A. 33°49N 84°10W 316 B5
Stone Park U.S.A. 41°53N 87°52W 119 B1
Stoneboro U.S.A. 41°20N 80°7W 312 E4
Stonebridge U.K. 51°32N 0°16W 125 A2
Stoneham U.S.A. 42°29N 71°5W 116 A2
Stonehaven U.K. 56°59N 2°12W 167 E6
Stonehenge Queens., Australia 24°22S 143°17E 280 C3
Stonehenge Wilts., U.K. 51°9N 1°45W 169 F6
Stonewall Canada 50°10N 97°19W 297 C9
Stongfjorden Norway 61°26N 5°10E 164 C2
Stonington U.S.A. 39°44N 89°12W 310 E7
Stony Brook Res. U.S.A. 42°15N 71°8W 116 B2
Stony Creek ➔ U.S.A. 41°38N 87°41W 119 C2
Stony Hill Jamaica 18°5N 76°48W 320 a
Stony I. U.S.A. 43°53N 76°19W 313 C8
Stony L. Man., Canada 58°51N 98°40W 297 B9
Stony L. Ont., Canada 44°30N 78°5W 312 B6
Stony Point U.S.A. 41°14N 73°59W 313 E11
Stony Pt. U.S.A. 43°50N 76°18W 313 C8
Stony Rapids Canada 59°16N 105°50W 297 B7
Stony River U.S.A. 61°47N 156°35W 303 F8
Stony Tunguska = Tunguska, Podkamennaya ➔ Russia 61°50N 90°13E 215 C10
Stonyford U.S.A. 39°23N 122°33W 306 F4
Stopnica Poland 50°27N 20°57E 185 H7
Storå Sweden 59°42N 15°6E 162 E9
Storå ➔ Denmark 56°20N 8°19E 163 H2
Stora Gla Sweden 59°30N 12°30E 162 E6
Stora Le Sweden 59°5N 11°55E 162 E5
Stora Lulevatten Sweden 67°10N 19°30E 160 C18
Stora Värtan Sweden 59°25N 18°7E 139 A2
Stóra-Vatnshorn Iceland 65°4N 21°33W 155 B5
Storavan Sweden 65°45N 18°10E 160 D18
Stord Norway 59°52N 5°23E 164 E2
Stordalen Norway 62°23N 7°0E 164 B4
Store Bælt Denmark 55°20N 11°0E 163 J4
Store Hareskov Denmark 55°46N 12°23E 118 A2
Store Heddinge Denmark 55°18N 12°23E 163 J6
Store Jukleggi = Høgeloft Norway 61°3N 8°12E 164 C5
Store Koldewey Greenland 76°30N 19°0W 154 B9
Store Magleby Denmark 55°35N 12°35E 118 B3
Store Mosse △ Sweden 57°18N 13°55E 163 G7
Store Sotra Norway 60°18N 5°4E 164 D1
Storebro Sweden 57°35N 15°52E 163 G9
Støren Norway 63°3N 10°18E 164 A7
Storerikvollen Norway 63°7N 11°58E 164 A8
Storfjellsætra Norway 61°40N 10°30E 164 C7
Storfjorden Norway 62°28N 6°35E 164 B3
Storfors Sweden 59°32N 14°17E 162 E8
Storholmen Sweden 59°23N 18°8E 139 A2
Stóridalur Iceland 63°38N 19°57W 155 D7
Stórinúpur Iceland 64°3N 20°10W 155 C6
Storkerson Pen. Canada 72°30N 106°30W 294 C10
Storkyrkan Stockholm, Sweden 139 c2
Storli Norway 62°42N 9°5E 164 B6
Storlien Sweden 63°19N 12°6E 162 A6
Storm B. Australia 43°10S 147°30E 281 G4
Storm Lake U.S.A. 42°39N 95°13W 308 D6
Stormberge S. Africa 31°16S 26°17E 270 D4
Stormsrivier S. Africa 33°59S 23°52E 270 D3
Stornoway U.K. 58°13N 6°23W 167 C2
Storo Italy 45°51N 10°35E 198 C7
Storozhinets = Storozhynets Ukraine 48°14N 25°45E 183 B10
Storozhynets Ukraine 48°14N 25°45E 183 B10
Storrs U.S.A. 41°49N 72°15W 313 E12
Storsjøen Hedmark, Norway 60°20N 11°40E 164 D8
Storsjøen Hedmark, Norway 61°30N 11°14E 164 C8
Storsjön Gävleborg, Sweden 60°35N 16°45E 162 D10
Storsjön Jämtland, Sweden 62°48N 13°7E 162 B7
Storsjön Jämtland, Sweden 63°9N 14°30E 162 A8
Storsølnkletten Norway 61°59N 10°16E 164 C7
Storstrømmen Greenland 76°17N 22°25W 154 B8
Storuman Sweden 65°5N 17°10E 160 D17
Storuman, L. Sweden 65°13N 16°50E 160 D17
Stóruvellir Iceland 65°30N 17°29W 155 B9
Storvätteshågna Sweden 62°6N 12°30E 162 B6
Storviglen Norway 62°32N 12°2E 164 B9
Storvik Sweden 60°35N 16°33E 162 D10
Storvreta Sweden 59°58N 17°44E 162 E11
Story City U.S.A. 42°11N 93°36W 310 B3
Stouffville Canada 43°58N 79°15W 312 C5
Stoughton Sask., Canada 49°40N 103°0W 297 D8
Stoughton Wis., U.S.A. 42°55N 89°13W 310 B8
Stour ➔ Dorset, U.K. 50°43N 1°47W 169 G6
Stour ➔ Kent, U.K. 51°18N 1°22E 169 F9
Stour ➔ Suffolk, U.K. 51°57N 1°4E 169 F9
Stourbridge U.K. 52°28N 2°8W 169 E5
Stout L. Canada 52°0N 94°40W 297 C10
Stove Pipe Wells Village U.S.A. 36°35N 117°11W 307 J9
Støvring Denmark 56°54N 9°50E 163 H3
Stow U.S.A. 41°10N 81°27W 312 E3
Stowbtsy Belarus 53°30N 26°43E 177 B14
Stowmarket U.K. 52°12N 1°0E 169 E9
Stoyka Russia 59°57N 30°25E 137 B2
Strabane U.K. 54°50N 7°27W 166 B4
Stracin Macedonia 42°13N 22°2E 202 D6
Stradella Italy 45°5N 9°18E 198 C6
Strahan Australia 42°9S 145°20E 281 G4
Straiton U.K. 55°53N 3°9W 121 B3
Strajitsa Bulgaria 43°14N 25°58E 203 C9
Strakonice Czech Rep. 49°15N 13°53E 180 B6
Straldzha Bulgaria 42°35N 26°40E 203 D10
Stralsund Germany 54°18N 13°4E 178 A9
Strand Hedmark, Norway 61°17N 11°17E 164 C8
Strand Western Cape, S. Africa 34°9S 18°48E 270 D2
Strand London, U.K. 125 b4
Stranda Møre og Romsdal, Norway 62°19N 6°58E 164 B3
Stranda Nord-Trøndelag, Norway 63°33N 10°14E 160 E14
Strandasýsla ☐ Iceland 65°45N 21°45W 155 B5
Strandby Denmark 57°30N 10°29E 163 G4
Strandfontein S. Africa 34°4S 18°34E 118 B2
Strangford L. U.K. 54°30N 5°37W 166 B6
Strängnäs Sweden 59°23N 17°2E 162 E11
Stranorlar Ireland 54°48N 7°46W 166 B4
Stranraer U.K. 54°54N 5°1W 167 G3
Strasbourg Sask., Canada 51°4N 104°55W 297 C8
Strasbourg Bas-Rhin, France 48°35N 7°42E 173 D14
Strasburg Germany 53°30N 13°43E 178 B9
Strășeni Moldova 47°8N 28°36E 183 C13
Strašnice Czech Rep. 50°4N 14°28E 135 B2
Stråssa Sweden 59°44N 15°12E 162 E9
Strassburg = Aiud Romania 46°19N 23°44E 183 D8
Strasstrudering Germany 48°6N 11°41E 131 B3
Stratford N.S.W., Australia 32°7S 151°55E 283 B9
Stratford Vic., Australia 37°59S 147°7E 283 D7
Stratford Ont., Canada 43°23N 81°0W 312 C4
Stratford N.Z. 39°20S 174°19E 284 F3
Stratford London, U.K. 51°33N 0°0 125 A4
Stratford Calif., U.S.A. 36°11N 119°49W 306 J7
Stratford Conn., U.S.A. 41°12N 73°8W 313 E11
Stratford Tex., U.S.A. 36°20N 102°4W 314 C3
Stratford-upon-Avon U.K. 52°12N 1°42W 169 E6
Strath Spey U.K. 57°9N 3°49W 167 D5
Strathalbyn Australia 35°13S 138°53E 282 C3
Strathaven U.K. 55°40N 4°5W 167 F4
Strathcona ⌓ Canada 49°38N 125°40W 296 D3
Strathfield Australia 33°52S 151°5E 139 B1
Strathmore Alta., Canada 51°5N 113°18W 296 C6
Strathmore Angus, U.K. 56°37N 3°7W 167 E5
Strathmore Calif., U.S.A. 36°9N 119°4W 306 J7
Strathnaver Canada 53°20N 122°33W 296 C4
Strathpeffer U.K. 57°35N 4°32W 167 D4
Strathroy Canada 42°58N 81°38W 312 D3
Strathy Pt. U.K. 58°36N 4°1W 167 C4
Strattanville U.S.A. 41°12N 79°19W 312 E5
Stratton U.S.A. 45°8N 70°26W 313 A14
Stratton Mt. U.S.A. 43°4N 72°55W 313 C12
Straubing Germany 48°52N 12°34E 179 G8
Straumnes Iceland 66°26N 23°8W 155 A3
Strausberg Germany 52°35N 13°54E 178 C9
Strawberry ➔ U.S.A. 40°10N 110°24W 304 F8
Strawberry Point U.S.A. 42°41N 91°32W 310 B5
Strážnice Czech Rep. 48°54N 17°19E 181 C10
Streaky B. Australia 32°48S 134°13E 281 E1
Streaky Bay Australia 32°51S 134°18E 281 E1
Streatham U.K. 51°25N 0°7W 125 B3
Streatham Vale U.K. 51°24N 0°8W 125 B3
Streator U.S.A. 41°8N 88°50W 311 C8
Strebersdorf Austria 48°17N 16°23E 142 A2
Středočeský ☐ Czech Rep. 49°55N 14°30E 180 B7
Streetsboro U.S.A. 41°14N 81°21W 312 E3
Streetsville Canada 43°35N 79°42W 312 C5
Strehaia Romania 44°37N 23°10E 183 F8
Strehlen = Strzelin Poland 50°46N 17°2E 185 H4
Strelcha Bulgaria 42°25N 24°19E 203 D8
Streng ➔ Cambodia 13°12N 103°37E 236 F4
Stresa Italy 45°52N 8°28E 198 C5
Střešovice Czech Rep. 50°5N 14°23E 135 B2
Streymoy Færoe Is. 62°8N 7°5W 160 E9
Strezhevoy Russia 60°42N 77°34E 214 C8
Stříbro Czech Rep. 49°44N 13°0E 180 A6
Strickland ➔ Papua N. G. 7°35S 141°36E 286 D1
Striegau = Strzegom Poland 50°58N 16°20E 185 H3
Strilky Ukraine 49°20N 22°59E 185 J9
Strimonas ➔ Greece 40°46N 23°51E 202 F7
Strip, The U.S.A. 36°7N 115°10W 124 B2
Střížkov Czech Rep. 50°7N 14°28E 135 B2
Stroeder Argentina 40°12S 62°37W 336 B4
Strofades Greece 37°15N 21°0E 204 D3
Strogino Russia 55°48N 37°24E 129 B2
Strokestown Ireland 53°46N 8°7W 166 C3
Stroma U.K. 58°41N 3°7W 167 C5
Strombeek-Bever Belgium 50°54N 4°21E 116 A2
Stromberg-Heuchelberg ⌓ Germany 49°2N 8°50E 179 F4
Strómboli Italy 38°47N 15°13E 201 D8
Stromeferry U.K. 57°21N 5°33W 167 D3
Strommen Norway 59°57N 11°0E 164 E7
Stromness U.K. 58°58N 3°17W 167 C5
Stromovka Czech Rep. 50°6N 14°25E 135 B2
Strömsbruk Sweden 61°52N 17°18E 162 C11
Stromsburg U.S.A. 41°7N 97°36W 308 E5
Strömsnäsbruk Sweden 56°35N 13°45E 163 H7
Strömstad Sweden 58°56N 11°10E 163 F5
Strömsund Sweden 63°51N 15°33E 160 E16
Stronghurst U.S.A. 40°45N 90°55W 310 D6
Strongili Greece 36°6N 29°42E 205 E11
Stróngoli Italy 39°16N 17°3E 201 C10
Strongsville U.S.A. 41°19N 81°50W 312 E3
Stronie Śląskie Poland 50°18N 16°53E 185 H3
Stronsay U.K. 59°7N 2°35W 167 B6
Stropkov Slovak Rep. 49°13N 21°39E 181 B14
Stroud U.K. 51°45N 2°13W 169 F5
Stroud Road Australia 32°18S 151°57E 283 B9
Stroudsburg U.S.A. 40°59N 75°12W 313 F9
Stroumbi Cyprus 34°53N 32°29E 207 F8
Štrpce Kosovo 42°14N 21°1E 202 D5
Struer Denmark 56°30N 8°35E 163 H2
Struga Macedonia 41°11N 20°44E 202 E4
Strugi Krasnyye Russia 58°21N 29°1E 188 C5
Strumica Macedonia 41°28N 22°41E 202 E6
Strumica ➔ Europe 41°20N 23°22E 202 E7
Strumok Ukraine 45°43N 29°27E 183 E14
Struthers U.S.A. 41°4N 80°39W 312 E4
Stryama Bulgaria 42°16N 24°54E 203 D8
Stryker U.S.A. 48°41N 114°46W 304 B6
Stryków Poland 51°55N 19°33E 185 G6
Stryn Norway 61°54N 6°43E 164 C3
Stryy Ukraine 49°16N 23°48E 177 D12
Strzegom Poland 50°58N 16°20E 185 H3
Strzelce Krajeńskie Poland 52°52N 15°33E 185 F2
Strzelce Opolskie Poland 50°31N 18°18E 185 H5
Strzelecki Cr. ➔ Australia 29°37S 139°59E 281 D2
Strzelecki Desert Australia 29°30S 140°0E 281 D3
Strzelin Poland 50°46N 17°2E 185 H4
Strzelno Poland 52°35N 18°9E 185 F5
Strzybnica Poland 50°28N 18°48E 185 H5
Strzyżów Poland 49°52N 21°47E 185 J8
Stuart Fla., U.S.A. 27°12N 80°15W 317 H9
Stuart Iowa, U.S.A. 41°30N 94°19W 310 C2
Stuart Nebr., U.S.A. 42°36N 99°8W 308 D4
Stuart ➔ Canada 54°0N 123°35W 296 C4
Stuart Bluff Ra. Australia 22°50S 131°52E 278 D5
Stuart I. U.S.A. 63°35N 162°30W 303 E7
Stuart L. Canada 54°30N 124°30W 296 C4
Stuart Mts. N.Z. 45°2S 167°39E 285 F2
Stuart Ra. Australia 29°10S 134°56E 281 D1
Stubbekøbing Denmark 54°53N 12°9E 163 K6
Stubbs St. Vincent 13°7N 61°9W 323 n
Stuben Austria 47°10N 10°8E 180 D3
Štubnianske Teplice = Turčianske Teplice Slovak Rep. 48°52N 18°52E 181 C11
Studen Kladenets, Yazovir Bulgaria 41°37N 25°30E 203 E9
Studenka Czech Rep. 49°44N 18°5E 181 B11
Studholme N.Z. 44°42S 171°9E 285 E6
Studio City U.S.A. 34°8N 118°24W 126 B2
Studley Park Trin. & Tob. 11°11N 60°40W 323 s
Stugudalen Norway 62°53N 11°53E 164 B8
Stugun Sweden 63°10N 15°40E 162 A9
Stuhlweissenburg = Székesfehérvár Hungary 47°15N 18°25E 182 C3
Stuhm = Sztum Poland 53°55N 19°1E 184 E6
Stuhr Germany 53°5N 8°44E 178 B4
Stull L. Canada 54°24N 92°34W 298 B1
Stung Treng = Stoeng Treng Cambodia 13°31N 105°58E 236 F5
Stupart ➔ Canada 56°0N 93°25W 298 A1
Stupava Slovak Rep. 48°17N 17°2E 181 C10
Stupino Russia 54°57N 38°2E 188 E10
Stureby Sweden 59°15N 18°4E 139 B2
Sturge I. Antarctica 67°26S 164°47E 151 C11
Sturgeon B. Canada 52°0N 97°50W 297 C9
Sturgeon Bay U.S.A. 44°50N 87°23W 308 C10
Sturgeon Falls Canada 46°25N 79°57W 298 C4
Sturgeon L. Alta., Canada 55°6N 117°32W 296 B5
Sturgeon L. Ont., Canada 50°0N 90°45W 298 C1
Sturgeon L. Ont., Canada 44°28N 78°43W 312 B6
Sturgis Sask., Canada 51°56N 102°36W 297 C8
Sturgis Mich., U.S.A. 41°48N 85°25W 311 C11
Sturgis S. Dak., U.S.A. 44°25N 103°31W 308 C2
Sturkö Sweden 56°5N 15°42E 163 H9
Štúrovo Slovak Rep. 47°48N 18°41E 181 D11
Sturt △ Australia 27°17S 141°37E 281 D3
Sturt Cr. ➔ Australia 19°8S 127°50E 278 C4
Sturt Stony Desert Australia 28°30S 141°0E 281 D3
Sturts Meadows Australia 31°18S 141°42E 282 A4
Stutterheim S. Africa 32°33S 27°28E 270 D4
Stuttgart Baden-W., Germany 48°48N 9°11E 179 G5
Stuttgart Ark., U.S.A. 34°30N 91°33W 314 D9
Stuttgart Echterdingen ✈ (STR) Germany 48°42N 9°11E 179 G5
Stutthof = Sztutowo Poland 54°20N 19°15E 184 D6
Stuvsta Sweden 59°15N 18°0E 139 B2
Stuyvesant U.S.A. 42°23N 73°45W 313 D11
Stykkishólmur Iceland 65°2N 22°40W 155 B4
Styria = Steiermark ☐ Austria 47°26N 15°0E 180 D8
Styrsö Sweden 57°37N 11°46E 163 G5
Su-no-Saki Japan 34°58N 139°45E 223 C11
Su Xian = Suzhou China 33°41N 116°59E 226 H9
Suakin Sudan 19°8N 37°20E 256 D4
Suakin Archipelago Sudan 18°42N 38°30E 256 D4
Suan N. Korea 38°42N 126°22E 224 C3
Suana Indonesia 8°44S 115°36E 231 K18
Süanhwa = Xuanhua China 40°40N 115°2E 226 D8
Suao Taiwan 24°36N 121°51E 225 B3
Suapure ➔ Venezuela 6°48N 67°1W 328 B4
Suar India 29°2N 79°3E 243 E8
Suau Papua N. G. 10°37S 150°2E 286 F6
Suavanao Solomon Is. 7°35S 158°47E 287 L10
Şubā Si. Arabia 27°10N 35°40E 246 E2
Subang Indonesia 6°34S 107°45E 235 D3
Subankhata India 26°48N 91°25E 241 B3
Subansiri ➔ India 26°48N 93°50E 241 B4
Subarnagiri India 19°50N 83°51E 244 E6
Subarnarekha ➔ India 22°34N 87°24E 243 H12
Subay', Urūq Si. Arabia 22°15N 43°5E 256 C5
Subayhah Si. Arabia 30°2N 38°50E 246 D3
Subcetate Romania 45°36N 23°0E 182 E8
Subhepur India 28°44N 77°15E 120 A2
Subi Indonesia 2°58N 108°50E 235 B3
Subiaco Italy 41°56N 13°5E 199 G10
Subic B. Phil. 14°44N 120°12E 232 D3
Subotica Serbia 46°6N 19°39E 182 D4
Suburban Canal U.S.A. 30°2N 90°11W 131 B1
Suca Ethiopia 6°31N 39°14E 257 F4
Sucat Phil. 14°27N 121°2E 127 C2
Suceava Romania 47°38N 26°16E 183 C11
Suceava ☐ Romania 47°37N 25°40E 183 C10
Suceava ➔ Romania 47°32N 26°32E 183 C11
Sucha-Beskidzka Poland 49°44N 19°35E 185 J6
Suchan = Partizansk Russia 43°8N 133°9E 215 E14
Suchań Poland 53°18N 15°18E 185 E2
Suchdol Czech Rep. 50°8N 14°22E 135 B2
Suchedniów Poland 51°3N 20°49E 185 G7
Suchil Mexico 23°39N 103°54W 318 C4
Suchou = Suzhou China 31°19N 120°38E 229 B13
Süchow = Xuzhou China 34°18N 117°10E 227 G9
Suchowola Poland 53°33N 23°3E 184 E10
Sucio ➔ Colombia 7°27N 77°7W 328 B2
Suck ➔ Ireland 53°17N 8°3W 166 C3
Suckling, Mt. Papua N. G. 9°49S 148°53E 286 E5
Sucre Bolivia 19°0S 65°15W 331 D4
Sucre Colombia 8°49N 74°44W 328 B3
Sucre ☐ Colombia 8°50N 75°40W 328 B2
Sucre ☐ Venezuela 10°25N 63°30W 329 A5
Sucuaro Colombia 4°34N 68°50W 328 C4
Sucumbíos ☐ Ecuador 0°6S 76°52W 328 D2
Sućuraj Croatia 43°10N 17°8E 199 E14
Sucuriju Brazil 1°39N 49°57W 332 A2
Sucuriú ➔ Brazil 20°47S 51°38W 331 E7
Sucy-en-Brie France 48°46N 2°31E 134 B4
Sud ☐ Cameroon 2°30N 11°45E 263 E7
Sud, Pte. Comoros Is. 11°53S 43°29E 272 a
Sud, Pte. du Canada 49°3N 62°14W 299 C7
Sud-Kivu ☐ Dem. Rep. of the Congo 3°0S 28°30E 268 C2
Sud-Ouest ☐ Cameroon 5°25N 9°20E 263 D6
Sud-Ouest, Pte. Qué., Canada 49°23N 63°36W 299 C7
Sud Ouest, Pte. Mauritius 20°28S 57°18E 272 e
Suda ➔ Russia 59°0N 37°40E 188 C9
Sudak Ukraine 44°51N 34°57E 189 K8
Sudan U.S.A. 34°4N 102°31W 314 D3
Sudan ■ Africa 15°0N 30°0E 257 E3
Sudauen = Suwałki Poland 54°8N 22°59E 184 D9
Sudbury Ont., Canada 46°30N 81°0W 298 C3
Sudbury Suffolk, U.K. 52°2N 0°45E 169 E8
Sûdd Sudan 8°20N 30°0E 257 F3
Suddie Guyana 7°8N 58°29W 329 B6
Sudeifel = Deutsch-Luxemburgischer ⌓ Germany 49°58N 6°12E 179 F2
Süderbrarup Germany 54°38N 9°45E 178 A5
Süderlügum Germany 54°52N 8°54E 178 A4
Süderoogsand Germany 54°27N 8°28E 178 A4
Sudeten Mts. = Sudety Europe 50°20N 16°45E 181 A9
Sudety Europe 50°20N 16°45E 181 A9
Súðavík Iceland 66°2N 23°0W 155 A3
Südheide ⌓ Germany 52°46N 10°10E 178 C6
Suður-múlasýsla ☐ Iceland 65°0N 14°30W 155 C12
Suður-þingeyjarsýsla ☐ Iceland 65°30N 17°0W 155 B9
Suðureyri Iceland 66°7N 23°32W 155 A3
Suðuroy Færoe Is. 61°32N 6°50W 160 F9
Sudi Tanzania 10°11S 39°57E 269 E4
Sudirman, Pegunungan Indonesia 4°30S 137°0E 231 E9
Sudiţi Romania 44°35N 27°38E 183 F12
Sudogda Russia 55°55N 40°50E 190 C5
Sudong, Pulau Singapore 1°13N 103°44E 237 d
Sudostroy = Severodvinsk Russia 64°27N 39°58E 186 B6
Sudova Vyshnya Ukraine 49°46N 23°22E 185 J10
Sudzha Russia 51°14N 35°17E 189 G8
Sue ➔ Sudan 7°41N 28°3E 257 F2
Sue, L. U.S.A. 28°34N 81°21W 133 A2
Sueca Spain 39°12N 0°21W 197 F4
Sŭedinenie Bulgaria 42°16N 24°33E 203 D8
Suemez I. U.S.A. 55°15N 133°20W 296 B2
Sueyoshi Japan 31°40N 131°5E 222 F3
Suez = El Suweis Egypt 29°58N 32°31E 256 B3
Suez, G. of = Suweis, Khalîg el Egypt 28°40N 33°0E 256 J8
Suez Canal = Suweis, Qanâ es Egypt 31°0N 32°20E 256 H8
Suffield Canada 50°12N 111°10W 296 C6
Suffolk U.S.A. 36°44N 76°35W 309 G15
Suffolk ☐ U.K. 52°16N 1°0E 169 E9
Şufiān Iran 38°16N 45°58E 213 C11
Suga-no-Sen Japan 35°25N 134°25E 222 B6
Şugag Romania 45°47N 23°37E 183 E8
Sugamo Japan 35°44N 139°43E 140 A3
Sugar ➔ U.S.A. 42°26N 89°12W 310 B7
Sugar Cr. ➔ Ill., U.S.A. 40°9N 89°38W 310 D7
Sugar Cr. ➔ Ind., U.S.A. 39°51N 87°21W 311 E9
Sugar Grove U.S.A. 41°59N 79°20W 312 E5
Sugar Hill U.S.A. 34°6N 84°2W 316 A5
Sugar Loaf Grenada 12°13N 61°36W 323 q
Sugar Loaf Mt. = Açúcar, Pão de Brazil 22°56S 43°9W 135 B2
Sugar Loaf Pt. St. Helena 15°54S 5°42W 153 h
Sugarcreek U.S.A. 41°25N 79°52W 312 E5
Sugarive ➔ India 26°16N 86°24E 243 F12
Sugbai Passage Phil. 5°22N 120°33E 233 J3
Suge Japan 35°37N 139°32E 140 B2
Sughd ☐ Tajikistan 40°0N 69°0E 217 E7
Sugihwaras Indonesia 4°1S 103°46E 234 C2
Suginami Japan 35°41N 139°37E 140 A2
Suğla Gölü Turkey 37°20N 32°0E 212 D5
Sugluk = Salluit Canada 62°14N 75°38W 295 E16
Sugō Japan 35°34N 139°33E 140 B2
Sugun China 39°53N 76°47E 217 E9
Suha Reke = Suva Reka Kosovo 42°21N 20°50E 202 D4
Suhaia, Lacul Romania 43°45N 25°15E 183 G10
Şuḩār Oman 24°20N 56°40E 247 E8
Sühbaatar Mongolia 50°17N 106°10E 218 A10
Sühbaatar ☐ Mongolia 45°30N 114°0E 226 B8

Suheli Par *India* 10°5N 72°17E 245 J1
Suhl *Germany* 50°36N 10°42E 178 E6
Şuhut *Turkey* 38°31N 30°32E 205 C12
Sui *Pakistan* 28°37N 69°19E 242 E3
Sui Sai Wan *China* 22°16N 114°14E 122 B1
Sui Xian *China* 34°25N 115°2E 226 G8
Suiá Missu → *Brazil* 11°13S 53°15W 331 C7
Šuica *Bos.-H.* 43°52N 17°11E 182 G2
Suichang *China* 28°29N 119°15E 229 C12
Suichuan *China* 26°20N 114°32E 229 D10
Suide *China* 37°30N 110°12E 226 F6
Suifenhe *China* 44°25N 131°10E 227 B16
Suihua *China* 46°32N 126°55E 219 B14
Suijiang *China* 28°40N 103°59E 228 C4
Suining *Hunan, China* 26°35N 110°10E 229 D8
Suining *Jiangsu, China* 33°56N 117°58E 227 H9
Suining *Sichuan, China* 30°26N 105°35E 228 B5
Suiping *China* 33°10N 113°59E 226 H7
Suippes *France* 49°8N 4°30E 173 C11
Suir → *Ireland* 52°16N 7°9W 166 D4
Suisse = Switzerland ■ *Europe* 46°30N 8°0E 179 J4
Suisun City *U.S.A.* 38°15N 122°2W 306 G4
Suita *Japan* 34°45N 135°30E 133 A2
Suitland *U.S.A.* 38°50N 76°55W 143 B4
Suixi *China* 21°19N 110°18E 229 G8
Suiyang *Guizhou, China* 27°58N 107°18E 228 D6
Suiyang *Heilongjiang, China* 44°30N 130°56E 227 B16
Suizhong *China* 40°21N 120°20E 227 D11
Suizhou *China* 31°42N 113°24E 229 B9
Sujangarh *India* 27°42N 74°31E 242 F6
Sujiatun *China* 41°39N 123°20E 227 D12
Sukabumi *Indonesia* 6°56S 106°50E 234 D3
Sukadana *Kalimantan Barat, Indonesia* 1°10S 110°0E 235 C4
Sukadana *Lampung, Indonesia* 5°5S 105°33E 234 D3
Sukadana, Teluk *Indonesia* 1°24S 109°50E 235 C3
Sukagawa *Japan* 37°17N 140°23E 221 F10
Sukamade *Indonesia* 8°30S 113°52E 235 D4
Sukamara *Indonesia* 2°43S 111°10E 235 C4
Sukaraja *Indonesia* 2°28S 110°25E 235 C4
Sukarnapura = Jayapura *Indonesia* 2°28S 140°38E 231 E10
Sukarno, Puntjak = Jaya, Puncak *Indonesia* 3°57S 137°17E 231 E9
Sukau *Malaysia* 5°32N 118°17E 235 A5
Sukawati *Indonesia* 8°35S 115°17E 231 K18
Sukchar *India* 22°42N 88°22E 124 A2
Sukch'ŏn *N. Korea* 39°22N 125°35E 224 C2
Sukhindol *Bulgaria* 43°11N 25°10E 203 C9
Sukhinichi *Russia* 54°8N 35°10E 188 E8
Sukhona → *Russia* 61°15N 46°39E 186 C6
Sukhothai *Thailand* 17°1N 99°49E 236 D2
Sukhumi = Sokhumi *Georgia* 43°0N 41°0E 191 J5
Sukkertoppen = Maniitsoq *Greenland* 65°26N 52°55W 154 D5
Sukkur *Pakistan* 27°42N 68°54E 242 F3
Sukkur Barrage *Pakistan* 27°40N 68°50E 242 F3
Sukma *India* 18°24N 81°45E 244 E5
Sukovo *Serbia* 43°4N 22°37E 202 C6
Sukri → *India* 25°4N 71°43E 242 G4
Sukumo *Japan* 32°56N 132°44E 222 E4
Sukunka → *Canada* 55°45N 121°15W 296 B4
Sul, Canal do *Brazil* 0°10S 48°30W 332 B2
Sula *Norway* 61°7N 4°54E 164 C1
Sula → *Ukraine* 49°40N 32°41E 189 H7
Sula, Kepulauan *Indonesia* 1°45S 125°0E 231 E7
Sulaco → *Honduras* 15°2N 87°44W 320 C2
Sulaiman Range *Pakistan* 30°30N 69°50E 242 D3
Sulak → *Russia* 43°20N 47°34E 191 J8
Sulakyurt *Turkey* 40°9N 33°43E 212 B5
Sūlār *Iran* 31°53N 51°54E 247 D6
Sulawesi *Indonesia* 2°0S 120°0E 235 C5
Sulawesi Barat □ *Indonesia* 3°0S 119°0E 235 C5
Sulawesi Sea = Celebes Sea *Indonesia* 3°0N 123°0E 231 D6
Sulawesi Selatan □ *Indonesia* 2°30S 120°0E 231 E6
Sulawesi Tengah □ *Indonesia* 1°30S 121°0E 231 E6
Sulawesi Tenggara □ *Indonesia* 3°50S 122°0E 231 E6
Sulawesi Utara □ *Indonesia* 1°0N 124°0E 231 D6
Suldalsheiene *Norway* 59°28N 7°10E 164 E3
Suldalsosen *Norway* 59°29N 6°29E 164 E3
Sulechów *Poland* 52°5N 15°40E 185 F2
Sulęcin *Poland* 52°26N 15°10E 185 F2
Sulei *Solomon Is.* 8°3S 159°34E 287 M10
Suleja *Nigeria* 9°10N 7°10E 263 D6
Sulejów *Poland* 51°26N 19°53E 185 G6
Sulejówek *Poland* 52°13N 21°17E 185 F8
Süleymanlı *Turkey* 38°58N 27°47E 205 C9
Sulima *S. Leone* 6°58N 11°32W 262 D2
Sulina *Romania* 45°10N 29°40E 183 E14
Sulina, Braţul → *Romania* 45°10N 29°40E 183 E14
Sulingen *Germany* 52°41N 8°48E 178 C4
Suliţa *Romania* 47°39N 26°59E 183 C11
Sulitjelma *Norway* 67°9N 16°3E 160 C17
Sułkowice *Poland* 49°50N 19°49E 185 J6
Sullana *Peru* 4°52S 80°39W 330 A1
Süller *Turkey* 38°9N 29°29E 205 C11
Sullivan *Ill., U.S.A.* 39°36N 88°37W 311 E8
Sullivan *Ind., U.S.A.* 39°6N 87°24W 311 E9
Sullivan *Mo., U.S.A.* 38°13N 91°10W 310 F5
Sullivan Bay *Canada* 50°55N 126°50W 296 C3
Sullivan I. = Lanbi Kyun *Burma* 10°50N 98°20E 237 G2
Sullom Voe *U.K.* 60°27N 1°20W 167 A7
Sullorsuaq *Greenland* 70°5N 53°0W 154 C5
Sully *U.S.A.* 41°34N 92°50W 310 C4
Sully-sur-Loire *France* 47°45N 2°20E 173 E9
Sulmierzyce *Poland* 51°37N 17°32E 185 G4
Sulmona *Italy* 42°3N 13°55E 199 F10
Süloğlu *Turkey* 41°44N 26°53E 203 E10
Sulphur *La., U.S.A.* 30°14N 93°23W 314 F8
Sulphur *Okla., U.S.A.* 34°31N 96°58W 314 D6
Sulphur Pt. *Canada* 60°56N 114°48W 296 A6
Sulphur Springs *U.S.A.* 33°8N 95°36W 314 E7
Sulsul *Ethiopia* 5°5N 44°50E 267 C5
Sultan *Ont., Canada* 47°36N 82°47W 298 C3
Sultan *Wash., U.S.A.* 47°52N 121°49W 306 C5
Sultan Dağları *Turkey* 38°20N 31°20E 212 C4
Sultan Hamud *Kenya* 2°1S 37°22E 268 C4
Sultan Kudarat *Phil.* 7°16N 124°18E 233 H5
Sultan Kudarat □ *Phil.* 6°30N 124°10E 233 H5
Sultan Naga Dimaporo *Phil.* 7°55N 123°44E 233 H4
Sultan sa Barongis *Phil.* 6°45N 124°35E 233 H5
Sultanābād = Arāk *Iran* 34°0N 49°40E 247 C6
Sultanahme Camil *Turkey* 41°0N 28°58E 122 B1
Sultanhisar *Turkey* 37°53N 28°9E 205 D10
Sultaniça *Turkey* 40°37N 26°8E 203 F10
Sultaniye *Turkey* 40°11N 28°12E 203 F12
Sultanpur *Mad. P., India* 23°9N 77°56E 242 H8
Sultanpur *Punjab, India* 31°13N 75°11E 242 D6
Sultanpur *Ut. P., India* 26°18N 82°4E 243 F10
Sulu □ *Phil.* 5°30N 120°30E 233 J3
Sulu Arch. *Phil.* 6°0N 121°0E 233 J3
Sulu Sea *E. Indies* 8°0N 120°0E 233 G3
Sülüklü *Turkey* 38°53N 32°20E 212 C5
Sululta *Ethiopia* 9°10N 38°43E 257 F4
Suluova *Turkey* 40°46N 35°32E 212 B6
Sulūq *Libya* 31°44N 20°14E 258 B4
Suluru *India* 13°42N 80°1E 245 H5
Sulzbach *Germany* 49°18N 7°3E 179 F3
Sulzbach-Rosenberg *Germany* 49°30N 11°44E 179 F7
Sulzberger Ice Shelf *Antarctica* 78°0S 150°0W 151 E13
Sumaco -Napo Galeras △ *Ecuador* 0°34S 77°38W 328 D2
Sumalata *Indonesia* 1°0N 122°31E 231 D6
Sumale □ *Ethiopia* 7°0N 45°0E 267 C6
Sumampa *Argentina* 29°25S 63°29W 334 B3
Sumapaz △ *Colombia* 3°49N 74°13W 328 C3
Sumaré *Brazil* 22°48S 47°17W 333 F2
Sumatera *Indonesia* 0°40N 100°20E 234 B2
Sumatera Barat □ *Indonesia* 1°0S 101°0E 234 B1
Sumatera Selatan □ *Indonesia* 3°0S 104°0E 234 C2
Sumatera Utara □ *Indonesia* 2°30N 98°0E 234 B1
Sumatra = Sumatera *Indonesia* 0°40N 100°20E 234 B2
Sumatra *U.S.A.* 30°1N 84°59W 316 E5
Sumava △ *Czech Rep.* 49°0N 13°49E 180 C6
Sumba *Angola* 6°15S 12°38E 265 D2
Sumba *Indonesia* 9°45S 119°35E 231 F5
Sumba, Selat *Indonesia* 9°0S 118°40E 231 F5
Sumbawa *Indonesia* 8°26S 117°30E 235 D5
Sumbawa Besar *Indonesia* 8°30S 117°26E 235 D5
Sumbe *Angola* 11°10S 13°48E 265 E2
Sumbu △ *Zambia* 8°43S 30°22E 269 D3
Sumburgh Hd. *U.K.* 59°52N 1°17W 167 B7
Sumdeo *India* 31°26N 78°44E 243 D8
Sumdo *China* 35°6N 78°41E 243 B8
Sumé *Brazil* 7°39S 36°55W 332 C4
Sumedang *Indonesia* 6°52S 107°55E 235 D3
Sümeg *Hungary* 46°59N 17°20E 182 D2
Sumeih *Sudan* 9°50N 27°39E 257 F2
Šumen = Shumen *Bulgaria* 43°18N 26°55E 203 C10
Sumenep *Indonesia* 7°1S 113°52E 235 D4
Sumgait = Sumqayıt *Azerbaijan* 40°34N 49°38E 191 K9
Sumida *Japan* 35°42N 139°49E 140 A3
Sumida → *Japan* 35°39N 139°45E 140 A3
Sumisu-Jima *Japan* 31°27N 140°3E 223 F12
Sumiyoshi *Japan* 34°36N 135°30E 133 B2
Sumiyoshi Shrine *Japan* 34°36N 135°30E 133 B1
Summer L. *U.S.A.* 42°50N 120°45W 304 E3
Summerland *Canada* 49°32N 119°41W 296 D5
Summerland Key *U.S.A.* 24°40N 81°27W 317 L8
Summerside *Canada* 46°24N 63°47W 299 C7
Summersville *U.S.A.* 38°17N 80°51W 309 F13
Summerton *U.S.A.* 33°36N 80°20W 316 B9
Summertown *U.S.A.* 32°45N 82°16W 316 C7
Summerville *Ont., Canada* 43°37N 79°33W 141 B1
Summerville *Ga., U.S.A.* 34°29N 85°21W 315 D12
Summerville *S.C., U.S.A.* 33°1N 80°11W 316 B9
Summit *Alaska, U.S.A.* 63°20N 149°7W 303 E10
Summit *Ill., U.S.A.* 41°47N 87°47W 119 C2
Summit Lake *Canada* 54°20N 122°40W 296 C4
Summit Peak *U.S.A.* 37°21N 106°42W 305 H10
Sumner *N.Z.* 43°35S 172°48E 285 D7
Sumner *Ill., U.S.A.* 38°42N 87°53W 311 F9
Sumner *Iowa, U.S.A.* 42°51N 92°6W 310 B4
Sumner *Wash., U.S.A.* 47°12N 122°14W 306 C4
Sumner, L. *N.Z.* 42°42S 172°15E 285 C7
Sumner Tunnel *Boston, U.S.A.* 116 a3
Sumoto *Japan* 34°21N 134°54E 222 C6
Sumpangbinangae *Indonesia* 4°24S 119°36E 235 C5
Šumperk *Czech Rep.* 49°59N 16°59E 181 B9
Sumprabum *Burma* 26°33N 97°36E 241 B6
Sumqayıt *Azerbaijan* 40°34N 49°38E 191 K9
Sumter *U.S.A.* 33°55N 80°21W 316 B9
Sumxi *China* 34°35N 80°22E 217 F10
Sumy *Ukraine* 50°57N 34°50E 189 G8
Sumy □ *Ukraine* 50°50N 33°50E 189 G7
Sun City *North West, S. Africa* 25°17S 27°3E 270 C4
Sun City *Ariz., U.S.A.* 33°35N 112°16W 305 K7
Sun City *Calif., U.S.A.* 33°42N 117°11W 307 M9
Sun City Center *U.S.A.* 27°43N 82°21W 317 H7
Sun Lakes *U.S.A.* 33°10N 111°52W 305 K8
Sun Prairie *U.S.A.* 43°11N 89°13W 310 A7
Sun Valley *U.S.A.* 43°42N 114°21W 304 E6
Sunagawa *Japan* 43°29N 141°55E 220 C10
Sunamachi *Japan* 35°40N 139°50E 140 A4
Sunan *N. Korea* 39°15N 125°40E 224 C2
Sunart, L. *U.K.* 56°42N 5°43W 167 E3
Sunburst *U.S.A.* 48°53N 111°55W 304 B8
Sunbury *Vic., Australia* 37°35S 144°44E 283 D6
Sunbury *Pa., U.S.A.* 40°52N 76°48W 313 F8
Sunbury-on-Thames *U.K.* 51°25N 0°26W 125 B1
Sunchales *Argentina* 30°58S 61°35W 334 C3
Suncheon *S. Korea* 34°52N 127°31E 224 E3
Suncho Corral *Argentina* 27°55S 63°27W 334 B3
Sunch'on *N. Korea* 39°25N 125°56E 224 C2
Suncook *U.S.A.* 43°8N 71°27W 313 C13
Sunda, Selat *Indonesia* 6°20S 105°30E 234 D3
Sunda Is. *Indonesia* 5°0S 105°0E 288 H2
Sunda Str. = Sunda, Selat *Indonesia* 6°20S 105°30E 234 D3
Sunda Trench = Java Trench *Ind. Oc.* 9°0S 105°0E 234 D2
Sundance *Man., Canada* 56°32N 94°4W 297 B10
Sundance *Wyo., U.S.A.* 44°24N 104°23W 304 D11
Sundar Nagar *India* 31°32N 76°53E 242 D7
Sundarbans *Asia* 22°0N 89°0E 241 E2
Sundarbans △ *India* 22°0N 88°45E 241 E2
Sundargarh *India* 22°4N 84°5E 244 C7
Sundays = Sondags → *S. Africa* 33°44S 25°51E 270 D4
Sundbyberg *Sweden* 59°22N 17°57E 139 A1
Sundbyerne *Denmark* 55°39N 12°36E 118 B3
Sunderland *Ont., Canada* 44°16N 79°4W 312 B5
Sunderland *Tyne & W., U.K.* 54°55N 1°23W 168 C6
Sundi Lutete *Dem. Rep. of the Congo* 4°34S 14°14E 265 C2
Sundown △ *Australia* 28°49S 151°38E 281 D5
Sundre *Canada* 51°49N 114°38W 296 C6
Sunds *Denmark* 56°13N 9°1E 163 H3
Sundsvall *Sweden* 62°23N 17°17E 162 B11
Sundsvallsbukten *Sweden* 62°21N 17°25E 162 B11
Sung Kong *China* 22°11N 114°17E 122 B2
Sungai Acheh *Malaysia* 5°8N 100°30E 237 c
Sungai Kolok *Thailand* 6°2N 101°58E 237 J3
Sungai Lembing *Malaysia* 3°55N 103°3E 237 L4
Sungai Petani *Malaysia* 5°37N 100°30E 237 K3
Sungai Siput *Malaysia* 4°49N 101°4E 234 B2
Sungaidurian *Indonesia* 0°6S 109°21E 235 C3
Sungaigerong *Indonesia* 2°59S 104°52E 234 C2
Sungailiat *Indonesia* 1°51S 106°8E 234 C3
Sungaipakning *Indonesia* 1°19N 102°8E 234 B2
Sungaipenuh *Indonesia* 2°1S 101°20E 234 C2
Sungari = Songhua Jiang → *China* 47°45N 132°30E 219 B15
Sungei Kadut Industrial Estate *Singapore* 1°24N 103°44E 138 A2
Sungei Selatar Res. *Singapore* 1°24N 103°51E 138 A3
Sungguminasa *Indonesia* 5°17S 119°30E 235 D5
Sunghua Chiang = Songhua Jiang → *China* 47°45N 132°30E 219 B15
Sungikai *Sudan* 12°20N 29°51E 257 E2
Sungsang *Indonesia* 2°22S 104°55E 234 C2
Sungu *Dem. Rep. of the Congo* 1°5S 17°21E 264 C3
Sungurlu *Turkey* 40°12N 34°21E 212 B6
Sunja *Croatia* 45°21N 16°35E 199 C13
Sunland Park *U.S.A.* 31°50N 106°40W 305 L10
Sunnansjö *Sweden* 60°13N 14°58E 162 D8
Sunndalsøra *Norway* 62°40N 8°33E 164 B5
Sunne *Sweden* 59°52N 13°5E 162 E7
Sunnemo *Sweden* 59°53N 13°44E 162 E7
Sunnfjord *Norway* 61°35N 5°45E 164 C2
Sunnmøre *Norway* 62°35N 6°30E 164 B3
Sunnyside *U.S.A.* 46°20N 120°0W 304 C4
Sunnyvale *U.S.A.* 37°23N 122°2W 306 H4
Sunrise *U.S.A.* 26°8N 80°14W 317 J9
Sunrise Manor *U.S.A.* 36°12N 115°4W 124 A2
Sunrise Mountain Natural Area *U.S.A.* 36°12N 114°58W 124 A2
Sunset Beach *U.S.A.* 21°40N 158°3W 302 J13
Sunset Park *N.Y., U.S.A.* 40°38N 73°59W 132 C2
Sunset Park *Nev., U.S.A.* 36°3N 115°6W 124 B2
Sunshine Coast *Australia* 26°30S 153°0E 276 F9
Suntar *Russia* 62°15N 117°30E 215 C12
Sunter *Indonesia* 6°7S 106°51E 122 A2
Sunter, Kali → *Indonesia* 6°10S 106°53E 122 B2
Suntrana *U.S.A.* 63°52N 148°51W 303 E10
Sunwi-do *N. Korea* 37°43N 125°16E 224 D2
Sunyani *Ghana* 7°21N 2°22W 262 D4
Suō-Nada *Japan* 33°50N 131°30E 222 D3
Suomenlinna *Finland* 60°9N 24°59E 121 C2
Suomenselkä *Finland* 62°52N 24°0E 160 E21
Suomi = Finland ■ *Europe* 63°0N 27°0E 160 E22
Suomussalmi *Finland* 64°54N 29°10E 160 D23
Suoyarvi *Russia* 62°3N 32°20E 188 A7
Supai *U.S.A.* 36°15N 112°41W 305 H7
Supamo → *Venezuela* 6°48N 61°50W 329 B5
Supaul *India* 26°10N 86°40E 243 F12
Superagüi △ *Brazil* 25°6S 48°18W 333 G2
Superior *Ariz., U.S.A.* 33°18N 111°6W 305 K8
Superior *Mont., U.S.A.* 47°12N 114°53W 304 C6
Superior *Nebr., U.S.A.* 40°1N 98°4W 308 E4
Superior *Wis., U.S.A.* 46°44N 92°6W 308 B7
Superior, L. *N. Amer.* 47°0N 87°0W 298 C2
Supetar *Croatia* 43°25N 16°32E 199 E13
Suphan Buri *Thailand* 14°14N 100°10E 236 E3
Suphan Dağı *Turkey* 38°54N 42°48E 213 C10
Supiori *Indonesia* 1°0S 136°0E 231 E9
Supraśl *Poland* 53°13N 23°19E 185 E10
Supraśl → *Poland* 53°11N 22°57E 185 E9
Supreme Court *Washington, D.C., U.S.A.* 143 b3
Supung *N. Korea* 40°27N 124°54E 224 B2
Supung Shuiku *China* 40°35N 124°50E 224 B2
Sūq' Abs *Yemen* 16°0N 43°12E 248 D3
Sūq ash Shuyūkh *Iraq* 30°53N 46°28E 246 D5
Sūq Suwayq *Si. Arabia* 24°23N 38°27E 246 E3
Şuqaylabīyah *Syria* 35°23N 36°23E 250 C7
Suqian *China* 33°54N 118°8E 227 H10
Suquṭra = Socotra *Yemen* 12°30N 54°0E 249 D6
Sūr *Lebanon* 33°19N 35°16E 250 E6
Şūr *Oman* 22°34N 59°32E 249 B7
Sur, C. *Chile* 27°12S 109°26W 330 b
Sur, Pt. *U.S.A.* 36°18N 121°54W 306 J5
Sur Bahr *West Bank* 31°44N 35°13E 123 B2
Sura *India* 22°33N 88°24E 124 B2
Sura → *Russia* 56°6N 46°0E 190 C8
Surab *Pakistan* 28°25N 66°15E 242 E2
Surabaja = Surabaya *Indonesia* 7°17S 112°45E 235 D4
Surabaya *Indonesia* 7°17S 112°45E 235 D4
Surahammar *Sweden* 59°43N 16°13E 162 E10
Suraia *Romania* 45°40N 27°25E 183 E12
Surakarta *Indonesia* 7°35S 110°48E 235 D4
Suraksan *S. Korea* 37°40N 127°4E 137 A2
Surallah *Phil.* 6°22N 124°44E 233 H5
Šurany *Slovak Rep.* 48°6N 18°10E 181 C11
Surat *Queens., Australia* 27°10S 149°6E 281 D4
Surat *India* 21°12N 72°55E 244 D1
Surat Thani *Thailand* 9°6N 99°20E 237 H2
Suratgarh *India* 29°18N 73°55E 242 E5
Surathkal *India* 12°58N 74°46E 245 H2
Suraxanı *Azerbaijan* 40°25N 50°1E 191 K10
Şuraymilā *Si. Arabia* 25°7N 46°7E 246 E5
Suraż *Poland* 52°57N 22°57E 185 F9
Surazh *Belarus* 55°25N 30°44E 188 E6
Surazh *Russia* 53°5N 32°27E 189 F7
Surbiton *U.K.* 51°23N 0°17W 125 B2
Surduc *Romania* 47°15N 23°25E 183 C8
Surduc Pasul *Romania* 45°21N 23°23E 183 E8
Surdulica *Serbia* 42°41N 22°11E 202 D6
Surendranagar *India* 22°45N 71°40E 242 H4
Suresnes *France* 48°52N 2°13E 134 A2
Surf *U.S.A.* 34°41N 120°36W 307 L6
Surfers Paradise *Australia* 28°0S 153°25E 281 D5
Surfside *U.S.A.* 25°52N 80°7W 128 A2
Surgana *India* 20°34N 73°37E 244 D1
Surgères *France* 46°7N 0°47W 174 B3
Surgut *Russia* 61°14N 73°20E 214 C8
Sùria *Spain* 41°50N 1°45E 196 D6
Suriapet *India* 17°10N 79°40E 244 F4
Suribachi Yama *Iwo Jima* 24°45N 141°17E 288 b
Surigao *Phil.* 9°47N 125°29E 233 G5
Surigao del Norte □ *Phil.* 9°40N 125°40E 233 G5
Surigao del Sur □ *Phil.* 8°45N 126°0E 233 G6
Surigao Str. *Phil.* 10°15N 125°23E 233 F5
Surin *Thailand* 14°50N 103°34E 236 E4
Surinam = Suriname ■ *S. Amer.* 4°0N 56°0W 329 C6
Surinam *Mauritius* 20°30S 57°30E 272 e
Suriname ■ *S. Amer.* 4°0N 56°0W 329 C6
Suriname → *Suriname* 5°50N 55°15W 329 B6
Surjagarh *India* 19°36N 80°25E 244 E5
Surma → *Bangla.* 24°34N 91°14E 241 C3
Sūrmaq *Iran* 31°3N 52°48E 247 D7
Sürmene *Turkey* 41°0N 40°1E 213 B9
Surna → *Norway* 62°59N 8°40E 164 B5
Surnadalsøra *Norway* 62°58N 8°40E 164 B5
Surovikino *Russia* 48°32N 42°55E 191 F6
Surquillo *Peru* 12°6S 77°1W 124 B2
Surrency *U.S.A.* 31°44N 82°12W 316 D7
Surrey *Canada* 49°7N 122°45W 306 A4
Surrey □ *Jamaica* 18°5N 76°34W 320 a
Surrey □ *U.K.* 51°15N 0°31W 169 F7
Surrey Hills *Australia* 33°53S 151°13E 139 B2
Sursand *India* 26°39N 85°43E 243 F11
Sursar → *India* 26°14N 87°3E 243 F12
Sursee *Switz.* 47°11N 8°6E 179 H4
Sursk *Russia* 53°3N 45°40E 190 D7
Surskoye *Russia* 54°30N 46°44E 190 C8
Surt *Libya* 31°11N 16°39E 258 B3
Surt □ *Libya* 30°0N 17°30E 258 B3
Surt, Al Ḩamādah al *Libya* 30°0N 17°50E 258 C3
Surt, Khalīj *Libya* 31°40N 18°30E 258 B3
Surtanahu *Pakistan* 26°22N 70°0E 242 F4
Surte *Sweden* 57°50N 12°1E 163 G6
Surtsey *Iceland* 63°20N 20°30W 155 D6
Surubim *Brazil* 7°50S 35°45W 332 C4
Sürüç *Turkey* 36°58N 38°25E 213 D8
Surud, Ras *Somali Rep.* 11°10N 47°30E 267 B6
Surud Ad *Somali Rep.* 10°42N 47°9E 267 B6
Suruga-Wan *Japan* 34°45N 138°30E 223 C10
Surulangun *Indonesia* 2°37S 102°45E 234 C2
Surumu → *Brazil* 3°22N 60°19W 329 C5
Surxondaryo □ *Uzbekistan* 38°0N 67°30E 217 E7
Susa = Sousse *Tunisia* 35°50N 10°38E 258 A2
Susa *Italy* 45°8N 7°3E 198 C4
Suså → *Denmark* 55°12N 11°42E 163 J5
Sušac *Croatia* 42°46N 16°30E 199 F13
Susaek *S. Korea* 37°34N 126°54E 137 B1
Susak *Croatia* 44°30N 14°18E 199 D11
Susaki *Japan* 33°22N 133°17E 222 D5
Susam-Adasi = Samos *Greece* 37°45N 26°50E 205 D8
Sūsangerd *Iran* 31°35N 48°6E 213 G13
Susanville *U.S.A.* 40°25N 120°39W 304 F3
Susch *Switz.* 46°46N 10°5E 179 J6
Suşehri *Turkey* 40°10N 38°6E 213 B8
Sušice *Czech Rep.* 49°17N 13°30E 180 B6
Susleni *Moldova* 47°25N 28°59E 183 C13
Susner *India* 23°57N 76°5E 242 H7
Susong *China* 30°10N 116°5E 229 B11
Susono *Japan* 35°10N 138°55E 223 B10
Susquehanna *U.S.A.* 41°57N 75°36W 313 E9
Susquehanna → *U.S.A.* 39°33N 76°5W 313 G8
Susques *Argentina* 23°35S 66°25W 334 A2
Süssenbrunn *Austria* 48°16N 16°29E 142 A2
Sussex *N.B., Canada* 45°45N 65°37W 299 C6
Sussex *N.J., U.S.A.* 41°13N 74°37W 313 E10
Sussex, E. □ *U.K.* 51°0N 0°20E 169 G8
Sussex, W. □ *U.K.* 51°0N 0°30W 169 G7
Sussex Inlet *Australia* 35°10S 150°36E 283 C9
Sustut → *Canada* 56°20N 127°30W 296 B3
Susuman *Russia* 62°47N 148°10E 215 C15
Susunu *Indonesia* 3°7S 133°39E 231 E8
Susurluk *Turkey* 39°54N 28°8E 205 B10
Susuz *Turkey* 40°46N 43°8E 213 B10
Susz *Poland* 53°44N 19°20E 184 E6
Sutay Uul *Asia* 46°35N 93°38E 218 B7
Sütçüler *Turkey* 37°29N 30°57E 212 D4
Şuteşti *Romania* 45°13N 27°27E 183 E12
Sutherland *N.S.W., Australia* 34°2S 151°4E 283 C9
Sutherland *Northern Cape, S. Africa* 32°24S 20°40E 270 D3
Sutherland *Highl., U.K.* 58°12N 4°50W 167 C4
Sutherland *Nebr., U.S.A.* 41°10N 101°8W 308 E3
Sutherland Falls *N.Z.* 44°48S 167°46E 285 E2
Sutherland Road *Barbados* 13°16N 59°39W 323 r
Sutherlin *U.S.A.* 43°23N 123°19W 304 E2
Suthri *India* 23°3N 68°55E 242 H3
Sutjeska △ *Bos.-H.* 43°50N 18°32E 182 G3
Sutlej → *Pakistan* 29°23N 71°3E 242 E4
Sutter *U.S.A.* 39°10N 121°45W 306 F5
Sutter Buttes *U.S.A.* 39°12N 121°49W 306 F5
Sutter Creek *U.S.A.* 38°24N 120°48W 306 G6
Sutton *Qué., Canada* 45°6N 72°37W 313 A12
Sutton *Dublin, Ireland* 53°23N 6°7W 120 A3
Sutton *N.Z.* 45°34S 170°8E 285 F5
Sutton *London, U.K.* 51°21N 0°11W 125 B2
Sutton *Nebr., U.S.A.* 40°36N 97°52W 308 E5
Sutton *W. Va., U.S.A.* 38°40N 80°43W 309 F13
Sutton → *Canada* 55°15N 83°45W 298 A3
Sutton Coldfield *U.K.* 52°35N 1°49W 169 E6
Sutton in Ashfield *U.K.* 53°8N 1°16W 168 D6
Sutton L. *Canada* 54°15N 84°42W 298 B3
Suttor → *Australia* 21°36S 147°2E 280 C4
Suttsu *Japan* 42°48N 140°14E 220 C10
Sutwik I. *U.S.A.* 56°34N 157°12W 303 H8
Suva *Fiji* 18°6S 178°30E 287 B2
Suva Gora *Macedonia* 41°45N 21°3E 202 E5
Suva Planina *Serbia* 43°10N 22°5E 202 C6
Suva Reka *Kosovo* 42°21N 20°50E 202 D4
Suvorov *Russia* 54°7N 36°30E 188 E9
Suvorov Is. = Suwarrow Is. *Cook Is.* 13°15S 163°5W 289 J11
Suvorove *Ukraine* 45°35N 28°59E 183 E13
Suvorovo *Bulgaria* 43°20N 27°35E 203 C11
Suwa *Japan* 36°2N 138°8E 223 A10
Suwa-Ko *Japan* 36°3N 138°5E 223 A10
Suwałki *Poland* 54°8N 22°59E 184 D9
Suwanee *U.S.A.* 34°3N 84°4W 316 A5
Suwannaphum *Thailand* 15°33N 103°47E 236 E4
Suwannee *U.S.A.* 29°20N 83°9W 317 F6
Suwannee → *U.S.A.* 29°17N 83°10W 317 F6
Suwannee Sd. *U.S.A.* 29°20N 83°15W 317 F6
Suwanose-Jima *Japan* 29°38N 129°43E 221 K4
Suwarrow Is. *Cook Is.* 13°15S 163°5W 289 J11
Suwayqīyah, Hawr as *Iraq* 32°40N 46°3E 213 G12
Suweis, Khalîg el *Egypt* 28°40N 33°0E 256 J8
Suweis, Qanâ es *Egypt* 31°0N 32°20E 256 H8
Suwon *S. Korea* 37°17N 127°1E 224 D3
Suyu *S. Korea* 37°37N 127°0E 137 B2
Suzaka *Japan* 36°39N 138°19E 223 A10
Suzdal *Russia* 56°29N 40°26E 188 D11
Suzhou *Anhui, China* 33°41N 116°59E 226 H9
Suzhou *Jiangsu, China* 31°19N 120°38E 229 B13
Suzu *Japan* 37°25N 137°17E 221 F8
Suzu-Misaki *Japan* 37°31N 137°21E 221 F8
Suzuka *Japan* 34°55N 136°36E 223 C8
Suzuka-Sammyaku *Japan* 35°5N 136°30E 223 B8
Suzukishinden *Japan* 35°43N 139°31E 140 A2
Suzun *Russia* 53°47N 82°18E 217 B10
Suzzara *Italy* 44°59N 10°45E 198 D7
Svalbard *Arctic* 78°0N 17°0E 154 B12
Svalbard Radio = Longyearbyen *Svalbard* 78°13N 15°40E 150 B8
Svalbarð *Iceland* 66°12N 15°43W 155 A11
Svalbarðseyri *Iceland* 65°45N 18°5W 155 B8
Svalöv *Sweden* 55°57N 13°8E 163 J7
Svalyava *Ukraine* 48°33N 22°59E 182 B7
Svaneke *Denmark* 55°8N 15°8E 163 J9
Svanemøllen *Denmark* 55°43N 12°34E 118 A3
Svängsta *Sweden* 56°16N 14°47E 163 H8
Svanskog *Sweden* 59°11N 12°33E 162 E6
Svappavaara *Sweden* 67°40N 21°3E 160 C19
Svärdsjö *Sweden* 60°45N 15°54E 162 D9
Svarstad *Norway* 59°27N 9°56E 164 E6
Svartå *Sweden* 59°8N 14°32E 162 E8
Svartárkot *Iceland* 65°20N 17°15W 155 B9
Svartevatn *Norway* 59°10N 6°56E 164 E3
Svartisen *Norway* 66°40N 13°59E 160 C15
Svartvik *Sweden* 62°19N 17°24E 162 B11
Svatove *Ukraine* 49°22N 38°15E 189 H10
Svatovo = Svatove *Ukraine* 49°22N 38°15E 189 H10
Svatsum *Norway* 61°20N 9°50E 164 C6
Svay Chek *Cambodia* 13°48N 102°58E 236 F4
Svay Rieng *Cambodia* 11°9N 105°45E 237 G5
Sveaborg = Suomenlinna *Finland* 60°9N 24°59E 121 C2
Svealand *Sweden* 60°20N 15°0E 162 D9
Svedala *Sweden* 55°30N 13°15E 163 J7
Sveg *Sweden* 62°2N 14°21E 162 B8
Sveindal *Norway* 58°29N 7°30E 164 F4
Sveinseyri *Iceland* 65°38N 23°51W 155 B3
Sveio *Norway* 59°33N 5°23E 164 E2
Svelgen *Norway* 61°46N 5°17E 164 C2
Svelvik *Norway* 59°37N 10°24E 164 E7
Svendborg *Denmark* 55°4N 10°35E 163 J4
Svene *Norway* 59°45N 9°31E 164 E6
Svenljunga *Sweden* 57°29N 13°5E 163 G7
Svenstavik *Sweden* 62°45N 14°26E 162 B8
Svenstrup *Denmark* 56°58N 9°50E 163 H3
Svenyhorodka *Ukraine* 49°4N 30°56E 189 H6
Sverdlov *Russia* 55°46N 37°36E 129 B3
Sverdlovsk = Yekaterinburg *Russia* 56°50N 60°30E 214 D7
Sverdlovsk *Ukraine* 48°5N 39°47E 189 H10
Sverdrup Chan. *Canada* 79°56N 96°25W 295 B12
Sverdrup Is. *Canada* 79°0N 97°0W 292 B10
Sverige = Sweden ■ *Europe* 57°0N 15°0E 161 H16
Svestad *Norway* 59°46N 10°36E 133 B2
Svetac *Croatia* 43°3N 15°43E 199 E12
Sveti Ivan = Zelina *Croatia* 45°57N 16°16E 199 C13
Sveti Nikola, Prokhad *Europe* 43°27N 22°6E 202 C6
Sveti Nikole *Macedonia* 41°51N 21°56E 202 E5
Sveti Rok *Croatia* 44°22N 15°39E 199 D12
Sveti Vrach = Sandanski *Bulgaria* 41°35N 23°16E 202 E7
Svetlaya *Russia* 46°33N 138°18E 220 A9
Svetlogorsk = Svyetlahorsk *Belarus* 52°38N 29°46E 177 B15
Svetlogorsk *Russia* 54°56N 20°10E 184 D7
Svetlograd *Russia* 45°25N 42°58E 191 H6
Svetlovodsk = Svitlovodsk *Ukraine* 49°2N 33°13E 189 H7
Svetlyy *Kaliningrad, Russia* 54°41N 20°8E 184 D7
Svetlyy *Orenburg, Russia* 50°48N 60°51E 216 B6
Svidník *Slovak Rep.* 49°20N 21°37E 181 B14
Svignaskarð *Iceland* 64°40N 21°42W 155 C5
Svilaja Planina *Croatia* 43°49N 16°31E 199 E13
Svilajnac *Serbia* 44°15N 21°11E 202 B5
Svilengrad *Bulgaria* 41°49N 26°12E 203 E10
Svinafell *Iceland* 63°59N 16°51W 155 D10
Svinö *Finland* 60°7N 24°44E 121 C1
Svir → *Russia* 60°30N 32°48E 188 B7
Sviritsa *Russia* 60°29N 32°51E 188 B7
Svishtov *Bulgaria* 43°36N 25°23E 203 C9
Svislach *Belarus* 53°3N 24°2E 185 E11
Svitava → *Czech Rep.* 49°11N 16°37E 181 B9
Svitavy *Czech Rep.* 49°47N 16°28E 181 B9
Svitlovodsk *Ukraine* 49°2N 33°13E 189 H7
Svizzera = Switzerland ■ *Europe* 46°30N 8°0E 179 J4
Svobodnyy *Russia* 51°20N 128°0E 215 D13
Svoge *Bulgaria* 42°59N 23°23E 202 D7
Svolvær *Norway* 68°15N 14°34E 160 B16
Svorkmo *Norway* 63°10N 9°46E 164 A6
Svoronata *Greece* 38°7N 20°31E 207 C2
Svratka → *Czech Rep.* 49°11N 16°38E 181 B9
Svrljig *Serbia* 43°25N 22°6E 202 C6
Svullrya *Norway* 60°25N 12°23E 164 D9
Svyatogorovsky Rudnik = Dobropole *Ukraine* 48°25N 37°2E 189 H9
Svyetlahorsk *Belarus* 52°38N 29°46E 177 B15
Swa *Burma* 19°15N 96°17E 241 F6
Swa Tende *Dem. Rep. of the Congo* 7°9S 17°7E 265 D3
Swabian Alps = Schwäbische Alb *Germany* 48°20N 9°30E 179 G5
Swaffham *U.K.* 52°39N 0°42E 169 E8
Swains I. *Amer. Samoa* 11°11S 171°4W 289 J11
Swainsboro *U.S.A.* 32°36N 82°20W 316 C7
Swakop → *Namibia* 22°38S 14°36E 270 B2
Swakopmund *Namibia* 22°37S 14°30E 270 B1
Swale → *U.K.* 54°5N 1°20W 168 C6
Swamihalli *India* 14°52N 76°38E 245 G3
Swan → *W. Austral., Australia* 32°3S 115°45E 279 F2
Swan → *Man., Canada* 52°30N 100°45W 297 C8
Swan Hill *Australia* 35°20S 143°33E 282 C5
Swan Hills *Canada* 54°43N 115°24W 296 C5
Swan Is. = Santanilla, Is. *Honduras* 17°22N 83°57W 320 C3
Swan L. *Man., Canada* 52°30N 100°40W 297 C8
Swan L. *Ont., Canada* 54°16N 91°11W 298 B1
Swan Ra. *U.S.A.* 48°0N 113°45W 304 C7
Swan Reach *Australia* 34°35S 139°37E 282 C3
Swan River *Canada* 52°10N 101°16W 297 C8
Swanage *U.K.* 50°36N 1°58W 169 G6
Swanley *U.K.* 51°23N 0°11E 125 B4
Swansea *N.S.W., Australia* 33°3S 151°35E 283 B9
Swansea *Tas., Australia* 42°8S 148°4E 281 G4
Swansea *Ont., Canada* 43°38N 79°28W 141 B2
Swansea *Swansea, U.K.* 51°37N 3°57W 169 F4
Swansea *S.C., U.S.A.* 33°44N 81°6W 316 B8
Swansea □ *U.K.* 51°38N 4°3W 169 F3
Swanton *U.S.A.* 41°35N 83°53W 311 C13
Swartberge *S. Africa* 33°20S 22°0E 270 D3
Swartmodder *S. Africa* 28°1S 20°32E 270 C3
Swartnossob → *Namibia* 23°8S 18°42E 270 B2
Swartruggens *S. Africa* 25°39S 26°42E 270 C4
Swarzędz *Poland* 52°25N 17°4E 185 F4
Swastika *Canada* 48°7N 80°6W 298 C3
Swat → *Pakistan* 34°40N 72°5E 243 B5
Swatow = Shantou *China* 23°18N 116°40E 229 F11
Swaziland ■ *Africa* 26°30S 31°30E 271 C5
Sweden ■ *Europe* 57°0N 15°0E 161 H16
Swedru *Ghana* 5°32N 0°41W 263 D4
Sweet Grass *U.S.A.* 48°59N 111°58W 304 B8
Sweet Home *U.S.A.* 44°24N 122°44W 304 D2
Sweet Springs *U.S.A.* 38°58N 93°25W 310 F3
Sweetwater *Nev., U.S.A.* 38°27N 119°9W 306 G7
Sweetwater *Tenn., U.S.A.* 35°36N 84°28W 315 D12
Sweetwater *Tex., U.S.A.* 32°28N 100°25W 314 E4
Sweetwater → *U.S.A.* 42°31N 107°2W 304 E10
Swellendam *S. Africa* 34°1S 20°26E 270 D3
Swider → *Poland* 52°6N 21°14E 185 F8
Świdnica *Poland* 50°50N 16°30E 185 H3
Świdnik *Poland* 51°13N 22°39E 185 G9
Świdwin *Poland* 53°47N 15°49E 184 E2
Świebodzice *Poland* 50°51N 16°20E 185 H3
Świebodzin *Poland* 52°15N 15°31E 185 F2
Świecie *Poland* 53°25N 18°30E 184 E5
Swierzawa *Poland* 51°1N 15°54E 185 G2
Świętokrzyski △ *Poland* 50°53N 20°59E 185 H7
Świętokrzyskie □ *Poland* 50°45N 20°45E 185 H7
Świętokrzyskie, Góry *Poland* 51°0N 20°30E 185 H7
Swift Current *Canada* 50°20N 107°45W 297 C7
Swift Current → *Canada* 50°38N 107°44W 297 C7
Swifts Creek *Australia* 37°17S 147°44E 283 D7
Swilly, L. *Ireland* 55°12N 7°33W 166 A4
Swinburne I. *U.S.A.* 40°33N 74°3W 132 C1
Swindon *U.K.* 51°34N 1°46W 169 F6
Swindon □ *U.K.* 51°34N 1°46W 169 F6
Swinemünde = Świnoujście *Poland* 53°54N 14°16E 184 E1
Swinford *Ireland* 53°57N 8°58W 166 C3
Świnoujście *Poland* 53°54N 14°16E 184 E1
Switzerland ■ *Europe* 46°30N 8°0E 179 J4
Swords *Ireland* 53°28N 6°13W 120 A2
Swoyerville *U.S.A.* 41°18N 75°53W 313 E9
Syasstroy *Russia* 60°9N 32°33E 188 B7
Sycamore *Ill., U.S.A.* 41°59N 88°41W 311 C8
Sycamore *Ohio, U.S.A.* 40°57N 83°10W 311 D13
Sychevka *Russia* 55°59N 34°16E 188 E8
Syców *Poland* 51°19N 17°40E 185 G4
Syddanmark □ *Denmark* 55°30N 9°0E 163 J2
Sydenham *S. Africa* 26°9S 28°5E 123 A2
Sydenham → *Canada* 42°33N 82°25W 312 D2
Sydney *N.S.W., Australia* 33°52S 151°12E 139 B2
Sydney *N.S., Canada* 46°7N 60°7W 299 C7
Sydney, Univ. of *Australia* 33°54S 151°11E 139 B2
Sydney Harbour △ *Australia* 33°50S 151°14E 139 B2
Sydney Harbour Bridge *Australia* 33°51S 151°12E 139 B2
Sydney Kingsford Smith ✈ (SYD) *Australia* 33°57S 151°11E 139 B2
Sydney L. *Canada* 50°41N 94°25W 297 C10
Sydney Mines *Canada* 46°18N 60°15W 299 C7
Sydney Opera House *Sydney, Australia* 139 a2
Sydprøven = Alluitsup Paa *Greenland* 60°30N 45°35W 154 E6
Sydra, G. of = Surt, Khalīj *Libya* 31°40N 18°30E 258 B3
Sydstranden *Denmark* 55°34N 12°38E 118 B3
Syeverodonetsk *Ukraine* 48°58N 38°35E 189 H10
Syfteland *Norway* 60°14N 5°27E 164 D2
Syke *Germany* 52°55N 8°50E 178 C4
Sykesville *U.S.A.* 41°3N 78°50W 312 E6
Sykkylven *Norway* 62°23N 6°35E 164 B3
Syktyvkar *Russia* 61°45N 50°40E 186 B9
Sylacauga *U.S.A.* 33°10N 86°15W 316 B3
Sylarna *Sweden* 63°2N 12°13E 164 A9
Sylhet *Bangla.* 24°54N 91°52E 241 C3
Sylhet □ *Bangla.* 24°50N 91°50E 241 C3
Sylt *Germany* 54°54N 8°22E 178 A4
Sylte *Norway* 62°18N 7°17E 164 B4
Sylvan Beach *U.S.A.* 43°12N 75°44W 313 C9
Sylvan Lake *Canada* 52°20N 114°3W 296 C6
Sylvania *N.S.W., Australia* 34°0S 151°7E 139 C1
Sylvania *Ga., U.S.A.* 32°45N 81°38W 316 C8
Sylvania *Ohio, U.S.A.* 41°43N 83°42W 311 C13
Sylvester *U.S.A.* 31°32N 83°50W 316 D6
Sym *Russia* 60°20N 88°18E 214 C9
Symphony Hall *San Francisco, U.S.A.* 136 c1
Synelnykove *Ukraine* 48°25N 35°30E 189 H8
Synevyr △ *Ukraine* 48°30N 23°40E 183 B8
Synevyrska Polyana *Ukraine* 48°35N 23°41E 183 B8
Synnervika *Norway* 62°25N 11°54E 164 B8
Synnfjell *Norway* 61°5N 9°46E 164 C6
Synnot Ra. *Australia* 16°30S 125°20E 278 C4
Syntagma Square *Athens, Greece* 112 b2
Synyak *Ukraine* 48°35N 22°51E 182 B7
Syon Park *U.K.* 51°28N 0°18W 125 B2
Syowa *Antarctica* 68°50S 12°0E 151 C5
Syracuse = Siracusa *Italy* 37°4N 15°17E 201 E8
Syracuse *Ind., U.S.A.* 41°26N 85°45W 311 C11
Syracuse *Kans., U.S.A.* 37°59N 101°45W 308 G3
Syracuse *N.Y., U.S.A.* 43°3N 76°9W 313 C8
Syracuse *Nebr., U.S.A.* 40°39N 96°11W 308 E5
Syrdarya → *Kazakhstan* 46°3N 61°0E 216 C6
Syria ■ *Asia* 35°0N 38°0E 213 E8
Syriam *Burma* 16°44N 96°19E 241 G6
Syrian Desert = Shām, Bādiyat ash *Asia* 32°0N 40°0E 246 C3
Syros = Ermoupoli *Greece* 37°28N 24°57E 204 D6
Sysslebäck *Sweden* 60°44N 12°52E 162 D6
Syvden *Norway* 62°5N 5°44E 164 B2
Syzran *Russia* 53°12N 48°30E 190 D9
Szabolcs-Szatmár-Bereg □ *Hungary* 48°2N 21°45E 182 B6
Szadek *Poland* 51°41N 18°59E 185 G5
Szamocin *Poland* 53°2N 17°7E 185 E4
Szamos → *Hungary* 48°7N 22°20E 182 B7
Szamotuły *Poland* 52°37N 16°33E 185 F3
Száraz → *Hungary* 46°10N 21°15E 182 D6
Szarvas *Hungary* 46°50N 20°38E 182 D5
Százhalombatta *Hungary* 47°20N 18°58E 182 C3
Szczawnica *Poland* 49°26N 20°30E 185 J7
Szczebrzeszyn *Poland* 50°42N 22°59E 185 H9
Szczecin *Poland* 53°27N 14°27E 184 E1
Szczecinek *Poland* 53°43N 16°41E 184 E3
Szczeciński, Zalew = Stettiner Haff *Germany* 53°47N 14°15E 178 B10
Szczekociny *Poland* 50°38N 19°48E 185 H6
Szczęśliwice *Poland* 52°12N 20°57E 142 B1
Szczucin *Poland* 50°18N 21°4E 185 H8
Szczuczyn *Poland* 53°36N 22°19E 184 E9
Szczyrk *Poland* 49°43N 19°2E 185 J6
Szczytna *Poland* 50°25N 16°28E 185 H3
Szczytno *Poland* 53°33N 21°0E 184 E7
Széchnenyi-hegy *Hungary* 47°29N 18°57E 117 B1
Szechuan Basin = Sichuan Pendi *China* 31°0N 105°0E 228 B5
Szechwan = Sichuan □ *China* 30°30N 103°0E 228 B5
Szécsény *Hungary* 48°7N 19°30E 182 B4
Szeged *Hungary* 46°16N 20°10E 182 D5
Szeghalom *Hungary* 47°1N 21°10E 182 C6
Székesfehérvár *Hungary* 47°15N 18°25E 182 C3
Szekszárd *Hungary* 46°22N 18°42E 182 D3
Szendrő *Hungary* 48°24N 20°41E 182 B5
Szentendre *Hungary* 47°39N 19°4E 182 C4
Szentes *Hungary* 46°39N 20°21E 182 D5
Szentgotthárd *Hungary* 46°58N 16°19E 182 D1
Szentlőrinc *Hungary* 46°3N 18°1E 182 D3
Széphalom *Hungary* 47°34N 18°57E 117 A1
Szeping = Siping *China* 43°8N 124°21E 227 C13
Szerencs *Hungary* 48°10N 21°12E 182 B6
Szigetszentmiklós *Hungary* 47°21N 19°3E 182 C4
Szigetvár *Hungary* 46°3N 17°46E 182 D2
Szikszó *Hungary* 48°12N 20°56E 182 B5
Szklarska Poreba *Poland* 50°50N 15°33E 185 H2
Szkwa → *Poland* 53°11N 21°43E 185 E8
Szlichtyngowa *Poland* 51°42N 16°15E 185 G3
Szob *Hungary* 47°48N 18°53E 182 C3
Szolnok *Hungary* 47°10N 20°15E 182 C5
Szombathely *Hungary* 47°14N 16°38E 182 C1
Szprotawa *Poland* 51°33N 15°35E 185 G2
Sztálinváros = Dunaújváros *Hungary* 46°58N 18°57E 182 D3
Sztum *Poland* 53°55N 19°1E 184 E6
Sztutowo *Poland* 54°20N 19°15E 184 D6
Szubin *Poland* 53°1N 17°45E 185 E4
Szydłowiec *Poland* 51°15N 20°51E 185 G7
Szypliszki *Poland* 54°17N 23°2E 184 D10

T

Ta Khli *Thailand* 15°15N 100°21E 236 E3
Ta Lai *Vietnam* 11°24N 107°23E 237 G6
Ta Phraya △ *Thailand* 14°11N 102°49E 236 E4
Ta Pieh Shan = Dabie Shan *China* 31°20N 115°20E 229 B10
Taakoka *Cook Is.* 21°15S 159°43W 289 h
Taal, L. *Phil.* 13°56N 121°0E 232 E3
Taal Volcano △ *Phil.* 14°1N 120°59E 232 D3
Taan *Taiwan* 24°22N 120°35E 225 B2
Taastrup *Denmark* 55°39N 12°18E 118 B1
Tab *Hungary* 46°44N 18°2E 182 D3
Tabacal *Argentina* 23°15S 64°15W 334 A3
Tabaco *Phil.* 13°22N 123°44E 232 E4
Tabagné *Ivory C.* 7°59N 3°4W 262 D4
Ţābah *Si. Arabia* 26°55N 42°38E 246 E4
Tabajara *Brazil* 8°56S 62°8W 331 B5
Tabalo *Papua N. G.* 1°24S 149°40E 286 A5
Tabalos *Peru* 6°26S 76°37W 330 B2
Tabanan *Indonesia* 8°32S 115°8E 231 K18
Tabang *Indonesia* 0°34N 116°1E 235 B5
Tabankort *Niger* 17°44N 0°20E 263 B5
Tabaquite *Trin. & Tob.* 10°23N 61°18W 323 t
Tabar I. *Papua N. G.* 2°56S 152°0E 286 B7
Tabar Is. *Papua N. G.* 2°50S 152°0E 286 B7
Tabarka *Tunisia* 36°56N 8°46E 258 A1
Ţabas *Khorāsān, Iran* 32°48N 60°12E 247 C9
Ţabas *Yazd, Iran* 33°35N 56°55E 247 C8
Tabasará, Serranía de *Panama* 8°35N 81°40W 320 E3

Tabasco □ Mexico 18°0N 92°40W 319 D6
Tabāsīn Iran 31°12N 57°54E 247 D8
Tabata Japan 35°44N 139°46E 140 A3
Tabatinga Brazil 4°16S 69°56W 330 A4
Tabatinga, Serra da Brazil 10°30S 44°0W 332 D3
Tabayin Burma 22°42N 95°20E 241 D5
Tabelbala Algeria 29°24N 3°15W 260 C4
Tabelbala, Kahal de Algeria 28°47N 2°0W 261 C4
Tabelembila Algeria 24°43N 4°16E 261 D5
Taber Canada 49°47N 112°8W 296 D6
Taberg Sweden 57°40N 14°6E 163 G8
Tabernacle St. Kitts & Nevis 17°23N 62°46W 322 d
Tabi Angola 8°10S 13°18E 265 D2
Tabina Phil. 7°28N 123°24E 233 H4
Tabira Brazil 7°35S 37°33W 332 C4
Tabiteuea Kiribati 1°25S 174°50E 277 A13
Tabla Niger 13°46N 3°1E 263 C5
Tablada Argentina 34°41S 58°32W 117 C1
Tablas de Daimiel △ Spain 39°9N 3°40W 195 F7
Tablas I. Phil. 12°25N 122°2E 232 E4
Tablas Str. Phil. 12°40N 121°48E 232 E3
Table, Pte. de la Réunion 21°14S 55°48E 272 f
Table B. Nfld. & L., Canada 53°40N 56°25W 299 B8
Table B. Western Cape, S. Africa 33°35S 18°25E 118 A1
Table C. N.Z. 39°6S 178°0E 284 F7
Table Grove U.S.A. 40°20N 90°27W 310 D6
Table I. Burma 14°12N 93°22E 245 G11
Table Mountain △ S. Africa 34°20S 18°28E 118 A1
Table Mt. S. Africa 33°58S 18°26E 118 A1
Table Rock L. U.S.A. 36°36N 93°19W 308 G7
Tableland Trin. & Tob. 10°16N 61°16W 323 t
Tabletop, Mt. Australia 23°24S 147°11E 280 C4
Taboão da Serra Brazil 23°36S 46°45W 137 B1
Tabocal Brazil 2°42S 57°40W 329 D6
Tabon Cave Complex Phil. 9°17N 118°5E 233 G2
Tábor Czech Rep. 49°25N 14°39E 180 B7
Tabora Tanzania 5°2S 32°50E 268 D3
Tabora □ Tanzania 5°0S 33°0E 268 D3
Tabou Ivory C. 4°30N 7°20W 262 E3
Tabrīz Iran 38°7N 46°20E 213 C12
Tabuaeran Kiribati 3°51N 159°22W 289 G12
Tabubil Papua N. G. 5°20S 141°15E 286 C1
Tabuenca Spain 41°42N 1°33W 196 D3
Tabuk Phil. 17°24N 121°25E 232 C3
Tabūk Si. Arabia 28°23N 36°36E 251 K7
Tabūk □ Si. Arabia 27°40N 36°50E 246 E3
Tabunifi Micronesia 9°28N 138°4E 287 S16
Taburno-Camposauro ⌓ Italy 41°8N 14°37E 201 A7
Tabwemasana, Mt. Vanuatu 15°20S 166°44E 287 E4
Täby Sweden 59°26N 18°2E 139 A2
Tacámbaro de Codallos Mexico 19°14N 101°28W 318 D4
Tacarigua Trin. & Tob. 10°38N 61°22W 323 t
Tacariqua, Laguna de Venezuela 10°15N 65°50W 328 A4
Tacheng Xinjiang Uygur, China 46°40N 82°58E 217 C10
Tacheng Taiwan 23°51N 120°19E 225 C2
Tach'i Taiwan 24°53N 121°17E 225 B3
Tachia Taiwan 24°25N 120°28E 225 B2
Tachia Hsi → Taiwan 24°20N 120°33E 225 B3
Tachibana-Wan Japan 32°45N 130°7E 222 E2
Tachikawa Japan 35°42N 139°25E 223 B11
Tachilek Burma 20°26N 99°52E 236 B2
Tach'ing Shan = Daqing Shan China 40°40N 111°0E 226 D6
Táchira □ Venezuela 8°7N 72°15W 328 B3
Tachiumet Libya 26°19N 10°3E 261 C7
Tachoshui Taiwan 24°20N 121°44E 225 B3
Tachov Czech Rep. 49°47N 12°39E 180 B5
Tácina → Italy 38°57N 16°55E 201 D9
Tacloban Phil. 11°15N 124°58E 233 F5
Tacna Peru 18°0S 70°20W 330 D3
Tacna □ Peru 17°40S 70°20W 330 D3
Tacoma U.S.A. 47°14N 122°26W 306 C4
Tacopaya = Zudañez Bolivia 19°6S 64°44W 331 D5
Tacuarembó Uruguay 31°45S 56°0W 335 C4
Tacuba Mexico 19°26N 99°11W 128 B1
Tacubaya Mexico 19°24N 99°10W 128 B1
Tacurong Phil. 6°40N 124°41E 233 H5
Tada-u Burma 21°49N 95°58E 241 E5
Tadahadi Solomon Is. 10°18S 161°35E 287 N11
Tademaït, Plateau du Algeria 28°30N 2°30E 261 C5
Tādepallegudem India 16°50N 81°30E 244 F5
Tadéra Niger 20°29N 8°18E 261 D6
Tadine N. Cal. 21°33S 167°52E 288 d
Tadio, L. Ivory C. 5°10N 5°15W 262 D3
Tadjerdjeri, O. → Algeria 26°0N 8°0E 261 C6
Tadjerouna Algeria 33°31N 2°3E 261 B5
Tadjettaret, O. → Algeria 21°20N 7°22E 261 D6
Tadjmout Laghouat, Algeria 33°52N 2°30E 261 B5
Tadjmout Saoura, Algeria 25°37N 3°48E 261 C5
Tadjoura Djibouti 11°50N 42°55E 257 E5
Tadjoura, Golfe de Djibouti 11°50N 43°0E 257 E5
Tadmor N.Z. 41°27S 172°45E 285 B7
Tadoba △ India 20°30N 78°20E 244 D4
Tadotsu Japan 34°16N 133°45E 222 C5
Tadoule L. Canada 58°36N 98°20W 297 B9
Tadoussac Canada 48°11N 69°42W 299 C6
Tadpatri India 14°55N 78°1E 245 G4
Tadrés ⌓ Niger 16°0N 7°10E 263 B6
Tadzhikistan = Tajikistan ■ Asia 38°30N 70°0E 217 E8
Tae-an S. Korea 36°45N 126°17E 224 D3
Tae-an Seashore Nat. Park △ S. Korea 36°40N 126°0E 224 D3
Taebaek S. Korea 37°10N 128°59E 224 D4
Taebaeksan S. Korea 37°5N 128°54E 224 D4
T'aebaeksanmaek S. Korea 37°40N 128°50E 224 D4
Taedong-gang → N. Korea 38°41N 125°15E 224 C2
Taedong-man N. Korea 38°4N 125°7E 224 C2
Taegu = Daegu S. Korea 35°50N 128°37E 224 E4
Taegwan N. Korea 40°13N 125°12E 224 B2
Taehung N. Korea 40°5N 126°56E 224 B3
Taehwa-do N. Korea 39°26N 124°36E 224 C2
Taejŏn = Daejeon S. Korea 36°20N 127°28E 224 D3
Tælavåg Norway 60°15N 4°58E 164 D1
Taen, Ko Thailand 9°22N 99°57E 237 b
Tafalla Spain 42°30N 1°41W 196 C3
Tafar Sudan 6°52N 28°15E 257 F2
Tafassasset, O. → Algeria 22°0N 9°57E 261 D6
Tafelbaai = Table B. S. Africa 33°35S 18°25E 118 A1
Tafelberg Curaçao 12°4N 68°50W 322 g
Tafelney, C. Morocco 31°3N 9°51W 260 B3
Tafermaar Indonesia 6°47S 134°10E 231 F8
Taffermit Morocco 29°37N 9°15W 260 C3
Tafi Viejo Argentina 26°43S 65°17W 334 B2
Tafīhān Iran 29°25N 52°39E 247 D7
Tafilalet Morocco 31°20N 4°45W 260 B4
Tafiré Ivory C. 9°4N 5°4W 262 D3
Tafjord Norway 62°14N 7°24E 164 B4
Tafnidilt Morocco 28°47N 10°58W 260 C2
Tafo Ghana 6°15N 0°20W 263 D4
Tafraoute Morocco 29°50N 8°58W 260 C3
Tafresh Iran 34°45N 49°57E 247 C6
Taft Iran 31°45N 54°14E 247 D7
Taft Phil. 11°57N 125°30E 233 F5
Taft Calif., U.S.A. 35°8N 119°28W 307 K7
Taft Fla., U.S.A. 28°25N 81°21W 133 B2
Taftan Pakistan 29°0N 61°30E 240 C1
Taftān, Kūh-e Iran 28°40N 61°0E 247 D9
Tafu Taiwan 23°37N 121°23E 225 C3
Tafwap India 7°23N 93°43E 245 L11
Taga Samoa 13°46S 172°28W 287 V19
Taga Dzong Bhutan 27°5N 89°55E 241 B2
Tagana-an Phil. 9°42N 125°35E 233 G5
Taganrog Russia 47°12N 38°50E 189 J10
Taganrogskiy Zaliv Russia 47°0N 38°30E 189 J10
Tagânt □ Mauritania 19°0N 10°0W 260 E3
Tagap Ga Burma 26°56N 96°13E 241 B6
Tagauayan I. Phil. 10°58N 121°13E 233 F3
Tagaung Burma 23°30N 96°2E 241 D6
Tagawa Japan 33°38N 130°51E 222 D2
Tagaytay Phil. 14°6N 120°56E 232 D3
Tagbilaran Phil. 9°39N 123°51E 233 G4
Tagdempt = Tiaret Algeria 35°20N 1°21E 261 A5
Tage Papua N. G. 6°19S 143°20E 286 D2
Tageren Canal Micronesia 9°33N 138°8E 287 R16
Tággia Italy 43°52N 7°51E 198 E4
Taghit Algeria 30°58N 2°0W 261 B4
Tagig → Phil. 14°31N 121°5E 127 B2
Tagish Canada 60°19N 134°16W 296 A2
Tagish L. Canada 60°10N 134°20W 296 A2
Tagkawayan Phil. 13°58N 122°32E 232 E4
Tagliacozzo Italy 42°4N 13°14E 199 F10
Tagliamento → Italy 45°38N 13°6E 199 C10
Táglio di Po Italy 45°0N 12°12E 199 D9
Tagna Colombia 2°24S 70°37W 328 D3
Tago Phil. 9°2N 126°13E 233 G6
Tago, Mt. Phil. 8°23N 125°5E 233 G5
Tagomago Spain 39°2N 1°39E 206 C2
Tagourāret Mauritania 17°45N 7°45W 262 B3
Tagpochau, Mt. N. Marianas 15°11N 145°44E 302 e
Taguatinga Distrito Federal, Brazil 16°12S 44°35W 333 E2
Taguatinga Tocantins, Brazil 12°27S 46°22W 333 D2
Tagudin Phil. 16°56N 120°27E 232 C3
Taguenout Chagguerет Mali 21°14N 0°48W 261 D4
Taguig Phil. 14°31N 121°4E 127 B2
Tagula Papua N. G. 11°22S 153°15E 286 F7
Tagula I. Papua N. G. 11°30S 153°30E 286 F7
Tagum Phil. 7°33N 125°53E 233 H5
Tagus = Tejo → Europe 38°40N 9°24W 195 F2
Tahakopa N.Z. 46°30S 169°23E 285 G4
Tahala Morocco 34°0N 4°28W 260 B4
Tahan, Gunung Malaysia 4°34N 102°17E 237 K4
Tahānah-ye sūr Gol Afghan. 31°43N 67°53E 240 C2
Tahara Japan 34°40N 137°16E 223 C9
Tahat Algeria 23°18N 5°33E 261 D6
Tāherī Iran 27°43N 52°20E 247 E7
Tahgong Pt. N. Marianas 15°6N 145°39E 302 e
Tahifet Algeria 22°58N 6°0E 261 D6
Tahiti French Polynesia 17°37S 149°27W 289 e
Tahlab → Pakistan 28°9N 62°45E 240 C1
Tahlequah U.S.A. 35°55N 94°58W 314 D7
Tahoe, L. U.S.A. 39°6N 120°2W 306 G6
Tahoe City U.S.A. 39°10N 120°9W 306 F6
Tahoka U.S.A. 33°10N 101°48W 314 E4
Taholah U.S.A. 47°21N 124°17W 306 C2
Tahora N.Z. 39°2S 174°49E 284 F3
Tahoua Niger 14°57N 5°16E 263 C6
Tahrūd Iran 29°26N 57°49E 247 D8
Tahsis Canada 49°55N 126°40W 296 D3
Tahta Egypt 26°44N 31°32E 256 B3
Tahtaköprü Turkey 39°57N 29°39E 203 G13
Tahtalı Dağları Turkey 38°20N 36°0E 212 C7
Tahu Taiwan 24°26N 120°52E 225 B2
Tahuamanú → Bolivia 11°6S 67°36W 330 C4
Tahuata, I. French Polynesia 9°57S 139°5W 289 f
Tahulandang Indonesia 2°27N 125°23E 231 D7
Tahuna Indonesia 3°38N 125°30E 231 D7
Taï Ivory C. 5°55N 7°30W 262 D3
Taï △ Ivory C. 5°25N 7°5W 262 D3
Tai Hu China 31°5N 120°10E 229 B12
Tai Lo Shan China 22°21N 114°13E 122 A2
Tai Mo Shan China 22°25N 114°7E 219 a
Tai O China 22°15N 113°52E 219 a
Tai Pang Wan China 22°33N 114°24E 219 a
Tai Po China 22°27N 114°10E 219 a
Tai Po Tsai China 22°20N 114°15E 122 A2
Tai Rom Yen △ Thailand 8°45N 99°30E 237 H2
Tai Seng Singapore 1°20N 103°53E 138 A3
Tai Shan China 36°25N 117°20E 227 F9
Tai Shui Hang China 22°24N 114°13E 122 A2
Tai Tam B. China 22°12N 114°13E 122 B2
Tai Tam Tuk Res. China 22°14N 114°13E 122 B2
Tai Wai China 22°22N 114°10E 122 A2
Tai Wan Tau China 22°17N 114°17E 122 B2
Tai Wo Hau China 22°21N 114°7E 122 A1
Tai Yue Shan = Lantau I. China 22°15N 113°56E 219 a
Tai'an China 36°12N 117°8E 227 F9
Taiarapu, Presqu'île de Tahiti 17°47S 149°14W 289 e
Taibai Shan China 33°57N 107°45E 226 H4
Taibei = T'aipei Taiwan 25°4N 121°29E 225 A3
Taibique Canary Is. 27°42N 17°58W 153 e1
Taibus Qi China 41°54N 115°22E 226 D8
Taichow = Taizhou China 32°28N 119°55E 229 A12
T'aichung Taiwan 24°9N 120°37E 225 B2
Taieri → N.Z. 46°3S 170°12E 285 G5
Taigu China 37°28N 112°30E 226 F7
Taihang Shan China 36°0N 113°30E 226 G7
Taihape N.Z. 39°41S 175°48E 284 F4
Taihe Anhui, China 33°20N 115°42E 226 H8
Taihe Jiangxi, China 26°47N 114°52E 229 D10
Taihoku = T'aipei Taiwan 25°4N 121°29E 225 A3
Taihsi Taiwan 23°51N 120°16E 225 C2
Taihu China 30°22N 116°20E 229 B11
Taijiang China 26°39N 108°21E 228 D7
Taikang China 34°5N 114°50E 226 G8
Taikkyi Burma 17°20N 96°0E 241 G6
Tailem Bend Australia 35°12S 139°29E 282 C3
Tailfingen Germany 48°15N 9°1E 179 G5
T'ailuko Taiwan 24°9N 121°37E 225 B3
T'aimali Taiwan 22°36N 121°0E 225 D2
Taimyr Peninsula = Taymyr, Poluostrov Russia 75°0N 100°0E 215 B11
Tain U.K. 57°49N 4°4W 167 D4
Tainaka Japan 34°36N 135°35E 133 B2
T'ainan Taiwan 23°0N 120°10E 225 D2
T'ainan □ Taiwan 23°15N 120°20E 225 C2
Tainggyo Burma 17°49N 94°29E 241 G5
Taining China 26°54N 117°9E 229 D11
Taiobeiras Brazil 15°49S 42°14W 333 E3
Taipa China 22°10N 113°35E 219 a
T'aipei Taiwan 25°4N 121°29E 225 A3
T'aipei □ Taiwan 24°50N 121°35E 225 B3
Taiping Anhui, China 30°15N 118°6E 229 B12
Taiping Malaysia 4°51N 100°44E 237 K3
Taipingchuan China 44°23N 123°11E 227 B12
Taipingzhen China 33°35N 111°42E 226 H6
Taipu Brazil 5°37S 35°36W 332 C4
Tairbeart = Tarbert U.K. 57°54N 6°49W 167 D2
Tairenpokpi India 24°39N 93°40E 241 C4
Tairua N.Z. 37°0S 175°51E 284 D4
Tais Indonesia 4°6S 102°34E 234 C2
Taisha Japan 35°24N 132°40E 222 B4
Taishan China 22°14N 112°41E 229 F9
Taishō Japan 34°38N 135°27E 133 B1
Taishun China 27°30N 119°42E 229 D12
Taita N.Z. 41°12S 174°57E 143 B2
Taita Hills Kenya 3°25S 38°15E 268 C4
Taitao, C. Chile 45°53S 75°5W 336 C1
Taitao, Pen. de Chile 46°30S 75°0W 336 C2
T'aitung Taiwan 22°43N 121°4E 225 D3
T'aitung □ Taiwan 23°0N 121°0E 225 D3
Taivalkoski Finland 65°33N 28°12E 160 D23
Taiwan ■ Asia 23°30N 121°0E 225 C3
Taiwan Strait Asia 24°40N 120°0E 229 E12
Taixing China 32°11N 120°0E 229 A13
Taiyara Sudan 13°12N 30°47E 257 E3
Taiyiba Israel 32°36N 35°27E 250 F6
Taiyuan China 37°52N 112°33E 226 F7
Taizhong = T'aichung Taiwan 24°9N 120°37E 225 B2
Taizhou Jiangsu, China 32°28N 119°55E 229 A12
Taizhou Zhejiang, China 28°40N 121°24E 229 C13
Taizhou Liedao China 28°30N 121°55E 229 C13
Ta'izz Yemen 13°35N 44°2E 248 D4
Tājābād Iran 30°2N 54°24E 247 D7
Tajapuru, Furo do Brazil 1°50S 50°25W 332 B1
Tajarḥī Libya 24°21N 14°28E 258 D2
Tajen Taiwan 22°17N 120°53E 225 D2
Tajikistan ■ Asia 38°30N 70°0E 217 E8
Tajima Japan 37°12N 139°46E 221 F9
Tajimi Japan 35°19N 137°8E 223 B9
Tajo = Tejo → Europe 38°40N 9°24W 195 F2
Tajrīsh Iran 35°48N 51°25E 141 A2
Tajumulco, Vol. Guatemala 15°2N 91°55W 320 C1
Tājūrā Libya 32°51N 13°21E 258 B2
Tak Thailand 16°52N 99°8E 236 D2
Takāb Iran 36°24N 47°7E 213 D12
Takabanare-shima Japan 26°22N 127°59E 288 a
Takabba Kenya 3°21N 40°13E 267 D5
Takachiho Japan 32°42N 131°18E 222 E3
Takachu Botswana 22°37S 21°58E 270 B3
Takada Japan 37°7N 138°15E 221 F9
Takahagi Japan 36°43N 140°45E 221 F10
Takahashi Japan 34°51N 133°39E 222 C5
Takaido Japan 35°40N 139°37E 140 A2
Takaishi Japan 35°36N 139°31E 140 B2
Takaka N.Z. 40°51S 172°50E 285 A7
Takaki = Yamato Japan 35°27N 139°25E 223 B11
Takalar Indonesia 5°28S 119°24E 235 D5
Takalous, O. → Algeria 22°36N 7°21E 261 D6
Takamaka Seychelles 4°50S 55°30E 272 c
Takamatsu Japan 34°20N 134°5E 222 C6
Takanabe Japan 32°8N 131°30E 222 E3
Takangkou Taiwan 23°28N 121°29E 225 C3
Takaoka Japan 36°47N 137°0E 223 A9
Takapau N.Z. 40°2S 176°21E 284 G5
Takapuna N.Z. 36°47S 174°47E 284 C3
Takarazuka Japan 34°47N 135°20E 133 A1
Takaroa French Polynesia 14°28S 144°58W 289 f
Takasago Japan 34°45N 134°48E 140 A4
Takasaki Japan 36°20N 139°0E 223 A11
Takashima Japan 35°24N 136°2E 223 B8
Takatsu Japan 35°36N 139°37E 140 B2
Takatsuki Japan 34°51N 135°37E 223 C7
Takaungu Kenya 3°38S 39°52E 268 C4
Takayama Japan 36°18N 137°11E 223 A9
Takayama-Bonchi Japan 36°0N 137°18E 223 B9
Take-Shima Japan 30°49N 130°26E 221 J5
Takefu Japan 35°50N 136°10E 223 B8
Takehara Japan 34°21N 132°55E 222 C4
Takengon Indonesia 4°45N 96°50E 234 B1
Takeo Cambodia 10°59N 104°47E 237 G5
Takeo Japan 33°12N 130°1E 222 D2
Tåkern Sweden 58°22N 14°45E 163 F8
Takeshima = Tokdo Asia 37°15N 131°52E 221 F5
Takeshita Japan 35°33N 139°32E 140 B2
Tākestān Iran 36°0N 49°40E 247 C6
Taketa Japan 32°58N 131°24E 222 E3
Takh India 33°6N 77°32E 243 C7
Takhār □ Afghan. 36°40N 70°0E 240 A3
Takhiatash Uzbekistan 42°20N 59°33E 216 D5
Takhmau Cambodia 11°29N 104°57E 237 G5
Takht-Sulaiman Pakistan 31°40N 69°58E 242 D3
Taki Papua N. G. 6°29S 155°52E 286 D8
Takiéta Niger 13°41N 8°32E 263 C6
Takikawa Japan 43°33N 141°54E 220 C10
Takinegawa Japan 35°45N 139°44E 140 A3
Takla L. Canada 55°15N 125°45W 296 B3
Takla Landing Canada 55°30N 125°50W 296 B3
Takla Makan China 38°0N 83°0E 217 E10
Taklamakan Shamo = Takla Makan China 38°0N 83°0E 217 E10
Takoma Park U.S.A. 38°58N 77°0W 143 B3
Takotna U.S.A. 62°59N 156°4W 303 E8
Taksim Turkey 41°2N 28°58E 122 B1
Taksimo Russia 56°20N 114°52E 215 D12
Taku Japan 33°18N 130°3E 222 D2
Taku → Canada 58°30N 133°50W 296 B2
Takua Thung Thailand 8°24N 98°27E 237 a
Takum India 27°47N 93°37E 241 B4
Takum Nigeria 7°18N 9°36E 263 D6
Takume French Polynesia 15°49S 142°12W 289 f
Takundi Dem. Rep. of the Congo 4°45S 16°34E 265 C3
Takutu → Brazil 3°1N 60°29W 329 C5
Takutu → Guyana 3°1N 60°29W 329 C5
Tal Halāl Iran 28°54N 55°1E 247 D7
Tala Uruguay 34°21S 55°46W 335 C4
Talachyn Belarus 54°25N 29°42E 188 E5
Talacogon Phil. 8°32N 125°39E 233 G5
Talagang Pakistan 32°55N 72°25E 242 C5
Talagante Chile 33°40S 70°50W 334 C1
Talahouhait Algeria 24°52N 1°5E 261 D5
Talaide Portugal 38°44N 9°18W 126 A1
Talaimannar Sri Lanka 9°6N 79°43E 245 K4
Talaïnt Morocco 29°41N 9°40W 260 C3
Talak Niger 18°0N 5°0E 263 B6
Talakag Phil. 8°16N 124°37E 233 G5
Talamanca, Cordillera de Cent. Amer. 9°20N 83°20W 320 E3
Talampaya △ Argentina 29°43S 67°42W 334 B2
Talangbetutu Indonesia 2°53S 104°41E 234 C2
Talant France 47°19N 4°58E 173 E11
Talara Peru 4°38S 81°18W 330 A1
Talas Kyrgyzstan 42°30N 72°13E 217 D8
Talas Turkey 38°41N 35°33E 212 C6
Talas □ Kyrgyzstan 42°20N 72°0E 217 D8
Talas → Kazakhstan 44°0N 70°20E 217 D8
Talas Ala Too Kyrgyzstan 42°15N 72°0E 217 D8
Talasea Papua N. G. 5°20S 150°2E 286 C6
Talasskiy Alatau = Talas Ala Too Kyrgyzstan 42°15N 72°0E 217 D8
Talâta Egypt 30°36N 32°20E 251 H3
Talata Mafara Nigeria 12°38N 6°4E 263 C6
Talaud, Kepulauan Indonesia 4°30N 126°50E 231 D7
Talaud Is. = Talaud, Kepulauan Indonesia 4°30N 126°50E 231 D7
Talavera de la Reina Spain 39°55N 4°46W 194 F6
Talavera la Real Spain 38°53N 6°46W 195 G4
Talawgyi Burma 25°4N 97°19E 241 C6
Talayan Phil. 6°52N 124°24E 233 H5
Talayuela Spain 39°59N 5°36W 194 F5
Talbandh India 22°3N 86°20E 243 H12
Talbert, Sillon de France 48°53N 3°5W 172 D3
Talbot Australia 37°10S 143°44E 282 D5
Talbot, C. Australia 13°48S 126°43E 278 B4
Talbotton U.S.A. 32°41N 84°32W 316 C5
Talbragar → Australia 32°12S 148°37E 283 B8
Talca Chile 35°28S 71°40W 334 D1
Talcahuano Chile 36°40S 73°10W 334 D1
Talcher India 21°0N 85°18E 244 D7
Talcho Niger 14°44N 3°28E 263 C5
Taldy Kurgan = Taldyqorghan Kazakhstan 45°10N 78°45E 217 C9
Taldyqorghan Kazakhstan 45°10N 78°45E 217 C9
Tālesh Iran 37°58N 48°58E 213 D13
Tālesh, Kūhhā-ye Iran 37°42N 48°55E 213 D13
Talgar = Talghar Kazakhstan 43°19N 77°15E 217 D9
Talghar Kazakhstan 43°19N 77°15E 217 D9
Talguharai Sudan 18°19N 35°56E 256 D4
Talguppa India 14°13N 74°56E 245 G2
Tali Post Sudan 5°55N 30°44E 257 F3
Taliabu Indonesia 1°50S 125°0E 231 E6
Taliao Taiwan 22°36N 120°23E 225 D2
Talibon Phil. 10°9N 124°20E 233 F5
Talichien Taiwan 24°58N 121°55E 225 B3
Taliganga India 22°30N 88°22E 124 B2
Talihina U.S.A. 34°45N 95°3W 314 D7
Talikota India 16°29N 76°17E 245 F3
Talikud I. Phil. 6°56N 125°41E 233 H5
Talin Taiwan 23°36N 120°27E 225 C2
Talipapa Phil. 14°41N 121°1E 127 A2
Talipaw Phil. 5°59N 121°7E 233 J3
Talipparamba India 12°3N 75°21E 245 H2
Talisay Phil. 10°44N 122°58E 233 F4
Talisayan Phil. 9°0N 124°55E 233 G5
Taliwang Indonesia 8°50S 116°55E 235 D5
Talkeetna U.S.A. 62°20N 150°6W 303 E10
Talkha Egypt 31°3N 31°22E 251 G2
Tálknafjörður Iceland 65°34N 24°0W 155 B2
Tall 'Afar Iraq 36°22N 42°27E 213 D10
Tall Kalakh Syria 34°41N 36°15E 250 D7
Tall Kayf Iraq 36°29N 43°7E 213 D10
Talla Egypt 28°5N 30°43E 256 B3
Talladega U.S.A. 33°26N 86°6W 316 B3
Tallaganda △ Australia 35°29S 149°37E 283 C8
Tallaght Ireland 53°17N 6°22W 120 B1
Tallahassee U.S.A. 30°27N 84°17W 316 E5
Tallangatta Australia 36°15S 147°19E 283 D7
Tallapoosa U.S.A. 33°45N 85°17W 316 B4
Tallapoosa → U.S.A. 32°30N 86°16W 316 C3
Tallard France 44°28N 6°3E 175 D10
Tallarook Australia 37°5S 145°6E 283 D6
Tallassee U.S.A. 32°32N 85°54W 316 C4
Tällberg Sweden 60°51N 15°2E 162 D9
Tallering Pk. Australia 28°6S 115°37E 279 E2
Talli Pakistan 29°32N 68°8E 242 E3
Tallinn Estonia 59°22N 24°48E 188 C3
Tallkrogen Sweden 59°16N 18°4E 139 B2
Tallmadge U.S.A. 41°6N 81°27W 312 E3
Tallulah U.S.A. 32°25N 91°11W 314 E9
Tălmaciu Romania 45°38N 24°19E 183 E9
Talmest Morocco 31°48N 9°21W 260 B3
Talmont-St-Hilaire France 46°27N 1°37W 174 B2
Talnakh Russia 69°29N 88°22E 215 C9
Talne Ukraine 48°50N 30°44E 189 H6
Talnoye = Talne Ukraine 48°50N 30°44E 189 H6
Taloda India 21°34N 74°11E 244 D2
Talodi Sudan 10°35N 30°22E 257 E3
Talofofo Guam 13°21N 144°45E 302 d
Tāloqān Afghan. 36°44N 69°33E 240 A3
Talovaya Russia 51°6N 40°45E 190 E5
Taloyoak Canada 69°32N 93°32W 294 D13
Talpa de Allende Mexico 20°23N 104°51W 318 C4
Talparo Trin. & Tob. 10°30N 61°17W 323 t
Talparo → Trin. & Tob. 10°34N 61°17W 323 t
Talquin, L. U.S.A. 30°23N 84°39W 316 E5
Talsi Latvia 57°10N 22°30E 184 A9
Talsi □ Latvia 57°20N 22°40E 184 A9
Talsinnt Morocco 32°33N 3°27W 261 B4
Taltal Chile 25°23S 70°33W 334 B1
Taltson → Canada 61°24N 112°46W 296 A6
Talu Indonesia 0°13N 99°58E 234 B1
Taluk Indonesia 0°31S 101°34E 234 C2
Talwood Australia 28°29S 149°29E 281 D4
Talyawalka Cr. → Australia 32°28S 142°22E 282 B5
Tam Dao △ Vietnam 21°45N 105°45E 236 B5
Tam Ky Vietnam 15°34N 108°29E 236 E7
Tam Quan Vietnam 14°35N 109°3E 236 E7
Tama Tōkyō, Japan 35°38N 139°26E 140 B1
Tama Iowa, U.S.A. 41°58N 92°35W 310 C4
Tama → Japan 35°32N 139°39E 140 B2
Tama ⌓ Ethiopia 5°55N 36°5E 257 F4
Tama Abu, Banjaran Malaysia 3°50N 115°5E 235 B5
Tama Kyūryō Japan 35°34N 139°30E 140 B2
Tamada Algeria 21°34N 3°20E 261 D5
Tamaden Japan 35°39N 139°38E 140 B2
Tamagawa-josui → Japan 35°41N 139°47E 140 A1
Tamakautoga Cook Is. 19°5S 169°55W 289 g
Tamalameque Colombia 8°52N 73°49W 328 B3
Tamale Ghana 9°22N 0°50W 263 D4
Taman Russia 45°14N 36°41E 189 K9
Taman Negara △ Malaysia 4°38N 102°26E 237 K4
Taman Sari Indonesia 6°8S 106°48E 122 A1
T'aman Shan Taiwan 24°42N 121°27E 225 B3
Tamana Japan 32°58N 130°32E 222 E2
Tamana Kiribati 2°30S 175°59E 277 A14
Tamana, Mt. Trin. & Tob. 10°28N 61°12W 323 t
Tamanar Morocco 31°1N 9°46W 260 B3
Tamanduateí → Brazil 23°37S 46°38W 137 B2
Tamanhint Libya 27°13N 14°37E 258 C2
Tamani Mali 13°20N 6°50W 262 C3
Tamano Japan 34°29N 133°59E 222 C5
Tamanrasset Algeria 22°50N 5°30E 261 D6
Tamanrasset □ Algeria 23°45N 4°40E 261 D5
Tamanrasset, O. → Algeria 22°0N 2°0E 261 D5
Tamanthi Burma 25°19N 95°17E 241 C5
Tamaqua U.S.A. 40°48N 75°58W 313 F9
Tamar → U.K. 50°27N 4°15W 169 G3
Támara Colombia 5°50N 72°10W 328 B3
Tamarac U.S.A. 26°12N 80°15W 317 J9
Tamarin Mauritius 20°19S 57°20E 272 e
Tamarinda Spain 39°55N 3°49E 206 B4
Tamarite de Litera Spain 41°52N 0°25E 196 D5
Tamaroa U.S.A. 38°8N 89°14W 310 F7
Tamashima Japan 34°32N 133°40E 221 G6
Tamási Hungary 46°40N 18°18E 182 D3
Tamaské Niger 14°49N 5°43E 263 C6
Tamatave = Toamasina Madag. 18°10S 49°25E 272 B2
Tamaulipas □ Mexico 24°0N 98°45W 319 C5
Tamaulipas, Sierra de Mexico 23°30N 98°20W 319 C5
Tamazula Mexico 24°57N 106°57W 318 C3
Tamazunchale Mexico 21°16N 98°47W 319 C5
Tamba-Dabatou Guinea 11°50N 10°40W 262 C2
Tambach Kenya 0°36N 35°31E 268 B4
Tambacounda Senegal 13°45N 13°40W 262 C2
Tambacounda □ Senegal 14°0N 13°0W 262 C2
Tambaram India 12°55N 80°7E 245 H5
Tambea Solomon Is. 9°16S 159°41E 287 M10
Tambelan, Kepulauan Indonesia 1°0N 107°30E 235 B3
Tambellup Australia 34°4S 117°37E 279 F2
Tambo Queens., Australia 24°54S 146°14E 280 C4
Tambo Peru 12°57S 74°1W 330 C3
Tambo → Peru 10°42S 73°47W 330 C3
Tambo de Mora Peru 13°30S 76°8W 330 C2
Tambobamba Peru 13°54S 72°8W 330 C3
Tamboerskloof S. Africa 33°56S 18°25E 118 A1
Tambohorano Madag. 17°30S 43°58E 272 B1
Tambopata → Peru 13°21S 69°36W 330 C4
Tambora Jakarta, Indonesia 6°8S 106°47E 122 A1
Tambora Nusa Tenggara Barat, Indonesia 8°12S 118°5E 235 D5
Tamboritha, Mt. Australia 37°31S 146°40E 283 D7
Tamboura C.A.R. 5°10N 25°12E 264 A5
Tambov Russia 52°45N 41°28E 190 D5
Tambov □ Russia 52°50N 41°20E 190 D5
Tambre → Spain 42°49N 8°53W 194 C2
Tambuku Indonesia 7°8S 113°40E 235 D4
Tambul Papua N. G. 5°54S 143°54E 286 C2
Tambunar Malaysia 5°43N 116°24E 235 A5
Tamburâ Sudan 5°40N 27°25E 257 F2
Tambuyukan, Gunong Malaysia 6°13N 116°39E 235 A5
Tâmchekket Mauritania 17°25N 10°40W 262 B2
Tame Colombia 6°28N 71°44W 328 B3
Tâmega → Portugal 41°5N 8°21W 194 D2
Tamegroute Morocco 30°15N 5°39W 260 B3
Tamelelt Morocco 31°50N 7°32W 260 B3
Tamenglong India 25°0N 93°35E 241 C4
Tamerza Tunisia 34°23N 7°58E 258 B1
Tamgak, Adrar Niger 19°12N 8°35E 259 E1
Tamgué, Massif du Guinea 12°0N 12°18W 262 C2
Tami Is. Papua N. G. 6°46S 147°55E 286 D4
Tamiahua, L. de Mexico 21°35N 97°35W 319 C5
Tamiami Canal U.S.A. 25°50N 81°0W 317 K8
Tamianglayang Indonesia 2°7S 115°10E 235 C5
Tamil Nadu □ India 11°0N 77°0E 245 J3
Tamis → Serbia 44°51N 20°39E 182 F5
Tamiya Egypt 29°29N 30°58E 256 J7
Tamlelt, Plaine de Morocco 32°30N 2°20W 261 B4
Tamluk India 22°18N 87°58E 243 H12
Tammerfors = Tampere Finland 61°30N 23°50E 188 B2
Tammisalo Finland 60°11N 25°5E 121 B3
Tammûh Egypt 29°55N 31°15E 117 B2
Tämnaren Sweden 60°10N 17°25E 162 D11
Tampa Angola 15°30S 13°27E 265 F2
Tampa Fla., U.S.A. 27°56N 82°27W 317 H7
Tampa, Tanjung Indonesia 8°55S 116°12E 231 K19
Tampa B. U.S.A. 27°50N 82°30W 317 H7
Tampa Int. ✈ (TPA) U.S.A. 27°59N 82°32W 317 H7
Tamparan Phil. 7°53N 124°20E 233 H5
Tampere Finland 61°30N 23°50E 188 B2
Tampico Tamaulipas, Mexico 22°13N 97°51W 319 C5
Tampico Ill., U.S.A. 41°38N 89°47W 310 C7
Tampin Malaysia 2°28N 102°13E 237 L4
Tampines Singapore 1°21N 103°56E 138 A3
Tampoi Malaysia 1°30N 103°39E 237 d
Tamrah Si. Arabia 20°24N 45°25E 248 B4
Tamri Morocco 30°49N 9°50W 260 B3
Tamrida = Qādub Yemen 12°37N 53°57E 249 D6
Tamsagbulag Mongolia 47°14N 117°21E 219 B12
Tamsweg Austria 47°7N 13°49E 180 D6
Tamu Burma 24°13N 94°12E 241 C5
Tamuja → Spain 39°38N 6°29W 195 F4
Tamuning Guam 13°29N 144°47E 302 d
Tamworth N.S.W., Australia 31°7S 150°58E 283 A9
Tamworth Ont., Canada 44°29N 77°0W 312 B8
Tamworth Staffs., U.K. 52°39N 1°41W 169 E6
Tan An Vietnam 10°32N 106°25E 237 G6
Tan Chau Vietnam 10°48N 105°12E 237 G5
T'an-do N. Korea 39°30N 124°41E 224 C2
Tan Hiep Vietnam 10°27N 106°21E 237 G6
Tan Iddah Algeria 26°33N 9°42E 261 C6
Tan-Tan Morocco 28°29N 11°1W 260 C2
Tan Yen Vietnam 22°4N 105°3E 236 A5
Tana → Coast, Kenya 2°32S 40°31E 268 C5
Tana → Finnmark, Norway 70°30N 28°14E 160 A23
Tana, L. Ethiopia 13°5N 37°30E 257 E4
Tana River Primate ⌓ Kenya 1°55S 40°7E 268 C5
Tanabe Japan 33°44N 135°22E 223 D7
Tanabi Brazil 20°37S 49°37W 333 F2
Tanacross U.S.A. 63°23N 143°21W 303 E12
Tanafjorden Norway 70°45N 28°25E 160 A23
Tanaga I. U.S.A. 51°48N 177°53W 303 L3
Tanaga Volcano U.S.A. 51°53N 178°8W 303 L3
Tanah Abang Indonesia 6°12S 106°48E 122 B1
Tanah Kusir Indonesia 6°15S 106°46E 122 B1
Tanah Merah Malaysia 5°48N 102°9E 237 K4
Tanahbala Indonesia 0°30S 98°30E 234 C1
Tanahgrogot Indonesia 1°55S 116°15E 235 C5
Tanahjampea Indonesia 7°10S 120°35E 231 F6
Tanahmasa Indonesia 0°12S 98°39E 234 C1
Tanahmerah Indonesia 6°5S 140°16E 231 F10
Tanahputih Indonesia 1°40N 101°3E 234 B2
Tanakpur India 29°5N 80°7E 243 E9
Tanakura Japan 37°10N 140°20E 221 F10
Tanamalwila Sri Lanka 6°26N 81°8E 245 L5
Tanami Desert Australia 18°50S 132°0E 278 C5
Tanana U.S.A. 65°10N 152°4W 303 D9
Tanana → U.S.A. 65°10N 151°58W 303 D10
Tananarive = Antananarivo Madag. 18°55S 47°31E 272 B2
Tananger Norway 58°57N 5°37E 164 F2
Tanannt Morocco 31°54N 6°56W 260 B3
Tanapag N. Marianas 15°14N 145°45E 302 e
Tánaro → Italy 44°55N 8°40E 198 D5
Tanauan Phil. 14°5N 121°10E 232 D3
Tanay Phil. 14°30N 121°17E 232 D3
Tanba-Sanchi Japan 35°7N 135°48E 223 B7
Tancheng China 34°25N 118°20E 227 G10
Tanch'ŏn N. Korea 40°27N 128°54E 224 B4
Tanda Ut. P., India 26°33N 82°35E 243 F10
Tanda Ut. P., India 28°57N 78°56E 243 E8
Tanda Ivory C. 7°48N 3°10W 262 D4
Tandag Phil. 9°4N 126°9E 233 G6
Tandaia Tanzania 9°25S 34°15E 269 D3
Tăndărei Romania 44°39N 27°40E 183 F12
Tandaué Angola 16°58S 18°5E 265 F3
Tandil Argentina 37°15S 59°6W 334 D4
Tandil, Sa. del Argentina 37°30S 59°0W 334 D4
Tandin Burma 19°33N 93°58E 241 F4
Tandjilé □ Chad 9°30N 16°30E 259 G3
Tandjilé → Chad 9°45N 15°50E 259 G3
Tandlianwala Pakistan 31°3N 73°9E 242 D5
Tando Adam Pakistan 25°45N 68°40E 242 G3
Tando Allahyar Pakistan 25°28N 68°43E 242 G3
Tando Bago Pakistan 24°47N 68°58E 242 G3
Tando Mohommed Khan Pakistan 25°8N 68°32E 242 G3
Tando-Zinze Angola 5°22S 12°30E 265 D2
Tandou-Bengou Congo 3°50S 11°44E 264 C2
Tandou L. Australia 32°40S 142°5E 282 B5
Tandoureh △ Iran 37°50N 59°0E 247 B8
Tandragee U.K. 54°21N 6°24W 166 B5
Tandsjöborg Sweden 61°42N 14°43E 162 C8
Tandubas Phil. 5°8N 120°20E 233 J3
Tandula → India 21°6N 81°14E 244 D5
Tandula Tank India 20°40N 81°12E 244 D5
Tandur Andhra Pradesh, India 19°11N 79°30E 244 E4
Tandur Andhra Pradesh, India 17°14N 77°35E 244 F3
Tane-ga-Shima Japan 30°30N 131°0E 221 J5
Taneatua N.Z. 38°4S 177°1E 284 E6
Tanen Tong Dan = Dawna Ra. Burma 16°30N 98°30E 236 D2
Tanew → Poland 50°29N 22°16E 185 H9
Tanezrouft Algeria 23°9N 0°11E 261 D5
Tanezzuft, W. → Libya 25°51N 10°19E 258 C2
Tang, Koh Cambodia 10°16N 103°7E 237 G4
Tang, Ra's-e Iran 25°21N 59°52E 247 E8
Tang Krasang Cambodia 12°34N 105°3E 236 F5
Tanga Tanzania 5°5S 39°2E 268 D4
Tanga □ Tanzania 5°20S 38°0E 268 D4
Tanga Is. Papua N. G. 3°20S 153°15E 286 B7
Tanga Langua Grenada 12°14N 61°39W 323 q
Tangail Bangla. 24°15N 89°55E 241 C2
Tangalla Sri Lanka 6°1N 80°48E 245 L5
Tanganyika = Tanzania ■ Africa 6°0S 34°0E 268 D3
Tanganyika, L. Africa 6°40S 30°0E 268 D3
Tangará da Serra Brazil 14°50S 57°47W 331 C6
Tangarare Solomon Is. 9°36S 159°41E 287 M10
Tangasseri India 8°53N 76°35E 245 K3
Tangaza Nigeria 13°19N 4°55E 263 C5
Tangelo Park U.S.A. 28°27N 81°26W 133 B2
Tangen Norway 60°37N 11°15E 164 D8
Tanger Morocco 35°50N 5°49W 260 A3
Tanger □ Morocco 35°43N 5°50W 260 A3
Tangerang Indonesia 6°11S 106°37E 234 D3
Tangerhütte Germany 52°26N 11°48E 178 C7
Tangermünde Germany 52°33N 11°58E 178 C7
Tanggu China 39°2N 117°40E 227 E9
Tanggula Shan China 32°40N 92°10E 218 E7
Tanggula Shankou China 32°42N 92°27E 218 E7
Tanghe China 32°47N 112°50E 226 H7
Tanghla Range = Tanggula Shan China 32°40N 92°10E 218 E7
Tangi India 19°56N 85°24E 244 E7
Tangier = Tanger Morocco 35°50N 5°49W 260 A3
Tangjia China 22°22N 113°35E 219 a
Tangjia Wan China 22°21N 113°36E 219 a
Tango-Hantō Japan 35°45N 135°10E 223 B7
Tangorin Australia 21°47S 144°12E 280 C3
Tangorombohitr'i Makay Madag. 21°0S 45°15E 272 C2
Tangra Yumco China 31°0N 86°38E 218 E6
Tangshan China 39°38N 118°10E 227 E10
Tangtou China 35°28N 118°30E 227 G10
Tangub Phil. 8°3N 123°44E 233 G4
Tanguen-Dassouri Burkina Faso 12°16N 1°42W 263 C4
Tanguiéta Benin 10°35N 1°21E 263 C5
Tangxi China 29°3N 119°25E 229 C12
Tangyan He → China 28°54N 108°19E 228 C7
Tangyin China 35°54N 114°21E 226 G8
Taniantaweng Shan China 31°20N 98°0E 228 B2
Taniao Taiwan 22°23N 120°53E 225 D2
Tanimbar, Kepulauan Indonesia 7°30S 131°30E 231 F8
Tanimbar Is. = Tanimbar, Kepulauan Indonesia 7°30S 131°30E 231 F8
Taninthari = Tenasserim Burma 12°6N 99°3E 237 F2
Tanis Egypt 31°0N 31°54E 251 H2
Tanjay Phil. 9°30N 123°5E 233 G4
Tanjong Pelepas Malaysia 1°21N 103°33E 237 d
Tanjong Po Malaysia 1°45N 110°30E 235 B4
Tanjore = Thanjavur India 10°48N 79°12E 245 J4
Tanjung Kalimantan Selatan, Indonesia 2°10S 115°25E 235 C5
Tanjung Nusa Tenggara Barat, Indonesia 8°21S 116°9E 231 J19
Tanjung Datu △ Malaysia 2°13N 109°3E 235 B3
Tanjung Duren Indonesia 6°10S 106°46E 122 B1
Tanjung Malim Malaysia 3°42N 101°31E 237 L3
Tanjung Priok Indonesia 6°6S 106°52E 122 A2
Tanjung Putung △ Indonesia 2°54S 111°59E 235 C4
Tanjung Tokong Malaysia 5°28N 100°18E 237 c
Tanjungbalai Kepulauan Riau, Indonesia 1°0N 103°25E 234 B2
Tanjungbalai Sumatera Utara, Indonesia 2°55N 99°44E 234 B1
Tanjungbatu Kalimantan Selatan, Indonesia 3°0S 116°13E 235 C5
Tanjungbatu Kalimantan Timur, Indonesia 2°23N 118°3E 235 B5
Tanjungbatu Kepulauan Riau, Indonesia 0°37N 103°25E 234 B2
Tanjungisui Indonesia 0°30S 116°8E 235 C5
Tanjungkarang Telukbetung = Bandar Lampung Indonesia 5°20S 105°10E 234 D3
Tanjungpandan Indonesia 2°43S 107°38E 235 C3
Tanjungpinang Indonesia 1°5N 104°30E 234 B2
Tanjungpriok Indonesia 6°8S 106°55E 234 D3
Tanjungraja Indonesia 3°21S 104°46E 234 C2
Tanjungredeb Indonesia 2°9N 117°29E 235 B5
Tanjungselor Indonesia 2°55N 117°25E 235 B5
Tank Pakistan 32°14N 70°25E 242 C4
Tankhala India 21°58N 73°47E 242 J5
Tankwa-Karoo △ S. Africa 32°14S 19°50E 270 D2
Tanlu Taiwan 22°12N 120°44E 225 D2
Tanna Vanuatu 19°30S 169°20E 287 J7
Tännäs Sweden 62°26N 12°42E 162 B6
Tannersville U.S.A. 41°3N 75°18W 313 E9
Tannis Bugt Denmark 57°40N 10°15E 163 G4
Tannu Ola Asia 51°0N 94°0E 217 B12
Tannum Sands Australia 23°57S 151°22E 280 C5
Tano → Ghana 5°7N 2°56W 262 D4
Tanombella Algeria 25°30N 5°49E 261 C6
Tanon Str. Phil. 10°20N 123°30E 233 F4
Tanout Niger 14°50N 8°55E 259 F1
Tanquinho Brazil 11°58S 39°6W 333 D4
Tanshui Taiwan 25°10N 121°28E 225 A3
Tanshui Kang → Taiwan 25°10N 121°25E 225 A3
Tansilla Burkina Faso 12°25N 4°23W 262 C4
Tanta Egypt 30°45N 30°57E 256 H7
Tantabin Burma 17°1N 95°59E 241 G5
Tantoyuca Mexico 21°21N 98°14W 319 C5
Tantung = Dandong China 40°10N 124°20E 224 B2
T'antzu Taiwan 24°13N 120°42E 225 B2
Tanuku India 16°45N 81°44E 244 F5
Tanum Norway 59°53N 10°28E 133 A1
Tanūmah Si. Arabia 18°58N 42°10E 248 C3
Tanumshede Sweden 58°42N 11°20E 163 F5
Tanunda Australia 34°30S 139°0E 282 C3
Tanur India 11°1N 75°52E 245 J2
Tanus France 44°8N 2°19E 174 D6
Tanzania ■ Africa 6°0S 34°0E 268 D3
Tanzawa-Sanchi Japan 35°27N 139°0E 223 B11
Tanzhou China 22°16N 113°28E 219 a
Tanzilla → Canada 58°8N 130°43W 296 B2
Tao, Ko Thailand 10°5N 99°52E 237 G2
Tao'an = Taonan China 45°22N 122°40E 227 B12

Tao'er He → China 45°45N 124°5E 227 B13
Taohua Dao China 29°50N 122°20E 229 C14
Taolanaro Madag. 25°2S 47°0E 272 D2
Taole China 38°48N 106°40E 228 E4
Taonan China 45°22N 122°40E 227 B12
Taora Solomon Is. 7°21S 157°30E 287 L9
Taormina Italy 37°51N 15°17E 201 E8
Taos U.S.A. 36°24N 105°35W 305 H11
Taoudenni Mali 22°40N 3°55W 260 B4
Taoudrart, Adrar Algeria 24°25N 2°24E 261 D5
Taounate Morocco 34°25N 4°41W 260 B4
Taounate □ Morocco 34°30N 4°50W 260 B4
Taourirt Algeria 26°37N 0°20E 261 C5
Taourirt Morocco 34°25N 2°53W 261 B4
Taouz Morocco 30°53N 4°0W 260 B4
Taoyuan Hunan, China 28°55N 111°16E 229 C8
T'aoyüan Kaohsung,
Taiwan 23°9N 120°46E 225 C2
T'aoyüan Yünlin, Taiwan 25°0N 121°4E 225 B3
T'aoyüan □ Taiwan 24°55N 121°15E 225 B3
Tapa Estonia 59°15N 25°50E 161 G21
Tapa Shan = Daba Shan
China 32°0N 109°0E 228 B7
Tapachula Mexico 14°54N 92°17W 319 E6
Tapada Portugal 38°49N 9°16W 126 A1
Tapah Malaysia 4°12N 101°15E 237 K3
Tapajós → Brazil 2°24S 54°41W 329 D7
Tapaktuan Indonesia 3°15N 97°10E 234 B1
Tapanahoni → Suriname 4°20N 54°25W 329 C7
Tapanila Finland 60°15N 25°2E 121 B3
Tapanui N.Z. 45°56S 169°18E 285 F4
Taparo Pt. Trin. & Tob. 10°3N 61°38W 323 t
Tapauá → Brazil 5°40S 64°20W 331 B5
Tapauá → Brazil 5°40S 64°21W 331 B5
Tapaz Phil. 11°16N 122°32E 233 F4
Tapes Brazil 30°40S 51°23W 335 C5
Tapeta Liberia 6°29N 8°52W 262 D3
Taphan Hin Thailand 16°13N 100°26E 236 D3
Tapia de Casariego Spain 43°34N 6°56W 194 B4
Tapiales Argentina 34°42S 58°30W 117 C1
Tapiantana Channel Phil. 6°22N 122°1E 233 H4
Tapiantana Group Phil. 6°20N 122°0E 233 H4
Tapiau = Gvardeysk
Russia 54°39N 21°5E 184 D8
Tapilon = Daanbantayan
Phil. 11°17N 124°2E 233 F5
Tapini Papua N. G. 8°19S 147°0E 286 E4
Tapiola Finland 60°10N 24°48E 121 B1
Tapirai Brazil 19°52S 46°1W 333 E2
Tapirapé → Brazil 10°41S 50°38W 332 D1
Tapirapecó, Serra Venezuela 1°10N 65°0W 329 C5
Taplan Australia 34°33S 140°52E 282 C4
Tapo-Capara △ Venezuela 7°55N 71°15W 328 B3
Tapoeripa Suriname 5°22N 56°34W 329 B6
Tapolca Hungary 46°53N 17°29E 182 D2
Tapsia India 22°32N 88°23E 124 B2
Tapti → India 21°8N 72°41E 244 D1
Tapu Taiwan 23°18N 120°35E 225 C2
Tapuae-o-Uenuku N.Z. 42°0S 173°39E 285 C8
Tapul Phil. 5°42N 120°55E 233 J3
Tapul Group Phil. 5°35N 120°50E 233 J3
Tapul I. Phil. 5°43N 120°55E 233 J3
Tapun Phil. 27°35N 96°22E 241 B6
Tapurucuará Brazil 0°24S 65°2W 328 D5
Taputapu, C. Amer. Samoa 14°20S 170°51W 302 f
Taputimu Amer. Samoa 14°21S 170°46W 302 f
Taqtaq Iraq 35°53N 44°35E 213 E11
Taquara Brazil 29°36S 50°46W 335 B5
Taquari → Brazil 19°15S 57°17W 331 D6
Taquaritinga Brazil 21°24S 48°30W 333 F2
Tara Queens., Australia 27°17S 150°31E 281 D5
Tara Ont., Canada 44°28N 81°9W 312 B3
Tara Maharashtra, India 19°5N 72°49E 130 A1
Tara Japan 33°2N 130°11E 222 D2
Tara Russia 56°55N 74°24E 214 D8
Tara Zambia 16°58S 26°45E 269 F2
Tara → Montenegro 43°21N 18°51E 202 C2
Tara △ Serbia 43°55N 19°30E 202 C3
Tara-Dake Japan 32°58N 130°6E 222 E2
Taraba □ Nigeria 8°0N 10°30E 263 D7
Taraba → Nigeria 8°30N 10°15E 263 D7
Tarabuco Bolivia 19°10S 64°57W 331 D5
Tarābulus Lebanon 34°31N 35°50E 250 D6
Tarābulus Libya 32°49N 13°7E 258 B2
Tarābulus N. Afr. 31°0N 13°0E 258 B2
Tarābulus □ Libya 32°53N 13°11E 261 B7
Tarabya Turkey 41°8N 29°3E 122 B2
Taraclia Taraclia, Moldova 45°54N 28°40E 183 E13
Taraclia Tighina, Moldova 46°28N 28°52E 183 D14
Taradale N.Z. 39°33S 176°53E 284 F5
Taradehi India 23°18N 79°21E 243 H8
Tarāghān Libya 26°0N 14°30E 258 C2
Taragi Japan 32°16N 130°56E 222 E2
Tarahouahout Algeria 22°41N 5°59E 261 D6
Tarajalejo Canary Is. 28°12N 14°7W 153 e2
Tarakan Indonesia 3°20N 117°35E 235 B5
Tarakit, Mt. Kenya 2°2N 35°10E 268 A4
Taralga Australia 34°26S 149°52E 283 C8
Tarama-Jima Japan 24°39N 124°42E 221 M2
Taramakau → N.Z. 42°34S 171°8E 285 C6
Taran, Mys Russia 54°56N 19°59E 184 D6
Taranagar India 28°43N 74°50E 242 E6
Taranaki □ N.Z. 39°25S 174°30E 284 F3
Taranaki, Mt. N.Z. 39°17S 174°5E 284 F3
Tarancón Spain 40°1N 3°1W 196 E1
Tarangire △ Tanzania 4°21S 36°7E 268 C4
Taransay U.K. 57°54N 7°0W 167 D1
Táranto Italy 40°28N 17°14E 201 B10
Táranto, G. di Italy 40°8N 17°20E 201 B10
Tarapacá Colombia 2°56S 69°46W 328 D4
Tarapacá □ Chile 20°45S 69°30W 334 A2
Tarapoto Peru 6°30S 76°20W 330 B2
Taraquá Brazil 0°6N 68°28W 328 C4
Tarare France 45°54N 4°26E 175 C8
Tararua Ra. N.Z. 40°45S 175°25E 284 G4
Tarasag Vanuatu 14°12S 167°36E 287 D5
Tarascon France 43°48N 4°39E 175 E8
Tarascon-sur-Ariège
France 42°50N 1°36E 174 F5
Tarashcha Ukraine 49°30N 30°31E 177 D16
Tarata Peru 17°27S 70°2W 330 D3
Tarauacá Brazil 8°6S 70°48W 330 B3
Tarauacá → Brazil 6°42S 69°48W 330 B4
Taravao Tahiti 17°43S 149°19W 289 e
Taravao, Isthme de Tahiti 17°43S 149°19W 289 e
Taravo → France 41°42N 8°49E 175 G12
Tarawa Kiribati 1°30N 173°0E 288 G9
Tarawai I. Papua N. G. 3°13S 143°15E 286 B2
Tarawera N.Z. 39°2S 176°36E 284 F5
Tarawera, Mt. N.Z. 38°13S 176°27E 284 E6
Taraz Kazakhstan 42°54N 71°22E 214 E8
Tarazona Spain 41°55N 1°43W 196 D3
Tarazona de la Mancha
Spain 39°16N 1°55W 197 F3
Tárbæk Denmark 55°46N 12°35E 118 A3
Tarbagatay, Khrebet
Kazakhstan 48°0N 83°0E 217 C10
Tarbaj Kenya 2°12N 40°8E 267 D5
Tarbat Ness U.K. 57°52N 3°47W 167 D5
Tarbela Dam Pakistan 34°8N 72°52E 242 B5
Tarbert Kerry, Ireland 52°34N 9°22W 166 D2
Tarbert Argyll & Bute, U.K. 55°52N 5°25E 167 F3
Tarbert W. Isles, U.K. 57°54N 6°49W 167 D2

Tarbes France 43°15N 0°3E 174 E4
Tarboro U.S.A. 35°54N 77°32W 315 D16
Tărcău, Munţii Romania 46°39N 26°7E 183 C11
Tarcento Italy 46°13N 13°13E 199 B10
Tarchomin Poland 52°19N 20°58E 142 B1
Tarcoola Australia 30°44S 134°36E 281 E1
Tarcoon Australia 30°15S 146°43E 281 E4
Tarcutta Australia 35°16S 147°44E 283 C7
Tardeo India 18°57N 72°48E 130 B1
Tardets-Sorholus France 43°8N 0°52W 174 E3
Tardoire → France 45°14N 0°28W 174 C4
Taredjerdja Algeria 25°12N 2°32E 261 C5
Taree Australia 31°50S 152°30E 283 A10
Tarella Australia 31°2S 143°2E 282 A5
Tarfa, Ras Morocco 35°40N 5°11W 260 A3
Tarfa, W. el → Egypt 28°25N 30°50E 256 B3
Tarfaya Morocco 27°55N 12°55W 260 C2
Tárgovişte Romania 44°55N 25°27E 183 F10
Targówek Poland 52°16N 21°3E 142 B2
Târgu Bujor Romania 45°52N 27°54E 183 E12
Târgu Cărbuneşti
Romania 44°57N 23°31E 183 F8
Târgu Frumos Romania 47°12N 27°2E 183 C12
Târgu Jiu Romania 45°5N 23°19E 183 E8
Târgu Lăpuş Romania 47°27N 23°52E 183 C8
Târgu Mureş Romania 46°31N 24°38E 183 D9
Târgu Neamţ Romania 47°12N 26°25E 183 C11
Târgu Ocna Romania 46°16N 26°39E 183 D11
Târgu Secuiesc Romania 46°0N 26°10E 183 E11
Targuist Morocco 34°59N 4°14W 260 B4
Târguşor Romania 44°27N 28°25E 183 F13
Tărhăus, Vf. Romania 46°40N 26°8E 183 C11
Tarhbalt Morocco 30°39N 5°20W 260 B3
Tarhūnah Libya 32°27N 13°36E 258 B2
Tari Papua N. G. 5°54S 142°59E 286 C2
Táriba Venezuela 7°49N 72°13W 328 B3
Tarif U.A.E. 24°3N 53°46E 247 E7
Tarifa Spain 36°1N 5°36W 195 J5
Tarigtig Pt. Phil. 16°25N 122°14E 232 C4
Tarija Bolivia 21°30S 64°40W 334 A3
Tarija □ Bolivia 21°30S 63°30W 334 A3
Tarik I. Micronesia 7°20N 151°46E 287 F18
Tariku → Indonesia 2°55S 138°26E 231 E9
Tarim Yemen 16°3N 49°0E 249 C5
Tarim Basin = Tarim Pendi
China 40°0N 84°0E 217 E10
Tarim He → China 39°30N 88°30E 217 E11
Tarim Pendi China 40°0N 84°0E 217 E10
Tarime Tanzania 1°2S 34°22E 266 E3
Taritatu → Indonesia 2°54S 138°27E 231 E9
Tarka → S. Africa 32°10S 26°0E 270 D4
Tarka La Bhutan 27°12N 89°44E 243 F13
Tarkastad S. Africa 32°0S 26°16E 270 D4
Tarkhankut, Mys Ukraine 45°25N 32°30E 177 E8
Tarko Sale Russia 64°55N 77°50E 214 C8
Tarkwa Ghana 5°20N 2°0W 262 D4
Tarlac Phil. 15°25N 120°35E 232 D3
Tarlac □ Phil. 15°30N 120°30E 232 D3
Tarm Denmark 55°56N 8°31E 163 J2
Tarma Peru 11°25S 75°45W 330 C2
Tarmiya Iraq 33°40N 44°23E 213 G11
Tarn □ France 43°49N 2°8E 174 E6
Tarn → France 44°5N 1°6E 174 D5
Tarn-et-Garonne □ France 44°8N 1°20E 174 D5
Tarna → Hungary 47°31N 19°59E 182 C4
Târnava Mare →
Romania 46°10N 23°43E 183 D8
Târnava Mică → Romania 46°9N 23°55E 183 D8
Târnăveni Romania 46°19N 24°13E 183 D9
Tarnica Poland 55°37N 12°35E 118 B3
Tarnobrzeg Poland 50°35N 21°41E 185 H8
Tarnogród Poland 50°22N 22°58E 185 H9
Tarnopol = Ternopil
Ukraine 49°30N 25°40E 177 D13
Tarnos France 43°32N 1°28W 174 E2
Târnova Moldova 48°10N 27°40E 183 B12
Târnova Romania 45°23N 21°59E 182 D6
Tarnów Poland 50°3N 21°0E 185 H8
Tarnowitz = Tarnowskie Góry
Poland 50°27N 18°54E 185 H5
Tarnowskie Góry Poland 50°27N 18°54E 185 H5
Tärnsjö Sweden 60°9N 16°56E 162 D10
Táro → Italy 45°2N 10°15E 198 C7
Taroko △ Taiwan 24°10N 121°33E 225 B3
Tárom Iran 28°11N 55°46E 247 D7
Taroom Australia 25°36S 149°48E 281 D4
Taroudannt Morocco 30°30N 8°52W 260 B3
Taroudannt □ Morocco 30°30N 8°0W 260 B3
Taroume Cook Is. 21°15S 159°45W 289 h
Tarp Germany 54°39N 9°24E 118 A5
Tarpeena Australia 37°37S 140°47E 282 D4
Tarpon Springs U.S.A. 28°9N 82°45W 317 G7
Tarqua Bay Nigeria 6°24N 3°23E 124 B2
Tarquinia Italy 42°15N 11°45E 199 A8
Tarra Bulga △ Australia 38°27S 146°31E 283 E7
Tarrafal C. Verde Is. 15°18N 23°39W 153 j
Tarragona Spain 41°5N 1°17E 196 D6
Tarragona □ Spain 41°0N 1°0E 196 D6
Tarraleah Australia 42°17S 146°26E 281 G4
Tarrasa = Terrassa Spain 41°34N 2°1E 196 D7
Tàrrega Spain 41°39N 1°9E 196 D6
Tarrytown Ga., U.S.A. 32°19N 82°34W 316 D7
Tarrytown N.Y., U.S.A. 41°4N 73°52W 313 E11
Tårs Denmark 57°23N 10°7E 163 G4
Tarshiha = Me'ona Israel 33°1N 35°15E 250 E6
Tarsus Turkey 36°58N 34°55E 250 B5
Tartagal Argentina 22°30S 63°50W 334 A3
Tartane Martinique 14°45N 60°55W 322 j
Tärtär Azerbaijan 40°20N 46°58E 191 K8
Tärtär → Azerbaijan 40°26N 47°20E 191 K8
Tartas France 43°50N 0°49W 174 E3
Tartu Estonia 58°20N 26°44E 188 C5
Tartūs Syria 34°55N 35°55E 250 D6
Tartūs □ Syria 35°0N 36°0E 250 D7
Tarumirim Brazil 19°16S 41°59S 333 E3
Tarumizu Japan 31°29N 130°42E 222 F2
Tarussa Russia 54°44N 37°10E 188 B9
Tarutao = Ko Tarutao △
Thailand 6°31N 99°26E 237 J2
Tarutao, Ko Thailand 6°33N 99°40E 237 J2
Tarutung Indonesia 2°0N 98°54E 234 B1
Tarutyne Ukraine 46°12N 29°9E 183 E14
Tarvísio Italy 46°30N 13°35E 199 B10
Tarxien Malta 35°52N 14°31E 206 F8
Taşagıl Turkey 36°58N 31°14E 250 B2
Tasahku Burma 26°25N 98°25E 241 A6
Tasaret, O. → Algeria 26°25N 1°59E 261 C5
Tasawah Libya 26°0N 13°30E 258 C2
Tasböget Kazakhstan 44°46N 65°33E 217 D7
Tasek Merimbun △
Brunei 4°31N 114°41E 235 B4
Taseko → Canada 51°58N 123°45W 296 C6
Tasgaon India 17°2N 74°28E 244 F2
Tash-Kömür Kyrgyzstan 41°40N 72°10E 217 D8
Tash-Kumyr = Tash-Kömür
Kyrgyzstan 41°40N 72°10E 217 D8
Tashauz = Dashoguz
Turkmenistan 41°49N 59°58E 216 D5
Tashi Chho Dzong = Thimphu
Bhutan 27°31N 89°45E 241 B2
Tashino = Pervomaysk
Russia 54°56N 43°58E 190 C6

Ţashk, Daryācheh-ye
Iran 29°45N 53°35E 247 D7
Tashkent = Toshkent
Uzbekistan 41°20N 69°10E 217 D7
Tashtagol Russia 52°47N 87°53E 217 B11
Tashu Taiwan 22°41N 120°25E 225 D2
Tasiilaq Greenland 65°40N 37°20W 154 D7
Tasik Bera Malaysia 3°5N 102°38E 234 D2
Tasik Kenyir Malaysia 5°5N 102°45E 234 A2
Tasikmalaya Indonesia 7°18S 108°12E 235 D3
Tåsinge Denmark 55°0N 10°35E 163 J4
Tåsjön Sweden 64°15N 15°40E 160 D16
Task Niger 14°56N 10°46E 299 F2
Taskan Russia 62°59N 150°20E 215 C16
Taşkent Turkey 36°55N 32°29E 250 B3
Taşköprü Turkey 41°30N 34°15E 212 B6
Taskul Papua N. G. 2°32S 150°27E 286 A6
Taşlıçay Turkey 39°38N 43°22E 213 C10
Taşlıçay Turkey 39°38N 43°22E 213 C10
Taşliçik Moldova 47°4N 29°24E 183 C14
Tasman □ N.Z. 41°3S 172°40E 285 D7
Tasman → N.Z. 43°48S 170°12E 285 D5
Tasman, Mt. N.Z. 43°35S 170°12E 285 D5
Tasman Abyssal Plain
Pac. Oc. 34°30S 153°15E 276 G9
Tasman B. N.Z. 40°59S 173°25E 285 A8
Tasman Basin Pac. Oc. 46°0S 158°0E 288 M7
Tasman Glacier N.Z. 43°45S 170°20E 285 D5
Tasman Mts. N.Z. 41°3S 172°25E 285 D7
Tasman Pen. Australia 43°10S 148°0E 281 G4
Tasman Sea Pac. Oc. 36°0S 160°0E 277 H10
Tasmania □ Australia 42°0S 146°30E 281 G4
Tasmanian Wilderness World
Heritage Area △
Australia 43°0S 146°0E 281 G4
Tăşnad Romania 47°30N 22°33E 182 C7
Taşova Turkey 40°45S 36°19E 212 B7
Tassili n' Ajjer Algeria 25°47N 8°1E 261 C6
Tassili n' Ajjer △ Algeria 25°47N 8°1E 261 C6
Tassili-Oua-n-Ahaggar
Algeria 20°41N 5°30E 261 D6
Taşucu Turkey 36°19N 33°52E 250 B4
Taşucu Körfezi Turkey 36°16N 33°56E 250 B4
Tat Ton △ Thailand 15°57N 102°2E 236 E4
Tata Hungary 47°37N 18°19E 182 C3
Tata Morocco 29°46N 7°56W 260 C3
Tatabánya Hungary 47°32N 18°25E 182 C3
Tatakoto French Polynesia 17°20S 138°23W 289 f
Tatamá △ Colombia 5°N 76°9W 328 B2
Tatamba Solomon Is. 8°21S 159°51E 287 M10
Tataouine Tunisia 32°57N 10°29E 258 B2
Tataouine □ Tunisia 32°0N 10°0E 261 B7
Tatar-Pazardzhik = Pazardzhik
Bulgaria 42°12N 24°20E 203 D8
Tatar Republic = Tatarstan □
Russia 55°30N 51°30E 190 C10
Tatarbunary Ukraine 45°50N 29°39E 183 E14
Tatarovo Russia 55°45N 37°24E 129 B2
Tatarsk Russia 55°14N 76°0E 217 D9
Tatarskiy Proliv Russia 50°0N 141°0E 215 D15
Tatarstan □ Russia 55°30N 51°30E 190 C10
Tatatúaros = Tata
Hungary 47°37N 18°19E 182 C3
Tatatua, Pte. Tahiti 17°44S 149°8W 289 e
Tatau Malaysia 3°23S 112°51E 235 B4
Tatau I. Papua N. G. 2°48S 151°57E 286 D6
Tatebayashi Japan 36°15N 139°32E 223 A11
Tateshina-Yama Japan 36°8N 138°11E 223 A10
Tateyama Japan 35°0N 139°50E 223 C11
Tateyama Japan 36°40N 137°35E 223 A8
Tathlina L. Canada 60°33N 117°39W 296 A5
Tathlith Si. Arabia 19°32N 43°30E 248 C3
Tathlith, W. → Si. Arabia 20°35N 44°20E 248 B4
Tathong Channel China 22°15N 114°16E 122 B2
Tathong Pt. China 22°14N 114°17E 122 B2
Tathra Australia 36°44S 149°59E 283 D8
Tatinnai L. Canada 60°55N 97°40W 297 A9
Tatitlek U.S.A. 60°52N 146°41W 303 F11
Tatkon Burma 20°7N 96°13E 241 E6
Tatla Lake Canada 52°0N 124°20W 296 C4
Tatlısu Turkey 40°24N 27°55E 203 F11
Tatnam, C. Canada 57°16N 91°0W 297 B10
Tatra = Tatry Slovak Rep. 49°20N 20°0E 181 B13
Tatranský △ Slovak Rep. 49°10N 20°0E 181 B13
Tatry Slovak Rep. 49°20N 20°0E 181 B13
Tatshenshini → Canada 59°28N 137°45W 296 B1
Tatsuno Hyōgo, Japan 34°52N 134°33E 222 C6
Tatsuno Nagano, Japan 35°58N 138°0E 223 B9
Tatuapé Brazil 23°32S 46°33W 127 A2
Tatuí Brazil 23°25S 47°53W 335 A6
Tatum U.S.A. 33°16N 103°19W 305 K12
Ta'ung = Datong China 40°6N 113°18E 228 D7
Tatura Australia 36°29S 145°16E 283 D6
Tatvan Turkey 38°31N 42°15E 213 C10
Ta'ū Amer. Samoa 14°15S 169°30W 302 g
Tau Rogaland, Norway 59°3N 5°56E 164 E2
Tauá Brazil 6°1S 40°26W 332 C3
Taubaté Brazil 23°0S 45°36W 335 A6
Tauberbischofsheim
Germany 49°37N 9°39E 179 F5
Taucha Germany 51°23N 12°29E 178 D8
Tauern Austria 47°15N 12°40E 180 D6
Tauern-tunnel Austria 47°0N 13°12E 180 D6
Taufikia Sudan 9°24N 31°37E 257 F3
Taufkirchen Germany 48°2N 11°36E 131 B2
Taulé France 48°37N 3°54W 172 D3
Taumarunui N.Z. 38°53S 175°15E 284 F4
Taumaturgo Brazil 8°54S 72°51W 330 B3
Taung S. Africa 27°33S 24°47E 270 D3
Taungdwingyi Burma 20°1N 95°40E 241 E5
Taunggyi Burma 20°50N 97°0E 241 F6
Taungtha Burma 21°12N 95°25E 241 E5
Taungup Burma 18°51N 94°14E 241 F5
Taungup Pass Burma 18°40N 94°45E 241 F5
Taunsa Pakistan 30°42N 70°39E 242 D4
Taunsa Barrage Pakistan 30°42N 70°50E 242 D4
Taunton Somst., U.K. 51°1N 3°5W 169 F4
Taunton Mass., U.S.A. 41°54N 71°6W 313 E13
Taunus Germany 50°13N 8°34E 179 E4
Taupo N.Z. 38°41S 176°7E 284 E6
Taupo, L. N.Z. 38°46S 175°55E 284 E5
Tauragė Lithuania 55°14N 22°16E 184 C9
Tauragė □ Lithuania 55°15N 22°17E 184 C9
Tauranga N.Z. 37°42S 176°11E 284 D6
Tauranga Harb. N.Z. 37°30S 176°5E 284 D5
Taureau, Rés. Canada 46°46N 73°50E 304 E4
Taurianova Italy 38°21N 16°1E 201 D9
Taurus Mts. = Toros Dağları
Turkey 37°0N 32°30E 250 B3
Taus = Domažlice
Czech Rep. 49°28N 12°58E 180 B5
Tauste Spain 41°58N 1°18W 196 D3
Tautira Tahiti 17°44S 149°9W 289 e
Tauyskaya Guba
Russia 59°20N 150°20E 215 D16
Tauz = Tovuz Azerbaijan 41°0N 45°40E 191 K7
Tavan Bogd Uul
Mongolia 49°10N 87°49E 217 C11
Tavares U.S.A. 28°48N 81°44W 317 G8
Tavares, I. dos Brazil 22°49S 43°6W 135 A2
Tavas Turkey 37°34N 29°4E 205 D11

Teaca Romania 46°55N 24°30E 183 D9
Teague U.S.A. 31°38N 96°17W 314 F6
Teahupoo Tahiti 17°50S 149°16W 289 e
Teaneck U.S.A. 40°53N 74°1W 132 A1
Teano Italy 41°15N 14°4E 201 A7
Teapa Mexico 17°33N 92°57W 319 D6
Teba Spain 36°59N 4°55W 195 J6
Tebakang Malaysia 1°6N 110°30E 235 B4
Tébarat Niger 14°49N 4°27E 263 C5
Teberau → Malaysia 1°30N 103°42E 237 d
Teberda Russia 43°30N 41°46E 191 J5
Tébessa Algeria 35°22N 8°8E 261 A6
Tébessa □ Algeria 35°0N 7°50E 261 B6
Tebet Indonesia 6°14S 106°50E 122 B2
Tebicuary → Paraguay 26°36S 58°16W 334 B4
Tebingtinggi Riau, Indonesia 1°0N 102°45E 234 B2
Tebingtinggi Sumatera Selatan,
Indonesia 3°36S 103°4E 234 C2
Tebingtinggi Sumatera Utara,
Indonesia 3°20N 99°9E 234 B1
Tébourba Tunisia 36°49N 9°51E 258 A1
Téboursouk Tunisia 36°29N 9°10E 258 A1
Tebulos Georgia 42°36N 45°17E 191 J7
Tecamachalco Mexico 18°52N 97°44W 319 D5
Tecate Mexico 32°34N 116°38W 307 N10
Tecer Dağları Turkey 39°27N 37°27E 212 C7
Tech → France 42°36N 3°3E 174 F7
Techiman Ghana 7°35N 1°58W 262 D4
Techirghiol Romania 44°4N 28°32E 183 F13
Techou = Dezhou China 37°36N 116°18E 226 F9
Tecka Argentina 43°29S 70°48W 336 E2
Tecomán Mexico 18°55N 103°53W 318 D4
Tecopa U.S.A. 35°51N 116°13W 307 K10
Tecoripa Mexico 28°37N 109°57W 318 B3
Tecuala Mexico 22°23N 105°27W 318 C3
Tecuci Romania 45°51N 27°27E 183 E12
Tecumseh Ont., Canada 42°19N 82°54W 312 D2
Tecumseh Mich., U.S.A. 42°0N 83°57W 311 B13
Tecumseh Okla., U.S.A. 35°15N 96°56W 314 D6
Ted Somali Rep. 4°24N 43°55E 267 D5
Ted=Tejen
Turkmenistan 37°23N 60°31E 216 E6
Tees → U.K. 54°37N 1°10W 168 C6
Tees B. U.K. 54°40N 1°9W 168 C6
Teeswater Canada 43°59N 81°17W 312 C3
Tefé Brazil 3°25S 64°50W 329 D5
Tefé → Brazil 3°35S 64°47W 329 D5
Tefenni Turkey 37°18N 29°45E 205 D11
Tegal Indonesia 6°52S 109°8E 235 D3
Tegallalang Indonesia 8°27S 115°17E 231 J18
Tegalsari Indonesia 8°25S 114°8E 231 J17
Tegel Germany 52°34N 13°16E 115 A2
Tegel, Berlin ✈ (TXL)
Germany 52°33N 13°14E 115 A2
Tegeler See Germany 52°34N 13°15E 115 A2
Tegelort Germany 52°34N 13°13E 115 A2
Tegernsee Germany 47°43N 11°46E 179 H7
Teggiano Italy 40°23N 15°32E 201 B8
Tegid, L. = Bala, L. U.K. 52°53N 3°37W 168 E4
Tegina Nigeria 10°5N 6°11E 263 C6
Tegua Vanuatu 13°15S 166°37E 287 D6
Tegucigalpa Honduras 14°5N 87°14W 320 D2
Teguidda i-n-Tessoum
Niger 17°25N 6°37E 263 B6
Teguise Canary Is. 29°4N 13°34W 153 e3
Tehachapi U.S.A. 35°8N 118°27W 307 K8
Tehachapi Mts. U.S.A. 35°0N 118°30W 307 L8
Tehamiyam Sudan 18°30N 36°32E 256 D4
Teheran = Tehrān Iran 35°41N 51°25E 141 A2
Tehilla Sudan 17°42N 36°6E 256 D4
Tehoru Indonesia 3°23S 129°30E 231 E7
Tehrān Iran 35°41N 51°25E 141 A2
Tehrān □ Iran 35°30N 51°30E 247 C6
Tehrān Mehrābād ✈ (THR)
Iran 35°41N 51°18E 141 A1
Tehrān Pārs Iran 35°44N 51°32E 141 A3
Tehri India 30°23N 78°29E 243 D8
Tehuacán Mexico 18°27N 97°23W 319 D5
Tehuantepec Mexico 16°21N 95°13W 319 D5
Tehuantepec, G. de
Mexico 15°50N 95°12W 319 D5
Tehuantepec, Istmo de
Mexico 17°15N 94°30W 319 D6
Tehuantepec Fracture Zone
Pac. Oc. 13°0N 97°0W 289 F19
Tei Tong Tsui China 22°16N 114°17E 122 B2
Teide, Pico de Canary Is. 28°15N 16°38W 153 e1
Teifi → U.K. 52°5N 4°41W 169 E3
Teign → U.K. 50°32N 3°32W 169 G4
Teignmouth U.K. 50°33N 3°31W 169 G4
Teius Romania 46°12N 23°40E 183 D8
Teixeira Brazil 7°8S 37°15W 332 C4
Teixeira Pinto Guinea-Biss. 12°3N 16°0W 262 C1
Tejakula Indonesia 8°8S 115°20E 231 J18
Tejam India 29°57N 80°11E 243 E9
Tejen Turkmenistan 37°23N 60°31E 216 E6
Tejen → Turkmenistan 37°24N 60°38E 247 B9
Tejo → Europe 38°40N 9°24W 195 F2
Tejo, Rio → Portugal 38°40N 9°24W 135 A1
Tejon Pass U.S.A. 34°49N 118°53W 307 L8
Tekamah U.S.A. 41°47N 96°13W 308 E5
Tekapo → N.Z. 44°10S 170°23E 285 E4
Tekapo, L. N.Z. 43°53S 170°33E 285 E4
Tekax Mexico 20°11N 89°18W 319 C7
Tekeli Kazakhstan 44°50N 79°0E 217 D9
Tekeze → Ethiopia 14°20N 35°50E 257 E4
Tekeze Dam Ethiopia 13°20N 38°45E 257 E4
Tekija Serbia 44°42N 22°26E 202 B6
Tekirdağ Turkey 40°58N 27°30E 203 F11
Tekirdağ □ Turkey 41°0N 27°0E 203 F11
Tekirova Turkey 36°32N 30°30E 205 D12
Tekkali India 18°37N 84°15E 244 E7
Tekke Turkey 40°24N 36°12E 212 B7
Tekman Turkey 39°38N 41°29E 213 C9
Teknaf Bangla. 20°52N 92°18E 241 F9
Tekoa U.S.A. 47°14N 117°4W 306 C5
Tekokota French Polynesia 17°18S 142°33W 289 f
Tekong Besar, Pulau
Singapore 1°25N 104°3E 237 d
Tekoulat, O. → Algeria 22°25N 2°35E 261 D5
Tekro Chad 19°32N 20°56E 259 D9
Tekstilyshchik Russia 55°42N 37°41E 129 B3
Tel → India 20°50N 83°54E 244 D6
Tel Aviv-Yafo Israel 32°4N 34°48E 250 C5
Tel Kauwhata N.Z. 37°25S 175°9E 284 D5
Tel Lakhish Israel 31°34N 34°51E 250 D5
Tel Megiddo Israel 32°35N 35°11E 250 C6
Tela Honduras 15°40N 87°28W 320 C2
Telanaipura = Jambi
Indonesia 1°38S 103°30E 234 C2
Telanaipura = Jambi
Indonesia 1°38S 103°30E 234 C2
Telašćica △ Croatia 43°53N 15°12E 198 B6
Telavi Georgia 42°0N 45°30E 191 J7
Telč Czech Rep. 49°11N 15°28E 180 B8
Telciu Romania 47°25N 24°24E 183 C9
Telde Canary Is. 27°59N 15°25W 153 e1
Telefomin Papua N. G. 5°10S 141°31E 286 C1

Telegraph Creek Canada 58°0N 131°10W 296 B1
Telegraph Hill San Francisco, U.S.A. 136 a2
Telekhany = Tsyelyakhany
Belarus 52°30N 25°46E 177 B13
Telemark □ Norway 59°15N 7°40E 161 G12
Telemark → Norway 59°25N 8°30E 164 E5
Télemsès Niger 15°34N 4°44E 263 B5
Telén Argentina 36°15S 65°31W 334 D2
Telén Argentina 36°15S 65°31W 334 D2
Teleorman □ Romania 44°0N 25°0E 183 G10
Teleorman → Romania 43°52N 25°26E 183 G10
Teles Pires → Brazil 7°21S 58°3W 331 B6
Telescope Pk. U.S.A. 36°10N 117°5W 307 J9
Telescope Pt. Grenada 12°7N 61°36W 323 q
Teletaye Mali 16°31N 1°30E 263 B5
Telford U.K. 52°40N 2°27W 169 E5
Telford and Wrekin □
U.K. 52°45N 2°27W 168 E5
Telfs Austria 47°19N 11°4E 180 D4
Telhal Portugal 38°46N 9°18W 126 A1
Telida U.S.A. 63°23N 153°16W 303 E9
Télimélé Guinea 10°54N 13°2W 262 C2
Teljo, J. Sudan 14°42N 25°26E 257 E2
Telkwa Canada 54°41N 127°5W 296 C3
Tell City U.S.A. 37°57N 86°46W 311 G10
Teller U.S.A. 65°16N 166°22W 303 D6
Tellicherry India 11°45N 75°30E 245 J2
Tellin Belgium 50°4N 5°13E 157 D6
Telluride U.S.A. 37°56N 107°49W 305 J10
Teloloapán Mexico 18°21N 99°51W 319 D5
Telpos Iz Russia 63°16N 59°13E 186 B10
Telsen Argentina 42°30S 66°50W 336 E3
Telšiai Lithuania 55°59N 22°14E 184 C9
Telšiai □ Lithuania 55°59N 22°15E 184 C9
Teltow Germany 52°23N 13°17E 115 B2
Teltow kanal Germany 52°25N 13°29E 115 B3
Teluk Anson = Teluk Intan
Malaysia 4°3N 101°0E 237 K3
Teluk Bahang Malaysia 5°28N 100°13E 237 c
Teluk Betung = Bandar Lampung
Indonesia 5°20S 105°10E 234 D3
Teluk Intan Malaysia 4°3N 101°0E 237 K3
Teluk Kumbar Malaysia 5°18N 100°14E 237 c
Telukbatang Indonesia 0°34S 109°46E 235 C3
Telukbayur Kalimantan Timur,
Indonesia 2°9N 117°24E 235 B5
Telukbutun Indonesia 4°13N 108°12E 235 B3
Telukdalam Indonesia 0°33N 97°50E 234 B1
Tema Ghana 5°41N 0°0 263 D5
Temagami, L. Canada 47°0N 80°10W 298 C3
Temasint Algeria 23°18N 7°40E 261 B6
Tematangi
French Polynesia 21°41S 140°40W 289 f
Temax Mexico 21°9N 88°56W 319 C7
Temba S. Africa 25°20S 28°17E 271 C4
Tembagapura Indonesia 4°20S 137°0E 231 E9
Tembe
Dem. Rep. of the Congo 0°16S 28°14E 268 C2
Tembe → S. Africa 26°51S 32°24E 271 C5
Tembesi → Indonesia 1°43S 103°6E 234 C2
Tembeling → Malaysia 4°4N 102°20E 234 B2
Tembilahan Indonesia 0°19S 103°9W 234 C2
Temblador Venezuela 8°59N 62°44W 329 B5
Tembleque Spain 39°41N 3°30W 194 F7
Temblor Range U.S.A. 35°20N 119°50W 307 K7
Tembo Aluma Angola 7°42S 17°17E 266 D3
Teme → U.K. 52°11N 2°13W 169 E5
Temecula U.S.A. 33°30N 117°9W 307 M9
Temengor, Tasik Malaysia 5°24N 101°18E 237 K3
Temerloh Malaysia 3°27N 102°25E 237 L4
Temiang Indonesia 0°19N 104°23E 234 B2
Teminabuan Indonesia 1°26S 132°1E 231 E8
Temir Kazakhstan 49°1N 57°14E 187 E10
Temir-Khan-Shura = Buynaksk
Russia 42°48N 47°7E 191 J8
Temirtau Kazakhstan 50°5N 72°56E 217 B8
Temirtau Russia 53°10N 87°30E 217 B11
Témiscamie → Canada 50°59N 73°5W 299 B5
Témiscaming Canada 46°44N 79°5W 298 C4
Témiscamingue, L.
Canada 47°10N 79°25W 298 C4
Temnikov Russia 54°40N 43°11E 190 D6
Temnikovo Russia 55°43N 38°11E 129 B6
Temo → Italy 40°17N 8°28E 200 B1
Temora Australia 34°30S 147°30E 283 C7
Temosachic Mexico 28°57N 107°51W 318 B3
Temósachic Mexico 28°57N 107°51W 318 B3
Tempe U.S.A. 33°24N 111°54W 305 K8
Tempelburg = Czaplinek
Poland 53°34N 16°14E 184 E3
Tempelhof Germany 52°28N 13°23E 115 B3
Temperance U.S.A. 41°47N 83°34W 311 C13
Tempino Indonesia 1°46S 103°30E 234 C2
Témpio Pausánia Italy 40°54N 9°6E 200 B2
Temple U.S.A. 31°6N 97°21W 314 F6
Temple B. Australia 12°15S 143°3E 281 A4
Temple City U.S.A. 34°6N 118°3W 126 B4
Temple Hills U.S.A. 38°48N 76°56W 143 C4
Temple of Heaven China 39°52N 116°23E 114 B2
Temple Mount Jerusalem 123 b3
Temple of the Dawn = Arun
Bangkok, Thailand 113 b1
Temple Terrace U.S.A. 28°2N 82°23W 317 G7
Templemore Ireland 52°47N 7°51W 166 D4
Templeogue Ireland 53°16N 6°18W 126 D2
Templeton U.S.A. 35°33N 120°42W 306 K6
Templeton → Australia 21°0S 138°40E 280 C2
Templin Germany 53°8N 13°31E 178 B9
Templo Mayor Mexico City, Mexico 128 b3
Tempoal de Sánchez
Mexico 21°31N 98°23W 319 C5
Temppeliaukio Church
Finland 60°10N 24°56E 121 B2
Tempué Angola 13°27S 18°49E 265 E3
Temryuk Russia 45°15N 37°24E 189 K9
Temse Belgium 51°8N 4°13E 157 C4
Temuco Chile 38°45S 72°40W 336 D2
Temuka N.Z. 44°14S 171°17E 285 E4
Ten Degree Channel India 10°0N 92°30E 245 K11
Ten Thousand Is. U.S.A. 25°45N 81°35W 317 K8
Tena Ecuador 0°59S 77°49W 328 D2
Tenabo Mexico 20°3N 90°14W 319 C6
Tenaha U.S.A. 31°57N 94°15W 314 F7
Tenakee Springs U.S.A. 57°47N 135°13W 296 B2
Tenali India 16°15N 80°35E 245 F5
Tenancingo de Degollado
Mexico 18°58N 99°36W 319 D5
Tenango del Valle Mexico 19°7N 99°33W 319 D5
Tenaro, Akra Greece 36°22N 22°27E 204 E4
Tenasserim □ Burma 14°0N 98°30E 236 F2
Tenasserim □ Burma 14°0N 98°30E 236 F2
Tenby U.K. 51°40N 4°42W 169 F3
Tenda, Colle di France 44°7N 7°36E 198 D4
Tendaho Ethiopia 11°48N 40°54E 257 E5
Tende France 44°5N 7°35E 175 D11

Tendelti *Sudan* 13°1N 31°55E **257** E3
Tendjedi, Adrar *Algeria* 23°41N 7°32E **261** D6
Tendō *Japan* 38°20N 140°30E **220** E10
Tendrara *Morocco* 33°3N 1°58W **261** B4
Tendrovskaya Kosa *Ukraine* 46°16N 31°35E **189** J6
Tendukhera *India* 23°24N 79°33E **243** H8
Teneguía, Volcanes de *Canary Is.* 28°28N 17°51W **153** e1
Teneida *Egypt* 25°30N 29°19E **256** B2
Tenenkou *Mali* 14°28N 4°55W **262** C4
Tenente Marques → *Brazil* 11°10S 59°56W **331** C6
Ténéré *Niger* 19°0N 10°30E **259** E2
Ténéré, Erg du *Niger* 17°35N 10°55E **259** E2
Tenerife *Canary Is.* 28°15N 16°35W **153** e1
Tenerife, Pico *Canary Is.* 27°43N 18°1W **153** e1
Tenerife Norte ✈ (TFN) *Canary Is.* 28°28N 16°17W **153** e1
Tenerife Sur ✈ (TFS) *Canary Is.* 28°3N 16°33W **153** e1
Ténès *Algeria* 36°31N 1°14E **261** A5
Teng Xian *Guangxi Zhuangzu, China* 23°21N 110°56E **229** F8
Teng Xian *Shandong, China* 35°5N 117°10E **227** G9
Tengah → *Singapore* 1°23N 103°43E **138** A2
Tengah, Kepulauan *Indonesia* 7°5S 118°15E **235** D5
Tengchong *China* 25°0N 98°28E **228** E2
Tengchowfu = Penglai *China* 37°48N 120°42E **227** F11
Tenggarong *Indonesia* 0°24S 116°58E **235** C5
Tengger Feng *China* 43°12N 86°48E **217** D11
Tengger Shamo *China* 38°0N 104°10E **226** F3
Tenggol, Pulau *Malaysia* 4°48N 103°41E **237** K4
Tengiz Köli *Kazakhstan* 50°30N 69°0E **217** B7
Tengzhou *China* 35°4N 117°9E **227** G9
Tenhult *Sweden* 57°41N 14°20E **163** G8
Teniente Enciso △ *Paraguay* 21°5S 61°8W **334** A3
Teniente Rodolfo Marsh *Antarctica* 62°30S 58°0W **151** C18
Tenille *U.S.A.* 29°46N 83°19W **316** F6
Tenino *U.S.A.* 46°51N 122°51W **306** D4
Tenkasi *India* 8°55N 77°20E **245** K3
Tenke *Katanga, Dem. Rep. of the Congo* 11°22S 26°40E **269** E2
Tenke *Katanga, Dem. Rep. of the Congo* 10°32S 26°7E **269** E2
Tenkodogo *Burkina Faso* 11°54N 0°19W **263** C4
Tenna → *Italy* 43°14N 13°47E **199** E10
Tennant Creek *Australia* 19°30S 134°15E **280** B1
Tennessee □ *U.S.A.* 36°0N 86°30W **315** D11
Tennessee → *U.S.A.* 37°4N 88°34W **315** C10
Tennille *U.S.A.* 32°56N 82°48W **316** C7
Tennoji *Japan* 34°39N 135°30E **223** B2
Teno, Pta. de *Canary Is.* 28°21N 16°55W **153** e1
Tenojoki = Tana → *Norway* 70°30N 28°14E **160** A23
Tenom *Malaysia* 5°4N 115°57E **235** A5
Tenosique *Mexico* 17°29N 91°26W **319** D6
Tenri *Japan* 34°39N 135°49E **223** B2
Tenryū *Japan* 34°52N 137°49E **223** C9
Tenryū-Gawa → *Japan* 35°39N 137°48E **223** B9
Tensift, Oued → *Morocco* 32°3N 9°28W **260** B3
Tente *Indonesia* 8°35S 118°41E **235** D5
Tenterden *U.K.* 51°4N 0°42E **169** F8
Tenterfield *Australia* 29°0S 152°0E **281** D5
Tenuaiur, Uad → *W. Sahara* 21°36N 16°0W **260** D1
Teo = A Ramallosa *Spain* 42°45N 8°30W **194** C2
Teófilo Otoni *Brazil* 17°50S 41°30W **333** E3
Tepa *Indonesia* 7°52S 129°31E **231** F7
Tepa Pt. *Cook Is.* 19°6S 169°55W **289** g
Tepalcatepec → *Mexico* 18°35N 101°59W **318** D4
Tepalcates *Mexico* 19°23N 99°3W **128** B2
Tepecik *Bursa, Turkey* 40°7N 28°25E **203** F12
Tepecik *Kütahya, Turkey* 39°32N 29°28E **205** B11
Tepehuanes *Mexico* 25°21N 105°44W **318** B3
Tepelenë *Albania* 40°17N 20°2E **202** F4
Tepequem, Serra *Brazil* 3°45N 61°45W **329** C5
Tepetongo *Mexico* 22°28N 103°9W **318** C4
Tepeyac △ *Mexico* 19°30N 99°7W **128** B2
Tepic = Nayarit □ *Mexico* 22°0N 105°0W **318** C4
Tepic *Mexico* 21°30N 104°54W **318** C4
Teplá *Czech Rep.* 49°59N 12°52E **180** B5
Teplice *Czech Rep.* 50°40N 13°48E **180** A6
Teplitz = Teplice *Czech Rep.* 50°40N 13°48E **180** A6
Teplyk *Ukraine* 48°40N 29°44E **183** B14
Tepoca, C. *Mexico* 30°20N 112°25W **318** A2
Tequila *Mexico* 20°54N 103°47W **318** C4
Ter → *Spain* 42°2N 3°12E **196** B8
Ter Apel *Neths.* 52°53N 7°5E **170** B7
Téra *Niger* 14°0N 0°45E **263** C5
Tera → *Spain* 41°54N 5°44W **194** D5
Tera Kora *Bonaire* 12°11N 68°16W **322** h
Teraina *Kiribati* 4°43N 160°25W **289** G12
Terakeka *Sudan* 5°26N 31°45E **257** F3
Téramo *Italy* 42°39N 13°42E **199** F10
Terang *Australia* 38°15S 142°55E **282** E5
Terang, Teluk *Indonesia* 8°44S 116°0E **231** K19
Terawhiti, C. *N.Z.* 41°16S 174°38E **284** H3
Terazit, Massif de *Niger* 20°2N 8°30E **259** D1
Tercan *Turkey* 39°47N 40°23E **213** C9
Terceira *Azores* 38°43N 27°13W **153** d1
Tercero → *Argentina* 32°58S 61°47W **334** C3
Terdal *India* 16°33N 75°3E **244** F2
Terebovlya *Ukraine* 49°18N 25°44E **177** D13
Teregova *Romania* 45°10N 22°16E **182** E7
Tereida *Sudan* 10°35N 31°17E **257** E3
Terek → *Russia* 44°0N 47°30E **191** J8
Terengganu □ *Malaysia* 4°55N 103°0E **237** K4
Terenos *Brazil* 20°26S 54°50W **331** E7
Terepaima △ *Venezuela* 9°58N 69°17W **328** B4
Tereshka → *Russia* 51°48N 46°26E **190** E8
Teresina *Brazil* 5°9S 42°45W **332** C3
Teresinha *Brazil* 0°58N 52°2W **329** C7
Terespol *Poland* 52°5N 23°37E **185** F10
Teressa *India* 8°15N 93°10E **245** K11
Teresva *Ukraine* 48°0N 23°42E **183** B8
Terewah, L. *Australia* 29°52S 147°35E **281** D4
Terges → *Portugal* 37°49N 7°41W **195** H3
Tergnier *France* 49°40N 3°17E **173** C10
Terhazza *Mali* 23°38N 5°22W **260** D3
Teridgerie Cr. → *Australia* 30°25S 148°50E **283** A8
Terijoki = Zelenogorsk *Russia* 60°12N 29°43E **188** B5
Terlizzi *Italy* 41°8N 16°32E **201** A9
Termas de Río Hondo *Argentina* 27°29S 64°52W **334** B3
Terme *Turkey* 41°11N 37°0E **212** B7
Termez = Termiz *Uzbekistan* 37°15N 67°15E **217** E7
Términi Imerese *Italy* 37°59N 13°42E **200** E6
Términos, L. de *Mexico* 18°37N 91°33W **319** D6
Termit, Massif de *Niger* 16°2N 11°20E **259** E2
Termiz *Uzbekistan* 37°15N 67°15E **217** E7
Térmoli *Italy* 42°0N 15°0E **199** F12
Ternate *Indonesia* 0°45N 127°25E **231** D7
Terneuzen *Neths.* 51°20N 3°50E **170** C3
Terney *Russia* 45°3N 136°37E **220** B8
Terni *Italy* 42°34N 12°37E **199** F9
Ternitz *Austria* 47°43N 16°2E **180** D9
Ternivka *Ukraine* 48°32N 29°58E **183** B14
Ternopil *Ukraine* 49°30N 25°40E **177** D13
Ternopil □ *Ukraine* 48°10N 25°10E **177** D13
Ternopol = Ternopil *Ukraine* 49°30N 25°40E **177** D13
Terowie *Australia* 33°8S 138°55E **282** B3
Terpni *Greece* 40°55N 23°26E **202** F7
Terra Bella *U.S.A.* 35°58N 119°3W **307** K7
Terra Nova △ *Canada* 48°33N 53°55W **299** C9
Terrace *Canada* 54°30N 128°35W **296** C3
Terrace Bay *Canada* 48°47N 87°5W **298** C2
Terracina *Italy* 41°17N 13°15E **200** A6
Terralba *Italy* 39°43N 8°39E **200** C1
Terranova di Sicilia = Gela *Italy* 37°4N 14°15E **201** E7
Terranova Pausania = Ólbia *Italy* 40°55N 9°31E **200** B2
Terrasini *Italy* 38°10N 13°4E **200** D6
Terrassa *Spain* 41°34N 2°1E **196** D7
Terrasson-la-Villedieu *France* 45°8N 1°18E **174** C5
Terrazzano *Italy* 45°32N 9°4E **129** A1
Terre-de-Bas *Guadeloupe* 15°51N 61°38W **322** e
Terre-de-Bas *Guadeloupe* 16°10N 61°7W **322** e
Terre-de-Haut *Guadeloupe* 15°52N 61°34W **322** e
Terre des Hommes *Canada* 45°31N 73°32W **130** A2
Terre Haute *U.S.A.* 39°28N 87°25W **311** E9
Terre Rouge *Mauritius* 20°7S 57°31E **272** e
Terrebonne B. *U.S.A.* 29°5N 90°35W **315** G9
Terrecht *Mali* 19°35N 0°22E **261** D4
Terrell *U.S.A.* 32°44N 96°17W **314** E6
Terrenceville *Canada* 47°40N 54°44W **299** C9
Terrick Terrick △ *Australia* 36°8S 144°13E **282** D6
Terrugem *Portugal* 38°41N 9°17W **126** A1
Terry *U.S.A.* 46°47N 105°19W **304** C11
Terrytown *U.S.A.* 29°54N 90°1W **131** B2
Terryville *U.S.A.* 41°41N 73°3W **313** E11
Terschelling *Neths.* 53°25N 5°20E **170** A5
Tersko-Kumskiy Kanal *Russia* 44°32N 44°38E **191** H7
Tertenia *Italy* 39°42N 9°34E **200** C2
Terter = Tärtär → *Azerbaijan* 40°26N 47°20E **191** K8
Teruel *Spain* 40°22N 1°8W **196** E3
Teruel □ *Spain* 40°48N 1°0W **196** E4
Tervel *Bulgaria* 43°45N 27°28E **203** C11
Tervola *Finland* 66°6N 24°49E **160** C21
Tervuren *Belgium* 50°49N 4°31E **116** B3
Tervuren, Park van *Belgium* 50°49N 4°31E **116** B3
Teryaweynya L. *Australia* 32°18S 143°22E **282** B5
Tešanj *Bos.-H.* 44°38N 18°1E **182** F3
Teschen = Cieszyn *Poland* 49°45N 18°35E **185** J5
Teseney *Eritrea* 15°5N 36°42E **257** D4
Tesha → *Russia* 55°38N 42°9E **190** C6
Teshekpuk L. *U.S.A.* 70°35N 153°26W **303** A9
Teshio *Japan* 44°53N 141°44E **220** B10
Teshio-Gawa → *Japan* 44°53N 141°45E **220** B10
Tešica *Serbia* 43°27N 21°45E **202** C5
Tesiyn Gol → *Mongolia* 50°40N 93°20E **218** A7
Teslić *Bos.-H.* 44°37N 17°54E **182** F2
Teslin *Canada* 60°10N 132°43W **296** A2
Teslin → *Canada* 61°34N 134°35W **296** A2
Teslin L. *Canada* 60°15N 132°57W **296** A2
Tesouro *Brazil* 16°4S 53°34W **331** D7
Tessalit *Mali* 20°12N 1°0E **261** D5
Tessaoua *Niger* 13°47N 7°56E **259** F1
Tessin *Germany* 54°2N 12°26E **178** A8
Tessit *Mali* 15°13N 0°18E **263** B5
Tessounfat *Mali* 22°53N 0°32E **261** D5
Test → *U.K.* 50°56N 1°29W **169** G6
Testa del Gargano *Italy* 41°50N 16°10E **199** G13
Testigos, Is. Los *Venezuela* 11°23N 63°7W **321** D7
Tét *Hungary* 47°30N 17°33E **182** C2
Têt → *France* 42°44N 3°2E **174** F7
Tetachuck L. *Canada* 53°18N 125°55W **296** C3
Tetas, Pta. *Chile* 23°31S 70°38W **334** A1
Tete *Mozam.* 16°13S 33°33E **269** F3
Tete □ *Mozam.* 15°15S 32°40E **269** F3
Tetenga, Caleta *Chile* 27°9S 109°19W **330** b
Tetepare *Solomon Is.* 8°45S 157°35E **287** M9
Teterev → *Ukraine* 51°1N 30°5E **177** C16
Teterow *Germany* 53°46N 12°34E **178** B8
Teteven *Bulgaria* 42°58N 24°17E **203** D8
Tethul → *Canada* 60°35N 112°12W **296** A6
Tetiyev *Ukraine* 49°22N 29°38E **177** D15
Tetlin *U.S.A.* 63°8N 142°31W **303** E12
Tetlin Junction *U.S.A.* 63°19N 142°36W **303** E12
Tetlin Nat. Wildlife Refuge ⌂ *U.S.A.* 62°40N 141°50W **303** E12
Tetlit Zheh = Fort McPherson *Canada* 67°30N 134°55W **294** D5
Teton → *U.S.A.* 47°56N 110°31W **304** C8
Tétouan *Morocco* 35°35N 5°21W **260** A3
Tétouan □ *Morocco* 35°35N 5°30W **260** A3
Tetovo *Macedonia* 42°1N 20°59E **202** D4
Tetschen = Děčín *Czech Rep.* 50°47N 14°12E **180** A7
Tetuán *Spain* 40°27N 3°42W **127** B1
Tetufera, Mt. *Tahiti* 17°40S 149°26W **289** e
Tetyukhe = Dalnegorsk *Russia* 44°32N 135°33E **220** B7
Tetyushi *Russia* 54°55N 48°49E **190** C9
Teuco → *Argentina* 25°35S 60°11W **334** B3
Teufelsberg *Germany* 52°29N 13°14E **115** B2
Teulada *Italy* 38°58N 8°46E **200** D1
Teulon *Canada* 50°23N 97°16W **297** C9
Teun *Indonesia* 6°59S 129°8E **231** F7
Teuri-Tō *Japan* 44°26N 141°19E **220** B10
Teutoburger Wald *Germany* 52°5N 8°22E **178** C4
Teutopolis *U.S.A.* 39°8N 88°29W **311** E8
Tevere → *Italy* 41°44N 12°14E **199** G9
Tevere ⌂ *Italy* 42°46N 12°14E **199** F9
Teverya *Israel* 32°47N 35°32E **250** C4
Teviot → *U.K.* 55°29N 2°38W **167** F6
Tewantin *Australia* 26°27S 153°3E **281** D5
Teweh → *Indonesia* 0°58N 114°54E **235** C5
Tewkesbury *U.K.* 51°59N 2°9W **169** F5
Texada I. *Canada* 49°40N 124°25W **296** D4
Texarkana *Ark., U.S.A.* 33°26N 94°2W **314** E7
Texarkana *Tex., U.S.A.* 33°26N 94°3W **314** E7
Texas *Australia* 28°49S 151°9E **281** D5
Texas □ *U.S.A.* 31°40N 98°30W **314** F5
Texas City *U.S.A.* 29°24N 94°54W **314** G7
Texel *Neths.* 53°5N 4°50E **170** A4
Texline *U.S.A.* 36°23N 103°2W **314** C3
Texoma, L. *U.S.A.* 33°50N 96°34W **314** E6
Teykovo *Russia* 56°55N 40°30E **188** D11
Teyvareh *Afghan.* 33°30N 64°24E **240** B2
Teza → *Russia* 56°32N 41°53E **190** B5
Tezin *Afghan.* 34°24N 69°30E **242** B3
Teziutlán *Mexico* 19°49N 97°21W **319** D5
Tezpur *India* 26°40N 92°45E **241** F18
Tezu *India* 27°55N 96°10E **241** B6
Tezzeron L. *Canada* 54°43N 124°30W **296** C4
Tha-anne → *Canada* 60°31N 94°37W **297** A10
Tha Deua *Laos* 17°57N 102°53E **236** D4
Tha Deua *Laos* 19°26N 101°50E **236** C3
Tha Li *Thailand* 17°37N 101°25E **236** D3
Tha Pla *Thailand* 17°48N 100°32E **236** D3
Tha Rua *Thailand* 14°34N 100°44E **236** E3
Tha Sala *Thailand* 8°40N 99°56E **237** H2
Tha Song Yang *Thailand* 17°34N 97°55E **236** D1
Thaba Putsoa *Lesotho* 29°45S 28°0E **271** C4
Thaba-Tseka *Lesotho* 29°32S 28°36E **271** C4
Thabana Ntlenyana *Lesotho* 29°30S 29°16E **271** C4
Thabaung *Burma* 17°2N 94°48E **241** G5
Thabazimbi *S. Africa* 24°40S 27°21E **271** B4
Thabeikkyin *Burma* 22°53N 95°59E **241** D5
Thādiq *Si. Arabia* 25°18N 45°52E **246** E5
Thai Binh *Vietnam* 20°35N 106°1E **228** G6
Thai Muang *Thailand* 8°24N 98°16E **237** H2
Thai Nguyen *Vietnam* 21°35N 105°55E **228** G5
Thailand ■ *Asia* 16°0N 102°0E **236** E4
Thailand, G. of *Asia* 11°30N 101°0E **237** G3
Thakhek *Laos* 17°25N 104°45E **236** D5
Thakurgaon *Bangla.* 26°2N 88°34E **241** B2
Thal *Pakistan* 33°28N 70°33E **242** C4
Thal Desert *Pakistan* 31°10N 71°30E **242** D4
Thala *Tunisia* 35°35N 8°40E **258** A1
Thala La = Hkakabo Razi *Burma* 28°25N 97°23E **228** C1
Thalabarivat *Cambodia* 13°33N 105°57E **236** F5
Thalang = Amphoe Thalang *Thailand* 8°1N 98°20E **237** a
Thalang *Thailand* 8°2N 98°20E **237** H2
Thalassery = Tellicherry *India* 11°45N 75°30E **245** J2
Thale Sap Songkhla *Thailand* 7°12N 100°28E **237** J3
Thalkirchen *Germany* 48°6N 11°32E **131** B2
Thallon *Australia* 28°39S 148°49E **281** D4
Thalu, Ko *Thailand* 9°26N 99°54E **237** b
Thalwil *Switz.* 47°17N 8°35E **179** H4
Tham Lot *Thailand* 19°34N 98°16E **236** C2
Thamarīt *Oman* 17°39N 54°2E **249** C6
Thames *N.Z.* 37°7S 175°34E **284** D4
Thames → *Ont., Canada* 42°20N 82°25W **312** D2
Thames → *U.K.* 51°29N 0°34E **169** F8
Thames → *Conn., U.S.A.* 41°18N 72°5W **313** E12
Thames, Firth of *N.Z.* 37°0S 175°25E **284** D4
Thames Ditton *U.K.* 51°23N 0°20W **125** B1
Thames Estuary *U.K.* 51°29N 0°52E **169** F8
Thamesford *Canada* 43°4N 81°0W **312** C4
Thamesmead *U.K.* 51°30N 0°7E **125** A4
Thamesville *Canada* 42°33N 81°59W **312** D3
Thāmit, W. → *Libya* 31°11N 16°8E **258** B3
Thamūd *Yemen* 17°18N 49°55E **249** C5
Than *India* 22°34N 71°11E **242** H4
Than Kyun *Burma* 9°49N 98°4E **237** H1
Than Uyen *Vietnam* 22°0N 103°54E **236** B4
Thana Cr. → *India* 19°4N 72°54E **130** A2
Thana Gazi *India* 27°25N 76°19E **242** F7
Thanbyuzayat *Burma* 15°58N 97°44E **241** G6
Thandaung *Burma* 19°4N 96°41E **241** F6
Thandla *India* 23°0N 74°34E **242** H6
Thandwe *Burma* 18°20N 94°30E **241** F5
Thane *India* 19°12N 72°59E **244** E1
Thanesar *India* 30°1N 76°52E **242** D7
Thanet, I. of *U.K.* 51°21N 1°20E **169** F9
Thangool *Australia* 24°38S 150°42E **280** C5
Thanh Hoa *Vietnam* 19°48N 105°46E **236** C5
Thanh Hung *Vietnam* 9°55N 105°43E **237** H5
Thanh Pho Ho Chi Minh *Vietnam* 10°58N 106°40E **237** G6
Thanh Thuy *Vietnam* 22°55N 104°51E **236** A5
Thanjavur *India* 10°48N 79°12E **245** J4
Thanlwin = Salween → *Burma* 16°31N 97°37E **241** G6
Thann *France* 47°48N 7°5E **173** E14
Thano Bula Khan *Pakistan* 25°22N 67°50E **242** G2
Thanya Buri *Thailand* 14°1N 100°45E **236** E3
Thaoge → *Botswana* 20°27S 22°36E **270** B3
Thaolintoa L. *Canada* 61°30N 96°25W **297** A9
Thaon-les-Vosges *France* 48°15N 6°24E **173** D13
Thap Lan △ *Thailand* 14°15N 102°16E **236** E4
Thap Sakae *Thailand* 11°30N 99°37E **237** G2
Thap Than *Thailand* 15°27N 99°54E **236** E2
Thar Desert *India* 28°0N 72°0E **242** F5
Tharad *India* 24°30N 71°44E **242** G4
Thargomindah *Australia* 27°58S 143°46E **281** D3
Tharp Fracture Zone *S. Ocean* 54°0S 135°0W **151** B14
Tharrawaddy *Burma* 17°38N 95°48E **241** G5
Tharrawaw *Burma* 17°41N 95°28E **241** G5
Tharthār, Buḩayrat ath *Iraq* 34°0N 43°15E **213** E10
Tharthār, L. = Tharthār, Buḩayrat ath *Iraq* 34°0N 43°15E **213** E10
Tharthār, W. ath → *Iraq* 34°32N 43°4E **213** E10
Thasopoula *Greece* 40°49N 24°45E **203** F8
Thasos *Greece* 40°40N 24°40E **203** F8
That Khe *Vietnam* 22°16N 106°28E **228** F6
Thatcher *Ariz., U.S.A.* 32°51N 109°46W **305** K9
Thatcher *Colo., U.S.A.* 37°33N 104°7W **305** H11
Thaton *Burma* 16°55N 97°22E **241** G6
Thau, Bassin de *France* 43°23N 3°36E **174** E7
Thaungdut *Burma* 24°30N 94°40E **241** C5
Thawatti *Burma* 19°32N 96°16E **241** F6
Thayawthadangy Kyun *Burma* 12°19N 98°0E **236** F1
Thayer *U.S.A.* 36°31N 91°33W **308** G8
Thayetmyo *Burma* 19°20N 95°10E **241** F5
Thazi *Magwe, Burma* 19°59N 95°3E **241** F5
Thazi *Mandalay, Burma* 21°0N 96°5E **241** E6
Thbeng Meanchey *Cambodia* 13°49N 104°58E **236** F5
The Broads *U.K.* 52°45N 1°30E **168** E9
The Everglades *U.S.A.* 25°50N 81°0W **317** K9
The Gulf = Persian Gulf *Asia* 27°0N 50°0E **247** E6
The Hague = 's-Gravenhage *Neths.* 52°7N 4°17E **170** B4
The Pas *Canada* 53°45N 101°15W **297** C8
The Wash *U.K.* 52°58N 0°20E **168** E8
The Weald *U.K.* 51°4N 0°20E **169** F8
Thebes = Thiva *Greece* 38°19N 23°19E **204** C5
Thebes *Egypt* 25°40N 32°35E **256** B3
Thedaw *Burma* 21°5N 96°4E **241** E6
Thedford *U.S.A.* 41°59N 100°35W **308** E3
Theebine *Australia* 25°57S 152°34E **281** D5
Thegon *Burma* 18°39N 95°25E **241** F5
Thekulthili L. *Canada* 61°3N 110°0W **297** A7
Thelon → *Canada* 64°16N 96°4W **297** A8
Thénezay *France* 46°44N 0°2W **172** F6
Thenon *France* 45°9N 1°4E **174** C5
Theodore *Queens., Australia* 24°55S 150°3E **280** C5
Theodore *Sask., Canada* 51°26N 102°55W **297** C8
Theodore *Ala., U.S.A.* 30°33N 88°10W **315** F10
Theodore Roosevelt △ *U.S.A.* 47°0N 103°25W **308** B2
Theodore Roosevelt L. *U.S.A.* 33°40N 111°10W **305** K8
Thepha *Thailand* 6°52N 100°58E **237** J3
Thérain → *France* 49°15N 2°27E **173** C9
Theresa *U.S.A.* 44°13N 75°48W **313** B9
Thermaïkos Kolpos *Greece* 40°15N 22°45E **202** F6
Thermopolis *U.S.A.* 43°39N 108°13W **304** E9
Thermopylae *Greece* 38°48N 22°35E **204** C4
Thesprotia □ *Greece* 39°27N 20°22E **204** B2
Thessalon *Canada* 46°20N 83°30W **298** C3
Thessalonica, Gulf of = Thessaloniki Kolpos *Greece* 40°15N 22°45E **202** F6
Theresa *U.S.A.*
Therma = Eagle Nest *U.S.A.* 36°33N 105°16W **305** H11
Thessaloniki *Greece* 40°38N 22°58E **202** F6
Thessaloniki □ *Greece* 40°45N 23°0E **202** F7
Thessaloniki ✈ (SKG) *Greece* 40°30N 23°0E **202** F7
Thessaloniki Kolpos *Greece* 40°15N 22°45E **202** F6
Thessaly □ *Greece* 39°25N 22°0E **204** B4
Thetford *U.K.* 52°25N 0°45E **169** E8
Thetford Mines *Canada* 46°8N 71°18W **299** C5
Theun → *Laos* 18°19N 104°0E **236** C5
Theunissen *S. Africa* 28°26S 26°43E **270** C4
Thevenard *Australia* 32°9S 133°38E **281** E1
Thiais *France* 48°46N 2°23E **134** B3
Thiamis → *Greece* 39°15N 20°6E **204** B2
Thibaud *Dominica* 15°36N 61°24W **323** k
Thiberville *France* 49°8N 0°27E **172** C7
Thibodaux *U.S.A.* 29°48N 90°49W **315** G9
Thicket Portage *Canada* 55°19N 97°42W **297** B9
Thief River Falls *U.S.A.* 48°7N 96°10W **308** A5
Thiel Mts. *Antarctica* 85°15S 91°0W **151** E16
Thiene *Italy* 45°42N 11°29E **199** C8
Thiérache *France* 49°51N 3°45E **173** C10
Thiers *France* 45°52N 3°33E **174** C7
Thiès *Senegal* 14°50N 16°51W **262** C1
Thiès □ *Senegal* 14°45N 16°50W **262** C1
Thiesi *Italy* 40°31N 8°43E **200** B1
Thika *Kenya* 1°1S 37°5E **268** C4
Thille-Boubacar *Senegal* 16°31N 15°5W **262** B1
Thimân, W. → *Egypt* 28°4N 33°45E **251** K4
Thimphu *Bhutan* 27°31N 89°45E **241** B2
Thina → *S. Africa* 31°18S 29°13E **271** D4
Thinadhoo *Maldives* 0°32N 72°56E **272** d
Thingangyun *Burma* 16°49N 96°12E **241** G6
Þingeyjarsýsla □ *Iceland* 65°40N 16°30W **155** B10
Þingeyri *Iceland* 65°52N 23°30W **155** B3
Þingmúli *Iceland* 65°22N 14°37W **155** B12
Þingvallavatn *Iceland* 64°11N 21°9W **155** C5
Þingvellir *Iceland* 64°15N 21°7W **155** C5
Þingvellir △ *Iceland* 64°16N 21°5W **155** C5
Thio *N. Cal.* 21°37S 166°14E **288** d
Thionville *France* 49°20N 6°10E **173** C13
Thira = Santorini *Greece* 36°23N 25°27E **205** E7
Thirasia *Greece* 36°26N 25°21E **205** E7
Third Cataract *Sudan* 19°42N 30°20E **256** D3
Thirsk *U.K.* 54°14N 1°19W **168** C6
Thiruvananthapuram = Trivandrum *India* 8°41N 77°0E **245** K3
Thiruvarur *India* 10°46N 79°38E **245** J4
Thisio *Athens, Greece* 112 c1
Thisted *Denmark* 56°58N 8°40E **163** H2
Þistilfjörður *Iceland* 66°18N 15°24W **155** A11
Thistle I. *Australia* 35°0S 136°8E **282** C2
Thistletown *Canada* 43°44N 79°34W **141** A1
Thitgy *Burma* 18°15N 96°13E **241** F6
Thithia = Cicia *Fiji* 17°45S 179°18W **287** A3
Thitpokpin *Burma* 19°24N 95°58E **241** F5
Thiva *Greece* 38°19N 23°19E **204** C5
Thiviers *France* 45°25N 0°54E **174** C4
Thizy *France* 46°2N 4°18E **173** F11
Þjórsá → *Iceland* 63°47N 20°48W **155** D6
Thlewiaza → *Canada* 60°29N 94°40W **297** A10
Thmar Puok *Cambodia* 13°57N 103°4E **236** F4
Tho Chu, Dao *Vietnam* 9°20N 103°28E **237** H4
Tho Vinh *Vietnam* 19°16N 105°42E **236** C5
Thoa → *Canada* 60°31N 109°47W **297** A7
Thoen *Thailand* 17°43N 99°12E **236** D2
Thoeng *Thailand* 19°41N 100°12E **236** C3
Thomas *U.S.A.* 35°45N 98°45W **314** D5
Thomas, L. *Australia* 26°4S 137°58E **281** D2
Thomas Circle *Washington, D.C., U.S.A.* 143 a1
Thomas Hill Res. *U.S.A.* 39°34N 92°39W **310** E4
Thomas Hubbard, C. *Canada* 82°0N 94°25W **295** A13
Thomaston *U.S.A.* 32°53N 84°20W **316** C5
Thomastown *Australia* 37°40S 145°2E **128** A2
Thomasville *Ala., U.S.A.* 31°55N 87°44W **315** F11
Thomasville *Ga., U.S.A.* 30°50N 83°59W **316** E6
Thomasville *N.C., U.S.A.* 35°53N 80°5W **315** D14
Thompson *Man., Canada* 55°45N 97°52W **297** B9
Thompson *Pa., U.S.A.* 41°52N 75°31W **313** E9
Thompson → *B.C., Canada* 50°15N 121°24W **296** C4
Thompson → *Mo., U.S.A.* 39°46N 93°37W **310** E3
Thompson Falls *U.S.A.* 47°36N 115°21W **304** C6
Thompson I. *U.S.A.* 42°19N 70°59W **116** B3
Thompson Pk. *U.S.A.* 41°0N 123°2W **304** F2
Thompson Sd. *N.Z.* 45°8S 166°46E **285** F1
Thompson Springs *U.S.A.* 38°58N 109°43W **304** G9
Thompsontown *U.S.A.* 40°33N 77°14W **312** F7
Thomson *Ga., U.S.A.* 33°28N 82°30W **316** B7
Thomson *Ill., U.S.A.* 41°58N 90°6W **310** C6
Thomson → *Australia* 25°11S 142°53E **280** C3
Thomson's Falls = Nyahururu *Kenya* 0°2N 36°27E **268** B4
Thon Buri *Thailand* 13°45N 100°29E **113** B1
Thônes *France* 45°54N 6°18E **175** C10
Thong Yang *Thailand* 9°28N 99°56E **237** b
Thongwa *Burma* 16°45N 96°33E **241** G6
Thonon-les-Bains *France* 46°22N 6°29E **173** F13
Thonze *Burma* 17°38N 95°47E **241** G5
Thoothukudi = Tuticorin *India* 8°50N 78°12E **245** K4
Thorez *Ukraine* 48°4N 38°34E **189** H10
Þórisjökull *Iceland* 64°32N 20°43W **155** C6
Þórisvatn *Iceland* 64°20N 18°55W **155** C8
Þórkötlustaðir *Iceland* 63°50N 22°24W **155** D4
Þorlákshöfn *Iceland* 63°51N 21°22W **155** D5
Thorn = Toruń *Poland* 53°2N 18°39E **185** E5
Thornaby on Tees *U.K.* 54°33N 1°18W **168** C6
Thornbury *Vic., Australia* 37°44S 145°1E **128** A2
Thornbury *Ont., Canada* 44°34N 80°26W **312** B4
Thornbury *N.Z.* 46°17S 168°9E **285** G3
Thorncliffe *Canada* 43°42N 79°20W **141** A2
Thorne *U.K.* 53°37N 0°57W **168** D7
Thornhill *Canada* 43°48N 79°25W **141** A2
Thornton *Ont., Canada* 44°16N 79°43W **312** B5
Thornton *Western Cape, S. Africa* 33°55S 18°32E **118** A2
Thornton *Colo., U.S.A.* 39°52N 104°58W **304** G11
Thornton *Iowa, U.S.A.* 42°57N 93°23W **310** B3
Thornton Heath *U.K.* 51°23N 0°6W **125** B3
Thorntown *U.S.A.* 40°8N 86°36W **311** D10
Thorold *Canada* 43°7N 79°12W **312** C5
Thorpes *Barbados* 13°9N 59°37W **323** r
Þórshöfn *Iceland* 66°12N 15°20W **155** A11
Thouarcé *France* 47°17N 0°30W **172** E6
Thouars *France* 47°0N 0°15W **172** F6
Thouet → *France* 47°17N 0°6W **172** E6
Thouin, C. *Australia* 20°20S 118°10E **278** D2
Thousand Islands *U.S.A.* 44°20N 76°0W **313** B9
Thousand Oaks *U.S.A.* 34°10N 118°50W **307** L8
Thrace *Turkey* 41°0N 27°0E **203** F10
Thrace, Sea of *Greece* 40°30N 25°0E **203** F8
Thredbo *Australia* 36°31S 148°20E **283** D8
Three Forks *U.S.A.* 45°54N 111°33W **304** D8
Three Gorges Dam *China* 30°45N 111°15E **229** B8
Three Gorges Res. = Sanxia Shuiku *China* 30°3N 107°58E **228** B6
Three Hills *Canada* 51°43N 113°15W **296** C6
Three Hummock I. *Australia* 40°25S 144°55E **281** G3
Three Oaks *U.S.A.* 41°48N 86°36W **311** D10
Three Pagodas Pass *Asia* 15°20N 98°30E **236** E2
Three Points, C. *Ghana* 4°42N 2°6W **262** E4
Three Rivers *Calif., U.S.A.* 36°26N 118°54W **306** J8
Three Rivers *Mich., U.S.A.* 41°57N 85°38W **311** C11
Three Rivers *Tex., U.S.A.* 28°28N 98°11W **314** G5
Three Sisters Is. *Solomon Is.* 10°10S 161°57E **287** N11
Three Springs *Australia* 29°32S 115°45E **279** E2
Threipmuir Res. *U.K.* 55°51N 3°19W **121** B2
Thrissur = Trichur *India* 10°30N 76°18E **245** J3
Throgs Neck *U.S.A.* 40°48N 73°49W **132** B3
Throssell, L. *Australia* 27°33S 124°10E **279** E3
Throssell Ra. *Australia* 22°3S 121°43E **278** D3
Thrumshing △ *Bhutan* 27°25N 90°50E **241** B3
Thrushton △ *Australia* 27°47S 147°40E **281** D4
Thu Dau Mot *Vietnam* 10°58N 106°39E **237** G6
Thua → *Kenya* 1°31S 39°30E **268** C4
Thuamal Rampur *India* 19°23N 82°56E **244** E6
Thuan Hoa *Vietnam* 8°58N 105°30E **237** H5
Thubun Lakes *Canada* 61°30N 112°0W **297** A6
Thueyts *France* 44°41N 4°9E **175** D8
Thuin *Belgium* 50°20N 4°17E **170** D4
Thuir *France* 42°38N 2°45E **174** F6
Thule = Qaanaaq *Greenland* 77°30N 69°10W **154** B4
Thule Air Base = Uummannaq *Greenland* 77°33N 68°52W **154** B4
Thun *Switz.* 46°45N 7°38E **179** J3
Thunder B. *U.S.A.* 45°0N 83°20W **312** B1
Thunder Bay *Canada* 48°20N 89°15W **298** C2
Thunderbolt *U.S.A.* 32°3N 81°4W **316** C8
Thunersee *Switz.* 46°43N 7°39E **179** J3
Thung Salaeng Luang △ *Thailand* 16°43N 100°50E **236** D3
Thung Song *Thailand* 8°10N 99°40E **237** H2
Thungyang △ *Thailand* 15°30N 98°40E **236** E2
Thunkar *Bhutan* 27°55N 91°0E **241** B3
Thuong Tra *Vietnam* 16°2N 107°42E **236** D6
Thur → *Switz.* 47°32N 9°10E **179** H5
Thurgau □ *Switz.* 47°34N 9°10E **179** H5
Thüringen □ *Germany* 51°0N 11°0E **178** D6
Thüringer Wald *Germany* 50°35N 11°0E **178** E6
Thuringowa △ *Australia* 19°18S 146°43E **280** B4
Thurles *Ireland* 52°41N 7°49W **166** D4
Thurn P. *Austria* 47°20N 12°25E **180** D5
Thurrock □ *U.K.* 51°31N 0°23E **169** F8
Thursday I. *Australia* 10°30S 142°3E **286** F2
Thurso *Qué., Canada* 45°36N 75°15W **298** C4
Thurso *Highl., U.K.* 58°36N 3°32W **167** C5
Thurso → *U.K.* 58°36N 3°32W **167** C5
Thurston I. *Antarctica* 72°0S 100°0W **151** D16
Thury-Harcourt *France* 48°59N 0°30W **172** D6
Thutade L. *Canada* 57°0N 126°55W **296** B3
Thy *Denmark* 56°52N 8°25E **163** H2
Thyborøn *Denmark* 56°42N 8°12E **163** H2
Þykkvabæjarklaustur *Iceland* 63°30N 18°22W **155** D8
Þykkvibær *Iceland* 63°45N 20°37W **155** D6
Thyolo *Malawi* 16°7S 35°5E **269** F4
Thyssen-Bornemisza, Museo *Madrid, Spain* **127** b3
Ti-n-Amzi → *Niger* 18°20N 4°32E **263** B5
Ti-n-Barraouene, O. → *Africa* 18°40N 4°5E **261** E5
Ti-n-Rerhoh *Algeria* 20°44N 4°2E **261** D5
Ti-n-Tanetfirt *Algeria* 24°49N 3°48E **261** D5
Ti-n-Tarabine, O. → *Algeria* 21°16N 7°25E **261** D6
Ti-n-Toumma *Niger* 16°4N 12°40E **259** E2
Ti-n-Zaouatene *Algeria* 19°55N 2°55E **261** E5
Ti-Tree *Australia* 22°5S 133°22E **280** C1
Tiadiaye *Senegal* 14°25N 16°40W **262** C1
Tiahuanaco *Bolivia* 16°33S 68°42W **330** D4
Tian Shan *Asia* 40°30N 76°0E **217** D9
Tian'anmen Square *Beijing, China* **114** c2
Tianchang *China* 32°40N 119°0E **229** A12
Tiancun *China* 39°54N 116°12E **114** B1
Tiandeng *China* 23°6N 107°7E **228** F6
Tiandong *China* 23°36N 107°8E **228** F6
Tian'e *China* 25°1N 107°9E **228** E6
Tianguá *Brazil* 3°44S 40°59W **332** B3
Tianhe *Guangdong, China* 23°7N 113°21E **121** B3
Tianhe *Guangxi Zhuangzu, China* 24°48N 108°40E **228** E7
Tianjin *China* 39°7N 117°12E **227** E9
Tianjin Shi □ *China* 39°8N 117°12E **227** E9
Tianjun *China* 38°0N 98°30E **218** D8
Tiankoura *Burkina Faso* 10°47N 3°17W **262** C4
Tianlin *China* 24°21N 106°12E **228** E6
Tianmen *China* 30°39N 113°9E **229** B9
Tianquan *China* 30°7N 102°43E **228** B4
Tianshifu *China* 41°17N 124°22E **224** B2
Tianshui *China* 34°32N 105°40E **226** G3
Tiantai *China* 29°10N 121°2E **229** C13
Tiantan Park *Beijing, China* **114** c3
Tianya *China* 18°18N 109°20E **236** C7
Tianyang *China* 23°42N 106°53E **228** F6
Tianyar *Indonesia* 8°12S 115°30E **231** J18
Tianzhen *China* 40°24N 114°5E **226** D8
Tianzhu *China* 26°54N 109°11E **228** D7
Tianzhuangtai *China* 40°43N 122°5E **227** D12
Tiarei *Tahiti* 17°32S 149°20W **289** e
Tiaret *Algeria* 35°20N 1°21E **261** A5
Tiaret □ *Algeria* 34°30N 1°30E **261** B5
Tias *Canary Is.* 28°57N 13°39W **153** e2
Tiassalé *Ivory C.* 5°58N 4°57W **262** D4
Tibagi *Brazil* 24°30S 50°24W **335** A5
Tibagi → *Brazil* 22°47S 51°1W **335** A5
Tibastī, Sarīr *Libya* 22°50N 18°30E **258** D3
Tibati *Cameroon* 6°22N 12°30E **263** D7
Tibe *Ethiopia* 9°2N 37°12E **257** F4
Tiber = Tevere → *Italy* 41°44N 12°14E **199** G9
Tiber Res. *U.S.A.* 48°19N 111°6W **304** B8
Tiberias = Teverya *Israel* 32°47N 35°32E **250** F6
Tiberias, L. = Yam Kinneret *Israel* 32°45N 35°35E **250** F6
Tibesti *Chad* 21°0N 17°30E **259** D3
Tibet = Xizang Zizhiqu □ *China* 32°0N 88°0E **217** F11
Tibet, L. *U.S.A.* 28°27N 81°31W **133** B1
Tibet, Plateau of *Asia* 32°0N 86°0E **210** E10
Tibiao *Phil.* 11°17N 122°2E **233** F4
Tibidabo *Spain* 41°25N 2°6E **114** A1
Tibiri *Niger* 13°34N 7°4E **263** C6
Ţibleş, Vf. *Romania* 47°32N 24°15E **183** C9
Ţibleşului, Munţii *Romania* 47°38N 24°5E **183** C9
Tibni *Syria* 35°36N 39°50E **213** E8
Tibooburra *Australia* 29°26S 142°1E **281** D3
Tibradden Mt. *Ireland* 53°15N 6°16W **120** B2
Tibro *Sweden* 58°28N 14°10E **163** F8
Tiburon *U.S.A.* 37°53N 122°27W **136** A2
Tiburón, I. *Mexico* 29°0N 112°25W **318** B2
Tiburtino *Italy* 41°54N 12°32E **136** B2
Ticao I. *Phil.* 12°31N 123°42E **232** E4
Tice *U.S.A.* 26°40N 81°49W **317** J8
Tichît *Mauritania* 18°21N 9°29W **262** B3
Tichla *Mauritania* 21°36N 14°58W **260** D2
Ticho *Ethiopia* 7°50N 39°32E **257** F4
Ticino □ *Switz.* 46°20N 8°45E **179** J4
Ticino → *Italy* 45°9N 9°14E **179** J4
Ticleni *Romania* 44°53N 23°24E **183** F8
Ticomán *Mexico* 19°31N 99°8W **128** A2
Ticonderoga *U.S.A.* 43°51N 73°26W **313** C11
Ticul *Mexico* 20°24N 89°32W **319** C7
Tidaholm *Sweden* 58°12N 13°58E **163** F7
Tidal Basin *Washington, D.C., U.S.A.* **143** c1
Tidan *Sweden* 58°34N 14°1E **163** F8
Tiddim *Burma* 23°28N 93°45E **241** D4
Tiden *India* 7°15N 93°33E **245** L11
Tiderïdjaouine, Adrar *Algeria* 23°0N 2°15E **261** D5
Tidikelt *Algeria* 26°58N 1°30E **261** C5
Tidioute *U.S.A.* 41°41N 79°24W **312** E5
Tidjikja *Mauritania* 18°29N 11°35W **262** B2
Tidmore = Seminole *U.S.A.* 35°14N 96°41W **314** D6
Tidore *Indonesia* 0°40N 127°25E **231** D7
Tiébissou *Ivory C.* 7°9N 5°10W **262** D3
Tiéboro *Chad* 21°20N 17°7E **259** D3
Tiefa *China* 42°28N 123°26E **224** A1
Tiefersee *Germany* 52°24N 13°3E **115** B1
Tiegang Shuiku *China* 22°37N 113°53E **219** a
Tiel *Neths.* 51°53N 5°26E **170** C5
Tiel *Senegal* 14°55N 15°5W **262** C1
Tieli *China* 46°57N 128°3E **219** B14
Tieling *China* 42°20N 123°55E **224** A1
Tielt *Belgium* 51°0N 3°20E **170** C3
Tien Shan = Tian Shan *Asia* 40°30N 76°0E **217** D9
Tien-tsin = Tianjin *China* 39°7N 117°12E **227** E9
Tien Yen *Vietnam* 21°20N 107°24E **236** B6
T'ienching = Tianjin *China* 39°7N 117°12E **227** E9
T'ienchung *Taiwan* 23°52N 120°35E **225** C2
Tienen *Belgium* 50°48N 4°57E **170** D4
Tiénigbé *Ivory C.* 8°11N 5°43W **262** D3
Tientsin = Tianjin *China* 39°7N 117°12E **227** E9
Tiergarten *Germany* 52°31N 13°20E **115** A3
Tieri *Australia* 23°2S 148°21E **280** C4
Tieroko, Tarso *Chad* 20°45N 17°52E **259** D3
Tierp *Sweden* 60°20N 17°30E **162** D11
Tierra Amarilla *Chile* 27°28S 70°18W **334** B1
Tierra Amarilla *N. Mex., U.S.A.* 36°42N 106°33W **305** H10
Tierra Colorada *Mexico* 17°11N 99°32W **319** D5
Tierra de Barros *Spain* 38°40N 6°30W **195** G4
Tierra de Campos *Spain* 42°10N 4°50W **194** C6
Tierra del Fuego □ *Argentina* 54°0S 67°45W **336** D3
Tierra del Fuego, I. Grande de *Argentina* 54°0S 69°0W **336** D3
Tierra del Fuego △ *Argentina* 54°50S 68°23W **336** D3
Tierralta *Colombia* 8°11N 76°4W **328** B2
Tiétar → *Spain* 39°50N 6°1W **194** F4
Tieté → *Brazil* 20°40S 51°35W **335** A5
Tifarati *W. Sahara* 26°9N 10°33W **260** C2
Tiffin *U.S.A.* 41°7N 83°11W **311** C13
Tiffin → *U.S.A.* 41°17N 84°23W **311** C12
Tiflèt *Morocco* 33°54N 6°20W **260** B3
Tiflis = Tbilisi *Georgia* 41°43N 44°50E **191** K7
Tifton *U.S.A.* 31°27N 83°31W **316** D6
Tifu *Indonesia* 3°39S 126°24E **231** E7
Tiga, Î. *N. Cal.* 21°7S 167°49E **288** d
Tiga Res. *Nigeria* 11°35N 8°30E **263** C6
Tigalda I. *U.S.A.* 54°6N 165°5W **303** J6
Tigaon *Phil.* 13°38N 123°30E **232** E4
Tigbauan *Phil.* 10°41N 122°27E **233** F4
Tiger Leaping Gorge = Hutiao Xia *China* 27°13N 100°9E **228** D3
Tighina *Moldova* 46°50N 29°30E **183** D14
Tigil *Russia* 57°49N 158°40E **215** D16
Tigiria *India* 20°29N 85°31E **244** D7
Tignall *U.S.A.* 33°52N 82°44W **316** B7
Tignish *Canada* 46°58N 64°2W **299** C7
Tigray □ *Ethiopia* 13°35N 39°15E **257** E4
Tigre → *Peru* 4°30S 74°10W **328** D3
Tigre → *Venezuela* 9°20N 62°30W **329** B5
Tigris = Dijlah, Nahr → *Asia* 31°0N 47°25E **246** D5
Tiguentourine *Algeria* 27°52N 9°8E **261** C6
Tigveni *Romania* 45°10N 24°31E **183** E9
Tigyaing *Burma* 23°45N 96°10E **241** D6
Tigzerte, O. → *Morocco* 28°10N 9°37W **260** C3
Tîh, Gebel el *Egypt* 29°32N 33°26E **256** B3
Tihodaine, Erg de *Algeria* 25°15N 7°15E **261** C6
Tihwa = Ürümqi *China* 43°45N 87°45E **217** D11
Tijara *India* 27°56N 76°31E **242** F7
Tijeberdef *S. Africa* 33°53S 18°36E **118** A2
Tijī *Libya* 32°0N 11°18E **258** B2
Tijuana *Mexico* 32°32N 117°1W **307** N9
Tijuca *Brazil* 22°56S 43°13W **135** B1
Tijuca, Pico da *Brazil* 22°56S 43°17W **135** B1
Tijuca △ *Brazil* 22°56S 43°14W **135** B1
Tikahau *French Polynesia* 15°0S 148°10W **289** f
Tikal *Guatemala* 17°13N 89°24W **320** C2
Tikamgarh *India* 24°44N 78°50E **243** G8
Tikaré *Burkina Faso* 13°15N 1°43W **263** C4
Tikchik Lakes *U.S.A.* 60°0N 159°0W **303** G8
Tikéi *French Polynesia* 14°58S 144°32W **289** f
Tikhonkaya = Birobidzhan *Russia* 48°50N 132°50E **219** B15
Tikhoretsk *Russia* 45°56N 40°5E **191** H5
Tikhvin *Russia* 59°35N 33°30E **188** C7
Tikirarjuaq = Whale Cove *Canada* 62°10N 92°34W **297** A10
Tikkadouine, Adrar *Algeria* 24°28N 1°30E **261** D5
Tikkurila *Finland* 60°17N 25°2E **121** B3
Tikmehdāsh *Iran* 37°16N 46°54E **213** D12
Tiko *Cameroon* 4°4N 9°20E **263** E6
Tikopia *Pac. Oc.* 12°19S 168°49E **277** C12
Tikrīt *Iraq* 34°35N 43°37E **213** E10
Tiksi *Russia* 71°40N 128°45E **215** B13
Tiladummati Atoll *Maldives* 7°0N 73°20E **272** d
Tilak Nagar *India* 28°38N 77°5E **120** B1
Tilamuta *Indonesia* 0°32N 122°23E **231** D6
Tilanqiao *China* 31°15N 121°29E **138** B1
Tilburg *Neths.* 51°31N 5°6E **170** C5
Tilbury *Ont., Canada* 42°17N 82°23W **312** D2
Tilbury *Essex, U.K.* 51°27N 0°22E **169** F8
Tilcara *Argentina* 23°36S 65°23W **334** A2
Tilden *U.S.A.* 42°3N 97°50W **308** D5
Tilemsi, Vallée du *Mali* 17°42N 0°15E **263** B5
Tilhar *India* 28°0N 79°45E **243** F8
Tilia, O. → *Algeria* 27°32N 0°55E **261** C5
Tilichiki *Russia* 60°27N 166°5E **215** C17
Tililane *Algeria* 27°49N 0°6W **261** C4
Tilin *Burma* 21°41N 94°6E **241** E5
Tilissos *Greece* 35°20N 25°1E **205** F7
Till → *U.K.* 55°41N 2°13W **168** B5
Tillabéri *Niger* 14°28N 1°28E **263** C5
Tillamook *U.S.A.* 45°27N 123°51W **304** D2
Tillanchong I. *India* 8°30N 93°37E **245** K11
Tillberga *Sweden* 59°40N 16°39E **162** E10
Tillia *Niger* 16°8N 4°47E **263** B5
Tillman *U.S.A.* 32°28N 81°6W **316** C8
Tillsonburg *Canada* 42°53N 80°44W **312** D4
Tillyeria *Cyprus* 35°6N 32°40E **207** E8
Tilogne *Senegal* 16°0N 13°40W **262** B2
Tilos *Greece* 36°27N 27°27E **205** E9
Tilpa *Australia* 30°57S 144°24E **282** A6
Tilrhemt *Algeria* 33°9N 3°22E **261** B5
Tilsit = Sovetsk *Russia* 55°6N 21°50E **184** C8
Tilt → *U.K.* 56°46N 3°51W **167** E5
Tilton *U.S.A.* 43°27N 71°36W **313** C13
Tiltonsville *U.S.A.* 40°10N 80°41W **312** F4
Tim *Denmark* 56°12N 8°19E **163** H2
Tima *Egypt* 26°54N 31°25E **256** B3
Timah, Bukit *Singapore* 1°21N 103°46E **138** A2

Timanah Asia 19°0N 41°0E 248 C3
Timanfaya △ Canary Is. 29°0N 13°46W 153 e2
Timanskiy Kryazh Russia 65°58N 50°5E 186 A9
Timaru N.Z. 44°23S 171°14E 285 E6
Timashevo Russia 53°22N 51°9E 190 D10
Timashevsk Russia 45°35N 39°0E 191 H4
Timau Kenya 0°4N 37°15E 268 B4
Timbaki Greece 35°4N 24°45E 207 E5
Timbaúba Brazil 7°31S 35°19W 332 C4
Timbedgha Mauritania 16°17N 8°16W 262 B3
Timber Creek Australia 15°40S 130°29E 278 C5
Timber Lake U.S.A. 45°26N 101°5W 308 C3
Timber Mt. U.S.A. 37°6N 116°28W 306 H10
Timbío Colombia 2°20N 76°40W 328 C2
Timbiquí Colombia 2°46N 77°42W 328 C2
Timbo Guinea 10°35N 11°50W 262 C2
Timbo Liberia 5°35N 9°45W 262 D3
Timboon Australia 38°30S 142°58E 282 E5
Timbué, Ponta Mozam. 18°47S 36°22E 269 F4
Timbuktu = Tombouctou Mali 16°50N 3°0W 262 B4
Timdjaouine Algeria 21°37N 4°30E 261 D5
Timeïaouine Algeria 20°27N 1°50E 261 D5
Timellouline Algeria 29°22N 8°55E 261 C6
Times Square New York, U.S.A. 132 c2
Timétrin Mali 19°19N 0°34W 263 B4
Timétrine, Mts. Mali 19°25N 1°0W 263 B4
Timfi Oros Greece 39°59N 20°45E 204 B2
Timfristos, Oros Greece 38°57N 21°50E 204 C3
Timgad Algeria 35°29N 6°28E 261 A6
Timhadit Morocco 33°15N 5°4W 260 B3
Timi Cyprus 34°44N 32°31E 207 F8
Tîmia Niger 18°4N 8°40E 259 E1
Timika Indonesia 4°47S 136°32E 231 E9
Timimoun Algeria 29°14N 0°16E 261 C5
Timimoun, Sebkha de Algeria 28°50N 0°46E 261 C5
Timiris, Râs Mauritania 19°21N 16°30W 262 B1
Timiryazev Park Russia 55°49N 37°33E 129 B3
Timiş = Tamis → Serbia 44°51N 20°39E 182 F5
Timiş □ Romania 45°40N 21°30E 182 E6
Timiskaming, L. = Témiscamingue, L. Canada 47°10N 79°25W 298 C4
Timişoara Romania 45°43N 21°15E 182 E6
Timmersdala Sweden 58°32N 13°46E 163 F7
Timmins Canada 48°28N 81°25W 298 C3
Timmonsville U.S.A. 34°8N 79°57W 316 A10
Timok → Serbia 44°10N 22°40E 202 B6
Timoleague Ireland 51°39N 8°46W 166 E3
Timon Brazil 5°8S 42°52W 332 C3
Timor Asia 9°0S 125°0E 231 F7
Timor Leste = East Timor ■ Asia 8°50S 126°0E 231 F7
Timor Sea Ind. Oc. 12°0S 127°0E 278 B4
Timrå Sweden 62°29N 17°18E 162 B11
Timucuan ⌓ U.S.A. 30°28N 81°27W 316 E8
Tîn, Ra's at Libya 32°37N 23°8E 258 B4
Tin Alkoum Algeria 24°42N 10°17E 261 D7
Tin Amzi, O. → Algeria 18°20N 4°32E 261 D6
Tin Atanai Algeria 25°52N 1°37E 261 C5
Tin Can Bay Australia 25°56S 153°0E 281 D5
Tin Can I. Nigeria 6°26N 3°21E 124 B2
Tin Ethisane Mali 19°3N 0°52W 263 B4
Tin Gornai Mali 16°38N 0°38W 263 B4
Tin Mt. U.S.A. 36°50N 117°10W 306 J9
Tina = Thina → S. Africa 31°18S 29°13E 271 D4
Tîna, Khalîg el Egypt 31°10N 32°40E 251 G3
Tinaca Pt. Phil. 5°30N 125°25E 233 J5
Tinaco Venezuela 9°42N 68°26W 328 B4
Tinajo Canary Is. 29°4N 13°42W 153 e2
Tinca Romania 46°46N 21°58E 182 D6
Tindal Australia 14°31S 132°22E 278 B5
Tindivanam India 12°15N 79°41E 245 H4
Tindouf Algeria 27°42N 8°10W 260 C3
Tindouf □ Algeria 27°25N 5°50W 260 C3
Tinée → France 43°55N 7°11E 175 E11
Tineo Spain 43°21N 6°27W 194 B4
Tinerhir Morocco 31°29N 5°31W 260 B3
Tinfouchi Algeria 28°52N 5°49W 260 C3
Tinfunque △ Paraguay 23°55S 60°17W 334 A3
Ting Jiang → China 24°45N 116°35E 229 E11
Ting Kau China 22°22N 114°4E 122 A1
Tinggi, Pulau Malaysia 2°18N 104°7E 237 L5
Tinghert, Ḥamādat Libya 29°0N 9°0E 258 C1
Tingi Mts. S. Leone 8°55N 10°47W 262 D2
Tingkan Taiwan 23°48N 120°52E 225 C2
Tingkawk Sakan Burma 26°4N 96°44E 241 B6
Tinglayan Phil. 17°15N 121°9E 232 C3
Tinglev Denmark 54°57N 9°13E 163 K3
Tingmerkpuk Mt. U.S.A. 68°34N 162°28W 303 B7
Tingo María Peru 9°10S 75°54W 330 B2
Tingrela Ivory C. 10°27N 6°25W 262 C3
Tingri China 28°34N 86°38E 218 F6
Tingsryd Sweden 56°31N 15°0E 163 H9
Tingstäde Sweden 57°44N 18°37E 163 G12
Tingvoll Norway 62°55N 8°12E 164 B5
Tingwon Group Papua N. G. 2°37S 149°42E 286 B5
Tinh Bien Vietnam 10°36N 104°57E 237 G5
Tinharé, I. de Brazil 13°30S 38°58W 333 D4
Tinian N. Marianas 15°0N 145°38E 302 e
Tinian Channel N. Marianas 14°54N 145°36E 302 e
Tinigua △ Colombia 2°30N 74°8W 328 C3
Tiniguiban Phil. 11°22N 119°30E 233 F2
Tinjar → Malaysia 4°4N 114°18E 235 B4
Tinkisso → Guinea 11°21N 9°10W 262 C3
Tinn = Atrå Norway 59°59N 8°45E 164 E5
Tinnevelly = Tirunelveli India 8°45N 77°45E 245 K3
Tinnoset Norway 59°43N 9°3E 164 E6
Tinnsjå Norway 59°55N 8°54E 164 E5
Tinogasta Argentina 28°5S 67°32W 334 B2
Tinos Greece 37°33N 25°8E 205 D7
Tiñoso, C. Spain 37°32N 1°6W 197 H3
Tinpahar India 24°59N 87°44E 243 G12
Tinputz Papua N. G. 5°33S 155°0E 286 C8
Tinrhert, Plateau du Algeria 29°30N 9°0E 258 C1
Tinsukia India 27°29N 95°20E 241 B5
Tinta Peru 14°3S 71°20W 330 C3
Tintamarre, Île St.-Martin 18°7N 63°2W 322 a
Tîntâne Mauritania 16°18N 10°10W 262 B2
Tintina Argentina 27°2S 62°45W 334 B3
Tintinara Australia 35°48S 140°2E 282 C4
Tintioulé Guinea 10°13N 9°12W 262 C3
Tinto → Spain 37°12N 6°55W 195 H4
Tinui N.Z. 40°52S 176°5E 284 G5
Tinwald N.Z. 43°55S 171°43E 285 D6
Tiobraid Árran = Tipperary Ireland 52°28N 8°10W 166 D3
Tioga N. Dak., U.S.A. 48°24N 102°56W 308 A2
Tioga Pa., U.S.A. 41°55N 77°8W 312 E7
Tioman, Pulau Malaysia 2°50N 104°10E 237 L5
Tione di Trento Italy 46°2N 10°43E 198 B7
Tionesta U.S.A. 41°30N 79°28W 312 E5
Tior Sudan 6°26N 31°11E 257 F3
Tiouliline Algeria 27°1N 0°2W 261 C4
Tipaza Algeria 36°35N 2°26E 261 A5
Tipaza □ Algeria 36°35N 2°25E 261 A5
Tipitapa Nic. 12°12N 86°5W 320 D2
Tipp City U.S.A. 39°58N 84°11W 311 E12
Tippecanoe → U.S.A. 40°30N 86°45W 311 D10
Tipperary Ireland 52°28N 8°10W 166 D3
Tipperary □ Ireland 52°37N 7°55W 166 D4
Tipton Calif., U.S.A. 36°4N 119°19W 306 J7
Tipton Ind., U.S.A. 40°17N 86°2W 311 D10
Tipton Iowa, U.S.A. 41°46N 91°8W 310 C5
Tipton Mo., U.S.A. 38°39N 92°47W 310 F4
Tipton Mt. U.S.A. 35°32N 114°12W 307 K12
Tiptonville U.S.A. 36°23N 89°29W 315 C10
Tiptur India 13°15N 76°26E 245 H3
Tiquié → Brazil 0°5N 68°25W 328 C4
Tiquina Bolivia 16°13S 68°50W 330 D4
Tira West Bank 31°52N 35°7E 123 A1
Tiracambu, Serra do Brazil 3°15S 46°30W 332 B2
Tirad Pass △ Phil. 17°3N 120°38E 232 C3
Tirahart, O. → Algeria 23°45N 3°10E 261 D5
Tīrān Iran 32°45N 51°8E 247 C6
Tīrān Si. Arabia 27°57N 34°32E 251 L5
Tiranë Albania 41°18N 19°49E 202 E3
Tiranë ✈ (TIA) Albania 41°57N 19°42E 202 E3
Tirano Italy 46°13N 10°10E 198 B7
Tirari Desert Australia 28°22S 138°7E 281 D2
Tiraspol Moldova 46°55N 29°35E 183 D14
Tiratimine Algeria 25°56N 3°37E 261 C5
Tirau N.Z. 37°58S 175°46E 284 D4
Tirdout Mali 16°7N 1°5W 263 B4
Tire Turkey 38°5N 27°45E 205 C9
Tirebolu Turkey 40°58N 38°45E 213 B8
Tiree U.K. 56°31N 6°55W 167 E2
Tiree, Passage of U.K. 56°30N 6°30W 167 E2
Tîrgovişte = Târgovişte Romania 44°55N 25°27E 183 F10
Tîrgu Jiu = Târgu Jiu Romania 45°5N 23°19E 183 E8
Tîrgu Mureş = Târgu Mureş Romania 46°31N 24°38E 183 D9
Tirgua △ Venezuela 10°5N 68°48W 328 A4
Tirich Mir Pakistan 36°15N 71°55E 240 A3
Tiriolo Italy 38°57N 16°30E 201 D9
Tiririca, Serra da Brazil 17°6S 47°6W 333 E2
Tiriro Guinea 10°27N 8°40W 262 C3
Tiris Zemmour □ Mauritania 24°0N 9°0W 260 D3
Tiritiri o te Moana = Southern Alps N.Z. 43°41S 170°11E 285 D5
Tirna → India 18°4N 76°57E 244 E3
Tirnavos Greece 39°45N 22°18E 204 B4
Tirodi India 21°40N 79°44E 244 D4
Tirol □ Austria 47°3N 10°43E 180 D3
Tiros Brazil 19°0S 45°58W 333 E2
Tirrukkovil Sri Lanka 7°7N 81°51E 245 L5
Tirsa Egypt 29°57N 31°12E 117 B2
Tirschenreuth Germany 49°53N 12°19E 179 F8
Tirschtiegel = Trzciel Poland 52°23N 15°50E 185 F2
Tirso → Italy 39°53N 8°32E 200 C1
Tirstrup Denmark 56°18N 10°42E 163 H4
Tirtagangga Indonesia 8°24S 115°35E 231 J18
Tirthahalli India 13°42N 75°14E 245 H2
Tirua Pt. N.Z. 38°25S 174°40E 284 E3
Tiruchchendur India 8°30N 78°11E 245 K4
Tiruchchirappalli India 10°45N 78°45E 245 J4
Tirukkoyilur India 11°57N 79°12E 245 J4
Tirumangalam India 9°49N 77°58E 245 K3
Tirumayam India 10°14N 78°45E 245 J4
Tirunelveli India 8°45N 77°45E 245 K3
Tirupati India 13°39N 79°25E 245 H4
Tiruppattur Tamil Nadu, India 10°8N 78°37E 245 J4
Tiruppattur Tamil Nadu, India 12°30N 78°30E 245 H4
Tiruppur India 11°5N 77°22E 245 J3
Tirur India 10°54N 75°55E 245 J2
Tiruttani India 13°11N 79°58E 245 H4
Tirutturaippundi India 10°32N 79°41E 245 J4
Tiruvadaimarudur India 11°2N 79°27E 245 J4
Tiruvalla India 9°23N 76°34E 245 K3
Tiruvallar India 13°9N 79°57E 245 H4
Tiruvannamalai India 12°15N 79°5E 245 H4
Tiruvettipuram India 12°39N 79°33E 245 H4
Tiruvottiyur India 13°10N 80°22E 245 H5
Tis Issat Ethiopia 11°25N 37°45E 257 E4
Tisa India 32°50N 76°9E 242 C7
Tisa → Serbia 45°15N 20°17E 182 E5
Tisdale Canada 52°50N 104°0W 297 C8
Tishomingo U.S.A. 34°14N 96°41W 314 D6
Tishrīyaa Iraq 33°18N 44°24E 113 B2
Tisjön Sweden 60°56N 13°0E 162 D7
Tisnaren Sweden 58°58N 15°56E 163 F9
Tišnov Czech Rep. 49°21N 16°25E 181 B9
Tisovec Slovak Rep. 48°41N 19°56E 181 C12
Tissamaharama Sri Lanka 6°17N 81°17E 245 L5
Tissān, Ḥasy Libya 28°14N 12°26E 261 C7
Tissemsilt Algeria 35°35N 1°50E 261 A5
Tissemsilt □ Algeria 35°45N 1°45E 261 A5
Tissint Morocco 29°57N 7°16W 260 C3
Tista → India 25°23N 89°43E 241 C2
Tistedal Norway 59°8N 11°27E 164 E8
Tisza = Tisa → Serbia 45°15N 20°17E 182 E5
Tiszaföldvár Hungary 46°58N 20°14E 182 D5
Tiszafüred Hungary 47°38N 20°50E 182 C5
Tiszalök Hungary 48°1N 21°20E 182 B6
Tiszavasvári Hungary 47°58N 21°18E 182 C6
Tit Ahaggar, Algeria 23°0N 5°10E 261 D6
Tit Tademait, Algeria 27°0N 1°29E 261 C5
Tit-Ary Russia 71°55N 127°2E 215 B13
Titabar India 26°36N 94°12E 241 B5
Titaguas Spain 39°53N 1°6W 196 F3
Titao Burkina Faso 13°45N 2°5W 263 C4
Titel Serbia 45°10N 20°18E 182 E5
Tithwal Pakistan 34°21N 73°50E 243 B5
Titicaca, L. S. Amer. 15°30S 69°30W 330 D4
Titikaveka Cook Is. 21°16S 159°45W 289 h
Titisee Germany 47°54N 8°10E 179 H4
Tititira Hd. N.Z. 43°36S 169°25E 285 D4
Tititut Burma 18°54N 95°16E 241 F5
Titiwa Nigeria 12°14N 12°53E 263 C7
Titlagarh India 20°15N 83°11E 244 D6
Tito Italy 40°35N 15°40E 201 B8
Titograd = Podgorica Montenegro 42°30N 19°19E 202 D3
Titova Korenica Croatia 44°45N 15°41E 199 D12
Titu Romania 44°39N 25°32E 183 F10
Titule Dem. Rep. of the Congo 3°15N 25°31E 268 B2
Titusville Fla., U.S.A. 28°37N 80°49W 317 G9
Titusville Pa., U.S.A. 41°38N 79°41W 312 E5
Tiu Keng Leng China 22°18N 114°15E 122 B2
Tivaouane Senegal 14°56N 16°45W 262 C1
Tivat Montenegro 42°28N 18°43E 202 D2
Tivedens △ Sweden 58°45N 14°35E 163 F8
Tiverton Ont., Canada 44°16N 81°32W 312 B3
Tiverton Devon, U.K. 50°54N 3°29W 169 G4
Tivoli Grenada 12°10N 61°37W 323 q
Tívoli Italy 41°58N 12°45E 199 G9
Tiwī Oman 22°45N 59°12E 249 B7
Tiwi ❂ Australia 11°33S 130°42E 278 B5
Tiyo Eritrea 14°41N 40°15E 257 E5
Tizapán Mexico 19°19N 99°13W 128 C1
Tizga Morocco 32°1N 5°9W 260 B3
Ti'zi N'Isli Morocco 32°28N 5°47W 260 B3
Tizi-Ouzou Algeria 36°42N 4°3E 261 A5
Tizi-Ouzou □ Algeria 36°35N 4°5E 261 A5
Tizimín Mexico 21°9N 88°9W 319 C7
Tiznados → Venezuela 8°16N 67°47W 328 B4
Tiznap He → China 38°21N 77°26E 217 E9
Tiznit Morocco 29°48N 9°45W 260 C3
Tiznit □ Morocco 29°35N 9°30W 260 C3
Tjæreborg Denmark 55°28N 8°36E 163 J2
Tjällmo Sweden 58°43N 15°21E 163 F9
Tjeggelvas Sweden 66°37N 17°45E 160 C17
Tjieggelvas = Tjeggelvas Sweden 66°37N 17°45E 160 C17
Tjirebon = Cirebon Indonesia 6°45S 108°32E 235 D3
Tjirrkarli ❂ Australia 26°0S 125°28E 279 E4
Tjluring Indonesia 8°25S 114°13E 231 J17
Tjøme Norway 59°8N 10°26E 164 E7
Tjörn Sweden 58°0N 11°35E 163 F5
Tjukayirla Roadhouse Australia 27°9S 124°34E 279 E3
Tjurabalan ❂ Australia 19°50S 128°0E 278 C4
Tkibuli = Tqibuli Georgia 42°26N 43°0E 191 J6
Tkvarcheli = Tqvarcheli Georgia 42°47N 41°42E 191 J5
Tlacotalpan Mexico 18°37N 95°40W 319 D5
Tlahualilo de Zaragoza Mexico 26°7N 103°27W 318 B4
Tlalnepantla → Mexico 19°30N 99°18W 128 A1
Tlalpan Mexico 19°18N 99°10W 128 C2
Tlaquepaque Mexico 20°39N 103°19W 318 C4
Tlaxcala Mexico 19°19N 98°14W 319 D5
Tlaxcala □ Mexico 19°25N 98°10W 319 D5
Tlaxiaco Mexico 17°25N 97°35W 319 D5
Tlemcen Algeria 34°52N 1°21W 261 B4
Tlemcen □ Algeria 34°38N 1°30W 261 B4
Tleta Sidi Bouguedra Morocco 32°16N 9°59W 260 B3
Tlokweng Botswana 24°40S 25°58E 270 B4
Tlumach Ukraine 48°51N 25°0E 183 B10
Tłuszcz Poland 52°25N 21°25E 185 F8
Tlyarata Russia 42°9N 46°26E 191 J8
Tmassah Libya 26°19N 15°51E 258 C3
To Bong Vietnam 12°45N 109°16E 236 F7
To Kwai Wan China 22°18N 114°11E 122 B2
To-Shima Japan 34°31N 139°17E 223 C11
Toa Payoh Singapore 1°20N 103°51E 138 A3
Toad → Canada 59°25N 124°57W 296 B4
Toad River Canada 58°51N 125°14W 296 B3
Toamasina Madag. 18°10S 49°25E 272 B2
Toamasina □ Madag. 18°0S 49°0E 272 B2
Toay Argentina 36°43S 64°38W 334 D3
Toba China 31°19N 97°42E 228 B1
Toba Japan 34°30N 136°51E 223 C8
Toba, Danau Indonesia 2°30N 98°30E 234 B1
Toba Kakar Pakistan 31°30N 69°0E 242 D3
Toba Tek Singh Pakistan 30°55N 72°25E 242 D5
Tobago Trin. & Tob. 11°10N 60°30W 323 s
Tobarra Spain 38°37N 1°44W 197 G3
Tobelo Indonesia 1°45N 127°56E 231 D7
Tobermory Ont., Canada 45°12N 81°40W 312 A3
Tobermory Argyll & Bute, U.K. 56°38N 6°5W 167 E2
Tobi Palau 2°40N 131°10E 231 D8
Tobi-Shima Japan 41°12N 139°34E 220 D9
Tobias Fornier = Dao Phil. 10°30N 121°57E 233 F3
Tobiishi Hana Iwo Jima 24°45N 141°17E 288 b
Tobin, L. Australia 21°45S 125°49E 278 D4
Tobin L. Canada 53°35N 103°30W 297 C8
Toblach = Dobbiaco Italy 46°44N 12°14E 199 B9
Toboali Indonesia 3°0S 106°25E 234 C3
Tobol → Russia 58°10N 68°12E 214 D7
Toboli Indonesia 0°38S 120°5E 231 E6
Tobolsk Russia 58°15N 68°10E 214 D7
Tobor Senegal 12°40N 16°15W 262 C1
Toboso Phil. 10°43N 123°31E 233 F4
Tobruk = Tubruq Libya 32°7N 23°55E 258 B4
Tobyhanna U.S.A. 41°11N 75°25W 313 E9
Tobyl = Tobol → Russia 58°10N 68°12E 214 D7
Tobyl Kazakhstan 52°41N 62°34E 216 B6
Tocache Nuevo Peru 8°9S 76°26W 330 B2
Tocantínia Brazil 9°33S 48°22W 332 C2
Tocantinópolis Brazil 6°20S 47°25W 332 C2
Tocantins □ Brazil 10°0S 48°0W 332 D2
Tocantins → Brazil 1°45S 49°10W 332 B2
Toccoa U.S.A. 34°35N 83°19W 315 D13
Toce → Italy 45°56N 8°29E 198 C5
Tochi → Pakistan 32°49N 70°41E 242 C4
Tochigi Japan 36°25N 139°45E 223 A11
Tochigi □ Japan 36°45N 139°45E 223 A11
Tocina Spain 37°37N 5°44W 195 H5
Töcksfors Sweden 59°31N 11°52E 162 E5
Točná Czech Rep. 49°58N 14°25E 135 C2
Toco Chile 22°5S 69°35W 330 E4
Toco Trin. & Tob. 10°49N 60°57W 323 t
Toco Hills U.S.A. 33°49N 84°20W 113 B2
Toconao Chile 23°11S 68°1W 334 A2
Tocopilla Chile 22°5S 70°10W 334 A1
Tocqueville = Râs el Oued Algeria 35°57N 5°2E 261 A6
Tocumwal Australia 35°51S 145°31E 283 C6
Tocuyo → Venezuela 11°3N 68°23W 328 A4
Tocuyo de la Costa Venezuela 11°2N 68°23W 328 A4
Todalen Norway 62°49N 8°44E 164 B5
Todd → Australia 24°52S 135°48E 280 C2
Todds Road Trin. & Tob. 10°28N 61°20W 323 t
Toddu Atoll Maldives 4°25N 72°57E 272 d
Todeli Indonesia 1°40S 124°29E 231 E6
Todenyang Kenya 4°35N 35°56E 268 B4
Todgarh India 25°42N 73°58E 242 G5
Todi Italy 42°47N 12°24E 199 F9
Todos os Santos, B. de Brazil 12°48S 38°38W 333 D4
Todos Santos Mexico 23°26N 110°13W 318 C2
Todt Hill U.S.A. 40°36N 74°6W 132 C1
Todtnau Germany 47°49N 7°56E 179 H3
Toe Hd. U.K. 57°50N 7°8W 167 D1
Toecé Burkina Faso 11°50N 1°16W 263 C4
Toekornstig Stuwmeer Suriname 4°45N 57°30W 329 C6
Toetoes B. N.Z. 46°42S 168°41E 285 G3
Tofield Canada 53°25N 112°40W 296 C6
Tofino Canada 49°11N 125°55W 296 D3
Töfsingdalen △ Sweden 62°10N 12°28E 162 B6
Tofte Norway 59°33N 10°34E 164 E7
Tofua Tonga 19°45S 175°5W 287 P13
Toga Vanuatu 13°26S 166°42E 287 C4
Tōgane Japan 35°33N 140°22E 223 B12
Togba Mauritania 17°26N 10°12W 262 B2
Togbo C.A.R. 6°0N 17°27E 264 A3
Togdheer □ Somali Rep. 9°20N 45°25E 267 C6
Togdheer → Somali Rep. 6°26N 48°39E 267 C6
Togiak U.S.A. 59°4N 160°24W 303 G7
Togiak Nat. Wildlife Refuge ⌓ U.S.A. 59°20N 160°15W 303 G7
Togian, Kepulauan Indonesia 0°20S 121°50E 231 E6
Togliatti Russia 53°32N 49°24E 190 D9
Togo ■ W. Afr. 8°30N 1°35E 263 D5
Togo Wichale Somali Rep. 9°22N 43°40E 267 C5
Tögrög Mongolia 47°25N 92°13E 217 C12
Togtoh China 40°15N 111°10E 226 D6
Tohiea, Mt. Moorea 17°33S 149°49W 289 e
Tohma → Turkey 38°29N 38°23E 212 C8
Tōhoku □ Japan 39°50N 141°45E 220 E10
Töhöm Mongolia 44°27N 108°2E 226 B5
Tohopekaliga, East L. U.S.A. 28°18N 81°15W 317 G8
Tohopekaliga, L. U.S.A. 28°12N 81°24W 317 G8
Toi Cook Is. 18°57S 169°51W 289 g
Toi Japan 34°54N 138°47E 223 C10
Toibalewe India 10°32N 92°30E 245 J11
Toiny St.-Martin 17°53N 62°47W 322 a
Toinya Sudan 6°17N 29°46E 257 F2
Toiyabe Range U.S.A. 39°30N 117°0W 304 G5
Tojikiston = Tajikistan ■ Asia 38°30N 70°0E 217 E8
Tojo Indonesia 1°20S 121°15E 231 E6
Tōjō Japan 34°53N 133°16E 222 C5
Tok U.S.A. 63°20N 142°59W 303 E12
Toka Guyana 3°58N 59°17W 329 C6
Tokaanu N.Z. 38°58S 175°46E 284 E4
Tokachi-Dake Japan 43°17N 142°5E 220 C11
Tokachi-Gawa → Japan 42°44N 143°42E 220 C11
Tōkagi Japan 35°42N 139°55E 140 A4
Tokai Japan 35°2N 136°55E 223 B8
Tokai Plantation S. Africa 34°3S 18°24E 118 B1
Tōkaichiba Japan 35°31N 139°30E 140 B2
Tokaj Hungary 48°8N 21°27E 182 B6
Tokala Indonesia 1°30S 121°40E 231 E6
Tōkamachi Japan 37°8N 138°43E 221 F9
Tokanui N.Z. 46°34S 168°56E 285 G3
Tokar Sudan 18°27N 37°56E 256 D4
Tokara-Rettō Japan 29°37N 129°43E 221 K4
Tokarahi N.Z. 44°56S 170°39E 285 E5
Tokarevo Russia 55°38N 37°54E 129 C5
Tokashiki-Shima Japan 26°11N 127°21E 221 L3
Tokat Turkey 40°22N 36°35E 212 B7
Tokat □ Turkey 40°15N 36°30E 212 B7
Tŏkch'ŏn N. Korea 39°45N 126°18E 224 C3
Tokdo Asia 37°15N 131°52E 221 F5
Tokeland U.S.A. 46°42N 123°59W 306 D3
Tokelau Is. ⧄ Pac. Oc. 9°0S 171°45W 277 B16
Toki Japan 35°18N 137°8E 223 B9
Toki Pt. Wake I. 19°19N 166°35E 302 b
Tokmak Kyrgyzstan 42°49N 75°15E 217 D9
Tokmak Ukraine 47°16N 35°42E 189 J8
Toko Ra. Australia 23°5S 138°20E 280 C2
Tokomaru Bay N.Z. 38°8S 178°22E 284 E7
Tokoname Japan 34°53N 136°51E 223 C8
Tokoro-Gawa → Japan 44°7N 144°5E 220 B12
Tokoroa N.Z. 38°13S 175°50E 284 E4
Tokorozawa Japan 35°47N 139°28E 223 B11
Toksook Bay U.S.A. 60°32N 165°0W 303 F6
Toksun China 42°47N 88°38E 217 D11
Toktogul Kyrgyzstan 41°50N 72°50E 217 D8
Toku Tonga 18°10S 174°11W 287 P13
Tokuji Japan 34°11N 131°42E 222 C3
Tokuno-Shima Japan 27°56N 128°55E 221 L4
Tokushima Japan 34°4N 134°34E 222 C6
Tokushima □ Japan 33°55N 134°0E 222 D6
Tokuyama Japan 34°3N 131°50E 222 C3
Tōkyō Japan 35°43N 139°45E 140 B3
Tōkyō □ Japan 35°40N 139°30E 223 B11
Tōkyō B. = Tōkyō-Wan Japan 35°25N 139°50E 140 B4
Tōkyō Disneyland Japan 35°37N 139°53E 140 B4
Tōkyō Haneda ✈ (HND) Japan 35°33N 139°46E 140 B3
Tōkyō Harbour Japan 35°38N 139°46E 140 B3
Tōkyō Narita ✈ (NRT) Japan 35°45N 140°25E 223 B12
Tōkyō-Wan Japan 35°25N 139°50E 140 B4
Tokzār Afghan. 35°52N 66°26E 240 B2
Tol I. Micronesia 7°20N 151°37E 287 U17
Tolaga Bay N.Z. 38°21S 178°20E 284 E7
Tolageak U.S.A. 70°3N 162°27W 303 A7
Tolbo Mongolia 48°25N 90°17E 217 C12
Tolbukhin = Dobrich Bulgaria 43°37N 27°49E 203 C11
Tolé C.A.R. 6°34N 16°1E 264 A3
Töle Bī Kazakhstan 43°42N 73°46E 217 D8
Toledo Brazil 24°44S 53°45W 335 A5
Toledo Phil. 10°23N 123°38E 233 F4
Toledo Spain 39°50N 4°2W 194 F6
Toledo Ill., U.S.A. 39°16N 88°15W 311 E8
Toledo Iowa, U.S.A. 42°0N 92°35W 310 C4
Toledo Ohio, U.S.A. 41°39N 83°33W 311 C13
Toledo Oreg., U.S.A. 44°37N 123°56W 304 D2
Toledo Wash., U.S.A. 46°26N 122°51W 304 C2
Toledo, Montes de Spain 39°33N 4°20W 195 F6
Toledo Bend Res. U.S.A. 31°11N 93°34W 314 F8
Tolentino Italy 43°12N 13°17E 199 E10
Tolfa Italy 42°9N 11°56E 199 F8
Tolga Algeria 34°40N 5°22E 261 B6
Tolga Queens., Australia 17°15S 145°29E 280 B4
Tolga Hedmark, Norway 62°26N 11°1E 164 B8
Tolhuaca △ Chile 38°15S 71°50W 336 A2
Toli China 45°57N 83°37E 217 C10
Toliara Madag. 23°21S 43°40E 272 C1
Toliara □ Madag. 21°0S 45°0E 272 C2
Tolima Colombia 4°40N 75°19W 328 C2
Tolima □ Colombia 3°45N 75°15W 328 C2
Tolitoli Indonesia 1°5N 120°50E 231 D6
Tolka → Ireland 53°21N 6°14W 120 A1
Tolkmicko Poland 54°19N 19°31E 184 D6
Tollarp Sweden 55°55N 13°58E 163 J7
Tollensesee Germany 53°30N 13°13E 178 B9
Tollhouse U.S.A. 37°1N 119°24W 306 H7
Tollygunge = Taliganga India 22°30N 88°22E 124 B2
Tolmachevo Russia 58°56N 29°51E 188 C5
Tolmezzo Italy 46°24N 13°1E 199 B10
Tolmin Slovenia 46°11N 13°45E 199 B10
Tolna Hungary 46°25N 18°48E 182 D3
Tolna □ Hungary 46°30N 18°30E 182 D3
Tolo Dem. Rep. of the Congo 2°55S 18°34E 264 C3
Tolo, Teluk Indonesia 2°20S 122°10E 231 E6
Tolo Harbour China 22°27N 114°12E 219 a
Tolochin = Talachyn Belarus 54°25N 29°42E 188 E5
Tolokiwa I. Papua N. G. 5°19S 147°37E 286 C4
Tolong B. Phil. 9°20N 122°49E 233 G4
Tolono U.S.A. 39°59N 88°16W 311 E8
Tolosa Spain 43°8N 2°5W 196 B2
Tolox Spain 36°41N 4°54W 195 J6
Toltén Chile 39°13S 74°14W 336 A2
Toluca México, Mexico 19°17N 99°40W 319 D5
Toluca Ill., U.S.A. 41°0N 89°8W 310 C7
Tolworth U.K. 51°22N 0°17W 125 B2
Tolyatti = Togliatti Russia 53°32N 49°24E 190 D9
Tom Burke S. Africa 23°5S 28°0E 271 B4
Tom Price Australia 22°40S 117°48E 278 D2
Toma Burkina Faso 12°45N 2°53W 262 C4
Tomah U.S.A. 43°59N 90°30W 308 D8
Tomahawk U.S.A. 45°28N 89°44W 308 C9
Tomai Moldova 46°34N 28°19E 183 D13
Tomakomai Japan 42°38N 141°36E 220 C10
Tomales U.S.A. 38°15N 122°53W 306 G4
Tomales B. U.S.A. 38°15N 123°58W 306 G3
Tomanivi Fiji 17°37S 178°1E 287 A2
Tomar Portugal 39°36N 8°25W 195 F2
Tomaros, Oros Greece 39°29N 20°48E 204 B2
Tomarza Turkey 38°27N 35°48E 212 C6
Tomás Barrón Bolivia 17°35S 67°31W 330 D4
Tomashevka Belarus 51°33N 23°36E 185 G10
Tomashpil Ukraine 48°32N 28°31E 183 B13
Tomaszów Lubelski Poland 50°27N 23°25E 185 H10
Tomaszów Mazowiecki Poland 51°30N 20°2E 185 G7
Tomatlán Mexico 19°56N 105°15W 318 D3
Tomb of the Kings Jerusalem 123 a2
Tomba di Nerone Italy 41°58N 12°26E 136 B1
Tombadonkéa Guinea 11°0N 14°25W 262 C2
Tombador, Serra do Brazil 12°0S 58°0W 331 C6
Tombe Sudan 5°53N 31°40E 257 F3
Tombeau Bay Mauritius 20°6S 57°30E 272 e
Tombel Cameroon 4°45N 9°40E 264 B1
Tombigbee → U.S.A. 31°8N 87°57W 315 F11
Tomboco Angola 6°48S 13°18E 265 D2
Tombouctou Mali 16°50N 3°0W 262 B4
Tombouctou □ Mali 20°0N 3°0W 262 B4
Tombstone U.S.A. 31°43N 110°4W 305 L8
Tombua Angola 15°55S 11°55E 265 F2
Tomé Chile 36°36S 72°57W 334 D1
Tome Japan 38°40N 141°20E 220 E10
Tomé-Açu Brazil 2°25S 48°9W 332 B2
Tomelilla Sweden 55°33N 13°58E 163 J7
Tomelloso Spain 39°10N 3°2W 195 F7
Tomil Micronesia 9°31N 138°9E 287 R16
Tomil Harbor Pac. Oc. 9°30N 138°10E 287 R16
Tomilino Russia 55°39N 37°55E 129 C5
Tomingley Australia 32°26S 148°16E 283 B8
Tomini Indonesia 0°30N 120°30E 231 D6
Tomini, Teluk Indonesia 0°10S 121°0E 231 E6
Tominian Mali 13°17N 4°35W 262 C4
Tomiño Spain 41°59N 8°46W 194 D2
Tomintoul U.K. 57°15N 3°23W 167 D5
Tomioka Japan 36°15N 138°54E 223 A10
Tomislavgrad Bos.-H. 43°42N 17°13E 182 G2
Tomkinson Ranges Australia 26°11S 129°5E 279 E4
Tommot Russia 59°4N 126°20E 215 D13
Tommy Thompson Park Canada 43°38N 79°20W 141 B3
Tomnop Ta Suos Cambodia 11°20N 104°15E 237 G5
Tomo Colombia 2°38N 67°32W 328 C4
Tomo → Colombia 5°20N 67°48W 328 B4
Tomobe Japan 36°20N 140°20E 223 A12
Tomra Norway 62°34N 6°56E 164 B3
Toms Place U.S.A. 37°34N 118°41W 306 H8
Toms River U.S.A. 39°58N 74°12W 313 G10
Tomsk Russia 56°30N 85°5E 214 D9
Tomtabacken Sweden 57°30N 14°30E 163 G8
Tömük Turkey 36°42N 34°23E 250 B5
Tona Spain 41°51N 2°14E 196 D7
Tonalá Chiapas, Mexico 16°4N 93°45W 319 D6
Tonalá Jalisco, Mexico 20°37N 103°14W 318 C4
Tonale, Passo del Italy 46°16N 10°35E 198 B7
Tonami Japan 36°40N 136°58E 223 A8
Tonantins Brazil 2°45S 67°45W 328 D4
Tonasket U.S.A. 48°42N 119°26W 304 B4
Tonate Fr. Guiana 5°0N 52°28W 329 C7
Tonawanda U.S.A. 43°1N 78°53W 312 D6
Tonb Iran 26°15N 55°15E 247 E7
Tonbo Burma 18°31N 95°5E 241 F5
Tonbridge U.K. 51°11N 0°17E 169 F8
Tonda Papua N. G. 8°55S 141°34E 286 E1
Tondabayashi Japan 34°30N 135°36E 223 C7
Tondano Indonesia 1°35N 124°54E 231 D6
Tondela Portugal 40°31N 8°5W 194 E2
Tønder Denmark 54°58N 8°50E 163 K2
Tondern = Tønder Denmark 54°58N 8°50E 163 K2
Tondi India 9°45N 79°4E 245 K4
Tondi Kiwindi Niger 14°28N 2°2E 263 C5
Tondibi Mali 16°39N 0°14W 263 B4
Tondo Phil. 14°36N 120°57E 127 B1
Tondoro Namibia 17°45S 18°50E 270 A2
Tone → Australia 34°25S 116°25E 279 F2
Tone-Gawa → Japan 35°44N 140°51E 223 B12
Tonekābon Iran 36°45N 51°12E 247 B6
Tong I. Papua N. G. 2°2S 147°47E 286 B4
Tong Xian China 39°55N 116°35E 226 E9
Tong-yeong S. Korea 34°50N 128°20E 224 E4
Tonga Cameroon 4°58N 10°42E 264 B2
Tôngâ Sudan 9°28N 31°3E 257 F3
Tonga ■ Pac. Oc. 19°50S 174°30W 287 P13
Tonga Trench Pac. Oc. 18°0S 173°0W 277 D16
Tongaat S. Africa 29°33S 31°9E 271 C5
Tongala Australia 36°14S 144°56E 283 D6
Tong'an China 24°37N 118°8E 229 E12
Tongareva = Penrhyn Cook Is. 9°0S 158°0W 289 H12
Tongariro, Mt. N.Z. 39°8S 175°38E 284 F4
Tongariro △ N.Z. 39°8S 175°33E 284 F4
Tongass Nat. Forest U.S.A. 54°45N 133°0W 303 J14
Tongatapu Tonga 21°10S 175°10W 287 Q13
Tongatapu Group Tonga 21°0S 175°0W 287 Q13
Tongbai China 32°20N 113°23E 229 A9
Tongbinggo S. Korea 37°31N 126°58E 137 B1
Tongcheng Anhui, China 31°4N 116°56E 229 B11
Tongcheng Hubei, China 29°15N 113°50E 229 C9
Tongchuan China 35°6N 109°3E 226 G5
Tongdao China 26°10N 109°42E 228 D7
Tongeren Belgium 50°47N 5°28E 170 D5
Tonggu China 28°31N 114°20E 229 C10
Tonggu Jiao China 22°22N 113°37E 219 a
Tongguan China 34°40N 110°25E 226 G6
Tonghai China 24°10N 102°53E 228 E4
Tonghua China 41°42N 125°58E 224 B2
Tongi = Tungi Bangla. 23°53N 90°24E 241 D3
Tongjiang Heilongjiang, China 47°40N 132°27E 219 B15
Tongjiang Sichuan, China 31°58N 107°11E 228 B6
Tongjosŏn Man N. Korea 39°30N 128°0E 224 C4
Tongking, G. of = Tonkin, G. of Asia 20°0N 108°0E 236 C7
Tongliang China 29°50N 106°3E 228 C6
Tongliao China 43°38N 122°18E 227 C12
Tongling China 30°55N 117°48E 229 B11
Tonglu China 29°45N 119°37E 229 C12
Tongnan = Anyue China 30°9N 105°50E 228 B5
Tongoa Vanuatu 16°54S 168°34E 287 F6
Tongobory Madag. 23°32S 44°20E 272 C1
Tongoy Chile 30°16S 71°31W 334 C1
Tongqiao China 31°21N 121°22E 138 A1
Tongquil I. Phil. 6°2N 121°51E 233 H3
Tongren China 27°43N 109°11E 228 D7
Tongres = Tongeren Belgium 50°47N 5°28E 170 D5
Tongsa Dzong Bhutan 27°31N 90°31E 241 B3
Tongsha Tao Taiwan 26°12N 128°28E 225 b
Tongshi China 18°30N 109°20E 236 C7
Tongue U.K. 58°29N 4°25W 167 C4
Tongue → U.S.A. 46°25N 105°52W 304 C11
Tongwei China 35°0N 105°5E 226 G3
Tongxiang China 30°39N 120°34E 229 B13
Tongxin China 36°59N 105°58E 226 F3
Tongyang N. Korea 39°9N 126°53E 224 C3
Tongyu China 44°45N 123°4E 227 B12
Tongzhou China 32°12N 121°2E 229 A13
Tongzi China 28°9N 106°49E 228 C6
Tonica U.S.A. 41°13N 89°4W 310 C7
Tonj Sudan 7°20N 28°44E 257 F2
Tonj → Sudan 7°31N 28°55E 257 F2
Tonk India 26°6N 75°54E 242 F6
Tonkawa U.S.A. 36°41N 97°18W 314 C6
Tonkin = Bac Phan Vietnam 22°0N 105°0E 228 G5
Tonkin, G. of Asia 20°0N 108°0E 236 C7
Tonlé Sap Cambodia 13°0N 104°0E 236 F5
Tonnay-Charente France 45°56N 0°55W 174 C3
Tonneins France 44°23N 0°19E 174 D4
Tonnerre France 47°51N 3°59E 173 E10
Tönning Germany 54°19N 8°56E 178 A4
Tono Japan 39°19N 141°32E 220 E10
Tonoas I. Micronesia 7°22N 151°52E 287 T18
Tonopah U.S.A. 38°4N 117°14W 305 G5
Tonoshō Japan 34°29N 134°11E 222 C6
Tonosí Panama 7°20N 80°20W 320 E3
Tons → Haryana, India 30°30N 77°39E 242 D7
Tons → Ut. P., India 26°1N 83°33E 243 F10
Tønsberg Norway 59°19N 10°25E 164 E7
Tonsina U.S.A. 61°39N 145°11W 303 F11
Tonstad Norway 58°40N 6°45E 164 F3
Tonto △ U.S.A. 33°39N 111°7W 305 K8
Tonumea Tonga 20°30S 174°30W 287 Q13
Tonya Turkey 40°53N 39°16E 213 B8
Tonzang Burma 23°36N 93°42E 241 D4
Tonzi Burma 24°39N 94°57E 241 C5
Toobanna Australia 18°42S 146°9E 280 B4
Toodyay Australia 31°34S 116°28E 279 F2
Tooele U.S.A. 40°32N 112°18W 304 F7
Toompine Australia 27°15S 144°19E 281 D3
Toomsboro U.S.A. 32°50N 83°5W 316 C6
Toora Australia 38°39S 146°23E 283 E7
Toora-Khem Russia 52°28N 96°17E 217 B13
Toorak Australia 37°50S 145°1E 128 B2
Tootias Somali Rep. 3°57N 43°57E 267 D5
Toowoomba Australia 27°32S 151°56E 281 D5
Top Springs Australia 16°37S 131°51E 278 C5
Topalu Romania 44°31N 28°3E 183 F13
Topanga State Park ⌓ U.S.A. 34°7N 118°31W 126 B1
Topaz U.S.A. 38°41N 119°30W 306 G7
Topeka U.S.A. 39°3N 95°40W 308 F6
Topkapı Turkey 41°1N 28°55E 122 B1
Topkapı Palaca Turkey 41°1N 28°59E 122 B1
Topl'a → Slovak Rep. 48°45N 21°45E 181 C14
Topley Canada 54°49N 126°18W 296 C3
Toplica → Serbia 43°15N 21°49E 202 C5
Toplița Romania 46°55N 25°20E 183 D10
Topo Azores 38°33N 27°45W 153 d1
Topo, Pta. do Azores 38°33N 27°46W 153 d1
Topocalma, Pta. Chile 34°10S 72°2W 334 C1
Topock U.S.A. 34°46N 114°29W 307 L12
Topola Serbia 44°17N 20°41E 202 B4
Topolčani Macedonia 41°14N 21°25E 202 E5
Topol'čany Slovak Rep. 48°35N 18°12E 181 C11
Topolnitsa → Bulgaria 42°11N 24°18E 203 D8
Topolobampo Mexico 25°36N 109°3W 318 B3
Topoloveni Romania 44°49N 25°5E 183 F10
Topolovgrad Bulgaria 42°5N 26°20E 203 D10
Topolvățu Mare Romania 45°46N 21°41E 182 E6
Topozero, Ozero Russia 65°35N 32°0E 160 D25
Toppenish U.S.A. 46°23N 120°19W 304 C3
Topraisar Romania 44°1N 28°27E 183 F13
Toprakkale Turkey 37°5N 36°8E 250 A7
Topusko Croatia 45°18N 15°59E 199 C12
Toquepala Peru 17°24S 70°25W 330 D3
Toqyraūyn → Kazakhstan 46°48N 75°24E 217 C9
Tor di Quinto Italy 41°56N 12°27E 136 B1
Tor Pignattara Italy 41°53N 12°31E 136 B2
Tor Sapienza Italy 41°53N 12°35E 136 B2
Torà Spain 41°49N 1°25E 196 D6
Tora Kit Sudan 11°2N 32°36E 257 E3
Toraka Vestale Madag. 16°20S 43°58E 272 B1
Toranomon Tokyo, Japan 140 c3
Torata Peru 17°23S 70°1W 330 D3
Torbalı Turkey 38°10N 27°21E 205 C9
Torbat-e Heydārīyeh Iran 35°15N 59°12E 247 C8
Torbat-e Jām Iran 35°16N 60°35E 247 C9
Torbay Canada 47°40N 52°42W 299 C9
Torbay □ U.K. 50°26N 3°31W 169 G4
Tørberget Norway 61°8N 12°7E 164 C9
Torbjörntorp Sweden 58°12N 13°36E 163 F7
Torcy France 48°51N 2°39E 134 A4
Tordesillas Spain 41°30N 5°0W 194 D6
Töreboda Sweden 58°41N 14°7E 163 F8
Torekov Sweden 56°26N 12°37E 163 H6
Torellò Spain 42°3N 2°16E 196 C7
Toreno Spain 42°42N 6°30W 194 C4
Torfaen □ U.K. 51°43N 3°3W 169 F4
Torfajökull Iceland 63°54N 19°0W 155 D7
Torgau Germany 51°34N 13°0E 178 D8
Torgelow Germany 53°37N 14°1E 178 B10
Torghay Kazakhstan 49°38N 63°29E 216 C6
Torghay → Kazakhstan 48°1N 62°45E 216 C6
Torghay Ustirti Asia 51°0N 63°0E 216 B6
Torghay Zhylghasy Kazakhstan 52°0N 64°30E 216 B6
Torgovaya = Salsk Russia 46°28N 41°30E 191 G5
Torhamn Sweden 56°6N 15°50E 163 H9
Torhout Belgium 51°5N 3°7E 170 C3
Torhovytsya Ukraine 48°36N 25°26E 183 B10
Tori Ethiopia 7°53N 33°35E 257 F3
Tori-Shima Japan 30°29N 140°19E 221 J10
Torigni-sur-Vire France 49°3N 0°58W 172 C6
Torija Spain 40°44N 3°2W 196 E1
Torilla Pen. Australia 22°29S 150°5E 280 C5
Torino Italy 45°3N 7°40E 198 C4
Torit Sudan 4°27N 32°31E 257 G3
Torkamān Iran 37°35N 47°23E 213 D12
Torkovichi Russia 58°51N 30°21E 188 C6
Tormac Romania 45°30N 21°30E 182 E6
Tormes → Spain 41°18N 6°29W 194 D4
Tornado Mt. Canada 49°55N 114°40W 296 D6
Tornal'a Slovak Rep. 48°25N 20°20E 181 C13
Torneå = Tornio Finland 65°50N 24°12E 160 D21
Torneälven → Europe 65°50N 24°12E 160 D21
Torneträsk Sweden 68°24N 19°15E 160 B18
Torngat Mts. Canada 59°0N 63°40W 295 F19
Tornio Finland 65°50N 24°12E 160 D21
Tornionjoki = Torneälven → Europe 65°50N 24°12E 160 D21
Tornquist Argentina 38°8S 62°15W 334 D3
Toro Baleares, Spain 39°59N 4°8E 206 B5
Toro Zamora, Spain 41°35N 5°24W 194 D5
Torö Sweden 58°48N 17°50E 163 F11
Toro, Cerro del Chile 29°10S 69°50W 334 B2
Toro ⌓ Uganda 1°5N 30°22E 268 C3
Toro Pk. U.S.A. 33°34N 116°24W 307 M10
Torodi Niger 13°7N 1°47E 263 C5
Torokina Papua N. G. 6°14S 155°3E 286 D8
Törökszentmiklós Hungary 47°11N 20°27E 182 C5
Toronto N.S.W., Australia 33°0S 151°30E 283 B9
Toronto Ont., Canada 43°39N 79°20W 141 B2
Toronto Ohio, U.S.A. 40°28N 80°36W 312 F4
Toronto, Univ. of Canada 43°39N 79°23W 141 B2
Toronto City Centre ✈ (YTZ) Canada 43°38N 79°24W 141 B2
Toronto Harbour Canada 43°38N 79°21W 141 B2
Toronto I. Canada 43°37N 79°23W 141 B2
Toronto Lester B. Pearson Int. ✈ (YYZ) Canada 43°46N 79°35W 141 A1
Toropets Russia 56°30N 31°40E 188 D6
Tororo Uganda 0°45N 34°12E 268 B3
Toros Dağları Turkey 37°0N 32°30E 250 B3
Toros Monumental, Templo de Barcelona, Spain 114 a3
Torotoro Bolivia 18°7S 65°46W 331 D4
Torotoro △ Bolivia 18°8S 65°46W 331 D4
Torpa India 22°57N 85°6E 243 H11
Torpo Norway 60°40N 8°43E 164 D5
Torquay Vic., Australia 38°20S 144°19E 282 E6
Torquay Torbay, U.K. 50°27N 3°32W 169 G4
Torquemada Spain 42°2N 4°19W 194 C6
Torrais, Pta. Azores 39°43N 31°7W 153 d2
Torrance U.S.A. 33°50N 118°20W 307 M8
Torrão Portugal 38°16N 8°11W 195 G2
Torre Annunziata Italy 40°45N 14°27E 201 B7

Tsurusaki *Japan* 33°14N 131°41E **222** D3
Tsushima *Ehime, Japan* 33°7N 132°32E **222** D4
Tsushima *Gifu, Japan* 35°10N 136°43E **223** B8
Tsushima *Nagasaki, Japan* 34°20N 129°20E **222** C1
Tsuyama *Japan* 35°3N 134°0E **222** B6
Tsvetkovo *Ukraine* 49°8N 31°33E **189** H6
Tsyelyakhany *Belarus* 52°30N 25°46E **177** B13
Tsz Wan Shan *China* 22°20N 114°11E **122** A2
Tu → *Burma* 21°50N 96°15E **241** E6
Tua *Dem. Rep. of the Congo* 3°38S 16°38E **264** C3
Tua → *Papua N. G.* 6°30S 144°28E **286** D3
Tua → *Portugal* 41°13N 7°26W **194** D3
Tuaheni Pt. *N.Z.* 38°43S 178°4E **284** E6
Tuai *N.Z.* 38°47S 177°10E **284** E6
Tuaim = Tuam *Ireland* 53°31N 8°51W **166** C3
Tuakau *N.Z.* 37°16S 174°59E **284** D3
Tual *Indonesia* 5°38S 132°44E **231** F8
Tualatin *U.S.A.* 45°23N 122°45W **306** E4
Tuam *Ireland* 53°31N 8°51W **166** C3
Tuamarina *N.Z.* 41°25S 173°59E **285** B8
Tuamotu, Îs.
French Polynesia 17°0S 144°0W **289** f
Tuamotu Arch. = Tuamotu, Îs.
French Polynesia 17°0S 144°0W **289** f
Tuamotu Ridge *Pac. Oc.* 20°0S 138°0W **289** K14
Tuan Giao *Vietnam* 21°35N 103°25E **236** B4
Tuanfeng *China* 30°38N 114°52E **229** B10
Tuangku *Indonesia* 2°10N 97°16E **234** B1
Tuanxi *China* 27°28N 107°8E **228** D6
Tuao *Phil.* 17°45N 121°22E **232** C3
Tuapa *Cook Is.* 18°57S 169°54W **289** g
Tuapse *Russia* 44°5N 39°10E **191** H4
Tuaran *Malaysia* 6°10N 116°13E **235** A5
Tuas *Singapore* 1°19N 103°39E **138** B1
Tuatapere *N.Z.* 46°8S 167°41E **285** G2
Tuba City *U.S.A.* 36°8N 111°14W **305** H8
Tuban *Indonesia* 6°54S 112°3E **235** D4
Tubani *Botswana* 24°46S 24°18E **270** B3
Tubarão *Brazil* 28°30S 49°0W **335** B6
Tūbās *West Bank* 32°20N 35°22E **251** F6
Tubas → *Namibia* 22°54S 14°35E **270** B2
Tubau *Malaysia* 3°10N 113°40E **235** B4
Tubbataha Reefs △ *Phil.* 8°53N 119°53E **233** G2
Tubigon *Phil.* 9°57N 123°58E **233** G4
Tübingen *Germany* 48°31N 9°4E **179** G5
Tubod *Phil.* 8°3N 123°48E **233** G4
Tubou *Fiji* 18°13S 178°48W **287** B3
Tubruq *Libya* 32°7N 23°55E **258** B4
Tubuai *French Polynesia* 23°18S 149°30W **289** f
Tubuaï, Îs. *French Polynesia* 25°0S 150°0W **289** f
Tuburan *Basilan, Phil.* 6°39N 122°16E **233** H4
Tuburan *Cebu, Phil.* 10°44N 123°49E **233** F4
Tuc Trung *Vietnam* 11°1N 107°12E **237** G6
Tucacas *Venezuela* 10°48N 68°19W **328** A4
Tucano *Brazil* 10°58S 38°48W **332** D4
T'uch'ang *Taiwan* 24°35N 121°29E **225** B3
Tuchitua *Canada* 60°55N 129°13W **296** A3
Tuchodi → *Canada* 58°17N 123°42W **296** B4
Tuchola *Poland* 53°33N 17°52E **184** E4
Tuchoměřice *Czech Rep.* 50°7N 14°16E **135** B1
Tuchów *Poland* 49°54N 21°1E **185** J8
Tuckahoe *U.S.A.* 40°56N 73°49W **132** A3
Tuckanarra *Australia* 27°7S 118°5E **279** E2
Tucker *U.S.A.* 33°51N 84°13W **316** B5
Tuckers Town *Bermuda* 32°20N 64°42W **153** a
Tucson *U.S.A.* 32°13N 110°58W **305** K8
Tucumán □ *Argentina* 26°48S 66°2W **334** B2
Tucumcari *U.S.A.* 35°10N 103°44W **305** J12
Tucunaré *Brazil* 5°18S 55°51W **331** B6
Tucupido *Venezuela* 9°17N 65°47W **328** B4
Tucupita *Venezuela* 9°2N 62°3W **329** B5
Tucuruí *Brazil* 3°42S 49°44W **332** B2
Tucuruí, Represa de *Brazil* 4°0S 49°30W **332** B2
Tucuruvi *Brazil* 23°28S 46°35W **137** A2
Tuczno *Poland* 53°13N 16°10E **185** E3
Tuddal *Norway* 59°46N 8°49E **164** E5
Tudela *Spain* 42°4N 1°39W **196** C3
Tudmur *Syria* 34°36N 38°15E **213** E8
Tudor, L. *Canada* 55°50N 65°25W **299** A6
Tudora *Romania* 47°31N 26°45E **183** C11
Tuella → *Portugal* 41°30N 7°12W **194** D3
Tuen Mun *China* 22°24N 113°59E **219** a
Tueré → *Brazil* 2°48S 50°59W **332** B1
Tufanbeyli *Turkey* 38°15N 36°13E **212** C7
Tufello *Italy* 41°56N 12°32E **136** B2
Tüffer = Laško *Slovenia* 46°10N 15°16E **199** B12
Tufi *Papua N. G.* 9°8S 149°19E **286** E4
Tufnell Park *U.K.* 51°33N 0°8W **125** A3
Tufsingdal *Norway* 62°18N 11°44E **164** B8
Tufts Abyssal Plain
Pac. Oc. 47°0N 140°0W **289** C14
Tufts Univ. *U.S.A.* 42°24N 71°7W **116** A2
Tufu Pt. *Amer. Samoa* 14°13S 169°30W **302** g
Tugaya *Phil.* 7°53N 124°10E **233** H5
Tugela → *S. Africa* 29°14S 31°30E **271** C5
Tughlakabad *India* 28°30N 77°16E **120** B2
Tugidak I. *U.S.A.* 56°30N 154°40W **303** H9
Tuguegarao *Phil.* 17°35N 121°42E **232** C3
Tugur *Russia* 53°44N 136°45E **215** D14
Tui *Spain* 42°3N 8°39W **194** C2
Tuileries, Jardin des *Paris, France* **134** b3
Tuineje *Canary Is.* 28°19N 14°3W **153** e2
Tukangbesi, Kepulauan
Indonesia 6°0S 124°0E **231** F6
Tukarak I. *Canada* 56°15N 78°45W **298** A4
Tukayyid *Iraq* 29°47N 45°36E **246** D5
Tûkh *Egypt* 30°21N 31°12E **256** H7
Tukhlya *Ukraine* 48°55N 23°28E **183** B8
Tukituki → *N.Z.* 39°36S 176°56E **284** F5
Tukobo *Ghana* 5°1N 2°47W **262** D4
Tūkrah *Libya* 32°30N 20°37E **258** B4
Tuktoyaktuk *Canada* 69°27N 133°2W **294** D5
Tuktuk *Indonesia* 2°37N 98°54E **234** B1
Tuktut Nogait △ *Canada* 69°15N 122°0W **294** D7
Tuku *Taiwan* 23°41N 120°23E **225** C2
Tukums *Latvia* 56°58N 23°10E **184** B10
Tukums □ *Latvia* 56°55N 23°0E **184** B10
Tukuran *Phil.* 7°51N 123°34E **233** H4
Tukuyu *Tanzania* 9°17S 33°35E **269** D3
Tula *Amer. Samoa* 14°15S 170°34W **302** f
Tula *Hidalgo, Mexico* 20°3N 99°21W **319** C5
Tula *Tamaulipas, Mexico* 23°0N 99°43W **319** C5
Tula *Nigeria* 9°51N 11°27E **263** D7
Tula *Russia* 54°13N 37°38E **188** E9
Tula □ *Russia* 53°45N 37°30E **188** F9
Tulach Mhór = Tullamore
Ireland 53°16N 7°31W **166** C4
Tulagi *Solomon Is.* 9°5S 160°10E **287** M11
Tulak *Afghan.* 33°55N 63°40E **240** B1
Tulan *Taiwan* 22°53N 121°13E **225** D3
Tulancingo *Mexico* 20°5N 98°22W **319** C5
Tulangbawang →
Indonesia 4°24S 105°52E **234** C3
Tulare *Serbia* 42°48N 21°28E **202** D5
Tulare *Calif., U.S.A.* 36°13N 119°21W **306** J7
Tulare Lake Bed *U.S.A.* 36°0N 119°48W **306** K7
Tularosa *U.S.A.* 33°5N 106°1W **305** K10
Tulbagh *S. Africa* 33°16S 19°6E **270** D2
Tulcán *Ecuador* 0°48N 77°43W **328** C2
Tulcea *Romania* 45°13N 28°46E **183** E13
Tulcea □ *Romania* 45°0N 28°30E **183** E13
Tulchyn *Ukraine* 48°41N 28°49E **183** B13
Tūledi Araldary
Kazakhstan 45°2N 50°16E **191** H10
Tūleh *Iran* 34°35N 52°33E **247** C7
Tulemalu L. *Canada* 62°58N 99°25W **297** A9
Tulghes *Romania* 46°58N 25°45E **183** D10
Tuli *Zimbabwe* 21°58S 29°13E **269** G2
Tulia *U.S.A.* 34°32N 101°46W **314** D4
Tuliszków *Poland* 52°5N 18°18E **185** F5
Tulita *Canada* 64°57N 125°30W **294** E6
Ţūlkarm *West Bank* 32°19N 35°2E **251** F6
Tulla *Ireland* 52°53N 8°46W **166** D3
Tullahoma *U.S.A.* 35°22N 86°13W **315** D11
Tullamarine *Australia* 37°41S 144°50E **128** A1
Tullamore *N.S.W.,*
Australia 32°39S 147°36E **283** B7
Tullamore *Offaly, Ireland* 53°16N 7°31W **166** C4
Tulle *France* 45°16N 1°46E **174** C5
Tulln *Austria* 48°20N 16°4E **180** C9
Tullow *Ireland* 52°49N 6°45W **166** D5
Tullus *Sudan* 11°7N 24°31E **257** E1
Tully *Queens., Australia* 17°56S 145°55E **280** B4
Tully *N.Y., U.S.A.* 42°48N 76°7W **313** D8
Ţulmaythah *Libya* 32°40N 20°55E **258** B4
Tulnici *Romania* 45°51N 26°38E **183** E11
Tulovo *Bulgaria* 42°33N 25°32E **203** D9
Tulsa *U.S.A.* 36°10N 95°55W **314** C7
Tulse Hill *U.K.* 51°26N 0°6W **125** B3
Tulsequah *Canada* 58°39N 133°35W **296** B2
Tulu Milki *Ethiopia* 9°55N 38°20E **257** F4
Tulu Welel *Ethiopia* 8°56N 34°47E **257** F3
Tuluá *Colombia* 4°6N 76°11W **328** C2
Tulucești *Romania* 45°34N 28°2E **183** E13
Tuluksak *U.S.A.* 61°6N 160°58W **303** F7
Tulun *Russia* 54°32N 100°35E **215** D11
Tulungagung *Indonesia* 8°5S 111°54E **235** D4
Tuluran I. *Phil.* 10°58N 119°16E **233** F2
Tuma *Russia* 55°10N 40°30E **188** E11
Tuma → *Nic.* 13°6N 84°35W **320** D3
Tumacacori ⌂ *U.S.A.* 31°35N 111°6W **305** L8
Tumaco *Colombia* 1°50N 78°45W **328** C2
Tumaco, Ensenada
Colombia 1°55N 78°45W **328** C2
Tumakuru = Tumkur
India 13°18N 77°6E **245** H3
Tumatumari *Guyana* 5°20N 58°55W **329** B6
Tumauini *Phil.* 17°17N 121°49E **232** C3
Tumba
Dem. Rep. of the Congo 3°10S 23°36E **264** C4
Tumba *Sweden* 59°12N 17°48E **162** E11
Tumba, L.
Dem. Rep. of the Congo 0°50S 18°0E **264** C3
Tumbangsamba *Indonesia* 1°27S 113°7E **235** C4
Tumbarumba *Australia* 35°44S 148°0E **283** C8
Tumbaya *Argentina* 23°50S 65°26W **334** A2
Tumbes *Peru* 3°37S 80°27W **330** A1
Tumbes □ *Peru* 3°50S 80°30W **330** A1
Tumbler Ridge *Canada* 55°8N 121°0W **296** B4
Tumbur *Sudan* 4°20N 31°34E **257** G3
Tumbwe
Dem. Rep. of the Congo 11°25S 27°15E **269** E2
Tumby Bay *Australia* 34°21S 136°8E **282** C2
Tumd Youqi *China* 40°30N 110°30E **226** D6
Tumen *China* 43°0N 129°50E **224** A4
Tumen Jiang → *China* 42°20N 130°35E **224** A5
Tumeremo *Venezuela* 7°18N 61°30W **329** B5
Tumindao I. *Phil.* 4°41N 119°24E **233** J2
Tumiritinga *Brazil* 18°58S 41°38W **333** E3
Tumkur *India* 13°18N 77°6E **245** H3
Tumon B. *Guam* 13°31N 144°48E **302** d
Tump *Pakistan* 26°7N 62°16E **240** D1
Tumpat *Malaysia* 6°11N 102°10E **237** J4
Tumsar *India* 21°26N 79°45E **244** D4
Tumu *Ghana* 10°56N 1°56W **262** C4
Tumucumaque, Serra *Brazil* 2°0N 55°0W **329** C7
Tumupasa *Bolivia* 14°9S 67°55W **330** C4
Tumut *Australia* 35°16S 148°13E **283** C8
Tumwater *U.S.A.* 47°1N 122°54W **306** C4
Tun *Sweden* 58°26N 12°43E **163** F6
Tuna *India* 22°59N 70°5E **242** H4
Tunapuna *Trin. & Tob.* 10°38N 61°24W **323** t
Tunas de Zaza *Cuba* 21°39N 79°34W **320** B4
Tunbridge Wells = Royal Tunbridge
Wells *U.K.* 51°7N 0°16E **169** F8
Tunçbilek *Turkey* 39°37N 29°29E **205** B11
Tunceli *Turkey* 39°6N 39°31E **213** C8
Tunceli □ *Turkey* 39°5N 39°35E **213** C8
Tunchang *China* 19°21N 110°5E **236** C8
Tuncurry *Australia* 32°17S 152°29E **283** B10
Tundla *India* 27°12N 78°17E **242** F8
Tundubai *Sudan* 18°36N 28°35E **256** D2
Tunduru *Tanzania* 11°8S 37°25E **269** E4
Tundzha → *Bulgaria* 41°40N 26°35E **203** E10
Tung Chung *China* 22°17N 113°57E **219** a
Tung Lung Chau *China* 22°15N 114°17E **122** B2
Tung O *China* 22°11N 114°8E **122** B1
Tunga → *India* 15°0N 75°50E **245** G2
Tunga Pass *India* 29°0N 94°14E **241** A5
Tungabhadra → *India* 15°57N 78°15E **245** G4
Tungabhadra Dam *India* 15°0N 75°50E **245** G2
Tungao *Taiwan* 24°31N 121°50E **225** B3
Tungaru *Sudan* 10°9N 30°52E **257** E3
Tungawan *Phil.* 7°30N 122°20E **233** H4
Tungchi Yü *Taiwan* 23°15N 119°40E **225** C1
Tungch'uan = Dongchuan
China 26°8N 103°1E **228** D4
Tungho *Taiwan* 22°58N 121°18E **225** D3
T'ungshiao *Taiwan* 24°29N 120°40E **225** B2
Tunghwa = Tonghua
China 41°42N 125°58E **224** B2
Tungi *Bangla.* 23°53N 90°24E **241** D3
Tungkang *Taiwan* 22°27N 120°26E **225** D2
Tungku *Malaysia* 5°1N 118°53E **235** A5
Tungla *Nic.* 13°24N 84°21W **320** D3
T'unglo *Taiwan* 24°30N 120°47E **225** B2
Tungnafellsjökull *Iceland* 64°45N 17°55W **155** C9
Tungsha Tao = Dongsha Dao
S. China Sea 20°45N 116°43E **229** G11
Tungshan *Taiwan* 24°38N 121°47E **225** B3
Tungshih *Changhua,*
Taiwan 24°12N 120°43E **225** B2
Tungshih *Chiai, Taiwan* 23°27N 120°8E **225** C2
Tungsten *Canada* 61°57N 128°16W **296** A3
Tungufell *Iceland* 64°17N 20°10W **155** C6
Tungurahua □ *Ecuador* 1°15S 78°35W **328** D2
Tunguska, Nizhnyaya →
Russia 65°48N 88°4E **215** C9
Tunguska, Podkamennaya →
Russia 61°50N 90°13E **215** C10
Tungyin Tao *Taiwan* 26°22N 128°29E **225** b
Tuni *India* 17°22N 82°36E **244** F6
Tunia *Colombia* 2°41N 76°31W **328** C2
Tunica *U.S.A.* 34°41N 90°23W **315** D9
Tunis *Baghdād, Iraq* 33°23N 44°21E **113** A2
Tunis *Tunisia* 36°50N 10°11E **258** A2
Tunis □ *Tunisia* 36°46N 10°10E **261** A7
Tunis ✕ (TUN) *Tunisia* 36°52N 10°14E **200** F3
Tunis, Golfe de *Tunisia* 37°0N 10°30E **258** A2
Tunisia ■ *Africa* 33°30N 9°10E **258** B1
Tunja *Colombia* 5°33N 73°25W **328** B3
Tunkhannock *U.S.A.* 41°32N 75°57W **313** E9
Tunliu *China* 36°13N 112°52E **226** F7
Tunnel Creek △
Australia 17°41S 125°18E **278** C4
Tunnsjøen *Norway* 64°45N 13°25E **160** D15
Tunø *Denmark* 55°57N 10°27E **163** J4
Tunstall *U.K.* 52°9N 1°27E **169** E9
Tuntatuliak *U.S.A.* 60°22N 162°38W **303** F7
Tunu □ *Greenland* 75°0N 30°0W **154** C7
Tununak *U.S.A.* 60°37N 165°15W **303** F6
Tunungayualok I. *Canada* 56°0N 61°0W **299** A7
Tunuyán *Argentina* 33°35S 69°0W **334** C2
Tunuyán → *Argentina* 33°33S 67°30W **334** C2
Tunxi = Huangshan
China 30°8N 118°9E **229** B12
Tuo Jiang → *China* 28°50N 105°35E **228** C5
Tuolumne *U.S.A.* 37°58N 120°15W **306** H6
Tuolumne → *U.S.A.* 37°36N 121°13W **306** H5
Tuomarila *Finland* 60°11N 24°41E **121** B1
Tüp *Kyrgyzstan* 42°45N 78°20E **217** D9
Tūp Āghāj *Iran* 36°3N 47°50E **213** D12
Tupã *Brazil* 21°57S 50°28W **335** A5
Tupaciguara *Brazil* 18°35S 48°42W **333** E2
Tupelo *U.S.A.* 34°16N 88°43W **315** D10
Tupik *Russia* 55°42N 33°22E **188** E7
Tupinambarana, I. *Brazil* 3°0S 58°0W **329** D6
Tupirama *Brazil* 8°58S 48°12W **332** C2
Tupiratins *Brazil* 8°23S 48°8W **332** C2
Tupiza *Bolivia* 21°30S 65°40W **334** A2
Tupižnica *Serbia* 43°43N 22°10E **202** C6
Tupman *U.S.A.* 35°18N 119°21W **307** K7
Tupper *Canada* 55°32N 120°1W **296** B4
Tupper L. *U.S.A.* 44°10N 74°32W **313** B10
Tupper Lake *U.S.A.* 44°14N 74°28W **313** B10
Tüpqarghan Muyis
Kazakhstan 44°40N 50°19E **191** H10
Tupungato, Cerro
S. Amer. 33°15S 69°50W **334** C2
Tuquan *China* 45°18N 121°38E **227** B11
Túquerres *Colombia* 1°5N 77°37W **328** C2
Tura *India* 25°30N 90°16E **241** C3
Tura *Russia* 64°20N 100°17E **215** C11
Turabah *Ḩā'il, Si. Arabia* 28°20N 43°15E **246** D4
Turabah *Makkah,*
Si. Arabia 21°15N 41°34E **248** B3
Turagua, Serranía
Venezuela 7°20N 64°35W **329** B5
Turakina *N.Z.* 40°3S 175°16E **284** G4
Turakina → *N.Z.* 40°5S 175°8E **284** G4
Turakirae Hd. *N.Z.* 41°26S 174°56E **284** H3
Turama → *Papua N. G.* 7°40S 143°50E **286** D2
Tūrān *Iran* 35°39N 56°42E **247** C8
Turan *Russia* 51°55N 94°0E **217** B12
Turan Lowland *Asia* 43°30N 62°0E **216** D6
Turangi *N.Z.* 38°59S 175°48E **284** E4
Ţurayf *Si. Arabia* 31°41N 38°39E **246** D3
Turbaco *Colombia* 10°21N 75°25W **328** A2
Turbacz *Poland* 49°30N 20°8E **185** J7
Turbat *Pakistan* 25°59N 63°4E **240** D1
Turbe *Bos.-H.* 44°15N 17°35E **182** F2
Turbeville *U.S.A.* 33°54N 80°1W **316** B9
Turbo *Colombia* 8°6N 76°43W **328** B2
Turčianske Teplice
Slovak Rep. 48°52N 18°52E **181** C11
Turco *Bolivia* 18°10S 68°11W **330** D4
Turcoaia *Romania* 45°7N 28°11E **183** E13
Turda *Romania* 46°34N 23°47E **183** D8
Tureberg *Sweden* 59°25N 17°55E **139** A1
Turéia *French Polynesia* 20°50S 138°32W **289** f
Turek *Poland* 52°3N 18°30E **185** F5
Turfan = Turpan *China* 43°58N 89°10E **217** D11
Turfan Basin = Turpan Pendi
China 42°40N 89°25E **217** D11
Turfan Depression = Turpan Pendi
China 42°40N 89°25E **217** D11
Turffontein *S. Africa* 26°14S 28°2E **123** B2
Turgayskaya Stolovaya Strana =
Torghay Ustirti *Asia* 51°0N 63°0E **216** B6
Turgeon → *Canada* 50°0N 78°56W **298** C4
Tŭrgovishte *Bulgaria* 43°17N 26°38E **203** C10
Tŭrgovishte □ *Bulgaria* 43°17N 26°38E **203** C10
Turgut *Turkey* 37°22N 28°4E **205** D10
Turgutlu *Turkey* 38°30N 27°43E **205** C9
Turgwe → *Zimbabwe* 21°31S 32°15E **271** B5
Turhal *Turkey* 40°24N 36°5E **212** B7
Turia → *Spain* 39°27N 0°19W **197** F4
Turiaçu *Brazil* 1°40S 45°19W **332** B2
Turiaçu → *Brazil* 1°36S 45°19W **332** B2
Turiec → *Slovak Rep.* 49°7N 18°55E **181** B11
Turin = Torino *Italy* 45°3N 7°40E **198** C4
Turinskaya Kultbaza = Tura
Russia 64°20N 100°17E **215** C11
Turka *Ukraine* 49°10N 23°2E **185** J10
Turkana, L. *Africa* 3°30N 36°5E **268** B4
Turkayef *Ethiopia* 8°7N 45°21E **267** C6
Türkeli *Turkey* 40°30N 27°30E **203** F11
Turkestan = Türkistan
Kazakhstan 43°17N 68°16E **217** D7
Turkestan Range *Asia* 39°35N 69°0E **217** E7
Túrkeve *Hungary* 47°6N 20°44E **182** C5
Turkey ■ *Eurasia* 39°0N 36°0E **212** C7
Turkey → *U.S.A.* 42°43N 91°2W **310** B5
Turkey Creek = Warmun
Australia 17°2S 128°12E **278** C4
Turkey L. *U.S.A.* 28°30N 81°28W **133** A2
Turkey Lake Park *U.S.A.* 28°30N 81°28W **133** A2
Turki *Russia* 52°0N 43°15E **190** D6
Türkistan *Kazakhstan* 43°17N 68°16E **217** D7
Türkmenabat *Turkmenistan* 39°6N 63°34E **247** B9
Türkmenbashi *Turkmenistan* 40°5N 53°5E **247** A7
Turkmenistan ■ *Asia* 39°0N 59°0E **216** E5
Türkmenli *Turkey* 39°45N 26°30E **205** B8
Türkoğlu *Turkey* 37°23N 36°50E **212** D7
Turks & Caicos Is. ☒
W. Indies 21°20N 71°20W **321** B5
Turks Island Passage
W. Indies 21°30N 71°30W **321** B5
Turku *Finland* 60°30N 22°19E **188** B2
Turkwel → *Kenya* 3°6N 36°6E **268** B4
Turlock *U.S.A.* 37°30N 120°51W **306** H6
Turnagain *Australia* 9°34S 142°17E **280** a
Turnagain → *Canada* 59°12N 127°35W **296** B3
Turnagain, C. *N.Z.* 40°28S 176°38E **284** G5
Turneffe Is. *Belize* 17°20N 87°50W **320** C2
Turner *U.S.A.* 48°51N 108°24W **304** B9
Turner Field *U.S.A.* 33°44N 84°23W **113** B2
Turner Pt. *Australia* 11°47S 133°32E **280** A1
Turner Valley *Canada* 50°40N 114°17W **296** C6
Turners Falls *U.S.A.* 42°36N 72°33W **313** D12
Turner's Pen. *S. Leone* 7°22N 12°24W **262** D2
Turnham Green *U.K.* 51°29N 0°16W **125** B2
Turnhout *Belgium* 51°19N 4°57E **170** C4
Türnitz *Austria* 47°55N 15°29E **180** D8
Turnor L. *Canada* 56°35N 108°35W **297** B7
Turnov *Czech Rep.* 50°34N 15°10E **180** A8
Tŭrnovo = Veliko Tŭrnovo
Bulgaria 43°5N 25°41E **203** C9
Turnu Măgurele *Romania* 43°46N 24°56E **183** G9
Turnu Roșu, P. *Romania* 45°33N 24°17E **183** E9
Turobin *Poland* 50°50N 22°44E **185** H9
Tuross Head *Australia* 36°3S 150°8E **283** D9
Turpan *China* 43°58N 89°10E **217** D11
Turpan Pendi *China* 42°40N 89°25E **217** D11
Turrawan *Australia* 30°28S 149°53E **283** A8
Turrës, Kala e *Albania* 41°10N 19°28E **202** E3
Turriff *U.K.* 57°32N 2°27W **167** D6
Tursaq *Iraq* 33°27N 45°47E **213** F11
Tursi *Italy* 40°15N 16°28E **201** B9
Tursunzoda *Tajikistan* 38°30N 68°13E **217** E7
Turtle Head I. *Australia* 10°56S 142°37E **286** F2
Turtle Is. *Phil.* 6°7N 118°14E **233** H2
Turtle Is. *S. Leone* 7°40N 13°0W **262** D2
Turtle Islands *Phil.* 6°13N 118°6E **235** A5
Turtle L. *Canada* 53°36N 108°38W **297** C7
Turtle Lake *U.S.A.* 47°31N 100°53W **308** B3
Turtleford *Canada* 53°23N 108°57W **297** C7
Turtucaia = Tutrakan
Bulgaria 44°2N 26°40E **203** B10
Turua *N.Z.* 37°14S 175°35E **284** D4
Turukhansk *Russia* 65°21N 88°5E **215** C9
Turyinskiye Rudniki =
Krasnoturinsk *Russia* 59°46N 60°12E **186** C11
Turzovka *Slovak Rep.* 49°25N 18°35E **181** B11
Tuscaloosa *U.S.A.* 33°12N 87°34W **315** E11
Tuscánia *Italy* 42°25N 11°52E **199** F8
Tuscany = Toscana □
Italy 43°25N 11°0E **198** E8
Tuscarawas → *U.S.A.* 40°24N 81°25W **312** F3
Tuscarora Mt. *U.S.A.* 40°55N 77°55W **312** F7
Tuscola *Ill., U.S.A.* 39°48N 88°17W **311** E8
Tuscola *Tex., U.S.A.* 32°12N 99°48W **314** E5
Tuscolana, Via *Italy* 41°52N 12°31E **136** B2
Tuscumbia *Ala., U.S.A.* 34°44N 87°42W **315** D11
Tuscumbia *Mo., U.S.A.* 38°14N 92°28W **310** F4
Tushino *Russia* 55°50N 37°24E **129** A2
Tuskegee *U.S.A.* 32°25N 85°42W **316** C4
Tusket Wedge = Wedgeport
Canada 43°44N 65°59W **299** D6
Tustna *Norway* 63°10N 8°5E **164** A5
Tuszyn *Poland* 51°36N 19°33E **185** G6
Tutak *Turkey* 39°31N 42°46E **213** C10
Tutayev *Russia* 57°53N 39°32E **188** D10
Tuticorin *India* 8°50N 78°12E **245** K4
Tutin *Serbia* 42°58N 20°20E **202** D4
Tutóia *Brazil* 2°45S 42°20W **332** B3
Tutong *Brunei* 4°47N 114°40E **235** B4
Tutova → *Romania* 46°7N 27°30E **183** D12
Tutrakan *Bulgaria* 44°2N 26°40E **203** B10
Tuttle Creek L. *U.S.A.* 39°15N 96°36W **308** F5
Tuttlingen *Germany* 47°58N 8°48E **179** H4
Tutuala *E. Timor* 8°25S 127°15E **231** F7
Tutuba *Vanuatu* 15°33S 167°16E **287** E5
Tutubeia *Papua N. G.* 9°34S 150°40E **286** E6
Tutuila *Amer. Samoa* 14°19S 170°50W **302** f
Tutuko, Mt. *N.Z.* 44°35S 168°1E **285** E3
Tutun *Egypt* 29°9N 30°46E **256** J7
Tütz = Tuczno *Poland* 53°13N 16°10E **185** E3
Tuul Gol → *Mongolia* 48°30N 104°25E **218** B9
Tuva □ *Russia* 51°30N 95°0E **217** B12
Tuvalu ■ *Pac. Oc.* 8°0S 178°0E **277** B14
Tuvuca *Fiji* 17°40S 178°48W **287** A3
Ţuwal *Si. Arabia* 22°17N 39°6E **248** B2
Tuxer Alpen *Austria* 47°10N 11°45E **180** D4
Tuxpan *Mexico* 20°57N 97°24W **319** C5
Tuxtla Gutiérrez *Mexico* 16°45N 93°7W **319** D6
Tuy = Tui *Spain* 42°3N 8°39W **194** C2
Tuy Duc *Vietnam* 12°15N 107°27E **237** F6
Tuy Phong *Vietnam* 11°14N 108°43E **237** G7
Tuya L. *Canada* 59°7N 130°35W **296** B2
Tuyen Hoa *Vietnam* 17°50N 106°10E **236** D6
Tuyen Quang *Vietnam* 21°50N 105°10E **228** G5
Tuymazy *Russia* 54°36N 53°42E **216** B4
Tūysarkān *Iran* 34°33N 48°27E **213** E13
Tuyün = Duyun *China* 26°18N 107°29E **228** D6
Ţuz Gölü *Turkey* 38°42N 33°18E **212** C5
Ţūz Khurmātū *Iraq* 34°56N 44°38E **213** E11
Tuzi *Montenegro* 42°22N 19°20E **202** D3
Tuzigoot △ *U.S.A.* 34°46N 112°2W **305** J7
Tuzla *Bos.-H.* 44°34N 18°41E **182** F3
Tuzla *Turkey* 36°42N 35°6E **250** B6
Tuzlov → *Russia* 47°17N 39°57E **189** J10
Tuzluca *Turkey* 40°3N 43°39E **213** B10
Tuzly *Ukraine* 45°54N 30°6E **183** E15
Tvååker *Sweden* 57°4N 12°25E **163** G6
Tvardița *Moldova* 46°9N 28°58E **183** D13
Tvedestrand *Norway* 58°38N 8°58E **164** F5
Tver *Russia* 56°55N 35°59E **188** D8
Tver □ *Russia* 56°50N 35°0E **188** D8
Tvrdošín *Slovak Rep.* 49°21N 19°35E **181** B12
Tvrdošovce *Slovak Rep.* 48°6N 18°4E **181** C11
Tvŭrditsa *Bulgaria* 42°42N 25°53E **203** D9
Twain *U.S.A.* 40°1N 121°3W **306** E5
Twain Harte *U.S.A.* 38°2N 120°14W **306** G6
Twardogóra *Poland* 51°23N 17°28E **185** G4
Twee Rivier *Namibia* 25°27S 19°27E **270** C2
Tweed *Canada* 44°29N 77°19W **312** B7
Tweed → *U.K.* 55°45N 2°0W **167** F6
Tweed Heads *Australia* 28°10S 153°31E **281** D5
Tweedsmuir ⌂ *Canada* 53°0N 126°20W **296** C3
Twelve Apostles *S. Africa* 33°58S 18°23E **118** A1
Twentieth Century Fox Studios
U.S.A. 34°4N 118°25W **126** B2
Twentynine Palms
U.S.A. 34°8N 116°3W **307** L10
Tweya
Dem. Rep. of the Congo 0°54S 18°58E **264** C3
Twickenham *U.K.* 51°26N 0°20W **125** B1
Twickenham Rugby Ground
U.K. 51°27N 0°20W **125** B1
Twillingate *Canada* 49°42N 54°45W **299** C9
Twin Bridges *U.S.A.* 45°33N 112°20W **304** D7
Twin City *U.S.A.* 32°35N 82°10W **316** C7
Twin Falls *Canada* 53°30N 64°32W **299** B7
Twin Falls *Idaho, U.S.A.* 42°34N 114°28W **304** E6
Twin Hills *U.S.A.* 59°23N 159°58W **303** G8
Twin Lakes *U.S.A.* 30°43N 83°13W **316** E6
Twin Peaks *U.S.A.* 37°45N 122°26W **136** B2
Twin Valley *U.S.A.* 47°16N 96°16W **308** B5
Twinnge *Burma* 23°10N 96°2E **241** D6
Twinsburg *U.S.A.* 41°19N 81°26W **312** E3
Twistringen *Germany* 52°48N 8°37E **178** C4
Twitchell Res. *U.S.A.* 34°59N 120°19W **307** L6
Two Boats Village
Ascension I. 7°56S 14°22W **153** g
Two Harbors *U.S.A.* 47°2N 91°40W **308** B8
Two Hills *Canada* 53°43N 111°52W **296** C6
Two Rivers *U.S.A.* 44°9N 87°34W **308** C10
Two Rock Mt. *Ireland* 53°15N 6°14W **120** B2
Two Rocks *Australia* 31°30S 115°35E **279** F2
Two Thumb Ra. *N.Z.* 43°45S 170°44E **285** D5
Twofold B. *Australia* 37°8S 149°59E **283** D8
Twyfelfontein *Namibia* 20°34S 14°22E **270** B1
Ty Ty *U.S.A.* 31°28N 83°39W **316** D6
Tyachiv *Ukraine* 48°1N 23°35E **177** D12
Tybee Island *U.S.A.* 32°1N 80°51W **316** C9
Tychy *Poland* 50°9N 18°59E **185** H5
Tyczyn *Poland* 49°58N 22°2E **185** J9
Tydal *Norway* 63°4N 11°34E **164** A8
Tyin *Norway* 61°18N 8°15E **164** C5
Tykocin *Poland* 53°13N 22°46E **185** E9
Tyler *Minn., U.S.A.* 44°17N 96°8W **308** C5
Tyler *Tex., U.S.A.* 32°21N 95°18W **314** E7
Tyligul → *Ukraine* 47°4N 30°57E **189** J6
Tylldal *Norway* 62°8N 10°48E **164** B7
Tymanivka *Ukraine* 48°34N 28°50E **183** B13
Tymon North *Ireland* 53°18N 6°20W **120** B1
Týn nad Vltavou
Czech Rep. 49°13N 14°26E **180** B7
Tynda *Russia* 55°10N 124°43E **215** D13
Tyndall *U.S.A.* 43°0N 97°50W **308** D5
Tyndinsky = Tynda
Russia 55°10N 124°43E **215** D13
Tyne → *U.K.* 54°59N 1°32W **168** C6
Tyne & Wear □ *U.K.* 55°6N 1°17W **168** B6
Týnec nad Sázavou
Czech Rep. 49°50N 14°36E **180** B7
Tynemouth *U.K.* 55°1N 1°26W **168** B6
Tynset *Norway* 62°17N 10°47E **164** B7
Tyonek *U.S.A.* 61°4N 151°8W **303** F10
Tyre = Sūr *Lebanon* 33°19N 35°16E **250** E6
Tyresta △ *Sweden* 59°12N 18°14E **162** E12
Tyrifjorden *Norway* 60°2N 10°8E **164** D7
Tyringe *Sweden* 56°9N 13°35E **163** H7
Tyristrand *Norway* 60°4N 10°6E **164** D7
Tyrnyauz *Russia* 43°21N 42°45E **191** J6
Tyrol = Tirol □ *Austria* 47°3N 10°43E **180** D3
Tyrone *U.S.A.* 40°40N 78°14W **312** F6
Tyrone □ *U.K.* 54°38N 7°11W **166** B4
Tyrrel Bay *Grenada* 12°27N 61°28W **323** q
Tyrrell → *Australia* 35°26S 142°51E **282** C5
Tyrrell, L. *Australia* 35°20S 142°50E **282** C5
Tyrrell L. *Canada* 63°7N 105°27W **297** A7
Tyrrhenian Sea *Medit. S.* 40°0N 12°30E **192** D6
Tysfjorden *Norway* 68°7N 16°25E **160** B17
Tysmenytsya *Ukraine* 48°54N 24°51E **183** B9
Tysnes *Norway* 60°1N 5°30E **164** D2
Tysnesøya *Norway* 60°0N 5°35E **164** D2
Tysons Corner *U.S.A.* 38°55N 77°13W **143** B2
Tysse *Norway* 60°23N 5°46E **164** D2
Tyssedal *Norway* 60°7N 6°35E **164** D3
Tystberga *Sweden* 58°51N 17°15E **163** F11
Tytuvėnai *Lithuania* 55°36N 23°12E **184** C10
Tyub Karagan, Mys = Tüpqarghan
Muyis *Kazakhstan* 44°40N 50°19E **191** H10
Tyuleni, Ostrova = Tūledi Araldary
Kazakhstan 45°2N 50°16E **191** H10
Tyuleniy *Russia* 44°28N 47°30E **191** H8
Tyuleniy, Mys *Azerbaijan* 40°12N 50°22E **191** K10
Tyulgan *Russia* 52°22N 56°12E **186** D10
Tyumen *Russia* 57°11N 65°29E **214** D7
Tyup = Tüp *Kyrgyzstan* 42°45N 78°20E **217** D9
Tywi → *U.K.* 51°48N 4°21W **169** F3
Tywyn *U.K.* 52°35N 4°5W **169** E3
Tzaneen *S. Africa* 23°47S 30°9E **271** B5
Tzermiado *Greece* 35°12N 25°29E **207** E6
Tzia = Kea *Greece* 37°35N 24°22E **204** D6
Tzoumérka, Óros = Athamanon
Oros *Greece* 39°30N 21°26E **204** B3
Tzukong = Zigong *China* 29°15N 104°48E **228** C5
Tzukuan *Taiwan* 22°46N 120°16E **225** D2
Tzupo = Boshan *China* 36°28N 117°49E **227** F9
Tzutung *Taiwan* 23°45N 120°30E **225** C2

U

U.S.A. = United States of America ■
N. Amer. 37°0N 96°0W **301** H20
U.S. Capitol *Washington, D.C., U.S.A.* **143** b3
U.S. Cellular Field *U.S.A.* 41°50N 87°37W **119** C3
U.S.S. Arizona ⌂
U.S.A. 21°22N 157°57W **302** K14
U.S.S. Constitution = Old Ironside
Boston, U.S.A. **116** a3
U.S. Virgin Is. ☒ *W. Indies* 18°20N 65°0W **321** C7
Ua Huka *French Polynesia* 8°55S 139°32W **289** f
Ua Pu *French Polynesia* 9°25S 140°0W **289** f
Uachadi, Sierra = Uasadi-jidi
Venezuela 4°54N 65°18W **329** C4
Uad Atui → *W. Sahara* 20°4N 15°59W **260** D2
Uad el Jat → *W. Sahara* 26°47N 13°3W **260** C2
Uainambi *Colombia* 1°43N 69°51W **328** C4
Uamba *Angola* 7°21S 16°10E **265** D3
Uanle Uen = Wanleweyne
Somali Rep. 2°37N 44°54E **267** D5
Uasadi-jidi *Venezuela* 4°54N 65°18W **329** C4
Uati-Paraná → *Brazil* 1°51S 65°37W **328** D4
Uatumã → *Brazil* 2°26S 57°37W **329** D6
Uauá *Brazil* 9°50S 39°28W **332** C4
Uaupés *Brazil* 0°8S 67°5W **328** D4
Uaupés → *Brazil* 0°2N 67°16W **328** C4
Uaxactún *Guatemala* 17°25N 89°29W **320** C2
Ub *Serbia* 44°28N 20°6E **202** B4
Ubá *Brazil* 21°8S 43°0W **333** F3
Uba *Nigeria* 10°29N 13°13E **263** C7
Ubai *Papua N. G.* 5°39S 150°38E **286** C6
Ubaitaba *Brazil* 14°18S 39°20W **333** D4
Ubajara △ *Brazil* 3°55S 40°50W **332** B3
Ubangi = Oubangi →
Dem. Rep. of the Congo 0°30S 17°50E **264** C3
Ubaté *Colombia* 5°19N 73°49W **328** B3
Ubauro *Pakistan* 28°15N 69°45E **242** E3
Ubay *Phil.* 10°3N 124°28E **233** F5
Ubaye → *France* 44°28N 6°18E **175** D10
Ubayyiḑ, W. al → *Iraq* 32°34N 43°48E **213** F10
Ube *Japan* 33°56N 131°15E **222** D3
Úbeda *Spain* 38°3N 3°23W **195** G7
Ubeidiya *West Bank* 31°43N 35°17E **123** B2
Uberaba *Brazil* 19°50S 47°55W **333** E2
Uberaba → *Brazil* 23°35S 46°41W **137** B2
Uberaba, L. *Brazil* 17°30S 57°50W **331** D6
Uberlândia *Minas Gerais,*
Brazil 19°0S 48°20W **333** E2
Uberlândia *Roraima, Brazil* 0°48N 59°20W **329** C6
Überlingen *Germany* 47°46N 9°10E **179** H5
Ubiaja *Nigeria* 6°41N 6°22E **263** D6
Ubin, Pulau *Singapore* 1°24N 103°57E **138** A3
Ubly *U.S.A.* 43°42N 82°55W **312** C2
Ubolratna Res. *Thailand* 16°45N 102°30E **236** D4
Ubombo *S. Africa* 27°31S 32°4E **271** C5
Ubon Ratchathani
Thailand 15°15N 104°50E **236** E5
Ubondo
Dem. Rep. of the Congo 0°55S 25°42E **268** C2
Ubort → *Belarus* 52°6N 28°30E **177** B15
Ubrique *Spain* 36°41N 5°27W **195** J5
Ubud *Indonesia* 8°30S 115°16E **231** J18
Ubuna *Solomon Is.* 10°11S 161°24E **287** N11
Ubundu
Dem. Rep. of the Congo 0°22S 25°30E **264** C5
Ucar *Azerbaijan* 40°31N 47°39E **191** K8
Ucayali → *Peru* 4°30S 73°30W **328** D3
Uccle *Belgium* 50°48N 4°22E **116** B2
Uchab *Namibia* 19°47S 17°42E **270** A2
Uchiko *Japan* 33°33N 132°39E **222** D4
Uchiura-Wan *Japan* 42°25N 140°40E **220** C10
Uchiza *Peru* 8°25S 76°20W **330** B2
Uchquduq *Uzbekistan* 41°50N 62°50E **216** D6
Uchte *Germany* 52°30N 8°54E **178** C4
Uchur → *Russia* 58°48N 130°35E **215** D14
Uckermark *Germany* 53°5N 13°30E **178** B9
Ucluelet *Canada* 48°57N 125°32W **296** D3
Ucua *Angola* 8°43S 14°8E **265** D2
Uda → *Russia* 54°42N 135°14E **215** D14
Uda Walawe △ *Sri Lanka* 6°20N 81°0E **245** L5
Udachnyy *Russia* 66°25N 112°24E **215** C12
Udagamandalam *India* 11°30N 76°44E **245** J3
Udainagar *India* 22°33N 76°13E **242** H7
Udaipur *Raj., India* 24°36N 73°44E **242** G5
Udaipur *Tripura, India* 23°32N 91°30E **241** D3
Udaipur Garhi *Nepal* 27°0N 86°35E **243** F12
Udala *India* 21°35N 86°34E **243** J12
Udalguri *India* 26°46N 92°8E **241** B4
Udayagiri *Andhra Pradesh,*
India 14°52N 79°19E **245** G4
Udayagiri *Orissa, India* 20°8N 84°23E **244** D7
Udbina *Croatia* 44°31N 15°47E **199** D12
Uddeholm *Sweden* 60°1N 13°38E **162** D7
Uddevalla *Sweden* 58°21N 11°55E **163** F5
Uddheden *Sweden* 59°57N 12°54E **162** E6
Uddjaure *Sweden* 65°56N 17°49E **160** D17
Udelnaya *Russia* 60°0N 30°18E **137** A2
Udelnoe *Russia* 59°58N 30°20E **137** B1
Uden *Neths.* 51°40N 5°37E **170** C5
Udgir *India* 18°25N 77°5E **244** E3
Udhampur *India* 33°0N 75°5E **243** C6
Udi *Nigeria* 6°17N 7°21E **263** D6
Údine *Italy* 46°3N 13°14E **199** B10
Udintsev Fracture Zone
S. Ocean 57°0S 145°0W **151** B13
Udlding *Germany* 48°15N 11°25E **131** A1
Udmurtia □ *Russia* 57°30N 52°30E **186** C9
Udon Thani *Thailand* 17°29N 102°46E **236** D4
Udong *Cambodia* 11°48N 104°45E **237** G5
Udot I. *Micronesia* 7°22N 151°42E **287** T17
Udskaya Guba *Russia* 54°50N 135°45E **215** D14
Udu Pt. *Fiji* 16°9S 179°57W **287** A3
Udumalaippettai *India* 10°35N 77°15E **245** J3
Udupi *India* 13°25N 74°42E **245** H2
Udva *India* 20°5N 73°0E **244** D1
Udvoy Balkan *Bulgaria* 42°50N 26°50E **203** D10
Udzungwa △ *Tanzania* 7°52S 36°35E **268** D4
Udzungwa Range *Tanzania* 9°30S 35°10E **269** D4
Ueckermünde *Germany* 53°44N 14°1E **178** B10
Ueda *Japan* 36°24N 138°16E **223** A10
Uedineniya, Os. *Russia* 78°0N 85°0E **150** B12
Uele →
Dem. Rep. of the Congo 3°45N 24°45E **264** B4
Uelen *Russia* 66°10N 170°0W **215** C19
Uelzen *Germany* 52°57N 10°32E **178** C6
Ueno *Mie, Japan* 34°45N 136°8E **223** C8
Ueno *Tōkyō, Japan* 35°42N 139°46E **140** A3
Uetersen *Germany* 53°40N 9°40E **178** B5
Uetze *Germany* 52°28N 10°11E **178** C6
Ufa *Russia* 54°45N 55°55E **186** D10
Ufa → *Russia* 54°40N 56°0E **186** D10
Uffenheim *Germany* 49°33N 10°14E **179** F6
Ugab → *Namibia* 20°55S 13°30E **270** B1
Ugalla → *Tanzania* 5°8S 30°42E **268** D3
Ugalla River △ *Tanzania* 5°50S 31°54E **268** D3
Uganda ■ *Africa* 2°0N 32°0E **268** B3
Ugento *Italy* 39°56N 18°10E **201** C11
Ugep *Nigeria* 5°53N 8°2E **263** D6
Ughelli *Nigeria* 5°33N 6°0E **263** D6
Ugie *S. Africa* 31°10S 28°13E **271** D4
Ugíjar *Spain* 36°58N 3°7W **195** J7
Ugine *France* 45°45N 6°25E **175** C10
Uglegorsk *Russia* 49°5N 142°2E **215** E15
Uglich *Russia* 57°33N 38°20E **188** D10
Ugljan *Croatia* 44°12N 15°10E **199** D12
Ugljane *Croatia* 43°35N 16°46E **199** E13
Ugolny = Beringovskiy
Russia 63°3N 179°19E **215** C18
Ugolny = Karpinsk *Russia* 59°45N 60°1E **186** C11
Ugolnye Kopi *Russia* 64°44N 177°42E **215** C18
Ugolnyye Kopi = Kopeysk
Russia 55°7N 61°37E **216** A6
Ugoofaaru *Maldives* 5°40N 73°0E **272** d
Ugra → *Russia* 54°30N 36°7E **188** E9
Ugürchin *Bulgaria* 43°6N 24°26E **203** C8
Uh → *Slovak Rep.* 48°37N 22°0E **181** C15
Uherské Hradiště
Czech Rep. 49°4N 17°30E **181** B10
Uherský Brod *Czech Rep.* 49°1N 17°40E **181** B10
Úhlava → *Czech Rep.* 49°45N 13°24E **180** B6
Uhlenhorst *Namibia* 23°45S 17°55E **270** B2
Uhniv *Ukraine* 50°22N 23°45E **185** H10
Úholičky *Czech Rep.* 50°9N 14°19E **135** B1
Uhrichsville *U.S.A.* 40°24N 81°21W **312** F3
Uhříněves *Czech Rep.* 50°2N 14°35E **135** B3
Uibhist a Deas = South Uist
U.K. 57°20N 7°15W **167** D1
Uibhist a Tuath = North Uist
U.K. 57°40N 7°15W **167** D1
Uíche *Angola* 12°2S 20°51E **265** E4
Uido *S. Korea* 34°36N 125°50E **224** E2
Uig *U.K.* 57°35N 6°21W **167** D2
Uíge *Angola* 7°30S 14°40E **265** D2
Uíge □ *Angola* 7°0S 16°0E **265** D3
Uiha *Tonga* 19°54S 174°25W **287** P13
Uijeongbu *S. Korea* 37°44N 127°2E **224** D3
Ŭiju *N. Korea* 40°15N 124°35E **224** D3
Uinta Mts. *U.S.A.* 40°45N 110°30W **304** F8
Uiryeong *S. Korea* 35°19N 128°15E **224** E4
Uis *Namibia* 21°8S 14°49E **270** B1
Uiseong *S. Korea* 36°21N 128°45E **224** D4
Uitenhage *S. Africa* 33°40S 25°28E **270** D4
Uithoorn *Neths.* 52°14N 4°50E **112** B1
Uithuizen *Neths.* 53°24N 6°41E **170** A6
Ujazd *Poland* 50°23N 18°21E **185** H5
Ujazdów *Poland* 52°13N 21°1E **142** B2
Ujazdowski Castle *Warsaw, Poland* **142** c3
Újfehértó *Hungary* 47°49N 21°41E **182** C6
Ujh → *India* 32°10N 75°18E **242** C6
Ujhani *India* 28°0N 79°6E **243** F8
Uji *Japan* 34°53N 135°48E **223** C7
Uji-guntō *Japan* 31°15N 129°25E **221** J4
Ujiyamada = Ise *Japan* 34°25N 136°45E **223** C8
Ujjain *India* 23°9N 75°43E **242** H6
Újpalota *Hungary* 47°32N 19°8E **117** A2
Újpest *Hungary* 47°35N 19°4E **117** A2
Újście *Poland* 53°3N 16°45E **185** E3
Újszász *Hungary* 47°19N 20°7E **182** C5
Ujung Kulon △ *Indonesia* 6°46S 105°19E **234** D3
Ujung Pandang = Makassar
Indonesia 5°10S 119°20E **235** D5
Uka *Russia* 57°50N 162°0E **215** D17
Ukai Sagar *India* 21°20N 73°43E **244** D1
Ukara I. *Tanzania* 1°50S 33°0E **268** C3
Uke-Shima *Japan* 28°2N 129°14E **221** K4
Ukerewe I. *Tanzania* 2°0S 33°0E **268** C3
Ukholovo *Russia* 53°47N 40°30E **190** D5
Ukhrul *India* 25°10N 94°25E **241** C5
Ukhta *Russia* 63°34N 53°41E **186** B9
Uki Ni Masi *Solomon Is.* 10°15S 161°47E **287** N11
Ukiah *U.S.A.* 39°9N 123°13W **306** F3
Ukita *Japan* 35°40N 139°51E **140** A4
Ukmergė *Lithuania* 55°15N 24°45E **188** E3
Ukraine ■ *Europe* 49°0N 32°0E **189** H7
Uku *Angola* 11°24S 14°22E **265** E2
Ukwi *Botswana* 23°29S 20°30E **270** B3
Ula *Turkey* 37°6N 28°25E **212** D3
Ulaan Nuur *Mongolia* 44°30N 103°40E **226** B2
Ulaan-Uul *Mongolia* 46°4N 100°49E **226** B6
Ulaanbaatar *Mongolia* 47°55N 106°53E **218** B10
Ulaangom *Mongolia* 50°5N 92°10E **217** B12
Ulaanjirem *Mongolia* 45°5N 105°30E **226** B3
Ulak I. *U.S.A.* 51°22N 178°57W **303** L3
Ulala = Gorno-Altaysk
Russia 51°50N 86°5E **217** B11
Ulalu I. *Micronesia* 7°23N 151°41E **287** T17
Ulamambri *Australia* 31°19S 149°23E **283** A8
Ulamba
Dem. Rep. of the Congo 9°3S 23°38E **265** D4
Ulamona *Papua N. G.* 5°0S 151°15E **286** C6
Ulan Bator = Ulaanbaatar
Mongolia 47°55N 106°53E **218** B10
Ulan Erge *Russia* 46°19N 44°53E **191** G7
Ulan Khol *Russia* 45°18N 47°4E **191** H8
Ulan Ude *Russia* 51°45N 107°40E **219** A10
Ulanhad = Chifeng
China 42°18N 118°58E **227** C10
Ulanhot = Horqin Youyi Qianqi
China 46°5N 122°3E **227** A12
Ulanów *Poland* 50°30N 22°16E **185** H9
Ulansuhai Nur *China* 40°53N 108°51E **226** D5
Ulaş *Sivas, Turkey* 39°26N 37°2E **212** C7
Ulaş *Tekirdağ, Turkey* 41°14N 27°42E **203** E11
Ulawa *Solomon Is.* 9°46S 161°57E **287** M11

Ulaya *Morogoro, Tanzania* 7°3S 36°55E **268** D4
Ulaya *Tabora, Tanzania* 4°25S 33°30E **268** C3
Ulcinj *Montenegro* 41°58N 19°10E **202** E3
Ulco *S. Africa* 28°21S 24°15E **270** C3
Ule älv = Oulujoki →
Finland 65°1N 25°30E **160** D21
Ule träsk = Oulujärvi
Finland 64°25N 27°15E **160** D22
Uleåborg = Oulu *Finland* 65°1N 25°29E **160** D21
Ulefoss *Norway* 59°17N 9°16E **164** E6
Ulëz *Albania* 41°46N 19°54E **202** E3
Ulfborg *Denmark* 56°16N 8°20E **163** H2
Ulhasnagar *India* 19°15N 73°10E **244** E1
Uliastay *Mongolia* 47°56N 97°28E **218** B8
Uljin *S. Korea* 36°59N 129°24E **224** D4
Uljma *Serbia* 45°2N 21°10E **182** E6
Ülken *Kazakhstan* 45°12N 73°58E **217** C8
Ülken Borsyq Qumy
Kazakhstan 47°0N 59°11E **216** C5
Ulla → *Spain* 42°39N 8°44W **194** C2
Ulladulla *Australia* 35°21S 150°29E **283** C9
Ullal *India* 12°48N 74°51E **245** H2
Ullapool *U.K.* 57°54N 5°9W **167** D3
Ullared *Sweden* 57°8N 12°42E **163** G6
Ulldecona *Spain* 40°36N 0°20E **196** E5
Ullerup *Denmark* 55°34N 12°36E **118** B3
Ulleungdo *S. Korea* 37°30N 130°30E **224** D5
Ullevål *Norway* 59°56N 10°46E **133** A3
Ullswater *Ont., Canada* 45°12N 79°29W **312** A5
Ullswater *Cumb., U.K.* 54°34N 2°52W **168** C5
Ulm *Germany* 48°23N 9°58E **179** G5
Ulmarra *Australia* 29°37S 153°4E **281** D5
Ulmeni *Buzău, Romania* 45°4N 26°40E **183** E11
Ulmeni *Maramureș,*
Romania 47°28N 23°18E **183** C8
Ulongué *Mozam.* 14°37S 34°19E **269** E3
Ulricehamn *Sweden* 57°46N 13°26E **163** G7
Ulrika *Sweden* 58°5N 15°23E **163** F9
Ulriksdal *Sweden* 59°23N 17°59E **139** A1
Ulsan *S. Korea* 35°20N 129°15E **224** E4
Ulsberg *Norway* 62°45N 10°0E **164** B6
Ulsta *U.K.* 60°30N 1°9W **167** A7
Ulsteinvik *Norway* 62°21N 5°53E **164** B2
Ulster □ *U.K.* 54°35N 6°30W **166** B5
Ulstrem *Bulgaria* 42°1N 26°27E **203** D10
Ultima *Australia* 35°30S 143°18E **282** C5
Ulu Temburong △ *Brunei* 4°27N 115°15E **235** B5
Ulubat Gölü *Turkey* 40°9N 28°35E **203** F12
Ulubey *Turkey* 38°25N 29°18E **205** C11
Uluborlu *Turkey* 38°4N 30°28E **205** C12
Uluçinar *Turkey* 36°24N 35°53E **250** B6
Uludağ *Turkey* 40°4N 29°13E **203** F13
Uludağ △ *Turkey* 40°5N 29°12E **203** F13
Uludere *Turkey* 37°28N 42°42E **213** D10
Uluggat *China* 39°48N 74°15E **217** E8
Uluguru Mts. *Tanzania* 7°15S 37°40E **268** D4
Ulukışla *Turkey* 37°33N 34°28E **212** D6
Ulundi *S. Africa* 28°20S 31°25E **271** C5
Ulungur He → *China* 47°1N 87°24E **217** C11
Ulungur Hu *China* 47°20N 87°10E **217** C11
Ulupalakua *U.S.A.* 20°39N 156°24W **302** C5
Uluru *Australia* 25°23S 131°5E **279** E5
Uluru-Kata Tjuta △
Australia 25°19S 131°1E **279** E5
Ulutau *Kazakhstan* 48°39N 67°1E **217** C7
Uluwatu *Indonesia* 8°50S 115°5E **231** K18
Ulva *U.K.* 56°29N 6°13W **167** E2
Ulverston *U.K.* 54°13N 3°5W **168** C4
Ulverstone *Australia* 41°11S 146°11E **281** G4
Ulvik *Norway* 60°35N 6°54E **164** D3
Ulya *Russia* 59°10N 142°0E **215** D15
Ulyanka *Russia* 59°50N 30°14E **137** B1
Ulyanovo *Russia* 54°50N 22°6E **184** D9
Ulyanovsk *Russia* 54°20N 48°25E **190** C9
Ulyanovsk □ *Russia* 54°5N 48°5E **190** C9
Ulyasutay = Uliastay
Mongolia 47°56N 97°28E **218** B8
Ulysses *Kans., U.S.A.* 37°35N 101°22W **308** G3
Ulysses *Pa., U.S.A.* 41°54N 77°46W **312** E7
Ulysses, Mt. *Canada* 57°20N 124°5W **296** B4
Ulysses S. Grant Nat. Historic Site ⌂
U.S.A. 38°33N 90°28W **310** F6
Ulyzhylanshyq →
Kazakhstan 48°51N 63°46E **216** C6
Um Al-Khanazir Island
Iraq 33°17N 44°22E **113** B2
Umag *Croatia* 45°26N 13°31E **199** C10
Umala *Bolivia* 17°25S 68°5W **330** D4
'Umān = Oman ■ *Asia* 23°0N 58°0E **249** B7
Uman *Ukraine* 48°40N 30°12E **177** D16
Uman I. *Micronesia* 7°17N 151°52E **287** U18
Umaria *India* 23°35N 80°50E **243** H9
Umarkhed *India* 19°37N 77°46E **244** E3
Umarkot *Pakistan* 25°15N 69°40E **242** G3
Umarpada *India* 21°27N 73°30E **244** D1
Umatac *Guam* 13°18N 144°39E **302** d
Umatilla *U.S.A.* 45°55N 119°21W **304** D4
Umba *Russia* 66°42N 34°11E **186** A5
Umbagog L. *U.S.A.* 44°46N 71°3W **313** B13
Umbakumba *Australia* 13°47S 136°50E **280** A2
Umbértide *Italy* 43°18N 12°20E **199** E9
Umboi I. *Papua N. G.* 5°40S 148°0E **286** C5
Umbrella Mts. *N.Z.* 45°35S 169°5E **285** F4
Umbria □ *Italy* 42°53N 12°30E **199** F9
Umeå *Sweden* 63°45N 20°20E **160** E19
Umeälven → *Sweden* 63°45N 20°20E **160** E19
Umeda *Japan* 34°41N 135°29E **133** A1
Umera *Indonesia* 0°12S 129°37E **231** E7
Umerkhadi *Mumbai, India* **130** b2
Umfuli → *Zimbabwe* 17°30S 29°23E **269** F2
Umfurudzi △ *Zimbabwe* 17°6S 31°40E **269** F3
Umgusa *Zimbabwe* 19°29S 27°52E **269** F2
Umgwenya → *Mozam.* 25°14S 32°18E **271** C5
Umiat *U.S.A.* 69°22N 152°8W **303** B9
Umiray *Phil.* 15°13N 121°25E **232** D3
Umiujaq *Canada* 56°33N 76°33W **298** A4
Umka *Serbia* 44°40N 20°19E **202** B4
Umkomaas *S. Africa* 30°13S 30°48E **271** D5
Umm ad Daraj, J. *Jordan* 32°18N 35°48E **251** F6
Umm al Arānib *Libya* 26°10N 14°43E **258** C2
Umm al Khashab
Si. Arabia 17°23N 42°32E **256** D5
Umm al Qaywayn *U.A.E.* 25°30N 55°35E **247** E7
Umm al Qittayn *Jordan* 32°18N 36°40E **251** F7
Umm al' Abīd *Libya* 27°31N 15°2E **258** C3
Umm Arda *Sudan* 15°17N 32°31E **257** D3
Umm Bāb *Qatar* 25°12N 50°48E **247** E6
Umm Badr *Sudan* 14°13N 27°58E **257** E2
Umm Bel *Sudan* 13°35N 28°0E **257** E2
Umm Birkah *Si. Arabia* 27°44N 36°31E **256** B4
Umm Boim *Sudan* 11°43N 25°27E **257** E2
Umm Dam *Sudan* 13°45N 30°59E **257** E3
Umm Debi *Sudan* 14°37N 30°23E **257** E3
Umm Dubban *Sudan* 15°23N 32°52E **257** D3
Umm Durman = Omdurmân
Sudan 15°40N 32°28E **257** D3
Umm el Fahm *Israel* 32°31N 35°9E **251** F6
Umm Gafala *Sudan* 13°22N 27°15E **257** E2
Umm Gimala *Sudan* 11°27N 28°12E **257** E2
Umm Inderaba *Sudan* 17°30N 33°13E **256** D3
Umm Isheirāt, G. *Egypt* 28°21N 34°18E **251** K5
Umm Keddada *Sudan* 13°33N 26°35E **257** E2
Umm Koweika *Sudan* 13°10N 32°16E **257** E3
Umm Lajj *Si. Arabia* 25°0N 37°23E **246** E3
Umm Merwa *Sudan* 18°4N 32°30E **256** D3
Umm Qantur *Sudan* 14°17N 31°22E **257** E3
Umm Qasr *Iraq* 30°1N 47°58E **246** D5
Umm Qurein *Sudan* 9°58N 28°55E **257** F2
Umm Ruwaba *Sudan* 12°50N 31°20E **257** E3
Umm Saiyala *Sudan* 14°25N 31°10E **257** E3
Umm Shanqa *Sudan* 13°14N 27°14E **266** B2
Umm Shugeira *Sudan* 13°34N 29°37E **266** B2
Umm Shutur *Sudan* 7°17N 33°14E **257** F3
Umm Sidr *Sudan* 14°29N 25°10E **257** E2
Umm Tais △ *Qatar* 26°7N 51°15E **249** A5
Umm Urūmah *Si. Arabia* 25°43N 36°35E **256** B4
Umm Zehetir *Egypt* 28°48N 32°31E **256** J8
Umnak I. *U.S.A.* 53°15N 168°20W **303** K5
Umniati → *Zimbabwe* 16°49S 28°45E **269** F2
Umpqua → *U.S.A.* 43°40N 124°12W **304** E1
Umpulo *Angola* 12°38S 17°42E **265** E3
Ümraniye *Turkey* 41°1N 29°4E **122** B2
Umred *India* 20°51N 79°18E **244** D4
Umreth *India* 22°41N 73°4E **242** H5
Umri *India* 19°2N 77°39E **244** E3
Umtata = Mthatha
S. Africa 31°36S 28°49E **271** D4
Umuahia *Nigeria* 5°31N 7°26E **263** D6
Umuarama *Brazil* 23°45S 53°20W **335** A5
Umuda I. *Papua N. G.* 8°29S 143°46E **286** E2
Umurbey *Turkey* 40°13N 26°36E **203** F10
Umvukwe Ra. *Zimbabwe* 16°45S 30°45E **269** F3
Umzimvubu *S. Africa* 31°38S 29°33E **271** D4
Umzingwane →
Zimbabwe 22°12S 29°56E **269** G2
Umzinto = eMuziwezinto
S. Africa 30°15S 30°45E **271** D5
Una *India* 20°46N 71°8E **242** J4
Una → *Bos.-H.* 45°0N 16°20E **199** D13
Unac → *Bos.-H.* 44°30N 16°9E **199** D13
Unaðsdalur *Iceland* 66°7N 22°36W **155** A4
Unadilla *Ga., U.S.A.* 32°16N 83°44W **316** C6
Unadilla *N.Y., U.S.A.* 42°20N 75°19W **313** D9
Unaí *Brazil* 16°23S 46°53W **333** E2
Unalakleet *U.S.A.* 63°52N 160°47W **303** E7
Unalaska *U.S.A.* 53°53N 166°32W **303** K6
Unalaska I. *U.S.A.* 53°35N 166°50W **303** K6
'Unayzah *Si. Arabia* 26°6N 43°58E **246** E4
'Unayzah, J. *Asia* 32°12N 39°18E **246** C3
Uncastillo *Spain* 42°21N 1°8W **196** C3
Uncía *Bolivia* 18°25S 66°40W **330** D4
Uncompahgre Peak
U.S.A. 38°4N 107°28W **304** G10
Uncompahgre Plateau
U.S.A. 38°20N 108°15W **304** G9
Undara Volcanic △
Australia 18°14S 144°41E **280** B3
Unden *Sweden* 58°45N 14°25E **163** F8
Underbool *Australia* 35°10S 141°51E **282** C4
Underground Atlanta
U.S.A. 33°45N 84°24W **113** B2
Underhill, L. *U.S.A.* 28°32N 81°20W **133** A3
Undersaker *Sweden* 63°19N 13°21E **162** A7
Underwood *Canada* 44°18N 81°29W **312** B3
Undredal *Norway* 60°57N 7°6E **164** D4
Unea I. *Papua N. G.* 4°53S 149°9E **286** C5
Unecha *Russia* 52°50N 32°37E **189** F7
Uneiuxi → *Brazil* 0°37S 65°34W **328** D4
Unětický potok →
Czech Rep. 50°9N 14°24E **135** B2
Unga I. *U.S.A.* 55°15N 160°40W **303** J7
Ungarie *Australia* 33°38S 146°56E **283** B7
Ungarisch-Hradisch = Uherské
Hradiště *Czech Rep.* 49°4N 17°30E **181** B10
Ungarisch-Ostra = Uherský Brod
Czech Rep. 49°1N 17°40E **181** B10
Ungarra *Australia* 34°12S 136°2E **282** C2
Ungat *Papua N. G.* 2°40S 150°15E **286** B6
Ungava, Pén. d' *Canada* 60°0N 74°0W **295** F17
Ungava B. *Canada* 59°30N 67°30W **295** F18
Ungeny = Ungheni
Moldova 47°11N 27°51E **183** C12
Unggi *N. Korea* 42°16N 130°28E **224** A5
Ungheni *Moldova* 47°11N 27°51E **183** C12
Unguala → *Ethiopia* 8°6N 41°9E **257** F5
Ungvár = Uzhhorod
Ukraine 48°36N 22°18E **182** B7
Ungwana B. *Kenya* 2°45S 40°20E **268** C5
Ungwatiri *Sudan* 16°52N 36°10E **257** D4
Unhos *Portugal* 38°49N 9°7W **126** A2
Uni *Russia* 57°46N 51°31E **190** B10
União *Brazil* 4°35S 42°52W **332** B3
União da Vitória *Brazil* 26°13S 51°5W **335** B5
União dos Palmares *Brazil* 9°10S 36°2W **332** C4
Uničov *Czech Rep.* 49°46N 17°8E **181** B10
Unidad Santa Fe *Mexico* 19°23N 99°13W **128** B1
Uniejów *Poland* 51°59N 18°46E **185** G5
Unije *Croatia* 44°40N 14°15E **199** D11
Unimak I. *U.S.A.* 54°45N 164°0W **303** J7
Unimak Pass. *U.S.A.* 54°15N 164°30W **303** J6
Unini → *Brazil* 1°41S 61°31W **329** D5
Union *Miss., U.S.A.* 32°34N 89°7W **315** E10
Union *Mo., U.S.A.* 38°27N 91°0W **310** F6
Union *Ohio, U.S.A.* 39°55N 84°12W **311** E12
Union *S.C., U.S.A.* 34°43N 81°37W **315** D14
Union City *Calif., U.S.A.* 37°36N 122°1W **306** H4
Union City *Ga., U.S.A.* 33°35N 84°33W **316** B5
Union City *New York, U.S.A.* **132** b1
Union City *Ohio, U.S.A.* 40°12N 84°48W **311** D12
Union City *Pa., U.S.A.* 41°54N 79°51W **312** E5
Union City *Tenn., U.S.A.* 36°26N 89°3W **315** C10
Union Dale *U.S.A.* 41°43N 75°29W **313** E9
Union Gap *U.S.A.* 46°33N 120°28W **304** C3
Union Grove *U.S.A.* 42°41N 88°3W **311** B8
Union I. *St. Vincent* 12°36N 61°26W **323** n
Union Park *U.S.A.* 28°34N 81°17W **317** G8
Union Point *U.S.A.* 33°37N 83°4W **316** B6
Union Port *U.S.A.* 40°48N 73°51W **132** b2
Union Springs *Ala., U.S.A.* 32°9N 85°43W **316** C4
Union Springs *N.Y.,*
U.S.A. 42°50N 76°41W **313** D8
Union Square *San Francisco, U.S.A.* **136** b2
Union Star *U.S.A.* 39°59N 94°36W **310** E2
Union Station *Toronto, Canada* **141** c2
Union Station *Chicago, U.S.A.* **119** c1
Union Station *Washington, D.C., U.S.A.* **143** b3
Union Station *Los Angeles, U.S.A.* **127** b3
Union Station *New Orleans, U.S.A.* **131** b1
Union Station Plaza
Washington, D.C., U.S.A. **143** b3
Uniondale *S. Africa* 33°39S 23°7E **270** D3
Uniontown *Ky., U.S.A.* 37°47N 87°56W **311** G9
Uniontown *Pa., U.S.A.* 39°54N 79°44W **309** F14
Unionville *Ga., U.S.A.* 31°26N 83°30W **316** D6
Unionville *Mo., U.S.A.* 40°29N 93°1W **310** D3
Unirea *Romania* 44°15N 27°35E **183** F12
United Arab Emirates ■
Asia 23°50N 54°0E **247** F7
United Arab Republic = Egypt ■
Africa 28°0N 31°0E **256** B3
United Center *U.S.A.* 41°53N 87°41W **119** B2
United Kingdom ■ *Europe* 53°0N 2°0W **165** E6
United Nations Headquarters
New York, U.S.A. **132** c3
United Provinces = Uttar Pradesh □
India 27°0N 80°0E **243** F9
United States of America ■
N. Amer. 37°0N 96°0W **301** H20
Unity *Canada* 52°30N 109°5W **297** C7
Universal Studios *Calif.,*
U.S.A. 34°9N 118°21W **126** B2
Universal Studios *Fla.,*
U.S.A. 28°29N 81°29W **133** B2
Universales, Mtes. *Spain* 40°18N 1°33W **196** E3
Universidad *Spain* 40°27N 3°44W **127** B1
University City *U.S.A.* 38°39N 90°18W **310** F6
University Park *Md.,*
U.S.A. 38°58N 76°56W **143** B4
University Park *N. Mex.,*
U.S.A. 32°17N 106°45W **305** K10
University Place *U.S.A.* 47°14N 122°33W **306** C4
Unjha *India* 23°46N 72°24E **242** H5
Unmet *Vanuatu* 16°8S 167°15E **287** F5
Unna *Germany* 51°32N 7°42E **178** D3
Unnao *India* 26°35N 80°30E **243** F9
Uno, Ilha *Guinea-Biss.* 11°15N 16°13W **262** C1
Unpongkor *Vanuatu* 18°50S 168°59E **287** H6
Unruhstadt = Kargowa
Poland 52°5N 15°51E **185** F2
Unsan *N. Korea* 40°6N 125°54E **224** B2
Unsengedsi → *Zimbabwe* 15°43S 31°14E **269** F3
Unst *U.K.* 60°44N 0°53W **167** A8
Unstrut → *Germany* 51°10N 11°48E **178** D7
Unter den Linden *Berlin, Germany* **115** a4
Unterbiberg *Germany* 48°6N 11°38E **131** B2
Unterdrauburg = Dravograd
Slovenia 46°36N 15°5E **199** B12
Unterföhring *Germany* 48°11N 11°38E **131** A3
Unterfranken □ *Germany* 50°0N 10°0E **179** F5
Unterhaching *Germany* 48°3N 11°37E **131** B2
Unterlaa *Austria* 48°8N 16°24E **142** B2
Untermenzing *Germany* 48°10N 11°28E **131** A1
Unterschleissheim
Germany 48°17N 11°34E **179** G7
Unuk → *Canada* 56°5N 131°3W **296** B2
Ünye *Turkey* 41°5N 37°15E **212** B7
Unzen-Amakusa △
Japan 32°15N 130°10E **222** E2
Unzen-Dake *Japan* 32°45N 130°17E **222** E2
Unzha *Russia* 58°0N 44°0E **190** A7
Unzha → *Russia* 57°49N 43°47E **190** B6
Uong Bi *Vietnam* 21°2N 106°47E **236** B6
Uozu *Japan* 36°48N 137°24E **223** A9
Upata *Venezuela* 8°1N 62°24W **329** B5
Upatoi Cr. → *U.S.A.* 32°22N 84°58W **316** C5
Upemba, L.
Dem. Rep. of the Congo 8°30S 26°20E **269** D2
Upemba △
Dem. Rep. of the Congo 9°0S 26°35E **269** D2
Upernavik *Greenland* 72°49N 56°20W **154** C5
Upington *S. Africa* 28°25S 21°15E **270** C3
Upleta *India* 21°46N 70°16E **242** J4
'Upolu *Samoa* 13°58S 172°0W **287** V20
Upolu Pt. *U.S.A.* 20°16N 155°52W **302** C6
Upper □ *Ghana* 10°30N 1°30W **263** C4
Upper Alkali L. *U.S.A.* 41°47N 120°8W **304** F3
Upper Arlington *U.S.A.* 40°0N 83°4W **311** E13
Upper Arrow L. *Canada* 50°30N 117°50W **296** C5
Upper Austria = Oberösterreich □
Austria 48°10N 14°0E **180** C7
Upper B. *U.S.A.* 40°40N 74°3W **132** C1
Upper Daly ◎ *Australia* 14°26S 131°3E **278** B5
Upper Darby *U.S.A.* 39°55N 75°16W **309** F16
Upper East Side *New York, U.S.A.* **132** b3
Upper Elmers End *U.K.* 51°23N 0°1W **125** B3
Upper Foster L. *Canada* 56°47N 105°20W **297** B7
Upper Hutt *N.Z.* 41°8S 175°5E **284** H4
Upper Klamath L.
U.S.A. 42°25N 121°55W **304** E3
Upper Lake *U.S.A.* 39°10N 122°54W **306** F4
Upper Liard *Canada* 60°3N 128°54W **296** A3
Upper Manilla *Australia* 30°38S 150°40E **283** A9
Upper Manzanilla
Trin. & Tob. 10°31N 61°4W **323** t
Upper Missouri Breaks ⌂
U.S.A. 47°50N 109°55W **304** C9
Upper Musquodoboit
Canada 45°10N 62°58W **299** C7
Upper New York B. = Upper B.
U.S.A. 40°40N 74°3W **132** C1
Upper Norwood *U.K.* 51°24N 0°6W **125** B3
Upper Peirce Res.
Singapore 1°22N 103°47E **138** A2
Upper Red L. *U.S.A.* 48°8N 94°45W **308** A6
Upper Sandusky *U.S.A.* 40°50N 83°17W **311** D13
Upper Senegal & Niger = Mali ■
Africa 17°0N 3°0W **262** B4
Upper Sydenham *U.K.* 51°26N 0°4W **125** B3
Upper Tooting *U.K.* 51°25N 0°9W **125** B3
Upper Volta = Burkina Faso ■
Africa 12°0N 1°0W **262** C4
Upper West Side *New York, U.S.A.* **132** a2
Uppharad *Sweden* 58°9N 12°19E **163** F6
Uppland *Sweden* 59°59N 17°48E **162** D12
Upplands-Väsby *Sweden* 59°31N 17°54E **162** E11
Uppsala *Sweden* 59°53N 17°38E **162** E11
Uppsala län □ *Sweden* 60°0N 17°30E **162** D11
Upshi *India* 33°48N 77°52E **243** C7
Upton *London, U.K.* 51°32N 0°1E **125** A4
Upton *Wyo., U.S.A.* 44°6N 104°38W **304** D11
Uptown *U.S.A.* 41°58N 87°40W **119** B2
Uqsuqtuuq = Gjoa Haven
Canada 68°38N 95°53W **294** D12
Ur *Iraq* 30°55N 46°25E **246** D5
Ur Kut *Somali Rep.* 3°31N 42°47E **267** D5
Ura-Tyube = Üroteppa
Tajikistan 39°55N 69°1E **217** E7
Urabá, G. de *Colombia* 8°25N 76°53W **328** B2
Urad Qianqi *China* 40°40N 108°30E **226** D5
Uraga-Suidō *Japan* 35°13N 139°45E **223** B11
Urahoro *Japan* 42°50N 143°40E **220** C11
Urakawa *Japan* 42°9N 142°47E **220** C11
Ural = Uralskiy □ *Russia* 64°0N 70°0E **214** C7
Ural = Zhayyq →
Kazakhstan 47°0N 51°48E **187** E9
Ural *Australia* 33°21S 146°12E **283** B7
Ural Mts. = Uralskie Gory
Eurasia 60°0N 59°0E **186** C10
Uralla *Australia* 30°37S 151°29E **283** A9
Uralmedstroy = Krasnouralsk
Russia 58°21N 60°3E **186** C11
Uralsk = Oral *Kazakhstan* 51°20N 51°20E **190** E10
Uralskie Gory *Eurasia* 60°0N 59°0E **186** C10
Uralskiy □ *Russia* 64°0N 70°0E **214** C7
Urambo *Tanzania* 5°4S 32°0E **268** D3
Uran *India* 18°53N 72°56E **130** B2
Urana *Australia* 35°15S 146°21E **283** C7
Urana, L. *Australia* 35°16S 146°10E **283** C7
Urandangi *Australia* 21°32S 138°14E **280** C2
Uranga *Australia* 30°31S 153°1E **283** A10
Uranium City *Canada* 59°34N 108°37W **297** B7
Urapuntja = Utopia
Australia 22°14S 134°33E **280** C1
Uraricaá → *Brazil* 3°20N 61°56W **329** C5
Uraricoera *Brazil* 3°27N 60°59W **329** C5
Uraricoera → *Brazil* 3°2N 60°30W **329** C5
Urasoe *Japan* 26°15N 127°43E **288** a
Uravakonda *India* 14°57N 77°12E **245** G3
Urawa = Saitama *Japan* 35°54N 139°38E **223** B11
Uray *Russia* 60°5N 65°15E **214** C7
Urayasu *Japan* 35°39N 139°53E **140** B4
'Uray'irah *Si. Arabia* 25°57N 48°53E **247** E6
Urbakh = Pushkino *Russia* 51°16N 47°0E **190** E8
Urbana *Ill., U.S.A.* 40°7N 88°12W **311** D8
Urbana *Ohio, U.S.A.* 40°7N 83°45W **311** D13
Urbandale *U.S.A.* 41°38N 93°43W **310** C3
Urbánia *Italy* 43°40N 12°31E **199** E9
Urbano Santos *Brazil* 3°12S 43°23W **332** B3
Urbe ✕ *Italy* 41°57N 12°30E **136** B2
Urbel → *Spain* 42°21N 3°40W **194** C7
Urbino *Italy* 43°43N 12°38E **199** E9
Urbión, Picos de *Spain* 42°1N 2°52W **196** C2
Urca *Brazil* 22°56S 43°9W **135** B2
Urcos *Peru* 13°40S 71°38W **330** C3
Urdaneta *Phil.* 15°59N 120°34E **232** D3
Urdinarrain *Argentina* 32°37S 58°52W **334** C4
Urdos *France* 42°51N 0°35W **174** F3
Ure → *U.K.* 54°5N 1°20W **168** C6
Uren *Russia* 57°35N 45°55E **190** B7
Urengoy *Russia* 65°58N 78°22E **214** C8
Ureparapara *Vanuatu* 13°32S 167°20E **287** C5
Ures *Mexico* 29°26N 110°24W **318** B2
Ureshino *Japan* 33°6N 129°59E **222** D1
Urewera △ *N.Z.* 38°29S 177°7E **284** E6
Urfa = Sanliurfa *Turkey* 37°12N 38°50E **213** D8
Urga = Ulaanbaatar
Mongolia 47°55N 106°53E **218** B10
Urganch *Uzbekistan* 41°40N 60°41E **216** D6
Urgench = Urganch
Uzbekistan 41°40N 60°41E **216** D6
Ürgüp *Turkey* 38°38N 34°56E **212** C6
Uri *India* 34°8N 74°2E **243** B6
Uri □ *Switz.* 46°43N 8°35E **179** J4
Uribante → *Venezuela* 7°25N 71°50W **328** B3
Uribe *Colombia* 3°13N 74°24W **328** C3
Uribia *Colombia* 11°43N 72°16W **328** A3
Uricani *Romania* 45°20N 23°9E **182** E8
Urimba *Angola* 10°56S 16°32E **265** D2
Uriondo *Bolivia* 21°41S 64°41W **334** A3
Urique *Mexico* 27°13N 107°55W **318** B3
Urique → *Mexico* 26°29N 107°58W **318** B3
Uritsk *Russia* 59°49N 30°10E **137** C1
Urk *Neths.* 52°39N 5°36E **170** B5
Urkiola ⌂ *Spain* 43°6N 1°2W **196** B2
Urla *Turkey* 38°20N 26°47E **205** C8
Urlați *Romania* 44°59N 26°15E **183** F11
Urmia = Orūmīyeh *Iran* 37°40N 45°0E **213** D11
Urmia, L. = Orūmīyeh,
Daryācheh-ye *Iran* 37°50N 45°30E **213** D11
Üröm *Hungary* 47°35N 19°1E **117** A2
Uromi *Nigeria* 6°42N 6°20E **263** D6
Uroševac *Kosovo* 42°23N 21°10E **202** D5
Üroteppa *Tajikistan* 39°55N 69°1E **217** E7
Uroyan, Montanas de
Puerto Rico 18°12N 67°0W **321** b
Urrampinyi Iltjiltarri ◎
Australia 24°20S 132°10E **278** D5
Urrao *Colombia* 6°20N 76°11W **328** B2
Urshult *Sweden* 56°31N 14°50E **163** H8
Ursus *Poland* 52°11N 20°52E **142** B1
Ursvik *Sweden* 59°23N 17°57E **139** A1
Uru Uru, L. *Bolivia* 18°6S 67°8W **330** D4
Uruaçu *Brazil* 14°30S 49°10W **333** D2
Uruanã *Brazil* 15°30S 49°41W **333** D2
Uruapan *Mexico* 19°24N 102°3W **318** D4
Uruará *Brazil* 3°42S 53°51W **329** D7
Uruará → *Brazil* 2°6S 53°38W **329** D7
Urubamba *Peru* 13°20S 72°10W **330** C3
Urubamba → *Peru* 10°43S 73°48W **330** C3
Urubaxi → *Brazil* 0°31S 64°50W **329** D5
Urubu → *Brazil* 2°55S 58°25W **329** D6
Urucará *Brazil* 2°32S 57°45W **329** D6
Uruçuí *Brazil* 7°20S 44°28W **332** C3
Uruçui, Serra do *Brazil* 9°0S 44°45W **332** C3
Uruçuí Prêto → *Brazil* 7°20S 44°38W **332** C3
Urucuia → *Brazil* 16°8S 45°5W **333** E2
Uruguai → *Brazil* 26°0S 53°30W **335** B5
Uruguaiana *Brazil* 29°50S 57°0W **334** B4
Uruguay ■ *S. Amer.* 32°30S 56°30W **334** C4
Uruguay → *S. Amer.* 34°12S 58°18W **334** C4
Urukthapel I. *Palau* 7°17N 134°25E **288** c
Urumchi = Ürümqi
China 43°45N 87°45E **217** D11
Ürümqi *China* 43°45N 87°45E **217** D11
Uruna ◎ *Australia* 24°3S 133°1E **278** D5
Urundi = Burundi ■ *Africa* 3°15S 30°0E **268** C3
Urup → *Russia* 45°0N 41°10E **191** H5
Urup, Ostrov *Russia* 46°0N 151°0E **215** E16
Urutaí *Brazil* 17°28S 48°12W **333** E2
Uryupinsk *Russia* 50°45N 41°58E **190** E5
Ürzhar *Kazakhstan* 47°5N 81°38E **217** C10
Urzhum *Russia* 57°10N 49°56E **190** B9
Urziceni *Romania* 44°40N 26°42E **183** F11
Usa *Japan* 33°31N 131°21E **222** D3
Usa → *Russia* 66°16N 59°49E **186** A10
Uşak *Turkey* 38°43N 29°28E **205** C11
Uşak □ *Turkey* 38°30N 29°0E **205** C11
Usakos *Namibia* 21°54S 15°31E **270** B2
Usborne, Mt. *Falk. Is.* 51°40S 59°55W **153** f
Ušće *Serbia* 43°30N 20°39E **202** C4
Usedom *Germany* 53°55N 14°2E **178** B10
Usedom ⌂ *Germany* 53°55N 14°0E **178** B10
Useless Loop *Australia* 26°8S 113°23E **279** E1
Usera *Spain* 40°22N 3°42W **127** B1
'Usfān *Si. Arabia* 21°58N 39°27E **256** C4
Ushakova, Ostrov *Russia* 82°0N 80°0E **215** A8
Ushakovo *Russia* 54°37N 20°16E **184** D7
Ushant = Ouessant, Î. d'
France 48°28N 5°6W **172** D1
Usharal *Kazakhstan* 46°10N 80°56E **217** C10
Ushashi *Tanzania* 1°59S 33°57E **268** C3
Ushat *Sudan* 7°59N 29°28E **257** F2
'Ushayrah *Ar Riyāḍ,*
Si. Arabia 25°35N 45°47E **246** E5
'Ushayrah *Makkah,*
Si. Arabia 21°46N 40°42E **256** C5
Ushibuka *Japan* 32°11N 130°1E **222** E2
Ushiku *Japan* 35°42N 139°44E **140** A3
Üshtöbe *Kazakhstan* 45°16N 78°0E **217** C9
Ushuaia *Argentina* 54°50S 68°23W **336** D3
Ushumun *Russia* 52°47N 126°32E **215** D13
Ushytsya → *Ukraine* 48°35N 27°8E **183** B12
Usina *Brazil* 22°57S 43°17W **135** B1
Usino *Papua N. G.* 5°32S 145°23E **286** C3
Usinsk *Russia* 65°57N 57°27E **186** A10
Usk *Canada* 54°38N 128°26W **296** C3
Usk → *U.K.* 51°33N 2°58W **169** F5
Uska *India* 27°12N 83°7E **243** F10
Uskedalen *Norway* 59°56N 5°53E **164** E2
Üsküb = Skopje *Macedonia* 42°1N 21°26E **202** D5
Üsküdar *Turkey* 41°1N 29°0E **122** B2
Uslar *Germany* 51°39N 9°38E **178** D5
Usman *Russia* 52°5N 39°48E **189** F10
Usoke *Tanzania* 5°8S 32°24E **268** D3
Usolye-Sibirskoye
Russia 52°48N 103°40E **215** D11
Usolye-Solikamskoye = Berezniki
Russia 59°24N 56°46E **186** C10
Usoro *Nigeria* 5°33N 6°11E **263** D6
Uspallata, P. de *Argentina* 32°37S 69°22W **334** C2
Uspenka = Kirovskiy
Russia 45°7N 133°30E **220** B6
Ussel *France* 45°32N 2°18E **174** C6
Usson-du-Poitou *France* 46°16N 0°31E **174** B4
Ussuri → *Asia* 48°27N 135°0E **215** E14
Ussuriysk *Russia* 43°48N 131°59E **220** C5
Ussurka *Russia* 45°12N 133°31E **220** B6
Ust-Aldan = Batamay
Russia 63°30N 129°15E **215** C13
Ust-Amginskoye = Khandyga
Russia 62°42N 135°35E **215** C14
Ust-Buzulukskaya *Russia* 50°8N 42°11E **190** E6
Ust-Chaun *Russia* 68°47N 170°30E **215** C18
Ust-Chorna *Ukraine* 48°19N 23°56E **183** B8
Ust-Donetskiy *Russia* 47°35N 40°55E **191** G5
Ust-Ilimpeya = Yukta
Russia 63°26N 105°42E **215** C11
Ust-Ilimsk *Russia* 58°3N 102°39E **215** D11
Ust-Ishim *Russia* 57°45N 71°10E **214** D8
Ust-Kamchatsk *Russia* 56°10N 162°28E **215** D17
Ust-Kamenogorsk = Öskemen
Kazakhstan 50°0N 82°36E **217** C10
Ust-Khayryuzovo
Russia 57°15N 156°45E **215** D16
Ust-Kut *Russia* 56°50N 105°42E **215** D11
Ust-Kuyga *Russia* 70°1N 135°43E **215** B14
Ust-Labinsk *Russia* 45°15N 39°41E **191** H4
Ust-Luga *Russia* 59°35N 28°20E **188** C5
Ust-Maya *Russia* 60°30N 134°28E **215** C14
Ust-Medveditskaya = Serafimovich
Russia 49°36N 42°43E **190** F6
Ust-Mil *Russia* 59°40N 133°11E **215** D14
Ust-Nera *Russia* 64°35N 143°15E **215** C15
Ust-Nyukzha *Russia* 56°34N 121°37E **215** D13
Ust-Olenek *Russia* 73°0N 120°5E **215** B12
Ust-Omchug *Russia* 61°9N 149°38E **215** C15
Ust-Port *Russia* 69°40N 84°26E **214** C9
Ust-Slavyanka *Russia* 59°51N 30°32E **137** C3
Ust-Sysolsk = Syktyvkar
Russia 61°45N 50°40E **186** B9
Ust-Tsilma *Russia* 65°28N 52°11E **186** A9
Ust-Urt = Ustyurt Plateau
Asia 44°0N 55°0E **216** D5
Ust-Usa *Russia* 66°2N 56°57E **186** A10
Ust-Vorkuta *Russia* 67°24N 64°0E **186** A11
Ust-Zhuya = Chara
Russia 56°54N 118°20E **215** D12
Ustaoset *Norway* 60°30N 8°2E **164** D5
Ustaritz *France* 43°24N 1°27W **174** E2
Ustecký □ *Czech Rep.* 50°30N 14°0E **180** A7
Uster *Switz.* 47°22N 8°43E **179** H4
Ústí nad Labem *Czech Rep.* 50°41N 14°3E **180** A7
Ústí nad Orlicí *Czech Rep.* 49°58N 16°24E **181** B9
Ustica *Italy* 38°42N 13°11E **200** D6
Ustinov = Izhevsk *Russia* 56°51N 53°14E **186** C9
Ustka *Poland* 54°35N 16°55E **184** D3
Ustroń *Poland* 49°43N 18°48E **185** J5
Ustrzyki Dolne *Poland* 49°27N 22°40E **185** J9
Ustupo *Panama* 9°27N 78°34W **328** B2
Ustyluh *Ukraine* 50°51N 24°10E **185** H11
Ustyurt Plateau *Asia* 44°0N 55°0E **216** D5
Ustyuzhna *Russia* 58°50N 36°32E **188** C9
Usu *China* 44°27N 84°40E **217** D10
Usuki *Japan* 33°8N 131°49E **222** D3
Usulután *El Salv.* 13°25N 88°28W **320** D2
Usumacinta → *Mexico* 18°24N 92°38W **319** D6
Usumbura = Bujumbura
Burundi 3°16S 29°18E **268** C2
Usure *Tanzania* 4°40S 34°22E **268** C3
Usutuo → *Mozam.* 26°48S 32°7E **271** C5
Uta *Indonesia* 4°33S 136°0E **231** E9
Utah □ *U.S.A.* 39°20N 111°30W **304** G8
Utah L. *U.S.A.* 40°12N 111°48W **304** F8
Utansjö *Sweden* 62°46N 17°55E **162** B11
Utara, Selat *Malaysia* 5°28N 100°20E **237** c
Utarni *India* 26°5N 71°58E **242** F4
Utatlan *Guatemala* 15°2N 91°11W **320** C1
Ute Creek → *U.S.A.* 35°21N 103°50W **305** J12
Utebo *Spain* 41°43N 1°0W **196** D3
Utegi *Tanzania* 1°19S 34°13E **266** E3
Uteke *Sweden* 59°24N 18°15E **139** A3
Utena *Lithuania* 55°27N 25°40E **188** E3
Utete *Tanzania* 8°0S 38°45E **268** D4
Uthai Thani *Thailand* 15°22N 100°3E **236** E3
Uthal *Pakistan* 25°44N 66°40E **242** G2
Utiariti *Brazil* 13°0S 58°10W **331** C6
Utica *N.Y., U.S.A.* 43°6N 75°14W **313** C9
Utica *Ohio, U.S.A.* 40°14N 82°27W **312** F2
Utiel *Spain* 39°37N 1°11W **197** F3
Utikuma L. *Canada* 55°50N 115°30W **296** B5
Utila *Honduras* 16°6N 86°56W **320** C2
Utinga *Brazil* 12°6S 41°5W **333** D3
Utkela *India* 20°6N 83°10E **244** D6
Utlängen *Sweden* 56°2N 15°48E **163** H9
Utne *Norway* 60°25N 6°37E **164** D3
Utnur *India* 19°22N 78°46E **244** E4
Uto *Japan* 32°41N 130°40E **222** E2
Utö *Sweden* 58°56N 18°16E **162** F12
Utopia *Australia* 22°14S 134°33E **280** C1
Utrata *Poland* 52°15N 21°4E **142** B2
Utrauía *India* 27°19N 82°25E **243** F10
Utrecht *Neths.* 52°5N 5°8E **170** B5
Utrecht *KwaZulu Natal,*
S. Africa 27°38S 30°20E **271** C5
Utrecht □ *Neths.* 52°6N 5°7E **170** B5
Utrera *Spain* 37°12N 5°48W **195** H5
Utria △ *Colombia* 5°57N 77°21W **328** B2
Utsira *Norway* 59°19N 4°53E **164** E1
Utsjoki → *Finland* 69°51N 26°59E **160** B22
Utsunomiya *Japan* 36°30N 139°50E **223** A11
Uttar Pradesh □ *India* 27°0N 80°0E **243** F9
Uttaradit *Thailand* 17°36N 100°5E **236** D3
Uttarakhand □ *India* 30°0N 79°30E **243** D8
Uttaranchal = Uttarakhand □
India 30°0N 79°30E **243** D8
Uttarpara *India* 22°39N 88°21E **124** B1
Utterslev Mose *Denmark* 55°42N 12°29E **118** A2
Utterson *Canada* 45°12N 79°19W **312** A5
Uttoxeter *U.K.* 52°54N 1°52W **168** E6
Utuado *Puerto Rico* 18°16N 66°42W **321** b
Uummannaq *Avannaarsua,*
Greenland 77°33N 68°52W **154** B4
Uummannaq *Kitaa,*
Greenland 70°58N 52°17W **150** B5
Uummannarsuaq = Nunap Isua
Greenland 59°48N 43°55W **154** F6
Uunartoq Qeqertoq
Greenland 71°33N 21°47W **154** C8
Uusikaarlepyy *Finland* 63°32N 22°31E **160** E20
Uusikaupunki *Finland* 60°47N 21°25E **188** B1
Uva *Russia* 56°59N 52°13E **190** B11
Uvá → *Colombia* 3°41N 70°3W **328** C4
Uvac → *Serbia* 43°35N 19°30E **202** C3
Uvalda *U.S.A.* 32°2N 82°31W **316** C7
Uvalde *U.S.A.* 29°13N 99°47W **314** G5
Uvarovo *Russia* 51°59N 42°14E **190** E6
Uvat *Russia* 59°5N 68°50E **214** D7
Uvdal *Norway* 60°17N 8°48E **164** D5
Uvéa, I. *Wall. & F. Is.* 13°18S 176°10W **277** C15
Uvinza *Tanzania* 5°5S 30°24E **268** D3
Uvira *Dem. Rep. of the Congo* 3°22S 29°3E **268** C2
Uvs □ *Mongolia* 49°38N 93°0E **217** C12
Uvs Nuur *Mongolia* 50°20N 92°30E **217** B12
Uwa *Japan* 33°22N 132°31E **222** D4
'Uwairidh, Ḥarrat al
Si. Arabia 26°50N 38°0E **246** E3
Uwajima *Japan* 33°10N 132°35E **222** D4
Uwanda ⌂ *Tanzania* 7°46S 32°0E **268** D3
Uweinat, Jebel *Sudan* 21°54N 24°58E **256** C2
Uxbridge *Canada* 44°6N 79°7W **312** B5
Uxin Qi *China* 38°50N 109°5E **226** E5
Uxmal *Mexico* 20°22N 89°46W **319** C7
Uyak *U.S.A.* 57°38N 154°0W **303** G9
Üydzin *Mongolia* 44°9N 107°0E **226** B4
Uyo *Nigeria* 5°1N 7°53E **263** D6
Uyu → *Burma* 24°51N 94°57E **241** C5
Üyüklü Tepe *Turkey* 37°5N 27°21E **205** D9
Uyûn Mûsa *Egypt* 29°53N 32°40E **251** J3
Uyuni *Bolivia* 20°28S 66°47W **330** E4
Uzbekistan ■ *Asia* 41°30N 65°0E **217** D7
Uzboy → *Turkmenistan* 39°30N 55°0E **247** B7
Uzen, Mal → *Kazakhstan* 49°4N 49°44E **191** F9
Uzerche *France* 45°25N 1°34E **174** C5
Uzès *France* 44°1N 4°26E **175** D8
Uzh → *Ukraine* 51°15N 30°12E **177** C16
Uzhgorod = Uzhhorod
Ukraine 48°36N 22°18E **182** B7
Uzhhorod *Ukraine* 48°36N 22°18E **182** B7
Uzhok *Ukraine* 48°59N 22°52E **182** B7
Užice *Serbia* 43°55N 19°50E **202** C3
Uzlovaya *Russia* 54°0N 38°5E **188** F10
Üzümlü *Turkey* 36°44N 29°14E **205** E11
Uzuncaburç *Turkey* 36°35N 33°57E **250** B4
Uzunköprü *Turkey* 41°16N 26°43E **203** E10
Uzunkuyu *Turkey* 38°17N 26°33E **205** C8

V

V.C. Bird Int. ✕ (ANU)
Antigua & B. 17°8N 61°47W **322** b
Vaal → *S. Africa* 29°4S 23°38E **270** C3
Vaal Dam *S. Africa* 27°0S 28°14E **271** C4
Vaalwater *S. Africa* 24°15S 28°8E **271** B4
Vaasa *Finland* 63°6N 21°38E **160** E19
Vabre *France* 43°42N 2°24E **174** E6
Vác *Hungary* 47°49N 19°10E **182** C4
Vacaos, Mare aux
Mauritius 20°22S 57°30E **272** e
Vacaria *Brazil* 28°31S 50°52W **335** B5
Vacata *Fiji* 17°15S 179°31W **287** A3
Vacaville *U.S.A.* 38°21N 121°59W **306** G5
Vaccarès, Étang de *France* 43°32N 4°34E **175** E8
Vach = Vakh → *Russia* 60°45N 76°45E **214** C8
Vache, Î. à *Haiti* 18°2N 73°35W **321** C5
Väckelsång *Sweden* 56°37N 14°58E **163** H8
Vaclavské náměstí *Prague, Czech Rep.* **135** b2
Vacoas *Mauritius* 20°18S 57°29E **272** e
Vada *India* 19°39N 73°8E **244** E1
Vadakara = Badagara
India 11°35N 75°40E **245** J2
Vadaul *India* 19°2N 72°55E **130** A2
Väddö *Sweden* 60°0N 18°50E **162** D12
Väderstad *Sweden* 58°19N 14°55E **163** F8
Vadheim *Norway* 61°13N 5°49E **164** C2
Vadnagar *India* 23°47N 72°40E **242** H5
Vado Ligure *Italy* 44°17N 8°26E **198** D5
Vadodara *India* 22°20N 73°10E **242** H5
Vadsø *Norway* 70°3N 29°50E **160** A23
Vadstena *Sweden* 58°28N 14°54E **163** F8
Vaduj *India* 17°36N 74°27E **244** F2
Vaduz *Liech.* 47°8N 9°31E **179** H5
Værlandet *Norway* 61°18N 4°44E **164** C1
Værøy *Norway* 67°40N 12°40E **160** C15
Vagalat *Albania* 39°44N 20°8E **206** B10
Vågåmo *Norway* 61°52N 9°6E **164** C6
Vágar *Færoe Is.* 62°5N 7°15W **160** E9
Vagarshapat = Yejmiadzin
Armenia 40°12N 44°19E **191** K7
Vaggeryd *Sweden* 57°30N 14°10E **163** G8
Vaghena *Solomon Is.* 7°25S 157°45E **287** L9
Vaghia *Greece* 38°19N 23°11E **204** C5
Vagia, Akra *Greece* 36°15N 28°11E **206** E12
Vagney *France* 48°1N 6°43E **173** D13
Vagnhärad *Sweden* 58°57N 17°33E **163** F11
Vagos *Portugal* 40°33N 8°42W **194** E2
Vågsfjorden *Norway* 68°50N 16°50E **160** B17
Váh → *Slovak Rep.* 47°43N 18°7E **181** D11
Vahitahi *French Polynesia* 18°44S 138°52W **289** f
Vahsel B. *Antarctica* 75°0S 35°0W **151** D1
Váhtjer = Gällivare
Sweden 67°9N 20°40E **160** C19
Vaï *Greece* 35°15N 26°18E **207** E7
Vaiaea *Cook Is.* 19°6S 169°54W **289** g
Vaigai → *India* 9°15N 79°10E **245** K4
Vaiges *France* 48°2N 0°30W **172** D6
Vaihingen *Germany* 48°54N 8°57E **179** G4
Vaihiria, L. *Tahiti* 17°40S 149°25W **289** e
Vaijapur *India* 19°58N 74°45E **244** E2
Vaikam *India* 9°45N 76°25E **245** K3
Vail *U.S.A.* 39°40N 106°20W **301** H18
Vailala → *Papua N. G.* 7°57S 145°25E **286** D3
Vailhau, Récif *Comoros Is.* 11°48S 43°2E **272** a
Vailly-sur-Aisne *France* 49°24N 3°31E **173** C10
Vailoatai *Amer. Samoa* 14°21S 170°46W **302** f
Vaippar → *India* 9°0N 78°25E **245** K4
Vairaatea *French Polynesia* 19°19S 139°20W **289** f
Vairao *Tahiti* 17°47S 149°17W **289** e
Vaires-sur-Marne *France* 48°52N 2°38E **134** A4
Vaisali → *India* 26°28N 78°53E **243** F8
Vaison-la-Romaine *France* 44°14N 5°4E **175** D9
Vaitogi *Amer. Samoa* 14°24S 170°44W **302** f
Vaitupu *Pac. Oc.* 7°28S 178°41E **277** B14
Vajpur *India* 21°24N 73°17E **244** D1
Vakaga → *C.A.R.* 9°48N 21°32E **264** A4
Vakarai *Sri Lanka* 8°8N 81°26E **245** K5
Vakarel *Bulgaria* 42°35N 23°40E **202** D7
Vakfıkebir *Turkey* 41°2N 39°17E **213** B8
Vakh → *Russia* 60°45N 76°45E **214** C8
Vakhtan *Russia* 57°53N 46°47E **190** B8
Vaksdal *Norway* 60°29N 5°45E **164** D2
Vakuta I. *Papua N. G.* 8°51S 151°10E **286** E6
Vál *Hungary* 47°22N 18°40E **182** C3
Val-de-Marne □ *France* 48°45N 2°28E **173** D9
Val-d'Isère *France* 45°27N 6°59E **175** C10
Val-d'Oise □ *France* 49°5N 2°10E **173** C9
Val-d'Or *Canada* 48°7N 77°47W **298** C4
Val Grande △ *Italy* 46°3N 8°25E **198** B5
Val Marie *Canada* 49°15N 107°45W **297** D7
Val Thorens *France* 45°20N 6°33E **175** C10
Valaam *Russia* 61°22N 30°57E **188** B6
Valadares *Portugal* 41°5N 8°38W **194** D2
Valahia *Romania* 44°35N 25°0E **183** F9
Valaichenai *Sri Lanka* 7°54N 81°32E **245** L5
Valais □ *Switz.* 46°12N 7°45E **179** J3
Valais, Alpes du *Switz.* 46°5N 7°35E **179** J3
Valandovo *Macedonia* 41°19N 22°34E **202** E6
Valašské Meziříčí
Czech Rep. 49°29N 17°59E **181** B10
Valatie *U.S.A.* 42°24N 73°40W **313** D11
Valaxa *Greece* 38°50N 24°29E **204** C6
Vålberg *Sweden* 59°23N 13°11E **162** E7
Valbo *Sweden* 60°40N 17°0E **162** D10
Valbondione *Italy* 46°2N 10°1E **198** B7
Valby *Denmark* 55°39N 12°29E **118** B2
Vâlcani *Romania* 46°0N 20°26E **182** D5
Valcannuta *Italy* 41°52N 12°25E **136** B1
Vâlcea □ *Romania* 45°0N 24°10E **183** F9
Valcheta *Argentina* 40°40S 66°8W **336** B3
Valdagno *Italy* 45°38N 11°18E **199** C8
Valdahon *France* 47°8N 6°21E **173** E13
Valdai Hills = Valdayskaya
Vozvyshennost *Russia* 57°0N 33°30E **188** D7
Valday *Russia* 57°58N 33°9E **188** D7
Valdayskaya Vozvyshennost
Russia 57°0N 33°30E **188** D7
Valdeazogues → *Spain* 38°45N 4°55W **195** G6
Valdecañas, Embalse de
Spain 39°45N 5°25W **194** F5
Valdelatas *Spain* 40°31N 3°42W **127** A1
Valdemarsvik *Sweden* 58°14N 16°40E **163** F10
Valdemoro *Spain* 40°12N 3°40W **194** E7

Valdepeñas Spain 38°43N 3°25W 195 G7
Valderaduey → Spain 41°31N 5°42W 194 D5
Valdérice Italy 38°4N 12°37E 200 D5
Valderrobres Spain 40°53N 0°9E 196 E5
Valdés, Pen. Argentina 42°30S 63°45W 336 B4
Valdez Ecuador 1°15N 79°0W 328 C2
Valdez Alaska, U.S.A. 61°7N 146°16W 303 F11
Valdgeym = Dobropole Ukraine 48°25N 37°2E 189 H9
Valdivia Chile 39°50S 73°14W 336 A2
Valdivia Colombia 7°11N 75°27W 328 B2
Valdivia Abyssal Plain S. Ocean 62°30S 70°0E 151 C6
Valdobbiádene Italy 45°54N 12°0E 199 C8
Valdosta U.S.A. 30°50N 83°17W 316 E6
Valdoviño Spain 43°36N 8°8W 194 B2
Valdres Norway 61°5N 9°5E 164 C6
Vale Georgia 41°30N 42°58E 191 K6
Vale Oreg., U.S.A. 43°59N 117°15W 304 E5
Vale Va., U.S.A. 38°55N 77°20W 143 B1
Vale of Glamorgan □ U.K. 51°28N 3°25W 169 F4
Valea lui Mihai Romania 47°32N 22°11E 182 C7
Valea Mărului Romania 45°49N 27°42E 183 E12
Valemount Canada 52°50N 119°15W 296 C5
Valença = Valença do Piauí Brazil 6°20S 41°45W 332 C3
Valença Brazil 13°20S 39°5W 333 D4
Valença Portugal 42°1N 8°34W 194 C2
Valença do Piauí Brazil 6°20S 41°45W 332 C3
Valençay France 47°9N 1°34E 173 E8
Valence France 44°57N 4°54E 175 D8
Valence d'Agen France 44°6N 0°53E 174 D4
Valencia Phil. 7°57N 125°3E 233 H5
Valencia Spain 39°27N 0°23W 197 F4
Valencia Trin. & Tob. 10°39N 61°11W 323 t
Valencia N. Mex., U.S.A. 34°48N 106°43W 305 J10
Valencia Venezuela 10°11N 68°0W 328 A4
Valencia □ Spain 39°20N 0°40W 197 F4
Valencia ✈ (VLC) Spain 39°20N 0°26W 197 F4
Valencia, G. de Spain 39°30N 0°20E 197 F5
Valencia de Alcántara Spain 39°25N 7°14W 195 F3
Valencia de Don Juan Spain 42°17N 5°31W 194 C5
Valencia I. Ireland 51°54N 10°22W 166 E1
Valenciennes France 50°20N 3°34E 173 B10
Văleni Romania 44°15N 24°45E 183 F9
Vălenii de Munte Romania 45°11N 26°2E 183 E11
Valensole France 43°50N 5°59E 175 E9
Valentigney France 47°27N 6°51E 173 E13
Valentim, Sa. do Brazil 6°0S 43°30W 332 C3
Valentin Russia 43°8N 134°17E 220 C7
Valentine Nebr., U.S.A. 42°52N 100°33W 308 D3
Valentine Tex., U.S.A. 30°35N 104°30W 314 F2
Valenton France 48°44N 2°27E 134 B3
Valenza Italy 45°1N 8°38E 198 C5
Våler Hedmark, Norway 60°41N 11°50E 164 D8
Våler Østfold, Norway 59°29N 10°51E 164 E7
Valera Piemonte, Italy 45°33N 9°3E 129 A1
Valera Venezuela 9°19N 70°37W 328 B3
Valesdir Vanuatu 16°47S 168°10E 287 F6
Valestrand Norway 59°40N 5°26E 164 E2
Valga Estonia 57°47N 26°2E 188 D4
Valguarnera Caropepe Italy 37°30N 14°23E 201 E7
Valier U.S.A. 48°18N 112°16W 304 B7
Valinco, G. de France 41°40N 8°52E 175 G12
Valjevo Serbia 44°18N 19°53E 202 B3
Valka Latvia 57°46N 26°3E 188 D3
Valkeakoski Finland 61°16N 24°2E 188 B2
Valkenswaard Neths. 51°21N 5°29E 170 C5
Vall de Uxó = La Vall d'Uixó Spain 39°49N 0°15W 196 F4
Valla Sweden 59°2N 16°20E 162 E10
Valladolid Yucatán, Mexico 20°41N 88°12W 319 C7
Valladolid Spain 41°38N 4°43W 194 D6
Valladolid □ Spain 41°38N 4°43W 194 D6
Vallata Italy 41°2N 15°15E 201 A8
Vallcarca Spain 41°25N 2°9E 114 A1
Valldemossa Spain 39°43N 2°37E 206 B3
Valldoreix Spain 41°27N 2°3E 114 A1
Valle Norway 59°13N 7°33E 164 E4
Valle d'Aosta □ Italy 45°45N 7°15E 198 C4
Valle de Aran Spain 42°50N 0°55E 196 C5
Valle de la Pascua Venezuela 9°13N 66°0W 328 B4
Valle de las Palmas Mexico 32°20N 116°43W 307 N10
Valle de Santiago Mexico 20°23N 101°12W 318 C4
Valle de Zaragoza Mexico 27°25N 105°50W 318 B3
Valle del Cauca □ Colombia 3°45N 76°30W 328 C2
Valle del Ticino ⌓ Italy 45°22N 9°0E 198 C6
Valle Fértil, Sierra del Argentina 30°20S 68°0W 334 C2
Valle Gran Rey Canary Is. 28°5N 17°20W 153 e1
Valle Hermoso Mexico 25°35N 97°40W 319 B5
Valle Nacional Mexico 17°47N 96°18W 319 D5
Vallecas Spain 40°22N 3°37W 127 B2
Vallecas, Cumbres de Spain 40°20N 3°33W 127 B2
Valledupar Colombia 10°29N 73°15W 328 A3
Vallegrande Bolivia 18°30S 64°10W 331 D5
Vallehermoso Canary Is. 28°10N 17°15W 153 e1
Vallejo U.S.A. 38°7N 122°14W 306 G4
Vallenar Chile 28°30S 70°50W 334 B1
Vallensbæk Denmark 55°38N 12°21E 118 B2
Vallensbæk Strand Denmark 55°36N 12°23E 118 B2
Vallentuna Sweden 59°32N 18°5E 162 E12
Vallentunasjön Sweden 59°27N 18°1E 139 A2
Valleranello Italy 41°46N 12°29E 136 C1
Valleraugue France 44°6N 3°39E 174 D7
Vallet France 47°10N 1°15W 172 E5
Valletta Malta 35°54N 14°31E 206 F8
Valley, The Anguilla 18°13N 63°4W 322 a
Valley Center U.S.A. 33°13N 117°2W 307 M9
Valley City U.S.A. 46°55N 98°0W 308 B5
Valley Falls Oreg., U.S.A. 42°29N 120°17W 304 E3
Valley Falls R.I., U.S.A. 41°54N 71°24W 313 E13
Valley Junction = West Des Moines U.S.A. 41°35N 93°43W 310 C3
Valley of Flowers △ India 30°50N 79°40E 243 D8
Valley of the Kings Egypt 25°41N 32°34E 256 B3
Valley Springs U.S.A. 38°12N 120°50W 306 G6
Valley Station U.S.A. 38°6N 85°52W 311 F11
Valley View U.S.A. 40°39N 76°33W 313 F8
Valley Wells U.S.A. 35°27N 115°46W 307 K11
Valleyview Canada 55°5N 117°17W 296 B5
Valli di Comácchio Italy 44°40N 12°15E 199 D9
Vallimanca, Arroyo Argentina 35°40S 59°10W 334 D4
Vallisaari Finland 60°7N 25°0E 121 C3
Vallo della Lucánia Italy 40°14N 15°16E 201 B8
Vallon-Pont-d'Arc France 44°24N 4°24E 175 D8
Vallorbe Switz. 46°42N 6°20E 179 J2
Valls Spain 41°18N 1°15E 196 D6
Vallvidrera Spain 41°24N 2°6E 114 A1
Vallvik Sweden 61°11N 17°10E 162 C11
Valmaseda = Balmaseda Spain 43°11N 3°12W 196 B1
Valmeyer U.S.A. 38°18N 90°19W 310 F6
Valmiera Latvia 57°37N 25°29E 188 D3
Valnera Spain 43°9N 3°40W 194 B7
Valognes France 49°30N 1°28W 172 C5
Valona = Vlorë Albania 40°32N 19°28E 202 F3
Valongo Portugal 41°8N 8°30W 194 D2
Valozhyn Belarus 54°3N 26°30E 177 A14
Valpaços Portugal 41°36N 7°17W 194 D3
Valparai India 10°22N 76°58E 245 J3
Valparaíso Chile 33°2S 71°40W 334 C1
Valparaíso Zacatecas, Mexico 22°46N 103°34W 318 C4
Valparaiso Fla., U.S.A. 30°29N 86°30W 317 E3
Valparaiso Ind., U.S.A. 41°28N 87°4W 311 C9
Valparaíso □ Chile 33°2S 71°40W 334 C1
Valpovo Croatia 45°39N 18°25E 182 E3
Valpoy India 15°32N 74°8E 245 G2
Valréas France 44°24N 5°0E 175 D9
Vals Switz. 46°39N 9°11E 179 J5
Vals → S. Africa 27°23S 26°30E 270 C4
Vals, Tanjung Indonesia 8°26S 137°25E 231 F9
Vals-les-Bains France 44°42N 4°24E 175 D8
Valsad India 20°40N 72°58E 244 D1
Valsamata Greece 38°10N 20°36E 207 C2
Valtellina Italy 46°11N 9°55E 198 B6
Valþjofsstaður Iceland 65°1N 14°59W 155 B12
Valti Greece 38°27N 21°7E 207 C3
Valuyki Russia 50°10N 38°5E 189 G10
Valverde Canary Is. 27°48N 17°55W 153 e1
Valverde del Camino Spain 37°35N 6°47W 195 H4
Valverde del Fresno Spain 40°15N 6°51W 194 E4
Valvidrera → Spain 41°25N 2°0E 114 A1
Vama Romania 47°34N 25°42E 183 C10
Vambori India 19°17N 74°44E 244 E2
Vamdrup Denmark 55°25N 9°17E 163 J3
Våmhus Sweden 61°7N 14°29E 162 C8
Vamizi, I. Mozam. 11°2S 40°40E 269 E5
Vammala = Sastamala Finland 61°20N 22°54E 188 B2
Vamos Greece 35°24N 24°13E 207 E5
Vamsadhara → India 18°21N 84°8E 244 E7
Van Turkey 38°30N 43°20E 213 C10
Van □ Turkey 38°30N 43°20E 213 C10
Van, L. = Van Gölü Turkey 38°30N 43°0E 213 C10
Van Alstyne U.S.A. 33°25N 96°35W 314 E6
Van Blommestein Meer Suriname 4°45N 55°5W 329 C6
Van Buren = Kettering U.S.A. 39°41N 84°10W 311 E12
Van Buren N.B., Canada 47°10N 67°55W 299 C6
Van Buren Ark., U.S.A. 35°26N 94°21W 314 D7
Van Buren Maine, U.S.A. 47°10N 67°58W 309 B20
Van Buren Mo., U.S.A. 37°0N 91°1W 308 G8
Van Canh Vietnam 13°37N 109°0E 236 F7
Van Diemen, C. N. Terr., Australia 11°9S 130°24E 278 B5
Van Diemen, C. Queens., Australia 16°30S 139°46E 280 B2
Van Diemen G. Australia 11°45S 132°0E 278 B5
Van Gogh Museum Amsterdam, Neths. 112 c1
Van Gölü Turkey 38°30N 43°0E 213 C10
Van Horn U.S.A. 31°3N 104°50W 314 F2
Van Horne U.S.A. 42°1N 92°5W 310 B4
Van Meter U.S.A. 41°32N 93°57W 310 C3
Van Ninh Vietnam 12°42N 109°14E 236 F7
Van Rees, Pegunungan Indonesia 2°35S 138°15E 231 E9
Van Tivu India 8°51N 78°15E 245 K4
Van Wert U.S.A. 40°52N 84°35W 311 D12
Van Yen Vietnam 21°4N 104°42E 228 G5
Van Zylsrus S. Africa 26°52S 22°4E 270 C3
Vanadzor Armenia 40°48N 44°30E 191 K7
Vanak Iran 35°45N 51°23E 141 A2
Vanavana French Polynesia 20°47S 139°9W 289 f
Vanavara Russia 60°22N 102°16E 215 C11
Vanceburg U.S.A. 38°36N 83°19W 311 F13
Vancouver B.C., Canada 49°15N 123°7W 306 A3
Vancouver Wash., U.S.A. 45°38N 122°40W 306 E4
Vancouver, C. Australia 35°2S 118°11E 279 G2
Vancouver, Mt. U.S.A. 60°20N 139°41W 303 F13
Vancouver I. Canada 49°50N 126°0W 306 B2
Vancouver Int. ✈ (YVR) Canada 49°10N 123°10W 306 A3
Vanda = Vantaa Finland 60°18N 24°56E 121 B2
Vandalia Ill., U.S.A. 38°58N 89°6W 310 F7
Vandalia Mo., U.S.A. 39°19N 91°29W 310 E5
Vandalia Ohio, U.S.A. 39°54N 84°12W 311 E12
Vandavasi India 12°30N 79°30E 245 H4
Vandeloos B. Sri Lanka 8°0N 81°45E 245 L5
Vandenberg Village U.S.A. 34°43N 120°28W 307 L6
Vandergrift U.S.A. 40°36N 79°34W 312 F5
Vanderhoof Canada 54°0N 124°0W 296 C4
Vanderkloof Dam S. Africa 30°4S 24°40E 270 D3
Vanderlin I. Australia 15°44S 137°2E 280 B2
Vänern Sweden 58°47N 13°30E 163 F7
Vänersborg Sweden 58°26N 12°19E 163 F6
Vang Norway 61°7N 8°34E 164 C5
Vang Vieng Laos 18°58N 102°32E 236 C4
Vanga Kenya 4°35S 39°12E 268 C4
Vangaindrano Madag. 23°21S 47°36E 272 C2
Vänge Sweden 59°50N 17°20E 162 E11
Vangede Denmark 55°45N 12°30E 118 A3
Vangsnes Norway 61°9N 6°39E 164 C3
Vanguard Canada 49°55N 107°20W 297 D7
Vangunu Solomon Is. 8°40S 158°5E 287 M10
Vanikoro Pac. Oc. 11°39S 166°54E 277 C12
Vaniköy Turkey 41°3N 29°3E 122 B2
Vanimo Papua N. G. 2°42S 141°21E 286 B1
Vanino Russia 48°50N 140°5E 215 E15
Vanivilasa Sagara India 13°45N 76°30E 245 H3
Vaniyambadi India 12°46N 78°44E 245 H4
Vânju Mare Romania 44°25N 22°52E 182 F7
Vankleek Hill Canada 45°32N 74°40W 313 A10
Vanløse Denmark 55°41N 12°28E 118 A2
Vännäs Sweden 63°58N 19°48E 160 E18
Vannes France 47°40N 2°47W 172 E4
Vannøya Norway 70°6N 19°50E 160 A18
Vanoise, Massif de la France 45°25N 6°40E 175 C10
Vanrhynsdorp S. Africa 31°36S 18°44E 270 D2
Vansada India 20°47N 73°25E 244 D1
Vansbro Sweden 60°32N 14°15E 162 D8
Vanse Norway 58°6N 6°41E 164 F3
Vansittart B. Australia 14°3S 126°17E 278 B4
Vansittart I. Canada 65°50N 84°0W 295 D15
Vantaa Finland 60°18N 24°56E 121 B2
Vantaankoski Finland 60°18N 24°50E 121 B2
Vantaanpuisto Finland 60°18N 24°53E 121 B2
Vanua Balavu Fiji 17°12S 178°55W 287 A3
Vanua Lava Vanuatu 13°50S 167°30E 287 C5
Vanua Levu Fiji 16°33S 179°15E 287 A2
Vanua Vatu Fiji 18°22S 179°15W 287 B3
Vanuatu ■ Pac. Oc. 15°0S 168°0E 287 E6
Vanves France 48°49N 2°17E 134 B2
Vanwyksvlei S. Africa 30°18S 21°49E 270 D3
Vao N. Cal. 22°39S 167°32E 288 d
Vapnyarka Ukraine 48°32N 28°45E 183 B13
Var □ France 43°27N 6°18E 175 E10
Var → France 43°39N 7°12E 175 E11
Vara Sweden 58°16N 12°55E 163 F6
Vara, Pico da Azores 37°48N 25°13W 153 d3
Varada → India 15°0N 75°40E 245 G2
Varades France 47°25N 1°1W 172 E5
Varáita → Italy 44°9N 7°53E 198 D4
Varaldsøy Norway 60°6N 5°59E 164 D2
Varalé Ivory C. 9°40N 3°17W 262 D4
Varallo Italy 45°49N 8°15E 198 C5
Varāmīn Iran 35°20N 51°39E 247 C6
Varāmīn □ Iran 35°18N 51°35E 247 B6
Varanasi India 25°22N 83°0E 243 G10
Varangerfjorden Norway 70°3N 29°25E 160 A23
Varangerhalvøya Norway 70°25N 29°30E 160 A23
Varano, Lago di Italy 41°53N 15°45E 199 G12
Varaždin Croatia 46°20N 16°20E 199 B13
Varazze Italy 44°22N 8°34E 198 D5
Varberg Sweden 57°6N 12°20E 163 G6
Varcar Vakuf = Mrkonjić Grad Bos.-H. 44°26N 17°4E 182 F2
Vardak □ Afghan. 34°0N 68°0E 240 B3
Vardar = Axios → Greece 40°57N 22°35E 202 F6
Varde Denmark 55°38N 8°29E 163 J2
Varde Å → Denmark 55°35N 8°19E 163 J2
Vardenis Armenia 40°10N 45°43E 191 K7
Vardø Norway 70°23N 31°5E 160 A24
Varedo Italy 45°35N 9°8E 129 A1
Varel Germany 53°23N 8°8E 178 B4
Varella, Mui = Nay, Mui Vietnam 12°54N 109°26E 236 F7
Varėna Lithuania 54°12N 24°30E 188 E3
Varennes-sur-Allier France 46°19N 3°24E 173 F10
Varennes-Vauzelles France 47°3N 3°9E 173 E10
Vareš Bos.-H. 44°12N 18°23E 182 F3
Varese Italy 45°48N 8°50E 198 C5
Vârfurile Romania 46°19N 22°31E 182 D7
Vårgårda Sweden 58°2N 12°49E 163 F6
Vargem Bonita Brazil 20°20S 46°22W 333 F2
Vargem Grande Brazil 3°33S 43°56W 332 B3
Varginha Brazil 21°33S 45°25W 335 A6
Vargön Sweden 58°22N 12°20E 163 F6
Varhaug Norway 58°37N 5°41E 164 F2
Vari Greece 38°24N 20°35E 207 C2
Varillas Chile 24°0S 70°10W 334 A1
Varkaus Finland 62°19N 27°50E 188 A4
Varkiza Greece 37°50N 23°49E 112 C2
Värmdölandet Sweden 59°20N 18°33E 162 E12
Värmeln Sweden 59°35N 12°54E 162 E6
Värmlands län □ Sweden 60°0N 13°20E 162 E6
Värmlandsbro Sweden 59°11N 13°0E 162 E7
Varna Bulgaria 43°13N 27°56E 203 C11
Varna □ Bulgaria 43°20N 27°30E 203 C11
Varna → India 16°48N 74°32E 244 F2
Värnamo Sweden 57°10N 14°3E 163 G8
Várnjárga = Varangerhalvøya Norway 70°25N 29°30E 160 A23
Varnsdorf Czech Rep. 50°55N 14°35E 180 A7
Varnville U.S.A. 32°51N 81°5W 316 C8
Várpalota Hungary 47°12N 18°8E 182 C3
Vars Ont., Canada 45°21N 75°21W 313 A9
Vars Hautes-Alpes, France 44°37N 6°42E 175 D10
Vartdal Norway 62°20N 6°8E 164 B3
Vartiokylä Finland 60°13N 25°6E 121 B3
Vartiosaari Finland 60°11N 25°5E 121 B3
Varto Turkey 39°10N 41°27E 213 C9
Varvarin Serbia 43°43N 21°20E 202 C5
Varysburg U.S.A. 42°46N 78°19W 312 D6
Varzaneh Iran 32°25N 52°40E 247 C7
Varzaqān Iran 38°29N 46°40E 213 C12
Várzea Alegre Brazil 6°47S 39°17W 332 C4
Várzea da Palma Brazil 17°36S 44°44W 333 E3
Várzea Grande Brazil 15°39S 56°8W 331 D6
Varzi Italy 44°49N 9°12E 198 D6
Varzo Italy 46°12N 8°15E 198 B5
Varzy France 47°22N 3°20E 173 E10
Vas □ Hungary 47°10N 16°55E 182 C1
Vasa = Vaasa Finland 63°6N 21°38E 160 E19
Vasa Barris → Brazil 11°10S 37°10W 332 D4
Vasamuseet Stockholm, Sweden 139 b3
Vásárosnamény Hungary 48°9N 22°19E 182 B7
Vascão → Portugal 37°31N 7°31W 195 H3
Vaşcău Romania 46°28N 22°30E 182 D7
Vasco S. Africa 33°54S 18°34E 118 A2
Vascongadas = País Vasco □ Spain 42°50N 2°45W 196 C2
Vasfanārd Iran 35°38N 51°20E 141 B2
Vashi India 19°4N 72°59E 130 A2
Vāshīr Afghan. 32°16N 63°51E 240 B1
Vashkivtsi Ukraine 48°23N 25°31E 183 B10
Vasht = Khāsh Iran 28°15N 61°15E 240 C1
Vasilevichi Belarus 52°15N 29°50E 177 B16
Vasiliki Greece 38°37N 20°36E 207 B2
Vasiliko = Michurin Bulgaria 42°9N 27°51E 203 D11
Vasiliko Greece 38°25N 23°40E 204 C5
Vasilikos Greece 37°43N 20°59E 207 D2
Vasilkov = Vasylkiv Ukraine 50°7N 30°15E 177 C16
Vasilyevskiy, Ostrov Russia 59°55N 30°16E 137 B1
Vasilyova Sloboda = Chkolovsk Russia 56°50N 43°10E 190 B6
Vasilyovo = Chkolovsk Russia 56°50N 43°10E 190 B6
Väskinde Sweden 57°40N 18°20E 163 G10
Vaslui Romania 46°38N 27°42E 183 D12
Vaslui □ Romania 46°30N 27°45E 183 D12
Väsman Sweden 60°9N 15°5E 162 D9
Vassar Man., Canada 49°10N 95°55W 297 D9
Vassar Mich., U.S.A. 43°22N 83°35W 309 D12
Vassfaret Norway 60°38N 9°28E 164 D6
Västerås Sweden 59°37N 16°38E 162 E10
Västerbotten Sweden 64°36N 20°4E 160 D19
Västerdalälven → Sweden 60°30N 15°7E 162 D8
Västergötland Sweden 58°0N 13°10E 163 F7
Västerhaninge Sweden 59°7N 18°6E 162 E12
Västervik Sweden 57°43N 16°33E 163 G10
Västmanland Sweden 59°45N 16°20E 161 G17
Västmanlands län □ Sweden 59°45N 16°20E 162 E10
Vasto Italy 42°8N 14°40E 199 F11
Västra Götalands Län □ Sweden 58°0N 13°0E 163 F6
Vasvár Hungary 47°3N 16°47E 182 C1
Vasylivka Ukraine 45°38N 28°50E 183 E13
Vasylkiv Ukraine 50°7N 30°15E 177 C16
Vat Phou Laos 14°51N 105°49E 236 E5
Vatan France 47°4N 1°50E 173 E8
Vaté = Efate, I. Vanuatu 17°40S 168°25E 287 G6
Vatersay U.K. 56°55N 7°32W 167 E1
Vathi Greece 38°41N 20°47E 207 B2
Vathia Greece 36°29N 22°29E 204 E4
Vati Greece 36°3N 27°53E 206 E11
Vatia Amer. Samoa 14°15S 170°40W 302 f
Vatican City ■ Europe 41°54N 12°27E 136 B1
Vaticano, C. Italy 38°37N 15°50E 201 D8
Vatili Cyprus 35°6N 33°40E 207 E9
Vatin Serbia 45°12N 21°20E 182 E6
Vatiu = Atiu Cook Is. 20°0S 158°10W 289 J12
Vatnajökull Iceland 64°30N 16°48W 155 C10
Vatnajökull △ Iceland 64°24N 16°48W 155 C10
Vatnås Norway 59°58N 9°37E 164 E6
Vatnsfjörður Iceland 65°56N 22°30W 155 B4
Vato Sweden 59°50N 19°0E 162 E12
Vatolakkos Greece 35°27N 23°53E 207 E4
Vatoloha Madag. 17°52S 47°48E 272 B2
Vatomandry Madag. 19°20S 48°59E 272 B2
Vatra-Dornei Romania 47°22N 25°22E 183 C10
Vatrak → India 23°9N 73°2E 242 H5
Vattaru Atoll Maldives 3°16N 73°25E 272 d
Vättern Sweden 58°25N 14°30E 163 F8
Vatu Vara Fiji 17°26S 179°31W 287 A3
Vatulele Fiji 18°33S 177°37E 287 B1
Vauclin, Mt. du Martinique 14°33N 60°53W 322 j
Vauclin, Pte. de Martinique 14°34N 60°49W 322 j
Vaucluse Australia 33°51S 151°15E 139 B2
Vaucluse □ France 43°50N 5°20E 175 E9
Vaucluse House Australia 33°51S 151°15E 139 B2
Vaucouleurs France 48°37N 5°40E 173 D12
Vaucresson France 48°50N 2°9E 134 A1
Vaud □ Switz. 46°35N 6°30E 179 J2
Vaudreuil-Dorion Canada 45°23N 74°3W 313 A10
Vaughan Canada 43°50N 79°32W 141 A1
Vaughn Mont., U.S.A. 47°33N 111°33W 304 C8
Vaughn N. Mex., U.S.A. 34°36N 105°13W 305 J11
Vauhallan France 48°44N 2°12E 134 B2
Vaujours France 48°56N 2°34E 134 A4
Vaujours L. Canada 55°27N 74°15W 298 A5
Vaupés = Uaupés → Brazil 0°2N 67°16W 328 C4
Vaupés □ Colombia 1°0N 71°0W 328 C3
Vauvert France 43°42N 4°17E 175 E8
Vauxhall Alta., Canada 50°5N 112°9W 296 C6
Vauxhall London, U.K. 125 c4
Vav India 24°22N 71°31E 242 G4
Vavatenina Madag. 17°28S 49°12E 272 B2
Vava'u Tonga 18°36S 174°0W 287 P14
Vava'u Group Tonga 18°40S 174°0W 287 P14
Vavoua Ivory C. 7°23N 6°29W 262 D3
Vavuniya Sri Lanka 8°45N 80°30E 245 K5
Vawkavysk Belarus 53°9N 24°30E 177 B13
Vaxholm Sweden 59°25N 18°20E 162 E12
Växjö Sweden 56°52N 14°50E 163 H8
Våxtorp Sweden 56°25N 13°8E 163 H7
Vayalpad India 13°39N 78°38E 245 H4
Vayenga = Severomorsk Russia 69°5N 33°27E 160 B25
Vaygach, Ostrov Russia 70°0N 60°0E 214 C7
Veadeiros Brazil 14°7S 47°31W 333 D2
Veaikevárri = Svappavaara Sweden 67°40N 21°3E 160 C19
Vechelde Germany 52°16N 10°22E 178 C6
Vechta Germany 52°44N 8°17E 178 C4
Vechte → Neths. 52°34N 6°6E 170 B6
Vecsés Hungary 47°26N 19°19E 117 B3
Vedaranniyam India 10°25N 79°50E 245 J4
Vedavågen Norway 59°17N 5°12E 164 E2
Veddige Sweden 57°17N 12°20E 163 G6
Vedea → Romania 43°42N 25°41E 183 G10
Vedi Armenia 39°54N 44°43E 213 C11
Vedia Argentina 34°30S 61°31W 334 C3
Vedrette di Ries-Aurina ⌓ Italy 46°54N 12°5E 199 B9
Vedum Sweden 58°11N 13°0E 163 F7
Veedersburg U.S.A. 40°7N 87°16W 311 D9
Veendam Neths. 53°5N 6°52E 170 A6
Veenendaal Neths. 52°2N 5°34E 170 B5
Vefsna → Norway 65°48N 13°10E 160 D15
Vega Nordland, Norway 65°40N 11°55E 160 D14
Vega Tex., U.S.A. 35°15N 102°26W 314 D3
Vega Alta Puerto Rico 18°25N 66°20W 321 b
Vega Baja Puerto Rico 18°27N 66°23W 321 b
Vega de Ribadeo = Vegadeo Spain 43°27N 7°4W 194 B3
Vegadeo Spain 43°27N 7°4W 194 B3
Vegårshei Norway 58°44N 8°51E 164 F5
Vegas Verde = North Las Vegas U.S.A. 36°11N 115°7W 124 A1
Veggli Norway 60°3N 9°9E 164 D6
Veglia = Krk Croatia 45°8N 14°40E 199 C11
Vegoritida, L. Greece 40°45N 21°45E 202 F5
Vegreville Canada 53°30N 112°5W 296 C6
Veiholmen Norway 63°31N 7°58E 164 A4
Veimandu Channel Maldives 2°10N 73°20E 272 d
Veinge Sweden 56°33N 13°4E 163 H7
Veisiejai Lithuania 54°6N 23°42E 184 D10
Vejbystrand Sweden 56°19N 12°45E 163 H6
Vejen Denmark 55°30N 9°9E 163 J3
Vejer de la Frontera Spain 36°15N 5°59W 195 J5
Vejle Denmark 55°43N 9°30E 163 J3
Vejle Fjord Denmark 55°40N 9°50E 163 J3
Vela Luka Croatia 42°59N 16°44E 199 F13
Velachha India 21°26N 73°1E 244 D1
Velanai I. Sri Lanka 9°45N 79°45E 245 K4
Velas Azores 38°41N 28°13W 153 d1
Velas, C. Costa Rica 10°21N 85°52W 320 D2
Velasco, Sierra de Argentina 29°20S 67°10W 334 B2
Velay, Mts. du France 45°0N 3°40E 174 D7
Velbert Germany 51°20N 7°3E 178 D3
Velddrif S. Africa 32°42S 18°11E 270 D2
Velebit ⌓ Croatia 44°30N 15°15E 199 D12
Velebit Planina Croatia 44°50N 15°20E 199 D12
Velebitski Kanal Croatia 44°45N 14°55E 199 D11
Veleka → Bulgaria 42°4N 27°58E 203 D11
Veleň Czech Rep. 50°10N 14°33E 135 A3
Velencei-tó Hungary 47°13N 18°36E 182 C3
Velenje Slovenia 46°23N 15°8E 199 B12
Veles Macedonia 41°46N 21°47E 202 E5
Veleslavin Czech Rep. 50°5N 14°21E 135 B2
Velestino Greece 39°23N 22°43E 204 B4
Vélez Colombia 6°1N 73°41W 328 B3
Vélez-Málaga Spain 36°48N 4°5W 195 J6
Vélez Rubio Spain 37°41N 2°5W 197 H2
Velhas → Brazil 17°13S 44°49W 333 E3
Velika Croatia 45°27N 17°40E 182 E2
Velika Gorica Croatia 45°44N 16°5E 199 C13
Velika Kapela Croatia 45°10N 15°5E 199 C12
Velika Kikinda = Kikinda Serbia 45°50N 20°30E 182 E5
Velika Kladuša Bos.-H. 45°11N 15°48E 199 C12
Velika Kruša Kosovo 42°19N 20°39E 202 D4
Velika Morava → Serbia 44°43N 21°3E 202 B5
Velika Plana Serbia 44°20N 21°4E 202 B5
Velikaya → Russia 57°48N 28°10E 188 D5
Velikaya Kema Russia 45°30N 137°12E 220 B8
Velikaya Lepetikha Ukraine 47°2N 33°58E 189 J7
Veliké Kapušany Slovak Rep. 48°34N 22°5E 181 C15
Velike Lašče Slovenia 45°49N 14°45E 199 C11
Veliki Jastrebac Serbia 43°25N 21°30E 202 C5
Veliki Kanal Serbia 45°45N 19°15E 182 E4
Veliki Popović Serbia 44°8N 21°18E 202 B5
Veliki Ustyug Russia 60°47N 46°20E 186 B8
Velikiye Luki Russia 56°25N 30°32E 188 D6
Veliko Gradište Serbia 44°46N 21°29E 202 B5
Veliko Tŭrnovo Bulgaria 43°5N 25°41E 203 C9
Veliko Tŭrnovo □ Bulgaria 43°5N 25°41E 203 C9
Velikonda Range India 14°45N 79°10E 245 G4
Vélingara Kolda, Senegal 13°12N 14°5W 262 C2
Vélingara Louga, Senegal 15°0N 14°40W 262 B2
Velingrad Bulgaria 42°4N 23°58E 202 D7
Velino, Mte. Italy 42°9N 13°23E 199 F10
Velizh Russia 55°36N 31°11E 188 E6
Vélizy-Villacoublay France 48°47N 2°11E 134 B2
Velka-Chuchle Czech Rep. 50°0N 14°23E 135 B2
Velké Karlovice Czech Rep. 49°20N 18°17E 181 B11
Velké Meziříčí Czech Rep. 49°21N 16°1E 180 B9
Velké Přilepy Czech Rep. 50°9N 14°19E 135 B1
Veľký Javorník Slovak Rep. 49°19N 18°22E 181 B11
Veľký Krtíš Slovak Rep. 48°12N 19°21E 181 C12
Veľký Meder Slovak Rep. 47°52N 17°46E 181 D10
Veľký Tribeč Slovak Rep. 48°28N 18°15E 181 C11
Vella G. Solomon Is. 8°0S 156°50E 287 M9
Vella Lavella Solomon Is. 7°45S 156°40E 287 L9
Vellar → India 11°30N 79°36E 245 J4
Velletri Italy 41°41N 12°47E 200 A5
Vellinge Sweden 55°29N 13°2E 163 J6
Vellmar Germany 51°22N 9°28E 178 D5
Vellore India 12°57N 79°10E 245 H4
Velopoula Greece 36°55N 23°27E 204 E5
Velsk Russia 61°10N 42°5E 188 B11
Velten Germany 52°42N 13°10E 178 C9
Veluwezoom △ Neths. 52°5N 6°0E 170 B6
Velva U.S.A. 48°4N 100°56W 308 A3
Velvendos Greece 40°15N 22°6E 202 F6
Velyka Mykhaylivka Ukraine 47°4N 29°52E 183 C14
Velyki Luchky Ukraine 48°25N 22°34E 182 B7
Velykyy Bereznyy Ukraine 48°54N 22°28E 182 B7
Velykyy Bychkiv Ukraine 47°58N 24°1E 183 C9
Vemb Denmark 56°21N 8°21E 163 H2
Vembanad L. India 9°36N 76°15E 245 K3
Vemdalen Sweden 62°27N 13°51E 162 B7
Ven Sweden 55°55N 12°45E 163 J6
Venaco France 42°14N 9°11E 175 F13
Venado Mexico 22°56N 101°6W 318 C4
Venado Tuerto Argentina 33°50S 62°0W 334 C3
Venafro Italy 41°29N 14°2E 201 A7
Venarey-les-Laumes France 47°32N 4°26E 173 E11
Venaría Italy 45°8N 7°38E 198 C4
Venčane Serbia 44°24N 20°28E 202 B4
Vence France 43°43N 7°6E 175 E11
Venda Seca Portugal 38°46N 9°15W 126 A1
Vendas Novas Portugal 38°39N 8°27W 195 G2
Vendée □ France 46°50N 1°35W 172 F5
Vendée → France 46°20N 1°10W 172 F5
Vendéen, Bocage France 46°40N 1°20W 174 B2
Vendeuvre-sur-Barse France 48°14N 4°28E 173 D11
Vendôme France 47°47N 1°3E 172 E8
Vendrell = El Vendrell Spain 41°10N 1°30E 196 D6
Vendsyssel Denmark 57°22N 10°0E 163 G4
Vendychany Ukraine 48°38N 27°48E 183 B12
Venelles France 43°35N 5°28E 175 E9
Véneta, L. Italy 45°23N 12°25E 199 C9
Venetian Islands U.S.A. 25°47N 80°9W 128 B2
Venetie U.S.A. 67°1N 146°25W 303 C11
Véneto □ Italy 45°30N 12°0E 199 C9
Venev Russia 54°22N 38°17E 188 E10
Venézia Italy 45°27N 12°21E 199 C9
Venézia, G. di Italy 45°15N 13°0E 199 C10
Venézia, Palazzo Rome, Italy 136 c2
Venézia Tridentina = Trentino-Alto Adige □ Italy 46°30N 11°20E 199 B8
Venezuela ■ S. Amer. 8°0N 66°0W 328 B4
Venezuela, G. de Venezuela 11°30N 71°0W 328 A3
Venezuelan Basin Cent. Amer. 14°0N 68°0W 321 C6
Vengurla India 15°53N 73°45E 245 G1
Vengurla Rocks India 15°55N 73°22E 245 G1
Venice = Venézia Italy 45°27N 12°21E 199 C9
Venice Calif., U.S.A. 33°59N 118°27W 126 C2
Venice Fla., U.S.A. 27°6N 82°27W 317 H7
Vénissieux France 45°42N 4°53E 175 C8
Venjan Sweden 60°57N 13°55E 162 D7
Venjansjön Sweden 60°54N 14°0E 162 D8
Venkatagiri India 14°0N 79°35E 245 H4
Venkatapuram India 18°20N 80°30E 244 E5
Venlo Neths. 51°22N 6°11E 170 C6
Vennachar Junction Canada 45°5N 77°14W 312 A7
Vennesla Norway 58°15N 7°59E 164 F4
Venosa Italy 40°58N 15°49E 201 B8
Venray Neths. 51°31N 6°0E 170 C6
Vent, Îs. du French Polynesia 17°30S 149°30W 289 f
Venta Lithuania 56°12N 22°42E 184 B9
Venta → Latvia 57°24N 21°33E 184 A8
Venta de Baños Spain 41°55N 4°30W 194 D6
Venta de Cardeña = Cardeña Spain 38°16N 4°20W 195 G6
Ventana, Punta de la Mexico 24°4N 109°48W 318 C3
Ventana, Sa. de la Argentina 38°0S 62°30W 334 D3
Ventas Spain 40°26N 3°40W 127 B1
Ventersburg S. Africa 28°7S 27°9E 270 C4
Ventersburgweg = Hennenman S. Africa 27°59S 27°1E 270 C4
Venterstad S. Africa 30°47S 25°48E 270 D4
Ventimíglia Italy 43°47N 7°36E 198 E4
Ventnor U.K. 50°36N 1°12W 169 G6
Ventorro del Cano Spain 40°23N 3°49W 127 B1
Ventoténe Italy 40°47N 13°25E 200 B6
Ventoux, Mt. France 44°10N 5°17E 175 D9
Ventspils Latvia 57°25N 21°32E 184 A8
Ventspils □ Latvia 57°20N 21°50E 184 A8
Ventuarí → Venezuela 3°58N 67°2W 328 C4
Ventucopa U.S.A. 34°50N 119°29W 307 L7
Ventura U.S.A. 34°17N 119°18W 307 L7
Venus U.S.A. 27°4N 81°22W 317 H8
Vénus, Pte. Tahiti 17°29S 149°29W 289 e
Venus B. Australia 38°40S 145°42E 283 E6
Venustiano Carranza Baja Calif., Mexico 30°25N 115°53W 318 A1
Venustiano Carranza Distrito Federal, Mexico 19°25N 99°5W 128 B2
Vera Argentina 29°30S 60°20W 334 B3
Vera Spain 37°15N 1°51W 197 H3
Veracruz Mexico 19°11N 96°8W 319 D5
Veracruz □ Mexico 19°0N 96°15W 319 D5
Veraval India 20°53N 70°27E 242 J4
Verbánia Italy 45°56N 8°33E 198 C5
Verbicaro Italy 39°45N 15°55E 201 C8
Verbier Switz. 46°6N 7°13E 179 J3
Vercelli Italy 45°19N 8°25E 198 C5
Verchovchevo Ukraine 48°32N 34°10E 189 H8
Vercors ⌓ France 45°0N 5°25E 175 D9
Verdalsøra Norway 63°48N 11°30E 160 E14
Verde → Argentina 41°56S 65°5W 336 B3
Verde → Goiás, Brazil 19°11S 50°44W 333 E1
Verde → Goiás, Brazil 18°1S 50°14W 333 E1
Verde → Mato Grosso, Brazil 11°54S 55°48W 331 C6
Verde → Mato Grosso do Sul, Brazil 21°25S 52°20W 331 E7
Verde → São Paulo, Brazil 23°29S 46°27W 137 A1
Verde → Chihuahua, Mexico 26°29N 107°58W 318 B3
Verde → Oaxaca, Mexico 15°59N 97°50W 319 D5
Verde → Veracruz, Mexico 21°10N 102°50W 318 C4
Verde → Paraguay 23°9S 57°37W 334 A4
Verde → Ariz., U.S.A. 33°33N 111°40W 300 J17
Verde, Cay Bahamas 23°0N 75°5W 321 B4
Verde Grande → Brazil 16°13S 43°49W 333 E3
Verde I. Phil. 13°33N 121°5E 232 E3
Verde Island Pass. Phil. 13°34N 120°51E 232 E3
Verde Pequeno → Brazil 14°48S 43°31W 333 D3
Verden Germany 52°55N 9°14E 178 C5
Verdi Athina, Greece 38°2N 23°40E 112 A2
Verdi Nev., U.S.A. 39°31N 119°59W 306 F7
Verdikoussa Greece 39°47N 21°59E 204 B3
Verdon → France 43°43N 5°46E 175 E9
Verdon ⌓ France 43°50N 6°5E 175 E10
Verdugo Mts. U.S.A. 34°10N 118°16W 126 A2
Verdun Qué., Canada 45°27N 73°35W 130 B2
Verdun Meuse, France 49°9N 5°24E 173 C12
Verdun-sur-le-Doubs France 46°54N 5°2E 173 F12
Vereeniging S. Africa 26°38S 27°57E 271 C4
Verga, C. Guinea 10°30N 14°10W 262 C2
Vergara Uruguay 32°56S 53°57W 335 C5
Vergato Italy 44°17N 11°7E 198 D8
Vergemont Cr. → Australia 24°16S 143°16E 280 C3
Vergennes U.S.A. 44°10N 73°15W 313 B11
Vergt France 45°2N 0°43E 174 C4
Vérhalom Hungary 47°31N 19°1E 117 A2
Veria Greece 40°34N 22°12E 202 F6
Verín Spain 41°57N 7°27W 194 D3
Verkhnedvinsk = Vyerkhnyadzvinsk Belarus 55°45N 27°58E 188 E4
Verkhnetulomskoye Vdkhr. Russia 68°36N 31°12E 160 B24
Verkhnevilyuysk Russia 63°27N 120°18E 215 C13
Verkhniy Baskunchak Russia 48°14N 46°44E 191 F8
Verkhovye Russia 52°55N 37°15E 189 F9
Verkhovyna Ukraine 48°9N 24°47E 183 B9
Verkhoyansk Russia 67°35N 133°25E 215 C14
Verkhoyansk Ra. = Verkhoyanskiy Khrebet Russia 66°0N 129°0E 215 C13
Verkhoyanskiy Khrebet Russia 66°0N 129°0E 215 C13
Verma Norway 62°21N 8°3E 164 B5
Vermelho → Brazil 23°30S 46°46W 137 B1
Vermenton France 47°40N 3°42E 173 E10
Vermilion Alta., Canada 53°20N 110°50W 297 C6
Vermilion Ohio, U.S.A. 41°25N 82°22W 312 E2
Vermilion → Alta., Canada 53°22N 110°51W 297 C6
Vermilion → Ill., U.S.A. 41°19N 89°4W 310 C7
Vermilion B. U.S.A. 29°42N 92°0W 314 G9
Vermilion Bay Canada 49°51N 93°34W 297 D10
Vermilion L. U.S.A. 47°53N 92°26W 308 B7
Vermillion U.S.A. 42°47N 96°56W 308 D5
Vermillion → Canada 47°38N 72°56W 298 C5
Vermont U.S.A. 40°18N 90°26W 310 D6
Vermont □ U.S.A. 44°0N 73°0W 313 C12
Vermont Knolls U.S.A. 33°57N 118°21W 126 C3
Vermosh Albania 42°35N 19°42E 202 D3
Verna U.S.A. 27°23N 82°16W 317 H7
Vernadsky Antarctica 65°0S 64°0W 151 C17
Vernal U.S.A. 40°27N 109°32W 304 F9
Vernalis U.S.A. 37°36N 121°17W 306 H5
Vernazza Italy 44°10N 9°45E 198 D6
Verner Canada 46°25N 80°8W 298 C3
Verneuil-sur-Avre France 48°45N 0°55E 172 D7
Verneukpan S. Africa 30°0S 21°0E 270 D3
Vernier Switz. 46°11N 6°12E 179 J2
Vérnio Italy 44°3N 11°9E 198 D8
Vernon B.C., Canada 50°20N 119°15W 296 C5
Vernon Eure, France 49°5N 1°30E 172 C8
Vernon Calif., U.S.A. 34°0N 118°13W 126 B3
Vernon Ill., U.S.A. 38°48N 89°5W 310 F7
Vernon Ind., U.S.A. 38°59N 85°36W 311 F11
Vernon Tex., U.S.A. 34°9N 99°17W 314 D5
Vernonia U.S.A. 45°52N 123°11W 306 E3
Vernou Guadeloupe 16°11N 61°39W 322 e
Verny = Almaty Kazakhstan 43°15N 76°57E 217 D9
Vero Beach U.S.A. 27°38N 80°24W 317 H9
Véroia = Veria Greece 40°34N 22°12E 202 F6
Véroli Italy 41°41N 13°25E 199 G10
Verona Ont., Canada 44°29N 76°42W 313 B8
Verona Italy 45°27N 10°59E 198 C7
Verona Wis., U.S.A. 42°59N 89°32W 310 B7
Verrès Italy 45°40N 7°42E 198 C4
Verrières-le-Buisson France 48°44N 2°16E 134 B2
Verron Ra. Papua N. G. 4°21S 152°46E 286 C7
Versailles B. Aires, Argentina 34°38S 58°31W 117 B1
Versailles Yvelines, France 48°48N 2°7E 134 B1
Versailles Ill., U.S.A. 39°53N 90°39W 310 E6
Versailles Ind., U.S.A. 39°4N 85°15W 311 E11
Versailles Ky., U.S.A. 38°3N 84°44W 311 F12
Versailles Mo., U.S.A. 38°26N 92°51W 310 F4
Versailles Ohio, U.S.A. 40°13N 84°29W 311 D12
Versalles Bolivia 12°44S 63°18W 331 C5
Versmold Germany 52°2N 8°9E 178 C4
Vert, C. Senegal 14°45N 17°30W 262 C1
Vertou France 47°10N 1°28W 172 E5
Vertus France 48°54N 4°2E 173 D11
Verulam S. Africa 29°38S 31°2E 271 C5
Verviers Belgium 50°37N 5°52E 170 D5
Vervins France 49°50N 3°53E 173 C10
Veržej Slovenia 46°34N 16°13E 199 B13
Verzy France 49°9N 4°10E 173 C11
Vescovato France 42°30N 9°27E 175 F13
Veselí nad Lužnicí Czech Rep. 49°12N 14°43E 180 B7
Veselie Bulgaria 42°18N 27°38E 203 D11
Veselovskoye Vdkhr. Russia 46°58N 41°25E 191 G5
Veshenskaya Russia 49°35N 41°44E 190 F5
Veshnyaki Russia 55°43N 37°48E 129 B4
Vesle → France 49°23N 3°28E 173 C10
Vesolyy Posolok Russia 59°53N 30°28E 137 B2
Vesoul France 47°40N 6°11E 173 E13
Vessigebro Sweden 56°58N 12°40E 163 H6
Vest-Agder □ Norway 58°30N 7°15E 164 F4
Vestbygd Norway 58°6N 6°34E 164 F3
Vesterålen Norway 68°45N 15°0E 160 B16
Vestfjorden Norway 67°55N 14°0E 160 C16
Vestfold □ Norway 59°15N 10°0E 164 E7
Vestfossen Norway 59°44N 9°52E 164 E6
Vestgrønland = Kitaa □ Greenland 70°0N 47°0W 154 C6
Vestmannaeyjar Iceland 63°27N 20°15W 155 D6
Vestnes Norway 62°39N 7°5E 164 B4
Vestra Finland 60°19N 24°46E 121 B1
Vestre Gausdal Norway 61°12N 10°8E 164 C7
Vestskoven Denmark 55°41N 12°23E 118 A2
Vestspitsbergen Svalbard 78°40N 17°0E 150 B8
Vestur-skaftafellssýsla □ Iceland 63°50N 18°30W 155 D8
Vestvågøya Norway 68°18N 13°50E 160 B15
Vesuvio Italy 40°49N 14°26E 201 B7
Vesuvius, Mt. = Vesuvio Italy 40°49N 14°26E 201 B7
Vesyegonsk Russia 58°40N 37°16E 188 C9
Veszprém Hungary 47°8N 17°57E 182 C2
Veszprém □ Hungary 47°5N 17°55E 182 C2
Vésztő Hungary 46°55N 21°16E 182 D6
Vetapalem India 15°47N 80°18E 245 G5
Vetlanda Sweden 57°24N 15°3E 163 G9
Vetluga Russia 57°53N 45°45E 190 B7
Vetlugu → Russia 56°36N 46°4E 190 B8
Vetluzhskiy Kostroma, Russia 58°23N 45°26E 190 A7
Vetluzhskiy Nizhniy Novgorod, Russia 57°17N 45°12E 190 B7
Vetovo Bulgaria 43°42N 26°16E 203 C10

Vladimirovac Serbia 45°1N 20°53E 182 E5
Vladimirovka = Yuzhno-Sakhalinsk Russia 46°58N 142°45E 219 B17
Vladimirovka Russia 48°27N 46°10E 191 F8
Vladimirovo Bulgaria 43°32N 23°22E 202 C2
Vladislavovka Ukraine 45°12N 35°29E 189 K8
Vladivostok Russia 43°10N 131°53E 220 C5
Vladykino Russia 55°51N 37°35E 129 A3
Vlăhiţa Romania 46°21N 25°31E 183 D10
Vlasenica Bos.-H. 44°11N 18°59E 182 F3
Vlašić Bos.-H. 44°19N 17°37E 182 F2
Vlašim Czech Rep. 49°40N 14°53E 180 B7
Vlasinsko Jezero Serbia 42°44N 22°22E 202 D6
Vlasotince Serbia 42°59N 22°7E 202 D6
Vlieland Neths. 53°16N 4°55E 170 A4
Vlissingen Neths. 51°26N 3°34E 170 C3
Vlorë Albania 40°32N 19°28E 202 F3
Vlorës, Gjiri i Albania 40°29N 19°27E 202 F3
Vltava ➜ Czech Rep. 50°21N 14°30E 180 A7
Vnukovo Russia 55°37N 37°17E 129 C1
Vo Dat Vietnam 11°9N 107°31E 237 G6
Vobarno Italy 45°39N 10°30E 198 C7
Voćin Croatia 45°37N 17°33E 182 E2
Vöcklabruck Austria 48°1N 13°39E 180 C6
Vodice Croatia 43°47N 15°47E 199 E12
Vodňany Czech Rep. 49°9N 14°11E 180 B7
Vodnjan Croatia 44°59N 13°52E 199 D10
Vodopyanovo = Donskoy Russia 53°55N 38°15E 188 F10
Voe U.K. 60°21N 1°16W 167 A7
Vogan Togo 6°23N 1°30E 263 D5
Vogar Iceland 63°58N 22°22W 155 D4
Vogel Pk. Nigeria 8°24N 11°47E 263 D7
Vogelkop = Doberai, Jazirah Indonesia 1°25S 133°0E 231 E8
Vogelsberg Germany 50°31N 9°12E 178 E5
Voghera Italy 44°59N 9°1E 198 D6
Voh N. Cal. 20°58S 164°42E 288 d
Vohibinany Madag. 18°49S 49°4E 272 B2
Vohilava Madag. 21°4S 48°0E 272 C2
Vohimarina = Iharana Madag. 13°25S 50°0E 272 A3
Vohimena, Tanjon' i Madag. 25°36S 45°8E 272 D2
Vohipeno Madag. 22°22S 47°51E 272 C2
Voi Kenya 3°25S 38°32E 268 C4
Void-Vacon France 48°40N 5°36E 173 D12
Voineşti Iaşi, Romania 47°5N 27°27E 183 C12
Voineşti Prahova, Romania 45°5N 25°14E 183 E10
Voinjama Liberia 8°25N 9°44W 262 D3
Voiron France 45°22N 5°35E 175 C9
Voisey B. Canada 56°15N 61°50W 299 A7
Voitsberg Austria 47°3N 15°9E 180 D8
Vojens Denmark 55°16N 9°18E 163 J3
Vojmsjön Sweden 65°0N 16°24E 160 D17
Vojnić Croatia 45°19N 15°43E 199 C12
Vojnik Italy 46°18N 15°19E 199 B12
Vojvodina □ Serbia 45°20N 20°0E 182 E5
Vokeo I. Papua N. G. 3°14S 144°2E 286 B3
Vokhtoga Russia 58°46N 41°8E 188 C11
Vokovice Czech Rep. 50°5N 14°21E 135 B2
Volary Czech Rep. 48°54N 13°52E 180 C6
Volborg U.S.A. 45°51N 105°41W 304 D11
Volcán de Colima △ Mexico 19°30N 103°40W 318 D4
Volcano U.S.A. 19°26N 155°14W 302 D6
Volcano Is. = Kazan-Rettō Pac. Oc. 25°0N 141°0E 288 E6
Volcans △ Rwanda 1°30S 29°26E 268 C2
Volcans d'Auvergne ⌂ France 45°20N 2°40E 174 C6
Volchansk = Vovchansk Ukraine 50°17N 36°58E 189 G9
Volchikha Russia 52°2N 80°23E 217 B10
Volchya ➜ Ukraine 48°32N 36°0E 189 H8
Volda Norway 62°9N 6°5E 164 B3
Volga = Privolzhskiy □ Russia 56°0N 50°0E 190 D9
Volga Russia 57°58N 38°16E 188 C10
Volga ➜ Russia 46°0N 48°30E 191 G9
Volga Hts. = Privolzhskaya Vozvyshennost Russia 51°0N 46°0E 190 E7
Volgelsdorf Germany 52°30N 13°44E 115 B5
Volgo-Baltiyskiy Kanal Russia 60°0N 38°0E 188 B9
Volgo-Donskoy Kanal Russia 48°40N 43°37E 191 F7
Volgodonsk Russia 47°33N 42°5E 191 G6
Volgograd Russia 48°40N 44°25E 191 F7
Volgograd □ Russia 49°40N 44°30E 190 F7
Volgogradskoye Vdkhr. Russia 50°0N 45°20E 190 E8
Volgorechensk Russia 57°28N 41°14E 190 B5
Volimes Greece 37°52N 20°39E 207 D2
Volintiri Moldova 46°26N 29°37E 183 D14
Volissos Greece 38°29N 25°54E 205 C7
Volkach Germany 49°52N 10°14E 179 F6
Völkermarkt Austria 46°39N 14°39E 180 E7
Volkhonka-Zil Russia 55°39N 37°37E 129 C3
Volkhov Russia 59°55N 32°15E 188 C7
Volkhov ➜ Russia 60°8N 32°20E 188 B7
Volkhovstroy = Volkhov Russia 59°55N 32°15E 188 C7
Völklingen Germany 49°15N 6°50E 179 F2
Volkovysk = Vawkavysk Belarus 53°9N 24°30E 177 B13
Volksrust S. Africa 27°24S 29°53E 271 C4
Voll Norway 62°31N 7°27E 164 B4
Vollen Norway 59°48N 10°27E 133 B1
Volnovakha Ukraine 47°35N 37°30E 189 J9
Volochanka Russia 71°0N 94°28E 215 B10
Volodarsk Russia 56°12N 43°15E 190 B6
Volodarskoye Russia 59°54N 30°23E 132 B2
Volodymyr-Volynskyy Ukraine 50°50N 24°18E 177 C13
Vologda Russia 59°10N 39°45E 188 C10
Vologda □ Russia 60°15N 39°0E 188 B10
Volokolamsk Russia 56°5N 35°57E 188 D8
Volokonovka Russia 50°33N 37°52E 189 G9
Volos Greece 39°24N 22°59E 204 B4
Vološinovo = Novi Bečej Serbia 45°36N 20°10E 182 E5
Volosovo Russia 59°27N 29°32E 188 C5
Volovets Ukraine 48°43N 23°11E 183 B8
Volovo Russia 53°35N 38°1E 188 F10
Volozhin = Valozhyn Belarus 54°3N 26°30E 177 A14
Volsk Russia 52°5N 47°22E 190 D8
Volta □ Ghana 7°0N 0°30E 263 D5
Volta ➜ Ghana 5°46N 0°41E 263 D5
Volta, L. Ghana 7°30N 0°0 263 D5
Volta Blanche = White Volta ➜ Ghana 9°10N 1°15W 263 D4
Volta Redonda Brazil 22°31S 44°5W 333 F3
Voltaire, C. Australia 14°16S 125°35E 278 B4
Volterra Italy 43°24N 10°51E 198 E7
Voltri Italy 44°26N 8°45E 198 D5
Volturno ➜ Italy 41°1N 13°55E 200 A6
Volubilis Morocco 34°2N 5°33W 260 B3
Volvi, L. Greece 40°40N 23°34E 202 F7
Volyn □ Ukraine 51°15N 24°30E 177 C13
Volyně Czech Rep. 49°10N 13°53E 180 B6
Volynkina-Derevnya Russia 59°53N 30°18E 137 B1
Volzhsk Russia 55°57N 48°23E 190 C9
Volzhskiy Russia 48°56N 44°46E 191 F7
Vomo Fiji 17°30S 177°15E 287 A1
Vonavona Solomon Is. 8°15S 157°5E 287 M9
Vondelpark Neths. 52°21N 4°52E 112 A2
Vondrozo Madag. 22°49S 47°20E 272 C2
Vonitsa Greece 38°55N 20°53E 207 B2
Vopnafjörður Iceland 65°45N 14°50W 155 B12
Vorarlberg □ Austria 47°20N 10°0E 180 D2
Voras Oros Greece 40°57N 21°45E 202 F5
Vorbasse Denmark 55°39N 9°6E 163 J3
Vorchdorf Austria 48°0N 13°55E 180 C6
Vorderrhein ➜ Switz. 46°49N 9°25E 179 J5
Vordingborg Denmark 55°0N 11°54E 163 J5
Vorë Albania 41°23N 19°40E 202 E3
Voreio Aigaio □ Greece 38°50N 25°30E 205 C7
Voreppe France 45°18N 5°39E 175 C9
Vori Greece 35°4N 24°49E 207 E5
Vorios Evoikos Kolpos Greece 38°45N 23°15E 204 C5
Vorkuta Russia 67°48N 64°20E 186 A11
Vorma ➜ Norway 60°9N 11°29E 164 D8
Vormsi Estonia 59°1N 23°13E 188 C2
Vorona ➜ Russia 51°22N 42°3E 190 E6
Voronezh Russia 51°40N 39°10E 189 G10
Voronezh Ukraine 51°47N 33°28E 189 G7
Voronezh □ Russia 51°30N 39°30E 190 E4
Voronezh ➜ Russia 51°32N 39°10E 189 G10
Vorontsovo-Aleksandrovskoye = Zelenokumsk Russia 44°24N 44°0E 191 H6
Voroshilov = Ussuriysk Russia 43°48N 131°59E 220 C5
Voroshilovgrad = Luhansk Ukraine 48°38N 39°15E 189 H10
Voroshilovsk = Alchevsk Ukraine 48°30N 38°45E 189 H10
Voroshilovsk = Stavropol Russia 45°5N 42°0E 191 H6
Vorpommersche Boddenlandschaft △ Germany 54°25N 12°32E 178 A8
Vorskla ➜ Ukraine 48°50N 34°10E 189 H8
Võrts järv Estonia 58°16N 26°3E 188 C4
Võru Estonia 57°48N 26°54E 188 D4
Vösendorf Austria 48°7N 16°20E 142 B2
Vosges France 48°20N 7°10E 173 D14
Vosges □ France 48°12N 6°20E 173 D13
Vosges du Nord ⌂ France 49°0N 7°30E 173 D14
Voskopojë Albania 40°35N 20°33E 202 F4
Voskresensk Russia 55°19N 38°43E 188 E10
Voskresenskoye Russia 56°51N 45°30E 190 B7
Voss Norway 60°38N 6°26E 164 D3
Vostochnyy Russia 55°49N 37°51E 129 B5
Vostok = Neftegorsk Russia 44°25N 39°45E 191 H4
Vostok Antarctica 78°30S 106°50E 151 D8
Vostok I. Kiribati 10°5S 152°23W 289 J12
Votice Czech Rep. 49°38N 14°39E 180 B7
Votkinsk Russia 57°0N 53°55E 186 C9
Votkinskoye Vdkhr. Russia 57°22N 55°12E 186 C10
Votsuri-Shima Japan 25°45N 123°29E 221 M1
Votuporanga Brazil 20°24S 49°59W 333 F2
Vouga ➜ Portugal 40°41N 8°40W 194 E2
Vouillé France 46°38N 0°10E 172 F7
Voula Greece 37°49N 23°45E 112 C2
Vouliagmeni Greece 37°50N 23°46E 112 C2
Voulkaria, L. Greece 38°52N 20°50E 207 B2
Voulou C.A.R. 8°33N 22°36E 264 A4
Vouxa, Akra Greece 35°37N 23°32E 207 E4
Vouzela Portugal 40°43N 8°7W 194 E2
Vouziers France 49°22N 4°40E 173 C11
Vovchansk Ukraine 50°17N 36°58E 189 G9
Vovodo ➜ C.A.R. 5°40N 24°21E 264 A4
Vowchyn Belarus 52°18N 23°18E 185 F10
Voyageurs △ U.S.A. 48°32N 93°0W 308 A7
Voynitsa Russia 65°10N 30°20E 160 D24
Voyvozh Russia 62°56N 54°56E 214 C6
Vozhe, Ozero Russia 60°45N 39°0E 188 B10
Vozhega Russia 60°29N 40°12E 188 B11
Voznesensk Ukraine 47°35N 31°21E 189 J6
Voznesenye Russia 61°0N 35°28E 188 B8
Vrå Denmark 57°21N 9°56E 163 G3
Vráble Slovak Rep. 48°15N 18°16E 181 C11
Vračevšnica Serbia 44°2N 20°34E 202 B4
Vrachneika Greece 38°10N 21°40E 204 C3
Vrådal Norway 59°20N 8°25E 164 E5
Vrancea □ Romania 45°50N 26°45E 183 E11
Vrancei, Munţii Romania 46°0N 26°30E 183 E11
Vrangel Russia 42°43N 133°5E 220 C6
Vrangelya, Ostrov Russia 71°0N 180°0E 215 B18
Vranica Bos.-H. 43°55N 17°50E 182 G2
Vranje Serbia 42°34N 21°54E 202 D5
Vranjska Banja Serbia 42°34N 22°1E 202 D6
Vranov nad Topl'ou Slovak Rep. 48°53N 21°40E 181 C14
Vransko Slovenia 46°17N 14°58E 199 B11
Vransko Jezero Croatia 43°53N 15°34E 199 E12
Vrapčište Macedonia 41°50N 20°53E 202 E4
Vratsa Bulgaria 43°15N 23°30E 202 C7
Vratsa □ Bulgaria 43°13N 23°30E 202 C7
Vråvatn Norway 59°20N 8°8E 164 E5
Vrbas Serbia 45°40N 19°40E 182 E4
Vrbas ➜ Bos.-H. 45°8N 17°29E 182 E2
Vrbnik Croatia 45°4N 14°40E 199 C11
Vrbovec Croatia 45°53N 16°28E 199 C13
Vrbovsko Croatia 45°24N 15°5E 199 C12
Vrchlabí Czech Rep. 50°38N 15°37E 180 A8
Vrede S. Africa 27°24S 29°6E 271 C4
Vredefort S. Africa 27°0S 27°22E 270 C4
Vredehoek S. Africa 33°57S 18°25E 118 A1
Vreden Germany 52°2N 6°50E 178 C2
Vredenburg S. Africa 32°56S 18°0E 270 D2
Vredendal S. Africa 31°41S 18°35E 270 D2
Vretstorp Sweden 59°1N 14°53E 162 E8
Vrgorac Croatia 43°12N 17°20E 199 E14
Vrhnika Slovenia 45°58N 14°15E 199 C11
Vriddhachalam India 11°30N 79°20E 245 J4
Vridi Ivory C. 5°15N 4°3W 262 D4
Vrigstad Sweden 57°22N 14°28E 163 G8
Vrindavan India 27°37N 77°40E 242 F7
Vrisses Greece 35°23N 24°13E 207 E5
Vrnograč Bos.-H. 45°10N 15°57E 199 C12
Vrondados Greece 38°25N 26°7E 205 C8
Vrpolje Croatia 45°13N 18°24E 182 E3
Vršac Serbia 45°8N 21°20E 182 E6
Vrsacki Kanal Serbia 45°15N 21°0E 182 E5
Vršovice Czech Rep. 50°4N 14°28E 135 B2
Vrútky Slovak Rep. 49°7N 18°55E 181 B11
Vryburg S. Africa 26°55S 24°45E 270 C3
Vryheid S. Africa 27°45S 30°47E 271 C5
Vsetín Czech Rep. 49°20N 18°0E 181 B11
Vu Liet Vietnam 18°43N 105°23E 236 C5
Vúcha ➜ Bulgaria 42°10N 24°26E 203 D8
Vučitrn Kosovo 42°49N 20°59E 202 D4
Vuga Sudan 5°21N 29°40E 257 F2
Vukovar Croatia 45°21N 18°59E 182 E3
Vuktyl Russia 63°52N 57°20E 214 C6
Vulcan Alta., Canada 50°25N 113°15W 296 C6
Vulcan Romania 45°23N 23°17E 183 E8
Vulcaneşti Moldova 45°41N 28°18E 183 E13
Vulcano Italy 38°24N 14°58E 201 D7
Vŭlchedruma Bulgaria 43°42N 23°27E 202 C7
Vulkaneshty = Vulcaneşti Moldova 45°41N 28°18E 183 E13
Vunduzi ➜ Mozam. 18°56S 34°1E 269 F3
Vung Tau Vietnam 10°21N 107°4E 237 G6
Vunidawa Fiji 17°50S 178°21E 287 A2
Vunisea Fiji 19°3S 178°10E 287 B2
Vuranggo Solomon Is. 6°39S 156°38E 287 L9
Vŭrbitsa Bulgaria 42°59N 26°40E 203 D10
Vŭrshets Bulgaria 43°13N 23°23E 202 C7
Vushtrri = Vučitrn Kosovo 42°49N 20°59E 202 D4
Vutcani Romania 46°26N 27°59E 183 D12
Vuzlove Ukraine 48°22N 22°24E 182 B7
Vwaza ⌂ Malawi 10°58S 33°25E 269 E3
Vyara India 21°8N 73°28E 244 D1
Vyartsilya Russia 62°8N 30°45E 188 A6
Vyatka = Kirov Russia 58°35N 49°40E 186 C8
Vyatka ➜ Russia 55°37N 51°28E 190 C10
Vyatskiye Polyany Russia 56°14N 51°5E 190 B10
Vyazemskiy Russia 47°32N 134°45E 215 E14
Vyazma Russia 55°10N 34°15E 188 E8
Vyazniki Russia 56°10N 42°10E 190 B6
Vyborg Russia 60°43N 28°47E 188 B5
Vyborgskaya Storona Russia 59°57N 30°22E 137 B2
Vychegda ➜ Russia 61°18N 46°36E 186 B8
Vychodné Beskydy Europe 49°20N 22°0E 181 B15
Vyerkhnyadzvinsk Belarus 55°45N 27°58E 188 E4
Vyg-ozero Russia 63°47N 34°29E 186 B5
Vyhoda Ukraine 48°56N 23°55E 183 B8
Vykhino Russia 55°42N 37°48E 129 B4
Vyksa Russia 55°19N 42°11E 190 C6
Vylkove Ukraine 45°28N 29°32E 183 E14
Vylok Ukraine 48°6N 22°50E 182 B7
Vynohradiv Ukraine 48°9N 23°2E 182 B8
Vypin India 10°10N 76°15E 245 J3
Vyrnwy, L. U.K. 52°48N 3°31W 168 E4
Vyšehrad Czech Rep. 50°3N 14°25E 135 B2
Vyshkiv Ukraine 48°44N 23°39E 183 B8
Vyshkove Ukraine 48°3N 23°25E 183 B8
Vyshniy Volochek Russia 57°30N 34°30E 188 D8
Vyshzha = imeni 26 Bakinskikh Komissarov Turkmenistan 39°22N 54°10E 247 B7
Vyškov Czech Rep. 49°17N 17°0E 181 B9
Vyskoye Belarus 52°22N 23°22E 185 F10
Vysoké Mýto Czech Rep. 49°58N 16°10E 181 B9
Vysokovsk Russia 56°22N 36°30E 188 D9
Vyšší Brod Czech Rep. 48°37N 14°19E 180 C7
Vytegra Russia 61°0N 36°27E 188 B9
Vyzhnytsya Ukraine 48°15N 25°11E 183 B10
Vyzhnytsya ⌂ Ukraine 48°7N 25°15E 183 B10

W

W du Benin △ Benin 11°57N 2°43E 263 C5
W du Burkina Faso △ Burkina Faso 11°52N 2°50E 263 C5
W du Niger △ Niger 13°31N 2°28E 263 C5
W.A.C. Bennett Dam Canada 56°2N 122°6W 296 B4
Wa Ghana 10°7N 2°25W 262 C4
Waag Amsterdam, Neths. 112 b3
Waal ➜ Neths. 51°37N 5°0E 170 C5
Waalwijk Neths. 51°42N 5°4E 170 C5
Waanyi-Garawa ◎ Australia 18°2S 137°33E 280 B2
Waat Sudan 8°10N 32°7E 257 F3
Wabag Papua N. G. 5°32S 143°40E 286 C2
Wabakimi △ Canada 50°43N 89°29W 298 B2
Wabana Canada 47°40N 53°0W 299 C9
Wabasca ➜ Canada 58°22N 115°20W 296 B5
Wabasca-Desmarais Canada 55°57N 113°56W 296 B6
Wabash U.S.A. 40°48N 85°49W 311 D11
Wabash ➜ U.S.A. 37°48N 88°2W 311 G8
Wabasso U.S.A. 27°45N 80°26W 317 H9
Wabawng Burma 26°20N 97°25E 241 B6
Wabi ➜ Ethiopia 7°45N 40°50E 257 F5
Wabigoon L. Canada 49°44N 92°44W 297 D10
Wabowden Canada 54°55N 98°38W 297 C9
Wąbrzeźno Poland 53°16N 18°57E 185 E5
Wabu Hu China 32°20N 116°50E 229 A11
Wabuda I. Papua N. G. 8°23S 143°37E 286 E2
Wabuk Pt. Canada 55°20N 85°5W 298 A2
Wabush Canada 52°55N 66°52W 299 B6
Waccasassa B. U.S.A. 29°10N 82°50W 317 F7
Wąchock Poland 51°4N 21°1E 185 G8
Wachterhof Germany 48°2N 11°42E 131 B3
Wächtersbach Germany 50°14N 9°17E 179 E5
Wacissa U.S.A. 30°22N 83°59W 316 E6
Waco U.S.A. 31°33N 97°9W 314 F6
Waconichi, L. Canada 50°8N 74°0W 298 B5
Wad Ban Naqa Sudan 16°32N 33°9E 257 D3
Wad Banda Sudan 13°10N 27°56E 257 E2
Wad el Haddad Sudan 13°50N 33°30E 257 E3
Wad en Nau Sudan 14°10N 33°34E 257 E3
Wad Hamid Sudan 16°30N 32°45E 257 D3
Wad Medanî Sudan 14°28N 33°30E 257 E3
Wad Thana Pakistan 27°22N 66°23E 242 F2
Wadai Africa 12°0N 19°0E 254 E5
Wadala India 19°1N 72°51E 130 A2
Wadayama Japan 35°19N 134°52E 222 B6
Wadbilliga △ Australia 36°25S 149°35E 283 D8
Waddān Libya 29°9N 16°10E 258 C3
Waddeneilanden Neths. 53°25N 5°10E 170 A5
Waddenzee Neths. 53°6N 5°10E 170 A5
Waddi, Chappal Nigeria 7°2N 11°43E 263 D7
Waddington U.S.A. 44°52N 75°12W 313 B9
Waddington, Mt. Canada 51°23N 125°15W 296 C3
Waddy Pt. Australia 24°58S 153°21E 281 C5
Wadebridge U.K. 50°31N 4°51W 169 G3
Wadena Sask., Canada 51°57N 103°47W 297 C8
Wadena Minn., U.S.A. 46°26N 95°8W 308 B6
Wädenswil Switz. 47°14N 8°40E 179 H4
Wadern Germany 49°32N 6°53E 179 F2
Wadestown N.Z. 41°16S 174°46E 143 B1
Wadeye Australia 14°28S 129°52E 278 B4
Wadgaon India 18°44N 73°39E 244 E1
Wadhams Canada 51°30N 127°30W 296 C3
Wadhwan = Surendranagar India 22°45N 71°40E 242 H4
Wadhwan India 22°42N 71°41E 242 H4
Wadi India 17°4N 76°59E 244 F3
Wadi al-Arayis West Bank 31°43N 35°15E 123 B2
Wādī Al Ḩayāt □ Libya 26°26N 12°30E 258 C2
Wādī as Sīr Jordan 31°56N 35°49E 251 G6
Wādī Ash Shāţi □ Libya 27°27N 13°37E 258 C2
Wâdi Feirân Egypt 28°42N 33°19E 251 K4
Wadi Fira □ Chad 15°0N 21°0E 259 F4
Wadi Fukin West Bank 31°42N 35°6E 123 B1
Wâdi Gemâl, J. Egypt 24°35N 35°10E 256 C4
Wadi Halfa Sudan 21°53N 31°19E 256 C3
Wādī Mūsá Jordan 30°19N 35°29E 251 H6
Wadi Rum △ Jordan 29°30N 35°20E 251 J6
Wadian China 32°42N 112°29E 229 A9
Wadlew Poland 51°31N 19°23E 185 G6
Wadley Ala., U.S.A. 33°7N 85°34W 316 B4
Wadley Ga., U.S.A. 32°52N 82°24W 316 C7
Wadowice Poland 49°52N 19°30E 185 J6
Wadsworth Nev., U.S.A. 39°38N 119°17W 304 G4
Wadsworth Ohio, U.S.A. 41°2N 81°44W 312 E3
Waduk Pluit Indonesia 6°5S 106°46E 122 A1
Waegwan S. Korea 35°59N 128°23E 224 E4
Wafangdian China 39°38N 121°58E 227 E11
Wafania Dem. Rep. of the Congo 1°23S 20°22E 264 C4
Wafrah Kuwait 28°33N 47°56E 246 D5
Wagadugu = Ouagadougou Burkina Faso 12°25N 1°30W 263 C4
Wagait ◎ Australia 13°1S 130°5E 278 B5
Wagener U.S.A. 33°39N 81°22W 316 B8
Wageningen Neths. 51°58N 5°40E 170 C5
Wageningen Suriname 5°50N 56°50W 329 B6
Wager B. Canada 65°26N 88°40W 295 D14
Wagga Wagga Australia 35°7S 147°24E 283 C7
Waggaman U.S.A. 29°55N 90°12W 131 B1
Waghai India 20°46N 73°29E 244 D1
Waghete Indonesia 4°10S 135°50E 231 E9
Wagin Australia 33°17S 117°25E 279 F2
Wagner U.S.A. 43°5N 98°18W 308 D4
Wagon Mound U.S.A. 36°1N 104°42W 305 H11
Wagoner U.S.A. 35°58N 95°22W 314 D7
Wągrowiec Poland 52°48N 17°11E 185 F4
Wah Pakistan 33°45N 72°40E 242 C5
Wah Fu China 22°15N 114°8E 122 B1
Wahai Indonesia 2°48S 129°35E 231 E7
Waharoa N.Z. 37°46S 175°45E 284 D4
Waḥda Iraq 33°18N 44°26E 113 B2
Wahiawā U.S.A. 21°30N 158°2W 302 K13
Wahiawā District U.S.A. 21°31N 157°58W 302 J14
Wahiawā Res. U.S.A. 21°30N 158°3W 302 K13
Wāḥid Egypt 30°48N 32°21E 251 H3
Wahnai Afghan. 32°40N 65°50E 242 C1
Wahni Ethiopia 12°40N 36°39E 257 E4
Wahoo U.S.A. 41°13N 96°37W 308 E5
Wahpeton U.S.A. 46°16N 96°36W 308 B5
Währing Austria 48°14N 16°20E 142 A2
Wahx, Ras il- Malta 35°56N 14°20E 206 F7
Wai India 17°56N 73°57E 244 F1
Wai'ale'ale U.S.A. 22°4N 159°30W 302 A2
Waialee U.S.A. 21°41N 158°1W 302 J13
Waialua U.S.A. 21°34N 158°8W 302 J13
Waialua B. U.S.A. 21°35N 158°5W 302 J13
Waialua District U.S.A. 21°35N 158°5W 302 J13
Wai'anae U.S.A. 21°27N 158°11W 302 K13
Wai'anae Coast U.S.A. 21°26N 158°11W 302 K13
Wai'anae District U.S.A. 21°28N 158°10W 302 K13
Wai'anae Range U.S.A. 21°30N 158°10W 302 K13
Waiao Taiwan 24°54N 121°51E 225 B3
Waiapu ➜ N.Z. 37°47S 178°29E 284 D7
Waiau N.Z. 42°39S 173°5E 285 C8
Waiau ➜ Canterbury, N.Z. 42°47S 173°22E 285 C8
Waiau ➜ Southland, N.Z. 46°12S 167°38E 285 G2
Waiawa ➜ U.S.A. 21°23N 157°59W 302 K14
Waiawe Ganga ➜ Sri Lanka 6°15N 81°0E 245 L5
Waibeem Indonesia 0°30S 132°59E 231 E8
Waiblingen Germany 48°49N 9°18E 179 G5
Waidhofen an der Thaya Austria 48°49N 15°17E 180 C8
Waidhofen an der Ybbs Austria 47°57N 14°46E 180 D7
Waidmannslust Germany 52°36N 13°20E 115 A3
Waigeo Indonesia 0°20S 130°40E 231 E8
Waihao ➜ N.Z. 44°47S 171°10E 285 E6
Waihao Downs N.Z. 44°48S 170°55E 285 E5
Waiheke I. N.Z. 36°48S 175°6E 284 C4
Waihi N.Z. 37°23S 175°52E 284 D4
Waihi Beach N.Z. 37°25S 175°57E 284 D4
Waihola N.Z. 46°1S 170°8E 285 G5
Waihola L. N.Z. 45°59S 170°8E 285 F5
Waihou ➜ N.Z. 37°15S 175°40E 284 D4
Waika Dem. Rep. of the Congo 2°22S 25°42E 264 C5
Waikabubak Indonesia 9°45S 119°25E 231 F5
Waikaia N.Z. 45°44S 168°51E 285 F3
Waikaka N.Z. 45°55S 169°1E 285 F4
Waikane U.S.A. 21°30N 157°51W 302 J14
Waikare, L. N.Z. 37°26S 175°13E 284 D4
Waikareiti, L. N.Z. 38°43S 177°10E 284 E6
Waikaremoana N.Z. 38°42S 177°12E 284 E6
Waikaremoana, L. N.Z. 38°49S 177°9E 284 E6
Waikari N.Z. 42°58S 172°41E 285 C7
Waikato ➜ N.Z. 37°23S 174°43E 284 D3
Waikelo Indonesia 9°24S 119°19E 278 A2
Waikerie Australia 34°9S 140°0E 282 C4
Waikiekie N.Z. 35°57S 174°16E 284 B3
Waikīkī U.S.A. 21°17N 157°50W 302 K14
Waikokopu N.Z. 39°3S 177°52E 284 F6
Waikoloa Village U.S.A. 19°55N 155°49W 302 D6
Waikouaiti N.Z. 45°36S 170°41E 285 F5
Waikouaiti Downs N.Z. 45°30S 170°30E 285 F5
Wailea-Makena U.S.A. 20°40N 156°27W 302 C5
Wailing Wall = Western Wall Jerusalem 123 b3
Wailua U.S.A. 22°3N 159°20W 302 A2
Wailuku U.S.A. 20°53N 156°30W 302 C5
Waimakariri ➜ N.Z. 43°24S 172°42E 285 D7
Waimalu U.S.A. 21°24N 157°57W 302 K14
Waimānalo U.S.A. 21°21N 157°43W 302 K14
Waimānalo B. U.S.A. 21°20N 157°40W 302 K14
Waimānalo Beach U.S.A. 21°21N 157°42W 302 K14
Waimangaroa N.Z. 41°43S 171°46E 285 B6
Waimano ➜ U.S.A. 21°25N 157°58W 302 K14
Waimarie N.Z. 41°35S 171°58E 285 B6
Waimate N.Z. 44°45S 171°3E 285 E6
Waimea Hawai'i, U.S.A. 21°58N 159°40W 302 B2
Waimea Hawai'i, U.S.A. 21°39N 158°3W 302 J13
Waimea B. U.S.A. 21°40N 158°5W 302 J13
Waimea Plain N.Z. 45°55S 168°35E 285 F3
Waingaenga ➜ India 18°50N 79°55E 244 E4
Waingapu Indonesia 9°35S 120°11E 231 F6
Waingmaw Burma 25°21N 97°26E 241 B6
Waini ➜ Guyana 8°20N 59°50W 329 B6
Wainuiomata N.Z. 41°17S 174°56E 143 B2
Wainuiomata ➜ N.Z. 41°20S 174°55E 143 B2
Wainwright Alta., Canada 52°50N 110°50W 297 C6
Wainwright Alaska, U.S.A. 70°38N 160°2W 303 A7
Waiotapu N.Z. 38°21S 176°25E 284 E5
Waiouru N.Z. 39°28S 175°41E 284 F4
Waipa ➜ N.Z. 38°16S 175°21E 284 E4
Waipahi N.Z. 46°6S 169°15E 285 G4
Waipahu U.S.A. 21°23N 158°1W 302 K13
Waipapa Pt. N.Z. 46°40S 168°51E 285 G3
Waipara N.Z. 43°3S 172°46E 285 D7
Waipawa N.Z. 39°56S 176°38E 284 F5
Waipi'o U.S.A. 21°25N 158°0W 302 K14
Waipi'o Acres U.S.A. 21°28N 158°1W 302 K13
Waipi'o Peninsula U.S.A. 21°20N 158°0W 302 K14
Waipiro N.Z. 38°2S 178°22E 284 E7
Waipiro Bay N.Z. 38°1S 178°21E 284 E7
Waipoua Forest N.Z. 35°39S 173°33E 284 B2
Waipu N.Z. 35°59S 174°29E 284 B3
Waipukurau N.Z. 40°1S 176°33E 284 G5
Wairakei N.Z. 38°37S 176°6E 284 E5
Wairarapa, L. N.Z. 41°14S 175°15E 284 H4
Wairau ➜ N.Z. 41°32S 174°7E 285 B9
Wairio N.Z. 45°59S 168°3E 285 F3
Wairoa N.Z. 39°3S 177°25E 284 F6
Wairoa ➜ Hawke's Bay, N.Z. 39°4S 177°25E 284 F6
Wairoa ➜ Northland, N.Z. 36°5S 173°59E 284 C2
Waisantiang Taiwan 23°20N 120°1E 225 C2
Waisisi Vanuatu 19°32S 169°22E 287 J7
Waitaki ➜ N.Z. 44°56S 171°7E 285 E6
Waitaki Plains N.Z. 44°22S 170°0E 285 E5
Waitangi N.Z. 35°16S 174°5E 284 B3
Waitara N.Z. 38°59S 174°15E 284 E3
Waitara ➜ N.Z. 38°59S 174°14E 284 E3
Waitiki Landing N.Z. 34°31S 172°50E 284 A1
Waitoa N.Z. 37°37S 175°35E 284 D4
Waitomo Caves N.Z. 38°16S 175°7E 284 E4
Waitotara N.Z. 39°49S 174°44E 284 F3
Waitotara ➜ N.Z. 39°51S 174°41E 284 F3
Waitsburg U.S.A. 46°16N 118°9W 304 C4
Waitzen = Vác Hungary 47°49N 19°10E 182 C4
Waiuku N.Z. 37°15S 174°45E 284 D3
Wajima Japan 37°30N 137°0E 221 F8
Wajir Kenya 1°42N 40°5E 268 B5
Waka Dem. Rep. of the Congo 1°1N 20°13E 264 B4
Waka Ethiopia 7°2N 37°20E 257 F4
Waka-Kungo Angola 11°21S 15°7E 265 E3
Wakarusa U.S.A. 41°32N 86°1W 311 C10
Wakasa Japan 35°20N 134°24E 222 B6
Wakasa-Wan Japan 35°40N 135°30E 223 B7
Wakatipu, L. N.Z. 45°5S 168°33E 285 F3
Wakaw Canada 52°39N 105°44W 297 C7
Wakaya Fiji 17°37S 179°0E 287 A2
Wakayama Japan 34°15N 135°15E 223 C7
Wakayama □ Japan 33°50N 135°30E 223 D7
Wake Japan 34°48N 134°8E 222 C6
Wake Forest U.S.A. 35°59N 78°30W 315 D15
Wake I. Pac. Oc. 19°18N 166°36E 302 b
WaKeeney U.S.A. 39°1N 99°53W 308 F4
Wakefield Jamaica 18°26N 77°42W 320 a
Wakefield N.Z. 41°24S 173°5E 285 B8
Wakefield W. Yorks., U.K. 53°41N 1°29W 168 D6
Wakefield Mass., U.S.A. 42°30N 71°5W 116 A2
Wakefield Mich., U.S.A. 46°29N 89°56W 308 B9
Wakema Burma 16°30N 95°11E 241 G5
Wākhān Afghan. 37°8N 73°4E 240 A4
Waki Japan 34°4N 134°9E 222 C6
Wakkanai Japan 45°28N 141°35E 220 B10
Wakkerstroom S. Africa 27°24S 30°10E 271 C5
Wakool Australia 35°28S 144°23E 282 C6
Wakool ➜ Australia 35°5S 143°33E 282 C5
Wakre Indonesia 0°19S 131°5E 231 E8
Waku Papua N. G. 6°5S 149°9E 286 D5
Wakuach, L. Canada 55°34N 67°32W 299 A6
Wakulla U.S.A. 30°14N 84°14W 316 E5
Wakunai Papua N. G. 5°52S 155°13E 286 C8
Walagunya ◎ Australia 23°10S 120°50E 278 D3
Walamba Zambia 13°30S 28°42E 269 E2
Wałbrzych Poland 50°45N 16°18E 185 H3
Walbury Hill U.K. 51°21N 1°28W 169 F6
Walcha Australia 30°55S 151°31E 283 A9
Walcheren Neths. 51°30N 3°35E 170 C3
Walcott U.S.A. 41°46N 106°51W 304 F10
Wałcz Poland 53°17N 16°27E 185 E3
Waldbröl Germany 50°52N 7°37E 178 E3
Waldburg Ra. Australia 24°40S 117°35E 279 D2
Waldeck Germany 51°12N 9°4E 178 D5
Walden Colo., U.S.A. 40°44N 106°17W 304 F10
Walden N.Y., U.S.A. 41°34N 74°11W 313 E10
Waldenberg = Wałbrzych Poland 50°45N 16°18E 185 H3
Waldesruh Germany 52°28N 13°37E 115 B4
Waldkirch Germany 48°5N 7°58E 179 G3
Waldkirchen Germany 48°43N 13°36E 179 G9
Waldkraiburg Germany 48°11N 12°24E 179 G8
Waldo U.S.A. 29°48N 82°10W 316 F7
Waldperlach Germany 48°4N 11°40E 131 B3
Waldport U.S.A. 44°26N 124°4W 304 D1
Waldron U.S.A. 34°54N 94°5W 314 D7
Waldtrudering Germany 48°6N 11°42E 131 B3
Waldviertel Austria 48°30N 15°30E 180 C8
Walebing Australia 30°41S 116°13E 279 F2
Walemale Ghana 10°30N 1°58W 262 C4
Walensee Switz. 47°7N 9°13E 179 H5
Wales U.S.A. 65°37N 168°5W 303 D5
Wales □ U.K. 52°19N 4°43W 169 E3
Wales I. Canada 68°1N 86°40W 295 D14
Walewale Ghana 10°21N 0°50W 263 C4
Walgett Australia 30°0S 148°5E 281 E4
Walgreen Coast Antarctica 75°15S 105°0W 151 D15
Walhalla Australia 37°56S 146°29E 283 D7
Walis I. Papua N. G. 3°14S 143°18E 286 B2
Walker Mich., U.S.A. 42°58N 85°46W 311 B11
Walker Minn., U.S.A. 47°6N 94°35W 308 B6
Walker, L. Canada 50°20N 67°11W 299 B6
Walker L. Man., Canada 54°42N 95°57W 297 C9
Walker L. Nev., U.S.A. 38°42N 118°43W 304 G4
Walkerston Australia 21°11S 149°8E 280 b
Walkerton Ont., Canada 44°10N 81°10W 312 B3
Walkerton Ind., U.S.A. 41°28N 86°29W 311 C10
Walkinstown Ireland 53°19N 6°20W 120 B1
Wall U.S.A. 44°0N 102°8W 308 C2
Wall Street New York, U.S.A. 132 f1
Walla Walla N.S.W., Australia 35°45S 146°54E 283 C7
Walla Walla Wash., U.S.A. 46°4N 118°20W 304 C4
Wallabout Bay New York, U.S.A. 132 f2
Wallace Idaho, U.S.A. 47°28N 115°56W 304 C6
Wallace N.C., U.S.A. 34°44N 77°59W 315 D16
Wallaceburg Canada 42°34N 82°23W 312 D2
Wallacetown N.Z. 46°21S 168°19E 285 G3
Wallachia = Valahia Romania 44°35N 25°0E 183 F9
Wallal Australia 26°32S 146°7E 281 D4
Wallam Cr. ➜ Australia 28°40S 147°20E 281 D4
Wallambin, L. Australia 30°57S 117°35E 279 F2
Wallan Australia 37°26S 144°59E 283 D6
Wallangarra Australia 28°56S 151°58E 281 D5
Wallaroo Australia 33°56S 137°39E 282 B2
Walldürn Germany 49°34N 9°22E 179 F5
Wallenhorst Germany 52°21N 8°1E 178 C4
Wallenpaupack, L. U.S.A. 41°25N 75°15W 313 E9
Wallerawang Australia 33°25S 150°4E 283 B9
Wallingat △ Australia 32°14S 152°25E 283 B10
Wallingford Conn., U.S.A. 41°27N 72°50W 313 E12
Wallingford Vt., U.S.A. 43°28N 72°58W 313 C12
Wallis & Futuna, Is. ☑ Pac. Oc. 13°18S 176°10W 277 C15
Wallowa U.S.A. 45°34N 117°32W 304 D5
Wallowa Mts. U.S.A. 45°20N 117°30W 304 D5
Walls U.K. 60°14N 1°33W 167 A7
Walls of Jerusalem △ Australia 41°56S 146°15E 281 G4
Wallsend Australia 32°55S 151°40E 283 B9
Wallula U.S.A. 46°5N 118°54W 304 C4
Wallumbilla Australia 26°33S 149°9E 281 D4
Walmsley L. Canada 63°25N 108°36W 297 A7
Walney, I. of U.K. 54°6N 3°15W 168 C4
Walnut U.S.A. 41°33N 89°36W 310 C7
Walnut Canyon ⌂ U.S.A. 35°15N 111°20W 305 J8
Walnut Creek U.S.A. 37°54N 122°4W 306 H4
Walnut Grove U.S.A. 34°4N 86°18W 316 A3
Walnut Hill U.S.A. 30°53N 87°30W 317 E2
Walnut Ridge U.S.A. 36°4N 90°57W 315 C9
Walpeup Australia 35°7S 142°2E 282 C5
Walpole W. Austral., Australia 34°58S 116°44E 279 F2
Walpole Mass., U.S.A. 42°9N 71°15W 313 D13
Walpole-Nornalup △ Australia 35°0S 116°45E 279 G2
Wals Austria 47°47N 12°58E 180 D5
Walsall U.K. 52°35N 1°58W 169 E6
Walsenburg U.S.A. 37°38N 104°47W 305 H11
Walsh U.S.A. 37°23N 102°17W 305 H12
Walsh ➜ Australia 16°31S 143°42E 280 B3
Walsingham Canada 42°40N 80°31W 312 D4
Walsrode Germany 52°51N 9°35E 178 C5
Walt Disney Concert Hall Los Angeles, U.S.A. 127 b1
Walt Disney World U.S.A. 28°22N 81°33W 133 B1
Waltair India 17°44N 83°23E 244 F6
Walter D. Stone Memorial Zoo U.S.A. 42°28N 71°6W 116 A2
Walter F. George Res. U.S.A. 31°38N 85°4W 316 D4
Walterboro U.S.A. 32°55N 80°40W 316 C9
Walters U.S.A. 34°22N 98°19W 314 D5
Waltershausen Germany 50°54N 10°33E 178 E6
Waltershausen Gletscher Greenland 73°54N 24°25W 154 C8
Waltham U.S.A. 42°23N 71°14W 116 A1
Waltham Forest □ U.K. 51°35N 0°0 125 A3
Walthamstow U.K. 51°34N 0°1W 125 A3
Waltman U.S.A. 43°4N 107°12W 304 E10
Walton Ky., U.S.A. 38°52N 84°37W 311 F12
Walton N.Y., U.S.A. 42°10N 75°8W 313 D9
Walton-on-Thames U.K. 51°23N 0°24W 125 B1
Walton-on-the-Naze U.K. 51°51N 1°17E 169 F9
Waltonville U.S.A. 38°13N 89°2W 310 F7
Walu Burma 26°28N 98°2E 241 B7
Walvis Bay Namibia 23°0S 14°28E 270 B1
Walvis Ridge Atl. Oc. 26°0S 5°0E 152 J12
Walvisbaai = Walvis Bay Namibia 23°0S 14°28E 270 B1
Walwa Australia 35°59S 147°44E 283 C7
Wamba Équateur, Dem. Rep. of the Congo 1°37S 22°30E 264 C4
Wamba Orientale, Dem. Rep. of the Congo 2°10N 27°57E 268 B2
Wamba Rift Valley, Kenya 0°58N 37°19E 268 B4
Wamba Nigeria 8°57N 8°42E 263 D6
Wamba ➜ Dem. Rep. of the Congo 3°56S 17°12E 265 C3
Wambardi ◎ Australia 16°2S 130°55E 278 C5
Wambeek Belgium 50°55N 4°30E 116 A3
Wamego U.S.A. 39°12N 96°18W 308 F5
Wamena Indonesia 4°4S 138°57E 231 E9
Wampana Karlantijpa ◎ Australia 17°45S 132°10E 278 C5
Wampaya ◎ Australia 17°20S 135°0E 280 B2
Wampsville U.S.A. 43°4N 75°42W 313 C9
Wamsutter U.S.A. 41°40N 107°58W 304 F10
Wamulan Indonesia 3°27S 126°7E 231 E7
Wan Chai China 22°16N 114°10E 122 B2
Wan Chai Lanes Hong Kong, China 122 c2
Wan Hat Burma 20°14N 97°53E 241 E6
Wan Kinghao Burma 21°34N 98°17E 241 E7
Wan Lai-kam Burma 21°21N 98°22E 241 E7
Wan Tup Burma 21°13N 98°42E 228 G2
Wan Xian China 38°47N 115°7E 226 E8
Wana Pakistan 32°20N 69°32E 242 C3
Wanaaring Australia 29°38S 144°9E 281 D3
Wanaka N.Z. 44°42S 169°9E 285 E4
Wanaka, L. N.Z. 44°33S 169°7E 285 E4
Wan'an China 26°26N 114°49E 229 D10
Wanani Comoros Is. 12°20S 43°47E 272 a
Wanapa Bonaire 12°7N 68°14W 322 h
Wanapitei L. Canada 46°45N 80°40W 298 C3
Wanbi Australia 34°46S 140°17E 282 C4
Wandaik Guyana 4°27N 59°35W 329 C6
Wandel Sea = McKinley Sea Arctic 82°0N 0°0 154 A11
Wandérama Ivory C. 8°37N 4°25W 262 D4
Wandhari Pakistan 27°42N 66°48E 242 F2
Wanding China 24°5N 98°4E 228 E2
Wandle ➜ U.K. 51°27N 0°12W 125 B2
Wando S. Korea 34°21N 126°41E 224 G3
Wandoan Australia 26°5S 149°55E 281 D4
Wandsworth □ U.K. 51°27N 0°11W 125 B2
Wandur Marine △ India 11°30N 92°30E 245 J11
Wanfu China 40°8N 122°38E 224 B1
Wang ➜ Thailand 17°8N 99°2E 236 D2
Wang Center, The Boston, U.S.A. 116 c2
Wang Kai Sudan 9°3N 29°23E 257 F2
Wang Noi Thailand 14°13N 100°44E 236 E3
Wang Saphung Thailand 17°18N 101°46E 236 D3
Wang Thong Thailand 16°50N 100°26E 236 D3
Wanga Dem. Rep. of the Congo 2°58N 29°12E 268 B2
Wangal Indonesia 6°8S 134°9E 231 F8
Wangan Taiwan 23°21N 119°29E 225 C1
Wanganella Australia 35°6S 144°49E 283 C6
Wanganui N.Z. 39°56S 175°3E 284 F4
Wanganui ➜ W. Coast, N.Z. 43°3S 170°26E 285 D5
Wanganui ➜ Wanganui-Manawatu, N.Z. 39°55S 175°4E 284 F4
Wangaratta Australia 36°21S 146°19E 283 D7
Wangary Australia 34°35S 135°29E 281 E2
Wangcang China 32°18N 106°20E 228 A6
Wangcheng China 28°22N 112°49E 229 C9
Wangcun China 36°41N 117°41E 227 F9
Wangdu China 38°40N 115°7E 226 E8
Wangdu Phodrang Bhutan 27°28N 89°54E 241 B2
Wangen Germany 47°41N 9°50E 179 H5
Wangerin = Węgorzyno Poland 53°32N 15°33E 184 E2
Wangerooge Germany 53°47N 7°54E 178 B3
Wangiwangi Indonesia 5°22S 123°37E 231 F6
Wangjiang China 30°10N 116°42E 229 B11
Wangjing China 40°0N 116°28E 114 B2
Wangkung Taiwan 23°57N 120°20E 225 C2
Wangmo China 25°11N 106°5E 228 E6
Wangolodougou Ivory C. 9°55N 5°10W 262 D3
Wangqing China 43°12N 129°42E 227 C15
Wani India 20°5N 78°55E 244 D4
Wanigela Papua N. G. 9°21S 149°9E 286 E5
Wanimiyn ◎ Australia 15°55S 130°49E 278 C5
Wanjina Wunggurr Wilinggin ◎ Australia 16°0S 127°0E 278 C4
Wanjung Taiwan 23°43N 121°25E 225 C3
Wankaner India 22°35N 71°0E 242 H4
Wankhede Stadium Mumbai, India 130 c2
Wanless Canada 54°11N 101°21W 297 C8
Wanleweyne Somali Rep. 2°37N 44°54E 267 D5
Wanli Taiwan 25°10N 121°41E 225 A3
Wanluan Taiwan 22°34N 120°34E 225 D2
Wanneroo Australia 31°42S 115°46E 279 F2
Wannian China 28°42N 117°4E 229 C11
Wanning China 18°48N 110°22E 236 C8
Wannoo Billabong Roadhouse Australia 27°25S 115°49E 279 E2
Wannsee Germany 52°25N 13°9E 115 B1
Wanon Niwat Thailand 17°38N 103°46E 236 D4
Wanqinsha China 22°43N 113°33E 219 a
Wanquan China 40°50N 114°40E 226 D8
Wanrong China 35°25N 110°50E 226 G6
Wansdorf Germany 52°38N 13°5E 115 A1
Wansen = Wiązów Poland 50°50N 17°10E 185 H4
Wanshan China 27°30N 109°12E 228 D7
Wanshan Qundao China 21°57N 113°45E 219 a
Wansheng China 28°57N 106°53E 228 C6
Wanstead N.Z. 40°8S 176°30E 284 G5
Wanstead London, U.K. 51°34N 0°1E 125 A1

Wantage *U.K.* 51°35N 1°25W **169** F6
Wantan *Taiwan* 22°35N 120°29E **225** D2
Wantouliu *Taiwan* 24°1N 120°41E **225** B2
Wanxian *China* 30°42N 108°20E **228** B7
Wanyin *Burma* 20°23N 97°15E **241** E6
Wanyuan *China* 32°4N 108°3E **228** A7
Wanzai *Guangdong, China* 22°12N 113°31E **219** a
Wanzai *Jiangxi, China* 28°7N 114°30E **229** C10
Wapakoneta *U.S.A.* 40°34N 84°12W **311** D12
Wapato *U.S.A.* 46°27N 120°25W **304** C3
Wapawekka L. *Canada* 54°55N 104°40W **297** C8
Wapello *U.S.A.* 41°11N 91°11W **310** C5
Wapikopa L. *Canada* 52°56N 87°53W **298** B2
Wapinda
Dem. Rep. of the Congo 3°41N 22°48E **264** B4
Wapiti ➔ *Canada* 55°5N 118°18W **296** B5
Wapping *U.K.* 51°30N 0°3W **125** A3
Wappingers Falls *U.S.A.* 41°36N 73°55W **313** E11
Wapsipinicon ➔ *U.S.A.* 41°44N 90°19W **310** C6
Wapusk △ *Canada* 57°46N 93°22W **297** B10
War Galoh *Somali Rep.* 6°17N 47°31E **267** C6
War in the Pacific Nat. Hist. Park △
Guam 13°24N 144°39E **302** d
Warab *Sudan* 8°8N 28°37E **257** F2
Warab □ *Sudan* 7°30N 28°30E **257** F2
Warabi *Japan* 35°49N 139°41E **223** B11
Warakurna *Australia* 24°59S 128°17E **279** D4
Warangal *India* 17°58N 79°35E **244** F4
Waraseoni *India* 21°45N 80°2E **243** J9
Waratah *Australia* 41°30S 145°30E **281** G4
Waratah B. *Australia* 38°54S 146°5E **283** E7
Warburg *Germany* 51°28N 9°11E **178** D5
Warburton *Vic., Australia* 37°47S 145°42E **283** D6
Warburton *W. Austral.,*
Australia 26°8S 126°35E **279** E4
Warburton ✪ *Australia* 26°7S 126°34E **279** E4
Warburton ➔ *Australia* 28°4S 137°28E **281** D2
Warburton Groove
Australia 28°18S 137°8E **281** A2
Warburton Ra. *Australia* 25°55S 126°28E **279** E4
Ward *N.Z.* 41°49S 174°11E **285** B9
Ward ➔ *Australia* 26°28S 146°6E **281** D4
Ward Hunt, C. *Papua N. G.* 8°2S 148°10E **286** E5
Ward Hunt Str. *Papua N. G.* 9°30S 150°0E **286** E6
Ward I. *N.Z.* 41°18S 174°54E **143** B2
Ward Mt. *U.S.A.* 37°12N 118°54W **306** H8
Wardang I. *Australia* 34°30S 137°20E **282** C2
Warden *S. Africa* 27°50S 29°0E **271** D4
Wardha *India* 20°45N 78°39E **244** D4
Wardha ➔ *India* 19°57N 79°11E **244** E4
Wardija Point *Malta* 36°2N 14°11E **206** E6
Wards I. *U.S.A.* 40°47N 73°55W **132** B2
Wardsville *Canada* 42°39N 81°45W **312** D3
Ware *Herts., U.K.* 51°49N 0°0 **169** F8
Ware *Mass., U.S.A.* 42°16N 72°14W **313** D12
Waregem *Belgium* 50°53N 3°27E **170** D3
Wareham *U.S.A.* 41°46N 70°43W **313** E14
Waremme *Belgium* 50°43N 5°15E **170** D5
Waren *Germany* 53°31N 12°40E **178** B8
Warendorf *Germany* 51°57N 8°1E **178** D4
Waresboro *U.S.A.* 31°15N 82°29W **316** D7
Waria ➔ *Papua N. G.* 7°49S 147°41E **286** D4
Warialda *Australia* 29°29S 150°33E **281** D5
Wariap *Indonesia* 1°30S 134°5E **231** E8
Warin Chamrap *Thailand* 15°12N 104°53E **236** E5
Warka *Poland* 51°47N 21°12E **185** G8
Warkopi *Indonesia* 1°12S 134°9E **231** E8
Warkworth *N.Z.* 36°24S 174°41E **284** C3
Warm Baths = Bela Bela
S. Africa 24°51S 28°19E **271** B4
Warm Springs *Ga., U.S.A.* 32°53N 84°41W **316** C5
Warm Springs *Nev.,*
U.S.A. 38°10N 116°20W **305** G5
Warman *Canada* 52°19N 106°30W **297** C7
Warmbad = Bela Bela
S. Africa 24°51S 28°19E **271** B4
Warmbad *Namibia* 28°25S 18°42E **270** C2
Warming I. = Uunartoq Qeqertoq
Greenland 71°33N 21°47W **154** C8
Warmińsko-Mazurskie □
Poland 54°0N 21°0E **184** D8
Warminster *Wilts., U.K.* 51°12N 2°10W **169** F5
Warminster *Pa., U.S.A.* 40°12N 75°6W **313** F9
Warmun *Australia* 17°2S 128°12E **278** C4
Warnberg *Germany* 48°4N 11°31E **131** B2
Warnemünde *Germany* 54°10N 12°4E **178** A8
Warner Brothers Studios
U.S.A. 34°9N 118°20W **126** B2
Warner Mts. *U.S.A.* 41°40N 120°15W **304** F3
Warner Robins *U.S.A.* 32°37N 83°36W **316** C6
Warnes *Bolivia* 17°30S 63°10W **331** D5
Warnow ➔ *Germany* 54°6N 12°9E **178** A8
Waroona *Australia* 32°50S 115°58E **279** F2
Warora *India* 20°14N 79°1E **244** D4
Warrabah △ *Australia* 30°31S 150°56E **283** A10
Warrabri ✪ *Australia* 21°1S 134°19E **280** C1
Warracknabeal *Australia* 36°9S 142°26E **282** D5
Warragul *Australia* 38°10S 145°58E **283** E6
Warrâq el 'Arab *Egypt* 30°4N 31°11E **117** A2
Warrego ➔ *Australia* 30°24S 145°21E **281** E4
Warrego Ra. *Australia* 24°58S 146°0E **280** C4
Warren *N.S.W., Australia* 31°42S 147°51E **283** A7
Warren *Ark., U.S.A.* 33°37N 92°4W **314** E8
Warren *Ill., U.S.A.* 42°29N 90°0W **310** B7
Warren *Ind., U.S.A.* 40°41N 85°26W **311** D11
Warren *Mich., U.S.A.* 42°28N 83°1W **311** B13
Warren *Minn., U.S.A.* 48°12N 96°46W **308** A5
Warren *Ohio, U.S.A.* 41°14N 80°49W **312** E4
Warren *Pa., U.S.A.* 41°51N 79°9W **312** E5
Warrenpoint *U.K.* 54°6N 6°15W **166** B5
Warrensburg *Ill., U.S.A.* 39°56N 89°4W **310** E7
Warrensburg *Mo., U.S.A.* 38°46N 93°44W **310** F3
Warrensburg *N.Y.,*
U.S.A. 43°29N 73°46W **313** C11
Warrenton *Northern Cape,*
S. Africa 28°9S 24°47E **270** C3
Warrenton *Ga., U.S.A.* 33°24N 82°40W **316** B7
Warrenton *Mo., U.S.A.* 38°49N 91°9W **310** F5
Warrenton *Oreg., U.S.A.* 46°10N 123°56W **306** D3
Warrenville *U.S.A.* 33°33N 81°48W **316** B8
Warri *Nigeria* 5°30N 5°41E **263** D6
Warringal Park *Australia* 37°45S 145°4E **128** A2
Warrington *N.Z.* 45°43S 170°35E **285** F5
Warrington *Warrington,*
U.K. 53°24N 2°35W **168** D5
Warrington *Fla., U.S.A.* 30°23N 87°17W **317** E2
Warrington □ *U.K.* 53°24N 2°35W **168** D5
Warriston *U.K.* 55°58N 3°11W **121** B2
Warrnambool *Australia* 38°25S 142°30E **282** E5
Warroad *U.S.A.* 48°54N 95°19W **308** A6
Warrumbungle △
Australia 31°18S 149°1E **283** A8
Warruwi *Australia* 11°36S 133°20E **280** A1
Warsa *Indonesia* 0°47S 135°55E **231** E9
Warsak Dam *Pakistan* 34°11N 71°19E **242** B4
Warsaw = Warszawa
Poland 52°14N 21°0E **142** B2
Warsaw *Ill., U.S.A.* 40°22N 91°26W **310** D5
Warsaw *Ind., U.S.A.* 41°14N 85°51W **311** C11
Warsaw *Ky., U.S.A.* 38°47N 84°54W **311** F12
Warsaw *Mo., U.S.A.* 38°15N 93°23W **310** F3
Warsaw *N.Y., U.S.A.* 42°45N 78°8W **312** D6
Warsaw *Ohio, U.S.A.* 40°20N 82°0W **312** F3
Warshiikh *Somali Rep.* 2°28N 45°55E **267** D6
Warstein *Germany* 51°26N 8°22E **178** D4
Warszawa *Poland* 52°14N 21°0E **142** B2
Warszawa ✈ (WAW)
Poland 52°9N 20°59E **142** B1
Warta *Poland* 51°43N 18°38E **185** G5
Warta ➔ *Poland* 52°35N 14°39E **185** F1
Wartenberg *Germany* 52°34N 13°31E **115** A4
Wartenburg = Barczewo
Poland 53°50N 20°42E **184** E7
Warthbrücken = Koło
Poland 52°14N 18°40E **185** F5
Warthe = Warta ➔
Poland 52°35N 14°39E **185** F1
Warthen *U.S.A.* 33°6N 82°48W **316** B7
Warthenau = Zawiercie
Poland 50°30N 19°24E **185** H6
Waru *Indonesia* 3°30S 130°36E **231** E8
Warud *India* 21°30N 78°16E **244** D4
Warumungu ✪ *Australia* 19°15S 134°44E **280** B1
Warwick *Queens.,*
Australia 28°10S 152°1E **281** D5
Warwick *Warks., U.K.* 52°18N 1°35W **169** E6
Warwick *Ga., U.S.A.* 31°50N 83°57W **316** D6
Warwick *N.Y., U.S.A.* 41°16N 74°22W **313** E10
Warwick *R.I., U.S.A.* 41°42N 71°28W **313** E13
Warwickshire □ *U.K.* 52°14N 1°38W **169** E6
Wasaga Beach *Canada* 44°31N 80°1W **312** B4
Wasagaming *Canada* 50°39N 99°58W **297** C9
Wasatch Ra. *U.S.A.* 40°0N 111°30W **304** F8
Wasbank *S. Africa* 28°15S 30°9E **271** C5
Wasco *Calif., U.S.A.* 35°36N 119°20W **307** K7
Wasco *Oreg., U.S.A.* 45°36N 120°42W **304** D3
Wase *Nigeria* 9°4N 9°54E **263** D6
Waseca *U.S.A.* 44°5N 93°30W **308** C7
Wasekamio L. *Canada* 56°45N 108°45W **297** B7
Wasgomuwa △ *Sri Lanka* 7°45N 81°0E **245** L5
Wash, The *U.K.* 52°58N 0°20E **168** E8
Washago *Canada* 44°45N 79°20W **312** B5
Washburn *Ill., U.S.A.* 40°55N 89°17W **310** D7
Washburn *N. Dak., U.S.A.* 47°17N 101°2W **308** B3
Washburn *Wis., U.S.A.* 46°40N 90°54W **308** B8
Washim *India* 20°3N 77°0E **244** D3
Washington *Bonaire* 12°17N 68°23W **322** h
Washington *Tyne & W.,*
U.K. 54°55N 1°30W **168** C6
Washington *D.C., U.S.A.* 38°53N 77°2W **143** B3
Washington *Ga., U.S.A.* 33°44N 82°44W **316** B7
Washington *Ill., U.S.A.* 40°42N 89°24W **310** D7
Washington *Ind., U.S.A.* 38°40N 87°10W **311** F9
Washington *Iowa, U.S.A.* 41°18N 91°42W **310** C5
Washington *Mo., U.S.A.* 38°33N 91°1W **310** F5
Washington *N.C., U.S.A.* 35°33N 77°3W **315** D16
Washington *N.J., U.S.A.* 40°46N 74°59W **313** F10
Washington *Pa., U.S.A.* 40°10N 80°15W **312** F4
Washington *Utah, U.S.A.* 37°8N 113°31W **305** H7
Washington □ *U.S.A.* 47°30N 120°30W **304** C3
Washington, Mt. *U.S.A.* 44°16N 71°18W **313** B13
Washington Court House
U.S.A. 39°32N 83°26W **311** E13
Washington Dulles Int. ✈ (IAD)
U.S.A. 38°57N 77°27W **143** B1
Washington Heights
U.S.A. 40°51N 73°56W **132** A2
Washington I. *U.S.A.* 45°23N 86°54W **308** C10
Washington Land
Greenland 80°30N 66°0W **154** A4
Washington Monument
Washington, D.C., U.S.A. **143** b1
Washington Park *U.S.A.* 41°47N 87°36W **119** C3
Washington Ronald Reagan Nat. ✈
(DCA) *U.S.A.* 38°51N 77°2W **143** B3
Washington Slagbaai △
Bonaire 12°16N 68°23W **322** h
Washougal *U.S.A.* 45°35N 122°21W **306** E4
Washpool △ *Australia* 29°22S 152°20E **281** D5
Washuk *Pakistan* 27°42N 64°45E **240** D2
Wasian *Indonesia* 1°47S 133°19E **231** E8
Wasilków *Poland* 53°12N 23°13E **185** E10
Wasilla *U.S.A.* 61°35N 149°26W **303** F10
Wasini Marine △ *Kenya* 4°33S 39°14E **268** C4
Wasior *Indonesia* 2°43S 134°30E **231** E8
Wāsiṭ □ *Iraq* 32°50N 45°50E **213** F11
Wasjabo *Suriname* 5°13N 57°11W **329** B6
Waskaganish *Canada* 51°30N 78°40W **298** B4
Waskaiowaka L. *Canada* 56°33N 96°23W **297** B9
Waskesiu Lake *Canada* 53°55N 106°5W **297** C7
Wassaw I. *U.S.A.* 31°53N 80°58W **316** D9
Wassaw Sd. *U.S.A.* 31°55N 80°55W **316** D9
Wasserburg *Germany* 48°3N 12°14E **179** G8
Wasserkuppe *Germany* 50°29N 9°55E **178** E5
Wassy *France* 48°30N 4°58E **173** D11
Wasu *Papua N. G.* 5°58S 147°12E **286** C4
Wasua *Papua N. G.* 8°18S 142°52E **286** E2
Waswanipi *Canada* 49°40N 76°29W **298** C4
Waswanipi, L. *Canada* 49°35N 76°40W **298** C4
Wat Pho *Bangkok, Thailand* **113** b1
Watagans △ *Australia* 33°0S 151°28E **283** B9
Watam *Papua N. G.* 3°55S 144°33E **286** B3
Watampone *Indonesia* 4°29S 120°25E **231** E6
Watamu *Kenya* 3°23S 40°0E **268** C5
Watansoppeng *Indonesia* 4°10S 119°56E **235** C5
Watarrka △ *Australia* 24°20S 131°30E **278** D5
Watee *Solomon Is.* 10°30S 162°2E **287** N12
Watenstadt-Salzgitter = Salzgitter
Germany 52°9N 10°19E **178** C6
Water of Leith ➔ *U.K.* 55°59N 3°10W **121** B1
Water Park Pt. *Australia* 22°56S 150°47E **280** C5
Water Tower Place *Chicago, U.S.A.* **119** a2
Water Valley *U.S.A.* 34°10N 89°38W **315** D10
Waterberg Plateau ⌂
Namibia 20°25S 17°18E **270** B2
Waterberge *S. Africa* 24°10S 28°0E **271** B4
Waterbury *Conn., U.S.A.* 41°33N 73°3W **313** E11
Waterbury *Vt., U.S.A.* 44°20N 72°46W **313** B12
Waterbury L. *Canada* 58°10N 104°22W **297** B8
Waterdown *Canada* 43°20N 79°53W **312** C5
Wateree ➔ *U.S.A.* 33°45N 80°37W **316** B9
Waterford *Ont., Canada* 42°56N 80°17W **312** D4
Waterford *Waterford, Ireland* 52°15N 7°8W **166** D4
Waterford *Calif., U.S.A.* 37°38N 120°46W **306** H6
Waterford *Mich., U.S.A.* 42°45N 83°32W **311** B13
Waterford *Pa., U.S.A.* 41°57N 79°59W **312** E5
Waterford *Wis., U.S.A.* 42°46N 88°13W **311** B8
Waterford □ *Ireland* 52°10N 7°40W **166** D4
Waterford Harbour *Ireland* 52°8N 6°58W **166** D5
Watergraafsmeer *Neths.* 52°21N 4°56E **112** A2
Waterhen L. *Canada* 52°10N 99°40W **297** C9
Waterland *Neths.* 52°26N 4°58E **112** A2
Waterloo *Belgium* 50°43N 4°25E **116** B2
Waterloo *Ont., Canada* 43°30N 80°32W **312** C4
Waterloo *Qué., Canada* 45°22N 72°32W **313** A12
Waterloo *Wellington, N.Z.* 41°13S 174°56E **143** B2
Waterloo *S. Leone* 8°26N 13°8W **262** D2
Waterloo *Trin. & Tob.* 10°28N 61°28W **323** t
Waterloo *London, U.K.* **125** b4
Waterloo *Ill., U.S.A.* 38°20N 90°9W **310** F6
Waterloo *Ind., U.S.A.* 41°26N 85°1W **311** C11
Waterloo *Iowa, U.S.A.* 42°30N 92°21W **310** B4
Waterloo *N.Y., U.S.A.* 42°54N 76°52W **312** D8
Waterloo *Wis., U.S.A.* 43°11N 88°59W **310** A8
Waterman *U.S.A.* 41°46N 88°47W **311** C8
Watermeal-Boitsfort
Belgium 50°48N 4°25E **116** B2
Watersmeet *U.S.A.* 46°16N 89°11W **308** B9
Waterton Lakes △
Canada 48°45N 115°0W **296** D6
Watertown *Conn., U.S.A.* 41°36N 73°7W **313** E11
Watertown *Fla., U.S.A.* 30°11N 82°36W **316** E7
Watertown *Mass., U.S.A.* 42°22N 71°10W **116** A1
Watertown *N.Y., U.S.A.* 43°59N 75°55W **313** C9
Watertown *S. Dak., U.S.A.* 44°54N 97°7W **308** C5
Watertown *Wis., U.S.A.* 43°12N 88°43W **311** A8
Waterval-Boven *S. Africa* 25°40S 30°18E **271** C5
Waterville *Qué., Canada* 45°16N 71°54W **313** A13
Waterville *Maine, U.S.A.* 44°33N 69°38W **309** C19
Waterville *N.Y., U.S.A.* 42°56N 75°23W **313** D9
Waterville *Pa., U.S.A.* 41°19N 77°21W **312** E7
Waterville *Wash., U.S.A.* 47°39N 120°4W **304** C3
Watervliet *Mich., U.S.A.* 42°11N 86°18W **311** B10
Watervliet *N.Y., U.S.A.* 42°44N 73°42W **313** D11
Wates *Indonesia* 7°51S 110°10E **235** D4
Watford *Ont., Canada* 42°57N 81°53W **312** D3
Watford *Herts., U.K.* 51°40N 0°24W **169** F7
Watford City *U.S.A.* 47°48N 103°17W **308** B2
Wathaman ➔ *Canada* 57°16N 102°59W **297** B8
Wathaman L. *Canada* 56°58N 103°44W **297** B8
Watheroo *Australia* 30°15S 116°5E **279** F2
Watheroo △ *Australia* 30°19S 115°48E **279** F2
Wating *China* 35°40N 106°38E **226** G4
Watîr, W. ➔ *Egypt* 29°0N 34°40E **251** K5
Watkins Glen *U.S.A.* 42°23N 76°52W **312** D8
Watkinsville *U.S.A.* 33°52N 83°25W **316** B6
Watling I. = San Salvador I.
Bahamas 24°0N 74°40W **321** B5
Watom I. *Papua N. G.* 4°7S 152°4E **286** C7
Watonga *U.S.A.* 35°51N 98°25W **314** D5
Watrous *Sask., Canada* 51°40N 105°25W **297** C7
Watrous *N. Mex.,*
U.S.A. 35°48N 104°59W **305** J11
Watsa *Dem. Rep. of the Congo* 3°4N 29°30E **268** B2
Watseka *U.S.A.* 40°47N 87°44W **311** D9
Watsi Kenga
Dem. Rep. of the Congo 0°49S 20°34E **264** C4
Watson *Canada* 52°10N 104°30W **297** C8
Watson Lake *Canada* 60°6N 128°49W **296** A3
Watsonia *Australia* 37°43S 145°5E **128** A2
Watsontown *U.S.A.* 41°5N 76°52W **312** E8
Watsonville *U.S.A.* 36°55N 121°45W **306** J5
Watt Mt. *Dominica* 15°19N 61°19W **323** k
Wattiwarriganna Cr. ➔
Australia 28°57S 136°10E **281** D2
Wattwil *Switz.* 47°18N 9°6E **179** H5
Watu *Dem. Rep. of the Congo* 3°18S 20°3E **264** C4
Watuata = Batuata
Indonesia 6°12S 122°42E **231** F6
Watubela, Kepulauan
Indonesia 4°28S 131°35E **231** E8
Watubela Is. = Watubela,
Kepulauan *Indonesia* 4°28S 131°35E **231** E8
Wau = Wâw *Sudan* 7°45N 28°1E **257** F2
Wau *Papua N. G.* 7°21S 146°47E **286** D4
Waubamik *Canada* 45°27N 80°1W **312** A4
Waubay *U.S.A.* 45°20N 97°18W **308** C5
Waubra *Australia* 37°21S 143°39E **282** D5
Wauchope *N.S.W.,*
Australia 31°28S 152°45E **283** A10
Wauchope *N. Terr.,*
Australia 20°36S 134°15E **280** C1
Wauchula *U.S.A.* 27°33N 81°49W **317** H8
Waukarlycarly, L.
Australia 21°18S 121°56E **278** D3
Waukeenah *U.S.A.* 30°25N 83°57W **316** E6
Waukegan *U.S.A.* 42°22N 87°50W **311** B9
Waukesha *U.S.A.* 43°1N 88°14W **311** B8
Waukon *U.S.A.* 43°16N 91°29W **308** D8
Waupaca *U.S.A.* 44°21N 89°5W **308** C9
Waupun *U.S.A.* 43°38N 88°44W **308** D9
Waurika *U.S.A.* 34°10N 98°0W **314** D6
Wausau *Fla., U.S.A.* 30°38N 85°35W **316** E4
Wausau *Wis., U.S.A.* 44°58N 89°38W **308** C9
Wauseon *U.S.A.* 41°33N 84°8W **311** C12
Wautoma *U.S.A.* 44°4N 89°18W **308** C9
Wauwatosa *U.S.A.* 43°2N 88°0W **311** A9
Wave Hill = Kalkarindji
Australia 17°30S 130°47E **278** C5
Wave Rock ⌂ *Australia* 32°26S 118°53E **279** F2
Waveland *U.S.A.* 39°53N 87°3W **311** E9
Waveney ➔ *U.K.* 52°35N 1°39E **169** E9
Waverley *N.S.W.,*
Australia 33°53S 151°15E **139** B2
Waverley *N.Z.* 39°46S 174°37E **284** F3
Waverley *Gauteng, S. Africa* 26°7S 28°4E **123** A2
Waverley *Mass., U.S.A.* 42°23N 71°10W **116** A1
Waverley Station *Edinburgh, U.K.* **121** b3
Waverly *Ala., U.S.A.* 32°44N 85°35W **316** C4
Waverly *Fla., U.S.A.* 27°59N 81°37W **317** H8
Waverly *Ga., U.S.A.* 31°6N 81°43W **316** D8
Waverly *Ill., U.S.A.* 39°36N 89°57W **310** E7
Waverly *Iowa, U.S.A.* 42°44N 92°29W **310** B4
Waverly *Mo., U.S.A.* 39°13N 93°31W **310** E3
Waverly *N.Y., U.S.A.* 42°1N 76°32W **313** E8
Waverly Hall *U.S.A.* 32°41N 84°44W **316** C5
Wavre *Belgium* 50°43N 4°38E **170** D4
Waw *Burma* 17°28N 96°41E **241** G6
Wâw *Sudan* 7°45N 28°1E **257** F2
Wāw al Kabīr *Libya* 25°20N 16°43E **258** C3
Wāw an Nāmūs *Libya* 24°55N 17°46E **258** D3
Wawa *Ont., Canada* 47°59N 84°47W **298** C3
Wawa *Nigeria* 9°54N 4°27E **263** D5
Wawa *Sudan* 20°30N 30°22E **256** C3
Wawanesa *Canada* 49°36N 99°40W **297** D9
Wawasee, L. *U.S.A.* 41°24N 85°42W **311** C11
Wawer *Poland* 52°13N 21°8E **142** B2
Wawoi ➔ *Papua N. G.* 7°48S 143°16E **286** D2
Wawona *U.S.A.* 37°32N 119°39W **306** H7
Wawrzyszew *Poland* 52°17N 20°53E **142** B1
Waxahachie *U.S.A.* 32°24N 96°51W **314** E6
Waxxari *China* 38°42N 87°9E **217** E11
Way, L. *Australia* 26°45S 120°16E **279** E3
Way Kambas △ *Indonesia* 4°54S 105°43E **234** C3
Waya *Fiji* 17°19S 177°10E **287** A1
Waycross *U.S.A.* 31°13N 82°21W **316** D7
Wayi *Sudan* 5°8N 30°10E **257** F3
Wayland *Mich., U.S.A.* 42°40N 85°39W **311** B11
Wayland *N.Y., U.S.A.* 42°34N 77°35W **312** D7
Wayne *Nebr., U.S.A.* 42°14N 97°1W **308** D5
Wayne *W. Va., U.S.A.* 38°13N 82°27W **309** F12
Wayne City *U.S.A.* 38°21N 88°35W **311** F8
Wayne County, Detroit ✈ (DTW)
U.S.A. 42°13N 83°21W **311** B13
Wayne Lakes *U.S.A.* 40°1N 84°40W **311** D12
Waynesboro *Ga., U.S.A.* 33°6N 82°1W **316** B7
Waynesboro *Miss.,*
U.S.A. 31°40N 88°39W **315** F10
Waynesboro *Pa., U.S.A.* 39°45N 77°35W **309** F15
Waynesboro *Va., U.S.A.* 38°4N 78°53W **309** F14
Waynesburg *U.S.A.* 39°54N 80°11W **309** F13
Waynesville *Mo., U.S.A.* 37°50N 92°12W **310** G4
Waynesville *N.C., U.S.A.* 35°28N 82°58W **315** D13
Waynesville *Ohio, U.S.A.* 39°32N 84°5W **311** E12
Waynoka *U.S.A.* 36°35N 98°53W **314** C5
Wayside *U.S.A.* 33°4N 83°37W **316** B6
Waza *Afghan.* 33°22N 69°26E **240** B3
Waza △ *Cameroon* 11°15N 14°38E **259** F2
Wazikhwah *Afghan.* 32°11N 68°21E **240** B3
Wāzin *Libya* 31°58N 10°40E **258** B2
Wazirabad *Delhi, India* 28°43N 77°13E **120** A2
Wazirabad *Pakistan* 32°30N 74°8E **242** C6
Waziristan *Pakistan* 33°0N 70°0E **242** C4
Wazīrīya *Iraq* 33°22N 44°23E **113** A2
Wazirpur *India* 28°41N 77°10E **120** A2
Wda ➔ *Poland* 53°25N 18°29E **184** E5
We *Indonesia* 5°51N 95°18E **234** A1
Wé *N. Cal.* 20°55S 167°16E **288** d
Weald, The *U.K.* 51°4N 0°20E **169** F8
Wealdstone *U.K.* 51°35N 0°17W **125** A1
Weam *Papua N. G.* 8°37S 141°8E **286** E1
Wear ➔ *U.K.* 54°55N 1°23W **168** C6
Weatherford *Okla., U.S.A.* 35°32N 98°43W **314** D5
Weatherford *Tex., U.S.A.* 32°46N 97°48W **314** E6
Weaubleau *U.S.A.* 37°54N 93°32W **310** G3
Weaverville *U.S.A.* 40°44N 122°56W **304** F2
Webb City *U.S.A.* 37°9N 94°28W **308** G6
Webequie *Canada* 52°59N 87°21W **298** B2
Weber *N.Z.* 40°24S 176°20E **284** G5
Weber Basin *Pac. Oc.* 6°0S 131°0E **276** B5
Webo = Nyaake *Liberia* 4°52N 7°37W **262** E3
Webster *Mass., U.S.A.* 42°3N 71°53W **313** D13
Webster *N.Y., U.S.A.* 43°13N 77°26W **312** C7
Webster *S. Dak., U.S.A.* 45°20N 97°31W **308** C5
Webster City *U.S.A.* 42°28N 93°49W **310** B3
Webster Springs *U.S.A.* 38°29N 80°25W **309** F13
Webuye *Kenya* 0°37N 34°46E **268** B3
Weda *Indonesia* 0°21N 127°50E **231** D7
Weda, Teluk *Indonesia* 0°20N 128°0E **231** D7
Weddell Abyssal Plain
S. Ocean 65°0S 20°0W **151** C2
Weddell I. *Falk. Is.* 51°50S 61°0W **153** f
Weddell Sea *Antarctica* 72°30S 40°0W **151** D1
Wedderburn *Australia* 36°26S 143°33E **282** D5
Weddin Mts. △ *Australia* 33°59S 148°0E **283** C8
Wedding *Germany* 52°32N 13°21E **115** A3
Wedel *Germany* 53°34N 9°42E **178** B5
Wedemark *Germany* 52°32N 9°43E **178** C5
Wedgeport *Canada* 43°44N 65°59W **299** D6
Wednesday I. *Australia* 10°31S 142°16E **286** F2
Wedowee *U.S.A.* 33°19N 85°29W **316** B4
Wedza *Zimbabwe* 18°40S 31°33E **269** F3
Wee Waa *Australia* 30°11S 149°26E **281** E4
Weed *U.S.A.* 41°25N 122°23W **304** F2
Weed Heights *U.S.A.* 38°59N 119°13W **306** G7
Weedsport *U.S.A.* 43°2N 76°33W **313** C8
Weedville *U.S.A.* 41°17N 78°30W **312** E6
Weehawken *New York, U.S.A.* **132** b1
Weeki Wachee *U.S.A.* 28°32N 82°35W **317** G7
Weel Shimbirro *Somali Rep.* 2°23N 44°14E **267** D5
Weenen *S. Africa* 28°48S 30°7E **271** C5
Weener *Germany* 53°9N 7°20E **178** B3
Weert *Neths.* 51°15N 5°43E **170** C5
Weesp *Neths.* 52°18N 5°2E **112** B3
Węgierska-Górka *Poland* 49°36N 19°7E **185** J6
Węgliniec *Poland* 51°18N 15°10E **185** G2
Węgorzewo *Poland* 54°13N 21°43E **184** D8
Węgorzyno *Poland* 53°32N 15°33E **184** E2
Węgrów *Poland* 52°24N 22°0E **185** F9
Wehda □ *Sudan* 8°30N 30°0E **257** F3
Wei He ➔ *Hebei, China* 36°10N 115°45E **226** F8
Wei He ➔ *Shaanxi, China* 34°38N 110°15E **226** G6
Weichang *China* 41°58N 117°49E **227** D9
Weichuan *China* 34°20N 113°59E **226** G7
Weida *Germany* 50°46N 12°2E **178** E8
Weiden *Germany* 49°41N 12°10E **179** F8
Weidling *Austria* 48°17N 16°18E **142** A1
Weidlingbach *Austria* 48°16N 16°15E **142** A1
Weifang *China* 36°44N 119°7E **227** F10
Weihai *China* 37°30N 122°6E **227** F12
Weihui *China* 35°25N 114°3E **226** G8
Weil *Germany* 47°35N 7°37E **179** H3
Weilburg *Germany* 50°28N 8°17E **178** E4
Weilheim *Germany* 47°50N 11°9E **179** H7
Weimar *Germany* 50°58N 11°19E **178** E7
Weinan *China* 34°31N 109°29E **226** G5
Weingarten *Germany* 49°3N 8°31E **179** F4
Weinheim *Germany* 49°32N 8°39E **179** F4
Weining *China* 26°50N 104°17E **228** D5
Weipa *Australia* 12°40S 141°50E **280** A3
Weir ➔ *Queens.,*
Australia 28°20S 149°50E **281** D4
Weir ➔ *Man., Canada* 56°54N 93°21W **297** B10
Weir, L. *U.S.A.* 29°0N 81°57W **317** F8
Weir River *Canada* 56°49N 94°6W **297** B10
Weirsdale *U.S.A.* 28°59N 81°55W **317** G8
Weirton *U.S.A.* 40°24N 80°35W **312** F4
Weiser *U.S.A.* 44°15N 116°58W **304** D5
Weishan *Shandong, China* 34°47N 117°5E **227** G9
Weishan *Yunnan, China* 25°12N 100°20E **228** E3
Weishan Hu *China* 34°35N 117°14E **227** G9
Weissenburg *Germany* 49°2N 10°58E **179** F6
Weissenfels *Germany* 51°11N 12°0E **178** D7
Weissensee *Germany* 52°33N 13°27E **115** A3
Weisskirchen = Hranice
Czech Rep. 49°34N 17°45E **181** B10
Weisswasser *Germany* 51°30N 14°36E **178** D10
Weistritz = Bystrzyca ➔ *Dolnośląskie,*
Poland 51°12N 16°55E **185** G3
Weistritz = Bystrzyca ➔ *Lubelskie,*
Poland 51°21N 22°46E **185** G9
Wéitra *Austria* 48°41N 14°54E **180** C7
Weixi *China* 27°10N 99°10E **228** D2
Weixin *China* 27°48N 105°3E **228** D5
Weiyuan *Gansu, China* 35°7N 104°10E **226** G3
Weiyuan *Sichuan, China* 29°35N 104°36E **228** C5
Weiz *Austria* 47°13N 15°39E **180** D8
Weizhou Dao *China* 21°0N 109°5E **228** G7
Wejherowo *Poland* 54°35N 18°12E **184** D5
Wekoewa Pt. *Bonaire* 12°13N 68°24W **322** h
Wekusko L. *Canada* 54°40N 99°50W **297** C9
Welch *U.S.A.* 37°26N 81°35W **309** G13
Welchman Hall *Barbados* 13°11N 59°34W **323** r
Weldya *Ethiopia* 11°50N 39°34E **257** E4
Welega *Ethiopia* 9°25N 34°20E **257** F3
Welford △ *Australia* 25°5S 143°16E **280** D3
Weligama *Sri Lanka* 5°58N 80°25E **245** M5
Welkite *Ethiopia* 8°15N 37°42E **257** F4
Welkom *S. Africa* 28°0S 26°46E **270** C4
Welland *Canada* 43°0N 79°15W **312** D5
Welland ➔ *U.K.* 52°51N 0°5W **169** E7
Wellawaya *Sri Lanka* 6°44N 81°6E **245** L5
Welles Harbor *Midway Is.* 28°13N 177°25W **302** c
Wellesley Hills *U.S.A.* 42°18N 71°16W **116** B1
Wellesley Is. *Australia* 16°42S 139°30E **280** B2
Wellesley Islands ✪
Australia 16°32S 139°23E **280** B2
Welling *U.K.* 51°27N 0°6E **125** B4
Wellingborough *U.K.* 52°19N 0°41W **169** E7
Wellington *N.S.W.,*
Australia 32°35S 148°59E **283** B8
Wellington *Ont., Canada* 43°57N 77°20W **312** C7
Wellington *N.Z.* 41°19S 174°46E **143** B1
Wellington *Western Cape,*
S. Africa 33°38S 19°1E **270** D2
Wellington *Somst., U.K.* 50°58N 3°13W **169** G4
Wellington *Telford & Wrekin,*
U.K. 52°42N 2°30W **169** E5
Wellington *Colo., U.S.A.* 40°42N 105°0W **304** F11
Wellington *Kans., U.S.A.* 37°16N 97°24W **308** G5
Wellington *Mass., U.S.A.* 42°24N 71°5W **116** A2
Wellington *Mo., U.S.A.* 39°8N 93°59W **310** E3
Wellington *Nev., U.S.A.* 38°45N 119°23W **306** G7
Wellington *Ohio, U.S.A.* 41°10N 82°13W **312** E2
Wellington *Tex., U.S.A.* 34°51N 100°13W **314** D4
Wellington □ *N.Z.* 40°8S 175°36E **284** G4
Wellington, I. *Chile* 49°30S 75°0W **336** C2
Wellington, L. *Australia* 38°6S 147°20E **283** E7
Wellington Chan. *Canada* 75°0N 93°0W **295** C13
Wellington Int. ✈ (WLE)
N.Z. 41°20S 174°50E **143** B1
Wellman *U.S.A.* 41°28N 91°50W **310** C5
Wells *Somst., U.K.* 51°13N 2°39W **169** F5
Wells *Maine, U.S.A.* 43°20N 70°35W **313** C14
Wells *N.Y., U.S.A.* 43°24N 74°17W **313** C10
Wells *Nev., U.S.A.* 41°7N 114°58W **304** F6
Wells, L. *Australia* 26°44S 123°15E **279** E3
Wells, Mt. *Australia* 17°25S 127°8E **278** C4
Wells Fargo Center *Los Angeles, U.S.A.* **127** b1
Wells Gray ⌂ *Canada* 52°30N 120°15W **296** C4
Wells-next-the-Sea *U.K.* 52°57N 0°51E **168** E8
Wells River *U.S.A.* 44°9N 72°4W **313** B12
Wellsboro *U.S.A.* 41°45N 77°18W **312** E7
Wellsburg *U.S.A.* 40°16N 80°37W **312** F4
Wellsford *N.Z.* 36°16S 174°32E **284** C3
Wellston = Warner Robins
U.S.A. 32°37N 83°36W **316** C6
Wellsville *Mo., U.S.A.* 39°4N 91°34W **310** E5
Wellsville *N.Y., U.S.A.* 42°7N 77°57W **312** D7
Wellsville *Ohio, U.S.A.* 40°36N 80°39W **312** F4
Wellsville *Utah, U.S.A.* 41°38N 111°56W **304** F8
Wellton *U.S.A.* 32°40N 114°8W **305** K6
Welmel, Wabi ➔ *Ethiopia* 5°38N 40°47E **257** F5
Welo *Ethiopia* 11°50N 39°48E **257** E4
Welo *Somali Rep.* 9°25N 48°55E **267** C6
Wels *Austria* 48°9N 14°1E **180** C7
Welshpool *Vic., Australia* 38°42S 146°26E **283** E7
Welshpool *Powys, U.K.* 52°39N 3°8W **169** E4
Weltevreden Park *S. Africa* 26°7S 27°56E **123** A1
Welungen = Wieluń
Poland 51°15N 18°34E **185** G5
Welwitschia = Khorixas
Namibia 20°16S 14°59E **270** B1
Welwyn Garden City *U.K.* 51°48N 0°12W **169** F7
Wem *U.K.* 52°52N 2°44W **168** E5
Wembere ➔ *Tanzania* 4°10S 34°15E **268** C3
Wembley *U.K.* 51°33N 0°17W **125** A2
Wemindji *Canada* 53°0N 78°49W **298** B4
Wemmel *Belgium* 50°55N 4°18E **116** A1
Wemmer Pan *S. Africa* 26°13S 28°3E **123** B2
Wemyss *Canada* 44°52N 76°23W **313** B8
Wen Xian *Gansu, China* 32°43N 104°36E **226** H3
Wen Xian *Henan, China* 34°55N 113°5E **226** G7
Wenatchee *U.S.A.* 47°25N 120°19W **304** C3
Wenceslas Square = Václavské
náměstí *Prague, Czech Rep.* **135** b2
Wenchang *China* 19°38N 110°42E **236** C8
Wencheng *China* 27°46N 120°4E **229** D13
Wenchi *Ghana* 7°46N 2°8W **262** D4
Wenchow = Wenzhou
China 28°0N 120°38E **229** D13
Wenchuan *China* 31°22N 103°35E **228** B4
Wenden *U.S.A.* 33°49N 113°33W **307** M13
Wendeng *China* 37°15N 122°5E **227** F12
Wendenschloss *Germany* 52°24N 13°35E **115** B4
Wendesi *Indonesia* 2°30S 134°17E **231** E8
Wendo *Ethiopia* 6°40N 38°27E **257** F4
Wendover *U.S.A.* 40°44N 114°2W **304** F6
Weng'an *China* 27°5N 107°25E **228** D6
Wengcheng *China* 24°22N 113°50E **229** E9
Wengen *Switz.* 46°37N 7°55E **173** F14
Wengyuan *China* 24°20N 114°9E **229** E10
Wenling *China* 28°21N 121°20E **229** C13
Wenlock ➔ *Australia* 12°2S 141°55E **286** G1
Wennington *U.K.* 51°30N 0°12E **125** A5
Weno *Pac. Oc.* 7°27N 151°52E **287** T18
Wenona *U.S.A.* 41°3N 89°3W **310** C7
Wenshan *China* 23°20N 104°18E **228** F5
Wenshang *China* 35°45N 116°30E **226** G9
Wenshui *China* 37°26N 112°1E **226** F7
Wensleydale *U.K.* 54°17N 2°0W **168** C6
Wensu *China* 41°15N 80°10E **217** D10
Wensum ➔ *U.K.* 52°40N 1°15E **168** E8
Wentworth *Australia* 34°2S 141°54E **282** C4
Wentzel L. *Canada* 59°2N 114°28W **296** B6
Wentzville *U.S.A.* 38°49N 90°51W **310** F6
Wenut *Indonesia* 3°11S 133°19E **231** E8
Wenxi *China* 35°20N 111°10E **226** G6
Wenzhou *China* 28°0N 120°38E **229** D13
Weott *U.S.A.* 40°20N 123°55W **304** F2
Wepener *S. Africa* 29°42S 27°3E **270** C4
Werda *Botswana* 25°24S 23°15E **270** C3
Werdau *Germany* 50°44N 12°22E **178** E8
Werder *Ethiopia* 6°58N 45°1E **267** C6
Werder *Brandenburg,*
Germany 52°23N 12°55E **178** C8
Werdohl *Germany* 51°15N 7°46E **178** D3
Wereilu *Ethiopia* 10°40N 39°28E **257** E4
Weri *Indonesia* 3°10S 132°38E **231** E8
Werneck *Germany* 49°58N 10°5E **179** F6
Werneuchen *Germany* 52°38N 13°44E **115** A5
Wernigerode *Germany* 51°50N 10°47E **178** D6
Werra ➔ *Germany* 51°24N 9°39E **178** D5
Werribee *Australia* 37°54S 144°40E **282** D6
Werrikimbe △ *Australia* 31°11S 152°15E **283** A10
Werrimull *Australia* 34°25S 141°38E **282** C4
Werris Creek *Australia* 31°18S 150°38E **283** A9
Werschetz = Vršac *Serbia* 45°8N 21°20E **182** E6
Wertach ➔ *Germany* 48°22N 10°54E **179** G6
Wertheim *Germany* 49°45N 9°32E **179** F5
Wertingen *Germany* 48°33N 10°41E **179** G6
Wesel *Germany* 51°39N 6°37E **178** D2
Weser ➔ *Germany* 53°36N 8°28E **178** B4
Weser-Ems □ *Germany* 53°0N 7°30E **178** C3
Weserbergland *Germany* 52°12N 9°17E **178** C5
Weserbergland Schaumburg
Hameln ⌂ *Germany* 52°8N 9°20E **178** C5
Wesermünde = Bremerhaven
Germany 53°33N 8°36E **178** B4
Wesiri *Indonesia* 7°30S 126°30E **231** F7
Weslaco *U.S.A.* 26°10N 97°58W **314** H6
Weslemkoon L. *Canada* 45°2N 77°25W **312** A7
Wesley *Dominica* 15°33N 61°18W **323** k
Wesleyville *Nfld. & L.,*
Canada 49°9N 53°33W **299** C9
Wesleyville *Pa., U.S.A.* 42°9N 80°1W **312** D4
Wessel, C. *Australia* 10°59S 136°46E **280** A2
Wessel Is. *Australia* 11°10S 136°45E **280** A2
Wesselburen *Germany* 54°13N 8°54E **178** A4
Wessington Springs
U.S.A. 44°5N 98°34W **308** C4
West *U.S.A.* 31°48N 97°6W **314** F6
West ➔ *U.S.A.* 42°52N 72°33W **313** D12
West Allis *U.S.A.* 43°1N 88°0W **311** B8
West Antarctica *Antarctica* 80°0S 90°0W **151** D15
West Baines ➔ *Australia* 15°38S 129°59E **278** C4
West Bank ■ *Asia* 32°6N 35°13E **251** F6
West Bend *U.S.A.* 43°25N 88°11W **308** D9
West Bengal □ *India* 23°0N 88°0E **243** H13
West Berkshire □ *U.K.* 51°25N 1°17W **169** F6
West Beskids = Západné Beskydy
Europe 49°30N 19°0E **181** B12
West Branch *U.S.A.* 44°17N 84°14W **309** C11
West Branch Susquehanna ➔
U.S.A. 40°53N 76°48W **313** F8
West Bromwich *U.K.* 52°32N 1°59W **169** E6
West Burra *U.K.* 60°5N 1°21W **167** A7
West Canada Cr. ➔
U.S.A. 43°1N 74°58W **313** C10
West Caroline Basin
Pac. Oc. 4°0N 138°0E **288** G5
West Carrollton *U.S.A.* 39°40N 84°17W **311** E12
West Chazy *U.S.A.* 44°49N 73°28W **313** B11
West Chester *U.S.A.* 39°58N 75°36W **313** G9
West Chicago *U.S.A.* 41°53N 88°12W **311** C8
West Coast △ *N.Z.* 43°15S 170°30E **285** D5
West Coast △ *Namibia* 21°53S 14°14E **270** B1
West Coast △ *S. Africa* 33°13S 18°0E **270** D2
West Columbia *S.C.,*
U.S.A. 33°59N 81°4W **316** B8
West Columbia *Tex.,*
U.S.A. 29°9N 95°39W **314** G7
West Covina *U.S.A.* 34°4N 117°54W **307** L9
West Des Moines *U.S.A.* 41°35N 93°43W **310** C3
West Don ➔ *Canada* 43°44N 79°24W **141** A2
West Drayton *U.K.* 51°30N 0°28W **125** A1
West Dunbartonshire □
U.K. 55°59N 4°30W **167** F4
West End *Bahamas* 26°41N 78°58W **320** A4
West End *Boston, U.S.A.* **116** b1
West End Village *Anguilla* 18°10N 63°10W **322** a
West Falkland *Falk. Is.* 51°40S 60°0W **153** f
West Fargo *U.S.A.* 46°52N 96°54W **308** B5
West Fiji Basin *Pac. Oc.* 17°0S 173°0E **288** J9
West Fjord = Vestfjorden
Norway 67°55N 14°0E **160** C16
West Fork Trinity ➔
U.S.A. 32°48N 96°54W **314** E6
West Frankfort *U.S.A.* 37°54N 88°55W **310** G8
West Grand L. *U.S.A.* 45°14N 67°51W **309** C20
West Green *U.S.A.* 31°37N 82°44W **316** D7
West Ham *U.K.* 51°31N 0°1E **125** A4
West Harrow *U.K.* 51°34N 0°21W **125** A1
West Hartford *U.S.A.* 41°45N 72°44W **313** E12
West Haven *U.S.A.* 41°17N 72°57W **313** E12
West Hazleton *U.S.A.* 40°58N 76°0W **313** F9
West Heath *U.K.* 51°29N 0°7E **125** B4
West Helena *U.S.A.* 34°33N 90°38W **315** D9
West Hill *Canada* 43°46N 79°10W **141** A3
West Hollywood *U.S.A.* 34°5N 118°21W **126** B2
West Hurley *U.S.A.* 41°59N 74°7W **313** E10
West I. *India* 13°35N 92°54E **245** H11
West Ice Shelf *Antarctica* 67°0S 85°0E **151** C7
West Indies *Cent. Amer.* 15°0N 65°0W **321** D7
West Jefferson *U.S.A.* 39°57N 83°17W **311** E13
West Jordan *U.S.A.* 40°36N 111°56W **304** F8
West Kensington *London, U.K.* **125** c1
West Kilburn *London, U.K.* **125** a1
West Lafayette *U.S.A.* 40°27N 86°55W **311** D10
West Lamma Channel
China 22°14N 114°4E **122** B1
West Liberty *Iowa, U.S.A.* 41°34N 91°16W **310** C5
West Liberty *Ky., U.S.A.* 37°55N 83°16W **311** G13
West Liberty *Ohio,*
U.S.A. 40°15N 83°45W **311** D13
West Linn *U.S.A.* 45°21N 122°36W **306** E4
West Lorne *Canada* 42°36N 81°36W **312** D3
West Los Angeles, Univ. of
U.S.A. 34°7N 118°23W **126** C2
West Lothian □ *U.K.* 55°54N 3°36W **167** F5
West Lunga ➔ *Zambia* 13°6S 24°39E **265** E4
West Lunga △ *Zambia* 12°49S 24°47E **265** E4
West MacDonnell △
Australia 23°38S 132°59E **278** D5
West Mariana Basin
Pac. Oc. 15°0N 137°0E **288** F5
West Medford *U.S.A.* 42°25N 71°7W **116** A2
West Memphis *U.S.A.* 35°8N 90°10W **315** D9
West Miami *U.S.A.* 25°45N 80°17W **128** B1
West Midlands □ *U.K.* 52°26N 2°0W **169** E6
West Mifflin *U.S.A.* 40°21N 79°52W **312** F5
West Milford *U.S.A.* 41°8N 74°22W **313** E10
West Milton *Ohio, U.S.A.* 39°58N 84°20W **311** E12
West Milton *Pa., U.S.A.* 41°1N 76°50W **312** E8
West Molesey *U.K.* 51°24N 0°22W **125** B1
West Monroe *U.S.A.* 32°31N 92°9W **314** E8
West New Britain □
Papua N. G. 5°0S 149°30E **286** C5
West New York *New York, U.S.A.* **132** a1
West Newton *U.S.A.* 40°14N 79°46W **312** F5
West Nicholson *Zimbabwe* 21°2S 29°20E **269** G2
West Odessa *U.S.A.* 31°50N 102°30W **314** F3
West of Twin Peaks
U.S.A. 37°43N 122°27W **136** B2
West Palm Beach *U.S.A.* 26°43N 80°3W **317** J9
West Palm Beach Canal
U.S.A. 26°40N 80°15W **317** J9
West Park *S. Africa* 26°9S 27°59E **123** A1
West Pensacola *U.S.A.* 30°25N 87°16W **317** E2
West Plains *U.S.A.* 36°44N 91°51W **308** G8
West Point *Ga., U.S.A.* 32°53N 85°11W **316** C4
West Point *Iowa, U.S.A.* 40°43N 91°27W **310** D5
West Point *Ky., U.S.A.* 37°59N 85°57W **311** G11
West Point *Miss., U.S.A.* 33°36N 88°39W **315** E10
West Point *N.Y., U.S.A.* 41°24N 73°58W **313** E11
West Point *Nebr., U.S.A.* 41°51N 96°43W **308** E5
West Point *Va., U.S.A.* 37°32N 76°48W **309** G15
West Point L. *U.S.A.* 33°8N 85°0W **316** B4
West Pt. = Ouest, Pte. de l'
Canada 49°52N 64°40W **299** C7
West Pt. *Australia* 35°1S 135°56E **282** C1
West Ra. *Papua N. G.* 4°15S 141°30E **286** C1
West Road ➔ *Canada* 53°18N 122°53W **296** C4
West Rouge *Canada* 43°48N 79°7W **141** A4
West Roxbury *U.S.A.* 42°16N 71°9W **116** B2
West Rutland *U.S.A.* 43°36N 73°3W **313** C11
West Salem *U.S.A.* 38°31N 88°1W **311** F8
West Schelde = Westerschelde ➔
Neths. 51°25N 3°25E **170** C3
West Seneca *U.S.A.* 42°51N 78°48W **312** D6
West Sepik □ *Papua N. G.* 3°30S 142°0E **286** B2
West Siberian Plain *Russia* 62°0N 75°0E **210** B9
West Springfield *U.S.A.* 38°47N 77°13W **143** C2
West Sussex □ *U.K.* 50°55N 0°30W **169** G7
West Terre Haute *U.S.A.* 39°28N 87°27W **311** E9
West-Terschelling *Neths.* 53°22N 5°13E **170** A5
West Town *U.S.A.* 41°53N 87°42W **119** B2
West Union *Iowa, U.S.A.* 42°57N 91°49W **310** B5
West Union *Ohio, U.S.A.* 38°48N 83°33W **311** F13
West Unity *U.S.A.* 41°35N 84°26W **311** C12
West Valley City *U.S.A.* 40°42N 111°58W **304** F8
West Virginia □ *U.S.A.* 38°45N 80°30W **309** F13
West-Vlaanderen □ *Belgium* 51°0N 3°0E **170** D2
West Walker ➔ *U.S.A.* 38°54N 119°9W **306** G7
West Wharf *Pakistan* 24°49N 66°58E **123** B1
West Wyalong *Australia* 33°56S 147°10E **283** B7
West Yellowstone *U.S.A.* 44°40N 111°6W **304** D8
West Yorkshire □ *U.K.* 53°45N 1°40W **168** D6
Westall, Pt. *Australia* 32°55S 134°4E **281** E1
Westbay *U.S.A.* 30°18N 85°52W **316** E4
Westbourne Green *London, U.K.* **125** a1
Westbrook *U.S.A.* 43°41N 70°22W **309** D18
Westbury *Australia* 41°30S 146°51E **281** G4
Westby *U.S.A.* 48°52N 104°3W **304** B11
Westchester *Calif.,*
U.S.A. 33°57N 118°23W **126** C2
Westchester *Ill., U.S.A.* 41°51N 87°53W **119** B1
Westchester *N.Y., U.S.A.* 40°51N 73°51W **132** A3
Westcliff *S. Africa* 26°10S 28°1E **123** B2
Westdene *S. Africa* 26°10S 27°59E **123** B1
Westende *Helsinki, Finland* 60°9N 24°48E **121** C1
Westend *Calif., U.S.A.* 35°42N 117°24W **307** K9
Wester Hailes *U.K.* 55°55N 3°16W **121** B2
Westerham *Germany* 48°3N 11°36E **131** B2
Westerland *Germany* 54°54N 8°17E **178** A4
Westerly *U.S.A.* 41°22N 71°50W **313** E13
Western □ *Ghana* 5°30N 2°30W **262** D4
Western □ *Kenya* 0°30N 34°30E **268** B3
Western □ *Papua N. G.* 7°30S 142°0E **286** D2
Western □ *S. Leone* 8°30N 13°0W **262** D2
Western □ *Zambia* 15°0S 24°4E **265** F4
Western Addition
U.S.A. 37°47N 122°25W **136** B2
Western Australia □
Australia 25°0S 118°0E **279** E2
Western Cape □ *S. Africa* 34°0S 20°0E **270** D3

Western Dvina = Daugava → Latvia 57°4N 24°3E 188 D3
Western Ghats India 14°0N 75°0E 245 H2
Western Highlands □ Papua N. G. 5°45S 144°30E 286 C3
Western Isles □ U.K. 57°30N 7°10W 167 D1
Western Sahara ■ Africa 25°0N 13°0W 260 D2
Western Samoa = Samoa ■ Pac. Oc. 14°0S 172°0W 287 V20
Western Sierra Madre = Madre Occidental, Sierra Mexico 27°0N 107°0W 318 B3
Western Wall Jerusalem 123 b3
Westernport U.S.A. 39°29N 79°3W 309 F14
Westerschelde → Neths. 51°25N 3°25E 170 C3
Westerstede Germany 53°15N 7°55E 178 B3
Westerwald Germany 50°38N 7°56E 178 E3
Westfield Ill., U.S.A. 39°27N 88°0W 311 E8
Westfield Ind., U.S.A. 40°2N 86°8W 311 D10
Westfield Mass., U.S.A. 42°7N 72°45W 313 D12
Westfield N.Y., U.S.A. 42°20N 79°35W 312 D5
Westfield Pa., U.S.A. 41°55N 77°32W 312 E7
Westgate La., U.S.A. 30°0N 90°13W 131 A1
Westgate Md., U.S.A. 38°57N 77°6W 143 B3
Westhill U.K. 57°9N 2°19W 167 D6
Westhope U.S.A. 48°55N 101°1W 308 A3
Westlake Western Cape, S. Africa 34°4S 18°26E 118 B1
Westlake Calif., U.S.A. 34°4N 118°15W 126 B3
Westlake Calif., U.S.A. 37°42N 122°29W 136 B2
Westland U.S.A. 42°15N 83°20W 311 B13
Westland △ N.Z. 43°16S 170°16E 285 D5
Westland Bight N.Z. 42°55S 170°5E 285 C5
Westlock Canada 54°9N 113°55W 296 C6
Westmar Australia 27°55S 149°44E 281 D4
Westmeath □ Ireland 53°33N 7°34W 166 C4
Westminster London, U.K. 51°30N 0°7W 125 A3
Westminster Calif., U.S.A. 33°45N 118°0W 307 M8
Westminster Colo., U.S.A. 39°50N 105°2W 304 G11
Westminster Md., U.S.A. 39°34N 76°59W 309 F15
Westmont U.S.A. 40°19N 78°58W 312 F6
Westmorland U.S.A. 33°2N 115°37W 307 M11
Westmount Canada 45°29N 73°35W 130 B2
Weston Ont., Canada 43°42N 79°30W 141 A1
Weston Ohio, U.S.A. 41°21N 83°47W 311 C13
Weston Oreg., U.S.A. 45°49N 118°26W 304 D4
Weston W. Va., U.S.A. 39°2N 80°28W 309 F13
Weston I. Canada 52°33N 79°36W 298 B4
Weston-super-Mare U.K. 51°21N 2°58W 169 F5
Westover U.S.A. 40°45N 78°40W 312 F6
Westphalia U.S.A. 38°26N 92°0W 310 F5
Westport Ont., Canada 44°40N 76°25W 313 B8
Westport Mayo, Ireland 53°48N 9°31W 166 C2
Westport N.Z. 41°46S 171°37E 285 B6
Westport Ind., U.S.A. 39°11N 85°34W 311 E11
Westport N.Y., U.S.A. 44°11N 73°26W 313 B11
Westport Oreg., U.S.A. 46°8N 123°23W 306 D3
Westport Wash., U.S.A. 46°53N 124°6W 306 D2
Westpunt Curaçao 12°22N 69°10W 322 g
Westray Man., Canada 53°36N 101°24W 297 C8
Westray Orkney, U.K. 59°18N 3°0W 167 B5
Westree Canada 47°26N 81°34W 298 C3
Westville Calif., U.S.A. 39°8N 120°42W 306 F6
Westville Fla., U.S.A. 30°46N 85°51W 316 E4
Westville Ill., U.S.A. 40°2N 87°38W 311 D9
Westville Ind., U.S.A. 41°32N 86°54W 311 C10
Westwego U.S.A. 29°54N 90°8W 131 B2
Westwood U.S.A. 40°18N 121°0W 304 F3
Westwood Lake U.S.A. 25°44N 80°23W 317 K9
Westwood Village U.S.A. 34°3N 118°26W 126 B2
Westzaan Neths. 52°28N 4°46E 112 A1
Wetar Indonesia 7°48S 126°30E 231 F7
Wetaskiwin Canada 52°55N 113°24W 296 C6
Wetherby U.K. 53°56N 1°23W 168 D6
Wethersfield U.S.A. 41°42N 72°40W 313 E12
Wetlet Burma 22°20N 95°53E 241 D5
Wetteren Belgium 51°0N 3°53E 170 D3
Wetton S. Africa 34°0S 18°31E 118 B2
Wetumpka U.S.A. 32°32N 86°13W 316 C3
Wetzlar Germany 50°32N 8°31E 178 E4
Wevok U.S.A. 68°53N 166°13W 303 B6
Wewahitchka U.S.A. 30°7N 85°12W 316 E4
Wewak Papua N. G. 3°38S 143°41E 286 B2
Wewoka U.S.A. 35°9N 96°30W 314 D6
Wexford Ont., Canada 43°45N 79°18W 141 A3
Wexford Wexford, Ireland 52°20N 6°28W 166 D5
Wexford □ Ireland 52°20N 6°25W 166 D5
Wexford Harbour Ireland 52°20N 6°25W 166 D5
Weybridge U.K. 51°22N 0°27W 125 B1
Weyburn Canada 49°40N 103°50W 297 D8
Weyer Markt Austria 47°51N 14°40E 180 D7
Weyhe Germany 52°58N 8°48E 178 C4
Weyib → Ethiopia 7°15N 40°15E 257 F5
Weymouth N.S., Canada 44°30N 66°1W 299 D6
Weymouth Dorset, U.K. 50°37N 2°28W 169 G5
Weymouth Mass., U.S.A. 42°13N 70°58W 313 D14
Weymouth, C. Australia 12°37S 143°27E 280 A3
Wezembeek-Oppem Belgium 50°51N 4°29E 116 A2
Wha Ti Canada 63°8N 117°16W 294 E8
Whakaari N.Z. 37°30S 177°13E 284 D6
Whakamaru N.Z. 38°23S 175°50E 284 E4
Whakatane N.Z. 37°57S 177°1E 284 D6
Whakatane → N.Z. 37°57S 177°1E 284 D6
Whale = Baleine → Canada 58°15N 67°40W 299 A6
Whale B. Burma 11°37N 98°38E 237 G2
Whale Cove Canada 62°10N 92°34W 297 A10
Whale Pt. Ascension I. 7°57S 14°18W 153 g
Whales, B. of Antarctica 78°0S 160°0W 151 D12
Whalsay U.K. 60°22N 0°59W 167 A8
Whangaehu → N.Z. 40°3S 175°6E 284 G4
Whangamata N.Z. 37°12S 175°53E 284 D4
Whangamomona N.Z. 39°8S 174°44E 284 F3
Whanganui △ N.Z. 39°17S 174°53E 284 F3
Whangaparaoa Pen. N.Z. 36°40S 174°45E 284 C4
Whangarei N.Z. 35°43S 174°21E 284 B3
Whangarei Harb. N.Z. 35°45S 174°28E 284 B3
Whangaroa Harb. N.Z. 35°4S 173°46E 284 B3
Whangaruru Harb. N.Z. 35°24S 174°23E 284 B3
Wharanui N.Z. 41°55S 174°6E 285 B9
Wharekauri = Chatham Is. Pac. Oc. 44°0S 176°40W 285 a
Wharfe → U.K. 53°51N 1°9W 168 D6
Wharfedale U.K. 54°6N 2°1W 168 C5
Wharton N.J., U.S.A. 40°54N 74°35W 313 F10
Wharton Pa., U.S.A. 41°31N 78°1W 312 E6
Wharton Tex., U.S.A. 29°19N 96°6W 314 G6
Wharton Basin Ind. Oc. 22°0S 92°0E 273 F8
Whataroa N.Z. 43°18S 170°24E 285 D5
Whataroa → N.Z. 43°7S 170°16E 285 D5
Whatcom = Bellingham U.S.A. 48°46N 122°29W 306 B4
Wheatfield U.S.A. 41°13N 87°4W 311 C9
Wheatland Calif., U.S.A. 39°1N 121°25W 306 F5
Wheatland Ind., U.S.A. 38°40N 87°19W 311 F9
Wheatland Wyo., U.S.A. 42°3N 104°58W 304 E11
Wheatley Canada 42°6N 82°27W 312 D2
Wheaton Ill., U.S.A. 41°52N 88°6W 311 C8
Wheaton Md., U.S.A. 39°3N 77°3W 309 F15
Wheaton Minn., U.S.A. 45°48N 96°30W 308 C5
Wheelbarrow Pk. U.S.A. 37°26N 116°5W 306 H10
Wheeler Oreg., U.S.A. 45°41N 123°53W 304 D2
Wheeler Tex., U.S.A. 35°27N 100°16W 314 D4
Wheeler → Canada 57°2N 67°13W 299 A6
Wheeler L. U.S.A. 34°48N 87°23W 315 D11
Wheeler Pk. N. Mex., U.S.A. 36°34N 105°25W 305 H11
Wheeler Pk. Nev., U.S.A. 38°57N 114°15W 304 G6
Wheeler Ridge U.S.A. 35°0N 118°57W 307 L8
Wheelersburg U.S.A. 38°44N 82°51W 309 F12
Wheeling U.S.A. 40°4N 80°43W 312 F4
Whernside U.K. 54°14N 2°24W 168 C5
Whiddy I. Ireland 51°41N 9°31W 166 E2
Whim Creek Australia 20°50S 117°49E 278 D2
Whirlwind Reef Papua N. G. 4°42S 148°16E 286 C5
Whiskey Jack L. Canada 58°23N 101°55W 297 B8
Whiskeytown-Shasta-Trinity ⌂ U.S.A. 40°45N 122°15W 304 F2
Whistleduck Cr. → Australia 20°15S 135°18E 280 C2
Whistler Canada 50°7N 122°58W 296 C4
Whitby Ont., Canada 43°52N 78°56W 312 C6
Whitby N. Yorks., U.K. 54°29N 0°37W 168 C7
Whitcombe Pass N.Z. 43°13S 170°55E 285 D5
White → Ark., U.S.A. 33°57N 91°5W 314 E9
White → Ind., U.S.A. 38°25N 87°45W 311 F9
White → S. Dak., U.S.A. 43°42N 99°27W 308 D4
White → Tex., U.S.A. 33°14N 100°56W 314 E4
White → Utah, U.S.A. 40°4N 109°41W 304 F9
White → Vt., U.S.A. 43°37N 72°20W 313 C12
White → Wash., U.S.A. 47°12N 122°15W 306 C4
White, L. Australia 21°9S 128°56E 278 D4
White B. Canada 50°0N 56°35W 299 C8
White Bird U.S.A. 45°46N 116°18W 304 D5
White Butte U.S.A. 46°23N 103°18W 308 B2
White City Fla., U.S.A. 29°53N 85°13W 316 F4
White City Oreg., U.S.A. 42°26N 122°51W 304 E2
White Cliffs Australia 30°50S 143°10E 282 A5
White Cloud Hill = Baiyun Hill China 23°3N 113°15E 121 B2
White Desert = Es Sahrâ al Beida Egypt 27°50N 28°45E 256 B2
White Hall U.S.A. 39°26N 90°24W 310 E6
White Haven U.S.A. 41°4N 75°47W 313 E9
White Horse, Vale of U.K. 51°37N 1°30W 169 F6
White House, The Washington, D.C., U.S.A. 143 b1
White I. = Whakaari N.Z. 37°30S 177°13E 284 D6
White I. Grenada 12°26N 61°28W 323 q
White L. Ont., Canada 45°18N 76°31W 313 A8
White L. La., U.S.A. 29°44N 92°30W 314 G8
White Lake Canada 45°21N 76°29W 313 A8
White Mountain U.S.A. 64°41N 163°24W 303 D7
White Mountain Peak U.S.A. 37°38N 118°15W 305 H4
White Mountains Nat. Recr. Area ⌂ U.S.A. 65°30N 147°40W 303 D11
White Mts. Alaska, U.S.A. 65°30N 146°30W 303 D11
White Mts. Calif., U.S.A. 37°30N 118°15W 306 H8
White Mts. N.H., U.S.A. 44°15N 71°15W 313 B13
White Mts. △ Australia 20°43S 145°12E 280 C4
White Nile = Nîl el Abyad → Sudan 15°38N 32°31E 257 D3
White Nile Dam = Khazzān Jabal al Awliyā Sudan 15°24N 32°20E 257 D3
White Oak U.S.A. 31°2N 81°43W 316 D8
White Otter L. Canada 49°5N 91°55W 298 C1
White Pass U.S.A. 46°38N 121°24W 306 D5
White Pigeon U.S.A. 41°48N 85°39W 311 C11
White Plains Ga., U.S.A. 33°28N 83°1W 316 B6
White Plains N.Y., U.S.A. 41°2N 73°46W 313 E11
White River Ont., Canada 48°35N 85°20W 298 C2
White River S. Dak., U.S.A. 43°34N 100°45W 308 D3
White Rock B.C., Canada 49°2N 122°48W 306 A4
White Rock N. Mex., U.S.A. 35°50N 106°12W 305 J10
White Russia = Belarus ■ Europe 53°30N 27°0E 177 B14
White Sands ⌂ U.S.A. 32°46N 106°20W 305 K10
White Sea = Beloye More Russia 66°30N 38°0E 186 A6
White Springs U.S.A. 30°20N 82°45W 316 E7
White Sulphur Springs Mont., U.S.A. 46°33N 110°54W 304 C8
White Sulphur Springs W. Va., U.S.A. 37°48N 80°18W 309 G13
White Swan U.S.A. 46°23N 120°44W 306 D6
White Volta → Ghana 9°10N 1°15W 263 D4
Whitechapel U.K. 51°31N 0°3W 125 A3
Whitecliffs N.Z. 43°26S 171°55E 285 D6
Whitecourt Canada 54°10N 115°45W 296 C5
Whiteface Mt. U.S.A. 44°22N 73°54W 313 B11
Whitefield U.S.A. 44°23N 71°37W 313 B13
Whitefish U.S.A. 48°25N 114°20W 304 B6
Whitefish B. U.S.A. 46°40N 84°55W 298 C3
Whitefish Bay U.S.A. 43°6N 87°54W 311 A9
Whitefish L. Canada 62°41N 106°48W 297 A7
Whitefish Pt. U.S.A. 46°45N 84°59W 309 B11
Whitegull, L. = Goélands, L. aux Canada 55°27N 64°17W 299 A7
Whitehall Dublin, Ireland 53°22N 6°16W 120 A2
Whitehall London, U.K. 125 b3
Whitehall Mich., U.S.A. 43°24N 86°21W 308 D10
Whitehall Mont., U.S.A. 45°52N 112°6W 304 D7
Whitehall N.Y., U.S.A. 43°33N 73°24W 313 C11
Whitehall Wis., U.S.A. 44°22N 91°19W 308 C8
Whitehaven U.K. 54°33N 3°35W 168 C4
Whitehorse Canada 60°43N 135°3W 296 A1
Whiteman Ra. Papua N. G. 5°55S 150°0E 286 C6
Whitemark Australia 40°7S 148°3E 281 G4
Whiteplains Liberia 6°28N 10°40W 262 D2
Whiteriver U.S.A. 33°50N 109°58W 305 K9
Whitesand → Canada 60°9N 115°45W 296 A5
Whitesands S. Africa 34°23S 20°50E 270 D3
Whitesboro N.Y., U.S.A. 43°7N 75°18W 313 C9
Whitesboro Tex., U.S.A. 33°39N 96°54W 314 E6
Whiteshell ⌂ Canada 50°0N 95°40W 297 D9
Whiteside, Canal Chile 53°55S 70°15W 336 D2
Whiteville U.S.A. 34°20N 78°42W 315 D15
Whitewater U.S.A. 42°50N 88°44W 311 B8
Whitewater B. U.S.A. 25°15N 81°0W 317 K9
Whitewater Baldy U.S.A. 33°20N 108°39W 305 K9
Whitewater L. Canada 50°50N 89°10W 298 B2
Whitewood Queens., Australia 21°28S 143°30E 280 C3
Whitewood Sask., Canada 50°20N 102°20W 297 C8
Whitfield Australia 36°42S 146°24E 283 D7
Whithorn U.K. 54°44N 4°26W 167 G4
Whitianga N.Z. 36°47S 175°41E 284 C4
Whiting U.S.A. 41°41N 87°30W 311 C9
Whitman U.S.A. 42°5N 70°56W 313 D14
Whitmore Village U.S.A. 21°31N 158°1W 302 J13
Whitney Ont., Canada 45°31N 78°14W 312 A6
Whitney Nev., U.S.A. 36°4N 115°5W 124 B2
Whitney, Mt. U.S.A. 36°35N 118°18W 306 J8
Whitney Point U.S.A. 42°20N 75°58W 313 D9
Whitstable U.K. 51°21N 1°3E 169 F9
Whitsunday I. Australia 20°15S 149°4E 280 b
Whitsunday Islands △ Australia 20°15S 149°0E 280 b
Whittemore U.S.A. 43°4N 94°26W 310 A2
Whittier Alaska, U.S.A. 60°47N 148°41W 303 F10
Whittier Calif., U.S.A. 33°58N 118°2W 126 C4
Whittlesea Australia 37°27S 145°9E 283 D6
Whitton U.K. 51°27N 0°21W 125 B1
Wholdaia L. Canada 60°43N 104°20W 297 A8
Whyalla Australia 33°2S 137°30E 282 B2
Wiang Kosai △ Thailand 17°54N 99°29E 236 D2
Wiang Sa Thailand 18°34N 100°45E 236 C3
Wiarton Canada 44°40N 81°10W 312 B3
Wiawso Ghana 6°10N 2°25W 262 D4
Wiay U.K. 57°24N 7°13W 167 D1
Wiązów Poland 50°50N 17°10E 185 H4
Wibaux U.S.A. 46°59N 104°11W 304 C11
Wichabai Guyana 2°57N 59°35W 329 C6
Wichian Buri Thailand 15°39N 101°7E 236 E3
Wichita U.S.A. 37°42N 97°20W 308 G5
Wichita Falls U.S.A. 33°54N 98°30W 314 E5
Wick U.K. 58°26N 3°5W 167 C5
Wickenburg U.S.A. 33°58N 112°44W 305 K7
Wickepin Australia 32°50S 117°30E 279 F2
Wickham Australia 20°42S 117°11E 278 D2
Wickham, C. Australia 39°35S 143°57E 281 F3
Wickliffe U.S.A. 41°36N 81°28W 312 E3
Wicklow Ireland 52°59N 6°3W 166 D5
Wicklow □ Ireland 52°57N 6°25W 166 D5
Wicklow Hd. Ireland 52°58N 6°0W 166 D6
Wicklow Mts. Ireland 52°58N 6°26W 166 C5
Wicklow Mts. △ Ireland 53°6N 6°21W 166 C5
Widawa Poland 51°27N 18°51E 185 G5
Widawka → Poland 51°27N 18°52E 185 G5
Wide B. Papua N. G. 5°55S 152°5E 286 C7
Widgeegoara Cr. → Australia 28°51S 146°34E 281 D4
Widgiemooltha Australia 31°30S 121°34E 279 F3
Widnes U.K. 53°23N 2°45W 168 D5
Wido S. Korea 35°35N 126°17E 224 E3
Więcbork Poland 53°21N 17°30E 185 E4
Wieden Austria 48°11N 16°22E 142 A2
Wiehengebirge = Nördlicher Teutoburger Wald-Wiehengebirge ⌂ Germany 52°18N 8°10E 178 C4
Wiehl Germany 50°56N 7°34E 178 E3
Wiek Germany 54°37N 13°17E 178 A9
Wielbark Poland 53°24N 20°55E 184 E7
Wieleń Poland 52°53N 16°9E 185 F3
Wielichowo Poland 52°7N 16°22E 185 F3
Wieliczka Poland 50°0N 20°5E 185 J7
Wielkopolski △ Poland 52°18N 16°45E 185 F3
Wielkopolskie □ Poland 52°10N 17°30E 185 F4
Wieluń Poland 51°15N 18°34E 185 G5
Wien Austria 48°12N 16°22E 142 A2
Wien-Schwechat ✈ (VIE) Austria 48°7N 16°35E 142 B3
Wiener Neustadt Austria 47°49N 16°16E 181 D9
Wienerberg Austria 48°9N 16°21E 142 B2
Wieprz → Poland 51°34N 21°49E 185 G8
Wieprza → Poland 54°26N 16°25E 184 D3
Wieruszów Poland 51°19N 18°9E 185 G5
Wierzbno Poland 52°11N 21°1E 142 B2
Wiesbaden Germany 50°4N 8°14E 179 E4
Wiesental Germany 49°13N 8°31E 179 F4
Wiesloch Germany 49°18N 8°41E 179 F4
Wiesmoor Germany 53°24N 7°47E 178 B3
Wieżyca Poland 54°14N 18°8E 184 D5
Wigan U.K. 53°33N 2°38W 168 D5
Wiggins Colo., U.S.A. 40°14N 104°4W 304 F11
Wiggins Miss., U.S.A. 30°51N 89°8W 315 F10
Wight, I. of U.K. 50°41N 1°17W 169 G6
Wigierski △ Poland 54°5N 23°5E 184 D10
Wigry, Jezioro Poland 54°2N 23°8E 184 D10
Wigston U.K. 52°35N 1°6W 169 E6
Wigton U.K. 54°50N 3°10W 168 C4
Wigtown U.K. 54°53N 4°27W 167 G4
Wigtown B. U.K. 54°46N 4°15W 167 G4
Wijde Wormer Neths. 52°28N 4°52E 112 A2
Wik and Wikway People ◎ Australia 13°55S 142°28E 280 A3
Wil Switz. 47°28N 9°3E 179 H5
Wilamowice Poland 49°55N 19°9E 185 J6
Wilanów Poland 52°10N 21°4E 142 B2
Wilanówka → Poland 52°13N 21°6E 142 C2
Wilber U.S.A. 40°29N 96°58W 308 E5
Wilberforce Canada 45°2N 78°13W 312 A6
Wilberforce, C. Australia 11°54S 136°35E 280 A2
Wilburton U.S.A. 34°55N 95°19W 314 D7
Wilcannia Australia 31°30S 143°26E 282 A5
Wilcox U.S.A. 41°35N 78°41W 312 E6
Wildbad Germany 48°44N 8°33E 179 G4
Wildcat Cr. → U.S.A. 40°28N 86°52W 311 D10
Wildenschwert = Ústí nad Orlicí Czech Rep. 49°58N 16°24E 181 B9
Wildeshausen Germany 52°54N 8°27E 178 C4
Wildeshauser Geest ⌂ Germany 52°54N 8°30E 178 C4
Wildon Austria 46°52N 15°31E 180 E8
Wildrose U.S.A. 36°14N 117°11W 307 J9
Wilds, The S. Africa 26°10S 28°2E 123 B2
Wildspitze Austria 46°53N 10°53E 180 E3
Wildwood U.S.A. 28°52N 82°2W 317 G7
Wilga → Poland 51°52N 21°18E 185 G8
Wilge → S. Africa 27°3S 28°20E 271 C4
Wilhelm, Mt. Papua N. G. 5°50S 145°1E 286 C3
Wilhelm II Coast Antarctica 68°0S 90°0E 151 C7
Wilhelmina Geb. Suriname 3°50N 56°30W 329 C6
Wilhelmina Top = Trikora, Puncak Indonesia 4°15S 138°45E 231 E9
Wilhelmsburg Austria 48°6N 15°36E 180 C8
Wilhelmshagen Germany 52°26N 13°42E 115 B5
Wilhelmshaven Germany 53°31N 8°7E 178 B4
Wilhelmstal Namibia 21°58S 16°21E 270 B2
Wilis Indonesia 7°51S 111°48E 235 D4
Wilkes-Barre U.S.A. 41°15N 75°53W 313 E9
Wilkes I. Wake I. 19°18N 166°34E 302 b
Wilkes Land Antarctica 69°0S 120°0E 151 D9
Wilket Creek Park Canada 43°43N 79°21W 141 A2
Wilkie Canada 52°27N 108°42W 297 C7
Wilkieston U.K. 55°54N 3°24W 121 B1
Wilkinsburg U.S.A. 40°26N 79°52W 312 F5
Wilkinson Lakes Australia 29°40S 132°39E 279 E5
Will Rogers State Historical Park ⌂ U.S.A. 34°2N 118°30W 126 B1
Willacoochee U.S.A. 31°20N 83°3W 316 D6
Willandra △ Australia 33°12S 145°0E 283 B6
Willandra Creek → Australia 33°22S 145°52E 282 B6
Willapa B. U.S.A. 46°40N 124°0W 304 C1
Willapa Hills U.S.A. 46°35N 123°25W 306 D3
Willard U.S.A. 41°3N 82°44W 312 E2
Willare Bridge Roadhouse Australia 17°43S 123°38E 278 C3
Willaumez Pen. Papua N. G. 5°15S 150°2E 286 C6
Willbriggie Australia 34°28S 146°2E 283 C7
Willbrook Ireland 53°17N 6°16W 120 B2
Willcox U.S.A. 32°15N 109°50W 305 K9
Willemstad Curaçao 12°5N 68°55W 322 g
Willenberg = Wielbark Poland 53°24N 20°55E 184 E7
Willesden U.K. 51°32N 0°15W 125 A2
Willesden Green U.K. 51°32N 0°13W 125 A2
Willi Willi △ Australia 30°57S 152°27E 283 A10
William → Canada 59°8N 109°19W 297 B7
William, Mt. Australia 37°17S 142°35E 282 D5
William 'Bill' Dannelly Res. U.S.A. 32°6N 87°24W 315 E11
William Creek Australia 28°58S 136°22E 281 D2
Williams W. Austral., Australia 33°2S 116°52E 279 F2
Williams Ariz., U.S.A. 35°15N 112°11W 305 J7
Williams Calif., U.S.A. 39°9N 122°9W 306 F4
Williams Harbour Canada 52°33N 55°47W 299 B8
Williams Lake Canada 52°10N 122°10W 296 C4
Williamsbridge U.S.A. 40°52N 73°51W 132 A2
Williamsburg Fla., U.S.A. 28°24N 81°26W 133 B2
Williamsburg Iowa, U.S.A. 41°40N 92°1W 310 C4
Williamsburg Ky., U.S.A. 36°44N 84°10W 309 G11
Williamsburg New York, U.S.A. 132 f3
Williamsburg Pa., U.S.A. 40°28N 78°12W 312 F6
Williamsburg Va., U.S.A. 37°16N 76°43W 309 G15
Williamsburg Bridge New York, U.S.A. 132 e2
Williamsfield U.S.A. 40°55N 90°1W 310 D6
Williamson N.Y., U.S.A. 43°14N 77°11W 312 C7
Williamson W. Va., U.S.A. 37°41N 82°17W 309 G12
Williamsport Ind., U.S.A. 40°17N 87°17W 311 D9
Williamsport Pa., U.S.A. 41°15N 77°1W 312 E7
Williamston Mich., U.S.A. 42°41N 84°17W 311 B12
Williamston N.C., U.S.A. 35°51N 77°4W 315 D16
Williamstown Vic., Australia 37°51S 144°52E 128 B1
Williamstown Ky., U.S.A. 38°38N 84°34W 311 F12
Williamstown Mass., U.S.A. 42°43N 73°12W 313 D11
Williamstown N.Y., U.S.A. 43°26N 75°53W 313 C9
Williamsville U.S.A. 39°57N 89°33W 310 E7
Willikies Antigua & B. 17°3N 61°42W 322 b
Willimantic U.S.A. 41°43N 72°13W 313 E12
Willingboro U.S.A. 40°3N 74°54W 309 E16
Willis, L. U.S.A. 28°23N 81°28W 133 B2
Willisburg U.S.A. 37°49N 85°8W 311 G11
Williston Northern Cape, S. Africa 31°20S 20°53E 270 D3
Williston Fla., U.S.A. 29°23N 82°27W 317 F7
Williston N. Dak., U.S.A. 48°9N 103°37W 308 A2
Williston S.C., U.S.A. 33°24N 81°25W 316 B8
Williston L. Canada 56°0N 124°0W 296 B4
Willits U.S.A. 39°25N 123°21W 304 G2
Willmar U.S.A. 45°7N 95°3W 308 C6
Willmore Wilderness ⌂ Canada 53°45N 119°30W 296 C5
Willoughby N.S.W., Australia 33°48S 151°12E 139 A2
Willoughby Ohio, U.S.A. 41°39N 81°24W 312 E3
Willoughby B. Antigua & B. 17°2N 61°44W 322 b
Willow U.S.A. 61°45N 150°3W 303 F10
Willow Bunch Canada 49°20N 105°35W 297 D7
Willow L. Canada 62°10N 119°8W 296 A5
Willow Springs U.S.A. 41°44N 87°51W 119 C1
Willow Tree Australia 31°40S 150°45E 283 A9
Willow Wall, The China 42°10N 122°0E 227 C12
Willowdale Ont., Canada 43°46N 79°25W 141 A2
Willowdale La., U.S.A. 30°0N 90°12W 131 A1
Willowick U.S.A. 41°38N 81°28W 312 E3
Willowlake → Canada 62°42N 123°8W 296 A4
Willowmore S. Africa 33°15S 23°30E 270 D3
Willows U.S.A. 39°31N 122°12W 306 F4
Willowvale = Gatyana S. Africa 32°16S 28°31E 271 D4
Wills, L. Australia 21°25S 128°51E 278 D4
Wills Cr. → Australia 22°43S 140°2E 280 C3
Willsboro U.S.A. 44°21N 73°24W 313 B11
Willunga Australia 35°15S 138°30E 282 C3
Wilma U.S.A. 30°9N 84°58W 316 E5
Wilmersdorf Berlin, Germany 115 c1
Wilmette U.S.A. 42°4N 87°42W 119 A2
Wilmington S. Austral., Australia 32°39S 138°7E 282 B3
Wilmington Kent, U.K. 51°25N 0°12E 125 B5
Wilmington Del., U.S.A. 39°45N 75°33W 309 F16
Wilmington Ill., U.S.A. 41°18N 88°9W 311 C8
Wilmington N.C., U.S.A. 34°14N 77°55W 315 D16
Wilmington Ohio, U.S.A. 39°27N 83°50W 311 E13
Wilmington Vt., U.S.A. 42°52N 72°52W 313 D12
Wilmslow U.K. 53°19N 2°13W 168 D5
Wilna = Vilnius Lithuania 54°38N 25°19E 188 E3
Wilpattu △ Sri Lanka 8°20N 79°50E 245 K4
Wilpena Australia 31°31S 138°37E 282 A3
Wilpena Cr. → Australia 31°25S 139°29E 282 A3
Wilsall U.S.A. 45°59N 110°38W 304 D8
Wilson N.C., U.S.A. 35°44N 77°55W 315 D16
Wilson N.Y., U.S.A. 43°19N 78°50W 312 C6
Wilson Pa., U.S.A. 40°41N 75°15W 313 F9
Wilson → Australia 16°48S 128°16E 278 C4
Wilson Bluff Australia 31°41S 129°0E 279 F4
Wilson Inlet Australia 35°0S 117°22E 279 G2
Wilson Str. Solomon Is. 8°0S 156°39E 287 M9
Wilsons Promontory Australia 38°59S 146°23E 283 E7
Wilsons Promontory △ Australia 38°59S 146°23E 283 D7
Wilster Germany 53°55N 9°23E 178 B5
Wilton Iowa, U.S.A. 41°35N 91°1W 310 C5
Wilton N. Dak., U.S.A. 47°10N 100°47W 308 B3
Wilton → Australia 14°45S 134°33E 280 A1
Wiltshire □ U.K. 51°18N 1°53W 169 F6
Wiltz Lux. 49°57N 5°55E 170 E5
Wiluna Australia 26°36S 120°14E 279 E3
Wimbledon U.K. 51°25N 0°13W 125 B2
Wimbledon Common U.K. 51°26N 0°14W 125 B2
Wimbledon Park U.K. 51°25N 0°11W 125 B2
Wimbledon Tennis Ground U.K. 51°25N 0°12W 125 B2
Wimborne Minster U.K. 50°48N 1°59W 169 G6
Wimereux France 50°45N 1°37E 173 B8
Wimmera → Australia 36°8S 141°56E 282 D4
Winam G. Kenya 0°20S 34°15E 268 C3
Winamac U.S.A. 41°3N 86°36W 311 C10
Winburg S. Africa 28°30S 27°2E 270 C4
Winchelsea Australia 38°10S 144°1E 282 E6
Winchendon U.S.A. 42°41N 72°3W 313 D12
Winchester N.Z. 44°11S 171°17E 285 E6
Winchester Hants., U.K. 51°4N 1°18W 169 F6
Winchester Conn., U.S.A. 41°53N 73°9W 313 E11
Winchester Idaho, U.S.A. 46°14N 116°38W 304 C5
Winchester Ill., U.S.A. 39°38N 90°27W 310 E6
Winchester Ind., U.S.A. 40°10N 84°59W 311 D12
Winchester Ky., U.S.A. 37°59N 84°11W 311 G12
Winchester Mass., U.S.A. 42°26N 71°8W 116 A2
Winchester N.H., U.S.A. 42°46N 72°23W 313 D12
Winchester Nev., U.S.A. 36°7N 115°7W 124 B2
Winchester Ohio, U.S.A. 38°56N 83°39W 311 F13
Winchester Tenn., U.S.A. 35°11N 86°7W 315 D11
Winchester Va., U.S.A. 39°11N 78°10W 309 F14
Wind → U.S.A. 43°12N 108°12W 304 E9
Wind Cave △ U.S.A. 43°32N 103°17W 308 D2
Wind Point U.S.A. 42°47N 87°46W 311 B9
Wind River Range U.S.A. 43°0N 109°30W 304 E9
Windamere, L. Australia 32°48S 149°51E 283 B8
Windau = Ventspils Latvia 57°25N 21°32E 184 A8
Windber U.S.A. 40°14N 78°50W 312 F6
Winder U.S.A. 34°0N 83°45W 316 A6
Windermere Western Cape, S. Africa 33°55S 18°30E 118 A2
Windermere Cumb., U.K. 54°23N 2°55W 168 C5
Windermere Fla., U.S.A. 28°29N 81°32W 133 B1
Windfall U.S.A. 40°22N 85°57W 311 D11
Windhoek Namibia 22°35S 17°4E 270 B2
Windidda ◎ Australia 26°23S 122°12E 279 E3
Windisch-Feistritz = Slovenska Bistrica Slovenia 46°24N 15°35E 199 B12
Windischgarsten Austria 47°42N 14°21E 180 D7
Windischgratz = Slovenj Gradec Slovenia 46°31N 15°5E 199 B12
Windjana Gorge △ Australia 17°51S 125°0E 278 C3
Windom U.S.A. 43°52N 95°7W 308 D6
Windorah Australia 25°24S 142°36E 280 D3
Window Rock U.S.A. 35°41N 109°3W 305 J9
Windrush → U.K. 51°43N 1°24W 169 F6
Windsor N.S.W., Australia 33°37S 150°50E 283 B9
Windsor N.S., Canada 44°59N 64°5W 299 D7
Windsor Ont., Canada 42°18N 83°0W 312 D2
Windsor N.Z. 44°59S 170°49E 285 E5
Windsor Gauteng, S. Africa 26°7S 27°59E 123 A1
Windsor Windsor & Maidenhead, U.K. 51°29N 0°36W 169 F7
Windsor Calif., U.S.A. 38°33N 122°49W 306 G4
Windsor Colo., U.S.A. 40°29N 104°54W 304 F11
Windsor Conn., U.S.A. 41°50N 72°39W 313 E12
Windsor Ill., U.S.A. 39°26N 88°36W 311 E8
Windsor Mo., U.S.A. 38°32N 93°31W 310 F3
Windsor N.Y., U.S.A. 42°5N 75°37W 313 D9
Windsor Vt., U.S.A. 43°29N 72°24W 313 C12
Windsor, Gare Montréal, Canada 130 c2
Windsor & Maidenhead □ U.K. 51°29N 0°40W 169 F7
Windsor Caves Jamaica 18°21N 77°39W 320 a
Windsor Hills U.S.A. 33°59N 118°22W 126 C2
Windsorton S. Africa 28°16S 24°44E 270 C3
Windward Grenada 12°31N 61°26W 323 q
Windward Is. W. Indies 13°0N 61°0W 321 D7
Windward Passage = Vientos, Paso de los Caribbean 20°0N 74°0W 321 C5
Windward Side Saba 17°38N 63°14W 322 a
Windy Arbour Ireland 53°18N 6°14W 120 B2
Winefred L. Canada 55°30N 110°30W 297 B6
Winejok Sudan 9°1N 27°30E 257 F2
Winfield Iowa, U.S.A. 41°7N 91°26W 310 C5
Winfield Kans., U.S.A. 37°15N 96°59W 308 G5
Winfield Mo., U.S.A. 39°0N 90°44W 310 F6
Wingate Mts. Australia 14°25S 130°40E 278 B5
Wingellina = Irrunytju Australia 26°3S 128°56E 279 E4
Wingham N.S.W., Australia 31°48S 152°22E 283 A10
Wingham Ont., Canada 43°55N 81°20W 312 C3
Winisk → Canada 55°17N 85°5W 298 A2
Winisk L. Canada 52°55N 87°22W 298 B2
Wink U.S.A. 31°45N 103°9W 314 F3
Winkler Canada 49°10N 97°56W 297 D9
Winklern Austria 46°52N 12°52E 180 E5
Winlock U.S.A. 46°30N 122°56W 306 D4
Winneba Ghana 5°25N 0°36W 263 D4
Winnebago U.S.A. 42°16N 89°15W 310 B7
Winnebago, L. U.S.A. 44°0N 88°26W 308 D9
Winnecke Cr. → Australia 18°35S 131°34E 278 C5
Winnemucca U.S.A. 40°58N 117°44W 304 F5
Winnemucca L. U.S.A. 40°7N 119°21W 304 F4
Winner U.S.A. 43°22N 99°52W 308 D4
Winnett U.S.A. 47°0N 108°21W 304 C9
Winnfield U.S.A. 31°56N 92°38W 314 F8
Winnibigoshish, L. U.S.A. 47°27N 94°13W 308 B6
Winning Germany 48°2N 11°37E 131 B2
Winnipeg Canada 49°54N 97°9W 297 D9
Winnipeg → Canada 50°38N 96°19W 297 C9
Winnipeg, L. Canada 52°0N 97°0W 297 C9
Winnipeg Beach Canada 50°30N 96°58W 297 C9
Winnipegosis Canada 51°39N 99°55W 297 C9
Winnipegosis L. Canada 52°30N 100°0W 297 C9
Winnipesaukee, L. U.S.A. 43°38N 71°21W 313 C13
Winnisquam L. U.S.A. 43°33N 71°31W 313 C13
Winnsboro La., U.S.A. 32°10N 91°43W 314 E9
Winnsboro S.C., U.S.A. 34°23N 81°5W 315 D14
Winnsboro Tex., U.S.A. 32°58N 95°17W 314 E7
Winokapau, L. Canada 53°15N 62°50W 299 B7
Winona Minn., U.S.A. 44°3N 91°39W 308 C8
Winona Miss., U.S.A. 33°29N 89°44W 315 E10
Winooski U.S.A. 44°29N 73°11W 313 B11
Winooski → U.S.A. 44°32N 73°17W 313 B11
Winschoten Neths. 53°9N 7°3E 170 A7
Winsen Germany 53°22N 10°13E 178 B6
Winsford U.K. 53°12N 2°31W 168 D5
Winslow = Bainbridge Island U.S.A. 47°38N 122°32W 306 C4
Winslow Ariz., U.S.A. 35°2N 110°42W 305 J8
Winslow Ind., U.S.A. 38°23N 87°13W 311 F9
Winslow Reef Kiribati 1°36S 174°57W 277 A16
Winsted U.S.A. 41°55N 73°4W 313 E11
Winston-Salem U.S.A. 36°6N 80°15W 315 C14
Winter Garden U.S.A. 28°34N 81°35W 317 G8
Winter Haven U.S.A. 28°1N 81°44W 317 G8
Winter Park U.S.A. 28°36N 81°20W 317 G8
Winterberg Germany 51°11N 8°33E 178 D4
Winterhaven U.S.A. 32°44N 114°38W 307 N12
Winters U.S.A. 38°32N 121°58W 306 G5
Winterset U.S.A. 41°20N 94°1W 310 C3
Wintersville U.S.A. 40°23N 80°42W 312 F4
Winterswijk Neths. 51°58N 6°43E 170 C6
Winterthur Switz. 47°30N 8°44E 179 H4
Winthrop U.S.A. 48°28N 120°10W 304 B3
Winton Queens., Australia 22°24S 143°3E 280 C3
Winton N.Z. 46°8S 168°20E 285 G3
Wintua Vanuatu 16°30S 167°26E 287 F5
Wipper → Germany 51°16N 11°12E 178 D7
Wirlyajarrayi ◎ Australia 21°45S 132°35E 278 D5
Wirraminna Australia 31°12S 136°13E 282 A2
Wirrulla Australia 32°24S 134°31E 281 E1
Wisbech U.K. 52°41N 0°9E 169 E8
Wisconsin □ U.S.A. 44°45N 89°30W 310 B7
Wisconsin → U.S.A. 43°0N 91°15W 310 A5
Wisconsin Rapids U.S.A. 44°23N 89°49W 308 C9
Wisdom U.S.A. 45°37N 113°27W 304 D7
Wiseman U.S.A. 67°25N 150°6W 303 C10
Wishaw U.K. 55°46N 3°54W 167 F5
Wishek U.S.A. 46°16N 99°33W 308 B4
Wisła Poland 49°38N 18°53E 185 J5
Wisła → Poland 54°22N 18°55E 184 D5
Wisłok → Poland 50°13N 22°32E 185 H9
Wisłoka → Poland 50°27N 21°23E 185 H8
Wismar Mecklenburg-Vorpommern, Germany 53°54N 11°29E 178 B7
Wismar Guyana 5°59N 58°18W 329 B6
Wisner U.S.A. 41°59N 96°55W 308 E5
Wissant France 50°52N 1°40E 173 B8
Wissembourg France 49°2N 7°57E 173 C14
Wissous France 48°44N 2°19E 134 B2
Wisznice Poland 51°48N 23°13E 185 G10
Witbank = eMalahleni S. Africa 25°51S 29°14E 271 C4
Witches Gorge = Wu Xia China 31°2N 110°10E 229 B8
Witdraai S. Africa 26°58S 20°48E 270 C3
Witham U.K. 51°48N 0°40E 169 F8
Witham → U.K. 52°59N 0°2W 168 E7
Withernsea U.K. 53°44N 0°1E 168 D8
Withlacoochee → Fla., U.S.A. 30°24N 83°10W 316 E6
Withlacoochee → Fla., U.S.A. 29°0N 82°45W 317 G7
Witjira △ Australia 26°22S 135°37E 281 D2
Witkowo Poland 52°26N 17°45E 185 F4
Witless Bay Canada 47°17N 52°50W 299 C9
Witney U.K. 51°48N 1°28W 169 F6
Witnica Poland 52°40N 14°54E 185 F1
Witnossob → Namibia 23°55S 18°45E 270 C3
Witriver S. Africa 25°20S 31°0E 271 C5
Wittdün Germany 54°38N 8°23E 178 A4
Witte Pan Bonaire 12°3N 68°17W 322 h
Witten Germany 51°26N 7°20E 178 D3
Wittenau Germany 52°35N 13°19E 115 A2
Wittenberge Germany 53°0N 11°45E 178 B7
Wittenburg Germany 53°31N 11°4E 178 B7
Wittenheim France 47°44N 7°20E 173 E14
Wittenoom Australia 22°15S 118°20E 278 D2
Witti, Banjaran Malaysia 5°11N 116°29E 235 A5
Wittingau = Třeboň Czech Rep. 49°1N 14°48E 180 B7
Wittingen Germany 52°44N 10°44E 178 C6
Wittlich Germany 49°59N 6°53E 179 F2
Wittmund Germany 53°34N 7°46E 178 B3
Wittow Germany 54°38N 13°20E 178 A9
Wittstock Germany 53°10N 12°28E 178 B8
Witu Kenya 2°23S 40°26E 268 C5
Witu Is. Papua N. G. 4°50S 149°25E 286 C5
Witvlei Namibia 22°23S 18°32E 270 B2
Witwatersrand, Univ. of S. Africa 26°11S 28°1E 123 B2
Witzenhausen Germany 51°20N 9°51E 178 D5
Wiwon N. Korea 40°54N 126°3E 224 B3
Wixom U.S.A. 42°32N 83°32W 311 B13
Wkra → Poland 52°27N 20°44E 185 F7
Władysławowo Poland 54°48N 18°25E 184 D5
Wleń Poland 51°2N 15°39E 185 G2
Wlingi Indonesia 8°5S 112°25E 235 D4
Włochy Poland 52°12N 20°54E 142 B1
Włocławek Poland 52°40N 19°3E 185 F6
Włodawa Poland 51°33N 23°31E 185 G10
Włoszczowa Poland 50°50N 19°55E 185 H6
Wo Mei China 22°21N 114°15E 122 A2
Wo Yi Hop China 22°23N 114°8E 122 A1
Woburn Ont., Canada 43°46N 79°13W 141 A3
Woburn Mass., U.S.A. 42°29N 71°9W 116 A2
Wodian China 32°50N 112°35E 226 H7
Wodonga Australia 36°5S 146°50E 283 D7
Wodzisław Śląski Poland 50°1N 18°26E 185 H5
Wœrth France 48°57N 7°45E 173 D14
Wohlau = Wołów Poland 51°20N 16°38E 185 G3
Woinbogoin China 32°51N 98°39E 228 A2
Woippy France 49°10N 6°8E 173 C13
Woitape Papua N. G. 8°33S 147°15E 286 E4
Wojcieszow Poland 50°58N 15°55E 185 H2
Wokam Indonesia 5°45S 134°28E 231 F8
Wokha India 26°6N 94°16E 241 B5
Woking U.K. 51°19N 0°34W 169 F7
Wokingham U.K. 51°24N 0°49W 169 F7
Wokingham □ U.K. 51°25N 0°51W 169 F7
Woko △ Australia 31°46S 151°49E 283 A9
Wola Poland 52°14N 20°57E 142 B1
Wolbrom Poland 50°24N 19°45E 185 H6
Wolcottville U.S.A. 41°32N 85°22W 311 C11
Wołczyn Poland 51°1N 18°3E 185 G5
Woldegk Germany 53°27N 13°34E 178 B9
Woldenberg = Dobiegniew Poland 52°59N 15°45E 185 F2
Woldenberg Park New Orleans, U.S.A. 131 b3
Wolf → Canada 60°17N 132°33W 296 A2
Wolf, Volcán Ecuador 0°2N 91°20W 330 a
Wolf Creek U.S.A. 47°0N 112°4W 304 C7
Wolf L. Canada 60°24N 131°40W 296 A2
Wolf Point U.S.A. 48°5N 105°39W 304 B11
Wolf Trap Farm Park U.S.A. 38°56N 77°17W 143 B2
Wolfe Creek Crater △ Australia 19°10S 127°47E 278 C4
Wolfe I. Canada 44°7N 76°20W 313 B8
Wolfeboro U.S.A. 43°35N 71°13W 313 C13
Wolfen Germany 51°39N 12°15E 178 D8
Wolfenbüttel Germany 52°10N 10°33E 178 C6
Wolfratshausen Germany 47°54N 11°24E 179 H7
Wolfsberg Austria 46°50N 14°52E 180 E7
Wolfsburg Germany 52°25N 10°48E 178 C6
Wolgast Germany 54°3N 13°44E 178 A9
Wolgok S. Korea 37°35N 127°1E 137 B2
Wolhusen Switz. 47°4N 8°4E 179 H4
Wolica Warszawa, Poland 52°9N 21°3E 142 C2
Wolica Warszawa, Poland 52°7N 20°51E 142 C1
Wolin Poland 53°50N 14°37E 184 E1
Woliński △ Poland 53°57N 14°28E 184 E1
Wollaston U.S.A. 42°15N 71°2W 116 B2
Wollaston, Is. Chile 55°40S 67°30W 336 E3
Wollaston Forland Greenland 74°25N 19°40W 154 C9
Wollaston L. Canada 58°7N 103°10W 297 B8
Wollaston Lake Canada 58°3N 103°33W 297 B8
Wollaston Pen. Canada 69°30N 115°0W 294 D9
Wollemi △ Australia 33°0S 150°30E 283 B9
Wollongong Australia 34°25S 150°54E 283 C9
Wolmar = Valmiera Latvia 57°37N 25°29E 188 D3
Wolmaransstad S. Africa 27°12S 25°59E 270 C4
Wolmirstedt Germany 52°14N 11°37E 178 C7
Wołomin Poland 52°19N 21°15E 185 F8
Wołów Poland 51°20N 16°38E 185 G3
Wolseley S. Austral., Australia 36°23S 140°54E 282 D4
Wolseley Western Cape, S. Africa 33°26S 19°7E 270 D2
Wolsey U.S.A. 44°25N 98°28W 308 C4
Wolstenholme, C. Canada 62°35N 77°30W 292 C12
Wolsztyn Poland 52°8N 16°5E 185 F3
Woltersdorf Germany 52°27N 13°44E 115 B5
Woluwe-St-Lambert Belgium 50°50N 4°24E 116 A2
Woluwe-St-Pierre Belgium 50°50N 4°25E 116 A2
Wolvega Neths. 52°52N 6°0E 170 B6
Wolverhampton U.K. 52°35N 2°7W 169 E5
Wondai Australia 26°20S 151°49E 281 D5
Wonenara Papua N. G. 6°48S 145°53E 286 D3
Wong Chuk Hang China 22°15N 114°10E 122 B2
Wong Chuk Wan China 22°23N 114°17E 122 A2
Wong Chuk Yeung China 22°24N 114°15E 122 A2
Wonga Wongué △ Gabon 0°29S 9°25E 264 C1
Wongalarroo L. Australia 31°32S 144°0E 282 A6
Wongan Hills Australia 30°51S 116°37E 279 F2
Wonju S. Korea 37°22N 127°58E 224 D3
Wonosari Indonesia 7°58S 110°36E 231 G14
Wonosobo Indonesia 7°22S 109°54E 235 D3
Wonowon Canada 56°44N 121°48W 296 B4
Wŏnsan N. Korea 39°11N 127°27E 224 C3
Wonthaggi Australia 38°37S 145°37E 283 E6
Wood Buffalo △ Canada 59°0N 113°41W 296 B6
Wood Green U.K. 51°36N 0°6W 125 A3
Wood Is. Australia 16°24S 123°19E 278 C3
Wood L. Canada 55°17N 103°17W 297 B8
Wood Ridge U.S.A. 40°50N 74°4W 132 A1

446 Wood River INDEX

Wood River U.S.A. 38°52N 90°5W 310 F6
Woodah, I. Australia 13°27S 136°10E 280 A2
Woodbine U.S.A. 30°58N 81°44W 316 E8
Woodbine Race Track Canada 43°43N 79°36W 141 A1
Woodbourne U.S.A. 41°46N 74°36W 313 E10
Woodbridge Ont., Canada 43°47N 79°36W 141 A1
Woodbridge Suffolk, U.K. 52°6N 1°20E 169 E9
Woodbridge B. Dominica 15°19N 61°25W 323 k
Woodburn N.S.W., Australia 29°6S 153°23E 281 A5
Woodburn Oreg., U.S.A. 45°9N 122°51W 304 D2
Woodbury U.S.A. 32°59N 84°35W 316 C5
Woodenbong Australia 28°24S 152°39E 281 D5
Woodend Australia 37°20S 144°33E 282 D6
Woodford Queens., Australia 26°58S 152°47E 281 D5
Woodford London, U.K. 51°36N 0°3E 125 A4
Woodford Bridge U.K. 51°36N 0°3E 125 A4
Woodford Green U.K. 51°36N 0°1E 125 A4
Woodfords U.S.A. 38°47N 119°50W 306 G7
Woodhaven U.S.A. 40°41N 73°51W 132 B2
Woodhouselee U.K. 55°52N 3°13W 121 B2
Woodlake U.S.A. 36°25N 119°6W 306 J7
Woodland Calif., U.S.A. 38°41N 121°46W 306 G5
Woodland Maine, U.S.A. 45°9N 67°25W 309 C20
Woodland Pa., U.S.A. 41°0N 78°21W 312 F6
Woodland Wash., U.S.A. 45°54N 122°45W 306 E4
Woodland Caribou △ Canada 51°0N 94°45W 297 C10
Woodlands Singapore 1°26N 103°46E 138 A2
Woodlands, The U.S.A. 30°9N 95°29W 314 F7
Woodlark I. Papua N. G. 9°10S 152°50E 286 E7
Woodmont U.S.A. 38°59N 77°5W 143 B3
Woodonga Australia 36°10S 146°50E 281 F4
Woodridge Canada 49°20N 96°9W 297 D9
Woodroffe, Mt. Australia 26°20S 131°45E 279 E5
Woods, L. Australia 17°50S 133°30E 280 B1
Woods, L. of the N. Amer. 49°15N 94°45W 297 D10
Woods Bay Canada 45°8N 79°59W 312 A5
Woodside S. Austral., Australia 34°58S 138°52E 282 C3
Woodside Vic., Australia 38°31S 146°52E 283 E7
Woodside London, U.K. 51°23N 0°4W 125 B3
Woodside N.Y., U.S.A. 40°44N 73°54W 132 B2
Woodson U.S.A. 39°37N 90°14W 310 E6
Woodstock N.S.W., Australia 33°45S 148°53E 283 B8
Woodstock Queens., Australia 19°35S 146°50E 280 B4
Woodstock N.B., Canada 46°11N 67°37W 299 C6
Woodstock Ont., Canada 43°10N 80°45W 312 C4
Woodstock Western Cape, S. Africa 33°55S 18°27E 118 A1
Woodstock Oxon., U.K. 51°51N 1°20W 169 F6
Woodstock Ga., U.S.A. 34°6N 84°31W 316 A5
Woodstock Ill., U.S.A. 42°19N 88°27W 311 B8
Woodstock N.Y., U.S.A. 42°2N 74°7W 313 D10
Woodstock Vt., U.S.A. 43°37N 72°31W 313 C12
Woodsville U.S.A. 44°9N 72°2W 313 B13
Woodview Canada 44°35N 78°8W 312 B6
Woodville N.Z. 40°20S 175°53E 284 G4
Woodville Fla., U.S.A. 30°19N 84°15W 316 E5
Woodville Ga., U.S.A. 33°40N 83°7W 316 B6
Woodville Miss., U.S.A. 31°6N 91°18W 314 F9
Woodville Ohio, U.S.A. 41°27N 83°22W 311 C13
Woodville Tex., U.S.A. 30°47N 94°25W 314 F7
Woodward U.S.A. 36°26N 99°24W 314 C5
Woody U.S.A. 35°42N 118°50W 307 K8
Woody → Canada 52°31N 100°51W 297 C8
Woolacombe U.K. 51°10N 4°13W 169 F3
Woolamai, C. Australia 38°30S 145°23E 283 E6
Woolbrook Australia 30°56S 151°25E 283 A9
Wooler U.K. 55°33N 2°1W 168 B5
Woolgoolga Australia 30°6S 153°11E 281 E5
Woollahra Australia 33°53S 151°15E 139 B2
Woolloomooloo Sydney, Australia 139 b2
Woolooware B. Australia 34°1S 151°8E 139 C1
Woolwich U.K. 51°29N 0°4E 125 B4
Woolworth Building New York, U.S.A. 132 e1
Woomargama △ Australia 35°50S 147°15E 283 C7
Woomera Australia 31°5S 136°50E 282 A2
Woonsocket R.I., U.S.A. 42°0N 71°31W 313 E13
Woonsocket S. Dak., U.S.A. 44°3N 98°17W 308 C4
Wooramel → Australia 25°47S 114°10E 279 E1
Wooramel Roadhouse Australia 25°45S 114°17E 279 E1
Wooroonooran △ Australia 16°25S 146°1E 280 B4
Wooster U.S.A. 40°48N 81°56W 312 F3
Woqooyi Galbeed □ Somali Rep. 10°0N 44°30E 267 C5
Woraksan △ S. Korea 36°50N 128°5E 224 D4
Worcester Western Cape, S. Africa 33°39S 19°27E 270 D2
Worcester Worcs., U.K. 52°11N 2°12W 169 E5
Worcester Mass., U.S.A. 42°16N 71°48W 313 D13
Worcester N.Y., U.S.A. 42°36N 74°45W 313 D10
Worcestershire □ U.K. 52°13N 2°10W 169 E5
Worden U.S.A. 38°56N 89°50W 310 F7
Wörgl Austria 47°29N 12°3E 180 D5
Worker's Stadium China 39°55N 116°25E 114 B2
Workington U.K. 54°39N 3°33W 168 C4
Worksop U.K. 53°18N 1°7W 168 D6
Workum Neths. 52°59N 5°26E 170 B5
Worland U.S.A. 44°1N 107°57W 304 D10
World Bank Washington, D.C., U.S.A. 143 b1
World Financial Center New York, U.S.A. 132 e1
World Financial Centre China 31°14N 121°30E 138 B2
World Trade Center, Site of former = Ground Zero New York, U.S.A. 132 e1
World War Two Memorial Washington, D.C., U.S.A. 143 b1
Worli India 19°1N 72°49E 130 A1
Wormhout France 50°52N 2°28E 173 B9
Worms Germany 49°37N 8°21E 179 F4
Worsley Canada 56°31N 119°8W 296 B5
Wörth Bayern, Germany 49°1N 12°24E 179 F8
Worth Ill., U.S.A. 41°41N 87°47W 119 C2
Wortham U.S.A. 31°47N 96°28W 314 F6
Wörther See Austria 46°37N 14°10E 180 E7
Worthing U.K. 50°49N 0°21W 169 G7
Worthington Ind., U.S.A. 39°7N 86°59W 311 E10
Worthington Minn., U.S.A. 43°37N 95°36W 308 D6
Worthington Ohio, U.S.A. 40°5N 83°1W 311 D13
Worthington Pa., U.S.A. 40°50N 79°38W 312 F5
Wosi Indonesia 0°15S 128°0E 231 E7
Wote Kenya 1°47S 37°38E 268 C4
Wotjalum ⊙ Australia 16°30S 123°45E 278 C3
Wotjobaluk ⊙ Australia 37°0S 142°0E 281 C3
Wou-han = Wuhan China 30°31N 114°18E 229 B10
Wour Chad 21°14N 16°0E 259 D3
Wousi = Wuxi China 31°33N 120°18E 229 B13
Wowoni Indonesia 4°5S 123°5E 231 E6
Woy Woy Australia 33°30S 151°19E 283 B9
Wrangel I. = Vrangelya, Ostrov Russia 71°0N 180°0E 215 B18
Wrangell U.S.A. 56°28N 132°23W 296 B2
Wrangell Mts. U.S.A. 61°30N 142°0W 303 F12
Wrangell-St. Elias △ U.S.A. 61°0N 142°0W 303 F12
Wrath, C. U.K. 58°38N 5°1W 167 C3
Wray U.S.A. 40°5N 102°13W 304 F12
Wrekin, The U.K. 52°41N 2°32W 169 E5
Wrens U.S.A. 33°12N 82°23W 316 B7
Wren's Nest U.S.A. 33°44N 84°25W 113 B2
Wrexham U.K. 53°3N 3°0W 168 D4
Wrexham □ U.K. 53°1N 2°58W 168 D5
Wriezen Germany 52°42N 14°7E 178 C10
Wright = Paranas Phil. 11°42N 125°2E 233 F5
Wright Fla., U.S.A. 30°27N 86°38W 317 E3
Wright Wyo., U.S.A. 43°45N 105°28W 304 E11
Wright Pt. Canada 43°48N 81°44W 312 C3
Wrightmyo India 11°47N 92°43E 245 J11
Wrightson, Mt. U.S.A. 31°42N 110°51W 305 L8
Wrightsville U.S.A. 32°44N 82°43W 316 C7
Wrightwood U.S.A. 34°22N 117°38W 307 L9
Wrigley Canada 63°16N 123°37W 294 E7
Wrigley Building Chicago, U.S.A. 119 b2
Wrigley Field U.S.A. 41°56N 87°39W 119 B3
Wrocław Poland 51°5N 17°5E 185 G4
Wronki Poland 52°41N 16°21E 185 F3
Września Poland 52°21N 17°36E 185 F4
Wschowa Poland 51°48N 16°20E 185 G3
Wu Hsi → Taiwan 24°9N 120°31E 225 B2
Wu Jiang → China 29°40N 107°20E 228 C6
Wu Kau Tang China 22°30N 114°14E 219 a
Wu Xia China 31°2N 110°10E 229 B8
Wu'an China 36°40N 114°15E 226 F8
Wubalawun ⊙ Australia 15°28S 133°1E 278 C5
Wubin Australia 30°6S 116°37E 279 F2
Wubu China 37°28N 110°42E 226 F6
Wuchang China 44°55N 127°5E 227 B14
Wucheng China 37°12N 116°20E 226 F9
Wuch'i Taiwan 24°16N 120°31E 225 B2
Wuchieh Taiwan 24°41N 121°47E 225 B3
Wuchow = Wuzhou China 23°30N 111°18E 229 F8
Wuchuan Guangdong, China 21°33N 110°43E 229 G8
Wuchuan Guizhou, China 28°25N 108°3E 228 C7
Wuchuan Nei Monggol Zizhiqu, China 41°5N 111°28E 226 D6
Wuda China 39°29N 106°42E 226 E4
Wudang Shan China 32°23N 111°2E 229 A8
Wuday'ah Si. Arabia 17°2N 47°7E 248 C4
Wudi China 37°40N 117°35E 227 F9
Wuding China 25°24N 102°21E 228 E4
Wuding He → China 37°2N 110°23E 226 F6
Wudinna Australia 33°0S 135°22E 281 E2
Wudongde Dam China 26°20N 102°15E 228 D4
Wudu China 33°22N 104°54E 226 H3
Wufeng Henan, China 30°12N 110°42E 229 B8
Wufeng Taiwan 24°4N 120°42E 225 B2
Wugang China 26°44N 110°35E 229 D8
Wugong Shan China 27°30N 114°0E 229 D9
Wuguishan China 22°25N 113°25E 219 a
Wugullar = Beswick Australia 14°34S 132°53E 278 B5
Wuhai China 39°39N 106°48E 226 E4
Wuhan China 30°31N 114°18E 229 B10
Wuhe China 33°10N 117°50E 227 H9
Wuhlgarten Germany 52°31N 13°34E 115 A4
Wuhsi = Wuxi China 31°33N 120°18E 229 B13
Wuhu China 31°22N 118°21E 229 B12
Wujiang China 31°10N 120°38E 229 B13
Wujiaochang China 31°18N 121°31E 138 B2
Wujih Taiwan 24°6N 120°38E 225 B2
Wukari Nigeria 7°51N 9°42E 263 D6
Wulai Taiwan 24°52N 121°33E 225 B3
Wulajie China 44°6N 126°33E 227 B14
Wulanbulang China 41°5N 110°55E 226 D6
Wular L. India 34°20N 74°30E 243 B6
Wulehe Ghana 8°39N 0°0 263 D5
Wulff Land Greenland 82°0N 49°0W 154 A6
Wulian China 35°40N 119°12E 227 G10
Wulian Feng China 27°48N 103°36E 228 D4
Wuliang Shan China 24°30N 100°40E 228 E3
Wuliaru Indonesia 7°27S 131°0E 231 F8
Wulicheng Taiwan 23°47N 121°0E 225 C3
Wuling Shan China 30°0N 110°0E 228 C7
Wulingyuan △ China 29°20N 110°32E 229 C8
Wulong China 29°22N 107°43E 228 C6
Wulong △ China 31°8N 103°5E 228 B4
Wulu Taiwan 23°10N 121°2E 225 C3
Wulumuchi = Ürümqi China 43°45N 87°45E 217 D11
Wum Cameroon 6°24N 10°2E 263 D7
Wumeng Shan China 26°48N 104°0E 228 D5
Wuming China 23°12N 108°18E 228 F7
Wun Rog Sudan 9°0N 28°20E 257 F2
Wundanyi Kenya 3°24S 38°22E 268 C4
Wuning China 29°17N 115°5E 229 C10
Wunna → India 20°18N 78°48E 244 D4
Wunnummin L. Canada 52°55N 89°10W 298 B2
Wunsiedel Germany 50°2N 12°0E 179 E8
Wunstorf Germany 52°25N 9°26E 178 C5
Wuntho Burma 23°55N 95°45E 241 D5
Wupatki △ U.S.A. 35°35N 111°20W 305 J8
Wuping China 25°5N 116°5E 229 E11
Wuppertal Nordrhein-Westfalen, Germany 51°16N 7°12E 178 D3
Wuppertal Western Cape, S. Africa 32°13S 19°12E 270 D2
Wuqia China 39°40N 75°7E 217 E9
Wuqing China 39°23N 117°4E 227 E9
Würm → Germany 48°8N 11°27E 131 B1
Würm-kanal Germany 48°13N 11°29E 131 A1
Wurralibi ⊙ Australia 15°43S 137°1E 280 B2
Wurtsboro U.S.A. 41°35N 74°29W 313 E10
Würzburg Germany 49°46N 9°55E 179 F5
Wurzen Germany 51°22N 12°44E 178 D8
Wushan China 34°43N 104°53E 226 G3
Wushi China 41°9N 79°13E 217 D9
Wushishi Nigeria 9°46N 6°7E 263 D6
Wusi Vanuatu 15°21S 166°40E 287 E4
Wusih = Wuxi China 31°33N 120°18E 229 B13
Wusong China 31°22N 121°29E 138 A1
Wutach → Germany 47°37N 8°15E 179 H4
Wutai China 38°40N 113°12E 226 E7
Wutai Shan China 39°3N 113°32E 226 E7
Wuting = Huimin China 37°27N 117°28E 227 F9
Wutong China 25°24N 110°4E 229 E8
Wutonghaolai China 42°50N 120°5E 227 C11
Wutongqiao China 29°22N 103°50E 228 C4
Wutung Papua N. G. 2°37S 141°1E 286 B1
Wuwei Anhui, China 31°18N 117°54E 229 B11
Wuwei Gansu, China 37°57N 102°34E 218 D9
Wuxi Jiangsu, China 31°33N 120°18E 229 B13
Wuxi Sichuan, China 31°23N 109°35E 228 B7
Wuxiang China 36°49N 112°50E 226 F7
Wuxuan China 23°34N 109°38E 228 F7
Wuxue China 29°52N 115°30E 229 C10
Wuyang China 33°25N 113°35E 226 H7
Wuyi Hebei, China 37°46N 115°56E 226 F8
Wuyi Zhejiang, China 28°52N 119°50E 229 C12
Wuyi Shan China 27°0N 117°0E 229 D11
Wuyishan China 27°45N 118°0E 229 D12
Wuyishan △ China 27°55N 117°54E 229 D11
Wuyo Nigeria 10°23N 11°50E 263 C7
Wuyuan Jiangxi, China 29°15N 117°50E 229 C11
Wuyuan Nei Monggol Zizhiqu, China 41°2N 108°20E 226 D5
Wuzhai China 38°54N 111°48E 226 E6
Wuzhi Shan China 18°45N 109°45E 236 C7
Wuzhong China 38°2N 106°12E 226 E4
Wuzhou China 23°30N 111°18E 229 F8
Wuzishan = Tongshi China 18°30N 109°20E 236 C7
Wyaaba Cr. → Australia 16°27S 141°35E 280 B3
Wyalkatchem Australia 31°8S 117°22E 279 F2
Wyalusing U.S.A. 41°40N 76°16W 313 E8
Wyandotte U.S.A. 42°12N 83°9W 311 B13
Wyandra Australia 27°12S 145°56E 281 D4
Wyangala, L. Australia 33°54S 149°0E 283 B8
Wyara, L. Australia 28°42S 144°14E 281 D3
Wycheproof Australia 36°5S 143°17E 282 D5
Wycliffe Well Australia 20°48S 134°14E 280 C1
Wyczółki Poland 52°9N 20°59E 142 C1
Wye → U.K. 51°38N 2°40W 169 F5
Wyemandoo Australia 28°28S 118°29E 279 E2
Wygoda Poland 52°15N 21°7E 142 B2
Wyk Germany 54°41N 8°33E 178 A4
Wymondham U.K. 52°35N 1°7E 169 E9
Wymore U.S.A. 40°7N 96°40W 308 E5
Wynberg S. Africa 34°2S 18°28E 118 B1
Wyndham W. Austral., Australia 15°33S 128°3E 278 C4
Wyndham N.Z. 46°20S 168°51E 285 G3
Wynne U.S.A. 35°14N 90°47W 315 D9
Wynyard Tas., Australia 41°5S 145°44E 281 G4
Wynyard Sask., Canada 51°45N 104°10W 297 C8
Wyola L. Australia 29°8S 130°17E 279 E5
Wyoming Ont., Canada 42°57N 82°7W 312 D2
Wyoming Ill., U.S.A. 41°4N 89°47W 310 C7
Wyoming Iowa, U.S.A. 42°4N 91°0W 310 B6
Wyoming Mich., U.S.A. 42°54N 85°42W 311 B11
Wyoming □ U.S.A. 43°0N 107°30W 304 E10
Wyomissing U.S.A. 40°20N 75°59W 313 F9
Wyong Australia 33°14S 151°24E 283 B9
Wyperfeld △ Australia 35°35S 141°42E 282 C4
Wyrzysk Poland 53°10N 17°17E 185 E4
Wyśmierzyce Poland 51°37N 20°50E 185 G7
Wysoka Poland 53°13N 17°2E 185 E4
Wysokie Poland 50°55N 22°40E 185 H9
Wysokie Mazowieckie Poland 52°55N 22°30E 185 F9
Wyszków Poland 52°36N 21°25E 185 F8
Wyszogród Poland 52°23N 20°9E 185 F7
Wytheville U.S.A. 36°57N 81°5W 309 G13
Wyżyna Małopolska Poland 50°45N 20°0E 185 H7

X

Xa-Cassau Angola 9°5S 20°15E 265 D4
Xa-Muteba Angola 9°34S 17°50E 265 D3
Xaafuun Somali Rep. 10°25N 51°16E 267 B7
Xaafuun, Ras Somali Rep. 10°27N 51°24E 267 B7
Xabregas Portugal 38°43N 9°6W 126 A2
Xaçmaz Azerbaijan 41°31N 48°42E 191 K9
Xaghra Malta 36°3N 14°16E 206 E7
Xai-Xai Mozam. 25°6S 33°31E 271 C5
Xaidulla China 36°28N 77°59E 217 E9
Xaignabouri = Sayaboury Laos 19°15N 101°45E 236 C3
Xainza China 30°58N 88°35E 218 E6
Xalapa Mexico 19°32N 96°55W 319 D5
Xalin Somali Rep. 9°6N 48°37E 267 C6
Xallas → Spain 42°54N 9°8W 194 C1
Xambioá Brazil 6°25S 48°40W 332 C2
Xangongo Angola 16°45S 15°5E 265 F3
Xankändi Azerbaijan 39°52N 46°49E 213 C12
Xanlar Azerbaijan 40°37N 46°12E 191 K8
Xanten Germany 51°39N 6°26E 178 D2
Xanthi Greece 41°10N 24°58E 203 E8
Xanthi □ Greece 41°10N 24°58E 203 E8
Xanthos Turkey 36°19N 29°18E 205 E11
Xanxerê Brazil 26°53S 52°23W 335 B5
Xapuri Brazil 10°35S 68°35W 330 C4
Xar Moron He → China 43°25N 120°35E 227 C11
Xarardheere Somali Rep. 4°33N 47°38E 267 D6
Xarrë Albania 39°44N 20°3E 206 B10
Xátiva Spain 38°59N 0°32W 197 G4
Xau, L. Botswana 21°15S 24°44E 270 B3
Xavantina Brazil 21°15S 52°48W 335 A5
Xayar China 41°13N 82°48E 217 D10
Xebert China 44°2N 122°0E 227 B12
Xenia U.S.A. 39°41N 83°56W 311 E13
Xeropotamos → Cyprus 34°42N 32°33E 207 F8
Xertigny France 48°3N 6°24E 173 D13
Xewkija Malta 36°2N 14°15E 206 E7
Xhora S. Africa 31°55S 28°38E 271 D4
Xhumo Botswana 21°7S 24°35E 270 B3
Xi Jiang → China 22°5N 113°20E 229 F9
Xi Ujimqin Qi China 44°32N 117°40E 227 B9
Xi Xian Henan, China 32°20N 114°43E 229 A10
Xi Xian Shanxi, China 36°41N 110°58E 226 F6
Xia Xian China 35°8N 111°12E 226 G6
Xiachengzi China 44°40N 130°18E 227 B16
Xiachuan Dao China 21°40N 112°40E 229 G9
Xiajiang China 27°30N 115°10E 229 D10
Xiajin China 36°56N 116°0E 226 F9
Xiamen China 24°25N 118°4E 229 E12
Xi'an China 34°15N 109°0E 226 G5
Xian Xian China 38°12N 116°6E 226 E9
Xianfeng China 29°40N 109°8E 228 C7
Xiang Jiang → China 28°55N 112°50E 229 C9
Xiang Khouang Laos 19°17N 103°25E 236 C4
Xiangcheng Henan, China 33°50N 113°27E 226 H7
Xiangcheng Sichuan, China 28°53N 99°47E 228 C2
Xiangdu China 23°13N 106°58E 228 F6
Xiangfan China 32°2N 112°8E 229 A9
Xianggang = Hong Kong □ China 22°11N 114°14E 229 F10
Xianghuang Qi China 42°2N 113°50E 226 C7
Xiangjiaba Dam China 28°37N 104°17E 228 C5
Xiangning China 35°58N 110°50E 226 G6
Xiangquan China 36°30N 113°1E 226 F7
Xiangquan He = Sutlej → Pakistan 29°23N 71°3E 242 E4
Xiangshan China 29°29N 121°51E 229 C13
Xiangshui China 34°12N 119°33E 227 G10
Xiangtan China 27°51N 112°54E 229 D9
Xiangxiang China 27°43N 112°28E 229 D9
Xiangyin China 28°38N 112°54E 229 C9
Xiangyun China 25°34N 100°35E 228 E3
Xiangzhou China 23°58N 109°40E 228 F7
Xianju China 28°51N 120°44E 229 C13
Xianning China 29°51N 114°16E 229 C10
Xianshui He → China 30°10N 100°59E 228 B3
Xiantao China 30°25N 113°25E 229 B9
Xianyang China 34°20N 108°40E 226 G5
Xianyou China 25°22N 118°38E 229 E12
Xiao Hinggan Ling China 49°0N 127°0E 219 B14
Xiao Xian China 34°15N 116°55E 226 G9
Xiaofeng China 30°35N 119°32E 229 B12
Xiaogan China 30°52N 113°55E 229 B9
Xiaogang Park China 23°6N 113°16E 121 B2
Xiaojin China 30°59N 102°21E 228 B4
Xiaolan China 22°38N 113°13E 229 F9
Xiaoping China 22°13N 113°13E 121 A2
Xiaoshan China 30°12N 120°18E 229 B13
Xiaowutai Shan China 39°51N 114°59E 226 E8
Xiaoyi China 37°8N 111°48E 226 F6
Xiapu China 26°54N 119°59E 229 D12
Xiasha chong China 23°8N 113°9E 121 B1
Xiashan = Zhanjiang China 21°15N 110°20E 229 G8
Xiawa China 42°35N 120°38E 227 C11
Xiayi China 34°15N 116°10E 226 G9
Xichang Guangdong, China 23°9N 113°13E 121 B2
Xichang Sichuan, China 27°51N 102°19E 228 D4
Xicheng Beijing, China 114 b1
Xichong China 30°57N 105°54E 228 B5
Xichou China 23°25N 104°42E 228 E5
Xichuan China 33°0N 111°30E 226 H6
Xidan China 39°52N 116°20E 114 B2
Xide China 28°8N 102°19E 228 C4
Xiemahe China 31°38N 111°12E 229 B8
Xifei He → China 32°45N 116°40E 226 H9
Xifeng Gansu, China 35°40N 107°40E 226 G4
Xifeng Guizhou, China 27°7N 106°42E 228 D6
Xifeng Liaoning, China 42°42N 124°45E 227 C13
Xifengzhen = Xifeng China 35°40N 107°40E 226 G4
Xigazê China 29°5N 88°45E 218 F6
Xihe China 34°2N 105°20E 226 G3
Xihua China 33°45N 114°30E 226 H8
Xilagani Greece 40°58N 25°28E 203 F9
Xili Shuiku China 22°36N 113°57E 219 a
Xiliao He → China 43°32N 123°35E 227 C12
Xilin China 24°30N 105°6E 228 E5
Xiling Gorge = Xiling Xia China 30°54N 110°48E 229 B8
Xiling Xia China 30°54N 110°48E 229 B8
Xilinhot China 43°52N 116°2E 226 C9
Xilokastro Greece 38°5N 22°38E 204 C4
Xiluodu Dam China 28°12N 103°34E 228 C4
Ximana Mozam. 19°24S 33°58E 269 F3
Xime Guinea-Biss. 11°59N 14°57W 262 C2
Ximeng China 22°50N 99°27E 228 F2
Ximiao China 40°59N 100°12E 218 C9
Xin Jiang → China 28°45N 116°35E 229 C11
Xin Xian = Xinzhou China 38°22N 112°46E 226 E7
Xin'anjiang Shuiku China 29°33N 118°56E 229 C12
Xinavane Mozam. 25°2S 32°47E 271 C5
Xinbin China 41°40N 125°2E 224 B2
Xincai China 32°43N 114°58E 229 A10
Xinchang China 29°28N 120°52E 229 C13
Xincheng Guangxi Zhuangzu, China 24°5N 108°39E 228 E7
Xincheng Jiangxi, China 26°48N 114°6E 229 D10
Xinchengzi China 42°2N 123°30E 224 A1
Xinfeng Guangdong, China 24°5N 114°16E 229 E10
Xinfeng Jiangxi, China 27°7N 116°11E 229 D11
Xinfeng Jiangxi, China 25°27N 114°58E 229 E10
Xinfengjiang Shuiku China 23°52N 114°30E 229 F10
Xing Xian China 38°27N 111°7E 226 E6
Xing'an Guangxi Zhuangzu, China 25°38N 110°40E 229 E8
Xingan Jiangxi, China 27°46N 115°20E 229 D10
Xingcheng China 40°40N 120°45E 227 D11
Xingguo China 26°21N 115°21E 229 D10
Xinghe China 40°55N 113°55E 226 D7
Xinghua China 32°58N 119°48E 227 H10
Xinghua Wan China 25°15N 119°20E 229 E12
Xinglong China 40°25N 117°30E 227 D9
Xingning China 24°3N 115°42E 229 E10
Xingping China 34°20N 108°28E 226 G5
Xingren China 25°24N 105°11E 228 E5
Xingshan China 31°15N 110°45E 229 B8
Xingtai China 37°3N 114°32E 226 F8
Xingu → Brazil 1°30S 51°53W 329 D7
Xingwen China 28°22N 104°50E 228 C5
Xingxingxia China 41°47N 95°0E 218 C8
Xingyang China 34°45N 112°52E 226 G7
Xingyi China 25°3N 104°59E 228 E5
Xinhe Hebei, China 37°30N 115°15E 226 F8
Xinhe Xinjiang Uygur, China 41°33N 82°37E 217 D10
Xinhua China 27°42N 111°13E 229 D8
Xinhuang China 27°21N 109°12E 228 D7
Xinhui China 22°25N 113°0E 229 F9
Xining China 36°34N 101°40E 218 D9
Xinjian China 28°37N 115°46E 229 C10
Xinjiang China 35°34N 111°11E 226 G6
Xinjiang Uygur Zizhiqu □ China 42°0N 86°0E 217 D11
Xinjin = Pulandian China 39°25N 121°58E 227 E11
Xinjin China 30°24N 103°47E 228 B4
Xinkai He → China 43°32N 123°35E 227 C12
Xinken China 22°39N 113°36E 219 a
Xinle China 38°25N 114°40E 226 E8
Xinlitun China 42°0N 122°8E 227 D12
Xinlong China 30°57N 100°12E 228 B3
Xinmin China 41°59N 122°50E 224 B1
Xinning China 26°28N 110°50E 229 D8
Xinping China 24°5N 101°59E 228 E3
Xinshao China 27°21N 111°26E 229 D8
Xintai China 35°55N 117°45E 227 G9
Xintian China 25°55N 112°13E 229 E9
Xinwan China 22°47N 113°40E 219 a
Xinxiang China 35°18N 113°50E 226 G7
Xinxing China 22°35N 112°15E 229 F9
Xinyang China 32°6N 114°3E 229 A10
Xinye China 32°30N 112°21E 229 A9
Xinyi Guangdong, China 22°25N 111°0E 229 F8
Xinyi Nei Monggol Zizhiqu, China 34°23N 118°21E 227 G10
Xinyu China 27°49N 114°58E 229 D10
Xinzhan China 43°50N 127°18E 227 C14
Xinzheng China 34°20N 113°45E 226 G7
Xinzhou Hainan, China 19°43N 109°17E 236 C7
Xinzhou Hubei, China 30°50N 114°48E 229 B10
Xinzhou Shanxi, China 38°22N 112°46E 226 E7
Xinzo de Limia Spain 42°3N 7°47W 194 C3
Xiongyuecheng China 40°12N 122°5E 227 D12
Xiping Henan, China 33°22N 114°5E 226 H8
Xiping Henan, China 33°25N 111°8E 226 H6
Xiping Zhejiang, China 28°16N 119°29E 229 C12
Xique-Xique Brazil 10°50S 42°40W 332 D3
Xiruá → Brazil 6°3S 67°50W 330 B4
Xisha Qundao = Paracel Is. S. China Sea 15°50N 112°0E 230 A4
Xishuangbanna China 22°5N 101°1E 228 F3
Xishui Guizhou, China 28°19N 106°9E 228 C6
Xishui Hubei, China 30°30N 115°15E 229 B10
Xitole Guinea-Biss. 11°43N 14°50W 262 C2
Xiu Shui → China 29°13N 116°0E 229 C10
Xiuning China 29°45N 118°10E 229 C12
Xiuren China 24°27N 110°12E 229 E8
Xiushan China 28°25N 108°57E 228 C7
Xiushui China 29°2N 114°33E 229 C10
Xiuwen China 26°49N 106°32E 228 D6
Xiuyan China 40°18N 123°11E 224 B1
Xixabangma Feng China 28°20N 85°40E 243 E11
Xixia China 33°25N 111°29E 226 H6
Xixiang Guangdong, China 22°34N 113°52E 219 a
Xixiang Shaanxi, China 33°0N 107°44E 226 H4
Xixón = Gijón Spain 43°32N 5°42W 194 B5
Xiyang China 37°38N 113°38E 226 F7
Xizang Zizhiqu □ China 32°0N 88°0E 217 F11
Xizhimen China 39°55N 116°19E 114 B1
Xlendi Malta 36°1N 14°12E 206 E6
Xochimilco, Parque Ecológico Mexico 19°18N 99°5W 128 C2
Xochob Mexico 19°21N 89°48W 319 D7
Xojayli = Khojayli Uzbekistan 42°29N 59°31E 216 D5
Xorazm □ Uzbekistan 43°0N 60°0E 216 D6
Xu Beihong Memorial Hall Beijing, China 114 a2
Xu Jiang → China 28°0N 116°25E 229 D11
Xuan Loc Vietnam 10°56N 107°14E 237 G6
Xuan'en China 30°0N 109°30E 228 C7
Xuanhan China 31°18N 107°38E 228 B6
Xuanhua China 40°40N 115°2E 226 D8
Xuanwei China 26°15N 103°59E 228 C5
Xuanwu Beijing, China 114 c1
Xuanzhou China 30°56N 118°43E 229 B12
Xuchang China 34°2N 113°48E 226 G7
Xudat Azerbaijan 41°38N 48°41E 191 K9
Xuddur Somali Rep. 4°11N 43°52E 267 D5
Xuefeng Shan China 27°5N 110°35E 229 D8
Xuejiaping China 31°39N 110°16E 229 B8
Xuhui China 31°11N 121°26E 138 B1
Xun Jiang → China 23°35N 111°30E 229 F8
Xun Xian China 35°42N 114°33E 226 G8
Xundian China 25°36N 103°15E 228 E4
Xunwu China 24°54N 115°37E 229 E10
Xunyang China 32°48N 109°22E 226 H5
Xunyi China 35°8N 108°20E 226 G5
Xupu China 27°53N 110°32E 229 D8
Xúquer → Spain 39°5N 0°10W 197 F4
Xushui China 39°2N 115°40E 226 E8
Xuwen China 20°20N 110°10E 229 G8
Xuyi China 32°55N 118°32E 229 A12
Xuyong China 28°10N 105°22E 228 C5
Xuzhou China 34°18N 117°10E 227 G9
Xylophagou Cyprus 34°54N 33°51E 207 F9

Y

Y.S. Falls Jamaica 18°9N 77°49W 320 a
Ya Xian = Sanya China 18°14N 109°29E 236 C7
Yaamba Australia 23°8S 150°22E 280 C5
Ya'an China 29°58N 103°5E 228 C4
Yaapeet Australia 35°45S 142°3E 282 C5
Yaba Nigeria 6°30N 3°22E 124 A2
Yabassi Cameroon 4°30N 9°57E 263 E6
Yabayo Ivory C. 5°56N 6°36W 262 D3
Yabelo Ethiopia 4°50N 38°8E 257 G4
Yabelo ⌂ Ethiopia 6°0N 37°50E 257 F4
Yablanitsa Bulgaria 43°2N 24°5E 203 C8
Yablonovyy Khrebet Russia 53°0N 114°0E 215 D12
Yablonovyy Ra. = Yablonovyy Khrebet Russia 53°0N 114°0E 215 D12
Yabluniv Ukraine 48°24N 24°57E 183 B9
Yablunytsya Ukraine 48°19N 24°29E 183 B9
Yabrai Shan China 39°40N 103°0E 226 E2
Yabrūd Syria 33°58N 36°39E 250 E7
Yabucoa Puerto Rico 18°3N 65°53W 321 b
Yacambú △ Venezuela 9°42N 69°27W 328 B4
Yacheng China 18°22N 109°6E 236 C7
Yackandandah Australia 36°18S 146°52E 283 D7
Yacuiba Bolivia 22°0S 63°43W 334 A3
Yacuma → Bolivia 13°38S 65°23W 331 C4
Yadgir India 16°45N 77°5E 244 F3
Yadkin → U.S.A. 35°23N 80°4W 315 D14
Yadong China 27°26N 88°56E 241 B2
Yadrin Russia 55°57N 46°12E 190 C8
Yadua Fiji 16°49S 178°18E 287 A2
Yaeyama-Rettō Japan 24°30N 123°40E 221 M1
Yafran Libya 32°4N 12°31E 258 B2
Yafran □ Libya 32°0N 12°20E 258 B2
Yaftābād Iran 35°37N 51°17E 141 B1
Yagaba Ghana 10°14N 1°20W 263 C4
Yagaji-shima Japan 26°39N 128°0E 288 a
Yagasa Cluster Fiji 18°57S 178°28W 287 B3
Yağcılar Turkey 39°25N 28°23E 205 B10
Yagodnoye Russia 62°33N 149°40E 215 C15
Yagoua Cameroon 10°20N 15°13E 259 F3
Yaguas → Peru 2°45S 70°10W 328 D3
Yahara Japan 35°44N 139°37E 140 A2
Yahila Orientale, Dem. Rep. of the Congo 0°13N 24°28E 264 B4
Yahila Orientale, Dem. Rep. of the Congo 1°48N 23°37E 264 B4
Yahk Canada 49°6N 116°10W 296 D5
Yaho Japan 35°40N 139°26E 140 A1
Yahotyn Ukraine 50°17N 31°46E 189 G6
Yahuma Dem. Rep. of the Congo 1°0N 23°10E 264 B4
Yahyalı Turkey 38°5N 35°2E 212 C6
Yaita Japan 36°48N 139°56E 221 F9
Yaiza Canary Is. 28°57N 13°46W 153 e2
Yaizu Japan 34°52N 138°20E 223 C10
Yajiang China 30°2N 100°57E 228 B3
Yajua Nigeria 11°27N 12°49E 263 C7
Yakacık Turkey 36°46N 36°11E 250 B7
Yakage Japan 34°37N 133°35E 222 C5
Yakamba Dem. Rep. of the Congo 2°42N 19°38E 264 B3
Yakapınar Turkey 36°57N 35°36E 250 B6
Yakeshi China 49°17N 120°44E 219 B13
Yakima U.S.A. 46°36N 120°31W 304 C3
Yakima → U.S.A. 46°15N 119°14W 304 C4
Yakire Japan 35°45N 139°54E 140 A4
Yakishiri-Jima Japan 44°26N 141°25E 220 B10
Yako Burkina Faso 12°59N 2°15W 262 C4
Yakobi I. U.S.A. 58°0N 136°30W 296 B1
Yakoma Dem. Rep. of the Congo 4°5N 22°27E 264 B4
Yakoruda Bulgaria 42°1N 23°39E 202 D7
Yakossi C.A.R. 5°37N 23°19E 264 A4
Yakovlevka Russia 44°26N 133°28E 220 B6
Yakovlevskoye = Privolzhsk Russia 57°23N 41°16E 190 B5
Yaksu S. Korea 37°34N 127°1E 137 B2
Yaku-Shima Japan 30°20N 130°30E 221 J5
Yakumo Japan 42°15N 140°16E 220 C10
Yakutat U.S.A. 59°33N 139°44W 303 G13
Yakutat B. U.S.A. 59°45N 140°45W 303 G12
Yakutia = Sakha □ Russia 66°0N 130°0E 215 C14
Yakutsk Russia 62°5N 129°50E 215 C13
Yakymivka Ukraine 46°44N 35°0E 189 J8
Yala Thailand 6°33N 101°18E 237 J3
Yala △ Sri Lanka 6°20N 81°30E 245 L5
Yalata Australia 31°59S 132°26E 279 F5
Yalata ⊙ Australia 31°35S 132°7E 279 F5
Yalboroo Australia 20°50S 148°40E 280 b
Yale U.S.A. 43°8N 82°48W 312 C2
Yalgorup △ Australia 32°39S 115°38E 279 F2
Yali Dem. Rep. of the Congo 0°4N 21°3E 264 B4
Yaligimba Dem. Rep. of the Congo 2°13N 22°56E 264 B4
Yalikanda Dem. Rep. of the Congo 0°23N 24°47E 264 B4
Yalinga C.A.R. 6°33N 23°10E 264 A4
Yalkabul, Pta. Mexico 21°32N 88°37W 319 C7
Yallahs Jamaica 17°53N 76°35W 320 a
Yallahs Hill Jamaica 17°54N 76°30W 320 a
Yalleroi Australia 24°3S 145°42E 280 C4
Yalobusha → U.S.A. 33°33N 90°10W 315 E9
Yaloké C.A.R. 5°19N 17°5E 264 A3
Yalong China 18°12N 109°42E 236 C7
Yalong Jiang → China 26°40N 101°55E 228 D3
Yalova Turkey 40°41N 29°15E 203 F13
Yalpirakinu ⊙ Australia 22°24S 132°15E 278 D5
Yalpuh, Ozero Ukraine 45°30N 28°41E 183 E13
Yalta Ukraine 44°30N 34°10E 189 K8
Yalu Jiang → China 39°55N 124°19E 224 C2
Yalvaç Turkey 38°17N 31°10E 212 C4
Yam Australia 9°54S 142°46E 280 a
Yam Ha Melah = Dead Sea Asia 31°30N 35°30E 251 G6
Yam Kinneret Israel 32°45N 35°35E 250 F6
Yamada Fukuoka, Japan 33°33N 130°49E 222 D2
Yamada Kanagawa, Japan 35°33N 139°37E 140 B2
Yamada Ōsaka, Japan 34°47N 135°32E 133 A2
Yamaga Japan 33°1N 130°41E 222 D2
Yamagata Japan 38°15N 140°15E 220 E10
Yamagata □ Japan 38°30N 140°0E 220 E10
Yamagawa Japan 31°12N 130°39E 222 F2
Yamaguchi Japan 34°10N 131°32E 222 C3
Yamaguchi □ Japan 34°20N 131°40E 222 C3
Yamal, Poluostrov Russia 71°0N 70°0E 214 B8
Yamal Pen. = Yamal, Poluostrov Russia 71°0N 70°0E 214 B8
Yamanaka Japan 36°15N 136°22E 223 A8
Yamanashi Japan 35°41N 138°40E 223 B10
Yamanashi □ Japan 35°40N 138°40E 223 B10
Yamantau, Gora Russia 54°15N 58°6E 186 D10
Yamasaki Japan 35°0N 134°32E 222 C6
Yamato Japan 35°27N 139°25E 223 B11
Yamato → Japan 34°36N 135°26E 133 B1
Yamato Ridge Sea of Japan 39°20N 135°0E 220 E7
Yamatotakada Japan 34°31N 135°45E 223 C7
Yamba Australia 29°26S 153°23E 281 D5
Yambarran Ra. Australia 15°10S 130°25E 278 C5
Yambata Dem. Rep. of the Congo 2°26N 21°58E 264 B4
Yambéring Guinea 11°50N 12°18W 262 C2
Yâmbiô Sudan 4°35N 28°16E 257 G2
Yambol Bulgaria 42°30N 26°30E 203 D10
Yambol □ Bulgaria 42°30N 26°30E 203 D10
Yamboyo Dem. Rep. of the Congo 0°40N 22°18E 264 B4
Yamburg Russia 68°21N 77°8E 214 C8
Yambuya Dem. Rep. of the Congo 1°17N 24°34E 264 B4
Yamdena Indonesia 7°45S 131°20E 231 F8
Yame Japan 33°13N 130°35E 222 D2
Yamethin Burma 20°29N 96°18E 241 E6
Y'Ami I. Phil. 21°6N 121°57E 232 A3
Yamma Yamma, L. Australia 26°16S 141°20E 281 D3
Yamoussoukro Ivory C. 6°49N 5°17W 262 D3
Yampa → U.S.A. 40°32N 108°59W 304 F9
Yampi Sd. Australia 16°8S 123°38E 278 C3
Yampil Moldova 48°15N 28°15E 177 D15
Yampol = Yampil Moldova 48°15N 28°15E 177 D15
Yamrat Nigeria 10°11N 9°55E 263 C6
Yamrukchal = Botev Bulgaria 42°44N 24°52E 203 D8
Yamuna → India 25°30N 81°53E 243 G9
Yamunanagar India 30°7N 77°17E 242 D7
Yamzho Yumco China 28°48N 90°35E 218 F7
Yan Nigeria 10°5N 12°11E 263 C7
Yan Kit Singapore 1°21N 103°58E 138 A3
Yan Oya → Sri Lanka 9°0N 81°10E 245 K5
Yana → Russia 71°30N 136°0E 215 B14
Yanagawa Japan 33°10N 130°24E 222 D2
Yanahara Japan 34°58N 134°2E 222 C6
Yanai Japan 33°58N 132°7E 222 D4
Yan'an China 36°35N 109°26E 226 F5
Yanaul Russia 56°25N 55°0E 186 C10
Yanbian China 26°47N 101°31E 228 D3
Yanbu China 23°5N 113°9E 121 B1
Yanbu 'al Baḩr Si. Arabia 24°0N 38°5E 246 F3
Yanchang China 36°43N 110°1E 226 F6
Yancheng Henan, China 33°35N 114°0E 226 H8
Yancheng Jiangsu, China 33°23N 120°8E 227 H11
Yanchep Australia 31°33S 115°37E 279 F2
Yanchi China 37°48N 107°20E 226 F4
Yanchuan China 36°51N 110°10E 226 F6
Yanco Australia 34°38S 146°27E 283 C7
Yanco Cr. → Australia 35°14S 145°35E 283 C6
Yandang Shan China 28°0N 120°25E 229 D13
Yandeyarra ⊙ Australia 21°17S 118°24E 278 D2
Yandicoogina Australia 22°49S 119°12E 278 D2
Yandina Solomon Is. 9°7S 159°13E 287 M10
Yandja Dem. Rep. of the Congo 1°41S 17°43E 264 C3
Yandongi Dem. Rep. of the Congo 2°51N 22°16E 264 B4
Yandoon Burma 17°0N 95°40E 241 G5
Yanfeng China 25°52N 101°8E 228 E3
Yanfolila Mali 11°11N 8°9W 262 C3
Yang Xian China 33°15N 107°30E 228 A6
Yang-yang S. Korea 38°4N 128°38E 224 C4
Yang-Yang Senegal 15°30N 15°20W 262 B1
Yangambi Dem. Rep. of the Congo 0°47N 24°24E 264 B4
Yangbi China 25°41N 99°58E 228 E2
Yangcheng China 35°28N 112°22E 226 G7
Yangcheon S. Korea 37°30N 126°51E 137 B1
Yangchow = Yangzhou China 32°21N 119°26E 229 A12
Yangch'ü = Taiyuan China 37°52N 112°33E 226 F7
Yangchüan = Yangquan China 37°58N 113°31E 226 F7
Yangchun China 22°11N 111°48E 229 F8
Yangdok N. Korea 39°13N 126°38E 224 C3
Yanggang-do □ N. Korea 41°15N 128°0E 224 B4
Yanggao China 40°21N 113°55E 226 D7
Yanggu China 36°8N 115°43E 226 F8
Yanghuayuan China 39°49N 116°18E 114 C1
Yangiyul Uzbekistan 41°0N 69°3E 217 D7
Yangjae S. Korea 37°29N 127°2E 137 C2
Yangjiang China 21°50N 111°59E 229 G8
Yangjiazhuang China 31°22N 121°25E 138 A1
Yangjing China 31°15N 121°32E 138 B2
Yangju S. Korea 37°47N 127°7E 224 D3
Yangliuqing China 39°2N 117°5E 227 E9
Yangmei Taiwan 24°55N 121°8E 225 B3
Yangmingshan △ Taiwan 25°9N 121°32E 225 A3
Yangon = Rangoon Burma 16°45N 96°20E 241 G6
Yangonde Dem. Rep. of the Congo 0°3N 22°43E 264 B4
Yangping China 31°12N 111°25E 229 B8
Yangpingguan China 32°58N 106°5E 228 A6
Yangpu China 31°16N 121°32E 138 B2
Yangpu Park China 31°17N 121°31E 138 B2
Yangquan China 37°58N 113°31E 226 F7
Yangsan S. Korea 35°20N 129°2E 224 E4
Yangshan China 24°30N 112°40E 229 E9
Yangshuo China 24°48N 110°29E 229 E8
Yangtse = Chang Jiang → China 31°48N 121°10E 229 B13
Yangtze Kiang = Chang Jiang → China 31°48N 121°10E 229 B13
Yangudi Rassa △ Ethiopia 10°50N 40°42E 257 E5
Yangxin China 29°50N 115°12E 229 C10
Yangyuan China 40°1N 114°10E 226 D8
Yangzhong China 32°22N 119°22E 229 A12
Yangzhou China 32°21N 119°26E 229 A12
Yanhe China 28°31N 108°29E 228 C7
Yanji China 42°59N 129°30E 227 C15
Yanjin China 28°5N 104°18E 228 C5
Yanjing China 29°7N 98°33E 228 C2
Yankari △ Nigeria 9°50N 10°28E 259 G2
Yankton U.S.A. 42°53N 97°23W 308 D5
Yankunytjatjara-Antakirinja ⊙ Australia 27°20S 134°30E 281 A1
Yannawa Thailand 13°43N 100°32E 113 B2

Yanonge *Dem. Rep. of the Congo* 0°35N 24°38E **264** B4
Yanov = Ivanava *Belarus* 52°7N 25°29E **177** B13
Yanqi *China* 42°5N 86°35E **217** D11
Yanqing *China* 40°30N 115°58E **226** D8
Yanshan *Hebei, China* 38°4N 117°22E **227** E9
Yanshan *Jiangxi, China* 28°15N 117°41E **229** C11
Yanshan *Yunnan, China* 23°35N 104°20E **228** F5
Yanshou *China* 45°28N 128°22E **227** B15
Yantabulla *Australia* 29°21S 145°0E **281** D4
Yantai *China* 37°34N 121°22E **227** F11
Yantarnyy *Russia* 54°52N 19°57E **184** D6
Yantian *China* 22°35N 114°16E **219** a
Yanting *China* 31°11N 105°24E **228** B5
Yantongshan *China* 43°17N 126°0E **227** C14
Yantra → *Bulgaria* 43°40N 25°37E **203** C9
Yanuca *Fiji* 18°24S 178°0E **287** B1
Yanununbeyan △ *Australia* 35°29S 149°24E **283** C8
Yanwa *China* 27°35N 98°55E **228** D2
Yanyuan *China* 27°25N 101°30E **228** D3
Yanzhou *China* 35°35N 116°49E **226** G9
Yao *Chad* 12°56N 17°33E **259** F3
Yao *Japan* 34°37N 135°36E **223** C7
Yao Noi, Ko *Thailand* 8°7N 98°37E **237** a
Yao Xian *China* 34°55N 108°59E **226** G5
Yao Yai, Ko *Thailand* 8°0N 98°35E **237** a
Yao'an *China* 25°31N 101°18E **228** E3
Yaoundé *Cameroon* 3°50N 11°35E **263** E7
Yaowan *China* 34°15N 118°3E **227** G10
Yap *Pac. Oc.* 9°30N 138°10E **287** R16
Yapacana △ *Venezuela* 3°49N 66°44W **328** C4
Yapehe *Dem. Rep. of the Congo* 0°13S 24°28E **264** C4
Yapei *Ghana* 9°10N 1°10W **263** D4
Yapen *Indonesia* 1°50S 136°0E **231** E9
Yapen, Selat *Indonesia* 1°20S 136°10E **231** E9
Yapero *Indonesia* 4°59S 137°11E **231** E9
Yappar → *Australia* 18°22S 141°16E **280** B3
Yapuparra ☼ *Australia* 27°15S 126°20E **279** E4
Yaqaga *Fiji* 16°35S 178°36E **287** A2
Yaqui → *Mexico* 27°37N 110°39W **318** B2
Yar-Sale *Russia* 66°50N 70°50E **214** C8
Yaracuy □ *Venezuela* 10°20N 68°45W **328** A4
Yaracuy → *Venezuela* 10°33N 68°15W **328** A4
Yaraka *Australia* 24°53S 144°3E **280** C3
Yaransk *Russia* 57°22N 47°49E **190** B8
Yarbasan *Turkey* 38°59N 28°49E **205** C10
Yardımcı Burnu *Turkey* 36°13N 30°25E **205** E12
Yare → *U.K.* 52°35N 1°38E **169** E9
Yaremcha *Ukraine* 48°27N 24°33E **183** B9
Yaren *Nauru* 0°33S 166°55E **288** H8
Yarensk *Russia* 62°11N 49°15E **186** B8
Yarfa *Si. Arabia* 24°37N 38°35E **256** C4
Yarí → *Colombia* 0°20S 72°20W **328** D3
Yarīm *Yemen* 14°20N 44°22E **248** D4
Yaritagua *Venezuela* 10°5N 69°8W **328** A4
Yarkand = Shache *China* 38°20N 77°10E **217** E9
Yarkant He → *China* 40°26N 80°59E **217** D10
Yarker *Canada* 44°23N 76°46W **313** B8
Yarkhun → *Pakistan* 36°17N 72°30E **243** A5
Yarlung Ziangbo Jiang = Brahmaputra → *Asia* 23°40N 90°35E **241** D3
Yarmouth *Canada* 43°50N 66°7W **299** D6
Yarmūk *Iraq* 33°18N 44°19E **113** B1
Yarmūk → *Syria* 32°42N 35°40E **250** F6
Yaroslavl *Russia* 57°35N 39°55E **188** D10
Yaroslavl □ *Russia* 59°20N 38°50E **188** C10
Yarra → *Trin. & Tob.* 10°48N 61°21W **323** t
Yarra Bend Park *Australia* 37°47S 145°0E **128** A2
Yarra Ranges △ *Australia* 37°40S 146°3E **283** D7
Yarra Yarra Lakes *Australia* 29°40S 115°45E **279** E2
Yarram *Australia* 38°29S 146°39E **283** E7
Yarraman *Australia* 26°50S 152°0E **281** D5
Yarras *Australia* 31°25S 152°20E **283** A10
Yarraville *Australia* 37°48S 144°53E **128** A1
Yarrawonga *Australia* 36°0S 146°0E **283** D7
Yarrie *Australia* 20°40S 120°12E **278** D3
Yartsevo *Sib., Russia* 60°20N 90°0E **215** C10
Yartsevo *Smolensk, Russia* 55°6N 32°43E **188** E7
Yarumal *Colombia* 6°58N 75°24W **328** B2
Yasa *Dem. Rep. of the Congo* 3°50S 21°25E **264** C4
Yasawa *Fiji* 16°47S 177°31E **287** A1
Yasawa Group *Fiji* 17°0S 177°23E **287** A1
Yaselda *Belarus* 52°7N 26°28E **177** B14
Yasen *Ukraine* 48°45N 24°10E **183** B9
Yashbum *Yemen* 14°19N 46°56E **248** D4
Yashi *Nigeria* 12°23N 7°54E **263** C6
Yashikera *Nigeria* 9°44N 3°29E **263** D5
Yashiro-Jima *Japan* 33°55N 132°15E **222** D4
Yashkul *Russia* 46°11N 45°21E **191** G7
Yasin *Pakistan* 36°24N 73°23E **243** A5
Yasinovataya *Ukraine* 48°7N 37°57E **189** H9
Yasinski, L. *Canada* 53°16N 77°35W **298** B4
Yasinya *Ukraine* 48°16N 24°21E **183** B9
Yasnyy *Russia* 51°1N 59°58E **216** B5
Yasothon *Thailand* 15°50N 104°10E **236** E5
Yass *Australia* 34°49S 148°54E **283** C8
Yasugi *Japan* 35°26N 133°15E **222** B5
Yāsūj *Iran* 30°31N 51°31E **247** D6
Yasuní △ *Ecuador* 1°19S 76°3W **328** D2
Yat *Niger* 20°28N 13°27E **259** D2
Yata → *Bolivia* 10°29S 65°26W **331** C4
Yata → *C.A.R.* 10°23N 22°45E **264** A4
Yata-Ngaya ⌓ *C.A.R.* 9°15N 23°25E **264** A4
Yatağan *Turkey* 37°20N 28°10E **205** D10
Yatakala *Niger* 14°50N 0°22E **263** C5
Yaté *N. Cal.* 22°9S 166°57E **288** d
Yates Center *U.S.A.* 37°53N 95°44W **308** G6
Yates Pt. *N.Z.* 44°29S 167°49E **285** E2
Yathkyed L. *Canada* 62°40N 98°0W **297** A9
Yathong *Australia* 32°37S 145°33E **283** B6
Yatolemu *Dem. Rep. of the Congo* 0°25N 24°35E **264** B4
Yatsuo *Japan* 36°34N 137°8E **223** A9
Yatsushiro *Japan* 32°30N 130°40E **222** E2
Yatsushiro-Kai *Japan* 32°30N 130°25E **222** E2
Yatta Plateau *Kenya* 2°0S 38°0E **268** C4
Yatua → *Venezuela* 1°30N 66°30W **328** C4
Yauca *Peru* 15°39S 74°35W **330** D3
Yauco *Puerto Rico* 18°2N 66°51W **321** b
Yauri *Peru* 14°47S 71°25W **330** C3
Yauya *Peru* 8°59S 77°17W **330** B2
Yauyos *Peru* 12°19S 75°50W **330** C2
Yauza → *Russia* 55°54N 37°43E **129** B4
Yaval *India* 21°10N 75°42E **244** D2
Yavarí → *Peru* 4°21S 70°2W **330** A3
Yávaros *Mexico* 26°42N 109°31W **318** B3
Yavatmal *India* 20°20N 78°15E **244** D4
Yavero → *Peru* 12°6S 72°57W **330** C3
Yavne *Israel* 31°52N 34°45E **251** G5
Yavoriv *Ukraine* 49°55N 23°20E **177** D12
Yavorov = Yavoriv *Ukraine* 49°55N 23°20E **177** D12
Yavuzeli *Turkey* 37°18N 37°24E **212** D7
Yawatahama *Japan* 33°27N 132°24E **222** D4
Yawnghwe *Burma* 20°39N 96°56E **241** E6
Yawri B. *S. Leone* 8°22N 13°0W **262** D2
Yaxi *China* 27°33N 106°41E **228** D6
Yaxian = Sanya *China* 18°14N 109°29E **236** C7
Yayama *Dem. Rep. of the Congo* 1°16S 23°7E **264** C4
Yayladağı *Turkey* 35°54N 36°3E **250** C7
Yazagyo *Burma* 23°30N 94°6E **241** D5
Yazd *Iran* 31°55N 54°27E **247** D7
Yazd □ *Iran* 32°0N 55°0E **247** D7
Yazd-e Khvāst *Iran* 31°31N 52°7E **247** D7
Yazdān *Iran* 33°30N 60°50E **240** B1
Yazıköy *Turkey* 36°40N 27°20E **205** E9
Yazman *Pakistan* 29°8N 71°45E **242** E4
Yazoo → *U.S.A.* 32°22N 90°54W **315** E9
Yazoo City *U.S.A.* 32°51N 90°25W **315** E9
Ybbs *Austria* 48°12N 15°4E **180** C8
Ybycuí △ *Paraguay* 26°5S 56°46W **334** B4
Ybytyruzú △ *Paraguay* 25°51S 56°11W **335** B4
Ye *Burma* 15°15N 97°15E **236** E1
Ye-ngan *Burma* 21°9N 96°27E **241** E6
Ye-u *Burma* 22°46N 95°26E **241** D5
Ye Xian = Laizhou *China* 37°8N 119°57E **227** F10
Ye Xian *China* 33°35N 113°25E **226** H7
Yea *Australia* 37°14S 145°26E **283** D6
Yeading *U.K.* 51°31N 0°23W **125** A1
Yebawmi *Burma* 25°15N 95°45E **241** C5
Yebbi-Souma *Chad* 21°7N 17°54E **259** D3
Yebyu *Burma* 14°15N 98°13E **236** E2
Yecheng *China* 37°54N 77°26E **217** E9
Yecheon *S. Korea* 36°39N 128°27E **224** D4
Yecla *Spain* 38°35N 1°5W **197** G3
Yécora *Mexico* 28°20N 108°58W **318** B3
Yedashe *Burma* 19°10N 96°20E **241** F6
Yedebub Biheroch Bihereseboch na Hizboch □ *Ethiopia* 12°0N 36°0E **257** F4
Yedigöller △ *Turkey* 40°55N 31°55E **212** B4
Yedikule *Turkey* 40°59N 28°55E **122** C1
Yedintsy = Edineţ *Moldova* 48°9N 27°18E **183** B12
Yedri *Chad* 22°25N 17°30E **259** D3
Yedseram → *Nigeria* 12°30N 14°5E **263** C7
Yeed *Somali Rep.* 4°33N 43°2E **267** D5
Yefremov *Russia* 53°8N 38°3E **188** F10
Yegguéba *Niger* 19°59N 12°52E **259** E2
Yeghegnadzor *Armenia* 39°44N 45°19E **213** C11
Yegorlyk → *Russia* 46°35N 41°57E **191** G5
Yegorlykskaya *Russia* 46°35N 40°35E **191** G5
Yegoryevsk *Russia* 55°27N 38°55E **188** E10
Yegri-Dere = Ardino *Bulgaria* 41°34N 25°9E **203** E9
Yegros *Paraguay* 26°20S 56°25W **334** B4
Yehbuah *Indonesia* 8°23S 114°45E **231** J17
Yehuda, Midbar *Israel* 31°35N 35°15E **251** G6
Yei *Sudan* 4°9N 30°40E **257** G3
Yei, Nahr → *Sudan* 6°15N 30°13E **257** F3
Yeji *Ghana* 8°13N 0°39W **263** D4
Yejmiadzin *Armenia* 40°12N 44°19E **191** K7
Yekaterinburg *Russia* 56°50N 60°30E **214** D7
Yekaterinenshtadt = Marks *Russia* 51°45N 46°50E **190** E8
Yekaterinodar = Krasnodar *Russia* 45°5N 39°0E **191** H4
Yekumbe *Dem. Rep. of the Congo* 1°2S 23°27E **264** C4
Yelan *Russia* 50°55N 43°43E **190** E6
Yelandur *India* 12°6N 77°0E **245** H3
Yelarbon *Australia* 28°33S 150°38E **281** D5
Yelatma *Russia* 55°0N 41°45E **190** C5
Yelcho, L. *Chile* 43°18S 72°18W **336** B2
Yelenovka = Sevan *Armenia* 40°33N 44°56E **191** K7
Yelenovskiye Karyery = Dokuchayevsk *Ukraine* 47°44N 37°40E **189** J9
Yelets *Russia* 52°40N 38°30E **189** F10
Yélimané *Mali* 15°9N 10°34W **262** B2
Yelin = Lingshui *China* 18°27N 110°0E **236** C8
Yelizavetgrad = Kirovohrad *Ukraine* 48°35N 32°20E **189** H7
Yelizovo *Russia* 53°11N 158°23E **215** D16
Yell *U.K.* 60°35N 1°5W **167** A7
Yell Sd. *U.K.* 60°33N 1°15W **167** A7
Yellamanchilli = Elamanchili *India* 17°33N 82°50E **244** F6
Yellandu *India* 17°39N 80°23E **244** F5
Yellapur *India* 14°58N 74°43E **245** G2
Yellareddi *India* 18°12N 78°2E **244** E4
Yellow = Huang He → *China* 37°55N 118°50E **227** F10
Yellow → *U.S.A.* 30°30N 87°0W **317** E3
Yellow Sea *China* 35°0N 123°0E **227** G12
Yellowhead Pass *Canada* 52°53N 118°25W **296** C5
Yellowknife *Canada* 62°27N 114°29W **296** A6
Yellowknife → *Canada* 62°31N 114°19W **296** A6
Yellowstone → *U.S.A.* 47°59N 103°59W **304** C12
Yellowstone △ *U.S.A.* 44°40N 110°30W **304** D8
Yellowstone L. *U.S.A.* 44°27N 110°22W **304** D8
Yelnya *Russia* 54°35N 33°15E **188** E7
Yelsk *Belarus* 51°50N 29°10E **177** C15
Yelwa *Nigeria* 10°49N 4°41E **263** C5
Yemanzhelinsk *Russia* 54°58N 61°18E **216** B6
Yemassee *U.S.A.* 32°41N 80°51W **316** C9
Yembongo *Dem. Rep. of the Congo* 3°12N 19°2E **264** B3
Yemen ■ *Asia* 15°0N 44°0E **248** D4
Yemin Moshe *Jerusalem* **123** b2
Yemmiganur *India* 15°44N 77°29E **245** G3
Yen Bai *Vietnam* 21°42N 104°52E **228** G5
Yenagoa *Nigeria* 4°58N 6°16E **263** E6
Yenakiyeve *Ukraine* 48°15N 38°15E **189** H10
Yenakiyevo = Yenakiyeve *Ukraine* 48°15N 38°15E **189** H10
Yenangyat *Burma* 21°6N 94°48E **241** E5
Yenangyaung *Burma* 20°30N 95°0E **241** E5
Yenanma *Burma* 19°46N 94°49E **241** F5
Yenbo = Yanbu 'al Baḩr *Si. Arabia* 24°0N 38°5E **246** F3
Yenchao *Taiwan* 22°46N 120°21E **225** D2
Yenda *Australia* 34°13S 146°14E **283** C7
Yende Millimou *Guinea* 8°55N 10°10W **262** D2
Yendéré *Burkina Faso* 10°12N 4°59W **262** C4
Yendi *Ghana* 9°29N 0°1W **263** D4
Yengisar *China* 38°56N 76°9E **217** E9
Yengo *Congo* 0°22N 15°29E **264** B3
Yengo △ *Australia* 33°0S 150°55E **283** B9
Yéni *Niger* 13°30N 3°1E **263** C5
Yeni Erenköy = Yialousa *Cyprus* 35°32N 34°10E **207** E10
Yeni-Pazar = Novi Pazar *Serbia* 43°12N 20°28E **202** C4
Yenice *Ankara, Turkey* 39°14N 32°42E **212** C5
Yenice *Aydın, Turkey* 37°49N 28°35E **205** D10
Yenice *Çanakkale, Turkey* 39°55N 27°17E **205** B9
Yenice *Edirne, Turkey* 40°42N 26°9E **203** F10
Yenice *Kahramanmaraş, Turkey* 37°0N 35°4E **250** B6
Yenice → *Turkey* 37°37N 35°33E **212** D6
Yenifoça *Turkey* 38°44N 26°51E **205** C8
Yenihisar *Turkey* 37°22N 27°16E **205** D9
Yenikapı *Turkey* 41°0N 28°56E **122** B1
Yeniköy *Bursa, Turkey* 40°31N 29°22E **203** F13
Yeniköy *Çanakkale, Turkey* 39°55N 26°10E **205** B8
Yeniköy *İstanbul, Turkey* 41°6N 29°3E **122** B2
Yeniköy *Kütahya, Turkey* 38°52N 29°17E **205** C11
Yenipazar *Turkey* 37°49N 28°11E **205** D10
Yenişehir *Turkey* 40°16N 29°38E **203** F13
Yenisey → *Russia* 71°50N 82°40E **214** B9
Yeniseysk *Russia* 58°27N 92°13E **215** D10
Yeniseyskiy Zaliv *Russia* 72°20N 81°0E **214** B9
Yenki = Yanji *China* 42°59N 129°30E **227** C15
Yenne *France* 45°43N 5°44E **175** C9
Yenotayevka *Russia* 47°15N 47°0E **191** G8
Yenpu *Taiwan* 22°45N 120°35E **225** D2
Yenshui *Taiwan* 23°19N 120°16E **225** C2
Yenyuka *Russia* 57°57N 121°15E **215** D13
Yeo → *U.K.* 51°2N 2°49W **169** G5
Yeo, L. *Australia* 28°0S 124°30E **279** E3
Yeo I. *Canada* 45°24N 81°48W **312** A3
Yeoju *S. Korea* 37°20N 127°35E **224** D3
Yeola *India* 20°2N 74°30E **244** D2
Yeon-gi *S. Korea* 36°35N 127°15E **224** D3
Yeoncheon *S. Korea* 38°5N 127°4E **224** C3
Yeong-am *S. Korea* 34°47N 126°42E **224** E3
Yeong-ilman *S. Korea* 36°4N 129°28E **224** D4
Yeong-wol *S. Korea* 37°11N 128°28E **224** D4
Yeong-yang *S. Korea* 36°39N 129°7E **224** D4
Yeongcheon *S. Korea* 35°58N 128°56E **224** E4
Yeongdeok *S. Korea* 36°24N 129°22E **224** D4
Yeongdeungpo *S. Korea* 37°31N 126°54E **137** B1
Yeongdong *Chungcheongbuk-do, S. Korea* 36°10N 127°46E **224** D3
Yeongdong *Seoul, S. Korea* 37°30N 127°1E **137** B2
Yeonggwang *S. Korea* 35°16N 126°30E **224** E3
Yeongheungdo *S. Korea* 37°15N 126°27E **224** D3
Yeongju *S. Korea* 36°50N 128°40E **224** D4
Yeongju △ *S. Korea* 35°45N 129°20E **224** D4
Yeosu *S. Korea* 34°47N 127°45E **224** E3
Yeotmal = Yavatmal *India* 20°20N 78°15E **244** D4
Yeouido *S. Korea* 37°31N 126°55E **137** B1
Yeovil *U.K.* 50°57N 2°38W **169** G5
Yepes *Spain* 39°55N 3°39W **194** F7
Yeppoon *Australia* 23°5S 150°47E **280** C5
Yerba Buena I. *U.S.A.* 37°48N 122°21W **136** B2
Yerbent *Turkmenistan* 39°30N 58°50E **216** E5
Yerbogachen *Russia* 61°16N 108°0E **215** C11
Yerevan *Armenia* 40°10N 44°31E **191** K7
Yerington *U.S.A.* 38°59N 119°10W **304** G4
Yerkesik *Turkey* 37°7N 28°19E **205** D10
Yerköy *Turkey* 39°38N 34°28E **212** C6
Yerla → *India* 16°50N 74°30E **244** F2
Yermo *U.S.A.* 34°54N 116°50W **307** L10
Yerólakkos *Cyprus* 35°11N 33°15E **207** E9
Yeropol *Russia* 65°15N 168°40E **215** C17
Yeroskipos *Cyprus* 34°46N 32°28E **207** F8
Yerres *France* 48°43N 2°30E **134** B4
Yershov *Russia* 51°23N 48°27E **190** E9
Yerupajá, Cerro *Peru* 10°16S 76°55W **330** C2
Yerushalayim = Jerusalem *Israel/West Bank* 31°47N 35°10E **123** B2
Yerville *France* 49°40N 0°53E **172** C7
Yes Tor *U.K.* 50°41N 4°0W **169** G4
Yesagyo *Burma* 21°38N 95°14E **241** E5
Yesan *S. Korea* 36°41N 126°51E **224** D3
Yeshin *Burma* 23°43N 95°6E **241** D5
Yeşikent = Erzin *Turkey* 36°57N 36°11E **250** B7
Yeşil → *Turkey* 37°20N 33°16E **250** A4
Yeşildere *Turkey* 37°9N 33°31E **250** A4
Yeşilhisar *Turkey* 38°20N 35°5E **212** C6
Yeşilırmak → *Turkey* 41°22N 36°37E **212** B7
Yeşilkent *Turkey* 36°57N 36°12E **212** D7
Yeşilköy *Turkey* 40°57N 28°49E **203** F12
Yeşilova *Turkey* 37°31N 29°46E **205** D11
Yeşilyurt *Manisa, Turkey* 38°22N 28°40E **205** C10
Yeşilyurt *Muğla, Turkey* 37°10N 28°20E **205** D10
Yeski Dzhumaya = Târgovişte *Romania* 44°55N 25°27E **183** F10
Yesnogorsk *Russia* 54°32N 37°38E **188** E9
Yeso *U.S.A.* 34°26N 104°37W **305** J11
Yessentuki *Russia* 44°5N 42°53E **191** H6
Yessey *Russia* 68°29N 102°10E **215** C11
Yeste *Spain* 38°22N 2°19W **197** G2
Yetman *Australia* 28°56S 150°48E **281** D5
Yetti *Mauritania* 26°10N 7°50W **260** C3
Yeu, Î. d' *France* 46°42N 2°20W **172** F4
Yevdokimovskoye = Krasnogvardeyskoye *Russia* 45°52N 41°33E **191** H5
Yevlakh = Yevlax *Azerbaijan* 40°39N 47°7E **191** K8
Yevlax *Azerbaijan* 40°39N 47°7E **191** K8
Yevpatoriya *Ukraine* 45°15N 33°20E **189** K7
Yeya → *Russia* 46°40N 38°40E **191** G4
Yeysk *Russia* 46°40N 38°12E **189** J10
Yezd = Yazd *Iran* 31°55N 54°27E **247** D7
Yezerishche *Belarus* 55°50N 30°0E **188** E5
Ygatimi *Paraguay* 24°5S 55°40W **335** A4
Yhati *Paraguay* 25°45S 56°35W **334** B4
Yhú *Paraguay* 25°0S 56°0W **335** B4
Yí → *Uruguay* 33°7S 57°8W **334** C4
Yi 'Allaq, G. *Egypt* 30°21N 33°31E **251** H4
Yi He → *China* 34°10N 118°8E **227** G10
Yi Xian *Anhui, China* 29°55N 117°57E **229** C11
Yi Xian *Hebei, China* 39°20N 115°30E **226** E8
Yi Xian *Liaoning, China* 41°30N 121°22E **227** D11
Yialiás → *Cyprus* 35°9N 33°44E **207** E9
Yialousa *Cyprus* 35°32N 34°10E **207** E10
Yibin *China* 28°45N 104°32E **228** C5
Yichang *China* 30°40N 111°20E **229** B8
Yicheng *Henan, China* 31°41N 112°12E **229** B9
Yicheng *Shanxi, China* 35°42N 111°40E **226** G6
Yichuan *China* 36°2N 110°10E **226** F6
Yichun *Heilongjiang, China* 47°44N 128°52E **219** B14
Yichun *Jiangxi, China* 27°48N 114°22E **229** D10
Yidu *China* 36°43N 118°28E **227** F10
Yidun *China* 30°22N 99°21E **228** B2
Yiexiu *China* 23°8N 113°16E **121** B2
Yifag *Ethiopia* 12°4N 37°46E **257** E4
Yifeng *China* 28°22N 114°45E **229** C10
Yigo *Guam* 13°32N 144°53E **302** d
Yiheyuan *China* 39°59N 116°15E **114** B1
Yihuang *China* 27°30N 116°12E **229** D11
Yijun *China* 35°28N 109°8E **226** G5
Yılanlıkale *Turkey* 36°59N 35°47E **250** B6
Yıldız Dağları *Turkey* 41°48N 27°36E **203** E11
Yıldız Park *Turkey* 41°2N 29°1E **122** B2
Yıldızeli *Turkey* 39°51N 36°36E **212** C7
Yilehuli Shan *China* 51°20N 124°20E **219** A13
Yiliang *Yunnan, China* 27°38N 104°2E **228** D5
Yiliang *Yunnan, China* 24°56N 103°11E **228** E4
Yilong *China* 31°34N 106°23E **228** B6
Yima *China* 34°44N 111°53E **226** G6
Yimen *China* 24°40N 102°10E **228** E4
Yimianpo *China* 45°7N 128°2E **227** B15
Yin Xu *China* 36°8N 114°10E **226** F8
Yi'nan *China* 35°31N 118°24E **227** G10
Yinchuan *China* 38°30N 106°15E **226** E4
Yindaik *Burma* 23°35N 95°22E **241** D5
Yindarlgooda, L. *Australia* 30°40S 121°52E **279** F3
Yindjibarndi ☼ *Australia* 22°0S 118°35E **278** D2
Ying He → *China* 32°30N 116°30E **226** H9
Ying Xian *China* 39°32N 113°10E **226** E7
Yingcheng *China* 30°56N 113°35E **229** B9
Yingde *China* 24°10N 113°25E **229** E9
Yingjiang *China* 24°41N 97°55E **228** E1
Yingjing *China* 29°41N 102°52E **228** C4
Yingkou *China* 40°37N 122°18E **224** B1
Yingkow = Yingkou *China* 40°37N 122°18E **224** B1
Yingpanshui *China* 37°26N 104°18E **226** F3
Yingshan *Hubei, China* 30°41N 115°32E **229** B10
Yingshan *Sichuan, China* 31°4N 106°35E **228** B6
Yingshang *China* 32°38N 116°12E **229** A11
Yingtan *China* 28°12N 117°0E **229** C11
Yingualyalya ☼ *Australia* 18°49S 129°12E **278** C4
Yinhangzhen *China* 31°20N 121°31E **138** A2
Yining *China* 43°58N 81°10E **217** D10
Yiningarra ☼ *Australia* 20°53S 129°27E **278** D4
Yinjiang *China* 28°1N 108°21E **228** C7
Yinmabin *Burma* 22°10N 94°55E **241** D5
Yioúra = Giaros *Greece* 37°32N 24°40E **204** D6
Yipinglang *China* 25°10N 101°52E **228** E3
Yirba Muda *Ethiopia* 6°12N 38°42E **257** F4
Yirga Alem *Ethiopia* 6°48N 38°22E **257** F4
Yirol *Sudan* 6°33N 30°30E **257** F3
Yirrkala *Australia* 12°14S 136°56E **280** A2
Yishan *China* 24°28N 108°38E **228** E7
Yishui *China* 35°47N 118°30E **227** G10
Yishun *Singapore* 1°26N 103°51E **138** A3
Yitong *China* 43°13N 125°20E **227** C13
Yiwu *China* 29°20N 120°3E **229** C13
Yixing *China* 31°21N 119°48E **229** B12
Yiyang *Henan, China* 34°27N 112°10E **226** G7
Yiyang *Hunan, China* 28°35N 112°18E **229** C9
Yiyang *Jiangxi, China* 28°22N 117°20E **229** C11
Yizhang *China* 25°27N 112°57E **229** E9
Yizheng *China* 32°18N 119°10E **229** A12
Ylästö *Finland* 60°17N 24°54E **121** B2
Yli-Kitka *Finland* 66°8N 28°30E **160** C23
Yliki, L. *Greece* 38°24N 23°15E **204** C5
Ylitornio *Finland* 66°19N 23°39E **160** C20
Ylivieska *Finland* 64°4N 24°28E **160** D21
Ymer Ø *Greenland* 73°9N 24°20W **154** C8
Yngaren *Sweden* 58°50N 16°35E **163** F10
Yoakum *U.S.A.* 29°17N 97°9W **314** G6
Yob ⌓ *Eritrea* 17°15N 37°50E **257** D4
Yobe □ *Nigeria* 12°0N 11°30E **263** C7
Yoboki *Djibouti* 11°30N 42°6E **267** B5
Yobuko *Japan* 33°32N 129°54E **222** D1
Yodo → *Japan* 34°45N 135°35E **133** A2
Yog Pt. *Phil.* 14°6N 124°12E **232** D5
Yoğuntaş *Turkey* 41°50N 27°4E **203** E11
Yogyakarta *Indonesia* 7°49S 110°22E **235** D4
Yogyakarta □ *Indonesia* 7°48S 110°22E **235** D4
Yoho △ *Canada* 51°25N 116°30W **296** C5
Yojoa, L. de *Honduras* 14°53N 88°0W **320** D2
Yok Don △ *Vietnam* 12°50N 107°40E **236** F6
Yokadouma *Cameroon* 3°26N 14°55E **264** B2
Yōkaichi *Japan* 35°6N 136°12E **223** B8
Yōkaichiba *Japan* 35°42N 140°33E **223** B12
Yokkaichi *Japan* 34°55N 136°38E **223** C8
Yoko *Cameroon* 5°32N 12°20E **263** D7
Yokohama *Japan* 35°27N 139°28E **223** B11
Yokosuka *Japan* 35°20N 139°40E **223** B11
Yokote *Japan* 39°20N 140°30E **220** E10
Yola *Nigeria* 9°10N 12°29E **263** D7
Yolaina, Cordillera de *Nic.* 11°30N 84°0W **320** D3
Yolombo *Dem. Rep. of the Congo* 1°36S 23°12E **264** C4
Ýolöten *Turkmenistan* 37°18N 62°21E **247** B9
Yom → *Thailand* 15°35N 100°1E **236** E3
Yombi *Gabon* 1°26S 10°37E **264** C2
Yona *Guam* 13°25N 144°46E **302** d
Yonago *Japan* 35°25N 133°19E **222** B5
Yonaguni-Jima *Japan* 24°27N 123°0E **221** M1
Yonaha-Dake *Japan* 26°43N 128°13E **288** a
Yŏnan *N. Korea* 37°55N 126°11E **224** D3
Yonezawa *Japan* 37°57N 140°4E **220** F10
Yong-in *S. Korea* 37°14N 127°12E **224** D3
Yong Peng *Malaysia* 2°0N 103°3E **237** M4
Yong Sata *Thailand* 7°8N 99°41E **237** J2
Yongama *Dem. Rep. of the Congo* 0°2N 24°35E **264** B4
Yongamp'o *N. Korea* 39°56N 124°23E **224** C2
Yong'an *China* 25°59N 117°25E **229** E11
Yongchang *China* 38°17N 102°7E **218** D9
Yongcheng *China* 33°55N 116°20E **226** H9
Yongchuan *China* 29°17N 105°55E **228** C5
Yongchun *China* 25°16N 118°20E **229** E12
Yongde *China* 24°5N 99°25E **228** E2
Yongdeng *China* 36°38N 103°25E **226** F2
Yongding *China* 24°43N 116°45E **229** E11
Yongdingman *China* 39°50N 116°20E **114** B2
Yonge Street *Toronto, Canada* **141** b3
Yongfeng *China* 27°20N 115°22E **229** D10
Yongfu *China* 24°59N 109°59E **228** E7
Yongfucun *China* 23°8N 113°17E **121** B2
Yonggyap Pass *India* 29°17N 95°37E **241** A5
Yonghe *China* 36°46N 110°38E **226** F6
Yonghong *India* 26°28N 94°58E **241** B5
Yŏnghŭng *N. Korea* 39°31N 127°18E **224** C3
Yŏnghŭng-man *N. Korea* 39°14N 127°30E **224** C3
Yongji *Jilin, China* 43°33N 126°13E **227** C14
Yongji *Shanxi, China* 34°52N 110°28E **226** G6
Yongjia *China* 28°10N 120°45E **229** C13
Yongkang *Yunnan, China* 24°9N 99°20E **228** E2
Yongkang *Zhejiang, China* 28°55N 120°2E **229** C13
Yongnian *China* 36°47N 114°29E **226** F8
Yongning *Guangxi Zhuangzu, China* 22°44N 108°28E **228** F7
Yongning *Ningxia Huizu, China* 38°15N 106°14E **226** E4
Yongping *China* 25°27N 99°38E **228** E2
Yongren *China* 26°4N 101°40E **228** D3
Yongsan *S. Korea* 37°32N 126°58E **137** B1
Yongshan *China* 28°11N 103°35E **228** C4
Yongsheng *China* 26°38N 100°46E **228** D3
Yongshun *China* 29°2N 109°51E **228** C7
Yongtai *China* 25°49N 118°58E **229** E12
Yongxin = Jinggangshan *China* 26°58N 114°15E **229** D10
Yongxing *China* 26°9N 113°8E **229** D9
Yongxiu *China* 29°2N 115°42E **229** C10
Yongzhou *China* 26°17N 111°37E **229** D8
Yonibana *S. Leone* 8°30N 12°19W **262** D2
Yonkers *U.S.A.* 40°56N 73°52W **132** A2
Yonne □ *France* 47°50N 3°40E **173** E10
Yonne → *France* 48°23N 2°58E **173** D9
Yopal *Colombia* 5°21N 72°23W **328** B3
York *W. Austral., Australia* 31°52S 116°47E **279** F2
York *Ont., Canada* 43°40N 79°26W **141** A2
York *York, U.K.* 53°58N 1°6W **168** D6
York *Ala., U.S.A.* 32°29N 88°18W **315** E10
York *Nebr., U.S.A.* 40°52N 97°36W **308** E5
York *Pa., U.S.A.* 39°58N 76°44W **309** F15
York, C. *Australia* 10°42S 142°31E **286** F2
York, City of □ *U.K.* 53°58N 1°6W **168** D6
York, Kap *Greenland* 75°55N 66°25W **154** B4
York, Vale of *U.K.* 54°15N 1°25W **168** C6
York I. *Antigua & B.* 17°2N 61°40W **322** b
York Mills *Canada* 43°45N 79°22W **141** A2
York Sd. *Australia* 15°0S 125°5E **278** C4
York Univ. *Canada* 43°43N 79°22W **141** A1
Yorke Pen. *Australia* 34°50S 137°40E **282** C2
Yorketown *Australia* 35°2S 137°33E **282** C2
Yorkshire Dales △ *U.K.* 54°12N 2°10W **168** C5
Yorkshire Wolds *U.K.* 54°8N 0°31W **168** C7
Yorkton *Canada* 51°11N 102°28W **297** C8
Yorkville *Calif., U.S.A.* 38°52N 123°13W **306** G3
Yorkville *Ga., U.S.A.* 33°55N 84°58W **316** B5
Yorkville *Ill., U.S.A.* 41°38N 88°27W **311** C8
Yoro *Honduras* 15°9N 87°7W **320** C2
Yoron-Jima *Japan* 27°2N 128°26E **221** L4
Yorosso *Mali* 12°17N 4°55W **262** C4
Yos Sudarso, Pulau = Dolak, Pulau *Indonesia* 8°0S 138°30E **231** F9
Yosemite △ *U.S.A.* 37°45N 119°40W **306** H7
Yosemite Village *U.S.A.* 37°45N 119°35W **306** H7
Yoshida *Japan* 34°40N 132°42E **222** C4
Yoshimatsu *Japan* 32°0N 130°47E **222** F2
Yoshino-Kumano △ *Japan* 34°12N 135°55E **223** C7
Yoshkar Ola *Russia* 56°38N 47°55E **190** B8
Yotala *Bolivia* 19°10S 65°17W **331** D4
Yotsuya *Tokyo, Japan* **140** a2
Yotvata *Israel* 29°55N 35°2E **251** J6
You Jiang → *China* 22°50N 108°6E **228** F6
You Xian *China* 27°1N 113°17E **229** D9
You'anmen *China* 39°51N 116°19E **114** B1
Youbou *Canada* 48°53N 124°13W **306** B2
Youghal *Ireland* 51°56N 7°52W **166** E4
Youghal B. *Ireland* 51°55N 7°49W **166** E4
Youkounkoun *Guinea* 12°35N 13°11W **262** C2
Young *N.S.W., Australia* 34°19S 148°18E **283** C8
Young *Sask., Canada* 51°47N 105°45W **297** C7
Young *Uruguay* 32°44S 57°36W **334** C4
Young I. *Antarctica* 66°25S 162°24E **151** C11
Young Ra. *N.Z.* 44°10S 169°30E **285** E4
Younghusband, L. *Australia* 30°50S 136°5E **282** A2
Younghusband Pen. *Australia* 36°0S 139°25E **282** D3
Youngsfield *S. Africa* 34°0S 18°30E **118** B1
Youngstown *Alta., Canada* 51°35N 111°10W **297** C6
Youngstown *Fla., U.S.A.* 30°22N 85°26W **316** E4
Youngstown *N.Y., U.S.A.* 43°15N 79°3W **312** C5
Youngstown *Ohio, U.S.A.* 41°6N 80°39W **312** E4
Youngsville *U.S.A.* 41°51N 79°19W **312** E5
Youngwood *U.S.A.* 40°14N 79°34W **312** F5
Youssoufia *Morocco* 32°16N 8°31W **260** B3
Youxi *China* 26°10N 118°13E **229** D12
Youyang *China* 28°47N 108°42E **228** C7
Youyu *China* 40°10N 112°20E **226** D7
Yozgat *Turkey* 39°51N 34°47E **212** C6
Yozgat □ *Turkey* 39°30N 35°0E **212** C6
Ypacaraí △ *Paraguay* 25°18S 57°19W **334** B4
Ypané → *Paraguay* 23°29S 57°19W **334** A4
Yport *France* 49°45N 0°15E **172** C7
Ypres = Ieper *Belgium* 50°51N 2°53E **170** D2
Ypsilanti *U.S.A.* 42°14N 83°37W **311** B13
Yreka *U.S.A.* 41°44N 122°38W **304** F2
Yrghyz *Kazakhstan* 48°37N 61°16E **216** C6
Yrghyz → *Kazakhstan* 48°6N 62°30E **216** C6
Ysabel Chan. *Papua N. G.* 2°0S 150°0E **286** B6
Yssingeaux *France* 45°9N 4°8E **175** C8
Ystabøhamn *Norway* 59°3N 5°23E **164** E2
Ystad *Sweden* 55°26N 13°50E **163** J7
Ysyk-Köl = Balykchy *Kyrgyzstan* 42°26N 76°12E **217** D9
Ysyk-Köl *Kyrgyzstan* 42°25N 77°15E **217** D9
Ysyk-Köl □ *Kyrgyzstan* 42°0N 78°0E **217** D9
Ythan → *U.K.* 57°19N 1°59W **167** D7
Ytre Arna *Norway* 60°27N 5°25E **164** D2
Ytre Enebakk *Norway* 59°44N 11°0E **164** E8
Ytre Rendal *Norway* 61°46N 11°8E **164** C8
Ytteran *Sweden* 63°16N 14°7E **162** A8
Ytterhogdal *Sweden* 62°12N 14°56E **162** B8
Yttermalung *Sweden* 60°35N 13°51E **162** D7
Ytyk-Kyuyel *Russia* 62°30N 133°45E **215** C14
Yu Jiang → *China* 23°22N 110°3E **228** F7
Yü Shan *Taiwan* 23°25N 120°52E **225** C2
Yü Shan △ *Taiwan* 24°45N 121°12E **225** C3
Yu Xian = Yuzhou *China* 34°10N 113°28E **226** G7
Yu Xian *Hebei, China* 39°50N 114°35E **226** E8
Yu Xian *Shanxi, China* 38°5N 113°20E **226** E7
Yuan Jiang → *Hunan, China* 28°55N 111°50E **229** C8
Yuan Jiang → *Yunnan, China* 22°20N 103°59E **228** F4
Yuan'an *China* 31°3N 111°34E **229** B8
Yüanch'ang *Taiwan* 23°39N 120°18E **225** C2
Yuanjiang *Hunan, China* 28°47N 112°21E **229** C9
Yuanjiang *Yunnan, China* 23°32N 102°0E **228** F4
Yüanli *Taiwan* 24°27N 120°39E **225** B2
Yüanlin *Taiwan* 23°58N 120°30E **225** C2
Yuanling *China* 28°29N 110°22E **229** C8
Yuanmingyuan Park *China* 40°0N 116°17E **114** A1
Yuanmou *China* 25°42N 101°53E **228** E3
Yuanping *China* 38°42N 112°46E **226** E7
Yuanqu *China* 35°18N 111°40E **226** G6
Yuanshan *Taiwan* 24°45N 121°43E **225** B3
Yuanxiatian *China* 23°12N 113°17E **121** A2
Yuanyang *Henan, China* 35°3N 113°58E **226** G7
Yuanyang *Yunnan, China* 23°10N 102°43E **228** F4
Yuat → *Papua N. G.* 4°10S 143°52E **286** C2
Yuba → *U.S.A.* 39°8N 121°36W **306** F5
Yuba City *U.S.A.* 39°8N 121°37W **306** F5
Yūbari *Japan* 43°4N 141°59E **220** C10
Yubdo *Ethiopia* 8°58N 35°24E **257** F4
Yūbetsu *Japan* 44°13N 143°50E **220** B11
Yubo *Sudan* 5°23N 27°25E **266** C2
Yucatán □ *Mexico* 20°50N 89°0W **319** C7
Yucatán, Canal de *Caribbean* 22°0N 86°30W **320** B2
Yucatán, Península de *Mexico* 19°30N 89°0W **292** H11
Yucatan Basin *Cent. Amer.* 19°0N 86°0W **320** C3
Yucatan Channel = Yucatán, Canal de *Caribbean* 22°0N 86°30W **320** B2
Yucca *U.S.A.* 34°52N 114°9W **307** L12
Yucca Valley *U.S.A.* 34°8N 116°27W **307** L10
Yucheng *China* 36°55N 116°32E **226** F9
Yüch'ih *Taiwan* 23°54N 120°56E **225** C2
Yuching *Taiwan* 23°7N 120°27E **225** C2
Yuci = Jinzhong *China* 37°42N 112°46E **226** F7
Yudu *China* 25°59N 115°30E **229** E10
Yuechi *China* 30°34N 106°25E **228** B6
Yuen Long *China* 22°26N 114°2E **219** a
Yuendumu *Australia* 22°16S 131°49E **278** D5
Yuendumu ☼ *Australia* 22°21S 131°40E **278** D5
Yueqing *China* 28°9N 120°59E **229** C13
Yueqing Wan *China* 28°5N 121°20E **229** D13
Yuexi *Anhui, China* 30°50N 116°20E **229** B11
Yuexi *Sichuan, China* 28°37N 102°26E **228** C4
Yuexiu Park *China* 23°8N 113°16E **121** B2
Yueyang *China* 29°21N 113°5E **229** C9
Yufu-Dake *Japan* 33°17N 131°33E **222** D3
Yugan *China* 28°43N 116°37E **229** C11
Yuğluk Dağı *Turkey* 36°59N 33°50E **250** B4
Yugo-Zarad *Russia* 55°40N 37°30E **129** B3
Yugorenok *Russia* 59°47N 137°40E **215** D14
Yuhalixqui, Volcan *Mexico* 19°19N 99°4W **128** C2
Yuhuan *China* 28°9N 121°12E **229** C13
Yühuan Dao *China* 28°5N 121°15E **229** C13
Yujiang *China* 28°10N 116°43E **229** C11
Yukhnov *Russia* 54°44N 35°15E **188** E8
Yūki *Japan* 36°18N 139°53E **223** A11
Yukon *U.S.A.* 35°31N 97°45W **314** D6
Yukon → *U.S.A.* 62°32N 163°54W **303** E7
Yukon-Charley Rivers ⌓ *U.S.A.* 65°15N 144°0W **303** D12
Yukon Delta Nat. Wildlife Refuge ⌓ *U.S.A.* 61°0N 163°0W **303** F7
Yukon Flats *U.S.A.* 66°40N 145°45W **303** C11
Yukon Territory □ *Canada* 63°0N 135°0W **294** E5
Yüksekova *Turkey* 37°34N 44°16E **213** D11
Yukta *Russia* 63°26N 105°42E **215** C11
Yukuhashi *Japan* 33°44N 130°59E **222** D2
Yulara *Australia* 25°10S 130°55E **279** E5
Yule → *Australia* 20°41S 118°17E **278** D2
Yuleba *Australia* 26°37S 149°24E **281** D4
Yulee *U.S.A.* 30°38N 81°36W **316** E8
Yuli *China* 41°19N 86°15E **217** D11
Yuli *Nigeria* 9°44N 10°12E **263** D7
Yüli *Taiwan* 23°20N 121°18E **225** C3
Yulin *Guangxi Zhuangzu, China* 22°40N 110°8E **229** F8
Yulin *Hainan, China* 18°10N 109°31E **236** C7
Yulin *Shaanxi, China* 38°20N 109°30E **226** E5
Yulong Xueshan *China* 27°6N 100°10E **228** D3
Yuma *Ariz., U.S.A.* 32°43N 114°37W **307** N12
Yuma *Colo., U.S.A.* 40°8N 102°43W **304** F12
Yuma, B. de *Dom. Rep.* 18°20N 68°35W **321** C6
Yumali *Australia* 35°32S 139°45E **282** C3
Yumbe *Uganda* 3°28N 31°15E **268** B3
Yumbi *Équateur, Dem. Rep. of the Congo* 1°53S 16°34E **264** C3
Yumbi *Maniema, Dem. Rep. of the Congo* 1°12S 26°15E **268** C2
Yumbo *Colombia* 3°35N 76°28W **328** C2
Yumen *China* 39°50N 97°30E **218** D8
Yumurtalık *Turkey* 36°45N 35°48E **250** B6
Yun Gui Gaoyuan *China* 26°0N 104°0E **228** E3
Yun Ling Shan *China* 27°0N 99°20E **228** D2
Yun Xian *Hubei, China* 32°50N 110°46E **226** H6
Yun Xian *Yunnan, China* 24°27N 100°8E **228** E3
Yuna *Australia* 28°20S 115°0E **279** E2
Yunak *Turkey* 38°49N 31°43E **212** C4
Yunan *China* 23°12N 111°30E **229** F8
Yunaska I. *U.S.A.* 52°38N 170°40W **303** K5
Yuncheng *Henan, China* 35°36N 115°57E **226** G8
Yuncheng *Shanxi, China* 35°2N 111°0E **226** G6
Yunfu *China* 22°50N 112°5E **229** F9
Yung Shue Wan *China* 22°13N 114°6E **122** B1
Yungan *Taiwan* 22°49N 120°12E **225** D2
Yungang Shiku *China* 40°5N 113°0E **226** D7
Yungas *Bolivia* 17°0S 66°0W **331** D4
Yungay *Chile* 37°10S 72°5W **334** D1
Yungay *Peru* 9°2S 77°45W **330** B2
Yungk'ang *Taiwan* 23°2N 120°15E **225** C2
Yungki = Jilin *China* 43°44N 126°30E **227** C14
Yungning = Nanning *China* 22°48N 108°20E **228** F7
Yunhe *China* 28°8N 119°33E **229** C12
Yunkai Dashan *China* 22°30N 111°0E **229** F8
Yunkanjini ☼ *Australia* 22°33S 131°6E **278** D5
Yünlin □ *Taiwan* 23°40N 120°20E **225** C2
Yunling Shan *China* 28°30N 98°50E **218** F8
Yunlong *China* 25°57N 99°13E **228** E2
Yunmeng *China* 31°2N 113°43E **229** B9
Yunnan □ *China* 25°0N 102°0E **228** E4
Yunotsu *Japan* 35°5N 132°21E **222** B4
Yunquera de Henares *Spain* 40°47N 3°11W **196** E1
Yunshui *Taiwan* 23°23N 120°31E **225** C2
Yunt Dağı *Turkey* 38°56N 27°13E **205** C9
Yunta *Australia* 32°34S 139°36E **281** E2
Yunxi *China* 33°0N 110°22E **226** H6
Yunxiao *China* 23°59N 117°18E **229** F11
Yunyang *Chongqing, China* 31°2N 108°51E **228** B7
Yunyang *Henan, China* 33°26N 112°42E **229** A9
Yupanqui Basin *Pac. Oc.* 19°0S 101°0W **289** J17
Yuping *China* 27°13N 108°56E **228** D7
Yupukarri *Guyana* 3°45N 59°20W **329** C6
Yuqing *China* 27°13N 107°53E **228** D6
Yuraygir △ *Australia* 29°45S 153°15E **281** D5
Yurga *Russia* 55°42N 84°51E **214** D9
Yurimaguas *Peru* 5°55S 76°7W **330** B2
Yurkiyka *Ukraine* 48°42N 28°35E **183** B13
Yurungkax He → *China* 38°5N 80°34E **217** E10
Yuryev = Tartu *Estonia* 58°20N 26°44E **188** C4
Yuryev-Polskiy *Russia* 56°30N 39°40E **188** D10
Yuryevets *Russia* 57°25N 43°2E **190** B6
Yuscarán *Honduras* 13°58N 86°45W **320** D2
Yûsef, Bahr → *Egypt* 28°25N 30°35E **256** B3
Yushan *China* 28°42N 118°10E **229** C12
Yushanzhen *China* 29°28N 108°22E **228** C7
Yushe *China* 37°4N 112°58E **226** F7
Yushu *Jilin, China* 44°43N 126°38E **227** B14
Yushu *Qinghai, China* 33°5N 96°55E **218** E8
Yūsofābād *Iran* 35°43N 51°24E **141** A2
Yusufeli *Turkey* 40°50N 41°33E **213** B9
Yutai *China* 35°0N 116°45E **226** G9
Yutian *Hebei, China* 39°53N 117°45E **227** E9
Yutian *Sinkiang-Uigur, China* 36°52N 81°42E **217** E10
Yütze = Jinzhong *China* 37°42N 112°46E **226** F7
Yüweng Tao *Taiwan* 23°36N 119°30E **225** C1
Yuxarı Qarabağ = Nagorno-Karabakh □ *Azerbaijan* 39°55N 46°45E **213** C12
Yuxi *China* 24°30N 102°35E **228** E4
Yuyao *China* 30°3N 121°10E **229** B13
Yuzawa *Japan* 39°10N 140°30E **220** E10
Yuzha *Russia* 56°34N 42°1E **190** B6
Yuzhno-Kurilsk *Russia* 44°1N 145°51E **215** E15
Yuzhno-Sakhalinsk *Russia* 46°58N 142°45E **219** B17
Yuzhno-Sukhokumsk *Russia* 44°40N 45°35E **191** H7
Yuzhnouralsk *Russia* 54°26N 61°15E **216** B6
Yuzhnyy □ *Russia* 44°0N 40°0E **191** H6
Yuzhou *China* 34°10N 113°28E **226** G7
Yuzovka = Donetsk *Ukraine* 48°0N 37°45E **189** J9
Yvelines □ *France* 48°40N 1°45E **173** D8
Yverdon-les-Bains *Switz.* 46°47N 6°39E **179** J2
Yvetot *France* 49°37N 0°44E **172** C7
Yzeure *France* 46°33N 3°22E **173** F10

Z

Zaandam *Neths.* 52°26N 4°49E **112** A1
Zaandijk *Neths.* 52°28N 4°49E **112** A1
Zaanstad *Neths.* 52°27N 4°50E **112** A1
Zab, Monts du *Algeria* 34°55N 5°0E **261** B6
Zāb al Kabīr → *Iraq* 36°1N 43°24E **213** D10
Zāb aş Şaghīr → *Iraq* 35°17N 43°29E **213** E10
Žabalj *Serbia* 45°21N 20°5E **182** E5
Žabari *Serbia* 44°22N 21°15E **202** B5
Zabarjad *Egypt* 23°40N 36°12E **256** C4
Zabaykalsk *Russia* 49°40N 117°25E **215** E12
Zabbar *Malta* 35°53N 14°32E **206** F8
Záběhlice *Czech Rep.* 50°3N 14°29E **135** B2
Zabīd *Yemen* 14°0N 43°10E **248** D3
Zabīd, W. → *Yemen* 14°7N 43°6E **248** D3
Zabki *Poland* 52°17N 21°6E **142** B2
Ząbkowice Śląskie *Poland* 50°35N 16°50E **185** H3
Žabljak *Montenegro* 43°18N 19°5E **202** C3
Zabłudów *Poland* 53°0N 23°19E **185** F9
Żabno *Poland* 50°9N 20°53E **185** H7
Zabol *Iran* 31°0N 61°32E **247** D9
Zābol □ *Afghan.* 32°0N 67°0E **240** C2
Zābolī *Iran* 27°10N 61°35E **247** E9
Zabolotiv *Ukraine* 48°28N 25°18E **183** B10
Zabolottya *Ukraine* 51°38N 24°16E **185** G11
Zabré *Burkina Faso* 11°12N 0°36W **263** C4
Zábřeh *Czech Rep.* 49°53N 16°52E **181** B9
Zabrze *Poland* 50°18N 18°50E **185** H5
Zabuzhzhya *Ukraine* 51°21N 23°42E **185** G10
Zabzuga *Ghana* 9°20N 0°30E **263** D5
Zacapa *Guatemala* 14°59N 89°31W **320** D2
Zacapu *Mexico* 19°50N 101°43W **318** D4
Zacatecas *Mexico* 22°47N 102°35W **318** C4
Zacatecas □ *Mexico* 23°0N 103°0W **318** C4
Zacatecoluca *El Salv.* 13°29N 88°51W **320** D2
Zacharo *Greece* 37°30N 21°39E **204** D3
Zachary *U.S.A.* 30°39N 91°9W **314** F9
Zachodnio-Pomorskie □ *Poland* 53°40N 15°50E **184** E2
Żacisze *Poland* 52°17N 21°4E **142** B2
Zacoalco de Torres *Mexico* 20°14N 103°35W **318** C4

Zacualtipán *Mexico* 20°39N 98°36W **319** C5
Zadar *Croatia* 44°8N 15°14E **199** D12
Zadawa *Nigeria* 11°33N 10°19E **263** C7
Zadetkyi Kyun *Burma* 10°0N 98°25E **237** G2
Zadonsk *Russia* 52°25N 38°56E **189** F10
Zafarqand *Iran* 33°11N 52°29E **247** C7
Zafra *Spain* 38°26N 6°30W **195** G4
Żagań *Poland* 51°39N 15°22E **185** G2
Zagaoua *Chad* 16°0N 21°10E **259** E4
Žagarė *Lithuania* 56°21N 23°15E **184** B10
Zagazig *Egypt* 30°40N 31°30E **256** H7
Zāgheh *Iran* 33°30N 48°42E **247** C6
Zaghouan *Tunisia* 36°23N 10°10E **258** A2
Zaghouan □ *Tunisia* 36°20N 10°0E **261** A7
Zaglou *Algeria* 27°17N 0°3W **261** C4
Zagnanado *Benin* 7°18N 2°28E **263** D5
Zagora *Greece* 39°27N 23°6E **204** B5
Zagora *Morocco* 30°22N 5°51W **260** B3
Zagorje *Slovenia* 46°8N 15°0E **199** B11
Zagórów *Poland* 52°10N 17°54E **185** F4
Zagorsk = Sergiyev Posad *Russia* 56°20N 38°10E **188** D10
Zagorsky = Krasnozavodsk *Russia* 56°27N 38°25E **188** D10
Zagórz *Poland* 49°30N 22°14E **185** J9
Zagreb *Croatia* 45°50N 15°58E **199** C12
Zagreb ✈ **(ZAG)** *Croatia* 45°45N 16°4E **199** C13
Zāgros, Kūhhā-ye *Iran* 33°45N 48°5E **247** C6
Zagros Mts. = Zāgros, Kūhhā-ye *Iran* 33°45N 48°5E **247** C6
Žagubica *Serbia* 44°15N 21°47E **202** B5
Zaguinaso *Ivory C.* 10°1N 6°14W **262** C3
Zagyva → *Hungary* 47°5N 20°4E **182** C5
Zahamena ⌓ *Madag.* 17°37S 48°49E **272** B2
Zāhedān *Fārs, Iran* 28°46N 53°52E **247** D7
Zāhedān *Sīstān va Balūchestān, Iran* 29°30N 60°50E **247** D9
Zahirabad *India* 17°43N 77°37E **244** F3
Zahlah *Lebanon* 33°52N 35°50E **250** E6
Zahna *Germany* 51°55N 12°49E **178** D8
Záhony *Hungary* 48°25N 22°11E **182** B7
Zahrā *Iraq* 33°22N 44°19E **113** A1
Ẓahrān *Si. Arabia* 17°40N 43°30E **248** C3
Zainsk *Russia* 55°18N 52°4E **190** C11
Zaïre = Congo → *Africa* 6°4S 12°24E **265** D2
Zaïre = Congo, Dem. Rep. of the ■ *Africa* 3°0S 23°0E **265** C4
Zaire □ *Angola* 7°0S 14°0E **265** D2
Zaječar *Serbia* 43°53N 22°18E **202** C6
Zaka *Zimbabwe* 20°20S 31°29E **271** B5
Zakamensk *Russia* 50°23N 103°17E **215** D11
Zakani *Dem. Rep. of the Congo* 2°33N 23°16E **264** B4
Zakarpattya □ *Ukraine* 48°20N 23°20E **183** B8
Zakataly = Zaqatala *Azerbaijan* 41°38N 46°35E **191** K8
Zakbayemé *Cameroon* 4°2N 10°34E **264** B2
Zakharkovo *Russia* 55°46N 37°18E **129** B1
Zakhodnaya Dzvina = Daugava → *Latvia* 57°4N 24°3E **188** D3
Zākhū *Iraq* 37°10N 42°50E **213** D10
Zakinthos = Zakynthos *Greece* 37°47N 20°54E **207** D2
Zakinthos, Diavlos *Greece* 37°50N 21°0E **207** D2
Zakopane *Poland* 49°18N 19°57E **185** J6
Zakouma *Chad* 10°54N 19°49E **259** F3
Zakouma △ *Chad* 10°52N 19°45E **259** F3
Zakroczym *Poland* 52°26N 20°38E **185** F7
Zakros *Greece* 35°6N 26°10E **207** E7
Zakynthos *Greece* 37°47N 20°54E **207** D2
Zakynthos □ *Greece* 37°47N 20°57E **204** D2
Zakynthos ✈ **(ZTH)** *Greece* 37°45N 20°50E **207** D2
Zala *Angola* 7°52S 13°42E **265** D2
Zala *Ethiopia* 6°28N 37°13E **257** F4
Zala □ *Hungary* 46°42N 16°50E **182** D1
Zala → *Hungary* 46°43N 17°16E **182** D2
Zalaegerszeg *Hungary* 46°53N 16°47E **182** D1
Zalakomár *Hungary* 46°33N 17°10E **182** D2
Zalalövő *Hungary* 46°51N 16°35E **182** D1
Zalamea de la Serena *Spain* 38°40N 5°38W **195** G5
Zalamea la Real *Spain* 37°41N 6°38W **195** H4
Zalantun *China* 48°0N 122°43E **219** B13
Zalari *Russia* 53°33N 102°30E **215** D11
Zalău *Romania* 47°12N 23°3E **182** C8
Žalec *Slovenia* 46°16N 15°10E **199** B12
Zaleshchiki = Zalishchyky *Ukraine* 48°45N 25°45E **183** B10
Zalesye *Russia* 54°50N 21°31E **184** D8
Zalew Wiślany *Poland* 54°20N 19°50E **184** D6
Zalewo *Poland* 53°50N 19°41E **184** E6
Ẓalīm *Si. Arabia* 22°43N 42°10E **248** B3
Zalingei *Sudan* 12°51N 23°29E **259** F4
Zalishchyky *Ukraine* 48°45N 25°45E **183** B10
Zalmah, J. az *Libya* 25°30N 24°40E **258** C4
Žalov *Czech Rep.* 50°10N 14°22E **135** A2
Zalṭan *Ajdābiyā, Libya* 28°51N 19°52E **258** C3
Zalṭan *Zuwārah, Libya* 32°57N 11°52E **258** B2
Zalṭan, Jabal *Libya* 28°46N 19°45E **258** C3
Zalun *Burma* 17°29N 95°34E **241** G5
Załuski *Poland* 52°9N 20°55E **142** C1
Zama L. *Canada* 58°45N 119°5W **296** B5
Zambales □ *Phil.* 15°20N 120°10E **232** D3
Zambales Mts. *Phil.* 15°45N 120°5E **232** D3
Zambeke *Dem. Rep. of the Congo* 2°8N 25°17E **268** B2
Zambeze → *Africa* 18°35S 36°20E **269** F4
Zambezi = Zambeze → *Africa* 18°35S 36°20E **269** F4
Zambezi *Zambia* 13°30S 23°15E **265** E4
Zambezi △ *Zimbabwe* 17°54S 25°41E **269** F2
Zambezia □ *Mozam.* 16°15S 37°30E **269** F4
Zambia ■ *Africa* 15°0S 28°0E **269** F2
Zamboanga *Phil.* 6°59N 122°3E **233** H4
Zamboanga del Norte □ *Phil.* 8°0N 123°0E **233** G4
Zamboanga del Sur □ *Phil.* 7°40N 123°0E **233** H4
Zamboanga Pen. *Phil.* 7°32N 122°16E **233** H4
Zamboanguita *Phil.* 9°6N 123°11E **233** G4
Zambrano *Colombia* 9°45N 74°49W **328** B3
Zambrów *Poland* 52°59N 22°14E **185** F9
Zamdorf *Germany* 48°8N 11°35E **131** B2
Zametchino *Russia* 53°30N 42°30E **190** D6
Zamfara □ *Nigeria* 12°10N 6°0E **263** C6
Zamfara → *Nigeria* 12°5N 4°2E **263** C5
Zamora *Ecuador* 4°4S 78°58W **328** D2
Zamora *Michoacan, Mexico* 19°59N 102°16W **318** D4
Zamora *Spain* 41°30N 5°45W **194** D5
Zamora □ *Spain* 41°30N 5°46W **194** D5
Zamora → *Ecuador* 2°59S 78°13W **328** D2
Zamora-Chinchipe □ *Ecuador* 4°15S 78°50W **328** D2
Zamość *Poland* 50°43N 23°15E **185** H10
Zamtang *China* 32°26N 101°6E **228** A3
Zamuro, Sierra del *Venezuela* 4°0N 62°30W **329** C5
Zamzam, W. → *Libya* 30°58N 14°48E **258** B2
Zan *Ghana* 9°26N 0°17W **263** D4
Zanaga *Congo* 2°48S 13°48E **264** C2
Záncara → *Spain* 39°18N 3°18W **197** F1
Zanda *China* 31°32N 79°50E **218** E4
Zanderij *Suriname* 5°20N 55°16W **329** B6
Zandu *Dem. Rep. of the Congo* 5°11S 18°16E **265** D3
Zandvoort *Neths.* 52°22N 4°32E **170** B4
Zanesville *U.S.A.* 39°56N 82°1W **312** G2
Zanevka *Russia* 59°55N 30°31E **137** B3
Zangābād *Iran* 38°26N 46°44E **246** B5
Zangliveri *Greece* 40°36N 23°15E **202** F7
Zangoza = Sangüesa *Spain* 42°37N 1°17W **196** C3
Zangue → *Mozam.* 17°50S 35°21E **269** F4
Zanjān *Iran* 36°40N 48°35E **213** D13
Zanjān □ *Iran* 37°20N 49°30E **247** B6
Zanjān → *Iran* 37°8N 47°47E **247** B6
Zannone *Italy* 40°58N 13°3E **200** B6
Zanow = Sianów *Poland* 54°13N 16°18E **184** D3
Zante = Zakynthos *Greece* 37°47N 20°54E **207** D2
Zanthus *Australia* 31°2S 123°34E **279** F3
Zanzibar *Tanzania* 6°12S 39°12E **268** D4
Zanzūr *Libya* 32°55N 13°1E **258** B2
Zaouatallaz *Algeria* 24°52N 8°30E **261** D6
Zaouiet El-Kala = Bordj Omar Driss *Algeria* 28°10N 6°40E **261** C6
Zaouiet Reggâne *Algeria* 26°32N 0°3E **261** C5
Zaoyang *China* 32°10N 112°45E **229** A9
Zaozernyy *Kazakhstan* 53°6N 71°9E **217** B8
Zaozhuang *China* 34°50N 117°35E **227** G9
Zap Suyu = Zāb al Kabīr → *Iraq* 36°1N 43°24E **213** D10
Zapadna Morava → *Serbia* 43°38N 21°30E **202** C5
Zapadnaya Dvina = Daugava → *Latvia* 57°4N 24°3E **188** D3
Zapadnaya Dvina *Russia* 56°15N 32°3E **188** D7
Západné Beskydy *Europe* 49°30N 19°0E **181** B12
Zapadni Rodopi *Bulgaria* 41°50N 24°0E **202** E7
Západočeský □ *Czech Rep.* 49°35N 13°0E **180** B6
Zapala *Argentina* 39°0S 70°5W **336** A2
Zapaleri, Cerro *Bolivia* 22°49S 67°11W **334** A2
Zapata *U.S.A.* 26°55N 99°16W **314** H5
Zapatón → *Spain* 39°0N 6°49W **195** F4
Zapiga *Chile* 19°40S 69°55W **330** D4
Zapolyarnyy *Russia* 69°26N 30°51E **160** B24
Zapopán *Mexico* 20°43N 103°24W **318** C4
Zaporizhzhya *Ukraine* 47°50N 35°10E **189** J8
Zaporizhzhya □ *Ukraine* 46°55N 35°50E **189** J8
Zaporozhye = Zaporizhzhya *Ukraine* 47°50N 35°10E **189** J8
Zapote *Phil.* 14°27N 120°56E **127** C1
Zappeion *Athens, Greece* **112** c2
Zaqatala *Azerbaijan* 41°38N 46°35E **191** K8
Zara *Turkey* 39°58N 37°43E **212** C7
Zarafshon *Uzbekistan* 41°34N 64°12E **216** D6
Zaragoza *Colombia* 7°30N 74°52W **328** B3
Zaragoza *Coahuila, Mexico* 28°29N 100°55W **318** B4
Zaragoza *Nuevo León, Mexico* 23°58N 99°46W **319** C5
Zaragoza *Spain* 41°39N 0°53W **196** D4
Zaragoza □ *Spain* 41°35N 1°0W **196** D4
Zarand *Kermān, Iran* 30°46N 56°34E **247** D8
Zarand *Markazī, Iran* 35°18N 50°25E **247** C6
Zărandului, Munţii *Romania* 46°14N 22°7E **182** D7
Zaranj *Afghan.* 30°55N 61°55E **240** C1
Zarasai *Lithuania* 55°40N 26°20E **188** E4
Zárate *Argentina* 34°7S 59°0W **334** C4
Zarautz *Spain* 43°17N 2°10W **196** B2
Zaraysk *Russia* 54°48N 38°53E **188** E10
Zaraza *Venezuela* 9°21N 65°19W **329** B4
Zard, Kūh-e *Iran* 32°22N 50°4E **247** C6
Zarechye *Russia* 55°41N 37°22E **129** B2
Zāreh *Iran* 35°7N 49°9E **247** C6
Zari *Nigeria* 13°4N 12°45E **263** C7
Zaria *Nigeria* 11°0N 7°40E **263** C6
Zarineh → *Iran* 36°17N 46°26E **213** D12
Zarinsk *Russia* 53°43N 84°55E **217** B10
Żarki *Poland* 50°38N 19°23E **185** H6
Zarko *Greece* 39°38N 22°6E **204** B4
Zarneh *Iran* 33°55N 46°10E **246** C5
Zărneşti *Romania* 45°33N 25°18E **183** E10
Zaros *Greece* 35°8N 24°54E **207** E5
Żarów *Poland* 50°56N 16°29E **185** H3
Zarqā', Nahr az → *Jordan* 32°10N 35°37E **251** F6
Zarrīn *Iran* 32°46N 54°37E **247** C7
Zarrinābād *Iran* 36°25N 48°17E **213** D13
Zaruma *Ecuador* 3°40S 79°38W **328** D2
Żary *Poland* 51°37N 15°10E **185** G2
Zarza de Granadilla *Spain* 40°14N 6°3W **194** E4
Zarzaïtine *Algeria* 28°15N 9°34E **261** C6
Zarzal *Colombia* 4°24N 76°4W **328** C2
Zarzis *Tunisia* 33°31N 11°2E **258** B2
Zas *Spain* 43°4N 8°53W **194** B2
Zashaghan *Kazakhstan* 51°11N 51°20E **216** B4
Zaskar → *India* 34°13N 77°20E **243** B7
Zaskar Mts. *India* 33°15N 77°30E **243** C7
Zastavna *Ukraine* 48°31N 25°51E **183** B10
Zastron *S. Africa* 30°18S 27°7E **270** D4
Žatec *Czech Rep.* 50°20N 13°32E **180** A6
Zaterechnyy *Russia* 44°48N 45°11E **191** H7
Zatishye = Elektrostal *Russia* 55°41N 38°32E **188** E10
Zator *Poland* 49°59N 19°28E **185** J6
Zatyshshya *Ukraine* 47°20N 29°51E **183** C14
Zavala *Bos.-H.* 42°50N 17°59E **202** D1
Zavāreh *Iran* 33°29N 52°28E **247** C7
Zave *Zimbabwe* 17°6S 30°1E **271** A5
Zaventem *Belgium* 50°53N 4°28E **116** A2
Zavetnoye *Russia* 47°13N 43°50E **191** G6
Zavidovići *Bos.-H.* 44°27N 18°10E **182** F3
Zavitaya = Zavitinsk *Russia* 50°10N 129°20E **215** D13
Zavitinsk *Russia* 50°10N 129°20E **215** D13
Zavodovski I. *Antarctica* 56°0S 27°45W **151** B1
Zavodskoy = Komsomolskiy *Russia* 54°27N 45°33E **190** C7
Zavolzhsk *Russia* 57°30N 42°3E **190** B6
Zavolzhye = Zavolzhsk *Russia* 57°30N 42°3E **190** B6
Zavolzhye *Russia* 56°37N 43°26E **190** B6
Zawady *Poland* 52°10N 21°6E **142** B2
Zawadzkie *Poland* 50°37N 18°28E **185** H5
Zawichost *Poland* 50°48N 21°51E **185** H8
Zawidów *Poland* 51°1N 15°1E **185** G2
Zawiercie *Poland* 50°30N 19°24E **185** H6
Zāwīyah, J. az *Syria* 35°45N 36°35E **250** C7
Zāwiyat al Bayḍā = Al Bayḍā *Libya* 32°50N 21°44E **258** B4
Zāwiyat Masūs *Libya* 31°35N 21°1E **258** B4
Zâwiyet Abû Musallam *Egypt* 29°56N 31°9E **117** B1
Zawrā' Park *Iraq* 33°18N 44°23E **113** B2
Zâwyet Shammas *Egypt* 31°30N 26°37E **256** A2
Zâwyet Um el Rakham *Egypt* 31°18N 27°1E **256** A2
Zâwyet Ungeîla *Egypt* 31°23N 26°42E **256** A2
Zāyā *Iraq* 33°33N 44°13E **246** C5
Zāyandeh → *Iran* 32°35N 52°0E **247** C7
Zaymah *Si. Arabia* 21°37N 40°6E **248** B3
Zaysan *Kazakhstan* 47°28N 84°52E **217** C10
Zaysan Köli *Kazakhstan* 48°0N 83°0E **217** C10
Zayü *China* 28°48N 97°27E **228** C1
Zazafotsy *Madag.* 21°11S 46°21E **272** C2
Zāzamt, W. → *Libya* 30°29N 14°30E **258** B2
Zazir, O. → *Algeria* 22°0N 5°40E **261** D6
Zázrivá *Slovak Rep.* 49°16N 19°7E **181** B12
Zbarazh *Ukraine* 49°43N 25°44E **177** D13
Zbąszyń *Poland* 52°14N 15°56E **185** F2
Zbąszynek *Poland* 52°16N 15°51E **185** F2
Zblewo *Poland* 53°56N 18°19E **184** E5
Zbraslav *Czech Rep.* 49°58N 14°23E **135** C2
Zbruch → 48°32N 26°27E **183** B11
Zbuzany *Czech Rep.* 50°1N 14°17E **135** B1
Ždár nad Sázavov *Czech Rep.* 49°34N 15°57E **180** B8
Zdiby *Czech Rep.* 50°9N 14°27E **135** B2
Zdolbuniv *Ukraine* 50°30N 26°15E **177** C14
Ždrelo *Serbia* 44°16N 21°28E **202** B5
Zduńska Wola *Poland* 51°37N 18°59E **185** G5
Zduny *Poland* 51°39N 17°21E **185** G4
Zearing *U.S.A.* 42°10N 93°18W **310** B3
Zeballos *Canada* 49°59N 126°50W **296** D3
Zebbug *Malta* 35°52N 14°26E **206** F7
Zebbug *Gozo, Malta* 36°4N 14°14E **206** E6
Zebediela *S. Africa* 24°20S 29°17E **271** B4
Zebila *Ghana* 10°55N 0°30W **263** C4
Zebulon *U.S.A.* 33°6N 84°21W **316** B5
Zeebrugge *Belgium* 51°19N 3°12E **170** C3
Zeehan *Australia* 41°52S 145°25E **281** G4
Zeekoevlei *S. Africa* 34°4S 18°31E **118** B2
Zeeland *U.S.A.* 42°49N 86°1W **311** B10
Zeeland □ *Neths.* 51°30N 3°50E **170** C3
Zeelandia *St. Eustatius* 17°30N 62°59W **322** a
Zeerust *S. Africa* 25°31S 26°4E **270** C4
Ẕefat *Israel* 32°58N 35°29E **250** F6
Zegdou *Algeria* 29°51N 4°45W **260** C4
Zege *Ethiopia* 11°43N 37°18E **257** E4
Zeggerene, Iracher *Mali* 16°49N 2°16E **263** B5
Zégoua *Mali* 10°32N 5°35W **262** C3
Zehak *Iran* 30°53N 61°42E **247** D9
Zehden = Cedynia *Poland* 52°53N 14°12E **185** F1
Zehdenick *Germany* 52°58N 13°20E **178** C9
Zehlendorf *Germany* 52°26N 13°16E **115** B2
Zeigler *U.S.A.* 37°54N 89°3W **310** G7
Zeil, Mt. *Australia* 23°30S 132°23E **278** D5
Zeila = Saylac *Somali Rep.* 11°21N 43°30E **267** B5
Zeist *Neths.* 52°5N 5°15E **170** B5
Zeitz *Germany* 51°2N 12°7E **178** D8
Zejtun *Malta* 35°51N 14°32E **206** F8
Żelechów *Poland* 51°49N 21°54E **185** G8
Zelena *Ukraine* 48°3N 24°45E **183** B9
Zelengora *Bos.-H.* 43°22N 18°30E **202** C2
Zelenodolsk *Russia* 55°55N 48°30E **190** C9
Zelenogorsk *Russia* 60°12N 29°43E **188** B5
Zelenograd *Russia* 56°1N 37°12E **188** D9
Zelenogradsk *Russia* 54°53N 20°29E **184** D7
Zelenokumsk *Russia* 44°24N 44°0E **191** H6
Zeleqa, W. → *Egypt* 29°7N 34°31E **251** J5
Železná Ruda *Czech Rep.* 49°8N 13°15E **180** B6
Železnik *Serbia* 44°43N 20°23E **202** B4
Zelfana *Algeria* 32°27N 4°15E **261** B5
Zelienople *U.S.A.* 40°48N 80°8W **312** F4
Želiezovce *Slovak Rep.* 48°3N 18°40E **181** C11
Zelina *Croatia* 45°57N 16°16E **199** C13
Zell *Baden-W., Germany* 47°42N 7°52E **179** H3
Zell *Rhld-Pfz., Germany* 50°1N 7°10E **179** E3
Zell am See *Austria* 47°19N 12°47E **180** D5
Zella-Mehlis *Germany* 50°39N 10°40E **178** E6
Zelmen = Rovnoye *Russia* 50°52N 46°3E **190** E8
Zelów *Poland* 51°28N 19°14E **185** G6
Zeltweg *Austria* 47°11N 14°45E **180** D7
Zelyony Dol = Zelenodolsk *Russia* 55°55N 48°30E **190** C9
Žemaitijos △ *Lithuania* 56°2N 21°55E **184** B8
Zembra, I. *Tunisia* 37°5N 10°56E **258** A2
Zemgale = Jelgava *Latvia* 56°41N 23°49E **184** B10
Zémio *C.A.R.* 5°2N 25°5E **264** A5
Zemlya Imperatora Nikolaya II = Severnaya Zemlya *Russia* 79°0N 100°0E **215** B11
Zemmora *Algeria* 35°44N 0°51E **261** A5
Zemmur *W. Sahara* 25°5N 12°0W **260** C2
Zemongo ⌓ *C.A.R.* 6°45N 25°5E **264** A5
Zemoul, O. → *Algeria* 29°15N 7°0W **260** C3
Zempelburg = Sępólno Krajeńskie *Poland* 53°26N 17°30E **184** E4
Zempléni-hegység *Hungary* 48°25N 21°25E **182** B6
Zemplínska širava *Slovak Rep.* 48°48N 22°0E **181** C15
Zempoala *Mexico* 19°27N 96°23W **319** D5
Zemun *Serbia* 44°51N 20°25E **202** B4
Zendeh Jān *Afghan.* 34°21N 61°45E **240** B1
Zengbé *Cameroon* 5°46N 13°4E **263** D7
Zengcheng *China* 23°13N 113°52E **229** F9
Zenica *Bos.-H.* 44°10N 17°57E **182** F2
Zenne → *Belgium* 51°4N 4°26E **116** A2
Zentsūji *Japan* 34°14N 133°47E **222** C5
Zenza → *Angola* 8°45S 13°24E **265** D2
Zenza do Itombe *Angola* 9°16S 14°13E **265** D2
Žepče *Bos.-H.* 44°28N 18°2E **182** F3
Zephyr Field *U.S.A.* 30°1N 90°5W **131** B1
Zephyrhills *U.S.A.* 28°14N 82°11W **317** G7
Zepu *China* 38°11N 77°16E **217** E9
Zeraf, Bahr ez → *Sudan* 9°42N 30°52E **257** F3
Żerań *Poland* 52°18N 20°58E **142** B1
Zerbst *Germany* 51°58N 12°5E **178** D8
Zerhamra *Algeria* 29°58N 2°30W **261** C4
Żerków *Poland* 52°4N 17°32E **185** F4
Zermatt *Switz.* 46°2N 7°46E **179** J3
Zernez *Switz.* 46°42N 10°7E **179** J6
Zernograd *Russia* 46°52N 40°19E **191** G5
Zernovoy = Zernograd *Russia* 46°52N 40°19E **191** G5
Zero Milestone *Washington, D.C., U.S.A.* **143** b1
Zerqan *Albania* 41°27N 20°20E **202** E4
Zerzeń *Poland* 52°12N 21°7E **142** B2
Zestaponi *Georgia* 42°6N 43°0E **191** J6
Zetel *Germany* 53°25N 7°58E **178** B3
Zetland = Shetland □ *U.K.* 60°30N 1°30W **167** A7
Zeulenroda *Germany* 50°39N 11°59E **178** E7
Zévallos *Guadeloupe* 16°18N 61°17W **322** e
Zeven *Germany* 53°17N 9°16E **178** B5
Zevenaar *Neths.* 51°56N 6°5E **170** C6
Zévio *Italy* 45°22N 11°8E **198** C8
Zeya *Russia* 53°48N 127°14E **215** D13
Zeya → *Russia* 51°42N 128°53E **215** D13
Zeyne *Turkey* 36°25N 33°31E **250** B4
Zeytinbaği *Turkey* 40°24N 28°47E **203** F12
Zeytinburnu *Turkey* 40°58N 28°53E **122** C1
Zeytindağ *Turkey* 38°58N 27°4E **205** C9
Zghartā *Lebanon* 34°21N 35°53E **250** D6
Zgierz *Poland* 51°50N 19°27E **185** G6
Zgorzelec *Poland* 51°10N 15°0E **185** G2
Zguriţa *Moldova* 48°8N 28°1E **183** B13
Zhabei *China* 31°16N 121°26E **138** B1
Zhabinka *Belarus* 52°13N 24°2E **185** F11
Zhabokrych *Ukraine* 48°23N 28°59E **183** B13
Zhalaghash *Kazakhstan* 45°5N 64°40E **216** C6
Zhalpaqtal *Kazakhstan* 49°42N 49°25E **190** F9
Zhaltyr *Kazakhstan* 51°37N 69°49E **217** B7
Zhambyl = Taraz *Kazakhstan* 42°54N 71°22E **217** D8
Zhambyl □ *Kazakhstan* 44°0N 72°0E **217** D8
Zhanatas *Kazakhstan* 43°35N 69°35E **217** D7
Zhangaly *Kazakhstan* 47°1N 50°37E **191** G10
Zhangaözen *Kazakhstan* 43°18N 52°48E **187** F9
Zhangaqala *Kazakhstan* 48°56N 49°36E **191** F9
Zhangaqazaly *Kazakhstan* 45°48N 62°6E **216** C6
Zhangatas = Zhanatas *Kazakhstan* 43°35N 69°35E **217** D7
Zhangbei *China* 41°10N 114°45E **226** D8
Zhangguangcai Ling *China* 45°0N 129°0E **227** B15
Zhangjiabian *China* 22°33N 113°28E **219** a
Zhangjiagang *China* 31°55N 120°30E **229** B13
Zhangjiakou *China* 40°48N 114°55E **226** D8
Zhangping *China* 25°17N 117°23E **229** E11
Zhangpu *China* 24°8N 117°35E **229** E11
Zhangshu *China* 28°4N 115°29E **229** C10
Zhangye *China* 38°50N 100°23E **218** D9
Zhangzhou *China* 24°30N 117°35E **229** E11
Zhanhua *China* 37°40N 118°8E **227** F10
Zhänibek *Kazakhstan* 49°25N 46°50E **190** F8
Zhanjiang *China* 21°15N 110°20E **229** G8
Zhannetty, Ostrov *Russia* 76°43N 158°0E **215** B16
Zhanyi *China* 25°38N 103°48E **228** E4
Zhanyu *China* 44°30N 122°30E **227** B12
Zhao Xian *China* 37°43N 114°45E **226** F8
Zhao'an *China* 23°41N 117°10E **229** F11
Zhaocheng *China* 36°22N 111°38E **226** F6
Zhaojue *China* 28°1N 102°49E **228** C4
Zhaoping *China* 24°11N 110°48E **229** E8
Zhaoqing *China* 23°0N 112°20E **229** F9
Zhaotong *China* 27°20N 103°44E **228** D4
Zhaoyang Hu *China* 35°4N 116°47E **226** G9
Zhaoyuan *Heilongjiang, China* 45°27N 125°0E **227** B13
Zhaoyuan *Shandong, China* 37°20N 120°23E **227** F11
Zhari Namco *China* 31°6N 85°36E **218** E6
Zharkent *Kazakhstan* 44°10N 80°0E **217** D10
Zharkovskiy *Russia* 55°56N 32°19E **188** E7
Zhashkiv *Ukraine* 49°15N 30°5E **177** D16
Zhashui *China* 33°40N 109°8E **226** H5
Zhaslyk *Uzbekistan* 43°58N 57°10E **216** D5
Zhayrang *Kazakhstan* 48°20N 70°10E **217** C8
Zhayylma *Kazakhstan* 51°37N 61°33E **216** B6
Zhayyq → *Kazakhstan* 47°0N 51°48E **187** E9
Zhdanov = Mariupol *Ukraine* 47°5N 37°31E **189** J9
Zhdanov *Russia* 55°44N 37°41E **129** B4
Zhecheng *China* 34°7N 115°20E **226** G8
Zhegao *China* 31°46N 117°45E **229** B11
Zhejiang □ *China* 29°0N 120°0E **229** C13
Zheleznodorozhnyy = Qŭnghirot *Uzbekistan* 43°2N 58°50E **216** D5
Zheleznodorozhnyy *Kaliningrad, Russia* 54°22N 21°19E **184** D8
Zheleznodorozhnyy *Komi, Russia* 62°35N 50°55E **186** B9
Zheleznodorozhnyy *Moskva, Russia* 55°45N 38°0E **129** B6
Zheleznogorsk *Russia* 52°22N 35°23E **189** F8
Zheleznogorsk-Ilimskiy *Russia* 56°34N 104°8E **215** D11
Zheltyye Vody = Zhovti Vody *Ukraine* 48°21N 33°31E **189** H7
Zhen'an *China* 33°27N 109°9E **228** A7
Zhenba *China* 32°34N 107°58E **228** A6
Zhenfeng *China* 25°22N 105°40E **228** E5
Zheng'an *China* 28°32N 107°27E **228** C6
Zhengding *China* 38°8N 114°32E **226** E8
Zhenghe *China* 27°20N 118°50E **229** D12
Zhengyang *China* 32°37N 114°22E **229** A10
Zhengyangguan *China* 32°30N 116°29E **229** A11
Zhengzhou *China* 34°45N 113°34E **226** G7
Zhenhai *China* 29°59N 121°42E **229** C13
Zhenjiang *China* 32°11N 119°26E **229** A12
Zhenkang *China* 23°58N 99°0E **228** F2
Zhenlai *China* 45°50N 123°5E **227** B12
Zhenning *China* 26°4N 105°45E **228** D5
Zhenping *Henan, China* 33°10N 112°16E **226** H7
Zhenping *Shaanxi, China* 31°59N 109°31E **228** B7
Zhenru *China* 31°16N 121°22E **138** B1
Zhenxiong *China* 27°27N 104°50E **228** D5
Zhenyuan *Gansu, China* 35°35N 107°30E **226** G4
Zhenyuan *Guizhou, China* 27°4N 108°21E **228** D7
Zhenyuan *Yunnan, China* 23°51N 100°59E **228** F3
Zherdevka *Russia* 51°56N 41°29E **190** E5
Zherebkove *Ukraine* 47°50N 29°52E **183** C14
Zhernovka *Russia* 59°56N 30°30E **137** B2
Zherong *China* 27°15N 119°52E **229** D12
Zhetiqara *Kazakhstan* 52°11N 61°12E **216** B6
Zhezdi *Kazakhstan* 48°3N 67°3E **217** C7
Zhezqazghan *Kazakhstan* 47°44N 67°40E **217** C7
Zhicheng *China* 30°25N 111°27E **229** B8
Zhicun *China* 23°0N 113°18E **121** B2
Zhidan *China* 36°48N 108°48E **226** F5
Zhigansk *Russia* 66°48N 123°27E **215** C13
Zhigulevsk *Russia* 53°28N 49°30E **190** D9
Zhijiang *Hubei, China* 30°28N 111°45E **229** B8
Zhijiang *Hunan, China* 27°27N 109°42E **228** D7
Zhijin *China* 26°37N 105°45E **228** D5
Zhilinda *Russia* 70°0N 114°20E **215** C12
Zhilino *Russia* 54°54N 21°54E **184** D8
Zhirnovsk *Russia* 50°57N 44°49E **190** E7
Zhirnovsky = Zhirnovsk *Russia* 50°57N 44°49E **190** E7
Zhirnoye = Zhirnovsk *Russia* 50°57N 44°49E **190** E7
Zhitomir = Zhytomyr *Ukraine* 50°20N 28°40E **177** C15
Zhizdra *Russia* 53°45N 34°40E **188** F8
Zhlobin *Belarus* 52°55N 30°0E **177** B16
Zhmerynka *Ukraine* 49°2N 28°2E **177** D15
Zhob *Pakistan* 31°20N 69°31E **242** D3
Zhob → *Pakistan* 32°4N 69°50E **242** C3
Zhodzina *Belarus* 54°5N 28°17E **177** A15
Zhokhova, Ostrov *Russia* 76°4N 152°40E **215** B16
Zholkev = Zhovkva *Ukraine* 50°4N 23°58E **177** C12
Zholkva = Zhovkva *Ukraine* 50°4N 23°58E **177** C12
Zhongba *China* 29°39N 84°10E **218** F5
Zhongdian *China* 27°48N 99°42E **228** D2
Zhongdong *China* 22°48N 107°47E **228** F6
Zhongdu *China* 24°40N 109°40E **228** E7
Zhongguancun *China* 39°59N 116°18E **114** B1
Zhongjiang *China* 30°53N 104°46E **228** B5
Zhongning *China* 37°29N 105°40E **226** F3
Zhongshan *Antarctica* 69°0S 39°50E **151** C6
Zhongshan *Guangdong, China* 22°26N 113°20E **229** F9
Zhongshan *Guangxi Zhuangzu, China* 24°29N 111°18E **229** E8
Zhongshan Park *Beijing, China* **114** c3
Zhongshan Park *Shanghai, China* 31°13N 121°24E **138** B1
Zhongshankong *China* 22°35N 113°29E **219** a
Zhongtiao Shan *China* 35°0N 111°10E **226** G6
Zhongwei *China* 37°30N 105°12E **226** F3
Zhongxian *China* 30°18N 107°58E **228** B6
Zhongxiang *China* 31°12N 112°34E **229** B9
Zhongyang *China* 37°20N 111°11E **226** F6
Zhorany *Ukraine* 51°19N 23°58E **185** G10
Zhosaly *Kazakhstan* 45°29N 64°4E **216** C6
Zhoucun *Guangdong, China* 23°11N 113°11E **121** A2
Zhoucun *Shandong, China* 36°47N 117°48E **227** F9
Zhoujiadu *China* 31°11N 121°29E **138** B1
Zhoujiazhen *China* 31°16N 121°33E **138** B2
Zhoukou *China* 33°38N 114°38E **226** H8
Zhoukoudian *China* 39°41N 115°56E **226** E8
Zhouning *China* 27°12N 119°20E **229** D12
Zhoushan *China* 30°1N 122°6E **229** B14
Zhoushan Dao *China* 30°5N 122°10E **229** C14
Zhouzhi *China* 34°10N 108°12E **226** G5
Zhouzhuangzi *China* 39°51N 116°16E **114** B1
Zhovkva *Ukraine* 50°4N 23°58E **177** C12
Zhovti Vody *Ukraine* 48°21N 33°31E **189** H7
Zhovtneve *Lubelskie, Ukraine* 50°42N 24°12E **185** H11
Zhovtneve *Mykolayiv, Ukraine* 46°54N 32°3E **189** J7
Zhu Jiang → *China* 22°45N 113°37E **229** F9
Zhuanghe *China* 39°40N 123°0E **224** C1
Zhucheng *China* 36°0N 119°27E **227** G10
Zhugqu *China* 33°40N 104°30E **226** H3
Zhuhai *China* 22°17N 113°34E **229** F9
Zhuji *China* 29°40N 120°10E **229** C13
Zhujiang Kou *China* 22°20N 113°45E **219** a
Zhukovka *Russia* 53°35N 33°50E **188** F7
Zhulebino *Russia* 55°42N 37°50E **129** B5
Zhumadian *China* 32°59N 114°2E **229** A10
Zhuo Xian = Zhuozhou *China* 39°28N 115°58E **226** E8
Zhuolu *China* 40°20N 115°12E **226** D8
Zhuozhou *China* 39°28N 115°58E **226** E8
Zhuozi *China* 41°0N 112°25E **226** D7
Zhushadi *China* 23°11N 113°22E **121** A3
Zhushan *China* 32°15N 110°13E **229** A8
Zhuxi *China* 32°25N 109°40E **228** A7
Zhuzhou *China* 27°49N 113°12E **229** D9
Zhvanets *Ukraine* 48°33N 26°30E **183** B11
Zhympīty *Kazakhstan* 50°16N 52°35E **216** B4
Zhytomyr *Ukraine* 50°20N 28°40E **177** C15
Zhytomyr □ *Ukraine* 50°50N 28°10E **177** C14
Zi Shui → *China* 28°40N 112°40E **229** C9
Žiar nad Hronom *Slovak Rep.* 48°35N 18°53E **181** C11
Ziarat *Pakistan* 30°25N 67°49E **242** D2
Zibo *China* 36°47N 118°3E **227** F10
Zichang *China* 37°18N 109°40E **226** F5
Zidarovo *Bulgaria* 42°20N 27°24E **203** D11
Zidi = Wandhari *Pakistan* 27°42N 66°48E **242** F2
Ziębice *Poland* 50°37N 17°2E **185** H4
Ziebingen = Cybinka *Poland* 52°12N 14°46E **185** F1
Ziegenhals = Głuchołazy *Poland* 50°19N 17°24E **185** H4
Zielenzig = Sulęcin *Poland* 52°26N 15°10E **185** F2
Zielona *Poland* 52°14N 21°11E **142** B3
Zielona Góra *Poland* 51°57N 15°31E **185** G2
Zielonka *Poland* 52°18N 21°9E **142** B2
Zierikzee *Neths.* 51°40N 3°55E **170** C3
Ziesar *Germany* 52°16N 12°17E **178** C8
Zifta *Egypt* 30°43N 31°14E **256** H7
Zīghan *Libya* 25°29N 22°8E **258** C4
Zigon *Burma* 18°20N 95°37E **241** F5
Zigong *China* 29°15N 104°48E **228** C5
Ziguéy *Chad* 14°43N 15°50E **259** F3
Ziguinchor *Senegal* 12°35N 16°20W **262** C1
Ziguinchor □ *Senegal* 12°45N 16°20W **262** C1
Zihuatanejo *Mexico* 17°39N 101°33W **318** D4
Zijin *China* 23°33N 115°8E **229** F10
Zile *Turkey* 40°15N 35°52E **212** B6
Žilina *Slovak Rep.* 49°12N 18°42E **181** B11
Žilinský □ *Slovak Rep.* 49°10N 19°0E **181** B12
Zillah *Libya* 28°30N 17°33E **258** C3
Zillertaler Alpen *Austria* 47°6N 11°45E **180** D4
Zima *Russia* 54°0N 102°5E **215** D11
Zimapán *Mexico* 20°45N 99°21W **319** C5
Zimba *Zambia* 17°20S 26°11E **269** F2
Zimbabwe *Zimbabwe* 20°16S 30°54E **269** G3
Zimbabwe ■ *Africa* 19°0S 30°0E **269** F3
Zimmi *S. Leone* 7°20N 11°20W **262** D2
Zimnicea *Romania* 43°40N 25°22E **183** G10
Zimovniki *Russia* 47°10N 42°25E **191** G6
Zina *Cameroon* 11°19N 14°54E **259** F2
Zinave △ *Mozam.* 21°35S 33°40E **271** B5
Zinder *Niger* 13°48N 9°0E **259** F1
Zinder □ *Niger* 15°0N 10°30E **263** C7
Zinga *C.A.R.* 3°49N 18°34E **264** B3
Zinga *Tanzania* 9°16S 38°49E **269** D4
Zingaro ⌓ *Italy* 38°6N 12°53E **200** D5
Zingst *Germany* 54°26N 12°39E **178** A8
Ziniaré *Burkina Faso* 12°35N 1°18W **263** C4
Zinnowitz *Germany* 54°4N 13°54E **178** A9
Zinovyevsk = Kirovohrad *Ukraine* 48°35N 32°20E **189** H7
Zion *St. Kitts & Nevis* 17°8N 62°33W **322** d
Zion *Ill., U.S.A.* 42°27N 87°50W **311** B9
Zion △ *U.S.A.* 37°15N 113°5W **305** H7
Zionsville *U.S.A.* 39°57N 86°16W **311** E10
Zipaquirá *Colombia* 5°0N 74°0W **328** C3
Zirbitzkogel *Austria* 47°4N 14°34E **180** D7
Zirc *Hungary* 47°17N 17°52E **182** C2
Žiri *Slovenia* 46°5N 14°5E **199** B11
Žirje *Croatia* 43°39N 15°42E **199** E12
Zirke = Sieraków *Poland* 52°39N 16°2E **185** F3
Zirl *Austria* 47°17N 11°14E **180** D4
Zirndorf *Germany* 49°27N 10°57E **179** F6
Ziros *Greece* 35°5N 26°8E **207** E7
Zirreh, Gowd-e *Afghan.* 29°45N 62°0E **240** C1
Zisterdorf *Austria* 48°33N 16°45E **181** C9
Zitácuaro *Mexico* 19°24N 100°22W **318** D4
Žitava → *Slovak Rep.* 48°14N 18°21E **181** C11
Žitište *Serbia* 45°30N 20°32E **182** E5
Zitong *China* 31°37N 105°10E **228** B5
Zitsa *Greece* 39°47N 20°40E **204** B2
Zittau *Germany* 50°53N 14°48E **178** E10
Zitundo *Mozam.* 26°48S 32°47E **271** C5
Živinice *Bos.-H.* 44°27N 18°36E **182** F3
Ziwa Maghariba = Kagera □ *Tanzania* 2°0S 31°30E **268** C3
Ziway *Ethiopia* 7°56N 38°43E **266** C4
Ziway, L. *Ethiopia* 8°0N 38°50E **257** F4
Zixi *China* 27°45N 117°4E **229** D11
Zixing *China* 25°59N 113°21E **229** E9
Ziyang *Shaanxi, China* 32°32N 108°31E **226** H5
Ziyang *Sichuan, China* 30°6N 104°40E **228** B5
Ziyuan *China* 26°2N 110°40E **229** D8
Ziyun *China* 25°45N 106°5E **228** E6
Ziz, Oued → *Morocco* 31°40N 4°15W **260** B4
Zizhong *China* 29°48N 104°47E **228** C5
Zizhuyuan Park *China* 39°54N 116°18E **114** B1
Žižkov *Czech Rep.* 50°5N 14°28E **135** B2
Zizur Mayor *Spain* 42°47N 1°41W **196** C3
Zlarin *Croatia* 43°42N 15°49E **199** E12
Zlatar *Croatia* 46°5N 16°3E **199** B13
Zlatar *Serbia* 43°25N 19°47E **202** C3
Zlataritsa *Bulgaria* 43°2N 25°55E **203** C9
Zlaté Moravce *Slovak Rep.* 48°23N 18°24E **181** C11
Zlatibor *Serbia* 43°45N 19°43E **202** C3
Zlatitsa *Bulgaria* 42°41N 24°7E **203** D8
Zlatna *Romania* 46°8N 23°11E **183** D8
Zlatna Panega *Bulgaria* 43°5N 24°9E **203** C8
Zlatni Pyasŭtsi *Bulgaria* 43°17N 28°3E **203** C12
Zlatograd *Bulgaria* 41°22N 25°7E **203** E9
Zlatoust *Russia* 55°10N 59°40E **186** C10
Zletovo *Macedonia* 41°59N 22°17E **202** E6
Zličín *Czech Rep.* 50°3N 14°17E **135** B1
Zlín *Czech Rep.* 49°14N 17°40E **181** B10
Zlínský □ *Czech Rep.* 49°20N 17°40E **181** B10
Ẓlītan *Libya* 32°32N 14°35E **258** B2
Złocieniec *Poland* 53°30N 16°1E **184** E3
Złoczew *Poland* 51°24N 18°35E **185** G5
Zlot *Serbia* 44°1N 21°58E **202** B5
Złotoryja *Poland* 51°8N 15°55E **185** G2
Złotów *Poland* 53°22N 17°2E **184** E4
Zmeinogorsk *Kazakhstan* 51°10N 82°13E **217** B10
Żmigród *Poland* 51°28N 16°53E **185** G3
Zmiyev *Ukraine* 49°39N 36°27E **189** H9
Znamenka = Znamyanka *Ukraine* 48°45N 32°30E **189** H7
Znamensk *Russia* 54°36N 21°16E **184** D8
Znamyanka *Ukraine* 48°45N 32°30E **189** H7
Żnin *Poland* 52°51N 17°44E **185** F4
Znojmo *Czech Rep.* 48°50N 16°2E **180** C9
Zobeyrī *Iran* 34°10N 46°40E **246** C5
Zobia *Dem. Rep. of the Congo* 3°0N 25°59E **268** B2
Zobten = Sobótka *Poland* 50°54N 16°44E **185** H3
Zócalo *Mexico City, Mexico* **128** b3
Zoetermeer *Neths.* 52°3N 4°30E **170** B4
Zogang *China* 29°55N 97°42E **228** C1
Zogno *Italy* 45°48N 9°40E **198** C6
Zografou *Greece* 37°58N 23°47E **112** B2
Zohreh → *Iran* 30°16N 51°15E **247** D6
Zolfo Springs *U.S.A.* 27°30N 81°48W **317** H8
Żoliborz *Poland* 52°16N 20°57E **142** B1
Zolochiv *Ukraine* 49°45N 24°51E **177** D13
Zolotonosha *Ukraine* 49°39N 32°5E **189** H7
Zolotyy Potik *Ukraine* 48°54N 25°20E **183** B10
Zomba *Malawi* 15°22S 35°19E **269** F4
Zongo *Dem. Rep. of the Congo* 4°20N 18°35E **264** B3
Zonguldak *Turkey* 41°28N 31°50E **212** B4
Zonguldak □ *Turkey* 41°20N 31°45E **212** B4
Zongyang *China* 30°42N 117°12E **229** B11
Zonnebloem *S. Africa* 33°56S 18°26E **118** A1
Zonqor Pt. *Malta* 35°52N 14°34E **206** F8
Zonza *France* 41°45N 9°11E **175** G13
Zoo Baba *Niger* 18°13N 13°2E **259** E2
Zorgo *Burkina Faso* 12°15N 0°35W **263** C4
Zorita *Spain* 39°17N 5°39W **195** F5
Zorleni *Romania* 46°14N 27°44E **183** D12
Zornitsa *Bulgaria* 42°23N 26°58E **203** D10
Zorritos *Peru* 3°43S 80°40W **330** A1
Żory *Poland* 50°3N 18°44E **185** H5
Zorzor *Liberia* 7°46N 9°28W **262** D3
Zossen *Germany* 52°13N 13°27E **178** C9
Zou Xiang *China* 35°30N 116°58E **226** G9
Zouan-Hounien *Ivory C.* 6°55N 8°15W **262** D3
Zouar *Chad* 20°30N 16°32E **259** D3
Zouérate = Zouîrât *Mauritania* 22°44N 12°21W **260** D2
Zouîrât *Mauritania* 22°44N 12°21W **260** D2
Zouri *Gabon* 1°1S 8°53E **264** C1
Zourika *Niger* 19°16N 7°52E **259** E1
Zourma *Burkina Faso* 11°20N 0°50W **263** C4
Zousfana, O. → *Algeria* 31°28N 2°17W **261** B4
Zoutkamp *Neths.* 53°20N 6°18E **170** A6
Zrenjanin *Serbia* 45°22N 20°23E **182** E5
Zuarungu *Ghana* 10°49N 0°46W **263** C4
Zuatá → *Venezuela* 7°52N 65°22W **329** B4
Zuba *Nigeria* 9°11N 7°12E **263** D6
Zubayr *Yemen* 15°3N 42°10E **248** D3
Zubin Potok *Kosovo* 42°54N 20°41E **202** D4
Zubtsov *Russia* 56°10N 34°34E **188** D8
Zudañez *Bolivia* 19°6S 64°44W **331** D5
Zuénoula *Ivory C.* 7°34N 6°3W **262** D3
Zuera *Spain* 41°51N 0°49W **196** D4
Zuetina = Az Zuwaytīnah *Libya* 30°58N 20°7E **258** B4
Ẓufār *Oman* 17°40N 54°0E **249** C6
Zug *Switz.* 47°10N 8°31E **179** H4
Zug *W. Sahara* 21°36N 14°9W **260** D2
Zugdidi *Georgia* 42°30N 41°55E **191** J5
Zugersee *Switz.* 47°7N 8°35E **179** H4
Zugliget *Hungary* 47°30N 18°59E **117** B1
Zugló *Hungary* 47°31N 19°8E **117** A2
Zugspitze *Germany* 47°25N 10°59E **179** H6
Zuhd, J. az *Si. Arabia* 28°20N 35°17E **251** K6
Zuid-Holland □ *Neths.* 52°0N 4°35E **170** C4
Zuidbeveland *Neths.* 51°30N 3°50E **170** C3
Zuiderwoude *Neths.* 52°26N 5°2E **112** A3
Zuidhorn *Neths.* 53°15N 6°23E **170** A6
Zújar *Spain* 37°34N 2°50W **195** H8
Zújar → *Spain* 39°1N 5°47W **195** G5
Żukowo *Poland* 54°21N 18°22E **184** D5
Zula *Eritrea* 15°17N 39°40E **257** D4
Zulia □ *Venezuela* 10°0N 72°10W **328** B3
Züllichau = Sulechów *Poland* 52°5N 15°40E **185** F2
Zülpich *Germany* 50°41N 6°39E **178** E2
Zülz = Biała *Poland* 50°24N 17°40E **185** H4
Zumaia *Spain* 43°19N 2°15W **196** B2
Zumárraga *Spain* 43°5N 2°19W **196** B2
Zumbi *Brazil* 22°49S 43°10W **135** A1
Zumbo *Mozam.* 15°35S 30°26E **269** F3
Zummo *Nigeria* 9°51N 12°59E **263** D7
Zumpango *Mexico* 19°48N 99°6W **319** D5
Zunderdorp *Neths.* 52°24N 4°58E **112** A2
Zundi *Angola* 10°28S 16°48E **265** E3
Zungeru *Nigeria* 9°48N 6°8E **263** D6
Zunhua *China* 40°18N 117°58E **227** D9
Zuni Pueblo *U.S.A.* 35°4N 108°51W **305** J9
Zunyi *China* 27°42N 106°53E **228** D6
Zuo Jiang → *China* 22°50N 108°6E **228** F6
Zuoquan *China* 37°1N 113°27E **226** F7
Zuozhou *China* 22°42N 107°27E **228** F6
Županja *Croatia* 45°4N 18°43E **182** E3
Žur *Kosovo* 42°13N 20°34E **202** D4
Zurbātīyah *Iraq* 33°9N 46°3E **213** F12
Zürich *Switz.* 47°22N 8°32E **179** H4
Zürich □ *Switz.* 47°26N 8°40E **179** H4
Zürichsee *Switz.* 47°18N 8°40E **179** H4
Żuromin *Poland* 53°4N 19°51E **185** E6
Zurrieq *Malta* 35°50N 14°28E **206** F7
Žut *Croatia* 43°52N 15°17E **199** E12
Zutphen *Neths.* 52°9N 6°12E **170** B6
Zuurberg △ *S. Africa* 33°12S 25°32E **270** D4
Zuvuvu → *Brazil* 23°40S 46°42W **137** C1
Zuwārah *Libya* 32°58N 12°1E **258** B2
Zūzan *Iran* 34°22N 59°53E **247** C8
Žužemberk *Slovenia* 45°52N 14°56E **199** C11
Zvanka = Volkhov *Russia* 59°55N 32°15E **188** C7
Zvečan *Kosovo* 42°54N 20°50E **202** D4
Zvenigorodka = Svenyhorodka *Ukraine* 49°4N 30°56E **189** H6
Zvezdets *Bulgaria* 42°6N 27°26E **203** D11
Zvishavane *Zimbabwe* 20°17S 30°2E **269** G3
Zvolen *Slovak Rep.* 48°33N 19°10E **181** C12
Zvonce *Serbia* 42°57N 22°34E **202** D6
Zvornik *Bos.-H.* 44°26N 19°5E **182** F4
Zwanenburg *Neths.* 52°23N 4°45E **112** A1
Zwedru = Tchien *Liberia* 5°59N 8°15W **262** D3
Zweibrücken *Germany* 49°15N 7°21E **179** F3
Zwenkau *Germany* 51°13N 12°20E **178** D8
Zwettl *Austria* 48°35N 15°9E **180** C8
Zwickau *Germany* 50°44N 12°30E **178** E8
Zwierzyniec *Poland* 50°36N 22°58E **185** H9
Zwiesel *Germany* 49°1N 13°13E **179** F9
Zwittau = Svitavy *Czech Rep.* 49°47N 16°28E **181** B9
Zwoleń *Poland* 51°21N 21°36E **185** G8
Zwölfaxing *Austria* 48°6N 16°28E **142** B2
Zwolle *Neths.* 52°31N 6°6E **170** B6
Zwolle *La., U.S.A.* 31°38N 93°39W **314** F8
Żychlin *Poland* 52°15N 19°37E **185** F6
Żyrardów *Poland* 52°3N 20°28E **185** F7
Zyryan *Kazakhstan* 49°43N 84°20E **217** C10
Zyryanka *Russia* 65°45N 150°51E **215** C16
Zyryanovsk = Zyryan *Kazakhstan* 49°43N 84°20E **217** C10
Zyuzino *Russia* 55°39N 37°34E **129** C3
Żywiec *Poland* 49°42N 19°10E **185** J6

KEY TO EUROPEAN MAP PAGES

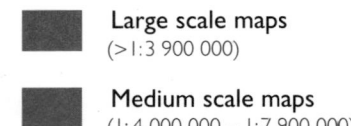

Large scale maps
(>1:3 900 000)

Medium scale maps
(1:4 000 000 – 1:7 900 000)

Small scale maps
(<1:8 000 000)

Paris p134 City maps

155

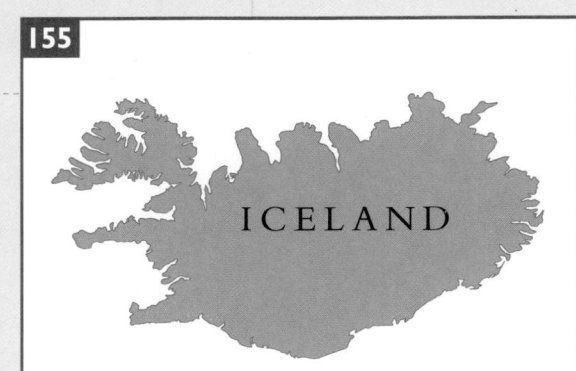

ICELAND

Arctic Circle

WORLD COUNTRY INDEX

Afghanistan	240	
Albania	202	
Algeria	260–261	
Angola	265	
Argentina	334, 336	
Armenia	213	
Australia	278–283	
Austria	180–181	
Azerbaijan	213	
Azores	153	
Bahamas	320–321	
Bahrain	249	
Bangladesh	241	
Barbados	322	
Belarus	188–189	
Belgium	170	
Belize	320	
Benin	263	
Bhutan	241	
Bolivia	330–331	
Bosnia-Herzegovina	198, 202	
Botswana	270	
Brazil	328–335	
Brunei	235	
Bulgaria	202–203	
Burkina Faso	262–263	
Burma (Myanmar)	236–237, 241	
Burundi	268	
Cambodia	236–237	
Canary Is.	153	
Cameroon	259, 264	
Canada	294–299	
Cape Verde Is.	153	
Central African Republic	264	
Chad	259	
Chile	330, 334, 336	
China	218–219, 226–229	
Colombia	328	
Comoros	272	
Congo	264–265	
Congo, Dem. Rep. of the	264–265, 268–269	
Costa Rica	320	
Croatia	182, 199	
Cuba	320–321	
Cyprus	207	
Czech Republic	180–181	
Denmark	163	
Djibouti	267	
Dominican Republic	321	
Ecuador	328	
Egypt	256	
El Salvador	320	
England	168–169	
Equatorial Guinea	264	
Eritrea	266–267	
Estonia	188	
Ethiopia	266–267	
Fiji	287	
Finland	160–161	
France	172–175	
French Guiana	329	
Gabon	264	
Gambia	262	
Georgia	213	

Germany	178–179	
Ghana	262–263	
Greece	202–205	
Greenland	154	
Guadeloupe	322	
Guatemala	320	
Guinea	262	
Guinea-Bissau	262	
Guyana	329	
Haiti	321	
Honduras	320	
Hungary	182	
Iceland	155	
India	241, 242–245	
Indonesia	230–231, 234–235	
Iran	246–247	
Iraq	246–247	
Irish Republic	166	
Israel	250–251	
Italy	198–201	
Ivory Coast	262	
Jamaica	320	
Japan	220–223	
Jordan	251	
Kazakhstan	216–217	
Kenya	268	
Korea, North	224	
Korea, South	224	
Kosovo	202	
Kuwait	246–247	
Kyrgyzstan	217	
Laos	236	
Latvia	188	
Lebanon	250	
Lesotho	271	
Liberia	262	
Libya	258	
Lithuania	188	
Luxembourg	170	
Macedonia	202	
Madagascar	272	
Malawi	269	
Malaysia	234–235	
Mali	260–263	
Malta	206	
Martinique	322	
Mauritania	260, 262	
Mauritius	272	
Mexico	318–319	
Moldova	183	
Mongolia	218–219	
Montenegro	202	
Morocco	260–261	
Mozambique	269, 271	
Namibia	270	
Nepal	243	
Netherlands	170	
New Zealand	284–285	
Nicaragua	320	
Niger	259, 263	
Nigeria	263	
Northern Ireland	166	
Norway	160–161, 164	

Oman	249	
Pakistan	240	
Panama	320	
Papua New Guinea	286	
Paraguay	334–335	
Peru	328, 330	
Philippines	232–233	
Poland	184–185	
Portugal	194–195	
Puerto Rico	321	
Qatar	249	
Réunion	272	
Romania	182–183	
Russia	186–191, 214–215	
Rwanda	268	
St. Lucia	322	
Samoa	287	
Saudi Arabia	246–249	
Scotland	167	
Senegal	262	
Serbia	182, 202	
Seychelles	272	
Sierra Leone	262	
Singapore	237	
Slovak Republic	181	
Slovenia	199	
Solomon Is.	287	
Somali Republic	267	
South Africa	270–271	
Spain	194–197	
Sri Lanka	245	
Sudan	256–257	
Suriname	329	
Swaziland	271	
Sweden	160–163	
Switzerland	179	
Syria	212–213	
Taiwan	225	
Tajikistan	217	
Tanzania	268–269	
Thailand	236–237	
Togo	263	
Tonga	287	
Trinidad and Tobago	323	
Tunisia	261	
Turkey	212–213	
Turkmenistan	216–217	
Uganda	268	
Ukraine	189	
United Arab Emirates	249	
United Kingdom	166–169	
USA	300–317	
Uruguay	334–335	
Uzbekistan	216–217	
Vanuatu	287	
Venezuela	328–329	
Vietnam	236–237	
Wales	168–169	
Yemen	248–249	
Zambia	265, 269	
Zimbabwe	269	

160

Færoe Is.

165

167

Shetland Is.

167

Orkney Is.

168

Edinburgh p121

166

UNITED KINGDOM

176

170

Dublin p120

IRELAND

Am
NE

192

171

London p125

172

174

FRANC

ANDORRA

Barcelona p114

194

196

SPAIN

206

PORTUGAL

Madrid p127

Lisbon p126

Baleari

Paris

MOROCCO

ALG

HOLLYWOOD
COSTUME

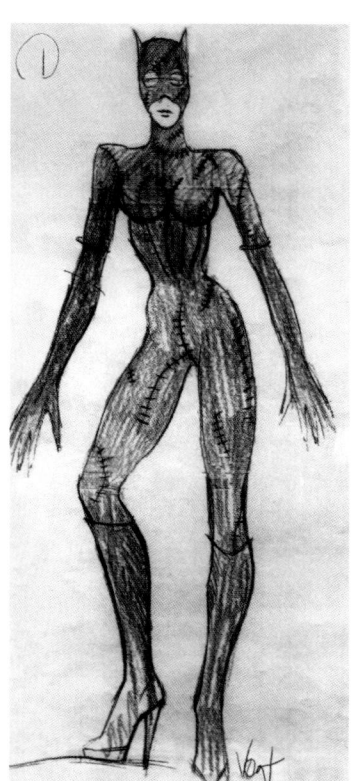
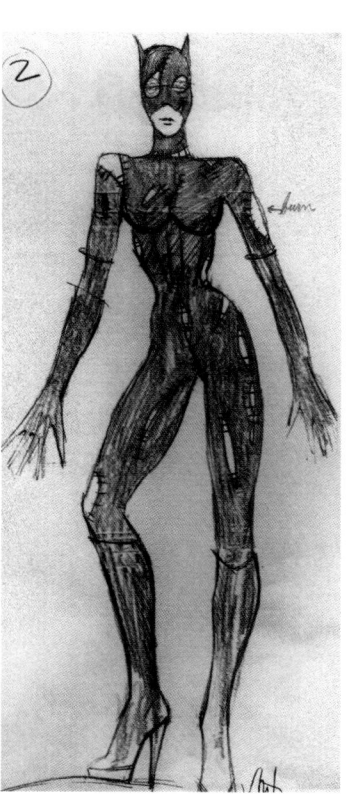
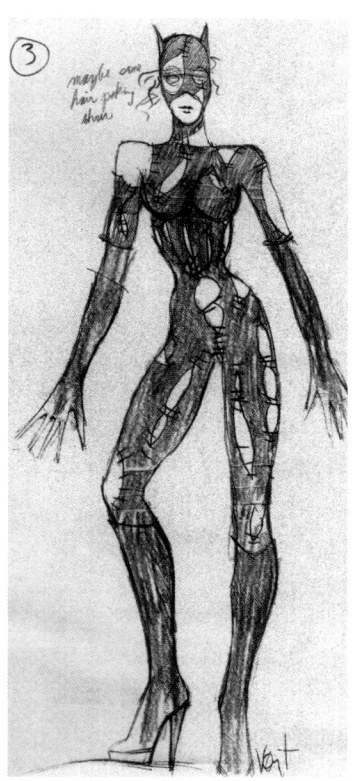

HOLLYWOOD

Edited by
DEBORAH NADOOLMAN LANDIS

COSTUME

ABRAMS, NEW YORK

Library of Congress Control Number: 2013935889

ISBN: 978-1-4197-0982-1

Copyright © 2013 The Board of the Trustees of the Victoria and Albert Museum

Originally published in 2012 by V&A Publishing

Published in 2013 by Abrams, an imprint of ABRAMS. All rights reserved. No portion of this book may be reproduced, stored in a retrieval system, or transmitted in any form or by any means, mechanical, electronic, photocopying, recording, or otherwise, without written permission from the publisher.

Printed and bound in China
10 9 8 7 6 5 4 3 2 1

Abrams books are available at special discounts when purchased in quantity for premiums and promotions as well as fundraising or educational use. Special editions can also be created to specification. For details, contact specialsales@abramsbooks.com or the address below.

THE ART OF BOOKS SINCE 1949

115 West 18th Street
New York, NY 10011
www.abramsbooks.com

Designer: Raymonde Watkins
Editor: Johanna Stephenson

New V&A photography by Richard Davis, V&A Photographic Studio

FRONT COVER:
Replica of the ruby slippers
The Wizard of Oz, 1939
Costume designer Adrian
Crafted by Mauricio Osorio/
Western Costume Company

BACK COVER:
Sir Frederick Barker, Maria Barker and Anthony Halton (Herbert Marshall, Marlene Dietrich and Melvyn Douglas)
Angel, 1937
Costume designer Travis Banton

ENDPAPERS (HARD BACK ONLY):
Designs for Cruella De Vil (Glenn Close)
102 Dalmations, 2000
Costume designer Anthony Powell
Illustrator Anthony Powell

PAGE 1:
Sketches for the three stages of Catwoman (Michelle Pfeiffer)
Batman Returns, 1992
Costume designers Bob Ringwood and Mary E. Vogt
Illustrator Mary E. Vogt

PAGES 2–3:
Catwoman (Michelle Pfeiffer)
Batman Returns, 1992
Costume designers Bob Ringwood and Mary E. Vogt

PAGE 5:
Mlle Amy Jolly (Marlene Dietrich)
Morocco, 1930
Costume designer Travis Banton

PAGES 6–7, LEFT TO RIGHT:
Detail of costume for the Emperor
The Last Emperor, 1987
Costume designer James Acheson
The Recorded Picture Company

Costume for Cleopatra
Cleopatra, 1934
Costume designer Travis Banton
The Collecton of Motion Picture Costume Design
Larry McQueen

Dick Tracy (Warren Beatty)
Dick Tracy, 1990
Costume designer Milena Canonero

Neytiri (Zoë Saldana)
Avatar, 2009
Costume designers Mayes C. Rubeo and Deborah L. Scott

PAGE 10:
Debbie Reynolds, 1950

PAGE 47:
Sketches for Tyler Durden (Brad Pitt)
Fight Club, 1999
Costume designer Michael Kaplan
Illustrator Pauline Annon

PAGE 93:
Cleopatra (Claudette Colbert)
Cleopatra, 1934
Costume designers Travis Banton and Madeleine Vionnet

PAGE 177:
Costume for Dorothy Gale (Judy Garland)
The Wizard of Oz, 1939
Costume designer Adrian

PAGES 262–3:
Jake Sully and Neytiri (Sam Worthington and Zoë Saldana)
Avatar, 2009
Costume designers Mayes C. Rubeo and Deborah L. Scott

CONTENTS

1 THE ART OF BECOMING

2 DEFINING THE CHARACTER

Sponsor's foreword 8

Preface 11
Debbie Reynolds

Setting the scene:
a short history of
Hollywood costume
design 1912–2012 12
Deborah Nadoolman Landis

What is costume design? 48
Deborah Nadoolman Landis

Moving pictures, silent movies
and the art of William Hogarth 56
Aileen Ribeiro

Designing *The Last Emperor* 68
James Acheson

The process of transformation 72
Kristin M. Burke

Designing for the Coen Brothers 76
Mary Zophres

Transformations: Johnny Depp 80
Keith Lodwick

Creative collaborations 84
    Edith Head and Alfred Hitchcock
    Martin Scorsese and Sandy Powell
    Mike Nichols and Ann Roth
    Tim Burton and Colleen Atwood

The costume of silent comedy 94
David Robinson

Sound comedy: louder and funnier 106
John Landis

Silhouettes of seduction 110
Jean L. Druesedow

Hollywood and history 126
Edward Maeder

Banton's beauties 132
Deborah Nadoolman Landis

Costume and fashion 138
Valerie Steele

Beaton's Fair Lady 146
Keith Lodwick

Unfashioning costume design 150
Booth Moore

Transformations: an interview with
Robert De Niro 158
Deborah Nadoolman Landis

Transformations: an interview with
Meryl Streep 162
Deborah Nadoolman Landis

Ann Roth in conversation 168
Peter Biskind

3 COLLECTORS & COLLECTING

4 NEW FRONTIERS

The exhibition odyssey 178
Deborah Nadoolman Landis

Looking behind the wizard's curtain 188
Christopher Frayling

The treasure hunt 202
Keith Lodwick

Showcasing the talent 212
Sam Gatley

A collectors' tale 216
Larry McQueen

The collecting imperative:
a studio perspective 228
Deidre Thieman

Actress and collector 236
Debbie Reynolds

Blades 242
Christopher Frayling

Gunslingers 246
Christopher Frayling

90027, Hollywood is a zip code:
the LA connection 252
Beth Werling

Afterlife: ensuring the enduring interest
of a web audience 264
Chris Laverty

Why design? 272
Jeffrey Kurland

Fantasy, sci-fi and superheroes 280
Jacob McMurray

The challenges of Mocap and CGI 294
Joanna Johnston

Notes 306

Further reading 309

Filmography 310

Picture credits 314

Acknowledgements 315

Index 316

SPONSOR'S FOREWORD

FOR OVER seven decades, the House of Harry Winston has been an integral part of Hollywood history and the jeweller of choice for the silver screen's most iconic stars. Revolutionizing modern red carpet glamour, Harry Winston was the first jeweller to loan diamonds to an actress for the Academy Awards, dressing Best Actress winner Jennifer Jones in 1944. Setting a new standard for Hollywood's most memorable night, a 'Jeweller to the Stars' was born.

Hollywood Costume speaks to the timeless magic of cinema's most beloved on-screen moments, and fits seamlessly with our brand heritage. We are extremely proud to support and be involved with this innovative exhibition. Through this partnership, we pay homage to the legacy of our founder Mr Harry Winston and our longstanding relationship with the red carpet. After all, it is a simple matter of fact – you cannot spell Hollywood without H.W.

Frédéric de Narp
President & CEO
Harry Winston Inc.

Andie Anderson (Kate Hudson)
wearing necklace by Harry Winston
How to Lose a Guy in Ten Days, 2003
Costume designer Karen Patch

PREFACE

Debbie Reynolds

I HAVE BEEN fortunate to have worked in the entertainment business for the past sixty years, and to have been part of Hollywood's Golden Age. I remember well the magic of costumes when, as a young actress from Burbank, I was overwhelmed by the dazzling variety and rich array of fabrics in the wardrobe department at Metro-Goldwyn-Mayer in 1950. When MGM held its first studio sale twenty years later, I was eager to save all I could for posterity: these costumes, props and related material were the physical embodiment of Hollywood's film history, and as such were irreplaceable. While we are still fortunate enough to have the legacy of classic movies left to us by previous generations, the nature of costumes in particular is to be part of the magic, to lead the viewer on as the plot unfolds on the silver screen. There is no replacement for coming face to face with the very costumes worn by the Hollywood stars – and they, in turn, are testament to the art of the unspoken heroes of Hollywood, the costume designers.

Over the next forty years my collection grew year by year, and in 2008 I was delighted to hear from Deborah Nadoolman Landis of her plans for an exhibition on the art of Hollywood costume, then at an early stage. Here was an important opportunity to put these historic pieces on display to the widest possible audience, in a major celebration of the costume designer's art over 100 years. My collection was sold in June 2011, but pieces were bought by collectors from all over the world and can now be seen by people across the globe. Meanwhile, the costumes gathered from far and wide for the exhibition represent a century of glorious Hollywood history.

Change is constant; as with fashion, things evolve with time. I believe that my efforts to save the costumes from our early Hollywood history have been appreciated. Now everyone must do their part to remember the past and preserve the work of those special talents who have gone before us.

Debbie Reynolds
Beverly Hills, California

❛ Everything begins with a story. ❜

JOSEPH CAMPBELL¹

SETTING THE SCENE
A SHORT HISTORY OF HOLLYWOOD COSTUME DESIGN 1912–2012

Deborah Nadoolman Landis

SINCE THE EARLIEST FILMS, costumes have served as a critical element of the storytelling process. While the purpose of costuming has remained the same over the past century, the process by which costumes are created for a film has changed significantly and now, a hundred years later, has come nearly full circle. These foundations of costume design, its history, its purpose and its practice, will be explored within *Hollywood Costume*.

THE SILENT ERA

The history of film-making in the United States begins in New York in the mid-1890s. One of the earliest 'film studios' in the country, the American Mutoscope and Biograph Company,² opened its doors in 1896. Throughout the next decade the American film industry and the film crafts quickly began to take shape as public demand grew. Concurrent with this development was the migration of actors and costume designers from the theatre to the newly emerging cinema community.

Costume design is one good example of the 'hit or miss' approach to pioneer film-making during the industry's formative years. The actors themselves provided most of their own costumes, although period and more ornate theatrical garments were obtained from Broadway theatrical costume rental houses. 'Those fortunate actresses who had extensive wardrobes of their own received more parts than more modestly dressed women', according to W. Robert LaVine. 'The point was to "make do" when it came to dressing for a film, and most films were a hodgepodge of apparel.'³ Contemporary stories were costumed off the backs of the actors. Applicants came dressed appropriately for an audition, hoping to win a role.

Unfortunately there is little discussion in the literature of costumes in new American cinema during the decade 1900–1910, but one can always watch the old films to evaluate them. Certainly costumes were not granted a significant amount of a film's budget. In a description of the depiction of Native Americans in early films, one author observes: 'In *Captain John Smith and Pocahontas* (1908) … obvious white actors smeared with brown make-up were dressed in long brown underwear and skull caps to which ordinary chicken feathers were attached!'⁴

There was a visual intelligence at work making immediate choices about style and character for each role, but whether this was the first assistant director, the cameraman or the director is difficult to glean from existing literature of the time. In this primitive world of early film-making no formal costume department existed. And as yet there were no fan magazines to report it.

The beginnings of the industry in California, and Hollywood, occurred concurrently with the heyday of the East Coast production companies. In 1907 California's first dramatic film, *The Power of the Sultan*, was produced by the Selig Company. Within a decade Hollywood had become synonymous with the film industry. Film-makers were drawn west for several reasons:

OPPOSITE
1 Pauline Garon, Cecil B. DeMille and Clare West discussing designs for *Adam's Rib*, 1923
Costume designer Clare West

RIGHT
2 'Faking' a snow scene in tropical California, 1920s
Mack Sennett Studios, Edendale, California

"Faking" a Snow Scene in Tropical California, Mack Sennett Studios, Edendale.

3 Sketch for Eleanor Bates (Claire Windsor)
For Sale, 1924
Costume designer and illustrator Clare West

4 Sketch for Ruth Lawrence (Norma Shearer)
His Secretary, 1925
Costume designer and illustrator André-ani

the sunny weather of southern California made it possible to film outside all year round (plate 2), and the variety of landscapes around Los Angeles provided an array of natural sets – 'every variety of mountain, valley, lake, seacoast, island, desert, countryside, and plain that a story might call for'.[5] New York City, by contrast, 'was a hopeless location for cowboys, Indians, Confederate soldiers, knights or South Seas aborigines'.[6]

When it came to costumes, Hollywood producers relied on the source they knew best from New York: the actresses. But two noted film visionaries – in quite divergent manners – began to create a new approach to costuming films in the 1910s. Producer Adolph Zukor introduced Americans to the concept of the film costume designer as a creative artist,[7] while director D. W. Griffith introduced the practice of creating costumes specifically for American-made films.[8] One of Zukor's best-known contributions to the emerging film industry was his 1912 purchase of the rights to the French film *The Loves of Queen Elizabeth*, which starred Sarah Bernhardt wearing clothing designed by the highly respected French couture designer Paul Poiret (plate 152).[9] One could argue that film wardrobe departments came into being largely through

the creative practices of Griffith, whose employment of film design was just one of his many innovations.

Film lore has it that a number of the costumes for *The Birth of a Nation* (1915) were made by actress Lillian Gish's mother, a source that could be considered a 'hybrid' of past and future costuming processes.[10] Indeed, the comments about Griffith's 'auditioning' practices made by his wife, Linda Arvidson, have often been quoted: '"I have no part for you, Miss Hart, but I can use your hat. I'll give you five dollars if you will let Miss Pickford wear your hat for this picture."'[11] Griffith chose a more structured path, however, in costuming his 1916 drama *Intolerance: Love's Struggles Through the Ages*, considered the first Hollywood film in which costumes were created for lead players and extras alike.[12]

Following Poiret, fashion designers started to design for films with some regularity.[13] This practice was less common at first in California than in New York, where the fashion houses clothed actresses both on and off screen. Couture designers of this era generally worked in tandem with particular performers and, as a rule, did not receive screen credit for their work.[14] Over time these firms, particularly Lucile Ltd, began to fulfil Hollywood's need for designers.[15] Early silent features had few credits, and none for costume designer. Until the creation of the executive studio designer in the mid-1920s, costume designer credits on films were rare. If acknowledged at all, some credits read 'Gowns by…', reflecting that designers were credited for the costumes of a single star.

In addition to fashion firms and the actresses' own closets, rental houses became an important source of costumes. As

However, a wonderful example of the connection between costume and character can be seen in Charlie Chaplin's Little Tramp, who first appeared in the 1914 film *Kid Auto Races at Venice*.[19] His signature outfit, which Chaplin purportedly scavenged from a communal studio dressing room,[20] was recognized by audiences as the embodiment of humour and pathos: 'The little tramp in a bowler hat, tight jacket and baggy pants, with a duck-like walk and carrying a cane, became immensely popular on screens throughout the world.'[21]

The silence of early films intensified the need for illustrative costumes. In discussing novelist and film producer Elinor Glyn, N. Fowler writes:

> In silent films, dressing the part and playing the part were one and the same, as Elinor and the other members of Hollywood's pioneer film industry instantly understood. A February 1916 article in *Photoplay* by actress Louise Howard is called 'How I Teach My Gowns to Act.' Dress had to place a character quickly and effectively in one symbolic sweep.[22]

By the end of the First World War Hollywood was firmly established as the home of the film business. The distinctive shape of the major Hollywood studios – an 'integrated' system that produced and distributed films to its affiliated theatre chains – was consolidating. The standard technique for costuming a film employed by the major studios was a blending of the approaches developed in the previous decade: merging the on-site wardrobe production facility with the creative talents and panache of the professional designer. According to Satch LaValley, 'The largest studios began to maintain enormous costume departments: the costume designer, heretofore anonymous for the most part, now began to assume a vital and well-publicized role'.[23]

early as 1912 the Western Costume Company in Los Angeles was providing wardrobes for Hollywood films. Western Costume grew out of the personal collection of Native American paraphernalia of L.L. Burns, a trader who accumulated hundreds of items as he travelled across the United States. By 1920 a standardized mode of production led to an accumulation of costumes in the studio costume departments: it made fiscal sense for the studio to retain all the costumes that they had already paid to produce. Furthermore, 'Bookkeepers wrote the cost of all sets and costume against the film for which they were made; as a result, any subsequent uses were free. This encouraged the reuse of sets [and costumes] and a return to the same genres.'[16]

As the output of the studios grew throughout the first decade of the twentieth century, the benefits of obtaining costumes quickly, easily and inexpensively became increasingly apparent and a few producers thus began employing costume designers on a full-time basis.[17] Costume designer Edith Head remembered that 'Most production companies didn't … have designers on staff until about 1918, when DeMille secured Clare West as head of costume design for his films'.[18] Other than what we can see on the screen, the use of costumes as storytelling vehicles during this time is poorly documented.

‘ Adrian was my favourite designer.
He and I had the same sense of 'smell' about what
clothes should do and what they should say. ’

KATHARINE HEPBURN

OPPOSITE
7 Tracy Lord
(Katharine Hepburn)
The Philadelphia Story, 1940
Costume designer Adrian

LEFT
8 Anni Pavlovitch
(Joan Crawford)
The Bride Wore Red, 1937
Costume designer Adrian

ABOVE
9 Joan Crawford with one
of Adrian's designs for
The Bride Wore Red, 1937

At the pinnacle of these studios, as a producer of quality films, a successful business enterprise and a unifier of skilled and dedicated professionals,[24] was Metro-Goldwyn-Mayer Studios. As the silent era was coming to a close, MGM's productive costume department was full of talented professionals and the studio was on the cusp of hiring Adrian, the designer who would lead the studio into the Golden Age of Hollywood.

The busy wardrobe department at Paramount was divided into two sections: women's costumes and character costumes. Paramount's wardrobe chief Howard Greer (plate 5) began his career in fashion design, as an assistant in the popular New York House of Lucile.[25] Greer joined Paramount in 1923 and was the studio's chief costume designer until 1928. In keeping with the practice at the time, as chief designer Greer only clothed the principal women in a film. Having worked in both fields Greer understood the distinction in purpose and scale between fashion and costume design, astutely observing that

> Overemphasis, as it applied to
> acting techniques and story treatments, was essential.
> If a lady in real life wore a train one yard long, her
> prototype in film wore one three yards long…. The most
> elegant Chanel of the early twenties was a washout on
> the screen. When you strip color and sound and the
> third dimension from a moving object, you have to make
> up for the loss with dramatic black-and-white contrasts
> and enriched surfaces.[26]

With an ever-growing quantity of costumes required to keep pace with the number of films in production at any one time, Paramount was constantly increasing its staff. When Greer hired Edith Head as a wardrobe sketch artist for $50 a week in 1923, he could not have dreamed how prolific she would be. Head recollected:

> I never got down on the set to see the clothes. I never
> met the stars. But gradually this changed … sometimes
> he would take me out in the workroom to watch him
> drape model figures with the garments made from these
> designs. It was like watching the drawings come to life.[27]

In 1928 couture-trained Travis Banton, acclaimed as a 'French' designer, took over as the head of Paramount's costume department.

The silent era was about to end by the time RKO (Radio-Keith-Orpheum) hired designer Walter Plunkett in 1926.[28] Plunkett recalled that at that time the studio's costume department was part of the drapery department:

> The men in charge of drapery went out and bought or
> rented clothes, or gave yardage to the maids who pinned
> it on…. The first day I went to work there, they told me
> that a girl who was playing a mysterious queen in a Tarzan
> picture was having trouble with her costume and they
> asked me if I would get to her dressing room and see what
> I could do. When I got there, I found her maid … trying
> to pin three or four yards of beaded chiffon. She had no
> idea what she was doing, so I pinned it onto the actress's
> bra and draped it around her and that was the costume for
> the day. It was the customary way of doing things.[29]

Of great concern to virtually everyone in the early American film industry were the strong opinions of certain conservative civic and religious groups. In a preemptive strike against federal legislation regulating films, 'Hollywood responded in 1922 by founding the Motion Picture Producers and Distributors of America Inc. [MPPDA], to operate a system of self-regulation'.[30] Led by Will H. Hays, a former Republican Postmaster General,

award for costume design would not be presented until 1948.

By the close of the 1920s Hollywood costume design had developed a template of normative practices based on economic efficiency. The popular rags-to-riches silent comedies and melodramas communicated character transformation most effectively through costume. The early in-house studio dressmakers were costume designers in all but title; their purpose was to create believable characters for the appreciative silent film-going audience. With the establishment of the executive costume designer in the mid-1920s, whose focus was the female stars, secondary designers or costume department supervisors costumed the male leads and supporting cast.

THE GOLDEN AGE

The creation of the talking picture is considered the birth of Hollywood's Golden Age and one of the most significant turning points in film history. The arrival of sound had an effect on virtually every aspect of the industry. The addition of direct sound impacted both the purpose and the practice of costume design: sensitive microphones suddenly amplified the noise of clicking heels and jangling jewellery, which meant that otherwise innocuous accessories had to be reconsidered (or taped or sewn to the garment), and 'Ruffles, taffeta skirts and the like were troublesome because they made too much noise'.[35] Sound, moreover, gave costumes a new role in the storytelling process: 'With the addition of dialogue, films gradually became more realistic, and less atmospheric.'[36]

On the introduction of sound, the MGM designer Adrian observed:

the MPPDA immediately began to create a list of plays and books that could not be used as the basis for films.[31] Costume designers, too, were affected:

> Censorship frequently forced last-minute changes. After 1923 the Hays office mandated an anti-cleavage rule; and while it was all right to show a man's navel, women's navels were taboo. The wardrobe department was often called upon to supply a diamond belt or pearls to hide a dancing girl's navel before shooting could resume.[32]

Hollywood movies had become tremendously popular by the end of the silent era. In 1926 some $120 million was spent making more than four hundred feature films.[33] In order to meet public demand, by the end of the decade 'every studio of rank had its own costume department, with a full-time staff of designers, milliners, tailors, and seamstresses … The last gap in the team of studio professionals had been filled.'[34] Yet while costume design was gaining attention within the studios and with the public, the newly founded Academy of Motion Picture Arts and Sciences ignored costuming at its inaugural Academy Awards ceremony. Excellence in film art direction and cinematography were honoured at the inception of the awards in 1929, yet the

> All the studio costume designers have been thinking in terms of dramatic moments instead of the genuine, real moments that occur in life. When sound came in, a great change came over movie fashions. With the entrance of the human voice actresses suddenly became human beings. A quality of mind came with the characterization and the story. Everything had to be more real. Roses became real roses. Chippendale chairs became real Chippendale. The clothes took on a genuine character.[37]

The factory-like environment born in the 1920s swung into full force at the major studios in the 1930s. Wardrobe departments grew to be small factories that employed as many as two hundred workers

(plates 10, 11).[38] 'The costume department of a Hollywood studio was hierarchically organized, supervised by a chief designer who was assisted by the head of wardrobe, several junior designers, sketch artists, period researchers, wardrobe assistants, and seamstresses.'[39] An on-site assembly line was simply the most efficient method of getting actors clothed. Moreover, wardrobe departments accumulated an ever-increasing number of completed costumes. As each film wrapped, the principal costumes were sorted and recycled on extras in future productions.[40]

In general the major studio costume designers of the 1930s did not suffer much at the hands of the Depression.[41] According to D. McCarthy, 'At the larger studios during Hollywood's Golden Age, costume designers had no fixed line in the production budget and they worked accordingly'.[42] One source estimates that over $6 million was spent by Hollywood studios on costumes in 1938.[43] This wonderful confluence of resources – materials, staff, costume stock and finances – was probably in greatest abundance at the very successful MGM studios.[44]

Adrian was the executive costume designer at MGM in the 1930s. Creating a credible character and mood was to Adrian central to his purpose as a costume designer. As a young designer working for Cecil B. DeMille, he reasoned that 'The dramatic situations in a picture must be costumed according to the feeling of a scene'.[45] Although his designs were often reproduced for the retail market by fashion manufacturers, Adrian recognized that the objectives of costume design and fashion design were completely different, and at times in conflict: 'there are some clothes that are not in good taste if worn off the set. They are put into the picture like futuristic scenery in some plays to help the drama and are out of place anywhere else.'[46]

At the height of his fame, Adrian understood that:

> Few people in an audience watching a great screen production realize the importance of any gown worn by the feminine star. They may notice that it is attractive, that they would like to have it copied, that it is becoming, but the fact that it was definitely planned to mirror some definite mood, to be as much a part of the play as the lines or the scenery, seldom occurs to them. But that most assuredly is true.[47]

An equally important aspect of Adrian's aim as a storyteller was his collaboration with an actress to portray her character. Looking back on her career, Katharine Hepburn said: 'Adrian was my favorite designer. He and I had the same sense of "smell" about what clothes should do and what they should say.'[48] Adrian's remarkable talent resulted in a great diversity of costuming feats, from the embroidered period gowns of *Marie Antoinette* (1938) to the whimsical costumes of *The Wizard of Oz* (1939).

As a starting point for *The Wizard of Oz* Adrian turned to the drawings he had made of the characters as a child, and he scanned the series of books for costume ideas. He made 3,210 individual costume sketches for the film, all painted to match early Technicolor requirements. Virtually every costume was fancifully colourful, and every garment was custom-made since nothing that might be appropriate for the Land of Oz could be found anywhere in costume stock in the MGM Wardrobe Department.[49]

For *Marie Antoinette*, researchers were sent to Europe to gather 'antique prints, folios of drawings, actual garments of the period, and rare accessories. Adrian carefully studied the objects and made hundreds of sketches for his staff. The MGM costume shop turned out twenty-five hundred costumes.'[50]

In later years, Joan Crawford recognized Adrian's contribution to her career: 'Adrian had a profound effect both on my professional life and personal life. He taught me so much about drama. He said nothing must detract. Everything must be simple, simple. Just your face must emerge. He made me conscious of simplicity.'[51]

At the height of the studio system, 'producers, not the directors, most often determined the look of the films. Costumes were frequently underway before a director and stars had been assigned to a production.'[52] Paramount chief Adolph Zukor 'spared nothing to see that his stars were dressed in the manner the public had come to expect'.[53] Zukor wanted substantive characters who

14 Travis Banton (seated) and Edith Head (far right)
at a costume fitting at Paramount Studios, *c.*1934

would resonate with audiences, but he also understood the value of style and packaging in the marketing of a film. In this respect the dedication and perfectionism of Travis Banton and Marlene Dietrich were legendary:

> When Marlene's clothes for *Morocco* [1930] were ready for fittings, she often spent as much as six hours at a stretch standing patiently on a padded platform while she and Travis pointed and pinched, and the fitters pinned and repinned. In those days, when every film showed their heroines in at least 20 different outfits, stars would be condemned to standing stock still for as many as 120 hours per film…. However long it took to get it right, she was ready to stand and endure.[54]

Edith Head assumed Banton's position as Head Designer of Paramount in 1937, where she was always busy during the studio's prolific war years. LaVine reports that for Head: 'It was normal … to have the wardrobes for three or four films in process simultaneously, a stack of new scripts awaiting her consideration, and fittings scheduled at fifteen-minute intervals.'[55] Head exemplified the costume designer as storyteller. For example, in describing her work on *Lady in the Dark* (1944), she said that the film 'depended enormously on the clothes to tell the story'.[56] She was also keenly aware that her purpose as a costume designer was not to create new fashionable styles:

> I do not consider a motion picture costume designer necessarily a fashion creator because we do what the script tells us to. If we do a period piece, then we re-create fashion that was done before, and if we have a character role, we do character clothes. It is only by the accident of a script that calls for fashion and an actress that can wear fashion that some of the beautiful clothes will emerge. I don't consider myself a designer in the sense of a fashion designer. I am a motion picture costume designer.[57]

This design process had become the normative practice that was followed by the top designers working in studio costume departments, such as Banton and Head at Paramount, and at Warner

15 Edith Head, Edward Stevenson, Howard Greer and Adrian, c.1942

16 Mary Stuart (Katharine Hepburn)
Mary of Scotland, 1936
Costume designer Walter Plunkett

Bros by Orry-Kelly, probably best remembered for his work with Bette Davis. In describing Orry-Kelly's designs for Davis for *Jezebel* (1938) and *The Little Foxes* (1941), McConathy noted that he

> depended more on detail than on flash to make his historical points. His psychological understanding of historical period, along with Davis's willingness to change her image entirely for a role, distinguished his beautifully executed ideas.... Bette Davis's classical period came … in the forties, when she began to play independent, contemporary women whose clothes were a far less obtrusive part of the characterization. Even in those pictures, Davis's collaboration with Orry-Kelly was evident, and the elements of reportage and timeliness were an integral part of her look.[58]

Orry-Kelly's determination to help the actor find her character is seen in his work with Davis for *The Private Lives of Elizabeth and Essex* (1939). He researched the Elizabethan period thoroughly, but when Hungarian-born director Michael Curtiz saw the costumes for her first tests, he pointed to the hoop skirts and the ruff around Davis's neck and said: 'Too beeg'. But the designer and the star had been around long enough to win their way. Two sets of costumes were made. Davis tested in the scaled-down gowns and wore the larger, historically correct clothes in the film![59] Bette Davis revived this favourite character much later in *The Virgin Queen* (1955; plate 17) with the size of ruff and her farthingale intact.

Davis recognized Orry-Kelly's unwavering commitment to character and costume over fashion: 'His contribution to my career was an enormous one. He never featured his clothes to such a degree that the performance was overshadowed.'[60]

Over at RKO, Walter Plunkett continued to act as an executive costume designer throughout most of the 1930s,[61] he preferred designing period films to creating costumes for contemporary ones because, in his words,

> Everyone wants to stick his nose into modern things – the directors' wives, secretaries, actresses with rather bad taste. It's far easier when you can tell them, 'I love your idea, but it's just wrong for the period.' That gets them the hell off the set and out of your hair.[62]

His costumes for David O. Selznick's *Gone with the Wind* (1939) were his crowning achievement, successful because they were realistic enough to be viewed as correct period attire but attractive enough to be embraced by a 1939 audience as evocative of the story's romantic, Southern fairytale quality. Describing his approach to the task, Plunkett stated that he read the novel several times,

> making notations of every line and passage containing a reference to clothes or related subjects. Then my secretary read the book to catch any items I might have missed, then we made a script of these notes, and it worked out that there would be almost 5,500 separate items, all of which would have to be made from scratch.[63]

Plunkett travelled to Atlanta to discuss his notes for the costumes with the book's author, Margaret Mitchell. Mitchell brought him to the homes of women who had kept heirloom clothing from the antebellum period and he cut fabric swatches from hems and made sketches as he went.[64] Of his design process, Plunkett stated:

> You don't first make a sketch and then go hunting for a fabric that will do what you want it to do. You get that piece of fabric and you hold it, you play with it, you

17 Queen Elizabeth I (Bette Davis)
The Virgin Queen, 1955
Costume designer Mary Wills

throw it around to see how it moves, how it reflects light, then you know how you are going to use it. It's like building a house, you have to know the materials you are going to use before you design the house.[65]

Looking back over his career, Plunkett said of *Gone with the Wind*:

> I don't think it was my best work, or even the biggest thing I ever did.... But that picture, of course, will go on forever, and that green dress, because it makes a story point, is probably the most famous costume in the history of motion pictures. So I am very glad I did it.[66]

The role of the costume designer is to create the best costume for the character within the context of the narrative and the visual style of the film. The most historically accurate costume may not be the most theatrically effective costume on camera. In a remark that illustrates the dichotomous role of the costume designer within highly pressured collaborative relationships, Plunkett gently complained of his *Gone with the Wind* director:

> Selznick wasn't interested in accuracy. I did research in the South because I thought it was necessary. Selznick was much more worried about being true to Margaret Mitchell. If he objected to a design, I'd only have to point out one of her descriptions in the novel and he was satisfied.[67]

During the 1930s everyone involved in the Hollywood film industry, particularly costume designers, paid close attention to the Hays Office of the Motion Picture Producers and Distributors of America (MPPDA), the censorship organization led by William H.

Hays. In 1930 the Hays Office authored a production code providing 'moral guidelines' for the content and language of films.[68] The censorship code published in 1927 had been largely ignored for the first several years of its passage: Edith Head reminisced that in the freewheeling 1920s and early 1930s, 'Our only rule ... was will it stay on? If dresses fell off, we just shot again'.[69]

The censors of the 1930s became intrusive. Every single dress had to be reviewed for modesty and a representative from the Hays Office, which also ensured compliance on the sets, studied all costume tests. No sign of pregnancy was permitted, no garters, and – heaven forbid! – no cleavage. Even the slightest shadow that suggested cleavage could suspend production. Designers were called to sets to adjust problematic necklines, and handkerchiefs and extra ruffles were always in great demand to camouflage bare skin.

Hollywood's Golden Age continued through the Second World War. Americans flocked to the cinema, 'with weekly attendance climbing from 80 million in 1940 to nearly 100 million in 1946'.[70] The war brought changes to the film industry, such as a shift toward more 'realistic' films,[71] reflecting both tightened budgets and the sober mood of the nation. The work of costume designers was affected by this change. Of more direct impact, however, was the new rationing of fabrics. In an effort to conserve resources in 1942, the United States government issued a directive known as L-85, which, according to Edith Head, 'drastically limited the amount of fabric that could be used in any garment construction – including Hollywood costumes. It meant no pleats, no cuffs, no ruffles, no long jackets, no extra frills.'[72]

By the mid-1940s resourceful costume designers had found economical ways to cope with wartime shortages while maintaining the integrity of their purpose to honour every script. The

18 Ringo Kid (John Wayne)
***Stagecoach*, 1939**
Costume designer Walter Plunkett

19 Delilah (Hedy Lamarr)
Samson and Delilah, 1949
Costume designers Edith Head,
Gile Steele, Dorothy Jeakins,
Gwen Wakeling and
Elois W. Jenssen
Delilah costume designed
by Edith Head

20 Sketch for Delilah
Samson and Delilah, 1949
Costume designers Edith Head,
Gile Steele, Dorothy Jeakins,
Gwen Wakeling and
Elois W. Jenssen
Illustrator Donna Kline

factory system at the major studios was in full swing, the amassing and recycling of costumes continued, and wardrobe stocks grew as pictures were produced in multiple genres. These well-worn costumes became vital assets when fabric shortages made new costume construction during the war impossible.

The Golden Age was a time of consolidation of the classical Hollywood style.[73] Under the management of the executive costume designer, the costume department was subdivided into costumers who worked on the set with finished costumes and those who toiled in the workroom manufacturing the costumes. The assembly-line process was streamlined and the internal hierarchy of the department became formalized.

Throughout the Golden Era, costume designers continued to design primarily for lead actresses. However, this procedure was to change forever with the arrival of Irene Sharaff, a veteran Broadway designer from New York. The overall responsibilities of the costume designer grew in the early 1940s, as Miss Sharaff wrote:

One fundamental difference, which I found at MGM in 1942 between designing costumes for the screen and for the stage illustrates a step in the changing role of designers. At that time there was an almost Victorian attitude in the separation of designing of men's costumes from those of the women. Hardly any attention was given to integrating the costumes of stars with the others, and little thought was given to a degree of coherence in the look of a scene and of the production as a whole.... The situation began to change in Hollywood, and I believe it soon became generally accepted that one designer was put on a picture and worked on all of the costumes on it.[74]

Before Sharaff's arrival in Hollywood most film designers analysed each script for the costumes they needed to design for individual actresses. But Irene Sharaff and Helen Rose, both designers with Broadway careers, introduced to Hollywood the concepts of an

OPPOSITE
21 Sketch for Cleopatra
Cleopatra, 1963
Costume designers Irene Sharaff, Nino Novarese and Renie
Illustrator Irene Sharaff

ABOVE
**22 Irene Sharaff arranging the costume for Cleopatra
(Elizabeth Taylor)**
Cleopatra, 1963
Costume designers Irene Sharaff, Nino Novarese and Renie

overall colour palette and the design integration of an entire cast of characters that were commonplace in the theatre. Thus designers began to work closely with the art director from the beginning of each production, approaching screenplays in the same way as their counterparts in the theatre. The immediate effect of the 'one designer' approach was a cohesive and integrated look for each film.

THE 1950s AND 1960s

The decline of the studio factory system did not mean the end of the Hollywood studio, nor did it mean the end of the Hollywood film, as both are still very much with us today. What began after the close of the Second World War was a slow dissolution of the 'studio system of moviemaking, the near-absolute power that the studio wielded over the American movie industry'.[75] Many events contributed to the demise of the studios' power, including a renewed zealousness of antitrust activity by the United States Justice Department and the growing popularity of television.[76]

No two studios were affected by these changes in precisely the same way. According to Thomas Schatz, MGM 'held out against the inevitable longer than any other company, turning out the last of Hollywood's studio-era productions'.[77] To costume designers this meant that for the moment they retained their regular studio positions, luxurious facilities and craftspeople. Certainly the wardrobe department at MGM retained a factory-like quality after the war, and the studio executives were still very interested in having their say about costumes. Chief designer Helen Rose and her staff remained at MGM, Twentieth Century-Fox retained Charles LeMaire as Executive Designer and head of wardrobe until 1959, and Jean Louis stayed at Columbia until 1958.[78] However, the studios were cutting back on contract staff during this transitional period. For most others, costume design became a freelance career.

It is axiomatic that costumes designed for Hollywood's post-war years retained their character-creating purpose and definition. Orry-Kelly's determination to create outrageous characters is seen in the classic comedy *Some Like It Hot* (1959), in which Monroe wears a series of sheer cocktail dresses. One story circulating at the time claimed that Marilyn Monroe wanted an even more revealing wardrobe for the film but, rising to the challenge, 'Kelly argued it was wrong for the character, saying "Sugar Kane is the kind of girl who will go so far and no further"'.[79]

By the 1950s the film director had emerged as the final stylistic authority as the power of the studios began to wane. Edith Head remembers her guidance in the 1950s coming solely from a director, Alfred Hitchcock. About her first Hitchcock film, *Notorious* (1946), Head remembers:

> He was very specific about costumes for his leading ladies. He spoke a designer's language, even though he didn't know the first thing about clothes. He specified colors in the script if they were important. If he wanted a skirt that brushed a desk as a woman walked by, he spelled that out too. For *Notorious*, he repeated many times that the clothes must not be a focal point, that Bergman was to be a believable secret agent.[80]

Hitchcock cared deeply about the clothes of the characters in his films, and they are very specific. He used costume to balance the frame with colour and scale, working out the look of the picture by using storyboards extensively. He worked closely with his Edith Head; prior to shooting he insisted on knowing how every costume would look in the frame (see p.85).

Constant and vigilant awareness of the censors' mandates continued to be one of the tasks of Hollywood costume designers. In 1956 the Motion Picture Production Code was revised, but most of its provisions remained virtually unchanged.[81] Irene Sharaff recalled:

> With the emphasis on bosoms at the time, the amount of cleavage permitted was left to the discretion of a man from the censorship office, whose OK was necessary for every dress and costume before it could be shot.... This taboo on crannies and expanses of flesh started a prodigious use in Hollywood of nude-colored soufflé under transparent materials, for so long as there was a covering, however thin, the studio could claim that the actress was fully clothed.[82]

An on-site censor was not uncommon. Head consulted at length with the studio specialist concerning Hedy Lamarr's scanty costumes for *Samson and Delilah* (1949; plates 19, 20), recalling that the censorship issue was so delicate that she was still visiting the set to consult with the censor on the last day of shooting.[83] Censorship reigned omniscient in the industry and was a thorn in the side of the costume designer in the post-war years, until the ratings system finally replaced the Hays Code in 1968.

In an attempt to heighten the appeal of films, the industry began experimenting with new ways to lure Americans back to the cinemas (and away from their television sets). One cause of flagging attendance – at least for big studio 'A' films – was the exodus of Americans to the suburbs, away from the downtown movie palaces, and the arrival of the drive-in theatre. Wider, deeper screens were developed to accommodate new methods of making bigger, more visually impressive films. One such innovation was CinemaScope, a technique that Twentieth Century Fox announced in 1953 would be applied to 'all future productions'.[84] The first Fox film produced in CinemaScope was *The Robe* (1953), originally scheduled as a black-and-white film designed by Charles LeMaire and Emile Santiago.

The films offered grandeur of scale – as seen in action, sets/location, and costumes – that simply did not project on the television screen. Therefore Hollywood focused on 'big' films in the 1950s as another way to attract an audience. Although the Western had always been a favourite with American audiences, it

was given a new life as a main feature:[85] until 1960, half of all films produced in Hollywood were Westerns. The Western had traditionally been the product of the smaller studios such as Republic, and although costume designers routinely contributed to them, the men's costumes for these films were generally pulled from costume stock by costume supervisors from the studio's wardrobe department. But with the rebirth of the Western as a high-budget commodity, the most established costume designers began to lend their skills to the genre. For example, Walter Plunkett designed costumes for Selznick's *Duel in the Sun* (1946) René Hubert designed costumes for Twentieth Century Fox's *Broken Arrow* (1950), and veteran Frank Beetson was credited as the costume designer for *The Searchers* (1956; plate 344).

The new wide screens were perfect for the 'epic' and the 1950s brought a host of gladiator, ancient history films, and musicals. With casts of thousands, it is not unexpected to see the label 'costume picture' applied to these epics, period and fantasy films. Approximately fifty thousand people appeared in *Ben-Hur* (1959),[86] the best of the 'sword-and-sandal' epics. Creating the costumes for these films required a tremendous amount of design and organization, and it was not uncommon to hire several costume designers for one picture. Five costume designers are credited on two DeMille/Paramount epics – *Samson and Delilah* (1949)[87] and *The Ten Commandments* (1956).[88] Hollywood also turned to lavish musicals to regenerate public interest, such as the classic *Singin' in the Rain* (1952), with costumes by Walter Plunkett.

'If any film made in the sixties symbolized the end of old Hollywood, it was *Cleopatra* [1963], the costs of which finally accelerated to $40 million.'[89] Irene Sharaff, who designed Elizabeth Taylor's costumes for the film (plates 21, 22), recalled that the magnitude of the project was complicated by the fact that the script and schedule were not complete when she started working:

> I had a rough breakdown of the scenes in which she [Taylor] appeared, by which to figure out what would be needed and which scenes were likely to be shot first. Since the ceremonial costumes were the most complicated to make and would need more time, I started them in Hollywood and also put into work three others, totaling sixteen. The rest of her costumes were made at the same costume house in Rome where additional costumes were being made for the new cast and for the crowd scenes.[90]

Cleopatra was a financial disaster, and although it was not the last epic-style production offered by Hollywood in the 1960s, the interest in smaller, more thematically complex films was on the rise by the middle of the decade. New American film-makers from both coasts – such as John Cassavetes, Arthur Penn, Roger Corman, Sam Peckinpah and Mike Nichols – were finding a voice, and experienced directors were exploring new approaches to storytelling. This casual approach to film craft and 'realness', coupled with the financial woes of the studios,[91] diminished the studios' willingness to spend money, hire costume designers or generate the energy to manufacture costumes. By the mid-1960s, 'budgets assumed major importance and the costume departments were one of the first places that expenses were cut'.[92] As Edith Head put it, 'the studio designer … was suddenly a thing of

the past'.[93] This was a dark foreshadowing of what would become in the next decade a fight for the very existence of the profession.

Although the status and prestige of the costume designer had grown in the late 1940s and early 1950s, with the first Academy Award for best costume design in 1948, the film industry's overall slump prompted a sharp reduction in feature releases, resulting in deep job cuts in the costume department. The studio workrooms were decimated and many studio designers lost their contracts. Edith Head, who left Paramount for Universal when her contract was not renewed in 1967, reflected that at that time: 'More and more contemporary costumes were simply being purchased in Los Angeles and Beverly Hills department stores – and that was a job for an increasingly important person in the wardrobe department, *the shopper*.'[94] 'The growing demand for utter realism required costumes that had a straight-from-the-rack look; indeed, countless films were so costumed, with a designer acting more as a "shopper" for suitable garments than as an artist who was an integral part of a carefully conceived production.'[95]

With the rise of super-naturalistic film-making, Hollywood costume budgets were reduced and the overall recognition of the costume designer was diminished. Directors such as Mike Nichols, Sidney Lumet and Arthur Penn continue to trust and collaborate with costume designers but the polished style of the Hollywood Golden Age was an anathema. With few exceptions, desire for a 'real' or 'raw' near-documentary style led costume designers to buying and coordinating costumes for modern films in boutiques, department stores and thrift shops. Costume designers lost ground in the late 1960s and early 1970s, when the perception grew among producers that contemporary costuming could be accomplished by 'anyone'.

Regardless of whether costumes were manufactured, pulled from costume stock or bought at a thrift shop, their core purpose – to realize the people in the story – remained a constant during the 1960s. Sadly there are only a handful of recollections and observations from those involved during this era. Costume design and character continued to be taken very seriously by the best film-makers and substantive conversations continued about the clothes. Authenticity continued to be the hallmark of great work. For the extras' costumes on *My Fair Lady* (1964), Cecil Beaton was asked by director George Cukor

> to start looking right now for old clothes to wear in Covent Garden – old used clothes, not just things that are dirtied up by the prop man, but real old, worn materials, and masses of them: vests and shirts and jersey and coats on coats, and lots of petticoats under skirts.[96]

Beaton was committed to the realization of his own childhood memory of Ascot:

> In this production there are virtually no 'extras' and, with the exception of the tails at the Ball, and the grey frock-coats at Ascot, there are no 'repeats'. Even the men in the cockney scenes are being created as individual characters…. Among the four hundred women at the Ball and at Ascot, there is not one

25 Fanny Brice (Barbra Streisand)
Funny Girl, 1968
Costume designer Irene Sharaff

26 Sketch for Fanny Brice
Funny Girl, 1968
Costume designer and illustrator Irene Sharaff

27 Virginia Hill and Bugsy Siegel
(Annette Bening and Warren Beatty)
Bugsy, 1991
Costume designer Albert Wolsky

28 Sketch for Virginia Hill
Bugsy, 1991
Costume designer Albert Wolsky
Illustrator Shawna Leavell Trpcic

costume that has not been specially designed, or recreated from museum sources, with the care and attention given to a principal's clothes.[97]

Janet Leigh, the star of Hitchcock's *Psycho* (1960), related her experience with the film's costume designer Helen Colvig and set costumer Rita Riggs:

> It was the practice at the time for wardrobe to be custom-made, but Mr Hitchcock insisted we shop in a regular ready-to-wear store. He asked us to buy Marion's two dresses off the rack and only pay what a secretary could afford. We all agreed.
>
> The slip mentioned in the novel and script became a bra and half-slip. For the opening love scene, a white bra and half-slip were chosen. Then after she steals the money and is changing for the ride to see Sam, we switched to a black bra and half-slip. Mr Hitchcock wanted even the wardrobe to reflect the good and evil each of us has lurking within our inner selves.[98]

At the end of the decade, costume designer Theadora Van Runkle was hired by Arthur Penn for her first picture, *Bonnie and Clyde* (1967; plate 29). When she showed her costume illustrations to Penn, he declared, 'If the film is as good as your drawings, it will be a hit'. Van Runkle said that 'the minute I opened the script, I saw ... everything everybody should wear as I read. And I never really deviated.'[99]

Some designers, such as William Travilla, were still creating couture clothes for every actress in the film, and often the result was a stage-bound, stilted affair harking back to an earlier era. Reflecting on *Valley of the Dolls* (1967), fashion critic Simon Doonan remembers:

> Individually, the clothes in this film weren't all that exceptional. It's more how they worked as a whole to define the three types of women – as well as to illustrate their transformations from prissy to tarty – that made these looks so memorable. When we look back at these girls they seem so sweet and composed in their very dressmaker-chic sixties outfits. The film is about druggies, about being addicted to pills and booze, yet the characters look like Lady Bird Johnson.[100]

The Hollywood studio entered the 1960s trying to find a cohesive identity in the new world of media conglomerates. Film historians consider the mid-1960s to be the absolute end of 'Old Hollywood'. By this time, '"the studio system" was all but gone. The studios would survive – as production plants, as distribution companies, as familiar trademarks – but the studio era had ended, and with it Hollywood's classical age.'[101] By decade's end the Hollywood film had been deconstructed and redefined.

Many inside and outside the industry feel that the true turning point came with the release of the costume designer-less *Easy Rider* (1969): 'The impact of *Easy Rider*, both on the film-makers and the industry as a whole, was no less than seismic.... To the Hollywood old guard, the good news was that after nearly a decade of floundering the films had finally *connected*, found a new audience.'[102]

The normative practices of costume design established fifty years earlier (whether practiced by a costume designer or someone else) survived as modern scripts were dissected for continuity, characters evaluated and diagnosed, sketches generated, and colour palettes devised and discussed with the art and camera departments. Actors continued to arrive at the studio or on location for fittings and to discuss the costumes for their characters, and purchased clothes were altered, adjusted, dyed and aged. Bought or borrowed, rented or manufactured, beautiful or ugly, vulgar or sophisticated, costumes continued to serve the script, the character, the frame and the director.

THE TWENTIETH CENTURY BOWS OUT

The mid-1970s was a time in Hollywood when the last veteran craftsmen of the studio system were on the cusp of retirement and the producers and executives who had entered the film business after the Second World War had taken over the management of the major studios. The craftspeople working both in studio workrooms and soundstages were an eclectic mix of the old guard and the new. Many film directors were now the youngest people on the crew.

29 **Sketch for Bonnie Parker (Faye Dunaway)**
***Bonnie and Clyde*, 1967**
Costume designer and
illustrator Theadora Van Runkle

30 Travis Bickle (Robert De Niro)
Taxi Driver, **1976**
Costume designer Ruth Morley

OPPOSITE
31 Indiana Jones (Harrison Ford)
Raiders of the Lost Ark, **1981**
Costume designer Deborah Nadoolman

32 Sketch for Indiana Jones
Raiders of the Lost Ark, **1981**
Costume designer Deborah Nadoolman
Illustrator Steven Spielberg

❝ In *Taxi Driver,* when I finally found
the plaid shirt Bobby wanted to wear,
when I found the army jacket, the pants,
well, *he wanted to wear them.* ❞

RUTH MORLEY, COSTUME DESIGNER

half of Hollywood…teetering on an economic tight-rope…. The way it looks for costume designers, they might as well jump. Their equilibrium, it seems, has been upset not only by the move to shoestring cinema but by a radical shift in how actors and actresses should look and who should help them look that way.[103]

But towards the end of the 1970s budgets grew, and greater risks were taken. The traditional role of the costume designer became solidly re-established in action and adventure, science fiction and fantasy films. Directors in these genres required full partnership with a costume designer in order to accomplish their vision. *Star Wars Episode IV: A New Hope* (1977) progenitor George Lucas said, 'On the first films I purposefully avoided intense design cultures. I kept the costumes very, very simple and the costumes were designed not to draw attention to themselves' (plate 33).[104] As the industry recovered, the studios were willing to spend more money for a greater return on their investment. Directors were given the tools to allow their imaginations full reign. At the suggestion of director Ridley Scott, designer John Mollo used an unlikely source of inspiration to create costumes for *Alien* (1979). Science fiction has a tradition of leveraging ethnography and world culture for invented worlds: rather than designing spacesuits based on gear worn by astronauts, Mollo's space travellers wore outfits derived from the armour of Japanese Samurai.[105]

Costume designers continued to produce valuable work in naturalistic stories as well. Among New York film-makers, character was king. Martin Scorsese collaborated with costume designer Ruth Morley to create a rough and recognizable New York story, *Taxi Driver* (1976; plate 30). This required total commitment by the actors; in Morley's words, 'I like working with actors who *care* more than with actors who say "Put something on me". In *Taxi Driver,* when I finally found *the* plaid shirt Bobby wanted to wear, when I found the army jacket, the pants, well, *he wanted to wear them.*'

By the 1980s the studio hierarchy had shifted to the new order and the structure of the film business had finally stabilized. It was a time when Hollywood regained its equilibrium. Although many sophisticated films for adults were produced, the primary target became the teen audience and the studios produced a flurry of 'high-concept', 'popcorn' films.[106] 'The eighties, goes the conventional wisdom, was the decade when Hollywood gave up any pretence of engaging the emotions and challenging the intellect, concentrating solely on meeting the demands of the marketplace', writes Jon Bernstein.[107]

When Steven Spielberg first gave me the script of *Raiders of the Lost Ark* (1981; plates 31, 32) he described it as a big 'B' film. In fact, Spielberg screened the 'B' film on which it was based, *The Secret of the Incas* (1954), in order to ascertain whether he could

The Hollywood studios entered the 1970s with an identity crisis, half-empty back lots, skeleton staffs and a few very confused and panic-stricken executives. Costume design had come full-circle in some respects. As in the early, primitive days of Hollywood, on low-budget independent modern films, actors might be asked to provide their own clothing as costumes if it worked for the part. It was common practice in the 1970s for costume designers to be hired to design a film and then be forced to depart after the commencement of principal photography – producers were not willing to keep the designers on the payroll for the run of the picture. The production component of the designer's role became radically foreshortened, missing the opportunity to continue to design new characters as they were cast in the film, check the principal actors' costumes on the set, and work with the assistant director and cinematographer to place the background talent to best advantage on the set and within the frame. By default, the costume supervisor gained as a result of the designer's demotion, shouldering more of the designer's responsibilities and decision-making power on the set, as the person ultimately responsible for the physical costumes and management of the department. According to an article in *The Los Angeles Times,* with

Indiana Jones

6' 1½"

Steven Spielberg
May 1/80

replicate the exciting and heroic Saturday morning serial experience of the film. Spielberg, echoing *Raiders* producer and *Star Wars* (1977) director George Lucas, had a male teenage audience in mind from the very beginning.

Although he was not the original choice for the role, Harrison Ford did more than wear the clothes that I designed; he inhabited Indiana Jones, saying:

> I intentionally keep my interpretation simple. I don't make up a character who could have a life without benefit of the specific story. Han Solo [*Star Wars*], Indiana Jones [*Raiders of the Lost Ark*], Rick Deckard [*Blade Runner*] – they wear different clothes and they live in different times. I'm not being glib when I say it's as simple as that.[108]

From the earliest days of the industry, some films had always been made outside the studios on distant locations. The 1980s saw the real beginning of production flight from the home base of Hollywood studios. Shooting in East Africa posed a serious challenge for designer Milena Canonero in creating costumes for Sidney Pollack's *Out of Africa* (1985; plate 225). Canonero's rigorous research had to include not only the details of the Belle Epoque clothing worn by Europeans in the 1910s, but also the tribal costume of the East Africans: 'It's not easy to find references in books showing what the Somalis wore in those days.'[109] Canonero was astonished that after its release, 'The costumes in *Out of Africa* had quite an impact on fashion. It was as though the fashion world was ready for the styles of the film; the costumes just caught something that was in the air.' But the fashion accolades did not reassure Meryl Streep who, accustomed to taking on the challenges of a new role, was unsure of her performance. On her portrayal of Danish writer Isak Dinesen, Streep said, 'It's hard to feel you're doing justice to the ghost. I always feel inadequate toward it. I'm intimidated by walking in someone else's shoes.'

The integrity of designing and manufacturing contemporary costumes survived the cutbacks of the 1970s and '80s. Purchased and sourced clothing was aged to look worn just as as custom-made clothes had been in the past. In the words of Milena Canonero,

> In contemporary films, often, our work is less obvious, but I try to find, beside the palette, something more satisfying … I hate it when people think that a contemporary film is not really costume-designed because so much is bought. It is like saying that a production designer does not 'art direct' because a film is shot on existing locations. I do believe that selections and choices constitute designing a look.[110]

The seamless integration of modern costume into the story was an imperative, the clothes telling the story quietly and with confident authority. Ultimately the clothes must never overwhelm the dialogue. Ellen Mirojnick, costume designer for *Wall Street* (1987; plate 372) and *Basic Instinct* (1992; plate 307), described the transformative effect that modern costumes have on performers (and on the audience): 'I get scared stiff the character will look like a cardboard cutout up there on the screen. Because, if the actor can't move *into* his or her clothes – the character's clothes – then the audience will notice the clothes, not the man, not the woman, not the body, and I've *failed*.'[111]

As the marketplace continued to evolve in the 1990s, directors maintained their role as authors of the film while stars gained ever more power. Deals were leveraged more and more on the drawing power of stars, based on the opening weekend box office grosses. Eager to offset risk, studios counted on fans wanting to see their favourite actors.

As the countdown to the end of the twentieth century began, studios continued to release full-length features as entertainment for all ages. Baby-boomers wanted to enjoy 'family' entertainment with their children. Full-length animated films were revitalized by the Michael Eisner and Jeffrey Katzenberg team at

33 Luke Skywalker, Princess Leia Organa and Han Solo (Mark Hamill, Carrie Fisher and Harrison Ford) *Star Wars Episode IV: A New Hope*, 1977 Costume designer John Mollo

Disney, and by Steve Jobs and director John Lasseter at Pixar. These witty, child-friendly multigenerational films, such as the Oscar-nominated *Beauty and the Beast* (1991) and the revolutionary *Toy Story* (1995), were novel in that they could also be enjoyed by parents. Costume designers were asked for the first time to design the costumes for animated characters – Joanna Johnston for Robert Zemeckis' early groundbreaking *Who Framed Roger Rabbit* (1988) and later, Isis Mussenden for *Shrek* (2001).

The turn of the century was also marked by the national reporting of weekly Hollywood box office returns in such industry papers as *Variety* and *The Hollywood Reporter* and read by the film going audience in the *New York Times*, *Wall Street Journal* and *USA Today*. This was the era of populist ratings (thumbs up or down) and the death of the long-suffering drive-in theatre. The huge opening-day profits and success of such films as *Titanic* (1997; plates 37–9) led to even greater opening weekend pressure on producers and studios seeking to top other studios – and themselves.

Although the James Cameron film was rumoured to be a production nightmare, with the costume department dealing with the challenge of hundreds of stunt people in period clothes jumping into the water, *Titanic* broke every worldwide box office record. The film attracted an adoring public. Its broad appeal included the legend surrounding the ship herself; the romantic storyline; the hit musical score; and the boatload of endearing characters, from first class to steerage. Winner of an Academy Award for Best Costume Design, Deborah L. Scott said that 'This was an era of great formality. People of wealth changed their wardrobe four and five times a day. Their clothes were so elaborate that personal maids and valets were absolutely necessary. The clothes were incredibly beautiful and detailed.'[112]

The formulaic blockbuster was bait to studio executives, luring the public to multiplexes with the new digital special effects, Dolby Sound and a spectacle that the small screen could not possibly offer. By 1999 the dye was set with the *Matrix* series, which also broke new boundaries with computer generated effects. Costume designer Kym Barrett approached this science fiction thriller as she would any film:

> I'm looking at the big picture of the whole film and
> every member of the cast and all the different conceptual
> worlds we move through. It's a very organic process we
> go through. Things are coming to me from all over the
> world and people are working in little shops all around
> the city or in different countries. It's like its own
> corporation almost.[113]

While many of the studios' films went on to gross over $100 million, the special effects-laden, high-concept scripts left the door wide open for audiences seeking edgy films like Ethan and Joel Coens' *The Big Lebowski* (1998; plates 75, 145). Jeff Dowd, who was the basis for Jeff Bridges' character 'The Dude' in the film, revealed that 'When my daughter saw a poster of the film, she said, "Daddy, where did they get all your clothes?"'[114] Such intimate, smaller-scale, character-driven narratives were often to be found in independent films, but these were not the films that studios were interested in making at the time. Their costume designers, such as the Coen Brothers' constant key collaborator Mary

Zophres, were overlooked at the Academy Award nominations for Best Costume Design. Independent films were most often made cheaply, on location, with a company of actors and minimal special effects. Their opening weekend box office expectations were modest and, with marketing and advertising budgets skyrocketing, they entertained a small but dedicated audience.

As they gained steam at the box office and attracted critical acclaim, Hollywood responded by institutionalizing the indies by acquiring them. The studios developed their own in-house 'independent' production arms. In the 1996 Academy Awards race, four of the five nominees for best picture were from independent studios. But earning studio-level grosses was a near necessity in the new economics of independent films. Every studio was looking for the next *Shakespeare in Love* (1998; plates 40, 42), which won the Academy Award for Best Picture, six more Oscars plus Best Costume Design for Sandy Powell.

As actors' fees grew ever higher, studios focused their interest on the stars they felt could guarantee a big opening weekend. In seeking less risk and more reward, they backed the stars to bring in the audiences. Costume budgets continued to shrink, alongside those in all below-the-line departments, to offset the overall cost of the cast.

Hollywood production ramped up as the twenty-first century dawned, and by the end of the 1990s the annual number of films produced (450–500) rivalled the Golden Age. Because of the exorbitant marketing and advertising costs of each film release, which cancelled out box office profits, much of this product was sold direct-to-video with no cinematic release at all. VHS and, subsequently, DVD rentals were big business and those studio departments thrived.

As to the effect on costume designers, by the turn of the century 'runaway production' became the plague that the Hollywood labour unions could not stop. President of the Directors Guild of America (DGA) Jack Shea defined the practice as 'US-developed feature films which are filmed in another country for economic reasons'. Runaway production came to mean that the designer and the costume supervisor had to rebuild the entire studio costume workroom for each production outside the studio and often outside California – or even the United States. Without the physical plant of the studio (vast quantities of clothes, stocks of fabrics, trims and notions), the support of a veteran costume workroom with seamstresses and tailors and an experienced costume crew, designers were under unprecedented pressure to be ever more resourceful.

THE DAWN OF THE TWENTY-FIRST CENTURY

The first decade of the 2000s was a time when the studios' demand for fashion designer labels on clothing in films became a recurrent obstacle for costume designers. Cross-promotion and 'synergy' were the new bywords. Imposed by studios seeking to offset production and marketing costs, product placement, always a minefield, threatened to sabotage authentic characterizations. In the word of costume designer Anthony Powell,

> I don't mind using a suit if it's right for the character,
> but if I have to use that name exclusively it bothers me
> terribly because nobody dresses that way. Nobody, unless

34 *The Addams Family*, 1991
Costume designer Ruth Myers

35 Charles Addams (1912–88), the Addams Family
standing in front of College Hall, University of Pennsylvania,
first published as the cover of
The Pennsylvania Gazette, March 1973
© 1973 Charles Addams
With permission Tee and Charles Addams Foundation

OPPOSITE
36 Costume for Morticia Addams (Anjelica Huston)
Addams Family Values, 1993
Costume designer Theoni V. Aldredge
The Collection of Motion Picture Costume Design Larry McQueen

it's a story point, dresses from head to toe with one designer all bought three weeks ago at Barneys. You wear something from five years ago, you have something favorite, you mix this, you mix that, something got a little tight on you, something's more worn than something else. That's what clothes are about. That's what we have to accomplish designing modern costumes.[115]

Fashion's ever-passionate love affair with Hollywood heated up. This symbiotic relationship benefits fashion designers by associating their name with a film and an actor and by giving them licence to market clothes popularized by a film; and it benefits the producer by providing cash to offset costs, clothing and free advertising. The sacrifice can be the integrity of the story and the film. The director and the costume designer may argue vigorously against the intrusion of fashion labels and product placement, while the producer may be faced with a choice between making art and making money. Most just try to do their best not to lose money.

Audiences continue to want to dress like their favourite stars. The green bias-cut gown created by costume designer Jacqueline Durran for *Atonement* (2007; plate 315) spawned thousands of copies, introducing bright green to the prom dress market seen at graduation parties everywhere in 2007. With a modern sensibility aimed at re-creating the height of the Golden Age, Durran said, 'We used a modern aesthetic with '30s shapes. We literally made everything for the '30s scenes, finding original costumes and using shapes from that era remade with modern fabrics.'[116]

The 2000s have provided Hollywood costume designers much to sing about. Colleen Atwood has continued her role as muse to directors Tim Burton and Rob Marshall. Of her collaboration with Marshall for *Chicago* (2002; plate 306) she has said:

Rob definitely had a vision of the film, but as far as specifics about the costumes, he was very open to what I thought. We tried to keep a contrast between the real world Roxie lived in and the imagined world of the stage. It's like a parallel universe.[117]

For *Dreamgirls* (2006), designer Sharen Davis worked closely with the film's stars:

Beyoncé said the costumes forced her into a position of such uprightness that it gave her absolute confidence in what she was doing as a performer, while Jennifer [Hudson] said it made her feel like a Barbie, and made her stand up straight, which she didn't like to do![118]

CONCLUSION

Over the past century Hollywood films have become part of our shared global mythology. During the Golden Age of Hollywood the talent and craftsmanship at work in the major studios were of such a high calibre that even the 'B-pictures' displayed a level of storytelling that remains unequalled. Costume designers today continue to work in motion pictures using the same creative process and values. It is the success or failure in telling a story that makes a film a classic or instantly forgettable. Whether it scared us, made us laugh or cry or just amazed us, the finished product, the film itself, is what makes these clothes in *Hollywood Costume* so special.

Mary Lea Bandy, retired director of the Film Department at the Museum of Modern Art, once asked me: 'Isn't there a better word for what you do than "costume"?' Her point hit home. The word 'costume' summons images of Halloween, carnival, circus and masked balls, where it is decorative, embellished, and an intrinsic part of spectacle. But cinema costuming aspires to be much more than superficial style. The characters are just like us – with a life lived before each film begins. Our clothes are inextricably part of our identity and our memory. The costume designer and actor search for that truth together. When Robert De Niro was honoured with an American Film Institute Lifetime Achievement Award, Martin Scorsese said: 'To be certain, he has an extraordinary genius to be able to transform himself, to undergo a metamorphosis, and to simply be, just BE the person he's playing.'

The clothes in *Hollywood Costume* are memorable because of the rich collaborative film-making process that creates great movies. Costumes are one tool that the film-maker has to tell the story. Nothing in the film frame is arbitrary and nothing is allowed to get in the way of the script. The 'best' costume design may be invisible. Director Sidney Lumet captured the essence when he said, 'Good style, to me, is unseen style. It is style that is felt.' Dorothy's gingham dress instantly brings that particular MGM picture to mind. The hat and leather jacket belonging to Indiana Jones and Holly Golightly's little black dress will always be identified with the films in which they appear (*Raiders of the Lost Ark* and *Breakfast at Tiffany's*) and the actors who played those characters (Harrison Ford and Audrey Hepburn). Our expectation is to be entirely seduced, and that is what the film-maker must deliver if he or she expects us to care about their journey, to love the film and to elevate the characters into icons.

OPPOSITE
37 Jack Dawson (Leonardo DiCaprio)
Titanic, 1997
Costume designer Deborah L. Scott

ABOVE
38 Rose DeWitt Bukater (Kate Winslet)
Titanic, 1997
Costume designer Deborah L. Scott

RIGHT
39 Sketch for Rose DeWitt Bukater
Titanic, 1997
Costume designer Deborah L. Scott
Illustrator David Le Vey

ABOVE LEFT
40 Sketch for Viola De Lesseps
Shakespeare in Love, 1998
Costume designer and illustrator
Sandy Powell

ABOVE RIGHT
41 Satine (Nicole Kidman)
Moulin Rouge!, 2001
Costume designers Catherine Martin
and Angus Strathie

LEFT
**42 Viola De Lesseps and
William Shakespeare
(Gwyneth Paltrow and
Joseph Fiennes)**
Shakespeare in Love, 1998
Costume designer Sandy Powell

OPPOSITE
43 Sketch for Satine
Moulin Rouge!, 2001
Costume designers Catherine Martin
and Angus Strathie
Illustrator Angus Strathie

1 THE ART OF BECOMING

FIGHT CLUB

"PORNO PRINT"
TANK TOP

w/ MUSKRAT
FAKE FUR COAT
—
POSTAL WORKER
PANTS

"CARMEL" PANTENT
LEATHER VINTAGE
GUCCI LOAFERS

BRAD PITT
AS
"TYLER DUR

WHAT IS COSTUME DESIGN?

Deborah Nadoolman Landis

FILMS are about people: they are at the emotional core and it is their story that moves us. It is the characters in the stories who hold our attention, provide the action and establish the framework for a screenplay. Although clues to the character are set within the script, it is the interpretation by the actor and the director and their key collaborators that breathes life and personality into each fictional being. Harrison Ford explains: 'The role of an actor is to serve as a mirror. My job is not to show you that the character and I have something in common. My job is to show you that you and the character – even one who may seem a little crazy – have something in common.' In the cinema, the actor must fully inhabit the character; the audience's suspension of disbelief is essential.

Costume design is not just about the clothes: in film, it has both a narrative and a visual mandate. Designers serve the script and the director by creating authentic characters and by using colour, texture and silhouette to provide balance within the composition of the frame. The costume designer must first know *who* the character is before approaching this challenge.

Over the past century costume designers have practised a discrete and formal design process, beginning with the written word of the screenplay, discussion with the director, collaboration with the actor and research. For each production costume designers compile a scrapbook of photos, historic text, family albums, home movies, yearbooks, hair and make-up styles, sketches, fabric swatches, and virtually any visual reference that they can acquire. This research volume, the designer's 'bible', may take the form of a binder, a notebook or a website. It is shared with all key creative collaborators – the director, actor, cinematographer and production designer, and with the hair and make-up artists. The costume designer will also use the 'bible' as the centrepiece for discussions with the costume crew. We do not simply make things up, we will need to justify each choice. Whatever the genre, whether the budget is low or high, whether or not the film becomes a classic, the costume designer approaches each production in the same way.

No matter in what the era the story is set, the audience is asked to believe that the people in the movie are real and that they had a life prior to the start of the action. We join our cast of characters at one moment in their life. Everything about them must ring true, including their clothes. In the same way, our own clothes take our life journey with us: we all wear an amalgam of stories, each item telling its own unique tale. Everything, including our earrings, shoes, socks, watch, trousers, shirt, necklace, jacket, ring and suit, have been purchased, inherited, gifted, stolen or borrowed at different moments of our life. We all wear a mix of clothes, some old and some new. People also wear tattoos and piercings, nail polish, crazy hair colour and cut. These details provide others with more than a clue about our own personal style. Our clothing can also reveal and conceal our moods, taste and personality, our social and economic aspirations and the time in which we live. Clothes function as social and emotional signposts.

In the same way costumes provide the audience with essential information. Attention to detail is the hallmark of great costuming. The audience's attention is focused on that which the director chooses to reveal. A close-up may emphasize or disclose details – a cuff, a lapel or a piece of jewellery – for a deliberate narrative purpose. The integrity of the story takes precedence over a gorgeous gown – glamorous clothes, when inappropriate, can sabotage a serious scene.

Regardless of whether a film is period, fantasy or modern, all require research. Designers are inspired by art, literature, photography, nature, music, childhood memories, other films, and freely associate all of these. For *Dreamgirls* (2006; plates 45, 46), a musical based on girl bands of the early 1960s, costume designer Sharen Davis remembers that she 'looked at magazines like *Ebony* and *Life*, and footage from the Motown era, and appearances on "American Bandstand"'. Janty Yates, longtime costume collaborator of director Ridley Scott, recalls: 'On *Gladiator* [2000], he suggested, "Look at Alma-Tadema for the crowd." Sir Lawrence Alma-Tadema painted Roman scenes in the late 1800s, using pastels – so I used pistachios, pinks, almonds and sky blue for the extras'. For the Coen Brothers' Western *True Grit* (2010), designer

Mary Zophres immersed herself in images and writings of the late nineteenth century: 'I found a lot of the written text to be more helpful than the photographs, which were often taken in studios where they were sometimes wearing the studio's clothes.'

Research is taken no less seriously in Hollywood comedies. For *Austin Powers* (1997), according to designer Deena Appel, 'researching 1967, when the first movie began, I found a lot of inspiration from the British music scene – primarily George Harrison, Mick Jagger, Jimi Hendrix'.

Most costume designers contend that contemporary costume is more difficult to design. Since everyone gets dressed in the morning, everyone considers themselves an expert on clothes. As Joanna Johnston said, 'Contemporary films depend on delicate and subtle design; it's a very fine line. The designers can go too far, or you can understate it and not make the point. The audience must be able to say, absolutely, "I recognize that person".' Costumes are considered successful if audiences *do not* notice the costumes, but are nonetheless deeply connected to the characters. Ellen Mirojnick contends that designing contemporary costumes means that 'you have to work doubly hard to make them disappear'.

Film-makers tell a visual story by marrying sight, sound and music to communicate with the audience. Production designers define the 'where' – the place and setting of the story – while cinematographers create the mood and tone of the action. Along with the costume designer, these key creative collaborators paint each frame of film as meticulously as a canvas in service of the story and the director. Together we make the world – and the characters that people it – come alive. Colour is a strong reference point from which to create a cinematic style, a powerful tool used to underscore the narrative, create a cohesive fictional space and provide an overarching palette for the narrative. Because they are worn by the actors, costumes dominate the foreground action. Costume designer Edith Head wrote: 'Alfred Hitchcock has a complete phobia about what he calls "eye-catchers", like a scene with a woman in bright purple or a man in an orange suit. Unless there is a story reason for a color, we keep the colors muted, because Hitchcock believes they can detract from an important action scene.' Hitchcock needed the audience to listen carefully, without distraction. If dialogue is the melody of a movie, colour provides the harmony.

Throughout Hollywood history, motion pictures have used a combination of designed, purchased, rented and manufactured clothes. Depending on the film, a designer may sketch and create, or shop and age the clothes. It is a common misperception that all modern costumes are 'shopped' by designers, reaching the big screen unaltered and fully accessorized, with fashion designers' labels intact from the boutique. But the role of the costume designer is defined by the requirements of each individual screenplay. Mark Bridges, costume designer of the modern silent film *The Artist* (2011; plates 47, 48), explains:

45 **Design for Lorrell Robinson, Deena Jones and Effie White**
Dreamgirls, **2006**
Costume designer Sharen Davis
Illustrator Felipe Sanchez

The creative path that I take depends on the character and is specific on a case-by-case basis. If I need to, I'll design all the pieces, but I don't have to make everything

for every movie. You're not going to find the right fabric, or be able to afford to make the clothes, or have the time to make them, on every film.

For *Fight Club* (1999; plate 44), Michael Kaplan explains that his job 'was to produce clothes that looked like they came from thrift shops … clothes that nobody would want', adding:

Brad [Pitt] didn't really know what Tyler Durden should look like. We were dealing with a level of unreality, people who weren't real. But they still had to look and seem real. I would make them new and then age them. I would break buttons, crack leather, and put things in the oven and wash them, so that they would look like they were 30 years old even though they were actually made the week before.

Nothing that appears on screen is casual or accidental – every single accessory and costume is a deliberate choice made by the designer and, ultimately, the director.

Costumes provide the means for actors to channel new characters, and actors often discover their character in the fitting room. After many discussions with Daniel Day-Lewis for *Gangs of New York* (2002), Sandy Powell describes how 'The minute he put the costume on he said he could see the character'. Glenn Close considers costume designer Anthony Powell to be an indispensable collaborator. Powell recalls designing Cruella De Vil for *101 Dalmatians* (1996): 'When I asked for her thoughts on the character, she [Glenn Close] said "You just design it, and at the end I shall look at myself in the mirror and then I shall decide how to play the part".' The actor is asked to fully inhabit a new person, the act of becoming 'Cruella' or 'Dorothy' or 'Captain Jack Sparrow' being not so much a change of clothes as a change of skin. This inhabiting of a character is the actor's profession as

46 Lorrell Robinson, Deena Jones and Effie White (Anika Noni Rose, Beyoncé Knowles and Jennifer Hudson) *Dreamgirls*, 2006 Costume designer Sharen Davis

they morph into hundreds of people in their professional careers. Meryl Streep is known for her complete commitment to her new characters: long-time collaborator Ann Roth describes how, in the fitting room, 'We wait for the third person to arrive'.

Costumes are so much more than clothes, embodying the psychological, social and emotional condition of the character at a particular moment in the script. Ang Lee, director of *Brokeback Mountain* (2005; plates 49, 50), said of his costume designer that 'Marit Allen clothed her characters, not to cover them with a preconceived image but to liberate them to express everything she dreamed they could become'. This key role of the costume designer has not changed in over a century of film-making and as

long as stories require realized characters it is unlikely that costume design will be affected by fashion, the economic exigencies of the film business or the changes wrought by new technology. Today's costume designers are now working in the extended non-three-dimensional worlds of animation, motion-capture and gaming. Infinitely resourceful, they must utilize digital technologies and unconventional solutions to challenges presented by the script, and pressurized working conditions, including truncated pre-production, late casting and reduced budgets.

Clothes sit close to our heart, containing our personality and carrying complex personal stories from our past and present. Costumes in films have to express all of that, and at the same time

47 **Design for**
Peppy Miller
The Artist, **2011**
Costume designer and
illustrator Mark Bridges

OPPOSITE
48 **Peppy Miller**
(Bérénice Bejo)
The Artist, **2011**
Costume designer
Mark Bridges

blend with the set and the lighting within the period and genre of the film. Costume designers need to be talented dressmakers, couturiers and fine artists. In a 1938 interview MGM costume designer Adrian said that

> Few people in an audience watching a great screen production realize the importance of any gown worn by the feminine star. They may notice that it is attractive, that they would like to have copied it, that it is becoming, but the fact that it was definitely planned to mirror some definite mood, to be as much a part of the play as the lines or the scenery, seldom occurs to them. But that most assuredly is true.

The costume designer gives the clothes to the actor, the actor gives the character to the director, and the director tells the story. When a character and a film capture the public's imagination, the costumes can ignite worldwide fashion trends and influence global culture. Cinematic icons are born when the audience falls deeply in love with the people in the story. And that's what movies, and costume design, are all about.

49 **Ennis Del Mar and Jack Twist (Heath Ledger and Jake Gyllenhaal)**
Brokeback Mountain, **2005**
Costume designer Marit Allen

OPPOSITE
50 **Costumes for Ennis Del Mar and Jack Twist**
Brokeback Mountain, **2005**
Costume designer Marit Allen
NBCUniversal Archives & Collections

MOVING PICTURES, SILENT MOVIES
AND THE ART OF WILLIAM HOGARTH

Aileen Ribeiro

CLOTHING is such an integral part of human existence that in the theatre – which of course is a reflection of life – it plays a crucial role. From the earliest forms of drama onwards, clothing *as costume tells* the audience before a word is spoken the rank and character of the role played by the actor. As Deborah Landis remarks, costume is able to 'define identity, ethnicity, economic and social status, as well as the personality and individuality of each character'.[1] The gestures and deportment of the actors who inhabit the clothes in the theatre or in films – movements which are often conditioned by the garments themselves – are equally important, effects which can rarely (if ever) be achieved in historical films. It is my contention that the present (which will obviously become the past) is the only way in which costume in any form of theatre can be truly authentic and real, an unselfconscious element of the stories which all drama tells. As the hero in David Lodge's novel *Therapy* (1986) says, 'in drama or film, everything is happening now. That's why stage directions are always in the present tense … the *telling* is happening in the present'.[2]

The past is a foreign country; they do things differently there. While the passions and emotions people feel may be universal, the material world of the past is not ours. The classic inter-war films set in the historical past are often little more than vehicles for the great stars (and for the designer), with little sense of historical accuracy, particularly the further back in time they are set; examples here might be *Queen Christina* (1933) and *Marie Antoinette* (1938), both costumed by Adrian. The former, although a triumph for the unique talents of Garbo, could not bring to life mid-seventeeth-century Sweden; the latter, in spite of a considerable

amount of research, and including silks woven specially in Lyon, was an overblown parody of French court life, where the costumes were the stars and not vice versa. Does authenticity matter? Films are entertainments above all, and not exercises in antiquarianism; in any case, it might be argued, if we cannot get back to a true knowledge of the past, should we try? Or should we accept that historical films are as much part of the period in which they were made as those with contemporary themes – that the stars of the moment (especially when young) need to relate to their own time?[3]

Films with major historical characters are inevitably hamstrung by the weight of visual tradition and expectation, whereas the costume designer working with fiction has, in theory, greater flexibility, far less need for 'statement' costumes. In *Portrait of a Lady* (1996; plate 53) Janet Patterson's costume designs reflect Henry James's novel, with dark and sombre tones. Dress is cleverly used to express emotion, notably in the snake-like pleated train worn by Nicole Kidman as Isabel Archer when she hurries upstairs, along floors, and out-of-doors; it appears to have a life of its own, reflecting her agitation and despair. This is costume that is both authentic (for the 1870s) *and* used as a dramatic device, clothing as real and as gesture, underlined by clever camera-work.

OPPOSITE
51 William Hogarth
***Before* (detail), c.1730–31**
Fitzwilliam Museum, Cambridge

RIGHT
52 William Hogarth
***The Four Times of Day: Morning* (detail),**
1736
Bearsted Collection, Upton House,
Warwickshire

It helps, perhaps, that we are more familiar and at ease with the dress of the later nineteenth century than with the perceived artifice of that of the *ancien régime*. In *Dangerous Liaisons* (1988; plate 56) James Acheson's designs for Glenn Close (and the other main characters in the film) are somewhat too opulent, often inappropriate for the occasions on which they appear; the choice of the 1760s as the period chosen does not reflect the sartorial subtleties of elite court life at the time of Laclos' great novel (1782).

The film that most respects the eighteenth century is *Barry Lyndon* (1975; plate 54). Perhaps because it is based on a nineteenth-century work (Thackeray's satirical novel *The Luck of Barry Lyndon*, 1844), Stanley Kubrick had more licence to create the essence of the eighteenth century, which he did mainly through painting. He spent as much time with the costume designers (Milena Canonero and Ulla-Britt Søderlund) as he did with the cameraman; every scene was posed and costumed as in paintings by a number of eighteenth-century artists, particularly Hogarth and Gainsborough. Hogarth inspired Kubrick's use of light and shadow and the arrangement of figures within a stage-like setting; Gainsborough's fashionable elite Englishwomen of the 1770s and 1780s with their pale, melancholy faces, vast, complex hairstyles and slightly fantastic dresses prompted the appearance of Marisa Berenson as Lady Lyndon.[4]

Artists, notes Anne Hollander, have a 'compelling interpretation of the look of the moment', and as such they create effects similar to 'the distinctive movie tradition of stylized reality'.[5] Landis makes a specific link between painting and film-making:

> 'Painting the frame' is a term of art that
> we use in relationship to the combined
> work of the cinematographer (the light),
> the production design (the where) and the
> costume designer (the who). No frame of
> film is accidental, it is always meticulously
> designed … Costume in painting telegraphs
> meaning as costume does in cinema …
> Put a baroque frame around our work and
> it's a painting.[6]

53 **Isabel Archer (Nicole Kidman)**
Portrait of a Lady, 1996
Costume designer Janet Patterson

One of the reasons why Kubrick selected Hogarth as a source for *Barry Lyndon* is the artist's skill in using dress not just to underscore character, personal relationships and the interplay between social classes in mid-eighteenth-century England, but the way in which it furthers the story by revealing motivations and serves to foster action, as in a novel or a play.

Hogarth is both a literary and a dramatic artist, inextricably linked in the 1740s with his friend the novelist Henry Fielding. Both had the same hatred of cruelty, hypocrisy and affectation, the same tastes in humour, the same love of theatre as a microcosm of society: 'Stage and Scene are by common Use as familiar

to us, when we speak of Life in general, as when we confine ourselves to dramatic Performances', claimed Fielding in *Tom Jones* (1749).[7] Both men wished 'to laugh Mankind out of their favourite Follies and Vices',[8] and Hogarth was determined to prove that art could do this as effectively as the novel; his work is the visualization of Fielding's texts, more film than theatre because of the imaginative way costume is used, and the way we are allowed to focus on details significant to character and plot. Fielding and Hogarth knew that great art and literature relied on a knowledge of how people lived, how they behaved, and the clothes they wore. Fielding repeatedly notes the importance of 'Human Nature' in his novels, which he perceived as 'Entertainment' where the subject was less important than 'the Author's Skill in dressing it up'.[9] He often refers to 'the inimitable pencil of my friend Hogarth' in his novels, either as specific references or in general terms of praise (in the preface to *Joseph Andrews* of 1742 he notes: 'his figures seem to breathe … [and] they appear to think'[10]). A well-known example of the former is the comment in *Tom Jones* about the hypocritical 'Old Maid' ('somewhat past the Age of 30'), Bridget Allworthy:

> I would attempt to draw her Picture; but this is done already by a more able Master, Mr. Hogarth himself, to whom she sat many Years ago, and had been lately exhibited by that Gentleman in his Print of a Winter's Morning, of which she was no improper Emblem, and may be seen walking (for walk she doth in the Print) to Covent-Garden Church, with a starved Foot-boy behind carrying her Prayer-book.[11]

In Hogarth's *Four Times of Day: Morning* (plate 52) we see the figure of a woman wearing an over-elaborate, formal (and rather old-fashioned) dress, a fan held up, presumably in disapproval, to her ridiculously patched face; the marks of the iron rings of her pattens (overshoes) can be seen in the snow, precisely the kind of touch made for cinema, the camera tracking across the frozen ground.

'We know the very minds of people by their dress', commented Hogarth in his *Analysis of Beauty* (1753),[12] and his observation applied to people of all kinds, in what he and Fielding referred to as High and Low Life. In his *Before and After* (c.1730–31) the first painting (plate 51) shows a young man stylishly dressed in a suit of shot silk (possibly a valet in his master's cast-off garments, an accepted perquisite of his job) about to seduce a pretty woman – also an indoor servant, of slightly lower rank – who wears a yellow silk gown over a humble red woollen skirt. The physical realities of the sexual act are reflected in the dishevelment of the clothing in the second painting (plate 55): the man's unbuttoned breeches reveal the absence of under-drawers (his shirt has to make do) and the young woman has lost her white kerchief (which lies on the ground in front of her), and the layers of her dress and petticoats are pushed up showing blue knitted silk hose gartered above the knee. This is drama without words, a sequence of events which tell a coherent narrative. *Before and After* depicts 'the immediate preliminaries to and the aftermath of a seduction. The interval carries the undisclosed climax of the event; hence, a perfect narrative incident is presented with its beginning, undisclosed middle, and end.'[13]

**54 Barry Lyndon and Lady Honoria Lyndon
(Ryan O'Neal and Marisa Berenson)
Barry Lyndon, 1975
Costume designers Milena Canonero
and Ulla-Britt Søderlund**

55 William Hogarth
After (detail), c.1730–31
Fitzwilliam Museum,
Cambridge

56 Marquise Isabelle de Merteuil
and Vicomte Sébastien
de Valmont (Glenn Close and
John Malkovich)
Dangerous Liaisons, 1988
Costume designer James Acheson

Hogarth claimed to treat his 'subjects as a dramatic writ-er'; he wished, he informs us, 'to compose pictures on canvas, similar to representations on the stage'.[14] In the journal *The Champion* (10 June 1740) Fielding admired the dramatic narrative of the 'ingenious Mr. Hogarth': 'In his excellent works you see the delusive Scene exposed with all the Force of Humour, and on casting your Eyes on another Picture, you behold the dreadful and fatal Consequence.' This is the *leitmotiv* of what Hogarth called his 'modern moral subjects'. He knew how pictures can often tell a story more effectively than words, and no more so than in his famous series of paintings entitled *Marriage à-la-Mode* (1743–5).

DRESSING THE PART: HOGARTH'S *MARRIAGE À-LA-MODE*

The story, invented by Hogarth, records in six scenes over a period of about three years the disaster of an arranged marriage based on money and not love, which in the end leads to murder and suicide. The first scene, *The Marriage Settlement* (plate 57), centres on the exchange of contracts between the Earl of Squander, an impoverished nobleman with expensive tastes, and an unnamed wealthy City merchant and alderman who wishes to purchase an entry into high society; but the indifference to each other evident in the affianced couple is underlined by the dog and bitch chained together nearby. After the wedding, husband and wife pursue their

own largely separate lives with extra-marital affairs. The title of the second scene, *The Tête à Tête* (plate 58), is an ironic comment on separate lives as while the newly married couple are depicted together in the same room, they are a world apart in reality – even the table laid for a late breakfast (the clock says 12.20) is only for one. The husband, Viscount Squanderfield, has spent the night with a prostitute, whose white cap pokes out from his pocket. His wife has held a whist party, the latest thing in up-to-date gambling (Edmond Hoyle's *Short Treatise on the Game of Whist*, published in 1742, lies on the floor), which has probably lasted until the early hours.

   Lord Squanderfield's taste for young prostitutes is evident

57 William Hogarth
Marriage à-la-Mode: The Marriage Settlement (detail), c.1743
The National Gallery, London

from the third scene, *The Inspection* (plate 59), where he visits an unsavoury quack doctor in search of a cure for syphilis. The scene is dominated by the doctor's terrifying and vulgar wife or mistress, a former whore in *Covent Garden* and with a criminal past ('FC' – Female Convict – is tattooed on her breast) with her patched face, far too showy in her dress with its vast hooped skirt and imitation gold lace edging her bright red silk apron.

Meanwhile, the Viscount's wife is pursuing a love affair with a lawyer, Silvertongue, first seen in *The Marriage Settlement* and then in the fourth scene, *The Toilette* (plate 60), as an intimate of Lady Squanderfield. The toilette or the morning levee, a custom imported from the French court at Versailles, was an occasion for receiving guests while the final stages of dressing and make-up were completed. The alderman's daughter is now a countess (there are earls' coronets displayed ostentatiously on top of the bed and the dressing-table mirror) and a mother, a fact we deduce from the child's teething coral hanging from a ribbon on the back of

her chair. Silvertongue invites his mistress to a masquerade, pointing to a screen behind him on which is painted such a scene, a familiar eighteenth-century trope for the pleasures and perils of disguise and sexual intrigue. Hogarth's 'camera' tells us without words the relationship between Silvertongue and the Countess: his portrait is prominently displayed on the wall to the left of the bed, and at the bottom right of the scene the fashionable black servant boy holds a statue of the horned Actaeon, an obvious reference to the cuckolding of the Earl.

The dénouement of the story occurs in the fifth scene, *The Bagnio* (plate 61), set in a place of assignation in Soho to which Silvertongue and the Countess have retired after the masquerade, their costumes and masks lying on the floor. The Earl, jealous of his 'honour' and having attended the masquerade himself with his wife's dressmaker, follows the couple to the *bagnio*, finds them

59 **William Hogarth**
Marriage à-la-Mode: The Inspection
(detail), c.1743
The National Gallery, London

in flagrante delicto, and is fatally stabbed by Silvertongue, who, dressed just in his shirt, makes his escape through the window. With a show of contrition, real or contrived, the Countess in her white satin dressing gown kneels before her dying husband.

In the final painting, *The Lady's Death* (plate 62), the scene is set in the gloomy and old-fashioned interior of the miserly alderman's house in the City of London (his gown hangs on pegs on the wall near the window). Silvertongue has been caught and hanged for the murder of the Earl, and on hearing this the Countess has taken poison (laudanum); the bottle lies at her feet next to the broadsheet announcing the execution of her lover. Wearing no mourning for the Earl, the Countess, simply but elegantly dressed in white satin and sage green silk, is embraced for the last time by their child, whose syphilitic black patch and leg irons reveal an inheritance of venereal disease, the sins of the father visited upon

the son and heir. Hogarth cleverly reveals the avarice of the alderman in two mini narratives within the scene, firstly in the removal of a valuable diamond ring from his daughter's hand before rigor mortis sets in, for suicides forfeited their goods, and secondly in the appearance of his idiot servant (presumably paid very little) dressed in a cheap second-hand livery coat far too big for him, with buttons missing, and with a comb and curling papers in his hair. On the far left, moving, so to speak, out of the final frame of the film, is a departing doctor in professional black (like the apothecary who blames the servant for handing the laudanum to

60 **William Hogarth**
Marriage à-la-Mode: The Toilette
(detail), *c.*1743
The National Gallery, London

the Countess), top-heavy in his self-important periwig and with a gold-topped cane, the sign of his office – in this case he can do nothing for the patient.

Each painting in the series is full of incident, of drama, of telling detail, a tragedy whose sadness and horror are leavened by comic touches; the characters and their passions are universal – 'to the garb and fashion of the moment … he adds story and sentiment for all time'.[15] As in a film, costume is used generally in Hogarth to create character and identity, to provide continuity, and to further the plot. The most obvious aim of costume in both arts is

to create personality via the visual. The French finery of the young Squanderfield (and as Earl Squander) is intended by Hogarth to suggest a fop and a debauchee; the dark, hooded, swirling cloak worn by Meryl Streep as *The French Lieutenant's Woman* in the famous opening scene of the film (1981; plate 234) symbolizes her mystery and unhappiness, and anticipates the stormy nature of the unfolding narrative. Costume can sometimes be essential to the plot, as Hogarth suggests in *Marriage à-la-Mode*, where the story is played out through appearance and disguise. An example of this in film is Hitchcock's *Vertigo* (1958), where the flawed hero (James Stewart), a man possessed by the image of a supposedly lost lover (Madeleine), is determined to recreate her dress and appearance (a ghostly figure with pale makeup, platinum blonde hair, and a tight-fitting grey pencil-line suit) in a new love (Judy). Madeleine/Judy (Kim Novak) seems only to exist in terms of what

61 **William Hogarth**
Marriage à-la-Mode: The Bagnio (detail), *c.*1743
The National Gallery, London

she wears (her costumes designed by Edith Head), not who she is, a typical fetishist theme in Hitchcock's work.

Clothing in itself can *be* life, with its own emotional resonance, as, lit up by the fireside on the far left in *The Bagnio* we see the Countess's discarded stays (corset), which mimic the shape of her body and symbolize her lost virtue. In the moving picture of the child prostitute in *The Inspection*, the 'camera' of Hogarth's sympathetic vision notes the absurd and pitiful second-hand clothes, far too long for a girl in her early teens. Her skirt and apron trail on the ground, and her velvet cape, instead of resting on her shoulders, reaches well below her waist. It may, of course, be the case that this choice of dress is deliberate, to provide an extra frisson for men who liked the pathetic and childish in their sexual encounters. Judy Egerton posits the notion that the virago is the 'madam' of a brothel and the child her daughter, citing as

evidence the identical brightly coloured brocaded silk worn as a bodice by the adult woman and as a skirt by the girl.[16] Such silks were expensive, and in a culture where clothes were constantly recycled, they were valuable goods.

As at the beginning of any theatrical experience, costume serves first to establish who the characters are and how they might behave as the drama unfolds. In *The Marriage Settlement*, which takes place in the Squander town house, the Earl, showing off his family tree which he claims can be traced back to William the Conqueror, reveals his aristocratic tastes and connections by

his gouty foot (popularly thought to derive from an excessive consumption of port), his rich velvet court suit and silver tissue waistcoat, and the elegance of the hand touching his lace-edged cravat. As for his son Viscount Squanderfield, he is shown as a fashion victim, completely in thrall to his own appearance and to the dictates of French style, from his powdered bag wig and his suit of Lyons silk to his red-heeled court shoes; his gesture (taking a pinch of snuff) and pose are dictated by the dancing master, the arbiter of genteel deportment in the mid-eighteenth century. But the darker side of his character is suggested by the black patch on his neck, covering a syphilitic sore. A contemporary poem notes that he is:

> An half-bred Fop, a Petit-Maitre,
> An English, French, Italian Creature,
> A young Narcissus, vain and dull,
> A wou'd-be Rake, yet half a Fool
> Brought up in Pride and Insolence[17]

In Squanderfield's abject obeisance to foreign vices and costume, Hogarth may have had in mind Fielding's description (poking fun at the breathless and over-detailed prose of fashion journalism) in *Joseph Andrews* of the foppish Bellarmine, 'dressed all in the French fashion', wearing 'a cut velvet coat of a cinnamon colour, lined with a pink satten, embroidered all over with gold; his waistcoat, which was of cloth of silver, was embroidered with gold likewise'.[18] That the elegance of pose and dress is little more than a veneer can be seen in *The Tête à Tête*, where the Viscount has lost control of his appearance: he sits, legs stretched out, hands in pockets, hair uncurled, waistcoat unbuttoned, and wrinkled stockings about to part company from his knee breeches. To the eighteenth-century mindset, slovenliness and disorder in dress and appearance indicated a similar state of mind. Lady Squanderfield's attire and manner are similarly inappropriate for the time of day and a formal drawing room, even one with such vulgar and expensive bad taste. Her hair is not properly dressed and her costume – a morning cap tied under the chin, a loose jacket and skirt – is too informal. But the household is in disarray (a slovenly servant yawns in the background and the steward, a mock-saintly nonconformist in a plain dark cloth suit, retires with a sheaf of unpaid bills), and the husband too far gone to care. Clearly indifferent to his presence, her body language expresses the 'lineaments of gratified desire', from 'the Adventures of the Night', presumably an assignation with Silvertongue: 'In Rapture with uplifted Arms, She spreads abroad a thousand Charms, Her Neck, her Breast, expanded Legs'.[19]

For Hogarth, foolish and sometimes vicious tastes were often symbolized by foreign customs and costume. Even before her marriage the alderman's daughter, 'affected, forward, pert and bold', has been taught to love 'French Taste and Airs' and 'Op'ra Tunes more than her Prayers'.[20] In *The Marriage Settlement*, where she is clearly more attracted to the lawyer Silvertongue than to her fiancé, she appears in French dress, a *robe à la française* of white silk with gold lace. Not only is this rich dress a sign of the wealth she brings to the straightened Squander finances, but it also marks the familiarity with French modes which will be necessary in her

new aristocratic life – as when we see her in *The Toilette* (sometimes called *The Countess's Morning Levee*) her hair being curled by a French hairdresser. During the levee, a custom taken from the court at Versailles (and decried by English critics as symbolic of French obsession with fashion), a fashionable man or woman entertained friends in the bedroom or boudoir, while finishing dressing, and discussing new clothes with tailor or dressmaker. In *Barry Lyndon*, there is a levee scene, where the eponymous 'hero' is shown adopting such a custom alien to his background, but indicative of his desire (unfulfilled) to be accepted by the English elite; in a velvet dressing gown, he sits in front of a dressing table while his hair is dressed, and the tailor shows him a coat. In *The Toilette* the company is being entertained by a castrato singer and Hogarth has much fun with his plump effeminacy, his bejewelled and exaggerated appearance, which he felt summed up a certain type of Italian personality; this scene from *Marriage à-la-Mode* was the inspiration for the Marschallin's levee in the first act of Richard Strauss's great opera *Der Rosenkavalier*.

Continuity plays a key role in all drama, and is especially important where – as in the 'silent movie' of Hogarth's *Marriage à-la-Mode* – the characters are identified by their appearance. Lawyers (barristers) can be identified, as today, in their black gowns and white tabs: we first see the lawyer Silvertongue so dressed in *The Marriage Settlement*, and again sprawling on the sofa in *The Toilette*. In *The Marriage Settlement* the lumpish alderman's bright red coat is old-fashioned when compared to the muted colours worn by the Earl and his son, and dates, we are told, from the reign of Queen Anne at the beginning of the century, along with his campaign wig (from Marlborough's wars) – which has been 'thrice in Fashion, thrice out' since that time.[21] The way he ties his cravat, the ends pushed through a buttonhole in his coat, dates from the battle of Steinkirk, a French victory over an Anglo-Dutch army in 1692, and can also be seen worn by the uncouth doctor in *The Inspection*. As in the first scene, so in the last: the alderman wears exactly the same costume in *The Lady's Death*, as he removes his daughter's ring, 'Shaking his Head with seeming Grief'.[22]

In terms of action, the characters in *Marriage à-la-Mode* are so identified with their costume that every aspect of what they wear and how they wear it can be seen to contribute to the plot. Each turn of events seems to lead inexorably to the last two tragic scenes, the catalyst being Silvertongue's invitation to the masquerade:

> What longing Wife, what melting Maid,
> Who sighs not for the Masquerade?[23]

In *The Bagnio* the masquerade costumes (domino gowns and masks) lie on the furniture and the floor, forgotten in the heat of the moment as the dying Earl slowly collapses in front of his wife whose white shift and dressing gown seem to mock her abandoned virtue. In the final scene, returning to her pre-marital home, all pretence and acquired aristocratic graces vanished, the dying Countess is simply dressed in English style, with plain linen. She is no longer a world removed from the humble and old-fashioned clothing of her father's old servant, perhaps the only character with any humanity in *Marriage à-la-Mode*.

To the essayist William Hazlitt, writing in *The Examiner*

(1814), Hogarth's work, and especially *Marriage à-la-Mode*, contain 'so much truth of Nature', representing 'the manners and humours of mankind in action, and their characters by individual expression. Everything in his pictures has life and motion in it'.[24] Painting by its very nature is of course inanimate, frozen for all time; but we might imagine that the figures in *Marriage à-la-Mode* come to life at night on the gallery wall, when no one sees them, to become moving pictures – silent movies. Costume is essential to our analysis and appreciation of figurative art, including films. In painting, however, we rarely find the exact clothing which artists depict (even in portraiture), whereas in films we have much extant clothing – its variety and extent revealed in this exhibition – to add an extra dimension, both to our enjoyment, and as a way of understanding one of the crucial creative processes that make up a great movie, that of the costumier.

62 **William Hogarth**
Marriage à-la-Mode: The Lady's Death
(detail), c.1743
The National Gallery, London

Aileen Ribeiro is Professor Emeritus of the History of Art at the Courtauld Institute of Art, London. She is author of numerous titles on the history of dress and appearance, the most recent being Facing Beauty: Painted Women and Cosmetic Art *(2011), and is currently researching a book on the relationships between art and fashion.*

DESONING *THE LAST EMPEROR*

James Acheson

I REMEMBER MEETING director Bernardo Bertolucci in London. He told me that he had seen half of a movie I had worked on; 'My wife has seen the other half', he explained later. The film was *Brazil* (1985), directed by Terry Gilliam. Bernardo had noticed that one of the characters in the film was wearing a pinstriped suit and that the stripes ran horizontally rather than vertically across the jacket. He seemed amused by this anachronism. I often think it was this tiny detail, which only he had noticed, that got me the job. I told him that asking me to design the costumes for *The Last Emperor* (1987) was like asking a Chinese designer to design the clothes for a film about the life of Queen Victoria.

Bertolucci insisted on a very close working relationship with his chief collaborators. His cinematographer, production designer, editor and costume designer were vital players in the planning of his films. He called us his 'lemons' and we would be 'squeezed every day'. He expected and demanded daily contributions to this enormous project. I have never had, before or since, the opportunity to sit down with a director for four days and go through the script page by page to find out – even at that early stage – how the costumes could and should contribute to the storytelling and serve the vision of the film he was about to make.

We started work in October 1985, in a tiny room in Great Cumberland Place, London. The film's finances were still not in place but as monies gradually became available we were able to start determining the costume requirements of the film. By the commencement of shooting, on 3 August 1986 at the Beijing Film Studios, we had constructed 10,500 costumes in workshops in Brighton, London, Rome, Spoleto, Hong Kong, Tokyo and Beijing.

To examine the many facets of the Ching Dynasty for *The Last Emperor* I was lucky enough to begin preparations, with my assistants, in London. At the V&A we discovered one of the finest collections of Ching costumes and artefacts in the world, and we were able to make invaluable use of the Museum's resources. Much work was also done in China and Hong Kong, researching and photographing existing examples of clothing from the period and looking at every contemporary photograph and painting that we could find.

Ching Dynasty imperial robes were often made of elaborately hand-embroidered silk, with detachable collars of heavily couched gold thread. In order to create the illusion of detailed, exquisitely hand-crafted clothes, for a fraction of the true cost, I was forced to find ways of cheating the eye of the camera. Many theatrical techniques were used to solve these problems. Much of the embroidery was modelled and sculpted in wax, cast in aluminum and then gold plated. Each individual piece was then hand stitched to the costume. Many of the imperial robes were created by using six-colour photographic silkscreen prints on cheap rayon of different colours. Larger motifs of swirling dragons were sculpted and then cast in a flexible glue, gold plated and stuck to the garment. 'Puffer paint' (much used at the time to give motifs on T-shirts a 'raised' look) became another useful way to create gold 'embroidery'. By making small, shallow lines of puff paint on the artwork of chosen motifs, we discovered that these tiny furrows of paint when heated looked just like gold embroidered couchwork.

While only 34 original antique pieces of Chinese silk-embroidered costume were used in the film, detailed embroidered elements from damaged and worn garments were carefully repaired and appliquéd on to stronger, newer

OPPOSITE
63 Costume for the Emperor
***The Last Emperor*, 1987**
Costume designer James Acheson
The Recorded Picture Company

ABOVE
64 Pu Yi (Richard Vuu) in the Forbidden City
***The Last Emperor*, 1987**
Costume designer James Acheson

LEFT
65 Centre: Wan Jung and Pu Yi
(Joan Chen and John Lone)
***The Last Emperor*, 1987**
Costume designer James Acheson

❛ To create the illusion of detailed, exquisitely hand-crafted clothes, for a fraction of the true cost, I was forced to find ways of cheating the eye of the camera. Many theatrical techniques were used to solve these problems. ❜

in the research, construction and coordination of the costumes for *The Last Emperor*. Creating costumes, like making films, is a close collaborative process. I would like to acknowledge the enormous skill and dedication of so many people who brought their extraordinary talents to this project. In particular, my thanks and admiration go to my three assistants, Thomas Casterline, Frank Gardiner and Gilly Hebden, and to Martin Adams and Shirley Cooper and their team who created the jewellery and headdresses. The late Annie Hadley and her team made many of the leading costumes; Margot Foster and Day Murch did much of the costume appliqué work; Michael Jones created the hats; and Ugo Pericoli and his team created the military costumes. I offer my heartfelt thanks and appreciation to these remarkable people – and to all of those talented hands that contributed in so many valuable ways to the costumes of *The Last Emperor.*

cloth. Everything from new silk-embroidered table-mats to damask tablecloths were used to fabricate the costumes for the film.

These days modern film technology can easily turn two hundred costumed extras into two thousand people using computer generated imaging (CGI). But in 1986 we needed to clothe every one of those thousands of people. We often used the Chinese Army for our production, and they can be seen briefly in the background of some of the bigger scenes in *The Last Emperor*. These extras wore simple cotton robes of varying colours and their Chinese hats were fashioned out of black vacuum-formed plastic. At lunchtime they could be seen turning over their hats to use as bowls from which to eat their lunch.

While the traditional wedding colour of red was used for the silk wedding robes in the film, the bride's headdress and veil were adaptations of the original Hann and Manchu form of headdress. Bertolucci decided that the face of Pu Yi's beautiful bride should be initially hidden from view. He wanted his camera, like his actor and his audience, to discover at the same moment what was hidden behind the veil.

We have estimated that more than 250 people in five different countries were employed

66 Eastern Jewel and Wan Jung (Maggie Han and Joan Chen)
The Last Emperor, **1987**
Costume designer James Acheson

RIGHT AND OPPOSITE
67, 68 Details of costume for the Emperor
The Last Emperor, **1987**
Costume designer James Acheson
The Recorded Picture Company

James Acheson began designing costume for the Doctor Who *TV series in the 1970s before moving in to film. He has won Academy Awards for costume for three films:* Restoration *(1995),* Dangerous Liaisons *(1988) and* The Last Emperor *(1987). His other work includes* Monty Python's The Meaning of Life *(1983),* Brazil *(1985) and* Spider-Man *(2002, 2004 and 2007).*

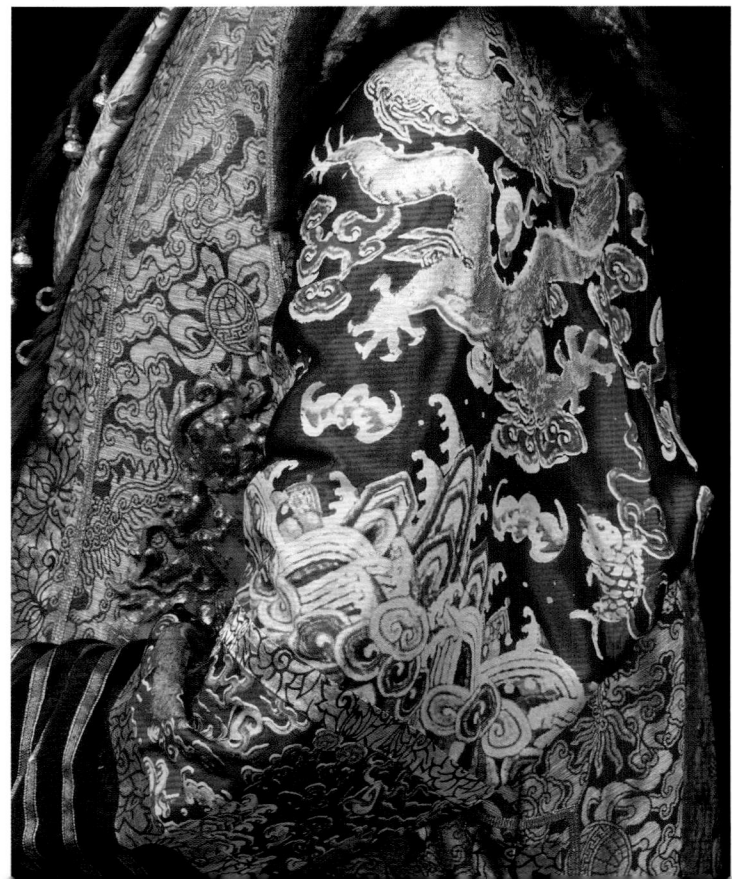

THE PROCESS OF TRANSFORMATION

Kristin M. Burke

IT IS a common misconception that the life of a Hollywood costume designer is glamorous and fabulous. The truth, however, is a far cry from convertible Bentleys and bottomless Beverly Hills credit accounts. We work, on average, seventy hours per week. We are not paid overtime. We miss birthdays, family reunions and graduations. We have aching feet and bad backs. We are constantly sleep-deprived. For every four job interviews we only book one job – if we are lucky. What compels us, then, to take on this kind of work? Certainly it is different for each individual, but at the core, the work is so fulfilling that we put up with its challenges. As costume designers we love the spiritual and artistic reward of creative work.

THE INTERVIEW

Generally three or four costume design candidates are called in for any project, picked from a tall stack of résumés. Once called for interview, we read the script, the story playing out in our mind's eye as we read. This visualization is the genesis of our ideas. We then put that vision into physical form, sketching, pulling tearsheets from magazines, researching the period or circumstances in which the story takes place. The aim is to have a rough outline of the costume changes in the script that can be presented with some authority at the interview.

The interview itself can range from very casual to highly formal. Costume designers are aware that we are often judged immediately by our physical appearance, specifically by our sartorial choices. Consequently, sometimes we dress 'in character' for interviews, to demonstrate our personal style and our grasp of the atmosphere and look of the film.

An interview can last for anything from thirty minutes to two hours, depending on how overscheduled the production has become. Usually we meet with the director and possibly a producer or two. We show them our research, tearsheets and sketches, hoping that our ideas are fresh and innovative and that they are also what the film-makers have in mind. We say goodbye – and then the waiting begins…

69, 70 Sketch and costume design for Penny (Keira Knightley) *Seeking a Friend for the End of the World*, 2012 Costume designer and illustrator Kristin M. Burke

THE DESIGN DEVELOPMENT PROCESS

Having booked the job, the real work begins. First we re-read the script to make sure that we know it like the backs of our hands. The designer then hires the costume supervisor, who is responsible for staffing, scheduling, budgeting and breakdowns for the costume department. 'Breaking down' requires that a supervisor must be intimately acquainted with all the details of the story and characters: together we comb over the minutiae, the big picture, the narrative arcs of both principal and supporting characters (that is, the status of each as the storyline unfolds), the stunts, and the overall orchestration of the costumes. It is at this point that the costume designer and costume supervisor begin to plan how the various different costumes will harmonize with each other to tell the story as one unified visual element.

Every film has a budget – some are quite lavish, while others are painfully austere – and every film has a unit production manager and

a line producer closely monitoring this budget to make sure the film stays on track. Together the costume designer and costume supervisor build a budget that we think we can reasonably achieve.

The costume designer then researches the sociological elements of the script: the people, the politics, economics, history, events, trends and social constructs. We talk to people who live, or have lived, in the world we are trying to re-create. We have long discussions with the director about his or her ideas, about what the world of the film means and about the significance of its dialogue and action. Based on these meetings, the costume designer will refine the focus of the research and sketches to develop costumes that function well within the constructs of the world we are trying to create together.

THE DESIGN PRESENTATION

The function of the design presentation is to start the discussion between the costume designer, the costume department and the director, and the art department, sound department, camera, stunts and props. Communication is central to our work, and a solid design presentation nips many conflicts in the bud. For the presentation we mount photographs, images, sketches and fabric swatches on black foam core boards hanging on the walls of our offices. These days sketches are often created using Adobe Illustrator or Photoshop – gone are the gouache-and-paper sketches of yesteryear.

Digitized sketching has helped us keep up with the frenetic pace of script and casting changes, and costume designers can create a sketch of the same dress in red, blue, orange, purple or silver sequins at the click of a button. Modern technology also allows us to post our design boards on the Internet so that creative collaborators and crew members may have our research images at their fingertips, accessible even when they are out buying or pulling costumes at rental houses. The technical revolution has forever changed the way costume designers work – for the better.

The first official presentation of the design boards is to the director. If a costume or characterization does not fit the director's vision, the image can be removed from the board before it is seen by anyone else. Once the director has approved the costumes, we go public with the boards so that the actors and crew are fully up to date. Ultimately our job is to bring the director's singular vision to life.

THE COSTUME TEAM IN ACTION

When contact details for members of the cast start to trickle in from their agents, the costume department leaps into action. The costume designer tries to speak to each actor in person, to discuss in detail the character and specific costume ideas put forward by the director. Costume is the 'skin' of the character, and it is often only at the costume fitting that the character begins to come to life.

When designers talk to the actors for the first time we make notes of their measurements and clothes sizes, their quirks and – most importantly – their ideas for the character. If there are any glaring conflicts with the director's vision, we note them immediately and try to mediate a discussion with the director. We run through the online design presentation process and the actor's individual costume breakdown with the character's arc. The costume supervisor sets up a fitting time, and the clock starts ticking.

The costume team is comprised of the costume supervisor, assistant costume designer, prep costumers (including shoppers), set costumers, fabrication costumers (including cutters, stitchers, tailors and ager-dyers), illustrators, production assistants and interns. Everyone's job is very specific in the United States – there are union rules dictating what each person can and cannot do. To a large extent the film's budget dictates how many of these team members are in the department. On a very small film there may be a total of just two or three crew members, in which case everyone must do a bit of everything.

The costume designer and costume supervisor check the filming schedule to see which scenes will be shot first, and this gives us our order of play. We check to see whether any costumes require a particularly long prep period, such as custom-made garments or costumes with special effects integration, and prioritize these. Additionally, if any garments are required for rehearsals, they are brought to the front of the queue. We keep running lists for shopping, pulling from rental houses, building and stitching, online sourcing, product placement, ageing and dyeing, and returns. The costume supervisor and designer tend to be the master plate-spinners, keeping track of everything at all times.

During this prep period the designer and assistant designer also collect and collate fabric swatches, and make muslin mock-ups and samples of garments that are being created by a cutter-fitter and tailor. If there is ageing and dyeing (tech) involved, we make samples of these garments for the director's approval. All of this work is done, wheels burning, leading up to the fitting with the actor.

THE FITTING

The objective of the fitting is to make sure that the garments fit the actor and look appropriate, and ultimately to breathe life into the character. It is truly a magical moment when an actor puts the garments on and starts to walk differently, talk differently, shift comportment and metamorphose into the character in front of the mirror.

Usually, the only people attending the fitting are the actor, the costume designer, a costumer and a tailor: the designer and actor talk while the costumer organizes the clothing and takes notes as each costume is tried on. Does it need alteration? More age/tech? Do the shoes need to be stretched? Do they need inner soles? There are myriad things to remember after a fitting, and without the costumer there to write it all down and tag the clothing with the notes, these things do not get done. Different colours of tags are used to represent the various actions that need to be taken: red for alteration, green for age/tech, and so on. Good tailors make their own notes in the form of pinning garments for alteration and marking with chalk. It is important that the garments are pinned by the same tailor and cutter-fitter responsible for sewing them.

Occasionally the fitting will need to be broken up into several sessions, if there are a large number of complex changes. If an actor is unavailable for fitting, we may hire a body-double (courtesy of extras casting) or make a dress form with the exact measurements of the actor, fit costumes to the dress form and photograph them for approval.

At the end of the fitting, the actor and the costume team review the costumes against the character breakdown to make sure that all the actor's questions have been answered and all fitting issues addressed. I usually send the actor home with a copy of the breakdown for reference, in case of any questions that may arise later. We then wrap the fitting room: the rack of 'keeper' costumes comes back to the costume office with a rainbow of tags, while the rejects are taken to another area to be separated and sorted for returns to costume rental houses and shops. The key at this point is to not lose anything: all it takes is one slippery hanger for panic to ensue when the costume has disappeared on the day of filming.

THE FEEDBACK

After the fitting, the main form of communication from the designer to the director is photographs, and occasionally video. It is essential that every image represents the costume and the actor at their best, so particular care is taken to ensure that they are appropriately lit. As soon as the day's fittings are done, the work of organizing, tweaking and sending photographs begins. Email has become the most efficient way of conferring at this point: the director can review the costumes in his or her own time, and respond directly, in the same email chain. Once the director has seen and approved the costume changes on the actor in this way, the approved images can be sent to the producers for their review and sign-off.

If there is conflict between the director and the producers, this is when it becomes apparent. Just when the costume designer thinks that the costumes have been approved and finalized

> ❦ Just when the costume designer thinks that the costumes have been approved and finalized we may get notes from production to make changes. Some changes are small, while others require us to 'scrap it and start again'. ❧

we may get notes from production to make changes. Some changes are small, while others require us to 'scrap it and start again'. If there is significant disagreement, we may have to mediate between the different factions until we can find a solution that pleases everyone. We make the changes, have another fitting and get the final approvals. From this point we send the approved photos to other department heads for reference, and we move forward with an eye on the camera test.

The camera test is a day of shooting on a sound stage to test the hair, make-up, special effects and costume on the actors. This is usually the first time the rest of the film crew meets the actors face-to-face: until this point, the only contact the actors have had with anyone from the production team is with the costume designer and the costume department. The costume designer and a set costumer are often the only department members who attend the camera test.

THE GALLOP TO THE FINISH

With the camera test approved, the costume moves to the next step in the design process. Ideas have become garments and garments

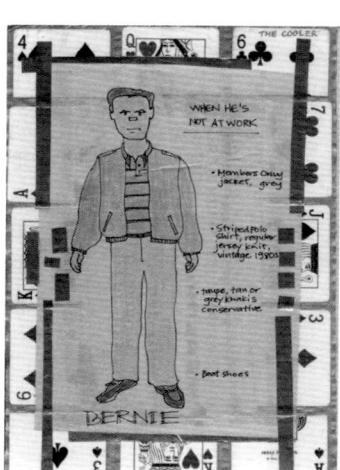

72 Sketches for Bernie Lootz
The Cooler, 2003
Costume designer and
illustrator Kristin M. Burke

73 Shelly Kaplow and
Bernie Lootz (Alec Baldwin
and William H. Macy)
The Cooler, 2003
Costume designer
Kristin M. Burke

74 Kristin M. Burke fitting
actor Joseph Bishara at
Warner Bros studio

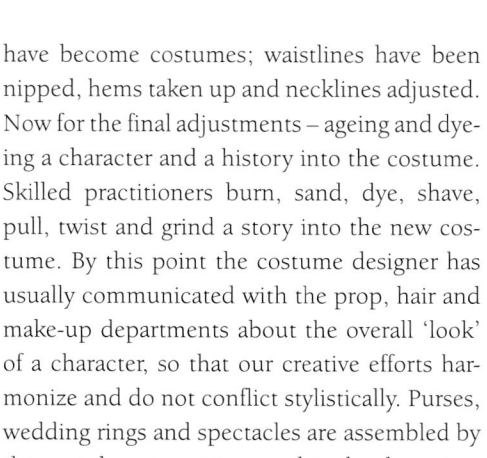

have become costumes; waistlines have been nipped, hems taken up and necklines adjusted. Now for the final adjustments – ageing and dyeing a character and a history into the costume. Skilled practitioners burn, sand, dye, shave, pull, twist and grind a story into the new costume. By this point the costume designer has usually communicated with the prop, hair and make-up departments about the overall 'look' of a character, so that our creative efforts harmonize and do not conflict stylistically. Purses, wedding rings and spectacles are assembled by the prop department to complete the character.

The costume department sews labels into the garments, indicating the character's name and the details of the garment – whether it is a 'hero' copy (worn only by the lead actor) or a 'stunt' copy, what stage of distress it is (how dirty, bloody, torn), and so forth. We have recently started to add the costume designer's personal label to the custom-made garments so that years from now, when the garment resurfaces, it is not remembered as just 'the dress from *Movie X*', but also as 'designed by …'.

Finally, the costume truck arrives and load-in of costumes begins. Costumes are organized, hung and tagged with meticulous care by the costumers. Drawers are loaded with sewing and office supplies and equipment. Everything is labelled and locked down. Costume continuity binders are created, with the breakdown serving as the grand road map for the rest of the shoot. The costume crew closes the doors and locks the trailer, knowing that the next time we all see the inside of the truck it will be Day One of a whole new adventure.

THE SHOOT

Everyone has first-day jitters, even the most seasoned among us; it is like the first day of

school all over again. We veterans come to expect changes, some of them drastic. Designers must arrive with 'hammer in hand', ready to tear down and rebuild anything. When the first assistant director finally calls 'roll sound!' we all hold our breath…

… and in the silence, something magical begins to happen. Characters ignite. A story other than our own, a world other than our own, comes to life. A scene plays before our eyes. It's enchanting. 'And CUT!'

We can breathe again.

THE FINISHED PRODUCT

Working on a film day after day, costume designers seldom think about what is going to happen when it is finished. We do our jobs, maintain our focus and deliver the film. But when the time comes for the first official screening, be it at a film festival or at a première, it can be a tremendously nervous time. We know what the film looked like on the monitor on the set, but how did it cut together? Will our work look good? Will the film 'work'?

Whether the movie succeeds or not is often inconsequential to costume designers:

❛ When the first assistant director finally calls 'roll sound!' we all hold our breath … and in the silence, something magical begins to happen. Characters ignite. A story other than our own, a world other than our own, comes to life. A scene plays before our eyes. It's enchanting. 'And CUT!' We can breathe again. ❜

ultimately, creative work is its own reward. In the end, if we feel satisfied with the quality of our work and with the friends we made along the way, the movie is a triumph. It is often with a great sigh of relief that the costume designer walks out of a first screening. Sometimes it feels as though one has given birth: and, in a strange way, one has. The dream factory has created a new baby – a film – and its story is only beginning

Kristin M. Burke has provided costume design for a diverse range of independent films such as The Cooler *(2003),* Insidious *(2010) and* Seeking a Friend for the End of the World *(2012). Her costume designs have also featured in music videos, commercials and television serials.*

DESIGNING FOR THE COEN BROTHERS

Mary Zophres

I BEGAN DESIGNING costumes for Joel and Ethan Coen in 1996, with their acclaimed *Fargo*, and have worked with them on every one of their films since. The process of working with the Coen Brothers is extraordinarily creative, fulfilling and challenging, and above all, collaborative. The Coens give their department heads the freedom to create, but they are always there to guide and advise. As decisive and fiscally responsible filmmakers they are ready to address any questions that arise and always aware of budget restraints.

Joel and Ethan will very often tell me about their next project while we are still shooting the current one – they are prolific filmmakers who have many stories to tell. Sometimes I receive the script as much as six months before I am scheduled to begin prep on the film; for a costume designer, having this time to contemplate the script, get ahead with research, start planning and then work up designs well in advance is extremely helpful.

The next stage is to have a phone conversation to exchange general ideas. At this point the Coens will share with me any thoughts that they have been living with while writing the script.

75 Jeffrey Lebowski 'The Dude'
(Jeff Bridges)
The Big Lebowski, 1998
Costume designer Mary Zophres

76 Marge Gunderson
(Frances McDormand)
Fargo, 1996
Costume designer Mary Zophres

Then I do my research and seek inspiration. I like to gather my ideas for all the characters and the various types of scene in the film set out on boards, with a combination of sketches and research photos. We then try to meet in person to discuss the boards, which are always a good way to start the conversation about converting the written word to the screen. At this point we discuss palette, season, mood, and any other questions I may have.

Coen Brothers scripts are like no other. Rather like great novels, they have a very strong sense of time and place, with fully developed characters who can be imagined in great detail. Although precise descriptions are not generally given of how character should be dressed, they are so convincingly drawn that it is an

easy matter to imagine how they should look. For the Dude (Jeff Bridges) in *The Big Lebowski* (1998; plate 75), for example, I based my approach on a single line in the script that said 'the Dude is terminally relaxed'. Everything about his costumes had to be casual and unstructured – elastic waist pants and stretchy knit shirts, Munsingwear briefs with the waistband poking out of the top of his pants. Furthermore, the Dude was a slob, with stains on his clothes – and certainly did not separate his darks from his whites when he did do his laundry; this, too, was reflected in his costumes. The script also stated that he lived in Venice, California. As always, I began with research and then combed thrift and vintage clothing stores; I shopped mostly in Venice and Santa Monica, where the

77 Anton Chigurh
(Javier Bardem)
*No Country for Old
Men*, 2007
Costume designer
Mary Zophres

78 Storyboard for
*No Country for Old
Men*, 2007
Costume designer
Mary Zophres

79 Pete, Delmar and Everett
(John Turturro, Tim Blake Nelson
and George Clooney)
O Brother, Where Art Thou?, 2000
Costume designer Mary Zophres

80 Storyboard for *True Grit*, 2010
Costume designer Mary Zophres

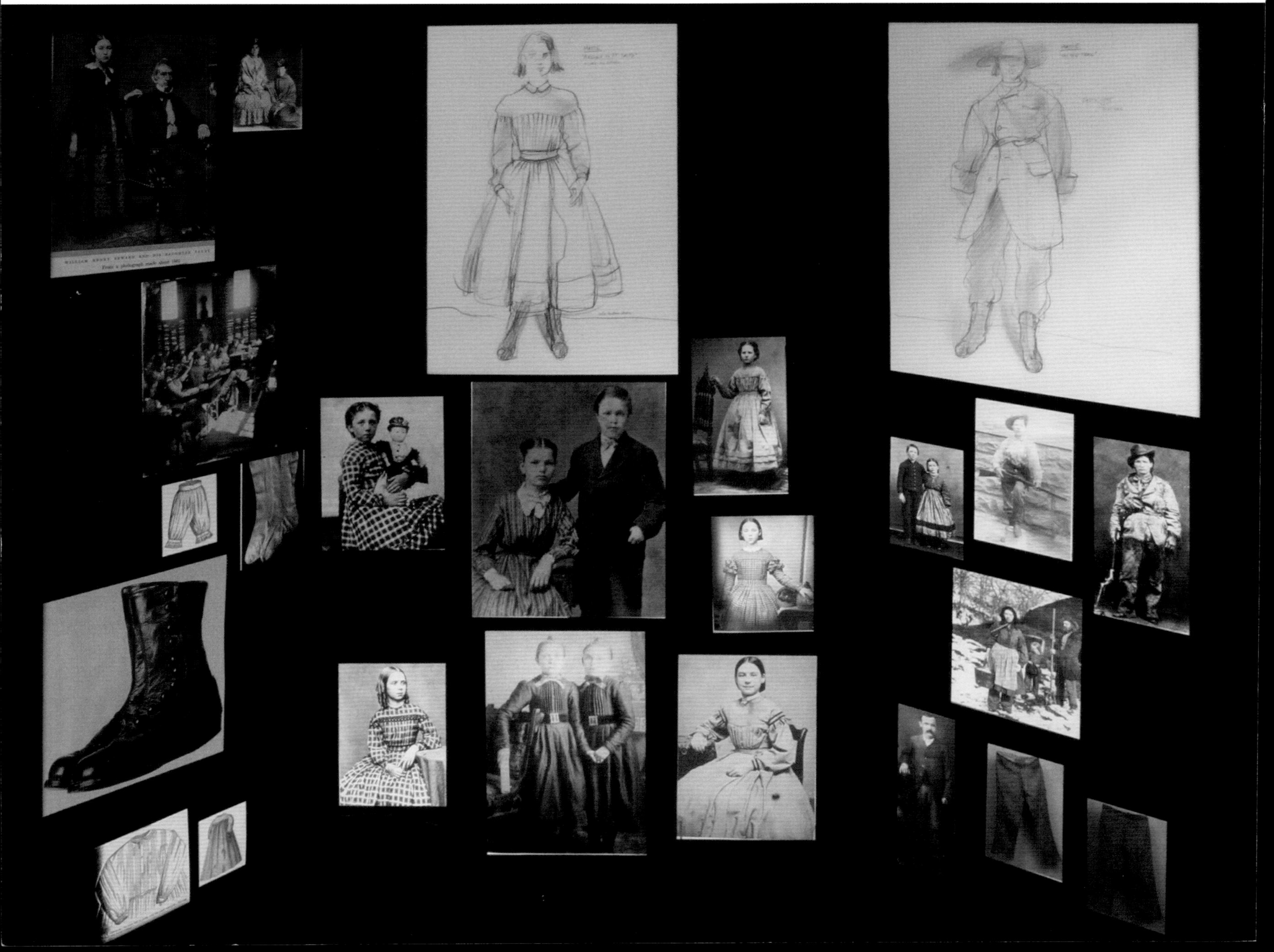

donated clothing can be very different from that on the east side of town. Here I found original pieces and then those garments that needed to be multiplied (such as his sweater) we had duplicated by manufacturers in Los Angeles.

My approach was quite different for Anton Chigurh (Javier Bardem) in *No Country for Old Men* (2007; plate 77). Unlike *The Big Lebowski*, in this case there was no clothing reference in the book or script; the character speaks very little but is a huge, evil presence and catalyst in the plot. I wanted him to be wearing the darkest end of the palette I had chosen for the film. Although an outsider, Anton tries to fit to his surroundings, not wishing to attract too much attention. I imagined that he would have purchased cowboy boots having arrived in Texas, but would no doubt have wanted them to look like a weapon – in my mind he had probably kicked someone to a pulp with the pointed toes of his crocodile boots. The idea for his distinctive haircut came from a piece of research I found in the Warner Brothers library in a 'prisoner' file. Here I found a photograph from the late 1970s of a prisoner who resembled Javier, who had an extreme side parting with a bit of a pageboy haircut. Then Paul LeBlanc (our fabulous hairdresser) took it even further.

❛ It helped so much to have him [Joel Coen] there in person: it meant we could discuss, for example, the exact length of her father's oversized coat and the style of her hat (the very first one I tried on her in a room full of at least fifty hats). ❜

Once each character has been meticulously analysed and planned in this way and the cast has been assembled, I begin costume fittings. At each fitting I take a series of photos and then discuss them with Joel and Ethan afterwards. These fitting photos are often a work in progress and may need interpretation – never a problem for the Coens. Occasionally they will be present for a costume fitting, especially if there is a special circumstance. For example, for *True Grit* (2010; plate 81) the role of Mattie Ross (Hailee Steinfeld) was cast rather late. We measured Hailee on a Saturday just three weeks before she was scheduled to start principal photography. We had our first fitting one week later. Joel happened to be in Los Angeles and was able come to the fitting. It helped so much to have him there in person: it meant we could discuss, for example, the exact length of her father's oversized coat and the style of her hat (the very first one I tried on her in a room full of at least fifty hats). We even decided that her hair should be in pigtails, and braided her hair, right there in the fitting. We then had to make the garments in multiples and age them appropriately.

Costume designer for a number of high-profile films, Mary Zophres has had a long collaboration with the Coen Brothers, her designs appearing in ten of their films.

81 Mattie Ross and Rooster Cogburn (Hailee Steinfeld and Jeff Bridges)
True Grit, **2010**
Costume designer Mary Zophres

TRANSFORMATIONS **JOHNNY DEPP**

Keith Lodwick

> ❛ I always picture it as this chest of drawers in your body – Ed Wood is in one, The Mad Hatter is in another, Edward Scissorhands is in another. ❜
>
> **JOHNNY DEPP**[1]

SINCE HIS BREAKTHROUGH role in *Edward Scissorhands* (1990), Johnny Depp has become one of Hollywood's most established and versatile actors. He has played an eclectic range of characters, from portrayals of real people such as 1950s cult film director Edward Wood Jr in *Ed Wood* (1994) and *Peter Pan* creator J.M. Barrie in *Finding Neverland* (2004), to characters of urban legend – *Sweeney Todd: The Demon Barber of Fleet Street* (2007) and Ichabod Crane in *Sleepy Hollow* (1999).

His success is complemented by the close rapport he has built up with the costume designers who have helped him bring his characters to the screen, and describes that moment of assuming a character through costume: 'It's always great to have that layer of the character's clothing – the skin. It helps you find your posture, how does the character stand?'[2]

Edward Scissorhands was designed by Colleen Atwood, whose long-term collaboration with Johnny Depp and director Tim Burton has lasted over twenty years. Burton credits Atwood with helping Depp fully realize the look for Edward: 'I can have an idea about something, and Johnny can have an idea, but especially with the more extreme characters, it really does take the costume to fully get the feeling of it.'[3] Atwood has described how she and Depp have created some of his most memorable characters, from cross-dressing Ed Wood to murderous Sweeney Todd: 'Johnny is the kind of artist that feels his costume so as soon as I see he's connecting with something, I go for it. As an artist he understands the process, so is always open to new ideas. His sense of play is unique.'[4]

Costume designer Renée Ehrlich Kalfus worked with Depp on two films, *What's Eating Gilbert Grape* (1993) and *Chocolat* (2000); she explains how they created the character of Gilbert Grape together:

Gilbert was the eldest son in a dysfunctional family, and was responsible for providing for them. They had very little money. A key part of Johnny's discovery of Gilbert came from an old pair of work boots that I bought from a customer in an Army Navy store. I traded him a new pair for his very beat up old pair. I brought these old used boots to Johnny along with many frayed vintage shirts and worn jeans. A transformation took place in the fitting room. There seemed to be a way these specific pieces felt on him, which he responded to. He talked about the costumes and how they felt right. It is really a thrill to see an actor walk into a dressing room and walk out as their character. Johnny liked how old and worn the costumes were and they helped him in his discovery of Gilbert.[5]

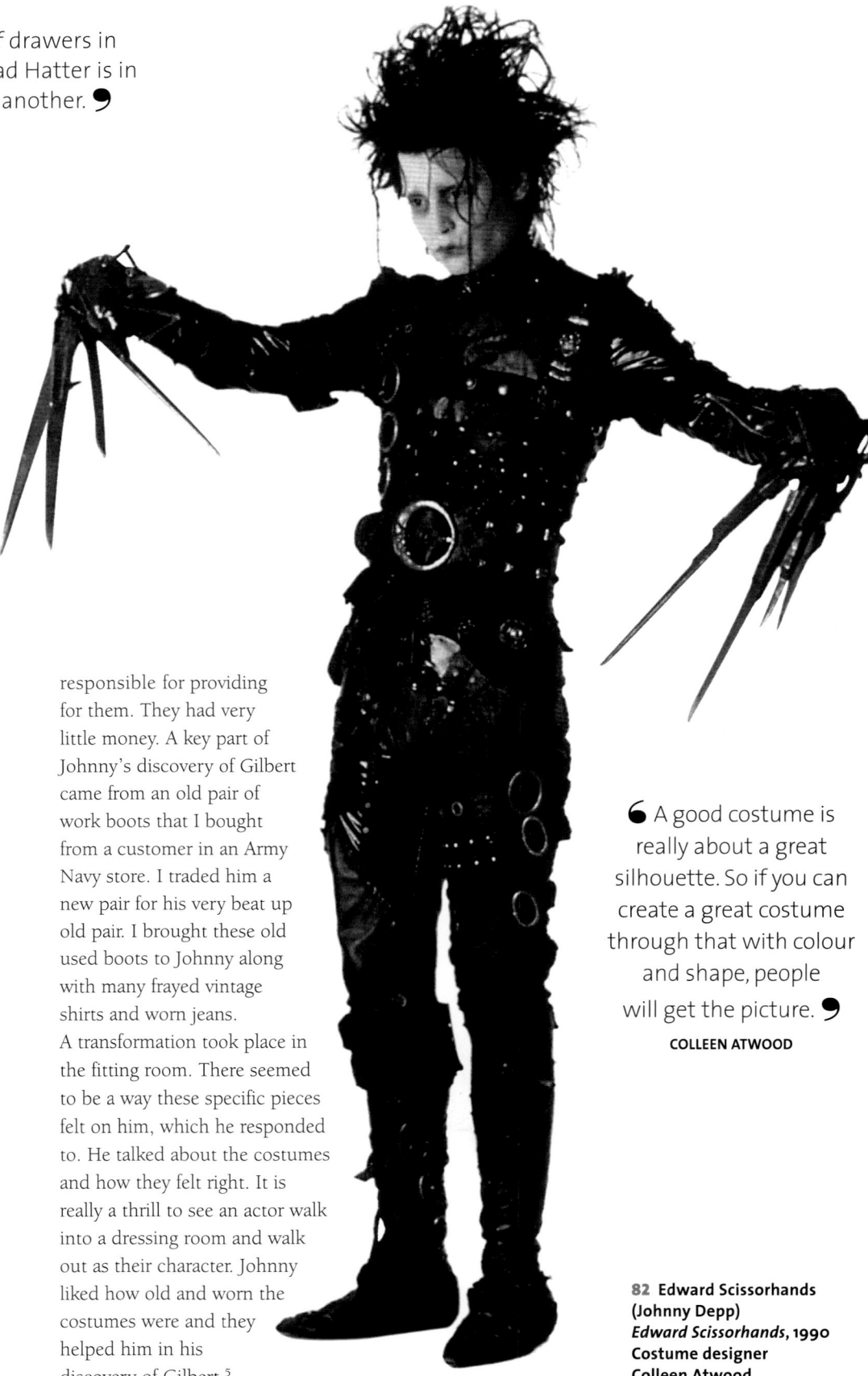

> ❛ A good costume is really about a great silhouette. So if you can create a great costume through that with colour and shape, people will get the picture. ❜
>
> **COLLEEN ATWOOD**

82 Edward Scissorhands
(Johnny Depp)
Edward Scissorhands, 1990
Costume designer
Colleen Atwood

83 Raoul Duke (Johnny Depp)
Fear and Loathing in Las Vegas, 1998
Costume designer Julie Weiss

84 Ed Wood (Johnny Depp)
Ed Wood, 1994
Costume designer Colleen Atwood

85 Sam and Juniper 'Joon' Pearl
(Johnny Depp and Mary Stuart Masterson)
Benny and Joon, 1993
Costume designer Aggie Guerard Rodgers

86 The Mad Hatter (Johnny Depp)
Alice in Wonderland, 2010
Costume designer Colleen Atwood

Depp's sense of character leads him to seek inspiration from the most cinematic of sources. For Ichabod Crane in Burton's *Sleepy Hollow* he was inspired by legendary screen actors Basil Rathbone, Roddy McDowall and even Angela Lansbury; the costumes won Atwood a BAFTA. Depp's admiration of Hollywood's silent era inspired him for both *Edward Scissorhands* and *Benny and Joon* (1993): 'The guys I always adored were mostly silent-film actors, Buster Keaton first, Lou Chaney Sr, and Charlie Chaplin of course – those three for me. And John Barrymore. The gods: those are the gods.'[6]

A new generation of cinemagoers associates Depp with his Oscar-nominated performance in the *Pirates of the Caribbean* series (2003–). His star turn as Jack Sparrow is in no small way helped by the enduring look he put together with costume designer Penny Rose:

> The actor's involvement is paramount to me. I knew Johnny was cast as Jack Sparrow so when we were introduced I said, 'What do you think of Jack Sparrow?', and he looked me in the eye and said, 'He's a rock-n-roller.' During the making of the film I was probably one of the few people who knew that Jack Sparrow was based on Keith Richards. At our first costume session, Johnny tried on maybe two or three frock coats, a couple of vests and some breeches and within about half an hour Jack Sparrow was born.[7]

Depp once again drew on a number of cultural references for Captain Jack, including Warner Bros Looney Tunes cartoon character Pepé Le Pew. For the role he had four of his teeth capped with gold and had a fake tattoo of a sparrow on his right arm. Over the course of the Pirates film series Rose has made very few changes to his costume:

> We decided to leave Captain Jack pretty much as he was, he has become so iconic. We've added some trinkets over time and a new waistcoat which we think Jack stole from a Spanish ship. He's added a shrunken head which he tells me is his mother! As an actor, he is acutely aware of his clothes and stepping into the costume is stepping into the character. He knows what he likes and what he doesn't like. For the first film, we put eight hats on the floor that we thought would make great pirate hats and he

picked up the leather one and said 'that's mine'. He knew instantly which was the correct hat for his character.[8]

For Depp's seventh collaboration with Tim Burton, a 3-D version of *Alice in Wonderland* (2010), he once again worked with Colleen Atwood and make-up artist Patty Duke to help create the bizarre but charismatic design for the Mad Hatter. Depp spent a lot of time developing the character's inner world, which Atwood expressed through her design. The hat itself was key, as Atwood explains:

> It needed to be something that had gone through a holocaust-y moment in his life; it was a remnant, as was his costume, of another time. I found a piece of charred, laser-cut leather embroidered

in gold thread, and bought it immediately. I thought it would be wonderful for the hat, instead of the usual felt. It just took it to a different place. Sometimes you give an actor a prop and they say, 'What am I supposed to do with this?' But Johnny knows how to use clothes.[9]

87 Costume for Captain Jack Sparrow *Pirates of the Caribbean: On Stranger Tides*, 2011 Costume designer Penny Rose Courtesy of Disney Pictures and Jerry Bruckheimer Films

OPPOSITE
88 Captain Jack Sparrow (Johnny Depp) *Pirates of the Caribbean: On Stranger Tides*, 2011 Costume designer Penny Rose

CREATIVE COLLABORATIONS

EDITH HEAD AND ALFRED HITCHCOCK

ALFRED HITCHCOCK and Edith Head had a long and productive working relationship, encompassing 11 films between 1946 and 1976. These included some of Hitchcock's most enduring classics and Head's most iconic looks, such as *Rear Window* (1954), *To Catch a Thief* (1955), *Vertigo* (1958) and *The Birds* (1963). Theirs was a symbiotic collaboration: Hitchcock had a strong vision of how his characters should be presented, and Head was able to successfully translate his ideas into specific costumes.

❛ Unless there is a story reason for a color, we keep the colors muted, because Hitchcock believes they can detract from an important action scene. He uses color, actually, almost like an artist, preferring soft greens and cool colors for certain moods. ❜

EDITH HEAD

92 Edith Head, Alfred Hitchcock and Ingrid Bergman during production of *Notorious*, 1946

❛ Blondes make the best victims. They're like virgin snow that shows up the bloody footprints. ❜

ALFRED HITCHCOCK

OPPOSITE
89 Alfred Hitchcock and Edith Head on the set of *Family Plot*, 1976

ABOVE
90 Judy Barton (Kim Novak) *Vertigo*, 1958
Costume designer Edith Head

LEFT
91 Costume for Judy Barton *Vertigo*, 1958
Costume designer Edith Head
The Collection of Motion
Picture Costume Design Larry McQueen

MARTIN SCORSESE AND SANDY POWELL

SANDY POWELL was already an established costume designer in her native UK, working with directors such as Derek Jarman, Neil Jordan and Sally Potter, before winning her first Academy Award for *Shakespeare in Love* in 1998. She first collaborated with Martin Scorsese on the epic *Gangs of New York* in 2002. Since then they have worked together on four films: *The Aviator* (2004), *The Departed* (2006), *Shutter Island* (2010), and *Hugo* (2011).

> ❛ Nearly every costume designed for a film has a story behind its creation ... Martin Scorsese once gave me an entire film to watch just to see the stripe on a collar. ❜
>
> **SANDY POWELL**

93 Jack Nicholson and Martin Scorsese on the set of *The Departed*, 2006

> ❛ [In *The Departed*] I wanted to strip away the complexity of colours, and for characters to come to the forefront. This idea was an homage, or reference, based on the noir genre. It's different in the sense that it takes place in the modern day, and the noir of today reflects a different culture and time in the world. ❜
>
> **MARTIN SCORSESE**

ABOVE
94 Dr Cawley, Chuck Aule and Teddy Daniels (Ben Kingsley, Mark Ruffalo and Leonardo DiCaprio) *Shutter Island*, 2010 Costume designer Sandy Powell

RIGHT
95 Howard Hughes (Leonardo DiCaprio) *The Aviator*, 2004 Costume designer Sandy Powell

> ❛ We've tried to be as authentic as possible and as close as possible to the character that we are portraying. I've looked at all of the things Howard Hughes actually wore, and really tried to re-create that ... The pictures I am looking at are in black and white most of the time, and we're doing colour, so I have to imagine what the colours would have been. ❜
>
> **SANDY POWELL**

'Sandy and I had a chance to meet in Dublin before we started shooting ... then we went our separate ways, and when I came back a month later, to my astonishment I found the rack of clothes she had created. I hadn't imagined Bill being such a peacock, but the discovery was a really wonderful one, a hooligan dandy. It made me think a little differently ... From the moment I tried on the costumes, I was utterly delighted.'

DANIEL DAY-LEWIS

ABOVE
96 Amsterdam Vallon, Bill 'The Butcher' Cutting and Johnny Sirocco (Leonardo DiCaprio, Daniel Day-Lewis and Henry Thomas)
Gangs of New York, 2002
Costume designer Sandy Powell

RIGHT
97 Sketch for Bill 'The Butcher' Cutting
Gangs of New York, 2002
Costume designer and illustrator Sandy Powell

LEFT
98 Isabelle and Hugo Cabret (Chloë Grace Moretz and Asa Butterfield)
Hugo, 2011
Costume designer Sandy Powell

'Everything [in *Hugo*] is seen as if through the eyes of a child, therefore I wanted to simplify the looks to just one, maybe two outfits for each character. I approached the actual costumes as if they were illustrations from a children's picture book, keeping the looks simple, graphic and colourful.'

SANDY POWELL

MIKE NICHOLS AND ANN ROTH

VETERAN COSTUME designer Ann Roth and director Mike Nichols have developed a close collaboration over four decades, both for screen and stage, starting with the original Broadway production of Neil Simon's *The Odd Couple* in 1965. Their film projects include *Silkwood* (1983), *Working Girl* (1988), *Postcards from the Edge* (1990), *The Birdcage* (1996) and *Closer* (2004), and they recently collaborated on the Broadway revival of *Death of a Salesman* opening in 2012.

❝ I have a long history with costume designer Ann Roth, whose sense of character and detail is magnificent. Ann's ability to make a metaphor out of the truth – out of accurate observations of what these people would wear and how they would live – is of immeasurable importance ... ❞

MIKE NICHOLS

TOP
99 Mike Nichols, 1990

RIGHT
100 Karen Silkwood, Drew Stephens and Dolly Pelliker (Meryl Streep, Kurt Russell and Cher)
***Silkwood*, 1983**
Costume designer Ann Roth

BELOW
101 Suzanne Vale and Doris Mann (Meryl Streep and Shirley MacLaine)
***Postcards from the Edge*, 1990**
Costume designer Ann Roth

❝ Mike is constantly reinventing as he works; he is always looking for something new. He is very demanding, very confident and mentally he never tires ... We will usually envision the script and the characters in the same way, only he's smarter ... We both have a love of improvisation. He likes a scene to take shape from an improvisational rehearsal and I like accidental problem-solving. ❞

ANN ROTH

LEFT
102 Albert Goldman
(Nathan Lane)
The Birdcage (1996)
Costume designer Ann Roth

BELOW
103 Dan and Alice
(Jude Law and
Natalie Portman)
Closer, 2004
Costume designer Ann Roth

❝ Ann Roth is a genius; she instinctively knows what everybody should wear, even when it's just t-shirts and shorts. But there's something about the way she conceives Nathan's character when he's in drag – especially when he's in drag for the family as Mrs Coleman – that made her a whole person with a specific identity. ❞

MIKE NICHOLS

❝ I went down to the bottom of the World Trade Center and sat there and watch people getting off the Staten Island ferry and walking in ... They usually don't come to Manhattan, but those girls who come and work as secretaries, getting off the boat, their shoes would be in their purses ... And they were sexy. That's the point. They were very sexy. ❞

ANN ROTH

104 Jack Trainer,
Tess McGill and Katharine
Parker (Harrison Ford,
Melanie Griffith and
Sigourney Weaver)
Working Girl, 1988
Costume designer Ann Roth

TIM BURTON AND COLLEEN ATWOOD

COLLEEN ATWOOD began designing film costumes in the 1980s, and was introduced to Tim Burton following her work on *Joe vs The Volcano*. Their first film together, *Edward Scissorhands* (1990), created an iconic look and marked their first collaboration with Johnny Depp. Since then, together, they have brought to the screen a league of extraordinary and memorable film characters including *Ed Wood* (1994), Ichabod Crane in *Sleepy Hollow* (1999) and *Sweeney Todd: The Demon Barber of Fleet Street* (2007) and Barnabas Collins in *Dark Shadows* (2012).

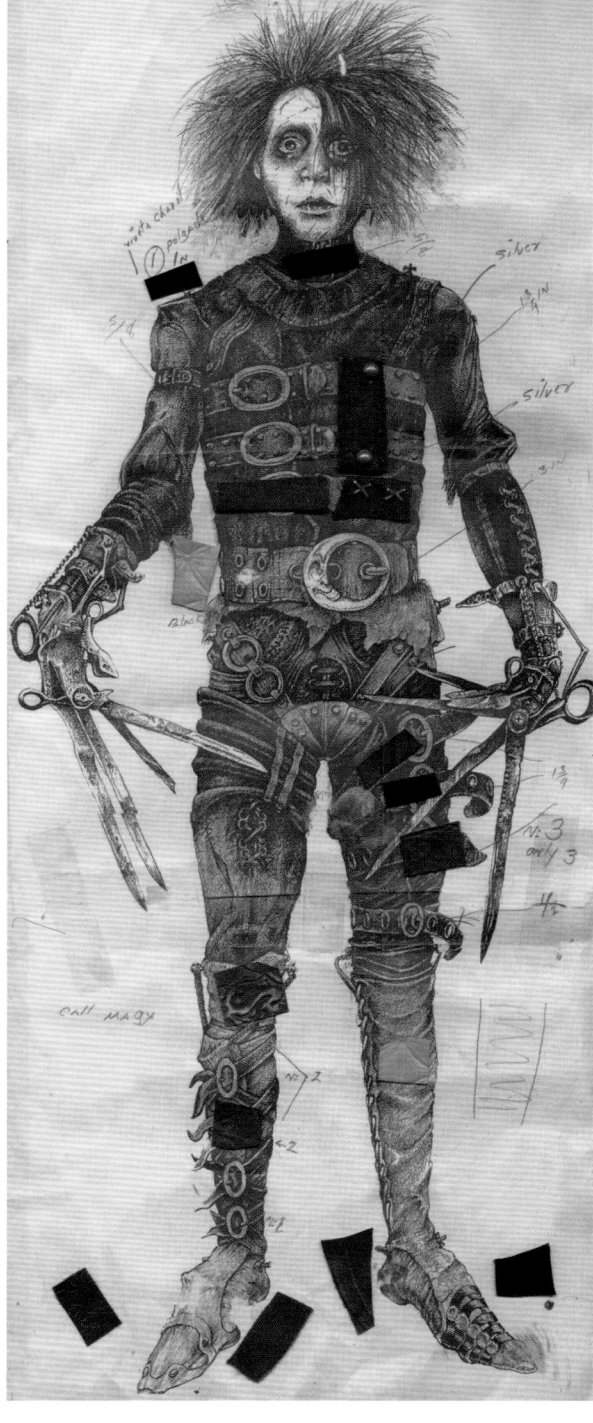

❝ I've worked with Colleen Atwood many, many times, and she's as important as anybody on a movie. Costumes are another character in the movie. Most of the great actors I've worked with, when they put on the costume they become the character. I help them find who the character is. ❞

TIM BURTON

❝ ... he really doesn't give me a drawing and say, 'This is what I want'. I think it's because he knows the other people working with him are artists, so he gets very excited and enthusiastic when we show him what we have. He has a wonderful eye himself, and so he'll give a little magical touch to something. ❞

COLLEEN ATWOOD

ABOVE, LEFT TO RIGHT
105 **Sketch for Martian Girl**
Mars Attacks!, 1996
Illustrator Tim Burton

106 **Martian Girl (Lisa Marie)**
Mars Attacks!, 1996
Costume designer Colleen Atwood

ABOVE
107 **Sketch for**
Edward Scissorhands
Edward Scissorhands, 1990
Illustrator Tim Burton

LEFT TO RIGHT
108 **Ping and Jing**
(Ada and Arlene Tai)
Big Fish, 2003
Costume designer Colleen Atwood

109 **Attar (Michael Clarke Duncan)**
Planet of the Apes, 2001
Costume designer Colleen Atwood

110 **Barnabas Collins (Johnny Depp)**
Dark Shadows, 2012
Costume designer Colleen Atwood

111 **Katrina Van Tassel**
(Christina Ricci)
Sleepy Hollow, 1999
Costume designer Colleen Atwood

❛ For the Red Queen, Helena's inspiration was Elizabethan ... We had a lot of challenges with her because of the head situation. [The actress's head was enlarged for the film using special effects.] The collar became really important because when your head gets big, your neck tends to disappear. So we had to slice the neck thinner and shave her waist away in visual effects and in the costume to make her head look bigger. She was a real piece of sculpture. ❜

COLLEEN ATWOOD

ABOVE
**112 Tim Burton and
Mia Wasikowska on the set
of *Alice in Wonderland*, 2010**

LEFT
**113 The Red Queen
(Helena Bonham Carter)
Alice in Wonderland, 2010
Costume designer Colleen Atwood**

BELOW
**114 Sweeney Todd and Mrs Lovett
(Johnny Depp and
Helena Bonham Carter)
Sweeney Todd, 2007
Costume designer Colleen Atwood**

❛ When I first spoke to Tim about *Sweeney Todd*, he wanted to create a world that felt mid-Victorian, without making it too precious, and tried to have a bit fun with it as well. ❜

COLLEEN ATWOOD

2 DEFINING THE CHARACTER

THE COSTUME OF SILENT COMEDY

David Robinson

THE COSTUME of comedy stands apart. In other film genres, actors wear clothes that identify their roles – by period, ethnicity, nationality, class or character – or enhance their personal allure. The comedian's clothes, on the contrary, are functional, tools of the trade, aiming in themselves to be a cause of laughter.

From the beginning, comedy followed a course of evolution different from other genres. While these had to wait to be invented, film comedy derived directly from a long heritage. Director Mack Sennett, wrote James Agee, 'took his comics out of music halls, burlesque, vaudeville, circuses and limbo, and through them he tapped in on that great pipeline of horsing and miming which runs back unbroken through the fairs of the Middle Ages at least to Ancient Greece'. Even before Sennett and Hollywood, the infant cinemas of France and Italy had recruited clowns from circus and popular theatre and won a world market with hundreds of five-minute, one-joke knockabout farces, generally culminating in a wild chase. The comedians brought their tricks and tumbles and grimaces from long-practised stage turns and played them before the cameras on the streets of Paris and Nice, Rome or Turin. As production became more organized and the films grew in length to 10 or 15 minutes, the companies discovered the strategy of producing them in series, each featuring an individual clown. Under their screen names – among the most famous of scores of them were Boireau, Prince, Onésime in France and Cretinetti (Boireau renamed), KriKri, Polidor, Robinet in Italy – they were the cinema's first true box-office stars (plates 116, 117).

These early clowns depended on their faces and their antics for laughter: few adopted recognizable characteristic costumes – any sufficiently extravagant variant on the day's fashions would do, so long as it was ready to be ripped, wrecked, hooked on fishing rods or soaked in paint, tar, treacle or any other malevolent substance.

The cinema's first recognizable comic costume is the most unexpected because in itself it is not comic at all. Max Linder (plate 119) began his career as a legitimate actor, but from 1905 eked out his income by playing in comedy films at the Pathé Studios for 20 francs a day plus compensation when his clothes were damaged. From 1910 Pathé featured Linder in his own *Max* series: in all he was to conceive, direct and star in some four hundred comedies. His output and invention were prodigious, establishing a huge repertoire of gags which was in large part to shape the whole future of visual film comedy: Chaplin, never inclined to admire other artists, called Linder 'The Master'.

The character that Linder created was a handsome and stylish young boulevardier. His hair was sleek, his moustache perfectly trimmed; he wore an elegant cutaway, a beautiful cravat, the fanciest of waistcoats, a gleaming silk hat and perfect shoes. He was smart, intelligent and resourceful, possibly living above his income and with an eye for the fair sex which was always getting him into some sort of trouble, out of which he generally extricated himself. The comedy lay in the contrast between this exquisite person and the ludicrous annoyances that assailed him in the shape of taking a bath, climbing a mountain, jealous husbands, dogs, cats and smelly feet. Remarkably, however extravagant the adventures, the costume was rarely impaired. Perhaps it was just too expensive to risk: one of the purely incidental pleasures of Max Linder comedies is to relish male couture of the Belle Epoque at its most exquisite.

Linder's recognition of the comic effect of juxtaposing supreme elegance with the absurd has been profitably exploited by comediennes from Mabel Normand and Marion Davies to Mae West, Lucille Ball and Marilyn Monroe, and by one notable male Hollywood comedy star, Raymond Griffith. Even his trim figure, smoothed hair and neat moustache recalled Linder. To the top hat, white tie and tails he added a watch-chain and opera cloak, and thus attired faced a hostile world, to which he generally proved serenely superior. In *Hands Up!* (1926; plate 120) the costume serves him in his role as a spy in the Civil War, variously faced by a firing squad (whose aim he distracts by tossing into the air plates conjured from beneath the cloak) and hostile Indians who are won over when he offers them a stylish Charleston as an improvement

ABOVE
116 André Deed as 'Cretinetti' (left) *Foolshead Pays his Debts*, **1909**

RIGHT
117 André Deed poster for his character, 'Toribio', c.1910

118 Ferdinand Guillaume as 'Polidor', c.1913

on their regular war dance. Sadly, this cool, sophisticated and unique clown who had learned his craft as a writer at the Mack Sennett studios, is today all but forgotten thanks to the disappearance of the greater part of his films.

A decade or more before Griffith, however, the major influence on the emergent American film comedy was vaudeville, still, in the years before the First World War, a flourishing industry, only just beginning to give way to the cinema as the most potent medium of popular entertainment, on both sides of the Atlantic. Vaudeville and music hall were international, with a regular exchange of artists between Britain and North America. Fundamental to performance in this singular genre of theatre was the presentation of character: artists' bylines would regularly boast ' … in characters true to life'. Every song was presented in character; every comedian established a character whose ethnic or social distinctions were expressed and exaggerated by a costume that was calculated in itself to provoke instant laughter of recognition. The cinema's first consistent borrowings from vaudeville, starting in the late 1890s, were the tramp characters which (reflecting contemporary social phenomena) proliferated both in vaudeville and comic strips and inspired scores of films centring on the tramp's plots to filch a piece of pie or a garment off the clothes-line, and his inevitable frustration and punishment

by ferocious dogs or virago cooks. Only one of the tramp figures of this vaudeville era is now remembered: W.C. Fields (plate 121), having embarked on his stage career as a juggler, first introduced comedy into his act in the costume, make-up and character of a tramp.

Almost all the other legendary clowns who emerged in silent cinema – Chaplin, Keaton, Harry Langdon, Raymond Griffith, Roscoe 'Fatty' Arbuckle, Charley Chase, Laurel and Hardy – also brought with them long experience in vaudeville. (The outstanding exception was Harold Lloyd, a refugee from an indifferent apprenticeship on the legitimate stage.) Of these, the majority were first recruited by Mack Sennett, boss of the Keystone Comedy Company and historically celebrated as the architect of American screen comedy. The celebration is not quite unanimous: no less a chronicler than Walter Kerr found Keystone comedies mirthless, comparing them to the learning antics of young chimpanzees:

> Perhaps we might have laughed too in 1914. At least we would have felt excitement … I say 'perhaps' we might have laughed, because I'm not entirely sure … There is very little in the Sennett films, for all their breakneck pace and bizarre manhandling of the universe, that one would care to call humor under analytic examination.[1]

TOP LEFT
119 Max Linder, 1910

TOP RIGHT
120 Jack (Raymond Griffith)
Hands Up!, 1926

ABOVE
121 W.C. Fields poster for his vaudeville act, 'Irwin's Burlesquers', _c._1910

122 **The Keystone Kops, c.1915**

123 **Poster for Keystone Comedy,
Western Import Company, c.1912**

Even though the Keystone films, like Sennett himself, were determinedly unrefined, Kerr's underestimation is extreme. Already in these films Chaplin, Mabel Normand and Arbuckle are evidently, if still intermittently, great comedians, and Ford Sterling, who preceded Chaplin as Keystone's male star, was not a bad one. With due respect to Kerr, we can still laugh at the supporting ensemble of idiots who are the studio's taskforce (plate 122). Cross-eyed Ben Turpin, Hank Mann, Billy Bevan, Mack Swain, Chester Conklin, Al St John, Charles Avery, Billy Gilbert, Edgar Kennedy, Slim Summerville were all funny men who went on to careers in their own rights. The comediennes Phyllis Allen, Alice Davenport and Alice Howell also gave as good as they got.

There was, however, nothing individual or distinctive about the ensemble couture. By and large the Keystone wardrobe seemed to supply clothes that might have been worn by working men on days off or nights out, with occasional ritzier outfits for toffs set up to be taken down a peg or two. The particular speciality of Keystone – which need to be regarded as costume accessories – were odious moustaches and whiskers. But if the outer clothing was unspectacular, underclothing always held out rich promise. As James Agee wrote,

The intimate tastes and secret hopes of these poor ineligible dunces were ruthlessly exposed whenever a hit stove, an electric fan or a bulldog took a dislike to their outer garments: agonizingly elaborate drawers, worked up on some lonely evening out of some Godforsaken lace curtain; or men's underpants with big round black spots on them.[2]

Besides underwear, Sennett's Keystone also appreciated the essential comicality of the costume of authority. The most mythical creation of Keystone remains its Kops, incompetents in tall, thimble-shaped helmets, brandishing batons, led by Ford Sterling with a 'Dutch' beard, cramming into the paddy-wagon or chasing after it in a human chain, to end up like lemmings over cliff edges. It is the Kops whom everyone believes he remembers from Keystones, though their appearances in the films were in fact only sporadic, generally dragged in ad hoc to fortify the climactic final chase. Every comic who was not otherwise engaged was recruited to the force, however: recently a long-lost film of 1914, *A Thief Catcher,* turned up with Chaplin himself taking a turn as Kop. Yet the Kops had some special appeal: their legend was established early, it seems, if we believe the claim that municipal police forces across

❝ I had no idea of the character. But the moment I was dressed, the clothes and the make-up made me feel the person he was. I began to know him, and by the time I walked on to the stage, he was born. **❞**

CHARLES CHAPLIN

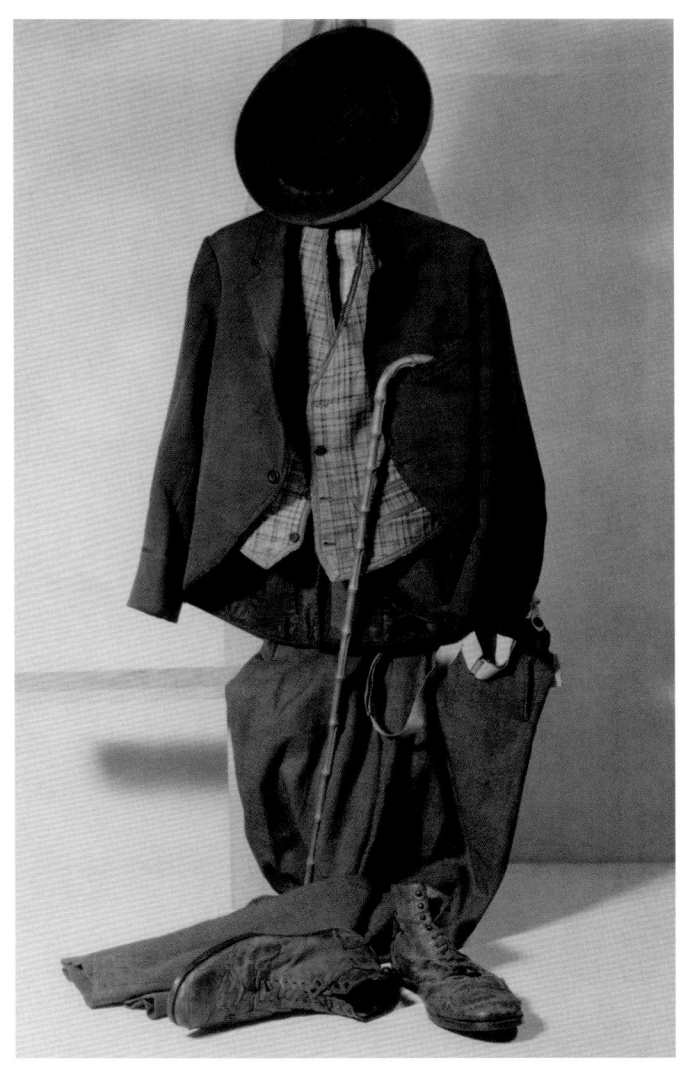

124 Charles Chaplin, *c.*1920
Photographer Jack Wilson

125 Costume for The Tramp
The Tramp, 1914
Costume designer Charles Chaplin

126 **Factory worker (Charles Chaplin)**
Modern Times, 1936

the United States altered their headgear to military-style caps, since Sennett slapstick had brought the old British-style helmets into popular ridicule.

It was, however, the Keystone wardrobe shed that supplied the world's most famous comedy costume. Charles Chaplin joined the studio in the first days of 1914, and his debut film, *Making a Living*, was released on 14 January of that year. Almost nothing in the character he plays anticipates the Chaplin we know. He is a character of dubious respectability who is trying to muscle in on a newsman's professional territory. He wears a grey top hat, coat, checked waistcoat, stiff collar, spotted cravat and monocle. A melancholy walrus moustache droops heavily at either side of his mouth. He manages a few nice gags but does not establish a character. The film was not bad, by the usual Keystone standards, but Chaplin hated it, feeling that the personage was not defined and that the director had wrecked his timing. For his second film, evidently, he determined to find a costume with character.

From all accounts, that costume, which was to be little modified in its 22-year career, was created almost spontaneously, without premeditation. The pervasive legend is that it was concocted one rainy afternoon in the communal male dressing room

at Keystone, where Chaplin borrowed Fatty Arbuckle's voluminous trousers, tiny Charles Avery's jacket, Ford Sterling's size 14 shoes, worn on the wrong feet to keep them from falling off, a too-small derby belonging to Arbuckle's father-in-law, and a moustache intended for Mack Swain's use, which Chaplin trimmed to toothbrush size. This neat and colourful version of the genesis of the tramp seems to have originated in the Keystone Studio, and was certainly never endorsed by Chaplin.

When he described the creation of the costume in his 1964 autobiography, the memory was undoubtedly coloured by half a century of rationalization and reading high-brow critical commentators. As he recalled it, Mack Sennett had told him: 'Put on a comedy make-up. Anything will do.'

> I had no idea what make-up to put on … However, on
> the way to the wardrobe, I thought I would dress in
> baggy pants, big shoes, a cane and a derby hat. I wanted

everything a contradiction: the pants baggy, the coat tight, the hat small and the shoes large. I was undecided whether to look old or young, but remembering Sennett had expected me to be a much older man, I added a small moustache, which I reasoned, would add age without hiding my expression. I had no idea of the character. But the moment I was dressed, the clothes and the make-up made me feel the person he was. I began to know him, and by the time I walked on to the stage he was fully born. When I confronted Sennett I assumed the character and strutted about, swinging my cane and parading before him. Gags and comedy ideas went racing through my mind.

Encouraged by Sennett's laughter, Chaplin began to explain the character:

> You know this fellow is many-sided, a tramp, a gentleman, a poet, a dreamer, a lonely fellow, always hopeful of romance and adventure. He would have you believe he is a scientist, a musician, a duke, a polo-player. However, he is not above picking up cigarette butts or robbing a baby of its candy. And of course if the occasion warrants it, he will kick a lady in the rear – but only in extreme anger.

Although we can probably disregard this instant verbal analysis of the character, we have other evidence for Chaplin's claim that 'the clothes and the make-up made me feel the person he was'. In 1984 the cameraman Fred Koenekamp, who had begun his career at Keystone, remembered:

> I can still see the little shack where he came out the dressing room. He'd come out and he'd kind of rehearse himself – that walk, the cane, the hat and things like that, you know.
> I can still see him when he came onto the set. He was supposed to be half drunk or something like that. He came into the lobby and tried to make eyes at women, and women ignored him and all that kind of stuff. I can remember that. Never forget that. So I really photographed the first scene he played in.
> Did it look funny there and then? Yes, it did. Well, it was, because it was 'fresh' … And his movements too. Wiggle the mouth and that moustache would kinda work. And the cane flapping around, swinging on his arm … and going around on one leg like he was skating.

The film was *Mabel's Strange Predicament* (1914), and at the end of the week's shooting Chaplin went on to use the costume for a quick improvisation filmed against the background of a Saturday afternoon sporting event, a competition for boys in soap-box cars, racing down a steep ramp. The film, *Kid Auto Races at Venice*, runs for only seven minutes, and turns upon a single joke – Charlie is a shabby nuisance whose eagerness to get in front of the lens infuriates the newsreel cameraman. Clearly its 20 shots were rapidly put together, so that it was released before *Mabel's Strange Predicament*, and can be counted the first appearance of the

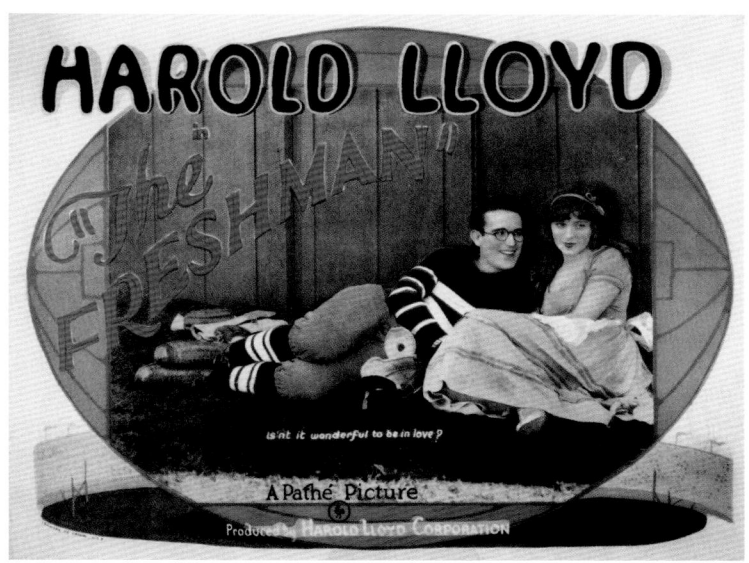

127 The Freshman (Harold Lloyd)
The Freshman, 1925
128 Poster for *The Freshman*, 1925

Chaplin character and costume. This, and the nature of the film, as an off-the-cuff record of a sporting event and of its spectators gives it an extraordinary documentary quality. At the moment it was shot, the Chaplin persona had never been seen on the screen. The spectators at the races were therefore the first people in the world to glimpse the figure that was soon to become universally famous (plates 115, 124). So we observe this first audience as they progress (the children first) from initial bewilderment and embarrassment at the antics of this obstreperous little vagabond, to uninhibited laughter as they realize he is a professional

entertainer. *Kid Auto Races* is a historical record of the world's first encounter with its greatest clown.

From that moment Chaplin's trajectory to universal fame was phenomenal. Within months he was the biggest attraction in the international cinema; within a year or two – certainly by the start of the 1920s – he was probably the best-known figure in the world. Of course his success, his popularity, his universal recognition went far deeper than the costume. James Agee defined his unique genius, with simple precision: 'Of all comedians he worked most deeply and most shrewdly within a realization of what a human being is, and is up against'. Chaplin's 1964 recollection that "by the time I walked onto the stage he was fully born" is another fallacy of hindsight. We know from the films that this was far from true; the character was to take a year or more to evolve its full dimensions and even then – which was its particular strength – it would evolve during the whole of the rest of his career. Nor was the costume consistent: the details changed and varied over the years, though the silhouette remained unmistakable. There was a fundamental symbolism:

the derby, the cane, the bow tie and close-trimmed moustache indicated brave but ineffectual pretensions to the dignity of the *petit bourgeois*. It was timeless: this little character would have been at home on the mean streets of Victorian London, which Chaplin knew painfully well from his boyhood, yet did not seem out of place in the automated new world of the 1930s and *Modern Times* (1936). Chaplin finally abandoned the character only because he considered this kind of homeless mendicant, living on the streets, was an anachronism. In the twenty-first century it no longer seems so.

Chaplin's instant triumph for a while inspired imitators – some better than others, but all eventually dispatched by legal action – and attempts to emulate the suggestiveness, the pitiful pretensions to gentility of the Chaplin costume. Harold Lloyd, in his early screen character 'Lonesome Luke', was influenced by the Chaplin costume in his choice of tightly pinching suits and a little moustache. Lloyd, however, was to give the cinema one of its most distinctive and minimalist comedy costumes when he adopted his round horn-rimmed glasses, which, whatever the

rest of the wardrobe, at once declared the prissy, eager, well-intentioned but disaster-prone go-getter. Lloyd was at the same time keenly alert to the comic possibilities of clothing. Making *The Freshman* (1925; plates 127, 128), he discovered the fundamental principle that the unfailing seat of comedy is the trousers. He had devised a gag in which a tuxedo snatched up before the tailor had finished it would disintegrate in the course of a dance. But at the preview, the laughs were few: only when he lowered the gag, so that it was the trousers which fell apart to leave him in shirt-tail and underpants, did the howls come.

Buster Keaton, too, discovered the single garment which would instantly define as his own any costume he wore, regardless of the place or period: the little flat pork-pie hat alone is still sufficient to evoke the memory of the stone face, deep eyes and uniquely expressive body. After the early shorts the hat was not invariable; but even when playing a Civil War soldier or a young millionaire adrift in *The Navigator* (1924; plate 129), some casually adopted headgear would just remind us.

Harry Langdon (plate 130) – neglected now, but regarded by Agee as one of the big four of silent comedy, alongside Chaplin, Keaton and Lloyd, never varied the costume he had brought with him from a long vaudeville career:

> His clothes are tell-tale. The trousers, overlong and ballooning at the cuffs, would seem to have been handed down from an older brother. Draping over the locked ankles, they sometimes make him seem a statue. His tie is never tied quite tightly at the neck, nor is it properly centered; some other kid has been tugging at it. His too-tight jacket is fastened high by a single enormous button, its tails flaring behind in seagull sweep. He uses his hat-brim as ballast; let the least wind stir and both hands fly to its edge, finding security in the firmness with which it rides his brow. One forelock slips beneath it. A five-year-old not gaining much on six.[3]

Langdon, wrote the demanding Walter Kerr, 'had one queerly toned, unique little reed. But out of it he could get incredible melodies'.

The English Stan Laurel (a colleague of Chaplin in British vaudeville days) and the stout Southerner Oliver Hardy were teamed in the last days of silence and, bridging the eras of silence and sound, looked forward to new styles of comedy clothing that would perhaps reflect a new social era. Their suits and overcoats and Derby hats and wives proclaim a dream of bourgeois respectability doomed always to frustration. By this time, too, W.C. Fields had long left behind his tramp costume, and in his sound films generally has an aspiring wife, a demanding family and a day job as small-town grocer, dentist or clerk to push him reluctantly to respectability. But like Walter Matthau after him, an ill-tied tie and a crooked collar will always proclaim misanthropy, mendacity and ultimate disreputability. The Marx Brothers were a special case of ensemble costume, but even here there is the permanent conflict between the suited but fraudulent social pretensions of Groucho and Zeppo, and Chico's menacing crushed headgear and Harpo's crazed curls, Mad Hat and tramp coat of inexhaustible capacity (plate 131).

A turning point in the appreciation of the unique visual comedy that had been born out of cinema came with James Agee's classic article 'Comedy's Greatest Era' in *Life* magazine, 6 September 1949. Shrewdly and brilliantly, Agee analysed the aesthetic principles that had blossomed unsought from the rough and tumble, and recalled the great comedy artists whose names by that time were all but forgotten. Of the great ones, only Langdon was then dead. Chaplin was still working, though under the shadow of McCarthyist harassment which would soon exile him from America. Harold Lloyd was rich, happy and retired. Keaton's reputation and career were renewed by Agee's article.

Agee defined that Greatest Era as the years 1912 to 1930, and saw everything that had come since as a decline:

The best of comedies these days hand out plenty of titters and once in a while it is possible to achieve a yowl without overstraining. Even those who have never seen anything better must occasionally have the feeling, as they watch the current run or, rather, trickle of screen comedy, that they are having to make a little cause for laughter go an awfully long way. And anyone who has watched screen comedy over the past 10 or 15 years is bound to realize that it has quietly but steadily deteriorated.... To put it unkindly, the only thing wrong with screen comedy today is that it takes place on a screen which talks.

131 The Marx Brothers, 1935

132 Poster for *Les vacances de Monsieur Hulot (Mr Hulot's Holiday)*, 1953

133 Monsieur Hulot (Jacques Tati) *Les vacances de Monsieur Hulot (Mr Hulot's Holiday)*, 1953

The most gifted comedians, explained Agee, 'learned to show emotion through it [the silent idiom], and comic psychology, more eloquently than most language has ever managed to, and they discovered beauties of comic motion which are hopelessly beyond reach of words'.

At the very moment when Agee's article was published, a new French film, *Jour de Fête* (1949), presented a comedian who fulfilled all Agee's expectations of the great silent stars. He was Jacques Tati. Agee lived long enough to see Tati's second feature, *Les vacances de Monsieur Hulot (Mr Hulot's Holiday*, 1953; plates 132, 133), which introduced the cinema's (until now) last great silent comic. Monsieur Hulot – subsequently to figure in *Mon Oncle* (1958), *Play Time* (1967) and *Trafic* (1971) – was a modest bourgeois battling with a world of escalating consumerism and dehumanizing automation. Insofar as his invariably well-intentioned activities constantly brought chaos and confusion to overturn this self-satisfied world, it was a battle which he won on behalf of every little man. This was also the last pure comedy costume, unmistakably declaring the character. The costume dis-covered the absurdity in the ordinary – Monsieur Hulot's large, self-absorbed face, was surmounted by an out-of-shape fedora. His beige mackintosh flared out to conical form. He wore a drooping bow tie, and his too-short trousers revealed striped socks and brown suede shoes. He was inseparable from his rolled umbrella. Yet it is not Monsieur Hulot who is absurd, but the world of which he is the centre – a world that is familiar, modern, yet revealed as a wonderland in which every chair and door and car and telephone and cushion is a joke. Tati lovingly, indulgently, uncomprehendingly watches the antics of the people who have made this world their own, and now scuttle about it with the in-turned pride of White Rabbits. Tati's view of our universe is unique in the history of film comedy, for it leaves us with the happy conviction that all men were made in the clown's image.

David Robinson has had a long and distinguished career as an editor, film critic and author. His books include Hollywood in the Twenties *(1968),* World Cinema *(1973) and* Chaplin: His Life and Art *(1985), considered the definitive biography of Charles Chaplin. He is director of* Le Giornate del Cinema Muto *(Pordenone Silent Film Festival).*

SOUND COMEDY LOUDER AND FUNNIER

John Landis

WHEN HE lay on his deathbed, actor Edmund Gwynne was asked if it was hard to die. He answered, 'Dying is easy, comedy is hard'. Although the story may be apocryphal, it speaks the truth. Comedy is unforgiving; either the audience laughs or it doesn't.

When making a modern comedy the costumes help create the people on screen, and sometimes the costumes themselves are the joke. The ways the characters dress in films like *Austin Powers: International Man of Mystery* (1997; plates 138, 139), *Legally Blonde* (2001, 2003; plates 140, 141) and *iThree Amigos!* (1986; plate 143) are visual punchlines, whereas the laid-back clothing of The Dude in *The Big Lebowski* (1998; plate 145) or the ill-fitting suit worn by *Borat* (2006; plate 144) help define not only the look but the personality of the characters.

In Billy Wilder's *Some Like It Hot* (1959), Marilyn Monroe as Sugar Kane Kowalczyk wears an outrageous dress designed by Orry-Kelly to showcase her breasts, which manages somehow to be both sexy and funny. Disney's *101* and *102 Dalmatians* (1996, 2000) were both based on the original animated film (1961) and actress Glenn Close re-created the over-the-top character of Cruella De Vil. Cruella is a wildly exaggerated fashionista and Anthony Powell's witty costumes brilliantly balance high-styled extravagance and just plain silliness (plates 136, 137).

John Belushi and Dan Aykroyd created the characters of Jake and Elwood Blues and would wear any pair of sunglasses and hats when performing on stage. When we made the film *The Blues Brothers* (1980), costume designer Deborah Nadoolman created a uniform look for their black suits and hats so they would have

OPPOSITE, TOP
**134 Elwood and Jake Blues (Dan Aykroyd
and John Belushi)**
The Blues Brothers, 1980
Costume designer Deborah Nadoolman

OPPOSITE, LEFT
135 John Blutarsky 'Bluto' (John Belushi)
National Lampoon's Animal House, 1978
Costume designer Deborah Nadoolman

ABOVE
136 Designs for Cruella De Vil
102 Dalmatians, 2000
Costume designer Anthony Powell
Illustrator Anthony Powell

RIGHT
137 Cruella De Vil (Glenn Close)
102 Dalmatians, 2000
Costume designer Anthony Powell

"AUSTIN POWERS."

FROZEN IN THE 60'S...THAWING SPRING '97, BABY!

OPPOSITE, FROM TOP LEFT

142 Billy Ray Valentine (Eddie Murphy)
Trading Places, 1983
Costume designer Deborah Nadoolman

143 Ned Nederlander, Lucky Day and Dusty Bottoms
(Martin Short, Steve Martin and Chevy Chase)
¡Three Amigos!, 1986
Costume designer Deborah Nadoolman

144 Borat (Sacha Baron Cohen)
*Borat: Cultural Learnings of America for Make
Benefit Glorious Nation of Kazakhstan*, 2006
Costume designer Jason Alper

145 Jeffrey Lebowski 'The Dude' and Walter Sobchak
(Jeff Bridges and John Goodman)
The Big Lebowski, 1998
Costume designer Mary Zophres

ABOVE

138 Sketch for Austin Powers
*Austin Powers: International
Man of Mystery*, 1997
Costume designer Deena Appel
Illustrator Michele Michel

139 Austin Powers (Mike Myers)
*Austin Powers: International Man
of Mystery*, 1997
Costume designer Deena Appel

RIGHT

140 Sketch for Elle Woods
*Legally Blonde 2: Red, White
and Blonde*, 2003
Costume designer Sophie de Rakoff
Ilustrator Anna Wyckoff

141 Elle Woods (Reese Witherspoon)
*Legally Blonde 2: Red, White
and Blonde*, 2003
Costume designer Sophie de Rakoff

a very specific silhouette (plate 134). Deborah told me at the time that to be a truly iconic character you must be easily recognizable just from your shadow (Steven Spielberg introduced the character of Indiana Jones in the most recent *Raiders* sequel by his silhouette alone). So she chose a certain type of sunglasses, Ray Ban Wayfarers (which at the time of production were no longer being manufactured) and 'snap brim' fedoras from Dobb's of Chicago to make Jake and Elwood's iconic look. Although they are not dressed in an extraordinary way, Jake and Elwood manage to stand out from everyone else in every scene.

Sometimes a costume worn by an actor in a film captures the public imagination and creates a fashion trend. This happens when the character, the story and the performer all connect with the zeitgeist. When we made *National Lampoon's Animal House* (1978) Deborah asked if I thought it would be funny if Bluto (John Belushi) wore a sweatshirt that simply said 'COLLEGE' on it (plate 135). The combination of that actor (John Belushi) in that part (Bluto) made such a powerful impression that 34 years later Universal Studios are still selling copies of that sweatshirt!

In contemporary comedies that take place in the real world, the costumes are not there to draw attention to the clothes, but rather to help define the people who are wearing them. Seamless costuming, as in *Trading Places* (1983), helps to tell the story. The bespoke suits of wealthy Philadelphia commodities traders Mortimer and Randolph Duke (Don Ameche and Ralph Bellamy) and Louis Winthorpe (Dan Aykroyd) contrast sharply with the torn sneakers, worn jeans and red hoodie worn by street hustler Billy Ray Valentine (Eddie Murphy; plate 142).

As a director I look to the costume designer to help me visually define the people the actors are portraying. The role of the costume designer remains constant regardless of genre. However, in comedy one of the most difficult, if invisible, aspects of costume design is that the audience understands the story and gets the joke. Whether the humour is broad slapstick or sophisticated repartee, whether the costume is an elegant evening gown or a gorilla suit, every article of clothing worn on screen is there for a reason.

Director John Landis's many films include Animal House, The Blues Brothers, Trading Places, An American Werewolf in London, ¡Three Amigos!, Coming To America, Burke and Hare, *and the groundbreaking* Michael Jackson's Thriller.

SILHOUETTES OF SEDUCTION

Jean L. Druesedow

FROM THE MOMENT when the early film studios discovered that their actors and actresses had a fan base and had become, in fact, film stars, their publicity departments set about creating exciting off-screen personas for these 'hot properties'. Covered extensively by fan magazines fed with endless press releases, film stars were moulded and their appearances managed to advance the studios' interests. Even a star like Katharine Hepburn, who rejected most image manipulation, created the public persona of a feisty but glamorous independent woman in slacks. She acknowledged that she worked diligently to keep this public image 'fascinating' throughout her 66-year career.

During much of the twentieth century the established public image of a film star usually determined the roles they were assigned (in the studio era) and the way they were presented on screen. For a successful and confident star, more liberties could be taken with the on-screen image and a broader range of characters could be portrayed while keeping their fans happy. However, powerful studio heads, such as Louis B. Mayer (MGM), Harry Cohn (Columbia) and Jack Warner (Warner Bros), continued to maintain control over their stars and their contract images. When Bette Davis rebelled against the lesser roles she was offered, Jack Warner sued her to force her to honour her contract. The end of the Hollywood studio system in the 1960s changed this power structure. Star power now determines the films that are made, and also how the star's persona is presented on screen. Instead of studio publicity departments creating the image, the star weighs in on aesthetic decisions, sometimes with more than just the character in mind. The costume designer must advance the story through creating the physical appearance of each character in the script and, if necessary, seamlessly merging the star's public persona and personality with the character to be played. To do this, the costume designer must keep in mind the expectations of the film-going public. Stars who are intent on looking the same

and cultivating the same image in every film will not be choosing scripts that do not further this goal.

The audience goes to the theatre to experience the story and to see the transformation of a favourite star whom they know through publicity. While they expect this transformation into a character they still enjoy seeing something of the familiar star, who may in turn make the character more accessible. In other words, costume designers must use the design tools at their disposal to seduce the audience into believing that their favourite star is the character in the context of the story. Of these creative tools, one of the most powerful is the use of line to establish the shape, or silhouette, of a character's costume. When a film is set in an historic period there is no pure re-creation of the costumes in a distant time and place. Contemporary aesthetic elements may mix with whatever historic aspects of dress and appearance the designer chooses. Without these critical design choices and blending of the historic and contemporary, films may lose their appeal for their intended audience. The concept of beauty changes constantly, as do ideas about what is 'historic'. We recognize at once whether a style is currently in fashion and whether it meshes with our idea of the past. Although costumes for historical, contemporary and futuristic films may use a fashionable silhouette, they are not 'fashion'. Costumes are designed for the specific context of the film and must meet all the requirements of the script – and sometimes the audience's expectations of the star. This does not imply that film costumes do not influence fashion after the film is released, for they often do.

The many twentieth-century Cleopatra films provide excellent examples of how Hollywood and history mix. Hollywood has dealt with the historic Cleopatra very much as painters and sculptors have presented her image since Roman times. There are no positively identified likenesses of the real Cleopatra: every image of her, whether on a coin, a statue or a painting, was invented by artists as dictated by the aesthetic of their own time. Similarly, in each film featuring Cleopatra, the temptress of the Nile is given a contemporary twist (plates 146, 149, 151). The 1917 *Cleopatra*, starring Theda Bara, is the first film credited to the costume designer George James Hopkins (plate 149). The film captured the imagination of the First World War audience

and catapulted its star to even more fame and infamy. Hopkins combined Egyptian decorative elements with the then fashionable hairstyle, silhouette and popular burlesque costumes of the day, to create a Queen of the Nile whom the audience of 1917 would find believable – and irresistible.

When Paramount costume designer Travis Banton was called in, at Claudette Colbert's insistence, to redesign her costumes for Cecil B. DeMille's 1934 *Cleopatra*, the fashionable silhouette was one of sinuous, body-skimming bias-cut gowns created by the French couturier Madeleine Vionnet (plate 150). If DeMille looked at Cleopatra (Claudette Colbert) as a femme fatale, Banton saw her lithe figure as perfect for the allure of the revealing bias cut that was the most glamorous look of the 1930s. The audience for this film would have identified immediately with the sensuousness of Banton's costumes for Colbert. In this instance, current fashion, the star and the character combined with history to evoke the idealized garments depicted in Ancient Egyptian art.

Costume designer Irene Sharaff confronted different issues when she designed the 1963 Academy Award-winning costumes for Elizabeth Taylor as Cleopatra. The actress had a voluptuous bosom, a tiny waist and round hips that Sharaff accentuated with revealing pleated silk jersey gowns and brilliantly adapted organza kaftans embroidered with Egyptian-style flourishes. The fashionable silhouette of the early 1960s was narrow and sculptural, as seen in the classic silk jersey gowns by Paris couturier Alix Grès. Irene Sharaff translated this look into costumes that referenced Ancient Egyptian art while at the same time retaining the hourglass shape preferred by Miss Taylor.

These three examples demonstrate how fashionable concepts of history, sexuality and beauty are transformed by cinema costume designers. Although George James Hopkins, Travis Banton and Irene Sharaff used Egyptian art as a starting point for their research, they could not escape the present and had to meet both the exigencies of the script and the expectations of the audience. Whether designing for black and white or colour films, all three designers created colourful garments that would support the work of the actresses by defining Cleopatra through her costume. All interpreted the past to create gowns with fashionable

silhouettes, thus contemporizing an iconic symbol of seduction in order to enchant and engage their modern audiences.

Costume designers re-creating Elizabeth I face quite a different design challenge. Unlike Cleopatra, for whom no actual portrait likeness exists, there are many formal portraits of Elizabeth I (plate 153). However, the imposing silhouette of late sixteenth-century court dress – stiff, padded, bejewelled and encumbering – has little that a contemporary audience finds attractive: the body is encased in a rigid bodice with exaggerated sleeves, the waist features an elongated point that reaches down to the genital area, and the ankle-length skirt is supported by a round farthingale or bum-roll that makes the figure look short and wide. Furthermore, the many portraits of the queen depict her with an 'official' face that changed little throughout her reign, whitened by make-up, with a plucked hairline and cradled by a large, starched ruff. Descriptions by her contemporaries were not especially flattering and included mention of a red wig, hooked nose and black, decaying teeth. These things have not discouraged costume designers from envisioning or actresses from playing the dramatic life events of the great English queen. The challenge is to make the character of Elizabeth I recognizable to a modern

LEFT
**150 Evening gown by Madeleine
Vionnet from *Vogue*, 10 November 1930
Photograph by Hoyningnen-Huene**

RIGHT
**151 Cleopatra (Claudette Colbert)
Cleopatra, 1934
Costume designer Travis Banton**

audience: no-one has yet attempted to replicate her historic personage in its glorious entirety, perhaps for fear of losing the audience.

When the French couturier Paul Poiret costumed Sarah Bernhardt as Elizabeth I in *Les amours de la reine Elisabeth* (*The Loves of Queen Elizabeth*, 1912), there was no attempt to mask the fashionable line of the day. Poiret famously took credit for ridding women of their corsets but hobbling them with narrow skirts. He retained the silhouette fashionable in 1912, adding large draped sleeves and ruffs to make his costume 'Elizabethan' (plate 152). However, when Bette Davis played Elizabeth I, careful attention was paid to details of her dress. Davis played the role twice, costumed by Orry-Kelly in 1939 (*The Private Lives of Elizabeth and Essex*; plate 156) and by Mary Wills in 1955 (*The Virgin Queen*; plate 155). In both films the costumes were softer and less extreme than those seen in portraits of the queen. The sleeves were not as high or rigid, the waist point was reduced to one more familiar from late nineteenth- and early twentieth-century evening gowns, the boned bodice was less stiff, and the floor-length skirt lacked the sharp edge of the wheel farthingale. The silhouette was modified for both appeal and movement: in addition to being appropriate for the character and meeting audience expectations, a film costume must also allow the actress to do what the part requires physically. During costume fittings Bette Davis would rehearse the repertoire of actions demanded by the script to test whether the costume would allow her to move.

152 Robert Devereux, Earl of Essex, and Queen Elizabeth I (Lou Tellegen and Sarah Bernhardt)
The Loves of Queen Elizabeth, 1912
Costume designer Paul Poiret

OPPOSITE
153 Attributed to George Gower (c.1540–96)
*The Armada Portrait of Elizabeth I, c.*1588
National Portrait Gallery, London

154 Queen Elizabeth I (Judi Dench)
Shakespeare in Love, 1998
Costume designer Sandy Powell

155 Design for Queen Elizabeth I
The Virgin Queen, 1955
Costume designer and illustrator Mary Wills

156 Queen Elizabeth I (Bette Davis)
The Private Lives of Elizabeth and Essex, 1939
Costume designer Orry-Kelly

Bette Davis

Mary Wills

The head-to-toe look of the character is essential to the realization of every role. Bette Davis was known for her willingness to undertake difficult roles that were not always glamorous, including wearing a bald cap for Elizabeth I. She fearlessly submerged both her own personality and her public image into the character. The other actress to play the role of Elizabeth twice, Cate Blanchett, progressed from youthful princess to aged queen through two films. For each, costume designer Alexandra Byrne evoked the period for the modern audience, first in the 1998 *Elizabeth*, and again for the 2007 Academy Award-winning costumes for *Elizabeth: The Golden Age*. In neither film did Byrne or the director, Shekhar Kapur, feel bound by historical accuracy. Byrne is quoted in the *Los Angeles Times* (21 November 2007) as saying that she referred to 'all kinds of images', from sixteenth-century fashions to the designs of modern couturiers such as Balenciaga and Vivienne Westwood. Similarly, designer Sandy Powell, who costumed Quentin Crisp for the 1992 *Orlando* (plate 157) and created Oscar-winning costumes for Judi Dench in *Shakespeare in Love* in 1998 (plate 154), was not constrained by historical detail. For *Shakespeare in Love*, Elizabeth I (Judi Dench) is a supporting character but has to be instantly recognizable by a single costume, so Powell gave her the exaggerated sixteenth-century silhouette. Powell believes that the costume designer's contribution to any film is to 'make some believable characters, that's all'. To do so, she focuses on the underpinnings that create her chosen silhouette. No matter what the strictures of any historical period, the film must speak to its own audience, and must be in some way modern.

As with portraits of Elizabeth I, Marie Antoinette was painted by the most renowned artists of her day. The more formal portraits by court painter Elisabeth-Louise Vigée-Lebrun (1755–1842) depict the elegance and luxury of formal eighteenth-century court dress, with the wide skirt and hooped petticoats providing one of the most recognizable silhouettes associated with the period (plate 160). Although many original garments exist in museum collections, almost nothing from the French court survived the aftermath of the French Revolution. The costume designers for both *Marie Antoinette* films – Adrian for the 1938 MGM version and Milena Canonero for the 2006 Columbia film – had access to portraits and original gowns. But just as with Cleopatra and Elizabeth I, they needed to adjust the mix of Hollywood and history. Even when the final effect of a film costume is to appear close to an authentic original, there is no need to replicate its construction. For example, the luxurious eighteenth-century Swedish royal wedding dress illustrated here (plate 166), in silver cloth trimmed with silver lace, has boning covering every centimetre of the bodice (plate 167). This would have forced the wearer's shoulders back and prevented full movement of her arms, while the heavily boned point at the centre front prevented her from bending forward at the waist. This would be a physically restrictive and highly uncomfortable costume for an actress to work in over a three-month film production. Adrian's meticulously detailed costumes for Marie Antoinette (Norma Shearer) and her court capture the eighteenth-century silhouette that the 1930s audience would have expected, including the high white wigs and expansive skirts associated with the period in the popular imagination (plates 161, 162). He gave his period silhouettes a contemporary flair with bold ornamentation echoing high fashion of the 1930s, to the delight of his audience. At the same period, Elsa Schiaparelli's Winter 1937–8 collection featured evening jackets with extravagant, 'eighteenth-century-style' embroidery, but paired with sleek evening gowns (plate 158).

Milena Canonero, costume designer for the 2006 version of *Marie Antoinette* directed by Sofia Coppola, had previously designed the Oscar-winning costumes (with Ulla-Britt Søderlund) for the eighteenth-century costume drama *Barry Lyndon* (1975), directed by Stanley Kubrick. Brilliantly true to the period, the costumes nonetheless appealed to popular taste of the mid-1970s. Lady Lyndon was played by Marissa Berenson, a high-profile fashion model who embodied the 1970s aesthetic. It was a tribute to both costume designer and the actress that in his review of the film Vincent Canby wrote: 'Marissa Berenson splendidly suits her costumes and wigs' (*New York Times*, 19 December 1975). Canonero and Søderlund had succeeded in creating costumes that were far removed from the androgynous, casual and in many ways

unkempt fashion of the day, yet they made Lady Lyndon (Marissa Berenson) sympathetic to a contemporary audience. In addition, Stanley Kubrick wished to maintain the ambience of the period and avoid artificial lighting as far as possible, so the designers had to consider the kinds of costume details that would reveal character to the audience under low or natural light (plate 165).

Director Sofia Coppola wanted the 2006 *Marie Antoinette* to appeal to audiences in their late teens and twenties. Her vision for the film was captured by Milena Canonero, whom she instructed to restrict her colour palette to the pastel shades of Ladurée macaroons (plate 163). This, combined with dresses made from feather-light silk tissue taffeta, successfully established an aura of youthful frivolity – in contrast to the richly ornamented silk brocades of the eighteenth-century French court (and Adrian's designs of 1938). Only the recognizable eighteenth-century silhouette was retained. The stiffly corseted bodices and encumbering skirts – so foreign to a young contemporary audience – made the strictures of court life realistically physical and gave the audience a sense of historical fact, while the rock and roll film score kept the film readily accessible. At times in production Kirsten Dunst, in the title role, chose not to wear a wig, so some of the high pomaded and powdered hairstyles of the 1770s and 1780s were abandoned in favour of hair dressed to evoke the period while relating more closely to the taste of a modern audience.

The connection between the film and its audience is made possible in large measure by effective costume design, the result of close collaboration by skilled individuals both behind and in front of the camera. Those participating in this exhilarating

160 Elisabeth-Louise Vigée-Lebrun
Portrait of Marie Antoinette, after 1778
Château de Versailles

161 Repairing costumes on the set of
Marie Antoinette, 1938
Costume designer Adrian

OPPOSITE
162 Marie Antoinette (Norma Shearer)
Marie Antoinette, 1938
Costume designer Adrian

OVERLEAF
163 *Marie Antoinette*, 2006
Costume designer Milena Canonero
Photoshoot for *Vogue*, 2006
© Annie Leibovitz/Contract Press

OPPOSITE
164 Costume for Marie Antoinette (Kirsten Dunst)
Marie Antoinette, 2006
Costume designer Milena Canonero
Courtesy of The One Srl, Rome

RIGHT
165 Lady Honoria Lyndon (Marisa Berenson)
Barry Lyndon, 1975
Costume designers Milena Canonero and Ulla-Britt Søderlund

BELOW
166, 167 Wedding dress of Edwige Elisabeth
Charlotte de Holstein-Gottorp, 1774,
with detail showing boning in bodice
Livrustkammeren, Stockholm

creative process must realize the director's vision while being ever mindful of the spirit of the time – and of what will make the film speak to the audience and connect them with the characters and the story. How the characters in a film are perceived is in many ways determined by a very personal and intimate visual response to costume. Actresses look the way they do on screen because the costume designer has used the tools of the craft to support their performance and define their character. In doing so the designer lures us out of our own time and into the world of the film.

Jean L. Druesedow, currently the Director of the Kent State University Museum, began her career on university faculties as a theatrical costume designer. She then joined the curatorial staff of the Costume Institute and later became the Associate Curator-in-Charge of that department at the Metropolitan Museum of Art, New York.

HOLLYWOOD AND HISTORY

Edward Maeder

THE WAY in which each generation views the world is shaped by the times in which it lives, and this is nowhere more evident than in period films. These present to a contemporary audience an interpretation of unfamiliar worlds through modern eyes, shaped by all the tastes and sensibilities of its own time. Certainly costume designers in the world of historic films strive for authenticity, to transcend contemporary fashion, creating costumes that will often appear to be faithful re-creations of clothes from an earlier era. Their audiences may not be aware, however, that these costumes reflect their own standards of style or ideas of beauty – that the cave-dwellers' costumes in *One Million B.C.* (1940) are cut to emphasize the 1940s silhouette, for example, as were the corsets and crinolines of *Gone with the Wind* (1939). These realizations only emerge with the passing of time, as tastes change with subsequent generations.

A second driving force behind costume design for historic films is the medium itself: the quest for authenticity must be tempered by the expectations and acceptance of the audience. Perhaps one of the most impressive depictions on film of ancient Egypt was the wildly successful *Cleopatra* (1934) starring Claudette Colbert as the renowned Queen of Egypt. The original designs were created in close consultation with a learned Egyptologist to ensure that they were historically 'authentic'; but they were rejected by Colbert. Creative genius and Paramount's chief costume designer Travis Banton was called in to save the day and his stunning gowns swept away the public. Colbert's pleated gown of glittering gold lamé could have been worn by any socialite to a grand evening party in 1934. The all-encompassing influence of *art moderne* can been seen in every aspect of the film, from the shape of the flowers to the curves of the Egyptian queen herself – and the effect on screen was breathtaking.

OPPOSITE
168 Rhett Butler (Clark Gable)
***Gone with the Wind*, 1939**
Costume designer Walter Plunkett

169 Wardrobe expert Otto Kottka adjusting John Barrymore's costume during production of *Marie Antoinette*, 1938
Costume designer Adrian

One of the most extravagant costume films in history was *Marie Antoinette* (1938; plate 169), with more than 2,500 costumes. Although endless research, including a number of trips to Europe to purchase fabrics and furnishings, had been carried out at great expense, the talented costume designer Gilbert Adrian employed the dressmaking practices of his time. He used bias-cut swags of silver tissue, even though dress trimmings in the eighteenth century were never cut on the bias. Even the towering white wigs (there were 22 for Marie Antoinette alone), also well researched by Sidney Guilaroff, the highly gifted and prolific wig master/designer for Metro-Goldwyn-Mayer, were purely in the style of nineteenth-century *ancien régime* revival. Norma Shearer, in the title role, had particularly beautiful shoulders and Adrian ensured that these were prominently displayed, even though

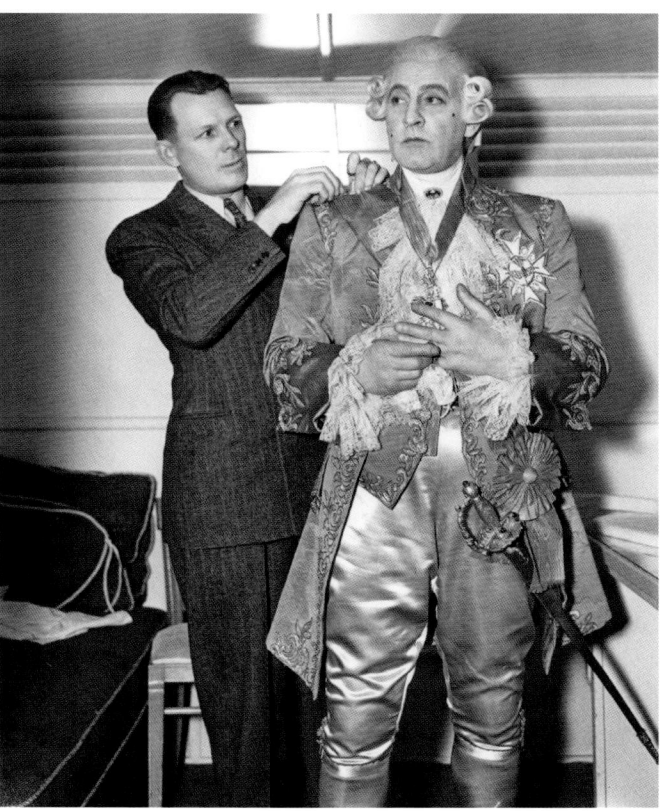

shoulders were rarely revealed in eighteenth-century court circles. Creative licence was also liberally applied to the famous 'minuet scene' in which dozens of couples were arranged in long rows that filled the huge ballroom. The investigative trips to Europe had confirmed that the Hall of Mirrors in Versailles was far too small for the kind of spectacular needed for the film, so a much larger Hall of Mirrors was built on the MGM sound stage in Culver City.

In designing the costumes for *Gone with the Wind* (1939; plates 168, 170–72) Walter Plunkett strove for authenticity, a re-creation of the way people looked in the American South during the Civil War period. He spent months researching styles, looking at fashion publications and travelling through the South, visiting plantations and interviewing survivors of the period. He was ushered into homes and proudly shown silk gowns that had belonged to grandmothers and great-grandmothers. In general the film's costumes met with critical acclaim – they were certainly extraordinarily beautiful. Viewers were convinced that they were seeing a true reflection of the past. But almost half a century later we can see that many aspects of the film's costume styles are rooted more in the 1930s than the 1860s. The hats designed by John Frederics for Scarlett O'Hara (Vivien Leigh) are not of a style worn in the Civil War: with silk ribbon bows tied under her right ear, they present an asymmetry that only became acceptable in the 1930s. In all the dresses for the film, bodices were cut to conform to the shape of the bosom, whereas in the 1860s the

170 Carreen, Scarlett and Suellen O'Hara (Ann Rutherford, Vivien Leigh and Evelyn Keyes)
Gone with the Wind, 1939
Costume designer Walter Plunkett

OPPOSITE
171 Scarlett O'Hara (Vivien Leigh) surrounded by admirers
Gone with the Wind, 1939
Costume designer Walter Plunkett

172 Walter Plunkett adjusting Leslie Howard's costume on set
Gone with the Wind, 1939
Costume designer Walter Plunkett

corset formed the basis for the fashionable shape and the bosom conformed to the corset. The crinolines in the film are exaggerated, designed in a dome-shaped style that is larger and wider than that found in surviving examples from the early 1860s. Even the men's suits in the film reflect the late 1930s cut, with broad extended shoulders, a fullness across the upper rib-cage and a narrower cut over the waist and hips. The style and cut of the lapels are strictly contemporary.

Anachronisms are found in almost every motion picture that portrays another period. While presenting an illusion of an earlier time, these films rarely replicate the exact look that prevailed; instead the costumes take elements from past styles and

combine them with aspects of contemporary fashion. The excesses that Hollywood went to are the stuff of legend. Film-makers went to great lengths to ensure that their films would be wondrous spectacles and that the actors would look gorgeous. A successful period costume, however, must be more than a beautiful work of art: it should help a film tell its story, enhance the character and contribute to the setting. Many period costumes require extensive research. Charles LeMaire worked with a curator at the Brooklyn Museum for two years as he gathered background information for the costumes in *The Egyptian* (1954). Other costume designers have spent months studying illustrations and paintings, scholarly works and historical documents. Historical sources can, however, be misleading. For example, for *Bride of Vengeance* (1949; plate 173), the story of Lucretia Borgia, Mitchell Leisen and Mary Grant based their costume designs on Italian paintings of the fifteenth century. Although the paintings show several layers in the women's gowns, the full chemise (an undergarment) was supposed to puff out through the openings in the seams left at the shoulders and elbows. In the costume these puffs are sewn into the seam, which superficially matches the painted portraits – but the garment would move quite differently if the various layers were truly independent.

In order to translate a painting into an exact replica of a period dress, a costume designer must transcend the contemporary aesthetic standard. But this is an impossible task because the costumes must appeal to the audience in an aesthetic language

173 Lucretia Borgia (Paulette Goddard)
Bride of Vengeance, 1949
Costume designers Mary Grant and Mitchell Leisen

that they will understand, yet remain consistent with the tone of the film. What is socially acceptable, beautiful or risqué varies dramatically for different periods. Compromise is also required when authenticity clashes with prevailing social mores. Attitudes about socially acceptable dress vary from period to period, and authenticity is often sacrificed when it clashes with contemporary views of decency and beauty. For *Bride of Vengeance*, for example, Mitchell Leisen wanted the actors to wear codpieces, pouches over the male genitals, for authenticity: 'We made them up … but the studio was not about to allow it and in the end they just wore tights.'

Finding authentic fabric is always a problem, as materials that were available in another time may no longer exist. To reproduce a perfect rendition of the garb of a North European lord or lady of the Middle Ages, for example, whose cloaks were

often lined with miniver – fur from the underbellies of hundreds, sometimes thousands, of squirrels – a replacement must be found. In developing turn-of-the-century costumes for *Hello, Frisco, Hello* (1943; plate 174) costume designer Helen Rose could not obtain flexible steel ribs, metal clasps and other materials needed for the construction of an authentic wasp-waisted corset because of wartime restrictions. In such situations the costume designer is forced to improvise, to adapt available materials and techniques to imitate historic ones. The designer's choices regarding accurate substitute are influenced by the contemporary aesthetic, and there is often a tendency towards the latest development in textiles.

While costumes may deviate from authenticity in silhouette, fabric and other aspects, they often include extremely precise reproductions of certain key details. In the 1962 film *Mutiny on the Bounty* (plate 175) costume designer Moss Mabry was so careful with details that he made sure to dress a number of the sailors in breeches with a drop front, the precedessor of modern fly fronts. For other sailors in the film he duplicated the striped trousers that were popular at the time of the French Revolution. For *Gone with the Wind* Walter Plunkett found a textile mill in Pennsylvania that still made authentic 1860s printed fabric, while for *That Forsyte Woman* (1949) he used colours such as 'stone' and 'ashes of roses' that were popular in the 1870s. In cases like this the costume designers' research might be described as 'costume archaeology'.

The costume designer, like the sculptor, painter or even the historian, works within physical, social and aesthetic limits to make a creation acceptable and comprehensible by contemporary standards. Because of these different factors, a work of art inevitably carries the stamp of its time, the response to the aesthetic of the day. Ultimately a viewer can distinguish between costumes from two *Cleopatra* films, one made in 1934, the other in 1963, just as a scholar of art history can distinguish between a sculpture of a Roman warrior from the first century AD and a sixteenth-century version of the same subject. Costumes for period films provide a fascinating source for understanding how each generation has looked at history, tempered by the contemporary fashion and convention, since the very beginning of the film industry.

Edward Maeder was formerly a curator at the Fashion Institute of Technology and at Los Angeles County Museum of Art, and Director of Exhibits and Curator of Textiles at Historic Deerfield, a complex of historic houses and other buildings in Western Massachusetts. He has lectured on costumes, textiles and conservation throughout the world, and is the author of Hollywood and History: Costume Design in Film *(1987).*

174 Trudy Evans (Alice Faye)
Hello, Frisco, Hello, 1943
Costume designer Helen Rose

175 First Lieutenant Fletcher Christian, Captain William Bligh, Seaman Edward Birkett, Seaman John Mills, John Williams and Michael Byrne (Marlon Brando, Trevor Howard, Gordon Jackson, Richard Harris, Duncan Lamont and Chips Rafferty)
Mutiny on the Bounty, 1962
Costume designer Moss Mabry

BANTON'S BEAUTIES

Deborah Nadoolman Landis

TRAVIS BANTON knew how to dress a woman. as one colleague remarked, 'Carole Lombard was just a tootsie when she came to Paramount, but Banton saw things in her that even she didn't know she had'. Now obscured by the substantial shadow of MGM's Adrian, costume designer and magician Travis Banton conjured the glamour of Paramount's Golden Age, creating luminous designs for legendary stars Mae West, Claudette Colbert, Carol Lombard and the extraordinary Marlene Dietrich. The 'less is more' treatment worked for the brassy blonde Lombard, who played comedy in understated clothes that were never funny. Colbert never looked more at ease than when practically naked in Banton's cut-to-the-waist gowns for *Cleopatra* (1934). And he could pile the jewels on Dietrich without ever gilding that lily. As Paramount's chief costume designer from 1927 to 1938, and with well over a hundred film credits to his name, Banton's ravishing work includes the timeless classics *Blonde Venus* (1932), *Belle of the Nineties* (1934) and *My Man Godfrey* (1936).

Heralded by Paramount co-founder Jesse Lasky as a 'famous Parisian designer', Banton was hired by the studio in 1924 to design *The Dressmaker from Paris* (1925), which Lasky promoted as 'a parade of fashion and beauty unprecedented in the history of films'. The studios of the day leveraged the allure of new fashions to seduce a female audience, but with his theatre background Banton understood that designing costumes was not all about being dressmaker. He insisted:

> My aim is for the legitimate. When a
> woman is required to dress for golf in
> a certain scene there is really no point
> in making her seem ready for a dance
> at the country club. When she is fitted
> with a bathing suit it should at least
> look suitable for water. Keeping this in
> mind … I then muster new fashions
> and modify and adjust them to the
> needs of the role.

Like Adrian, Banton created distinctive personas for each actress while enabling them to fully

176 Travis Branton and Marlene Dietrich on the set of *Angel*, 1937

177 Travis Branton and Carole Lombard on the set of *Rumba*, 1935

OPPOSITE
178 Carole Lombard, 1933

inhabit the characters in the story. Because he was responsible for so many memorable gowns, it may come as a surprise that Banton believed that 'character' comes first. But his creative process always included his star:

> I unfailingly discuss their reactions
> to a role – how they wish to look
> for the part; and between the stars'
> own conception of character and
> their own intrinsic personalities
> a very satisfactory result is attained.
> Each star has her own particular
> idiosyncrasies, I might say,
> 'hallucinations,' as to her defects
> and best points. These must
> be tactfully and diplomatically
> approached and overcome.

Hollywood columnist Hedda Hopper remarked that before Dietrich met Travis, she looked more like a *hausfrau*. Banton worked tirelessly with Dietrich and director Joseph Von Sternberg to craft her public image; they were a team for whom the

179 Mademoiselle Amy Jolly (Marlene Dietrich)
Morocco, 1930
Costume designer Travis Banton

180 Concha Perez (Marlene Dietrich)
The Devil is a Woman, 1935
Costume designer Travis Banton

181 Shanghai Lily (Marlene Dietrich)
Shanghai Express, 1932
Costume designer Travis Banton

only acceptable outcome was perfection. Dietrich's daughter Maria Riva remembered that 'Day in and day out, [Dietrich and Banton] worked, sometimes for 12-hour stretches. My mother never tired, such normal things as breaking for food, bathroom, and rest did not exist while Banton prepared the clothes for a film.'

A superb illustrator and sketch artist, Banton mapped out each costume meticulously in his head: 'I have always made only one sketch of any costume I create and I don't bother with roughs. I think of the character as I sketch, so I know just

where I want a fold to fall or a neckline to drop.'

Travis Banton was an international trendsetter and considered a style superstar by contemporary fashion and fan publications – indeed, the Paramount publicity department made certain that he was available to offer advice and counsel to his adoring female audience. Eternally elegant, he resisted when Technicolor revolutionized the big screen in the late 1930s. He was famous for the purity of his bias-cut dresses and use of contrast, especially white. A contemporary article noted: 'White was not admitted on

ABOVE
**182 Sketch for
Ruby Carter
Belle of the Nineties, 1934
Costume designer and
illustrator Travis Banton**

RIGHT
**183 Sketch for
Concha Perez
The Devil is a Woman, 1935
Costume designer and
illustrator Travis Banton**

the set until Travis Banton gowned Pola Negri in white, a color that she loves more than all others…'. As the trend towards colour accelerated, Banton complained:

> Hollywood will meet any sudden demand for exotic color in film costumes. Although I have always used colors that I considered most becoming to the star, I will abandon as many colored costumes as possible in any Technicolor film … I tend to tone down the coloring of my costumes so that there will be a minimum of color.

He died in 1958 at the age of 64, leaving behind a glittering legacy steeped in the glamour of the 1930s, a legacy that lives on the films he designed. These unforgettable images of Colbert, Dietrich, Lombard and Mae West have taken their place in popular culture. Imbued with his wit, imagination, and pitch-perfect taste, Travis Banton's incomparable costumes have influenced generations of designers.

184 Ruby Carter (Mae West)
Belle of the Nineties, 1934
Costume designer Travis Banton

OVERLEAF
185 Cleopatra (Claudette Colbert)
Cleopatra, 1934
Costume designer Travis Banton

186 Costume for Cleopatra
Cleopatra, 1934
**Costume designer Travis Banton
The Collection of Motion
Picture Costume Design Larry McQueen**

COSTUME AND FASHION

Valerie Steele

DEBORAH NADOOLMAN LANDIS has long been frustrated by what she calls 'the mellifluous but misleading moniker "fashion in film"'.[1] Deborah is a costume designer while I am a fashion historian and curator, so we approach the subject from somewhat different perspectives. Nevertheless, I agree that to talk about 'fashion and film' is problematic, since the relationship between fashion and film costume is complex and often ambiguous.

Actors obviously wear *clothes* on stage or screen, often fashionable-looking clothes, and sometimes even clothes created by fashion designers (as opposed to costume designers), but it is probably not legitimate to describe such clothes as 'fashion'. Fashion is usually defined as the prevailing style of dress at any given time, with the implication that it is characterized, above all, by change. As Shakespeare put it, 'The fashion wears out more apparel than the man'. Fashion is also a verb, referring to the way things are made, and the changing forms they take. More generally, there are fashions in food, music, and even the names we give our children. It could be said, therefore, that fashion is 'a matter of taste'.[2]

When I launched my journal *Fashion Theory*, I proposed a new definition of fashion as 'the cultural construction of the embodied identity', placing the emphasis on bodies and identities, and deliberately including all forms of self-fashioning, including street styles such as punk, and body modifications such as tattooing, as well as modish clothes created by professional fashion designers. Like fashion, film costume involves the creation of identity, but it is the identity of a particular character within the film. Although certain fashion designers do think of a particular 'type' of woman who wears their clothes, and may even imagine her doing certain things, rather like a character in a film, inevitably the reality is more complicated and the identity of the women who buy and wear the clothes impinges on the designer's fantasies.

Fashion is also a *system*, involving not only the production and consumption of fashionable clothes, but also discourses and imagery. It seems to me that 'costume' refers to more limited categories of clothing – especially theatrical costume (and, by extension, film costume), and perhaps also certain types of ceremonial and festival costume. While film undoubtedly constitutes a system as well, complete with a superstructure of film history and film theory, film costume is only a component of this system. The work of the costume designer is subordinate to the vision of the film director, and may also be modified in collaboration with the actor.

By the eighteenth century Paris had been established as the centre of fashion, and actresses were among the leading trendsetters. At this time most actresses wore their own fashionable clothes on stage, regardless of the character they played or the period within which the action was set. Indeed, as late as the beginning of the 1920s many actresses still wore their own clothes on screen or stage. Over time, however, professional costume designers began creating theatrical costumes that were regarded as appropriate for the play (or film) and the part. For example, when Norma Shearer appeared in the film *Marie Antoinette* (1938) she wore clothes by the famous Hollywood costume designer Gilbert Adrian. Although Adrian did a great deal of research into eighteenth-century fashion (and court dress, which was a slightly antiquated and ceremonial type of fashion), and the studio even had special fabrics woven to replicate historical prototypes, Shearer's costumes only superficially resembled actual eighteenth-century fashions.

Although Adrian's costumes looked authentic to most viewers *at the time*, today it is easier to see how the historical silhouette was compromised in accordance with 1930s aesthetic values. Both the neckline and the torso of Shearer's gowns, for example, are typical of fashionable dress of the later 1930s, not the 1770s. To point this out is not to criticize Adrian, since strict historical accuracy is not the purpose of film costume. Nevertheless, it is worth drawing attention to the relationship between fashion as it actually existed in the past and what is known as 'period costume'.

When Sofia Coppola directed her film *Marie Antoinette* (2006), she instructed costume designer Milena Canonero to use

fresh, bright pastel colours, like macaroons from Ladurée, to create a sugary sweet image of youth and frivolity. Canonero duly stylized and simplified the heavy fabrics and rich ornament of eighteenth-century court fashion, deliberately avoiding the look of a period film. Coppola's *Marie Antoinette* received extensive favourable publicity in the fashion press. In particular, Kirsten Dunst appeared on the cover of the September 2006 issue of *Vogue*, wearing a bright pink dress, which was apparently designed by Canonero especially for this photograph since it did not actually appear in the film (plate 187). The headline read: 'Kirsten Dunst as the Teen Queen Who Rocked Versailles'. Fashion photographer Annie Leibovitz also photographed Dunst as Marie Antoinette for *Vogue*, wearing romantic fashions such as a pink and grey taffeta evening dress by Alexander McQueen and a black ballgown by John Galliano for Christian Dior Haute Couture. Reporting on the *Vogue* photo shoot, some journalists appeared to think that McQueen and Galliano had actually designed the film's costumes. This type of mistake, which is not rare, must be deeply discouraging to professional costume designers.

Despite the extensive coverage in *Vogue*, it is not clear to what extent Canonero's film costumes influenced fashion that season. Coppola's friend Marc Jacobs claimed to be influenced by the film, but this is not immediately apparent. Anna Sui's spring 2007 Pirate collection was also, she says, partly inspired by Coppola's *Marie Antoinette*, but also by several other films, including *Golden Earrings* (1947), *All Dolled Up: A New York Dolls Story* (2005), *The Pirate* (1948) and *Captain Blood* (1935). Nevertheless, Coppola's film may well exert an indirect influence on fashion designers in the future, if only because Marie Antoinette is widely regarded as a

historical fashion icon with at least some contemporary relevance (Madonna had already dressed up as Marie Antoinette in 1990).

Under what circumstances do film costumes influence contemporary fashion? The short answer might be whenever fashion designers are inspired by the costumes in a particular film. This happens, but probably less often today than in the past. Certain veteran fashion designers, such as Giorgio Armani, Valentino and Ralph Lauren, have often described being greatly influenced by films, and especially by the glamorous stars of the 1930s through to the 1950s, whose on- and off-stage style was created by the studios and in-house costume designers. More recent fashion designers tend to draw on a wider range of visual sources, of which film is only one of many, although they also often say that they are attracted to the look and style of particular actresses, such as Elizabeth Taylor, Faye Dunaway and Charlotte Rampling.

Among contemporary fashion designers who claim to be influenced by film, Anna Sui has cited a wide variety of films as inspiration for her collections. Her autumn 1996 Bloomsbury collection was partly inspired by *Carrington* (1995); her spring 1997 Ballet collection by *A Midsummer Night's Dream* (1935); her spring 1999 Glam collection by *Velvet Goldmine* (1998), *Lisztomania* (1975) and *Born to Boogie* (1972); her autumn 2001 Pop collection by *Chelsea Girls* (1966) and *Midnight Cowboy* (1969); her spring 2004 Beach collection by *Beach Blanket Bingo* (1965), *Gidget Goes Hawaiian* (1961) and *How to Stuff a Wild Bikini* (1965); her spring/summer 2010 Circus collection by *Doctor Dolittle* (1967; plates 189, 190), *La Strada* (1954) and *Trapeze* (1956), and so on.[3] As these examples indicate, however, the old paradigm that a newly released film has costumes that can immediately influence the world of fashion is no longer very relevant. Although Anna Sui sometimes appears to have seen a recent film and to have been inspired by its costumes, more often she draws on old films, perhaps partly because she has an idea (such as the circus) which then leads her to look at a range of circus films on DVD. Even when she is inspired by a newly released film, it is often set in the past and so fits well with her use of retro fashion references.

In general, it is surprisingly difficult to demonstrate that particular film costumes have actually had an important influence on fashion. It is sometimes even difficult to determine *who* was responsible for the clothes in a certain film. For example, for Blake Edwards's *Breakfast at Tiffany's* (1961) the French couturier Hubert de Givenchy designed Audrey Hepburn's wardrobe, including the iconic black dress (plate 192), which has entered fashion history. Patricia Neal's wardrobe was designed by Pauline Trigère, and the other costumes in the film were designed by Edith Head, who was head of the costume department. Very often costume designers are quite anonymous to the general public –

188 **Marie Antoinette (Norma Shearer)**
Marie Antoinette, 1938
Costume designer Adrian

OPPOSITE
189 **Circus collection, spring/summer 2010**
Inspired by *Doctor Dolittle*, 1967
Designer Anna Sui

190 **Dr John Dolittle (Rex Harrison)**
Doctor Dolittle, 1967
Costume designer Ray Aghayan

especially when they collaborate with a fashion designer. A case in point is Luis Buñuel's *Belle de Jour* (1967), which featured an incredibly chic wardrobe designed for Catherine Deneuve by the great French couturier Yves Saint Laurent. Although Deneuve's clothes worked well as film costume to help create the character of Séverine Serizy, a repressed bourgeois housewife moonlighting as a prostitute, they also functioned beautifully as contemporary fashion by a master of the art. But Saint Laurent was not the costume designer for *Belle de Jour*; he dressed only the title character. The name of the costume designer, Hélène Nourry, was little known except to film experts.

Hollywood costume designer Theadora Van Runkle has received credit for the terrific 1930s-inspired suits, dresses, and accessories worn by Faye Dunaway in *Bonnie and Clyde* (1967; plate 191). Her berets and scarves certainly launched a trend for these accessories, as documented in fashion periodicals; but what about the rest of Bonnie's costumes? In fact, these also

influenced fashion that year, no doubt partly because fashion trendsetters were already scouring thrift stores for vintage 1930s clothes. After the film was released, manufacturers jumped on the fashion bandwagon and began producing midi-skirts, slinky bias-cut dresses and – yes – berets.

In other words, film costume has an impact when it is in sync with other trends in fashion. But this seems to be happening much less frequently today than in previous decades. As recently as the 1970s and 1980s, manufacturers produced clothes and accessories adapted from film costumes. Santo Loquasto's costume designs for *Desperately Seeking Susan* (1985), for example, had Madonna in lace gloves, hair accessories, black leggings, and a brassière worn over her clothes – all of which launched, or rather reinforced, trends in fashion. Underwear as outerwear already existed in the fashion world: Vivienne Westwood showed brassières worn over clothing as early as 1983. When the style appeared in a film, it gained greater traction.

Very few current films have the kind of vivid and instantaneous impact on fashion that *Bonnie and Clyde* did, and fewer still feature the high fashion of *Belle de Jour*. This is not to say that there are no longer stylish films that create indelible images – think of Uma Thurman in *Pulp Fiction* (1994; plate 196), although for most viewers their lingering memory is not so much of Betsy Heimann's costumes (except perhaps the white blouse) as of Uma's dark bobbed hair – and the desire to purchase her Chanel Rouge Noir nail polish.

There is, of course, an entire genre of films *about* fashion, from *Funny Face* (1957) to *The Devil Wears Prada* (2006; plate 194). While to the uninitiated such films as *Funny Face* and *Breakfast at Tiffany's* appear to epitomize the relationship between film and fashion, fashion designers are much more likely to cite obscure, cult films as influential to them. So says Simon Doonan, window dresser extraordinaire and now Ambassador-at-Large for Barneys New York, who recently curated the 'Fashion in Film' event at the Museum of Art and Design, New York. For this Doonan selected a number of cult films, some of which, such as the horror film *Eyes of Laura Mars* (1978; plate 193), are set in the world of fashion, while others, such as Russ Meyer's cult exploitation flick *Faster, Pussycat! Kill! Kill!* (1965), are not. But all are characterized by a certain 'deranged' sensibility (in Doonan's words). *Eyes of Laura Mars* is about a fashion photographer who 'sees' murders being committed whenever she looks through her camera lens. I used to show this film to my fashion history students because of the way it evoked the 'terrorist chic' of late 1970s fashion photography. The film did not set the trend, but it exposed it to an audience beyond people who read *Vogue* and were already familiar with the sexy, violent images of photographers such as Helmut Newton, Guy Bourdin, and Chris Von Wangenheim.

Doonan's film series also featured legendary fashion photographer William Klein's wickedly satiric film *Qui êtes-vous, Polly Maggoo?* (*Who Are You, Polly Maggoo?*, 1966; plate 195), which concerns the strange world of a fashion model working in 1960s Paris. Klein knew all about this world through his work as a fashion photographer, and his film features various types familiar to fashion

193 *Eyes of Laura Mars*, 1978
Costume designer Theoni V. Aldredge
Photographer Rebecca Blake

194 Miranda Priestly (Meryl Streep)
***The Devil Wears Prada*, 2006**
Costume designer Patricia Field

OPPOSITE
195 Polly Maggoo (Dorothy McGowan)
***Qui êtes-vous, Polly Maggoo?*, 1966**
Costume designer Janine Klein

196 Vincent Vaga and Mia Wallace (John Travolta and Uma Thurman)
***Pulp Fiction*, 1994**
Costume designer Betsy Heimann

people. There is the arrogant French fashion designer, apparently based on Paco Rabanne, who creates metal garments which gash the models' flesh. Sycophantic fashion journalists wait for a cue from their queen bee before applauding; based on Diana Vreeland, this alpha fashion editor rises slowly to her feet before exclaiming (in execrable French): '*C'est formidable!*' – thus unleashing a torrent of applause. There is even a professor who pontificates for a television crew about the hidden meaning of the Cinderella story, triumphantly concluding: 'So there you are: fetishism, mutilation, pain. Fashion in a nutshell.'

Fashion is like a giant vacuum cleaner that sucks up all manner of visual material – from cinema, art, sub-culture and pornography to old copies of *National Geographic*. Within their mental image files fashion designers may certainly store many film stills, but not necessarily those one might expect – and they tend to be conceptually divorced from their original function within the film. Similarly, film costumes are 'read' by fashion designers simply as fashion images, no more or less than famous fashion photographs. In short, what begins as film costume is transformed, whether the costume designer likes it or not, into fashion.

Director and chief curator of the Museum at the Fashion Institute of Technology, New York, Valerie Steele is also editor-in-chief of Fashion Theory and author of more than a dozen books on the history of fashion.

BEATON'S FAIR LADY

Keith Lodwick

SIR CECIL BEATON (1904–80) was one of Great Britain's most influential twentieth-century theatre and film designers, socialite, photographer and writer of remarkable memoirs. He was deeply immersed in the Edwardian period – in which *My Fair Lady* (1964) was set – and this shaped his conception of luxury and elegance. He had a profound understanding of the colour, texture and fabric of the period, which lent his designs an air of authenticity.

Beaton had a long association with *My Fair Lady*. He was the costume designer for the 1956 Lerner and Loewe Broadway production starring Julie Andrews and Rex Harrison, for which he won the Tony Award for Best Costume Design. The production ran for 2,717 performances, a Broadway record at the time.

When Warner Bros bought the film rights, Beaton was hired as the costume designer and art director, a rare opportunity as the roles are normally split. As a consequence, he was responsible for the visual style of the entire production. Warner Bros chief Jack Warner cast Audrey Hepburn as Eliza Doolittle, with Rex Harrison reprising his stage success as Henry Higgins. Hepburn was famous for her elegance in such iconic roles as *Sabrina* (1954) and Holly Golightly in *Breakfast at Tiffany's* (1961), so transforming her from a Covent Garden ragamuffin into Higgins's 'fair lady' was a particular challenge for Beaton and his team. Hepburn's elfin beauty was hard to suppress, even under layers of de-glamorizing make-up:

> Audrey herself was waiting for me to direct the various hairstyles she should wear in the interim stages between being the cockney flower-seller and the resplendent butterfly. Tough going. Tests were made with no make-up, with a pale, opalescent foundation, then a strong make-up, with lips, without lips, with dirt, without dirt and hair matted and covered in with dust.[1]

Throughout the production Beaton worked closely with the wardrobe department at Warner Bros, which he clearly relished:

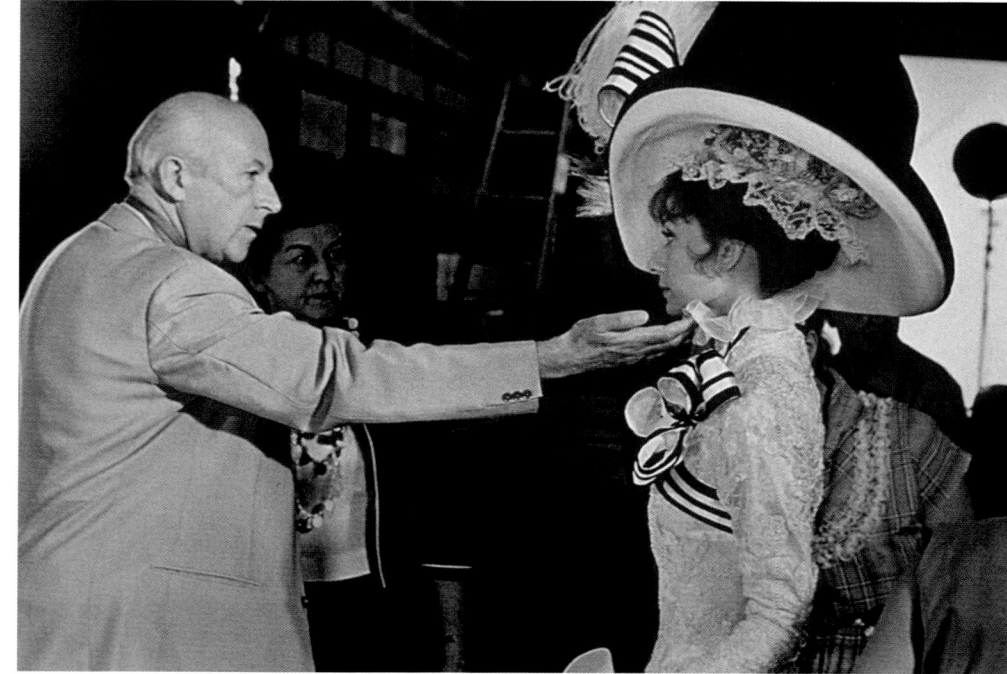

197 Cecil Beaton checking Audrey Hepburn's costume on the set of *My Fair Lady*, 1964

198 Eliza Doolittle and Professor Henry Higgins (Audrey Hepburn and Rex Harrison) *My Fair Lady*, 1964 Costume designer Cecil Beaton

OPPOSITE
199 Rex Harrison and Audrey Hepburn (on slant boards) during production of *My Fair Lady*, 1964

In the workrooms, a row of toiles of the Ascot costumes were on stands for my inspection and criticism. They left nothing to be desired. Hundreds of yards of material and trimmings were chosen, and forthwith ordered, and the enthusiasm of Anne Laune and her staff was infectious.[2]

Eleanor Abbey was Beaton's assistant on the film:

> Eleanor has found, among a collection of old clothes some oddly assorted garments that vaguely resemble the rough, pencilled suggestions I gave her. These she has re-cut and pinned together to create a poignant first appearance for Eliza. When Audrey saw Eliza's thin green coat, drab skirts and black boater, she was so moved by compassion that she gulped.[3]

Creating a suitably different costume for Eliza in her first public appearance as the transformed flower-girl was a major challenge. Director George Cukor had expressed his desire for Hepburn to look 'clean, slightly comic, but not

chic'.[4] Beaton responded in style. His black-and-white dress for Eliza is a most impressive re-creation of Edwardian costuming, constructed from silk with a hand-embroidered flower motif to symbolize the girl's blossoming. When Hepburn appeared on the set, Beaton 'yelled with laughter',[5] delighted that the dress was 'funny, elegant and just right for the scene'.[6]

The Royal Ascot races scene, with over four hundred costumes, was one of the biggest design challenges of the production. Having written an article for *Vogue* in 1930 entitled 'Ascots of the Past', Beaton had been in a sense artistically prepared for this all his professional life. For his film designs he fused historical descriptions of the famous Black Ascot of 1911, the first

Ascot racing season after the death of King Edward VII, with eyewitness accounts. When he consulted his friend Lady Diana Cooper to discover what her mother, the Duchess of Rutland, wore at Ascot, Lady Diana replied:

Certainly *cream*. A straw hat trimmed, of course, by herself with little bits of

bird's breast and/ or ribbon in dirty pink, wide-ish brimmed and fairly shallow. Cream skirt to the ground and cream shirt, lace scarves around the neck. Good beige gloves (long), very high heeled shoes she hoped didn't show, parasol of course.[7]

Beaton recalled Audrey's first appearance during preparations for the Ascot scene:

in the middle of the crowds of racegoers Audrey appeared to be tested in her ballroom dress and coiffure.

Never has she more lived up to her name, and never was her allure more obvious than now as she smiled radiantly or shyly, flickering her eyelids, lowered her lashes, blinked, did all the tricks of allure with enormous assurance. She gyrated in front of the camera while two hundred extras watched. She was vastly entertained that some of them were scrutinising her through their race glasses.[8]

Audrey Hepburn wearing Cecil Beaton's stunning black-and-white creation for the Royal Ascot scene remains one of the film's most

ABOVE
200 Sketch of Eliza Doolittle, *My Fair Lady*, 1964 **Costume designer and illustrator Cecil Beaton**

BELOW
201 Colonel Hugh Pickering, Professor Henry Higgins and Eliza Doolittle (Wilfrid Hyde-White, Rex Harrison and Audrey Hepburn) on the set of *My Fair Lady*, 1964

OPPOSITE
202 Eliza Doolittle (Audrey Hepburn) *My Fair Lady*, 1964 **Costume designer and photographer Cecil Beaton**

enduring images. When the costume came up for auction in 2011 (sold as part of the Debbie Reynolds collection), it fetched the unprecedented sum of $3.7 million.

During the course of shooting the film Beaton took every opportunity to photograph Hepburn. In one famous two-day session he photographed her in each of the costumes that were to be worn by the extras in the Ascot scene. Beaton and Hepburn's collaboration thus resulted in some of the most iconic photographic records of a motion picture production. Hepburn was thrilled with the results and wrote to Beaton afterwards:

Dearest C.B.
Ever since I can remember I have always so badly wanted to be beautiful. Looking at those photographs last night I saw that, for a short time at least, I am, because of you, Audrey[9]

The film – and its costumes – were a huge critical and commercial success. Released in 1964, *My Fair Lady* was nominated for twelve Academy Awards and won eight. Beaton won two of them, for Color Art Direction and Color Costume Design, the only designer ever to win in both categories.

UNFASHIONING COSTUME DESIGN

Booth Moore

THERE HAS always been a tension between fashion and costume design. Costume design is regarded as a creative art, and fashion design as a creative industry. But as the fashion critic of the *Los Angeles Times*, I have a front row seat to both, and have learned how they frequently intersect.

On the surface, they are different disciplines. Fashion designers are beholden to sales, and costume designers are beholden to stories, a notion held so dear that the latter chafes at appearing in the fashion section of the newpaper with the former. But they both deal in fantasy – and reality. And, if you appreciate the art of fashion, you should appreciate the art of costume design.

Fashion designers pull inspiration from the ether and translate the zeitgeist. Their currency is desire, and their stage is the catwalk. They build a brand image, sometimes even a whole luxury lifestyle, in hopes that the public will take notice. Costume designers pull inspiration from the script and translate the director's vision. Their currency is truth and they set the stage. They build characters, creating a whole world of time and place, in hopes that it looks effortless. That makes costume design fashion design's brainier cousin – more purposeful, steeped in historical research and obsessed with details, even ones the audience never sees.

Costume designers create clothing to help an actor find a character (Charlie Chaplin's choice of a tight coat, baggy pants, derby hat and oversized shoes helped him find *The Tramp*). Certainly glamour, and creating standout pieces, is part of the job. (Edith Head's mink-skirted sequinned gown worn by Ginger Rogers in the 1944 film *Lady in the Dark* [plates 205, 206], touted as the most expensive film costume at the time, would be a prime example.) But far more often the job is to make the costumes

OPPOSITE
203 Alex Owens (Jennifer Beals)
***Flashdance*, 1983**
Costume designer Michael Kaplan

RIGHT
204 Letty Lynton (Joan Crawford)
***Letty Lynton*, 1932**
Costume designer Adrian

OVERLEAF
205 Liza Elliot (Ginger Rogers)
***Lady in the Dark*, 1944**
Costume designer Edith Head

206 Costume for Liza Elliot
***Lady in the Dark*, 1944**
Costume designer Edith Head
Collection BFI Archive

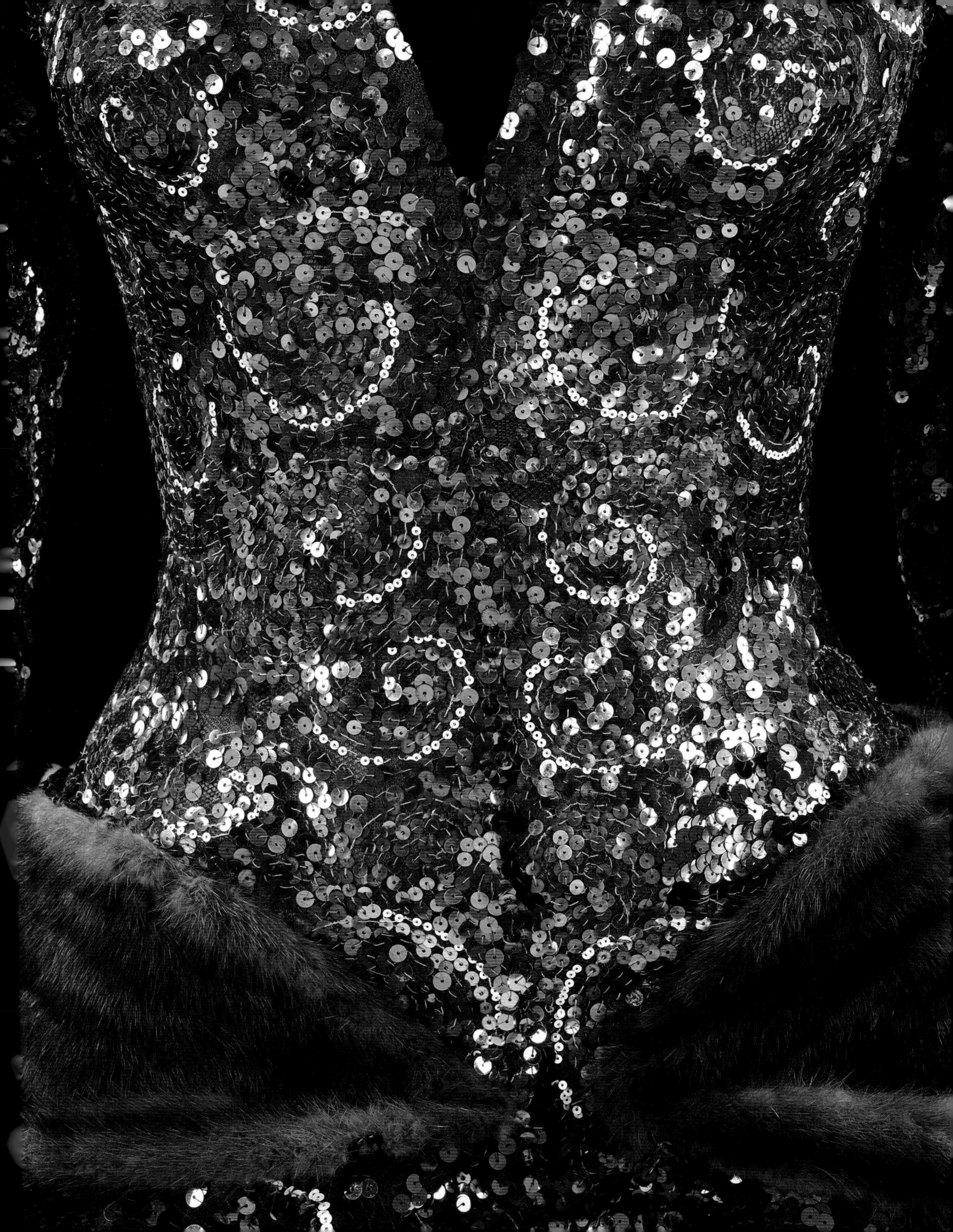

207 Effie Trinket (Elizabeth Banks)
The Hunger Games, 2012
Costume designer Judianna Makovsky

realistic enough that they simultaneously further the story and disappear into the film.

For costume designers, every decision must be justifiable, taking into account the fabrics and materials that were in use – and in fashion – in a given time and place. Take the 2010 film *True Grit*, Joel and Ethan Coen's take on the 1968 novel about a headstrong young girl named Mattie Ross (Hailee Steinfeld) who sets out to avenge her father's murder in 1870s-era Indian Territory. Ross hits the trail, wearing her father's oversized coat cinched with a belt (plate 81). The only problem was that men did not wear belts at that period. Costume designer Mary Zophres justified the decision thus: men used leather straps to cinch saddle rolls, and that is how Mattie would have acquired a belt.

To see film costumes in this context is a reminder of the role that style – not fashion – plays in everyday life, and the subtle cues given off by choosing to wear one thing or another – French cuffs versus barrel cuffs, for example, or a narrow spread versus a widespread collar. For fictional film characters and real people alike, clothing is an amalgam of personal stories and style choices.

Of the two disciplines, fashion is the one that is supposed to be rooted in reality, but catwalk collections are exercises in pure fantasy – Hollywood-worthy productions, such as Alexander McQueen's human chessboard (plate 209) and underwater world of Atlantis, which spin intoxicating stories to sell perfume and other affordable luxuries to a world watching on the Internet. (No wonder that so many of today's fashion designers are referred to as 'creative directors'.)

Costume designers, on the other hand, strive for reality to sell a fantasy. But the two disciplines are not mutually exclusive. Fashion designers Coco Chanel, Yves Saint Laurent, Giorgio Armani and Kate and Laura Mulleavy of Rodarte have all worked as costume designers. And there is cross-pollination. What appears on screen influences the catwalk and the street. Indeed, film costume design may be Los Angeles' most profound contribution to fashion. For example, *Annie Hall* (1977) helped establish men's wear as a chic alternative for women in the late 1970s (plate 208). Ruth Morley was the costume designer on the film, though the baggy trousers, waistcoats, neckties and floppy hats were sourced from second-hand and vintage shops all over New York's East Village. The 1983 film *Flashdance* (plate 203) set off a craze for ripped sweatshirts and legwarmers, but Michael Kaplan's

costumes also reflected the fitness-wear-as-fashion trend of the time. And Audrey Hepburn's two distinct looks in the 1954 film *Sabrina* (plates 210, 211) – she played the tomboy in Capri pants and a bateau top and the sophisticate in a strapless gown with detachable train – proved how a fashion designer (Hubert de Givenchy) and a costume designer (Edith Head) both can make worthy contributions to creating lasting sartorial images on screen.

And yet, when it comes to inspiring others, costume designers rarely get credit – or remuneration, even when films and TV shows spin off commercial cosmetics and clothing lines based on their work, such as the *Mad Men* collection for Banana Republic and *The Hunger Games* Capitol Colours collection of nail polishes for China Glaze. It is no wonder that, after seeing so many of his designs for screen adapted for retail (Macy's sold thousands of copies of his stunning white cotton organdy gown with ruffled puffed sleeves from the 1932 film *Letty Lynton* [plate 204]), costume designer Adrian decided to open a fashion salon of his own after his retirement from MGM in 1942.

But fashion designers are the pop culture celebrities, the subject of solo museum exhibitions and the source of endless fascination in books and magazines. When costume designers do their job, they leave no fingerprints – until now, when at last a spotlight will be shone on an art form that by its very nature is in the shadows.

Booth Moore is the Los Angeles Times *Fashion Critic. She lives in Los Angeles where she has been covering Hollywood and style for 15 years.*

BELOW
209 Alexander McQueen's human chessboard, spring/ summer collection 2005
Designer Alexander McQueen

OVERLEAF
210, 211 Sabrina Fairchild (Audrey Hepburn)
***Sabrina*, 1954**
Costume designers Hubert de Givenchy and Edith Head

208 Annie Hall and Alvy Singer
(Diane Keaton and Woody Allen)
***Annie Hall*, 1977**
Costume designer Ruth Morley

TRANSFORMATIONS **AN INTERVIEW WITH ROBERT DE NIRO**

Deborah Nadoolman Landis

THE AMERICAN actor, producer and director Robert De Niro is best known for his roles as the young Vito Corleone in *The Godfather, Part II* (1974), cab driver Travis Bickle in *Taxi Driver* (1976), Michael Vronsky in *The Deer Hunter* (1978), casino director Sam 'Ace' Rothstein in *Casino* (1995) and, more recently, as Jack Byrnes in *Meet the Parents* (2000) and *Meet the Fockers* (2004). De Niro has produced more than thirty films and directed two, *A Bronx Tale* (1993) and *The Good Shepherd* (2006).

De Niro's immersion into his characters is legendary, assisted by his close collaboration with production and costume designers. He is also known for valuing costumes more than many actors: he personally keeps his own cos-

tumes after his films, donating them and supporting ancillary material to the Harry Ransom Center at the University of Texas in Austin, enabling future generations to study and enjoy the art of costume design.

Deborah Nadoolman Landis *When did you begin collecting?*
Robert De Niro I used the jacket and the boots from Paul Schrader, they put [the army jacket] in some Hard Rock café and I tried to get it back. When I was at Western Costume and working on movies like *The Godfather*, I'd see the boots from *Bonnie and Clyde* and they had them to put on somebody else. Then when I did *New York, New York* there were things that disappeared and I thought: let me hold onto

stuff myself because otherwise it just becomes nothing. I'd collected some things before then, over the years. Later I did it very consistently and consciously – you might as well try to keep it together.

DNL *When you first get a script and you read the part, do you see the person in your mind's eye?*
RDN Sometimes I do. Sometimes I try to look for a real example in a person or people and then I see what they would be wearing and often it's not what you would think it would be. It's almost a cliché but when they're wearing it, it's real and so how do you make it as real? And what are they doing that makes it real when they're wearing it – like being worn a lot, rather than being aged by the wardrobe department.

LEFT
212 Sketch for Vito Corleone
The Godfather, Part II, 1974
Costume designer and illustrator Theadora Van Runkle

ABOVE
213 Vito Corleone (Robert De Niro)
The Godfather, Part II, 1974
Costume designer Theadora Van Runkle

DNL *How do you start becoming that person?*
RDN Sometimes when you put something on it just feels right and it helps you get a sense of who you are as a character. Maybe it's something you associate with that you can't even remember, that subconsciously connects to trip something off in your mind to make you feel more like that character or what that character gives off. It helps you believe who you are as that character.

DNL *You played real people in* Casino *and* Raging Bull. *Do you try to be them?*
RDN No, some people can but we are doing our interpretation of what he [Jake La Motta] was and what his life was, and so you have to make it your own. You don't necessarily want to

TOP
**214 Rupert Pupkin
(Robert De Niro)
The King of Comedy, 1983
Costume designer
Richard Bruno**

ABOVE
**215 Michael Vronsky
(Robert De Niro)
The Deer Hunter, 1978
Costume designer
Eric Seelig**

RIGHT
**216 Travis Bickle
(Robert De Niro)
Taxi Driver, 1976
Costume designer
Ruth Morley**

FAR RIGHT
**217 Jake La Motta
(Robert De Niro)
Raging Bull, 1980
Costume designers
John Boxer
and Richard Bruno**

LEFT
218 Sam 'Ace' Rothstein
(Robert De Niro)
Casino, 1995
Costume designers Rita Ryack
and John Dunn
Suit designed by Rita Ryack

BELOW
219 Frankenstein's Monster
(Robert De Niro)
Mary Shelley's Frankenstein, 1994
Costume designer James Acheson

BOTTOM, LEFT TO RIGHT
220 Al Capone (Robert De Niro)
The Untouchables, 1987
Costume designer Marilyn
Vance-Straker

221 Henry Hill, James Conway,
Paul Cicero and Tommy DeVito
(Ray Liotta, Robert De Niro,
Paul Sorvino and Joe Pesci)
Goodfellas, 1990
Costume designer Richard Bruno

222 Conrad Brean (Robert De Niro)
Wag the Dog, 1997
Costume designer Rita Ryack

make a clone, like a carbon copy – you're making an interpretation of what you think the character is going through. We tried to get as much as we could from Jake and his surroundings, and he was very helpful. But at the end of the day we had to make certain decisions and choices. He understood.

DNL *When you look out at other people from your character's point of view, do you look around when everybody's dressed, and think 'I'm here'?*

RDN Yeah, you help create or you feel like you're in that world. The clothes are an expression of the people there. They mean a lot – they have great significance. The shoes have to be a certain way, the socks, the tie all has to be a certain way. It's all very important. There is a reason behind why certain people wear certain things and as an actor you fill that history in and try and get it as right as you can.

DNL *Do you like the director in the fitting room with you?*

RDN Yeah, I always like the director there or at least be available if needed. Sometimes I'm not sure myself what their vision and they can help give an objectivity to it.

DNL *And have you changed in the way you deal with costumes through the arc of your life?*

RDN Depends on what it is – if you have a good costume designer. As I get older I like to see what they're going to come up with. That helps give it a bit more latitude or objectivity: 'Let me try that, let me see'. That's why I say you've got to put everything on because you'll try something and it's right, and you don't know that until you've put it on. As you get older, you get more practical – will it fit right? Not afraid to try things that are less familiar to you and if it's not right to make the adjustment.

DNL *What about the way you move in costume too – the choreography of the person?*

RDN With Frankenstein, I had these things that were half moon this way/half moon that way, boot sneakers that are like stilts when you walk on them. So we messed around with them, and they gave me more height and a certain spring – a particular kind of walk. In *Flawless*, the guy had had a stroke, so I put weights on my arm and strapped them on my legs.

DNL *When do you think a costume is most successful?*

RDN When the whole thing works. The character, the story, it all comes together and you don't feel like you're playing the costume. It's not that obvious. Again, it depends on the character. It should all complement each other: the performance and the costume, the costume and the performance and all the other things.

223 Jimmy Doyle (Robert De Niro)
New York, New York, 1977
Costume designer Theadora Van Runkle

224 Sketch for Jimmy Doyle
New York, New York, 1977
**Costume designer and illustrator
Theadora Van Runkle**

TRANSFORMATIONS **AN INTERVIEW WITH MERYL STREEP**

Deborah Nadoolman Landis

MERYL STREEP is considered by many to be the leading film actress of her generation. Her success is partly the result of her remarkable versatility – embracing comedy, tragedy, singing and dancing – and her extraordinary ear for speech patterns. Her talent is matched by a chameleon-like ability to transform her appearance, assisted by her close and successful relationships with costume designers.

Deborah Nadoolman Landis   When you read the script, do you visualize the person?
Meryl Streep   I don't see a different person, but I see things about me that I'm going to shift or move or emphasize or de-emphasize to make this character.

DNL   *For* The Iron Lady *I can imagine what your*

preparation in the fitting room must have been for the body that would be underneath those clothes.
MS   That's really true. As an actor you don't want to commit to anything so early in the process as a costume fitting. And yet I knew that I was going to have to commit to a certain marriage to gravity that I have been resisting most of my life, so I would have to stand and be a certain way. So we padded out and brought all that to the fittings right at the beginning, which forced me to find that character earlier than normal.

DNL   *So chronologically, we talk to the director and make contact with the costume designer and go to the fitting.*
MS   Yes. In *The French Lieutenant's Woman* there were two stories concurrent. There's the modern story of the actress in the film and then

OPPOSITE
225   Karen Blixen (Meryl Streep)
Out of Africa, **1985**
Costume designer Milena Canonero

BELOW
226   Sister Aloysius Beauvier (Meryl Streep)
Doubt, **2008**
Costume designer Ann Roth

227   Susan Traherne (Meryl Streep)
Plenty, **1985**
Costume designer Ruth Myers

there's the French Lieutenant's Woman herself. This woman of the nineteenth century was constrained in every way. Tom Rand decided that she would have pretty much one dress, as people often did. You had one very good dress that was well made, as was my dress. It was green,

228 Sketch for Aunt Josephine
Lemony Snicket's A Series of Unfortunate Events, 2004
Costume designer Colleen Atwood
Illustrator Felipe Sanchez

229 Aunt Josephine (Meryl Streep)
Lemony Snicket's A Series of Unfortunate Events, 2006
Costume designer Colleen Atwood

*Lemony Snicket...
A Series of
Unfortunate
Events...*

dark forest green, sort of wool. But it was warm for the summer; it also kept me warm in the misty autumn evenings when we were shooting.

DNL *And the beautiful hood and the long red hair.*
MS I was looking at the Pre-Raphaelites when I was getting ready to do this and I thought this is a woman who has a romance about herself. She's obsessed with becoming something that's

she's not allowed to become. I was looking at that famous painting of Ellen Terry as Ophelia with that reddish wiggly hair and I wanted to have that, I wanted it to be very romantic. I also have lots of freckles and an English grandmother so I thought, we might bring that out a little bit more. Not be so afraid to go out in the sun and just let them pop.

DNL *Hats are fantastic for silhouette and so powerful for stature.*
MS The haberdashery on *Out of Africa* was spectacular. The film was a magical experience but very difficult in terms of costume because it spanned so many years. And Isak Dineson was an aristocrat – she thought of herself with a certain outline of style, of female importance that was manifest in her clothes. We had many choices

of what to wear but I found it difficult to make that choice in the morning before shooting an important scene. But that was the way Milena Canonero liked to work. Racks would be rolled in and I was to decide. I like things to be a little more cut and dry – so that was weird and hard.

DNL *Did you read the* Lemony Snicket *books to your kids?*
MS They were a little older but I read the books because they were really fun. Very witty and detailed. Aunt Josephine was described quite specifically, but what Colleen brought to these costumes was an infinite attention to detail that makes you feel more dressed in the moment and in the person. It was really the marriage of the idea of a character and the actuality of it.

DNL *What about the little bits: does everything have to have a story, from your pedicure to everything else…?*
MS Everything is eloquent, everything is character, everything is story. Or at least it should be, it seems to me. I'm a real pain in the ass for every costume designer to work with because I took my degree in costume design. My thesis in college was costume design. I have a lot of ideas about my character and what she should wear or what might be wrong for her to wear. So it can be painful I'm sure for people to work with me, but for the ones who like that, the

230 Miranda Priestly (Meryl Streep)
The Devil Wears Prada, 2006
Costume designer Patricia Field

231 Meryl Streep and Patricia Field on
the set of *The Devil Wears Prada*, 2006

BELOW
232 Margaret Thatcher (Meryl Streep)
The Iron Lady, 2011
Costume designer Consolata Boyle

233 Sketch for Margaret Thatcher
The Iron Lady, 2011
Costume designer and illustrator
Consolata Boyle

234 Sarah (Meryl Streep)
The French Lieutenant's Woman, 1981
Costume designer Tom Rand

235 Joanna Kramer (Meryl Streep)
Kramer vs. Kramer, 1979
Costume designer Ruth Morley

BELOW
236 Lindy Chamberlain (Meryl Streep)
A Cry in the Dark, 1988
Costume designer Bruce Finlayson

237 Corrine Whitman (Meryl Streep)
Rendition, 2007
Costume designer Michael Wilkinson

back and forth and the collaborative thing, we have a lot of fun.

DNL *We should talk about* Mamma Mia! *What was it like doing that?*

MS *Mamma Mia!* was Ann Roth's chance to do what she had always wanted to do with me, which is try to make me sexy and fun. Her theory about that show was that there should be a little sparkle everywhere, even in daytime clothes. There were a lot of sequins, you may not even notice them, but there was sparkle, bright clothes, the feeling of vacation and weddings and happiness. The very last scene, where we all do the big number, was not going to be shot, it wasn't in the budget or the schedule. We made a plea early on, we said you have to have the curtain call: it's like permission to join this thing that's looks like so much fun. Gradually as the footage came in and they saw what was shaping up, they said 'Oh go ahead, shoot the ending'. That was our wrap day, the beginning of the party, which is the key to the good humour in it.

DNL *I heard that it was your idea to have the grey wig for* The Devil Wears Prada.

MS It's really a white wig, some salt and pepper at the nape, the way hair goes sometimes. There is only really one older model in the United States and her name is Carmen, I was intrigued with that shocking willingness to be her age and make it into something completely stylish and indelible. I was trying to make an indelible character, and was not interested in being Anna Wintour or replicating the book.

DNL *When you work with Patricia Field was it the same, is it always the same with a costume designer?*

MS With Patricia it was all about the clothes so I've never done so many fittings. I think I did a minimum of sixty hours, sixty more of fitting – or maybe it was sixty days of fitting. It was a lot. I remember thinking will it never end? Everybody always says it must have been fun to do *Devil Wears Prada*. But it was like torture, a different pair of torturous heels every day. It was really interesting because Patricia has a great eye and she's fast, she decides, yes, no, no, no, yes. We had to be: we had no time and no money, all the clothes were borrowed, it was really masterful on her part.

238 Eleanor Shaw (Meryl Streep)
The Manchurian Candidate, 2004
Costume designer Albert Wolsky

239 Julia Child (Meryl Streep)
Julie and Julia, 2009
Costume designer Ann Roth

LEFT
240 Robert Kincaid and Francesca Johnson
(Clint Eastwood and Meryl Streep)
The Bridges of Madison County, 1995
Costume designer Colleen Kelsall

DNL *How does costume help you transform?*
MS Costume is incredibly important. It's just
like when you get dressed in the morning and
you go into your closet and you put on something and then you go make coffee and then you
grab your briefcase, and you look at yourself and
say no, no, no, no and go change. That's costume, that's decision, that's your inner world
manifesting because you just don't feel right in
the wrong thing.

ANN ROTH IN CONVERSATION

Peter Biskind

ANN ROTH has had an illustrious fifty-year career designing costumes for screen and stage, and is still going strong into her sixth professional decade, working, as always, non-stop. With approximately two hundred film and theatre credits, she has forgotten more than most designers will ever know, and it is tempting to fill up an introductory essay like this one by listing them all because they speak for themselves, including as they do many of the most significant productions of the post-Second World War era. In the course of the frantic pace she maintains, she has been nominated for four Tony and two Emmy Awards, winning one for *Angels in America* (2003). She has also been nominated for Academy Awards four times, winning once, for *The English Patient* in 1996.

Timing is all, or almost all, and Roth appeared on the scene in the mid-1960s, a propitious moment, when the Old Hollywood's venerable studio system was crumbling, about to be replaced by the brash movie brats of the New Hollywood. In costume design, this meant a turn towards a dressed-down new realism. Roth has always been an enemy of prettiness and glamour for its own sake. As she once put it, costuming 'is not fashion ... I've never been near a catwalk'.

A new generation of film-makers like John Schlesinger, Martin Scorsese and Robert Altman were fleeing the back lots with their artificial sets, preferring location shooting instead, which lent their films a new immediacy. Roth's hallmarks were 'authenticity' and 'character', as well as a peculiarly postmodern use of found objects and materials used in unexpected combinations. She was a perfect fit for film-makers who were determined to destroy the hoary conventions that governed how movies were made, smash taboos, and jettison spectacle in favour of personal film-making, story and narrative. Roth, who has a gift for the apt phrase as well as an eye for attire, once summed up her approach by saying: 'I don't dress movie stars. I dress actors who are playing characters'.

Its impossible to give an overview of a career as long and various as hers in a short space, so what follows is no more than a sampler, in which she speaks about her 'process' and some of her favourite films.

OPPOSITE
241 Joe Buck and Ratso Rizzo (Jon Voight and Dustin Hoffman)
***Midnight Cowboy*, 1969**
Costume designer Ann Roth

LEFT
242 Ann Roth (centre) at the Warner Bros studio with costumes from *Klute*, 1971

243 Bree Daniels (Jane Fonda)
Klute, 1971
Costume designer Ann Roth

PB   *When did you first realize you wanted to be a costume designer?*
AR   As a young girl playing dress-ups, naturally. I'm Pennsylvania Dutch. I grew up in Hanover, Pennsylvania, a farm town. If you had visions of a more glamorous life, you weren't ever going to realize it there. I saw myself with a cigarette holder and a big hat. Actually, I didn't want to be a theatrical costumer. I saw myself as somebody to do scenery. When I went to work at the Bucks County Playhouse, the die was cast. Jean Rosenthal, a very famous lighting designer and a Balanchine person, came down there while we were doing *On Your Toes*. She said, 'I'm going to recommend you to work for Irene Sharaff'.

PB   *You must have been excited. Irene Sharaff was one of the great designers. She started with* Meet Me in St Louis *[1944] and ended with* Mommie Dearest *[1981], and did many great films in between, including* The King and I *[1956],* West Side Story *[1961],* Cleopatra *[1963],* Who's Afraid of Virginia Woolf? *[1966]. When did you go out to LA?*
AR   After college. I drove out in an ancient MG. Everyone in LA had these giant baby blue Oldsmobile convertibles. At first I loved it. I was invited everywhere. I remember the [Sam] Jaffes, who were part of this group of rarefied Austrian Jews that left Vienna in the late 1930s. I had never seen this kind of glamour. Not Hollywood glamour, not lavish, not disgusting, but classical music glamour: trios and quartets and perfect little lunches. They talked about Neutra and Ray and Charles Eames. I had never met people like them before [laughs], and they were so highly exotic for me that I knew that's where I wanted to be, in that world: 'Just leave me here. I'm very happy.'

PB   *Tell me about Irene Sharaff.*
AR   Irene was tall and thin, had a sensational figure. Her clothes were made by Arthur Falkenstein, known just as 'Falkenstein'. She smoked like a fiend and she wore kohl around her eyes and white rice powder, and her hair was pulled back very severely.

Sharaff had worked for Aline Bernstein, who was Thomas Wolfe's benefactress 'with benefits', I believe, and a pioneering female theatrical designer. When Sharaff went away I stayed and worked for Miles White. He designed *Oklahoma* [1943], and *Around the World in 80 Days* [1956]. I was his assistant on that. So that combination is very important to me. Irene is the one who said to me, 'Ann, don't pursue scenery, because you'll have a lot of trouble as a woman'. So I did costumes with her.

She had so many rules. For instance, she would never, ever tell anybody where she got her fabric samples. She wouldn't tell anybody where her paper came from that her drawings were done on. When we were doing the born-in-the-trunk sequence for *A Star is Born* in 1954, she made these terrific bows on the back of the bustle dresses. They were made out of real snakeskins that had been tanned and then metallized. People would say, 'They're fantastic. Where did you get those snake skins?' You'd have to kill her to get that information. And I, in a way, have that. I don't share. Now, I'm not a mean person, but I just don't.

When I worked for Sharaff, we were at Western Costume

> ❢ I had her hair cut like that, the shag, and, of course, that cut became a sensation. It never occurred to me to tell the director. It never dawned on me that this might be a rash thing. I just knew how I saw this character. ❢

Company and I was surrounded by these incredible talents, with loads of skills and training. It made you feel worthy, to be doing something so silly as a costume that required so much classical learning. The studios had the finest craftsmen and women in the world: beaders and embroiderers, milliners and shoemakers and armourers. The finest handwork and drapers and tailors. It was beyond fabulous. There were women from Spain who could make lace. There were French women and there were Italians and Austrians. And there were dress forms at all of these studios that exactly fit the measurements of the stars. When I was a little kid, I didn't get to the movies very often, but I had seen Sonja Henie in a movie and I thought she was just spectacular. One day when I was working at Western and I was up on a ladder when I put my hand

244 Doris (Barbra Streisand)
The Owl and the Pussycat, 1970
Costume designer Ann Roth

BELOW
245 Doralee Rhodes, Franklin M. Hart Jr, Violet Newstead
and Judy Bernly
(Dolly Parton, Dabney Coleman, Lily Tomlin and Jane Fonda)
Nine to Five, 1980
Costume designer Ann Roth

Eventually I designed ninety to a hundred Broadway shows. And a lot of Hollywood directors called me. Jerry Hellman, the producer, asked me to do *The World of Henry Orient* [1964], which we made in New York. In California you were told how to do everything. You were treated like a child or like a factory employee. But in New York there was a more of a renegade quality. You were on your own. That sort of charged the blood. So I designed *The World of Henry Orient* for George Roy Hill. Often if I don't know the director, and he says so what are we going to do here, I say, 'I don't know. We'll wing it'. That doesn't mean I don't have the vision. I do have the vision. But it's more I just don't feel like explaining it because I'm not good with words. There was a lot of winging it on that movie.

PB *But eventually you went back to Hollywood.*
AR I went to work at Warner Brothers – this was around 1967 – and they asked me to join the bowling team. I said, 'No, thank you'. And then apparently it spread around the lot that I wasn't being a part of the family. I didn't realize [laughs] that I had upset them.

Hollywood had a very established way of doing things. If you were doing, say, Joan Fontaine – let's say for *Rebecca* [1940] – that was Paramount – the designer would design the leading lady, period. The wardrobe people would do Mrs Danvers. They would find something in stock and depending – I mean, if it was Hitchcock and he said, 'I want her to have a navy blue housekeeper dress', and they didn't have one, then they'd make one for her.

Well, when I got there, I said, 'Just a minute, everybody, if I'm designing the picture, I'm designing the picture'. That meant I'm not just designing the leading lady, I'm designing the mother-in-law, the janitor, the secretary, and so on. And that was not the way that system worked. A lot of them took great offence. I didn't

in a box and in there was a Sonja Henie costume. It was in a box because the beads were so heavy it couldn't hang on a hanger. It was the kind of work that simply isn't done anymore. The expertise was so profound that you didn't want to do anything ever for the rest of your life except that. I mean, you wanted to just dig deeper and deeper and deeper.

But I had a tough time in Hollywood because I was this kid who came out of the East – very arty, and my costumes were unconventional and bohemian. And the studio system was just that, a system. They were the best facilities with the greatest collection of craftspeople. But they were factories.

I was at Disney once because I had helped with *The Two Mouseketeers* [1951]. I was in the cafeteria. And they're pouring gravy in mashed potatoes with a breaded veal cutlet and I said, 'No, this isn't the way designers eat. This is the way they eat at the Prudential Insurance Company. Get me out of here'. I knew I was in the wrong place. So I went home. I came back East and went to work in New York.

I designed some small plays, and then *The Disenchanted* for Budd Schulberg. That was a big deal. I got some good notices.

realize it, but they really disliked me enormously. And, I mean, they did everything possible to thwart me, like hide clothes.

PB *Because you're a woman?*

AR No. There was a way of doing things that was extremely entrenched. When the wardrobe ladies would get high up in the echelons of stardom, like Linda Darnell's wardrobe lady when Linda was a big, big deal, those women did nothing. They had assistants who would hand Ms Darnell her bra or whatever. It was an extremely complicated caste system and division of labour.

PB *That was pretty nervy, to change the way things were done.*

AR I didn't think of it that way. I just had my idea of what it all looked like and that vision extended across the entire cast. It actually extends across the entire frame, but what can you do? I went to design a Neil Simon piece with Marsha Mason and Richard Dreyfuss – *The Goodbye Girl* [1977]. There's a scene where they go Off-Broadway and Richard Dreyfuss is going to play Richard the III. And I was in my element and did some of my best work ever designing this experimental Off-Broadway Shakespeare company. But the California wardrobe man assumed that I would do Marsha and he was going to do Dreyfuss. And he came to me – I know that they decided, 'Let's just be nice to her. We'll let her look at our selections' – I mean, he had a hundred pairs of blue jeans there, like they do in Hollywood. You say, 'I want a pair of brown loafers' and there are 75 different pairs of brown loafers there, and [laughs] you say, 'Oh, no, no!'

I was designing a picture featuring Sandy Dennis [*Sweet November*, 1968] who had been on the cover of *Time* magazine. But I was also designing either an opera or some Chekhov play in San Francisco. And never in the history of Hollywood, had someone designed two things at one time. That was just the worst thing you could possibly do to Jack Warner.

Mr Warner was this weird, adorable man. He was so funny looking that you had to just love him. I was always there at night because that's when you have quiet. And he would always be there too, walking around in the dark, turning all the lights out in the various places. Sandy was wearing something in the picture that had New York cutting-edge quality, and he didn't like that at all. I was called into this screening room where he was watching dailies so he could have a word with me. It was pouring with rain and I didn't have proper clothes, but I had a cowboy hat. It was dark, but in there was this man with a cigar. I sat down next to him, 'You wanted to see me Mr. Warner?' and the water poured off my hat and put his cigar out. I will never forget it as long as I live. He didn't think it was funny. It was funny, though [laughs].

PB *Paramount declined to renew Edith Head's contract in 1967, symbolically marking the end of the era of the studio system. The best example of the new anti-glamour costuming of the late 1960s and early '70s is* Midnight Cowboy, *released in 1969. How did you approach that?*

AR I had an image for Ratso Rizzo [plate 241]. I had pretended that maybe this was a guy who slept on pool tables on 42nd Street, but he fantasized himself as a sort of Marcello Mastroianni character, because that's whose name was on a couple of billboards. And in all these photographs, Marcello Mastroianni was wearing a white suit. And he, being Ratso Rizzo, had this Italianate sensibility about

246 **Peter Fallow, Maria Ruskin and Sherman McCoy (Bruce Willis, Melanie Griffith and Tom Hanks)**
The Bonfire of the Vanities, **1990**
Costume designer Ann Roth

himself. And being a small, unattractive, crippled boy, this was as good a fantasy as he could come up with, and it was a pretty good one at that. In front of the Port Authority bus terminal there was always a table of clothes for sale. There were stacks of white polyester piqué trousers, continental cut. Cha-cha pants. Then I saw a guy get out of the back of a limo right on 42nd Street looking like he was coming from his prom, dump his jacket, obviously a rental, in a garbage can. I think he'd thrown up on it. I designed an awful lot of off-Broadway shows, and I wanted to dress the actors in real clothes. Out of throwaway stuff. I was the first person to use what they now call vintage clothes, which made me very unfashionable in Los Angeles. So I took that jacket. I had it cleaned, and that was Ratso's costume.

This is my process. I'll sit down with the actor and we'll have a cup of coffee and we'll talk about his or her character, the back-story. How much money do you think he has? He says, 'Well, he's a substitute teacher, blah, blah, blah. And he lives with his grandmother's sister or something in Brooklyn.' When he takes off his clothes at night, where does he put them? Who does his laundry? Does he go to a laundromat? Does he wear jockey shorts or boxers? There's a reason for everything.

The point of the exercise is that when somebody, especially an actor I don't know, is coming in for a fitting, the idea is that he and I, or she and I, will find this character together. Now Dustin Hoffman was the kind of actor who had to feel that he had invented

his character and his costume. But I have a vision of what I want. Otherwise, I wouldn't know in which direction to go, would I? So the goddamn costume is hidden in my fitting room. He walks in, I've already got it, and I'm about to force it on the actor. It's not a very nice thing to do [laughs], so you have to make him feel like he chose it himself. How you do that is the key to costuming, because most people say, 'So, what do you want? Do you think it should be yellow?' That's not the way to do it. You do it with words. 'Let's try this, and see if this works. I have a bunch of stuff here. Do me a favour and just be a mannequin, a dummy. Just stand in front of the mirror and don't say anything, don't form an opinion, and let me play.' In half an hour the floor is covered with crap, shirts, pants, hats, and none of them are the real thing. They are all play.

So there's junk all over the floor. And the kicker is, you put something on the actor that he never thought of. It takes hold, and suddenly, in front of you, is a different person. For Dustin, that turned out to be the shoes. They were these cockroach-in-the-corner shoes, cucaracha shoes, very pointed toes. I had had the heels built up, and I had one of them weighted. So when he got them on, it threw him into a different posture, and suddenly there was somebody in front of me who was nothing like Dustin Hoffman. It's a very nice thing to happen in the fitting room, and that's what I enjoy doing.

PB *Klute?*

AR Around 1968 or 1969, Alan Pakula asked me to design *Klute* [1971]. The first thing I did was I took Jane [Fonda] over to East 8th Street. And there was a guy who cut hair over there. And I had her hair cut like that, the shag, and, of course, that cut became a sensation [plate 243]. It never occurred to me to tell the director. It never dawned on me that this might be a rash thing. I just knew how I saw this character. In retrospect, that was really and truly typical of me. I did that nose on Nicole Kidman for *The Hours* [2002; plate 250]. Of course, that nose could've come off. But you couldn't put the hair back on Jane [laughs].

I had a vision of her being sort of dark and provocative, but still, she could walk down the street and people would only turn to look at her not because of her clothes, but just her carriage, and then her unhappiness in her personal life at home. I wanted her to be like a scared bird in a nest. And I always had her in flannel pyjamas. And that was basically my key. Because they're warm and cozy. They're not sexy, and her life was sex.

PB *So you dressed her against character, or against her profession.*
AR Yeah, exactly. If there's such a thing as a theme in my approach, it is pretty much that.

PB *You were saying that you made the clothes with the little boy in* Extremely Loud and Incredibly Close *[2011] a little bit off-kilter.*
AR He's supposed to be 'on the spectrum'. His clothes are off. His trousers are a little too short. You understand something about him that you wouldn't have understood if his costumes were correct. The off thing usually works. I saw the picture the other day, and afterwards I leaned over to my assistant and said, 'Those pants are too narrow on the child'. It was a mistake. Later, Stephen Daldry, the director, said, 'Ann, I really thank you for making me go with those weird clothes. Every single one was right.' I said, 'No, it wasn't.' If it's wrong, if there's something that's not consistent with the wrongness that I impose, it's like falling in a pothole for me.

PB *You designed* Hair *in 1979?*
AR Well, *Hair* I love. But if somebody said they're going to ask you to do the movie *Hair*, I would've said, 'You're insane!' It's like asking me to design *Mamma Mia*. I was not suited to do *Hair*. I suppose I was a bohemian, but that '60s vibe never got to me. I was not a wild child by a long shot. I was a working woman. To this day, I don't know if I did a really good job on that movie.

**247 Frank, Possum and Edna Spalding and Moze
(Yankton Hatton, Gennie James, Sally Field and Danny Glover)**
Places in the Heart, **1984
Costume designer Ann Roth**

PB *Among the shows you designed in the 1980s, among many, many others, was* Places in the Heart, *in 1984.*

AR I know I did a good job on *Places in the Heart* [plate 247]. I knew just where to take that. The Depression, the South. I knew that when those women have two dresses and an apron and they're darning socks, they have a girdle on under there. I knew that if I put two pairs of pants on Danny Glover, he'd lose his form, and that's a look that I like. It's more real. If you're an actor, you often like to preserve yourself, and here's a certain consciousness you have about your body. But if you take some of that away, one pair of pants on top of another, you're able to remove the actor from himself, free him to become someone else.

PB *In the 1990s, you designed two films with Anthony Minghella,* The English Patient *and then* The Talented Mr Ripley *in 1999.*

AR *The English Patient* [plate 249], whenever it was – '96, I guess – was a very, very difficult job because I had to do so much research, and it doesn't show in the movie. I had a third of the amount of money that I needed. At one point I was taking the shirt off one soldier and putting it on another. The most important costume in it was Kristen Scott Thomas's dress. I found a beautiful white tablecloth that was maybe 12ft long. It was huge. And I wanted to make a dress for Kristen out of it for when she comes to him to his hotel after they've been stuck out in the desert a long time and they're starting their forbidden affair. And she's all fresh and clean and he still has sand all over him. But I knew that the tablecloth was not big enough to have three dresses made out it, which is what they usually want, at the very least. So in the scene, Ralph Fiennes pushes his face onto her breast and down the front of her dress, and he is covered in fricking Italian makeup. And of course, this exquisite dress of the finest of inserted laces and linens is ruined. Anthony says, 'Do you have another one?' I said, 'I have one more, Anthony.' Anthony got very testy about it. It was very tense.

PB *But not so testy that he didn't want you for* Ripley?

AR I felt good about *Ripley*. I think it's maybe one of the best jobs I've done.

PB *How did you approach the costumes?*

AR From my life [laughs].

PB *Meaning –*

AR Closing my eyes and remembering [laughs]. It was set in the end of the '50s, the early '60s, and I just sort of knew all those people. It was a familiar territory. Matt Damon's character, Ripley, comes to the beach, Portofino or somewhere, and he has no bathing suit. He has to borrow one. I found bright, screaming green wool bathing trunks for him [plate 248]. His skin is cottage cheese white and everybody else is golden and beautiful. And he has to walk across the beach in this green bathing suit. I said to Matt, 'If you have the guts to wear this suit in this movie, you will win a million awards and kisses.' And he did. And I truly admired him for doing it because nobody could look good in those bathing trunks. I had a great time on that picture. It's very, very rare that I have a good time while working.

PB The Hours *in 2002?*

❝ I said to Matt, 'If you have the guts to wear this suit in this movie, you will win a million awards and kisses.' And he did. ❞

AR I remember finding in a drawer in my house a box of notepaper that was designed by Vanessa Bell, who was a painter and interior designer and a member of the Bloomsbury group. It was this rusty orange and blue and gold, some black. I did that entire picture in those colours. It might look a little self-conscious, but it was for me a wonderful palette. I loved the way it looked.

I remember going into the very fancy costume house in London to do the costumes for Stephen Dillane, who plays Leonard Woolf. I got a lot of attitude when I said, 'Listen, I want to rent an old coat that should look like it hangs in the mud room, you know, an old barn coat.' They thought that was ridiculous, and they said, 'Mr Dillane wouldn't wear that.' They said that to me twice. They said he wouldn't wear the shoes I picked out for him. So I said, 'Oh, well, then you design Mr Dillane's clothes', and I left – because I'm not doing Stephen Dillane's clothes, I'm doing Leonard Woolf's costume. And then I called Stephen that night and I said, 'Listen, I have to start over with you'. And that's the way it went.

On the other hand, I went to a shoemaker to have some shoes made for Kidman, and the shoemaker said to me, 'I hope that actress who's playing Mrs Woolf has her beautiful and distinctive voice'. And I thought, 'How do you know what she sounded like?' And he told me that when he was a kid she read stories or something over the radio and he heard her. Now, I defy you to find a shoemaker in America who knows what a female author sounds like. I was so impressed by that that. I thought, I have to come up to these expectations. And I do admire the British for their appreciation of their theatrical heritage. But I had a hard time with it [laughs].

PB Mildred Pierce [2011] *that you designed for HBO? How did you deal with the wonderful costumes in the Joan Crawford original?*

AR I wasn't allowed to. I mean, Todd Haynes was so absolutely insane about it not being any kind of nod to Michael Curtiz's version that we changed everything about it. Todd's *Mildred Pierce* was not a murder story. It buried James Cain. It starts in 1931, ends

OPPOSITE
248 **Tom Ripley (Matt Damon)**
The Talented Mr Ripley, **1999**
Costume designers Ann Roth and Gary Jones

RIGHT
249 **Katharine Clifton (Kristen Scott Thomas)**
The English Patient, **1996**
Costume designers Ann Roth and Gary Jones

BELOW
250 **Virginia Woolf (Nicole Kidman)**
The Hours, **2002**
Costume designer Ann Roth

in 1941, and there's only a bit of 1941 there. Most of it is set in the Depression.

Todd said the strangest thing. He forbade, absolutely forbade shoulder pads. In my subconscious I knew that Schiaparelli arrived with the shoulder pads in 1936/37 in Paris and Milan, and if she did that, then they got to New York probably that year, and to Hollywood the following year. So don't tell me there were no shoulder pads. But I always had to do these sort of mouse dresses. There were no power dresses.

At one point I found this beautiful coat that I wanted Kate Winslet to walk on the beach in, and it had shoulder pads. She looked sensational in it, so I said, 'Let's just try it'. But Todd said, 'Absolutely not!' – he really did call the shots on that. He did not want the slightest bit of Joan Crawford.

PB *You've designed almost every single picture Mike Nichols has directed. What's the connection there?*

AR He and I have the same sense of humour. That was also true of John Schlesinger. Humour is everything for me. And when we walk into a room we both see the same thing. From the beginning, when Mike and I did *The Odd Couple* on Broadway, we both got it. And he's very, very appreciative. Meryl Streep told me that what she loved about Mike – Meryl and I were doing this movie, *Great Hope Springs* [2012], and David Frankel was the director. She said

'you know, I can hear David cackling back there, while I'm acting.' And that's what Mike does, but Mike does it better. And he's not doing it for anybody, he's just enjoying it. He enjoys it and I enjoy it, and that's it.

PB *And one last question, which is, your career has spanned – I don't know – five decades. What's it like for you to work with young pups?*

AR Directors that are now coming to the surface – a lot of them are intimidated by the likes of my generation, let's say. They're more comfortable with designers who don't have my history, are younger and they think more malleable. And, of course, there's a new system in movie making, and it's about product placement and stylists. But there are plenty of young directors who appreciate my experience. Boaz Yakin – I love him. And he's just asked me to design his next picture, so I guess I'm not totally antiquated. An actor in *Great Hope Springs* – he played a tiny part, but he was spectacular in it. And he came in for his fitting in New York and he called me a 'legend'. Well, I've heard that before in kidding from my gang, but I don't like it. I seriously don't like it. The word 'legend' is not what you want in the movie business. Or any art. What you want is fresh and new and exciting, not a legend, which conjures up the phrase, 'been there, done that'. There. I've said it.

PB *You're still designing plays and films back to back. Do you ever think about calling it quits?*

AR I'm going to keep on going until I do something that I really, really am mad about, a wonderful picture that I really want to do. And there is one, if Mike Nichols will do it. Then I'll stop.

Peter Biskind is a contributing editor to Vanity Fair, *the author of several books, including* Easy Riders, Raging Bulls *(1999), and is currently working on a new one called* The Eve of Destruction: Adventures in Extreme Culture.

3 COLLECTORS & COLLECTING

THE EXHIBITION ODYSSEY

Deborah Nadoolman Landis

WHERE DO THE HOLLYWOOD COSTUMES COME FROM?

The clothes in the *Hollywood Costume* exhibition have been assembled over a period of five years. It has felt, sometimes, like Howard Carter's search for the tomb of Tutankhamun in the Valley of the Kings. As I write these words I am still pursuing an iconic costume held by an unknown collector in the Middle East and negotiating with the new owners of a certain pair of red shoes. Some of the most famous Hollywood costumes either no longer exist or are not where they are supposed to be. Walter Plunkett's costumes for *Singin' in the Rain* (1952) should be together at their home in the MGM Wardrobe Department, but nothing could be further from the truth. The 1970 MGM auction decimated the 50-year-old costume collection of that defunct studio, leaving the costumes for the leading ladies and the chorus line spread over the entire globe.

With more than sixty lenders, *Hollywood Costume* is a major endeavour accomplished with the generosity and cooperation of a worldwide network of public and private collections. In the hands of a growing band of avid costume collectors, what was once no more than a hobby has expanded well beyond souvenir hunting at flea markets and yard sales. Film memorabilia auctions now command serious public interest and an international audience, and prices have spiralled upwards. From the original film production to the auction house to the archive and collection, each costume included in the *Hollywood Costume* exhibition has made its own fascinating journey to the V&A galleries.

WHAT HAPPENS TO THE COSTUMES AFTER SHOOTING FINISHES?

In the Golden Age of Hollywood, when the big studios were film factories, upon the completion of principal photography the costumes would be placed among the thousands already hanging in

OPPOSITE
**251 Replica of ruby slippers
for Dorothy Gale (Judy Garland)
The Wizard of Oz, 1939
Costume designer Adrian
Crafted by Mauricio Osorio/
Western Costume Company**

the wardrobe department costume stock to await their next role on camera. When they were needed for a new film these same clothes would be altered, dyed, aged, re-trimmed and substantially remade, rendering them unrecognizable for the next screen character. Decades ago costume designer Edith Head described the process:

> Usually the costumes are put in stock. If they are used on a secondary character, a different collar is put on. The third time around we will shorten a skirt and put a ruffle on it. After that, the costumes go to the background [extras]. [2]

With few exceptions, reuse and recycling have remained been the professional practice and culture in cinema costuming.

The life expectancy for a costume extended when Warner Bros created an archive and studio museum (1996) on its lot in Burbank. This was a turning point in Hollywood costume design history. Until the founding of this archive the head of the wardrobe department had the sole responsibility for these clothes. Previously studios had no archivist or professional textile curator safeguarding their historic assets. Because thousands of garments were in storage, historic inventories of the costume stock were piecemeal or non-existent. With the renovation and beautification of the Paramount, Universal, Sony and Warner Bros lots in the 1990s, the studios requisitioned the old centrally located wardrobe departments for new executive office space. With their relocation on the studio lot there was more pressure to reduce costume stock as the real estate they occupied became more valuable. [3] This move also presented the studios with the opportunity to assess the value of their costume holdings.

As the film business turned to smaller independent producers such as Miramax, New Line and Lionsgate, these companies were eager to liquidate their assets and recover their costs as soon as possible. Many jettisoned their costumes as soon as a film finished shooting without waiting until it was released in theatres. New Line listed Deena Appel's costumes from *Austin Powers: The Spy Who Shagged Me* (1999) on its own auction site as soon as the film opened. [4] Paying storage fees for costumes was impossible

for these companies, which thrived on low-budget financing and movable office space. For the past thirty years many independent Hollywood companies have made modern clothes available for purchase by the cast and the crew at 50% of their cost price after the production wraps. The rest is sold to shops in Los Angeles that specialize in film clothes. 'It's a Wrap', a vintage shop in the San Fernando Valley, remains the repository of thousands of items from contemporary films and television productions. Searching for a specific modern costume from a recent film at a costume rental house and vintage emporium is like looking for the proverbial needle in a haystack.

Period costumes, with all their accoutrements, take a different path when the filming ends. These clothes are cleaned, sized, tagged and placed in the costume stock on a rail labelled with the correct date. These clothes are entirely dismantled, which makes reassembly incredibly challenging. Ruffs, caps and fichus are thrown into the ruff, cap and fichu boxes, gloves into the correct-length glove box, corsets with the matching period corsets, crinolines and petticoats with those of the correct size and shape for each period. Buckles may be removed from belts, while hatpins, ribbons, buttons and exquisite ornaments will be saved for another star and another close-up. Period storage is generally organized in a tight chronological maze. In this way, costume designers can mix styles from the previous decade or two, accomplishing a more naturalistic blend of garments for a given period. With an abundance of palaces and castles the location for many a Hollywood film, the costume houses of Europe have clothed royal courts, Roman armies and caped crusaders.

After working in their costumes for months during long days of filming, few actors want to wear them home. They may ask the director or the producer for a souvenir but it is more common for the clothes to be sent to costume house storage or to studio stock. Contrary to popular myth, very few actors have their costumes included in their contract. A few have assembled private costume collections that represent their entire careers in cinema. Among these are Glenn Close, who maintains her own costume archive, while The Harry Ransom Center at the University of Texas, Austin, holds Robert De Niro's personal costume collection. De Niro's fastidiousness has enabled the *Hollywood Costume* exhibition to show the complexity of his madmen, monsters and ordinary individuals by gathering them together in one gallery.

WHY HAVE SO FEW HISTORIC COSTUMES SURVIVED?

In 1979, at the newly named Burbank Studios,[5] I was designing the costumes for Steven Spielberg's Second World War comedy *1941* (1979). Although I was thrilled to be working there, the studio itself was in serious disrepair. The studio lot had become a decrepit anachronism, with no money being reinvested into the infrastructure of the specialist departments, including the wardrobe department. The value of the clothes, studio assets, lay in the fact that they could be reused and rented since the studio amortized their original costs across many productions. The wardrobe department was, and is, expected to turn a profit. Management and staff coped as best they could but their thousands of costumes had long outgrown their 1930s-era storage. Costumes were cached in every corner of the studio. An entire soundstage was littered with caps, helmets, braid, epaulettes, medals, boots and uniforms of every nation, packed in cardboard boxes arranged in no certain order. There were enough clothes to provision legions of cavalry and troops from every war and service. Costumers with long memories were depended upon to remember where a specific costume resided or to 'Find the hat that we used on Steve McQueen two years ago'. Adjacent to the wardrobe department was 'The Barn', a windy, leaky wooden building built in the 1920s. Here rows of woolly sheepskin cowboy chaps, waistcoats, studded leather gun belts, holsters, bandoleros and long western canvas dusters of every description hung on wooden pegs.[6] Hundreds of classic A and B Westerns had been outfitted from the cowboy stock in The Barn.

Burbank Studios' (Warner Bros) rich costume stock also included coats, suits and gowns with the labels of such stars as Bette Davis and Rita Hayworth and other Warner stars of the 1930s, '40s and '50s. In true Hollywood tradition, I reused many of these star costumes for the extras in *1941*. At Burbank Studios there did exist a 'star closet' for a few costumes of exceptional provenance and workmanship. These had been retrieved from general stock by the dedicated and highly knowledgeable staff costumers and the head of wardrobe.[7] Many of the 'best' costumes were hanging in locked wooden wardrobes, some with wire hangers poking through torn dress sleeves. Clothes were packed so tightly that it was impossible to stick your hand between the garments. There was simply no more room.

Thus studio costume departments in the 1970s had become 50-year-old repositories of gorgeous period fabrics, feathers, buttons and notions, handbags, parasols, fans, shoes and marvellous Egyptian, Roman, Victorian, art nouveau and art deco jewellery. Hats and bonnets would be constantly re-trimmed by the resident milliner and miraculously come back to life after a good steaming. These treasure houses were mined by generations of designers.

'Star closets' also remained available for rental at an inflated price. The rental stock of costumes at Burbank Studios included those unforgettable black-and-white gowns and hats designed by Cecil Beaton for *My Fair Lady* (1964; plates 267, 268), including the white lace 'Ascot' dress worn by Audrey Hepburn. It was there that I tried on all those fabulous hats in 1978. At the time they were crushed into storage boxes. There was no respect, not even a line item in the studio budget for the preservation of important clothing – as much as the costume department chief may have wished to protect them. Thankfully, professional conservators in the excellent Warner Bros archives now safeguard Beaton's gowns.

It was rare for costumes to be set apart because of their historic value. With no studio archive founded until the 1990s, there was no designated person to decide which costume would be significant. This was impossible to guess: heavily promoted film releases were not guaranteed to be hits or memorable movies; only time would tell which characters would be meaningful to generations of audiences and therefore worth saving for posterity. Clothes were reused and rented unless the film became recognized as a classic. The cycle from original production to recognition as sufficiently 'culturally, historically, or aesthetically significant' to be included in the National Film Registry of the United States Library of Congress could take decades. For the costume, exhausted from repeated rentals and revision, this honour usually came too late.

252 Angels The Costumiers warehouse, London

There was also a clandestine movement to save costumes at the studios. Sometimes 'rescue' meant that costumers secreted these precious and worn-out artefacts in their cars in order to save them from further destruction. This nefarious practice was widespread during the 1970s and '80s. A group of these activists brazenly called themselves 'Robin Hoods', arguing that they were saving precious relics for future generations. With no studio archives or Hollywood museum, it is thanks to these passionate 'collectors' (and thieves) that many of the famous Golden Age clothes have survived.[8]

In the Golden Age of Hollywood, as now, costume designers did not use personal labels.[9] In the wardrobe department it was impossible to tell an 'Adrian' (MGM), 'Travis Banton' (Paramount) or 'Orry-Kelly' (Warner Bros) simply by looking inside the gown to establish the name of the designer. Actresses' names were written in pen or typed on a studio or Western Costume label, often with a costume change number, and sewn into a garment (plates 256, 260). Costumes that were costly to make, with lavish beading, lace, feathers or fur, resided in a locked storage closet. Ironically, the more unusual and recognizable the design of the costume, such as the Ascot gowns for *My Fair Lady*, the more unlikely it was that the clothes would be reused on another production and therefore the more likely that they would survive unscathed. The vast majority of period and modern suits, dresses, hats, gowns, overcoats and shoes were used for production after production. Garments were cut and redesigned until they became unrecognizable from their original pattern. White wedding gowns were hemmed and dyed to become cocktail dresses; cuffs came and went. Costumes were rented until they disintegrated and were then discarded.[10]

At the end of the 1960s companies like MGM and Twentieth Century Fox were eager to leverage every studio asset to offset their losses. They sold their back lots and auctioned huge quantities of historically significant props and costumes. In 1969 MGM held a public auction of its warehouses of costumes (including the ruby slippers from *The Wizard of Oz*) and its extraordinary collection of props, furniture and weaponry in what resembled a fire sale. This irreplaceable treasure trove of Hollywood history grossed MGM ten million dollars. Debbie Reynolds made significant purchases at the auction and with them founded her famous private Hollywood costume collection.[11] The historic sale signalled a 'gold rush' of Hollywood memorabilia and heralded the emergence of the modern memorabilia collector. The MGM sale is what now passes as 'provenance' in the costume collecting community. It was also a low-point in Hollywood history.

HOLLYWOOD COSTUME COMES TO LIFE

In 1974, as a graduate student, I visited *Romantic and Glamorous Hollywood Design*, the landmark exhibition curated by Diana Vreeland at the Costume Institute at the Metropolitan Museum of Art in New York. The show broke attendance records at the Met, was extended twice and ran for nearly a year. Its focus was on the glamour of Golden Age Hollywood, sidelining cinema storytelling and leaving naturalistic characters out in the cold. Although unpublicized at the time, the exhibition also featured some newly manufactured reproductions of classic costumes.[12] Reviewing Diana Vreeland's object list revealed that when an iconic costume she desired for the exhibition was lost or destroyed, she boldly took the liberty of re-creating it. The Costume Institute exhibition created a surge of interest in Hollywood costume design and the survey books that it generated are still valued today.[13]

It was another 12 years before the next major exhibition, *Hollywood and History: Costume Design in Film*, opened at the Los Angeles County Museum of Art, curated by Edward Maeder (Curator of Costumes and Textiles 1979–94). Maeder's exhibition attempted to look beyond the glamorous. He contended that film designers may aspire to the correct silhouette but that historically accurate costumes may be too distracting for the audience. Maeder argued that historical authenticity in costume, hair and make-up is

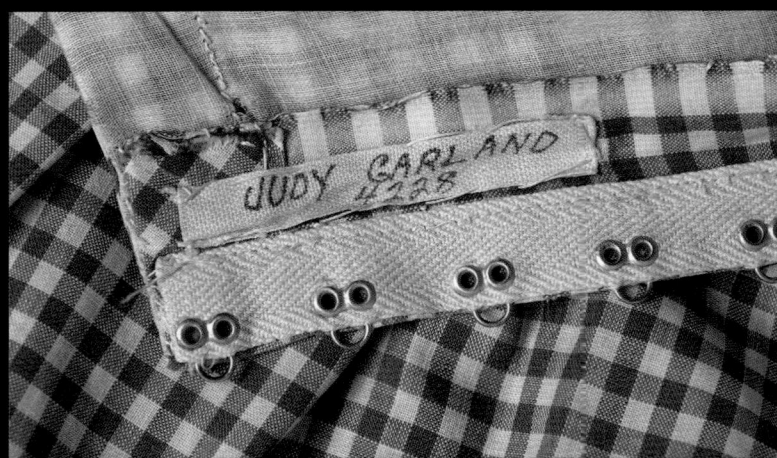

253 Preparing the textile conservation report for the pinafore

253 In the bank vault, curators and conservators inspect the pinafore

255 Dorothy Gale (Judy Garland)
The Wizard of Oz, 1939
Costume designer Adrian

256 Original MGM garment label, Judy Garland, with handwritten MGM production number

often unattractive to contemporary eyes, and that period stories are told most effectively and unobtrusively when the costumes (of any period) mirror the fashion of the day.[14]

The idea of *Hollywood Costume* as a designer-focused exhibition came as a natural extension of my professional life as a costume designer. After finishing my doctorate at the Royal College of Art I was more convinced than ever that the general public as well as my colleagues in the entertainment industry profoundly misunderstand the role of the costume designer. An exhibition was needed that would place costume at the centre of cinema storytelling. Designers collaborate with the writer, actor and director to create the people who populate the screen. Regrettably, because we also design and source the clothes worn by the actors, costume designers are often confused with personal stylists, denigrated as 'frock queens' and dismissed as shoppers. The fashion press frequently

sees films as a product placement provider for fashion labels, their advertisers. The fashion and film theorists who cultivate the philosophy of spectatorship neatly supersede the costume practitioners who actually make it all appear on screen.

In 2006 I pitched a cinema costume exhibition to Mary Lea Bandy, Director of the Department of Film at the Museum of Modern Art in New York. *Hollywood Costume* was always conceived as a film exhibition, not just another couture show. After a long discussion Mary Lea firmly corrected my movie industry usage of the word 'craft' in association with costume. This would be the 'art of costume design': Bandy pointed out that the American Craft Museum was 'across the street. This is the Museum of Modern Art'. With heavy heart we decided that the film department located in the basement of MoMA could not accommodate the large survey exhibition that *Hollywood Costume* demanded.

Sir Christopher Frayling[15] (who had been my doctoral advisor at the Royal College of Art) agreed with me that the V&A, as the greatest design museum in the world and home to a distinguished collection of theatre and performance costumes, was the most appropriate venue for the show. It took over a year for the exhibition to be approved by the V&A Public Programme Group. In the spring of 2008 my newly assembled V&A team[16] travelled to Hollywood and the search for the costumes commenced. Together we visited studio and private archives all over Los Angeles, as well as the famed Debbie Reynolds collection near San Luis Obispo, California.

CHALLENGING CHOICES AND THE OBJECT LIST

The first *Hollywood Costume* object list, which I sourced from past exhibitions, museum inventories and auction catalogues with the help of my long-time assistant Natasha Rubin, read like a long wish-list of 'The Greatest Cinema Costumes Ever Created'. Polling cinephiles, lists were created of 'must have' costumes from the 'greatest' and 'most popular' Hollywood films of every genre. I asked people of all ages who they felt was most important to include and which characters they most wanted to see. Natasha and I followed every plausible lead on the Internet, along with tips from costume designers, costumers and collectors. The professional costume houses are filled with vintage clothes from every era. After a century of mistreatment, between the unsecured studio costume departments and the practice of insider trading among costume collectors, it was impossible to determine the whereabouts of many iconic costumes. It became clear that these clothes were scattered all over the world.

As with paintings and fine art, private and public collections hold many reproductions of star costumes masquerading as the real thing. Whether or not the costume in the collections was authentic or whether the costumes on the wish list were still in existence was often anyone's guess. With dubious provenance, reputable auction houses may or may not be deliberately deceiving their buyers with counterfeits. With prices for celebrity costume skyrocketing, the opportunity for fraud exists. Disturbingly, some of the fakes (made with contemporary fabrics) were furnished with convincing vintage studio labels bearing the star's name penned in ink. With a vacuum in cinema costume scholarship and few experts to authenticate the clothes, the prevailing warning for private collectors is 'caveat emptor'.

In addition, the eccentric world of collecting made finding original costumes in good condition more challenging. Many clothes fall into disrepair because their owners do not have the budget, the ability or the knowledge to care for them properly. Some collectors confuse restoration and textile conservation, having their fragile historic costumes repaired (and sometimes remade) at local tailor shops and dry cleaners. In contrast to more sophisticated private archives, there are enthusiastic collectors who wear and enjoy the clothes on a daily basis. There is also a huge corporate collection gracing the walls of restaurants in Los Angeles, London and hundreds of hotel rooms in Las Vegas. The search for the *Hollywood Costume* object list thus became a major scavenger hunt.

257 **The Tramp (Charlie Chaplin)**

258 **Charlie Chaplin, 'The Tramp', boots and cane**
Courtesy of Julien's Auctions, Darren Julien

The unpicking of this puzzle led us to clothes sourced from the collections all over the United States. Hollywood has been making films and manufacturing costumes in Europe since the beginning of cinema. Some costumes on the wish-list were found in Rome,[17] where costume houses are filled with gladiatorial gear and ravishing period dress. Tough choices where made when it was clear that designer Piero Tosi's magnificent costumes from *The Leopard* (1963) and *Death in Venice* (1971) would not be a good fit for a Hollywood show. The London costume houses, with their racks of Jane Austen gowns, are lenders to the exhibition[18] and there were unhappy exclusions of purely British productions. The Deutsche Kinemathek in Berlin safeguards the Marlene Dietrich Collection and the Cinémathèque Française has over a thousand Hollywood, French and international costumes thanks to the foresight of its founder, Henri Langlois. Our hunt uncovered the first costume change of an actress in Rome, her second change in London, and the third in a private Los Angeles collection. Doubles and triples of costumes are also commonly found in separate international collections.

DESIGN DILEMMAS

As a practitioner as well as a scholar, my goal is to present as clear a picture as possible of the purpose, function and process of costume design in cinema. *Hollywood Costume* presented the opportunity to examine the art of costume design in a way that the public had never considered. Using my lesson plan as a template, the exhibition reflects the chronology of the designer's work, starting with the screenplay. This approach differs from exhibitions that have treated clothes as decorative artefacts, for beauty must take second place. Costuming is first and foremost an intellectual pursuit. Here, the emphasis is on the designer's conversation with the two key collaborators, the director and the actor. In films the clothing is not the final artwork but just one element of storytelling.

Costumes suffer when they are removed from their narrative and visual mandate. A colleague once complained that film costume in a museum gallery was a very bad idea and had never been wholly successful: 'Dead frocks on dummies!' he cried. After all, cinema costumes are created to be seen projected on a screen, lit a certain way, for a very particular moment in the story. They are not well served by being displayed and it it is arguably unfair to do so, since they rarely look as they do on screen. Without the actor, costumes can be very disappointing on a lifeless mannequin. The *Hollywood Costume* galleries needed to channel the kinetic experience of film. For a character and a film to capture our imagination, the suspension of disbelief must be complete. As Producer Jerry Bruckheimer said, 'We are in the transportation business because we move the audience from one place to another'.

Early in 2008 I discussed this design problem with my UCLA colleague and the Chief Creative Executive of Walt Disney Imagineering,[19] Bruce Vaughan. Walt Disney invented the immersive entertainment environment at his then revolutionary 'theme park', Disneyland, in 1955. The challenge for *Hollywood Costume* (and the effect that would guarantee its success) was to put the character back into the costumes and to bring the magic of the movies to the galleries. Mellissa Berry, a creative executive at Imagineering, flew to London to walk the V&A galleries with me. Later that year, Christopher Frayling, Natasha Rubin and I were treated to an unforgettable day-long charette (an intense workshop with participants engaged to solve design challenges) with Mellissa at Walt Disney Imagineering, together with Imagineers, artists and screenwriters. Although no specific ideas from that session survived in the final gallery design, it was enormously stimulating to engage in problem-solving with Disney's master designers.

In 2009, after discussions with Christopher Frayling, Keith Lodwick and the exhibition designers Casson-Mann, *Hollywood Costume* began to emerge. The exhibition grew into three galleries and evolved into three distinct 'acts': 'Dialogue', 'Deconstruction' and 'Finale'. With this conceit the show became a dramatic 'show' to mirror a screenplay. To complete the parallel an original score was composed to carry the visitor through the galleries with music. Theatrical lighting was designed to replace the traditional museum lighting of individual garments. After years of deliberation, *Hollywood Costume* became an experiential installation. The cinematic context was replaced by a strong visual and narrative structure. The costumes on display became just one part of the overall story of costume design, thus lifting a burden from these clothes that were never created to play a solo.

These classic costumes assumed a new role in the exhibition galleries. They were all included for a purpose, to tell the story of their creation. It is my great pleasure to honour my past and present colleagues and to share their gifts with the public. There are costumes that got away – those that ceased to exist almost immediately after being created, like many from my own films that are gone forever. *Hollywood Costume* demonstrates that costume design is linked inextricably to human stories. The art of costume unifies identity and imagination to create people who are real enough to make us believe they exist, even though we know that it is 'only a movie'. Let us hope that the exhibition does the job and that the status and art of the cinema costume designer will be finally appreciated.

LOOKING BEHIND THE WIZARD'S CURTAIN

Christopher Frayling

IN AUTUMN 1956 Lindsay Anderson – then an angry young documentary filmmaker and critic – wrote a characteristically trenchant review of an exhibition called *The Observer Film Exhibition: Sixty Years of Cinema*, which had recently been displayed in a prefabricated plaster-and-metal building on the north side of Trafalgar Square, and visited by more than 200,000 people. Anderson's review was headlined: 'Stand up! Stand up!'[1] The exhibition had been selected from a much more extensive show, curated in June to September the previous summer by Henri Langlois at the Musée d'Art moderne in Paris, to celebrate the sixtieth anniversary of the Lumière Brothers' first screening in Paris, the official origin of cinema in 1895.[2] The London version was abridged and redesigned by Richard Buckle – critic, ex-editor of *Ballet* magazine, exhibition designer – following the success of his *Diaghilev* exhibition at the Edinburgh Festival and in London some eighteen months before.[3] Buckle's main contribution was to display the pieces of equipment, optical toys, models of studios and sets, posters and designs, photographs, re-creations of props – and film costumes – in installations created specially by visual artists and graphic designers. These included a façade by Hugh Casson; silhouettes by Lotte Reiniger (plate 272); an animated cartoon room by Osbert Lancaster; a pageant of 'America since 1929' by Leonard Rosoman; a shadow theatre by John Piper; a photomontage of stars at home 'seen through the arches of a Spanish Colonial colonnade'; and, after the exhibition had been running for seven weeks, an added 'Hall of Glamour' with blow-up photographs on easels 'from Valentino to Dors!'. In the catalogue, Buckle explained why:

> The pleasure many people said they had from the Diaghilev Exhibition, which I drifted into organising almost by accident, made me think that here and now we might invent a new kind of exhibition, a show where people had fun (whether they wanted instruction or not) and were carried out of themselves, as they are in the theatre.[4]

271 Dorothy Gale (Judy Garland)
***The Wizard of Oz*, 1939**
Costume designer Adrian

Lindsay Anderson's review took particular exception to this paragraph:

> Of particular interest here is the careful profession of amateurism: 'The Diaghilev Exhibition, which I drifted into organising almost by accident…' Thus Mr Buckle avoids from the start any possible accusation of being over-serious: the implied assumption is that if you are serious, you are probably also boring. It is no coincidence that the word 'fun' appears twice before the end of the paragraph. Just as, in this context, words like 'instruction', 'culture' and even 'art' acquire connotations of pretentiousness and gloomy didacticism, so the idea of pleasure dwindles into that of 'fun'… Granted this basic attitude, it was inevitable that the exhibition should take the form it did: an orthodox, unadventurous choice of [material]…disposed in a series of sophisticated decors which tended to 'kill' rather than set off the material on display.[5]

Anderson thought it significant that Buckle had 'started off with Nanny'. This was a reference to the opening words of the catalogue's Introduction:

> It was a fine day and I must have been three or four, when Nanny popped me into a charabanc and took me off to Blackpool to see my first film. I remember a woman's huge face in a picture hat. Perhaps it was Lillian Gish…[6]

It was seriousness versus camp; pleasure versus fun; players versus gentlemen; commitment versus dilettantism; renewal versus complacency; esteem versus denigration; reflection versus being 'carried out of themselves'; exhibits with a point to them versus exhibits as a galleried facsimile of the theatre experience. It was also a plea to stop apologizing for film, and to treat film at its best unashamedly as one of the seven arts, with the same 'claim to attention as literature, music, painting or any of the arts' – to embrace film within mainstream culture. Sixty years

after the Lumière Brothers' first screening, wasn't it about time? The amateurishness, the theatricality, the over-designed installations, the emphasis on graphic displays rather than on film, the camp arrangement of star portraits, all these were to Anderson clear evidence of a lack of confidence in the subject, a feeling that film was not considered quite worthy of the cultural first eleven. The exhibition had started life in the Musée d'Art moderne; now it had been demoted to a prefab in Trafalgar Square.

Lindsay Anderson was, however, prepared to concede that there was one section of the show which was challenging, and which did indeed involve an element of curatorial discrimination:

> In the darkest corner of the room [Piper's shadow theatre, the final gallery] there is a shelf. On this rests a large book. Peering at a typewritten notice on the wall, you learn that this contains stills from the twenty-five best films ever made. But there is no light by which to see them…[7]

What he omitted to mention in his review was that, with Lawrence Alloway, as one of the 'historical advisors' he had helped to select the stills.

Museums and film have always had a strained relationship – at least since film pioneer Robert Paul offered in 1896–7 to donate his films to the British Museum, only to have his offer turned down, partly on the grounds that the powers-that-were could not fit 'film' into their traditional museological categories, and partly because of outright cultural snobbery about this upstart medium.[8] Museums *in* film have had a far more fruitful relationship – in

the sound era, since Alfred Hitchcock had Donald Calthrop run through the galleries of the British Museum, chased by the police, and fall through its domed roof at the climax of the first British talkie, *Blackmail* (1929). Museums have served as treasure-houses to be robbed in heist movies; as cabinets of curiosities; as places for lovers to meet and show off to one another; as shelters from the rain, leading to chance encounters; as places where haunted exhibits (usually ancient Egyptian or Aztec) come to life when the genie is let out of the bottle; as galleries containing portraits which feed dark obsessions; as the cluttered workplaces of eccentric antiquarians in half-moon spectacles; and so on. But museums *and* film have never got on so well.

One of the most important statements about the relationship between the two remains social and cultural critic Walter Benjamin's essay, first written in Paris autumn 1935, and called *The Work of Art in the Age of its Technical Reproducibility* (more popularly known, after paperback circulation in the 1960s, as *The Work of Art in the Age of Mechanical Reproduction*), which was centrally concerned with the impact of photography and film on the appreciation of works of art.[9] When art reproductions are available to everyone – as postcards, posters, illustrations or increasingly in films – the originals they refer to, he said, eventually take on new meanings and shed their cult value in the process. According to Benjamin, the original work of art, unlike its photographic reproductions, has a certain aura about it – a slippery term, which for him combines the work's presence, the physical fact of it, its location, its uniqueness, scale, authority, its place in tradition, and its ritual function: all part of the electric current, as it were, that flows from picture or sculpture to viewer. 'That

which withers in the age of technical reproducibility is the *aura* of the work of art…'; for the first time in world history, technical reproducibility 'emancipates the work of art from its dependence on ritual', and makes it available as a secular, insubstantial image in the public realm. Benjamin used several examples from 1920s films – especially those of Abel Gance – to illustrate his argument. His concern, though, was with the influence of reproduction *on art* rather than the other way round. It did not occur to him that photography and film might possibly be arts in their own right, with their own place in an art museum. Their invention may have redefined 'art', but not *that* much…

Poet, novelist and arts commentator André Malraux's essay *Museum Without Walls*, published as *Le musée imaginaire* in 1947, was in some ways a more detailed elaboration of Benjamin's central concerns.[10] He had met Benjamin in Paris in the mid-1930s, when Benjamin was mulling over *The Work of Art*. Malraux, too, was focused on the work of art – as traditionally defined – and on how perceptions had shifted in the age of photographic and filmic reproduction. Most public museums, he suggested, started life as responses to industrialization, which separated art from everyday life and placed it in dedicated institutions. This tended to diminish the age-old religious value of the arts. But in the modern *Museum Without Walls*, wrote Malraux, even a religious icon or a stained-glass window becomes merely a 'picture' – shedding what was left of its artistic, social and historical significance in the process: a picture placed next to any other picture, and all of them printed about the same size. A miniature becomes the size of a large painting; a panel the size of a building; a minor work seems major; an imperfect finish looks like a bold style; a fragment or detail becomes a 'fictitious work of art', a new work created by

the means of reproduction. The work of art thus reproduced – in print or as film – has turned into something else: '[This] will carry infinitely further than that revelation of the world of art, limited perforce, the "real" museums offer us within their walls.' Malraux called this 'the virus of the art book', though he was later to edit an influential series of picture books on art. The plus was that more people would have access to art more easily; the minus was that in the process art would lose much of its traditional meaning and value. The role of the museum nevertheless remained as a site 'which gives us the highest idea of man'.

He had much to say, too, about the impact of film – and especially on editing/constructing a sequence rather than in the frame – on 'the world of art': 'cinema acquired the status of an art only when the director … was emancipated from the limitations of the theatre'. 'The status of an art', note, rather than a place *within* 'the world of art'. For both Benjamin and Malraux, photographic reproduction – still *and* moving – would have a profound impact on artists' understanding of the arts (they could, in principle, 'be acquainted with all of art'), on the display of art in museum settings, and on public perception/understanding of the visual arts. But 'the arts' as a category still remained entirely separate from the media of their reproduction. For Malraux, film had earned the *status* of an art – post-montage – but *museums* of art were about something else. The key issue was the impact of new media on the citadel of the arts, as traditionally defined. Neither of these radical intellectuals could even imagine that a time might come when film would find its way into an art museum, even a 'Museum Without Walls'. There were *art* museums – art with a capital A – and there was *film*, which Malraux reckoned had taken over from narrative painting and was 'the ideal medium for

273 Musée du Cinéma Palais du Chaillot, Paris Gallery view showing the characteristic juxtaposition of costumes, equipment and objects

pictorializing the anecdote' as he put it. He was very supportive of French film – for example, giving Truffaut's career a big boost – but that was a different thing.

It is not difficult to see why, with their notion of an art museum as keeper of the aura, they could not encompass the idea. And if it was unthinkable to these two radical thinkers, it is not difficult to imagine the position of the museum establishment of the day. As recently as 1967, twenty years after Malraux's essay, a UNESCO report on 'Film in Museums' concluded that:

> With the projection of film one sinks to a level that is otherwise energetically opposed, the visitors are overfed with visual stimuli, of which they get quite enough through the illustrated press, cinema, and television. This favours the distraction of interests instead of striving for spiritual concentration, and it thus helps those powers one is usually fighting against…[11]

This position – high/low, individual/mass, concentration/distraction, spiritual/material, eternal/commercial, museums as defences against 'mass culture'/museums as reflections of or on the arts in society – a distant echo of the work of the Frankfurt School of social critics from the 1930s (of which Benjamin was a distinguished affiliate), is still taken as a given in many parts of 'the art world' where it is wrongly confused with dumbing down. As a result, it has not – or not enough – been seriously examined.

The point of a museum was to provide contact with the original, with the aura of the original. Where film, the seventh art, was concerned, what was the original? As someone once said of Action Painting: 'how do you hang an event on the wall?' To put it another way, 'how on earth do you hang a motion picture?' Film is an experience, normally projected at 24 individual frames per second. While in film pioneer Robert Paul's day films only ran for a minute or so – and could credibly be projected complete in a gallery – feature films since the 1920s have tended to run for about an hour and a half, and many of them a lot longer than that. So, if the 'aura' resided in the film itself – if film was to be treated as a museum artefact – this raised some immediate practical problems. As film historian Richard Koszarski has written, about New York's Museum of Modern Art and its early promotion of film as art through a 'film library' and through touring programmes,

> In the first place, there was no original object to valorize, and unlike prints or photographs, which also exist as multiples, 'owning' a copy of a film (when possible) did not necessarily bestow on the possessor the right to show it to anyone. And even if one did own such a print, was the 'film' (the original object of interest) really just that roll of celluloid in a can? Or was it more akin to software, only coming alive when processed mechanically for performance?[12]

The Museum of Modern Art, concluded Koszarski, did indeed bestow 'the imprimatur of high art' on film 'through its very association with the Museum' from 1934 onwards, and its touring programmes did help to professionalize cinema studies – but

some of the big questions still remained unanswered. MoMA championed a *certain kind of film* (especially Soviet cinema), its own canon, in line with the museum's particular philosophy of Modernism – '[pushing] aside competing narratives'. The film experience happened in a viewing theatre, on the model of the London Film Society of the late 1920s, with the occasional small exhibition around the entrance. It was a kind of lean-to, attached to the main museum building.

I can remember taking part in a seminar in the mid-1990s – one of an extensive series of consultations in preparation for the opening of the then-new Tate Modern at Bankside – about film and photography and their place in the art gallery of tomorrow. Maybe the 'Tate Moment' would provide an opportunity to redefine the boundaries of the arts – as a spectrum rather than a set of discrete categories dating back to the Industrial Revolution – and to include the moving image side by side with the other visual arts. As it transpired, the seminar revealed that in some circles the debate had not moved on much since the mid-1930s, and in some ways it had taken several steps backwards.

An art critic opened the discussion with the statement that if we were talking about feature films, then they rightly belonged in archives for presentation purposes, in libraries for borrowing purposes, or in their own film museums, rather than in a major museum of art. He could imagine them featuring in the gallery's education programmes or in the lecture theatre, but that was about it. Someone interjected that he had omitted to mention theme parks, hamburger joints and Madame Tussauds in his list. What was the opposite of fine art? Was it 'coarse art'? A curator seemed to endorse this by adding that feature films of the 'Golden Age' were in the end *industrial* products, created by large teams of people in quasi-factory conditions (Hollywood, like Bollywood or equivalents), and as such they did not belong in the cultural canon of individual works of art made *by* individuals *for* individuals. So if a film was made by, say, Man Ray or Marcel Duchamp or Salvador Dalí and projected in gallery-like conditions, that was one thing – but if it had emerged from a Hollywood studio to be screened in a cinema, that was quite another.

The concept of the film director as 'author' was in the end a metaphorical one, promoted by the critic/film-makers of *Cahiers du cinéma* magazine in the early 1950s, who liked to see themselves as authors. Where *film* films as distinct from artists' films (themselves distinct from 'art films') were concerned, they should be filed under 'the popular arts' – maybe on a par with carnival or circus or music hall, which certainly had an impact on the visual arts (think Toulouse Lautrec and the music hall or Picasso and the circus) but from well *outside* the art world. Surely 'the art world' was a sociological concept, said an intense research student, not an aesthetic one? Even if that was the case, replied the curator, film belonged in a different sociological world.

Someone added that it was time the discussion became more practical: if the *film* was the museum artefact, how on earth was it to be screened in the gallery? Yes, it was becoming the norm for museums to present informational images on screens, side by side with the artefacts themselves (at least in *this* respect, the debate had moved on since that UNESCO report of 1967), but the maximum attention span of the viewer was about four minutes and in blockbuster exhibitions considerably lower. So at

274 **Musée du Cinéma**
Palais du Chaillot, Paris

what price feature films? The only practicable mode of exhibition in galleries was through film *clips* – where they would inevitably lack context, and so would surely diminish rather than enhance the understanding of film: there would be no narrative or emotional or even authorial context. Plus, the medium of display in galleries tended to be video rather than celluloid, another problem if the film *print* was to be the artefact. All in all, if the museum artefact were the film itself, there would be a series of insuperable problems for curators. This all arose through a confusion between an experience and an artefact.

A conservator asked how museums and galleries were expected to take seriously the preservation and exhibition of film, when the industry itself had been so uninterested in the afterlife of its products once their commercial potential had been exhausted – at least up until the era of video and studio tours, when the back-catalogue was radically revalued. The classic example of this had been the transition from silent to sound, when countless films had been junked because they were thought to be beyond their sell-by date. Yes, I responded, if museums had been around to take film more seriously in the 1920s – if they had helped to draw political and public attention to their cultural value – then perhaps many of these silent films might have been saved. The reply to this was that museum artefacts were on the whole made to last:

but what about the famous 18-day MGM auction of May 1970, when the studio sold off warehouses full of props and costumes and fixtures and fittings as part of its business plan? Didn't that speak volumes about the attitude of the industry to its own past?

In the end, as the tone of this seminar seemed to me to predict, the boundaries of the arts and 'the art world' were not to be significantly challenged or redefined by this great new gallery, except occasionally at the margins. At the Tate Modern Edward Hopper exhibition in summer 2004, reproductions of stills from feature films which had been decisively influenced by Hoppers' paintings – notably his *Nighthawks* (1942), a key influence on noir films, and *The House by the Railroad* (1925, which inspired the house in *Psycho* [1960]) – were to be stuck to the wall of the cafeteria area rather than in the galleries themselves. The *Dalí and Film* exhibition of summer 2007 was quietly to drop the '… *and Film*' part of its title to lower case on the posters, for fear of putting off the art crowd: 'Dalí at Tate Modern' sounded so much more reassuring. But films by Andy Warhol, for example (in spring 2002), were allowed into the pantheon, and everyone seemed comfortable with that. And so – occasionally – were photographs by professional photographers rather than 'fine artists', in thematic exhibitions.

André Malraux in his *Museum Without Walls* phase would no doubt have agreed with this policy, as a way of protecting the 'highest ideas of man' against lower ones. It was the same André Malraux who, as de Gaulle's Minister of Cultural Affairs – the first in France – dismissed Henri Langlois from his post as

275 Installation showing alien costume and painted
background from George Méliès' film *Le Voyage dans
la Lune (A Trip to the Moon)*, 1902
Musée du Cinéma
Palais du Chaillot, Paris

head of the Cinémathèque française (which he had co-founded)
in February 1968 – leading to the 'affaire Langlois': demonstrations and petitions, François Truffaut mobilizing the *Cahiers du
cinéma* magazine network, Langlois' eventual reinstatement in
April 1968 as Secretary-General of the Cinémathèque – albeit
with a reduced budget and strict conditions attached. Malraux
had been a supporter of Langlois and his aspirations, but by the
late 1960s had become exasperated with him. The '*affaire*' was
in many ways a dry run for the subsequent '*événements*' of May
1968. François Truffaut wrote: 'The demonstrations for Langlois
were to the events of May '68 what the trailer is to the feature
film coming soon.'[13]

Langlois had since the mid-1930s – around the time that
MoMA's touring programmes were instituted – worked tirelessly
to rescue discarded films, especially silents (some of which he
called 'works of art essential to our intellectual patrimony'). He
had also dreamed of creating a '*grand musée du cinéma*', a 'Louvre
of the cinema', a 'Cathedral of Chartres made of 50,000 films,
not stones', or even 'an Acropolis of the Seventh Art'. For him,

the screenings at the Cinémathèque were a parallel experience,
'part of what Malraux would have called the "museum without
walls"'. His exhibition at the Musée d'Art moderne, from July
to September 1955 – which has been dubbed his 'masterwork'
– gave him the opportunity to experiment with ways of making
the artefacts 'come alive' to viewers, and with variations on the
idea that an exhibition about film can itself become a work of
art – a three-dimensional film, almost – an idea that Richard
Buckle would take considerably further and in a different direction in his London version.[14] This was followed in autumn 1961
by an exhibition in the Louvre itself, to mark the centenary of
the birth of pioneer film-maker and animator Georges Méliès,
and in June 1972 by the grand opening of the Musée du Cinéma
in the long and narrow galleries recently created by the Musée
national des Arts et Traditions populaires in the east wing of the
Palais de Chaillot (plates 273–5). Langlois' close colleague Lotte
Eisner said that at first they pretended that the takeover of the
space was a temporary expedient, that they were '*comme squatter*', hoping that in time they would be left alone.[15] She was to
be proved right. Jean Cocteau referred to Henri Langlois as 'the
dragon who watches over our treasure'.

But his approaches to making a 'living museum of cinema'
were not without controversies. They involved juxtaposing pictures and objects in period or ethnic settings, with an emphasis on
antique apparatus, pre-cinema gadgets, scripts, designs, posters,

stills, programmes – and costumes on mannequins. These were juxtapositions rather than instructional connections,[16] with specially constructed sections of sets and models of stages in studios. Vivien Leigh's greying ball-gown from *Gone with the Wind* (1939) was draped near Esther Williams's pearl bathing costume and across the way from Delphine Seyrig's Chanel-designed costume from *L'Année dernière à Marienbad* (*Last Year at Marienbad*, 1961). A section of the set for *The Cabinet of Dr Caligari* (1920), reconstructed by Hermann Warm, one of its three original designers, led to the robot Maria from *Metropolis* (1927) reproduced by its creator, sculptor Walter Schulze-Mittendorf, and some Expressionist drawings and posters. For Langlois, the aura lay in the overall visitor experience – in 'creating the atmospheres', as he called it, or 'recreating an ambience' or 'a book which is no book' – and in the certain knowledge that the objects if not the environments were the originals or reconstructed by the *originals*: 'for ten years most people have considered me a madman; I was the gentleman who bought scraps of paper.' The controversies were about exhibiting film or exhibiting 'associated materials'; about Langlois' idiosyncratic and sometimes baffling approach to 'creating the atmospheres'; about the paucity of captions and information boards in favour of 'the overall experience'; about the relative significance of technologies (pre-cinema gadgets; early cameras and projectors' lenses) and of artefacts associated with specific films; about the 'waxwork' or 'relic' feel of the mannequins; and the emphasis on early cinema (the displays to all intents and purposes ended around 1940), which for Langlois justified the inclusion of the material in a museum setting. Anything more modern had not yet stood the test of time, had to prove itself as 'intellectual patrimony' and might even be seen as promotional. Also, the films were still fresh in peoples' minds so there was less need to 'evoke' them in a museum setting.

François Truffaut, for one, was far from convinced. 'Who cares about seeing a lot of old projectors?' he asked, and thought some of the juxtapositions (a Garbo costume next to Mom's mummified skull from *Psycho*, for example) were merely 'a gimmick for tourists'. It was in the end a question of resource allocation:

> Personally, I see little value in displaying a dress worn by Greta Garbo. The Cinémathèque's major function must be the preservation of films, especially nitrate-based prints ... The money spent on the museum would have enabled at least 500 nitrate prints to have been copied on safety stock.[17]

Joseph Losey agreed with him. He called the museum 'a fine testimony to the futility of trying to preserve a transient art'.[18] But other film-makers wrote or said how 'helpful' they thought it was to see the original set designs or costumes or storyboards of well-known films. 'Associated materials' could sometimes be very instructive.[19]

Where such materials were concerned, Sabine Lenk – Director of the Filmmuseum in Düsseldorf – has written in their defence:

> As it is almost impossible to present film as *film* in a fully satisfactory way, film museums have to look for other

ways to exhibit the subject. This is mostly achieved with a selection of objects related to film technology (cameras, projectors), items that demonstrate principles of cinematography (illusion of movement, elements of film language), and artefacts documenting aspects of the film business, including star portraits, lobby-cards, and merchandising.[20]

The main objectives of a film museum or of films in museums, she writes, is to help visitors to 'get in touch with the original' – to trigger memories, enhance knowledge and interpretation, redefine the films' signification as culture, and remind visitors of the pleasure of watching particular films. But in a museum or gallery setting this cannot mean sitting down for 90 minutes or more to watch complete films. So the 'aura' must be transferred to associated objects:

> ... film as an object is just a celluloid strip in a can. Put in a display cabinet it looks like decoration. The 'aura of the original' is much better provided by associated objects, especially those which a movie star or director has once used. Mentally projecting recollections of scenes from the film into the object, the spectator's imagination recreates the flair of Hollywood ... thus creating the object's aura.[21]

Certainly, of the estimated 123 public and private film museums – or significant film collections within more broadly based institutions, such as museums of science and technology, or even natural history museums – listed in a worldwide survey of 2006, a significant majority interpret 'the aura of the original' as meaning the technologies of film: scientific instruments, kaleidoscopes, optical tricks, magic lanterns, pre-cinema and film apparatus illustrating the principles and practices of the moving image.[22] The next largest category of 'associated objects' consists of exhibits relating to the cinema as industry: posters, stills, press books, programmes, paper materials promoting individual films: nearly always flat works. The third largest category is about film stars: either museums devoted to particular actors (Laurel and Hardy in Solingen as 'Dick und Dorf' – and Ulverston; John Wayne, James Stewart, Tom Mix, Will Rogers, and William S. Hunt in the United States, usually in their home towns) or galleries evoking their significance – through costumes, magazines, merchandising, promotional materials, personal objects and documents. Most film museums started life as private collections – as, of course, did many art museums: the difference of emphasis here is that in the case of the film museums, the very survival of the material (at times when few others valued it) often depended on private collectors and their obsessions. According to this survey, in 2006 the countries with the most film museums were the USA (25), France and Germany (17), and Italy and the UK (10). The largest are publicly funded; the monographic museums tend to be private and run by enthusiasts. Several of the museums on the 2006 list are no longer in existence. In Hollywood there has been talk of establishing a major film museum for years, countering the criticism that the industry is not interested enough in its own past.

276, 277, 278 *Romantic and Glamorous Hollywood Design* exhibition, 1974–5 Metropolitan Museum of Art, New York

Lenk concludes that even if documents, artefacts and words can never be a substitute for the experience of watching a film, it is better to 'keep the memory alive indirectly through artefacts' than to lose it through 'lack of contact'. For Henri Langlois, film costume played a key role in this project. Film historian and critic David Robinson has recalled their strong presence in the original 1955 exhibition *300 années de cinématographie, 60 ans de cinéma*, which was adapted for Trafalgar Square:

> Langlois understood the excitement of the three-dimensional, full-colour reality of the two-dimensional monochrome images on the screen. Here were costumes that had once clad Asta Nielsen, W.S. Hart, Charlie Chaplin, Lon Chaney, Clara Bow, Greta Garbo, Mae West, Fairbanks and Stroheim, Tom Mix and Harold Lloyd; Jean-Louis Barrault's Pierrot costume from *Les Enfants du Paradis* and Gregory Peck's coat from *Moby Dick*; most glamorous of all, the cloak, shimmering with silver embroidery, worn by Napierkowska as Antinea in Feyder's *L'Atlantide*.[23]

This was effectively the first major international exhibition of film costumes – though the design process was not one of its explicit themes. Langlois was more interested in stars and directors (as were most *cinéastes* at the time). He wrote to them, begged, borrowed and … sometimes omitted to return their loans until reminded several times. In response to the suspicion that some

of his enthusiasm for old clothes and scraps of paper smacked of fetishism and collector-mania rather than curatorial detachment, Langlois later replied (about his Musée du Cinéma at the Palais de Chaillot):

> What interests us about costumes is less who wore them than their characteristic and educational value. Certainly we have James Dean's jacket in the exhibition [it subsequently disappeared], but clearly it will be more evocative once it has ceased to be a present-day garment – it will no longer be a fetishistic garment, but an illustration of an era.[24]

For Langlois, the 'educational value' of the costumes was to do with their social and cultural resonance. Buster Keaton's hat made sense when placed next to a small portrait of Keaton by the French comedian Pierre Étaix. Directors and stars – even cinematographers and production designers – were credited, but costume designers on the whole were not. In part, this was because the distinctive contribution of the designers was not yet understood outside the industry itself. In 1979, the designer and photographer Cecil Beaton was still complaining about this:

It is true to say that Hollywood introduced a new sense of fashion and beauty to the world and – sad to say – also true that the designers of the clothes worn by famous Hollywood stars were never really given their full credit.[25]

Beaton's point was about the status and public understanding of the costume designer in film. In the silent era, the designers did not usually feature on the credit titles at all. Historical costumes were in the early days carried over from theatre. In the studio era, the credit tended to go to the supervising head of the studio costume department – or the executive designer who dressed the female principals. The producer, more than the director, had the last word on design matters. And the designers were curiously anonymous: Edith Head wrote that 'we did what we were hired to do. We were professionals, and if we did what we were supposed to do, why should anyone say anything?'[26] Then, when the distinctive contribution of costume designers began to be recognized by the industry, there were for a time two Academy Awards for film costume – one for black and white and one for colour – until 1967, when the categories were merged. At this point that particular Award was demoted until after the advertising break on television – buried in the 'craft' sections. Only since the late 1950s and the rise of the 'auteur' theory have directors and designers really developed a close creative relationship.

When Henri Langlois set up his museum, countless books had been written about film directors, actors and screenwriters, and a few on cinematographers and production designers, but hardly anything of substance had been written about the people who designed or made the costumes. There were a few celebrity autobiographies – Edith Head, Howard Greer, Cecil Beaton on *My Fair Lady* – and some books or essays about fashion designers who occasionally worked in the movies (not at all the same thing as professional costume designers): Pierre Balmain, Coco Chanel, Christian Dior, Erté, Norman Hartnell, Elsa Schiaparelli and Paul Poiret. But in 1974, two years after Henri Langlois opened his museum in Paris, there was a large and influential exhibition at the Metropolitan Museum in New York, under the aegis of Diana Vreeland's Costume Institute, called *Romantic and Glamorous Hollywood Design* (plates 276–8).[27]

The operative word here was 'glamour', a word that Hollywood had done so much to popularize. As Vreeland gushed in her introduction to the unassuming little catalogue in November 1974,

> Glamorous and romantic Hollywood design. The glorification of heroes and heroines. Beautiful women, handsome men. Everything was larger than life. The diamonds were bigger, the furs were thicker and more. The silks, velvets, satins and chiffons, and miles of ostrich feathers. Everything was an exaggeration of history, fiction and the whole wide extraordinary world. The basis was perfect designing and incredible workmanship…[28]

These sentiments were repeated in the elaborate coffee-table book *Hollywood Costume – Glamour! Glitter! Romance!* published two years later, following the success of the exhibition. *Romantic and Glamorous Hollywood Design* consisted of 146 costumes. At its core were many exhibits from the MGM sale – by now in private hands – and from the still-existing Paramount wardrobe. As Vreeland added, in her catalogue,

> [of] the entire galaxy of Hollywood designers – Gilbert Adrian, Travis Banton, Walter Plunkett, Orry-Kelly, Edith Head, Irene Sharaff – the most luminous were Adrian and Banton.[29]

Adrian stood out for his 'MGM style' as a costume designer, Banton for his 'Paramount workmanship'. In particular, the exhibition focused on Adrian and Greta Garbo, Banton and Marlene Dietrich, and, apart from these luminaries, on the surviving work of the contracted heads of department at the major studios who had dressed the (usually female) stars from the 1930s to the 1950s. By 1974 only one Hollywood studio still had a full-time costume designer under contract, and that was Edith Head at Universal. So the exhibition also marked the end of an era. The final section was devoted to the costumes designed for Cher and Carol Burnett in their television shows.

One major problem in researching the exhibition, wrote Vreeland, was that 'many of the finest examples of Hollywood design have disappeared', especially those from her beloved Golden Age:

> Once a movie was completed, the costumes were generally considered expendable. For the most part, costumes made for the stars were the property of the studios. Some were redesigned for use in other movies. Many were casually stored, and have vanished. Others have deteriorated from sheer neglect … a sizeable number of those that have survived now belong to private collectors who have acquired them out of sentiment and nostalgia or as rentals for costume balls and Mardi Gras.[30]

According to Dale McConathy in the retrospective book, sentiment also played a large part in the exhibition's success:

> For many, it was clearly a sentimental journey; for others, a splendid anatomy of what made Hollywood romantic and glamorous. One visitor exclaimed as she neared the portion of the gallery devoted mainly to Greta Garbo: 'I never thought I'd get so close to a star!' For the young, taken with films perhaps seen only on television, the exhibit wakened a new sense of the great care and extravagance lavished on the visual object in the most powerful days of the Hollywood Dream Factory…[31]

But five years after this, Cecil Beaton – who had designed *Gigi* in 1958 and *My Fair Lady* six years later, both in heightened period style – was still asking why the role of the costume designer for film had been so relatively neglected. The Metropolitan Museum of Art exhibition had been very strong on 'Hollywood fashion', glamour and femininity – less strong on the distinctive contribution of the designer as a member of the creative team,

on what the designer actually *does*. Quite apart from the costume designer's contribution to the overall look of the film, the characterizations and the story, there was the fact that film costumes are, give or take a few props, the only material culture of film there is – not the technology, the preparatory material or the post-production marketing, but the material culture as featured in the film itself. The *Hollywood Costume* exhibition provides an excellent opportunity to ask Cecil Beaton's question again, reaching beyond glamour and status and star quality.

Apart from the museological debates discussed earlier, there seem to be many reasons for this relative neglect. The very word 'costume' has unhelpful connotations of fancy dress, not helped by the fact that Academy Awards have tended to go to period costumes which have self-evidently been 'designed'. The word also helps to confuse the craft with fashion design, and continues to be too often associated with the designer/star relationship rather than with performances. The Metropolitan Museum of Art exhibition did not help here either. And where the actual costumes are concerned, as Diana Vreeland pointed out, there is the low-life expectancy of many of the artefacts themselves – which have in the past only survived in private collections, costume stores where they have been made over for subsequent projects, in basements, or on the Internet. When they do survive being reworked, discarded, sold or stolen, to be exhibited in museum settings, they have seldom been credited to the designer: usually the caption includes instead the title of the film, the name of the studio and

279 Wardrobe racks at MGM Studios during production of *The Wizard of Oz*, 1939

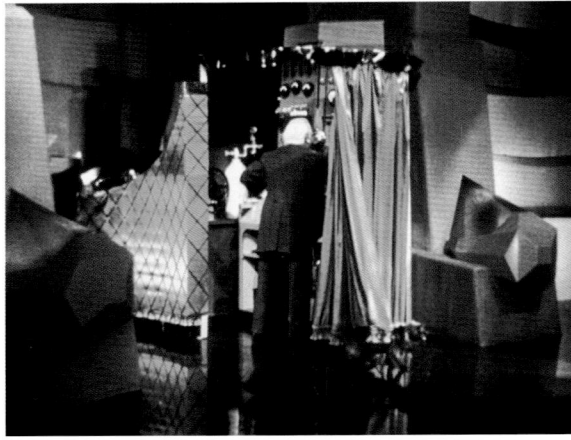

the star, the date and the director. Until very recently this was the case with Indiana Jones's outfit from *Raiders of the Lost Ark* now at the Smithsonian in Washington – and in 2004 with one of the *Troy* costumes at the British Museum. In the exhibition of costumes *Marilyn – Hollywood Icon* at the American Museum in Bath (March to October 2011) the captions listed the films and the directors but not the designers.

The scholars and commentators writing about film costume since the mid-1970s and the pioneering exhibition at the Metropolitan Museum of Art have in some ways matched the trajectory of design history in general. First of all they discussed named designer-heroes from the fashion industry; then pioneers and design managers from the film industry, their names given in the credits; then the designer-star relationship; then the craft as embedded in the studio system; then thematic rearrangements from within the heroic period – with reference to the 'look' of individual studios; then the impact of film costume on the world of fashion (costume and high-street), and vice versa – from producers to consumers; then, in the 1990s and 2000s, clothes as texts about identity. Only now is the distinctive role of the professional costume designer as part of the creative team, whether in-house or freelance, at last acknowledged. Today there is a growing realization that costume design for film is not about fashion design or fancy dress, or even about theatre design – but about helping to develop a character and contribute to a story. Garments are designed to 'work' at a particular moment, worn by a particular person, lit in a particular way, at a particular stage in the script as interpreted by a particular director – a kind of production design for the body, of form follows function – that is not quite like any other form of design. This form of design depends on a presumed understanding – by director and designer, on behalf of the audience – of how garments will 'read': what they will say about class, income group, taste, biography, back-story, psychology, mood and more. Charlie Chaplin put this well, in his autobiography of 1964, when recalling a key moment in the life of his Tramp in early February 1914 – albeit with the benefit of hindsight and a bit of poetic licence:

> The moment I was dressed, the clothes and the makeup made me feel the person he was. I began to know him and by the time I walked onto the stage he was fully born.[32]

This was one version of the origin of Chaplin's screen image which actually took some time to develop to its complete state. There were several other versions. The point, though, was that wearing the clothes made Chaplin the actor 'feel the person he was'. And the resulting interplay of actor, clothing and performance became in the eyes and minds of the audience, one of the best-known screen images in the world – up there with Mickey Mouse's ears Alfred Hitchcock's silhouette, Boris Karloff's Monster make-up Humphrey Bogart's trenchcoat – and Judy Garland's ruby slippers. Many other actors have since confirmed that an essential way into the character is through wearing the clothes – which in turn, when the film is released, can make a strong emotional connection with the audience as well as being 'read' in character-specific ways. But, where scholars and museums are concerned, this is a very recent realization.

The classic example of a single artefact from a film, which raises many of the reasons why it has taken so long for the penny to drop, is the case of the ruby slippers from *The Wizard of Oz* (MGM's production no.1060, 1939).[33] The film version has entered the history books as *the* classic Hollywood product, in many ways an allegory of the film-making process itself: a Depression farm-girl from Kansas, whose world is in black and white, dreams of a three-strip Technicolor land of Oz beyond the rainbow where the flora and fauna are larger-than-life, the costumes cartoonish, and where the Emerald City resembles a Hollywood studio – complete with props room and sound stage. The wonderful Wizard himself does not possess real magic powers – cannot really give the Scarecrow a brain, the Tin Man a heart, the Lion some courage – but he can pretend to. So, like the fairground huckster he is, he gives the Scarecrow a degree certificate, the Tin Man a heart-shaped clock and the Lion a medal, making Uncle Henry's farm-hands (in the film version) *feel* better about themselves. It is, as a critic has written, as if 'a Marxist had rewritten the last scene of *The Tempest*'.[34] The Wizard cannot give them the real thing, so instead he restores through illusion their faith in themselves. *The Wizard of Oz* is at the same time an exposé and a celebration of the Hollywood dream factory. Dorothy just wants to go home, on the other side of the rainbow, back to the grey washes of Kansas.

And this is where the artefact comes in – her bridge between Depression monochrome and Hollywood Technicolor. In L. Frank Baum's book of 1900 and the earliest drafts of the script, Dorothy Gale's magic shoes were silver. But in his script dated 14 May 1938, British screenwriter Noel Langley changed the stage direction 'C.U. Silver Shoes' to 'C.U. Ruby Shoes' – and added:

'The ruby shoes appear on Dorothy's feet, glittering sparkling in the sun.' Silver shoes would not have provided enough of a contrast with the yellow brick of the road, they would have looked dull, and that was not good enough in a three-million-dollar film which was pushing the possibilities of Technicolor. So the ruby slippers were born; they have since become, over the years, one of *the* icons of Hollywood. Christie's East catalogue, dated 24 May 2000, called them 'the most recognizable shoes in the world'.[35] Close your eyes and tap your heels together three times and think to yourself: 'There's no place like home.' There are also the poignant associations with the tragic and archetypical showbiz life of Judy Garland, who died in June 1969; the ruby slippers seem to put us back in touch with lost innocence.

Lot W-1048, the 'red sequinned "ruby" shoes (Adrian) – Judy Garland, *The Wizard of Oz*' were auctioned at 8pm on Sunday 17 May 1970, as part of the MGM sale of 30,000 lots, on Stage 27 – the very same stage on which Judy Garland had followed the yellow brick road in 1939. They were carried in on a tasselled velvet cushion and sold for $15,000, a much higher figure than expected. Today the figure would probably be in excess of $2 million. Although everyone knew that more than one pair of ruby slippers must have been made in 1938–9 – for standing and dancing, walking and skipping, wide-shots and close-ups, for the stand-in, as a substitute if the first pair was damaged, and so on – it was assumed on the day of the auction that this was the only pair, size 5C, to have survived.[36] Then, following the auction, other authenticated pairs started surfacing. Four pairs used in the film, are now known to have survived. One slipper, it has been claimed, was chewed to pieces by Toto. The colourful story of how these pairs of ruby slippers happen to have survived – a story involving wardrobe departments, studio stores, costume rental houses, auction rooms, used clothing stores and memorabilia shops, replicas and originals, and a cast of several film fans who became obsessed with them – has been well told in Rhys Thomas's book *The Ruby Slippers of Oz*. Since then there have been one theft, several rumoured sightings and a record price at auction. The story continues...

Which is the 'original' pair? Does it matter? Why was the studio so uninterested in its own history? Why did no museums even bid for the slippers in 1970? Why did it take a small dedicated group of film buffs to protect the shoes from being discarded? Why have the ruby slippers been canonized since as *the* artefacts? Is it because of *The Wizard of Oz*, because of Judy Garland, because of their iconic status in the gay community, or because more generally they stand for lost innocence? Or because the film has been shown so often on television since 1956, or because of the music, and especially 'Over the Rainbow'? What exactly do the slippers represent? Are they interesting as pieces of design – or only by association? What should the caption say? In museum terms, what story do they tell? They certainly did their job well as contributors to the screen story.

L. Frank Baum's 'modernized fairy-tale', *The Wonderful Wizard of Oz*, was first published in 1900, the same year as Freud's *Interpretation of Dreams*...

Cultural historian and broadcaster Sir Christopher Frayling has written widely on the subject of cinema. He was until recently Rector of the Royal College of Art, the longest-serving trustee of the V&A and Chairman of the Royal Mint Committee, as well as Chairman of Arts Council England and the Design Council. He served a term as a Governor of the British Film Institute until January 2012.

OPPOSITE
**280 Professor Marvel/
The Wizard of Oz (Frank Morgan)**
The Wizard of Oz, 1939
Costume designer Adrian

LEFT
281 Dorothy Gale (Judy Garland)
The Wizard of Oz, 1939
Costume designer Adrian

THE TREASURE HUNT

Keith Lodwick

ASSEMBLING OBJECTS for an exhibition is one of the most fascinating and challenging roles for a curator. The process of sourcing, identifying and choosing items for the *Hollywood Costume* exhibition was particularly complex. This is the story of how the exhibition was put together.

An exhibition celebrating film costume design was first proposed to the V&A in 2006 by Deborah Nadoolman Landis, herself a distinguished costume designer with an impressive list of major motion pictures to her name. This exhibition would not only be a testimony to her years of research into the art of costume design on film, but also an opportunity to examine and explain the often misunderstood role of the costume designer. The challenge for the curators was to appeal to film and costume fans alike: to display the finest and most enduring cinema costumes from 1912 to the present day, while describing the costume designer's process from script to screen. Early in the development of the exhibition, Deborah told me that this would be like assembling 'the biggest jigsaw puzzle in film history' – but without the finished picture for reference or all the pieces to hand. Since the exhibition would be made up entirely of loaned objects, this assembly job required a long process of often frustrating but sometimes rewarding paper trails and gossip which occasionally led to a hidden gem – and then, of course, careful negotiation with private, public and studio lenders.

Deborah has herself acknowledged the difficulties of research in this field:

> Not long after a movie has wrapped, its entire costume department disappears. A wealth of prosaic paperwork – costume budgets, continuity photographs, costume change breakdowns and fabric swatch books – is dumped after a film has been released and the need for re-shoots has ended.[1]

OPPOSITE
282 Melanie Daniels (Tippi Hedren)
***The Birds*, 1963**
Costume designer Edith Head

One of the most frequent questions asked of a costume designer is: 'What happens to the costume after filming?' During the 1930s, '40s and '50s, when the era of the Hollywood studio system was at its peak, once a film production was complete the costumes would be removed to the studio's vast costume storage – as stock. Costumes were considered a studio asset and subsequently rented, remade and re-styled for new productions; they had no intrinsic value beyond shooting, and were thought to have no historic significance. Following the decline of the studio system in the 1960s and '70s, researching the costumes that we wanted for this exhibition was therefore a real challenge, not only in terms of locating the costumes that helped our narrative, but finding out whether they still existed at all. To compound the problem of tracing particular pieces, there has never been a tendency to document or collate film costume. Perhaps Hollywood's relationship with its own history has never been one of looking back: the film industry is more focused on looking forward – to the next box office hit, sequel or film franchise.

The decline in studio production, mounting debts and changes in the corporate structure of the Hollywood studio system in the late 1960s resulted in many of the studios selling off their back lots for real estate, and subsequently their costumes, props and archive assets. The most famous of the studio sales occurred in 1970 (plate 286). Metro-Goldwyn-Mayer (MGM) had been the richest of the Hollywood studios, with its famous catchline 'more stars than there are in heaven'. Its roll-call of stars during its golden age in the 1930s and '40s included Clark Gable, Greta Garbo, Spencer Tracy, Joan Crawford, Norma Shearer, Judy Garland and Gene Kelly. But in 1970 MGM held a series of public auctions and the entire stock of furniture, props and costumes from over fifty years of film-making went under the hammer. The studio raised the staggering sum of nearly ten million dollars – but this is nothing to what these pieces would be worth today.

> These precious assets represented nearly seventy years of movie making and symbolized nothing less than the cultural iconography of Hollywood itself. Irreplaceable memorabilia and ephemera, relics and remnants of Hollywood's Golden Age were scattered to the winds.[2]

As a consequence of the MGM and later studio sales, the all-important ephemera that accompany costume, such as drawings, notebooks, trade pamphlets and catalogues, were also sold or destroyed.

Early in the planning process for the *Hollywood Costume* exhibition we conducted a feasibility study which demonstrated that original film costumes dating back to the silent film era did still exist. Most of these were in the hands of passionate private collectors, who had lovingly taken care of them, and at the Natural History Museum of Los Angeles County. These collections became the start of the exhibition. We were now faced with a unique opportunity to reunite these icons of cinema in one place; to examine the costume designers' creative journey in the process of film-making; and to explore how, through innovative exhibition design, costumes could be 'brought to life'. The challenge for Deborah Landis as chief curator, representing her peers in the film industry, was to communicate the role of the designer in the film-making process, which is not well documented:

> The exhibition is not really about the clothes – that's the hardest endeavour. Our role is misunderstood by the public, the industry and even our friends … Costumes in the movies are supposed to disappear so how are we supposed to display something that's designed to

disappear? For me, the question is what did that costume do to move the story forward? How was that costume the conduit to a new person or character? So this is the most elusive part of my challenge.[3]

The story of how the 'jigsaw puzzle' has been assembled represents over five years of sourcing, identifying and securing objects. The provenance of film costume has always been a murky area for film costume collectors: there were more than one pair (possibly as many as ten) of Dorothy's ruby slippers from *The Wizard of Oz* (1939); costume designers make duplicates of costumes; labels are missing or have been removed over time; test dresses are made that do not make it on to the screen. Each of the more than forty lenders to the V&A exhibition has a story of how or why they came to own each of their costumes. Our treasure hunt has been an extraordinary journey through costume design and cinema history.

The collectors who have made loans to this exhibition range from major motion picture studios, public museums and archives to private individuals. We have met a series of fascinating people and discovered film costumes in the most unusual places. I was delighted to visit Quentin Tarantino's home in Los Angeles to see the yellow jumpsuit worn by Uma Thurman in the two-part *Kill Bill* action thriller (2003–4), and to travel to Paris, Berlin and Rome, where collectors generously offered their costumes. The Cinémathèque française in Paris has a rich collection of American and French film costume dating back to the silent era. The major Hollywood Studios (Disney, Paramount, Sony, Twentieth Century Fox, Universal and Warner Bros) all offered costumes from their collections, including some important recent films such as the *Harry Potter* series (2001–11). But a great number of the costumes from the Golden Age of Hollywood from the 1930s, '40s and '50s simply do not exist. What does survive is in museums scattered around the world or in private hands. Some of these costumes are too fragile to be displayed and others selected for the exhibition have required extensive conservation. Finding costumes to illustrate the history of Hollywood costume involved a mixture of tenacity, relentless investigation, careful negotiation – and luck.

PRIVATE COLLECTORS

The gingham pinafore worn by Judy Garland as Dorothy in *The Wizard of Oz* was offered to the V&A in a phone call from a private collector. The costume was being held in a secure bank vault in London's Fleet Street. In June 2010 Deborah Landis, a V&A textile conservator and I were ushered through the depths of the bank, past corridors

283 Inez Schroedt at MGM Studios works on a dress for *Marie Antoinette*, 1938
Costume designer Adrian

on a long search for one of the pairs of ruby slippers that were worn with it. These have taken on iconic status since the 1970 MGM auction, when a single pair was sold for $15,000. No one quite knows how many shoes remain in existence. At one point the V&A was in negotiation with two owners concurrently, and during the making of the exhibition one of these announced that he was putting his pair of slippers up for auction. Once again the possibility of including these iconic shoes was hanging in the balance.

As news of the exhibition began to circulate around the world of private cinema costume collectors, one contact invariably led to another and to the discovery of other important costumes. For many collectors this was the once-in-a-generation opportunity to be involved in a major retrospective. Larry McQueen (see pp.217–27) has been a generous lender to the exhibition; for him this was a chance both to see some of his collection on display and to celebrate the costume designer's art and contribution to popular culture. Larry's main focus has always been on the artistry and imagination of costume designers, and on communicating the story of how factors come together to create pieces that in some cases can never be created again.

with glass cases containing ledgers dating back to the seventeenth century. Once we were safely inside the large vault, two security men appeared carrying a huge box. As the lid was removed, we gathered around to watch Deborah remove reams of tissue paper to reveal one of the most iconic costumes in film history: Dorothy's blue and white pinafore dress from *The Wizard of Oz* (plates 253–6). For the exhibitions team it was a 'holy grail' moment. One of the most enduring and cherished films of all time would now be part of the *Hollywood Costume* exhibition.

For collector Heather Porter, *The Wizard of Oz* is one of her greatest passions. In 2005 Dorothy's blue and white gingham dress came up for auction at Bonham's, London. For Porter, the possibility of owning the very dress worn by Garland was an opportunity not to be missed. As the price of the dress rose she pulled out of the bidding, although she did acquire some of the film's promotional material instead. Unbeknownst to her, the successful bidder was her own husband! Heather Porter continues to collect material relating to the Frank L. Baum novel and the 1939 MGM film. She also runs a charitable foundation called, naturally, The Red Shoes Charitable Trust. She is delighted that, after years of storage in a bank vault, at last Dorothy's dress can be viewed and enjoyed by the wider public.

Having secured the loan of the dress, Deborah and I embarked

Collector Norman Tipton has amassed an important collection of Hollywood costumes from the Golden Age to the modern day, including pieces from celebrated films such as *Marie Antoinette* (1938), *Mildred Pierce* (1945), *Funny Girl* (1968) and *102 Dalmatians* (2000). He began collecting as a young man, buying film posters from a shop in San Diego. When he discovered that his posters had significantly increased in value over time, he began to trade them, sometimes exchanging them for props and costumes: 'Initially I was trying to match my posters to the costume, for display purposes: my original collection was posters, then it became props and costumes.'[4] His experience as a collector reveals the journey that film costumes sometimes make once filming is over. Joan Crawford's wedding dress in *I Live My Life* (1935) ended up as a prize awarded to the leading debutante at President Roosevelt's birthday ball, having been donated by MGM. When he heard that the family was looking to part with the costume, Tipton traded some posters and received the gown.

Part of Norman Tipton's work has been the conservation of costumes acquired for his collection. One of Norma Shearer's dresses from the 1938 production of *Marie Antoinette* was in poor

285 Milo Anderson
and Joan Crawford on
the set of *Mildred Pierce*,
1945
Costume designer
Milo Anderson

286 Sale catalogue for
the MGM public auction,
2 May 1970

condition when he acquired it from another private collector. Having hung on a wire hanger for a long time, it had suffered severe hanger rot and had to be completely disassembled. The shattered sleeves had the appearance of broken glass: the conservators embroidered these to muslin to close them back up again. Tipton's collection is carefully stored in conservation boxes: the care of his costumes is his utmost priority. Each garment is stuffed and padded with tissue so that the fabric is properly supported. The costumes are kept in large containers lined with acid-free tissue and stored in a darkened room. From time to time selected costumes are put out on display, but only for short periods, to avoid the perils of damage from gravity, dirt and exposure to light.

Prices for costumes and props have escalated recently as film memorabilia have become highly sought after. Larry McQueen hopes that this will bring renewed respect for film costume and ensure that they will be preserved for future generations.

THE UNIVERSITY COLLECTION: THE HARRY RANSOM CENTER AT THE UNIVERSITY OF TEXAS AT AUSTIN

The David O. Selznick Archive at the Harry Ransom Center, University of Texas, holds dresses from one of the enduring films of all time, *Gone with the Wind* (1939). The Center also has an extensive collection of rare books, manuscripts, photography, film and art, and an especially rich collection of material relating to the American film industry including the archives of some of the most important film-makers, actors, screenwriters and production designers of the twentieth century. Its origins go back

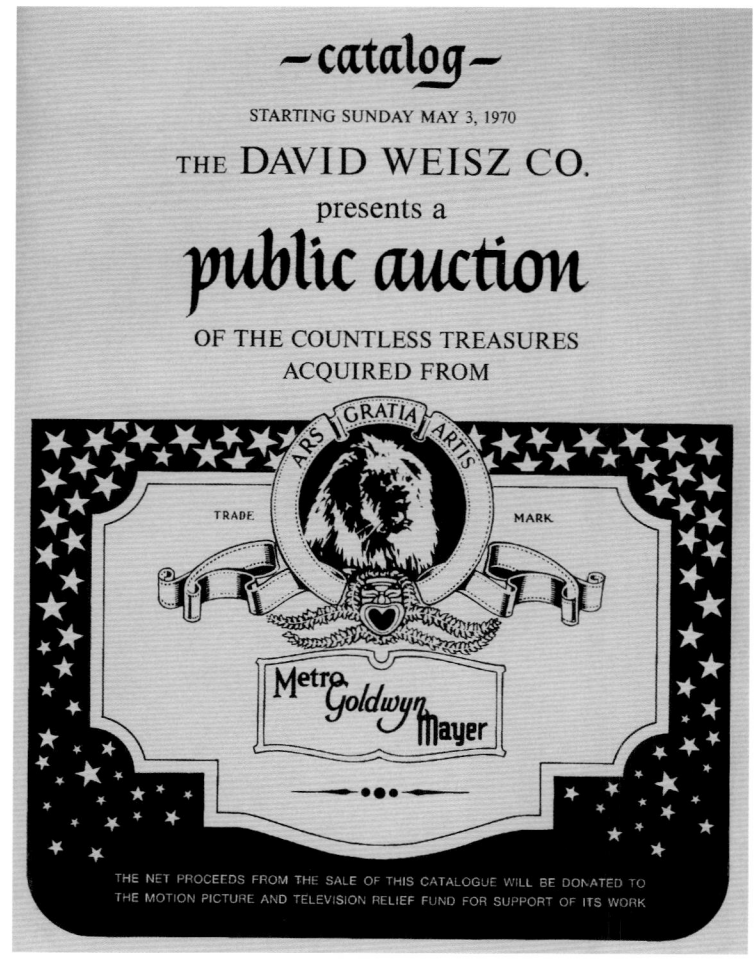

~catalog~

STARTING SUNDAY MAY 3, 1970

THE DAVID WEISZ CO.

presents a

public auction

OF THE COUNTLESS TREASURES
ACQUIRED FROM

ARS GRATIA ARTIS

TRADE   MARK

Metro
Goldwyn
Mayer

• • •

THE NET PROCEEDS FROM THE SALE OF THIS CATALOGUE WILL BE DONATED TO
THE MOTION PICTURE AND TELEVISION RELIEF FUND FOR SUPPORT OF ITS WORK

to 1941, with the collection of film director King Vidor. The collection was really established with the acquisition of the archive of David O. Selznick, legendary producer of *Gone with the Wind*, in 1980. The Selznick archive is still the largest collection at the Ransom Center, and includes the safety film from Selznick's personal library, as well as five dresses from *Gone with the Wind*. The collection is in constant use by scholars and students and has in turn attracted other collections such as the archives of screenwriter Paul Schrader (including the *Taxi Driver* [1976] costume included in the *Hollywood Costume* exhibition).

The Robert De Niro collection at the Ransom Center is one of the most exceptional collections held anywhere in the world relating to a single actor's body of work on screen. In the words of Steve Wilson, Curator of Film at the Center,

> De Niro told me a very interesting story about why he began to keep his props and costumes. It was sometime in the late 1970s and he was at Western Costume in California going through racks of costumes, looking for something to help build a character. He came across a costume from *Bonnie and Clyde* [1967]. It bothered him that they were recycling a costume from that classic film instead of preserving it. So he started keeping his costumes and his other material that he used in his work. That was what prompted him to start the collection. He didn't know what students and scholars might be interested in, so he just kept everything. Later, he was looking for a home for his collection and approached us. It took us quite some time to really work it out, but eventually we agreed to accept the collection and all the responsibilities that go with that – and it has worked out really well. We now have students from the University of Texas and other universities coming here to study and work with the costumes. In short, the collection and related archive have got as much use as we could ever have hoped for.[5]

During preparations for the *Hollywood Costume* exhibition the Harry Ransom Center launched an appeal to raise $30,000 to conserve the five *Gone with the Wind* dresses. The campaign received unprecedented results, with donations from all over the world, an indication of the degree of international interest in the film and in Scarlett O'Hara, its heroine. This enabled two of the costumes (the famous green velvet 'curtain' dress, plate 292, and the burgundy ballgown, plate 287) to travel to London for the exhibition, the first time these costumes have been displayed outside the United States since the early 1940s.

Jill Morena, Collection Assistant for Costumes and Personal Effects at the Harry Ransom Center, describes the conservation work as a constant balance between preservation and access. With the burgundy ballgown it

was decided to remove certain material that was not original to the dress. For example, the lead weights sewn into a compartment in the hem of the train were removed but saved. The conservators photographed and documented which weight came from which compartment, ensuring that the alterations were all reversible. They also discovered that several feathers that were not original had been added to the dress over time, giving an overly fussy look. It was easy to see which ones were not original: their colour was different and they lacked the wonderful volume and shape of the originals. Even just removing some of those non-original feathers made an enormous difference, and the dress can now be seen in its original glory.

287 **Costume for Scarlett O'Hara (Vivien Leigh)**
***Gone with the Wind*, 1939**
Costume designer Walter Plunkett

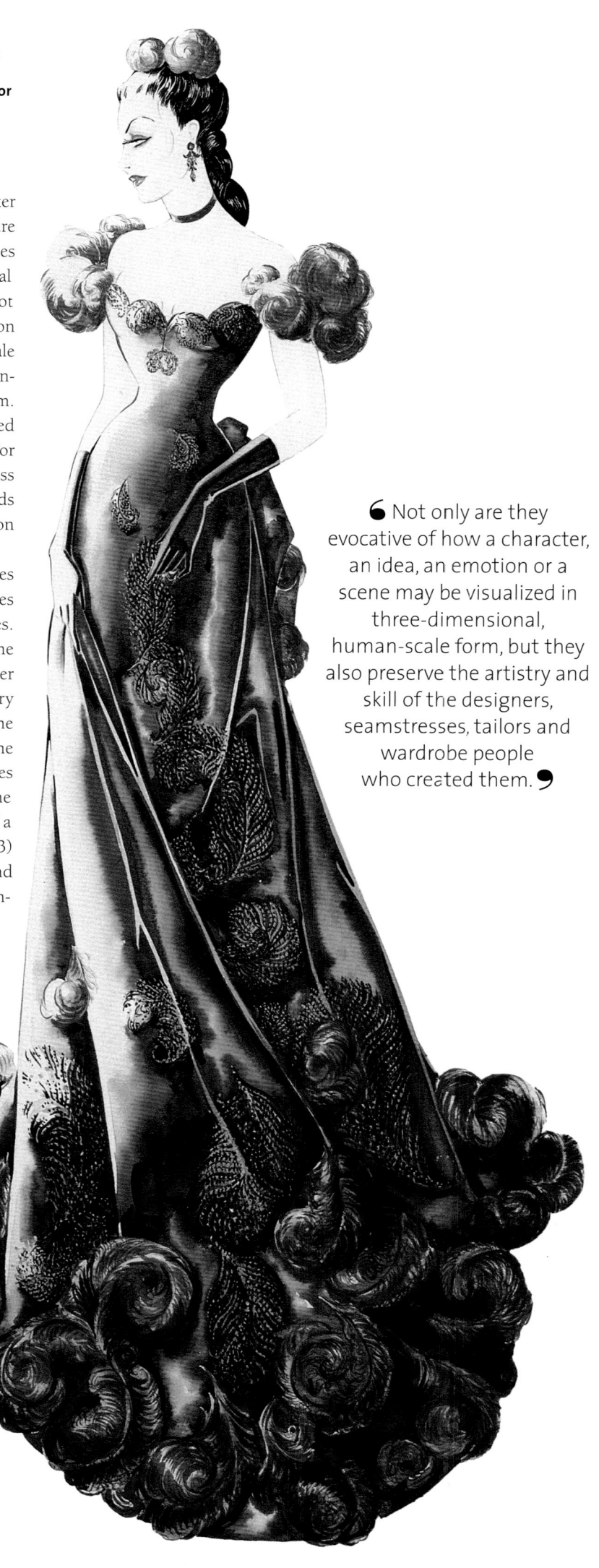

Steve Wilson describes the goals of the Ransom Center as to collect material and preserve these collections for future generations of scholars of film history. In recent years costumes have come to be recognized increasingly as objects of cultural and historical value, with meaning in and of themselves. Not only are they evocative of how a character, an idea, an emotion or a scene may be visualized in three-dimensional, human-scale form, but they also preserve the artistry and skill of the designers, seamstresses, tailors and wardrobe people who created them.

During the exhibition research, Deborah and I discovered that accessories were often separated from their counterparts. For example, the green velvet hat that accompanies the 'curtain' dress from *Gone with the Wind* was in the collection of Debbie Reynolds on loan from Daniel Selznick. The *Hollywood Costume* exhibition reunites the two pieces.

Sourcing, contacting and eventually identifying costumes for the exhibition was a long, drawn-out process, sometimes leading to dead ends and sometimes to unexpected surprises. One of these was Newbridge Silverware. Established in 1934, the Newbridge Silverware Company in Dublin is Ireland's premier giftware brand, its vast product line includes jewellery, cutlery and homeware. At the Newbridge Silverware Visitor Centre, the Museum of Style Icons attracts thousands of visitors per year. The museum exhibits a permanent collection of signature costumes worn by Audrey Hepburn, Grace Kelly and Marilyn Monroe. The collection was started in 2006, with the purchase at auction of a classic dress by Hubert de Givenchy from the film *Charade* (1963) worn by Audrey Hepburn. The costume was put on display and the public reaction was so great, with thousands of visitors coming to see this one piece, that the collection has been developed to include almost five hundred costumes. The museum's Edith Head collection includes the suit worn by Tippi Hedren in Alfred Hitchcock's *The Birds* (plate 282), which was purchased from Christie's in 2007 and is a key piece in the *Hollywood Costume* exhibition.

THE COSTUME HOUSE: ANGELS THE COSTUMIERS

Unlike the costume archive or personal collection, for professional costume houses film costumes are their business. The oldest costume house in London, Angels provides the film, theatre, TV and opera industry with costumes. Founded in 1840 by Morris Angel, the collection began with a barrow in the heart of London's theatreland, from which good-quality second-hand clothes were sold. Morris and his son Daniel Angel eventually moved to premises on Shaftesbury Avenue, where Daniel opened a bespoke department in this new,

❛ Not only are they evocative of how a character, an idea, an emotion or a scene may be visualized in three-dimensional, human-scale form, but they also preserve the artistry and skill of the designers, seamstresses, tailors and wardrobe people who created them. ❜

TOP
289 Walter Plunkett during production of
Gone with the Wind, 1939

ABOVE
290 Walter Plunkett at a fitting during
production of *Gone with the Wind*, 1939
Costume designer Walter Plunkett

ABOVE RIGHT
291 Scarlett O'Hara (Vivien Leigh)
Gone with the Wind, 1939
Costume designer Walter Plunkett

respectable environment. The quality and style of the clothes was
high, and soon theatrical managers were seeking his services for
their West End shows. At the beginning of the twentieth century
Angels began a relationship with the film industry that lasts to
this day, starting with making the costumes for the film *Maid of
the Mountains* (1913). Angels is now one of the largest costume
houses in the world, with around six million costumes hanging
on over eight miles of rails (plate 252). Its collection could dress
every section of society and every military operation, and is a living history of dress. The 'star' costumes in the collection are kept
in an archive, from which the Academy Award-winning costumes
designed by Sandy Powell for *Shakespeare in Love* (1998; plates
40, 42) have been loaned to the *Hollywood Costume* exhibition.

THE FILM STAR: DEBBIE REYNOLDS

During the course of assembling the exhibition, film costume was
front page news with the sale of Debbie Reynolds' collection.
Debbie Reynolds is a pioneer in saving film memorabilia and has
been a collector for most of her career. She purchased assets from
the 1970 sale at MGM – the studio where she began her career
in the late 1940s. Early in the exhibition's feasibility stage we had

**292 Costume for Scarlett O'Hara
(Vivien Leigh)**
Gone with the Wind, **1939**
Costume designer Walter Plunkett

visited Debbie's vast collection, which was stored on her son Todd Fisher's ranch, a three-hour drive from Los Angeles. Debbie's collection was legendary among film costume collectors, so to have the opportunity to see some of the treasures that she had amassed during her career was an unforgettable experience. Debbie's vision was to open a museum celebrating the history of Hollywood; sadly, her dream was not to be. On Saturday 18 June 2011, over the course of eleven hours, almost six hundred costumes, props and posters were sold as one of the most important collections of film memorabilia was dispersed. With no museum to display these objects and no offer to purchase the entire collection, Debbie's archive from the silent era to the modern age went under the hammer. The auction created some interesting twists of fate: Paramount Pictures, for example, bought back costumes that the studio had originally created in 1949. Hedy Lamarr's peacock dress worn in *Samson and Delilah* (1949; plates 259–63) was purchased by Paramount, enabling the V&A to reunite the dress with the peacock-feathered cape borrowed from the Cecil B. DeMille Foundation.

THE PRIVATE FILM FOUNDATION:
THE CECIL B. DEMILLE FOUNDATION

Cecilia DeMille Presley is a film historian, documentary maker and a key player in film preservation; she is also the granddaughter of film pioneer and legendary film director Cecil B. DeMille. The Cecil B. DeMille Foundation is a testament to the great film director's passion for all the elements that create moving pictures. He was especially interested in set and costume design, and in archiving his work.

> When Grandfather died, he had saved everything from his movies. When the studios would simply throw things away, he recognized that they were history and brought them home. When he died, Brigham Young University was very interested in collections of motion picture people, so we gave them over 44,000 pieces of art, sketches and everything from his motion pictures. Our archives contain art, costume and memorabilia. My grandfather kept a place called 'Paradise', a beautiful ranch with lots of animals. He was not a hunter – he never could kill anything – and no-one was allowed there with a gun. The peacocks roamed freely, as did the deer. He loved it when the peacocks spread their tails – absolutely beautiful.[6]

LEFT
293 Scarlett O'Hara (Vivien Leigh)
Gone with the Wind, 1939
Costume designer Walter Plunkett

RIGHT
294 Sketch for Scarlett O'Hara
Gone with the Wind, 1939
Costume designer and illustrator Walter Plunkett

DeMille's 1949 blockbuster *Samson and Delilah* required five costume designers. Edith Head, Paramount's principal designer, was assigned to create the costumes for the film's star, Hedy Lamarr.

> Cecil wanted something special for the scene where Delilah sits on the throne just before Samson tears down the walls of the temple. Her costume was to be nothing like the scant things she had worn in the more erotic scenes. Here she has to demonstrate the power of her position: she was to be beautiful, but not a seductress. I designed a long, draping cape covered with real plumage and DeMille liked my idea very much. DeMille informed me that he had several peacocks on his ranch so we waited until moulting season and then my wardrobe people trudged up to his ranch to collect almost two thousand feathers. The cape, which attached at the shoulder formed a train several yards long was covered with the iridescent feathers, each hand-sewn or glued in place.[7]

Paramount Pictures, already a lender to the exhibition, was delighted to see the cape and dress reunited. Restoration and preservation are now very much a part of the studio's work, although the idea that costumes were more than just things to be rented for a production is a relatively new concept. According to Andrea Kalas, Head of Corporate Archives at Paramount, costumes from new feature films are collected, conserved and archived, and exhibited from time to time. The studio also re-acquires key costumes when they come up for auction, in order to rebuild its core collection. The aim of the archive department is to be the one place in which the materials and the history of the studio – including films, publicity stills and other photographs, artwork and posters – are preserved and conserved. Paramount has recently embarked on restoring key costumes and props from the studios back-catalogue of important feature films, including Cecil B. DeMille's epic, *The Ten Commandments* (1956):

> *The Ten Commandments* is a significant film. So when we began the film restoration we knew that some of the costume elements were squirreled away in one of the buildings on the Paramount lot, basically what was left of the jewellery rental part of the costume department. Some of the intrepid archaeological staff trawled through various drawers and cupboards and discovered a variety of treasures, so apart from the film we restored the jewellery too. The detail that was put into that is just incredible.[8]

From the Hollywood studio warehouses and private collectors in Los Angeles, via the museums of New York and Paris to the costume houses of London and Rome, the jigsaw puzzle began to assemble itself. With a rich object list which now included some of the most cherished and important films from a hundred years of film-making, the V&A was finally able to stage this historic show celebrating costume design in film. The extraordinary range of objects in the *Hollywood Costume* exhibition make this an unprecedented event in the exhibiting of motion picture design. From research to conservation, from lighting to object mounting, it has been a team effort. But put simply, without the collectors there would be no exhibition. From the major Hollywood studios to the individual private collector, the exhibition is testament to their generosity and spirit.

Keith Lodwick trained as a set and costume designer and has designed more than thirty stage productions. He is currently a curator for the V&A Theatre & Performance Department and worked on the new Theatre & Performance Galleries which opened in March 2009. Keith contributed to Oliver Messel: In the Theatre of Design *(2011).*

SHOWCASING THE TALENT

Sam Gatley

FROM THE very early stages of working on the *Hollywood Costume* exhibition the V&A conservation studio was aware that the display mannequins had to reflect the characters inhabiting each costume. We needed a display solution that could imbue the iconic costumes with as much life and verve as possible.

Although mannequins and dress stands can be purchased easily, they are rarely the right size or shape to accurately support and interpret a costume, and adaptations to the basic figure are often necessary. For *Hollywood Costume* the V&A mounting team was tasked with creating bespoke mounts for each ensemble that not only served to ensure the longevity of each garment by minimizing stress and strain on the fabrics, but also to present the costumes with as

much interpretive movement as possible.

Many of the costumes from Hollywood's Golden Age are extremely fragile. The dress and duster jacket designed by Travis Banton for Carole Lombard as Irene Bullock in *My Man Godfrey* (1936) is constructed from tiers of glass bugle beads stitched to a fine silk georgette. In order for the splendour of the costume to be truly appreciated, it needed to be displayed on a full-figure mannequin. However, the fine silk ground could not support the weight of the beading when displayed on a standing figure: too much stress was placed on the shoulder seams as the dress became increasingly heavy towards the hemline. Conservation of the dress had been carried out in Los Angeles prior to its arrival at the V&A. The original ground silk

was further reinforced by the V&A Conservation Studio before mounting. However, it was still not deemed strong enough to support its own weight over a prolonged display period. Consequently it was decided that the mannequin, when posed, should appear to lounge whilst on display. A reclining figure would support the entire length of the dress, and padded underpinnings would control the drape of the beaded fabric. So that Ms Lombard's mannequin would not be lying upon her own fragile dress, the figure needed to support itself by the exposed hands and feet only. This was achieved by cutting away the mannequin's hips. Although Irene Bullock is never seen to recline wearing this dress in the film, it was felt that the pose was in the decadent spirit of the film and a reasonable compromise for the sake of preserving the garments whilst on display.

With the more modern and robust costumes featured in the exhibition, it was imperative that the dynamic stances of Uma Thurman as the sword-wielding bride in *Kill Bill* (2003) or Johnny Depp as Captain Jack Sparrow in *Pirates of the Caribbean: On Stranger Tides* (2011) accommodated proper support of the fabrics, and each mannequin's pose was carefully discussed and reviewed by the curatorial and conservation departments prior to mounting. Undergarments for each costume component were painstakingly made to follow and support the lines and folds of each crease or area of stress that a bent arm or twisted upper torso might induce. This ensured that any potential damage to the costumes was significantly minimized.

Working on the *Hollywood Costume* exhibition has allowed the V&A textile conservation team to develop new and intricate display methods in order to sensitively bring this diverse and iconic collection of characters to life.

Sam Gatley is a textile display specialist at the V&A textile conservation studio.

295 Irene Bullock (Carole Lombard)
My Man Godfrey, 1936
Costume designers Travis Banton and Brymer
Gown and duster jacket designed by Travis Banton

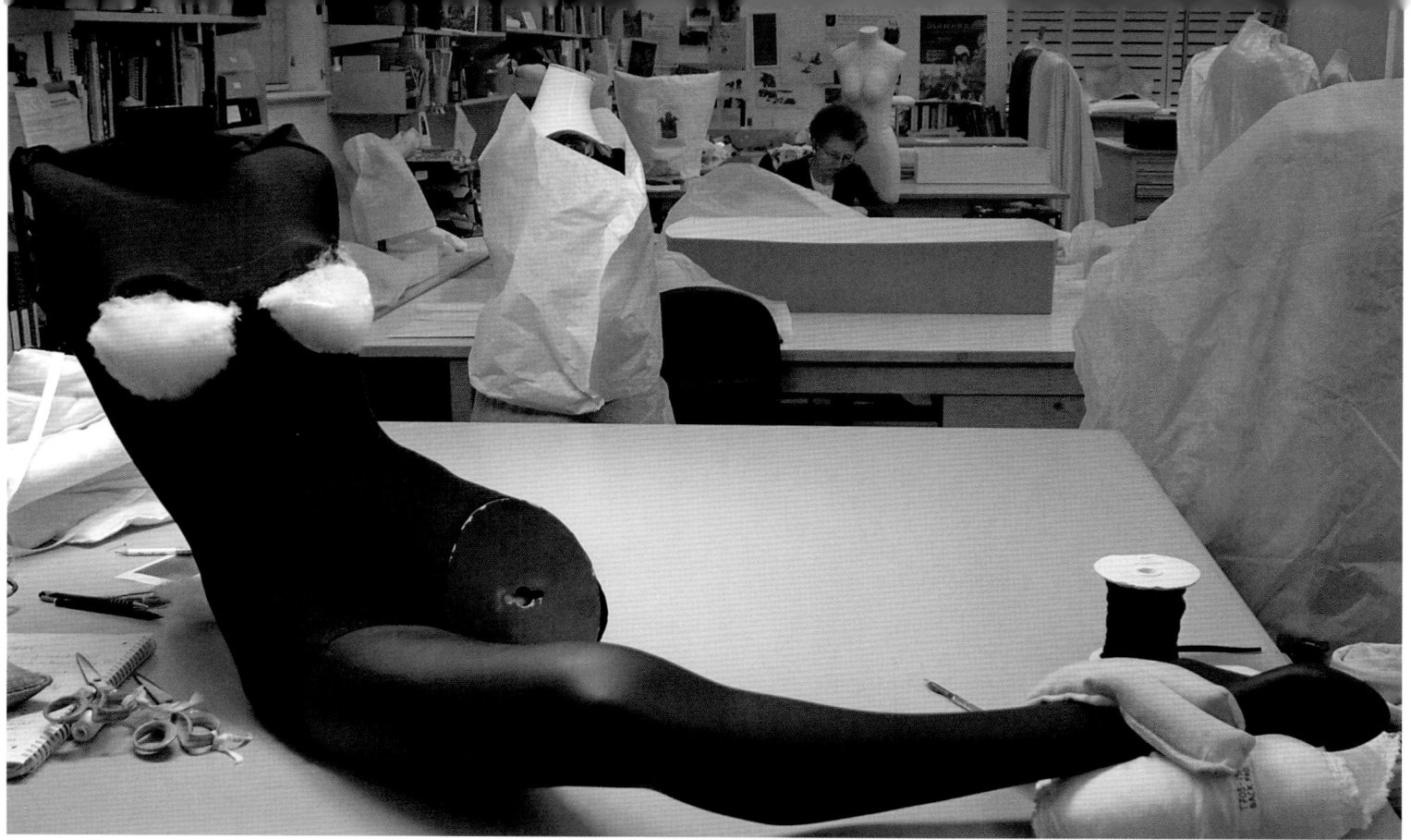

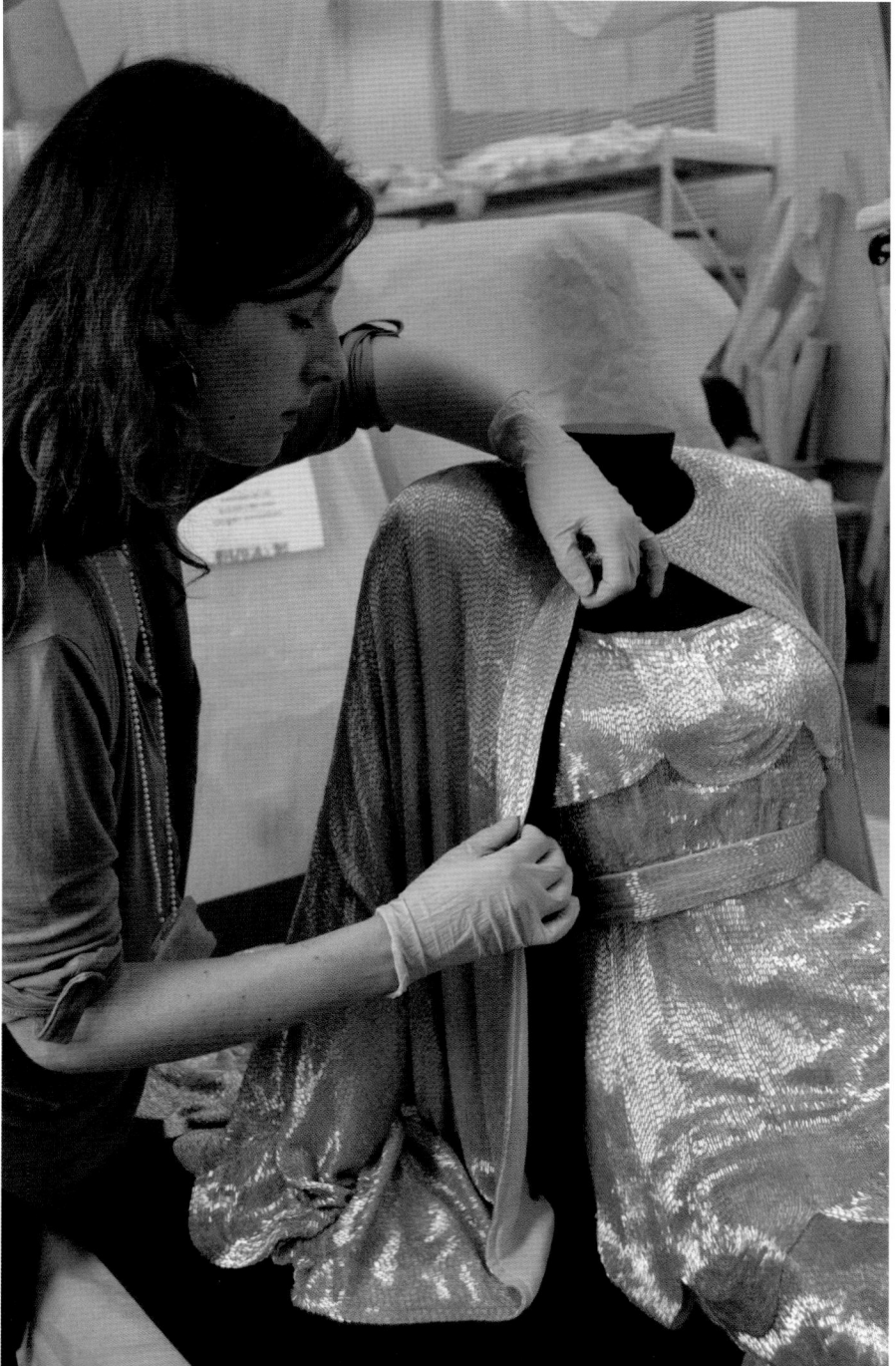

TOP
296 Mannequin modification for
My Man Godfrey

LEFT
297 Sam Gatley dressing the duster jacket on
to supportive undergarments

ABOVE
298 Costume detail showing glass bugle beaded scalloped edge

OVERLEAF
299 Costume for Irene Bullock
My Man Godfrey, 1936
Costume designers Travis Banton and Brymer
Gown and duster jacket designed by Travis Banton
The Collection of Motion Picture Costume Design Larry McQueen

213

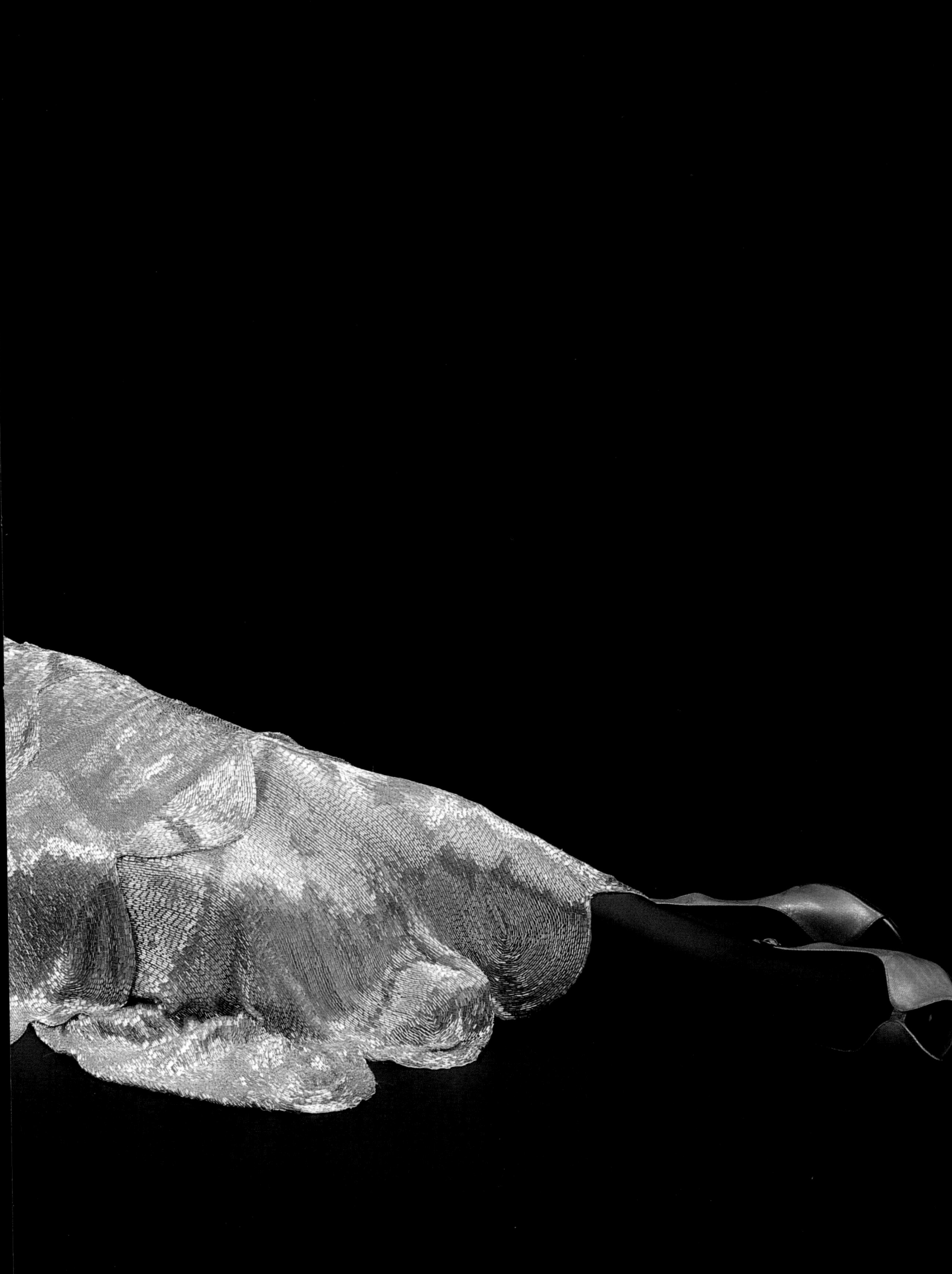

A COLLECTOR'S TALE

Larry McQueen

M Y FIRST impression of the world of costumes was at the age of ten, enthralled by a stage production of *The King and I* in my small home town in Colorado. Years later, working as a stage manager on a similar production, I learned that the Western Costume Co. had purchased the costumes from the 1956 film and then rented them out for such productions. I was shocked to see that some of the amazing gowns worn by Anna Leonowens (Deborah Kerr) in the film were held together with tape. The majority of the costumes were in poor condition because they had been rented until they literally fell apart. Years later I purchased two costumes, two masks and a headdress from the 'Uncle Tom's Cabin' production number from the same film, and felt that I had come full circle.

Collecting costumes and props used in film-making began when the industry itself was born, when members of the cast or crew might keep a favourite memento from the production. The stars often paid for their wardrobe themselves: in the fledgling business, actresses with the best personal wardrobe often received the best parts, and to that end in the 1920s they frequently had their gowns designed by Paris designers. Thus they amassed considerable private collections, some of which were given to museums or sold in estate sales. The studios themselves also had regular public sales when wardrobe departments were 'spring-cleaned', and filmgoers would flock to them in the hope of finding something originally worn by their favourite star.

My own involvement with film costume collecting began in 1978, when I first met Bill Thomas, then aged 18, who later became my best friend and business partner. I was fascinated by Bill's hobby of collecting film costumes. I was aware that he was a junior member of the 'Robin Hoods', a group of studio employees who 'rescued' items from the studios to save them from the auction block (and ruin) – although he took great pains to keep me away from them, and was finding it increasingly difficult to justify their practices. He was concerned that that his desire for individual items was destroying his love of the field in general, so on 13 December 1984 he sold his considerable collection at Christie's, New York. This was the first auction to consist entirely of film costumes.

But Bill's love of film costumes certainly had not been destroyed, and it was at this point that I got involved. In 1989 the superbly opulent court gown worn by Greta Garbo in *Queen Christina* (1933; plate 305) came up for auction at Christie's, New York. We had seen the piece at auction about five years earlier, and were dismayed to see that it was falling apart; since then it had gone through major restoration for an exhibition at the Smithsonian Museum. Bill and I decided to combine our resources to purchase it. The fact that we had no intention of ever re-selling it meant that we were no longer casual collectors: this was the beginning of The Collection of Motion Picture Costume Design. Our plan was to assemble costumes based on their historic and fashion significance rather than their commercial value, and we were determined to share our collection with the public.

In order to finance our collection we began to work with auction houses that saw the commercial value of movie memorabilia. I have been fortunate to work with such companies and collections as Camden House Auctioneers, Inc., in Los Angeles, the first auction house to deal specifically in movie memorabilia; Christie's East, New York, while researching a major collection of movie wardrobe to be auctioned by Paramount Studios (1992); Butterfield & Butterfield Auction Company, Los Angeles, working on the star collection of movie wardrobe auctioned by Western Costume Co. (1992 and two successive auctions) and in inventorying the collection of costume and props from the *Star Trek* franchise (2002); and Julien Entertainment, Los Angeles, in researching the Edith Head collection (2004). I have also worked with private estates, costume houses, individual collectors, designers and others in the course of researching and valuing items. Since 1999 I have been creating an archive for MGM/UA,

OPPOSITE
**300 Sir Frederick Barker,
Maria Barker and
Anthony Halton
(Herbert Marshall,
Marlene Dietrich and
Melvyn Douglas)**
Angel, **1937
Costume designer
Travis Banton**

OVERLEAF
301, 303 Costume for Maria Barker
Angel, **1937
Costume designer Travis Banton
The Collection of Motion
Picture Costume Design Larry McQueen**

302 Sketch for Maria Barker
Angel, **1937
Costume designer and illustrator
Travis Banton**

304 **Stage performance of the 'Uncle Tom's Cabin' number from Rodgers and Hammerstein's *The King and I*, c.1951**

BELOW
305 **Queen Christina, Oxenstierna and Antonio (Greta Garbo, Lewis Stone and John Gilbert) *Queen Christina*, 1933 Costume designer Adrian**

OPPOSITE
306 **Roxie Hart (Renée Zellweger) *Chicago*, 2002 Costume designer Colleen Atwood**

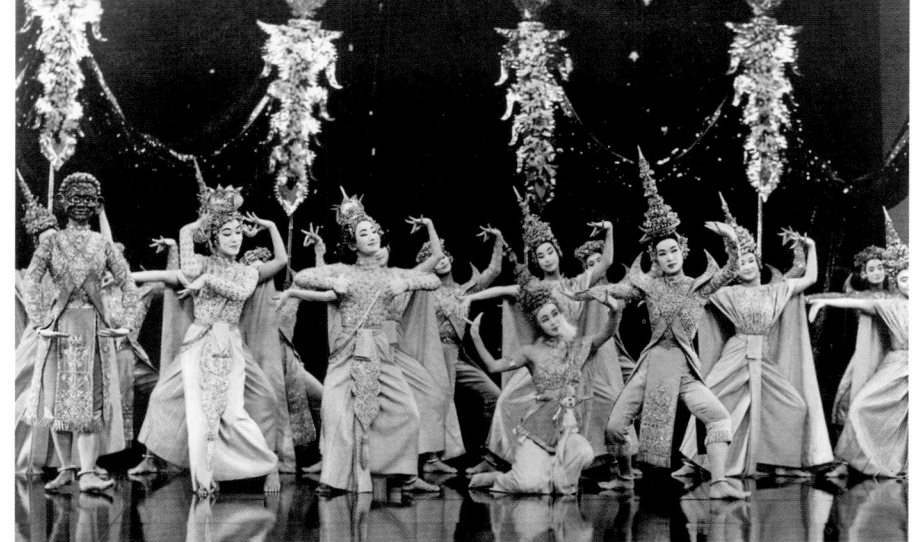

compiling, maintaining, documenting and storing a collection of film-related costumes and props as a physical record of the story of film-making at MGM studios. Regrettably, changing times have led to the decision to liquidate this archive, so another important historical record will be lost to future generations.

Although the majority of the clothes in The Collection have been purchased at public auctions of movie memorabilia, which have changed dramatically since the time when costumes were a mere novelty, I acquired my first film costume, a grey wool period dress, from a second-hand clothing store in Hollywood one Halloween. This, I discovered, was from the 1955 film *The Virgin Queen*. Years later, in April 1992, we purchased a red wool period gown with caplet worn by Bette Davis from the same film from the gift shop at Bally's Hotel in Las Vegas. Previously the MGM Grand Hotel, the building had suffered a major fire and significant water damage in 1980. A handful of costumes had been bagged and forgotten in the storeroom: when we purchased the Bette Davis gown it was covered in mould and the fur trim was decaying, but it emerged from cleaning and restoration flawless, without a moth hole or stain.

Some of our pieces, such as the sequin trouser suit worn by Susan Hayward in *Valley of the Dolls* (1967; plates 23, 24), were purchased from private collectors. My favourite method of gleaning from other collectors is by trading pieces, the transaction thus becoming less about monetary worth and more about the value of the pieces to our respective collections. For example, as part of a series of pieces from *Chicago* (2002), the long black dress worn by Renée Zellweger (plate 306) was traded for a selection of costumes from *Stargate* (1994).

Other costumes in our collection have been acquired from estate sales: the Louise Glaum spider web dress from *Sex* (1920; plate 308), for example, was purchased at her estate sale in 1985.

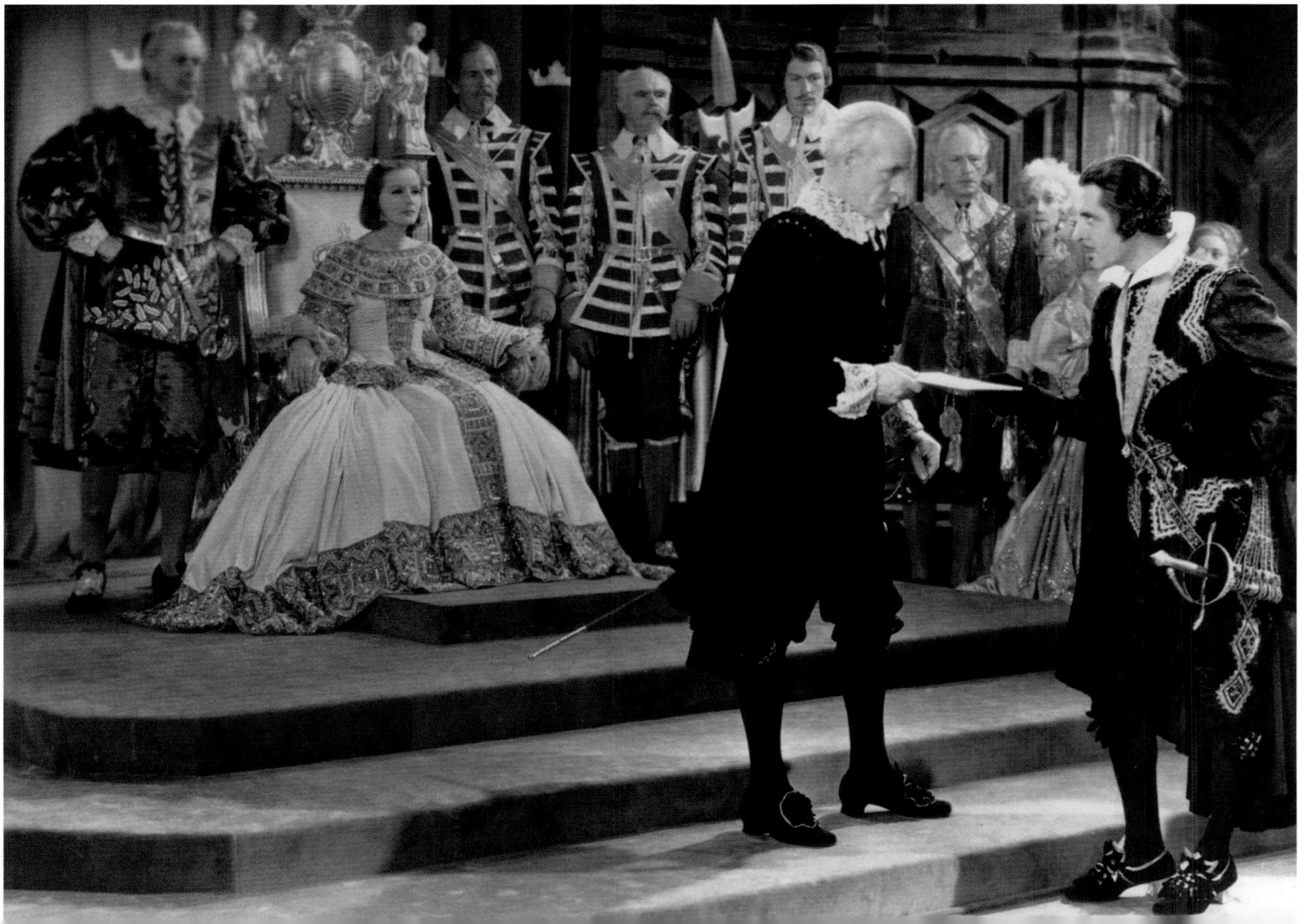

One of my great regrets is not having been at the early estate sales of Mary Pickford and Charlie Chaplin, two pioneer performers who retained much of their film wardrobe, understanding the importance of imagery in building their careers. Fortunately many items from these two sales were donated to museums, and Miss Pickford's clothes reside at the Los Angeles County Museum of Natural History.

From time to time the studios themselves hold public sales. One brilliant campaign on the part of Paramount was to offer potential buyers the chance to prove the identities of unknown costumes, whereupon they would give each a valuation and possibly offer it for sale. The green costume worn by Kim Novak in *Vertigo* (1958; plate 91) and a costume worn by Grace Kelly in *Rear Window* (1954), which was exhibited at the V&A in 2010, were both purchased from Paramount in an online auction. I have also worked with Warner Brothers archives and have traded costumes worn in Warner Brothers films for others in their collection, such as those worn by Vivien Leigh and Laurence Olivier in *That Hamilton Woman* (1941).

Companies that dispose of production wardrobe have been

OPPOSITE
307 Catherine Tramell (Sharon Stone)
Basic Instinct, 1992
Costume designer Ellen Mirojnick

TOP
308 Unknown dancer and Adrienne Renault
(Louise Glaum)
Sex, 1920
Costume designer (uncredited) Louise Glaum

ABOVE
309 Publicity photograph for *Sex* from
the *Green Book* magazine, c.1920

a useful source for contemporary pieces, such as the white dress worn by Sharon Stone in the 'interview' scene in *Basic Instinct* (1992; plate 307). When acquiring contemporary costume, one of the most interesting challenges for the collector is determining which film will withstand the test of time and become tomorrow's classic, and which actors tomorrow's stars.

Occasionally collectors are lucky enough to be presented with a piece by a designer or someone in the industry who wants to ensure that the costumes are respected and shared with the public. One of our most gratifying such gifts was from the Australian designer Janet Patterson and Miramax, comprising six costumes from *The Piano* (1993), including the black dress, hat and parasol belonging to Ada McGrath (Holly Hunter).

I have been fortunate to have had thousands of film costumes and props pass through my hands over the years. I can recognize studio construction and I trust my instincts as to what may or may not be an important film piece. In 1992, for example, I discovered a sceptre with an Egyptian motif in an antique shop and purchased it without knowing what it was. It was a most unexpected delight to discover later that it was used by Charlton Heston in *The Ten Commandments* (1956). Other such discoveries are still waiting to be made. I have a rack of unidentified items: there is nothing more exciting than watching a film and seeing something from that rack appear on the screen.

From time to time costumes provide an opportunity to make a truly visceral connection with Hollywood history. In December 1990, at an auction of 'star wardrobe' from Paramount

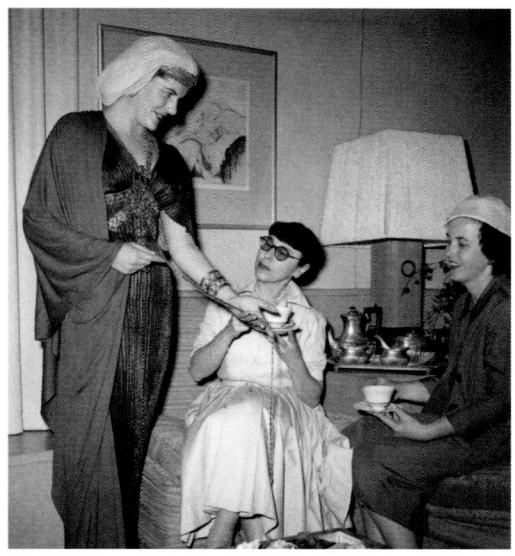

at Christie's, New York, Bill and I were overwhelmed to see one of the most spectacular film costumes ever created up for sale. The golden gown with train and fur-trimmed stole, embroidered with millions of gold beads, pearls, rhinestones, gold bullion, gold sequins and faux ruby and emeralds, was designed in 1936 by Travis Banton for Marlene Dietrich, for the film *Angel* (1937; plates 301–3). At $8,000 (over $100,000 in today's money), this was the most expensive gown Banton had ever designed. Dietrich loved the gown and asked the studio if she could keep it. It is said that she was so angry at being refused that she stormed off the set – and did not return to Paramount until a decade later. Having retained the gown, Paramount put it to good use. Reusing costumes was common practice among film studios to maintain an opulent look for background characters without the expense of creating new clothes. It is not known exactly how many times the Dietrich gown was reused, but it appeared in a number of films, undergoing numerous alterations in the process.

When we acquired the iconic gown in 1990, our excitement soon gave way to dismay when the reality of its condition dawned. Weakened by age, poor storage conditions and multiple alterations, it could never be dressed on a mannequin because it was unable to support its own weight. In 1999, four years after Bill's death, I consulted museum experts in conservation and restoration and we debated whether we should tamper with the integrity

of the gown – however poor. We finally decided that instead of leaving the gown as it was – a box of unshowable beads – the ensemble should be restored. I employed Getson/Eastern embroidery, the firm that had embroidered the original costume for Travis Banton and still had many of the beads, sequins and stones.

The restoration process proved far more difficult than planned: the gown had only taken a few weeks to create, but it took years to restore. Every inch of beadwork had to be attached to new silk backing, the patterns pulled into shape and lightly tacked before hand-stitching in place, with missing stones or beads being replaced during the process. Previous poor repairs were removed, missing areas replaced, broken silk threads reinforced, and so on. Using enlarged photographs of Dietrich wearing the gown, it was possible to determine how the patterns had been altered; templates were made to re-create the originals. The task involved working inch by inch over thousands of hours – and at great expense.

After a year we were having difficulty finding qualified people with the time and patience to spend on the garment, and most of the work was now being carried out by the owner of Getson/Eastern, Annie Denderian. I decided that the best way forward was to take over the bulk of the hands-on restoration myself. Mentored by Ms Denderian, learning and perfecting the techniques to painstakingly re-attach the patterns, I felt a strong

sense of connection with the people who originally created the garment. I could tell when one was having a bad day and cutting corners, or when another was struck with genius; I learned to distinguish between different beaders; I marvelled at the time spent on details in areas that no-one could see. The gown is now truly a testament to the artistry of early Hollywood: the care, attention and thousands of hours spent on its restoration would make its original creators proud.

Just before Bill's death in 1995, he told me that he wanted me to pass on his passion. The night before he died I attended an initial meeting to discuss our first international exhibition, *Cinema Fashion and Hollywood Designers*, to be mounted in Tokyo later the same year. Bill knew that our dream would become a reality. Words cannot express my appreciation for all I learned from Bill Thomas, for his innate passion, knowledge and respect for the field of film costumes, and for the opportunities that were to follow.

From the very conception of The Collection, our desire was always to share our pieces via public exhibition and to communicate the magic that they created in the films in which they appeared. There are often unforeseen difficulties associated with such an ambition. For example, the costumes were created to 'move' across the silver screen, and I have to admit that seeing live models moving in them is an exciting concept; but the sight of a model stepping on the hem of a 1930s period gown at one such show and ripping the skirt off at the waist made me realize that this was a bad idea.

In compiling The Collection our focus has been on representing different time periods and fashion trends while including as many stars and designers associated with them as we can. We have concentrated on costumes with popular appeal and, wherever possible, in good enough condition to retain their original magic while withstanding the rigours of exhibition. Because some – like Dietrich's *Angel* gown – have undergone alterations and were stored in poor conditions, this is not always easy. We have never worked from a specific 'wish-list', not knowing whether certain costumes actually still exist, whether they are in a condition that can be shown, or whether we can afford them. Certainly mistakes have been made and pieces have come up for sale at the wrong time, when I was unprepared either financially or mentally to make a commitment; no doubt I shall be haunted by those forever. But that is the nature of collecting and you have to move on.

When costumes are purchased in less than perfect condition, decisions must be made concerning their conservation, restoration and cleaning. Consultation and restraint are important to ensure that the garment does not become a copy of the original, and to avoid more damage during the course of restoration. Above all, any changes to the garment are meticulously documented. There are also responsibilities associated with collecting textiles, and I must often forego the purchase of new costumes in order to finance the care of The Collection. Storage is a major concern: the use of acid-free boxes and tissue and maintaining a temperature and humidity-controlled environment are essential. Maintenance of the costumes is also a vital part of assuring that they may continue to be be exhibited: the Adrian *Queen Christina* gown, for example, underwent 450 hours of strengthening and securing the beadwork for exhibition.

As for the future, I have accepted the responsibility that

313 Marilyn Monroe and Orry-Kelly at a fitting for *Some Like it Hot*, 1959
Costume designer Orry-Kelly

OPPOSITE
314 Sugar Kane Kowalczyk (Marilyn Monroe)
***Some Like it Hot*, 1959**
Costume designers Orry-Kelly

goes with being the caretaker of these costumes and ensure that these fragile and uniquely beautiful parts of film history will survive. I wish I could honestly say that I believe in the possibility of a world-class museum that tells the Hollywood story and is supported by the industry itself. It is a fascinating story that has helped shape our culture, and I would like to believe that the renewed energy created by the memorabilia market would bring focus and help to keep it alive. But, as with other collectable artwork, the field has entered a new international marketplace and the Hollywood story is being dissipated across the world. Some of the studios are frantically trying to acquire back some of those lost memories, but often too late. The nature of the industry is (and probably always was) an ever-advancing money-making business focused on the next box office hit. It is not a single, supportive, cohesive industry, but one made up of numerous companies competing to out-manoeuvre one other. But they all have one thing in common: their shared history of wonderful artistry based on a rich imagination that touches us all. With the demise of collections such as Debbie Reynolds' in June 2011, and of historic records such as the MGM/UA archive, the legacy of a hundred years of Hollywood costumes now rests in our hands.

A highly respected collector of vintage film costumes, Larry McQueen regularly loans pieces for exhibitions from his extensive Collection of Motion Picture Costume Design.

THE COLLECTING IMPERATIVE
A STUDIO PERSPECTIVE

Deidre L. Thieman

N 30 APRIL 1912 the Universal Film Manufacturing Company was incorporated in New York by Carl Laemmle (affectionately known as Uncle Carl), a German immigrant who arrived in America with $50 to his name. Laemmle opened his first nickelodeon in Chicago in 1906 and by 1909 moved into producing motion pictures for his own use. The famous San Fernando Valley chicken ranch that became one of the world's largest studios officially opened in 1915. Now, a hundred years after Universal's founding, NBCUniversal Archives & Collections is thrilled to be participating in the exhibition celebrating Hollywood costume at the Victoria and Albert Museum.

Archives & Collections originated with the work of Carla Ash, former Corporate Art Curator for Seagram in 1996–7, when that company owned Universal. The department was formally established in 1998 with objects discovered in Ash's original historical survey of the studio and included items such as set plans, photography, corporate records, matte paintings and, of course, costumes and props. The eight pieces loaned from our archives are not only part of the way we are celebrating our Centennial, but this display – and others like it – is also our way of sharing NBCUniversal's contribution to global cultural history.

WHY DO WE COLLECT?

It often strikes people as unusual for a corporation to maintain an archive, particularly one that contains artefacts and textiles more commonly found in museum settings, but there is practical value to doing so. NBCUniversal Archives & Collections is maintained for a number of reasons. First and foremost, it allows us to share with worldwide audiences what we do and how we create our productions. As such, wardrobe is only a single facet of an archive which also includes corporate history, publicity and marketing materials, theme park collections, props, art department materials and visual effects assets from feature films and television shows.

Secondary to its mission of outreach, Archives & Collections also exists to help NBCUniversal produce, publicize and market quality entertainment in a variety of ways. Our collections are used to maintain continuity in sequels, prequels, spin-offs and remakes that are so much a part of film history. Entertainment assets in the archives are used to help market and publicize our films when they are displayed during premières, in theatre lobbies and used for photo shoots at the time of a film's release. The

OPPOSITE
315 Cecilia Tallis (Keira Knightley)
***Atonement*, 2007**
Costume designer
Jacqueline Durran

RIGHT
316 Sketch for Cecilia Tallis
***Atonement*, 2007**
Costume designer and
illustrator
Jacqueline Durran

OVERLEAF, LEFT
317, 318 Costume Department,
Universal Studios, 1940

OVERLEAF, RIGHT
319 Sketch artists at work,
Costume Department,
Universal Studos, 1940

320 Costume Workroon,
Costume Department,
Universal Studios, 1940

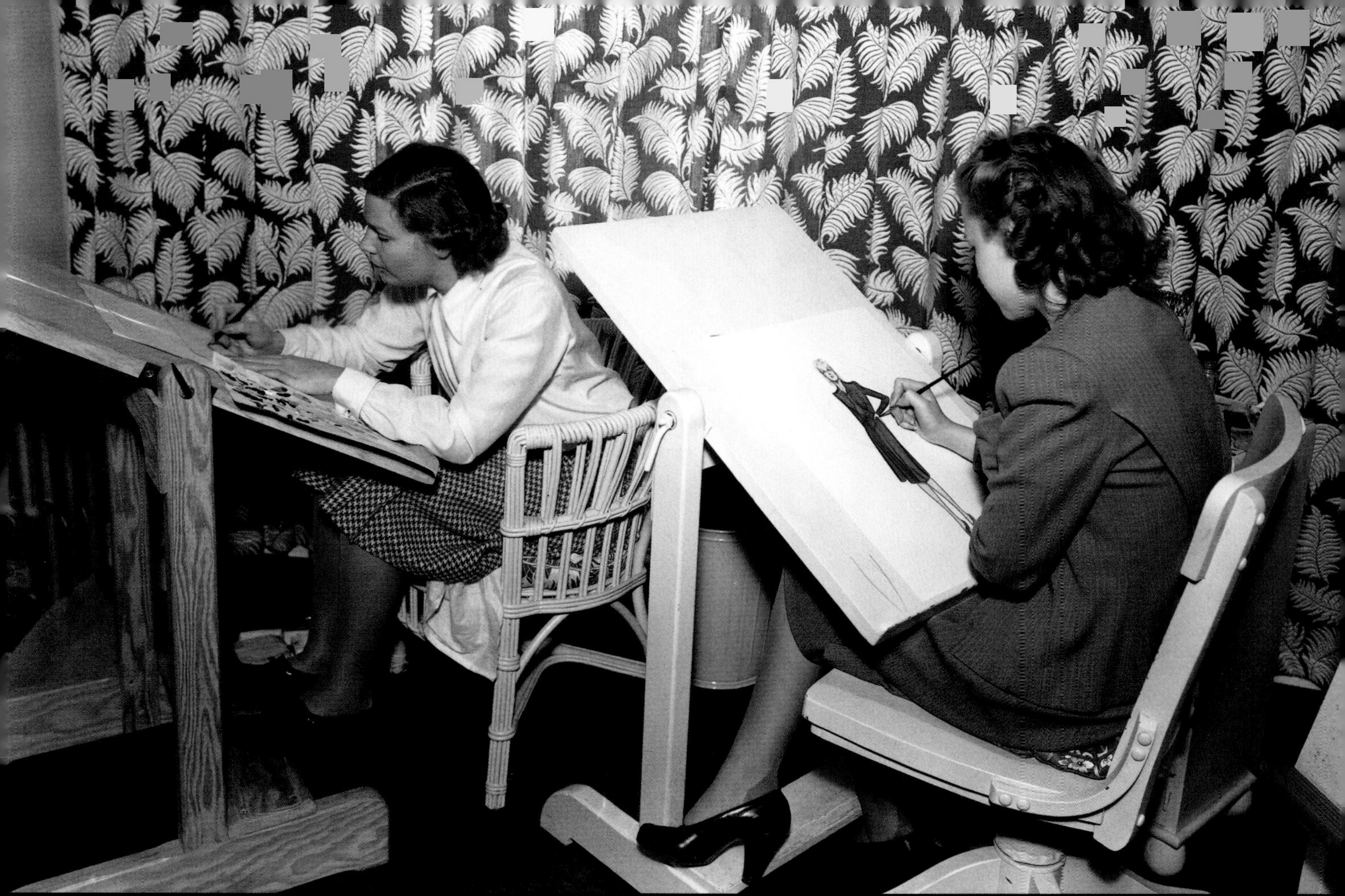

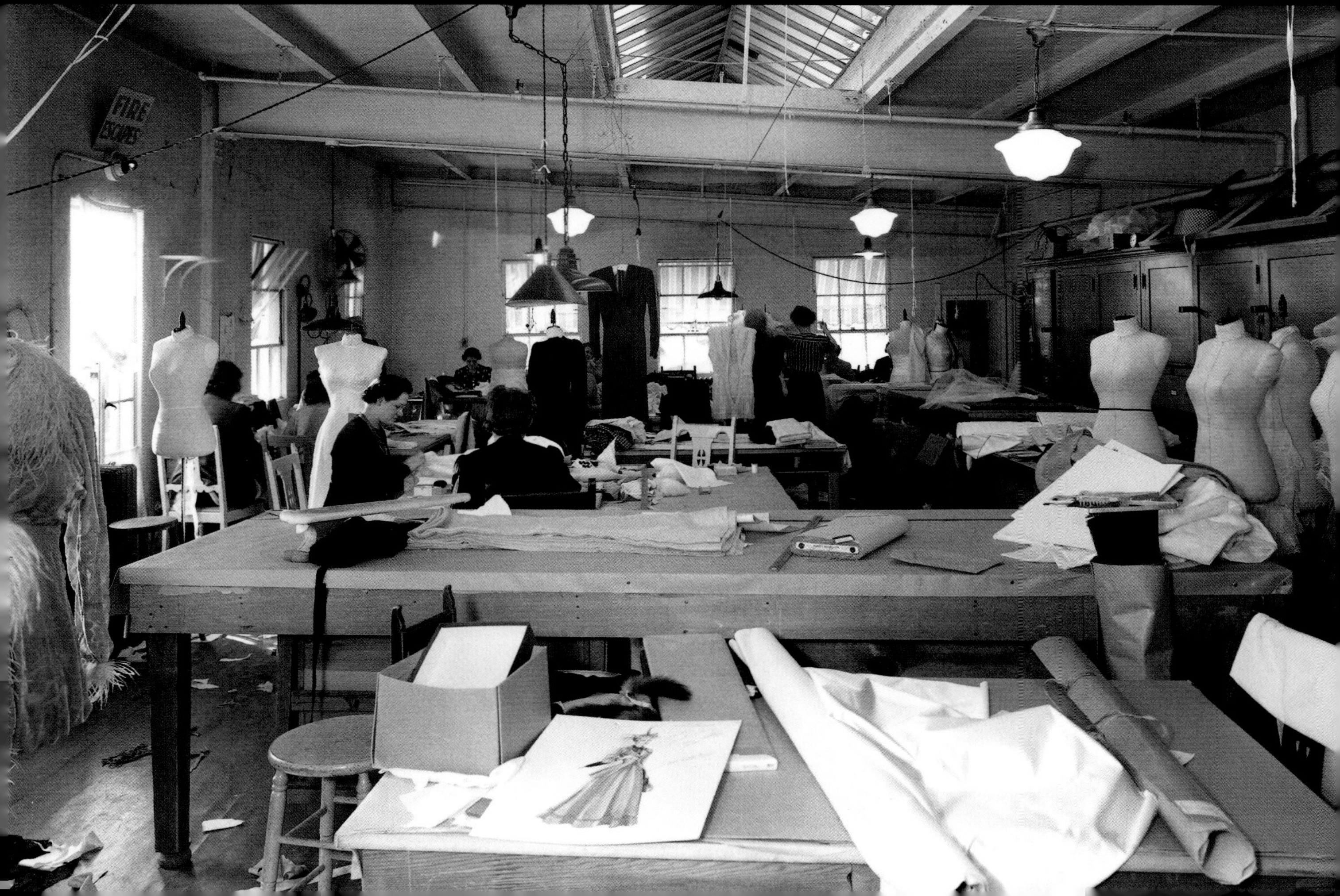
FIRE
ESCAPES

831:—THE LARGEST MOVING PICTURE STUDIO IN THE WORLD, UNIVERSAL CITY, CALIFORNIA.

321 Entrance to
Universal Studios,
late 1910s–1920s

archives are often referred to during the development of new consumer products, for licensing requests and to enhance the extras, or Added Value Features, on DVDs and videos.

HOW DO WE OBTAIN WARDROBE FROM OUR PRODUCTIONS AND DECIDE WHAT TO KEEP?

All of the archives' collecting activities are governed by a collections development policy which was designed by determining what materials best document the creative process, and by analysing user requests over a period of years in order to discover which materials were most frequently requested. The policy states that archivists should seek specific materials for permanent preservation, including using the following criteria for feature titles:

Wardrobe (select hero)
● Due to size and storage considerations, Television & Feature wardrobe acquisition will be limited by choosing a representative sample of the materials that are the most significant in the production.
● Wardrobe will be selected on the basis of its representation of characters, its ability to illustrate change in characters and production and its ability to be displayed.
● Normal parameters for wardrobe are 2–3 changes for main cast, 1–2 changes for supporting cast and 1 change for significant cameos. Exceptions are made for period films or science fiction/fantasy productions where wardrobe may be more distinctive than for contemporary comedies or dramas. For these films, numerical limitations will be increased or rendered inapplicable.

There is no practical way to save everything, so representative sampling is used to control the volume of collecting, while ensuring the preservation of those items that best represent the production as a whole.

Every production by Universal Pictures & Focus Features, as well as those by Universal Television and Universal Cable Productions, undergoes a formal process that allows the archive to select and preserve a representative sample so that it is available for future use. This process has six basic stages, handled by a variety of staff members:

1 **Appraisal** (Manager – Production Archives)
Script review to generate costume, prop and set-dressing breakdowns.
2 **Reappraisal** (Manager – Production Archives)
Refining the request using continuity books, publicity photographs and/or a viewing of a near-to-final cut of the film in order to determine which pieces are available and best represent the film.
3 **Submission to Feature Assets**
(Manager – Production Archives)
This department is responsible for the disposal of all the assets from a film. Assets listed in their database are requested and approval given for distribution to the archives and other departments.
4 **Accessioning** (Archivist and Assistant Archivist)
Some items are received directly from Productions (Continuity, Art Department, etc.) in case they are needed for re-shoots or inserts before picture lock, the stage in the editing process where all changes to the production have been made and approved. The remainder is retrieved from Feature Assets' storage facility, where they are held until it is certain they will no longer be needed for Production. Once the wardrobe (and all other assets) enters our building the transfer of materials is formally documented or accessioned in our database. After this (Temp Items), very basic box level records with locations, are entered.
5 **Physical Processing** (Archivist, Assistant Archivists and interns)
Upon release or request, the each item is processed. Every asset

is packed according to proper archival and museum methods and stored in a temperature-controlled environment to prevent damage and deterioration. A series level record is created for the wardrobe in the database.

6 Cataloguing (Archivist, Assistant Archivists and Interns)
The wardrobe series is then broken down into file unit records, each containing a still of the change from the film; a continuity photo of the whole change; information about the pieces which make up the change, such as how they are worn (dressing notes), the scene in which the change is used, the actor who wears it, the designer who created it, and any other information that applies to the whole change or outfit. Item records are then created for every individual element of the change, containing specific information about that piece – its measurements, brand, full description, photos, and so on. Once these records are complete, assets have locations assigned in the database and are put away. All this work helps contribute to the preservation of the collection: the detailed catalogue records minimize the need to handle physical garments.

WHY DON'T WE HAVE IT?

When working with reference or loan requests we may be asked why we do not have a particular item in the archive. There are four primary responses to this question. The first is the history of the Archives department, which was founded long after the studio itself. At NBCUniversal we have had a working wardrobe department since the founding of Universal City in 1915 and even before this property was purchased, there was a wardrobe department

at the company's first production studio in Fort Lee, New Jersey, dating from 1912. From time to time the department's wardrobe managers have donated notable historic pieces from their stock to the archives. As a result we have pieces dating back to the 1930s and '40s, from such stars as Rock Hudson, Abbott and Costello, Maureen O'Hara and Deanna Durbin. The oldest wardrobe element in the collection is a brocade tunic worn by Basil Rathbone in *Tower of London* (1939). Other pieces have not survived the passage of time or were sold long ago, and are now cared for by other cultural, educational institutions and by private collectors.

For current productions, costumes are often rented from a variety of rental houses and then returned to them afterwards. This was the case with the shoes worn by Cate Blanchett in *Elizabeth: The Golden Age* (2007) to accompany the orange dress in the present exhibition, by costume designer Alexandra Byrne (plates 323–5). Accessories and costumes used in contemporary films are frequently subject to product placement deals, in which a manufacturer supplies goods for a production in return for the publicity generated by their appearance in the film or associated advertising. Since part of our mission is to document how films are created, the absence of pieces can actually help us explain this. The creative people involved in a production will sometimes maintain assets in their private collections if they have negotiated for this in their contracts. Finally, costumes may be auctioned by marketing departments to generate publicity for a film. For example, the two 'hero' shirts from the end of *Brokeback Mountain* were sold at a charity auction: those included in this exhibition are versions of the shirts, from earlier in the film. Even though costumes may appear identical throughout a film, there are often multiple versions used in different scenes, with levels of distressing (ageing) to reflect the action. Other versions may be worn by stunt people and stand-ins. The Archives department sometimes collects multiple hero versions of costumes to reflect this process. All the pieces in the present exhibition are hero pieces, worn by the principal cast member during the film.

322 Tanya, Donna and Rosie (Christine Baranski, Meryl Streep and Julie Walters) *Mamma Mia!*, 2008
Costume designer Ann Roth

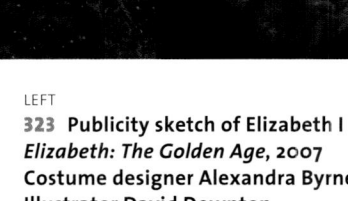

LEFT
323 Publicity sketch of Elizabeth I
Elizabeth: The Golden Age, 2007
Costume designer Alexandra Byrne
Illustrator David Downton

ABOVE
324 Elizabeth I (Cate Blanchett)
Elizabeth: The Golden Age, 2007
Costume designer Alexandra Byrne

OPPOSITE
325 Costume for Elizabeth I
Elizabeth: The Golden Age, 2007
Costume designer Alexandra Byrne
NBCUniversal Archives & Collections

Some, like the dance costume designed by Ann Roth and worn by Donna (Meryl Streep) for the final credits of *Mamma Mia!* (2006; plate 322) are one of a kind, and no copies exist.

THE ADVANTAGE OF STUDIO-BASED COLLECTING

The greatest advantage of studio-based collecting is that it provides costume historians with context. Because an archive like ours is not limited to costumes, we are able to place each piece alongside associated props, to document how it was used in a production and what version of the change it was. Our records contain details of, for example, original values for insurance purposes. We can place the costumes in the context of the history of the studio that created the productions, and we can provide stills that show it in the film along with documentation of its creation – continuity books, costume plots and sometimes original sketches. Perhaps our greatest asset is a sure and certain record of the costume's provenance. Our formal collecting policy, with procedures to document everything in our catalogue, means that everything in the archive is demonstrably authentic. There are many replicas of Hollywood costume out there, and they are not always clearly identified as such.

A primary part of our mission is to share film history and the work of the great costume designers who help create it, and we are delighted to have this opportunity to celebrate Universal's Centenary by sharing part of our collections with visitors to the *Hollywood Costume* exhibition.

The Manager, Production Archives, Deidre Thieman is responsible for the acquisition, cataloguing, processing, preservation and exhibition of wardrobe and other assets from film and television productions at NBCUniversal. Costumes in her charge include those featured here from Brokeback Mountain *(2005),* Elizabeth: The Golden Age *(2007),* Gladiator *(2000),* The Blues Brothers *(1980),* Mamma Mia! *(2006),* Atonement *(2007) and* The Bourne Ultimatum *(2007).*

ACTRESS AND COLLECTOR

Debbie Reynolds

MY LOVE of Hollywood costumes was formed at Metro-Goldwyn-Mayer Studios. When I arrived in 1950, signed to the studio as a contract player, I was a child in Wonderland, in awe of everything there – especially the costume department. As a teenager from a poor family in Burbank, California, my closet contained one pair of blue jeans, a white blouse and one grey skirt that my mother made me. Imagine how it felt to walk into an entire building full of the most beautiful clothing in the world. I had never seen dresses or suits so stunning. The fabrics were dazzling. The many seamstresses and designers paid attention to every stitch, seam and adornment. The great costume creator Walter Plunkett made our costumes for *Singin' in the Rain* (1952). Prior to that he had designed the costumes for many classic films, including *Gone with the Wind* (1939) and *Little Women* (1949), and had won an Academy Award for *An American in Paris* (1951). When I wore Mr Plunkett's beautiful costumes, I felt like a grown-up young lady for the first time.

At MGM the actors were under contract to make films. We were also required to learn all the crafts that were part of the creative process of film-making. We took singing lessons, dancing classes, learned make-up techniques, lighting and set design, and took part in endless wardrobe fittings. MGM was very kind to me during my early years there. They allowed my mother to come to the studio to study pattern making for a year in the wardrobe department. Mother was so happy to learn from these experts.

The costume designer who had the most influence on me was Helen Rose (plate 330). A small, delicate person, Helen was the most feminine of ladies, as well as a brilliant artist. Helen was fanatical about details. She supervised the construction of every seam and pleat; every button had to pass her inspection.

Helen designed my wedding gown when I married Eddie Fisher (plate 329). She made wedding gowns for Elizabeth Taylor, Ava Gardner, Lana Turner and Grace Kelly (plate 331). We kept her busy with all our marriages. When I watched the wedding of Prince William to Kate Middleton, I was thrilled when I saw the bride's gloriously graceful dress (plate 332). It was reminiscent of the gown that Helen Rose had designed for Grace Kelly's marriage to Prince Rainier of Monaco so long ago. It was nice to see Helen Rose's influence reach across the years to the wedding of this lovely royal couple.

For my first big Hollywood party, Helen made a sketch of a dress for me to wear. The fitted bodice had a V-neck, three-quarter-length sleeves and was made of black velvet. The full cocktail-length skirt was made of beautiful white lace. My mother took the sketch home and she and our neighbour, Mrs Kropf, made the pattern and sewed the dress. Jane Powell loaned me her white mink stole and pearl handbag. My teacher and mentor at MGM, Lillian Burns Sidney, loaned me her emerald ring. The actor Hugh O'Brian was my date for this magnificent party at the home of Marion Davies and her husband, Captain Horace Brown.

OPPOSITE
**326 Johnny Brown and Molly Brown
(Harve Presnell and Debbie Reynolds)
The Unsinkable Molly Brown, 1964
Costume designer Morton Haack**

RIGHT
**327 Morton Haack sketching designs
for *The Unsinkable Molly Brown*, 1964**

It was a splendid evening with several orchestras, lavish refresh-
ments and many glamorous people. As I danced the night away,
I felt so mature and attractive in my Helen Rose creation that had
been lovingly assembled by my family and friends.

Of the many beautiful costumes I wore in my films, one
of my favourites was in *The Unsinkable Molly Brown* (1964; plate
326). Morton Haack created an opulent red gown for Molly with
feathers at the shoulders and bead rosettes on the skirt. It was
the perfect costume for a country girl who went to Denver and
tried to fit into their high society. Morton's vision for my character
enhanced my performance.

In 1970, while still under contract, I read in *The Hollywood
Reporter* that MGM was going to be holding an auction. I called
Jim Aubrey, who was the President of MGM at the time, and
asked him about the announcement. He told me that the studio

had decided to sell Lot 2 and all its other assets, including props,
costumes and set pieces. I was shocked. Lot 2 was where *Singin' in
the Rain* had been filmed. So many other famous movies were shot
there. Today it is a block of condominiums. This was incredible
news to me. MGM had always been so strict about their costumes
– we were not even allowed to borrow them to wear to a party.
Now they planned to sell everything but the main real estate. I
had been around these amazing costumes since I was a teenager.
I knew the actors who wore them to create their famous roles.

ABOVE, LEFT TO RIGHT
329 Eddie Fisher and Debbie Reynolds, 1952
Gown designed by Helen Rose

330 Helen Rose, 1948

BELOW, LEFT TO RIGHT
331 Grace Kelly and Prince Rainier
of Monaco, 1956
Gown designed by Helen Rose

332 The Duke and Duchess
of Cambridge, 2011
**Gown designed by Sarah Burton for
Alexander McQueen**

333 Debbie Reynolds with costumes from
Cleopatra (1963)

OPPOSITE
334 Debbie Reynolds in her costume from
The Unsinkable Molly Brown, with gowns from
Conquest (1937) and *The Virgin Queen* (1955)
Photoshoot for the *Franklin Mint* magazine, 1996
Photographer Mark Lynn

This was our Hollywood history. I was overcome by the need to save everything I could.

My husband at the time, Harry Karl, and I went to see Al Hart at Citibank in Beverly Hills, to borrow money to buy up the studio property. Harry thought I was crazy but he indulged me. We explained the situation to Mr Hart. 'We should turn Lot 2 into another Disneyland', I said. 'People will come to see the things that belonged to their favourite stars.' The bank inspected the land and agreed to a loan of five million dollars. I made an offer to Jim Aubrey but somehow the deal didn't go through and the property was sold to someone else. Everything else went up for grabs. I asked Mr Aubrey if I could bid for things before the public auction. He told me to find a seat and bid with everyone else.

So I did. I couldn't believe the waste and destruction that went on at the studio. I was so upset. Every day I was tearful at the wilful disregard for film history. Films were being burned in rubbish barrels, including remnants of classic MGM movies with extra scenes that had been cut from the original releases. All those wonderful musical numbers and footage, up in smoke. Reams of sheet music and arrangements from the Music Department were sold as landfill. Photo stills were trashed. Clothes were tossed into boxes. Costumes that cost $25,000 to build in 1970 were bundled in groups of thirty and sold to costume houses all over the country for very little money. I didn't sleep for three weeks. I went every day and bought everything I could. I bought suites of costumes – assemblies of clothes worn by all the actors in a scene and the props or set pieces that belonged with them. I sat

in the auction room intimidating people who tried to outbid me. My collecting life began – in a big way.

The following year the same thing happened at 20th Century Fox. This time my friend Jerry Wunderlich, the set designer, got permission from the President of Fox for me to buy items before the sale. That was when I bought the famous Marilyn Monroe costumes that became the centerpiece of my collection.

In only a year my collection had grown. I housed it at the Karz building on Hollywood Boulevard, next door to Grauman's Chinese Theatre. It was my first attempt to build a museum for the public enjoyment of our film history. Over the next forty years I tried unsuccessfully to open a permanent home for my ever-expanding collection.

Many years later I was able to display part of the collection at my hotel in Las Vegas. After I lost the hotel (that's a story for another time) I entered into an agreement to build a museum at the new Hollywood & Highland complex. When that fell through, I planned to house the collection at a special museum in Pigeon Forge, Tennessee, near Dolly Parton's famous Dollywood theme park. When this plan was not approved, I contacted the Academy of Motion Picture Arts and Sciences and offered to allow them to display my collection at their proposed museum. They turned me down. I asked every wealthy film producer, director and businessperson I know to help me build a home for my collection, without success.

Ironically, although Hollywood – where all those wonderful and famous costumes were created and preserved forever on film – did not want them, the world did. In 2008 Deborah Nadoolman Landis and I met to discuss the present exhibition, and it was my pleasure to agree to loan her about a dozen costumes from my collection. The following year, a team from the V&A visited my son Todd Fisher in California, spending the day taking pictures of the pieces that were to be displayed in London. All these plans evaporated in the beginning of June 2011, when I was forced to sell my beloved collection and part of it was then moved to the Paley Media Center in Beverly Hills as an exhibition prior to being auctioned. As soon as the doors opened, throngs of fans filled the Paley Center to overflowing. In the next three weeks, before the auction on 18 June, thousands of people came for a last look at the costumes I had collected over the years. People used to make fun of me for saving everything, but I knew that people would love to see these treasures – because I'm a fan of movies too. The exhibition was bittersweet for me as I saw the popularity of the costumes, but the success of the auction has been a wonderful validation of my dream to save our film history. Now all the glorious Hollywood history they represent can be seen in every corner of the world.

Actress, singer and dancer with a career spanning six decades, Debbie Reynolds began collecting film costumes and memorabilia in 1970; by 2011 her Hollywood Motion Picture Museum was the largest collection of its kind in the world.

BLADES

Christopher Frayling

THE GENERIC LABEL for film stories set in the past often refers to the costumes: 'costume dramas', 'swords and sandals', 'peplums' or 'pepla', and of course 'swashbucklers' – a reference, apparently, to the swashing sound made by a side-sword as it leaves or strikes the buckler. So, 'costume' equals 'historical'. But the costumes worn by swordspeople of the screen, whenever the story happens to be set, tend – as in all historical feature films – to be as much about the present as the past. The art historian Ernst Gombrich once wrote that visions of the future tell us about the world of the present – and its attitudes – as well as the world of the future, but that these distinctions only become really noticeable in retrospect. The same goes for the past, whether the historical period is 26 AD (*Ben-Hur*, 1959), 175–180 AD (*Gladiator*, 2000), thirteenth-century Scotland (*Braveheart*, 1995) or early seventeenth-century Spain (*The Adventures of Don Juan*, 1949).

Of course, the costume designers engaged in a great deal of research for all these films, sifting through visual evidence such as paintings, sculptures and prints, and written evidence such as memoirs and novels, and, in the case of big-budget films, this research even became part of the ballyhoo surrounding the film's initial release. The important thing was – and is – for the costumes to *seem* to be a recreation of historical dress. But the tailoring, the way the garment is worn, the silhouette, the materials, the colours, the demands of the narrative – all of these are as much about the present, distilled into the film experience. The costumes must 'read' to the audience as credible garments. This phenomenon used sometimes to be known as the 'Tarzan's hairdo' syndrome: whenever the story is set, in the past or in the present, the hairstyle of the hero will tell you exactly when the film was made. Sometimes this is evident on first release; sometimes, with more sophisticated films, as Gombrich observed it only becomes apparent with the passage of time.

When he was making *Ben-Hur* at Cinecitta studio in Rome, actor Charlton Heston noticed that one of the elderly extras was wearing the costume worn by Leo Genn as Petronius in *Quo Vadis* (1951), which had been made at the same studio. *Quo Vadis* was set in 64–8 AD rather

337 Sketch for Don Juan de Marana
The Adventures of Don Juan, 1949
Costume designers Leah Rhodes,
William Travilla and Marjorie Best
Illustrator William Travilla

338 Don Sebastian and
Don Juan de Marana
(Jerry Austin and Errol Flynn)
The Adventures of Don Juan, 1949
Costume designers Leah Rhodes,
William Travilla and Marjorie Best

than half a century before, and Petronius was a patrician rather than a proletarian spectator at a chariot race. But it *looked* right. It 'worked'.

The research for *Ben-Hur* was famously extensive: Elizabeth Haffenden and her team made over eight thousand costume sketches; but the colours still looked 1950s. In the heyday of Hollywood on the Tiber, when *Ben-Hur* was filmed, the Roman armour was made by Italian craftspeople working in traditional materials – one of the attractions of working at Cinecitta. By the time of *Gladiator*, Janty Yates and her team designed the armour for Maximus Decimus Meridius (Russell Crowe) out of lighter materials – foam coated in leather – because of the physical demands of the role (plates 339, 340). The film had several historical advisers and was explicitly inspired by the nineteenth-century paintings of Alma-Tadema and Gerome, among others, but had just as much to do with previous epic films such as *Spartacus* (1960; plate 335) and *The Fall of the Roman Empire* (1964; plate 336) as with daily life in

the era of Marcus Aurelius and Commodus. The scenes in and around the Colosseum were filmed as if they were the Superbowl.

For the warriors in *Braveheart* (1995) Charles Knode designed belted plaid or plaid shawls draped over leather jerkins – neither of which seem to have been actually worn by the Scots in the thirteenth century. But, again, it looked just right for a story about brawny Scottish nationalists versus the effete court of King Edward I of England – it 'worked' spectacularly well, playing on the audience's knowledge of the subsequent history of Scotland. In *The Adventures of Don Juan* (1949; plates 337, 338), designed by Leah Rhodes, Travilla and Marjorie Best, Errol Flynn's Spanish nobleman is a professional swordsman – he is fencing instructor to the National Academy (cue much synchronized swordplay) – and, according to Edward Maeder, 'the men's costumes are historically accurate in both cut and fabrics, featuring diagonal-patterned velvets common in the period dress', whereas the women's costumes

are much more of the late 1940s. Flynn's out-fits also looked good in motion, as when he – in a celebrated moment – leaped from the top of a long staircase, as was only to be expected of the star of *Captain Blood* (1935) and *The Sea Hawk* (1940).

Uma Thurman's costume for the action-packed climax of *Kill Bill* (2003; plates 341, 342) – a manga-style yellow two-piece karate jump-suit with a black stripe, designed by Catherine Marie Thomas and Kumiko Ogawa – became the corporate symbol for the entire film, featured on countless yellow and black colour-coded posters, usually with a samurai sword laid across it.

The costume designs for *Ben-Hur*, *Don Juan* and *Gladiator* deservedly won Academy Awards; *Braveheart*, too, was nominated. The Academy has by tradition been good at recognizing the special qualities of 'costume dramas'. Such films seem more obviously *designed*, and based on detailed visual research, than dramas set in the present day. Actually of course 'cos-tume dramas' are *really* about the present – while contemporary dramas often involve just as much care, attention and research on the part of designers.

RIGHT
341 The Bride (Uma Thurman)
Kill Bill: Volume 1, **2003**
Costume designers Kumiko Ogawa
and Catherine Marie Thomas

BELOW
342 Sketch for the showdown at
the House of Blue Leaves
Kill Bill: Volume 1, **2003**
Costume designers Kumiko Ogawa
and Catherine Marie Thomas
Illustrator Catherine Marie Thomas

❛ The tailoring, the way the garment is worn, the silhouette, the materials, the colours, the demands of the narrative – all of these are as much about the present, distilled into the film experience. ❜

C.D. 3924
COSTUME DESIGNER

SIGNATURE

GUNSLINGERS

Christopher Frayling

SOMETHING SERIOUS happened to the action hero in the 1960s. The traditional heroic virtues of chivalry, modesty, romance and belief in a cause made way for pure style: the hero became a focus for the projection of the audience's dreams, rather than a role-model for the audience to emulate. This transformation – from chivalry to efficiency, from warmth to cool or even coldness, from affection to affectlessness, from life experience to lifestyle, from behaviour to look – seems to have accelerated in films, in advertising and marketing, and in popular music, during the era of James Bond (first appearance, in a dinner-jacket of course, in *Dr No*, 1962), Pop Art (Andy Warhol and 'famous for fifteen minutes') and 'The Man With No Name' (first appearance, riding on a mule in a Mexican-style poncho, in A *Fistful of Dollars*, 1964, costumes and sets designed by Carlo Simi). As Sergio Leone said of the bounty-hunter played by Clint Eastwood in this film, he was more interested as a director in his cigarillo, his designer stubble, his poncho and his shrunk-to-fit jeans than in anything to do with 'the inner person'. This was the hero with no answers; a survivor rather than a crusader.

By the 1980s, the new-style hero had become the cornerstone of a vast growth industry: the hero as style warrior, as corporate image and as site for consumption. Deyan Sudjic has speculated in *Cult Heroes* (1989), his book about the phenomenon:

> Perhaps the nature of the change can be explained partly by the isolation and anonymity of life in the big cities. There is an apparent yearning for hero figures [of the new breed] … To service that demand, a handful of individuals has moved beyond celebrity to become cult heroes. They have a presence, whether it is created artificially or not, which has a powerful economic role … The heroes who last are the ones who have the stamina to adapt to adjusting circumstances. Partly it is a question of substance … but it is also a *stylistic* issue…

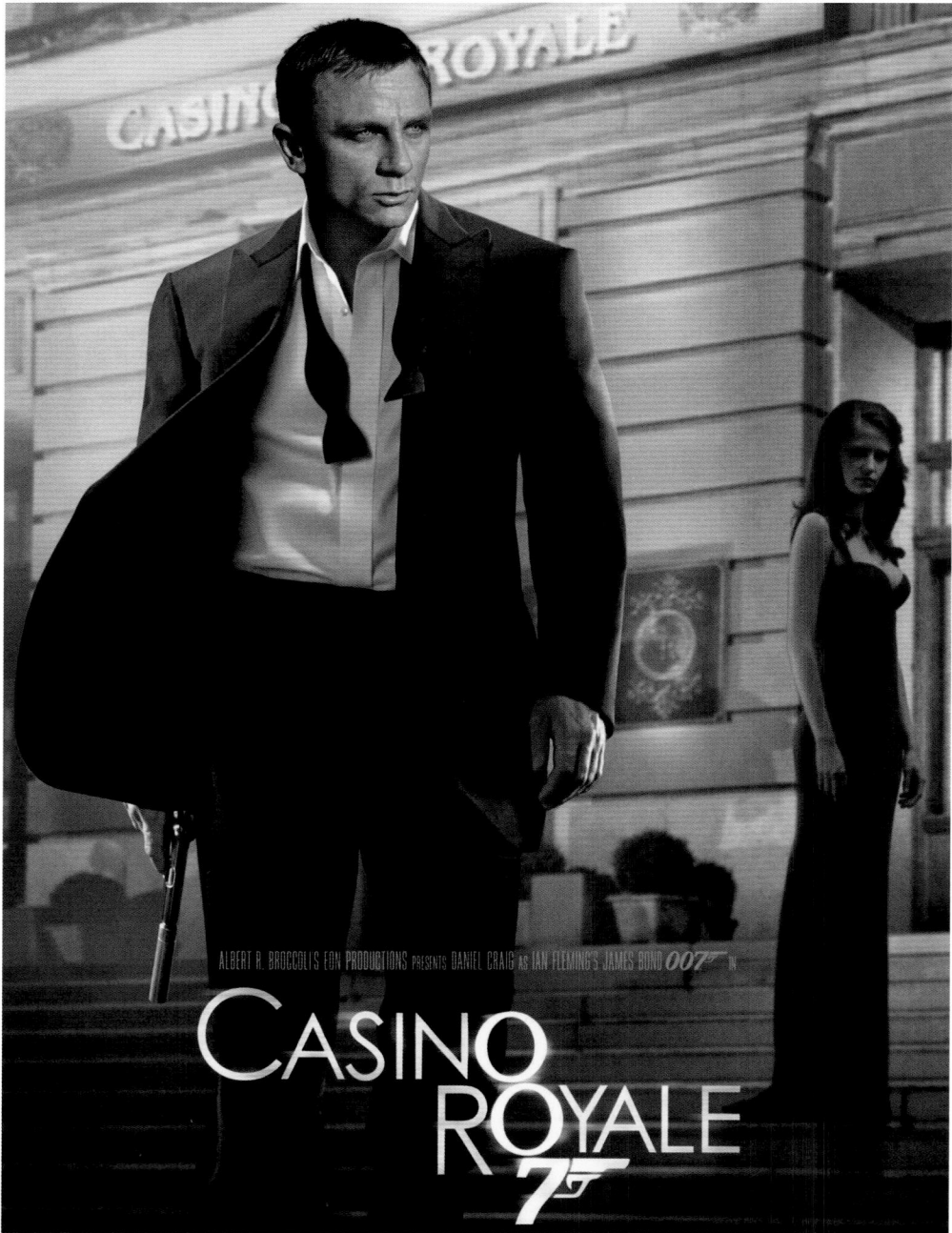

It is a transformation which was predicted by philosophers of culture at least as far back as Friedrich Nietzsche, who wrote in *Untimely Meditations* (1873–8) that cultural forms have a tendency to travel from high art/myth and romance (when the artists mean it) to the ironic (when in an age of 'oversaturation' the artists mean it and do not mean it, both at the same time).

So irony and parody and outward appearance begin to ride the range… *Dr No* led to the longest-running franchise in the history of cinema (24 films and still counting), and from *Goldfinger* (1964) onwards began to place the emphasis away from Cold War certainties towards smart one-liners, elaborate gadgets and sets, tourist destinations and cartoon-style violence.

OPPOSITE
343 James Bond (Daniel Craig)
Promotional poster for *Casino Royale*, 2006
Costume designer Lindy Hemming

LEFT
344 Ethan Edwards (John Wayne)
The Searchers, 1956
Costume designers Frank Beetson
and Ann Peck
Ethan Edwards' costume designed
by Frank Beetson

BELOW
345 Monco (Clint Eastwood)
For a Few Dollars More, 1965
Costume designer Carlo Simi

Casino Royale (2006), based surprisingly closely at times on Ian Fleming's first Bond novel, published in 1953, set out to re-boot the established 007 formula which had accumulated over the past 45 years, by deliberately taking it apart while playing to audience expectations. So when Daniel Craig as James Bond, in the bar of a hotel in Montenegro, is asked by the bartender whether he wanted his vodka martini shaken or stirred – the most famous drinks order in the movies – he growls in reply: 'Do I look like I give a damn?' Clearly, by now he did *not* give a damn. But he did wear a perfect-fitting dinner-jacket, designed by Lindy Hemming and tailored by Brioni Roma

– even if the garment was beaten up as often as he was. This Bond was more athletic, less sophisticated, not so bright, he did not have Miss Moneypenny and Q to look after him back at the office – and he came out of the sea, in his bathing trunks, as if he was trying to be Ursula Andress in *Dr No*, who was originally trying to do a Botticelli birth of Venus.

Bruce Willis in *Die Hard* (1988) would not be seen dead in a dinner-jacket, let alone an up-market cocktail bar. As super-tough cop John McClane of the New York Police Department, his preferred attire is a dirty, torn T-shirt (plate 346) and his style is parody Wild West hero: as he likes to say to the crisply-dressed terrorist

bad guys in moments of high stress – usually involving a big blast – 'yippie-kai-yay!' He is an over-the-top action figure with a twinkle in his eye – and in inverted commas.

Independence Day (1996, advertising tagline 'don't make plans for August'), with Will Smith as US Marine Corps pilot and all-round regular guy Steven Hiller (plate 351), is parodic in a different way: it fuses, on a much grander scale as whole cities are reduced to rubble this time, 1970s multi-character disaster movies – especially those produced by Irwin Allen, such as *The Poseidon Adventure* (1972) and *The Towering Inferno* (1974) – and 1950s science fiction stories about alien attacks from the skies. Producer

LEFT

350 Captain John Miller (Tom Hanks)
Saving Private Ryan, 1998
Costume designer
Joanna Johnston

BELOW

351 Captain Steven Hiller and David Levinson (Will Smith and Jeff Goldblum)
Independence Day, 1996
Costume designer
Joseph A. Porro

OPPOSITE

352 Dick Tracy (Warren Beatty)
Dick Tracy, 1990
Costume designer
Milena Canonero

353 Costume for Dick Tracy
Dick Tracy, 2007
Costume designer
Milena Canonero
The Collection of Motion Picture Costume Design Larry McQueen

354 Sketch for Dick Tracy
Dick Tracy, 1990
Costume designer
Milena Canonero

Warren Beatty's *Dick Tracy* (1990; plates 352–4) finds its retro visual sources in the decade before the Second World War – the comic strips by Chester Gould which started in 1931, featuring a square-jawed detective fighting organized crime in the modern city – and the film's overall 'look' was intended to evoke the feel of period comics, with a limited colour palette, larger-than-life prosthetic make-up for the bad guys, and fixed frames rather than a moving camera. The dialogue ('Mind if I call you Dick?' asks the nightclub singer Breathless Mahoney, played by Madonna; 'Eat lead, copper', shouts one of the baddies) is a late 1980s take on the speech bubbles of half a century before. Dick Tracy's yellow overcoat and fedora turn the character into a post-Roy Lichtenstein visual statement about style. In the 1930s he still meant it.

By extreme contrast, the central character in the Hitchcock-like Jason Bourne series (played by Matt Damon; plate 347) has lost his identity and his memory, and is determined somehow to piece them together again, despite a conspiracy against him involving the CIA and the mysterious 'Operation Treadstone'. He is an Everyman of a different kind, a character in search of a character – an unusual challenge to the costume designer – with anonymity as his trademark: his clothes and his outward appearance must reflect this. As costume designer Pierre-Yves Gayraud has recalled, 'he has a very simple look … his clothes must never draw attention to themselves … he wears practical clothes, the kind you might buy in a military clothing store, and later a simple long black coat'. The action hero has completely shed the traditional heroic virtues, to the point where this has become the purpose of the story.

Dean Devlin called the Will Smith character 'the Everyman in America, the good GI Joe, like you would have seen in old World War Two movies'. In one spectacular sequence, he pilots an F-18 fighter-jet through the Grand Canyon, pursued by an alien Attacker shaped like a pizza. And on 4 July – when else? – accompanied only by a computer boffin, he destroys the alien Mother Ship and saves the world. 'Didn't I promise you fireworks?' he says knowingly at one point. Yes, he did.

There were very different fireworks in *Saving Private Ryan* (1998; plate 350), in which a squad of eight American soldiers under Captain John Miller (Tom Hanks) endures the troop landings at Omaha Beach, Normandy, on 6 June 1944 – reconstructed in spectacularly gory detail, semi-documentary style with de-saturated colours on a beach in Wexford Ireland – to go behind enemy lines and rescue Private James Ryan (Matt Damon), the only survivor of four brothers. The squad had to wear combat uniforms, handguns, rifles and packs – and wear them convincingly – while being stormed at by shot and shell (costumes designed by Joanna Johnston, a Steven Spielberg and Tom Hanks regular). The heroism of the soldiers emerged less from what they said than from the carnage which surrounded them. As the Military Adviser on the film Captain Dale Dye USMC (retd) put it, 'the more horrible we can show it, the more people will understand the nobility of the sacrifice that those men made'.

90027, HOLLYWOOD IS A ZIP CODE
THE LA CONNECTION

Beth Werling

WHAT IS Hollywood? To most of the world it is symbolized by the Hollywood sign, representing not just film-making, but also Los Angeles and even California at large. To tourists seeking Hollywood, it is the footprints in front of Grauman's Chinese Theatre. But to Angelenos, it is simply 'the Industry'.

According to film historians, it was Manifest Destiny that film-makers should settle in Hollywood with its never-ending sunshine, warm temperatures and variety of terrain. While climate and topography did play a key role in relocating film production from the East Coast, there were also often overlooked financial advantages, specifically Los Angeles's open-shop, anti-union labour practices which provided a cheap, readily available workforce. In many respects it seems almost inevitable that this maverick industry should have found itself in the last outpost of the American frontier. Since the Gold Rush, California had been depicted by promoters to the rest of the world as a Garden of Eden, where people could reinvent themselves outside the confines of the Victorian home or of the newly emerging factories. Screenwriter Anita Loos claimed, 'I sometimes think that if the movies had developed in San Francisco when they moved from New York they might have grown out of their infancy in a fraction of the time it took in the south'.[1] Loos was a Bay Area native, and therefore a biased eyewitness to the founding of the film industry in Hollywood; what is significant about her recollections, however, is that she described the event in pioneer terms:

> There will always be an abyss dividing Los Angeles from San Francisco … we of the north are descendants of Argonauts in whom initiative and physical courage were requisites before they ever started their dangerous

adventure. But the Angeleno came to his city after the railroad had been built, his trip generally a timid retreat from some community of the Middle West where he wasn't smart enough to make a living. On reaching his goal, the migrant found himself competing with others no smarter than himself, so he was able to prosper and, groggy with the astonishment of unmerited success, and titillated by perpetual sunshine, he blossomed forth, manufactured gaudy clothing, freak architecture, rowdy exhibitionist religions, and all the other devices which only a brain devoid of moral stamina and good taste could conjure up.[2]

There are many who would still agree with Loos' assessment of Southern Californians.

Loos was correct that San Francisco would have made a more logical home for the film industry. As the cultural capital of California at the beginning of the twentieth century it had a large theatrical population, along with the support industries upon which the burgeoning film industry relied, including costume rental agencies. When film-makers arrived in Los Angeles they discovered few costume rental houses, department stores or even

OPPOSITE
355 **Harold Rosson, Victor Fleming, Mary Astor, Clark Gable and Jean Harlow on the set of *Red Dust*, 1932**
Costume designer Adrian

356 **Hollywoodland sign marking the centre of America's film industry, Los Angeles, 1925**

second-hand clothing shops to supply actors with screen attire. While many continued to rely on their own wardrobes to provide costumes for modern-dress pictures, the studios had no alternative but to quickly develop wardrobe departments to purchase and make military uniforms, period attire and other specialized costume. Instead of the simple racks of used clothing found in East Coast studios, Hollywood wardrobe departments grew more rapidly into vast depositories of all types of clothing.

This is not to say that costume was not important to early Hollywood: quite to the contrary. By 1914 there were more than seventy studios in and around Hollywood, but by the 1930s these had consolidated into the Big Eight: Metro-Goldwyn-Mayer (MGM), Paramount, Radio-Keith-Orpheum (RKO), Columbia, Fox, Universal, Warner Bros and United Artists. Just as the in-

dustry immigrated to California, so did the people. This is where Loos got it wrong. The heads of the Big Eight were for the most part Eastern European Jews with a background in manufacturing or selling clothing. Although they arrived in Los Angeles by train, they had originally immigrated to the East Coast as a result of religious persecution or poverty back home. These early moguls were of the hardy 'argonaut' stock Loos praised, willing to gamble their money and uproot their families to achieve the American Dream in California.

What was the dream they pursued? Charlie Chaplin, himself an immigrant from the slums of London, depicted it best In *Modern Times* (1936). The Tramp as a prisoner of the factory in his striped overalls caught in the cogs of a machine is one of the indelible images of American cinema, but equally important is his

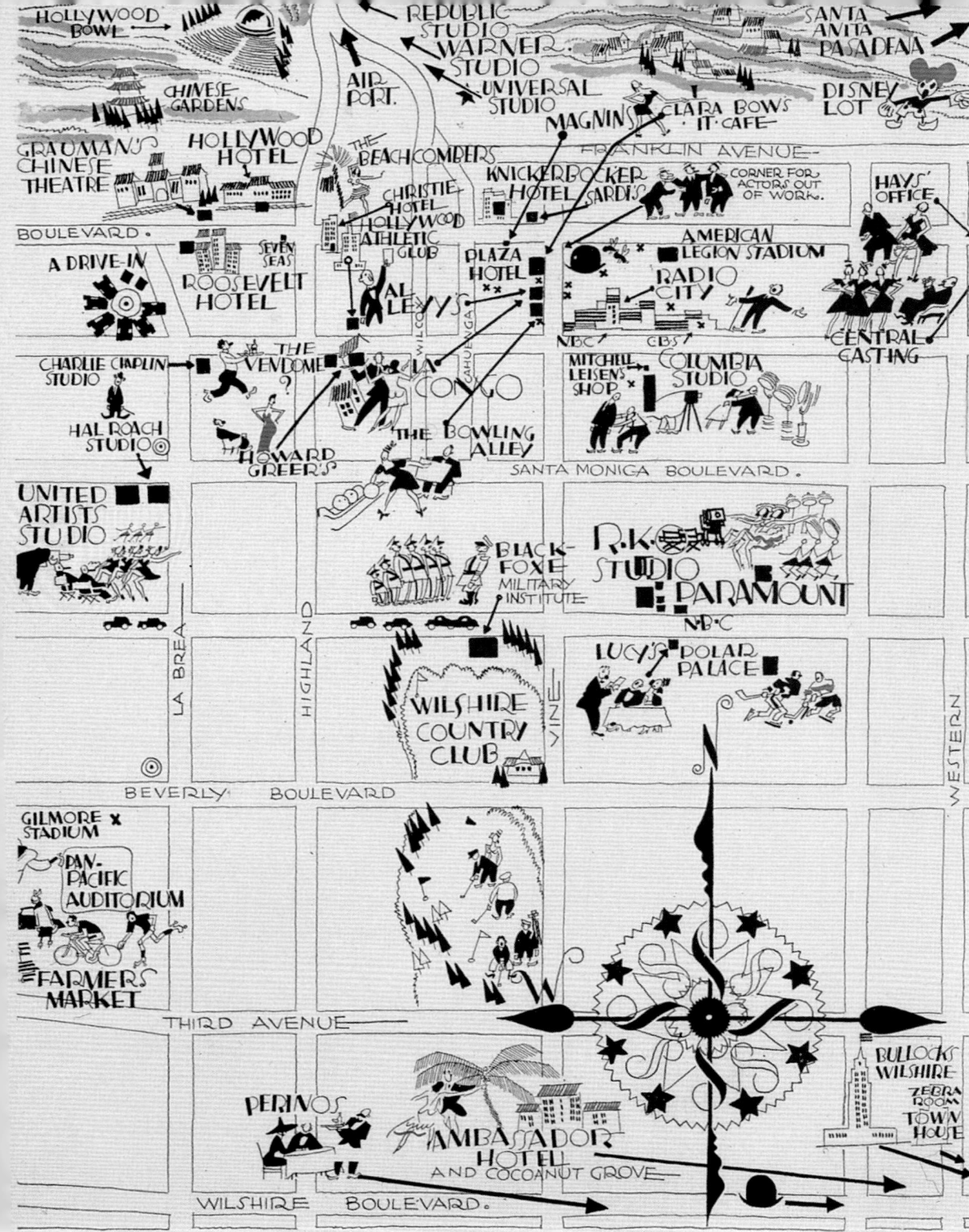

escape to the 'garden landscape of a typical Los Angeles suburb', where he 'fantasizes about what life would be like in such a garden home … to open the front door and a cow walks up to deliver fresh milk. Bunches of grapes hang invitingly close, and oranges grow right outside the living room window, ripe for plucking.'[3] This is the California Dream the early studio heads pursued and depicted on screen for the rest of the world.

They were not only marketing dreams, however, but product as well. With their retail background, the early studio heads realized that they could sell more than tickets to the films: they were selling a lifestyle, complete with clothing. From the swimsuits worn by Mack Sennett's Bathing Beauties to the film magazine articles about the stars' personal attire, costume design was at the forefront of Hollywood's consumer campaign. During the 1910s

and early 1920s articles in *Photoplay* and other fan magazines promoted couture clothing by designers such as Lucile (Lady Duff Gordon), whose creations were worn on screen and off by Mary Pickford and Lillian Gish, among others.

Costume began to change in the 1920s, reflecting the California lifestyle as the industry began to establish roots in Los Angeles. Although Mary Pickford was trapped in little girl roles for much of the decade, her then husband Douglas Fairbanks Sr personified the 'Californication' of clothing. On and off screen he promoted a healthy outdoor lifestyle, appearing in casual sports clothes with open shirts displaying his bare, tanned chest. Fairbanks's smiling, tanned image seduced a young British acrobat, Archibald Leach, to reinvent himself in his idol's image – as Cary Grant.[4]

For women, skirts shortened and morals loosened. The Jazz

358 Metro-Goldwyn-Mayer Studio, Culver City,
California, late 1920s/early 1930s

359 Paramount Famous Lasky Studio,
Hollywood, California, 1920s/early 1930s

PARAMOUNT FAMOUS LASKY STUDIO. HOLLYWOOD. CALIF. A-94

Baby was born, celebrated on screen in *Chicago* (2002; costume designer Colleen Atwood). D.W. Griffith's virginal Lillian Gish heroine was swept away by Cecil B. DeMille's vamp Gloria Swanson. DeMille summed up costuming in the 1920s best in his directive to designer Howard Greer: 'I want clothes that will make people gasp when they see them. I don't want to see any clothes anybody could possibly buy in a store'.[5] It was a principal DeMille would stick to throughout his career, culminating in the peacock feather cape designed by Edith Head for Delilah (Hedy Lamarr) in *Samson and Delilah* (1949; plates 262, 263).

Howard Greer was also part of the wave of change. He was a fashion designer trained on the East Coast and in Europe under Lucile and Paul Poiret, who had dabbled in theatrical costume when he was hired by Paramount in 1924. The isolation of Los Angeles from the design centres in New York and Chicago created a need for costume designers locally. The studios, realizing that costume helped sell films, were willing to spend time and money transforming their wardrobe racks into costume departments complete with designers, fitters, embroiderers and even armourers.

By the late 1920s Hollywood had developed a sense of itself and began to define glamour to its audience – that is, the rest of the world. No matter what your ethnic or socio-economic background, everyone went to the cinema. Instead of borrowing couture or expecting actresses to provide their own, studios began to create magnificent costumes to rival gowns produced in Paris and New York. DeMille's over-the-top creations were refined, emerging as the sensual allure found in the designs of Adrian. Studios packaged and marketed glamour as a commodity. Despite the Depression, opulence sold and costume designers were expected to aid the cause by creating tasteful but luxurious costumes

that also served to hide a star's physical flaws when necessary. It was standard procedure to design and create everything in-house for a star, even garments as simple as a bathrobe. The costumes created by Hollywood designers are so powerful that even today they serve as the definition of Hollywood glamour, representing the region 'as home to the most beautiful and alluring people in the world'.[6]

The industry also began to be recognized as a major cultural and economic force in the region. The Los Angeles County Museum of History, Art and Science (founded in 1910) started collecting and exhibiting artefacts from the movies in 1930. Surprisingly it was the History rather than the Art Department of the institution that first grasped the importance of film, not as an art form but as a business. The acknowledgement of the economic and social significance of the industry defined the collecting parameters. Curatorial staff sought everything required to create and promote a film. The timing could not have been better. Most studios were in the process of jettisoning their silent film equipment and the Museum was the beneficiary. All the items needed to produce a film, including banks of mercury vapour lights, were collected.

While MGM's Adrian is best remembered for the beaded gowns he created for Crawford and his period costumes for Garbo, his most remarkable work was for *The Wizard of Oz* (1939). This was his charge to suspend and heighten the element of make-believe with costume as diverse as the ruby slippers to Dorothy's pinafore to the Munchkins' attire. It was the responsibility of others, however, to execute Adrian's vision. It took a whole village to break down the script into the number and kinds of costumes needed, and to attach a price to each for budget purposes. After Adrian completed his designs it was up to the seamstresses, fitters, embroiderers, shoemakers and others to execute his vision. The film required 124 Munchkin costumes and 300 costumes for the citizens of the Emerald City – and these were just the extras! Vera Mordaunt, then head of MGM's dyeing department remembered colouring the Munchkin shoes green to be the worst part of the process:

And there were *boxes* of shoes! Satin shoes, dance shoes, things that had been used in other pictures and were left over. I had this new girl and I thought, 'Well, she's new, so she can do it.' I brought her the spray gun and showed her how to mix the dye. She worked … and about two days later somebody said, 'Aren't you getting bored to death with those shoes?' She looked up so surprised and said, 'I was just thinking how wonderful it was. To be doing this and getting paid for it!'[7]

The transition to sound was documented by early sound effects devices donated by animator Charles Mintz and RKO Studios. Costume also reflected the change. The stiffer fabrics used in the attire for 1921's *Black Beauty*, whose rustling would have been recorded by primitive microphones, were replaced by the quieter bias-cut garments of the 1930s, all of which were collected by the Museum. Only Adrian's sleek gowns for silent screen clotheshorse Mae Murray could be mistaken for wardrobe for the sound era in the Museum's closets.

The Museum considered costume an integral part of the film-making process and the History Department gathered it along with props, cameras, editing equipment, animation cels, models and miniatures, set designs, scripts, projectors, posters and stills. Objects were solicited from primary sources: the studios, inventors, moguls, actors, cameramen, designers and animators. Charlie Chaplin donated his Tramp costume; Douglas Fairbanks his swashbuckling props, Mary Pickford her golden curls, Harold Lloyd his glasses, Walt Disney the animation stand used to create the first Mickey Mouse cartoons, and Willis O'Brien provided King Kong's hand.

Even after the Art Department separated in 1965 (becoming the Los Angeles County Museum of Art), the History Department which remained with the Science Department in the newly renamed Natural History Museum continued to actively collect and preserve Hollywood's history. Recent additions, including Christina Ricci's gothic gown from *Addams Family Values* (1993) and Betty Bronson's Peter Pan costume from the 1924 version of the film.

It takes a village of curators, collection staff, conservators, preparators and registrars to house, preserve, and display these materials. And costume is among the most fragile and ephemeral items. They were meant to last for only a few minutes on screen, not for generations of visitors to view.

Creating the costumes, though, was often just as difficult as saving them. It took a factory to produce Hollywood's polished image; glamour and fantasy were not easy to create and maintain.

Experiencing the Hollywood Dream had not disillusioned this young assistant, but others were beginning to experience the dark side of the dream, and depicting it on screen.

The 1930s witnessed the arrival of the hard-core detective novel, translated in Hollywood to the Film Noir in the 1940s, exploring the seamy underside of life in Los Angeles. One of the films depicting this disillusionment is *Mildred Pierce* (1945). Suburban Los Angeles housewife Mildred Pierce (Joan Crawford) is determined that her daughter Veda, the apple of her eye, should have everything she desires. Mildred will take on any job, no matter how menial, in order to provide Veda with luxury goods representing the kind of life she never had. Veda proves ungrateful and unloving, a worm in Eden's apple. At the end of the film her mother, by now wiser and tougher, leaves Veda to rot in jail. Money and success in Los Angeles have not brought them happiness; instead, the pursuit of the California Dream has destroyed her family. Was this the beginning of the end of the Dream in Hollywood's eyes?

This cynical view of the California Dream can also be seen in *Double Indemnity* (1944), among numerous films of the period. Costumes reflected this new sobriety. Wartime fabric restrictions meant that slimmer silhouettes with less trim were the norm until Dior launched his 'New Look' in 1947, and suddenly Hollywood was following a fashion trend instead of leading it, with the tight bodices and voluminous skirts of 1950s. Not all film-makers

LEFT
365 Stewart Graff
(Charlton Heston)
Earthquake, 1974
Costume designers Burton Miller
and Edith Head

BELOW
366 Rick Deckard
(Harrison Ford)
Blade Runner, 1982
Costume designers Michael
Kaplan and Charles Knode

followed the trend, however. Alfred Hitchcock requested that designer Edith Head continue dressing his leads in simple wool suits and dresses in earth-tones of green and tan, as witnessed in *Vertigo* (1958) and *Marnie* (1964): Kim Novak and Tippi Hedren used costume to some extent to masquerade as ladies. Their predatory successor is another cool blonde who certainly wielded costume – or the lack thereof – to remarkable effect: Sharon Stone in *Basic Instinct* (1992; costume designer Ellen Mirojnick).

Films took on a new, atomic twist in the 1950s, with Los Angeles being destroyed by everything from ants (*Them!*, 1954) to Martians (*The War of the Worlds*, 1953). By the 1970s this view had morphed into apocalyptical Los Angeles, starting when the 'Big One' hit in 1974: *Earthquake*, followed by *Blade Runner* (1982), *Escape from L.A.* (1996), *Independence Day* (1996) and *Volcano* (1997). There has been a shift in tone to these films, as Mike Davis has pointed out in relation to *Independence Day*: 'when the aliens turn to Los Angeles … There is a comic undertone of "good riddance" when kooks like these are vaporized by the earth's latest ill-mannered guests'.[8] Whether destroyed by aliens or nature, there is a sense that the destruction of Los Angeles will be no great loss to Western Civilization.

These films depicting the death of California, however, are only one genre the industry was turning out in the years immediately following the Second World War. In most respects Hollywood was revelling in its power as the major producer of the world's dominant form of mass culture, excelling at promoting itself and the sunnier vision of the California Dream. At the same time as giant ants were attacking Los Angeles through its sewer system (*Them!*), Gidget was surfing in Malibu (*Gidget* [1959]). As Dana Polan describes it, 'what is perhaps most Californian about Hollywood films is not necessarily the specific representation of California locales or experiences but the very ability of the place, indoors or outdoors, to represent any experience whatsoever'.[9] Hollywood's craftsmen pride themselves on being able to create any era or location. Most Americans growing up in the twentieth

century learned about the South from *Gone with the Wind* (1939) and New York City from musicals such as *The Broadway Melody* (1929) or more recently from comic book films: *Superman* (1978) *Batman* (1989) and *Spider-Man* (2002).

No matter what the message or where the location of a film, costume still remains one of the key visual methods a filmmaker uses to tell his story. Although today's films deal primarily with modern times, the costumer designer's role and methodology have stayed the same. What is important to remember, however, is where these designers are researching and shopping; like most of us, they do so close to home. Costume designers not only work in Los Angeles, but they live and experience their own version of the Hollywood Dream here. Their experiences are reflected in the contributions they make to film. Hollywood is still, a century later, the industry's home and, as such, its inspiration.

Collections Manager for Material Culture at the Natural History Museum of Los Angeles County, Beth Werling specializes in the history of the motion picture industry and lectures widely on the subject. She recently participated in the BBC 2 programme 'Shooting the Hollywood Stars' made by leading fashion photographer Rankin and published an essay in Mary Pickford, Queen of the Movies (2012).

4 NEW FRONTIERS

AFTERLIFE
ENSURING THE ENDURING INTEREST
OF A WEB AUDIENCE

Chris Laverty

FASCINATION with costume design has been inestimably heightened by the Internet. Whether this is entirely advantageous is dependent on communicating a better understanding of costume to a wider public. The price of increased coverage is that it is generally indiscriminate; costume tends to be regarded in the press as 'film fashion'. But costume is categorically not fashion, even if the Internet is guilty of promoting it as such: unfortunately, to many, the silver screen has become a $100-million catwalk.

Conversely, this renaissance of interest in costume design has stimulated no more than minor influence on fashion. More knowledge relevant to the creation of costume is available than

ever before, but this is largely in period dramas and fantasy rather than contemporary costume design. In this context, 'interest' may be defined as preoccupation with costume exclusively as aesthetic display, independent of narrative. That costume retains its appeal away from film is undeniable, and yet without the context for which it was created it loses its function. Costume remains covetable if it has been validated – as, for instance, in the case of the black whale-cord frock coat worn by Robert Downey Jr as Sherlock Holmes (2009). Disregard the historical setting; costume as fashion is motivated by endorsement. If fashionistas did not exactly start wearing frock coats after watching *Sherlock Holmes*, they were certainly inspired by them. Robert Downey Jr, an A-list Hollywood actor in a fantastically successful film, is enough to legitimize a garment perhaps only previously viewed as fancy dress (plate 371).

Jenny Beavan's costumes for *Sherlock Holmes* are particularly interesting as, far from seeking period authenticity, they are merely suggestive of their setting (late nineteenth-century London), a kind of 'Bohemian Victorian' look, which audiences concerned with fashion were swift to appreciate. The same can be said of Penny Rose's costumes in the *Pirates of the Caribbean*

OPPOSITE
**367 Nina Sayers
(Natalie Portman)**
Black Swan, 2010
**Costume designers Amy Westcott,
Laura and Kate Mulleavy
Black Swan costume designed
by Laura and Kate Mulleavy**

BELOW
368 Costume fitting for
Black Swan, 2010

**369 Thomas Leroy and
Nina Sayers (Vincent Cassel
and Natalie Portman)**
Black Swan, 2010
**Costume designers Amy Westcott,
Laura and Kate Mulleavy**

series (2003–). This is not how seventeenth-century pirates dressed; this is how we want them to have dressed, based on the archetypal Hollywood swashbucklers of the 1950s. Rose satisfies our expectations, creating costume as wish fulfilment; style transcends character.

Nowhere is this concept more apparent than with Ellen Mirojnick's costume design for *Wall Street* (1987), specifically that of corporate antagonist Gordon Gekko (Michael Douglas; plate 372). According to Mirojnick, during an interview conducted with the costume designer herself for *Clothes on Film*, until she created Gekko's radical look of wide-shouldered double-breasted suit, patterned silk tie, coloured braces and shirt with contrasting collars and cuffs, those working on real Wall Street were broadly conservative in their dress.

Mirojnick appropriated their subtle elements of rebellion, namely colourful braces, and established them as emblematic first of Gekko's character and then, later in the story, of patsy Bud Fox (Charlie Sheen). Soon Gekko's look was copied by brokers all over the world. 'Gekko style' had come to represent power and, ironically, individuality. It was of no consequence that Gekko was fundamentally a criminal: he was fiercely intelligent and immaculately attired – and, more importantly to his emulators, sought financial success at any cost. Thirty years and a world economic crisis later, the Internet is still overflowing with images of those desperate to resurrect the sartorial ghost of Gekko. Interestingly,

Wall Street's sequel, *Money Never Sleeps* (2010) is far less imitated for its costume design. Perhaps the simple reason for this is that fashionistas buy into more than a look. Even ignoring the true motives of character, the politics of the era are essential.

Atonement (2007) further alludes to this idea that clothing trends can be dictated by cinema. Costume designer Jacqueline Durran created the slinky silk evening gown worn by Keira Knightley (plate 315) as 1930s socialite Cecilia Tallis from scratch, its distinctive colour a combination of Lin black, green organza and green chiffon. While historically accurate, the dress is also a heightened form of perfection in that flawlessness is given even greater significance than realism. Green alludes to temptation, and yet to ascribe absolute definition to any colour is impossible. As such it becomes mysterious by proxy, as does Cecilia. Such mystery and delicate beauty add to the romance of the dress. This captured the imagination of audiences enough for it to be voted the Best Costume of All Time in 2008.[1]

While fashion can be viewed as a potential gateway to costume design – indeed, several contemporary costume designers, such as Leesa Evans and Christine Wada (*Bridesmaids*, 2011), previously worked in the fashion industry – nevertheless costume design deserves greater appreciation as a semiotic art. Costume shapes our viewing experience by subtle communication, drip-feeding information so vital to the narrative that, paradoxically, we scarcely notice it is happening.

When FBI agent Melvin Purvis (Christian Bale) begins tracking Prohibition-era bank robber John Dillinger (Johnny Depp) in *Public Enemies* (2009; plate 370), his entire investigation is triggered by a misplaced overcoat. The overcoat in question is 'Shragge Quality', a 32-oz double-breasted garment in charcoal grey wool. That it is so unremarkable speaks volumes about how costume may deliberately manipulate narrative rather than simply serve its own ends – the role of all visual media – to be seen. This coat helps shapes the plot; remove it, and the film makes no sense. However, for all the attention Colleen Atwood's faithfully reproduced 1930s costumes attracted in the press, which at the time of release was largely focused on Depp's Optimo fedoras, little reference was made to this vital plot point. Although the overcoat is crucial to the set-up, its role in the narrative remains subtextual. Like all memorable costume, the coat exemplifies function over form. It also acts as a metaphor for flawed masculinity, Dillinger only abandoning the garment, and thus incriminating himself, when he uses it to protect a female kidnap victim from the cold weather outside.

While costume does not directly form part of the story in *Black Swan* (2010), it indirectly reflects the internal journey of its main character, striving ballet dancer Nina Sayers (Natalie Portman). Costume designer Amy Westcott adhered to a strict colour palette throughout the film. initially using pink and white to symbolize Nina's perpetually enforced adolescence, gradually bleeding into black and grey as darkness floods her soul (plates 367, 369). This is costume design carefully constructed with a clear intention of being read by its audience. *Black Swan* also incorporates present-day theatre fashion, with designers Kate and Laura Mulleavy designing the principals' *Swan Lake* stage costumes. With so many elements contributing to the overall aesthetic – overt and subtextual interpretation, high-end fashion collaboration, fantasy costume and contemporary dress – *Black Swan* lends itself to study as a costume template. The film has been seen as a 'way in' for those previously unfamiliar with costume design, perhaps drawing more attention to the art – beyond that of large-scale period dramas – than any major feature film of recent years.

372 Gordon Gekko (Michael Douglas)
***Wall Street*, 1987**
Costume designer Ellen Mirojnick

TOP

373 Megan, Becca, Helen, Rita, Lillian
and Annie (Melissa McCarthy, Ellie Kemper,
Rose Byrne, Wendi McLendon-Covey,
Maya Rudolph and Kristen Wiig)
Bridesmaids, 2011
Costume designers Leesa Evans and
Christine Wada

ABOVE

374 Frances 'Francie' Stevens and
John Robie (Grace Kelly and Cary Grant)
To Catch a Thief, 1955
Costume designer Edith Head

❛ Costume shapes our viewing experience
by subtle communication, drip-feeding
information so vital to the narrative that,
paradoxically, we scarcely notice
it is happening. ❜

If the use of costume to enrich narrative is more readily discernible in *Black Swan*, it is no less effective as character discourse in *To Catch a Thief* (1955). The narrative cleverly plays on star Grace Kelly's natural femininity in the role of debutante Frances Stevens (plate 374). After suffering a humiliating verbal attack by younger woman while swimming in a plain black bathing costume, Frances changes into a coral pink crêpe silk top and calf-length skirt for her picnic date with ageing playboy John Robie (Cary Grant). She regains her authority by accentuating that which stabilizes her image.

Having returned to her feminine comfort zone, Frances then proceeds to undermine Robie's expectations by driving recklessly on a mountain pass, then bluntly accusing him of being the Riviera cat burglar. Director Alfred Hitchcock and costume designer Edith Head worked closely together, envisaging each of Kelly's costumes. Just by this fairly rudimentary two-piece ensemble, Frances' role as incidental to the central plot was abandoned and suddenly she became essential to the story progression.

The rise of interest in film costume is not merely due to a new enthusiasm for deciphering semiotics, but the result of open access to information about film-making via the Internet. This has led in turn to a curiosity about other aspects of film-making, from musical score to production design. It is no longer necessary to wait for information to be sourced and printed by the press, weeks or even months after the event: answers and, more importantly, discussions are available at the touch of a button. When the film *Inception* was released in 2010, admittedly following a deluge of hype, there was considerable interest in Jeffrey Kurland's costume designs – accessibly stylish and contemporary, yet shrewdly intertwined with visual narrative (plate 375). Internet fervour over who designed the costumes and what they meant in context of the story led to Jeffrey Kurland becoming a well-known name. Such immediate acclaim would have been inconceivable twenty years ago; before the present web explosion it is unlikely that even devoted filmgoers could name more than one costume designer; today, many have a favourite designer. A similarly enthusiastic reaction to costume design followed the release of *Black Swan* – moreover, controversy surrounding the film's final credit, that Amy Westcott was usurped in the press by Kate and Laura Mulleavy for her contribution, was investigated and resolved entirely thanks to the Internet. Audiences

know and understand more about the role of costume design than ever before.

Since the advent of the Internet no genre has grown in popularity more than the superhero or comic-book film, and this interest shows no sign of abating. The practical realities of interpreting superhero costume for cinema are fraught with challenges. Costume designers are more scrutinized for this genre than any other, apart from period dramas – of necessity, their contribution is highly visible in both. Here costume designers face a delicate balancing act of retaining a semblance to the often elaborately attired hero, even though in some cases (such as Batman and Superman) their costume was originally conceived in comic strips published over seventy years ago. Crucially, the superhero costume, with its body armour and hidden weapons, must be credible to a modern audience in the context of the story. Awe-inspiring can be just one over-moulded pectoral or codpiece away from ridiculous. Louise Mingenbach's costumes for *X-Men* (2000) established a new standard in how to meet hard-core fan expectation without alienating newcomers or, worse still, causing them to laugh. In what was for some an unfamiliar community of bizarre humanoid mutants with names such as 'Wolverine' and 'Storm', Mingenbach recreated workable hero costumes that were, to all intents and purposes, believable in our own world.

Occasionally such demands are too difficult to achieve, practically, and computer-generated imagery must be employed. Ngila Dickson's costume for Hal Jordan (Ryan Reynolds) in *Green Lantern* (2011), for example, was entirely computer generated

375 **Arthur (Joseph Gordon-Levitt)**
Inception, 2010
Costume designer Jeffrey Kurland

LEFT
376 Green Lantern (Ryan Reynolds)
Green Lantern, 2011
Costume designer Ngila Dickson

BELOW
377 Emma Frost (January Jones)
X-Men: First Class, 2011
Costume designer Sammy Sheldon

OPPOSITE
378 Wolverine (Hugh Jackman)
X-Men: The Last Stand, 2006
Costume designers Judianna Makovsky
and Lisa Tomczeszyn

(plate 376). This is a new frontier for costume that will continue to be explored in the future.

Superhero costume is best received when combined elegantly with that of the alter ego (think Clark Kent/Superman). If this is fairly contemporary, it is more likely to influence fashion on the street, and this is what brings awareness of costume to a wider public. *X-Men: First Class* (2011) was greeted with enthusiasm for its 'Swinging Sixties' civilian wear designed by Sammy Sheldon (plate 377). A stylish period setting cannot be underestimated in drawing attention to costume, even if this attention remains superficial. This facilitates increased knowledge, though perhaps not a deeper understanding. In this respect the web still has a lot to achieve. Only with sustained interest in the craft, and the continued enthusiasm of costume designers to talk about their work in detail, can such an objective be accomplished. This is not simply a matter of more information, but the right information. The more willing practitioners are to objectively discuss and promote costume design, the more the public will understand it.

Chris Laverty has written for numerous magazines and websites, and his work has been featured on television and radio. In 2009 he launched his website, Clothes on Film, its purpose to analyse and identify costume in film.

WHY DESIGN?

Jeffrey Kurland

I T IS sometimes easy to forget that all films are the result of creativity, and to a greater or lesser extent show the originality of the artists involved, whether scriptwriters, actors, directors or any of the many other people on the creative team. The role of the costume designer is to bring the cast to life, starting with the script and transforming words on the page into living characters on the screen.

The contribution of the costume designer – indeed of all players in the filmmaking game – varies from one film to another. In some cases the director has a very strong idea of what is required of the costumes. Sometimes the actors will bring with them a very firm idea of their roles. In other cases, the lion's share falls to the costume designer to shape the characters. In my experience, I tend to be left to my own devices, developing the characters and discussing them in detail with the actors and directors who inhabit them. This is the way I have always worked. With Woody Allen, for instance, although he had a great deal to say about it all, I was left to do my business. We would talk, I went to work, we tested (with Woody, I always tested wardrobe before we starting shooting), and then after viewing the tests we talked about what might be a problem. Then we moved on. I always try to give a lot of leeway, designing with a broad stroke early on, rather than attempting to dictate specifics. I believe that my role is to create a very large picture into which everybody can fit. Then we hone down, hone down, hone down until, in the end, we're picking out the ring they're going to wear, and what's in the wallet. This does not mean that one cannot begin with definite ideas – it's good to have a strong starting point, but offering up too much can be as muddy as not having enough. The process of honing down enables us to arrive at the best conclusion.

Erin Brockovich (2000) was a very interesting film from the point of view of design because the title character is a real person (plates 382, 383). Thorough research is important for any film, of course; but when the main subject is a living person it is possible to sit with them and ask direct questions, face to face. I gained an enormous amount of factual information from talking to Erin Brockovich: she was extremely forthcoming, and a fascinating character. For an actor, playing somebody living presents particular challenges: of truthfully embodying the person while at the same time bringing an element of interpretation into creating their character on screen – rather than simply mimicking them. When Julia Roberts was cast, my role was to interpret Julia's version of Erin Brockovich, while knowing very well who the real Erin Brockovich was – bringing together all the factual knowledge that I had gained from my research and from conversations with Erin herself, and incorporating this into Julia's creation of his character.

In biographical films a director will not necessarily attempt to cast actors who look like the person they are playing. Thus Steven Soderbergh felt that it was important to create Erin's look without actually producing a 'lookalike' – it was the essence of who she was that was most significant. Much of Erin's physical persona was connected with how she used her body: her flirtatiousness, her daring way of dressing and her subtle use of physicality to lure people in order to achieve her own aims. Julia Roberts's body is very different from Erin Brockovich's; Erin was very curvaceous. She invariably wore 5-inch heels (she called them her 'cha-cha heels'), very short skirts and low-cut tops to reveal her impressive cleavage. These were all elements that Julia wanted to incorporate into the character. So a new, fuller body had to be created that looked entirely convincing. This was a complex engineering task: a range of prosthetic pieces were used to fill the clothes in the right places, pressing outward from Julia's own body. The plan was to construct her body and then put the clothes over it – success! Finally, Julia's hair was bleached to emulate Erin's – a grown-out peroxide blonde with dark roots. Thus in a very literal way Julia Roberts slipped into Erin Brockovich's skin – her very body – because the character's physicality was so much a part of her persona.

The film was highly topical at the time. The other characters were also based on real people and the process of finding out what they were about was fascinating. For example, I met Ed Masry, Erin Brockovich's boss, played in the film by Albert Finney, and noticed that he wore very unusual shoes. I said to him: 'These

ABOVE
380 Hannah, Lee and Holly (Mia Farrow,
Barbara Hershey and Dianna Wiest)
Hannah and her Sisters, 1986
Costume designer Jeffrey Kurland

BELOW
381 Linda Ash and Lenny (Mira Sorvino
and Woody Allen)
Mighty Aphrodite, 1995
Costume designer Jeffrey Kurland

shirts are amazing; where do you get them?' And he said: 'I have them made in Singapore. I found this place years ago: they charge me $8 a shirt, I order them and they send them to me.' This personality point was a gift: I was able to produce some designs that I felt were right for the character played by Albert Finney, but the source for this idea was the very person I was aiming to create.

When I was designing contemporary pieces for Woody Allen earlier in my career, my mental and artistic process was much the same as it is now. I have always tended to deal with characters in the same way: I read the script, talk to the writer and the director (in my case, often the same person), and flesh out how we feel a given character should appear. Once I have understood the director's vision for the character, I meet with the actor. Some costume designers will produce a number of choices and discuss with the actor which works best. However, I prefer a more focused approach: too many alternatives can muddy the waters. Design, I believe, is in the end very finite; the right thing is the right thing, although there may be many ways to get there. I like to talk to the director, do research, make drawings, and compile tear sheets, to come to a conclusion on what this character is. I then talk to the actor and have a conversation informed by any material we have garnered from the writer/director. The actor's opinion is then added to the mix. In this way, I always start with the director's vision and move on to include the artist's needs.

What has changed for me, as a result of having moved from New York to California, is my process of creating costumes. Resources in New York are vastly richer and more varied than they are in California. In California where resources are more restricted, it is invariably impossible to find exactly what is needed for a given costume – particularly for a contemporary character. Much more

has to be made from scratch. The advantage of this, of course, is that it gives the designer total control over colour, style and texture, and the chance to create subtle nuances through design. But our budgets often prevent our creating individual elements in this way, and we more often find ourselves searching for existing items to be incorporated into a costume to reveal the essence of a character. Truthfully, I still prefer to make everything – apart from the fact that it is harder to find exactly the right manufactured items in California – it can be unsatisfactory having to depend on what the market offers rather than taking complete control as a designer. Both approaches are legitimate, however, and will depend to a large extent on the circumstances, requirements and budget of a particular project.

When I read the script for *Inception* (2010; plates 385, 386), I immediately felt that it was the perfect film for me: everything in the film would have to be designed and custom made in order to bring to life the incredible world created by Christopher Nolan. It needed to have a unique look, and each character needed to exude the power written into the story. Christopher Nolan's only instruction was that I should keep him informed at every stage of the design process, day by day. We had just 12 weeks to work up the design, so I began at once to visualize the characters. At the same time we discussed ideas, batting them back and forth, throwing out ideas and catching them again, slightly changed. As things began to take shape, I could start drawing. After initial discussions, I like to create a palette of each character and then the entire group – usually a large board of colours, tones and images. These are then discussed with the production designer, so that everybody can begin to work together.

Creating costumes for contemporary characters can be very much more complex than designing for a period picture. With a period film the look can be researched and reproduced – and

an audience will often be more accepting when clothing is not familiar to them. Certainly it is acceptable to adapt for effect, to distill the essence of a period but move slightly away from absolute historical accuracy if necessary. However, when the audience is familiar with a period the constraints are much tighter – and the requirements may be more demanding. For example, in *Inception* I had seven men in a relatively contemporary setting, all in their thirties and forties and all wearing suits and ties; I had to create an individual 'look' for each one of them. How should they be characterized? A suit is not just a suit; what would this man wear? How should his suit and tie differ from another man's? As I have said, I find that designing and making a range like this allows much more latitude than having to depend on what can be found in the marketplace: the nuances of colour and style can only really be achieved by making the garments, as opposed to buying them 'off the rack', enabling me to distinguish one personality from another by texture, line and style.

The same was true of *Collateral* (2004), another male-dominated film. It is much harder to dress men interestingly and uniquely than it is women. You can get away with so much more with women, whereas with men the challenge is to communicate a character with a palette restricted to, for example, trousers, shirt and jacket. But what makes Vincent (Tom Cruise; plate 379) look and dress the way he does? Who is this ghost-like character who looks nondescript and yet must be noticed? He wears a grey suit to match his grey hair – a monochrome, one-colour character, grey and ghost-like. His style is not necessarily of today, yet not out of the ordinary: his suit should, as director Michael Mann would say, look as if it had been made in a day, ten years ago, by a tailor in Asia or the Far East for $70. The effect was reminiscent of

Roger Thornhill (Cary Grant) in *North by Northwest* (1959): again, one grey suit for the entire film – just as the action of the film all takes place in a single night. The suit is like Vincent's 'second skin' and, although monochrome, the fabric – chosen after much testing – is significant. Its black and white heathery tones, visible in close-up, gave it texture and depth, and there were shadows within the fabric. It was a great way of marking about this character: always in the shadows.

Another challenge for this particular film was that it was one of the first high-definition films, so depth perception – everything that would normally turn into a beautiful blur in the background – was crystal clear. So I had to be very careful about the detail of the clothes of the other characters – even if they were reasonably far away from Vincent or in the deep background – which on film is much less of an issue.

Having worked closely with Steven Soderbergh on *Erin Brockovich*, I was very interested when he called me to talk about *Ocean's Eleven*, his 2001 remake of the 1960 Rat Pack film. *Ocean's Eleven* and the Rat Pack were a major cultural force in the 1960s, and Frank Sinatra and Dean Martin were cult figures – so the idea of a remake was very appealing. Right from the start I made it clear that I was not interested in making this a retail extravaganza, or speaking to a plethora of suit manufacturers who might want to dress George Clooney or Brad Pitt. I felt that the style should be created for the film, and was very relieved and happy when Steven's reaction was 'That's why I want you to do this' – despite the fact that he was no doubt deluged by offers from any number of manufacturers. Steven believed – like me – that the film required a certain theatricality. Our job was to lift the drama above reality: although it had to look real, his plan was to heighten the

384 Julianne Potter and Kimberly Wallace
(Julia Roberts and Cameron Diaz)
My Best Friend's Wedding, 1997
Costume designer Jeffrey Kurland

narrative through his direction. That, for me, was manna from heaven – it was the perfect approach.

At my first meeting with Steven for the film he laid down his mandate. He was looking for a heightened reality: we were not making a period 1960s film, but we had to bring the essence of the Rat Pack into our own era. George Clooney, Brad Pitt and Matt Damon were already cast at this point, as was Julia Roberts; the rest of the cast were signed later on. Having met with George and Brad, I produced a large number of drawings to be approved by Steven and the producer, Jerry Weintraub. Then we looked at swatches for colour and texture, in discussion with the production designer Phil Messina, until we had a colour board for the entire picture. We broke these down methodically into individual sets, and then for each character. Thus everything was drawn out, swatched and painted, discussed with the director, the producer, and then with each individual actor. The next stage would be challenging: these were people with very heavy schedules who came and went at various times, so meetings and fittings had to be arranged as they were available.

Ted Griffin's script had no specific character descriptions for wardrobe, other than through the locations and action. For example, at the beginning of the film Danny Ocean (George Clooney) is in prison, so wears prison uniform; then he leaves prison and goes to Atlantic City, and then moves on. I referred to the script repeatedly: it was essential to know precisely what the actors were going to wear at every point in the action. Part of my job was to design each individual – to physicalize the script, decide who the characters were and how their clothes would bear this out.

At the top of the pyramid is Danny Ocean, played by George Clooney: as the film's starting point Danny sets the style and starts the action, and the rest of the characters develop from him. He leaves prison in a tuxedo – he had been arrested in a nightclub, wearing a tuxedo, so that was the suit he wore when he went to prison and the suit in which he leaves. The next time we see him he's in Atlantic City wearing a very well cut jacket and pants – sharp but not exaggerated, just great-looking. This use of Danny's image to introduce the rest of the cast was crucial: the same heightened style characterizes the whole production, but without his character to set the pace, this would feel entirely false – whereas our aim was a well-rounded, stylish piece. Danny Ocean is a rakish man about town, a gambler and a risk-taker, and this had to be evident in the clothes. I assumed that his wardrobe would be well made but not necessarily new: after all, he had been in prison for some time. However, I wanted him to have a very classic look: sharp two-button suits with notch lapels, tapered jackets with a strong shoulder to emphasise his personal strength. Similarly, his shirts, made by ANTO of Beverly Hills, are designed to emphasise his physique – rather than the clothes themselves standing out. My assumption was that Danny would have had his clothes made when he had money, and he kept them – there was no reason not to. Nothing was brand new, everything had a bit of a patina to it, but it was all classic.

By contrast, Rusty Ryan (Brad Pitt) is much more avant-garde: he is still a successful gambler, and spending money on himself. His clothes are designed to bring out the best in his appearance – he is meant to make you swoon. His suits are single and double breasted, each with a different cut and line, all very original. His single-button French cuffs are always open across his knuckles. His collars are also open, framing his face and his jaw. Ryan is the party-boy, friend of hookers and regular at strip clubs – intelligent, not frivolous, but a party-boy nevertheless. Danny, by contrast, is the more serious character – older and wiser, married and divorced, he has lived a life. Different though they are, the two men are still close friends. All these factors needed to be shown through their clothes.

The suits for the film were all tailor-made. Danny's clothes were made by Dominic Geraldi, a very traditional tailor whose style is, as it were 'Saville Row Italian' – stylish but conservative. Rusty's suits were made by Dennis Kim, whose cut was much more minimalist; he cut a narrower frame, which was appropriate for what I envisioned for Rusty. For Las Vegas casino owner Terry Benedict (Andy Garcia) I designed slim-cut suits but showing Asian influence, so Mr Kim made these as well. For Reuben Tishkoff (Elliott Gould), wealthy former casino owner and friend of Danny and Rusty, I wanted more traditional clothes, but still with flair. Again I commissioned Dominic to make these, knowing that his cut and tailoring would have unmistakable style, no matter what.

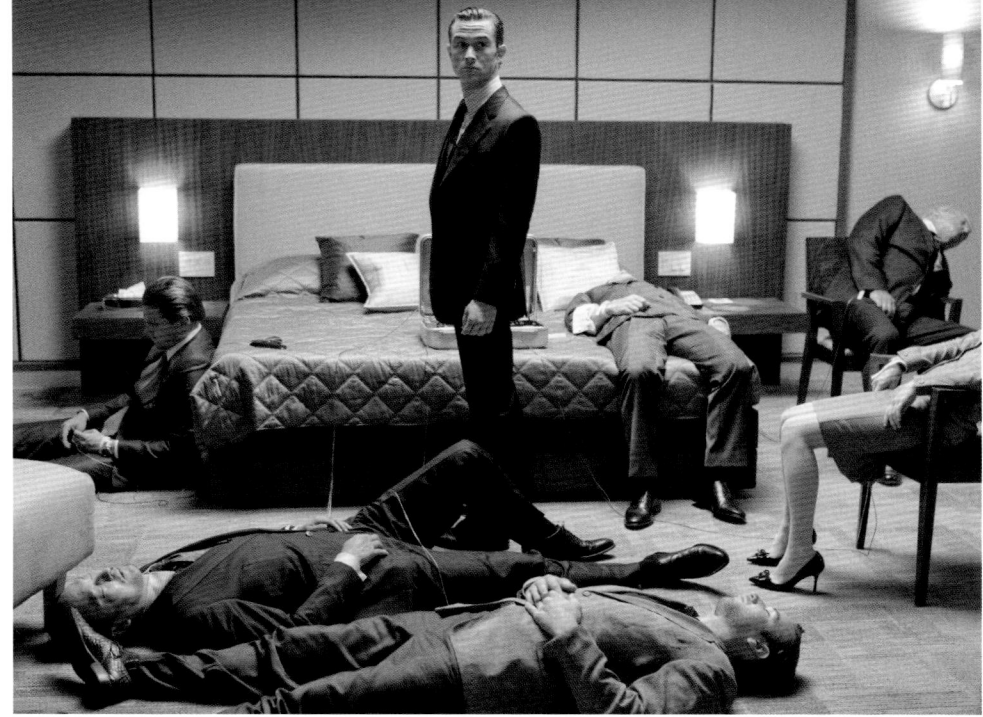

LEFT
385 Arthur (Joseph Gordon-Levitt)
***Inception*, 2010**
Costume designer Jeffrey Kurland

BELOW
386 Cobb (Leonardo DiCaprio)
***Inception*, 2010**
Costume designer Jeffrey Kurland

Linus Caldwell (Matt Damon), a gifted young pickpocket from Chicago, is the young turk who is the last to join the group as they plan their casino raid. Self-assured, even cocky, Linus nevertheless shows a vulnerability: he's the youngest and most inexperienced, but is learning from the best. My challenge was to show his youth and immaturity, although Matt Damon is actually not much younger than George and Brad. Thus his shirt, jacket and trousers were more youthful and much less structured than the suits worn by the others: it is only later in the film that he joins the suit-and-tie crowd. When we first see Linus in Chicago, he is a young guy, and I had vintage-style clothes made for him, complete with baseball cap to emphasise his youth. His loose, relaxed clothes reflect his personality: laid-back, self-assured and comfortable with himself. For the sake of realism I had to give his cap a badge, but wanted to avoid using a team or city badge. So I made a badge showing the hat itself and put that on the hat – it's a badge of the hat on the hat!

Working with the actors involved a good deal of collaboration and conversation. Each of them had a very different approach. Brad Pitt is businesslike, with discussions in front of a mirror about fabrics, colour, cut and line and where things are going to fit during movement. With George Clooney I spent more time looking at the drawings, fabrics and colours, deciding what would be most appropriate for the amalgam that was Danny Ocean and George. As for Matt Damon, the simplicity of the clothing instantly gave away his character, so agreeing on his clothes was the quickest of all: the leather jacket, the old tweed overcoat he wears in Chicago, the hat, all communicated his character with remarkable ease.

My favourite character in *Ocean's Eleven* is Reuben Tishkoff (Elliot Gould). When I read the script I felt that I knew this guy so well – in fact, to a certain extent I based him on old friends and members of my own family. In the 1960s Las Vegas was all

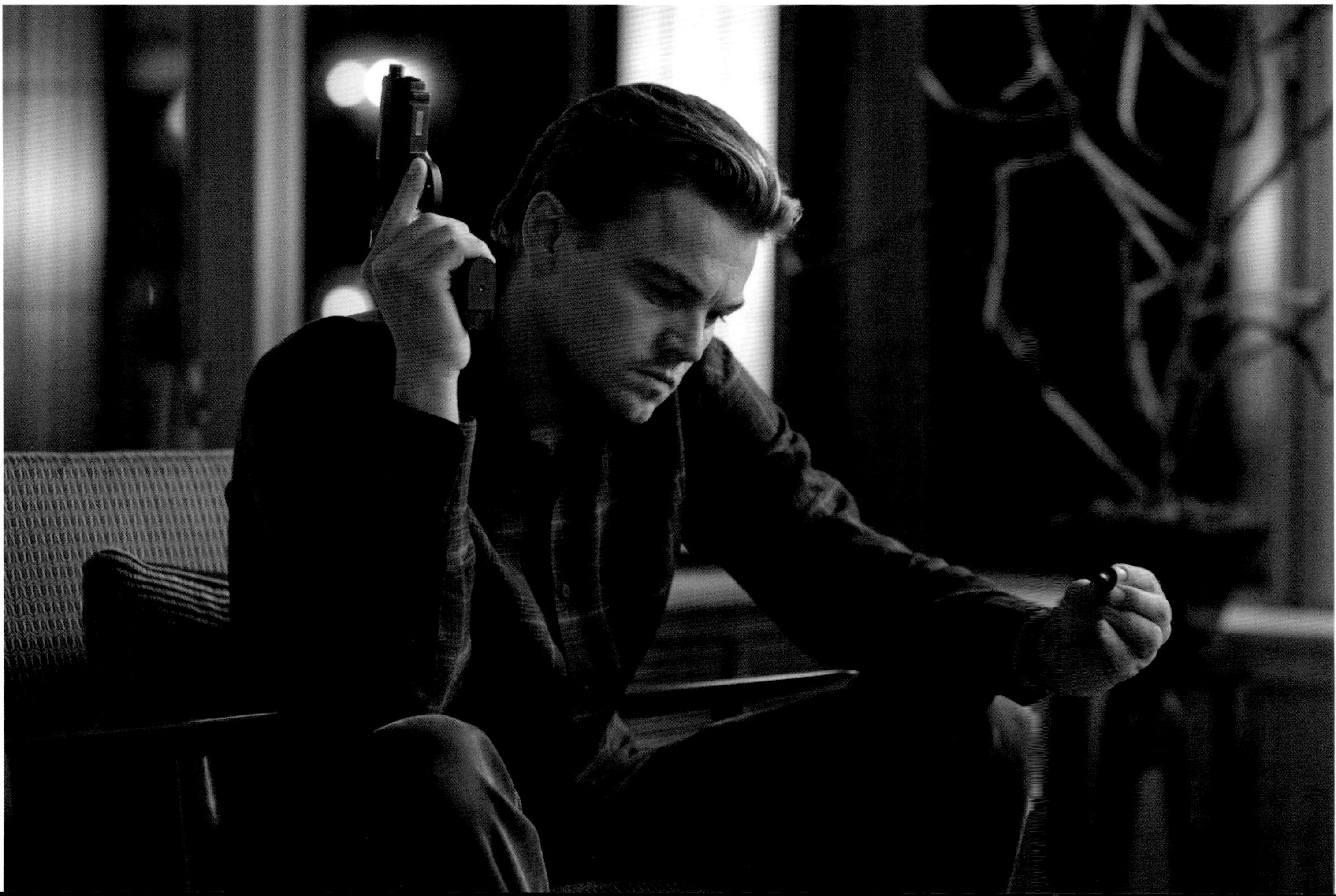

387, 388, 389 Sketches for Danny Ocean, Reuben Tishkoff and Rusty Ryan
Ocean's Eleven, 2001
Costume designer Jeffrey Kurland
Illustrators Jeffrey Kurland and Haleen K. Holt

RIGHT
390 Danny Ocean, Rusty Ryan, Linus Caldwell, Reuben Tishkoff and Basher Tarr
(George Clooney, Brad Pitt, Matt Damon, Elliott Gould and Don Cheadle)
Ocean's Eleven, 2001
Costume designer Jeffrey Kurland

the rage, and I can remember some of my relatives going there a lot: my father would tell me about the guys who would set visitors up in hotels and encourage them to gamble. These were the Tishkoff characters, the players of Vegas – wealthy, quick talking and cigar chewing. So Tishkoff's glasses and jewellery, his monogrammed bathrobes and slippers are all based on people from my own past. I knew he was the kind of person who would have had a haberdasher and a tailor, so although I was making every character's clothes for the film, I wanted to make Tishkoff's look especially created for him. This was a larger-than-life character who exuded originality. Elliott Gould's height and size were a major advantage: he could wear anything. So I made him a burgundy velvet zip-fronted jumpsuit, a Western-style sports jacket with a bolo tie, and a big tweed overcoat, with a hat – topped off with those big glasses, rings and jewellery. The first time we see Tishkoff he is sitting poolside, wearing a terrycloth and silk bathrobe with matching bathing suit – again, based on my own memories as a small child of family friends

in the Catskills and later in Vegas, in their matching suits and robes. I wanted Tishkoff's character to be instantly recognizable, with his matching outfit, glasses and heavy gold jewellery. This first impression is made in a few seconds, but then has to be continued through the entire film: his personality follows a narrative arc from this starting point, develops through the screenplay and arrives at an endpoint.

Don Cheadle played the character of Basher Tarr, the explosives expert, and he told Steven Soderbergh that he wanted to play him as a cockney. For his character, therefore, I looked at English styles of different eras. It was important to decide at the same time how old this character might be and what sort of fashion would influence his personal style. We looked at late 1960s and 1970s coats and jackets – maxi-coats, tight clothes as worn by Herman's Hermits and other British musicians of that era. In the end Basher wore turtlenecks, slim-fit trousers and beetle-boots, and, for most of the film, a 1970s-style brown leather coat. (He wears a different jacket at the beginning of the film, when he is

caught during the failed bank robbery – for this scene I made him a leather work-jacket with many pockets for his dynamite and fuses.) Finally, the scarf around his neck seemed to add a bit of panache and fitted his character well. With his cockney accent, he stood apart from the rest of the group – and this individuality was exactly what I wanted to achieve for all the characters, while at the same time, working together as a group.

The action of *Ocean's Eleven* takes place over a short time-span and there are few stunts or action scenes where clothes might be damaged. So for this film, other than shirts I made very few doubles. This is not always the case: for *Inception* (2010), many multiples of suits had to be made. For *Collateral* (2004) I made 26 copies of Tom Cruise's suit alone – and there were three stuntmen, all of whom were shooting and falling and needed multiple suits. As a rule, however, I only make what is necessary, and only make multiples if there is a need – and if money in the budget.

My approach to costume design has always been to create

original things for an original script. This gives more control to the artist, which for me works much better than having to adapt another artist's creation. I can thus control palette and, to an extent, fashion – in the case of Rusty Ryan (Brad Pitt), for example, the character wears fashion, but a fashion created for that character. And the assumption by the viewer is that Rusty created this fashion himself: his clothes show his own taste and decisions. The physical presentation of characters should be as original as their creation – the script, ideas, production and direction. We should not forget that iconic films that we now consider period pieces, made in the 1930s, '40s and 50s, were contemporary in their day, with all elements created for each particular film. The role of the costume designer is to create, whatever the production, period or contemporary, fact or fantasy.

Jeffrey Kurland is a celebrated film costume designer and a Governor of the Academy of the Motion Picture Academy of Arts & Sciences. His Oscar-nominated designs have appeared in exhibitions worldwide and he frequently gives lectures on the art of costume design.

FANTASY, SCI-FI AND SUPERHEROES

Jacob McMurray

PEOPLE have always been drawn to fantastic stories of heroes and villains with incredible powers and prowess, born out of magic, science, or natural ability. Part of this attraction derives from our need to find a meaningful context in a world in which individuals rarely enjoy total control over their destiny. In evolutionary terms, *homo sapiens* is not far from the cradle and there are Big Questions that have eternally confounded us. Countless creation myths, religions, song cycles, and tall tales have been built around these anxieties and serve to connect us to the universe and the unknown.

As complex social creatures with a unique mix of desires, needs and affinities, we have natural conflict within ourselves: try as we might to be good, we've all done a little bad. There are everyday heroes and villains, but they pale in comparison to the exploits of the characters that inhabit our fiction. The fact is that we need our heroes, villains, caped crusaders and superhumans, because they are singularly able to mete out awesome justice and terrifying evil. While we may not meet them in our daily lives,[1] we encounter them – both admirable and despicable – in novels, comics, games, and the movies. And – oh, yeah – their costumes are really cool.

Across the film spectrum costume design helps to define the characters, and in genre films these characters become archetypal and demand to be dressed accordingly. What would Darth Vader be without his iconic helmet and vestments? The Wicked Witch of the West without her pointy black hat? Superman without his primary-colour underpants? With fantastic film, in many ways the costume *is* the character.

Fantasy is the oldest genre of storytelling, with myths and legends appearing in the earliest texts. With the advent of

OPPOSITE
391 Batman (Christian Bale)
***The Dark Knight Rises*, 2012**
Costume designer Lindy Hemming

RIGHT
392 Sketch for Batman
***The Dark Knight Rises*, 2012**
Costume designer and illustrator Lindy Hemming

393 Count Dracula (Gary Oldman)
Bram Stoker's Dracula, 1992
Costume designer Eiko Ishioka

394 Sketch for Count Dracula
Bram Stoker's Dracula, 1992
Costume designer and illustrator Eiko Ishioka

cinema, fantasy film borrowed heavily from stories of ages past, with costumes referencing styles from across historical periods. Sword-and-Sorcery films looked to Roman gladiatorial outfits and 'barbarian' couture. The costume of the titular character in *Conan the Barbarian* (1982) is a fur Speedo and a sword blessed by the god Crom, filled out by Arnold Schwarzenegger's impressive physique. For a barbarian from the frozen antediluvian land of Cimmeria it is not exactly practical, but it fulfills popular conceptions of the dress of Huns, Picts, Celts, Vandals, Visigoths, and other hordes of historical times.

High fantasy, a common setting for fantasy film that has exploded in literature, film and computer and tabletop gaming, heavily references a spectrum of quasi-medieval and Renaissance-era styles, replete with magical bits and bobs as necessary to evoke sufficient atmosphere. Fantastic adventure tales took inspiration from swashbuckling themes and exotic fashions from non-Western cultures, accentuating a character's otherness. Johnny Depp's Captain Jack Sparrow from the *Pirates of the Caribbean*

films (2003–) strides across multiple worlds, with his British Navy-inspired tricorn hat and coat, Rastafarian dreadlocks and Romani jewellery. While most fantasy films look to the past for inspiration, the steady rise of contemporary and urban fantasy films show characters wearing costumes inspired from everyday youth fashion. In the *Harry Potter films* (2001–11), Harry (Daniel Radcliffe) and the Scooby Gang attend Hogwarts School of Witchcraft and Wizardry wearing traditional English school clothes under their wizard robes (they pull out their wands and owls when they need to), while in the *Twilight* films (2008–12), Edward Cullen (Robert Pattinson, plate 397) wears similarly casual street clothes (despite his sparkly vampire nature), as the human he adores, Bella Swan (Kristen Stewart), goes through requisite teenage angst-ridden melodrama. Fantasy costume can now mean *anything*.

The science fiction film has taken a similar path, but instead of clinging to myths of bygone eras, its focus is on outer space and the future. In these films blasters have taken the place of swords, face shields of steel helmets, and uniforms of woven space-age materials replace leather doublets. Harrison Ford's Han Solo in *Star Wars Episode IV: A New Hope* (1977) is a space-cowboy, a swashbuckling mercenary, while Jane Fonda in the title role of *Barbarella* (1968) updates the classic fantasy princess as a sexualized galactic wayfarer dressed in skimpy silver lamé futurewear.

Paradoxically, given the futuristic settings explored, sci-fi films often feel like products of their time – Barbarella's get-ups

ABOVE

395 **Sketch for Harry Potter**
Harry Potter and the Philosopher's Stone, 2001
Costume designer and illustrator Judianna Makovsky

396 **Harry Potter (Daniel Radcliffe)**
Harry Potter and the Philosopher's Stone, 2001
Costume designer Judianna Makovsky

LEFT

397 **Edward Cullen (Robert Pattinson)**
Twilight, 2008
Costume designer Wendy Chuck

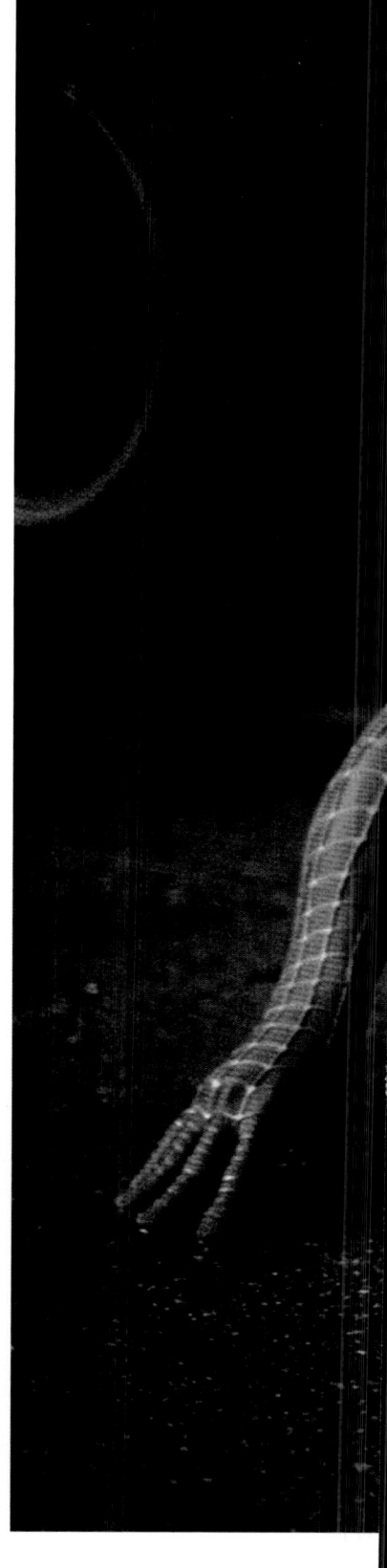

TOP
398 Concept design for *Spider-Man 2*, 2004
Costume designer James Acheson
Concept artist Warren Manser

ABOVE
399 Spider-Man (Tobey Maguire)
Spider-Man 2, 2004
Costume designers James Acheson and Gary Jones
Spider-Man costume designed by James Acheson

RIGHT
400 Spider-Man (Tobey Maguire)
Spider-Man, 2002
Costume designer James Acheson

could only have happened in the Swingin' Sixties, while Harrison Ford's shaggy hairdo and vest would not feel out of place in the mid-1970s. There are many factors at play, including the current popular conception of 'the future', to name but one. The futuristic velour mini-dress worn by Lieutenant Nyota Uhura (Nichelle Nichols) in the television series *Star Trek* (1966–9) illustrates the potential advantages of asynchronous sci-fi costuming. In the case of *Star Trek*, the costumes directly connected to contemporary fashions of the time, allowing viewers to imagine themselves aboard the USS *Enterprise*.

In the 1930s and '40s, the moon and stars were the next frontier. Between the wars a sense of wonder and manifest destiny suffused our culture, and future visions were promoted by pulp magazines such as Amazing Stories and films and serials such as *Things to Come* (1936), *Buck Rogers* (1939) and others. There was hopefulness that science could boost humanity to previously undreamed-of heights and create a technology-driven paradise on earth coupled with a future for humanity among the stars.

Enthusiasm for all things intergalactic continued in the 1950s, but became tempered with economic and technical realities as the ambitious US space programme began separating science fact from science fiction. Costumes in films from this period, such as *Destination Moon* (1950), began to reflect our growing awareness of the constraints of space travel.[2] If fantasy adapts history and science fiction looks towards the future, the superhero genre is a decidedly contemporary beast, with the action taking place in an urban setting. With global troubles like the Great Depression, the pressures of society and existential malaise were immense, and superheroes acted as champion for the masses.[3] Superman was created in 1932, first appearing in *Action Comics* no.1 in June 1938, and remains one of the most iconic superheroes in history, throughout a wide array of media.

From the 1960s, with the war in Vietnam and social unrest in the United States an idealized future seemed increasingly remote. Economics can put a damper on unbridled technology, slowing progress. With humanity's naïveté bubble bursting, costume design began to reference more earthly visions: Arnold Schwarzenegger's robot-as-rebel leatherwear in the *Terminator* movies (1984–2003), the cyber-fetish outfits worn by Neo (Keanu Reeves) in *The Matrix* (1999; plates 407, 408), and the 1940s noir/new-wave/pan-Asian costume design of *Blade Runner* (1982).

The comic artists who conceived of early superheroes were inspired by the durability and practicality of athletic clothing and the showmanship of outfits worn

405 Trinity (Carrie-Anne Moss)
The Matrix, 1999
Costume designer Kym Barrett

406 Sketch for Trinity
The Matrix, 1999
Costume designer Kym Barrett
Illustrator Ed Natividad

407 Neo (Keanu Reeves)
The Matrix, 1999
Costume designer Kym Barrett

408 Sketch for Neo
The Matrix, 1999
Costume designer Kym Barrett
Illustrator Ed Natividad

by circus acrobats, strongmen and wrestlers. Allowing for freedom of movement, these stretchy, form-fitting, brightly coloured costumes helped to define a superhero in the public eye. For many superheroes, costumes are also a means of disguising their true identity – a concept at the centre of the superhero *Weltanschauung*. In order for superheroes to maintain their *otherness* from the rest of humanity, they have to keep their true identity secret. Time and time again discovering a superhero's true identity revealed the key to their power – and their weakness. Christopher Reeve as the Caped and Colourful One in *Superman* (1978) is rendered weak by matter from his home planet Krypton, revealing him as Kal-El, a normal being of his species. Bruce Wayne's suave playboy in *Batman* (1997–2012) is quite exposed in his tuxedo compared to the seemingly invincible Batman, in his darkly cowled, menacing batsuit (plate 391).

Superhero costumes augment the superior physicality of their owners – who are imbued with special attributes and abilities and are paragons of human physicality. Superheroes and villains are amplified toward the light or dark, in all ways reflecting our inner desires, dreams and fears. Peter Parker in *Spider-Man* (2001–12) is a baby-faced, kindly nerd, but as Spider-Man, he has the physique of

409 Superman (Christopher Reeve)
Superman: The Movie, **1978**
Costume designer Yvonne Blake

a god and the athletic prowess of a Cirque du Soleil acrobat (plates 398–400). Catwoman's skin-tight black latex catsuit in *Batman Returns* (1992; plate 415) oozes overt athletic sexuality and sells at the box office.

We are entering an age where nearly anything that could be imagined can now be visualized on the screen. Many of the most popular computer games place you as the protagonist in science fiction, fantasy and superhero settings. In popular franchises such as *World of Warcraft, Elder Scrolls, Second Life* and countless film or comic tie-ins, gamers are compelled to spend considerable time outfitting their characters, dressing them in various armour and clothing. It is a natural part of the process of merging with a character. Players become one with their avatar, united in their quest. The trend has become such an ingrained part of gaming today that whole economies have been built around players paying real-world money in exchange for in-game equipment, clothing

and weapons. Such is the power of our human desire to become something greater than ourselves. We desire to control our destiny.

'Clothes make the man. Naked people have little or no influence on society.' Mark Twain certainly never played *World of Warcraft*, fought alongside Aragorn, son of Arathorn, to secure Minas Tirith against advancing hordes, watched Batman beat the crap out of baddies, or rode in an X-wing fighter toward the Death Star, but his adage still applies. The role and visibility of costume design (in the digital or real world) is immense, acting as a prime signifier for the characters, their powers, personal histories, and motivations. Media in the realms of fantasy, sci-fi and superheroes continue to push the costume designer's art to new heights, bringing fantastic visions of mythical worlds and other planets to life on a screen near you.

Senior Curator at EMP, the science fiction museum in Seattle, Jacob McMurray has organized numerous exhibitions examining the relationship between costume and science fiction in films. He is also an independent arts curator, graphic designer and writer.

410 Sketch for Rachel
Blade Runner, 1982
Costume designers Michael Kaplan
and Charles Knode
Illustrator Michael Kaplan

411 Rachel (Sean Young)
Blade Runner, 1982
Costume designers Michael Kaplan
and Charles Knode

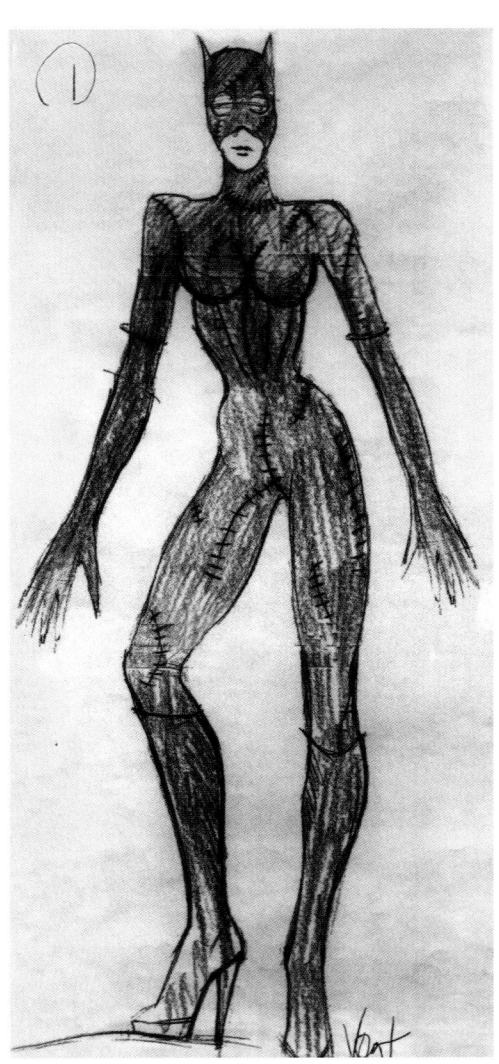 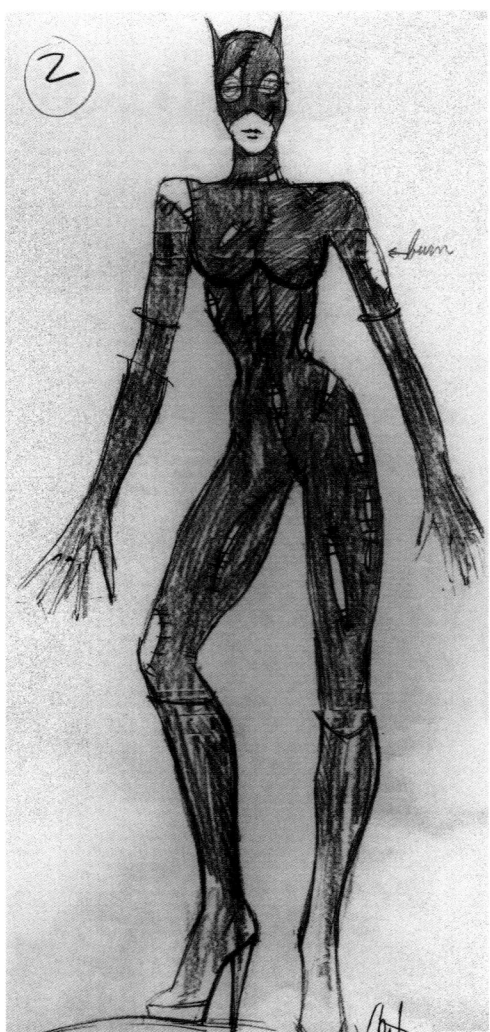 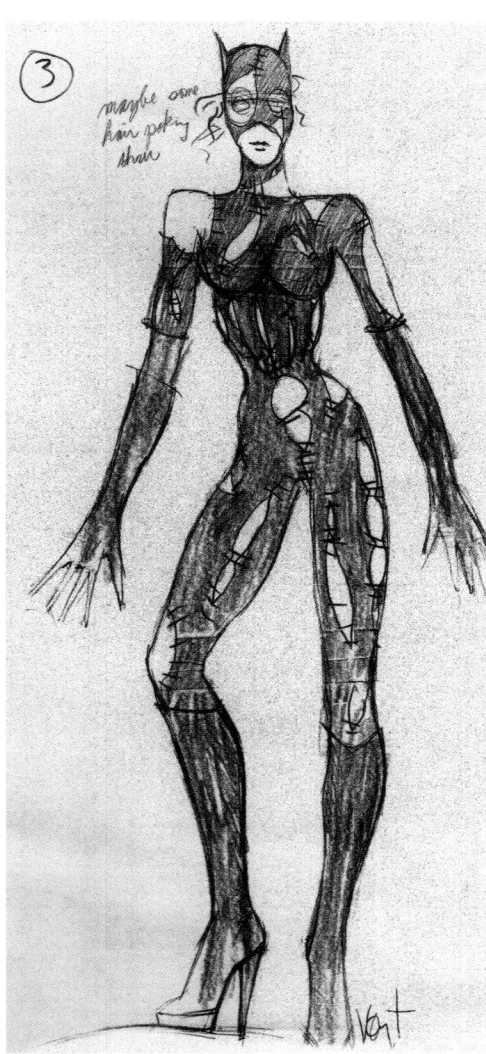

412, 413, 414 Sketches for the three stages of Catwoman
Batman Returns, 1992
Costume designers Bob Ringwood and Mary E. Vogt
Illustrator Mary E. Vogt

415 Catwoman (Michelle Pfeiffer)
Batman Returns, 1992
Costume designers Bob Ringwood
and Mary E. Vogt

THE CHALLENGES OF MOCAP AND CGI

Joanna Johnston

THE GROWTH of computer-generated imagery (CGI) and motion capture (mocap) technology in recent years has presented costume designers with an ever-increasing array of challenges. The first film to combine live action with animation was *Anchors Aweigh* (1945), in which Gene Kelly dances with an animated mouse. The combination of animated and live actors reappeared in various films over the following forty years, such as *Mary Poppins* (1964) and *Bedknobs and Broomsticks* (1971), but the animated characters invariably appeared almost as separate and two-dimensional life-form, lacking depth and shadow. The last twenty years have seen extraordinary developments in this area of film-making, beginning with *Who Framed Roger Rabbit* (1988), directed by Robert Zemeckis, which can be seen as a springboard between the old world and the new. I remember seeing an early screen test by Industrial Light & Magic (ILM), with Eddie Valiant (played in the film by Bob Hoskins) on

a metal staircase with an animated rabbit. As the rabbit tumbled down the stairs the effect was entirely convincing. One could completely accept that the rabbit was an integral part of the scene.

Roger Rabbit required an extraordinary combination of skills: the broad strokes of old-world animators, the latest computer-generated imagery then being developed by ILM, and the tools of old-fashioned film-making to put it all together. The animators would create the animation, leaving a void for us on set where the cartoons were meant to be. At first we worked with a scaled rubber Roger Rabbit that had to be picked up and moved from place to place. Then Bob Hoskins requested a real rabbit – something that moved, rather than this inanimate rubber model. So the stand-up comedian Charlie Fleischer (who voiced the character of Roger Rabbit) came on set, I made a rabbit outfit for him and he spent all day being Roger on the set. Thus there could be real interaction between him and Bob Hoskins – or

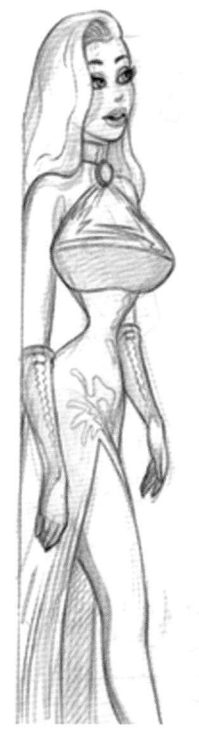

OPPOSITE
**416 Jessica Rabbit
(Kathleen Turner)**
***Who Framed Roger Rabbit*, 1988**
**Costume designer
Joanna Johnston**

RIGHT
417 Sketch for Jessica Rabbit
***Who Framed Roger Rabbit*, 1988**
**Early concept design
Richard Williams**

**418 Eddie Valiant, Judge Doom
(Bob Hoskins, Christopher Lloyd)
and Toons**
***Who Framed Roger Rabbit*, 1988**
**Costume designer
Joanna Johnston**

whoever else was with the rabbit – which brought him to life. I made Charlie's costume quickly and cheaply and it soon became very dilapidated as he trailed around in it all day. For the Ink and Paint Club scenes puppeteers operated the props, including real trays with real drinks. For more detailed or complex choreography, such as when we needed small arms undoing somebody's tie, we employed dwarfs and the animators would then draw over the top of these stand-ins. Anything that was going to be animated we called a 'toon', and the rest was called 'real'. Every day on set was an adventure trail, a pooling of ideas as we worked out how each scene could be made to work. The process was highly experimental and definitely pioneering. Bob Zemeckis always raised the bar and used many complicated camera moves, which made the work of the animators, led by associate producer Don Hahn, extremely complex. The huge visual effects crew, under Ken Ralston, also faced major challenges every hour.

The cartoons were designed by Richard Williams, an eminent animator, and he was responsible for creating all the animated characters and their costumes. As costume designer I was not to be involved in the animated characters: my responsibility was confined to the live action, although in the end I did contribute designs to the cartoons. First, I helped give a more period effect to the weasels, and then I became involved with designing Jessica Rabbit. Jessica represents a classic film goddess, the perfect woman. Bob Zemeckis was unsure about the design of her original gown, a sixties-style halter-neck, and I was asked to redesign her costume. I was inspired by costume designer Jean Louis's glamorous strapless gown for Rita Hayworth as the ultimate *femme fatale* in *Gilda* (1946). I felt that Jessica should defy gravity in an extreme way. The original plan was to have her in a fully sequined hot pink gown with a very low back. This design was embraced, but the animators said that it would be too expensive for Jessica's gown to be sequined throughout the film. This was disappointing, as I wanted her to be constantly shimmering, but they agreed that she would be sequined only when appearing singing on stage. As a reference to show the effect of sequins reflecting on the faces of the audience I produced a sample piece

of sequined fabric; for the rest of the film Jessica was drawn wearing a plain, unsequined satin gown.

Animators very often become totally enraptured by the creatures they create. When Richard Williams handed over Jessica Rabbit's designs to me it was clearly difficult as he had become so emotionally involved with Jessica as a character.

As films become more techically advanced the costume designer needs to be aware of certain constraints imposed by new CGI technology, and of what is planned in the post-production process. Sometimes this has a lesser effect on costume design, such as in the designs for *Forrest Gump* (1994), when the head of Tom Hanks as Forrest is superimposed onto old footage (plate 419), or *Death Becomes Her* (1992), when Madeline (Meryl Streep) appears with her head on back to front (plate 420). In most cases it is critical that the costume designer understands what will happen in post-production and keep an open dialogue with the visual effects team and the director. For *Back to the Future II* (1989) and *III* (1990) I interacted frequently with Ken Ralston, the visual effects supervisor. In *Back to the Future III*, which goes back to the 1880s, blue screen was used extensively. At that time it was important to avoid the same electric blue in the costumes, but I wanted to use a strong violet colour on Clara Clayton (Mary Steenburgen) for a portion of the film. We tested the colour and found that it contained a lot of blue; anyone other than Ken Ralston would have said 'no', but he agreed to let us try. Working alongside the visual effects team and developing an understanding of their requirements and constraints is increasingly important for any costume designer.

The Polar Express (2004; plates 422–8) presented me with even more sophisticated challenges. This was the second-ever feature-length film to use motion capture (mocap) for all the actors (the first was *Final Fantasy: The Spirits Within*, 2001), and was based on a children's book by Chris Van Allsburg. Director Bob Zemeckis wanted to keep closely to the original illustrations, which were very beautiful. The plan was to shoot the film using brand-new mocap technology, where actors inhabit the characters but the rest – the set, scenery and so on – is created by computer.

My brief was to design all the costumes with different levels of complexity. The principals were not a problem, but for all the supporting characters, including the children on the train, I had to avoid fussiness and embellishment, such as frills on the clothes. Everything in a scene was described according to three levels of complexity; anything over-dimensional, which was not flat and therefore caused complications, was described as level 3. If an outfit did have any embellishment, I had to tone it down to a certain degree. Another unexpected difficulty was that heads and bodies of characters were sometimes switched in what I call the 'decapitation' process. We had a huge cast of children, and their heads were frequently moved from one body to another. I found this confusing as I would be designing for one child and then find that it had been given a completely different head! Tom Hanks created the range of motions and therefore the character of four people within the film: Conductor, Hero Boy, Hobo and Santa Claus.

This was a curious, completely new world for me, but this pioneering process was enormously enjoyable. First I made the costumes for the children and adults and they were filmed in a range of motions as a reference for the computer animators: jumping, skipping, lying down, sitting still, arms up and down. Next was the process of three-dimensional scanning using the Gentle Giant cyber scanner. This is a mobile device that scans the actor's entire body, building up a shape of the body in a leotard, then the next layer of clothing and so on, to provide the computer animators with all the information they need to build up the layers required for the computer.

Nothing was filmed 'in costume' for motion capture: actors wore leotards with reflective stripes and balls stuck on them. In this very early stage of the evolution of the mocap process, hundreds of tiny balls had to be stuck all over the characters' faces in order to capture each expression, carefully placed with tweezers by the make-up team. This technique is now a thing of the past. It was fascinating and exciting being part of this changing world, where the set and everything about it was completely new and unfamiliar. We worked on a sound stage entirely blank, with camera rigs that could move through 360 degrees. The props were wire frameworks, representing non-solid outlines: a chair, for instance, was reduced to a see-through wire frame. So the action took place on a very dead stage and everything being filmed was logged in three-dimensional form by operators on banks of computers.

We made all the costumes as they would appear in the film, and then gave them to the computer operators so that they could study them and translate them into their final, animated form. Techniques have undoubtedly improved since 2004: the effect then was rather solid and doll-like with no sense of air underneath the clothing. The costume designer's role was to give a point of reference and an inspiration rather than a final design: once we had handed over the costume to the computer team they were out of our hands. Being part of a technical 'conveyor belt' process, with no consultation or regular updates, can be a hard thing for a costume designer: while the production designer continues to work with the computer designer, the costume designer's involvement definitely stops at hand-over point. For me the great thing about *The Polar Express* was having all the fun of designing the costumes without the stress of film making: the mocap suit

BELOW LEFT
420 Madeline Ashton (Meryl Streep)
Death Becomes Her, 1992
Costume designer Joanna Johnston

BELOW RIGHT
421 Mary Steenburgen and director Robert Zemeckis between takes on the set of *Back to the Future III*, 1990

ABOVE RIGHT
**422 Hero Boy, Hero Girl and Bill
(Tom Hanks, Nona Gaye and
Peter Scolari)**
The Polar Express, 2004
Costume designer Joanna Johnston

ABOVE AND RIGHT
**423, 424, 425 Sketches for
Hero Boy, Smokey and Steamer**
The Polar Express, 2004
Costume designer
Joanna Johnston
Illustrator Robin Richesson

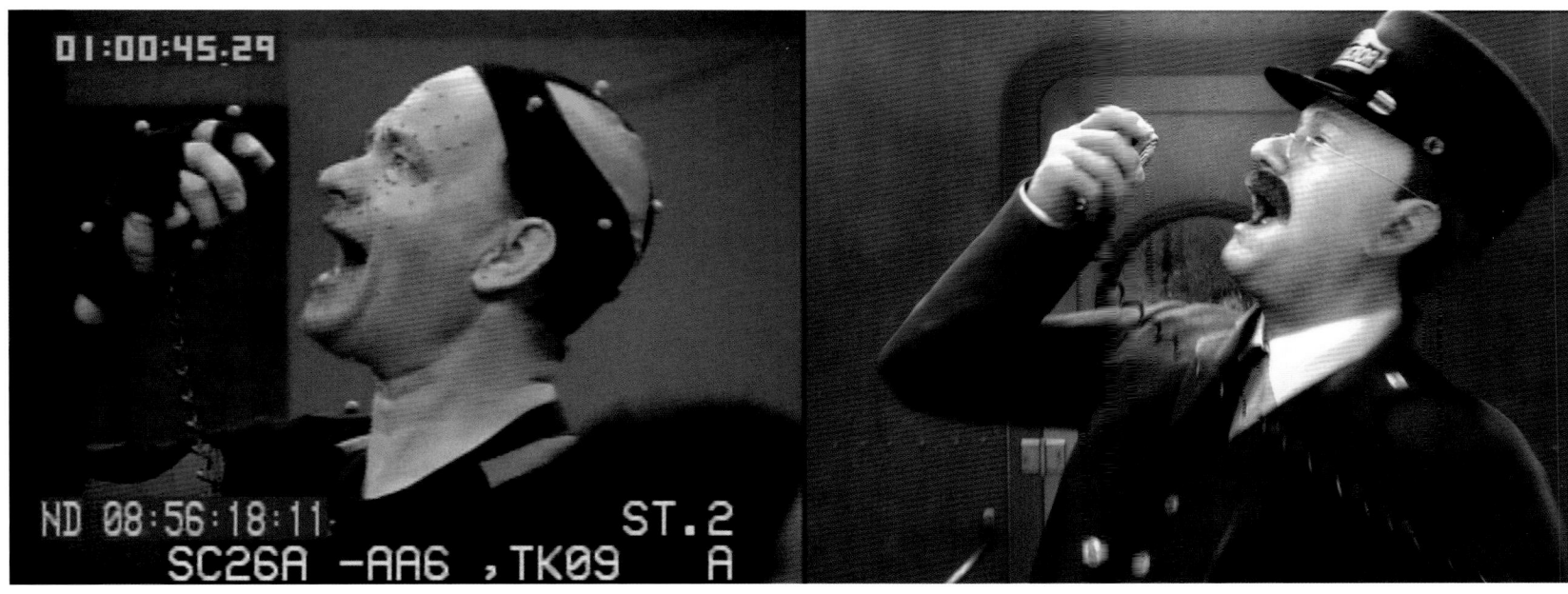

426, 427 **Tom Hanks filming motion capture (left)
and final animation (right) for *The Polar Express*, 2004**
Costume designer Joanna Johnston

428 **Sketch for Conductor**
***The Polar Express*, 2004**
Costume designer Joanna Johnston
Illustrator Robin Richesson

was maintained by the people on the set who had the rather worrying responsibility of ensuring all the balls were in the right place.

The Spiderwick Chronicles (2008) was another film that combined CGI and mocap technology. To prepare the costume designs I was supplied with maquettes of the tiny forest creatures on which to build the clothes, and these were then used as blueprint for the final designs. This was a thoroughly enjoyable process. For the computer animators having a detailed three-dimensional object, with all its texture, colour and character, provided a useful starting-point from which to create the final characters. For the animator it can also be extremely useful to see a real-life, fabric costume as a reference for the drape and texture of fabric and the air space between garment and body. While I was designing the costumes for *War Horse* (2011) I supplied a few fabric samples which were sent to Peter Jackson's company in New Zealand as a reference for *The Adventures of Tintin: The Secret of the Unicorn* (2011).

For Bryan Singer's mocap *Jack the Giant Killer* (2012) I was asked to design clothing for the 30-ft computer-generated giants as well as the costumes for the film. I provided the computer team with a selection of textural references and drawings – the giants were too large to construct as full figures. The idea was that the giants were ancient creatures who had existed since the Stone Age, evolving into hideous crustacean forms over the years. Their flesh had become almost indistinguishable from the rotting fabric covering them, so that they became live creatures encased in dead and rotting matter. It was interesting to be part of an organic process in this way: the work of the costume designer once again became the starting-point for the animators.

429 Sketch for Neytiri
Avatar, 2009
Costume designers Mayes
C. Rubeo and Deborah L. Scott

OPPOSITE
430 Neytiri (Zoë Saldana)
Avatar, 2009
Costume designers Mayes
C. Rubeo and Deborah L. Scott

ABOVE
434 Goblins in
the kitchen scene
*The Spiderwick
Chronicles*, 2008
Costume designer
Joanna Johnston

LEFT
435, 436 Sketches
for Thimbletack
and Redcap
*The Spiderwick
Chronicles*, 2008
Costume designer
Joanna Johnston
Illustrator Robin
Richesson

Although I have worked on a wide variety of genres, from sci-fi, fantasy, mocap and CGI to period films such as *War Horse* and *Lincoln* (2012), my skill set – the design process and costume building blocks – have remained fundamentally the same. But the ability to be flexible in light of fast-developing technology is now more important than ever. Certainly the techniques and requirements vary enormously from one film to the next, which makes the work of the costume designer invariably interesting and challenging. Working with collaborative film-makers and directors with innovative ideas has enabled me to be part of a broadening world. Going forward with new technology, the world of film will always have a place for a costume designer, even if only as a springboard to inspire the animators to build their characters with clothing – and in understanding the texture and behaviour of cloth.

Joanna Johnston works as a costume designer and has collaborated with directors such as Bob Zemeckis and Steven Spielberg. Her costume design credits include such blockbusters as Saving Private Ryan *(1998),* The Sixth Sense *(1999),* Love Actually *(2003),* The Boat that Rocked *(2009),* War Horse *(2011),* Lincoln *(2012) and* Jack the Giant Killer *(2013).*

ABOVE
437 Captain Haddock and Tintin (Andy Serkis and Jamie Bell)
***The Adventures of Tintin: The Secret of the Unicorn,* 2011**
Costume designer Lesley Burkes-Harding

LEFT
438 Sketch for Tars Tarkas
***John Carter,* 2012**
Costume designer Mayes C. Rubeo

OPPOSITE
439 Concept design for *Jack the Giant Killer,* 2013
Costume designer Joanna Johnston
Concept artist Colin Marks

NOTES

SETTING THE SCENE: A SHORT HISTORY OF HOLLYWOOD COSTUME DESIGN 1912–2012

1   Campbell 1949.
2   A mutoscope is a 'simple form of animated-picture viewing device in which the series of views is printed on paper and mounted around the periphery of a wheel' (*Webster's New International Dictionary*, 2nd edn (Cambridge, MA, 1934).
3   LaVine 1980, pp.12–13.
4   Spears 1971, p.365.
5   MacGowan 1965, p.139.
6   Spehr 1977, p.45.
7   Wollen 1995, p.14.
8   McConathy and Vreeland 1976, p.31.
9   Wollen 1995, p.14. See also MacGowan 1965, p.158.
10 Engelmeier and Einzig 1990, p.18.
11 Glynn 1978, p.72.
12 LaVine 1980, p.4; Schreier 1998, p.30.
13 Bordwell, Staiger and Thompson 1985, p.149.
14 Leese 1991, p.12.
15 Hollywood designers Howard Greer and Robert Kalloch began their careers with Lucile; Bernard Newman had been head designer at Bergdorf Goodman (Berry 2000, p.14). Travis Banton began his career at Mme Francis, a custom dressmaker in New York; after the First World War he, too, worked for Lucile (LaVine 1980, p.170).
16 Bordwell, Staiger and Thompson 1985, p.145.
17 Chierichetti 1976, p.12.
18 Head and Calistro 1983, p.13.
19 MacGowan 1965, p.209.
20 Ibid., p.209.
21 LeBrun 1996, p.57.
22 Fowler 1996, pp.98–9.
23 LaValley 1987, p.86.
24 Howard Strickling, Introduction to Part III, 'MGM', in Rose 1976, p.47.
25 Greer 1949, pp.3–4.
26 Ibid., p.219.
27 Head and Calistro 1983, p.7.
28 Walter Plunkett began his show business career as an actor on Broadway. He had no formal training as a designer, yet he is 'generally acknowledged to be Hollywood's foremost designer of period clothes' (LaVine 1980, p.227).
29 Quoted in Finch and Rosenkrantz 1980, p.68.
30 Robinson 1994, p.37.
31 Hirschhorn 1979, p.18.
32 Davis 1993, p.215.
33 Hirschhorn 1979, p.18.
34 Engelmeier and Einzig 1990, p.18.
35 Bailey 1982, p.64.
36 Gutner 2001, p.7.
37 Ibid., pp.7–8, quoting *Modern Screen* no.1 (April 1930), p.36.
38 LaVine 1980, p.27. It should be noted that the phrase 'major studio', as used in connection with Hollywood in the 1930s and early 1940s, generally refers to Metro-Goldwyn-Mayer (MGM), Paramount, Radio-Keith-Orpheum (RKO), Warner Bros and Twentieth Century Fox. 'These five studios … were the supreme powers in the industry' (Schatz 1988, p.11).

39 Balio 1993, p.92.
40 LaVine 1980, p.28; Bailey 1982, p.262.
41 The Depression crept up on Hollywood as the studios slowly lost their value during the early 1930s. The industry was quickly revived by President Roosevelt's National Industrial Recovery Act (NIRA), which promoted recovery 'by sanctioning certain monopoly practices'. The studios took full advantage of the legislation. Although the NIRA was declared unconstitutional in 1935, the consolidation of the studios' power would take many years to unravel. Ultimately, 'Hollywood was a Depression-era success story' (Schatz 1988, p.160).
42 McConathy and Vreeland 1976, pp.27–8.
43 'Each dress, each costume was unique and designed for one star or one extra' (Bailey 1982, p.56).
44 'Of all the Hollywood studios, MGM was least affected by the stock market crash and ensuing Depression' (Schatz 1988, p.98).
45 Gutner 2001, p.22, quoting *Motion Picture*, no.183 (May 1926), p.42.
46 Ibid.
47 Watts 1938, p.57.
48 Gutner 2001, p.54, quoting an interview with Calvin Klein, Program for the 1985 Council of Fashion Designers of America Awards.
49 Ibid., p.62.
50 Balio 1993 p.93.
51 Tapert 1998, p.53.
52 McConathy and Vreeland 1976, pp.27–8.
53 LaVine 1980, p.64. Zukor's interest in apparel may have stemmed in part from his previous profession as a fur trader (Eames 2004, p.7). In fact, many Hollywood moguls had earlier careers in the garment industry.
54 Fowler 1996, p.140.
55 LaVine 1980, p.206.
56 Head and Calistro 1983, p.59.
57 Quoted in Bailey 1982, p.8.
58 McConathy 1976, p.176.
59 Stine and Davis 1980, p.176.
60 Ibid., pp.190–91.
61 Plunkett served as the studio's head of wardrobe from 1926 to 1930 and 1932 to 1935 (Leese 1991, p.105). After leaving the wardrobe post he designed costumes for RKO films until 1939.
62 Quoted in Finch and Rosenkrantz 1980, p.70.
63 Haver 1986, p.7.
64 Ibid., p.9.
65 Quoted in Bailey 1982, p.20.
66 Quoted in Chierichetti 1976, p.166.
67 McConathy and Vreeland 1976, pp.164–6.
68 Doherty 1999, pp.357–8.
69 Schumach 1964, p.168.
70 Schatz 1988, p.298.
71 'The year 1940 marked the beginning of a more serious decade of film-making' (LaVine 1980, p.99). 'By 1940 Hollywood had crossed an important threshold…. [with the making of interventionist films] the departure from a sole reliance on "the pleasant and profitable course of entertainment" marked a significant shift in thinking' (Koppes and Black 1987, p.32).
72 Head and Calistro 1983, p.50.

73 The classical style refers to the period in Hollywood after 1917, when 'the system was complete in its basic narrative and stylistic premises' (Bordwell, Staiger and Thompson 1985, p.157).
74 Sharaff 1976, p.66.
75 Schatz 1988, p.4.
76 Ibid., pp.411–12.
77 Ibid., p.440.
78 Leese 1991, pp.70–75.
79 Chierichetti 1976, p.90.
80 Head and Calistro 1983, p.58.
81 Schumach 1964, p.34.
82 Sharaff 1976, pp.60–61.
83 Head and Calistro 1983, p.82.
84 MacGowan 1965, p.449.
85 One writer notes that with the end of the Second World War, 'the search for a new national identity was mirrored in the search for individual identity in a complex and hostile world. It is not surprising that Americans sought escape in the old West' (Hyams 1983, p.76).
86 Eames 1975, p.291.
87 The notoriety of the costume designers for *Samson and Delilah* – Edith Head, Dorothy Jeakins, Eloise, Gile Steele and Gwen Wakeling – competes with that of the film's cast. Internet Movie Database (www.imdb.com), credits for *Samson and Delilah* (1949), 10 May 2002. The film won the Academy Award for costume design for a colour picture.
88 For *The Ten Commandments* the studio enlisted Arnold Friberg, Edith Head, Dorothy Jeakins, John Jensen and Ralph Jester. Internet Movie Database (www.imdb.com), credits for *The Ten Commandments* (1956), 10 May 2002. *The Ten Commandments* was nominated for an Academy Award for costume design for a colour picture.
89 Shindler 1983, p.35.
90 Sharaff 1976, p.107.
91 The Hollywood studios were largely in debt by the mid-1960s (LeBrun 1996, p.656).
92 LaVine 1980, p.137.
93 Head and Calistro 1983, p.143.
94 Ibid.
95 LaVine 1980, p.137.
96 Beaton, Cecil, *Cecil Beaton's Fair Lady* (New York 1964), p.32.
97 Ibid., p.41.
98 Leigh and Nickens 1995, pp.43–4.
99 Deborah Nadoolman Landis interview with Theadora Van Runkle on 7 May 2002 (for Landis 2003).
100 Doonan, Simon, 'Best Wardrobe in a Supporting Role', *InStyle Magazine*, vol.10, issue 3 (March 2003), p.236.
101 Schatz 1988, p.481.
102 Biskind 1998, pp.74–5.
103 Krier, B.A., 'Costume Design Revolution', *Los Angeles Times* (18 March 1971), part IV, p.1.
104 DVD: *Dressing a Galaxy: The Costumes of Star Wars* (San Rafael, CA, 2005).
105 Chierichetti, David, 'How to dress Buck Rogers – and other sci-fi tales', *Los Angeles Times Fashion '79*, 26 October 1979, p.9.
106 Medavoy and Young 2002, p.151.
107 Bernstein 1996, p.2.

108 Rochelle Levy Lazar, 'Harrison Ford: In His Own Words', American Film Institute (http://www.fathom.com/feature/190179/index.html).

109 Betty Goodwin, 'Authenticity Sparks "Out of Africa" Costume Designs', Los Angeles Times, 3 January 1986, p.G6.

110 Landis 2003, p.32

111 C. Troy, 'Ellen Mirojnick and the Inner Game of Costume: "Can You Imagine Them Making Love?"', American Film, no.138 (June 1989), p.51.

112 http://www.titanicmovie.com/present/bts_index.html

113 DVD: The Matrix Revisited, Collector's Edition, Warner Bros Entertainment Inc. (Burbank, CA, 2004).

114 Ivana Redwine, interview: 'Jeff Dowd and The Big Lebowski' (http://homevideo.about.com/od/dvdsvideosbytitle/a/JDowdBLebowskia.htm), About, Inc., 2005.

115 Interview with Albert Wolsky for Screencraft by Deborah Nadoolman, 12 March 2002, audiocassette transcript pp.35–6.

116 Elizabeth Snead, '"Atonement": The past made new', Los Angeles Times, 12 December 2007, pp.S24–5.

117 Keith Bush, 'From Sleepy Hollow to Chicago, Colleen Atwood creates beautiful costumes for beastly characters' (www.keithbush.com).

118 Emanuel Levy, 'Dreamgirls: Creating Authentic Look through Costumes, Makeup and Hair', 2004–7 (http://www.emanuellevy.com/article.php?articleID=3901).

1 THE ART OF BECOMING

MOVING PICTURES, SILENT MOVIES AND THE ART OF WILLIAM HOGARTH

1 Landis 2007, p.xviii.

2 David Lodge, Therapy (London 1996), p.285.

3 As, for example, in The Leopard (1963), where the style of the early 1960s can be seen in the appearance of the young lovers – the tight trousers worn by Alain Delon as Tancredi and the make-up of Claudia Cardinale as Angelica. The eponymous hero of Lampedusa's novel, played by Burt Lancaster, is costumed accurately for the early 1860s, when the story mainly takes place.

4 Kubrick was also inspired by the detailed costume plates made from 1775 to 1783, by the French artist Jean-Michel Moreau, published in 1789 as the Monument du Costume Physique et Moral de la fin du Dix-huitième siècle.

5 Hollander 1978, pp.350, 345. The British director Peter Greenaway has a particularly close relationship with fine art in his work; trained as an artist, his films are imbued with a painterly quality.

6 Personal communication from Deborah Landis, 22 February 2011

7 Fielding 1749, vol.II, pp.1–2.

8 Ibid., p.viii. It has to be said that there is more artistic mileage and greater interest in the depiction of human depravities than in the portrayal of uncomplicated and perfect lives; we prefer paradise lost to paradise regained. Hogarth was aware of this in his great moral cycles, where he reveals how much an addiction to pleasure, to sexual gratification and avid consumerism (venial sins perhaps) can lead to cruelty, crime, murder and insanity. I have particularly in mind here his Rake's Progress (1732–3), which has inspired a number of works, such as Stravinsky's opera of the same name (1951), and the film Boogie Nights (1997; directed by Paul Thomas Anderson, costume designer Mark Bridges), the story of a young man's adventures in the world of Californian pornography in the 1970s and 1980s. In The Rake's Progress Hogarth lays the story out as an entertainment, un-judgementally, for us to observe (and, inevitably, judge for ourselves); as in Boogie Nights, a materialist obsession with outward show and fashionable pursuits, sex, prostitution and debt inevitably lead to downfall and disaster.

9 Ibid., vol.I, p.3.

10 Henry Fielding, Joseph Andrews (London 1742), p.iii.

11 Fielding 1749, vol.I, p.42.

12 Hogarth 1997 edn, p.128.

13 Robert Cowley, Marriage à-la-Mode. A Re-view of Hogarth's narrative art (Manchester 1983), p.5. Matthew Craske notes: 'Hogarth came to regard the idea of telling a story through a series of images as the greatest innovation of his career' (William Hogarth, London, 2000, p.7).

14 Nichols 1833, pp.8–9.

15 Ibid., p. 88; the author is Allan Cunningham, an early nineteenth-century Scottish writer.

16 Judy Egerton, Hogarth's Marriage à-la-Mode (London 1997), p.30. It could equally be the case that the girl is unrelated and employed as a child whore in the adult woman's establishment.

17 Marriage à-la-Mode (1746), p.5. No author has been credited with this poetic commentary on Hogarth's six paintings, but I suggest Fielding as a possibility. A 'Petit Maitre' is a fop. Black patches worn by men to cover the evidence of syphilis were obvious signs of vice, but they were also worn, though less frequently, as a fashionable cosmetic device, as women did. In both instances they were accredited to French decadence, and as such the men and women, lavishly costumed and with made-up faces, are seen wearing them in the gambling scenes of Kubrick's Barry Lyndon.

18 Henry Fielding, ed. A.R.Humphreys, Joseph Andrews and Shamela (London, 1975), p.76.

19 Marriage à-la-Mode (1746), pp.15–16.

20 Ibid., p.7.

21 Ibid., pp.6–7.

22 Ibid., p.59.

23 Ibid., p.28.

24 Nichols 1833, pp.91–2.

TRANSFORMATIONS: JOHNNY DEPP

1 Johnny Depp, Vanity Fair interview with Patti Smith, January 2011, p.98.

2 Johnny Depp, Pirates of the Caribbean: Curse of the Black Pearl, DVD Extra.

3 Tim Burton, Daily Variety, February 2006.

4 Colleen Atwood, Seattle Times, December 2010.

5 Renée Ehrlich Kalfus, personal communication, January 2012.

6 Johnny Depp, Vanity Fair interview with Patti Smith, January 2011, p.98.

7 Penny Rose in Landis 2004.

8 Penny Rose, interview with the author, January 2012.

9 Colleen Atwood, Seattle Times, December 2010.

2 DEFINING THE CHARACTER

THE COSTUME OF SILENT COMEDY

1 Kerr 1975.

2 James Agee, 'Comedy's Greatest Era', Life, 26 September 1949.

3 Ibid.

COSTUME AND FASHION

1 Landis 2007, p.xvi.

2 Lieberson 2000.

3 Anna Sui in conversation with Valerie Steele and Deborah Nadoolman Landis at the Morgan Library, New York, 15 June 2011.

BEATON'S FAIR LADY

1 Beaton 1964, p.62.

2 Ibid., p.55

3 Ibid., p.52

4 Hugo Vickers, Cecil Beaton: The Authorised Biography (London 1985), p.463.

5 Ibid., p.180

6 Beaton 1964, p.67.

7 Ibid., p.39.

8 Ibid., p.05.

9 Ibid., p.54.

TRANSFORMATIONS: ROBERT DE NIRO

Interview with Deborah Nadoolman Landis, New York, July 2012

TRANSFORMATIONS: MERYL STREEP

Interview with Deborah Nadoolman Landis, New York, July 2012

3 COLLECTORS & COLLECTING

THE EXHIBITION ODYSSEY

1 From a speech delivered by Sir Joshua Reynolds at the Royal Academy of Arts on 11 December 1780, etched above the main entrance to the V&A.

2 Head 1973, p.36.

3 Paramount, Universal, and Warner Bros all moved their wardrobe departments in the 1990s.

4 Graser 1999

5 The Warner Bros lot in Burbank. Columbia Studios sold its studio on Gower in Hollywood and moved only its executive offices onto the Warner Bros Burbank lot, subsequently renamed Burbank Studios.

6 The prop department provided the guns.

7 Costumers work with clothes on the set and in the costume department. They work with a costume designer.

8 See Thomas 1989 for a contemporary examination of the Robin Hood culture.

9 Adrian later had a couture clothing line and his designs featured his signature on his label.

10 Recycling clothing has a long tradition. London streets such as Petticoat Lane were the sites of busy used-clothing markets. Clothes too expensive to be purchased new for most people were re-fashioned until the garment was ready for the ragman and his cart.

11 In turn, Doble Reynolds' 'Profiles in History' auction in June 2011 made over 22 million dollars for the actress.

12 See McConathy and Vreeland 1976, which showcases photographs from the exhibition, published two years after it opened. The book notes that several of the costumes on show were copies, including Jean Louis's black gown for Rita Hayworth in Gilda (1946), Adrian's costume for Greta Garbo in Mata Hari (1931) and Travilla's design for Marilyn Monroe's pleated white dress in The Seven Year Itch (1955).

13 Chierichetti 1976, Leese 1977 (2nd edn 1991), LaVine 1980 and Prichard 1981.

14 See Maede 1987.

15 Rector of the Royal College of Art and longest-serving Trustee of the V&A.

16 Geoffrey Marsh and Victoria Broakes, of the Theatre and Performance department at the

V&A; Keith Lodwick, Assistant Curator of *Hollywood Costume*; and Sam Gatley of the V&A Conservation Department.

17 At Tirelli Costumi, Peruzzi, Farani, GP11 and Anamode.
18 Cosprop, Angels Costumiers and Sands Films.
19 Imagineering is the company that conceives and designs the attractions in Disney theme parks around the world.

LOOKING BEHIND THE WIZARD'S CURTAIN

This article has benefited from numerous invaluable conversations about the art and craft of costume design for film with Deborah Nadoolman Landis, while she was preparing her doctoral thesis at the Royal College of Art (which I supervised), and while she turned aspects of the thesis into books (Landis 2003 and 2007). The article is also indebted to the special issue of *Film History: An International Journal*, edited by Richard Koszarski, vol.18, no.3 (September 2006), pp.237–51, on film museums.

1 *Sight and Sound*, vol.2 (autumn 1956), esp. pp.63–6. On Lindsay Anderson's stance as a critic, see Hedling 1998, pp.26–37).
2 On the Langlois version, see Roud 1983, pp.94–5. Also Robinson 2006.
3 See Buckle 1956, pp.3–22.
4 Ibid., pp.3–4.
5 Anderson 1956, p.65. See also Robinson 2006, pp.249–50.
6 Buckle 1956, p.3.
7 Anderson 1956, p.66.
8 See Bottomore 1995. In the end, the museum agreed to accept just one film.
9 See Benjamin 2002, pp.101–33, and for the better-known version of the essay, Benjamin 1999, pp.211–44. It was originally intended to be part of a much larger project about reproducibilty in a range of media and its wider implications. Sadly, Benjamin never completed the project in this form.
10 Malraux 1974.
11 Quoted in Lenk 2006.
12 Richard Koszarski, book review of Wasson 2005, in *Film History*, vol.18, no.3 (September 2006), pp.350–51.
13 François Truffaut, Foreword in Roud 1983, p.viii. Truffaut resigned from the Council of the Cinémathèque in February 1973.
14 On the 1955 exhibition, see note 1.
15 Lotte Eisner, Preface to Myrent 1984, p.5.
16 See Roud 1983, pp.175–86; Robinson 2006, pp.244–6; Mannoni 2006; and the Musée catalogue, Myrent 1984, pp.18–71.
17 Cited in Roud 1983, p.178.
18 Cited ibid., p.185.
19 See, for example, Roud 1983, pp.179–81

and Mannoni 2006, pp.283–4.
20 Lenk 2006, p.320.
21 Ibid., p.320.
22 For the 2006 survey, see Bottomore 2006.
23 See Robinson 2006.
24 Mannoni 2006, p.280.
25 Cited in Landis 2003, p.8.
26 Cited in McConathy and Vreeland 1976, p.28.
27 Vreeland 1974. The cover of the catalogue shows a leaping Fred Astaire in white tie and tails, although nearly all the pieces in the exhibition were in fact costumes for female stars.
28 Vreeland 1974, p.1. See also Vreeland, 'Make it big!', in McConathy and Vreeland 1976, p.21.
29 Vreeland 1974, p.5.
30 Ibid., p.9.
31 Dale McConathy, 'The ruby slippers, the trenchcoat, and the lion's suit', in McConathy and Vreeland 1976, p.25). The Metropolitan Museum of Art exhibition was an important stimulus to scholarship and fact-gathering on Hollywood costume design – especially in the studio era. See, for example, Chierichetti 1976; Leese 1991, originally published in 1976, with an emphasis on 'couture on the screen'; and Delpierre, Fleury and Lebrun 1988, with much material on French fashion designers working in Hollywood. Much more recently there has been a biography of Adrian (Gutner 2001) and an updated survey of Edith Head's Hollywood (Head and Calistro 2008). For the most recent scholarly approach to questions of clothing and identity' – currently the big issue in the academy – see (among many others) Bruzzi 1997; Geraghty 2000; and Moseley 2005.
32 Cited in Robinson 1985, p.114.
33 This account of *The Wizard of Oz* was inspired by Harmetz 1989, esp. pp.181–6, 206–42; Fricke, Scarone and Stillman 1989, esp. pp.18–122; Hearn 1974; and Thomas 1989.
34 See Harmetz 1989, p.58 for lyricist Yip Harburg's version of this.
35 Lot 148: 'A pair of "ruby slippers" made for Judy Garland in the 1939 MGM film *The Wizard of Oz*' (entry by Rhys Thomas, 'A Century of Hollywood' auction cat., Christie's, New York, 24 May 2000, pp.59–61).
36 Rhys Thomas gives a thorough description of all the known pairs of slippers – and speculates about some of the unknown ones too. See Thomas 1989, Appendix I, pp.219–26.

THE TREASURE HUNT

1 Landis 2007, Introduction p.xvi.

2 Ibid., p.247.
3 Deborah Nadoolman Landis, interviewed by Keith Lodwick, 5 October 2011.
4 Norman Tipton, interviewed by Keith Lodwick, 15 August 2011.
5 Steve Wilson, interviewed by Keith Lodwick, 25 August 2011.
6 Cecilia DeMille Presley, interviewed by Keith Lodwick, 19 August 2011.
7 Head 1983, p.117.
8 Andrea Kalas, interviewed by Keith Lodwick, 21 September 2011.

90027, HOLLYWOOD IS A ZIP CODE: THE LA CONNECTION

1 Loos 1966, p.45.
2 Ibid.
3 Sackman 2005, pp.265–6.
4 Torregrossa 2006, p.31.
5 Chierichetti 1976, p.46.
6 Bernstein 2000, p.131.
7 Harmetz 1989, p.237.
8 Davis 1998, p.277.
9 Polan 2000, p.134.

4 NEW FRONTIERS

AFTERLIFE: ENSURING THE ENDURING INTEREST OF A WEB AUDIENCE

1 http://www.thestar.com/article/297215

FANTASY, SCI-FI AND SUPERHEROES

1 In my hometown of Seattle, you actually can meet them – there is a real superhero, Phoenix Jones, who dresses up in quasi-X-Men garb and metes out justice Batman-style across the city.
2 Interestingly enough, one classic film from this period, *Forbidden Planet* (1956), had an indelible influence on future youth fashion. Costume designer Helen Rose created an assemblage of exceedingly short dresses for actress Anne Francis as teenage space girl Altaira Morbius, presaging by several years the miniskirt craze of the 1960s.
3 With our recent global recession, superheroes are popular again. The United States is fighting wars in several countries with real enemies as well as more abstract concepts, such as the all-paralyzing 'terror'. It is no wonder that facets of the US population increasingly view the world with a simplistic moral outlook – us against them, good against evil – the classic superhero world view.

FURTHER READING

Anderson, Lindsay, 'Stand Up! Stand Up!', *Sight and Sound* (autumn 1956), p. 65

Bailey, Margaret J., *Those Glorious Glamour Years* (Secaucus, NJ, 1982)

Balio, Tino, ed. *History of the American Cinema*, vol.5: *Grand Design: Hollywood as a Modern Business Enterprise, 1930–1939* (New York 1993)

Beaton, Cecil, *Cecil Beaton's Fair Lady* (New York 1964)

Beaton, Cecil, *Cecil Beaton's Diaries: 1955–1963: The Restless Years* (London 1976)

Benjamin, Walter, *Illuminations* (London 1999)

Benjamin, Walter, *Selected Writings vol. 3 1935–1938*, ed. H. Eiland and M.W. Jennings (Harvard 2002)

Bernstein, Jonathan, *Pretty in Pink: The Golden Age of Teenage Movies* (New York 1996)

Bernstein, Shari, 'Contested Eden 1920–40', in *Made in California: Art, Image, and Identity* (Los Angeles County Museum of Art in association with University of California Press, Berkeley, 2000)

Berry, Sarah, *Screen Style: Fashion and Femininity in 1930s Hollywood* (Minneapolis 2000)

Biskind, Peter, *Easy Riders, Raging Bulls: How the Sex-Drugs-and-Rock 'n' Roll Generation Saved Hollywood* (New York 1998)

Bordwell, David, Janet Staiger and Kristin Thompson, *The Classical Hollywood Cinema: Film Style and Mode of Production to 1960* (New York 1985)

Bottomore, Stephen, '"The Collection of Rubbish": Animatographs, Archives and Arguments – London 1896–1897', *Film History*, vol.7, no.3 (autumn 1995), pp. 291–7

Bottomore, Stephen, 'Cinema museums: A worldwide list', *Film History*, vol.18, no.3 (September 2006), pp.261–73

Bruzzi, Stella, *Undressing Cinema* (London 1997)

Buckle, Richard, *The Observer Film Exhibition: Sixty Years of Cinema, presented in association with the British Film Institute and La Cinémathèque Française*, exh. cat., British Film Institute (London 1956)

Burns, Bob, and John Michlig, *It Came From Bob's Basement* (San Francisco 2000)

Campbell, Joseph, *The Hero with a Thousand Faces* (New York 1949)

Chierichetti, David, *Hollywood Costume Design* (New York 1976)

Cole, Holly and Kristin Burke, *Costuming for Film: The Art and the Craft* (Los Angeles 2005)

Davis, Mike, *Ecology of Fear* (New York, 1998)

Davis, Ronald L., *The Glamour Factory: Inside Hollywood's Big Studio System* (Dallas, TX, 1993)

Delpierre, Madeleine, Marianne de Fleury and Dominique Lebrun, *French Elegance in the Cinema*, exh. cat., Musée de la mode et du costume (Paris 1988)

Doherty, Thomas, *Pre-Code Hollywood* (New York 1999)

Eames, John Douglas, *The MGM Story: The Complete History of Fifty Roaring Years* (New York 1975)

Eames, John Douglas, *The Paramount Story* (New York 2004)

Engelmeier, Regine, Peter W. Engelmeier and Barbara Einzig, *Fashion in Film* (Munich and New York 1990)

Esquevin, Christian, *Adrian: From Silver Screen to Custom Label* (New York 2008)

Fiamini, Roland, *Scarlett, Rhett and a Cast of Thousands: The Filming of Gone with the Wind* (London 1976)

Fielding, Henry, *The History of Tom Jones, a Foundling* (Dublin 1749)

Finch, Christopher and Linda Rosenkrantz, *Gone Hollywood: The Movie Colony in the Golden Age* (London 1980)

Fowler, Marian, *The Way She Looks Tonight: Five Women of Style* (New York 1996)

Fricke, John, Jay Scarone and William Stillman, *The Wizard of Oz* (New York 1989)

Geraghty, Christine, *British Cinema in the Fifties: Genders, Genre and the 'New Look'* (London 2000)

Glynn, Prudence with Madeleine Ginsburg. *In Fashion: Dress in the Twentieth Century* (Oxford 1978)

Greer, Howard, *Designing Male* (New York 1949)

Gutner, Howard, *Gowns by Adrian: The MGM Years 1928–1941* (New York 2001)

Hajdu, David, *The Ten-Cent Plague: The Great Comic-Book Scare and How It Changed America* (New York 2009)

Harmetz, Aljean, *The Making of The Wizard of Oz* (New York 1989)

Haver, Ronald, *David O. Selznick's Gone with the Wind* (New York 1986)

Hayes, Kevin J., ed., *Martin Scorsese's Raging Bull*, Cambridge 2005

Head, Edith, and Paddy Calistro, *Edith Head's Hollywood* (New York 1983)

Hearn, Michael Patrick (ed.), *The Annotated Wizard of Oz* (New York 1974)

Hedling, Erik, *Lindsay Anderson: Maverick film-maker* (London 1998)

Hogarth, William, *The Analysis of Beauty*, ed. R. Paulson (New Haven and London 1997)

Hollander, Anne, *Seeing Through Clothes* (New York 1978)

Hirschhorn, Clive, *The Warner Bros Story* (New York 1979)

Hyams, Jay, *The Life and Times of the Western Movie* (New York 1983)

Johnstone, Iain, *Streep: A Life in Film* (Godalming 2009)

Kerr, Walter, *The Silent Clowns* (New York 1975)

Koppes, C.R. and G.D. Black, *Hollywood Goes to War: How Politics, Profits and Propaganda Shaped World War II Movies* (New York 1987)

Koszarski, Richard: book review of Haidee Wasson, *Museum Movies*, California, 2005, in *Film History*, vol.18, no.3 (September 2006), pp.350–51

Landis, Deborah Nadoolman, *Screencraft: Costume Design* (Oxford 2003)

Landis, Deborah Nadoolman, *50 Designers/50 Costumes: Concept to Character* (Los Angeles 2004)

Landis, Deborah Nadoolman, *Dressed: A Century of Hollywood Costume Design* (New York 2007)

LaValley, Satch, 'Hollywood and Seventh Avenue: The Impact of Period Films on Fashion', in Maeder 1987, pp. 78–96

LaVine, W. Robert, *In a Glamorous Fashion: The Fabulous Years of Hollywood Costume Design* (New York 1980)

LeBrun, Dominique, *Hollywood* (Corte Madera, CA, 1996)

Leese, Elizabeth, *Costume Design in the Movies: An Illustrated Guide to the Work of 157 Great Designers*, 2nd edn (New York 1991)

Leigh, Janet, and Christopher Nickens, *Psycho: Behind the Scenes of the Classic Thriller* (New York 1995)

Lenk, Sabine, 'Collections on display: exhibiting artifacts in a film museum, with pride', *Film History* vol.18, no.3 (September 2006), pp.320–21

Lieberson, Stanley, *A Matter of Taste: How Names, Fashions, and Culture Change* (New Haven and London 2000)

Loos, Anita, *A Girl Like I* (New York 1966)

McConathy, Dale, and Diana Vreeland, *Hollywood Costume: Glamour! Glitter! Romance!* (New York 1976)

MacGowan, Kenneth, *Behind the Screen: The History and Techniques of the Motion Picture* (New York 1965)

Maeder, Edward, *Hollywood and History: Costume Design in Film*, exh. cat., Los Angeles County Museum of Art (Los Angeles and London 1987)

Malraux, André 'Museum Without Walls', in *Voices of Silence* (London 1974), pp.11–128

Mannoni, Laurent, 'Henri Langlois and the Musée du Cinéma', *Film History*, vol.18, no.3 (September 2006), pp.274–87

Marriage à-la-Mode: An Humorous Tale in Six Cantos, in Hudibrastic Verse; being an Explanation of the Six Prints lately published by the Ingenious Mr Hogarth (London 1746)

Medavoy, Mike and Josh Young, *You're Only as Good as Your Next One: 100 Great Films, 100 Good Films, and 100 for Which I Should Be Shot* (New York 2002)

Moseley, Rachel (ed.), *Fashion and Film Stars: Dress, Culture, Identity* (London 2005)

Myrent, Glenn, *Musée du cinéma Henri Langlois*, cat. (Paris 1984)

Nichols, J.B. (ed.). *Anecdotes of William Hogarth, Written by Himself* (London 1833)

Polan, Dana, 'California Through the Lens of Hollywood', in *Reading California: Art, Image and Identity, 1900–2000* (Los Angeles County Museum of Art in association with University of California Press, Berkeley, 2000)

Prichard, Susan Perez, *Film Costume: An Annotated Bibliography* (New Jersey and London 1981)

Reynolds, Debbie (with David Patrick Columbia), *My Life* (New York 1988)

Robinson, David, *Chaplin: His Life and Art* (London 1985)

Robinson, David, 'The Chronicle of Cinema, 1895–1995', vol. 2: '1920–1940. Murnau's "Nosferatu" to Ford's "Stagecoach"' supplement to *Sight & Sound*, vol.4 (1994)

Robinson, David, 'Film museums I have known and (sometimes) loved', *Film History: An International Journal*, vol.18 no.3 (September 2006), pp.242–3

Rose, Helen, *Just Make Them Beautiful: The Many Worlds of a Designing Woman* (Santa Monica, CA, 1976)

Roud, Richard *A Passion for Films: Henri Langlois and the Cinémathèque Française* (New York 1983)

Sackman, Douglas C., 'A Garden of Worldly Delights', in *Land of Sunshine* (Pittsburgh, PA, 2005)

Schatz, Thomas, *The Genius of the System: Hollywood Filmmaking in the Studio Era* (New York 1988)

Schreier, Sandy, *Hollywood Dressed and Undressed: A Century of Cinema Style* (New York 1998)

Schumach, Murray, *The Face on the Cutting Room Floor: The Story of Movie and Television Censorship* (New York 1964)

Sharaff, Irene, *Broadway and Hollywood: Costumes Designed by Irene Sharaff* (New York 1976)

Shindler, Colin 'Bleak House: The harsh winds of economic reality', in A. Lloyd and D. Robinson (eds), *Movies of the Sixties* (London 1983), pp.35–7

Spears, Jack, *Hollywood. The Golden Era* (New York 1971)

Spehr, Paul C., *The Movies Begin: Making Movies in New Jersey, 1887–1920* (Newark, NJ, 1977)

Stine, Whitney, with Bette Davis, *Mother Goddam* (New York 1990)

Tapert, Annette, *The Power of Glamour: The Women Who Defined the Magic of Stardom* (New York 1998)

Thomas, Rhys, *The Ruby Slippers of Oz* (Los Angeles 1989)

Torregrossa, Richard, *Cary Grant: A Celebration of Style* (New York 2006)

Vreeland, Diana, *Romantic and Glamorous Hollywood Design*, exh. cat., Metropolitan Museum of Art (New York 1974)

Wasson, Haidee, *Museum Movies: The Museum of Modern Art and the Birth of Art Cinema* (Los Angeles 2005)

Watts, Stephen (ed.), *Behind the Screen: How Films Are Made* (London 1938)

Wollen, Peter, 'Strike a Pose', *Sight and Sound* 5, no. 3 (March 1995), pp.10–15

FILMOGRAPHY

Release dates and costume designers are given in parentheses

101 Dalmatians (1961)
101 Dalmatians (1996; Rosemary Burrows and Anthony Powell)
102 Dalmatians (2000; Anthony Powell)
1941 (1979; Deborah Nadoolman)
A Bronx Tale (1993; Rita Ryack)
Addams Family Values (1993; Theoni V. Aldredge)
A Fistful of Dollars (1964; Carlo Simi)
Alice in Wonderland (2010; Colleen Atwood)
Alien (1979; John Mollo)
All Dolled Up: A New York Dolls Story (2005)
A Midsummer Night's Dream (1935; Max Rée and Milo Anderson)
Analyze This (1999; Aude Bronson-Howard)
An American in Paris (1951; Walter Plunkett, Orry-Kelly and Irene Sharaff)
An American Werewolf in London (1981; Deborah Nadoolman)
Anchors Aweigh (1945; Irene)
Angel (1937; Travis Banton)
Angels in America (2003; Ann Roth)
Anna Karenina (2012; Jacqueline Durran)
Annie Hall (1977; Ruth Morley)
Arabian Nights (1917; Lucile)
A Room with a View (1986; Jenny Beavan and John Bright)
Around the World in 80 Days (1956; Miles White)
A Star is Born (1954; Jean Louis, Mary Ann Nyberg and Irene Sharaff)
A Thief Catcher (1914)
Atonement (2007; Jacqueline Durran)
Austin Powers: International Man of Mystery (1997; Deena Appel)
Austin Powers: The Spy Who Shagged Me (1999; Deena Appel)
Avatar (2009; Mayes C. Rubeo and Deborah L. Scott)
Back to the Future II (1989; Joanna Johnston)
Back to the Future III (1990; Joanna Johnston)
Barbarella (1968; Jacques Fonteray and Paco Rabanne)
Barry Lyndon (1975; Ulla-Britt Søderlund and Milena Canonero)
Basic Instinct (1992; Ellen Mirojnick)
Batman (1989; Bob Ringwood)
Batman Returns (1992; Bob Ringwood and Mary E. Vogt)
Batman and Robin (1997; Ingrid Ferrin and Robert Turturice)
Batman Begins (2005; Lindy Hemming)
Beach Blanket Bingo (1965; Marjorie Corso)
Beauty and the Beast (1991; Dan Haskett)
Bedknobs and Broomsticks (1971; Bill Thomas)
Belle de Jour (1967; Hélène Nourry and Yves Saint Laurent)
Belle of the Nineties (1934; Travis Banton)
Ben-Hur (1959; Elizabeth Haffenden)
Benny and Joon (1993; Aggie Guerard Rodgers)
Big Fish (2003; Colleen Atwood)
Birth of a Nation (1915; Robert Goldstein and Clare West)
Black Beauty (1921)
Blackmail (1929)
Black Swan (2010; Amy Westcott, Kate Mulleavy and Laura Mulleavy)
Blade Runner (1982; Michael Kaplan and Charles Knode)
Blonde Venus (1932; Travis Banton)
Bonnie and Clyde (1967; Theadora Van Runkle)

Boogie Nights (1997; Paul Thomas Anderson)
Borat: Cultural Learnings of America for Make Benefit Glorious Nation of Kazakhstan (2006; Jason Alper)
Born to Boogie (1972)
Bram Stoker's Dracula (1992; Eiko Ishioka)
Braveheart, 1995; Charles Knode)
Brazil (1985; James Acheson)
Breakfast at Tiffany's (1961; Hubert de Givenchy, Edith Head and Pauline Trigere)
Bride of Vengeance (1949;Mary Grant and Mitchell Leisen)
Bridesmaids (2011; Leesa Evans and Christine Wada)
Broadway Melody (1929; David Cox)
Brokeback Mountain (2005; Marit Allen)
Broken Arrow (1950; René Hubert)
Buck Rogers (1939)
Bugsy (1991; Albert Wolsky)
Burke and Hare (2010; Deborah Nadoolman)
Burn After Reading (2008; Mary Zophres)
Camelot (1967; John Truscott)
Camille (1937; Adrian)
Captain Blood (1935; Milo Anderson)
Captain John Smith and Pocahontas (1908)
Carrington (1995; Penny Rose)
Casino (1995; Rita Ryack and John Dunn)
Casino Royale (2006; Lindy Hemming)
Charade (1963; Hubert de Givenchy)
Charley's Aunt (1941; Travis Banton)
Charlie and the Chocolate Factory (2005; Gabriella Pescucci)
Chelsea Girls (1966)
Chicago (2002; Colleen Atwood)
Chocolat (2000; Renée Ehrlich Kalfus)
City Lights (1931)
Cleopatra (1917; George James Hopkins)
Cleopatra (1934; Travis Banton)
Cleopatra (1963; Irene Sharaff, Nino Novarese and Renie)
Closer (2004; Ann Roth)
Collateral (2004; Jeffrey Kurland)
Coming to America (1988; Deborah Nadoolman)
Conan the Barbarian (1982; John Bloomfield)
Cover Girl (1944; Travis Banton)
Dangerous Liaisons (1988; James Acheson)
Dark Shadows (Colleen Atwood)
Death Becomes Her (1992; Joanna Johnston)
Death in Venice (1971; Piero Tosi)
Desire (1936; Travis Banton)
Desperately Seeking Susan (1985; Santo Loquasto)
Destination Moon (1950)
Dick Tracy (1990; Milena Canonero)
Die Hard (1988; Marilyn Vance-Straker)
Dinner at Eight (1933; Adrian)
Doctor Dolittle (1967; Ray Aghayan)
Double Indemnity (1944; Edith Head)
Doubt (2008; Ann Roth)
Dr No (1962; Tessa Wellborn)
Dreamgirls (2006; Sharen Davis)

Duel in the Sun (1946; Walter Plunkett)

Earthquake (1974; Burton Miller and Edith Head)

Easy Rider (1969)

Ed Wood (1994; Colleen Attwood)

Edward Scissorhands (1990; Colleen Atwood)

Elizabeth (1998; Alexandra Byrne)

Elizabeth: The Golden Age (2007; Alexandra Byrne)

Erin Brockovich (2000; Jeffrey Kurland)

Escape from L.A. (1996; Robin Michel Bush)

Extremely Loud and Incredibly Close (2011; Ann Roth)

Eyes of Laura Mars (1978; Theoni V. Aldredge)

Family Plot (1976; Edith Head)

Fargo (1996; Mary Zophres)

Faster, Pussycat! Kill! Kill! (1965)

Fear and Loathing in Las Vegas (1998; Julie Weiss)

Fight Club (1999; Michael Kaplan)

Final Fantasy: The Spirits Within (2001; Shuko Murase)

Finding Neverland (2004; Alexandra Byrne)

Flashdance (1983; Michael Kaplan)

Flash Gordon: Space Soldiers (1936)

Foolshead Pays His Debts (1909)

For a Few Dollars More (1965; Carlo Simi)

Forbidden Planet (1956; Walter Plunkett and Helen Rose)

Forrest Gump (1994; Joanna Johnston)

For Sale (1924; Clare West)

Funny Face (1957; Edith Head and Hubert de Givenchy)

Funny Girl (1968; Irene Sharaff)

Gangs of New York (2002; Sandy Powell)

Gidget (1959)

Gidget Goes Hawaiian (1961)

Gigi (1958; Cecil Beaton)

Gilda (1946; Jean Louis)

Gladiator (2000; Janty Yates)

Golden Earrings (1947; Mary Kay Dodson)

Goldfinger (1964; Elsa Fennell)

Gone with the Wind (1939; Walter Plunkett)

Goodfellas (1990; Richard Bruno)

Great Hope Springs (2012; Ann Roth)

Green Lantern (2011; Ngila Dickson)

Hair (1979; Ann Roth)

Hands Up! (1926)

Hannah and her Sisters (1986; Jeffrey Kurland)

Harry Potter and the Philosopher's Stone (2001; Judianna Makovsky)

Harry Potter and the Chamber of Secrets (2002; Lindy Hemming)

Harry Potter and the Prisoner of Azkaban (2004; Jany Temime)

Harry Potter and the Goblet of Fire (2005; Jany Temime)

Harry Potter and the Order of the Phoenix (2007; Jany Temime)

Harry Potter and the Half-Blood Prince (2009; Jany Temime)

Harry Potter and the Deathly Hallows, parts 1 and 2 (2010–11; Jany Temime)

Heartburn (1986; Ann Roth)

Heat (1995; Deborah L.Scott)

Hello Dolly! (1969; Irene Sharaff)

Hello, Frisco, Hello (1943; Helen Rose)

His Secretary (1925; André-ani)

How to Lose a Guy in 10 Days (2002; Karen Patch)

How to Stuff a Wild Bikini (1965; Richard Bruno)

Hugo (2011; Sandy Powell)

I Live My Life (1935; Adrian)

Inception (2010; Jeffrey Kurland)

Independence Day (1996; Joseph A. Porro)

Indiana Jones and the Temple of Doom (1984; Anthony Powell)

Indiana Jones and the Last Crusade (1989; Joanna Johnston and Anthony Powell)

Indiana Jones and the Kingdom of the Crystal Skull (2008; Mary Zophres)

Insidious (2010; Kristen M. Burke)

Intolerable Cruelty (2003; Mary Zophres)

Intolerance: Love's Struggle Through the Ages (1916; D.W Griffith and Clare West)

Jack the Giant Killer (2012; Joanna Johnston)

Jezebel (1938; Orry-Kelly)

Joan of Arc (1948; Dororthy Jeakins and Barbara Karinska)

Joe vs. the Volcano (1990; Colleen Atwood, Robert Chase and Sue Moore)

John Carter (2012; Mayes C. Rubeo)

Jour de Fête (1949; Jacques Cottin)

Julie and Julia (2009; Ann Roth)

Kid Auto Races at Venice (1914)

Kill Bill: Volume I (2003; Kumiko Ogawa and Catherine Marie Thomas)

Kill Bill: Volume II (2004; Kumiko Ogawa and Catherine Marie Thomas)

Klute (1971; Ann Roth)

Kramer vs. Kramer (1979; Ruth Morley)

Lady in the Dark (1944; Edith Head)

L'Année dernière à Marienbad (*Last Year at Marienbad*, 1961; Bernard Evein and Chanel)

La Strada (1954; Margherita Marinari)

L'Atlantide (1921; Manuel Orazi)

Legally Blonde (2001; Sophie de Rakoff)

Legally Blonde 2: Red, White and Blonde (2003; Sophie de Rakoff)

Lemony Snicket's A Series of Unfortunate Events (2004; Colleen Atwood)

Les amours de la reine Elisabeth (*The Loves of Queen Elizabeth*, 1912; Paul Poiret)

Les enfants du Paradis (*Children of Paradise*, 1945; Antoine Mayo)

Les vacances de Monsieur Hulot (*Mr Hulot's Holiday*, 1953)

Letty Lynton (1932; Adrian)

Lincoln (2012; Joanna Johnston)

Lisztomania (1975; Shirley Russell)

Little Annie Rooney (1925)

Little Women (1949; Walter Plunkett)

Love Actually (2003; Joanna Johnston)

Mabel's Strange Predicament (1914)

Mad Dog and Glory (1993; Rita Ryack)

Magnificent Doll (1946; Travis Banton)

Maid of the Mountains (1913)

Making a Living (1914)

Mamma Mia! (2008; Ann Roth)

Marie Antoinette (1938; Adrian)

Marie Antoinette (2006; Milena Canonero)

Marnie (1964; Edith Head)

Mars Attacks! (1996; Colleen Atwood)

Mary of Scotland (1936; Walter Plunkett)

Mary Poppins (1964; Tony Walton)

Mary Shelley's Frankenstein (1994; James Acheson)

Max (series, 1910–25)

Meet Me in St Louis (1944; Irene Sharaff)

Meet the Fockers (2004; Carol Ramsey)

Meet the Parents (2000; Daniel Orlandi)

Metropolis (1927; Aenne Willkomm)

Midnight Cowboy (1969; Ann Roth)

Midnight Run (1988; Gloria Gresham)

Mildred Pierce (1945; Milo Anderson)

Mildred Pierce (2011; Ann Roth)

Mighty Aphrodite (1995; Jeffrey Kurland)

Moby Dick (1956; Elizabeth Haffenden)

Modern Times (1936)

Mommie Dearest (1981; Irene Sharaff)

Mon Oncle (1958; Jacques Cottin)

Monty Python's The Meaning of Life (1983; James Acheson)

Morocco (1930; Travis Banton)

Moulin Rouge! (2001; Catherine Martin and Angus Strathie)

Mutiny on the Bounty (1962; Moss Mabry)

My Best Friend's Wedding (1997; Jeffrey Kurland)

My Fair Lady (1964; Cecil Beaton)

My Man Godfrey (1936; Travis Banton and Brymer)

National Lampoon's Animal House (1978; Deborah Nadoolman)

New York, New York (1977; Theodora Van Runkle)

No Country for Old Men (2007; Mary Zophres)

North by Northwest (1959; Harry Kress)

Notorious (1946; Edith Head)

O Brother, Where Art Thou (2000; Mary Zophres)

Ocean's Eleven (2001; Jeffrey Kurland)

Ocean's Thirteen (2007; Louisa Frogley)

Oklahoma (1943; Miles White)

One Million B.C. (The Cave Dwellers) (1940; Harry Black)

Orlando (1992; Sandy Powell and Dien van Straalen)

Out of Africa (1985; Milena Canonero)

Paranormal Activity 2 (2010; Kristin M. Burke)

Peter Pan (1924)

Pirates of the Caribbean: The Curse of the Black Pearl (2003; Penny Rose)

Pirates of the Caribbean: Dead Man's Chest (2006; Penny Rose)

Pirates of the Caribbean: At World's End (2007; Penny Rose)

Pirates of the Caribbean: On Stranger Tides (2011; Penny Rose)

Places in the Heart (1984; Ann Roth)

Planet of the Apes (2001; Colleen Atwood)

Play Time (1967; Jacques Cottin)

Plenty (1985; Ruth Myers)

Portrait of a Lady (1996; Janet Patterson)

Postcards from the Edge (1990; Ann Roth)

Psycho (1960; Helen Colvig)

Public Enemies (2009; Colleen Atwood)

Pulp Fiction (1994; Betsy Heimann)

Queen Christina (1933; Adrian)

Queen Elizabeth (1912; Paul Poiret)

Qui êtes-vous, Polly Maggoo? (Who Are You, Polly Maggoo?, 1966; Janine Klein)

Quo Vadis (1951; Herschel McCoy)

Raging Bull (1980; John Boxer and Richard Bruno)

Raiders of the Lost Ark (1981; Deborah Nadoolman)

Rear Window (1954; Edith Head)

Rebecca (1940; Irene)

Red Dust (1932; Adrian)

Restoration (1995; James Acheson)

Rocky III (1982; Tom Bronson)

Roman Holiday (1953; Edith Head)

Rumba (1935; Travis Banton)

Running Scared (2006; Kristin Burke)

Sabrina (1954; Hubert de Givenchy and Edith Head)

Samson and Delilah (1949; Edith Head, Gile Steele, Dorothy Jeakins, Gwen Wakeling and Elois W. Jenssen)

Saturday Night Fever (1977; Patrizia Von Brandenstein)

Saving Private Ryan (1998; Joanna Johnston)

Secret of the Incas (1954; Edith Head)

Seeking a Friend for the End of the World (2012; Kristin Burke)

Sex (1920; Louise Glaum)

Shakespeare in Love (1998; Sandy Powell)

Shanghai Express (1932; Travis Banton)

Sherlock Holmes (2009; Jenny Beavan)

Sherlock Holmes: A Game of Shadows (2011; Jenny Beavan)

Shrek (2001; Isis Mussenden)

Shrek 2 (2004; Isis Mussenden)

Shutter Island (2010; Sandy Powell)

Silkwood (1983; Ann Roth)

Singin' in the Rain (1952; Walter Plunkett)

Sleepy Hollow (1999; Colleen Atwood)

Some Like It Hot (1959; Orry-Kelly and Bert Henrikson)

Sophie's Choice (1982; Albert Wolsky)

Spartacus (1960; Valles and William Ware Theiss)

Spider-Man (2002; James Acheson)

Spider-Man 2 (2004; James Acheson and Gary Jones)

Stagecoach (1939; Walter Plunkett)

Stargate (1994; Joseph A. Porro)

Star Wars Episode IV: A New Hope (1977; John Mollo)

Star Wars Episode VI: Return of the Jedi (1983; Aggie Guerard Rodgers and Nilo Rodis-Jamero)

Superman: The Movie (1978; Yvonne Blake)

Superman IV: The Quest for Peace (1987; John Bloomfield)

Sweeney Todd: The Demon Barber of Fleet Street (2007; Colleen Atwood)

Sweet November (1968; Ann Roth)

Taxi Driver (1976; Ruth Morley)

Terminator (1984; Hilary Wright)

Terminator 2: Judgment Day (1991; Marlene Stewart)

Terminator 3: Rise of the Machines (2003; April Ferry)

That Forsyte Woman (1949; Walter Plunkett and Valles)

That Hamilton Woman (1941; René Hubert)

The Addams Family (1991; Ruth Myers)

The Adventures of Don Juan (1949; Leah Rhodes, William Travilla and Marjorie Best)

The Adventures of Tintin: The Secret of the Unicorn (2011; Lesley Burkes-Harding)

The Artist (2011; Mark Bridges)

The Aviator (2004; Sandy Powell)

The Big Lebowski (1998; Mary Zophres)

The Birdcage (1996; Ann Roth)

The Birds (1963; Edith Head)

The Birth of a Nation (1915; Robert Goldstein and Clare West)

The Blues Brothers (1980; Deborah Nadoolman)

The Boat that Rocked (2009; Joanna Johnston)

The Bonfire of the Vanities (1990; Ann Roth)

The Bourne Identity (2002; Pierre-Yves Gayraud)

The Bourne Ultimatum (2007; Shay Cunliffe)

The Bride Wore Red (1937; Adrian)

The Bridges of Madison County (1995; Colleen Kelsall)

The Broadway Melody (1929; David Cox)

The Cabinet of Dr Caligari (1920; Walter Reimann)

The Canary Murder Case (1929; Travis Banton)

The Chelsea Girls (1966)

The Cooler (2003; Kristin Burke)

The Dark Knight (2008; Lindy Hemming)

The Dark Knight Rises (2012, Lindy Hemming)

The Deer Hunter (1978; Eric Seelig)

The Departed (2006; Sandy Powell)

The Devil is a Woman (1935; Travis Banton)

The Devil Wears Prada (2006; Patricia Field)

The Dressmaker from Paris (1925; Travis Banton)

The Egyptian (1954; Charles LeMaire)

The English Patient (1996; Ann Roth and Gary Jones)

The Fall of the Roman Empire (1964; Veniero Colasanti and John Moore)

The French Lieutenant's Woman (1981; Tom Rand)

The Freshman (1925)

The Godfather (1972; Anna Hill Johnstone)

The Godfather, Part II (1974; Theadora Van Runkle)

The Goodbye Girl (1977; Ann Roth)

The Good Shepherd (2006; Ann Roth)

The Hobbit: An Unexpected Journey (2012; Ann Maskrey and Richard Taylor)

The Hours (2002; Ann Roth)

The Hunger Games (2012; Judianna Makovsky)

The Iron Lady (2011; Consolata Boyle)

The Iron Strain (A Modern Taming of the Shrew) (1915)

The King and I (1956; Irene Sharaff)

The King of Comedy (1983; Richard Bruno)

The Ladykillers (2004; Mary Zophres)

The Last Days of Pompeii (1935; Aline Bernstein)

The Last Emperor (1987; James Acheson)

The Leopard (1963; Piero Tosi)

The Little Foxes (1941; Orry-Kelly)

The Lord of the Rings: The Fellowship of the Ring (2001; Ngila Dickson and Richard Taylor)

The Lord of the Rings: The Two Towers (2002; Ngila Dickson and Richard Taylor)

The Lord of the Rings: The Return of the King (2003; Ngila Dickson and Richard Taylor)

The Loves of Queen Elizabeth (1912; Paul Poiret)

Them! (1954; Moss Mabry)

The Maltese Falcon (1941; Orry-Kelly)

The Manchurian Candidate (2004; Albert Wolsky)

The Man Who Wasn't There (2001; Mary Zophres)

The Matrix (1999; Kym Barrett)

The Matrix Reloaded (2003; Kym Barrett)

The Matrix Revolutions (2003; Kym Barrett)

The Navigator (1924)

The Owl and the Pussycat (1970; Ann Roth)

The Philadelphia Story (1940; Adrian)

The Piano (1993; Janet Patterson)

The Pirate (1948; Tom Keogh)

The Polar Express (2004; Joanna Johnston)

The Poseidon Adventure (1972; Paul Zastupnevich)

The Power of the Sultan (1907)

The Private Lives of Elizabeth and Essex (1939; Orry-Kelly)

The Prodigal (1955; Herschel McCoy)

The Queen (2006; Consolata Boyle)

The Reader (2008; Donna Maloney and Ann Roth)

The Robe (1953; Charles LeMaire and Emile Santiago)

The Scarlet Empress (1934; Travis Banton)

The Sea Hawk (1940; Orry-Kelly)

The Searchers (1956; Frank Beetson)

The Secret of the Incas (1954; Edith Head)

The Sixth Sense (1999; Joanna Johnston)

The Spanish Dancer (1923; Howard Greer)

The Spiderwick Chronicles (2008; Joanna Johnston)

The Strange Case of Clara Deane (1932)

The Talented Mr Ripley (1999; Ann Roth and Gary Jones)

The Ten Commandments (1956; Arnold Friberg, Edith Head, Ralph Jester, Dorothy Jeakins and John Jensen)

The Tourist (2010; Colleen Atwood)

The Towering Inferno (1974; Paul Zastupnevich)

The Tramp (1915)

The Twilight Saga: New Moon (2009; Tish Monaghan)

The Twilight Saga: Eclipse (2010; Tish Monaghan)

The Twilight Saga: Breaking Dawn, parts 1 and 2 (2011–12; Michael Wilkinson)

The Two Mouseketeers (1951)

The Unsinkable Molly Brown (1964; Morton Haack)

The Untouchables (1987; Marilyn Vance-Straker)

The Virgin Queen (1955; Charles LeMaire and Mary Wills)

The War of the Worlds (1953; Edith Head)

The Wizard of Oz (1939; Adrian)

The Women (1939; Adrian)

The World of Henry Orient (1964; Ann Roth)

Things to Come (1936; John Armstrong, René Hubert, Cathleen Mann and Sam Williams)

¡Three Amigos! (1986; Deborah Nadoolman)

Titanic (1997; Deborah L. Scott)

To Catch a Thief (1955; Edith Head)

Tower of London (1939; Vera West)

Toy Story (1995; Tom Holloway, Steve Johnson, Bud Luckey, Bob Penley and Andrew Stanton)

Trading Places (1983; Deborah Nadoolman)

Trafic (1971; Jacques Esterel)

Trapeze (1956; Veniero Colasanti)

Troy (2004; Bob Ringwood)

True Grit (2010; Mary Zophres)

Twilight (2008; Wendy Chuck)

Valley of the Dolls (1967; William Travilla and Charles LeMaire)

Velvet Goldmine (1998; Sandy Powell)

Vertigo (1958; Edith Head)

Volcano (1997; Kirsten Everberg)

Wall Street (1987; Ellen Mirojnick)

Wall Street: Money Never Sleeps (2010; Ellen Mirojnick)

Wag the Dog (1997; Rita Ryack)

War Horse (2011; Joanna Johnston)

West Side Story (1961; Irene Sharaff)

What's Eating Gilbert Grape (1993; Renée Ehrlich Kalfus)

Who Framed Roger Rabbit (1988; Joanna Johnston)

Who's Afraid of Virginia Woolf? (1966; Irene Sharaff)

Working Girl (1988; Ann Roth)

X-Men (2000; Louise Mingenbach)

X-Men: The Last Stand (2006; Judianna Makovsky and Lisa Tomczeszyn)

X-Men: First Class (2011; Sammy Sheldon)

PICTURE CREDITS

A Band Apart/Miramax/Kobal Collection: 341
© 1973 Charles Addams/With permission Tee & Charles Addams Foundation: 35
© AF Archive/Alamy: 41, 119, 171, 393, 422
Alamy/Photos 12: 420
Amblin/Malpaso/Kobal Collection/Ken Regan: 240
AMPAS/From the Leonard Stanley Collection, Margaret Herrick Library: 288, 294, 302
AMPAS/From the Albert Wolsky Collection, Margaret Herrick Library: 28
AMPAS/From the collections of the Margaret Herrick Library: 1, 9–11, 20, 22, 29, 92, 121, 161, 169, 172, 176, 231, 242, 261–2, 279, 284, 312, 314, 327, 361
Courtesy of Deena Appel: 138
Courtesy of Colleen Atwood: 228
Photograph courtesy of Autumn de Wilde: 368
Courtesy of Kim Barrett: 406, 408
Courtesy of Bazmark: 43
© Bettmann/Corbis: 147
Photo © Boltin Picture Library/Bridgeman Art Library: 148
Courtesy of Consolata Boyle/Pathé Productions Ltd: 233
Bridgeman Art Library: 52, 55, 160
Courtesy of Mark Bridges: 47
British Film Institute: 272
Bryna/Universal/Kobal Collection: 335
Jaap Buitendijk © 2011 GK Films LLC. All Rights Reserved: 98
Courtesy of Kristin M. Burke: 69, 70–72, 74
Courtesy of Alexandra Byrne: 323
Cady/Discina/Kobal Collection: 132
Cannon/Kobal Collection: 236
Courtesy of Milena Canonero: 354
© Stephanie Cardinaie/People Avenue/Corbis: 209
Carolco/Kobal Collection: 307, 349
Castle Rock/Shangri-La Entertainment/Kobal Collection: 426, 427
Chaplin/United Artists/Kobal Collection: 126
© CinemaPhoto/Corbis: 127
Cinémathèque Française/© Jean-Pierre Jolly: 273–4
Cinémathèque Française/© Littoz: 275
La Classe Americaine/uFilm/France 3/Kobal Collection: 48
Courtesy of Murray Close: 207
Columbia/Kobal Collection: 25, 30, 101, 103, 193, 216, 235, 244
Columbia/Marvel/Kobal Collection: 400
Columbia/Tri-Star/Kobal Collection/Zade Rosenthal: 108
Condé Nast Archive/Corbis: 202
Content Film/Dog Pond/Lionsgate/Kobal Collection: 73
Courtesy of David C. Copley: 200
Courtesy of Sharen Davis: 45
Courtesy of Sophie de Rakoff: 140
David O' Selznick Collection/Harry Ransom Humanities Research Center/The University of Texas at Austin: 287, 289, 292
Delpire Productions/Kobal Collection: 195
© 2012 Digital Image Museum Associates/LACMA/Art Resource NY/Scala Florence: 155
© Disney: 438
www.doctormacro.com: 269, 271
Dreamworks/Amblin/Universal/Kobal Collection: 350
Dreamworks/Kobal Collection: 433
Dreamworks/Kobal Collection/David James: 46
Dreamworks/Paramount/Kobal Collection/

Frank Connor: 379
Dreamworks/Universal/Kobal Collection/Jaap Buitendijk: 340
Dreamworks/Warner Bros/Kobal Collection/Leah Gallo: 114
Courtesy of Jacqueline Durran: 316
EMI/Columbia/Warner Bros/Kobal Collection: 215
Eon/Danjaq/Sony/Kobal Collection: 343
Courtesy Christian Esquevin/Silver Screen Modiste: 4
Everett Collections/Rex Features: 56, 76, 219
Famous Players/Lasky/Kobal Collection: 120
Courtesy of April Ferry: 348
Film 4/Kobal Collection: 232
Fitzwilliam Museum, University of Cambridge/Bridgeman Art Library: 51
Collection of Forrest Paulette and Robert Evanko: 26, 337
Forward Pass/Kobal Collection: 370
Getty Images: 189, 201, 356, 383
Courtesy of Lindy Hemming: 392
Histrionic Film/Kobal Collection: 152
Hulton-Deutsch Collection/Corbis: 131
© The Estate of Irene Sharaff/Planned Parenthood Federation of America, Inc./Yales School of Drama: 21
Courtesy of Eiko Ishioka: 394
ITV Global/Kobal Collection: 336
Courtesy of Joanna Johnston: 423–5, 428, 435–6
Courtesy of Joanna Johnston/Illustrated by Colin Marks: 439
John Springer Collection/Corbis: 130
Courtesy of Michael Kaplan: page 47, 410
Keystone Film Company/Kobal Collection: 122
Kobal Collection: 15, 99, 257, 286, 329, 331, 360
Courtesy of Jeffrey Kurland: 387–9
Ladd Company/Warner Bros/Kobal Collection: 411
Courtesy of John Landis: 143
Courtesy of Deborah Nadoolman Landis: 32, 105
© Annie Leibovitz/Contact Press Images/photographed for Vogue: 163, 187
Lucasfilm Ltd/Paramount/Kobal Collection: 31
Lucasfilm Ltd/20th Fox Film Corporation/Kobal Collection: 33, 403–4
Courtesy of Judianna Makovsky: 395
Marvel/Sony Pictures/Kobal Collection/Melissa Moseley: 399
Courtesy of Larry McQueen: page 7 (left), 151, 185, 304, 308, 338, 352
© The Metropolitan Museum of Art/Al Mozell: 277–9
MGM/ Kobal Collection: 8, 12, 85, 175, 305, 326, 328, 330
MGM/ Kobal Collection/Eric Carpenter: 255
MGM/ Kobal Collection/Sam Emerson: 141
MGM/ Kobal Collection/George Hurrell: 204
MGM/ Kobal Collection/Clarence Sinclair Bull: 7
MGM/ Kobal Collection/Laszlo Willinger: 162, 188
MGM/Photofest: 129, 281, 293
Miramax/Buena Vista/Kobal Collection: 196
Miramax Films/Dimension Films/Kobal Collection/Mario Tursi: 96
Miramax Films/Kobal Collection: 306
Miramax Films/Kobal Collection/Andrew Schwartz: 226
Miramax Films/Universal/Kobal Collection: 154
Miramax Films/Universal/Kobal Collection:

Laurie Sparham: 42, 154
Moviestore Collection Ltd/Alamy 157, 430
Moviestore Collection Ltd/Rex Features: 44, 311, 351, 381
Mptv images: 197, 295
Courtesy of Isis Mussenden: 431–2
© The National Gallery, London: 57–62
© National Portrait Gallery, London: 153
NBCUniversal Archives and Collections: 49, 315, 317–20, 322
New Line Cinema/Kobal Collection/Sam Emerson: 237
New Line Cinema/Tribeca/Kobal Collection: 222
Nickelodeon Movies/Kobal Collection: 434
Marcel Noecker/Sygma/Corbis: 333
Orion/Kobal Collection/Brian Hamill: 380
Orion/Paramount Pictures/Kobal Collection: 34
© 2002–3 Paramount Pictures: page 9
Paramount/Columbia/Wingnut/Amblin/Kobal Collection: 437
Paramount/Everett/Rex Features: 419
Paramount/ Kobal Collection: back cover, 14, 19, 90, 94, page 93, 142, 173, 177, 180–84, 192, 203, 210, 211, 213, 220, 263, 300, 401
Paramount/ Kobal Collection/Ken Regan: 238
Paramount/ Kobal Collection/E.R. Richee: page 5, 5, 13, 178, 179
Paramount/ Kobal Collection/A.L. 'Whitey' Schafer/Colour: Paul Faherty: 205
Paramount/Mandalay Pictures/ Kobal Collection/Clive Coote: 111
Paramount/Miramax/ Kobal Collection: 77
Paramount/Miramax/ Kobal Collection/Clive Coote: 250
Paramount/Photofest: 229, 248, 374
Paris Pierce/Alamy: 123
Philadelphia Museum of Art: Gift of Mme Elsa Schiaparelli, 1969: 158
Pictorial Press Ltd/Alamy: 128, 133, 139, 416
Polygram/Propaganda/ Kobal Collection: 53
Polygram/Working Title/Kobal Collection/Merrick Morton: 75
Popperfoto/Getty Images: page 11
Courtesy of Anthony Powell: endpapers, 136
Courtesy of Sandy Powell: 40, 97
Pressman Productions/ Kobal Collection/Frank Connor: 227
Private collection: 286
Prod. Eur. Assoc./Gonzalez/Constantin/Kobal Collection: 345
Protozoa Pictures/Phoenix Pictures/ Kobal Collection: 367, 369
Rex Features/Heathcliff O'Malley: 332
Courtesy of Debbie Reynolds: 334
RKO/ Kobal Collection: 16
Courtesy of David Robinson: 116–18, 124
From the archives of the Roy Export Company Establishment: 94, 115, 125
Royal Armoury, Stockholm: 166–7
Courtesy of Mayes C. Rubeo: 429
Courtesy of Deborah L. Scott: 39
Scott Rudin Productions/Kobal Collection: 239
Seaver Center for Western History Research, Natural History Museum of Los Angeles County: 2, 3, 321, 355, 357–9, 362–6
Selznick/MGM/Kobal Collection: 168, 170, 290
Silver Pictures/Kobal Collection: 371
Skydance Productions/Kobal Collection/Lorey Sebastian: 81
Snap/Rex Features: 225, 291
Spider-Man 2 © 2004 Columbia Pictures

Industries Inc., Spider-Man character ® & © 2004 Marvel Characters, Inc. All rights reserved. Courtesy of Warren Manser: 398
Summit Entertainment/Kobal Collection: 397
Courtesy of Catherine Thomas: 342
Tiger Moth/Miramax Pictures/Kobal Collection: 249
Courtesy of Norman Tipton: 283
Touchstone/Amblin/Kobal Collection: 418
Touchstone/Kobal Collection: 84
Touchstone/Universal/Kobal Collection: 79, 145
Tri-Star/Kobal Collection: 27, 245, 247, 384
Turner Entertainment Company (S12): 280
20th Century Fox/Kobal Collection: page 7 (right), 17, 23, 82, 100, 104, 144, 146, 149, 159, 174, 190, 214, 346, pages 262–3, 372, 378
20th Century Fox/Kobal Collection/Brigitte Lacombe: 230
20th Century Fox/Kobal Collection/Barry Wetcher: 194
20th Century Fox/Marvel/ Kobal Collection: 377
20th Century Fox/Paramount/ Kobal Collection: 37, 38
20th Century Fox/Zanuck Co./ Kobal Collection: 109
United Artists/Everett/Rex Features: 102
United Artists/Kobal Collection: 6, 18, 208, 217, 223, 234, 241
United Artists/Photofest: 313
Universal Studios: 282
Universal/Kobal Collection: 89, 134–5, 213, 402, 421
Universal/Kobal Collection/Jasin Boland: 347
Universal/Kobal Collection/Suzanne Hanover: 373
Universal/The Kobal Collection/Bob Marshak: 382
Universal/Kobal Collection/Peter Mountain: 83
Universal/Studio Canal/Working Title/Kobal Collection/Greg Williams: 324
Courtesy of University of Michigan Library: 309
Courtesy of Theadora Van Runkle: 212, 224
Image © Victoria and Albert Museum: Front cover, page 6 (right and left), 24, 36, 50, 63, 67–8, 87, 91, 164, 186, 206, page 177, 251, 296–9, 301, 303, 310, 325, 353
© Vogue 1930/Courtesy of Condé Nast: 150
Courtesy of Mary E. Vogt: page 1, 412–4
Walt Disney Pictures/Kobal Collection: 86, 88, 112–13, 137
Warner Bros/DC Comics/Kobal Collection: pages 2–3, 376, 409, 415
Warner Bros. Entertainment Inc. 391
Warner Bros/First National/Kobal Collection: 156
Warner Bros/Kobal Collection: 54, 95, 110, 165, 191, 198–9, 243, 246, 264, 268, 344, 375, 385–6, 396
Warner Bros/Kobal Collection/Jasin Boland: 405, 407
Warner Bros/Kobal Collection/Andrew Cooper: 93
Warner Bros/Kobal Collection/Milton Gold: 285
Warner Bros/Kobal Collection/Dirck Halsted: 221
Warner Bros/ Kobal Collection/Bob Marshak: 390
Warner Bros/Kobal Collection/Bruce Talamon: 106
Courtesy of Western Costume: 107, 251
Yanco/Tao/The Recorded Picture Company/Kobal Collection: 64–6
Courtesy of Janty Yates: 339
Courtesy of Mary Zophres: 78, 80

ACKNOWLEDGEMENTS

THE *Hollywood Costume* exhibition and book have been made possible by the support and generosity of the following individuals and institutions. The exhibition was created at the V&A over a period of six years (2007–12) and was the beneficiary of a lifetime of close personal and professional relationships.

Hollywood Costume brings together costumes from all over the world, and the exhibition would not have been possible without the support of our sponsors, particularly Harry Winston and my gracious friend David C. Copley whose generosity equals his passion for life and for enabling the scale and vision of this project to be realized. I am also grateful to the Blavatnik Family Foundation, the American Friends of the V&A, American Airlines and Samsung. I gratefully acknowledge the support of our lenders and I would especially like to thank The Chaplin Family, The DeMille Collection: Cecilia DeMille Presley and Helen Cohen, Margie Duncan, David Elkouby and Hal Ornstein, Christian Esquevin, Hani Farsi, Todd Fisher, Romaine Gavras, Dorian Hannaway, Dan Lanigan, Larry McQueen, Morning Glory Antiques & Jewelry: Jane H.Clarke, Heather Porter, Debbie Reynolds, Quentin Tarantino and Pilar Savone, Norman Tipton and Jerry Wallace.

Numerous curators, scholars and archivists at the following institutions have generously given their time and expertise:Academy of Motion Picture Arts & Sciences: Dawn Hudson, Heather Cochran, Julio Vera, Randy Haberkamp, Ellen Harrington, Maryrose McMahon, Matt Severson, Rich Miller, Margaret Herrick Library Linda Mehr, Anne Coco; Angels the Costumiers: Tim Angel OBE, Shelley Thompson; Annamoda: Simone Bessi; Costume for *The Artist* (2011) courtesy, Bérénice Bejo; BFI: Michael Caldwell, Nigel Arthur, Nathalie Morris, Claire Smith, Justin Johnson; Blackframe: Juliana Riberio, Margo Schneier, Kevin Brownlow; Cinémathèque Française Paris: Serge Toubieff, Costa Gavras, Marianne de Fleury, Danielle Kenzey, Jacques Ayroles, Charlyne Carrere; COSPROP: John Bright, Christine McSweeney; Costumi d'Arte, Rome: Guiseppe Peruzzi, Carolina Destito; Deutsche Kinemathek Museum für Film und Fernsehen, Berlin: Silke Ronneburg, Barbara Schröter, Anett Sawall; Dreamworks Archive: Michelle Fandeti, Andrew Jackson; The E. Land World, Ltd: Justine Kang, Monica Park; EON Productions: Barbara Broccoli, Michael Wilson, Meg Simmonds, Stephanie Wenborn; Experience Music Project, Seattle: Jasen Emmons, Jacob McMurray, Therese Littleton; Farani Costume House: Luigi Piccolo; The Museum at F.I.T.:Dr Valerie Steele, Jennifer Farley; G.P.11: Gabriele Mayer, Andrea Sorrentino; Harry Ransom Center at the University of Texas, Austin, David O. Selznick Archive: Steve Wilson, Jill Moreno; Kobal Picture Desk: Lauretta Dives, Martin Dives, Dave Kent, Phil Moad, Paul Faherty; Library of Congress, National Film Archive: Director Pat Lochney; Natural History Museum Los Angeles: William D. Estrada, Ph.D., John Cahoon, Beth Werling; Lucas Film Ltd Archives: George Lucas, Laela French, Joanee Honour; Museo del Traje, Madrid: Andrés Carretero Pérez, Amalia Descalzo, Concha Herranz, Rafael Garcia Serrano; Museum of the Moving Image, New York: Executive Director Carl Goodman, Dr. Barbara Miller; NBCUniversal: Craig Kornblau, Josh Goldstine, NBCUniversal Archives: Deidre Thieman; Newbridge Silverwear: Phil Donnolly; Paramount: Andrea Kalas, Randall Thropp, Jaci Rohr; Pathé Films UK: Sophie Glover; Pompeii Shoes: Carlo Pompeii; Private Textile Conservators: Fionn Zarubica, Cara Varnell, Janie Lightfoot; The Prop Store: Stephen Lane, Tim Lawes; The Recorded Picture Company: Jeremy Thomas, Karin Padgham, David Robinson; Roy Export Company Establishment: Kate Guyonvarch; Sands Films: Olivier Stockman, Christine Edzard; Daniel Mayer Selznick; SONY: Colin Greene, Karen Boysen; Stephen Jones Millinery: Stephen Jones; Summit Entertainment: Sabrina Lamb; Tirelli: Dino Trapetti, Laura Nobile; Turner Classic Movies: Robert Osborne, Charles Tabesh, Darcy Hettrich; Twentieth-Century Fox: Victoria Snow, Mike Voght; Vulcan Inc. Archive: Paul Allen, Tom Venditti, Deborah Gunn;Walt Disney Studios: Michael Mark Snovell, Walt Disney Imagineering: Bruce Vaughn, Melissa Berry, Joseph Garlington, Christopher M. Mais, Mark Page, Tom Child; Warner Bros. Archive & Costume Dept.: Leith Adams, Elaine Patton, Steve Bingen, Elaine Maser; Western Costume Co.: Bill Haber, Eddie Marks, Bobi Garland, José Bello, Mauricio Osorio; Wisconsin Center for Film & Television: Maxine Ducey; Costume for *Legally Blonde* (2003) courtesy Reese Witherspoon.

The essay authors have been far more than contributors to the book; their commitment and expertise all combine to highlight one aspect above any other in filmmaking: that the audience must connect and care about the people in the movie. Naturally, this whole project highlights the invaluable contribution of costume designers to filmmaking in Hollywood today and grateful thanks to those who shared their expertise, experiences and sketches: James Acheson, Jason Alper, Deena Appel, Colleen Atwood, Kym Barrett, Jenny Beavan, Yvonne Blake, John Bloomfield, Mark Bridges, Consolata Boyle, John Bright, Aude Bronson-Howard, Alexandra Byrne, Milena Canonero, Shay Cunliffe, Sharen Davis, Jean Druesdow, John Dunn, Jacqueline Durran, April Ferry, Hubert de Givenchy, Lindy Hemming, Joanna Johnston, Michael Kaplan, Jeffrey Kurland, Judianna Makovsky, Catherine Martin, Ellen Mirojnick, John Mollo, Tish E. Monaghan, Kate and Laura Mulleavy, Isis Mussenden, Kumiko Ogawa, Karen Patch, Joseph Porro, Anthony Powell, Sandy Powell, Sophie de Rakoff, Tom Rand, Bob Ringwood, Penny Rose, Ann Roth, Mayes C. Rubeo, Rita Ryack, Deborah L. Scott, Angus Strathie, Jany Temime, Catherine Thomas, Marilyn Vance, Mary E. Vogt, Patrizia Von Brandenstein, Amy Westcott, Albert Wolsky, Janty Yates, Mary Zophres.

My warmest thanks to the following individuals for their friendship: Sarah Bailey, Mary Lee Bandy, Cari Beauchamp, Marshall Bell, Jim Bissell, Dwight Block-Bowers, Susan and William Boyd, Joan Boyle, Rosemary Brandenburg, Kristin M. Burke, David Burton, Tim Burton, James Cameron, Robert De Niro, Jeffrey Deitch, Marina Draghici, Alice and Jon Flint, Sir Christopher and Lady Helen Frayling, Nancy and Sid Ganis, Josh Goldstine, Nick Grace at Royal College of Art, Rapid Form Studio, John Gray, Judith Harris and Dr. Robert Singer, Tippi Hedren, Alexander Jaffe, Darren Julien at Julien's Auctions, Kate Krukiel, Jon Landau, Deirdre Lawrence, Jennifer Levy, Edward Maeder, Michelle Matland, Daryl, Maxwell, Julie McLean, Lori and Michael Milken, Lady Grania and Sir Alan Munro, Mike Nichols, Laura and Milton Nadoolman, Dr Wolffe Nadoolman, Abram Nalibotsky, at Olswang: Lisbeth Savill and Tariq Mirza, Gwyneth Paltrow, Simon Pegg, Annie Philbin, Patrizia Pitt, at Profiles in History: Joe Maddalena, at the Autry Center: Jeffrey Richardson, Dr Aileen Ribeiro, David Robertson, Professor Bob Rosen, Jared Rosen, Jane Rosenthal, J.K. Rowling, Brenda Royce-Posada, Karen and David Sachs, Jasha and Maurice Salter, Martin Scorsese, Terry Semel, Andy Serkis, Shambala Preserve: The Roar Foundation, Andrew Shelton, Steven Spielberg, Dr Valerie Steele, Meryl Streep, David Sulzberger, Jenny Agutter Tham and John Tham.

I owe a huge thanks to my colleagues and students at UCLA:Dean Teri Schwartz, Chair Michael Hackett, Leighton Bowers, Caitlin Talmage, Anthony Tran and Hannah Greene.

Among current and former staff at the V&A, I would like to thank all those for their contributions in bringing this exhibition to life: Paul Ruddock, Sir Mark Jones, Martin Roth and Damien Whitmore. In Exhibitions, Charlotte Allan, Stephanie Cripps, Claire Everitt, Matthew Cowpe, Poppy Hollman, Rebecca Lim, Linda Lloyd-Jones, Zoe Louizos, Shona Connechen; Donatella Barbieri, Victoria Broackes, Vanessa Eyles and Geoffrey Marsh in Theatre and Performance Collections; Glenn Adamson, Christopher Breward. Katy Conover, Liz Miller, Helen Woodfield, Oliver Winchester, David Caamano, Adrián Villaseñor in the Research department; James Stevenson, Richard Davis, Peter Kelleher and Maike Zimmerman in the Photographic Studio; Eleanor Appleby, Andrea Carr, Olivia Colling, Zoe Franklin, Elinor Hughes, Katy Towse in Public Affairs; Kathleen Dowling, Lara Flecker, Sam Gatley, Roisin Morris in Conservation; Alison Pearce in Sculpture, Metalwork, Ceramics and Glass department, Jenny Lister in Furniture, Textiles and Fashion department, Andrea Davies in Public Affairs; Jo Ani, Camilla Graham, Kate Brier, Jane Lawson, Laura Sears in Development; Mark Eastment, Liz Edmunds, Vicky Haverson, Jo Prosser, Sarah Sevier and Matt Thomas in V&A Enterprises. Dinah Casson, Roger Mann, Gary Shelley, Virna Di Schiavi, Poppy Watson at Casson-Mann brought their innovative edge and talent to the exhibition design. The three year long collaboration with Casson Mann was one of the great joys of mounting Hollywood Costume; and Sue Joly, our AV producer has brought together all the extraordinary visuals in the galleries.

My special and heartfelt thanks to Max and Rachel without whose love, nothing is accomplished; my own John Landis, resident film historian, agent, editor, collaborator, and patron of the arts; Christopher Frayling, who launched me on this path; Anjali Bulley, Johanna Stephenson, Ray Watkins, the V&A Publishing dream team for this astonishing volume; my dogged Copley Center assistant and brilliant friend Natasha Rubin, who provided the basic research for *Hollywood Costume* and every one of my past, present and future costume design history projects; and curator Keith Lodwick, whose constant assistance and enthusiasm for the movies provided the encouragement and the energy to endure the long flights back and forth from Hollywood to London.

DEBORAH NADOOLMAN LANDIS

INDEX

Page numbers in *italic* refer to plate captions

101 Dalmatians 51, 106
102 Dalmatians 106, *107*, 205
1941 180
Abbey, Eleanor 146
Abbott and Costello 233
Academy Awards 19, 32, 39, 198, 199, 244
Acheson, James *4*, 58, *60*, 69–70, *69*, *70*, 160, 284
Adams, Martin 70
Adam's Rib 13
Addams Family, The 40
Addams Family Values 260
Adrian *4*, *16–18*, 18, 19, *19*, *20*, 21, 23, 54, 57, 118, 120, *120*, 127–8, *127*, 132, 139, *140*, 151, 155, *179*, 181, *182*, 198, 201, *204*, 220, 226, 253, 257, 260
Adventures of Don Juan, The 242, 243–4, *243*
Adventures of Tintin, The: The Secret of the Unicorn 299, *304*
Agee, James 95, 98, 102, 104–5
Aghayan, Ray *140*
Aldredge, Theoni V. *40*, 144
Alice in Wonderland *81*, 82, 91
Alien 36
All Dolled Up 140
Allen, Irwin 249
Allen, Marit 52, *54*
Allen, Woody 155, 273, 274, *274*
Alloway, Lawrence 190
Alma-Tadema, Sir Lawrence 48
Alper, Jason *108*
Altman, Robert 169
Ameche, Don 109
American in Paris, An 237
Anchors Aweigh 295
Anderson, Lindsay 189–90
Anderson, Milo *186*, 206
André-ani 14
Andress, Ursula 249
Andrews, Julie 146
Angel *132*, 217, 225–6
Angels in America 169
Angels The Costumiers 181, 208–9
Année dernière à Marienbad, L' 195
Annie Hall 154, *155*
Annon, Pauline *4*
Appel, Deena 50, *108*, 179
Arabian Nights 112
Arbuckle, Roscoe 'Fatty' 97, 98, 100
Armani, Giorgio 140, 154
Around the World in 80 Days 170
Artist, The 50–51, *52*
Ash, Carla 229
Astor, Mary *253*
Atlantide, L' 196
Atonement 42, *229*, 266
Atwood, Colleen *42*, 80, *80*, *81*, 82, 90–91, *90–91*, 163–4, *164*, 220, 257, *266*, 267
Aubrey, Jim 238, 240
Austin, Jerry *243*
Austin Powers 50, 106, *108*, 179
Avatar *4*, *300*
Aviator, The 86, *86*
Aykroyd, Dan 106, *107*, 109

Back to the Future 296, *297*
Baldwin, Alec 75
Bale, Christian 267, *281*

Balenciaga 118
Ball, Lucille 95
Balmain, Pierre 198
Bandy, Mary Lea 42, 182
Banks, Elizabeth *154*
Banton, Travis *4*, 18, *21*, 22, 23, 112, *114*, 127, 132–5, *132–7*, 181, 198, 212, *212–15*, 217, 225
Bara, Theda 111, *112*
Baranski, Christine 233
Barbarella 282–7, *287*
Bardem, Javier 77, 79
Barrault, Jean-Louis 196
Barrett, Kym 39, *288–9*
Barry Lyndon 58, *59*, 118–20, *125*
Barrymore, John 82, 127
Basic Instinct 38, 223, *223*, 261
Batman films *4*, 261, 269, 281, 290, 292
Beach Blanket Bingo 140
Beals, Jennifer *151*
Bearsted Collection, Upton House 57
Beaton, Cecil 32–5, 146–8, *146–9*, 180, 187, *196–9*
Beatty, Warren *4*, *34*, *143*, 250, *250*
Beauty and the Beast 39
Beavan, Jenny 265, *266*
Bedknobs and Broomsticks 295
Beetson, Frank 32, *247*
Bejo, Bérénice 52
Bell, Jamie *304*
Bellamy, Ralph 109
Belle de Jour 143, 144
Belle of the Nineties 132, *135*
Belushi, John 106, *107*, 109
Ben-Hur 32, 225, 242–3, 244
Bening, Annette 34
Benjamin, Walter 190–91, 192
Benny and Joon *81*, 82
Berenson, Marisa 58, *59*, 118–20, *125*
Bergman, Ingrid 30, *85*
Bernhardt, Sarah 14, 116, *116*
Bernstein, Aline 170
Berry, Melissa 186
Bertolucci, Bernardo 69–70
Best, Marjorie 243, *243*
Beyoncé 42, *51*
BFI Archive *151*
BFI Collection 187
Big Fish 90
Big Lebowski, The 39, 76–9, *76*, 106, *108*
Birdcage, The 89
Birds, The 85, *203*, 208
Birth of a Nation, The 14
Bishara, Joseph 75
Black Beauty 260
Black Swan 265, 267–8, 269
Blackmail 190
Blade Runner 38, 261, *261*, 287, 291
Blake, Yvonne 290
Blanchett, Cate 118, 233, *234*
Blonde Venus 132
Blues Brothers, The 106–9, *107*
Bogart, Humphrey 200
Bonfire of the Vanities, The 172
Bonham Carter, Helena 91
Bonnie and Clyde 35, *35*, 143, *143*, 144, 207
Borat 106, *108*
Born to Boogie 140
Bourdin, Guy 144
Bourne Ultimatum, The 248, 250
Bow, Clara 196

Boxer, John 159, *159*
Boyle, Consolata *165*, 166
Bram Stoker's Dracula 282
Brando, Marlon *131*, 158
Braveheart 242, 243, 244
Brazil 69
Breakfast at Tiffany's 42, 140, *143*, 144, 146
Bride of Vengeance 129, 130, *130*
Bride Wore Red, The 17
Bridesmaids 266, 268
Bridges, Jeff 39, 76, *76*, 79, 108
Bridges, Mark 50–51, *52*
Bridges of Madison County, The 167
Brioni Roma 249
Broadway Melody, The 187, 261
Brockovich, Erin 275
Brokeback Mountain 52, 54, 233
Broken Arrow 32
Bronson, Betty 260
Bronx Tale, A 158, 161
Bruckheimer, Jerry 186
Bruno, Richard 159, *159*
Brymer *212–15*
Buck Rogers 287
Buckle, Richard 189, 194
Bugsy 34
Buñuel, Luis 143
Burbank Studios 180
Burke, Kristin M. 72–5, *72*, *74*, 75
Burkes-Harding, Lesley *304*
Burnett, Carol 198
Burns, L.L. 15
Burton, Tim 42, 80, 82, 90–91, *90–91*
Butterfield, Asa 87
Butterfield & Butterfield Auction Company 217
Byrne, Alexandra 118, 233, *234*
Byrne, Rose 268

Cabinet of Dr Cagliari, The 195
Calthrop, Donald 190
Camden House Auctioneers 217
Cameron, James 39
Canonero, Milena *4*, 38, 58, *59*, 118–20, *120*, 125, 139–40, *139*, 163, 164–6, *250*
Captain Blood 140
Captain John Smith and Pocahontas 13
Carrington 140
Casino 158, *160*, 161
Casino Royale 247, 249
Cassavetes, John 32
Cassel, Vincent 265
Casson, Hugh 189
Casson-Mann 187
Casterline, Thomas 70
Chanel, Coco 154, 195, 198
Chaney, Lon Sr 82, 196
Chaplin, Charlie 15, 82, 95, *95*, 97, 98, *99*, 100–102, *100*, 104, 151, *183*, 196, 200, 222, 254–5, 260
Charade 208
Chase, Charley 97
Chase, Chevy *108*
Cheadle, Don 278–9, *278*
Chelsea Girls 140
Chen, Joan 69, *70*
Cher *88*, 198
Chicago 42, 220, *220*, 257
Chocolat 80
Christie's East, New York 217

Chuck, Wendy 283
Cimino, Michael 158
Cleopatra (1917) 111–12, *112*
Cleopatra (1934) *4*, 112, *114*, 127, 131, 132, *135*
Cleopatra (1963) 28–9, 32, *111*, 112, 131, *240*
Clooney, George 78, 275–7, *278*
Close, Glenn 51, 58, *60*, 106, *107*, 180
Closer 89
Cocteau, Jean 194
Coen Brothers 39, 48–50, 76–9, 154
Cohn, Harry 111
Colasanti, Veniero 242
Colbert, Claudette *4*, 112, *114*, 127, 132, 135, *135*
Coleman, Dabney *171*
Collateral 273, 275, 279
Collection of Motion Picture Costume Design, The
    30, *40*, *85*, *135*, *213*, 217, 217–26, *225*, 250
Columbia 30
Colvig, Helen 35
Conan the Barbarian 282
Conquest 240
Cooler, The 74, *75*
Cooper, Lady Diana 147–8
Cooper, Shirley 70
Coppola, Sofia 118, 120, 139–40
Corman, Roger 32
Cox, David *187*
Craig, Daniel 247, 249
Crawford, Joan *17*, 21, *151*, 174–5, *186*, 203, 205,
    206, 260
Crisp, Quentin 118, *118*
Crowe, Russell *243*, *244*
Cruise, Tom 273, 275, 279
Cry in the Dark, A 166
Cukor, George *21*, 32, 146–7
Cunliffe, Shay 248
Curtiz, Michael 24, 174

Daldry, Stephen 173
Dalí, Salvador 192, *193*
Damon, Matt *174*, *175*, 248, 250, 276, 277, *278*
Dangerous Liaisons 58, *60*
Dark Knight Rises, The, 280, 281
Dark Shadows 90
Darnell, Linda *172*
Davies, Marion 95
Davis, Bette 24, *25*, 111, 116–18, *116*, *118*, 180, 220
Davis, Sharen 42, 48, *50*, 51
Day-Lewis, Daniel 51, 87, *87*
De Niro, Robert *36*, 42, 158–61, *158–61*, 180, 207
de Rakoff, Sophie *108*
Death Becomes Her 296, *297*
Death in Venice 186
Deed, André 96
Deer Hunter, The 158, *159*
DeMille, Cecil B. *13*, 15, 21, 32, 112, *184*, 210–11,
    257
Dench, Judi *116*, 118
Denderian, Annie 225
Deneuve, Catherine 143
Dennis, Sandy 172
Departed, The 86, *86*
Depp, Johnny 80–82, *80–83*, 90, *90*, *91*, 212, *266*,
    267, 282
Desperately Seeking Susan 143
Destination Moon 287
Devil is a Woman, The 134, *135*
Devil Wears Prada, The 144, *144*, *165*
Devlin, Dean 250
Diaghilev, Sergei 189
Diaz, Cameron 276, 302
DiCaprio, Leonardo *43*, *86*, 87, 277
Dick Tracy 4, 250, *250*
Dickson, Ngila 269–70, *270*
Die Hard 248, 249
Dietrich, Marlene *4*, 23, 132–4, *132*, *134*, 135, 186,
    198, 217, 225, 226
Dillane, Stephen 174

Dinner at Eight 21
Dior, Christian 140, 198, 260
Disney Pictures 82
Disney, Walt 39, 186, 260
Doctor Dolittle 140, *140*
Dr No 246, 249
Doonan, Simon 35, 144
Double Indemnity 260
Doubt 163
Douglas, Kirk 242
Douglas, Melvyn *217*
Douglas, Michael 266, *267*
Dowd, Jeff 39
Downey, Robert Jr 265, *266*
Downton, David 234
Dreamgirls 42, 48, *50*, 51
Dressmaker from Paris, The 132
Dreyfuss, Richard 172
Duchamp, Marcel 192
Duel in the Sun 32
Duke, Patty 82
Dunaway, Faye 35, 140, 143, *143*
Duncan, Michael Clarke 90
Dunn, John *160*, 161
Dunst, Kirsten 120, *125*, *139*, 140
Durbin, Deanna 233
Durran, Jacqueline 42, *229*, 266
Dye, Captain Dale 250

Earthquake 261, *261*
Eastwood, Clint 167, 246, 247
Easy Rider 35
Ed Wood 80, *81*, 90
Edward Scissorhands 80, *80*, 82, 90, *90*
Edwards, Blake 140
Egerton, Judy 65
Egyptian, The 129
Eisner, Lotte 194
Eisner, Michael 38–9
Elizabeth I, Queen 112–18
Elizabeth: The Golden Age 118, 233, *234*
Enfants du Paradis, Les 196
English Patient, The 169, 174, *175*
Ephron, Nora 166
Erin Brockovich 273–4, 275, *275*
Erté 198
Escape from L.A. 261
Evans, Leesa 266, *268*
Extremely Loud and Incredibly Close 173
Eyes of Laura Mars 144, *144*

Fairbanks, Douglas Sr 196, 254, 257, 260
Falkenstein, Arthur 170
Fall of the Roman Empire, The 243
Family Plot 85
Fargo 76, *76*
Farrow, Barbara 274
Faster, Pussycat! Kill! Kill! 144
Faye, Alice *131*
Fear and Loathing in Las Vegas 81
Ferry, April 248
Field, Patricia *144*, *165*
Field, Sally 173
Fielding, Henry 58–60, 66
Fields, W.C. 97, *97*, 104
Fiennes, Joseph 44
Fiennes, Ralph 174
Fight Club 4, 48, 51
Finding Neverland 80
Finlayson, Bruce *166*
Finney, Albert 273–4, 275
Fisher, Carrie *38*, 287
Fisher, Eddie 237, *239*
Fistful of Dollars, A 246
Fitzwilliam Museum 57, *60*
Flash Gordon: Space Soldiers 287
Flashdance *151*, 154–5
Fleischer, Charlie 295–6

Fleming, Ian 249
Fleming, Victor 253
Flynn, Errol 243–4, *243*
Foch, Nina 225
Fonda, Jane *170*, *171*, 173, 282, 287
Fontaine, Joan 171
Fonteray, Jacques 287
Foolshead Pays His Debts 96
For a Few Dollars More 247
For Sale 14
Ford, Harrison *36*, 38, *38*, 42, 48, *89*, *261*, 282,
    287, *287*
Forrest Gump 296, *296*
Foster, Margot 70
Frankel, David 175
Frayling, Sir Christopher 182, 186, 187
Frederics, John 128
French Lieutenant's Woman, The 64, *166*
Freshman, The 100, 103
Friberg, Arnold 225
Funny Face 144
Funny Girl 33, 205

Gable, Clark *127*, 203, *253*
Gainsborough, Thomas 58
Galliano, John 140
Gangs of New York 51, 86, 87, *87*
Garbo, Greta 57, 195, 196, 198, 203, 217, 220, 260
Garcia, Andy 276
Gardiner, Frank 70
Gardner, Ava 237
Garland, Judy *179*, *182*, *188*, 200, 201, *201*, 203,
    204–5
Garon, Pauline *13*
Gatley, Sam 212, *213*
Gaye, Nona 298
Gayraud, Pierre-Yves 250
Genn, Leo 242
Geraldi, Dominic 276
Getson/Eastern embroidery 225
Gidget 261
Gidget Goes Hawaiian 140
Gigi 198
Gilbert, John 220
Gilda 296
Gilliam, Terry 69
Gish, Lillian 254, 257
Givenchy, Hubert de 140, *143*, 155, *155*, 208
Gladiator 48, 242, 243, 244, *244*
Glaum, Louise 220
Glover, Danny *173*, 174
Glyn, Elinor 15
Goddard, Paulette *130*
Godfather, The, Part II 158, *158*
Goldblum, Jeff 250
Golden Earrings 140
Goldfinger 246
Gombrich, Ernst 242
Gone with the Wind 24–6, *127*, *127*, 128, *128*, 131,
    195, 206–8, *207–11*, 237, 261
Good Shepherd, The 158
Goodbye Girl, The 172
Goodfellas 160
Goodman, John *108*
Gordon-Levitt, Joseph 269, 277
Gould, Chester 250
Gould, Elliott 276, 277–8, *278*
Gower, George 116
Grant, Cary 254, 268, *268*, 275
Grant, Mary 129, *130*
Grauman's Chinese Theatre, Los Angeles 253, 260
Great Hope Springs 175
Green Lantern 269–70, *270*
Greer, Howard 15, 18, 23, 198, 257
Grès, Alix 112
Griffin, Ted 276
Griffith, D.W. 14, 257
Griffith, Melanie *89*, 172

Griffith, Raymond 95–6, 97, *97*
Guilaroff, Sidney 127
Guillaume, Ferdinand *96*
Gwynne, Edmund 106
Gyllenhaal, Jake *54*

Haack, Morton *237*, 238
Hadley, Annie 70
Haffenden, Elizabeth 225, 243
Hahn, Don 296
Hair 173
Hamill, Mark *38*
Han, Maggie *70*
Hands Up! 95–6, 97
Hanks, Tom *172*, 250, *250*, 296, *296*, *298–9*
Hannah and Her Sisters 274
Harareet, Haya 225
Harlow, Jean *21*, 253
Harris, Richard *131*
Harrison, Rex *140*, 146, *146*, 148
Harry Potter films 204, 282, *283*
Hart, W.S. 196
Hartnell, Norman 198
Hatton, Yankton *173*
Haynes, Todd 174–5
Hays, Will H. 18–19, 26
Hays Office 18–19, 26, 30
Hayward, Susan *30*, 220
Hayworth, Rita *180*, 296
Hazlitt, William 66–7
Head, Edith 15, 18, 22, 23, *23*, 26, 27, 30, 32, 50, 65, 85, *85*, 140, *143*, 151, *151*, 155, *155*, 172, 179, *184*, 198, *203*, 208, 211, 217, 225, 257, 261, *261*, 268, *268*
Heartburn 166
Hebden, Gilly 70
Hedren, Tippi *203*, 208, 261
Heimann, Betsy 144, *144*
Hellman, Jerry 171
Hello, Frisco, Hello 130, *131*
Hemming, Lindy 247, 249, *281*
Henie, Sonja 170–71
Hepburn, Audrey *42*, 140, *143*, 146–8, *146–9*, 155, *155*, 180, *187*, 208
Hepburn, Katharine *16–17*, 21, 24, 111
Hershey, Barbara 274
Heston, Charlton 223, 225, 242, 261
Hill, George Roy 171
His Secretary 14
Hitchcock, Alfred 30, 35, 50, 64–5, 85, *85*, 171, 190, 200, 208, 261, 268
Hoffman, Dustin *169*, 172–3
Hogarth, William 57, 58–67, *60–65*, 67
Hollander, Ann 58
Holt, Haleen K. 278
Hopkins, George James 111–12, *112*
Hopper, Edward 193
Hopper, Hedda 132
Hoskins, Bob 295, *295*
Houghton, Hal 184
Hours, The 164, 173, 174, *175*
How to Lose a Guy in Ten Days 9
How to Stuff a Wild Bikini 140
Howard, Leslie *128*
Howard, Trevor *131*
Hubert, René 32
Hudson, Jennifer 42, *51*
Hudson, Kate 9
Hudson, Rock 233
Hugo 86, 87, *87*
Hunger Games, The 154, *155*
Hunt, William S. 195
Hunter, Holly 223
Huston, Anjelica *40*
Hyde-White, Wilfrid *148*

I Live My Life 205
Inception 269, *269*, 274–5, 277, 279

Independence Day 249–50, *250*, 261
Industrial Light & Magic (ILM) 295
Intolerance 14
Iron Lady, The 163, *165*, 166
Ishioka, Eiko *282*

Jack the Giant Killer 299
Jackman, Hugh *270*
Jackson, Gordon *131*
Jackson, Peter 299
Jacobs, Marc 140
James, Gennie *173*
James, Henry 57
Jarman, Derek 86
Jeakins, Dorothy 27, *184*, 225
Jensen, John 225
Jenssen, Elois W. 27, *184*
Jerry Bruckheimer Films 82
Jester, Ralph 225
Jezebel 24
Jobs, Steve 39
John Carter 304
Johnston, Joanna 39, 50, *250*, *250*, 295–304, *295–9*, *303–5*
Jones, Gary *175*, 284
Jones, January *270*
Jones, Michael *70*
Jordan, Neil 86
Jour de Fête 105
Julie and Julia 164, 167
Julien Entertainment 217
Julien's Auctions 183

Kalas, Andrea 211
Kalfus, Renée Ehrlich 80
Kaplan, Michael 4, 48, 51, *151*, 154–5, *261*, 291
Kapur, Shekhar 118
Karloff, Boris 200
Katzenberg, Jeffrey 38–9
Keaton, Buster 82, 97, *102*, 104, 196
Keaton, Diane 155
Kelly, Gene 203, 238, 295
Kelly, Grace 208, 222, 237, *239*, 268, *268*
Kelsall, Colleen *167*
Kemper, Ellie 268
Kennedy, John F. *296*
Kerr, Deborah 217
Keyes, Evelyn *128*
Keystone Comedy Company 97–101, *98*
Kid Auto Races at Venice 15, 101–2
Kidman, Nicole *44*, 57, *58*, 173, *174*, *175*
Kill Bill 204, 212, 244, *245*
Kim, Dennis 276
King and I, The 217, *220*
King of Comedy, The 159
Kingsley, Ben 86
Klein, Janine *144*
Klein, William *144*
Klute *169*, *170*, 173
Knightley, Keira *72*, *229*, 266
Knode, Charles 243, *261*, 291
Knowles, Beyoncé *42*, 51
Koenekamp, Fred 101
Koszarski, Richard 192
Kottka, Otto 127
Kramer vs. Kramer 166
Kubrick, Stanley 58, 118–20
Kurland, Jeffrey *269*, 269, 273–9, *273–9*

Lady in the Dark 23, 151, *151*
Laemmle, Carl 229
Lamarr, Hedy 27, 30, *184*, 210, 211, 257
Lamont, Duncan *131*
Lancaster, Osbert 189
Landis, Deborah Nadoolman *36*, 57, 58, 106–9, *107*, 108, *187*, 203, 204–5, 240
Landis, John 106–9
Lane, Nathan *89*

Langdon, Harry 97, 103, 104
Langley, Noel 200–202
Langlois, Henri 189, 193–5, 196, 198
Lansbury, Angela 82
Lasky, Jesse 132
Lasky Studio 256
Lasseter, John 39
Last Days of Pompeii, The 257
Last Emperor, The 4, 69–70, *69–71*
Laurel and Hardy 97, 104, 195
Lauren, Ralph 140
Law, John Philip 287
Law, Jude *89*, 266
LeBlanc, Paul 79
Ledger, Heath *54*
Lee, Ang 52
Legally Blonde 106, *108*
Leiber, Fritz 112
Leibovitz, Annie 140
Leigh, Janet 35
Leigh, Vivien 128, *128*, 195, 207, 209–11, 222
Leisen, Mitchell 129, 130, *130*
LeMaire, Charles 30, 129
Lemony Snicket's A Series of Unfortunate Events 163–4, *164*
Lenk, Sabine 126, 195
Leone, Sergio 246
Leopard, The 186
Lerner and Loewe 146
Letty Lynton 151, 155
Le Vey, David, 43
Lincoln 304
Linder, Max 95, 97
Liotta, Ray *160*
Lisztomania 140
Little Annie Rooney 15, 257
Little Foxes, The 24
Little Women 237
Livrustkammeren, Stockholm *125*
Lloyd, Christopher 295
Lloyd, Harold 97, *100*, 102–3, 104, 196, 260
Lloyd, Phyllida 166
Lodge, David 57
Lombard, Carole 132, *132*, 135, 212, *212*
Lone, John *69*
Loos, Anita 253, 254
Loquasto, Santo 143
Los Angeles County Museum of History, Art and Science 257–60
Losey, Joseph 195
Louis, Jean 30, 296
Love, Bessie 187
Loves of Queen Elizabeth, The 116, *116*
Lucas, George 36, 38
Lucile 14, 18, *112*, 254, 257
Lumet, Sidney 32, 42

Mabel's Strange Predicament 101
Mabry, Moss 131, *131*
McCarthy, Melissa 268
McConathy, Dale 198
McDormand, Frances *76*
McDowall, Roddy 82
McGowan, Dorothy *144*
MacLaine, Shirley 88
McLendon-Covey, Wendi 268
McQueen, Alexander 140, 154, *155*
McQueen, Larry *30*, *40*, 85, *135*, 205, 206, *213*, *217*, 217–26, 225, *250*
Macy, William H. 75
Mad Dog and Glory 161
Mad Men 155
Madonna 140, *143*, 250
Maeder, Edward 181–2
Maid of the Mountains 209
Making a Living 100
Makovsky, Judianna *154*, 270, *283*

Malkovich, John *60*
Malraux, André 191–2, *193–4*
Mamma Mia! 164, 166, 173, *233*, 234
Manchurian Candidate, The 167
Mann, Michael 275
Man Ray 192
Manser, Warren *284*
Marie, Lisa *90*
Marie Antoinette (1938) *19*, 21, 57, 118, *120*, 127–8, *127*, 139, *140*, *204*, 205–6
Marie Antoinette (2006) 118, 120, *120*, *125*, 139–40, *139*
Marks, Colin *304*
Marnie 261
Mars Attacks! 90
Marshall, Herbert *217*
Marshall, Rob *42*
Martin, Catherine *44*
Martin, Dean 275
Martin, Steve *108*
Marx Brothers 104, *104*
Mary Poppins 295
Mary of Scotland 24
Mary Shelley's Frankenstein 160
Mason, Marsha *172*
Masterson, Mary Stuart *81*
Mastroianni, Marcello *172*
Matrix, The 39, 287, 288–9
Matthau, Walter 104
Mayer, Louis B. 111
Meet the Fockers 158
Meet the Parents 158
Méliès, George 194, *194*
Messina, Phil 276
Metro-Goldwyn-Mayer (MGM) 18, 30, 179, 181, 193, *199*, 203–4, *205*, *206*, 217–20, 237–40, *256*, *257*, 260
Metropolis 195
Metropolitan Museum of Art, New York *196*, 198–9, 200
Meyer, Russ 144
Michel, Michele *108*
Middleton, Charles *287*
Middleton, Kate (Duchess of Cambridge) 237, *239*
Midnight Cowboy 140, *169*, 172–3
Midnight Run 161
Midsummer Night's Dream, A 140
Mighty Aphrodite 274
Mildred Pierce (1945) 174, *186*, 205, *206*, 260
Mildred Pierce (2011) 174–5
Miller, Burton *261*
Mingenbach, Louise 269
Minghella, Anthony 174
Mintz, Charles 260
Miramax 223
Mirojnick, Ellen 38, 50, *223*, 261, 266, *267*
Mix, Tom 195, *196*
Moby Dick 196
Modern Times 100, *102*, 254–5
Mollo, John 36, *38*, *287*
Money Never Sleeps 266
Monroe, Marilyn 30, 95, 106, 200, 208, *226*, 240
Moore, John 242
Mordaunt, Vera 260
Moretz, Chloë Grace *87*
Morgan, Frank *201*
Morley, Ruth 36, *36*, 154, *155*, 158, *159*, *166*
Morocco 4, 23, *134*
Moss, Carrie-Anne *288*
Motion Picture Producers and Distributors of America Inc. (MPPDA) 18–19
Motion Picture Production Code 18–19, 26, 30
Moulin Rouge! 44
Mulleavy, Kate and Laura 154, *265*, 267, 269
Murch, Day 70
Murphy, Eddie *108*, 109, *302*
Murray, Mae 260
Musée du Cinéma, Palais du Chaillot, Paris *191*, *193*, 194–5, *196*
Museum of Modern Art, New York 192
Mussenden, Isis *39*, *302*
Mutiny on the Bounty 131, *131*
My Best Friend's Wedding 276
My Fair Lady 32–5, *146–9*, 180, *181*, *187*, 198
My Man Godfrey 132, 212, *212–15*
Myers, Mike *108*, *302*
Myers, Ruth 40, *163*

Nadoolman, Deborah *see* Landis, Deborah Nadoolman
National Gallery, London *61–5*, 67
National Portrait Gallery, London *116*
National Lampoon's Animal House 107, 109
Natividad, Ed *288*, *289*
Navigator, The *102*, 103
NBCUniversal Archives & Collections *54*, 229–34, *234*
Neal, Patricia 140
Negri, Pola *15*, 135
Nelson, Tim Blake *78*
New York, New York 161
Newbridge Silverware 208
Newman, E. de B. 257
Newton, Helmut 144
Nichols, Mike 32, 88–9, 175
Nichols, Nichelle *287*
Nicholson, Jack *86*
Nielsen, Asta 196
Nietzsche, Friedrich 246
Nine to Five 171
No Country for Old Men 77, 79
Nolan, Christopher 274
Normand, Mabel 95, 98
North by Northwest 275
Notorious 30, 85
Nourry, Hélène 143
Novak, Kim 64–5, *85*, 222, 261
Novarese, Nino *29*, *111*

O Brother, Where Art Thou? 78
O'Brien, Willis 260
Ocean's Eleven (2001) 275–9, *278*
O'Connor, Donald *238*
Odd Couple, The 175
Ogawa, Kumiko 244, *245*
O'Hara, Maureen 233
Oklahoma 170
Oldman, Gary 282
Olivier, Laurence 222
One Million B.C. 127
O'Neal, Ryan *59*
Orlando 118, *118*
Orry-Kelly 24, 30, 106, 116, *116*, 181, *226*
Out of Africa 38, *163*, 164–6
Owl and the Pussycat, The 171

Pakula, Alan 173
Paley Media Center, Beverly Hills 240
Paltrow, Gwyneth *44*
Paramount Pictures 18, 211, 222, 223–5, *256*
Parker, Peter 290
Parton, Dolly *171*
Patch, Karen *9*
Patterson, Janet 57–8, *58*, 223
Pattinson, Robert 282, *283*
Paul, Robert 190, 192
Peck, Ann *247*
Peck, Gregory 196
Peckinpah, Sam 32
Penn, Arthur 32, 35
Pericoli, Ugo 70
Pesci, Joe 160
Pfeiffer, Michelle *4*, *292*
Philadelphia Story, The 17
Piano, The 223
Pickford, Mary *15*, 222, 254, *255*, 257, 260
Piper, John 189, *190*

Pirate, The 140
Pirates of the Caribbean 82, *82*, 212, 265–6, 282
Pitt, Brad *4*, *48*, 51, 275–7, *278*, 279
Pixar 39
Places in the Heart *173*, 174
Planet of the Apes 90
Plenty 163
Plummer, Christopher 242
Plunkett, Walter 18, 24–6, *24*, *26*, 32, 127, 128, *128*, 131, 179, *207–11*, 237, 238
Poiret, Paul 14, 116, *116*, 198, 257
Polan, Dana 261
Polar Express, The 296–9, *298–9*
Pollack, Sidney 38
Porro, Joseph A. *250*
Porter, Heather 205
Portman, Natalie *89*, 265, 267
Portrait of a Lady 57–8, *58*
Poseidon Adventure, The 249
Postcards from the Edge 88
Potter, Sally 86
Powell, Anthony *39*–42, 51, 106, *107*
Powell, Sandy 39, *44*, 51, 86–7, *86–7*, 116, 118, *118*, 209
Power of the Sultan, The 13
Presley, Cecilia DeMille 210
Presnell, Harve 237
Private Lives of Elizabeth and Essex, The 24, 116, *116*
Prowse, David 287
Psycho 35, 193, 195
Public Enemies *266*, 267
Pulp Fiction 144, *144*

Quayle, Anthony *242*
Queen Christina 57, 217, 220, 226
Queen Elizabeth 1*4*
Qui êtes-vous, Polly Maggoo? 144, *144*
Quo Vadis 242–3

Rabanne, Paco 144, 287
Radcliffe, Daniel *282*, 283
Rafferty, Chips *131*
Raging Bull 159, *159*
Raiders of the Lost Ark 36–8, *36*, 42, 200
Ralston, Ken 296
Rampling, Charlotte 140
Rand, Tom 166
Ransom (Harry) Center, University of Texas at Austin 206–8
Rathbone, Basil 82, 233
Rear Window 85, 222
Rebecca 171
Recorded Picture Company, The *69–70*
Red Dust 253
Reeve, Christopher 290, *290*
Reeves, Keanu *287*, 289
Reininger, Lotte 139, *190*
Rendition 166
Renie *29*, *111*
Reynolds, Debbie *4*, 11, 181, 209–10, 237–40, *237–40*
Reynolds, Ryan 269–70, *270*
Rhodes, Leah 243, *243*
Ricci, Christina *90*, 260
Richesson, Robin *298*, 299, *303*
Riggs, Rita 35
Ringwood, Bob *4*, *292*
RKO 18, 260
Robe, The 30
Roberts, Julia 273, *275*, 276, *276*
Robinson, David 196
Rodarte 154
Rogers, Ginger 151, *151*
Rogers, Will 195
Rose, Anika Noni *51*
Rose, Helen 27–30, 130, *131*, 237–8, *239*
Rose, Penny 82, *82*, 265–6
Rosenthal, Jean 170

Rosoman, Leonard 189
Rosson, Harold 253
Roth, Ann 52, 88–9, *88–9*, *163*, 164, 166, *167*, 169–75, *169–75*, 233, 234
Rubeo, Mayes C. *4*, *300*, *304*
Rudolph, Maya *268*
Ruffalo, Mark *86*
Rumba 132
Russell, Kurt *88*
Rutherford, Ann *128*
Ryack, Rita *160*, 161

Sabrina 146, 155, *155*
Saint Laurent, Yves 143, 154
Saldana, Zoë *4*, *300*
Samson and Delilah 27, 30, 32, *184*, 210, 211, 257
Sanchez, Felipe *50*, *164*
Santiago, Emile 30
Saving Private Ryan 250, *250*
Schiaparelli, Elsa 118, *118*, 175, 198
Schlesinger, John 169, 175
Schrader, Paul 207
Schroedt, Inez *204*
Schulberg, Budd 171
Schulze-Mittendorf, Walter 195
Schwartz, David 161
Schwarzenegger, Arnold *248*, 282, 287
Scolari, Peter *298*
Scorsese, Martin 36, 42, 86–7, *86*, 158, 159, 161, 169
Scott, Deborah L. *4*, 39, *43*, *300*
Scott, Ridley 36, 48
Scott Thomas, Kristen 174, *175*
Searchers, The 32, 247
Second World War 26–7
Secret of Madame Blanche, The 257
Seeking a Friend for the End of the World 72, 73
Seelig, Eric 158, *159*
Selznick, David O. 24, *26*, 32, 207
Sennett, Mack *13*, 95, 96, 97–101, 254
Serkis, Andy *304*
Sex 220, 223
Seyrig, Delphine 195
Shakespeare in Love 39, 44, 86, *116*, 118, 209
Shanghai Express 134
Sharaff, Irene 27–30, *28–9*, 30, 32, *33*, *111*, 112, 170
Shea, Jack 39
Shearer, Norma *14*, 118, *120*, 127–8, 139, *140*, 203, 205–6
Sheen, Charlie 266
Sheldon, Sammy 270, *270*
Sherlock Holmes 265, *266*
Short, Martin *108*
Shrek films 39, 302
Shutter Island 86, *86*
Silkwood 88, 164
Simi, Carlo 246, *247*
Simon, Neil 172
Sinatra, Frank 275
Singer, Bryan 299
Singin' in the Rain 32, 179, 237, 238, *238*
Sleepy Hollow 80, 82, 90, *90*
Smith, Will 249–50, *250*
Soderbergh, Steve 273, 275–6, 278
Søderlund, Ulla-Britt 58, *59*, 118–20, *125*
Some Like It Hot 30, 106, 226
Sorvino, Mira 274
Sorvino, Paul *160*
Spanish Dancer, The 15
Spartacus 242, 243
Spider-Man films *4*, 261, 284, 290
Spiderwick Chronicles, The 299, *303*
Spielberg, Steven 36–8, *36*, 109, 180, 250
Stagecoach 26
Star is Born, A 170
Star Trek 217, 287
Star Wars films 36, 38, *38*, 282, 287

Stargate 220, 223
Steele, Gile 27, *184*
Steenburgen, Mary 296, 297
Steinfeld, Hailee 79, *79*, 154
Sterling, Ford 98, 100
Stevenson, Edward 23
Stewart, James 64, 195
Stewart, Kristen 282
Stewart, Marlene 248
Stone, Lewis 220
Stone, Sharon 223, *223*, 261
Strada, La 140
Strathie, Angus *44*
Strauss, Richard 66
Streep, Meryl 38, 52, 64, *88*, *144*, 163–6, *163–7*, 175, *233*, 234, 296, 297
Streisand, Barbra *33*, 171
Sudjic, Deyan 246
Sui, Anna 140, *140*
Superman 261, 269, 270, 281, 287, 290, *290*
Swanson, Gloria 257
Sweeney Todd: The Demon Barber of Fleet Street 80, 90, *91*
Sweet November 172

Tai, Ada and Arlene *90*
The Talented Mr Ripley 174, *175*
Tarantino, Quentin 204
Tati, Jacques 105, *105*
Taxi Driver 36, *36*, 158, *159*, 207
Taylor, Elizabeth *29*, 32, *111*, 112, 140, 237
Taylor, Ruth *21*
Tellegen, Lou *116*
Ten Commandments, The 32, 211, 223, 225
Terminator films *248*, 287
That Forsyte Woman 131
That Hamilton Woman 222
Them! 261
Thief Catcher, A 98
Things to Come 287
Thomas, Bill 217, 225, 226, 242
Thomas, Catherine Marie 244, *245*
Thomas, Henry 87
¡Three Amigos! 106, *108*
Thurman, Uma *144*, *144*, 204, 212, 244, *245*
Tipton, Norman 205–6
Titanic 39, 43
To Catch a Thief 85, 268, *268*
Tomczeszyn, Lisa 270
Tomlin, Lily *171*
Tosi, Piero 186
Tower of London 233
Towering Inferno, The 249
Toy Story 39
Tracy, Spencer 203
Trading Places 108, 109
Tramp, The 99, 151, *183*
Trapeze 140
Travilla, William 30, 35, 243, *243*
Travolta, John *144*
Trigere, Pauline 140, *143*
Troy 200
Trpcic, Shawna Leavell *34*
True Grit (2010) 48–50, 78, 79, *79*, 154
Truffaut, François 192, 194, 195
Turner, Kathleen 295
Turner, Lana 237
Turturro, John *78*
Twentieth-Century Fox 30, 181, 240
Twilight 282, 283

Universal Studios 229–34, *229*, *232*
Unsinkable Molly Brown, The 237, 238, *240*
Untouchables, The 159–61, *160*

vacances de Monsieur Hulot, Les 105, *105*
Valentino 140

Valles *242*
Valley of the Dolls 30, 35, 220
Van Runkle, Theadora 35, *35*, 143, *143*, *158*, 161
van Straalen, Dien *118*
Vance-Straker, Marilyn *160*, 248
Vaughan, Bruce 186
Velvet Goldmine 140
Versailles, Château de *120*
Vertigo 64–5, 85, *85*, 222, 261
Vidor, King 207
Vigée-Lebrun, Elisabeth-Louise 118, *120*
Vionnet, Madeleine *4*, 112, *114*
Virgin Queen, The 24, 25, 116, *116*, 118, 220, 240
Vogt, Mary E. *4*, 292
Voight, Jon *169*
Volcano 261
Von Sternberg, Joseph 132–4
Von Wangenheim, Chris 144
Vreeland, Diana 144, 181, 198, 199
Vuu, Richard 69

Wada, Christine 266, *268*
Wag the Dog 160, 161
Wakeling, Gwen 27, *184*
Wall Street 38, 266, 267
Walters, Julie 233
War Horse 299, 304
War of the Worlds, The 261
Warhol, Andy 193, 246
Warm, Hermann 195
Warner, Jack 111, 146, 172
Warner Brothers 179, 180, 222
Wasikowska, Mia *91*
Wayne, Bruce 290
Wayne, John 26, 195, 247
Weaver, Sigourney 89
Weintraub, Jerry 276
Weiss, Julie *81*
West, Clare 13, *14*, 15
West, Mae 95, 132, 135, *135*, 196
Westcott, Amy 265, 267, 269
Western Costume Company 15, 170–71, 181, 217
Westwood, Vivienne 118, 143
What's Eating Gilbert Grape 80
White, Miles 170
Who Framed Roger Rabbit 39, 295–6, *295*
Wiest, Dianna 274
Wiig, Kristen *268*
Wilcoxon, Henry *184*
Wilder, Billy 106
Wilkinson, Michael *166*
Williams, Esther 195
Williams, Richard 295, 296
Willis, Bruce *172*, 248, 249
Wills, Mary 25, 116, *116*, 118
Windsor, Claire *14*
Winslet, Kate 43, 175
Witherspoon, Reese *108*
Wizard of Oz, The *4*, 21, *179*, 181, *182*, 199, 200–201, *201*, 204–5, 260
Wolsky, Albert 34, *167*
Women, The 18
Working Girl 89
World of Henry Orient, The 171
Worthington, Sam *4*
Wyckoff, Anna *108*

X-Men 269, 270, *270*

Yakin, Boaz 175
Yates, Janty 48, 243, *244*
Young, Sean *291*

Zellweger, Renée 220, *220*
Zemeckis, Robert 39, 295–6, 297
Zophres, Mary 39, 50, 76–9, *76–9*, *108*, 154
Zukor, Adolph 14, 21–3

Se 1 - 4

Se 5 - 15A

Se 18

① Se 1-4

② Se 5-15A

②A

⑧ ⑨ ⑩

⑪

⑫

⑬

Se 31-44
(She changes
back from Ella
to Cruella.)

Se 45-46

Se 47-50

Se 59.